International
WHO'S WHO in

2002

Popular
MUSIC

International WHO'S WHO in

2002

Popular
MUSIC

Fourth Edition

First published 1996

© **Europa Publications Limited 2002**
11 New Fetter Lane, London, EC4P 4EE, England
(A member of the Taylor & Francis Group)

ISBN: 1 85743 161 8

Editor: Andy Gregory

Series Editor: Elizabeth Sleeman
Associate Editor: Alison Neale

Researchers:

Jak Knowles

Justin Lewis

Mark Stevens

Mike Hingston

Jennifer Byrne

Jon Philibert

Paul Swing

Simon Gitter

Technology Editor: Ian Preston
Technical Support: Terry Brett, Terry Carter

Typeset by Bibliocraft Ltd, Dundee

Printed and bound by St Edmundsbury Press, Bury St Edmunds

Foreword

The fourth edition of the INTERNATIONAL WHO'S WHO IN POPULAR MUSIC (formerly International Who's Who in Music, Volume Two – Popular Music) provides biographical information on over 5,000 prominent people from pop, rock, folk, jazz, dance, world and country music, including instrumentalists, singers, writers, producers and managers. The biographies include, where available, personal details and information on career, recordings, compositions, publications and honours.

For this edition existing entrants were given an opportunity to make necessary amendments and additions to their biographies, while potential new entrants were asked to provide biographical details. Supplementary research was done by the Editor, a team of researchers and the Europa Publications editorial department in order to ensure that the book is as up to date as possible on publication.

In addition to the biographical information, appendices provide details of record companies, management companies, agents and promoters, music publishers, festivals and events, and music organizations.

The assistance of the individuals and organizations included in this publication in providing up-to-date material is much appreciated.

March 2002

CONTENTS

ABBREVIATIONS

AB	Alberta	CT	Connecticut
ACT	Australian Capital Territory		
Admin.	Administrator, Administrative	d.	daughter(s)
AG	Aktiengesellschaft (Joint Stock Company)	DC	District of Columbia; Distrito Central
AIDS	acquired immunodeficiency syndrome	DE	Delaware
AK	Alaska	Dec.	December
a.k.a.	also known as	demo	demonstration
AL	Alabama	Dept	Department
AM	amplitude modulation	devt	development
Apdo	Apartado (Post Box)	DF	Distrito Federal
approx.	approximately	Dir	Director
Apt	Apartment	DIY	do-it-yourself
apto	apartamento	DJ	Disc Jockey
A & R	Artists and Repertoire	DMus	Doctor of Music
AR	Arkansas	DN	Distrito Nacional
ASCAP	American Society of Composers, Authors and Publishers	dpto	departamento
		Dr(a)	Doctor(a)
Asscn	Association	Dr.	Drive
Assoc.	Associate		
Asst	Assistant	E	East(ern)
Aug.	August	EC	European Community
Avda	Avenida (Avenue)	Ed.	Editor
Ave	Avenue	Edif.	Edificio (Building)
AZ	Arizona	Edn	Edition
		e.g.	exempli gratia (for example)
b.	born	ENO	English National Opera
BA	Bachelor of Arts	EP	Extended Play
BAFTA	British Academy of Film and Television Arts	esq.	esquina (corner)
		etc.	et cetera
BBC	British Broadcasting Corporation	EU	European Union
BC	British Columbia	eV	eingetragener Verein
Bdwy	Broadway	Exec.	Executive
BEd	Bachelor of Education		
BFI	British Film Institute	f.	founded
Bldg	Building	fax	facsimile
Blvd	Boulevard	Feb.	February
BMus	Bachelor of Music	FL	Florida
BP	Boîte postale (Post Box)	FM	frequency modulation
bros	brothers	fmr(ly)	former(ly)
c.	circa; child, children	GA	Georgia
CA	California	Gdns	Gardens
CBC	Canadian Broadcasting Corporation	Gen.	General
C.B.E.	Commander of (the Order of) the British Empire	GmbH	Gesellschaft mit beschränkter Haftung (Limited Liability Company)
		GMT	Greenwich Mean Time
CBS	Columbia Broadcasting System	GPO	General Post Office
CD	Compact Disc		
CD-ROM	compact disc read-only memory	h.c.	honoris causa
CEO	Chief Executive Officer	HI	Hawaii
Chair.	Chairman, Chairwoman	HIV	human immunodeficiency virus
Cia	Companhia	Hon.	Honorary; Honourable
Cía	Compañía	Hons	Honours
Cie	Compagnie	Hwy	Highway
circ.	circulation		
c/o	care of	IA	Iowa
Co	Company; County	IBA	Independent Broadcasting Authority
CO	Colorado	ID	Idaho
Col.	Colonia, Colima	i.e.	id est (that is to say)
COO	Chief Operating Officer	IL	Illinois
Corpn	Corporation	IN	Indiana
CP	Case Postale; Caixa Postal; Casella Postale (Post Box)	Inc	Incorporated
		incl.	including
Cres.	Crescent	ITA	Independent Television Authority
Ct	Court	ITV	Independent Television

ABBREVIATIONS

Jan.	January	PO Box	Post Office Box
Jr	Junior	PR	Public Relations
		Pres.	President
km	kilometre(s)	PRO	Public Relations Officer
KS	Kansas	Prod.	Producer
KY	Kentucky	Prof.	Professor
		promo	promotional
LA	Louisiana	pt.	part
L.A.	Los Angeles	Pty	Proprietary
LP	Long Playing record		
Ltd	Limited	QC	Québec
LW	long wave	q.v.	quod vide (to which refer)
m.	married; million	R & B	Rhythm and Blues
MA	Massachusetts; Master of Arts	Rd	Road
Man.	Manager; Managing	Rep.	Republic
MB	Manitoba	retd	retired
M.B.E.	Member of (the Order of) the British Empire	RI	Rhode Island
		rpm	revolutions per minute
MC	master of ceremonies; music cassette	RSC	Royal Shakespeare Company
MD	Maryland; Music Director		
ME	Maine	S	South(ern); San
mem.	member	s.	son(s)
MI	Michigan	SA	Société Anonyme, Sociedad Anónima (Limited Company); South Australia
MMus	Master of Music		
MN	Minnesota	SC	South Carolina
MO	Missouri	SD	South Dakota
MP	Member of Parliament	SE	South-east(ern)
MS	Mississippi	Sec.	Secretary
MT	Montana	Sept.	September
MTV	Music Television	SK	Saskatchewan
MW	medium wave	SL	Sociedad Limitada
		Sq.	Square
N	North(ern)	Sr	Senior
NB	New Brunswick	St	Street; Saint
NBC	National Broadcasting Corporation	Sta	Santa
NC	North Carolina	Ste	Sainte
ND	North Dakota	str	strasse
NE	Nebraska; North-east(ern)	SW	South-west(ern); short wave
NF	Newfoundland		
NH	New Hampshire	tel.	telephone
NJ	New Jersey	TN	Tennessee
NM	New Mexico	Treas.	Treasurer
no.	number	TV	television
Nov.	November	TX	Texas
nr	near		
NS	Nova Scotia	u.	utca (street)
NSW	New South Wales	UHF	ultra-high frequency
NT	Northwest Territories; Northern Territory	UK	United Kingdom
		ul.	ulitsa (street)
NU	Nunavut Territory	UN	United Nations
NV	Nevada	UNESCO	United Nations Educational, Scientific and Cultural Organization
NW	North-west(ern)		
NY	New York	UNICEF	United Nations Children's Fund
NZ	New Zealand	Urb.	Urbanización (urban district)
		US	United States
O.B.E.	Officer of (the Order of) the British Empire	USA	United States of America
		USSR	Union of Soviet Socialist Republics
Oct.	October	UT	Utah
Of.	Oficina (Office)		
OH	Ohio	VA	Virginia
OK	Oklahoma	VHF	very high frequency
ON	Ontario	VI	(US) Virgin Islands
OR	Oregon	Vol.(s)	Volume(s)
		VT	Vermont
p.	page		
PA	Pennsylvania	W	West(ern)
PE	Prince Edward Island	WA	Western Australia; Washington (state)
PEN	Poets, Playwrights, Essayists, Editors and Novelists (Club)		
		WI	Wisconsin
PF	Postfach (Post Box)	WV	West Virginia
Pkwy	Parkway	www	world-wide web
Pl.	Place	WY	Wyoming
PLC	Public Limited Company		
PMB	Private Mail Bag	YT	Yukon Territory

INTERNATIONAL TELEPHONE CODES

To make international calls to telephone and fax numbers listed in the book, dial the international code of the country from which you are calling, followed by the appropriate country code for the organization you wish to call (listed below), followed by the area code (if applicable) and telephone or fax number listed in the entry.

	Country code	+ or − GMT*		Country code	+ or − GMT*
Afghanistan	93	+4½	Burundi	257	+2
Albania	355	+1	Cambodia	855	+7
Algeria	213	+1	Cameroon	237	+1
Andorra	376	+1	Canada	1	−3 to −8
Angola	244	+1	Cape Verde	238	−1
Antigua and Barbuda	1 268	−4	Central African Republic	236	+1
Argentina	54	−3	Chad	235	+1
Armenia	374	+4	Chile	56	−4
Australia	61	+7 to +10	China, People's Republic	86	+8
Australian External Territories:			Special Administrative Regions:		
Christmas Island	61	+10	Hong Kong	852	+8
Cocos (Keeling) Islands	61	+10	Macao	853	+8
Norfolk Island	672	+11½	China (Taiwan)	886	+8
Austria	43	+1	Colombia	57	−5
Azerbaijan	994	+5	Comoros	269	+3
The Bahamas	1 242	−5	Congo, Democratic Republic	243	+1
Bahrain	973	+3	Congo, Republic	242	+1
Bangladesh	880	+6	Costa Rica	506	−6
Barbados	1 246	−4	Côte d'Ivoire	225	0
Belarus	375	+2	Croatia	385	+1
Belgium	32	+1	Cuba	53	−5
Belize	501	−6	Cyprus	357	+2
Benin	229	+1	'Turkish Republic of		
Bhutan	975	+6	Northern Cyprus'	90 392	+2
Bolivia	591	−4	Czech Republic	420	+1
Bosnia and Herzegovina	387	+1	Denmark	45	+1
Botswana	267	+2	Danish External Territories:		
Brazil	55	−3 to −4	Faroe Islands	298	0
Brunei	673	+8	Greenland	299	−1 to −4
Bulgaria	359	+2	Djibouti	253	+3
Burkina Faso	226	0	Dominica	1 767	−4

INTERNATIONAL TELEPHONE CODES

	Country code	+ or − GMT*		Country code	+ or − GMT*
Dominican Republic	1 809	−4	India	91	+5½
Ecuador	593	−5	Indonesia	62	+7 to +8
Egypt	20	+2	Iran	98	+3½
El Salvador	503	−6	Iraq	964	+3
Equatorial Guinea	240	+1	Ireland	353	0
Eritrea	291	+3	Israel	972	+2
Estonia	372	+2	Italy	39	+1
Ethiopia	251	+3	Jamaica	1 876	−5
Fiji	679	+12	Japan	81	+9
Finland	358	+2	Jordan	962	+2
Finnish External Territory:			Kazakhstan	7	+6
Åland Islands	358	+2	Kenya	254	+3
France	33	+1	Kiribati	686	+12
French Overseas Departments:			Korea, Democratic People's		
French Guiana	594	−3	Republic (North Korea)	850	+9
Guadeloupe	590	−4	Korea, Republic		
Martinique	596	−4	(South Korea)	82	+9
Réunion	262	+4	Kuwait	965	+3
French Overseas Collectivités			Kyrgyzstan	996	+5
Territoriales:			Laos	856	+7
Mayotte	269	+3	Latvia	371	+2
Saint Pierre and Miquelon	508	−3	Lebanon	961	+2
French Overseas Territories:			Lesotho	266	+2
French Polynesia	689	−10	Liberia	231	0
New Caledonia	687	+11	Libya	218	+1
Wallis and Futuna Islands	681	+12	Liechtenstein	423	+1
Gabon	241	+1	Lithuania	370	+2
The Gambia	220	0	Luxembourg	352	+1
Georgia	995	+4	Macedonia, former Yugoslav		
Germany	49	+1	Republic	389	+1
Ghana	233	0	Madagascar	261	+3
Greece	30	+2	Malawi	265	+2
Grenada	1 473	−4	Malaysia	60	+8
Guatemala	502	−6	Maldives	960	+5
Guinea	224	0	Mali	223	0
Guinea-Bissau	245	0	Malta	356	+1
Guyana	592	−4	Marshall Islands	692	+12
Haiti	509	−5	Mauritania	222	0
Honduras	504	−6	Mauritius	230	+4
Hungary	36	+1	Mexico	52	−6 to −7
Iceland	354	0	Micronesia, Federated States	691	+10 to +11

	Country code	+ or − GMT*		Country code	+ or − GMT*
Moldova	373	+2	Saint Vincent and the		
Monaco.	377	+1	Grenadines.	1 784	−4
Mongolia	976	+8	Samoa	685	−11
Morocco	212	0	San Marino	378	+1
Mozambique.	258	+2	São Tomé and Príncipe	239	0
Myanmar	95	+6½	Saudi Arabia	966	+3
Namibia.	264	+2	Senegal	221	0
Nauru.	674	+12	Seychelles.	248	+4
Nepal	977	+5¾	Sierra Leone.	232	0
The Netherlands.	31	+1	Singapore	65	+8
Netherlands Dependencies:			Slovakia	421	+1
Aruba	297	−4	Slovenia	386	+1
Netherlands Antilles	599	−4	Solomon Islands	677	+11
New Zealand	64	+12	Somalia	252	+3
New Zealand's Dependent and			South Africa	27	+2
Associated Territories:			Spain	34	+1
Cook Islands	682	−10½	Sri Lanka.	94	+5½
Niue	683	−11	Sudan.	249	+2
Nicaragua.	505	−6	Suriname	597	−3
Niger	227	+1	Swaziland.	268	+2
Nigeria.	234	+1	Sweden.	46	+1
Norway.	47	+1	Switzerland	41	+1
Norwegian External Territory:			Syria	963	+2
Svalbard	47	+1	Tajikistan.	992	+5
Oman.	968	+4	Tanzania	255	+3
Pakistan.	92	+5	Thailand.	66	+7
Palau	680	+9	Togo.	228	0
Panama	507	−5	Tonga.	676	+13
Papua New Guinea.	675	+10	Trinidad and Tobago	1 868	−4
Paraguay	595	−4	Tunisia.	216	+1
Peru.	51	−5	Turkey	90	+2
The Philippines	63	+8	Turkmenistan.	993	+5
Poland	48	+1	Tuvalu	688	+12
Portugal.	351	0	Uganda	256	+3
Qatar	974	+3	Ukraine	380	+2
Romania.	40	+2	United Arab Emirates	971	+4
Russia	7	+2 to +12	United Kingdom.	44	0
Rwanda	250	+2	United Kingdom Crown		
Saint Christopher and			Dependencies	44	0
Nevis	1 869	−4	United Kingdom Overseas Territories:		
Saint Lucia.	1 758	−4	Anguilla	1 264	−4

INTERNATIONAL TELEPHONE CODES

	Country code	+ or − GMT*		Country code	+ or − GMT*
Ascension Island	247	0	United States Virgin		
Bermuda	1 441	−4	Islands	1 340	−4
British Virgin Islands	1 284	−4	Uruguay	598	−3
Cayman Islands	1 345	−5	Uzbekistan	998	+5
Falkland Islands	500	−4	Vanuatu	678	+11
Gibraltar	350	+1	Vatican City	39	+1
Montserrat	1 664	−4	Venezuela	58	−4
Saint Helena	290	0	Viet Nam	84	+7
Turks and Caicos Islands .	1 649	−5	Yemen	967	+3
United States of America . . .	1	−5 to −10	Yugoslavia	381	+1
United States Commonwealth Territories:			Zambia	260	+2
Northern Mariana Islands.	1 670	+10	Zimbabwe	263	+2
Puerto Rico	1 787	−4			
United States External Territories:					
American Samoa	684	−11			
Guam	1 671	+10			

* The times listed compare the standard (winter) times in the various countries. Some countries adopt Summer (Daylight Saving) Time-i.e. +1 hour-for part of the year.

A

3-D (Robert Del Naja); b. 21 Jan. 1965, Brighton, England. Vocalist. *Career:* Member: Massive Attack; Numerous club shows and parties; Collaborations: Shara Nelson; Tricky; Horace Andy; Madonna; Tracey Thorn, Everything But the Girl; Liz Fraser, Cocteau Twins; Damon Albarn, Blur; One Day At a Time features on soundtrack to Ordinary Decent Criminal film, 2000. *Recordings:* Singles: Daydreaming (with Shara Nelson), 1990; Safe From Harm EP, 1991; Sly, 1994; Protection, 1995; Karmacoma, 1995; Risingson, 1997; Teardrop (with Liz Fraser); Inertia Creeps; Angel/Group Four, 1998; Albums: Blue Lines, 1991; Protection, 1994; No Protection (Massive Attack vs Mad Professor), 1995; Mezzanine, 1998; Singles Collection Box Set 1990–98, 1998. *Honours:* Brit Award, Best British Dance Act, 1996. *Internet:* www.massiveattack.co.uk.

AALTONEN Juhani 'Junnu'; b. 12 Dec. 1935, Finland. Musician (saxophones, flutes). *Musical Education:* Flute, Sibelius Academy, Helsinki; Berklee College of Music, Boston, USA, 1970. *Career:* Played with drummer Edward Vesala, 1965–; Played with Arils Andersen's quartet, 1970s; Work in radio, television and studio recordings; Featured soloist, Suomi (jazz suite), Heikki Sarmanto; Crossing, Jukka Linkola; Played in reed section, UMO (New Music Orchestra), 1975–; Former member, jazz rock group Tasavallan Presidentti; Concentrated on flute, as beneficiary of government grant, late 1980s–; Duo with pianist-composer Heikki Sarmanto; Recital of solo improvisations on flute, Tampere Biennale, 1990. *Recordings:* Several with Arild Andersen, 1970s; Nana, Edward Vesala, 1970; with Heikki Sarmanto: Hearts, 1995; Solo: Springbird, 1979. *Honour:* Yrjö Award, Finnish Jazz Federation, 1968. *Address:* Kukintie 10, 01620 Vantaa, Finland.

AARONSON Paul; b. 16 March 1955, Queens, New York, USA. Sales and Marketing Dir. m. Sharon Stern, 14 Aug. 1994. *Education:* BA, University of Florida, 1976; MBA, St John's University, 1981. *Career:* Salesman, Record Shack, New York, 1978–81; Sales Manager, Important Record Distributors, 1981–86; Owner, One Up Promotions, 1987–90; Director of Marketing, Domino Records, 1991–92; Director, Sales and Marketing, Viceroy Music, 1992. *Recordings:* with John Mooney: Testimony, 1992; with Cowboy Mouth: Mouthing Off, 1993; with Sunset Heights: Texas Tea, 1994; with Savoy Brown: Bring It Home, 1995; Rattlesnake Guitar, The Music of Peter Green, 1995. *Leisure interests:* Watching and playing basketball. *Current Management:* c/o Viceroy Music Group, 547 W 27th St, Sixth Floor, New York, NY 10001, USA.

ABA YAZEED Mohamed Mounir; b. 10 Oct. 1954, Aswan. Singer; Actor. *Education:* Faculty of Applied Arts (Cinematography). *Career:* Films: Bitter Day, Sweet Day; An Egyptian Story; Destiny (total of 11 films): Stage: The King is the King; King of the Beggars; Goodnight Egypt; Television film: Tales of the Stranger. *Recordings:* 11 albums including: Windows; Talk; In the Middle of the Circle; From First Touch. *Publications:* Windows, 1981; Talk, 1985; In the Middle of the Circle, 1987; From First Touch, 1996. *Honour:* Second Prize in The Festival of Arab Television, 1995–96. *Memberships:* Syndicate of Musicians; Syndicate of Actors. *Leisure interest:* Music. *Address:* 13 Fl-Bergass St, Garden City, Cairo, Egypt.

ABADIE Claude; b. 15 Jan. 1920, Paris, France. Musician (clarinet); Bandleader. m. Chantal Bertin, 8 Oct. 1958, two s., one d. *Education:* Engineer. *Career:* Leader, first Dixieland Revival Band, France, early 1940s; Modern jazz musician, late 1960s; Leader, own jazz tentette. *Recordings:* Album: Blues Pour Boris; Revival New Orleans Sur Seine; Vivement Le 15 Novembre. *Publications:* Le Jazz: Comment Ça Fonctionne, Diaphonie, March 1994. *Membership:* Union des Musiciens de Jazz. *Leisure interest:* Hockey. *Address:* 16 Domaine des Hocquettes, 92150 Suresnes, France.

ABATÉ Gregory; b. 31 May 1947, Fall River, Massachusetts, USA. Musician (saxophone, flute). m. Denise Marie Forcina, 10 April 1988, two s., one d. *Musical Education:* Berklee College of Music, Boston. *Career:* Major tours of US and Europe; Radio appearances on about 200 stations throughout USA; Selmer Saxophone Clinician. *Recordings:* with Greg Abaté Quartet: Bop City Live At Birdland; Straight Ahead; Bird Lives; with Greg Abaté Quintet: Live At Chans, featuring Richie Cole; Bop Lives with Kenny Barron Trio and Claudio Roditi; Happy Samba; It's Christmastime, 1995; My Buddy, 1996; Boulevard of Broken Dreams, the Greg Abate Quintet, 1996; As sideman: Samba Manhattan Style, with Claudio Ruditi, 1996; Blue Chip Jazz, with Mark Soskin, Harvie Swartz. *Publications:* Jazz Times; Penguin Guide To Jazz; Sax Journal; Other trade and national newspapers. *Honours:* Arts International Grant, 1992. *Membership:* International Asscn of Jazz Adjudicators. *Leisure interests:* Ocean activities; Being outdoors. *Current Management:* Abby Hoffer Enterprises, 223 E 48th St, New York, NY 10017, USA; Entertainment

Exclusives, 403 Commonwealth, Boston, MA 02215, USA. *Address:* 14 Blaine St, Cranston, RI 02920, USA.

ABBEY John E; b. 8 July 1945, London, England. Record Co Exec. *Career:* Editor and founder, Blues and Soul Magazine, London, 1966–85; President and founder, Contempo Records, London, 1971–78; President and co-founder, Ichiban Records Inc, 1985. *Current Management:* Ichiban Records Inc, PO Box 724677, Atlanta, GA 31139, USA.

ABBOTT Jacqueline; b. 10 Nov. 1973, Merseyside, England. Vocalist. *Career:* Member: The Beautiful South, 1994–2000; Numerous television appearances, live gigs and festival appearances. *Recordings:* Singles: Good As Gold, 1994; Everybody's Talkin', 1994; One Last Love Song, 1994; Pretenders To The Throne, 1995; Rotterdam (Or Anywhere), 1996; Don't Marry Her, 1996; Liar's Bar, 1997; Perfect 10, 1998; Dumb, 1999; How Long's a Tear Take To Dry, 1999; The River, 2000; Albums: Miaow, 1994; Carry On Up The Charts (compilation), 1994; Blue Is The Colour, 1996; Quench, 1998; Painting It Red, 2000; Solid Bronze: Great Hits (compilation), 2001.

ABDOU Saabou; b. 28 Dec. 1963, Maradi. Musician. m. Hassana, 5 s., 2 d. *Career:* Live Concert At Various Places. *Compositions:* Saadou; Bori; Carnaval; Tchoun Koussouma. *Recordings:* Carnaval; Tchoun Koussouma. *Honours:* Best Musician of The Year, 1998; Certificate of Honour, 1997. *Memberships:* ANACIM. *Leisure interests:* Traveling; Music; Film Watching. *Current Management:* Band Leader, Carnaval Maradi, Niger.

ABDUL Paula; b. 19 June 1963, Los Angeles, California, USA. Singer; Dancer; Choreographer. *Education:* Television and Radio Studies, Cal State, Northridge College. *Musical Education:* Studied jazz and tap dance. *Career:* Choreographer, LA Laker basketball cheerleaders; Scenes in films: Bull Durham; Coming To America; The Waiting Game; Appeared in a Saturday Night Live sketch with David Duchovny; Choreographer, pop videos including: The Jacksons and Mick Jagger: Torture; George Michael: Monkey; with Janet Jackson: Nasty; When I Think of You; What Have You Done For Me Lately; Fitness video, Cardio Dance; World-wide performances as singer include: Tours throughout US, UK, Japan and Far East; Prince's Trust Rock Gala, London Palladium, 1989; America Has Heart (earthquake and hurricane benefit concert), 1989; LIFEbeat's Counteraid (AIDS benefit concert), 1993; Own dance company, Co Dance; US No. 1 singles include: Straight Up; Forever Your Girl; Cold Hearted; Opposites Attract; Rush Rush; The Promise of a New Day. *Recordings:* Albums: Forever Your Girl (No. 1, USA), 1989; Shut Up and Dance (The Dance Mixes), 1990; Spellbound (No. 1, USA), 1991; Head Over Heels, 1995; Greatest Hits, 2000; features on: For Our Children (Disney charity album), 1991. *Honours:* MTV Video Award, Best Choreography, Janet Jackson's Nasty, 1987; Emmy, Best Choreography, for Tracey Ullman Show, 1989; Rolling Stone Awards, including Best Female Singer, 1989; American Music Awards include: Favourite Pop/Rock Female Vocalist, 1989, 1992; Billboard Magazine, Top Female Pop Album, 1990; Grammy, Best Music Video, Opposites Attract, 1991; Star on Hollywood Walk of Fame, 1993; Humanitarian of the Year, Starlight Foundation, Los Angeles, 1992; Numerous Gold and Platinum discs.

ABERCROMBIE John; b. 16 Dec. 1944, Portchester, New York, USA. Jazz Musician (guitar). *Musical Education:* Berklee School of Music, Boston, USA. *Career:* Musician with Johnny 'Hammond' Smith; Dreams (with Michael and Randy Brecker); Chico Hamilton Band; Gil Evans; Gato Barbieri; Billy Cobham's Spectrum; Founder, own trio Timeless; Founder, trio Gateway (with Jack DeJohnette and Dave Holland), 1975; Leader, own quartet, 1978; Also worked with: Ralph Towner; Michael Brecker; Jan Garbarek; Jack DeJohnette's New Directions; Jan Hammer. *Recordings:* Albums include: Timeless, 1974; Gateway, 1975; Characters, 1977; Night, 1984; Current Events, 1985; Getting There, 1988; While We're Young, 1992; Speak of The Devil, 1993; Gateway: Homecoming, 1994; Farewell, 1995; Tactics Live, 1996; Open Land, 1999.

ABILDGAARD Bertel; b. 2 April 1955, Soborg, Denmark. Entertainer; Actor; Songwriter; Musician. m. 14 July 1984, 1 s., 2 d. *Career:* Member, cabaret group, 5XKAJ, 1982–; Main character, Tony, in comedy, Room Service; Many television, radio appearances, radio plays; Solo artist, 1995. *Recordings:* Kajsynger Pop, 1984; Agte Kærlighed, 1987; Alle Bornene, 1991; Krumme Tær-sang, 1992; Films include: Kajs Fosdeldag, 1990. *Honour:* Se Og Hors Humor Pris, 1988. *Membership:* DPA (Danske Populærautører). *Current Management:* Erik Morbo/Vagn Moller, Dansk Dirma Og Hotel, Underholding Aps, Rosenyparken 81, 2670 Greve, Denmark.

ABORG Carl Anders; b. 24 March 1952, Malmö, Sweden. Musician; Journalist; Radio Prod.; Teacher. Divorced, 2 s., 1 d. *Education:* University Degree in Ethnology, Swedish and Media Communication. *Musical Education:* Self-taught musician. *Career:* Group, Aston Reymers Rivaler, 1979–85; Television, Own Show, 1981, Nygammalt, 1982; Stage, Roskilde, 1982; Film, Alska mig, 1984; Numerous Radio. *Compositions:* Sambo; Hall mig hart; Vi bygger om; Rosa-Lill; Grannens Fru. *Recordings:* With the Group, Aston Reymers Rivaler: Fran Myggjagare till fotrata, 1979; Kraal, 1980; Tval, 1981; Aston!, 1983; I grodornas land, 1984; Masterverk, 1995; With the Group Drompojkarna, Drompojkarna, 1978; With the Group OJJ!600, OJJ!600, 1986; With Prins Lätt, Nåt att guaga på, 1999. *Honours:* Munich Youth Prize for Film Animation, 1988. *Memberships:* MCHK; SKAP; BMW-Klubben. *Address:* Mariestadsvägen 17, 12150 Johanneshov, Sweden.

ABRAHAMS Mick; b. 7 April 1943, Luton, Bedfordshire, England. Musician (guitar). *Career:* Guitarist with Neil Christian; Dickie Pride; Toggery Five; McGregor's Engine; Member, Jethro Tull, 1967–69; Concerts include: Support to Pink Floyd, Hyde Park, 1968; Sunbury Jazz and Blues Festival, 1968; Founder, Blodwyn Pig; Solo artiste, 1971–; Financial consultant, 1970s-80s; Reformed Blodwyn Pig, 1988. *Recordings include:* with Jethro Tull: This Was, 1968; Love Story, 1969; with Blodwyn Pig: Ahead Rings Out, 1969; Getting To This, 1970; All Said and Done, 1991; Lies (A New Day), 1993; Solo albums: Mick Abrahams, 1971; A Musical Evening With Mick Abrahams, 1971; At Last, 1982. *Current Management:* Serious Bob Promotions, 250 W 85th St, Suite 11D, New York, NY 10024, USA.

ACE (Martin Ivor Kent); b. 30 March 1967, Cheltenham, Gloucestershire, England. Musician (Guitar). *Career:* Founder Member, Skunk Anansie, 1994; Signed to indie label One Little Indian, 1994; Numerous live appearances and appearances at festivals, on television and radio. *Recordings:* Singles: Little Baby Swastika; Weak; Brazen (Weep), 1997; Charlie Big Potato, 1999; Albums: Paranoid and Sunburnt, 1995; Stoosh, 1996; Post Orgasmic Chill, 1999.

ADA Paul; b. 22 Feb. 1962, Istanbul, Turkey. Composer; Singer; Musician (piano); Lyricist; Songwriter. *Musical Education:* Academy of Music of Anderlecht, Brussels; Piano Lessons. *Career:* Composer and Singer, Rever D'Aventures, Spirou and Fanfasio; cartoon; Working partners: Ralph Benatar, Serge Frances (lyrics), Michel de Neve (producer). *Compositions:* Songs for Belgian singers Paul Severs; Yasmine Art Sulivan; Caroline Jokris; Maria Mouzon (Africa); Evy Furman (Germany); Garcia del Valle (Spain). *Recordings:* Maryel Epps: Sing For Me; Curro Savoy: Songs for Whistle (Hollywood); Marc Garcia del Valle: Pienso enti, South America and Spain. *Publications:* Music of the Ballet; King Solomon and The Queen of Sheba, 1997; Music and Dreams: The Musical, 1995. *Honour:* Honour Student, Academy of Music. *Memberships:* Flight Case Music; Recording Student. *Leisure interest:* Swimming. *Address:* Rue Limnander 37, 1070, Brussels, Belgium.

ADAM F (Adam Fenton); b. 8 Feb. 1972, Liverpool, England. Prod.; Remixer; DJ. *Career:* Started career in a funk band; Moved into producing drum and bass for Lucky Spin Records, London; Released debut album, 1997; Started working with US rappers, producing Hip Hop, 2000; Collaborations: Redman; M.O.P.; Everything But The Girl. *Recordings:* Albums: Colours, 1997; Kaos, 2001; Singles: Circles, 1995; F-Jam, Metropolis, 1996; Music In My Mind, 1998; Smash Sumthin' (with Redman), Stand Clear (with M.O.P.), 2001. *Honours:* MOBO Award, Best Album, Colours, 1997. *Address:* c/o EMI Records, EMI House, 43 Brook Green, London, W6 7EF, England.

ADAMS (David) Ryan; b. 5 Nov. 1974, North Carolina, USA. Vocalist; Musician (guitar, piano); Songwriter. *Career:* Member of alternative country band Whiskeytown formed in Raleigh, North Carolina, 1994; Band split after the recording of Pneumonia album, 1998 (not released until 2001); solo career 2000-. *Recordings:* with Whiskeytown: Singles: Angels, 1995; Bloodshot Singles, 1997; Car Songs, 1997; Albums: Faithless Street, 1996; Rural Free Delivery, 1997; Stranger's Almanac, 1997; Pneumonia, 2001; solo: Single: New York, New York, 2001; Albums: Heartbreaker, 2000; Gold, 2001; features on: Real – The Tom T Hall Project, 1998; Return of The Grievous Angel, 1999; Timeless – Hank Williams Tribute, 2001. *Honours:* Brit Award, Best International Male nominee, 2002. *Current Management:* FCC Management, 209 10th Ave S, Nashville TN 37203, USA.

ADAMS Ben, (Benjamin Anthony Edward Stevens); b. 22 Nov. 1981, Middlesex, England. Vocalist; Musician (piano, violin, oboe); Songwriter. *Career:* Former head chorister, St Margaret's, Westminster Abbey; Sang solos on two albums and performed in front of Pope John Paul II and Queen Elizabeth II; Joined A1 pop group; Signed recording contract, 1999; Sell-out theatre tours of South-East Asia and UK, 2000–01. *Recordings:* Albums: Here We Come, 1999; The A List, 2000; Singles: Be The First To Believe, Summertime of Our Lives, Ready Or Not/Everytime, 1999; Like A Rose,

Take On Me, Same Old Brand New You, 2000; No More, 2001; Caught In The Middle, 2002. *Honours:* Brit Award, Best Newcomer, 2001; Also honoured at MTV Mandarin Music Awards. *Current Management:* c/o Byrne Blood Ltd. *Internet:* www.a1-online.com.

ADAMS Bob; b. 10 March 1922, Dalkeith, Scotland. Musician (saxophones, clarinet, bass clarinet, flute). m. Audrey Mason, 30 April 1948, 2 s. *Musical Education:* Choir boy, Duke of Buccleuch's Private Chapel; Taught by parents. *Career:* Geraldo Orchestra, 1947–55; Jack Parnell Orchestra, ATV 1956–63; Emigrated to South Africa, 1963–80; MD, Guys and Dolls; Fiddler On The Roof; Cabaret in Johannesburg; Conductor for many artistes visiting South Africa including: Englebert Humperdinck; Marlene Deitrich; Frankie Laine; Johnny Mathis; Jerry Lewis; Eartha Kitt; Kenneth McKellar. *Compositions:* Scored 4 films for 20th Century Fox Studios, South Africa; Composition: When I See a Rainbow, chosen for World Song Festival, Tokyo, 1975; Chappells Music and Boosey and Hawkes Music Library. *Recordings:* Switched On Sax; Let's Party With Bob; Upon a Time; Tales For Children. *Membership:* Musicians' Union. *Leisure interest:* Music. *Address:* 50 Brick Farm Close, Richmond, Surrey TW9 4EG, England.

ADAMS Bryan; b. 5 Nov. 1959, Kingston, Ontario, Canada. Vocalist; Songwriter; Musician (guitar). *Career:* International recording artist; Numerous world-wide tours; Album sales have exceeded 40m. copies. *Recordings:* Albums: Bryan Adams, 1980; You Want It You Got It, 1981; Cuts Like a Knife, 1983; Reckless, 1984; Into The Fire, 1987; Waking Up The Neighbours, 1991; So Far So Good, 1993; Live! Live!, 1995; 18 'Til I Die, 1996; MTV Unplugged, 1987; On a Day Like Today, 1998; Best of Me, 2001; Singles include: Summer of '69, 1985; Heaven, 1985; Run To You, 1985; Can't Stop This Thing We Started, 1991; There Will Never Be Another Tonight, 1991; It's Only Love (with Tina Turner); Everything I Do I Do It For You (theme from Robin Hood-Prince of Thieves), 1991; All I Want Is You, 1992; Please Forgive Me, 1993; All For Love (with Sting and Rod Stewart), 1993; Have You Ever Really Loved a Woman, 1995; I Finally Found Someone (with Barbra Streisand), 1996; Star, 1996; The Only Thing That Looks Good On Me Is You, 1996; Let's Make a Night To Remember, 1996; On a Day Like Today, 1998; When You're Gone (with Melanie C), 1998. *Honours:* Longest standing No. 1 in UK singles chart, 16 weeks, Everything I Do, I Do It For You, 1991; 15 Canadian Juno Awards; Grammy Award; American Music Award; 3 Academy Award nominations for film soundtracks. *Current Management:* Bruce Allen Talent, Suite 406, 68 Water St, Vancouver, British Columbia V6B 1A4, Canada.

ADAMS Faye Ann; b. 24 March 1952, Allentown, Pennsylvania, USA. Certified Music Specialist in Voice; Musical (piano, band and orchestral) Instructor. m. Ronald G Adams, 19 Oct. 1974, 2 d. *Education:* BSc; Masters Degree, Elementary Education, Kutztown State University. *Musical Education:* Mansfield State University School of Music. *Career:* Soprano; Piano accompanist; Proprietor and Instructor, Willing Hearts, Hands and Voices Music Studio; Former Head Music Specialist, Reading City School District; Singer and Soloist in Pennsylvania German Dialect, Soloist, German Festival (Heemt Fescht). *Publication:* Events at Allemangel: Historic research on Berks County history, 1995. *Honour:* Zeswitz Music Award for Music Achievement, 1973, 1974. *Leisure interest:* Singing Christian music in German dialect. *Address:* 42 George Rd, Lenhartsville, PA 19534, USA.

ADAMS Michael; b. 20 May 1951, Birmingham, Alabama, USA. Musician. m. Marsha Adams, 1 s., 2 d. *Musical Education:* BS, Music Education, Tennessee State University; MM, Percussion, Roosevelt University, Chicago, Illinois. *Career:* Played with Skokie Valley Symphony, Chicago Civic Orchestra, New York City Ballet, Merit Music Programme, Lyric Opera of Chicago and Von Freeman (jazz). *Composition:* Sonata Ico for Marimba Quintet. *Recording:* Misled, song on album Mirror Town, Ronnie Laws. *Contribution to:* Chicago Sun Times, 1989. *Memberships:* Phi Mu Alpha; Sinfonia; Percussive Arts Society. *Address:* 15505 Cottage Grove, Dolton, IL 60419, USA.

ADAMS Oleta; b. Seattle, Washington, USA. Vocalist. *Career:* Leader, own trio, 1980s; Cabaret singer, Kansas; Discovered by Tears For Fears, 1985; Singer with Tears For Fears, album and tours, 1987; Solo artiste, 1990-. *Recordings:* Albums: Circle of One, 1990; Evolution, 1993; Never Knew, 1995; Movin' On, 1995; Come Walk With Me, 1997; The Very Best Of..., 1998; All The Love, 2001; Singles: Rhythm of Life, 1990; Get Here, 1991; Circle of One, 1991; Don't Let The Sun Go Down On Me, 1992; I Just Had To Hear Your Voice, 1993; Tracks with Tears For Fears: Woman In Chains, Badman's Song, on album, The Seeds of Love, 1989. *Honours:* Grammy nomination, 1991. *Current Management:* Morey Management Group, 335 N 345 N Maple Dr., Suite 351, Beverly Hills, CA 90210, USA.

ADDISON Ben; Musician (drums). *Career:* Former Member, Boys Wonder; Formed Corduroy, for one-off gig; Decided to continue and obtained record deal; Several UK top ten hits. *Recordings:* Singles: Something In My Eye; The Frighteners; London, England; The Joker is Wild; Overhauls; Albums:

Dad Man Cat, 1992; High Havoc, 1993; Out of Here, 1994; The New You, 1997.

ADDISON Scott; Musician (keyboards); Singer. *Career:* Former Member, Boys Wonder; Member, Corduroy; Played one-off gig as Corduroy, decided to continue; Obtained record deal; Several UK top ten hits. *Recordings:* Singles: Something in My Eye; The Frighteners; London, England; The Joker is Wild; Albums: Dad Man Cat, 1992; High Havoc, 1993; Out of Here, 1994; The New You, 1997.

ADE King Sunny; b. 1 Sept. 1946, Oshogbo, Nigeria. Singer. *Career:* Played with semi-professional juju bands, Nigeria; Lead guitarist, Rhythm Dandies, 1964; Also played with Tunde Nightingale; Formed the Green Spots, 1966; Renamed the African Beats, late 60s; Formed own label, Sunny Alade Records, 1975; Established the Ariya, own juju nightclub, Lagos, Nigeria; Also owns an oil firm, a mining company and a film and video production company; Founded the King Sunny Ade Foundation for young musicians and performers, Lagos; Formed supergroup, The Way Forward, 1996; Tours include UK, US and Japan; African Beats dissolved; Currently playing in Nigeria, with new group Golden Mercury; Appeared in films: Juju Music, 1988; Live At Montreux, 1990; Roots of Rhythm, 1997. *Recordings:* Numerous albums include: Alanu Loluwa, 1967; Sunny Ade Live Play, 1976; In London, 1977; Festac 77, 1978; The Message, 1981; Ariya Special, 1982; Conscience, 1982; Juju Music, 1982; Synchro System, 1983; Aura, 1984; Otito, 1985; Saviour, 1986; Funmilayo, 1989; Live At The Hollywood Palace, 1992; E Dide, 1995; Odu, 1998; Singles include: Challenge Cup, 1967. *Address:* c/o Atomic Communications Group, 6226 1/2 Manchester Ave, Los Angeles, CA 90045, USA.

ADEDAYO Shola, (Olu-Shola); b. 27 April 1964, Nigeria. Singer. *Education:* Trained as nurse. *Musical Education:* Studio programmer. *Career:* Many ventures with African band Leke Leke, 1990–93; Member, all-girl dance band Orage; Managing Director, recording company. *Recordings:* Album: with Leke Leke: Leke Leke; Single: with Orage: Body and Soul. *Memberships:* Musicians' Union; BASCA; Music of Black Origin. *Leisure interests:* Writing lyrics. *Current Management:* Taurus Records (UK). *Address:* 12 Queen Adelaide Rd, Penge, London SE20 7DX, England.

ADEJUMO Shade; b. 12 Aug. 1963, Paddington, London, England. Singer; Songwriter. *Career:* Backing vocalist with: Carroll Thompson; Lavine Hudson; Take That; Mica Paris; Sting; Yazz; David Grant; Television appearances: Richard Littlejohn Show; Michael Ball Show; The White Room; The South Bank Show; The Brit Awards; Concerts include: Wembley Arena; The Grand; The Marquee; The London Palladium; Radio broadcast: BBC2. *Membership:* Musicians' Union. *Leisure interests:* Jogging; Reading. *Address:* 32 Red Post Hill, Herne Hill, London SE24 9JQ, England.

ADKINS Trace (Tracy Deryl); b. 13 Jan. 1962, Sarepta, Louisiana, USA. Country vocalist; Musician (guitar). *Musical Education:* Louisiana Tech, music student. *Career:* After graduation, worked on an oil rig for several years before deciding to pursue musical career; Joined gospel quartet the New Commitments; After two albums, decided upon a solo career, early 1990s; Signed to Capitol Nashville by label president Scott Hendricks after discovery in Nashville; Survived 1994 shooting incident and two car crashes; Made steady progress on both Billboard's country album and singles charts, including a #1 single (This Ain't) No Thinkin' Thing, 1997; Sentenced to two days in jail after pleading guilty to drunk driving charges, 2001. *Compositions include:* The Rest of Mine. *Recordings include:* Every Light In The House, 1996; (This Ain't) No Thinkin' Thing, I Left Something Turned On At Home, The Rest of Mine, 1997; Lonely Won't Leave Me Alone, 1998; Albums include: Dreamin' Out Loud, 1996; Big Time, 1997; More, 1999; Chrome, 2001. *Address:* c/o The Country Music Asscn, Nashville, Tennessee, USA. *Internet:* www.traceadkins.com.

ADLER Richard; b. 3 Aug. 1921, New York City, USA. Composer; Lyricist; Prod. *Career:* Collaborator with Jerry Ross, music and lyrics for musicals: Pajama Game, 1954; Damn Yankees, 1955; Composer, lyricist, Kwamina, 1961; Television productions: Little Women, 1959; Gift of The Magi, 1959; Produced White House shows, salutes and galas for President Kennedy and President Johnson, 1962–65; Composer, lyricist, producer: A Mother's Kisses, 1968; Revival of Pajama Game, 1973; Rex, 1976; Commissions include: Wilderness Suite, for Dept of Interior; The Lady Remembers, Retrospectrum, for Statue of Liberty/Ellis Island; Eight By Adler, for Chicago City Ballet; Chicago (ballet), for City of Chicago; Fanfare and Overture, US Olympic Festival, for Olympic Committee, 1987; Producer of several Broadway shows. *Honours include:* Variety Critics Poll Winner, The Pajama Game, 1954; 3 Pulitzer Prize Nominations; Inducted into Songwriters Hall of Fame, 1984. *Memberships:* Dramatists Guild; Songwriters Guild of America; Trustee, John F Kennedy Center For The Performing Arts, 1964–77.

ADOLFSSON Jorgen; b. 14 March 1951, Hallingeberg, Sweden. Musician; Composer. m. Vered Adolfsson Mann, 13 April 1994, 1 s., 1 d. *Education:* Art and Film History, Stockholm University; Classical Violin, 1961–69. *Career:* Member, Archimedes Badkar, Ramlosa Kvallar, Iskra, Vargavinter, Bitter Funeral Beer Band, Karl Brothers, Uroboro; Performer of Music for Modern Choreographers including Kenneth Kvarnstrom, Cristina Caprioli, Bogdan Szyber, Carina Reich, Greta Lindholm, Efva Lilja; Television and Radio Productions; Performed with Don Cherry, Mongezi Feza, Johnny Dyani, Jon Rose, Lars Gullin, Raymond Strid, Tommy Adolfsson. *Compositions:* Grodsymfonin, 1976; Ancient Evenings, Future Mornings, 1984; Exhibo Suite, 1990; Syrinx Svit, 1991; Music in Sand, 1991; Fem Danser, 1995; Digger Dog, 1995. *Recordings:* With Iskra, Allemansratt, Besvarjelser, Fantasies; Luft; With Bitter Funeral Beer Band, Bitter Funeral Beer; With Karl Brothers, Air Change; With Vargavinter, S/T, Roster Fran Alla Land; With Archimedes Badkar, II, Tre, Afro 70; with Per Tjernberg: Universal Riddim. *Honours:* Grand Prix, International Video Danse/Carina Ari, 1992. *Memberships:* STIM; FSJ; SKAP; Fylkingen. *Current Management:* Musikcentrum, Chapmansgatan 4, 11236 Stockholm, Sweden. *Address:* Selmedalsringen 8 4 tr, 129 36 Hagersten, Sweden.

ADOLFSSON Tommy C; b. 21 Oct. 1953, Ljusdal, Halsingland, Sweden. m. Cecilia Johansson, 1 d. *Education:* Economy College, 1969–72; Development Studies, Sussex University, England, Sweden, Tanzania, Malawi, Zambia, Madagascar, 1976–78; Marketing courses for artists, 1991, 1995. *Musical Education:* Trumpet Studies, Music School, 1963–70; Trumpet Studies, Stockholm Music Conservatory, 1970–74; Music Studies, England, 1976; Music Studies, Senegal, Tanzania, 1976; Music Studies, Theory and Ensemble play, Birkagarden Music College, 1980–82; Music Studies, Bali and Java, 1983; Music Studies, India, 1984; Japanese Taiko Drum music studies, 1990. *Career:* Archimedes Bathtube, world music group, 1974–82; ISKRA, free improvised music, 1980–85; Bitter Funeral Beer Band, afro-jazz, 1980–86; Half Nelson, brassband, 1985–88; DAST, Quartet, South African music and poetry, 1985–90; Kenneth Kvarnstrom Danscompany, modern ballet, 1989–91; Swedish Radio jazz group, 1990–94; Peter Bryngelsson Project, 1992; Cristina Caprioli Danscompany, 1992–93; Tuomo Hapaalas Waterorchestra, Stockholm Waterfestival, 1994; Jazz group Krakatau, Finland, 1995–96. *Compositions:* Wet Fantasy, ISKRA; Three Voices on a White Line; Echoes Beyond Joy and Despair; Baptismal Song; IA; Syrinx Suite, CD, Karl Brothers; Ballet Music: 1989–91: XXX; Exhibo; Trio, Duo, Solo: 1992: Ubergang; Damp; Luege, 1993; Theatre Music: 1996: The Jurt, A Stormy History; The Dolphin. *Recordings:* Archimedes Bathtube, Three, 1975–78; Bitter Funeral Beer Band, 1981; ISKRA, Fantasies, 1984; Bitter Funereal Beer Band 2, Praise Drumming, 1986; Karl Brothers, Air Change, 1994. *Honours:* Academy of Art Awards, 1985, 1991, 1993, 1994, 1997; STIM Award, 1995. *Memberships:* STIM; SAMI; SKAP. *Leisure interests:* Cooking food from different cultures; Travel; Going to modern dance performances. *Address:* Torkel Knutssonsgatan 39, 2 tr, 118 49 Stockholm, Sweden.

ADSHEAD Christopher John; b. 3 April 1966. Musician (Bass guitar). 1 d. *Career:* Joined RAF Central Band, 1984; QEII World Cruise, 1990; Summer season in Devon, 1991; Moved to London, worked at Talk of London nightclub, played in shows including Cats at the New London Theatre and the Cats British tour, 1993–95; Played in Joseph and the Amazing Technicolour Dreamcoat with Phillip Schofield at Hammersmith Apollo, 1995–96; Played on Grease British tour with Shane Ritchie, 1996–97; Played in Boogie Nights with Shane Ritchie, 1997–99; Television credits include Pebble Mill at One, Richard and Judy Tonight, The Six O'clock Show, Talking Telephone Numbers, Going Live/Live and Kicking, Night Fever; Radio credits include Paul Jones Blues Night, Friday Night is Music Night; Concerts include The Monaghan Blues Festival with Out of the Blue. *Recordings:* Marilla Ness: From Where I Stand; Shane Ritchie: The Album; Boogie Nights: Cast Album. *Leisure interests:* Reading; West Ham football club. *Address:* 72 Clarkes Dr., Uxbridge, Middlesex UB8 3UL, England.

AERTS Raymond Benedict Charles; b. 12 April 1966, Amsterdam, Netherlands. Theatre and Concert Prod.; Artist Agent and Man. m. Sarah Frances Kate Reÿs-Smith, 1 Aug. 1992. *Education:* Marketing Communications. *Musical Education:* School of Music, piano. *Career:* with Charles Aerts Theatre Productions International, concert and theatre productions for: Liza Minelli; Ray Charles; Shirley Bassey; Bold and Beautiful In Concert; Lionel Hampton; Don McLean; Oklahoma!; Elvis; Annie Get Your Gun; Maria de Lourdes; Artists represented include: Charles Aznavour; Gilbert Bécaud; Nana Mouskouri; Julien Clerc; Lionel Hampton; Maria Callas; Don McLean; Shirley Bassey. *Honours:* with Charles Aerts Theatre Productions International: Ridder, Orde van Oranje Nassau, Netherlands; Chevalier, Ordre des Arts et des Lettres, France; Vecta Mem. of Honour; Cultural awards and honours from: Brazil; Hungary; Bulgaria; Indonesia. *Membership:* Vecta. *Leisure interests:* Sports; Film; Music.

AGERSKOV Flemming Michael; b. 29 Sept. 1963, Holstebro, Denmark. 2 d. *Musical Education:* Studied Classical Trumpet, Conservatory in Aarhus, 1983–85; Japanese Music, Kyoto, Japan, 1985–86. *Career:*

Played with Marc Johnson, Eliane Elias, Marilyn Mazur, Jonas Johansen, Jon Balke, Martin France, Joakim Milder, Fredrik Lundin; Ray Charles; Iain Bellamy; Josefine Cronholm; Formed own group, Face to Face, with Martin France, Julian Argüelles; Jesper Nordenstroem and Hans Andersson, 1997. *Compositions:* Arctic Views; With Closed Eyes. *Recordings:* CV Joergensen: Sjaelland; Kim Kristensen: A Jazzpar 93 Project on Storyville; Ane Ramlose Sextet: Days Without Make Up; Takuan, Takuan; Face to Face, 1999. *Honours:* Trumpet Player of the Year, 1991; Danish Music Award, Push To Participate, Takuan, 2001. *Address:* Holbergsgade 18, 1 TV, 1057 Copenhagen K, Denmark. *Internet:* www.face2face.dk.

AGUILAR Pepe; b. San Antonio, Texas. Vocalist. *Career:* Son of Antonio Aguilar and Flor Silvestre; Began singing, aged 3; Collaborations include: Rocio Durcal; Vikki Carr; Has produced for Jose Julian; Guadalupe Pineda; Antonio Aguilar. *Recordings:* Recuerdame Bonito, 1992; Chiquilla Bonita, 1995; Con Tambora, 1995; Que Bueno Mariachi, 1995; Exitos Con Banda, 1997; Por Mujeres Como Tu, 1998; Por El Amor De Siempre, Por Una Mujer Bonita, 1999; Grande De Los Grande, 2000; Mejor De Nosotros, Tambora 2 – Cautiva Y Triste, 2001. *Internet:* www.pepeaguilar.com.

AGUILERA Christina Maria; b. 18 Dec. 1980, Staten Island, New York, USA. Vocalist. *Career:* Appeared on US Star Search TV talent show aged 8; Joined cast of Orlando-based TV show The New Mickey Mouse Club aged 12; Intensive world-wide promotional touring since 1997; Signed recording contract in 1998 following inclusion on Disney's Mulan OST; Numerous TV appearances including Christmas At The White House spectacular, 1999 and Super Bowl 2000 half-time show. *Recordings:* Albums: Christina Aguilera, 1999; Mi Reflejo, 2000; My Kind of Christmas, 2000; Singles: All I Wanna Do (with Keizo Nakanishi), 1997; Reflection (from Mulan), 1998; Genie In A Bottle, 1999; What A Girl Wants, 1999; Come On Over Baby (All I Want Is You), 2000; I Turn To You, 2000; Lady Marmalade (with Lil' Kim, Mya and Pink), 2001. *Honours:* Grammy, Best New Artist, 2000; ALMA Award, Best New Entertainer, 2000; Billboard Award, Female Vocalist of The Year, 2000; Billboard Latin Music Award, Best Pop Album of The Year, Mi Reflejo, 2001. *Address:* c/o Irving Azoff, 3500 W Olive Ave, Suite 600, Burbank, CA 91505, USA.

AHLIN Tina; b. 6 July 1967, Stockholm, Sweden. Musician (Piano); Singer; Arranger; Composer. *Career:* Several big pop acts and pop tours around Scandinavia; Lisa Wilsson, Orup, Tomas Dileva; Musician, lots of records; worked with several television productions and television orchestra; Written arrangements to Swedish Radio Symphony Orchestra, Choirs, Big Bands; Work with lots of Jazz and Pop Concerts. *Address:* Ehrensvardsg 2, 3 tr, 112 35 Stockholm, Sweden.

AHROLD Robert Liam (Ro bbin); b. 29 Sept. 1943, Washington, USA. Copyright Exec. m. Kyle Warren, 20 March 1972, 2 d. *Education:* BSc, Foreign Service School, Georgetown University. *Career:* Reporter, Time Magazine, 1967–71; Various positions, Home Box Office, including Director, Special Programming; Director, Corporate Public Relations, 1974–82; Producer, Executive producer, Celebration, first pay television Rock Series, 1975; Vice President, Corporate Relations, RCA Records, 1982–87; Various pay television music specials for HBO including: Country In New York, 1976; Vice President, Corporate Relations, Broadcast Music Inc, 1987–. *Publications:* Editor, publisher, Musicworld (quarterly membership magazine for BMI). *Honours:* Vice President, Board of Governors, New York Chapter, NARAS; NATAS; Country Music Asscn; Gospel Music Asscn; National Academy Popular Music. *Leisure interests:* Photography; Art; Scuba; Cycling. *Address:* c/o Broadcast Music Inc, 320 W 57th St, New York, NY 10019, USA.

AHVENLAHTI Olli; b. 6 Aug. 1949, Finland. Composer; Musician (piano, keyboards). *Education:* Musicology, English Philology, Helsinki University, 1968–73. *Musical Education:* Piano from age 7; Sibelius Academy from age 11; Berklee College of Music, Boston, US. *Career:* First jazz concert, Hasse Walli-Make Lievonen Sextet, 1969; Collaborated with Mike Koskinen, Pekka Pöyry, Esko Rsnell; Founding member, The Group, 1970s; Represented Finland, Nordring radio contest; Formed quintet with trumpeter Markku Johansson, 1970s; Chief conductor, TV1, Finnish Broadcasting Company, 1990–; Pianist, backing singer Vesa-Matti Loiri. *Compositions:* Composer, arranger for UMO (New Music Orchestra); Music for theatre, film, television dramas; Piece based on texts from Herman Hesse's Glass Bead Game. *Honour:* Yrjö Award, Finnish Jazz Federation, 1975.

AIREY Don; b. 21 June 1948, Sunderland, England. Musician (Keyboards); Arranger; Conductor. m. Doris, 25 March 1977, 2 s., 1 d. *Education:* Nottingham University, England. *Musical Education:* Royal Manchester College of Music. *Career:* Member of Groups: Colosseum II, 1975–78; Rainbow, 1978–81; Ozzy Osbourne, 1982–85; Jethro Tull, 1986–87; Whitesnake, 1988–90; Gary Moore Blues Band, 1990–91; Session Player, Arranger, 1992–95; ELO, 1996–97; Conducted winning entry, Eurovision Song Contest. *Compositions:* Numerous co-writes on

various heavy metal albums. *Recordings:* Down to Earth, Rainbow; Blizzard of Oz, Ozzy Osbourne; Whitesnake 87, Whitesnake; Still Got the Blues, Gary Moore; Variations, Andrew Lloyd Webber; 20 Years of Jethro Tull, Jethro Tull, 1988; Back To The Light, Brian May, 1993; Solo album, K2, Tales of Triumph and Tragedy, Don Airey. *Honour:* Eurovision 97. *Membership:* BASCA; PRS. *Leisure interests:* Cricket; Photography; Football Supporter (Sunderland). *Current Management:* Sound Evision Enterprises Ltd. *Address:* 4 Hardwick Rd Ind Pk, Gt Gransden, Sandy, Bedfordshire SG19 3BJ, England.

AITKEN Matt; b. 25 Aug. 1956. Songwriter; Prod. *Career:* Member, pop band Agents Aren't Aeroplanes, with Mike Stock and Pete Waterman, 1980s; Member, songwriting/production team Stock Aitken Waterman (SAW), 1984–93; Co-founder, PWL label, 1988; Co-producer with Mike Stock, Love This Records, 1994-. *Recordings:* Albums: Hit Factory, 1987; Hit Factory, Vol. 2, 1988; Hit Factory, Vol. 3, 1989; The Best of Stock Aitken and Waterman, 1990; Single: Roadblock, 1987; As co-writer, producer, hit singles include: You Spin Me Round, Dead Or Alive (No. 1, UK), 1984; So Macho, Sinitta, 1986; Respectable, Mel and Kim (No. 1, UK), 1987; Never Gonna Give You Up, Rick Astley, 1987; with Kylie Minogue: I Should Be So Lucky (No. 1, 12 countries), 1988; Got To Be Certain, 1988; The Locomotion, 1988; Hand On Your Heart (No. 1, UK), 1989; Better The Devil You Know, 1990; with Robson Green and Jerome Flynn: Unchained Melody (No. 1, UK), 1995; I Believe/Up On The Roof (No. 1, UK), 1995; What Becomes of The Broken Hearted (No. 1, UK), 1996; Other recordings with: Jason Donovan; Sonia; Brother Beyond; Big Fun; Donna Summer; Divine; Hazell Dean. *Honours:* Brit Award, Best Producer, Stock Aitken Waterman, 1988. *Address:* c/o Love This Records, Hundred House, 100 Union St, London SE1 0NL, England.

AJAO Steven John; b. 1 Oct. 1952, Birmingham, England. Musician (blues guitar, saxophone). 1 s. *Education:* Moseley School of Art, Lanchester Polytechnic (Art). *Musical Education:* Self-taught. *Career:* Mainly blues guitarist to 1981; Started to play alto and tenor saxophone; Numerous jazz club appearances; Played with: Red Rodney, Brighton, 1987; Bude Jazz Festival, 1988; Le Puy Peace Festival, 1989; Recorded sessions for Ali Campbell (UB40); Slade; Mickey Greaney. *Leisure interests:* Drawing; Painting; Sculpture. *Current Management:* Bob Lamb. *Address:* 122a Highbury Rd, Kings Heath, Birmingham B14 7QP, England.

AKENDENGUE Pierre Claver; b. 25 April 1943, Aouta, Gabon. Psychologist; Musician. m. Michelle Ossouach, 31 Aug. 1997, 6 s., 3 d. *Education:* Physiotherapy, 1968–69. *Musical Education:* PhD, Psychology, Sorbonne, 1987; Musicology; Ethnomusicology. *Career:* Many compositions and recordings; Concerts world-wide including Africa, Europe, Canada, West Indies, Japan. *Compositions:* Nandipo Nkere, Powe; Owende; Africa Obota; Awana; Silence; Maladalite; Piroguier Lambarena. *Recordings:* Nandipo, 1974; Africa Obota, 1976; Awana, 1982; Silence, 1990; Lambarena, 1995; Maladalite, 1995; Espoir a Soweto, 1997; Passe Compose, 1997. *Honours:* Prize, Young Singers, SACEM, 1976; Best Film Music Award, FESCAPO, 1985; RFI Trophy, 1989. *Memberships:* Founder, Gabonese Asscn of Artists and Performers. *Leisure interest:* Reading. *Current Management:* Melodie, 50 rue Stendhal, 75020 Paris, France. *Address:* PO Box 13, 305 Libreiville, Gabon.

AKIYOSHI Toshiko; b. 12 Dec. 1929, Dairen, Manchuria, China. Musician (piano); Composer. m. (1) Charlie Mariano; (2) Lew Tabackin. *Musical Education:* Classically-trained piano; Berklee College of Music, Boston, USA. *Career:* Successful jazz pianist, Japan; Recorded for Norman Granz; Moved to USA; Member, various groups including Charlie Mariano; Charles Mingus; Became composer, especially for big bands; Worked with saxophonist (later her husband) Lew Tabackin, Los Angeles, early 1970s; Leader own small group; Subject, documentary film Toshiko Akiyoshi, Jazz Is My Native Language, 1984. *Recordings:* Toshiko's Piano, 1953; Amazing Toshiko Akiyoshi, 1954; The Toshiko Trio, 1954; Jam Session For Musicians III: The Historic Mocambo Session '54, 1954; Toshiko Her Trio, 1956; Toshiko Her Quartet, 1956; The Many Sides of Toshiko, 1957; United Nations, 1958; Toshiko Meets Her Old Pals, 1961; Country and Western Jazz Pianos (with Steve Kühn), 1963; Mariano-Toshiko Quartet, 1963; Toshiko Akiyoshi, 1965; Toshiko At The Top of The Gate, 1968; Toshiko Akiyoshi Quartet Vols I-III, 1970–71; Solo Piano, 1971; Dedications, 1976–77; Plays Billy Strayhorn, 1978; Finesse, 1978; Interlude, 1987; Remembering Bud, Cleopatra's Dream, 1990; Carnegie Hall Concert Live, 1991; Albums with Lew Tabackin: Kogun, 1974; Long Yellow Road, 1974–75; Tales of a Courtesan, 1975; Road Time, 1976; Insights, 1976; March of The Tadpoles, 1977; Dedications II, 1977; Live At Newport '77, 1977; Sumi-e, 1979; Farewell To Mingus, 1980; From Toshiko With Love, 1981; Tanuki's Night Out, 1981; European Memoirs, 1982; Carnegie Hall Concert Live, 1991; Live At Maybeck Recital Hall, 1995.

AKKERMAN Jan; b. 24 Dec. 1946, Amsterdam, Netherlands. Musician (guitar, lute); Composer; Arranger. *Musical Education:* Gradutate, Music Lyceum, Amsterdam. *Career:* Member, groups including: Johnny and The

Cellar Rockers, 1958; The Hunters; Brainbox, 1969; Focus, 1969–76; Solo artiste, 1973–; Periodic reunions with Focus; Member, side project Forcefield, with Ray Fenwick and Cozy Powell, 1988–89. *Recordings:* Albums: with Focus: In and Out of Focus, 1971; Moving Waves, 1971; Focus III, 1972; At The Rainbow, 1973; Hamburger Concerto, 1974; Mother Focus, 1975; Focus Con Proby, 1977; House of The King, 1983; Pass Me Not, 1995; Solo albums: Profile, 1973; Tabernakel, 1974; Eli, 1977; Jan Akkerman, 1978; Arunjuez, 1978; Live, 1979; 3, 1980; It Could Happen To You, 1985; Can't Stand Noise, 1986; Pleasure Point, 1987; The Noise of Art, 1990; Heartware, 1998; with Forcefield: The Talisman, 1988; To Oz and Back, 1989; Singles: with Focus: House of The King, 1971; Hocus Pocus, 1971; Sylvia, 1972. *Honours:* Melody Maker Poll Winner, Best Guitarist, 1973. *Address:* c/o Bert Bijlsma, P/A Hamrikkerweg 4, 9943 TB, NW Scheemda, Netherlands.

AKYUZ Osman Refik; b. 16 June 1974, Istanbul, Turkey. Recording Engineer; Prod.; Musician (Vocals, Bass Guitar, Keyboards). *Musical Education:* Capital University; The Recording Workshop, USA; Ulster County College; Timur Selcuk Music School. *Career:* Video Clips, Happy, Let Me Be, Major Radio Stations in Turkey; Süüpeermeen. *Compositions:* Happy; Aydede; Let Me Be; Sunday Morning; The Land of Sand; Ascend; A Sail To Sky. *Recordings:* Atonall; Iksir. *Leisure interests:* Cycling; Photography; Travel. *Address:* Zergerdan SOK, No. 22 80850 Emirgan, Istanbul, Turkey.

ALAKOTILA Timo Pekka; b. 15 July 1959, Finland. Musician (Piano). *Education:* Conservatory of Helsimes. *Career:* Member of Several Groups Including, JPP, Maria Kalamehi and Aldargaz, Troka, Luwa Nova; Performed in Man countries Including, USA, England, France, Germany, Sweden, Finland, Canada. *Compositions:* Folkmoods West; About 60 Pieces for Diferent Groups. *Recordings:* 6 Records with JPP; 3 Records with Maria Kalamehi and Aldargaz; 3 Records with Opera Singer; 2 Records with Troka. *Honours:* Album of the Year, 1988; Nvor Svom Prize, 1995. *Current Management:* Howdown, Laivurinrinne, Helsinki. *Address:* Impilinnankatu, 3C 52 FIN 05800 Hyvinkaa, Finland.

ALAN Mark; b. 14 Sept. 1939, Elizabeth, New Jersey, USA. Personal Man.; Agent. 1 s., 1 d. *Education:* BSc, Masters, Speech and Theatre. *Career:* Premier Talent Agency, New York City, 1965–68; President, New Beat Management, New York City, 1968–71; Artists included: Tommy James and the Shondells; The Illusion; Robin McNamara; The Sidekicks; Exile; Worked with Jeff Barry and Tommy James; Manager, Andre Cymone; Airkraft; Zwarte; President and owner, National Talent Associates, Minneapolis; President, Mark Alan Agency, 1988–; Manager for Illerazzum, Every Mother's Nightmare and Peter Phippen. *Recordings:* As manager include: The Dance Electric, Andre Cymone; Did You See Her Eyes, The Illusion; Lay A Little Lovin' On Me, Robin McNamara; with Tommy James: Draggin the Line; Come to Me; Ball and Chain; She; Ball of Fire; Sweet Cherry Wine; Crimson and Clover; Crystal Blue Persuasion; with Zwarte: Zwarte; Hit the Road; Easy Street; with Peter Phippen: Book of Dreams; Albums: with The Illusion: The Illusion; Together (As a Way of Life); withHow Does It Feel; Tommy James: Crimson and Clover; Best of Tommy James and The Shondells; Travelin'; Tommy James; LP, Tommy James; with Robin McNamara: Lay A Little Lovin' On Me; with Andre Cymone: AC. *Current Management:* Mark Alan Agency, PO Box 21323, St Paul, MN 55121, USA.

ALBARN Damon; b. 23 March 1968, Whitechapel, London, England. Vocalist; Songwriter. *Education:* Drama School, Stratford East, 1 year. *Musical Education:* Part-time Music course, Goldsmith's College. *Career:* First solo concerts, Colchester Arts Centre; Member: Blur; Gorillaz; Numerous television and radio appearances, include: Later With Jools Holland; Top of The Pops; Loose Ends, Radio 4; Later With. . . Britpop Now; Extensive tours, concerts include: Alexandra Palace, Reading Festival, 1993; Glastonbury, 1994; Mile End, 1995; V97, 1997; UK Arena Tour, 1997; Glastonbury, 1998; T in the Park, 1999; Reading and Leeds Festival, 1999; Actor, film, Face, 1997. *Recordings:* Albums: with Blur: Leisure, 1991; Modern Life Is Rubbish, 1993; Parklife, 1994; The Great Escape, 1995; Blur, 1997; 13, 1999; The Best of Blur, 2000; with Gorillaz: Gorillaz, 2001; Singles: with Blur: She's So High, 1990; There's No Other Way, 1991; Bang, 1991; Popscene, 1992; For Tomorrow, 1993; Chemical World, 1993; Sunday Sunday, 1993; Girls and Boys, 1994; To The End, 1994; Parklife, 1994; End of a Century, 1994; Country House, 1995; The Universal, 1995; Stereotypes, 1996; Charmless Man, 1996; Beetlebum, 1997; Song 2, 1997; On Your Own, 1997; MOR, 1997; Tender, 1999; Coffee and TV, 1999; No Distance Left To Run, 1999; Music Is My Radar, 2000; with Gorillaz: Clint Eastwood, 2001; 19–2000, 2001; Rock The House, 2001; solo: Original film scores: Ravenous, directed by Antonia Bird, with Michael Nyman, 1998; Ordinary Decent Criminal, directed by Thasseus O'Sullivan, 1999; 101 Reykjavik, directed by Baltasar Kormákur, with Einar Örn Benediktsson, 2000. *Honours:* Mercury Music Prize nominations with Blur and Gorillaz; Platinum album, Parklife; Brit Awards: Best Single, Video, Album and Band, 1995; Q Awards, Best Album, 1994, 1995; Mercury Music Prize nomination, 1999; Platinum

albums. *Current Management:* CMO Management, Unit 32, Ransome Dock, 35–37 Parkgate Rd, London SW11 4NP, England.

ALBERTO José, (José Alberto Justiniano); b. 22 Dec. 1958, Santo Domingo, Dominican Republic. Singer; Bandleader. *Musical Education:* Studied music at Antilles Military Academy, Puerto Rico. *Career:* Club circuit singer, New York; Recording artiste, 1976–; Known as 'El Canario' (The Canary); Member, Típica 73, 1978–81; Bandleader, 1984–; Appearances include: Debut UK performance, with Celia Cruz, 1978; New Orleans Jazz and Heritage Festival, with Celia Cruz, 1990; New York Salsa Festival, Madison Square Garden, 1990. *Recordings:* Albums: with Tito Rodríguez?, 1976; with Típica 73: Salsa Encendida, 1978; Típica 73 En Cuba, Intercambio Cultural, 1979; Charangueando Con La Típica 73, 1980; Into The 80s, 1981; Solo: Tipicamente, 1984; Canto Canario, 1985; Latino Style, 1986; Sueño Contigo, 1988; Mis Amores, 1989; Dance With Me, 1991. *Current Management:* Ralph Mercado Management, 568 Broadway, Suite 806, New York, NY 10012, USA.

ALBERTS Al, (Al Albertini); b. 19 Aug. 1922, Philadelphia, USA. Musician; Television Presenter. m. Stella Zippi, 6 June 1953, 2 s. *Education:* BS, Temple University, 1951. *Career:* Lead singer, The Four Aces, 1946–58, 1975–85; President, Alstel Television Productions Inc, Chester, Pennsylvania, 1958–; Executive producer, television host, Al Alberts Showcase Station, Philadelphia, 1968–; President, Al Alberts Onstage Ltd, Chester, 1988-. *Recordings include:* It's No Sin; Tell Me Why; Stranger In Paradise; Three Coins In The Fountain; Love Is A Many Splendoured Thing; Mr Sandman; Dream; Heart and Soul; A Woman In Love; Heart of My Heart; Garden In The Rain; It's A Woman's World; Lazy, Hazy, Crazy Days of Summer. *Honours include:* Inducted into Music Hall of Fame, 1988. *Address:* Al Alberts Onstage Ltd, 15 E Eighth St, Chester, PA 19013, USA.

ALBINI Steve; b. USA. Vocalist; Musician (guitar); Record Prod. *Career:* Founder, Big Black, 1982–88; Founder, Rapeman, 1988; Record producer, for artists including The Pixies; The Wedding Present; Tad; The Breeders; Formed Shellac with Bob Weston and Todd Trainer, 1993; Toured with Shellac 1993–95. *Recordings include:* Albums: with Big Black: Racer X, 1985; Atomizer, 1986; The Hammer Party, 1986; Sound of Impact, 1987; Big Black, Live, 1989; Rich Man's Track, 1989; Pigpile, 1992; with Rapeman: Two Nuns and a Pack Mule, 1988; with Shellac: At Action Park, 1994; Terraform, 1998; 1000 Hurts, 2000; As producer include: Surfer Rosa, The Pixies; Pod, The Breeders; Salt Lick, Tad; Seamonsters, The Wedding Present; Bush; Storm and Stress; Melt Banana; PW Long.

ALBURO Francisco; b. 19 July 1953, Legaspi City, Philippines. Singer; Musician (keyboards); Singer. m. Minerva de Leon, 7 May 1977, 2 s., 2 d. *Musical Education:* Course, Melody School of Music, Stamford House, London. *Career:* Formed group, The Spider's Webb (first Phillipino band), 1973; Member, PI Sea Dust, 1976–82; Partime singer, Memoza Club, 1983; Bass guitar, Pula't Asul Band, 1990; Solo singer, 1991–95.

ALDRIDGE Chris, (B B / Beebé Aldridge); b. 14 March 1976, Walsall, England. Musician (saxophone, flute); Composer; Teacher. *Musical Education:* University of Wolverhampton, Music, BA (Hons); Apprentice Lead Alto Saxophonist: Walsall Jazz Orchestra; Midland Youth Jazz Orchestra. *Career:* Performed at London Marathon, 1997; London Jazz Festival, Reading Rock Festival, 1998; Montreux Jazz Festival, 1989; sell-out appearances at Ronnie Scott's and Rock City; Played on Intimate with a Stranger film soundtrack; Colloborations include: Bud Shank; John Dankworth; Kenny Baker; Victor Mendoza; Bobby Shew; Roy Wood; Hot Chocolate; The Christians; Various musical instrument manfacturer endorsements. *Compositions:* Original music for The Biome Dome (prize-winning entry at BBC Gardeners World Live, 2000). *Recordings include:* Waddaman by Mother; Home Turf by Gold Blade; 1000 Nudes by Divine Sounds; Stereoman by Bizarre Inc; solo: Chris Aldridge, 1997; featured soloist on Montreux Jazz Festival compilation, 1999; Holy Island (as Beebé), 2001. *Honours:* Lead Alto Saxophonist of BBC Big Band Competition Winners, Walsall Jazz Orchestra, 1995. *Membership:* Musicians' Union. *Current Management:* Caldridge Music, PO Box 2377, Walsall, WS8 7YB, England. *Address:* 19 Bransdale Rd, Swingbridge Park, Clayhanger, Brownhills, West Midlands, WS8 7SD, England. *Internet:* www.big-it-up.com.

ALDRIDGE Roger Merle; b. 18 Sept. 1946, Kansas City, Missouri, USA. Jazz Composer; Research Analyst. m. Nancy Sherwood, 9 Jan. 1999, 1 s., 2 d. *Education:* CSP, Institute for the Certification of Computer Professionals, 1985. *Musical Education:* Jazz Studies, Berklee College of Music, Boston, 1964–68; Advanced Composition Studies, Washington University, 1969; BA, Music Composition, McKendree College, 1972; MA, Music Composition, Highlands University, 1974. *Career:* Performed with Smoky Robinson, Diahann Carroll, 1970–72; Composed Multi-Media theatre music and jazz works, 1972–77; Instructor of Muisc, Fontbonne Colege, 1974–77; Adjunct Professor, Montgomery College, 1988–99; Composed many works including contemporary jazz pieces, rags, blues and traditional style fiddle tunes, 1989-. *Compositions include:* Farewell to the Goslings; Atlantic Flyway; Winter's Woods; Pipes of Peace; October Morn; Treasure the Chesapeake; Appalachian Twilight; Autumn Walk; Anne's Lullaby; Spring Beauties; Young Henry's Wild Ride; Buzzards in Love; Appalachian Awakening; Desperate Measures; Salt Marsh Rag; Spirit Journeys Suite. *Recordings include:* Earth's Essence; A Celtic Portrait; Michigan's Heritage; Buzzards in Love, Appalachian Awakening; Spirit Journeys. *Honours:* Research Grant, Institute of Scientific Studies, 1973; Montie Award, Best Music in a Video, 1992; Award and Grant, Fannie Mae Foundation, 1994; Award, Chesapeake Bay Foundation, 1995. *Memberships:* BMI; American Music Center; Chesapeake Bay Foundation. *Leisure interests:* Tae kwando; Chi kung; Hiking. *Address:* 4205 Gelding Lane, Olney, MD 20832, USA.

ALEMAÑY Jesús, (Jesús Alemañy Castrillo); b. 14 Oct. 1962, Guanabacoa, Cuba. Musician (Trumpet); Composer. *Musical Education:* Conservatoire Guillermo Tomas, Guanabacoa. *Career:* began studying trumpet at the Conservatoire, aged 13; Invited to join Sierra Maestra, Cuba's leading contemporary ensemble specializing in the roots style of salsa known as son, featuring the trumpet as solo instrument, aged 16; Played with Sierra Maestra for over a decade, recording 11 albums; Relocated to London, 1992; Organized (with Paris-based Cuban pianist Akfredo Rodriguez) a Descarga jam session in Paris to honour percussionist Patato Váldez, 1994; Impressed Hannibal Records boss Joe Boyd; Both musicians invited to record in Cuba with some of the top Cuban musicians; Project became the band ¡Cubanismo!; Remains as band leader after Rodriguez's departure; Subsequent releases were a straight Latin album, Reencarnación, and a collaboration with New Orleans musicians, Mardi Gras Mambo. *Recordings:* Albums include: with ¡Cubanismo!: Jesús Alemañy's ¡Cubanismo!, 1996; Malembe, 1997; Reencarnación, 1998; Mardi Gras Mambo, 2000; with Sierra Maestra: Son Highlights From Cuba, 1993; ¡Dundunbanza!, 1994; features on: Wild Mood Swings, The Cure, 1996; Cuba Linda, Alfredo Rodriguez, 1997; Curtains, Tindersticks, 1997. *Internet:* www.jesusalemany.com.

ALESSANDRO; b. 26 Nov. 1959, Venice, Italy. Singer; Musician (guitar); Entertainer. *Education:* Cosmologist; Linguist. *Career:* With Los Primos, tour of Japan, 1988; With Ole, Italy, 1989; Australia; Singapore; Hong Kong; Russia; Canada; Presently touring UK with solo show Passion, Grace, Fire; Television appearances: Wogan; Just For Laughs; Edinburgh Nights; Television commercials: Canale 5. *Recordings:* Wrote and performed Lorca's Women, for Royal Shakespeare Company; with Los Primos: Paul's Lurking Grapefruit, Latino-comedy. *Honours:* Time Out Magazine, Pick of The Fringe, 1989; Winner, Covent Garden Street Festival, 1989; British Gas Best Newcomer, Edinburgh Festival, 1992. *Membership:* Musicians' Union. *Leisure interests:* Astronomy; Cosmology; Flying; Skiing. *Current Management:* Wizard Entertainments, 102 Euston St, London NW1 2HA. *Address:* 14B Vicarage Grove, London SE5 7LW, England.

ALEXANDER Dennis; b. 7 May 1953, Fyvie, Aberdeenshire, Scotland. Entertainer; Musician (acoustic guitar). m. Isobel, 3 Aug. 1974, 1 s., 1 d. *Education:* Member, 1st Purchase and Supply, Hand Promotions Events Management. *Musical Education:* Self-taught. *Career:* Lead singer, Crooked Jack; Writer, producer, Crooked Jack's Giant Jeely Piece Show; Appearances, Edinburgh Festival Fringe; Major folk festivals in Scotland. *Recordings:* Tomorrow Must Wait; The Giant Jeely Piece Show (video); An Audience with Crooked Jack. *Membership:* Musicians' Union. *Leisure interests:* Running café and joke/fancy dress hire in Kirkcaldy. *Current Management:* Crooked Jack Promotions. *Address:* 16 Moray Court, Auchtertool, Kirkcaldy, Fife KY2 5XS, Scotland.

ALEXANDER John Eric; b. 10 Feb. 1962, Elizabeth, New Jersey, USA. Composer. m. Ellen Greiss, 3 Aug. 1986, 1 s. *Education:* BFA, Parsons School of Design, 1983. *Career:* Associate Producer, Iris Films Inc, New York, 1975–83; Producer, Sam Alexander Productions, New York, 1983–86; John Eric Alexander Music Inc, New York, 1986-. *Compositions:* Composer, music producer, film soundtracks: The Fly, 1986; Red Heat, 1987; Predator, 1987; The Mosquito Coast, 1987; Witches of Eastwick, 1988; Flatliners, 1990; Lethal Weapon II, 1990; Bird On A Wire, 1990; Die Hard II, 1990; Silence of The Lambs, 1991; Point Break, 1991; Ricochet, 1991. *Honours:* Cannes Film Festival Award, Witches of Eastwick, 1988. *Membership:* AFofM.

ALEXANDER Otis Douglas; b. 1 June 1949, Virginia, USA. Musician (French Horn, Piano). *Education:* BA, MS, University of The District of Columbia; MLS, Ball State University; Norfolk State University; University of Toledo; Studied French Horn With Hermann Suehs; Piano With Hildred Roach; Voice With Nelda Ormond, Robert Porter; Opera With Gloria Amos. *Career:* Original Choreography In Tribute To World Renowned Poet Andre Lorde, Brooklyn Academy of Music; Danced In Oscar Brown Jr and Lonnie Levister's, Slave Song; Performed Principal Role In William Grant Stills Opera, Highway I; Recitalist, Whim Great House Museum; Recitalist, Cuttington University College and Harrison

Opera House. *Compositions:* Queen Mary: Folk Play With Music. *Publications:* Virgin Islands and Caribbean Communities: An Afro Treasure Chest. *Honours:* Plaque and Certificate, Outstanding Musical Performance and Directing, 1996. *Memberships:* Phi Delta Kappa; Omega Psi Phi. *Leisure interests:* Choreography; Collecting Folktales; Fishing. *Address:* PO Box 8052, Christiansted, St Croix, VI 00823, USA.

ALEXANDER Van; b. 2 May 1915, New York City, USA. Music Arranger; Composer; Conductor; Author. m. Beth Baremore, 22 Sept. 1938, 2 d. *Education:* Columbia University. *Musical Education:* Studied with Otto Cesana, New York City; with Mario Tedsco, California; (Orchestration, Conducting, Composition). *Career:* Worked with Chick Webb at The Savoy Ballroom, New York; Benny Goodman; Paul Whiteman; Les Brown; Formed own band, played on radio, The Fitch Bandwagon; Morey Amsterdam's Laugh and Swing Club; Played ballrooms, theatres throughout US, including: New York Paramount, Loews State; Capitol, New York; Earle, Philadelphia; The Stanley, Pittsburg; Arranger/conductor for Dinah Shore; Doris Day; Dean Martin; Gordon and Sheila MacRae; Kay Starr; Peggy Lee; Dakota Staton; Patty Andrews. *Compositions include:* 22 feature films; Co-writer, arranger, A-Tisket-A-Tasket, hit for Ella Fitzgerald; Hundreds of television segments include; The Wacky World of Jonathan Winters; Gene Kelly's Wonderful World of Girls; The Goldiggers Chevy Show; Composer, conductor, NBC's 50th Anniversary Show, A Closer Look; Dom De Luise specials; 1969 Emmy Awards; The Guy Mitchell Show Series; Scoring credits: Hazel; I Dream of Jeanie; Bewitched; Donna Reed; Dennis The Menace. *Recordings:* Swing Staged For Stereo; Savoy Stomp; The Last Dance; Numerous albums with Gordon MacRae; Kay Starr; Dakota Staton; Dorothy Kirsten (all on Capitol Records). *Publication:* First Arrangement (a learning method for the novice arranger). *Honours:* Irwin Kostal Award, 1995; 3 Emmy Nominations; NARAS Hall of Fame Award, for A-Tisket-A-Tasket, 1986; Los Angeles Jazz Society, Composer/Arranger Award, 1997; Pacific Pioneer Broadcasters, Diamond Circle Award, 1996. *Memberships:* ASCAP; ASMAC; NARAS; Big Band Academy of America; Academy of Motion Picture Arts and Sciences; Hon. mem. of SPERDVAC (Society to Preserve and Encourage Radio Drama), Variety and Comedy, 1993; National Sheet Music Society, 1988. *Leisure interests:* Golf; Reading; Watching grandchildren grow up.

ALFORD Clem; b. 2 Oct. 1945, Glasgow, Scotland. Musician. Divorced. *Career:* Major Recitals, Radio in India; Toured Europe, Far East, including Japan; Major concert appearances with Laxshmi Shankar, Royal Albert Hall; Many Sessions with Major Musical Personalities, Lulu, Maurice Jarre, John Williams. *Compositions:* The Electronic Sitar of Clem Alford; Magic Carpet; Sangeet Sagar; Pop Explosion, Sitar Style; K.P.M.; One More Magic Carpet II; Akasa, Staying On. *Recordings:* The Electronic Sitar of Clem Alford; Magic Carpet; Sangeet Sagar; Pop Explosion, Sitar Style; K.P.M.; One More Magic Carpet II; Monsoon, Akasa, Jewell in the Crown; Mirror Image, 1974; Once Moor, 1996. *Publications:* The Sitar Manual; The Sitar Book. *Honours:* Jr Sangeet Ratnakar, West Bengal; Sangeet Sudhakar, Calcutta; Sur-Mani, Bombay. *Memberships:* PRS; MCPS; PAMRA; Indian Music Congress. *Leisure interest:* Recording. *Address:* 9 Tavistock Mansions, 16 Tavistock Pl., London WC1H 9RA, England.

ALIFANTIS Nicu; b. 31 May 1954, Braila, Romania. Singer; Composer; Musician (guitar). *Career:* Wrote music for theatre, 10 film soundtracks; 19 recitals; 5000 concerts, tours: Romania; Bulgaria; Czechoslovakia; Germany; Israel; England; Italy; Hungary; Holland. *Recordings:* 3 singles; 6 albums; 2 CDs, 1 in France, produced by Radio France International; 8 albums with other singers. *Honours:* 3 awards, Theatre Music, 1986, 1991, 1993; First awards for Singer of The Year, 1993. *Memberships:* Romanian Union of Composers; International Union of Theatre, UNIMA. *Leisure interests:* Autos; Tennis; Books. *Current Management:* Aurel Mitram, PO Box 26–54, Bucharest, Romania.

ALLDIS Dominic William; b. 15 April 1962, London, England. Musician (Piano); Singer; Composer. *Career:* Debut at Purcell Room, London, 1985; Recitals at major festivals with Midi grand piano, 1986–89; Performances at jazz clubs, jazz festivals, 1990–; Formed trio, 1996; Teaching Staff, Royal Academy of Music, 1993; Gives presentations to companies and businesses using music as metaphor for business concerns, 1998-. *Recordings:* Night Music, original composition for piano and synthesizers, 1989; Turn Out the Stars, vocal jazz album, 1996; If Love Were All, The Songs of Noël Coward. *Publication:* A Classical Approach to Jazz Piano. *Honours:* Royal Academy of Music, honorary associate. *Memberships:* Asscn of British Jazz Musicians; Musicians Union. *Leisure interests:* Skiing; Tennis; Food. *Current Management:* Canzona Music. *Address:* 122 Dawes Rd, Fulham, London SW6 7EG, England. *Internet:* www.dominicalldis.com.

ALLEN David Andrew Wells; b. 1 June 1953, Toronto, Ontario, Canada. Lecturer; Musician (guitar, bass, classical guitar); Composer. m. 26 May 1975, 2 s., 1 d. *Musical Education:* Bachelor of Music, Master of Music, Manchester. *Career:* Concerts as soloist and in duos/trios, 1978–88; Tours and concerts: London; Manchester; Liverpool; Canada, 1981–88;

Broadcasts: Radio 3; Granada Television; Lecturer, Popular Music, NEWI Wrexham, 1988–94; Course Co-ordinator, Performing Arts, Yale College, Wrexham, 1995. *Compositions:* Sequencing, Theatr Clwyd, 1990; The Roots of Rhythm, 1993; Theatr Clwyd/BBC Children in Need Commission. *Memberships:* Musicians' Union; IASPM. *Leisure interests:* Swimming; Gardening; Camping. *Address:* 31 Birch Hall Lane, Manchester M13 0XJ, England.

ALLEN Duane David; b. 29 April 1943, Taylortown, Texas, USA. Singer; Songwriter. m. Norah Lee Stuart, 22 Sept. 1969, 2 s. *Musical Education:* BS, Music, East Texas University, 1965. *Career:* Radio DJ, Paris, Texas, 1963–65; Lead singer, US gospel/country group Oak Ridge Boys, 1966–; Co-owner, president, Silverline/Goldline Music Publishing; Owner, president, Superior Sound Studios. *Compositions:* He Did It All For Me; Here's A Song For The Man; How Much Further Can We Go; I Will Follow The Sun. *Recordings:* Singles include: Priase the Lord and Pass the Soup; I'll Be True To You; Y'All Come Back Saloon; Elvira; Bobbie Sue; Leavin' Louisiana In The Broad Daylight; Trying To Love Two Women; American Made; Make My Life With You; I Guess It Never Hurts To Hurt Sometime; Come On In; Albums include: International, 1971; Light, 1972; Hymns, 1973; Street Gospel, 1973; Gospel Gold Heartwarming, 1974; Oak Ridge Boys, 1974, Super Gold, 1974; Sky High, 1975; Old Fashioned..., 1976; Y'All Come Back Saloon, 1977; Room Service, 1978; The Oak Ridge Boys Have Arrived, 1979; Together, 1980; Greatest Hits, 1980; Fancy Free, 1981; Bobbie Sue, 1982; Oak Ridge Boys Christmas, 1982; Friendship, 1983; American Made, 1983; The Oak Ridge Boys Deliver, 1984; Greatest Hits II, 1984; Step On Out, 1985; Seasons, 1985; Christmas Again, 1986; Where The Fast Lane Ends, 1986; Monongahela, 1987; New Horizons, 1988; American Dreams, 1989; Greatest Hits III, 1989; Unstoppable, 1991; The Long Haul, 1992. *Publications:* Co-author, The History of Gospel Music, 1971. *Honours:* Grammies, 1970–77; 12 Gospel Music Asscn Dove Awards; American Music Award, Best Country Group of the Year, 1982; Country Music Asscn Award, Vocal Group of the Year, 1978; Academy of Country Music Awards, Best Vocal Group 1977, 1979; Numerous Gold discs. *Memberships:* CMA; Gospel Music Asscn; AFTRA; National Academy Recording Arts and Sciences; Academy of Country Music. *Current Management:* Don Light Talent. *Address:* PO Box 120308, Nashville, TN 37212, USA.

ALLEN Geri; b. 1957, Detroit, Michigan, USA. Jazz Musician (piano). *Musical Education:* Jazz Studies Degree, Howard University, Washington, 1979; Masters Degree, Ethnomusicology, University of Pittsburgh, 1982; Studied piano with Kenny Barrow. *Career:* Formed own trio with Ron Carter, Tony Williams; Also played with: Ornette Coleman; Wallace Roney; Jack DeJohnette; Betty Carter; Dave Holland; Marcus Belgrave; Steve Coleman; Lester Bowie. *Recordings:* The Printmakers; Twilight Time; The Nurturer; Maroons; Twenty One; Etudes and Segments (with Charlie Haden, Paul Motian); Feed The Fire (with Betty Carter, Jack DeJohnette, Dave Holland); Solo: Sound Museum, 1996; Gathering, 1998. *Honours:* Howard University Alumni Award; SESAE Special Achievement Award; Eubie Blake Award; Downbeat Critics Poll, Talent Deserving Wider Recognition, 1993, 1994. *Current Management:* Blue Note. *Address:* 1290 Avenue of the Americas, 35th Floor, New York, NY 10104, USA.

ALLEN Henry Kaleialoha; b. 11 June 1933, Honolulu, HI, USA. Master Artist, Hawaiian Steel Guitar; Recording Artist; Show Prod. m. Sherron Allen, 1971, 1 s., 2 d. *Musical Education:* Studied Jazz, Los Angeles, Music Theory, Composition, Johnny Smith, Alex Keck; Hawaiian Music Institute, Teaching Hawaiian Steel Guitar for County of Maui, Hawaii. *Career:* Music parts in films; Hawaiian Eye; Blue Hawaii; Barnaby Jones; Mama's Family; Regular guest on Home Shopping Channel Network; QVC and produces Hawaiian shows and music for their 50th state tours; Show Producer, own shows; Music is played, inflight, American Airlines; Opened up Planet Hollywood with Music in Maui, 1995; Own record label, Rainbow Records. *Compositions include:* Lahaina; Walking in the Sand; Hookipa (Jazz) Noalani; Koele Mist; We Say Aloha; Goodbye; Lanikai; Hawaii, Islands in the Sky; Kalele; Swinging. *Recordings:* Albums: Memories of Hawaii; Magic of Steel Guitar; Blue Hawaii. *Publications:* Learning to Play the Hawaiian Way, 1991; Book of Songs, Hawaiian Steel Guitar, 1993. *Honours:* Awards, State Foundation/Culture and the Arts, 1995, 1996; Master Artist Grants; ASCAP Awards, 1996, 1997; County of Maui Grant for Music Work Musicians Asscn of Hawaii (Lifetime Mem.); ASCAP Mem.; HSGA Mem. *Leisure interests:* Jazz; Golf; Wine Tastings; Travel. *Current Management:* Own Manager, Polynesian Promotions, Rainbow Records. *Address:* 5161-D, Kohi St, Lahaina, Maui, Hawaii 96761, USA.

ALLEN Peter Raymond; b. 23 Nov. 1954, Newbury, Berkshire, England. *Career:* Formed Pete Allen Jazz Band, 1978; Regular television and radio shows followed including: Pebble Mill at One, BBC Television; Jazzin Around, HTV Series; Most BBC Radio Two Programmes including five broadcasts for Friday Night is Music Night and own six week series for Radio Two. *Compositions:* Beau Sejour; Mystic Gypsy; St Louis Street Stomp; Riverside Rag; Springtime Swing; Black Lion Rag; At the Upton Mardi Gras. *Recordings:* Turkey Trot, 1978; Down in Honky Tonk Town, 1979; Gonna Build a Mountain, 1980; Beau Sejour, 1987; Big Chief, Loose

Tie, 1996; All Aboard for Alabama, 1997; Oh Play That Thing, 1998; Reeds 'n' Rhythm, 1998; Movin' On, 1999. *Honours:* World Wide All Stars, Sacramento, USA, 1984; Hon. Citizenship of New Orleans, 1992; European Top Eight Jazz Band, Germany. *Memberships:* Performing Rights Soc; Lions International. *Leisure interests:* Football; Travel. *Address:* PO Box 505, Chippenham, Wiltshire SW15 3WS, England.

ALLEN Rick; b. 1 Nov. 1963, Sheffield, England. Musician (drums). *Career:* Drummer, Def Leppard, 1978–; Concerts include: Support tours to Sammy Hagar; AC/DC; Ted Nugent; Reading Rock Festival, 1980; Lost left arm in car crash, 1984; Returns to perform with custom-built electronic drum kit, 1985; Monsters of Rock festivals, including Castle Donington, 1986; Royal Albert Hall, 1989; Freddie Mercury Tribute Concert, Wembley Stadium, 1992; Television interview, Fighting Back, BBC1, 1992. *Recordings:* Albums: On Through The Night, 1980; High 'n' Dry, 1981; Pyromania, 1983; Hysteria, 1987; Adrenalize, 1992; Retroactive, 1993; Vault 1980–95, 1995; Slang, 1996; Euphoria, 1999; Singles include: Hello America, 1980; Photograph, 1983; Rock of Ages, 1983; Foolin', 1983; Animal, 1987; Pour Some Sugar On Me, 1987; Armageddon It, 1988; Love Bites (No. 1, USA), 1988; Rocket, 1989; Let's Get Rocked (No. 2, UK), 1992; Make Love Like A Man, 1992; Have You Ever Needed Someone So Bad, 1992; Heaven Is, 1993; Two Steps Behind (featured in film soundtrack The Last Action Hero), 1993; Action, 1994; When Love and Hate Collide (No. 2, UK), 1995; All I Want Is Everything, 1996; Promises, 1999. *Honours include:* American Music Awards: Favourite Heavy Metal Album, Favourite Heavy Metal Artists, 1989. *Current Management:* Q-Prime Inc. *Address:* 729 Seventh Ave, 14th Floor, New York, NY 10019, USA.

ALLEN Terry, (Terry L Comp); b. 1 Sept. 1947, Niles, Michigan, USA. Entertainer; Vocalist; Musician (bass, rhythm guitar). m. Barbara Sweets, 23 April 1995, 4 s., 4 d. *Education:* Aircraft Maintenance Diploma. *Career:* Tours USA and Canada, playing private and public clubs and military bases; Numerous television and radio appearances, state and county fairs, 1969–81; Currently, Director of Marketing for Gf Mac Management Inc. *Recordings:* CB Duck; A Little Love, 1978; Time Has; Footprints; Good Old Days, 1989. *Honours:* NE Country Music Hall of Fame, Achievement and Performance Award, 1987. *Leisure interests:* Horses; Camping; Fishing; Hunting. *Current Management:* Blackhawk International, Dalton Fuller Management. *Address:* Rt1 Box 200, Rising City, NE 68658, USA.

ALLEYNE Cheryl Louise; b. 4 Sept. 1963, North London, England. *Musical Education:* Royal School of Music, England. *Career:* Freelance Drummer; Appeared On BBC Television, Mad About Music, Blue Peter, Top of The Pops, MTV Spring Break Jams; Interviewed On Jazz FM, Womens Hour, Radio 4. *Composition:* Solar Breeze. *Recordings:* Include, The Human Groove, 1989; Chameleon, 1993; Magic of Olmec, 1995; Gail Thompson's Jazz Africa, 1995; Somewhere Out There, 1996; Tomorrows Path, 1997. *Publications:* Best of British Publications; Best of British Women. *Honours:* Most Promising Musician of The Year, 1986. *Leisure interests:* Art; Painting; photography; Astronomy. *Address:* 9 Croxford Gardens, Wood Green, London N22 5QU, England.

ALLISON Bernard; b. 26 Nov. 1965, Chicago, Illinois, USA. Musician (Guitar); Vocalist; Arranger; Composer. 1 d. *Career:* Documentary Film, The Next Generation; France, Grand de Sable, Paris Premier; Live at the New Morning. *Recordings:* The Next Generation; Hang On; Low Down and Dirty; Playin' A Losin' Game; No Mercy; Funkifino; Born with the Blues; Times Are Changing. *Honours:* New Artist of the Year, Atlanta, Georgia, 1998; Nominee, New Artist of the Year, WC Handy, 1999. *Membership:* SCEM. *Leisure interests:* Basketball; Fishing. *Current Management:* Blue Sky Artists World-wide. *Address:* 761 Washington Ave N, Minneapolis, MN 55401, USA.

ALLISON Jim (James H); b. 13 Feb. 1959, Gettyburg, Pennsylvania, USA. Songwriter; Music Publisher; Prod. *Education:* Master's Penn State University, Gettysburg College, BA. *Musical Education:* Learned Trumpet in high school; Self-taught: Guitar, Piano. *Career:* Began writing songs aged 13; High school English teacher for 2 years; Musician and bandleader for 20 years; Set up own music publishing and production company, 1985; Studio owner and producer; Recorded and helped launch country music career of Billy Ray Cyrus. *Compositions:* What Am I Gonna Do About You, Reba McEntire; Fade To Blue, LeAnn Rimes; Cowboys Don't Cry, Daron Norwood. *Recordings:* Razzy Bailey; Earl Thomas Conley; Mickey Gilley; Brenda Lee; Jo Dee Messina; Del Reeves; Connie Smith; Jett Williams; Lee Ann Womack. *Publications:* 1001 Song Ideas Vols 1 and 2, 1999; Million Dollar Ideas – Inventions Creations and Opportunities, 2000. *Honours:* Nashville Songwriters Asscn award, What Am I Gonna Do About You, 1987; Billboard Song Contest, Nobody Loves Me Like The Blues, Winner, 1992. *Memberships:* CMA. *Leisure interests:* Hiking; Re-modelling properties. *Current Management:* AlliSongs Inc. *Address:* 1603 Horton Ave, Nashville, Tennessee 37212, USA. *Internet:* www.allisongs.com.

ALLISON Mose; b. 11 Nov. 1927, Tippo, Mississippi, USA. Vocalist; Musician (piano); Lyricist. *Education:* Chemical engineering; English; Philosophy. *Career:* Influenced by Louis Jordan, Louis Armstrong and Nat 'King' Cole, started out playing trumpet then switched to piano; After college and the army, appeared professionally for the first time, 1950; Returned to college shortly after; Recorded with Al Cohn and Bobby Brookmeyer for Prestige Records, 1956; Signed own deal, 1957; Joined Columbia in 1960 for 2 years before a 14-year stint with Atlantic; After a 6-year recording hiatus re-emerged briefly on Elektra before current deal with Blue Note; Tours extensively throughout North America, Britain and Europe. *Compositions include:* Ain't You A Mess; Certified Senior Citizen; Ever Since I Stole The Blues; The Fool Killer; Gimcracks and Gewgaws; How Does It Feel To Be Good Looking?; Natural Born Malcontent; Parchman Farm; What Do You Do After You Ruin Your Life?; You're Mind Is On Vacation. *Recordings:* Albums include: Back Country Suite, 1957; I Love The Life I Live, 1960; I Don't Worry About A Thing, 1962; I've Been Doin' Some Thinkin', 1968; Your Mind Is On Vacation, 1976; Middleclass White Boy, 1982; Gimcracks and Gewgaws, 1997; The Mose Chronicles #1, 2000; The Mose Chronicles #2, 2001. *Current Management:* The Blues Agency, 323 Beale St, Suite 2000, Memphis, Tennesee, USA.

ALLMAN Gregg; b. 8 Dec. 1947, Nashville, Tennessee, USA. Musician. m. Cher Bono, 1975, (divorced 1979), 1 c. *Career:* Co-founder, Hour Glass; Support to Eric Burdon and the Animals, 1967; Co-founder, singer, Allman Brothers (with brother Duane), 1969–76, 1978–81, 1989–; Solo artiste, 1973–; Also recorded with wife Cher, 1976–79; Appearances include: Atlanta International Pop Festival, with Jimi Hendrix, Jethro Tull, B B King, 1979; Fillmore East, New York, 1971; Mar Y Sol Festival, Puerto Rico, 1972; Watkins Glen Raceway, with Grateful Dead and the Band (largest-ever concert of 600,000), 1973; Knebworth Festival, 1974; New Orleans Jazz and Heritage Festival, 1993; Actor, film Rush, 1991. *Recordings:* Albums with Hour Glass: Hour Glass, 1967; Power of Love, 1968; with The Allman Brothers: Allman Brothers Band, 1970; At Fillmore East, 1971; Eat A Peach, 1972; Brothers and Sisters, 1973; Win Lose Or Draw, 1975; The Road Goes On Forever, 1976; Wipe The Windows, Check The Oil, Dollar Gas, 1976; Enlightened Rogues, 1979; Brothers of the Road, 1981; The Best of the Allman Band, 1981; Dreams, 1989; Seven Turns, 1989; Shades of Two Worlds, 1991; Second Set, 1995; Fantastic Allman Brothers Original Hits, 1999; Solo albums: Laid Back, 1973; The Gregg Allman Tour, 1974; Playin' Up A Storm, 1977; I'm No Angel, 1987; Just Before The Bullets Fly, 1988; Searchin' For Simplicity, 1997; with Cher: Allman and Woman, 1976; Two The Hard Way, 1977.

ALLOUCHE Joël; b. 6 Nov. 1960, Bougie, Algeria. Musician (drums, percussion). m. 24 Dec. 1988, 1 s., 1 d. *Career:* Professional with pop bands, singers, 1975–; Jazz, 1980–; Played in Japan; Canada; New York; Africa; England; India; With musicians including: John Suriman; Kenny Whecks; Palle Danielsson; Enrico Rava; Urs Leimgruber; Don Friedman; Maurice Magnoni; Palle Danielsson; Marc Ducret; François Jeanneau; Michel Portal; Michel Marre; Doudou Gouirand; Don Cherry; Antonello Salis; Concerts, festivals with Coincidence, the group of the Llabador brothers; International concerts with trio of guitarist Philippe Caillat, concerts in Berlin; Copenhagen; Hamburg; Hungary; Member, Reflexionen, 1983; Maurice Magnoni Quintet, 1987; Marc Ducret Trio, 1988; Pandémonium; François Jeanneau Quartet; Michel Portal's New Unit, 1990. *Recordings:* French Connection, Philippe Caillat, 1981; Fire Brigade, Philippe Caillat, 1982; with J P Llabador: Coincidence, 1984; Brussels, 1987; Forgotten Tales, Doudou Gouirand, with Don Cherry, 1985; with Urs Leimgruber: Reflexionen, 1986; Live, 1986; Remember To Remember, 1987; Andata Senza Ritorno, Maurice Magnoni, 1988; Superbe Déménagement, 1989; Gris, Marc Ducret, 1990; Lato Sensu, Philippe Gareil, 1991; Beatles Stories, Gérard Panseanel/Antonello Salis, 1992; Maloya Transit, François Jeanneau and Trio Tambours, 1992; Paolo Damiani, with Kenny Wheeler, 1992; Nguyên Lê, with Art Lande, Paul McCandless, 1992; Dominique Pifarely, with Ricardo del Fra, F Couturier, 1993; Birds Can Fly, Jean Pierre Llabador, 1995; Orchestra Improvista, Nino Rota-Fellini (Gouvirand, Pansanel), 1995; Tales From Vietnam, Nguyen Lê, 1996; Few Notes, Jean Bardy, 1998; Tamborea, Engergypsy, 1999. *Leisure interest:* Sport. *Address:* 8 bis rue du Professeur Lombard, 34000 Montpellier, France.

ALLPASS Soma; b. 9 July 1968, Copenhagen, Denmark. Musician (cello, piano, guitar); Singer; Songwriter; Arranger. *Musical Education:* Private lessons in Cello playing, 10 years; Royal Academy of Music, Copenhagen, 5 years; Lessons in piano and singing; Self-taught guitar. *Career:* Cellist and Backing Singer, Trains and Boats and Trains, rock band, 1989–94; Co-arranger, Roskilde Festival, 1992, 1993, 1994; Tours in Denmark, Norway, Sweden, Germany, England, Finland and New York; New Music Seminar, 1992. *Compositions:* Working on solo CD. *Recordings:* Trains and Boats and Trains, 1990; Hum, mini LP, 1990; Engulfed, LP, CD, 1991; I Like Cars, single, CD, 1992; Minimal Star, LP, CD, 1992. *Honour:* Rodovre Music Prize, 1996. *Memberships:* KODA; Danish Musicians Union. *Leisure interests:* Yoga; Breathing; Favourite Music: Neil Young and Van

Morrison. *Current Management:* Jim Holm, Klarboderne 3, 1001, KBH K, Denmark. *Address:* Brofogedvej 2, 2th, 2400 KBH NV, Denmark.

ALL-STAR FRESH; b. 1 Aug. 1965, Amsterdam, Netherlands. Prod.; Rapper; Remixer; Composer. *Musical Education:* Self-taught. *Career:* Leader, producer, King Bee. *Compositions include:* (co-writer) Cappella: Move On Baby; Move Your Body; U and Me. *Recordings:* Back By Dope Demand; Must Be The Music. *Honours:* Dance Artist Award, 1991, 1992. *Leisure interest:* Music. *Current Management:* Hans Van Pol Management. *Address:* PO Box 9010, 1006 AA Amsterdam, Netherlands.

ALLWRIGHT (Sydney) Graeme; b. 7 Nov. 1926, Lyall Bay, New Zealand. Singer; Author; Composer. m. Catherine Dasté, 8 June 1951, 3 s., 1 d. *Education:* Short period university. *Musical Education:* Self-taught. *Career:* 30 years professional stage work, television, radio; Concerts include: Nyons Festival, Switzerland; Le Printemps de Bourges; Les Francofolies à la Rochelle, France; L'Olympia, Palais des Sports. *Recordings:* 19 albums. *Publications:* Song books. *Membership:* SACEM; ADAMI. *Leisure interests:* Woodwork; Gardening. *Current Management:* Claire Bataille. *Address:* 13 Pl. D'Aligre, 75000 Paris, France.

ALMEIDA Joaquim; b. 24 July 1931. Singer; Composer; Musician (Trumpet). m. Alice Almeida, 2 s., 1 d. *Musical Education:* Music Conservatoire. *Career:* Starlet In SVicente; Singing and Playing In Clubs; Performed in Adega Machadol Founded, Vozde Cadoverde, Toured Around Europe, Africa. *Compositions:* size; Cretchu Di Cei; Amorde Mai; Wibovente Year 2000. *Recordings:* Includes CD Un Creole In France. *Honours:* Prize of Recognition for Best Cabovermnteau Artist. *Memberships:* SACEM. *Leisure interests:* Basketball; Swimming. *Current Management:* Edition 4, Paris. *Address:* 3 Allee Maurice Chevalier, 93100 Montreuil, France.

ALMOND (Peter) Marc; b. 9 July 1959, Southport, Lancashire, England. Vocalist; Lyricist. *Education:* College, Southport; Fine Arts, Leeds Polytechnic. *Career:* Member: Soft Cell, 1979–84, reformed 2001; Also recorded as Marc and the Mambas; Solo artiste, 1984–; Major concerts include: Future 2 Science Fiction Music Festival, 1980; Terrence Higgins Trust benefit concert, 1990; Red Hot and Dance AIDS benefit concert, Barcelona, 1991; Royal Albert Hall, London; Philharmonic Hall, Liverpool, 1992. *Recordings:* Singles: with Soft Cell: Singles include: Tainted Love (No. 1, UK), 1981; Bedsitter; Say Hello Wave Goodbye; Torch; Soul Inside; Solo singles include: I Feel Love (medley), with Bronski Beat; Something's Gotten Hold of My Heart; Jacky; My Hand Over My Heart; The Days of Pearly Spencer; Adored and Explored; Glorious; Albums: with Soft Cell: Some Bizarre Album, 1981; Non-Stop Erotic Cabaret, 1981; Non-Stop Ecstatic Dancing, 1982; The Art of Falling Apart, 1983; As Marc and the Mambas: Untitled, 1982; Torment and Toreros, 1983; This Last Night In Sodom, 1984; As Marc Almond and the Willing Sinners: Vermin In Ermine, 1984; Solo albums: Mother Fist and Her Five Daughters, 1987; Enchanted, 1990; Tenement Symphony, 1991; 12 Years of Tears, Live At The Albert Hall, 1993; Fantastic Star, 1996; Live In Concert, 1998; Open All Night, 1999; Stranger Things, 2001. *Honours:* Best Selling Selling of The Year, Tainted Love, 1981; BRIT award, Best British Single, Tainted Love, 1982; Billboard Magazine, New Wave Band of The Year, 1982.

ALPERT Herb; b. 31 March 1935, Los Angeles, California, USA. Musician (trumpet); Songwriter; Arranger; Record Co Exec. m. Lani Hall, 1 s., 2 d. *Education:* University of Southern California. *Career:* Three television specials; Leader, own group Tijuana Brass; Multiple world tours; Owner, Dore Records; Manager, Jan and Dean; Co-founder with Jerry Moss, A & M Records (formerly Carnival), 1962–89; Artists have included: The Carpenters; Captain and Tennille; Carole King; Cat Stevens; The Police; Squeeze; Joe Jackson; Bryan Adams. *Compositions include:* Wonderful World, Sam Cooke (co-writer with Lou Adler). *Recordings:* The Lonely Bull; A Taste of Honey; Spanish Flea; Tijuana Taxi; Casino Royale; This Guy's In Love With You, 1968; Rise (No. 1, USA), 1979; Albums include: The Lonely Bull, 1963; Tijuana Brass, 1963; Tijuana Brass Vol. 2, 1964; South of The Border, 1965; Whipped Cream and Other Delights, 1965; Going Places, 1966; SRO, 1967; Sounds Like Us, 1967; Herb Alpert's Ninth, 1968; The Best of The Brass, 1968; Warm, 1969; Rise, 1979; Keep Your Eyes On Me, 1979; Magic Man, 1981; My Abstract Heart, 1989; Midnight Sun, 1992; Second Wind, 1996; Passion Dance, 1997; Colors, 1999; Definitive Hits, 2001. *Honours:* Numerous Grammy Awards. *Leisure interests:* Painting; Sculpting. *Current Management:* c/o Kip Cohen, La Brea Tours, Inc, 1414 Sixth St, Santa Monica, CA 90401, USA.

ALQUERES Gabriela; b. 1 Sept. 1972, Sao Paulo, Brazil. Musician (guitar); Songwriter. m. Pete Whittard, 23 Nov. 1992. *Musical Education:* The Guitar Institute. *Career:* Played with David McAlmont supporting Cyndi Lauper; Venues played include the Royal Albert Hall; Radio appearances include GLR. *Membership:* Musicians' Union. *Leisure interest:* Aerobics. *Address:* 7 Cambridge Gardens, Muswell Hill, London N10 2LL, England.

ALSOU (Alsou Tenisheva); b. 27 June 1983, Bugulma, Tatarstan, Russia. Vocalist. *Career:* Relocated to Moscow, Russia, aged 9; Educated in and resident of England from age 13; Discovered by manager Valeriy Belotserkovsky, 1998; Russia's most popular teen star by end of 1999; Many Russian concerts throughout 2000–01; Became first Russian pop artist ever to sign with international record company following appearance at Eurovision Song Contest, 2000. *Recordings:* Albums: Alsou, 1999; Greatest Hits, Alsou (world-wide release), 2001; Singles: Winter Dream, 1999; Solo, You're My No. 1 (with Enrique Iglesias), 2000; Before You Love Me, 2001. *Honours:* Eurovision Song Contest, second place, Solo, 2000; Presented with award for largest Russian single sales ever, You Are My Number One (136,000 copies), 2001. *Address:* c/o Universal Music Group, Russia. *Internet:* www.alsouonline.com.

ALTERHAUG Bjorn; b. 3 June 1945, Mo i Rana, Norway. Asst Prof.; Jazz Musician (bass). m. Anne-Lise Alterhaug, 1 Jan. 1968, 1 s., 1 d. *Education:* University. *Musical Education:* Self-taught. *Career:* Played as jazz soloist with: Ben Webster; Lucky Thompson; Chet Baker; Clark Terry; Numerous television and radio performances; Festival composer, Silver Jubilee of North Norway Festival, 1989. *Compositions:* For big band and symphony-setting. *Recordings:* Solo albums: Moments, 1979; A Ballad, 1986; Constellations, 1991. *Publications:* Articles on improvisation and communication. *Honours:* Buddy Award, Norwegian Jazz Federation (highest honour). *Memberships:* Norwegian Jazz Federation; NOPA. *Leisure interests:* Football; Walking in the mountains.

ALTMAN John Neville Rufus; b. 5 Dec. 1949, London, England. Composer; Conductor; Arranger; Orchestrator; Musician (saxophone). m. Rita Pukacz, 30 Oct. 1977, 3 s., 1 d. *Education:* BA Hons, University of Sussex; Birkbeck College, London. *Career:* Recorded as keyboard player with Eric Clapton; Sting; Phil Collins; Saxophonist with Muddy Waters; Little Richard; Ben E King; Jimmy Page; John Lennon; Dr John; Slim Gaillard; Musical Director for Van Morrison, late 1970s; Regular conductor, Royal Philharmonic Orchestra. *Compositions:* Films include: Funny Bones; Bhaji On The Beach; Hear My Song; Bad Behaviour; Devlin; Camilla; Titanic; RKO 281; The Lost Empire; Fidel; Beautiful Joe; Television includes: Peak Practice; Miss Marple; Shadowlands; First and Last; Comic Relief, 1995; By The Sword Divided; Composer, arranger, producer of over 3000 commercials including: British Airways; ATandT; Pan Am; General Motors; Stella Artois; Rover; Intercity; British Telecom; Films as arranger, orchestrator, conductor include: Monty Python's Life of Brian; Erik The Viking; Just A Gigolo; Foreign Bodies; The Sheltering Sky; Leon (a.k.a. The Professional); Golden Eye; Little Voice. *Recordings:* Arranger, conductor, producer: Singles: Downtown Train, Rod Stewart; Kissing A Fool, George Michael; That Ole Devil Called Love, Alison Moyet; Always Look On The Bright Side of Life, Monty Python; Walking In The Air, Aled Jones; Love Is On Our Side, Tom Jones; It's Oh So Quiet, Björk; Albums: Streetfighting Years, Simple Minds; Hey Manhattan, Prefab Sprout; A Very Special Season, Diana Ross; Wildest Dreams, Tina Turner; Closing credits, song for film: Innocent Lies, Patricia Kaas. *Honours:* BAFTA, Anthony Asquith Award for Best Original Film Score nominee, Hear My Song, 1992; TRIC Award, 1995; Primetime Emmy Award, Outstanding Music Composition for a Drama or Miniseries, RKO 281, 2000;. *Memberships:* PRS; ASCAP; BASCA; ASMAC. *Leisure interest:* Cricket. *Current Management:* SMA, 8938 Keith Ave, West Hollywood, CA 90069, USA.

ALU Steve; b. 13 July 1957, Beckenham, Kent, England. Front of House Sound Engineer; Tour Man.; Studio Sound Engineer. *Career:* 15 years practical experience engineering, production and tour management; Credits: One The Juggler; AirHead; Bolshoi; Eddie And The Hotrods; N-Joi; Senser; OMD; Jason Rebello; Bush Telegraph; Phil Manzanera; Loise Goffin; Royal Festival Ballet; Limelight/Hippodrome clubs; Concorde Agency; Elevator Man. *Leisure interests:* Computers; Videos. *Address:* Flat F, 78 Deptford High St, Deptford, London SE8 4RT, England.

AMA Shola, (Mathurin Campbell); b. 8 March 1979, Willesden, London, England. Vocalist. *Career:* Solo recording artiste, 1997–; Television appearances including Top of the Pops; Tour with Fugees, 1997; Tour with Jamiroquai's Jam in the Park; UK Rhythm Nation tour. *Recordings include:* Albums: Much Love, 1997; In Return, 1999; Singles: You Might Need Somebody, 1997; You're The One That I Love, 1997; Who's Loving My Baby, 1997; Much Love, 1998; Taboo (with Glamma Kid), 1999; Imagine, 2000. *Honours include:* Nominated for 3 MOBO Awards, won Best R & B Artist and Best Newcomer, 1997; Nominated, 2 Brit Awards, won Best Female, 1998. *Leisure interests:* Oil painting; Swimming; Writing. *Current Management:* 1 2 One Management. *Address:* c/o 20 Damien St, London E1 2HX, England.

AMBROSE (Edmund) David; b. 11 Dec. 1945, Highgate, London, England. Record Co Exec.; Musician (bass). m. Angela, 3 Sept. 1975, 2 s., 1 d. *Education:* Brymshaw College of Art; London College of Printing. *Career:* Musician with: Shotgun Express; Julie Driscoll; Brian Auger and Trinity; Arthur Brown; Cat Stevens; Numerous television and radio appearances; Concerts include: Royal Albert Hall and Fairfield Hall; Director of Planet 3 Records; Publishing for: Sex Pistols; Vapors; Dexy's Midnight Runners; Duran Duran; Pet Shop Boys; Transvision Vamp; Love City Groove. *Recordings:* with Shotgun Express: Shotgun Express, 1969; with Brian Auger and The Trinity: Open, 1967; Definitely What, 1968; Steetnoise, 1968; Befour, 1970; Genesis, 1975. *Memberships:* Chelsea Arts Club; Rye Art Gallery. *Leisure interests:* Sailing; Painting; Songwriting; Tennis. *Address:* 71 Finlay St, Fulham, London SW6 6HF, England.

AMENT Jeff; Rock Musician (bass). *Career:* Musician in Seattle SubPop scene, 1980s; Member, Green River, 1987–89; Mother Love Bone, 1989; Pearl Jam, 1990–; Concerts with Pearl Jam: Support to Alice In Chains, 1991; Lollapalooza Festival 92 tour, 1992; Drop In The Park concert, Seattle, 1992; European tour, 1992; Bridge School Benefit, with Neil Young, Elton John, Sammy Hagar, James Taylor, 1992; Support to Keith Richards and The Expensive Winos, New York, 1992; Concert appearances with Neil Young; Group appearance in film Singles, 1992; Also member, Temple of The Dog project, 1991. *Recordings:* Albums: with Green River: Rehab Doll (EP), 1988; with Mother Love Bone: Shine (EP), 1989; Apple, 1990; with Pearl Jam: Ten (No. 2, US), 1991; Vs. (No. 1, USA), 1993; Vitalogy, 1994; No Code, 1996; Live On Two Legs, 1998; Yield, 1998; with Temple of The Dog: Temple of The Dog, 1991; Singles: with Pearl Jam: Alive, 1992; Even Flow, 1992; Jeremy, 1992. *Honours:* American Music Award: Favourite New Artist, 1993; Rolling Stone Readers' Awards, Best New American Band, Best Video, 1993; 4 MTV Awards, 1993; Highest 1-week album sales total in history, Vs., 1993. *Current Management:* Curtis Management, 1423 34th Ave, Seattle, WA 98122, USA.

AMIGO Vicente; b. 25 March 1967, Guadalcanal, Sevilla, Spain. *Career:* Paris Guitar Festival; International Festival of Cordoba; First on David Bowie Spanish tour, Ballet Nacional de España tour, USA; L'Ete de Nimes, France; Legends of Guitar Festival, Sevilla; International Guitar Festival, La Habana; Mestres Da Guitarra, Paco de Lucia, John McLaughlin. *Compositions:* De mi corazón al aire, 1991; Poeta, Concierto flamenco para un marinero en tierra, orchestra; Vivencias imaginadas, 1995. *Honours:* Icaro, 1991; Ateneo de Cordoba, 1992; Best Flamenco Guitarist (Guitar Player), 1993. *Current Management:* Intercambio de Cultura y Arte (ICARI). *Address:* c/o Carretas, 14–5-I-5, 28012 Madrid, Spain.

AMOS Tori; b. 22 Aug. 1963, North Carolina, USA. Vocalist; Songwriter; Musician (piano). *Education:* Scholarship, Peabody Institute, Baltimore, USA. *Musical Education:* Church choir, piano from age 4. *Career:* Singer, piano bars as teenager; Solo recording artiste, 1987–; British tour, 1991; Tour with Alanis Morissette, 1999. *Recordings:* Albums: Y Kant Tori Read, 1988; Me and My Gun (EP), 1991; Little Earthquakes, 1991; Under The Pink, 1994; Boys For Pele, 1995; From The Choirgirl Hotel, 1998; To Venus and Back, 1999; Strange Little Girls, 2001; Singles include: Cornflake Girl; Caught A Lite Sneeze; Professional Widow (No. 1, UK) 1997; Talula, 1998; Jackie's Strength, 1999; Bliss, 1999; featured track on: Tower of Strength (Leonard Cohen tribute), 1995. *Honours include:* Q Award, Best New Act, 1992; Grammy Nominations, Best Alternative Music Performance (To Venus and Back), Best Female Rock Vocal Performance (Bliss), 2000. *Current Management:* Spivak Entertainment, 11845 W Olympic Blvd, Suite 1125, Los Angeles, CA 90064, USA.

AMRAM David Werner; b. 17 Nov. 1930, Philidelphia, USA. Composer; Conductor; Musician. m. Loralee Ecobelli, 1 s., 2 d. *Musical Education:* Oberlin Conservatory Music, 1948–49; Manhattan School of Music, 1955–56; BA, George Washington University, 1952; LLD, Moravian College, PA, 1979; MusD, Muhlenberg College, 1988; University Hartford, 1989; DMus, St Lawrence University, 1994. *Career:* Head Free Schooltime Concert Series, Philharmonic Orchestra, 1971–; Leo Block Chair, Arts and Humanities, University; Conductor, Soloist with 14 orchestras; Composer, incidental music for productions, Broadway plays, films and television; Recording Artist; Conductor; Composer; Multi Instrumentalist; Music Director, International Jewish Arts Festival. *Compositions include:* (for orchestras) Ode to Lof Buckley; (Opera) The Final Ingredient, 12th Night. *Publications:* Vibrations: Adventures and Musical Times of David Amram; At Home Around The World. *Honours:* Include, Obie Award. *Current Management:* Ed Keane Associate, 32 Saint Edward Rd, Boston, MA 02128, USA.

AMSALLEM Franck; b. 25 Oct. 1961, Oran, Algeria. Musician (piano); Composer; Prod. *Musical Education:* Nice Conservatory of Music; Berklee College of Music; Manhattan School of Music. *Career:* Performed with Gerry Mulligan, Charles Lloyd, Bobby Watson, Joe Chambers, Harry Belafonte, Blood Sweat and Tears, Bob Belden, Tim Ries, Peter King, Didier Lockwood; Featured on French National Radio. *Compositions:* Out A Day; Chanson Triste; After; Running After Eternity; Nuits, 1994. *Recordings:* Out A Day; Regards; Is That So; Years Gone By; New York Stories; On Second Thoughts, 2000. *Honours:* Fondation de la Vocation, 1989; NEA Competition Fellowship, 1990; Ascap Award for Young Composers, 1991. *Leisure interests:* Tennis; Wine and Food. *Current*

Management: FRAM Music. *Address:* 100 Ocean Parkway #6K, Brooklyn, NY 11218, USA. *E-mail:* sallemjazz@yahoo.com.

AMSTELL Billy; b. 20 Aug. 1911, London, England. Musician (saxophone, clarinet); Composer; Author. m. Tessa, 19 June 1938. *Musical Education:* 2 Certificates for Piano, Royal College of Music, aged 10. *Career:* 11 years with Ambrose Orchestra; 2 years with Geraldo Orchestra, radio and records; 8 years with Stanley Black on BBC Radio shows: Much Binding In The Marsh; The Goon Show; Ray's A Laugh; Life With The Lyons; With wife, presented to HRH Princess Anne; Played twice at Buckingham Palace; Sergeant i/c Station Band, RAF Wittering, Lincs. *Compositions:* At least 30 compositions (Peter Maurice, Music Coy, Keith Prowse, Bosworth). *Recordings:* Over 1000 with: Ambrose; Geraldo; Stanley Black; Geoff Love; Video: Don't Fuss, Mr Ambrose. *Publications:* Memoirs: Don't Fuss, Mr Ambrose. *Honours:* Guild of Freeman of the City of London; Hon. Citizen of New Orleans (USA). *Memberships:* Musicians' Union (Hon); PRS; Academy of Songwriters and Authors; Hon. mem. of the Clarinet and Saxophone Society of Great Britain; Life Mem., Bomber Command Asscn; Associate Hon. Mem., Pathfinders Asscn. *Leisure interest:* Writing for magazines. *Address:* Billy Amstell, 40 Ebrington Rd, Kenton, Harrow, Middlesex HA3 0LT, England.

AMYOT Robert; b. 25 July 1953, Montréal, Canada. French Bagpipes. 2 d. *Education:* Traditional Singing French State Diploma. *Career:* Played with Jean Blanchard and Evelyne Girardon in Beau-Temps-Sur-La-Province; La Grande Bande de Cornemuse; Le Quintette deCornemuse; Major folk festivals around the world, St-Chartier. *Compositions:* Le Brandevin; Le Loriot de Baltimore; Le Harfang des Neiges; Marie Miville; L'Anniversaire. *Recordings:* Sur La Vignolon; Trappeur Courtois; Le Grand Festin; La Grande Bande de Cornemuse; Le Quintette de Cornemuse. *Publications:* Cornemuse; Souffles Infinis Souffles Continus, collection Moda, article, 1991. *Honours:* First Prize, Cornemuse in Anost, France, 1987; President, St-Chartier Jury, 1990–96. *Membership:* APMT, France. *Leisure interests:* French Baroque Culture; French Food and Wines. *Current Management:* Cie du Beau Temps, 20 Cours Suchet, 69002 Lyon, France. *Address:* Le Bourgeal Dessous, 74130 Brizon, France.

ANASTACIA (Anastacia Newkirk); b. 17 Sept. 1973, Chicago, USA. Vocalist; Songwriter. *Education:* Professional Children's School, Manhattan, graduate. *Career:* Cabaret singer father and musical theatre actress mother; Worked as a dancer on pop videos and TV prior to being discovered as vocalist on MTV talent show The Cut; Career developed in Europe prior to USA success; Performed alongside Michael Jackson at historic United We Stand benefit concert, 2001. *Compositions:* Boom, chosen as official song of World Cup, 2002. *Recordings:* Albums: Not That Kind, 2000; Freak of Nature, 2001; Singles: I'm Outta Love, Not That Kind, 2000; Cowboys and Kisses, Made For Lovin' You, Paid My Dues, 2001. *Honours:* World Music Award, Best New International Artist, 2001; MTV Europe Music Award, Best Pop Act, 2001. *Current Management:* Lisa Braude, Braude Management, PO Box 7249, San Diego, CA 92167, USA. *Internet:* www.anastacia.com.

ANCHEV Emil; Vocalist. *Career:* Founder member, lead vocalist, Concurant, 1986; Numerous concerts, television and radio programmes, Bulgaria. *Recordings:* Rock For Peace, 1988; Rock Festival In Mitchurin, 1989; The Black Sheep (rock collection), 1992; Something Wet (best-selling album, Bulgaria), 1994; The Best of Bulgarian Rock, 1995. *Honours:* First prizes: Top Rock Band, Youth Festival Vidin, 1989; Rock Ring, Sofia, 1990; Top Rock Composition: The Cavalry, 1991; Top Rock Singer, Bulgaria, 1994; Group of The Year, The Darik Radio Countdown, 1994. *Address:* 40 St Stambolov Blvd, 1202 Sofia, Bulgaria.

ANDERSEN Arild; b. 27 Oct. 1945, Oslo, Norway. Jazz Musician (bass); Bandleader; Composer. *Musical Education:* Studied with Karel Netolicka and George Russell. *Career:* Touring musician with George Russell; Jan Garbarek, Karin Krog, Edward Vesala, 1966–73; Also worked with Don Cherry; Stan Getz; Sam Rivers; Paul Bley; Leader, own quartet, 1974; Member, Norwegian quintet Masquelero, 1983-. *Compositions include:* Sagn (series of works based on traditional folk songs), premiered at Vossajazz Festival, 1990. *Recordings:* Albums: Clouds In My Head, 1975; Shimri, 1976; Green Shading Into Blue, 1978; Lifelines, 1980; A Molde Concert, 1981; Sagn, 1990; Masquelero, 1983; Bande A Part, 1985; If You Look Far Enough (with Nana Vasconcelos, Ralph Towner), 1993; Kritin Lavransdatter, 1995; Hyperborean, 1997.

ANDERSEN Torfinn Nergaard; b. Norway. Music Co-Exec. *Career:* Director, Groovy Management; Owner, Record label, Rec 90 (Norway); Manager for Butterfly Garden (Norway). *Membership:* FONO. *Current Management:* Groovy Management, PO Box 1291, 5001 Bergen, Norway.

ANDERSON Beth; b. 3 Jan. 1950, Kentucky, USA. Composer, Musician (Piano). m. Elliotte Rusty Harold. *Education:* BA, University of California; MFA, MA, Mills College; PhD, New York University. *Career:* Wrote Music For, Off Off Boradway Musicals, Nirvana Manor; Elizabeth Rex: Or The

Well Bred Mother Goes to Camp; Fat Opera. *Compositions:* Minnesota Swale; Trio: Dream in 'd'; Net Work. *Recordings:* Belgian Tango; Revel. *Publications:* Beauty is Revolution; The Internet for Women In Music. *Honours:* National Endowment for the Arts; National Public Radio Satellite Program Development Fund Grant. *Memberships:* New York Women Composers; International Alliance of Women in Music; Poets and Writers. *Leisure interests:* Yoga; Astrology. *Address:* 135 Eastern Parkway #4D, Brooklyn, NY 11238, USA.

ANDERSON Bill (James William III); b. 1 Nov. 1937, Columbia, South Carolina, USA. Country vocalist; Songwriter; Musician (guitar, harmonica); Actor; Presenter. *Career:* Began career as sports writer; Later DJ in Commerce, Georgia; After early writing success, signed by Decca Records as a performer, 1958; Joined the Grand Ole Opry, 1961; US country and pop successes for five decades as both writer and performer; Written hits for artists including: Ivory Joe Hunter; Jerry Lee Lewis; Dean Martin; Ray Price; Collin Raye; Debbie Reynolds; Connie Smith; Porter Wagoner; Steve Wariner; Lawrence Welk; Kitty Wells; Faron Young; Ken Dodd; As artist, over 80 Billboard country chart singles, 1958–91; Movie appearances include: Forbidden Island, 1959; Gold Guitar, 1966; Las Vegas Hillbillies, 1966; Forty Acre Feud, 1968; From Nashville With Love, 1969; Hosted own TV show, 1966; Also US TV game shows: The Better Sex, 1977–78; Fandango, 1983–89; Currently hosting Opry Backstage; Idiosyncratic monologues on record earned the nickname Whispering Bill. *Compositions include:* Cincinnati Ohio; City Lights; Eight By Ten; Face To The Wall; Five Little Fingers; Get A Little Dirt On Your Hands; Happy Birthday To Me; Happy State of Mind; I Can't Remember; I Don't Love You Anymore; I Get The Fever; I Love You Drops; I May Never Get To Heaven; I Missed Me; I Never Once Stopped Loving You; I've Enjoyed As Much of This As I Can Stand; If It's All The Same To You; Losing Your Love; Mama Sang A Song; My Life (Throw It Away If I Want To); Nobody But A Fool Would Love You; Once A Day; Peel Me A Nanner; Po' Folks; River Boat; Saginaw Michigan; Still; That's What It's Like To Be Lonesome; Then and Only Then; Tip of My Fingers; Two Teardrops; Walk Out Backwards; We All Missed You; When Two Worlds Collide; Wild Weekend; Wish You Were Here; You and Your Sweet Love. *Recordings include:* Mama Sang A Song, 1962; Still, 1963; I Get The Fever, 1966; For Loving You (with Jan Howard), 1967; My Life (Throw It Away If I Want To), 1969; Where Have All Our Heroes Gone, 1970; Always Remember, 1971; World of Make Believe, 1973; Sometimes (with Mary Lou Turner), 1975; I Can't Wait Any Longer, 1978; Albums: I Love You Drops, 1966; Greatest Hits, 1967; For Loving You (with Jan Howard), 1968; My Life/But You Know I Love You, 1969; Sometimes (with Mary Lou Turner), 1976. *Publications:* I Hope You're Living As High On The Hog As The Pig You Turned Out To Be (anecdotes), 1983; Whispering Bill (autobiography), 1989. *Honours:* various including: Nashville Songwriters Hall of Fame, 1975; Georgia Music Hall of Fame, 1985; Vocal Event of the Year, Too Country (with Brad Paisley, George Jones and Buck Owens), 2001; Country Music Hall of Fame, 2001. *Address:* c/o Sony/ATV Tree Music, 8 Music Sq. W, Nashville, TN 37203, USA.

ANDERSON Billy (William John); b. 5 March 1946, Colinsburgh, Fife, Scotland. Musician (piano accordion); Radio Presenter; Tutor. m. Elizabeth W Hannah, 12 Aug. 1966, 3 s., 1 d. *Education:* Piano-accordion as a boy. *Career:* Composer; Arranger; Producer; Broadcast with BBC Radio, television, 1969–; Tours: USA; Canada; United Arab Emirates; Oman; Brunei; North Malaysia; Germany; Netherlands; Italy; Australia. *Recordings:* 7 with Albany (own group), mainly American appearances; CD, Sonas, released October 1999. *Publications:* 5 compositions published. *Memberships:* Musicians Union; PRS. *Leisure interests:* Walking; MIDI computing. *Address:* 4 Kingsloan Court, Largoward, Leven, Fife KY9 1JH, Scotland.

ANDERSON Brett; b. 26 Sept. 1967. Vocalist; Songwriter. *Career:* Founder member: Geoff, 1985; Suave and Elegant, 1989; Suede, 1989–; Television appearances include: Top of The Pops, BBC1; BRIT Awards, Alexandra Palace, London, 1993; The Beat, ITV; Later With Jools Holland, BBC2; The Tonight Show, NBC Television; Concerts include: Phoenix Festival; Glastonbury Festival; Tours, Europe, America and Japan. *Recordings:* Albums: Suede (No. 1, UK), 1993; Dog Man Star, 1994; Coming Up, 1996; Sci-Fi Lullabies, 1997; Head Music, 1999; Sessions CD (fan club release), 2000; Singles include: The Drowners, 1992; Metal Mickey, 1992; Animal Nitrate, 1993; So Young, 1993; Stay Together, 1994; We Are The Pigs, 1994; New Generation, 1995; Trash, 1996; The Beautiful Ones, 1996; Film Star, 1997; Lazy, 1997; Saturday Night, 1997; She's In Fashion, 1999; Everything Will Flow, 1999; Can't Get Enough, 1999; Contributor, Shipbuilding, to War Child charity album, 1995. *Honours include:* Mercury Music Prize, 1993; Q Award, Best New Act, 1993. *Current Management:* Interceptor Enterprises, The Greenhouse, 34–38 Provost St, London N1 7NG, England.

ANDERSON Carleen; b. 10 May 1957, Houston, Texas, USA. Vocalist; Songwriter. 1 s. *Musical Education:* Music Education Studies, University of Southern California; Graduate, Music Performance, Los Angeles City College. *Career:* Country and Western session singer, 1976–79; Joined

Black Widow as lead singer, 1976–77; Joined Family Funkton, lead singer, 1978; Worked as bank teller and office clerk; Singer and Songwriter, Young Disciples, 1990–92; Solo work; Work with Paul Weller, Bryan Ferry, Doctor John; Joined Brand New Heavies, 1999. *Recordings:* Singles: Apparently Nothin' (with Young Disciples), 1991; Mama Said, 1993; Nervous Breakdown, True Spirit, 1994; Let It Last, 1995; Maybe I'm Amazed, Woman In Me, 1998; Apparently Nothing (with Brand New Heavies), 2000; Albums: True Spirit, 1994; Blessed Burden, 1998.

ANDERSON Chris(topher William); b. 22 Sept. 1956, Los Angeles, California, USA. Musician (guitar); Singer; Songwriter. m. Sharon Ann Cooper, 11 May 1991, 1 s., 1 d. *Musical Education:* Self-taught. *Career:* Leader, own Chris Anderson Band; Tours with artists including: Allman Brothers; Stevie Ray Vaughan; Double Trouble; Lynyrd Skynyrd; Bad Company; Government Mule; Outlaws; Marshall Tucker; Charlie Daniels; Wet Willie; Concerts include: Radio City Music Hall; Television: Throw, Fox Television; Commercials: Bush Radio; Budweiser; Videos: Srascle, Outlaws. *Recordings:* Old Friend, Chris Anderson Band; Trouble On The Tracks, Double Trouble; Right On Time, Grinder Switch; Floyd Miles. *Honour:* Inducted into Rock and Roll Hall of Fame. *Memberships:* AFTRA; AFofM. *Leisure interests:* Motorcycles; Mountain biking. *Current Management:* Doc Field, Creative Action Music Group. *Address:* 865 Bellevue Rd, Suite E-12; Nashville, TN 37221, USA.

ANDERSON Dave; b. 21 Nov. 1949, Essex, England. Musician (bass); Studio Owner; Record Co Owner; Record Prod. and Engineer. 1 s., 2 d. *Career:* Worked with Nick Lowe; Amon Düül II; Hawkwind; Bob Calvert; Groundhogs; Library Music for Chappell Music Publishers. *Recordings:* Albums with the above artists. *Membership:* PRS; MCPS; PPL. *Leisure interests:* Flying. *Address:* Foel Studio, Llanfair Caeeinion, Powys SY21 0DS, Wales.

ANDERSON Emma Victoria Jane; b. 10 June 1967, Wimbledon, London, England. Musician (guitar); Songwriter. *Education:* BA (Hons) Humanities, Ealing College of Higher Education, 1986–90. *Career:* Bass player, The Rover Girls, 1986–88; Lead guitarist, songwriter, Lush, 1988–96; Signed to 4AD Records; World-wide tours include rock festival tour Lollapalooza, 1992; Guitarist, Songwriter, Sing-Sing, 1998-. *Recordings:* Singles: with Lush: Mad Love (EP), 1990; Sweetness and Light, 1990; For Love, 1992; Single Girl, 1996; Ladykillers, 1996; 500 (Shake Baby Shake), 1996; with Sing-Sing: Feels Like Summer, 1998; I'll Be, 2000; Tegan, 2001; Albums: with Lush: Scar (mini-album), 1989; Gala, 1990; Spooky, 1992; Split, 1994; Lovelife, 1996; Ciao! Best of Lush, 2000; with Sing-Sing: The Joy of Sing-Sing, 2001. *Memberships:* PRS; Musicians' Union; PAMRA. *Current Management:* Ifan Thomas, 23 Management, 1308 Factory Pl., Studio 504, Los Angeles, CA 90013, USA. *E-mail:* ifan@23-studios.com.

ANDERSON Ian; b. 26 July 1947, Weston-Super-Mare, England. Writer; Broadcaster; Musician (guitar, slide guitar). m. Hanitra Rasoanaivo, 2 May 1990, 1 step-d. *Musical Education:* Self-taught. *Career:* Solo musician, 1967–72; Member of duo Hot Vultures, 1972–79; English Country Blues Band, 1979–83; Tiger Moth, 1983–89; Editor of Folk Roots Magazine, 1979–; Radio presenter, BBC and ILR, 1984-. *Recordings:* 5 solo albums include: Stereo Death Breakdown, 1969; 3 albums with Hot Vultures include: Up The Line, 1979; 2 albums with English Country Blues Band, compiled as Unruly, 1993; 2 albums with Tiger Moth, compiled as Mothballs, 1995. *Publications:* Folk Roots Magazine. *Leisure interests:* Music; Photography. *Current Management:* Folk Music Services. *Address:* c/o Folk Music Services, PO Box 337, London N4 1TW, England.

ANDERSON Ian Scott; b. 10 Aug. 1947, Dunfermline. Musician; Songwriter. m. Shona, 1 s., 1 d. *Career:* 30 years, 60m. albums, countless radio and television appearances. *Compositions include:* Living In The Past; Aqualung; Thick As A Brick. *Recordings:* Numerous including Living In The Past; Aqualung; Thick As A Brick; Minstrel In The Gallery; The Best of Jethro Tull; Songs From The Wood; Heavy Horses; Celtic Experience. *Honours:* US Grammy Award, 1988. *Memberships:* PRS; Composers Guild. *Leisure interests:* Growing Chile Peppers; Study of Wild Cats; Painting; Photography. *Address:* Jethro Tull Production Ltd, PO Box 159, Witney, Oxon OX8 6JP, England.

ANDERSON James Noel; b. 23 Dec. 1951, Butler, Pennsylvania, USA. Recording Engineer; Prod.; Radio Consultant. m. Phoebe Ferguson, 10 Oct. 1982, 2 s. *Musical Education:* BS, Music Education, Duquesne University, 1973; Postgraduate, 1974; Postgraduate, Eastman School of Music, 1976; Postgraduate, Audio Engineering, Berlin, 1978. *Career:* Audio engineer, radio stations, Pittsburgh, Washington, 1973–80; Prowse James Anderson Audio (radio consultant), New York, 1980; Radio programmes: Taylor Made Piano, with Billy Taylor, 1981; Co-producer, Segovia! (radio documentary), 1983 Television programme: Segovia At The White House, with Andres Segovia, 1980. *Recordings:* Albums as recording engineer: Live At Fat Tuesdays, Pepper Adams, 1983; Sweet and Lovely, James Moody, 1989; Uptown/Downtown, McCoy Tyner, 1989. *Honours include:* Emmy

Nomination, Segovia At The White House, 1981; Peabody Award, Taylor-Made Piano, 1982; 3 Grammy Award Nominations; EBU Prix Futura Award, 1986. *Memberships:* Audio Engineering Society; NARAS; Audio Independents in Radio.

ANDERSON John, (John David Alexander); b. 13 Dec. 1954, Orlando, Florida, USA. Country vocalist; Songwriter; Musician (guitar, harmonica). *Career:* Formed bands the Weed Seeds and the Living End during teens; Moved to Nashville and sang with sister Donna, 1972; Staff writer for Al Gallico Music; First recorded for Ace of Hearts, 1974; Signed toWarner Bros Records, 1977; Over 50 country chart entries for Warner Bros, MCA, BNA and Mercury include: Black Sheep, co-written by film-maker Robert Altman; Swingin', biggest selling country single in Warner Bros history (1.4m.). *Compositions include:* Swingin' Goin' Down Hill; I Wish I Could've Been There. *Recordings:* Wild and Blue, 1982; Black Sheep, Swingin', 1983; Money In The Bank, 1993; Straight Tequila Night, 1991; Albums: Wild and Blue, 1982; All The People Are Talkin', 1983; Eye of a Hurricane, 1984; Seminole Wind, 1992. *Honours:* CMA, Horizon Award, 1983; CMA, Single of The Year, Swingin', 1983. *Leisure interests:* Fishing; Hunting. *Address:* c/o The Bobby Roberts Company Inc, 909 Meadowlark Lane, Goodlettsville, TN 37072, USA.

ANDERSON Jon; b. 25 Oct. 1944, Accrington, Lancashire, England. Vocalist. *Career:* Member, The Warriors, late 1960s; Co-founder, UK progressive rock group Yes, 1968–80; 1991–; Duo with Vangelis as Jon and Vangelis, 1980–; Concerts include: Support to Cream, Royal Albert Hall, 1968; Support to Janis Joplin, Royal Albert Hall, 1969; Montreux Television Festival, 1969; Support to The Nice, Royal Festival Hall, 1970; Tours, UK and USA, 1970–; Reading Festival, 1975; Evening of Yes Music, US tour, 1989; Yesshows '91, Round The World In 80 Dates tour, 1991. *Recordings:* Albums: with Yes: Yes, 1969; Time and A Word, 1970; Fragile, 1971; Close To The Edge, 1972; Yessongs, 1973; Tales From The Topographic Oceans, 1973; Relayer, 1974; Yesterdays, 1975; Going For The One, 1977; Tormato, 1978; 90125, 1983; 9012 Live, The Solos, 1986; Union, 1991; Yesstory, 1991; Symphonic Music of Yes, 1993; History of The Future, 1993; Open Your Eyes, 1998; Ladder, 1999; with Jon and Vangelis: Short Stories, 1980; Jon and Vangelis, 1980; Private Collection, 1983; The Best of Jon and Vangelis, 1984; Solo albums: Olias of Sunhillow, 1976; Song of Seven, 1980; Animation, 1982; Three Ships, 1985; Change We Must, 1994; The More You Know, 1998; Simply Christmas, 2001; with Anderson Bruford Wakeman Howe: Anderson Bruford Wakeman Howe, 1989; Contributor, Shine, Mike Oldfield; Legend, Tangerine Dream; Wintertime Is On, Whole World Band (proceeds to Down's Syndrome Association, Sickle Cell Society); Singles: with Yes include: Roundabout, 1972; Wondrous Stories, 1977; Owner of a Lonely Heart (No. 1, USA), 1983; Leave It, 1984; with Vangelis: I Hear You Now, 1980; I'll Find My Way Home, 1982; Whatever You Believe, with Steve Harley, Mike Batt (charity single), 1988. *Honours:* Gold Ticket, Madison Square Garden, 1978; Grammy Award, Best Rock Instrumental Performance, Cinema, 1985. *Current Management:* Big Bear Management, 9 Hillgate St, London W8 7SP, England.

ANDERSON Laurie P; b. 5 June 1947, Illinois, USA. Performance Artist; Musician (keyboards, violin). *Education:* MFA, Columbia University; BA, Barnard College. *Career:* Major performances: Stories From The Nerve Bible; Voices From The Beyond; Empty Places; Talk Normal; Natural History; United States; Films, videos: Carmen; Personal Service Announcements; Beautiful Red Dress; Talk Normal; Alive From Off Center; What You Mean We?; Language Is A Virus; Home of The Brave; This Is The Picture; Sharkey's Day; O Superman; Dear Reader; Puppet Motel (CD-Rom), 1995. *Recordings include:* O Superman, 1981; Big Science, 1982; Mister Heartbreak, 1984; United States Live, 1985; Home of The Brave, 1986; Strange Angels, 1989; Bright Red, 1994; The Ugly One With The Jewels and Other Stories, 1995; Film scores: Swimming To Cambodia; Monster In A Box. *Publications:* Stories From The Nerve Bible, 1994; Empty Places; Postcard Book; United States; Words In Reverse. *Honours:* Distinguished Alumna Award, Columbia School of The Arts; Hon. Doctorates, Art Institute of Chicago, Philadelphia College of the Arts. *Current Management:* Original Artists, 853 Broadway, Suite 1901, New York, NY 10003, USA.

ANDERSON Lynn Rene; b. 26 Sept. 1947, Grand Forks, North Dakota, USA. Country Singer. m. (1) Glenn Sutton, 1968, divorced; (2) Harold Stream III, divorced. *Career:* Former success as horse rider; Singer, recording artist, 1966–; Television appearances include: Lynn Anderson specials; Resident guest, Lawrence Welk Show, 1967–70; Grand Ole Opry; Ed Sullivan Show. *Recordings:* US Country No. 1 hit singles: Rose Garden; You're My Man; How Can I Unlove You?; Keep Me In Mind; What A Man My Man Is; Other hits include: If I Kiss You (Will You Go Away); That's A No No; Top of The World; Rocky Top; Encore; Duets include: with Gary Morris: You're Welcome To Tonight; with Ed Bruce: Fool For Each Other; with Billy Joe Royal: Under The Boardwalk; Numerous albums include: Ride Ride Ride, 1967; With Love From Lynn, 1969; No Love At All, 1970; Cry, 1972; Singing My Song, 1973; Smile For Me, 1974; All The King's Horses, 1976; From The Inside, 1978; Lynn Anderson Is Back, 1983; What

She Does Best, 1988; Greatest Hits, 1992; Cowboy's Sweetheart, 1993. *Honours:* Gold discs; Over 700 horse riding trophies. *Current Management:* Anders Productions. *Address:* 4925 Tyne Valley Blvd, Nashville, TN 37220, USA.

ANDERSON Moira; b. 5 June 1940, Kirkintilloch, Scotland. Vocalist. *Career:* Singer, traditional Scottish folk music; Also interpretations of popular standards and light operatic works; Regular UK television appearances, especially religious programmes. *Recordings:* Numerous albums include: Moira Anderson's Scotland, 1970; This Is Moira Anderson, 1971; The Auld Scotch Songs, 1975; Someone Wonderful, 1978; Golden Memories, 1981; The Love of God, 1986; A Land For All Seasons, 1988; 20 Scottish Favourites, 1990. *Honours:* OBE, Services to music industry. *Address:* International Artistes Ltd, Mezzanine Floor, 235 Regent St, London W1R 8AX, England.

ANDERSON Roger Lee; b. 6 Jan. 1955, Peoria, Illinois, USA. Musician (Keyboards); Songwriter. m. Pegeen Conners, 10 June 1996. *Education:* Bradley University, Peoria, Illinois, two years. *Recordings:* Eargazm, album; Tumblin' Dice, cassette; Knight Crawler, CD. *Honours:* Best Pop Artist, Prairie Sun Midwest Readers' Poll, 1983; Best Keyboardist, Twin Cities Blues News Readers' Poll, 1997; Nominee, Best Rock CD, for Knight Crawler, Best Rock Artist and Best Keyboardist, Minnesota Music Awards, 1997–98. *Memberships:* Minnesota Music Movement; NARAS. *Current Management:* Artist Representation and Management. *Address:* 1257 Arcade St, St Paul, MN 55106, USA.

ANDERSON Terry Randall; b. 25 Dec. 1956, Louisberg, North Carolina, USA. Songwriter; Musician (drums, guitar). m. Grace Brummett, 29 April 1989, 1 s. *Education:* 2 years college, Sandhills Community College, Southern Pines, North Carolina, USA. *Career:* Two European tours; Drums with: Don Dixon; Marti Jones. *Compositions:* Battleship Chains, recorded by Georgia Satellites; I Love You Period; Co-wrote 4 songs on Dan Baird's solo record. *Recordings:* Solo record on ESD (Minn, Minn). *Membership:* ASCAP. *Leisure interests:* Golf; Following UNC (Carolina) basketball; Painting. *Current Management:* Harry Simmons, Simmons Management. *Address:* 5214 Western Blvd, Raleigh, NC 27606, USA.

ANDERSSON G B Benny; b. 16 Nov. 1946, Stockholm, Sweden. Composer; Musician (keyboards). m. Mona Nörklit, Dec. 1981, 2 s., 1 d. *Career:* Member and songwriter; Abba; Composer: musical, Chess, with Tim Rice, Björn Ulvaeus; Kristina Från Duvemåla, musical based on Vilhelm Moberg's epic novels, Utvandrarna; Abba songs also inspired musical Mamma Mia! stage show, opened London 1999. *Recordings:* Albums: Waterloo, 1974; Abba, 1976; 8 number 1 in album charts: Greatest Hits, 1976; Arrival, 1976; The Album, 1978; Voulez-Vous, 1979; Greatest Hits Vol. 2, 1979; Super Trouper, 1980; The Visitors, 1981 The Singles, The First Ten Years, 1982; also: Thank You For The Music, 1983; Absolute Abba, 1988; Abba Gold, More Abba Gold, 1994; Thank You For The Music, 1995; Forever Gold, 1998; The Singles Collection, 2001. *Leisure interests:* Thoroughbred breeding and racing. *Address:* Södra Brobänken 41A, 111 49 Stockholm, Sweden.

ANDERSSON Mats Lennart; b. 2 Jan. 1964, Stockholm, Sweden. Drums. *Education:* Member, bob hund, 1991; More than 300 gigs in Scandinavia; Played at famous Roskilde, Lollipop, Ruisrock, Quartfestivalen and Hultsfred. *Compositions:* I Stället för Musik: Förvirring, 1996; Düsseldorf, 1996. *Recordings:* bob hund, 1993; Edvin Medvind, 7, 1994; I Stället för Musik: förvirring, 1996; Omslag: Martin Kann, 1996; Düsseldorf 3:53, 1996; Ett fall och en lösning, 1997; Nu är det väl revolution på gång?, 1998; Jag rear ut min själ! Allt skal bort!!!, 1998; Helgen V.48, 1999; Sover aldrig, 1999. *Honours:* Grammy, best live act, 1994; Grammy, best lyrics, 1996. *Memberships:* STIM; SAMI. *Leisure interests:* Music; Books; Food; Drinking. *Address:* c/o bob hunds förlag, Råsundavägen 150, 169 36 Solna, Sweden.

ANDRE Peter; b. 1973, England. Vocalist. *Career:* Moved to Australia, aged 10; Solo artiste, 1990–; Australian tours as support act to Madonna and Bobby Brown; Collaborations: Coolio; Montell Jordan; Brian McKnight; Fugees. *Recordings:* Albums: Natural, 1996; Time, 1997; Peter Andre, 1997; Singles: Turn It Up, 1995; Mysterious Girl, 1995; Only One, 1996; Flava (No. 1, UK), 1996; I Feel You (No. 1, UK), 1996; Lonely, 1997; All About Us, 1997; Natural, 1997; All Night All Right (with Warren G), 1998; Kiss The Girl, 1998. *Honours include:* Winner, talent contest to win recording contract, Australia, 1990; Best Selling Single in Australia, 1993; Highest Australian Chart Performer, Most Popular Australian Dance Act, Most Popular Australian Act, Coca Cola Awards, Australia, 1993; Best Australian Pop Dance release, Aria Awards, 1993; Best Selling Independent Single, Mysterious Girl, 1996; Best Selling Independent Album, Natural, 1996; Best International Male Singer, National TV2 Plus, Denmark, 1996; Best Male Singer, TV Hits Magazine, 1996; Best MMale Singer, Best Album Cover, Smash Hits Poll Winners Party, 1996; Best Dude Singer, Capital Slammers, 1996; Best Singer, Best Single, CITV Awards, 1996; Best Male in the Whole World, Otto Award Bravo 1997,

Germany; Best Newcomer, Popcorn Awards, Greece, 1997; Best International Artist, Irma's Ireland, 1997; World's Bestselling Australian Artist of the Year, 1996. *Address:* c/o Sue Harris, Blitz, Edwarebury Farm, Edwarebury Lane, Edgware, Middlesex HA8 8QX, England.

ANDREA Mihallaq; b. 17 July 1949, Korce, Albania. Musician (Guitar, Organ); Composer. m. Irena Cironaku, 21 Nov. 1988, 1 s., 1 d. *Career:* Appearances at National Festivals, Kenget e Stines (The Songs of the Season); The Geologist; Appearance, Serenata Korcare Festival. *Compositions:* Margarita; Serenata; Kitare E Dashur (My Dearly Beloved Guitar); Eja, Eja (Come, Come); Ne Kinema (At The Cinema). *Recordings:* The above; Fatkeqesia (The Misfortune). *Honours:* First Place, the music of the drama, The Geologist, 1984; First Place, Serenata Korcare Festival, 1999. *Membership:* Chair, Musical Society, Serenata Korcare. *Leisure interests:* Has written poems and novels for young people. *Address:* Petro Saro, No. 9 Lagjja 3, Korce, Albania.

ANDREA Nanni; b. 20 May 1963, Porretta Terme, Italy. Prod.; Promoter. m. Cristina Baisi, 27 April 1998. 1 c. *Career:* Music Producer, mainly Soul, Funk and R & B; Recordings for many labels. *Address:* Via Giardini 81, 41026 Pavullo, Modena, Italy.

ANDREASSEN Preben; b. 23 Aug. 1944, Aalborg, Denmark. Organist; Choir Dir. m. 2 s. *Musical Education:* Royal Danish Music Academic, Copenhagen; Diploma Degree, Church Organ and Choir Direction, 1974. *Career:* Concerts in Germany, Sweden, Norway, Holland, Greece, USA Los Angeles and Denmark; Television: Danich Channe 1, Before Sunday, 1992, 1993, 1998; Youth Services, 1991, 1995; Christmas Services, 1993; Gospel Services, 1998, 2000. *Compositions:* Choir works at Publisher Edition EGTVED: Before Sunday, 1992; Christmas Songs, 1994; New Danish Hymnbook, 1994; Music for Meditation, 1998; Hymns in different collection. *Recordings:* Christmas Music, 1982; Before Sunday, MC, VCR; CD Life is Living, 1992; Gospel Music, 1997, 1998. *Publications:* Brondbyvester Church Organ History, 1987; Christmas Songs, edition EGTVED, 1994. *Honour:* Intl Choir Fest, Veldhoven, Holland, First Prize, 1989. *Memberships:* Danich Organist Society; Danich Director Society. *Leisure interest:* Wood Carving. *Address:* Brondbyvester Church as Organist, Pianist, Choir Director and Composer, started in 1975.

ANDREWS Bob 'Derwood'; b. 17 June 1959, Fulham, London, England. Musician (guitar); Songwriter. *Career:* Guitarist, punk band Generation X, 1976–79; Formed Empire, early 80s; Formed Westworld, 1986; Tours with Generation X; Westworld; Appeared on Top of The Pops, and reached No. 11, UK charts, with both bands; Formed Moondogg, 1994; Album due 1995. *Recordings:* Albums: with Generation X: Generation X; Valley of The Dolls; Unreleased third album; with Westworld: Where The Action Is; Beatbox Rock 'N' Roll; Movers and Shakers; with Empire: Expensive Sound; with Jimmy Pursey: Imagination Camouflage. *Membership:* PRS. *Leisure interests:* Motorcycles; Speedway; Native American life. *Current Management:* Moondogg. *Address:* PO Box 163, Cave Creek, AZ 85331, USA.

ANDREWS Harvey; Singer; Songwriter. *Career:* Performer, songwriter for over 30 years; Appearances include: 36 major festivals, UK, North America, including 5 Cambridge festivals; Tours throughout Europe; Canada; US; Belize; Played venues throughout UK; Television includes: Old Grey Whistle Test; Rhythm On Two, BBC; Pebble Mill At One; Two television specials: The Camera and The Song; The Same Old Smile; 2 specials, Holland and Ireland; Radio includes: John Peel; Stuart Hall; Alan Freeman; Host, Folk On Two, BBC; Music presenter, BBC Radio Stoke. *Compositions:* Songs covered by artists including: Christy Moore; Mary Hopkin; Max Boyce; Ian MacIntosh; Lyrics used in GCSE English Language examination. *Recordings include:* Faces and Places; Writer of Songs; Friends of Mine; Margarita; Someday; Fantasies From A Corner Seat; Brand New Day; Old Mother Earth; PG; 25 Years On The Road; Spring Again; Snaps (The Family Album). *Current Management:* c/o Jim McPhee, Acorn Entertainments. *Address:* Winterfold House, 46 Woodfield Rd, Kings Heath, Birmingham B13 9UJ, England.

ANDREWS Julie, (Julia Wells); b. 1 Oct. 1935, Walton-on-Thames, Surrey, England. Singer; Actress. m. (1) Tony Walton, 10 May 1959, divorced, 1 d., (2) Blake Edwards, 1969. *Musical Education:* Voice lessons with Lillian Stiles-Allen. *Career:* As actress: Debut, Starlight Roof, London Hippodrome, 1947; Appeared: Royal Command Performance, 1948; Broadway production, The Boyfriend, NYC, 1954; My Fair Lady, 1956–60; Camelot, 1960–62; Putting It Together, 1993; Film appearances include: Mary Poppins, 1964; The Americanization of Emily, 1964; Torn Curtain, 1966; The Sound of Music, 1966; Hawaii, 1966; Thoroughly Modern Millie, 1967; Stark, 1968; Darling Lili, 1970; The Tamarind Seed, 1973; 10, 1979; Little Miss Marker, 1980; S.O.B., 1981; Victor/Victoria, 1982; The Man Who Loved Women, 1983; That's Life!, 1986; Duet For One, 1986; Television debut, 1956; Host, The Julie Andrews Hour, 1972–73; Julie (comedy series), ABC Television, 1992; Television films include Our Sons, 1991. *Recordings:* Albums: A Christmas Treasure, 1968; The Secret of

Christmas, 1977; Love Me Tender, 1983; Broadway's Fair, 1984; Love Julie, 1989; Broadway: The Music of Richard Rogers, 1994; Here I'll Stay, 1996; Nobody Sings It Better, 1996; with Carol Burnett: Julie and Carol At Carnegie Hall, 1962; At The Lincoln Center, 1989; Cast and film soundtacks: My Fair Lady (Broadway cast), 1956; Camelot (Broadway cast), 1961; Mary Poppins (film soundtrack), 1964; The Sound of Music (film soundtrack), 1965; The King and I (studio cast), 1992. *Publications:* Mandy (as Julie Edwards), 1971; The Last of The Really Great Whangdoodles, 1974. *Honours:* Academy Award, Mary Poppins, 1964; Golden Globe Awards, Hollywood Foreign Press Asscn, 1964, 1965; BAFTA Silver Mask, 1989.

ANDREWS Patti; b. 16 Feb. 1920, Minnesota, Louisiana, USA. Singer. *Career:* Lead singer, vocal group The Andrews Sisters (with sisters Laverne and Maxene), 1938–53; Occasional reunions until Laverne's death, 1967; Solo artiste, 1953–; Film appearances include: Argentine Nights, 1940; Buck Privates; Hollywood Canteen, 1944; Stage appearances include: Broadway musical, Over Here, 1974; Currently singing with Glenn Miller Orchestra. *Recordings:* Hits include: with The Andrews Sisters: Bei Mir Bist Du Schon; Hold Tight, Hold Tight; Roll Out The Barrel; Boogie Woogie Bugle Boy; Says My Heart; Say Si Si; I'll Be With You At Apple Blossom Time; Three Little Sisters; Strip Polka; Collaborations with: Bing Crosby; Burl Ives; Les Paul; Ernest Tubbs; Carmen Miranda; Solo hit: I Can Dream, Can't I? (No. 1, USA), 1949; Albums include: with The Andrews Sisters: Curtain Call, 1956; By Popular Demand, 1957; Dancing Twenties, 1958; The Andrews Sisters Present, 1963; The Andrews Sisters Go Hawaiian, 1965; with Maxene Andrews: Over Here (cast recording), 1974; Numerous compilations and greatest hits collections.

ANDRIES Alexandru Braesti; b. 13 Oct. 1954, Brasov, Romania. Singer; Songwriter; Musician (electric guitar, acoustic guitar, keyboards, harmonica); Architect; Lecturer. *Education:* Graduate, Institute of Architecture, 1980; PhD in progress. *Musical Education:* Self-taught. *Career:* Guest, most Romanian jazz festivals including: Sibiu; Costinesti; Cluj; Constanta; Bucharest, 1979–; Tours throughout Romania; Concerts include: Palace Hall, Bucharest; Polivalenta Hall, Bucharest; Special guest, concerts at American Cultural Center, Bucharest; Guest, British Council, 1989; Appearances, most jazz and blues clubs in Romania: Club A, Bucharest; Constanta; Timisoara; Tirgu-Mures; Iasi; Special guest star, Golden Stag Festival, Brasov, Romania, with Kylie Minogue, Dionne Warwick, 1993; Guest, most Romanian radio stations: ProFM; Contact; Total; Independent television stations. *Recordings:* Albums: Interiors 1, 1984; Interiors 2, 1985; Country and Western Greatest Hits, 1986; Rock 'N' Roll, 1987; On Distance, 1988; Three Mirrors, 1989; Censored, 1990; Today, 1991; Appetite Rises Eating, 1992; My She-Neighbours 1, 2, 3, 1992; How Far Away, 1993; Nothing New On The Eastern Front, 1993; Slow Burning Down, 1994; Alexandru Andries, 1994; Hocus Pocus, 1995; White Album, 1996; Home, 1996; Ungra, 1996; Silence of the Heart, 1996; In Concert, 1997; All By Myself, 1997; Bluntly, 1998; Secret Colours, 1998; Black and White, 1999; Texteriors, 1999; Songs for the Princess, 1999; Bad Weather, 2000; Live, 2001; Singles: Waiting For Maria, 1990; Wait 'Til Tomorrow, 1992; Dream With Angels, 1994; Watercolours, 1999; Bingo Romania, 2000; Videos: How Far Away, 1992; 21 Decembrie 1995/Teatrul Bulandra, 1996; In Concert, 1997; Blues Alive, The Most Beautiful Day, 2000; Live, 2001. Publicatons: Home Alone, short stories, 1992; Waiting For Maria, 1990; Happy Birthday Mr Dylan (Romanian translations from Bob Dylan's songs), 1991. *Honours:* Voted Best Singer/Songwriter, Vox, Pop, Rock (Romanian musical newspaper), 1990–; Golden Record Award, 1991; Best Singer, 1992; The Pro FM Contact Radio Awards, Best Singer, Songwriter, 1994. *Memberships:* Romanian Union of Composers; Romanian Union of Writers; Romanian Union of Architects; The Mickey Mouse Club, 1993. *Leisure interests:* Art shows; Exhibitions of photography and paintings; Films; Theatre; Concerts; Reading. *Current Management:* Aurel Mitran Management, Calea Victorei 48–50, Sc.B, Apt 73, Sector 1, Bucharest 70102, Romania. *Address:* Soseaua Stefan Cel Mare 26, Blvd 24A, Apt 26, Sector 2, Bucharest 71158, Romania.

ANDRST Lubos; b. 26 July 1948, Prague, Czech Republic. Musician; Composer. m. 11 July 1974, 1 s. *Education:* Autodidact. *Career:* Musician with J Stivin, E Viklicky, R Dasek, M Svoboda, V Misik, M Prokop; Founder, Energit, 1973; Founder, Lubos Andrst Blues Band, 1980. *Compositions:* Capricornus; November; Ikebana; La Bodeguita Dez Medio; Imprints; Encountering; White Landscape; Follow Your Heart; Europe Blues; Wide-Open Door. *Recordings:* Energit 1975; Piknik, 1978; Capricornus, 1981; Plus-Minus Blues, 1988; Imprints, 1992; L Andrst With Friends, 1996; L Andrst Acoustic Set, 1996. *Publications:* Guitar Book, Jazz Rock Blues, 1988; Redaction, 1995. *Memberships:* Czech Jazz Asscn; Ochranny svoz Autorsky; OSA. *Leisure interest:* Canoeing. *Current Management:* ARTA Music, Lubzanska 57, 120 00 Prague 2, Czech Republic. *Address:* Hvozdnice 8, 25205 Prague-Zapad, Czech Republic.

ANDRUSZKOW Life; b. 22 Sept. 1955, Copenhagen, Denmark. Singer; Composer; Musician (guitar, multi-instrumentalist). m. 2 c. *Musical Education:* Private lessons in classical music on trumpet and cornet by

conductor Jorgen Clausen and piano by Professor Anker Blyme; Self-taught in pop-rock-avantegarde composition and guitar; Private lessons in vocal by tutor Jens Christian Smith, (Denmark), tutor Ian Adams, (London) and by various tutors at Musicians Institute, London. *Career:* Performed with pop-rock-bands since 1979 The Law, Art Exist, The Act and Life; Performed on Ringe Festival, 1984 and Roskilde Festival, 1985. *Recordings:* Own releases: Aubaude Dolorose, maxi-single, 1985; Heaven Cries For No One, video, 1988; Dreams Without Reality, video, 1988; Tones of An Outsider, novel-video, 1989; Dancing In Burning Silhouettes, video, 1990; Europe After The Rain, CD, 1996; Promises, CD and video, 1998; Composing scores for radio-play: Sincerely, National Radio, 1984; for theatre: Images, Musical, 1986; Film soundtrack: Vertical, 1995; Lyrics for artists Michael Westwood: Bromskij Garden, CD, 1994; Live For It All, CD, 1996; My Living Dawn, CD, 1998. *Current Management:* Out of Eden Records, Sankt Pauls Gade 42, DK 1313 Copenhagen K, Denmark.

ANGELOPULO Charles; b. 8 Dec. 1954, Pretoria, South Africa. Singer; Composer. m. 6 May 1978, 1 s., 1 d. *Career:* Title role, Jesus Christ Superstar, 1990; Lead singer: Web; Cafe Society; Blasé. *Compositions:* Over 65 recorded and released titles include: Helen of Troy, The Rock Opera; I Love Africa; Good Time Girls; When You Gonna Love Me; Nothing Anybody Can Say. *Honour:* Finalist, South African Music Awards, 1995. *Memberships:* SAMRO; ASAMI. *Leisure interest:* Motor sport. *Address:* 433 16th Ave, Rietfontein, Pretoria 0084, South Africa.

ANGER Darol; b. 7 May 1953, Seattle, Washington, USA. Musician (violin, mandolin, guitar); Publisher; Author; Educator. *Education:* UC at Santa Cruz. *Musical Education:* Informal study with David Grisman; David Baker. *Career:* Member, Montreux Band, 1984; Founding member, David Grisman Quintet (DGQ); Played with artists including Stéphane Grappelli; Bela Fleck; Tony Rice; Mark O'Connor; Vassar Clements; Bill Keith; Richard Greene; Mike Marshall; Tony Trischka; Todd Phillips; Leader, Turtle Island String Quartet; Co-leader (with Mike Marshall), Psychograss; Co-founded the Anger/Marshall Band; Works with the Heritage Folk Music Project; Continues appearances with previous groups; Works as a producer and arranger for other artists; Featured soloist on film soundtracks, including Best Offer; A Shock To The System; Country; Annual seminars at US colleges; Instructor at Mark O'Connor Fiddle Camps. *Recordings include:* with Montreux Band: Sign Language; Let Them Say; Montreux Retrospective; with David Grisman: The David Grisman Quintet; Hot Dawg; Acoustic Christmas; with Turtle Island String Quartet: Turtle Island String Quartet; Metropolis; Skylife; On The Town; Spider Dreams; A Night In Tunisia, A Week In Detroit; By The Fireside; with Pyschograss: Like Minds; Anger/Marshall and Psychograss; with Mike Marshall: The Duo; Chiaroscuro; with Barbara Higbie: Tideline; Live At Montreux; Solo albums include: Fiddlistics; Jazz Violin Celebration; Also appears on: Harvest, 1996; When No One's Around, 1997; Heritage, 1998; View From Here, 1998; Heritage, 1999; With A Little Luck, 1999; Featured on recordings by: Suzanne Vega; Thomas Dolby; Henry Kaiser; Bela Fleck; Tony Trischka; John Gorka. *Publications:* Grant Wood and Street Stuff; Songs For Turtle Island; The Turtle Island Workbook; Darol Anger Originals; Fiddle Tunes. *Memberships:* NARAS; String Chair, International Asscn of Jazz Educators (IAJE); Sonneck Society. *Leisure interest:* Driving. *Current Management:* BZ Productions, PO Box 19297, Oakland, CA 94619, USA.

ANGUS Colin; b. 24 Aug. 1961, Aberdeen, Scotland. Musician. *Education:* Aberdeen University. *Career:* Member: Alone Again Or; Founder member: The Shamen, 1986-. *Recordings:* Albums: Drop, 1987; In Gorbechev We Trust, 1989; Phorward, 1989; En-Tact, 1990; Progeny, 1991; Boss Drum, 1992; SOS, 1993; Axis Mutatis, 1995; Hempton Manor, 1996; UV, 1998; On Air, The BBC Sessions (compilation), 1998; Singles include: Christopher Mayhew Says, 1987; Jesus Loves Amerika, 1988; Pro Gen, 1990; Move Any Mountain (Pro Gen '91), 1991; L.S.I., 1992; Ebeneezer Goode (No. 1, UK), 1992; Boss Drum, 1992; Phorever People, 1992; Destination Eschaton, 1995; Hemp, 1996; Universal, 1998; U Nations, 1998. *Current Management:* Moshka Management, PO Box 102, London E15 2HH, England.

ANKA Paul; b. 30 July 1941, Ottowa, Ontario, Canada. Vocalist; Composer. m. Marie Ann Alison de Zogheb, 16 Feb. 1963, 5 d. *Career:* Live and television appearances world-wide, 1956–; Actor, films: Girls Town; The Private Lives of Adam and Eve; Look In Any Window; The Longest Day. *Compositions include:* It Doesn't Matter Any More, for Buddy Holly, 1959; Co-writer (with Johnny Carson), Theme for Tonight Show, NBC Television, 1962–; My Way, for Frank Sinatra, 1969; She's A Lady, for Tom Jones, 1971. *Recordings:* Numerous singles include: Diana; I Love You Baby; You Are My Destiny; Crazy Love; (All of a Sudden) My Heart Sings; Lonely Boy; Put Your Head On My Shoulder; It's Time To Cry; Puppy Love; My Home Town; Summer's Gone; The Story of My Love; Tonight My Love Tonight; Dance On Little Girl; Love Me Warm and Tender; A Steel Guitar and A Glass of Wine; Eso Beso (That Kiss!); Albums include: Paul Anka Sings His Big 15, 1960; Anka At The Copa, 1960; Young Alive and In Love!, 1962; Let's Sit This One Out, 1962; Golden Hits, 1963; Goodnight My Love, 1969; Life Goes On, 1969; Paul Anka, 1972; Jubilation, 1972; Paul Anka

Gold, 1974; Feelings, 1975; Times of Your Life, 1976; The Painter, 1976; The Music Man, 1977; Listen To Your Heart, 1978; Both Sides of Love, 1978; Walk A Fine Line, 1983; Paul Anka Five Decades, 1992; A Body of Work, 1998; Christmas With Paul Anka, 2000. *Honours:* Numerous BMI Awards, for Most Performed Songs and Over 1 Million Plays; 15 Gold discs; Inducted, Songwriters Hall of Fame, 1993. *Membership:* BMI. *Address:* c/o Paul Anka Productions, 10573 W Pico Blvd, Suite 159, Los Angeles, CA 90064, USA.

ANNIES Nicholas Charles; b. 23 Jan. 1971, Kettering, England. Photographer; Graphic Artist. m. Lauren Kelly Behan, 4 Aug. 1996, 1 d. *Musical Education:* Self-taught. *Career:* Manager, record labels: Reality Recordings, c. 1990; ADI Records, 1991; Paradise Records, 1992; Co-manager, Village of Experimental Sound Studios, Cambridge; PA Engineer, including Caister Weekenders, 1987–91; Graphic Designer; Professional website designer; Managing Director: Once Click Solutions Ltd. *Recordings:* Singles: Armageddon (12), co-produced by Shades of Rhythm, 1991; with 39 Orbits: 2 12 releases, 1993–94; Music For A Mono Nation, due 2002. *Publications:* Underworld, monthly magazine, Peterborough City, 1990–93. *Memberships:* Musicians' Union; Society of Amateur Artists; Media Records Italy. *Leisure interests:* Painting; Making friends.

ANNISETTE (Annisette Hansen); b. 29 Aug. 1948, Denmark. Singer; Songwriter; Composer; Lyricist. m. Thomas Koppel, 1971, 2 d. *Career:* Lead Singer, The Savage Rose, 1967–; Numerous tours: Denmark; Europe; USA; Middle East; Newport Festival, 1969; Numerous international television appearances; Title role in her own musical drama with Thomas Koppel, Bella Vita, 1997; Vocal Soloist on the occasion of the 50th Anniversary of Denmark's Liberation from Nazi Army, 1995, in Symphony 2 by Thomas Koppel. *Compositions:* Several songs, Savage Rose; Lyrics for: Bella Vita, Thomas Koppel, 1997; Symphony No2, Thomas Koppel, 1995; Script for musical drama Bella Vita, 1996–97. *Recordings:* Savage Rose, 18 albums; Triumph of Death (ballet), Thomas Koppel, Bella Vita, 1993; Black Angel, 1995;. *Honours:* Several Grammy nomincations 1989–96; Several Gold, Platinum and Double Platinum Awards, 1968–97; Prize of Honour, Danish Songwriters; Union, 1995; Nomination for Music Award of the Nordic Council, 1996; Grammy, 1996. *Memberships:* Danish Artist's Union; Danish Jazz, Beat and Folk Authors' Society; Authors' Union. *Current Management:* South Harbor Productions, Frederikshíj 114, DK 2450 Copenhagen SV, Denmark.

ANSELMO Phil; b. USA. Rock Vocalist; Songwriter. *Career:* Lead vocalist, lyricist, US heavy rock group Pantera, 1986–; Also, lead vocalist with side-project Down, 1995-. *Recordings:* Albums: with Pantera: Power Metal, 1988; Cowboys From Hell, 1990; A Vulgar Display of Power, 1992; with Down: Nola, 1995; Singles with Pantera include: Cowboys From Hell; Mouth For War. *Current Management:* Concrete Management, 301 W 31st St, Suite 11-D, New York, NY 10019, USA.

ANSEMS Tony; b. 9 March 1940, Tilburg, Netherlands. Musician (guitar); Songwriter. m. Rita, 8 April 1964, 3 s. *Education:* American College, Bryn Mawr, Pennsylvania. *Career:* Guitarist with Breakaway; Songwriter; President, Songwriters of Wisconsin. *Compositions:* with Danny Mack: Old Rockers Never Die. *Memberships:* NSA; NAS; ASCAP. *Leisure interest:* Football. *Address:* PO Box 1027, Neenah, WI 54957–1027, USA.

ANSTICE-BROWN Sam; b. 24 July 1963, Sherborne, Dorset, England. Musician (drums); Arranger. *Musical Education:* BMusic Hons, Berklee College of Music, Boston, USA. *Career:* Tours, gigs with: Georgie Fame; Barbara Thompson; Mornington Lockett; Guy Barker; Jean Toussant; Iain Bellamy; Tony Wjan; John Etheridge; Zoot Money; Dick Morissey; Don Weller; Dave Newton; Alan Skidmore; Bobby Wellins. *Recordings:* Take It Or Leave It, Giladatzmon; Back To Square One, Organix. *Membership:* Musician's Union. *Leisure interests:* Music. *Address:* 2 Church St, Kingsbury, Martock, TA12 6AU, England. *Internet:* www.sambrown.co.uk.

ANT Adam (Stuart Leslie Goddard); b. 3 Nov. 1954, Marylebone, London, England. Vocalist; Songwriter; Actor. *Career:* Founder, lead singer, Adam and The Ants, 1977–82; Early tours with Siouxsie and The Banshees; X-Ray Spex; Desolation Angels; The Slits; Regular British tours, 1979–; Solo artiste, 1982–86, 1992–; Appeared at Live Aid, Wembley Stadium, 1985; Numerous television and radio appearances; Member, all-star Peace Choir, 1991; Actor, 15 films, including World Gone Wild; Sunset Heat; Numerous television series including: Northern Exposure; The Equalizer. *Compositions:* Numerous songs with co-writer Marco Pirroni; Songs covered by: Elastica; Nine Inch Nails. *Recordings:* Albums: with Adam and The Ants: Dirk Wears White Sox, 1979; Kings of The Wild Frontier, 1980; Prince Charming, 1981; solo: Friend Or Foe, 1982; Strip, 1983; Vive Le Rock, 1985; Hits, 1986; Manners and Physique, 1990; Wonderful, 1995; Antbox (career box set), 2001; Singles include: Ant Music; Dog Eat Dog; Kings of The Wild Frontier (No. 2, UK); Stand and Deliver (No. 1, UK); Prince Charming (No. 1, UK); Ant Rap (No. 3, UK); Goody Two Shoes (No. 1, UK); Puss In Boots; Apollo 9; featured tracks on

film soundtracks including: Jubilee; Metropolis. *Honours:* Ivor Novello Award, Songwriters of Year, with Pirroni, 1982; BRIT Award, Best British Album, Kings of The Wild Frontier, 1982. *Current Management:* UK/LA Management. *Address:* Bugle House, 21a Noel St, London W1V 3PD, England.

ANTHONY Marc, (Marco Antonio Muniz); b. 16 Sept. 1968, New York City, New York, USA. Vocalist; Songwriter. *Career:* Sang back-up on demos and TV commercials, aged 12; Started writing songs in high school including Boy I've Been Told, a hit for SaFire, 1988; Starred in the film East Side Story, 1988; Teamed up with composer of the film score, Louie Vega; Resulting album When The Night Is Over, 1990; Release featured many Latin musicians, awakening interest in salsa; Signed to Sony and released first solo album, Otra Nota, 1993; Starred in Paul Simon's Broadway musical The Capeman, 1998. *Recordings:* Otra Nota, 1993; Todo A Su Tiempo, 1995; Contra La Corriente, 1997; Marc Anthony, 1999; Libre, 2000. *Honours:* Latin Grammy Award, Song of The Year, Dimelo (I Need To Know), 2000. *Internet:* www.marcanthony.net.

ANTHONY Michael; b. 20 June 1955, Chicago, Illinois, USA. Musician (bass). *Career:* Member, Snake; Bass player, US rock group Van Halen, 1974–; Support tours with UFO; Santana; Black Sabbath; Regular US and world-wide tours; Major concerts: California Music Festival, 1979; US Festival, 1982; 1983; Monsters of Rock Festival, Castle Donington, 1984; Monsters of Rock US tour (with Metallica, Scorpions), 1988; Texxas Jam, 1988; Co-host, radio show with Sammy Hagar, Radio Westwood One, 1992. *Recordings:* Albums: Van Halen, 1978; Van Halen II, 1979; Women and Children First, 1980; Fair Warning, 1981; Diver Down, 1982; 1984, 1984; 5150 (No. 1, USA), 1986; OU812 (No. 1, USA), 1988; For Unlawful Carnal Knowledge (No. 1, USA) 1991; Right Here Right Now, 1993; Balance, 1995; Van Halen III, 1998; Van Halen 1978–84 (retrospective box set), 2000; Singles include: You Really Got Me, 1978; Running With The Devil, 1978; Dance The Night Away, 1979; And The Cradle Will Rock, 1980; (Oh) Pretty Woman, 1981; Dancing In The Street, 1982; Jump (No. 1, USA), 1984; Panama, 1984; I'll Wait, 1984; Hot For Teacher, 1984; Why Can't This Be Love, 1986; Dreams, 1986; Love Walks In, 1986; When It's Love, 1988; Finish What Ya Started, 1988; Feels So Good, 1989; Poundcake, 1991; Top of The World, 1991; Right Now, 1992; Appears on: Heart of Stone, Cher, 1989; Trash, Alice Cooper, 1989; Fresh Outta P University; 1997; R, R Kelly, 1998; I Do, Blaque, 1999; Ain't Talkin' Bout Dub, Apollo Four Forty; Post-Mersh Vol. 3, Minutemen. *Honours:* Platinum discs; Grammy Award, Best Hard Rock Performance, 1992; MTV Music Video Awards, 1984, 1992; Band awarded Gold Ticket, Madison Square Garden, 1988; American Music Award, Favourite Album, 1992. *Current Management:* SRO Management Inc, 189 Carlton St, Toronto, ON M5A 2K7, Canada.

ANTILL Danny Terrance; b. 8 Sept. 1959, Johannesburg, South Africa. Musician (keyboards, flute); Prod.; Arranger. m. 6 Feb. 1982, 1 s., 2 d. *Musical Education:* Eighth Grade classical piano, flute (Royal Academy of Music). *Career:* Toured with Stingray throughout South Africa; Appeared on national television 1, 2, 3; Solo piano albums released throughout Europe; Playlisted on German national radio. *Recordings:* Stingray; Danny Antill, 3 solo albums released throughout Europe; Amaduduzo, Siyabamukela; Amaduduzo, Exotic Voices and Rhythms; Producer, arranger, 17 Gold records; Composer, theme song for local blockbuster film Boetie Gaan Bordertoe. *Honours:* 17 Gold records; Top 5 3 years consecutively; South African OKTV Award Nomination, Best Producer, Arranger, Jingle and television themes writer. *Membership:* SAMRO. *Leisure interests:* Golf; Fishing; Diving. *Current Management:* Brettian Productions. *Address:* Brettian Productions, PO Box 96395, Brixton 2019, Johannesburg, South Africa.

APACHE INDIAN, (Steven Kapur); b. Birmingham, England. Vocalist. *Career:* Solo singer, 1992–; International tours include Middle East; India; Japan. *Recordings:* Albums: No Reservations, 1992; Make Way For The Indian, 1995; Real People, 1998; Wild East, 1998; Best of Apache Indian, 2000; Singles: Boom-Shack-A-Lack, 1993; features on Wreck Shop, Wreckx 'N' Effect, 1993. *Address:* c/o Island Records, 22 St Peters Sq., London W6 9NW, England.

APELBAUM Morris Moishe; b. 13 July 1957, Haifa, Israel. Prod.; Engineer. m. 1 s. *Education:* BSc; BA; DipEd; Dip Admin. *Recordings:* Producer: Oliver Jones: Many Moods; Lights of Burgundy; Tim Brady: Scenarios; Imaginary Guitars; Inventions; Double Variations. *Honours:* 3 Juno Nominations; 2 Adisq Nominations; 1 Juno Award. *Memberships:* CARAS; SOCAN. *Current Management:* Silent Sound. *Address:* 3880 Clark St, Montréal, QC H2W 1W6, Canada.

APHEX TWIN (Richard D James), (Polygon Window, AFX, Caustic Window, Powerpill); b. 18 Aug. 1971, Republic of Ireland. Prod.; Remixer; DJ. *Career:* Based in Cornwall, started producing tracks on own custom-made equipment; First recordings (including Analogue Bubblebath) released on Exeter's Mighty Force Records; Debut album on Belgium's R & S Records; Subsequent releases on Warp Records; Collaborations: Mike

Paradinas; Luke Vibert; LFO; Remixed: Baby Ford; Saint Etienne; Beck; Wagon Christ. *Recordings:* Albums: Selected Ambient Works 85–92, 1993; Surfing On Sine Waves (as Polygon Window), 1993; Selected Ambient Works II, 1994; I Care Because You Do, 1995; Richard D James LP, 1996; Drukqs, 2001; Singles: Analogue Bubblebath, 1991; Digeridoo, 1992; Pac-Man (as Powerpill), 1992; Quoth (as Polygon Window), 1993; Gak (as Gak), 1994; Donkey Rhubarb, 1995; Ventolin EP, 1995; Come To Daddy, 1997; Windowlicker, 1999. *Honours:* Brit Award, Best Album nominee, Drukqs, 2002. *Address:* c/o Warp Records, Spectrum House, 32–34 Gordon House Rd, London, NW5 1LP, England.

APPLE Fiona, (Fiona Apple Maggart); b. 13 Sept. 1977, New York, New York, USA. Vocalist. *Career:* Obtained recording contract; Numerous television appearances and live dates. *Recordings:* Singles: Criminal, 1998; Shadowboxer, 1998; Paper Bag, 1999; Fast As You Can, 2000; Albums: Tidal, 1996; When the Pawn Hits..., 2000. *Honours:* Best New Artist, MTV Video Music Awards, 1997; Grammy nominations, Best New Artist, Best Female Rock Vocal Performance, Best Rock Song, 1998.

APPLETON Natalie; b. 1974. Vocalist. *Career:* Joined female vocal group All Saints, 1995; group split 2001; Feature film, Honest, released 2000. *Recordings:* Singles: I Know Where It's At, 1997; Never Ever (No. 1, UK), 1997; Under The Bridge (No. 1, UK), 1998; Lady Marmalade (No. 1, UK), 1998; Bootie Call (No. 1, UK), 1998; War of Nerves, 1998; Pure Shores (No. 1, UK), 2000; Black Coffee (No. 1, UK), 2000; All Hooked Up, 2001; Albums: All Saints, 1997; Saints and Sinners, 2000; All Hits (compilation), 2001. *Honours:* Brit Award, Best Single, Never Ever, 1998. *Current Management:* John Benson.

APPLETON Nicole; b. 1976. Vocalist. *Career:* Joined female vocal group All Saints, 1995; group split 2001; Feature film, Honest, released 2000. *Recordings:* Singles: I Know Where It's At, 1997; Never Ever (No. 1, UK), 1997; Under The Bridge (No. 1, UK), 1998; Lady Marmalade (No. 1, UK), 1998; Bootie Call (No. 1, UK), 1998; War of Nerves, 1998; Pure Shores (No. 1, UK), 2000; Black Coffee (No. 1, UK), 2000; All Hooked Up, 2001; Albums: All Saints, 1997; Saints and Sinners, 2000; All Hits (compilation), 2001. *Honours:* Brit Award, Best Single, Never Ever, 1998. *Current Management:* John Benson.

APRIL Johnny; b. 27 March 1965, Enfield, Connecticut, USA. Musician (bass guitar). *Career:* Former cook and car repair man; Gained rock group experience with Maniax and Mostly Holy prior to appointment as bassist with Staind; First gig with Staind, 1995; Released self-financed debut album, 1996; Album sold 4000 copies; Discovered by Fred Durst, 1997; Signed to Flip/Elektra; Presented to rock cognoscenti at Limp Bizkit gold record party for Three Dollar Bill Y'All $, 1998; Major breakthrough with unscheduled smash US #1 radio hit Outside; Appeared on bill for Korn-founded Family Values tours, 1999 and 2001; Headlined MTV's Return of The Rock tour, 2000. *Recordings:* Albums: Tormented, 1996; Dysfunction, 1999; Break The Cycle, 2001; Singles: Mudshovel, Just Go, 1999; Home, Outside, 2000; It's Been Awhile, Fade, 2001. *Honours:* Break The Cycle certified quadruple platinum by RIAA; It's Been Awhile topped Billboard Modern Rock Singles Chart for record-equalling 16 weeks; VH-1 Award, Your Song Kicked Ass But Was Played Too Damn Much prize, 2001. *Address:* c/o The Firm, Inc, 9100 Whilshire Blvd, Suite 400W, Beverly Hills, CA 90212, USA. *Internet:* www.staind.com.

AQUAMANDA (Amanda Greatorex); b. Matlock, Derbyshire, England. Vocalist; Musician (keyboards); Writer; Prod. *Education:* BA Hons, Fashion Textile Design (Fashion Designer), Leicester. *Career:* Vocalist, lyricist, Knights of The Occasional Table; Breathe track on compilation album Shamanarchy In The UK; Album and cover design, Knees Up Mother Earth, 1993; Session on John Peel, 1994; Now solo as Aquamanda; Runs record label Fairy Cake Universe with partner Dr Tony Hare. *Compositions:* Lyricist, vocalist, composer, Knees Up Mother Earth. *Recordings:* Album: Knights of The Occasional Table, 1993; Solo single: Free Your Spirit (12 vinyl), 1995. *Memberships:* PRS; MCPS; PPL; Musicians' Union. *Leisure interests:* Scuba diving; Tama-Do. *Current Management:* Dr Tony Hare, FCU Records. *Address:* Fairy Cake Universe, PO Box LB621, London W1A 5EB, England.

ARAGAO Monique Cavalcanti de; b. 10 Nov. 1960, Rio de Janeiro, Brazil. Composer; Musician (piano); Arranger. m. David Ganc, 1 s. *Musical Education:* BA, Music, University of Rio de Janeiro; Piano with Undine de Mello and Linda Bustani and voice with Carol McDavit, Clarice Szajmbrum. *Career:* Television: Monique Aragao Special, TVE, 1990; Special, Dentro and Fora do Compasso, TVE, 1994; Guest appearance, New Year's Eve special, TV Globe, 1993; Radio: Radio Roquete Pinto; Radio Mec; Radio Journal do Brasil; Radio Nacional. *Recordings:* Solo: Monique Aragao, 1991; Canoas, 1993; Ventos do Brasil, 1995; Original soundtracks for theatre, films, ballet. *Publications:* Coral Hoje; Choral Pieces. *Honours:* Contests Alcina Navarro, 1970; Liddy Mignone, Lucia Branco, 1976; Sharp Prize, 1992. *Membership:* AMAR (RJ). *Leisure interests:* Painting; Tap dance. *Current Management:* Zillion Artistic Productions.

ARAM Vicki; b. 31 Dec. 1935, Stanley, County Durham, England. Musician (piano); Vocalist. m. David Wager, 28 Sept. 1957, 1 s., 2 d. *Education:* Sunderland Art College. *Musical Education:* ALCM, aged 15. *Career:* Became professional rehearsal pianist with Dino Shafeek in Action 5; Vocalist, pianist, resident at Mortons, playing to audience including Rod Stewart; David Essex; Marc Bolan; Richard and Grace Jones; Played in many London hotels, jazz venues include: Pizza Express; Pizza On The Park; Worked with the best jazz musicians; Resident at The Canteen, 1980; Filled in between sets by great American jazz musicians; Now studying astrology and painting idealised style portraits. *Address:* 43 Baronsmere Rd, East Finchley, London N2 9QG, England.

ARCARI Dave; b. 14 Aug. 1964, Glasgow, Scotland. Musician (guitar); Prod.; Publicist. m. Anne, 5 Feb. 1993. *Education:* Fife College. *Career:* Ex-member, band Summerfield Blues; Numerous live sessions for BBC Radio; Television appearances, European Cable Shows; Member of the Radiotones. *Compositions:* Ain't Crying, 1993; 24 Hours, 1993; Uncle Jack, 1995; Journeytime is Over, 1997; You Oughta Know, 1997. *Recordings:* with Summerfield Blues: Devil and The Freightman; Let's Scare The Posh People; Little Miss Behavin'; with Denim Elliots: Gooseberry Rain; with Radiotones: Radiotones; Whiskey'd Up. *Honours:* Scottish Blues Band of The Year, 1993. *Membership:* Musicians' Union. *Leisure interests:* Technology; American Roots music. *Current Management:* Buzz Artist Management, Perth, Scotland. *Address:* 14 Corsiehill Rd, Perth, PH2 7BZ, Scotland.

ARCH David; b. 25 Oct. 1962, Watford, England. Composer; Musician (keyboards); Arranger. m. Katherine, 2 Jan. 1991, 1 s., 1 d. *Education:* King James College, Henley. *Musical Education:* Guildhall School of Music, GGSM. *Career:* In NYJO whilst at college; MD for Dash, Hot Shoe Show (Wayne Sleep); Session keyboard player, many films, television, album projects; Started composing, joined Joe and Co, 1988; Now writing, mainly advertisements and television music. *Compositions:* GMTV logos; LWT logos; Numerous commercials. *Recordings:* Played on soundtracks for Notting Hill, Return of the Jedi, The Avengers, An Ideal Husband, Goldeneye, The Saint. *Memberships:* PRS; MCPS; Academy of Composers and Songwriters. *Leisure interests:* Travel; Cars. *Current Management:* Joe and Co. *Address:* Denholm House, Pinner Hill, Pinner, Middlesex HAS 3XX, England.

ARCHER Gem; Musician (Guitar); Singer. *Career:* Singer and Guitarist, Heavy Stereo; Numerous tours; Joined Oasis as Guitarist, 1999. *Recordings:* With Heavy Stereo: Sleep Freak, 1995; Mouse in a Hole, 1996; Smiler, 1996; Album: Deja Voodoo; With Oasis: Album forthcoming.

ARCHER Martin Walker; b. 9 March 1957, Sheffield, England. Musician (saxophone, electronics, composer). *Education:* Law degree, Nottingham University, 1978. *Musical Education:* Self-taught instrumentalist, composer. *Career:* Leader, Composer, Hornweb, 1983–93; Current member, Transient v Resident, ASK, Closed Order; Owner of Discus Record Label. *Recordings:* Albums: with Hornweb Saxophone Quartet: Kinesis, 1986; Sixteen, 1987; Universe Works, 1989; Solo recordings: Wild Pathway Favourites, 1988: Ghost Lily Cascade, 1994; 88 Enemies, 1998; Winter Pilgrim Arriving, 2000; With Transient v Resident: Electrical Shroud, 1995; Dharma Day, 1998; WKCR, 1999; Medulla, 1999; With Simon H Fell: Pure Water Construction, 1998; with Geraldine Monk: Angel High Wires, 2001; Compiler of the Network miniatures series: Vol. I, 1994; Vol. II, 1995; The Music is Silent, 1996; Sound Gallery, 1997. *Honours:* Wire Magazine World Top 25 album, Wild Pathway Favourites, 1988. *Memberships:* Sonic Arts Network; Society for Promotion of New Music. *Leisure interests:* Music; Film; Theatre; Fresh air. *Current Management:* Discus. *Address:* Discus, PO Box 658, Sheffield S10 3YR, England.

ARCHER Tasmin Angela; b. 3 Aug. 1963, Bradford, England. Vocalist; Songwriter. *Career:* Solo artiste, 1992–; Tours of USA, United Kingdom, Europe. *Recordings:* Singles: Sleeping Satellite (No. 1, UK), 1992; In Your Care; Lords of The New Church; Arriene; Shipbuilding; One More Goodnight With The Boys; Albums: Great Expectations, 1992; Bloom, 1995; Premium Gold Collection (compilation), 2000. *Honours:* Brit Award, Best Newcomer, 1993. *Membership:* Musicians' Union. *Leisure interests:* Reading; Exercise. *Current Management:* Ian McAndrew, Wildlife Entertainment. *Address:* 21 Heathmans Rd, Parsons Green, London SW6 4TJ, England.

ARDEN-GRIFFITH Paul; b. 18 Jan. 1952, Stockport, England. Opera, Music-Theatre, Concert, Cabaret Singer (tenor). *Musical Education:* Royal Manchester College of Music; Cantica Voice Studio. *Career:* Concert, theatre singer, 1971–; Opera singer, 1973–; Major operas include: Midsummer Night's Dream; The Rake's Progress; Of Mice and Men; Carmina Burana; The Barber of Seville; Music, theatre performances include: The Merry Widow; Phantom of The Opera; The Legendary Lanza; Babes In The Wood; Gilbert and Sullivan to Lloyd Webber- The

Great British Musicals; German production of Sunset Boulevard; Concerts, cabarets include: London: Dorchester Hotel; Hyde Park Intercontinental; Picadilly Theatre; The Belfry Club; Savoy Hotel; Tramshed; Theatre Royal Drury Lane; The Limelight Club; Internationally: Wexford (Eire); Hong Kong; Sydney; Singapore; Palm Springs (California); Television appearances include: Wozzeck; A Christmas Carol; The Cleopatras; The Comic Strip; The Bill; Pebble Mill At One; Save The Children Christmas Special. *Recordings:* Paul Arden Griffith, The Song Is You, 1986; Phantom of The Opera (original cast album), 1987; An Evening With Alan Jay Lerner, 1987; Minstrel Magic (Black and White Minstrel cast album), 1993; A Minstrel On Broadway, 1994; Encore!, Paul Arden-Griffith In Concert, 1995; The Classic Collection, 1995; Accolade!, 1996; Video: On Stage At The Hackney Empire, 1989. *Honours:* Gwilym Gwalchmai Jones Scholarship For Singing, 1974. *Memberships:* British Actors Equity Asscn; Musicians' Union; Barezzi Theatre School, president. *Leisure interests:* Travel; Hiking; Swimming; Painting. *Current Management:* Geoff Stanton, Brunskill Management, UK. *Address:* c/o Ken Spencer Personal Management, 138 Sandy Hill Rd, London SE18 7BA, England.

ARENA Tina; b. 1 Sept. 1967, Melbourne, Australia. Vocalist. *Career:* Former member, Young Talent Time, Australia; Other performances include: Nine, 1987; Soul Dynamite, 1989; Joseph and His Amazing Technicolour Dreamcoat, 1992. *Recordings:* Albums: Tiny Tina, 1977; Strong As Steel, 1990; Don't Ask, 1995; In Deep, 1997; Singles: Chains, 1995; Heaven Help My Heart, 1995; Show Me Heaven, 1995; Sorrento Moon (I Remember), 1996; Burn, 1997; If I Didn't Love You, 1997; Now I Can Dance, 1997; I Want To Know What Love Is, 1998; If I Was A River, 1998; Whistle Down The Wind, 1998; I Want To Spend My Lifetime Loving You, 1998; Live For The One I Love, 2000. *Honours:* Performer and Rock Performer of the Year MO Awards, 1996; 1995 Aria Best Pop Release, Chains, 1995 Aria Song the Year, Chains; Aria Female Artist of the Year, 1995; Aria Album of the Year, Don't Ask, 1995; Variety Club Entertainer of the Year, 1995; Advance Australia Foundation Award, 1996; APRA Song of the Year, Wasn't It Good, 1996; World Music Award for World's Highest Selling Female Artist, Highest Selling Female Artist in Australian History, 1996. *Address:* c/o RCM International, Lennox House, 229 Lennox St, Richmond, Vic 3121, Australia.

ARGENT Rod; b. 14 June 1945, St Albans, Hertfordshire, England. Musician (keyboards); Vocalist. *Career:* Founder, The Zombies, 1963–69; Founder, own group Argent, 1970s; Also solo artiste and record producer; Appearances include: New York, 1964; British tour, with Dusty Springfield, The Searchers, 1965; Caravan of Stars US tour, 1965; Production partnerships with Chris White and Peter Van Hooke, 1980s. *Recordings:* Albums: with the Zombies: The Zombies, 1965; Begin Here, 1965; Odyssey and Oracle, 1967; with Argent: Argent, 1970; Ring of Hands, 1971; All Together Now, 1972; In Deep, 1973; Nexus, 1974; Encore, 1974; Circus, 1975; Counterpoints, 1975; Anthology, 1976; Hold Your Head Up, 1978; Rock Giants, 1982; Music From The Spheres, 1991; Solo: Moving Home, 1978; Ghosts, 1982; Shadowshow, 1985; Red House, 1988; Rescue, 1991; with Nanci Griffith: Late Night Grande Hotel, 1991; MCA Years, 1993; also: Into The West, 1993; Painted Desert Serenade, 1993; Sun Ain't Gonna Shine Anymore, 1994; Healing Bones, 1994; On Nights Like This, 1996; Martyrs and Madmen, 1997; Dick Bartley Presents.., 1998; Salty Heaven, 1999; Singles include: with the Zombies: She's Not There (No. 2, US), 1964; Tell Her No, 1965; with Argent: Hold Your Head Up, 1971; God Gave Rock and Roll To You, 1973; with Colin Blunstone: Sanctuary, 2001; Co-producer, debut album by Tanita Tikaram, 1988.

ARGÜELLES Julian; b. 28 Jan. 1966. Musician (saxophones, various woodwinds); Composer. *Musical Education:* Studied briefly at Trinity College of Music. *Career:* Various youth bands; Loose Tubes, including a Proms performance; Mike Gibbs Orchestra; Kenny Wheeler Big Band; Chris McGregor's Brotherhood of Breath; The Very Big Carla Bley Band; Hermeto Pascoal; Django Bates' Delightful Precipice; Performed Concerto for piano, percussion and saxophone, by Mario Lagina. *Recordings:* with Julian Argüelles Quartet: Phaedrus; Home Truths; Scapes, 1996; Skull View, 1997; Escapade, 1999; Various recordings with: Steve Argüelles, Django Bates, Kenny Wheeler, Mike Gibbs, Mario Laginha. *Honours:* Pat Smyth Award; Various BBC Awards; Commission by BBC Radio 3 for Octet; Jazz Composers Alliance, Julius Hemphill Award (USA), 1999. *Leisure interests:* Reading. *Address:* 12B Balchier Rd, London SE22 0QN, England.

ARMAOU Lyndsay Gael Christian; b. 18 Dec. 1980, Athens, Greece. Singer; Musician (piano, guitar). *Career:* Member, B*Witched; Numerous tours and television appearances; Several hit singles. *Recordings:* Singles: C'est La Vie, 1998; Rollercoaster, 1998; To You I Belong, 1998; Blame it on the Weatherman, 1998; Jesse Hold On, 1999; Albums: B*Witched, 1998; Awake and Breathe, 1999.

ARMATAGE John Sinclair; b. 5 Aug. 1929, Newcastle Upon Tyne, England. Musician (drums). m. Ann Johnston, 9 May 1975. *Musical Education:* Self-taught. *Career:* Member, Wally Fawkes Band; Bruce

Turner Jump Band; Alan Elsdon Band; Pete Allen Band; Terry Lightfoot Band; Tours with Don Byas; Ben Webster; Earl Hines; Red Allen; Pee Wee Russell; Films: Living Jazz; Plenty; Television and radio apppearances. *Recordings:* Albums with: Bruce Turner; Alan Elsdon; Bud Freeman; Terry Lightfoot. *Leisure interests:* Model railways; Reading; Walking. *Current Management:* Ann Armatage. *Address:* 1 Keable Rd, Wrecclesham, Farnham, Surrey GU10 4PW, England.

ARMATRADING Joan; b. 9 Dec. 1950, Basseterre, St Kitts. Vocalist; Songwriter; Musician (guitar). *Musical Education:* Self-taught piano and guitar. *Career:* Songwriting, performing partnership, with Pam Nestor, 1969–73; Solo artiste, 1973–; Appearances include: Regular international tours; Concerts include: Prince's Trust Gala, Wembley Arena, 1986; Nelson Mandela's 70th Birthday Tribute, Wembley Stadium, 1988; Numerous world tours, 1973–96. *Compositions include:* Down To Zero; Willow, 1977. *Recordings:* Singles: Love and Affection, 1976; Rosie, 1980; Me Myself I, 1980; All The Way From America, 1980; I'm Lucky, 1981; Drop The Pilot, 1983; Perfect Day, 1997; Albums include: Whatever's For Us, 1973; Joan Armatrading, 1976; Show Some Emotion, 1977; Stepping Out, 1979; Me Myself I, 1980; Walk Under Ladders, 1981; The Key, 1983; Track Record, 1983; The Shouting Stage, 1988; The Very Best Of..., 1991; What's Inside, 1995; Living For You; Greatest Hits, 1996; Love and Affection, 1997; 20th Century Masters, The Millennium Edition (compilation), 2000; The Collection (compilation), 2001; Also appears on: Listen To The Music: 70's Females, 1996; Carols of Christmas Vol. 2, 1997; Prince's Trust 10th Anniversary Birthday, 1997; Film soundtrack, The Wild Geese, 1978. *Honour:* BASCA Ivor Novello Award for Outstanding Contemporary Collection, 1996. *Address:* c/o F Winter and Co, Ramillies House, 2 Ramillies St, London W1V 1DF, England.

ARMSTRONG Billie Joe; b. 17 Feb. 1972, San Pablo, California, USA. Vocalist; Musician (guitar). *Career:* Formed early band Sweet Children, became Green Day; Numerous tours and television appearances; Side projects, Pinhead Gunpowder and Screeching Weasel; Gained major label deal; Provided track for soundtrack to film Godzilla; Appeared in cartoon King of the Hill as The Stubborn Stains. *Recordings:* Singles: Slappy EP, 1990; Welcome to Paradise, 1992; Longview, 1994; Basket Case, 1994; Geek Stink Breath, 1995; Stuck With Me, 1996; Brain Stew, 1996; Hitchin' A Ride, 1998; Time of Your Life, 1998; Nice Guys Finish Last, 1999; Minority, 2000; Waiting, 2001; Albums: Kerplunk, 1992; Dookie, 1994; Insomniac, 1995; Live, 1995; Nimrod, 1997; Foot in Mouth, 1998; Warning, 2000; International Superhits (compilation), 2001.

ARMSTRONG Gerry; b. 28 Oct. 1929, Detroit, Michigan, USA. Folk Singer; Storyteller. m. George D Armstrong, 24 April 1954, (deceased 1993), 2 d. *Education:* College. *Musical Education:* The oral tradition. *Career:* I Come For To Sing, weekly programme with Studs Terkel, Big Bill Broonzy and others, 1953–; Folk clubs, festivals, churches, schools, radio and television, films, 1960s-70s; Sometimes play with 3 generations of Armstrong family on stage together, 1990s. *Recordings:* Simple Gifts, Folkways (now Smithsonian); Wheel of The Year, Flying Fish (now Rounder); Golden Ring; Five Days Singing, Vols 1 and 2 (Folk-legacy); My Singing Bird (tape); Once Upon a Time..., tape of stories; Music in My Mother's House, CD. *Publications:* 3 children's books: The Magic Bagpipe; The Boat On The Hill; The Fairy Thorn; Many stories in school readers, Cricket magazine. *Memberships:* Old Town School of Folk Music; The Aural Tradition; Sacred Harp Singers. *Leisure interests:* Quilting and other crafts; Cornhusk dolls; Dream catchers; Gods Eyes; Paper pretties. *Address:* 1535 Lake Ave, Wilmette, IL 60091-1637, USA.

ARMSTRONG Tim(othy Lockwood); b. 1966. Singer; Musician (guitar). m. Brody, March 1998. *Career:* Member, Operation Ivy; Joined Downfall; Started Rancid, with Matt Freeman; Numerous live shows; Started own record label, Hellcat Records, 1996. *Recordings:* Singles: Rancid, 1993; Radio, Radio, Radio, 1994; Roots Radicals, 1995; Time Bomb, 1995; Ruby Soho, 1996; Bloodclot, 1998; Hooligans, 1998; Brad Logan, 1998; Albums: Rancid, 1993; Let's Go, 1994; And Out Come the Wolves, 1995; Life Won't Wait, 1998.

ARMSTRONG Timothy Paul; b. 10 Feb. 1961, Birmingham, England. Singer; Songwriter. 2 s., 1 d. *Musical Education:* 2 years piano, SC Music. *Career:* Member, band The Politicians, 1981–86; Appearances: Telethons, 1981–85; Shazam Television Special, 1985; NZ Today, 1992–93. *Recordings:* Singles: Down In Baghdad, 1983; Energy, 1985; Christmas Day/Photograph, 1986; Albums: Relationships, 1992; Breaking Hearts, 1993; Wondering Why, 1995. *Honours:* Waikato Rock Awards: Best Male Vocalist, Best Recorded Work. *Leisure interest:* Local politics. *Current Management:* Tim Armstrong. *Address:* 11 Beatrice Pl., Hamilton, New Zealand.

ARNESEN Dag S; b. 3 May 1950, Bergen, Norway. Musician (piano); Composer. m. Wenche Gausdal, 17 Oct. 1986. *Education:* Teacher training (Music). *Musical Education:* Music Conservatory, Bergen, classical piano. *Career:* Norwegian television (NRV) appearances: with own group: Ny Bris;

with project for Vossa Jazz, 8 piece band includes Elvin Jones, drums, Jon Surman, saxophone, Palle Danielson, bass; with Joe Henderson, Woody Shaw Quintet. *Recordings:* Albums: Ny Bris, 1982; Renascent, 1984; The Day After, 1990; Photographs, 1992; Movin', 1994; Wandering Around Grieg, 1996; Inner Lines, 1998. *Honours:* The Vossa Jazz Prize, 1992; The Grieg Prize, 1994. *Memberships:* FNJ; NOPA; GRAMART. *Leisure interest:* Walking in the mountains. *Address:* Gutenbergs V6 18, 5035 B6 Sandviken, Norway.

ARNOLD Cheryl Christine; b. 23 April 1951, Seattle, Washington, USA. Country Singer. m. 23 June 1979, Michael Stipek, 3 s. (triplets). *Education:* Washington University, 1970–73. *Career:* Country singer, 1980–; Support act for country artistes including: Lorrie Morgan, 1982; Hoyt Axton, 1984; Loretta Lynn, 1984; Ricky Nelson, 1985; Johnny Cash, 1988; Reba McEntire, 1989; Glen Campbell, 1990. *Memberships:* ACM; CMA.

ARNOLD David Michael; b. 21 April 1958, Maidstone, Kent, England. Singer; Composer. 1 s. *Education:* Technical School; Hackney and Hastings Colleges. *Musical Education:* Self-taught. *Career:* Various radio appearances, 1980–94; Formed own record label, appearances, 1980–94; Meridian Television, 1993, 1995. *Recordings:* High Upon The Rhythm; Hallelujah; Valentine; National Health Tender. *Publications:* Various (International). *Memberships:* PRS; MCPS. *Leisure interests:* Art; Poetry; Performance; Writing. *Current Management:* Happy House; Dead Happy Records. *Address:* 3B Castledown Ave, Hastings, East Sussex TN34 3RJ, England.

ARNOLD Eddy (Richard Edward); b. 15 May 1918, Madisonville, Tennessee, USA. Country Singer. m. Sally Arnold, 28 Nov. 1941, 1 s., 1 d. *Musical Education:* Self-taught guitar. *Career:* Member, Pee Wee King's Golden West Cowboys, 1940–43; Radio appearances: WSM Radio, Nashville, as solo artist The 'Tennessee Plowboy'; Co-host, Grand Ole Opry, 1943–48; Host, Checkerboard Square, 1947–55; Television appearances: Milton Berle Show, 1949; Host, Eddy Arnold Time, 1950s; Guest on all major shows including Ed Sullivan; Jackie Gleason; Johnny Carson; Dean Martin; Television specials: Profile From The Land, 1968; Kraft Music Hall Specials, 1967–71; Appeared films: Feudin' Rhythm, 1949; Hoedown, 1950: One of first country artists to play Carnegie Hall, 1966; Performed with symphony orchestras of Hartford; Nashville; Memphis, 1960s. *Recordings:* Record sales total over 80m. (one of most successful artists in history); Over 145 country hits including 21 US Country No. 1s, 1945–55; Hits include: Please Stay Home With Me; That's How Much I Love You; Bouquet of Roses; Anytime; I'll Hold You In My Heart; Just A Little Lovin' Will Go A Long Way; Cattle Call; Tennessee Stud; What's He Doing In My World?; Make The World Go Away; The Last Word In Lonesome Is Me; Misty Blue; Turn The World Around; Albums: Memories Are Made of This, 1995; Christmas Time, 1997; Songs I Love To Sing; Then You Can Tell Me Goodbye; I Need You All The Time. *Publications:* It's A Long Way From Chester Country, 1969. *Honours:* Inducted into Country Music Hall of Fame, 1966; Entertainer of The Year, 1967; Pioneer Award, Academy of Country Music, 1984; President's Award Songwriter's Guild, 1987. *Current Management:* Gerald W. Purcell Associates. *Address:* 964 Second Ave, New York, NY 10022, USA.

ARNOLD Kristine; b. California, USA. Singer. m. Leonard Arnold, 2 d. *Career:* Member, duo Sweethearts of The Rodeo with sister Janis Gill; Signed to Columbia Records; Sugar Hill Records; Winners, Wrangler Country Showcase, 1985. *Recordings:* Sweethearts of The Rodeo, 1986; Top 20 hits include: Since I Found You; Midnight Girl/Sunset Town; Satisfy You; Chains of Gold, 1987; Rodeo Waltz, 1993; Video: Things Will Grow. *Honours:* CMA's Vocal Duo, 9 consecutive years; Music City News Award, Best Vocal Duo; TNN Viewers Choice Awards, Favourite Group; NAIRD Award, Best Country Album, 1994. *Current Management:* M Hitchcock Management. *Address:* PO Box 159007, Nashville, TN 37214, USA.

ARRIALE Lynne; b. 29 May 1957, Milwaukee, Wisconsin, USA. Composer; Jazz Musician (piano). *Musical Education:* BMus, MMus, Classical Piano. *Career:* Tour of Japan with 100 Golden Fingers (featuring 10 great jazz pianists); Tours of Europe and North America with the Lynne Arriale Trio. *Recordings:* Albums: The Eyes Have It; When You Listen; With Words Unspoken, 1996; Long Road Home, 1997; Melody, 1999; Live At The Montreux Jazz Festival (Lynne Arriale Trio), 2000. *Honours:* First Prize, Great American Jazz Piano Competition, 1993; Great American Piano Competition, winner. *Memberships:* International Asscn of Jazz Educators. *Current Management:* Suzi Reynolds and Associates, 200 Rector Pl. 7H, New York, NY 10280, USA; Promotion Aktiv, Gerold Merkle, Zirbenweg 52, 87448 Waltenhoffen, Germany. *E-mail:* promotionaktiv.jazzgentur@online.de.

ARROYO Joe (Alvaro José); b. 1955, Cartagena, Colombia. Singer; Songwriter. *Musical Education:* Soloist, school choir. *Career:* Nightclub singer from age 12; Formed La Protesta, 1970; Singer, Fruko Y Sus Tesos, 1971–81; South American and US tours; Numerous hits; Formed own group, La Verdad (15 piece band), 1981–; Concerts include: Empire

Leicester Square, London 1992; Founder, own band, Son Caribeno (the Caribbean Sound). *Recordings:* Hit singles: with Fruko y sus Tesos: Manyoma; Tania; El Ausente; with La Verdad: Tumbatecho, 1986; Rebelión (considered all-time Latin classic), UK release 1991; Numerous hit albums with La Verdad include: En Acción; Musa Original; Toque de Clase; Fire in my Mind; Fuego; Reinando en Vida; Deja que te Cante; Cruzando el Milenio; Noche. *Honours:* Over 100 music awards; Conga de Oro, Barranquila Carnival; 13 Golden Bongo Awards. *Address:* c/o Jenny Adlington, World Circuit Records, 106 Cleveland St, London W1P 5DP, England.

ARTHUR Davey; b. 24 Sept. 1954, Edinburgh, Scotland. Musician (multi-instrumentalist); Vocalist. *Career:* Member, The Buskers; Member, Tam Linn; Apperaed at the Cambridge Folk Festival; Later became the Fureys and Davey Arthur, 1980-. *Recordings:* The Cisco Special, 1960; Songs of Woody Guthrie, 1961; I Ain't Got No Home, 1962; The Sound of The Fureys and Davey Arthur, 1981; When You Were Sweet Sixteen, 1982; Steal Away, 1983; In Concert, 1984; Golden Days, 1984; At The End of a Perfect Day, 1985; The First Leaves of Autumn, 1986; The Fureys Finest, 1987; The Fureys Collection, 1989; The Scattering, 1989; The Very Best Of, 1991; The Winds of Change, 1992; Singles include: When You Were Sweet Sixteen, 1981. *Current Management:* Park Promotions, 20 Raleigh Park Rd, N Hinksey, Oxford OX2 9AZ, England.

ARTHURS Paul 'Bonehead'; b. 23 June 1965, Manchester, England. Musician (guitar). *Career:* Formed Rain; Changed name to Oasis, recruited Noel and Liam Gallagher; Numerous support slots, to The Milltown Brothers, BMX Bandits, The Verve, Liz Phair, The Real People, Dodgy; Obtained record deal with Creation; Numerous tours and television appearances; Festival dates; Left band, 1999, during recordings for 2000 album Standing On The Shoulder of Giants. *Recordings:* Singles: Supersonic; Whatever; Cigarettes and Alcohol; Shakermaker; Live Forever; Some Might Say; Wonderwall; Roll With It; Champagne Supernova; Don't Look Back in Anger; D'You Know What I Mean; Stand By Me; All Around the World; Albums: Definitely Maybe, 1994; What's the Story (Morning Glory), 1995; Be Here Now, 1997; The Masterplan, boxed set, 1999.

ARTIST The (Prince Rogers Nelson), (Prince, TAFKAP, Symbol); b. 7 June 1958, Minneapolis, Minnesota, USA. Vocalist; Songwriter; Prod. m. Mayté, 1996. *Career:* Previously billed as Prince, The Artist Formerly Known as Prince (AFKAP) and Symbol; Leader, Prince and The Revolution; Singer, with own backing group the New Power Generation, 1991–; Numerous tours, concerts; Own recording studio and record label, Paisley Park; Currently billed as The Artist. *Recordings:* Singles include: I Wanna Be Your Lover, 1979; 1999, 1983; Little Red Corvette, 1983; When Doves Cry (No. 1, USA), 1984; Purple Rain, 1984; Let's Go Crazy (No. 1, USA), 1984; Raspberry Beret, 1985; Kiss, 1986 (No. 1, USA); Sign O' The Times, 1987; If I Was Your Girlfriend, 1987; U Got The Look, 1987; I Could Never Take The Place of Your Man, 1987; Alphabet Street, 1988; Batdance, (No. 1, USA), 1989; Thieves In The Temple, 1990; Gett Off!, 1991; Cream (No. 1, USA), 1991; Money Don't Matter 2 Nite, 1992; Sexy MF, 1992; Controversy, 1993; The Most Beautiful Girl In The World (No. 1, UK), 1994; Gold, 1995; Betcha By Golly Wow, 1996; The Greatest Romance Ever Sold, 1999; Albums include: For You, 1978; Dirty Mind, 1979; Controversy, 1979; Prince, 1979; 1999, 1983; Purple Rain, 1984; Around The World In A Day, 1985; Parade, 1986; Sign O' The Times, 1987; Lovesexy, 1988; Batman (soundtrack), 1989; Graffiti Bridge (soundtrack), 1990; Diamonds and Pearls, 1991; Symbol, 1992; Hits 1 and 2 (compilations), 1993; Come, 1994; The Black Album (recorded 1987), 1994; The Gold Experience, 1995; Emancipation, 1996; Chaos and Disorder, 1996; New Power Soul, 1998; Rave Un2 The Joy Fantastic, 1999; The Very Best of Prince (compilation), 2001; As producer: Child of The Sun, Mayté, 1996. *Honours include:* Academy Award, Best Original Score, Purple Rain, 1984; 3 Grammy Awards, 1985; Brit Awards: Best International Artist, Best Soundtrack (Purple Rain), 1985; Best Soundtrack (Batman), 1990; Best International Male Artist, 1992, 1993, 1995, 1996; Q Award, Best Songwriter, 1990. *Current Management:* Paisley Park Enterprises, 7801 Audoban Rd, Chanhassen, MN 55317, USA.

ASHBAKER Jeffrey Carton; b. 10 May 1954, Alamagordo, New Mexico, USA. Singer; Songwriter; Musician (Guitar). m. Betty Ashbaker, 1 s., 2 d. *Education:* BA, Business Studies. *Career:* Stage performances in local night clubs, fairs and fiestas throughout Southern California. *Compositions:* I Never Thought I'd Ever Feel This Good; First Date Blues; Cradled With Love; Riding My Way; Riding Free. *Recordings:* Albums: I Never Thought I'd Ever Feel This Good, 1996; The Other Brothers, 1997; The Other Brothers and a Sister, 1998. *Publication:* I Never Thought I'd Ever Feel This Good, 1998. *Honour:* Hon. Mention, Billboard Song Contest, 1988. *Address:* Redlands, CA 92373, USA.

ASHCROFT Richard; Vocalist; Songwriter; Musician (guitar). *Career:* Vocalist, The Verve; Concerts include: Lollapalooza Tour, USA, 1994; British tours, 1994–95; Support to Oasis, Paris, 1995; Glastonbury

Festival, 1995; Solo career, 2000-. *Compositions include:* On Your Own; Drive You Home; History; No Knock On My Door. *Recordings:* Albums: with The Verve: A Storm In Heaven, 1993; A Northern Soul, 1995; Urban Hymns, 1997; solo: Alone With Everybody, 2000; Singles: with The Verve: This Is Music, 1995; On Your Own, 1995, 1995; History, 1995; Bitter Sweet Symphony, 1997; The Drugs Don't Work, 1997; Sonnet, 1998; Lucky Man, 1998; solo: Song For The Lovers, 2000; Money To Burn, 2000; C'mon People (We're Making It Now), 2000. *Honours:* Brit Awards: Best British Group; Best British Album (Urban Hymns), 1998. *Current Management:* Larrikin Management, 8391 Beverly Blvd #298, Los Angeles, CA 90048, USA.

ASHER James; b. 4 Sept. 1950, Eastbourne, Sussex, England. Composer; Prod.; Musician (keyboards, drums). *Musical Education:* Grade VI violin. *Career:* Sound engineer, R G Jones studio, London. *Compositions:* Wrote and recorded over 20 albums library music; Films and television include: La Filiere Chinoise, Cinema Euro Group; Gems, Thames Television; The Boat Show, BBC2; The Plant, Screen One; Television station idents for: Central; Granada; MTV, USA; Future Television, Lebanon; European Superchannel; Television themes for: Ulster Television news; Channel 4 rugby programme. *Recordings:* Single: Peppermint Lump (produced by Pete Townshend); Albums: The Great Wheel; Globalarium (used by The Clothes Show, BBC1); Dance of The Light; Rivers of Life; Feet in the Soil; Tigers of the Raj; Tigers of the Remix; Raising the Rhythms; Colours of Trance, with harpist Madeleine Doherty; As drummer: Empty Glass, Pete Townshend; Producer for: Ritchie; John 'Rabbit' Bundrick; Ritchie; Asha. *Memberships:* APC; REPRO. *Address:* 34 Starfield Rd, London W12 9SW, England.

ASHER Peter; b. 22 June 1944, London, England. Man.; Record Prod.; Vocalist; Musician (guitar). m. Wendy Worth, 20 May 1983, 1 d. *Education:* Philosophy, King's College, London University. *Career:* Member, duo, Peter and Gordon, 9 top records, 3 Gold discs, 1964–68; Head of A & R, Apple Records, 1968–70; Produced, signed, James Taylor; Founder, Peter Asher Management, USA; Began management, production of Linda Ronstadt; Today represents: Peter Blakeley; Chicano Soul'n Power; Iris DeMent; The Innocence Mission; Little Feat; Kirsty MacColl; Maria Fatal; Mariachi Los Campaneros de Nati Cano; Randy Newman; Over The Rhine; Linda Ronstadt; Laura Satterfield; James Taylor; Williams Brothers; Warren Zevon; Department for management of major record producers, engineers, including Phil Ramone, George Massenburg. *Recordings:* Albums produced include: with 10,000 Maniacs: In My Tribe, 1987; Blind Man's Zoo, 1989; with Linda Ronstadt: Canciones de mi padre, 1987; Cry Like A Rainstorm, Howl Like the Wind, 1989; Frenesi, 1992; with Mary's Danish: American Standard, 1992; with Neil Diamond: The Christmas Album, 1992; The Christmas Album, Vol. 2, 1994; with Randy Newman: Faust, 1995; Albums or tracks for: Paul Jones; Barbara Keith; Tony Kosinec; Jo Mama; John Stewart; Kate Taylor; Tony Joe White; Andrew Gold; John David Souther; Bonnie Raitt; Ronin; Cher; Peter Blakeley; Maria McKee; Williams Brothers; Diana Ross; Julia Fordham; Ringo Starr; Olivia Newton-John; Laura Satterfield; Dixie Chicks. *Honours:* 31 Gold, 19 Platinum albums, USA; 8 Grammy winning records; 2 Grammys, Producer of The Year, 1978, 1989. *Address:* 644 N Doheny Dr., Los Angeles, CA 90069, USA.

ASHER Phil; b. 3 Jan. 1966, London, England. Prod.; Remixer; DJ. *Career:* World-wide DJ; Compiler of Jazz In The House album series for Kickin' Music; Member: Restless Soul, Pascal's Bongo Massive, Two Shiny Heads, Electric Soul; Collaborations: Orin Walters, Luke McCarty, Nathan Haine. *Recordings:* Albums: Sound Travels (with Nathan Haines), 2001; Singles: Pascal's Bongo Massive Vol. 1, 1991; Vol. 2, 1992; Vol. 3, 1993; Let Go (with Two Shiny Heads), 1992; Dub House Disco (with Two Shiny Heads), 1992; Mama (with Restless Soul), 1997; Psykodelik (with Restless Soul), 1997; Phlash 3000 Parts 1 and 2 (as Phlash), 2000; Earth Is The Place (with Nathan Haines), 2001. *Current Management:* c/o Phlash Music, Suite B, 2 Tunstall Rd, London, SW9 2DA, England.

ASHFORD Nickolas (Nick); b. 4 May 1942, Fairfield, South Carolina, USA. Songwriter; Musician; Vocalist. m. Valerie Simpson, 1974. *Career:* Member, performing, recording, songwriting duo with Valerie Simpson; Later joined by Jo Armstead. *Compositions:* Co-writer, Never Had It So Good, Ronnie Milsap; One Step At A Time, Maxine Brown, The Shirelles; Let's Go Get Stoned, Ray Charles; Songs: Ain't No Mountain High Enough; You're All I Need To Get By; Reach Out and Touch Somebody's Hand; Remember Me. *Recordings:* with Valerie Simpson: Keep It Comin', 1973; Gimme Something Real, 1973; I Wanna Be Selfish, 1974; Come As You Are, 1976; So, So Satisfied, 1977; Send It, 1977; Is It Still Good To Ya?, 1978; Stay Free, 1979; A Musical Affair, 1980; Performance, 1981; Street Opera, 1982; High-Rise, 1983; Solid, 1984; Real Love, 1986; Love Or Physical, 1989; I'm On Your Side, 1991; Live Wire! The Singles, 1993; Emperors of Soul, 1994; Best of Smokey Robinson and The Miracles, 1995; Best of Diana Ross and The Supremes, 1995; Ultimate Collection, Gladys Knight, 1997; Hit singles: It Seems To Hang On, 1978; Found A Cure, 1979; Solid, 1984; Babies, 1985. *Current Management:* Hopsack and Silk Productions, 254 W 72nd St, Suite 1A, New York, NY 10023, USA.

ASHILAAKO BILANSO MBO Djonimbo; b. 3 July 1969, Bolobo, Congo. Country Singer; Musician (Guitar, flute); Composer; Interpreter; Artist. 2 s. *Education:* Degree in secondary studies. *Career:* Numerous appearances on national television and radio, 1984–; Playing character in stories for the Francohone Photo Magazine, Amina; Singer with Planete Lolingo Band, 1976; Tout Grand Nania Band, 1979; Credo Band, 1980; Fa-Sol Band, 1983–. *Compositions:* Si Bonne, Si Belle, Si Compliquée... La Vie, 1989; Bosso Bikali, 1993. *Recording:* La Vie est Belle et Compliquée, 1996. *Honours:* First Prize, Radio Challenge for Family Planning, 1986; Third Prize, poetry and song challenge, Goethe Institute, 1987; First Prize, National Song Festival, 1991; Second Prize, Song Festival, French Embassy, 1998. *Membership:* National Society of Artists. *Leisure interests:* Books; Cinema; Walking. *Address:* B P 18525 Kinshasa 13, Democratic Republic of the Congo.

ASHLEY Steve (Stephen Frank); b. 9 March 1946, Perivale, London, England. Singer; Songwriter; Musician (guitar, bouzouki, harmonica, whistle). m. Elizabeth Mary Holborow, 1 d., 1 s. *Education:* DipAD (Hons), Maidstone. *Career:* Founder member, Albion Country Band, 1972; Formed Ragged Robin, 1973; Solo tours of Europe and USA; Television and radio appearances, 1974–79, including Family Album (performed with members of Fairport Convention); Peace Songs for CND; Formed Steve Ashley Band, 1983; Tours of Europe, including festivals at Glastonbury, Cambridge and Cropredy. *Compositions:* Songs: Fire and Wine; The Rough With The Smooth; Original music: Ballad of the Ten Rod Plot, 1991; Stable Lads, for Anglia Television, 1993. *Recordings:* Stroll On, 1974; Speedy Return, 1975; Demo Tapes, 1980; Family Album, 1981; More Demo Tapes, 1983; Mysterious Ways, 1990; The Test of Time, 1999; Stroll on Revisited, 1999. *Honour:* Contemporary Folk Album of the Year, for Stroll On, Folk Review, 1974. *Memberships:* MCPS; PRS; PAMRA. *Leisure interests:* Painting; Photography. *Current Management:* Elizabeth Jones Entertainments. *Address:* 87 Prestbury Rd, Cheltenham, Gloucestershire GL52 2DR, England.

ASHTON Bill (William Michael); b. 6 Dec. 1936, Blackpool, Lancashire, England. Musician (saxophones, clarinet); Composer; Bandleader; Songwriter; Journalist. *Education:* St Peter's College, Oxford; Degree, Modern Languages, DipEd. *Career:* Founder, University Dance Band The Ambassadors; OU Big Band; Founder, secretary, OU Modern Jazz Club; Taught in France, 1960–61; Played US bases with The Stardust Combo, Caveau Des Fouleurs, Chateaudun, France; Worked in Red Bludd's Bluesicians, London; Co-founder with Pat Evans, The London Schools Jazz Orchestra, later renamed The London Youth, then The National Youth Jazz Orchestra (NYJO); Worked full-time with NYJO, 1973–; With NYJO, played world-wide, made numerous television appearances, and recorded over 30 albums; Royal Variety Performance, 1978; Toured twice with Shorty Rogers, John Dankworth, John Williams, and many singers; Formed own publishing company, Stanza Music, 1967; Numerous compositions for NYJO. *Recordings:* with National Youth Jazz Orchestra, Live at London Weekend Television, 1975; These Are The Jokes, 1996; View From The Hill, 1996; In Control, 1999; also; Live At The Blue Note, with Irvin Mayfield and Chico Freeman, 1999. *Honours:* MBE; Inter-University Jazz Band Competition Award, 1962; Critics Choice, 1992, 1995; British Jazz Award, Best British Big Band, 1993, 1995; BBC Radio 2 Award, Services to Jazz, 1995; Fellow, Leeds College of Music, 1995. *Address:* NYJO Records, 11 Victor Rd, Harrow, Middlesex HA2 6PT, England.

ASHWORTH Stephanie; Musician (bass guitar). *Career:* Resides in Australia; Joined group Sandpit, 1995; Replaced bassist Toby Ralph in Melbourne-based trio Something For Kate, 1998; Band gradually broke nationally, then internationally with first US/Japan tour, 2000; Big sell-out Australian shows including Mythology and Echo-la-la-lalia tours plus Powderfinger support slots, 2001; Group subject of JJJ radio station special, 2001. *Recordings:* Albums: with Sandpit: On Second Thought (compilation), 1998; with Something For Kate: Beautiful Sharks, 1999; QandA With Dean Martin (compilation), 2000; Echolalia, 2001; Singles: with Sandpit: Lessons In Posture (EP), 1995; Tyranny of Creeps (EP), 1997; Along The Moors, 1998; with Something For Kate: Harpoon/Clint, 1998; Electricity, Hallways, Whatever You Want, 1999; The Astronaut, 2000; Monsters, Three Dimensions, Twenty Years, 2001. *Honours:* Australian Music Industry Critics Awards, Album of the Year, 2000; Australian Live Music Awards, Best Live Act, 2000; Australian Record Industry Awards, 7 nominations, 2001; JJJ Listeners' Poll, Best Album, 2001. *Current Management:* Carlene Albronda, Catapult Management, Sydney, Australia. *E-mail:* carlene@presto.net.au. *Internet:* www.somethingforkate.com.

ASQUITH Stuart Andrew; b. 23 Sept. 1971, Wakefield, England. Songwriter; Entertainer; Keyboards. *Musical Education:* Piano lessons, 4–8 years old; Moved on to keyboard lessons. *Career:* Made White Label dance record, under name, Mind Vacation, 1992; Changed name of band to: Lost In Process; Made demos, signed to Ouch! Records, 1995. *Recordings:* Aint We Funky/Sustain The Pressure; Pacemaker/We Can Do This; Rock

On; Made In Rio; All recorded 1995. *Membership:* Musicians Union. *Leisure interests:* Cars; Quad Racing; Socialising; Clubbing. *Current Management:* Ouch! Records. *Address:* Ouch! Records, Unit 5, Bowhouse Business Centre, 153–159 Bow Rd, London E3 2SE, England.

ASTBURY Ian; b. 14 May 1962, Heswall, Merseyside, England. Vocalist. *Career:* Founder, Southern Death Cult, 1982; Re-named Death Cult, 1983; Re-named The Cult, 1984–95; Formed Holy Barbarians, 1996–99; Reformed The Cult, 1999–; Headline tours include: UK, Europe, North America, Japan; Also tours with: Bauhaus, 1983; Big Country, 1984; Billy Idol, 1987; Guns N'Roses, 1987; Metallica, 1989; Lenny Kravitz, 1991; Major concerts include: Futurama Festival, Leeds, 1983; A Gathering of The Tribes Festival, California, 1990; Kick Out The Jams Festival, Detroit, 1992; Cult In The Park '92 Festival, Finsbury Park, London, 1992; Guns N' Roses concert, Milton Keynes, 1993. *Recordings:* Albums: Southern Death Cult, 1983; Dreamtime, 1984; Love, 1985; Electric, 1987; Sonic Temple, 1989; Ceremony, 1991; Pure Cult (No. 1, UK), 1993; The Cult, 1994; Ghost Dance, 1996; High Octane Cult, 1996; Cream, 1996; Celebrity Deathmatch, 1999; Zen Mafia, 1999; Best of Rare Cult (compilation), 2000; Beyond Good and Evil, 2001; Singles include: Fat Man, 1983; Spiritwalker, 1984; She Sells Sanctuary, 1985; Rain, 1985; Love Removal Machine, 1987; Lil' Devil, 1987; Wild Flower, 1987; Fire Woman, 1989; Edie (Ciao Baby), 1989; Sweet Soul Sister, 1990; Wild Hearted Son, 1990; Rise, 2001. *Current Management:* Deluxe Entertainment, 12750 Ventura Blvd, Suite 202, Studio City, CA 91604, USA.

ASTLEY Jon; b. 22 Jan. 1951, Manchester, England. Record Prod. 2 d. *Career:* Producer, 1978–; 2 own records released as solo artist, songwriter, 1986, 1988. *Recordings:* Producer for: The Who; Eric Clapton; Phil Collins; Corey Hart; The Rolling Stones; Debbie Harry; The Eagles; Pete Townesend; LSO and LPO; Loz Netto; Johnny Be Good; Orphan; Own recordings; Remixing and remastering extensive catalogues: The Who; Eric Clapton; Bob Dylan; Joni Mitchell; Pete Townesend; Tropicana; Tori Amos. *Memberships:* MCPS; PRS. *Current Management:* A-Sharp Publishing Co. *Address:* 2 Embankment, Twickenham, TW1 3DH, England.

ASTON Michael Philip; b. 22 Aug. 1957, Bridgend, South Wales. Musician; Artist; Singer. m. Margaret La Guardia, 23 June 1992. *Career:* Lead vocalist: Gene Loves Jezebel; Toured: USA; Europe; world; MTV Live At Ritz, NY; MTV New Tears Eve Ball; John Peel sessions, UK; Joan Rivers Show (Fox); Television: Japan; Italy; France; Argentina; Songs, various films; Film Role: She's Having A Baby, by John Hughes, 1986. *Recordings:* Gene Loves Jezebel: Promise; Immigrant; Discover; House of Dolls; From The Mouth of Babes; Love Lies Bleeding; Voodoo Dollies; Albums: Edith Grove, 1995; Why Me Why This Why Now, 1995. *Publications:* Gothic Rock (Black book); Various A-Z Rock. *Honours:* T J Martel MVP, 1995; Song of Year, Desire, College USA, 1986. *Leisure interests:* Art; Record sleeves; Paintings. *Current Management:* William Morris (US). *Address:* 1419 N Hayworth Ave, Los Angeles, CA 90046, USA.

ASTRAUSKAS Rimantas; b. 9 April 1954, Kaunas, Lithuania. Ethnomusicologist; Prod. *Musical Education:* Kaunas J. Gruodis Higher Music School, 1973; MA, Lithuanian State Conservatoire, 1978; Dr of Humanities, Musicology, Lithuanian Academy of Music, 1993. *Career:* Producer, Lithuanian State Television and Radio Committee, 1978–88; Lecturer, Lithuanian Academy of Music, 1988–; Associate Professor of Ethnomusicology, 1993-. *Compositions:* Author, over 500 television and radio broadcasts on various musical topics and events; Co-author, Documentary Film, Išaudes Šokio Rašta. *Publications:* Typological Classification of Tunes, editor, 1996; Ritual and Music, editor, 1999; Over 30 articles on Lithuanian Traditional Music. *Honour:* Special Award, Best Broadcast at International Contest of Musical Broadcasts in Kishinew, 1982. *Memberships:* International Organization of Folk Art; International Council for Traditional Music; European Seminar in Ethnomusicology; Lithuanian Composers' Union. *Leisure interests:* Computers; Travel. *Address:* V. Grybo 1/29–11, 2055 Vilnius, Lithuania.

ATB, (Andre Tanneberger); b. 1973, Freiberg, Germany. Prod.; Remixer; DJ. *Career:* Resident DJ at Tarm Center, Bochum, Germany; World-wide DJ; Collaborations with York; Remixes for Moby, Rank 1, Sash, Blank and Jones, Enigma. *Recordings:* Albums: Movin' Melodies, 2000; Two Worlds, 2001; Singles: 9PM (Till I Come), 1999; Don't Stop, 2000; Killer, 2000; Fields of Love (with York), 2001; Let U Go, 2001. *Current Management:* c/o Ministry of Sound Recordings Ltd, 103 Gaunt St, London, SE1 6DP, England.

ATKINS Bobby Lee; b. 22 May 1933, Surrey Country, USA. Musician (guitar); Singer. m. Judy Smit, 4 April 1961, 6 s., 1 d. *Musical Education:* Self-taught. *Career:* Began with Bill Monroe and the Bluegrass Boys; Played with Charlie Monroe, Flint Hill Playboys; Played with Joe Stone for 15 years; Played with Joe and the Dixie Mountaineers all over USA; Formed own band, Bobby Atkins and The Countrymen, 1967; Rated among the ten best banjo players in the world; Songwriter; Composer; Arranger; Music Publisher, Bob's Special Music Publishing Co; 2 film scores;

Performed on stage with: Mac Wiseman; Clyde Moody; Jim Fanes; Radio with: Flatt and Scruggs; Don Reno; Red Smiley. *Recordings:* over 60 albums and two film scores including: Crimes of the Heart; Gold Hill Gold; The Best of Bobby Atkins, Mark Albin and the Country; The Country Side of Bobby Atkins. *Honours:* Songwriter of The Year, Hawaii; Represented in Bluegrass Hall of Fame, Nashville, Tennessee; Top Male Vocal, Top Band, Top Musician; Top Songwriter; Living Legend Award, 1995; Country Music Organisation of America, Songwriter of the Year, Male Vocalist and Album of the Year, Vallejo. *Memberships:* Country and Bluegrass Music Asscn; Wall of Fame, New York, New York. *Leisure interests:* Garden; Working in yard. *Current Management:* c/o Jolene Caudill, 1109 Cleburne St, Greensboro, NC 27408, USA. *Address:* PO Box 251, Summerfield, NC 27358, USA.

ATKINS Juan, (Model 500, Infiniti); b. 12 Sept. 1962, Detroit, Michigan, USA. Prod.; Remixer; DJ. *Career:* Techno innovator; credited with inventing the Techno genre as part of the Belleville Three (with Derrick May and Kevin Saunderson); Member: Cybotron; Collaborations: Derrick May, Kevin Saunderson, Maurizio. *Recordings:* Albums: Enter (with Cybotron), 1983; Sonic Sunset, 1994; Deep Space, 1995; Skynet (as Infiniti), 1998; Mind and Body, 1999; Singles: Clear (with Cybotron), 1983; as Model 500: No UFO's, 1985; Night Drive (Thru Babylon), 1985; Technicolor, 1986; Sound of Stereo, 1987; Interference, 1988; The Chase, 1989; Ocean To Ocean, 1990; Jazz Is The Teacher, 1993; The Flow, 1995; I Wanna Be There, 1996; Be Brave, 1999; Game One (as Infiniti), 1996. *Current Management:* c/o Metroplex Records, Detroit, Michigan, USA.

AUBUT Lise; b. 29 Aug. 1943, Lévis, Québec, Canada. Songwriter; Impresario. *Education:* CEGEP. *Career:* Songwriter, 15 musical albums and over 150 songs. *Compositions include:* Hit songs: Paquetville, sung by Edith Butler; Un Million de Fois Je T'aime. *Honours:* 3 Felix Awards; 3 Platinum discs. *Memberships:* SPACQ; SODRAC; SACEM. *Leisure interests:* Computers. *Address:* 86 Côte Ste Catherine, Outremont, QC H2V 2A3, Canada.

AUCH Greg; b. 28 Jan. 1967, Charlotte, NC, USA. Country Musician; Singer. m. Linda Auch, 3 s. *Career:* Drummer, The Moody Brothers, 1987–98; Played Guitar and Drumms, Disneyland Paris, 1992–98; On Stage for TNN; Sang At The White House for George Bush, Take Pride In America Campaign. *Honours:* Nominated For The Grammy Award Twice. *Memberships:* National Academy of Recording Arts and Sciences. *Address:* 5900 Oakwielde Ct, Charlotte, NC 28227, USA.

AUGER Brian Albert Gordon; b. 18 July 1939, London, England. Musician (organ, piano); Composer; Prod. m. Ella Natale, 14 Nov. 1968, 1 s., 2 d. *Musical Education:* Mainly self-taught; 1 year, College of Marin, San Francisco, California. *Career:* Professional musician, 1963–; Performed with: Brian Auger Trinity; Brian Auger's Oblivion Express; Eric Burdon/ Brian Auger Band; World-wide tours; Major television shows in UK; Europe; USA; Japan; Czechoslovakia; Hungary; Greece; Radio appearances world-wide. *Recordings:* No. 1 single: This Wheel's On Fire, 1968; Albums: Brian Auger Trinity and Julie Driscoll: Open, 1967; Definitely What, 1968; Streetnoise, 1969; Brian Auger Trinity: Befour, 1970: Brian Auger's Oblivion Express: Oblivion Express, 1970; A Better Land, 1971; Second Wind, 1972; Closer To It, 1973; Straight Ahead, 1974; Reinforcements, 1977; Live Oblivion, Vol. 1, 1975; Vol. II, 1976; Happiness Heartaches, 1977; Encore, 1978; Planet Earth Calling, 1981; Here and Now, 1983; Keys To The Heart, 1987; Eric Burdon/Brian Auger Band: Access All Areas, 1993; The Best of Brian Auger, 1997; Voices of Other Times, 2000. *Honours:* Poll Winner, Jazz Piano and New Star categories, UK Melody Maker magazine, 1963; German Rock and Folk Best Jazz and Best Rock Organist, 1970; Best Jazz Organist, USA Keyboard Magazine, 1976, 1977. *Current Management:* Steve Zelenka, Resource Management, 1341 Ocean Ave #456, Santa Monica, CA 90401, USA.

AUSTEN Ed, (Edward John Roberts); b. 22 Dec. 1942, London, England. Musician (guitar, bass, mandolin); Vocalist. *Musical Education:* 1 year classical guitar; Then self-taught. *Career:* Worked with: The Who; Free; Derek and The Dominoes; Eric Clapton; The Hollies; Dave Dee; Cliff Bennett; Robert Fripp; Andy Summers; Many artistes on country music circuit. *Membership:* Musicians' Union. *Leisure interests:* Martial arts (judo, karate, kendo); Leathercraft; Fishing; Photography. *Address:* 417 Wimbourne Rd E, Ferndown, Dorset BH22 9L2, England.

AUSTIN Dallas; Prod.; Songwriter. *Recordings include:* Troop, Attitude, musician, producer, 1989; Oooooooh... On the TLC Tip, arranger, producer, 1992; White Men Can't Jump, producer, drummer, 1992; DJ Jazzy Jeff and the Fresh Prince, Code Red, composer, producer, 1993; Hi Five, Faithful, producer, 1993; Joi, Pendulum Vibe, vocalist, producer, 1994; Madonna, Bedtime Stories, producer, 1994; Berry Gordy, Music, The Magic, The Memories, producer, 1995; Michael Jackson, History: Past, Present and Future, keyboards, producer, 1995; Boyz II Men, II: Yo Te Voy a Amar, producer, 1995; Fishbone, Chim Chim's Bad Ass REvenge, producer, 1996; Nutty Professor soundtrack, producer, 1996; Indigo Girls,

Shaming of the Sun, vocals, 1997; Michael Jackson, Blood on the Dance Floor, keyboards, producer, 1997; Aretha Franklin, Rose is Still a Rose, arranger, producer, 1998; Brandy, Never Say Never, producer, 1998; N'Dea Davenport, producer, 1998; Monica, Boy is Mine, producer, 1998; TLC, Fanmail, arranger, vocals, 1999.

AUSTIN Patti; b. 10 Aug. 1948, California, USA. Vocalist. *Career:* Child performer from age 3; Appearances included Sammy Davis Jr television show; Theatre performances: Lost In The Stars; Finian's Rainbow; Tours with Quincy Jones, age 9; Harry Belafonte, age 16; Recording debut, age 17; Singer, television jingles, session work, 1970s; Worked with: Paul Simon; Billy Joel; Frankie Valli; Joe Cocker; George Benson; Roberta Flack; Marshall Tucker; Steely Dan; The Blues Brothers; Continued to work with Quincy Jones. *Recordings:* Albums: End of a Rainbow, 1976; Havana Candy, 1977; Live At The Bottom Line, 1979; Body Language, 1980; Every Home Should Have One, 1981; Patti Austin, 1984; Gettin' Away With Murder, 1985; The Real Me, 1988; Love's Gonna Get You, 1990; Carry On, 1991; Live, 1992; That Secret Place, 1994; In and Out of Love, 1998; Street of Dreams, 1999; On The Way To Love, 2001; Singles: Family Tree, 1969; Every Home Should Have One; Razzmatazz (with Quincy Jones), 1981; The Dude, 1982; with James Ingram: Baby Come To Me, theme for television series General Hospital (No. 1, USA), 1983; Film themes: Two of a Kind, 1984; Shirley Valentine, 1988; Soldier Boy, 1991; Givin' In To Love, 1991; Reach, 1994; I'll Keep Your Dreams Alive, 1995; Why You Wanna Be Like That?, 1998; Guest vocalist, album George Gershwin songs, Hollywood Bowl Orchestra, 1992. *Honour:* Grammy Award, The Dude, 1982.

AVALON Frankie, (Francis Avallone); b. 18 Sept. 1939, Philadelphia, Pennsylvania, USA. Vocalist; Musician (trumpet); Actor. m. Kay Avalon, 4 s., 4 d. *Career:* Began playing trumpet with Rocco and The Saints; Television appearances include: Patti Duke Show; Ed Sullivan Show; Pat Boone Show; Perry Como Show; Milton Berle Show; American Bandstand; Hullaballoo; Steve Allen Show; Dinah Shore Show; Film appearances include: Jamboree, 1957; Guns of The Timberland, 1960; The Alamo, 1960; Sail A Crooked Ship, 1962; Voyage To The Bottom of The Sea, 1962; Beach Party, 1963; Bikini Beach, 1964; Muscle Beach Party, 1964; The Carpetbaggers, 1964; Beach Blanket Bingo, 1965; I'll Take Sweden, 1965; Sergeant Deadhead, 1966; Fireball 500, 1966; How To Stuff A Wild Bikini, 1966; Skidoo, 1968; The Take, 1974; Grease, 1978; Back To The Beach, 1987; Appearances include: Alan Freed's New York Christmas Rock 'n' Roll Spectacular, 1959; Saturday Night At The London Palladium, ITV, 1967; American Bandstand's 20th Anniversary Special, ABC, 1973; Easy Does It, Starring Frankie Avalon, CBS, 1976. *Recordings include:* De De Dinah, 1957; Venus, 1959; Bobby Sox To Stockings, 1959; A Boy Without a Girl, 1959; Just Ask Your Heart, 1959; Why (No. 1, USA), 1960; When The Good Guys Used To Win, 1999; Albums include: Swingin' On A Rainbow, 1960; A Whole Lotta Frankie, 1961; Frankie Avalon's Christmas Album, 1962; Venus, 1978; Fabulous Frankie Avalon, 1991; Good Guys, 1999; The EP Collection, 2000. *Honours include:* Star on Hollywood Walk of Fame, 1992. *Current Management:* Fox Entertainment, 1650 Broadway, Suite 503, New York, NY 10019, USA.

AVELLA Vicente G; b. 27 Nov. 1970, Caracas, Venezuela. Composer; Musician (Piano). m. Kirsten Sollek-Avella, 27 Dec. 1996. *Musical Education:* BM, Piano Performance, Indiana University, 1995; MM, Composition, Eastman School of Music, 1998. *Career:* Score to animations, A Spring Day, 1997, Up The Tree, 1999, by Glenn Ehlers; Outdone, by Dan Pejril; Score to independent film, A Night Less Ordinary, by John Rockefeller, 1999; Score to industrial video by The Greater Rochester Visitors Association; Performances by ALEA III, Boston, 1997, and Academic Octet of Caracas, Venezuela, 1998; Score to animation by Val Perkins, Bibbily Bobbily Job, 2000; Score to animation by Shaun Forster, The Diestmobile, 2000; Score to short film by E. Hannois, The Shell, 2001. *Compositions:* Different Beginnings, concerto for 2 drums and orchestra, 1998; Vegetaciones and In the Forestial Depths of the Day, songs for mezzosoprano and chamber ensemble; String Quartet; Winter's Cold Light, for brass quintet; Songs of Sand, a set of songs for mezzosoprano and piano, 2000. *Honours:* Second Place, 15th International Composition Competition for Young Composers, 1997; Bernard and Rose Sernoffsky Competition Prize, 1998. *Memberships:* ASCAP; The Society of Composers and Lyricists. *Leisure interest:* Nature trips. *Current Management:* Westwood Entertainment Group. *Address:* 162 Chestnut St, Suite 2, Rutherford, New Jersey, NJ 07070, USA.

AVON Alan; b. 25 Dec. 1945, England. Vocalist; Actor; Songwriter. *Musical Education:* Private Music; Drama Tuition. *Career:* Backing and session vocalist, London, 1960s; Lead vocalist, Hedgehoppers Anonymous; Toured Europe, Southern Africa, UK, 1965–72; Solo artiste, 1972–; Numerous radio, television, and record apperances; Now presenter, commercial radio. *Recordings:* Hit single: Good News Week, Hedgehoppers Anonymous, 1965; Compositions featured on other artists' albums. *Honours:* 3 SARI Awards: Best Male Vocalist; Best Album; Best British Group, 1972. *Memberships:* Equity; British Academy of

Songwriters, Composers and Authors. *Leisure interest:* Music. *Current Management:* Dinosaur Promotions. *Address:* 5 Heyburn Cres., Westport Gardens, Stoke On Trent, Staffordshire ST6 4DL, England.

AYALA Jose (Joey); b. 1 June 1956, Philippines. Songwriter; Performer; Musician. m. Maria Jessie G Sorongon, 2 s. *Education:* AB, Economics. *Musical Education:* Self-taught Musical Education. *Career:* School Based Theatre Artist; Independent, Alternative Album Production; Entertainment World, Neo-Ethnic Icon. *Compositions:* modern dance, Encantada, 1992; Noche Buena, 1995; I Hotel/The Fall, 1997. *Recordings:* Panganay Ng Umaga, 1982; Magkabilaan, 1986; Mga Awit ng Tanod-lupa, 1991; Lumad Sa S'yudad, 1992; Lupa't Langit, 1997. *Honours:* Ten Outstanding Young Men, 1991; Awit Awards, 1992, 1993, 1997; Katha Award, 1997; Datu Bago Citation, 1998. *Leisure interests:* Reading; Learning. *Current Management:* Ma Jessie S Ayala, Bagong Lumad Productions. *Address:* 11 St Lucia St, Rosalia Compound, Tandang Sora, QCMM, Philippines.

AYERS Ben; Musician (multi-instrumentalist); Songwriter. *Career:* Musician and singer, Cornershop. *Recordings include:* Elvis Sex Change, 1993; Hold On It Hurts, 1994; Woman's Gotta Have It, 1995; I Was Born For The Seventh Time, 1997; Hit single: Brimful of Asha (No. 1, UK), 1998. *Address:* c/o Oasis Productions, 909 Hudson St, Suite 2, Hoboken, NJ 07030, USA.

AYERS Nigel; b. 3 July 1957, Tideswell, Derbyshire, England. Composer; Visual Artist. *Education:* BA Hons, Fine Art, Sculpture, 1977. *Musical Education:* Self-taught. *Career:* Founder pioneering multi-media performance group Nocturnal Emissions, 1978; Business ventures: Record labels: Sterile Records, 1978; Earthly Delights, 1987–; Tours: Europe; USA; Canada, including performances with Butch Dance Company: Poppo and the GoGo Boys; Exhibitions of video work in Tate Gallery and ICA, London; Soundtracks for film work by Charlotte Bill. *Recordings include:* Tissue of Lies, 1978; Drowning In A Sea of Bliss, 1982; Viral Shedding, 1983; Befehlsnotstand, 1984; Spiritflesh, 1988; Magnetized Light, 1993; Glossalalia, 1994; Imaginary Time, 1995. *Publications:* Network News, Vegetation Flesh, 1995. *Honour:* Meet The Composer, New York City, 1992. *Memberships:* MCPS; PRS; PPL. *Leisure interests:* Reading; Walking; Inventing. *Current Management:* Earthly Delights. *Address:* PO Box 2, Lostwithiel, Cornwall PL22 OYY, England.

AYERS Roy; b. 10 Sept. 1940, Los Angeles, California, USA. Musician (vibraphone). m. Argerie J Ayers, 20 July 1973, 2 s., 1 d. *Musical Education:* Self-taught musician. *Career:* Appeared on Merv Griffin, Johnny Carson, Jay Leno and most Jazz festivals throughout the world; Live on BBC Hammersmith Odeon London, many times; Live film, Ronnie Scotts Jazz House London. *Compositions:* Everybody Loves The Sunshine; Running Away; Love Will Bring Us Back; Searching; Most Sampled Composer, by most major Rap Groups, 1988–97. *Recordings:* Recorded 80 albums including: Wayne Henderson, 1980; Music of Many Colors, 1980; Pre-Mixture, 1981; Center of The World, 1981; Feeling Good, 1982; Lots of Love, 1983; Silver Vibrations, 1983; Drivin' On Up, 1983; In The Dark, 1984; You Might Be Surprised, 1985; I'm The One, 1987; Searchin', 1991; Drive, 1992; Vibesman Live At Ronnie Scott's, 1995; Essential Groove Live, 1996; Spoken Word, 1998; Singles include: Get On Up Get On Down, 1978; Heat of The Beat (with Wayne Henderson), 1979; Don't Stop The Feeling, 1980; Poo Poo La La, 1984; Expansions (with Scott Grooves), 1998. *Publications:* Leonard Feather, Encyclopedia of Jazz, second edition, 1960–65. *Honours:* New Star on Vibes Downbeat Mag, 1966; American Music Award, 1977; Louis Armstrong Award, 1978; Best Song of Year, Get Money, 1997. *Memberships:* ASCAP; Local 802; American Federation of Musicians. *Leisure interests:* Plays Chess; Running. *Current Management:* Roy Ayers, PO Box 1219, New York, NY 10023, USA.

AYICK Paul; b. 28 May 1947, Paterson, New Jersey, USA. Musician (trumpet); Composer. m. Rose Marie Kissel, 6 Jan. 1984, 1 d. *Musical Education:* NYCOM, 1967–69; NYU, 1969–71. *Career:* Trumpeter with Ray Fernandez, 1972–75; Hugh Brodie, 1975–78; Leader, Paul Ayick Quintet, 1978–88; Co-leader with Ira Sullivan, 1990; Also appeared with: Les Elgant; Ray Anthony; John Spider Martin; Little Anthony; Paul Cohen; Gene Krupa Band. *Recordings:* Currently recording project for trumpet, synthesiser. *Publications:* Photographer, contributor, journals and magazines. *Membership:* AFofM. *Leisure interest:* Photography. *Current Management:* Gemini Productions. *Address:* 4800 SW 70th Terrace, Davie, FL 33314, USA.

AYRES Mark Richard; b. 28 Dec. 1960, London, England. Composer. m. Nicola Jane, 11 Sept. 1993, 2 s. *Musical Education:* BSc Hons, Music, Electronics, University of Keele. *Career:* Composer of music for films including: The Innocent Sleep; Television including: Doctor Who, BBC Television, 1988–89. *Compositions:* Soundtracks: The Innocent Sleep, for soprano, orchestra; Doctor Who; Numerous arrangements of film, television themes, for album release. *Memberships:* British Academy of Composers and Songwriters; Musicians' Union; PRS; MCPS. *Leisure interest:* Meeting deadlines. *Address:* London, England.

AZNAVOUR Charles, (Varenagh Aznavourian); b. 22 May 1924, Paris, France. Singer; Actor. m. (1) Micheline Rugel, 1946, (2) Evelyene Plessis, 1955, (3) Ulla Thorsel, 1967, 5 c. (1 deceased). *Education:* Ecole Centrale de TSF. *Career:* Centre de Spectacle, Paris; Jean Dasté Company, 1941; Les Fâcheux, Arlequin, 1944; Numerous film appearances, 1964-. *Compositions include:* Songs: Il Pleut; Le Feutre Tropez; Jezebel (all recorded by Edith Piaf); Hier Encore (Yesterday When I Was Young); The Old Fashioned Way; She (theme for ITV series, The Seven Faces of Woman); What Makes A Man; Happy Anniversary. *Recordings:* Albums include: Charles Aznavour Sings, 1963; Qui, 1964; Et Voici, 1964; Sings His Love Songs In English, 1965; Encore, 1966; De T'Avoir Aimée, 1966; Désormais, 1972; Chez Lui A Paris, 1973; A Tapestry of Dreams, 1974; I Sing For You, 1975; In Times To Be, 1983; Aznavour, 1990; En Espanol, Vols I-III, 1991; The Old Fashioned Way, 1992; Jezabel, 1993; Toi Et Moi, 1994; Il Faut Savior, 1995; Paris Palais Des Congres, 1996; Jazznavour, 1999. *Honours:* Chevalier Légion d'Honneur, Des Arts et Lettres; Grand Prix National de la Chanson, 1986. *Address:* c/o Lévon Sayan, 76–78 Ave des Champs Elysées, Bureau 322, 75008 Paris, France.

AZRAK Janice; b. 12 Dec. 1951, Brooklyn, New York, USA. Record Co Exec. *Career:* Publicist, MCA Records, New York, 1971–76, SIR Productions, New York, 1976–77; Vice-president, Creative Services/Artist Development, Warner Brothers Records, Nashville, 1977-. *Membership:* Vice-President, Board of Directors, Academy of Country Music, 1985–86. *Address:* c/o Warner Brothers Records, 20 Music St E, Nashville, TN 37203, USA.

AZZI María Susana**;** b. 12 Oct. 1952, Buenos Aires, Argentina. Social Anthropologist. *Education:* Licenciada en Ciencias Antropòlógicas, Universidad de Buenos Aires, 1987; Columbia University, New York, 1986; MBA, Escuela Superior de Economía y Administración de Empresas, Buenos Aires; Piano Lessons with Teresa Eichelbaum, 1984–92, Vera Anosova, 1992–95. *Career:* Professor, Board Member, Academia Nacional del Tango, Buenos Aires; Lecturer on the Tango and Astor Piazzolla in Argentina, USA, Europe, Australia, Mexico and Korea; Television and radio appearances in Argentina and UK; Consultant work for: Sony Classical (US), Dance Perspectives Foundation and Metropolitan Museum of Art, Metropolitan Museum of Art, New York; Smithsonian Institution, Washington DC; Fundación Astor Piazzolla and Instituto Nacional de Antropología, Buenos Aires, Argentina. *Publications include:* Italian Immigration and Their Impact On The Tango In Argentina, 1997; Tango Album by Yo-Yo Ma, 1997; Tango Argentino, 1998; Asphalt, by Paolo Ziegler, liner notes, 1998; Tango Ballad, by Gidon Kremer, liner notes, 1999; Le Grand Tango: A Biography of Astor Piazzola, forthcoming. *Memberships include:* Academia Nacional del Tango; Society for Ethnomusicology; American Anthropological Asscn; International Council for Traditional Music; International Asscn for the Study of Popular Music. *Leisure interest:* Golf. *Address:* Posadas 1612 8°, Buenos Aires 1112, Argentina.

B

BABULJAK Karel; b. 5 Oct. 1957, Prague, Czech Republic. Musician (Keyboards, Zither, Guitar, Drums); Composer; Poet. m. (1) Barbora, 1982, (2) Tereza, 22 June 1996, 2 s., 1 d. *Career:* Broadrange Musician and Composer, rock reggae, new age, made demonic experiments; Founder Member of Groups: Relaxace, 1979; Ma'ma Bubo, 1983; Vopruz, 1983; Sajkedelik Sraml Band, 1992; Karel Babuljak and His Band of Dreams, 1999; Member of groups: Babalet, 1983–; Hypnotix, 1988–90; Boothill 1998–; Cooperation with Theatre Prague 5. *Recordings include:* Solo Albums: A Mass of Lany; Billiard Blues; Bubol's Shouts from Darkness; A Man With a Knapsack; Albums with groups: Mama Bubo: Ball-Shapedness, 1983–85; Planet Haj, 1985; So thet they Love One Another; Relaxace: Dhjana, 1991; Kadael, 1993; Flower Reggae, 1995; Sound and Silence, 1996; Boothill: Sister, 1999. *Leisure interests:* Sport; Gardening; Work of all kinds. *Current Management:* Lubos Fendrych, Nad Koulkon 21, 15000 Prague 5 Czech Republic. *Address:* Na'drazní 213, 33805 My'to v Cecha'ch, Czech Republic. *E-mail:* karelbabuljak@netscape.net.

BACA Susana; b. Chorrillos, Peru. Vocalist. m. Ricardo Pereira. *Career:* Formed experimental group combining poetry and song; Researched Afro-Peruvian tradition and formed the Instituto Negrocontinuo with husband. *Recordings:* Albums: Susana Baca, 1997; Eco De Sombras, 2000; Lamento Negro (earlier Cuban recordings), 2001.

BACAR Zena; b. Ilha de Mocambique, Mozambique. Vocalist; Songwriter. *Career:* Fisher woman; Founding member and lead singer of Eyuphuro, 1981; Recorded the first international release for a Mozambican group, Mama Mosambiki, 1989; Toured Europe, late 1980s/early 1990s; Disbanded shortly after; Reunited, 1998. *Recordings:* Albums; Parado de Sucessos; Mama Mosambiki, 1990; Yellela, 2001. *Address:* c/o World Music Network/ Riverboat Records, 6 Abbeville Mews, 88 Clapham Park Rd, London SW4 7BX.

BACCHUS Brian Michel; b. 8 Aug. 1957, New York, New York, USA. Record Co Exec.; Record Prod. *Education:* AB, Syracuse University, 1980. *Career:* National Jazz Promotions Co-ordinator, Polygram Records, New York, 1986–87; Manager, National Jazz Promotions, 1987–88; Director, Jazz Promotion, 1988–90; Director, Antilles Records/Island Records, New York, 1990–. *Recordings:* Producer of albums: Remembrance, The Harper Brothers, 1990; Music Inside, Joyce, 1990; Amazon Secrets, Ricardo Silveira, 1990; Kenny Drew Jr, 1991; with Randy Weston: Spirits of Our Ancestors, 1991; Volcano Blues, 1993; Khepara, 1998; Sanctified Shells, Steve Turre, 1992; Ann Dyer and The No Good Time Fairies, 1995; Timepeace, Terry Callier, 1998. *Honours:* Billboard Award, Top Jazz Album, Remembrance, 1990. *Address:* c/o Antilles Records, 825 Eighth Ave, New York, NY 10019, USA.

BACCINI John; b. 31 March 1947, Luton, Bedfordshire, England. Musician. *Career:* Played electric bass guitar in clubs and pubs, 1960–; First recording at Abbey Road studios; Played in Germany, 1964; Played in clubs and on radio and television, 1966–70; Numerous BBC radio sessions and shows with various bands, also performing backing and lead vocals; Over 40 records for major labels, to date; Engineer, up to 4000 sessions, from rhythm section work to orchestral and 60 piece choir, all musical styles; Producer, 1970–; Music Publisher, 1973–; Songwriter, currently writing and with record deal. *Memberships:* PRS; MCPS. *Leisure interests:* Music; Clothes; Sports; Karate; Yoga; Women; Life. *Current Management:* Don Larking, Hitchin. *Address:* Everyday Music, 14–15 Cam Sq., Wilbury Way, Hitchin, Hertfordshire SG4 0TZ, England.

BACH Sebastian, (Sebastian Bierk); b. 3 April 1968, Bahamas. Rock Vocalist; Lyricist. m. Maria Aquinar, 1992. *Career:* Lead singer, US rock group Skid Row, 1986–98; Major appearances include: Support to Bon Jovi, US tour, 1988; Support to Guns 'N' Roses, US tour, 1991; European tour, 1992; US tour, 1992; Earth Pledge Concert, Central Park, New York, 1992; South American tour, 1992; Monsters of Rock Festival, Castle Donington, 1992; Japanese tour, 1992; Took title role in Broadway production of Jekyll and Hyde, 2000. *Recordings:* Albums: Skid Row, 1989; Slave To The Grind (No. 1, USA), 1991; B-Sides Ourselves, 1992; Subhuman Race, 1995; Scream, 1996; Working Man, 1996; 12 Picks, 1997; Forty Seasons…, 1998; Loaded Deck, 1998; Bring 'Em Bach Alive, 1999; Singles: Youth Gone Wild, 1989; 18 and Life, 1989; I Remember You, 1990; Monkey Business, 1991; Slave To The Grind, 1991; Wasted Time, 1991. *Honours include:* Gold discs; American Music Awards, Favourite New Hard Rock Artist, 1990. *Current Management:* Doc McGhee, McGhee Entertainment, 8730 Sunset Blvd, Suite 175, Los Angeles, CA 90069, USA.

BACH YEN, (Bach Yen Tran, Blanche Hirondelle); b. 12 June 1942, Soc Trang, Viet Nam. Pop and Folk Singer. m. Tran Quang Hai, 17 June 1978, 1 d. *Career:* Started performing in Paris, 1961, in the style of Edith Piaf; Tour of Europe including Belgium, Germany and Austria; Visited USA, 1965; Appeared on Ed Sullivan TV Show; Appearances on other television shows and appearances with Bing Crosby, Joey Bishop, Mike Douglas, Pat Boone; Toured in 46 US states and also visited Canada, Mexico, Caracas, Panama, Bogotá, Curaçao, alongside Jimmy Duranti, Liberace and Frankie Avalon; Sang for John Wayne film, The Green Berets; Returned to Paris; Met Musician and Ethnomusicologist Tran Quang Hai and worked with traditional Vietnamese folk music; Performed in over 2000 concerts. *Recordings:* Recorded 7 albums with Tran Quang Hai. *Honour:* Grand Prix du Disque, Académie Charles Cros in 1983. *Address:* 12 rue Gutenberg, 94450 Limeil Brevannes, France.

BACHARACH Burt; b. 12 May 1928, Kansas City, Missouri, USA. Composer; Arranger; Conductor; Musician (piano). m. (1) Paula Stewart, (2) Angie Dickinson, (3) Carole Bayer Sager, 1982, 1 s., 1 d. *Musical Education:* Composition and Theory, McGill University, Montréal; Music Academy West, Santa Barbara. *Career:* Jazz musician, 1940s; Accompanist, arranger, conductor, various artists including Vic Damone; Marlene Dietrich; Joel Gray; Steve Lawrence. *Compositions:* Popular songs, film music and stage musicals; Regular collaborations with Hal David, 1962–70; Carole Bayer Sager, 1981–; Numerous hit songs as co-writer include: with Hal David: The Story of My Life, Marty Robbins; Magic Moments, Perry Como; Tower of Strength, Frankie Vaughan; Wives and Lovers, Jack Jones; 24 Hours From Tulsa, Gene Pitney; What The World Needs Now Is Love, Jackie DeShannon; Walk On By; Trains and Boats and Planes; Do You Know The Way To San Jose?; Alfie (all by Dionne Warwick); Anyone Who Had A Heart, Cilla Black; There's Always Something There To Remind Me, Sandie Shaw; Make It Easy On Yourself, Walker Brothers; What's New Pussycat?, Tom Jones; This Guy's In Love With You, Herb Alpert; Raindrops Keep Fallin' On My Head, Sacha Distel; Close To You, The Carpenters; Numerous film scores include: The Man Who Shot Liberty Valence; Wives and Lovers; What's New Pussycat?; Alfie; Casino Royale; Butch Cassidy and The Sundance Kid; with Carole Bayer Sager: Making Love, Roberta Flack; Heartlight, Neil Diamond; That's What Friends Are For, Dionne Warwick and Friends (AIDS charity record); On My Own, Patti Labelle and Michael McDonald; with Carole Bayer Sager, Peter Allen and Christopher Cross: Arthur's Theme, Christopher Cross. *Recordings:* Albums include: Hit Maker, 1965; Reach Out, 1967; Make It Easy On Yourself, 1969; Burt Bacharach, 1971; Portrait In Music, 1971; Living Together, 1973; Greatest Hits, 1974; Futures, 1977, 1999; Woman, 1979; Walk On By, 1989; Butch Cassidy and The Sundance Kid, 1989. *Publications:* Numerous song books. *Honours:* Entertainers of The Year, with Hal David, Cue Magazine, 1969; 3 Academy Awards; Several Academy Award Nominations; 4 Grammy Awards; 2 Emmy Awards; 1 Tony Award. *Address:* c/o McMullen and Co, Hollywood, CA, USA.

BACHCHAN Amitabh Harivanshrai; b. 11 Oct. 1942, Alahabad, India. Vocalist; Actor. m. Jaya Bhaduri. *Career:* Primarily Indian film actor but unusually, in an industry dominated by actors lip-synching to playback singers, does much of own singing; First film, Saat Hindustani, not a great success; Became one of the most popular Indian film actors as a new type of hero ('Angry Young Man' figure); Retired from acting and became involved in politics; Returned to film as head of production company; Acting comeback, 1997; Named the Superstar of the Millennium by BBC Online poll, defeating many Hollywood legends such as Alec Guinness and Marlon Brando, 1999; Host of record-breaking quiz show Kaun Banega Crorepati (Indian version of Who Wants To Be A Millionaire?) and had a critically acclaimed role in film Mohabbatein, 2000; Also became the first living Asian to have a statue of his likeness installed in Madame Tussaud's waxwork museum, London. *Recordings include:* It's My Choice (compilation), 1997; Bachchan Blast (remixes), 2000. *Honours:* Filmfare, Lifetime Achievement Award, 1991; BBC, Superstar of the Millennium, 1999; Filmfare, Star of the 20th Century, 2000.

BACHMAN Randy; b. 27 Sept. 1943, Winnipeg, Manitoba, Canada. Vocalist; Musician (guitar); Songwriter. *Career:* Father of singer-songwriter Tal Bachman; Member, Guess Who; Founder member, Brave Belt; Reformed as Bachman-Turner Overdrive, 1972–76; Solo career, 1977–79; Founder member, Ironhorse, 1979; Union, 1981; Solo artist, 1981–; Tours with reformed Guess Who, 1984. *Compositions include:* You Ain't Seen Nothing Yet. *Recordings:* with Bachman-Turner Overdrive: Singles: Let It Ride, 1974; Takin' Care of Business, 1974; You Ain't Seen Nothing Yet (No. 1, USA), 1974; Roll On Down The Highway, 1975; Hey You, 1975; Albums: Bachman-Turner Overdrive, 1973; Bachman-Turner Overdrive 2, 1974; Not Fragile (No. 1, USA), 1974; BTO As Brave Belt, 1975; Four-Wheel Drive, 1975; Head On, 1976; The Best of BTO (So Far), 1976; Bachman-Turner Overdrive, 1984; Solo albums: Axe, 1972; Survivor,

1978; Any Road (featuring Neil Young), 1993; with Ironhorse: Ironhorse, 1979; Everything Is Grey, 1979; with Union: on Strike, 1981; CD, Merge, 1996; Randy Bachman Song book, 1999. *Honour:* Prairie Music Hall of Fame, Manitoba, Canada, 1999. *Current Management:* c/o Marty Kramer Bachman Headquarters, 10331 Steveston Hwy, Richmond, BC V7A 1N3, Canada.

BACKER Matthew De Bracey; b. New Orleans, Louisiana, USA. Musician (guitar); Vocalist; Songwriter. m. Elisa Richards, 5 Jan. 1994. *Education:* BA Hons, University of Warwick. *Musical Education:* Berklee College of Music, Boston, USA. *Career:* Recordings, performances, television appearances with: Sinéad O'Connor; Elton John; Marcella Detroit; Aimee Mann; Emmylou Harris; Mica Paris; Joe Cocker; Swing Out Sister; Beautiful South; Sarah Jane Morris; Michael Ball; Suzanne Rhatigan; Jools Holland; Kate Saint John; Daniel Cartier; Soundtrack work for television programmes including Equinox; Cracker; Spitting Image; Knowing Me Knowing You; Rory Bremner; Solo and collaborative singing/songwriting, and session work. *Membership:* Musicians' Union.

BADLEY Bill; b. Wiltshire, England. Musician (guitar, banjo, mandolin, lute); Vocalist. *Education:* Medieval Studies, Exeter University. *Musical Education:* Lute, Royal College of Music. *Career:* Played with: The Consort of Musicke; The New London Consort; The Dufay Collective; Own group, Arcadia; Film work includes: Lady Jane; Caravaggio; Member, The Carnival Band, 1984–; First performance, Burnley Canalside Festival, 1984; Play material from: Sweden; Croatia; US; Bolivia; Spain; UK; France; Appearances include: festivals, arts theatres and centres; Barbican Centre; Glasgow Cathedral; Birmingham Symphony Hall; Assistant producer, Thames Television. *Recordings include:* Album with Maddy Prior: Christmas Carols. *Current Management:* c/o Jim McPhee, Acorn Entertainments. *Address:* Winterfold House, 46 Woodfield Rd, Kings Heath, Birmingham B13 9UJ, England.

BADLY DRAWN BOY (Damon Gough); b. 2 Oct. 1970, Bolton, England. Vocalist; Musician (guitar, keyboards); Songwriter. *Career:* Collaborated with UNKLE, 1998; Runs Twisted Nerve record label with Andy Votel. *Recordings:* Singles: EP1, 1997; EP2, EP3, 1998; It Came From The Ground, Once Around The Block, 1999; Another Pearl, Disillusion, 2000; Pissing In The Wind, 2001; Silent Sigh, 2002; Albums: The Hour of Bewilderbeast, 2000; About A Boy OST, 2002. *Honours:* Mercury Music Prize, The Hour of Bewilderbeast, 2000. *Current Management:* Big Life Management. *Internet:* www.badlydrawnboy.co.uk.

BADU Erykah; b. 26 Feb. 1972, Dallas, Texas, USA. Vocalist; Songwriter. 1 s. *Education:* Graduated in Theatre, Grambling State University, Louisiana. *Career:* Performances with cousin Free, in Erykah Free; Turned solo, obtained recording deal; Appeared in interview in numerous publications including Time and Rolling Stone; Support slots to numerous artists including Wu Tang Clan; Collaborations: Omar; OutKast; Guru. *Recordings:* Singles: Next Lifetime, 1997; Tyrone, 1997; Apple Tree, 1997; On and On, 1997; Southern Girl, 1999; You Got Me (with The Roots), 1999; Bag Lady, 2000; Didn't Cha Know, 2001; Albums: Baduizm, 1997; Live, 1997; Heartache, 1998; Mama's Gun, 2000. *Honours:* Grammy Award, Best Rap Performance By Duo Or Group, You Got Me (with The Roots), 2000; Further Grammy nominations, 2000/2001; MOBO Award nominations, 2000.

BAEZ Joan; b. 9 Jan. 1941, Staten Island, New York, USA. Singer. m. David Harris, 26 March 1968, divorced 1974, 1 s. *Education:* Boston University, 1958; Dr Humane Letters, Antioch University, 1980; Rutgers University, 1980. *Recordings:* Albums include: Joan Baez, 1960; Joan Baez, Vol. 2, 1961; In Concert, part 2, 1963; 5, 1964; Farewell Angelina, 1965; Noel, 1966; Joan, 1967; Baptism, 1968; Any Day Now, 1968; David's Album, 1969; One Day At A Time, 1969; First Ten Years, 1970; Carry It On (soundtrack), 1971; Ballad Book, 1972; Come From The Shadows, 1972; Where Are You Now My Son?, 1973; Hits, Greatest and Others, 1973; Gracias A La Vida, 1974; Contemporary Ballad Book, 1974; Diamonds and Rust, 1975; From Every Stage, 1976; Gulf Winds, 1976; Blowin' Away, 1977; Best Of, 1977; Honest Lullaby, 1979; Very Early Joan, 1982; Recently, 1987; Diamonds and Rust In The Bullring, 1989; Speaking of Dreams, 1989; Play Me Backwards, 1992; Rare Live and Classic, 1993; Ring Them Bells, 1995; Gone from Danger, 1997; Dreams, 1997; Best Of..., 1997; 20th Century Masters: The Millenium, 1999. *Publications:* Joan Baez Song Book, 1964; Daybreak, 1968; Coming Out (with David Harris), 1971; And Then I Wrote (song book), 1979; And A Voice To Sing With: A Memoir, 1987. *Honours:* 8 Gold albums; 1 Gold single; Joan Baez Day In Atlanta, Georgia, 2 Aug 1975; Thomas Merton Award, 1976; Public Service, Third Annual Rock Music, 1977; Best Female Vocalist, Bay Area Music, 1978, 1979; ACLU Awards, 1979, 1989; Jefferson Award, 1980; Lennon Peace Tribute, 1982; ADA Award, 1982; Sane Education Fund Peace, 1983; Chevalier, Legion of Honour, France, 1983; Academy Charles Cros (France), 1983; Death Penalty Focus, California, 1992. *Memberships include:* Founder, Institute Study Nonviolence, 1965; Founder, President,

Humanitas International Human Rights Committee, 1979–92. *Address:* PO Box 1026, Menlo Park, CA 94026, USA.

BAGGE Nigel; b. 6 June 1953, London, England. Musician (guitarist); Singer; Songwriter. *Musical Education:* Self-taught. *Career:* Extensive gigging, bands include: Cold Comfort, 1970s; Highway 61, 1985–90; Duck Soup, 1990–; Bag Band, 1992–93; Juice On The Loose, 1990; Nicky Moore's Blues Corporation, 1993–97; Angela Brown and The Mighty 45s, 1997–; Various session work. *Recordings:* Albums: Cold Comfort: In The Can; Highway 61: Talk To Me; Further Up The Road; Nicky Moore's Blues Corporation: I Just Got Back; Holding On; Angela Brown and the Mighty 45s: Thinking Out Loud. *Membership:* Musicians' Union. *Current Management:* A.R.M., PO Box 177, New Malden, Surrey KT3 6YT, England.

BAHRI Mamdouh; b. 31 July 1957, Sfax, Tunisia. Musician (guitar). m. Geva Nouyrit, 24 July 1993, 1 s., 1 d. *Education:* Maths, technical studies. *Musical Education:* Swiss Jazz School; Seminars with Joe Diorio, Jim Hall, John Abercrombie. *Career:* Festival Jazz D'0-Beziers, 1989; Bastia Festival, 1990; Carthage Music Festival, Tunisia, 1991; New Yok, Blue Note, 1992, 95; Romans Festival, 1993; Pori Jazz Festival, Finland, 1995; Sweet Basil, 1995; Appearances in USA: New York; Alabama; Connecticut; Maryland. *Recordings:* From Tunisia With Love, The Spirit of Life Ensemble, 1992; Mamoudh Bahri, Nefta, 1993; Inspirations, 1993; Feel The Spirit, 1994; Live At The S Spot, 1995. *Memberships:* SACEM; SPEDIDAM; ADAMI. *Address:* 4 Lot Bonnier D'Alco, 34990 Juvignac, France.

BAIKIE Pete; b. 17 April 1957, Edinburgh, Scotland. Composer; Writer; Comedian; Musician (guitar, piano); Actor. *Education:* Edinburgh University. *Musical Education:* Self-taught. *Career:* Actor, writer, BBC Radio 4 series In Other Words... The Bodgers, 1985; Actor, singer/ musician, BBC Radio 4 series Bodgers, Banks and Sparkes, 1986; Actor, singer, musician, writer, CH4 television series, Absolutely, 1989–93; Actor, writer, CH4 television series, Squawkie Talkie, 1995; Actor, role of Bandleader, Swing Kids (Disney film); Producer, HTV/Paramount television series Barry Welsh Is Coming, 1996–; Bandleader/musician, Channel 5 UK television series The Jack Docherty Show, 1997; Co-presenter, BBC Radio 2 series Saturday Night Jack, 2000–01; Co-founder, Absolutely Productions, 1989–. *Compositions:* Television themes for: It's Only TV But I LIke It (BBC1), Vic and Bob's Shooting Stars, Two Fat Ladies, Bang Bang It's Reeves and Mortimer, Stressed Eric (all BBC2); Barbara, 2DTV (both ITV1); Absolutely; mr don and mr george; Squawkie Talkie; Teenage Health Freak (all CH4); Radio themes for: Labour Exchange; If You're So Clever; The Preventers, BBC Radio 4. *Memberships:* Musicians' Union; BASCA. *Leisure interests:* Snorkelling. *Current Management:* Michael Foster/ICM and Leah Schmidt. *Address:* Absolutely Productions, 6/7 Fareman St, London W1V 3AH, England.

BAILEY Derek; b. 29 Jan. 1930, Sheffield, Yorkshire, England. Musician (guitar). 1 s. *Musical Education:* Music with C H C Biltcliffe; Guitar with George Wing, Jack Duarte, and others. *Career:* Orchestral guitarist, 1951–65; Soloist, 1965–; Performed solo concerts in most of world's cultural centres; Played with most of the musicians associated with freely improvised music. *Recordings:* Recorded over 100 albums on many labels; Recorded with: Company; Cecil Taylor; Han Bennink; Anthony Braxton; Steve Lacy. *Publications:* Improvisation, Its Nature and Practice. *Current Management:* Incus Records. *Address:* 14 Downs Rd, London E5 8DS, England.

BAILEY Jim; b. 10 Jan. 1948, Philadelphia, USA. Singr; Actor; Entertainer. *Musical Education:* Voice, piano, Philadelphia Conservatory of Music. *Career:* Concerts world-wide include: Carnegie Hall, Las Vegas; Top casinos; London Palladium; Specials: Superbowl; Olympics; Peoples Choice Awards; Royal Variety (twice); Television shows: about 40 include: Here's Lucy; Vegas; Rockford Files; Carol Burnett Show; Ed Sullivan; Tonight Show; Des O'Connor; Russell Harty; Pebble Mill. *Recordings:* Jim Bailey Live At Carnegie Hall; Jim Bailey Sings, 1998; Also performed for 3 US presidents. *Honours:* Las Vegas Entertainer of The Year, 4 times; Peoples Choice Award; IPA Award, 2 times; Many theatre awards. *Leisure interests:* Film and book collector; Pool. *Current Management:* Stephen Campbell Management. *Address:* 350 N Crescent Dr., Suite 105, Beverly Hills, CA 90210, USA.

BAILEY Philip; b. 8 May 1951, Denver, Colorado, USA. Vocalist; Musician (percussion); Prod. *Career:* Musical director, gospel group The Stovall Sisters; Member, Friends and Love; Member, Earth Wind and Fire, 1972–84, 1987–; Solo recording artiste, 1983–86; Peformances include: Opened for Sly and The Family Stone, Madison Square Gardens, 1974; Featured as rock band in film, Shining Star, 1975; Tours, USA, Europe, Asia, 1979; Music for UNICEF Concert, UN, New York, 1979; Earth Pledge Concert, Central Park, New York, 1992. *Recordings:* Albums: Last Days and Time, 1972; Head To The Sky, 1973; Open Our Eyes, 1973; That's The Way of the World, 1975; Gratitude, 1976; Spirit, 1976; All 'N' All, 1978; The Best Of, Vol. 1, 1979; I Am, 1979; Faces, 1980; Raise, 1981; Powerlight,

1983; Chinese Wall, 1985; The Wonders of His Love, 1984; Inside Out, 1986; Triumph, 1986; Wonders of Love, 1988; Family Affair, 1990; Philip Bailey, 1994; Dreams, 1999; Singles include: Getaway, 1976; Saturday Nite, 1977; Serpentine Fire, 1978; Fantasy, 1978; Got To Get You Into My Life, 1978; September, 1979; Runnin', 1979; Boogie Wonderland, 1979; After The Love Has Gone, 1979; Star, 1979; Let's Groove, 1981; Here With Me, 1994; Solo: Easy Lover (duet with Phil Collins, No. 1, UK), 1985. *Honours:* American Music Awards, Favourite Band, Soul/Rhythm and Blues, 1977, 1979; Grammy, Best R & B Vocal Performance, All 'N' All, 1979; After The Love Has Gone, 1980; Best R & B Instrumental, Boogie Wonderland, 1980; Gold Ticket, Madison Square Garden, 1979; MTV Music Video, 1985; Ivor Novello Award, Easy Lover, 1986; Grammy Award, Best Gospel Performance, 1987. *Current Management:* Bob Cavallo, Third Rail Entertainment. *Address:* 9169 Sunset Blvd, Los Angeles, CA 90069, USA.

BAILEY Roy; b. 20 Oct. 1935, London, England. Folk Singer; Musician (guitar); Academic. m. Val Turbard, 10 Aug. 1963, 1 s., 1 d. *Education:* BA Hons, Social Science. *Career:* Professional singer, 1960–; Radio, television, tours, in: UK; Switzerland; Canada; USA; Australia; Appearances include festivals in: UK; Canada; Switzerland; Belgium; Australia; Professor of Sociology and Social Work, Sheffield Hallam University, 1988. *Recordings:* Smoke and Dust Where The Heart Should Have Been, 1965; Oats and Beans and Kangaroos, 1966; Cobweb of Dreams, 1967; Roy Bailey, 1970; That's Not The Way It's Got To Be (with Leon Rosselson), 1975; New Bell Wake, 1976; Love Loneliness and Laundry (with Leon Rosselson) 1977; If I Knew Who The Enemy Was (with Leon Rosselson) 1978; Hard Times, 1982; Freedom Peacefully, 1985; Leaves From A Tree, 1989; Why Does It Have To Be Me, 1990; Never Leave A Story Unsung, 1992; What You Do With What You've Got, 1993; Business As Usual, 1994; Rhythm and Reds (with Band of Hope), 1994; New Directions in the Old, 1997; Past Masters, 1998. *Publications:* Contemporary Social Problems in Britain (with Jock Young), 1973; Radical Social Work (with Mike Brake), 1975; Radical Social Work and Practice (with Mike Brake), 1980; Theory and Practice In Social Work (with Phil Lee), 1982. *Honours:* Fellow, Royal Society of Arts, 1989; Emeritus Professor, Sheffield Hallam University, 1990. *Current Management:* Brass Tacks Music Agency, PO Box 1162, Sheffield S8 9JY, England.

BAIN Aly; b. 15 May 1946, Lerwick, Shetland, Scotland. Musician (violin). *Musical Education:* Began playing aged 11; Taught by Tom Anderson. *Career:* Member, Boys of The Lough, 1988; Television includes: Presenter, Down Home, series on spread on fiddle music from Scotland and Ireland to North America, BBC, 1991; Series, The Shetland Set, BBC, 1991. *Recordings:* Aly Bain-Mike Whelans, 1971; The Silver Bow (with Tom Anderson), 1976; Shetland Folk Fiddling Vol. 2 (with Tom Anderson), 1978; Aly Bain, 1985; Down Home Vol. 1, 1986; Down Home Vol. 2, 1986; Aly Meets The Cajuns, 1988; The Pearl, 1995; Follow The Moonstone, 1996; Lonely Bird, 1996; Ruby, 1998.

BAIYEWU Tunde; b. London, England. Vocalist. *Education:* Newcastle University. *Career:* Singer, The Lighthouse Family, 1994–; Television includes: Top of The Pops. *Recordings:* Albums: Ocean Drive, 1995; Postcards From Heaven, 1997; Whatever Gets You Through The Day, 2001; Singles: Lifted, 1995; Ocean Drive (for film soundtrack Jack and Sarah), 1995; Goodbye Heartbreak, 1996; Loving Every Minute, 1996; Raincloud, 1997; High, 1998; Lost In Space, 1998; Question of Faith, 1998; Free/One, 2001. *Current Management:* Kitchenware, 7 The Stables, St Thomas St, Newcastle-Upon-Tyne, Tyne and Wear NE1 4LE, England.

BAJTALA Janos; b. 5 Dec. 1944, Budapest, Hungary. Singer; Composer; Arranger; Musician (piano). 1 s. *Musical Education:* Diploma, Jazz Academy, Budapest. *Career:* Formed Jazz/Soul Trio, 1965; Television and radio shows in Hungary, 1965–71; Tours with soul bands The Bandwagon, Foundation, 1974; Co-arranger, West End hit musical, The Black Mikado, 1975–76; Tours with reggae group Chosen Few, 1981–88; Tours with Boney M, 1991–98; Tours with Jimmy Ruffin (Motown), 1999–; First appearance in 24 years in Hungary, broadcast on national television, 1995. *Recordings:* Gipsy Girl (own composition), charted in Hungary, 1968; Keyboards, Black Mikado cast album, 1975; Keyboards on album Bad Weathers, Vivian Weathers, 1980; Various recordings with Chosen Few, 1981–88. *Honours:* First prize, nationwide pop and jazz contest, 1967; Best soloist, Hugarian International Jazz Festival, 1971. *Memberships:* PRS. *Leisure interests:* Computers; Flying. *Address:* 176 Weedington Rd, London NW5 4QQ, England.

BAKALA Bretislav; b. 18 June 1957, Brno, Czech Republic. Musician (keyboard). m. Marta Srvtova, 8 Sept. 1984, 1 s., 1 d. *Education:* Diploma, College of Technology, Brno, Faculty of Electronics; Folk Art School. *Career:* Keyboard in Jazz Duo Brno; Good Company, Dancing 19, in Norway, Germany, Switzerland, Mallorca, Austria, 1987–97; Immerwieder, 1 CD, Just Friends, 2 CD, Composer, Keyboards, Sound Studio. *Compositions:* Warum Lieb'ich Dich Allein; Lift Me Up; You're Crossing My Life; New Day; Zeit, Du Heilst Wunden. *Recordings:* Immer Wieder, CD, 1994; Just Friends, CD, 1996. *Leisure interests:* Computer;

Music; Swimming. *Current Management:* Good Sound CZ. *Address:* 2a Gymnaziem 2448, 39701 Pisek, Czech Republic.

BAKER Anita; b. 20 Dec. 1957, Detroit, USA. Vocalist. m. Walter Bridgforth, 24 Dec. 1988, 1 s. *Career:* Lead vocalist, soul group Chapter 8, 1976–80; Solo singer, 1983–; Appearances include: Nelson Mandela International Tribute, Wembley, 1990; Radio City Music Hall, 1990; Compositions tour, 1990; Television appearances include: Christmas in Washington, NBC, 1991; A Call To Action In The War Against AIDS, ABC, 1992. *Recordings:* Albums: with Chapter 8: Chapter 8; Solo albums: The Songstress, 1983; Rapture (No. 1, USA R & B chart), 1986; Giving You The Best That I Got (No. 1, USA), 1988; Compositions, 1990; Rhythm of Love, 1994; Singles: No More Tears; Angel; You're The Best Thing Yet; Sweet Love; Caught Up In The Rapture; Same Ole Love; No One In The World; Just Because; Giving You The Best That I Got; Talk To Me; Soul Inspiration; Fairy Tales; Live In London; Body and Soul; I Apologize; It's Been You; When You Love Someone; featured on: Rubáiyát (Elektra Records 40th Anniversary compilation), 1990; Barcelona Gold, 1992. *Honours:* Grammy Awards: 5 consecutive Best Female R & B Vocal Performances, 1987–91; Best R & B Song, Sweet Love, 1987; Giving The Best That I Got, 1989; Best Soul/Gospel Performance, 1988; Soul Train Awards: Best Single, Female, 1987; Best R & B Single, Best R & B Album, Best R & B Song, 1989; American Music Awards: Favourite Female Soul/R & B Artist, 1988, 1990; Favourite Female Soul/R & B Album, 1988; NAACP Image Award, Best Female Artist, 1990. *Current Management:* Sterling/Winters Co, 1640 Ave of the Stars, Los Angeles, CA 90067, USA.

BAKER Carroll Anne; b. 4 March 1949, Nova Scotia, Canada. Country Singer; Songwriter. *Musical Education:* Self-taught. *Career:* British tour with Slim Whitman; Recorded duets with daughter Candace; Eddie Eastman; Jack Scott; Roger Whittaker; Concert with Canada Pops Orchestra; Television includes: 3 Carroll Baker super specials, CBC TV; Mini-series, 7 half-hour shows, CBC; Guest appearances: Hee Haw; New Country; Nashville Now; The Tommy Hunter Show; Lifetime; Canada AM; Headlined for Regent Holiday Tours, Carroll Baker's Country Cruise, 1989. *Compositions include:* I'm An Old Rock and Roller (Dancin' To A Different Beat). *Recordings:* I Should Have Put A Hold On Love (Canadian Country No. 2), 1990. *Honours:* Entertainer of The Year, Country Award, Canada; 3 Platinum, 6 Gold albums; 5 Gold Singles; JUNO Awards: 1975–78; Big Country Awards, 1975–81; 1987; BMI Award, 1977; RPM Programmer Award, 1978, 1981; Procan Award, 1983; 14 consecutive No. 1 singles, Canadian country charts, 1975–81; Top Country Female, Canadian Country Music, 1985; Martin Guitar Award, 1989; Lifetime Achievement, Canadian Country Music Awards, 1991; JUNO Award Nominations, 1974–92; Inductee, Canadian Country Music Hall of Honour, 1992. *Memberships:* AFofM; ACTRA; SOCAN. *Leisure interests:* Charities; General home life. *Current Management:* John Beaulieu, Carroll Baker Enterprises Inc. *Address:* 210 Dimson Ave, Guelph, ON N1G 3C8, Canada.

BAKER Ginger (Peter); b. 19 Aug. 1939, Lewisham, London, England. Musician (drums). *Career:* Drummer with Terry Lightfoot; Acker Bilk; Alexis Korner's Blues Incorporated, 1962; Graham Bond Organisation, 1963; Member, Cream, 1966–68; Blind Faith, 1969; Airforce, 1970–72; Salt (Nigeria); Baker-Gurvitz Army; Energy; Short spells with Atomic Rooster and Hawkwind; Ginger Baker's Nutters; Solo recording artiste, and leader of own trio (with Bill Frisell and Charlie Haden); Collaboration with Masters of Reality, 1993; Performances include: with Cream: Jazz and Blues Festival, Windsor, 1966, 1967; 2 US tours, 1967; Madison Square Garden, New York, 1968; Royal Albert Hall, London, 1968; with Blind Faith: Hyde Park, London, 1969; Madison Square Garden, New York, 1969. *Recordings:* Albums: with Cream: Fresh Cream, 1967; Disraeli Gears, 1967; Wheels of Fire, 1968; Goodbye, 1969; The Best of Cream, 1969; Live Cream, 1970; Live Cream Vol. 2, 1972; Heavy Cream, 1972; 20th Century Masters (compilation), 2000; with Blind Faith: Blind Faith (No. 1, UK and US), 1969; with Airforce: Airforce, 1970; Airforce 2, 1972; Solo: The Best Of, 1973; 11 Sides of Baker, 1977; From Humble Origins, 1983; Horses and Trees, 1987; In Concert, 1987; African Force, 1980s; In Concert, 1987; Middle Passage, 1992; The Album, 1992; The Alternative Album, 1992; Unseen Rain, 1993; with Ginger Baker Trio: Going Back Home, 1995; Falling Off The Roof, 1995; Do What You Like, 1998; Coward of The County, 1999; Singles with Cream include: I Feel Free, 1967; Strange Brew, 1967; Sunshine of Your Love, 1968; White Room, 1968. *Current Management:* Kron Management, 41489 Frontier Rd, Parker, CO 80134, USA.

BAKER Ronald; b. 21 Nov. 1968, Baltimore, Maryland, USA. Musician (trumpet); Singer. m. Patricia Labeau, 26 Feb. 1994, 1 d. *Musical Education:* BA, Music Education. *Career:* Appearances on Radio France; Played in film, Le Nouveau Monde; Opened concerts for: André Ceccarelli; Black Label; Roy Haynes; Benny Waters; Major festivals include: Montlouis; Montpellier; Orléans; Concert at Virgin Megastore. *Recordings:* Oberlin Jazz Ensemble; Perry-Boulanger Duo; Oppossum Gang. *Leisure interests:* Squash; Juggling. *Address:* 1 Passage Des Grillons, 37390 La Membrolle, France.

BAKER Toni; b. 24 Feb. 1949, Littleborough, Lancashire, England. Musician (keyboards); MD; Arranger. m. Stephanie, 12 Dec. 1986, 1 s., 1 d. *Musical Education:* Piano lessons, aged 5–14; Then involved in bands. *Career:* Played American bases, in soul music apprenticeship; Television shows include: Opportunity Knocks, 1971–76; Formed: Shabby Tiger, pop/rock band; No. 1 hits in Denmark, Netherlands, Belgium; Session work, freelance; Now playing with The Dakotas. *Compositions:* Eat You Up (No. 3, Japan); 5 album tracks for Shabby Tiger include: Nancy; Shabby Tiger; 20th Century Cowboy. *Memberships:* Musicians' Union; Equity. *Leisure interests:* Photography; Travelling; Skiing; Being a Dad. *Current Management:* Freelance Studio Director/Owner. *Address:* Moose Studio, 351 Holcombe Rd, Greenmount, Bury, Lancashire BL8 4DT, England.

BALDAN Bebo; b. 16 April 1966, Venice, Italy. Prod., Musician (drums, percussion, electronics); Composer. *Musical Education:* Studied with Percussione Ricerca Ensemble, Conservatory of Venice, Nana Vasconcelos, Trilok Gurtu. *Career:* Played in: Italy (Interzone Festival, RAI Television, Videomusic Television); France (Sacre du Printemps); England; Switzerland; Brazil; New York (and KPEL Radio, Berkeley, California); Tallinn Jazz Festival, Estonia; Tour of Mexico, Venezuela and Scandinavia; Played with Eugenio Bennato, DMA, Max M'Bass Ado, Andrea Braido, Luis Rizzo, Estasia, Duck Baker, Tolo Marton, Stephen James, Eddy C Campbell, Pitura Freska. *Compositions:* The Armenian Island, 1999; Soundtracks: Macbeth, film by Claudio Misculin; Aqua Nostra Igniset, film by Anselmo de Filippis. *Recordings:* As composer: Bebo Baldan: Vapor Frames; with Stephen James: Soniasikri-Sub Rosa, 1992; with David Torn: Diving Into The World, 1995; Earthbeat, 1995; Tantra, featuring David Torn, 1999; Jaya, 1998; Maya, 2000. *Publications:* Ethnos, featuring Gilberto Gil, 1999; Passion of Scotland; Anima, Private Music, Light from the Abyss by P Zennaro and Carolyn Carlson, 1999. *Membership:* SIAE. *Leisure interests:* Ethnic music; Oriental Phylosophy, Electronics. *Current Management:* Exit. *Address:* Via Antelao, 18 Mestre, Venice, Italy.

BALDASSARI Butch (Jerome Donald); b. 12 Nov. 1952, Scranton, Pennsylvania, USA. Musician (Mandolin). m. L Sinclair Dickey, 19 March 1993, 1 s. *Musical Education:* Self-taught, Mandolin; Studied Guitar and Violin privately, Pennsylvania and Nevada; 1 Semester, Berklee School of Music, Boston. *Career:* Appearances, CBS, This Morning, Prairie Home Companion, CNN Showbiz, Tennessee Crossroads; Adjunct Associate Professor, Mandolin, Blair School of Music. *Compositions:* What's Drivin'; Jack Rabbit Trail; Old Town; Slocum Hollow; Consider This; It's Raining the Blues; King Wilkie. *Recordings:* Gifts, Plectrasonics and All the Rage, with Nashville Mandolin Ensemble; Travellers, Reflections, Cantabile, New Classics, American Portraits, Old Town, Evergreen, solo. *Publications:* You Can Play Bluegrass Mandolin, Vols 1 and 2 (Video); 30 Fiddle Tunes for Mandolin. *Honours:* 2 Grammy Nominations, Bluegrass, 1992, 1998; Co-Producer, Recorded Event of the Year, IBM, 1994. *Memberships:* BMI; IBMA; CMSA; NARAS. *Leisure interest:* Snow skiing.

BALDOUS Bernard; b. 12 Dec. 1951, Montpellier, France. Musician (acoustic bass). *Musical Education:* Conservatoire de Musique, Montpellier, 1977; Berklee College of Music, Boston, USA, 1979. *Career:* Plays bass with: R Anouillez; S Baldous; J Blanton; J Benayoun; V Espinieto; Fanfan Sanchez; E Goldstein; M Levine; A Marcos; C McBride; J Neves; F Nicolas; J Peiffer; V Perez; P Pellegati; D Ragot; G Reilles; P Rosengoltz; Sega Seck; P Torreglosa; F Urtado; S Wilson; A Woygnet. *Compositions:* Fantome; Gigi; BB Blues. *Recordings:* Bernard Baldous Trio, 1993; Concerto for Jazz Band and Symphony Orchestra, 1994; Instant Jazz Quintet, 1995. *Membership:* Jazz Action Montpellier. *Address:* 3 Pl. Coluche, 34670 Baillargues, France.

BALDRY Long John; b. 12 Jan. 1941, Haddon, Derbyshire, England. Singer. *Career:* Member, R & B groups: Cyril Davies' All-Stars; Ramblin' Jack Elliot; Member, Alexis Korner's Blues Incorporated, 1961; Worked with Horace Silver Quintet, Cyril Davies' R & B All-Stars, 1962; Founder, the Hoochie Coochie Men, 1964; British tour, with Chuck Berry, Moody Blues, 1965; National Jazz and Blues Festival, 1965; Member, Steampacket, 1965–66; Member, Bluesology, 1966–67; Soloist, Rolling Stones '66, 1966; Solo artiste, 1967–; Becomes manager of Stuart A Brown (Bluesology), 1968; First US tour, 1971; Moved to Canada, 1980. *Recordings:* Hit singles include: Let The Heartaches Begin (No. 1, UK), 1967; When The Sun Comes Shinin' Thru, 1968; Mexico, 1968; It's Too Late Now, 1969; Albums: with Alexis Korner: R & B From The Marquee, 1962; with The Hoochie Coochie Men: Long John's Blues, 1964; Solo: It Ain't Easy, 1971; Everything Stops For Tea, 1971; Out!, 1979; Silent Treatment, 1986; It Still Ain't Easy, 1991; The Best of Long John Baldry, 1991; On Stage Tonight, 1994; Let Rock The Heartaches Begin, 1995; A Thrill's A Thrill, 1996; With The Best, 1996; Right To Sing The Blues, 1996. *Current Management:* S L Feldman, 1505 W Second Ave, Suite 200, Vancouver, BC V6H 3Y4, Canada.

BALKE Jon Georg; b. 7 June 1955, Hamar, Norway. Musician (piano, keyboards); Composer. *Career:* Started professional career with Arild

Andersen's quartet, 1974; Tours of Europe; Recordings for ECM Records; Later established as composer for groups such as Oslo 13; Masqualero; Jokleba; Magnetic North Orchestra; Also composer of chamber music and theatre. *Recordings:* Nonsentration, 1992; Further, 1994; Rotor, 1998; Solarized, 1999. *Honours:* Buddy Award, Norwegian Jazz Federation, 1985; Jazz Musician of Year, 1994. *Memberships:* Norwegian Composers Asscn; Norwegian Jazz Forum. *Leisure interests:* Paragliding; Skiing. *Address:* Hegermannsgt 15, 0478 Oslo, Norway.

BALL Daryl; b. 9 May 1974, Ballymena, County Antrim, Northern Ireland. Songwriter; Musician (guitar, bass). *Career:* Started playing guitar aged 15 with school band; Joined The Norwegians; Formed Stripped; Regulars on local radio throughout Ireland and numerous international stations; Television appearance, The Next Big Thing, US television; Forthcoming local television appearances. *Recordings:* The Norwegians, Turn it On, 1991; With Stripped: 4 Walls, 1998; The Girl With Cartoon Eyes, 1999; Compilations: Burbs, 1999; Blue and Grey Vol. 4, forthcoming. *Honours:* Finalist, Fourth Annual Song for Peace, 1999; Regularly featured as Artist of the Month on Internet music sites. *Membership:* Musicians' Union. *Leisure interests:* Ju Jitsu; Science Fiction; Reading. *Address:* 37 Mount St, Ballymena, County Antrim BT43 6BW, Northern Ireland.

BALL David; b. 3 May 1959, Blackpool, Lancashire, England. Musician (synthesizer); Composer. m. Ginny. *Career:* Formed Soft Cell (with Marc Almond), 1979–84, reformed 2001; Concerts include: Futurama 2 Festival, Leeds, 1980; British tours, 1982–84; Member, The Grid, with Richard Norris, 1990–; Written and produced for: Kylie Minogue; Billie Ray Martin. *Composition:* Score for stage revival, Suddenly Last Summer, 1983. *Recordings:* Albums: with Soft Cell: Non-Stop Erotic Cabaret, 1981, 1996, 1998; Non-Stop Ecstatic Dancing, 1982; The Art of Falling Apart, 1983; The Last Night In Sodom, 1984; Wasted, 1995; Compilations: The Singles Album, 1986; Memorabilia, The Singles (remixed by Ball), 1991; Hit singles: Tainted Love (World-wide No. 1), 1981; Bedsitter, 1981; Say Hello Wave Goodbye, 1982; Torch, 1982; What, 1982; Solo album: In Strict Tempo, 1983; Singles with The Grid: Floatation, 1990; Beat Called Love, 1990; Texas Cowboys, 1993; Swamp Thing, 1994; Rollercoaster, 1994; Diablo, 1995. *Honours:* Billboard Award, New Wave Band of The Year, 1981; BRIT Award, Best British Single, Tainted Love, 1982.

BALL David (Taif); b. 23 Jan. 1957, Weston, England. 1 s. *Musical Education:* Leeds College of Music. *Career:* Touring and recording, 1981–. *Compositions:* Voodoocult Music, Steve Hackett. *Recordings:* Barbara Thompson, Pure Fantasy; Lloyd Cole; John Martyn; Foundations: Jools Holland; How We Live: Killing Joke; Voodoocult. *Leisure interests:* Crosswords; Gardening; Walking. *Current Management:* Claire Baggett, Serendipity, Heol y Nant, Barry CF63 1SF. *Address:* 16 Park Cres., Barry, Vale of Glamorgan, CF62 6HD.

BALL Ian E; b. 1974, Southport, England. Musician (guitar, bass, percussion, harmonica); Vocalist. *Career:* Member, Gomez; Numerous live dates and television appearances. *Recordings:* Singles: 78 Stone Wobble, 1998; Whippin' Piccadilly, 1998; Get Myself Arrested, 1998; Bring It On, 1999; Rhythm and Blues Alibi, 1999; We Haven't Turned Around (featured on American Beauty OST), 1999; Machismo EP, 2000; Albums: Bring It On, 1998; Liquid Skin, 1999; Abandoned Shopping Trolley, 2000; Further collaboration: Hobotalk, Beauty In Madness, 2000. *Honours:* Mercury Music Prize winner, Bring It On, 1998; Brit Awards nominations, 1999–2000.

BALL Kenny Daniel; b. 22 May 1930, Ilford, Essex, England. Jazz Musician (trumpet). m. Michelle, 28 Dec. 1984, 1 s., 4 d. *Career:* Played with Charlie Galbraith; Sid Phillip; Eric Delaney; George Chisholm; Terry Lightfoot; Al Fairweather; Formed own dixieland band, Kenny Ball's Jazzmen, 1958–; Film debut, Live It Up (with Gene Vincent), 1963; Film, Trad Dad; Television appearances: Easy Beat, 3 series; Morcambe and Wise, 6 series; Saturday Night at the Mill, 4 series; Numerous foreign tours; UK concerts with: Acker Bilk; Kenny Baker; Lonnie Donegan; George Chisholm; Played at wedding reception, HRH the Prince and Princess of Wales, 1981. *Composition:* Midnight In Moscow, arrangement. *Recordings:* Albums include: Kenny Ball and His Jazzmen, 1961; The Kenny Ball Show, 1962; The Big Ones, Kenny Ball Style, 1963; Jazz Band Ball, 1964; Trubute To Tokyo, 1964; The Sound of Kenny Ball, 1968; King of The Swingers, 1969; At The Jazz Band Ball, 1970; Fleet Street Lightning, 1970; Saturday Night With Kenny Ball and His Band, 1970; Pixie Dust (A Tribute To Walt Disney), 1971; My Very Good Friend... Fats Waller, 1972; Have A Drink On Me, 1972; Let's All Sing A Happy Song, 1973; A Friend To You, 1974; Titillating Tango, 1976; In Concert, 1978; Way Down Yonder, 1977; Soap, 1981; Ball, Barber and Bilk Live At The Royal Festival Hall (with Chris Barber and Acker Bilk), 1984; Kenny Ball and His Jazzmen Play The Movie Greats, 1987; On Stage, 1988; Dixie, 1989; Kenny Ball Plays British, 1989; Jazz Classics, 1990; Kenny Ball Now, 1990; The Ultimate! (with Chris Barber and Acker Bilk), 1991; Singles include: Samantha; Midnight In Moscow; March of The Siamese Children;

The Green Leaves of Summer; Sukiyaki. *Honours:* 3 Carl Alan Awards; Billboard Best Band. *Memberships:* PRS; MCPS; BASCA; MU. *Current Management:* John Martin Promotions. *Address:* Warmans Farm, Burton End, Stansted, Essex CM24 8UQ, England.

BALL Malcolm; b. 8 Aug. 1953, Ilford, England. Musician (percussion, keyboards); Composer. *Musical Education:* Royal College of Music, London. *Career:* Specializing in contemporary music of all kinds; BBC Radio broadcasts with Geoff Warren Quartet for Jazz in Britain, Jazz Today; Arts Council tours of Hungary, Yugoslavia; Workshops with Graham Collier; Head of Percussion, London Borough of Redbridge; Examiner for GSM, London; Writer for Avant, contemporary music magazine; Author, articles on Stockhausen on the Internet. *Compositions:* Close Your Eyes and See, for orchestra, 1995; Many used for library music; O-taiko-Do, Terror Nova, for percussion ensemble. *Recording:* Close Your Eyes and See, in New British Music, Vol. 1. *Publications:* Percussive Perspectives (IMP). *Honours:* Licentiate, Royal Academy of Music, London. *Memberships:* Royal Society of Musicians of Great Britain; Musicians' Union; Stockhausen Society; British Harry Partch Society. *Leisure interests:* Travel; Food. *Address:* 79 Chalgrove Cres., Ilford, Essex IG5 0LX, England.

BALL Michael Ashley; b. 27 June 1962, Bromsgrove, Hereford and Worcester, England. Singer; Entertainer. *Education:* Plymouth College. *Musical Education:* Guildford School of Acting, 1981–84. *Career:* The Pirates of Penzance, 1984; Les Miserables, West End, 1985; Phantom of the Opera, West End, 1987; Aspects of Love, West End and New York, 1989–90; Represented UK, Eurovision Song Contest, 1992; British tours, 1992, 1993, 1994, 1996, 1999; Television appearances: Host, own series, Michael Ball, 1993, 1994; Film appearance, England My England, 1995. *Recordings:* Albums: Michael Ball, 1992; Always, 1993; West Side Story, 1993; One Careful Owner, 1994; The Best of Michael Ball, 1994; First Love, 1996; Michael Ball: The Musicals, 1996; The Movies, 1998: Singles include: Love Changes Everything; The First Man You Remember; It's Still You; One Step Out of Time; Sunset Boulevard; From Here to Eternity; The Lovers We Were; Wherever You Are; Something Inside So Strong; Appears on cast albums: Les Miserables; Aspects of Love; Encore!, Andrew Lloyd Webber collection; West Side Story; Passion; Sang on Rugby World Cup album. *Honours:* 10 Gold albums; 1 Platinum album; Variey Club of Great Britain, Recording Artiste of 1998; Theatre Goers Club of Great Britain Award, Most Popular Muscial Actor over the last 21 years, 1999. *Leisure interest:* Cars. *Current Management:* Michael Ball Enterprises, PO Box 173, Hampton, TW12 1HF, England. *E-mail:* mbe@michaelball.co.uk. *Internet:* www.michaelball.co.uk.

BALL Tom; b. 24 Oct. 1950, Los Angeles, California, USA. Singer; Musician (harmonica, guitar); Writer. m. Laurie Linn, 2 Oct. 1983, 1 d. *Education:* Santa Monica College. *Career:* Singer, harmonica player, Yerba Buena Blues Band, 1965–67; Freelance musician, 1968–79; Member duo, Tom Ball and Kenny Sultan, 1979–; Business Venture: Good Time Blues Pub (BMI); Studio work on over 80 recordings, films, television shows. *Recordings:* Albums: Confusion, 1981; Who Drank My Beer, 1983; Bloodshot Eyes, 1986; Guitar Music, 1988; Too Much Fun, 1990; Filthy Rich, 1993; Double Vision, 1996. *Publications:* Author: Blues Harmonica, 1993; Nasty Blues, 1994; Sonny Terry Licks, 1995. *Honours:* NARAS MVP Nomination, 1983; Telly Award Winner, 1994. *Memberships:* NARAS; AFTRA; AFofM; Folk Alliance. *Current Management:* Mercer Management. *Address:* PO Box 20156, Santa Barbara, CA 93120, USA.

BALLAMY Iain Mark; b. 20 Feb. 1964, Guildford, Surrey, England. Musician (saxophone); Composer. *Musical Education:* City and Guilds Musical Instrument Technology; Self-taught; Piano lessons as child. *Career:* Worked with groups include: Loose Tubes; Delightful Precipice; Human Chain; Bill Bruford's Earthworks; Balloon Man; Dewey Redman; Gil Evans; Hermeto Pascoal, 1982–; Karnatica College of Percussion, Voice of God; Tours: USA; Canada; Japan; Hong Kong; India; Europe; Scandinavia; Morocco; Turkey; Toronto; Saskatoon; Brecon; Glasgow; Edinburgh; Willisau; Leverkusen; Soho; Cork; Festivals: Berlin; Montreux; Frankfurt; Monterey; Montréal; Copenhagen; Molde; Istanbul; World-wide television and radio broadcasts and appearances including The Tube, Bergerac, Right to Reply and Wogan; Performances at Ronnie Scott's, Knitting Factory, Royal Festival Hall, Royal Albert Hall, Barbican and most international jazz festivals; Appeared in Out There, musical theatre production, 1995–96. *Compositions:* Commissions for Apollo Saxophone Quartet, Salford College, Birmingham Jazz, Food Cheltenham Jazz Festival, Bath International Festival. *Recordings:* All Men Amen; Balloon Man; with Django Bates: Summer Fruits; Winter Truce; 4 albums with Bill Bruford's Enthusiasts; Appeared on 45 CDs. *Honours:* John Dankworth Cup, 1985; BT British Jazz Award, best ensemble, 1995. *Memberships:* Musicians' Union; PRS; MCPS; GVL. *Leisure interests:* Metal detecting; Riding. *Address:* 4 Old Queen Anne House, London, England.

BALLARD Hank (Henry); b. 18 Nov. 1936, Detroit, Michigan, USA. Singer; Songwriter. *Career:* Lead singer, the Royals (later called the Midnighters), 1953–62; Solo artiste, 1962–; Also worked with James

Brown, 1962-. *Compositions include:* Work With Me, Annie; Finger Poppin' Time; The Twist (also recorded by Chubby Checker), 1960. *Recordings:* Singles: with the Midnighters: Work With Me, Annie, 1954; Sexy Ways, 1954; Annie Had A Baby, 1955; Annie's Aunt Fanny, 1955; Teardrops On Your Letter, 1959; Finger Poppin' Time, 1960; The Twist, 1960; Let's Go, Let's Go, Let's Go, 1960; The Hoochi-Coochi-Coo, 1961; Let's Go Again, 1961; The Continental Walk, 1961; The Switch-A-Roo, 1961; Albums include: Their Greatest Hits, 1954; The Midnighters Vol. 2, 1957; Great Juke Box Hits, 1958; Singin' and Swingin', 1959; The One and Only, 1960; Mr Rhythm and Blues, 1960; Sing Along, 1961; Let's Go Again, 1961; Jumpin' Hank Ballard, 1962; Twistin' Fools, 1962; The Sound of 1963, 1963; Stars In Your Eyes, 1964; Those Lazy Days, 1965; Glad Songs, Sad Songs, 1965; You Can't Keep A Good Man Down, 1969; Live At The Palais, 1986; Sexy Ways, The Best of Hank Ballard and The Midnighters, 1993; Naked In The Rain, 1993; From Love To Tears, 1998. *Honours:* Inducted into Rock and Roll Hall of Fame, 1970; Rhythm and Blues Foundation Award, New York, 1990. *Address:* c/o David Harris Enterprises, 24210 E Fork Rd, Suite 9, Star Route 1, Azusa, CA 91702, USA.

BALLARD Kaye; b. 20 Nov. 1926, Cleveland, Ohio, USA. Actress; Singer. *Career:* Television: The Mothers-in-Law; Perry Como Show; Doris Day Show; over 150 performances on the Tonight Show; Films: The Ritz; The Girl Most Likely; House Is Not A Home; Eternity; Which Way To The Front; Modern Love; Tiger Warsaw; Falling In Love Again; Freaky Friday; Concerts include: 2 Royal Command Performances; Hello Dolly; Nymph Errant; Stage performances include: Nunsense; Gypsy; Annie Get Your Gun; High Spirits; Odd Couple; Ziegfield Follies (touring companies); Top Bananas; Three To Make Ready; Touch and Go; Wonderful Town; She Stoops To Conquer; Golden Apple; Carnival; Molly (Broadway); One woman shows: Working 42nd Street At Last; Hey Ma. *Recordings include:* Nymph Errant; Songs From Hey Ma; Fanny Brice; Then and Again; Unsung Sondheim; Ladies Who Wrote The Lyrics; Long Time Friends; Golden Apple; Gershwin Rarities; Follies; Peanuts. *Memberships:* SAG; AFTRA; Equity. *Current Management:* Mark Sendroff c/o Gottlier, Schiff, Bonsee and Sendroff. *Address:* c/o Lee S Mimms, 2644 E Chevy Chase Dr., Glendale, CA 91206, USA.

BALTAZANIS Kostas; b. 20 Feb. 1965, Patras, Greece. Musician (guitar); Music Educator; Writer. *Musical Education:* Bachelor of Music, Performance; Professor Music, Berklee College of Music, Boston, USA. *Career:* Artistic Director, Nakas Conservatory, Athens, Greece; Studio musician, clinician for Berklee College of Music; Writer of music education books. *Recordings:* Two forthcoming albums. *Publications:* Jazz Harmony; Music Theory and Ear Training; Electric Guitar. *Address:* 25 25th Martiou Str, 16233 Athens, Greece.

BANDY Moe (Marion); b. 12 Feb. 1944, Meridian, Mississippi, USA. Country vocalist; Musician (guitar). *Career:* Played guitar in father's band The Mission City Playboys, San Antonio, Texas; Rodeo rider; Debut single Lonely Lady, Satin Records, 1964; Regular on San Antonio TV show Country Corner, 1973; Signed to GRC Records, 1974; Many Billboard country hits mostly on Columbia Records, including some with Joe Stampley, 1974–89; Moe and Joe collaborations included controversial parody of Boy George, Where's The Dress, 1984; Americana, 1988, used by George Bush Sr as presidential theme song; Opened own 900 seater Moe Bandy Americana Theatre in Branson, Missouri. *Recordings:* Hank Williams You Wrote My Life, 1975; Just Good Ol' Boys (with Joe Stampley), I Cheated Me Right Out of You, It's A Cheatin' Situation, 1979; She's Not Really Cheatin' (She's Just Getting' Even), 1982. *Honours:* CMA, Vocal Duo of the Year (with Joe Stampley), 1980. *Leisure interests:* Hunting; Golf. *Address:* c/o The Moe Bandy Americana Theatre, Branson, MO, USA; c/o The Bobby Roberts Company Inc, 909 Meadowlark Lane, Goodlettsville, TN 37072, USA.

BANGALTER Thomas; b. 1 Jan. 1975, Paris, France. Prod.; Remixer; DJ. *Career:* Formed Daft Punk with school friend Guy Manuel De Homem Christo, 1992; Debut single released on Scotland's Soma Records, 1994; Found commercial success with the release of Da Funk; Signed to Virgin Records and released debut album Homework; Founder: Roule Records; Collaborations: Bob Sinclair; Alan Braxe; Remixed: Gabrielle; Ian Pooley; Chemical Brothers. *Recordings:* Albums: Homework, 1996; Discovery, 2001; Alive 1997, 2001; Singles: Da Funk, 1995; Musique, Trax On Da Rocks, 1996; Around The World, Burnin', 1997; Revolution 909, Music Sounds Better With You (with Stardust), 1998; One More Time, 2000; Aerodynamic, 2001; Harder Better Faster Stronger, 2001. *Honours:* Brit Award, nominees: Best International Group; Best International Album, Discovery, 2002. *Address:* c/o Virgin Records, Kensal House, 553–579 Harrow Rd, London, W10 4RH, England.

BANKS Mike; b. Detroit, Michigan, USA. Musician (bass guitar); Prod. *Career:* Former session bass guitarist with Parliament; Founder: Underground Resistance (techno collective and label), Submerge Distribution and record shop in Detroit; Collaborations: Jeff Mills, Robert Hood, Suburban Knight, Octave One; Member: Members of The House,

L'Homme Van Renn. *Recordings:* Albums: Sonic Destroyer (as X101), 1991; BXA (as X102), 1992; Interstellar Fugitives (with Underground Resistance), 1998; Singles: As Underground Resistance: Final Frontier, 1991; Nation To Nation, 1991; Living For The Night (featuring Yolanda Reynolds), 1991; Riot EP, 1991; World To World, 1991; Galaxy 2 Galaxy, 1992; Codebreaker, 1997; Turning Point, 1998; Hardlife, 2001. *Current Management:* c/o Submerge Distribution, 2030 Grand River, Detroit, Michigan, USA.

BANKS Nick; b. 28 July 1965, Rotherham, Yorkshire, England. Musician (Drums). *Career:* Joined Pulp, 1987; Numerous tours, television appearances and festival dates; Contributed track to soundtrack of film Mission Impossible, 1996. *Recordings:* Singles: My Legendary Girlfriend, 1990; O.U. (Gone, Gone), 1992; Lipgloss, 1993; Do You Remember The First Time, 1994; The Sisters EP, 1994; Common People (No. 2, UK), 1995; Mis-Shapes/ Sorted For E's and Wizz (No. 2, UK), 1995; Disco 2000, 1995; Help The Aged, 1998; This Is Hardcore, 1998; A Little Soul, 1998; Party Hard, 1998; The Trees/Sunrise, 2001; Albums: Separations, 1992; Intro (compilation), 1994; His 'N' Hers, 1994; Different Class (No. 1, UK), 1995; This Is Hardcore (No. 1, UK), 1998; We Love Life, 2001. *Honours:* Mercury Music Prize nominee, 1994; Mercury Music Prize, winner, 1995; Brit Award, 1996.

BANKS Paul; b. 1973, England. Musician (guitar). *Career:* Member, Shed Seven; Numerous television appearances and live tours. *Recordings:* Singles: Mark, 1994; Dolphin, 1994; Speakeasy, 1994; Ocean Pie, 1994; Where Have You Been Tonight?, 1995; Getting Better, 1996; Bully Boy, 1996; On Standby, 1996; Chasing Rainbows, 1996; She Left Me On Friday, 1998; The Heroes, 1998; The Devil In Your Shoes, 1998; Disco Down, 1999; Cry For Help, 2001; Albums: Change Giver, 1996; A Maximum High, 1996; Let It Ride, 1998; Going For Gold, The Best of Shed Seven, 1999; Truth Be Told, 2001.

BANKS Tony; b. 27 March 1950. Musician (keyboards). *Career:* Musician, Genesis, 1970–; Solo artiste, 1979–; Numerous world-wide tours, include concerts at: Philharmonic Hall, New York; Giants Stadium, New York; Madison Square Gardens, New York; L A Forum; Rainbow Theatre, London; Wembley Arena; World tour, played to 3m. people, 1987. *Recordings:* Albums: with Genesis: Foxtrot, 1972; Selling England By The Pound, 1973; Genesis Live, 1973; The Lamb Lies Down On Broadway, 1974; Trick of The Tail, 1976; Wind and Wuthering, 1977; Seconds Out, 1977; And Then There Were Three, 1978; Duke, 1980; Abacab, 1981; Three Sides Live, 1982; Genesis, 1983; Invisible Touch, 1986; We Can't Dance, 1991; Genesis Live, 1992; Calling All Stations, 1997; Archives Vol. 1, 1998; Not About Us, 1998; Demo Mix Down On Broadway, 1998; Turn It On Again, 1999; Archive Vol. 2, 2001; solo: A Curious Feeling; The Fugitive; The Wicked Lady; Soundtracks; Bankstatement; Still: with Mike and The Mechanics: Living Years, 1988; Singles: with Genesis: Abacab; Follow You Follow Me; Mama; Illegal Alien; Invisible Touch; Land of Confusion; Tonight Tonight Tonight; That's All; Turn It On Again. *Honours:* Golden Ticket, Madison Square Gardens, 1986; First group with 5 US Top 5 singles from one album, 1986; Band of Year, Rolling Stone Readers Poll, 1987. *Current Management:* Hit and Run Music, 30 Ives St, London SW3 2ND, England.

BANNISTER Brian; Vocalist; Musician (banjo, mandolin, harmonica). *Career:* Founder member, Salty Dog; Winner, Birmingham songwriting competition; Performed official Olympic bid record; Resident topical songwriter for John Tainton Show, BBC; Member, The Debonairs, including television and radio appearances; Founder member, Mack and The Boys, 1989; Member, The New Bushbury Mountain Daredevils, 1992–; Work includes: Backing vocalist, Slade album; Producer, songwriter, dance artists. *Recordings:* with The Debonairs: Hoochey Coochey Man; with Sub Zero: Out of The Blue; with The Balti Brothers: Balti; with Mack and The Boys: Mack and The Boys; Downtime Love; with The New Bushbury Mountain Daredevils: Bushwacked; The Yellow Album; Bushbury Mountain. *Current Management:* c/o Jim McPhee, Acorn Entertainments. *Address:* Winterfold House, 46 Woodfield Rd, Kings Heath, Birmingham B13 9UJ, England.

BANTON Pato, (Patrick Murray); b. Birmingham, England. Reggae Vocalist; Songwriter. *Career:* Tours throughout USA and South America with own eight-piece group The Reggae Revolution; Now solo recording artiste. *Recordings:* Albums include: Never Give In, 1987; Visions of The World, 1989; Wize Up!, 1990; Mad Professor Recaptures Pato Banton, 1990; Live and Kickin' All Over America, 1991; Universal Love, 1992; Collections, 1995; Stay Positive, 1996; Time Come, 1999; Go Pato, 2000; Live In Brazil, 2000; Singles include: Hello Tosh; Baby Come Back, with UB40 (No. 1, UK); Pato and Roger Come Again; Beams of Light; Tudo de Bom; Spirits In The Material World; Cowboy Song, with Sting; Bubbling Hot; Legalise It!. *Current Management:* Atomic Communications Group, 10553 W Jefferson Blvd, Culver City, CA 90232, USA.

BARBEAU Mark Jerome; b. 20 Sept. 1961, San Francisco, California, USA. Event Production; Production Consultant; Screen Writer; Graphic Artist. *Education:* San Francisco City College. *Career:* Personal manager for: Anton Barbeau, pop singer; Produced touring scenery for Primus, Fishbone, Babes In Toyland, during Lollapalooza '93 tour; Formerly Account Executive for FM Productions on tours for: U2; Pink Floyd; Metallica; Guns N' Roses; ZZ Top; Rolling Stones; Currently Operations Manager, Key Events, and runs own company Runlikehell Productions, San Francisco, focussing on artist management and tour production; Currently personal manager for San Francisco Rock Band, Handfullaflowers. *Publications:* Pop artist in The Art of Rock, edited by Paul Gruskin. *Leisure interests:* Pool; Bowling; Reading; Travel; Writing fiction. *Address:* 2269 Chestnut St, PMB #143, San Francisco, CA 94123, USA.

BARBER (Daniel) Chris(topher); b. 17 April 1930, Welwyn Garden City, Hertfordshire, England. Jazz Musician (trombone, trumpet, horn, double bass); Bandleader; Composer. *Musical Education:* Trombone, bass, Guildhall School of Music. *Career:* Leader, various amateur jazz bands; Formed first band with Lonnie Donegan, Monty Sunshine, 1940s; Leader, Chris Barber Jazzband (later changed to Chris Barber Jazz and Blues Band), 1954–; International tours and concerts include: 1954 line-up reformed for 40th Anniversary concerts: Royal Festival Hall, 100 Club, Netherlands, Germany, 1994; Also played with Ken Colyer; Joe Harriott; Wild Bill Davis; Mac Rebenneck; Helped promote US artists in UK, including Brownie McGhee; Muddy Waters; Louis Jordan. *Compositions:* Numerous works with Richard Hill, including Jazz Elements; Concerto For Jazz Trombone (both premiered in Berlin). *Recordings:* Numerous albums include: Ragtime, 1960; Getting Around, 1963; Live In East Berlin, 1968; Sideways, 1974; Take Me Back To New Orleans, 1980; Everybody Knows, 1987; Stardust, 1988; Essential Chris Barber, 1990; Get Yourself To Jackson Square, 1990. *Honour:* OBE, 1991. *Current Management:* Vic Gibbons, Cromwell Management, 4/5 High St, Huntingdon, Cambridgeshire PE18 6TE, England.

BARBER Tony; b. 20 April 1963, Edmonton, London, England. Musician (guitar, bass, drums, synthesiser); Prod. m. Nathalie, 1 d. *Musical Education:* Self-taught. *Career:* Musician with Lack of Knowledge, 1979–85; Boys Wonder, 1987–88; Buzzcocks, 1992–; Solo recordings as Airport; Appeared on records by other artists, 1986-. *Compositions:* Sirens are Back, with Lack of Knowledge, 1984; Lift Off with Airport, as Airport, 2000. *Recordings:* Wandering Sickness, 1979; Sirens Are Back, 1984; Goodbye James Dean, 1987; Pied Piper of Feedback, 1990; Trade Test Transmissions, 1993; Troublemaker, 1995; Denim On Ice, 1996; Powersurge, 1996; Modern, 1999; Instant Wigwam and Igloo Mixture, 1999; Lift Off With Airport, 2000. *Memberships:* PRS; PAMRA; PPL. *Leisure interest:* Football (Data FC). *Current Management:* 26 Charlton Rd, Edmonton, London, N9 8EJ, England; Damage Productions, 130 Seigel St, Fourth Floor, Brooklyn, NY 11206, USA.

BARBIER Denis; b. 22 April 1954, Paris, France. Composer; Musician (flute). 1 d. *Musical Education:* Conservatories, Montreux, Vincennes. *Career:* Flute soloist, National French Jazz Orchestra; US tour, with Big Band Lumière, 1991; Tour, Europe, with Gil Evans and Big Band Lumière, 1986; Concerts on Radio France with Lumière; National French Orchestra; Chute Libre; Moravagine; France Culture with Shi Pei Pou (Peking). *Compositions include:* Music for theatre; Jazz on the Moon, for symphonic orchestra and solo alto saxophone, 1996. *Recordings:* Piece Pour Voix, Cordes Et Hautbois, 1998; Sous Le Signe Du Cheval (wind quintet and piano), 1995; Work For 30 Musicians and Rhythm Section In 4 Movements, 1995; Film music: L'Alibi En Or, with Charles Aznavour, 1993; Fausto (A La Mode, USA), 1993; Bosna, 1994; Music for television serial, 1984–; documentaries with Serge Moat; From the Sea to the Land, for two harps, 1996; Television films: Barbe Bleue, with Samy Frey; Jazz records: PRAO with Mino Cinelu and Brothers; Denis Barbier Jazz Group; Chute Libre and Moravagine with Mino Cinelu; National French Jazz Orchestra. *Memberships:* SACEM; SACD. *Leisure interests:* Kites; Sailing. *Current Management:* Éditions des Alouettes. *Address:* 8 rue Jules Vallés, 75011 Paris, France.

BARBIERI Richard; b. 30 Nov. 1957. Musician (keyboards). *Career:* Member, Japan, 1977–83; Member, The Dolphin Brothers (with Steve Jansen), 1987; Member, Rain Tree Crow (with 3 former members of Japan), 1992; Member, The Porcupine Tree, 1993–; British tours include: Support to Blue Öyster Cult, 1978; Backing musician, No-Man, 1992; Record producer, Swedish group Lustans Lakejer, 1982. *Recordings:* Albums with Japan: Adolescent Sex, 1978; Obscure Alternatives, 1978; Life In Tokyo, 1979; Quiet Life, 1980; Gentlemen Take Polaroids, 1980; Assemblage, 1981; Tin Drum, 1981; Oil On Canvas, 1983; Exorcising Ghosts, 1984; with The Dolphin Brothers: Catch The Fall, 1987; with Rain Tree Crow: Rain Tree Crow, 1991; with Steve Jansen: Stone To Flesh, 1995; Changing Hands, 1998; with Porcupine Tree: Signify, 1997; Stupid Dream, 1999; Singles include: The Art of Parties, 1981; Quiet Life, 1981;

Visions of China, 1981; Ghosts, 1982; Cantonese Boy, 1982; Life In Tokyo, 1982; Night Porter, 1982; Canton, 1982.

BARBOSA Chris; Prod.; Remixer. *Career:* Produced or performed production remixes for many artists including: Shannon; Robin Gibb; Billy Idol; George Michael; New Kids on the Block; The Spinners; Lisa Fischer; George Lammond; Nolan Thomas; Andru Donalds; Safire; Cynthia; Judy Torres; Monet; Alisha. *Recordings include:* Bad of The Heart, George Lamond, 1978; Hot Power Mixes, 1987; I Wasn't Born Yesterday, Safire, 1990; No More Games, New Kids On The Block, 1991; Best of Freestyle, 1992; Bass Bomb: Latin Hip Hop, 1993; Freestyle Greatest Hits, 1994; Essential, Shannon, 1995; Wherever The Rhythm Takes Me, Alisha, 1996; Absolutely: The Very Best Of..., 1997; Freestyle Explosion, 1998. *Honour:* ASCAP Pop Award. *Address:* CBM Entertainment Corp, 185 Ardsley Loop, Suite 1B, Brooklyn, NY 11239, USA.

BARCODE; b. 6 Dec. 1971, Barcelona, Spain. Programmer; Songwriter; Musician (keyboards, synthesisers). *Career:* Numerous concerts with band HED include: Phoenix Festival, 1994; Glastonbury Festival, 1995; Les Confort Moderne, 10th anniversay, Poitiers, France, 1995; Strawberry Fayre Festival, Cambridge, 1995; Megatripolis, London, 1995. *Recordings:* HED: Reigndance, 1994; Reigndance remix, Unity compilation album, 1994; Folklaw, 1995; New Dance, 1996; New Dance Remix, 1997. *Membership:* Musicians' Union. *Leisure interests:* Juggling; Collecting Town Lego. *Current Management:* David Crompton, Timebomb. *Address:* c/o Timebomb, Box No. 15, 63 Camden High St, London NW1 7JL, England.

BARD Alexander; b. 17 March 1961, Vaestra Ny, Sweden. Artist; Record Prod.; Songwriter. *Education:* Masters Degree, Economics, Geography. *Recordings:* with Army of Lovers: Disco Extravaganza, 1990; Massive Luxury Overdose, 1991; The Gods of Earth and Heaven, 1993; Glory Glamour and Gold, 1994; Les Greatest Hits, 1995; Crucified, 1999; with Vacuum: The Plutonium Cathedral, 1997; Seance At The Chaebol, 1998; Also: Abba A Tribute, 1999. *Membership:* Co-owner, Stockholm Records. *Leisure interests:* Practising Zoroastrian; Internet guru; Breeder of racehorses. *Current Management:* Tra La La Productions. *Address:* c/o Tra La La Productions, Naerkesgatan 1, 11640 Stockholm, Sweden.

BARDY Jean; b. 3 March 1957, Soisy, Montmorency, France. Musician (bass, guitar, trumpet); Composer. *Musical Education:* Conservatoire de Musique d'Eubonne. *Career:* Professional jazz bass player, playing Be-Bop in clubs including: River Bop; Petit Opportun; Cardinal Paf; Throughout France; Played with artists including: Guy Lafitte; René Urtreger; Martial Solal; Laurent Cugny; Barney Wilen; Laurent de Wilde; Pepper Adams; Roy Haynes; Steve Grossman; Sonny Stitt; Chet Baker (1 year in France, Europe); Nat Adderley; Johnny Griffin; Harold Danko; Dee Dee Bridgwater. *Compositions:* Received grant: Léonard de Vinci, from French government to write original music while in the USA. *Recordings:* Live In Paris, Antoine Hervé; Sud, Antoine Illouz; Naif; Rhythm-A-Ning, Laurent Cugny, Gil Evans, 1987; Samya Cynthia, François Chassagnite; César Le Chien; Chansons, Jean Bardy, 1991; Anna Livia Plurabelle, André Hodeir. *Honours:* Prix Django Reinhardt for: Live In Paris; Rhythmning; Prix de l'Academie du Disque. *Leisure interests:* Golf; Tennis. *Address:* 7 rue de l'Elysic-Ménilmontant, 75020 Paris, France.

BARE Bobby (Robert Joseph); b. 7 April 1935, Ironton, Ohio, USA. Country Singer; Songwriter. *Career:* Prolific recording artist, 1955–; Club, television and radio station appearances; Television includes: Grand Ole Opry; Host, Bobby Bare and Friends; Film appearance, A Distant Trumpet, 1964. *Recordings:* Singles include: All American Boy; Detroit City; 500 Miles Away From Home; Miller's Cave; A Dear John Letter; Come Sundown; Please Don't Tell Me How The Story Ends; Marie Laveau; Daddy What If; The Jogger; Tequila Sheila; Numbers; Numerous albums include: Detroit City, 1963; 500 Miles Away From Home, 1963; The Travelling Bare, 1964; Tender Years, 1965; Talk Me Some Sense, 1966; Folsom Prison Blues, 1968; Lincoln Park Inn, 1969; This Is Bare Country, 1970; I'm A Long Way From Home, 1971; What Am I Gonna Do, 1972; Memphis Tennessee, 1973; Lullabys, Legends and Lies, 1974; Cowboys and Daddys, 1975; The Winner and Other Losers, 1978; Bare, 1979; Down and Dirty, 1980; Drunk and Crazy, 1980; As Is, 1981; Ain't Got Nothing To Lose, 1982; Bobby Bare-The Mercury Years 1970–72, 1987; Country Store, 1988; I Love An Old Fashioned Christmas, 1995; Hard Time Hungrys, 1998; Live At Gilley's, 1999; with Skeeter Davis: Tunes For Two, 1965; Your Husband, My Wife, 1970; with The Hillsiders: The English Countryside, 1967; with Norma Jean and Liz Anderson: The Game of Triangles, 1967. *Honour:* Grammy, Detroit City, 1963. *Current Management:* Bare Enterprises, PO Box 2422, Hendersonville, TN 37077, USA.

BARKER Aaron G Sr; b. 3 May 1953, San Antonio, Texas, USA. Songwriter. *Compositions:* for George Strait: Baby Blue, 1988; Love Without End, 1990; Easy Come, Easy Go, 1990; I Know She Still Loves

Me, 1995; I'd Like To Have That One Back, 1995; I Can Still Make Cheyene, 1997; for Doug Supernaw: Honky Tonkin' Fool, 1993; Not Enough Hours, 1995; for Clay Walker: Watch This, 1997; You're Beginning to Get to Me, 1998; for George Strait: Peace of Mind, 1998; Christmas Cookie, 1999; Old Time Christmas, 1999; I Am a Cowboy, for Bill Enquall, 1998; What About Now, for Lonestar, 1998; I'm Leaving, 1998. *Recording:* Feelin' Like Freedom. *Honours:* Voted No. 1 in all three trades, Cash Box, 1988; Songwriters Award, Music City News, 1990. *Memberships:* Country Music Asscn; NSAI; Academy of Country Music. *Leisure interest:* Woodwork. *Current Management:* OTex Music, 1000 18th Ave S, Nashville, TN 37212, USA.

BARKER Guy; b. 26 Dec. 1957, London, England. Jazz Musician (trumpet). *Musical Education:* Royal College of Music. *Career:* Member, National Youth Jazz Orchestra; Major concerts include: Cleveland Jazz Festival, 1978; South Bank Jazz Festival, 1989; Leader, own quintet, British tour, 1978; Also played with: Gil Evans; John Dankworth; Chris Hunter; Stan Tracey's Hexad; Hubbard's Cubbard; Ornette Coleman; Peter King; Jim Mullen; Jack Sharpe Big Band; Featured soloist, London Symphony Orchestra; Played in backing groups with artists including: Sammy Davis Jr; Mel Tormé; Liza Minnelli; Lena Horne; British tour with Frank Sinatra, 1991; Far East tour with Georgie Fame; Tribute tours to Chet Baker and Bix Beiderbecke. *Recordings:* Albums include: Holly J, 1989; Isn't It, 1991; with Hubbard's Cubbard: Hubbard's Cubbard, 1983; Nip It In The Bud, 1985; with Clark Tracey: Suddenly Last Tuesday, 1986; Stiperstones, 1987; with Peter King: Brother Bernard, 1988; Featured on soundtracks: Insignificance, 1985; Absolute Beginners, 1986; The Living Daylights, 1987; Also featured on recordings with Paul McCartney; Grace Jones; Joan Armatrading; XTC; Sting; Erasure; The The; The Beautiful South.

BARKER Paul; b. 8 Feb. 1950, Palo Alto, California, USA. Musician (Bass, Keyboards). *Career:* Member, Ministry, 1986–; Numerous side projects including Pigface, including Steve Albini, Jello Biafra, Chris Connelly and Dwayne Goettell; Numerous tours including Lollapalooza; Covered the Grateful Dead's song Friend of the Devil for the Neil Young Bridge School Benefits album. *Recordings:* Halloween Remix, 1987; Stigmata, 1988; Burning Inside, 1989; Jesus Built My Hotrod, 1991; N.W.O., 1992; Just One Fix, 1992; The Fall, 1995; Lay Lady Lay, 1996; Bad Blood, 1995; Albums: Twitch, 1985; The Land of Rape and Honey, 1988; The Mind Is a Terrible Thing to Taste, 1989; In Case You Didn't Feel Like Showing Up (Live), 1990; Psalm 69: The Way To Succeed and the Way to Suck Eggs, 1992; Filth Pig, 1996; Dark Side of the Spoon, 1999.

BARKER Travis Landon; b. 14 Nov. 1975, Fontana, California, USA. Musician (drums). *Career:* Former member of punk-pop groups The Vandals and The Aquabats; Replaced Scott Raynor as Blink-182 drummer, 1998–; Numerous TV appearances and concerts world-wide including: The Enema Strikes Back '99 tour, released on CD as The Mark Tom and Travis Show; 11-week US Summer tour, 2001; Cameo appearance with group in American Pie film, 1999. *Recordings:* Albums: Enema of The State, 1999; The Mark Tom and Travis Show (live), 2000; Take Off Your Pants and Jacket, 2001; Singles: What's My Age Again, All The Small Things, 1999; Adam's Song, Man Overboard, 2000; The Rock Show, Stay Together For The Kids, 2001. *Honours:* World-wide sales of 1999 album in excess of 7m. *E-mail:* travis@loserkids.com. *Internet:* www.blink182.com.

BARLOW Eric; Vocalist; Musician (guitar). *Musical Education:* Classical training. *Career:* Member, The New Bushbury Mountain Daredevils, 1992–; Backing vocals, Slade; Producer, songwriter for various dance artists; Topical songs for radio. *Compositions include:* Songs recorded by artists including: Jaki Graham; Asia Blue; Several songs at number 1, Europe and Africa, including: Heartbreaker, Rozalla. *Recordings:* Solo: You Betta Run; with Rozalla: Heartbreaker; Sunny; The Perfect Kiss; Spirit of Africa; with Mack and The Boys: The Unknown Legends; with The New Bushbury Montain Daredevils: Bushwacked; The Yellow Album; Bushbury Mountain; Banjo Spiders, 1999. *Current Management:* c/o Jim McPhee, Acorn Entertainments. *Address:* Winterfield House, 46 Woodfield Rd, Kings Heath, Birmingham B13 9UJ, England.

BARLOW Gary; b. 20 Jan. 1971, Fradham, Cheshire, England. Vocalist; Songwriter. *Career:* Songwriter, singer, UK all-male vocal group, Take That, 1991–96; Television includes: Take That and Party, C4, 1993; Take That Away documentary, BBC2, 1993; Take That In Berlin, 1994. *Recordings:* with Take That: Albums: Take That and Party, 1992; Everything Changes, 1993; Nobody Else, 1995; Greatest Hits, 1996; with Take That: Hit singles: It Only Takes A Minute, 1992; I Found Heaven, 1992; A Million Love Songs, 1992; Could It Be Magic, 1993; Why Can't I Wake Up With You, 1993; UK No. 1 hits: Pray, 1993; Relight My Fire (with Lulu), 1993; Babe, 1993; Everything Changes, 1993; Sure, 1994; Back For Good, 1995; Never Forget, 1995; How Deep Is Your Love, 1996; Solo Album: Open Road, 1997; Solo Singles: Forever Love, 1996; Love Won't Wait, 1997; So Help Me Girl, 1997; Open Road, 1997; Stronger, 1999. *Publications:*

Numerous videos, books, magazines. *Honours:* 7 Smash Hit Awards, 1992; BRIT Award, Best British Single, 1994; BRIT Award Nominations, Best Single, Best Video, 1996. *Current Management:* Simon Fuller, 19 Management, Unit 32, Ransomes Dock, 35–37 Parkgate Rd, London SW11 4NP, England.

BARLOW Thomas; b. 30 Sept. 1961, Manila, Philippines. Musician (saxophone). *Education:* BA Hons, University of Kent; PGCE, De Montfort University. *Career:* Founder member, The Larks; Aztec Camera, UK, Europe tour, 1988; Tommy Barlow Quartet; Butterfield 8; Founder member, Deptford Dance Orchestra (later Jools Holland Big Band); Matt Bianco; Holly Johnson; Swordfish. *Recordings:* 3 singles, 1 EP, with The Larks; Recording sessions with: Aztec Camera (No. 3 UK charts), 1988; Jools Holland; Deptford Dance Orchestra; BBC Education Programme; Swordfish. *Memberships:* Musicians' Union; PRS. *Leisure interests:* Cycling; Basketball. *Address:* 161A Southampton Way, Camberwell, London SE5 7EJ, England.

BARNACLE Gary; b. 3 April 1959, Nicosia, Cyprus. Musician (saxophone, flute); Songwriter. *Career:* Toured with The Ruts; Elvis Costello; Soft Cell; Marc Almond; Tina Turner; Level 42; Jamiroquai; Played at various Prince's Trust concerts; Nelson Mandela Tribute, Wembley Stadium; Midge Ures's All Star Band; Numerous television, radio appearances in UK and abroad, include 40 Top of The Pops. *Compositions:* Co-writer, Jazzmasters album; Space Clav, Jamiroquai; Leisure Process Tracks; Ruts D C tracks. *Recordings:* Gold and Platinum discs with artists including: Tina Turner (4 albums); Phil Collins; Paul McCartney; David Bowie; The Clash; Swing Out Sister; The Beautiful South; Jamiroquai (2 albums); Björk (2 albums); Soul II Soul; James Brown; Five Star; Yazz; T'Pau (including hit single China In Your Hand); Elvis Costello; Pet Shop Boys; Massive Attack. *Memberships:* MCPS; PRS; Musicians' Union; GVL (Germany); SENA (Netherlands). *Leisure interests:* Squash; Football; Collecting old records, films. *Address:* 160 Queenstown Rd, Battersea, London SW8 3QE, England.

BARNACLE Steve; b. 27 Sept. 1956, Aldershot, Hampshire, England. Musician (bass guitar, guitar); Composer; Prod. m. Lesley Lacey-Smith, 10 July 1989, 1 s., 2 d. *Musical Education:* Self-taught. *Career:* Numerous world tours; Most television and radio shows with artists including: Tina Turner; Pete Townshend; Deborah Harry; Spear of Destiny; Rick Wakeman; Julien Clerc (France only). *Compositions:* Co-writer, co-producer, Beat Boy album, Visage; Co-writer: Dream City, Samantha Fox; Juanita, Iron Maiden; Numerous writing and production credits. *Memberships:* PRS; Musicians' Union; MCPS. *Leisure interests:* Reading; Sport; Anything creative. *Address:* 65 Natal Rd, Streatham, London SW16 6JA, England.

BARNARD Robert Graeme; b. 24 Nov. 1933, Melbourne, Australia. m. Danielle Ann Barnard, 22 July 1993, 2 s., 1 d. *Career:* Regular appearances on variety television; Co-Compere for ABC Television Jazz Programme; Featured Soloist, Queensland Symphony Orchestra; Tours extensively. *Compositions:* Many pieces recorded over the years. *Recordings:* Lord of the Rings, with John Sangster; Many with Graeme Bell; About 300 under own name including: Bob Barnard-With Strings. *Honours:* Order of Australia, 1990; Advance Australia Award, 1991; Received prestigious, MO Award, 1993, 1997. *Membership:* Professional Musicians Club. *Leisure interest:* Golf. *Address:* 8/9 Hume St, Crows Nest, Sydney, 2065, Australia.

BARNES Alan Leonard; b. 23 July 1959, Altrincham, Cheshire, England. Musician (Saxophone, Clarinet). m. Clare Hirst, 31 July 1995, 1 s., 1 d. *Musical Education:* Leeds Music College, First Class Diploma in Jazz and Light Music, 1977–80. *Career:* Pasadena Roof Orchestra, 1980–82; Tommy Chase Quartet, 1983–86; Coled Jazz Renegades, 1986–88; Humphrey Lyttelton Band, 1988–92; Freelance Musician with bands by Mike Westbrook, Kenny Baker, Don Weller, Warren Vache, Freddie Hubbard; Own quartet and duo with David Newton. *Compositions:* Blues on the Beach; The Hawk; Side-Steppin'; Freedom Samba; Below Zero. *Recordings:* Below Zero, with David Newton Trio; Like Minds; Thirsty Work; Days of Wine and Roses, with Tony Coe; A Dotty Blues; Shine, with Warren Vaché; Memories of You. *Honours:* British Jazz Awards: Alto Sax, 1995, 1997, 1999, Clarinet, 1994, 1996, 1998, Baritone Sax, 1998. *Address:* 146 Kings Ave, London SW12 0BA, England.

BARNES Jimmy; b. Scotland. Musician (guitar); Vocalist. *Career:* Lead singer, Australian group, Cold Chisel, 1979–83; Solo artiste, 1984-. *Recordings:* with Cold Chisel: Breakfast At Sweethearts, 1979; East, 1980; Circus Animals, 1982; The Last Wave of Summer, 1998; Solo albums: Body Swerve, 1984; Jimmy Barnes, 1985; Freight Train Heart, 1987; Barnestorming, 1988; Two Fires, 1990; Heat, 1993; Psychlone, 1995; Hits: The Best of Jimmy Barnes, 1996. *Current Management:* Michael Long Management, PO Box 136, Double Bay 2028, New South Wales, Australia.

BARNES John; b. 15 May 1932, Manchester, England. Musician (Saxophone, Clarinets); Vocalist. m. Patricia Ann Barnes, 1 March 1958.

Recordings: Alex Welsh Band; Humphrey Lyttelton Band. *Honours:* 10 times Winner, British Jazz Awards, Baritone Saxophone, 1987–99; Winner, Baritone, Downbeat Magazine, 1966. *Leisure interests:* Music; Cricket. *Address:* 16 Worton Rd, Isleworth, Middlesex TW7 6HN, England.

BARNES Neil; b. 6 Aug. 1960, London, England. Prod.; Remixer. *Career:* Co-founder Hard Hands Records with Paul Daley; World-wide DJ; Member of Leftfield, split 2002; Collaborations: Djum Djum, Afrika Bambaataa, Roots Manuva, John Lydon. *Recordings:* Albums: Leftism, 1995; Rhythm and Stealth, 1999; Singles: Not Forgotten, 1990; Release The Pressure, 1992; Song of Life, 1992; Open Up (with John Lydon), 1993; Original, 1995; Afrika Shox (with Afrika Bambaataa), 1999. *Current Management:* c/o Hard Hands Recordings, The Courtyard, Saga Centre, 326 Kensal Rd, London, W10 5BZ, England.

BARNHOLDT Ole; b. 14 Feb. 1958, Hvorup, Denmark. Composer. *Musical Education:* Graduate, Film Music Composition, Dick Grove School of Music, Los Angeles, USA, 1988; Masters degree, Music, University of Aalborg, Denmark, 1990. *Career:* Scored various film, television, video projects, 1988-. *Compositions:* For Denmark's Radio Symphony Orchestra: Valley Heart; Siciliano For Maria. *Publications:* Music Design. *Membership:* KODA (Denmark). *Current Management:* Whiteheart Music Ltd. *Address:* Whiteheart Music Ltd, 100 Edenbridge Rd, Enfield EN1 2HT, England.

BARRATT Bob; b. 22 March 1938, Croydon, Surrey, England. Record Prod. m. Annette Key, 24 Sept. 1960, 3 d. *Musical Education:* Self-taught piano. *Career:* Wrote songs as child; Office boy, EMI Records, 1959; Trained as record producer by Norman Newell and Norrie Paramor; Artist roster included: Max Boyce; Pam Ayres; Wurzels; Basil Brush; King's Singers; Fivepenny Piece; Gene Vincent; Chris Barber; Vince Hill (Edelweiss); Ran own label, Grasmere Records, featuring specialist music, 1984-. *Compositions:* 400 songs and instrumentals; 7 songs used in films; Many used by recorded libraries; 450 recordings of own compositions made by artists including: Gene Vincent; Dick Haymes; Roger Whittaker; King's Singers; Big Daddy; Brigitte Bardot. *Recordings:* Produced hundreds of records including: We All Had Doctor's Papers, Max Boyce (number 1 album, UK charts); Combine Harvester, Wurzels (number 1 single, UK charts). *Honours:* 4 Gold discs, 12 Silver discs; Twice winner of Gibraltar Song Festival, as songwriter. *Leisure interests:* Travel, especially in mountainous regions; Buses and trams. *Address:* c/o Grasmere Music Ltd, PPG House, 290–292 Brighton Rd, South Croydon, Surrey CR2 6AG, England.

BARRET Eric; b. 5 May 1959, Le Havre, France. Musician (saxophone); Composer. *Career:* Played with J P Mas, A Ceccarelli, 1983; Barret, Romano Texier, 1985; Orchestre National de Jazz, 1986; D Humair, 1988; Quartet with M Ducret, 1988; Also played with: A Hervé, R Urtreger, S Swallow, J Griffin, K Wheeler, A Farmer, L Bennett, S Grossman, F Hubbard; Professor, Bagneux Music Conservatory, 1991–; Member, Roy Haynes 4tet, 1997; Orchestre National de Jazz, 1997. *Recordings:* Barret, Romano Texier, 1987; Eric Barret Quartet, 1989; L'Echappe Belle, 1992. *Publications:* Etudes Jazz Pour Saxophone, 2 Vols; Gammes Et Arpèges Pour Le Jazz, 1987. *Honour:* Boris Vian Price; Bien débuter le saxophone, 1997. *Leisure interests:* Wine; Bicycles; Books; Modern art; Painting; Plants. *Current Management:* Hélène Manfredi, Atout Jazz. *Address:* 118 rue du Chateau des Rentiers, 75013 Paris, France.

BARRETT Andrew; b. 19 Aug. 1953, Oceanside, New York, USA. Musician (keyboards); Arranger; Composer. m. Kathleen Anna McGinley, 22 Sept. 1980. *Musical Education:* Mus B, Indiana University, 1975. *Career:* Musician, arranger for various artistes including: Diana Ross; Irene Cara; Sister Sledge, 1981–82; Consultant, Cats Shubert Organization, 1982–; Synthesizer consultant, New York stage productions including: Cats, 1987; Me and My Girl, 1987; Les Miserables, 1988; Phantom of The Opera, 1988; Miss Saigon, 1989. *Compositions:* Contributor, film soundtracks: Nightmare On Elm Street, Part II, 1987; National Lampoon's Christmas Vacation, 1990; Shattered, 1991. *Memberships:* ASCAP; NARAS.

BARRETT Brian; b. 9 Feb. 1968, Murfreesboro, Tennessee, USA. Recording Artist; Songwriter. m. Katrina Startin Barrett. *Education:* Hardin-Simmons University, Abilene, Texas. *Career:* Appearances: Concert of The Age Tour; Television includes: TBN (Gospel America with Pat Boone); Carman's Time 2, TBN; Z-TV; TNN; CCM-TV (Family Channel); ACTS TV Network; Nashville's Talk of The Town (WTVF CBS Affiliate); Radio: CCM Radio; Dawson McAllister's Praise Him In Your Youth; 20: The Countdown Magazine; The Best Country Countdown. *Recordings:* Albums: Brian Barrett, 1993; Nailed In Stone, 1995; Also appeared on: Child's Christmas, Revel Players, 1993; Tribute: The Songs of Andrae Crouch, 1996; Should've Been Gone, Empty Grave, 1999. *Honours:* Dove Award Nominations, Country Song of Year, Country Album of Year, 1995; CCM Readers Awards, Favourite Country Artist, Favourite Country Album. *Memberships:* Gospel Music Asscn; Alpha Psi Omega (Theatrical

Society). *Leisure interests:* Photography; Fishing; Swimming. *Current Management:* Michael Smith and Associates. *Address:* 1024 17th Ave S, Nashville, TN 37212, USA.

BARRETT James Charles; b. 4 Dec. 1970, London, England. Musician (Bass guitar, programming). *Career:* Co-Founder, Member, Rock/dance group Senser, 1989–99; Numerous television and radio appearances including The Word (Channel 4), The Beat (Channel 4), Raw Soup, Naked City, MTV's Most Wanted, Glastonbury Live, Chart Show, numerous European shows; John Peel session on Radio 1; Toured extensively throughout Europe, USA, Japan; Numerous festivals. *Recordings:* Singles include: Eject; The Key/No Comply; Switch; Age of Panic; Adrenalin; Breed; Harry Moss Mix; Albums: Stacked Up; Asylum. *Leisure interests:* Kung fu; Information technology. *Current Management:* Space Management. *Address:* 24 Gibson Gardens, Stoke Newington London N16 7HB, England.

BARRETT Mark Vincent; b. 27 Jan. 1959, Bishops Stortford, England. Musician (guitar); Sound Engineering. 1 s., 1 d. *Education:* Fine Art Degree, Stourbridge College of Art. *Musical Education:* Acton Guitar Institute. *Career:* Member, East Orange, 1983; Q Lazzarus, 1988; Guitarist for Janey Lee Grace; Radio broadcasts: GLR; Regional BBC stations; Various US stations; Major US tour; Television, Tricks and Tracks, BBC. *Recordings:* with Q Lazzarus: Don't Let Go; Goodbye Horses, from film The Silence of The Lambs; Mexico 70; Albums: Dust Has Come To Stay; Sing When You're Winning; Singles: Everywhere; Worthless. *Membership:* Musicians' Union. *Leisure interests:* Drawing and painting; Surfing; White water canoeing. *Current Management:* Diamond Sounds Management. *Address:* Fox and Punch Bowl, Burfield Rd, Old Windsor, Berkshire, England.

BARRETT Paul; b. 8 Aug. 1954, Dublin, Ireland. Prod.; Musician Arranger (Keyboards, Brass); Composer. *Musical Education:* Trinity College, Dublin (Mus B); Royal Irish Academy of Music. *Career:* Trombone, RTE Symphony Orchestra, 1970–74; Musical Arranger, EMI Records, 1975–76; Keyboards, arranger, composer, trombonist, RTE Television, radio, 1975–89; Founder, bands: Sleepless Knights, 1976–77; Metropolis, 1979–82; Junta, 1982; Founder, STS, 1983; 24 track studio with Fairlight CMI; Performed with artists including: U2; Marianne Faithfull; The Edge; Sinead O'Connor; Brian Eno; Tom Robinson; Bono; Hazel O'Connor; Steve Lillywhite; Luka Bloom; Flood; Hothouse Flowers; Bill Whelan; Christy Moore; Now composing film music; Producing records for U2; Hazel O'Connor; Hothouse Flowers; Luka Bloom; Bono; The Stars of Heaven; Carole King; Coosh; Equation; Quincy Jones; Boyzone. *Recordings:* with U2: Desire; Joshua Tree; Unforgettable Fire; Rattle and Hum; Achtung Baby; Night and Day; Passengers; Best Of, 1980–90; with Hothouse Flowers: Home; with Hazel O'Connor: Private Wars; with Frank Sinatra and Bono: I've Got You Under My Skin; Contributed to recordings for: Quincy Jones; Frank Sinatra; Jim Sheridan; Stevie Wonder; Marvin Gaye; Johnny Cash; Ray Charles; Leonard Cohen; Willie Nelson. *Honours:* Platinum discs, Desire; Rattle and Hum; Joshua Tree; Unforgettable Fire; Gold disc, Home. *Memberships:* PRS; MCPS; AYIC; PAMRA. *Leisure interest:* Sailing. *Current Management:* STS. *Address:* c/o STS, Ballyward Stud, Oldcourt, Manor Kilbride, Co Wicklow, Ireland.

BARRETT Paul Frank Stalin; b. 14 Dec. 1940, Blackwood, Wales. Booking Agent; Promoter; Personal Man. m. Lorraine Jayne Booth, 27 July 1972, 1 s., 1 d. *Career:* Owner, Paul Barrett Rock 'n' Roll Enterprises; 30 years as promoter, booking agent, personal manager, representing among others: The Jets; Crazy Cavan and the Rhythm Rockers; Freddie 'Fingers' Lee and His Trio; Matchbox; Jean Vincent; Earl Jackson and The Jailbreakers; Wee Willie Harris; The Rimshots; Jack Scott; Tommy Sands; Numerous personal appearances, television, radio; Film appearances: Blue Suede Shoes; Bloody New Year. *Recordings:* Spirit of Woodstock; I Told You So; Punk; Girl Please Stay; Solo vocals, Superstar, featured on Gold album. *Honours:* Bop Cat of High Standing, Carl Perkins Fan Club. *Memberships:* PRS; MCPS. *Leisure interests:* Films; Books; Rock 'n' Roll (50s) music. *Address:* 16 Grove Pl., Penarth CF64 2ND, South Wales.

BARRETT Tina Ann; b. 16 Sept. 1976, West London, UK. Vocalist; Actor. *Education:* Trained in classical ballet at London's Arts Educational School. *Career:* Appeared in fashion shows, pantomimes and TV advertisements; Danced professionally in UK and overseas for various pop artists prior to joining S Club 7; Group quickly achieved international success following sales of TV series Miami 7 (1999), LA 7 (2000) and Hollywood 7 (2001) featuring the band's music to nearly 100 countries; Also made nature TV series S Club 7 Go Wild (2000) and various TV specials; First British tour with S Club 7, 2001. *Recordings:* Albums: S Club, 1999; 7, 2000; Sunshine, 2001; Singles: Bring It All Back, 1999; S Club Party, 1999; Two In A Million/You're My Number One, 1999; Reach, 2000; Natural, 2000; Never Had A Dream Come True, 2000; Don't Stop Movin', 2001; Have You Ever, 2001. *Honours:* Brit Award, Best British Newcomer, 2000. *Current Management:* 19 Management, Unit 32, Ransomes Dock, 35–37 Parkgate Rd, London, SW11 4NP, England.

BARRON Andy; b. 4 June 1962, Doncaster, England. Musician (drums). m. Anne Braymand, 22 Aug. 1992. *Education:* College. *Musical Education:* Privately taught; Doncaster Youth Jazz Orchestra. *Career:* Played, recorded or toured with Dominic Miller; Nigel Kennedy; Mark King; Mike Lindup; Julia Fordham; Kenny Wheeler; John Scofield; Rick Margitza; Kenny Werner; Stan Sultzman; Marcia Maria; Eurojazz; ORJ (Orchestra Regional de Jazz Rhone Alpes); John Surman; Pierre Drevet; Mario Stantchev; London Contemporary Dance. *Memberships:* ORJ; AIMRA. *Leisure interests:* Sports. *Address:* 50 rue de la Convention, 38200 Vienne, France; Garden Flat 27, Rye Hill Park, London SE15 3JN, England.

BARRON Chris; b. 1968. Vocalist. *Musical Education:* Music theory, New York's New School College. *Career:* Founder member, funk/rock group The Spin Doctors, 1988–; Tours, performances include: Horizon of Blue Developing Everywhere tour, 1992; Saturday Night Live, 1992; MTV Drops The Ball '93, 1992; Late Night Show With David Letterman, CBS Television, 1993. *Recordings:* Singles include: Little Miss Can't Be Wrong, 1992; Two Princes, 1993; Albums: Homebelly Groove, 1990; Pocket Full of Kryptonite, 1992; Turn It Upside Down, 1994; You've Got To Believe In Something, 1996; Here Comes The Bride, 1999; Just Go Ahead Now (compilation), 2000; Can't Be Wrong, 2001; solo: Shag, 2001. *Address:* c/o DAS Communications, 83 Riverside Dr., New York, NY 10024, USA.

BARRON Christine Angela; b. 9 May 1949, Birmingham, England. Composer; Musician; Author; Music Teacher. *Education:* Moseley School of Art, Birmingham. *Musical Education:* School of Contemporary Pop and Jazz. *Career:* Began as freelance percussionist, including work with Birmingham Symphony Orchestra; Theatre, cabaret musician with top entertainers including: Bruce Forsyth; Des O'Connor; Leslie Crowther; Val Doonican; Part-time lecturer, percussion and composition; North Warwickshire and Hinkley College of Technology and Art, Nuneaton, Warwickshire; Well known in the UK for innovative percussion workshops and master classes featuring percussion; Adjudicator and Member, British Federation for Music, Dance and Speech. *Compositions include:* Television signature tunes: Shut That Door (also released as single); Where Are They Now; Commissioned by Chappell Music Library for album, short pieces as jingles, theme, incidental music for television, radio, films (distributed world-wide); Collaboration with Boosey and Hawkes Music Publishers on albums, including album recorded by Royal Philharmonic Orchestra; Also wrote for their educational catalogue under pseudonyms: Chris Barron, Christine Barron. *Publications:* 2 comprehensive tutors with cassette for Learn As You Play series: Learn As You Play Drums; Learn As You Play Tuned Percussion and Timpani; Learn As You Play Drums Cassette. *Memberships:* The British Academy of Composers and Songwriters; British Federation of Festivals for Music, Dance and Speech. *Leisure interests:* Art; Swimming; Travel. *Current Management:* Boosey and Hawkes Music Publishers Ltd. *Address:* 27 Madeira Croft, Coventry, Warwickshire CV5 8NX, England.

BARRON Jay; b. 24 Feb. 1957, Yokusuka, Japan. Artist Man.; Concert Tour Prod. m. Leann Barron, 2 May 1990, 1 d. *Career:* Artist manager; International concert tour producer, Barron Entertainment. *Memberships:* CMA; ACM; AFofM; NARAS. *Leisure interest:* Collecting antique American Indian Art. *Address:* Barron Entertainment, 1600 Linden Ave, Nashville TN 37212, USA.

BARROW Geoff; b. 9 Dec. 1971, Walton in Gordano, Bristol, England. Musician (drums, programming). *Career:* Member, Portishead; Tape Operator, Coach House Studio, Bristol; Worked on Massive Attack's Blue Lines; Wrote track for Neneh Cherry's Home Brew album; Remixed work for Primal Scream, Paul Weller, Depeche Mode; Massive Attack; Earthling; Met Beth Gibbons on a Government Enterprise Allowance Scheme, 1991; Joined with Adrian Utley and Dave McDonald; Signed to Go!Beat Records as Portishead; Short Feature Film, To Kill A Dead Man shown at cinemas and projected on the MI5 building in London, 1995; Glastonbury Festival appearance, 1995; Internet concert broadcast, New York, 1997. *Recordings:* Singles: Sour Times, 1994; Numb, 1994; Glory Box, 1995; All Mine, 1997; Cowboys EP, 1997; Over, 1997; Cowboys; Albums: Dummy, 1994; Portishead, 1997; PNYC, 1998. *Publication:* Straight Outta Bristol: Massive Attack, Portishead, Tricky and the Roots of Trip Hop, Phil Johnson, 1995. *Honours:* Mercury Music Prize, 1994.

BARRY Daemion; b. 20 Nov. 1960, London, England. Musician; Composer. 1 s. *Education:* First Class Hons degree, Exeter University. *Compositions:* Television credits: Signs and Wonders, BBC; The English Wife, Meridian; Chandler and Co, BBC; My Good Friend, Anglia; A Woman's Guide To Adultery, Carlton Television; Friday On My Mind, BBC; Thicker Than Water, BBC; Reportage, BBC2; Go Wild, ITV; Gamesmaster, CH4; The Farm, TVE; Cinema credits: The Duke of Edinburgh Award Scheme; Commercial: Robinsons Orange Drinks; McCallum; Dalziel and Pascow. *Honours:* BAFTA Award, Best Original Music Score, Friday On My Mind; Golden Gate Award (US), Friday On My Mind. *Memberships:* PRS; British Songwriters; BAFTA; Groucho. *Current*

Management: Soundtrack Music Associates, 22 Ives St, Chelsea, London SW3 2ND, England.

BARRY James M; b. 16 Jan. 1952, Chicago, Illinois, USA. Songwriter. m. Emma Fontes, 1 July 1992, 1 s., 1 d. *Education:* Illinois Wesleyan University, BFA Theatre Cum Laude. *Musical Education:* Musical Theatre. *Compositions:* Colors of Grey, for award winning CBS documentary; If I Could Only Say Goodbye, David Hasselhoff, Baywatch; Step By Step, Groove U. *Publication:* Hear The Quiet. *Memberships:* EMI Music Publishing; ASCAP; Songwriters Guild of America. *Leisure interests:* Martial Arts; Skiing; Cooking; Travel. *Address:* 389 S Many Lakes Dr., Kalispell, MT 59901, USA.

BARRY John, (Jonathan Barry Prendergast); b. 3 Nov. 1933, York, Yorkshire, England. Composer. *Career:* Leader, John Barry Seven, 1960–62; Composer, film soundtrack music. *Recordings:* Singles: What Do You Want, Adam Faith (as arranger), 1959; with John Barry Seven: Hit and Miss (theme for Juke Box Jury, BBC), 1960; Walk Don't Run, 1960; As composer: From Russia With Love, Matt Monro, 1963; Goldfinger, Shirley Bassey, 1964; You Only Live Twice, Nancy Sinatra 1967; Down Deep Inside (theme from The Deep), Donna Summer, 1977; Albums (as performer, composer, arranger or conductor): Oh Boy, 1958; Drumbeat, 1959; Beat Girl, 1959; Stringbeat, 1961; Dr No, 1962; Man In The Middle, 1962; It's All Happening, 1963; Zulu, 1963; Elizabeth Taylor In London, 1963; From Russia With Love, 1963; The Man In The Middle, 1964; Sophia Loren In Rome, 1965; King Rat, 1965; Four In The Morning, 1965; Thunderball, 1965; Passion Flower Hotel, 1965; The Wrong Box, 1966; The Chase, 1966; The Quiller Memorandum, 1966; You Only Live Twice, 1967; The Lion In Winter, 1968; On Her Majesty's Secret Service, 1969; Midnight Cowboy, 1969; Diamonds Are Forever, 1971; Lolita My Love, 1971; Mary Queen of Scots, 1971; The Persuaders, 1971; Alice's Adventures In Wonderland, 1971; A Doll's House, 1973; The Man With The Golden Gun, 1974; Robin and Marian, 1976; King Kong, 1976; Moonraker, 1979; Frances, 1982; Body Heat, 1983; Out of Africa, 1985; Jagged Edge, 1985; A View To A Kill, 1985; Peggy Sue Got Married, 1986; Howard The Duck, 1986; The Deep, 1977; The Living Daylights, 1987; Dances With Wolves, 1990; Ruby Cairo; Indecent Proposal; Chaplin; Moviola II-Action and Adventure, 1995; The Scarlet Letter, 1995; King Rat, 1995; Beyondness of Things, 1999; Playing By Heart, 2000; The Last Valley, 2001; Robin and Marian, 2001. *Honours include:* Academy Awards: Midnight Cowboy; Born Free; Out of Africa; Dances With Wolves; Academy Award nomination, Chaplin.

BARRY Mark Anthony Luke; b. 26 Oct. 1978, Manchester, England. Vocalist; Songwriter. *Career:* Co-founder: BBMak pop group, 1996; Signed to UK company Telstar; Gained large US popularity after licence deal with Hollywood/Disney; Performed to over 100m US viewers through group's own TV specials; Supported Britney Spears on sell-out US tour followed by 28-date first headline US tour, 2000; UK shows with The Corrs, 2001. *Recordings:* Albums: Sooner Or Later, 2000; Singles: Back Here, Still To Your Side, 2000; Ghost of You and Me, 2001. *Honours:* Debut LP sales of over 1m. copies. *Address:* c/o Diane Young. *E-mail:* DaytimeENT@aol.com. *Internet:* www.bbmak.co.uk.

BARTHOLOMEW Simon James; b. 16 Oct. 1965, Woolwich, London, England. Musician (rhythm, lead guitar). *Education:* BA (Hons) Fine Art, Polytechnic of East London. *Career:* Guitarist, The Brand New Heavies; The Akimbo Band; Session musician for Mother Earth; Jamiroquai; Samuel Purdey; Mr X. *Recordings:* Albums: with The Brand New Heavies: The Brand New Heavies; The Heavy Rhyme Experience; Brother Sister; Akimbo on Top; Shelter. *Honours:* Platinum disc, Brother Sister album. *Memberships:* Musicians' Union; MCPS; PRS. *Leisure interests:* Painting; Filming; Gardening; Design. *Current Management:* Wildlife Entertainment. *Address:* Unit F, 21 Heathmans Rd, Parsons Green, London, England.

BARTON Bart; b. USA. Songwriter; Record Prod.; Man. m. Pat McKool, 9 Oct. 1975. *Education:* College. *Musical Education:* Vocal Education; Piano. *Career:* Songwriter; Record Producer; President, Canyon Creek Records; President, Nashville Bekool Music; Owner, Lemonsquare Music and Friends of the General Music. *Recordings:* She's Sitting Pretty, Top Record of the Year, Canada, 1989; Also recorded on Super Country 89 Album, one of Top 10 Records of the Year, Canada, 1989; Co-Producer and writer of 4 songs on album A Tribute to the American Veterans, featuring Charley Pride, Moe Bandy, BJ Thomas, Bobby Bare, Freddie Hart, Billy Walker, Billy Parker, The Kendalls, Johnny Rodriguez, Johnny Paycheck, Jeff Moore, Riders in the Sky and others. *Honours:* Candian Country Music Asscn, Outstsanding International Support Award. *Memberships:* CMA; CCMA; GMA; CARAS; NARAS. *Leisure interest:* Geneology. *Address:* 23 Music Sq. E, Suite 101, Nashville, TN 37203, USA.

BARTON James L; b. 12 June 1948, Memphis, Tennessee, USA. Musician (trumpet, flugel horn, piccolo trumpet, cornet); Musical Dir.; Arranger. m. Lorraine McKenna, 8 Dec. 1990, 2 s. *Education:* MSE, BSE, University of Michigan, Ann Arbor, 1966–72; De Anza College, Cupertino, California,

1974–76. *Musical Education:* Private instruction with Claude Gordon, 1974–80. *Career:* Played with The Platters; Little Anthony; The Shirells; Tommy Rowe; K. C. and The Sunshine Band; Bo Diddley; Musicals, London's West End: Cats; Sophisticated Ladies; Grease; Starlight Express; Into The Woods; Also performed in Assassins, Ronnie Scott's, London. *Composition:* Looking Back, 1989. *Honours:* John Phillips Sousa Award, 1966, 1969, 1970. *Memberships:* AFofM; Musicians' Union (UK). *Leisure interests:* Golf; Snooker; Movies. *Current Management:* Musical Director, West End Theatres, London. *Address:* Flat 2, 56 Upper Berkeley St, London W1H 7PP, England.

BARTON Lou Ann; b. 17 Feb. 1954, Fort Worth, Texas, USA. Singer. *Career:* Live concerts for television: MTV; Austin City Limits; Texas Connection; Member of bands: Fabulous Thunderbirds, 1975; Triple Threat Review and Double Trouble (both as lead singer with Stevie Ray Vaughan), 1977–80; Solo artist, Lou Ann Barton Band, 1981–95; Featured vocalist with Jimmie Vaughn supporting Eric Clapton, Royal Albert Hall, 1993. *Recordings:* Old Enough, 1982; Austin Rhythm and Blues Christmas, 1983; Forbidden Tones, 1988; Read My Lips, 1989; Dreams Come True with Angela Strehli, Marcia Ball, 1990; Sugar Coated Love, 1998. *Honours:* 4 times winner, Austin Chronicle Music Awards include 3 years Female Vocalist of Year; Inducted Texas Hall of Fame, 1992. *Current Management:* Davis McLarty Agency. *Address:* PO Box 3156, Austin, TX 78764, USA.

BARTON Tim; b. 27 March 1959, Melbourne, Australia. Singer; Musician; Comedian. m. Jane O'Brien, 30 Aug. 1992. *Musical Education:* Grade 5 guitar, Bruce Clarke Jazz School, Australia. *Career:* Tours: INXS; Men At Work; Midnight Oil; Concerts: Rolf Harris; Yothu Yindi; Jeff St John; Television: Touralla Telefon; Tours: Europe; Australia; Radio: Gary Crowley Show, GLR; Currently touring extensively with Tim Barton's All Star Six. *Recordings:* with Tim Bartons's All Star Six: T-BASS; Solo: So Called Thing Called Love. *Memberships:* PRS; Musicians' Union. *Leisure interest:* Ceramics. *Current Management:* Job Management. *Address:* 71a Penwith Rd, London SW18 4PX, England.

BARZEN Dietmar; b. 18 Oct. 1958, Oberhausen, Germany. Prod.; Composer. m. 31 May 1994, 1 d. *Education:* Dipl-kfm, Dr rer pol in Business Administration and Marketing; Composer. *Compositions:* Songs into the Light, Chris Sutton; Friday Night, Kent; Sky High, Far Side Gallery; Piano Dreams, David Warwick; Number One, SES. *Recordings:* Approximately 150 published and released titles. *Membership:* Marketing Club. *Leisure interests:* Jogging; Skiing. *Address:* Mail Box 4502241, 50877 Cologne, Germany.

BASA Andrej; b. 10 Feb. 1950, Ljubljana, Croatia. Composer; Musician (keyboards); Prod.; Arranger. m. 27 Nov. 1977, 1 s. *Musical Education:* Academy of Music, Ljubljana. *Career:* Australia; America; Canada; 25 years on television; More than 1200 compositions, 2000 arrangements. *Recordings:* Suite for orchestra; Music for 3 films; Album: Between The Sky and The Earth (instrumental music); As producer, arranger, sound engineer: over 180 albums with variuos artists. *Honours:* Eurovision Song Contest, 1993; 6 Festival awards. *Membership:* HDS, Croatia. *Leisure interest:* Yachting. *Address:* 51215 Kastav, Rubesi 139A, Croatia.

BASIA (Basia Trzetizelewska); b. Warsaw, Poland. Vocalist; Songwriter. *Career:* Singer, Matt Bianco, until 1986; Solo artiste, 1986–; Concerts include: Broadway. *Recordings:* Solo albums: Time and Tide; London, Warsaw, New York; The Sweetest Illusion; A New Day; Brave New Hope; Basia On Broadway; Clear Horizon-The Best of Basia, 1998; Singles: with Matt Bianco: Get Out of Your Lazy Bed, 1984; solo: Until You Come Back; Brave New Hope; Drunk On Love; Third Time Lucky; Contributor, film soundtrack, Pret-A-Porter. *Current Management:* BTB Management, PO Box 3509, Westport, CT 06880, USA.

BASS Lance (James Lansten); b. 4 May 1979, Laurel, MI, USA. Vocalist. *Career:* Aged 11 joined local community choir; First engagement with the Mississippi Show Stoppers; Toured USA with Attache choir; Member of boy band *N Sync signed to BMG Ariola Munich, 1997; First headline US tour, 1998; Created own Pop and Country record label Free Lance Entertainment, 2000; Released own film production On The Line, 2001. *Recordings:* Albums: *N Sync, 1998; Home For Christmas, 1998; No Strings Attached, 2000; Celebrity, 2001; Singles include: I Want You Back, 1997; Tearin' Up My Heart, 1997; Let The Music Heal Your Soul (various artists charity single credited to Bravo All Stars), 1999; Music of My Heart (with Gloria Estefan), 1999; Bye, Bye, Bye, 2000; I'll Never Stop, 2000; It's Gonna Be Me, 2000; This I Promise You, 2000; Pop, 2001; Gone, 2001. *Honours:* *N Sync reported as music industry's biggest earners in 2000 (estimated $184m); Recognition at MTV and Billboard Awards; Presented with keys to City of Orlando, 2000. *Address:* c/o Wright Entertainment Group, PO Box 590009, Orlando, FL 32859–0009, USA. *Internet:* www.wegmusic.com.

BASSEY Shirley; b. 8 Jan. 1937, Tiger Bay, Cardiff, Wales. Vocalist; Entertainer. m. (1) Kenneth Hume; (2) Sergio Novak. *Career:* Variety and revue singer, 1950s; Headlined concerts in New York, Las Vegas, early

1960s; Concerts and regular television appearances world-wide; Semi-retirement, 1981-. *Recordings:* Hit singles include: Banana Boat Song; Kiss Me Honey Honey, Kiss Me; As I Love You (No. 1, UK), 1959; As Long As He Needs Me; Big Spender; You'll Never Know; I'll Get By; (I) Who Have Nothing; Bond film themes: Goldfinger; Diamonds Are Forever; Moonraker; Numerous albums include: The Bewitching Miss Bassey, 1959; Fabulous Shirley Bassey, 1960; Shirley, 1961; Shirley Bassey, 1962; Let's Face The Music, 1962; Shirley Bassey Belts The Best!, 1965; I've Got A Song For You, 1966; Twelve of Those Songs, 1968; Live At The Talk of The Town, 1970; Something, 1970; Something Else, 1971; Big Spender, 1971; It's Magic, 1971; What Now My Love, 1971; I Capricorn, 1972; And I Love You So, 1972; Never, Never, Never, 1973; Live At Carnegie Hall, 1973; Broadway, Bassey's Way, 1973; Nobody Does It Like Me, 1974; Good Bad and Beautiful, 1975; Love Life and Feelings, 1976; Thoughts of Love, 1976; You Take My Heart Away, 1977; The Magic Is You, 1979; As Long As He Needs Me, 1980; As Time Goes By, 1980; I'm In The Mood For Love, 1981; Love Songs, 1982; All By Myself, 1984; I Am What I Am, 1984; Playing Solitaire, 1985; I've Got You Under My Skin, 1985; Sings The Songs From The Shows, 1986; Born To Sing The Blues, 1987; Let Me Sing and I'm Happy, 1988; Her Favourite Songs, 1988; Keep The Music Playing, 1991; New York, New York, 1991; Love Album, 1994; Songs of Andrew Lloyd Webber, 1995; Birthday Concert, 1997; Power of Love, 1998; Let Me Sing and I'm Happy, 1998; Sings The Movies, 1998; Great Shirley Bassey, 1999; Greatest Hits, 2001; Various compilations; Collaborations with: Yello (The Rhythm Divine, 1987), Propellerheads (History Repeating, 1997). *Honours include:* 20 Gold discs; 14 Silver discs; TV Times Award, Best Female Singer, 1972; Britannia Award, Best Female Solo Singer In The Last 50 Years, 1977; American Guild of Variety Artists Award, Best Female Entertainer, 1976. *Current Management:* c/o Stan Scottland, JKES Services, 404 Park Ave S, 10th Floor, New York, NY 10016, USA.

BASTOS Waldemar; b. 1954, Sao Salvador do Congo, Angola. Vocalist; Songwriter. *Career:* Began performing, 1961; Formed Jovial in Kabinda; Fled Angola, 1982; Now based in Lisbon. *Recordings:* Estamos Juntos (featuring Chico Buarque and Martinho da Vila), 1983; Angola Minha Namorada (featuring Jorge Degas), 1990; Pitanga Madura, 1992; Pretaluz, 1998. *Internet:* www.luakabop.com.

BATES Django Leon; b. 2 Oct. 1960, Beckenham, Kent, England. Musician (keyboards, horn); Composer. m. Beverley Hills, 26 Aug. 1988 1 s., 1 d. *Musical Education:* CYM/Full time Young Musicians (Morley College); Self-taught jazz. *Career:* Formed Human Chain, 1981; Co-founder, Loose Tubes, 1983; Formed Delightful Precipice, 1992; Toured over 30 countries with these bands and others: Europe; USA; South America; Japan; Scandinavia; Television includes: 1 In A Million, BBC Television, 1996. *Compositions include:* Writing commissions for Evelyn Glennie; J McGregor; London Sinfonietta. *Recordings:* Summer Fruits/Unrest; Autumn Fires/Green Shoots; Winter Truce/Homes Blaze; Spring Is Here/Shall We Dance? Good Evening… Here Is The News; Like Life; Quiet Nights; Contributor, All Men Amen, Iain Ballamy, 1995. *Publications:* Quarterly newsletter, available from management. *Honours:* 3 UK Wire Awards, All Music, 1987; German Stern Des Jahres, 1993; French Academie Du Jazz, 1994; Danish Jazz Par Nominee, 1996. *Leisure interests:* Compiling 'To Do' lists; Curry; Good books; World news; Beer. *Current Management:* Peter Luxton, Partnerships. *Address:* 5 Dryden St, London WC2E 9NW, England.

BATES Simon Dominic; b. 24 Aug. 1964, London, England. Musician (saxophone, clarinet, flute, wind synthesiser, programmer). *Musical Education:* BA Hons, Colchester Institute; LGSM (Jazz), Guildhall SMD. *Career:* Yamaha Saxophone; Wind Synthesiser endorsee and clinician; Musician with: Simon Bates Quartet; Sax Appeal; Peter Erskine; Chaka Khan; Lulu; Billy Ocean; D:ream; Eddie Floyd; Tony Remy; The Great Googly Moogly; The Diplomats; Zig Zag; Dominic King. *Recordings:* Television, radio, library sessions; Albums and singles with: D:ream; The Diplomats; EKO; Sasha/Brian Transeau. *Membership:* Musicians' Union. *Leisure interests:* Computing; Jaguar cars; Recorded music; Music programming. *Address:* 1 Erin Close, Bromley, Kent BR1 4NX, England.

BATES Stuart; b. 19 Sept. 1967, Orpington. Musician. *Musical Education:* Canterbury Cathedral Choir School; Lancing College Music School; Royal Holloway and Bedford New College; University of London. *Career:* Hammond, Keyboards, Accordion, The Divine Comedy, 1996–; Shows Across Europe and Japan, Collaboration and Performances with Michael Nyman, 1997; Trombone with Elvis Da Costa and The Imposter, 1996; Television Includes Top of the Pops, TFI Friday, Later with Jools Holland, The Big Breakfast, The Late Late Show; The Hot Press Awards; Radio Includes, Radio 1, Capital Radio, GLR, Virgin Radio, Radio France. *Recordings:* Casanova; A Short Album About Love; Fin de Siecle; Tomorrow's World Theme. *Membership:* The Musicians Union. *Leisure interests:* Mountain Walking; Football; Cricket; Backgammon. *Current Management:* Divine Management, Top Floor, 1 Cowcross St, London EC1M 6DR, England.

BATSFORD Richard; b. 25 Oct. 1969, Birmingham, England. Musician; Promoter. *Education:* Durham University. *Career:* Singer, National Youth Choir, City of Birmingham Symphony Orchestra; Vocalist; Session Keyboard Player. *Membership:* Musicians Union. *Current Management:* The GAG Club. *Address:* 2 Valentine Court, Valentine Rd, Kings Heath, Birmingham, B14 7AN, England.

BATT Mike; b. 6 Feb. 1950. Songwriter; Composer; Prod.; Arranger; Vocalist. *Career:* Began as A & R man for Liberty/UA Records, producing Groundhogs, Big Joe Williams, leaving to pursue independent career as Artist, Writer Producer; Produced Linda Lewis (All Around My Hat), Elkie Brooks (Lilac Wine), David Essex (Oh What a Circus); Wrote, sang and produced The Wombles (8 UK hits, 4 gold albums) and solo albums Schizophonia, Tarot Suite and others; Produced and composed for Vanessa Mae's album The Violin Player, 1995; Worked with Bond and Becky Taylor, 2000–01. *Compositions include:* Caravans, film score; Bright Eyes, for Art Garfunkel, (No 1, UK); A Winter's Tale, David Essex; I Feel Like Buddy Holly, Alvin Stardust; Please Don't Fall in Love, Cliff Richard; Solo hit singles: Summertime City; The Ride to Agadir; Lady of the Dawn; The Winds of Change; Theatrical project The Hunting of the Snark, starring Cliff Richard, Roger Daltrey, Deniece Williams, John Hurt, Sir John Gielgud, Captain Sensible, Art Garfunkel; Produced Phantom of the Opera hit (Steve Harley and Sarah Brightman); Composer of many commissioned pieces, including the opening of the Channel Tunnel for HM the Queen, also for 50th Wedding Anniversary of HM the Queen in 1997 a piece for massed bands of the Guards and 100 pipers. *Memberships:* PRS, council; Vice President, BASCA. *Address:* c/o Artbeat Ltd, PO Box 214, Farnham, Surrey GU10 5XZ, England.

BATTEUX Slim; b. 11 July 1949, La Fère, Aisne, France. Backing Singer; Singer; Musician (Hammond B3). Divorced, 2 d. *Career:* Backing singer for: Diane Tell; Eddy Mitchell; Michel Jonasz; Patricia Kaas; Bill Deraime; Johnny Halliday; Jean-Jacques Goldman; Dicks Rivers; Francis Cabrel; Florent Cagny; Hughes Aufrey; Veronique Samson; Percy Sledge; Billy Paul; Recordings with most of the above artists. *Recordings include:* Ellis Island: Voices of America; Ray Charles; Garry Christian. *Publication:* Je parle Sioux-Lakota. *Memberships:* SPEDIDAM; ADAMI; SACEM. *Leisure interest:* Lakota Sioux language of culture. *Address:* 9 bis, rue Descombes, 75017 Paris, France.

BATTLE Nicholas Nigel; b. 14 Aug. 1957, Dartmouth, Devon, England. Music Publisher; Musician; Man. m. Lynn, 12 Aug. 1989. *Musical Education:* Classical violin, led Sheffield Youth Orchestra; Self-taught guitar, bass, piano. *Career:* Bass player, After The Fire; Bass player, Writz; Also worked with Godley and Creme, Kajagoogoo; Currently General Manager, Windswept Pacific Music Ltd. *Recordings:* Songs recorded by Cliff Richard: First Date; Front Page; Producer, Falling In Love Again, Techno Twins. *Memberships:* PRS; BASCA; MPA Pop Publishers Committee; IPA Council. *Leisure interests:* Family life; Local Church. *Address:* 27 Queensdale Pl., Holland Park, London W11 4SQ, England.

BAUER Johannes; b. 22 July 1954, Halle, East Germany. Musician. *Education:* Trombone Studies, Berlin, 1971–77. *Career:* Freelance Improvisational Musician, 1979–; Duo with Barry Gay, Trio with Annick Nozati and Fred Van Hove Doppelmoppel (with Konrad Bauer, Joe Sachse, Uwe Kropinski) Slawterhaus (with Dietmar Diesner, Jon Rose, Peter Hellinger), Ulrich Gumpert Trio, Peter Brötzmann Alarm Orchester, März Combo, Tony Oxleys Contemporary Music Ensemble, Globe Unity Orchestra, Derek Baileys Company, Cecil Taylor European Big Band; Leader of Various Workshop Bands. *Recordings:* Round About Mittweida; ALARM; Nr.12; Cecil Taylor in Berlin '88; Slawterhaus Live a Victoriaville; Organo Pleno; Bauer Bauer; In The Tradition; The Wild Man's Band. *Address:* Dannecker Str 6, Berlin 10245, Germany.

BAUER Judah; b. 1973, Appleton, Wisconsin, USA. Musician (guitar, harmonica). *Career:* Member, Twenty-Miles, with brother; Member, Jon Spencer Blues Explosion. *Recordings:* Singles: The Sound of the Future is Here Today, 1992; Son of Sam, 1992; Big Yule Log Boogie, 1992; Train 3, 1993; Bellbottoms, 1995; Get With It, 1996; 2 Kindsa Love, 1996; Wail, 1997; Rocketship, 1997; Talk About the Blues, 1998; Albums: The Jon Spencer Blues Explosion, 1992; Crypt-Style, 1992; Extra Width, 1993; Mo' Width, 1994; Orange, 1994; Experimental Remixes, 1995; Not I Got Worry, 1996; Controversial Negro, 1997; Rocketship, 1997; ACME, 1998.

BAUER William Henry (Billy); b. 14 Nov. 1915, Bronx, New York, USA. Musician (banjo, guitar). m. Marion V Cos, 15 March 1941, 1 s., 1 d. *Musical Education:* Mostly self-taught; Harmony and theory in college. *Career:* Woody Herman, 1942–45; Lennie Tristano, 1946–49; Teacher, Conservatory of Modern Music, 1946–49; NBC Staff Musician, 1950–58; Benny Goodman, 1958; Brussels Worlds Fair, Sherwood Inn, 1960–62; Ice Capades, 1963–67; Broadway Theatre, 1968–69; Billy Bauer Guitar School, 1970-. *Recordings:* Freelance recording musician for about 10 years; Guitar solos recorded: Blue Mist; Purple Haze; Short Stories; Greenway;

Impressions; Pam, for Woody Herman; Marionette; Blue Boy, both for Lennie Tristano; Duet for saxophone and guitar recorded by Lee Konitz. *Publications:* Jazz Lines, by Lennie Tristano, Lee Konitz, Warne Marsh; Author, Guitar Instructor Series; Sideman: Autobiography of Billy Bauer, 1997. *Honours:* Metronome All Star Poll, 1947–51; Down Beat Award, 1949–50. *Membership:* ASCAP. *Leisure interest:* Writing instruction books for guitar. *Current Management:* William H Bauer Inc.

BAY Hans Henrik; b. 26 Dec. 1963, Copenhagen, Denmark. Guitar Player; Composer. m. Susanne Bechmann, 1 s., 1 d. *Musical Education:* Rhythmic Music Conservatory, Copenhagen. *Career:* Tour in Denmark with Jorgen Emborg, 1988–89; Tour in Denmark with Ensemble NEW and Billy Cobham, 1997; Played with James Moody, Ed Neumeister, Jukkis Outtila, Tomas Franck, Bob Rockwell and Jesper Lundgaard. *Composition:* Crescent 434, 6/8, In the Bar. *Recordings:* Jorgen Emborg Septet: Keyword, 1989; Ensemble New with Billy Cobham, 1998. *Memberships:* Danish Music Union; Danish Jazz Beat Folk Autorer. *Current Management:* Ole Cristensen, vendersgade 28, 7000 Fredericia, Denmark. *Address:* Bredager 32, 7120 Vejle O, Denmark.

BAYLIS Christopher Edward; b. 7 July 1954, Reading, Berkshire, England. Prod.; Musician (guitar). *Education:* BSc Hons, University of Surrey. *Musical Education:* Self-taught. *Career:* Founder member, Siam, 1980; Formed The Guitar Orchestra, 1989; Production credits include: Maddy Prior; Davey Arthur; Automatic Dlamini. *Recordings:* The Guitar Orchestra, 1991; Interpretations, The Guitar Orchestra, 1994. *Memberships:* PRS; MCPS; Musicians' Union. *Leisure interests:* Antiques; Furniture design. *Current Management:* Park Records. *Address:* 20 Raleigh Park Rd, Oxford OX2 9AZ, England.

BAYNE Iain; b. 22 Jan. 1960, St Andrews, Fife, Scotland. Musician (drums, percussion, piano). *Career:* Member, Scottish folk group Runrig, 1980–; International concerts include: Canada, 1987; Support to U2, Murrayfield Stadium, Edinburgh, 1987; Royal Concert Hall, Glasgow; Open-air concert, Loch Lomond. *Recordings:* Albums: Play Gaelic, 1978; Highland Connection, 1979; Recovery, 1981; Heartland, 1985; The Cutter and The Clan, 1987; Once In A Lifetime, 1988; Searchlight, 1989; The Big Wheel, 1991; Amazing Things, 1993; Transmitting Live, 1995. *Current Management:* Marlene Ross Management, 55 Wellington St, Aberdeen AB2 1BX, Scotland.

BAYNHAM Frank; b. 29 May 1942, Warrington, England. Musician (English concertina, bodhran). m. Sherry, 5 Jan. 1972, 3 s. *Musical Education:* BEd, Hons, Lancaster University, Art, Music. *Career:* Founder member, Wigan Folk Club; Played solo and with various individuals, bands; Formed current band Kings of Puck, 1993. *Honours:* Guinness Best Entertainment of Puck Fair, Killorglin, Co Kerry, Ireland, with Steve Ashton, Dave Mann, 1993. *Membership:* Musicians' Union. *Leisure interests:* Snooker; Boules; Irish history; Mythology. *Current Management:* Ricky McCabe Entertainments Ltd. *Address:* 26 Crosby Rd N, Waterloo, Liverpool L22 4QF, England.

BAYNTON-POWER David; b. 29 Jan. 1961, England. Musician (Drums). *Career:* Member, James, 1990–; Numerous tours, festival dates and television appearances. *Recordings:* Singles: Born of Frustration; Sound; Sometimes (Lester Piggott); Laid; Say Something; Sit Down '98; She's A Star; Tomorrow; Destiny Calling; I Know What I'm Here For; Just Like Fred Astaire; Albums: Seven, 1992; Laid, 1993; Wah Wah, live, 1994; Whiplash, 1997.

BAYSHAW Debbie; b. 5 Feb. 1958, Chapeau, Québec, Canada. Singer. m. Peter Komisar Jr, 1 s., 3 d. *Musical Education:* 4 years classical guitar. *Career:* Performed coast to coast, Canada; Appeared several major television shows; Host, 3 part variety mini series, CBC Television, Toronto. *Recordings:* Albums: Time To Move Along; Mixed Emotions. *Honours:* Winner, Canadian Open Country Singing Contest; CBC TV Contest, Look Out World Here We Come. *Membership:* AFofM. *Leisure interests:* Cycling; Mending; Craft making. *Current Management:* Big Peach Records. *Address:* RR2, Grand Valley, Ontario L0N 1G0, Canada.

BEACHILL Peter C; b. 1 Feb. 1961, Barnsley, Yorkshire, England. Musician (trombone). *Musical Education:* Leeds College of Music. *Career:* Studio musician; Various television shows: Royal Variety; Barrymore; BAFTA Awards; BBC, LWT Shows; Tours with James Last; Natalie Cole; Shirley Bassey; Pete Townsend; Cliff Richard; Chris Rea; Eric Clapton; Oasis. *Recordings:* Albums with: Paul McCartney; Sting; Pet Shop Boys; Diana Ross; Rod Stewart; James Last; Shirley Bassey; Cliff Richard; Peter Gabriel; Eric Clapton; Grace Jones; Pink Floyd; Led Zeppelin; Pete Townshend. *Honour:* BBC Don Lusher Trombone Award. *Membership:* Royal Society of Musicians. *Leisure interest:* Sport. *Address:* 16 Coniston Rd, Muswell Hill, London N10 2BP, England.

BEAKER Norman; b. 21 June 1950, Manchester, England. Musician (guitar, piano); Vocalist; Composer; Prod. m. Sept. 1977, divorced 1985, 1 s. *Musical Education:* College of Music (Northern). *Career:* Concerts with Alexis Korner; Eric Clapton; Jack Bruce; B B King; Lowell Fulsom; Graham Bond; Buddy Guy; Television and radio appearances include: Old Grey Whistle Test; The Tube; So It Goes; Radio 1 in Concert; Paul Jones R & B Show Radio 2; Capital Radio with Jack Bruce; First blues band to tour East Germany, 1977. *Recordings:* Into The Blues, Norman Beaker Band; Modern Days Lonely Nights; I Was Once A Gambler (Phil Guy); Theme music, World In Action; Theme music, Stand Up. *Publications:* Freelance writer on R & B, various magazines and journals. *Honour:* Blues Guitarist of The Year, 1989. *Memberships:* PRS; MCPS. *Leisure interests:* Tennis; Walking. *Current Management:* Actual Music.

BEARD Frank; b. 11 June 1949, Frankston, Texas, USA. Musician (drums). *Career:* Joined The Warlocks, 1967; Band name changed to The American Blues, 1968; Founder member, ZZ Top, 1970–; Toured regularly, 1970–; Tours include Eliminator tour, 1984; Afterburner tour, 1985–87; Recycler tour, 1990; Rock The Bowl '91, Milton Keynes, 1991. *Recordings:* Albums include: 2 with The American Blues, 1968; with ZZ Top: ZZ Top's First Album, 1970; Rio Grande Mud, 1972; Tres Hombres, 1973; Fandango, 1975; Tejas, 1977; The Best Of, 1978; Deguello, 1979; El Loco, 1981; Eliminator, 1983; Afterburner, 1985; Recycler, 1990; Greatest Hits, 1992; Antenna, 1994; XXX, 1999; Singles include: La Grange, 1974; Tush, 1975; Gimme All Your Lovin', 1983; Sharp Dressed Man, 1983; Legs, 1984; Sleeping Bag, 1985; Stages, 1986; Rough Boy, 1986; Velcro Fly, 1986; Doubleback, from film Back To The Future Part III, 1990; Viva Las Vegas, 1992. *Honours include:* Several MTV Video Awards; ZZ Top Day, Texas, 1991; Silver Clef Award, Nordoff-Robbins Music Therapy Foundation, 1992. *Current Management:* Lone Wolf Management, PO Box 163690, Austin, TX 78716, USA.

BEARD Susan Stephanie (Sue); b. 25 Feb. 1961, London, England. Jazz Singer; Songwriter; Actress; Writer; Stand-up Comic; Musician (piano, oboe, ukelele). *Education:* Bristol University postgraduate certificate in film. *Musical Education:* BA Hons, Music, York University, 1983. *Career:* Comic/satirical jazz singer; Television appearances: Les Dawson Show, BBC1; Pebble Mill, BBC1; The Happening, with Jools Holland, CH4 Television; Numerous radio broadcasts include: Loose Ends; Pick of The Week, BBC Radio 4; BBC Radio 2; JFM; Many commercial stations; Concerts include: Live at London's Comedy Store; Ronnie Scott's; Pizza On The Park; Astoria; One Woman Show Tour including Edinburgh Festival; Kuala Lumpur; Arezzo, Paris. *Compositions:* Spooks! (children's musical), 1995; Composer, performer, many topical, satirical and jazz songs for radio, television, live performances. *Leisure interests:* Films; Coaching drama students in singing and performance. *Current Management:* Nick Young, Crawfords. *Address:* 2 Conduit St, London W1R 9TG, England.

BÉART Guy; b. 16 July 1930, Cairo, Egypt. Singer; Composer; Engineer; Author. 2 d. *Education:* Ecole Nationale des Ponts et Chaussées. *Career:* Cabaret, recitals and concerts, Paris; Author, producer, television series Bienvenue, 1966–72. *Compositions:* Songs for artists including: Zizi Jeanmaire; Juliette Greco; Patachou, Maurice Chevalier; Film music includes: L'Eau Vive; Pierrot La Tendresse; La Gamberge. *Honours:* Chevalier, Légion d'Honneur; Officier, Ordre National du Mérite; Commandeur des Arts et des Lettres; Grand Prix, Academy du Disque, 1957; Academy Charles Cros, 1965; Grand Prix de la Chanson, SACEM, 1987; Prix Balzac, 1987. *Address:* Editions Temporel, 2 rue du Marquis de Morès, 92380 Garches, France.

BEASLEY Walter; b. California, USA. Musician (alto/soprano saxophones); Songwriter. *Career:* Jazz Explosion's Just The Sax tour. *Recordings:* Albums: Walter Beasley, 1988; Just Kickin' It, 1989; Intimacy, 1992; Private Time, 1995; Live and More, 1996; Tonight We Love, 1997; For Your Pleasure, 1998; Won't You Let Me Love You, 2000; Rendez Vous, 2002; Call Me; I'm So Happy; Jump On It; Nothin' But A Thang; On The Edge; Tenderness; Where; Singles: You Are The One; If You Ever Loved Someone; Don't Say Goodbye. *Current Management:* c/o Preston Powell, Jazzateria Inc, 112 W 72nd St, #2F, New York, NY 10023, USA.

BEAUFORD Carter; b. 2 Nov. 1957, USA. Musician (drums). *Education:* Shenandoah Conservatory, Winchester, Virginia, studied occupational therapy. *Musical Education:* Self-taught. *Career:* Son of a jazz trumpeter; Attended schools in North Carolina prior to becoming full-time musician; Resides in Charlottesville, California; Moonlights as session player including guest appearance on a Carlos Santana album; First gig with jazz-fusion outfit led by local luminary Big Nick Nicholas, aged 9; Played with Secrets band 1984–90; Four year residency as pianist on Ramsey Lewis' BET on Jazz show; Drummer for The Dave Matthews Band, 1991–; Rapid growth of fanbase through touring schedules; First album released on group's own Bama Rags label certified gold by RIAA; First national US tour in support of RCA debut album, 1994; Many world-wide concerts and festival appearances since including 2001 album tour; Group permits fans to tape-record shows for personal use; I Did It single officially released through Napster, 2001. *Recordings:* Albums: Remember Two Things (live), 1993; Under The Table and Dreaming, 1994; Crash, 1996; Live At Red

Rocks 8–15–95, 1997; Before These Crowded Streets, 1998; Listener Supported (live), 1999; Everyday, Live In Chicago 12–19–98, 2001; Singles: Recently (EP), 1994; What Would You Say, Jimi Thing, Ants Marching, 1995; So Much To Say, Too Much, 1996; Don't Drink The Water, 1997; Satellite, Crash Into Me, Crush, 1998; I Did It, The Space Between, Everyday, 2001. *Honours:* Grammy Awards: Best Rock Performance By A Duo Or Group With Vocal, 1997; US VH-1 Awards: Favourite Group; Must Have Album; Song of The Year, 2001; Top-grossing touring band in US, 2000. *Address:* c/o Red Light Communications, 3305 Lobban Pl., Charlottesville, VA 22903, USA. *E-mail:* info@rlc.net. *Internet:* www.dmband.com.

BEAUPRE Jhan; b. 29 April 1950, Dallas, Texas, USA. Songwriter; Musician (Guitar). m. Joyce Ann Beaupre, 10 July 1983, 6 d. *Education:* Degree in Nursing, Southwestern Union College, 1978. *Musical Education:* Self-taught. *Career:* Founded The Sound System, age 15; Played with various bands for 7 years; As songwriter, numerous awards and nominations; Business venture, Sound Illusions, promoting and recording new artists and songwriters. *Compositions include:* She Can Make A Man Cry; A Good Guitar; There's A Flame. *Honours:* 3 Trail Blazer Award Nominations, Nashville, USA; Semi-finalist, Austin Songwriters; Placed 2 times, Wisconsin Songwriters. *Memberships:* BMI; Austin Song Writers Group; Secretary, Johnson County Asscn; Song Writers of Wisconsin; Fort Bend S W Group. *Leisure interests:* Music; Art; Writing. *Current Management:* Davis and Davis Music, 5755 June Lane, Winston-Salem, NC 27127, USA.

BEAUSSIER Daniel Gérard Jacques; b. 2 June 1957, Valenciennes, Nord, France. Musician; Composer; Teacher; Prod. m. Aesa Sigurjonsdottir, 22 Aug. 1987, 3 s., 1 d. *Education:* Engineer, ICAM. *Musical Education:* First prize, CNR, Lille, France. *Career:* Tour, Europe, with Carla Bley, 1988; with Nana Vasconcellos, Paris Jazz Festival, 1991; Hozan Yamamoto, 1995; Monica Passos; Charlélie Couture; Shiro Daimon; Astrolab Collectif; Correspondances with D Beaussier (150 concerts). *Recordings:* Fleur Carnivore, Carla Bley; Lueurs Bleues, Daniel Goyone, Trilok Gurtu; Sans(e)krit, Daniel Beaussier; Casamento, Monica Passos; Chambre 13, Lydia Domancich; You Are Here, Uman. *Publications:* Analysis of solos in Findings, My Experience With Saxophone, by Steve Lacy. *Memberships:* UMJ; FNEIJ; IAJS; Director, EDIM, Creative Music School, Paris. *Current Management:* EDIM Productions. *Address:* 24 Ave d'Alembert, 92160 Antony, France.

BEAVERS Les; b. 23 Nov. 1934, Manchester, England. Musician (guitar). m. Terry Burton, 23 Jan. 1963. *Musical Education:* Mainly self-taught. *Career:* Played at various ballrooms, 1956–59; Played with BBC Northern Dance Orchestra, 1959–68; Bob Sharples, Thames Television, 1963–78; Appearances on Granada Television and sessions on STV, among others; Also theatre tours. *Membership:* Musicians' Union. *Leisure interests:* Golf; Trout fishing. *Address:* 7 Sandown Rd, Sunny Bank, Bury, Lancashire BL9 8HN, England.

BEBEK Zeljko; b. 16 Dec. 1945, Sarajevo, Croatia. Singer. m. Sandra Bebek, 2 Oct. 1982, 2 d. *Education:* University of Civil Rights. *Career:* Hundreds of concerts and television shows, over 20 years; 2m. recordings; Many concerts of Townsends and Townsends Peoples in Zagreb, Sarajevo; Tours: Europe; USA; Canada. *Recordings:* (Singing in Croatian language) Bosanac; Selma; Na Zadnjem Sjedistu; Da Je Srece Bilo; Dabogda Te Voda Odnijela; Sta Je Meni Ovo Trebalo; A Svemir Miruje; Odlazim; Tijana. *Membership:* Hrvatska Glazbewa Unija (HGU). *Leisure interests:* Skiing; Tennis. *Current Management:* Song Agency, Split, Croatia. *Address:* Crnciceva 41, 41000 Zagreb, Croatia.

BECK (Beck Hansen); b. 8 July 1970, Los Angeles, California, USA. Musician; Vocalist. *Career:* Early performances at local parties in Los Angeles; Worked with producers Karl Stephenson, and later the Dust Brothers; Numerous tours and live appearances including Glastonbury Festival, England, 1997; Collaborated with Snoop Doggy Dogg; Air; Remixed: Air; Jon Spencer Blues Explosion; Bjork; David Bowie; Covered Bowie's Diamond Dogs for Moulin Rouge OST, 2001. *Recordings:* Singles: Loser, 1994; Beercan EP, 1994; Devil's Haircut (remixed by Noel Gallagher), 1996; Where It's At, 1996; The New Pollution, 1997; Jack Ass, 1997; Sissyneck, 1997; Deadweight, 1998; Tropicalia, 1999; Nobody's Fault But My Own EP, 1999; Sexxlaws, 1999; Mixed Bizness, 2000; Albums: Mellow Gold, 1994; One Foot in the Grave, 1994; Stereopathic Soul Manure, 1994; Odelay, 1996; Mutations, 1998; Midnite Vultures, 1999. *Honours:* Grammy Award, Alternative Music Performance (Mutations), 2000; Brit Award, Best International Male, 1997, 1999, 2000.

BECK Jeff; b. 24 June 1944, Surrey, England. Musician (guitar); Composer; Vocalist. *Education:* Wimbledon Art College. *Career:* Member, Screaming Lord Sutch; The Tridents; Guitarist, The Yardbirds, 1965–66; Appearances include: Tours with the Kinks, 1965; The Beatles, Paris, 1965; Manfred Mann, 1965; Rolling Stones '66 tour, 1966; Leader, Jeff Beck Group, 1967–; Concerts include: National Jazz and Blues Festival, 1967,

1968; Newport Jazz Festival, 1969; Secret Policeman's Other Ball, London (Amnesty benefit), 1981; Prince's Trust Rock Gala, Royal Albert Hall, 1983; US tour with Stevie Ray Vaughn, 1989. *Recordings:* Hit singles include: with the Yardbirds: Heart Full of Soul; For Your Love; Evil Hearted You/ Still I'm Sad; Shapes of Things; Over Under Sideways Down; with Jeff Beck Group: Hi-Ho Silver Lining; Tallyman; Love Is Blue; Albums include: with the Yardbirds: For Your Love, 1965; Having A Rave Up With The Yardbirds, 1965; The Yardbirds with Sonny Boy Williamson, 1966; Yardbirds, 1966; Over Under Sideways Down, 1966; with Jeff Beck Group/solo: Truth, 1968; Beck-Ola, 1969; Rough and Ready, 1971; Jeff Beck Group, 1972; Jeff Beck, Tim Bogert and Carmine Appice, 1973; Blow By Blow, 1975; Wired, 1976; Jeff Beck With The Jan Hammer Group Live, 1977; There and Back, 1980; Flash, 1985; Jeff Beck's Guitar Shop With Terry Bozzio and Tony Hymas, 1989; Crazy Legs, 1993; Up, 1995; The Best of Beck, 1995; Blow By Blow, 1995; Shapes of Things, 1998; Who Else! 1999; You Had It Coming, 2001; Beck-Ola Cosa Nostra; Contributor, film soundtracks: The Pope Must Die, 1991; Honeymoon In Vegas, 1992; Contributor, Blaze of Glory, Jon Bon Jovi, 1990; Amused To Death, Roger Waters, 1992; Tribute To Muddy Waters, 1993; Stone Free-A Tribute To Jimi Hendrix, 1993. *Honours:* Grammy Awards: Best Rock Instrumental Performance, 1986, 1990; BAFTA Award, Best Original Television Music, Frankie's House, with Jed Leiber, 1993. *Current Management:* c/o Ernest Chapman, Equator Music, 17 Hereford Mansions, Hereford Rd, London W2 5BA, England.

BECKER Irene; b. 30 March 1951, Aalborg, Denmark. Musician (piano); Composer. m. Pierre Dorge, 24 Aug. 1985. *Musical Education:* Cand Phil. in Music, University of Copenhagen. *Career:* Member, Pierre Dorge's New Jungle Orchestra, 1980–; Member, Trio: Dorge, Becker, Carlsen; Performs with singer Sainkho Namtclylak, Austria; Composer, film music. *Recordings:* Albums: New Jungle Orchestra, 10 albums; Dancing On The Island, Irene Becker and Sainkho. *Memberships:* DJBFA; Danish Musicians Union. *Current Management:* Copenhagen Concerts, Holmbladsgade 35, 2300 Copenhagen S, Denmark.

BECKER Jason; Rock Musician (guitar). *Musical Education:* Classical guitar. *Career:* Guitarist, US rock group Cacophony (with Marty Friedman), 1986–90; Also solo artiste; Guitarist, David Lee Roth, 1991–. *Recordings:* Albums: with Cacophony: Speed Metal Symphony, 1987; Go Off, 1989; solo: Perpetual Burn, 1988; Perspective, 1996; Raspberry Jams, 1999; with David Lee Roth: A Little Ain't Enough, 1991.

BECKER Walter; b. 20 Feb. 1950, New York, USA. Musician (guitar, bass); Record Prod. 1 s., 2 step-s. *Career:* Founder member, Steely Dan, 1972–81, 1993–; Record producer, 1980–; Solo recording artiste; Tours of US; Japan; Europe; Australia. *Recordings:* Albums: Can't Buy A Thrill, 1973; My Sportin' Life, 1973; Countdown To Ecstasy, 1973; Pretzel Logic, 1974; Katy Lied, 1975; The Royal Scam, 1976; Aja, 1978; Greatest Hits, 1979; Metal Leg, 1980; Gaucho, 1981; Reelin' In The Years, 1985; Do It Again, 1987; Remastered-The Best of Steely Dan, 1993; Citizen Steely Dan 1972–80, 1993; Alive In America, 1995; Two Against Nature, 2000; solo: 11 Tracks of Whack, 1995; Singles include: Dallas; Show Biz Kids; My Old School; Black Friday; Kid Charlemagne; Haitian Divorce; Deacon Blues; FM (No Static At All); Rikki Don't Lose That Number; As producer: Flaunt The Imperfection, China Crisis, 1985; Flying Cowboys, Rickie Jones, 1989; Jazz recordings for: LeeAnn Ledgerwood; Andy Laverne; Jeff Beal; Jeremy Steig; David Kikosi; Lorraine Feather; Sam Butler; Donald Fagen. *Honours:* Platinum disc; Grammy Awards, Aja, 1978; Two Against Nature, 2001; Inducted into Hollywood's Rock Walk, 1993. *Current Management:* HK Management, 8900 Wilshire Blvd, Suite 300, Beverly Hills, CA 90211, USA.

BECKERS (Ludo) Lazy Lew; b. 27 March 1957, Molenstede, Belgium. Musician (Harmonica). m. 27 March 1981, 1 s., 1 d. *Musical Education:* Self-taught Harmonica; Jazz Theory Lessons, Halewÿnstichting, Antwerp, Belgium. *Career:* Harmonica Player (sometimes Singer); The Zoots, 1984–86; The Sultans, 1987; Medford Slim Band, 1990–94; Brothers in Blues, 1990–96; European Tours with Zora Young, R L Burnside, Big Lucky Carter, Calvin Jackson. *Recordings:* The Zoots and Louisiana Red; The Sultans; Medford Slim Band; P Vansant. *Honours:* Nominated for W C Handy Award, Category Best Bluesband Foreign (The Zoots), 1987. *Membership:* SABAM. *Leisure interest:* Freelance Journalism. *Address:* 77 Te Boelaarlei, 2140 Borgerhout, Belgium.

BECKHAM Victoria, (Posh Spice); b. 7 April 1975, Cuffley, England. Vocalist. m. David Beckham, 4 July 1999, 1 s. *Career:* Member, Spice Girls; Numerous television and radio appearances, magazine interviews; Film, Spiceworld: The Movie, 1997; World tour including dates in UK, Europe, India and USA. *Recordings:* Singles: Wannabe, 1996; Say You'll Be There, 1996; 2 Become 1, 1996; Mama/ Who Do You Think You Are, 1997; Step To Me, 1997; Spice Up Your Life, 1997; Too Much, 1997; Stop, 1998; (How Does It Feel To Be) On Top of the World, with England United, 1998; Move Over/ Generation Next, 1998; Viva Forever, 1998; Goodbye, 1998; Holler/Let Love Lead The Way, 2000; solo: Out of Your Mind (with True Steppers/Dane

Bowers), 2000; Not Such An Innocent Girl, 2001; Albums: Spice, 1996; Spiceworld, 1997; Forever, 2000; solo: Victoria Beckham, 2001. *Honours:* Brit Awards: Best Single, Wannabe, 1997; Outstanding Contribution, 2000.

BEDER Mark; b. 16 Nov. 1959, London, England. Record Prod.; Music Publisher; Artist Man. 1 s., 1 d. *Career:* A & R Dept, Carlin Music Publishers; A & R Manager, Polydor and Virgin Records; Currently Managing Director for Pumphouse Music; Pumphouse Sounds; Pumphouse Songs; FXU Records; Manager of: D:ream; X-Avia; Tri; Siren; D J Peer; Recordings by artists listed above. *Honours:* Best Newcomers; Best Dance Act; Radio One Tune of The Year, 1992; Official Labour Party Anthem, Things Can Only Get Better. *Memberships:* PRS; MCPS; MPA; IMF. *Leisure interests:* Music; Fun and games. *Address:* FXU, G T Studios, 97 Scrubs Lane, London NW10 6QU, England.

BEEBY John; b. 18 Nov. 1945, Nuneaton, Warwickshire, England. Musician (guitar); Songwriter; Prod. m. 16 Nov. 1974, 1 s. *Musical Education:* Taught by father. *Career:* Tour, Germany, 1963–64; The Zephyrs, 1964; Toured with: Del Shannon; Jerry Lee Lewis; Billy Fury; Pretty Things; Count Prince Miller, 1968; Tony Gregory; Horace Faith; Television appearances include: Ready Steady Go; Top of The Pops; Scene At 6.30; Wogan; Pebble Mill; Film appearances: Be My Guest (with Jerry Lee Lewis, Steve Marriot); Primitive London; Ice Cream Dream; Business Ventures: John Beeby's Music Place, 1975; Worked freelance with various artists; Worked with Eurythmics' Dave Stewart as songwriter, producer, 1980s; Co-writer, Dreamtime, with Daryl Hall, 1986; Co-writer, producer, with Brian Hodgson, Why Do I Always Get It Wrong (UK entry, Eurovision Song Contest), No. 2, 1989; Worked in Nashville, USA, with various artists including Robert Ellis Orral, Larry Henley, Roger Cook, 1989. *Recordings:* She's Lost You, 1964; Wonder What I'm Gonna Do, 1965; A Little Bit of Soap, 1965; Dreamtime, 1986; Why Do I Always Get It Wrong, 1989; Take A Chance On Me, 1989. *Honours:* BMI Dreamtime, USA; BMI Dreamtime, UK. *Memberships:* PRS; BASCA. *Leisure interest:* Speedway. *Address:* Crouch End, London N8, England.

BEECHER Franny; b. Philadelphia, Pennsylvania, USA. Musician (guitar). *Musical Education:* Worked with Benny Goodman. *Career:* Original member, Bill Haley's Comets, 1952–62; Invented rock 'n' roll music; First rock band to headline a film; Worked with Buddy Grecco. *Recordings:* Rock Around The Clock; See You Later Alligator; Crazy Man Crazy; Shake Rattle and Roll; Rock The Joint; Mabo Rock; Rudy's Rock; Florida Twist; Skinnie Minnie; Capitol 50th Anniversary Jazz Box; Undercurrent Blues; From The Original Master Tapes; Back To A Better Time; Decca Years and More; Bring Back The Music; Rock-A-Billy Son. *Publications:* Rock Around The Clock; Stage Clear; We're Gonna Party; Never Too Old To Rock. *Honours:* Best Vocal Group, 1954; Best Instrumental Group, 1956; Best Guitar Player; Rock and Roll Hall of Fame; Gold Records. *Address:* Rock It Concerts, Bruno Mefer Platz 1, 80937 Munich, Germany.

BEEDLE Ashley, (Daddy Ash, Black Jazz Chronicles, Delta House of Funk); b. 25 Nov. 1962, Hemel Hempstead, England. Prod.; Remixer; DJ. *Career:* Worked in record shops Black Market and Flying Records in London; Formed X-Press 2 with Rocky and Diesel, 1993; Signed to Junior Boy's Own label; Member: Ballistic Brothers; Black Science Orchestra; Disco Evangelists; Founder: Afro Art Records; Collaborations: David Holmes; Marc Woolford; Remixed: Fatboy Slim; River Ocean; Richard Blackwood; D-Influence; Gabrielle; East 17. *Recordings:* Albums: Walter's Room (with Black Science Orchestra), 1994; Ballistic Brothers vs The Eccentric Afros, 1995; London Hooligan Soul (with Ballistic Brothers), 1995; Future Juju (as Black Jazz Chronicles), 1998; Xpress-2 album forthcoming, 2002; Singles: Where Were You (with Black Science Orchestra), 1992; Muzik X-Press, London X-Press, 1993; Altered States EP (with Black Science Orchestra), Rock 2 House, 1994; The Sound, 1995; Tranz Euro Express, 1996; Blacker (with Ballistic Brothers), 1997; AC/DC, 2000; Smoke Machine, Muzikizum, 2001. *Honours:* Muzik Awards, Best Producers, X-Press 2, 2001. *Membership:* MCPS/PRS. *Address:* c/o Skint Records, 73A Middle St, Brighton, Sussex, BN1 4BA, England.

BEGGS Nick; b. 15 Dec. 1961, Winslow, Bucks, England. Musician (bass guitar, chapman stick); Prod.; Writer; Arranger. 1 d. *Musical Education:* Self-taught. *Career:* Kajagoogoo; Ellis Beggs and Howard Iona; Belinda Carlisle. *Compositions:* White Feathers; Islands; Crazy People's Right to Speak; Homelands; The Book of Kells; Beyond These Shores. *Recordings:* Big Bubbles No Troubles, Ellis Beggs and Howard; A Woman and A man, Belinda Carlisle; The Thunderthief, John Paul Jones, 2001. *Publication:* Too Shy, Kajagoogoo, 1983. *Memberships:* Musicians' Union; MCPS; PPL; PRS. *Leisure interest:* Flying Gliders. *Address:* 61 Atheldene Rd, London SW18 3BN, England.

BEGLEY Seamus; b. Dingle, County Kerry, Ireland. Vocalist; Musician (button accordion). *Career:* Brother of Eilin Begley, Maire Begley, Seosaimhin Ni Bheaglaoich and Breandan Begley; Started playing for local dances, aged 14; Long-term collaboration with Steve Cooney.

Recordings: Albums include: An Ciarraioch Mallaithe (with sister Maire), 1972; Plancstai Bhaile Na Buc (with Maire), 1989; features on Vinnie Kilduff, 1990; Meiteal (with Steve Cooney), 1997; Water From The Well, The Chieftains, 2000. *Honours:* Ireland National Entertainment Awards, Most Popular Traditional Act (with Steve Cooney), 1997.

BEIJBOM Lars; b. 1 Aug. 1950, Sweden. Composer; Arranger; Drums. 1 s. *Musical Education:* Berklee College of Music, composition, arranging diploma, 1975. *Career:* Composer and arranged music for large number of radio/television programmes; Big Bands Symphony Orchestra's, Pop/Rock/Jazz; Played, arranged and composed music for artists including: George Russell, Dorothy Donegan, Tomas Ledin, Maritza Horn, Tre Damer, The Swedish Radio Jazz Group, The Danish Radio Big Band, NDR-band; Musical Arranger, Danish star Stig Rossen, 1997-. *Compositions:* Three for Daniel; The Swinging Triangle; In the Long Run; Eat Your Heart Out; Up Your Alley; The Goose is Out; Sweet Sadness; The Fire Within; Alpha and Omega; 11 Peterborough Street. *Recordings:* Subway Baby, 1977; White Orange, 1980; Bright Orange-The Goose is Out, 1983; Beijbom Kroner Big Band, Live in Copenhagen, 1996; Beijbom Kroner Big Band, Opposites Attract, 1998; Tredamer, Duke, We Love You Madly, 1999. *Honour:* Jazz CD of the Year, Danish Jazz Special Critics Choice, for Live in Copenhagen, 1997. *Memberships:* STIM; SKAP; SAMI. *Address:* Flygel 4, 22472 Lund, Sweden.

BEINS Burkhard; b. 22 Oct. 1964, Celle, Germany. Percussionist. *Career:* Various punkbands and experimental music for taped material and percussion, 1980–90; Concerts, Festivals: Second LMC Festival, London; Musique Action, Vendoeuvre; Symposium For Contemporary Music, Kopenhagen; 2:13 Club Festival, Berlin; Recordings with contemporary improvised and composed music; Currently active groups: Activity Center, NUNC, Yarbles, 2:13 Ensemble, Das Kreisen, Sowari, Perlon; Worked With Keith Rowe, John Butcher, Fred Frith, Maggie Nicols, John Bisset, Sven Ake Johansson. *Recordings:* Relay III; NUNC; Yarbles; Activity Center; Perlon. *Current Management:* 2:13 Music, 139 Gibson Gardens, London N16 7HH. *Address:* Ackerstr 2, 10115 Berlin, Germany.

BELAFONTE Harry (Harold George); b. 1 March 1927, Harlem, New York, USA. Singer; Actor; Prod.; Human Rights Activist. m. (1) Marguerite, 1948; (2) Julie Robinson, 1957, 1 s., 3 d. *Education:* Dramatic Workshop of The New School For Social Research. *Career:* Member, American Negro Theater, late 1940s; Performer, New York clubs, early 1950s; Singer, actor, Broadway, 1953; Recording artist, actor, 1954; World-wide tours: UK; Europe; USA; Canada; Australia; New Zealand; Jamaica; Cuba; Actor, films: Bright Road, 1952; Carmen Jones (television version), 1955; Island In The Sun, 1957; Odds Against Tomorrow, 1959; Buck and The Preacher, 1971; Uptown Saturday Night, 1974; First Look, 1984; The Player, 1992; Television appearances include: A Time For Laughter, 1967; Harry and Lena (with Lena Horne), 1969; Tonight With Belafonte, 1960; As producer: Strolling Twenties; Beat Street; Producer, stage: To Be Young Gifted and Black, 1969; Performer, co-ordinator, We Are The World, USA For Africa charity recording, 1985. *Recordings:* Songs include: Banana Boat Song; Matilda; Island In The Sun; Mary's Boy Child; Numerous albums include: Calypso, 1956; Porgy and Bess (with Lena Horne), 1959; Streets I Have Walked, 1963; Don't Stop The Carnival, 1972; Belafonte '89, 1989; Also recorded with Miriam Makeba; Nana Mouskouri. *Honours:* Tony Award, John Murray Anderson's Almanac, Broadway, 1953; Emmy Award (first black recipient), Tonight With Belafonte, 1960; Grammy Award, We Are The World, 1985; American Music Award, We Are The World, 1985; Cultural adviser, Peace Corps (first entertainer chosen), 1988; National Conference of Black Mayors Tribute, 1991; UNICEF's Danny Kaye Award, 1989; Mandela Courage Award (Inaugural presentation), 1990; UNICEF Goodwill Ambassador, 1987. *Address:* c/o William Morris Agency, 1325 Avenue of the Americas, New York, NY 10019, USA.

BELASCO Pete; b. 1 July 1966, Queens, NY, USA. Vocalist; Songwriter; Saxophonist. m. 3 Oct. 1991, 1 d. *Education:* Rutgers University, New Jersey. *Career:* Today, show appearance with Kim Carnes. *Composition:* Lap of Luxury, sung by Diane Wild-Island. *Recordings:* Debut: Get it Together. *Membership:* BMI. *Current Management:* Avenue Management Group, Bruce Garfield, 250 W 57th St Suite 407, New York, NY 10019, USA.

BELCHEV Mikhail Ivanov; b. 13 Aug. 1946, Sofia, Bulgaria. Singer; Composer; Lyricist; Musician (guitar); Dir. m. Christina Konstantinova Belcheva, 15 April 1988, 1 s. *Education:* Hons degrees in: Mining, Geology Engineering; Theatre Directing; Television Directing. *Musical Education:* Bodra Smyana Bulgarian National Youth Choir. *Career:* Solo artiste since 1967–; Tours: Italy, 1970; Spain, 1982; France, 1983; West Berlin, 1986; USA, 1987; Canada, 1988; USSR; Germany; Poland; Czechoslovakia; Romania. *Recordings:* Albums: Where Are Your Friends, 1972; Counterpart, 1977; Re-Qualification, 1988; Cricket On The Pavement, 1993; Man To Hug (lyrics by Mikhail Belchev) 1994; Television biographical musical films: Where Are You Friends, 1973; Counterpart, 1977. *Publications:* Poetry: At First Cock-Crow, 1987; A Man To Hug, 1994.

Honours: Cyril and Methodius Order Highest degree, Golden Orpheus Festival, many awards; Awards, Bratislava and Sopot Festivals. *Memberships:* Bulgarian Artiste Asscn; The Music Author Board of Directors. *Leisure interests:* Collection of paintings and bronze/brass plastic art works.

BELEW Adrian; Musician (guitar); Vocalist; Songwriter; Prod. *Career:* Session musician, 1980s; Singer, guitarist, King Crimson, 1981–84, 1993–; Solo artiste, 1982–; Founder, The Bears, 1986; Producer, Jars of Clay, 1966. *Recordings:* Albums: Solo: Lone Rhino, 1982; Twang Bar King, 1983; Mr Musichead, 1989; Young Lions, 1990; Inner Revolution, 1990; Desire Caught By The Tail, 1991; The Acoustic Adrian Belew, 1995; with King Crimson: Discipline, 1981; Beat, 1982; Three of a Perfect Pair, 1984; Vroom, 1995; Thrak, 1995; B'Boom, 1995; with The Bears: The Bears, 1987; As session musician: with Laurie Anderson: Mister Heartbreak, 1984; Home of The Brave, 1986; with David Bowie: Stage, 1978; Lodger, 1979; Another Face, 1981; with Talking Heads: Remain In Light, 1980; The Name of This Band Is, 1982; with Frank Zappa: In New York, 1978; Sheik Yerbouti, 1979; Yer Are What You Is, 1982; You Can't Do That On Stage Anymore, 1988; The Key, Joan Armatrading, 1983; The Catherine Wheel, David Byrne, 1981; Maybe It's Live, Robert Palmer, 1982; Zoolook, Jean-Michel Jarre, 1984; True Colors, Cyndi Lauper, 1986; Strange Little Girls, Tori Amos, 2001. *Current Management:* Umbrella Artists, PO Box 8385, 2612 Erie Ave, Cincinnati, OH 45208, USA.

BELL Andrew Piran; b. 11 Aug. 1970, Cardiff, Wales. Musician (guitar); Songwriter. m. Idha Övelius, 12 Feb. 1992. *Education:* Banbury Art School, 1988–89. *Musical Education:* Self-taught. *Career:* Singer, songwriter and lead guitarist, rock band Ride, 1988–96; Session musician with Idha, 1992–; Member, Hurricane #1, 1997–99; Member, Oasis, 1999–. *Recordings:* Nowhere, Ride, 1990; Going Blank Again, Ride, 1992; Carnival of Light, Ride, 1994; Melody Inn, Idha, 1994; Tarantula, Ride, 1996; Hurricane #1, 1997; Only The Strongest Will Survive, Hurricane #1, 1999; Familiar To Millions (live), Oasis, 2000; OX4, Ride, 2001.

BELL Andy; b. 25 April 1964. Vocalist; Songwriter. *Career:* Vocalist, Void; Lead vocalist, pop duo Erasure (with Vince Clarke), 1985–; Regular UK and international tours; Performances include: Support to Duran Duran, US tour, 1987; Prince's Trust Rock Gala, NEC Birmingham, 1989; Red Hot and Dance AIDS benefit concert, 1991; Duet with k d lang, BRIT Awards, 1993. *Recordings:* Albums: Wonderland, 1986; The Circus, 1987; Two Ring Circus, 1987; The Innocents, 1988; Wild!, 1989; Chorus, 1991; Pop!-The First 20 Hits, 1992; I Say I Say I Say, 1994; Erasure, 1995; Cowboy, 1996; Loveboat, 2000; Moon and The Sky Plus, 2001; Singles include: Sometimes, 1986; Victim of Love, 1987; Ship of Fools, 1988; A Little Respect, 1988; Drama!, 1989; Chorus, 1991; Love To Hate You, 1991; Breath of Life, 1992; Abba-esque EP (No. 1, UK), 1992; Stay With Me, 1995; Freedom, 2000; Contributor to: Red Hot and Blue (AIDS benefit record); Tame Yourself (animal rights benefit record). *Honours:* BRIT Award, Best British Group, 1989; Ivor Novello Award, Most Performed Work of 1990, Blue Savannah, 1991. *Address:* c/o Mute Records, 429 Harrow Rd, London W10 4RE, England.

BELL Chris; b. 26 Aug. 1960, London, England. Musician (drums). *Career:* Joined Thompson Twins, 1979–82; Tour with King Trigger, 1982; Joined Spear of Destiny, 1982–83; Work with Specimin, 1985; Joined Gene Love Jezebel, 1986–91; Tour, USA, Japan, 1986; Television includes: MTV Awards, Joan Rivers Show, 1986; Tours: UK/Europe, USA, Japan, South America, UK, 1988; USA, supporting Echo and The Bunnymen, New Order, 1987; USA, Europe, UK, supporting Billy Idol, 1990; USA, 1990; Tours, recordings, television, with Big Country, 1991–92; Tour, recording, Nan Vernon, 1992; Tours with Hugh Cornwall, UK, Europe, 1993; France, 1994; UK, 1994; Live work with Phantom Chords, 1994–95; Various sessions, 1995; Live work with Gene Loves Jezebel, 1995. *Recordings:* Albums with Thompson Twins: A Product Of, 1981; Set, 1982; Single: In The Name of Love; Grapes of Wrath, Spear of Destiny, 1982; Single: Ain't That Always The Way, Edwyn Collins, 1985; with Gene Loves Jezebel, The Immigrant, 1985; House of Dolls; Kiss of Life, 1989; Album with Nan Vernon, 1993; Album with Hugh Cornwell, 1995. *Leisure interest:* Checking out places missed when touring. *Address:* 2 Bolingbroke Rd, London W14 OAL, England.

BELL Colin Stewart; b. 11 Sept. 1952, Carrickfergus, County Antrim, Northern Ireland. Record Co Exec. *Education:* BA Hons Drama. *Career:* Publicist, Rogers and Cowan; Manager, Tom Robinson Band; Head of Press, Phonogram UK Ltd; Managing Director, London Records, 1991–98; Manager, Elton John. *Honours:* Leslie Perrin P R Award; Music Week Marketing Award. *Leisure interest:* Theatre. *Current Management:* Elton John Management, 7 King St Cloisters, London W6 0GY, England.

BELL Dennis Lawrence; b. 4 Dec. 1941, New York City, USA. Record Prod.; Musician (keyboard); Music Educator; Personal Man.; Arranger; Conductor; Composer. m. Claudette Washington, 28 April 1979, 1 s., 3 d. *Musical Education:* BM, NYU; Master of Arts, Composition, Queens

College; Piano, arranging, composition, conducting with variety of teachers. *Career:* Television appearances include: Joan Rivers; BBC, One World One Voice; Top of The Pops; with U2: Madison Square Garden; Carnegie Hall; Rattle and Hum; Commercials: Pizza Hut with Aretha Franklin; Roy Rogers; Drakes Company; Give Peace A Chance; Keep Rising To The Top; Videos. *Recordings:* with Tom Browne; Dave Valentine; Doug E. Fresh; U2; Celia Cruz; Give Peace A Chance; Touché; Lee Ritenour; Scrooged film soundtrack. *Publication:* Music Alive. *Honours:* Boystown for Public Service; Bronx Boro President's Award for Community Service. *Memberships:* BMI; National Asscn of Jazz Educators. *Leisure interests:* Cooking; Golf.

BELL Eric; b. 3 Sept. 1947, Belfast, Northern Ireland. Musician (guitar); Singer; Songwriter. *Musical Education:* Self-taught. *Career:* Musician with Van Morrison, Northern Ireland, 1967; Founder member, rock group Thin Lizzy, 1969–74; Co-arranger, Whiskey In The Jar; Television appearance: Top of The Pops; Joined Noel Redding Band, 1976–78. *Recordings:* with Thin Lizzy: Whiskey In The Jar; The Rocker; Collection; Soldier of Fortune; Dedication: The Very Best…; Remembering. *Honours:* Gold album, The Adventures of Thin Lizzy; Silver single, Whiskey In The Jar. *Leisure interests:* Reading; Listening to music. *Address:* 115 Pembroke Ave, Enfield, Middlesex EN1 4EZ, England.

BELL Mark, (Fawn, Clarke); b. Leeds, West Yorkshire, England. Prod.; Remixer. *Career:* Formed LFO with production partner Gez Varley, 1990; Signed to Warp Records; Released debut album, 1991; Collaborations: Bjork; Depeche Mode; Richie Hawtin; Remixed: Art of Noise; Yellow Magic Orchestra; Erasure; Radiohead. *Recordings:* Albums: Frequencies, 1991; Advance, 1996; Singles: LFO, 1990; What Is House, 1991; Tied Up, 1995; Lofthouse EP (as Clarke), 1996. *Address:* c/o Warp Records, Spectrum House, 32–34 Gordon House Rd, London, NW5 1LP, England.

BELL Philip; b. 21 May 1965, Finsbury Park, London, England. Musician (guitar, bass). *Musical Education:* Guitar Institute of Technology, Wapping, London. *Career:* Guitarist, Brothers Like Outlaw; European Tour supporting Arrested Development, 1993; Also festivals including: Fest'in Bahia, Salvador, Brazil, 1992; Citta D'ella Musica, Bari, Italy, 1992; Metropolis, Rotterdam, Netherlands, 1992; Jazz In Sardinia, 1992; Radio and television: Chart Show, 1993; BBC Radio 1 session; Member, Vibe Tribe; Concerts include Phoenix Festivals, UK, 1993–94; with The Filberts, Glastonbury Festival, 1993; Television: TXT, 1994; with Leena Conquest: European Tour supporting Bryan Ferry, 1994. *Recordings:* with Vibe Tribe: Johnny; Our Purpose, 1993; with FM Inc: Call Me Anytime, 1992; Fresh 'n' Funky; Chill Me, 1993; African Wonderland, 1996. *Publications:* Music Journalist, Sounds, 1980–84. *Memberships:* Musicians' Union; PRS; MCPS. *Leisure interest:* Spiritual development. *Address:* 17A Northbrook Rd, London N22 4YQ, England.

BELLAMY David; b. 16 Sept. 1950, Darby, Florida, USA. Vocalist; Songwriter. *Career:* Played R & B clubs, backing Eddie Floyd, Percy Sledge, Little Anthony and the Imperials; Played throughout Southeast USA, with own band, Jericho; Wrote Spiders and Snakes for Jim Stafford, 3m. sales world-wide; Cut demos with Neil Diamond's band; Formed Bellamy Brothers with brother Howard; Most successful duo in country music history; Tours with Loggins and Messina; Doobie Brothers; Beach Boys; Conway Twitty; Collaborated as songwriter with Costas, Don Schlitz and Bobby Braddock; Formed Bellamy Brothers Records; Initiated annual Snake Rattle and Roll Jam, 1989, major charity fundraiser. *Compositions include:* Spiders and Snakes; Sugar Daddy; Do You Love As Good As You Look; Old Hippie; Kids of The Baby Boom. *Recordings:* Singles include: Let Your Love Flow, 1976 (No. 1 in charts in ten countries); If I Said You Had A Beautiful Body Would You Hold It Against Me, 1979; Sugar Daddy, Dancin' Cowboys, 1980; Do You Love As Good As You Look, 1981; For All The Wrong Reasons, 1982; Redneck Girl, 1982; When I'm Away From You, 1983; I Need More of You, 1985; Feelin' The Feelin,' 1985; Too Much Is Not Enough, 1986; Kids of The Baby Boom, 1986; Crazy From The Heart, 1987; Rip Off The Knob, 1993; Dancin', 1996; Lonely Planet, 1999; The 25 Year Collection Vols 1 and 2 (compilations), 2001; 22 albums, 1976–94. *Honours:* Platinum albums, UK, Scandinavia; Gold albums, USA, Austria, Germany, UK, Norway, Sweden; Consistently nominated Duo of the Year, CMA, ACM, 1979–; Record of the Year, If I Said You Had A Beautiful Body, England, 1979; Independent Video of Year, Cowboy Beat, CMT. *Memberships:* ASCAP; AFTRA; AFofM. *Leisure interests:* Collecting Western and Indian artifacts; Travel; Swimming. *Current Management:* Refugee Management International. *Address:* 209 10th Ave S, Suite 347, Nashville, TN 37203, USA.

BELLAMY Howard; b. 2 Feb. 1946, Darby, Florida, USA. Vocalist; Songwriter. m. Ilona. *Career:* Played R & B Clubs, backing Eddie Floyd, Percy Sledge, Little Anthony and the Imperials; Played Southeast USA with own band, Jericho; Became Jim Stafford's road manager; Cut demos with Neil Diamond's band; Formed The Bellamy Brothers with brother David; Most successful duo in country music history; Toured USA with Loggins and Messina; Doobie Brothers; Beach Boys; Conway Twitty; 14

number 1 singles in US country charts; Collaborated with Costa, Don Schlitz and Bobby Braddock; Formed Bellamy Brothers Records; Initiated annual benefit concert, Snake Rattle and Roll Jam, 1989, major local charity fundraiser. *Recordings:* Singles include: Let Your Love Flow, 1976 (No. 1 in charts in ten countries); If I Said You Had A Beautiful Body Would You Hold It Against Me, 1979; Sugar Daddy, 1980; Dancin' Cowboys, 1980; Do You Love As Good As You Look, 1981; For All The Wrong Reasons, 1982; Redneck Girl, 1982; When I'm Away From You, 1983; Old Hippie, 1985; I Need More of You, 1985; Feelin' The Feelin', 1985; Too Much Is Not Enough, 1986; Kids of The Baby Boom, 1986; Crazy From The Heart, 1987; You'll Never Be Sorry, 1989; Rip Off The Knob, 1993; Dancin', 1996; Lonely Planet, 1999; The 25 Year Collection Vols 1 and 2 (compilations), 2001; 22 albums, 1976–94. *Honours:* Consistently nominated Duo of the Year, CMA, ACM, since 1979; Platinum albums, England, Scandinavia; Gold albums, USA, Austria, Germany, UK, Norway, Sweden; Record of the Year, If I Said You Had A Beautiful Body, UK, 1979; Independent Video of 1992, Cowboy Beat, CMT. *Memberships:* ASCAP; AFTRA; AFofM. *Leisure interests:* Travel; Swimming; Collecting Western and Indian artifacts. *Current Management:* Refugee Management, 209 10th Ave S, Suite 347, Nashville, TN 37203, USA.

BELLAMY Matthew James; b. 9 June 1978. Vocalist; Musician (guitar). *Musical Education:* Self-taught. *Career:* Formed group Gothic Plague in adopted hometown of Teignmouth, aged 13; Group became Fixed Penalty then Rocket Baby Dolls before finally settling on name Muse; Released two 1000-copy EPs on UK independent label Dangerous; Signed to Madonna's US label Maverick following lauded UK In The City '98 and New York CMJ festival appearances; Rapid rise to fame followed; Live shows include: Ill-fated Woodstock '99 US festival; Headline slots at UK's Leeds, Reading and T In The Park festivals, 2000; European tours, 2001. *Recordings:* Albums: Showbiz, 1999; Origin of Symmetry, 2001; Singles: Muse EP, 1998; Muscle Museum EP, Uno, Cave, 1999; Sunburn, Unintended, 2000; Plug In Baby, New Born, Bliss, Hyper Music/Feeling Good, 2001. *Honours:* NME Award, Best Newcomer, 2000; Kerrang! Award, Best British Band, 2001. *Current Management:* Taste Media/SJP Management, 263 Putney Bridge Rd, London, SW15 2PU, England. *Internet:* www.muse-official.com.

BELLEST Christian; b. 8 April 1922, Paris, France. Musician (trumpet); Arranger. m. Sally Pearce, 9 Jan. 1962, 1 s. *Education:* CEP. *Musical Education:* Musical studies, harmony, counterpoint, fugas. *Career:* Accompanist, arranger, for singers including Edith Piaf; Yves Montand; Michel Berger; Veronique Sanson; Paul Anka; Television series and films. *Recordings with:* Django Reinhardt; Aux Combelle; Jazz de Paris; Jacques Helian. *Publications:* Co-author, Le Jazz for collection Que Sais-Je; Articles for Les Cahiers Du Jazz. *Membership:* Academie Du Jazz. *Leisure interest:* Home studio. *Address:* 9 rue Victorien Sardou, 75016 Paris, France.

BELLOW Roger David; b. 15 April 1950, Chicago, Illinois, USA. Musician (guitar, violin, mandolin, banjo, bass); Teacher. m. Judy Golombeck, 25 Sept. 1977, divorced. *Education:* BA University of Tennese; Antioch College; Foreign study, Bogotá, Colombia. *Musical Education:* Old Town School of Folk Music, Chicago. *Career:* Cas Walker, TV Show, Knoxville, Tennessee, 1968–70; Kennedy Center Concert, Washington, DC, 1976; Kaustinen International Folk Festival, Finland, 1981; Belize Tour, 1983; University of Chicago, Folk Festival, 1986; Faculty of Augusta Heritage Center, Elkins, W Virginia, 1989–; SC Arts Comm Resident Artist, 1987–; Host, Vintage Country Radio Program, public radio, 1987–2001; Japan Tour, 1993; University of Chicago Folk Festival, 1999; Performing at the Encuentro de Dos Tradiciones in Mexico, March 2000; Performance on Radio México, 2001. *Recordings:* with Revonah: Get In Line Brother, 1980; with Flying Fish: Success Street, 1988; On The Road To Prosperity, 1991; (Japanese recording) The Bay Quintet, 1993; with Augusta Faculty Band: Zombies of Swing, 1994; Allons a Grand Kaplan, with Paul Dudley Kershaw, 1998; Cross Country Swing, with Paul Anastasio, 1999; Snetimental Journey, with Ann Caldwell, 2001. *Publications:* Research published in Bluegrass Unlimited and Journal of Country Music. *Honours:* South Carolina Folk Heritage Award, 1995; SC Grant for Research in Country Music. *Memberships:* AFofM; ROPE (Reunion of Professional Entertainers). *Leisure interest:* Record collecting. *Current Management:* Town and Country Music.

BELMONDO Lionel; b. 19 Aug. 1963, Hyères, France. Musician (saxophones, flute). *Musical Education:* Jazz, Piano and saxophone studies, Conservatory de Toulon. *Career:* Director, School of Music, Centre Vas; Professor in other schools, 1982–90; Moved to Paris, 1990; Sideman for concerts with Michel Legrand; Phil Woods; Toots Thielemans; Dee Dee Bridgewater; Horace Silver; Lew Tabackin; Own quintet with brother Stéphane; Leader, Belmondo Big Band, with brother Stéphane; Television: Belmondo In Concert, on Jazz 6, at M6, 1995. *Recordings include:* Belmondo Quintet; For All Friends, Belmondo Quintet; Love and Peace, Dee Dee Bridgewater; Face The Challenge In Music, 1996; Cyclades, Jean-Loup Longnon, 1996; Jazz Singers 1919–94, 1998. *Honour:* Prix Django Reinhardt, Best French Musician (with brother Stéphane), 1994.

Current Management: KSM (Karen Strugg Management). *Address:* 17 rue des Ecoles, 75005 Paris, France.

BELMONDO Stéphane; b. 8 July 1967, Hyères, France. Musician (trumpet, flugelhorn). m. Elisabeth Kontomanou (singer), 1 s. *Musical Education:* Conservatory, Toulon, Marseilles. *Career:* Member, Big Band Lumiere, conducted by Gil Evans; Sideman and concerts with Michel Legrand Big Band; Chet Baker; Tom Harrell; David Liebman; Dee Dee Bridgewater; Horace Silver; Own quintet with brother Lionel Belmondo; Own Belmondo Big Band, with brother Lionel; Television: Belmondo In Concert, Jazz 6 at M6, 1995. *Recordings:* Belmondo Quintet JAR; For All Friends, Belmondo Quintet; Sideman: Big Band Band Lumiere with Gil Evans; Love and Peace, Dee Dee Bridgewater; Parapluies de Cherbourg, 1996; Face The Challenge In Music, 1996; Cyclades, Jean-Loup Longnon, 1996; Soley Glase, Ziskakan, 1997; Jazz Singers 1919–94, 1998; Moon and Sand, Tom Harrell. *Honour:* Django Reinhardt Award, Best French Musician, with brother Lionel, 1994. *Current Management:* KSM (Karen Strugg Management). *Address:* 17 rue des Ecoles, 75005 Paris, France.

BEN Besiakov; b. 27 Oct. 1956, Copenhagen, Denmark. Musician (Piano and Organ). 1 s. *Composition:* Choo Choo, with Lennart Ginman and Mike Clark. *Recordings:* You Stepped Out of a Dream, 1990; Raney, with Doug Raney, 1996; The Red Light, with Bent Jaedig, 1996; When Granny Sleeps, with Dave Liebman, 1995; Human Beat Boxer, with Niclas Knudsen and Adam Nussbaum, 1997. *Honours:* Ben Webster Prize, 1990; Jasa Prize, 1993. *Membership:* Danish Musicians Asscn. *Leisure interest:* Model flyes. *Address:* GL Vartov Vej 21, 2900 Hellerup, Denmark.

BEN Jorge, (Jorge Duílio Menezes, Jorge Ben Jor); b. 1940, Rio de Janeiro, Brazil. Vocalist; Musician (guitar); Composer; Songwriter. *Career:* Fuses different musical traditions, both Brazilian and international; Music is rhythmically very creative with an African feel combined with rock, samba, baião (music based on northeastern Brazilian folkloric forms) and maracatu (an Afro-Brazilian processional dance); Career started in the early 1960s, when bossa nova was the dominant music, but gained more recognition during MPB (Música Popular Brasileira) era when experimentation and fusing of styles was more accepted; First big hit Mas Que Nada in 1963 covered by Sergio Mendes, who had US hit with the song; Mas Que Nada revived and entered UK chart when the Tamba Trio's recording was used in Nike advertisement during soccer World Cup, 1998; Had many hits in Brazil which firmly established career, 1969–72; Toured internationally many times and has worked with artists including: King Sunny Ade; Os Mutantes; Timbalada. *Compositions:* Mas Que Nada. *Recordings:* Single: Mas Que Nada, 1963; Albums include: Samba Esquema Novo, 1963; Sacundin Ben Samba, 1964; O Bidú, 1967; Jorge Ben, 1969; Forca Bruta, 1970; Ben, 1972; Dez Anos Depois, 1973; A Tabú De Esmerelda, 1974; Samba Nova, 1975; Africa Brasil, 1976; A Banda Do Ze Pretinho, 1978; Salve Simpatia, 1979; Alo Alo Como Vai?, 1980; Dadiva, 1983; Benjor, 1989; Ao Vivo No Rio, 1992; 23, 1993; Homo Sapiens, 1995; Musicas Para Tocar Em Elevador, 1997; Puro Suingue, 2000.

BENATAR Pat, (Patricia Andrzejewski); b. Brooklyn, New York, USA. Vocalist. m. (1) Dennis Benatar, 1972, divorced 1979; (2) Neil Geraldo, 20 Feb. 1982, 1 d. *Education:* Studied health education. *Musical Education:* Brief training opera singer. *Career:* Singer, Holiday Inns, Virginia, 1972–74; Singing waitress in New York Club, Catch A Rising Star; Solo artiste, 1979-. *Recordings:* Singles include: Heartbreaker; You Better Run; Treat Me Right; Love Is A Battlefield; Hell Is For Children; Invincible (soundtrack to film Legend of Billie Jean); Hit Me With Your Best Shot; Sex As A Weapon; We Belong; All Fired Up; Albums include: In The Heat of The Night, 1979; Crimes of Passion, 1980; Precious Time, 1981; Get Nervous, 1982; Live From Earth, 1983; Tropico, 1984; Seven The Hard Way, 1985; Wide Awake In Dreamland, 1988; True Love, 1991; Gravity's Rainbow, 1993; Best of Pat Benatar Vols 1 and 2, 2001; Christmas In America, 2001. *Honours:* 4 Grammy Awards, Best Female Rock Vocal Performance, 1981–84; Grammy Nomination, Female Rock Vocal Performance, Invincible, 1986; Numerous Gold discs. *Current Management:* Lookout Management, 2644 30th St, First Floor, Santa Monica, CA 90405, USA.

BENBOW Steve (Stephen George); b. 29 Nov. 1931, London, England. Singer; Musician (Guitar). m. Sandra Estelle Benbow, 10 Feb. 1976. *Career:* Television appearances on BBC Focus, Blue Peter, Late Night Line Up, Muses with Milligan and Plectrum; Radio appearances on BBC Guitar Club, Saturday Skiffle Club, Saturday Club, Easy Beat, Radio Luxembourg series Have Guitar Will Travel; Stage Show, Spike Milligan meets Steve Benbow, Lyric Theatre, London. *Compositions:* You Can Have Him; Madrid; Pickin' and Grinnin'; I Travel The World. *Recordings:* Admiral Benbow, 1962; I Travel the World, 1963; This, That and the Other, 1964; Irish Songs, double album, 1965; Of Situations and Predicaments, 1967; Friendly Folk, 1971. *Publication:* Guitar Tutor, Folk Music Accompaniment for Guitar, 1965. *Memberships:* Equity; PRS; PAMRA; Musicians' Union. *Leisure interests:* Breeding Old English mastiffs, goats, donkeys, ponies and poultry. *Address:* 55 St Marks Rd, Old Hanwell, London W7 2PN, England.

BENDIX Nicky; b. 22 March 1969, Odense, Denmark. Musician (piano, keyboard); Music Teacher; Composer; Arranger. *Musical Education:* Self-taught; Piano lessons. *Career:* Started composing and playing at age 15; Performed in Jazz/fusion settings with the Danish Radio Big Band, Rudi Smith, Jorge Degas, Uffe Markussen, Henrik Bolberg and Bent Jædig; Own composition, Suite for Mankind, performed on TV2, Denmark in September 1997; Since 1993 has composed and performed music for contemporary dance and multimedia events; Multimedia performer, The Pillar of Shame, 1997; Composed and recorded the music score for the film En Sidste gang, by Jesper Bernt. *Recordings:* Trancework, 1994; with Sunset Yellow: Sunset Yellow, 1995; with Sunset: Sunzet, 1998. *Honour:* Jazz Musician of the Year, FYN, Denmark, 1995. *Membership:* Dansk Musiker Forbund. *Leisure interest:* Gardening. *Current Management:* NB Music. *Address:* Andekæret 160, 5300 Kekteminde C, Denmark.

BENEDETTI Peter Sergio (Pepe); b. 15 July 1938, Greenock, Scotland. Jazz Blues Singer; Musician (tenor saxophone, clarinet). m. Lorna Magner, 14 Feb. 1980, divorced 1983, 1 d. *Education:* College Commerce, 1988–89. *Musical Education:* Mabel Fletcher School of Music-Drama, Liverpool, 1990. *Career:* Musician, Robert Bros Circus, 6 months, 1978; Promotional tour, London, Tony Conn Rockabilly Artiste, 1979; Support Jack Bruce Tour, 1985; Played for: The Undertakers, Liverpool, Played 3 day concerts, Hamburg, West Germany, 1990–91; 6 week tour, Sonny Curtis, Denmark, 1991. *Compositions:* Songwriting: Country/rock; Blues; Rock 'n' roll. *Honours:* Elgin Music Festival (Jazz), Best Male Singer, 1958. *Membership:* Musicians' Union. *Leisure interests:* Swimming; Photography; Films; Cat shows; Flower shows. *Current Management:* Rock/Fairisle Music.

BENET Eric; b. Milwaulkee, Wisconsin, USA. Vocalist. *Career:* Began career as part of Gerard in the late '80s; Formed Benet and released debut album, 1992; Solo career, 1999–; Collaborations: Faith Evans; Tamia; Roy Ayers; Me'Shell Ndegeocello. *Recordings:* Albums: Benet (with Benet), 1992; True To Myself, 1996; A Day In The Life, 1999; Singles: Spiritual Thang, 1996; Georgy Porgy, Why You Follow Me, Spend My Life With You, 1999. *Address:* c/o Warner Music, The Warner Building, 28 Kensington Church St, London, W8 4EP, England.

BÉNEY Jean-Christophe; b. 2 Oct. 1969, Boulogne, Billancourt, France. Jazz Musician (saxophone). *Musical Education:* Conservatoire National Supérieure de Musique, Paris. *Career:* Le Pom (Scene et Marnaise de Création Musicale); Orchestra co-directed by François Jeanneau, Patrice Caratini; Philippe Macé; Andy Emler; Jean-Christophe Béney Quartet (Pierre de Bethmann, Jules Bikoko; Benjamin Hénocq); Laurent Coq Quartet; Belmonder Big Band; Antoine Heuve Big Band; Nicolas Folmer Quintet. *Recordings:* Hard Scores, Patrice Caratini, 1996; Le Pom, 1997; Sérénade, Philippe Sellam, 1997; Le Pom, 1997; Tenor Joke, with Jean-Christophe Béney Quartet, 1998; Jaywalker, with Laurent Coq Quartet, 1998. *Honours:* Prix de Soloiste, Concours National de Jazz de la Défense, 1995; Nominated, Django d'Or, 1998. *Memberships:* SACEM; ADAMI; SPEDIDAM. *Current Management:* C C PRoduction, 70 Ave du 11 novembre, 94170 Le Perreux-sur-Marne, France. *Address:* 2 rue Cyrano de Bergerac, 75018 Paris, France.

BENHAMOU Lionel; b. 27 Aug. 1956, Paris, France. Musician (guitar). m. Helene Ruyer, 30 Oct. 1987, 1 s., 1 d. *Musical Education:* Music school, harmony with Mr Weber. *Career:* Tours with: Gil Evans; Martial Solal; Bernard Lubat; Many festivals in Europe; Plays with Orchestre National de Jazz, directed by Laurent Cugny. *Recordings:* with Lionel Benhamou Trio: Fruits Cuits, Fruits Crus; 5 albums with Orchestre National de Jazz; Yestenow, conducted by Laurent Cugny; Rhythm-A-Ning, with Gil Evans; Santander, Laurent Cugny; Golden Hair, Gil Evans; 20 Ans de Jazz En France. *Publications:* 10 Themes et Improvisations Pour Le Saxophone. *Membership:* UMJ. *Leisure interests:* Computers; Mycology; Cycling. *Address:* 75 rue de Turenne, 75003 Paris, France.

BENNETT Allan Charles; b. 12 March 1968, London, England. Musician (tenor, soprano saxophones); Singer; Songwriter. 1 d. *Musical Education:* Grade 5 Practical, Grade 5 Theory, Music O Level; Sound Engineering Foundation Course. *Career:* Waltham Forest Assembly Hall, oboist, Waltham Forest Intermediate Band, 1976; Saxophonist, community reggae band Reality, 1987; Lead saxophonist, reggae band Jimmy Mac, 1991; Polish Club Manchester; Palm Tree Club, Tottenham; Singer, songwriter, saxophonist, Tusu, 1989; Marquee; Porter House, Nottinghamshire; Lead saxophonist, Tribal Union, 1994; Sydenham Wells Park; Amersham Arms the gig; Allan B Promotions and live shows, 1992–; Solo saxophonist, Allan and Lea, 1994; Kingshead Theatre Pub. *Recordings:* with Jimmy Mac: Little Bit of Your Time, 1991; with Tusu: August The Two (songs include: Dream Crazy; Catch 66; Fascination); Slipping Away, 1992; Gone To Earth: Be The Dub, 1994; Humanoia: Nothing More, Nothing Less, 1992. *Membership:* Musicians' Union. *Leisure interests:* Weight training; Swimming; Football; Travel; Sightseeing; Theatre; Restaurants. *Address:* 22 Gaitskill House, The Drive, Walthamstow, London E17 3DD, England.

BENNETT Brian Laurence; b. 9 Feb. 1940, London, England. Musician (drums); Composer. m. Margaret Tuton, 2 s., 1 d. *Musical Education:* Self-taught. *Career:* Backed Gene Vincent, Eddie Cochran on tour; Drummer, Cliff Richard and The Shadows, 1961–; Session drummer, 1970s-80s; Composer of film and television music; Arranger, producer; Brian Bennett Band support to Cliff Richard, UK, Japan, USSR, 1970s; Played with Hank Marvin as The Shadows, Knebworth, 1990; British tour, joined by Hank Marvin, also son Warren Bennett on keyboards. *Compositions include:* Film themes: Summer Holiday; Wonderful Life; Finders Keepers; The Harpist, 1997; Score: The Boys; Soundtrack: French Dressing; The American Way; Terminal Choice; Television soundtracks: Dallas; Knots Landing; Ruth Rendell Mysteries; Nomads of The Wind, BBC2; Pulaski; The Knock; The Sweeney; Minder; Global Sunrise, BBC, 1997; Living Britain, BBC 2; Dirty Work, BBC, 2000. *Honours:* 3 Ivor Novello Awards: Summer Holiday, 1962; 25 Years in British Music, 1983; Best TV Theme, Ruth Rendell Mysteries, 1989. *Memberships:* PRS; MCPS; APC; MPA; SODS. *Leisure interest:* Golf. *Address:* 91 Tabernacle St, London EC2A 4JN, England.

BENNETT Easther; Vocalist. m. Shane Lynch, 1998. *Career:* Singer, UK all-female vocal group Eternal, 1992-. *Recordings:* Albums: Always and Forever, 1993; Power of a Woman, 1995; Before The Rain, 1997; Greatest Hits, 1998; Eternal, 1999; Essential Eternal (compilation), 2001; Singles: Stay, 1993; Power of a Woman, 1995; I Am Blessed, 1995; Good Thing, 1996; Secrets, 1996; Don't You Love, 1997; I Wanna Be The Only One (No. 1, UK), 1997; Angel of Mine, 1997; What'cha Gonna Do, 1999; Mind Odyssey. *Honours:* BRIT Award Nominations: Best Group, Best Newcomers, Best Album, Best Dance Act, 1995; Best Dance Act, 1996; Smash Hits Award; International Dance Award, Dance Act of The Year, 1995; Only UK act to have 6 Top 15 hits from debut album.

BENNETT Phil; b. 28 Sept. 1958, Singapore. Singer; Songwriter; Musician (Keyboards). m. Fifi, 4 July 1992. *Career:* Band Member: Helicopters, mid 1980s; Love Bites, 1990s; Witness, 1997; Support shows with: Duran Duran, Elvis Costello, Joe Jackson, Wreckless Eric, Sandi and the Sunsets, Midnight Oil, Church, Gang Gajang, Models, Jimmy Barnes; Member, PillBox, 1998. *Compositions:* Eyewitness, 1997; Carved in Stone, 1997. *Recordings:* Albums: The Helicopters, 1982; Great Moments in Aviation, 1984; Never Seen Eyes, solo, 1990; Kiss the Feet, 1995; Stories from the South, Witness, 1998; Singles: Eyewitness, Lovebites, 1997; Eyewitnes, Witness, 1998; Carved in Stone, Witness, 1998. *Honours:* Sonics Magazine on Cue Award, 1990; Australia Day Award, 1993. *Membership:* Australian Performing Rights Asscn. *Leisure interests:* Rolling Stones; Rhinos. *Current Management:* Mischief Management, 8 Michael Court, Shelley 6148, West Australia.

BENNETT Rex; b. 16 Dec. 1920, Victoria, London. Musician (Drums). m. Olive Rosa Bennett, 1 May 1946, 1 d. *Musical Education:* Self-taught. *Recordings:* Sandie Shaw; Brotherhood of Man; Crispin St Peter; Ray Conniff in Britain; Singalong with Max; Bring Me Sunshine, Morecambe and Wise; Dave Dee Dozy Mick and Tich; Jonathan King; Anita Harris; Everly Bros; Kenny Ball; Acker Bilk; Johnny Halliday; Mike Batt; Harold Geller; Vince Hill; Shirley Bassey; Maynard Ferguson with Strings; Matt Monro; Tony Blackburn; Cliff Richard; George Martin; Madmovies for Bob Monkhouse; Numerous backing tracks for most American jazz musicians. *Leisure interests:* Jazz; Sailing. *Address:* 1 Ellery Close, Cranleigh, Surrey, GU6 8DF, England.

BENNETT Richard; b. 1951, Chicago, IL, USA. Musician (Guitar); Prod.; Arranger; Writer. *Musical Education:* Taught by Forrest Skaggs. *Career:* Record Producer, Musician – Session and touring; Recording and touring with Neil Diamond in Los Angeles, 1971–88. *Recordings:* The Red Road, Bill Miller, 1994; Raven In the Snow, Bill Miller, 1995; A Native Suite, Bill Miler, 1995; Kim Richey, Kim Richey, 1995; Silvertone, Steve Earle, 1995; Capitol, High and Dry, Marty Brown; Wild Kentucky Skies, Marty Brown; Cryin', Lovin', Leavin', Marty Brown; Hillbilly Rock, Marty Stuart; Tempted, Marty Stuart; This One's Gonna Hurt You, Marty Stuart; Come on Joe, Jo-El Sonnier; Have A Little Faith, Joe-El Sonnier; Lost and Profound, Lost and Profound; Memory Thieves, Lost and Profound; A Joyful Noise, The Sullivan's; Music Makin' Mama, Jim Silvers; Everybody Knows, Prairie Oyster; Plectrasonics, Nashville Mandolin Ensemble; Sessions: Billy Pilgrim, 1994; Mark Knopfler and Neil Diamond, 1995. *Current Management:* Dennis Muirhead, Muirhead Management, 202 Fulham Rd, Chelsea, London SW10 9PJ, England.

BENNETT Tony; b. 3 Aug. 1926, Queens, New York, USA. Vocalist. *Education:* High School of Industrial Arts, Manhattan; Vocal Studies, American Theater Wing School. *Career:* Debut in nightclub, 1946; Spotted by Bob Hope; Numerous live and television appearances, hit singles and awards. *Recordings:* Singles: Because of You; Rags to Riches; Cold, Cold Heart; I Wanna Be Around; The Good Life; Who Can I Turn To (When Nobody Needs Me); I Left My Heart in San Francisco; Albums: Forty Years: The Artistry of Tony Bennett, 1997; All Time Hall of Fame Hits, 1997; If I Ruled the World: Songs for the Jet Set, 1997; All-time Greatest

Hits, 1997; Tony Bennett at Carnegie Hall, 1997; This is Jazz, 1998; The Playground, 1998; Bennett Sings Ellington/Hot and Cool, 1999; Playin' With My Friends, 2001. *Publications:* What My Heart Has Seen, paintings, 1996; The Good Life, autobiography, 1998. *Honours:* Eight Grammy Awards; Emmy Award; Cable Ace Award for television special. *Memberships:* Save the Rainforest; Project for Walden Woods; Juvenile Diabetes Foundation; American Cancer Society.

BENNETT Vernie; b. 1972. Vocalist. *Education:* Studied law. *Career:* Singer, UK all-female vocal group Eternal, 1992-. *Recordings:* Albums: Always and Forever, 1993; Power of a Woman, 1995; Greatest Hits, 1997; Before The Rain, 1997; Power of a Woman, 1998; Eternal, 1999; Essential Eternal (compilation), 2001; Singles: Stay, 1993; Power of a Woman, 1995; I Am Blessed, 1995; Secrets, 1996; Good Thing, 1996; Angel of Mine, 1997; Don't You Love, 1997; I Wanna Be The Only One (No. 1, UK), 1997; What'cha Gonna Do, 1999. *Honours:* BRIT Award Nominations: Best Group, Best Newcomers, Best Album, Best Dance Act, 1995; Best Dance Act, 1996; International Dance Award, Dance Act of The Year, 1995; Smash Hits Award; Only UK act to have 6 top 15 hits from debut album.

BENNETT Warren; b. 4 July 1962, Palmers Green, London, England. Composer; Musician. m. Jane Catherine, 18 May 1991, 2 d. *Career:* Music for television includes Wuthering Heights, London's Burning, Ambassador, The Knock, Staying Alive, Birds of a Feather; Arranger, Hank Marvin albums Into the Light, Heartbeat, Plays Cliff, Plays Holly, Plays Lloyd-Webber and Tim Rice; Arranger, Darren Day album Summer Holiday; Concert tours with Hank Marvin, 1994, 1995, 1997, 1998. *Recordings:* Solo: Secrets of The Heart; Pathways To Love; Close to the Hedge, with Mark Griffiths; Classical Guitar Moods, with Mirage. *Address:* Waffles Music Ltd, 91 Tabernacle St, London EC2A 2BA, England.

BENNETT Willie P; b. 26 Oct. 1951, Toronto, Ontario, Canada. Songwriter; Musician (harmonica, mandolin, guitar). *Musical Education:* Self-taught. *Career:* Radio appearances: CBC Radio National, Toronto: The Entertainers; Morningside; Prime Time; Six Days On the Road; Swingin' On A Star, Murray Mclaughlin; Touch The Earth; CFTO TV: Lifetime; CFPL TV: Morning Break; CBCTV: Ninety Minutes Live, Peter Gzowsky; Festivals: Ontario: Canadian Music; Carlisle Bluegrass; Festival of Friends; Home Country Folk; Mariposa Folk; Northern Lights; Northwinds; Ottawa Folk; Summerfolk; Alberta: Calgary Folk; Edmonton Folk; Northwest Territories: Folk On The Rocks; Saskatchewan: Redberry Folk and Country; British Columbia: Vancouver Folk; Manitoba: Winnipeg Folk. *Recordings:* As artist: Trying To Start Out Clean; Blackie and The Rodeo King; Hobo's/Taunt; The Lucky Ones; Collectibles; Take My Own Advice; As musician with artists: Fred J Eaglesmith; Robert Atyeo; Joe Hall; The Dixie Flyers; Also appears on: Slightly Haunted, 1996; She and She and She, 1996; Flying Jenny, 1997; Lipstick, Lies and Gasoline, 1997; Painter Passing Through, 1998; Industrial Lullaby, 1998. *Honours:* CCMA Award Song of the Year: Hello, So Long Goodbye, 1990; CCMA Nomination Special Instrument: Harmonica, 1994. *Memberships:* AFofM; ACTRA; Canadian Country Music Asscn. *Leisure interests:* Running; Painting; Travelling. *Current Management:* Dark Light Music Ltd. *Address:* 51 Bulwer St, Toronto, ON M5T 1A1, Canada.

BENNINGTON Chester; b. 20 March 1976, Phoenix, Arizona, USA. Vocalist. m. Samantha. *Career:* Vocalist with Grey Daze group prior to successful audition for California-based act Xero; Became Hybrid Theory and signed to Warner Bros, Spring 2000; Band immediately sent to professional studio; Further name change to Linkin Park prior to first record releases; Incessant promotional activity since release of album; Live shows include: Family Values and Ozzfest tours; KROQ Acoustic Christmas Concert 2001; many international dates; TV specials include: Live At The Fillmore; Reverb; Currently resides in Los Angeles, California. *Recordings:* Albums: with Grey Daze: Wake Me, 1994; No Sun Today, 1997; with Linkin Park: Hybrid Theory, 2000; Singles: Hybrid Theory (Acoustic EP), 2000; One Step Closer, Crawling, Papercut, In The End, 2001. *Honours:* Over 10m. world-wide sales of debut album to end of 2001; Billboard Award, Best Modern Rock Artist, 2001; Rock Bear Awards: Best International Band; Best International Album, 2001; Kerrang! Award, Best International Newcomer, 2001; Rolling Stone Award, Best Hard Rock/ Metal Band, 2001. *Current Management:* Andy Gould Management, 8484 Wilshire Blvd #425, Beverly Hills, CA 90211, USA. *Internet:* www.linkinpark.com.

BENOIT Blue Boy, (Benoît Billot); b. 24 May 1946, Paris, France. Singer; Musician (harmonica, guitar). 2 d. *Education:* Ecole Des Beaux Arts, Paris. *Career:* Harmonica with: Stevie Wonder; Carole King; James Taylor; Albert King; 1970–72; Plays with Zachery Richard, 1972; First band: Benoît Blue Boy and The Tortilleurs, 1978. *Recordings:* Benoît Blue Boy, 1978; Original, 1979; Le Blues du Vendeur de Blues, 1981; Plaisir Simple, 1982; Tortillage, 1986; BBB et les Toit Cleurs, 1988; Parlez Vouz Français?, 1990; Plus Tard Dans La Soirée, 1992; Couvert de Bleus, 1994. *Memberships:* SACEM; ADAMI. *Leisure interest:* Antiquities. *Current Management:* Denis Leblond. *Address:* c/o Musiques Bleues, 16 rue Jacquemunt, 75017 Paris, France.

BENOIT Tab; b. 17 Nov. 1967, Baton Rouge, Louisiana, USA. Blues/Rock Singer; Musician (Guitar, Harmonica). *Career:* Guitarist, various country, rock and blues bands, Houma, Louisiana, 1986–89; Solo Career, New Orleans, Louisiana, 1990–; Appears on Strike a Deep Chord compilation CD, 1991; TV Debut on Baywatch Nights, 1993; Songs featured on TV in Melrose Place, Party of Five, Northern Exposure, Beverly Hills 90210, Baywatch. *Recordings:* Strike a Deep Chord: Blues Guitars for the Homeless, 1991; Nice and Warm, 1992; What I Live For, 1994; Standing on the Bank, 1995; Live: Swampland Jam, 1997; Homesick for the Road, 1999. *Membership:* Screen Actors Guild. *Leisure interests:* Auto racing; Golf. *Current Management:* Thunderbird Management Group LLC. *Address:* c/o 1245 Park Ave, Suite 10 E, New York, NY 10128, USA.

BENSON George; b. 22 March 1943, Pittsburgh, Pennsylvania, USA. Musician (guitar); Vocalist. *Career:* Session musician, Pittsburgh; Guitarist with Brother Jack McDuff; Session work with Herbie Hancock, Wes Montgomery, 1966; Solo artist, 1966–; Regular world-wide tours; Major concerts include: Rock In Rio Festival, 1983; JVC Jazz Festival, Newport, USA, 1990; North Sea Jazz Festival, Netherlands, 1991; Guitar Legends, Seville, Spain, 1991. *Recordings:* Singles include: This Masquerade; Nature Boy; Give Me The Night; Love X Love; Turn Your Love Around; On Broadway; Love Ballad; Moody's Mood; In Your Eyes; Love All The Hurt Away (duet with Aretha Franklin); Never Give Up On A Good Thing; The Greatest Love of All; Lady Love Me; Feel Like Makin' Love; Shiver; Albums: Its Uptown, 1966; Benson Burner, 1966; Giblet Gravy, 1967; Tell It Like It Is, 1969; The Other Side of Abbey Road, 1970; Beyond The Blue Horizon, 1972; Good King Bad, 1973; Bad Benson, 1974; Supership, 1975; Breezin' (No. 1, USA), 1976; Benson and Farrell (with jazz flautist Joe Farrell), 1976; George Benson In Concert – Carnegie Hall, 1977; In Flight, 1977; Weekend In LA, 1978; Livin' Inside Your Love, 1979; Give Me The Night, 1981; George Benson Collection, 1981; In Your Eyes, 1983; 20/ 20, 1985; The Love Songs (No. 1, UK), 1985; While The City Sleeps, 1986; Collaboration, 1987; Twice The Love, 1988; Tenderly (No. 1, USA Jazz chart), 1989; Big Boss Band, 1990; Midnight Moods – The Love Collection, 1991; Love Remembers, 1993; The Most Exciting New Guitarist On The Jazz, 1994; Take Five, 1995; Live and Smokin', 1995; California Dreamin', 1996; That's Right, 1996; Lil' Darlin', 1996; Talkin' Verve, 1997; Essentials, 1998; Standing Together, 1998; Masquerade, 1998; Masquerade Is Over, 1999; Love and Jazz, 1999; Live At Casa Caribe, 2000; Absolute Benson, 2000; All Blues, 2001; Guest musician, Back On The Block, Quincy Jones, 1991. *Honours include:* Grammy Awards: Best R & B Instrumental, 1976, 1980; Record of the Year, 1976; Best Pop Instrumental, 1976, 1984; Best R & B Male Vocal Performance, 1978, 1980; Best Jazz Voval Performance, 1980; Best Jazz Instrumental Performance, 1991. *Current Management:* Ken Fritz Management, 648 N Robertson Blvd, Los Angeles, CA 90069, USA.

BENSON Ray; b. 16 March 1951, Philadelphia, Pennsylvania, USA. Musician (guitar); Vocalist; Record Prod.; Actor; Man. m. Diane Carr, 27 March 1983, 2 s. *Education:* 1 year Antioch College. *Career:* Leader, lead singer, Asleep At The Wheel, for 25 years; Producer, 9 Asleep At The Wheel albums, 1973–93; Also producer for George Strait; Ricky Van Shelton; Sweethearts of the Rodeo; k d lang; Aaron Neville and Rob Wasserman; Bruce Hornsby and Willie Nelson; Darden Smith; Don Walser; 8 film scores; Commercials include: Anheuser-Busch products, Coors, Delta Airlines, Pepsi Cola, Levi's Jeans; Actor, 4 music videos; Numerous television appearances include: Austin City Limits, with band Asleep At The Wheel; Wild Texas Wind; Nashville Now; Johnny Carson; Executive Director and Co-Producer, Texas Festival, Kennedy Centre, 1991. *Recordings:* Albums: Coming Right At Ya, 1973; Asleep At The Wheel, 1974; Texas Gold, 1975; The Wheel, 1977; Served Live, 1979; Framed, 1980; Drivin', 1980; Pasture Prime, 1985; Asleep At The Wheel 10, 1987; Western Standard Time, 1988; Keepin' Me Up Nights, 1990; Live and Kickin', 1992; Route 66, 1992; The Swingin' Best of Asleep At The Wheel, 1992; Tribute To The Music of Bob Wills and The Texas Playboys, 1993; Still Swingin', 1994; The Wheel Keeps On Rollin', 1995; Minstrel Man From Georgia, 1996; Texas Top Hand, 1996; Way Out West, 1996; Swing, 1997; Live Back to the Future Now, 1997; Down At The Sky-Vue Drive In, 1998; Horse Whisperer, 1998; Songs of Forbidden Love, 1998; Fiddle Fire, 1998; Global Voices, 1998; More, 1999. *Honours:* Academy of Country Music Award, 1977; Buddy Award, 1985; 4 Grammy Awards; 3 Grammy Nominations; CMA Nominations, 1975–80, 1994; Western Swing Society Hall of Fame, 1994; Academy of Country Music Nomination, 1994. *Memberships:* Trustee, NARAS; Board Mem., R & B Foundation. *Leisure interest:* Golf. *Current Management:* Bismeaux Productions, PO Box 463, Austin, TX 78767, USA.

BENSUSAN Pierre; b. 30 Oct. 1957, Oran, French Algeria. Musician (guitar); Singer; Composer. m. Doatea Cornu, 22 June 1985, 1 s. *Musical Education:* Self-taught. *Career:* Festivals include: Montreux, Nyon, (Switzerland); Musiques Métisses d'Angouleme (France); Jazz Festivals: Montréal; Edmonton (Canada); Brussels; Guitar Festivals: Liege, Grand, (Belgium); Milwaukee (USA): Tel-Aviv (Israel); Paris, Nice (France); Festival Inter-Celtic de Lorient (France); Zenith-Paris (as Jacques

Higelin's guest); Boston; Germany (Stockfish tour); Bern; Lanzburg; Eppalinges (Switzerland); Summer Banks Festival, London; Vancouver, Toronto (Canada); Polymusicales de Bollene; Bergamo (Italy); Rotterdam (Netherlands); Flanders Festival, Grand (Belgium); Appeared with or played with artistes including: Suzanne Vega; Jacques Higelin; Paco de Lucia; Carla Bley; Larry Corryell; Philip Catherine; Doc Watson; John Renbourn and David Bromberg; Nana Vasconcelos; Oregon; Uzeb; Taj Mahal; Alan Stivell; Al Stewart; Bobby Thomas; Didier Malherbe. *Recordings:* Près de Paris; Pierre Bensusan 2; Musiques; Solilai; Spices; Wu Wei; Live an a New Morning; Nice Feeling. *Publications:* The Guitar Book; Dagad Music; 3 videos: The Guitar of Pierre Bensusan, Vol. 1 and 2; Pierre Bensusan in Concert, A World of Celtic Fingerstyle Guitar. *Honours:* Grand Prix du Disque, Montreux Festival, 1976. *Address:* B P 232, 02406 Chateau Thierry Cedex, France.

BENTZON Nikolaj; b. 21 Feb. 1964, Copenhagen, Denmark. Jazz Musician (piano); Composer. m. Agnethe Koch, 3 July 1993, 1 s., 2 d. *Musical Education:* Performance Diploma, Berklee College of Music, Boston, USA. *Career:* Member of Danish Radio Jazz Orchestra, 1990–; Leader of Nikolaj Bentzon Trio, 1989; Nikolaj Bentzon and The Scandinavian Connection, 1992–; The Nikolaj Bentzon Brotherhood, 1995; Nikolai Bentzon Constitution, 1997 with Herbie Hancock Headhunters' rhythm section Paul Jackson (bass) and Mike Clarke (drums); 3 years with Ernie Wilkin's Almost Big Band; Debut performance of Bob Brookmeyer's November Music, written for Nikolaj Bentzon, 24 Nov 1994, Radio House, Copenhagen. *Recordings:* Albums: with Nikolaj Bentzon Trio: Pianoforte, Between Us, Triskelos, Nexus; 1 album with Nikolaj Bentzon and The Scandinavian Connection; 1 album with Nikolaj Bentzon Brotherhood; 1 album featuring Mike Clark and Paul Jackson; Bentzon album featuring Headhunter greats Paul Jackson, Mike Clarke, 1998. *Honours:* Best soloist, Dunkerque Jazz Festival, 1983; Jacob Gade Award, 1983; Oscar Peterson Jazz Award, 1985; Danish Society for Jazz, Rock and Folk Music Hon. Award, 1991. *Current Management:* Anders Tidemann, Word of Mouth. *Address:* Grundtvigsvej 27B, suite 4mf, 1864 Copenhagen, Denmark.

BERAUD Marie Laure; b. 22 Jan. 1959, Lyon, France. Singer. 2 s. *Education:* Degree Languages and History of Arts, University, Paris. *Career:* Four-month tour including France; Belgium; Netherlands; Germany; Switzerland; USA (Ballroom Club, New York), 1992; Television apperances include: Nulle Part Ailleurs, with Antoine de Gaunes, 1992. *Recordings:* Album: Turbigo 12–12, 1992; Singles: Viens Simon; Les Immortelles; Macadam Ramdam, 1992. *Honour:* Academie Charles Cros First Album Prize, 1992. *Membership:* SACEM. *Leisure interests:* Painting; Poetry; Drawings. *Current Management:* Cyril Prieur, Talent Sorcier. *Address:* Talent Sorcier, 3 rue des Petites Écuries, 75010 Paris, France.

BERENGUER José; b. 21 Oct. 1955, Barcelona, Spain. Musician (guitar). *Education:* PhD, Clinical Psychology, Medicine. *Musical Education:* Composer, computer, electroacoustical music. *Career:* Autumno Musicale, Como, Italy; Internationale Fenienkurse-Danmstadt, Germany; Synthèse, Bourges, France; Festival International de Músicadel Segle XX, Barcelona, Spain; Puntope En Cuentro, Madrid, Spain; Para Lelo Madrid. *Recordings:* Klängé, 1993; Antropometria Don Quichotte; Spira; Constellacions; Silence. *Honours:* TIME of CIM/UNESCO; Electroacoustic Music Prize, Bourges. *Memberships:* Chairman of Ascociacion de Musica Electroacoustica de Espana; Vice-chairman of Associaó Catacana de Compositors; International Electroacoustic Music Academy of Bourges. *Current Management:* Côchlea. *Address:* Sardeeva 516 6e 2a, 08024 Barcelona, Spain.

BERESFORD Steve; b. 6 March 1950, Wellington, Shropshire. Musician (Piano). *Education:* BA, York University. *Career:* Worked on a large number of film soundtracks, concerts, recordings. *Compositions:* I Was There; Unremarkable; Thanks to Minnie; My Hawaiian Bath Tub Melody; Pentimento; Avril Brisé. *Recordings:* Cue Sheets; Short in the UK; The Bath of Surprise; Museum of Towing and Recovery; Fish of the Week. *Memberships:* PRS; MCPS; PAMRA; MU. *Address:* 62 Oxford Gardens, London, W10 5UN, England.

BERG Shelton Glen; b. 18 Aug. 1955, Cleveland, OH, USA. Pianist; Educator; Composer; Arranger. *Education:* MM, Piano Performance, University of Houston, 1979; BM, Piano Performance, University of Houston, 1977. *Career:* Chair, Jazz Studies, University of Southern California, 1991–; Composer: Fudge, ABC Television Series, A League of Their Own, CBS Television; Orchestra for Film: Edwards and Hunt; President: International Association of Jazz Education, 1996–98. *Compositions:* Numerous compositions for Jazz Combos, Chorus and Big Band. *Recordings:* as Pianist: The Joy, with Bill Watrons; A Time for Love; Space Available. *Publications:* Jazz Improvisation: The Goal – Note Method, 1989; Numerous articles in Jazz Educators Journal and Piano and Keyboard Magazines. *Honours:* Finalist, 1988 Great American Jazz Piano Competition; Commission – Theme Song of 1986 US Olympia

Festival. *Memberships:* IAJE; MENC. *Current Management:* Open Door Management. *Address:* 3545 Downing Ave, Glendale, CA 91208, USA.

BERG Terje; b. 24 Jan. 1972, Trondheim, Norway. Musician (bass). *Education:* College. *Career:* Started Hedge Hog, 1989; Toured Europe, 1994, 1995. *Recordings:* Erase, 1992; Surprise, 1992; Primal Gutter, 1993; Mercury Red, 1994; Mindless, 1994; The Healing EP, 1995; Thorn Cord Wonder, 1995. *Leisure interest:* Paragliding. *Current Management:* Martin Aam, Hedge Hogment. *Address:* Hedge Hog, PO Box 683, 7001 Trondheim, Norway.

BERGGREN Jonas 'Joker'; b. Sweden. Musician (keyboards); Songwriter; Vocalist. *Career:* Member, Ace of Base, 1990-. *Recordings:* Albums: Happy Nation, 1993; The Bridge, 1995; Made In Sweden, 1996; Cruel Summer, 1998; Flowers, 1999; Greatest Hits, 2000; Singles: Wheel of Fortune; All That She Wants (No. 1, UK), 1993; Lucky Love; The Sign, Don't Turn Around, Cruel Summer, Life Is A Flower, Always Have Always Will; No. 1 records in UK; US; Canada; Australia; New Zealand; Israel; Argentina; Europe. *Honours:* Highest-ever world-wide sales for a debut album (Happy Nation, 19m.); Platinum discs world-wide. *Current Management:* Siljemark Production AB, Gårdsvägen 4, 171 52 Solna, Sweden.

BERGGREN Linn (Malin); b. 1970, Sweden. Vocalist. *Career:* Singer, Ace of Base, 1990-. *Recordings:* Albums: Happy Nation, 1993; The Bridge, 1995; Made In Sweden, 1996; Cruel Summer, 1998; Flowers, 1999; Greatest Hits, 2000; Singles: Wheel of Fortune; All That She Wants (No. 1, UK), 1993; Lucky Love; The Sign, Don't Turn Around, Cruel Summer, Life Is A Flower, Always Have Always Will; No. 1 records in UK; US; Canada; Australia; New Zealand; Israel; Argentina; Europe. *Honours:* Highest-ever world-wide sales for a debut album (Happy Nation, 19m.); Platinum discs world-wide. *Current Management:* Siljemark Production AB, Gårdsvägen 4, 171 52 Solna, Sweden.

BERGH Totti; b. 5 Dec. 1935, Oslo, Norway. Musician (tenor, soprano, alto saxophones). m. Laila Dalseth, 1 June 1963, 2 d. *Career:* Jazz artist; Television and radio appearances in Scandinavia; Concerts include: Playboy Jazz Festival; Sacramento Jazz Festival; Caribbean Cruises; Molde Jazz Festival; Oslo Jazz Festival; Jakarta Jazz Festival; Currently fronting own group with singer (wife) Laila Dalseth. *Recordings:* with Bengt Hallberg's Swinging Swedes: We Love Norway, 1977; with Laila Dalseth/Louis Stewart Quintet: Daydreams, 1984; I Hear A Rhapsody, 1985; with Al Cohn: Tenor Gladness, 1986; with George Masso, Major Holley: Major Blues, 1990; with Plas Johnson: On The Trail, 1992; with Joe Cohn: Remember, 1995; with Laila Dalseth/Philip Catherine Sextet: A Woman's Intuition, 1995.

BERGMAN Alan; b. Brooklyn, New York, USA. Lyricist; Writer. m. Marilyn Keith, 2 d. *Musical Education:* BA, Music, University of North Carolina. *Career:* Collaborated with Marilyn Bergman; Michel Legrand; Dave Grusin; Marvin Hamlisch; Henry Mancini; Johnny Mandel; John Williams; David Shire; Neil Diamond; James Newton Howard; Quincy Jones; Lew Spence; Sammy Fain; Billy Goldenberg; Lalo Schifrin; Norman Luboff; Sergio Mendes. *Compositions:* Songs include: That Face; Yellow Bird; Nice 'n' Easy; The Windmills of Your Mind; The Way We Were; The Summer Knows; What Are You Doing The Rest of Your Life?; Summer Me, Winter Me; So Many Stars; You Must Believe In Spring; Places That Belong To You; You Don't Bring Me Flowers; Little Boy Lost; In The Heat of The Night; The Hands of Time; I Love To Dance; I Believe In Love; Sweet Gingerbread Man; The Last Time I Felt Like This; I'll Never Say Goodbye; Make Me Rainbows; Like A Lover; The Island; All His Children; Marmalade, Molasses and Honey; If We Were In Love; It Might Be You; How Do You Keep The Music Playing; Papa Can You Hear Me? The Way He Makes Me Feel; Ordinary Miracles; Where Do You Start? Most of All You; The Girl Who Used To Be Me; Michel Legrand Album; Live At Donte's; Broadway scores: Something More; Ballrooom; Film/TV scores: Yentl; Queen of The Stardust Ballroom; Sybil; TV themes: Maude; Good Times; Alice; Brooklyn Bridge; The Powers That Be. *Honours:* 3 Academy; 2 Emmy; 2 Golden Globe; 2 Grammy; Inducted into Songwriters Hall of Fame, 1979. *Memberships:* ASCAP; AMPAS; Songwriters Guild of America; Society of Composers and Lyricists. *Leisure interests:* Art and antique collecting; Tennis. *Current Management:* Gorfaine Scwartz. *Address:* 3301 Barham Blvd #201, Los Angeles, CA 90068, USA.

BERGMAN Barry; b. 24 Aug. 1944, New York, USA. Artist Man.; Music Publisher. *Education:* BS, New York University, 1966. *Career:* Vice President, Marks Music, 1975–79; Vice President, Creative Affairs, United Artists Music, 1979–81; Owner, Barry Bergman Management, 1982–; Ellymax Music, 1985-, Wood Monkey Music, 1986–; Artist manager for: Keven Jordan; Marc Ribler; Rob Friedman; Kings Country; Publisher of music by: Cher; Kiss; Michael Bolton; Kathy Mattea. *Contributions to:* Billboard Magazine, Narm Sounding Board. *Honour:* ASCAP Pop Award, 1989. *Memberships:* ASCAP; Broadcast Music Inc; Founder, President, International Managers Forum, USA. *Current*

Management: Barry Bergman Management, 350 E 30th St, Suite 4D, New York, NY 10016, USA.

BERGMAN Marilyn; b. Brooklyn, New York, USA. Lyricist; Writer. m. Alan Bergman, 1 d. *Education:* New York University. *Musical Education:* High School of Music and Art. *Career:* Collaborators: Alan Bergman; Michel Legrand; Dave Grusin; Marvin Hamlisch; Henry Mancini; Johnny Mandel; John Williams; David Shire; Neil Diamond; James Newton Howard; Quincy Jones; Lew Spence; Sammy Fain; Billy Goldenberg; Lalo Schifrin; Norman Luboff; Sergio Mendes. *Compositions include:* Yellow Bird; Nice 'n' Easy; The Windmills of Your Mind; The Way We Were; The Summer Knows; What Are You Doing For The Rest of Your Life?; Summer Me Winter Me; So Many Stars; You Must Believe In Spring; Places That Belong To You; You Don't Bring Me Flowers; Little Boy Lost; In The Heat of The Night; The Hands of Time; I Love To Dance; I Believe In Love; Sweet Gingerbread Man; The Last Time I Felt Like This; I'll Never Say Goodbye; Make Me Rainbows; Like a Lover; The Island; All His Children; Marmalade, Molasses and Honey; If We Were In Love; It Might Be You; How Do You Keep The Music Playing; Papa Can You Hear Me?; The Way He Makes Me Feel; Ordinary Miracles; Where Do You Start?; Most of All You; The Girl Who Used To Be Me; Portrait Edition; Michel Legrand Album; Live At Donte's; Broadway scores: Something More; Ballroom; Film/TV scores, Yentl; Queen of The Stardust Ballroom; Sybil. *Honours include:* 3 Academy; 2 Golden Globe; 2 Emmy; 2 Grammy; Inducted into Songwriters Hall of Fame, 1979; Crystal Award, Women In Film, 1986. *Memberships:* (Chairman) ASCAP; AMPAS; Society of Composers and Lyricists; Songwriters Guild of America. *Leisure interests:* Antique and art collecting. *Current Management:* Gorfaine/Scwartz.

BERGSTEIN Scott; b. 8 June 1952, Midland, Michigan, USA. Record Co Exec. m. Elisa Fegarido, 18 Nov. 1989, 1 s. *Education:* BA Communications, American University, Washington DC. *Career:* Head Buyer, Wherehouse Records; International Operations Manager, Casablanca Records; Director of Artist Development, Allegiance Records; Marketing Manager, Chameleon Music Group; Senior Vice President, Higher Octave Music. *Memberships:* NARAS; NARM; AFIM. *Address:* 23852 Pacific Coast Hwy #2C, Malibu, CA 90265, USA.

BERLIOZ Gérard; b. 15 March 1943, Paris, France. Musician (percussion, tympanon, cymbalum); Music Educator. m. 11 April 1964, 1 s., 1 d. *Musical Education:* Prix de Percussion du Mans; Prix de Percussion, Conservatoire National Supérieur de Music de Paris. *Career:* Professor, several conservatoires in Paris region; Worked with symphony orchestras: Radio-France; Radio-Moscow; Leningrad; Prague; Music Hall concerts at Moulin Rouge; Casino de Paris; Olympia; Theatres, operas, ballet companies include: Paris; Rouen; Vichy; Nice; Toulouse; Grenoble (others in France); Monte Carlo; Canada; Japan; Festivals all over France; International tours with: Mikis Theodorakis; Lorin Maazel; Jerry Lewis (Europe, North Africa, South Africa, USA, Canada, Japan, Thailand, South America, Israel, Australia); Musician accompanying: Claude Bolling; Tom Jones; Ginger Rogers; Ray Charles; Charles Aznavour; Gilbert Bécaud; Mireille Mathieu; Catherine Ribeiro; Music for films, musical comedies and recordings with: Michel Legrand; Maurice Jarre; Claude Nougaro; Mikis Theodakaris; Jean Claude Naude; Guy Defatto; Mireille Mathieu; Catherine Ribeiro. *Publications:* Director, Percussion Collection; Chronicler, Journal: Tam Tam Percussion; Author, several instruction manuals; Author, numerous articles on percussion. *Membership:* L'Ordre National Des Musiciens. *Leisure interests:* Collecting drums and percussion instruments.

BERNARD Alain; b. 8 Sept. 1952, Algeria. Jazz Musician (piano, synthesizer). *Education:* English studies, Paris University, 1971–72. *Musical Education:* Private lessons until 1985; CIM Diploma, orchestration, arrangement, composition. *Career:* Musician, 1977–; Sideman for French musicians including: R Guérin; Gérard Badini Swing Machine; Ornicar big-band; American musicians include: F Foster; E L Davis; Joe Henderson; J Newman; Dee Dee Bridgewater; Jazz festivals at Nice and Dresden; Founder, own trio, 1987; Plays in France and Germany. *Recordings:* Mais Où Est Donc Ornicar, with Joe Henderson; Mr Swing Is Still Alive, Gérard Badini Super Swing Machine; Jazz Cartoon; L'Incroyable Huck. *Memberships:* SACEM; SPEDIDAM; ADAMI. *Address:* rue de l'Ile Irus, Tourlarec, 56870 Baden, France.

BERNARD Claude Camille; b. 5 Oct. 1945, Paris, France. Musician (alto saxophone); Bandleader. Widower, 2 s., 2 d. *Education:* Conservatoire Artistique Cardinal Lemoine. *Musical Education:* Jean Ledieu, Professor, alto saxophone, soloist, Conservatoire National, Nancy. *Career:* Festivals: Chateauvallon, 1976; Vansovin, 1977; Suse den Netherlands; Yugoslavia, Turkey, 1994; China, Africa, 1995; Played with: Steve Lacy; Michael Smith; Lavelle; Mickey Baker; Wei Wei; Specializes in improvisation, solo and accompanied. *Recordings:* Quebella Promenade; Brin de Laine; Facett'vega. *Publications:* Olympic Games Atlanta centennial with Wei Wei and Michael Smith Band, 1996. *Memberships:* Syndicat des Chefs d'Orchestre; SACEM; SACD; Centre International de Musicotherapie. *Address:* 48 Ave du Maréchal Foch, 78400 Chatou, France.

BERNASCONI Justin Anthony; b. 29 Sept. 1972, Croydon, Surrey, England. Singer; Songwriter; Musician (guitar, keyboards, banjo, bass). *Musical Education:* Anglia Polytechnic, Cambridge, 2 years music, philosophy; 4 years guitar tuition including advanced guitar lessons with Richard Newman. *Career:* Played Cambridge Folk Festival, 1993, 1994; Appeared as country rock guitarist, Roy Waller's Radio Norfolk Show; Anglia TV featuring The Fen Blows debut album, local news programme. *Recordings:* Debut album: The Fen Blows, 8 songs on historical events and fables of Cambridgeshire; Composed all own material. *Honour:* Best Guitarist Award, East Anglian Rock Competition, 1991. *Memberships:* Musicians' Union; Cambridge Folk Club. *Leisure interests:* Reading; Poetry; Novels; Local History. *Address:* 17 Mill Green, Warboys, Huntingdon, Cambs PE17 25A, England.

BERRY Bill; b. 31 July 1958, Hibbing, Minnesota, USA. Musician (drums). *Career:* Member, R.E.M., 1980–97; World-wide tours; Member, side project, Hindu Love Gods, 1986–90. *Recordings:* Albums: with R.E.M.: Chronic Town (mini-album), 1982; Murmur, 1983; Reckoning, 1984; Fables of The Reconstruction, 1985; Life's Rich Pageant, 1986; Dead Letter Office, 1987; Document, 1987; Eponymous, 1988; Green, 1988; Out of Time, 1991; The Best of REM, 1991; Automatic For The People, 1992; Monster, 1995; with Hindu Love Gods: Hindu Love Gods, 1990; Also appears on: Beat The Retreat, 1994; I'll Sleep When I'm Dead, 1996; Live On Letterman, 1997; Singles: with R.E.M.: The One I Love, 1987; Stand, 1989; Orange Crush, 1989; Losing My Religion, 1991; Shiny Happy People, 1991; Near Wild Heaven, 1991; Radio Song, 1991; Drive, 1992; Man On The Moon, 1992; The Sidewinder Sleeps Tonite, 1993; Everybody Hurts, 1993; Crush With Eyeliner; Nightswimming; What's The Frequency Kenneth?; Tracks featured on film soundtracks: Batchelor Party, 1984; Until The End of The World, 1991; Coneheads, 1993; Recordings with: Indigo Girls; Warren Zevon; Love Tractor; Contributor, albums: Tom's Album; I'm Your Fan. *Honours:* Earth Day Award, 1990; Numerous MTV Music Video Awards; Billboard Awards: Best Modern Rock Artists, Best World Album, 1991; BRIT Awards: Best International Group, 1992, 1993, 1995; Grammy Awards, Best Pop Performance, Alternative Music Album, Music Video, 1992; Atlanta Music Awards: Act of The Year, Rock Album, Video, 1992; IRMA, International Band of The Year, 1993; Rolling Stone Critics Awards: Best Band, Best Album; Q Awards: Best Album, 1991, 1992; Best Act In The World, 1991, 1995. *Current Management:* REM/Athens Ltd, 250 W Clayton St, Athens, GA 30601, USA.

BERRY Chuck (Charles); b. 18 Oct. 1926, San Jose, California, USA. Rock 'n' Roll Singer; Musician (guitar). *Career:* Member, Johnny Johnson Trio, 1947; Renamed Chuck Berry Trio; Established Berry Park, Wentzville, Missouri (home and country club); Owner, nightclub The Bandstand, St Louis; Hundreds of world-wide concerts including: Newport Jazz Festival, 1958; New York Folk Festival, 1965; Toronto Rock 'n' Roll Revival, 1969; UK Rock 'n' Roll Revival, Wembley, 1972; White House concert, for President Carter, 1979; 60th Birthday concert, Fox Theatre, St Louis, 1986; Film appearances: Rock Rock Rock, 1956; Jazz On A Summers Day, 1958; Go Johnny Go, 1959; American Hot Wax, 1978; Hail! Hail! Rock 'n' Roll!, 1987. *Recordings:* Numerous albums include: Chuck Berry, 1963; Chuck Berry On Stage, 1963; His Latest and Greatest, 1964; Chuck Berry's Greatest Hits, 1964; St Louis To Liverpool, 1965; Chuck Berry In London, 1965; Chuck Berry's Golden Decade, 1968; Back Home, 1970; St Louis To Frisco To Memphis, 1972; Golden Decade Vol. 2, 1973; Motorvatin', 1977; Rock! Rock! Rock 'N' Roll, 1980; Chuck Berry – The Chess Box, 1990; Anthology, 2000; Singles include: Maybellene, 1955; Roll Over Beethoven, 1956; School Day, 1957; Rock and Roll Music, 1957; Sweet Little Sixteen, 1958; Johnny B Goode, 1958; Memphis Tennessee, 1963; Nadine (Is It You?), 1964; No Particular Place To Go, 1964; You Never Can Tell, 1964; My Ding A Ling, 1972. *Publication:* Chuck Berry – The Autobiography, 1988. *Honours include:* Grammy, Lifetime Achievement Award, 1985; Inducted into Rock and Roll Hall of Fame, 1986; Hollywood Walk of Fame, 1987; Inducted into Songwriters Hall of Fame, 1986; Maybellene inducted into NARAS Hall of Fame, 1988; St Louis Walk of Fame, 1989; Johnny B Goode, featured on Voyager Interstellar Record, NASA's Voyager satellite, 1989; Roll Over Beethoven inducted into NARAS Hall of Fame, 1990. *Current Management:* Ira Okun Enterprises, 211 S Beverly Dr., Suite 103, Beverly Hills, CA 90212, USA.

BERRY Dave; b. 6 Feb. 1941, Sheffield, England. Vocalist. m. Marthy Van-Lopik, 20 Feb. 1967, 1 d. *Musical Education:* Father a semi-professional drummer. *Career:* Tours with Rolling Stones, 1964–65; Television: Top of The Pops; Ready Steady Go; Lucky Stars; Song Festival, Knokke, Belgium; Gran Gala, Netherlands; Concert tours, 60's package with other artists, 1985–95. *Recordings:* Memphis Tennessee, 1963; Crying Game, 1964; Baby Its You, 1964; This Strange Effect, 1965; Little Things, 1965; Mama, 1966; Albums: Dave Berry, 1964; Can I Get It From You, 1965; A Dozen Berry's, 1966; Special Sound Of, 1968; 68, 1968; Remembering, 1976; The Crying Game, 1983; This Strange Effect, 1986; A Totally Random Evening With, 1992; The Very Best Of, 1999. *Honour:* Press Prize, Knokke, Belgium. *Leisure interests:* Travel; Hiking. *Current*

Management: Brian Gannon Management. *Address:* PO Box 106, Rochdale, England.

BERRY Jan; b. 3 April 1941, Los Angeles, California, USA. Vocalist. m. Gertie Filip, 1991. *Career:* Member, duo Jan and Dean (with Dean Torrence), 1957–66; 1973–; Career interrupted by serious accident, 1966; Performances include: Dick Clark's stage show, Michigan State Fair, with Frankie Avalon, Duane Eddy, The Coasters, 1959; American Bandstand, ABC-TV, 1964; New York, with The Animals, Chuck Berry, Del Shannon, 1964; California Surfer's Stomp Festival, 1973; Subject of biopic, Dead Man's Curve, ABC-TV, 1978. *Recordings:* Albums: Jan and Dean Take Linda Surfin', 1963; Surf City and Other Swinging Cities, 1963; Drag City, 1964; Dead Man's Curve/The New Girl At School, 1964; The Little Old Lady From Pasadena, 1964; Ride The Wild Surf (film soundtrack), 1964; Command Performance/Live In Person, 1965; Jan and Dean Meet Batman, 1966; One Summer Night – Live, 1982; Various compilations; Live recordings include: Center Stage, 2000; Surf City, 2001; Singles include: with Jan and Dean: Linda, 1963; Surf City (No. 1, USA), 1963; Honolulu Lulu, 1963; Dead Man's Curve, 1964; The Little Old Lady (From Pasadena), 1964; Ride The Wild Surf, 1964; Catch A Wave, 1964; You Really Know How To Hurt A Guy, 1965; Solo albums: Mother Earth, 1972; Don't You Just Know It, 1972; Tinsel Town, 1974. *Current Management:* Bill Hollingshead Productions, 1720 N Ross St, Santa Ana, CA 92706, USA.

BERRY John; b. 14 Sept. 1959, Aiken, South Carolina, USA. Singer; Songwriter. m. Robin Calvert, 2 s., 1 d. *Career:* Moved to Nashville, 1990; Tours, concerts with own band; Television includes: Music City Tonight; The Ralph Emery Show; CBS This Morning; NBC Weekend Today; Entertainment Tonight; The Road; Exclusively Leeza; Conan O'Brian. *Recordings:* John Berry, 1995; Standing On The Edge, 1995; O Holy Night, 1995; Faces, 1996; Better Than A Biscuit, 1998; Wildest Dreams, 1999; Singles: Your Love Amazes Me (No. 1); Standing On The Edge of Goodbye; I Think About It All The Time; If I Had Any Pride Left At All, 1995; Change My Mind, 1996; She's Takin' A Shine, 1997. *Honours include:* 2 Gold albums; 1 Platinum album, John Berry, 1995; Platinum single, Your Love Amazes Me; Grammy Awards: Best Male Country Performance, 1995, 1996. *Memberships:* AFofM; CMA; NARAS; ACM. *Leisure interest:* Motorcycles. *Current Management:* Corlew – O'Grady Management. *Address:* 1503 17th Ave S, Nashville, TN 37212, USA.

BERRYMAN Guy; b. 12 April 1978, Fife, Scotland. Musician (bass guitar); Songwriter. *Education:* University College, London. *Career:* Member: Coldplay, 1998-. *Recordings:* Albums: Parachutes, 2000; Singles: The Safety EP, 1998; Brothers and Sisters, The Blue Room EP, 1999; Shiver, Yellow, Trouble, 2000. *Honours:* Brit Award, Best Album, 2001; Mercury Music Prize, nominee, 2000. *Current Management:* Phil Harvey. *Internet:* www.coldplay.com.

BERRYMAN Peter Anthony; b. 22 June 1945, Redruth, Cornwall, England. Musician (Guitar); Composer; Teacher. 2 s., 1 d. *Musical Education:* Self-taught musically. *Career:* Tours With Famous Jug Band, 1969–71; Mormos, Africa, 1973; Julie Felix, Australasia, 1974; Bridget St John, UK, 1976; Brenda Wootton, France, 1985–90; Blue Ticket, 1987–93; Solo, UK, Europe, 1972–; Radio Includes, John Peel; Andy Kershaw; Television Includes Old Grey Whistle Test, BBC2; Festivals, Cambridge; Hyde Park; Glastonbury; L'Orient; Womad; Guitar Teacher, 1982–; Music for Kneehigh Theatre; Theatre Rotto; The Barneys. *Recordings:* Spiral Staircase, 1968; Sunshine Possibilities, 1969; Chameleon, 1970; Legendary Me; Magical Flight; Sky In My Pie; Past, Present and Future; Under A Summer Sky; Best of British Folk; Picture Rags; The Electric Muse; Duet, with Adrian O'Reilly, 1999. *Publication:* Silver Harvest, 1998. *Membership:* PRS. *Leisure interests:* Walking; Cornish Language; The Sea. *Address:* Hill Cottage, Lanwithan Rd, Lostwithiel, Cornwall PL22 0LA, England.

BERT Eddie; b. 16 May 1922, Yonkers, New York, USA. Musician (trombone). m. Mollie Petrillo, 21 Aug. 1940, 3 d. *Musical Education:* Manhattan School of Music, Bachelor and Master of Music. *Career:* Orchestras include: Illinois Jacquet's Big Band; Thelonius Monk; Charles Mingus; Elliot Lawrence; Lionel Hampton; Stan Kenton; Benny Goodman's Orchestra; Charlie Barnet; Woody Herman; Red Norvo; Broadway shows include: Bye Bye Birdie, 1960; How To Succeed In Business, 1961; Golden Boy, 1964; Pippin, 1972–77; Ain't Misbehavin', 1978–82; Human Comedy, 1984–85; Uptown It's Hot, 1986; Films: Jam Session With Charlie Barnet Orchestra, 1943; The French Connection; School Daze (Spike Lee), 1987; Television: Dick Cavett Show, 1968–72; Associate Professor, Essex College, 1981–82; Bridgeport University, 1984–86; Tours include: USSR, France, Denmark, 1975; Spain, 1986; Netherlands, 1987; Italy, 1987; Japan, with Walt Levinsky's Great American Swing Band, 1988–89; Five Continents with Gene Harris-Philip Morris Superband, 1989; Performances: Dick Gibson's Jazz Party, Denver, Colorado, 1979, 1981; Florida Jazz Festival, 1981, 1982; Carnegie Hall Jazz Festival, 1980–84. *Recordings include:* As Eddie Bert: Like Cool, 1955; East Coast Jazz, 1955; Encore, 1955; Musician of The Year, 1955; Kaleidoscope, 1987; The Human Factor, Eddie Bert Sextet, 1987; Live At Birdland, Eddie Bert Quintet, 1991; Also appears on:

Ellington Masterpieces, 1988; Just A-Settin' and A-Rockin', 1990; Music of Jimmie Lunceford, 1992; Monk On Monk, 1997; This Is Living!, 1997; Complete Blue Note 50s Sessions, 1998; Star Wars and Other Galactic Funk, 1999. *Publications:* Eddie Bert Trombone Method; Eddie Bert Lead Sheet Book. *Honours:* Brass Conference Salute, Hotel Roosevelt, New York City, 1990. *Membership:* NARAS. *Leisure interest:* Photography.

BERTHELSEN Claus Gymoese; b. 28 Sept. 1958, Copenhagen, Denmark. Songwriter; Author; Singer. 1 d. *Education:* Bachelor of Economics. *Musical Education:* Copenhagen Boys Choir. *Career:* Founder, own group Naïve; Several gigs in Denmark including: The Roskilde Festival (twice); Numerous Danish television appearances with Naïve; Actor in Gangway I Tyrol. *Compositions:* Songs: Carry On; Marble Afternoon. *Recordings:* Albums: with Naïve: Fish; Careless; Absolution Music. *Membership:* DJBFA. *Leisure interests:* Writing video screenplays for: Heinrich Von Hinten, underground video team (members include: Henrik Balling; Peter Ravn; Renee Paschburg; Asger G Larsen; Arne Siemsen; Thomas Arnoldi). *Current Management:* Allan Graunkjaer, Record Music Denmark. *Address:* Wilkensvej 25, 2000 Frederiksberg, Denmark.

BERTRAM Dominique; b. 8 Aug. 1954, Alger, Algeria. Musician (electric bass). m. Florence Faisan, 6 Nov. 1991, 1 s., 1 d. *Musical Education:* Self-taught. *Career:* Worked with singers: Michael Jonasz; Veronique Sanson; Catherine Lara; Patrick Bruel; Al Jarreau. *Recordings:* Michael Jonasz; Veronique Sanson; Dominique Bertram: Chinese Paradise, 1985; Bass Now, 1992. *Publications:* Method Up Bass, 1990; Jouer de la Basse C'est Facile, 1994. *Memberships:* SACEM; Spedidam; ADAMI. *Leisure interests:* Cycling; Backgammon. *Address:* 101 rue de Mont-Cenis, 75018 Paris, France.

BERTRAM Hans-Dieter 'Sherry'; b. 20 May 1936, Leipzig, Germany. Musician (drums, percussion). m. Dagmar, 16 Sept. 1969, 2 s. *Education:* Study of Engineering, Berlin, 1959. *Musical Education:* Berlin Conservatory, 1959–65. *Career:* Freelance Musician; Graphic Designer, Moderator for Rias Radio Station, 1957–89; Concerts and recordings, Berlin Philarmonic Orchestra, 1962; Deutsche Oper Berlin, 1962, 1967, 1972, 1993–95; Musicals and music for theatre; Studio musician for television, radio, films, jingles, records, Rias Live Talk Show, 1969–89; CA 1000 Programs; Jazz drummer with own groups, bigbands; Percussion teacher at Leo-Borchard Music School. *Membership:* Landesmusikrat Berlin, Jazz Department. *Leisure interests:* Swimming; Cycling; Ice Skating. *Current Management:* Orchester Bertram GmbH. *Address:* Rudolstaedter Strasse 123, 10713 Berlin, Germany.

BERTRAND Plastic; b. 24 Feb. 1954, Brussels, Belgium. Vocalist; Composer; Writer; Prod. m. Evelyne Van Daele, 1979, 1 s., 1 d. *Musical Education:* Conservatoire Royal de Musique de Bruxelles (university level musical High School). *Career:* Singer, drummer, punk band: Hubble Bubble, 1977–; Solo career, 1977–; 8 albums; International tours world-wide; Appears in own television shows: France (TF Jackspot); Italy (Due per tutti); Belgium (Supercool). *Recordings:* Wrote, produced: Ça Plane Pour Moi; Tout Petite La Planète; Stop Ou Encore; Sentimentale-Moi; Hula Hoop; Slave To The Beat; Plastic Hits (compilation), 1995. *Honours:* 15 Gold, 5 Platinum records world-wide; Billboard Award; Grand Prix de l'Académie Française Du Disque. *Membership:* SABAM. *Leisure interests:* Antiques. *Current Management:* MMD, Broodthaers Pierrette. *Address:* 38 rue Fernand Bernier, 1060 Brussels, Belgium.

BESEMANN Robyn; b. 19 Jan. 1954, Reed City, Michigan, USA. Singer; Songwriter; Public Speaker; Author. m. Ivan L Besemann, 1 s., 1 d. *Career:* Gospel recording artist signed with Incubator Records for 2 years; Executive Director, co-founder of LIFE Aerobics, 1980–88; Franklin Graham Crusades; Regular tours. *Recordings:* In His Name, 1993; For His Glory, 1995. *Membership:* Gospel Music Asscn (GMA). *Leisure interests:* Travel; Music; Boating; Going to the coast.

BEST Matthew; b. 26 Jan. 1961, London, England. Musician (drums, keyboards); DJ; Record Prod. *Education:* West London Institute of HE. *Musical Education:* Self-taught. *Career:* Studio drummer, Captain Sensible, 1977–80; Formed Carcrash International, 1983–84; Played live for UK Subs and Anti-Nowhere League; Formed Urban Dogs; Pressure Point (featuring P P Arnold); Simultaneously member of Psychic TV, 1986–; Formed Greedy Beat Syndicate; Play live with techno band Yum Yum. *Recordings:* 2 albums, Urban Dogs; 12 albums, Psychic TV; 2 albums, Greedy Beat Syndicate. *Membership:* Musicians' Union. *Leisure interests:* Music; Records; Usual vices associated therewith. *Current Management:* Colleen Sanders, 1–7 Boundary Row, London SE1, England. *Address:* 19 Irving St, London WC2H 7AU, England.

BETTENCOURT Nuno; b. 20 Sept. 1966, Azores, Portugal. Musician (guitar); Prod. *Career:* Member, Sinful; Guitarist, US funk/rock group Extreme, 1985–; Played Boston club circuit, 1985–88; World-wide appearances include: British tour, 1991; A Concert For Life, Tribute to Freddie Mercury, Wembley, 1992; American Dream concerts, London,

1992; Support to Bryan Adams, European tour, 1992. *Recordings:* Singles include: Get The Funk Out, 1991; More Than Words (No. 1, USA), 1991; Decadence Dance, 1991; Hole-Hearted, 1991; Song For Love, 1992; Stop The World, 1992; Albums: Extreme, 1989; Extreme II Pornograffitti, 1991; III Sides To Every Story, 1992; Very Special Christmas Vol. 2, 1992; Shaved and Dangerous, 1993; Ultimate Rock Vol. 1, 1993; There Is No God, 1994; Kiss My Ass, 1994; Honey, 1994; Waiting For The Punchline, 1995; Flesh, 1995; Schizophonic, 1997; Mourning Widows, 1999. *Honours:* Boston Music Awards: Act of Year; Outstanding Rock Single, Hole Hearted; Outstanding Pop Single; Outstanding Song/Songwriter, More Than Words; Outstanding Instrumentalist, 1992. *Current Management:* Andon Artists, 79 Fairview Farm Rd, West Redding, CT 06896, USA.

BETTIS John; b. 24 Oct. 1946, Long Beach, California, USA. Lyricist. *Career:* Co-founder, The Carpenters; 38 songs recorded by them, 1970–; Other artists: Michael Jackson; Madonna; Whitney Houston; Diana Ross; 180m. records sold. *Compositions include:* Top of The World; Yesterday Once More; Only Yesterday; Goodbye To Love; Human Nature; Crazy For You; Slow Hand; One Moment In Time; When You Tell Me That You Love Me. *Honours:* Grammy Nomination; Academy Award; Golden Globe; Emmy.

BEVAN Alonza; b. 24 Oct. 1970, London, England. Musician (bass). *Career:* Formed The Objects of Desire with Crispian Mills and Paul Winterhart; Became The Kays, and then formed Kula Shaker with Jay Darlington, 1995–99; Member, Johnny Marr's Healers, 2000–; Numerous TV appearances and appearances at rock festivals. *Recordings:* Singles: Tattva, 1996; Hey Dude, 1996; Govinda, 1996; Hush, 1997; Sound of Drums, 1998; Albums: K, 1996; Peasants, Pigs and Astronauts, 1999.

BEVAN Bev(erley); b. 24 Nov. 1946, Birmingham, England. Musician (drums). *Career:* Member, groups: Carl Wayne and The Vikings; Denny Laine and The Diplomats; Danny King and The Mayfair Set; Drummer, The Move, 1966–72; Appearances include: National Jazz and Blues Festival, 1966; Support to The Rolling Stones, Paris, 1967; Art Festival Ball, Brighton, 1967; Isle of Wight Festival, 1968; Reading Festival, 1972; Drummer, Electric Light Orchestra (ELO), 1972–; Concerts include: Heartbeat '86 benefit, Birmingham, 1986; Brief spell, drummer, Black Sabbath, including Reading Festival, 1983. *Recordings:* Albums: with the Move: Move, 1968; Shazam, 1970; Looking On, 1970; Message From The Country, 1971; Great Move: The Best of The Move, 1993; with ELO: Electric Light Orchestra, 1972; On The Third Day, 1973; Eldorado, 1974; The Night The Light Went On In Long Beach, 1974; Face The Music, 1975; Olé ELO, 1976; A New World Record, 1976; Out of The Blue, 1977; Discovery (No. 1, UK), 1979; ELO's Greatest Hits, 1979; Xanadu (film soundtrack), 1980; Time, 1981; Secret Messages, 1983; Balance of Power, 1986; Greatest Hits, 1989; Afterglow, 1990; Electric Light Orchestra, 1991; Moment of Truth, 1994; One Night Live In Australia, 1997; Live At Wembley '78, 1998; Flashback 2000; Also appears on: Twang! A Tribute, 1996; Supernatural Fairy Tails, 1996; Under Wheels of Confusion, 1996; Singles: with the Move include: I Can Hear The Grass Grow; Flowers In The Rain; Fire Brigade; Blackberry Way (No. 1, UK); Hello Susie; Curly; Brontosaurus; California Man; with ELO: Roll Over Beethoven; Showdown; Can't Get It Out of My Head; Strange Magic; Evil Woman; Lovin' Thing; Rockaria!; Do Ya; Telephone Line; Turn To Stone; Mr Blue Sky; Wild West Hero; Shine A Little Love; Don't Bring Me Down; Xanadu (No. 1, UK); Hold On Tight; Rock 'n' Roll Is King; Calling America; Solo: Let There Be Drums. *Honours include:* Outstanding Contribution to British Music, Ivor Novello Award, 1979.

BEX Emmanuel Jean; b. 8 June 1959, Caen, France. Musician (Hammond organ). m. Sophie Simon, 31 Aug. 1991, 1 s., 1 d. *Musical Education:* Conservatory of Caen; Conservatory of Paris. *Career:* Member, quintet The Bex'tet, 1991; Sideman with: Babick Reinhardt; Barney Wilen; Philippe Catherine; New Group, Steel Bex, with E Bex and Steel Band, 1997; New Group, Bex Machine, E Bex Quartet, 1997; New Group, Bex, with Philip Catherine and Aldo Romano, 1998; New Group, Bex, with Glenn Ferris and Simon Goubert, 2000. *Recordings:* Bex and Jouvelet In Public, 1983; with Ray Lema: Bwana Zoulu, 1987; with Bex, Pino, Teslard: Triple Idiome, 1988; with Xavier Jouvelet: Blues Congo, 1988; with La Bande à Badauld: Vacances Au Soleil, 1988; Caravanserail, 1989; with Bertrand Renaudin: Interplay, 1990; Miscellaneous Song, 1991; with Carl Schlosser: Texas Sound, 1992; with Babick Reinhardt: Histoire Simple, 1992; with Marais, Bex, Romano: Poissons Nageurs, 1993; with Bex'tet: Enfance, 1991; Organique, 1993; Rouge Et Or, 1995; with Barney Wilen: Nitty Gritty, 1993; Steel Bex, Emmanuel Bex, 1996; Due des Lowbards, Christian Escoudé Trio, 1997; '3' with trios: Bex/Romano/Catherine, Bex/Huchard/Barthelmy, Bex/Ceccareli/Lagrene, 1997; Mauve, 2000; Here and Now, Bex/Ferris/Goubert, 2001. *Honour:* Prix Django Reinhardt, Academy of Jazz, 1995. *Current Management:* Sophie Simon Management. *Address:* 8 Impasse Chanut, 93200 Saint Denis, France.

BEZ (Mark Berry); b. 18 April 1964, Manchester, England. Musician (Percussion); Dancer. *Career:* Member, Happy Mondays; Joined Black Grape with Shaun Ryder, 1993; Numerous live gigs and festival appearances; Left, 1995; Rejoined Happy Mondays, 1999. *Recordings:* with Happy Mondays: Singles: 24 Hour Party People, 1987; WFL (Wrote For Luck), 1988; Madchester Rave On EP, 1989; Step On, 1990; Kinky Afro, 1990; Loose Fit, 1991; Judge Fudge, 1991; The Boys Are Back In Town, 1999; with Black Grape: Reverend Black Grape, 1995; In The Name of The Father, 1995; Kelly's Heroes, 1995; England's Irie, 1996; Fat Neck, 1996; Get Higher, 1997; Marbles, 1998; Albums: with Happy Mondays: Squirrel and G-Man, 1987; Bummed, 1988; Pills Thrills 'N' Bellyaches, 1990; Yes Please!, 1992; Loads, 1995, Greatest Hits, 2001; with Black Grape: It's Great When You're Straight... Yeah, 1995; Stupid Stupid Stupid, 1997.

BHAMRAH Kulwant Singh; b. 11 Feb. 1955, India. Bhangra Singer; Songwriter. m. Satvinder Bhamrah, 3 March 1979, 1 s., 1 d. *Education:* Civil engineer. *Musical Education:* Hobby developed into profession. *Career:* Singer, Bhangra Folk Panjabi band Apna Sangeet; Performed in: UK; Kenya; Tanzania; Canada; America; Singapore; India; Television appearances include: BBC; ITV; CH4; TV Asia; Star TV; Appeared on all official Asian broadcasting radio stations. *Compositions:* Writes own songs. *Recordings:* Albums include: Toor India; Mera Yaar; Chack Dey Phattay; Desi Rytham; Musicblasters; Mini Blasters; Mister Blaster; Hi-Kiddaw. *Honours:* Asian Pop Awards, Best Band, 1988; Best Songwriter, 1992; Best Live Band, 1994. *Memberships:* PRS; MCPS; Musicians' Union; British Actor Equity. *Leisure interests:* Formerly singing; Sport; Television; Keep fit.

BHATIA Anjali; b. 15 Oct. 1968, Chiswick, London, England. Singer; Musician (guitar, former drummer); Songwriter. *Education:* Kingsway Princeton College, BTec, Art and Design; Goldsmiths College, degree in textiles design, Art and critical theory. *Musical Education:* Certificate in Music Technology, Islington Music Workshop; Classical guitar training, Grade 4. *Career:* Festivals: Reading, Phoenix; Radio: 3 John Peel sessions; Solo Artist, Producer and Engineer. *Recordings:* Singles: Supermodel/Superficial; Kenuweehead; f is for fame; Eat The Gems; Album: Chocolate Revenge; Sheer Witchery, singles compilation, 1999. *Memberships:* PRS; Musicians' Union. *Leisure interests:* Art; Food; Travel; Painting. *Address:* c/o Beggars Banquet/Wiija Records, 17–19 Alma Rd, London SW18 1AA, England.

BHEAGLAOICH Seosaimhín Ní; b. West Kerry, Gaeltacht, Ireland. Singer; Broadcaster. *Education:* BA (Mod) Hons Trinity College Dublin. *Career:* Presenter, television series The Mountain Lark, RTE; Broadcaster with Raidio-Na-Gaeltachta; Numerous television appearances, RTE, Ireland; Presenter, As I Roved Out, BBC Ulster. *Recordings:* Solo album: Taobh Na Gréine (Under The Sun), Gael-Linn; Sings title track: Mná Na h-Éireann, on Macalla, all-woman group's first album; Also sings on Macalla 2. *Leisure interests:* Travel; Walking. *Current Management:* Gael-Linn. *Address:* Gael-Linn, 26 Cearnóg Mhuirfean, Bac 2, Ireland.

BHOSLE Asha; b. 1933, Satara, Maharashtra, India. Vocalist; Composer. *Career:* Indian film playback singer; Sister of Lata Mangeshkar; Has recorded thousands of songs in 14 Indian languages; First film Chunaria, 1948; First solo number in Raat Ki Rani, 1949; Sang in styles influenced by Latin American and American Big Band Jazz; Worked extensively with Kishore Kumar in the 1970s; First Indian Singer to be nominated for a Grammy Award. *Recordings include:* Albums: soundtracks: Dus Lakh, 1967; Shikhar, 1968; Hare Rama Hare Krishna, 1972; Naina, 1973; Pran Jaye Par Vachan Na Jaye, 1974; Don, 1977; Umrao Jaan, 1981; Ijazat, 1986; Dilwale Dulhania Le Jayeng, 1995; Rangeela, 1996; solo: Songs of My Soul – Rare and Classic Vol. 1, Songs of My Soul – Rare and Classic Vol. 2, 2001. *Honours:* Filmfare Award, 1967, 1968, 1971, 1972, 1973, 1974, 1977, 1996; Filmfare Special Award, Rangeela Re, 1996; Filmfare Lifetime Achievement Award, 2001; National Award, 1981, 1986; Nightingale of Asia, 1987; Lata Mangeshkar Award, Madhya Pradesh Govt, 1989; Screen Videocon Award, 1997; MTV Award, 1997; Channel V Award, 1997; Grammy Award Nomination, 1997; Lata Mangeshar Award, Maharashtra Govt, 1999; Singer of the Millennium, Dubai, 2000; Kolhapuri Bhushan Award, 2000; Sangli Bhushan Award, 2000; Omega Excellence Lifetime Achievement Award, 2000; Dada Saheb Phalke Award, 2001; Dayawati Modi Award, 2001; Hon. Doctrates from the University of Amravati and Jalgaon in Literature.

BICKERSTETH John Dennis; b. 27 June 1954, Constantine, Cornwall, England. Musician (piano, keyboards); Singer; Composer; Entertainer. *Musical Education:* Choral Scholar, Truro Cathedral; Organ, piano, John Winter and Guillaume Ormond. *Career:* Member of: Cruiser; Ian and The Muscletones; The Barneys; Ian Dunlop's Babylon Babies; Daniel Rovai and Friends; Ton and Kirschen Theatre (Potsdam); Chip Bray Show (Amsterdam Lido); MD, Back On Stage, UFA Fabrik, Berlin; MD, Stewart and Ross; Live television: Japan; Ireland; Germany; M'Toto; J B Band; Botticelli Angels. *Recordings:* Album: Ian and The Muscletones. *Membership:* Musicians' Union. *Leisure interests:* Jazz; Blues guitar; Classical music; Vintage cars. *Current Management:* Wouter de Boer,

Streetwise, Oosterburger voorstraat 88, 1018 MR Amsterdam, The Netherland. *Address:* Tregarth, Bissoe, Truro, Cornwall TR4 8RJ, England.

BICKERTON Wayne; b. 11 July 1941, Rhyl, Wales. Songwriter; Music Publisher; Prod. m. Carole Da-Silva. *Career:* Lee Curtis and the All Stars; Pete Best Four; Songwriting in partnership with Tony Waddington, hits with: Bing Crosby; Jose Feliciano; The Bachelors; Tom Jones; Andy Williams; Decca Records, producer/head of DERAM, 1967–70; Polydor/ Polygram, Divsional Manager, 1970–74; Odyssey Group/State Records and State Music, Founder, 1974–78; Performing Rights Society, Chairman and Acting Chief Executive, 1978–96; SESAC, Consultant, 1996; SESAC, Chairman, 1997; Reliable Source Music, Chairman and Managing Director. *Recordings:* Singles (as producer/co-writer): Sugar Baby Love, Rubettes, 1974; Juke Box Jive, Rubettes, 1974; Sugar Candy Kisses, Mac and Katie Kissoon, 1975; I Can Do It, Rubettes, 1975. *Honours:* Songwriter of the Year (joint), Ivor Novello Awards, 1975; Top British Record Producer by British Phonographic Industry, 1976; Fellow of Liverpool University, 1996; Dr of Laws LL.D (Hons), 1997; Ambassador for Merseyside, 1997. *Memberships:* PRS, Chairman, 1993; MCPS; BASCA (UK); ASCAP; BMI (USA). *Leisure interest:* Tennis. *Current Management:* Reliable Source Music. *Address:* 6 Kenrick Pl., London, W1H 3FF, England. *Internet:* www.reliable-source.co.uk.

BICKNELL Robert David; b. 7 Dec. 1957, Jersey, St Helier, Channel Islands. Singing Teacher. *Career:* Tosca, Aida, Carmen, Hello Dolly, Rocky Horror Show, Godspell, Many pantomimes; TV, Robin Hood, Lenny Henry Show, Doctor Who, Saturday Night Live; TV as Singing Coach, Big Breakfast Show, 16 months; Richard and Judy; Ozone; This Morning; Musical Director, Royal Albert Hall, Wembley Arena; Teacher: Redroofs Theatre School; Goldsmiths University of London. *Recordings:* Love Can Build a Bridge; Film, The Matchmaker. *Contributions to:* Daily Mail. *Honour:* BMus, London. *Memberships:* Equity; British Voice Asscn; Incorporated Society of Musicians. *Leisure interests:* Horseriding; Gym. *Address:* 69 Lower Flat, Acre Lane, London SW2 5TN, England.

BIDDLE Elizabeth Rosina; b. 29 April 1952, Pontypridd, South Wales. Record Prod.; Music Agent; Musician (bassoon). *Musical Education:* Aberystwth University, BA Hons Music; Guildhall School of Music and Drama, City University, MA Music Performance Studies. *Career:* Director of Music, Comprehensive School, 1984; Bassoon tutor at Christs Hospital, Horsham, 1984–99; Founded Upbeat Management, 1986; Founded Upbeat Recordings, 1989. *Recordings:* Producer for The Temperance Seven; Terry Lightfoot; Ken Colyer; Carey Blyton. *Publications:* Writer for Musical Opinion for 3 years. *Memberships:* IAMA; BPI. *Leisure interests:* Playing bassoon for local operatic societies; Bird watching. *Address:* 6 Carleton Ave, Wallington, Surrey SM6 9LN, England.

BIET Remi; b. 1 Oct. 1958, Dieppe, France. Musician (saxophones, flute). m. Brigitte Tailleux, 2 d. *Education:* Ecole Normale d'Instituteurs. *Musical Education:* DE and CA of Jazz (self-taught). *Career:* Tours: USA (New Orleans, San Francisco, Chicago); Italy; Madagascar; Sicily; Germany; Television: Syria; Jordan; France; Italy. *Recordings:* ONJ: Badault; A Plus Tard, 1991; Mingus, Monk Ellington, 1992; Bouquet Final, 1993. *Membership:* UMJ. *Leisure interests:* Golf; Chess; Stunt kite. *Address:* 7 Parc de l'Andelle, 76130 Mt St Aignan, France.

BIG YOUTH (Manley Augustus Buchanan); b. 19 April 1949, Jamaica. Reggae DJ; Record Co Owner. *Career:* Former cab driver and mechanic; Leading reggae DJ, Kingston, 1970s; Founder, Negusa Nagast and Augustus Buchanan record labels, 1973. *Recordings:* Albums: Screaming Target, 1973; Reggae Phenomenon, 1974; Dreadlocks Dread, 1975; Natty Cultural Dread, 1976; Hit The Road Jack, 1976; Isaiah First Prophet of Old, 1978; Everybody Skank – the Best of Big Youth, 1980; Some Great Big Youth, 1981; The Chanting Dread Inna Fine Style, 1983; Live at Reggae Sunsplash, 1984; A Luta Continua, 1985; Manifestation, 1988; Jamming In the House of Dread, 1991; Higher Ground, 1997; Also appears on: Escape Artist, 1981; Holy Ground, 1990; Legends of Reggae Music, 1998. *Address:* c/o Zoe Productions, 450 Broome St, Eighth Floor, New York, NY 10013, USA.

BIKEL Theodore; b. 2 May 1924, Vienna, Austria. Actor; Lecturer; Musician (Guitar, singer). m. Rita Bikel, 2 s. *Education:* Royal Academy of Dramatic Art. *Career:* Theatre and Film Including Fiddler On The Roof, Le Gazza Ladra. *Compositions:* My Side of The Mountain. *Recordings:* 20 Albums. *Publications:* Folk-songs and Footnotes; Theo. (Autobiography). *Honours:* Hon. Doctorate, University of Hartford; Nominee Academy Award; Emmy Award, 1988. *Memberships:* American Federation of Musicians; Actors Equity; Screen Actors Guild; AFTRA; AGMA; Asscn of Actors and Artists of America. *Current Management:* Honeyhill Productions Inc, 94 Honey Hill Rd, CT 06897, USA. *Address:* Associated Actors and Artists of America, Suite 500, 165 W 46th St, New York, NY 10036, USA.

BILA Vera; b. 22 May 1954, Rokycany, Czechoslovakia. 1 s. *Career:* Appeared on 8pm TV News, France 2, Canal and RAI; Theatre Des Bouffes Du Nord, Paris, France, 6 days; Festivals, Jazz, Montréal, Bourges, Paleo-Nyon, Arezzo, Rennes. *Compositions:* E Daj Nasval'i on compilation of festivals: Transmusical Rennes, 1996; Arezzo Wave, 1997. *Recordings:* CDRom Pop, 1996; Kake Kolore, 1998. *Publications:* Article in Liberation; Article in Les Inrockuptibles. *Honour:* Record of the Year, 1996. *Leisure interest:* Children. *Current Management:* Jiri Smetana Management, Paris, France. *Address:* c/o Jiri Smetana, Vinohradska 168, 13000 Prague, Czech Republic.

BILAL (Bilal Sayeed Oliver); b. Philadelphia, Pennsylvania, USA. Vocalist. *Musical Education:* Mannes Music Conservatory, New York City, classically-trained. *Career:* Approached by Moyo Entertainment, moved to Brooklyn and started gigging; Demo tape heard by Erykah Badu; Contribute to her Mama's Gun album; Released debut album on Interscope Records, 2001; Member of the Soulaquarians collective which includes: Talib Kweli; D'Angelo; Jill Scott; Questlove; James Poyser; Collaborations: Common; Erykah Badu; Mos Def; Guru. *Recordings:* Albums: First Born Second, 2001; Singles: Soul Sista, 2001. *Address:* c/o Interscope Records, 825 Eighth Ave, New York, USA. *Internet:* www.bilal-the-man.com.

BILEZIKJIAN John; b. 1 Feb. 1948, California, USA. Musician; Composer. m. Helen Louise Bilezikjian. *Education:* AA, Los Angeles Valley College, 1968; BA, Northridge, 1970. *Career:* Mission Impossible; I Spy; Apples Way; KPFK; KCRW; KFAC; The Postman Aways Rings Twice; Anastasia; Schindlers List; The Prince of Egypt. *Compositions:* Preludio Primo; Jemilleh; Eastern Fantasy; Ansial; Taksim Opus 10; Taksim Opus 20; The Land of Noah's Ark; I Love You Baby; Music for Film, Television and Stage. *Recordings:* America's Oud Virtuoso; the Art of The Oud; The Neo Classical Oud; The Magic of John Bilezikjian; Music of the Armenian Diaspora; Dantz Fever; Armenian Connection; Moonlight Sonata; 1001 Nights; Dream of Scheherazade; Sirocco; Tapestry of the Dance. *Publication:* Thesis, Gail Schwartz. *Honours:* Gen Awards, 1994, 1995; Most Outstanding Musician. *Memberships:* Musicians Union. *Leisure interests:* Antique Car Restoring; Fishing.

BILK Acker (Bernard Stanley); b. 28 Jan. 1929, Pensford, Somerset, England. Musician (clarinet); Composer; Bandleader. m. Jean, 1 s., 1 d. *Career:* Began playing clarinet in Royal Engineers, 1948; Clarinet, Ken Colyer's Band; Formed Bristol Paramount Jazz Band; Currently freelance artiste; Guest musician on numerous records; Tours world-wide, now with Paramount Jazz Band; Played with Reunion Paramount Jazz Band, Isle of Bute Jazz Festival, 1995; Owner 2 publishing companies. *Recordings:* Singles include: Somerset; Aria; Stranger On The Shore (No. 1, USA and UK, 1961); Albums include: The One For Me; Sheer Magic; Evergreen; Chalumeau-That's My Home; Three In The Morning (with Humphrey Lyttelton, John Barnes, Dave Green, Dave Cliff, Bobby Worth); Giants of Jazz (with Paramount Jazz Band, Kenny Ball and his Jazzmen, Kenny Baker Don Lusher All Stars); Chris Barber and Acker Bilk, That's It Then!; Clarinet Moods With Acker Bilk, Acker Bilk with string orchestra; Acker Bilk – The Oscars; Clarinet Moods with Acker Bilk; All the Hits and More; The Christmas Album; Acker Bilk and His Paramount Jazz Band; Acker Bilk In Holland; It Looks Like A Big Time Tonight; Hits Blues and Class; Great Moments; Best of Acker Bilk. *Leisure interests:* Painting; Walking. *Current Management:* Acker's International Jazz Agency. *Address:* 53 Cambridge Mansions, Cambridge Rd, London SW11 4RX, England.

BILLINGTON Scott Thomas; b. 27 Oct. 1951, Melrose, Massachusetts, USA. Record Prod.; Musician (harmonica). 1 d. *Career:* Produced over 100 albums of roots-orientated music for labels including: Rounder; Columbia; Sire; Real World. *Recordings include:* Alright Again, Clarence Gatemouth Brown; Pictures and Paintings, Charlie Rich; Voodoo, The Dirty Dozen Brass Band; Turning Point, Buckwheat Zydeco; Johnny Adams, One Foot in the Blues, 1996; Beau Jocque and the Zydeco Hi-Rollers, 1996; Bill Morrissey, You'll Never Get to Heaven, 1996; Ruth Brown, R & B = Ruth Brown, 1997; Irma Thomas, The Story of My Life, 1997; Irma Thomas, Marcia Ball and Tracy Nelson, Sing It!, 1998; Davell Crawford, The B-3 and Me, 1998; Ruth Brown, A Good Day for the Blues, 1999. *Honours:* 2 Grammy Awards; 7 Nominations; Grand Prix Du Disque; 2 W C Handy Awards; Producer of the Year, Offbeat Magazine, New Orleans, 1997. *Memberships:* NARAS; BMI. *Address:* 47 Forrester St, Newburyport, MA 01950, USA.

BILOUS Edward; Composer; Conductor. *Musical Education:* BM, Composition and Conducting, Manhattan School of Music; MM DMA, Composition, Juilliard School. *Career:* After graduation, joined Juilliard School, Music, Drama, Liberal Arts Department, Lincoln Center Institute; Co-chairman of Literature, Music Department at Juilliard; Artisitic Director of Music Advancement Program; Director, Consultant of Music Education programme by Juilliard and Berkley Learning Technologies. *Compositions:* Film, television music: Sleepaway Camp; Le Bain; Tribeca; Anna Sorror; Urban Fairy Tales; The Last Romantic; Theme for Monaco

Film Festival, 1993; Mixing Nia by Ethan Coen, 1998; Orchestrator, arranger for: Carnegie Hall Tribute to Pete Townshend (with Roger Daltrey, Alice Cooper, Sinead O'Connor, The Spin Doctors, Eddie Vedder); CD-ROM tour of Beauborg Museum, Pompidou Center, Paris; Juilliard Music Adventure; Educational Adventure Game; Circus!. *Honours:* Joseph Machlis Award for Excellence, Juilliard School; Best Public Service Announcement Award (Elephant Slaughter), Cannes, 1989. *Current Management:* SESAC. *Address:* 55 Music Sq. E, Nashville, TN 37203, USA.

BILY Antonin; b. 7 May 1939, Prague, Czech Republic. Composer; Arranger; Pianist. m. Jitka Bila, 31 Aug. 1972, 2 s. *Education:* Conservatory of Prague and J Jezek Conservatory. *Career:* Pianist and Composer, Traditional Jazz Studio, Prague, 1960–; Teacher and Head of Composition/Conducting Section, J Jezek Conservatory, Prague, 1986–. *Compositions:* Metamorphoses of Time, 1986; Modus Vivendi, 1991; Fine Stagione; A Town So Strange; On the Seventh Floor. *Recordings:* CCA 20 albums with traditional Jazz Studio, some recorded with Benny Waters, Tonny Scot, Albert Nicholas, Beryl Breyden. *Honours:* First awards: Jazz Festival Düsseldorf, 1968; International Contest of Composition for Jazz bigband, Barga, Italy, 1989; Asscn of Music Artist and Scientists; Czech Music Society; Czech Jazz Society. *Leisure interests:* Enthnomology; Nature. *Address:* 2 Roskotova 4/1692, Prague 4, Czech Republic.

BINDING Philip Robert; b. 20 March 1960, Barry, South Wales. Composer; Prod.; Writer; Musician (piano-synthesiser). m. Helen Garnett, 23 Nov. 1990, 1 d. *Education:* Ravensbourne Art College, 1978–80. *Musical Education:* Piano, Theory. *Career:* Sound Engineer, 1980–91; Formed Boom Productions with Simon Moore, producing music for TV, film, 1991. *Compositions:* TV themes; Incidental music includes Gladiators; International Gladiators; You Bet; Pop Quiz; What's My Line; ITV Sport; Missing; Expert Witness; Strange But True; Beadle's About; Love and Marriage; ITV Promotions; World Cup '98 theme tune; C5 News; Moment of Truth; Gladiators; Survivor; HTV News. *Memberships:* Musicians' Union; BASCA; PRS; MCPS. *Address:* Boom! Music Ltd, Tanglewood, 16 Blackwood Close, West Byfleet, Surrey KT14 6PP, England.

BINDZI Lucien; b. Cameroon. Artist Man.; Music Promoter. *Education:* Industrial Electricity Diploma. *Career:* Service Leader, Director, Kilo Brother; Rhénaly Péchiney, Alsace; Radio Host and nightclub DJ, Brittany; Founder, President, producer of shows of African music, dance and culture, Africa Music International, 1986–; Manager, group The Veterans, specialising in traditional Bikutsi music; Numerous tours throughout Africa; Frequent No. 1 hits, African charts. *Recordings:* Albums with The Veterans include: Min Sounga Mi Kabard, 1975; Me Ne Ngon Oyap, 1983; Wa Dug Ma, 1984; Au Village, 1985; Traditions, 1986; Les Veterans Presentent Ahanda, 1988; Toss Difference, 1993. *Address:* Africa Music International, 15 rue Charles Gounod, 56100 Lorient, France.

BINNS Henry; b. 1971, London, England. Prod.; Remixer. *Career:* Started as studio engineer; Began remixing with partner Sam Hardaker under the name Zero 7; Produced own material as Zero 7; Released debut album, 2001; Also successful as a live act; Collaborations: Sia Furler; Sophie Barker; Remixed: Terry Callier; Radiohead; Lenny Kravitz. *Recordings:* Albums: Simple Things, 2001; Singles: EP 2, 2000; Destiny (featuring Sia and Sophie), I Have Seen, 2001. *Honours:* Mercury Music Prize nominee, Simple Things, 2001; Muzik Award, Best New Artist, 2001. *Membership:* PRS. *Address:* c/o Ultimate Dilemma Records, 1 Shorrolds Rd, London, SW6 7TR, England.

BIRCH Rob (Rob B); b. 11 June 1961, Nottingham, England. Vocalist; Rapper. *Career:* Founded Gee Street Studio and Record Label; Formed Stereo MCs; Gigs on indie dance scene including support to Happy Mondays; Live shows with extended band and extra vocalists; Numerous remixes including U2, PM Dawn, Queen Latifah, Disposable Heroes of Hiphoprisy, Monie Love, Electronic, Madonna – Frozen, Jungle Brothers. *Recordings:* Singles: Elevate My Mind, 1990; Lost In Music, 1991; Connected, 1992; Step It Up, 1993; Creation, 1993; Deep Down and Dirty, 2001; We Belong In This World Together, 2001; Albums: Supernatural, 1990; Connected, 1992; Stereo MCs, 1993; Deep Down and Dirty, 2001. *Honours:* Brit Awards: Best British Group; Best British Album, Connected, 1994.

BIRGÉ Jean-Jacques Gaston; b. 5 Nov. 1952, Paris, France. Composer; Musician (synthesizer); Film Dir. 1 d. *Education:* IDHEC Diploma, National Film School. *Musical Education:* Self-taught. *Career:* Live music on 23 silent films including: Caligari; Fall of The House of Usher; Jeanne d'Arc; The Man With The Camera; J'Accuse; Le K (with Richard Bohringer); Il Etait Une Fois La Fête Fotaine; The Extraordinary Museum, Japan; EuroPrix, Austria; The Alphabet, CD-ROM, 1999. *Recordings:* Trop D'Adrénaline Nuit, 1977; Rideau!, 1980; A Travail Égal Salaire Égal, 1981; Carnage, 1985; L'Hallali, 1988; Qui Vive?, 1990; Kind Lieder, 1991; Urgent Meeting, 1992; Opération Blow Up, 1993; Sarajevo Suite, 1994; Carton, enhanced CD, 1997; Machiavel, enhanced CD, 1998.

Publication: The Sniper. *Honours:* Nomination, Victoires de la Musique, for Le K, 1994; British Academy Award for TV Arts, 1994; Video Grand Prize at Locarno Festival for Sarajevo, A Street Under Siege (collective). *Memberships:* Un Drame Musical Instantané; Les allumés du jazz. *Leisure interest:* Resistance. *Address:* 60 rue René Alazard, 93170 Bagnolet, France.

BIRGE Jodle (Birge Lonquist); b. 6 Nov. 1945, Sebbersund, Denmark. Musician (guitar). m. Inger-Lise, 1 s., 1 d. *Education:* Butcher. *Career:* Wembley Arena, London, England; Jonkobing Ice-stadium, Sweden; Tivoli Gardens, Copenhagen, Denmark; Fan Fair, Nashville, USA; Spruce Meadows, Calgary, Canada; Television shows, Denmark; USA; Canada; First Dane to perform at Grand Ole Opry at Nashville, Tennessee, 1998. *Recordings:* Rigtige Venner (Best Buddies), Platinum disc; Tre Hvide Duer, (Three White Doves), Platinum disc; Tusinde Rode Roser (Garden Full of Roses), Platinum disc; 89 albums released in Denmark, sales of more than 2m. *Honours:* Silver, Gold, Platinum discs. *Leisure interest:* Hunting wild animals. *Current Management:* Calle Nielsen, CB and Ole B Booking Aps, Denmark. *Address:* Jordsmonnet 4, PO Box 224, 8900 Randers, Denmark.

BIRKBY Peter Richard; b. 30 Nov. 1957, England. Composer; Musician (percussion). *Musical Education:* Leeds College of Music. *Career:* BBC Radio; Television from Pebble Mill; Tours with Shirley Bassey; Vic Damone; Gene Pitney; Dave Willetts; Jesus Christ Superstar. *Recordings:* Three Movements for Orchestra, Queen Elizabeth Hall, 1994; With own group, Legends: Special Edition, 1986. *Publications:* Over 80 pieces for Percussion (solo and ensemble); 6 for Orchestra; 20 for Jazz Orchestra. *Memberships:* PRS; MCPS; Musicians' Union. *Leisure interests:* Swimming; Cinema. *Address:* PO Box 7, South Kirkby, Pontefract, West Yorkshire WF9 3XJ, England.

BIRKETT Chris; b. 14 April 1953, Aldershot, Hampshire, England. Record Prod.; Composer; Musician (guitar); Singer. m. Janet Susan Hewett, 25 Jan. 1981, 1 s., 1 d. *Career:* Guitarist with: Ann Peebles; Rufus Thomas; Gene Knight; Love Affair; Singer with Omaha Sherif; Producer: Sinead O'Connor; Buffy Sainte-Marie; Talitha MacKenzie; Television, radio: Wogan; Pebble Mill; BBC News; Radio: Radio1; GLR; Capital. *Compositions include:* The album: Men From The Sky. *Recordings:* As producer/mixer/writer: Sinead O'Connor: Nothing Compares 2U; Album: I Do Not Want; Kiss of Life, Mandinka/Put 'Em On Me; Siedah Garrett; Copperhead Road, Steve Earle; with Five Star: Silk and Steel; Luxury of Life; Love Letters/That Old Devil, Alison Moyet; Nothing But Flowers, Talking Heads; Movements, Osibisa; Johnny Come Lately, Pogues; Holding Up Half The Sky: Voices of Celtic Women; Also with artists: Sting; Buffy Sainte-Marie; Laurie Freelove; Darden Smith; Cry Sisco; The Bible; Randy Remet; Hernandez; Mango Grove; Mr Big; Ice Cold In Alice; Richard Jon Smith; John Otway; Roman Holiday; Precious Wilson; John Kongos; Siobhan McCarthy; Mondino; The Soul Brothers; Talitha MacKenzie; Guo Yue and Joji Hirota. *Publications:* Articles in Billboard, Studio Engineer. *Honours:* Ampex Golden Reel Awards: Gold Star and Mango Grove; Platinum discs: Nothing Compares 2U, Sinead O'Connor. *Memberships:* PRS; MCPS; Musicians' Union. *Leisure interests:* Inventing; Electronics; Building studios; Wine growing. *Current Management:* Einstein Brothers, Toronto, Canada.

BIRO Daniel Andrew; b. 29 Jan. 1963, Johannesburg, South Africa. Composer; Songwriter; Musician (piano). *Musical Education:* 8 years, Jazz Conservatory, Monaco; 3 years Nice University, France. *Career:* As keyboard player, World tours with: The Truth, 1987; Big Bam Boo, 1989; Bandleader, songwriter with L'Orange, 1993–; Arranger, musicals by Henry Lewis include: Joan of Kent; The End of The World Show; Co-founder, Lust, multi-arts performance organization; Business venture, record label, Sargasso Records, (Experimental New Music). *Compositions:* For dance: Beauty and The Beast, 1992; Desert, 1995; For film: Lessons In How To Wear Red, 1994; Mu, 1995; For lust: Through The Mirror, 1993; The Pinocchio Tapes, 1994; Beba In White, 1995. *Recordings:* Albums: Soho Square, 1993; The Comparative Anatomy of Angels, 1996; Elegant Enigmas, 1999. *Memberships:* Musicians' Union; SACEM (France); SPNM. *Leisure interests:* Travel; Cinema; Chocolate. *Address:* PO Box 10565, London N1 8SR, England.

BIROSIK P J; b. 2 Sept. 1956, New York, New York, USA. Music Industry Consultant. *Education:* MA, Columbia, 1977. *Career:* Formed Musik International Corporation, 1977; Services offered include: Market planning; Media promotion; Media relations; A & R/label development; Previous clients include: Ozzy Osbourne; Black Sabbath; Van Halen; Nils Lofgren; Paul McCartney and Wings; Kiss; Uriah Heep; Blondie; David Soul; Virgin; Lol Creme and Kevin Godley; Fleetwood Mac; Rod Stewart; Stevie Nicks; Herbie Hancock; Sony Records; Guns 'N' Roses; Journey; Japan; David Sylvian; Amii Stewart; Studio 54; The Doobie Brothers; Rickie Lee Jones; Art of Persuasion; Max Million; Chuck E; New World Music; Earth Wave Productions; New Earth Records. *Publications:* Monthly columns in magazines and newspapers. *Honours:* Gold records, Independent Promotion: Journey: Look Into The Future; Al Wilson: Show and Tell; Nomination, Inland Empire Awards: Best Air Personality, 1976; Billboard Magazine: Best College Station, 1977; First Place, Inland Empire Awards: Best Jazz Programming, 1977. *Memberships include:* Voting mem., NARAS, 1980–95; NAIRD, 1994, 1995; Judge, NAIRD Indie Awards, 1993–95; Founder, New Age Music Network; International Platform Asscn; CMC; IMA: ED; ABA. *Leisure interests:* Monitoring start-up international record companies. *Current Management:* Musik International. *Address:* 154 Betasso Rd, Boulder, CO 80302, USA.

BIRTLES Gary; b. 10 June 1955, Leicester, England. Musician (saxophone); Singer. 2 s. *Musical Education:* Self-taught. *Career:* Singer, own band, The Swinging Laurels; 2 UK support tours with Culture Club; Saxophone session player for Funboy 3; Member, brass section, The Beautiful South, 1990–; Currently singer, Country/Pop band Yellowbelly; Television appearances include: Top of The Pops, with Funboy 3 and The Beautiful South. *Recordings:* Singles: with The Swinging Laurels: Peace of Mind, 1980; Rodeo, 1982; Lonely Boy, 1983; Zoom, 1984. *Membership:* PRS. *Leisure interests:* Songwriting; Computers; Tai Chi. *Address:* 138 Howard Rd, Leicester LE2 1XJ, England.

BISHOP Michael Joseph; b. 14 June 1951, Santa Monica, California, USA. Recording Engineer; Record Prod. m. Wendy LaTessa, 22 Sept. 1979, 2 d. *Career:* Record producer, recording engineer, 1972–. *Recordings:* As recording engineer: Play That Funky Music, Wild Cherry, 1986; Live At Carnegie Hall, Liza Minnelli, 1987; The Sound of Music, Cincinnati Pops Orchestra, 1988; Big Band Hit Parade, Dave Brubeck/Cab Calloway/Gerry Mulligan/Doc Severensen, 1988; To Diz with Love, Dizzy Gillespie, 1992; The Great Fantasy Adventure Album, Cincinnati Pops Orchestra, 1995; Seven Steps to Heaven, Ray Brown Trio, 1996; Come On In This House, Junior Wells, 1996; Live at Buddy Guys, Junior Wells, 1997; Copland: Music of America, Cincinnati Pops Orchestra, 1997; Tribute at Town Hall, Oscar Peterson, 1996; So What's New?, Dave Brubeck, 1998. *Honours:* Grammy Award and Nominations. *Membership:* Audio Engineering Society; NARAS; MPGA; ASCAP; AQHA; NRHA. *Address:* Telarc International Corp, 23307 Commerce Park Rd, Cleveland, OH 44122, USA.

BISMUT Michel; b. 20 April 1954, Tunis, Tunisia. Composer; Musician (contrebass). m. Agnes Berger, 17 Oct. 1992, 1 s., 1 d. *Education:* Engineer, Computer Science and Management. *Musical Education:* Self-taught; Classic Conservatoire, Avignon-France. *Career:* Jazz festivals and clubs throughout France; Also UK; Germany; Spain; Israel; Appearances, French local television and national radio. *Recordings:* Socco, 1991; UR, 1996. *Memberships:* SACEM (French Composers' Society). *Current Management:* Condorcet Productions. *Address:* 21 rue Tour Gayraud, 34000 Montpellier, France.

BISSET John; b. 3 Nov. 1960, Stockport, England. Musician (Guitar). 2 s. *Education:* Fine Art Degree, Ravensbourne College of Art. *Career:* Improviser, Composer and Arranger; Work with London Electric Guitar Orchestra; Toured England with Billy Jenkins; Appearances at Relay, live shows; Performances at 2:13 Club run with Burkhard Beins, 1994098; Brush 'n' Strings with Rhodri Davies and Marcus Heesch, improvised music with live painting; Tha Arc, English tour, 1999; Go! daily radio show for children compiled by John Bisset and presented with children; Arranger and Performer, Happy Happy; Arranger of Purcell for dance piece Vivre d'Amour; Invited Artist, Real Time Music Meeting, Hamburg, 1998; Tours with Burkhard Beins on drums; Fairplay '98 Festival. *Recordings:* Flying Fish (without wings); Funny Old World; Ralay OOO Random Play 2; Kneel Down Like A Saint Gorilla and Stop; Dervish; Holly; 13 Lumps of Chease, with London Electric Guitar Orchestra. *Membership:* PRS. *Address:* 139 Gibson Gardens, London N16 7HH, England.

BJELLAND Kat; b. Woodburn, Oregon, USA. Vocalist; Musician (guitar). *Career:* Member, bands with Courtney Love (Hole) and Jennifer (L7); Founder, all-girl rock group Babes In Toyland, 1987–97. *Recordings:* Albums: With Babes In Toyland: Spanking Machine, 1990; To Mother (mini-album), 1991; Fontanelle, 1992; Peel Sessions, 1992; Painkiller, 1993; Nemesisters, 1995; Devil (compilation), 2000; Also appears on: Teriyaki Asthma, 1991; Fast Track To Nowhere, 1994; Spirit of '73, 1995; Reading '95, 1995; Screwed, 1996; Honky, 1997; Songs of The Witchblade, 1998; River of Song, 1998. *Address:* c/o Pinnacle Entertainment Inc, 83 Riverside Dr., New York, NY 10024, USA.

BJÖRK (Björk Gudmunsdottir); b. 21 Nov. 1965. Reykjavik, Iceland. Vocalist. *Career:* Solo release, aged 11; Singer, various Icelandic groups include: Exodus; Tappi Tikarras; Kukl; Singer, The Sugarcubes, 1987–92; Solo artiste, 1992–; Recent appearances include Reading Festival, 1995. *Recordings:* with The Sugarcubes: Life's Too Good, 1988; Here Today Tomorrow Next Week, 1989; Stick Around For Joy, 1992; It's It, 1992; solo: Björk, 1977; Debut, 1993; Post, 1995; Telegram, 1996; Homogenic, 1997; Selmasongs, 2000; Vespertine, 2001; Singles: with The Sugarcubes: Birthday; solo: Venus As A Boy; Violently Happy; Human Behaviour; Big Time Sensuality; Play Dead; Army of Me; Isobel; It's Oh So Quiet; Possibly Maybe; I Miss You/Cover Me; Hyperballad; Hunter; Bachelorette; All Is

Full of Love; Alarm Call; Pagan Poetry; Other recordings: Gling-Go, Trio Gudmundar Ingolfssonar, 1990; Ex-El, Graham Massey, 1991; Tank Girl, 1995; Mission Impossible, 1996; Nearly God, 1996; Archive, 1997; Tibetan Freedom Concert, 1997; Not For Threes, 1998; Great Crossover Potential, 1998; Y2K Beat The Clock Version 1, 1999. *Honours:* Brit Awards: Best International Newcomer, 1994; Best International Female Artist, 1994, 1996, 1997; Platinum and Gold records. *Current Management:* Insane Artists Management, 7218 Beverly Blvd, Los Angeles, CA 90036, USA. *Address:* c/o One Little Indian, 250 York Rd, London SW11 3SJ, England.

BJÖRKENHEIM Raoul Melvin; b. 11 Feb. 1956, Los Angeles, California, USA. Musician (guitar). m. Päivi Björkenheim (Määttä), 1 s. *Musical Education:* Helsinki Conservatory, 1977–78; Berklee College of Music, Boston, USA, 1978–81. *Career:* Founder member, own jazz groups Arbuusi and Roommushklahn, 1980–83; Member, Edward Vesala's Sound and Fury, 1984–86; with Sielun Veljet, 1989; Member, Krakatau, 1987–; Tours throughout Finland with above. *Compositions:* For big band: Other Places; Some; Primal Mind; For symphony orchestra: Whales; Ballando; For electric guitar orchestra: Apocalypso. *Recordings:* with Edward Vesala: Bad Luck Good Luck; Kullervo; Lumi; with Krakatau: Ritual, 1988; Alive, 1990; Volition, 1992; Matinale, 1994. *Honours:* Yrjö Award, Finnish Jazz Federation, 1984; Emma Prize, Best Jazz Record, Volition, 1993. *Leisure interests:* Literature; Photography; Swimming; Walking; Thinking. *Current Management:* Gunnar Pfabe. *Address:* Heinsbergstrasse 30, 50674 Cologne, Germany.

BJORNS Siggi; b. 26 June 1955, Iceland. Musician (guitar, harmonica). *Musical Education:* Self-taught. *Career:* Former fisherman, 14 years; Professional musician, 1988–; Performed in clubs and halls in more than 20 countries; Television apperances in Denmark and Iceland; Radio broadcasts in Denmark, Iceland, Norway and New Zealand. *Compositions:* Bubbinn; Kotturinn; Beitningartremmi; One Gentle Touch. *Recordings:* Albums: Blues On Both Sides, 1993; Live At Sorens, 1993; Bisinn a Trinidad, 1994; Smoke 'n' Perfume, 1995; Road, 1998. *Memberships:* Dansk Musikerforbund (Danish Musicians' Union); KODA; GRAMEX; DJBIA. *Leisure interest:* Kayaking. *Current Management:* Tusund Tjalir, Iceland. *Address:* Brammersgade 2A-3, 8000 Århus C, Denmark.

BLACHMAN Thomas; b. 2 April 1963, Copenhagen, Denmark. Musician (drums); Composer; Bandleader; Prod.; Label Man. *Musical Education:* Jazz Composition, Berklee College of Music, Boston, USA. *Career:* Co-founder, jazz quintet Page One; Tours of Europe, USA, 1986–90; Played drums for Lee Konitz, Joe Henderson; Solo artist, 1991-. *Recordings:* Albums: with Page One: Beating Bop Live, 1988; Live At Ronnie Scott's, 1989; Solo albums: Love Boat, 1991; Blachman Meets Al and Remee, 1994; Blachman Introduces Standard Jazz and Rap Vol. 1, Billie Koppel, 1995; Caroline Henderson, 1995. *Honours:* 3 Grammy Awards, 1991, 1995. *Leisure interest:* Swimming. *Current Management:* Mega Records. *Address:* Capella India Kaj 1, Frihavnen, 2100 O Copenhagen, Denmark.

BLACK Barry; b. 1 July 1950, Newcastle-upon-Tyne, England. Musician (drums, percussion). m. Barbara Ann, 1 s., 1 d. *Musical Education:* Personal tutors, aged 10–16; Further studies for LTCL, LGSM. *Career:* Member, John Miles Band, 1973–83; Tours: Europe, US, Canada; Support tours with: Elton John; Fleetwood Mac; Aerosmith; Jethro Tull; Tour with Beckett (later renamed Back Street Crawler); 2 albums, with Splinter; Television appearances: Top of The Pops; Magpie; Blue Peter; Mike Mansfield television specials; Tonite Show. *Compositions:* Do It Anyway, John Miles; Madness Money and Music, Sheena Easton; Take My Love and Run, The Hollies. *Recordings:* All John Miles albums and singles, up to early 1980's; Also: Barry Black, 1995; Tragic Animal Stories, 1997. *Memberships:* PRS; Equity; Musicians' Union.

BLACK Charlie; b. Cheverly, Maryland, USA. Country Music Songwriter. *Career:* Staff Writer, Terrace Music, Nashville, 1970–; Songwriter, Warner Chappell Music, 1977–88; Own company, Five-Bar-B Songs, 1989–; Songs recorded by: Roy Orbison; Anne Murray; Paul Anka; Dan Seals; Kenny Rogers; K T Oslin; Eddy Raven; Bobby Bare; Bellamy Brothers; Charlie Rich. *Compositions:* No. 1 Country Hit Singles: Anne Murray: Shadows In The Moonlight; A Little Good News; Blessed Are The Believers; Reba McEntire: You Lie; K T Oslin: Come Next Monday; T G Shepard: Slow Burn; Strong Heart; Bellamy Brothers: Do You Love As Good As You Look; Tommy Overstreet: I Don't Know You Anymore; Earl Thomas Conley: Honor Bound; Gary Morris: 100% Chance of Rain; Also appears on: At Last, Dirk Hamilton, 1977; Simple Little Words, Cristy Lane, 1979; Twist of Fate, Cee Cee Chapman, 1988; More I Learn, Ronna Reeves, 1992. *Honours:* Country Music Writer of Year, SESAC, 1979; Country Music Writer of Year, ASCAP 1983, 1984; Elected to NSAI Songwriters Hall of Fame, 1991; Grammy Nominations for: A Little Good News; Come Next Monday. *Membership:* ASCAP Southern Advisory Board. *Current Management:* Poker Productions. *Address:* 1618 16th Ave S, Nashville, TN 37212, USA.

BLACK Clint; b. 4 Feb. 1962, USA. Singer; Songwriter; Prod. m. Lisa Hartman Black, 20 Oct. 1991. *Career:* Film: Maverick; Television: Wings episode; Half-time performance, Superbowl XXXVIII; Performed National Memorial Day Celebration, Washington DC, 1994. *Recordings:* Killing Time, 1989; Put Yourself In My Shoes, 1990; The Hard Way, 1992; No Time To Kill, 1993; One Emotion, 1994; Nothin' But the Taillights, 1997; D'Lectrified, 1999. *Honours:* CMA's Horizon Award, 1989; CMA's Top Male Vocalist, 1990; AMA's Favourite New Country Artist, 1990; Music City News: Star of Tomorrow, Album of The Year, 1990; ACM's Album of The Year, Single of The Year; Best New Vocalist; Best Male Vocalist, 1990. *Current Management:* Mark Hartley. *Address:* c/o Fitzgerald/Hartley, 50 W Main St, Ventura, CA 93001, USA.

BLACK Frances; b. 25 June 1960, Dublin, Ireland. Singer. m. Brian Allen, 1 s., 1 d. *Education:* Rathmines College. *Career:* Member of Arcady, Woman's Heart Tour; Toured with Kieran Goss; Solo career; Tours in USA, Australia, England, Ireland. *Recordings:* Albums with The Black Family: The Black Family, 1986; Time For Touching Home, 1988; What A Time, 1996; With Arcady: After the Ball, 1991; With Kieran Goss: Black and Goss, 1994, 1995; Solo: Talk to Me, 1994; The Sky Road, 1995; Smile on Your Face, 1996; Don't Get Me Wrong, 1998; Also appears on: Woman's Heart, 1993; Celtic Twilight Vol. 3, 1996; Loving Time, 1997; Songs of The Irish Whistle Vol. 2, 1999; Holding Up Half The Sky, 1999; Singles/EPs: Fear Is The Enemy of Love and Children, 1994; Stranger On The Shore, 1996; Love Me Please, 1997. *Honours:* Most Popular Irish Entertainer; National Entertainment Awards, 1995; Best Female, 1995, 1996, IRMA. *Current Management:* Pat Egan/Brian Allen. *Address:* c/o Merchants Court, 24 Merchants Quay, Dublin, Ireland.

BLACK Frank, (Black Francis, Charles Michael Kitteridge Thompson IV); b. 1965, Long Beach, California, USA. Singer; Songwriter; Musician (Guitar). *Education:* Studied Anthropology, University of Massachusetts. *Career:* Formed The Pixies; Early support slots with Throwing Muses; Numerous tours and festival dates; Some television appearances; Support on U2's Zoo TV tour; Band disbanded, 1993; Some solo releases and live gigs. *Recordings:* with The Pixies: Singles: Gigantic; Monkey Gone To Heaven; Here Comes Your Man; Velouria; Dig For Fire; Planet of Sound; Alec Eiffel; Head On; Debaser; Albums: Come On Pilgrim, 1987; Surfer Rosa, 1988; Doolittle, 1989; Bossanova, 1990; Trompe Le Monde, 1991; Death To The Pixies (boxed set), 1997; Pixies At The BBC (sessions), 1998; Complete B-Sides, 2001; solo: Singles include: Hang On To Your Ego, 1993; Headache, 1994; Albums: Frank Black, 1993; Teenager of The Year, 1994; The Cult of Ray, 1996; Frank Black and The Catholics, 1998; Pistolero, 1999; Dog In The Sand, 2001.

BLACK Mary; b. 23 May 1955, Dublin, Ireland. Vocalist. *Career:* Folk singer, Dublin folk clubs; Member, De Dannan; Also solo career; Appearance, television series Bringing It All Back Home, with Emmylou Harris, Dolores Keane, Nashville; Also with Van Morrison on Celtic Heartbeat; Tours, USA, UK, Japan. *Recordings:* Mary Black, 1983; Collected, 1984; Without The Fanfare, 1985; The Black Family, with the Black Family, 1986; By The Time It Gets Dark, 1987; Time For Touching Home (with the Black Family), 1989; No Frontiers, 1989; Babes In The Wood (No. 1, Ireland), 1991; The Best of Mary Black, 1991; The Collection, 1992; The Holy Ground, 1993; Circus, 1995; Looking Back, 1995; One and Only, 1997; Shine, 1997; Song For Ireland, 1999; Songs of The Irish Whislte, 1999; Speaking With The Angel, 2000. *Honours:* Best Female Artist, Irish Rock Music Awards Poll, 1987, 1988. *Current Management:* Dara Management, Dublin; Big Advance Management, 12 Oval Rd, London NW1 7DH, England.

BLACKBURN Paul; b. 1974, Southport, England. Musician (guitar, bass, percussion, omnichord). *Career:* Member, Gomez; Numerous live dates and television appearances. *Recordings:* Singles: 78 Stone Wobble, 1998; Whippin' Piccadilly, 1998; Get Myself Arrested, 1998; Bring It On, 1999; Rhythm and Blues Alibi, 1999; We Haven't Turned Around (featured on American Beauty OST), 1999; Machismo EP, 2000; Albums: Bring It On, 1998; Liquid Skin, 1999; Abandoned Shopping Trolley Hotline, 2000.

BLACKMORE Ritchie (Richard Hugh); b. 14 April 1945, Weston-Super-Mare, Avon, England. Rock Musician (guitar); Composer. *Musical Education:* Thompson School of Music, 1 year. *Career:* Musician, toured with: Mike Dee and The Jaywalkers, 1961–62; Screaming Lord Sutch and His Savages, 1962; Gene Vincent; Jerry Lee Lewis; The Outlaws; The Musketeers; The Dominators; The Wild Boys, 1964; Neil Christian's Crusaders; The Roman Empire; Mandrake Root, 1967; Founder member, UK rock group Deep Purple, 1968–75; Founder, Ritchie Blackmore's Rainbow, 1975–84; Reformed Deep Purple, 1984-. *Recordings:* Albums: with Deep Purple: Shades of Deep Purple, 1968; The Book of Taliesyn, 1969; Deep Purple, 1969; Concerto For Group and Orchestra, 1970; Deep Purple In Rock, 1970; Fireball, 1971; Machine Head, 1972; Made In Japan, 1972; Purple Passages, 1972; Who Do You Think We Are?, 1973; Burn, 1974; Stormbringer, 1974; 24 Carat Purple, 1975; Come Taste The Band,

1975; Made In Europe, 1976; Last Concert In Japan, 1977; Perfect Strangers, 1985; House of Blue Light, 1987; Nobody's Perfect, 1988; Slaves and Masters, 1990; Stranger In Us All, 1995; with Rainbow: Ritchie Blackmore's Rainbow, 1975; Rainbow Rising, 1976; Live On Stage, 1977; Long Live Rock and Roll, 1978; Live In Germany, 1976, 90; Down To Earth, 1979; Difficult To Cure, 1981; Straight Between The Eyes, 1982; Bent Out of Shape, 1983; Finyl Vinyl, 1986; Blackmore's Night: Shadow of the Moon, 1996; Under a Violet Moon, 1999; Fires At Midnight, 2001. *Honours:* Grammy Nomination, Best Instrumental, Snowman, 1982; Numerous magazine poll wins, as Best Band; Best Guitarist; Best Album; Best Song. *Memberships:* ASCAP; BMI; PRS. *Leisure interests:* Football; Seances. *Current Management:* Carole Stevens at Minstrel Hall Music. *Address:* PO Box 735, Nesconset, NY 11767, USA.

BLACKSTOCK Narvel Wayne; b. 31 Aug. 1956, Fort Worth, Texas, USA. Artist Man.; Entertainment Co Exec. m. Reba McEntire, 3 June 1989, 4 c. (3 from previous marriage). *Career:* Personal Manager: Vice President, Starstruck Entertainment, Nashville, 1988–; Clients include: Reba McEntire; Rhett Atkins; Linda Davis; Brett James; Gary Oliver. *Memberships:* NARAS; Country Music Asscn; Academy of Country Music. *Address:* Starstruck Entertainment, PO Box 121996, Nashville, TN 37212, USA.

BLACKWELL Chris; b. 22 June 1937, London, England. Record Co Exec. *Career:* Founder, chairman, Island Records, 1962–97; Issued masters from Jamaican producers; Signings to Island include: Jimmy Cliff; Bob Marley; Millie Small (My Boy Lollipop, sold 6m. copies); Spencer Davis Group; Steve Winwood; John Martyn; Robert Palmer; Nick Drake; Cat Stevens; Free; Mott The Hoople; Spooky Tooth; Fairport Convention; B-52's; Toots and The Maytals. *Address:* c/o Island Records, 400 Lafayette St, New York, NY 10003, USA.

BLACKWELL Otis; b. 1931, Brooklyn, New York, USA. Songwriter; Musician. *Career:* One of major songwriters of rock 'n' roll era; Also recording artist. *Compositions:* for Derek Martin: Daddy Rolling Stone; for Little Willie John: Fever, 1956 (Later hit for Peggy Lee); for Elvis Presley include: All Shook Up (first UK No. 1); Don't Be Cruel, 1956; Paralysed, 1957; Return To Sender, 1962; One Broken Heart For Sale; for Jerry Lee Lewis: Breathless; Great Balls of Fire, 1958; for Dee Clark: Hey Little Girl; Just Keep It Up, 1959; for Jimmy Jones: Handy Man, 1960; for Cliff Richard: Nine Times Out of Ten, 1960. *Recordings:* Album: Singing The Blues, 1956; All Shook Up, 1976; These Are My Songs, 1978; Also appears on: You're OK I'm OK, 1978; Lovin' Bird Vol. 2, 1989.

BLACKWOOD James Webre; b. 4 Aug. 1919, Ackerman, Mississippi, USA. Gospel Singer. m. Miriam Grantham, 4 May 1939, 2 s. *Musical Education:* Doctorate in Music, Golden State University. *Career:* Appeared in film Sing a Song for Heaven's Sake; Appeared on Arthur Godfrey talent show on CBS, 1954, 1956; Appeared on all major TV and radio networks in USA; Recorded for over 21 years. *Composition:* Have You Talked to the Man Upstairs. *Recordings:* Numerous. *Honours:* Nominated for 30 Grammy Awards, Winner of 9; 7 Dove Awards, Gospel Music Asscn; Favourite Gospel Songs and Spirituals placed in Grammy Hall of Fame, 1999. *Memberships:* National Academy of Recording Arts and Sciences; American Federation of TV and Radio Artists. *Leisure interest:* Grandchildren. *Address:* 4411 Sequoia Rd, Memphis, TN 38117, USA.

BLACKWOOD Sarah; b. Halifax, England. Vocalist. *Career:* Singer, Dubstar, 1994–2000; British tour, 1996. *Recordings:* Albums: Disgraceful, 1995; Goodbye, 1997; Make It Better, 2000; Singles: Stars, 1995; Anywhere, 1995; Not So Manic Now, 1996; Elevator Song, 1996; Cathedral Park, 1997; I Will Be Your Girlfriend, 1997; No More Talk, 1997; Anxious, 1998; I (Friday Night), 2000. *Address:* c/o Food Records, 43 Brook Green, London W6 7EF, England.

BLADES Jack; Singer; Musician (bass guitar). *Career:* Member, Night Ranger, 1981–88; Concerts include: supports to Santana; Judas Priest; Doobie Brothers; Member, Damn Yankees, 1989–; US tour with Bad Company, 1990; Member, side project Shaw Blades (with Tommy Shaw), 1995. *Recordings:* Albums: with Night Ranger: Dawn Patrol, 1982; Midnight Madness, 1983; Seven Wishes, 1985; Big Life, 1987; Man In Motion, 1988; Live In Japan, 1990; Neverland, 1997; Seven, 1998; with Damn Yankees: Damn Yankees, 1991; Don't Tread, 1992; with Shaw Blades: Hallucination, 1995; with Tommy Shaw: 7 Deadly Zens, 1998; Singles: with Night Ranger: Sister Christian; Sentimental Street; with Damn Yankees: Coming of Age; High Enough; Come Again; Where You Goin' Now; Silence Is Broken, from film Nowhere To Run, 1993. *Honours:* Motor City Music Award, Outstanding National Rock Pop Single, 1992. *Current Management:* Madhouse Management, PO Box 15108, Ann Arbor, MI 48106, USA.

BLADES Rubén; b. 16 July 1948, Panama City, Panama. Singer; Bandleader; Composer; Actor. *Education:* University of Panama; Harvard Law School, USA. *Career:* Vocalist, groups Conjunto Latino, Los Salvjes del

Ritmo, 1966–69; Lawyer, National Bank of Panama, 1969–74; Joined Ray Barretto's band, 1974; Renamed Guarare, 1975; Member, Fania All-Stars, 1976–80; Songwriter, numerous Latin artistes, 1970s; Subject of television documentary, The Return of Rubén Blades, 1986; Leader, group Seis del Solar, 1984–; Film appearances include: Crossover Dreams, 1985; Critical Condition, 1987; The Milagro Beanfield War, 1988; The Lemon Sisters; The Two Jakes; Dead Man Out, 1989. *Recordings:* Albums include: with Pete Rodríguez, De Panama a Nuevo York, 1970; with Ray Barretto: Barretto, 1975; Barretto Live – Tomorrow, 1976; with Fania All-Stars: Tribute To Tito Rodríguez, 1976; with Larry Harlow: La Raza Latina, 1977; with Louie Ramírez: Louie Ramírez y Sus Amigos, 1978; with Willie Colón: The Good, The Bad, The Ugly, 1975; Metiendo Mano!, 1977; Siembra, 1978; Maestra Vida (parts 1 and 2), 1980; Canciones del Solar de los Arburridos, 1981; The Last Fight, 1982; Solo: El Que La Hace La Paga, 1983; Buscando America, 1984; Mucho Mejor, 1984; Crossover Dreams (film soundtrack), 1985; Escenas, 1985; Agua de Luna, 1987; Doble Filo, 1987; Nothing But The Truth, 1988; Antecedente, 1988; Rubén Blades y Son del Solar... Live!, 1990; Caminando, 1991. *Honours:* Gold discs; Grammy Award, Antecedente, 1988; Grammy Nomination, 1983; ACE Award, Dead Man Out, 1989; Composer of The Year, Latin NY magazine, 1976. *Current Management:* Morra, Brezner, Steinberg and Tenenbaum, 345 N Maple Dr., Suite 200, Beverly Hills, CA 90210, USA.

BLAKE Adam James Wyndham; b. 30 July 1960, Lincoln, England. Singer; Songwriter; Musician (guitar, bass); Teacher. m. Catherine Ramage, 31 Aug. 1991, 1 d. *Musical Education:* Self-taught. *Career:* Played with many groups including: The Cannibals; Treatment; Mumbo-Jumbo; The Hipshakers; Raw, 1976–; Bassist, Natacha Atlas; Guitarist, Errol Linton. *Recordings:* Restless; Put You Behind Me; Waiting For Love; Even If You Hadn't; Friends. *Publications:* Numerous articles published in periodicals. *Memberships:* PRS; Musicians' Union; PAMRA. *Leisure interests:* Literature; Cinema. *Address:* 77 Linden Gardens, London W2 4EU, England.

BLAKE Ian; b. 9 Dec. 1955, London, England. Composer; Prod.; Musician (Woodwinds, Keyboards, Bass). *Education:* Degree Course, London University; Member of London Boy Singers, 1968–71; Piano, organ, clarinet and lute lessons. *Career:* Tours and recording with Pyewackett, 1980–88; with Mike Jackson, 1988–93; Backing Musician for June Tabor, Michelle Shocked, Eric Bogle; Musician, National Theatre, London, 1987; Tours with Mellstock Band, 1988; Writer and Musician, The Crusades, Barossa Festival, 1992. *Compositions:* Persephone, 1995; Spirit of Place, 1996; The Gathering of the Animals, 1998. *Recordings:* Producer and Musician, Eric Bogles' Small Miracles, 1997; Writer, Producer, Musician, over 20 children's albums; Contributor, albums by Martin Simpson, Andrew Cronshaw, June Tabor. *Publication:* The Really Easy Cello Book, 1989. *Honours:* ARIA Nomination, 1992; Gold Disc, 1995; TDK Talking Book Award Nomination, 1996. *Memberships:* APRA; Musicians' Union of Australia. *Current Management:* Serpentine Productions, PO Box 1750, Canberra, ACT 2601, Australia. *Address:* 4 Rudall St, Latham, ACT 2615, Australia.

BLAKE Karl Antony; b. 5 Dec. 1956, Reading, Berkshire, England. Musician; Filmaker; Lyricist. *Education:* BA Hons, Fine Art and Mixed Media, 1991–94. *Career:* Formed Lemon Kittens, 1978; Joined as duo by Danielle Dax, 1979–82; Formed Shock Headed Peters, 1982–87; Formed British Racing Green, 1987; Formed Evil Twin with David Mellor; Reformed Shock Headed Peters, 1990–; Currently member of all 3 groups; Small roles in films, Chariots of Fire, Caravaggio, Voice of Silence. *Recordings:* with Lemon Kittens: 2 EPs; 2 albums: We Buy A Hammer For Daddy; The Big Dentist; with Shock Headed Peters; 3 EPs; 5 albums: Not Born Beautiful; Fear Engine; Several Headed Enemy; Fear Engine II; Tendercide, 1996; 2 EPs as member, Alternative TV with Mark Perry, 1985–86; Solo: 1 EP, 1 album as The Underneath, 1986–87; 9 short films, poetry in compilation; 2 solo archive albums as Karl Blake. *Address:* BM Swarf, London WC1N 3XX, England.

BLAKE Norman; b. 20 Oct. 1965, Bellshill, Scotland. Musician (guitar); Vocalist. 1 d. *Career:* Member, The Boy Hairdressers; Founder member, Teenage Fanclub, 1989-. *Recordings:* Albums: A Catholic Education, 1990; Bandwagonesque, 1991; Thirteen, 1993; Grand Prix, 1995; Mobile Safari, 1995; Sharks Patrol These Waters, 1995; Life Goes On, 1995; Reading '95 Special, 1995; Songs From Northern Britain, 1997; Howdy, 2000. *Address:* c/o Creation Records, 109 Regents Park Rd, London NW1 8UR, England.

BLANCHARD Pierre; b. 24 May 1956, Saint-Quentin, France. Musician (violin); Composer; Arranger. 1 s. *Musical Education:* Conservatoire de St Quentin; Université Musicale International de Paris; 6 months study in New York. *Career:* Lived in Paris, 1977–; Professor CIM, 1979–81; Violinist, Martial Solal's Big Band, 1981–86; Played throughout Europe; Played with Stéphane Grappelli, Antibes and Paris Festivals, 1988; Formed Gulf String, 1989; Director of Jazz class, CNR D'Aubervilliers – La Courneuve, 1992–; Formed Quintette A Cordes de Pierre Blanchard, 1994; Other festivals include: Halle That Jazz, 1993; Presences, 1994;

Banlieues Bleues, 1995; Also worked with: Bernard Lubat, Jacques Thollot, Rene Urtreger. *Recordings:* Solo albums: Each One Teach One, 1985; Music For String Quartet, Jazz Trio, Violin and Lee Konitz, 1987; Gulf String, 1993; 2 albums with Martial Solal Big Band; with Raphael Fays: Voyages, 1988; Gipsy Touch, 1991; with Pierre Michelot: Bass and Bosses, 1989; Other albums with René Urtreger, Eric Le Lann, Post Image, Jazzogene Big Band; Also appears on: Compact Jazz, 1992; Turtle's Dream, 1994; Voyage Aux Amériques, 1995; Ca Va Ca Va, 1996; Lagoa, 1998. *Honour:* Stéphane Grappelli donated the violin of M Warlop, 1984. *Leisure interests:* Drawing caricatures; Cooking; Travel; Chess. *Current Management:* Claudette de San Isidoro. *Address:* 93 bis rue de Montreux, 75011 Paris, France.

BLANCHARD Terence; b. 13 March 1962, New Orleans, Louisiana, USA. Musician. *Education:* Studied jazz with Ellis Marsalis and classical trumpet with George Jensen, 1978; Graduated; New Orleans Center of Creative Arts; Attended, Rutgers University, 1980. *Career:* Toured with Lionel Hampton, 1980; Joined Art Blakey and the Jazz Messengers, world-wide tours, 1982; Formed Harrison-Blanchard, 1990; Began work on first solo album; Worked on Spike Lee's film Malcolm X, and made first screen appearance; Tours throughout USA, Canada, Japan and Europe, 1991. *Compositions:* Caveman's Valentine, motion picture score, 2001; Original Sin, motion picture score, 2001. *Recordings include:* With Art Blakey: Dr Jeckyle, 1992; New Year's Eve at Sweet Basil, 1992; Art Blakey's Jazz Messengers: Live in Leverkeusen, 1995; Harrison-Blanchard: New York Second Line, 1984; Discernment, 1986; Crystal Stair, 1987; Black Pearl, 1988; Solo: Mo' Better Blues, 1990; Terence Blanchard, 1991; Simply Stated, 1992; Malcolm X Jazz Suite, 1993; Malcolm X: Original motion picture score, 1993; Billie Holliday Songgbook, 1994; Romantic Defiance, 1995; Clockers, motion picture score, 1995; The Heart Speaks, 1995; Summer of Sam, motion picture score, 1999; Jazz in Film, 1999; Let's Get Lost, 2001; Wandering Moon, 2001. *Publications:* Contributor of articles in professional journals and magazines. *Honours:* Winner, Grand Prix du Disque, 1984; Grammy Nomination, Best Jazz Instrumental Performance by a Group, 1990; Emmy Nomination, Best Original Score for a Documentary, 1995; Grammy Nomination, Best Latin Jazz Performance, 1996; Grammy nomination, Best Jazz Instrumental Solo for 'I Thought About You', 2001. *Current Management:* Burgess Management, 3225 Prytania St, New Orleans, LA 70115, USA.

BLAND Bill; b. 6 Feb. 1962, Wirral, Merseyside, England. Musician (African and Latin percussion). *Education:* Anthropology, School of Oriental and African Studies, London; Studied Cuban percussion with Oscar Valdes and African percussion with Emmanuel Tagoe. *Career:* Radio and TV appearances with Ebo Iye, with Peter Badejo, 1991; Roberto Plas's Latin Ensemble, 1992; Orquesta la Clave featuring Jesus Alemany, 1993; London Afro Blok, Commonwealth Games, Canada, 1994; Palenke, 1996; Yoruba Jazz People, 1998; Kevin Haynes Grupo Elegoua, 1999. *Recording:* Alex Wilson, Afro Saxon. *Leisure interests:* Orisha studies; IFA divination; African dance. *Address:* 33 Macbeth House, Ivy St, Hoxton, London N1 5JG, England.

BLAND Bobby (Robert); b. 27 Jan. 1930, Rosemark, Tennessee, USA. Singer. *Career:* Former valet for B B King, 1949; Member, The Beale Streeters; Gospel and blues vocalist; Early recordings with Ike Turner, 1952; Performances on US R & B circuit, 1957–; Ann Arbor Jazz and Blues Festival, 1973; First British tour, 1982; Regular tours with B B King, 1990s. *Recordings:* Hits include: Farther Up The Road, 1957; I'll Take Care of You, 1960; I Pity The Fool, 1961; Don't Cry No More, 1961; Turn On Your Love Light, 1962; Stormy Monday Blues, 1962; Call Me / That's The Way Love Is, 1963; Sometimes You Gotta Cry A Little, 1963; Ain't Nothing You Can Do, 1964; This Time I'm Gone For Good, 1974; Albums include: Here's The Man, 1962; Call On Me/That's The Way Love Is, 1963; Ain't Nothing You Can Do, 1964; His California Album, 1974; Dreamer, 1974; Together For The First Time... Live (with B B King), 1974; Get On Down With Bobby Bland, 1975; Together Again... Live (with B B King), 1976; Reflections In Blue, 1977; Come Fly With Me, 1978; I Feel Good, I Feel Fine, 1979; You've Got Me Loving You, 1984; Members Only, 1985; After All, 1986; Blues You Can Use, 1988; Midnight Run, 1989. *Honour:* Inducted into Rock and Roll Hall of Fame, 1992. *Address:* It's Happening Now Presents, PO Box 8073, Pittsburg, CA 94565, USA.

BLANDAMER Oscar Stewart Van; b. 8 May 1947, Weymouth, England. Songwriter; Musician (saxophone, guitar). m. Dianne Harrington, 16 July 1966, 1 s., 1 d. *Musical Education:* 1 year saxophone lessons. *Career:* Member: Orphesians, 1963–66; Jimmy James and the Vagabonds, 1969–72; Curly, 1973–75; Flirtations, Johnny Wakelin, 1976–78; Q-Tips, 1978–81; Adam Ant, 1981–83; Funk Bros, 1984-. *Compositions:* Darling, recorded by over 30 artists (3 No. 1 singles, US country chart); Songs covered by: Kim Wilde; Q-Tips; Paul Young; Tom Jones; Cliff Richard; Phil Everly. *Recordings:* with: Status Quo, 1973; Stiff Little Fingers, 1979; Wishbone Ash, 1979; Ray Minnhinnett's Bluesbusters, 1990; Video with Paul McCartney, 1984. *Honours:* 3 ASCAP Awards. *Memberships:*

Musicians' Union; BASCA; PRS; MCPS. *Leisure interest:* Travel. *Current Management:* Hyperfunk Productions.

BLANT David; b. 21 Nov. 1949, Burton-On-Trent, England. Musician (bass guitar, accordion); Teacher. m. Jennifer Gow, 27 March 1971, 1 s., 1 d. *Musical Education:* Dartington College of Arts. *Career:* Various bands from age 13; Member of: Yeah Jazz (Indie band); R Cajun and the Zydeco brothers, 1985–; Number of appearances, BBC Radio 2. *Recordings:* with R Cajun: Pig Sticking; In Arcadia; Out of The Swamp; Don't Leave The Floor; No Known Cure; That Cajun Thing. *Memberships:* Musicians' Union; PRS. *Current Management:* Swamp Management. *Address:* PO Box 94, Derby DE22 1XA, England.

BLATNY Pavel; b. 14 Sept. 1931, Brno, Czech Republic. m. Danuse Spirková, 19 June 1982, 1 s., 1 d. *Musical Education:* Musicology, University of Brno, 1958; Berklee School of Music, USA, 1968. *Career:* Composer; Conductor; Pianist; Chief, Music Department, Czech Television, to 1992; Professor, Janácek's Academy, Brno, to 1990. *Compositions include:* Concerto for Jazz Orchestra, 1962–64; Roll-call; Willow; Christmas Eve; Noonday Witch; Bells; Twelfth Night, based on Shakespeare's play, 1975; Two Movements for Brasses, 1982; Signals for Jazz Orchestra, 1985; Prologue for mixed choir and jazz orchestra, 1984; Per organo e big band, 1983; Ring a Ring o' Roses, for solo piano, 1984. *Honours:* Prize of Leos Jánácek, 1984; Antiteatro D'Argento for the whole work, Nepal, Italy, 1988. *Membership:* President, Club of Moravian Composers. *Leisure interest:* Write literature (stories). *Address:* 62400 Brno, Absolonova 35, Czech Republic.

BLATT Melanie; b. 1976. Vocalist. *Career:* Founding member, female vocal group All Saints, 1993–2000; Film, Honest, released 2000; Collaboration, Artful Dodger. *Recordings:* Singles: Silver Shadow; I Know Where It's At, 1997; Never Ever (No. 1, UK), 1997; Under The Bridge (No. 1, UK), 1998; Lady Marmalade (No. 1, UK), 1998; Bootie Call (No. 1, UK), 1998; War of Nerves, 1998; Pure Shores (No. 1, UK), 2000; Black Coffee (No. 1, UK), 2000; All Hooked Up, 2001; Albums: All Saints, 1997; Band Alert, 1998; Saints and Sinners, 2000; All Hits (compilation), 2001. *Honours:* Brit Award, Best Single, Never Ever, 1998. *Current Management:* John Benson.

BLAZEVIC Kresimir; b. 27 Jan. 1958, Slavonski Brod, Croatia. Prof. of Literature; Musician (guitar); Composer; Lyricist; Singer; Concert Hall Programme Man. m. Matea Banoza, 18 May 1991, 1 d. *Education:* University, Ethnology and Literature. *Musical Education:* Primary musical school, violin, guitar. *Career:* Over 500 concerts; Over 100 television and radio appearances. *Compositions:* 60 published works, music and lyrics; Girls in City Clothes, 1996. *Recordings:* 6 albums with The Animator, latest, The Dream Book; Hit singles include: Summer's Back To Town; I'll Stay Always Young; Summer Rendevous; Angels Asking Us To Take Away Their Wings. *Memberships:* HGU (Croatian Musical Union); Croatian Composers Society. *Address:* 10000 Zagreb, Buzanova 14, Croatia.

BLEY Carla Borg; b. 11 May 1938, Oakland, California, USA. Composer; Arranger. m. (1) Paul Bley, 27 Jan. 1959, divorced 1967; (2) Michael Mantler, 29 Sept. 1967, divorced 1992, 1 d. *Career:* Freelance jazz composer, 1956–; Pianist, Jazz Composers Orchestra, New York, 1964–; European concert tours, Jazz Realities, 1965–66; Founder, WATT, 1973–; Toured Europe with Jack Bruce Band, 1975; Leader, Carla Bley Band, touring USA, Europe, 1977-. *Compositions:* Composed and recorded: A Genuine Tong Funeral (with Charlie Haden), 1967; Liberation Music Orchestra, 1969; Escalator Over The Hill (opera), 1970–71; Tropic Appetites, 1973; Composer, Chamber Orchestra 3/4, 1974–75; Film scores, Mortelle Randonée, 1983. *Recordings:* Dinner Music, 1976; with The Carla Bley Band: European tour, 1977; Musique Mecanique, with Nick Mason, 1979; Fictitious Sports, 1980; Social Studies, 1980; Carla Bley Live!, 1981; Heavy Heart, 1984; I Hate To Sing, 1985; Night Glo, 1985; Sextet, 1987; Duets, 1988; Fleur Carnivore, 1989; The Very Big Carla Bley Band, 1991; Go Together, 1993; Big Band Theory, 1993; Songs With Legs (with Andy Sheppard), 1995; Goes to Church, 1996; Fancy Chamber Music, 1998; Are We There Yet?, 1999. *Honours include:* Guggenheim Fellowship, 1972; Oscar du Disque de Jazz, 1973; Composition grants, 1970s; New York Jazz Award, Arranger, 1979; Grammy Nominations, 1984, 1995; Deutscher Schallplattenpreis, 1985; Downbeat Poll, Best Composer, 1980s; Jazz Times, Composer, 1990; Hi Fi Vision, Jazz Musician of Year, 1990; Prix Jazz Moderne, 1991; Downbeat Poll, Composer/Arranger, 1990–94. *Membership:* NARAS. *Current Management:* Watt Works Inc. *Address:* c/o Watt Works Inc, PO Box 67, Willow, NY 12494, USA.

BLEY Paul; b. 10 Nov. 1932, Montréal, Québec, Canada. Musician (piano, synthesizer); Bandleader; Composer; Record Prod. m. (1) Carla Bley, (2) Annette Peacock. *Career:* Leader, own trio and quintet (latter included Ornette Coleman, Don Cherry, Charlie Haden, Billy Higgins); Also played with: Pat Metheny; Jaco Pastorius; Charlie Parker; Jackie McLean; Donald Byrd; Art Blakey; Charles Mingus; Bill Evans; Don Ellis; Jimmy Giuffre; John Gilmore; Formed own label, IAI, 1970s. *Recordings:* Albums include:

Introducing Paul Bley, 1954; Paul Bley, 1955; Solemn Meditation, 1958; Footloose, 1963; Barrage, 1965; Closer, 1966; Touching, 1966; Ramblin', 1967; Blood, 1967; Paul Bley In Haarlem, 1967; Mr Joy, 1968; The Fabulous Paul Bley Quintet, 1969; Paul Bley Trio In Canada, 1969; Ballads, 1970; The Paul Bley Synthesizer Show, 1971; Improvise, 1971; Dual Unity, 1972; Paul Bley and Scorpio, 1973; Open To Love, 1973; Paul Bley/NHOP, 1974; Alone Again, 1975; Copenhagen and Haarlem, 1975; Turning Point, 1975; Virtuosi, 1975; Bley, Metheney, Pastorius, Ditmus, 1975; Japan Suite, 1976; Axis, 1978; Sonor, 1983; Tango Palace, 1983; Tears, 1984; Questions, 1985; Hot, 1986; My Standard, 1986; Fragments, 1986; The Paul Bley Quartet, 1988; Solo, 1988; Solo Piano, 1988; Floater Syndrome, 1989; The Nearness of You, 1990; Bebop, 1990; Rejoicing, 1990; Blues For Red, 1991; Live At Sweet Basil, 1991; Indian Summer, 1991; Right Time Right Place, 1991; Memoirs, 1990; Changing Hands, 1991; Lyrics, 1991; In The Evenings Out There, 1991; Plays Carla Bley, 1991; If We May, 1993; Fabulous Paul Bley Quintet, 1994; Modern Chant, 1994; Speachless, 1995; Chaos, 1998; Not Two, Not One, 1999; Also recorded with Annette Peacock; Paul Motian; Jesper Lundgaard; Chet Baker; Jimmy Giuffre; Gary Peacock; As producer: albums for artists including Sun Ra; Marion Brown; Sam Rivers.

BLICHFELDT Anders; b. 9 Nov. 1963, Copenhagen, Denmark. Singer; Musician (guitarist). m. Marina, 20 Aug. 1988, 2 s. *Education:* Piano Tuner. *Career:* Lead singer, Big Fat Snake; Approximately 300 concerts, 1991–94 including Roskilde Festival, 1991, 1994; Midfyn Festival, 1991, 1992, 1994; Skanderborg Festival, 1991, 1992; Several national television and radio shows, 1991–94. *Recordings:* Big Fat Snake, 1991; Born Lucky, 1992; Beautiful Thing, 1994; Midnight Mission, 1995. *Honours:* Grammy Nomination, Best Male Vocalist, 1995. *Memberships:* DJBFA; Dansk Artist Forbund. *Leisure interests:* Friends and family. *Current Management:* Aarhus Musikkontor. *Address:* Mindegade 10, 8000, Aarhus C, Denmark.

BLIGE Mary J; b. 11 Jan. 1971, New York, USA. Vocalist. *Career:* Solo recording artiste; Support to Jodeci, British tour, 1995. *Recordings:* Albums: What's The 411, 1992; My Life, 1994; Mary Jane, 1995; Share My World, 1997; The Tour, 1998; Mary, 1999; No More Drama, 2001; Ballads, 2001; Singles: What's The 411, 1992; Sweet Thing, 1993; My Love, 1994; You Bring Me Joy, 1995; All Night Long, 1995; Not Gon' Cry, 1996; Love Is All We Need, 1997; Everything, 1997; Seven Days, 1999; All That I Can Say, 1999; As (with George Michael), 1999; Also appears on: Father's Day, 1990; Changes, 1992; Close To You, 1992; Panther, 1995; Show, 1995; MTV Party To Go, 1995; Waiting To Exhale, 1995; Nutty Professor, 1996; Case, 1996; Ironman, 1996; Love and Consequences, 1998; Miseducation of Lauryn Hill, 1998; Nu Nation Project, 1998. *Honours:* Grammy nominations: Female R & B Vocal Performance, All That I Can Say; R & B Vocal Performance By Duo Or Group, Don't Waste Your Time (with Aretha Franklin), 2000. *Current Management:* Steve Lucas Associates, 156 W 56th St, New York, NY 10019, USA.

BLIZARD H Ralph; b. 5 Dec. 1918, Kingsport, Tennessee, USA. Musician (fiddle). 2 s. *Musical Education:* Self-taught. *Career:* Smithsonian Institute Festival; Kingsport Symphony Orchestra; American Festival of Fiddle Tunes; Swannond Gathering, Asheville, North Carolina; Augusta Heritage Festival; Hudson River Clearwater Revival Festival, Croton, New York; Festival, American Fiddle Tunes, Port Townsend, Washington; Tampa Center, Performing Arts, Tampa, Florida; Good Morning America, ABC; PBS Appearances; Charles Karult, Sunday Morning, CBS; Library of Congress. *Recordings:* Blizard Train; Ralph Blizard Fiddles; Blue Highway; Green Grass Cloggers: Through The Ears; Southern Ramble; Old Time Music On The Air; American Fogies. *Honours:* Mount Airy Fiddle Championship, 3 years. *Membership:* Appointed by Governor to Tennessee Arts Committtee, 1987–92. *Leisure interest:* Violin making. *Address:* 1084 State Route #37, Blountville, TN 37617, USA.

BLOMSTROM John Paul Snr; b. 19 April 1949, Miami, Oklahoma, USA. Artist Agent; Musician (drums). m. Cheryl Ann Byrd, 28 Dec. 1978, 1 s., 2 d. *Career:* Artist manager for The Tonyans (family group), 1970's; Vince Vance and the Valiants; Lic and Stiff, 1980; First promoter to bring Pat Benatar to Houston; Also promoter of artists including Muddy Waters; Hall and Oates; Prince; The Police; Agent for artists including Madam X. *Publications:* Writer for Music News. *Memberships:* Various. *Leisure interests:* Horse riding; Weight training; Baseball; Basketball. *Current Management:* American Bands Management. *Address:* PO Box 840607, Houston, TX 77284–0607, USA.

BLONDIN Ludivine (Josette Edmee); b. 10 Oct. 1958, Lyon, France. Actress; Singer; Model. Partner, John Phil Wayne, 1 d. *Career:* Singer, musical act/films: L'Art de la Fugue with Bernard Haller and Maurice Biraud; William Tell with Will Lyman; Drole D'Endroit Pour Une Rencontre, with Gerard Depardieu; La Petite Maison Dans La Prairie, with Michael Landon; Interview of John Phil Wayne for France 3 TV and TLM TV; Introduction portrait of John Phil Wayne as video. *Recordings:*

Fairy Tales For Fauve; Recording for French radio and television as animator: Les Jeux de 20 Heures; Les Jeux Du Dimanche; La Soupiere a Des Oreilles; Maurice Bejart à Arles. *Membership:* AZ Production, France. *Leisure interests:* Movies; Modern jazz dancing; Swimming; Painting; Travel; Reading. *Current Management:* Longsongs Music Ltd, 21–23 Greenwich Market, London SE10 9HZ, England.

BLONDY Alpha; b. 1953, Dimbokoro, Ivory Coast. Reggae Vocalist; Bandleader. *Education:* Columbia University, USA, 1980–81. *Career:* Leading West African reggae vocalist and bandleader, 1980s. *Recordings:* Albums: Cocody Rock, 1984; Jah Glory, 1985; Jerusalem, 1986; Revolution, 1987; Apartheid Is Nazism, 1987; The Prophets, 1989; SOS Tribal War, 1991; Masada, 1992; Live Au Zenith, 1992; Dieu, 1994; Yitzhak Rabin, 1998. *Current Management:* MA Chetata Management, 105 W 28th St, Third Floor, New York, NY 10001, USA.

BLOOM Eric; b. 1 Dec. 1944. Singer; Musician (guitar, keyboards). *Career:* Singer, guitarist, keyboard player, US rock group Blue Öyster Cult, 1971–; Regular US tours including support to Alice Cooper, 1972; World tour, 1978; Monsters of Rock Festival, Castle Donington, 1981; British tour, 1989. *Recordings:* Albums: Blue Öyster Cult, 1972; Tyranny and Mutation, 1973; Secret Treaties, 1974; Live On Your Feet Or On Your Knees, 1975; Agents of Fortune, 1976; Spectres, 1978; Some Enchanted Evening, 1978; Mirrors, 1979; Cultosaurus Erectus, 1980; Fire of Unknown Origin, 1981; ETL (Extra-Terrestrial Live), 1982; The Revolution By Night, 1983; Club Ninja, 1986; Imaginos, 1988; Career of Evil – The Metal Years, 1990; Bad Channels, 1992; Live 1976, 1994; Cult Classic, 1994; Summerdaze, 1997; Singles include: (Don't Fear) The Reaper, 1976; In Thee, 1979; Burnin' For You, 1981; Film soundtrack, Bad Channels, 1992. *Honour:* Platinum disc, (Don't Fear) The Reaper. *Current Management:* Steve Schenck, 415 Madison Ave, New York, NY 10017, USA.

BLUE Barry; b. 4 Dec. 1950, London, England. Songwriter; Prod.; Singer. m. Lynda Blue, 20 May 1974, 1 s., 2 d. *Career:* First television appearance: Stubby Kaye's Silver Star Show, age 11; First major concert: Split Festival, Yugoslavia singing his own composition, 1969; First radio appearance: Bassist, Spice (later became Uriah Heep), John Peel Show; First major tour: Solo artist singer with Queen and Status Quo, 1973; Staff Producer, CBS Records, 1976–; Producer, composer numerous hit records for artists including: Bananarama; Five Star; Heatwave; Diana Ross; Celine Dion; Opened Aosis Recording Studios, where albums produced for artists include: Sinead O'Connor, Bronski Beat, Depeche Mode, Fine Young Cannibals, 1984–88; Owner of Escape Records. *Recordings include:* Dancin' On A Saturday Night (sold 1m.); Sugar Me, Lynsey de Paul; Boogie Nights, Heatwave; Always and Forever, Heatwave; Over 30 UK Chart singles as singer, producer and writer. *Honours:* Carl Allan Award, 1973; Producer of The Year, 1977; 6 BMI, ASCAP Awards. *Memberships:* Councillor, BASCA; PRS. *Leisure interests:* Writing; Lyrics; Computers. *Current Management:* The Escape Artist Company. *Address:* PO Box 31, Bushey, Hertfordshire WD2 2PT, England.

BLUE EAGLE; b. 4 March 1962, Philadelphia, Pennsylvania, USA. Singer; Songwriter; Musician; Prod. 1 d. *Musical Education:* Sang in school choir from elementary school to high school; Self-taught. *Honour:* President Elect for 2 years, All Philadelphia Boys Choir. *Memberships:* ASCAP; All Philadelphia Boys Choir. *Leisure interests:* Art; Reading. *Current Management:* Jackie Paul. *Address:* c/o Jackie Paul, 559 Wanamaker Rd, Jenkintown, PA 19046, USA.

BLUE Sam, (Simon Blewitt); b. 21 Aug. 1959, Newcastle upon Tyne, England. Singer; Songwriter; Actor. 1 s., 1 d. *Education:* Technical College. *Career:* Backing artists: Lulu; Michael Ball; 1991–93; Giant Killers, 1995; Sang on many television, radio, cinema commercials; Toured Britain, Europe, former Soviet Union, with Ya-Ya, 1987–89; Ultravox, 1993–95; Also television, radio with these groups; Appeared (acting) in Spender, television series; Co-wrote Hollywood Men theme tune for Carlton TV, 1996. *Recordings:* Emerson single: Something Special, 1984; Lead singer, Ya-Ya album, 1988; Ultravox: Ingenuity, 1994–95; Live, 1995; Eternal 12 single: So Good, 1994; GTS: Tracks From The Dust Shelf, 1995; GTS, Time Stood Still, 1996; Chorus work on Evita, film and soundtrack; Solo single: For The Life You Don't Yet Know, 1997; Backing Vocalist on Montserrat Caballe album, Friends for Life, 1997. *Memberships:* PRS; MCPS. *Leisure interests:* Watching and playing football; Golf. *Current Management:* Christine Poundford, Hobsons Singers. *Address:* 62 Chiswick High Rd, London W4 1SY, England.

BLUMBERG Stuart Lester; b. 27 Oct. 1947, Detroit, Michigan, USA. Musician (trumpet). m. Dorothy Ebeling, 1 s. *Education:* AA, Los Angeles Valley College, 1969; California State University, Northridge. *Career:* Toured with Don Ellis; Louis Bellson; First trumpet, numerous Broadway performances; Music Contractor, Shubert Theatre, Los Angeles, 1991; Recorded numerous television and radio commercials, film soundtracks. *Recordings:* with various artists including: Frank Sinatra; Barbra Streisand; Lou Rawls; Lionel Richie; The Osmonds; Joe Cocker; Dionne

Warwick; The Rolling Stones; Barry Manilow; Beach Boys; The Commodores; The Pointer Sisters; Steppenwolf; Jermaine Jackson; Carly Simon; Talking Heads; Air Supply; Blood, Sweat and Tears. *Membership:* NARAS.

BLUMENTHAL Laurent Pierre; b. 21 Dec. 1964, Paris, France. Musician (saxophone). m. Marianne, 11 Aug. 1992, 2 d. *Musical Education:* Diploma, CNR Lyons (saxophone, harmony), 1983; 2 months at Eastman School of Music, Rochester, New York, 1986. *Career:* Concerts and tours: with La Velle and Orj: Tour of USSR, 1991; with Tourmaline: Tour of Québec, 1991; Festival de Montréal, 1992; with L'Orchestre National de Jazz: Germany; Italy; Portugal; France, 1993–94; with Dimitrinaiditch / Laurent Blumenthal Duo: Tour of Germany, 1995; Played all French jazz festivals, 1990–; Performed with own quintet, septet, and artistes including: Johnny Griffin; Ernie Watts; Michel Colombier; ORJ; Henri Texier; Daniel Humair; Mario Stanchev; L'Orchestre National de Jazz, with Denis Badault (ONJ Badault); Also performed with Tito Puente; Nicole Croisile; Louis Sclavis. *Recordings:* Il Était Une Fois La Révolution, ORJ, 1988; Shakok, Shakok, 1989; Johnny Griffin et l'ORJ, ORJ, 1990; Sozopol, Mario Stanchev, 1990; Parcours, Aira Works, 1990; Kaleidodscope, Mario Stanchev, 1992; Monk Mingus Ellington, ONJ Badault, 1993; Bouquet Final, ONJ Badault, 1994. *Honours:* First prize, National Saxophone Competition, 1987; First Prize, Festival de Vienne, with Shakok, 1988; First prize, Festival de Sorgues, 1993; Second prize (soloist), Third prize (group), with Dimitri Naiditch, Concours de la Défense, 1993. *Leisure interests:* Tennis; Squash; Swimming. *Current Management:* Dominique Camard. *Address:* 12 rue Justin Godart, 69004 Lyon, France.

BLUNSTONE Colin; b. 24 June 1945, Hatfield, Hertfordshire, England. Vocalist. *Career:* Singer, the Zombies, 1963–67; Solo career, 1969–; Reformed the Zombies, 1991; Appearances include: with The Shangri-Las, The Nashville Teens, US, 1964; with Dusty Springfield, The Searchers, UK 1965; Support to Herman's Hermits, US Caravan of Stars tour, 1965; Film appearance, Bunny Lake Is Missing, 1966. *Recordings:* Albums: with the Zombies: The Zombies, 1965; The Zombies – Begin Here, 1965; Odessey and Oracle, 1967; New World, 1991; Solo albums: One Year, 1971; Ennismore, 1973; Journey, 1974; Planes, 1976; Never Even Thought, 1978; Late Nights In Soho, 1979; I Don't Beleive In Miracles, 1982; Sings His Greatest Hits, 1991; Echo Bridge, 1995; Live At The BBC, 1996; Light Inside, 1998; Hit singles with the Zombies: She's Not There (No. 2, US), 1964; Tell Her No, 1965; with the Alan Parsons Project: Pyramid, 1978; Eye of The Sky, 1982; Ammonia Avenue, 1984; Vulture Culture, 1985; Definitive Collection, 1997; Other albums include: Walk On Water, Mae McKenna, 1977; Tarot Suite, Mike Batt, 1979; Exiled, Exiled, 1980; Keats, Keats, 1984; Greatest Show On Earth, Martin Darville and Friends, 2000. *Address:* c/o Permanent Records, 22–23 Brook Mews, London W2 3BW, England.

BOBEK Pavel; b. 16 Sept. 1937, Prague, Czech Republic. Singer; Musician. m. Marta Pokorna, 10 Oct. 1978, 1 s., 1 d. *Education:* Architecture, Prague Institute of Technology, 1961; Private Lessons, Piano. *Career:* Member, Olympic Rock and Roll Group, 1963–66; Actor, Singer, The Prague Semafor Theatre, 1967–90; Solo Singer, Founder of Band, 1982-. *Recordings:* First Singles, 1963; Six albums, 1975–93; Seven compilation albums; The Best of Pavel Bobek Vols I and II. *Honours:* Platinum Record, 1993. *Memberships:* OSA; SAI. *Leisure interests:* Aviation; Gardening; Architecture. *Current Management:* Venkow Records, Ovenecka 6, 170 00 Prague 7, Czech Republic. *Address:* ul 8 Listopadu 45, 169 00 Prague 6, Czech Republic.

BOBINEC Ivica; b. 16 Sept. 1937, Zagreb, Croatia. Radio Station Exec. m. Visnja Kolina, 1 July 1961, 1 s., 1 d. *Education:* Graduated ethnologist, University of Zagreb. *Musical Education:* Musical Academy, Zagreb. *Career:* Singer, bass guitar player, Combo 5 (orchestra), 1973–86; International concert tours across Europe, 1966–69; Split Festival, Zagreb Festival of Popular Music, 1971–77; Radio and television appearances 1958–95, including Eurovision Song Contest, Luxembourg, 1984; Bergen, Norway, 1986; General Manager, Cibona Radio Station. *Compositions:* Cibona (music and lyrics), anthem of the Croatian National Basketball Team, 1990. *Recordings:* Solo: Pijem Da Zaboravim Nju, 1973. *Membership:* Glazbena Unija (Music Society of Croatia). *Leisure interest:* Tennis. *Current Management:* Agency Estrada Zagreb, Croatia.

BOCK Jerry (Jerrold Lewis); b. 23 Nov. 1928, New Haven, Connecticut, USA. Composer. m. Patricia Faggen, 1950, 1 s., 1 d. *Education:* University of Wisconsin. *Career:* Composer, scores for high school and college musicals; Author for television, 1951–54; Member, New York board Educiradio broadcasts, 1961-. *Compositions:* Film score: Wonders of Manhattan, 1956; Music for show Mr Wonderful, 1956; with Sheldon Harnick: The Body Beautiful, 1958; Fiorello, 1959; Tenderloin, 1960; She Loves Me, 1963; Fiddler On The Roof, 1964; The Apple Tree, 1966; The Rothschilds, 1970; Jerome Robbins Broadway, 1989. *Honours:* Songwriters Hall of Fame, 1990; Theatre Hall of Fame, 1990. *Membership:* Broadcast Music Inc.

BOCKER Ingemar; b. 6 May 1934, Stockholm, Sweden. Jazz Musician; Transcriber. 1 d. *Musical Education:* Self-taught; Musicology Degree, Stockholm University. *Career:* Toured Sweden Extensively; Toured American Forces Clubs in West Germany, 1953–55, 1960–62; Toured with Rock and Rhythms Blues Groups; Joined Swedish Folk Rockband Kebnekaise 1972; Archivist, Swedish Centre for Folk Music Research, 1987–; Tour of Sweden with Stan Hasselgard Story, 1998. *Compositions:* Comanche Spring; Ballad of Blackberries and Melon; Galliarde Moderne; Wet Paint. *Recordings:* Kebnekaise II and III; Electric Mountain. *Publications:* Lars Gullin 8 Compositions Transcribed by I Bocker, 1998; Several articles in professional journals and magazines. *Memberships:* Swedish Jazz Musicians Organization; Lars Gullin Society; SKAP; STIM-NCB. *Address:* Tenstavagen 94, 16365 Spanga, Sweden.

BODDIE Don O'Mar; b. 22 Nov. 1944, St Louis, Missouri, USA. m. Paula R Boddie, 27 July 1991, 4 s., 2 d. *Education:* BS, Management, 1988; BS, Business Administration, 1988. *Musical Education:* BA, Music Arts, St Louis Musical Institute, 1968; BA, Music Management, JR College District, St Louis, Missouri, 1974; MBS, Music Production, 1975. *Career:* Super Sonic Attractions; Stars Spectacular; Salem Spirit Festival; Vocal Music Director, Martin Luther King Middle School, 1992–93, Clay CEC, 1997–98. *Compositions:* Can't Stop the Fire, 1982; Passing Fancy. *Recordings:* Two Piece Love; True Love; Dreams; Lets Be Lovers; Satisfaction; Legend of O'Mar the Grand Master; Lover Pt 1 and 2; As I Go, 1997; Clay School Song, 1997; Clay Code of Honor, 1997. *Publications:* Lets Be Lovers, 1982, released, 1988; Can't Stop the Fire, 1992; Dreams, 1997. *Memberships:* Friends of Black Music Society; MAM of Missouri. *Leisure interests:* Martial Arts; Basketball; Recording Productions.

BODILSEN Jesper Vejbaek; b. 5 Jan. 1970, Haslev, Denmark. Bass Player (Double Bass/Electric Bass). *Musical Education:* Rhythmical Diploma Degree, Royal Academy of Music, Aarhus; Played Cornet in Balleskolens Brass Band, 1980–89; Lessons in Big Band Arranging, Line Writing. *Career:* Pori Jazz, Beijing Jazz Festival, Scandinavian Jazz Quartet, 1994; Concerts with Ed Thigpen, Duke Jordan, Janusz Carmello, Bent Jaedig, 1994; James Moody, 1996; Fred Wesley, 1996; Horace Parlan, 1996; Ulf Wakenius, 1997; Tours with Beibom/Kroner Big Band, 1996–97; Katrine Madsen, 1998; Stig Rossen, 1997; Member, Ed Thigpen Trio, 1997; Jazzpar Concerts with Erling Kroner, Dino Saluzzi, 1998. *Compositions:* Dedication, 1994. *Recordings:* Contributor, albums: Come Rain Or Come Shine, Hanne Romer, 1994; New Deal, Scandinavian Jazz Quartet, 1994; A Night in Bilbao, Scandinavian Jazz Quartet, 1996; Giving It Away, Helle Hansen, 1995; Red Letter Days, Harvest Moon, 1995; I'm Old Fashioned Katrine Madsen, 1996; Dream Dancing, Katrine Madsen, 1997. *Address:* Godthaabsvej 36 B, 2 TV, 2000 Frederiksberg, Denmark.

BODINAT Henri de; b. 15 July 1948, Paris, France. Co Pres. m. Clèmence de Lasteyrie, 12 Sept. 1989, 2 s., 2 d. *Education:* Masters, Social Sciences; PhD, Economy, Harvard Business School. *Career:* Chief Executive Officer, Sony Music, France, 1985–94; Managing Director, Club Mediterrannée, 1994–94; Executive, Sony Software Europe, 1994; President, Musisoft SA, 1997-. *Publications:* Influence in the Multinational Corporation, 1977; The State: A Paranthesis in History?, 1996. *Address:* Musisoft, 85 rue Fondary, 75015 Paris, France.

BOGGUSS Suzy Kay; b. 30 Dec. 1956, Aledo, Illinois, USA. Country vocalist. *Education:* Art degree. *Career:* Country singer, 1986-. *Recordings:* Songs include: I Want To Be A Cowboy's Sweetheart; Night Rider's Lament; I Don't Want To Set The World On Fire; Somewhere Between, 1989; Moment of Truth, 1990; Aces, 1991; Voices In The Wind, 1992; Sorry Seems To Be The Hardest Word, 1994; Give Me Some Wheels, 1996; No Way Out, 1996; Somebody To Love, 1998; Albums: Somewhere Between, 1988; Moment of Truth, 1990; Aces, 1991; Voices In The Wind, 1992; Somethin' Up My Sleeve, 1993; Simpatico, 1994; Nobody Love, Nobody Gets Hurt, 1998; It's A Perfect Day, 1999; Greatest Hits Vols 1 and 2 (compilations), 2001; Other recordings: Happy Trails, with Michael Martin Murphey, 1990; Hopelessly Yours, with Lee Greenwood. *Honours:* CMA Horizon Award, Most Promising Artist, 1992. *Address:* Left Bank Organization, 1018 17th Ave S, Suite 10, Nashville, TN 37212, USA.

BOGLE Eric; b. 23 Sept. 1944, Peebles, Scotland. Songwriter; Musician (guitar). m. Carmel, 29 Jan. 1972. *Education:* Accountant until 1980; Full-time musician, 1980–; Various tours, television appearances. *Recordings:* The Band Played Waltzing Matilda; The Green Fields of France/No Man's Land; Albums include: Scraps of Paper, 1981; When The Wind Blows, 1985; Singing In The Spirit Home, 1987; Something of Value, 1988; Song Book, 1990; Voices In The Wilderness, 1991; I Wrote This Song, 1995; Hard Hard Times, 1997; Emigrant and The Exile, 1997; Small Miracles, 1998. *Publications:* Five song books, 12 CDs, 1980-. *Honours:* United Nations Peace Medal, 1986; APRA Gold Award, 1986; Order of Australia Medal, 1987. *Membership:* Full mem., APRA. *Leisure interests:* Reading; Television. *Address:* PO Box 529, Magill, Adelaide, South Australia 5072, Australia.

BOGLIUNI Mario; b. 24 May 1935, Svetvincenat-Pula, Croatia. Composer; Musician (piano); Arranger. m. Maria Adler, 24 Aug. 1973, 1 s. *Musical Education:* Conservatorium of Music Art. *Career:* Concerts and tours, Croatia; European countries; Australia, 1969; USA, 1970; Russia, 1974; Editor, several series on pop music; Compositions for theatre and film. *Compositions:* Songs: Running Out of World; Why Do I Love You; Sailors Cha Cha Cha; Three Friends; Serenade. *Honours:* 25 Croatian and international festival awards. *Membership:* Music Asscn of Croatia (DHS). *Leisure interests:* Collector of antiquities; Tennis. *Current Management:* Mr Finderle Vigor, Agency Adriatic, Opatijska 45, 51000 Rijeka, Croatia. *Address:* Sestinski Dol 121 A, 41000 Zagreb, Croatia.

BOIC Drazen; b. 11 April 1931, Zagreb, Croatia. Musician (piano); Composer; Arranger. m. Anita, 23 Sept. 1967, 1 s., 1 d. *Education:* Dr of Medicine. *Musical Education:* Secondary Music School, Zagreb. *Career:* 45 years, love for jazz, playing jazz, commercial music; Leader, own trio, quartet, quintet, sextet; Croatian Zagreb Radio Orchestra, 1954–58; Playing for US Air Forces, 1957–64; Tours in Russia, 1967–80; Pianist, ballet school, Zagreb, 1980–90; Piano player, Hotel Esplanade, Zagreb, 1980-. *Compositions include:* Tiho i Mirno; Ljetni Ritam; Anita Fedor; Petra. *Membership:* Croatian Musicians Union, Zagreb. *Leisure interests:* Photography; Listening to music; Swimming; Eating. *Address:* Cvijica 17, Zagreb, Croatia.

BOIC Fedor; b. 17 Oct. 1968, Zagreb, Croatia. Composer; Prod.; Musician (keyboards). *Musical Education:* Primary, secondary music school, music academy. *Career:* Playing in theatre, Komedija; With Tereda Kesouija: ITD Band; Aerodrom; Novi Fosili; Many Croatian television and radio shows; Currently playing keyboards in Prijavo Kazaliste; Producer, sound engineer, JM Sound Studio-Zagreb on over 30 LPs for artists including: ITD Band; Jasna Zlokic; Sanja Dolezal; Novi Fosili; Jasmin Stauros; Venera; Vesna Ivic; Duka Caic; Prljavo Kazaliste. *Publications:* Suzy; Jugoton; Ofej. *Honours:* 3 Gold records; 1 Gold CD; 10 Silver records; Porin. *Memberships:* HDS, Croatian Composer Society; HGU, Croatian Musician Society. *Leisure interests:* Reading; Listening to music; Watching films; Bike riding. *Current Management:* Branko Paic, Crno Bijeli Suijet CBS Croatia. *Address:* Brace Cvijica 17, 41000 Zagreb, Croatia.

BOJSEN-MOLLER Cai; b. 7 March 1966, Copenhagen, Denmark. Composer; Musician (Drums, Keyboards, Composer). m. Anna Reumert, 20 April 1986, 1 s., 1 d. *Education:* General Certificate of Education A-Level. *Musical Education:* Copenhagen Boys Choir. *Career:* Musician, Gangway; Musician for Busstop, Paris-Paris, Naive, Lisa Nilsson and Louise Hoffsten; Composer, Solo Performer, 1990; International concerts in England, Japan and Germany; Performed Roskilde Festival, 1997. *Compositions:* Solo albums: A Bit of Something, 1997; Super Sonic Jazzy Session, 1998; Singles: A Night in the Pit, 1996; Revertrhythm, 1996; Bits, 1997. *Recordings:* Compilations: Get Lost, 1996; Past, Present and Future, 1997; Further Adventures in Techno Soul, 1998. *Publications:* Film/Art Videos: Talk Like Whales, 1994; Pets, 1995. *Honours:* 4 Grammy Awards, Gangway, 1993. *Leisure interests:* Runner; Japanese Food; Science Fiction Movies; Computer Games; Jazz Music.

BOLAM Frank; b. 22 April 1949, Glasgow, Scotland. Musician (guitars). m. Jeanette Morrison, 13 May 1967, 1 s., 1 d. *Musical Education:* Studied under Iain McHaffie and Ron Moore, main guitar teachers in Scotland. *Career:* Professional since age 21; Major productions, theatre, musicals including: Hair, Glasgow Metropole Theatre; West Side Story; Chess; Television appearances include: Ronnie Scott's The Jazz Series; Radio recordings include: The Jazz Train; Extensive professional and session work; Full time teacher, Glasgow schools; Teacher, lecturer, Strathclyde University. *Publications:* Complete guitar courses (all styles and levels) for exam syllabus for Glasgow and Renfrew Education Department, commissioned by Strathclyde Education Department. *Memberships:* Glasgow Society of Musicians; Musicians' Union; EIS. *Leisure interest:* Music. *Address:* 47 Coltmuir St, Glasgow G22 6LU, Scotland.

BOLGER Leslie; b. 11 Aug. 1947, Liverpool, England. Musician (guitarist); Lecturer. m. Claire Holland, 21 April 1970, 3 d. *Education:* Certificate in Education (with distinction), University of Manchester. *Musical Education:* Studied with world renowned jazz guitarist George Gola, Australia. *Career:* Jazz performances with artistes including: Martin Taylor; Louis Stewart; Ike Isaacs; Gary Potter; Kenny Baker; Don Rendal; Many television and radio broadcasts; Arranger, Music Adviser, Granada Television; Session guitarist, Arranger, Piccadilly Radio and Radio Merseyside; Backing guitarist for many top cabaret artists including: Russ Abbott; Joe Longthorne; Bob Monkhouse; Vince Hill. *Honours:* Many first places with honours or distinction for Les Bolger Jazz Guitar Ensemble. *Membership:* Musicians' Union. *Leisure interests:* Reading; Computer Programming. *Current Management:* Claire Bolger. *Address:* 12 Firbank Close, Daresbury View, Runcorn, Cheshire WA7 6NR, England.

BOLLING Claude; b. 10 April 1930, Cannes, France. Jazz Musician (piano); Composer; Bandleader; Orchestra Conductor. m. Irène Dervize-

Sadyker, 1959, 2 s. *Musical Education:* Private teachers including Bob Colin, Earl Hines, Willie The Lion Smith; Maurice Duruflé. *Career:* As jazz pianist worked with: Dizzy Gillespie; Stéphane Grappelli; Rex Stewart; Roy Eldridge; Sidney Bechet; Albert Nicholas; Lionel Hampton; The Ellingtonians; Carmen McRae; Jo Williams; Formed group Les Parisiennes; Claude Bolling Big Band; Many jazz and variety shows. *Compositions include:* Sonatas 1 and 2 for two pianists; Suites for flute, violin, cello, chamber orchestra; Guitar Concerto; Picnic Suite; Toot Suite; More than 100 film soundtrack scores include: Le Jour et l'Heure; Borsalino; Lucky Luke; Le Magnifique; Willie and Phil; California Suite; La Mandarine; L'Homme en Colère; Flic Story; Le Mur de l'Atlantique; On Ne Meurt Que Deux Fois; Television: Jazz Memories; Le Brigades du Tigre; Chantecler. *Honours:* Gold Records, Canada, USA; Medaille d'Or Maurice Ravel; Officier Arts et Lettres; Chevalier Ordre Nationale du Mérite; Chevalier de la Légion d'Honneur; Los Angeles and New Orleans Honour Citizen; SACEM, Gold Medal and Grand Prix, 1984. *Leisure interests:* Ecology; Model railroading. *Address:* 20 Ave de Lorraine, 92380 Garches, France.

BOLO Yammie, (Roland Maclean); b. 1970, Kingston, Jamaica. Reggae Vocalist. *Career:* Began as Singer with Sugar Minott's Youth Promotion sound system; Solo singer, 1985–; Founder, Yam Euphony record label, 1992. *Recordings:* Numerous singles include: When A Man's In Love, 1985; Jah Made Them All, 1986; Roots Pon Mi Corner, 1986; Free Mandela, 1987; Ransome of a Man's Life, 1987; Tell Me Why Is This Fussing and Fighting, 1988; Love Me With Feeling, 1989; Poverty and Brutality, 1989; Poor Man's Cry, 1990; Struggle in Babylon, 1990; Turbo Charge, 1991; Blood A Run, 1991; Iniquity Worker, 1991; Jah Jah Loving, 1991; It's Not Surprising, 1992; Joe the Boss, 1992; Be Still, 1992; Revolution; Bowl Mus Fall; Albums: Ransom, 1989; Jah Made Them All, 1989; Who Knows It Feels It, 1991; Up Life Strcct, 1992; Cool and Easy, 1993; with Lloyd Hemmings: Meets Lloyd Hemmings, 1993. *Address:* c/o Free World Music Inc, 230 12th St, Suite 117, Miami Beach, FL 33139–4603, USA.

BOLTON Michael, (Michael Bolotin); b. 26 Feb. 1953, New Haven, Connecticut, USA. Vocalist; Songwriter; Prod. 3 d. *Career:* Singer, US rock group Blackjack, 1978–82; Collaborator, Glasnost album as member of US songwriting team in Moscow, 1988; Solo recording artiste, formerly under name Michael Bolotin; Appearances include: Support to Heart, US, 1988; Support to Ozzy Osbourne, US, 1988; US tour with Kenny G, 1990; US tour with Celine Dion, 1992; Songwriter for Barbra Streisand, Cher, KISS, Kenny G and Peabo Bryson; World Tour, 1993–95; Christmas in Vienna, 1997; Numerous television appearances include TV special, This Is Michael Bolton, NBC, 1992. *Compositions include:* How Am I Supposed To Live Without You, Laura Branigan, 1983; I Found Someone, Cher, 1988; Co-writer (with Paul Stanley), Forever, Kiss, 1990; Co-writer (with Bob Dylan), Steel Bars, 1992. *Recordings:* Singles include: That's What Love's All About, 1987; Dock of The Bay, 1988; How Am I Supposed To Live Without You, 1990; How Can We Be Lovers, 1990; When I'm Back On My Feet Again, 1990; Georgia On My Mind, 1990; Love Is A Wonderful Thing, 1991; Time, Love and Tenderness, 1991; When A Man Loves A Woman, 1991; Missing You Now, with Kenny G, 1992; Steel Bars, 1992; To Love Somebody, 1993; Drift Away, 1993; Said I Loved You… But I Lied, 1993; A Love So Beautiful, 1995; Can I Touch You… There, 1995; The Best of Love, 1997; Safe Place From The Storm, 1998; Reach Out I'll Be There, 1999; Albums include: Michael Bolton, 1983; Everybody's Crazy, 1985; The Hunger, 1987; Soul Provider, 1989; Time Love and Tenderness (No. 1, USA), 1991; Timeless – The Classics (No. 1, USA), 1992; The One Thing, 1993; All That Matters, 1997; My Secret Passion, 1998; Timeless Vol. 2, 1999; Greatest Hits 1985–95, 1995; Contributor, Pavarotti and Friends (charity record) for Bosnia relief), 1996; Go The Distance, theme from Disney film Hercules; This Is The Time – The Christmas Album, 1996; All That Matters, 1997; My Secret Passion, 1998; Timeless – The Classics Vol. 2, 1999; Live From Catania, 2001. *Publication:* The Secret of the Lost Kingdom, children's book, 1997. *Honours include:* New York Music Award, Best R & B Vocalist, 1988; ASCAP Airplay Awards, 1989; Pollstar Tour of the Year, 1990; Grammy Awards: Best Pop Vocal Performance, 1990, 1992; American Music Awards: Favourite Male Pop/Rock Artist, Favourite Album, 1992, 1993; BMI Song of The Year, 1991; Gold and Platinum discs; Hitmakers Award, National Songwriters Hall of Fame, 1995; Five times winner, BMI Million Perforamcne Song Award. *Membership:* BMI. *Current Management:* Louis Levin Management, 130 W 57th St #10-B, New York, NY 10019, USA.

BOLVIG Palle P S; b. 25 Nov. 1932, Copenhagen, Denmark. Musician (trumpet, flugelhorn); Composer; Arranger. m. Jytte, 12 July 1969, 1 s., 3 d. *Musical Education:* Private study. *Career:* Member, Ib Glindemann Orchestra, 1951–61; Member, International Band, Newport Festival, 1958; Member, Danish Radio Big Band, 1964-. *Compositions:* Easy Mood, 1961; Gosty Day, 1970; Zabacoot, 1970; Portrait of Cordoba, 1971; Back To Tenderness, 1971; Child of Pain, 1985; Blue January, 1999. *Recordings:* Newport International Band, 1958; Brownsville Trolley Line, Danish Radio Big Band, 1969; Ben Webster and the Danish Radio Big-Band, 1970; Thad Jones and the Danish Radio Big-Band, 1978; Ernie Wilkins Almost Big-

Band, 1981; Aura, Miles Davis, 1985; with the Danish Radio Band: Little Bit of Duke, 1994; First British tour, 1995; Suite For Jazz Band, 1995; Also: Captain Coe's Famous Racearound, 1996; Like Life, Django Bates, 1998; Impulsive, the Danish Radio Jazz Orchestra, 1997; Ways of Seeing, the Danish Radio Jazz Orchestra, 1999; Blues, Blues and All That Jazz, Allan Bo Bard, 1999. *Honours:* Selected, Newport International Jazz Band, 1958. *Memberships:* The Danish Trumpet Societies. *Leisure interest:* Cycling in the countryside. *Address:* Danmarks Radio P2 Jazz, 1999 Frederiksberg C, Denmark.

BOM-BANE Jane (Bayley); b. 11 Sept. 1953, Leek, Staffordshire, England. Singer; Composer; Lyricist; Musician (harmonium). m. André Schmidt, 20 Dec. 1982, divorced, 1 s. *Education:* BA Hons, French, Cultural Studies, PGCE, English, French, Spanish, Warwick University. *Musical Education:* History of Music (part of degree); Piano lessons as child. *Career:* Appearances include: Bracknell Festival, 1993; Edinburgh Fringe Festival, 1994, 1995; Glasgow Mayfest, GFT, 1995; Television and radio includes: Usual Suspects, BBC Radio Scotland, 1994; Don't Look Down, STV, 1994; We Stayed In With Jungr and Parker, BBC Radio 2, 1994; Russian State television. *Recordings:* Away/Mantovani, The Swinging Cats, 1980; Boy/Yob, The Round-a-way Wrong Chamber, 1984; Solo albums: Round-a-way Wrong Songs, 1993; It Makes Me Laugh, 1995; Soundtrack: The Man From Porlock, 1995. *Memberships:* Musicians' Union; PRS. *Leisure interests:* Collecting harmoniums; Swimming. *Current Management:* Round-a-way Wrong Music. *Address:* PO Box 8416, London SW9 92B, England.

BON JOVI Jon, (John Bongiovi); b. 2 March 1962, Sayreville, New Jersey, USA. Vocalist; Songwriter; Musician (guitar). m. Dorothea Hurley, May 1989, 1 s., 1 d. *Career:* Singer, local bands: Raze; Atlantic City Expressway; Singer, founder member, US rock group Bon Jovi, 1984–; 40m. albums sold world-wide to date; Numerous world-wide tours, including US, UK, Europe, USSR, South America, Australia, Japan, 1984–; Support tours with Kiss; Scorpions; .38 Special; Headliners, Donington Monsters of Rock Festival, 1987; Moscow Music Peace Festival, 1989; Numerous television, radio and video appearances world-wide; Own management company, BJM; Own record label Jambco. *Recordings:* US No. 1 singles include: You Give Love A Bad Name, 1986; Living On A Prayer, 1987; Bad Medicine, 1988; I'll Be There For You, 1989; Solo: Blaze of Glory, 1990; Destination Anywhere, 1997; Midnight In Chelsea Pt 1, 1997; Real Life Pt 1, 1999; Real Life Pt 2, 1999; Numerous other hits include: Wanted Dead Or Alive; Lay Your Hands On Me; Living In Sin; Born To Be My Baby; Keep The Faith; In These Arms; I'll Sleep When I'm Dead; Bed of Roses; Always; I Believe; Someday I'll Be Saturday Night; This Ain't A Love Song; Lie To Me; These Days; Hey God; One Road Man; Albums: Bon Jovi, 1984; 7800° Fahrenheit, 1985; Slippery When Wet (13m. copies sold), 1986; New Jersey, 1988; Keep The Faith, 1991; Crossroad (Best Of), 1994; These Days, 1995; Crush, 2000; One Wild Night 1985–2001 (live compilation), 2001; Solo album: Blaze of Glory (film soundtrack, Young Guns II); Contributor, Stairway To Heaven/Highway To Hell charity record, 1989; Two Rooms (Elton John/Bernie Taupin tribute album), 1991. *Honours:* American Music Awards, Favourite Pop/Rock Band, 1988; Favourite Pop/Rock Single, 1991; Bon Jovi Day, Sayreville, 1989; Silver Clef, Nordoff-Robbins Music Therapy, 1990; All albums Gold or Platinum status; Golden Globe, Best Original Song, Blaze of Glory, 1991; Academy Award nomination, Blaze of Glory; Best Selling Album of Year, Crossroad, 1994; BRIT Award, Best International Group, 1996. *Current Management:* c/o BJM, 809 Elder Circle, Austin, TX 78733, USA.

BONDS Gary 'US', (Gary Anderson); b. 6 June 1939, Jacksonville, Florida, USA. Vocalist; Songwriter; Prod. *Career:* Member, group The Turks; Solo artiste, 1960–; Co-writer, producer with Bruce Springsteen and Steve Van Zandt, 1978–; Appearances include: British tour, 1962; Richard Nader's second Rock 'n' Roll Revival concert, with Bill Haley, Jackie Wilson, 1969; Nuclear Disarmament rally, with Bruce Springsteen, James Taylor, Linda Ronstadt, Jackson Browne, Central Park, New York, 1982; Radio City Music Hall, New York, WCBS Radio's 20th Anniversary Concert, 1992. *Recordings:* Singles include: New Orleans, 1960; Quarter To Three (No. 1, USA), 1961; School Is Out, 1961; Dance Til Quarter To Three, 1961; Dear Lady Twist, 1962; Twist, Twist Señora, 1962; This Little Girl (written by Bruce Springsteen), 1981; Out of Work (also written by Springsteen), 1982; Albums: Dedication, 1978; On The Line, 1982; Standing In The Line of Fire, 1984; Take Me Back To New Orleans, 1995; King Biscuit Flower Hour Presents Gary US Bonds Live, 2001; Producer for artistes including: Johnny Paycheck; ZZ Hill.

BONE Greg; b. 21 Jan. 1962, Hartlepool, England. Musician (guitar). 1 s. *Musical Education:* Self-taught. *Career:* Played with Terry Ronald; Support tours with Hall and Oates, 1990; Robert Palmer, 1991; Television: Harry (drama series); Performances with Bros on Wogan; Top of The Pops; Going Live; Polish Music Festival; Radio sessions with One Word and Terry Ronald; Numerous television and radio appearances with Band of Thieves (now known as Thieves Like Us). *Recordings:* with the Pet Shop Boys: Discography, 1991; Was It Worth It? 1991; DJ Culture, 1991; Bilingual,

1996; Clive Griffin, Clive Griffin, 1993; Nobody Else, Take That, 1995; Sole Purpose, Secret Life, 1995; Warehouse Grooves Vol. 5, 1998; Love and The Russian Winter, Simply Red, 1999; Reload, Tom Jones, 1999; Killing Time, Tina Cousins, 2000; Steptacular, Steps, 2000. *Membership:* Musicians' Union. *Leisure interests:* Music; Cars; Guitars.

BONET Maria Del Mar; b. 27 April 1947, Palma, Majorca, Spain. Singer; Songwriter; Musician (guitar). *Career:* Began singing with Els Setze Jutges, Barcelona, 1967; Performed in: France; Denmark; England; Switzerland; Venezuela; Mexico; Argentina; Chile; Portugal; Poland; Italy; Sweden; Germany; Greece; Tunisia; Netherlands; Belgium; Former USSR; Japan; Annual concerts, Plaça del Rei, Barcelona; Recorded and toured, France and Spain, with Ensemble de Musique Traditionelle de Tunís, 1985; Toured Spain, with Brazilian Milton Nascimiento, 1986; Presented Arenal, with choreographer, dancer, Nacho Duato, 1988; International Peralada Music Festival, 1992; Performed show, The Greece of Theodorakis, 1993; Performed in Cants d'Abelone, 1994; Performed show, Merhaba, Summer Festival, Barcelona, 1994; Edinburgh International Festival, 1995. *Recordings include:* Maria del Mar Bonet, 1974; A L'Olympia, 1975; Maria del Mar Bonet, 1976; Cançons de Festa, 1976; Alenar, 1977; Saba de Terrer, 1979; Quico-Maria del Mar, 1979; Cançons de la Nostra Mediterranea, 1980; L'Aguila Negra, 1981; Jardí Tancat, 1981; Sempre, 1981; Breviari d'Amor, 1982; Maria del Bonet, 1983; Anells d'Aigua, 1985; Gavines i Dragons, 1987; Ben A Prop, 1989; Bon Viatge Faci la Cadernera, 1990; Coreografies, with Nacho Duato, 1990; Ellas, Maria del Mar Bonet Canta a Theodorakis, 1993; Salmaia, 1995; El Cor el Temps, 1997; Cavall de Foc, 1999. *Publications:* Antología de la Nova Cançó Catalana, 1968; Maria del Mar Bonet, 1976; La Nova Cançó, 1976; Tretze que Cantan, 1982; Veinte Años de Canción en España, 1984; Una Història de la Cançó, 1987; 25 Anys de Cançó a Mallorca, 1987; Secreta Veu (poems and watercolours), 1987; Maria del Mar Bonet (biography), Joan Manresa, 1994; Quadern de Viatge, poems and watercolours, 1998. *Honours:* Spanish Gold disc, 1971; French Government Charles Cross Academy Award, Best Foreign Record, 1984; Cross of St George, Catalan Government Prize, 1984; Catalan Government National Prize, 1992. *Memberships:* Societat General d'Autors i Editors (SGAE); Associació de Cantants i Intèrprets Professionals en Llangua Catalana (ACIC). *Leisure interests:* Poetry; Writing; Pottery; Painting. *Current Management:* Jordi de Ramon. *Address:* Sepúlveda, 147–149 Principal 1a, 08011 Barcelona, Catalonia, Spain.

BONFILS Tony; b. 27 Jan. 1948, Nice, France. Musician (bass guitar, double bass); Vocalist. 3 s., 1 d. *Education:* Licence de Psychologie. *Musical Education:* Prix de Contre Basse; Medaille de Solfege. *Career:* Bass player with: Dee Dee Bridgewater; Sacha Distel; Charles Aznavour; Also studio musician.

BONGA Ntshukumo (Ntshuks); b. 1 Oct. 1963, Johannesburg, South Africa. Musician (alto saxophone, clarinet); Engineer. *Education:* BSc (Hons), Aeronautical Engineering and Design. *Musical Education:* Self-taught. *Career:* Appearances include: Reithalle, Berne, Switzerland; Purcell Room, South Bank Centre; London Jazz Festival, 1994; London ICA, 1996; WOMAD Festival, 1997; Performances with Robyn Hitchcock; Radio broadcasts: Interview BBC World Service, Network Africa, 1993; Interview, session, BBC Radio 3, Impressions, 1994; PM Live, Radio South Africa. *Recordings:* Album: Urban Ritual, Ntshuks Bonga's Tshisa; Moss Elixir, Robyn Hitchcock. *Honour:* Debut Album, Urban Ritual, voted No 6, Wire magazine Jazz/Improvised Music Poll, 1995. *Memberships:* Musicians' Union; PRS; London Musicians Collective. *Leisure interests:* Cinema; World travel; Astronomy. *Address:* 22 Norcott Rd, Stoke Newington, London N16 7EL, England.

BONHAM Jason; b. 1967, England. Musician (drums, percussion). m. Jan Charteris, 5 May 1990. *Musical Education:* Played drums from age 4; Taught by father, John Bonham. *Career:* Member, Airrace, 1984; Founder member, Virginia Wolf, 1986; Worked with members of Led Zeppelin, 1987–88; Concert, Atlantic Records 40th Anniversary concert, Madison Square Garden, 1988; US tour with Jimmy Page, 1988; Founder, own group, Bonham, 1990-. *Recordings:* Albums: with Airrace: Shaft of Light, 1984; with Virginia Wolf: Virginia Wolf, 1986; with Jimmy Page: Outrider, 1988; with Bonham: The Disregard of Timekeeping, 1989; Madhatter, 1992; with Motherland: Peace For Me, 1994; with Red Blooded Blues: Red Blooded Blues, 1995; Also contributed to: Rock Star OST, 2001; Solo Albums: In The Name of My Father Zepset, 1997; When You See The Sun, 1997. *Current Management:* Part Rock Management, Suite 318, 535 Kings Rd, London SW10 0SZ, England.

BONIN Nathalie; b. 17 Nov. 1971, San Francisco, USA. Musician (Violin). *Musical Education:* Aaron Copland School of Music, 1985–86; McGill University, 1987–88, 1993. *Career:* Composer Director, Ca Se Soigne, 1998; Producer Co-ordinator, String Festival 1998; Duke Ellington Tribute Concert, 1998; Valentino Orchestra, 1998; Said Mesnaoui, Arabic Violin and Percussion, 1998. *Recordings:* Moist; Excentricus; Cineparc; Clair de Lune; Mendelssohn: Concerto for Violin Nos 1 and 2; Beethoven Symphony No. 3; Verismo; Enfants Retour; Prokofieff: Pierre et le Loup;

Korngold. *Honours:* Québec Arts Council Grant; Deans Honour List, McGill; First Prize Winner, Darius Milhaud Competition; Winner Canadian Music Competition; First Prize Winner, CW Post Summer Chamber Music Festival Concerto Competition. *Memberships:* AFM; SOCAN. *Leisure interests:* Cycling; Reading; Computers. *Address:* 6410 Chabot St, Montréal, QC H2G 2TZ, Canada.

BONN Stanley; b. 3 Feb. 1924, Freeport, Illinois, USA. Owner, Record Label/Publishing Co; Prod.; Dir. m. Eva L Bonn, 5 Aug. 1947, 1 s., 1 d. *Career:* Owner, ESB Records, Gather Round Music, Bonnfire Publishing; Worked with Bobby Lee Caldwell, John P Swisshelm, Rob Lynn, Jeff Ashbaker, Eddie Sheppard. *Composition:* The Sounds of the Universe. *Recordings:* The Gold in this Ring; Janie's Song; Highway 44; She's a Dance Hall Lady; Don't Watch Me Fall Apart; West Texas Lady; Ten Minutes After Five; The Sounds of the Universe; All the Tears; Toe Tappin' Country Man; Three Reasons; 2nd Wind; First Date Blues. *Honours:* Song of the Year, five times; Record Label of the Year, 1991, 1992, 1994; Golden Eagle Award, California Country Music Asscn, 1994. *Memberships:* Country Music Asscn of America; California Country Music Asscn; Greater Southern Country Music Asscn. *Leisure interest:* Fishing. *Address:* ESB Records, PO Box 6429, Huntington Beach, CA 92615–6429, USA.

BONNEY Simon; b. 3 June 1961, Sydney, Australia. Vocalist; Songwriter. m. 15 June 1984, 1 s., 1 d. *Career:* Performed in film Wings of Desire (Wim Wenders), with Crime and the City Solution; Contributor to film scores: To The Ends of The World (Wim Wenders); Faraway So Close (Wim Wenders); Gas Food and Lodgings (Alison Anders); Underworld (Roger Christian); Also appeared on MTV Road Hog. *Recordings:* Albums: with Crime and the City Solution: Just South of Heaven, 1985; Room of Lights, 1986; Shine, 1988; The Bride Ship, 1989; Paradise Discotheque, 1990; The Adversary – Live; Solo albums: Forever, 1992; Everyman, 1995; Also featured on film soundtrack albums: Wings of Desire; To The Ends of The World; Faraway So Close; Underworld. *Membership:* PRS. *Current Management:* c/o Ted Gardner, Larrkin Management, 8391 Beverly Blvd #298, Los Angeles, CA 90048, USA.

BONO (Paul Hewson); b. 10 May 1960, Dublin, Ireland. Vocalist; Lyricist. m. Alison, 2 d., 1 s. *Career:* Founder member, lead singer, rock group U2, 1978–; Regular national, international and world-wide tours; Major concerts include: US Festival, 1983; The Longest Day, Milton Keynes Bowl, 1985; Live Aid, Wembley, 1985; Self Aid, Ireland, 1986; A Conspiracy of Hope (Amnesty International US tour), 1986; Smile Jamaica (hurricane relief concert), 1988; Very Special Arts Festival, White House, 1988; New Year's Eve Concert, Dublin (televised throughout Europe), 1989; Yankee Stadium, New York (second concert ever), 1992; Group established own record company, Mother Records. *Compositions include:* Co-writer, Jah Love, Neville Brothers; Lyrics, Misere, Zucchero and Pavarotti; Screenplay, Million Dollar Hotel. *Recordings:* Albums: with U2: Boy, 1980; October, 1981; War (No. 1, UK), 1983; Under A Blood Red Sky, 1983; The Unforgettable Fire (No. 1, UK), 1984; Wide Awake In America, 1985; The Joshua Tree (No. 1, UK and US), 1987; Rattle and Hum, also film (No. 1, USA), 1988; Achtung Baby (No. 1, USA), 1991; Zooropa (No. 1, UK and US), 1993; Passengers (film soundtrack), with Brian Eno, 1995; Pop, 1997; The Best of 1980–90 (compilation), 1998; All That You Can't Leave Behind, 2001; Hit singles include: Out of Control (No. 1, Ireland), 1979; Another Day (No. 1, Ireland), 1980; New Year's Day, 1983; Two Hearts Beat As One, 1983; Pride (In The Name of Love), 1984; The Unforgettable Fire, 1985; With Or Without You (No. 1, USA), 1987; I Still Haven't Found What I'm Looking For (No. 1, USA), 1987; Where The Streets Have No Name, 1987; Desire (No. 1, UK), 1988; Angel of Harlem, 1988; When Love Comes To Town, with B B King, 1989; All I Want Is You, 1989; The Fly (No. 1, UK), 1991; Mysterious Ways, 1992; One, 1992; Even Better Than The Real Thing, 1992; Who's Gonna Ride Your Wild Horses, 1992; Stay, 1993; Hold Me, Thrill Me, Kiss Me (from film soundtrack Batman Forever), 1995; Discotheque (No. 1, UK), 1997; Staring At The Sun, 1997; If God Will Send His Angels, 1998; Sweetest Thing, 1998; Beautiful Day (No. 1, UK), 2000; Stuck In A Moment You Can't Get Out Of, 2001; Walk On, 2001; Contributor, Do They Know It's Christmas?, Band Aid, 1985; Sun City, Little Steven, 1985; In A Lifetime, Clannad, 1986; Mystery Girl, Roy Orbison, 1988; Special Christmas, charity album, 1987; Folkways – A Vision Shared (Woody Guthrie tribute), 1988; Live For Ireland, 1989; Red Hot + Blue (Cole Porter tribute), 1990; Tower of Song (Leonard Cohen tribute), 1995; Pavarotti and Friends, 1996; Forces of Nature, 1999. *Honours:* Grammy Awards: Album of The Year, Best Rock Performance, The Joshua Tree, 1987; Best Rock Performance, Desire, 1989; Best Rock Vocal, 1993, Record of The Year, Song of The Year, Best Rock Performance By Duo Or Group, Beautiful Day, 2001; Brit Awards: Best International Group, 1988–90, 1992, 1998, 2001; Best Live Act, 1993; Outstanding Contribution To The British Music Indstury, 2001; World Music Award, Irish Artist of The Year, 1993; Juno Award, International Entertainer of The Year, 1993; Q Awards: Best Act In The World, 1990, 1992, 1993; Merit Award, 1994; Numerous poll wins and awards, Billboard and Rolling Stone magazines; Gold and

Platinum discs. *Current Management:* Principle Management, 30–32 Sir John Rogersons Quay, Dublin 2, Ireland.

BONSALL Joseph Sloan Jr; b. 18 May 1948, Philadelphia, Pennsylvania, USA. Singer. m. Barbara Holt, 1969. *Career:* Member, gospel singing groups, 1966–73; Member, gospel/country group The Oak Ridge Boys, 1973–; Co-owner, Silverline/Goldline Music Publishing. *Recordings:* Singles: Y'All Come Back Saloon; I'll Be True To You; Leavin' Louisiana In The Broad Daylight; Trying To Love Two Women; Elvira; Bobbie Sue; American Made; Love Song; I Guess It Never Hurts To Hurt Sometime; Come On In; Make My Life With You; Albums: Oak Ridge Boys, 1974; Sky High, 1975; Old Fashioned..., 1976; Live, 1977; Y'All Come Back Saloon, 1977; Room Service, 1978; The Oak Ridge Boys Have Arrived, 1979; Together, 1980; Greatest Hits, 1980; Fancy Free, 1981; Bobbie Sue, 1982; Christmas, 1982; Very Best, 1982; American Made, 1983; The Oak Ridge Boys Deliver, 1983; Friendship, 1983; Greatest Hits II, 1984; Seasons, 1985; Step On Out, 1985; Where The Fast Lane Ends, 1986; Christmas Again, 1986; Monogahela, 1987; New Horizons, 1988; American Dreams, 1989; Greatest Hits III, 1989; Unstoppable, 1991; The Long Haul, 1992. *Honours:* Numerous Gospel Music Asscn Dove Awards; Grammy Awards, 1970–77; CMA Vocal Group of The Year, 1978; ACM Awards, Best Vocal Group, 1977, 1979; American Music Award, Best Country Group, 1982; Gold discs. *Memberships:* Academy of Country Music; NARAS; AFTRA; Country Music Asscn. *Current Management:* Don Light Talent, PO Box 120308, Nashville, TN 37212, USA.

BOO Betty, (Alison Moira Clarkson); b. 6 March 1970, Kensington, London, England. Rapper; Vocalist; Songwriter. *Career:* Member, rap group the She-Rockers; Duo, Hit 'n' Run; Guest singer with Beatmasters; Solo artiste, 1990-. *Compositions:* co-writer: Pure and Simple, number 1 UK hit for Hear'Say; tracks for artists including: Louise, 2000; Tweenies, 2001. *Recordings:* Albums: Boomania, 1990; Grrr...It's Betty Boo!, 1992; Hit singles: with Beatmasters: Hey DJ (I Can't Dance To That Music You're Playing), 1989; Solo: Doin' The Do, 1990; Where Are You Baby, 1990; 24 Hours, 1990; Let Me Take You There, 1992; I'm On My Way, 1992. *Honours:* Numerous dance music awards. *Current Management:* Big Life Management, 15 Little Portland St, London W1N 5DE, England.

BOOHORISHVILI Mehab; b. 15 June 1972, Batumi, Georgia. Folksinger; Musician (Guitar). *Musical Education:* Batumi Music College. *Career:* Turkey Folklore Festival, 1995; Eshme, group, Spain; Legames International Folklore Festival, 1997; GIEZA International Folk Festival, Spain, 1997; Bravo Festival, Tblisi, Georgia, 1998; Ariola, Otello, Turker; Festival of Arpendos; Leader, Folk Song Trio; Member, Batume folk song group; Singer, Batumi State Opera. *Recordings:* Interpretations of major Georgian folk songs with Batami State folk song group. *Honours:* Prize, GIEZA Festival, Spain, 1997; Prize, Spara Festival, 1997. *Leisure interest:* Singing. *Address:* S Khimstiashvili St No. 6 Apt 11, Batumi, Georgia.

BOONE Debby (Deborah Ann); b. 22 Sept. 1956, Hackensack, New Jersey, USA. Vocalist; Actress. m. Gabriel Ferrer, 1979, 2 s., 2 d. *Career:* singer with (father) Pat Boone and family group, 1970–; Recording artist, 1977–; Numerous television appearances include: Sins Of The Past, ABC-TV, 1984; Stage performances: Seven Brides For Seven Brothers, national tour, 1981–82; Sound of Music, national tour, 1987–88. *Recordings:* You Light Up My Life (No. 1, USA), 1977; Midstream, 1978; Love Has No Reason, 1980; Friends For Life, 1987; Reflections, 1988; Choose Life, 1992; Surrender, 1992; With My Song, 1992; Home For Christmas, 1993; Greatest Hymns, 2000; You Light Up My Life – Greatest Inspirational Songs, 2001. *Publications:* Debby Boone – So Far; Bedtime Hugs For Little Ones (children's book), 1988; Co-author, Tomorrow Is A Brand New Day, 1989. *Honours:* American Music Award, Song of The Year; Grammy Awards: Best New Artist, 1977; CMA Best New Country Artist, 1977; Singing Star of Year, AGVA, 1978; Dove Awards, 1980, 1984; Best Inspirational Performance, 1980; Best Gospel Performance, Keep The Flame Burning, 1984; Best New Personality, National Asscn Theatre Owners. *Current Management:* c/o Sparrow Communications Group, 101 Winners Circle, Brentwood, TN 37024, USA.

BOONE Pat; b. 1 June 1934, Jacksonville, Florida, USA. Singer; Actor. m. Shirley Foley, 14 Nov. 1953, 4 d. *Education:* North Texas State Teachers College; David Liscomb College; Gradute magna cum laude, Columbia, 1958. *Career:* Appearances include: Ted Mack TV Show, 1953; Arthur Godfrey Show, CBS, 1954–55; Own television show, 1957; Numerous other television appearances include: Moonlighting; Co-host, Wish You Were Here, Nashville Network, 1988–; Film appearances include: Bernadine, 1957; April Love, 1957; Mardi Gras, 1958; Journey To The Centre of The Earth, 1959; All Hands On Deck, 1961; State Fair, 1962; Main Attraction, 1962; Yellow Canary, 1963; Greatest Story Ever Told, 1965; Perils of Pauline, 1967; The Cross and The Switchblade, 1971; Owner, Lamb and Lion Records. *Publications include:* Twixt Twelve and Twenty, 1958; Between You and Me and The Gatepost, 1960; The Real Christmas, 1961; Care and Feeding of Parents, 1967; A New Song, 1971; Joy, 1973; A Miracle A Day Keeps the Devil Away; My Faith, 1976; Pat Boone Devotional Book,

1977; The Honeymoon Is Over, 1977; Together – 25 Years With The Boone Family, 1979; Pray To Win – God Wants You To Succeed, 1980. *Honours:* Listed in Top Ten Attractions, 1957; Listed in Top Fifteen Namepower Stars, 1959. *Current Management:* Tim Swift, Cossette Productions. *Address:* 8899 Beverly Blvd, Los Angeles, CA 90048, USA.

BOOTH Tim; b. 4 Feb. 1960, Leeds, England. Vocalist; Lyricist. 1 s. *Education:* University of Manchester. *Career:* Lead singer, James, 1982–2001; Early support slots to The Smiths; Numerous tours and television appearances. *Recordings:* Singles include: Jimone, 1983; Hymn from a Village, 1985; Come Home, 1989; Sit Down (No. 2, UK), 1991; Sound, 1991; Born of Frustration, 1992; Sometimes (Lester Piggott), 1993; Laid, 1993; Say Something, 1994; She's A Star, 1997; Tomorrow, 1997; Destiny Calling, 1998; Sit Down '98, 1998; I Know What I'm Here For, 1999; Just Like Fred Astaire, 1999; Getting Away With It (All Messed Up), 2001; Albums include: Stutter, 1986; Strip-Mine, 1988; One Man Clapping, live, 1989; Gold Mother, 1990; Seven, 1992; Laid, 1993; Wah Wah, live, 1994; Whiplash, 1997; The Best of James (compilation), 1998; Millionaires, 1999; Pleased To Meet You, 2001; One-off solo project: Booth and The Bad Angel, 1996 (with Angelo Badalementi). *Current Management:* Rudge Management, 1 Star St, London W2 1QD, England.

BORDEN David; b. 25 Dec. 1938, Boston, Massachusetts, USA. Composer; Musician (Piano, Synthesizer). m. (2) Rebecca Godin, 12 Aug. 1994, 1 s. *Musical Education:* BM, Eastman School of Music; MM, ESM, MA, Music Composition, Harvard University; Fulbright Student, Hochschule für Musik, Berlin, Germany. *Career:* WBAI Free Music Store, The Kitchen, The Knitting Factory, Dance Theatre Workshop, Town Hall, Lincoln Center, New York City; Tivoli Konzert Halle, Copenhagen; Barbican Centre, London; Portsmouth Festival, England; New Music America, Montréal, Canada. *Compositions:* The Continuing Story of Counterpunt; Easter, Enfield in Winter; The Birthday Variations; Variations on a Theme of Philip Glass; Angels. *Recordings:* The Continuing Story of Counterpunt; Place, Times and People; Cayuga Nightmusic; Another Mallard's Portable Masterpiece. *Membership:* American Music Center. *Address:* PO Box 842, Ithaca, NY 14851, USA.

BORLAND Wes; b. 7 Feb. 1975, Nashville, USA. Musician (guitar). m. Heather McMillan, April 1998. *Musical Education:* Learnt blues/country guitar at father's church; Douglas Anderson School of The Arts, studied jazz guitar for three years. *Career:* Sang and played guitar for own band in Jacksonville when recruited for Limp Bizkit, 1994; Signed to Flip/Interscope on strength of demo tape; Striking live shows at concerts and festivals; Group spearheaded 'nu-metal' breakthrough in Europe, 2001; Worked with side-project group Big Dumb Face whilst member of Limp Bizkit; Left Limp Bizkit, October 2001. *Recordings:* Albums: Three Dollar Bill, Y'All $, 1997; Significant Other, 1999; Chocolate Starfish and The Hot Dog Flavored Water, 2000; New Old Songs (remix album), 2001; Duke Lion Fights The Terror (with Big Dumb Face), 2001; Singles: Faith, 1997; Nookie, Rearranged, 1999; Break Stuff, Take A Look Around (from Mission Impossible 2 OST), My Generation, 2000; Rollin', My Way, Boiler, 2001. *Honours:* Second and third albums both debuted at #1 on US chart; Significant Other sales in excess of 6m. *Address:* c/o Geffen Records, USA. *Internet:* www.geffen.com.

BORN 2 B (Colin Crook); b. 29 Jan. 1971, London, England. Rapper; Prod.; Songwriter. *Education:* Woolwich Polytechnic, 1982–87. *Musical Education:* Self-taught whilst working for a South London Sound System. *Career:* Kiss FM Tour, including The Jazz Rap Weekender, London; The Wag Club, London; Juliana's, Istanbul, Turkey; The Brain Club, London, 1990; Interview on ITV London, Thames News programme, 1992; Numerous television appearances on MTV Europe, and in Germany, Turkey and Japan; UK radio appearances on Kiss FM; Capital Radio; Jazz FM, London. *Compositions:* Kings of the Ring, 1992; Live at Energy Radio Pt 1 and 2, 1997; The Band Played the Boogie/Can We Start Over, 1997. *Recordings:* Moments In Love, 1990; Aquarian House, 1990; Turkish Delight, 1992; The Band Played The Boogie, 1992–93; Debut album The Last Guv'nor, 1998; Single: Livin' Blue, 1998. *Publications:* Contributor of numerous articles in the music press. *Honour:* Official Music Week Top 60 Dance Singles, 1992. *Memberships:* Musicians' Union; MCPS; Performing Rights Society. *Leisure interests:* Music; Keeping fit; Restaurants; Clubs.

BORUM Stefan; b. 21 Aug. 1954, Viborg, Denmark. Composer; Musician (piano). 2 s., 1 d. *Musical Education:* 1 term, Creative Music Studio, Woodstock, New York, USA, 1980. *Career:* Member: Blue Sun, 1975–78; Concerts include: Roskilde Festival, 1977; Member, Lost Kids, 1979–80; Created Sun Quartet; Concerts include: Italian tour, 1984–85; First Prize winner, Jazz On The Oder, 1987; Jazz Jamboree, Warsaw, 1987; Autumn Rhythms, Leningrad, 1988; Member, Shades of Blue, 1987–; Concerts include: Djurs Bluesland, 1988, 1990, 1992; Notoddon Blues Festival, 1991. *Recordings:* It's All Money Johnny, Blue Sun, 1976; Sun Quartet, Sun Quartet, 1987; On A Mission From Muddy Waters, Shades of Blue, 1992. *Memberships:* DMF (Danish Musicians Union); DJFBA.

BOSCO João, (Joao Bosco De Freitas Mucci); b. 1946, Ponte Nova, Minas Gerais, Brazil. Vocalist; Musician (guitar); Composer. *Education:* Ouro Preto University, Civil Engineering, 1972. *Career:* From musical family: mother, violinist; father, samba singer; sister, concert pianist; brother, composer; University collaboration with lyricist Vinicius de Morais; Began long association with ex-psychiatrist Aldir Blanc, late 1970s-late 1980s; Supplied Elis Regina with much of her best material; After her early death, became known as a performer of own material; Struggled with censorship during military dictatorship in Brazil; 1977 composition O Bebaido e a Equilibrista (The Drunkard and the Tightrope Walker) became Amnesty International theme song; Influenced by many styles including: samba; jazz; African; Cuban; rock; In addition to Portuguese, lyrics use languages including: English; French; Spanish; Yoruban; International stage appearances include: Lee Ritenour, 1988; Montreux Jazz Festival; First major tour of USA, early 1990s. *Recordings:* João Bosco, 1973 Caca A Raposa, 1975; Galos De Briga, 1976; Tiro De Misericordia, 1977; Linha De Passe, 1979; Bandalhismo, 1980; Essa E A Sua Vida, 1981; Comissão De Frente, 1982; Ao Vivo 100th Apresentacao, 1983; Gagabirô, 1984; Cabeca De Nego, 1986; AiAiAi De Mim, 1986; Na Onda Que Balanca, 1987; Bosco, 1989; Zona De Fronteira, 1991; Afrocanto, 1992; Da Licenca Men Senhor, 1996; Benguele OST, 1998; Na Esquinha, 2000; features on: Festival, Lee Ritenour, 1988.

BOSKOV Ole; b. 31 Aug. 1963, Copenhagen, Denmark. Musician (piano, acoustic guitar, keyboards); Vocalist; Songwriter. m. Tina, 5 Sept. 1992. *Musical Education:* Piano lessons for 16 years, organ lessons for 2 years, and guitar lessons for 4 years. *Career:* No. 1 hit single in Denmark with Danish version of MC Hammer's Can't Touch This; Debut album of own compositions, 1996. *Compositions include:* Listen To The Wind; Pennsylvania; Going Crazy. *Recordings:* Backing vocals for Ester Brohus; Solo albums: Listen To The Wind, 1996; Mr Romance, 1998. *Membership:* Danish Songwriters Guild. *Leisure interests:* Football; Skiing; Spiritual enhancement. *Address:* Rolfsvej 22 st th, 2000 Frederiksberg, Denmark.

BOSTIC Earl; b. 4 June 1947. Musician (Bass). m. Maria Kottmair, 2 d. *Education:* BA, Wayne State University, Detroit, Michigan, USA, 1971. *Career:* Leo Wright Quartet, 1980–84; Played with Sarah Leander at Theater des Westens, 1980; Played with Eartha Kitt at the Groschenoper, Frankfurt, Germany, 1988; Rudy Stevenson Band, 1994–98; Harry's Freilach, 1994–98; Bregenz Music Festival in Porgy and Bess Stageband, 1997, 1998. *Recordings:* Wayne Martin: Hometown Boy; Klesmer Tov; Lia Ander: This Masquerade. *Address:* Karlsruherstr 16, 10711 Berlin, Germany.

BOSTOCK Chris; b. 23 Nov. 1959, Hillingdon, London, England. Songwriter; Prod.; Musician (bass, keyboards). *Career:* Songwriter and Bassist with Vic Godard's Subway Sect, 1981–82 and JoBoxers, 1983–86; 3 hit singles, 1 hit album; Touring in UK, USA, Canada, Australia, New Zealand and with Dave Stewart and Spiritual Cowboys, 1990–92; 2 albums; Touring in Europe; Sessions for OMD, Shakespeare's Sister, Style Council, Sandie Shaw; Produced albums for Savage World, 1993; Clint Bradley, 1997; Film soundtracks: Bad Girl, with Jane Horrocks, 1992; Dad Savage, with Patrick Stewart, 1998. *Compositions:* Hit Singles: Just Got Lucky; Johnny Friendly; Is This Really the First Time. *Recordings:* Boxerbeat, 1983; Just Got Lucky, 1983; Johnny Friendly, 1983; Is This Really the First Time, 1985; Spiritual Cowboys and Honest albums by Dave Stewart and the Spiritual Cowboys; Goodbye Cruel World, Shakespeare's Sister; Cafe Bleu, album, Style Council. *Memberships:* Re-Pro; PRS; Musician's Union. *Current Management:* Clive Banks Ltd, 1 Glenthorne Mews, 115a Glenthorne Rd, London W6 0JL, England. *Address:* 6 Cherry Tree Court, 54 Grove Hill, London E18 2JE, England.

BOTH Robert Allen; b. 10 Nov. 1952, Montclair, New Jersey, USA. Recording Engineer; Prod.; Musician. m. Karen Sue Cody, 2 March 1987, 1 s. *Education:* Art School, Ridgewood. *Musical Education:* Guitar and piano lessons. *Career:* A & R, Polydor Records, New York City, 1971–72; A & R Director, Recording engineer, producer, James Brown Enterprises, New York City, 1972–76; Staff engineer, Delta Recording, 1976–77; Staff engineer, Quad Recording, 1979; Owner, Chief engineer, Twain Recordings, New Jersey, 1976–; Audio instructor, Ramapo College of New Jersey, 1993; Audio Instructor, William Paterson University, New Jersey, 1995–; Audio Instructor, County College of Morris, New Jersey, 1997-. *Recordings:* with The JB's: Doin' It, 1973; with Maceo Parker, US, 1974; with James Brown: Get On The Good Foot, 1972; Reality, 1974; The Payback, 1974; Hell, 1974; Sex Machine Today, 1975; Hot, 1975; with Lyn Collins: Check Me Out, 1975; with The JB's Damn Night, 1974; Breakin' Bread, 1974; Hustle with Speed, 1975; JB's Reunion, 1999; Soul of the Funky, 1999. *Publications:* Articles in the music press. *Honours:* 3 RIAA Gold Records Awards for work with James Brown. *Membership:* Music Producers Guild of America. *Address:* Twain Recording, 18 Hiawatha Pass, West Milford, NJ 07480, USA.

BOTSCHINSKY Allan; b. 29 March 1940, Copenhagen, Denmark. Musician (trumpet, flugelhorn); Composer. *Musical Education:* Royal Danish Conservatory at age 14; Studied trumpet under Cecil Collins at the Manhattan School of Music, New York; Private studies of classical composition with Professor Svend Erik Werner and Bo Holten. *Career:* Professional at age 16, playing in leading groups of Copenhagen's Jazz Scene, with, among others, Oscar Pettiford, Stan Getz, Dexter Gordon and Ben Webster; Member of Jazz Quintet '60 and the Danish Radio Jazz Group; Played with and conducted The Danish Radio Big Band, whose guest conductors included Thad Jones, Oliver Nelson, Stan Kenton, Dizzy Gillespie, Maynard Ferguson and George Russell; Regular tours and recordings with Peter Herbolzheimer's Rhythm Combination and Brass and Ali Haurand's European Jazz Ensemble and European Trumpet Summit. *Compositions:* Numerous compositions and arrangements include: Sentiments, prizewinning suite for large orchestra and voice; Exercises For Jazz Orchestra; Synergy, piece for string quartet and jazz quintet; A Jazz Sonata, for trumpet and piano; Jazz-Antiphony, brass octet; Fantasia, piece for solo trumpet and symphony orchestra. *Recordings include:* Duologue, 1987; The Night, 1988; Jazzpar 95, 1995; Last Summer, 1992; I've Got Another Rhythm, 1995; Also appears on: Conversations, Sahib Shihab, 1963; Ben Webster Plays Duke Ellington, 1967; Akili, Akili, 1987; She Touched Me, Thomas Clausen, 1988; Lee Konitz and The Jazzpar All Stars, 1992; Axen, Bent Axen, 1996. *Honours include:* Ben Webster Prize, 1983; Special television tribute entitled The Music of Allan Botschinsky, 1984. *Address:* 64 Gilbey House, 38–46 Jamestown Rd, London NW1 7BY, England.

BOTTUM Roddy; b. 1 July 1963, Los Angeles, California, USA. Musician (keyboards). *Musical Education:* Classically-trained pianist. *Career:* Member, US rock group Faith No More, 1980–98; Leader, alternative pop band Imperial Teen, 1994–; Appearances include: Brixton, London (recorded for live video), 1990; Reading Festival, 1990; Monsters of Rock Festivals, Italy and France, 1990; Supported Robert Plant, US, 1990; Day On The Green, San Francisco, 1991; Rock In Rio II Festival, Brazil, 1991; Phoenix Festival, 1993, 1995. *Recordings:* Singles include: with Faith No More: We Care A Lot, 1988; Epic, 1990; Falling To Pieces, 1990; From Out of Nowhere, 1990; Midlife Crisis, 1992; A Small Victory, 1992; Everything's Ruined, 1992; I'm Easy, 1993; Falling, 1994; Ricochet, 1995; Evidence, 1995; Ashes To Ashes, 1997; I Started A Joke, 1998; Albums: with Faith No More: Faith No More, 1985; Introduce Yourself, 1987; The Real Thing, 1989; Live At Brixton Academy, 1991; Angel Dust, 1992; King For A Day... Fool For A Lifetime, 1995; Album of The Year, 1997; with Imperial Teen: Seasick, 1996; What Is Not To Love, 1998; Additional work: with Fenix TX, Lechuza, 2001. *Honours:* Grammy Nomination, Best Heavy Metal Performance, 1990; Bammy Awards: Outstanding Group, Best Keyboardist, 1991; MTV Video Award, Best Special Effects, 1991; Bay Area Award, Outstanding Keyboardist, 1993. *Current Management:* Warren Entner Management, 5550 Wilshire Blvd, Suite 302, Los Angeles, CA 90036, USA.

BOUBLIL Alain Albert; b. 5 March 1941, Tunis, Tunisia. Author; Dramatist. *Career:* Author, dramatist and lyricist. *Publications:* Wrote libretto and lyrics for: La Révolution Française, 1973; Les Misérables, 1980; Abbacadabra, 1984; Miss Saigon, 1989; Le Journal d'Adam et Eve (play), 1994; Martin Guerre, 1996. *Honours:* 2 Tony Awards, 2 Grammy Awards, 2 Victoire de la Musique Awards, Molière Award (all for Les Misérables); Evening Standard Drama Award (for Miss Saigon); Laurence Olivier Award (for Martin Guerre). *Address:* c/o Cameron Mackintosh Ltd, 1 Bedford Sq., London WC1B 3RA, England.

BOUCOUM Afel; b. 1955, Niafunke, Mali. Vocalist; Musician (guitar); Songwriter. *Education:* Won scholarship to study at government agricultural college in Mali. *Musical Education:* Learned music at home from father, a well-known local musician. *Career:* Began by accompanying father to his performances; At 13 joined Ali Farka Toure's band, ASCO, 1968; Agricultural advisor by profession; Joined Orchestre Diaba Regional, 1982; Toured internationally with Toure since 1991; Formed Alkibar, early 1980s; Involved in Damon Albarn's Mali Music project. *Recordings:* The Source, Ali Farka Toure, 1992; Alkibar, 1999; The Rough Guide To The Music of Mali and Guinea, 2000; The Music of Mali, 2001. *Honours:* Mali's Biennale, second place, 1972. *Address:* c/o World Circuit Ltd, 138 Kingsland Rd, London, E2 8DY, England.

BOULIANE Daniel G; b. 26 Oct. 1963, Hull, Québec, Canada. Prod.; Composer; Keyboards; Drums; Vocals; Percussions. m. Lise Roy, 1981, 1 s., 1 d. *Education:* Université du Québec; Collège Alexandre. *Career:* Soundtracks for NFB documentaries; Soundtracks for TV series; Soundtracks for Moving the Mountain; Soundtracks for many national ads. *Compositions:* for Nadia: Free Free; Live on Love; Shine On; Beatman; for Roxxy: Love Set Us Free; I Feel You; For Us to Be; for Nathalie Page: This is the Time. *Recordings:* New World, 1994; Nomad, 1996; Remember, 1998; Image Compilation, 1992. *Publications:* Titles of Dak: New World, 1994; Nomad, 1996; Remember, 1998. *Honours:* Reel Award Nominee, 1992–94; Gémeaux Award Nominee, 1995. *Membership:* Academic of Canadian Cinema and Television. *Leisure interests:* Astronomy; Fishing; Walking in the woods.

BOURASSA Francois; b. 26 Sept. 1959, Montréal, Canada. Jazz Musician (piano). *Musical Education:* Bachelor's Degree, Composition, McGill University; Master's Degree, Jazz, Academic Honours and Distinction in Performance, New England Conservatory of Music, Boston. *Career:* Concerts in Canada, USA, Europe (France, Belgium, Spain), Korea, Moscow, Mexico; Canadian tours of jazz festivals; Concert with Dave Brubeck; Celebration of Charles Dutoit's birthday, Radio France, Radio Canada. *Compositions:* Reflet 1; Jeune Vieux Jeune; Echo; Tour of France. *Recordings:* Reflet 1, 1986; Jeune Vieux Jeune, 1993; Echo, 1996; Cactus, 1998; Trio François Bourassa Et André LeRoux – Live, 2001. *Honours:* Canada and Québec Arts Council Compositions Grants; Winner, 1985 Montréal International Jazz Festival's Competition. *Current Management:* Fleming Artists Management, 4102 St Urbain, Montréal, QC H2W IV3, Canada.

BOURDE Hervé; b. 12 July 1951, Marseilles, France. Musician (saxophone, flute, piano); Composer. 1 d. *Career:* Tours, France and Europe, 15 years; Concepts for jazz festivals. *Recordings:* 6 solo records; 10 as soloist, composer. *Honours:* First prize, City of Marseilles Conservatoire. *Memberships:* SPEDIDAM; ADAMI. *Leisure interests:* Reading; Cooking; Music.

BOURDON Rod; b. 20 Jan. 1979, Calabasas, California, USA. Musician (drums). *Career:* Inspired to play drums during elementary school years after seeing Aerosmith concert; Once worked as a waiter; Teamed up with school friends in Xero group; Became Hybrid Theory and signed to Warner Bros, Spring 2000; Band immediately sent to professional studio; Further name change to Linkin Park prior to first record releases; Incessant promotional activity since release of album; Live shows include: Family Values and Ozzfest tours; KROQ Acoustic Christmas Concert 2001; many international dates; TV specials include: Live At The Fillmore; Reverb. *Recordings:* Albums: Hybrid Theory, 2000; Singles: Hybrid Theory (Acoustic EP), 2000; One Step Closer, Crawling, Papercut, In The End, 2001. *Honours:* Over 10m. world-wide sales of debut album to end of 2001; Billboard Award, Best Modern Rock Artist, 2001; Rock Bear Awards: Best International Band; Best International Album, 2001; Kerrang! Award, Best International Newcomer, 2001; Rolling Stone Award, Best Hard Rock/ Metal Band, 2001. *Current Management:* Andy Gould Management, 8484 Wilshire Blvd #425, Beverly Hills, CA 90211, USA. *Internet:* www.linkinpark.com.

BOURGOIN Patrick G; b. 16 Dec. 1948, Paris, France. Musician (saxophones, flute, clarinet, EWI). *Musical Education:* Autodidacte. *Career:* Has played with many French artists including Gino Vanelli in Paris and Manu Dibango on world tour, 1971-. *Recordings include:* With many French artists; Music for films; 1 album with Duran Duran. *Honour:* Nomination for Victoires de La Musique, 1988. *Memberships:* SACEM; SPEDIDAM. *Leisure interests:* Sport; Photography. *Address:* 80 Bd Gambetta, 94130 Nogent sur Marne, France.

BOUSSAGUET Pierre-Michel-André; b. 12 Nov. 1962, Albi, France. Jazz Musician (string bass player); Composer; Arranger. Divorced, 2 d. *Musical Education:* End of Studies Certificate. *Career:* with Guy Lafitte, 1986-; Tours, world-wide with artists including: Wynton Marsalis; Joe Pass; Didier Lockwood; Monty Alexander. *Compositions:* Impressions III, Creation for symphonic orchestra and jazz quartet; Symphonic and jazz pieces, 1997. *Recordings:* 2 Bass hits (with Ray Brown), 1988-; P Boussaguet Quintet featuring Tom Harrell, 1992; Charme, 1998; duet with Guy Lafitte, Crossings, 1999; current trio featuring H Sellin and A Queen, Charme, 1999. *Memberships:* SACEM; UMJ. *Leisure interests:* Golf; Aerobatic flying; Wine tasting. *Current Management:* B Hopper Management. *Address:* 52 rue Pierre Mourgues, 81000 Albi, France.

BOVA Jeffrey Stephen; b. 22 June 1953, District of Columbia, USA. Musician (keyboards); Composer. *Musical Education:* Berklee College of Music, 1971–72; Manhattan School of Music, 1972–75. *Career:* Musician, composer, 1975-; Assistant composer, arranger, Herbie Hancock, 1987–88; Cyndi Lauper, 1987–89; Ryuichi Sakamoto, 1988–89; Musician, composer, Distance, 1988-. *Compositions:* Composer, arranger, film soundtracks: Colors, 1989; The Handmaid's Tale, 1990; Pretty Woman, 1990. *Recordings:* Keyboard player on numerous albums including: The Bridge, Billy Joel, 1986; True Colors, Cyndi Lauper, 1986; Love, Aztec Camera, 1987; The Hunger, Michael Bolton, 1987; Cher, Cher, 1987; Foreign Affair, Tina Turner, 1989; Journeyman, Eric Clapton, 1989; Bat Out of Hell II – Back Into Hell, Meat Loaf, 1993; Welcome To The Neighbourhood, Meat Loaf, 1995; Falling Into You, Celine Dion, 1996; Still Waters, The Bee Gees, 1997; Other recordings by Average White Band; Ian Hunter; Robert Hart; Hall and Oates; Mick Jones. *Honours:* Numerous Platinum discs. *Membership:* ASCAP.

BOVEE Bob (Robert); b. 17 Feb. 1946, Omaha, Nebraska, USA. Musician (guitar, harmonica, banjo, autoharp); Singer. m. Gail A Heil, 8 Dec. 1988. *Education:* BA, History, University of Nebraska, 1969. *Career:* Six tours, Western Europe; Regular tours USA, 1971-; Iowa Public TV; Prairie Home

Companion; River City Folk; Rural Route 3; Other syndicated radio shows; Festival of American Fiddle Tunes. *Recordings:* Pop Wagner and Bob Bovee, 1977; The Roundup, 1979; For Old Time's Sake, 1985; Behind The Times, 1986; Come All You Waddies, 1988; Rebel Voices, 1988; Come Over and See Me, 1991; Rural Route 2, 1996. *Publications:* Numerous articles, reviews, American traditional music. *Memberships:* North American Folk Music and Dance Alliance. *Leisure interests:* Reading; Vintage record collecting. *Address:* Bob Bovee and Gail Heil, RT 2 Box 25, Spring Grove, MN 55974, USA.

BOWEN Lorraine; b. 31 Oct. 1961, Gloucestershire, England. Musician; Performer; Songwriter. *Musical Education:* BMus (Hons) Surrey University. *Career:* Singing teacher to Billy Bragg; Played piano on National television; Songwriter for Loose Ends, BBC Radio 4; Member, group The Dinner Ladies; Writer, singer, The Lorraine Bowen Experience; Songwriter; International songwriter and performer of lounge hits and comedy songs. *Compositions:* Julie Christie; Crumble Song; Bicycle Adventure; I Love London; Space; Spinach. *Recordings:* with The Dinner Ladies: These Knees Have Seen The World, 1989; with Billy Bragg: The Internationale, 1990; Don't Try This At Home, 1991; Bloke On Bloke, 1997; with The Lorraine Bowen Experience: Greatest Hits Vol. I, 1995; Vol. II, 1998; Bossy Nova, 2001; Oh! What A Star!, 2002. *Memberships:* MCPS; Musicians' Union; PRS. *Leisure interests:* Swimming; Coastal walking. *Current Management:* Sequin Skirt Management. *Address:* c/o 6 Stannard Rd, London E8 1DB, England.

BOWIE David, (David Jones); b. 8 Jan. 1947, Brixton, London, England. Vocalist; Actor. m. (1) Angela Barnet, divorced, 1 s., (2) Iman, 24 April 1992. *Career:* Solo recording artist, 1970-; Lead singer, Tin Machine, 1989–91; Actor, films, 1976-; World tours, concerts, television and radio appearances, many as Ziggy Stardust and Aladdin Sane; Performances include: Beckenham Free Festival (also organizer), 1969; Glastonbury Festival, 1971; Carnegie Hall, 1972; Royal Festival Hall, 1972; Earls Court, 1973; Madison Square Garden, 1978; Live Aid, Wembley, 1985; Dodger Stadium, Los Angeles, 1990; A Concert For Life (Freddie Mercury Tribute), 1992; Film appearances include: The Man Who Fell To Earth, 1976; Christiane F, 1980; Cat People, 1982; The Hunger, 1983; Merry Christmas Mr Lawrence, 1983; Ziggy Stardust, 1983; Labyrinth, 1986; Absolute Beginners, 1986; The Last Temptation of Christ, 1988; Theatre includes: The Elephant Man, 1980. *Recordings:* Numerous solo albums include: David Bowie, 1969; The Man Who Sold The World, 1971; Hunky Dory, 1971; The Rise and Fall of Ziggy Stardust..., 1972; Aladdin Sane (No. 1, UK), 1973; Pin-Ups (No. 1, UK), 1973; Diamond Dogs (No. 1, UK), 1974; David Live, 1974; Young Americans, 1975; Station To Station, 1976; Low, 1977; Heroes, 1977; Lodger, 1979; Scary Monsters (No. 1, UK), 1980; Let's Dance (No. 1, UK), 1983; Ziggy Stardust – The Motion Picture, 1983; Tonight (No. 1, UK), 1984; Never Let Me Down, 1987; Changesbowie (compilation; No. 1, UK), 1990; Black Tie White Noise (No. 1, UK), 1993; The Singles Collection (compilation), 1993; Outside, 1995; Earthling, 1997; Hours, 1999; Bowie At The Beeb (compilation of radio sessions and concerts), 2000; with Tin Machine: Tin Machine, 1989; Tin Machine II, 1991; Numerous solo hit singles include: Space Oddity, 1969 (No. 1, UK, 1975); The Man Who Sold The World, 1971; Starman, 1972; The Jean Genie, 1972; Drive-In Saturday, 1973; Life On Mars?, 1973; Sorrow, 1973; Rebel Rebel, 1974; Diamond Dogs, 1974; Young Americans, 1975; Fame (No. 1, USA), 1975; Golden Years, 1975; Sound and Vision, 1977; Heroes, 1977; Boys Keep Swinging, 1979; Ashes To Ashes (No. 1, UK), 1980; Fashion, 1980; Wild Is The Wind, 1981; Cat People, 1982; Let's Dance (No. 1, UK and US), 1983; China Girl, 1983; Modern Love, 1983; Blue Jean, 1984; Absolute Beginners, 1986; Fame 90, 1990; Real Cool World, 1992; Jump They Say, 1993; The Heart's Filthy Lesson, 1995; Strangers When We Meet/The Man Who Sold The World, 1995; Hallo Spaceboy, 1996; Little Wonder, 1997; Dead Man Walking, 1997; Seven Years In Tibet, 1997; I Can't Read, 1998; Growin' Up; Pretty Things Are Going To Hell, 1999; Thursday's Child, 1999; Seven, 2000; with Bing Crosby: Peace On Earth/ Little Drummer Boy, 1977 (UK hit, 1982); with Mick Jagger: Dancing In The Street (No. 1, UK), 1985; with Queen: Under Pressure (No. 1, UK), 1981; with Pat Metheny Group: This Is Not America, 1985; Other projects include: Theme for When The Wind Blows, 1986; Music for The Buddha of Suburbia (BBC TV), 1993; Other collaborators include: Goldie, Lou Reed, Nine Inch Nails, Iggy Pop. *Honours include:* Music Video Awards; Silver Clef Award for Outstanding Achievement, 1987; Ivor Novello Awards include: Outstanding Contribution To British Music, 1990; Q Magazine Inspiration Award (with Brian Eno), 1995; BRIT Award, Outstanding Contribution To Music, 1996. *Current Management:* Isolar Enterprises, 641 Fifth Ave, Suite 22Q, New York, NY 10022, USA.

BOWLS Richard John (Ric); b. 13 July 1950, Rantoul, Illinois, USA. Recording Engineer; Musician (violin, guitar, keyboards). *Education:* Graduate, University of California, Riverside. *Musical Education:* Private lessons from age 8; Also played in numerous orchestras. *Career:* Touring musician, 1975–77; Independent sound engineer, 1977-; Sound engineer, Total Expereince Records, 1986–88; Sound engineer, programmer, MIDI Studio Systems, 1988-; Technical consultant, Music Suite, 1992-;

Designer, builder, various recording studios and keyboard systems; Guest speaker, lecturer on Electronic music; Owner/designer, Sendit Electronics; Owner, It's Only Plastic, music recording studios, 1999; Chief Engineer, Studio 56 Entertainment, 2001–; Recording engineer, films: Apocalypse Now; Darkman; Halloweeen; The Fog; Television credits as engineer and/or synth programming include: War and Rememberance; Knots Landing; Dallas; The Incredible Hulk; Little House On The Prairie; Wonder Woman; Love Boat; Hawaii 5–0; Moonlighting; Baywatch; Star Trek-The Next Generation; Mission Impossible; Brady Bunch; Recordings and/or live credits include: Giorgio Moroder (11 albums); Donna Summer (5 albums); Cher; Michael Nesmith; Berlin; Gap Band; Oingo Boingo; Ahmad Jamal; Yarborough and Peoples; ELO; Deniece Williams; Earth Wind and Fire; The Crusaders; Frank Zappa; Stephen Stills; Barbra Streisand; George Clinton; David Bowie; Carl Palmer; Jean Luc-Ponty; Aretha Franklin; Peter Frampton; Sly Stone; Tom Jones; Lalo Schifrin; Cityscrapes film score; Co-productions with Carmine Appice. *Honours:* Academy Award, Apocalypse Now; Platinum disc, Donna Summer; 2 Gold discs, Cher; Grammy Award, Best Music Video, Michael Nesmith; Emmy Award, Golden Globe, People's Choice Award, all for War and Rememberance, 1989. *Membership:* NARAS. *Current Management:* Neil Scotti and Associates, 415 N Camden Dr, Beverly Hills, CA 90210, USA. *Address:* 1722 Rogers Pl. #25E, Burbank, CA 91504–3668, USA.

BOWN Alan; b. 21 July 1942, Slough, Berkshire, England. Musician (trumpet); Man. m. Jean, 7 March 1964, 1 s., 1 d. *Musical Education:* S/M/RAF School of Music; RAF bandsman, 1956–60. *Career:* Started playing with The John Barry Seven; Recorded 5 albums over 10 years with own band The Alan Bown; Tours with: The Who; Yes; Moody Blues; Cream; Television appearances: Top of the Pops; Ready Steady Go; Old Grey Whistle Test. *Recordings:* All compositions on own albums: Live At The Marquee, 1963 (first album); Outward Bown; Listen. *Membership:* PRS. *Leisure interests:* Music; Bands. *Address:* 71 Shaggy Calf Lane, Slough, Berks SL2 5HN, England.

BOWN Andrew Steven; b. 27 March 1946, City of London, England. Musician (keyboards, bass guitar, guitar, harmonica); Vocalist. m. Caroline Attard, 4 June 1971, 1 s., 1 d. *Musical Education:* Piano, Grade 6; Recorder to Grade 6. *Career:* Musician with: The Herd; Status Quo; Pink Floyd; Appearances include: Live Aid; Knebsworth Festival; Prince of Wales Trust; Last Tattoo in Berlin for HM Queen. *Compositions:* with Status Quo: Burning Bridges; Come On You Reds; Whatever You Want. *Recordings:* The Herd, Paradise Lost, 1968; The Final Cut, Pink Floyd, 1983; All albums with Status Quo, 1970–; including: In The Army Now, 1986; Ain"t Complaining, 1988; Rockin' All Over The Years (compilation), 1990; Don't Stop, 1996; Famous In the Last Century, 2000; Recordings with other artistes include: Jerry Lee Lewis; Roger Waters; Tim Hardin; Lesley Duncan; Johnny Halliday; Paul McCartney; Wendy James; Dusty Springfield. *Honours:* Silver Clef, 1981; Ivor Novello Award, 1983; BRIT Award, 1991. *Memberships:* Musicians' Union; PRS; Equity. *Leisure interests:* Green bowling; Wine; Cooking. *Current Management:* David Walker, Handle Artistes Ltd.

BOX Mick; b. 8 June 1947, Walthamstow, London, England. Vocalist; Musician (guitar). *Career:* Founder member, UK rock band, Uriah Heep, 1970–; Extensive international tours; First western heavy rock group to perform in Moscow, 1987. *Recordings:* Albums: Very 'Eavy, Very 'Umble, 1970; Salisbury, 1971; Look At Yourself, 1971; Demons and Wizards, 1972; The Magician's Birthday, 1972; Uriah Heep Live, 1973; Swweet Freedom, 1973; Wonderworld, 1974; Return To Fantasy, 1975; High and Mighty, 1976; The Best of Uriah Heep, 1976; Firefly, 1977; Innocent Victim, 1978; Fallen Angel, 1978; Conquest, 1980; Abnominog, 1982; Head First, 1983; Equator, 1985; Anthology, 1986; Live In Moscow, 1988; Raging Silence, 1989; The Uriah Heep Story, 1990; Still 'Eavy, Still Proud, 1990; Different World, 1991; Rarities, 1991; Sea of Light, 1995; Time of Revelation, 1996; Classic Heep, 1998; Spellbinder, 1999; Future Echoes of The Past, 2001; Electrically Driven (with Ian Anderson), 2001.

BOY GEORGE (George O'Dowd); b. 14 June 1961, Eltham, Kent, England. Vocalist; Songwriter; DJ. *Career:* Singer, Bow Wow Wow (under name Lieutenant Lush); Founder member, singer, Culture Club, 1982–89, reformed 1998; Solo artiste, 1987–; Numerous tours world-wide, including Artists Against Apartheid, 1988. *Compositions:* Numerous collaborations with John Themis. *Recordings:* Albums: with Culture Club: Kissing To Be Clever, 1982; Colour By Numbers (No. 1, UK and US), 1983; From Luxury To Heartache, 1986; Don't Mind If I Do, 1998; Solo albums: Sold, 1987; Tense Nervous Headache, 1988; High Hat, 1989; Martyr Mantras, 1991; Cheapness and Beauty, 1995; Hit singles with Culture Club: Do You Really Want To Hurt Me; (No. 1, UK), 1982; Church of The Poisoned Mind, 1983; Karma Chameleon (No. 1, UK and US), 1983; Victims, 1983; It's A Miracle, 1984; Move Away, 1986; Solo singles: Il Adore; The Crying Game (film theme) with Pet Shop Boys, 1992; Everything I Own (No. 1, UK), 1987; When Will You Learn, 1999. *Publications:* Take It Like A Man (autobiography). *Honours:* Brit Awards: Best British Newcomer, 1983;

Best British Group, 1984. *Current Management:* Wedge Music, 63 Grosvenor St, London W1X 9DA, England.

BOYD Brandon; b. 15 Feb. 1976, Van Nuys, California, USA. Vocalist; Musician (percussion). *Career:* Formed group Incubus with school friends in Calabasas, California, 1991; Initially played small parties, graduating to support slots in Hollywood, California; Circulated demo tapes of Closet Cultivation and Incubus before independent album release, 1995; Group signed by Immortal/Epic; Built US and European following support slots on tours with: Sugar Ray; Black Sabbath; Korn; Drive reached #1 on US Modern Rock Chart, 2001; First Japanese and Australian live dates, 2001. *Recordings:* Albums: Fungus Amongus, 1995; S.C.I.E.N.C.E., 1997; Make Yourself, 1999; Morning View, 2001; Singles: Enjoy Incubus EP, 1997; Pardon Me, 1999; Stellar, When Incubus Attacks Vol. 1 EP, 2000; Drive, Wish You Were Here, 2001. *Honours:* Make Yourself album certified double platinum by RIAA; Billboard Award, Modern Rock Single of The Year, 2001. *Current Management:* Steve Rennie, REN Management, California, USA. *Internet:* www.enjoyincubus.com.

BOYES Derrick; b. 13 June 1955, Bridlington, England. Musician (bass); Songwriter. *Education:* BA, Hons/DB, Plymouth Polytechnic, 1980; Open University, 1986–87. *Career:* Summer season at Butlins in Filey, 1966; Bass Player, 1982–; Worked on Joan Jett album, 1999; Recommencing career after ill health. *Compositions:* 1959; The Night They Drove Old Dixie Down; Rolling Stone; Can the Can; 48 Crash; Stupid Girl; If God Had A Name. *Honour:* Hull Piano Composition Competition, Winner, 1962. *Membership:* Musicians' Union. *Leisure interests:* Computers; Local politics. *Address:* 4 Church Rest Houses, Westgate, Driffield, East Yorkshire YO25 6TE, England.

BOYLAN John Patrick; b. 21 March 1941, New York, USA. Prod. *Education:* BA, Bard College. *Career:* Executive Producer, CBS Records, 1976–80; Vice President, CBS, 1980–86; President, Great Eastern Music Co, 1986-. *Recordings:* Producer for numerous acts including: Boston; The Charlie Daniels Band; Linda Ronstadt; Little River Band; Nelson; Carly Simon; As producer, film soundtracks: Nightshift; Urban Cowboy; Footloose; Born On The Fourth of July; The Simpsons Sing The Blues. *Honours:* Numerous Platinum and Gold discs. *Memberships:* NARAS; AFTRA; AFofM. *Address:* Great Eastern Music Co, 5750 Wilshire Blvd, Los Angeles, CA 90036, USA.

BOYLE Dee (Diarmuid); b. Rotherham, England. Musician (Drums). *Career:* Member, Chakk, 1985–88; The Longpigs; Left band, 1999. *Recordings:* Singles: Happy Again; She Said, 1995/1996; Jesus Christ, 1995; Far, 1996; On and On, 1996; Lost Myself, 1996; Blue Skies, 1999; Albums: The Sun Is Often Out, 1996; Mobile Home, 1999. *Honours:* Brit Award Nomination, 1997.

BOZIC Petar Vedran; b. 21 May 1947, Zadar, Croatia. Musician (Guitars, Piano, Vocals, Harp). m. Majstorovic-Bozic Nada, 9 Sept. 1972, 1 s. *Education:* Studied Mathematics. *Musical Education:* Self-taught guitar, bass, harp; Musical schools, 10 years. *Career:* Played piano, amateur groups, 1963; Played guitar professionally, 1965; Played in famous Croatian groups: Gresnici, Roboti, Wheels of Fire, MI, BP Convention, Time, Boomerang, Parni Valjak; Countless stage, TV, radio appearances; Toured all over Europe; Studio Musician, Telephon Blues Band (formerly Call 66). *Compositions:* Several. *Recordings:* Studio Musician, recorded over 200 LPs or CDs, 1972-. *Honours:* HGU (Croatian Musicians' Union), Status prize for Best Guitar Player of the Year, 2000; Stari Macak (critics award), Lifetime Achievement in Rock and Roll Music, 2001. *Membership:* HGU. *Leisure interest:* Ski Sport Travelling. *Address:* Livadarskiput 3, 10000 Zagreb, Croatia.

BRAAM Michiel; b. 17 May 1964, Nijmegen. Musician (Piano); Composer; Bandleader. *Education:* Conservatory Hogeschool Voor de Kunsten Arnhem. *Career:* Leader, Pianist, Composer, Bik Bent Braam, Bentje Braam, Trio Braamdejoodevatcher; All Kinds of Projects In The Field of Modern Jazz and Improvised Musicians; Many television and radio appearances. *Compositions:* Het Xyr Der Bik Bent Braam; The Second Coolbook; The Hobbit. *Recordings:* Bik Bent Braam-Howdg; Benjie Braam-Playing The Second Coolbook; Trio Braamdejoodevatcher-Monk Materials; Solo-Oeps. *Publications:* Tetterettet, 1996; New Dutch Swing, 1998. *Honours:* Dutch Most Important Encouragement Prize, 1989, 1996, 1997. *Memberships:* Dutch Union of Improvising Musicians. *Current Management:* St Bik Bent Braam. *Address:* Spoorstraat 32, 5451 GB Mill, Netherlands.

BRADFIELD James Dean; b. 21 Feb. 1969, Newport, Gwent, Wales. Musician (guitar); Vocalist. *Career:* Formed Betty Blue, became Manic Street Preachers; Numerous sell-out tours, many festival appearances; TV and radio appearances; First Western group to play concert in Cuba since 1979, February 2001. *Recordings:* Singles: New Art Riot EP, 1990; You Love Us, 1991; Motorcycle Emptiness, 1992; Theme From M.A.S.H., 1992; From Despair To Where, 1993; La Tristessa Durera, 1993; Roses in the

Hospital, 1993; Faster/PCP, 1994; She Is Suffering, 1994; A Design for Life, 1996; Everything Must Go, 1996; Kevin Carter, 1996; Australia, 1996; If You Tolerate This Your Children Will Be Next (No. 1, UK), 1998; The Everlasting, 1998; You Stole The Sun From My Heart, 1999; Tsunami, 1999; The Masses Against The Classes (No. 1, UK), 2000; So Why So Sad, 2001; Found That Soul, 2001; Ocean Spray, 2001; Let Robeson Sing, 2001; Albums: Generation Terrorists, 1992; Gold Against the Soul, 1993; The Holy Bible, 1994; Everything Must Go (No. 1, UK), 1996; This Is My Truth, Tell Me Yours (No. 1, UK), 1998; Know Your Enemy, 2001; Also featured on: Lopez (with 808 State), 1997; I'm Left, You're Right, She's Gone (duet with Tom Jones), 1999; Producer for Northern Uproar, 1996; producer and co-writer of Some Kind of Bliss, Kylie Minogue, 1997. *Honours:* Brit Awards: Best British Group, 1997, 1999; Best British Album, 1997, 1999. *Current Management:* Martin Hall.

BRADFIELD Marian; b. 31 Dec. 1953, Waterford, Ireland. Singer; Songwriter; Musician (guitar). m. Robert Bradfield, 17 Aug. 1974, 2 d. *Career:* Began career with Young Generation Choir, Waterford; Formed own group Peace; Performed at George Doherty's Folk Club, Donegal; Support concerts with: Mary Black; The Fureys; Davey Arthur; Concert with Sharon Shannon and Mick Hanley, Forum, Waterford, 1994; Performed with Altan, Belfast Festival; Showcase in Austin, Texas; Numerous television appearances include: Kenny Live, RTE; Bibi Show; Anderson On The Box, BBC; Mike Moloney; Alan Corcoran; Numerous radio appearances on FM 2, BBC Ulster and local radio (Christmas Eve Special). *Recordings:* Albums: Marian, 1993; Tonight Is Just For Us, 1994; The Emperor's Field, 1998. *Honours:* Hot Press and Smithwick's Nomination, Best Solo Performer, 1993; Voted one of Ireland's Top 10 singers, Hot Press Readers, 1993; IRMA Award Nomination, Tonight Is Just For Us, 1995.

BRADLEY Stuart; b. 23 Sept. 1965, London, England. Musician (6 string bass guitar, double bass); Teacher. m. Elizabeth Allen, 1 April 1995. *Musical Education:* Private study with father, Desmond Bradley, aged 4–16 years; Studied double bass to Grade 8 with Clive Brown; Currently studying for LTCL, Trinity College of Music; Studying Composition with John Thomas, and also studying with Kevin Rundell. *Career:* Major tours with Take That; Gary Glitter; Roger Taylor; Television and radio appearances include: The Word; 01-For-London; 6 O'Clock News; The Mix, Radio 5; Principal bass instructor, Academy of Contemporary Music until 1996; Member of Examiners Panel, Grades for bass, drums and guitar, Rockschool; Appearance on TV in National Lottery Dreamworld; Freelance musician. *Compositions:* Brass Septet, 1997; Piece for chamber orchestra, 1998. *Recordings:* Why Can't I Wake Up With You?, Take That; Happiness, Roger Taylor; Piaf, Elaine Page; Up and Over, Edwin Starr. *Honour:* LTCL (MusEd), 1998. *Memberships:* Musicians' Union; PAMRA; Rockschool Ltd; British and International Brass Forum. *Address:* 65 Spring Rd, Lower Feltham, Middlesex TW13 7JA, England.

BRADY Paul; b. 19 May 1947, Strabane, County Tyrone, Northern Ireland. Folk Singer; Songwriter; Musician (multi-instrumentalist). *Career:* Member, The Kult; Planxty; Duo with Andy Irvine; Solo artiste, 1978–; Tours, including support to Dire Straits; Eric Clapton; Recent performance, Cambridge Folk Festival, 1995. *Compositions:* Songs include: Crazy Dreams (recorded by Roger Chapman, Dave Edmunds); Night Hunting Time (recorded by Santana); Steel Claw; Paradise Is Here (both recorded by Tina Turner); Film soundtrack, Cal, with Mark Knopfler; 2 tracks, Luck of The Draw, Bonnie Raitt, 1991. *Recordings:* Albums: Andy Irvine/Paul Brady, 1976; The High Part of The Road (with Tommy Peoples), 1976; Welcome Here Kind Stranger, 1978; Hard Station, 1981; True For You, 1983; Full Moon, 1984; Back To The Centre, 1986; Molloy, Brady, Peoples (with Matt Molloy, Tommy Peoples), 1986; Primitive Dance, 1987; Paradise Is Here, 1989; Trick Or Treat, 1991; Spirits Colliding, 1995; Oh What A World, 2001; Singles include: Crazy Dreams (No. 1, Ireland); Theme music, UK television series, Faith In The Future, 1995. *Current Management:* c/o Ed Bicknell, Damage Management, 16 Lambton Pl., London W11 2SH, England.

BRADY Philip; b. 4 March 1939, Liverpool, England. Singer; Musician (guitar). m. Barbara Ann Shaw, 6 March 1942, 1 s., 1 d. *Musical Education:* Self-taught. *Career:* Tommy Collins tour, Bill Clifton Show, 1963; Ernest Tubb Record Shop, Porter Waggonmaster Show, 1968; Jeannie Sealey, Hank Cochran tour, Germany; First Country Music Awards Show, Wembley Stadium; Bill Anderson, Loretta Lynn, Conway Twitty, George Hamilton IV; Buck Owens Tour, Liverpool Empire; London Palladium, Country Meets Folk, 1969; Hank Snow, Willie Nelson tour, Liverpool Empire, Bellevue Manchester, Lyceum Ballroom London, 1970; Nightride BBC; Slim Whitman Tour, all ABC theatres nationwide, 1972; Tours: Germany; Italy; Norway; Netherlands; Saudi Arabia. *Recordings:* Singles: American Sailor At The Cavern/Sidetracked; Little Rosa/One More Time; Rambling Boy; Lonesome For You; Let The Whole World Sing It With Me; Brady Country; Songs of Nashville; A Little Bit Country; Live At Gunton Hall; Bobby McGee and Other Favourites; 7 albums. *Honour:* BCMA Award, presented by Roy Orbison, 1970. *Membership:* Equity. *Leisure*

interests: Fishing; Reading. *Current Management:* Mike Hughes Entertainment. *Address:* 96 Bold St, Liverpool, England.

BRAGG Billy; b. 20 Dec. 1957. Vocalist; Songwriter; Musician (guitar). *Recordings:* Singles include: Between The Wars, 1985; Levi Stubbs Tears, 1986; She's Leaving Home (with Cara Tivey; No. 1, UK), 1988; Sexuality, 1991; Albums include: Life's A Riot With Spy vs Spy, 1983; Brewing Up With Billy Bragg, 1984; Talking With The Taxman About Poetry, 1986; Back To Basics, 1987; Workers Playtime, 1988; The Internationale, 1990; Don't Try This At Home, 1991; William Bloke, 1996; Mermaid Avenue (with Wilco), 1998; Mermaid Avenue Vol. 2 (with Wilco), 2000; Also collaborated with: Kirsty MacColl, Beats International. *Current Management:* Sincere Management. *Address:* 421 Harrow Rd, London W10 4RD, England.

BRAKE Marita; b. Springfield, Illinois, USA. Singer; Songwriter; Musician (guitar). m. Gil Moore, 11 Sept. 1982. *Education:* BS, Theatre, Illinois State University. *Musical Education:* Private lessons, seminars, workshops. *Career:* Community concerts tour; Carnegie Hall; Canterbury Festival, Canterbury, England; Television broadcasts on BBC and PBS. *Composition:* The Marita Brake In Concert Song Book, 1997. *Recordings:* Albums: The Road I Took To You, 1989; Gypsy Moon, 1996. *Publications:* Contributor of articles in magazines and reviews. *Honours:* Performance for Presidential Inauguration, 1997; Woman of Distinction Award for Excellence in the Arts. *Memberships:* Nashville Songwriters Asscn; Folk Alliance; Gospel Music Asscn.

BRAMERIE Thomas; b. 18 Sept. 1965, Bergerac, France. Musician (acoustic bass). m. Edith Vuillon, 22 Aug. 1992. *Musical Education:* Various private lessons; Self-taught. *Career:* Sideman with various international jazz musicians in Europe, 1987–; Played with: Chet Baker; Toots Thielemans; Johnny Griffin; Frank Wess; Tom Harrell; Joshua Redman; European tour, with Jimmy Scott, 1994; Festival appearances: Nice; Montreux; Newport; Northsea; Permanent member, Belmondo Quintet; Michele Hendricks Quintet; Dédé Ceccarelli Quartet; Regular member of Dee Dee Bridgewater's Band, 1997; Several world tours, Japan, Europe, South America, USA, Canada. *Recordings:* Live In Paris, Teddy Edwards Quartet, 1994; For All Friends, Belmondo Quintet, 1994; From The Heart, Dédé Ceccarelli Quartet, 1996; Ted Nash European Quartet, 1996. *Address:* 641 E 11th St, Suite 4A, New York, NY 10009, USA.

BRAMLETT Paul Kent; b. 31 May 1944, MS, USA. Attorney; Singer; Record Prod. m. Shirley, 2 s. *Education:* BA, David Lipsund University, 1966; JD, University of MS, 1969. *Career:* Performed on Stage as Singer, USA, European Countries. *Recordings:* 2 Albums, 1984, 1991. *Honours:* BA Hons; Special Guest Student, Niville Symphony, 1966. *Leisure interests:* Performing; Travel. *Address:* PO Box 150734, Nashville, TN 31215 0734, USA.

BRANCH Alan; b. 22 Jan. 1962, London, England. Sound Engineer; Musician (guitar); Prod.; Programmer. m. 4 May 1988, 2 d. *Education:* City and Guilds, and Advanced City and Guilds Carpentry, Lime Grove College. *Musical Education:* Goldsmiths University, General Musicianship. *Career:* Live, session guitarist; Student; Tape operator at Topic Records; Engineer at The Works Studio; Engineer at Roundhouse Studios; Chief Engineer, Roundhouse Recording Studios. *Recordings:* Artists: M People; De La Soul; D:ream; Jamiroquai; Living Colour; Ruby Turner; Boy George; Omar; On U Sound; Adrian Sherwood; Primal Scream; Lighthouse Family; Eternal; Simply Red; Depeche Mode; Nine Inch Nails; Sinead O'Connor; The Popes; Various other artists. *Membership:* Musicians' Union. *Leisure interests:* Playing music; Family; Computers. *Address:* 69 Lateward Rd, Brentford, Middlesex TW8 0PL, England.

BRAND Oscar; b. 7 Feb. Winnipeg, Manitoba, Canada. Composer; Folk Singer; Musician (guitar); Writer. m. Karen Grossman, 14 June 1970, 3 s., 1 d. *Education:* BS Brooklyn College, 1942; Laureate History, Fairfield University, 1974. *Musical Education:* Self-taught. *Career:* Presenter, Folk-song Festival, New York Public Radio, (oldest continuous radio show in history), 1945–; On credits of 75 documentary films; Hundreds of radio and television shows include: Host, Let's Sing Out, Canadian series; Music Director, Sunday Show, NBC; Exploring; Treasure Chest; Host, composer, First Look; Spirit of '76, NBC; Performer for children on television, records and film; Member, advisory panel which created television programme Sesame Street; Curator of Songwriters Hall of Fame; President, Gypsy Hill Music; Lecturer on Dramatic Writing, Hofstra University, Hempstead, New York; Artistic Director, Project America, 1998–2000. *Compositions include:* Songs for: Doris Day; Ella Fitzgerald; Harry Belafonte; The Smothers Brothers; Mormon Tabernacle Choir; Scripted, scored ballets for Agnes DeMille and Michael Bennett; Commercials include: Maxwell House; Oldsmobile; Log Cabin; Rival; Songs in films: The Fox; Sybil; The Long Riders; Blue Chips; Music for: In White America; Score for: How To Steal An Election; Music and lyrics with Paul Nassau for Broadway shows: A Joyful Noise; The Education of Hyman Kaplan; Wrote, scored Kennedy Center's Bicentenniel musical, Sing America Sing; 2 new musicals in progress: Thunder Bay; Fun and Games. *Recordings:* Over 90 albums, latest being: I Love Cats, 1994; Get A Dog, 1995; Campaign Songs 1789–1996, 1999. *Publications:* Author, several best-selling books including: When I First Came To This Land; The Ballad Mongers (autobiography); Party Songs; Singing Holidays; Bawdy Songs; Songs of '76; Western Guitar; Celebrate; Bridge of Hope. *Honours:* Laureate, Fairfield University, 1972; Peabody Awards, 1982, 1996; Hon. PhD, University of Winnipeg, 1989; Radio Pioneers of America, 1991; Awards for film credits: Venice, Edinburgh, Golden Reel, Valley Forge, Freedoms Foundation; Scholastic; Golden Lion; Peabody; Ohio State; Edison; Emmy. *Memberships:* SAG; AFTRA; ACTRA; Dramatists Guild; AFofM. *Leisure interests:* Sailing; Carpentry.

BRANDY (Brandy Norwood); b. 11 Feb. 1979, McComb, Mississippi USA. Vocalist. *Education:* Major in Psychology and Music, Pepperdine University, California, USA. *Career:* Began singing when a child in the local church; Competed in numerous talent shows; Obtained record deal at age 14; Numerous live appearances and TV appearances; Many acting TV roles. *Recordings:* Singles: Make it Right, 1990; Sittin' Up in My Room, 1995; Missing You, 1996; Top of the World, 1998; The Boy is Mine (with Monica; No. 1, USA), 1998; Have You Ever, 1999; Almost Doesn't Count, 1999; What About Us, 2002; Albums: De Faida Cortita, 1995; Brandy, 1995; Never Say Never, 1998; Full Moon, 2002; Also appears on: Michael Jackson, Invincible, 2001; Big Punisher, Endangered Species, 2001.

BRANHAM (Robert) Shon; b. 27 Dec. 1960, Orange, Texas, USA. Maintenance Engineer. m. JoAnn LaPointe, 27 Oct. 1984, 2 d. *Career:* Appearances on local TV station; Won Male Vocalist from Texas; Appeared in Las Vegas in national contest, for Country Music Association of America. *Recordings:* Tape: This Country Boy is Green, 1994; Two Steppin' Heaven, 1995. *Honour:* Male Vocalist from Texas, CMAA, 1993. *Membership:* International Fan Club Organization, Nashville. *Leisure interests:* Plants; Fishing; Hunting. *Address:* Rt 1, Box 186, Kirbyville, TX 75956, USA.

BRANN Chris, (P'Taah, Feral, Ananda Project); b. Atlanta, Georgia, USA. Prod.; Remixer; DJ. *Career:* Formed Wamdue Kids, 1994; Has recorded for many labels including Strictly Rhythm; Collaborations: Gaelle Adisson; Remixed: Boney James; Bebel Gilberto; Everything But The Girl. *Recordings:* Albums: Resource Toolbox Vol. 1 (with Wamdue Kids), 1996; These Branching Moments (with Wamdue Kids), 1997; Program Yourself (with Wamdue Kids), 1998; Release (as Ananda Project), 2001; Singles: Deep Dreams (with Wamdue Kids), 1996; King of My Castle (UK #1 with Wamdue Project), 1997; Cascades of Color (as Ananda Project), 1999; You're The Reason (with Wamdue Project), 1999; Glory Glory (as Ananda Project), 2000. *Address:* c/o Universal Music, 8 St James's Sq., London, SW1Y 4JU, England.

BRAUN Rick; b. 6 July 1955, Allentown, Pennsylvania, USA. Musician (trumpet); Composer; Prod. m. Laura Hunter, 18 Oct. 1992. *Musical Education:* Eastman School of Music, Rochester, New York. *Career:* Montreux Jazz Festival, 1979; 3 world tours with Rod Stewart, 1989–90; 1991–92; 1995; Tonight Show, 1991; Featured soloist with Sade, 1994. *Compositions:* Co-writer, Here With Me, REO Speedwagon, 1989. *Recordings:* Intimate Secrets, 1993; Christmas Present, 1994; Nightwalk, 1994; Beat Street, 1995; Body and Soul, 1996; Full Stride, 1998; Best of Braun, 1999; Featured soloist; Album, Tina Turner, 1994; Born A Rebel, Tom Petty, 1984. *Honour:* BMI Top 100 Songs of The Year, Here With Me, 1990. *Memberships:* BMI; AFofM. *Leisure interests:* Tennis; Skiing; Billiards; Basketball; Woodworking. *Current Management:* Chapman and Co Management. *Address:* PO Box 5549, Santa Monica, CA 90409, USA.

BRAXTON Anthony; b. 4 June 1945, Chicago, Illinois, USA. Jazz Musician (alto saxophone, clarinet). *Education:* Wilson Jr College. *Career:* Played clarinet and alto saxophone, US Army; Joined musician's co-operative, AACM, Chicago, 1966; Formed own group, The Creative Construction Company (CCC), 1968; Co-founder, Circle (with Chick Corea, Dave Holland, Barry Altschul), 1970; Played in France with various European improvisers; Member, Globe Unity Orchestra; Performed at Derek Bailey's Company Festivals; Performed with own quartet; Duo with drummer Max Roach, 1970s; Teacher, Wesleyan College, Connecticut, 1980s-. *Compositions:* Approximately 400 include: Series of 12 operas, Trillium; Quartet (London), 1985; Quartet (Birmingham), 1985; Quartet (Willisau), 1991. *Recordings:* Over 70 albums as bandleader; Appeared on numerous other recordings by artistes including Joseph Jarman; George Lewis; Max Roach; Derek Bailey; Muhal Richard Abrams; CCC; ROVA Saxophone Quartet; London Jazz Composers Orchestra. *Publications:* Tri-axium Writings, 1985; Composition Notes (5 vols), 1988..

BRAXTON Toni; b. 1969, Philadelphia, Pennsylvania, USA. Vocalist. *Career:* Member of female vocal group with sisters Tamar, Trin and Tavanda, 1990; Solo recording artiste. *Recordings include:* Solo albums: Toni Braxton, 1993; Secrets, 1996; The Heat, 2000; Snowflakes, 2001; Hit singles: Breathe Again, 1994; Another Sad Love Song, 1994; Unbreak My

Heart (No. 1, USA), 1996; You're Making Me High (No. 1, USA), 1996; I Don't Want To, 1997; How Could An Angel Break My Heart (with Kenny G), 1997; He Wasn't Man Enough, 2000; Spanish Guitar, 2000. *Honours:* Grammy Award, Best Female R & B Vocal Performance, He Wasn't Man Enough, 2001. *Address:* c/o Stiefel Entertainment, Suite 6120, 9255 Sunset Blvd, Los Angeles, CA 90069, USA.

BRAZIER Graham Philip (The Brazz); b. 6 May 1952, Auckland, New Zealand. Vocalist; Composer; Musician (guitar, saxophone, harmonica). m. Alexandra, 13 Nov. 1993, 1 s., 1 d. *Musical Education:* Self-taught. *Career:* Appearances, national New Zealand and Australian television on video clips, interviews, Film: Queen City Rocker; Played support to Dire Straits; Eurythmics; Fleetwood Mac; Bryan Ferry; Marianne Faithfull; Canned Heat; Bo Diddley; Gerry Harrison; Many major Australian acts. *Recordings:* Albums include: 4 Hello Sailor studio albums; 2 solo albums; 1 live album; Numerous compilations, EPs and singles. *Honours:* Vocalist of Year; Best Song; Runner-up for APRA Silver Scroll 3 times. *Membership:* APRA (voting mem.). *Leisure interests:* Reading; Collecting books; Antique curios. *Current Management:* James Rowe (Strawberry Fields), PO Box, Raglan, New Zealand. *Address:* 13 Taupata St, Mt Eden, Auckland 3, New Zealand.

BRAZIER Roy; b. 28 Jan. 1965, Walthamstow, London, England. Bandleader; Musician (saxophone, blues harp); Vocalist. *Musical Education:* Self-taught, alto, tenor saxophones, blues harmonica. *Career:* Founder member, Darktown, 1987, for parties, functions; Performed for Williams Grand Prix Engineering; Concerts supporting Mud; The Troggs; Desmond Dekker; Jools Holland; Television and video appearances: Ridin' High, Robert Palmer (full length album video); Television commercial for News of The World, Greystoke Productions; Performed 309 gigs, 1994; Television advertisement for Cross and Blackwell, 1996; Television appearance on Top Gear, BBC TV, 1997. *Recordings:* with Darktown: Blues, Jazz and Other Animals. *Honours:* Voted in Top Ten Blues Harp players, UK, 1995; Certificate of Excellence for Blues Harmonica at the European Harmonica Festival, Germany, 1996. *Membership:* Musicians' Union. *Leisure interests:* Surfing; Painting; Building classic cars. *Address:* 227 Monks Walk, Buntingford, Hertfordshire SG9 9DY, England.

B-REAL (Louis Freeze); b. 2 June 1970, South Gate, Los Angeles, USA. Vocalist; Rapper. *Career:* Member, Cypress Hill; Numerous tours including Lollapalooza; Collaboration with Pearl Jam on soundtrack to film Judgement Night, 1993; Remix of Insane the Brain by Jason Nevins, 1999. *Recordings:* Singles include: Phuncky Feel One, 1991; Hand On The Pump, 1991; Latin Lingo, 1991; Insane In The Brain, 1993; We Ain't Goin' Out Like That EP, 1995; Throw Your Set In The Air, 1995; Boom Biddy Bye Bye, 1996; Unreleased and Revamped, 1996; Illusions, 1996; Tequila Sunrise, 1998; Rap Superstar, 2000; Albums: Cypress Hill, 1991; Black Sunday, 1993; Cypress Hill III, Temples of Boom, 1995; IV, 1998; solo: The Psycho Realm; additional collaborations: Eat At Whitey's (with Everlast), 2000; No Retreat (with Dilated Peoples), 2000; Xplosion (with OutKast), 2000; Deadly Assassins (single; with Everlast), 2001.

BRECHIN Sandy; b. 20 April 1969, Edinburgh, Scotland. Musician; Composer; Label Owner. *Education:* MA, Languages, Edinburgh University. *Musical Education:* Private accordion and piano lessons; Self-taught guitar and banjo. *Career:* Toured all over the world with the bands, Burach, Seelyhoo and the Sandy Brechin Band, as well as a variety of solo, teaching and session work; Many appearances on BBC TV and Radio, STV and Channel 4, including, The Lottery Show Live – A Song for Britain, 1997; Also several appearances on European TV and Radio and in the USA and Far East; Scottish Folk Festival Tour of Germany, 1996 with Aly Bain and Phil Cunningham; Recent appearances: STV's Boxed Set, 2000, with Donnie Munro and Karen Mathieson; Channel 4's Tartan Jam, 2000, with Martyn Bennet and Natalie Macmaster; Toured USA, Canada, South America, Scandinavia, Iceland, Spain, France, Netherlands, Italy, Germany, Czech Republic, Turkey, Hong Kong, Thailand and Middle East; Owner, Brechin All Records. *Recordings:* With Burach – The Weird Set, 1995; Born Tired, 1997; Deeper, 2000; With Seelyhoo: The First Caul, 1995; Leetra, 1998; Solo Albums: Out of his Box, 1996; Out of His tree, 1999; On the West Side, Donnie Munro, 2000; Also appears on over 30 other albums and compilations; Tuitional Video: Learn Scottish Accordion with Sandy Brechin, 2000. *Publication:* How to Get (The Best) Out of Your Box, book of own compositions, 2000. *Memberships:* Musician's Union; Equity; MCPS/PRS; TMSA. *Leisure interests:* Running; Weightlifting; Skiing; Cooking; Reading. *Current Management:* Brechin All Records. *Address:* 5 The Square, Kirkliston, West Lothian, EH29 9AX, Scotland.

BRECKER Michael; b. 29 March 1949, Philadelphia, Pennsylvania, USA. Musician (saxophone, horns); Bandleader. *Career:* Member, Billy Cobham's band, 1970s; Founder, group Dreams; The Brecker Brothers (with Randy Brecker); Bandleader, 1987–; Also played with Horace Silver; James Taylor; Yoko Ono; David Sancious; Prolific session musician. *Recordings:* Albums: with Billy Cobham: Crosswinds, 1974; Total Eclipse, 1974; Shabazz, 1975; A Funky Thide To Sings, 1975; Inner Conflicts, 1978;

with The Brecker Brothers: The Brecker Brothers, 1975; Back To Back, 1976; Don't Stop The Music, 1977; Heavy Metal Be-Bop, 1978; Detente, 1980; Straphangin', 1981; Blue Montreux, 1989; Collection, Vol. I, 1990; Vol. II, 1992; Big Idea, 1992; Return of The Brecker Brothers, 1992; Out of The Loop, 1994; Solo albums: City Scape, 1983; Mike Brecker, 1987; Don't Try This At Home, 1989; Now You See It, Now You Don't, 1991; Tales from Hudson, 1997; Two Blocks from the Edge, 1998; Time Is of The Essence, 1999; Nearness of You – The Ballad Book, 2001; with Randy Brecker: Toe To Toe, 1990; In The Idiom, 1991; Score, 1993; with Herbie Hancock: The New Standard, 1996; Also recorded with numerous artists including: Dreams; Steps Ahead; Charles Mingus; John Lennon; Eric Clapton; Paul Simon; Pat Metheny; John Abercrombie. *Publications:* Michael Brecker Artist Transcription Books, Vols I and II. *Honours:* 7 Grammy Awards including Best Jazz Instrumental Performance, 1996, 1997, Best Jazz Instrumental Solo, 1997. *Current Management:* Depth of Field Management, 1501 Broadway, Suite 1304, New Tork, NY 10036, USA.

BRECKER Randy (Randall Edward); b. 27 Nov. 1945, Philadelphia, Pennsylvania, USA. Musician (trumpet, saxophone, horns); Arranger. m. Eliane Elias, 1 d. *Education:* Indiana University, 1963–66. *Musical Education:* Classical trumpet studies at school. *Career:* Professional trumpeter, 1966–; Prolific freelance musician; Played with: Blood, Sweat and Tears; Horace Silver; Clark Terry; Janis Joplin; Stevie Wonder; James Brown; Larry Coryell; Billy Cobham; Charles Mingus; Lew Tabakin; Bandleader/arranger, 1975–; Formed Dreams with brother Michael; The Brecker Brothers (also with Michael); Leader, Randy Brecker Band; Arranger for numerous artists include: George Benson; Diana Ross; Chaka Khan; Clinician, National Association of Jazz Educators. *Recordings:* Albums: with The Brecker Brothers: The Brecker Brothers, 1975; Back To Back, 1976; Don't Stop The Music, 1977; Heavy Metal Be-Bop, 1978; Detente, 1980; Straphangin', 1981; Blue Montreux, 1989; Collection, Vol. I, 1990; Collection, Vol. 2, 1992; Big Idea, 1992; Return of The Brecker Brothers, 1992; Out of The Loop, 1994; Solo albums: Toe To Toe, 1989; In The Idiom, 1991; Live At Sweet Basil, 1992; Score, 1993; Into The Sun, 1995; Hanging In The City, 2001; with Horace Silver: You Gotta Take A Little Love, 1969; with Billy Cobham: Crosswinds, 1974; Total Eclipse, 1974; Shabazz, 1975; A Funky Thide To Sings, 1975; Inner Conflicts, 1978; with Charles Mingus: Me, Myself and Eye, 1978; Also on albums by numerous artists including: George Benson; Carla Bley; Eric Clapton; Dire Straits; Billy Joel; Elton John; Rickie Lee Jones; B B King; Manhattan Transfer; John Mayall; Lou Reed; Diana Ross; Todd Rundgren; Carly Simon; Paul Simon; Bruce Springsteen; Steely Dan; James Taylor; Tina Turner; Luther Vandross; Steve Winwood; Frank Zappa. *Membership:* AFofM. *Current Management:* Depth of Field Management. *Address:* 1501 Broadway, Suite 1304, New York, NY 10036, USA.

BRENNAN Dave; b. 24 Dec. 1936, Rotherham, England. Bandleader; Musician (banjo, guitar, parade drums); Vocalist; Master of Ceremonies; Broadcaster. m. (1) 2 s., (2) Val Hudson, 28 Sept. 1996. *Education:* CEng; M I MechE. *Career:* Own jazz programme, BBC Radio Sheffield, 17 years; Bandleader, 1960–; Leader: Jubilee Jazz Band; Jubilee New Orleans Brass Band; Heritage New Orleans Brass Band; Big Easy New New Orleans Parade Band; Toured widely including: USSR (twice), Russia and Siberia; Toured Europe with the International Jazz Band, 1997. *Recordings:* Mardi Gras in New Orleans; Take Me To The Mardi Gras; Rags, Stomps and Dreamy Melodies; Inn Swinger; Amazing Grace; Bouncing Around; Let's Get This Show On The Road with Alton Purnell; Swinging At Swinden, with Louis Nelson; International Jazz Band; Several recordings with Chris Blount Jazz Band, Ken Colyer and Sarah Spencer's Rue Conti Jazz Band. *Memberships:* Musicians' Union; MI Mech E; Labour Party; SIMA. *Leisure interests:* Record collecting; New Orleans music; Opera; Great singers of the past; Cricket. *Address:* Tanglewood, Marcliff Lane, Wickersley, Rotherham, S66 2AZ, England.

BRENNAN John Wolf; b. 1954, Dublin, Ireland. Musician (piano, organ); Composer; Conductor. m. Béatrice, 2 d. *Musical Education:* Musicology, Film and Literature, University of Fribourg; Piano (with Eva Serman), Lucerne Conservatory; Organ, Conducting, Academy of School and Church Music; Composition (with Karl Berger), CMS Woodstock/New York and (with James Wilson) Royal Irish Academy of Music, Dublin; Masterclasses with Edison Denisov, Ennio Morricone, Klaus Huber and Heinz Holliger. *Career:* Concert tours in Western and Eastern Europe, Russia, Japan, Canada and USA; Recording projects include: Pago Libre (pan-European jazz quartet with Arkady Shilkloper, Tscho Theissing and Daniele Patumi); Trio Aurealis (with Robert Dick and Daniele Patumi); Pipelines (with Hans Kennel and Marc Unternährer); Momentum (with Gene Coleman, Christian Wolfarth and Alfred Zimmerlin); Entropology (with Eddie Prévost and Simon Picard); HeXtet (with Julie Tippetts, Evan Parker, Chris Cutler, Paul Rutherford and Peter Whyman); Nisajo (with Nicky Heinen and Alexander Alexandrov); Many other collaborations include: Alex Cline; Gabriele Hasler; Norma Winstone; Christy Doran; Urs Leimgruber; Corin Curschellas; Lindsay Cooper; Margrit Rieben; Reto Senn; Member of Swiss composers' group, Groupe Lacroix; Has composed for piano; glockenspiel; chamber ensemble; a capella choir; choir, orchestra

and alphorn. *Compositions include:* The Well-Prepared Clavier; Silly Blooze; Sonata Pentatonica; KLA4; Zigfing; Frictions; Euratorium; Bestiarium; Through The Ear of a Raindrop; Sculptural Sonorities; Morgenstern Hat Gold Im Mund; Epithalamium; Alef Bet – An Ori-ental Peace Piece; A Golly Gale's Way To Galway Bay; Nearly Charming; The Age of Anxiety. *Recordings include:* Aurealis, 1997; Through the Ear of a Raindrop, 1998; The Well-Prepared Clavier, 1998; Brink Man Ship, 1998; Minute Age, 1999; Momentum, 1999; Entropology – The Science of Sonic Poetry, 2000; Pipelines, 2000; Momentum 2, 2000; Cinémagique, 2001. *Honours:* Werkjahr, Dienemann Foundation, Lucerne, 1989; Förderpreis, Sarna Jubilee Foundation, 1991; Stipendium of BINZ39 Art Foundation Zurich, 1993; Prize, National Flute Asscn, USA, 1993; Award, Jubilee Foundation of Union Bank of Switzerland, 1994; Miglior Disco Del Anno, Jazzpoll of MusicaJazz, Milano, 1994; Album of the Year, Jazzthetik, 1996; Invitation by Hindemith Foundation to write octet, 1997; London Fellowship, Zuger Kulturstiftung Landis and Gyr, 1997; Markant Foundation Fellowship and opera commission, 2000. *Memberships:* AIC; CMC; STV; SMS. *Current Management:* Musaic Artist Management, Claudia Julina, 1016 S B St, San Mateo, CA 94401, USA. *Address:* Hofmattstrasse 5, 6353 Weggis, Lucerne, Switzerland. *E-mail:* johnwolf@brennan.ch. *Internet:* www.brennan.ch.

BRENNAN Maire (Maire Ni Bhraonain); b. 4 Aug. 1952, Dublin, Ireland. Vocalist; Musician (harp). *Career:* Founder member, singer, harpist, folk group Clannad, 1970–; Regular Irish and international tours include: Germany, 1975; US, 1979; Europe, 1983; UK, 1986, 1991; Concerts include: Cambridge Folk Festival, 1991; Scottish Fleadh, Glasgow, 1992; Fleadh '92, Finsbury Park, London, 1992; Royal Albert Hall, 1993; Television includes: Clannad In Donegal, CH4 documentary, 1991; Hostage – Tribute To Brian Keenan, BBC, 1991; The Tonight Show, NBC, 1993. *Compositions include:* Television and film music: Harry's Game, ITV, 1982 (also used in film soundtrack Patriot Games and Volkswagen television commercial); Robin of Sherwood, ITV, 1984; The Atlantic Realm, BBC1, 1988. *Recordings:* Albums: Magical Ring, 1983; Legend, 1984; Macalla, 1986; Sirius, 1987; Atlantic Realm, 1989; Pastpresent, 1989; Clannad The Collection, 1989; Anam, 1993; Banba, 1993; Lore, 1996; Landmarks, 1998; Solo albums: Maire, 1992; Misty-Eyed Adventures, 1995; Perfect Time, 1998; Whisper To The Wild Water, 1999; Solo album: Maire, 1992; Singles include: Theme From Harry's Game, 1982; Robin (The Hooded Man), 1984; In A Lifetime, 1986; Both Sides Now, with Paul Young (used in film soundtrack Switch), 1991. *Honours:* Ivor Novello Award, Best Theme From A Television Or Radio Production, Theme From Harry's Game, 1983; British Academy Award, Best Soundtrack of Year, Robin of Sherwood, 1985. *Current Management:* Upfront Management, 4 Windmill Lane, Dublin 2, Ireland.

BRESLIN Paul; b. 27 June 1950. Singer; Composer; Lyricist; Musician (guitar). m. Cathy Liegeois, 14 Feb. 1989, 1 s. *Education:* Reed College. *Musical Education:* Self-taught. *Career:* Bandleader, on stage and live television, for Percy Sledge, 1994–95; Bandleader for Billy Paul, Europe, 1995; Played all major French jazz festivals with Eddy Louiss (Hammond organ). *Compositions:* Music and lyrics for Ray Charles: Separate Ways; Good Thang. *Recordings:* Solo albums: Hot Lunch; Rikitikitak; Musician on recordings by: Gilbert Becaud; Serge Gainsbourg; Michel Columbier; Françoise Hardy; Catherine Deneuve; Eddy Louiss; France Gall; Michel Berger. *Current Management:* Delabel-Chrysalis. *Address:* 24 Pl. des Voges, 75003 Paris, France.

BRETT Martin; b. 29 March 1959, Dorking, Surrey, England. Musician (bass guitar, guitar, piano). 2 s. *Musical Education:* Self-taught. *Career:* Bass guitar, Voice of The Beehive; World-wide tours; Television includes: 6 Top of The Pops; Currently in songwriting partnership with VOTB for new album and singles; Formed own music production company (Brett Dempsey Music) with Michael Dempsey (former Cure member); Studio in Sussex; Martin Brett and Michael Dempsey compose for films, television and commercials. *Recordings:* Albums: Let It Bee; Honey Lingers; Sex and Misery; Singles include: Don't Call Me Baby; Monsters and Angels; Angel Come Down. *Memberships:* PRS; PAMRA; Musicians' Union; MCPS. *Leisure interest:* Work. *Address:* Wimbledon, London SW20, England.

BREWER Neil; b. 15 July 1952, Berkhamsted, England. Musician (guitar, bass guitar); Vocalist. *Musical Education:* Self-taught. *Career:* Several major tours and radio shows: Television appearance with band Druid, Old Grey Whistle Test, 1975; Currently solo artist, guitarist and lead vocalist, with self-programmed/arranged computerised backing. *Recordings:* Albums: Toward The Sun, 1975; Fluid Druid, 1976; Druid 1; Singles: Modern Women, Splash; 2 singles, Frame By Frame. *Memberships:* Musicians' Union; PRS. *Leisure interests:* Music; Life. *Address:* 45 Melsted Rd, Boxmoor, Hemel Hempstead, Hertfordshire HP1 1SX, England.

BREWER Teresa; b. 7 May 1931, Toledo, Ohio, USA. Vocalist. m. Bob Thiele, 24 Oct. 1972, 4 d. (previous marriage). *Career:* Played with: Count Basie; Duke Ellington; Benny Carter; Stéphane Grappelli; Earl Hines; Ruby Braff; Dizzy Gillespie; Television appearances: Co-host, Summertime

USA, with Mel Tormé, 1953; Co-host, Perry Presents, with Tony Bennett, 1959; Ed Sullivan Show, 39 times; Film appearances include: Those Redheads From Seattle, 1953; Concerts include: Carnegie Hall, New York City, 1978; Montreux Jazz Festival, Switzerland, 1983. *Recordings:* 75 albums and 125 singles; Recorded over 600 songs; 43 songs in US charts including: Music! Music! Music!; Till I Waltz Again With You; Ricochet; A Sweet Old Fashioned Girl; Let Me Go Lover!; A Tear Fell; The Original Sound of Miss Music! Music! Music!, 2001. *Honours:* 6 Gold records. *Membership:* Society of Singers. *Current Management:* Bob Thiele. *Address:* c/o Bill Munroe, 584 Prospect St, New Haven, CT 06511, USA.

BREWIS David; b. 3 June 1957, Sunderland, England. Musician (guitar, bass, keyboards); Record Prod.; Songwriter. *Musical Education:* Newcastle College (diploma). *Career:* Member, Kane Gang; UK and European tours; Television appearances include Solid Gold (US); Top of the Pops; Whistle Test; The Tube; Co-writer of theme for BAFTA Award-winning children's series Byker Grove (Zenith for BBC-TV, 1988-). *Recordings:* Albums: with the Kane Gang: Bad and Lowdown World, 1985; Miracle, 1987; Hit singles: Small Town Creed, 1984; Closest Thing To Heaven, 1984; Respect Yourself, 1984; Gun Law, 1985; Motortown, 1987; Don't Look Any Further (US Billboard No. 1), 1988; As Producer: Prefab Sprout albums: Swoon, 1984; tracks for compilation Life of Surprises, 1992; As Guitarist: Andromeda Heights, Prefab Sprout album, 1997; Ocean Drive, Lighthouse Family album, 1995. *Memberships:* PRS; BMI. *Leisure interest:* Toy collecting. *Address:* Soul Kitchens, St Thomas Workshops, Newcastle Upon Tyne NE1 4LE, England.

BREWSTER Cori; b. 1960, Canada. Musician (guitar); Vocalist. *Career:* Major Canadian festivals, television shows. *Recordings:* Album: One More Mountain, 1994. *Honours:* Female Recording Artist Nomination in Alberta, Canada, 1994. *Current Management:* Horton Management and Publishing. *Address:* PO Box 48165, 595 Burrard St, Vancouver, BC V7X 1N8, Canada.

BREZOVSKY Ali; b. 26 Feb. 1940, Slovakia. m. Vlasta Brezovska, 8 Dec. 1963, 1 s., 1 d. *Education:* Faculty of Pedagogy, Bratislava, Slovakia. *Career:* Various projects including scores to Slovak films, Smoliari, 1978; Losers, Zázracny Autobus, 1981; Magic Bus; Scores to theatre plays, many songs (pop and rock) and instrumental compositions. *Compositions:* Rozpravkovi Stopari, fairy-tale; Hitchhikers, LP, for children; Cengá Do Triedy (School Bell is Ringing); Let/Flight – Songs for LP of a popular Slovak Rock Group. *Recordings:* CD, original soundtracks of Ali Brezovsky, 1996. *Honours:* Third Place, International Music Festival, Bratislavska, Lyra, 1974, 1985; Award for Original Soundtrack, 1978; Smoliari; Summer Film Festival. *Memberships:* Slovak Music Asscn; Soza/Slovak Union of Authors. *Leisure interests:* Sports; Swimming.

BRIGHT Anna Lia; b. 25 Feb. 1952, West Palm Beach, Florida, USA. Songwriter; Singer; Poet. *Musical Education:* Studied under Napoleon Bright and Bengt Lindskog. *Career:* Appearances on Danish television and radio; Singer in piano bars, clubs, cafés and concert halls in Holland, Spain, Scandinavia and the Canary Islands; Currently Songwriter for various artists; Tours schools with her show Stand Up Poetry (poetry, song and storytelling). *Recordings:* As songwriter, Wind and Fire, by Frank Ryan, You Better Believe, by Zapp Zapp and Walk The Walk; As singer and songwriter, That's Lambada; To This Planet. *Publication:* Undiscovered Days, poetry, 1996. *Honours:* Editors Choice Award for OutstandingAchievement in Poetry, National Library of Poetry, 1997; Hon. Mention for short stories entered in Daily City Short Story Contest; Certificate of Achievement, university song contest for Border Line Affair. *Memberships:* KODA; NCB; DJBFA. *Leisure interests:* Music; Hiking. *Address:* Mosedalvej 9 2 th, 2500 Valby, Copenhagen, Denmark.

BRIMLEY Robert George; b. 11 March 1943, Kent, England. Musician (jazz guitar, piano, keyboards). m. Indra, 1989, 2 s. *Education:* Technical College. *Musical Education:* Classical trained, since 9 years of age. *Career:* Played most jazz venues, jazz festivals. *Compositions:* Music written for television documentary Corporate Video work; Jingles; Kitty To The Cape; Aldabra Underwater Documentary; Air Ambulance Theme; Lands End Theme; Film including: A Year In Cornwall; Geeyor Tin Mine; Songs Loving You; Love With A Stranger. *Memberships:* PRS; BASCA; Musicians' Union. *Leisure interests:* Walking; Swimming; Music; Record producer; Studio engineer; Computer programming. *Current Management:* Cot Valley Music. *Address:* Cot Valley Lodge, Cot Valley, St Just, Penzance, Cornwall, England.

BRINCK Lars; b. 30 March 1957, Copenhagen, Denmark. Musician (keyboards); Composer; Arranger. m. Karen-Lis Kristensen, 18 Aug. 1984, 4 s. *Musical Education:* Royal Academy of Music, Aarhus, Denmark. *Career:* Keyboard player for: Arvid Hunter; Gary Snider; Poul Krebs; Jette Torp; Tomas Kellerup; Erik Grip; Lene Siel; Television appearances, Denmark, 1989–91. *Recordings with:* Arvid Hunter, 1989; Tomas Kellerup, 1990–92; Gary Snider, 1992; Erik Grip, 1993; Lene Siel, 1994; Jette Torp, 1995; Lars Brinck Jam Session, 1997. *Publications:* Numerous piano teaching manuals. *Honours:* Royal Academy Annual

Award, three times. *Memberships:* DJBFA; Gramex. *Address:* c/o LB Productions, Ludvig Holbergsvej 13, 8230 Aabyhoej, Denmark.

BRINK VAN DEN Bert; b. 24 July 1958, Geldrop, Netherlands. m. Medy Doves, 1 s. *Musical Education:* Private lessons, since age 5 years; Conservatory Utrecht Classical Music, by Herman Uhlhorn; Jazz, self-taught; Composer; Arranger. *Career:* Teacher, Jazz music at Conservatory, Utrecht; Composer; Arranger; Played with Dee Dee Bridge Water, Toots Thielemans, Denise Jannah, Philip Catherine, Chet Baker, Nat Adderly, Rick Margitza, Charlie Mariano. *Composition:* Wondering Why. *Recordings:* Live at Montréal Dee Dee Bridgewater, 1990; Deepest to Dearest, solo album; Hazy Hugs, Amstel Octet with Guest Chet Baker; Denise Jannah Albums; Also appears on: In Montreux, Dee Dee Bridgewater; Live, Philip Catherine; Dialogues, Lee Konitz; Chez Toots, Toots Thielemans. *Honour:* First Prize, International Concours for Visually Handicapped Musicians, Hungary. *Current Management:* Brink Productions BV, Akkerse Straat 6A, 4061 BH, Ophemert, The Netherlands. *Address:* Brink Productions BV, Akkerse Straat 6A, 4061 BH, Ophemert, The Netherlands.

BRISLIN Kate (Young); b. 19 Feb. 1946, Portsmouth, Ohio, USA. m. (1) Tom Brislin, 8 June 1968; (2) Jody Stecher, 29 July 1987. *Education:* BA, English, University of Guam. *Career:* Appearance, Prairie Home Companion, May 1994; As backing singer: with Laurie Lewis: Restless Rambling Heart, 1986; Earth and Sky, 1997; Third Annual Farewell Reunion, Mike Seeger, 1994; Pieces of My Heart, Alice Gerrard, 1994; with Jody Stecher: Going Up On The Mountain, 1976; Rasa, 1980; Out On The Rolling Sea, 1994; Heartsong, 1997; Oh The Wind and The Rain, 1999. *Recordings:* with Arkansas Sheiks: Whiskey Before Breakfast, 1975; with The Blue Flame Stringband, 1982; with the Any Old Time Stringband, 1978; I Bid You Goodnight, 1996; with Any Old Time: Ladies Choice, 1980; Duets with Jody Stecher: A Song That Will Linger, 1989; Blue Lightning, 1991; Our Town, 1993; Stay Awhile, 1995; Duet with Katy Moffatt: Sleepless Nights, 1996; Heart Songs, 1997; Also appears on: Young Fogies Vol. 2, 1995; Use A Napkin, 1995; American Fogies Vol. 2, 1996; Rounder Bluegrass Guitar, 1996. *Honour:* Grammy Nomination, 1994. *Memberships:* IBMA; North American Folk Alliance. *Leisure interests:* Knitting; Gardening; Reading. *Address:* 133 Lake St, San Francisco, CA 94118, USA.

BRITT Michael Wayne; b. 15 June 1966, Fort Worth, Texas, USA. Country vocalist; Musician (guitar). *Education:* University of Texas, Pharmacy and English. *Career:* Received first guitar, aged 15; Played in various school bands; Joined Santa Fe and had minor hits on independent label 16th Avenue as member of Canyon, 1988–90; Formed Texasee with Dean Sams, Keech Rainwater, Richie McDonald and John Rich, 1992; Group became resident house band at the Wildhorse Saloon, Nashville; After subsequent name change to Lonestar, came to the attention of BMG and were signed to their BNA subsidiary; Released promotional six-track live CD, recorded at the Wildhorse; First country chart entry No News/ Tequila Talkin' from debut album Lonestar, 1996; Single, Amazed, from third album became huge international hit and career record to date, 1999; By early 2000s, Lonestar estimated to be the most successful country group in the world. *Compositions include:* Runnin' Away With My Heart. *Recordings include:* No News, Tequila Talkin', 1996; Come Cryin' To Me, You Walked In, 1997; Say When, Everything's Changed, 1998; Amazed, Smile, 1999; I'm Already There, 2002; Albums include: Lonestar, 1995; Crazy Nights, 1997; Lonely Grill, 1999; I'm Already There, 2001. *Leisure interests:* Writing songs; Reading; Playing guitar; Listening to music; Photography; Computers. *Address:* c/o The Country Music Asscn, Nashville, Tennessee, USA.

BRITTON Reginald L; b. 19 Nov. 1964. Musician (Drums). 3 c. *Education:* School marching bands; Bellville Black Knight Drum Corps. *Career:* Young Americans; Tash and Country Magic; Eddie Snows Snow Flakes; G Sharp Band; Tom Irwin Band; Oysters Rockefeller. *Compositions:* 63 Blues; Mind My Own Business; Hooked on Something; Too Stupid; Little Bit Crazy; Every Now and Then; Gone to Long; Loving Ways. *Recordings:* Past and Present; Oysters Rockefeller. *Publications:* 63 Blues, 1996; Mind Your Own Business, 1998; Hooked on Something, 1998; Every Now and Then, 1998. *Memberships:* Central Illinois Blues Club; American Federation of Musicians. *Current Management:* Oyster Sound Management and Record Corp. *Address:* PO Box 20656 Springfield, IL 62708, USA.

BRITTON Simon, (Balance); b. 22 Jan. 1971, Bristol, England. Record Prod.; Re-Mixer; Vocalist; Musician (keyboards). *Musical Education:* Trained vocalist; Studied classical music. *Career:* Vocalist under name 'Balance', major recording success in Europe; Featured vocalist, several Top 10 UK Dance Music hits; Producer, several Dance Music hits; Featured vocalist with Black Box (major Italian production team). *Recordings:* Backing vocalist for artists including Tears For Fears; Scritti Politti; Massive Attack. *Membership:* Musicians' Union. *Leisure interests:* Nightclubs; Producing; Fashion. *Current Management:* Leisure UK.

Address: Suite 404, Victory House, Somers Rd N, Portsmouth, Hampshire PO1 1PJ, England.

BROCHET Marc; b. 3 April 1956, Soissons, Aisne, France. Composer; Musician; Teacher. m. Dominique Hemard, 11 Dec. 1981, 1 s., 2 d. *Musical Education:* First Prize d'Harmonie; Orchestration; Conservatoire Superieur de Paris. *Career:* Concerts with vocal jazz group Vox Office; Festivals include: Nice; Vienna; Tel Aviv; Televised concert for M6; Teacher in musical writings, Conservatoire National d'Enseignement Superieur de Poitiers. *Compositions:* Music for theatre and dance. *Recordings:* Boppin' In French, Vox Office. *Publications:* for television and radio. *Leisure interests:* Zen Buddhism; Astrology.

BROCK Dave; b. Isleworth, Middlesex, England. Vocalist; Musician (guitar). *Career:* Founder member, UK rock group Hawkwind, 1969–; Regular UK and US tours; Concerts include: Glastonbury Fayre, 1971, 1981; Reading Festival, 1975, 1977, 1986; Futurama Festival, Leeds, 1979; Stonehenge Festival, 1981, 1984; Monsters of Rock, Castle Donington, 1982. *Recordings:* Albums: Hawkwind, 1970; In Search of Space, 1971; Doremi Fasol Latido, 1972; Space Ritual, 1973; Hall of The Mountain Grill, 1974; Warrior On The Edge of Time, 1975; Astounding Sounds and Amazing Music, 1976; Road Hawks, 1976; Masters of The Universe, 1977; Quark Strangeness and Charm, 1977; 25 Years On, 1978; PXR-5, 1979; Live 1979, 1980; Levitation, 1980; Sonic Attack, 1981; Church of Hawkwind, 1982; Choose Your Masques, 1982; Zones, 1983; The Chronicle of The Black Sword, 1985; Angels of Death, 1987; Spirit of The Age, 1988; The Xenon Codex, 1988; Space Bandits, 1990; Stasis, 1990; Electric Tepee, 1992; It Is The Business of The Future, 1993; The Business Trip, 1994; New World's Fair, 1995; Alien 4, 1996; In Your Area, 1999; Weird Tapes Vols 1–6, 2000; Spacebrock, 2001; Singles include: Silver Machine, 1972; Urban Guerila, 1973. *Current Management:* Doug Smith Associates, PO Box 2098, London W12 9RZ, England.

BRODERICK Michael; b. 21 April 1941, Dumfries, Scotland. Folk Singer; Musician (bodhran). m. Irene Masia, 3 Sept. 1976, 1 s., 1 d. *Career:* Founder member of folk group The Whistlebinkies; Appearances include: John Cage's Scottish Circus, 1991; Toured extensively including: France, Germany, Italy, Sweden and China; Played at numerous festivals including Edinburgh International Festival and The Hong Kong Folk Festival; Television appearances: Celtic Weave, 1994; Celtic Connection, 1994. *Recordings:* The Whistlebinkies 1–5; Anniversary (compilation); Inner Sound. *Memberships:* Equity; PRS. *Leisure interest:* Hill walking. *Address:* Eddie McGuire, 13 Lawrence St, Glasgow G11 5HH, Scotland.

BRODY Lane (Lynn Connie Voorlas); b. Oak Park, Illinois, USA. Singer; Songwriter. m. Edward H Bayers Jr, 14 Nov. 1994. *Musical Education:* Private study. *Career:* Singer; Commercials include: Wrigley's; Johnson Wax; McDonalds; Tours world-wide with: John Anderson; Willie Nelson; Steve Wariner; Tom Bresh; Lee Greenwood; Television appearances: Taxi; Heart of The City; OSO TV Special; Lee Greenwood TV Special; Today Show; Austin City Limits. *Compositions include:* Tough Enough; Hottest Night of the Year, Anne Muray (co-wrote); All The Unsung Heroes; Yellow Rose (co-wrote). *Recordings:* Tender Mercies theme; The Gift of Life theme; Country Gold soundtrack; Yellow Rose title track; All The Unsung Heroes title song; Tough Enough, title track. *Honours include:* Academy Award Nomination, Over You; ACM Nomination, Top New Female Vocalist; Emmy Nomination, Gift of Life; BMI Award, Yellow Rose; American Film Festival Video Documentary of the Year; Numerous awards, Military and Charity organizations. *Memberships:* SAG; AFTRA; NARAS; CMA; ACM. *Leisure interests:* Gardening; Nutrition; Animals. *Current Management:* Lane Brody Global Fan Club. *Address:* PO Box 24775, Nashville, TN 37202, USA.

BROFSKY Howard; b. 2 May 1927, New York, USA. Musician; Musicologist. m. Robin Westen, 2 s., 1 d. *Education:* PhD, New York University. *Career:* Assistant Professor, University of Chicago, 1960–67; Professor, Queens College, Graduate School, City University of New York, 1967–92; President, Vermont Jazz Center. *Recordings:* Georgie Johnson, Paris, 1955; Larry Rivers and The East 13th Street Band, 1985. *Publication:* The Art of Listening: Developing Musical Perception. *Honours:* Fulbright Fellowship, 1953, 1972. *Memberships:* IAJE; AMS; International Musicological Society.

BROKENSHIRE Frederick; b. 21 April 1952, Toronto, Ontario, Canada. Music Industry Exec. 2 s., 1 d. *Education:* 2 years, Memorial University of Newfoundland. *Career:* Entered music business, 1972; President, majority shareholder, The Duckworth Group; Atlantica Music and Distribution Ltd; Duckworth Distribution Ltd; Latitude Records Inc; FRB Productions; Wildshore Music Inc; Atlantica Musique et Distribution Ltee; Fred's Records Ltd; Atlantic Canada's leading music companies; Engaged in record production, distribution, artist management, concert promotion, retail, with offices in: St John's; Halifax; Moncton; Toronto; Canada. *Memberships:* Founding mem., president, Music Industry Asscn, Newfoundland; Director, East Coast Music Asscn; Mem., regional

representative, Canadian Country Music Asscn; Canadian Academy Recording Arts and Sciences; Mem., Music Industry Asscn of Nova Scotia. *Leisure interests:* Sailing; Skiing. *Address:* The Duckworth Music Group, 198 Duckworth St, St John's, Newfoundland A1C 1G5, Canada.

BROKOP Lisa; b. 6 June 1973, Surrey, British Columbia, Canada. Singer; Songwriter; Musician (guitar, keyboards). *Career:* Singer, Rhythm guitarist, keyboardist, Marty Gillan and the Sweetwater Band, 1988; Formed own band, 1989; Toured with Clay Walker and George Strait; Film role: Harmony Cats; Performed CCMA Awards Show, Canada, and CMA Awards Show Nashville, 1992. *Recordings:* Albums: Every Little Girl's Dream, 1994; Lisa Brokop, 1995; Singles: Give Me A Ring Sometime, 1994; Take That, 1994; Who Needs You, 1995; She Can't Save Him, 1995; Before He Kissed, 1996; How Do I Let Go, 1998; When You Get To Be You, 1998. *Honours:* Horizon Award (Best New Artist), Gospel Performer of Year, British Columbia Country Music Asscn (BCCMA), 1990; Princess Margaret Order of Lion, Special Ambassador, 1991; CKWX Songwriter's Contest, 1991; Female Vocalist of Year, BCCMA, 1992; Youth Achievement Award, Vocal Excellence, YTV, 1992; Female Vocalist of Year, International Achievement Award, BCCMA, 1993; Vocal Collaboration Award with Johner Brothers, Saskatchawan Country Music Asscn, 1994; Worldfest Houston Gold Award, 1994; Female Vocalist of Year, International Achievement Award, Single of Year, BCCMA, 1994. *Memberships:* SOCAN; CCMA; CMA; ACM; AFofM. *Leisure interests:* Golf; Swimming. *Current Management:* Mascioli Entertainment Corporation. *Address:* 11 Music Circle S, First Floor, Nashville, TN 37203, USA.

BROM Gustav; b. 22 May 1921, Velké Leváre, Czech Republic. Jazz Band Conductor; Musician (violin, clarinet, saxophone). m. Marie Bromová-Gergelová, 1 s., 1 d. *Musical Education:* Music school; Private study. *Career:* Jazz band leader, 5 years; 300 concerts home and abroad; Jazz festivals; Rated among 10 best world jazz bands in world. *Recordings:* 175 albums; About 100 singles; About 30 CDs; 20 own compositions. *Publications:* My Life With Jazz-band. *Honours:* Czechoslovak State Award. *Leisure interests:* Sport: Football, hockey, tennis. *Address:* Preslova 28, 602 00 Brno, Czech Republic.

BROM Rafael; b. 13 Aug. 1952, Prague, Czech Republic. Singer; Musician (multi-instrumentalist); Composer; Prod.; Performer. *Education:* Graphic Art; Fine Art; Computer Graphics. *Career:* Appearances: Radio stations, USA, Canada; 9 albums, 2 singles. *Recordings:* Albums: Rafael Brom 1, 1983; Lord Hamilton-Padre Pio, 1985; Peace of Heart, 1986; The Sounds of Heaven, 1989; Dance For Padre Pio, 1991; The True Measure of Love, 1992; Music For Peace of Mind, 1993; The Christmas Songs; You'll Never Walk Alone. *Honours:* ASCAP Special Award. *Membership:* ASCAP. *Leisure interests:* Tennis; Videos; Books; Metaphysics; Political Science. *Current Management:* Cosmotone Records. *Address:* PMB 412, 3350-A Hwy 6, Sugarland, TX 77478, USA.

BRON Gerry; b. 1 March 1933, London, England. Man.; Prod.; Co Dir. m. 8 July 1982, 2 s. *Musical Education:* Clarinet, Harmony, Composition, Trinity College of Music, London. *Career:* Family Business, 1949; Manager: Gene Pitney; Manfred Mann; Uriah Heep; Formed Bronze Records, 1971; Built Roundhouse Recording Studios, 1974. *Recordings:* Productions include: Manfred Mann; Bonzo Dog Doo Dah Band; Colosseum; Juicy Lucy; Osibisa; Gene Pitney; Uriah Heep. *Leisure interests:* Music; Computers; Aviation. *Address:* 17 Priory Rd, London NW6 4NN, England.

BRONZE David; b. 2 April 1952, Billericay, Essex, England. Musician (bass). m. Julie, 1 s., 1 d. *Career:* Member of groups: Procul Harum; Robin Trower Band; Dr Feelgood; Art of Noise; Duane Eddy Band; Barbara Dickson Band; Mickey Jupp Band; Chris Farlowe and The Thunderbirds; Eric Clapton Band; With Paul Carrack Band. *Recordings:* As producer, mixer, musician, Down At The Doctors, Dr Feelgood, 1994; On the Road Again, Dr Feelgood, 1996; As musician: with Eric Clapton: From The Cradle, 1994; Pilgrim, 1998; with Procol Harum: Prodigal Stranger, 1991; with Paul Carrack: Beautiful World, 1997; with Gary Barlow: Open Road, 1997; with Nik Kershaw: 1997, 15 Minutes, 1999; To Be Frank, 2001; with Eric Bibb: Home To Me, 1997; Painting Signs, 2001; with S.A.S. Band: Show, 2001; Many sessions with various artists. *Memberships:* PRS; Musicians' Union; PAMRA. *Leisure interests:* Tennis; Cooking. *Address:* c/o 107A High St, Canvey, Essex, England.

BROOKS (Troyal) Garth; b. 7 Feb. 1962, Tulsa, Oklahoma, USA. Country vocalist; Songwriter; Musician (guitar). m. Sandra Mahl, 1986, 2 d. *Education:* BS, Journalism and Advertising, Oklahoma State University, 1985. *Career:* Television specials include: This Is Garth Brooks, 1992; This Is Garth Brooks Too!, 1994; Garth Brooks – The Hits, 1995; Best selling country album ever, No Fences (over 13m. copies). *Recordings:* Albums: Garth Brooks, 1989; No Fences, 1990; Ropin' The Wind, 1991; The Chase, 1992; Beyond The Season, 1992; In Pieces, 1993; The Hits, 1994; Fresh Horses, 1995; Sevens, 1997; In The Life of Chris Gaines, 1999; The Colors of Christmas, 1999; Scarecrow, 2001; Singles: If Tomorrow Never Comes,

1989; Tour EP, 1994; To Make You Feel My Love, 1998; One Heart At A Time, 1998; Lost In You, 1999. *Honours:* Grammy Award; CMA Horizon Award, Video of the Year, 1990; CMA Awards: Best Single, Best Album 1991; Music City News/TNN Award, Video of Year, 1991; CMA Entertainer of the Year, 1991–92; Numerous ACM Awards include: Music Entertainer of the Year, 1991–94, Best Single 1991, Best Album 1991; ASCAP Voice of Music Award, 1992; 9 People's Choice Awards; Top-selling solo artist in American music history, RIAA. *Memberships:* Inducted into Grand Ole Opry; ASCAP; CMA; ACM. *Leisure interests:* Horse riding; Sports (hockey, basketball). *Current Management:* Scott Stern, GB Management Inc, 1111 17th Ave S, Nashville, TN 37212, USA.

BROOKS Anthony Lewis; b. 20 April 1956, Treorchy, Rhondda, Wales. Prod.; Composer; Performer. 1 s. *Education:* Electrical Engineering, Nayland Technical College. *Musical Education:* Piano, Brass, Percussion, Bass, University of Wales; Music Degree, IRCAM; Sound Design Degree, Institute of Research Computers and Music, Paris. *Career:* Executives, British tours; Artatak, British tours, Television and Radio; ICA London Performance, 1975; Europe, USA Tours with Various Groups; Darts 2, British tours; Olympic Culture Event, Centre for Performing Arts, Atlanta, 1996; Danish Television, Tony Brooks Is Orchestra Soundscapes; Culture City Europe, Copenhagen, 1996; The World Is One Festival, Seoul, 1996; The Oedipus Production, Seoul, 1997; Designed Coil Interactive Sound and Image Room installation, leading museums for modern art, Scandinavia, 1998–99; Performance for Danish Institute for Electroacoustic Music, 1998; Performed at Malmö, Sweden Statensteater, 1997; Performed and composed Oedipus Trilogy, Seoul, South Korea; Performed, Exit Festival, Sweden, 1999; Behind the Wall, International Aarhus Festival, Denmark, 1999; Danish Newave and New York Festival, 1999. *Compositions:* Heaven People; Earth Tribe, 1, 2, and 3. *Recordings:* Tony Brooks Is Earth Tribe, 1, 2, and 3; Heaven People. *Memberships:* Danish Music Union; Danish Jazz Beat and Folk Authors; IRCAM, Paris. *Leisure interests:* Golf; Sun and Beach; Scuba Diving. *Current Management:* Pappagallo, Schleppegrellesgade 8, 8000 Aarhus, Denmark. *Address:* Heibergsgade 21 kld, 800 Aarhus C, Denmark.

BROOKS Clyde Scott; b. 16 Jan. 1948, Milwaukee, USA. Musician (percussion, drums); Record Prod. m. Geri Brooks, 13 May 1988. *Musical Education:* Berklee College of Music, Boston, 1968–70. *Career:* Session musician for: Dolly Parton; Kenny Rogers; Ronnie Milsap; Don Henley; Oak Ridge Boys; Johnny Winter; Jerry Lee Lewis; Barbara Mandrell; George Strait; Ted Nugent; Little Richard; B J Thomas. *Recordings:* Record producer for recordings by: Nancy Brooks; Lynn Anderson; The Headlights; B B Watson; Ronna Reeves. *Publication:* Author, The Recording Drummer, 1974. *Memberships:* AFTRA; Country Music Asscn; AFofM.

BROOKS David John; b. 6 June 1951, Sheffield, England. Singer; Songwriter; Musician (guitar, keyboards). m. Anthia Stephens, 19 Feb. 1985. *Musical Education:* Wells Cathedral School. *Career:* Opening solo act for many bands on various tours including: Fairport Convention; Georgie Fame; Chris Farlowe; Steve Gibbons Band; Ronnie Lane's Slim Chance. *Compositions:* Theme and incidental music, BBC television series: The Family, 1974; Story of Ruth, 1978; Romers Egypt, 1980; Breakaway Girls, 1978; Vox Pop, 1983; One Day, 1988; In Solidarity, 1989; Forty Minutes, 1993. *Recordings:* Family Theme, 1974; Vox Pop, 1983. *Memberships:* BASCA; PRS; Musicians' Union. *Leisure interests:* Cricket; Gardening; Rum. *Current Management:* Anthia Brooks. *Address:* 82 Lambton Rd, London SW20 0LP, England.

BROOKS Elkie, (Elaine Bookbinder); b. 25 Feb. 1946, Salford, Manchester, England. Vocalist. *Career:* Toured with Eric Delaney Band, 1960s; Joined jazz-rock act Dada (later became Vinegar Joe), 1970–74; Solo artiste, 1974-. *Recordings:* Albums: Rich Man's Woman, 1975; Two Days Away, 1977; Shooting Star, 1978; Live and Learn, 1979; Pearls, 1981; Pearls II, 1982; Minutes, 1984; Screen Gems, 1984; No More The Fool, 1986; The Very Best of Elkie Brooks, 1986; The Early Years 1964–66, 1987; Bookbinder's Kid, 1988; Inspiration, 1989; Round Midnight, 1993; Pearls III, 1993; Circles, 1995; Nothin' But The Blues, 1996; Round Midnight, 1996; From The Heart, 1996; Pearls Concert Live, 1999; We've Got Tonight, 2000; Singles include: Hello Stranger; The Way You Do The Things You Do; Pearl's A Singer, 1977; Sunshine After Rain, 1977; Fool If You Think It's Over, 1982; Nights In White Satin, 1982; No More The Fool, 1986. *Address:* c/o Barry Collings Entertainments, 21a Clifftown Rd, Southend-on-Sea, Essex SS1 1AB, England.

BROOKS Kix (Leon Eric III); b. 12 May 1955, Shreveport, Louisiana, USA. Country vocalist; Musician (guitar); Songwriter. *Career:* Member, Brooks and Dunn (with Ronnie Dunn). *Compositions include:* Brand New Man; I'm Only In It For The Love; My Next Broken Heart; That Ain't No Way To Go; Whiskey Under The Bridge; You're Gonna Miss Me When I'm Gone. *Recordings:* solo: Baby When Your Heart Breaks Down, 1983; Sacred Ground, 1989: as Brooks and Dunn: Brand New Man, 1991; My Next Broken Heart, 1991; Neon Moon, 1992; Boot Scootin' Boogie, 1992; Hard

Workin' Man, 1993; We'll Burn That Bridge, 1993; She Used To Be Mine, 1993; Rock My World (Little Country Girl), 1993; That Ain't No Way To Go, 1994; She's Not The Cheatin' Kind, 1994; Little Miss Honky Tonk, 1995; You're Gonna Miss Me When I'm Gone, 1995; Whiskey Under The Bridge, 1995; My Maria, 1996; I Am That Man, 1996; A Man This Lonely, 1996; He's Got You, 1997; Honky Tonk Truth, 1997; How Long Gone, 1998; Husbands and Wives, 1998; I Can't Get Over You, 1999; You'll Always Be Loved By Me, 2000; Ain't Nothing 'Bout You, 2001; Only In America, 2001; The Long Goodbye, 2002; Albums include: Brand New Man, 1991; Hard Workin' Man, 1993; Waitin' On Sundown, 1994; Borderline, 1996; The Greatest Hits Collection, 1997; If You See Her, 1998; Tight Rope, 1999; Steers and Stripes, 2001. *Honours:* various including: CMA, Vocal Duo of the Year, 1993–98. *Internet:* www.brooks-dunn.com.

BROOKS Meredith; b. Corvallis, Oregon, USA. Vocalist; Songwriter; Musician (guitar). *Career:* Member, all-female group The Graces, 1990; Solo recording artist, 1991-. *Recordings include:* Albums: Blurring The Edges, 1997; See It Through My Eyes, 1997; Deconstruction, 1999; Hit Singles: Bitch, 1997; What Would Happen, 1998. *Honours:* Brit Award Nomination, 1998. *Current Management:* Lori Leve Management, 151 N Almont Dr., Suite 305, Beverly Hills, CA 90211, USA.

BROOKS Nikki (Nichola Jane); b. Bristol, England. Musician (keyboards, bass guitar, clarinet); Vocalist. *Education:* BPharm, Degree. *Musical Education:* All grades Theory and Practical, Guildhall School of Music, Associate and Licentiate, London College of Music Diplomas. *Career:* ECT, Ch4, 1985; Lead vocalist, McCoy, 1985; Lead vocalist, Wild!, 1986–87; Lead and backing vocalist, bass, keyboards in various covers bands; Currently in Adam and The Ants covers band, and session musician; Played with members of: Gillan; Iron Maiden; UFO; Wild Horses; Pat Travers Band; Gary Moore Band; Tours, festivals in UK and Europe; Vocal sessions include: Dreamboys, LA Centrefold Videos; Currently writing material with songwriting partner. *Recordings:* Wrote and recorded 4 song session for BBC Radio 1 Rock Show (Tommy Vance). *Honour:* Prize for Grade 3 Guildhall Practical Piano. *Membership:* Musicians' Union; PRS. *Leisure interests:* Music; Cookery; Films. *Address:* Flat C, 49 Roxborough Park, Harrow-On-The-Hill, Middlesex HA1 3BA, England.

BROSCH Christopher; b. 9 April 1957, Munich, Germany. Promoter; Agent. m. Kerstin Estherr Brosch, 20 June 1991, 1 d. *Education:* Law studies, Cologne. *Career:* Freelance tour manager for various German tour promoters, 1980–85; Talent Booker for Peter Rieger Koncertagentur, Cologne, acts include: Peter Gabriel; Joe Cocker; Run-DMC; Beastie Boys; Changed to Hamburg based company, Blinffish Promotion, as talent booker for new bands; Started own company: Bizarre Productions, 1992; Acts promoted include: Beastie Boys; Portishead; Hole; Cocteau Twins; Oasis; Beastie Boys; Portishead; Hole; Foo Fighters; Daft Punk; New talent outdoor festival in the summer. *Leisure interests:* Travel; Golf. *Address:* Buelaustr 8, 20099 Hamburg, Germany.

BROUDIE Ian; b. 4 Aug. 1958. Vocalist; Songwriter; Musician (guitar); Prod. *Career:* Member, Original Mirrors, late 1970s; Member, Big In Japan, 1977; Member, duo, Care, mid-1980s; Founder, The Lightning Seeds, 1990–; Record producer, 1980s-; Numerous television and radio appearances; Concerts include: Glastonbury Festival, 1995. *Recordings:* Albums: Cloudcuckooland, 1991; Sense, 1992; Jollification, 1994; Dizzy Heights, 1996; Like You Do... The Best Of, 1997; Tilt, 1999; Singles: with The Lightning Seeds: Pure, 1989; Joy, 1990; Life of Riley, 1992; Sense, 1992; Lucky You, 1994; Change, 1995; Marvellous, 1995; Perfect, 1995; Ready Or Not, 1996; What If, 1996; Sugar Coated Iceberg, 1997; You Showed Me, 1997; What You Are, 1997; Life's Too Short, 1999; Singer, songwriter, Three Lions (Official England Squad's Euro '96 theme), with David Baddiel and Frank Skinner (No. 1, UK), 1996/1998; Record producer, numerous artists include: Echo and The Bunnymen; The Fall; Wah!; Icicle Works; The Primitives; Alison Moyet; Frank and Walters; Dodgy; Sleeper. *Honour:* Brit Award Nomination, Best British Group, 1996. *Current Management:* JPR Management, The Powerhouse, 70 Chiswick High Rd, London W4 1SY, England.

BROUWER Leovigildo; b. 1939, La Habana, Cuba. Orchestra; Conductor; Composer; Guitarist; Violoncellist; Clarinettist; Pianist; Percussionist. *Musical Education:* Studied Guitar with Isaac Nicola; Studied at Peyrellade Conservatoire, La Habana; Self-taught, Juilliard School of Music, New York; Hartford University. *Career:* Directed Music Department, Instituto Cubano, 1960; Created the Experimentacion of Sounds with Silvio Rodriguez and Pablo Milanes, 1968; Composed music for more than 100 films all around the world. *Compositions:* Conductor, Orquesta de Cuba. *Honour:* Hon. Mem., Cim of UNESCO, 1987. *Current Management:* Intercambio de Cultura y Arte. *Address:* Carreteras, 14–5-I-5, 28012 Madrid, Spain.

BROWN Alex; b. 17 Jan. 1967, Glynde, England. Singer; Musician (piano, trumpet, guitar, drums). *Musical Education:* Grade 8 trumpet; Music and Drama at college. *Career:* Lead singer, Macho Frog, 1985–88; UK (South

East) tour, 1987; Signed to Brown Bear Records, 1990–; Tours: Austria, Germany, 1991; Belgium, England; Appearances at: Radio 1 FM Roadshows; Atlantic 252 Roadshows; BBC Children In Need Show. *Recordings:* That's What It Takes, 1993; Supernatural Love, 1994; Life Is Just Worth Living, 1994; Halfway To Heaven, 1994; Too Far Away, 1995; What I Like, 1995; I've Been Missing You, 1995. *Memberships:* PRS; Musicians' Union; PPL; VPL; Umbrella. *Leisure interest:* Tennis. *Current Management:* Brown Bear Records. *Address:* 123A Wilton Rd, Victoria, London SW1V 1JZ, England.

BROWN Andy; b. 1 Nov. 1968, Auckland, New Zealand. Singer; Songwriter. *Career:* Mainstage NZ Festival, 1991; Shelterbelt Festival, 1992; New Zealand Tour; Australian Tour, 1993; Parachute Music Festivals, 1992, 1994, 1995; New Zealand tour, 3 months; Tear Fund, Hope and Justice Tour, 1995; World Tour, Europe and USA, 1996. *Recordings:* Albums: Surge, 1991; Nice Moon, 1994; Merge, 1996; Pakajam, 1998. *Honours:* Nice Moon, 10 Best of '94, Audio Video magazine, NZ. *Membership:* Australasian Performing Rights Asscn. *Current Management:* Mantis Productions, c/o Rowdy Disc, PO Box 16298, Sandringham, Auckland, New Zealand.

BROWN Angie; b. 13 June 1963, Clapham, London, England. Vocalist; Actor. *Musical Education:* Private drama lessons; 4 years intensive singing lessons with Annette Batram. *Career:* Solo singer; Television appearances include: Jonathan Ross, 1990; America's Top Ten, 1992; Dance Energy, 1993; Top of the Pops, 3 times, 1992–93; Big World Cafe, 1990; The Beat; Dublin Two; Pebble Mill; Currently vocalist of Ramona 55. *Composition:* Took My Love. *Recordings:* Singles: with Bizarre Inc (No. 2, UK) 1992; I'm Gonna Get You (No. 3, UK), 1992; Took My Love, 1993; You Got It; Album: An Album I Thought I Could Only Dream Of!, with Ramona 55, 1994; Also appears on: Bizarre Inc, Energique, 1992; Midge Ure, If I Was, 1993; Mark Morrison, Return of The Mack (No. 1, UK), 1996; Anthony Thistlethwaite, Crawfish and Caviar, 1997; Other session work includes: Heaven 17, Sarah Cracknell, Holly Johnson, Londonbeat, Freak Power. *Memberships:* Equity; Performing Rights Society; Musicians' Union; PAMRA. *Leisure interests:* Driving; Belly Laughing; Red Wine; Smoked Salmon; Cinema; Sauna; Working out. *Current Management:* Laurie Jay. *Address:* LJE, 32 Willesden Lane, Kilburn, London NW6 7ST, England.

BROWN Bobby; b. 5 Feb. 1969, Roxbury, Massachusetts, USA. Vocalist. m. Whitney Houston, 18 July 1992, 1 d. *Career:* Founder member, New Edition, 1981–85, reformed 1995; Solo artiste, 1985–; Film appearance, Ghostbusters II, 1989; Established Bosstown recording studio and record label. *Recordings:* New Edition singles include: Candy Girl (No. 1, UK), 1983; Cool It Now, 1984; Mr Telephone Man, 1985; Solo albums: King of Stage, 1986; Don't Be Cruel (No. 1, USA), 1989; Dance... Ya Know It!, 1989; Bobby, 1992; B Brown Posse, 1993; NBA Jam Session, 1993; Remixes N The Key of B, 1993; Forever, 1997; Greatest Hits, 2000; Singles include: Girlfriend, 1986; Girl Next Door, 1987; Don't Be Cruel, 1988; My Prerogative (No. 1, USA), 1989; Roni, 1989; Every Little Step, 1989; On Our Own, from film Ghostbusters II, 1989; Rock Wit' Cha, 1989; Humpin' Around, 1992; Good Enough, 1992; Get Away, 1993; That's The Way Love Is, 1993; Two Can Play That Game, 1995; Feelin' Inside, 1997; with Glenn Medeiros: She Ain't Worth It (No. 1, USA), 1990; Contributor, Voices That Care charity single (for Red Cross Gulf Crisis). *Honours:* various including: Regular winner, SKC Boston Music Awards, 1989–; Soul Train Music Award, Best R & B/Urban Contemporary Album of the Year; Regular winner, American Music Awards, 1990–; Grammy, Best Male R & B Vocal Performance, Every Little Step, 1990; Coca-Cola Atlanta Music Award, Outstanding Male Vocalist, 1992. *Current Management:* Tommy Brown, 2160 N Central Rd, Fort Lee, NJ 08014, USA.

BROWN Chris; b. Stockport, Cheshire, England. Recording Engineer; Record Prod. *Career:* Senior Engineer, Abbey Road Studios, London. *Current Management:* Townhouse Management. *Address:* 150 Goldhawk Rd, London W12 8HH, England.

BROWN Chris (Christopher M); b. 1 July 1954, Evanston, Illinois, USA. Composer; Prod.; Recording Engineer. *Musical Education:* Oberlin College Conservatory of Music. *Career:* Long affiliation with Paul Winter and The Winter Consort, 26 albums in nearly 20 years; Several nominated for Grammy Awards; Scores for: television; film; industrial videos; Recorded, edited or mixed numerous albums, CDs, films and video scores. *Recordings include:* Prayer for the Wild Things, Paul Winter, 1995. *Honour:* Grammy Award, 1995. *Memberships:* NARAS; AFofM. *Leisure interest:* Dinghy sailing. *Current Management:* Image-Net, Goshen, CT, USA. *Address:* 1401 Rt 35, South Salem, NY 10590, USA.

BROWN Errol; b. 12 Nov. 1948, Kingston, Jamaica. Vocalist; Songwriter. *Career:* Lead vocalist, Hot Chocolate, 1969–87; Solo artiste, 1987–; Mixing Engineer and Producer 1980's-90's. *Compositions:* Think About Your Children, Mary Hopkin; Bet Yer Life I Do, Herman's Hermits; Hits for Hot Chocolate include: Every 1's A Winner; Girl Crazy; It Started With A Kiss; Tears On The Telephone. *Recordings:* Albums: with Hot Chocolate:

Cicero Park, 1974; Hot Chocolate, 1975; Man To Man, 1976; Hot Chocolate's Greatest Hits, 1976; Every 1's A Winner, 1978; Going Through The Motions, 1979; 20 Hottest Hits, 1979; Class, 1980; Mystery, 1982; Love Shot, 1983; The Very Best of Hot Chocolate, 1987; Their Greatest Hits, 1993; Solo albums: That's How Love Is, 1989; Secret Rendevous 1992; Still Sexy, 2000; 30 hit singles with Hot Chocolate include: Love Is Life, 1970; I Believe (In Love), 1971; Brother Louie (No. 1, USA), 1973; Emma, 1974; Disco Queen, 1975; A Child's Prayer, 1975; You Sexy Thing, 1976; Don't Stop It Now, 1976; Man To Man, 1976; Heaven In The Back Seat of My Cadillac, 1976; So You Win Again (No. 1, UK), 1977; Put Your Love In Me, 1977; Every 1's A Winner, 1979; No Doubt About It, 1980; Girl Crazy, 1982; It Started With A Kiss, 1982; Tears On The Telephone, 1983; I Gave You My Heart (Didn't I), 1984. *Current Management:* Richard Martin Management, Agency House, 6 The Steyne, Worthing, West Sussex BN11 3DS, England.

BROWN Ian; b. 20 Feb. 1963, Ancoats, Greater Manchester, England. Vocalist; Songwriter; Musician (bass). *Career:* Formed Patrol, 1980; Name changed to English Rose, 1983; Became the Stone Roses, 1984–96; Tours include: British tour, 1989; European tour, 1989; Japanese tour, 1989; Concert, Alexandra Palace, 1989. *Recordings:* with the Stone Roses: Albums: The Stone Roses, 1989; Turn Into Stone, 1992; Second Coming, 1994; Singles: Made of Stone, 1989; She Bangs The Drums, 1989; Fool's Gold/What The World Is Waiting For, 1989; Elephant Stone, 1990; One Love, 1990; I Wanna Be Adored, 1991; Waterfall, 1992; I Am The Resurrection, 1993; Love Spreads, 1994; Ten Storey Love Song, 1995; Begging You, 1995; Solo Albums: Unfinished Monkey Business, 1998; Golden Greats, 1999; Music of The Spheres, 2001; Solo singles: My Star, 1998; Love Like A Fountain, 1999; Dolphins Were Monkeys, 2000.

BROWN James; b. 3 May 1928, Barnwell, South Carolina, USA. Soul Vocalist; Broadcasting Exec. m. (1) Deidre Jenkins, (2) Adrienne Brown, deceased 1996. *Career:* Singer with, then leader of own backing group Famous Flames, 1956–68; Solo performer, recording artist, 1969–; President, JB Broadcasting Ltd, 1968–; James Brown Network, 1968–; Film appearances include: Ski Party, 1964; Come To The Table, 1974; The Blues Brothers, 1980; Concerts include: The Biggest Show of Stars tour, 1963; The TAMI Show, 1964; Newport Jazz Festival, 1969; Festival of Hope, Garden City, 1972; Grand Ole Opry, Nashville, 1979; Montreux Jazz Festival, 1981; Coca-Cola Music Festival, Essex, 1992; Pori Jazz, Finland, 1995; Owner, several US radio stations; Co-owner, Brown Stone Records, 1992-. *Compositions include:* Film scores: Black Caesar, 1972; Slaughter's Big Rip Off, 1972. *Recordings:* Over 75 albums include: Live At The Apollo, 1963; I Can't Stand Myself, 1968; Hot Pants, 1971; The Payback, 1974; I'm Real, 1988; Universal James, 1992; Try Me, 1996; I'm Back, 1998; Hit singles include: Please, Please, Please, 1956; Out of Sight, 1964; Papa's Got A Brand New Bag, 1965; I Got You (I Feel Good), 1966; It's A Man's Man's Man's World, 1966; Cold Sweat, 1967; I Got The Feelin', 1968; Say It Loud, 1968; Give It Up Or Turn It Loose, 1969; Get Up, I Feel Like Being A Sex Machine, 1970; Super Bad, 1970; Get On The Good Foot, 1972; Get Up Offa That Thing, 1976; Living In America (used in film Rocky IV), 1986; I'm Real, 1988; Soul Jubilee, 1990; Love Over-Due, 1991; Love Power Peace, 1992; Funky Christmas, 1995; Hookedonbrown, 1996; Say It Live and Loud, 1998; On Stage Live, 1999. *Honours:* Inducted, Rock 'n' Roll Hall of Fame, 1986; Grammy Awards: Best R & B Recording, 1965; Best R & B Performance, 1987; 44 Gold discs; Award of Merit, American Music Awards, 1992; NARAS Lifetime Achievement Award, 1992; Lifetime Achievement Trophy, Rhythm and Blues Foundation Pioneer Awards, 1993; Lifetime Achievement Award, National Ass001 of Black Owned Broadcasters' Awards, 1993. *Current Management:* Brothers Management Associates. *Address:* 141 Dunbar Ave, Fords, NJ 08863, USA.

BROWN James Kofi; b. 15 Feb. 1949, Kumasi, Kwadaso, Ghana. Musician (guitar); Singer; Composer; Arranger. m. Comfort Peprah Aman Fo, 4 April 1992, 3 s. *Musical Education:* O Level Music, Ghana; Self-taught. *Career:* Many concerts in Ghana and 2 in Paris, France; Various radio and television appearances including: TV 5, Radio France International, Radio Africa No 1, Radio GBC 2, Ghana Broadcasting Corporation. *Recordings:* Time Is So Hard; Riot (That's Too Bad); I'm In The Mood For Love; Life Is A Stage; Be My Girl; I've Found A New Lover (Georgina); Let's Be Together. *Honour:* Best video clip, festival in Paris, France. *Memberships:* SACEM; SDRM French Musical Society. *Leisure interests:* Composing; Dancing. *Address:* 229 Ave D'Argenteuil, 92270 Bois Colombes, France.

BROWN James Lee; b. 7 Oct. 1953, Rocky Mt, North Carolina, USA. Musician (alto, tenor and soprano saxophones, keyboards). m. Angela Y Brown, 8 Aug. 1982, 2 s., 2 d. *Education:* 2 years college. *Musical Education:* Peabody study. *Career:* Appearances: WSMU-TV Nashville, Tennessee; Howard University WHUR-Radio; WEAA Radio Morgan State University. *Recordings:* Saxophonic Praises; Manifestation. *Honours:* ASCAP Award for Songwriting. *Leisure interests:* Weightlifting; Jogging; Biking. *Current Management:* Saxophonic Praises Inc. *Address:* 4714 Keppler PL, Temple Hills, MD 20748, USA.

BROWN Jim Ed (James Edward); b. 1 April 1934, Sparkman, Arkansas, USA. Country vocalist; Songwriter; Musician (guitar). *Career:* Featured on own radio show on KCLA, Pine Bluff, Arkansas with elder sister Maxine, late 1940s; Won talent contest on Barnyard Frolics, KLRA radio, Little Rock, Arkansas, early 1950s; Five singles on Fabor Records from 1954 onwards; Joined by sister Bonnie and became the Browns, 1955; Eighteen hits for RCA including number one pop and country hit The Three Bells, 1959; Recorded solo as Jim Edward Brown, 1965–67; Changed recording name to Jim Ed Brown, 1967–; Hit singles for RCA (including many with singer Helen Cornelius) until 1981; Host of TV shows: You Can Be A Star; Going Our Way (with wife Becky); Continued appearances on Grand Ole Opry; Opened The Jim Ed Brown Theater in Nashville, late 1980s. *Compositions include:* Looking Back To See. *Recordings include:* I Don't Want To Have To Marry You (with Helen Cornelius), 1976; Lying In Love With You, 1979; Saying Hello – Saying I Love You – Saying Goodbye (with Helen Cornelius), 1976; Pop A Top, 1967; Fools, 1979; Albums: Alone With You, 1966; I Don't Want To Have To Marry You (with Helen Cornelius), 1976. *Honours:* CMA, Duo of the Year, 1976; Music City News, Album of the Year, I Don't Want To Have To Marry You, 1976. *Memberships:* Grand Ole Opry, 1983. *Address:* c/o Billy Deaton Talent, 1300 Division, Suite 102, Nashville, TN, 37203, USA.

BROWN Kevin John; b. 19 July 1960, Nottingham, England. Musician (saxophone). *Career:* Member, The Beautiful South; Numerous tours: UK, Ireland, Europe, USA, Canada, Japan, 1989–94; Television appearances: Wogan; Top of The Pops; The Word; MotorMouth; Dennis Miller Show; Live performances recorded for television/video include: Feile Festival Live, Ireland, 1992, 1994; Bourges Festival Live, France; Live session, The Kelly Show, Ireland; Phoenix Festival, Stratford Upon Avon; Later with Jools Holland; Radio appearances include: Live session, Emma Freud, Radio 1; The Secret Gig, Radio 1. *Recordings:* Albums: with The Beautiful South: Choke, 1990; 0898, 1992; Carry On Up The Charts, 1994 (No. 1, UK); Rubaiyat (Elektra Records 40th anniversary), 1990; with The Miracle Drug: Imperial 66, 1993. *Honours:* Platinum Discs, Choke, Carry On Up The Charts; Gold Disc, 0898. *Membership:* Musicians' Union. *Address:* 136B Portland Rd, Hucknall, Nottingham NG15 7SA, England.

BROWN Lester Valentine; b. 27 Feb. 1958, Jamaica. Songwriter. 3 s., 2 d. *Musical Education:* Singing; Music business training (NBT). *Career:* Various public appearances, overseas tours (Caribbean); Own independent record label: Black Nation Music Productions. *Recordings:* I Want You To Want Me, cover of My Love Is True. *Membership:* Musicians' Union. *Leisure interests:* Music; Songwriting; Performing. *Current Management:* Broad Lane Music and Artist Management. *Address:* 14 St Peters House, Cunningham Rd, London N15 4DT, England.

BROWN Michael; b. 29 April 1968, Grimsby, South Humberside, England. Songwriter; Musician (saxophone, bass guitar, keyboards). *Musical Education:* Self-taught. *Career:* Saxophonist, Illustrious GY, 1988–93; Signed major recording contract, Arista, 1991; Toured nationally as support act with Arista, 1991; Television appearances on: Going Live (BBC), Mar 1993; Live and Kicking (BBC), 1993; Played acoustically, Steve Wright Show (BBC Radio 1), 1993; Illustrious GY disbanded, 1994; Formed new band: Giant Killers, as songwriter; Signed record contract with MCA, and publishing deal with Windswept Pacific, 1995. *Recordings:* Illustrious GY: Twenty Questions, 1993; Anytime At All, 1993; I'm Ugly, 1993; Album: No, No, No, 1993. *Membership:* Musicians' Union. *Leisure interest:* Keen football player. *Current Management:* Jonathon Cooke, Fat Cat Management. *Address:* 81 Harley House, Marylebone Rd, London NW1 5HT, England.

BROWN Norman; b. Shreveport, Louisiana, USA. Musician (guitar). *Musical Education:* Musicians Institute, Hollywood, California, USA. *Career:* World-wide touring, world-wide radio airplay. *Recordings:* Albums: Just Between Us; After The Storm; Better Days Ahead; Celebration. *Honours:* Soul Train Award: Best Jazz Album, BMI, 1995. *Current Management:* Bruce Kramer, Anchor Entertainment, 3522 Moore St, Los Angeles, CA 90066, USA.

BROWN Robert Jackson; b. 17 Oct. 1935, Framingham, Massachusetts, USA. Prod.; Composer; Lyricist; Arranger; Singer; Musician (piano, string bass). m. Belva Rousseau, 12 May 1956, divorced 1971, 1 s., 1 d. *Education:* Kimball Union Academy (College Preparation); Colby College. *Musical Education:* Piano lessons from age 7; Violin, clarinet, voice, music courses, Colby College, Boston Conservatory of Music; Harvard University. *Career:* Founded Upstarts, vocal/instrumental quintet, 1961; Studio singer, jingle writer, vocal arranger, lounge performer, Boston, 1961–64; New York City, 1964–86; Creative Producer, Mark Century Corporation, New York City, 1966–69; Music Director, Herb Mendelsohn Associates, New York City, 1969–71; President, Creative Director, Hunter Productions Inc; BMK Productions; BMK Records, Inc; Badito Productions Inc, 1970–78, all in New York City; Owner, Chief Engineer, Brownsound Recording Studios, New York City, 1978–83; Formed the Badito Brothers Band, 1974; Lead singer, conductor, music director, The Four Lads vocal

group, 1983–86; Lounge performer, Tampa Bay area, Florida, 1986–; Music director, Russ Byrd Music and Entertainment, St Petersburg, Florida, 1989–91; Singer, Pied Pipers vocal group, pianist, Warren Covington Orchestra, 1993–94; Pianist, The Jimmy Dorsey Orchestra, 1995; Music Director, First United Methodist Church, Largo, 1997–98; Music Director, St Paul's Lutheran Church, Clearwater, 1998; 9-week concert tour with the Pied Pipers vocal group, with the Jimmy Dorsey Orchestra, 1999. *Publications:* Talking To Joscelynne, National Library of Poetry, 1995. *Honour:* Editor's Choice Award, National Library of Poetry, 1995. *Memberships:* Screen Actors Guild; American Federation of Television and Radio Artists. *Address:* PO Box #5253, Largo, FL 33779–5253, USA.

BROWN Sam; b. 7 Oct. 1964, Stratford, London, England. Vocalist; Musician (keyboards). 1 s., 1 d. *Career:* Backing Vocalist, In the Shade, Small Faces, 1976; Numerous sessions as backing vocalist and keyboardist; Recording deal with AandM, 1986; Numerous tours and promotional activities; Released second album independently, 1993; Backing Vocalist, The Division Bell, Pink Floyd, and world tour, 1994, appeared on live album, P.U.L.S.E.; Worked with Jools Holland's Big Band; Duet with Fish on new album; Appeared on Nordoff-Robbins Rock Therapy record, and contributed Hammond organ, 1996; Numerous shows with Jools Holland R & B orchestra, 1996; Performed with Joe Brown (father) on The Subway Soopa Stringz, 1996. *Recordings:* Singles: Stop!, 1988 (reissued 1989); This Feeling, 1989; Can I Get A Witness, 1989; With a Little Love, 1990; Kissing Gate, 1990; Albums: Stop!, 1988; April Moon, 1990; 43 Minutes..., 1992; Box, 1997; Reboot, 2001; Appearances on: Before I Forget, Jon Lord, 1982; Too Rye Ay, Dexy's Midnight Runners, 1982; About Face, David Gilmour, 1984; Lowdown, Kane Gang, 1985; CD of JB, James Brown, 1985; Break Every Rule, Tina Turner, 1986; Division Bell, Pink Floyd, 1994, Pulse, 1995; Blood Brother, Tom Robinson, 1997; 56 and Taller Than You Think, Joe Brown, 1997; Prince's Trust 10th Anniversary Birthday Album; Small World Big Band, Jools Holland's Rhythm 'n' Blues Orchestra, 2001.

BROWN T Graham (Anthony Graham); b. 1954, Arabi, Georgia, USA. Country Singer; Songwriter. *Career:* Founder, Rio Diamond, 1976; Founder, T Graham Brown's Rock of Spam, 1979; Demo singer, Nashville, 1982; Recorded commercials for Budweiser; McDonalds; Solo artiste, 1985-. *Recordings:* Hit singles: US Country No. 1 hits: Hell Or High Water; Don't Go To Strangers; Darlene; Albums include: I Tell It Like It Used To Be, 1986; Brilliant Conversationalist, 1987; Come As You Were, 1988; Bumper To Bumper, 1990; You Can't Take It With You, 1991. *Current Management:* Starbound Management, 128 Volunteer Dr., Hendersonville, TN 37075, USA.

BROWN Tony Ersic; b. 11 Dec. 1946, Greensboro, North Carolina, USA. Record Co Exec.; Songwriter; Prod.; Musician (keyboards). m. (1) Janie Breeding (divorced), (2) Gina Morrison, 19 April 1979. *Career:* Songwriter, Silverline Music, 1972; Musician with: Oak Ridge Boys, 1972–75; Elvis Presley, 1975–77; Emmylou Harris, 1977–80; Roseanne Cash, 1980–83; A & R Executive, RCA Records, 1978–84; A & R Executive, MCA Records, 1984-. *Recordings:* Albums include: with Emmylou Harris: Blue Kentucky Girl, 1979; Christmas Album, 1979; Evangeline, 1981; Cimarron, 1981; White Shoes, 1983; with Guy Clark: Better Days, 1983; Also appears on: Guitar Town, 1986; Pontiac, 1987; Little Love Affairs, 1988; Lyle Lovett and His Large Band, 1989; Hardin County Line, 1990; For My Broken Heart, 1991; Love and Danger, 1992; Reba McEntire Greatest Hits Vol. 2, 1993; 8 Seconds, 1994; Strait Out of The Box, 1995; Step Right Up, 1996; Horse Whisperer, 1998. *Honours:* Dove Award, Gospel Music Asscn, 1972; Grammy Awards, 1980, 1983, 1985; Producer of the Year, NARAS, 1991. *Memberships:* NARAS; Nashville Entertainment Asscn; CMA; ACM; Gospel Music Asscn. *Address:* c/o MCA Records, 60 Music Sq. E, Nashville, TN 37203, USA.

BROWNE Jackson; b. 9 Oct. 1948, Heidelberg, Germany. Vocalist; Songwriter; Musician (guitar, piano). *Career:* Brief spell with Nitty Gritty Dirt Band, 1966; Solo singer, songwriter, musician, 1967–; Tours and concerts with Joni Mitchell; The Eagles; Bruce Springsteen; Neil Young; Trisha Yearwood; Major concerts include: Musicians United For Safe Energy (MUSE), Madison Square Garden (instigated by Browne and Bonnie Raitt), 1979; Glastonbury Festival, 1982; Montreux Jazz Festival, 1982; US Festival, 1982; Benefit concerts for: Amnesty International, Chile, 1990; Christie Institute, Los Angeles, 1990; Victims of Hurricane Inki, Hawaii, 1992; Various concerts for other environmental causes; Nelson Mandela Tributes, Wembley Stadium, 1988, 1990; Sang with Bonnie Raitt and Stevie Wonder, memorial service for Stevie Ray Vaughan, Dallas, Texas, 1990. *Compositions:* Songs recorded by Tom Rush; Nico; Linda Ronstadt; The Eagles; Co-writer with Glenn Frey, Take It Easy. *Recordings:* Albums: Jackson Browne, 1972; For Everyman, 1973; Late For The Sky, 1974; The Pretender, 1976; Running On Empty, 1978; Hold Out (No. 1, USA), 1980; Lawyers In Love, 1983; Lives In The Balance, 1987; World In Motion, 1989; I'm Alive, 1993; Looking East, 1996; Also featured on No Nukes album, 1980; Sun City, Artists United Against Apartheid, 1985; For Our Children, Disney AIDS benefit album, 1991; The Next Voice You Hear: The Best of Jackson Browne, 1997; Singles include: Doctor My

Eyes, 1972; Here Come Those Tears Again, 1977; Running On Empty, 1978; Stay, 1978; That Girl Could Sing, 1980; Somebody's Baby, used in film Fast Times At Ridgemont High, 1982; Tender Is The Night, 1983; You're A Friend of Mine, with Clarence Clemons, 1986; For America, 1987. *Current Management:* Donald Miller, 12746 Kling St, Studio City, CA 91604, USA.

BROWNE Michael Jerome; b. 9 April 1960, Indiana, USA. Singer; Musician (guitar, banjo, fiddle, mandolin, harmonica). *Career:* Solo Performer, Coffee Houses and Street Corners, Canada, US, UK, 1974–84; Lead singer, Guitarist, Stephen Barry Band, 1984–99; Accompanist, Vann Walls and Visiting Blues Artists. *Compositions:* Co Written with B A Markus, Blacktop; You're For Me. *Recordings:* In The Evening, with Vann Walls, 1997; Michael Jerome Browne, 1998; The Gold Record, 1998. *Honours:* Real Blues Award, Best Canadian Acoustic Blues Artist, 1998. *Memberships:* American Federation of Musicians. *Address:* 4840 St Laurent Blvd, Montréal, QC, H2T 1R5, Canada.

BRUBECK David Warren; b. 6 Dec. 1920, Concord, California, USA. Jazz Musician; Composer. m. Iola Whitlock, 1942. 5 s., 1 d. *Education:* BA, University of Pacific; Composition with Darius Milhaud, Mills College. *Career:* Leader, Dave Brubeck Octet, Trio, Quartet, 1946–; Formed Dave Brubeck Quartet, 1951; Played colleges, festivals, clubs, symphony orchestras; 3 month tour, Middle East, Europe, for State Department; Frequent tours, Europe, Australia, Japan, USSR. *Compositions:* Ballets; Points On Jazz; Glances; Orchestral; Elementals; They All Sang Yankee Doodle; Flute and Guitar; Tritonis; Piano; Reminiscences of The Cattle Country; Four By Four; Oratorios; The Light In The Wilderness; Beloved Son; Voice of The Holy Spirit; Cantatas; Gates of Justice; Truth; La Fiesta de la Posada; Chorus and Orchestra; Pange Lingua Mass; To Hope; I See; Satie; Four New England Pieces; Lenten Tryptich; Over 100 jazz compositions: Blue Rondo A La Turk; In Your Own Sweet Way; The Duke. *Recordings include:* Stardust, 1951; Jazz At Oberlin, 1953; Time Out, 1959; Time Further Out, 1961; The Dave Brubeck Quartet At Carnegie Hall (live), 1963; The Last Time We Saw Paris, 1967; Brubeck and Desmond Duets, 1975; Paper Moon, 1981; One Alone, 2000. *Honours:* Hon. doctorates from: University of Pacific; Fairfield University; University of Bridgeport; Mills College; Niagara University; BMI Jazz Pioneer Award, 1985; Compostela Humanitarian Award, 1986; Connecticut Arts Award, 1987; American Eagle Award, National Music Council, 1988; Duke Ellington Fellow, Yale University. *Current Management:* Derry Music Company. *Address:* PO Box 216, Wilton, CT 06897, USA.

BRUCE Hal Nelson; b. 27 May 1952, Halifax, Nova Scotia, Canada. Musician (guitars, piano, harmonica). 1 s., 1 d. *Education:* Cartography (mapping). *Musical Education:* Self-taught. *Career:* Began playing in first rock 'n' roll band aged 14; Full-time player, 1982–; Entertained 3 years running on Canadian Country Awards Show; Nominated twice for Canada's Vista Rising Star Award; Opened for Beach Boys 1989, Parlee Beach, Canada, 70,000 people. *Recordings:* The First Time, 1988; Goin' Home, 1992; On Our Way, 1998. *Honours:* Male Vocalist of the Year, 1991, Nova Scotia; Winner, talent search, Nova Scotia; Winner, Entertainer, Male Vocalist, Band, Video, Songwriter of the Year, Nova Scotia Country Music Awards. *Memberships:* Atlantic Federation of Musicians; Nova Scotia Country Music Asscn; Atlantic Federation of Musicians; Songwriters Asscn of Nova Scotia; Canadian Country Music Asscn; Music Industry Asscn of Nova Scotia. *Leisure interests:* White water canoeing; Collecting Beatles memorabilia. *Address:* 18 Bellefontaine Court, Lawrencetown, NS B2Z 1L3, Canada.

BRUCE Jack; b. 14 May 1943, Glasgow, Scotland. Musician (bass); Vocalist. *Musical Education:* Piano, Royal Scottish Academy of Music. *Career:* Member, Alexis Korner Blues Incorporated, 1962; Graham Bond Organisation, 1963; John Mayall's Bluesbreakers, 1965; Manfred Mann, 1965–66; Founder member, Cream (with Ginger Baker, Eric Clapton), 1966–68; Solo artiste, 1969–; Played in Tony Williams' Lifetime; Member, West Bruce and Laing; Leader, Jack Bruce and Friends (with Larry Coryell and Mitch Mitchell); Member, John McLaughlin's Mahavishnu Orchestra; Jack Bruce Band; Collaboration with Robin Trower, Bill Lordan, in BLT, 1981; Performances include: with Cream: National Jazz and Blues Festival, Windsor, 1967; Madison Square Garden, 1968; Royal Albert Hall, London, 1968. *Recordings:* Albums: with Cream: Fresh Cream, 1967; Disraeli Gears, 1967; Wheels of Fire, 1968; Goodbye, 1969; Live Cream, 1970; Live Cream, Vol. 2, 1972; Heavy Cream, 1972; Solo albums: Songs For A Tailor, 1969; Things We Like, 1970; Harmony Row, 1971; Jack Bruce At His Best, 1972; Out of The Storm, 1974; How's Tricks, 1977; I've Always Wanted To Do This, 1980; Greatest Hits, 1980; Truce, 1982; Automatic, 1987; Willpower, 1989; A Question of Time, 1990; with West Bruce and Laing: Why Dontcha, 1972; with Jack Bruce and Friends: Live At The Bottom Line, 1992; Something Else, 1993; Cities of The Heart, 1994; And Friends, 1994; Monkjack, 1995; Sitting On Top of The World, 1997; Shadows In The Air, 2001; Singles: with Cream: Wrapping Paper, 1966; I Feel Free, 1967; Strange Brew, 1967; Sunshine of Your Love, 1968; Anyone For Tennis (theme for film The Savage Seven), 1968; White Room, 1968.

BRUFORD Bill; b. 17 May 1949, Sevenoaks, Kent, England. Musician (drums, percussion). m. Carolyn, 2 March 1973, 2 s., 1 d. *Education:* Leeds University. *Musical Education:* Mainly self-taught, some lessons from Lou Pocock, Royal Philharmonic Orchestra. *Career:* Member of Yes; Genesis; UK; King Crimson; Gong; Sideman to USA and Japanese leaders; Solo career as bandleader with Bruford and Earthworks; World-wide tours since 1968. *Compositions:* 160 shared or solo; Writer for BBC TV and Buddy Rich Orchestra. *Recordings:* Over 80 album releases, 1968–; Solo albums include: Feels Good To Me, 1978; One of a Kind, 1978; The Bruford Tapes, 1980; Gradually Going Tornado, 1980; Earthworks, 1987; Dig?, 1989; All Heaven Broken Loose, 1991; Heavenly Bodies, 1997; If Summer Had Its Ghosts, 1997; A Part and Yet Apart, 1999; Sound of Surprise, 2001; Upper Extremities, 2001. *Publications:* When In Doubt, Roll; numerous magazine articles. *Honours:* Modern Drummer Magazine Hall of Fame; Gold records. *Memberships:* Percussive Arts Society; PRS; BASCA.

BRUN Christian; b. 24 Dec. 1965, Antibes, France. Musician (guitar); Composer. *Education:* Masters degree, Physics. *Musical Education:* Music school, lessons with Tal Farlow. *Career:* Performances with Lou Bennett; Turk Mauro; Big Band 31 and Dee Dee Bridgewater; Andre Villeger; Daniel Huck; Performed at festivals: Marciac; Albijazz; Jazz sur son 31; Jazz Sous les Pommiers. *Recordings:* Houseful; Samantha's Dance, with Steve Mabry; Brooklyn Session, with D Kikoski, L Plaxico, T Campbell. *Honour:* Winner, Radio France Concourse, 1991. *Memberships:* SACEM; SPEDIDAM. *Leisure interests:* Sailing; Food; Wines; Girls. *Address:* Les Campanules, 29 rue des Boulets, 75011 Paris, France.

BRUNBORG Tore; b. 20 May 1960, Trondheim, Norway. Jazz Musician (tenor, soprano saxophone). 1 s., 1 d. *Musical Education:* Music Conservatory in Trondheim. *Career:* Toured, recorded, with Masqualero, 1982–92. *Compositions:* Comission for Vossa Jazz, 1989; Music for big band, small groups. *Recordings:* 3 recordings with Masqualero; Also with: Bo Stieff; Rita Marcotulli; Jon Balke; Arild Anderson; Anders Jormin; Chick Lyall; Appears on: Bande A Part, 1985; Aero, 1988; Re-enter, 1991; Nonsentration, 1992; Hyperborean, 1997; North Story, 1998. *Honours:* Reenskaugprisen; Spelemannsprisen (3 times with Masqualero). *Membership:* Norwegian Musicians' Union. *Leisure interests:* Skiing; Cycling. *Address:* Billingstadveien 52, 1362 Billingstad, Norway.

BRUNEAU Thierry; b. 28 July 1949, Paris, France. Musician (alto saxophone, bass clarinet, bassoon, flute, tenor and baritone saxophones). m. Päivi Hernala, 30 Oct. 1971. *Education:* Anthropology; Ethnomusicology. *Musical Education:* CIM (jazz school); Private lessons with Allen Eager, Buddy Collette, Chris Woods; Conservatoire of Music (bassoon, flute). *Career:* Member, Big Bands: Alan Silva Celestrial Communication Orchestra; Laurent Cugny Big Band Lumiere; Quintet with Charles Tyler, 1987; Tours: Scandinavia, 1989–90; Japan, 1989; Europe with local rhythm sections, Mal Waldron, 1988–93; Ken McIntyre, 1990–92, 1996; Anthony Ortega, 1991–92, 1995; Concerts with: Richard Davis, 1990; Dennis Charles, 1994; Also played with: Duke Jordan; Han Bennink; Frank Lowe; Scriptwriter, actor, composer, film Last Date (Hans Hylkema's film about Eric Dolphy); Founder, own record label, Serene, 1989; Released some Eric Dolphy material (the Uppsala Concert); Played festivals at: Turku, Finland; Gothenburg, Sweden; Vienne, Tourcoing, Montpellier, TBB, Jazz Valley (France). *Recordings:* Live At De Kave, Thierry Bruneau Quartet featuring Mal Waldron; Tribute, Ken McIntyre/Thierry Bruneau Quintet featuring Richard Davis; Anthony Ortega/Thierry Bruneau – 7 Standards and A Blues, Anthony Ortega. *Publication:* Book on Eric Dolphy in preparation. *Leisure interests:* Films; Literature; Painting; Photography. *Address:* Saincy, 77510 Bellot, France.

BRUNET Alain; b. 6 March 1947, Saint Sorlin, Drome, France. Musician (trumpet). *Education:* Master, Literature, Musicology. *Musical Education:* Musicology, Sorbonne University, Paris National Conservatory. *Career:* Founder, Module, 1974; Founder, Alain Brunet Quartet; Played with: Martial Solal; René Utreger; Jean-Louis Chautemps; Lee Konitz; Sonny Stitt; Georges Wein; Swing Limited Corporation; Machi-oul Big Band; Michel Graillier; Richard Raux; Al Grey; Stéphane Grappelli; Bernard Lubat; Didier Lockwood; Festivals: Vienna, 1983; Paris, 1984; Montpellier, 1988–90; Nevers, 1988; Nice, 1989–90, 1992–93; Montreux, 1992; New Orleans, 1992; Midem, 1993; Halle That Jazz Paris, 1993; Montréal, 1993; Newport, Saratoga, 1993; Invited to numerous international festivals including: East Africa; Tunisia; Greece; Belgium; Germany; Italy; Russia; Poland; Finland; Appearances on French television, 1975–; Hosted with Eve Ruggieri, Musiques Au Coeur (Jazz News), France 2 TV; Adviser to President, Fifth TV Channel; Tour, USA includes: Boston, San Francisco, Los Angeles, 1995; Appeared Midem, Cannes, 1994. *Recordings:* with Machi-oul Big Band, 1975; Module, 1982; Rominus, with Didier Lockwood, 1991; Alain Brunet Plays Serge Gainsbourg, 1993; French Melodies in LA, Alain Brunet, 1997. *Membership:* SACEM. *Current Management:* Azimuth, 14 rue Bleue, 75009 Paris, France.

BRUNNING Bob; b. 29 June 1943, Bournemouth, Dorset, England. Musician (bass); Writer. m. Halina, 8 Aug. 1977, 2 s., 1 d. *Education:*

College of St Mark and St John, Chelsea, 3 year course qualified teacher, 1967; Now headteacher. *Career:* Began in Bournemouth with Tony Blackburn; College band, 1964–67; Fives Company (3 singles); Member, Fleetwood Mac, 1967; Savoy Brown, 1967; Own bands: Brunning Sunflower Blues Band, 1968–71; Tramp, 1971–74; The DeLuxe Blues Band, 1981–95. *Recordings:* 26 albums with all above, several recordings with visiting blues legends; Latest recording, DeLuxe Blues Band; Other collaborations include: Jo Ann Kelly, Memphis Slim. *Publications:* Blues: The British Connection; Behind The Mask: Biography of Fleetwood Mac; Blues In Britain: The 50s To The 90s. *Leisure interests:* Travel; Reading. *Current Management:* BB Management. *Address:* 55 Cavendish Rd, Colliers Wood, London SW19 2ET, England.

BRUNTON Gary; b. 9 March 1968, Burnley, Lancashire, England. Jazz Musician (double bass). m. Beatrice Welter, 18 Sept. 1993. *Education:* Modern Languages, Business Studies, University College, Swansea. *Musical Education:* Bass, double bass, CIM; Classical bass with Thierry Barbé; Private studies with: Henri Texier; Pierre Michelot; Ray Brown; Dave Holland; Gary Peacock, Paris Conservatory. *Career:* with Upper Space Group: Duc des Lombards; Sunset; Festival de Django Reinhardt, 1995; with Edouard Ferlet Trio: Petit Opportun; Festival de Jazz de Parthenay, 1994; Hotel Adagio; Hotel Lutecia; Trilogie: Salle André Marechal, 1994; with Guitar Hell: Tours, Germany, 1994, 1995; Sunset; Hot Club de Lyon; La Tour Rose; Performances with: Trio Bojan Zulfikarpasic: Radio France Inter; with Trio Michel Grailler: Le Petit Journal Montparnasse; Le Houdon; with Jonathan Lewis Quartet: Jazz Parade, BBC Radio; Brecon Jazz Festival, Tour, Britain, 1990; Elizabeth Kontamanu Quartet, Rumanian tour, 1992; Stephanie Crawford Quartet; Michelle Hendricks; Paulo Fresu; Stéphane Belmondo; François Théberge; Pete Osbourne; Jeannot Rabeson; Patrice Galas; Philippe Soirat; Simon Goubert; Sangoma Everett; Olivier Hutman; Charles Bellonzi; Craig Handy. *Recordings with:* Lucide Beausonge; Laure Milena; Bruno Joubrel; Patrick Husson; Commercial television; Film track, Tom Est Tout Seul, La Bande Son, Canal+. *Membership:* UMJ (Union Musiciens de Jazz). *Address:* 37 Bld Ornano, 75018 Paris, France.

BRUNTON Richard McNaughton; b. 3 Oct. 1949, Newcastle-Upon-Tyne, England. Musician (guitars, keyboards); Composer. 1 s., 2 d. *Musical Education:* Piano lessons age 8–12; Guitar self-taught. *Career:* Own R & B band, Newcastle, 1964–68; Moved to London, freelance guitarist, 1969; Recorded over 200 records for artists including: Gerry Rafferty; Dr John; Barbara Dickson; Greg Lake; Pete Sinfield; Numerous television and film soundtracks. *Recordings include:* Pete Sinfield, Still, 1973; with Gerry Rafferty: Night Owl, 1979; Snakes and Ladders, 1980; Best of..., 1989; with Steve Jolliffe: Journeys Out of The Body, 1982; Doorways To The Soul, 1988; Richard Thompson, Sweet Talker, 1992; Supernatural Fairy Tales, 1996; Greg Lake, From The Beginning, 1997; BBC television soundtracks: The Grass Arena; Life and Loves of a She-Devil. *Memberships:* Musicians' Union; PRS; BASCA. *Leisure interests:* Electro-mechanical engineering; Aviation.

BRYAN Kelle; b. 1976. Vocalist. *Career:* Singer, UK all-female vocal group, Eternal, 1992–98. *Recordings:* Albums: with Eternal: Always and Forever, 1993; Power of a Woman, 1995; Before The Rain, 1997; Greatest Hits, 1998; Essential Eternal (compilation), 2001; solo: Breakfast In Bed, 2000; Singles: with Eternal: Stay, 1993; Power of a Woman, 1995; I Am Blessed, 1995; Good Thing, 1996; Secrets, 1996; Don't You Love, 1997; I Wanna Be The Only One (No. 1, UK), 1997; Angel of Mine, 1997; solo: Higher Than Heaven, 1999; I Wanna Know, 2000. *Honours:* BRIT Award Nominations: Best Group, Best Newcomers, Best Album, Best Dance Act, 1995; Best Dance Act, 1996; Smash Hits Award; International Dance Award, Dance Act of The Year, 1995; Only UK act to have 6 Top 15 hits from debut album. *Current Management:* First Avenue Management, The Courtyard, 42 Colwith Rd, London W6 9EY, England.

BRYANT Colin; b. 20 Nov. 1936, Poole, Dorset, England. Musician (clarinet, saxophones). m. (1) 1 s., 2 d., (2). *Musical Education:* Privately taught; Later, Royal Marines School of Music. *Career:* Professional musician since leaving school; Principal clarinet, Band of Royal Marines, 1950s; Clarinet saxophone with Nat Gonnella, late 1950s; Toured with Louis Armstrong All Stars, 1962; Tours, performances, throughout Europe; Featured in film with Joe Darensburg (Louis Armstrong's clarinetist); Jazzband leader, The Hot Rhythm Orchestra, Cunard QE2, 1975–97; Cruises every year for 21 years; Many BBC Radio and ITV performances; Only jazzband invited to play at The Houses of Parliament; Director of Entertainment Agency; Numerous recordings on own Hot Rhythm label. *Honours:* Melody Maker Poll Winner, Best Jazz Clarinet, 1963. *Membership:* Musicians' Union. *Leisure interests:* Ships; Birds. *Current Management:* C B Entertainments. *Address:* 24 Bushmead Dr., Ringwood, Hants BH24 2HU, England.

BRYANT Dana; b. 2 May 1965, New York City, USA. Spoken word artist. *Education:* BA, Brandeis University. *Career:* Jazz festivals: Vienna, 1992; Berlin Jazz, 1992; Brighton Jazz Bop, 1993; Television: The Charlie Rose

Show, 1992; Fighting Wordz, MTV, 1992; Spoken Word Unplugged, 1993; The South Bank Show, Ch 4, 1994; The Girlie Show, London, Ch 4, 1996. *Recordings:* Dominican Girdles Heat, 1993; Wishing From The Top, 1996; Also appears on: Quiet Revolution, 1993; Time and Love, 1997; Adventures of Bread and Butter, 1998; Jazzonia, 1998. *Publication:* Song of The Siren, 1995. *Membership:* ASCAP. *Current Management:* Knitting; Fencing; Cycling. *Address:* c/o The Groove Academy, 62 White St, Suite 312, New York, NY 10013, USA.

BRYANT Gerry; b. 30 April 1965, Portsmouth, England. Musician (bass guitar). *Education:* Technical Colleges. *Career:* Bass guitarist, group Mega City Four, touring throughout Europe including Scandinavia, Japan, US and Canada, 1988–; Appeared on Peel Sessions, 1988–93; The Word, Ch4, 1992; Concerts include: Reading Festival, 1990–92; Glastonbury Festival, 1993; Phoenix Festival, 1994; Sound Engineer and Tour Manager, 1996–2001; Tours of: USA; New Zealand; Australia; Europe/UK; Director: The Rooms Rehearsal Studios Ltd. *Recordings:* with Mega City Four: Tranzophobia, 1988; Who Cares Wins, 1989; Terribly Sorry Bob, 1990; Sebastopol Road, 1992; Inspiringly Titled... (live album), 1992; Magic Bullets, 1993; Soulscraper, 1996; with Serpico: Everyone Vs Everyone, 2001. *Publication:* Tall Stories and Creepy Crawlies, Mega City Four biography, 1994. *Membership:* Musicians' Union. *Leisure interests:* Going to concerts; Football; British stately homes and castles; Travel. *Current Management:* Paul Bolton, ICM/Fair Warning. *Address:* 12 Orwell Close, Farnborough, Hnats, GU14 9LR, England.

BRYANT Teri; b. 2 May 1961, Walgrave, Northamptonshire, England. Musician (drums, percussion). m. Juliet, 3 Oct. 1992, 1 d. *Musical Education:* Self-taught. *Career:* Member, group Iona, 1992–; Toured, recorded with artists from UK and USA including: Steve Taylor; Cliff Richard; Darrell Mansfield; Sheila Walsh; Lies Damned Lies; Ben Okafor; Graham Kendrick; Ishmael; Phil and John (The Woodthieves); Iona; Richard Darbyshire; Martin Smith; Noel Richards; Dave Bilbrough; Adrian Snell; Paul Field; Others including 6 years with Peter Murphy (ex-Bauhaus), including 3 albums, extensive tours, USA, Japan, Israel, Europe. *Recordings:* Love Hysteria, 1987; Deep, 1989; Don't Look Now, 1989; Iona, 1990; Holy Smoke, 1991; Book of Kells, 1992; Beyond These Shores, 1994; Journey Into The Morn, 1995; Heaven's Bright Sun, 1997; Arms of Mercy, 1998; Solo: Psalm, 1995; Timbrel, 1999. *Honours:* GMA International Artist Award: The Book of Kells, 1993. *Membership:* Musicians' Union. *Address:* PO Box 5229, Ealing, London W5 2GD, England.

BRYCE Owen; b. 8 Aug. 1920, Woolwich, London, England. Musician (trumpet, piano); Writer; Lecturer. m. Iris Edith, 22 Dec. 1945, 1 s., 3 d. *Career:* Founder member, George Webb's Dixielanders, many records, broadcasts; Own band, 1956–; Many broadcasts, appearances include Savoy Hotel; Lecturer for many organizations, county councils, colleges, summer schools; First speaker on Jazz on BBC Schools Service; Teacher, pupils include Chris Barber; Cy Laurie. *Publications:* Let's Play Jazz 1–4; Book on British Jazz Scene 1942–55, to be published. *Honours:* Diploma Polish Music Festival; Freeman of New Orleans. *Membership:* Musicians' Union. *Leisure interests:* Croquet; Stamp collecting. *Address:* 58 Pond Bank, Blisworth, Northants NN7 3EL, England.

BRYDOY Eivind; b. 20 June 1964, Levanger, Norway. Artist Man. *Education:* MBA, Norwegian School of Economics; University of New Orleans; UMIST, Manchester, England. *Career:* Stageway, 3 years; Controller, Stageway Record Company, 1 year; Agency Dept, Stageway, 2 years; Manager, Artistpartner, own company, 4 years. *Publication:* Eureka Collaborative Agreements, 1992. *Membership:* General Secretary, International Managers Forum, Norway. *Leisure interest:* Sailing. *Current Management:* Cecilia, Ephemera Cornflakes, Baba Nation, Trang Fodsel, Di Derre. *Address:* Grini Naeringspark 17, 1345 Osteraas, Norway.

BRYNGELSSON Hans Inge Peter; b. 17 Sept. 1955, Vetlanda, Sweden. Musician; Composer. m. Anita Malmguist Bryngelsson, 11 Dec. 1986, 1 s. *Education:* Vallehilde Folkhojskole Dramatic Institute; Private courses in composition. *Career:* Leader of the Band Ragnarö, 1972–84, 4 albums; Leader, Triangulus, 1985–89, 2 albums; Guitarsis, Music for 10 guitars, Urban Turban, 1993–; Composed music for film, theatre, expositions, radio and TV. *Compositions:* Via, 1990; Happy Starr, 1992; Sound of Glass, 1995; Guitarrsis, Music for 10 guitarists; Katabasis, Music for 5 bass instr. *Recordings:* Ragnarö, 1976; King Tung, 1979; Via, 1990; Urban Turban, 1994; Urban Turban Overtime, 1996; Astro Turf, 1998. *Publications:* Ode to the Stone, TV-film, 1991; The Other Shore Michael Wiström, TV-film, 1992; Snalast, TV-film, 1997. *Honours:* 3 grammy nominations in Sweden, 1990, 1993, 1997; STIM's Musical Prize, SKAPs Musical Prize. *Memberships:* STIM; SKAP; SAMI. *Leisure interests:* Ski vacations; Tennis; Crosswords; Contemporary Art.

BRYSON (Robert) Peabo; b. 13 April 1951, Greenville, South Carolina, USA. Soul Vocalist; Prod. *Career:* Former member, Moses Dillard; Tex-Town Display; Michael Zager's Moon Band, 1976–78; Solo artiste, 1979–.

Recordings: Albums: Reaching For The Sky, 1978; Crosswinds, 1978; We're The Best of Friends (with Natalie Cole), 1979; Live – and More (with Roberta Flack), 1980; Paradise, 1980; I Am Love, 1981; Turn The Hands of Time, 1981; Don't Play With Fire, 1982; Born To Love (with Roberta Flack), 1983; The Peabo Bryson Collection, 1984; Straight From The Heart, 1984; Quiet Storm, 1986; Take No Prisoners, 1987; Positive, 1988; All My Love, 1989; Can You Stop The Rain, 1991; Tonight I Celebrate My Love, 1992; Through The Fire, 1994; Peace On Earth, 1997; Family Christmas, 1998; Unconditional Love, 1999; Singles: Closer Than Close; Lost In The Night; Shower You With Love; Why Goodbye; How Wonderful We Are; Light The World; with Michael Zager's Moon Band: Reaching For The Sky; I'm So Into You; Solo: If Ever You're In My Arms Again, 1984; Duets: Gimme Some Time, with Natalie Cole, 1979; Tonight I Celebrate My Love, with Roberta Flack (No. 2, UK), 1983; Beauty and The Beast, with Celine Dion, 1992; Other duets with Melissa Manchester; Regina Belle; Other collaborations include: Kenny G, Barry Mann, Minnie Riperton; Contributor, Color and Light – Jazz Sketches On Sondheim, 1995. *Current Management:* David M. Franklin and Associates, 999 Peachtree St, Suite 2680, Atlanta, GA 30309, USA.

BRYSON David; b. 5 Oct. 1961, San Francisco, California, USA. Musician (Guitar). *Career:* Formed acoustic duo with Adam Duritz; Became Counting Crows; Numerous headlining tours and TV appearances including MTV. *Recordings:* Singles: Round Here, 1994; Mr Jones, 1994; Rain King, 1994; Angels of the Silence (live), 1996; Albums: August and Everything After, 1993; Recovering the Satellites, 1996; Across a Wire: Live in New York, 1998; Long December, 1999; Daylight Fading, 1999; Guest Appearances: Steve Walsh, Schemer-Dreamer, 1980; Wild Flowers, Tales Like These, 1990; Faith No More, Angel Dust, 1992; Steve Taylor, Squint, 1993; Sordid Humor, Light Music for Dying People, 1994; Train: Train, 1998, Meet Virginia, 1999; Better Days, Leaving The Blue, 2001; Blue Druids, Roadsigns Towards Antiquity, 2001.

BRYSON William Shields; b. 10 Nov. 1946, Evanston, Illinois, USA. Musician (bass); Singer. m. Anne Jeanine Bailey, 24 July 1976. *Career:* Bass player, Bluegrass Cardinals; Country Gazette; Doug Dillard Band; The Long Riders with Ry Cooder, 1980–84; The Desert Rose Band, 1984-. *Recordings:* Albums include: What A Way Earn A Living, Country Gazette, 1977; Long Riders (film soundtrack), Ry Cooder, 1980; Jackrabbit, Doug Dillard, 1980; Home Coming and Family Reunion, The Dillards, 1980; with The Desert Rose Band: The Desert Rose Band, 1987; Running, 1988; Pages of Life, 1990; True Love, 1991; A Dozen Roses, 1991. *Honours:* Grammy Nominations, 1987, 1989; ACM Awards: Bass Player of the Year, 1990; Touring Band of the Year, Desert Rose Band, 1988–90. *Memberships:* Screen Actors Guild; AFTRA; AFofM.

BRZEZICKI Mark; b. 21 June 1957, Slough, Berkshire, England. Musician (drums, percussion). *Education:* City and Guilds, HNC, Aircraft Engineering, Brooklands Technical College. *Career:* Member of Big Country, 1981–; Tours include: Fish, 1990–91; Midge Ure, 1991–92; Procol Harum, USA 1991, Europe, 1992; Major concerts include: Mandela Concert, Wembley Stadium, 1989; Annual Princes Trust Rock Galas, 1985–88; Procol Harum European Festivals, 1992; Chieftains, Midge Ure, Roger Daltrey show, 1994; Television appearances include: Children in Need, 1989, BBC; ITV Telethon Live, 1992; BBC Breakfast Time; Phil Collins' This Is Your Life; Appearances with Sting; Nils Lofgren; Procol Harum; The Cult; Tears For Fears; Fish; Midge Ure; Big Country. *Recordings:* Big Country albums including: The Crossing, 1983; Steeltown (No. 1, UK), 1984; The Seer, 1986 and 7 others; also 5 albums with Pete Townshend; 3 with Midge Ure; 4 Prince's Trust Rock Gala Compilations; Also appeared on albums by artists including: Roger Daltrey; Simon Townshend; Procol Harum; Love and Money; The Cult; Fish; Nils Lofgren; Joan Armatrading; Ultravox; Howard Jones; Nik Kershaw; Steve Harley; Go West; Tom Robinson; Played on film soundtracks: Quick Silver Lightning; Rambo 3; Restless Natives; White City. *Honours:* Invited Special Guest, World Drum Festival, Canada, 1987; 2 Grammy Nominations, 1984; Zildjian Musician Poll, Best Rock/Pop mainstream drummer UK, 1988–90; Making Music Poll, 1988; Pearl Drummers Club, Best UK Rock/Pop drummer, 1990; Princes Trust Award, 1984; Numerous Platinum, Gold and Silver records. *Memberships:* Prince's Trust; GISM; PRS. *Leisure interest:* Boating. *Current Management:* Ian Grant Management. *Address:* Owl House, Byers Lane, South Godstone, Surrey RH9 8JL, England.

BT (Brian Transeau), (Libra; Elastic Chakra); b. Washington DC, USA. Prod.; Remixer. *Musical Education:* Berklee School of Music, Boston, USA. *Career:* Played synthesiser on a Salt 'N 'Pepa album; Started producing for Deep Dish's label; Signed to Perfecto, 1995; Began remixing, notably on his reworking of Tori Amos' Blue Skies; Collaborations: Deep Dish; Sasha; Tsunami One; Remixed: Billie Ray Martin; Madonna; Seal; Mike Oldfield. *Address:* c/o Pioneer Entertainment, Pioneer House, Hollybush Hill, Stoke Poges, Slough, SL2 4QP, England.

BUARQUE Chico; b. 1944, Rio de Janeiro, Brazil. Vocalist; Musician (guitar); Songwriter. *Career:* Brother of vocalist Miucha, uncle of Bebel Gilberto; Dropped out of University of Sao Paulo to absorb local Bossa Nova scene and began writing songs; Came to prominence when compositions recorded by vocalist Nara Leao; Made first record Pedro Pedriero, 1965; Wrote and scored the play Roda Vida, 1968; Recorded Construction, containing more political works, 1971; Subsequently forced to submit work to government censorship board; Virtually all compositions rejected by 1975; Freely performs, records, writes songs, books and plays as well as scoring films, 1980s-. *Compositions:* Pedro Pedreiro; A Banda; Carolina; Roda Viva; Saiba; Construcao; Folhetim; Vai Passar. *Recordings:* Albums include: Chico Buarque De Hollanda, 1966; Construcao, 1971; Vida, 1980; Chico Buarque, 1984; Caetano E Chico Juntos E Ao Vivo, 1993; Chico Buarque En Espanol, 1997; As Cidades, 1999; Chico Buarque Song Book #8, 2001. *Internet:* www.uol.com.br/chicobuarque.

BUCHANAN Margo; b. 3 Feb. 1955, Lanark, Scotland. Vocalist. m. Paul Wickens, 31 Jan. 1992. *Career:* Television: European promotional tour, Billy Idol, 1986; Concert By The Lake, with Eric Clapton, Phil Collins, Steve Winwood, 1988; Amnesty International Concert, with Dave Gilmour, Seal, Tom Jones, 1990; Concert with Billy Bragg, Hugh Cornwall, London Palladium, 1990; The Great Music Experience, with Joni Mitchell, Bob Dylan, Bon Jovi, 1994. *Recordings:* with Tina Turner: Break Every Rule, 1987; with Mink Deville: Silver Bullets; Recording/writing with Sam Brown: This Feeling; Your Love Is All; It Makes Me Wonder; With A Little Love; As One; with Jools Holland: No-One's To Blame. *Memberships:* Musicians' Union; Equity. *Leisure interests:* Concerts; Dolls houses; Films; Gardens. *Current Management:* One Management, 43 St Albans Ave, London W4 5JS, England.

BUCHANAN Wallis; b. 27 Nov. 1965, London, England. Musician (didgeridoo, vibraphone). *Career:* Member, Jamiroquai; Numerous tours and TV appearances. *Recordings:* Singles: When You Gonna Learn, 1993; Too Young To Die, 1993; Blow Your Mind, 1993; Emergency On Planet Earth, 1993; Space Cowboy EP, 1994; Half The Man, 1994; Stillness In Time, 1995; Virtual Insanity, 1996; Cosmic Girl, 1996; Light Years, 1996; Alright, 1997; Deeper Underground (No. 1, UK), 1998; High Times, 1997; Canned Heat, 1999; Little L, 2001; Albums: Emergency on Planet Earth (No. 1, UK), 1993; Travelling Without Moving, 1996; Synkronized, 1999; A Funk Odyssey, 2001. *Honours:* Gold and Platinum Albums; Several MTV Video Music Awards.

BUCHANAN-HINDLEY Aileen; b. 26 July 1964, Kippen, Stirlingshire, Scotland. Musician (accordion). m. Guy Hindley, 6 July 1996. *Education:* Accordion lessons with W Campbell. *Career:* Lead Accordion with Carousel Ceilidh Band, 1997–; Winter season work with Inversnaid Hotel, Loch Lomond, Scotland, 1977. *Leisure interests:* Musician for team of Morris dancers; Various accordion clubs. *Address:* 32 Tuxford Rd, Ansdell, Lytham St Annes, Lancashire FY8 4BH, England.

BUCHWALD Martyn Jerel; b. 30 Jan. 1942, Cincinnatti, USA. m. Karen Deal, Aug. 1989, 2 d. *Career:* 52 years in the music business. *Compositions:* Miracles; Count on Me; Runaway; Atlanta Lady; Comin Back to Me. *Recordings:* Airplane; Starship; PKA Marty Balin. *Honours:* Rock and Roll Hall of Fame; BAM Award; BMI Award. *Memberships:* AFM; AFTRA; SAG. *Leisure interests:* Reading; Travel; Painting; Music. *Address:* 436 Bevedere St, San Francisco, CA 94117, USA.

BUCK Gary Ralph; b. 21 March 1940, Thessalon, Ontario, Canada. Singer; Record Prod.; Songwriter. m. Deb Way, 2 s., 3 d. *Career:* Singer, most major Country Music television and radio shows, US and Canada; Tours throughout USA, Canada (Calgary Exhibition promotion), England, New Zealand (Miss NZ Pageant); Publisher, composer, songwriter for Calgary's Olympic bid; Music for commercials include: Pepsi, Molson's Export Ale, Kelloggs' Raisin Bran, Mastercard, Ford; Television appearances include: Gary Buck Show, CKCO TV, 1965–67; Host, Maritime Telethon, 3 times; Founder, President, Canadian Country Music Hall of Fame; Manager, Capitol Records Publishing Division, 3 years; Started Broadland Publishing Co; Became Broadlands International Records, 1991; International Director, Country Music Association, Nashville, 10 years; Founding Director, Academy of Country Music Entertainment, now known as Canadian Country Music Association; Literary Agent for Hank Snow; Producer of over 100 albums, launched careers of Wayne Rostad; Family Brown; Dallas Harms; Lee Roy Anderson; Currently producer for Gene Watson; Billie Jo Spears; George Hamilton IV. *Honours:* Top Male Singer, Canada, 5 times; Top Country Record Producer, 1975; Medal of Merit, City of Sault Ste Marie, for contributions to music industry, 1990.

BUCK Peter; b. 6 Dec. 1956. Musician (guitar); Prod. *Career:* Member, R.E.M., 1980–; International tours; Also member, side-project, Hindu Love Gods, 1986–90. *Recordings:* Albums: with R.E.M.: Chronic Town (mini-album), 1982; Murmur, 1983; Reckoning, 1984; Fables of The Reconstruction, 1985; Life's Rich Pageant, 1986; Dead Letter Office,

1987; Document, 1987; Eponymous, 1988; Green, 1988; Out of Time (No. 1, UK and US), 1991; The Best of R.E.M., 1991; Automatic For The People (No. 1, UK), 1992; Monster (No. 1, UK), 1994; New Adventures In Hi-Fi, (No. 1, UK) 1996; Up, 1998; Star Profiles, 1999; Reveal (No. 1, UK), 2001; with Hindu Love Gods: Hindu Love Gods, 1990; Singles include: with R.E.M.: It's The End of The World As We Know It (and I Feel Fine), 1987; The One I Love, 1987; Finest Worksong, 1988; Stand, 1989; Orange Crush, 1989; Losing My Religion, 1991; Shiny Happy People, 1991; Near Wild Heaven, 1991; Radio Song, 1991; Drive, 1992; Man On The Moon, 1992; The Sidewinder Sleeps Tonite, 1993; Everybody Hurts, 1993; Nightswimming, 1993; What's The Frequency, Kenneth?, 1994; Bang and Blame, 1994; Crush With Eyeliner, 1995; Strange Currencies, 1995; Tongue, 1996; E-Bow The Letter, 1996; Bittersweet Me, 1996; Electrolite, 1996; Daysleeper, 1998; Lotus, 1998; At My Most Beautiful, 1999; The Great Beyond, 2000; Imitation of Life, 2001; All The Way To Reno (You're Gonna Be A Star), 2001; Tracks featured on film soundtracks: Bachelor Party, 1984; Until The End of The World, 1991; Coneheads, 1993; Man On The Moon, 1999; Other recordings: with Indigo Girls; Warren Zevon; Billy Bragg; The Dream Academy; eels; Robyn Hitchcock; Liz Phair; Contributor, albums: Tom's Album; I'm Your Fan; Time Inbetween; Producer, albums by Uncle Tupelo; Vigilantes of Love. *Honours:* Earth Day Award, 1990; Numerous MTV Music Video Awards; Billboard Awards; Best Modern Rock Artist, Best World Album, 1991; BRIT Awards: Best International Group, 1992, 1993, 1995; Grammy Awards: Best Pop Performance, Alternative Music Album, Music Video, 1992; Atlanta Music Awards: Act of The Year, Rock Album, Video, 1992; IRMA, International Band of The Year, 1993; Rolling Stone Critics Awards: Best Band, Best Album, 1993; Q Awards: Best Album, 1991, 1992; Best Act In The World, 1991, 1995. *Current Management:* REM/Athens Ltd, 250 W Clayton St, Athens, GA 30601, USA.

BUCKINGHAM Lindsey; b. 3 Oct. 1947. Musician (guitar); Vocalist; Songwriter. *Career:* Member, rock band Fritz, 1960s; Duo, Buckingham Nicks (with Stevie Nicks), 1971–74; Member, Fleetwood Mac, 1975–87; Solo artiste, 1981–; Appearances include: Regular US tours; Madison Square Garden; US Festival, 1982. *Compositions:* with Fleetwood Mac: Second Hand News; Tusk; Go Your Own Way; Big Love; Oh Diane. *Recordings:* Albums: with Buckingham Nicks: Buckingham Nicks, 1973; with Fleetwood Mac: Fleetwood Mac, 1975; Rumours, 1977; Tusk, 1979; Live, 1980; Mirage (also producer), 1982; Tango In The Night, 1987; Behind The Mask, 1990; Time, 1995; Dance, 1997; Solo albums: Law and Order, 1981; Go Insane, 1984; Out of The Cradle, 1992; Singles with Fleetwood Mac: Over My Head; Rhiannon (Will You Ever Win); Say You Love Me; Dreams; You Make Loving Fun; Tusk; Sara; Think About Me; Trouble; Gypsy; Solo singles: Soul Drifter, 1992; Countdown, 1992; Don't Look Down, 1993; Also appears on: Building The Perfect Beast, Don Henley, 1984; Behind The Sun, Eric Clapton, 1985; Songs and Music, Tom Petty, 1996; Unchained, Johnny Cash, 1996; Show Must Go On, Leo Sayer, 1996; Guilty: 30 Years of Randy Newman, 1998; Trouble In Shangri-La, Stevie Nicks, 2001. *Honours:* Grammy Award, Fleetwood Mac, Rumours, 1977; American Music Awards: Favourite Pop/Rock Group, Favourite Album, 1978. *Current Management:* Michael Brokaw Management, 2934 Beverly Glen Circle #383, Bel Air, CA 90077, USA.

BUCKLAND Jon; b. 11 Sept. 1978, Mold, Wales. Musician (guitar); Songwriter. *Education:* University College, London. *Career:* Member: Coldplay, 1998-. *Recordings:* Albums: Parachutes, 2000; Singles: The Safety EP, 1998; Brothers and Sisters, The Blue Room EP, 1999; Shiver, Yellow, Trouble, 2000. *Honours:* Brit Award, Best Album, 2001; Mercury Music Prize, nominee, 2000. *Current Management:* Phil Harvey. *Internet:* www.coldplay.com.

BUCKLEY Steve; b. 6 Jan. 1959, Orpington, Kent, England. Musician (saxophones, bass clarinet, tin whistle). *Education:* Leeds University degree. *Musical Education:* Classical clarinet tuition at school. *Career:* Tours, recordings with Loose Tubes; Delightful Precipice; Human Chain; Numerous television and radio appearances with these bands; Long association with South American, African London-based bands; Current projects include Buckley Batchelor, impro trio with Steve Noble and Oren Marshall. *Recordings:* Open Letter, Loose Tubes; Third Policeman, Django Bates; Summer Fruits, Delightful Precipice; Winter Truce, Delightful Precipice; Whole and The Half, Buckley Batchelor; Pyrotechnics, Human Chain; Life as We Know It, Buckley Batchelor; Barrel Organ Far From Home, Huw Warren. *Address:* 140 Amelia St, London SE17 3AR, England.

BUDD Stephen; b. 25 Dec. 1958, London, England. m. 6 June 1986, 1 d., 1 s. *Career:* Started Torch Records, age 20, 1979; Signed: The Sound; The Cardiacs; Big Sound Authority; Manager: The Sound, Big Sound Authority; Sally Oldfield, 1980–85; Managed producers, Tony Visconti, Arthur Baker, 1985–88; Started Stephen Budd Management, managing producers: Martyn Ware; Mike Hedges; Rick Nowels; Rafe McKenna; Arthur Baker, Steve Levine, Charlie Rapino, Gary Katz and others 1988–; Formed Morrison Budd Music Publishing, with partner Bryan Morrison, 1993–; Formed Supervision Management with Paul Craig, for artists Lloyd Cole, Heaven 17, The Webb Brothers, Dark Flower, Seventh Son, Screaming

Orphans, Sherena Dugani, 1999-. *Honours:* Numerous Gold, Platinum discs. *Memberships:* Board mem., International Managers Forum; Chairman, Producer Managers Group. *Leisure interests:* Eating; Arsenal Football Club; Films of Russ Meyer. *Current Management:* Stephen Budd Management, 109B Regents Park Rd, London NW1 8UR, England.

BUDDE Martin; b. 25 Oct. 1966, Aarhus, Denmark. Musician (Drums, Organ). *Career:* Drummer, Godless Wicked Creeps, 1991–; Organist, The Defectors, 1997-. *Recordings:* with Godless Wicked Creeps: Victim of Science; Hellcoholic; Hystereo; with Defector: Allright Girl; Album, Let Me. *Membership:* Danish Music Society. *Address:* Laessoesgade 53 2th8000 Aarhus, Denmark.

BUDTS Danny; b. 12 May 1958, Wilrijk, Belgium. Production Officer. m. Machteld de Muynck, 6 Nov. 1982, 2 s. *Musical Education:* Self-taught guitar, synthesizer, studio equipment, singer, songwriter, composer, producer. *Career:* Lead Guitar, Cold Turkey, 1970s; Syndromeda, own midi studio, 1990; Different interviews on local radios. *Recordings:* Mind Trips, 1997; Circles of Life, 1997; The Legacy of God, 1998; Birth of a Black Hole, 1999; Tracks on: Truth or Dare; Movements; Sequences 14 and 19. *Honour:* Movements, CD, composition contest, 1997. *Leisure interests:* Music, Music and Music. *Current Management:* Groove Unlimited, PO Box 2171, 8203 AD, Lelystad, Netherlands. *Address:* Pastoryveld 28, 2180 Ekeren, Belgium.

BUDWEISEROVA Irena; b. 8 Nov. 1957, Rokycany, Czech Republic. Singer. m. Pavel Barta, 4 Jan. 1986, 1 d. *Education:* Conservatoire. *Career:* Member, Folk/Jazz group, Spiritual Kvintet, 1980–; Own Band, Budweiserova and Friends, Jazz, Blues, Soul, 1988–; Performed in 4 musicals, 2 on stage in Prague, 1993–; Speak About the Music, Czech Radio, 1997–98; Professor, Conservatoire of Jaroslav Jezek, Prague, 1998–; Concerts with Classical Guitar, Jan Zacek, Germany; Jazz concerts; Tour of Europe, Canada, USA, South America, Australia. *Recordings:* 15 CDs with Spiritual Kvintet; With own group: Blue Soul, 1993; Moment, 1995; Taking of the Skin, 1996; Guest on CDs: Walking and Talking, Josef Vejvoda Big Band, The Raven with ASPM Group; 2 CDs with Rangers; 2 CDs from musicals Bastard and Babylon. *Honours:* Female Vocalist of the Year, 1983; Nominated, Jazz CD in 1993, Prague; Nomination, Prize, Thalia, 1998. *Memberships:* Federation of Authors in Interprets; Czech Jazz Company. *Leisure interests:* Music; Dancing; Theatre; Films; Travel. *Current Management:* Pavel Barta Agency. *Address:* Varsavska 29, 120 00 Prague 2, Czech Republic.

BUFFETT Jimmy; b. 25 Dec. 1946, Pascagoula, Mississippi, USA. Country Singer; Songwriter. m. Jane Slagsvol, 27 Aug. 1977. *Education:* BS, History, Journalism, University of Southern California, 1969. *Career:* Former freelance journalist, Inside Sports Outside magazine; Billboard magazine; Solo artiste, 1970s-; Formed Coral Reef Band, 1975. *Compositions include:* Railroad Lady (recorded by Merle Haggard); He Went To Paris (recorded by Waylon Jennings); Margaritaville; Come Monday; Cheeseburger In Paradise. *Recordings:* Albums: Down To Earth, 1972; High Cumberland Jubilee, 1972; A White Sport Coat and A Pink Crustacean, 1973; Living and Dying In 3/4 Time, 1974; A1A, 1974; Rancho Deluxe (film soundtrack), 1975; Havana Daydreaming, 1976; Changes In Latitudes, Changes In Attitudes, 1977; Son of a Son of a Sailor, 1978; You Had To Be There, 1978; Volcano, 1979; Coconut Telegraph, 1980; Somewhere Over China, 1981; One Particular Harbour, 1983; Riddles In The Sand, 1984; Last Mango In Paris, 1985; Songs You Know By Heart, 1986; Floridays, 1986; Hot Water, 1988; Off To See The Lizard, 1989; Live Feeding Frenzy, 1991; Before The Beach, 1993; Fruitcakes, 1994; Margaritaville Cafe, 1995; Barometer Soup, 1995; Late Night Gumbo, 1995; Banana Wind, 1996; Christmas Island, 1996; Don't Stop The Carnival, 1998; Biloxi, 1998; Beach House On The Moon, 1999. *Publication:* Tales From Margaritaville, 1989. *Honours:* Platinum and Gold discs. *Memberships:* Hon. director, Greenpeace; Founder mem., Cousteau Society. *Current Management:* Howard Kaufman, HK Management, 8900 Wilshire Blvd, Suite 300, Beverly Hills, CA 90211, USA.

BUHRER Rolf Marcel; b. 28 June 1932, Zurich, Switzerland. Musician (valve-bone, upright string bass). 1 s. *Career:* Member of bands: Laferrière; Claude Luter; Mixim Saury; Played with: Albert Nicolas; Mezz Mezzrow; Harry 'Sweets' Edison; Eddie Davis; Moustache; Tours: France, Germany, North Africa; Numerous recordings. *Membership:* UMJ (Union Musician de Jazz).

BUIRETTE Michele Jeanne; b. 4 March 1949, Boulogne Sur Seine, France. Musician (accordion). 1 d. *Education:* Maitrise de Psychologie. *Career:* Jazz Festivals: Le Mans; Berlin; Grenoble; Tours, Europe: Germany; Netherlands; Switzerland; Italy; Croatia; Slovenia. *Recordings:* with Pied de Poule: Indiscretion; Café Noir; Jamais Tranquille!; Solo: La Mise En Plis. *Membership:* SACEM. *Current Management:* Edna Fainaru. *Address:* 63 Blvd de Ménilmoutant, 75011 Paris, France.

BUKEM LTJ (Danny Williamson), (Apollo); b. 1967, Watford, Hertfordshire, England. Prod.; Remixer; DJ. *Career:* Started career as DJ, late 1980s; Got break playing at the Biology raves; Founder: Good Looking Records; Promoter: Logical Progression and Speed club nights in London; World-wide DJ; Club residency at The End, London; Collaborations: MC Conrad; Peshay; Remixed: Jodeci; The Shamen; Grace; Michelle Gayle. *Recordings:* Albums: Journey Inwards, 2000; LTJ Bukem – Producer, 2001; Singles: Demon's Theme, 1993; Music, 1994; Horizons, 1995; Rhodes To Freedom, 1999; Sunrain, 2000. *Membership:* PRS. *Address:* c/o Good Looking Records, 84 Queen's Rd, Watford, Hertfordshire, WD17 2LA, England. *Internet:* www.thegoodlookingorganisation.co.uk.

BUKOVSKY Petr; b. 1 April 1947, Prague, Czech Republic. Divorced, 1 s., 1 d. *Musical Education:* Self-taught guitar, piano. *Career:* Songwriter, Radio, TV, Gramophone Companies (Pop, Rock, Brass and Dance Music), 1970-. *Recordings:* The Angel Ship, 1970; The Lime, The Lime My, 1974; Today We Will Polka Play to You, 1974; Lidice Warns, 1975; The Easter Rod, 1975; The Gamekeeper's Lodge, 1982; I Know, 1995; Today For the Last Time, 1997; I Can't Call You, 1997; The Caravan, 1998; I Have the Cottage, 1998; We Dance Tango, 1998. *Honours:* Today We Will Polka Play to You, 1974; The Easter Rod, 1975. *Membership:* OSA, Czech Republic. *Leisure interests:* Literature; Music; Sports. *Address:* Bukovsky Petr, Vitosska 3415/11, 14300 Prague 4, Modrany, Czech Republic.

BULOW Harry Timothy; b. 19 Feb. 1951, Des Moines, Iowa, USA. Composer; Conductor; Musician (Saxophone). m. Ellen Bulow, 18 June 1992, 1 s., 1 d. *Musical Education:* BA, Music, San Diego State University, 1975; MA, 1978, PhD, 1983, University of California at Los Angeles. *Career:* Composer of film scores, popular songs and jazz. *Compositions:* Film music: The Burglar, 1979–80; Popular songs: Touch My Life; He Is The Lord; All The Love I Had For You; I Don't Know Why; It's Jesus; Jazz: Kickback; Crystal Cove; Milpas Street Blues; Sola Street Strut; Hilo Bay; Distant Memory. *Recordings:* Numerous. *Honour:* Henry Mancini Award for Film Music Composition, 1980. *Memberships:* ASCAP; Society of Composers; Southeastern Composers League, USA. *Address:* PO Box 806, Mooresville, NC 28117, USA.

BUNDRICK John Douglas, (Rabbit); b. 21 Nov. 1948, Baytown, Texas, USA. Musician (keyboards, piano, hammond organ); Composer. m. Susan Elizabeth Vickers, 17 Sept. 1989. *Musical Education:* Piano lessons, age 7; School and college music. *Career:* Musical Director, composer, Johnny Nash, Sweden, 1971; Moved to UK, 1971; Member, Free, 1972; Eric Burdon, 1975; Co-founder, Crawler, 1976–79; The Who, 1979–; Concerts include Live Aid Concert, Wembley, 1985; Pete Townshend, US tour, 1993; Roger Daltrey, Carnegie Hall Concert, US tour, 1994; Television: Garth Brooks, BBC TV; Jay Leno Show, Los Angeles; Prolific session musician. *Recordings:* Numerous albums include: with The Who: Face Dances; Who's Better Who's Best; The Singles; Join Together; Live Aid; with Johnny Nash: I Can See Clearly Now; Celebrate Life; Here Again; My Merry Go Round; with Free: Heartbreaker; Free Story; The Best of Free; with Pete Townshend: Rough Mix; Empty Glass; Psychoderelict; White City; with Andy Fairweather-Low: La Booga Rooga; Be Bop 'N' Holla; with Rabbit: Dream Jungle; Broken Arrows; Dark Saloon; Run For Cover; Same Old Story; Solo albums include: Moccasin Warrior, 1997, Moccasin Warrior II, 1998; Echoes of Africa, 1999; The Fairy Garden, 1999; Welcome to America, 2001; Other recordings include: Catch A Fire, Bob Marley; Solid Air, John Martyn; Show Some Emotion, Joan Armatrading; Catfish Rising, Jethro Tull; Back Street Crawler, Paul Kossoff; Cosmic Wheels, Donovan; Survivor, Eric Burdon; Highway To The Sun, Snowy White; A Celebration-The Music of Pete Townshend, Roger Daltrey; She's The Boss, Mick Jagger; Bebop The Future, David Essex; Live At The Albert Hall, David Gilmore; Amused To Death, Roger Waters; Other recordings with artistes including Tom Robinson; Backstreet Crawler; Claire Hamill; Sandy Denny; Suzi Quatro; Toots and the Maytals; Russ Ballard; Peter Frampton; Hank Wangford; Bill Wyman; Richard Thompson; Barbara Dickson; Boo Hewerdine; Kossoff, Kirke, Tetsu and Rabbit; Film soundtracks: Rocky Horror Picture Show; King Ralph; McVicar; Bad Timing. *Memberships:* PRS; Musicians' Union. *Leisure interests:* Gardening; Music; Animals. *Address:* c/o David Clayton, 39 Staverton Rd, Bilborough, Nottingham NG8 4ET, England.

BUNFORD Huw, (Bunf); b. 15 Sept. 1967, Cardiff, Wales. Musician (guitar). *Career:* Member, Super Furry Animals; Early releases on small indie label; Obtained major indie label deal; Numerous international tours, and many festival appearances. *Recordings:* Singles: Llanfairpwllgwyngyllgogerychwyndrobwl... EP, 1995; Moog Droog EP, 1995; God! Show Me Magic, 1996; If You Don't Want Me To Destroy You, 1996; The Man Don't Give A Fuck, 1996; Hometown Unicorn, 1996; Something 4 The Weekend, 1996; The International Language of Screaming, 1997; Hermann Loves Pauline, 1997; Demons, 1997; Play It Cool, 1997; Ice Hockey Hair, 1998; Northern Lights, 1999; Fire In My Heart, 1999; Do Or Die, 2000; Juxtaposed With You, 2001; Albums: Fuzzy Logic, 1996; Radiator, 1997; Outspaced (compilation), 1998; Guerrilla, 1999; Mwng, 2000; Rings Around The World, 2001.

BUNN Roger; b. Norwich, England. Musician (guitar, bass); Music Exec. *Musical Education:* Self-taught musician and composer. *Career:* Guitarist, bassist, Ken Stevens, Val Merril, Denny Mann big bands; Lead guitarist, numerous jazz quartets, Beatles, Djinn, Roger Bunn and Endjinn; Various recordings with Roxy Music, Daevid Allen, Billy Idol, Arthur Brown, Alexis Korner; MEC Blues Band, with Boz Burrell; Stagecoach with Roy Babbington; Bassist, Marianne Faithfull, Peggy Seeger, Pete Brown and Piblokto; Various stage and touring shows; Work on Mike McGear album Women; Session work in UK and abroad; Executive and Journalist; Editor, Tiger Alert; Director, Policy and Publishing Office, Music Industry Human Rights Association. *Compositions include:* Songs written with Pete Brown on Piblokio, 1971; Bare Arms, broadcast on Internet. *Recordings:* Solo album: Piece of Mind, 1971. *Honours:* Hon. Chief, African National Congress; Patron, Professional Golfers Assen European Tour; Runs golf course website. *Address:* MIHRA, 192 Chiswick Village, London W4 3DG, England.

BUNTON Emma Lee, (Baby Spice); b. 21 Jan. 1976, London, England. Vocalist. *Career:* Actress, including appearances in EastEnders; Member, Spice Girls; Numerous TV and radio appearances, many magazine interviews; Film, Spiceworld: The Movie, 1997; World tour including dates in UK, Europe, India and USA; Presenter on TV and radio including Radio 1 and satellite TV show; Solo date on Breast Cancer Awareness concert. *Recordings:* Singles: with Spice Girls: Wannabe (No. 1, UK and US), 1996; Say You'll Be There (No. 1, UK), 1996; 2 Become 1 (No. 1, UK), 1996; Mama/Who Do You Think You Are (No. 1, UK), 1997; Step To Me, 1997; Spice Up Your Life (No. 1, UK), 1997; Too Much (No. 1, UK), 1997; Stop, 1998; (How Does It Feel To Be) On Top of The World, 1998; Move Over/Generation Next, 1998; Viva Forever (No. 1, UK), 1998; Goodbye (No. 1, UK), 1998; Holler/Let Love Lead The Way (No. 1, UK), 2000; solo: What I Am (with Tin Tin Out), 1999; What Took You So Long? (No. 1, UK), 2001; Take My Breath Away, 2001; We're Not Gonna Sleep Tonight, 2001; Albums: with Spice Girls: Spice (No. 1, UK), 1996; Spiceworld (No. 1, UK), 1997; Forever, 2000; solo: A Girl Like Me, 2001. *Honours:* Brit Awards: Best British Single, Wannabe, 1997; Best-Selling British Album Act, 1998; Outstanding Contribution, 2000.

BURCH Bruce; b. Georgia, USA. Songwriter. m. Cindy. *Education:* College degree, University of Georgia. *Musical Education:* Self-taught guitar. *Career:* Football Coach, Gainsville High School; Signed to Combine Music, Nashville, to develop songwriting, then Famous Music; Co-founder, Burch Brothers Music (with brother David). *Compositions:* Hits include: Reba McEntire: Rumor Has It; T Graham Brown: The Last Resort; Billy Joe Royal: Out of Sight and On My Mind; Other songs recorded by: Reba McEntire; Aaron Tippin; George Fox; Dan Seals; Barbara Mandrell; Oak Ridge Boys. *Membership:* SESAC. *Address:* c/o SESAC, 55 Music E, Nashville, TN 37203, USA.

BURDON Eric; b. 11 May 1941, Walker, Newcastle, Tyne and Wear, England. Vocalist. *Education:* Newcastle College of Art and Industrial Design. *Career:* Member, The Pagans; Member, The Animals, 1963–67; Became Eric Burdon and The New Animals, 1968; Eric Burdon and War, 1970; Solo artiste, 1971–; Also, leader, Eric Burdon Band; Tours world-wide; Major concerts include: Monterey Pop Festival, 1967; Reading Festival, 1973; Film appearances: Top Gear, 1965; Stranger In The House, 1967; Joe Vs The Volcano, 1990. *Recordings:* Hit singles include: with The Animals: House of The Rising Sun (No. 1, UK and US), 1964; I'm Crying, 1964; Don't Let Me Be Misunderstood, 1965; Bring It On Home To Me, 1965; We've Gotta Get Out of This Place, 1965; It's My LIfe, 1965; Inside Looking Out, 1966; Don't Bring Me Down, 1966; Good Times, 1967; San Franciscan Nights, 1967; Albums: with the Animals: The Animals, 1964; Animal Tracks, 1965; The Animals On Tour, 1965; The Best of The Animals, 1966; The Most of The Animals, 1966; Animalisms, 1966; Animalization, 1966; Help Me Girl, 1967; When I Was Young, 1967; Best of (Vol. 2), 1967; Winds of Change, 1967; The Twain Shall Meet, 1968; Every One of Us, 1968; Love Is, 1969; Before We Were So Rudely Interrupted, 1977; Ark, 1983; Rip It To Shreds, 1984; with Eric Burdon and War: Eric Burdon Declares War, 1970; Black Man's Burdon, 1971; Solo/ Eric Burdon Band: Eric Is Here, 1967; Guilty, 1971; Ring of Fire, 1974; Sun Secrets, 1975; Stop (with Jimmy Witherspoon), 1975; Survivor, 1978; Gotta Find My Baby, 1979; Last Drive, 1980; Live, 1982; Comeback, 1982; I Used To Be An Animal, 1988; Wicked Man (with Jimmy Witherspoon), 1988; Crawling King Snake, 1992; Lost Within The Halls of Fame, 1995; Misunderstood, 1995; Soldier of Fortune, 1997; The Ultimate Comeback, 2001. *Publication:* Autobiography, I Used To Be An Animal, But I'm All Right Now, 1986. *Current Management:* c/o Denis Vaughan, Bond St House, 14 Clifford St, London W1X 2JD, England.

BURFORD Ian James; b. 14 Jan. 1963, Leicester, England. Musician (Guitar, Bass, Keyboards); Composer; Tutor of Music. m. Sandra Higginson, 15 May 1993, 1 s., 1 d. *Career:* Founder Member, Quasar, with David Hone, 1980–82; Solo Artist and Composer, 1982–; Guitar Tutor and Part-Time College Tutor of Music, 1996–; Composer, New Age Music, 1997-. *Compositions:* The Industrial City, 1985; Satellites, 1986; Nowhere to Go, 1986; Strangers, 1986; Fatal Escpoure, 1987; Touch Down, 1991. *Recordings:* New Age Albums: Spirit of the Nile, 1997; Passage Through Time, 2000; Pathfinder, forthcoming. *Membership:* Musicians' Union. *Leisure interests:* Golf; Family; Steam engine rallies; Craft fairs.

BURGESS John Edward; b. 8 March 1932, London, England. Record Prod.; Studio Owner. m. Jean Horsfall, 5 Sept. 1964, 3 s. *Career:* Press, promotion, publicity, EMI Records, 1951; Production assistant to Norman Newell; Founder member, AIR Group of Companies with George Martin, 1965; AIR Studios opened 1969; Merged with Chrysalis, 1974; Managing Director, Air Studios, Montserrat, West Indies, 1979; Managing Director, Air Studios, London, 1969–90, Lyndhurst, 1990-. *Recordings:* Producer for: Adam Faith; Manfred Mann; Peter and Gordon; Freddie and the Dreamers; John Barry Seven; Cast albums: Barnum; Guys and Dolls. *Address:* 2 Sudbury Hill, Harrow on the Hill, Harrow, Middlesex HA1 3SB, England.

BURGESS Tim; b. 30 May 1967, Salford, Manchester, England. Vocalist. *Career:* Lead singer, The Charlatans; Sold-out concerts at Manchester Nynex Arena and London Docklands Arena, 1997. *Recordings:* Albums: Some Friendly (No. 1, UK), 1990; Between 10th and 11th, 1992; Up To Our Hips, 1994; The Charlatans (No. 1, UK), 1995; Tellin' Stories (No. 1, UK), 1997; Melting Pot (singles compilation), 1998; Us and Us Only, 1999; Wonderland, 2001; Singles include: Indian Rope, 1990; The Only One I Know, 1990; Then, 1990; Me In Time, 1991; Over Rising, 1991; Weirdo, 1992; Tremelo Song, 1992; Can't Get Out of Bed, 1994; I Never Want An Easy Life If Me and He Were Ever To Get There, 1994; Jesus Hairdo, 1994; Crashin' In, 1994; Just Lookin', 1995; Just When You're Thinkin' Things Over, 1995; One to Another, 1996; North Country Boy, 1997; How High, 1997; Tellin' Stories, 1997; Forever, 1999; My Beautiful Friend, 1999; Impossible, 2000; Love Is The Key, 2001; A Man Needs To Be Told, 2001; with Saint Etienne: I Was Born On Christmas Day, 1993; with The Chemical Brothers: Life Is Sweet, 1995. *Honours:* Gold, Silver and Platinum discs; Cover version of Time for Living by Sly and the Family Stone on the 'Help' Bosnia charity album, 1995; Raised money for charity Missing Persons Helpline at the Brixton Academy, 1997. *Current Management:* Steve Harrison Management, 2 Witton Walk, Northwich, Cheshire CW9 5AT, England.

BURGH Steven Lawrence; b. 17 Dec. 1950, Trenton, New Jersey, USA. Record Prod.; Musician (guitar). m. Jamie Reisch, 26 Feb. 1983, 1 s., 1 d. *Career:* Musician with: Phoebe Snow; Steve Forbert; Gladys Knight; Billy Joel; Producer, engineer, Baby Monster Studios, New York, 1986-. *Recordings:* As musician: with Phoebe Snow: Phoebe Snow, 1974; It Looks Like Snow, 1976; Never Letting Go, 1978; with Billy Joel: 52nd Street; with Steve Forbert: Alive In Arrival, 1978; Steve Forbert, 1982; Film soundtrack, Tender Mercies, 1982. *Honours:* Grammy, 52nd Street, 1978; Academy Award, Tender Mercies, 1982.

BURLEY Philip George (Pip); b. 31 Dec. 1943, Croydon, Surrey, England. Musician (keyboards) Composer; Television Prod. m. Christine Komaromy, 10 June 1974, 3 d. *Career:* Freelance keyboard player, composer, arranger; Played with: Sydney Lipton; Joe Loss; Ken Mackintosh; Cabaret with The Semitones; Television producer, 1987–; Credits include: Darling Buds of May; A Touch of Frost; Pride of Africa. *Compositions:* Music for television includes: Musicround; Darling Buds of May; Score for Romeo and Juliet, 1993; The Comedy of Errors, 1995. *Honours:* Ivor Novello Award, 1991. *Memberships:* PRS; Chief Barker, Variety Clubs of Great Britain, 1999-. *Leisure interests:* Golf; Theatre. *Address:* Heathwoods, Dorking Rd, Tadworth, Surrey KT20 7TJ, England.

BURMAKA Maria; b. 16 June 1970, Kharkiv, Ukraine. m. Dmytro Nebesiftchuk, 27 Nov. 1993, 1 d. *Education:* Kharkiv State University. *Musical Education:* Music School. *Career:* Won Grand Prix, all Ukrainian festivals: Oberig; Chervona Ruta; Many concerts in Ukraine; Concerts: France; Germany, 1992; Canada; Poland; USA, 1989–93; Songs at MB top national hit parade 7 times, 1993–94. *Recordings:* Cassette: Don't Blossom Spring, 1990; CD, Maria, 1992; CD: Hope Remains, 1994. *Honours:* Laureate, Ukrainian festivals, 1989–93; Album, Hope Remains, Best In Ukraine, Council of New Stars of Old Year Festival, 1993–94. *Current Management:* Dmytro Nebesijtchuk. *Address:* Schuseva St 36 #12, 254060 Kiev, Ukraine.

BURN Chris; b. 13 March 1955, Epping, Essex, England. Musician (piano). *Musical Education:* Surrey University, BMus. *Career:* British tours, 1985, 1987, 1990, 1992, 1994; Festivals: Bochum; Berlin; Copenhagen; Ulrichsberg; Cologne; Victoriaville, 1996; Radio 3 broadcasts: 1989, 1992, 1994; WDR-TV, radio. *Recordings:* A Fountain Replete; Ensemble; A Henry Cowell Concert; Music for Three Rivers. *Publications:* Various articles. *Honours:* ACGB, 1988, 1990, 1992, 1994. *Memberships:* PRS; MCPS. *Leisure interest:* 5-a-side-football. *Current Management:* ACTA. *Address:* 11 Marits Ave, Ongar, Essex CM5 9AY, England.

BURNEL Jean-Jacques; b. 21 Feb. 1952, London, England. Vocalist; Musician (bass). *Education:* History degree, Bradford University. *Career:* Founder member, UK rock group The Stranglers, 1976–; Headline tours, Europe; UK; USA; Canada; International concerts include: Support to Patti Smith, 1976; Climax Blues Band, 1977; Loch Lomond Festival, 1979; Reading Rock Festival, 1983; Alexandra Palace, 1970; Support to Simple Minds, 1991; Dartmoor Prison (first band ever to do so), 1992. *Recordings:* Albums include: Rattus Norvegicus, 1977; No More Heroes, 1978; Black and White, 1978; Live (X Cert), 1979; The Raven, 1979; Themeninblack, 1981; La Folie, 1982; The Collection, 1982; Feline, 1983; Aural Sculpture, 1984; Dreamtime, 1986; All Live and All of The Night, 1988; 10, 1990; Greatest Hits, 1991; In The Night, 1992; Saturday Night, Sunday Morning, 1993; About Time, 1995; Written In Red, 1997; The Hit Men (singles compilation), 1997; 5 Live 01, 2001; Solo album: Euroman Cometh, 1979; with Dave Greenfield, Fire and Water, 1983; Hit singles include: Peaches, 1977; Something Better Change, 1977; No More Heroes, 1977; Five Minutes, 1978; Nice 'n' Sleazy, 1978; Duchess, 1979; Golden Brown (No. 2, UK), 1982; Strange Little Girl, 1982; European Female, 1983; Skin Deep, 1984; Always The Sun, 1986; All Day and All of The Night, 1987. *Honour:* Ivor Novello Award, Most Performed Work of 1982, Golden Brown, 1983. *Current Management:* Cruisin' Music. *Address:* c/o 21 Gay St, Bath BA1 2PD, England.

BURNETT T-Bone (John Henry); b. 18 Jan. 1945, St Louis, Missouri, USA. Musician (guitar); Songwriter; Prod.; Vocalist. *Career:* Touring musician with Delaney and Bonnie; B-52s; Bob Dylan's Rolling Thunder Revue, 1970s; Founder, Alpha Band, 1976–79; Solo recording artiste, 1972, 1980–; Worked with Richard Thompson; Elvis Costello, 1980s. *Recordings:* Albums: J Henry Burnett, 1972; Truth Decay, 1980; Proof Through The Night, 1983; Behind The Trap Door, 1984; T-Bone Burnett, 1986; The Talking Animals, 1988; The Criminal Under My Own Hat, 1992; with Alpha Band: Alpha Band, 1977; Spark In The Dark, 1977; Statue Makers of Hollywood, 1978; with Bob Dylan: Hard Rain, 1976; Blowin' In The Wind, 1985; with Los Lobos: How Will The Wolf Survive, 1984; By The Light of The Moon, 1987; La Pistola Y El Corazon, 1988; with Roy Orbison: In Dreams, 1987; Mystery Girl, 1989; Friends – Black and White Night, 1988; Other recordings with: Willie Dixon; Kinky Friedman; Emmylou Harris; Golden Palaminos; Producer, albums with Bruce Cockburn; Leo Kottke; Bo Deans; Nitty Gritty Dirt Band; Elvis Costello, Spike, 1989; Counting Crows, August and Everything After, 1993; Gillian Welch, Revival, 1996; Wallflowers, Bringing Down The Horse, 1996; Natalie Merchant, Motherland, 2001. *Current Management:* Addis, Wechsler and Associates. *Address:* 955 S Carillo Dr., Third Floor, Los Angeles, CA 90048, USA.

BURNS Christian Anthony; b. 18 Jan. 1976, Liverpool, England. Vocalist; Musician (guitar); Songwriter. *Career:* Co-founder: BBMak pop group, 1996; Signed to UK company Telstar; Gained large US popularity after licence deal with Hollywood/Disney; Performed to over 100m US viewers through group's own TV specials; Supported Britney Spears on sell-out US tour followed by 28-date first headline US tour, 2000; UK shows with The Corrs, 2001. *Recordings:* Albums: Sooner Or Later, 2000; Singles: Back Here, Still On Your Side, 2000; Ghost of You and Me, 2001. *Honours:* Debut LP sales of over 1m. copies. *Address:* c/o Diane Young. *E-mail:* DaytimeENT@aol.com. *Internet:* www.bbmak.co.uk.

BURNS Patty; b. 16 Aug. 1967, Köln, Cologne, Germany. *Career:* Belgian support act for Scorpions; Performing alongside Marillion, Magnum, Erasure, Kent Festival, England, Sopot Festival, Poland, Bregenz Festival, Austria, Jurmala Festival, Russia. *Compositions:* Fast Traveller; Too Late; Explode Your Nature; Reach the Sky. *Recordings:* Just Remember (Trust Me); Ready for Duty, CD; Evening News, CD; These Boots, CD. *Honours:* Winner, Belgian National Rock Meeting; Graduate, Jurmala Festival and Bregenz. *Leisure interests:* Dance; Sport. *Current Management:* Life for Music, Belgium. *Address:* 96 Basilique Ave, 1089 Brussels, Belgium.

BURNS Robert Beverley; b. 16 May 1923, Toronto, Ontario, Canada. Musician (saxophones, clarinets). m. Enid Lambert Burns, 30 Oct. 1991, 1 s., 2 d. *Musical Education:* Toronto Conservatory; Tuition with William Matthews ARCM; Hiram and Walter Lear, London, Bournemouth. *Career:* One of few jazz and classical musicians; RCAF HQ Band, Europe; Returned Canada, 1946; Played with Maynard Ferguson, Ellis McClintock; Mart Kenney, and studio work, Toronto; Returned to England, 1948; Played, recorded with Ted Heath, Ambrose, Lew Stone, Jack Parnell's first band; Theatre, studio freelancing until 1989; Led jazz groups, productions at the National Theatre; Played Triparte by Robert Farnon, commissioned by Musicians' Union for May Day Concert at Festival Hall, Concerto for 3 saxophones played by 1 player; Toured with Tony Bennett, recorded at Albert Hall; Tours, 4 times with Benny Goodman, Ireland, Europe; Soloist, film tracks: The Spy Who Came In From The Cold; Dance With A Stranger; Shot In The Dark; Two For The Road. *Compositions:* Love theme, I Believe In You; Small jazz groups for Frank Cordell film music. *Recordings include:* with Benny Goodman: Today; London Date; Directions In Jazz, Bill Le Sage; Great Jazz Solos Revisited, Bernie Cash; As House Band, HMV

Studios titles include: When I'm Sixty-Four; Albums with Robert Farnon; Frank Chacksfield; Eric Rogers; Frank Sinatra In London, Robert Farnon; 25 years recording ITV artists including: Lene Horne; Ella Fitzgerald; Peggy Lee; Vic Damone; Vera Lynn; Petula Clark; Barbra Streisand; Also many classical recordings with the four major orchestras; Films and music as soloist with Bill McGuffie; House band with major labels; Albums with The Beatles including solo on When I'm Sixty-Four; Albums with Vanessa Redgrave and Noel Coward. *Honours:* Winner, All Canadian Jazz Poll (saxophone), ARCM. *Membership:* Musicians' Union, Canada, England. *Leisure interests:* Reading; Music studies; Swimming; Travel. *Address:* 124 Pearl St, Sarnia, ON N7T 5G5, Canada.

BURNS Robert George Henry; b. 24 Feb. 1953, London, England. Musician (bass guitar); Composer; Educator. m. Elizabeth Chennells, 14 Jan. 1991, 1 s. *Musical Education:* Guildhall School of Music and Drama; Brunel University College; Rhodesian College of Music. *Career:* Tours, live dates, recordings with: Sam and Dave; Edwin Starr; Lene Lovich; Isaac Hayes; Pete Townshend; Eric Burdon; David Gilmour; Albert Lee; James Burton; Jerry Donahue; Viv Stanshall; Zoot Money; Formed Robert Burns Music, 1987. *Compositions:* Soundtracks for clients including: Lonrho; Sunday Times; IBM; MTV; P & O. *Recordings:* Television: Red Dwarf; Mr Bean; 2 Point 4 Children; Alas Smith and Jones; Lenny Henry; Blackadder III; Not The Nine O'Clock News; Three of a Kind. *Publications:* The Rock File; Columnist for Bassist and Musician magazines; Syllabus for Trinity/ Rockschool graded exams for bass guitar, 1992. *Honours:* Appointed Principal Examiner, Bass Guitar, Trinity College of Music, 1992; Head, Bass Guitar Studies, BASStech/Thames Valley University, 1994. *Leisure interests:* Cinema; Literature; Music research. *Address:* Crouch End, London N8, England.

BURONFOSSE Marc; b. 6 May 1963, Soissons, France. Musician (upright acoustic bass). m. Jennifer Forse, 22 May 1993, 1 d. *Education:* 3 year degree, Sound Engineering. *Musical Education:* Prize, Union Des Conservatoires de Paris. *Career:* Japanese tour with Las Solistes de Versailles (chamber orchestra); Fellowship to study at the New School of Music, New York; Tour of Central Africa with Sylvain Kassap Quartet; European tours with Sylvain Kassap Quartet and Bojan Z Quartet; Television and radio appearances. *Recordings:* Sylvain Kassap Quartet Quixote; Bojan Z Quartet. *Honours:* First prize, Concours de la Défense, 1992; Concours Etrechy, 1995. *Memberships:* ADAMI; SACEM; SPEDIDAM. *Leisure interests:* Skiing; Cinema.

BURRELL Boz; b. 1 Aug. 1946, Holbeach, England. Musician (Bass Guitarist); Vocalist. *Career:* King Crimson; founder member, UK Rock Group Bad Company, 1973–83; founder member, Snape; toured world-wide; concerts include: Madison Square Gardens with Bad Company; headlined Hyde Park Gig with King Crimson, 1971. *Compositions:* Include: Smokin'45; Whiskey Bottle; Gone, Gone, Gone. *Recordings:* Albums: with King Crimson, Islands, 1971; Earthbound, 1972; Accidentally Born in New Orleans, 1972; Live At Jackson; Young Boys Guide to King Crimson, 1976; BBC Sessions, 1994; Beginners' Guide To The King Crimson Collectors' Club, 2000; with Amazing Blundle: Albums: Blundle, 1973; Musgrave Street, 1974; with Bad Company: Albums: Bad Company, 1974; Straight Shooter, 1975; Run With The Pack, 1976; Burnin' Sky, 1977; Desolation Angels, 1979; Rough Diamonds, 1982; 10 From 6, 1985; Fame and Fortune, 1986; with Snape and Alexis Korner: Album: On The Move, 1996; The 'Original' Bad Company Anthology, 1999; Singles: Can't Get Enough; Feel Like Makin' Love; Young Blood; Movin' On; Hey Hey; Hammer of Love; also played with: Graham Bond; Gary Brooker; Eric Burdon; Roger Chapman; Dick Heckstall-Smith; Tim Hinkley (Hinkley's Heroes); Ronnie Lane; Alvin Lee; Lulu; Zoot Money; Esther Phillips; Pete Townsend; Ruby Turner; Ronnie Wood; currently playing with Tam White/ Boz Burrell Band. *Honours:* Gold, Platinum Albums with Bad Company; Grammy Award, 1975; Hon. Col of Louisiana, with Bad Company, 1977. *Membership:* Musicians Union. *Leisure interests:* Music; Gardening; Fishing; Flying Kites; Jazz. *Address:* c/o Gremlin Productions, PO Box 216, Diss, Norfolk, IP22 2TY.

BURRELL Kenny; b. 31 July 1931, Detroit, Michigan, USA. Jazz Musician (guitar). *Musical Education:* Classical guitar, 1952–53; BMus, Wayne University, Detroit, 1955. *Career:* Played with Candy Johnson Sextet; Yusef Lateef; Tommy Flanagan; Dizzy Gillespie, 1951; Oscar Peterson Trio, 1955; Hampton Hawes Trio, 1956; Benny Goodman, 1957; Association with organist Jimmy Smith; Recorded with John Coltrane, Sonny Rollins, Coleman Hawkins; Leader, own trio. *Recordings:* Albums include: The Cats, 1957; Kenny Burrell – John Coltrane, 1958; At The Five Spot Cafe Vol. 1, 1959; Midnight Blue, 1960s; Live At The Village Vanguard, 1960s; Guitar Forms, 1965; For Charlie Christian and Benny Goodman, 1967; Handcrafted, 1978; Kenny Burrell In New York, 1981; Night Song, 1982; Listen To The Dawn, 1983; Bluesin' Around, 1984; A La Carte, 1986; Generations, 1987; Blue Lights Vols 1 and 2, 1989; Togethering, 1989; Recapitulation, 1989; Guiding Spirit, 1989; Sunup To Sundown, 1991; Soulero, 1996; Love Is The Answer, 1998. *Current*

Management: Tropix International. *Address:* 163 Third Ave, Suite 206, New York, NY 10003, USA.

BURROUGHS Gary Stuart; b. 3 April 1953, Doncaster, England. Musician (drums, percussion, multi-instrumentalist); Singer; Songwriter; Prod.; Engineer. m. Lyn Acton, 26 Nov. 1976, 1 s. *Education:* Hull Technical College. *Musical Education:* Lead tenor, school, 1961; Tenor horn, cornet, Askern Siver Prize Band, 1963; Self-taught drums, 1967. *Career:* Drummer with: Soul Image; The Pink; Listen; The Weazles; Johnny Duncan and the Bluegrass Boys; Rock and Roll Circus; Rock Orchestrals; Johnny Johnson and the Bandwagon; Snake Eye; The Killers; Jackal; Buster Crab; Sarah Gordans All American Soul Show; Sheer Elegance; Roy Wood – Wizzo; Christie; Nosmo King; Luggage; Export; Earthman Liberation; What Katy Did Next; Tiffanys; Gimmex; Stork Club; Bertice Redding; Lionel Bart; Simon Townshend; Resistdance; Marino; NGO; Fila Brazillia; Derek Bailey; Naked Orange, 1968–; Tour Manager, Limmie and The Family Cookin', 1976; Sound Engineer, Fairview Music, 1979; Derek Bailey; Lead singer with: Techno Pop; Marino; Listen; Blitzkrieg; The Weazles; The Choirboys; NGO; Drummer with: American Sweet Sound Tour; Simon Townshend; Support, West Coast Tour, Pretenders; Support, Duran Duran World tour, 1984; Television: Saturday Superstore, BBC1; Lift Off with Ayshea; Regional television, BBC2; Televised live concerts: Syracuse, USA; Seattle, USA; Baltimore, USA; Producer for: Smash live, Top of The Pops, BBC1, 1994; Various radio; Business ventures: DIG for music, Midem, 1991; Wall 2 Wall Records, 1990; Wall 2 Wall Studios, 1992. *Recordings:* Single: Year of The Tiger, 1975; Session drummer, vocalist, various singles, albums, 1976–98; As solo artist: Single: Paint It Black, 1980; Album: Sacred Places; with Marino: Blues For Lovers, 1991. *Honours:* Blues Album of The Year, Paris, France, 1992. *Memberships:* PRS; Equity. *Leisure interests:* Writing; Walks in the country; Cycling. *Current Management:* Wall 2 Wall.

BURTON Gary; b. 23 Jan. 1943, Anderson, Indiana, USA. Jazz musician (vibraphone, piano). *Musical Education:* Self-taught piano; Berklee College of Music, Boston. *Career:* Member, George Shearing's Group, 1963; Played with Stan Getz, 2 years; Formed own bands, 1960s-; Leader, various bands featuring artists including: Larry Coryell; Roy Haynes; Pat Metheny; Eberhard Weber; Also recorded with Stéphane Grappelli; Carla Bley; Keith Jarrett; Chick Corea; Michael Brecker; Peter Erskine; Teacher, Berklee College of Music, 1971-. *Recordings include:* Albums: Duster, 1967; Lofty Fake Anagram, 1967; Country Roads and Other Places, 1968; Green Apple, 1969; Hotel Hello, 1974; Matchbook, 1974; Dreams So Real, 1975; Easy As Pie, 1980; Picture This, 1983; Real Life Hits, 1984; Whiz Kids, 1986; Times Like These, 1988; Cool Nights, 1990; Six Pack, 1993; Live In Cannes, 1996; Astor Piazzolla Reunion, 1996; Departure, 1997; Like Minds, 1998; Libertango – The Music of Astor Piazzolla, 2000; For Hamp, Red, Bags and Cal, 2001; with Carla Bley: A Genuine Tang Funeral, 1968; with Stéphane Grappelli: Paris Encounter, 1969; with Keith Jarrett: Gary Burton and Keith Jarrett, 1970; with Eberhard Weber, Ring, 1974; Passengers, 1976; with Chick Corea: Crystal Silence, 1972; Duet, 1978; with Ralph Towner: Slide Show, 1976; with Pat Metheny: Reunion, 1989; with Paul Bley: Right Time Right Place, 1991; with Makoto Ozone: Face To Face, 1995. *Current Management:* Ted Kurland Associates, 173 Brighton Ave, Boston, MA 02134, USA.

BURTON Paddy (Patrick Henry); b. 19 Aug. 1961, Stockport, Cheshire, England. Musician (percussion); Musical Instrument Maker (slitdrums, multiplayer giant xylophones). 2 s. *Education:* Newcastle University. *Career:* Musical Director for theatre companies; Performing musician with local bands, 1978–86; Pineapple Agogo, 1986–90; Musician in Residence, City of Edinburgh District Council, 1990–92; Player with Amadeus, 1993–; Jack Drum Arts; Dodgy Clutch; The Fabulous Salami Brothers. *Recordings:* Trashcan Gamelan Edinburgh, 1992; Black Diamonds, Black Gold, 1993; Fish Xylophone, 1994. *Memberships:* Musicians' Union; Sound Sense; Equity. *Leisure interests:* Gardening; World travel. *Address:* 43–44 Gladstone Terrace, Sunniside, Bishop Auckland, County Durham DL13 4LS, England.

BUSH John; b. 24 Aug. 1963, Los Angeles, California, USA. Vocalist. *Career:* Lead Singer, Anthrax, 1992–; Lead Singer, Armored Saint; Appeared with Anthrax on episode of TV Show, News Radio; Recorded with Armored Saint in film Hellraiser 3. *Compositions:* With Anthrax: Only; Black Lodge; Fueled; Inside Out; With Armored Saint: Can U Deliver; Over the Edge; Reign of Fire. *Recordings:* Albums: with Anthrax: Sound of White Noise, 1993; Stomp 442, 1995; Vol. VIII – The Threat Is Real, 1998; Madhouse – The Very Best of Anthrax, 2001; with Armored Saint: March of The Saint, 1984; Delirious Nomad, 1985; Symbol of Salvation, 1991. *Membership:* AFTRA. *Leisure interests:* Basketball; Reading; Travelling. *Current Management:* Concrete Management. *Address:* 10074 Sully Dr., Sun Valley, CA 91352, USA.

BUSH Kate (Catherine); b. 30 July 1958, Bexleyheath, Kent, England. Vocalist; Songwriter. *Education:* Voice, dance and mime lessons. *Career:* Limited live performances include: Tour of Life, Europe, 1979; Secret

Policeman's Third Ball, London, 1987; Television appearances include: Bringing It All Back Home documentary, 1991; Writer, director, actress, film The Line, The Cross and The Curve, 1994. Recordings (mostly self-composed): Albums: The Kick Inside, 1978; Lionheart, 1978; Never For Ever (No. 1, UK), 1980; The Dreaming, 1982; Hounds of Love (No. 1, UK), 1985; The Whole Story (No. 1, UK), 1986; The Sensual World (No. 2, UK), 1989; This Womans Work, 1990; The Red Shoes (No. 2, UK), 1993; Contributor, Games Without Frontiers, Peter Gabriel, 1980; Two Rooms – Celebrating The Songs of Elton John and Bernie Taupin, 1991; Singles include: Wuthering Heights (No. 1, UK), 1978; The Man With The Child In His Eyes, 1978; Wow, 1979; Breathing, 1980; Babooshka, 1980; Army Dreamers, 1980; Sat In Your Lap, 1981; Running Up That Hill, 1985; Cloudbusting, 1985; Hounds of Love, 1986; Experiment IV, 1986; Don't Give Up, duet with Peter Gabriel, 1986; This Woman's Work (from film soundtrack She's Having A Baby), 1988; The Sensual World, 1989; Moments of Pleasure, 1993; Rubberband Girl, 1993; Man I Love, 1994; The Red Shoes, 1994. *Honours:* Ivor Novello Award, Outstanding British Lyric, The Man With The Child In His Eyes, 1979; Brit Award, Best British Female Artist, 1987; Q Award, Inspiration Award, 2001. *Current Management:* c/o Reluctant Management, 10603 Rochester Ave, Los Angeles, CA 90024, USA.

BUSHWACKA! (Matthew Stuart Benjamin); b. 2 Aug. 1972, London, England. Prod.; Remixer; DJ. *Career:* DJ with Ratpack; Resident DJ at The End, London; Engineer at Mr C's Watershed Studio, London; Member: Makesome Breaksome, Mashupheadz; Collaborations: Layo Paskin, Nathan Coles; Co-founder Plank/Oblong Records with Lewis Copeland. *Recordings:* Albums: Wak'd (as Plantastik), 1998; Low Life (with Layo), 1999; Cellar Dwellas, 2000; Singles: Deep South (with Layo), 1999; Monster, 2000; Healer, 2000. *Current Management:* c/o End Recordings, 18 W Central St, London, WC1A 1JJ, England.

BUSSCHOTS Patrick Eugéne; b. 18 Dec. 1953, Mortsel, Belgium. Man.-Dir. m. Lydia, 28 Oct. 1978, 2 d. *Education:* Jeweller; Various business courses. *Career:* Retail, wholesale, production, publishing; Currently holding, grouping all activities with ARS Productions. *Recordings:* with Technotronic: Pump Up The Jam; Material with: Faith No More; Gipsy Kings. *Honours:* World Music Award, Monte Carlo, 1990. *Membership:* IFPI. *Leisure interests:* Music; Sports; Outdoor dining. *Address:* ARS Productions, Singel 5, 2150 Kontich, Belgium.

BUSTA RHYMES (Trevor Smith); b. 1972, Brooklyn, New York, USA. Rapper; Prod. 2 s., 1 deceased. *Career:* Co-founder, Leaders of the New School; Obtained record deal; Guest artist on albums by artists including Boyz II Men, Mary J Blige, TLC and A Tribe Called Quest; Involvement in various film projects including Higher Learning; Began to release solo recordings; Formed own record company, Flipmode Entertainment; Started own clothing line, Bushi; Provided voice of Reptar in Rugrats film, and contributed one song, On Your Marks, Get Set, Ready, Go, to soundtrack; Duets with Ozzy Osbourne and Janet Jackson on third album; Appeared in remake of film Shaft, 2000; Several tours. *Recordings:* Singles: Woo Hah Got You All In Check, 1996; It's a Party, 1996; Put Your Hands Where My Eyes Could See, 1997; Dangerous, 1997; Turn It Up, 1998; One/Rhymes Galore, 1998; What's It Gonna Be, 1999; Gimme Some More, 1999; Get Out, 2000; Fire, 2000; Break Ya Neck, 2001; As I Come Back, 2001; Albums: The Coming, 1996; When Disaster Strikes, 1997; Extinction Level Event, 1998; Anarchy, 2000; Genesis, 2001. *Honours:* Grammy Nomination, Best Rap Solo Performance; Soul Train Nomination, Best R & B/Soul of Rap Music Video.

BUTCHER John Bernard; b. 25 Oct. 1954, Brighton, England. Musician (saxophone). *Education:* PhD, Theoretical Physics. *Musical Education:* Self-taught. *Career:* Worked mainly in jazz, late 1970s; Improvisation and new-music, early 1980s; Regular groups include: News From The Shed; Embers; Frisque Concordance; Ensemble; Festival appearances include: Berlin Total Music Meeting; Du Maurier Jazz (Canada); Knitting Factory (New York); Company (London); Head of ACTA Records. *Recordings:* Fonetiks, 1985; Conceits, 1987; News From The Shed, 1989; Cultural Baggage, 1990; Thirteen Friendly Numbers, 1992; Spellings, 1993; Respiritus, 1995; Concert Moves, 1995; London and Cologne, 1998. *Address:* 28 Aylmer Rd, London W12 9LQ, England.

BUTCHER Simon David; b. 21 Dec. 1975, Mansfield, Nottinghamshire. Musician (Vocals, Guitars, Violin, Keyboards). *Musical Education:* Self-taught. *Career:* Professional musician; Interviewed and played on Trent FM, BBC Radio Nottingham, Sherwood Radio, Radio Mansfield, BBC Radio Cambridge, Radio Hallam, BBC Radio Sheffield, Ashfield Community Radio; BBC East Midland Television performing Buzzer; Clarendon Cable Television, NTL Cable 7, acoustic set and interview; XFM Demo Call. *Compositions:* Soon You Will; Next Stage; Roadrunner. *Recordings:* Dual Carriageway; Bitch; Indignant; Soon You Will; Next Stage; Roadrunner. *Honours:* Delirium Win Band of The Year, 1995; signed To Roadrunner Records, 1997; signed to www.peoplesound.com, 1999. *Memberships:* PRS; MCPS; PPL; Musicians Union; BASCA; IMF;

AURA. *Leisure interests:* Drawing; Reading; Computers; Comic Collection; Music. *Current Management:* First Step Management, David Butcher, 96 George St, Mansfield, Nottinghamshire NG19 6SB, England.

BUTINA Roman; b. 5 Aug. 1937, Zagreb, Croatia. Musician (organ, keyboards); Composer. m. Ljerka Miladinov, 4 June 1960, 1 s., 1 d. *Education:* Dr of Medicine. *Musical Education:* Dip, Intermediate Music School. *Career:* Member, Dalmatia vocal group, 12 years; Tours former Yugoslavia, Eastern, Western Europe; Leader, organist, The Blue Stars group, 1970–72; Performer, Hammond Organ, Electric Piano, Laguna Hotel, occasionally Zagreb-Intercontinental Hotel, 1973. *Compositions:* recorded and published, numerous popular tunes and songs. *Publications:* As Editor: With Song Through Zagorje, 1960; Greetings Tyrol, 1969; Ancient Croatian Songs, 1972; World Folk Songs, 1975. *Honours:* Second Prize, Zagreb Festival, 1971. *Memberships:* Croatian Composers Asscn; Union of Artists of Croatia, Zagreb. *Leisure interest:* Philately. *Address:* Turopolska 36, 10000 Zagreb, Croatia.

BUTLER Bernard; b. 1 May 1970, Stamford Hill, London, England. Musician (guitar, keyboards); Songwriter. m. Elisa. *Education:* History, Queen Mary College, London, 1 year. *Musical Education:* Studied violin and piano; Self-taught guitar. *Career:* Member, Suede, 1989–94; Television appearances include: Top of The Pops, BBC1; BRIT Awards; Later With Jools Holland, BBC2; The Tonight Show, NBC TV; Concerts include Glastonbury Festival; Tours, Europe, America, Japan; Member, duo McAlmont and Butler (with David McAlmont), 1994–95. *Recordings:* Albums: with Suede: Suede (No. 1, UK), 1993; Dog Man Star, 1994; with McAlmont and Butler: The Sound of McAlmont and Butler, 1995; Solo albums: People Move On, 1998; Friends and Lovers, 2000; Singles include: with Suede: The Drowners, 1992; Metal Mickey, 1992; Animal Nitrate, 1993; So Young, 1993; Stay Together, 1994; We Are The Pigs, 1994; Wild One, 1994; New Generation, 1995; with McAlmont and Butler: Yes, 1995; You Do, 1995; Solo singles include: Stay, 1998; Not Alone, 1998; I'd Do It Again If I Could, 2000; Also recorded with Bryan Ferry; Edwyn Collins; Aimee Mann; Sparks; Eddi Reader; Neneh Cherry. *Honours:* Mercury Music Prize, 1993. *Current Management:* Geoff Travis.

BUTLER Clara G; b. 28 Oct. 1938, Greenville, South Carolina, USA. Songwriter; Dancer; Record Co Exec. m. Jojo St Mitchell, 18 May 1993, 1 s., 1 d. *Education:* 1 year college. *Musical Education:* 7 years with management team and songwriting team. *Career:* Arthur Murray Dance Awards; Dancing Instructor; CEO of record company, Notary Public; Music publisher and songwriter; Real estate owner; Executive producer of recording artists. *Compositions:* Songs: I Must Be Gettin' Older Now; It's You For Me; Executive Producer for groups: Destination Unknown; Safari. *Honours:* Business Leader; Ballroom Dancing Awards. *Memberships:* Broadcast Music Inc; Antithesis Music. *Leisure interests:* Reading; Dancing; Cooking; Crafts; Art; Poetry; Antiques. *Current Management:* The Amethyst Group Ltd.

BUTLER Edith; b. 27 July 1942, Paquetville, New Brunswick, Canada. Singer; Musician (guitar). *Education:* BA, Arts, Pedagogie; MA, Literature. *Musical Education:* Taught by mother. *Career:* Tours: Canada; USA; Japan; Olympia Theatre of Paris, France; Place des Arts, Montréal; All major television and radio shows, Canada, France, last 25 years. *Recordings:* 25 albums; 250 songs. *Honours:* 3 Platinum records; 3 Gold records; 3 Felix Awards; Nelly Award; Charles-Cros Award; Ordre National du Mérite, France, 1998; Helen Creighton Acheivement Award. *Memberships:* SOCAN; SACEM; SODRAC. *Leisure interests:* Gardening; Walking. *Current Management:* Lise Aubut. *Address:* 86 Côte Ste Catherine, Montréal, QC H2V 2A3, Canada.

BUTLER Geezer (Terry); b. 17 July 1949, Birmingham, England. Musician (bass). *Career:* Bass player, UK heavy rock group Black Sabbath, 1967–; Numerous concerts world-wide include: Madison Square Garden, New York, 1975; Live Aid, Philadelphia, 1985. *Recordings:* Singles include: Paranoid; Iron Man; War Pigs; Never Say Die; Albums: Black Sabbath, 1969; Paranoid, 1970; Masters of Reality, 1971; Sabbath Bloody Sabbath, 1973; Sabotage, 1975; Technical Ecstasy, 1976; Never Say Die, 1978; Heaven and Hell, 1980; Mob Rules, 1981; Live Evil, 1983; Born Again, 1983; Seventh Star, 1986; The Eternal Idol, 1987; Headless Cross, 1990; Tyr, 1990; Dehumanizer, 1992; Cross Purposes, 1994; Ozzmosis, 1995; Alive and Dead, 1996; Black Science, 1997; Reunion, 1998; Contributed to Big Country albums Driving To Damascus, 1999; One In A Million, 2001; Numerous compilations. *Current Management:* Gloria Butler Management, PO Box 2686, Knowle B94 5NQ, England.

BUTLER Jonathan Kenneth; b. 10 Oct. 1961, Cape Town, South Africa. Musician (guitar); Vocalist; Songwriter. m. Barenese Vanessa, 28 Jan. 1983, 2 d. *Musical Education:* Self-taught. *Career:* Three-month US tour with Whitney Houston; Three weeks with Eric Clapton, Albert Hall; Extensive touring in own right of USA, Japan, Europe, South America, South Africa; Television: Carson; Jay Leno; David Letterman; Top of The Pops; Mandela Birthday Concert, Wembley. *Recordings:* Albums:

Introducing Jonathan Butler, 1977; Jonathan Butler, 1987; More Than Friends, 1988; Heal Our Land, 1990; Head To Head, 1994; Do You Love Me? 1997; Story of Life, 1999; The Source, 2000; EP: Deliverance; Singles: with Ruby Turner, If You're Ready (Come Go With Me), 1986; Solo: Lies, 1987; Sarah, Sarah, 1989; Sing Me Your Love, 1990; I'm On My Knees, 1994; Can We Start All Over Again, 1995; Lost To Love, 1998; features on: Millie Jackson, Tide Is Turning, 1988; Marcus Miller, Sun Don't Lie, 1993; Will Downing, Invitation Only, 1997; George Duke, Is Love Enough?, 1997; Rachelle Ferrell, Individuality, 2000. *Honours:* 2 Grammy Nominations; NAACP Award; 5 ASCAP Awards. *Memberships:* Musicians' Union; PRS; AFTRA. *Current Management:* Running Dog Management. *Address:* Minka, Lower Hampton Rd, Sunbury, Middlesex TW16 5PR, England.

BUXTON Felix; b. England. DJ; Prod. *Career:* Member, Basement Jaxx; Founded Atlantic Jaxx records, 1994; Remixes for acts including Pet Shop Boys, Roger Sanchez, Lil' Mo Yin Yang; Worked with vocalist Corrina Josephs; Numerous gigs and television appearances. *Recordings:* Singles: Samba Magic, 1995; Fly Life, 1997; Same Old Show/Automatic, 1998; Red Alert, 1999; Rendez-vu, 1999; Jump 'n' Shout, 1999; Bingo Bango, 2000; Romeo, 2001; Where's Your Head At?, 2001; Albums: Atlantic Jaxx (compilation) 1997; Remedy, 1999; Rooty, 2001. *Honours:* Mercury Music Prize nomination, 2001.

BYERS Rodney; Musician (Guitar). *Career:* Member, The Specials; Early tours supporting The Clash; Formed own record label, 2-Tone; Debut album produced by Elvis Costello; Numerous tours and television appearances. *Recordings:* Singles: Gangsters; A Message to You, Rudi; Too Much Too Young; Rat Race; Stereotype; Do Nothing; Ghost Town; Racist Friend; Free Nelson Mandela; Albums include: The Specials, 1979; More Specials, 1980; The Singles Collection, 1991; Too Much Too Young, 1993; Today's Specials, 1996; Guilty 'Til Proved Innocent, 1998; Blue Plate Specials Live, 1999.

BYFORD Bill; b. 24 May 1955, Castleford, West Yorkshire, England. Music Publisher; Songwriter; Musician (guitar). m. Honor Mary Eastwood, 29 Aug. 1977, 1 d. *Education:* MA, Film and Media; BEd (Hons). *Career:* Publisher and Managing Director, Palace of Fun Music, 1980–; Member, songwriter with The Rhythm Sisters, 1986–92; Currently working with Steve Tilston and Maggie Boyle; Featured artist on film soundtracks including: Patriot Games; Before The Fall; Music journalist with NME; Melody Maker; The Guardian, 1973-. *Memberships:* BASCA; PRS; MPS. *Leisure interest:* Leeds United Football Club. *Current Management:* Palace of Fun Management. *Address:* 16 Elm View, Huddersfield Rd, Halifax, West Yorkshire HX3 0AE, England.

BYRD Donald; b. 9 Dec. 1932, Detroit, Michigan, USA. Jazz Musician (trumpet); Educator. *Musical Education:* Studied trumpet and composition. *Career:* Recorded with John Coltrane; Sonny Rollins; Art Blakey; Dexter Gordon; Kenny Clarke; Pepper Adams; Educator, Rutgers University and Howard University. *Recordings:* Long Green, 1955; Two Trumpets, 1956; The Young Bloods, 1956; September Afternoon, 1957; At Newport, 1957; X-tacy, 1957; Jazz Eyes, 1957; Byrd In Paris, Vols 1 and 2, 1958; 10 To 4 At The 5 Spot, 1958; Off To The Races, 1958; Byrd In Flight, 1960; Royal Flush, 1961; Chant, 1961; Groovin' For Nat, 1962; Mustang, 1966; The Creeper, 1967; Electric Byrd, 1970; Black Byrd, 1973; Street Lady, 1974; Steppin' Into Tomorrow, 1975; Places and Spaces, 1975; Caricatures, 1977; Thank You... For F U M L (Funking Up My Life), 1978; Love Byrd, 1981; Words Sounds Colours Shapes, 1982; Harlem Blues, 1987; Getting Down

To Business, 1989; A City Called Heaven, 1991; Jazz Lab, 1995; with Kenny Clarke: Bohemia After Dark, 1955; with Art Blakey: The Jazz Messengers, 1956; with John Coltrane: Lush Life, 1958; with Dexter Gordon: One Flight Up, 1964; with Kenny Burrell and Herbie Hancock, A New Perspective, 1964. *Address:* c/o Department of Music, Rutgers University, New Brusnwick, NJ 08903, USA.

BYRNE David; b. 14 May 1952, Dumbarton, Scotland. Vocalist; Songwriter; Composer; Film Dir; Photographer. m. Adelle Lutz, 1987. *Education:* Rhode Island School of Design, 1970–71; Maryland Institute College of Art, 1971–72. *Career:* Co-founder, singer, songwriter, Talking Heads, 1974–88; Recorded 10 albums, numerous world-wide concerts, television and radio appearances; Solo artiste, producer, composer, 1980–; Founder, Luaka Bop record label, 1988; Also artist, stage and lighting designer, album covers/posters designer. *Compositions include:* Film/stage scores: The Knee Plays, 1984; Alive From Off Center, 1984; Sounds From True Stories, 1986; The Forest, 1986; Something Wild, 1986; The Catherine Wheel, 1988; The Last Emperor, 1988; The Giant Woman and The Lightning Man, 1990; A Young Man's Dream and A Woman's Secret, 1990. *Recordings include:* with Talking Heads: Talking Heads '77, 1977; More Songs About Buildings and Food, 1978; Fear of Music, 1979; Remain In Light, 1980; The Name of This Band Is Talking Heads, 1982; Speaking In Tongues, 1983; Stop Making Sense, 1984; Little Creatures, 1985; True Stories, 1986; Naked, 1988; Popular Favourites – Sand In The Vaseline, 1992; ; with Brian Eno: My Life In The Bush of Ghosts, 1981; Solo albums: The Forest, 1988; Rei Momo, 1989; Uh-Oh, 1992; David Byrne, 1994; Feelings, 1997; Look Into The Eyeball, 2001; Solo singles: Forestry, 1991; Angels, 1994; As producer: Mesopotamia, B-52's; Waiting, Fun Boy 3; Elegibo, Margareth Menezes (2 tracks). *Honours include:* Academy Award, Golden Globe, and Hollywood Foreign Press Asscn Award, Best Original Score, The Last Emperor, 1987; Film Critics Award, Best Documentary, 1985; MTV's Video Vanguard Award, 1985; Music Video Producers Asscn, 1992. *Memberships:* Musicians' Union; Screen Actors Guild. *Address:* PO Box 652, Cooper Station, New York, NY 10276, USA.

BYRNE Nicholas Bernard James Adam; b. 9 Oct. 1978, Dublin, Ireland. Vocalist. *Career:* Member, Westlife; Numerous television appearences and hit singles. *Recordings:* Singles: Swear It Again (No. 1, UK), 1999; Flying Without Wings (No. 1, UK), 1999; Seasons in the Sun/I Have a Dream(No. 1, UK) 1999; Fool Again (No. 1, UK), 2000; Against All Odds (with Mariah Carey; No. 1, UK), 2000; My Love (No. 1, UK), 2000; What Makes A Man, 2000; Uptown Girl (in aid of Comic Relief charity; No. 1, UK), 2001; Queen of My Heart (No. 1, UK), 2001; World of Our Own (No. 1, UK), 2002; Albums: Westlife, 1999; Coast To Coast (No. 1, UK), 2000; World of Our Own (No. 1, UK), 2001. *Honours:* Brit Awards, Best Pop Act, 2001, 2002.

BYWATER Richard; Musician (string bass). *Career:* Founder member, Mack and The Boys, tours throughout Europe, 1990–93; Headlined Birmingham's largest ever concert, 100,000 audience; Member, The New Bushbury Mountain Daredevils, 1992–; Backing vocals for Slade; Production, songwriting for dance artists; Topical songs for radio. *Recordings:* with Mack and The Boys: Mack and The Boys; Downtime Love; The Unknown Legends; with The New Bushbury Mountain Daredevils: Bushwacked; The Yellow Album; Bushbury Mountain. *Current Management:* Jim McPhee, Acorn Entertainments. *Address:* Winterfold House, 46 Woodfield Rd, Kings Heath, Birmingham 0B13 9UJ, England.

C

CABBLE Lise; b. 10 Jan. 1958, Copenhagen, Denmark. Songwriter; Singer; Musician (guitar). *Career:* Founder member, all-girl punk band Clinic Q, 1981; Founder member, singer, guitarist, songwriter, rock band Miss B Haven, 1986; Tours: England; France; Netherlands; Germany; Denmark. *Recordings:* with Miss B Haven: Ice On Fire, 1987; On Honeymoon, 1988; Nobody's Angel, 1990; Miss B Haven, 1991; Suk and Stads, 1994. *Honours:* Danish songwriter and singer awards; Several awards with Miss B Haven. *Leisure interests:* Reading; Backgammon. *Current Management:* Ernst Mikael Jorgensen, PDH. *Address:* Katrinebjerg 10, Morkov, Denmark.

CABLE Stuart; b. 19 May 1970, Aberdare, Wales. Musician (drums). *Career:* Ex-school caterer and bulding site worker; Member of King Katwalk before joining Tragic Love Company, 1991; Name change to Stereophonics prior to joining Richard Branson's newly-formed V2 records, 1996; Toured UK, Europe and USA supporting acts including: Manic Street Preachers; Ocean Colour Scene; The Who; Aerosmith; Headlined various UK gigs and festivals including: Hillsborough Benefit Concert, 1997; Cardiff Castle, 1998; Reading Leeds and Glasgow Festivals, 2000; Donington, Chepstow, T In The Park, 2001. *Recordings:* Singles: Looks Like Chaplin, 1996; Local Boy In The Photograph, More Life In A Tramp's Vest, A Thousand Trees, Traffic, 1997; The Bartender and The Thief, 1998; Just Looking, Pick A Part That's New, I Wouldn't Believe Your Radio, Hurry Up and Wait, 1999; Mama Told Me Not To Come (with Tom Jones), 2000; Mr Writer, Have A Nice Day, Step On My Old Size Nines, Handbags and Gladrags, 2001; Albums: Word Gets Around, 1997; Performance and Cocktails, 1999; Just Enough Education To Perform, 2001. *Honours:* Brit Award, Best Newcomer, 1998; Kerrang: Best New Band, 1998; Best Band, Best Album, 1999; Q Awards, Best Live Act, 1999; BAFTA Cymru, Best Music Programme, Stereophonics – Live At Morfa, 1999. *Current Management:* Marsupial Management Ltd, Unit 3, Home Farm, Welford, nr Newbury, Berkshire, RG20 8HR. *E-mail:* marsupial@btinternet.com. *Internet:* www.stereophonics.com.

CACCI Neil 'Guitar Man', (Neil Cacciottolo); b. 9 Nov. 1953, Evergreen Park, Illinois, USA. Studio Musician; Arranger; Business Rep. *Education:* 3 years college, Southwest College; Graduate, Omega School of Communications, Media Communications/Journalism. *Musical Education:* Graduate, Carnvale School of Music, Chicago. *Career:* Prepares budgets, various recording projects; Supervisor, all aspects studio production; Public relations services, major and independent artists; Studio musician, involved with recording background music, demo production for song catalogues, commercial recordings; Professional career, 1969-. *Recordings:* Part Time Love; Rhonda Lee; Bye Bye Baby; Lonely Highway; Loves Touch; Enchanted Meadow; Country Life; The Happy Traveller; Melinda. *Publications:* The Do's and Don'ts of The Music Industry. *Honours:* CMA Record Promoter and Company of the Year Award, 1992; International Indie Gold Record Awards. *Memberships:* AFofM; Production Signatory; CMA; GMA; NARAS; ASCAP (writer and publisher); Publisher, Harry Fox Agency. *Leisure interests:* Golf; Reading; Cooking. *Current Management:* Central Management, Nashville. *Address:* 9359 S Kedzie Ave, 42807, Evergreen Park, IL 60805, USA and 1205 Division St, #205, Nashville, TN 37203, USA.

CACIA Paul Scott; b. 20 June 1956, Santa Ana, California, USA. Musician (trumpet); Bandleader; Prod. m. Janine Cameo, 1978, 2 d. *Musical Education:* Studied with Claude Gordon, 1970–74. *Career:* Musician with: Calvin Jackson, 1972; Louis Bellson Big Band, 1973; Stan Kenton College Neophonic, 1974; Buddy Miles Express, 1975; Don Ellis Electric Orchestra, 1976; Ray Anthony, 1978; Al Hirt Big Band, 1979; Independent musician and producer, 1979–84; Bandleader, The New Age Orchestra, 1984–; Director, Don Ellis Estate, 1984–87; Lecturer, Besson trumpets, 1984–; Chairman, Stan Kenton Scholar Fund. *Recordings:* Albums include: Unbelievable, 1977; Big Band Portrait, 1979; All In Good Time, 1982; Believe It!, Mormon Tabernacle Choir, 1983; Hardcore Jazz, Shelley Manne and Phil Woods, 1986; Alumni Tribute To Stan Kenton, 1987. *Membership:* AFofM.

CADBURY Richard (Dik) Benjamin; b. 12 June 1950, Selly Oak, Birmingham, England. Musician (bass, guitar); Vocalist; Composer. m. Barbara, 21 March 1979, 2 d. *Musical Education:* Violin to Grade 5; School Chorus and Church choral singing; Guitar self-taught. *Career:* Toured, recorded with Decameron, 1973–76; Member, Steve Hackett (bass and vocals), 1978–80; Tours include: Reading Festival, 1979; UK; Europe; North America, 1980; Owner, Millstream Recording Studio, 1978–88. *Compositions include:* Saturday, for Third Light (with Dave Bell). *Recordings:* Albums: with Decameron, Mammoth Special; Tomorrow's Pantomime, Third Light; with Steve Hackett: Spectral Mornings,

Defector; First solo album: About Time, 1999. *Memberships:* Musicians' Union; PRS. *Leisure interests:* Tending 6 acres of woodland; Playing guitar. *Address:* c/o Voiceatility, Hilcot House, Stanley Rd, Cheltenham, Glos GL52 6PF, England.

CAENS Thierry-Gerard; b. 24 Sept. 1958, Dijon, France. Musician (trumpet). m. Noëlle Diebold, 15 Sept. 1984, 2 s., 1 d. *Musical Education:* Paris National Superior Conservatory with Maurice André. *Career:* Former solo trumpet with Lyon Orchestra; Former solo cornet with Paris Opera Orchestra; Tours of Japan; Creator, William Sheller Trumpet Concerto, Pleyel, Paris, 1992; Soloist, Cyrano, B O Music by Jean-Claude Petit; Duo with Jean Guillou, Organ. *Recordings:* Tangos and Milongas; Haydn; Bach Brandenburg Concerts; Haydn; Jericho. *Publications:* Leduc-Hamelle publishers in Paris. *Honours:* First prize, Paris Conservatory; Victoires de la Musique. *Memberships:* Artistic Director, Camerata de Bourgogne; Music Festival of Great Wine of Burgundy. *Leisure interests:* Gastronomy; Wine; Films. *Current Management:* Jacques Thelen; Salle Pleyel.

CAFFREY Leon; Musician (drums). *Career:* Member, The Farm; Hunkpapa; Played with Squeeze and China Crisis; Joined Space, 1998; Numerous tours and television appearances. *Recordings:* Singles: The Ballad of Tom Jones (with Cerys Matthews), 1998; Begin Again, 1998; Bad Days, 1998; Diary of a Wimp, 2000; Album: Tin Planet, 1998; Greatest Hits, 2002.

CAIN Jonathan; b. 26 Feb. 1950, Chicago, Illinois, USA. Musician (keyboards); Songwriter; Prod. *Career:* Member, The Babys; Member, US rock group Journey, 1981–87; Member, Bad English, 1988–91; Member, Hardline, 1992–; Concerts include: Mountain Aire Festival, 1981, 1986; Support to Rolling Stones, US tour, 1981; Concert, Oakland Alameda County Coliseum, with Santana, The Tubes, Toto, 1982; US tour, supported by Bryan Adams, 1983. *Recordings:* Albums: with Journey: Escape, 1981; Frontiers, 1983; Raised On Radio, 1986; Greatest Hits, 1989; Trial By Fire, 1996; When You Love A Woman, 1996; Remember Me, 1998; Arrival, 2001; with Bad English: Bad English, 1989; Backlash, 1991; Solo albums: Back To The Innocence, 1995; Piano With A View, 1995; Body Language, 1997; For A Lifetime, 1998; Singles: with Journey: Still They Ride; Who's Crying Now; Separate Ways (Worlds Apart); Faithfully; After The Fall; Send Her My Love; Be Good To Yourself; Suzanne; Girl Can't Help It; I'll Be Alright; with Bad English: When I See You Smile (No. 1, USA) 1990; Straight To Your Heart, 1991. *Address:* c/o Hemming Morse, 650 California St, Suite 900, San Francisco, CA 94108, USA.

CAINES Ronald Arthur; b. 13 Dec. 1939, Bristol, England. Artist; Musician (saxophonist). m. Susan Weaver, 21 April 1958, 1 s., 2 d. *Education:* West of England College of Art. *Musical Education:* Self-taught, mainly listening to jazz records. *Career:* Worked extensively in Europe, especially France, Switzerland, UK college circuit; Played in Keith Tippett's Big Band, Ark; Also with: Julie Tippett; Evan Parker, in 1970s; Played improvised and Latin based music, led modern jazz quartet. *Compositions include:* Northern Hemisphere; Bathers of Lake Balaton; Isadora; Music for film Laughter In The Dark, 1969. *Recordings:* Mercator Projected; SNAFU; The World of East of Eden. *Memberships:* PRS; Musicians' Union (Delegate). *Leisure interests:* Travel; Politics. *Current Management:* Ben Williams, Vital Communications. *Address:* 15 Highbury Villas, Kingsdown, Bristol B52 8BX, England.

CAIRNS Andy; b. Ireland. Vocalist; Musician (guitar). *Career:* Singer, musician, Irish rock group Therapy?, 1989–; Appearances include Top of The Pops, BBC1. *Recordings:* Albums: Baby Teeth, 1991; Pleasure Death (mini-album), 1992; Nurse, 1993; Troublegum, 1994; Infernal Love, 1995; Semi-Detached, 1998; Shameless, 2001; EPs: Shortsharpshock, 1993; Face The Strange, 1993; Opal Mantra, 1993; Singles: Die Laughing, 1994; Nowhere, 1994; Trigger Inside, 1994; Stories, 1995; Loose, 1995; Diane, 1995; Church of Noise, 1998; Lonely, Cryin' Only, 1998; Hate Kill Destroy, 2000. *Honour:* Mercury Music Prize Nomination, 1995. *Current Management:* DCG Management, 89 Upper Georges St, Dun Laoghaire, Dublin, Ireland.

CALAZANS Teca; b. 27 Oct. 1940, Vitoria, Espirito Santo, Brazil. Composer; Singer. m. Philippe Lesage, 15 June 1991, 1 d. *Career:* Former actress; Moved to France, 1970; Recorded 6 discs, performed at Olympia, with Claude Nougaro, return to Brazil, 1979–88; 5 solo albums, compère television show, 3 years; Appearances include: Festival de Jazz de Vienne, 1991; 60 Villes pour les jeunesses Musicales de France, 1992; Festival de la Guitare, 1992; Festival de Chateauvallon, 1992; Festival de Jazz Zurich au Moods, 1994; Passage Du Nord Ouest, Paris, 1994; Soiree Jazz 94, Nice Jazz Festival, 1995; Guitar master de Paul, 1995. *Compositions:* Côco

Verde; Gabriel; Caíco (sung by Milton Nascimento); Firuliu (sung by Nara Leâo); Atras da luminosidade (sung by Gal Costa). *Recordings:* Musigues et Chants du Brasil, 1974; Caminho das Aguas, 1975; Cade o Povo, 1975; Desafio de Viola, 1978; Povo Daqui, 1980; Eu Nao Sou Dos, 1981; Teca Calazans, 1982; Mário Trezentos, 350, 1983; Jardin Exotique, 1983; Mina do Mar, 1985; Teca Calazans Chante Villa Lobos, 1990; Pizindim, 1991; Intuiçao, 1993; O Samba dos Bambas, 1994. *Leisure interest:* Swimming. *Current Management:* Rita Sá Rego, Cirandas. *Address:* 3 Ave Mathilde, 95210 Sainte-Gratien, France.

CALE J J (John Weldon); b. 5 Dec. 1938, Oklahoma City, Oklahoma, USA. Vocalist; Songwriter; Musician (guitar). *Career:* Singer, songwriter, pioneer of 'Tulsa sound'; Leader, Johnny Cale and the Valentines; Toured briefly with Grand Ole Opry road company; Backing musician to Red Sovine, Little Jimmy Dickens; Studio engineer, guitarist, Los Angeles, 1964; Played with artists including: Leon Russell; Delaney and Bonnie. *Compositions include:* Crazy Mama; Cajun Moon; Travelin' Light; Don't Cry Sister; Don't Go To Strangers; Songs covered by other artists include: After Midnight; Cocaine; I'll Make Love To You (all recorded by Eric Clapton); Mr Breeze (Johnny Cash, Lynyrd Skynyrd, The Allman Brothers); Clyde (Waylon Jennings); Bringing It Back (Kansas, Lynyrd Skynyrd); Same Old Blues (Bryan Ferry, Captain Beefheart); Magnolia (Deep Purple, Poco, Chris Smither, Jose Feliciano); The Sensitive Kind (John Mayall, Santana); Film scores include: La Femme de Mon Pote (My Best Friend's Girl), 1984. *Recordings:* Albums: A Trip Down Sunset Strip (recorded under the name The Leathercoat Minds), 1967; Naturally, 1972; Really, 1973; Okie, 1973; Troubadour, 1976; #5, 1979; Shades, 1981; Grasshopper, 1982; #8, 1983; Travel Log, 1989; #10, 1992; Closer To You, 1994; Guitar Man, 1996; Anyway the Wind Blows: The Anthology, 1997; The Very Best of JJ Cale, 1998; Live, 2001; Producer, albums by John Hammond: Got Love If You Want It; Trouble No More; Contributor, Rhythm of The Saints, Paul Simon, 1990; The Tractors, The Tractors, 1994; Fish Tree Water Blues, 1999. *Current Management:* Mike Kappus. *Address:* The Rosebud Agency, PO Box 170429, San Francisco, CA 94117, USA.

CALE John; b. 9 March 1942, Garnant, Wales. Vocalist; Musician (bass, keyboards, viola); Prod. *Musical Education:* Classical training. *Career:* Member, The Dream Syndicate; Founder member, The Velvet Underground, 1964–68, 1993; Solo artiste, 1970–; Residency, Café Bizarre, Greenwich Village, 1966; House band, Andy Warhol's Factory arts collective, New York, 1966; Reunion, with Lou Reed, Nico, 1972; Reunion with Velvet Underground, European Tour, 1993; Production includes: Nico: The Marble Index, 1969, Desert Shore, 1970, The End, 1974; Iggy Pop: The Stooges, 1969; Patti Smith: Horses, 1975; Jonathan Richman: Modern Lovers, 1975; Squeeze: Squeeze, 1977; Happy Mondays: Squirrel and G Man, 1987; Siouxsie and The Banshees: Rapture, 1995. *Recordings:* Albums: with The Velvet Underground: The Velvet Underground and Nico, 1967; White Light, White Heat, 1968; Live MCMXCIII, 1993; Solo albums include: Vintage Violence, 1970; Church of Anthrax, 1971; Academy in Peril, 1972; Paris 1919, 1973; Fear, 1974; June 1 1974, 1974; Slow Dazzle, 1975; Helen of Troy, 1975; Guts, 1977; Animal Justice, 1977; Sabotage, 1979; Honi Soit, 1981; Music For A New Society, 1982; Caribbean Sunset, 1984; Comes Alive, 1984; Artificial Intelligence, 1985; Words For The Dying, 1989; Fragments of a Rainy Season, 1992; Walking on Locusts, 1996; Dance Music, 1998; Le Vent de la Nuit, 1999; Close Watch, 1999; with Lou Reed: Songs For Drella, 1990; with Brian Eno: Wrong Way Up, 1991; with Bob Neuwirth: Last Day On Earth, 1994; Collaborated on: Small World, Big Band, Jools Holland's Rhythm 'n' Blues Orchestra, 2001; Film scores: Sid and Nancy, 1982; Paris S'Eveille, 1991; La Naissance de l'Amour, 1993; Antartida, 1995; N'oublie pas que tu vas mourir, 1996; I Shot Andy Warhol, 1997; Eat and Kiss, 1997. *Honours:* Inducted into Rock 'n' Roll Hall of Fame (with Velvet Underground), 1996; Honor Fellow, Goldsmiths College, London, 1997. *Current Management:* Firebrand Management, Suite 1.3, 12 Rickett St, London SW6 1RU, England.

CALHOUN Dave; b. 11 Feb. 1969, Whitehaven, Cumbria, England. Musician (guitar); Singer; Songwriter. *Musical Education:* Self-taught. *Career:* Played guitar alongside Dave Fenton of The Vapors, 1990; Played with Moondigger at many London venues including the Marquee, 1993–96; Currently writing and recording with Zenshoppers. *Recordings:* 423, Moondigger, 1993; Guitarist of The Year Album, 1994; Sorrows Wedding, single, Zenshoppers; Relax, album, Brian Green. *Publications:* Currently working on two guitar tuition books. *Honours:* Guitarist of the Year, 1994–95. *Memberships:* Musicians' Union; PRS; MCPS. *Leisure interest:* Carp fishing. *Current Management:* John Glover, 34 Lotts Rd, Chelsea, London SW10, England. *Address:* 15 Broughton Rd, Thornton Heath, Surrey CR7 6AG, England.

CALHOUN William; b. 22 July 1964, Brooklyn, New York, USA. Musician (Drums). *Career:* Member, Living Colour, 1984–95; Backed Mick Jagger of Primitive Cool album, 1986; Demo produced by Mick Jagger obtained them record deal; Support slots to live dates with Rolling Stones. *Recordings:*

Singles: Cult of Personality, 1988; Glamour Boys, 1988; Type, 1990; Love Rears Its Ugly Head, 1990; Solace of You, 1991; Talkin' Loud and Sayin' Nothing, 1991; AuslSnder, 1993; Bi, 1993; Sunshine of Your Love, 1994; Albums: Vivid, 1988; Time's Up, 1990; Biscuits, 1993; Stain, 1993; Pride (compilation), 1995; Also collaborated with: BB King; Cynthia Jane.

CALLE Ed (Eduardo Joaquin); b. 10 Aug. 1959, Caracas, Venezuela. Musician (saxophone); Composer; Arranger; Teacher. *Education:* Senior Mathematics Major. *Musical Education:* Masters degree Music, University of Miami. *Career:* Sony recording artist; Recorded and toured with international artistes including Frank Sinatra; Gloria Estefan; Vicki Carr; Julio Iglesias; Arturo Sandoval; Regina Belle. *Recordings:* Solo albums (original compositions and arrangements): Nightgames, 1985; Double-talk, 1996; Sunset Harbor, 1999. *Publications:* Working on books for the saxophone; Many published arrangements. *Membership:* NARAS. *Leisure interests:* Athletics; Mathematics; Films; Reading. *Current Management:* Carl Valldejulli, Turi's Music/Quiet Storm. *Address:* Turi's Music, 103 Westward Dr., Miami Springs, FL 33166, USA.

CALLIS Jo; b. 2 May 1955, Rotherham, Yorkshire, England. Musician; Songwriter. *Education:* Edinburgh College of Art. *Musical Education:* Self-taught. *Career:* Member of bands including: The Human League; The Rezillos; Shake; Boots For Dancing; Co-writer with many other artistes. *Recordings:* Albums: with The Human League: Dare (No. 1, UK), 1981; Love and Dancing, 1982; Hysteria, 1984; Octopus, 1995; with The Rezillos: Can't Stand The Rezillos; Singles: with The Human League: Don't You Want Me (No. 1, UK and US), 1981; Open Your Heart, 1981; Mirror Man, 1982; (Keep Feeling) Fascination, 1983; The Lebanon, 1984; Life On Your Own, 1984; Louise, 1984; with The Rezillos: Top of The Pops, 1978. *Honours:* ASCAP Awards, Don't You Want Me, (Keep Feeling) Fascination. *Membership:* BASCA. *Leisure interests:* Collecting old toys; Toy soldiers. *Address:* 3A Rochester Terrace, Edinburgh EH10 5AA, Scotland.

CALZADO David, (Sergio David Calzado Almenares); b. 1957, Cuba. Vocalist; Musician (violin); Songwriter; Prod. *Musical Education:* Escuela Nacional de Arte, Cuba, 1978. *Career:* Born into a musical family; Grandfather was a Trovador and father was a member of the Orquesta Estrellas Cubana; After graduating in music, played with father's band and Orquesta Ritmo Oriental; Produced records for Cuban record company Egrem; Became first violin at the Tropicana in Havana where approached to form a band for the summer season at the Sporting Club of Monaco; Band became La Charanga Habanera; During five years of summer stints in Monaco, supported stars including: Whitney Houston; Barry White; Charles Aznavour; Band had classic charanga line-up of flutes, violins, bass piano and percussion but re-launched with brass and reduced violin section, 1993; Spectacular live show included elaborate costumes and choreography; Charanga Habanera split, 2000; Retained right to the act name and put together a younger group under the same name.

CAMARA DE LANDA Enrique Guillermo; b. 3 May 1951, Buenos Aires, Argentina. Enthomusicologist. *Education:* Philosophy Doctorate, University of Valladolid, Spain, 1994. *Musical Education:* Degree in Musical Pedagogy, 1977, Degree in Musicology, 1979, Argentinian Catholic University, Buenos Aires; Piano degree, 1972. *Career:* Currently Professor of Ethnomusiclogy at the Universidad de Valladolid, Spain. *Publications:* Tango de ida y vuelta, 1992; Argentina: Charnada y chamamé, 1992; Argentina: Carnaval, 1994; L'arrivée du tango en Italie, 1995; Proyecciones de la baguala, 1996; Erkencho, 1995. *Memberships:* Vice-President, SIbE (Sociedad Ibérica de Etnomusicología); SEdEM (Sociedad Española de Musicología): IASPM; AAM (Asociación Argentina de Musicología). *Address:* Azorín 5, 4°A, 47005 Valladolid, Spain.

CAMBUZAT François R; Singer; Musician (Guitar); Composer. *Recordings:* With the Kim Squad: Young Bastards, 1987; Solo: Notre-Dame des Naufragés, 1988; Uccidiamo Kim, 1990; With Il Gran Teatro Amaro: Port-Famine, 1991; Hôtel Brennesel, 1993; Piazza Orphelins, 1995; With F R Cambuzat et les Enfants Rouges: Swinoujscie-Tunis, 1995; Reus-Ljubljana, 1998; Taurisano-Cajarc, 1998; Various compilations. *Membership:* SACEM. *Current Management:* Les Enfants Rouges. *Address:* 202 rue du Berger, 5350 Ohey, Belgium.

CAMERON Chris; b. England. Musician (keyboards); Arranger; Prod. *Career:* Worked with: Hot Chocolate; Wham!; George Michael (also his musical director); Stevie Nicks; Terence Trent D'Arby; Breathe; Take That; Presumptos Implicados; Pepsi and Shirlie; A1; Gary Barlow; Joe Cocker; Randy Crawford, Chris De Burgh, Will Downing; Stephen Duffy; Elton John; John Martyn; 911; Pet Shop Boys; Steps; Tina Turner. *Current Management:* The Liaison and Promotion Co. *Address:* 70 Gloucester Pl., London W1H 3HL, England.

CAMERON John Allan; b. 16 Dec. 1938, Inverness, Cape Breton, Nova Scotia. Singer; Songwriter; Musician. *Education:* BEd, St Francis Xavier University, Antignoish, Nova Scotia, Canada. *Career:* Professional, 1968;

Toured and performed throughout world from Arctic to Middle East; Appeared in Las Vegas and on Grand Ole Opry; Toured with Anne Murray for several years; Hosted TV shows, CBC and CTV Networks. *Recordings:* Here Comes John Allan Cameron, 1968; Get There By Dawn, 1975; Lord of the Dance, 1977; Weddings, Wakes and Other Things, 1979; Free Born Man, 1987; Good Times, 1990; Wind Willow, 1991; Glencoe Station, 1996. *Honours:* East Coast Music Asscn's Lifetime Achievement Award, 1995; Hon. Dr of Letters, University College, Cape Breton, 1998. *Memberships:* AFofM; SOCAN. *Current Management:* Joella Foulds, Rave Entertainment Inc. *Address:* Rave Entertainment Inc, 363 Charlotte St, Suite 1, Sydney, NS, B1P 1E1, Canada.

CAMERON Kate; b. 14 Nov. 1965, Hemel Hempstead, Hertfordshire, England. Singer; Songwriter; Entertainer; Musician (piano, french horn). *Musical Education:* Theory: Grade V; French Horn: Grade VIII; Piano: Grade VII; O and A Level, Grade A. *Career:* Lead vocalist, backing vocalist, vocal arranger, writer with GMT, 1990–92; Worked with Doug Wimbish, Bob Jones, John Waddell, Q; Host of Singers Nightclub; Musical Director, Minx, all-female cabaret acapella group, 1993–95; Session singer for artists including Norman Cook, 1994. *Recordings:* P.A.S.S.I.O.N.; Jon of The Pleased Wimmin, 1995; with Freak Power (backing vocals): Rush; Get In Touch, 1994. *Memberships:* Musicians' Union; Variety Artiste's Association. *Leisure interests:* Reading; Golf; Badminton; Cooking. *Current Management:* The Vocal Agency. *Address:* 43 Windsor Dr., East Barnet, Herts EN4 8UE, England.

CAMERON Matt; b. 28 Nov. 1962, San Diego, California, USA. Musician (drums). *Career:* Appeared in film Attack of the Killer Tomatoes, 1970s; Member, Soundgarden, 1986–97; Temple of The Dog, 1992; Hater, 1993; Wellwater Conspiracy, 1997–; Pearl Jam, 2000–; Numerous tours and festival appearances. *Recordings:* with Soundgarden: Singles: Nothing to Say, 1987; Flower, 1989; Loud Love, 1990; Hands All Over/Get On the Snake EP, 1990; Jesus Christ Pose, 1992; Outshined, 1992; Rusty Cage, 1992; Spoonman, 1994; The Day I Tried to Live, 1994; Black Hole Sun, 1994; Fell on Black Days, 1995; Pretty Noose, 1996; Burden in My Hand, 1996; Blow Up the Outside World, 1996; Ty Cobb, 1996; Bleed Together, 1996; Albums: Ultramega OK, 1988; Louder than Love, 1989; Badmotorfinger, 1991; Superunknown (No. 1, USA), 1994; Down on the Upside, 1996; A-Sides, 1997; with Temle of The Dog: Album: Temple of The Dog, 1992; with Hater: Single: Circles, 1993; Album: Hater, 1993; with Wellwater Conspiracy: Albums: Declaration of Conformity, 1997; Brotherhood of Electric: Operational Directives, 1999; Scroll and Its Combinations, 2001; with Pearl Jam: Binaural, 2000; Live 2000 (series of live albums), 2000. *Honours:* Grammy Award for Black Hole Sun, 1994.

CAMILLERI Claude Anthony Paul Francis Xavier; b. 9 Nov. 1963, Malta. Audio Engineering and Production Lecturer; Engineering Prod. m. Sharon, 16 June 1988, 1 s., 2 d. *Education:* Maynooth University, Ireland, 1984. *Musical Education:* Piano and guitar; Synthesis / Music Technology. *Career:* Considered leading pioneer in training audio engineers and producers, 1986–; Lectures, various universities and colleges world-wide; Founder, Alchemea; Work for Sony; Polygram; Virgin; EMI; Chrysalis; Acid-Jazz; Motor-Germany; Various productions for independent labels. *Recordings:* Producer for various record labels; Own albums on own label; Various collaborations. *Publications:* Various papers on production and sound/audio engineering; Two books due for publication in 1996. *Honour:* National Training Award for Achievements in field of training and education. *Memberships:* APRS; Producer's Guild. *Leisure interests:* Cooking; Chess; Research; Family. *Current Management:* c/o Hari Voyantzis, Alchemea Records. *Address:* The Windsor Centre, Windsor St, The Angel, Islington, London N1 8QH, England.

CAMILO Michel; b. 4 April 1954, Santo Domingo, Dominican Republic. Jazz Musician (piano); Composer; Conductor. m. Sandra Camilo, 22 Feb. 1975. *Education:* Universidad Autonoma de Santo Domingo (VASD). *Musical Education:* National Conservatory, Dominican Republic; Juilliard School of Music; Mannes School of Music. *Career:* Appearances include: Carnegie Hall debut, 1986; Berlin Jazz Festival, 1987; Musical director, Heineken Jazz Festival, Dominican Republic, 1987–; Newport Jazz Festival; North Sea Jazz Festival; Pori Jazz Festival; Grande Parade du Jazz; Copenhagen Jazz Festival; New Orleans Jazz Festival; Madrid and Barcelona Jazz Festivals; San Sebastian and Andorra Jazz Festival; Lugano Jazz Festival; Film: Two Much, 1996. *Recordings:* Why Not, 1986; Suntan/Michel Camilo in trio, 1987; Michel Camilo, 1988; On Fire, 1991; On The Other Hand, 1991; Rendezvous, 1993; One More Once, 1994; Two Much (soundtrack), 1996; Rhapsody For Two Pianos and Orchestra, 1992; Thru My Eyes, 1996. *Honours:* Emmy Award, 1986; Voted among Top Jazz Artists of Year, Billboard magazine, 1989, 1991; Hon. Professorship (VASD), 1992; Dr h.c. (Utesa), 1993. *Memberships:* AFofM; RMA; American Music Center. *Leisure interests:* Reading; Movies; Computers; Music. *Current Management:* Sandra Camilo, Redondo Music. *Address:* PO Box 216, Katonah, NY 10536, USA.

CAMISON Mathias (Mat); b. 5 Aug. 1941, Algeria. Composer; Arranger; Musician (keyboards). *Musical Education:* Conservatory. *Career:* Musician on tour: All French stars; Artists including Jimmy Cliff; The Four Tops; Film (France): Black and White In Color; Many hits, England, USA as Pepper Box; Television music for: Canal; Sport; Music on France 1; Horses races. *Recordings include:* Hits with Pepper Box; Love Me Baby, Sheila B Devotion; We've Got A Feeling, with Chris Waddle and B Boli. *Honours:* Academy Award; Molière. *Memberships:* SACEM; SPEDIDAM; ADAMI. *Leisure interests:* Tennis; Football; Sailing. *Address:* 5 rue de la Tuilierie, 92150 Suresnes, France.

CAMOZZI Christopher Alan; b. 1 May 1957, Burlingame, California, USA. Musician (guitar). *Musical Education:* Private study. *Career:* Musician for Michael Bolton tours: Soul Provider; Time, Love and Tenderness; Timeless, The Classics; The One Thing tours; Television: Tonight Show; Arsenio Hall; Billboard Music Awards; American Music Awards; VH-1 Honours; Oprah Winfrey Show; Donahue; NBC TV; Specials; VH2 Unplugged; with Mariah Carey: Grammy Awards; Tonight Show. *Recordings:* with Michael Bolton: Soul Provider; Time, Love and Tenderness; Timeless, The Classics; with Mariah Carey: Mariah Carey; with Barbra Streisand: Greatest Hits and More; with Whitney Houston: I'm Your Baby Tonight. *Publications:* Guitar Player; Peavey Monitor. *Membership:* Musicians' Union. *Leisure interest:* Golf. *Address:* 3341 Abbey Lane, Palmdale, CA 93551, USA.

CAMP Manel; b. 20 April 1947, Manresa, Barcelona, Spain. Musician (piano); Arranger; Composer; Concert and Recording Dir. *Musical Education:* Professional diploma, piano; Contemporary composition, orchestration, Language and methodology of Jazz, Berklee College of Music, Boston. *Career:* As solo pianist: International festivals: Grenoble, France; Brirstonas, Lithuania; Cheboksari and Yaroslav, Russia; Buenos Aires, Argentina; Caracas, Venezuela; Boston, USA; Barcelona, Madrid, San Sebastian and Granada, Spain. *Compositions:* Petita Suite; Simbols; Canigo; Ressorgir; El Llibre de les Besties. *Recordings:* Minorisa, Fusion; Poesia Secreta; Primer Viatge; La Meva Petita Terra; Escàndols; El Complot Dels Anells; Viu; Ben A Prop; Diàlegs; Ressorgir; Duets; Contrast; Coratge; Rosebud; Complicitats; Canço; Canigo; L'Ultime Frontera. *Publications:* Scores of first two albums. *Honours:* Best Recording Composition, Generalitat de Catalunya, 1985; Best Musical Performance, Radio Nacional, 1988; Best Soloist, International Festival Jazz, San Sebastian, 1986; National Cinematographyc Award, Generalitat, 1992; Premi Altaveu, 1996; Premi, Iniciativa, 1997. *Memberships:* Associación Catalana de Compositors; Associación de Musica de Jazz de Catalunya. *Current Management:* Madma. *Address:* c/o de la Mel, 23, 2n, 08240 Manresa, Barcelona, Spain.

CAMP Richard; b. 16 April 1956, Ipswich, Suffolk, England. Singer; Musician (guitar). *Career:* Lead singer, guitarist, with Blind Dog Beerbelly Blues Band; Live performances include: Diana Luke Show, Greater London Radio, 1994; Guitarist with groups: Click Click; Savage Bees; World Circus; Eclipse. *Recordings:* Single: Leave Well Alone, Savage Bees, 1978; EP: Reanimate, Click Click, 1983; Album: Blue Guitar, Blind Dog Beerbelly Blues Band, 1996. *Membership:* Musicians' Union. *Leisure interests:* Blues history; Guitar collecting; Graphic design; Reading; Socialising. *Address:* PO Box 4039, Dunstable, Bedfordshire LU5 4DG, England.

CAMPBELL Ali (Alistair); b. 15 Feb. 1959, Birmingham, England. Vocalist; Musician (guitar). *Career:* Member, UK reggae group, UB40, 1979–; Also solo artiste; Concerts include: Tour with the Pretenders, 1980; Support to the Police, Rockatta De Bowl, Milton Keynes, 1980; Nelson Mandela's 70th Birthday Tribute, Wembley Stadium, 1988; Film, Dance With The Devil, 1988; Television film: UB40 – A Family Affair, C4, 1991. *Recordings:* Albums: with UB40: Signing Off, 1980; Present Arms, 1981; The Singles Album, 1982; UB44, 1982; UB40 Live, 1983; Labour of Love (No. 1, UK), 1983; Geffrey Morgan, 1984; Baggariddim, 1985; Rat In The Kitchen, 1986; CCCP – Live In Moscow, 1987; The Best of UB40 Vol. 1, 1987; Labour of Love II, 1990; Promises and Lies (No. 1, UK), 1993; Anansi, 1995; Guns In The Ghetto, 1997; Labour of Love II, 1998; Very Best of UB40, 2000; Solo: Big Love, 1995; Singles include: King/Food For Thought, 1980; My Way of Thinking, 1980; The Earth Dies Screaming, 1980; One In Ten, 1981; Love Is All Is Alright, 1982; Red Red Wine (No. 1, UK), 1983 (also No. 1, US, 1988); Please Don't Make Me Cry, 1983; Many Rivers To Cross, 1983; Cherry Oh Baby, 1984; If It Happens Again, 1984; I Got You Babe, duet with Chrissie Hynde (No. 1, UK), 1985; Don't Break My Heart, 1985; Sing Our Own Song, 1986; Rat In Mi Kitchen, 1987; Maybe Tomorrow, 1987; Breakfast In Bed, duet with Chrissie Hynde, 1988; Homely Girl, 1989; Kingston Town, 1990; I'll Be Your Baby Tonight, with Robert Palmer, 1990; The Way You Do The Things You Do, 1990; Here I Am (Come and Take Me), 1991; Can't Help Falling In Love, used in film soundtrack Sliver (No. 1, UK and US), 1993; Higher Ground, 1993; Bring Me Your Cup, 1993; Way You Do The Things You Do, 1993; C'est La Vie, 1994; Come Back Darling, 1998; Train Is Coming, 1999; Light My Fire, 2000; Solo: That Look In Your Eyes, 1995. *Current Management:* David

Harper, What Management, 12B South Bar, First Floor, Banbury, Oxon OX16 9AA, England.

CAMPBELL David; b. 22 Oct. 1969, Glasgow, Scotland. Musician (drums, percussion); Songwriter; Musical Arranger; Prod. *Musical Education:* Clydebank College. *Career:* Drummer, percussionist, writer, arranger, producer with: Parksorch, 1987–88; Kiss 'N' Tell, 1988–92; Ragged Laughter, 1992–94; Raglin Street Rattle, 1994–; Concerts and tours include: Beat The Clyde, 1987; Prince of Wales Gala Concert, 1989; Solo American tour of Southern states, 1993; US Coast to Coast tour, 1994; TV Special, Live at The Festival, 1988. *Compositions include:* Need A Lover, 1992; State of Confusion, 1993, On Brilliant Wings, 1994, She Called My Name, 1995; Seize the Day, Moment in White, 1999. *Recordings include:* Cava Sessions, 1988; The Word Is Out... The Time Is Now, 1992; Raglin Street Rattle, 1995; Dog on Wheels, EP, with Belle and Sebastian, 1996; Year Zero, 1999. *Honour:* Premier Student of The Year, Clydebank College, 1990. *Membership:* PRS. *Leisure interests:* Photography; Motor sport; World travel. *Address:* 8 Whitslade St, Provanhall, Glasgow G34 9PY, Scotland.

CAMPBELL Eddie; b. 6 July 1965, Scotland. Musician (Keyboards). *Career:* Member, Texas; Numerous tours, festival appearances and TV appearances. *Recordings:* Singles include: I Don't Want a Lover, 1989; Tired of Being Alone, 1993; Say What You Want, 1997; Halo, 1997; Put Your Arms Around Me, 1997; Black Eyed Boy, 1997; In Our Lifetime, 1999; Summer Son, 1999; In Demand, 2000; Inner Smile, 2001; Albums: Southside, 1989; Mother's Heaven, 1991; Rick's Road, 1993; White on Blonde (No. 1, UK), 1997; The Hush (No. 1, UK) 1999; The Greatest HIts (No. 1, UK), 2000.

CAMPBELL Glen Travis; b. 22 April 1936, Delight, Arkansas, USA. Singer; Musician (guitar). *Career:* Member, Dick Bills Band, 1954; Founder, Glen Campbell and The Western Wranglers, 1958; Session musician, Los Angeles; Replaced Brian Wilson touring with the Beach Boys; Television work; Film appearances include: True Grit, 1969; Norwood, 1970; Duets with Anne Murray, Rita Coolidge, Tanya Tucker; Tours, television appearances, late 1970s. *Recordings:* Hit singles include: Gentle On My Mind; By The Time I Get To Phoenix; Wichita Lineman; Galveston; Rhinestone Cowboy; Southern Nights; Albums include: Too Late To Worry, Too Late To Cry, 1963; The Astounding 12-String Guitar of Glen Campbell, 1964; Gentle On My Mind, 1967; By The Time I Get To Phoenix, 1967; Hey Little One, 1968; A New Place In The Sun, 1968; Galveston, 1969; Try A Little Kindness, 1970; Oh Happy Day, 1970; Norwood (soundtrack), 1970; The Last Time I Saw Her, 1971; Anne Murray/Glen Campbell, 1971; I Knew Jesus (Before He Was A Star), 1973; Reunion (The Songs of Jimmy Webb), 1974; Rhinestone Cowboy, 1975; Bloodline, 1976; Southern Nights, 1977; Basic, 1978; Somethin' About You Baby I Like, 1980; It's The World Gone Crazy, 1981; Old Home Town, 1983; Letter To Home, 1984; Just A Matter of Time, 1986; No More Night, 1988; Still Within The Sound of My Voice, 1988; Walkin' In The Sun, 1990; Unconditional Love, 1991; Favourite Hymns, 1992; Somebody Like That, 1993; Phoenix, 1994; Christmas with Glen Campbell, 1995; Branson City Limits, 1998; In Concert (Live), 1999. *Honours:* Grammy, Best Country and Western Recording, Gentle On My Mind, 1967. *Current Management:* Girsey, Schneider and Co, 10351 Santa Monica Blvd #300, Los Angeles, CA 90025, USA.

CAMPBELL Isobel; b. 27 April 1976. Vocalist; Musician (cello); Songwriter. *Career:* Member: Belle and Sebastian, 1996–; The Gentle Waves 1998–; Collaborations: Arab Strap; Snow Patrol Curated Bowlie Weekend Festival with other Belle and Sebastian band members, 1999. *Recordings:* Albums: with The Gentle Waves: The Green Fields of Foreverland, 1999; Swansong For You, 2000; with Belle and Sebastian: Tigermilk, If You're Feeling Sinister, 1996; The Boy With The Arab Strap 1998; Fold Your Hands Child – You Walk Like A Peasant, 2000; Singles: with The Gentle Waves: Weathershow, 1999; Falling From Grace, 2000; with Belle and Sebastian: Dog On Wheels EP, Lazy Line Painter Jane EP, 3–6–9 Seconds of Light EP, 1997; This Is Just A Modern Rock Song EP, 1998; Legal Man, 2000; Jonathan David, I'm Waking Up To Us, 2001. *Honours:* Brit Award, Best Newcomer, 1999. *Current Management:* Banchory Management, PO Box 25074, Glasgow G2 6YL, Scotland. *Internet:* www.belleandsebastian.co.uk.

CAMPBELL John; b. 16 April 1953, Reigate, Surrey, England. Music Publisher; Artist Man. m. Sue, 7 April 1984. *Career:* Chairman JC Music; Publisher, Manager for: Richard Feldman; Nick Trevisick; Jeff Paris; Michael Graves; Mike Moran; Howard New; Lowcraft; Akure; Santessa; Bachelor Number One; Mikey Graham; Artist Manager for: Marcella Detroit; Shakespear's Sister; Lena Fiagbe; Oui 3; Clementines; Nut. *Recordings:* Stay, Shakespear's Sister (No. 1, 8 weeks, UK charts); Gotta Get It Right, Lena Fiagbe; I Believe, Marcella Detroit. *Memberships:* Pegs Club; Liberal Party; Groucho Club. *Leisure interest:* Fiscal philosophy. *Address:* 84 Strand on the Green, (Studio at rear), London W4 3PU, England.

CAMPBELL Junior (William); b. 31 May 1947, Glasgow, Scotland. Composer; Arranger; Musician; Vocalist; Conductor. m. (1) Margaret Hutcheson, 7 Jan. 1967, (2) Susan Chibnall, 18 March 1989, 1 s., 1 d. *Musical Education:* Studied orchestration, composition, conducting with Eric Gilder and Max Saunders, RCM. *Career:* Founder member, Gaylords, 1961; Later became Marmalade, many hits, 1968–71; Solo artist, singer, 1972–74; Record producer, songwriter, 1974–80; Produced many artists including Barbara Dickson; Film and television composer including Bafta Award drama: Taking Over The Asylum; Composer on 104 Thomas The Tank Engine Films. *Recordings:* with Marmalade: Lovin' Things, 1968; Ob-La-Di Ob-La-Da (No. 1), 1969; Reflections of My Life, 1970; Rainbow, 1970; Compilation: Reflections of The Marmalade, 2001; Solo: Hallelujah Freedom, 1972; Sweet Illusion; Second Time Around, 2001. *Memberships:* BASCA; PRS; MCPS. *Leisure interests:* Eating out; 2 Labrador dogs; Played showbiz charity football for many years (now retired gracefully); Squash. *Address:* Greyfriars Lodge, Greyfriars Dr., Ascot, Berks SL5 9JD, England.

CAMPBELL Rita; b. 28 Sept. 1968, London, England. Singer. *Career:* Backing singer for: D:ream; Take That tour; Kenny Thomas, British tour; Act of Faith, British tour; Brand New Heavies, European tour; Billie Ray Martin; China Black; Carleen Anderson; X-Avia; Ronnie Simon; Bell Curtis; Angie Brown; Mary Pearce; Dream Academy; Rin Tin Tin; Cindy Jackson; Perception; Television includes: Smash Hits Awards; Dance Energy; In The Air Tonight (Virgin's 21st); Top of The Pops; The James Whale Show; Later with Jools Holland; TFI Friday. *Recordings:* with: Pauline Henry; Sly and Robbie; Bizarre Inc; Odyssey; Act of Faith; Glamma Kid; Kavana; Cleopatra; Dream Academy; Perception; Medalling Thieves; Commercials: Ribena Spring; Audi; American Airlines; Gordons Gin; Heineken Beer; Pepsi; Sugar Puffs. *Membership:* Musicians' Union. *Leisure interests:* Films; Photography; Art; Eating out; Travel. *Current Management:* Hobsons Singers; Session Connection; Simon Harrison. *Address:* 21 Ruckholt Close, Leyton, London E10 5NX, England.

CAMPBELL Robin; b. 25 Dec. 1954, Birmingham, England. Musician (guitar); Vocalist. *Career:* Lead guitarist, vocalist, UK reggae group, UB40, 1979–; Concerts include: Tour with the Pretenders, 1980; Support to The Police, Rockatta De Bowl, Milton Keynes, 1980; Nelson Mandela's 70th Birthday Tribute, Wembley Stadium, 1988; Film, Dance With The Devil, 1988; Television film: UB40 – A Family Affair, C4, 1991. *Recordings:* Albums with UB40: Signing Off, 1980; Present Arms, 1981; The Singles Album, 1982; UB44, 1982; UB40 Live, 1983; Labour of Love (No. 1, UK), 1983; Geffrey Morgan, 1984; Baggariddim, 1985; Rat In The Kitchen, 1986; CCCP – Live In Moscow, 1987; The Best of UB40 Vol. 1, 1987; Labour of Love II, 1990; Promises and Lies (No. 1, UK), 1993; Anansi, 1995; Guns In The Ghetto, 1997; Labour of Love III, 1998; Very Best of UB40, 2000; Singles include: King/Food For Thought, 1980; My Way of Thinking, 1980; The Earth Dies Screaming, 1980; One In Ten, 1981; Love Is All Is Alright, 1982; Red Red Wine (No. 1, UK), 1983 (also No. 1, US, 1988); Please Don't Make Me Cry, 1983; Many Rivers To Cross, 1983; Cherry Oh Baby, 1984; If It Happens Again, 1984; I Got You Babe, duet with Chrissie Hynde (No. 1, UK), 1985; Don't Break My Heart, 1985; Sing Our Own Song, 1986; Rat In Mi Kitchen, 1987; Maybe Tomorrow, 1987; Breakfast In Bed, duet with Chrissie Hynde, 1988; Homely Girl, 1989; Kingston Town, 1990; I'll Be Your Baby Tonight, with Robert Palmer, 1990; The Way You Do The Things You Do, 1990; Here I Am (Come and Take Me), 1991; Can't Help Falling In Love, used in film soundtrack Sliver (No. 1, UK and US), 1993; Higher Ground, 1993; Bring Me Your Cup, 1993; Way You Do The Things You Do, 1993; C'est La Vie, 1994; Come Back Darling, 1998; Train Is Coming, 1999; Light My Fire, 2000. *Current Management:* David Harper, What Management, 12B South Bar, First Floor, Banbury, Oxon OX16 9AA, England.

CAMPBELL Simon John; b. 9 Jan. 1958, Bury, Lancashire, England. Musician (guitar); Vocalist; Prod. m. Angela Mary Campbell, 5 Sept. 1982, 2 s. *Education:* Degree in Chemistry. *Musical Education:* Self-taught. *Career:* Tours, 1 single, 1 EP with rock band Whitefire, 1975–81; National tours with R & B band Roadrunner, 1981–85; Tours with pop band Gilt Edge, Cutting Edge, 1985–86; International tours, 1 album with pop band Little Brother, 1986–89; 1 album with Disciples, 1990–92; with The Method, 1992–94; with Simon Campbell Band, 1994–95; Featured artist with The 1995 7. *Membership:* Musicians' Union. *Leisure interests:* Children; Food and drink. *Current Management:* Music Business Management, International House, Drake St, Rochdale OL16 1PN, England.

CAMPBELL Vivian; b. Belfast, Northern Ireland. Rock musician (guitar). *Career:* Guitarist, Dio, 1983–87; Whitesnake, 1987–88; Guitarist, Trinity; Riverdogs; Guitarist, Shadow King, 1991; Def Leppard, 1992–; Major international tours and concerts include Freddie Mercury Tribute Concert, Wembley Stadium, 1992. *Recordings:* Albums: with Dio: Holy Diver, 1983; The Last In Line, 1984; Sacred Heart, 1985; with Whitesnake: Whitesnake, 1987; with Shadow King: Shadow King, 1991; with Def Leppard: Adrenalize (No. 1, UK and US), 1992; Retroactive, 1993; Vault 1980–95, 1995; Slang, 1996; Euphoria, 1999; Singles: with Def Leppard:

Let's Get Rocked (No. 2, UK), 1992; Make Love Like A Man, 1992; Have You Ever Needed Someone So Bad, 1992; Stand Up (Kick Love Into Motion), 1992; Heaven Is, 1993; Tonight, 1993; Two Steps Behind, used in film soundtrack The Last Action Hero, 1993; When Love and Hate Collide (No. 2, UK), 1995; Slang, 1996; All I Want Is Everything, 1996; Guest musician, Long Hard Look, Lou Gramm, 1989; Brunel's LA Zoo, with Bunny Brunel, 1998; Fear of Flying, with PJ Smith, 2001. *Current Management:* Q-Prime Inc, 729 Seventh Ave, 14th Floor, New York, NY 10019, USA.

CAMPI Ray; b. 20 April 1934, New York, New York, USA. Musician (guitar, bass, dobro steel). *Education:* BFA, University of Texas, Austin, TX, USA, 1957. *Career:* Austin City Limits, national public TV; Tomorrow Show, NBC TV; Texas Saturday Night, BBC II TV, 1991, BBC Radio, 1977; Echo's Show. *Compositions:* Rockin' At the Ritz; Caterpillar; A Little Bit of Heartache; Kick Da Bukkit. *Recordings:* 35 or more CDs and albums on Rollin' Rock Records, 1956–96. *Publications:* Rolling Stone, 1980; Dynamite, 1995; Now Dig This, 1996. *Membership:* Austin Federation of Musicians. *Leisure interest:* Old car collecting. *Current Management:* Paul Barrett, Rock 'n' Roll Enterprises. *Address:* 2872 W Ave 35, Los Angeles, CA 90065, USA.

CANAPE Jean-François; b. 1 Dec. 1945, Lagny, France. Jazz Musician (trumpet, key bugle, flute). m. Bathany Jeanne, 26 March 1988, 1 s. *Musical Education:* Versailles Conservatory. *Career:* Several international festivals and tours: Montreux; Newport; Paris; Berlin; Babylon; Tokyo; Brazaville; India; Boulogne (played with Dave Liebman); Member, Orchestre National de Jazz, 1989–91; Played and composed for cinema, theatre, contemporary and classical music. *Recordings:* KONPS, Jean-François Canape Trio; Participated in: Jack-Line; Claire, with ONJ; Katchinas, Gerard Marais. *Leisure interests:* Cinema; Fishing. *Current Management:* Sylvie Caqué. *Address:* 18 rue des Plantes, 75014 Paris, France.

CANIBOL Heinz; b. 3 July 1951, Gelsenkirchen, Germany. Man.-Dir. m. Brigitte Canibol, 3 Feb. 1984. *Education:* Degree in Economics. *Career:* Product Manager and Marketing Director, CBS Records, Germany, 1977–89; Managing Director, Sony Music, Austria, 1989–91; Managing Director and Vice President G/A/S, MCA Music Entertainment, Germany, 1992-. *Leisure interests:* Music; Reading; Gardening. *Address:* c/o MCA Music Entertainment, Winterhuder Weg 27, 22085 Hamburg, Germany.

CANN Judith Leonie; b. 3 April 1958, Perth, Western Australia. Composer; Musician (keyboard). m. David George Hunt, 14 June 1986, 1 s., 1 d. *Education:* BA degree (majoring in film making); One year at Australian Film and TV school; Exchange student, National Film School, UK. *Musical Education:* Post-graduate diploma in conducting (Surrey University). *Career:* Composed, performed synthesized scores and music for use in the film, television, video industry. *Recordings:* 25 library tracks with Chappell; 175 library tracks with Carlin; Scored music for 1492 The Shattered Utopia (short film); Making Ends Meet; Network Europe; Channel Tunnel videos; Television series: A Tale of 4 Market Towns; World In Action; Laser, video, fireworks display in China. *Publications:* Article in APV magazine, Videomaker. *Honours:* Stemra Award, Netherlands, Most Impressive Use of Library Music, 1994. *Memberships:* PRS; Musicians' Union. *Leisure interests:* Drawing; Painting; Gardening. *Address:* 82 Bushey Hall Rd, Bushey, Herts WD2 2EQ, England.

CANONGE Mario-Laurent; b. 5 Sept. 1960, Fort de France, Martinique. Musician (Piano, Keyboards). 2 d. *Musical Education:* Bachelor Degree in Musicology; Classical Music, Conservatoire Haute de Seine, 2 years. *Career:* TV: Sur le Pont des Artistes; Rien a Cine, France Inter; Top Live, Europe I; Cerde de Minuit, Pintenne 2; Jazz 6; Jazz a Vienne; Concerts: New Morning, Zenith de Paris; Bataclan; Casino de Paris. *Compositions:* Pei Mwen Jodi; Pogo; Yélé Congo; L'esé; Palé; Si on sa Révé; Vidé Bo Kay; Echapaya; Dimanoua; Non Muoia; Sé Kon Ca; Bam Ti Bonjou. *Recordings:* Retour Aux Sources, 1991; Trait D'Union, 1993; Hommage A Marius Cultier, 1994; Aromes Caraibes, 1995. *Honours:* Best Pianist, Prix de la Défense, 1983; Best Album, Best Composer, SACEM Martinique, 1992–94, Best Album, 1996; Musical Research Prize, 1995. *Leisure interests:* The Sea; Friends; Music. *Current Management:* c/o François Post, Vivienne Sicnasi Promotion, 6 Pl. George Sand, 91130, Ris Orangis, France.

CANOVILLE Katherine; b. 13 Jan. 1965, Hillingdon, Middlesex, England. Co Dir; Group Man. m. Stephen Carrington, 7 July 1995. *Career:* Concert promoter, 1979–81; Artist Manager, 1981–95; Managing Director, Buzz Magazine, 1986–89; Co-founder, Nation Records, 1988; Managing Director, Nation Records, 1990–; Sole Trader, QFM Promotions, 1994. *Publications:* Ex-writer for Oracle/Teletext World Music Page, until 1992. *Membership:* BMIA BRIT Award Committee. *Leisure interests:* Music; Computing.

CANTRELL Jerry; b. 18 March 1966, Tacorna, Washington, USA. Musician (Guitar); Vocals. *Career:* Member, Alice in Chains; Numerous

tours and TV appearances including MTV Unplugged session. *Recordings:* Sap EP, 1992; Would?, 1993; Them Bones, 1993; Angry Chair, 1993; Down In A Hole, 1993; Grind, 1995; I Stay Away, 1995; Heaven Beside You, 1996; Fear The Voices, 1999; Bank Heist, 1999; Again, 2001; Albums: Facelift, 1990; Dirt, 1992; Sap, 1992; Jar of Flies (No. 1, USA), 1994; Alice in Chains (No. 1, USA), 1995; I Stay Away, 1995; Unplugged, 1996; Nothing Safe, 1999; Music Bank, 1999; Live, 2000; Greatest Hits, 2001; Solo Album: Boggy Depot, 1998.

CAPALDI Jim; b. 2 Aug. 1944, Evesham, Herefordshire, England. Musician (drums); Vocalist. *Career:* Member, The Helions; Deep Feeling; Traffic, 1967–69, 1970–74, reformed 1994; Also solo artiste. *Recordings:* Albums: with Traffic: Mr Fantasy, 1968; Traffic, 1968; Last Exit, 1969; Heaven Is In Your Mind, 1969; Best of Traffic, 1969; John Barleycorn Must Die, 1970; Low Spark of High-Heeled Boys, 1971; Welcome To The Canteen, 1971; Shoot Out At The Fantasy Factory, 1973; When The Eagle Flies, 1974; Far From Home, 1994; Feelin' Alright (The Very Best of Traffic), 2000; Solo albums: Oh How We Danced, 1972; Whale Meat Again, 1974; Short Cut Draw Blood, 1976; Fierce Heart, 1983; Some Came Running, 1989; Prince of Darkness, 1995; Let Thunder Cry, 1999; Singles with Traffic include: Paper Sun, 1967; Hole In My Shoe, 1967; Here We Go Round The Mulberry Bush (film title theme), 1967; No Name No Face No Number; Solo single: Love Hurts, 1975; Guest, Alone Together, Dave Mason, 1970. *Address:* c/o Freedom Songs, PO Box 272, London N20 0BY, England.

CAPLIN Arnold Stewart; b. 8 May 1929, New York, USA. Record Co Exec.; Record Prod. m. Barbara Stein, 29 June 1950, 2 s. *Career:* President, Biograph Records, 1964–; Consultant, advisor, Historic Records. *Recordings:* Albums: As producer for Thad Jones; George Gershwin; Scott Joplin; James P Johnson; Mel Lewis; Benny Goodman. *Honours:* Numerous Grammy Nominations, 1967-. *Memberships:* ASCAP; Broadcast Music Inc; NARAS (fellow); NAIRD; World Jazz Federation. *Address:* c/o Biograph Records, 35 Medford St, Somerville, MA 02143–4242, USA.

CAPONE Franco; b. 11 Jan. 1968, Rome, Italy. Author; Composer; Musician (guitar); Arranger; Language Teacher. m. Rita Tenan, 7 Sept. 1991. *Education:* Masters of Arts, Languages; PGCE Education. *Career:* Founder, French group, Melody, 1987–88; Moved to England, 1989; Worked on first album, 1991; Founded group, Open Arms, 1992; Recorded two albums, tours, Scotland, Ireland, Italy, Belgium, 1992–95; New album due 1996. *Recordings:* The World My Home, 1991; with Open Arms: Walking With Us, 1992; Back To The World, 1994. *Membership:* Musicians' Union. *Leisure interests:* Football; Tennis; Chess. *Current Management:* PPS Communications / Culture-Music, Villaverla, Italy.

CAPTAIN HOLLYWOOD (Tony Harrison); b. 9 Aug. 1962, Newark, New Jersey, USA. Singer; Rapper; Prod. *Musical Education:* Self-taught. *Career:* Choreographer, major German television programme; Artist, performing and producing: The Mixmaster; Twenty 4 Seven, 1986–90; Captain Hollywood Project, 1991-. *Recordings:* Albums: Love Is Not Sex, 1993; Singles: More and More, 1991; All I Want, 1993; Only With You, 1993; Rhythm of Life, 1994. *Publications:* Grand Piano; I Can't Stand It; More and More. *Honours:* 14 Gold records; 1 Diamond award; 1 Platinum. *Membership:* GEMA, Germany. *Leisure interests:* Cars; Basketball. *Current Management:* Susanne Foecker, D-Town Management. *Address:* Schündelnhöfe 8, 41751 Viersen, Germany.

CAPTAIN SENSIBLE (Ray Burns); b. 24 April 1954, Croydon, Surrey, England. Vocalist; Musician (lead guitar, bass). *Musical Education:* Self-taught. *Career:* Invented punk as member of The Damned; Many tours; Numerous television appearances include several on Top of The Pops. *Compositions:* Writes most of own material. *Recordings:* Albums: Solo albums, 1982- include: Women and Captain First, 1982; The Power of Love, 1983; Sensible Singles, 1984; Revolution Now, 1989; Live At The Milky Way (Amsterdam), 1995; Meathead, 1995; The Universe of Geoffrey Brown, 1998; Singles include: Happy Talk (No. 1, UK), 1982; Wot (No. 1, France, 7 weeks), 1982 ; Glad It's All Over, 1984; Come On Down, 1985; Revolution Now, 1987; Smash It Up Part 4, 1990; Wot 93, 1994. *Memberships:* PRS; Musicians' Union. *Leisure interest:* Public transport systems of the world. *Current Management:* Forward Agency Booking (FAB). *Address:* Humbug Records, Suite 4N, Leroy House, Essex Rd, Islington, London, England.

CARA Irene; b. 18 March 1959, Bronx, New York, USA. Vocalist; Actor; Dancer. *Career:* Stage appearances: Maggie Flynn, Broadway, 1968; The Me Nobody Knows, 1970; Via Galactica, New York, 1972; Got To Go Disco, 1979; Ain't Misbehavin'; Film appearances: Aaron Loves Angela, 1975; Sparkle, 1976; Fame, 1980; DC Cab, 1980; City Heat, 1984; A Certain Fury, 1985; Busted Up, 1986; Killing 'Em Softly, 1985; The Man In 5-A; Collaborations: George Duke; The Brecker Brothers; Oleta Adams; Giorgio Moroder. *Recordings:* Singles: Fame (No. 1, UK), 1980; Flashdance… What A Feeling (No. 1, USA), 1983; Why Me, 1983; Out Here On My Own; The Dream, from film DC Cab, 1984; Breakdance, 1984; All My

Heart, 1996; Albums: Anyone Can See, 1982; What A Feelin', 1983; Carasmatic, 1987. *Honours:* Obie Award; Academy Awards: Best Song, Fame; Best Song, Flashdance... What A Feeling. *Memberships:* Equity; Screen Actors Guild. *Address:* c/o Talent Consultants International Ltd, 1560 Broadway, Suite 1308, New York, NY 10036, USA.

CARCELES RUIZ Lola; b. 8 June 1960, Murcia, Spain. Singer. m. 25 May 1978, 2 s., 1 d. *Musical Education:* 5 years at conservatory. *Career:* Performed throughout Spain, 10 years; Television and radio work; Performed in USA, 1995. *Honours:* First Prize, Spanish Song Contest. *Leisure interest:* Singing. *Current Management:* Francisco Ferrer Montoya. *Address:* c/o Augustin Lara N, 10, 5°B, Vistalegre, Murcia, Spain.

CAREY Mariah; b. 22 March 1970, Long Island, New York, USA. Vocalist; Songwriter. m. Tommy Mottola, 5 June 1993. *Career:* Backing singer, Brenda K Starr, New York, 1988; Solo recording artiste, 1988–; 80m. albums sold to date; Concerts world-wide; Numerous television appearances include: Tonight Show; Arsenio Hall Show; Saturday Night Live; Top of The Pops; Wogan; Movie: Glitter, 2001. *Recordings:* Albums: Mariah Carey (No. 1, USA), 1990; Emotions, 1991; MTV Unplugged EP, 1992; Music Box (No. 1, USA and UK), 1993; Merry Christmas, 1994; Daydream (No. 1, UK), 1995; Butterfly, 1997; #1s, 1998; Rainbow, 1999; Glitter, 2001; Greatest Hits, 2001; Singles: Vision of Love (No. 1, USA), 1990; Love Takes Time (No. 1, USA), 1990; Someday (No. 1, USA), 1991; I Don't Wanna Cry (No. 1, USA), 1991; Emotions (No. 1, USA), 1991; Can't Let Go, 1992; Make It Happen, 1992; I'll Be There (No. 1, USA), 1992; Dreamlover (No. 1, USA), 1993; Hero (No. 1, USA), 1993; Without You (No. 1, UK), 1994; Anytime You Need A Friend, 1994; Endless Love (with Luther Vandross), 1994; All I Want For Christmas Is You, 1994; Fantasy (No. 1, USA), 1995; One Sweet Day (with Boyz II Men; No. 1, USA), 1995; Always Be My Baby (No. 1, USA), 1995; Open Arms, 1996; Honey (No. 1, USA), 1997; Butterfly, 1997; Breakdown, 1997; My All (No. 1, USA), 1998; When You Believe (Prince of Egypt) (with Whitney Houston), 1998; I Still Believe, 1999; Heartbreaker, 1999; Thank God I Found You, 2000; Can't Take That Away, 2000; Against All Odds (with Westlife; No. 1, UK), 2000; Loverboy, 2001; Never Too Far, 2001. *Honours:* 2 Grammy Awards: Best Female Pop Vocal and Best Artist, 1991; Rolling Stone Award, Best Female Singer, 1991; 3 Soul Train Awards, 1991; 6 Billboard Music Awards, 1991–92; 4 American Music Awards, 1992–93; 3 Citations BMI Pop Awards, 1993; International Dance Music Award, Best Solo Artist, 1996; Numerous platinum and gold records. *Current Management:* Hoffman Entertainment, 20 W 55th St, 11th Floor, New York, NY 10022, USA.

CARLISLE Belinda; b. 17 Aug. 1958, Hollywood, California, USA. Vocalist. m. Morgan Mason, 12 April 1986, 1 s. *Career:* Singer, all-girl group The Go-Gos (formerly the Misfits), 1978–85; Numerous tours world-wide; Solo artiste, 1986–94; Support to Robert Palmer, US tour, 1986; Solo tour, US and Canada, 1988; Re-formed Go-Gos, 1994–; Television includes: Late Night With David Letterman; Top of The Pops; Summer Scene; The O-Zone; Stage performance, Grease, 1983; Film appearance, Swing Shift, 1984; Model, Almay Cosmetics. *Recordings:* Singles: with The Go-Gos: Our Lips Are Sealed; We Got The Beat; Head Over Heels; The Whole World Lost Its Head; Solo: Mad About You, 1986; Heaven Is A Place On Earth (No. 1, UK and US), 1987; I Get Weak (No. 2, US), 1988; Circle In The Sand, 1988; I Feel Free, 1988; World Without You, 1988; Leave A Light On, 1989; Summer Rain, 1990; Runaway Horses, 1990; We Want The Same Thing, 1990; Live Your Life Be Free, 1991; Do You Feel Like I Feel, 1991; It's Too Real, 1993; Band of Gold, 1996; All God's Children, 1999; Albums: with the Go-Gos: Beauty and The Beat (No. 1, USA), 1981; Vacation, 1982; Talk Show, 1984; Return To The Valley of The Go-Gos, 1994; Solo albums: Belinda, 1986; Heaven On Earth, 1988; Runaway Horses, 1989; Live Your Life Be Free, 1991; Greatest Hits, 1992; Contributor, Rainbow Warriors, 1989; Tame Yourself (animal rights benefit album), 1991; Real, 1993; A Woman and A Man, 1996; Runaway Live, 2000. *Honour:* Grammy Nomination, Heaven Is A Place On Earth, 1988. *Current Management:* c/o Gold Mountain Entertainment, 3575 Cahuenga Blvd W, Los Angeles, CA 90068, USA.

CARLOTTI Jan-Mari; b. 23 June 1948, Meknès, Morocco. Singer; Musician (guitar); Writer; Composer. *Education:* Medieval History; Ethnology; Sanskrit. *Musical Education:* Self-taught. *Career:* Singer, solely in Occitan (Provençal language); Formed Mont Jóia, 1974–83; Solo artist, 1983; Also worked with Anita/Anita, Michel Marre. *Recordings:* 5 albums with Mont Jóia; 6 albums as solo artist or in other groups; Latest: Chants des Troubadours, with Michel Marre, 1995. *Publications include:* Anthologie De La Nouvelle Chanson Occitanie, 1984. *Honours:* Grand Prix, Academie Charles Cros, 1978, 1994; First Prize, International Artist, Turin Folk Competition, 1989; Best Solo Artist, Trad Magazine, 1991. *Leisure interests:* Mediterranean culture; The organization Rescontres de la Mer. *Current Management:* Ass Mont Jóia, Ostau de Provença, Parc Jourdan, 13100 Aix, France. *Address:* 2 bis Imp Fleury-Proudhon, 13200 Arles, France.

CARLYLE Mary Theresa, (Mary McLeish); b. 18 March 1938, Glasgow, Scotland. Musician (piano); Entertainer; Singer; Songwriter. m. Dick Le Claire, 15 Feb. 1968, 5 s. *Musical Education:* Privately, Frank McLeish (uncle), MA, ARCM; Violet Stewart, LRAM, ARCM. *Career:* Carroll Levis Discoveries, age 16; Variety; Moss Empires Tour, Scotland; Concert Parties; Rep; Reviews; BBC TV STV Drama, variety; Summer season Jersey's Sunshine Hotel, 1960; Winter, Manchester Clubland; US Forces Club Piani/bar, Frankfurt; Return Jersey, Formed trio, 1964; Played residencies, main hotels, clubs, also solo work; One of original (and current) resident musicians, Blue Note Club, Jersey. *Compositions include:* Jersey Suite, co-writer, Jack Duff; All I Got Was You; Jersey (all profits to J A Monday Club, childrens charity); I'll Think of You This Christmas; The Faceless Face; I'll Never Cry; How Can I Write A Song For You?. *Memberships:* Equity; Musicians' Union. *Leisure interests:* Charity work, Jersey Artists Monday Club; Variety Club, Jersey Tent 52; Writing; Composing; Sewing. *Current Management:* Dick Ray Organisation Ltd, Jersey. *Address:* 40 Seaton Pl., St Helier, Jersey JE2 3QL, Channel Islands.

CARMEN Eric; b. 11 Aug. 1949, Cleveland, Ohio, USA. Vocalist; Songwriter. *Musical Education:* Classical singing, Cleveland Institute of Music. *Career:* Singer, various groups, Cleveland, 1960s; Lead singer, The Choir, 1968; Name changed to Raspberries, 1971–75; Solo recording artiste, 1975–80, 1985–; Over 15m. record sales. *Recordings include:* Albums with: The Raspberries: The Raspberries, 1971; Fresh, 1972; Side 3, 1973; Starting Over, 1975; Solo albums: Eric Carmen, 1975; Boats Against The Current, 1977; Change of Heart, 1978; Tonight You're Mine, 1980; Eric Carmen, 1985; The Best of Eric Carmen, 1988; Winter Dreams, 1998; Someone That You Loved Before, 1998; All By Myself (compilation), 2000; Singles: with The Raspberries: Go All the Way, 1972; Overnight Sensation, 1974; All By Myself (No. 2, US); Never Gonna Fall In Love Again, 1976; Sunrise, 1976; Change of Heart, 1978; It Hurts Too Much, 1980; I Wanna Hear It From Your Lips, 1985; Solo: Hungry Eyes, used in film soundtrack Dirty Dancing, 1988; Make Me Lose Control, 1988; Reason To Try (used for Olympics Games coverage, NBC-TV), 1988; My Heart Stops, 1992; All By Myself, 1993; Make Me Lose Control, 1993. *Current Management:* QBQ Entertainment Inc, 341 Madison Ave, 14th Floor, New York, NY 10017, USA.

CARMICHAEL Anita; b. 17 Sept. 1964, Upminster, Essex, England. Musician (saxophone, alto); Vocalist. m. Michael Tanousis, 27 Aug. 1993, 1 s. *Musical Education:* Guildhall School of Music. *Career:* Tours with: The Communards; Jonathan Butler; Fay Weldon; Imagination; M-People; Television, radio: Woman's Hour (BBC Radio 4); BBC World Service; TV: Pebble Mill; Cue The Music; Womens' Jazz Archive (BBC GLR); Concerts: Antibes Festival; Brecon; Glastonbury; Jakarta; Montreux; Ronnie Scott's Club; Jazz Cafe; Red Sea; JVC Capital Jazz; Live TV and BBC Radio 2, 3, 5. *Recordings:* Live At The Premises (EP), 1993; The Unadulterated, 1994; Plays Dinner Jazz (EP), 1995; Saxotronix, 1995; Lipstick On My Reed, 1996; Video: Sax Skills With Anita Carmichael, 1995. *Honours:* Wire magazine, Newcomer of the Year, 1987. *Memberships:* Musicians' Union; PRS; MCPS; Ronnie Scott's. *Leisure interests:* Watching EastEnders; Tennis; Horse riding. *Current Management:* Saxology Records. *Address:* 49E St Pauls Rd, London N1 2LT, England.

CARMICHAEL Jim; b. 21 Feb. 1971, Sevenoaks, Kent, England. Musician (drums); Songwriter; Prod. *Education:* Design and Communication. *Musical Education:* Berklee College of Music, Boston, USA, 1989. *Career:* Principal percussionist in winning orchestra at National Festival For Youth, 1988; Drummer, acid jazz group, K-Creative, 1991–93; Member: Freak Power; Every Day People (EDP), 2000–; Played with Les Rhythmes Digitales, Barry Adamson, Mandalay, Regular Fries, Izit, K-Creative. *Composition:* QED, with K Creative, 1992. *Recordings:* with K-Creative: QED, 1992; with Izit: The Whole Affair, 1993; Imaginary Man, 1995; with Freak Power: Drive Thru Booty, 1994; More of Everything for Everybody, 1996; Carmichael's Crunchy Nut Loops, 1997; Mandalay: Empathy, 1998; with EDP: Sweet Music, 2001. *Address:* Flat 2, 3 College Terrace, Brighton BN2 2EE, England.

CARNEIRO Fernando (Nando); b. 26 June 1953, Belo Horizonte, Brazil. Nora Kholki, 10 July 1997, 2 s. *Musical Education:* Classical Guitar; Classical Piano; Composition and Orchestration. *Career:* A Barca Do Sol, own group; Recordings with singers: Olivia Byington and Beth Goulart; World tours with E Gismonti, 1986, 1990, 1991, 1993, 1994, 1995, 1996. *Compositions:* Kiss of the Spider Woman, soundtrack, Co-writer. *Recordings:* Topazio, Visom; Infancia, Gismonti; Zig-Zag, Gismonti; Glimpse, T Gurtu; Brassileiro, Brassil. *Honour:* Fiat Prize, Os Povos Da Floresta, 1989. *Leisure interests:* Computer; Internet. *Current Management:* Maquinando Music. *Address:* Igarapaua, 59–301 Leblon, Rio de Janeiro, RJ, Brazil.

CARNES Kim; b. 20 July 1945, Los Angeles, California, USA. Singer; Songwriter. m. Dave Ellington. *Career:* Member, New Christy Minstrels, 1960s; Solo artiste; Success as songwriter with husband Dave Ellington. *Compositions include:* Songs recorded by artists including Frank Sinatra;

Barbra Streisand; Kenny Rogers. *Recordings:* Albums: Rest On Me, 1972; Kim Carnes, 1975; Sailin', 1976; St Vincent's Court, 1979; Romance Dance, 1980; Mistaken Identity, 1981; Voyeur, 1982; Cafe Racers, 1983; Lighthouse, 1986; View From The House, 1988; Gypsy Honeymoon – The Best Of, 1993; Crazy In The Night, 1990; Back To Back, 1998; Mistaken Identity Collection; King Biscuit Flower Hour, 1998; Sweet Love Song of My Soul, 1999; Singles: Bette Davis Eyes (No. 1, USA); Draw of The Cards; What About Me (with Kenny Rogers, James Ingram), 1984; Make No Mistake He's Mine (with Barbra Streisand); Speed of The Sound of Loneliness (with Lyle Lovett, 1988); Contributor, We Are The World, USA For Africa, 1985. *Address:* c/o William Morris Agency, 2100 West End Ave, Suite 1000, Nashville, TN 37203, USA.

CARPENTER Mary Chapin; b. 21 Jan. 1958, Princeton, New Jersey, USA. Country / Folk vocalist; Musician (guitar); Songwriter. *Education:* Degree, American civilization. *Career:* Winner, numerous local music competitions; Solo recording artiste, 1986-. *Compositions:* Songs recorded by Tony Tice; Joan Baez. *Recordings:* Singles include: Right Now, 1991; I Feel Lucky, 1992; Albums: Home Town Girl, 1987; State of The Heart, 1989; Shooting Straight In The Dark, 1990; Come On Come On, 1992; Stones In The Road, 1994; A Place In The World, 1996; Party Doll and Other Favourites, 1999; Time Sex Love, 2001; Also appears on recordings by: Joan Baez; Roseanne Cash; The Chieftains; Shawn Colvin; Indigo Girls; Patty Loveless; Dolly Parton; The Rankin Family; Ricky Skaggs; Dusty Springfield; Pam Tillis; Trisha Yearwood. *Honours:* 5 Washington Area Music Awards; CMA Vocalist of The Year, 1992. *Current Management:* Studio One Artists, 7010 Westmoreland Ave #100, Takoma Park, MD 20912, USA.

CARPENTER Richard Lynn; b. 15 Oct. 1946, New Haven, Connecticut, USA. Vocalist; Composer; Arranger; Musician (piano). m. Mary Rudolph, 1984, 2 s. *Career:* Co-member, The Carpenters (with sister Karen), 1969–83; Group demise with death of Karen, 1983; Composer, numerous hits; World-wide tours, countless television, radio appearances; Advisor, television film The Karen Carpenter Story. *Recordings:* Singles include: (They Long To Be) Close To You (No. 1, USA), 1970; We've Only Just Begun, 1971; Rainy Days and Mondays, 1971; Goodbye To Love, 1972; Yesterday Once More, 1973; Top of The World (No. 1, USA), 1973; Please Mr Postman (No. 1, USA), 1975; Calling Occupants of Interplanetary Craft, 1977; Albums: Offering (a.k.a. Ticket To Ride), 1969; Close To You, 1970; Carpenters, 1971; A Song For You, 1972; Now and Then, 1973; Horizon, 1975; A Kind of Hush, 1976; Live At The Palladium, 1977; The Singles 1974–78; Christmas Portrait, 1978; Made In America, 1979; Voice of The Heart, 1983; Yesterday Once More, 1984; An Old Fashioned Christmas, 1985; Lovelines, 1990; Christmas Portrait, 1991; From The Top, 1991; Only Yesterday, 1993; Solo albums: Time, 1987; Pianist Arranger Composer Conductor, 1998. *Honours:* Numerous gold discs; Group of Year, 1971; 3 Grammy Awards; American Music Award, 1973. *Memberships:* ASCAP; National Academy of Songwriters; NARAS. *Leisure interest:* Collecting cars. *Address:* PO Box 1084, Downey, CA 90240, USA.

CARR Andy; b. 6 Dec. 1967, Kirkcaldy, Fife, Scotland. Musician (bass guitar, guitar); Vocalist; Songwriter. *Education:* Fife College of Further and Higher Education. *Musical Education:* Self-taught. *Career:* Lead vocalist and bass guitar with Summerfield Blues with live sessions on Annie Webster Show for BBC Scotland, on BBC Radio Tweed and on various independent radio stations. *Recordings:* with Summerfield Blues: Devil and The Freightman, Let's Scare The Posh People (EP) and Little Miss Behavin'. *Honours:* Nominated for Best Blues Album for British Blues Connection, Edinburgh International Festival; Scottish Blues Band of The Year, 1993–94. *Memberships:* PRS; Musicians' Union. *Leisure interests:* Playwriting; Caving; Socialising. *Current Management:* Dave Arcari. *Address:* 192 Glasgow Rd, Perth, Scotland.

CARR Budd; b. 5 Sept. 1945, Jersey City, New Jersey, USA. Music Supervisor. m. Jeanne, 4 Oct. 1970, 2 s., 1 d. *Education:* BA, MA, University of Illinois. *Career:* Began as music agent with CMA; Acts handled include: James Taylor; Bob Seger; Blind Faith; Carole King; Crosby Stills and Nash; Moved to IFA, acts handled: Eric Clapton Comeback Tour; Queen; Jefferson Starship; Stephen Stills; Left agency, signed band Kansas; Became personal manager, started management company, 1980; Joined forces with Wil Sharpe in Carr/Sharpe Entertainment Services, 1990; Clients include: Slaughter; Boxing Gandhis; The Buddah Heads; Eric Gales Band; John Wetton; After 25 films as a music supervisor, joined Joel Sill, Windswept Pacific Entertainment, whose catalogue includes: John Mellencamp; Rod Stewart; Willie Nelson; Numerous hits songs of 50s, 60s, 70s; Film credits include: Music consultant: The Terminator, 1984; Return of The Living Dead, 1985; Music supervisor: Salvador, 1986; Platoon, 1986; Wall Street, 1987; Talk Radio, 1988; Alien Nation, 1988; Born On The Fourth of July, 1989; Executive Music Producer: The Doors, 1991; JFK: 1991; Heaven and Earth, 1993; Natural Born Killers, 1994; Copycat, 1995; Nixon, 1995; Twister, 1996; Speed 2, 1997; I Know What You Did Last Summer, 1997;

Stigmata, 1999. *Address:* Carr Sharpe Entertainment, 9320 Wilshire Blvd, Suite 200, Beverly Hills, CA 90212, USA.

CARR Ian (Henry Randell); b. 21 April 1933, Dumfries, Scotland. Musician (trumpet); Composer; Author; Broadcaster. m. (1) Margaret B Bell, 28 June 1963 (deceased 1967), 1 d, (2) Sandra L Major, 9 Dec. 1972 (divorced 1993). *Education:* BA Hons, English Language and Literature, King's College, Newcastle-on-Tyne, 1952–56. *Musical Education:* Early piano lessons; Self-taught as trumpeter and composer. *Career:* Emcee Five, 1960–62; Rendell-Carr Quintet, 1962–69; Ian Carr's Nucleus, 1969–88; Ian Carr Group, 1989–92; United Jazz and Rock Ensemble, 1975–; Many international radio and television appearances. *Compositions:* Solar Plexus, 1970; Labyrinth, 1973; Out of The Long Dark, 1978; Awakening, 1980; Old Heartland, 1988; Sounds and Sweet Airs, 1992; Shhh, 1995; Fyace, 1997. *Recordings:* Numerous professional recordings. *Publications:* Music Outside, 1973; Miles Davis, A Critical Biography, 1982; Keith Jarrett, The Man and His Music, 1991; Co-author, Rough Guide to Jazz, 1995. Contributions to: Jazz Feature Writer for BBC Music Magazine, 1992-. *Honours:* Italian Calabria Award for Outstanding Contribution in the Field of Jazz, 1982. *Memberships:* Royal Society of Musicians of Great Britain; Professor, Guildhall School of Music; PRS; APC. *Leisure interests:* Literature; Art; travel; Swimming. *Current Management:* Barbara Levy, England. *Address:* Flat 1, 34 Brailsford Rd, London SW2 2TE, England.

CARR Martin; b. 29 Nov. 1968, Thurso, Scotland. Musician (guitar); Songwriter. *Career:* Member, The Boo Radleys, 1989–99; Televison includes: Top of the Pops; With the Boo Radleys; White Room; The Word. *Compositions include:* Lazarus, 1993; Wake Up Boo, 1994; Ride the Tiger, 1995. *Recordings:* Albums: Ichabod and I, 1989; Everything's Alright Forever, 1992; Giant Steps, 1993; Learning To Walk, 1994; Sharks Patrol These Waters, 1995; Wake Up, 1995; C'mon Kids, 1996; with Eggman, First Fruits, 1996; King Size, 1998; Hit single: Wake Up Boo, 1995. *Publications:* Front cover of Melody Maker, 3 times, 1995; Front cover of NME, 1993, 1995. *Honours:* NME Brat Award, Best Album, 1994; Select Magazine, Best Album of the Year, 1994; Liverpool Echo, Album of the Year, 1995. *Current Management:* CEC Management, 4Warren Mews, London W1P 5DJ, England.

CARR Vikki, (Florencia Bisenta De Casillas Martinez Cardona); b. 19 July 1941, El Paso, Texas, USA. Vocalist; Actress. *Career:* Appearances include: Television shows with: Dean Martin; Ed Sullivan; Jackie Gleason; Jerry Lewis; Carol Burnett; Bob Hope; Danny Kaye; Glen Campbell; Johnny Carson; Hostess of Tonight Show, several times; 5 TV specials; Concerts in US, Europe, Australia, Japan; Stage actress, South Pacific, Kansas City; Unsinkable Molly Brown, Ohio; I'm Getting My Act Together and Taking It On The Road, St Louis; Hostess, Mrs America Pageant, 1981–87; Mrs World Pageant, 1984–87; Founder and Chairman, Vikki Carr Scholarship Foundation, 1971; TV appearances in Baywatch; Bilingual TV special, Memorias, Memorias, 1998. *Recordings:* Albums include: It Must Be Him, 1967; For Once In My Life, 1969; Nashville By Carr, 1970; Vikki Carr Y El Amore, 1980; Cosas Del Amor, 1990; Reta Manda Y Provoca, 1998; Memorias Memorias, 1999; Vikki Carr Christmas Album, 2000. *Honours:* Hon. doctorates: St Edwards University, 1974; University of San Diego, 1975; Woman of Year, LA Times, 1970; Visiting Entertainer of Year, Mexico City, 1972; Singer of the Year, American Guild Variety Artists, 1972; Woman of The World, 1974; Humanitarian Award, Nosotros, 1981; Woman of the Year, League United Latin American Citizens, 1983; Hispanic Woman of The Year, 1984; Grammy Award, Best Mexican-American Performance, 1985; Silver Achievement, YWCA, 1989; Golden Eagle, Nosotros, 1989; 3 times Grammy Winner, 1985, 1992, 1995; Founder of Hope Award, City of Hope, Los Angeles, 1990; Career Achievement Award, Asscn of Hispanic Critics, 1990; Key Girl Scouts of America Award, 1991; Hispanic Heritage Award, Washington CD. *Current Management:* Vi-Car Entertainment Inc. *Address:* c/o Peter Shukat, 111 W 57th St, Suite 1120, New York, NY 10019, USA.

CARRACK Paul; b. 22 April, 1951, Sheffield, Yorkshire, England. Vocalist; Songwriter; Musician (keyboards). *Career:* Member: Ace; Squeeze, 1980–81; Mike and The Mechanics, 1986–; Concerts include: Prince's Trust Rock Gala, Birmingham, 1989; Also solo artiste, 1980–; Collaborations: Nick Lowe; Carlene Carter; John Hiatt; Phil Manzanera; The Pretenders; Roxy Music; Elvis Costello; The Undertones; The Smiths; Eric Clapton; Elton John; Roger Waters. *Recordings:* Albums include: with Squeeze: East Side Story, 1981; with Mike and The Mechanics: Mike and The Mechanics, 1986; The Living Years, 1988; Word of Mouth, 1991; Beggar On A Beach of Gold, 1995; Hits, 1996; solo: The Nightbirds, 1980; Suburban Voodoo, 1982; One Good Reason, 1987; Ace Mechanic, 1987; Carrack Collection, 1988; Groove Approved, 1989; Carrackter Reference, 1991; Blue Views, 1996; Beautiful World, 1997; Satisfy My Soul, 2000; Singles include: with Squeeze: Labelled With Love, 1981; with Mike and The Mechanics: Silent Running, 1986; All I Need Is A Miracle, 1986; The Living Years (No. 1, USA), 1989; Over My Shoulder, 1995; solo: How Long?,

1996. *Current Management:* Hit and Run Music, 30 Ives St, London SW3 2ND, England.

CARRASCO Joe 'King', (Joe Teutsch); b. 6 Dec. 1953, Dumas, Texas, USA. Musician (guitar). Divorced, 1 s. *Education:* University of Texas, 1972. *Career:* Son of Stiff tour, 1980; Saturday Night Live, 1981; Austin City Limits, 1981. *Recordings:* Albums include: Bandido Rock, 1988; Tales From The Crypt (with The Crowns), 2000. *Honour:* Mem. of Texas Music Hall of Fame. *Membership:* ASCAP. *Leisure interest:* Mexican surfing. *Current Management:* IKC Productions. *Address:* PO Box 12233, Austin, TX 78711, USA.

CARRINGTON Terri Lyne; b. 4 Aug. 1965, Medford, Massachusetts, USA. Musician (drums); Songwriter; Singer. *Musical Education:* Berklee College of Music, Boston. *Career:* Original house drummer, Arsenio Hall Show; Toured with: Al Jarreau; Herbie Hancock; David Sanborn; Joe Sample; Stan Getz; Wayne Shorter; Gerald Albright; Lalah Hathaway. *Compositions:* Reach For Your Dreams, for 1996 Olympics; Josa Lee, for Dianne Reeves; Whatcha Gonna Do, Patrice Rushen. *Recordings:* As a leader: Real Life Story. *Honours:* Grammy Nomination; Boston Music Award, 1989, 1990. *Membership:* NARAS. *Leisure interests:* Films; Cooking; Pool. *Address:* 366 W California Ave #1, Glendale, CA 91203, USA.

CARROLL Dina; b. 21 Aug. 1968; Cambridge, England. Vocalist; Songwriter. *Career:* Lead vocalist, Quartz, 1990; Solo artiste, 1992–; British tours, 1993, 1994; Concerts include: Support to Luther Vandross, Wembley, 1993. *Compositions:* Co-writer with producer, Nigel Lowis. *Recordings:* Albums: So Close, 1993; Only Human, 1996; Very Best Of, 2001; Singles: with Quartz: It's Too Late, 1991; solo: Ain't No Man, 1992; Special Kind of Love, 1992; So Close, 1992; This Time, 1993; Express, 1993; Don't Be A Stranger, 1993; The Perfect Year (co-written by Andrew Lloyd-Webber), 1993; Escaping, 1996; Only Human, 1996; One Two Three, 1998. *Honours:* First-ever million-selling debut album for UK female, So Close, 1993; BRIT Award, Best Female Artist, 1994; BRIT Award Nominations: Best Newcomer, 1993; Best Album, 1994; Best Single, 1994; Mercury Music Prize, 1993; 3 International Dance Awards, 1994; Great Britain Variety Award, Best Performing Artist; Silver Clef Award, Best Newcomer, 1994. *Current Management:* First Avenue Management, The Courtyard, 42 Colwith Rd, London W6 9EY, England.

CARRON-SMITH Patricia; b. 3 April 1952, Llantrisant, Wales. Singer; Musician. *Career:* Member, Welsh traditional music group Swansea Jack, 1977–78; Member, Welsh traditional music group Calennig, 1978–; Television includes: Torth y Fara, S4C, 1982; Folk On The Move, HTV, 1983; Trade Winds, BBC Wales, 1985; Fastest To Frisco, BBC Wales, 1986; Evening News, Dunedin, New Zealand, 1990; Celtic Magic, HTV, 1990; Gwerin y Werin, S4C, 1995. *Recordings:* with Swansea Jack: The Seven Wonders, 1978; with Calennig: Songs and Tunes From Wales, 1980; You Can Take a White Horse Anywhere, 1983; Dyddiau Gwynion Ionawr, 1985; Dwr Glan, 1990; Trade Winds, 1994; A Gower Garland, 2000; Numerous compilations. *Memberships:* Equity; Musicians' Union; PRS; PAMRA; CDdWC; COTC. *Leisure interests:* Music; Theatre; Travel; Welsh studies. *Address:* 1 Ty Clwyta Cottages, Cross Inn, Llantrisant Cynon Raf CF72 8AZ, Wales.

CARSON Jeff; b. 16 Dec. 1963, Tulsa, Oklahoma, USA. Singer; Songwriter; Musician (guitar, harmonica). m. Kim Cooper, 14 Dec. 1987. *Recordings:* Albums: Jeff Carson, 1995; Butterfly Kisses, 1997; Shine On, 1998; Singles: Yeah Buddy, 1995; Not On Your Love, 1995; The Car, 1995; Holdin' On to Something, 1996; That Last Mile, 1996; Do It Again, 1997; Butterfly Kisses, 1997; Here's the Deal, 1997; Shine On, 1998. *Honour:* Academy of Country Music, Video of the Year, The Car, 1996. *Leisure interests:* Fishing; Hunting; Woodwork; Collecting Police Memorabilia. *Current Management:* Marv Dennis and Associates. *Address:* 1002 18th Ave S, Nashville, TN 37212, USA.

CARSTEA Elena; b. 26 Feb. 1963, Agnita, Sibiu County, Romania. Musician (guitar). *Musical Education:* Classic Singing. *Career:* Television shows include: Golden Orpheus, 1993; Stars Duel, 1993; Mamaia Festival; Five O'Clock Tea; Golden Stag; Radio and television concerts. *Recordings:* Your Eyes, 1988; Tomorrow; Some Day, 1990; Ballad For Sandra, 1994. *Honours:* Public Prize for Composition, Your Eyes, 1983; Best Vocal Soloist of the Year, 1994. *Membership:* Radio Contact. *Leisure interests:* Parapsychology; Cycling; Men. *Current Management:* Doru Costea. *Address:* 61 Buzesti St A6, Third Floor, Apt 18, Sector 1, Bucharest, Romania.

CARTER Benny (Bennett Lester); b. 8 Aug. 1907, New York, New York, USA. Musician (saxophone, clarinet, trumpet); Composer; Conductor. *Career:* Musician, arranger, with bands including: Charlie Johnson, Fletcher Henderson, Chick Webb, Horace Henderson, 1925–32; Leader, own band, 1932–35, 1938–46; Arranger, BBC studio orchestra, 1936–38; Film appearance: Snows of Kilimanjaro, 1952; Conductor, workshops, US universities, 1970–; Member, music advisory panel, NEA, 1976–79; Artist

in residence, Rutgers University, 1986. *Compositions include:* Film scores: Stormy Weather, 1943; As Thousands Cheer, 1943; Panic In The Streets, 1950; Snows of Kilimanjaro, 1952; The Five Pennies, 1959; Guns of Navarone, 1961; A Man Called Adam, 1966; Buck and The Preacher, 1972; Cosmic Eye, 1985. *Recordings:* Albums include: Ridin' In Rhythm, 1933; Jazz Giant, 1957; Further Definitions, 1961; The Benny Carter 4: Montreux '77, 1977; Central City Sketches, 1987; In The Mood For Swing, 1987; Over The Rainbow, 1989; All That Jazz, 1990; All of Me, 1991; Song Book, 1995; Advanced Swing, 1996. *Honours include:* Silver Award, Esquire, 1943; Gold award, 1946; Grammy Lifetime Achievement Award, 1987; Aggie Award, Songwriters Guild, 1988; Downbeat Awards; ASMAC Golden Score Award. *Address:* PO Box 870, Hollywood, CA 90028, USA.

CARTER Carlene, (Rebecca Carlene Smith); b. 26 Sept. 1955, Nashville, Tennessee, USA. Country vocalist; Songwriter. m. (1) Joe Simpkins, divorced, 1 d., (2) Jack Routh, divorced, 1 s., (3) Nick Lowe, divorced. *Musical Education:* Piano lessons; Guitar lessons with Carl Perkins. *Career:* Country singer, 1974–; Concerts include: Wembley Country Music Family, with Carter family, 1981; Film appearance: Too Drunk To Remember, London Film Festival; Stage performance: Pump Boys and Dinettes, with Kiki Dee, Paul Jones, London, 1985. *Compositions:* Easy From Now On; Appalachian Eyes; Guardian Angel. *Recordings:* Albums: Carlene Carter, 1978; Two Sides To Every Woman, 1979; Musical Shapes, 1980; Blue Nun, 1981; C'est Bon, 1983; I Fell In Love, 1990; Little Acts of Treason, 1995; Hindsight 20/20, 1996; Contributor, The Junkie and The Juicehead Minus Me, Johnny Cash, 1974; Lost Dogs and Mixed Blessings, John Prine, 1995; Also recorded with members of Squeeze; Dave Edmunds; Kiki Dee; Albert Lee; Jim Kettner. *Current Management:* Fitzgerald-Hartley Co, 1212 16th Ave S, Nashville, TN 37203, USA.

CARTER Deana; b. 1964, Nashville, Tennessee, USA. Vocalist; Songwriter; Musician (guitar). *Career:* British tour support to Jimmy Nail, 1995; Recording Artists, extensive tours of USA and Canada. *Recordings:* Debut album, Did I Shave My Legs For This?, 1995; Did I Shave My Legs For This, 1996; Everything's Gonna Be Alright, 1998; Father Christmas (with Fred Carter Jr), 2001. *Honours:* Did I Shave My Legs for This, Quadruple Platinum album; Everything's Gonna Be Alright, Gold Album; CMA Single of the Year, for Strawberry Wine, 1997; Orville H Gibson Award, Best Country Guitarist, 1999. *Memberships:* Country Music Asscn; ASCAP. *Current Management:* The Left Bank Organization, 6609 Currywood Dr., Nashville, TN 37205, USA.

CARTER Derrick, (Sound Patrol, Tone Theory, Oneiro, The Unknown); b. 21 Oct. 1969, Chicago, Illinois, USA. Prod.; Remixer; DJ. *Career:* Started to DJ, aged 9; Worked for Curtis Jones' Cajual label; First release, 1987; First break with Symbols and Instruments, 1989; Co-founder: Classic Records (with Luke Solomon); World-wide DJ; Club residency at The End, London; Collaborations: Mark Farina; Chris Nazuka; Basement Jaxx; Cajmere; Remixes: Blaze; Tortoise; Slam; Modjo. *Recordings:* Albums: Sweetened – No Lemon (as Sound Patrol), 1995; Singles: Mood (with Symbols and Instruments), 1989; Dream States (with Cajmere), 1993; Tripping Amongst The Stars (as Sound Patrol), 1995; Limbo of Vanished Possibilities (as Tone Theory), 1995; Wear A Pair, 1996; Mo Pschidt EP, 2000; Shh! (as Oneiro), 2001. *Current Management:* Mumbo Jumbo Management, 2A Southam St, London, W10 5PH, England.

CARTER Kent; b. 12 June 1939, Hanover, New Hampshire, USA. m. June 1981, 4 s. *Musical Education:* Berklee School of Music, Boston; Private study, piano, cello, bassoon (as child), bass. *Career:* Participated in October Revolution, New York, early 1960s; Performed with Jazz Composers Guild Orchestra; Toured, recorded with artistes including: Paul Bley; Carla Bley; Michael Mantler; Steve Lacy; Don Cherry; Gato Barbieri; Alan Silva; Mal Waldron; Michael Smith; Bobby Bradford; Max Roach; Enrico Rava; Roswell Rudd; Derek Bailey; John Stevens; Trevor Watts; Steve McCall, 1964–; Member, co-founder, Tok Trio, including tours, Europe and Japan; Member, Steve Lacy Quintet, including tour, USA, 1970–81; Most major European jazz festivals; Radio WDR Köln, Germany; Radio France; Radio RAI, Italy; Founder, leader, chamber group Kent Carter String Trio, with Carlos Zingaro, Francois Dreno; Played major music festivals, Europe; Collaboration with Michala Marcus (dance) in productions including Dance Music Image, 1975-. *Compositions include:* Collaboration with choreographer Jean Pomares in ballet Paysages Avec Couple. *Recordings:* Beauvais Cathedral; Kent Carter Solo With Claude Bernard; Suspensions; La Contrebasse; Album: The Willisau Suites, 1999. *Leisure interest:* Recording. *Address:* Riviere, 16320 Juillaguet, France.

CARTER Mel; b. 22 April 1939, Cincinnati, Ohio, USA. Singer. *Musical Education:* Cincinnati Conservatory of Music. *Career:* Leading soloist, Assistant Director, Greater Cincinnati Youth and Young Adult Choral Union; Moved to Hollywood, 1960; Appearances include: Ciro's, with Dinah Washington; The Crescendo, with Bessie Griffin's Gospel Pearls; Guest on Ed Sullivan Show; Opened at The Flamingo, Las Vegas, with Damita Jo; First hit single led to touring with Dick Clark Caravan of Stars, sharing bill with Sonny and Cher, Tom Jones, others; Headlined nightclubs across USA, Canada; Appearances include: Slate Brothers, Hollywood; Cocoanut Grove; La Fiesta, Mexico; Hotel Americana, New York; Fairmont, Dallas; Played Sportin' Life in concert of Porgy and Bess; Starred in Glitter Palace; Successful actor, films include: Prime Time; No Way Out; Television includes: American Bandstand; Hullaballoo; Tonight Shows; New Love American Style; CHiPs; Many commercials; TV and film soundtracks; Tour of Japan; Engagements: Trump Castle; Taj Mahal; Merv Griffin's Resorts Casino Hotel, Atlantic City; Performance in Fly Blackbird Revisited, early 1990s. *Recordings include:* Albums: When A Boy Falls In Love; My Heart Sings; Hold Me, Thill Me, Kiss Me; Enter Laughing; Easy Listening; Be My Love; This Is My Life; Willing; Raise The World/ The Album of Life – Title Song; Live In Hollywood; The Best Of; Hit singles include: When A Boy Falls In Love, 1963; Hold Me, Thrill Me, Kiss Me, 1965; All of a Sudden My Heart Sings, 1965; Band of Gold, 1966; You, You, You, 1966; Take Good Care of Her, 1966. *Honours include:* LA Weekly's La Wee Award; NAACP Image Award Nomination, Best Performance in A Musical, Glitter Palace; Grammy Nomination, Willing album; Gold record.

CARTER Nick(olas Gene); b. 28 Jan. 1980, Jamestown, New York, USA. Vocalist; Musician (drums). *Career:* Brother of vocalist Aaron Carter; Acted in commercials on TV; Vocalist for Tampa Buccaneer's pregame show; Member, Backstreet Boys; Numerous television appearances, tours and hit singles. *Recordings:* Singles: We've Got It Goin' On, 1995; Quit Playing Games, 1998; I'll Never Break Your Heart, 1998; Everybody, 1998; As Long As You Love Me, 1998; Anywhere for You, 1998; All I Have to Give, 1998; I Want It That Way (No. 1, UK), 1999; Shape of My Heart, 2000; More Than That, 2001; Albums: Backstreet Boys, 1996; Live in Concert, 1998; Backstreet's Back, 1998; Millennium, 1999; Black and Blue (No. 1, USA), 2000; The Hits: Chapter One, 2001. *Honours:* Grammy Award nominations, 2000, 2001. *Leisure interests:* Boating; Fishing; Drawing; Collecting football cards; Video games.

CARTER Ronald; b. 4 May 1937, Ferndale, Michigan, USA. Jazz Musician (bass); Educator. m. Janet Hosbrouck, 7 June 1958, 2 s. *Musical Education:* BMus, Eastman School of Music, 1959; MusM, Manhattan School of Music, 1962. *Career:* Bass player, college orchestras; Bass player for Chico Hamilton Quintet; Don Ellis; Cannonball Adderley; Thelonious Monk; Eric Dolphy; Miles Davis, 1963–68; Wynton Marsalis; Formed own quartet, 1975; Also prolific freelance musician for numerous artists including George Benson; Sonny Rollins; VSOP Band (with Herbie Hancock and Tony Williams); McCoy Tyner; Freddie Hubbard; George Duke; Aretha Franklin; Lena Horne; Jazz teacher, universities in Buffalo, St Louis, New York. *Recordings:* Albums: Out Front, 1966; Uptown Conversation, 1970; Blues Farm, 1973; All Blues, 1974; Magic, 1975; Spanish Blue, 1975; Anything Goes, 1975; Yellow and Green, 1976; Pastels, 1977; Song For You, 1977; Parade, 1979; New York Slick, 1980; Patrao, 1980; Heart and Soul, 1982; Etudes, 1983; Live At Village West, 1984; All Alone, 1989; with Eric Dolphy: Out There, 1960; with Don Ellis: How Time Passes, 1960; with Miles Davis: Seven Steps To Heaven, 1963; Miles In The Sky, 1968; with Herbie Hancock: Maiden Voyage, 1965; Also on numerous recordings by: Roy Ayers; Gato Barbieri; George Benson; Billy Cobham; Chick Corea; Larry Coryell; Miles Davis; Roberta Flack; The Four Tops; Freddie Hubbard; Billy Joel; Quincy Jones; Manhattan Transfer; Diana Ross; Tom Rush; Paul Simon; Grace Slick; Jimmy Smith. *Publications:* Author, books on jazz and classical bass. *Honours:* Downbeat Critics Award, International Jazz Bassist of Year, 1965; Readers Poll Winner, 1973–75, 1983; Detroit Free Press, Jazz Bassist of Decade, 1966; Japan All-Star Jazz Poll Winner, 1969–70; Grammy, Best Jazz Instrumental Composition, 1987. *Membership:* Jazz Musicians' Asscn. *Current Management:* c/o JoAnne Jimenez, The Bridge Agency, 110 Salem Rd, Pound Ridge, NY 10576, USA.

CARTHY Eliza Amy Forbes; b. 23 Aug. 1975, Scarborough, England. Musician (violin); Folk vocalist; Songwriter. *Career:* Pro, sang with Watersons Cambridge Festival, 1988; Waterdaughters Vancouver Folk Music Festival, 1989; Tours of USA, Australia, England, Germany; TV appearances: Secombe on Sunday, TV Ballads, London Cable 1, later with Jools Holland; ABC Arts Show, Australia; Mountain Stage, USA; Headlined Sidmouth Folk Festival, 1999; Signed major recording deal, 1998. *Compositions:* By Then; The Wrong Favour; Time In the Sun; Peggy; Accordion Song, 1998; Russia, 1998; Red Rice, 1998; Fallen Leaves, 1998. *Recordings:* Eliza Carthy and Nancy Kerr, 1993; Waterson: Carthy, 1994; Heat, Light and Sound, 1995; Norma Waterson, 1996; Common Tongue, 1997; Eliza Carthy and the Kings of Calicutt, 1997; Red Rice, 1998; Angels and Cigarettes, 2000. *Honour:* Nominated for Mercury Music Prize, 1998. *Memberships:* Musician's Union; PRS; Labour Party. *Leisure interests:* Dying hair; Clog dancing; Yoghurt weaving. *Current Management:* Nigel Morton, Moneypenny Management, 35 Britannia Row, London, England.

CARTHY Martin; b. 21 May 1940, Hatfield, Hertfordshire, England. Vocalist; Musician (guitar). m. Norma Waterson. *Career:* Member, skiffle group, The Thameside Four; solo folk artiste, 1963–; Resident musician, Troubadour folk club, London; Member, Three City Four; regular

recordings, tours, with Dave Swarbrick; Member, Steeleye Span, 1969–72; Member, Brass Monkey; The Watersons; Keith Hancock Band. *Recordings:* Martin Carthy, 1965; Second Album, 1966; Byker Hill, 1967; But Two Came By (with Dave Swarbrick), 1968; Prince Heathen (with Dave Swarbrick), 1969; Landfall, 1971; This Is Martin Carthy, 1972; Sweet Wivelsfield, 1974; Shearwater, 1975; Crown of Horn, 1976; Because It's There, 1979; Out of The Cut, 1982; Right of Passage, 1989; Life and Limb (with Dave Swarbrick), 1990; Skin and Bone (with Dave Swarbrick), 1992; Kershaw Sessions, 1995; Signs of Life, 1999; Both Ears and The Tail, 2001.

CARTWRIGHT Deirdre Josephine; b. 27 July 1956, London, England. Musician (guitar); Composer; Author; Teacher. 1 d. *Musical Education:* Self-taught. *Career:* Guitar Presenter of both series of BBC TV's Rockschool, shown world-wide; Toured 17 countries with guest stars, national tours with own group Deirdre Cartwright Group, 1994–95; Arts Council tour with her eight-piece band, 1996; Concerts, Germany, Switzerland, 1996–97; Co-runs weekly jazz club, Blow the Fuse, at Vortex, North London; Presents new record releases for Jazz Notes, Radio 3; Advisory Panel, Jazz Services. *Recordings:* with The Guest Stars: The Guest Stars; Out At Night; Live In Berlin; One Night Stands, as featured artist, jazz compilation; Debut by with The Deirdre Cartwright Group; Play, second solo CD with Steve Lodder, Annie Whitehead, 1998. *Publications:* Rockschool Books; Rock Guitar Method; The Rockschool Sessions; The Rockfile. *Honours:* Arts Council Composition Award, 1991; Arts Council funded commission, 1996. *Memberships:* Musicians' Union; PRS. *Leisure interests:* Music; Walking; Reading; Woodwork; Family. *Current Management:* Blow The Fuse Records.

CARTY John; b. 7 Jan. 1962, London, England. Musician (Fiddle, Banjo, Flute). m. Maureen Brennan, 23 May 1987, 1 s., 1 d. *Musical Education:* Taught by Brendan Mulkere, Traditional Irish Music. *Career:* Moved to Ireland, 1991; First album on banjo, 1994, led to 3 album deal; Fiddle release, Last Night's Fun, Multi-instrumentalist playing fiddle, banjo and flute; Leading Member of band, At the Racket. *Compositions:* Jimmy Batty's, recorded on The Cat That Ate the Candle; Seanamhas Tube Station, recorded on At the Racke. *Recordings:* The Cat That Ate the Candle, banjo, album, 1994; Last Night's Fun, fiddle, album, 1996; At the Racket, 1997. *Current Management:* Racket Management. *Address:* Knockroe, Boyle, Co Roscommon, Ireland.

CASABLANCAS Julian; b. 23 Aug. 1978, New York City, USA. Vocalist; Songwriter. *Education:* L'Institut Le Rosey, Switzerland; Dwight School, Manhattan. *Career:* Member: The Strokes, 1998–. *Recordings:* Albums: Is This It, 2001; Singles: The Modern Age, Hard To Explain/New York City Cops, Last Nite/When It Started, 2001. *Honours:* Brit Award, Best International Newcomer, 2002; NME Awards: Band of The Year; Best New Act; Album of The Year, 2001. *Current Management:* Ryan Gentles, Wiz Kid Management. *Internet:* www.thestrokes.com.

CASADY Jack (John); b. 13 April 1944, Washington DC, USA. Musician (bass). *Education:* Montgomery College, Maryland. *Career:* Member, The Triumphs; Member, Jefferson Airplane, 1966–72, 1992; Also member, side project, Hot Tuna, 1968–78; Member, Kantner Balin Casady (KBC) Band, 1985–88, 1992–; Performances include: Berkeley Folk Festival, 1966; Monterey Jazz Festival, 1966; Monterey Pop Festival, 1967; Newport Pop Festival, 1968; Isle of Wight Festival, 1968; Atlantic City Pop Festival, 1969; Woodstock Music and Art Fair, 1969; Altamont Speedway, with Rolling Stones, 1969; Bath Festival, 1970. *Recordings:* Albums: with Jefferson Airplane: Jefferson Airplane Takes Off, 1966; After Bathing At Baxter's, 1968; Crown of Creation, 1968; Volunteers, 1969; Blows Against The Empire, 1970; Bark, 1970; Jefferson Airplane, 1989; Jefferson Airplane Loves You, 1992; with Hot Tuna: Burgers, 1972; The Phosphorescent Rat, 1974; America's Choice, 1975; Yellow Fever, 1975; Hopkorov, 1976; Double Dose, 1977; Pair A Dice Found, 1990; Live At Sweetwater, 1992; Best Of, 1998; And Furthermore, 1999; with KBC Band: KBC Band, 1986; with Jefferson Starship; Deep Space, 1995; Windows of Heaven, 1999; Ignition, 2001; Guest musician: If Only I Could Remember My Name, David Crosby, 1972. *Current Management:* Bill Thompson Management, 2051 Third St, San Francisco, CA 94107, USA.

CASALS Manu; b. 9 May 1970, France. Sound Engineer; Technical Man. *Education:* University of Nantes; University of Brest. *Career:* Sound Engineer, Live Concerts, Calvin Russel, Denez Prigent, Festival des Vieilles Charrues, Les Fiestas des Hesperides Festival; Sound Engineer, Studio. *Recordings:* Denez Prigent Albums; Philmarie, Matmathah albums; Major Mix in Festival. *Current Management:* La Chapelle and GAM Recording Studio. *Address:* 5 rue du Bac, 4950 Waimes, Belgium and 50 rue des Châlets, 72000 Le Mans, France.

CASEY Al (Albert A); b. 15 Sept. 1915, Louisville, Kentucky, USA. Musician (guitar). m. Athena Casey, 18 Sept. 1937, 1 s. *Musical Education:* 2 Years at musical school. *Career:* Guitarist for artists including: Fats Waller, Teddy Wilson, King Curtis. *Honour:* Esquire

Magazine Award, 1943–44. *Membership:* AFofM, New York City. *Current Management:* Al Wolman, New York, USA. *Address:* 404 W 54th St, Apt 3J, New York, NY, USA.

CASEY Harry Wayne; b. 31 Jan. 1951, Hialeah, Florida, USA. Musician (keyboards); Vocalist; Prod.; Arranger. *Career:* Founder member (as KC), KC and the Sunshine Band, 1973; Writer, arranger, producer, KC and the Sunshine Band; George McCrae; Career interrupted by severe injuries in car crash, 1982. *Recordings:* Albums: Do It Good, 1974; KC and The Sunshine Band, 1975; The Sound of Sunshine, 1975; Part Three, 1976; I Like To Do It, 1977; Who Do Ya Love, 1978; Do You Wanna Go To Party, 1979; Greatest Hits, 1980; Painter, 1981; All In A Night's Work, 1983; The Best Of, 1990; Solo albums: Space Cadet, Wayne Casey/KC, 1981; KC Ten, 1984; US No. 1 hit singles: Get Down Tonight, 1975; That's The Way (I Like It), 1975; Shake Shake Shake, 1976; I'm Your Boogie Man, 1977; UK No. 1 hit single: Give It Up, 1983; Other hits include: Queen of Clubs; Boogie Shoes; Please Don't Go; Yes I'm Ready, duet with Teri De Sario (No. 2, US). *Current Management:* Saquier Management. *Address:* 4770 Biscayne Blvd, Suite 900, Miami, FL 33137, USA.

CASEY Howie (Howard William); b. Liverpool, England. Musician (saxophones). m. Sheila, 19 Sept. 1980, 1 d. *Musical Education:* Army Band Kings Regiment; Mostly self-taught. *Career:* Recording, live concerts with: Paul McCartney; Wings (Over The World), 1975–76, 1980; The Who; ABC; Chuck Berry; Jimmy Ruffin; Cliff Richard; Lee Dorsey; PAL (Plaice, Ashton, Lord); Roy Young Band; Mark Bolan; Les Humphries Singers. *Recordings:* with Wings: Band On The Run; Wings At The Speed of Sound; Back To The Egg; Wings Over America; Rockestra; Albums with: ABC; Marc Bolan; PAL; Gilbert O'Sullivan; Cliff Richard; Elkie Brooks; Ashton, Gardner, Dyke; The Who. *Memberships:* PRS; Musicians' Union. *Address:* 36 R L Stevenson Ave, Bournemouth, Dorset BH4 8EG, England.

CASEY Karan; b. 5 April 1968, Waterford, Ireland. Vocalist. *Career:* Began performing in Waterford; Moved to Dublin, 1987; Relocated to New York, 1993; Joined Solas, 1997–; Solo artist, 1997–; Involved with Africans in America TV documentary; Currently touring. *Recordings:* with Solas: Solas, 1996; Sunny Spells and Scattered Showers, 1997; The Words That Remain, 1998; solo: Songlines, 1997; Fused (with Mike McGoldrick), 2000; The Seal Maiden, 2000; The Winds Begin To Sing, 2001. *Honours:* Won 3 NAIRD/AFIM indie awards with Solas; Grammy Award, Best New Age Album, Celtic Solstice, Paul Winter and Friends, 2000. *Current Management:* Tom Sherlock Management, Carysfort Ave, Blackrock, County Dublin, Ireland. *E-mail:* sherlock@altan.ie. *Internet:* www.karancasey.com.

CASH Johnny (John R); b. 26 Feb. 1932, Kingsland, Arkansas, USA. Country Vocalist; Musician (guitar); Songwriter; Entertainer; Actor. m. June Carter, 1968, 1 s., 4 d. (by previous marriage). *Education:* HHD, Gardner Webb College, 1971; National University, San Diego, 1975. *Career:* Composer, solo recording artist, 1955–; Also member of occasional side-project The Highwaymen (with Kris Kristofferson, Waylon Jennings, Willie Nelson), 1985–; Television includes: Johnny Cash Show, 1969–71; Subject of documentaries including: Johnny Cash, The Man, His World, His Music; Johnny Cash At San Quentin; Actor, films: A Gunfight; North and South; Stagecoach; Television films: The Baron and The Kid; The Last Days of Frank and Jesse; Other television appearances: Columbo; Dr Quinn – Medicine Woman; President, House of Cash Inc; Songs of Cash Inc; Vice President, Family of Man Music Inc; Collaborations: Ray Charles; Rodney Crowell; Bob Dylan; Emmylou Harris; Kris Kristofferson; Mark O'Connor; Marty Stuart; U2. *Compositions include:* The True West (documentary record); The Gospel Road (co-writer, producer, narrator); Movie soundtracks: I Walk The Line; Little Fauss and Big Halsy. *Recordings:* Over 150 albums, live recordings and compilations, 1957–; Albums include: The Fabulous Johnny Cash, 1959; Ring of Fire, 1963; Johnny Cash At Fulsom Prison, 1968; Johnny Cash At San Quentin (No. 1, USA), 1969; Hello, I'm Johnny Cash, 1970; Man In Black, 1971; One Piece At A Time, 1976; Water From The Wells of Home, 1988; The Mystery of Life, 1991; American Recordings, 1994; Unchained, 1996; Just As I Am, 1999; American III – Solitary Man, 2000; with The Highwaymen: The Highwayman, 1985; Highwaymen 2, 1990; Hit singles include: I Walk The Line, 1956; There You Go, 1957; Ballad of a Teenage Queen, 1958; Guess Things Happen That Way, 1958; Ring of Fire, 1963; A Boy Named Sue, 1969; If I Were A Carpenter (duet with June Carter Cash), 1970; A Thing Called Love, 1972. *Publications:* Man In Black, 1975; Man In White (novel), 1986. *Honours:* CMA Award, Best Album, 1968; Grammy Awards: Best Country Duet (with June Carter Cash), 1968, 1971; Best Country Vocal Performance, 1969, 1970; Best Country Song, 1970, 1986; Best Album Notes, 1969, 1970; Best Spoken Word Recording, 1987; Living Legend Award, 1990; 4 UK Country Music Awards, 1970; Special Award of Merit, American Music Awards, 1977; LHD (Hon), National University San Diego, 1976; Inducted into Country Music Hall of Fame, 1980; Aggie Award, Songwriters Guild of America, 1989; Inducted into Rock 'n' Roll Hall of Fame, 1992. *Membership:* Country Music Asscn. *Address:* Suite 118, 5743 Corsa Ave, Westlake Vill, CA 91362, USA.

CASH June Carter; b. 23 June 1929, Maces Springs, Virginia, USA. Vocalist; Actress. m. Johnny Cash, 1 March 1968, 1 s., 6 d. *Musical Education:* Actor's Studio, New York. *Career:* Singer, Carter family, 1939–43; Carter Sisters, 1943–; Solo artiste; Duo with Johnny Cash, 1963–; Television include: Johnny Cash Show; Grand Ole Opry; Tennessee Ernie Show; Television films: Stagecoach; The Baron; Gospel Road; Road To Nashville; Television special: The Best of The Carter Family; Television series: Dr Quinn – Medicine Woman (played Dr Ruth); Entertains as singer, actress, musician (guitar, banjo, auto-harp), comedienne. *Recordings:* Songs include: Baby It's Cold Outside; Music Music Music; Love Oh Crazy Love; Let Me Go Lover; Contributions to recordings by Johnny Cash including: Jackson Duo; If I Were A Carpenter; with Carter family: Wabash Cannon; May The Circle Be Unbroken; Solo album: Press On, 1999. *Publications:* Author: Among My Kledaments, 1979; From The Heart, 1987; Wildwood Flower, screenplay, 1990; Mother Maybelle's Cookbook, 1992; Co-author, Ring of Fire. *Honours:* HHD (Hon), National University, San Diego, 1977; Civic Award, Nashville Women Executives, 1980; Grammy Awards: Best Country Duo Performance (with Johnny Cash), 1968, 1971; CMA Duet Artists of The Year, with Johnny Cash; Virginian of Year, 1989. *Memberships:* ASCAP; Grand Ole Opry; Country Music Asscn. *Current Management:* Lou Robin, Artist Consultants Productions, Suite 670, 11777 San Vicente Blvd, Los Angeles, CA 90049, USA.

CASH Roseanne; b. 24 May 1955, Memphis, Tennessee, USA. Vocalist. m. Rodney Crowell, 1979, divorced. *Education:* Drama, Vanderbilt University; Method acting, Lee Strasberg's Institute, Los Angeles. *Career:* Worked 3 years with (father) Johnny Cash's road show; Worked with Rodney Crowell, Nashville; Recording artiste, 1979–; Collaborations include: Mary Chapin Carpenter; Marc Cohn; Vince Gill; John Hiatt; Lyle Lovett; Carly Simon. *Recordings:* Hit singles include: No Memories Hangin' Round (with Bobby Bare); Couldn't Do Nothin' Right; Take Me Take Me; Never Be You; I Don't Know Why You Don't Want Me (co-written with Rodney Crowell); The Way We Make A Broken Heart; Tennessee Flat Top Box; If You Change Your Mind; Rainway Train; Albums include: Roseanne Cash, 1978; Right Or Wrong, 1979; Seven Year Ache, 1981; Somewhere In The Stars, 1982; Rhythm and Romance, 1985; King's Record Shop, 1988; Hits 1979–89, 1989; Interiors, 1990; The Wheel, 1993; Retrospective, 1995; 10 Song Demo, 1996; What Kinda Girl (live), 1999. *Honours:* Grammy, Best Country Vocal Performance Female, 1985; Top Single Artist Award, Billboard, 1988. *Current Management:* Side One Management, 1026A Third Ave, New York, NY 10021, USA.

CASH Tommy; b. 5 April 1940, Dyess, Arkansas, USA. Professional Entertainer; Musician (rhythm guitar). m. (1) Barbara Wisenbaker, 18 Aug. 1961, 1 s., 1 d.; (2) Pamela Dyer, 12 March 1978. *Education:* Radio Broadcast School; Real estate school (Realtor); College courses: Tennessee Tech. *Career:* All major country music television shows, many network television programmes; Radio announcer, 1959–64, including: American Forces Network, Germany, 1959–62; Music publisher, 1965–; Professional entertainer, 1965–; Songwriter, songs recorded by: Conway Twitty; Kitty Wells; Faron Young; Jean Sheppard; Johnny Cash; Loretta Lynn; Music published by Tomcat Music, BMI. *Recordings:* More than 20 albums, approximately 65 songs, 1965–; Hits include: Six White Horses, 1970; Rise and Shine; That Certain One; So This Is Love; Gypsy Woman; Gospel album: This Happy Heart of Mine, 1995. *Honours:* Two BMI Awards for Songwriting, 1965, 1975; Music City News Most Promising Vocalist, 1970. *Memberships:* AFofM, Nashville; AFTRA, Nashville; National Asscn of Realtors; ROPE Inc. *Leisure interests:* Golf; Softball; Gardening. *Current Management:* Joe Taylor, AGN Nashville; Billy Deaton Talent Nashville. *Address:* Hendersonville, Tennessee, USA.

CASSIDY David; b. 12 April 1950, New York, New York, USA. Actor; Vocalist. *Career:* Actor, The Partridge Family television series; Lead vocalist, Partridge Family recordings; Solo artiste, 1971–; Actor, Joseph and The Amazing Technicolour Dreamcoat; Lead role, musical, Time, 1987. *Recordings:* Albums: Cherish, 1972; Could It Be Forever, 1972; Rock Me Baby, 1972; Dreams Are Nothin' More, 1973; Cassidy Live, 1974; The Higher They Climb, 1975; Greatest Hits, 1977; Romance, 1985; His Greatest Hits, Live, 1986; Didn't You Used To Be..., 1992; Old Trick, New Dog, 1998; Then and Now, 2001; Singles include: with The Partridge Family: I Think I Love You (No. 1, USA), 1970; Solo: Cherish (No. 1, USA), 1971; Could It Be Forever, 1972; How Can I Be Sure? (No. 1, UK), 1972; I Am A Clown, 1973; Daydreamer/The Puppy Song (No. 1, UK), 1973; The Last Kiss, 1985. *Current Management:* c/o Larry Lerner, 20501 Ventura Blvd, Suite 392, Woodland Hills, CA 91364, USA.

CASSWELL Michael; b. 18 June 1966, Romford, Essex, England. Musician (guitar). *Education:* Art College. *Career:* Signed to RCA America, album, 1986; MCA Records, 2 albums, 1989; Toured in Brian May Band, Back to the Light tour, 1992. *Recordings:* Heroes, 1986; Walk On Fire, 1989. *Memberships:* PRS; Musicians' Union. *Leisure interests:* Cars; Guitars. *Current Management:* Agent: Session Connection, Brenda

Brooker, RAK Records. *Address:* Angel Cottage, Manor Rd, Lambourne End, Romford, Essex RM4 1NH, England.

CASTLE Pete; b. 25 Feb. 1947, Ashford, Kent, England. Folk Singer; Musician (Guitar); Storyteller. m. Sue Brown, 27 April 1967, 1 s., 1 d. *Education:* Maidstone Technical High School; Bretton Hall College of Education. *Career:* Organizer of Luton Folk Festival, 1976–78; Solo artist, working at clubs, festivals, in schools and on community projects, 1978–; Presenter, Chiltern Radio Folk Show, 1981–87; Collaboration with Aroti Biswas, 1987; Mountsorrel Community Play, 1993; Launched the occasional band Popeluc, 1994. *Recordings include:* Bedfordshire Folk Songs, 1981; Rambling Robin, 1982; Punk's Delight, 1985; One Morning By Chance, 1989; Cottage By the Shore, 1992; Two Tongues One Voice, 1994; Keys of Canterbury, 1994; Maramures Et Cetera, 1994; Falsewaters, 1995; Blue Dor, 1996. *Memberships:* Musicians' Union; PRS; MCPS; Society for Storytelling. *Leisure interests:* Music; Walking; Cinema. *Address:* 190 Burton Rd, Derby, DE1 1TQ, England.

CASTLE-HOTEA Lucy Katherine; b. 15 Feb. 1970, Lincolnshire, England. Musician (Ethohusicologist, Fiddler). m. Ioan Castle-Hotea, 1 d. *Education:* BSc, City University, London. *Career:* Founded, Trio Popeluc with Father Pete Casre an Romanian Musician Ioan Pop, Toured Britain, Romania; Teacher of Violin; Performs with her Husband. *Recordings:* The Broken Pledge; Maramures Et Cetera; Popeuic Live; Blue Dor. *Membership:* ESTA. *Current Management:* Steel Carpet Music, 190 Burton Rd, Derby DE1 1TQ. *Address:* 6A Darley St, Darley Abbey, Derby, DE22 1DX.

CATER Pete; b. 8 Feb. 1963, Lichfield, Staffordshire, England. Musician (drums); Bandleader; Teacher. *Musical Education:* Self-taught. *Career:* Tour world-wide, with Elaine Delmar in Thank You Mr Gershwin; Played with Arturo Sandoval Quintet; Pete Cater Big Band; Sheena Davis Group; Spike Robinson Group; Rickey Woodard Quartet; Charlie Byrd Trio; Gene Bertoncinni Trio; Freelance session player with: BBC; ITV; C4; BBC Big Band; NYJO; A Ross; Val Doonican; Dave Willetts; S Maughan; Herb Miller Orchestra. *Recordings:* Upswing, with Pete Carter Big Band; Playing With Fire, with Pete Carter Big Band. *Honours:* Outstanding drummer, BBC Radio 2 National Big Band Competition, 1980, 1991; Best Big Band, British Jazz Awards, 2000. *Membership:* Faculty mem., Musician's Institute, London. *Address:* PO Box 123, Borehamwood, Herts WD6 3ZG, England.

CATLEY Bob; Vocalist. *Career:* Founder member, lead vocalist, UK rock group Magnum, 1972–; Support tours with: Judas Priest; Whitesnake; Blue Öyster Cult; Def Leppard; Own headline tours world-wide. *Recordings:* Albums: Kingdom of Madness, 1978; Magnum II, 1979; Marauder, 1980; Chase The Dragon, 1982; The Eleventh Hour, 1983; On A Storyteller's Night, 1985; Vigilante, 1986; Wings of Heaven, 1988; Goodnight LA, 1990; The Spirit, 1991; Rock Art, 1994; Stronghold, 1997; Archive, 2000; Numerous compilation albums; Singles include: Kingdom of Madness, 1978; Just Like An Arrow, 1985; On A Storyteller's Night, 1985; Midnight, 1986; Days of No Trust; 1988; Start Talking Love, 1988; It Must Have Been Love, 1988; Rocking Chair, 1990.

CATLEY Marc; b. 3 Nov. 1959, Birmingham, England. Singer; Songwriter; Musician (guitar); Satirist. *Education:* Liverpool University; London Bible College. *Career:* First solo progressive rock album Classical Acoustic Rock, 1986; Numerous radio interviews and airplay in Europe and US; 4 albums, religious satire with band The Flaming Methodists, 1991–; Television and radio appearances include: Granada TV and Radio 4; Formed progressive rock band Paley's Watch, 1993. *Composition:* Char, 1996. *Recordings:* Progressive rock albums: with Geoff Mann: The Off The End of The Pier Show, 1991; Fine Difference, 1992; with Paley's Watch: November, 1994; Satirical albums: Peel of Hope, 1991; Make The Tea, 1992; Hot Air For Jesus, 1993; No Tomorrow, 1994. *Memberships:* MCPS; PRS; BASCA; Musicians' Union. *Current Management:* Plankton Records; Sandcastle Productions. *Address:* 236 Sebert Rd, Forest Gate, London E7 0NP, England.

CATO Pauline; b. 14 Dec. 1968, Ashington, Northumberland, England. Musician (Northumbrian pipes, keyboards). *Education:* BA (Hons) Modern Languages, Sheffield University, 1991; PGCE 1992, Sheffield University. *Musical Education:* Grade 8 piano; Taught Northumbrian Pipes by Richard Butler, piper to the Duke of Northumberland. *Career:* Member, Border Spirit, 1988–90; Solo artiste, 1990–94; Cullercoats Tommy (opera), with Northern Sinfonia Orchestra, 1993; Became full-time musician, 1993; Also working in duo with fiddler Tom McConville; Television and radio appearances: Small Folk, YTV/Channel 4, 1989; Several Radio 2/3 features; Performed on BBC drama series soundtrack, Badger. *Recordings:* Hindley Steel, Border Spirit, 1988; Solo albums: The Wansbeck Piper, 1992; Changing Tides, 1994; Various recordings as session musician; By Land and Sea, with Tom McConville, 1996; The Surprise, with Tom McConville, Chris Newman and Maggie Boyle, 1999. *Publication:* Pauline Cato's Northumbrian Choice, with recordings, 1997.

Honours: Appointed Piper to Mayor of Gateshead, 1989; Hon. Mem., Northumbrian Pipers Society, for Services to Piping; Young Tradition Award Finalist, BBC, 1990; Daily Telegraph Folk Album of the Year, 1996, 1999. *Address:* Tomcat Music, PO Box 2100, Sheffield S36 9BW, England.

CATTERMOLE Paul; b. 7 March 1977, St Albans, UK. Vocalist; Actor. *Education:* Trained at Mountview Drama School and National Youth Music Theatre. *Career:* Former member of rock band Skua; Acted in numerous stage productions prior to joining S Club 7; Group quickly achieved international success following sales of TV series Miami 7 (1999), LA 7 (2000) and Hollywood 7 (2001) featuring the band's music to nearly 100 countries; Also made nature TV series S Club 7 Go Wild (2000) and various TV specials; First British tour with S Club 7, 2001. *Recordings:* Albums: S Club, 1999; 7, 2000; Sunshine, 2001; Singles: Bring It All Back, 1999; S Club Party, 1999; Two In A Million/You're My Number One, 1999; Reach, 2000; Natural, 2000; Never Had A Dream Come True, 2000; Don't Stop Movin', 2001; Have You Ever, 2001. *Honours:* Brit Award, Best British Newcomer, 2000. *Current Management:* 19 Management, Unit 32, Ransomes Dock, 35–37 Parkgate Rd, London, SW11 4NP, England.

CATTINI Clem; b. 28 Aug. 1939, London, England. Musician (drums). m. Anna, 17 May 1958, 3 d. *Career:* Member, Johnny Kidd and the Pirates; Tornados; Top of The Pops Orchestra (12 years); Toured with: Sir Cliff Richard; Kids From Fame; Lulu; Grace Kennedy; The Drifters; Liza Minnelli; Sandie Shaw; Tom Jones; Engelbert Humperdinck; Television: Michael Barrymore; Lulu; Michael Jackson; Stevie Wonder; Gladys Knight. *Recordings:* Johnny Kidd and the Pirates: Please Don't Touch, 1960; Shakin' All Over, 1971; Tornados: Sound Of; Telstar; More Sounds From; Tornado Rock; Away From It All, 1962–64; Everlasting Love; Devil Woman; Musician on: Roy Harper: Folkjokeopus, 1969; Joe Cocker: With A Little Help From My Friends, 1969; P J Proby: 3 Week Hero, 1969; Bee Gees: To Whom It May Concern, 1972; Lou Reed: Lou Reed, 1972; Phil Everly: Phil's Diner, 1974; Recorded with: Kinks; Dusty Springfield; Lulu; Tom Jones; Engelbert Humperdinck; Gene Pitney; Other albums by: Cliff Richard; Hank Marvin; Justin Hayward; Brian Auger; Claire Hamill; Jimmy Page; Albert Lee; John Paul Jones; Alan Price; Played on 42 No. 1s. *Honours:* Gold Disc, Gold Globe (Telstar); Cup NME Poll Winners (Tornados). *Memberships:* Musicians' Union; PRS; MCPS. *Leisure interests:* Golf; Football. *Address:* 15 Blenheim Close, London N21 2HQ, England.

CAUDEL Stephen; b. 29 June 1955, Sheffield, South Yorkshire, England. Composer; Musician (guitar). m. Shelagh Quinn, 17 Dec. 1983, 1 s. *Musical Education:* O Level, A Level Music; Studies Classical, Jazz, Light Music, at City of Leeds College of Music. *Career:* Numerous television and radio appearances; Concert tours: UK including Royal Albert Hall; Overseas tours including Japan. *Compositions:* Wine Dark Sea (rock symphony, world premiere, London, 1983); Edel Rhapsody, for Wagner Tuba and Orchestra, (world premiere, Carlisle, 1993). *Recordings:* Albums: Wine Dark Sea; Bow of Burning Gold; Impromptu Romance; The Earth In Turquoise; Featured guitarist on Hooked On Classics II, with Royal Philharmonic Orchestra. *Memberships:* PRS; MCPS; Musicians' Union. *Leisure interests:* Films; Books; Theatrical Magic. *Current Management:* Mr Laurie Mansfield. *Address:* International Artistes Ltd, Mezzanine Floor, 235 Regent St, London W1R 8AX, England.

CAUTY Jimi; b. 1954. Musician (guitar). *Career:* Member, Brilliant, 1983–86; Co-founder, KLF Communications, with Bill Drummond, 1987–92; Organized music projects under names: JAMs; Disco 2000; The Justified Ancients of Mu Mu; The Timelords; KLF; Founder, own recording studio, Trancentral, 1988; Appearances include DMC European Convention, Amsterdam, 1990; Film: The White Room, 1988. *Recordings:* Albums: with Brilliant: Kiss The Lips of Life, 1985; as JAMs: 1987, 1987; Shag Times (compilation), 1989; as KLF: The What Time Is Love Story, 1989; Chill Out, 1990; The White Room, 1991; Solo album (as Space): Space, 1990; Singles include: with Brilliant: It's A Man's Man's Man's World, 1985; Love Is War, 1986; Somebody, 1986; as JAMs: All You Need Is Love, 1987; Whitney Joins The Jams, 1987; Downtown, 1987; Who Killed The JAMs, 1988; as Disco 2000: I Gotta CD, 1987; Uptight, 1989; as The Timelords: Doctorin' The Tardis (No. 1, UK), 1988; as KLF: Burn The Beat, 1988; Kylie Said To Jason, 1989; What Time Is Love, 1990; 3AM Eternal (No. 1, UK), 1991; Last Train To Trancentral, 1991; as The Justified Ancients of Mu Mu: It's Grim Up North, 1991; Justified and Ancient, with Tammy Wynette, 1992; as 2K: Fuck The Millennium, 1997; Other collaborations: The Orb, 1989–91; The Black Dog, 1999. *Publication:* The Manual (How To Have A Number One Hit The Easy Way), 1988. *Honour:* Brit Award, Best British Group (shared with Simply Red), 1992.

CAVALERA Max; b. 4 Aug. 1969, Belo Horizonte, Brazil. Rock Musician (guitar, percussion); Vocalist. m. Gloria Cavalera, 6 June 1993, 4 s., 1 d. *Musical Education:* Self-taught. *Career:* Member, Brazilian heavy rock group Sepultura, 1984–97; World-wide tours including US, Brazil, Russia, Indonesia; Support tours with The Ramones, Ministry, Ozzy Osbourne; Concerts include: Rock in Rio, Brazil; Hollywood Rock, Brazil;

Monsters of Rock Festival, Castle Donington, UK; Dynamo Open Air Festival, Netherlands; Roskilde Festival, Denmark; Television appearances: The Word (UK); MTV Most Wanted (UK); Side project, Nailbomb 1994–95; Formed new band, Soulfly, 1997-. *Compositions:* Bleed; Tribe; Eye for an Eye. *Recordings:* Albums: with Sepultura: Morbid Visions, 1985; Schizophrenia, 1988; Beneath The Remains, 1989; Arise, 1991; Chaos AD, 1993; Roots, 1996; Nativity In Black (Black Sabbath tribute); Virus 100 (Dead Kennedys tribute); Tales From The Crypt (soundtrack); Under the Sun, for Nativity in Black II; Nailbomb albums: Point Blank, 1994; Proud To Commit Commercial Suicide, 1995; with Soulfly: Soulfly, 1998; Primitive, 2000. *Honours:* 2 MTV South America Awards; Best Album, Kerrang! magazine, UK, 1994; Best New Band, France. *Memberships:* ASCAP; National Wildlife Organization; Co-Founder, Iggy Diabetes Fund. *Leisure interests:* Football; Tattoos; Visiting rainforests. *Current Management:* Gloria Cavalera, Oasis Management, 3010 E Bloomfield, Phoenix, AZ 85032, USA.

CAVALERI Nathan Michael; b. 18 June 1982, Camden, NSW, Australia. Musician (guitar). *Education:* St Gregory's College, Campbelltown, NSW, Australia. *Musical Education:* Taught by father. *Career:* San Francisco Blues Festival, with Albert Collins, 1992; Toured with B B King, special guest, 1995; 25th Birthday for Guitar Player magazine; Kennedy Lifetime Achievement Awards, honouring B B King, 1995; Out In The Green Festival, Zurich, 1995; Tours, with Jimmy Barnes of Diesel, Australia; Appeared on: Arsenio Hall; Inside Edition; Good Morning America; Conan O'Brian; CNN; Hey Hey It's Saturday Australia; Midday Australia; MMM Network; Radio Australia; Camp Nowhere The Film; Baywatch Nights; Australia Music Awards; Entertainment Network Australia; Commercial for MacDonalds with B B King, 1995. *Compositions include:* Song, Lou's Blues, used in Free Willy 2 film soundtrack. *Recordings:* Albums: Jammin' With The Cats (5 co-written songs), 1994; Nathan (6 co-written songs). *Honours:* Variety Club, Australia, Young Variety award, 1993; BMW Jazz and Blues Best New Talent, 1993; Young Australian Achiever, 1994. *Membership:* SAG. *Leisure interests:* Drums; Bodyboarding; Computer Games. *Current Management:* CAA Agency, Linchpin-Russell Hayward, Los Angeles, California. *Address:* 2512 Zorada Dr., Los Angeles, CA 90046, USA.

CAVANAUGH Page; b. 26 Jan. 1922, Cherokee, Kansas, USA. Musician (piano); Singer; Entertainer. *Musical Education:* Private teachers. *Career:* Performed as pianist, vocalist, in films: Record Party, 1947; Romance On The High Seas (2 songs on screen with Doris Day), 1947; A Song Is Born (1 song with Virginia Mayo), 1947; Big City (2 songs with Betty Garret), 1947; Lullaby of Broadway (Song with: Gene Nelson: Zing Went The Strings of My Heart; with Doris Day and Gene: You're Getting to Be A Habit With Me), 1950. *Recordings:* Albums: with Michael Feinstein: Crazy Rhythm; Pure Imagination; with Page Cavanaugh Trio: Digital Page; Page One; Page Two, 1993; The Three Bears; All of Me; Walking My Baby Back Home; Page Cavanaugh Plays For The Cocktail Hour; Something's Happening At Page Cavanaugh's. *Memberships:* NAOL; Society of Singers. *Leisure interests:* Cooking; Gardening. *Address:* 5442 Woodman Ave, Sherman Oaks, CA 91401, USA.

CAVE Nick; b. 22 Sept. 1957, Australia. Vocalist; Songwriter; Actor. *Career:* Member, Birthday Party (formerly Boys Next Door), early 1980s; Founder, Nick Cave and The Bad Seeds; Actor, films include: Wings of Desire, 1987; Ghosts of The Civil Dead, 1989. *Recordings:* Albums: with Birthday Party: Prayers On Fire, 1981; Junkyard, 1982; The Bad Seed/ Mutiny, 1989; Hee-Haw, 1989; with The Bad Seeds: From Here To Eternity, 1984; The First Born Is Dead, 1985; Kicking Against The Pricks, 1986; Your Funeral, My Trial, 1986; Tender Prey, 1988; Ghost of The Civil Dead, 1989; The Good Son, 1990; Henry's Dream, 1992; Live Seeds, 1993; Let Love In, 1994; Murder Ballads, 1996; The Boatman's Call, 1997; The Very Best of Nick Cave and The Bad Seeds, 1998; No More Shall We Part, 2001; Albums of poetry: The Secret Life of The Love Song/The Flesh Made Word, 1998; And The Ass Saw The Angel; Singles: with Birthday Party: Fiend Catcher; Release The Collaborations, with Lydia Lunch and Einsturzende Neubaten; with the Bad Seeds: In The Ghetto, 1984; Tupelo, 1985; The Singer, 1985; The Mercy Seat, 1988; Oh Deanna, 1988; The Ship Song, 1990; The Weeping Song, 1990; Straight To You, 1992; I Had A Dream Joe, 1992; What A Wonderful World, duet with Shane MacGowan, 1992; Do You Love Me?, 1994; Loverman, 1994; Red Right Hand, 1994; Where The Wild Roses Grow, duet with Kylie Minogue, 1995; Henry Lee, duet with PJ Harvey, 1996; Into My Arms, 1997; Are You The One That I've Been Waiting For?, 1997; As I Sat Sadly By Her Side, 2001; Fifteen Feet of Pure White Snow, 2001; Contributor, film soundtrack, Batman Forever, 1995. *Publications:* and The Ass Saw The Angel (novel), 1989; King Ink (collection of lyrics and verse); King Ink II. *Current Management:* Rayner Jesson at Tender Prey, Studio 4, Ivebury Court, 325 Latimer Rd, London W10 6RA, England.

CAZES Henrique; b. 2 Feb. 1959, Rio de Janeiro, Brazil. Musician (cavaquinho – small 4-stringed guitar); Prod.; Arranger. m. Maria A C L Fernandes, 2 s. *Musical Education:* Self-taught acoustic guitar, cavaquinho,

banjo; Classes in harmony and arrangement with Ian Guest. *Career:* Worked with Radames Gnatelli, 7 years; Tours as cavaquinho soloist: Japan, 1985–90; USA, 1988, 1990; Europe, 1993; Founder member, Orchestra Brazilian Strings; Creator, director, Brasília Orchestra; Carrefour Mondial de la Guitare, Martinique. *Recordings include:* Henrique Cazes, 1988; Henrique Cazes – Tocando Waldir Azevado, 1990; Henrique Cazes – Waldir Azevado, Pixinguinha, Hermeto and Cia, 1992; Cristina Buarque e Henrique Cazes Sem Tostao, 1994; Henrique Cazes and The Guitar Family – Since The Choro Is Choro, 1995; Also appears on: Deixa Clarear, 1996; Rhythm and Romance, 1998. *Publications:* Text book Escola Moderna de Cavaquinho. *Honours:* Sharp Awards: 1991, 1992, 1995; Number One Cavaquinho of The World, Japan, 1990. *Membership:* AMAR (Brazilian Asscn of Arrangers and Conductors). *Current Management:* C Fernandes. *Address:* Paulo Barreto, No. 25/802 Botafogo, 22280–010 Rio de Janeiro, RJ, Brazil.

CECCARELLI Andre; b. 5 Jan. 1946, Nice, France. Musician (drums). m. Marcelle Ritling, 8 April 1968, 1 s. *Musical Education:* Music Academy of France. *Career:* Member, Les Chats Suavages, 1961; Worked with Aime Barelli, Monte Carlo, 1964; Played with Rocky Roberts and the Piranas, 1966–68; Freelance musician, 1968–; Worked with artists including: Brian Auger; Tania Maria; Tina Turner; Michel Legrand; Bireli Lagrene; Mike Stern; Tom Harle. *Recordings:* with Ceccarelli Trio: Hat Snatcher; Three Around The Floor; with Dee Dee Bridgewater: Keeping Traditions; Love and Peace; with Tina Turner: Love Explosion; with Tania Maria: Live In Copenhagen; with M Portal: Turbulence; Also recorded with: Michel Legrand and Stéphane Grappelli; Aretha Franklin; Tom Harrell and Bob Berg; Paul Mauriat; Bireli Lagrene and NHOP; Enrico Pieranunzi and H Van De Glyn; Brian Auger; Johnny Mercer; Richard Galliano. *Honours:* Django D'Or, Best Jazz Group, 1993; Victoire de la Musique, Best Jazz Album, 1993; Aigle D'Argent, Nice. *Memberships:* SACEM; ADAMI; SPEDIDAM. *Leisure interest:* Music. *Current Management:* Isoard Christiane and Sola Thierry. *Address:* 22 rue Ernest Revillon, 77630 Barbizon, France.

CECH Christoph; b. 29 June 1960, Vienna, Austria. Composer; Arranger; Musician (keyboards, orchestral percussion). m. Ursula, 5 March 1988, 3 s. *Education:* Matriculation/studies in Architecture, Technical University, Vienna. *Musical Education:* Studies in piano, rhythmic, orchestral percussion, jazz theory, composition, Vienna Conservatory. *Career:* Jazz fairy tale, F F Company and Co (co-composer with Christian Mühlbacher), 1987; TV production, (ORF), 1993; Concert number 1 for piano and orchestra, radio production (ORF), 1994; Suite for doublebass, bass clarinet and 15 players, The Musikvereinshall, Vienna; Many tours with different ensembles; Teacher, Harmonics and Counterpoint, University of Music, Vienna, 1998–; Leader, Jazz and popular music, Bruckner Conservatory, Linz, 1999-. *Compositions:* Chamber opera, Die Befreiung Des Modulors, State Theatre Schwerin, Germany, 1988; Protophantasm, Concerto Grosso for big band and orchestra; Opera, Aus Allen Blüten Bitternis, Chamber Opera, Vienna, 1996; B.A.C.H. Kantate, Dom St Pölten, 1997; Requiem, 1998; Bruckner Festival, Linz, 1998; Cantata das lied der lieder, 1999; Music Actual; Triple Concerto, Musikvereins Hall, Vienna. *Recordings:* with Nouvelle Cuisine Big Band: Flambée, 1988, 1989; Elephant Terrine, 1990; Phrygian Flight, 1994; Ultimate Sentences, 1997; with Striped Roses: Bonsai Beat, 1990; Insection, 1994; Tulpen, 1997; Solo: Mondautos, 1993; with Jubilo Elf: Missing Link, 1991; with Camerata Obscura, Batpulse, 1997; in duo with Bertl Mütter, Lohgesang, 1997; Requiem, 1998. *Publication:* Keyboard 1–4, 1991. *Honours:* Stipendium for Composition, City of Vienna, 1987, 1995; First Prize, Kunstpreis Leibnitz, Austria, 1994; State Stipendium, Austrian Republic, 1995; Austro Mechana Publicity Prize, 1997. *Leisure interests:* Eating; Drinking; Sleeping. *Address:* Schottenfeldgasse 61/16, 1070 Vienna, Austria.

CECH Vladimir; b. 22 March 1944, Brno. m. Alena Benesová, 29 Aug. 1975, 1 s. *Education:* Diploma Engineer, Technical University, Brno, 1970; Graduated, Faculty of Musicology and Theatrology, Brno, Masaryka University. *Career:* Regular programmes on Musical and Theatre Life, Radio Brno; Author, Speaker, public playbacks of classical and pop music; Contributions: Regularly to Brno, Prague, Vienna newspapers, especially Slovo, BT – Rovnist, Opus Musicum. *Publications:* Regular reports on music life in Czech Republic, Vienna. *Honour:* Prize, Czech Music Foundation, 1984–90. *Leisure interests:* Travel; Sport. *Address:* Drobného 16, 602 00 Brno, Czech Republic.

CELLIER Marcel; b. 29 Oct. 1925, Zurich, Switzerland. Musical Editor. m. Catherine, 15 May 1953, 3 s. *Musical Education:* Studied cello and Ethnomusicology about Eastern Europe. *Career:* Producer, Radio Suisse Romande, 1961–95, ORTF/Radio France, BR Munich, RDRS Zurich-Berne, WDR Cologne; Producer of 4 sound carriers with Gheorghe Zamfir as well as 4 with Mystère des Voix Bulgares. *Recordings:* Albanian, Hungarian, Romanian and Bulgarian folk music and vocal art. *Honours:* Grand Prix et Disque d'or de l'Academie Ch Cros, Paris; Critics Prize, Music Critics of Germany; Grand Prix Audiovisuel de l'Academie Française du Disque;

Grammy Award, 1990. *Memberships:* Rotary; ICTM; Vice-President, GVS Gesellschaft für Volksmusik in der Schweiz. *Leisure interests:* Gypsey music; Improvisations with friends. *Address:* Rue du Bourg-de-Plait, 1605 Chexbres, Switzerland.

CERMAK Zappa (Johann Leopold); b. 7 July 1949, Heidenreichstein, Austria. Musician (guitar, drums, percussion, harmonica); Vocalist. m. Erika. *Education:* VSA; HSA; Forestry technician. *Career:* Began as: Blues Zappa, 1974–76; Original member, Bluespumpm, 1975; Parallel project with Fritz Glatzl as Blues Zappa and Pumpm Fritz (also with Johannes Müller); Major tours, most European countries; Radio, television: Austria; Slovakia; Slovenia; Hungary; Czech Republic. *Recordings:* with Bluespumpm: Albums: Bluespumpm, 1979; Edlau, 1980; Village, 1981; Live With Friends, 1985; The 5th Ten Years Jubilee, 1987; Live At Utopia, 1988; Live With Friends, 1991; Birthday, 1991; Live In Vienna, 1992; The 5th, 1992; Living Loving Riding, 1994; Singles: Wolfgang Session and Song, 1980; Train and Quick Shoes, 1985; Men From Milwaukee, 1993; with Blues Zappa: Albums: Gitarrero, 1985; Blue Balance, 1987; Glaskar, 1987; Andy Bartosh and Radio 1, 1994; Single: Der Letzte Zug, 1987. *Honours:* Silbenes Ehrenzeichen, 1992; Third Best Blues Album, Rot-Weis-Role Critics Poll, Live In Vienna, 1992. *Memberships:* AKM; AUME; LSG. *Leisure interests:* Elephant collecting; Living life. *Current Management:* Peter Steinbach, RGG Management. *Address:* Favoritenstr 53/2/6/18, 1100 Vienna, Austria.

CERVENKOVA Helena; b. 3 March 1937, Slavicin, Czech Republic. Musician (Cimbal). m. Jaroslav Cervenka, 1958, 1 s., 1 d. *Career:* BROLN, radio broadcasting orchestra, Brno, Soloist, Folk Music, 35 years; Presentation of contemporary Czech music – radio, tv. *Recordings:* Vychodoslovenská Karicka; Romo Slavonica; Jak Kukacka Kuká; Fantasie; Ked sa Janko na Vojnu Bral. *Honours:* Festival of Folk Music in Wales, Third Prize as Soloist, 1958; Best Soloist of Radio, Czech Repub, 1967. *Membership:* Cimbal World Asscn. *Address:* Lerchova 26, 602 00 Brno, Czech Republic.

CETERA Peter; b. 13 Sept. 1944, Chicago, Illinois, USA. Vocalist; Musician (bass). *Career:* Bassist, The Exceptions; Member, Chicago (formerly Big Thing, Chicago Transit Authority), 1967–85; Solo artiste, 1985–; Regular world-wide tours; Concerts include: Support to Janis Joplin, Jimi Hendrix, 1969; Atlantic Pop Festival, 1969; Isle of Wight Festival, 1970; First rock group to play Carnegie Hall, New York, 1971; Madison Square Garden, New York, 1977. *Compositions include:* Wishin' You Were Here; Baby What A Big Surprise; Hard To Say I'm Sorry (co-writer with David Foster); You're The Inspiration (co-writer with David Foster). *Recordings:* Albums: with Chicago: Chicago Transit Authority, 1969; Chicago II, 1970; Chicago III, 1971; Chicago At Carnegie Hall, 1971; Chicago V, 1972; Chicago VI, 1973; Chicago VII, 1974; Chicago VIII, 1975; Chicago X, 1976; Chicago XI, 1978; Hot Streets, 1978; Chicago 13, 1979; Chicago XIV, 1980; Chicago 16, 1982; Chicago 17, 1984; Chicago 18, 1987; Chicago 19, 1988; Chicago 21, 1991; Various compilations and greatest hits collections; Solo albums: Peter Cetera, 1981; Solitude/ Solitaire, 1986; One More Story, 1988; World Falling Down, 1992; One Clear Voice, 1995; Another Perfect World, 2001; Singles: with Chicago: Does Anybody Really Know What Time It Is; Beginnings; Colour My World; If You Leave Me Now (No. 1, USA and UK), 1976; Hard To Say I'm Sorry (No. 1, USA), 1982; Solo singles: Glory of Love (No. 1, USA), 1986; The Next Time I Fall (duet with Amy Grant)(No. 1, USA), 1986; I Wasn't The One Who Said Goodbye (duet with Agnetha Fältskog); One Good Woman; After All (duet with Cher, 1989; Restless Heart; Feels Like Heaven (duet with Chaka Khan); Even A Fool Can See; Forever Tonight; Faithfully; You're The Inspiration; Contributor, Voices That Care, Gulf Crisis Fund benefit record, 1991. *Honours include:* Grammy Award, 1977; American Music Award, 1977; Gold Ticket, Madison Square Garden, 1977. *Address:* c/o Agency for the Performing Arts, 9000 Sunset Blvd 12th Floor, Los Angeles, CA 90069, USA.

CETINIC Meri; b. 15 June 1953, Split, Croatia. Singer; Musician (piano); Composer. 1 d. *Career:* 20 years of singing world-wide, including: USA; Canada; Former USSR; Australia; TV, radio shows; humanitarian concerts; State awards for different ways in music. *Recordings:* Albums: The Sea; Meri; I'm A Woman; By The Way; Road Dust; Ace; Golden Dreams; Meri (6); Why Do I Love You; Look For Me. *Honours:* Singer of the Year, 1981–82; 5 Gold albums. *Membership:* Croatian Composer's Society. *Leisure interests:* Swimming; Home recording. *Current Management:* ZG Zoe Cetinic, Rendiceva 28, 10000 Zagreb, Croatia. *Address:* Meri Cetinic, Getaldiceva 27, 58000 Split, Croatia.

CHABRIER Jean-Claude; b. 10 Nov. 1931, Neuilly-sur-Seine, France. Musicologist. 1 s., 1 d. *Education:* Studied sciences and Medicine, 1950; Plastic Surgery training, 1956; HIMT, Electrology, 1959; Dr of Medicine, 1959; Erotology and Sexology, 1999; Studied Oriental Languages, Middle Eastern Civilization and Turkish, Paris; Doctorate in Musicology and Islamic Studies, Sorbonne, 1976; Doctorate in History of Music, Sorbonne, 1995. *Career:* Researcher, CNRS, Paris; Teacher, New

University of the Sorbonne, Paris-Sorbonne. *Compositions:* Ten Arabesques. *Recordings:* Ten Arabesques recital album; Anthology of oriental recitals; 10 albums, 1974–84. *Publications:* Analysis of Traditional Music: Identification, Representation, Paris Arabesques, 2 Vols; Over 200 analyses. *Honours:* Five Times Winner, Grand Prix, Academie du disque français, Paris, 1975, and Academie Charles Cros, Paris, 1980. *Memberships:* Société française d'Analyse musicale; International Musicology Society; Society for Music Theory; International Council for Traditional Musics; Society for Ethnomusicology; Euro-Seminar for Ethnomusicology. *Address:* 213 Ave de Versailles, 75016 Paris, France.

CHAD Dominic; b. 5 June 1974, Cheltenham, Gloucestershire, England. Musician (guitar). *Career:* Formed Grey Lantern with Paul Draper and Stove King; Changed name to Mansun; Joined by Andy Rathbone on drums; Numerous live tours and TV appearances. *Recordings:* Singles: Take It Easy Chicken, 1996; Egg Shaped Fred, 1996; Stripper Vicar, 1996; Wide Open Space, 1997; Legacy, 1998; Six, 1999; I Can Only Disappoint You, 2000; Electric Man, 2000; Fool, 2001; Albums: Attack of the Grey Lantern (No. 1, UK), 1997; Six, 1999; Little Kix, 2000.

CHADIMA Mikolas; b. 9 Sept. 1952, Cheb, Czech Republic. Composer; Musician (Saxaphone, Guitar, Vocals). m. Marta Zelinkova. *Education:* Karel Velebnr's Jazz School, 1974–78. *Career:* Elektrobus, 1974–76; Extempore Band, 1976–81; MCH Band, 1982–; Kilhets Improvising Group, 1979–80; Prague Jazz Days, 1977, 1979; Concert for Armenia, 1989; Karot, Festival, Budapest, 1990; Alternativa, Prague, 1993, 1996. *Compositions:* The City; We Are Well and We Feel Fine; Es Reut Mich F...; Exodus. *Recordings:* Kilhets, 1979; Extempore, The City, 1980–81; We Are Well and We Feel Fine, 1983; Es Reut Mich F..., 1988; Pseudemokritos, 1996; Transparent People, 1998. *Honours:* First Place, Extempore Band, Jazz Bulletin, 1981. *Memberships:* OSA; SAI; Svaz Hudebniku. *Leisure interests:* History of XX Century; Literature. *Address:* Mikolas Chadima, Cechova 24, 170 00 Prague 7, Czech Republic.

CHADWICK James Manfred; b. 16 Oct. 1966, Lusaka, Zimbabwe. Jazz Musician (guitar). m. 31 March 1995. *Education:* Shiplake College, Henley-on-Thames. *Musical Education:* Welsh College of Music and Drama. *Career:* Appeared on live TV programme Heno in 1993; Member of Enrico Quartet performing at 3 venues in Italy in 1994; Various appearances throughout Britain; Tour of Northern England in 1995. *Recording:* In The Bag, with James Chadwick Quartet, 1992. *Membership:* Musicians' Union. *Address:* 91 Moy Rd, Roath, Cardiff CF2 4TE, Wales.

CHADWICK Mark; Vocalist; Musician (guitar); Songwriter. *Career:* Singer, guitarist, The Levellers, 1990–; Concerts include: Glastonbury Festival, 1992; Regular UK and European concerts; Support to REM, Eastern Europe. *Recordings:* Singles: 15 Years, 1992; One Way, 1992; Far From Home, 1992; This Garden, 1993; Just The One, 1995; Exodus (Live), 1996; What A Beautiful Day, 1997; Celebrate, 1997; Dog Train, 1997; Too Real, 1998; Bozos, 1998; Happy Birthday Revolution, 2000; Albums: A Weapon Called The Word, 1990; Levelling The Land, 1992; Levellers, 1993; Zeitgeist (No. 1, UK), 1995; Mouth to Mouth, 1997; One Way of Life (Best of compilation), 1998; Special Brew, 2000; Hello Pig, 2000. *Publication:* The White Book (directory of action groups). *Address:* Levellers, 55 Canning St, Brighton BN2 2EF, England.

CHAKROBARTY Mridul Kanti; b. Sunamganj. *Musical Education:* Bachelor of Music; Master of Music; PhD. *Career:* Enlisted Artist, Radio Bangladesh, Dhaka; Regular Artist, Bangladesh television. *Compositions:* Sources of Rabindranath Tagore Songs in Western Folk Music; Modifier and Developer, Folk Instrumental Dotara: Surasree. *Recordings:* Tagore Songs: Odhora Madhura; Songs of Hason Raja; Surasree, Folk Instrumental. *Publications:* Hason Raja: His Mystic Songs, 1992; Evolution and Development of Bengali Music, 1993; Ganer Jhorna Tolay, research articles on Tagore songs and folk songs, 1997; Folk Music, 1999. *Honours:* Yuv '77, India; Loknath Award, 1998. *Memberships:* Life Mem., National Academy (Bangla Academy); International Council for Traditional Music. *Leisure interest:* Listening to and collecting classical and world folk music. *Address:* Department of Theatre and Music, University of Dhaka, Dhaka 1000, Bangladesh.

CHALMERS Thomas; b. 4 Dec. 1930, Glasgow, Scotland. Musician (saxophone, clarinet, flute). m. Jeanette D McGhee, 21 Dec. 1950, 3 s., 1 d. *Musical Education:* Tutored by member of BBC S V Orchestra. *Career:* Played with Military Band, 1949–54, Ken Stevens Orchestra, 1960–66, Tommy Sampson Orchestra, 1970–86; Member of Fat Sam's Band, Edinburgh, 1986–96; Freelance musician with Bobby Wishart groups and Strathclyde Youth Jazz Orchestra. *Recordings:* with Fat Sam's Band: Boogie On Down; Jive On Down; Ring Dem Bells; Fat Sam's Band Live At. *Membership:* Musicians' Union. *Leisure interests:* Gardening; Walking. *Address:* 5 Beauly Dr., Craigshill, Livingston, West Lothian EH54 5LG, Scotland.

CHAMBERLIN Jimmy; b. 10 June 1964, Joliet, Illinois, USA. Musician (drums). *Career:* Jazz Drummer; Joined Smashing Pumpkins 1988; Numerous headlining tours, TV and radio appearances; Sacked from band, 1995, rejoined 1998; band split 2000; Also member of The Last Hard Men. *Recordings:* with Smashing Pumpkins: Singles: Lull EP, 1992; Today, 1994; Cherub Rock PEP, 1994; Disarm, 1994; I Am One EP, 1994; Bullet With Butterfly Wings, 1995; Thirty Three, 1996; Zero, 1996; Albums: Gish, 1991; Siamese Dream, 1993; Mellon Collie and the Infinite Sadness (No. 1, USA), 1995; MACHINA/The Machines of God, 2000; with The Last Hard Men: Album: The Last Hard Men, 1998.

CHAMBERS Guy; Prod.; Songwriter; Musician (keyboards). *Career:* Member: The Waterboys; World Party, 1986–91; The Lemon Trees; Co-writer and producer for Robbie Williams, 1997–; Various tours with Williams; Collaborations: Jimmy Nail; Cathy Dennis; Frances Ruffelle; Tom Jones; Holly Johnson, Blast; Julian Cope, Fried. *Compositions:* Co-writer of hits for Robbie Williams: Singles: Lazy Days, 1996; South of The Border, 1997; Angels, 1997; Let Me Entertain You, 1998; Millennium (No. 1, UK), 1998; No Regrets, 1998; Strong, 1999; She's The One (No. 1, UK), 1999; Rock DJ (No. 1, UK), 2000; Kids (duet with Kylie Minogue), 2000; Supreme, 2000; Let Love Be Your Energy, 2001; Eternity/The Road To Mandalay (No. 1, UK), 2001; Albums: Life Thru A Lens, 1997; I've Been Expecting You (No. 1, UK), 1998; Sing When You're Winning (No. 1, UK), 2000; Your Disco Needs You, Kylie Minogue, 2000. *Recordings:* Albums: with World Party: Private Revolution, 1986; Goodbye Jumbo, 1990; with Lemon Trees: Open Book, 1993; Singles: with Lemon Trees: The Way I Feel, 1992; Love Is In Your Eyes, 1992; Child of Love, 1993; I Can't Face The World, 1993; Let It Loose, 1993. *Honours:* Brit Awards: Best Single, Angels (co-writer), 1999; Rock DJ (co-writer), 2001. *Memberships:* Musicians' Union; PRS. *Current Management:* One Management, 43 St Alban's Ave, London W4 5JS, England.

CHAMBERS Martin Dale; b. 4 Sept. 1951, Herford, England. Musician (drummer). 1 s., 1 d. *Education:* Hereford College of Art. *Career:* Drummer, Pretenders, 1979–85; 1994–; Linda McCartney Tribute, Royal Albert Hall, London; Doug Stewart Spiritual Cowboys; Miss World. *Recordings:* Singles: Kid, 1979; Brass In Pocket (No. 1, UK), 1980; Talk of The Town, 1980; I Go To Sleep, 1981; Back On The Chain Gang, 1982; 2000 Miles, 1983; I'll Stand By You, 1994; Popstar, 1999; Albums include: Pretenders (No. 1, UK), 1980; Pretenders II (No. 1, UK), 1981; Learning To Crawl, 1984; The Singles, 1987; Last of the Independents, 1994; The Isle of View, 1995; Viva El Amor, 1999; Greatest Hits, 2000; Other work includes: Paul McCartney; Pete Townsend; Roger Daltrey. *Leisure interests:* Music; Nature. *Current Management:* Gail Force Management, 30 Ives St, London SW3 2ND.

CHAMBERS Wendy Mae; b. 24 Jan. 1953. Composer; Musician. m. Rajesh Karki. *Education:* BA, Barnard College; MA, SUNY. *Career:* CNN; BBC Television; NPR; WWL Television, New Orleans; WWOZ Radio, New Orleans. *Compositions:* 4 CDs; Symphony of The Universe; A Mass For Mass Trombones. *Honours:* NEA Grant, 1983, 1986; American Composers Forum Commission, 1998; CAPS Grant. *Memberships:* American Music Center; American Composer Forum. *Leisure interests:* Oil Painting; Photography; Tap Dancing. *Address:* 13 E Seventh St, Harvey Ledars, NJ 08008, USA.

CHAMPION Will; b. 21 July 1977, Southampton, England. Musician (drums); Songwriter. *Education:* University College, London. *Career:* Member: Coldplay, 1998-. *Recordings:* Albums: Parachutes, 2000; Singles: The Safety EP, 1998; Brothers and Sisters, The Blue Room EP, 1999; Shiver, Yellow, Trouble, 2000. *Honours:* Brit Award, Best Album, 2001; Mercury Music Prize, nominee, 2000. *Current Management:* Phil Harvey. *Internet:* www.coldplay.com.

CHANA Shan; b. 4 March 1969, Plymouth, Devon, England. Musician (drums, percussion, latin, timpani). *Musical Education:* London College of Music, England; GLCM (Hons). *Career:* West End shows: Crazy For You, Prince Edward Theatre; Grease, Dominion Theatre; Sunset Boulevard, Adelphi Theatre; She Loves Me, Savoy Theatre; Fame, Cambridge Theatre. *Recordings:* Fame, original cast album, Maison Rouge Studios, London; Major sessions at Snake Ranch Studios, London; CTS Studios, London; Sawmills Studios, Cornwall; ICC Studios, Eastbourne. *Honour:* Henry Bromley Derry Music Performance Prize, 1990. *Membership:* Musicians' Union. *Leisure interest:* Surfing. *Address:* 8 Juniper Court, 71 Mulgrove Rd, Sutton, Surrey SM2 6LY, England.

CHANDLER Gene, (Eugene Dixon); b. 6 July 1937, Chicago, Illinois, USA. Vocalist. *Career:* Lead singer, Gene Chandler and The Dukays; Solo artiste. *Recordings:* Singles include: Duke of Earl (No. 1, USA), 1962; Rainbow, 1963; Man's Temptation, 1963; Just To Be True, 1964; Nothing Can Stop Me, 1965; Groovy Situation, 1970; Solo single: Get Down, 1990; Albums: The Duke of Earl, 1962; Just Be True, 1964; The Girl Don't Care, 1967; There Was A Time, 1968; The Two Sides of Gene Chandler, 1969; The Gene Chandler Situation, 1970; Get Down, 1978; When You're Number One, 1979; 80, 1980; Live At The Regal, 1965; Soul Master, 1995; The Soul

Of, 1996; Numerous compilations and live albums, most recently: The Best of The Duke of Earl, 2000. *Address:* 8829 S Bishop, Chicago, IL 60620, USA.

CHANDLER Kerri, (Gate-Ah, Paper Mache, Kerri 'Kaoz 6.23' Chandler); b. East Orange, New Jersey, USA. Prod.; Remixer; DJ. *Career:* Started DJ career aged 13; Started producing in the late '80s; Set up own label, Express Records; Debut single Superlover/Get It Off released by Atlantic Records, 1991; Founder: Madhouse; Sfere Records; Collaborations: Jerome Sydenham; Dee Dee Brave; Dennis Ferrer; Arnold Jarvis; Byron Stingily; Remixed: Femi Kuti; Shawn Christopher; Ultra Nate; Ce Ce Rogers. *Recordings:* Albums: Hemisphere, 1996; Singles: Superlover/Get It Off, 1991; The Shelter (as Gate-Ah), 1992; Inspiration (with Arnold Jarvis), 1994; Ionosphere EP, 1995; See Line Woman (with The Songstress), 1998; My Old Friend, 1999. *Address:* c/o Champion Records, 181 High St, Harlesden, London, NW10 4TE, England.

CHAO Manu, (Oscar Tramor); b. 26 June 1961, Paris, France. Vocalist; Songwriter. *Musical Education:* Self-taught. *Career:* As teenager played in various bands including Les Hot Pants; Formed Mano Negra; First single earned group contract with Virgin; Toured Latin America; Moved to Spain, 1995; Formed Radio Bemba Sound System; Spent next few years recording in South and Central America; King of Bongo recording featured on soundtrack to Madonna's The Next Big Thing film; British tour, 2002. *Recordings:* with Mano Negra: Patchanka, 1988; Puta's Fever, 1989; King of The Bongo, 1991; Hell of Patchinko, 1992; Casa Babylon, 1994; solo: Clandestino, 1999; Proxima Estacion – Esperanza, 2001. *Honours:* BBC Radio 3 Award for World Music, Innovator award, 2002. *Internet:* www.manuchao.net.

CHAPIN Tom, (Thomas Forbes); b. 13 March 1945, Charlotte, North Carolina, USA. Vocalist; Songwriter; Musician (guitar, banjo, autoharp); Actor. m. Bonnie Chapin, 5 June 1976, 2 d., 1 step-s., 1 step-d. *Education:* College graduate, State University of New York, Plattsburgh. *Musical Education:* Self-taught. *Career:* Host, Make A Wish, ABC TV (award-winning children's show), 1971–76; Broadway: Pump Boys and Dinettes, 1983; Host, National Geographic Explorer, TV TBS, 1986–89; Thousands of concerts (mainly in North America) over last 30 years. *Recordings:* Children's recordings: Family Tree; Moonboat; Mother Earth; Billy The Squid; Zag Zig; Just For Kids; In My Hometown; Great Big Fun For The Very Little One, 2001; Adult's recordings: Life Is Like That; In The City of Mercy; Let Me Back Into Your Life; So Nice To Come Home; Join The Jubilee; Other collaborations include: Cherish The Ladies, John McCutcheon. *Publication:* Book/cassette: Sing A Whale Song, storybook for children. *Honours:* Peabody Award, Make A Wish, 1972, Emmy, Make A Wish, 1975; Harry Chapin Award for Contributions to Humanity, NACA, 1990. *Memberships:* AFofM; SAG; AFTRA; NARAS; NAS. *Leisure interests:* Tennis; Basketball; Reading. *Current Management:* Sundance Music. *Address:* Sundance Music, 100 Cedar St, Suite B-19, Dobbs Ferry, NY 10522, USA.

CHAPMAN Mike; b. 15 April 1947, Queensland, Australia. Songwriter. *Career:* Member, Tangerine Peel; Songwriting partnership with Nicky Chinn; Producer for Blondie hits; Founder, Dreamland label (with Nicky Chinn), 1979–81. *Compositions:* Hits include: Kiss You All Over, Exile (No. 1, USA), 1978; Hot Child In The City, Nick Gilder (No. 1, USA), 1979; Mickey, Toni Basil (No. 1, USA), 1982; Other hits for: Sweet; Gary Glitter; Mud; Suzi Quatro; Smokie; Patti Smith; Lita Ford. *Recordings:* as producer: with Blondie: Heart of Glass (No. 1, UK and US), 1979; Sunday Girl (No. 1, UK), 1979; Atomic (No. 1, UK), 1980; The Tide Is High (No. 1, UK), 1980; Rapture (No. 1, USA), 1981; with The Knack: My Sharona (No. 1, USA), 1979; Also for Patti Smith; Lita Ford; Blondie; Pat Benatar.

CHAPMAN Tracy; b. 30 March 1964, Cleveland, Ohio, USA. Singer; Songwriter. *Education:* BA, Anthropology and African Studies, Tufts University. *Career:* Performer on Boston Folk circuit, 1986; Recording artiste, 1987–; Major concerts include: Nelson Mandela 70th Birthday Tribute, Wembley Stadium, 1988; Human Rights Now world tour, with Peter Gabriel, Bruce Springsteen, Sting, Youssou N'Dour, 1988; AIDS benefit concert, Oakland, California, 1989; Nelson Mandela International Tribute, Wembley Stadium, 1990; Martin Luther King Celebration, Minneapolis, 1991; Bill Graham Memorial concert, San Francisco, 1991; Bob Dylan 30th Anniversary celebration, Madison Square Garden, 1992; Farm Aid V with Living Colour's Vernon Reid, 1992; Regular US and British tours; Television: Motown 30- What's Goin' On, CBS TV, 1990; True Stories – Too White For Me, Ch4, 1992; The Tonight Show, NBC TV, 1992; In Concert, ABC TV, 1992. *Recordings:* Albums: Tracy Chapman (No. 1, UK and US), 1988; Crossroads (No. 1, UK), 1989; Matters of The Heart, 1992; New Beginning, 1995; Telling Stories, 2000; Collection (compilation), 2001; Singles include: Fast Car, 1988; Talkin' 'Bout A Revolution, 1988; Baby Can I Hold You, 1988 (covered by Boyzone, 1996); Crossroads, 1989; New Beginning, 1995; Smoke and Ashes, 1995; Give Me One Reason, 1996. *Honours:* American Music Award, Favourite New Pop/Rock Artist, 1989; BRIT Awards, Best International Artist Female, Best International Newcomer, 1989; Grammy Awards include: Best Female Pop Vocal

Performance, Best Contemporary Folk Recording, Best New Artist, 1989; Boston Music Awards include: Best Female Vocalist, Top Song, Rock Album, 1989. *Current Management:* Gold Mountain Entertainment, Suite 450, 3575 Cahuenga Blvd W, Los Angeles, CA 90068, USA.

CHARLES Debbie; b. 9 Aug. 1966, London, England. Vocalist; Songwriter. *Career:* Backing vocalist with Fine Young Cannibals; Al Green; Bob Geldof; Gabrielle; Alison Moyet; Lighthouse Family; Member, accapella sextet Mint Juleps. *Membership:* PRS. *Leisure interests:* Writing; Poetry; Swimming. *Address:* 10 Pemell House, Pemell Close, London E1 4JY, England.

CHARLES Ray (Ray Charles Robinson); 23 Sept. 1930, Albany, Georgia, USA. Vocalist; Musician (piano); Composer. *Musical Education:* Piano and clarinet, St Augustine's School for Deaf and Blind, Orlando. *Career:* Blind since age 7 (glaucoma); Member, various groups, Florida; Founder, McSon Trio, 1948; Musical director, Lowell Fulson, 1949–51; Bandleader, own group, 1953–; Concerts include: Newport Jazz Festival, 1958; New York Jazz Festival, 1967; Soul Bowl '69, Houston Astrodome, 1969; Royal Festival Hall, London, 1970; Ann Arbor Jazz and Blues Festival, 1973; Kool Jazz Festival, New York, 1983; John Lennon Tribute Concert, Liverpool, 1990; Playboy Jazz Festival, 1991; Television special, Ray Charles – 50 Years In Music, Fox-TV, 1991; Film appearances: Ballad In Blue, 1964; The Blues Brothers, 1980; Other cameo roles, US television shows: Moonlighting; St Elsewhere; Who's The Boss. *Recordings:* Singles include: It Should Have Been Me, 1954; Don't You Know, I Got A Woman, 1954; This Little Girl of Mine, 1954; What'd I Say, 1959; Georgia On My Mind (No. 1, USA), 1960; One Mint Julep, 1961; Hit The Road Jack (No. 1, USA), 1961; Unchain My Heart, 1962; I Can't Stop Loving You (No. 1, USA), 1962; You Don't Know Me, 1962; Take These Chains From My Heart, 1963; Busted, 1963; Cryin' Time, 1966; Seven Spanish Angels, duet with Willie Nelson (US Country No. 1), 1985; I'll Be Good To You, duet with Chaka Khan, 1990; I'll Take Care Of, 1990; Fresh Out of Tears, 1991; Living Without You, 1991; I'll Be There, 1993; Numerous albums include: Ray Charles, 1957; Ray Charles At Newport, 1958; Soul Brothers (with Milt Jackson), 1959; The Genius of Ray Charles, 1960; In Person, 1960; The Genius Hits The Road, 1960; Dedicated To You, 1961; Genius + Soul = Jazz, 1961; What'd I Say, 1961; The Genius After Hours, 1961; Ray Charles and Betty Carter, 1961; The Genius Sings The Blues, 1961; Do The Twist, 1962; Modern Sounds In Country and Western Music Vols 1 and 2, 1962; The Ray Charles Story, 1962; Ingredients In A Recipe For Soul, 1963; Sweet and Sour Tears, 1964; Live In Concert, 1965; Rays Moods, 1966; A Man and His Soul, 1967; Ray Charles Invites You To Listen, 1967; A Portrait of Ray, 1968; Volcanic Action of My Soul, 1971; A Message From The People, 1972; Renaissance, 1975; Porgy and Bess (with Cleo Laine), 1976; Heart To Heart, 1980; Friendship, 1985; Back On The Block, 1990; Ray Charles – The Living Legend, 1993; My World, 1993; Strong Love Affair, 1996; Hit The Road, Ray, 1996; In Concert, 1998; Dedicated To You, 1998; Blues Is My Middle Name, 2001; Several greatest hits collections; Contributor, We Are The World, USA For Africa (No. 1, UK and US), 1985. *Honours include:* Numerous Grammy Awards, 1961–; Inducted into Rock 'n' Roll Hall of Fame, 1986; NARAS Lifetime Achievement Grammy Award, 1988; Legend Award, Rhythm and Blues Foundation, 1991; Atlanta Celebrity Walk, 1991; Los Angeles Distinguished Service Medal, 1992; Black History Honoree Award, Los Angeles, 1992; Songwriters Hall of Fame Lifetime Award, 1993. *Membership:* Rhythm and Blues Foundation, Washington. *Address:* Ray Charles Enterprises, 2107 Washington Blvd, Los Angeles, CA 90018, USA.

CHARLESON William (Bill); b. 20 June 1940, Oldham, Lancashire, England. Educator; Composer; Arranger; Musician (saxophone). m. Diane Margaret Fox, 18 Aug. 1965, 1 s., 1 d. *Musical Education:* Royal Manchester College of Music; University of York; Director of Studies, Leeds College of Music. *Career:* Appearances with: Ken Mackintosh and Orchestra; BBC Northern Dance Orchestra; BBC Northern Symphony Orchestra; Hallé Orchestra; Royal Liverpool Philharmonic Orchestra; Theatre and cabaret accompanying major British and American artistes; Radio appearances and television sessions for: Granada TV; Yorkshire TV; BBC TV; Consultancy, Open University. *Compositions:* Jazz compositions for National Youth Jazz Orchestra; Brass Band arrangements, compositions recorded by all major bands. *Recordings:* with Joe Jackson: Tucker-A Man and His Dream soundtrack. *Publications:* Jazz Sax 1 (Co-author with J R Brown); Articles for: Crescendo International; British Education Music Journal. *Honours:* YTV/MU Peter Knight Award, 1989; BBC Rehearsal Band Competition: Arranging Prize, 1989. *Membership:* PRS. *Leisure interest:* Collector of old toys. *Address:* 144 Sunnybank Rd, Mirfield, West Yorkshire WF14 0JQ, England.

CHARLTON Michael Anthony (Mad Dog Santini); b. 27 Feb. 1964, South Shields, Tyne and Wear, England. Musician (drums, percussion, keyboards). 1 d. *Musical Education:* BA Hons, Music, University of Northumbria, Newcastle. *Career:* Television, radio and live appearances include: The Tube; TX45; Mainline; Live 95; Worday Open Air Concert; Gypsies Green Stadium; Metro FM; Wear FM; 7FM; Radio Newcastle; The

Riverside; Temple Park Leisure Centre. *Recordings:* No More War; Is That It; Smooth Funk; Scratch It; Addicted; Devils In Heaven. *Memberships:* PRS; Musicians' Union; Equity. *Leisure interests:* Volunteer lifeguard; Keep fit. *Current Management:* Hardy Ismail, Axis Promotions. *Address:* 55 Marsden Lane, South Shields, Tyne and Wear, England.

CHARMASSON Rémi; b. 3 May 1961, Avignon, France. Musician (guitar). m. Audrey Faure, 22 Sept. 1990, 2 d. *Education:* Baccalaureat Philosophy. *Musical Education:* Gold Medal in Jazz, Avignon Conservatory. *Career:* Began with André Jaume, Jimmy Giuffre; Played clubs and festivals with: Charlie Mariano; Charles Tyler; Buddy Colette; Dennis Charles; Tony Coe; Freddie Studer; Jean Frantois; Jenny Clarke; Larry Schneider; Randy Kaye; Barry Altschul; Riccardo Del Fra. *Recordings:* Cinoche, with André Jaume, Rémi Charmasson, Claude Tchamitchian, 1989; Piazza Di Luna, with André Jaume, Rémi Charmasson, Jean-Marc Montera, Fredy Studer, Claude Tchamitchian, Tavagna singers, 1989; FollyFun Music Magic, with Charles Tyler, Rémi Charmasson, Jean Pierre Jullian, Bernard Santacruz, Christian Zagaria, 1990; Caminanado, duo with Claude Tchamitchian, 1990; A Scream For Charles Tyler, with Rémi Charmasson, Dennis Charles, Bernard Santacruz; Casa Blu, with Thierry Maucci; Nemo, trio with F Studer, Jenny Clarke; 10 records in 5 years, 1993; Current recordings with: André Jaume, Charlie Mariano Quintet; A Jaume and Groupes de Gamelans Indonésiens; A Soler and Larry Schneider. *Honours:* Diapason D'Or, from music newspaper: Diapason. *Leisure interest:* Fishing. *Current Management:* Asscn Jazz et Musique Improvisée (AJMI), Avignon, France. *Address:* La Manutention, 4 rue Scalier Ste Anne, PO Box 452, 84072 Avignons Cedex, France.

CHASE Katharine Ann; b. 29 April 1963, Ridgecrest, CA, USA. Vocalist; Songwriter; Musician. *Musical Education:* BA, Classical Voice, University of California, Los Angeles; Self-taught Bass and Rhythm Guitars. *Career:* Solo appearances with Hootie and the Blowfish; Mary Lou Lord; Exene Cervankova, Elliot Smith; Co-Founder Spanking Violets, 1992; Founder, Katharine Chase Band, 1994; Co-founder, Kindness, 1999. *Compositions:* Cake; The Blasters; Southern Culture On The Skids; Tripping Daisy. *Recordings:* Albums: solo: Loverman, 1994; Band albums: Spanking Violets, 1994; The Truth, 1995; The Truth, 1997; with Kindness: Welcome To Planet Excellent; Contributor, albums: Bigger Better Faster More, 1992; Trinket, 1996; Starene, 1997. *Publications:* Reviews and Interviews, 1995; San Francisco Chronicle, 1997; Bay Magazine, 1996. *Honours:* 12 Gold Medals, Regional Texas State Flute Competitions, 1980–86. *Memberships:* BMI; NARAS. *Current Management:* Midnight Sun, 382c Union Ave, Campbell, CA 95008, USA.

CHASEZ JC (Joshua Scott); b. 8 Aug. 1976, Washington, DC, USA. Vocalist; Songwriter. *Career:* Former presenter on TV's The Mickey Mouse Club; Honed vocal/songwriting talents working for free in LA and Nashville; Instigator and member of *N Sync vocal quintet signed to BMG Ariola Munich, 1997; First headline US tour, 1998. *Recordings:* Albums: *N Sync, 1998; Home For Christmas, 1998; No Strings Attached, 2000; Celebrity, 2001; Singles include: I Want You Back, 1997; Tearin' Up My Heart, 1997; Let The Music Heal Your Soul (various artists charity single credited to Bravo All Stars), 1999; Music of My Heart (with Gloria Estefan), 1999; Bye, Bye, Bye, 2000; I'll Never Stop, 2000; It's Gonna Be Me, 2000; This I Promise You, 2000; Pop, 2001; Gone, 2001. *Honours:* *N Sync reported as music industry's biggest earners in 2000 (estimated $184m); Recognition at MTV and Billboard Awards; Presented with keys to City of Orlando, 2000. *Address:* c/o Wright Entertainment Group, PO Box 590009, Orlando, FL 32859–0009, USA. *Internet:* www.wegmusic.com.

CHASSAGNITE François; b. 21 June 1955, Ussel, Correze, France. Musician (trumpet, flugelhorn). *Education:* Ex-veterinary doctor. *Career:* Member, Antoine Hervé Big Band; Gerard Badini Big Band; Jean Loup Lognon Big Band; François Jeanneau's Pandemonium; Orchestre National de Jazz; Laurent Cugny Big Band (2 records and a tour in Europe under Gil Evans direction); Festivals Nice, Juan les Pins; Mariac; Paris. *Recordings:* 2 records with Antoine Hervé; 3 with Frantois Jeanneau; 2 with Laurent Cugny; 1 with G Badini; 1 with Jean Loup Longnon; Several with small combos; 2 with own band Samya Cynthia, 1989; Chazzeology, 1996; With Sorgho: Savane, 1996; Kess-Kess, 1998. *Memberships:* SACEM; SPEDIDAM; ADAM. *Leisure interest:* Fly fishing. *Address:* 143 Chemin de la Sine, 06140 VENCE, France.

CHAUDAGNE Remy; b. 26 Aug. 1959, Melun, France. Composer; Musician (electric bass). m. Cora, 13 Jan. 1994, 1 s. *Musical Education:* Piano, saxophone, double bass, electric bass. *Career:* Tour, France, India, Indonesia, Viet Nam, Philippines, Cambodia, Sudan; Performances with: David Liebman; Scott Henderson; F Corneloup; Claude Barthelemy; Andy Sheppard. *Compositions:* Music for short films, theatre, saxophone quartet, Creation with jazz orchestra (24 musicians) or classical (13 musicians). *Recordings:* 7 albums as leader, including last in trio with Peter Erskine and Andy Sheppard: 3 Colors. *Honours:* First Prize, Villembourne Festival, music for film Sem Cor with Katie Adler. *Leisure interest:* Family. *Current*

Management: Benoit Lebon. *Address:* 4B rue de la Convention, 94270 Kremlin Bicêtre, France.

CHAULK (Lloyd) Wayne; b. 10 June 1950, Corner Brook, Newfoundland, Canada. Composer; Arranger; Musician; Prod. m. Denise, 29 March 1975, 1 d. *Education:* Bachelor of Commerce degree; Engineering technician; Real Estate license. *Musical Education:* Self-taught. *Career:* Canadian Broadcasting Corporation television features, 1993; Over 20 radio interviews, 1992–93; Music featured on international airlines, world-wide; Music played on over 4,000 US premises and on over 400 radio stations; Over 200 original compositions and 18 CDs produced. *Recordings:* Albums: Dreamer's Themes, 1991; New Directions and Christmas Keyboards, 1992; No Regrets, 1993; The Christmas to Remember, 1996; Nature's Splendour, 1996; Journey Home, 1997. *Honours:* Billboard Certificate of Achievement: Your Love Is My Song, 1992; Best Light Rock (Pop) Artist On Record, Aria, 1994, 1995; Albums rated among best instrumentals, Adult Contemporary Music Research Group, US, 1993–94; Juno Award Nomination, Instrumental Artist of The Year, Canada, 1995. *Membership:* SOCAN. *Leisure interests:* Golf; Tennis; Nature. *Current Management:* Distributor, Holborne Distribution Inc, Canada. *Address:* c/ o Ambassador Music, Deer Valley, PO #43029, Calgary, AB T2J 7A7, Canada.

CHAUTEMPS Jean-Louis; b. 6 Aug. 1931, Paris, France. Musician (saxophone); Composer. Divorced, 1 s., 1 d. *Education:* Philosophy; Musicology. *Career:* Member, Claude Bolling Orchestra, 1952; Also played with Sydney Bechet; Django Reinhardt; Zoot Sims; Lester Young; Bobby Jaspar; Albert Ayler; Roy Eldridge; Don Byas; European tour with Chet Baker; 3 years as saxphone player, musical arranger, Kurt Edelhagen Orchestra, Cologne, Germany; Played Paris jazz clubs, early 1960s; Played with Kenny Clarke; Martial Solal; Slide Hampton; Eddy Louiss; René Urtreger; Johnny Griffin; Dexter Gordon; Daniel Humair; Composer for films; Teacher, improvisation; Worked with the Ensemble InterContemporain, extensive tours USA with Musique Vivante, early 1970s; Leader, jazz workshop, The Sorbonne, 1975; Founder, Rhizome, 1976; Concerts, tours include Dizzy Gillespie; World premier, Périples For Solo Saxophone by Paul Méfano; Soloist, leader, Albert Mangelsdorff band, 2 years; Member, Martial Solal Big Band; Works for classical and avant garde orchestras; Works with computers and synthesisers; Played at the Guggenheim Museum, New York, with Quatuor de Saxophones, 1987; 3 jazz concerts, Opéra-Bastille, 1992; Also with Ensemble Contrechamps, 1994; Musical director, The Threepenny Opera, Théâtre National de Chaillot, 1995. *Compositions:* Film music includes Les Coeurs Verts; L'Ombre de la Pomme; Music for theatre, television and films. *Recordings:* Album: Chautemps, 1988. *Honours:* Chevalier des Arts et Lettres, Ordre National du Mérite; Prix du Jazz SACEM. *Membership:* Vice-President de l'Assafra. *Leisure interests:* Music; Computers. *Current Management:* Agnès Lupovici.

CHAYANNE (Elmer Figueroa Alce); b. 28 June 1968, Puerto Rico. Vocalist; Actor; Dancer. *Career:* First group: Los Chicos; Moved to Mexico to start a solo career, aged 17; Solo recording debut, 1986; Appeared in first Spanish language commercial on American network TV for Pepsi, 1989; Film appearances include: Dance With Me, 1998; Linda Sara, 1994; Los Chicos En Conexion Caribe; Las Divorciadas (mini series). *Recordings:* Albums include: Chayanne, 1989; Tempo De Vals, 1990; Provocame, 1992; Influencas, 1994; Volver A Nacer, 1996; Atado A To Amor, 1998; Simplemente, 2000. *Honours:* 49 gold and platinum sales awards; Grammy Award, Best Latin Pop Performance nominee, Atado A Tu Amor, 1989; MTV Award, Best Internaional Video, Este Ritmo Se Baila Asi, 1989.

CHEB FAUDEL, (Faudel Bellula); b. 6 June 1978, Mantes la Jolie, France. Vocalist; Songwriter. *Musical Education:* Began learning music within family. *Career:* Formed the Rai Stars (Les Étoiles du Raï), aged 12; Performed at local parties and weddings; Within three years was opening for MC Solaar and Cheb Khaled; Featured in two French TV shows: Saga Cities; Les Enfants du Raï, 1995; Selected to participate in Festival du Printemps de Bourges, 1996; Sold more than 300000 copies of Baida; Tours internationally. *Recordings:* Baida, 1998; Samra, 2001; 1 2 3 Soleils (with Khaled and Rachid Taha), 2001. *Honours:* Victoires de la Musique award, 1999. *Internet:* www.faudel.com.fr.

CHEB MAMI, (Mohamed Khelifati); b. 11 July 1966, Saïda, Algeria. Vocalist; Songwriter. *Musical Education:* Self-taught. *Career:* Started singing at weddings; Runner-up in televised talent contest Alhan wa Chabab, 1982; Recorded a few cassettes, early 1980s; Served in Algerian military; Relocated to Paris following discharge, 1985; First act to perform at Paris's L'Olympia, 1989; First rai singer to perform in US or record an album outside France or Algeria; First internationally distributed album released, 1989; Collaborations: Sting; K-Mel; Gordon Cyrus; Simon Law; Performed at Grammy Awards, 2000, and with Sting at the SuperBowl, 2001. *Recordings:* Albums include: Douni El Bladi, 1986; Prince of Rai, 1989; Let Me Rai, 1990; Saida, 1994; Let Me Cry, 1998; Meli Meli, 1999;

Dellali, Lazrag Saani, Saida, 2001; Single: Desert Rose (with Sting), 2000. *Honours:* Prince of Rai went gold in France; Victoires de la Musique Awards, Best Traditional or World Music Album nominations: Meli Meli, 1999; Dellali, 2001; World Music Award, Best Selling Arabic Artist, 2001. *Internet:* www.chebmami.net.

CHECKER Chubby (Ernest Evans); b. 3 Oct. 1941, South Carolina, USA. Singer. *Career:* Television appearances: The Dick Clark Saturday Night Show, ABC-TV, 1960; Ed Sullivan Show, 1961; Ready Steady Go, 1965; Featured in films: Twist Around The Clock, 1961; Don't Knock The Twist, 1962; Numerous world-wide tours; Featured artist, Dick Clark's Caravan of Stars, 1961; Performed at Nelson Mandela's 70th Birthday Tribute, Wembley, 1988. *Recordings:* Singles include: The Twist (No. 1, USA), 1960, 1962 (only song ever to reach US No. 1 on two occasions); The Hucklebuck, 1960; Pony Time (No. 1, USA), 1961; Dance The Mess Around, 1961; Let's Twist Again, 1961; The Fly, 1961; Jingle Bell Rock, duet with Bobby Rydell, 1961; Twistin' USA, 1961; Slow Twistin', 1962; Teach Me To Twist, duet with Bobby Rydell, 1962; Dancin' Party, 1962; Limbo Rock, 1962; Birdland, 1963; Loddy Lo, 1963; Let's Limbo Some More, 1963; Hooka Tooka, 1964; The Twist (Yo' Twist), with the Fat Boys, 1988; Doin The Zombie, 1997; Albums: Twist With Chubby Checker, 1960; It's Pony Time, 1961; For Twisters Only, 1962; Your Twist Party, 1962; Bobby Rydell/ Chubby Checker, 1962; For Teen Twisters Only, 1962; Twistin' Round The World, 1962; Don't Knock The Twist (film soundtrack), 1962; All The Hits (For Your Dancin' Party), 1961; Limbo Party, 1963; Chubby Checker's Biggest Hits, 1963; Let's Limbo Some More, 1963; Beach Party, 1963; Chubby Checker In Person, 1963; Chubby Checker's Greatest Hits, 1973; The Change Has Come, 1982; Still Twistin', 1986; In Deutschland, 1988; Mister Twist, 2000. *Honours include:* Grammy Award, Best Rock and Roll Recording, Let's Twist Again, 1961. *Current Management:* Twisted Entertainment, 320 Fayette St, 2nd Floor, Conshohocken, PA 19428, USA.

CHENEOUR (Ian) Paul; b. 19 April 1952, Southsea, Hampshire, England. Musician (flute). *Musical Education:* Guildhall School of Music and Drama, with Professor Rainer Schielein. *Career:* Member, Dutch Jazz Quintet, France; Leader, own 7 piece group The Cornish Connection; Leader, jazz fusion quartet, Cheneour, 1983–; Leader, The Aeona Flute Quartet, 1991–; Leader, Impromptu, 1993; Freelance musician for films, radios and documentaries; Numerous tours, UK; Europe; Middle East; North America; Canada; Greece, Turkey, 1997; Masterclasses in Improvisation and Composition, and flute playing; New Duo, Paul Cheneour and Dilly Meah, flutes and tabla, 1997. *Recordings:* Solo albums: Chenour Live I, 1987; The Time Has Come, 1995; with Impromptu: Sweet Kafka, 1994; Ocean of Dreams, 1996; Reiki Healing Symbols in Sound, 1997; This Being Human, 1998; Dance in the Fire, 1998; Between Silence, 1998; Feng Shui Soundworld. *Memberships:* Musicians' Union; PRS; MCPS; PPL. *Leisure interests:* Eating; Sleeping. *Current Management:* Red Gold Music Ltd. *Address:* 87A Queens Rd, East Grinstead, West Sussex RH19 1BG, England.

CHENEVIER Guigou; b. 21 Nov. 1955, La Tronche, France. Musician (percussions); Composer. 2 s. *Education:* University of Literature. *Musical Education:* Mostly self-taught, including piano and drum lessons. *Career:* More than 400 concerts world-wide, include 3 US tours, with Etron Fou Leloublan, 1973–86; Drummer, composer, with Les Batteries; Octavo; Encore Plus Grande; Volapék, 1986–95; Les Figures, collaboration with Maguy Marin, 1996. *Recordings:* Demesure Révolutionnaire, Les Batteries; Reedition, Etron Fou LeLoublan, 1991; Des Pieds et Des Mains, Octavo, 1992; Le Diapason Du Père Ubu, 1993; Le Feu Du Tigre, Volapék, 1995; Slang, 1997; Les Rumeurs de la Ville, 1998. *Current Management:* Inouï Productions. *Address:* 3A Maison IV De Chiffre, 26 rue des Teinturiers, 84000 Avignon, France.

CHENG Sammi, (Cheng Sau Man, Twinnie Cheng); b. 19 Aug. 1972, Hong Kong. Vocalist. *Education:* Tang Shui Kin Victoria Technical School. *Career:* Honoured at seventh Hong Kong Amateur Singing Contest, 1998; Initially signed to local Capital Artists label; Career blossomed following move to Warner Music, 1995; Many film appearances including: Needing You, 2000; Fighting For Love, 2001. *Recordings:* Albums: Sammi, 1990; Holiday, 1991; Never Too Late, 1992; Happy Maze, Big Revenge, 1993; Ten Commandments, Time Place People, Sammi, 1994; After, It's About Time, Can't Let You Go, 1995; Never Want To Let You Go, Worth It, Passion, Sammi X Live, 1996; Waiting For You, Our Theme Song, Life's Language, Sammi Star Show 97, Feel So Good, 1998; Listen To Sammi, I Deserved, Really Love You, Arigatou, Loving Deeply, Love Stories, ¡Concert, 1999; To Love, Ladies First, Mei Fei Seik Mo, Love Is…, Taipei Concert 2000, 2001; Complete, Shocking Pink, 2001. *Honours:* Asian CCTV-MTV Music Award, Best Female Artist, 2000; Singapore Golden Hits Award, Most Popular Female Artist, 2001. *Address:* c/o Warner Music (HK) Ltd, 12/F Peninsula Office Tower, 18 Middle Rd, TST, Kowloon, Hong Kong. *E-mail:* sammi@warnermusic.com.tw.

CHÉNIER Jacques Jake Pierre Roger; b. 31 July 1961, St Boniface, Winnipeg, Manitoba, Canada. *Education:* 1 year, University of Winnipeg;

Graphic Arts Degree, Red River Community College, 1986. *Career:* Winnipeg International Children's Festival, 1988–99; Winnipeg Folk Festival; Stan Rogers Memorial Folk Festival; Ottawa Children's Festival, 1994, 1997; Over 600 school performances; Fred Penner's Place, CBC TV; Dancing With the Dinosaurs, Multimedia planetarium show. *Compositions:* Buzz Buzzity Buzz; Dinosaurs; Ghost in the House; Pizza Paradise; Lobster Twist. *Recordings:* Dancing with the Dinosaurs, 1989; Pizza Paradise, 1992; Content d'être moi, 1994; Walking in the Sun, 1996. *Honours:* Juno Award Nominee, Best Children's Recording, 1996; John Lennon Songwriting Contest, Grand Prize Winner, 1997. *Memberships:* SOCAN; Manitoba Audio Recording Industry Asscn. *Leisure interests:* Wilderness camping and hiking. *Current Management:* Sandcastle Music. *Address:* PO Box 47025, RPO Marion, Winnipeg, Manitoba R2H 3G9, Canada.

CHER (Cherilyn Sarkisian LaPierre); 20 May 1946, El Centro, California, USA. Vocalist; Actor; Entertainer. m. (1) Sonny Bono, 1964, divorced, deceased, 1 d., (2) Gregg Allman, 1975, divorced, 1 s. *Career:* Worked with Sonny Bono in duo Sonny and Cher, 1964–74; Also solo artiste, 1964–; Performances include: Hollywood Bowl, 1966; Newport Pop Festival, 1968; Television includes: Sonny and Cher Comedy Hour, CBS, 1971; Cher, CBS, 1975–76; Sonny and Cher Show, CBS, 1976–77; Vocalist with rock group Black Rose, including US tour supporting Hall and Oates, 1980; Actress, films: Good Times, 1967; Chastity, 1969; Come Back To The Five and Dime, Jimmy Dean Jimmy Dean, 1982; Silkwood, 1984; Mask, 1985; The Witches of Eastwick, 1987; Moonstruck, 1987; Suspect, 1987; Mermaids, 1989. *Recordings include:* Singles: with Sonny and Cher: I Got You Babe (No. 1, UK and US), 1975; Baby Don't Go, 1965; Just You, 1965; But You're Mine, 1965; What Now My Love, 1966; Little Man, 1966; The Beat Goes On, 1967; All I Ever Need Is You, 1971; A Cowboy's Work Is Never Done, 1972; Solo hit singles include: All I Really Want To Do, 1965; Bang Bang, 1966; Gypsies Tramps and Thieves (No. 1, USA), 1971; The Way of Love, 1972; Half Breed (No. 1, USA), 1973; Dark Lady (No. 1, USA), 1974; Take Me Home, 1979; Dead Ringer For Love, duet with Meatloaf, 1982; I Found Someone, 1987; We All Sleep Alone, 1988; After All, duet with Peter Cetera (for film soundtrack Chances Are), 1989; If I Could Turn Back Time, 1989; Jesse James, 1989; Heart of Stone, 1990; The Shoop Shoop Song (from film soundtrack Mermaids) (No. 1, UK), 1991; Love and Understanding, 1991; Oh No Not My Baby, 1992; Love Can Build A Bridge (with Neneh Cherry and Chrissie Hynde; No. 1, UK), 1995; Walking In Memphis, 1995; One By One, 1996; Paradise Is Here, 1996; Believe (No. 1, UK and US), 1998; Strong Enough, 1999; The Music's No Good Without You, 2001; Albums: with Sonny and Cher: Look At Us, 1965; All I Really Want To Do, 1965; The Wondrous World of Sonny and Cher, 1966; Sonny and Cher Live, 1972; Solo albums include: All I Really Want To Do, 1965; The Sonny Side of Cher, 1966; With Love, 1967; Backstage, 1968; Jackson Highway, 1969; Gypsies Tramps and Thieves, 1972; Foxy Lady, 1972; Greatest Hits, 1974; Stars, 1975; I'd Rather Believe In You, 1976; Take Me Home, 1979; I Paralyze, 1984; Cher, 1988; Heart of Stone, 1989; Love Hurts, 1991; Cher's Greatest Hits 1965–92, 1992; It's A Man's World, 1995; Believe, 1999; Black Rose, 1999; The Greatest Hits, 1999; Living Proof, 2001. *Honours include:* Academy Award, Best Actress, Moonstruck, 1988; Academy Award nomination, Best Supporting Actress, Silkwood, 1984; Grammy Award, Best Dance Recording (Believe), 2000. *Current Management:* Bill Sammeth Organisation, PO Box 960, Beverly Hills, CA 90213, USA.

CHERONE Gary; b. 24 July 1961, Malden, Massachusetts, USA. Vocalist; Songwriter. *Career:* Member, Dream; Singer, funk/rock group Extreme, 1985–; Played club circuit, Boston, 1985–88; World-wide appearances include: Regular US tours; American Dream concerts, London, 1992; Concert For Life, Tribute to Freddie Mercury, Wembley, 1992; Support to Bryan Adams, European tour, 1992; Lead singer, Van Halen, 1998-. *Recordings:* with Extreme: Singles: More Than Words (No. 1, USA), 1991; Get The Funk Out, 1991; Decadence Dance, 1991; Hole-Hearted, 1991; Song For Love, 1992; Rest In Peace, 1992; Stop The World, 1992; Tragic Comic, 1993; There Is No God, 1994; More Than Words, 1995; Albums: Extreme, 1989; Extreme II – Pornograffiti, 1991; III Sides To Every Story, 1992; Waiting For The Punchline, 1994; Running Gag, 1998; Accidental Collision, 1998; Best of Extreme, 2000; with Van Halen: 3, 1998. *Honours:* Winners, MTV Video contest, 1987; Boston Music Awards: Act of Year; Outstanding Rock Single, Hole-Hearted; Outstanding Pop Single; Outstanding Singer/Songwriter, More Than Words, 1992. *Current Management:* SRO Management, 189 Carlton St, Toronto, ON M5A 2K7, Canada.

CHERRY Eagle Eye; b. 1970, Skåne, Sweden. Musician; Singer; Songwriter. *Education:* New York School of the Performing Arts. *Career:* Played drums in band for his father, Don Cherry; Worked as model and acted in several US TV shows; Wrote and performed debut album including duet with half-sister Titiyo and remixed by Cameron McVey. *Recordings:* Singles: Save Tonight, 1998; Falling in Love Again, 1998; Are You Still Having Fun, 2000; Long Way Around, 2001; Promises Made, 2001; Albums: Desireless, 1998; Living In The Present Future, 2000.

CHERRY Neneh, (Neneh Mariana Karlsson); b. 10 March 1964, Stockholm, Sweden. Singer. *Career:* Moved to London; Early band, The Cherries; Joined Rip, Rig and Panic until band broke up; Began solo work and signed record deal; Worked with Cameron McVey and Tim Simenon; Contributed one track, I've Got You Under My Skin for AIDS Benefit Red Hot + Blue, 1990; Worked on second album with Michael Stipe, Gang Starr and Geoff Barrow. *Recordings:* Singles: Buffalo Stance, 1988; Manchild, 1989; Kisses On The Wind, 1989; I've Got You Under My Skin, 1990; Money Love, 1992; 7 Seconds, with Youssou N'Dour, 1994; Trouble Man, 1995; Love Can Build A Bridge, with Chrissie Hynde and Cher (No. 1, UK), 1995; Woman, 1996; Buddy X (with Dreem Team) 1999; Albums: With Rip Rig and Panic: God, 1981; I Am Cold, 1982; Attidue, 1983; Solo: Raw Like Sushi, 1989; Homebrew, 1992; Man, 1997; Also appeared on The The's Infected, 1986; Eagle Eye Cherry's Living In The Present Future, 2000.

CHESCOE Laurie; b. 18 April 1933, London, England. Musician (drums). m. Sylviane Yanou Chescoe, 5 Aug. 1960, 1 s., 1 d. *Musical Education:* Tutor. *Career:* Teddy Layton Band, 1957; Monty Sunshine, 1960; Dick Charlesworth, 1964; Bruce Turner, 1965; Bob Wallis, 1966; Alan Elsdon, 1976 (14 years); Midnite Follies Orchestra, 1978; Alex Welsh Band, 1979; Formed own band, Laurie Chescoe's Good Time Jazz, 1990; Performed at all major festivals, television and radio. *Recordings:* Albums: 2 with Midnite Follies; 2 with Keith Nicholls; 78s with Eric Allendale New Orleans Knights; Teddy Layton Band; Albums with own band; 3 albums with Benny Walters, Ralph Sutton. *Membership:* Musicians' Union. *Leisure interests:* DIY; Francophile. *Current Management:* John Boddy Agency. *Address:* 10 Southfield Gardens, Twickenham TW1 4SZ, England.

CHESLIN Mat; b. 28 Nov. 1970, Wordsley, West Midlands, England. Musician (bass). *Career:* Founder member, Neds Atomic Dustbin, 1987–95. *Recordings:* Albums: Grey Cell Green, 1991; God Fodder, 1991; Are You Normal?, 1993; Brainbloodvolume, 1995; The Best of Ned's Atomic Dustbin, 2000. *Membership:* Musicians' Union. *Leisure interests:* Football; Squash. *Current Management:* Paul Bolton, Chris 'Tank' Gilks. *Address:* Stourbridge, West Midlands, England.

CHESNUTT Mark Nelson; b. 6 Sept. 1963, Beaumont, Texas, USA. Country vocalist; Musician (guitar, drums). *Career:* Played with father Bob Chesnutt's band around Beaumont region before pursuing solo career, aged 15; Landed a residency at Cutter's Bar, where the house band included Tracy Byrd; Recorded locally successful singles for several independent labels, notably Axbar, mid 1980s; Tape sent to regional promotions director of MCA Records in Houston, who passed it to MCA chief executive Tony Brown in Nashville; Brown flew to Beaumont to see live performance, resulting in record deal, 1990; Supported country legend Geoge Jones live and appeared on his Live In Tennessee video, 1994; Jones was a guest on second album; Continued to chart regularly throughout 1990s; Regularly tours with own New South Band. *Compositions include:* It's A Little Too Late; Let It Rain. *Recordings include:* Brother Jukebox, Too Cold At Home, 1990; Almost Goodbye, It Sure Is Monday, 1993; I Don't Want To Miss A Thing, 1998; Albums include: Longnecks and Short Stories, 1992; Almost Goodbye, 1993; Greatest Hits, 1996. *Honours:* CMA, Horizon Award, 1993; Amusement and Music Operators Asscn, Rising Star of the Year. *Leisure interests:* Collecting old country records; Fishing; Hunting. *Address:* c/o The BDM Co, 1106 16th Ave S, Nashville, TN 37212, USA. *E-mail:* nutthouse1@aol.com. *Internet:* www.markchesnutt.com.

CHESTER Ed; b. 24 Oct. 1971, Darlington, England. Musician (Drums). *Career:* Member, Bluetones; Early releases on own label; Secured major label deal; Numerous tours and many TV appearances. *Recordings:* Singles: Are You Blue Or Are You Blind, 1995; Bluetonic, 1995; Slight Return, 1996; Cut Some Rug, 1996; Marblehead Johnson, 1996; Solomon Bites the Worm, 1998; If…, 1998; Sleazy Bed Track, 1998; 4-Day Weekend, 1998; Keep The Home Fires Burning, 2000; Autophilia, 2000; Mudslide EP, 2001; Albums: Expecting to Fly (No. 1, UK), 1996; Return to the Last Chance Saloon, 1998; Science and Nature, 2000. *Honour:* Brit Award Nomination, 1997.

CHESTER Johnny; b. 26 Dec. 1941, Melbourne, Victoria, Australia. m. Larraine, 29 Sept. 1964, 3 d. *Musical Education:* Self-taught. *Career:* TV Host, Teen Scene, ABC TV, 1964–65; TV Host, Country Road, ABC TV, 1977–78; DJ, Radio 3U2, Melbourne, 1966–69; Presenter, Radio Australia, 1989–91; Toured Australia and New Zealand with The Beatles, 1964; Australia with Kenny Rogers, 1984; Tammy Wynette, 1992; Performed in Viet Nam, 1968; with own show, Australia Wide, 1961-. *Compositions:* World Greatest Mum; My Kind of Woman; Highway 31; I Love You So Rebecca; Lord I'd Forgotten. *Recordings:* Over 200 song titles released, 1961-. *Honours:* Male Vocalist of the Year, 1981, 1982, 1983; Australia CM Awards. *Memberships:* APRA; TSA; CMAA; CMA (US). *Leisure interest:* Fishing. *Current Management:* Ian B Allen, Dynamic Management, PO Box 101, Seaford, Victoria 3198, Australia.

CHEVALLIER D; b. 13 Jan. 1969, Ris Orangis, France. Musician (electric and acoustic guitar); Composer. *Musical Education:* Classical guitar, Conservatoire National De Région de Paris. *Career:* Concerts, Rome;

Berlin; New York; Rochester; Hartford; Richmond; Prague (EBU big band); Paris Jazz Festival; Nord Jazz Festival (Germany); Festival of Montpellier; Festival of Assier; Souillac; Ramatuelle and Montréal Jazz Festival, July 1996. *Recordings:* Migration, with Daniel Humoir, Yves Robert; Nilxa: State of Grace; Terre Nova: Danses. *Memberships:* SACEM; SPEDIDAM. *Leisure interest:* Photography. *Current Management:* Celia Productions. *Address:* 2 Pl. Beaumarchais, 91600 Savigny, S/Orge, France.

CHIARELLI Robert C; b. 13 Jan. 1963. Mixer; Remix Prod. *Musical Education:* University of Miami, Florida. *Recordings:* Producer and/or Mixer for numerous recordings including: Will Smith, The Temptations, Madonna, Janet Jackson, K-Ci and JoJo, Christina Aguilera, Jennifer Paige, The Corrs, Boyz II Men. *Honours:* 60 Platinum and Gold discs. *Memberships:* American Federation of Musicians; National Academy of Recording Arts and Sciences. *Address:* 2219 W Olive Ave #102, Burbank, CA 91506, USA.

CHIASSON Warren; b. 17 April 1934, Cheticamp, Nova Scotia, Canada. Jazz Musician (vibraphone, piano) Composer. *Education:* St Francis Xavier University, Antigonish, Nova Scotia. *Musical Education:* Jazz with Lenny Tristano; George Russell; Classical violin lessons for 6 years. *Career:* George Shearing Quintet, 1959–61, 1972–74; Clubs, concerts, tours with Chet Baker, Tal Farlow, Roberta Flack, 1975–82; Broadway show, Hair (composed the percussion), 1968–72. *Compositions:* Ultramarine; Bossa Nova Scotia; Bedouin; Hazel Eyes; Bravel; Festival. *Recordings:* Good Vibes For Kurt Weill; Point Counterpoint; Quartessence; Blues and Jazz, B. B. King. *Publications:* The Contemporary Vibraphonist. *Honours:* One of the Top Six Outstanding Jazz Vibraphonists over the last half-century, NY Times, 1989. *Memberships:* ASCAP; Recording Musicians of America; NARAS. *Leisure interests:* Ice hockey; Classical literature and poetry; Fine dining. *Current Management:* Abby Hoffer Enterprises. *Address:* 223 E 48th St, New York, NY 10017, USA.

CHIAVOLA Kathy; b. 7 March 1952, Chicago, Illinois, USA. Artist; Vocalist; Musician (guitar). *Musical Education:* Oberlin Conservatory, BM, MM; Indiana Conservatory, postgraduate work. *Career:* Sang opera professionally; Moved to Nashville, 1980; Toured with The Doug Dillard Band, Vassar Clements, The Country Gazette; Formed The Lucky Dogs; Toured Eastern Europe with Douglas and Mark O'Connor, USIA tour: The Nashville Masters; UK debut tour, 1993; Voice of State Farm Insurance, television commercial; McDonalds commercial on radio. *Recordings:* Albums: Labor of Love, 1990; The Harvest, 1995; Appeared on Emmylou Harris video, Thanks To You; Recorded with: Garth Brooks; Emmylou Harris; Vince Gill; Kathy Mattea; Ricky Skaggs. *Honour:* Nammie Award, Backup Vocalist of The Year, 1995. *Memberships:* IBMA; AFofM; AFTRA; NARAS. *Leisure interests:* Gardening; Her dog Lucy; Walking.

CHILD Desmond; b. 28 Oct. 1953, Miami, Florida, USA. Songwriter; Prod.; Musician (keyboards). *Career:* Formed Desmond Child and Rouge, 1975; Concentrated on songwriting, 1980s. *Compositions:* Hit songs include: You Give Love A Bad Name, Bon Jovi, 1986; Livin' On A Prayer, Bon Jovi, 1986; I Was Made For Loving You, Kiss, 1979; Livin' La Vida Loca, Ricky Martin, 1999; Who Let The Dogs Out, Baha Men, 2001; Other songs for: Cher; Michael Bolton; Alice Cooper; Jimmy Barnes. *Recordings:* Albums: Desmond Child and Rouge, 1978; Runners In The Night, 1979; Desmond Child Discipline, 1991; Singles: You're The Story of My Life, 1991; Love On A Rooftop, 1991; Obsession, 1992. *Current Management:* C Winston Simone Management, 1790 Broadway, 10th Floor, New York, NY 10019, USA.

CHILDERS Elsie T; b. 26 Sept. 1924, Henderson, Kentucky, USA. Studio Owner; Songwriter. 2 s. *Education:* Business, Midway College, 1941–42. *Musical Education:* Studied: Snare drum; Piano; Choral; Orchestra; Band; Marching band; Composition. *Career:* Owner, Manager: Trusty Tuneshop Recording Studio; Pianist and soloist for Johnson Island Baptist church 1950–; various radio and cable TV performances. *Compositions:* 380 songs published, over 100 recorded, artists include: Jennifer Nelson, 1991; Barry Russell, 1998; Jeremy Scott Busby, 2000. *Publications:* Instant Knowhow, 1971; Newsletter, 1978–98. *Honours include:* Country Music Organizations of America, Song of the Year; Record Label Promoter of the Year; Artist Promoter of the Year; CD of the Year; Record Label of the Year, 2000. *Memberships:* CMA; CMOA; Rotary Club. *Leisure interests:* Dancing; Surfing the internet; Fishing; Reading. *Current Management:* Trusty International. *Address:* 8771 Rose Creek Rd, Nebo, KY 42441, USA. *E-mail:* trusty@wko.com.

CHILDISH Billy; b. 1 Dec. 1959, Chatham, Kent. *Career:* The Pop Rivets Live At Detling Village Hall, 1977; The Headcoats Live At Royal Festival Hall, 1999. *Compositions:* The Cheeky Cheese; Plump Prizes and Little Gems; Hendrix Was Not The Only Musician. *Recordings:* The Pop Rivets Greatest Hits; Talkin' Bout Milkshakes; Acropolis Now; Ypres 1917 Overture; Which Dead Donky Daddy; In Tweed We Trust. *Publications:* My Fault, Novel, 1996; Notebooks of a Naked Youth, Novel, 1997; I'd Rather You'd Lied, Poetry, 1999; Chatham Town Welcomes Desperate Men,

Novel, 2001. *Memberships:* Worshipful Order of Ancient Headcoats. *Address:* 11 Boundary Rd, Chatham, Kent, ME4 6TS.

CHILDS Robert Alexander; b. 23 April 1961, London, England. Musician (guitar, steel guitar); Singer; Songwriter; Music Journalist. *Career:* Member, country band Greta and The Stray Shots; Major concerts: Johnny Cash Show; Americana Fest; Morecombe International Festival; Television: Country By The Sea, BBC; Radio: Live In Concert, BBC Essex. *Recordings:* Greta and The Stray Shots: EP: Your Foolish Heart, 1988; Albums: Live, 1987; Above and Beyond, 1990; Livewire, 1991; Playtime, 1993; Inclusion of track: I Didn't Mean To Do It, on Declaration of Independence, The Best of British Country, 1994. *Publications:* Articles for: Making Music; Country Music Gazette; International Country Music News. *Membership:* Performing Rights Society. *Leisure interests:* Equestrianism; Motor Racing; Watching TV, video. *Current Management:* New Cut Records. *Address:* 40 Fielding Way, Hutton, Essex, England.

CHILDS William Edward; b. 8 March 1957, Los Angeles, California, USA. Composer; Musician (piano). m. Holly Hamilton, 30 June, 1991, 1 s. *Education:* University. *Musical Education:* BM, Composition, University of Southern California (USC). *Career:* Six years with Freddie Hubbard, 1978–84; Played with J J Johnson, 1977; Played with: Allan Holdsworth; Dianne Reeves; Branford Marsalis; Bobby Hutcherson; Played twice as leader, North Sea Jazz Festival; Twice, Monterey Jazz Festival. *Compositions:* Two performed by Los Angeles Philharmonic; One for Akron Symphony Orchestra; One (strings, bass, rhythm section), performed at Monterey Jazz Festival, part of commission series; One at Grenoble Jazz Festival. *Recordings:* Albums: Take For Example This; Twilight Is Upon Us; His April Touch; Portrait of a Player; I've Known Rivers; Child Within, 1996; Skim Coat; Sideman with: Freddie Hubbard; Dianne Reeves; Allan Holdsworth; Eddie Daniels; Kevyn Lettau; Various selections in: New Real Book. *Honours:* Australian Film Institute nomination: Best Original Score (My Forgotten Man), 1993; Composition Department Award (USC). *Leisure interests:* Basketball; Reading; Aerobic Exercise. *Current Management:* Open Door Management, 865 Via de la Paz, Suite 365, Pacific Palisades, CA 90272-3618, USA.

CHILTON John; b. 16 July 1932, London, England. Musician (trumpet); Arranger; Bandleader; Writer. *Career:* Leader, own band, mid 1950s; Member, arranger, Bruce Turner Jump Band, 1958–63; Played with Alex Welsh and Mike Daniels, early 1960s; Co-leader, the Feetwarmers, late 1960s; Sole bandleader, 1974–; Musical director, George Melly, 1974–; Tours, recordings, broadcasts, as George Melly and John Chilton's Feetwarmers, 1974–; Writer and researcher into jazz history. *Publications:* Who's Who of Jazz: Storyville To Swing Street; Louis – The Louis Armstrong Story; Jazz; Billie's Blues, partial biography of Billie Holiday; Historical accounts of: the Jenkins Orphanage bands; McKinney's Cotton Pickers; The Bob Crosby Bobcats; Biographies of: Sidney Bechet; Coleman Hawkins; Louis Jordan; Henry 'Red' Allen; Who's Who of Jazz (Storyville to Swing Street); Who's Who of British Jazz. *Current Management:* Jack L Higgins, Pear Tree Cottage, Weymarks, Bradwell-On-Sea, Essex CM0 7JB, England.

CHIWESHE Stella Rambisai; b. 8 July 1946, Harare, Zimbabwe. m. (1) 2 d., (2) Peter Reich, 27 Jan. 1988. *Career:* Member, National Dance Company of Zimbabwe, Mbira Soloist, Actress and Dancer, 1981–84; Solotours in Germany, Great Britain and Italy, 1984; Tour through Germany, 1985; Introduction of marimbas for mbira music, 1986; Recording and publication of Ambuya?; Triumphant concert at Hackney Empire, London at Beat Apartheid Road Festival, 1987; European Tour, 1988; Tour in Europe with concerts in Slovenia, Switzerland, Austria, Great Britain, Italy, Poland and Germany, with trio and the Earthquake Band, 1995; Tour in Europe with concerts in the Netherlands, Belgium, Germany, Austria, Hungary, Great Britain and Ireland, 1996; Tour of USA, Netherlands, Germany and Italy, 1998; Appeared at Global Interchange Conference, New York, 1999; Directed music theatre performance of Chiedza – Light, in Cologne, 1999; Forthcoming workshop session for Dimensions Theatre Oakland, USA, 2000. *Compositions:* Kasahwa; Chaa!; Nsuzu Chamakuwende; Mapere. *Recording:* CD, Tapera, 1999. *Honour:* Billboard Music Award, 1993. *Membership:* GEMA. *Leisure interests:* Travel; Reading; Swimming. *Current Management:* Alba Kultur-Aktionen, Birgit Ellinghaus. *Address:* Alba Kulturaktionen, Justinianstr 16, 50679, Koeln, Germany.

CHOLET Jean-Christophe; b. 11 May 1962, Böhl, Germany. Musician (piano); Composer; Arranger. Divorced, 1 s., 1 d. *Musical Education:* University diploma, piano (schola cantorum), harmony, counterpoint and fugue. *Career:* Concerts, festivals: Radio France (Paris); Coutances; Couches; Sorgues; Toutplellier; Vienna (Austria); Tous le Savnièr; Worms; Mainz; Bonn; Trier, Germany; Le Havre; Avignon. *Recordings:* with Odéjy: Osti Natologie; Suite Alpestre; with Mathias Rüegg and Michel Portal: Third Dream. *Honours:* First Prize, Soloist, Composition and Orchestra, International Festival of Jazz, La Défense, Paris. *Membership:* Union of Jazz Musicians. *Leisure interests:* Cooking; Wine; Nature; Cinema;

Travel. *Current Management:* Odéjy, Route de St Georges, 8900 Perigny, France. *Address:* 295 Chemin de la Motte, 45200 Paulcourt, France.

CHOLEWA Tom Mike Werner; b. 4 June 1958, Copenhagen, Denmark. Conductor; Musician (French horn). m. Ellen, 1983, 2 d. *Musical Education:* Degree in Classical Music, Royal Danish Music Academy; French Horn and Musicology, University of Copenhagen. *Career:* Bandmaster of Zealand Life Regiment, 1989–96; Freelance conductor and musician; Music Educator. *Recording:* Conductor, television production Dagen vi aldrig glemmer, with the Danish vocal group Swing Sisters and Band of Zealand Life Regiment. *Honour:* Second Prize, march competition for Prince Joachim, Denmark. *Membership:* Danish Conductors Asscn. *Address:* Folkevej 19, 2820 Gentofte, Denmark.

CHRIS Jo; b. 12 Nov. 1960, Balengou, Cameroon. Musician (Piano). m. Ngandjeu Iavre, 6 Aug. 1984, 1 s., 3 d. *Musical Education:* Professor of Music, Lycee de Newbell; Music studies with Billy Mussango. *Compositions:* 17 published songs, arranged by Billy Mussango. *Membership:* Socimada. *Leisure interests:* Cookery; Ballads. *Address:* c/o Billy Mussango, PO Box 8363 Yaounde, Cameroon.

CHRISSY BOY (Chris Foreman); b. 8 Aug. 1958, London, England. Musician (guitar, keyboards). m. (1) 1976, 1 s., (2) 1992, 1 s. *Musical Education:* Self-taught. *Career:* Founder member, group Madness; Numerous appearances on television programmes including Top of The Pops; Band split in 1987; Became The Madness until 1989; Formed group The Nutty Boys, releasing album Crunch!, 1990; Madness reformed sporadically, 1992–. *Recordings:* with Madness: Albums include: One Step Beyond, 1979; Absolutely, 1980; 7, 1981; Complete Madness (No. 1, UK), 1982; The Rise and Fall, 1982; Madness, 1983; Keep Moving, 1984; Mad Not Mad, 1985; Peel Sessions, 1986; Utter Madness, 1986; The Madness, 1988; Divine Madness (compilation; No. 1, UK), 1992; Madstock (live), 1993; Wonderful, 1999; Singles include: One Step Beyond, 1979; My Girl, 1980; Baggy Trousers, 1980; Embarrassment, 1980; The Return of The Los Palmas 7, 1981; Grey Day, 1981; Shut Up, 1981; It Must Be Love, 1981; House of Fun (No. 1, UK), 1982; Driving In My Car, 1982; Our House, 1982; Tomorrow's Just Another Day, 1983; Wings of a Dove, 1983; The Sun and The Rain, 1983; Michael Caine, 1984; One Better Day, 1984; Yesterdays Men, 1985; Uncle Sam, 1985; Waiting For The Ghost Train, 1986; Lovestruck, 1999; Drip Fed Fred (with Ian Dury), 2000; with The Nutty Boys: Album: Crunch!, 1990; Singles: Magic Carpet; It's OK I'm A Policeman; Pop My Top. *Honours:* Gold discs; Ivor Novello Award, as songwriter, Our House. *Memberships:* PRS; VPL; Musicians' Union. *Leisure interests:* Films; Books. *Address:* c/o PO Box 3087, London NW5 3DZ, England.

CHRISTENSEN Nikolaj; b. 19 Feb. 1966, Copenhagen, Denmark. Singer; Actor. *Career:* Major films: Christian, director, Gabrial Axel; Hjerter I Slor, Jesper W Nielsen. *Recordings:* Piloter, 1990; Jimmy and Vicky, 1991; Hen Over Jorden, 1994; Vi Er På Vej, 1996. *Honour:* Grammy, Best New Artist, 1990. *Membership:* DJBFA. *Leisure interests:* Giraffe pictures/paintings. *Address:* Kick Musik, Energivej 42B, 2750 Ballerup, Denmark.

CHRISTENSEN Soren; b. 6 June 1963, Copenhagen, Denmark. Musician (Drums). *Musical Education:* Public Music School, Percussion, 1979; Berklee School of Music, 1980; Numerous trips to New York; Private tuition in Copenhagen. *Career:* Appearances in major festivals throughout Scandinavia; Many appearances on national TV and radio; Appearance in film The Naked Trees. *Recordings:* With EV's Youth Big Band, 1984, 1985; Hens Winther, The Planets; Claus Waidtlow, Claustrophobia; CD of own band, Drumscapes, forthcoming. *Honour:* The Planets, Grammy Award Winner, 1995. *Leisure interests:* Cycling; Triathlon (hobby level); Cooking; Nature. *Current Management:* Native Music, Denmark. *Address:* Nyelandsvej 7, U T H, 2000 Frederiksburg, Denmark.

CHRISTENSEN Thomas Hass; b. 15 March 1961, Frederiksberg, Denmark. Musician (saxophone); Composer. *Musical Education:* Self-taught. *Career:* Played: 2 weeks, Ronnie Scott's, 1989; Montréal Jazz Festival, with Page One, 1989; Toured with soloists as a sideman. *Recordings:* with Page One: Beating Bop; Live At Ronnie Scott's; Notes In Time, Thomas Hass; A Matter of Fact, The End. *Honour:* The European Jazz Federation Prize, 1977. *Memberships:* DMF; DJBFA. *Address:* Sollerod Park, bl 13 no 20, 2840 Holte, Denmark.

CHRISTI Ellen; b. 7 March 1958, Chicago, Illinois, USA. Vocalist; Composer; Arranger; Prod. *Musical Education:* BA, Music and Arts Management; Studied Composition, Technique and Arranging with Jaki Byard, bello canto technique with Virginia Davidson and Galli Campi. *Career:* Radio appearances in New York, Boston, Chicago, Los Angeles, San Francisco, Washington DC, North and South Carolina, Switzerland, Italy, France, Senegal, Germany, England, Austria, Japan, Australia; TV appearances in Senegal, Milan, Zurich, Munich, Hamburg, Nice. *Compositions:* I'm A Fan (of Every Man); Japanese Twilight; Midnight Moon; Senza Parole; Open Your Eyes; Anna Speaks. *Recordings:* I'm A Fan; Aliens' Talk; Instant Reality; Reconstruction of Sound; Vocal Desires; Piece of the Rock. *Leisure interests:* Working out; Working in recording studio late at night; Composing and playing. *Current Management:* Bliss Corporation, Italy. *Address:* 320 W 83rd St 6H, New York, NY 10024, USA.

CHRISTIAN Garry; b. 27 Feb. 1955, Liverpool, England. Vocalist. *Career:* Member, The Christians, 1984–95; reformed 2000; Appearances include: Liver Aid Ethiopian Famine benefit, Liverpool, 1985; Support to Fleetwood Mac, British tour, 1988; John Lennon Tribute Concert, Merseyside, 1990; Regular UK and European tours. *Recordings:* Albums: The Christians (No. 2, UK), 1987; Colour (No. 1, UK), 1990; Happy In Hell, 1992; The Best of The Christians, 1993; Singles include: Forgotten Town, 1987; Hooverville (They Promised Us The World), 1987; When The Fingers Point, 1987; Ideal World, 1988; Born Again, 1988; Harvest For The World, 1988; Words, 1989; What's In A Word, 1992; The Bottle, 1993; Contributor, Ferry 'Cross The Mersey, Hillsborough football disaster benefit record (No. 1, UK), 1989; solo: Your Cool Mystery, 1997. *Current Management:* Eternal Management, 55 Lark Lane, Liverpool, Merseyside L17 8UW, England.

CHRISTIAN James John; b. Milford, Connecticut, USA. Singer; Songwriter; Musician (guitar, drums, keyboards); Record Prod. *Career:* Lead singer, LA Rocks; Lead singer, House of Lords; World tours, opened for acts including: Ozzy Osbourne; Queensryche; Cheap Trick; Scorpions; Tesla; Producer, writer, solo musician; Lead singer, tour of Japan with Pata (lead guitarist with Japanese band X), 1993; Opened own recording studio, Bodeo Rodeo Records. *Compositions include:* Les Ideos Noires, platinum hit single for Julie Masse; Songs for group, Alias. *Recordings:* 3 albums with House of Lords include: House of Lords; Sahara; Solo album: Rude Awakening; Singles include: Can't Find My Way Home; As producer: Album: A Contre Jour, Julie Masse. *Current Management:* John Dubuque, Dublen Entertainment Group, 330 Merwin Ave, Unit #F1, Milford, CT 06460, USA.

CHRISTIAN Rick; b. 22 Sept. 1951, Romford, Essex, England. Singer; Songwriter; Musician (6 and 12 string guitars). m. Gillian Mary Moore, 11 April 1981. *Career:* Professional musician since 1987; Many radio appearances include: Capital; LBC; BBC and independent local radio stations including Essex, Suffolk, Kent, Bedford, Shropshire; Festivals include: South Downs, Broadstairs; Walton; Co-presenter, Essex Folk, BBC Essex, 1986–94; Organizer, Maldon Folk Club and Maldon Folk Festival; Supported artists including: Jim Couza; Fred Wedlock; Harvey Andrews; Played charity event alongside Griff Rhys Jones, 1990; Tours, Denmark, 1994, 1995; Arizona USA, 1999. *Recordings:* Albums: Reason Enough, 1983; Looking For Signs, 1990; These Things Happen, 1996. *Publications:* Major contributor: Guinness Who's Who of Folk Music; Guinness Encyclopedia of Popular Music. *Memberships:* Musicians' Union; PRS; PPL; EFDSS. *Leisure interests:* Photography; Walking; Swimming; Music; Reading; Films. *Address:* PO Box 4099, Maldon, Essex CM9 4YQ, England.

CHRISTIAN Roger; b. 13 Feb. 1950, Liverpool, Merseyside, England. Vocalist. *Career:* Member, The Christians, 1984–87; Solo artiste, 1989–; Appearances include: Liver Aid Ethiopian Famine benefit, Liverpool, 1985; British tour, 1986. *Recordings:* with The Christians: The Christians (No. 2, UK), 1987; Solo album: Checkmate, 1989; Singles: with The Christians: Forgotten Town, 1987; Hooverville (They Promised Us The World), 1987; When The Fingers Point, 1987; Solo: Take It From Home, 1989. *Current Management:* Eternal Management, 55 Lark Lane, Liverpool, Merseyside L17 8UW, England.

CHRISTIAN Russell; b. 8 July 1956, Liverpool, Merseyside, England. Vocalist. *Career:* Member, The Christians, 1984–95; Appearances include: Live Aid Ethiopian Famine benefit, Liverpool, 1985; Regular UK and European tours; Support to Fleetwood Mac, British tour, 1988; John Lennon Tribute Concert, Merseyside, 1990. *Recordings:* Albums: The Christians (No. 2, UK), 1987; Colour (No. 1, UK), 1990; Happy In Hell, 1992; The Best of The Christians, 1993; Singles include: Forgotten Town, 1987; Hooverville (They Promised Us The World), 1987; When The Fingers Point, 1987; Ideal World, 1988; Born Again, 1988; Harvest For The World, 1988; Words, 1989; What's In A Word, 1992; The Bottle, 1992; Contributor, Ferry 'Cross The Mersey, Hillsborough football disaster benefit (No. 1, UK), 1989. *Current Management:* Eternal Management, 55 Lark Lane, Liverpool, Merseyside L17 8UW, England.

CHRISTIANE Kelvin; b. 16 March 1958, Watford, Hertfordshire, England. Jazz Musician (saxophones, flute, clarinet, keyboards, percussion); Composer. Divorced, 1 s. *Musical Education:* Watford School of Music; City of Leeds College of Music. *Career:* Television appearances, Blue Mercedes, Afrique; Toured Europe and India with: Afrique, 1980; The Flyers, 1981–84; Frequent radio broadcasts promoting albums with Kelvin Christiane band; Toured with Tess Garraway in the Bernard 'Pretty' Purdie band, 1998. *Recordings:* Albums: with Kelvin Christiane Band: Awakening, 1992; Soho, 1993; Great Spirit, 1994; Salute the Sun, 1997;

Tribute to Roland Kirk, 1998; Peggy's Back, a toast to Peggy Lee with Tess Garraway, 1999. *Honour:* GDLM. *Membership:* Musicians' Union. *Leisure interest:* Swimming. *Address:* 43a Grove Rd, Eastbourne, East Sussex BN21 4TX, England.

CHRISTIDES Konstantinos; b. 30 April 1973, Thessaloniki, Greece. Composer; Musician (Piano). *Musical Education:* Studied Harmony, Counterpoint, Fugue, Macedonian Conservatoire, Thessaloniki, Greece, 1984–93; Bachelor in Piano and Composition, London College of Music, 1993–96; Postgraduate Diploma in Scoring for Film and TV, London College of Music, 1997; Graduate Diploma in Scoring for Film and TV, University of Southern California, 1998. *Career:* Scoring for Puzzle Box, short film; The Footsteps of Apostle John, short film; Scoring Assistant to Christopher Young including films Playing by Heart, 1998; Entrapment, 1999; The Big Kahuna, 1999; In Too Deep, 1999; Bless the Child, Wonderboys, The Hurricane, all forthcoming. *Compositions:* Measure for Measure, 1997; Olympic Fanfare, 1998; Out of the Ruins, 1998. *Honours:* Henry Purcell Prize for Composers, 1996; Wilfred Joseph's Prize for Composers, 1997; Sir Malcolm Arnols President's Award, 1997; University of Southern California International Students' Award, 1998. *Memberships:* Society of Composers and Lyricists, USA; American Musicians' Union, Los Angeles. *Leisure interest:* Soundtrack collector. *Address:* 1007 S Stanley Ave 104, Los Angeles, CA 90019, USA.

CHRISTIE Lou, (Lugee Alfredo Giovanni Sacco); b. 19 Feb. 1943, Glenwillard, Pennsylvania, USA. Singer; Songwriter; Prod. m. Francesca Winfield, Nov. 1971, 1 s., 1 d. *Musical Education:* Studied voice and classical music, with Miss Joliann Williams, 1957–58; Voice, music arranging/production, with Lennie Martin, 1961–62. *Career:* Leader, The Crewnecks, 1957–58; The Classics, 1959 60; Lugee and the Lions, 1961–62; Sang backgrounds, Marcy Jo, 1961; Solo artist, 1962–; Concerts: Dick Clark Caravan of Stars, 1963–66; First British tour, 1966; Tour, UK, Germany, Netherlands, 1969; Record Star Show, Wembley, 1970; Cabaret tour, UK, 1970; NME Poll Winners Concert, Wembley, 1970; Club tour, UK, 1972; Tours, USA, 1981–; Television: American Bandstand, 1963–66; Where The Action Is, 1966; Joey Bishop, 1969; Mike Douglas, 1969; The Dating Game, 1969; Top of The Pops, 1970; Midnight Special, 1974; Entertainment Tonight, 1985; Church Street Station, 1986; Nashville Now, 1989. *Recordings:* The Gypsy Cried, 1962; Two Faces Have I, 1963; Have I Sinned, 1964; Lightnin' Strikes, 1965; Rhapsody In The Rain, 1966; Painter, 1966; Wild Life's In Season, 1966; Don't Stop Me, 1967; Genesis and The Third Verse, 1968; I'm Gonna Make You Mine, 1969; Beyond The Blue Horizon, 1973; Guardian Angels, 1981; Enlightnin'ment, 1988; Glory River: The Buddah Years, 1968–72, 1992; Beyond The Blue Horizon: More of the Best of Lou Christie, 1994; Pledging My Love, 1997; The Complete Co and Ce/Roulette Recordings, 1998; Beyond the Blue Horizon/Hey You Cajun, 1998; Lou Christie Strikes Again, 1999; Egyptian Shumba (compilation), 2001; Film soundtracks include: Mondo Trasho, 1969; Rain Man, 1988; Dutch, 1990; A Home of Our Own, 1993; Barcelona, 1994; Before Sunrise, 1995; Burnzy's Last Call, 1995; Waiting for Guffman, 1996; Nick and Jane, 1997; The Last Days of Disco, 1998. *Honours:* 4 Gold records (USA); BMI Citation, 1966; 1 Gold (Japan), 1971; BMI Award, 1994. *Leisure interest:* Painting. *Current Management:* Dick Fox Management, 1650 Broadway, New York, NY 10019, USA.

CHUCK D (Carlton Ridenhour); b. 1 Aug. 1960, Long Island, New York, USA. Rapper. *Education:* Graphic Design, Adelphi University. *Career:* Super Special Mix Show, radio WBAU, 1982; Own mobile DJ and concert promotion company, Spectrum City; Founder member, US rap group, Public Enemy, 1984–; Concerts include: Support to the Beastie Boys, US, 1987; Support to LL Cool J, European tour, 1987; Tour of a Black Planet, 1990; British tour, 1990; Apocalypse '91 US tour, with Anthrax, 1991; Headliners, The World's Greatest Rap Show, 1992; Madison Square Garden, 1992; Greenpeace Stop Sellafield concert with U2, Manchester, England, 1992; Reading Festival, England, 1992; Support to U2, Zooropa tour, 1992; Manager, promoter, The Entourage (hip-hop venue), Long Island, New York, 1986. *Recordings:* Albums: Yo! Bum Rush The Show, 1987; It Takes A Nation of Millions To Hold Us Back, 1988; Fear of a Black Planet, 1990; Apocalypse '91 – The Enemy Strikes Back, 1991; Greatest Misses, 1992; Muse Sick 'n' Hour Mess Age, 1994; There's A Poison Goin' On, 1999; Solo releases include: No, 1996; Autobiography of Mistachuck, 1996; Singles include: Rebel Without A Pause, 1987; Bring The Noise, 1988; Don't Believe The Hype, 1988; Night of The Living Baseheads, 1988; Fight The Power, theme for film Do The Right Thing, 1989; Welcome To The Terrordome, 1990; 911 Is A Joke, 1990; Brothers Gonna Work It Out, 1990; Can't Do Nuttin For Ya Man, 1990; Bring The Noise (with Anthrax), 1991; Can't Truss It, 1991; Shut 'Em Down, 1992; Nighttrain, 1992; Give It Up, 1994; So Whatcha Gonna Do Now, 1995; He Got Game, 1998. *Honours include:* Platinum discs; Best Rap Group, Rolling Stone Readers Picks awards, 1991; Best Rap Album, Soul Train Music Awards, 1992. *Current Management:* Malik Entertainment, 3 Third Pl., Roosevelt, NY 11575, USA.

CHURCH Joseph; b. 25 Nov. 1957, New York, USA. Music Dir; Conductor; Composer; Prof.; Arranger; Musician. 1 d. *Education:* BA, Swarthmore College, 1978; MM, University of Illinois, 1980; DA, New York University, 1996. *Career:* Music Director, Conductor, Include National Tour, Little Shop of Horros, 1984–86; Radio City Music Halls Christmas Special, 1988–89; Promenade Theatre, Catch Me If I Fall, 1990; Giuseppe Verdi Society Chorus and Orchestra, Italy, 1991; St James Theatre, Broadway, The Who's Tommy, 1992–95; La Jolla Playhouse, California, 1995–97; Music Director, Conductor, The Lion King, New Amsterdam Theatre; Music Supervisor, The Lion King, London, Japan, Toronto; Adjunct Professor of Music, New York University School of Education, 1998–; Television appearances include The Late Show with David Letterman, The Today Show, Theatre Talk. *Compositions:* Les Fables; Sonata For Two Pianos; Vibrachrome; Mock Opera; Soggiorno; Duo For Vilin and Viola. *Honours:* Drama Logue Award; ASCAP Composition Award. *Memberships:* ASCAP; American Music Center; College Music Society. *Address:* 305 W 98th St, Apt 3E N, New York, NY 10025, USA.

CHURCHLEY Richard Allen; b. 13 Nov. 1952, Birmingham, England. Songwriter; Singer; Musician (accordion, guitar, mandolin). m. Prue Dobell, 18 Jan. 1975, 2 s. *Education:* BA Hons, German, Reading University, England. *Career:* Appearances with various bands on Folk and acoustic music circuits including: Harry-Ca-Nab; Peaky Blinders; Barker's Knee; Mind Your Own Business; Oh-Cajunal Playboys; Also radio appearances on local radio and BBC Radio 2. *Compositions:* Various Folk songs. *Recordings include:* Mega-Maggot, Harry-Ca-Nab, 1990. *Membership:* Musicians' Union. *Leisure interest:* Cricket. *Current Management:* Ashtree Agency. *Address:* 1293 Evesham Rd, Astwood Bank, Redditch, Worcestershire B96 6AY, England.

CIARAN Cian; b. 16 June 1976, Bangor, Wales. Musician (keyboards). *Career:* Member, Super Furry Animals; Early releases on small indie label, then obtained major indie label deal; Numerous British and international tours; Many festival appearances. *Recordings:* Singles: Llanfairpwllgwyngyllgogerychwyndrobwl... EP, 1995; Moog Droog EP, 1995; God! Show Me Magic, 1996; If You Don't Want Me To Destroy You, 1996; The Man Don't Give A Fuck, 1996; Hometown Unicorn, 1996; Something 4 The Weekend, 1996 The International Language of Screaming, 1997; Hermann Loves Pauline, 1997; Demons, 1997; Play It Cool, 1997; Ice Hockey Hair, 1998; Northern Lights, 1999; Fire In My Heart, 1999; Do Or Die, 2000; Juxtaposed With You, 2001; Albums: Fuzzy Logic, 1996; Radiator, 1997; Outspaced (compilation), 1998; Guerrilla, 1999; Mwng, 2000; Rings Around The World, 2001.

CINGL Pavel; b. 1962, Teplice, Czech Republic. Violinist. m. Katerina, 15 July 1989, 2 s. *Education:* Conservatory of Jaroslav Jezek, Prague. *Career:* Support to Alan Stivell in Prague; Tours in Germany, Austria, France, Netherlands, Belgium, Denmark; Regular Czech television and radio appearances. *Recordings:* 16 records with Czech bands. *Honours:* Several nominations of Rock and Pop Magazine. *Leisure interest:* Travel. *Current Management:* EXUPERY Art Agency, Krizeneckeho nam 322, 15250 Prague 5, Czech Republic. *Address:* Podlipneho 7, 180 00 Prague 8, Czech Republic.

CISAR Miroslav; b. 2 Dec. 1929, Prague, Czech Republic. Composer; Conductor. 2 s. *Career:* Member of Symphonic Orchestra; Conductor, Brass Bands and Folk Groups; Composer; Arrange; Publisher. *Compositions:* 150 recordings on Radio Prague; 20 LPs and EP of Folk music; Compositions and Arrangements on 24 cassettes and CDs. *Publications:* Compositions Published by Supraphon, Panton in Prague, 1955–58; Germany by Olbert Musikverlag and Musikverlag Ewoton, 1971–89. *Honours:* Winner in Radio Competition; Winner Compositions for Children and Sportsmen. *Memberships:* Company of Brass Music; Group Composers Czech Republic. *Leisure interest:* Gardening. *Address:* Hronovska 205, 542 33 Rtyne v Podkrkonosi, Czech Republic.

CISAR Zbynek; b. 6 March 1954, Prague, Czech Republic. Music School Dir. Alena Cisarova. *Musical Education:* Music College of Jaroslav Jezek, Masaryk University, Brno; Yamaha Music School. *Career:* Songs; Orchestra Pieces; Songs for Children; Amateur Theatre. *Compositions:* April School, Radio and Theatre Musical for Children. *Recordings:* April School; Childrens' Note. *Publications:* Text Books; Collection of Songs for Children. *Honours:* Childrens' Note, first, second and third places. *Memberships:* Copyright Organization of Musicians. *Leisure interests:* Music; Sport and Games; Books; Farming. *Current Management:* Music School. *Address:* Vobcanskem Domove 1, Prague 4 14000, Czech Republic.

CISSOKHO Malang; b. 27 May 1962, Thies, Senegal. Musician (Singing; Kora; Guitar; Bass; Percussion); Singer; Songwriter. m. Pirjo Saastamoinen, 24 Nov. 1989, 1 s. *Musical Education:* Traditional Musicial Education of Mandinko Griot. *Career:* Kaustinen Folk Music Festival, 1988, 1989, 1995; Jyvaskyla Summer Festival, 1989; Pori Jazz Festival, 1989, 1996; Joensuu Festival, 1994, 1996; Ruisrock, 1996. *Compositions:* Mun-Mun, 1982; Warale, 1985; Yendi, 1985; Touba, 1985;

Foroya, 1997; Kano, 1997; Alimaton Salia, 1990. *Recordings:* Solo albums: Lotus, 1990; Foroya, 1997; Dialia, 1997; Contributor: Super Etoile II de Dakar: Náteel Weerwi, Piirpanke: Tuku Tuku; Kristian Blak: Addeq; Rinne Radio: Rok; The Cool Sheiks: Serve Cool, Trance Planet Vol. 3; J Karjalainen and Electric Sauna: Electric Sauna; Piirpauke: Metamorphosis. *Honour:* Emma Award, 1996. *Membership:* Finnish Musician Asscn. *Address:* Haapalahdenkatu 5 G44, 00300 Helsinki, Finland.

CLACKETT Matthew James; b. 24 Aug. 1972, Dover, Kent, England. Musician (alto, tenor, soprano saxophone). *Musical Education:* Double music A levels, classical training to age 16. *Career:* Numerous session appearances and live concerts include: Roachford; Philip Bent; Peter Maas (Freeez); Worked in: USA; Canada; Japan. *Recordings:* Album: Take One, 1989; Second album due release 1995. *Membership:* Musicians' Union. *Leisure interests:* Motor racing; Travel. *Address:* 2 Kew Green, Richmond, Surrey TW9 3BH, England.

CLAIR Mark, (Mark Mac, Cold Mission); b. London, England. Prod.; Remixer; DJ. *Career:* Member: 4 Hero; Manix; Jacob's Optical Stairway; Co-founder: Reinforced Records, 1990; Collaborations: Jill Scott; Ursula Rucker; Terry Callier. *Recordings:* Albums: with 4 Hero: In Rough Territory, 1991; Parallel Universe, 1995; Jacob's Optical Stairway (with Jacob's Optical Stairway), 1996; Two Pages, 1998; Creating Patterns, 2001; Singles: Mr Kirk's Nightmare, 1991; Earth Pioneers, 1997; Escape That, 1999; Les Fleurs, 2001. *Honours:* Mercury Music Prize nominee, Two Pages, 1998. *Address:* c/o Reinforced Records, 387–389 Chapter Rd, London, NW2 5NG, England.

CLAPTON Eric, (Eric Patrick Clapp); b. 30 March 1945, Ripley, Surrey, England. Musician (guitar); Singer; Songwriter. m. Patti Boyd, 1979, divorced, 1 s., deceased. *Career:* Guitarist with groups: The Roosters, 1963; The Yardbirds, 1963–65; John Mayall's Bluesbreakers, 1965–66; Cream, 1966–68; Blind Faith, 1969; Derek and the Dominoes, 1970; Delaney and Bonnie, 1970–72; Solo artiste, 1972–; Concerts include: Concert for Bangla Desh, 1971; Last Waltz concert, The Band's farewell concert, 1976; Live Aid, 1985; Record series of 24 concerts, Royal Albert Hall, 1991; Japanese tour with George Harrison, 1991; Film appearance: Tommy, 1974. *Compositions include:* Presence of The Lord; Layla; Badge (with George Harrison). *Recordings include:* Albums: Disraeli Gears, 1967; Wheels of Fire, 1968; Goodbye Cream, 1969; Layla, 1970; Blind Faith, 1971; Concert For Bangladesh, 1971; Eric Clapton's Rainbow Concert, 1973; 461 Ocean Boulevard, 1974; E C Was Here, 1975; No Reason To Cry, 1976; Slowhand, 1977; Backless, 1978; Just One Night, 1980; Money and Cigarettes, 1983; Behind The Sun, 1985; August, 1986; Journeyman, 1989; 24 Nights, 1992; MTV Unplugged, 1992; From The Cradle, 1994; Rainbow Concert, 1995; Crossroads 2, 1996; Live In Montreux, 1997; Pilgrim, 1998; with Jimmy Page and Jeff Beck, 1999; Riding With The King, 2000; Reptile, 2001; Soundtracks include: Tommy; The Color of Money; Lethal Weapon; Rush; Hit singles include: I Shot The Sheriff; Layla; Lay Down Sally; Wonderful Tonight; Cocaine; Behind The Mask; Tears In Heaven; Contributed to numerous albums by artists including: Phil Collins; Bob Dylan; Aretha Franklin; Joe Cocker; Roger Daltrey; Dr John; Rick Danko; Ringo Starr; Roger Waters; Christine McVie; Howlin' Wolf; Sonny Boy Williamson; The Beatles: The White Album (listed as L'Angelo Mysterioso). *Honours:* numerous including: 6 Grammy Awards, 1993; Q Magazine Merit Award, 1995; Grammy Award, Best Rock Performance By Duo Or Group, The Calling (with Santana), 2000; Grammy Award, Traditional Blues Album, Riding With The King (with BB King), 2001. *Current Management:* Roger Forrester Management, 18 Harley House, Marylebone Rd, Regents Park, London NW1 5HE, England.

CLARIN Bjorn A F; b. 15 Dec. 1936. Songwriter; Composer; CD Prod.; Television Scriptwriter. m. Marianne, 26 April 1958, 2 s., 2 d. *Education:* Piano, Flute, Guitar. *Career:* Over 500 appearances, mostly in children's programmes. *Compositions:* Over Sixty Songs with Lyrics by Harry Martinson. *Recordings:* Twenty Five LP and CD Productions of Popular Swedish Music. *Honours:* Fred Winter Scholarship; Swedish Scholarship of Music. *Address:* Hampakersvagen 14, 55 339 Lerum, Sweden.

CLARK Anne; b. 14 May 1960, London, England. Poet; Songwriter; Performer. *Musical Education:* Piano, violin, viola. *Career:* 10 albums; Major tours, Europe, North America, 1980–; Co-editor, Paul Weller's Riot Stories. *Recordings:* 10 albums; Live album: Psychometry, 2000; Singles: Our Darkness; Sleeper In Metropolis; Abuse. *Publications:* Hard Lines; Notes Taken, Traces Left. *Memberships:* PRS; MCPS; GVL. *Leisure interests:* Music; Cinema; Reading; Clubbing. *Address:* 55 Fulham High St, London SW6 3JJ, England.

CLARK Colin; b. 6 June 1953, Hurstpierpoint, England. Vocalist. m. Solveig Clark. *Musical Education:* Self-taught. *Career:* Apperances on Meridian Television Pier Programme BBC Radio Sussex; Radio Kent; Radio BBC World Service; Radio Huset, Denmark; Mercury; Radio West Point, Denmark, Belgium; Performed at Copenhagen Country Music Club,

1997; Appearances in Denmark including Scandinavian Country Club Festival, Silkeborg, 1998; Numerous radio interviews in Denmark; Guest with Bendix Band, Leif Kerstein and Winchesters and Tomboola Band, 1998; Appearance with The Nashvilles in Denmark, January 2000. *Compositions:* Black Train; Trail of Tears; You Hold The Key To My Heart; Those City Lights Called Your Name. *Recordings:* Songs on forthcoming album: Standing On The Edge of Lonely; That Number's Been Changed; You Haunt The Shadows of My Mind; This Old Honky Tonk; I'm Outta Here; Black Train; Special Kind of Lady; The Price For Loving You; Boogie Woogie Thang; It's Time I Settled Down; Isom Dart, 1998; Those City Lights Called Your Name, 1999. *Address:* Valhíjs Allé 91, 7 tv, 2610 Rídovre, Denmark.

CLARK Graeme; b. 15 April 1966, Glasgow, Scotland. Musician (bass). *Career:* Member, Wet Wet Wet, 1982–; Performances include: Greenpeace charity concert, Royal Albert Hall, 1986; Support to Lionel Richie, British tour, 1987; Prince's Trust Rock Gala, Royal Albert Hall, 1988–90; John Lennon Tribute Concert, Merseyside, 1990; Edinburgh Castle, 1992; Live At The Royal Albert Hall 1992, 1993. *Recordings:* Albums: Popped In Souled Out, 1987; Sgt Pepper Knew My Father, 1988; The Memphis Sessions, 1988; High On The Happy Side, 1992; Wet Wet Wet Live At The Royal Albert Hall, 1993; End of Part One (Their Greatest Hits), 1993; Picture This, 1995; 10, 1997; Singles include: Wishing I Was Lucky, 1987; Sweet Little Mystery, 1987; Angel Eyes (Home and Away), 1988; With A Little Help From My Friends (No. 1, UK), 1988; Temptation, 1988; Sweet Surrender, 1989; Hold Back The River, 1990; Stay With Me Heartache, 1990; Goodnight Girl (No. 1, UK), 1992; More Than Love, 1992; Lip Service, 1992; Shed A Tear, 1993; Cold Cold Heart, 1993; Love Is All Around (No. 1, UK), 1994; She's All On My Mind, 1995; Julia Says, 1995; Don't Want To Forgive Me Now, 1995; Somewhere Somehow, 1995; Morning, 1996; If I Never See You Again, 1997; Strange, 1997; Yesterday, 1997. *Honours include:* Brit Award, Best British Newcomer, 1988. *Current Management:* The Precious Organisation, The Townhouse, 1 Park Gate, Glasgow G3 6DL, Scotland.

CLARK Guy; b. 6 Nov. 1941, Rockport, Texas, USA. Singer; Songwriter. *Career:* Former photographer; Guest singer, artists including: Emmylou Harris; Rodney Crowell; Steve Earle; Jerry Jeff Walker; Hoyt Axton; Waylon Jennings; Don Everly; Gordon Payne; KT Oslin; Rosanne Cash; Vince Gill; Recent concerts include Cambridge Folk Festival, 1995. *Compositions include:* LA Freeway, Jerry Jeff Walker; Desperados Waiting For A Train, Tom Rush; Texas 1947, Johnny Cash; The Last Gunfighter Ballad; Virginia's Real; Heartbroke, Ricky Skaggs; Co-writer with Rodney Crowell: The Partner Nobody Chose; She's Crazy For Leavin'. *Recordings:* Old No 1, 1975; Texas Cookin', 1976; Guy Clark, 1978; The South Coast of Texas, 1981; Better Days, 1983; Old Friends, 1989; Boats to Build, 1992; Dublin Blues, 1995; Craftsmen, 1995; Keepers, 1997; Cold Dog Soup, 1999. *Current Management:* Side One Management, 1026a Third Ave, New York, NY 10021, USA.

CLARK Lenny; b. 3 March 1958, Blackmoor, Hampshire, England. Country Singer; Musician (guitar); Harmony Vocalist. *Musical Education:* Self-taught. *Career:* Appeared with many of Britain's country bands; Guest on several albums; Backed many visiting artistes from USA; Toured Europe and Far East; Featured on CMR and radio stations nationwide; Currently fronting his 5-piece band, Preacher. *Recordings include:* Dyin' Ain't Much of a Living; Preacher. *Membership:* Equity. *Leisure interests:* Radio ham; Gliding. *Address:* Seminole, The St, Preston, Canterbury, Kent CT3 1EB, England.

CLARK Nicholas; b. 13 April 1963, Gillingham, Kent, England. Musician (guitar). *Education:* OND, HND, Business Studies. *Musical Education:* Guitar Institute, Intermediate. *Career:* Bands, including sessions: Konstructivitis; Talkies; Elliot Lewis Band; Bazooka Joe. *Recordings:* Session: Black December, Konstructivitis. *Membership:* Musicians' Union. *Leisure interests:* Music; Recording. *Address:* 45 Hazelwood Dr., Maidstone, Kent ME16 0EA, England.

CLARK Petula, (Sally Olwen); b. 15 Nov. 1934, Epsom, Surrey, England. Singer; Actress. m. Claude Wolff, 1961, 1 s., 2 d. *Musical Education:* Taught to sing by mother. *Career:* Stage and screen actress, aged 7; Own radio programme, 1943; Numerous film appearances, 1944–; Films include: Medal For The General, 1944; Here Come The Huggetts, 1948; Finian's Rainbow, 1968; Goodbye Mr Chips, 1969; Stage appearances include: Sound of Music, 1981; Someone Like You (also writer), 1989; Blood Brothers, Broadway, 1993–; Host, own BBC television series; US television special Petula, NBC, 1968; Solo singing career, 1964–; Sold over 30m. records to date. *Recordings:* Hit singles include: Ya-Ya Twist, 1960; Downtown (No. 1, USA and throughout Europe), 1964; The Other Man's Grass; My Love; I Know A Place; Downtown; Oxygen; Albums: Petula Clark Sings, 1956; A Date With Pet, 1956; You Are My Lucky Star, 1957; Pet Clark, 1959; Petula Clark In Hollywood, 1959; In Other Words, 1962; Petula, 1962; Les James Dean, 1962; Downtown, 1964; I Know A Place, 1965; The New Petula Clark Album, 1965; Uptown With Petula

Clark, 1965; In Love, 1966; Hello Paris, Vols I and II, 1966; I Couldn't Live Without Your Love, 1966; Hit Parade, 1967; The Other Man's Grass Is Always Greener, 1968; Petula, 1968; Portrait of Petula, 1969; Just Pet, 1969; Memphis, 1970; The Song of My Life, 1971; Warm and Tender, 1971; Live At The Royal Albert Hall, 1972; Now, 1972; Live In London, 1974; Come On Home, 1974; I'm the Woman You Need, 1975; Don't Sleep in the Subway, 1995; Wind of Change, 1998; With All My Heart, 2001; Spirit of Today, 2001. *Honours include:* 2 Grammy Awards; Grand Prix Du Disque, 1960; More Gold discs than any other UK female artist. *Current Management:* John Ashby, Hindsworth Management Ltd, 235 Regent St, London W1R 7AG, England.

CLARK Roy Linwood; b. 15 April 1933, Meherrin, Virginia, USA. Singer; Songwriter; Musician (guitar, banjo, mandolin). *Career:* Winner, National Banjo Championship, aged 16; Former professional boxer; Radio appearances include: Ozark Jubilee; Town and Country Time; Television: Guest, Country Style (Washington TV show), 1955; Host of show, early 60s; Actor, The Beverly Hillbillies; Host, television series Swingin' Country; Co-host, Hee Haw, CBS, 1969–; Lead guitarist, Wanda Jackson; Concerts include: Russia, 1976; Concert with Boston Pops Orchestra, 1976; Carnegie Hall, 1977; Film appearances include: Uphill All The Way, 1986; Member, Grand Ole Opry, 1987–; Later involvement in ranching, publishing, advertising, property. *Recordings:* Albums include: The Lightning Fingers of Roy Clark, 1962; The Tip of My Fingers, 1963; Happy To Be Unhappy, 1964; Guitar Spectacular, 1965; Sings Lonesome Love Ballads, 1966; Stingin' Along With The Blues, 1966; Roy Clark, 1966; Live, 1967; Do You Believe This Roy Clark, 1968; In The Mood, 1968; Urban, Suburban, 1968; Yesterday When I Was Young, 1969; The Everlovin' Soul of Roy Clark, 1969; The Other Side of Roy Clark, 1970; I Never Picked Cotton, 1970; The Magnificent Sanctuary Band, 1971; The Incredible Roy Clark, 1971; Roy Clark Country!, 1972; Family Album, 1973; Superpicker, 1973; Come Live With Me, 1973; Family and Friends, 1974; The Entertainer, 1974; Roy Clark, 1974; So Much To Remember, 1975; Heart To Heart, 1975; In Concert, 1976; Hookin' It, 1977; My Music and Me, 1977; Labour of Love, 1978. *Honours:* CMA Awards: Instrumentalist of The Year, 1977, 1978, 1980. *Address:* Roy Clark Productions, 3225 South Norwood, Tulsa, OK 74135, USA.

CLARK Terri; b. 5 Aug. 1968, Montréal, Québec, Canada. Singer; Songwriter; Musician. *Career:* Tour with George Strait, played dates with Clay Walker and Aaron Tippin, 1994; Performed on Prime Time Country; Recorded At The Ryman; Played on the Grand Ole Opry, 1994; Tour with George Strait, 1996; Tours played to over 1.5m. people, 1996; Appearing in Primestar Presents Clay Walker's Four Star Blowout Tour, 1997; Featured Artist, Calgary Stampede; Tours throughout Canada, 1997. *Recordings:* Better Things To Do; When Boy Meets Girl; If I Were You; Suddenly Single; Poor Poor Pitiful Me; Emotional Girl; Just the Same; Now That I Found You; Albums: Terri Clark; Just the Same; How I Feel; Ugly Duckling. *Honours:* Numerous including: Billboard Music Award, Top New Female Artist, 1995; Nominated Best New Female Vocalist, Academy of Country Music, 1996; Best Female Vocalist, Big Country Awards, 1997; Three Awards, Canadian Country Music Assen Awards, 1997. *Memberships:* AFofM; Broadcast Music Inc; Country Music Assen; Academy of Country Music. *Leisure interests:* Working out, physical training. *Current Management:* Woody Bowles, Woody Bowles Management, 1114 17th Ave S, Nashville, TN 37212, USA. *Address:* 5420 Camelot Rd, Brentwood, TN 37027, USA.

CLARK W.C.; b. 16 Nov. 1939, Austin, Texas, USA. Singer; Songwriter; Musician (guitar). 1 s., 1 d. *Career:* Toured with Joe Tex Band, 1960s; Member, Southern Feeling, with Angela Strehli, Denny Freeman; Worked on Triple Threat Revue, with Stevie Ray Vaughan, Lou Ann Barton, Mike Kindred; Support tours to B. B. King; Bobby Bland; Also performed with Albert Collins; Buddy Guy; Johnny Taylor; Lowell Fulsom; Joe Turner; Lou Rawls; Brooks Benton; Freddie King; Alvin Bishop; George Thorogood; James Brown; Matt Murphy; Jimmy Vaughan; Clarence Holliman; Carol Fran; Appeared at Austin City Limits, 1990. *Compositions:* Cold Shot, co-author; Standing Here at the Crossroads. *Recordings include:* Something For Everybody, 1987; Heart of Gold, 1994; Texas Soul, 1996; Lover's Plea, 1998. *Honours:* Austin Chronicle Music Awards: Best Blues Band, Best Soul Band; Inducted into Texas Music Hall of Fame, 1990; W C Handy Award, Best Blues/Soul Album, 1997; W C Handy Award for first time cotaegory: Artist Most Deserving Wider Recognition, 1999. *Membership:* BMI. *Current Management:* Vicky Gay Moerbe, Crossfire Productions, 304 Braeswood Rd, Austin, TX 78704-7200, USA. *E-mail:* vicky@wcclark.com.

CLARKE 'Fast' Eddie; b. 5 Oct. 1950, Isleworth, Middlesex, England. Rock Musician (guitar). *Career:* Guitarist, Continuous Performance; Guitarist, blues band, Curtis Knight; Guitarist, UK heavy rock group Motörhead, 1976–82; Support to Hawkwind, UK 1977; British tours, 1978–80; Heavy Metal Barn Dance, Stafford, UK, 1980; Co-founder, Fastway (with Pete Way), 1982-. *Recordings:* Albums: with Motörhead: Motörhead, 1977; Overkill, 1979; Bomber, 1979; Ace of Spades, 1980; No Sleep 'Til Hammersmith (No. 1, UK), 1981; Iron Fist, 1982; No Class, 2001;

with Fastway: Fastway, 1983; All Fired Up, 1984; Waiting For The Roar, 1986; The World Waits For You, 1986; Trick Or Treat, 1987; On Target, 1988; Bad Bad Girls, 1989; Solo album: It Ain't Over Till It's Over, 1994; Singles: with Motörhead include: Louie Louie; Bomber; No Class; Motörhead; Overkill; Ace of Spades; Iron Fist; The Golden Years EP; Beer Drinkers and Hell Raisers EP; St Valentine's Day Massacre EP (with Girlschool).

CLARKE Dave, (Pig City, Directional Force); b. 1968, Sussex, England. Prod.; Remixer; DJ. *Career:* Founder: Directional Force records; Recorded for: Stress Records; Deconstruction; Skint Records; World-wide DJ; Remixed: DJ Hell; DJ Rush; Chemical Brothers; Gary Numan; New Order; Faithless. *Recordings:* Albums: Archive 1, 1995; Singles: Red 1, Red 2, 1994; Red 3, Southside, 1995; No-One's Driving, 1996; Shake Your Booty, 1997; The Compass, 2001. *Honours:* Muzik Award, Best Essential Mix, 2000. *Membership:* PRS. *Address:* c/o Skint Records, 73A Middle St, Brighton, Sussex, BN1 4BA, England.

CLARKE David Roger; b. 28 Jan. 1948, Essex, England. Musician (guitar, keyboards); Songwriter; Record Co Owner. m. Patricia, 16 Dec. 1966, 1 s., 1 d. *Education:* BSc, MSc, Mathematics. *Musical Education:* Piano. *Career:* Joined Sapphires aged 13, 1961; Band renamed Blue Angels, 1963; Major USA, European tours, television appearances, 1975–78; Joined Royal Navy, active service Falkland Islands war, HMS Fearless, retired as Commander, 1979–92; Formed Mouse Records, 1993; Tours: Scandinavia; Germany; New Zealand, 1993–94; Lead vocalist, guitarist, keyboards, principal songwriter, producer on majority of recordings. *Recordings:* 2 singles as Danny Clyve and the Blue Angels, 1964; Album as Dave Carlsen: Pale Horse, 1974; Lead vocals, as Chester Baynes, hit single, 1972; Producer, Gaylords single: Hit Me With Music, 1974; with Noel Redding Band: 2 singles, 2 albums, 1975–76; Album, 1994; with Jimmy McCulloch and White Line, 2 singles, 1976, album, 1994; Album as Frigate, 1981; 4 releases as Shut Up Frank, with members of: The Kinks; The Animals; Jimi Hendrix Experience, 1993–97; Dream Machine album, 1995. *Memberships:* PRS; MCPS; PPL; PAMRA; Institute of Management. *Leisure interest:* Music. *Current Management:* Mouse Records. *Address:* 28 Breamore Rd, Seven Kings, Essex IG3 9NB, England.

CLARKE Kim Annette; b. 14 Nov. 1954, New York, USA. Musician (bass). *Education:* BA, Communications, CUNY, 1978. *Musical Education:* BA, Music, Long Island University, 1990. *Career:* Freelance musician, 1978–; Bass player, Yusef Lateef Quartet; Defunkt; Lester Bowie's Brass Fantasy; George Gruntz; Joe Henderson Quartet; Kit McLure; Also played with: Billy Taylor; Art Blakey; Lionel Hampton; Sarah Vaughn; Branford Marsalis; Betty Carter; Mike Manieri; Robert Palmer; Napoleon Revels-Bey.

CLARKE Kory; b. USA. Rock Vocalist; Songwriter. *Career:* Vocalist, lyricist, US heavy rock group Warrior Soul, 1988–95; subsequently member, Space Age Playboys; Tours and concerts include: Support to Metallica, European tour, 1990; Support to Queensryche, Empire tour, 1991; European tour, 1993; UK and European tours, 1995; European festivals, 1995. *Recordings:* Albums: Last Decade, Dead Century, 1989; Drugs God and The New Republic, 1991; Salutations From A Ghetto Nation, 1992; Chill Pill, 1994; Space Age Playboys, 1995; Odds and Ends, 1996; New Age Underground, 1998; Live In London, 1999. *Current Management:* Q-Prime Inc, 729 Seventh Ave, 14th Floor, New York, NY 10019, USA.

CLARKE Paul Frazer; b. 25 Sept. 1962, Leicester, England. Songwriter; Prod.; Musician (keyboards, drums, guitar). *Education:* Wyggeston Queen Elizabeth I College, Leicester. *Career:* Recording artist (Epic), British tours, 1987; with November One, London's Burning (LWT film/series), 1988; Writer, Warner Chappell, 1987–91; Co-writes with/for Glenn Nightingale; Angie Brown; Rick Astley; Other television appearances include: Rock Goes To College, BBC TV; Wide Awake Club, ITV; Hit Man and Her, LWT; Director, Fast Floor Multimedia Ltd; Writer, MCA, 1996–98; Film/TV Writer, 1998-. *Recordings:* Albums: Deja Vu, Magna Charta; Quest For Intelligence, Fast Floor; Purveyors of the New Groove, Earl Grey; The Eternal Dream, Fast Floor. *Memberships:* PRS; MCPS. *Leisure interests:* Football; Cricket; Walking. *Current Management:* c/o Christian Ulf-Hansen, BMI. *Address:* 79 Harley House, Marylebone Rd, London, England.

CLARKE Sharon D; b. 28 May 1965, London, England. Actress; Vocalist. *Career:* Performances: First British actress to play The Voice of Audrey II in The Little Shop of Horrors, London Bubble Theatre, Leicester Haymarket; The Singing Detective, Dennis Potter, BBC TV; 6 appearances, Top of the Pops, with Nomad; Guest presenter DJ, Saturday Morning Mayhem; Sunset Radio, Manchester; Princess of Wales Birthright Charity Trust; Lead vocalist, Royal Albert Hall; Lead vocalist, Stonewall Concert, Royal Albert Hall, 1995; Played opposite Chaka Khan, Mama I Want To Sing, Mama Winter, Cambridge Theatre, London. *Recordings:* I Wanna Give You (Devotion), Nomad (No. 2, UK charts; World-wide No. 1 club hit); Happiness, Serious Rope (No. 1 club hit, UK). *Honours:* Nominations: Manchester Evening News, Best Supporting Performer, A Taste of Honey, 1989; Laurence Olivier Awards, Best Supporting Performer in a Musical, Once On This Island, 1995. *Membership:* Equity. *Address:* 102 Ranelagh Rd, Tottenham, London, England.

CLARKE Simon C; b. 9 May 1955, Sheffield, South Yorkshire, England. Arranger; Musician (baritone, tenor, alto, flute, piccolo saxophones). m. Helen Sykes, 20 Aug. 1988. *Education:* BA Hons, York University. *Musical Education:* Serious flute playing to age 21, switched to saxophone. *Career:* Tours with Pete Townshend's Deep End, 1985; The Who, 1989–90; The Waterboys, 1990; Eric Clapton, 1993–95. *Recordings:* session work includes: Blur; China Crisis; Communards; Deacon Blue; Dubstar; Terence Trent D'Arby; Geri Halliwell; Tom Jones; Rolling Stones; Suede; Spiritualized. *Leisure interests:* Marathon running; Claret drinking.

CLARKE Stanley; b. 21 July 1951, Philadelphia, Pennsylvania, USA. Musician (bass). *Musical Education:* Philadelphia Musical Academy. *Career:* Member, various funk groups; Played jazz with Horace Silver; Joe Henderson; Pharoah Sanders; Chick Corea and Return To Forever Band; Partnership with George Duke. *Recordings:* Albums: Stanley Clarke, 1974; Journey To Love, 1975; School Days, 1976; Modern Man, 1978; I Wanna Play For You, 1979; Rocks Pebbles and Sand, 1980; Time Exposure, 1984; Find Out, 1985; Hideaway, 1986; Shieldstone, 1987; If This Bass Could Only Talk, 1988; with Pharoah Sanders: Black Unity, 1972; with George Duke: The Clarke/Duke Project, 1981; The Clarke/Duke Project II, 1983; 3, 1990; with Return To Forever: Return To Forever, 1972; with Aziza Mustafa Zadeh: Dance of Fire, 1995; with Al DiMeola, Jean-Luc Ponty: The Rite of Strings, 1996; Portrait Stanley Clarke, 2000. *Address:* c/o Baker, Winokur, Ryder Public Relations, 405 S Beverly Dr., Fifth Floor, Beverly Hills, CA 90212, USA.

CLARKE Vince; b. 3 July 1960, Basildon, Essex, England. Musician (keyboards, synthesizers); Songwriter. *Career:* Musician, groups: No Romance In China; Depeche Mode, 1980–81; Yazoo (with Alison Moyet), 1982–83; Erasure (with Andy Bell), 1985–; Support to Duran Duran, US tour, 1987; US tour, 1988; Prince's Trust Rock Gala, Birmingham, 1989. *Recordings:* Albums: with Depeche Mode: Speak and Spell, 1981; with Yazoo: Upstairs At Eric's, 1982; You and Me Both (No. 1, UK), 1983; with Erasure: Wonderland, 1986; The Circus, 1987; Two Ring Circus, 1987; The Innocents (No. 1, UK), 1988; Wild! (No. 1, UK), 1989; Chorus (No. 1, UK), 1991; Pop! – The First 20 Hits (No. 1, UK), 1992; I Say I Say I Say (No. 1, UK), 1994; Erasure, 1995; Cowboy, 1997; Loveboat, 2000; with Martyn Ware: The Clarke and Ware Experiment, 2000; Pretentious, 2000; Singles: with Depeche Mode: New Life, 1981; Just Can't Get Enough, 1981; with Yazoo: Only You, 1982; Don't Go, 1982; The Other Side of Love, 1983; Nobody's Diary, 1983; with The Assembly: Never Never, 1983; with Erasure: Sometimes, 1986; It Doesn't Have To Be, 1987; Victim of Love, 1987; Circus, 1987; Ship of Fools, 1988; Chains of Love, 1988; A Little Respect, 1988; Crackers International EP, 1988; Drama!, 1989; You Surround Me, 1989; Blue Savannah, 1990; Chorus, 1991; Love To Hate You, 1991; Breath of Life, 1992; Abba-esque EP (No. 1, UK), 1992; Who Needs Love (Like That) remix, 1992; Stay With Me, 1995; Fingers and Thumbs, 1996; Rock Me Gently, 1996; Don't Say Your Love Is Killing Me, 1997; Rain, 1998; EBX, 1999; Freedom, 2000; Contributor, Red Hot + Blue, AIDS benefit album, 1990; Tame Yourself, animal rights benefit album, 1991. *Honours:* BRIT Awards: Best British Newcomer, Yazoo, 1983; Best British Group, Erasure, 1989; Ivor Novello Award, Most Performed Work of 1990, Blue Savannah, 1991. *Address:* c/o Mute Records, 429 Harrow Rd, London W10 4RE, England.

CLARKIN Tony; Musician (guitar); Songwriter. *Career:* Founder member, guitarist, UK rock group Magnum, 1972–; Regular tours include support tours with Judas Priest; Whitesnake; Blue Oyster Cult; Def Leppard; Own headline tours world-wide. *Recordings:* Albums: Kingdom of Madness, 1978; Magnum II, 1979; Marauder, 1980; Chase The Dragon, 1982; The Eleventh Hour, 1983; On A Storyteller's Night, 1985; Vigilante, 1986; Wings of Heaven, 1988; Goodnight LA, 1990; The Spirit, 1991; Rock Art, 1994; Stronghold, 1997; Archive, 2000; Numerous compilation albums; Singles include: Kingdom of Madness, 1978; Just Like An Arrow, 1985; On A Storyteller's Night, 1985; Midnight, 1986; Days of No Trust, 1988; Start Talking Love, 1988; It Must Have Been Love, 1988; Rocking Chair, 1990.

CLARKSON Ian Christopher; b. 7 May 1964, Ormskirk, England. Musician (trumpet); Vocalist. m. Grazia Bevilacqua, 29 Dec. 1993. *Musical Education:* Self-taught. *Career:* Front man, vocalist and trumpet, with the Jive Aces; Prior to That, Aces of Rhythm, The Emperors of Rhythm; Television: Opportunity Knocks, BBC; Monte Carlo TV; Kenny Live RTE (Dublin); Concerts: Royal Albert Hall; Theatre Royal; Many many European tours, at least 250 gigs per year; Apollo Theatre, Harlem, with Doug E Fresh; Appeared with John Travolta, Lisa Marie Presley and Isaac Hayes, Church of Scientology event, and also Hollywood Palladium, Cotton

Club and The Derby, Los Angeles; 25 city tour of US swing clubs and tribute to Louis Prima guest starring trombone player James 'Little Red' Blount. *Compositions:* Blues 4 U; Still; Planet Jive; Imagination or Something Else; Junky Joe. *Recordings:* Albums: Jumping With The Aces; Bolt from the Blue; Planet Jive; Single: Blues 4 U/Heybarberebop. *Leisure interests:* Sports; Films; Dianetics; Spiritual philosophy. *Current Management:* Jive Aces. *Address:* St Hill Manor, East Grinstead, West Sussex, England.

CLASTRIER Valentin; b. 14 Feb. 1947, Nice, France, Musician. *Musical Education:* Classical guitar; Singing. *Career:* Guitar player with Jacques Brel, 1968–69; Guitar, Ricet Barrier, 1975–82; Composer for Hurdy Gurdy (acoustic, electro-acoustic), 1970–; Hurdy Gurdy teacher in training course, Master class, France and abroad. *Recordings:* Vielle à Roue de l'Imaginaire, 1984; Esprit de la Nuit, 1986; Grands Maîtres de la Vielle à Roue, 1988; Hérésie, 1992; Le Bûcher des Silences, 1994; Palude, 1995; Hurdy-Gurdy from Land of Cathars, 1997. *Publication:* Anthology For Hurdy Gurdy, 1985. *Honours:* Chevalier dans L'Ordre des Arts et des Lettres; Grand Prix de l'Académie Charles Cros; Grand Prix Audiovisuel de l'Europe. *Address:* Gué de la Pierre, 18380 Ennordres, France.

CLAUSELL Deborah Deloris; b. 16 July 1951, Mobile, Alabama, USA. Musician (guitar). *Education:* University of South Alabama, 1984. *Career:* CBS, Afternoon School; Special Emmy Hit; Tuesday Night At The Movies. *Compositions:* The Fewest Words I Need To Say; Major John Pelham; Willing Willie; He Is. *Recordings:* Strong Feeling of Love; Success In Christ; Angels; The Happier I Am In Thee The Greater I Am; Life. *Publications:* The Encyclopedia of Living Artist; Contemporary Art. *Memberships:* VFM; US Naval Institute; National Trust For Historic Preservation. *Leisure interests:* Guitar; Harmonica; Swimming; Reading; Singing. *Address:* 5859 N Reams Dr., Mobile, AL 36608, USA.

CLAUSEN Thomas; b. 5 Oct. 1949, Copenhagen, Denmark. Composer; Musician (piano, keyboards). m. (1) Pi Sveistrup, divorced, 2 d., (2) Tove Bornhift, 1999. *Musical Education:* Private lessons; 3 years, Royal Conservatory, Copenhagen. *Career:* Musician for Dexter Gordon; Palle Mikkelborg; Ben Webster; Jan Garbarek; Leader, own groups 1978-, including Mirror, quartet; Own trio, with NHOP, 1980–83; Trio with Mads Vinding and Alex Riel, 1987-. *Compositions:* Prism, 1975; Sonata for Oboe, Cello, Harp, 1989; Woods and Lakes, 1993; Danish Weather, 1996. *Recordings:* Mirror, 1979; Rain, 1980; The Shadow of Bill Evans, 1983; She Touched Me, 1988; Piano Music, 1989; Café Noir, 1990; Flowers and Trees, 1991; Psalm, 1995. *Honours:* Radio Jazz Prize, 1988; Ben Webster Prize, 1989; JASA Prize, 1990; Danish Grammy, 1991; Fanfare Prize, 1992. *Memberships:* KODA; NCB; DJFBA; Danish Arts Foundation, 1998. *Leisure interests:* Family; Nature; Films; Theatre. *Address:* Rastestedet 5, 3500 Vaerlose, Denmark.

CLAXTON Andrew; b. 22 Jan. 1950, London, England. Composer; Musician. 1 s. *Musical Education:* National Youth Orchestra of Great Britain; Royal Academy of Music; Bretton Hall College; University of Reading. *Career:* Freelance Composer, Instrumentalist, 1966–; Recorded, Toured With Dead Can Dance, 1987–93; Director, Peacock Epoch, 1985–; Recorded, Toured With Meltdown, 1998–; Musical Director, Gintare, 1999-. *Compositions:* Elements, 1988; Fall of The House of Usher, 1992; Six, 1996; Spires and Spirits, 1997; Silent Spaces, 1998. *Recordings:* Liar, 1995; The Big Sleazy, 1996; Drug Raped, 1998; Silent Spaces, 1998; Inside Polygamy, 1999; The Forbidden Journey, 1999; Collaborations: Dead Can Dance Albums, Within The Realm of a Dying Sin, 1987; Toward The Within, 1994; The Mirror Pool, 1995; Dead Can Dance 1981–98 (compilation), 2001. *Honours:* Winner, Oxford Town Hall Centenary Composers Competition, 1997; Finalist, Best Re-Recorded Music Category, British Television Advertising Craft Awards, 1998. *Memberships:* BACS; PRS; PCAM. *Current Management:* Ms Joan Gardner, Ivony, Cumnor Hill, Oxford, Oxfordshire OX2 9JA, England.

CLAYDERMAN Richard (Philippe Pages); b. 1954, Paris, France. Musician (piano); Composer. *Musical Education:* Paris Conservatory. *Career:* Former bank clerk; Became successful performer and recording artist; Played with French pop stars including Johnny Halliday; Michel Sardou; Top album seller, France, South Africa, Japan, early 1980s; Sellout UK concerts, 1982; Numerous television appearances; Concerts include: Japan; Brazil; Australia. *Recordings:* Albums: Ballade Pour Adeline (The Love Song), 1981; Dreaming (Traumereien), 1981; Dreaming (Traumereien), 3, 1981; Richard Clayderman, 1982; A Comme Amour, 1982; Lettre A Ma Mere, 1982; Musiques De L'Amour, 1982; The Music of Richard Clayderman, 1983; A Pleyel, 1983; Marriage of Love, 1984; The Music of Love, 1984; Christmas, 1984; The Classic Touch (with The Royal Philharmonic), 1985; Hollywood and Broadway, 1986; Songs of Love, 1987; A Little Night Music, 1988; Eleana, 1988; The Love Songs of Andrew Lloyd Webber, 1989; Together At Last, 1991; A Little Romance, 1994; Romance of. . ., 1995; Christmas Album, 1998; Con Amor, 2000; Amor Latino, 2000; Lettre A Ma Mere, 2001; Concerto For You, 2001. *Current Management:*

Gurtman and Mutha Associates, 450 Seventh Ave, #603, New York, NY 10123–10101, USA.

CLAYSON Alan; b. 3 May 1951, Dover, Kent, England. Composer; Author; Musician (keyboards, guitar); Vocalist. m. Inese Pommers, 31 July 1979, 2 s., 1 d. *Education:* Farnborough Technical College; University of Reading. *Musical Education:* Self-taught. *Career:* Member, Turnpike, 1971–74; Average Joe and the Men in the Street, 1974–75; Billy and The Conquerors, 1972–75; Portsmouth Sinfonia, viola, 1975; Clayson and The Argonauts, 1975–86; Toured UK, Europe, BBC Radio In Concert show, 1977; Solo performer, 1985–; USA debut, 1992; Worked with: Wreckless Eric; Twinkle; Screaming Lord Sutch; Dave Berry's Cruisers; Dick Taylor (Rolling Stone/Pretty Things); Writer and Presenter, Death Discs, BBC Radio 2, 1996. *Compositions include:* Moonlight Skater with Jim McCarty for Dave Berry and Stairway's Raindreaming album; Sol Nova, 1985; The Landlocked Sailor, for Poacher's Pocket, 1992; Man of the Moment, 1995; Angelette, 1997. *Recordings:* with The Argonauts: Single, The Taster, 1978; Last Respects (EP), 1982; Album, What A Difference A Decade Made, 1985; Producer, main songwriter, Dave Berry album Hostage To The Beat, 1986; 2 tracks, compilation album Beat Merchants, 1995; Album, Soiree, 1997; 2 tracks on compilation album Ne Me Quitte Pas, 1998. *Publications:* Books: Call Up The Groups! The Golden Age of British Beat, 1985; Back In The High Life – A Biography of Steve Winwood, 1988; Only The Lonely – The Life and Artistic Legacy of Roy Orbison, 1989; The Quiet One – A Life of George Harrison, 1990; Ringo Starr – Straight Man Or Joker, 1991; Death Discs, 1992; Backbeat, with Pauline Sutcliffe, 1994; Aspects of Elvis (edit) with Spencer Leigh, 1994; Beat Merchants, 1995; Jacques Brel, 1996; Hamburg: The Cradle of British Rock, 1997; Serge Gainsbourg: View from the Exterior, 1998; The Troggs File: The Official Story of Rock's Wild Things, 1999; Over Under Sideways Down: The Flight of the Yardbirds, 2000; George Harrison (paperback), 2001; Ringo Starr (paperback), 2001; Articles for: Record Collector; The Times; Goldmine; Medieval World; The Independent; Folk Roots; Country Music People; Mojo; The Beat Goes On; Gold; The 'Schoolkids' Oz; Erotic Review; Ugly Things; Discoveries. *Membership:* PRS. *Leisure interests:* Swimming; Animal welfare; Calligraphy. *Address:* 18 South St, Caversham, Berkshire RG4 8HY, England.

CLAYTON Adam; b. 13 March 1960, Chinnor, Oxfordshire, England. Musician (bass). *Career:* Founder member, bass player, rock group U2, 1978–; Regular national and world-wide tours; Major concerts include: US Festival, 1983; The Longest Day, Milton Keynes, 1985; Live Aid, Wembley, 1985; Self Aid, Dublin, 1986; A Conspiracy of Hope (Amnesty International Tour), 1986; Smile Jamaica, 1988; Very Special Arts Festival, Washington, 1988; New Year's Eve concert, Dublin (broadcast live to Europe), 1989; Yankee Stadium, New York (second-ever concert there), 1992. *Recordings:* Albums: Boy, 1980; October, 1981; War (No. 1, UK), 1983; Under A Blood Red Sky, 1983; The Unforgettable Fire (No. 1, UK), 1984; Wide Awake In America, 1985; The Joshua Tree (No. 1, USA and UK), 1987; Rattle and Hum, also film (No. 1, USA), 1988; Achtung Baby (No. 1, USA), 1991; Zooropa (No. 1, UK and US), 1993; Passengers film soundtrack (with Brian Eno), 1995; Pop, 1997; The Best of 1980–90 (compilation), 1998; All That You Can't Leave Behind, 2001; Hit singles include: Out of Control (No. 1, Ireland), 1979; Another Day (No. 1, Ireland), 1980; New Year's Day, 1983; Two Hearts Beat As One, 1983; Pride (In The Name of Love), 1984; The Unforgettable Fire, 1985; With Or Without You (No. 1, USA), 1987; I Still Haven't Found What I'm Looking For (No. 1, USA), 1987; Where The Streets Have No Name, 1987; Desire (No. 1, UK), 1988; Angel of Harlem, 1988; When Love Comes To Town, with B. B. King, 1989; The Fly (No. 1, UK), 1991; Mysterious Ways, 1992; Even Better Than The Real Thing, 1992; Who's Gonna Ride Your Wild Horses, 1992; Hold Me, Thrill Me, Kiss Me (from film Batman Forever), 1995; Discotheque (No. 1, UK), 1997; Staring At The Sun, 1997; If God Will Send His Angels, 1997; The Sweetest Thing, 1998; Beautiful Day (No. 1, UK), 2000; Stuck In A Moment That You Can't Get Out Of, 2001; Walk On, 2001; Guest appearances on recordings by: Nanci Griffith, Daniel Lanois, Little Steven, Robbie Robertson, Sharon Shannon. *Honours include:* Grammy awards: Album of The Year, 1987; Best Rock Performance, 1987, 1989; Best Rock Vocal, 1993; Record of The Year, Song of The Year, Best Rock Performance By Duo Or Group (all for Beautiful Day), 2001; BRIT Awards: Best International Act, 1988–90, 1992, 1998, 2001; Best Live Album, 1993; Outstanding Contribution To The British Music Industry, 2001; World Music Award, 1993; Q Awards: Best Act In The World, 1990, 1992, 1993; Merit Award, 1994; Juno Award, 1993; Gold and Platinum discs. *Current Management:* Principle Management, 30–32 Sir John Rogersons Quay, Dublin 2, Ireland.

CLAYTON Eddy; b. 6 May 1931, Watford, Hertfordshire, England. Musician (drums); Bandleader. m. Margaret Clayton, 20 March 1953, 1 s. *Musical Education:* Studied with Charles Botterill (drummer with Mantovani). *Career:* Formed own band at age 14; Member, RAF Skyliners Dance Band, 1949–51; Leader of own Big Band, 1950's-60's; Currently leader of own quartet performing mainly dance music and jazz. *Memberships:* Branch Secretary, Jazz Committee Delegate, Vice Chair of District Council, Musicians' Union; ABJM; Film Artists Asscn, Equity.

Leisure interests: Cars; Caravans. *Current Management:* Margaret Clayton. *Address:* Rainbow House, 3 Goodwood Ave, Watford, Hertfordshire WD2 5LA, England.

CLAYTON-THOMAS David (Thomsett); b. 13 Sept. 1941, Surrey, England. Vocalist. *Career:* Vocalist, Blood Sweat and Tears, 1969–; Performances include: Newport Jazz Festival, 1969; Atlanta Pop Festival, 1969; US State Department sponsored tour, Eastern Europe, 1970; US tour, 1992; Le Festival Les Heros Sont Immortals, Calais, France; 2 reunion concerts, New York. *Recordings:* Albums include: with Blood Sweat and Tears: Blood, Sweat and Tears (No. 1, USA), 1969; Blood, Sweat and Tears 3 (No. 1, USA), 1970; B, S and T – 4, 1971; Mirror Image, 1974; Brand New Day, 1977; Nuclear Blues, 1980; Live and Improvised, 1991; You've Made Me So Very Happy (compilation), 2001; Solo albums: David Clayton-Thomas, 1972; Tequila Sunrise, 1972; Harmony Junction, 1973; Clayton, 1977; Blue Plate Special, 1998; Singles: You've Made Me So Very Happy, 1969; Spinning Wheel, 1969; And When I Die, 1969; Hi-De-Ho, 1970; Music for film The Owl and The Pussycat, 1971. *Honours:* Grammy Awards: Best Album, Best Contemporary Instrumental Performnce, 1970.

CLEGG Johnny; b. 13 July 1953, Rochdale, Lancashire, England. Vocalist; Composer. *Education:* Social Anthropology, Wits University, South Africa. *Career:* Moved to South Africa, 1959; Duo, Johnny and Sipho (with Sipho Mchunu), 1972; Founder, sextet Juluka, 1976–85; Tours, UK, Europe and US; Leader, Savuka, 1986; Tours, South Africa and overseas. *Recordings:* Albums: with Juluka: Universal Men, 1979; African Litany, 1981; Ulshule Bemvelo, 1982; Scatterlings of Africa, 1982; Work For All, 1983; Musa Ukungilandela, 1984; The Hope Concerts, 1985; Solo: Johnny Clegg Third World Child, 1986; with Savuka: Savuka, 1987; Freedom, 1989; Heat Dust and Dreams, 1993; In My African Dreams, 1994; Anthology, 2000; Singles: Woza Friday, Juluka, 1978; Cruel Crazy Beautiful World, 1990; Life Is A Magic Thing, 1992; I Can Never Be, 1993. *Current Management:* HR Music, 6430 Sunset Blvd, Los Angeles, CA 90028, USA.

CLEMONS Clarence; b. 1 Nov. 1942, Norfolk, Virginia, USA. Musician (saxophone); Entertainer. 3 s. *Education:* University of Maryland. *Musical Education:* Music minor, University of Maryland. *Career:* Member, groups including Bruce Springsteen and E Street Band; Television: Numerous talk shows including David Letterman; Concerts include: Amnesty International tour; Leader, own group West Coast Red Bank Rockers; Films: New York New York; Bill and Ted's Excellent Adventure. *Recordings:* Solo albums: Rescue, 1981; Night With Mr C, 1983; Hero, 1985; Adventure; Peacemaker, 1995; Get It On, 1995; Peace makers, 1995; Albums with Bruce Springsteen include: Greetings From Astbury Park, 1973; The Wild, The Willing and The E-Street Shuffle, 1973; Born To Run, 1975; Darkness On The Edge of Town, 1978; The River, 1980; Born In The USA, 1984; Tunnel of Love, 1987; Live In New York City, 2001; Recent session work: Bad and Blue, Jimmy Dillon, 2000; Ringo Starr's All Starr Band, 2001. *Honours:* Bay Area Music Awards: Outstanding Reed Player, 6 times winner. *Membership:* Musicians' Union. *Leisure interests:* Fishing; Golf. *Current Management:* Alan Niven.

CLEVELAND Ashley Alexander; b. 2 Feb. 1957, Knoxville, Tennessee, USA. Vocalist; Musician (guitar); Songwriter. m. Kenny Greenberg, 27 April 1991, 1 s., 2 d. *Education:* University of Tennessee, Knoxville, 2 years. *Musical Education:* Self-taught. *Career:* Featured on US television series The Road; Performed on televised Dove Awards, 1993; Member of John Hiatt's band, 1990–; Performed on Saturday Night Live, David Letterman and Arsenio Hall shows; Appearances in clubs, theatres and festivals. *Recordings:* Albums: Big Town, 1991; Bus Named Desire, 1993; Lesson of Love, 1995. *Honour:* Nashville Area Music Award, Best Contemporary Christian Album, 1995; Grammy Award, Best Contemporary Rock Album, Lesson of Love, 1996. *Memberships:* NARAS; GMA; CMA. *Leisure interests:* Children; Gardening; Reading; Cooking. *Current Management:* Blanton and Harrell Entertainment. *Address:* 2910 Poston Ave, Nashville, TN 37203, USA.

CLIFF Jimmy (James Chambers); b. 1948, Jamaica. Reggae Singer; Composer. 1 s. *Career:* Singer, songwriter, 1960s–; Backing vocalist, London, 1963; Tours world-wide, especially US, Europe, South America, Africa; Concerts include: Montreux Jazz Festival, 1980; World Music Festival, Jamaica, 1982; Rock In Rio II, Brazil, 1991; Worlds Beat Reggae Festival, Portand, USA, 1992; Actor, films: The Harder They Come (also on film soundtrack), 1972; Bongo Man, 1980; Club Paradise (also on film soundtrack), 1986; Formed own record label, Cliff Records, 1989; Own production company, Cliff Sounds and Films, 1990. *Compositions include:* You Can Get It If You Really Want, Desmond Dekker; Let Your Yeah Be Yeah, The Pioneers; Trapped, Bruce Springsteen, for USA For Africa album. *Recordings:* Singles include: Dearest Beverley, 1962; Hurricane Hattie, 1962; Waterfall, 1968; Wonderful World Beautiful People, 1969; Many Rivers To Cross, 1969; Vietnam, 1969; Wild World, 1970; I Can See Clearly Now (featured on film soundtrack Cool Runnings), 1993; Higher and Higher, 1994; Hakuna Matata, 1995; Breakout, 1997; Albums: Hard Road, 1967; Jimmy Cliff, 1969; Can't Get Enough, 1969; Wonderful World, 1970; Another Cycle, 1971; The Harder They Come, 1972; Struggling Man, 1974; Follow My Mind, 1975; Give Thanx, 1978; I Am The Living, 1980; Give The People What They Want, 1981; Special, 1982; The Power and The Glory, 1983; Cliff Hanger, 1985; Hanging Fire, 1988; Images, 1990; Breakout, 1992; 100% Pure Reggae, 1997; Shout for Freedom, 1999; Humanitarian, 1999; Live and In The Studio, 2000; Wanted (compilation), 2000; Best of Jimmy Cliff, 2001; Contributor, Sun City, Artists Against Apartheid, 1985. *Honour:* Grammy Award, Best Reggae Recording, 1985; Grammy Nomination, Best Reggae Recording, 1984. *Address:* c/o DAS Communications, 83 Riverside Dr., New York, NY 10024, USA.

CLIFFORD (Brisley) Grieg; b. 31 Aug. 1971, Gillingham, Kent, England. Musician (drums). *Education:* Diploma, Photography. *Career:* Drummer with Hit 'n' Run, hard rock band, 1989–94; Tours Britain, Europe; Sessions, airplay, most countries; College radio, USA; Album, 1992; Member, If 6 Was 9 (3 piece rock band), first EP released 1995; Many sessions, studio and live work, for many Rock/Funk bands, notably Suicide Ride; Sessions by singer Mark Lehman, include 2 videos for MTV and National TV; Live sessions for Suicide Ride offshoot band: Creed. *Recordings:* with Hit 'n' Run: Hit 'n' Run, 1992; Suicide Ride session recordings, 1994; with If 6 Was 9: Out of the Fire; Silent Nights; Your Heart Somebody, 1995; Grieg Clifford: Funky Rock Drum Loops. *Membership:* Musicians' Union. *Leisure interests:* Photography; Art. *Current Management:* Groovytime Promotions. *Address:* 23 Harsfold Rd, Rustington, West Sussex BN16 2QE, England.

CLIFTON Bill (William August Marburg); b. 5 April 1931, Riderwood, Maryland, USA. Performing Artist; Singer; Musician (guitar, autoharp). m. Trijntje B Labrie, 31 Oct. 1978, 4 s., 6 d. *Education:* Graduate degree, Business Administration, University of Virginia. *Career:* Extensive work in radio late 1940s to mid 1950s; Recordings 1953–; Organized first all-bluegrass festival, Luray, Virginia, July 4 1961; Founding director, Newport Folk Festival; Compere, weekly BBC Show, Cellar Full of Folk; First bluegrass performer to earn living entirely in Europe, Asia, Africa, Australia, New Zealand. *Compositions:* Little White-Washed Chimney; Mary Dear; Where The Rainbow Finds Its End; Happy Days (instrumental); Recent albums include: Bill Clifton: The Early Years; Autoharp Centennial Celebration; Where The Rainbow Finds Its End; River of Memories. *Publications:* Bill Clifton's 150 Old-time Folk and Gospel Songs; Video: Grassroots to Bluegrass, recorded in Nashville, 1999. *Honours:* Award of Merit, International Bluegrass Music Asscn, 1992; Preservation Hall of Greats, SPBGMA, 1993. *Memberships:* International Bluegrass Music Asscn; Birthplace of Country Music Alliance. *Leisure interests:* Coin collector (British and American); Camping; Hiking; Cycling. *Address:* PO Box 69, Mendota, VA 24270, USA.

CLINTON George; b. 22 July 1940, Kannapolis, North Carolina, USA. Singer; Bandleader. 1 s. *Career:* Founder, leader, The Parliaments, 1950s–; Changed name to Funkadelic, 1969; Parliament/Funkadelic, 1970–; Solo artiste, 1982–; Owner, Bridgeport Music; Regular world-wide concerts and tours; Featured in Graffiti Bridge, Prince, 1990. *Recordings:* Albums: Funkadelic, 1969; Osmium, 1970; America Eats Its Young, 1972; Cosmic Stop, 1973; Standing On The Verge of Getting It On, 1974; Chocolate City, 1975; Mothership Connection, 1976; The Clones of Dr Funkenstein, 1976; Parliament Live/P Funk Earth Tour, 1977; Funkentelechy v. The Placebo, 1977; One Nation Under A Groove, 1978; Motor Booty Affair, 1978; Brides of Funkenstein, 1978; Underjam, 1979; Gloryhallastoopid (Pin The Tale On The Funky), 1979; The Electric Spanking of War Babies, 1981; Computer Games, 1982; You Shouldn't Nuf Bit, Fish!, 1984; Some of My Best Friends Are Jokes, 1985; R & B Skeletons In The Closet, 1986; The Cinderella Theory, 1989; Hey Man... Smell My Finger, 1993; Dope Dogs, 1994; The Music of Red Shoe Diaries, 1995; A Fifth of Funk, 1995; Mortal Kombat (film soundtrack), 1996; TAPOAFOM, 1996; Testing Positive, 1996; Live and Kickin', 1997; Funkadelic – Funk Gets Stronger, 2000; Singles include: One Nation Under A Groove; (Not Just) Knee Deep; Atomic Dog; Walk The Dinosaur, used in film soundtrack Super Mario Brothers. *Address:* c/o Ciccel Enterprises, Suite 102, 1830 S Robertson Blvd, Los Angeles, CA 90035, USA.

CLIVILLES Robert; b. 1964, New York, USA. DJ; Prod. *Education:* Business management at college. *Career:* DJ, member of production team, C and C Music Factory (with the late David Cole); Club DJ, performances world-wide; Collaborations: Mariah Carey, Aretha Franklin, Ultra Nate. *Recordings:* Numerous C and C recordings including: Gonna Make You Sweat (Everybody Dance Now) (No. 1, USA), 1991; Things That Make You Go Hmmm..., 1991; Pride In The Name of Love, 1992; A Deeper Love, 1992; Do You Wanna Get Funky, 1994.

CLOONEY Rosemary; b. 23 May 1928, Maysville, Kentucky, USA. Singer. *Career:* Early appearances with sister Betty; Joined saxophonist Tony Pastor's band, 1945; Solo recording artiste, 1946–; Films include: The Stars Are Singing, 1953; Here Come The Girls, 1954; Red Garters, 1954;

Deep In My Heart, 1954; White Christmas, 1954; Played at Carnegie Hall, 1991. *Recordings:* Numerous albums include: Deep In My Heart (film soundtrack), 1954; Hollywood's Best, 1955; Blue Rose, 1956; Clooney Times, 1957; Ring A Round Rosie, with the Hi-Lo's, 1957; Swing Around Rosie, 1958; Fancy Meeting You Here, with Bing Crosby, 1958; The Ferrers At Home, 1958; Hymns From The Heart, 1959; Rosemary Clooney Swings Softly, 1960; A Touch of Tabasco, 1960; Clap Hands, Here Comes Rosie, 1960; Rosie Solves The Swingin' Riddle, 1961; Country Hits From The Past, 1963; Love, 1963; Thanks For Nothing, 1964; That Travelin' Two Beat, 1965; Look My Way, 1976; Nice To Be Around, 1977; Here's To My Lady, 1979; Rosemary Clooney Sings Harold Arlen, 1983; My Buddy, 1983; Rosemary Clooney Sings The Lyrics of Johnny Mercer, 1987; Rosemary Clooney Sings The Music of Jimmy Van Heusen, 1987; Show Tunes, 1989; Everything's Coming Up Rosie, 1989; Girl Singer, 1992; Do You Miss New York?, 1992; Still on the Road, 1993; Dedicated to Nelson, 1995; Seventieth Birthday Celebration, 1998; Brazil, 2000; Sentimental Journey, 2001; A Very Special Christmas, 2001; Let It Snow, 2001; Various compilations; Singles include: You're Just In Love; Beautiful Brown Eyes; Come On – My House; Tenderly; Half As Much (No. 1, UK); Botcha Me; Too Old To Cut The Mustard (with Marlene Dietrich); The Night Before Christmas Song, with Gene Autry; Hey There (No. 1, UK); This Ole House (No. 1, UK), 1954; Mambo Italiano (No. 1, UK), 1955; Mangos. *Publication:* This For Remembrance. *Address:* c/o Production Central, 3500 W Olive, Suite 1420, Burbank, CA 91505, USA.

CLOUT Tony; b. 25 Feb. 1945, Danbury Palace, Chelmsford, England. Arranger; Copyist; Composer; Musician (bass guitar, guitar). m. Julia Anne Lamprell, 15 Aug. 1977, 4 s., 2 d. *Musical Education:* Self-taught. *Career:* Guitar with Paul Raven (Gary Glitter), 1960; with The Transatlantics, 1965–69; Recorded 6 singles; Television appearances include: 5 o'Clock Club; Thank Your Lucky Stars; BBC Light Programme, Easy Beat; Saturday Club; Bank Holiday Specials with The Beatles; with The Ross Mitchell Band, 1972; with The Ray McVay Band, 1975–83; Television, radio, records, touring, society functions include Prince Charles' 30th Birthday at Buckingham Palace; Musical Director, Circus Tavern cabaret club, Essex, 1983–93; British tour with Michael Barrymore, Stutz Bear Cats, Roly Polys, 1985; Arranger, copyist, West End Shows: Blood Brothers; Only The Lonely; Good Rockin' Tonite; Provincial Shows: Harry's Web; Thank You For The Music; Shows for BBC Radio 2, artists including: Charles Augins; Warren Mitchell; Chas 'n' Dave; Marti Caine; Bobby Crush; John Inman; Marty Webb and Elaine Paige tours. *Compositions:* La Concordia; Paso Doble De Cadiz; Spring's the Time, 1996. *Recordings:* Singles: Many Things From Your Window; Don't Fight It; Run For Your Life; Albums: Ray McVay dance albums; Pan Pipe Moods; Chas 'n' Dave's Street Party albums. *Membership:* British Music Writer's Council; PaMRA. *Leisure interests:* Steam locomotives; 18th Century architecture; Art; Gardens. *Address:* 36 Shirley Gardens, Hornchurch, Essex RM12 4NH, England.

CLOVER Val, (Valerie Ann Cope); b. 17 Sept. 1952, Liverpool, England. Singer; Songwriter; Model; Actress. *Musical Education:* Self-taught. *Career:* Joined Girl Trio, The Cherolees, 1968; Lead Singer, The Wheels of Fortune, 1969–70; Joined recording band, Justine, 1970; Concerts include: Earls Court Olympia and Buxton Festival; Appearances on Disco 2 (BBC TV) and Sounds of the Seventies (BBC Radio); Solo career, 1976; Sessions; Voice-overs and numerous TV, film and pop videos as Actress; Rock/Pop Reviewer for Disability Times. *Compositions:* Co-Writer, single, Don't Make My White Christmas Blue, by Iris Williams, 1982; Co-Writer, Oikotie Sydameen, Scandinavian Triple Platinum Album, Tahtikaaren Taa, by Aikakone, 1995; English Lyricist, Children of the Sea, Estonian entry in Eurovision Song Contest, 1998. *Recordings:* Band Member, Justine, album, 1970; Band Member, Justine, She Brings The Morning With Her, single, 1970. *Memberships:* PRS; MCPS; N(c)B; BASCA; Equity. *Leisure interests:* Music; Tennis; Gardening. *Current Management:* Mouse Records. *Address:* 28 Breamore Rd, Seven Kings, Essex IG3 9NB, England.

COATES Bruce Brian Gilbert; b. 3 July 1972, Birmingham, England. Musician (saxophone – alto tenor, soprano, melody); Writer; Lecturer. *Education:* North East Worcestershire College, Bromsgrove. *Musical Education:* BA Hons, Performing Arts (Music); MA, De Montfort University, 1998. *Career:* Music for Island, dance piece by Jo Walker (with Zo Sosinka and Craig Vear), Phoenix Theatre, Leicester, 1992; Contributed improvisations and ambient sound environment for Modal Spaces – A Sound/Architecture Project, (large-scale musical performance by Andrew Hugill), Queens Building, Leicester, 1994; Performance of Burdocks by Christian Wolff (with Zo Sosinka, Christian Wolff, Dave Smith), 25th Anniversary Concert of the Scratch Orchestra, ICA, 1994; Formed Lusus Naturae, trio with Jamie Smith and Zo Sosinka, 1996. *Composition:* Solos and Accompaniments, with Lusus Naturae, for improvisers, commission, 1996. *Recordings:* Sound Score/Tape Collage for She Ain't Jumping Off That Bridge (touring physical theatre piece), Conscious Opera Association, premiered Birmingham Dance Centre, 1994; Lusus Naturae-View, 1999. *Publications:* Lol Coxhill, Transcending Boundaries, in Rubberneck, 1995; Liner Notes, Dunmall/Sanders/Adams,

Ghostly Thoughts, 1997. Contributions to: Rubberneck; Jazz on CD; Avant, 1995-. *Address:* The Octagon, 16 Beeches Farm Dr., Northfield, Birmingham B31 4SD, England.

COATES Donald Denison; b. 23 March 1935, Orange, New Jersey, USA. Jazz Musician (piano); Composer. m. (1) Jacqueline Dorsey, divorced, (2) Dorothy Hering, 26 June 1988, 1 d. *Education:* Williams College, 1953–57. *Career:* Freelance jazz pianist, 1960–82; Played for: Jack Teagarden; Wild Bill Davison; Newport Jazz Festival All-Stars; Eddie Condon; Roy Eldridge; Solo pianist at: Windows On The World, Waldorf Astoria; Musician with vocalists including Maxine Sullivan, 1980–; Music Advisor, Entertainment Development Network, 1987. *Compositions:* Numerous songs, music for radio and television commercials. *Publications:* Contributor, articles of jazz instruction and history. *Membership:* AFofM. *Address:* 442 W 57th St, New York, NY 10019, USA.

COBBI Daniel; b. 3 May 1953, Paris, France. Musician (piano); Jazz Composer. 1 d. *Education:* Architecture. *Musical Education:* Boulogne Conservatory, classical piano studies. *Career:* Tours, Italy; Spain; Belgium; Switzerland; Television concert, 1988; Many concerts, Radio France; France Musique; France Culture; Free radio's special solo piano; Played in USA, 1978; Many festivals, Europe. *Recordings:* Music For The Blue Bar, 1980; Eighteen Surprises For Christmas, 1981; Ayanamsa, 1982; Dilation, 1985; For Camille, 1995. *Honour:* First Command in France of the Culture Ministère, 1982. *Leisure interests:* Astronomy; Spirituality. *Address:* 27 Ave d'Italie, 75013 Paris, France.

COBHAM Bill (William Emmanuel) Jr; b. 16 May 1944, Panama. Musician (drums). m. Marcia Ann McCarthy, 1 s., 1 d. *Musical Education:* High School of Music and Arts, New York, 1962. *Career:* Musician with: Billy Taylor's New York Jazz Sextet, 1967; Dreams, with Michael and Randy Brecker, 1969; Miles Davis, 1971; John McLaughlin's Mahavishnu Orchestra, 1972; Founder member, Spectrum, 1975–; Prolific recording artist and regular guest musician; Taught at numerous drum clinics; Own television series, Billy Cobham's World of Rhythm. *Recordings:* Albums: Spectrum, 1973; Total Eclipse, 1974; Crosswinds, 1974; Shabazz, 1975; A Funky Thide of Sings, 1975; Life and Times, 1976; Live In Europe, 1976; Magic, 1977; Inner Conflicts, 1978; Simplicity of Expression, 1978; BC, 1979; The Best Of, 1980; Flight Time, 1982; Observatory, 1982; Smokin', 1983; Warning, 1985; Powerplay, 1986; Picture This, 1987; Best Of, 1986; Stratus, 1988; Billy's Best Hits, 1988; By Design, 1992; Rudiments – The Billy Cobham Anthology, 2001; with Horace Silver: Serenade To A Soul Sister; with Miles Davis: Directions; Big Fun; Live Evil; Tribute To Jack Johnson; Circle In The Round; On The Cover; with John McLaughlin and Mahavishnu Orchestra: My Goals Beyond; The Inner Mounting Flame; Birds of Fire; Love Devotion and Surrender; Between Nothingness and Surrender; Electric Guitarist; with Ron Carter: Blues Farm; All Blues; Spanish Blue; Yellow and Green; Also featured on albums by: George Benson; Stanley Clarke; McCoy Tyner; Grover Washington; Larry Coryell; Milt Jackson. *Current Management:* The Cameron Organization, 2001 W Magnolia Blvd, Burbank, CA 91506, USA.

COBRIN Spencer James; b. 31 Jan. 1969, Paddington, London, England. Musician (drums, piano). *Musical Education:* Private lessons, trumpet, drums, piano. *Career:* Played London club circuit, 1986–91; International tours as drummer with Morrissey, 1991–; Television performances include: Tonight Show with Johnny Carson; Saturday Night Live; MTV; Tonight Show with Jay Leno; Later With Jools Holland. *Recordings:* Albums: with Morrissey: Your Arsenal, 1992; Southpaw Grammar, 1995; Maladjusted, 1997; Videos: Live In Dallas; Malady Lingers On (compilation). *Publications:* Featured in: Morrissey Shot, by Linder Sterling. *Membership:* Musicians' Union. *Leisure interests:* Piano; Composition.

COCCIANTE Richard (Riccardo); b. Saigon, Viet Nam. Composer; Singer; Musician (piano); Arranger. m. Catherine Boutet, 1 s. *Musical Education:* Self-educated. *Career:* Composer, solo artist, 1972–; World-wide television, radio appearances; Tour venues include: Gran Teatro La Fenice, Venice, 1988; Sporting Club, Monaco, 1988, 1990, 1995; Teatro dell'opera Caracalla, Rome, 1991; Vina del Mar Festival, Chile, 1994; Olympia, Paris, 1994, 1996; Zenith, Paris, 1994; Taj Mahal, Atlantic City, 1995; Teatro Sistina, Rome, 1988, 1993, 1995, 1997; Théâtre St Denis, Montréal, 1994, 1996; Stadsschouwberg, Amsterdam, 1995; Vienna Rathaus, 1997; Collaborated with producers including: Paul Buckmaster; Humberto Gatica, Ennio Morricone, James Newton-Howard; Vangelis; Participated in album World War II, interpreting Michelle with London Symphony Orchestra; soundtrack of Patrice Leconte's film, Tandem, France, 1987; Album, Sand et les Romantiques, interpreting the role of Chopin; Soundtrack of Franco Zeffirelli's film, Storia di una capinera (Sparrow), international release, 1994; soundtrack of Walt Disney's film, Toy Story, Italy, 1996; concert, Christmas In Vienna, with Placido Domingo, Sarah Brightman and Helmut Lotti, 1997; soundtrack of Claude Berri's film, Astérix and Obélix contre César, Italy, 1999; 2000 (Hymne pour la ville de Lyon commissioned by Raymonde Barre, Mayor of Lyon to celebrate the new millenium. *Compositions:* Notre Dame de Paris, the musical, 1998–99;

Solo albums: 16 Italian including: Mu, 1972, Poesia, 1973; Anima, 1974; L'alba, 1975; Concerto per Margherita, 1976; Riccardo Cicciante, A Mano A Mano, 1978; …E Io Canto, 1979; Cervo a Primavera, 1981; Cocciante, (Celeste Nostalgia) 1982; Sincerità, 1983; Il Mare dei Papaveri, 1985; La Grande Avventura, 1987; Se Stiamo Insieme, 1991; Eventi e Mutamenti, 1993; Un Uomo Felice, 1994; Innamorato, 1997; 10 French including: Atlanti, 1973; Quand un Amour, 1974; Concerto pour Marguerite, 1978; Je Chante, 1979; Au Clair de tes Silences, 1980; Vieille, 1982; Sincérité, 1983; L'Homme qui vole, 1986; Empreinte, 1993; L'Instant Présent, 1995; 10 Spanish; 3 English; Some albums common to all four languages. *Recordings:* International hits: Bella Senz' Anima (Italy)/Bella Sin Alma (Spain, Spanish South America), 1973; Quand un Amour (France, Belgium, Canada), 1974; Margherita (Italy)/Marguerite (France, Belgium, Canada)/ Margarita (Spain, Spanish South America), 1976–78; Coup de Soleil (France, Belgium), 1980; Cervo a Primavera (Italy)/Yo Renascere (Spain, Spanish South America), 1980; Sincéritié (France)/Sincerità (Italy, Holland)/Sinceridad (Spain, Spanish South America)/Sincerity (USA), 1983; Questione di Feeling – duet with Mina (Italy)/Question de Feeling – duet with Fabienne Thiebeault (France, Belgium, Canada)/Cuestion de Feeling – duet with Melissa (Spain, Spanish South America), 1985–86; Se Stiamo Insieme (Italy, Belgium, Holland, Brazil), 1991; Pour Elle (France)/ Per Lei (Italy, Brazil)/I'd Fly (Italy, France, Belgium, Holland)/Por Ella (Spanish South America)/Voorbij (Holland), 1993–95; Il ricordo di un istante (Italy, France, Belgium, Canada, Holland); Belle, Le Temps des Cathédrales, Vivre – excerpts from musical Notre Dame de Paris (France, Belgium, Canada), 1998–99. *Honours:* Rose d'Or Award (Greece), 1981; Rino Gaetana Award (Italy), 1982; Winner, Sanremo Festival (Italy), 1991; Telegatto (Italy), 1991; Notre Dame de Paris – the musical: Felix 98 Award (Canada) for Album of the Year, 1998; Medaille de la Ville de Paris (France), 1998; Victoire de la Musique Award (France) for Song of the Year, 1999; Victoire de la Musique Award (France) for Show of the Year, 1999; Grande ufficiale della Repubblica Italiana (Italy), 1999; World Music Award (Monaco) for Best-selling French Artists/Group, 1999; Rolf Marbot Award (France) for Song of the Year, 1999; Felix 1999 Award (Canada) for Song of the Year, Felix 99 Award (Canada for Show of the Year, 1999; Felix 99 Award (Canada) for Best-selling Album, 1999; Felix 99 Award (Canada) for Album of the Year, 1999. *Leisure interest:* Music. *Current Management:* Boventoon BV. *Address:* Blue Toon/Boventoon B.V. Information Office, 4 rue Chauveau Lagarde, 75008 Paris, France.

COCHRAN Hank; b. 2 Aug. 1935, Isola, Mississippi, USA. Songwriter. m. (1) Shirley Kay Foster, 24 July 1954, divorced, 3 s.; (2) Marilyn Jean Seely, 15 June 1969, divorced, 1981; (3) Susan Booth Calder, 18 Aug. 1982, 1 step-d. *Career:* Co-owner, song plugger, writer, Pamper Music Inc, 1950–67; Writer, professional consultant, Tree International, 1967–89; Co-owner, writer, professional consultant, Co-Heart Music Group, 1989-. *Compositions include:* A Little Bitty Tear, 1961; He's Got You, 1962; Funny Way of Laughing, 1962; Tears Break Out On Me, 1962; Make The World Go Away, 1963; You Comb Her Hair, 1963; Make The World Go Away, 1963; Don't Touch Me, 1966; It's Not Love But It's Not Bad, 1973; Can I Sleep In Your Arms, 1973; Why Can't He Be You, 1978; Make the World Go Away (sung by Willie Nelson in the film Honeysuckle Rose, 1979); That's All That Matters To Me, 1980; I Fall To Pieces, 1982; What Would Your Memories Do, 1984; The Chair, 1985; Ocean Front Property, 1988; Set 'Em Up Joe, 1989; Who You Gonna Blame It On This Time, 1989; Don't You Ever Get Tired of Hurting Me, 1989; Right In The Wrong Direction, 1990; Is It Raining At Your House, 1991; I Want To Go With You. *Honours:* Country Music Asscn Walkway of Stars, 1967; Nashville Songwriters Asscn Hall of Fame, 1974; Betty Clooney Foundation, Singer's Salute to Country Songwriter Award, 1993.

COCKBURN Bruce; b. 1945, Canada. Singer; Songwriter. 1 d. *Career:* Singer, songwriter, reflecting Christian beliefs and environmental issues. *Recordings:* Albums include: Bruce Cockburn, 1970; High Winds White Sky, 1971; Sunwheel Dance, 1972; Night Vision, 1973; Hand Dancing, 1974; Salt, Sun and Time, 1974; Joy Will Find A Way, 1975; Further Adventures, 1976; In The Falling Dark, 1976; Circles In The Stream, 1977; Dancing In The Dragon's Jaws, 1979; Humans, 1980; Resume, 1981; Inner City Front, 1981; Stealing Fire, 1984; World of Wonders, 1984; Trouble With Nowhere, 1985; Rumours of Glory, 1986; Waiting For A Miracle, 1987; Big Circumstance, 1989; Live, 1990; Nothing But A Burning Light, 1991; Christmas, 1993; Dart to the Heart, 1994; Charity of Night, 1997; Breakfast In New Orleans, 1999; Anything Anytime Anywhere, 2002. *Current Management:* Finkelstein Management Co, 260 Richmond St W, Suite 501, Toronto, ON M5V 1W5, Canada.

COCKER Jarvis Branson; b. Sept. 1962, Sheffield, South Yorkshire, England. Singer; Songwriter. *Education:* BA, Film studies, St Martin's College of Art, London, 1988–91. *Career:* Lead singer, Pulp, 1980–; Major concerts include: Headline act, Glastonbury Festival, 1995; Heineken Festival, Leeds, 1995; Television includes: Later With… Britpop Now, BBC2, 1995 Guest presenter, Top of The Pops, 1995. *Recordings:* Albums: It, 1983; Freaks, 1986; Separations, 1989 (released 1992); His 'N' Hers, 1994; Different Class (No. 1, UK) 1995; This Is Hardcore (No. 1, UK), 1998;

We Love Life, 2001; Singles: Little Girl (With Blue Eyes), 1985; Dogs Are Everywhere (EP), 1986; My Legendary Girlfriend, 1990; Countdown, 1991; OU, 1992; Babies, 1992; Razzmatazz, 1993; Lipgloss, 1993; Do You Remember The First Time?, 1994; The Sisters (EP), 1994; Sorted For E's and Whizz/Misshapes (No. 2, UK), 1995; Disco 2000, 1995; Common People (No. 2, UK), 1995; Something Changed, 1996; Help the Aged, 1997; This Is Hardcore, 1998; Party Hard, 1998; A Little Soul, 1998; The Trees/Sunrise, 2001; Other collaborations: Barry Adamson, All Seeing I. *Honours:* BRIT Award Nomination, Best Group, 1996. *Current Management:* Rough Trade Management, 66 Golborne Rd, London W10 5PF, England.

COCKER Joe; b. 20 May 1944, Sheffield, South Yorkshire, England. Singer; Songwriter. *Career:* Singer, Northern club circuit with group The Grease Band, 1965–69; Solo artiste, 1968–; Regular world-wide tours; Major concert appearances include: National Jazz and Blues Festival, 1968; Denver Pop Festival, 1969; Newport '69 Festival, 1969; Woodstock Festival (filmed), 1969; Isle of Wight Festival, 1969; Co-headliner with Beach Boys, Crystal Palace Garden Party, 1972; Prince's Trust Rock Gala, 1988; Nelson Mandela's 70th Birthday Tribute, Wembley Stadium, 1988; Rock In Rio II Festival, 1991; Guitar Legends, Seville, Spain, 1991; Montreux Jazz Festival, filmed for MTV's Unplugged series, 1992; Blues Music Festival, with B. B. King, 1992; Numerous television and radio broadcasts world-wide. *Recordings:* Hit singles include: With A Little Help From My Friends (No. 1, UK), 1968; Delta Lady, 1969; The Letter, 1970; Cry Me A River, 1970; You Are So Beautiful, 1975; Unchain My Heart, 1987; When The Night Comes, 1990; Night Calls, 1993; Simple Things, 1994; Could You Be Loved, 1998; with Jennifer Warnes: Up Where We Belong (No. 1, USA), theme to film An Officer and A Gentleman, 1982; Contributions to film soundtracks include: Edge of a Dream, for film Teachers, 1984; You Can Leave Your Hat On, for film 9 1/2 Weeks, 1986; Love Lives On, for film Bigfoot and The Hendersons, 1987; (All I Know) Feels Like Forever, for film The Cutting Edge, 1992; Trust In Me, duet with Sass Jordan, for film The Bodyguard, 1992; Albums include: With A Little Help From My Friends, 1969; Joe Cocker, 1970; Mad Dogs and Englishmen, 1970; Cocker Happy, 1971; Something To Say, 1972; I Can Stand A Little Rain, 1974; Jamaica Say You Will, 1975; Live In Los Angeles, 1976; Stingray, 1976; Joe Cocker's Greatest Hits, 1977; Luxury You Can Afford, 1978; Sheffield Steel, 1982; Civilized Man, 1984; Cocker, 1986; Unchain My Heart, 1987; Nightriding, 1988; One Night of Sin, 1989; Joe Cocker Live, 1990; Night Calls, 1992; The Legend – The Essential Collection, 1992; Have A Little Faith, 1994; Organic, 1996; Across from Midnight, 1997; No Ordinary World, 1999; Contributor, Two Rooms (tribute album to Elton John and Bernie Taupin), 1991. *Honours:* Grammy, Best Pop Vocal Performance, Up Where We Belong, 1983; Academy Award, Best Film Song, Up Where We Belong, 1983; Grammy Nomination, One Night of Sin, 1989. *Current Management:* Roger Davies Management, 15030 Ventura Blvd #772, Sherman Oaks, CA 91403, USA.

CODLING Neil John; b. 5 Dec. 1973, Stratford-on-Avon, England. Musician (Keyboards). *Career:* Joined Suede, 1995; Numerous tours and TV appearances; Festival dates in Britain and Europe. *Recordings:* Singles: Trash, 1996; Filmstar, 1996; Lazy, 1996; Beautiful Ones, 1996; Electricity, 1999; She's In Fashion, 1999; Everything Will Flow, 1999; Albums: Coming Up (No. 1, UK), 1996; Sci-Fi Lullabies, 1997; Head Music, 1999.

COE Tony (Anthony George); b. 29 Nov. 1934, Musician (clarinet, alto and tenor saxophone); Composer. *Career:* Jazz saxophonist and clarinettist; Worked with many ensembles led by musicians including: Joe Daniels; Humphrey Lyttelton; John Dankworth; Clarke-Boland Big Band; John Picard; Derek Bailey; Mike Gibbs; Stan Getz; Dizzy Gilespie; Bob Brookmeyer; Stan Tracey; Leader of many groups including: Axel and Coe; Wheeler and Co (with Kenny Wheeler); Toured Europe with United Jazz and Rock Ensemble; Recorded with Bob Moses and Norma Winstone; Collaborated with Henry Mancini as the soloist on early Pink Panther film soundtracks, 1970s; Other appearances on soundtracks: Superman II; Victor Victoria; Performed under Pierre Boulez and worked with Matrix (small ensemble formed by clarinettist Alan Hacker); Appearances on pop and rock albums by artists including: CCS; Caravan; Spencer Davis Group; Georgie Fame; The Hollies; Joe Jackson. *Compositions:* Film scores: Mer De Chine; Camomile; Peau de Pêche; Works recorded by: Matrix; Danish Radio Big Band; Metropole Orchestra; Skymasters; Wrote Zeitgeist, an orchestral work fusing jazz and rock elements with techniques from European Art Music, 1975. *Recordings:* Albums include: Swingin' Til The Girls Come Home, 1962; Tony Coe With The Brian Lemon Trio, 1971; Zeitgeist, 1976; Nutty On Willisau (with Tony Oxley), 1983; Le Chat Se Retourne, 1984; Canterbury Song, 1989; Captain Coe's Famous Racearound, 1996. *Honours:* Danish Jazzpar Prize, Hon. D Mus, 1995; BT British Jazz Award, Clarinet, 1997.

COFFEY Cath(erine Muthomi); b. 1965, Kenya. Vocalist. *Career:* Member, Stereo MCs; Numerous gigs and TV appearances. *Recordings:* Singles: Elevate My Mind, 1990; Lost In Music, 1991; Connected, 1992; Step It Up, 1993; Ground Level, 1993; Creation, 1993; Deep Down and Dirty, 2001; We Belong In This World Together, 2001; Albums: 33–45–78,

1989; Supernatural, 1990; Connected, 1992; Deep Down and Dirty, 2001; Solo Single: Wild World, 1997; Tell Me, 1997; Solo Album: Mind The Gap, 1997; Also appeared on: Tricky, Nearly God, 1996. *Honours:* Brit Awards: Best British Album; Best British Group, 1993.

COGHILL Jon; b. 26 Aug. 1971. Musician (drums). *Education:* University of Queensland, Botany student. *Career:* Joined Brisbane-based rock group Powderfinger, 1992; Steadily built reputation on many Australian tours/ festival appearances; International breakthrough with Odyssey Number Five album; Constant world-wide touring throughout 2000–01 ending with New Suburban Fables 2001 Australian shows. *Recordings:* Albums: Parables For Wooden Ears, 1994; Double Allergic, 1996; Internationalist, 1998; Odyssey Number Five, 2000; Singles: Powderfinger Blue (EP), Transfusion (EP), 1993; Tail, Grave Concern, 1994; Save Your Skin, Mr Kneebone (EP), 1995; Pick You Up, D.A.F., Living Type, 1996; Take Me In, 1997; The Day You Come, Don't Wanna Be Left Out/Good-Day Ray, 1998; Already Gone, Passenger, 1999; My Happiness, 2000; Like A Dog, The Metre, 2001. *Honours:* ARIA Awards: Album of The Year; Song of The Year; Best Rock Album; Best Cover Artwork, 1999; six times platinum fourth album on Australian chart for 67 weeks by end of 2001; Only home-grown act ever to play more than 3 consecutive nights at Festival Hall, Australia. *Address:* c/o Republic Records, Australia. *Internet:* www.powderfinger.com.

COHEN Leonard; b. 21 Sept. 1934, Montréal, Québec, Canada. Singer; Songwriter. *Education:* McGill University. *Career:* Founder, Country and Western group, The Buckskin Boys, 1951; Novelist; Poet; Solo singer; Subject of BBC documentary. *Compositions include:* Suzanne; Priests (both recorded by Judy Collins); Sisters of Mercy; Hey, That's No Way To Say Goodbye; Story of Isaac; Bird On A Wire. *Recordings:* Albums: The Songs of Leonard Cohen, 1968; Songs From A Room, 1969; Songs of Love and Hate, 1971; Live Songs, 1973; New Skin For The Old Ceremony, 1974; Greatest Hits, 1975; The Best of Leonard Cohen, 1976; Death of a Ladies Man, 1977; Recent Songs, 1979; Various Positions, 1985; I'm Your Man, 1988; The Future, 1992; More Best Of, 1997; Live Songs, 1998; Ten New Songs, 2001. *Publications:* Poetry: Let Us Compare Mythologies; Novels: The Favourite Game, 1963; Beautiful Losers, 1966. *Honours include:* McGill Literary Award for Let Us Compare Mythologies. *Current Management:* Stranger Music. *Address:* Suite 91, 419 N Larchmont Blvd, Los Angeles, CA 90004, USA.

COKE Charles M; b. 15 March 1943, San Jose, California, USA. Record Prod. 2 s., 1 d. *Career:* Toured USA for 20 years; Local television and radio shows. *Recordings:* Producer for: Tiggi Clay; Fizzy Quick; Derrick Hughes; Workforce; II Big; Bedroom Cowboys; John Payne; CP Salt; NVS; Baby Fat with Big Mitch. *Membership:* Musicians' Union (local, San Francisco). *Leisure interest:* Music. *Current Management:* Up Front Management. *Address:* 1906 Seward Dr., Pittsburg, CA 94565, USA.

COLBERT Laurence John; b. 27 June 1970, Kingston, Surrey, England. Musician (drums). *Musical Education:* Self-taught. *Career:* Member: Ride 1988–96; Animal House, 1999–; Concerts include: Royal Albert Hall; Reading Festival; Glastonbury; Television includes: The Word; Top of The Pops; BBC Radio 1 sessions: John Peel; Mark Goodier. *Recordings:* Albums: with Ride: Nowhere, 1990; Going Blank Again, 1992; Carnival of Light, 1994; Live Light, 1995; Tarantula, 1996; with Animal House: The Animal House EP, 1999; Ready To Receive, 2000. *Honours:* Silver discs: Nowhere, 1990; Going Blank Again, 1992. *Membership:* PRS. *Leisure interest:* Sailing. *Current Management:* Dave Newton. *Address:* PO Box 479, Headington, Oxford OX3 7QW, England.

COLBURN Richard; b. 25 July 1970. Musician (drums, percussion). *Career:* Member: Belle and Sebastian, 1996–; Collaborations: Snow Patrol; Hefner; Curated Bowlie Weekend Festival with other band members, 1999. *Recordings:* Albums: Tigermilk, If You're Feeling Sinister, 1996; The Boy With The Arab Strap 1998; Fold Your Hands Child – You Walk Like A Peasant, 2000; Singles: Dog On Wheels EP, Lazy Line Painter Jane EP, 3–6–9 Seconds of Light EP, 1997; This Is Just A Modern Rock Song EP, 1998; Legal Man, 2000; Jonathan David, I'm Waking Up To Us, 2001. *Honours:* Brit Award, Best Newcomer, 1999. *Current Management:* Banchory Management, PO Box 25074, Glasgow G2 6YL, Scotland. *Internet:* www.belleandsebastian.co.uk.

COLBY Mark Steven; b. 18 March 1949, Brooklyn, New York, USA. Musician (saxophone). m. (1) Janet McIntyre, divorced 1970; (2) Mary Deacon, 21 April 1977, 1 s., 3 d. *Musical Education:* MusB, University of Miami, 1972; MusM, 1975. *Career:* Musician with: Maynard Ferguson, 1975–77; Bob James, 1977–83; Freelance musician, 1980–; Teacher, jazz saxophone, De Paul University, Chicago, 1983–; Clinic musician for Selmer musical instruments, 1987-. *Recordings:* Solo albums: Serpentine Fire, 1978; One Good Turn, 1979; Mango Tango, 1990; Playground, 1991; Reunion with Vince Maggio, 1999; Other recordings include: with Bill Wyman: Monkey Grip, 1974; Stone Alone, 1976; Destively Bonaroo, Doctor John, 1974; Real Life Ain't This Way, Jay Ferguson, 1979; Cat In The Hat, Bobby Caldwell, 1980; Marbles, Software, 1981.

COLDWELL Terry, (Terence Mark Coldwell); b. 21 July 1974, Islington, London, England. Vocalist. *Career:* Member, East 17; Numerous television and live appearances. *Recordings:* Singles: House of Love, 1992; Deep, 1993; West End Girls, 1993; It's Alright, 1993; Around The World, 1994; Steam, 1994; Stay Another Day (No. 1, UK), 1994; Let It Rain, 1995; Thunder, 1995; Do U Still, 1996; If You Ever, with Gabrielle, 1996; Hey Child, 1997; Each Time, 1998; Betcha Can't Wait, 1999; Albums: Walthamstow, 1993; Steam, 1994; Up All Night, 1996; Around the World – The Journey So Far, 1996; Resurrection, 1998.

COLE B J (Brian John); b. 17 June 1946, North London, England. Musician (pedal steel guitar); Prod. *Career:* Musician, Country Music circuit, London, 1964–; Pedal steel guitar player, Cochise; Founder member, producer, Hank Wangford Band; Leading exponent of instrument in UK; Currently prolific session musician and solo artiste; Leader, own group Transparent Music Ensemble; Replacement guitarist for the Verve, 1998-. *Recordings:* Solo albums: New Hovering Dog, 1972; Transparent Music, 1989; The Heart of The Moment, 1995; Stop The Panic (with Luke Vibert), 2000; As session musician: Tiny Dancer, Elton John, 1970; Wide Eyed and Legless, Andy Fairweather-Low, 1975; No Regrets, Walker Brothers, 1976; City To City, Gerry Rafferty, 1978; Everything Must Change, Paul Young, 1984; Silver Moon, David Sylvian, 1986; Diet of Strange Places, k d lang, 1987; Montagne D'Or, The Orb, 1995; Possibly Maybe, Björk, 1995; with Hank Wangford: Hank Wangford, 1980; Live, 1982; Other recordings with: Johnny Nash; Deacon Blue; Level 42; Danny Thompson; Alan Parsons Project; Shakin' Stevens; Beautiful South; John Cale; Echobelly; Dot Allison; Richard Ashcroft; Pet Shop Boys; Eliza Carthy; REM; David McAlmont; Robbie Williams; Spiritualized.

COLE Freddy (Lionel F Cole); b. 1931, Chicago, Illinois, USA. Musician (piano); Singer. *Musical Education:* Roosevelt Institute; Juilliard School of Music; New England Conservatory. *Career:* Younger brother of Nat 'King' Cole; Performed with numerous jazz musicians, New York, 1950s; Festival performances, US, Japan, Europe; Toured with own quartet, 1997–98; Appearances at Carnegie Hall; Voiceovers for numerous TV commercials. *Recordings include:* Latest albums: Always, 1995; Circle of Love, 1996; To the Ends of the Earth, 1997; Love Makes the Changes, 1998; Le Grand Freddy Sings The Music of Michel Legrand, 2000; Merry Go Round, 2000; Rio De Janeiro Blue, 2001; Contributor, All My Tomorrows, Grover Washington Jr, 1994. *Current Management:* Maxine S Harvard Unlimited, 7942 W Bell Rd, #C5–501, Glendale, AZ 85308, USA.

COLE Gardner; b. 7 Feb. 1962, Flint, Michigan, USA. Singer; Musician (keyboards, drums, guitar). *Musical Education:* 1 year, Berklee College of Music, Boston. *Career:* Two solo albums, 1988, 1991; Drummer with ABC; Keyboard player with A-Ha! on Grammies; Toured as opening act for Toni Tony Tone, 1991. *Compositions:* 60 songs recorded by various artists including Amy Grant, Al Jarreau, Tom Jones, Madonna, Michael McDonald, Brenda Russell, Vonda Shepard, 3T, Jody Watley, Jane Wiedlin. *Recordings include:* Open Your Heart (No. 1, USA), Madonna, 1987; Most of All and Everything, Jody Watley, 1991; Barrier, Tina Turner; Tear It Up, Michael McDonald. *Honours:* BMI Million-Air Award; 3 BMI Pop Awards; 18 Gold and Platinum records. *Memberships:* AFTRA; SAG. *Leisure interests:* Gardening; Automobile Restoration. *Current Management:* Bennett Freed, One Love Management. *Address:* 5410 Wilshire Blvd, Suite #806, Los Angeles, CA 90036, USA.

COLE Holly; b. 1963, Halifax, Nova Scotia, Canada. Vocalist. *Musical Education:* Studied classical piano as a child. *Career:* Started singing jazz at 15 after hearing Sarah Vaughan; Moved to Toronto and sang in a big band, early 1980s; Formed own trio, 1985; Debut album released Alert Records (Manhattan label outside Canada), 1990; Continues to record and regularly tours Canada, USA, Japan and Europe. *Recordings:* Girl Talk, 1990; Blame It On My Youth, 1991; Don't Smoke In Bed, 1993; Temptation, 1995; It Happened One Night, 1996; Dark Dear Heart, 1997; Romantically Helpless, 2000; Baby It's Cold Outside, 2001. *Current Management:* W Tom Berry, Alert Music Inc, 41 Britain St, Suite 305, Toronto, ON, M5A 1R7, Canada. *Internet:* www.hollycole.com.

COLE Lloyd; b. 31 Jan. 1961, Buxton, Derbyshire, England. Singer; Songwriter. *Career:* Leader, Lloyd Cole and The Commotions, 1984–88; Solo artiste, 1989-. *Recordings:* Albums: with the Commotions: Rattlesnakes, 1984; Easy Pieces, 1985; Mainstream, 1987; Solo albums: Lloyd Cole, 1989; Don't Get Weird On Me Babe, 1991; Bad Vibes, 1993; Love Story, 1995; Singles: Perfect Skin, 1984; Brand New Friend, 1985; Lost Weekend, 1985; Like Lovers Do, 1995; features on: Naked Self, The The, 2000. *Current Management:* John Reid Enterprises Ltd, Singers House, 32 Galena Rd, London W6 0LT, England.

COLE M J, (Matthew James Colman); b. 24 Sept. 1973, London, England. Prod.; Musician (keyboards); Remixer. *Musical Education:* Classically trained at Royal College of Music. *Career:* Competitor in BBC Young Musician of The Year; Became engineer at SOUR studios in London; Set up Prolific Records, 1998; Collaborations: Elisabeth Troy; Jason Kaye;

Remixed: Incognito; Jill Scott; Nitin Sawhney; Masters At Work. *Recordings:* Albums: Sincere, 2000; Singles: Sincere, 1998; Crazy Love, 2000; Hold On To Me, 2000. Mercury Music Prize nominee, Sincere, 2000. *Address:* c/o Talkin' Loud Records, Chancellor's House, 72 Chancellor's Rd, London, W6 9QB, England.

COLE Natalie Maria; b. 6 Feb. 1950, Los Angeles, California, USA. Singer. m. (1) Marvin J Yancy, 30 July 1976, divorced, (2) Andre Fischer, 17 Sept. 1989, divorced. *Education:* BA, Child Psychology, University of Massachusetts, 1972. *Career:* Stage debut, 1962; Solo recording artist, 1975–; Major concerts world-wide include: Tokyo Music Festival, 1979; Nelson Mandela 70th Birthday Concert, Wembley, 1988; Nelson Mandela tribute, Wembley, 1990; John Lennon Tribute Concert, Liverpool, 1990; Homeless benefit concert with Quincy Jones, Pasadena, 1992; Rainforest benefit concert, Carnegie Hall, 1992; Commitment To Life VI (AIDS benefit concert), Los Angeles, 1992; Television appearances include: Sinatra and Friends, 1977; Host, Big Break, 1990; Motown 30, 1990; Tonight Show, 1991; Entertainers '91, 1991. *Recordings:* Hit singles: This Will Be, 1975; Sophisticated Lady, 1976; I've Got Love On My Mind, 1977; Our Love (No. 1, USA R & B chart), 1977; Gimme Some Time (duet with Peabo Bryson), 1980; What You Won't Do For Love (duet with Peabo Bryson), 1980; Jump Start, 1987; I Live For Your Love, 1988; Pink Cadillac, 1988; Miss You Like Crazy (No. 1, USA R & B charts), 1989; Wild Women Do, from film Pretty Woman, 1990; Unforgettable (duet with father Nat 'King' Cole), 1991; Smile Like Yours, 1997; Albums: Inseparable, 1975; Natalie, 1976; Unpredictable, 1977; Thankful, 1978; Natalie... Live!, 1978; I Love You So, 1979; Don't Look Back, 1980; Happy Love, 1981; Natalie Cole Collection, 1981; I'm Ready, 1982; Dangerous, 1985; Everlasting, 1987; Good To Be Back, 1989; Unforgettable... With Love (No. 1, USA), 1991; The Soul of Natalie Cole, 1991; Take A Look, 1993; Holly and Ivy, 1994; Stardust, 1996; This Will Be, 1997; Snowfall on the Sahara, 1999; Love Songs (compilation), 2000; with Peabo Bryson: We're The Best of Friends, 1980. *Honours:* Numerous Grammy Awards include: Best New Artist, 1976; Best Female R & B Vocal Performance, 1976, 1977; 5 Grammy Awards for Unforgettable, including Best Song, Best Album, 1992; 5 NAACP Image Awards, 1976, 1988, 1992; American Music Awards: Favourite Female R & B Artist, 1978; Favourite Artist, Favourite Album, 1992; Soul Train Award, Best Single, 1988; Various Gold discs. *Memberships:* AFTRA; NARAS. *Current Management:* Dan Cleary Management Associates, Suite 1101, 1801 Ave of The Stars, Los Angeles, CA 90067, USA.

COLE Pamela; b. 1 Jan. 1959, Edmonton, Alberta, Canada. Musician (bass guitar, acoustic guitar). 1 s., 1 d. *Education:* BA, Criminology. *Musical Education:* Self-taught. *Career:* Member, Country band Quickdraw; Performances include: Calgary Stampede, televised on Calgary Cable 10, 1994; Interviewed live, CKUA Radio, Edmonton, Alberta; Third place, fourth Annual Country Hootenanny, Claresholm, Alberta; International Country Music Grand Prix, Norway, 1 of 10 finalists with: Next To Nothing, 1995. *Recordings:* Change of Heart; Just A Guess; Winning Was The Only Thing; Weekend Cowboy; Next To Nothing; An Angel Told Me So. *Publications:* 2 chapbooks of poetry: In A Corner of My Room; Between Friends. *Honours:* Hon. mention from Billboard Magazine for Eye On Me; Alberta Music Project Award, 1992; Winner, 960 CFAC Country Showdown, with band Headin' West. *Memberships:* SOCAN; ASCAP; ARIA; NCMO 1994. *Leisure interests:* Reading; Walking; Dog training. *Address:* 5610 Trelle Dr. NE, Calgary, AB T2K 3V4, Canada.

COLE Paula; b. 1970, USA. Singer; Songwriter. *Musical Education:* Berklee College of Music. *Career:* Singer, Peter Gabriel's Secret World Tour, 1995; Solo Artiste, 1996-. *Recordings:* Albums: Harbinger, 1996; This Fire, 1997; Amen, 1999; Hit Single: Where Have All The Cowboys Gone? (EP), 1997; I Don't Want to Wait, 1999; I Believe In Love, 1999. *Address:* c/o Monterey Peninsula Artists, 509 Hartnell St, Monterey, CA 93940, USA.

COLEMAN Cy; b. New York, USA. Composer; Prod.; Musician (piano); Songwriter. *Career:* Began performing on piano aged 6; Played New York clubs, 1950s; Composed songs before writing for musical theatre; Began as producer with Barnum, 1980; President, Notable Music Co. *Compositions include:* Contributions to revues: John Murray Anderson's Almanac; Ziegfeld Follies; Broadway musicals: Wildcat, 1960; Little Me, 1962; Sweet Charity, re-run on Broadway, 1986; Seesaw; On The Twentieth Century; I Love My Wife; Barnum; City of Angels, 1990; The Will Rogers Follies, 1992; The Life, 1997; Television specials for Shirley MacLaine: If My Friends Could See Me Now; Gypsy In My Soul; Film scores: Father Goose; Power; Garbo Talks; Family Business; Sweet Charity; Songs include: Witchcraft; The Best Is Yet To Come; Hey Look Me Over (from Wildcat); I've Got Your Number (from Wildcat); Real Live Girl (from Little Me); Big Spender (from Sweet Charity); If My Friends Could See Me Now (from Sweet Charity). *Recordings:* Albums include: Cy Coleman, 1955; Flower Drum Song, 1959; Comin' Home, 1963; Barnum, 1980; The Life, 1996; It Started With A Dream, 2002. *Honours include:* Academy Award nomination, Sweet Charity; 3 Emmys, Shirley MacLaine's Television specials; 2 Grammys: Record Producer, Composer, 1992; 15 Grammy Nominations; Numerous Tony awards, including 6 Tonys, City of Angels,

1990; 6 Tonys, Will Rogers Follies, 1992; Johnny Mercer Award, Songwriters Hall of Fame; Doctorate, Music, Long Island University, 1994; Irvin Field Humanitarian Award, National Conference, Christians and Jews; Tribute, Avery Fisher Hall. *Memberships:* Vice President, mem., Board of Directors, ASCAP. *Address:* c/o Notable Music Co Inc, 441 E 57th St, New York, NY 10022, USA.

COLEMAN George Edward; b. 8 March 1935, Memphis, Tennessee, USA. Musician (tenor, alto, soprano saxophones). m. (1) Gloria Bell, 3 Aug. 1959, divorced, 1 s., 1 d., (2) Carol Hollister, 7 Sept. 1985. *Musical Education:* Self-taught; Privately from older Memphis musicians. *Career:* Played with: B B King Blues Band, 1952–53; Max Roach Quintet, 1958–59; Miles Davis Quintet, 1963–64; Lionel Hampton 1965–66; Lee Morgan Quintet, 1969; Elvin Jones Quartet, 1970; George Coleman Quartet and Octet, 1971–; NYU, 1984; New School, 1987; LI University, 1987; Consultant, Lenox Jazz School, Massachusetts, 1988. *Compositions:* 5/4 Thing; You Mean So Much To Me; Blondies Waltz; Amsterdam After Dark; Music in Free Jack. *Recordings:* My Horns of Plenty; Live At Yoshi's; Manhattan Panorama; Duo, with Tete Montelui; with Cedar Walton: Eastern Rebellion; with Miles Davis: My Funny Valentine; My Horns of Plenty; I Could Write a Book. *Honours:* International Jazz Critics Poll, 1958; Artist of the Year, Record World Magazine, 1969; Knight of Mark Twain, 1972; AWD Contribution to Music, Beale Street Asscn, 1977; Tip of the Derby Awards, 1978, 1979; Jazz Audience Award, 1979; Good Note Jazz Award, 1985; Key to City of Memphis, 1991; Grantee, National Endowment for the Arts, 1975, 1985; Lifetime Achievement Award, Jazz Foundation of America, 1996. *Leisure interests:* Body building; Sports. *Current Management:* Abby Hoffer Enterprises. *Address:* 63 E Ninth St, New York, NY 10003, USA.

COLEMAN Jaz (Jeremy); b. Cheltenham, Gloucestershire, England. Singer; Musician (keyboards). *Musical Education:* Piano lessons; Grade 8 violin; Cathedral choir. *Career:* Lead singer, keyboard player, UK rock band Killing Joke, 1980–; Numerous tours world-wide, television and radio appearances; Arranged Nigel Kennedy's Riders On The Storm, The Doors Concerto, 2000; Collaboration with Hinewehi Mohu on Oceania, 2000. *Compositions include:* 1 symphony. *Recordings:* Albums with Killing Joke: Killing Joke, 1980; What's This For?, 1981; Revelations, 1982; Fire Dances, 1983; Night Time, 1985; Brighter Than A Thousand Suns, 1986; Extremities, Dirt and Various Repressed Emotions, 1990; Pandemonium, 1994; Solo: with Anne Dudley, Outside the Gate, 1988; Songs from the Victorious City, 1998.

COLEMAN Lisa Annette; b. 17 Aug. 1960, Los Angeles, California, USA. Musician (piano, keyboards); Composer; Prod. *Career:* Appeared on numermous US and European TV shows and Merv Griffin Show with Waldorf Salad at the age of 12; Joined Prince's band at 19 years of age as keyboard player, 1980; Toured and recorded extensively; Featured in film Purple Rain; Part of recording Duo Wendy and Lisa with Wendy Melvoin; Numerous TV appearances in Europe and the USA; Collaborations include: Seal; Joni Mitchell; kd lang; MeShell NdegeOcello; Victoria Williams; Neil Finn. *Compositions:* Scores for films including Dangerous Minds, Soul Food, Hav Plenty. *Recordings:* Albums: Wendy and Lisa, 1987; Fruit At The Bottom, 1988; Eroica, 1990; Girl Bros, 1998; Appears on Prince albums: Dirty Mind, 1980; Controversy, 1981; 1999, 1982; Purple Rain (No. 1, USA), 1984; Around The World In A Day (No. 1, USA), 1985; Parade, 1986; Sign O' The Times, 1987. *Current Management:* Gold Mountain Entertainment. *Address:* Renata Kanclerz, 3575 Cahuenga Blvd W, Suite 450, Los Angeles, CA 90068, USA.

COLEMAN Ornette; b. 19 March 1930, Fort Worth, Texas, USA. Jazz Musician (saxophone, trumpet, violin); Composer. *Musical Education:* Lennox School of Jazz, Trumpet and violin studies; Studied theory. *Career:* Member, bands with Red Connors, 1946; Pee Wee Clayton, 1949; Own Coleman Quartet (Don Cherry, Charlie Haden, Billy Higgins); Residency at Five Spot Café, New York, 1958–63; Trio with David Izenzon and Charles Moffett, 1965; Created own group, Prime Time, mid 1970s-. *Recordings:* Albums include: Something Else!, 1958; Tomorrow Is The Question, 1959; The Shape of Jazz To Come, 1959; Change of The Century, 1960; This Is Our Music, 1960; Free Jazz, 1961; Ornette!, 1961; Ornette On Tenor, 1961; The Town Hall Concert, 1962, 1963; Chappaqua Suite, 1965; The Great London Concert (a.k.a. An Evening With Ornette Coleman), 1966; At The Golden Circle, Vols 1 and 2, 1966; The Empty Foxhole, 1966; Music of Ornette Coleman (a.k.a. Saints and Soldiers), 1967; New York Is Now, 1968; Love Call, 1968; Ornette At 12, 1969; Crisis, 1969; Friends and Neighbours, 1970; The Art of Improvisation, 1970; Science Fiction, 1972; Skies of America, 1972; Twins, 1972; Dancing In Your Head, 1976, 1976; Body Meta, 1976; Paris Concert, 1977; Coleman Classics, Vol. One, 1977; Soapsuds (with Charlie Haden), 1977; Broken Shadows, 1982; Opening The Caravan of Dreams, 1985; Prime Time/Time Design, 1985; Song X (with Pat Metheny), Song X, 1986; In All Languages, 1987; Virgin Beauty, 1988; Live In Milano, 1968, 1989; Jazzbuhne Berlin 88, 1990; Naked Lunch, 1992; Tone Dialing, 1995; Colors: Live from Leipzig, 1996; Complete Science Fiction Sessions, 2000; Guest musician: Old and New

Gospel, Jackie McLean; Tale of Captain Black, James Blood Ulmer. *Address:* c/o Monterey International Inc, 200 W Superior, Suite 202, Chicago, IL 60610, USA.

COLEMAN Steve; b. Chicago, Illinois, USA. Jazz Musician (saxophone). *Musical Education:* Music performance at: Wesleyan University; Chicago Music College. *Career:* Moved to New York, 1978; Toured USA, Europe with: Slide Hampton; Sam Rivers; Cecil Taylor; Doug Hammond; Formed Steve Coleman and Five Elements, 1982; Formed M-Base. *Recordings:* Albums: Solo: Motherland Pulse; Five Elements: Black Science; Rhythm People; On The Edge of Tommorrow; World Expansion; Sine Die; Rhythm in Mind; The Tao of Mad Phat Fringe Zones; Curves of Life; The Sonic Language of Myth; Played on recordings by: Dave Holland; Branford Marsalis; Geri Allen; Cassandra Wilson; Greg Osby. *Honours:* Regular winner, Downbeat polls. *Current Management:* SESAC. *Address:* 55 Music Sq. E, Nashville, TN 37203, USA.

COLINET Paul Marie Marcel; b. 27 Jan. 1954, Elisabethville, Belgian Congo. Composer (Classic and Folk); Pianotuner; Violin and Viola Player; Diatonic Accordion. m. Segers Yvonna, 14 Aug. 1982. *Musical Education:* Private lessons, violin and harmony; Self-taught composition and other instruments (viola, cello, mandola, esraj, lyra, accordion). *Career:* Piano Tuner; Orchestra, viola; Chamber Music; Member, Trio Michel Terlinck. *Compositions:* 2 mandolin concerts; 1 violin concerto; 4 suites, mandolin, solo; 48 diatonic dances for diatonic accordion; Some compositions for folk instruments including bagpipes, hurdy-gurdy and lyra. *Publications:* 37 own editions of own compositions. *Honours:* First Prize, Instrument Building, Viola d'amore, 1995. *Membership:* SABAM. *Leisure interests:* Reading; Mushrooms; Instrument Building; Photography; Indian Music (sarangi); Winemaking. *Address:* Blvd E Bockstael 294, 1020 Brussels, Belgium.

COLLAZO Steven André; b. 24 Jan. 1960, Brooklyn, NY, USA. Recording Engineer; Arranger; Composer; Artist; Prod.; Keyboardist. m. Linda Susan Dodson, 22 Aug. 1995. *Musical Education:* Self-taught in Music and Audio Engineering. *Career:* Nine piece band, formed in High School, appeared throughout New York City; Joined Warner Recording Act, Undisputed Truth; Toured USA with Natalie Cole, The Isleys, Smokey Robinson; Toured UK and Europe with Odyssey, 1981; Appeared on TOTP, 1981. *Compositions:* I've Got to Wonder, 1982; Keep You Comin' Back, 1990s; Do You Right, 1990s; Paradise, 1990s; Waverly Radio, 1997. *Recordings:* Back to My Roots, classic remake of 80s hit, appeared on CH5 Fives Company, 1997; Producer, several Odyssey classics and new material due for release. *Publications:* Sound on Sound, 1997; Mentions in SOS; The Mix and Future, demos and progs, 1996, 1997. *Honour:* Demo Reviews, Sound on Sound, Top Tape, 1997. *Memberships:* American Society of Composers, Authors and Publishers. *Leisure interests:* Dancing; Board Games Yahtzee; Scrabble. *Address:* 60 Russell Rd, Salisbury, Wiltshire, SP2 7LR, England.

COLLEN Phil; b. 8 Dec. 1957, Hackney, London, England. Rock Musician (guitar); Vocalist. *Career:* Guitarist, Girl, 1979–82; Guitarist, Def Leppard, 1982–; Concerts include: World tour, 1983; Monsters of Rock Festival, Castle Donington, 1986; BRIT Awards, Royal Albert Hall, 1989; Freddie Mercury Tribute Concert, Wembley Stadium, 1992. *Recordings:* Albums: with Girl: Sheer Greed, 1980; Wasted Youth, 1982; Live At The Marquee, 2001; with Def Leppard: Pyromania, 1983; High and Dry, 1984; Hysteria (No. 1, USA), 1987; Adrenalize (No. 1, UK and US), 1992; Retroactive, 1993; Vault 1980–95, 1995; Slang, 1996; Singles include: with Def Leppard: Photograph, 1983; Rock of Ages, 1983; Foolin', 1983; Animal, 1987; Pour Some Sugar On Me, 1987; Armageddon II, 1987; Love Bites (No. 1, USA), 1988; Rocket, 1989; Let's Get Rocked, 1992; Make Love Like A Man, 1992; Heaven Is, 1992; Two Steps Behind, featured in film soundtrack The Last Action Hero, 1993; When Love and Hate Collide, 1995. *Honours include:* American Music Awards: Favourite Heavy Metal Album, Favourite Heavy Metal Artists, 1989. *Current Management:* Q-Prime Inc, 729 Seventh Ave, 14th Floor, New York, NY 10019, USA.

COLLIE John Maxwell; b. 21 Feb. 1931, Melbourne, Australia. Musician (trombone). Divorced, 3 s., 2 d. *Career:* Band Leader in Melbourne Max Collie Jazz Bandits, 1948, then Max Collie Jazz Kings, 1952; Came to England, Joined Melbourne New Orleans Jazz Band, 1962; Joined London City Stompers, 1963; Founder, Max Collie Rhythm Aces, 1966; Played at Festivals, Concerts and Theatres in England, Scotland, Wales, Ireland, Germany, France, Spain, Denmark, Belgium, Holland, Switzerland, Austria, Norway, Sweden, Poland, Yugoslavia, USA, Canada, Finland, Japan; Several radio and television appearances. *Recordings include:* Battle of Trafalgar, 1973; World Champions of Jazz, 1976; New Orleans Mardi Gras, 1984; Latest and Greatest, 1993; On tour in the USA; Live in Stuttgart, 1998. *Honours:* Winner, World Championship of Jazz, 1975. *Memberships:* Musicians Union; MCPS; PRS; PPL. *Leisure interests:* Jazz; Archaeology. *Address:* 26 Wendover Rd, Bromley, Kent BR2 9JX, England.

COLLIER Neil Vaughn Robert; b. 25 April 1951, Watford, Hertfordshire, England. Record Co Exec. 1 s., 1 d. *Career:* Play Away,

BBC TV; Opportunity Knocks; Proprietor, Priory Records. *Membership:* M Inst M. *Leisure interests:* Football; Cricket. *Address:* Priory Records, Unit 9B, Upper Wingbury Courtyard, Wingrave, Bucks HP22 4LW, England.

COLLIER Pat; b. 20 Oct. 1951, London, England. Record Prod. m. Jill, 1 s., 2 d. *Recordings:* Wonderstuff, 3 albums; Kingmaker, 2 albums; Soft Boys, several albums; Robyn Hitchcock, several albums; House of Love, Primal Scream; Katrina and the Waves; New Model Army; The Senators; Voice of The Beehive; Sultans of Ping FC; The Wonder Stuff; The Men They Couldn't Hang; The Wildhearts; The Oyster Band. *Current Management:* Graham Carpenter, Pachuco Management. *Address:* Priestlands, Letchmore Heath, Herts, WD2 8EW, England.

COLLIER Tom W; b. 30 June 1948, Puyallup, Washington, USA. Musician (drums, vibraphone); Bandleader. m. Cheryl Zilbert, 31 May 1970, 2 d. *Education:* BA, MusB, University of Washington, 1971. *Career:* Northwest Jazz Quintet, 1972–80; Freelance musician, various artists including: Bud Shank; Barbra Streisand; Ry Cooder; Sammy Davis Jr; Olivia Newton-John; Paul Williams; Johnny Mathis; Diane Schuur; Earl Hines; The Beach Boys; Jermaine Jackson; Jazz vibraphonist, duo Collier/Dean, 1977–; Director, N W Percussion Institute, Seattle University, 1989-. *Recordings:* Whistling Midgets, 1981; Illusion, 1987; Pacific Aire, 1991. *Publications:* Jazz Improvistion and Ear Training, 1983. *Honours:* Outstanding Service Award, National Asscn of Jazz Educators, 1980. *Memberships:* ASCAP; Percussive Arts Society; National Asscn of Jazz Educators. *Address:* University of Washington School of Music, Seattle, Washington, USA.

COLLING Jonathon; b. 28 May 1968, England. Programmer; Engineer; Record Prod. *Education:* College; Polytechnic. *Career:* Record producer, Rumour Records/X-Clusive; All types of dance music, including: house, Euro, jungle; Also jingles for radio/television and radio idents for BBC and local radio. *Recordings:* Rhythm Nation, 1993; Inner State, 1993; Prohibition Groove, 1994; Music Is My Life; Remixes for X-clusive Records, under name of Proof. *Memberships:* Musicians' Union; PRS. *Leisure interests:* Badminton; Car maintenance; Music. *Address:* 9 Egerton Rd, Hale, Cheshire WA15 8EE, England.

COLLINS Bootsy (William); b. 26 Oct. 1951, Cincinnati, Ohio, USA. Musician (bass). *Career:* Musician with James Brown's backing group the JBs, 1969–71; Member, George Clinton's Parliament/Funkadelic, 1972–; Also leader, own groups, Bootsy's Rubber Band; Bootzilla Orchestra. *Recordings:* Albums: with Parliament/Funkadelic: America Eats Its Young, 1972; Cosmic Slop, 1973; Up For The Down Stroke, 1974; Standing On The Verge of Getting It On, 1974; Chocolate City, 1975; Let's Take It To The Stage, 1975; Mothership Connection, 1976; The Clones of Dr Funkenstein, 1976; Parliament Live, 1977; Funkentelechy v. The Placebo Syndrome, 1977; Player of The Year, 1978; One Nation Under A Groove, 1978; Motor Booty Affair, 1978; Underjam, 1979; Gloryhallastoopid (Pin The Tale On The Funky), 1979; Trombipulation, 1980; The Electric Spanking of War Babies, 1981; Computer Games, 1982; Dope Dogs, 1994; Solo: Stretchin' Out, 1976; Ahh... The Name Is Bootsy Baby, 1977; Player of The Year, 1978; Keepin' Dah Funk Alive 4 1995, 1995; Fresh Outta P University, 1997; Glory B – Da Funk's On Me, 2001; Singles include: Tear The Roof Off The Sucker (Give Up The Funk); Flash Light; One Nation Under A Groove; I'm Leaving; Party Lick-A-Ble's; Back to Good. *Address:* c/o Bootzilla Productions, PO Box 44158, Cincinnati, OH 45244, USA.

COLLINS Charlie; b. 26 Sept. 1952, Sheffield, South Yorkshire, England. Musician (saxophone, clarinet, flute, synthesizer); Composer; Prod. *Career:* Member, jazz, improvised an dmixed media groups, 1969–; Clock DVA, 1979–81; The Box, 1981–85; The Bone Orchestra, 1985–88; Company Week, 1988; Arts Council Tours, 1988, 1990, 1992; Left Hand Right Hand, 1992–; Solo and production work. *Recordings:* with Clock DVA: Thirst; White Souls In Black Suits; All recordings with The Box; with Hornweb: Sixteen; with Martin Archer: Wild Pathway Favourites; Telecottage; Left Hand Right Hand; Shockheaded Peters; Ideals of Freedom, Arts Council Funded Composer, 1990. *Address:* c/o The Sound Kitchen, 13 Headland Dr., Sheffield S10 5FX, England.

COLLINS Edwyn; b. 1959, Edinburgh, Scotland. Singer; Musician (guitar); Prod. 1 s. *Career:* Founder, lead singer, Orange Juice (formerly the Nu-Sonics), 1977–84; Solo artiste, 1985–; International tours, including Europe, Japan, Australia; Phoenix Festival, 1995; Owner, recording studio. *Recordings:* Albums: with Orange Juice: You Can't Hide Your Love Forever, 1982; Rip It Up, 1982; Texas Fever, 1984; Orange Juice, 1984; The Esteemed Orange Juice, 1992; Ostrich Churchyard, 1992; The Heather's On Fire, 1993; Best of collections; Solo albums: Hope and Despair, 1989; Hell Bent On Compromise, 1990; Gorgeous George, 1995; I'm Not Following You, 1997; Hit singles with Orange Juice: Rip It Up, 1982; Solo singles: A Girl Like You (No. 1, several countries), 1995; If You Could Love Me, 1995; The Magic Piper (of Love), 1997; Producer for: Astrid; Terrorvision. *Honours:* Brit Award Nominations: Best Male Artist; Best

Single, 1996. *Address:* c/o The Agency Group, 370 City Rd, London EC1V 2QA, England.

COLLINS Glenn; b. 7 Feb. 1968, Emsworth, Hampshire, England. Musician (drums). *Career:* First drummer, The Auteurs, 18 months; Tour, America, France; Played at: Glastonbury Festival, 1993; Roskilde Festival, Denmark, 1993; Toured UK twice, including support to Suede; Television: Late Show; 2 times, Chart Show; The Beat with Gary Crowley; Radio: Mark Goodier session, Radio 1, 1993; Sheffield Sound City, 1993; Live Broadcast, Radio 1. *Honour:* Mercury Music Prize Nomination, Top 10 shortlist, 1993. *Leisure interest:* New band. *Address:* 83 Coleridge Rd, Crouch End, London N8 8EG, England.

COLLINS John; b. April 1970. Musician (bass guitar). *Career:* Worked as book salesman; Joined Brisbane-based rock group Powderfinger, 1992; Steadily built reputation on many Australian tours/festival appearances; International breakthrough with Odyssey Number Five album; Constant world-wide touring throughout 2000–01 ending with New Suburban Fables 2001 Australian shows. *Recordings:* Albums: Parables For Wooden Ears, 1994; Double Allergic, 1996; Internationalist, 1998; Odyssey Number Five, 2000; Singles: Powderfinger Blue (EP), Transfusion (EP), 1993; Tail, Grave Concern, 1994; Save Your Skin, Mr Kneebone (EP), 1995; Pick You Up, D.A.F., Living Type, 1996; Take Me In, 1997; The Day You Come, Don't Wanna Be Left Out/Good-Day Ray, 1998; Already Gone, Passenger, 1999; My Happiness, 2000; Like A Dog, The Metre, 2001. *Honours:* ARIA Awards: Album of The Year; Song of The Year; Best Rock Album; Best Cover Artwork, 1999; six times platinum fourth album on Australian chart for 67 weeks by end of 2001; Only home-grown act ever to play more than 3 consecutive nights at Festival Hall, Australia. *Address:* c/o Republic Records, Australia. *Internet:* www.powderfinger.com.

COLLINS Judy Marjorie; b. 1 May 1939, Seattle, Washington, USA. Folk Singer; Songwriter. m. Peter A Taylor, divorced, 1 s. *Musical Education:* Private piano study with Dr Antonia Brico, 1953–56. *Career:* Debut as professional folk singer, 1959; Appearances, numerous clubs, USA and world-wide; Concerts include: Newport Folk Festival; Worked with: Joni Mitchell; Joshua Rifkin; Stephen Stills; Radio and television include: Judy Collins: From The Heart, HBO special, 1989; Actress, Peer Gynt, New York Shakespeare Festival, 1969; Producer, director, documentary Antonia – A Portrait of The Woman, 1974. *Compositions include:* Albatross; Since You've Asked; My Father; Secret Gardens; Born To The Breed; Suite – Judy Blue Eyes. *Recordings:* Singles include: Both Sides Now, 1968; Amazing Grace, 1971; Send In The Clowns, from musical A Little Night Music, 1975; Albums: A Maid of Constant Sorrow, 1961; The Golden Apples of The Sun, 1962; Judy Collins #3, 1964; The Judy Collins Concert, 1964; Judy Collins' 5th Album, 1965; In My Life, 1966; Widlflowers, 1967; Who Knows Where The Time Goes, 1968; Recollections, 1969; Whales and Nightingales, 1970; Living, 1971; Colours of The Day, 1972; True Stories and Other Dreams, 1973; Judith, 1975; Bread and Roses, 1976; So Early In The Spring (The First Fifteen Years), 1977; Hard Times For Lovers, 1979; The Most Beautiful Songs of Judy Collins, 1979; Running For My Life, 1980; Time of Our Lives, 1982; Home Again, 1984; Amazing Grace, 1985; Trust Your Heart, 1987; Trust Your Heart, 1987; Sanity and Grace, 1989; Fires of Eden, 1991; Just Like A Woman, 1993; Live at Newport, 1994; Forever: An Anthology, 1997; Both Sides Now, 1998; Very Best of Judy Collins, 2001. *Publications:* Trust Your Heart (autobiography), 1987; Shameless (novel), 1994. *Honours:* Grammy, Best Folk Performance, 1968; Six Gold albums; Academy Award Nomination, 1974; Silver Medal, Atlanta Film Festival; Blue Ribbon Award, American Film Festival, New York City; Christopher Award; BMI Performance Award, Both Sides Now, 1990. *Current Management:* Gurtman and Murtha Associates, 450 Seventh Ave, Suite 603, New York, NY 10123–0101, USA.

COLLINS Mike (Michael Edmond); b. 25 July 1949, Manchester, England. MIDI Programmer. *Musical Education:* MSc (with Distinction), Music Information Technology; BSc Electro-Acoustics with Music; Private tuition by Oliver Hunt, guitar, keyboards. *Career:* Guitarist, songwriter with jazz-funk band Light of The World; Top 40 success, Ride The Love Train, 1981; Songwriter, producer, Chappell Music, 1982–83; Dick James Music, 1984–85; Session musician, Top of The Pops, and other music television shows, 1985–86; MIDI programmer for records and films, 1987–. *Recordings:* Album: Loops, Music For Multi Media, 1993. *Contributions to:* Sound On Sound; Audio Media; Future Music; PCW; Mac World. *Memberships:* Re-Pro; AES; PRS. *Leisure interests:* Reading; Walking. *Address:* Flat 1c, 28 Pellatt Grove, Wood Green, London N22 5PL, England.

COLLINS Phil(ip); b. 30 Jan. 1951, London, England. Singer; Songwriter; Musician (drums); Prod.; Actor. m. (1) 1976, divorced, 1 s., 1 d., (2) Jill Tavelman, 1984, divorced, 1 d. *Education:* Barbara Speake Stage School. *Career:* Member, various groups, 1967–70; Drummer, 1970–96, singer, 1975–96, UK group Genesis; Solo recording artiste, 1981–; Numerous world-wide tours, Genesis and solo; Major concerts for charities include Prince's Trust and Live Aid; Record producer for various artists; Film appearances include: Buster, lead role, 1988; Frauds, 1993. *Recordings:* Albums include: with Genesis: Nursery Cryme, 1971; Foxtrot, 1972; Selling England By The Pound, 1973; Genesis Live, 1973; The Lamb Lies Down On Broadway, 1974; A Trick of The Tail, 1976; Wind and Wuthering, 1977; Seconds Out, 1977; And Then There Were Three, 1978; Duke, 1980; Abacab, 1981; Three Sides Live, 1982; Genesis, 1983; Invisible Touch, 1986; We Can't Dance, 1991; Archive Vol. 1, 1999; Archive Vol. 2, 2001; Solo albums: Face Value, 1981; Hello, I Must Be Going, 1982; No Jacket Required, 1985; But Seriously, 1989; Serious Hits Live, 1991; Both Sides, 1993; Dance into the Light, 1996; Numerous hit singles include: I Missed Again, 1981; In The Air Tonight, 1981; You Can't Hurry Love, 1982; I Can't Dance, 1991; Groovy Kind of Love, 1988; Two Hearts, 1988; Easy Lover, with Philip Bailey, 1984; Other collaborations include: Marilyn Martin, David Crosby. *Honours include:* LVO, 1994; 7 Grammy Awards; 6 Ivor Novello Awards; 4 BRIT Awards; 2 Silver Clef Awards; 2 Variety Club of Great Britain Awards. *Membership:* Trustee, Prince's Trust. *Current Management:* Hit and Run Music, 30 Ives St, London SW3 2ND, England.

COLMAN Stuart; b. 19 Dec. 1944, Harrowgate, West Yorkshire, England. Prod.; Presenter. m. Janet, 22 Sept. 1973, 1 s., 2 d. *Career:* Producer for: Jeff Beck; The Big Town Playboys; Billy Swan; Cliff Richard; Phil Everly; Duane Eddy; Shakin' Stevens; Little Richard; The Shadows; Gary Glitter; Billy Fury; Kim Wilde; The Hank Wangford Band; Rich Sharp; Presenter, London American, BBC Radio 2, 1999. *Publication:* They Kept On Rockin'. *Honours:* Music Week Award, Top Singles Producer, 1981. *Memberships:* Musicians' Union; Country Music Asscn; Nashville. *Current Management:* Dennis Muirhead, Muirhead Management, 202 Fulham Rd, London SW10 9PJ, England.

COLQUHOUN Tom; b. 24 Oct. 1968, Linwood, Scotland. Musician (guitar). *Musical Education:* Self-taught. *Career:* Guitarist, specialising in solo and small group projects; composer and arranger; performances include playing two guitars simultaneously. *Composition:* Wrote and performed theme music for BBC short film, When I'm 21. *Membership:* Musicians' Union; SPNM. *Leisure interests:* Reading; Fitness; UFO Research; Music. *Address:* 14 Barshaw Pl., Paisley PA1 3HJ, Scotland.

COLT Johnny; b. 1966, Cherry Point, North Carolina, USA. Musician (bass). *Career:* Member, Black Crowes; Numerous tours and TV and radio appearances. *Recordings:* Singles: She Talks to Angels, 1990; Seeing Things, 1991; Twice as Hard, 1991; Sting Me, 1992; One Mirror Too Many, 1996; Only A Fool, 1999; Soul Singing, 2001; Lickin', 2001; Albums: Shake Your Money Maker, 1990; The Southern Harmony and Musical Companion, 1992; Amorica, 1994; Three Snakes and One Charm, 1996; By Your Side, 1999; Lions, 2001.

COLTART Robert Alexander Hendry; b. 20 Dec. 1956, West Molesey, Surrey, England. Vocalist; Musician (guitar, bass guitar); Songwriter. m. Angela Gausden, 20 Aug. 1983, 1 d. *Musical Education:* Self-taught. *Career:* Member, Badge, 1972–75; Bass guitar for Peter Noone (Herman's Hermits), 1975; Whispering Wind, 1976–78; Solo artiste, 1978–80; Life 'N' Soul, 1979; Arthur Kay and The Originals, 1980; Vocalist, guitarist, Maroondogs, 1981; Chuck Berry European Tour, 1988; GLR Nina Myskow Show, with Maroondogs, 1989; Mort Shuman Memorial Concert, 1991; Berlin SKA Festival with Arthur Kay, 1995; Backing Chris Andrews, recording with him, 1992–95; Recording and writing with George Williams, 1997. *Recordings:* Various television and radio commercials; Dark Nights Falling, 1984; Volcanoes, Skatoon Time, 1989; No-One But You; The Chozen I, 1994. *Memberships:* PRS; MCPS; Musicians' Union. *Leisure interests:* Reading; Walking; Swimming; Football. *Address:* 1 Foord Rd, Folkstone, Kent CT20 1HH, England.

COLTER Jessi (Miriam Johnson); b. 25 May 1943, Phoenix, Arizona, USA. Singer; Musician (piano); Songwriter. m. (1) Duane Eddy, divorced 1968, (2) Waylon Jennings, 26 Oct. 1969, 1 d. *Career:* Church pianist, aged 11; Solo artiste, also with Waylon Jennings, late 1960s–. *Compositions include:* No Sign of The Living (recorded by Dottie West); You Hung The Moon; Storms Never Last; Jennifer; Co-writer (with Waylon Jennings), I'm Not Lisa. *Recordings:* Singles include: Lonesome Road; Guitar On My Mind, with Duane Eddy; I'm Not Lisa; Suspicious Minds; Storms Never Last; The Union Mare and The Confederate Grey; Solo albums: A Country Star Is Born, 1970; I'm Jessi Colter, 1975; Jessi, 1976; Diamond In The Rough, 1976; Mirriam, 1977; That's The Way A Cowboy Rock 'n' Rolls, 1978; Ridin' Shotgun, 1982; Rock 'n' Roll Lullaby, 1984; Albums with Waylon Jennings: Wanted – The Outlaws (with Waylon Jennings and Willie Nelson), 1975; White Mansions, 1978; Leather and Lace, 1981; Right for the Time, 1996; Closing in on the Fire, 1998; Film soundtrack, The Pursuit of D B Cooper, 1982. *Address:* c/o Buddy Lee Attractions, 38 Music Sq. E, Suite 300, Nashville, TN 37203, USA.

COLTRANE Chi; b. 16 Nov. 1952, Racine, Wisconsin, USA. Singer; Songwriter; Prod.; Musician (multi-instrumentalist). *Musical Education:* Vocal instruction; Choir and Musical Notation. *Career:* Las Vegas; Tours throughout USA; Special guest star representing USA at International

Song Festival, Rio De Janeiro; Many television appearances USA and Europe including: Tonight Show; Johnny Carson; Merv Griffin; Superstars of Rock; Numerous television specials, including Chi Coltrane in Concert with the Edmonton Symphony, 1995; Multiple tours of Europe, approximately 300 concerts in one year; Raised money for South American rain forest project; Worked with: Gary Brooker (Procol Harum); Barry McGuire; Jennifer Rush; Nina; Future tours include: USA and Russia. *Compositions:* Thunder and Lightning; Go Like Elijah; You Were My Friend; Wheel of Life; Who Ever Told You; Ooh Baby; I'm Gonna Make You Love Me. *Recordings:* Chi Coltrane, 1972; Let It Ride, 1973; Special Chi Coltrane, 1975; Best of Chi Coltrane, 1975; Road To Tomorrow, 1977; Silk and Steel, 1981; Ready To Roll, 1983; Chi Coltrane Live, 1982; The Message, 1986; Golden Classics, 1996; Recording featured in film Beaches. *Honours:* Gold Hammer, Silver Hammer, Best Female Artist: Germany; Switzerland; Austria; Netherlands. *Memberships:* AFTRA; AFM; ASCAP; SUISA. *Leisure interests:* Painting (oils, watercolours); Reading; All animals (especially cats, horses); Horse riding; Gymnastics; Dance. *Current Management:* Nick Joseph, Stellar Artists Management, 505 S Beverly Dr., Suite 166, Beverly Hills, CA 90212, USA.

COLVILLE (Creighton) Randolph (Victor); b. 23 May 1942, Glasgow, Scotland. Musician (clarinet, saxophone); Composer; Arranger; Musical Dir; Teacher. m. Joan Winifred Pym, 23 May 1970, 1 s., 1 d. *Musical Education:* Northern School of Music, 1962–66, appointed to teaching staff, 1966. *Career:* Teaching and Freelancing, 1966–75; Permanent Teacher and Conductor, Kent Music School, 1975; Numerous television appearances at home and abroad, including television film Buddy Bolden's Children; Many radio broadcasts for BBC Jazz Club, Jazz Parade, Sounds of Jazz; Frequent engagements as featured soloist at South Bank; Played the Mozart and Brahms Clarinet Quintets at Kenwood House, 1991. *Compositions:* Mantovani Mix-Up; S'Okay; Fuss Pot. *Recordings:* Jungle Nights In Harlem, Midnite Follies Orchestra, 1981; Echoes of The Duke, Humphrey Lyttelton and Helen Shapiro, 1984; The World of Buddy Bolden, Humphrey Lyttelton, 1986; Hot and Cool, Colville Collection, 1992; Hotter Than That, A Elsdon, 1986; Keepers of The Flame, A Elsdon, 1994; Various other recordings including with Keith Nichols Groups. *Honour:* British Jazz Award, Best Clarinettist, 1988. *Memberships:* Musicians' Union; Performing Rights Society; The British Music Writers Council; The British Jazz Musicians Society. *Leisure interests:* Reading; Travel; Crosswords; Cooking. *Current Management:* Shirley Walker. *Address:* 28 Childscroft Rd, Rainham, Gillingham, Kent ME8 7SS, England.

COLVIN Shawn; b. 1956, Vermillion, South Dakota, USA. Singer; Songwriter; Musician (guitar). *Musical Education:* Guitar lessons from age 10. *Career:* 15 years as bar musician. *Recordings:* Albums: Steady On, 1989; Fat City, 1992; Cover Girl, 1994; A Few Small Repairs, 1996; Holiday Songs and Lullabies, 1998; Whole New You, 2001. *Honours:* Grammy Awards, Steady On, 1990, Song of the Year, Record of the Year, for Sunny Came Home, 1997. *Current Management:* AGF Entertainment, 30 W 21st St, Seventh Floor, New York, NY 10010–6905, USA.

COMBELLE Philippe Alix François; b. 14 July 1939, Paris, France. Musician (drums). m. Françoise Ruiz, 4 May 1964, 1 s., 1 d. *Education:* Postgraduate studies. *Musical Education:* Studies with father Alix Combelle (Alix Combelle Big Band), piano, saxophone, drums, tabla. *Career:* Jazz concerts and clubs: Europe; USA; UK; Japan; Africa; Russia; Turkey; Thailand; India; Viet Nam; Israel; Martinique; Guadaloupe; Syria; Jordan; Yemen; Oman; Teacher, Marly Conservatory of Music; International Music School, Paris. *Recordings:* Recorded with: Don Byas; Sonny Criss; Memphis Slim; Willie Dixon; Christian Escoudé; Toots Thielemans; Cat Anderson; Barclay; Buck Clayton; Buddy De Franco; Jimmy Gourley; Marc Johnson; Lavelle; OMD with Ray Brown; Eddie Harris; Guy Lafitte; Alix Combelle; Jimmy Gourley; Rene Mailhes; Bernard Maury Trio; Pierre Michelot; Daniel Colin. *Membership:* SACEM. *Address:* 36 rue Sibuet, 75012 Paris, France.

COMBS Sean, (Puff Daddy, P Diddy); b. 1970, Harlem, New York, USA. Rap Performer; Prod.; Remixer. *Career:* Began work at R & B label Uptown; Talent spotter for artistes such as Jodeci and Mary J Blige; Produced many top acts including Ma$e, Sting, MC Lyte, Faith Evans, The Lox, Mariah Carey; Launched Bad Boy Entertainment label, 1994; Produced records for Notorious BIG before his death; Remixed and reworked songs by many artists including Sting and The Police; Worked with Jimmy Page for the soundtrack to the film Godzilla; Remixes include the Jackson 5, Goldie, Trent Reznor. *Recordings:* I'll Be Missing You, with Faith Evans; Been Around the World, 1997; Roxanne; Can't Nobody Hold Me Down, 1997; Victory, 19998; Come With Me, 1998; It's All About the Benjamins, 1998; P.E., 2000, 1999; Albums: No Way Out, 1997; Forever, 1999; As Producer: Life After Death, by Notorious BIG, 1997; Cold Rock A Party, MC Lyte; Cupid, 112; Mo Money Mo Problems, Notorious BIG; Honey, Mariah Carey; Feel So Good, Ma$e. *Honours:* Grammy Awards, Best Rap Album and Best Rap Performance by a Duo or Group, 1998.

COMMON (Lonnie Lynn), (Common Sense); b. Chicago, Illinois, USA. Rapper. *Career:* Started recording as Common Sense, releasing debut album Can I Borrow A Dollar, 1992; Involved in court case resulting in name change to simply Common; Recorded second album for Sony; Third for MCA, 2000; Collaborations: Bilal; Slum Village; D'Angelo; Chantay Savage. *Recordings:* Albums: Can I Borrow A Dollar, 1992; One Day It'll All Make Sense, 1997; Like Water For Chocolate, 2000; Singles: Resurrection, 1995; Reminding Me (of Sef), 1997; The Sixth Sense, 2000; The Light, 2000. *Address:* c/o MCA Records, 60 Music Sq. E, Nashville, Tennessee, USA.

COMPAGNO Tony; b. 16 Nov. 1966, Cork City, Ireland. Singer; Songwriter. *Career:* Appearances: RTE Cúrsaí; RTE 89FM; Tours, 1989, 1992, 1994; Cork multichannel, video, 1992. *Recordings:* Debut album: Tony Compagno, 1994; Guest artist to: Jimmy MacCarthy; Hazel O'Connor; Luka Bloom; Cutting Crew; Maura O'Connell; Mary Coughlan; Davy Spillane. *Leisure interests:* Swimming; Listening to music; People. *Current Management:* Denis Desmond Promotions. *Address:* Thompson House, MacCurtain St, Cork City, Ireland.

CONLEE John; b. 11 Aug. 1946, Versailles, Kentucky, USA. Country Singer; Songwriter. *Career:* Played guitar on radio, aged 10; Singer, Versailles barbershop group; DJ, Nashville, mid-1970s; Recording artiste, 1978–; Also licensed embalmer, farm owner. *Compositions include:* Rose-Coloured Glasses; Backside of Thirty. *Recordings:* US Country No. 1 hits: Lady Lay Down; Backside of Thirty; Common Man; I'm Only In It For The Love; In My Eyes; As Long As I'm Rockin' With You; Got My Heart Set On You; Conley Country; Songs for the Working Man; Fellow Travelers; Live at Billy Bob's. *Current Management:* John Conlee Enterprises Inc, 38 Music Sq. E 117, Nashville, TN 37203, USA.

CONLEY Earl Thomas; b. 17 Oct. 1941, Portsmouth, Ohio, USA. Country Singer; Songwriter; Musician. *Career:* First artist to have 4 hits from 1 album, 1984; Recorded 18 US Country No. 1 hits. *Compositions include:* Smokey Mountain Memories, Mel Street; This Time I've Hurt Her More, Conway Twitty. *Recordings:* US Country No. 1 hits include: Fire and Smoke; Somewhere Between Right and Wrong; Don't Make It Easy For Me, Your Love's On The Line; Angel In Disguise; Holding Her and Loving You; Duets include: Too Many Times, with Anita Pointer; We Believe In Happy Endings, with Emmylou Harris; Albums: Blue Pearl, 1980; Fire and Smoke, 1981; Somewhere Between Right and Wrong, 1982; Don't Make It Easy For Me, 1983; Treadin' Water, 1984; Greatest Hits, 1985; Too Many Times, 1986; The Heart of It All, 1988; Yours Truly, 1991. *Current Management:* Artists International Management Inc, 9850 Sandalfoot Blvd, Suite 458, Boca Raton, FL 33428, USA.

CONNELLY Chris(topher John); b. 11 Nov. 1964, Edinburgh, Scotland. Singer; Musician (guitar). *Musical Education:* Choir, George Heriots School. *Career:* World tours with Ministry; Revolting Cocks; Solo tours, USA. *Recordings:* with Ministry: Mind Is A Terrible Thing To Taste; Psalm 69; Ministry Greatest Fits, 2001; with Revolting Cocks: Beers, Steers and Queers; Solo: Shipwreck; Ultimate Seaside Companion. *Memberships:* BMI; PRS. *Leisure interests:* Jazz; Thinking; Writing; Staring. *Address:* PO Box 472, 1573 N Milwaukee Ave, Chicago, IL 60622, USA.

CONNICK Harry Jr; b. 11 Sept. 1967, New Orleans, Louisiana, USA. Jazz Musician (piano); Singer; Actor. *Musical Education:* New Orleans Center For the Creative Arts; Studied with Ellis Marsalis; Student, Hunter College, Manhattan School of Music. *Recordings:* Albums: Harry Connick Jr, 1987; 20, 1988; When Harry Met Sally (film soundtrack), 1989; We Are In Love, 1990; Blue Light, Red Light, 1991; Lofty's Roach Souffle, 1990; 25, 1992; When My Heart Finds Christmas, 1993; She, 1994; Imagination, 1994; Whisper Your Name, 1995; Star Turtle, 1995; All of Me, 1996; To See You, 1997; Come by Me, 1999; When My Heart Finds Christmas, 2000; 30, 2001; Songs I Heard, 2001; Contributions to other film soundtracks: Memphis Belle (also actor in film), 1990; Little Man Tate, 1991. *Honour:* Grammy Award, Male Jazz Vocal Performance, When Harry Met Sally, 1990. *Current Management:* Wilkins Management, 323 Broadway, Cambridge, MA 02139, USA.

CONNIFF Ray; b. 6 Nov. 1916, Attleboro, Massachusetts, USA. Musician (trombone); Conductor; Composer; Arranger. *Musical Education:* Juilliard School of Music; Taught trombone by father. *Career:* Trombone player, arranger, orchestras of: Bunny Berigan, 1936; Bob Crosby's Bobcats; Artie Shaw, 4 years; Harry James; Arranger, composer, conductor, solo recording artist, 1954–; Worked with Johnny Ray; Rosemary Clooney; Marty Robbins; Guy Mitchell. *Recordings include:* Lara's Theme, for film Doctor Zhivago, 1965; As composer/arranger: Band of Gold, Don Cherry, 1954; Numerous hit albums include: S'Wonderful, 1957; Say It With Music, 1960; Memories Are Made of This, 1961; Somewhere My Love, 1966; Evergreens, 1973; Sentimental Journey, 1978; Amor Amor, 1984; Always In My Heart, 1988; 16 Most Requested Songs, 1993; Many Moods of, 1995; Pure Country, 1996; I Love Movies, 1997; We Wish You A Merry Christmas, 2000; The Big Band Years, 1939–47, 2001. *Address:* PO Box 46395, Los Angeles, CA 90046, USA.

CONROY Patricia; b. 30 Jan. 1957, Montréal, Québec, Canada. Songwriter; Singer. *Career:* Television specials, Canadian networks, TNN; CMT; NCN; CBC. *Recordings:* Albums: Blue Angel, 1990; Bad Day For Trains, 1992; You Can't Resist, 1994. *Honours:* CCMA Album of the Year, 1993; CCMA Female Vocalist of the Year, 1994. *Membership:* AFM. *Current Management:* Tim Rathert, Tony Gottlieb, Morning Star Management. *Address:* PO Box 1770, Hendersonville, TN 37075, USA.

CONSTANTIN François; b. 2 Dec. 1961, Paris, France. Musician (percussion, drums). m. 10 May 1986, 2 d. *Musical Education:* Normal School of Music of Paris. *Career:* In Jazz and others: Lavel; Arturo Sandoval; Francis Lockwood; Veronique Sanson; France Gall; Elsa; Louis Chedid; Johnny Hallyday; Patrick Bruel; Jean-Patrick Capdeviel; Michel Sardoux; Fabian. *Recordings:* Live records with the above artists; Sessions with Jannick Top; Florent Pagny; Jean Marc Jafet; Own group Latin Jazz. *Leisure interests:* Sports; Judo; Fitness; Humour. *Address:* 53 rue du Petit Bois, 77200 Torcy, France.

CONSTANTINOU Chris, (Chris De Niro); b. 20 July 1957, London, England. Musician (bass guitar, guitar, flute); Singer; Actor. *Musical Education:* Flute, bass at school; Mainly learned playing live. *Career:* First record with Punk band The Drill and Hollywood Exiles, produced by Chas Chandler, 1976; Joined Adam Ant, as Chris De Niro, 1981–86; Several world tours, playing all major venues; Television appearances include: Saturday Night Live, USA; Solid Gold, USA; American Bandstand; Top of The Pops; Wogan; Russell Harty; Live Aid; Dick Clarke Show; Formed S.F.Go; Formed band and songwriting partnership with Annebella Lwin, ex-Bow Wow Wow singer, with record deal; Currently singer/writer, own band, Jackie On Assid; Film appearances: Lead actor, Touch, BBC2; Play Dead, by Danny Cannon; Shopping, by Paul Anderson. *Recordings:* Drill; Vive Le Rock, Apollo 9, Adam Ant; Do What You Do, with Annabella Lwin; Other hit singles and videos. *Memberships:* PRS; MCPS; Equity; Musicians' Union; AFTRA; PAMRA. *Current Management:* Jackie Management. *Address:* PO Box 18106, London, England.

CONTE Paolo; b. 6 Jan. 1937. Vocalist; Musician (piano, guitar, vibraphone); Composer; Songwriter. *Education:* University of Parma, Law Degree. *Career:* Began career as Jazz musician in various bands; Recorded The Italian Way to Swing with the Paolo Conte Quartet, 1962; Began composing songs, 1960s; Had a number one hit when Adriano Celentano recorded La Coppia piu' Bella Del Mondo, 1967; Songs recorded by artists including: Patty Pravo; Enzo Jannacci; Johnny Hallyday; Shirley Bassey; Solo career, 1974-. *Compositions:* La Coppia piu' Bella Del Mondo. *Recordings:* The Italian Way To Swing, 1962; Paolo Conte, 1974; Gelato Al Limon, 1979; Paris Milonga, 1981; Appunti Di Viaggio, 1982; Concerti, 1985; Aguaplano, 1987; Live, 1988; A Macchina, 1990; 900, Tournée, 1993; Una Faccia In Prestito, 1995; Tournée 2, 1998; Razmataz, 2000.

CONWAY Tony (James Anthony); b. Bardstown, Kentucky, USA. Entertainment Co Exec. m. Nancy Schaefer, 1976, 1 s., 1 d. *Education:* Graduate, Northwood College, Southern Indiana. *Career:* Opened first talent agency, Lexington, Kentucky; Moved to Nashville; Agent for Buddy Lee Attractions, Inc, 1975; President, Buddy Lee Attractions, Inc 1987–; Over 30 clients include: Willie Nelson; Emmylou Harris; Ricky Van Shelton; Clay Walker; Mark Chestnutt; Waylon Jennings; Lorrie Morgan; Handles special event department in offices in Nashville, Kansas City, Los Angeles; Director Services of Main Stage Production Enterprises Inc, producing major events, festivals, state fairs, North America; First agent in Nashville to develop new breed of country acts; Artists signed include: George Strait; Mary Chapin Carpenter; Patty Loveless; Garth Brooks; John Anderson; Sawyer Brown; Talent Co-ordinator, FarmAid Concerts, Illinois, Texas; Co-ordinated, booked, Highwayman I and II tours, with: Willie Nelson; Waylon Jennings; Johnny Cash; Kris Kristofferson; Handles international tours for all clients. *Honours:* CMA Agent of the Year, SRO Convention, 1990, 1991; Country Agent of the Year, Performance Magazine Readers Poll, 1992, 1993. *Address:* 38 Music Sq. E, Suite 300, Nashville, TN 37203, USA.

COODER Ry (Ryland Peter); b. 15 March 1947, Los Angeles, California, USA. Musician (guitar, slide guitar); Composer. *Career:* Member, Jackie DeShannon's backing group, aged 17; Member: The Rising Sons, 1966; Captain Beefheart's Magic Band, 1967; Session guitar work included: Everly Brothers; Paul Revere and The Raiders; Randy Newman; Rolling Stones; Solo recording artist, 1970–; Formed Little Village with Nick Lowe, John Hiatt, Jim Keltner, 1991; Film music writer, 1980s-. *Recordings include:* Solo albums: Ry Cooder, 1971; Into The Purple Valley, 1972; Boomer's Story, 1972; Paradise and Lunch, 1974; Chicken Skin Music, 1976; Live Show Time, 1977; Bop Till You Drop, 1979; Why Don't You Try Me Tonight?, 1986; Get Rhythm, 1987; Pecos Bill, with Robin Williams, 1988; Music By Ry Cooder, 1995; with Little Village: Little Village, 1992; with The Gabby Pahinui Hawaiian Band: The Gabby Pahinui Hawaiian Band and Ry Cooder Vol. 1, 2000; Film soundtracks include: Performance Candy; Blue Collar (with Captain Beefheart); Film scores as composer: The Long Riders, 1980; The Border, 1982; Paris Texas, 1985; Alamo Bay, 1985;

Crossroads, 1986; Blue City, 1986; Johnny Handsome, 1989; Geronimo, 1993; Music by, 1995; Buena Vista Social Club, 1997. *Honours include:* Grammy Award, Best Recording For Children, 1989. *Address:* c/o Warner Bros Records, 129 Park St, London W1Y 3FA, England.

COOK David Lynn; b. 11 Nov. 1965, Pascagula, Mississippi, USA. Singer; Charity Spokesman; Model. *Education:* Masters, Business; Doctorate, Child Psychology, Divinty. *Musical Education:* Masters, Music; Doctorate, Musical Composition. *Career:* Member, The Cook Family Singers; David L Cook and the Trinidetts; Performs religious songs; Performed at White House for Ronald Reagan, 1986; Appearances in: Japan; Israel; England; Russia; Netherlands; China; Australia; Television apppearances include: 700 Club; Host of The Prestigious Manitoba Awards, 1987, 1988, 1995; Sesame Street; Jerry Lewis Telethon; Night of 100 Stars; Walt Disney World's 35th Anniversary; White House Celebration, 1986. *Recordings include:* Album: Come Follow Me; Singles: My Song; Lift Him Up. *Honours include:* 3 Prestigious Manitoba Awards; AMAAA Male Vocalist of Year, 1986–87; AMAAA Composer of Year, 1987–90; ABG Rising Star Award, 1989; 5 Dove Award Nominations, 1995; Numerous Robi Awards, 1986–90; Gospel Music Humanitarian Award, ARAMA, 1995; 4 Gold Albums; Sacred Music USA Award, Contemporary Christian Artist of the Year, 1996. *Memberships:* GMA; NARAS; CMA; AMARA; SAG; SESAC. *Current Management:* Daylyn Ware, American Musical Academy of Arts Assembly. *Address:* 1336 Cheshire Ave, Charlotte, NC 28208, USA.

COOK Eddie; b. 18 April 1928, Billericay, Essex, England. Publisher; Writer; Musician (saxophone). m. Patricia Mary Beale (deceased), 26 March 1955, 1 s., 1 d.; m. (2) Janet Eva Job, 5 Dec. 1986. *Musical Education:* Taught by mother; Later studied tenor saxophone with Les Evans. *Career:* Amateur and semi-professional musical work, music industry (buying, selling, repairing musical instruments); Publisher, 1960–; Publisher, Jazz Journal, 1979–; Editor, 1983-. *Publications:* Jazz Journal International (also numerous earlier non-music publications). *Leisure interests:* Bicycle racing; Playing Jazz; Gardening. *Address:* Jazz Journal Ltd, 3 and 3A Forest Rd, Loughton, Essex IG10 1DR, England.

COOK Jeff; b. 27 Aug. 1949, Fort Payne, Alabama, USA. Vocalist; Musician (guitar). *Career:* Founder member, country music group Wild Country, 1969–; Changed name to Alabama, 1977–; Worked with Lionel Richie, 1986. *Recordings:* Albums: Alabama, 1980; My Home's In Alabama, 1980; Feels So Right, 1981; Mountain Music, 1982; The Closer You Get, 1983; Roll On, 1984; 40 Hour Week, 1985; The Touch, 1986; Greatest Hits, 1986; Just Us, 1987; Southern Star, 1989; Pass It On Down, 1990; Greatest Hits Vol. 2, 1991; American Pride, 1992; Cheap Scats, 1993; In Pictures, 1995; From The Archives Vol. 1, 1996; Live at Ebbets Field, 1997; For the Record, 1998; Singles include: I Want To Be With You; Tennessee River; Feels So Right; Love In The First Degree; Pass It On Down. *Current Management:* Dale Morris and Associates, 818 19th Ave S, Nashville, TN 37203, USA.

COOK Norman, (Quentin Cook); b. 31 July 1963, Brighton, England. Musician (guitar); Prod.; DJ. m. Zoë Ball, 20 Aug. 1999, 1 s. *Career:* Joined The Housemartins, 1985; Numerous television appearances and tours including Red Wedge concerts; Band split, 1988; Worked with Billy Bragg, 1989; Formed Beats International; Formed Freakpower, hit Turn On Tune In Cop Out used for Levi's advertisement; Released records under guises of Pizzaman and Mighty Dub Katz; Now recording as Fatboy Slim; Remix of Cornershop's No 1 Brimful of Asha and Wildchild's Renegade Master; Numerous DJ sets including appearances at Millennium gigs for Radio 1. *Recordings:* With The Housemartins: Singles: Sheep, 1986; Happy Hour, 1986; Think for a Minute, 1986; Caravan of Love (No. 1, UK), 1986; Five Get Over Excited, 1987; Me and the Farmer, 1987; Build, 1987; There is Always Something There to Remind Me, 1988; Albums: London 0 Hull 4, 1986; The People Who Grinned Themselves to Death, 1987; Now That's What I Call Quite Good, double album, 1988; Solo Single: For Spacious Lies, 1989; With Beats International: Single: Dub Be Good to Me (No. 1, UK), 1990; Album: Excursion on the Version; With Freakpower: Single: Turn On Tune In Cop Out, 1994; Album: Drive Thru Booty, 1994; As Pizzaman: Singles: Happiness, 1995; Trippin' on Sunshie, 1996; Hello Honky Tonks, 1996; Gottaman, 1997; As Mighty Dub Katz: Magic Carpet Ride, 1997; As Fatboy Slim: Singles: Everybody Needs a 303, 1993; Punk to Funk, 1996; Going Out of My Head, 1997; The Rockefeller Skank, 1998; Gangster Trippin', 1998; Praise You (No. 1, UK), 1999; Right Here, Right Now, 1999; Sunset (Bird of Prey), 2000; Demons, with Macy Gray, 2000; Star 69, 2001; Ya Mama, 2001; Albums: Better Living Through Chemistry, 1996; Let's Hear It, 1998; You've Come A Long Way Baby (No. 1, UK), 1998; Halfway Between The Gutter and The Stars, 2000; A Break From The Norm (mix album), 2001. *Honours:* Brit Award, Best British Dance Act, 1999, 2001; Grammy Nomination, Best Dance Recording, Praise You, 2000.

COOK Paul; b. 20 July 1956, London, England. Musician (drums). *Career:* Drummer, UK punk group, The Sex Pistols, 1975–78; Performances include: First gig, St Martin's School of Art, London, 1975; Screen On The Green Special, London, 1976; 100 Club punk rock festival, 1976;

Anarchy In The UK Tour, 1976; Tours, Europe, 1977; US, 1978; Plays dates with Johnny Thunders, 1978; Member band, The Professionals, 1979; Sex Pistols reunion concert, 1996; Collaborations: Edwyn Collins, 1992–97. *Recordings:* Albums: Never Mind The Bollocks – Here's The Sex Pistols, 1977; The Great Rock 'n' Roll Swindle, 1979; Some Product – Carri On Sex Pistols, 1979; Flogging A Dead Horse, 1980; Kiss This, 1992; Singles: God Save The Queen, 1977; Pretty Vacant, 1977; Holidays In The Sun, 1977; Something Else, 1979; Silly Thing, 1979; C'mon Everybody, 1979; The Great Rock 'n' Roll Swindle, 1979; with Steve Jones and Ronnie Biggs: No One Is Innocent (A Punk Prayer By Ronnie Biggs), 1978.

COOK Sean; b. 16 April 1969, England. Musician (bass, harmonica). *Career:* Joined Spiritualized, 1993; Formed Lupine Howl, 1999; Numerous live dates including world tour; Concerts at Royal Albert Hall and CN Tower in Toronto. *Recordings:* Singles: Let It Flow, 1995; Electricity, 1997; I Think I'm In Love, 1998; Come Together, 1998; Abbey Road EP, 1998; with Lupine Howl: 125, 2000; Albums: Lazer Guided Melodies, 1992; Pure Phase, 1995; Ladies and Gentlemen We Are Floating In Space, 1997; Royal Albert Hall October 10 1997 (live), 1998; with Lupine Howl: The Carnivorous Lunar Activities Of..., 2001.

COOKE Mick; b. 15 Dec. 1973. Musician (trumpet, guitar). *Career:* Member: Hardbody, mid 1990s; Belle and Sebastian, 1996–; Amphetameanies; Collaborations: Mojave 3; Ex-Cathedra; Curated Bowlie Weekend Festival with other Belle and Sebastian band members, 1999. *Recordings:* Albums: Tigermilk, If You're Feeling Sinister, 1996; The Boy With The Arab Strap 1998; Fold Your Hands Child – You Walk Like A Peasant, 2000; Singles: Dog On Wheels EP, Lazy Line Painter Jane EP, 3–6–9 Seconds of Light EP, 1997; This Is Just A Modern Rock Song EP, 1998; Legal Man, 2000; Jonathan David, I'm Waking Up To Us, 2001. *Honours:* Brit Award, Best Newcomer, 1999. *Current Management:* Banchory Management, PO Box 25074, Glasgow G2 6YL, Scotland. *Internet:* www.belleandsebastian.co.uk.

COOKE Paul Anthony; b. 18 Dec. 1961, Hull, England. Musician (drums); Singer; Songwriter; Man. m. Susan Lesley Jarvis, 9 Sept. 1991, 2 s., 1 d. *Musical Education:* Self-taught. *Career:* Drummer, Pride, 1981–82; Founder member, drummer, Sade, 1982–84; Tours: Danceteria, New York City, 1982; U4, Vienna, 1983; Television and radio appearances include: Switch, 1983; Loose Talk, 1983; Top of the Pops, 1984; Radio 1, Peter Powell Sessions, 1983; Singer, Songwriter, Esposito, 1985–86; Papa Divine, 1987–88; Songwriter, Producer, MBDK, 1989–90; Solo artist, 1991–93; Singer, songwriter, P Eye Eye, 1994; Major concerts include: Esposito, Royal Albert Hall, 1986; Papa Divine, Brighton Pavillion, 1987; Business Ventures: P R Clarke Management; PSP Productions; IVI Records Ltd; IVI Management; Artist Manager for Esposito; Papa Divine; MBDK; Buff Meaba; Proud; P Eye Eye. *Compositions:* Singles: Co-writer, Smooth Operator and Your Love Is King, Sade, 1984. *Recordings:* Message In A Melody, Esposito, 1986; You Don't Have To Say You Love Me, Paul Cooke, 1991; Emma, Paul Cooke, 1991; Lost At Sea, P Eye Eye, 1994; Album: Diamond Life, Sade, 1984; Pop Life, Bananarama, 1991; Best of Sade, 1994. *Honours:* BPI Award; Triple Platinum record, Diamond Life, 1984. *Memberships:* PRS; MCPS. *Leisure interests:* Martial arts; Film making. *Current Management:* IVI Management. *Address:* 6 Cheyne Walk, Hornsea, North Humberside HU18 1BX, England.

COOL Tré, (Frank Edwin Wright III); b. 9 Dec. 1972, Willits, California, USA. Musician (Drums). *Career:* Joined Green Day, 1992; Numerous tours and TV appearances; Obtained major label deal, 1994; Side projects, Pinhead Gunpowder and Screeching Weasel; Provided track for film soundtrack Godzilla; Appeared in cartoon King of the Hill as The Stubborn Stains. *Recordings:* Singles: Longview, 1994; Geek Stink Breath, 1995; Stuck With Me, 1996; Brain Stew, 1996; Hitchin' A Ride, 1998; Time of Your Life, 1998; Nice Guys Finish Last, 1999; Minority, 2000; Waiting, 2001; Albums: Dookie, 1994; Insomniac, 1995; Live, 1995; Nimrod, 1997; Foot in Mouth, 1998; Warning, 2000; International Superhits (compilation), 2001.

COOLIDGE Rita; b. 1 May 1944, Nashville, Tennessee, USA. Singer. m. Kris Kristofferson, 1973, divorced 1979. *Career:* Radio commercials with sister, Memphis, Tennessee; Session singer with artists including Eric Clapton, Stephen Stills, mid-1960s; Tours with Delaney and Bonnie; Leon Russell; Solo artiste, 1970–; British tour with Kristofferson, including Royal Albert Hall, 1978; Music for UNICEF Concert, New York, 1979. *Recordings:* Hit singles: Higher and Higher; We're All Alone; The Way You Do The Things You Do; All Time High, theme to film Octopussy; Duets with Kris Kristofferson include: Lovin' Arms; A Song I'd Like To Sing; From The Bottle To The Bottom; Albums: Rita Coolidge, 1971; Nice Feelin', 1971; Lady's Not For Sale, 1972; Fall Into Spring, 1974; It's Only Love, 1975; Anytime Anywhere, 1977; Love Me Again, 1978; Satisfied, 1979; Heartbreak Radio, 1981; Never Let You Go, 1983; Inside The Fire, 1988; Cherokee, 1995; Out of the Blues, 1996; Walela, native American recording, 1997; with Kris Kristofferson: Full Moon, 1974; Breakaway, 1975; Natural Act, 1979; Thinkin' About You, 1998. *Honours:* Grammy Awards: Best

Country Duo/Group Vocal Performance, with Kristofferson, 1974, 1975. *Current Management:* ShoCorp International, 11684 Ventura Blvd #899, Studio City, CA 91604, USA.

COOLIO (Artis Ivey Jr); b. 1 Aug. 1963, Compton, California, USA. Rapper; Vocalist; Prod. 5 c. *Career:* Rapper from age 15; Former fireman; Joined briefly WC and The Maad Circle; Began Solo rap career, 1994; Collaborations include 40 Thevz; Began own record label, Crowbar, 1997. *Recordings:* Singles: County Line EP, 1993; Fantastic Voyage, 1994; I Remember, 1994; Gangsta's Paradise, used in film soundtrack Dangerous Minds (No. 1, UK and US), 1995; Too Hot, 1995; It's All The Way Live (Now), 1996; 1, 2, 3, 4 (Sumpin' New), 1996; C U When U Get There, 1997; Ooh La La, 1997; Tuff Jam Uvm Dub, 1997; Winner, 1997; Albums: It Takes A Thief, 1994; Gangsta's Paradise, 1995; My Soul, 1997; Fantastic Voyage – Greatest Hits, 2001; Guest Appearances: WC and The Maad Circle: Ain't A Damn Thang Changed (vocalist), 1991; Quincy Jones: Q's Jook Joint, 1994; Clueless, 1995; Phat Beach, 1996; George Clinton: Greatest Funkin' Hits (vocals), 1996; Forty Thevz: Honor Among Thevz, 1997; 17 Reasons (producer), 1998; Coolio's Crowbar Records Presents, 1999. *Honours:* Brit Award, Best International Male Artist nominee, 1996; International Dance Music Award, Best Rap 12 Single, 1996. *Current Management:* Powermove, 8489 W Third St, Suite 1007, Los Angeles, CA 90048, USA.

COOMBES Bob; b. 27 April 1972, Oxford, England. Musician (Keyboards). *Career:* Member, Supergrass, 1995–; Numerous tours, festival dates and TV appearances. *Recordings:* Singles: Lenny, 1996; Richard III, 1997; Sun Hits the Sky, 1997; Late in the Day, 1997; Pumping on Your Stereo, 1999; Albums: In It For The Money, 1997; Supergrass, 1999.

COOMBES Gaz (Gareth); Singer; Musician (guitar). *Career:* Member, The Jennifers; Lead singer, guitarist, Supergrass, 1994–; Major concerts include: Support to Blur, Alexandra Palace, 1994; British tour with Shed Seven, 1994; T In The Park Festival, Glasgow, 1995. *Recordings:* Albums: I Should Coco (No. 1, UK), 1995; In It for the Money, 1997; Supergrass, 1999; Singles: Caught By The Fuzz, 1994; Mansize Rooster, 1995; Lenny, 1995; Alright, 1995; Going Out, 1996; Richard III, 1997; Sun Hits the Sky, 1997; Late In The Day, 1997; Pumping On Your Stereo, 1999; Moving, 1999; Mary, 1999. *Honours:* Q Award, Best New Act, 1995; Brit Award, Best British Newcomer, 1996. *Current Management:* Courtyard Management, 22 The Nursery, Sutton Courtenay, Abingdon, Oxon OX14 4UA, England.

COONEY Steve; b. Melbourne, Australia. Musician (guitar, bass, didgeridoo), Songwriter. *Career:* Started playing music, aged 17; Member of Australian bands: Bushwackers; Red Gum; Fruitcake; Moved to Ireland, 1981; Joined Stockton's Wing; Long-term musical partnership with Seamus Begley; Other collaborations include: Sharon Shannon; Altan; Martin Hayes; Mary Black; Kirsty MacColl; Recently established FACE with Laoise Kelly. *Recordings:* Albums include: Meiteal (with Seamus Begley), 1997; Rabhlai Rabhlai, 1998; features on The Chieftains Albums: Long Black Veil, 1995; Santiago, 1996; on Mary Black Albums: Speaking With The Angel, 2000; The Best of Mary Black, 2001; Under the Moon, Martin Hayes, 1995; Way Out Yonder, Andy Irvine, 2001; on Altan Albums: Island Angel, 1993; Blackwater, 1996; Runaway Sunday, 1997; Another Sky, 2000; Lemonade and Buns, Kila, 2000; The Best of Donal Lunny, 2000; on Sharon Shannon Albums: Sharon Shannon, 1991; Each Little Thing, 1997; Spellbound, 1998; The Diamond Mountain Sessions, 2000. *Honours:* Ireland National Entertainment Awards, Most Popular Traditional Act (with Seamus Begley), 1997.

COOPER Alice, (Vincent Furnier); b. 4 Feb. 1948, Detroit, Michigan, USA. Vocalist. m. Sheryl Goddard, 1 s., 2 d. *Career:* First to stage theatrical rock concert tours; Among first to film conceptual rock promotional videos (pre-MTV); Considered among originators and greatest hard rock artists; Known as King of Shock Rock; Many film, television appearances. *Recordings:* Singles include: I'm Eighteen; Poison; No More Mr Nice Guy; I Never Cry; Only Women Bleed; You and Me; Under My Wheels; Bed of Nails; Albums include: School's Out, 1972; Billion Dollar Babies, 1973; Welcome To My Nightmare, 1976; From The Inside, 1978; Constrictor, 1986; Raise Your Fist and Yell, 1987; Trash, 1988; Hey Stoopid, 1991; Last Temptation, 1994; He's Back, 1997; The Definitive Alice Cooper, 2001; Dragontown, 2001. *Publications:* Wrote foreword to short story book: Shock Rock. *Honour:* Foundations Forum, Lifetime Achievement Award, 1994. *Memberships:* BMI; NARAS; SAG; AFTRA; AFofM. *Leisure interest:* Watching low budget horror films. *Current Management:* Alive Enterprises. *Address:* PO Box 5542, Beverly Hills, CA 90211, USA.

COOPER Douglas; b. 3 Sept. 1929, Weymouth, Dorset, England. Musician (drums). m. Blanche, 23 April 1977, 1 s., 1 d. *Musical Education:* London School of Music. *Career:* Worked with: Geraldo; Joe Loss; Tito Burns; Eric Winstone; Edmundo Ross; Paul Fenoulhet; Also worked in USA with Al Grey, Jimmy Forest, Count Basie musicians; Decca sessions for Ray Martin, Norrie Paramor, 1950s; Accompanied many top artists including: Frankie Vaughan; Peter Knight Singers; Matt Monro;

Current member, Bournemouth Big Band; Southampton Allstars; Also with own group at local jazz club. *Membership:* Musicians' Union. *Leisure interest:* Golf. *Address:* 2 Gloucester St, Weymouth, Dorset DT4 7AP, England.

COOPER Geoffrey Richard; b. 19 March 1955, Stoke Newington, London, England. Composer; Musician (drums). *Musical Education:* Various private tutors; Hailybury College, Hertfordshire. *Career:* with Mothers Ruin; Session work includes many radio and television sessions; with Voyeur (unsigned); Sessions for: Kenny Ball; Michael Schenker; Three Degrees; Tim Rice; Mike Berry; Broken English; Member, The Counterfeit Stones, now left to resume session career. *Memberships:* Musicians' Union; PRS; MCPS. *Leisure interests:* Squash; Cycling; Country walking. *Address:* 15 Lilac Rd, Hoddesdon, Herts EN11 0PG, England.

COOPER Giles Richard; b. 6 Oct. 1968, Amersham, Buckinghamshire, England. Singer; Songwriter; Musician (guitar, bass, keyboards). *Career:* Live concerts throughout London, include Marquee/100 Club; Various bands include Kindred Spirit; Misbeat; Splinter. *Recordings:* Painted Sun; That Was The Year That Was; Fly Away; Don't Play Those Games; Minds Eye. *Memberships:* Musicians' Union; International Songwriters Asscn; Guild of International Songwriters and Composers. *Current Management:* A J Promotions. *Address:* Ground Floor, 108 Inderwick Rd, Hornsey, London N8 9JY, England.

COOPER Paul Joseph; b. 27 Dec. 1959, Liverpool, Merseyside, England. Musician (bass guitar, guitar). m. Jacqueline Ann Iveson, 5 Aug. 1989, 1 s., 1 d. *Career:* Glastonbury Festival; Royal Albert Hall; Wembley Stadium; London Palladium; Budokan Stadium, Tokyo, Japan; Television and radio: Blue Peter; Kaleidoscope; Radio 4; Newsnight. *Recordings:* (own composition) All of The Time, 1983. *Leisure interest:* Football. *Current Management:* Bootleg Beatles.

COOTE Anthony William John; b. 29 March 1961, Hilderborough, Kent, England. Musician (guitar, bass guitar); Vocalist. *Education:* Canterbury College. *Musical Education:* Kent Music School, guitar, tenor horn. *Career:* with Ruby Blue: major tours, UK; Television: Rock Steady, C4; James Whale Show (ITV); Daytime Live (BBC1); Garden Party (BBC1); Festivals: Glastonbury; Reading; WOMAD; Rebecca Pidgeon: Recording and touring in USA; Animals That Swim: Recording, touring UK, Europe; Tours with Bjorn Again. *Compositions:* Down From Above; The Raven. *Recordings:* Ruby Blue: Down From Above; Virginia Astley: All Shall Be Well; Rebecca Pidgeon: The Raven; Animals That Swim: Workshy; Singles: Ruby Blue: So Unlike Me; Because; Bloomsbury Blue; Stand Together; The Quiet Mind; Primitive Man; Can It Be; John Martyn: Deny This Love; Animals That Swim: Madame Yevonde; Pink Carnations; Animals that Swim: I Was the King, I Really Was the King; Rebecca Didgeon: New York Girls Club; Cinerama: Va Va Voom; Bjorn Again Live at the Albert Hall; Holiday Suite; Cinerama: Disco Volante, 2000; This Is Cinerama, 2000; Videos: Ruby Blue: The Quiet Mind; Primitive Man; Animals That Swim: Madame Yevonde. *Membership:* Musicians' Union. *Leisure interest:* Cycling. *Current Management:* c/o Elemental Records. *Address:* 64 Mount Grove Rd, London N5 2CT, England.

COPANI Ignacio Anibal; b. 25 Oct. 1959, Buenos Aires, Argentina. Musician (guitar, piano); Composer; Singer. m. Nora Krichmar, 10 March 1981, 3 d. *Career:* Major concerts at main theatres throughout Argentina including: Opera Theatre; Luna Park; Excursionistas Football Stadium; Tours: Argentina; Uruguay; Chile; Colombia; Numerous radio, TV programmes; Own 2 hour daily radio programme. *Recordings:* Ignacio Copani, 1988; Ya Vendram Temps Mejores, 1989; Copani, 1994; Copani Completo, 1992; Afectos Especiales, 1993; Puerto, 1994; Salvese Quien Pued'a, 1995; Compromiso, 1995. *Honours:* Nomination: Martin Fiero, 1992; Ace, 1994; Winner, Previsario, 1993; Konex, 1995. *Memberships:* SADAIC (composers); SADEM (musicians). *Leisure interests:* Computers; Football. *Current Management:* Nuevo Canto Producciones. *Address:* 1605 Lavalle St, 4, 8, Buenos Aires, Capital Federal, Argentina.

COPE Julian; b. 21 Oct. 1957, Bargoed, Wales. Singer; Musician (guitar, bass). m. Dorian, 2 d. *Career:* Member, The Crucial Three; Lead singer, musician, The Teardrop Explodes, 1978–82; Concerts include: Futurama Festival, Leeds, 1979; Opening of Club Zoo, Liverpool, 1980; Solo artiste, 1983–; Performances include: British tours, 1987–; Glastonbury Festival, 1987; Phoenix Festival, 1993. *Recordings:* Albums: with The Teardrop Explodes: Kilimanjaro, 1980; Wilder, 1981; Everybody Wants To Shag The Teardrop Explodes, 1990; The Greatest Hit (compilation), 2001; Singles: with The Teardrop Explodes: Treason, 1980; Reward, 1981; Passionate Friend, 1981; Solo albums include: World Shut Your Mouth, 1984; Fried, 1984; St Julian, 1987; My Nation Underground, 1988; Skellington, 1990; Peggy Suicide, 1991; Jehovah Kill, 1992; Floored Genius, 1992; 20 Mothers, 1995; Ritey, 1997; Leper Skin, 1999; Solo singles: World Shut Your Mouth, 1986; Beautiful Love, 1991. *Publications:* Head On (Vol. 1 of autobiography), 1991; Kraut Rock Sampler (Guide to German Music 1968-), 1995; The Modern Antiquarian,

1996); Repossessed (Vol. 2 of autobiography), 1999. *Current Management:* Seb Shelton Management, 13 Lynton Rd, London N8 8SR, England.

COPELAND Stewart; b. 16 July 1952, Alexandria, Egypt. Musician (drums, percussion); Singer; Composer. *Career:* Drummer, Curved Air; Drummer, The Police, 1977–86; Numerous world-wide tours, television and radio appearances with The Police; Founder, Animal Logic with Deborah Holland, Stanley Clarke, 1989. *Compositions:* Score for films: Rumble Fish; Wall Steet; Talk Radio; Hidden Agenda; First Power; Men At Work; Ballet: King Lear (for San Francisco Ballet), 1982; Opera: Holy Blood and Crescent Moon, for Cleveland Opera, 1989. *Recordings:* Hit singles include: With The Police: Can't Stand Losing You, 1978; Roxanne, 1979; Message In A Bottle (No. 1, UK), 1979; Walking On The Moon (No. 1, UK), 1979; So Lonely, 1980; Don't Stand So Close To Me (No. 1, UK), 1980; De Do Do Do De Da Da, 1980; Invisible Sun, 1981; Every Little Thing She Does (No. 1, UK), 1981; Spirits In The Material World, 1981; Every Breath You Take (No. 1, UK and US), 1983; Wrapped Around Your Finger, 1983; Synchronicity II, 1983; King of Pain, 1983; Albums: with the Police: Outlandos D'Amour, 1978; Regatta De Blanc (No. 1, UK), 1979; Zenyatta Mondatta (No. 1, UK), 1980; Ghost In The Machine (No. 1, UK), 1981; Synchronicity (No. 1, UK and US, 1983; Solo album: The Equalizer and Other Cliff Hangers, 1988; Noah's Ark, 1990; Leopard Son, 1996; Four Days In September, 1998; Simpatico, 2000. *Current Management:* Firstars, 3520 Hayden Ave, Culver City, CA 90232, USA.

COPLAND Clive Rowan; b. 6 June 1956, Hampton Court, England. Musician (guitar). m. Linda Copland, 2 s. *Musical Education:* Grade 3 classical, studied with Andre Edmonds, Kevin Stacey, John Mizarli. *Career:* First band, London soul band The Strutters, 1974; Later worked with Ray Shields Orchestra; Herb Miller Orchestra (brother of Glen Miller); Now freelance musician. *Recordings:* Played on film soundtrack to Yanks; Recording sessions with: Hurricane Smith; John Miller; 4 records with Herb Miller. *Membership:* Asociation of Motion Picture Sound. *Leisure interests:* Outdoors; Walking; Swimming. *Address:* 3 Defoe Ave, Kew, Richmond, Surrey TW9 4DL, England.

COPPEL Michael Henry; b. 1 Oct. 1949, Melbourne, Australia. Concert Promoter. m. Michelle Coppel, 15 Feb. 1981, 1 s., 3 d. *Education:* Bachelor of Laws (honour), Bachelor of Commerce, Melbourne University. *Career:* Concerts promoted in last 15 years include: AC/DC, 1981; Narara '83, 3 day Music Festival, Old Sydney Town, 1983; Narara '84, 1984; Whitney Houston tour, 1986; Eurythmics, Revenge Tour, 1987; U2 and B B King, Love Comes To Town Tour, 1989; Tina Turner's Simply The Best Tour, 1993; U2, Zoo TV Tour, 1993; Garth Brooks, 1994; Other tours include: Michael Bolton; UB40; Salt 'n' Pepa; Pet Shop Boys; Pantera; Tori Amos, 1994; Janet Jackson Tour, 1995; Alternative Nation, international and Australian alternative music groups, 1995; Tours for The Cranberries; Violent Femmes; Slayer with Biohazard; Jamiroquai; M People; Sheryl Crow, 1995; Tours for Green Day, Björk, Celine Dion, Smashing Pumpkins, Alanis Morissette, Emmylou Harris, Simply Red, Herbie Hancock, The Fugees; The Corrs, Tina Turner, LeAnn Rimes, Marilyn Manson, Cardigans, Ben Elton, Korn, Sheryl Crow, Victoria Wood, 1997; Joe Cocker, Oasis, Natalie Imbruglia, Metallica, Massive Attack, Public Enemy, 1998; Apollo '98 Dance Festival featuring Fluke, Daft Punk, Ultra Nate, Basement Jaxx, Jimmy Somerville, 1998; Hole, Elvis Costello, Catatonia, UB40, Placebo, Garbage, Reba McEntire, 1999. *Honours:* Australian Concert Promoter of The Year, 1993, 1994. *Membership:* EIEA, Executive Councillor. *Address:* 716–718 High St, Armadale, Victoria 3143, Australia.

COPPIN Johnny; b. 5 April 1946, South Woodford, London, England. Singer; Songwriter; Musician (guitar, piano); Anthologist. m. Gillian Mary Wall, 2 June 1990, 1 s. *Education:* Diploma in Architecture, Gloucester College of Art and Design, 1971. *Musical Education:* School choirs; Semi-professional and college rock bands; Self-taught guitar and piano. *Career:* Lead singer, songwriter with Decameron, 1969–76; Solo performer, 1976–; Support to Jasper Carrott and Gerry Rafferty; Many European festivals and concert tours; Television appearances: Song of Gloucestershire, BBC2, 1986; Stars In A Dark Night, C4, 1990; Songwriters, HTV, 1995; Radio appearances: Kid Jensen Show, BBC Radio 1, 1981; Kaleidoscope Special, BBC Radio 4, 1989; West Country Christmas, BBC Radio 2, 1993. *Recordings:* 4 albums with Decameron; Solo albums: Roll On Dreamer, 1978; No Going Back, 1979; Get Lucky, 1982; Forest and Vale and High Blue Hill, 1983; Line of Blue, 1985; English Morning, 1987; Edge of Day, with Laurie Lee, 1989; West Country Christmas, 1990; Force of The River, 1993; A Country Christmas, 1995; The Shakespeare Songs, 1997; A Journey, 1999. *Publications:* Forest and Vale and High Blue Hill, 1991; Between The Severn and The Wye, 1993; A Country Christmas, 1996. *Honour:* Hon. Fellow, Cheltenham and Gloucester College of Higher Education, 1997. *Memberships:* BASCA; Equity; PRS; MCPS. *Leisure interests:* Walking; Art; Architecture; Poetry. *Current Management:* CTM. *Address:* c/o Red Sky Records, PO Box 27, Stroud, Gloucestershire GL6 0YQ, England. *Internet:* www.johnnycoppin.co.uk.

CORBI Rafel; b. 30 July 1966, Palafrugell, Costa Brava, Spain. Radio Personality. m. Mariona Viella, 20 June 1987, 1 s., 1 d. *Career:* Worked in radio since age of 16; Worked for numerous prestigious Spanish newspapers; Featured in all major country music magazines world-wide; Managing Director for RPEM.FM; President, European Country Music Association; President, Spanish Academy of Country Music; Host, WCMN Radio syndicated show. *Honours:* Radio Personality of the Year, 1994, 1997, 1998; Nashville Award, Country Music's European Man of the Year, Airplay Internatinal, 1998; American Eagle Awards, Country Music Asscn of America. *Memberships:* CMA, Nashville; European CMA. *Leisure interest:* Reading and studying the history of Catalonia. *Address:* c/o Ample 35, Palafrugell 17200, Costa Brava, Spain.

CORDA Mike; b. 8 July 1921, New York City, USA. Record Co Exec.; Composer. m. Helen Marie Wheeler, 7 Dec. 1952, 3 d. *Musical Education:* New York College of Music. *Career:* Bassist, Honolulu Symphony Orchestra, 1945–46; Bassist, original company, Kiss Me Kate, Broadway, 1948–51; Songwriter, various US record companies, 1952–; President, New Horizon Productions, Las Vegas; Record producer, Bluebirds Over The Mountain, Ersel Hickey, 1958; Composer, producer for Mickey Rooney; Robert Goulet; Bill Haley and The Comets; Gloria Lynne; Joe Williams. *Composition:* America, I Love You So, 1995. *Membership:* ASCAP. *Address:* Corda Music Inc, 3398 Nahatan Way, Las Vegas, NV 89109, USA.

CORDERO Jorge Luis; b. 12 May 1952, Holguin, Cuba. Singer; Composer; Bandleader. m. Anne Nielsen Cordero, 21 Aug. 1976, 1 s., 1 d. *Education:* Technical College. *Musical Education:* Percussion ISA and AMI. *Career:* Bandleader, Los Gran Daneses; Concerts, tours include: Germany; Cuba; Poland; Sweden; Norway; Spain; Calle 8 Festival (Miami), 1992; Television and radio, USA, 1993-. *Recordings:* Que Vida, 1975; Salsa Na'ma, 1981; Diferente, 1988; Rompiendo el Hielo, 1994; Del Morte y Tropical, 1996; Al Tiempo, 1999. *Honour:* Representing Denmark in Berlin, 1994. *Memberships:* DMF; DJBFA. *Current Management:* Rock On. *Address:* Mondrupsvej 8, 8260 Viby, Denmark.

CORDIER Thierry; b. 29 May 1963, Mont Saint Martin, France. Writer; Composer; Musician (guitar, keyboards). m. Joëlle Cordier, 9 Sept. 1989, 2 d. *Musical Education:* Self-taught. *Career:* One album with Charles Baudelaire, 1986; 200 concerts in France, Luxembourg, Belgium; 2 hits on compilation Coup de Pauce '95; Television includes: FR3: L'Heure du Ci; Radio includes: France Culture, Fun, Nostalgia. *Recordings:* Correspondances, 9 hits; Tableau Noir, Charles Baudelaire (dedicated to Les Fleurs Du Mal), 1986; Human; Garcon d'Café; Compilat; Coup d'Pauce '95; Noirs et Couleurs; 1./kri/; Single: Aéroport, 1995. *Memberships:* SACEM; ADAMI. *Leisure interests:* Sport; Jogging. *Current Management:* Un Poisson Dans L'Desert. *Address:* 7, rue de la Chappelle, 54400 Longwy, France.

COREA Chick, (Armando Corea); b. 12 June 1941, Chelsea, Massachusetts, USA. Musician (piano); Composer. m. Gayle Moran, 1 s., 1 d. *Musical Education:* Juilliard School of Music, 1961. *Career:* Pianist with artistes including: Mongo Santamaria, 1962; Blue Mitchell, 1965; Stan Getz, 1966–68; Miles Davis, 1969–71; Sarah Vaughan, 1970; Founder member, leader, pianist with group, Return To Forever, 1971–; Founder, The Elektric Band, 1986. *Recordings:* Piano Improvisations 1 and 2; Leprechaun; My Spanish Heart; Mad Hatter; Delphi 1, 2 and 3; Light As A Feather; Romantic Warrior; Hymn of The Seventh Galaxy; Music Magic; Voyage (with Steve Kujala), 1984; The Chick Corea Akoustic Band, 1989; Elektric Band Inside Out, 1990; Chick Corea Akoustic Band Alive!, 1991; Elektric Band Beneath The Mask, 1991; Time Warp, 1995; Remembering Bud Powell, 1997; Native Sense, 1997; Solo Piano: Standards, 2000; Past Present and Futures, 2001; Numerous appearances on albums with other groups. *Honours include:* 9 Grammy Awards; 28 Grammy Nominations; Numerous magazine awards from Downbeat, Keyboard Magazine; Jazz Life Musician of World, Jazz Forum Music Poll, 1974; Best Electric Jazz group, 1990; Best Acoustic Pianist, 1990; Top Jazz Pianist, 1990. *Current Management:* Ron Moss Management, 2635 Griffith Park Blvd, Los Angeles, CA 90039, USA.

CORGAN Billy; b. 17 March 1967. Singer; Musician (multi-instrumentalist). *Career:* Lead singer, Smashing Pumpkins, 1989–2000; Concerts include: Reading Festival, 1992, 1995. *Recordings:* Singles include: Lull EP, 1992; Today, 1994; Cherub Rock PEP, 1994; Disarm, 1994; I Am One EP, 1994; Bullet With Butterfly Wings, 1995; Thirty Three, 1996; Zero, 1996; End is the Beginning is the Eng, 1997; Perfect, 1998; Stand Inside Your Love, 2000; Try Try Try, 2000; Albums: Gish, 1992; Hut Recordings – The Peel Sessions, 1992; Siamese Dream, 1993; Pisces Iscariot, 1994; Mellon Collie and The Infinite Sadness (No. 1, USA), 1995; MACHINA/The Machines of God, 2000; Rotten Apples, 2001; Joined New Order as additional guitarist, 2001: Singles: Crystal, 2001; 60 Miles An Hour, 2001; Album: Get Ready, 2001; Featured on film soundtrack, Singles, 1992. *Current Management:* Coffer/Gershon Management, 26 Park Rd, Bushey, Herts WD2 3EQ, England.

CORKETT Paul Alexander; b. 31 Oct. 1964, Hammersmith, London, England. Sound Engineer; Prod. m. Rachel, 19 May 1990. *Education:* Shiplake College. *Career:* Worked at Jacobs Studio and Trident Studio; Now freelance engineer, producer. *Recordings:* Albums: As producer: Smart, Sleeper; Time For The Rest of Your Life, Strangelove; As engineer: Jehovakill, Julian Cope; Violently Happy, Björk; Also worked with: Terrorvision, The Cure, Placebo, Nick Cave, Juliet Roberts. *Current Management:* 140dB Management. *Address:* 1 McCrone Mews, Belsize Village, London NW3 5BG, England.

CORMIER John Paul; b. 23 Jan. 1969, London, Ontario, Canada. Musician (Fiddle, Guitar, Banjo, Mandolin); Singer; Songwriter. m. Hilda Chiasson, 1994. *Musical Education:* Self-taught on guitar, fiddle, banjo, mandolin, dobro, bass and piano. *Career:* Regular Guest, Up Home Tonight, ATV; Studio, stage and session work with Travis Tritt, Waylon Jennings, Marty Stuart, Carl Perkins and Steve Warner; Major Folk and Celtic Festivals including: Tonder Festival, Denmark; Celtic Connections, Scotland; Celtic Colours, CB-NS; Touring extensively in Canada and US. *Compositions:* Another Morning; Highland Dream; The Island; Gone; Kelly's Mountain; Long for the Sea. *Recordings:* Out of the Blue, 1986; North Wind, 1989; The Fiddle Album, 1990; The Gift, 1992; When January Comes, 1993; Lord of the Dance, 1993; Return to the Cape, 1995; Another Morning, 1997. *Honours:* Canadian Open Guitar Champion, 1986; Maritime Fiddle Champion, 1995; East Coast Music Award Winner, Roots/Traditional Vocal Artist of the Year, 1998; Juno Nomination, 1998. *Memberships:* AFofM; SOCAN; CMRRA. *Current Management:* Max McDonald. *Address:* Rave Entertainment Inc, 363 Charlotte St, Sydney, Nova Scotia, B1P 1EI, Canada.

CORNELIUS Claes; b. 14 May 1949, Copenhagen, Denmark. A & R Man.; Publisher; Musician (guitar, keyboards). 1 s. *Education:* Art Academy, Venice, Italy. *Musical Education:* Piano lessons, various seminars. *Career:* Professional musician, late 1960s, Italy; Studio session musician; Music publishing, Denmark, early 1970s; With Mega Scandinavia, 1983–; Managing Director of Megasong Publishing A/S, 1999. *Recordings:* Countless studio sessions in Italy including Finardi; Claudio Rocchi; Caterina Caselli; Fausto Leali; Also member of Art Class LP. *Honour:* Shared Critics Prize for production in Italy. *Leisure interests:* Art installations; Music. *Address:* Gronnegade 3, 1107, Kopenhagen K, Denmark.

CORNELIUS Helen Lorene; b. 6 Dec. 1941, Hannibal, Missouri, USA. Singer; Songwriter. m. Jerry Garren, 22 June 1981, 2 s., 1 d. *Career:* Songwriter, 1970–; Recording artist, 1975–80; Television appearances include: Nashville On The Road; Host, Helen Cornelius Show, 1976–; Stage performances: Annie Get Your Gun, US touring production, 1984. *Recordings:* Hit single: Lying In Love With You, with Jim Ed Brown; Albums include: Helen Cornelius; Born Believer; I Don't Want To Have To Marry You. *Honour:* CMA Vocal Duo of the Year, 1977. *Memberships:* Broadcast Music Inc; AFTRA; CMA; National Asscn of Songwriters; West Coast Academy of Country Music. *Address:* c/o Morningstar Pubic Relations, PO Box 83, Brentwood, TN 32027, USA.

CORNELL Chris; b. 20 July 1964, USA. Vocalist; Songwriter; Musician (guitar). m. Susan Silver. *Career:* Vocalist, US heavy rock group Soundgarden, 1984–97; Concerts include: Support to Metallica, US, 1991; Support to Guns 'n' Roses, US tour, 1991; Lollapalooza II tour, 1992; Reading Festival, 1995; Lollapalooza VI, 1996; Member, tribute group, Temple of The Dog, 1991; Soundgarden, 1984–97; Began solo career 1997. *Recordings:* Albums: Ultramega OK, 1989; Louder Than Love, 1989; Badmotorfinger, 1991; Superunknown (No. 1, USA), 1994; Down on the Upside, 1996; with Temple of The Dog: Temple of The Dog, 1991; solo: Euphoria Morning, 1999; Singles: Flower; Loud Love; Jesus Christ Pose; Outshined; Black Hole Sun, 1994; Spoonman, 1994; Burden in my Hand, 1996; Sunshower, 1998; solo: Can't Change Me, 1999. *Honours:* 2 Grammy Awards, 1995. *Membership:* NARAS. *Current Management:* Jim Guerinot, Rebel Waltz Management, 31652 2nd Ave, Laguna Beach, CA 92651, USA.

CORNWELL Hugh; b. 28 Aug. 1949, London, England. Vocalist; Musician (guitar). *Education:* Chemistry graduate. *Career:* Former science teacher; Founder member, UK rock group The Stranglers, 1976–90; Headline tours, Europe; UK; Canada; US; International concerts include: Supports to Patti Smith, 1976; Climax Blues Band, 1977; Loch Lomond Festival, 1979; Reading Rock Festival, 1983, 1987; Alexandra Palace, 1990; Solo artiste, 1991–; Also worked with Roger Cook and Andy West, 1992. *Recordings:* Albums: Rattus Norvegicus, 1977; No More Heroes, 1978; Black and White, 1978; Live (X Cert), 1979; The Raven, 1979; Themeninblack, 1981; La Folie, 1982; The Collection, 1982; Feline, 1983; Aural Sculpture, 1984; Dreamtime, 1986; All Live and All of The Night, 1988; 10, 1990; Solo albums: Nosferatu, 1979; Wolf, 1988; Wired, 1993; Black Hair, Black Eyes, Black Suit, 1999; First Bus to Babylon, 1999; Hi-Fi, 2000; with Cornwell, Cook and West: C C W, 1992; Singles: with The Stranglers: Get A Grip On Yourself, 1977; Peaches, 1977; Something Better Change, 1977; No More Heroes, 1977; Five Minutes, 1978; Nice 'n' Sleazy, 1978; Walk On By, 1978;

Duchess, 1979; Golden Brown (No. 2, UK), 1982; Strange Little Girl, 1982; European Female, 1983; Skin Deep, 1984; Always The Sun, 1986; All Day and All of The Night, 1987; Solo: One In A Million, 1985; Another Kind of Love, 1988. *Publication:* Inside Information. *Honours:* Ivor Novello Award, Most Performed Work of 1982, Golden Brown, 1983.

CORONADO Gilles; b. 26 Oct. 1966, Avignon, France. Musician (guitar); Composer. *Education:* Superior Technical Brevet of technical drawing. *Musical Education:* Different School, Banff Jazz Workshop, Canada; Self-taught. *Career:* Various bands (jazz, funk, rock), South of France; Moved to Paris, 1991; Active member, HASK collective (musicians association, Paris); Founder, leader, quartet Urban Mood; Played various festivals: Germany; Belgium; Portugal; France; Collaborator with Dance Performances, 1993–; Teacher. *Recordings:* Urban Mood record due 1996. *Membership:* SACEM. *Leisure interests:* Arts performances; Cooking; Parties; Life. *Address:* Cité Internationale des Arts, 18 rue de l'Hotel de Ville, 75004 Paris, France.

CORR Andrea Jane; b. 17 May 1974, Dundalk, Co Louth, Ireland. Singer; Musician (Tin Whistle). *Career:* Member, The Corrs; Performed at Boston World Cup for Irish Ambassador, 1994; Signed recording deal; Numerous TV appearances and live shows; Several festival appearances; Acted in film The Commitments and Evita. *Recordings:* Singles: Forgiven Not Forgotten, 1996; Right Time, 1996; So Young, 1998; What Can I Do, 1998; Dreams, 1998; Runaway, 1999; Only When I Sleep, 1999; Radio, 1999; Breathless (No. 1, UK), 2000; Irresistible, 2000; Give Me The Reason, 2001; Would You Be Happier, 2001; Albums: Forgiven, Not Forgotten, 1996; Talk On Corners (No. 1, UK), 1998; Corrs Live, 1998; MTV Unplugged, 1999; In Blue (No. 1, UK), 2000; Best of The Corrs (compilation), 2001. *Honours:* Brit Award, Best International Group, 1999; Grammy Award Nominations, Pop Performance By A Duo Or Group (Breathless), Pop Instrumental Performance (Rebel Heart) 2001.

CORR Caroline; b. 17 March 1973, Dundalk, Co Louth, Ireland. Musician (Drums, Bodhran). *Career:* Member, The Corrs; Performed at 1994 World Cup in Boston for Irish Ambassador; Signed recording contract; Numerous TV appearances and live shows; Many festival appearances. *Recordings:* Singles: Forgiven Not Forgotten, 1996; Right Time, 1996; So Young, 1998; What Can I Do, 1998; Dreams, 1998; Runaway, 1999; Only When I Sleep, 1999; Radio, 1999; Breathless (No. 1, UK), 2000; Irresistible, 2000; Give Me The Reason, 2001; Would You Be Happier, 2001; Albums: Forgiven, Not Forgotten, 1996; Talk On Corners (No. 1, UK), 1998; Corrs Live, 1998; MTV Unplugged, 1999; In Blue (No. 1, UK), 2000; Best of The Corrs (compilation), 2001. *Honours:* Brit Award, Best International Group, 1999; Grammy Award Nominations, Pop Performance By A Duo Or Group (Breathless), Pop Instrumental Performance (Rebel Heart) 2001.

CORR James Steven (Jim); b. 31 July 1968, Dundalk, Co Louth, Ireland. Musician (Guitar, Keyboards). *Career:* Member, The Corrs; Performed for the Irish Ambassador at the 1994 World Cup in Boston; Secured major label recording contract; Numerous TV and live appearances; Many festival dates in Britain and Europe. *Recordings:* Singles: Forgiven Not Forgotten, 1996; Right Time, 1996; So Young, 1998; What Can I Do, 1998; Dreams, 1998; Runaway, 1998; Only When I Sleep, 1999; Radio, 1999; Breathless (No. 1, UK), 2000; Irresistible, 2000; Give Me The Reason, 2001; Would You Be Happier, 2001; Albums: Forgiven, Not Forgotten, 1996; Talk On Corners (No. 1, UK), 1998; Corrs Live, 1998; MTV Unplugged, 1999; In Blue (No. 1, UK), 2000; Best of The Corrs (compilation), 2001. *Honours:* Brit Award, Best International Group, 1999; Grammy Award Nominations, Pop Performance By A Duo Or Group (Breathless), Pop Instrumental Performance (Rebel Heart) 2001.

CORR Sharon; b. 24 March 1970, Dundalk, Co Louth, Ireland. Musician (Violin). *Career:* Member, The Corrs; Performed at 1994 World Cup in Boston for the Irish Ambassador; Secured record contract; Numerous TV appearances and live shows; Many festival dates. *Recordings:* Singles: Forgiven Not Forgotten, 1996; Right Time, 1996; So Young, 1998; What Can I Do, 1998; Dreams, 1998; Runaway, 1999; Only When I Sleep, 1999; Radio, 1999; Breathless (No. 1, UK), 2000; Irresistible, 2000; Give Me The Reason, 2001; Would You Be Happier, 2001; Albums: Forgiven, Not Forgotten, 1996; Talk On Corners (No. 1, UK), 1998; Corrs Live, 1998; MTV Unplugged, 1999; In Blue (No. 1, UK), 2000; Best of The Corrs (compilation), 2001. *Honours:* Brit Award, Best International Group, 1999; Grammy Award Nominations, Pop Performance By A Duo Or Group (Breathless), Pop Instrumental Performance (Rebel Heart) 2001.

CORRIGAN Briana; *Career:* Member, The Beautiful South, 1989–93; Left to pursue solo career. *Recording:* Singles: with Beautiful South: You Keep It All In, 1989; A Little Time (No. 1, UK), 1990; My Book, 1990; Bell Bottomed Tear, 1992; solo: Love Me Now, 1996; Albums: with Beautiful South: Welcome To The Beautiful South, 1989; Choke, 1990; 0898, 1992; Carry On Up The Charts (compilation; No. 1, UK), 1994; Solid Bronze – Great Hits (compilation), 2001; solo: When Your Arms Wrap Around Me, 1996.

CORSBY Dave; b. 29 June 1938, Hounslow, Middlesex, England. Composer; Arranger; Musician (saxophones; flute; clarinet; keyboards). m. Jill Corsby, 16 July 1992. *Career:* Founder member, Cave Jazz Club, Ramsgate, Kent, 1955; Co-organizer of Thanet Jazz Festival, 1982, 1983; Baritone saxophonist, John Burch Octet, 1986–; Radio, television, film and record sessions; Appeared at Dunkirk Jazzopale, 1994; Hot Club of Lyons, 1995; Arts Council tour with John Burch Octet, 1994–95; Ramsgate Spring Festival, 1999; Bandleader, Doctor Crotchet's Good Time Jazz (band for functions); Dave Corsby Quartet (modern jazz group); Mission Impossible Big Band; Business ventures: Carpe Diem Arts; Carpe Diem Music; Lincoln Studios; Played Canterbury Festival, 1998. *Compositions:* The Subterraneans; Rajans Banquet; Samuel Pepys Jazz Suite; Tale of Two Cities Jazz Suite (Arts Council Commission); Seven Deadly Sins, jazz musical; The Endeavour Experience, film score, 1994; Cinque Ports Jazz Suite, Sandwich Festival commission, 1997. *Recordings:* Tale of Two Cities Jazz Suite; Samuel Pepys Jazz Suite; The Seven Deadly Sins; Roll Call. *Memberships:* Musicians' Union; Performing Rights Society; Art Pepper Society; Asscn of British Jazz Musicians. *Current Management:* Carpe Diem Arts. *Address:* Lincoln Studios, 8 Lincoln Gardens, Birchington-on-Sea, Kent CT7 9SW, England.

CORSO Terry (Terence); b. 28 Nov. 1971, Riverside, California, USA. Musician (guitar). *Musical Education:* Learnt drums and guitar at band workshop programme sponsored by local music store. *Career:* Played with local bands Sinister Fiend, Brother Vibe, Wallop; Member: Alien Ant Farm, 1996–; Self-financed independent LP released to acclaim, 1999; Signed to Papa Roach's New Noize label; Second album released in conjunction with DreamWorks label, leading to major international breakthrough, 2000–01. *Recordings:* Albums: Greatest Hits, 1999; ANThology, 2001; Singles: $100 EP, 1996; Love Songs EP, 1998; Movies, Smooth Criminal, 2001. *Honours:* L.A. Music Award, Best Independent Album, 1999. *Address:* c/o New Noize, 2022 Cliff Dr #123, Santa Barbara, CA 93109, USA. *E-mail:* info@newnoize.com. *Internet:* www.alienantfarm.com.

CORTEZ Alberto, (Jose Alberto Garcia Gallo); b. 11 March 1940, Rancul, Argentina. Singer; Composer. m. Renee Govaerts, 2 June 1964. *Musical Education:* Chopin Conservatory, Mendoza, Argentina. *Career:* Performances include: Teatro de la Zarzuela, Madrid, 1967; Lincoln Center, New York, 1990; Teatro Colon, Buenos Aires, 1992. *Compositions:* Over 250 songs include: Distancia; Callajero; En Un Rincon Del Alama; El Abuelo; Cuando Un Amigo Se Va; Mi Arbol y Yo; Castillos En El Aire; Eran Tres; Equipaje; A Partir De Mañana. *Recordings:* Albums: Mr Sucu Sucu, 1960; Welcome To The Latin Club, 1961; Boleros, 1965; Poemas y Canciones, Vol. 1, 1967, Vol. 2, 1968; El Compositor, El Cantante, 1969; Distancia, 1970; No Soy De Aqui, 1971; Ni Poco... Ni Demasiado, 1973; Como El Ave Solitaria, 1974; A Mis Amigos, 1975; Soy Un Charlatan De Feria, 1976; Pensares y Sentires, 1977; En Vivo Desde Madrid, 1978; A Partir De Mañana, 1979; Castillos En El Aire, 1980; Como El Primer Dia, 1983; Gardel... Como Yo Te Siento, 1984; En Vivo, 1985; Sueños y Quimeras, 1986; Como La Marea, 1987; Almafuerte, 1989; Coincidencias, 1990; Si Vieras Que Facil, 1991; Aromas, 1993; Lo Cortez No Quita Lo Cabral, 1994; Lo Cortez No Quita Lo Cabral Vol. II, 1988; A Todo Corazon, 1996. *Publications:* 4 books: Equipaje; Soy Un Ser Humano; Almacen De Almas; Desde Un Rincon Del Alma, 1996. *Membership:* SGAE (Spain). *Leisure interests:* Computers; Football. *Current Management:* Raul Arribas. *Address:* c/o Pedro Teixeira 10, 28020 Madrid, Spain.

CORYELL Larry; b. 12 April 1943, Galveston, Texas, USA. Musician (guitar); Composer. m. Molly Shueler, 3 Sept. 1987, 2 s., 1 d. *Education:* University of Washington. *Musical Education:* Studied with Jerry Gray, Leon Bolotine, New York City, 1965. *Career:* Jazz guitarist, 1966–; Musician with: Chico Hamilton, 1966; Gary Burton, 1967; Founder, fusion band, Free Spirits; Leader, Eleventh House, 1969; Touring solo guitarist, also in duos with: Philip Catherine; Alphonse Mouzon; Steve Kahn; Emily Remier. *Recordings:* Albums include: Out of Sight and Sound, 1967; Lady Coryell, 1968; Spaces, 1969; Introducing The 11th House, 1974; The Restful Mind, 1975; Aspects, 1976; Basics, 1976; The Lion and The Ram, 1977; Standing Ovation, 1978; Bolero, 1981; Comin' Home, 1984; A Quiet Day In Spring, 1984; Equipoise, 1986; The Dragon Gate, 1989; Twelve Frets To The Octave, 1991; Fallen Angel, 1993; Dynamics, 1994; I'll Be Over You, 1994; Sketches of Coryell, 1996; Spaces Revisited, 1997; Major Jazz Minor Blues, 1998; Cause and Effect, 1998; Monk, Trane, Miles and Me, 1999; Private Concert (live), 1999; At Montreux (with The 11th House), 2000; Barefoot Boy, 2000; Inner Urge, 2001; Also recordings with Michael Urbaniak, Chet Baker, Gary Burton, Sonny Rollins and Laurindo Almeida. *Current Management:* Ted Kurland. *Address:* c/o Ted Kurland Associates, 173 Brighton Ave, Boston, MA 02167, USA.

COSGROVE Mike; b. 7 Nov. 1975, Long Beach, California, USA. Musician (drums). *Career:* Played with local bands Out of Order, Wallop, Brother Vibe, Tyemus; Member: Alien Ant Farm, 1996–; Self-financed independent LP released to acclaim, 1999; Signed to Papa Roach's New Noize label; Second album released in conjunction with DreamWorks label, leading to

major international breakthrough, 2000–01. *Recordings:* Albums: Greatest Hits, 1999; ANThology, 2001; Singles: $100 EP, 1996; Love Songs EP, 1998; Movies, Smooth Criminal, 2001. *Honours:* L.A. Music Award, Best Independent Album, 1999. *Address:* c/o New Noize, 2022 Cliff Dr #123, Santa Barbara, CA 93109, USA. *E-mail:* info@newnoize.com. *Internet:* www.alienantfarm.com.

COSTA Gal, (Maria da Graça Costa Pena Burgos); b. 1945, Salvador, Bahia, Brazil. Vocalist. *Career:* Part of Tropicália movement; Remained in Brazil whilst Gilberto Gil and Caetano Veloso were in exile, recording their songs; Has toured internationally and made many TV appearances. *Recordings include:* Albums: Domingo (with Caetano Veloso), 1967; Gal Costa, 1969; Gal, 1969; Gal A Todo Vapor, 1971; India, 1973; Gal Canta Caymmi, 1975; Caras E Bocas, 1977; Gal Tropical, 1979; Aquarel Do Brasil, 1980; Gal Costa, 1981; Fantasia, 1981; Plural, 1983; Baby Gal, 1983; Lua De Mel Como O Diabo Gosta, 1984; Bem Bom, 1985; Gal Canta Tom Jobim, 1999; Bem Bom, 2001. *Honours:* Shell Prize, 1984. *Address:* c/o BMG, Bedford House, 69–79 Fulham High St, London, SW6 3JW, England.

COSTEA Constantin; b. 1 Nov. 1931, Bucharest, Romania. Writer; Dance; Folklore Researcher; Record Prod. *Education:* Liceul Teoretic; Liceul Coregrfie; Special Master of Ballet Courses (3 years). *Career:* Numerous radio and television appearances; Tours, shows: Hungary; Czechoslovakia; Austria; Finland; Germany; France; Netherlands; UK; Sweden; Denmark; Iran. *Recordings:* As producer, series of 6 albums: Romanian Folk Dances, 1978–82. *Publications:* Numerous research studies. *Membership:* ICTM. *Address:* Bucaresti, 78468 Str, Moldovei, Nr 40, Sect 1, Romania.

COSTELLO Elvis, (Declan McManus); b. 25 Aug. 1955, London, England. Singer; Songwriter; Musician; Prod. m. Cait O'Riordan, 1 c. (from previous marriage). *Career:* Lead singer, Elvis Costello and The Attractions, 1977–; Appearances include: British tour, 1977; US tour, 1978; Grand Ole Opry, 1981; Royal Albert Hall, with Royal Philharmonic, 1982; Cambridge Folk Festival, 1995; Television includes: Appearance in Scully, ITV drama, 1985; Also worked with The Specials; Paul McCartney; Aimee Mann; George Jones; Roy Orbison; Wendy James; Robert Wyatt; Jimmy Cliff; Co-organizer, annual Meltdown festival, South Bank Centre, London. *Compositions include:* Alison, 1977; Watching The Detectives, 1977; (I Don't Want To Go To) Chelsea, 1979; Crawling To The USA, 1978; Radio Radio, 1978; Stranger In The House, 1978; Girls Talk, 1979; Oliver's Army, 1979; Boy With A Problem, 1982; Every Day I Write The Book, 1983; Music for television series (with Richard Harvey): G.B.H., 1991; Jake's Progress, 1995; Other songs for artists including Johnny Cash; June Tabor. *Recordings:* Albums include: My Aim Is True, 1977; This Years Model, 1978; Armed Forces, 1979; Get Happy, 1980; Trust, 1980; Almost Blue, 1981; Taking Liberties, 1982; Imperial Bedroom, 1982; Goodbye Cruel World, 1984; Punch The Clock, 1983; Goodbye Cruel World, 1984; The Best Of, 1985; Blood and Chocolate, 1986; King of America, 1986; Spike, 1989; Mighty Like A Rose, 1991; My Aim Is True, 1991; The Juliet Letters, with the Brodsky Quartet, 1993; Brutal Youth, 1994; The Very Best of Elvis Costello and The Attractions, 1995; Kojak Variety, 1995; Deep Dead Blue, Live At Meltdown (with Bill Frisell), 1995; All The Useless Beauty, 1996; Terror and Magnificence, 1997; Painted From Memory, 1998; The Sweetest Punch: The Songs of Costello, 1999; Best of Elvis Costello, 1999; For The Stars, with Anne Sofie von Otter, 2001. *Honours include:* BAFTA Award, Best Original Television Music, G.B.H., 1992; MTV Video, Best Male Video, 1989; Rolling Stone Award, Best Songwriter, 1990. *Current Management:* Jill Taylor, By Eleven Management, 12 Tideway Yard, 125 Mortlake High St, London SW14 8SN, England.

COTTLE Laurence; b. 16 Dec. 1961, Swansea, Wales. Musician (bass guitar). m. Alison Hooper, 16 April 1994. *Career:* Currently touring with Jim Mullen (GTR); Played most jazz festivals with Jim Mullen; Tours with Laurence Cottle Quintet include: America; Cuba; Germany; France; Spain; Italy; Collaborations include: Eric Clapton; Labi Siffre; James Taylor Quartet; Jason Rebello; Hue and Cry; Seal; Tom Jones; Rhythm and Blues (with Mark Feltham). *Recordings:* Solo album: Five Seasons; with Laurence Cottle Quintet: Live At 33, 1995. *Membership:* Musicians' Union. *Address:* 1 Harriet Walter Way, Rickmansworth, Hertfordshire WD3 2RT, England.

COULAM Roger Keith; b. 21 Aug. 1940, Blackburn, Lancashire, England. Musician (piano, organ, keyboards). m. Susan Chadwick, 19 Sept. 1961, 1 s., 2 d. *Musical Education:* Piano, harmony, London Guildhall School of Music and Drama, LGSM. *Career:* Backing Helen Shapiro, 1963; Duane Eddy, 1979; Johnny Howard's Band, Radio 1, Easybeat, 1966; Founder member, Blue Mink, 1969–73; Albert Hall Concert; Tour with Booker T and the MG's; Star Cabaret; Talk of The Town; Television includes: Top of The Pops; Prominent record, radio, television and film musician, 1966–; Sessions include: Tina Turner; Sammy Davis Jr; The Italian Job; Organist on Je T'Aime. *Compositions:* Co-writer several Blue Mink album tracks and B sides including chart single Sunday; Library music 1970, used for various radio, film, television series, including: Budgie; Vision On. *Recordings:* Solo albums: Organ In Orbit, 1966; Blow Hot, Blow Cool, 1969;

All Blue Mink recordings, 1969–73; Blue Mink Greatest Hits, 2000. *Honours:* Silver disc, Melting Pot, Blue Mink. *Memberships:* Musicians' Union; BMWC; PRS; MCPS; BASCA.

COULOMBE Daniel; b. 11 May 1960, Québec City, Canada. Music Prod. *Education:* University Communication. *Career:* Recording Producer; Remix Engineer; Radio Producer. *Recordings:* B-52's, Party Mix, 1981, Best of the B-52's: Dance This Mess, 1990, Party Mix/Mesopotamia, 1991; Icehouse; Indochine; Mitsou. *Leisure interests:* Mountain biking; Golf; Skiing; Swimming.

COUPLAND Gary; b. 27 March 1964, Dumfries, Scotland. Musician (accordion, keyboards). m. Karen Chaisson, 18 Sept. 1987, 3 d. *Education:* Dumfries Academy. *Musical Education:* Napier College, Edinburgh, Scotland. *Career:* Musical Director with The Singing Kettle, Scotland's Theatre Box Office Record Breakers, London Palladium and Sadler's Wells; 4 series for Children's BBC TV; Folk musician at Cambridge Folk Festival, Stage 1, 1992. *Recordings:* Appears on Ian Hardie, Ecosse: A Breath of Scotland, 1994; Brian McNeill, No Gods, 1996; Holding Up Half the Sky, Holding Up Half the Sky, 1997. *Publications:* 6 videos. *Honour:* BAFTA, Scotland, Best Children's TV Show. *Memberships:* Musicians' Union; Equity. *Address:* 12 Stanley St, Edinburgh EH15 1JJ, Scotland.

COURTOIS Vincent; b. 21 March 1968, Paris, France. m. Muriel, 1990, 1 s. *Career:* Played with: Michel Petrucciani; Niels Lan Doky; Tour with Michel Petrucciani, 1994–95. *Recordings:* Cello News; Pleine Lune; Pendulum Quartet; appears on Cheb Khaled, N'ssi N'ssi, 1993; Sahra, 1996; Philippe Eidel, Mammas, 1997; Imuhar, 1999. *Current Management:* Laurence Voiturier, Artalent. *Address:* 15 Passage de la Main d'Or, 75011 Paris, France.

COUSENS Peter William Light; b. 2 Nov. 1955, Tamworth, NSW, Australia. Singer; Actor. m. Suzanne Roylance, 9 Dec. 1984, 3 d. *Education:* National Institute of Dramatic Art Graduate, 1978. *Career:* Musicals: Camelot (Mordred), with Richard Harris, 1983; Blood Brothers (Eddie), 1987; The Mikado, The Australia Opera, 1986; Les Miserables (Marius), 1989–91; Aspects of Love (Alex), Phantom of the Opera, 1992; Sydney (Raoul), 1993–94; Miss Saigon (Chris), 1995–96; West Side Story (Tony), 1996; London (The Phantom), 1997; Australia Showboat, Ravenal, 1998. *Recordings:* First Album, Corner of the Sky, 1994; Second, From a Distance, 1996; International Symphonic Recording Miss Saigon (Chris), 1996; Are We Nearly There Yet, MBF Childrens with Noni Hazelhurst. *Honour:* Variety Club of Australia Heart Award, 1996. *Leisure interest:* Parenting. *Current Management:* International Casting Service, 147A King St, Sydney. *Address:* c/o ICS, 147A King St, Sydney, 2000, Australia.

COUSIN Andy; b. 28 June 1963, Lincoln, England. Musician (bass guitar); Vocalist. *Career:* Musician with: All About Eve; The Mission. *Recordings:* All About Eve: All About Eve, 1988; Scarlet and Other Stories, 1989; Touched By Jesus, 1991; Ultraviolet; Winter Words; Live At Glastonbury; Fairy Night Lights Vol. 1, 2000; Live and Electric At The Union Chapel, 2001; The Mission: Neverland. *Address:* 65 Vale Rd, Finsbury Park, London N4 1PP, England.

COVACI Nicu (Nicolae); b. 19 April 1947, Timisoara, Romania. Musician (6 and 12 string guitar); Vocalist. m. (1) 1976–78; (2) 1980–89. *Education:* High School of Arts; Academy of Arts. *Musical Education:* 4 years piano and guitar. *Career:* National Student Festival, Iasi, 1968; National Student Festival, Bucharest, 1969–71; Sopot Festival Poland, 1973; Romanian television: Tops of The Week; Romanian radio. *Recordings:* Vremuri (EP), 1968; Floarea Stincilor (EP), 1969; Cei Ce Ne-Au Dat Nume, 1971; Mesteroul Manole (EP), 1973; Mugur De Fluier, 1974; Cantafabule, 1975; Transsylvania, 1980; Symphoenix, 1992; Phoenix-Evergreens, 1995. *Honours:* First prize, National Student Festival, Iasi, 1968; Awards for: Composition and Creativity, Bucharest, 1969–71; Originality, Bratislawskalyra, Czechoslovakia, 1973. *Memberships:* GEMA; OCMR. *Leisure interests:* Painting; Diving; Motorcycles. *Address:* Im Dütetal 2, 49078 Osnabrück, Germany.

COVERDALE David; b. 22 Sept. 1949, Saltburn-By-The-Sea, Cleveland, England. Singer; Songwriter. m. Tawny Kitaen, 17 Feb., 1989. *Career:* Vocalist, Government; Lead singer, UK rock group Deep Purple, 1973–76; Founder, lead singer, UK heavy rock group Whitesnake, 1977–91; Solo artiste, 1991–; Member, Coverdale/Page, with Jimmy Page, 1993; Regular international tours; Concerts include: Reading Festival, 1979, 1980; Monsters of Rock, Castle Donington, 1981, 1983, 1990; Texas World Music Festival, 1987; Super Rock '90 Festival, Germany, 1990. *Recordings:* Albums: with Deep Purple: Burn, 1974; Stormbringer, 1974; 24 Carat Purple, 1975; Come Taste The Band, 1975; Live At The California Jam, 1996; King Biscuit Flower Hour, 1996; California Jam '74, 1996; with Whitesnake: Whitesnake, 1977; Northwinds, 1978; Trouble, 1979; Ready An' Willing, 1980; Live In The Heart of The City, 1980; Come An' Get It, 1981; Saints 'n' Sinners, 1982; Slide It In, 1984; Whitesnake 1987, 1987; Slip of The Tongue, 1989; Whitesnake's Greatest Hits, 1994; with

Coverdale/Page: Coverdale/Page, 1993; solo: Into The Light, 2000; Hit singles: with Whitesnake: Fool For Your Loving, 1980 (re-recorded, 1989); Don't Break My Heart Again, 1981; Here I Go Again, 1982 (re-recorded, No. 1, US, 1987); Give Me More Time, 1984; Still of The Night, 1987; Is This Love, 1987; Give Me All Your Love, 1987; The Deeper The Love, 1990; with Coverdale/Page: Take Me For A Little While, 1993. *Current Management:* H. K. Management, 8900 Wilshire Blvd #300, Beverly Hills, CA 90211, USA.

COWELL Harry Edmund (Sir); b. 4 Sept. 1960, Dorking, Surrey, England. Artist Man. m. Anita Harriet, 25 Feb. 1995, 1 d. *Career:* Management partner of Simon Napier-Bell; Clients include: Yardbirds; Japan; Marc Bolan; Wham!; Recent success with bands: Asia; Ultravox. *Recordings include:* Hokey Cokey, Captain Sensible, 1994, (for Great Ormond Street Hospital Childrens' Fund). *Leisure interest:* Polo. *Address:* 66 Prince Georges Ave, West Wimbledon, London SW20 8BH, England.

COWEN Jeanine M; b. 4 April 1965, Bettendorf, Iowa, USA. Composer; Musician (Percussion). m. Sara Whitman, 2 March 1991, 3 c. *Education:* Northwestern University. *Musical Education:* Berklee College of Music. *Career:* Film work as Composer: Home Before Dark, 1997; My Father's Love, 1998; Killing the Badge, 1999; A Far Distant Place, 2000; Killing Cinderella, 2000; Sandy 'Spin' Slade: Beyond Basketball, 2001. *Memberships:* IAWM; ASCAP; SCL; WIFVNE. *Address:* PO Box 66297, Auburndale, MA 02466, USA.

COWX Timothy; b. 23 Sept. 1975, Chester, England. Folk Singer; Musician (Guitar); Songwriter. *Career:* Acting in various local productions, lead roles in Bugsy Malone, Importance of Being Earnest; Formed Dicey Riler, 1996; Became Solo Artist, playing folk venues; Appeared at International Eistedffod Fringe, Llangollen. *Recordings:* Fabian Folk, 1997; Sanity EP, 1999; Dictonic, 1999. *Membership:* Musicians' Union. *Leisure interests:* Motor sport; Snooker; Walking. *Current Management:* M.G.E. *Address:* Glan Llyn, Glan Llyn Rd, Bradley, Wrexham, LL11 4BB, Wales.

COX Carl; b. 29 July 1962, Manchester, England. DJ; Prod.; Remixer; Label Owner. m. Rachel Turner, 19 March 1994. *Career:* DJ, 1980–; Sunrise Rave, 1989; Afterward known as '3 Deck Wizard'; One of top DJs on Rave scene, 1989–93; Signed album deal with Perfecto/BMG, 1991; Presently resident, top UK House/Techno clubs including Cream, Liverpool; Final Frontier, London; Also DJ in Germany; Tours: Australia; US; Japan; France; Switzerland; Austria; Ibiza; Started Ultimate Music Management (managing DJs from around the world), 1993; Started own MMR record label, 1994; Appeared in film Human Traffic, 1998. *Recordings:* Own albums: I Want You Forever, 1991; Does It Feel Good To You, 1992; At The End of The Cliché, 1996; Phuture 2000, 1999; Own record label releases include (own compositions): with Stone Circle: Deep In You; Tonight; with Conquer: Self Destruction; War Path; Solo: Anthemia; Motorway; Det 29–62; Remixed tracks by: Art of Noise; Sunscreen; Cuba Gooding; Yello; Stone Roses; Robert Owens; Patti Day; Jam and Spoon. *Honours:* DJ Magazine, No. 1 Rave DJ, 1992; Stepping Out, Top UK DJ, 1992, 1993; International Dance Awards: DJ of The Year, 1994, 1995; Frontpage Magazine, Top Overseas DJ, Germany, 1994. *Membership:* Musicians' Union. *Leisure interest:* Work. *Address:* 49 Highlands Rd, Horsham, West Sussex RH13 5LS, England.

COX Deborah; b. 1974, Canada. Singer; Songwriter. *Musical Education:* Performing Arts School. *Career:* Singer, commercials and local club circuit, Toronto, age 12; R & B singer, and songwriting partnership with Lascelles Stephens; Tour with Celine Dion; Concerts in Europe; Japan; Asia. *Recordings:* Debut album, 1995; One Wish, 1998; Singles: Sentimental, 1995; The Sound of My Tears, 1996; Nobody's Supposed To Be Here, 1998; It's Over Now, 1999; Appears on: Dan Hill, Greatest Hits and More, 1994; BeBe Winans, 1998; Trina and Tamara, Trina and Tamara, 1999; duet with Whitney Houston, Same Script Different Cast, 2000. *Current Management:* c/o Stiletto Entertainment, 5443 Beethoven St, Los Angeles, CA 90066, USA.

COX Doc, (Robert Cox); b. 1 July 1946, Sheffield, Yorkshire, England. Singer; Songwriter; Musician (ukelele). *Education:* Trained as teacher. *Musical Education:* 8 cello lessons; Several years under Bert Weedon book. *Career:* Semi-pro rock 'n' roll bands, 1960s, 70s; Top Twenty record, under name of Ivor Biggun (No. 1, Indie-Punk charts), 1978; 2 top 50 placings; Regular on That's Life, BBC TV, lots of BBC Radio. *Compositions include:* Ketchup Bottle Blues, sung by Marion Montgomery on BBC TV, Radio. *Recordings include:* The Winker's Song, banned by BBC, 1978; The Majorca Song, 1987; Compilation: The Fruity Bits, 1999. *Publications:* Rock Talk; Newspaper, magazine articles. *Honours:* Worthing Tourism Promotions Award. *Membership:* Musicians' Union. *Leisure interests:* Record collecting; Feeding cats. *Current Management:* Wendy Downes, 96 Broadway, Bexleyheath, Kent DA6 7DE, England.

COX Graham Kenneth; b. 24 Nov. 1965, Hammersmith, London, England. Journalist; Singer; Songwriter; Prod.; Man. *Education:* Sound Engineer, Detla Akustik and Vibration, Copenhagen. *Career:* Support for Depeche Mode, 1980s; A Void Citadel Tour, 1980s; Zenon Tour, Denmark, Infinity Tour, Denmark, late 1980s; Manager, Suspected Hippies in Transit, Mushroom Season 94 Tour; Singer, Producer, Low Flying Object, Plant More Trees; Owner, Director, Navajo Records, 1998-. *Compositions:* Plant More Trees; Low Flying Object; Crazy Horse. *Recordings:* Dragons; Folklore, Low Flying Object; Maxi CD, Plant More Trees. *Publications:* Several articles in professional magazines. *Address:* Damhusvej 27 st tv, 5000 Odense C, Denmark.

COX Peter; b. 17 Nov. 1955. Vocalist; Songwriter; Musician (guitar, keyboards). *Career:* Songwriting partnership with Richard Drummie, ATV Music; Founder member, duo Go West, 1982–; Solo career, 1997-. *Compositions include:* One Way Street (for film soundtrack Rocky IV). *Recordings:* Albums: Go West, 1985; Bangs and Crashes, 1986; Dancing On The Couch, 1987; Indian Summer, 1992; Best of Go West, 2000; Solo album, Peter Cox, 1997 Singles: We Close Our Eyes, 1985; Call Me, 1985; Don't Look Down, 1985; The King of Wishful Thinking, 1990; Solo single, Ain't Gonna Cry Again, 1997. *Current Management:* Blueprint Management, 134 Lots Rd, London SW12 0RJ, England.

COX Rachel Elizabeth; b. 15 April 1972, British Columbia, Canada. Co Dir. m. Carl Cox, 19 March 1994. *Career:* Director of Flying Records UK Ltd, 1990–92; Founder and Director of Ultimate Music Management, 1993-. *Address:* 49 Highlands Rd, Horsham, West Sussex RH13 5LS, England.

COXON Graham Leslie; b. 12 March 1969, Rinteln, Germany. Musician (guitar, saxophone). *Education:* Art and Design Diploma; N Essex School of Art; Goldsmiths College. *Musical Education:* Saxophone lessons at school. *Career:* Member, Blur; Television, radio appearances include: Top of the Pops; Later With Jools Holland; Extensive tours include: Alexandra Palace; Reading Festival, 1993; Glastobury Festival, 1994; Mile End, 1995; V97, 1997; UK Arena tour, 1997; Glastonbury, 1998; T in the Park, 1999; Reading/Leeds Festival, 1999. *Recordings:* Blur: Albums: Leisure, 1991; Modern Life Is Rubbish, 1993; Parklife (No. 1, UK) 1994; The Great Escape (No. 1, UK), 1995; Blur (No. 1, UK) 1997; 13 (No. 1, UK), 1999; The Best of Blur, 2000; Solo: The Sky is Too High, 1998; The Golden D, 2000; Crow Sit On Blood Tree, 2001; Singles: She's So High, 1990; There's No Other Way, 1991; Bang, 1991; Popscene, 1992; For Tomorrow, 1993; Chemical World, 1993; Sunday, Sunday, 1993; Girls and Boys, 1994; To The End, 1994; Parklife, 1994; End of a Century, 1994; Country House (No. 1, UK), 1995; The Universal, 1995; Stereotypes, 1996; Charmless Man, 1996; Beetlebum (No. 1, UK), 1997; Song 2, 1997; On Your Own, 1997; MOR, 1997; Tender, 1999; Coffee and TV, 1999; No Distance Left To Run, 1999; Music Is My Radar, 2000. *Honours:* Mercury Prize Nomination, 1999; Platinum Albums: Parklife, Blur, 13; BRIT Awards: Best Single, Album, Video, Band, 1995; Q Awards, Best Album, 1994, 1995. *Current Management:* CMO Management, Unit 32, Ransome Dock, 35–37 Parkgate Rd, London SW11 4NP, England.

COZENS Chris; b. 3 June 1959, England. Programmer. m. Mel, 5 Nov. 1988, 1 d. *Musical Education:* City of Leeds College of Music. *Career:* Keyboard player; Composed and performed music for new production: The Rise and Fall of The City of Mahogany, by Brecht; Spent year in Canada, with own band, Long Distanz; Returned to UK, joined Johnny Mars Band; Worked as arranger, orchestrator, session keyboard player, for: John Parr; Cozy Powell; Jan Akkerman; Barry Humphries; Graham Bonnett; Harry Nilsson; Francis Rossi; Demis Roussos; Jon English; producer Terry Britten; Programmer, musician, recording of Paris, rock opera by Jon English and Dave Mackay, with London Symphony Orchestra, Royal Philharmonic Orchestra, 1989; Toured Australia, MD for Jon English; Co-writer, 2 Australian television series, including All Together Now; Collaborated with Alan Parker, Dave Mackay, on incidental music for scores; Writer, portfolio of library music; Working with Alan Attfield on Facades (musical); Produced, recorded series of albums for Telstar Records under name Project D; Credits include: Films and television: What's Eating Gilbert Grape?; Wild Justice; To Be The Best; Voice of The Heart; Red Fox; Van Der Valk; Minder, by Alan Parker; 99 To 1, by Mike Gibbs; Coasting, West Beach, Making Out, by Dave Mackay; Bullseye, John Du Prez; Composer, incidental music, Children's Ward, 1994; Bridge To The Past, 1994; Music for documentary, Burning Rubber. *Recordings include:* Album: Synthesiser Greats, 1994; Lights Camera Action, 2001. *Memberships:* PRS; MCPS. *Current Management:* Soundtrack Music Management. *Address:* 22 Ives St, Chelsea, London SW3 2ND, England.

COZENS Spencer James; b. 11 Feb. 1965, Weston-Super-Mare, England. Musician (piano, keyboards); Composer; Prod. *Musical Education:* East Notts Music School; Newark Technical College; Goldsmiths College, 1987–91; B Mus degree. *Career:* Tours with Julia Fordham; Producing, touring with John Martyn, 1990–; Writer, producer, albums with Miles Bould (percussion) as Peoplespeak; Also with Jacqui McShee (vocals) Gerry Conway (drums), album: About Thyme; Writer, musician with Carol

Decker; Toured with Jacqui McShee's Pentangle. *Recordings:* Albums: with John Martyn: Cooltide (as producer, musician); As Co-producer and Musician: No Little Boy; Couldn't Love You More (as musician); The Church with One Bell (as musician); with Steps Ahead: Yin Yang; With Jacqui McShee's Pentangle: Passé Avant (writer, producer, musician); Albums by: Peoplespeak and About Thyme (as producer, writer, musician); John Martyn, And, co-producer, musician; Miten; David Hughes: 50 Yards of David Hughes (musician). *Memberships:* PRS; MCPS; PAMRA. *Address:* 72 Nottingham Rd, Bingham, Nottinghamshire NG13 8AW, England.

CRACKNELL Sarah; b. 12 April 1967, Chelmsford, Essex, England. Vocalist. *Musical Education:* Italia Conti Stage School; Drama Studio; Tona De Brett. *Career:* Singer, St Etienne; Television includes: Top of The Pops, five appearances; The Word, two appearances; Later With Jools Holland; Concerts include: Glastonbury; Tours of UK; Europe; Japan; US. *Recordings:* with St Etienne: Albums: Fox Base Alpha, 1991; So Tough, 1993; You Need A Mess of Help To Stand Alone, 1993; Tiger Bay, 1994; Too Young to Die, 1995; Casino Classics, 1996; Lipslide (solo), 1997; Good Humour, 1998; Singles: Nothing Can Stop Us, 1991; Join Our Club/People Get Real, 1992; Avenue, 1992; You're In A Bad Way, 1993; Who Do You Think You Are?/Hobart Paving, 1993; I Was Born On Christmas Day, 1993; Pale Movie, 1994; Like A Motorway, 1994; Hug My Soul, 1994; He's On The Phone, 1995; Gone (with David Holmes), 1995; Anymore (solo), 1997; Sylvie, 1998; The Bad Photographer, 1998; How We Used To Live, 2000; Heart Failed (In The Back of a Taxi), 2000; Boy Is Crying, 2001. *Honour:* Mercury Music Prize, runner-up. *Membership:* British Actors Equity. *Leisure interests:* Surfing; Snow-boarding. *Current Management:* Martin Kelly, Heavenly Management. *Address:* 72 Wardour St, London W1, England.

CRADDOCK Billy 'Crash' (William Wayne); b. 16 June 1939, Greensboro, North Carolina, USA. Singer. *Career:* Talent shows from age 10; Rock/country recording artiste, 1957-. *Recordings:* US Country No. 1 hits: Rub It In; Ruby Baby; Broken Down In Tiny Pieces; Other hit singles include: Boom Boom Baby; Knock Three Times; Dream Lover; You Better Move On; Ain't Nothin' Shakin'; I'm Gonna Knock On Your Door; I Cheated On A Good Woman's Love; Sea Cruise; Love Busted; Numerous albums include: I'm Tore Up, 1964; Knock Three Times, 1971; You Better Move On, 1972; Still Thinkin' About You, 1975; Crash, with Janie Frickie, 1976; Changes, 1980; Back On Track, 1989; Boom Boom Baby, 1992; Numerous greatest hits compilations including: Crash's Smashes: The Hits of Billy Crash, 1996. *Honours:* Cashbox Award, New Find of Year, 1972. *Address:* c/o Ace Productions, PO Box 292725, Nashville, TN 37229–2725, USA.

CRADOCK Steve; b. 22 Aug. 1969, Birmingham, England. Musician (guitar, keyboards). *Career:* Member, The Boys; Joined The Fanatics with Simon Fowler and Damon Minchella; Later joined Ocean Colour Scene; Joined Paul Weller's tour, 1993, and subsequent backing band, while still in Ocean Colour Scene; Played on Paul Weller's album Wild Wood; Band had support slot to Oasis 1994 tour; Numerous TV appearances and much radio airplay; Riverboat Song used as theme to TV Show TFI Friday; Several headlining tours. *Recordings:* Singles: with The Boys, Happy Days EP; Sway, 1990; with OCS: Yesterday Today, 1990; Giving It All Away, 1992; Do Yourself A Favour, 1992; Riverboat Song, 1996; The Day We Caught The Train, 1996; You've Got It Bad, 1996; The Circle, 1996; 100 Mile High City, 1997; Travellers Tune, 1997; Better Day, 1997; It's A Beautiful Thing, 1998; July/I Am The News, 2000; Albums: Ocean Colour Scene, 1992; Moseley Shoals, 1996; B-Sides, Seasides and Freerides, 1997; Marchin' Already (No. 1, UK), 1997; One From The Modern, 1999; Mechanical Wonder, 2001; Songs For The Front Row (compilation), 2001.

CRAIG Carl, (Paperclip People, 69, BFC, Psyche, Innerzone Orchestra); b. 1969, Detroit, Michigan, USA. Prod.; Remixer; DJ. *Career:* Protégé of Derrick May; Founder: Retroactive, Planet-E Recordings; Organizer: 2001 Detroit Electronic Music Festival; Remixed: Maurizio, Tori Amos, Gus Gus, Incognito; Collaborations: Derrick May. *Recordings:* Albums: Landcruising, 1995; More Songs About Food and Revolutionary Art, 1997 ; The Secret Tapes of Dr Eich (as Paperclip People), 1997; Programmed (with Innerzone Orchestra), 2000; Singles: Crackdown (as Psyche), 1990; Bug In The Bassbin (as Innerzone Orchestra), 1992; Throw (as Paperclip People), 1994; The Climax (as Paperclip People), 1995; 4 Jazz Funk Classics (as 69), 1994; People Make The World Go Round (as Innerzone Orchestra), 2000. *Current Management:* c/o Talkin' Loud Records, Chancellor's House, 72 Chancellor's Rd, London, W6 9QB, England.

CRAIG David Mark; b. 4 April 1969, Leeds, West Yorkshire, England. Musician (guitar); Songwriter. *Education:* BA Hons Historical Studies (undergraduate). *Musical Education:* Self-taught. *Career:* Guitarist with Drill, 1990–91; Television: Elements, Channel 4/Tyne Tees, 1990–91; Skin Down, voted album of the wwek on BBC Network, 1991; Recently formed The Sojourners, 1994. *Compositions:* Currently writing material with The Sojourners. *Recordings:* Drill: Skin Down, 1991. *Memberships:* Musicians'

Union. *Leisure interests:* Watching Newcastle United Football Club; Five-a-side football; Reading. *Address:* 13 St Joseph's Court, Heburn, Tyne and Wear NE31 2EN, England.

CRAIG Jay; b. 15 Oct. 1958, Bellshill, Scotland. Musician (baritone saxophone). *Musical Education:* Napier College, Edinburgh; Berklee College of Music, Boston, USA. *Career:* Member, National Youth Jazz Orchestra, 1976–81; Tommy Sampson Orchestra, Glasgow, 1979–82; Buddy Rich Band, 1984–87; BBC Big Band, 1992–; Performances with: Frank Sinatra; Tony Bennett; Sarah Vaughan; Jack Jones; Natalie Cole; Shirley Bassey; Vic Damone; Buddy Greco; Al Martino; Anita O'Day; Syd Lawrence Orchestra; BBC Scottish Radio Orchestra; Various West End shows. *Recordings:* 4 NYJO albums; with Buddy Rich: Live on King Street, San Francisco, 1985; Live In Leonberg, 1986; session work with: Terrorvision; Wet Wet Wet; George Martin. *Leisure interest:* Making model aeroplanes. *Address:* 3 Park Way, Ruislip, Middlesex HA4 8PJ, England.

CRAIG Mikey; b. 15 Feb. 1960, London, England. Musician (bass). *Career:* Member, with Boy George, In Praise of Lemmings; Became Sex Gang Children, then Culture Club; Numerous TV appearances and live dates; Band split, 1987; Worked as Record Producer; Band reformed, 1998. *Recordings:* Singles: Do You Really Want To Hurt Me (No. 1, UK), 1982; Time (Clock of the Heart), 1982; Church of the Poisoned Mind, 1983; Karma Chameleon (No. 1, UK and US), 1983; Victims, 1983; It's A Miracle, 1983; The War Song, 1984; The Medal Song, 1984; Move Away, 1986; God Thank You Woman, 1986; I Just Wanna Be Loved, 1998; Your Kisses Are Charity, 1999; Albums: Kissing to be Clever, 1982; Colour By Numbers (No. 1, UK), 1983; Waking Up With the House on Fire, 1984; From Luxury To Heartache, 1986; Greatest Moments (Live), 1998; Don't Mind If I Do, 1999. *Honours include:* Brit Awards: Best British Newcomer, 1983; Best British Group, 1984; Best-Selling British Single, Karma Chameleon, 1984.

CRANITCH Matt; b. 27 March 1948, Cork, Ireland. Traditional Musician (fiddle); Lecturer; Musicologist. m. Liz MacNamara, 17 July 1973, 2 s. *Education:* BE (Electrical Engineering), University College, Cork, Ireland. *Musical Education:* Cork School of Music, Ireland; BMus, University College, Cork. *Career:* Numerous concert performances as soloist, with Na Fili, with Any Old Time, with Sliabh Notes; Festival appearances include: Belfast; Brest; Cambridge; Clifden; Cologne; Copenhagen; Cork; Cornwall; Derry; Dingle; Dublin; Exeter; Killarney; Kilkenny; Galway; Inverness; Lenzburg; Loughborough; New York; Norwich; Nyon; Orkney; Paris; Penzance; Quimper; Rome; Rotterdam; Shetland; Sligo; Swansea; Vienna; Radio and television shows include: Bring Down The Lamp; Cúrsaí; The Humours of Donnybrook; The Late Late Show; Live From The Cork Opera House; The Pure Drop; As I Roved Out; Bringing It All Back Home; Sult; Geantraí; Lectures, workshops, master-classes in Ireland and abroad; Research work, ongoing, Irish World Music Centre, University of Limerick; Director, Chairman, Cork Arts Fest, 1993–98. *Recordings include:* with Dave Hennessy and Mick Daly: Any Old Time, 1982; Phoenix, 1987; Crossing, 1995; Solo: Éistigh Seal, 1984; Take A Bow, 1992; Give It Stick, 1996; with Dónal Murphy and Tommy O'Sullivan: Sliabh Notes, 1995; Gleanntán, 1999. *Publications:* The Irish Fiddle Book, 1988, third edition, 1996; contributions to several books on Irish Traditional Music. *Memberships:* Folk Music Society of Ireland; Irish Traditional Music Archive; Irish Music Rights Organisation. *Address:* Kerry Pike, Co Cork, Ireland.

CRAVEN Beverly; b. 28 June 1963, Sri Lanka. Singer; Songwriter; Musician (piano). *Musical Education:* Piano lessons. *Career:* Solo artiste, 1990–; British tour, 1993. *Recordings include:* Albums: Promise Me, 1990; Love Scenes, 1993; Mixed Emotions, 1999; Single: Promise Me, 1990. *Honour:* Brit Award, Best British Newcomer, 1992. *Current Management:* Blueprint Management, 134 Lots Rd, London SW12 0RJ, England.

CRAWFORD Randy (Randall Hugh); b. 16 Jan. 1953, Grand Rapids, Michigan, USA. Publisher; Cartoonist; Musician (Guitar). *Education:* Private instruction, guitar. *Career:* Wrote and acted in stage play Time Capsule; Wrote play Good Old Spot, performed at Grand Rapids Arts Fair; Interviews on TV to promote film Comic Book Confidential. *Compositions:* Autumn; Bothered; Sick; Black Velvet Elvis; Children of the Night. *Recordings:* Produced cassette box cover art, Acid Orangutan; CD cover art, Bloodsucking Mosquitos; Producer, Crooked Foot Live; Assembled compilations, Glove Box Sampler, Bad Exampler Sampler, Black Paper Packages. *Publications:* Issues on numerous magazines; Comic strip artist, The Three Pals. *Honour:* Student Award, Haiku, 1971. *Membership:* BMG Music Service, 1986-. *Leisure interests:* Drawing; Writing; Painting; Cooking; Correspondence; Playing guitar; Collecting comics; Music; Pornography. *Current Management:* Nice Day. *Address:* 911 Park St SW, Grand Rapids, MI 49504, USA.

CRAWFORD Randy (Veronica); b. 18 Feb. 1952, Macon, Georgia, USA. Singer. *Career:* Singer, 1967–; Appearances include: World Jazz Association tribute concert to Cannonball Adderley, 1968; Montreux Jazz Festival, 1982; 2 concerts with London Symphony Orchestra, Barbican

Centre, London, 1988. *Recordings:* Singles include: Street Life (with The Crusaders), 1979; One Day I'll Fly Away, 1980; You Might Need Somebody, 1981; Rainy Night In Georgia, 1981; Almaz (own composition), 1987; Knockin' On Heaven's Door, used in film soundtrack Lethal Weapon 2, 1989; Guest vocalist, Diamante, Zucchero, 1992; Albums: Everything Must Change, 1976; Miss Randy Crawford, 1977; Raw Silk, 1979; Now We May Begin, 1980; Secret Combination, 1981; Windsong, 1982; Nightline, 1983; Casino Nights (with Al Jarreau), 1983; Miss Randy Crawford – The Greatest Hits, 1984; Abstract Emotions, 1986; The Love Songs, 1987; Rich and Poor, 1989; The Very Best Of, 1993; Don't Say It's Over, 1993; Naked and True, 1995; Every Kind of Mood – Randy Randi Randee 1998; Play Mode, 2001; Permanent, 2001; Guest vocalist on albums: Please Don't Touch, Steve Hackett, 1977; Marching In The Streets, Harvey Mason, 1978; Street Life, The Crusaders, 1979; Hard To Hold, Rick Springfield, 1984; Lethal Weapon 2, 1989; Best of Smooth Jazz, 1997; Jackie Brown, Music from the Motion Picture Soundtrack, 1997; Funky Jazz Party, 1998; Crusaders, Priceless Jazz, 1998; Classic Gold Vol. 2: The Love Song, 1999; Barry Williams, Return of Johnny Bravo, 1999. *Honour:* Brit Award, Best Female Artist, 1982. *Current Management:* Gross Management Organisation, 930 Third St, Suite 102, Santa Monica, CA 90403, USA.

CRAWFORD Stephanie; b. 30 Aug. 1942, Detroit, Michigan, USA. Singer; Artist; Educator. *Education:* BA, Fine Arts, Wayne State University, Detroit, Michigan, USA. *Musical Education:* Barry Harris; Frank Foster, New York City. *Career:* Plays clubs and festivals including: Crest Jazz Festival; Aix-En-Provence Jazz Festival; Film appearance, La Vie En Rouge, 1995; Voice teacher, Centre d'Informations Musicales; Institut d'Art, Culture et Perception, Paris. *Recordings:* The Art of Romance, 1990; A Time For Love, 1991; The Gift, 1992. *Honour:* Django D'Or, Best Jazz Vocal, 1993. *Address:* 47 rue Piat, 75020 Paris, France.

CRAY Robert William; b. 1 Aug. 1953, Columbus, Georgia, USA. Blues Musician (guitar); Singer; Songwriter. *Career:* Began playing guitar aged 12; Member, Albert Collins' band, 1973–75; Formed Robert Cray Band, 1975–; Appearances include: Chuck Berry's 60th Birthday Concert, 1986; US tour as Bad Influence, 1987; Support to Tina Turner, European tour, 1987; Support to Eric Clapton, Royal Albert Hall, London, 1990; Concert with Eric Clapton and Stevie Ray Vaughan (his last), East Troy, Wisconsin, 1990; Guitar Legends, Seville, Expo '92, 1991; Tour with B B King, 1992; Festival appearances include: Glastonbury Festival; North Sea Jazz Festival; Newport Jazz Festival; Monterey Jazz Festival; Montreux Jazz Festival; San Francisco Blues Festival; New Orleans Jazz and Heritage Festival; Other concert performances with: The Rolling Stones; Muddy Waters; John Lee Hooker; Willie Dixon; Bonnie Raitt; The Grateful Dead; Film appearances: Animal House; Hail! Hail! Rock and Roll. *Compositions:* Songs covered by other artists include: Bad Influence, Eric Clapton; Old Love (co-writer with Eric Clapton); Phone Booth, Albert King; Playin' With My Friends, BB King. *Recordings:* Albums: Who's Been Talking, 1980; Bad Influence, 1983; False Accusations, 1985; Strong Persuader, 1986; Don't Be Afraid of The Dark, 1988; Midnight Stroll, 1990; I Was Warned, 1992; Shame and A Sin, 1993; Some Rainy Morning, 1995; Sweet Potato Pie, 1997; In Concert (Live), 1999; Take Your Shoes Off, 1999; Shoulda Been Home, 2001; Singles include: Smoking Gun, 1987; Right Next Door (Because of Me), 1987; Forecast, 1990; Contributor, recordings by artists including: Albert Collins; Eric Clapton; Tina Turner; BB King; John Lee Hooker; Chuck Berry; Johnny Copeland; The Memphis Horns; Katie Webster. *Honours include:* National Blues Awards, 1983, 1986; NAIRD Award, Best Blues Album, 1985; Grammy Awards, 1985, 1986, 1988; 8 Grammy Nominations; Numerous W.C. Handy Awards, 1984-, including 6 (Best Male Blues Artist, Vocalist of the Year, Single of the Year, Band of the Year, Song of the Year, Best Contemporary Blues Album), 1987; Numerous magazine awards, from Billboard; Downbeat; Rolling Stone; Esquire; Living Blues. *Current Management:* Eric Hanson, The Rosebud Agency, PO Box 170429, San Francisco, CA 94117, USA.

CREASEY Jason M; b. 23 July 1969, Andover, Hampshire, England. Record Prod.; Remixer; Composer; Arranger; Musician. *Musical Education:* GCE A Level Music and Practical Music; Piano, Grade 8 (Trinity College of Music); Trumpet, Grade 8 (AB). *Career:* Extensive work in areas of writing, arranging, producing for various artists; Music to film; Keyboards and drum programming; Most recent productions in partnership with Hamish Hutchison (also known as remix duo Hiss and Hum for Absolute Basic Productions). *Recordings:* Producer (including arranging) for: Chesney Hawkes; Big Fun; Glen Goldsmith; Think 2wice (including writing); Deni Lew (additional production only); Remixer for: PJ and Duncan; Love City Groove; Jack 'n' Chill; Chesney Hawkes. *Memberships:* PRS; MCPS; Musicians' Union. *Address:* 7 St John's St, Aylesbury, Buckinghamshire HP20 1BS, England.

CREME Lol; b. 19 Sept. 1947, Manchester, Lancashire, England. Musician (guitar); Vocalist; Songwriter; Prod.; Video and Film Dir. *Education:* Graphic design, art college. *Career:* Founder member, guitarist, songwriter, Hotlegs, 1970–71; 10cc, 1972–76; Appearances include:

Reading Festival, 1974; Knebworth Festival, 1976; Tours of UK, USA; Producer, songwriter, member, duo Godley and Creme (with Kevin Godley), 1976–; Debut feature film, Howling At The Moon, 1988; Film director, The Lunatic, 1992; Joined Art of Noise, 1998-. *Recordings:* Albums: with Hotlegs: Thinks: School Stinks, 1970; with 10cc: 10cc, 1973; Sheet Music, 1974; The Original Soundtrack, 1975; How Dare You?, 1976; with Godley and Creme (mostly self-written and produced): Consequences, 1977; L, 1978; Music From Consequences, 1979; Freeze Frame, 1979; Ismism, 1981; Birds of Prey, 1983; The History Mix Vol. 1, 1985; The Changing Faces of 10cc and Godley and Creme, 1987; Goodbye Blue Sky, 1988; Images, 1994; Hit singles: with Hotlegs: Neanderthal Man (No. 2, UK), 1970; with 10cc: Donna, 1972; Rubber Bullets (No. 1, UK), 1973; The Dean and I, 1973; Wall Street Shuffle, 1974; Life Is A Minestrone, 1975; Art For Arts Sake, 1976; I'm Not In Love (No. 1, UK, No. 2, US), 1976; I'm Mandy Fly Me, 1976; Singles: Under Your Thumb, 1981; Wedding Bells, 1981; Cry, 1985; with Art of Noise: Album: The Seduction of Claude Debussy, 1999; Other session work includes: Tina Turner, Rod Stewart, Producer, Long Distant Romancer, Mickey Jupp, 1981; Director, videos including: Every Breath You Take, The Police; Rockit, Herbie Hancock; Feel The Love, 10cc; Relax, Frankie Goes To Hollywood; Two Tribes, Frankie Goes To Hollywood. *Honours:* Ivor Novello Awards: Best Beat Song, Rubber Bullets, 1974; Most Performed British Work, Best Pop Song, International Hit of The Year, I'm Not In Love, 1976; 5 MTV Music Video Awards, Rockit, 1984; MTV Video Vanguard Award (shared), 1985.

CRESSWELL Guy; b. 17 May 1963, Bournemouth, England. Musical Entrepeneur; Musician (bass guitar, flute); Vocalist. m. Kate Snoswell. *Education:* 4 year Engineering diploma. *Career:* Six-month tour Europe, R & B band, 1983; Move to London, joined Innocent Party, 1984; Nationwide tours with TSB Rockschool teaching Hi tech, 1985–86; Worked as music demonstrator, Roland UK Ltd, 1986–95; Television appearances with: The Sweet; Jools Holland; Midge Ure; Ton of Joy, 1991–94. *Recordings:* with Playing For Time: With My Heart, 1990; Six Weeks In July; with Ton of Joy: Revealed Part 1. *Memberships:* PRS; Musicians' Union. *Leisure interests:* Mac computers; Reading; Fish keeping. *Current Management:* Promus Productions. *Address:* The Barley Mow Centre, 10 Barley Mow Passage, Chiswick, London W4 4PH, England.

CRETU Michael; b. 18 May 1957, Bucharest, Romania. Musician (keyboards); Arranger; Prod.; Composer. m. Sandra Lauer, 1988. *Musical Education:* Piano Lyzeum No 2, Bucharest, 1966; Academy of Music, Frankfurt, 1975. *Career:* Studio musician, 1978–; Writer, producer, musician, Moti Special; Mike Oldfield; Sylvie Vartan; Sandra, 1985–; Founder member, Enigma, 1990-. *Recordings:* Albums: Solo album: Legionare, 1983; with Enigma: MCMXC AD, 1990; The Cross of Changes, 1993; Le Roi Est Mort, Vive Le Roi!, 1996; Screen Behind The Mirror, 2000; Love, Sensuality and Devotion (compilation), 2001; 6 albums with Sandra; Singles include: with Enigma: Sadeness (No. 1 across Europe), 1990; Return To Innocence, 1994; Maria Magdelena, Sandra (No. 1 in 30 countries); C'est Fatale, Sylvie Vartan; Writer, arranger, tracks for film soundtrack Sliver. *Honours:* Numerous Platinum and Gold discs as producer. *Current Management:* Nizzari Artist Management, 410 W 25th St, Suite 5A, New York, NY 10001, USA.

CRISS Peter, (Peter Crisscoula); b. 27 Dec. 1947, Brooklyn, New York, USA. Musician (drums); Singer; Songwriter. *Career:* Founder member, US rock group Kiss, 1973–80, rejoined 1995; Debut, Academy of Music, New York, with Blue Öyster Cult; Iggy Pop; Teenage Lust; Tours include UK, 1976; Solo artiste, 1980–82; Member, Balls of Fire. *Recordings:* Albums with Kiss: Kiss, 1974; Hotter Than Hell, 1974; Dressed To Kill, 1975; Alive, 1975; Destroyer, 1976; The Originals, 1976; Rock and Roll Over, 1976; Kiss Alive II, 1977; Love Gun, 1977; Double Platinum, 1978; Dynasty, 1979; MTV Unplugged, 1996; Psycho Circus, 1998; Solo albums: Peter Criss, 1978; Out of Control, 1980; Let Me Rock You, 1982; Criss Cat #1, 1994. *Publications:* The Kiss Comic Book, Marvel Comics. *Honours:* Platinum albums; Footprints outside Grauman's Chinese Theatre, Hollywood, 1976; Gold Ticket, Madison Square Garden, New York. *Current Management:* GHR Entertainment Co, Suite 506, 16601 Ventura Blvd, Encino, CA 91436, USA.

CROISILLE Nicole; b. 9 Oct. 1936, Neuilly-Sur-Seine, France. Singer; Actress. *Career:* Tour with mime artist, Marcel Marceau; Lead role, musical, L'Apprenti Fakir; First record, 1961; Worked in USA with Lester Wilson, Lalo Schifrin; Un Homme Et Une Femme (A Man and A Woman), 1966; Olympia, Paris, 1976, 1978; Theatre des Champs-Elysées, Paris, 1981; Bataclan, Paris, 1988; Casino de Paris, 1991; Lead role, Hello Dolly, Thèatre du Chatelet, Paris, 1992–93; Actress, Les Miserables du XXe Siècle, 1995; Appearances: Canada; Latin America; Poland; Morocco; New show at Espace Pierre Cardin Theatre, Paris, 1997. *Recordings include:* Un Homme Et Une Femme; Parlez-Moi De Lui; Femme Avec Toi; T'arrai Voulu Etre Un Artiste; Albums: Croiselle Jazzille; Croiselle Black Et Blanche. *Honours:* Chevalier des Arts et des Lettres. *Membership:* SACEM. *Leisure interests:* Dance; Gymnastics; Travel. *Current Management:* Bertrand

Tallec, Showstop Management. *Address:* 64 Château Trompette, 78950 Gambais, France.

CROKER Brendan; b. 15 Aug. 1953, Bradford, Yorkshire, England. Musician (guitar). *Education:* Studied sculpture, art school. *Career:* Formed duo, Nev and Norris, with fellow guitarist Steve Phillips; Formed own band, the 5 O'Clock Shadows, early 1980s; Member, Notting Hillbillies (with Mark Knopfler, Guy Fletcher, Steve Phillips), 1990; British tour, 1990. *Recordings:* Albums: Close Shave, 1986; Brendan Croker and The 5 O'Clock Shadows, 1989; The Great Indoors, 1992; The Kershaw Sessions, 1996; Not Just A Hillbilly, 2000; with the Notting Hillbillies: Missing. . . Presumed Having, 1990; Guest musician, Ancient Heart, Tanita Tikaram; Singles: That's The Way All My Money Goes, 1986. *Current Management:* Paul Crockford Management, 56–60 Islington Park St, London N1 1PX, England.

CROMPHOUT Francis; b. 24 Oct. 1947, Antwerp, Belgium. Singer; Songwriter; Musician (Saxophone, Clarinet, Flute). m. Alejandra Anfossi, 20 Jan. 1994, 2 d. *Education:* University Degree in Roman Languages, Ghent State University. *Career:* Several performances in Jazz, Blues and Latin music; Creator and Performer, En Avian La Zizique, song programme around Boris Vian; Founder, Band Leader, Cuisine Cajun and Café con Leche; Songwriter, Cuisine Cajun, Café con Leche and Catherine Delasalle; Concerts in Holland, Germany, Belgium, France; Emmissions in VRT Radio and the RTBF Television. *Compositions include:* Allons au Fais-Do-Do; Le Grand Dérangement, Cofé Bon Dieu, Démarche, (Pigalle). *Recording:* Le Grand Dérangement, 1996. *Publication:* Als un pas vernielde stad, poetry, 1978. *Honours:* Nominee of the CAWAB Award, 1997, 1998, 1999; Chevalier dans l'Ordre des Palmes Académiques. *Memberships:* SABAM, Belgian Asscn of Authors and Composers; Country and Western Asscn of Belgium. *Leisure interests:* Journalist for Knack Magazine; Poetry (publication in several literary magazines). *Current Management:* Berkenhof 7, 9050 Ghent, Belgium. *Address:* Berkenhof 7, 9050 Ghent, Belgium.

CRONIN Kevin; b. 6 Oct. 1951, Evanston, Illinois, USA. Singer; Songwriter. *Career:* Lead vocalist, US rock group REO Speedwagon, 1972; 1976–; Solo artiste, 1973–76; Regular US and international concerts include: Anti-drug Users Are Losers concert, Miami, 1990. *Compositions include:* Keep On Loving You; Can't Fight This Feeling; Hard To Believe, for Home Front Trust (for families of Gulf War casualties). *Recordings:* Albums: with REO Speedwagon: R.E.O. T.W.O., 1972; R.E.O., 1976; REO Speedwagon Live/You Get What You Play For, 1977; You Can Tune A Piano But You Can't Tuna Fish, 1978; Nine Lives, 1979; A Decade of Rock 'N' Roll 1970–80, 1980; Hi Infidelity (No. 1, USA), 1981; Good Trouble, 1982; Wheels Are Turning, 1984; Best Foot Forward, 1985; Life As We Know It, 1987; The Hits, 1988; The Earth, A Small Man, His Dog and A Chicken, 1990; A Second Decade of Rock 'N' Roll, 1981–91, 1991; Building the Bridge, 1996; Ballads, 1999; Live Plus, 2001; Hit singles include: Time For Me To Fly, 1978; Keep On Loving You (No. 1, USA), 1981; Take It On The Run, 1981; Don't Let Him Go, 1981; Keep The Fire Burnin', 1982; I Can't Fight This Feeling (No. 1, USA), 1985; One Lonely Night, 1985; That Ain't Love, 1987; In My Dreams, 1988. *Honours:* Platinum and Gold discs. *Current Management:* Baruck-Consolo Management, 15003 Greenleaf St, Sherman Oaks, CA 91403, USA.

CRONK William Henry; b. 28 Aug. 1928, Fort Lee, New Jersey, USA. Musician (bass violin, electric bass); Arranger. m. Mary Reisinger, 10 Dec. 1947, divorced, 1 s., 1 d. *Musical Education:* Bass, with M. Hinton, G Duvivier, Robert Brennand; Arranging, with Sy Oliver, Hugo Winterhalter. *Career:* 52nd Street, NYC, with Don Byas, 1945; Tony Pastor, Ray Anthony, Ralph Flanagan, 1946; Joined Tommy Dorsey, 1950; United with Jimmy Dorsey to form The Fabulous Dorseys, 1952; Became associated with Jackie Gleason Show, 1950s; Recorded with: Tommy Dorsey; Jimmy Dorsey; Ray Anthony; Ralph Flanagan; Ray McKinley; Bobby Hackett; Joined Louis Armstrong, early 1960s; Playboy Resort Hotel, New Jersey, 1970s; Playboy In Atlantic City, 1980s; Formed own band for the Meyer Davis Off. *Memberships:* AFofM (New York and New Jersey). *Leisure interests:* Owning and racing Thoroughbred and Standardbred horses. *Current Management:* Own company, Bel-Cron Music. *Address:* William H Cronk Sr, 400 W 43rd St, Apt 44R, New York, NY 10036, USA.

CROOK (William) Roger; b. 13 Aug. 1942, Forfar, Scotland. Teacher; Semi-professional Singer (tenor); Instrumentalist. m. Nancy, 19 Aug. 1968, 1 s., 1 d. *Musical Education:* RSAMD Diplomas: DRSAM (singing teacher); DRSAM (singing performer); ARCM (singing teacher). *Career:* Broadcasts of Scottish songs, classical material; Leader, Thistle Ceilidh Band; Member, Quatrain; Arranger of Scottish material for voices and orchestra; Musician, accordion, fiddle, piano, for Scottish Dance Bands; Conductor. *Recordings:* An Evening of Scottish Songs; An Evening of Light Music; Songs We Love; Sound of The Sea. *Honours:* Officer, St John's Asscn for Musical Charity Work. *Leisure interests:* Walking; Hospital and Hospice entertaining. *Current Management:* The Entertainment Company, Edinburgh. *Address:* 11 Barbour Grove, Dunfermline, Fife KY12 9YB, Scotland.

CROOK Jenny; b. 16 Jan. 1971, Bath, Avon, England. Musician (non-pedal harp); Vocalist. *Education:* BA Hons, Performance Arts, Middlesex University. *Career:* Folk clubs and Festivals; Television appearances include: Pebble Mill; Summer In The City; Radio appearances in sessions for Folk On 2; Kaleidoscope; Played incidental music, David Attenborough's television series, The Private Life of Plants, BBC; Played at Barbican Festival; Current band, Madigan; Composed theme tune for S4C Club Gweryn series; Session musician and recording artist; Member of Duo, Jenny Crook and Henry Sears; Cythara, duo with Maclaine Colston (hammered dulcimer, vocals), 1991–95. *Recordings:* Evolving Tradition; Cythara, 1992; Pluckin' Hammered, 1995; Uncorked, 1997. *Honour:* Young Tradition Award Finalist, BBC Radio 2, 1993. *Memberships:* Musicians' Union; PRS; PAMRA; Clarsach Society. *Address:* 8 Walcot Terrace, London Rd, Bath BA1 6AB, England.

CROSBY David, (David Van Cortland); b. 14 Aug. 1941, Los Angeles, California, USA. Vocalist; Musician (guitar). m. Jan Dance, 15 May 1987. *Career:* Member, Les Baxter's Balladeers; The Byrds, 1964–67; Crosby Stills and Nash, 1968–; Also, Crosby Stills Nash and Young; Performances include: with the Byrds: Monterey Pop Festival, 1967; with Crosby Stills and Nash: Woodstock Festival, 1969; Altamont Speedway, with the Rolling Stones, 1969; Royal Albert Hall, 1970; Wembley Stadium, 1974; Anti-nuclear concert, Madison Square Garden, New York, 1979; Peace Sunday concert, Rose Bowl, Pasadena, 1982; Live Aid, Philadelphia, 1985; Madison Square Garden, 1988; Amnesty International benefit, Chile, 1990; Farm Aid IV, 1990; Royal Albert Hall, 1992; Film, No Nukes, 1980; Television: guest, Roseanne, ABC-TV, 1992; The Simpsons, Fox-TV, 1993; Collaborations include: Jeff Bridges; Jackson Browne; Phil Collins; Bob Dylan; Art Garfunkel; Carole King; Joni Mitchell; Stevie Nicks; Neil Young. *Recordings:* Albums include: with the Byrds: Mr Tambourine Man, 1965; Turn! Turn! Turn!, 1965; Fifth Dimension, 1966; Younger Than Yesterday, 1967; with Crosby Stills and Nash include: Crosby Stills and Nash, 1969; Déja Vu, 1970; 4-Way Street, 1971; So Far, 1974; Daylight Again, 1982; ; Looking Forward, 1999; with Graham Nash: Graham Nash/David Crosby, 1972; Wind On The Water, 1975; Whistling Down The Wire, 1976; Crosby/ Nash Live, 1977; The Best Of, 1978; Another Stoney Evening, 1998; Solo albums: If Only I Could Remember My Name, 1971; Oh Yes I Can, 1989; Now It's All Coming Back To Me, 1995; King Biscuit Flower Hour, 1996; Live, 2000; Singles include: with the Byrds: Mr Tambourine Man (No. 1, UK and US), 1965; All I Really Want To Do, 1965; Eight Miles High, 1966; 5D (Fifth Dimension), 1966; Mr Spaceman, 1966; So You Want To Be A Rock 'n' Roll Star, 1967; with Crosby Stills and Nash: Woodstock, 1970; Teach Your Children, 1970; Ohio, 1970; Just A Song Before You Go, 1977; Wasted On The Way, 1982; Southern Cross, 1982. *Publications include:* Stand Up and Be Counted, 2000. *Honours:* Grammy, Best New Artists, Crosby Stills and Nash, 1970; Best International Group, Melody Maker Poll, 1971; MusiCares Man of The Year, NARAS, 1991. *Current Management:* Management Network Inc, 14930 Ventura Blvd #205, Sherman Oaks, CA 91403, USA.

CROSS Christopher, (Christopher Geppert); b. 3 May 1951, San Antonio, Texas, USA. Musician (guitar); Vocalist; Songwriter. *Career:* Member, rock group Flash; Support for acts including Led Zeppelin, Jefferson Airplane, Deep Purple; Formed band for own compositions, 1975; Recording artist, 1978; Own publishing company, Pop 'n' Roll, 1978. *Compositions include:* Co-writer (with Burt Bacharach, Carole Bayer Sager, Peter Allen): Arthur's Theme (Best That You Can Do), for film Arthur, 1981. *Recordings:* Albums include: Christopher Cross, 1980; Another Page, 1983; Every Turn of The World, 1985; Back of My Mind, 1988; Rendezvous, 1992; Window, 1995; Walking in Avalon, 1998; Greatest Hits Live, 1999; Red Room, 2000; Singles include: Ride Like The Wind, 1980; Sailing (No. 1, USA), 1980; Never Be The Same, 1980; Say You'll Be Mine, 1981; Arthur's Theme (No. 1, USA), 1981; All Right, 1983; No Time To Talk, 1983; Think of Laura, 1983; A Chance For Heaven (used as swimming theme for Los Angeles Olympics), 1984; Contributor, Pearls – Songs of Goffin and King, Carole King, 1980; Film soundtrack, Nothing In Common, 1986; As co-producer: Long Time Friends, Alessi Brothers, 1982. *Honours:* Grammy Awards: Album of The Year, Christopher Cross; Best New Artist; Record of The Year, Sailing; Song of The Year, Sailing; Best Arrangement, Sailing, (all) 1981; Academy Award, Best Song From A Film, Arthur's Theme, 1982. *Current Management:* Baruck/Consolo, 15003 Greenleaf St, Sherman Oaks, CA 91043, USA.

CROSSLEY Syd; b. 10 Aug. 1961, Ilford, East London, England. Musician (saxophones, flute, keyboards, guitars); Vocalist; Programmer. 1 s. *Musical Education:* Self-taught. *Career:* Songwriter, saxophone, Bastard Bros Band, 1986; Songwriter, saxophone, lead vocalist, The Never Again With Rob Barham Band, 1987; Vocalist, co-songwriter, saxophone, Trip Cadets, 1988–91; Co-songwriter, saxophone, The Rubber Club, 1991; Co-songwriter, saxophone, Fat Cat Band, 1992–93; Co-songwriter, artist, programmer, Boom Devils, 1994–95; Co-songwriter, programmer, artist, King Kooba Triptet, 1995, appearances on various King Kooba tracks; Remixes for Senser; Co-songwriter and programmer in geko and itones. *Recordings:* Life's A Bummer EP, Trip Cadets, 1991; Albums: Saxophonist,

Seven, James (No. 1, UK), 1992; Currently completing albums: One Minute Away From Perfection, and Metamorphosis, Boom Devils; The Dub Commander Lands On The Kooba Twins, King Kooba Triptet; Roof Top Dub, Itones; King Kooba Triptet EP; Single remix, Utah Saints. *Memberships:* Musicians' Union; Founder mem., The Rubber Club. *Leisure interests:* Inventing instruments; Making sound effects. *Current Management:* Boom Devil Productions. *Address:* 236 Canbury Park Rd, Kingston upon Thames, Surrey, England.

CROUCHER Piers; b. 1 Nov. 1969, Minehead, Somerset, England. Musician (drums, percussion, guitar). Partner, Sadie Doyle. *Musical Education:* Tommy Cuncliffe, Jersey. *Career:* Member, Zapf The Band; Air Stream Stream Trailer; The Bar Flies; Summer seasons, Jersey; Lucy and Freud. *Recordings:* 2 EPs: Lucy and Freud; Field Day. *Memberships:* Equity; Musicians' Union. *Leisure interests:* Acting; Television; Motor scooters. *Current Management:* Robert Smith, Bristol. *Address:* 16 Poundfield Rd, Minehead, Somerset TA24 5EP, England.

CROW Bill; b. 27 Dec. 1927, Othello, Washington, USA. Musician (bass). m. Aileen Armstrong, 1965, 1 s. *Career:* Bassist, various artists including: Stan Getz; Claude Thorhill; Marian McPartland; Gerry Mulligan; Zoot Sims; Bob Brookmeyer; Clark Terry; Benny Goodman; Walter Norris; Peter Duchin; Musician, Broadway shows, 1975–89. *Publications:* Contributor, The Jazz Review; Jazz Letter; Author: Jazz Anecdotes, 1990. *Membership:* AFofM. *Address:* c/o American Federation of Musicians, New York, USA.

CROW Sheryl; b. 11 Feb. 1962, Kennett, Missouri, USA. Singer; Songwriter; Musician (guitar). *Musical Education:* Classical Music degree, Missouri State University; Organ and piano lessons; Self-taught guitar. *Career:* Backing singer, Michael Jackson tour, 18 months; Also backing singer for Joe Cocker; Rod Stewart; Don Henley; Songwriter, solo performer, mid 1980s-; International concerts and tours with John Hiatt; Crowded House; Big Head Todd; Support tours to Bob Dylan; Eagles, 1994; Joe Cocker, Wembley Arena, 1994; Performed at Woodstock II, 1994. *Recordings:* Solo album: Tuesday Night Music Club, 1993; Sheryl Crow, 1996; The Globe Sessions, 1998; Sheryl Crow and Friends: Live in Central Park, 1999; Singles include: All I Wanna Do, 1994; Leaving Las Vegas, 1994; Strong Enough, 1994; Can't Cry Anymore, 1995; If It Makes You Happy, 1996; Everyday Is A Winding Road, 1996; My Favorite Mistake, 1998; There Goes The Neighbourhood, 1998; Anything But Down, 1999; Sweet Child O' Mine, 1999; Contributor, albums: The End of Innocence, Don Henley, 1989; Late Night, Neal Schon, 1989; Other recordings by Eric Clapton; Wynnona Judd; Contributor, film soundtracks: Kalifornia, 1994; Leaving Las Vegas, 1995. *Honours:* 3 Grammy Awards, Tuesday Night Music Club, 1995; Brit Award, Best International Female Artist, 1997. *Current Management:* Weintraub Management, 80 Varick St #6B, New York, NY 10013, USA.

CROWE Mark Robert; b. 22 May 1958, Wolverhampton, England. Musician (Saxophone, Clarinet, Flute, Oboe); Arranger. m. Dolores Petrovich, 26 April 1986, divorced, Dec. 1995. *Education:* Wulfrun College, Wolverhampton; GDLM, City of Leeds College of Music; LGSM, Guildhall School of Music; LTCL, Trinity College; PGCE, University of Central England; MA, Monash University, Melbourne, Australia. *Career:* Summer Seasons, 1978–79; P & O Cruising, 1980; QE2 Orchestra, 1983–85; Freelance, London, 1985–89; Theatre Musician and Teacher, Melbourne, 1989–95, including Cats, La Cage aux Folles, Aspects of Love; QE2 Orchestra, 1996–98; P & O Arcadia, 1998. *Compositions:* Same Time Same Place, 1980; Chaser 1, 1982; Smallbrook Queensway, 1982; Spyro Tap, 1994. *Recordings:* Midland Youth Jazz Orchestra, 1975; Mick Urry Orchestra, 1985; Australia Cotton Club Orchestra, Rhapsody in Red, 1993. *Membership:* Musicians' Union. *Leisure interests:* Sailing; Travel. *Address:* 10 Trentham Close, Paignton, Devon TQ3 3GF, England.

CROWELL Rodney; b. 7 Aug. 1950, Houston, Texas, USA. Country Singer; Songwriter; Musician (guitar); Prod. 4 d. *Career:* Member, songwriter, Emmylou Harris' Hot Band, 1974–79; Worked with Willie Nelson; Ry Cooder; Jim Keltner; Solo artiste, and with own band, 1978-. *Compositions:* 10 US Country No. 1 hits; Songs for Emmylou Harris include: Bluebird Wine, 1974; Till I Gain Control Again, 1975; I Ain't Living Long Like This, 1979; Leaving Louisiana In The Broad Daylight, 1979; 250 versions of own compositions recorded by artists including: Willie Nelson; Foghat; Bob Seger; The Dirt Band; Waylon Jennings; George Jones. *Recordings:* US Country No. 1 hits include: It's Such A Small World, with Roseanne Cash; I Couldn't Leave You If I Tried; She's Crazy For Leaving; Albums: Ain't Living Long Like This, 1978; But What Will The Neighbours Think, 1980; Rodney Crowell, 1981; Street Language, 1986; Diamonds and Dirt, 1988; The Rodney Crowell Collection, 1989; Keys To The Highway, 1989; Life Is Messy, 1992; Jewel of The South, 1995; Soul Searchin, 1995; The Houston Kid, 2001; As producer: recordings for: Guy Clark; Albert Lee; Carl Perkins; Jerry Lee Lewis; Bobby Bare; Roseanne Cash; Lari White; Brady Seals; Beth Nielsen Chapman. *Honours include:* Grammy Award, Best Country Song, After All This Time, 1990. *Memberships:* CMA; Nashville Songwriters' Asscn; NARAS. *Leisure* *interests:* Outdoor activities; Family; Films; Travel; Athletics; Music. *Current Management:* Gold Mountain Entertainment, Suite 450, 3575 Cahuenga Blvd W, Los Angeles, CA 90068, USA. *Address:* c/o Beth Torrell, RC One, PO Box 120576, Nashville, TN 37212, USA.

CRUCIAL BANKIE (Ian Veira); b. 23 Nov. 1965, St Kitts. Musician (guitar, keyboard); Vocalist. 1 s. *Musical Education:* Self-taught. *Career:* Bunny Wailer First Antigua Show; Numerous radio broadcasts; Reggae Sunsplash, with Sagittarius Band, 1986, Stud Band, 1988; Performed with: Leroy Horsemouth Wallace; Jose Whale Brigadier Jerry; Buju Banton; Legendary Bunny Wailer. *Recordings:* Just A Sting, 1978; Sweet Reggae Muzik, 1994; Film: Uptown, soundtrack. *Publication:* The New Music of Reviews. *Membership:* ASCAP. *Leisure interests:* Travel; Basketball; Cricket. *Current Management:* African Shrine Management. *Address:* 196 Fourth Ave, Suite 2L, Brooklyn, NY 11217, USA.

CRUST Geoffrey Leonard; b. 30 March 1945, Boston, Lincolnshire, England. Songwriter; Publisher; Musician (guitars, keyboards). m. 5 Oct. 1984, 2 d. *Musical Education:* Privately taught, plus cadet musician, as drummer. *Career:* Songs on Songwriter Round Up albums, 1–4, featuring Ray Jones; Albums: Modern Country Melodies; USA/UK album; Country Headaches. *Compositions:* 67 published songs, both in UK, USA; Songs on 4 American albums with Music Room Records; Sollie Sunshine Records, USA. *Publications:* 15A Magazines, Brum Country Magazine, Spain, Denmark. *Memberships:* PRS; MCPS; TMA; ISA; BCMA; PPL Umbrella. *Leisure interests:* Writing songs, helping new writers, Heartbeat Music Publishing Company. *Current Management:* Thatch Records (own publishing company and record label). *Address:* 31 Tower St, Boston, Lincolnshire, England.

CRUZ Celia; b. 21 Oct. 1924, Havana, Cuba. Singer. m. Pedro Knight, 14 July 1962. *Education:* Teacher training. *Musical Education:* Classes at National Conservatory of Music, Havana. *Career:* First prize, Cuban radio talent show; Member, group Gloria Mantecera; Tours, Mexico, Venezuela, with Roderico Neyra's dance troupe, Las Mulatas de Fuego; Lead vocalist, Sonora Matancera, Radio Progreso, 1950; Recording artiste, 1951–; Collaborations with Tito Puente; Johnny Pacheco; Album debut with Fania All Stars, 1975; UK debut, 1976; Tours with Fania All Stars, Africa; Europe; Regular UK appearances with Tito Puente, 1984–; Subject, television documentary My Name Is Celia Cruz, Arena, BBC TV, 1988; Film appearances: Salsa, 1976; The Mambo Kings Play Songs of Love, 1991. *Recordings:* Numerous albums include: La Excitante Celia Cruz!, 1968; Etc Etc Etc, 1970; Tremendo Caché, 1975; Azuca Negra, 1993; with Tito Puente: Cuba y Puerto Rico Son, 1966; Son Con Guaguanco, 1966; Quimbo Quimbumbia, 1969; Alma Con Alma, 1971; Algo Especial Para Recordar, 1972; Hoenaje A Beny Moré Vol. III, 1985; Siempre Vivire, 2000; with Willie Colón: Only They Could Have Made This Album, 1977; Celia y Willie, 1981; The Winners, 1987; with Memo Salamanca: Bravo, 1967; A Ti Mexico, 1968; Serenata Guajira, 1968; Nuevos Exitos de Celia Cruz, 1971; with Johnny Pacheco: Celia and Johnny, 1974; Recordando El Ayer, 1976; Eternos, 1978; De Nuevo, 1985; with Ray Barretto: Tremendo Trio!, 1983; Ritmo En El Corazón, 1988; with Sonora Matancera: Feliz Encuentro, 1982; Live! From Carnegie Hall – 65th Anniversary Celebration, 1989; Azucar Negra, 1993; Homenaje A Los Santos, 1994; Double Dynamite, 1995; Fieston Tropical, 1998. *Honours include:* Hon. doctorate, Yale University, 1989; Grammy Award, 1990; Star on Hollywood Walk of Fame, 1990. *Current Management:* Ralph Mercado Management, 568 Broadway, Suite 806, New York, NY 10012, USA.

CUBER Ronnie; b. 25 Dec. 1941, Brooklyn, New York, USA. Musician (Baritone Saxophone). m. Roberta Arnold, 2 s. *Musical Education:* Brooklyn Conservatory of Music. *Career:* Film: Borgia Stick; TV appearances, Saturday Night Live, 1979–85; Appearances on BBC Radio, National public radio; Played at every majr jazz festival in Europe, USA and Japan; Masterclasses and clinics. *Compositions:* Airplay; Passion Fruit; Waltz Furgeralous. *Recordings:* Cuber Libre, 1976; The Eleventh Day of Aquarius, 1978; New York Jazz, 1981; Passion Fruit, 1985; Two Brothers King, 1985; Pin Point, 1985; Best of Ronnie Cuber, 1985; Live At Blue Note, 1986; Scean is Clean, 1993; Three Baritone Saxophone Band, 1998. *Honour:* Talent Deserving Greater Recognition, 1964. *Memberships:* DARAS; AFM. *Leisure interests:* Playing jazz; Writing jazz music; Snorkelling; Yoga. *Current Management:* Roberta Arnold. *Address:* 5219 N 24 St, Phoenix, AZ 85016, USA.

CUGNY Laurent; b. 14 April 1955, La Garenne-Colombes, France. Bandleader; Arranger; Musician (piano). m. Philippe Joëlle, 8 Feb. 1992, 1 s., 1 d. *Education:* BA, Economics, Cinema. *Musical Education:* Piano lessons, aged 10–14. *Career:* Founder, Lumière Big Band, 1979; European tour, Lumière and Gil Evans, 1987; Director, Orchestre National de Jazz (ONJ), 1994–97; European tour, ONJ and Lucky Peterson, 1995. *Recordings:* with Lumière and Gil Evans: Rhythm-A-Ning, 1988; Golden Hair, 1989; with Lumière: Santander, 1991; Dromesko, 1993; with ONJ: Yesternow, 1994; with Abbey Lincoln: A Turtle's Dream, 1995; With Orchestra National de Jazz: Reminiscing, 1995; In Tempo, 1995; Merci,

Merci, Merci, 1996. *Publications:* Las Vegas Tango – Une Vie De Gil Evans, 1989; Electrique Miles Davis, 1993. *Honours:* Django Reinhardt Award, Jazz Academy, 1991; Charles-Cros Academy Award, 1991. *Leisure interest:* Volleyball. *Current Management:* Memo, 17 rue de l'Abbé Carton, 75014 Paris, France. *Address:* 5 rue Leon Giraud, 75019 Paris, France.

CUILLERIER Philippe 'Doudou'; b. 5 Sept. 1961, Versailles, France. Musician (guitar); Lyricist. *Musical Education:* Saxophone from age 7; Guitar from age 17; Lessons with Eric Boell, Frederic Sylvestre. *Career:* Guitar teacher, 1983–; Backing guitarist with: Angelo Debarre; Romane Quintet; Lead guitarist, vocalist with Fernando Jazz Gang; Little Big Man (blues). *Recordings:* with Fernando Jazz Gang: Gipsy Violin, Swing Guitars; Gipsy Songs; with Romane Quartet: Quintet. *Address:* 2 Ruelle des Poulies, 78490 Montfort-l'Amaury, France.

CULLAZ Alby; b. 25 June 1941, Paris, France. Musician (double bass). 1 s., 1 d. *Musical Education:* Classical professors for piano and bass; Self-taught for jazz. *Career:* Backing for soloists: J Griffin; D Gordon; K Drew; Kenny Clark; H Mobley; Slide Hampton; Philly Joe Jones; Steve Grossman; René Urtreger; Chet Baker; Dee Dee Bridgewater; Alain Jean Marie; Art Farmer; Eric Lelann; Christian Escoude; Jean Luc Pouty; Michel Graillier; Art Taylor. *Recordings:* The Flip, with H Mobley, 1969; Reflections, with Steve Grosman and Simon Goubert, 1990; Duo with Christian Escoude; Jeff Gilson Big Band; Michel Grailler Trio; Christian Escoude Octet; Tac Tic, J. P. Foughet; Recidive, René Urtreger; Pure Be-Bop, 1998. *Honour:* Django Reinhardt Prize, 1973. *Address:* 52 rue du General Delestraint, 75016 Paris, France.

CULLAZ Pierre Maurice Louis; b. 21 July 1935, Paris, France. Musician (guitar); Teacher. m. Rita Castellano, 24 Feb. 1964. *Musical Education:* Classical, Jazz music, guitar. *Career:* Studio work; Jazz clubs; Tours with many singers; Contemporary classical music; Currently, extensive teaching, mainly jazz guitar. *Publication:* A Guitar Method, edited by Alphonse Leduc. *Leisure interests:* Concerts; Theatre; Sports. *Address:* 1 rue Charlot, 75003 Paris, France.

CULLIMORE Stan; b. 6 April 1962, Hull, England. Musician (bass). *Career:* Member, The Housemartins; Obtained recording contract; Numerous television appearances; Live dates including Red Wedge tour; Band split, 1988; Latterly author of children's books. *Recordings:* Singles: Flag Day, 1985; Sheep, 1986; Happy Hour, 1986; Think for a Minute, 1986; Caravan of Love (No. 1, UK) 1986; Five Get Over Excited, 1987; Me and the Farmer, 1987; Build, 1987; There is Always Something There to Remind Me, 1988; Albums: London 0 Hull 4, 1986; The People Who Grinned Themselves To Death, 1987; Now That's What I Call Quite Good, 1988. *Publications include:* The Turtle Who Danced With A Crane; Spider Boy; Long Live The Boy King; Where's Blinky?.

CUMMINGS Daniel; Musician (percussion); Musical Dir. 1 s. *Career:* Colaborations: Dire Straits, On Every Street, Tour, 1991–92; Tina Turner; George Michael; Simply Red, Life, album; Bon Jovi, Sophie B Hawkins; Brian Kennedy; Incognito; A1; Bryan Adams; Associates; Clannad; Depeche Mode; Tim Finn; Elton John; Lighthouse Family; John Martyn; Pet Shop Boys; Pulp; David Sylvian; The The. *Recordings:* Albums: Dire Straits, On Every Street, UK No 1; Tina Turner, Foreign Affair, UK No 1; George Michael: Without Prejudice, UK No 1; Careless Whisper, UK No 1; Wham, Make It Big!, UK No 1; Holly Johnson, Blast, UK No 1. *Membership:* Musicians' Union. *Current Management:* One Management, 43 St Alban's Ave, London W4 5JS, England.

CUMMINS Paul; b. 13 Oct. 1953, Portsmouth, Hampshire, England. Artist Man. m. Janice Bellamy, 25 June 1988. *Career:* Tour manager, 1975–79; Artists: Talking Heads; Andy Fairweather-Low; Jesse Winchester; XTC; Gallagher and Lyle; Manager, tour manager, Dire Straits, 1979-. *Leisure interests:* Fishing; Walking; Bird spotting; Cooking; Music; Pottery. *Current Management:* Damage Management, 16 Lambton Pl., London W11 4LQ, England.

CUNNAH Peter; b. 30 Aug. 1966, Belfast, Northern Ireland. Singer; Songwriter; Performer; Musician (guitar). *Education:* York St Art College, University of Ulster. *Career:* Singer, songwriter with D:ream; songwriter for A1, 2000; Tours and concerts: Support tour with Take That, UK and Europe; UK, 1993, 1994; Australia, 1994; Gay Pride, London; T In The Park, Glasgow; Fri Rock Festival, Copenhagen; Stonewall, Royal Albert Hall, London; Fleadh Festival, London; Gay Games, New York. *Recordings:* Albums: D:ream On Vol. 1, 1993; World, 1995; The Best of D:ream, 2000; Singles include: U R The Best Thing, 1992 (re-released 1994); Things Can Only Get Better, (No. 1, UK), 1993 (re-released 1997); Unforgiven, 1993; Star/I Like It, 1993; Take Me Away, 1994; Shoot With Me Your Love, 1995; Party Up The World, 1995; The Power (of All The Love In The World), 1995; Remixes for: Deborah Harry; Duran Duran; EMF. *Honours:* IDA Best Dance Act, 1993. *Current Management:* Mark Beder, FXU Records, 97A Scrubs Lane, London NW10 6QU, England.

CUNNINGHAM Christopher John; b. 7 June 1970, Droylsden, Manchester, England. Musician (acoustic guitar, electric guitar, electronic guitar). *Musical Education:* Tameside College of Technology. *Career:* Toured Ireland and Ulster with Indie guitar band, Poors of Reign; Guitarist for Gavin Friday, 1992–95; Several appearances, mostly musical and some theatrical, on local and national television including Juice, for Granada TV. *Compositions:* Over 200 songs written for guitar, bass and drums. *Recording:* Concerto De Piezo for guitar synthesizer. *Membership:* Musicians' Union. *Leisure interests:* Theatre; Cinema; Reading. *Current Management:* James Joseph Cunningham. *Address:* 37 Wordsworth Ave, Droylsden, Greater Manchester M43 6GA, England.

CUNNINGHAM Déirdre Mary Gerradine; b. 31 May 1956, Sutton, Surrey, England. Singer; Songwriter; Musician (acoustic guitar). m. Liam Cunningham, July 1977, 1 s. *Education:* Secretarial. *Musical Education:* Self-taught. *Career:* Tours: France; Germany; Netherlands; Ireland; Switzerland; Sweden; Denmark; Finland; Norway; England; Wales; Radio broadcasts: RTE Radio; BBC Radio; First single playlisted on national and local radio; Current album play-listed; Regular appearances on Irish national television, Welsh national television; Tour of Japan, Singapore and Philippines, 1998. *Recordings:* Albums: City of Tribes, 1996; Sunny Days; Cry From the Heart, 1998; Singles: Take Me For A Fool; Hurry Make Love. *Publications:* City of Tribes; Sunny Days; Irish Contemporary Songs; In progress, new album Song of the River. *Memberships:* IASC; ISA; IMRO; MCPS. *Leisure interests:* Mountain walking; Kayaking; Mountain biking; Windsurfing; Basketball; Swimming; Reading. *Current Management:* Lake Records, Cootehall, Boyle, Co Roscommon, Ireland.

CUNNINGHAM Philip Martin; b. 27 Jan. 1960, Edinburgh, Scotland. Composer; Accordionist; Music Dir; Prod. m. Donna Macrae, 24 Dec. 1982, 1 d. *Musical Education:* Private tuition from age 3. *Career:* Tours of UK, Europe and USA; Music Director of four series, over 4 years, of Talla A' Bhaile, for BBC Scotland; Music Director, Presenter, Hogmonay Live, for BBC, 1991–94; Co-presenter of weekly radio series, Live From The Lemon Tree, for BBC. *Compositions:* Music for Bill Bryden theatre productions, The Ship and The Big Picnic; Orchestral Suite, premiered 1996; Compositions used for film soundtrack Last of The Mohicans. *Honour:* Hon. Citizen, Reading, Pennsylvania, USA; M.B.E., 2002. *Membership:* Musicians' Union. *Leisure interests:* Clay Pigeon shooting; Scuba diving; Golf. *Current Management:* Donna Cunningham. *Address:* Cunningham Audio Productions Ltd, Crask of Aigas, By Beauly, Inverness IV4 7AD, Scotland.

CUNNINGHAM Tom; b. 22 June 1965, Glasgow, Scotland. Musician (drums). *Career:* Member, Wet Wet Wet, 1982–97; Formed The Sleeping Giants, 1999; Performances include: Greenpeace charity concert, Royal Albert Hall, London, 1986; Support to Lionel Richie, British tour, 1987; Prince's Trust Rock Gala, Royal Albert Hall, 1988–90; John Lennon Tribute Concert, Merseyside, 1990; Children In Need, BBC, 1991; Edinburgh Castle, 1992; Live At The Royal Albert Hall, C4, 1993. *Recordings:* Albums: Popped In Souled Out, 1987; Sgt Pepper Knew My Father, 1988; The Memphis Sessions, 1988; Holding Back The River, 1989; High On The Happy Side, 1992; Wet Wet Wet Live At The Royal Albert Hall, 1993; End of Part One (Their Greatest Hits), 1993; Picture This, 1995; 10, 1997; Singles include: Wishing I Was Lucky, 1987; Sweet Little Mystery, 1987; Angel Eyes (Home and Away), 1987; Temptation, 1988; With A Little Help From My Friends (No. 1, UK), 1988; Sweet Surrender, 1989; Broke Away, 1989; Hold Back The River, 1990; Make It Tonight, 1991; Goodnight Girl (No. 1, UK), 1992; Lip Service, 1992; More Than Love, 1992; Shed A Tear, 1993; Cold Cold Heart, 1994; Love Is All Around (No. 1, UK), 1994; She's All On My Mind, 1995; Julia Said, 1995; Don't Want To Forgive Me Now, 1995; Somewhere Somehow, 1995; Morning, 1996. *Honours:* Brit Award, Best British Newcomer, 1988. *Current Management:* The Precious Organisation, The Townhouse, 1 Park Gate, Glasgow G3 6DL, Scotland.

CUOMO Rivers; b. USA. Singer; Songwriter; Musician (guitar). *Career:* Singer, songwriter, Weezer. *Recordings:* Albums: Weezer – The Album, 1994; Pinkerton, 1996; Meet the Deedles, 1998; Hit single: Undone. *Current Management:* Third Rail Entertainment, 9169 Sunset Blvd, Los Angeles, CA 90069, USA.

CURNIN Cy; b. 12 Dec. 1957, Wimbledon, England. Vocalist. m. Peri, 7 Nov. 1985, 2 d. *Education:* Wimbledon College, London. *Musical Education:* Self-educated. *Career:* Vocalist with Fixx; US tours throughout 1980s; Tour with The Police, 1983; Appearances on: Saturday Night Live; Old Grey Whistle Test; In Concert (BBC); MTV; VH1. *Recordings:* Shuttered Room, 1981; Reach The Beach (Platinum US), 1983; Hits include: Stand Or Fall, 1982; Red Skids, 1982; One Thing Leads To Another, 1983; Further albums: Phantoms, 1984; Walkabout, 1986; Calm Animals, 1988; Ink, 1990; King Biscuit Flower Hour, 1996; Real Time Stood Still, 1997; Elemental, 1998; 1011 Woodland, 1999; with Tina Turner: What's Love Got To Do With It, 1993. *Honours:* ASCAP; 2m. plays, 1983, 1984. *Memberships:* PRS; ASCAP. *Leisure interests:* Fishing; Reading. *Current Management:* Jeff Nebin, USA.

CURRIE Justin; b. 11 Dec. 1964, Glasgow, Scotland. Singer; Songwriter; Musician (bass guitar, piano). *Career:* Founder, Del Amitri, 1981–; Concerts include: UK and international tours; Appearance at Woodstock Festival, 1994. *Recordings:* Singles: Kiss This Thing Goodbye, 1989; Nothing Ever Happens, 1990; Move Away Jimmy Blue, 1990; Spit In The Rain, 1990; Always The Last To Know, 1992; Be My Downfall, 1992; Just Like A Man, 1992; When You Were Wrong, 1993; Here and Now, 1995; Driving With The Brakes On, 1995; Roll To Me, 1995; Not Where It's At, 1997; Don't Come Home Too Soon, 1998; Cry To Be Found, 1998; Albums: Del Amitri, 1985; Waking Hours, 1989; Change Everything, 1992; Twisted, 1995; Some Other Suckers Parade, 1997; Crossroads, 1997; Daisy, 1997; Hatful of Rain, 1998. *Current Management:* JPR Management, The Power House, 70 Chiswick High Rd, London W4 1SY, England.

CURSON Theodore; b. 3 June 1935, Philadelphia, Pennsylvania, USA. Musician (trumpet). m. Marjorie Goltry, 1 April 1967, 1 s., 1 d. *Musical Education:* Granoff Music Conservatory, Philadelphia, 1952–53. *Career:* Trumpeter with Charlie Mingus; Max Roach; Philly Joe Jones; Cecil Taylor; Eric Dolphy, 1960–63; Concerts and jazz festivals include: North Sea; Nice; Antibes; Monterey; Newport; Concerts: Europe; USA; India; Middle East; North Africa; Director, Blue Note Open Jam, 1984–; President, Nosruc Publishing Company, 1961-. *Recordings include:* Plenty of Horn, 1961; Fire Down Below, 1963; New Thing and Blue Thing, 1965; The Urge, 1966; Ode To Booker Ervin, 1970; Pop Wine, 1972; Quicksand, 1975; Jubilant Power, 1976; Tears For Delphy, 1976; Blue Piccolo, 1976; Flip Top, 1977; Typical Ted, 1977; The Trio, 1979; I Heard Mingus, 1980; Snake Johnson, 1981; 'Round Midnight, 1990; Several film scores. *Honours:* New Star, Monterey Jazz Festival, 1962; Downbeat Critics Poll Winner, 1966; Readers Poll Winner, 1978; Long Island Musicians Society Award, 1970; Pori City Standard, Finland, 1978. *Membership:* AFofM.

CURTIS Catie; b. 22 May 1965, Biddeford, Maine, USA. Singer; Songwriter. *Education:* BA, Brown University. *Career:* Soundtrack work for TV, Dawson's Creek, Chicago Hope; Film, Annie O, A Slipping Down Life; Performances at clubs in the USA, Lilith Fair and other festivals; Theatre tour with Mary Chapin Carpenter, 1998–99. *Recordings:* Truth From Lies, 1996; Catie Curtis, 1997; A Crash Coursse in Roses, 1999; My Shirt Looks Good On You, 2001. *Honour:* GLAMA Album of the Year, 1998. *Membership:* AFTRA. *Leisure interest:* Basketball. *Current Management:* Gold Mountain. *Address:* Gold Mountain Entertainment, 3575 Cahuenga Blvd W, Suite 450, Los Angeles, CA 90068, USA.

CURTIS Mac; b. 16 Jan. 1939, Fort Worth, Texas, USA. Singer; Musician (guitar); Songwriter. m. Peggy, 3 March 1967, 3 s. *Education:* Graduated, Army Information and Broadcasting School, 1958; Graduated, Anthony School of Real Estate, 1975; Moorpark Community College Real Estates Course, Moorpark, California, USA, 1975–76; Licensed Real Estate Associate California, 1975–80. *Musical Education:* Self-taught. *Career:* Recorded for King records, 1956; Guest, Big D Jambouree and National Radio Show, 1956; Co-star, Alan Freed Rock 'n' Roll Revue, New York, 1956; Toured as Rock 'n' Roll Rockabilly, until 1960; Country Music DJ, Dallas Radio Station; Recorded Country for Epic and GRT Dj Atlanta, Nashville, LA, 1971. *Compositions:* I'd Run a Mile for Lynn Anderson; Give Us One More Chance. *Recordings:* The King Original Rockabilly Masters; Blue Jean Heart, CD; The Rollin' Rock series, 3 albums; Rollin' Rock Singles CD, Rollin' Rock Switzerland; Rockabilly Ready, with The Rimshots. *Publication:* Goldmine Magazine, Vol. 9, Issue 10, 1983; We Wanna Boogie, 1988. *Honours:* Golden Ear Awards, Country Survey News, 1969; ASCAP Chartbuster Award, 1972. *Membership:* American Society of Composers, Authors and Publishers, 1970-. *Leisure interests:* Music; Writing; International Travel. *Current Management:* Rock 'n' Roll Enterprises, 16 Grove Pl., Penarth, Vale of Glamorgan, CF64 2ND, South Wales.

CURTOLA (Robert Allen) Bobby; b. 14 April 1943, Thunder Bay, Ontario, Canada. Singer; Songwriter. m. Ava, 21 Sept. 1975, 2 s. *Career:* Singer, Rock 'n Roll; Co-Host, After Four, TV series, Canada, 1965–66; Own TV series on CTV, Shake, Rock and Roll; Own Christmas Special in Canada; Performer on Bob Hope Show; Guest, numerous national and regional talk and variety specials in Canada and USA; Headlined in Las Vegas for many years; Rock 'n' Roll Blast, 1999. *Composition:* The Real Thing, 1966. *Recordings include:* Fortune Teller; Aladdin; 3 Rows Over; Corrina. *Honours:* Winner, Jingle Award for North America, Things Go Better with Coke; Canada's First RPM Top Male Vocalist Juno Award, 1965; Inducted into Canadian Music Industry Hall of Fame, 1996; Order of Canada, 1998; Gold record status for 22 singles and 13 albums. *Memberships:* ACTRA; ARIA; AFofM; CARAS; SOCAN. *Current Management:* Mr Robert Hubbard. *Address:* PO Box 5359, Edmonton, AB T5P 4C5, Canada.

CUSSON Michel; b. 22 Jan. 1957, Drummondville. Guitarist; Composer. m. Michelle Alie, 2 d. *Musical Education:* College Degree in Pop Music; CEGEP, Drumondville, one session, McGill University Montréal; 4 months at Boston's Berklee College of Music. *Career:* Composed soundtrack for

Omertà, La loi du silence, television series, 1996, 1997, 1998; Composed soundtrack for films: La Comtesse de Baton Rouge (Amdré Forcier), 1997, and L'Automne Sauvage (Gabriel Pelletier), 1992; Numerous themes for Canadian television shows; Music themes for advertising campaigns; Created jazz-world beat group Michel Cusson and the Wild Unit in 1991 and jazz-fusion group UZEB in 1976. *Recordings:* 2 albums with Michel Cusson and the Wild Unit; 10 albums wwith UZEB. *Honours:* Felix Awards, 1983, twice 1984, 1987, 1990, twice 1992; Gemeaux Awards, 1989, 1996; Socan Awards, 1990, 1993, 1995, 1996; Music Plus Award, 1991; Oscar Peterson Trophy, 1991. *Address:* c/o Productions Flash Rose, 3867 rue Saint Denis, Montréal, QC H2W 2M4, Canada.

CUSTER Beth; b. 25 Feb. 1958, South Bend, Indiana, USA. Composer; Musician (clarinet, piano, trumpet, percussion); Vocalist. *Musical Education:* Bachelor Degree, Music Performance, SUNY, Potsdam, 1980; Masters Degree, Performance, Michigan and San Francisco State Universities, 1981–85; Clarinet Teachers, Rosario Mazzeo, Suzanne Stephens, Else Ludewig-Verdeht, Don Carroll, James Pyne, Frank Wanger. *Career:* Composer for TV, film, dance and theatre; Member, numerous new music, jazz and trip-hop groups; Collaborated, MacCarthur Fellow; Created soundtracks for independent films; Resident Composer, Joe Goode Performance Group, 1992–96. *Compositions include:* Film and TV: The Twisted Tales of Felix the Cat; Sherlock Jr; Oranges are Not the Only Fruit; Dance: The Maverick Strain; This is Where I Am Now; Stark Night; Theatre: Kingfish; Hamlet; 12 Angry Men; Flathead Flamenco; Buckets of Blood Slash/Play; Commissions: Arranger with Kronos Quartet, The Penguin; Earplay Suite. *Recordings:* with Eighty Mile Beach: Inclement Weather; Arboleda de Manzanitas; There Are No Right Angles Found In Nature; Solo: The Shirt I Slept In; Trance Mission: Head Light; Meanwhile...; Trance Mission; Club Foot Orchestra: Buster Keaton's Sherlock Jr; Metropolis; Nosferatu; The Cabinet of Dr Caligari; Kidnapped; Wild Beasts; Connie Champagne: La Strada; Dona Luz 30 Besos (with City of Tribes), 2000; Vinculum Symphony, 2000. *Honours:* Isadora Duncan Award; First Place, Berlin Film Festival; WAMMIE Music Awards; GOLDIE Award, Bay Guardian Award for composition; NEA Interarts Grant; Arts International Grant. *Address:* 88 Lundy's Lane, San Francisco, CA 94110, USA.

CYPORYN Dennis; b. 1 Feb. 1942, Detroit, Michigan, USA. Musician (banjo); Composer. 1 s., 1 d. *Education:* Oakland University, second year. *Musical Education:* Theory. *Career:* Dennis Cyporyn Band; Composes own music for band; Showcased at Detroit Music Awards, Motor City Music Awards; Won Best Instrumentalist 2 years, also Group Deserving Wider Recognition and Best Folk Group; Currently with Lonesome and Blue, bluegrass band. *Recordings:* Nashville Alley, 1991; I Must Be Dreaming, 1992; Deja Vu Debut, 1994; Duet to Quintet, 1997. *Publications:* The Bluegrass Song Book, 1972. *Honours:* 5 Awards, 12 Nominations, IBMA, MCMA, DMA. *Memberships:* IBMA; MCMA. *Leisure interest:* Sailing. *Address:* Krypton Records, PO Box 372, Highland, MI 48357, USA.

CYRKA Jan Josef; b. 31 Oct. 1963, Halifax, West Yorkshire, England. Musician (guitar); Composer. *Musical Education:* Self-taught. *Career:* Member, Max and the Broadway Metal Choir, 1984; Recording engineer, E-Zee Studios, 1985; Member, Zodiac Mindwarp and the Love Reaction, 1986–89; Tours, USA and Canada, supporting Guns N' Roses; Solo artist, 1989–; Session musician, television commercials; Partner, Take It For Granted PR Company; Producer and contributor, cover-mount CD for Guitarist magazine. *Composition:* Three library albums: Rock Guitar Album, Rock Attitude, Boom; Wrote most of music for BBC Horizon, Great Balloon Race, 1997. *Recordings:* Max and The Metal Choir, 1985; Tattooed Beat Messiah, Zodiac Mindwarp, 1987; Solo albums: Beyond The Common Ground, 1992; Spirit, 1993; Prickly Pear, 1997; Session guitarist, At This Moment, Tom Jones; Co-producer, All Day Long I Shouted, Carmel. *Memberships:* Musicians' Union; PRS; MCPS; BMI. *Leisure interests:* Walking; Building and expanding home recording studio. *Current Management:* Andrew Farrow, Northern Music Company. *Address:* Cheapside Chambers, 43 Cheapside, Bradford, West Yorkshire BD1 4HP, England.

CYRUS Billy Ray; b. 25 Aug. 1961, Flatwoods, Kentucky, USA. Country Singer. *Career:* Formed own group, Sly Dog, 1983; Worked as car salesman; Solo recording artiste, 1992-. *Recordings:* Singles: Achy Breaky Heart, 1992; Could've Been Me, 1992; In the Heart of a Woman, 1993; Words by Heart, 1994; Trail of Tears, 1996; Time for Letting Go, 1998; Albums: Some Gave All (No. 1, USA), 1992; It Won't Be The Last, 1993; Storm in the Heartland, 1994; Trail of Tears, 1996; Shot Full of Love, 1998; Southern Rain, 2000. *Current Management:* McFadden Artist Corp. *Address:* 818 18th Ave S, Nashville, TN 37203, USA.

CZ; b. 25 June 1969, Charleroi, Belgium. Singer; Guitar; Compositer. *Musical Education:* Self-taught musician. *Career:* Many concerts in Belgium and France under name of Candy Stripe, 1989–92, and Bloodminded, 1992-. *Recordings:* As Above So Below, Candy Stripe, 8 tracks vinyl LP, 1990; Hypocrisy, Blood Minded, 5 tracks tape, 1993; Demons for Tea, Bloodminded, 11 tracks tape, 1996; Rock in Belgium, Vol. 1, 2 tracks CD compilation, 1996; Rock in Belgium, Vol. 2, 2 tracks CD compilation, 1997; Bloodyminded CD, to be released 1998. *Memberships:* SABAM, Brussels, Belgium; Ciney Music Session, Arts Agency, Belgium. *Leisure interests:* Slot Racing; Moolelism. *Current Management:* PED Records, rue Vertevoie 13A, 5590 Ciney, Belgium. *Address:* Bloodminded, rue Jean Friot 91, 6180 courcelles, Belgium.

D

D Brenda (Brenda D Boyd); b. 30 Dec. 1936, Surrey, England. Vocalist; Actress. m. Jerry Haymes, 1 Aug. 1961, 1 s., 1 d. *Education:* Finishing school; Schools of Modelling. *Musical Education:* Church of England; Self-taught vocalist. *Career:* Film and television actress; Appearances include original Robin Hood series; Opened in England with Fess Parker as Davy Crockett; Toured USA and Europe; First British female singer to perform Country music on BBC; First British female Country singer to perform at Grand Ole Opry. *Recordings:* Major songs: Will You Still Love Me Tomorrow; Little Bitty Tear; Love You More Than I Can Say; Just Enough To Keep Me Hanging On. *Honours:* CMA International Award; Female Vocalist, Art and Entertainment Council; A and E Film Actress Award. *Memberships:* Screen Actors Guild; Arts and Entertainments Council. *Leisure interests:* Dog breeder, handler; Raises horses. *Current Management:* Umpire Entertainment Enterprises, J Haymes. *Address:* 1507 Scenis Dr., Longview, TX 75604, USA.

DA SILVA Rui, (Doctor J; 4 Elements; Teimoso); b. 25 April 1968, Lisbon, Portugal. Prod.; Remixer; DJ. *Career:* Began DJ career in Lisbon as member of Underground Sound of Lisbon; Signed to Tribal Records; Relocated to London, 2000; Collaborations: Terry Farley; Chris Coco; DJ Vibe. *Recordings:* with Underground Sound of Lisbon: Albums: Etno City, 2001; Singles: So Get Up, 1994; Are You Looking For Me, 1998; solo: Touch Me (with Cassandra Fox), 2000. *Honours:* Muzik Award, Best Single, Touch Me, 2001. *Membership:* MCPS/PRS. *Address:* c/o Arista Records, Cavendish House, 423 New Kings Rd, London, SW6 4RN, England.

DADAWA (Zhe Zheq); b. 1974, Guangzhou, China. Singer. *Career:* Solo artist, New Age music; Debut concerts: Midem Asia, Hong Kong, 1995; London Showcase, 1995. *Recordings:* Albums with He Xuntian: Yellow Child, 1991; Sister Drum, 1995; Voices from the Sky, 1998. *Address:* c/o Warner Records.

DADDY FREDDY (Samuel Small); b. Kingston, Jamaica. Rapper. *Career:* Television appearances include: Blue Peter; Record Breakers; BBC Summer TV; Big Breakfast; Radio includes: Tim Westwood, BBC Radio 1. *Recordings:* Albums: Ragamuffin Hip Hop; Ragga House; Pain Killa; Stress; Raggamuffin Soldier; Singles: Crown, 1991; Daddy Freddy's in Town, 1991; Haul and Pull, 1992; Respect Due, 1993; Old School New School. *Honour:* Guinness Book of Records, World's Fastest Rapper. *Membership:* PRS. *Address:* c/o 20 Hanway St, London W1P 9DD, England.

DADDY-G (Grant Marshall); b. 18 Dec. 1959, Bristol, England. Vocalist. *Career:* Member, Massive Attack; Started with collective The Wild Bunch, featuring Tricky, Goldie, Neneh Cherry and Nellee Hooper; Formed Massive Attack with 3-D and Mushroom, 1986; Collaborations: Shara Nelson; Tricky; Horace Andy; Madonna; Tracey Thorn, Everything But The Girl; Liz Fraser, Cocteau Twins; Numerous gigs in clubs and parties. *Recordings:* Singles: Daydreaming, with Shara Nelson; Unfinished Sympathy, with Shara Nelson, 1991; Safe From Harm EP, 1991; Sly, 1994; Protection, 1995; Karmacoma, 1995; Risingson, 1997; Teardrop, with Liz Fraser, 1998; Inertia Creeps, 1998; Angel/Group Four, 1998; Albums: Blue Lines, 1991; No Protection: Massive Attack vs Mad Professor, 1995; Mezzanine (No. 1, UK), 1998; DVD compilation of singles promos, 2001. *Honours:* Brit Award, Best British Dance Act, 1996. *Internet:* www.massiveattack.co.uk.

DADSWELL Melvyn John; b. 8 Jan. 1946, Uckfield, Sussex, England. Musician (saxophone); Lecturer; Teacher. m. He Feng Qin, 26 Sept. 1990, 2 s., 2 d. *Education:* BA Hons, Exeter University. *Musical Education:* Self-taught. *Career:* Began playing jazz, 1959; Teacher, jazz harmony, rhythm to undergraduate music students (privately); Many club concerts and British tours, with band Anthropology; 3 recordings Devon Air Jazz; Occasional session work; Bath Festival, 1988; Moscow, 1990; Schooled Red Army Orchestra in jazz, 1990–91. *Membership:* Musicians' Union. *Leisure interest:* Teaching languages: Russian; English; Polish. *Current Management:* Phil-Seong Huh. *Address:* Five Poplars, Ford Farm, Chudleigh-Knighton, Newton Abbot, South Devon TQ13 0ET, England.

DAGARA Hamouka; Musician. *Career:* Appearances on television in Nigeria, 1987; 8 years successful run in show, West Africa. *Compositions include:* Bori-Badossa; Yellerou; Dawa; Boujé Baka Baka; Malta Panther; Zicika la... Soyaka. *Recordings:* Bori Badossa; Yellerow; Boujé Baka Baka; Malta Panther; Album: Bakandarnia. *Honours:* First Prize, Music Competition, Niger, 1990; Third Prize, competition in Niger, 1992; 20th Place, Africa Palmarest, 1997. *Memberships:* Gominak; Somair; Sonichar; Societies of Air Mines; Palais Congrés. *Address:* Orchestre Carnayal, De Maradi, DDTSC, Republic of Niger.

DAGLEY Christopher; b. 23 June 1971, Solihull, West Midlands, England. Musician (drums). *Musical Education:* Grade 8 drumming. *Career:* National Youth Orchestra; BBC Big Band; Various theatre shows; Gemini; Paz; Brian Dee; Various groups. *Recordings:* 10 albums, NYJO; Dancing In The Park, Paz. *Membership:* Musicians' Union. *Leisure interest:* Weight lifting. *Address:* 439A Alexandra Ave, Rayners Lane, Harrow, Middlesex HA2 9SE, England.

DAGNELL John Richard; b. 2 Aug. 1956, Oxford, England. Music, Entertainment Promoter; Record Co Exec.; Music Publisher. m. Nicola, 30 July 1983, 1 s., 1 d. *Career:* Promoted various concert tours by: Maddy Prior; The Carnival Band; Gilbert O'Sullivan. *Recordings:* Albums: Maddy Prior; Steeleye Span; Gilbert O'Sullivan; Davey Arthur; Guitar Orchestra; Wild Willy Barrett; New recordings by Kathryn Tickell, Pentangle; New recordings by Lindisfarne. *Memberships:* PRS; ILA; PPL. *Address:* Park Records, PO Box 651, Oxford OX2 9RB, England.

DALE Chris; b. 4 Sept. 1967, London, England. Musician (bass guitar); Vocalist. *Musical Education:* Self-taught, and attended Musicians' Academy, Wapping, London, 1989–90. *Career:* Bassist with funk/rock band Atomseed, 1989–93; Extensive tours in United Kingdom and Europe; Several recordings; Bassist for Bruce Dickinson, tours of UK, Europe, USA, South America and Japan, 1994–96; Bassist and singer, Sack Trick, 1997-. *Compositions:* Co-writer, singles for Atomseed, Rebel; Get in Line; Dead Happy; Co-writer for Bruce Dickinson, various B-sides and album tracks; Music and lyrics for Sack Trick album Mystery Rabbits. *Recordings:* With Atomseed: Get in Line, 1990; Hard Sell Paranoia, 1992; With Bruce Dickinson: Alive in Studio A, 1995; Skunkworks, 1996; With Sack Trick: Mystery Rabbits, 1999; Penguins on the Moon, 2000; track on compilation Any Colour As Long As It's Black, 2000. *Address:* PO Box 16432, London W6 08Q, England.

DALE Colin; b. 14 April 1963, London, England. Prod.; Remixer; DJ. *Career:* Started as a soul/disco DJ on London pirate station Kiss in the '80s; Stayed with licensed Kiss FM presenting weekly Abstrakt Dance show until 2000; Moved to internet station Groovetech, 2001; Founder: Abstrakt Dance Records; Collaborations: Gareth Oxby; Haris Custovic; Access 58; Affie Yusseff. *Recordings:* Singles: Upstate Feeling (with Civil Attack), 1996; Make You High (with Kleer), 2001. *Address:* c/o Abstrakt Dance Records, 78 Mount Nod Rd, Streatham Hill, London, SW16 2lJ, England. *E-mail:* colindale@groovetech.com. *Internet:* www.abstraktdance.co.uk.

DALE Micky; b. 22 March 1968. Musician (keyboards, percussion). *Career:* Member, Embrace; Obtained major label deals in UK and USA; Released debut single independently; Support slot with Manic Street Preachers, 1997; Headline tours and TV appearances. *Recordings:* Singles: Fireworks EP, 1997; One Big Family EP, 1997; All You Good Good People, 1997; Come Back To What You Know, 1998; My Weakness Is None of Your Business, 1998; The Good Will Out, 1999; Hooligan, 1999; You're Not Alone, 2000; Save Me, 2000; I Wouldn't Wanna Happen To You, 2000; Make It Last, 2001; Wonder, 2001; Album: The Good Will Out, 1998; Drawn From Memory, 2000; If You've Never Been, 2001. *Address:* c/o PO Box 7, Brighouse, HD6 4UR, England. *Internet:* www.embrace.co.uk.

DALEY Paul; b. 23 Dec. 1962, Margate, Kent, England. Prod.; Percussion; Remixer; DJ. *Career:* Co-founder Hard Hands Records with Neil Barnes; World-wide DJ; Member of Leftfield, split 2002; Collaborations: A Man Called Adam, Afrika Bambaataa, Roots Manuva, John Lydon. *Recordings:* Albums: Leftism, 1995; Rhythm and Stealth, 1999; Singles: Not Forgotten, 1990; Release The Pressure, 1992; Song of Life, 1992; Open Up (with John Lydon), 1993; Original, 1995; Afrika Shox (with Afrika Bambaataa), 1999. *Current Management:* c/o Hard Hands Recordings, The Courtyard, Saga Centre, 326 Kensal Rd, London, W10 5BZ, England.

DALGLEISH Lou (Louise); b. 19 Oct. 1967, Birmingham, England. Singer; Songwriter; Musician (piano). *Education:* BA, Hons First Class, Arts Practice and Cultural Policy. *Musical Education:* Grade 8 classical piano and theory. *Career:* Professional dancer, theatre, film, including Steven Spielberg's Indiana Jones and the Temple of Doom; Singer-Songwriter, including headline residencies at Ronnie Scott's, Birmingham; Support act to Wet Wet Wet, NEC, Birmingham; Bryan Ferry, Dutch tour; Guestings, Brian Kennedy; National television performances include: BBC and ITV (UK); Belgium; Festival appearances: SXSW Austin, Texas, USA; Lowlands, Waterpop, Valkos, Netherlands; Phoenix, England; National radio sessions include BBC Radio 2 and 5; Netherlands; Belgium. *Recordings:* Singles: Orange Plane, 1995; Sold Out, 1995; Charlie Girl, 1996; EP: Loud Music, 1998; Album: Lou Dalgleish, 1995; Live Album, solo acoustic at Ronnie Scott's, 1997; Calmer,

1999; backing vocals on: The Good Sons, Happiness, 2001. *Memberships:* Equity; Musicians' Union. *Current Management: c/o* Ronnie Scott's Club. *Address: c/o* Ronnie Scotts, Broad St, Birmingham B1 2HF, England.

DALLIO Patricia; b. 3 Nov. 1958, Chaumont, France. Musician (piano); Composer. *Career:* Tours throughout Europe with Art Zoyd. Concerts include: Berlin; Milan; New York; London, Hong Kong, Adelaide, Mexico, Stockholm, and Yokohama Festivals; Live shows and films include: Nosferatu; Faust; Häxan Composer, Dance theatre, videos. *Recordings:* Procession; Champs de Mars; La Ronce N'est Pas Le Pire; D'où vient l'eau des puits; Barbe Bleue; Que personne ne bouge; Ubique, 2001. *Membership:* Soundtrack (Composer Asscn). *Address:* 11 rue de la Liberté, 52000 Chaumont, France. *E-mail:* dallio.patricia@libertysurf.fr.

DALSETH Laila; b. 6 Nov. 1940, Bergen, Norway. Jazz Singer. m. Totti Bergh, 1 June 1963, 2 d. *Career:* Solo Jazz artist; Television and radio appearances: Scandinavia; Germany; Yugoslavia; England; Scotland; Concerts include: Playboy Jazz Festival; Nice Jazz Festival; Sacramento Jazz Festival; Caribbean Jazz Cruises; Copenhagen Jazz Festival; Molde Jazz Festival; Jakarta Jazz Festival; Currently fronting own group with saxophonist (husband) Totti Bergh. *Recordings include:* Laila Dalseth/Wild Bill Davidson, 1974; with Bengt Hallberg, Arne Domnerus: Glad There Is You, 1978; with Louis Stewart: Daydreams, 1984; with Red Mitchell Quartet: Time For Love, 1986; with Al Cohn: Travelin' Light, 1987; Woman's Intuition, 1995; with Milt Hinton, Derek Smith, B Rosengarden, B Pizarelli: The Judge and I, 1992; with Joe Cohn, Totti Bergh: Remember, 1995; with Philip Catherine, Egil Kapstad: A Woman's Intuition, 1995; One of a Kind, 2000. *Honours:* 3 times Spellemannspris (Norwegian Grammy).

DALTON Lacy J (Jill Byrem); b. 13 Oct. 1948, Bloomsburg, Pennsylvania, USA. Country Singer. *Career:* Club singer, California, 12 years; Singer, psychedelic group Office, under name Jill Croston; Solo artiste, 1979–; Worked with Earl Scruggs, George Jones and Bobby Bare. *Recordings:* Hit singles: Crazy Blue Eyes; Tennessee Waltz; Hard Times; 16th Avenue; Working Class Man; Albums: As Jill Croston: Jill Croston, 1978; As Lacy J Dalton: Lacy J Dalton, 1979; Hard Times, 1980; Takin' It Easy, 1981; 16th Avenue, 1982; Dream Baby, 1983; Greatest Hits, 1983; Can't Run Away From Your Heart, 1985; Highway Diner, 1986; Blue Eyed Blues, 1987; Survivor, 1989; Lacy J, 1990; Crazy Love, 1991; Chains On The Wind, 1992; Somethin Special, 1995. *Current Management: c/o* Aaron Anderson, Lacy J Dalton Enterprises, PO Box 1109, Mount Juliet, TN 37122, USA.

DALTREY David Joseph; b. 30 Dec. 1951, London, England. Session Musician (guitar); Tutor (guitar); Composer. m. Helen McIldowie, 20 July 1989, divorced. *Education:* Mid Hertfordshire College. *Musical Education:* Guildhall School of Music and Drama; Studied with Rogers Covey-Crump; Private studies with Ike Isaacs and Jimmy Page. *Career:* Recording artist; Worked for BBC; Numerous compositions and recordings for various artists; Currently a session guitarist, tutor and composer. *Recordings:* Lead vocalist and guitarist, Joseph and The Amazing Technicolour Dreamcoat, 1969, 1971; Tales of Justine, Albert/Monday Morning, 1967; Petals From A Sunflower, 1998. *Memberships:* Musicians' Union; ISM. *Address:* Pilgrims Rest, 34 Guildhall St, Bury St Edmunds, Suffolk IP33 1QF, England.

DALTREY Roger; b. 1 March 1944, Hammersmith, London, England. Singer; Actor. *Career:* Member, UK rock group The Who, 1964–84; Appearances include: National Jazz and Blues Festivals, 1965, 1966, 1969; Monterey Pop Festival, 1967; Rock At The Oval, 1972; Farewell tour, 1982–83; Live Aid, Wembley, 1985; 25th Anniversary Reunion tour, 1989; Solo artiste, 1984–; Actor in films, including Tommy, 1974; Lisztomania, 1975; The Legacy, 1979; McVicar, 1980; Threepenny Opera, 1989. *Recordings:* Albums: My Generation, 1965; A Quick One, 1966; The Who Sell Out, 1968; Direct Hits, 1968; Tommy (rock opera), 1969; Live At Leeds, 1970; Who's Next, 1971; Meaty Beefy Big and Bouncy, 1971; Quadrophenia, 1973; Odds and Sods, 1974; The Who By Numbers, 1975; The Story of The Who, 1976; Who Are You, 1978; The Kids Are Alright (film soundtrack), 1979; Face Dances, 1981; Hooligans, 1982; It's Hard, 1982; Rarities Vols 1 and 2, 1983; Once Upon A Time, 1983; The Singles, 1984; Who's Last, 1984; Who's Missing, 1985; Two's Missing, 1987; Who's Better Who's Best, 1988; Joined Together, 1990; 30 Years of Maximum R & B, 1994; The BBC Sessions, 2000; Solo albums: Daltrey, 1973; Ride A Rock Horse, 1975; One of The Boys, 1977; Best Bits, 1982; If Parting Should Be Painless, 1984; Under A Raging Moon, 1985; I Can't Wait To See The Movie, 1987; Rocks in the Head, 1992; McVicar, 1996; Martyrs and Madmen, 1997; Singles include: I Can't Explain, 1965; Anyway Anyhow Anywhere, 1965; My Generation (No. 2, UK), 1965; Substitute, 1966; I'm A Boy (No. 2, UK), 1966; Happy Jack, 1967; Pictures of Lily, 1967; I Can See For Miles, 1967; Pinball Wizard, 1969; See Me Feel Me, 1970; Won't Get Fooled Again, 1971; Join Together, 1972; Who Are You, 1978; You Better You Bet, 1981; Contributor, Rock and Roll, Rock Aid Armenia, 1991. *Honours include:* Gold Ticket, Madison Square Garden, 1979; Ivor

Novello Award, Outstanding Contribution To British Music, 1982; BRIT Award, Outstanding Contribution to British Music, 1988; Group inducted into Rock 'n' Roll Hall of Fame, 1990. *Current Management:* Trinifold Management, 22 Harley St, Marylebone Rd, London NW1 4PR, England.

DALY Stan; b. 27 Nov. 1929, Grays Inn Road, London. Jazz Musician (drums); Band leader. m. 3 Aug. 1957, 1 s., 3 d. *Musical Education:* Royal Air Force. *Career:* Played in top dance orchestras of Lou Preager, Frank Weir, Jack Nathan, 1950s-60s; Drummer, Harry Gold's Pieces of Eight, for 15 years; Broadcasting, television, concerts; Own band Sonny Dee All-Stars playing Chicago/mainstream jazz; Worked on West Coast America with Wild Bill Davison, Dick Cathcart, Eddie Miller, Bob Enevoldson; Played with: Harry Parry's Radio Sextet; Freddy Randall; Pasadena Roof Orchestra; Sandy Brown; Played almost every top international jazz festival world-wide. *Recordings:* Drummer, many albums. *Address:* 92 Greenway, Totteridge, London N20 8EJ, England.

DAMBRY Stephane; b. 7 March 1959, Barentin, France. Singer. *Education:* Teacher. *Musical Education:* Self-taught guitarist, singer. *Career:* Lead singer, Little Big Band, 1987–97; Solo artist, 1991-. *Recordings:* Talk To The Mirror, 1991; The Fatal Glass of Beer, 1994; The Welsh Rare Beat, 1994; with Little Big Band: Hey! Doc, 1994. *Current Management:* L'Echo du Kazoo Management. *Address:* 1 rue C Nicole, 76800 st Etienne du Rouvray, France.

DAMEN Paul; b. 26 Jan., The Netherlands. Musician (Drums). *Career:* Mid 80s Leading Dutch Top 40 Band accompanying major Dutch Artists, 1989; Toured in Holland, The Trammps; Jimmy Bo Horne; Dutch Group, Haitai; Numerous jingles and commercials (studio) for : Mercedes; SAAB; General Motors; L'Oreal Cosmetics; TV appearances with Gloria Estefan; Toured with popular Dutch Artist Rob Janszen; Toured with International Artist, CB Milton, 1995; National Studio/Session Drummer, currently. *Recordings:* Promo; Endorser for Remo, Drums and Drumheads. *Current Management:* De Otter and De Vries, Entertainment Productions BC, Hertogin Juliana Singel 34 055, The Netherlands. *Address:* Hogehofstraat 26, 5366 CC Megen, Holland.

DAMINESCU Adrian; b. 2 Oct. 1956, Timisoara, Romania. Musician (cello, piano, guitar, bass guitar); Vocalist. m. Francis Susan Walker, 30 June 1990, divorced. *Musical Education:* Department of voice music and composition, Academy of Music. *Career:* Concerts, tours and recitals throughout Romania; Israel; USSR; Germany; China; Japan; Canada; USA; Czechoslovakia; Television and radio appearances: National Romanian television station; The Stars Duel; 10 weeks in Top 3–2–1; Hit Studio, London 1990; Cable TV; Gloria Hunniford, BBC1; Voice of America; National Radio Station. *Compositions:* Romania; You're Still Beautiful; Looking In My Teacup; Stop; Pleading For Michael Jackson; I Miss My Home; Final Day; Praying For Mercy; Midnight. *Recordings:* I Will Love You (Eu Te Voi Iubi); Pieces of Me (Bucati Din Mine). *Publications:* Currently writing memoirs: Music and My Life. *Honours:* Great Prize, Bucharest Festival, 1986; Most Beautiful Voice of the Festival, Bratislava, 1986; 3 times Great Prize winner as singer, Mamaia National Festival, 1986–88; Second Prize, Golden Orpheus Festival, Bulgaria, 1988; 3 Mamaia National Festival Awards as composer: First, 1989; Third, 1991; Second, 1992. *Leisure interests:* Fishing; Painting; Sculpting. *Address:* Constanta 8700, 45 Gen Manu St, Romania.

DAMMERS Jerry (Gerald Dankin); b. 22 May 1954, Coventry, Warwickshire, England. Musician (keyboards). *Career:* Founder member, Coventry Automatics, 1977; Name changed to Coventry Specials, then Special AKA, then the Specials, 1979–; Support to the Clash, British tour, 1978; Designer, record label 2-Tone, marketed by Chrysalis Records, 1979; Kampuchea benefit concert, with The Who, the Pretenders, London, 1979; Film, Dance Craze, 1981; Formed Artists Against Apartheid, 1986; Organizer, Nelson Mandela 70th Birthday Tribute, Wembley, 1990. *Recordings:* Singles include: Gangsters, 1979; A Message To You, Rudy, 1979; Too Much Too Young EP (No. 1, UK), 1980; Rat Race, 1980; Stereotype, 1980; Do Nothing, 1981; Ghost Town (No. 1, UK), 1981; Nelson Mandela, 1984; Albums: Specials, 1979; More Specials, 1980; Dance Craze, 1981; In The Studio, 1984; The Specials Singles, 1991; Live – Too Much Young, 1992; Live At The Moonlight Club, 1992; Two Tone Compilation, 1993; Rebirth of Cool Vol. 2, 1994; Fearless, 1998; Stereotypical – As Bs and Rarities (box set), 2000.

DAMONE Vic, (Vito Farinola); b. 12 June 1928, Brooklyn, New York, USA. Singer; Actor. m. (4) Diahann Carroll, 1 s., 3 d. *Musical Education:* Singing lessons. *Career:* Winner, Arthur Godfrey's Talent Scouts, CBS, 1946; Singer, La Martinique nightclub, New York; Recording artiste, 1947–; Own CBS radio show, Saturday Night Serenade, late 1940s; Film apperances include: Rich Young and Pretty, 1951; The Strip (featuring Mickey Rooney, Jack Teagarden, Louis Armstrong), 1951; Hell To Eternity; Athena, 1954; Deep In My Heart, 1954; Hit The Deck, 1955; Kismet, 1955; Crash Boat; Own television series, 1956–57; Regular concert tours, UK, US and Australia, 1980s-. *Recordings:* Albums: Athena (soundtrack), 1954;

Rich Young and Pretty (soundtrack), 1955; The Voice of Vic Damone, 1956; That Towering Feeling, 1956; The Stingiest Man In The World (soundtrack), 1956; The Gift of Love (soundtrack), 1958; Closer Than A Kiss, 1959; Angela Mia, 1959; This Game of Love, 1959; On The Swingin' Side, 1961; Linger Awhile With Vic Damone, 1962; Strange Enchantment, 1962; The Lively Ones, 1962; My Baby Loves To Swing, 1963; The Liveliest, 1963; On The Street Where You Live, 1964; You Were Only Fooling, 1965; Stay With Me, 1976; Damone's Feeling 1978, 1979; Now, 1981; Make Somone Happy, 1981; Now and Forever, 1982; Vic Damone Sings The Great Songs, 1983; The Damone Type of Thing, 1984; Christmas With Vic Damone, 1984; The Best of Vic Damone, Live, 1989; The Glory of Love, 1984; Tender Is the Night, 1995; Best of The Mercury Years, 2001; Various compilations; Hit singles (sold 1m.): Again; You're Breaking My Heart; On The Street Where You Live (No. 1, UK), 1958; Other hits include: I Have But One Heart; You Do; Tzena Tzena Tzena; Cincinnati Dancing Pig; My Heart Cries For You; My Truly Truly Fair; Here In My Heart; April In Portugal; Eternally; Ebb Tide; An Affair To Remember; You Were Only Fooling (While I Was Falling In Love). *Publications:* Recipes For Lovers cookbook. *Current Management:* c/o Stan Scottland, JKE Services Inc, 404 Park Ave S, 10th Floor, New York, NY 10016, USA.

DAMRON Dick; *Career:* Starday Studios, Recording Country Rockabilly Records with Tommy Hill, 1961; Teamed up with Producer Joe Bob Barnhill, Soldier of Fortune Album, 1971. *Recordings:* Include, Countrified, 1971; Susan Flowers; Jesus Its Me Again; Still Countrified; Dick Damron: The Anthology. *Honours:* 4 Times Top Canadian Country Singer; Best Country Record of 1977; Top Canadian Songwriter; Artist of the Year; Country Gospel Album of the Year, 1996; 7 Times Winner, Outstanding Contribution to Canadian Music; 2 Times Winner, Province of Alberta Award; Country Music Man of the Year; 5 Texas Proud Awards. *Address:* PO Box 270, Bentley, AB Canada T0C 0J0.

DANA (Rosemary Brown); b. 30 Aug. 1951, Belfast, Northern Ireland. Singer. *Career:* Winner, Eurovision Song Contest, with All Kinds of Everything (No. 1, UK, South Africa, Ireland, Australia), 1970; Over 1m. sales world-wide; Actress, television and pantomime. *Recordings:* Hit singles: All Kinds of Everything, 1970; Who Put The Lights Out, 1971; It's Gonna Be A Cold Christmas, 1975; Please Tell Him That I Said Hello, 1975; Fairy Tale, 1976; Albums: All Kinds of Everything, 1970; World of Dana, 1975; Have A Nice Day, 1977; Love Songs and Fairy Tales, 1977; The Girl Is Back, 1979; Totally Yours, 1982; Everything Is Beautiful, 1980; Let There Be Love, 1985; No Greater Love, 1988; Dana's Ireland, 1991; Lady of Knock, 1992; Say Yes, 1993; Gift of Love, 1996; Best Travelin' Tunes, 1997; Heavenly Portrait, 1999. *Current Management:* The Brokaw Company, 9255 Sunset Blvd, Suite 804, Los Angeles, CA 90069, USA.

DANCE Stanley (Frank); b. 15 Sept. 1910, Braintree, England. Writer. m. Helen Oakley, 30 Jan. 1947, 2 s., 2 d. *Education:* Framlingham College, 1925–28. *Career:* Reviewer, Jazz Journal, London, 1948–96; Saturday Review, New York City, 1967–72; Music Journal, New York City, 1962–79; Jazz Times, Silver Spring, Maryland, 1980–98. *Publications:* Editor, Jazz Era, 1961; The World of Duke Ellington, 1970; The Night People, with Dicky Wells, 1971; The World of Swing, 1974; The World of Earl Hines, 1977; Duke Ellington in Person, with Mercer Ellington, 1978; The World of Count Basie, 1980; Those Swinging Years, with Charlie Barnet, 1984; Jazz Talking, with Max Jones, 2000. *Honour:* Deems Taylor Award, American Society of Composers, Authors and Publishers, 1979. *Address:* 1745 Bittersweet Hill, Vista, CA 92084–7621, USA.

DANDO Evan; b. 4 March 1967, USA. Singer; Musician (guitar); Songwriter. *Career:* Founder member, The Lemonheads, 1986–97; Numerous world-wide concerts include: Solo tour, Australia, 1992; Solo acoustic concert, Ronnie Scott's, London, 1992; Reading Festival, 1994; Collaborations include: The Blake Babies; Kirsty MacColl; Juliana Hatfield; Godstar. *Recordings:* Albums: Hate Your Friends, 1987; Creator, 1988; Lick, 1989; Lovey, 1990; It's A Shame About Ray, 1992; Come On Feel The Lemonheads, 1993; Car Button Cloth, 1996; Best of the Lemonheads, 1998; Singles include: It's A Shame About Ray; Mrs Robinson (from film soundtrack, 25th Anniversary wide-screen release of The Graduate, 1993); Confetti; Into Your Arms; It's About Time; Contributor, Sweet Relief (Victoria Williams benefit album), 1993. *Honour:* Boston Music Awards, Outstanding Modern Rock Act, Single of The Year, 1993. *Current Management:* Gold Mountain Entertainment. *Address:* 3575 Cahuenga Blvd W, Suite 450, Los Angeles, CA 90068, USA.

DANE Phil; b. 31 Oct. 1961, Leeds, Yorkshire, England. Prod.; Engineer; Songwriter. *Musical Education:* City of Leeds, College of Music. *Career:* Mixes and/or productions of: Back To The Planet; Bomb The Bass; Boy George; B T: Darkman; D:ream; East 17; Julia Fordham; Innocence; James; Mike Oldfield; Robert Palmer; Diana Ross; Rozalla; Salt 'n' Pepa; Sasha; Utah Saints; Worlds Apart; Yazz; Aswad; Madonna; Paul Oakenfold; Robbie Williams; Lighthouse Family; Republica; Matt Bianco. *Memberships:* Musicians' Union; PRS. *Leisure interests:* Motorcycling;

Gym training. *Current Management:* 750 cc. *Address:* 152 Vaughan Rd, Harrow HA1 4EB, England.

DANGAIN Guy; b. 12 July 1935, Sains-en-Gohelle, France. 1 d. *Musical Education:* First Prize, Conservatoire National Superieur de Musique, Paris, studied clarinet with Professor Ulysse Delecluse; First Prize, Chamber Music, with Professor Ferrand Oubradous. *Career:* Soloist, clarinet, with National Orchestra of France, 1963–93; Professor, Ecole Normale, Paris; Professor, Conservatoire National Superieur du Musique, Paris; Director, International Festival, Haut Bugey. *Compositions:* Over 50 collections of compositions. *Recordings:* Brahms Sonata; Debussy, Rhapsody; Rhapsody with National Orchestra of Martinon; Repertoire from young clarinettist H Mundi; Creation du Monde, du Bernstein; Hommage à Louis Ca Huzoc; Guisganolerie: Hommage à Guisganol; Quinette et Two Songs. *Publications:* Prestige de la clarinette, 1987; A propos de la clarinette, 1991. *Honour:* Chevalier des Arts et des Lettres. *Leisure interest:* Philosophy. *Address:* 14 Ruelle à Potier, Nerville la forêt, 95590 France.

D'ANGELO (Michael Archer); b. 11 Feb. 1974, Richmond, Virginia, USA. Singer; Songwriter; Musician (multi-instrumentalist); Prod. *Career:* Recording artiste, 1992-. *Compositions:* Co-writer, producer, U Will Know, Black Men United. *Recordings:* Solo Albums: Brown Sugar, 1995; Live at the Jazz Cafe, 1998; Voodoo, 1999; Singles: Brown Sugar, 1995; Cruisin', 1996; Lady, 1996; Me and Those Dreaming Eyes of Mine, 1996; Left and Right, 1999. *Honours:* Harlem Apollo Talent Contest Winner, 3 times; Grammy Awards: Best R & B Male Vocal Performance, Untitled – How Does It Feel?; Best R & B Album, Voodoo, 2001. *Address:* c/o William Morris Agency, 1325 Ave of the Americas, New York, NY 10019, USA.

DANIELS Bob (Robert T Hahn); b. 2 March 1959, Milwaukee, Wisconsin, USA. Musician (banjo). m. Denise Blank, 1 s., 2 d. *Education:* College. *Musical Education:* Various private teachers. *Career:* Professional musician for 20 years; Played in bands: The Nashville Cats; The Nashtown Ramblers; Backroads; Johnny Rodriguez Backup Band; Played with artists including: Charley Colllins; Bashful Brother Oswald; Earl Scruggs; Jethro Burns; Duane Stuermer; Jack Grassel; Warren Wiegratz; Infamous Ramblin' Rick Trudell; Grand Old Opry, Opry Land, 1976; Broadway production, 1979; Live radio music appearances, WMIL FM 106, late 1980s; Associate songwriter for BMI; Composes for other singers, commercials, theatre. *Recordings:* Single: Back Home To Yesterday, 1988; Albums: Bob Daniels and A Milwaukee All-Star Pot Pourri, 1990; Bob Daniels, Rick Trudell, Best Banjo, 1995; Bob Daniels, Rick Trudell, Rough Cuts, 1995; Best Banjo, 1995. *Honour:* Rated by HFR as one of top 5 improvisational 5-string banjo players, USA. *Membership:* AFofM. *Leisure interest:* Fishing. *Current Management:* D J Blank. *Address:* 606 W Wisconsin Ave, Suite 1100, Milwaukee, WI 53203, USA.

DANIELS Charlie; b. 28 Oct. 1937, Wilmington, North Carolina, USA. Country Singer; Songwriter; Musician (multi-instrumentalist). *Career:* Played guitar from age 15; Founder, bluegrass band The Misty Mountain Boys; Changed name to The Jaguars, 1959; Regular session work, Nashville, 1968–; Partnership with Earl Scruggs; Formed Charlie Daniels Band, 1970–; Started Volunteer Jam (became annual event), 1974; Featured on film soundtrack Urban Cowboy; Recorded film theme for Stroker Ace. *Compositions include:* It Hurts Me, Elvis Presley, 1964. *Recordings:* Hit singles include: Uneasy Rider, 1973; The South's Gonna Do It, 1973; The Devil Went Down To Georgia, 1979; Albums: To John, Grease and Wolfman, 1970; Charlie Daniels, 1970; Honey In The Rock, 1973; Way Down Yonder, 1974; Fire On The Mountain, 1975; Nightrider, 1975; Teach Yourself Rock Guitar, 1976; Saddletramp, 1976; High Lonesome, 1976; Volunteer Jam, 1976; Midnight Wind, 1977; Volunteer Jam 3 and 4, 1978; Million Miles Reflections, 1979; Volunteer Jam VI, 1980; Full Moon, 1980; Volunteer Jam VII, 1981; Windows, 1982; A Decade of Hits, 1983; Me and The Boys, 1985; Powder Keg, 1987; Renegade, 1991; Same Ol Me, 1995; By the Light of the Moon, 1997; Tailgate Party, 1999; Road Dogs, 2000; with Bob Dylan: Nashville Skyline, 1969; Self Portrait, 1970; New Morning, 1970; Other recordings with Ringo Starr; Marty Robbins; Hank Williams Jr. *Publication:* Book of short stories, 1986. *Current Management:* High Lonesome Management Inc, 17060 Central Pike, Lebanon, TN 37087, USA.

DANIELS Luke; b. 18 Nov. 1973, Reading, England. Musician (button accordion). *Musical Education:* Self-taught. *Career:* Accordion player with Scarp, formerly with De Danann; Major concerts include: St Chartier Festival, 1993; Philadelphia Festival of Folk Music, 1993; Pebble Mill TV, 1994; Theatre de Ville, Paris, 1995; Accordionist with Riverdance; Composer for English National Opera. *Compositions include:* Musette À Térésa; The Snoring Barber; Wednesday's Tune; Gallowstree Sonata; The King of Prussia; This Love; Breath Without a Sigh. *Recordings:* Tarantella, 1994; Scarp, 1995; Across The Waters; Reeltime (compilation); features on: Kissing Fishes, Broderick, 2000; Broad Street Ballads, Ray Hearne, 2001; Cara Dillon, Cara Dillon, 2001. *Honours:* Young Tradition Award, Folk Musician of the Year, BBC Radio 2, 1992. *Memberships:* MU. *Leisure* *interests:* Walking. *Current Management:* Acoustics. *Address:* 4 Lea Rd, Sonning Common, Reading, Berkshire RG4 9LJ, England.

DANIELZ; b. 25 Nov. 1957, Hong Kong. Vocalist; Musician (guitar). *Musical Education:* Self-taught. *Career:* Lead guitarist with T Rextasy, T Rex tribute group; Tours include: UK arena tour as support to Gary Glitter; Tour with Sweet and Slade, Germany, 1995; Japan, 1995; British tour with Sweet, 1997; VH1 shows T Rextasy concert footage from Cambridge Corn Exchange Bolan birthday show, 1997; major British theatre tour with Slade, 1999; Television appearances: Unplugged, MTV/VHI, 1995; Glam-Doc documentary, Ch4, 1995. *Recordings:* with T Rextasy: Baby Factory, 1994; Trip and Glide In The Ballrooms of T Rextasy, 1995 (UK and Japan); Album: Savage Beethoven, 1997; Major record deal in Japan. *Publication:* Wilderness of The Mind, biography of Marc Bolan, 1992; Marc Bolan – T Rex, published in Japan, 1999. *Memberships:* Musicians' Union; PRS. *Leisure interests:* Rock and Pop Music; Reading; Writing. *Current Management:* Mark Lundquist, 2 The Woodlands, Woking, Surrey GU22 7RU, England. *Address:* 8 Moriatry Close, Holloway, London N7 0EF, England.

DANKO Harold; b. 13 June 1947, Sharon, Pennsylvania, USA. Musician (piano); Composer; Educator. *Musical Education:* Dana School of Music, 1965–69; BME, Youngstown State University, Ohio, 1969; Additional studies, Juilliard School of Music, 1970. *Career:* Tours, concerts and recordings, 1972–; Pianist with various artistes including: Woody Herman; Chet Baker; Thad Jones and Mel Lewis; Lee Konitz; Gerry Mulligan; Leader, Harold Danko Trio, 1980–; Leader, Harold Danko Quartet, 1990–; Festival appearances include: JVC, New Haven and Clearwater (USA); Montréal (Canada); Metz, TBB and Fort Napoleon (France); Marca and Riva (Italy); Gouvy (Belgium) and North Sea Jazz Festival (Netherlands); Featured artist, Meet The Artist series, Lincoln Center, and Performing Arts Society series, JFK Center; Concert series, Manhattan School of Music, New York funded by NEA fellowship; President, Aaychdee Music; Founder, Jazz Haven (Jazz society); Current music educator, Manhattan School of Music, New York, Hartt School of Music, Hartford, Connecticut and Neighborhood Music School, New Haven. *Compositions include:* Tidal Breeze; Alone But Not Forgotten; Ink and Water Suite; Chasin' The Bad Guys; Shorter By Two; Music for theatre and television. *Recordings:* Coincidence, 1979; Mirth Song, 1982; Shorter By Two, 1983; Alone But Not Forgotten, 1985; The First Love Song, 1988; Next Age, 1993; After The Rain, 1994; New Autumn, 1995; The Feeling of Jazz, 1996; Tidal Breeze, 1997; This Isn't Maybe, 1999; Stable Mates, 2000. *Publication:* Author, The Illustrated Keyboard Series, 1982; Video: Jazz Concepts for Keyboard (Brazil). *Honours:* Awards from ASCAP and National Asscn of Concert and Cabaret Acts (NACCA); Outstanding Service to Jazz Education award, International Asscn of Jazz Educators; Distinguished Alumni award, Youngstown State University; Fellowship, National Endowment for the Arts, 1995. *Memberships:* AFofM; ASCAP. *Leisure interest:* Humour. *Address:* 172 Alden Ave, New Haven, CT 06515, USA.

DANKWORTH Alec (Alexander William); b. 14 May 1960, London England. Musician (double bass, acoustic bass guitar). *Musical Education:* Berklee School of Music, Boston, USA. *Career:* Son of John Dankworth and Cleo Laine, brother of singer Jacqui; Played clarinet before taking up double bass; Worked and toured internationally with parents, 1981–91; During this period also worked with: Tommy Chase; Dave O'Higgins; Tommy Smith; Jean Toussaint; Buddy De Franco; Nigel Kennedy; Stephane Grappelli; Michael Garrick; Began long associations with Clark Tracey and Pizza Express Modern Jazz Sextet, late 1980s; Accompanied many visiting American jazz musicians; Toured Europe and South Africa with Abdullah Ibrahim, 1993; Played in the Dankworth Generation Band; Toured and recorded with Van Morrison and Georgie Fame, mid 1990s, and Dave Brubeck, 1999; Collaborations: Julian Joseph; Martin Taylor; Pete King; Pat Crumley; Tommy Smith; Guy Barker. *Recordings:* Albums: We've Been Expecting You (Clark Tracey Quintet), 1992; Nebuchadnezzar (with John Dankworth), 1994; Rhythm Changes (with John Dankworth), 1995; features on: Bartók – Solo Violin Sonata/ Ellington – Mainly Black, Nigel Kennedy, 1986; What Goes Around, Jean Toussaint, 1992; Spirit of Django, Martin Taylor, 1994; How Long Has This Been Going On, Van Morrison and Georgie Fame, 1995; Into The Blue, Guy Barker, 1995; Beasts of Scotland, Tommy Smith, 1996; The Healing Game, Van Morrison, 1997; Gold, Martin Taylor, 1997; Brubeck's Back, Dave Brubeck, 1999; Deep Water Drop Off, Sin É, 1999.

DANKWORTH Jacqui (Jaqueline Caryl); b. 5 Feb. 1963, UK. Vocalist; Actress. *Career:* Daughter of John Dankworth and Cleo Laine, sister of Alec; Acted with the Royal Shakespeare Company; Stage appearances in London's West End include: Sophisticated Ladies (Ellington revue); Into The Woods (Stephen Sondheim); Les Liaisons Dangereuses; Formed Alec and Jacqui Dankworth Quartet, 1993; First solo album, First Cry, released, 1994; Current ensemble named after second release, Field of Blue. *Recordings:* Albums: First Cry, 1994; Field of Blue, 1996; Still (with Field of Blue), 2000.

DANKWORTH John Philip William; b. 20 Sept. 1927, Walthamstow, London, England. Composer; Musician (saxophone, clarinet). m. Cleo Laine, 18 March 1958, 2 s., 1 d. *Musical Education:* Royal Academy of Music. *Career:* Involved in post-war development of British Jazz, 1947–60; Formed Jazz orchestra, 1953; Pops Music Director, London Symphony Orchestra, 1985–90; Principal Guest Pops Conductor, San Francisco Symphony Orchestra, 1987–89; Numerous film scores and albums; With Cleo Laine, founded performing arts centre, Wavendon Stables, 1970-. *Compositions:* Improvisations (with Matyas Seiber), 1959; Escapade, 1967; Tom Sawyer's Saturday, 1967; String Quartet, 1971; Piano Concerto, 1972; Grace Abounding, 1980; Dialogue and Songs For Colette, starring Cleo Laine, 1980; The Diamond and The Goose, 1981; Reconciliation (for Silver Jubilee of Coventry Cathedral), 1987; Woolwich Concerto (Clarinet Concerto for Emma Johnson), 1995; Dreams '42 (string quartet) for 1997 Kidderminster Festival; Double Vision, 1997 world premiere by BBC Big Band at BBC Proms; Objective 2000 (for the combined orchestras of the Harpur Trust Schools), 2000. *Recordings:* Albums include: 5 Steps T Dankworth, 1958; England's Ambassador of Jazz, 1960; Jazz From Abroad, 1963; Echoes of Harlem, 1988; Generation Big Band, 1995. *Publications:* Sax from the Start, 1996; Jazz in Revolution, 1998. *Honours:* CBE, 1974; Hon MA, Open University, 1975; Hon DMus, Berklee College of Music, 1982; Hon DMus, York University, 1993; Honourary Fellow, Leeds College of Music, 1999; Variety Club of Great Britain Show Business Personality Award, with Cleo Laine, 1977; ISPA Distinguished Artists Award, 1999. *Membership:* Fellow of Royal Academy of Music. *Leisure interests:* Driving; Household maintenance. *Current Management:* Dankworth Management. *Address:* The Old Rectory, Wavendon, Milton Keynes MK17 8LT, England.

DANNENBERG Roger; b. 9 March 1955, Houston, Texas, USA. Composer; Musician (Trumpet). m. Frances Dannenberg, 1 s. *Education:* BSEE, 1977, MSCE, 1979, Rice University; PhD, Carnegie Mellon University, 1982; Studied Trumpet With Nelson Hatt, Frank Tripani, Anthony Pasquarelli; Composition With Paul Cooper. *Career:* Trumpet With George Gee Orchestra, Apollo Theatre, 1986; Greenwich Village Jazz Festival, 1988; Stuck With Each Other, NBC Television Movie, 1989; Trumpet, Composer, Nitely News, World Affairs Conference, 1996; In Transit, Guanajuato, 1997. *Compositions:* Ritual of The Science Makers, 1990; Nitely News, 1992; The Words Are Simple, 1994; Aura, 1998. *Publications:* Combining Instrument and Performance Models For High Quality Music Synthesis, 1998. *Honours:* ICMA Board of Directors; Pittsburgh New Music Ensemble Board of Directors. *Memberships:* International Computer Music Asscn. *Address:* 6529 Aylesboro Ave, Pittsburgh, PA 15217, USA.

DANTER John; b. 3 Sept. 1946, Birmingham. Musician; Composer. 1 s. *Education:* MA, Reading University. *Career:* Toured as guitarist with various groups, Germany, Turkey, Greece, USA, 1960's and 70's; Session work on 'Jingles', 1970's; Writing songs, 1980's-90's; Commissioned music for production companies and songwriting for the American country market. *Compositions include:* Have You Ever Been In Love; Making Your Mind up; The Perfect Kiss; Started So Well; Another Beautiful Guy; Daddy Said. *Recordings:* About 1500 Television and Radio Jingles. *Publication:* Sound As Inspiration-Study In Improvisation. *Honours:* Ivor Novello Award, Best Song, musically and lyrically, 1983; Eurovision Song Contest Winner, 1981. *Memberships:* PRS; The Lute Society; West Bromwich Albion Supporters Club. *Leisure interests:* Music; Travelling; Property development; Flamenco.

DANTZLER Russ; b. 5 Dec. 1951, Ainsworth, Nebraska, USA. Agent; Artist Man.; Record Prod. *Education:* Business, University of Nebraska. *Career:* Began Hot Jazz Management and Production as hobby, to preserve the Swing tradition, 1974; Hot Jazz became full-time career, New York City, 1989; Clients include: Claude 'Fiddler' Williams; Earl May; Red Richards; Benny Waters; Al Grey; The Duke's Men with Arthur Baron; Carrie Smith; Bross Townsend; Norris Turney; Ken Peplowski; Bill 'Mr Honkey Tonk' Doggett; Contracting work for the Smithsonian Jazz Oral History Department, and Jazz Foundation of America. *Recordings:* Produced: Claude Williams, Live At J's, Vols 1 and 2, 1993; Swingtime In New York, with Claude Williams, Sir Roland Hanna, Bill Easley, Earl May, Joe Ascione, 1995. *Publications:* Columnist, Jam/Jazz Ambassadors Magazine (Kansas City); Scrapple From The Apple, 1993-. *Honours:* Produced recording placing on critic's polls; Asked to write remembrance of Haywood Henry for the Alabama Jazz Hall of Fame archives. *Memberships:* Jazz Journalists Asscn; Kansas City Jazz Ambassadors; American Federation of Jazz Societies; Duke Ellington Society; New York Chapter, National Jazz Service Organization. *Leisure interests:* Photography (credits: Bulletin of the Hot Club of France; New York Times; Downbeat); All music; Travel. *Address:* Hot Jazz, 328 W 43rd St, Suite 4F, New York, NY 10036, USA.

DANZIG Glenn (Glen Anzalone); b. 23 June 1955, Lodi, New Jersey, USA. Rock vocalist. *Career:* Vocalist, US punk groups, The Misfits; Samhain; Founder, vocalist, Danzig, 1987-. *Recordings include:* Albums:

with the Misfits: Beware, 1979; Walk Among Us, 1982; Static Age, 1995; Collection II, 1995; Box Set, 1996; with Danzig: Danzig, 1988; Danzig II – Lucifage, 1990; Danzig III – How The Gods Kill, 1992; Danzig 4, 1994; Blackacidevil, 1996; Satan's Child, 1999; Live On The Black Hand Side, 2001. *Current Management:* Big FD Management, 10801 National Blvd, Suite 530, Los Angeles, CA 90064, USA.

DAPOGNY James; b. 3 Sept. 1940, Illinois, USA. Prof. of Music; Musician (Jazz Pianist); Bandleader. *Education:* University of Illinois. *Career:* Professor of Music, University of Michigan, 1966–; Jazz Pianist, Leader, James Dapogny's Chicago Jazz Band, 1975–; Touring; Recording; Radio and television. *Compositions:* West of The Mississippi; Santa Passed My House By This Christmas; Shortstory; Lobogo; Miles From Home. *Recordings:* Laughing At Life; Original Jelly Blues; Hot Club Stomp; On The Road; Whatcha Gonna Swing Tonight. *Honours:* Grammy Nomination. *Current Management:* Zajonc/Valenti Management. *Address:* 1154 Olden Rd, Ann Arbor, MI 48103, USA.

D'ARBY Terence Trent; b. 15 March 1962, New York, USA. Singer; Songwriter; Prod. 1 d. *Education:* Journalism, University of Central Florida. *Career:* Singer, Touch, Germany, 1982; Solo artiste, 1986–; Concerts include: British tour, support to Simply Red, 1987; Artists Against Apartheid, Royal Albert Hall, 1987; Hardline Introduction, British tour, 1987; British tour, support to David Bowie, 1987; US tour, 1988; Nelson Mandela tribute, Wembley, 1990; John Lennon tribute, Liverpool, 1990; Concerts with Bruce Springsteen, New York, 1993; Concerts with Duran Duran, Mexico, 1993; Television includes: Motown 30 – What's Goin' On, CBS, 1990. *Recordings:* Singles include: If You Let Me Stay, 1987; Wishing Well (No. 1, USA), 1987; Dance Little Sister, 1987; Sign Your Name, 1988; Do You Love Me Like You Say, 1993; Delicate (with Des'ree), 1993; She Kissed Me, 1993; Let Her Down Easy, 1993; Holding On To You, 1995; O Divina, 2001; Albums: Introducing The Hardline According To... (No. 1, UK), 1987; Neither Fish Nor Flesh, 1989; Symphony Or Damn – The Tension Inside The Sweetness, 1993; Vibrator, 1995; Wildcard, 2001; Contributor track to: Music of Quality and Distinction Vol. 2, British Electric Foundation, 1991. *Honours:* Brit Award, Best International Newcomer, 1988; Grammy nomination, Best New Artist, 1988; Platinum disc, Introducing The Hardline, 1988; Grammy Award, Best R & B Vocal Performance, Introducing, 1989; Best Vocal Performance by Duo or Group, with Booker T and the MG's, 1995. *Current Management:* Lippman Entertainment, 8900 Wilshire Blvd, Suite 340, Beverly Hills, CA 90211–1906, USA.

D'ARCY Doug; b. 23 Feb. 1946, Hull, England. Record Co Exec. m. Catherine Williams, May 1974, 1 s., 1 d. *Education:* Manchester University. *Career:* Chrysalis Records, 1968–89; Managing Director, Dedicated Records, 1990–95. *Leisure interests:* Tennis; Reading; Painting; Cooking. *Current Management:* Songlings Ltd. *Address:* c/o PO Box 20206, London NW1 7FF, England.

DARLING Helen; b. 5 May, Baton Rouge, Louisiana, USA. Singer; Songwriter. m. Dennis Darling. *Education:* Bachelor Degree, Organizational Communication, University of Texas, Austin, Texas. *Career:* Jingle singer, Chicago; Demo singer, Nashville; Female vocalist on Garth Brooks' The Red Strokes; Co-writer with: Bob DiPiero; John Scott Sherill; Karen Staley; Chuck Jones; Michael Omartian. *Compositions include:* Track for own album, co-written with Tena Clark, Gary Prim: When The Butterflies Have Flown Away. *Recordings:* Song: It's So Easy, College Vocal Group Album: Ensemble 109; Single: Jenny Come Back, 1995; Album: Helen Darling, 1995. *Current Management:* Chip Peay, PBH Entertainment.

DARLINGTON Jay; b. 3 May 1969, Sidcup, England. Musician (keyboards). *Career:* Joined The Kays; Became Kula Shaker, 1995–99; Numerous live tours and TV appearances; Many festival appearances. *Recordings:* Singles: Tattva, 1996; Hey Dude, 1996; Govinda, 1996; Hush, 1997; Sound of Drums, 1998; Albums: K (No. 1, UK), 1996; Peasants Pigs and Astronauts, 1999. *Honours:* Brit Award, Best British Newcomer, 1997.

DAURAT Jean-Sebastien; b. 11 Feb. 1961, Neuilly Sur Seine, France. Musician (guitar). 2 s. *Education:* 3 years art school. *Musical Education:* Self-taught, also private lessons. *Career:* Television: Sideman for H Leonard; Corine Marchand; Maria Glen; Marion Montgomery; Erchy Lawson; Own group, Jazz Oil Quintet; Plays in numerous clubs, Paris (international pop, rock, funk, jazz, Latin jazz); 150 more dates in 1998; Bass player on stage for Amarande Story, theatre production; On tour each year in South of France. *Compositions:* St Emilion, 1997; Fête de l'Humanité, 1999. *Recordings:* On Ne Discute Pas, 1997; On ne Panique pas, 1998; Jazz Oil Spirit, 1999; Un Jour, le lendemain, 1999. *Publication:* Jazz Hot Magazine, 1997; La Teste de Buche, 1999. *Membership:* SACEM. *Leisure interests:* Writing; Painting; Travel; Cinema; Theatre; Surfing. *Current Management:* Jules Music, Night and Day Records. *Address:* 86 Ave de Gournay, 94800 Villejuif, France.

DAVENPORT Bob; b. 31 May 1932, Newcastle-Upon-Tyne, England. Singer. *Education:* 4 years, St Martins College of Art, London (sculpture). *Career:* Member, Bob Davenport and The Rakes; Solo folk artist; Appeared at Newport Folk Festival, with Joan Baez, Phil Ochs, Bob Dylan, Tom Paxton, 1963; Guest on Pete Seegers Central Park and Tanglewood concerts, 1967; Took break from scene, 1980s; Currently singing in clubs. *Recordings:* Wor Geordie, 1962; The Iron Muse, 1963; Farewell Nancy, 1964; Northumbrian Minstrelcy, 1964; Bob Davenport and The Rakes, 1965; Bob Davenport, 1971; Bob Davenport and The Marsden Rattlers, 1971; Pal of My Cradle Days, 1974; Down The Long Road, 1975; Postcards Home, 1977; With The Rakes, 1977; The Good Old Way – British Folk Music Today, 1980; Will's Barn, 1990; From The Humber To The Tweed, 1991; With the Rakes, The Rakes, 1976; Guest on albums by David Essex; Mike Harding; Watersons; Flowers and Frolics. *Publication:* Cuitanovitch's Road To Wigan Pier documentary, for Thames TV. *Membership:* Equity. *Address:* 14 Calthorpe St, London WC1X 0JS, England.

DAVERNE Gary Michiel; b. 26 Jan. 1939, Auckland, New Zealand. Musical Dir; Composer; Educator. *Education:* Auckland University; Auckland Teachers' College, Diploma Teaching, 1959. *Musical Education:* Trinity College of Music, London, FTCL (Composition), 1969; LRSM, 1965. *Career:* Self-employed, international conductor, composer, arranger, record producer, over 40 albums, including 1 Platinum, 2 Gold discs; Conductor and arranger of music for television, film, radio; Formerly teacher, economics, accountancy, 1962–77; Composer in Schools, 1978–79; President, Composers' Association, New Zealand, 1979; Musical director, Auckland Symphony Orchestra, 1975–; Director of Music, Waitangi Day celebrations (before Queen Elizabeth II); Musical Director, Military Searchlight Tattoo, New Plymouth, 1997; Musical Director, premiere of Jewish oratorio Hear! O Israel by Cormac O'Duffy to celebrate Israel's 50th National birthday; Produced record for Sir Howard Morrison; Arranger/ Producer, Kylie Harris's Country Album of the Year, 1998. *Compositions include:* Over 100 pop songs; Operettas; Songs for children; 3 rock operas; Concert accordion music; Many symphonic works for orchestra (recorded by NZSO) include: Rhapsody For Accordion and Orchestra; Over 600 television and radio jingles, film soundtracks. *Honours:* Officer of the New Zealand Order of Merit (ONZM), 1996. *Leisure interests:* Chess; Bridge; Fishing; Films; Travel.

DAVEY Rick; b. 11 Jan. 1952, Devon, England. Music Publisher; Record Label Owner; Prod. *Education:* BA Hons Philosophy, London University. *Musical Education:* ABRSM Grade VIII (Theory). *Career:* Jazz/blues musician, saxophone and keyboards, since age 15; Music consultant, Tomorrows World, BBC; Artist management for Silver Bullet; Tour manager for Big Youth/Alton Ellis; Studio manager, Machelle Alexander; Acts and labels controlled include: Custers Last Stand Records (Kissing The Pink); Black Cat Records (Jungle/Reggae); Flowsound Ltd publish Zion Train; Terence McKenna (Shamen); KOTOT, Dennis Alcapone; Tour manager, Black Uhuru, Mindlink, Justin Hinds, Jonny Osbourne. *Recordings:* New Era, on Face film with Damon Albarn (Blur); Bible and the Gun, Devon Russell; UTE; Black Cat; Tassoulla. *Memberships:* PRS; MCPS. *Current Management:* Flowsound Ltd; Black Cat RPM. *Address:* Unit C, Imperial Works, Perren St, London NW5 7EE, England.

DAVID Craig (Ashley); b. 5 May 1981, Southampton, England. Vocalist; Songwriter. *Education:* Southampton City College, NVQ Electronics student. *Career:* Worked as club DJ and pirate radio presenter before meeting with local musician (and Artful Dodger member) Mark Hill; Provided vocals for Artful Dodger duo, scoring massive UK hit single; Signed solo contract, 1999; Sell-out British tour, 2000; Developed international fanbase 2001. *Recordings:* Albums: Born To Do It, 2000; Singles: Re-Rewind (with Artful Dodger), 1999; Fill Me In (No. 1, UK), Woman Trouble (with Artful Dodger), 7 Days (No. 1, UK), Walking Away, 2000; Rendezvous, 2001. *Honours:* MOBO Awards: Best Newcomer, Best R & B Act, Best UK Single, 2001; Debut album multi-certified by record industries world-wide. *Current Management:* Colin Lester, Wildstar Management. *Internet:* www.craigdavid.co.uk.

DAVID Hal; b. 25 May 1921, Brooklyn, New York, USA. Lyricist. m. Eunice Bernstein, 2 s. *Career:* Songwriter, collaborations with Burt Bacharach; Henry Mancini; Joe Rapaso; Record producer for Dionne Warwick. *Compositions include:* Raindrops Keep Fallin' On My Head; The Look of Love; What's New Pussycat?; Alfie; Wives and Lovers; It Was Almost Like A Song; What The World Needs Now Is Love; To Love A Child; To All The Girls I've Ever Loved Before (recorded by Julio Iglesias, Willie Nelson); Broadway show, Promises Promises; Films include: April Fools. *Honours include:* Academy Award, Raindrops Keep Fallin' On My Head; Grammy Award, Promises Promises; Tony Award Nomination: Promises Promises; Inducted into Songwriters Hall of Fame; Nashville Songwriters Hall of Fame International; NARM Presidential Award; Creative Achievement Award, B'Nai B'rith. *Memberships:* ASCAP; Songwriters Guild of America; Lyricists Guild of America; Dramatists Guild; Authors League.

DAVID Joel; b. 22 Dec. 1948, Blackburn, Lancashire, England. Musician; Singer; Actor. m. Maureen Seaberg, 10 July 1984. *Musical Education:* Self-taught. *Career:* Actor: Brideshead Revisited, GTV, 1981; Strangers, Granada, 1983; Coronation Street, 1981; 3–4–7–9, GTV; Prime Suspect, GTV, 1989; Nature of The Beast, British Screen, CH4, 1987; Singer: Victoria Wood Show, GTV; Radio: Live At Golders Green Hippodrome, BBC Radio Two, Live With The BBC Big Band, 1990; Nightride, BBC Radio 2, 1988–91; We'll Meet Again, BBC Radio 2, 1994; The David Jacobs Show, BBC Radio 2; The Charlie Chester Show, BBC Radio Two, 1994–95. *Recordings:* Old Bones, 1987; Be My Valentine Tonight, 1988; Dance To The End of Love, 1990; Paws For Love, 1995. *Membership:* British Actors Equity Asscn. *Leisure interests:* Eating out; Driving own Rolls Royce; Foreign travel. *Current Management:* Maureen Seaberg. *Address:* Old Records, 17 Moor Close, Darwen, Lancashire BB3 3LG, England.

DAVIDS Brent Michael; b. 4 June 1959, Madison, Wisconsin, USA. Musician (Quartz Crystal Flutes). *Musical Education:* Master of Music Degree, Composition. *Career:* Appearance on Sunday Morning with the Kronos Quartet, CBS, feature on Sunday Morning, 1997; Performed with Kronos Quartet at Brooklyn Academy of Music, Lincoln Center Out-of-Doors, 1996, 1999; Performed with Joffrey Ballet, 1998–99; Performed with New Mexico Symphony Orchestra, 1999. *Compositions:* Pauwau, for New Mexico Symphony Orchestra; Moon of the Falling Leaves for Joffrey Ballet; Singing Woods; Turtle People, and Native American National Anthem, for Kronos Quartet; Night Chant, for Chanticleer. *Recordings:* Ni-Tcang, CD; Brent Michael Davids; Joe and the Blue Butterfly, forthcoming. *Honours:* ASCAP, 1989; International Music Festival, 1990; National Endowments for the Arts Grant, 1994; Rockefeller Fellowship, 1998; Sundance Institute Composer Fellowship, 1998. *Memberships:* American Composers Forum; American Music Center; Society of Composers Inc; ATLATL. *Leisure interests:* Canoeing; Biking; Camping. *Current Management:* Blue Butterfly Group. *Address:* 3049 10th Ave S, Minneapolis, MN 55407, USA.

DAVIES Bruce William; b. 25 Nov. 1955, Kirkcaldy, Fife, Scotland. Musician; Singer; Songwriter; Entertainer; Radio Presenter. m. (1), 3 s., (2) Anne, 18 Sept. 1993. *Musical Education:* Briefly at Royal Scottish Academy of Music and Drama. *Career:* With folk duo Beggars Mantle, 1983–90; Solo artist, 1990–; Television appearances: BBC Network; Scottish; Border; Grampian; Ulster; numerous US channels; Performances mainly in Scotland, also: UK; Europe; Africa; USA; Canada; Taking accessible but unique style of folk music to audiences both in and out of the folk field. *Recordings:* Numerous; 5 albums currently available; Numerous recordings as session musician; Arranger and producer for other artists. *Leisure interests:* Music (all aspects); Watching football. *Current Management:* Rothes Recordings. *Address:* PO Box 7, Glenrothes, Fife KY6 2TA, Scotland.

DAVIES Gail Patricia; b. 5 June 1948, Broken Bow, Oklahoma, USA. Country Singer; Musician. m. (3) Robert Victor Price, 1 s. *Career:* Own touring band featuring husband and son; Appearances on TV including CBS Morning News Show, The Today Show; Featured in TV Special, The Women of Country; Tours with Neil Young, Willie Nelson, Carl Perkins, Glen Campbell, Don Williams; Toured with Roger Miller; Appearance on Merv Griffin Show; Formed Country-Rock Band, Wild Choir; Staff Producer, Liberty Records, 1991, developed new acts; Founder, Little Chickadee Records, 1995; Writer and producer of albums. *Compositions:* Bucket to the South, for Ava Barber, 1977; single and album tracks. *Recordings:* Singles include: No Love Have I; Someone Is Looking For Someone Like You; It's A Lovely Lovely World, with Emmylou Harris; Round the Clock Lovin'; Grandma's Song; Singing the Blues; You Turn Me On I'm a Radio; You're A Hard Dog To Keep Under The Porch; Boys Like You; Break Away; Jagged Edge of a Broken Heart; Unwed Fathers, featured Dolly Parton; Albums: Gail Davies, 1978; The Game, 1980; Blue Heartache; I'll Be There, 1980; Giving Herself Away, 1982; Where Is A Woman To Go, 1984; Pretty Words, 1989; The Other Side of Love, 1990; The Best of Gail Davies, 1991; Gail Davies' Greatest Hits, 1998; Live and Unplugged At The Station Inn, 2001. *Honours:* Best New Female Vocalist, DJ's of America; Nominee, Academy of Country Music. *Address:* PO Box 120545, Nashville, TN 37212, USA.

DAVIES Mark John; b. 19 Nov. 1969, Ampthill, Bedfordshire, England. Musician (keyboards); Vocalist; Record Prod.; Remixer. *Education:* BA Hons, German, University of East Anglia, 1988–92. *Musical Education:* Violin/viola, to Grade 6, Theory, Grade 4. *Career:* Keyboards, vocals with Messiah, 1990–; Album released, worked with Ian Astbury (of the Cult) and Precious Wilson; Television includes: 2 appearances Top of The Pops, 1992; O-Zone; 5 times on Radio One Roadshow; Major concerts include: Los Angeles, 1992; Scotland; Guernsey, 1993; London. *Recordings:* Album: 21st Century Jesus, 1994; Singles include: There Is No Law (No. 1, USA College Chart), 1991; Temple of Dreams, 1992; I Feel Love, 1992; Thunderdome, 1994; Creator, with Ian Astbury, Peace and Tranquility; 20,000 Hardcore Members (No. 4, UK Dance Charts), 1990; Law of The Night, Marc Almond. *Membership:* Musicians' Union. *Leisure interests:* CAD; Computer games; Football; Herpetology; Skiing; Fashion. *Current Management:* Stevo

Pearce, Some Bizarre. *Address:* 124 New Bond St, London W19 9AE, England.

DAVIES Neol Edward; b. 26 April 1952, Coventry, England. Songwriter; Musician (guitar); Teacher (guitar). *Musical Education:* Self-taught. *Career:* Founded 2 Tone Records with The Specials; Founder member, The Selecter; Tours included: The 2 Tone Tour, 1979; Tours of USA, Europe, Japan, supporting Talking Heads, Blondie, Elvis Costello, The Skatalites, and Prince Buster; Current member, Selecter Instrumental (8-piece instrumental ska band); Television and radio appearances include: Top of the Pops; Old Grey Whistle Test; BBC Radio 1. *Recordings:* The Selecter, 1979; On My Radio, 1979; Three Minute Hero, 1980; Too Much Pressure, 1980; Missing Words, 1980; The Whisper, 1980; Celebrate The Bullet, 1981; Selecter Greatest Hits, 1996; Cruel Britannia, 2000. *Membership:* MU. *Current Management:* Roger Lomas Productions and Management. *Address:* 35 Dillotford Ave, Coventry CV3 5DR, England.

DAVIES Peter Max Crofts; b. 30 Nov. 1950, Salisbury, Wiltshire, England. Luthier; Instrument Designer; Musician (guitar). m. Patricia Anne, 28 Feb. 1981, 1 s., 1 d. *Musical Education:* Learned piano as a child; Self-taught on guitar. *Career:* R and D consultant to: Goodfellow Guitars; Patrick Eggle Guitars, to 1993; Guitar technician to major artists, 1987–; Consultant for care and preservation of Jimi Hendrix' Black Stratocaster guitar; Currently involved in design of new MIDI musical interface, Tonepool; Built guitars for Queen video The Miracle, 1989; Invented Melodic Table and Tonepool instrument, and associated new ways to play and learn music; Currently researching playing techniques for Tonepool and preparing for the manufacture of the instrument. *Honours:* Bachelor of Arts; Guild of Master Craftsmen Nomination. *Leisure interests:* Music; Blues and rock guitar; Painting; Writing. *Current Management:* C-thru Music Ltd. *Address:* 6 Pleasant Row, Woodford, Kettering, Northamptonshire NN14 4HP, England.

DAVIES Ray; b. 21 June 1944, Muswell Hill, London, England. Singer; Songwriter; Musician (guitar); Prod. m. 1) Rasa Didztpetris, 12 Dec. 1964, 2 d., 2) Yvonne, 1 d. with Chrissie Hynde. *Education:* Hornsey Art College; Theatre Design, Croydon College of Art. *Career:* Founder, Ray Davies Quartet, aged 16, later named The Ravens; Group became The Kinks, 1963–; UK debut, London, 1963; US debut, Academy of Music, New York, 1965; Concerts and tours world-wide include: Madison Square Garden, New York, 1981; US Festival, San Bernardino, 1981; Earth Day Concert, Foxborough, 1992; Glastonbury Festival, 1993; Royal Albert Hall, 1993. *Recordings:* Numerous albums include: Kinks, 1964; Kinda Kinks, 1965; Face to Face, 1966; Something Else, 1967; Sleepwalker, 1977; Misfits, 1978; Low Budget, 1979; One for the Road, 1980; Glamour, 1981; Give the People What They Want, 1981; State of Confusion, 1983; Think Visual, 1987; Phobia, 1993; To the Bone, 1994; BBC Sessions 1964–77, 2001; Numerous compilations, live albums and greatest hits collections; Solo albums: Return to Waterloo, 1985; The Storyteller, 1998; Hit Singles: Long Tall Sally, 1964; You Really Got Me, (No. 1, UK), 1964; All Day and All of the Night, 1964; Tired of Waiting For You (No. 1, UK), 1965; Everybody's Gonna Be Happy, 1965; Set Me Free, 1965; See My Friend, 1965; Till the End of the Day, 1966; A Well-Respected Man, 1966; Dedicated Follower of Fashion, 1966; Sunny Afternoon (No. 1, UK), 1966; Dead End Street, 1966; Waterloo Sunset, 1967; Autumn Almanac, 1967; Days, 1968; Lola, 1980; Apeman, 1971; Supersonic Rocket Ship, 1972; Come Dancing, 1983; Contributions as songwriter to: The Virgin Soldiers, film soundtrack, 1969; Chorus Girls, play, 1981; Actor, Absolute Beginners, film, 1986. *Honours* include: Inducted into Rock 'n' Roll Hall of Fame, 1990; Ivor Novello Award for Special Contribution to Music, 1990. *Address:* c/o Asgard, 125 Parkway, London, NW1 7PS, England.

DAVIES Rhodri John; b. 19 Dec. 1971, Aberystwyth, Wales. Musician (Harp); Improviser; Composer. *Education:* BMus (Hons), University of Sheffield; Postgraduate Certificate in Performance, Trinity College of Music, London; Masters in Music, University of Huddersfield. *Career:* Freelance Harpist, London, 1995–; Worked with Derek Bailey, Evan Parker, Chris Burn, John Butcher, Phil Durrant, John Russell, Orphy Robinson, Pat Thomas, Simon Fell, Mark Wastell, Charlotte Church; TV Appearances: Prince of Wales's 50th Birthday, Carlton TV, 1998; Sunday Night with Fiona Phillips, LWT, 1998. *Compositions:* Lle y bwriaf Angor, 1996; Wstrws, 1998; Eleanor's Song, Mrs Bradley Mystery, BBC Drama, 1998; Still Point, 2001; Decalogue (Es I Wacan Gyda'r Jesu), 2001. *Recordings:* Anagrams to Avoid, 1997; Navigations, Chris Burn's Ensemble, 1997; Ghost Notes, 1998; Assumed Possibilities, 1998; Simon H Fell Composition No 30, 1998; Chris Born's Ensemble, Navigations, 1998; String, with Evan Parler, 2001; Vortices and Angels, 2001; Company in Marseille, 2001. *Membership:* London Musicians Collective. *Address:* 40 Stanley Rd, Bounds Green, London N11 2LE, England.

DAVIES Saul; b. 28 June 1965, England. Musician (guitar, violin, percussion); Vocalist. *Career:* Member, James, 1990-. Singles include: Sound, 1991; Born of Frustration, 1992; Sometimes (Lester Piggott), 1993; Laid, 1993; Say Something, 1994; She's A Star, 1997; Tomorrow,

1997; Destiny Calling, 1998; Sit Down '98, 1998; I Know What I'm Here For, 1999; Just Like Fred Astaire, 1999; Getting Away With It (All Messed Up), 2001; Albums: Seven, 1992; Laid, 1993; Wah Wah, 1994; Whiplash, 1997; The Best of James (compilation), 1998; Millionaires, 1999; Pleased To Meet You, 2001. *Current Management:* Rudge Management, 1 Star St, London, W2 1QD, England. *Internet:* www.jamestheband.com.

DAVIS Chip; Songwriter; Composer. *Career:* New Age Music composer; Formed Mannheim Steamroller; Created American Gramaphone record label; Compositions used extensively on television and radio, including: The Today Show; The Rush Limbaugh Show. *Compositions:* Wrote hit single: Convoy, under pen-name, C W McCall; Series of New Age albums: Fresh Aire 1–7; Music for television documentary: Saving The Wildlife; Several Christmas albums. *Leisure interests:* Nature and Environmental conservation. *Current Management:* SESAC. *Address:* 55 Music Sq. E, Nashville, TN 37203, USA.

DAVIS Copeland; b. 16 Aug. 1950, Orlando, Florida, USA. Pop and Jazz Musician (piano); Entertainer. m. Mary Birt Norman, 23 Aug. 1987. *Education:* BFA, Florida Atlantic University. *Musical Education:* Degree in Composition, Arranging, BFA. *Career:* Arranger for The Fifth Dimension; Conductor for Barbara McNair; Arranger, guest artist, Florida Symphonic Pops Orchestra; Television: Tonight Show; Good Morning America; Three Copeland Davis TV Specials; Newly signed with Atlantic Records. *Honours:* Emmy Nomination: Copeland Davis at Crystal Tree. *Membership:* BMI. *Leisure interests:* Computers; Cycling. *Current Management:* Herbert Moon. *Address:* Bowen Agency, 504 W 168th St, New York, NY 10032, USA.

DAVIS Eddy Ray; b. 26 Sept. 1940, Greenhill, Indiana, USA. Composer; Conductor; Musician. *Education:* Purdue University; Chicago University. *Musical Education:* Cosmopolitan Conservatory; Chicago School of Music. *Career:* Appearances include: Mike Douglas Show; Tonight Show; Carnegie Hall; Jazz and Heritage festivals throughout the world including: Japan; Europe; Australia; Russia; Brazil; Records and tours with Woody Allen; Tours with (film star) George Segal; Tours, recordings with Leon Redbone and Tom Waits; Musical Director, Best of Spike Jones; Makin Whoppee; Warren G; Jazz Leggs. *Compositions include:* Penny Candy; Play For Me A Love Song; Now I'm Blue. *Recordings:* Soundtracks: Radio Days; Fried Green Tomatoes (with Patti Labelle); Sophie's Choice. *Publications:* The Theory Behind Chord Symbols. *Honours:* First place, Fretts Magazine Poll for Four String Banjo; Award from Berliner Theatretaler. *Memberships:* The New York Society for the Preservation of Illegitimate Music; The Bunk Project; The New York Banjo Ensemble. *Current Management:* New York Jazz Productions; Sky King Productions. *Address:* 260 Fifth Ave, New York, NY, USA.

DAVIS Jean Michel; b. 2 March 1956, Suresnes, Paris, France. Musician (drums, vibraphone, percussion). m. Cynthia Stone, March 1985, 1 s., 1 d. *Musical Education:* Conservatoire de Montreux, Paris; Berklee College of Music, Boston, USA. *Career:* Drummer, vibraphone player, in clubs: New Morning; Hot Brass; Freelance percussionist playing with: Modulations, (contemporary music ensemble of composer Philippe Durville); Les Primitifs Du Futur; Big bands; Paris opera: Die Soldaten de Zimmerman; Television appearances: Stravinsky's Histoire du Soldat, with the Campagnol theatre troupe (FR3); (France 2); Played with rock group Au Bonheur des Dames, 1997; Studio sessions with various artists; Advertising jingles and cartoon theme tunes; Plays with the Broadway Musical Company, tour of Japan, 1998. *Recordings:* Albums with: Les Primitifs Du Futur; The François Fichu Jazz Gang; Cordes Et Lames: Accordion Madness; Paris Scat; Au Bonheur des Dames, Paris Musette 3. *Publications:* 10 ètudes De Vibraphone Jazz (Salabert); Association Française de Percussion. *Leisure interests:* Family; Hiking. *Address:* 172 Ave de Choisy, 75013 Paris, France.

DAVIS Jonathan; b. 1971. Vocalist; Musician (guitar, percussion, bagpipes). *Career:* Member, Korn; Numerous tours and radio appearances. *Recordings:* Singles: No Place to Hide; Good God; A.D.I.D.A.S., 1997; Got the LIfe, 1998; Freak on a Leash, 1999; Albums: Korn, 1995; Life is Peachy, 1996; Quorn Box, 1998; Follow the Leader, 1998; French Remixes, 1999; Freak on a Leash, 1999; Issues, 1999.

DAVIS Keith; b. 28 Dec. 1946, Bristol, England. Musician (guitar, dobro, banjo). m. Susan Carole Wilson, 14 Dec. 1984, 1 s. *Education:* Reading University. *Musical Education:* Self-taught. *Career:* Played on national and local radio; Concerts include: Various clubs; Sidmouth International Festival; Burnley National Blues Festival; Warwick Festival; Tutor at London College of Music. *Recordings:* On The Streets, 1987; Wireless, 1992; Smoke and Mirrors, 1995; Snake Root, 1999. *Publication:* Swagbag Folk Magazine. *Memberships:* Musicians' Union; Royal Institution of Chartered Surveyors. *Current Management:* Susie Davis, Ferndale Management. *Address:* 6 North St, Downend, Bristol BS16 5SY, England.

DAVIS Lena; b. 8 March 1938, London, England. Personal Man.; Songwriter; Publicist. 1 s. *Career:* Discovered Ricky Valance, had hit with Tell Laura I Love Her, aged 22; Joined Noel Gay Agency as Personal Manager; Later, freelance artist manager. *Compositions:* Hits for Joe Brown; Kathy Kirby; Polly Perkins; Theme music for BBC TV. *Recordings include:* Tell Laura I Love Her. *Publications:* Currently contributes to 5 magazines. *Leisure interests:* Photography; Animals. *Address:* Cotton's Farmhouse, Whiston Rd, Cogenhoe, Northants NN7 1NL, England.

DAVIS Linda Kaye; b. 26 Nov. 1962, Carthage, Texas, USA. Vocalist; Entertainer. m. Lang Jeffrey Scott, 24 Aug. 1984, 2 d. *Career:* Opened shows for superstars including: Garth Brooks; George Strait; Currently touring with Reba McEntire's show; Dream Catcher Recording Artist. *Recordings:* Duet with Reba McEntire: Does He Love You; Album: In a Different Light, 1991; Linda Davis, 1992; Shoot For The Moon, 1994; Some Things Are Meant to Be, 1996; I'm Yours, 1998. *Honours:* CMA Award, 1993; Music City News/TNN Award, 1993; Grammy, 1993. *Memberships:* ASCAP; CMA; ACM; AFTRA. *Leisure interests:* Trap and Skeet Shooting; Being with family; Eating out. *Current Management:* Dream Catcher Entertainment, PO Box 767, Hermitage, TN 37076, USA.

DAVIS Mac; b. 21 Jan. 1942, Lubbock, Texas, USA. Singer; Songwriter. m. Lisë Kristen Gerard, 1983, 3 s. *Education:* Emory University; Georgia State College. *Career:* Manager, Metric Music, 1966–68; Solo singer, 1969–; Television and film performer, 1978–; Screen performances include: North Dallas Forty, 1979; Cheaper To Keep Her, 1980; The Sting II, 1983. *Compositions:* numerous. *Recordings:* Albums include: Mac Davis, 1973; Baby Don't Get Hooked On Me, 1973; Forever Lovers, 1978; Thunder In The Afternoon, 1978; Midnight Crazy, 1981; Texas In My Rear View Window, 1981; Soft Talk, 1984; 20 Golden Greats, 1984; Till I Made It With You, 1986; I Sing the Hits, 1995; The Best of Mac Davis, 2000. *Address:* c/o Gallin Morey Associates, 8730 Sunset Blvd W, Los Angeles, CA 90069, USA.

DAVIS Paul; b. 21 April 1944, Cumberland, England. Record Prod.; Music Publisher; Author; Journalist. m. Hazel, 20 March 1965, 1 s., 2 d. *Career:* Presenter/producer, BBC Radio and local radio; Chairman, RTM Radio; Commercial Manager, Word Records; Owner, New Music Enterprises. *Recordings:* Producer for George Hamilton IV; Wes Tracks; Jerry Arhelger; Pat Boone; Cliff Barrows; Burl Ives; George Beverly Shea. *Publications:* New Life In Country Music (book); Editor, Publisher, New Music Magazine; Books: The Blackwood Brothers, authorised biography of James and Cecil Blackwood; International Ambassador, authorised biography of George Hamilton IV; Pat Boone's authorised biography; Articles, various music and Christian journals. *Memberships:* MCPS; PRS; European Director, Gospel Music Asscn. *Leisure interests:* Church Work. *Address:* Meredale, Reach Lane, Heath and Reach, Bedfordshire LU7 0AL, England.

DAVIS Richard; b. 15 April 1930, Chicago, Illinois, USA. Musician (bass); Teacher. *Musical Education:* MusB, Vanderbrook College of Music, 1952; Postgraduate, Manhattan School of Music, 1964–66. *Career:* Bandleader, own quartet, 1980–; Performed at: Berkeley Jazz Festival; New Orleans Jazz Heritage Festival; Fletcher Henderson Memorial Concert; International tours with: Elvin Jones; Lalo Schrifin; McCoy Tyner; Sun Ra; Archie Shepp; Don Cherry; Associated Professor, Full Tenured Professor of Music, University of Wisconsin, 1976–; Owner, Sympatico Music Publications Inc; Founder, Richard Davis Foundation for Young Bassists. *Recordings:* Albums: with Richard Davis Quartet: With Understanding, 1975; Epistrophy, 1981; Way Out West, 1981; Harvest, 1988; As One; One for Frederick, 1989; Live at Sweet Basil, 1990; The Bassist – Homage To Diversity, 2001; Other recordings with numerous artist including Janis Ian; Herbie Mann; Van Morrison; Freddie Hubbard; Bo Diddley; Laura Nyro; Melissa Manchester; George Benson; Quincy Jones; Judy Collins; Elvin Jones; Charlie Mingus; Bonnie Raitt; Jimmy Smith; Bruce Springsteen; Loudon Wainwright III; Paul Simon; Carly Simon; Manhattan Transfer. *Publications:* Author, The Bass Tradition, with M.C. Gridley, 1984; Jazz Styles, 1985; Contributor to numerous journals. *Honours:* Downbeat Awards: Readers Poll Winner, 1967–72; Critics Poll Winner, 1967–74; ASCAP Popular Award, 1979–83, 1984–85. *Memberships:* International Composers Society; International Society of Bassists; ASCAP; NARAS; National String Artists; American Jazz Foundation; Screen Actors Guild; National Asscn of Jazz Educators. *Address:* University of Wisconsin, Madison, WI 53706, USA.

DAVIS Skeeter (Mary Frances Penick); b. 30 Dec. 1931, Dry Ridge, Kentucky, USA. Singer. *Career:* Duo, The Davis Sisters, with Betty Jack Davis, on radio, television and recordings, 1949–53; Solo career, 1955–; Worked with Eddy Arnold; Elvis Presley; Regular member, Grand Ole Opry, 1959; Toured extensively, US, Canada, Europe, Far East; Regular performances with Duke Ellington. *Recordings:* Hit singles include: I Forgot More Than You'll Ever Know, with Betty Jack Davis; Set Him Free; Can't Help You, I'm Falling Too; My Last Date; The End of The World; A Dear John Letter, with Bobby Bare; For Loving You, with Don

Bowman; Let's Get Together, with George Hamilton IV; Albums include: with The Davis Sisters: Hits, 1952; Jealous Love, 1952; Solo: I'll Sing You A Song…, 1961; Here's The Answer, 1961; The End of The World, 1961; Cloudy With Occasional Tears, 1963; I Forgot More Than You'll Ever Know, 1964; Written By The Stars, 1965; Sings Buddy Holly, 1967; What Does It Take, 1967; Why So Lonely, 1968; Mary Frances, 1969; Skeeter, 1971; Love Takes A Lot of My Time, 1971; Foggy Mountain Top, 1971; Sings Dolly, 1972; Bring It On Home, 1972; I Can't Believe That It's All Over, 1973; The Hillbilly Singer, 1973; He Wakes Me With A Kiss Every Morning, 1974; Heartstrings, 1984; She Sings They Play, 1985; Stars 3, 1994; The Essential Skeeter Davis, 1996; Other albums with: Porter Wagoner; Bobby Bare; Don Bowman; George Hamilton IV; NRBQ. *Address:* c/o Joe Taylor Artist Agency, 2802 Columbine Pl., Nashville, TN 37204, USA.

DAVIS Spencer; b. 17 July 1941, Swansea, Wales. Musician (guitar). *Education:* Birmingham University. *Career:* Founder, Spencer Davis Group, 1963–69; Solo artist and duo with Peter Jameson, 1971; Record company executive, Island Records; Played in Blues Reunion, 1988; Reformed Spencer Davis Group, 1990; Film appearances: The Ghost Goes Gear, 1966; Here We Go Round The Mulberry Bush, 1967; Collaborations include: Keith Moon; Todd Rundgren; Paul Williams; Country Joe McDonald. *Recordings:* Albums: with The Spencer Davis Group: Their First LP, 1965; The Second Album, 1966; Autumn 66, 1966; Gimme Some Lovin', 1967; I'm A Man, 1967; Solo albums: It's Been So Long; Mousetrap; Crossfire, 1984; Singles include: with the Spencer Davis Group: I Can't Stand It, 1964; Strong Love, 1965; Keep On Running (No. 1, UK), 1966; Somebody Help Me (No. 1, UK), 1966; When I Come Home, 1966; Gimme Some Lovin', 1966; I'm A Man, 1967; Mr Second Class, 1968. *Honour:* Carl Alan Award, Most Outstanding Group, 1966. *Current Management:* Richard Martin Management, Agency House, 6 The Steyne, Worthing, West Sussex BN11 3DS, England.

DAVIS Teresa Jane (T J); b. Leeds, West Yorkshire, England. Singer; Musician. *Education:* Diploma, Wakefield Performing Arts College; Leeds College of Music, Jazz and Light Music. *Career:* Lead Vocals: Shiva, Album and Live Gigs including Phoenix, 1996, Tribal Gathering, 1996, Northern Exposure, 1996, Featured Artist on Single, Brilliant Feeling, Full Monty All Stars; Backing Vocals: D:ream, Album, World, Featured Artist on Single, Power, 2 UK Headlining Tours, 1 Australian Headlining Tour, Various Television including TOTP, Steve Wright Show; Walkon and Appearances in EastEnders, The Bill, 1991; Backing Singer for Gary Numan, 2 Tours, 1993; Backing Vocals for Lisa Stansfield, ABC, Playing Role of Frida in Bjorn Again, International Tours, 1997–98. *Recordings:* Lead and Backing Vocals for Sonic R (Sega Game), 1997; Blur, P J Proby/ Marc Almond, Album Sigue Sigue Sputnik; Bjorn Again Live At The Royal Albert Hall, 1998. *Memberships:* Equity; Musicians Union; PAMRA.

DAVISON Peter; b. 26 Oct. 1948, Los Angeles, California, USA. Composer; Orchestrator; Conductor; Arranger. m. Iris Pell, 21 Sept. 1984, 1 d. *Musical Education:* BA, MA, Music Composition, California State University, Northridge; Film Scoring Workshops, Earle Hagan, BMI; Fred Karlin, ASCAP; Travel to Bali to study Gamelan music. *Career:* Composed/ arranged television series and documentaries, including: Seaquest; Batman – The Animated Series; John Denver Tour Special; Films; Interactive media; Commercials including: Hilton Hotels; India; videos. *Recordings:* As composer, arranger, producer, artist: Winds of Space, 1987; Glide – Star Gazer, 1987; Forest – Mountain, 1994; Traces – Music On The Way, 1994; Adagio For Yoga (soundtrack), 2000; Adagio: Music For Relaxation, 2000. *Memberships:* SCL (Society of Composers and Lyricists); ASMA (American Society Music Arrangers); IFP/West; IDA (International Documentary Asscn).

DAWNE Cliff; b. 13 March 1950, Sask, Canada. Songwriter; Singer; Musician (Guitar, Keyboard, Drums). *Career:* Entertainment Showcase, Baton Broadcasting, Shamrock Profile, Broadcasting Ltd; You Can Be A Star Contest, Nashville. *Compositions:* Ever Been Lonely; Before She Said Goodbye. *Recordings:* Boomerang; Heaven; Physical Attraction; The Strength of My Weakness; Ever Been Lonely. *Publication:* The Voice of Country Music In Canada. *Honours:* Finalist, You Can Be A Star Contest, 1987. *Memberships:* Socan Canada; Broadcast Music Inc; American Musicians Asscn. *Current Management:* Little Big Productions, #3 W Broadway Mall, 504 Broadway St, West Yorkton, Sask, Canada.

DAWSON Dana; b. 1975, New York, USA. Singer. *Career:* Performed on Broadway, aged 8; Solo artiste, 1993–; Early success in France; Concerts include: Radio 1's Massive Music tour, 1995. *Recordings:* Albums: Black Butterfly, 1995; Got to Give Me Love, 1995; Singles: Tell Me Bonita, 1991; 3 Is Family, 1995; How I Wanna Be Loved, 1996. *Current Management:* First Avenue Management, The Courtyard, 42 Colwith Rd, London W6 9EY, England.

DAWSON Mary A; b. 6 April 1944, Chicago, Illinois, USA. Songwriter; Music Publisher; Radio Talk Show Host. m. David L Dawson, 15 April 1966, 2 s., 2 d. *Education:* BS, Education; 14 years of piano study. *Career:*

Published songwriter; Music Publisher, President, CQK Music; Host, nationally syndicated radio programme, I Write the Songs, also available on Internet; Songs broadcast on numerous television shows. *Compositions:* Lifelong Friend; The Serenity Prayer; Long Distance Christmas. *Recording:* The Serenity Songs Project: Twelve Steps to Freedom. *Publications:* How to Get Somewhere in the Music Business from Nowhere with Nothing, 1997; Columnist for 4 online magazines on songwriting. *Membership:* Music Women International. *Leisure interests:* Jogging; Interior decorating. *Address:* CQK Music/ I Write the Songs, PMB 208, 2250 Justin Rd, Suite 108, Highland Village, TX 75077, USA.

DAY Doris, (Doris Mary Anne von Kapelhoff); b. 3 April 1924, Cincinnati, Ohio, USA. Singer; Actress. m. (1) Al Jorden, March 1941, divorced 1943, 1 s., (2) George Weilder divorced 1949, (3) Marty Melcher, 3 April 1951, deceased 1968. *Career:* Former dancer, Cincinnati; Singer, shows including: Karlin's Karnival, WCPO-Radio; Bob Hope NBC Radio Show, 1948–50; Doris Day CBS Show, 1952–53; Solo recording artist, 1950–; Actress, numerous films including: Tea For Two, 1950; Lullaby of Broadway, 1951; April In Paris, 1952; Pajama Game, 1957; Teacher's Pet, 1958; Pillow Talk, 1959; Midnight Lace, 1960; Jumbo, 1962; That Touch of Mink, 1962; The Thrill of It All, 1963; Send Me No Flowers, 1964; Do Not Disturb, 1965; The Glass Bottom Boat, 1966; Caprice, 1967; The Ballad of Josie, 1968; Where Were You When The Lights Went Out, 1968; Own television series, The Doris Day Show, 1970–73; Doris Day and Friends, 1985–86; Doris Day's Best, 1985–86; TV special, The Pet Set, 1972. *Recordings:* Hit songs include: Sugarbush, 1952; Secret Love (No. 1, UK and US), 1954; The Black Hills of Dakota, 1954; If I Give My Heart To You, 1954; Ready Willing and Able, 1955; Whatever Will Be Will Be (Que Sera Sera) (No. 1, UK), 1956; Move Over Darling, 1964. *Honours:* Winner (with Jerry Doherty), Best Dance Team, Cincinnati; Laurel Award, Leading New Female Personality In Motion Picture Industry, 1950; Top audience attractor, 1962; American Comedy Lifetime Achievement Award, 1991.

DE BETHMANN Pierre; b. 21 April 1965, Boulogne Billancourt, France. Musician (piano). m. Christel Hua, 22 Sept. 1990, 2 c. *Education:* Baccalauréat C (Science), 1982; ESCP (Paris Graduate School of Management), 1987. *Musical Education:* Classical piano, 1971–87; Private lessons, jazz piano, 1975–; Some self-training; Berklee College of Music, 1989. *Career:* Management consultant, 1990–94; Professional musician, 1994–; Member, 4 regular groups, including PRYSM, trio with Christophe Wallemme and Benjamin Henocq, 1994; Numerous gigs in most Parisian clubs, various international festivals; Numerous radio and television appearances with PRYSM; Occasionally played with: Vincent Herring; Rick Margitza; Willie Williams; Vanessa Rubin; Sylvain Beuf; Philip Catherine; George Brown; Jean-Loup Longnon; François Jeauneau; François Théberge; Aldo Romano. *Recordings:* PRYSM, PRYSM, 1995; Quoi de Neuf Docteur, Big Band; La Femme Du Bouc èmissaire; 51 Below, 1996. *Honour:* First Prize, La Defense National Jazz Contest, 1994. *Memberships:* SACEM; UMJ (Union des Musiciens de Jazz). *Current Management:* Renaud di Matteo, Paris. *Address:* 16 Cité de Trévise, 75009 Paris, France.

DE BURGH Chris, (Christopher Davison); b. 15 Oct. 1948, Argentina. Singer; Songwriter. *Education:* Trinity College, Dublin. *Career:* Irish tour with Horslips, 1973; Solo artiste, 1974–; Album sales, 40m.; Sell-out concerts world-wide; Performances include: Carol Aid, London, 1985; The Simple Truth, benefit concert for Kurdish refugees, Wembley, 1991; Royal Albert Hall, London. *Recordings:* Singles include: Flying, 1975; Patricia The Stripper, 1976; A Spaceman Came Travelling, 1976; Don't Pay The Ferryman, 1982; High On Emotion, 1984; Lady In Red (No. 1, UK), 1986; Love Is My Decision, theme from film Arthur 2, 1988; Missing You, 1988; So Beautiful, 1997; Albums: Far Beyond These Castle Walls, 1975; Spanish Train and Other Stories, 1975; At The End of a Perfect Day, 1977; Crusader, 1979; Eastern Wind, 1980; Best Moves, 1981; The Getaway, 1982; Man On The Line, 1984; The Very Best of Chris De Burgh, 1985; Into The Light, 1986; Flying Colours, 1988; From A Spark To A Flame – The Very Best of Chris De Burgh, 1989; High On Emotion – Live From Dublin, 1990; Power of Ten, 1992; This Way Up, 1994; Beautiful Dreams, 1995; The Love Songs, 1997; Quiet Revolution, 1999; Notes From Planet Earth, 2001. *Honours:* ASCAP Award, The Lady In Red, 1985, 1987, 1988, 1990, 1991, 1997; IRMA Awards, Ireland, 1985–90; Berliner Award, Germany; BAMBI Award, Germany; Midcm Trophy, France. *Current Management:* Kenny Thomson, 754 Fulham Rd, London SW6 5SH, England.

DE DAVRICHEWY Irakli; b. 1 Feb. 1940, Paris, France. Bandleader; Musician (trumpet). 1 s., 2 d. *Musical Education:* Early studies, violin, piano; Self-taught trumpet. *Career:* Formed first orchestra, 1958; Leader, own groups: The Swing Orchestra; French All-Stars; Jazz Four; Also soloist; Worked as accompanist to: Barney Bigard; Cozy Cole; Arvell Shaw; Claude Hopkins; Wallace Davenport; Christian Morin; Moustache; Numerous television broadcasts for J. C. Averty, with Victoria Spivey; Edith Wilson; Claude Bolling; Also with the Orchestra of Marc Lafferière; with Moustache et les Petits Français: accompanied Buddy Tate; Harry Edison; Al Grey; Cat Anderson; Jimmy Forrest; Eddie Vinson; Jimmy Witherspoon; Dorothy Donnegan; Played with Lionel Hampton; Dizzy

Gillespie; Joe Newman; Jo Jones; Sam Woodyard; Joe Muranyi; Tours: Sweden; Netherlands; Germany; Switzerland; Jazz festivals include: Antibes; Coulombs; Breda; Nice; Andernos; Montauban; Hamburg; Concerts include: First part, Louis Armstrong concert, Palais des Sports, Paris, 1965; Numerous concerts for the Hot Club de France, 1984. *Recordings:* Abide With Me, Irakli Quartet, 1971; Les Petits Français with G Brassens, 1979; Le Vieux Truc, Raymond Fonsèque, 1984; Mack The Knife, Irakli Swiss All-Stars, 1985; Chicago Southside Sound, Irakli Jazz Four, 1994; Irakli At The Hot Club de Rouen, 1995. *Publications:* Producer, record and booklets for Media 7: Masters of Jazz, Louis Armstrong complete and chronological. *Honours:* Jazz Hot Award, 1959, 1962; Academie du Jazz, 1972. *Memberships:* President of the Louis Armstrong Asscn, France; Creation, Paris, Louis Armstrong Square, with City of Paris. *Leisure interests:* Golf; France's leading Louis Armstrong archivist. *Address:* 10 Ave Fleury, 92700 Colombes, France.

DE GROOTE Geeraard Albert; b. 3 Sept. 1958, Blankenberge, Belgium. Songwriter; Musician (saxes, guitar, bass); Vocalist. *Education:* School of Economics, Accounting and Modern Languages; Academy of Music, Bruges; Jazz Studio, Antwerp; Jazz Academy, Knokke-Heist. *Career:* Studio recordings and TV appearances with various Belgian artists and bands; TV appearances with Tom Robinson and Tony O'Malley; Belgian concerts with Tom Robinson. *Compositions:* Start Again with Blond. *Recordings:* with Hideaway: Billy Goat Riders; Cly-an; Blond; Rhythm Deep, various Belgian artists. *Leisure interests:* Literature; Travelling; Cars; Girls; Sport. *Address:* Westmoere 50, 8490 Snellegem, Jabbeke, Belgium.

DE JOHNETTE Jack; b. 4 Aug. 1942, Chicago, Illinois, USA. Jazz Musician, (piano, drums); Bandleader; Composer. m. Lydia, 8 Sept. 1968, 2 d. *Musical Education:* Chicago Conservatory of Music. *Career:* Performed and recorded with John Coltrane, Thelonious Monk, Miles Davis, Stan Getz, Bill Evans, Herbie Hancock, Betty Carter; currently with Keith Jarrett Trio; Pat Metheny; Gateway Trio with Dave Holland and John Abercrombie; Also leads own group. *Composition:* Silver Hollow. *Recordings:* Albums: New Directions Live; Parallel Realities; Earth Walk; Music For The Fifth World; Special Edition; Untitled; Pictures; New Rags; Tin Can Alley; Inflation Blues; Album Album. *Honours:* Grand Prix Du Disque, Academy of Jazz, Paris, 1978; Best Jazz Album of Year, Album Album; NEA Fellow, 1978; CAPS Composers Grantee, 1980; Winner, Downbeat Readers Poll, 13 consecutive years; Numerous drum magazine awards; Swing Journal Video Award; Hon. Doctorate of Music, Berklee College of Music, 1990. *Current Management:* Alison Loerke, 1245 N E 88 St, Seattle, WA 98115, USA.

DE LA ROCHA Zach; b. 12 Jan. 1970, Long Beach, California, USA. Vocalist. *Career:* Member, Rage Against The Machine; Former member of early bands Headstance, Farside and Inside Out; Obtained major recording deal; Involved in various causes such as Fairness and Accuracy in Reporting, Rock for Choice and Refuse and Resist; Numerous tours including Lollapalooza; Tour with Wu Tang Clan; Contributed to soundtrack of film Godzilla, 1998. *Recordings:* Singles: Killing In The Name, 1993; Bullet In The Head, 1993; Freedom, 1994; Bombtrack Plus Live, 1994; Bulls On Parade, 1996; People of the Sun EP, 1997; Albums: Rage Against the Machine, 1992; Evil Empire, 1996; The Battle of Los Angeles, 1998; Renegades, 2000. *Honours:* Grammy Award, Hard Rock Performance, Guerrilla Radion, 2001.

DE LONGE Tom (Thomas Matthew); b. 15 Dec. 1975, San Diego, California, USA. Vocalist; Musician (guitar). m. Jennifer Jenkins, May 2001. *Career:* Co-founder: Blink-182, 1993; Built popularity with string of popular independent 7 singles; Signed to MCA through Cargo Music/MCA joint venture deal, 1997; Numerous TV appearances and concerts worldwide including: The Enema Strikes Back '99 tour, released on CD as The Mark Tom and Travis Show; 11-week US Summer tour, 2001; Cameo appearance with group in American Pie film, 1999. *Recordings:* Albums: Fly Swatter (mini-LP), 1993; Cheshire Cat, 1994; Buddah, 1995; Dude Ranch, 1997; Enema of The State, 1999; The Mark Tom and Travis Show (live), 2000; Take Off Your Pants and Jacket, 2001; Singles: Short Bus (split 7 with The Iconoclasts), 1996; They Came To Conquer Uranus (7 EP), Lemmings (split 7 with Swindle), 1997; Dick Lips, Dammit (Growing Up), I Won't Be Home For Christmas, 1997; Josie, 1998; What's My Age Again, All The Small Things, 1999; Adam's Song, Man Overboard, 2000; The Rock Show, Stay Together For The Kids, 2001. *Honours:* World-wide sales of 1999 album in excess of 7m. *E-mail:* tom@loserkids.com. *Internet:* www.blink182.com.

DE LUCIA Paco, (Francisco Sanchez Gomez); b. 21 Dec. 1947, Algeciras, Spain. Musician (flamenco guitar); Composer. *Career:* Debut on Radio Algeciras, 1958; Member: Paco de Lucia Sextet with brothers (including flamenco guitarist Ramon de Algeciras and vocalist Pepe de Lucia); Accompanied many flamenco singers in the 1960s before long-term association with Camaron de la Isla, 1968–; Worked with dancer Jose Greco and flamenco troupe Festival Flamenco Gitano; Live debut at Carnegie Hall, 1970; Experimented with mixing musical elements in the 1970s,

laying the foundations of Nuevo Flamenco; Collaborations with jazz musicians: Chick Corea; John McLaughlin; Larry Coryell; Al DiMeola; Has also performed Spanish classical guitar repertoire. *Compositions:* Soundtracks for films: La Sabina; The Hit; Carmen; Montoyas y Tarantos; Sevillanas. *Recordings include:* Los Chiquitos de Algeciras, 1961; Dos Guitarras Flamencas, Doce Canciones de Garcia Lorca (both with Ricardo Mondrego), 1965; Dos Guitarras Flamencas En America (with Ramon de Algerciras), La Fabulosa guitarra de Paco de Lucia, 1967; Hispanoamerica, Fantasia Flamenca, 1969; Recital de Guitarra, 1971; Fantasia Flamenca de Paco de Lucia, El Duende Flamenco, 1972; En Vivo – Desde El Teatro Real, Fuente Y Caudel, 1975; Almoraima, 1976; Paco de Lucia performs Manuel de Falla with Dolores, 1978; Castro Marin, Friday Night In San Francisco (with John McLaughlin and Al DiMeola), Solo Quiero Caminar, 1981; Passion Grace and Fire (with Al DiMeola and John McLaughlin), 1983; Live... One Summer Night, 1987; Siroco, 1987; Zyryab, 1990; Concierto de Aranjuez, 1991; Live in America, 1993; The Guitar Trio (with Al DiMeola and John McLaughlin), 1996; Luzia 1998. *Honour:* Jerez Flamenco Competition, Special Prize, 1958. *Address:* International Music Network, Fourth Floor, 2 Main St, Gloucester, MA 01930, USA. *Internet:* www.pacodelucia.org.

DE MAEYER Marc; b. 23 April 1966, Willebroek, Belgium. 1 d. *Musical Education:* Academy of Music, Mechelen, Belgium; Self-taught keyboards. *Career:* Keyboards and backings in Hardrockband, Rubicon, keyboards and vocals in Flemish Pop Band, Van Gogh; Producer of Demotapes, Prime Mover and Herve and Anton Menke; Writing for Petra, Yasmine and Barbara Dex; Television appointments: Tien omtezien; BRT, Man. b t Lond; Radio appointments: BRT; RSJ. *Compositions:* Elsje; Jij Bent Voor Mij; Icecubes and Diamonds; Shadow King; Moonlite; Een Nachtje Slapen. *Recordings:* Alles Draait Om Haar; Vers Bloed, demotape; Prime Mover, demotape. *Publication:* Alles Draait om Haar, 1994. *Honour:* Semi-final, Rock in Flanders, 1990. *Leisure interest:* Travelling. *Address:* De Maeyer Marc, Heufstraat 49, BE 3350 Overhespen, Belgium.

DE MARCOS GONZÁLEZ (CARDENAS) Juan; b. 1954, Havana, Cuba. Musician (Tres, Guitar); Vocalist; Composer; Arranger; Bandleader. *Education:* Studied Russian and Hydraulic Engineering at university; Agronomic Science Institute, Doctorate, 1989. *Career:* Formed Sierra Maestra, styled on the traditional Cuban septeto group, 1978; Director, arranger and conductor for Afro-Cuban All-Stars; Consultant, co-ordinator, conductor and musician on the sessions for the Buena Vista Social Club series of recordings which featured: Afro-Cuban All-Stars; Rubén Gonzaléz; Ibrahim Ferrer; Compay Segundo; Omara Portuonda; Eliades Ochoa; Barbarito Torres; Guajiro Mirabel; Ry Cooder; Appeared in Wim Wenders' documentary film Buena Vista Social Club; Formed Ahora (own production company in Cuba). *Recordings:* recent Albums: ¡Dundunbanza! (Sierra Maestra), 1994; Tibiri Tabara (Sierra Maestra), Buena Vista Social Club, A Toda Cuba Le Gusta (Afro Cuban All-Stars), Introducing Rubén Gonzaléz, 1997; Buena Vista Social Club Presents Ibrahim Ferrer, Distinto Diferente (Afro Cuban All-Stars), 1999. *Address:* c/o World Circuit Ltd, First Floor, Shoreditch Stables, 138 Kingsland Rd, London, E2 8DY, England.

DE MASURE Geoffrey; b. 16 May 1969, Tourcoing, France. Musician (trombone). *Musical Education:* Musical study in Avignon, 1984–89, with André Jaume in Paris, 1989, in New York and at Banff, Canada, with Steve Coleman, Robin and Kevin Eubanks, Marvin Smith, Kenny Wheeler and Rufus Reid. *Career:* Founder, Tribu; Appearances at La Défense, Concours de jazz d'Etréchy, 1996, Orchestre National de Jazz, 1997; Appearances with Tribu at Centre Culturel Jean Cocteau, Etréchy, Centre Culturel de Marines, théâtre de Vanves, festival de Radio France de Montpellier, Jazz Club d'Auxerre, Cave Dimière à Argenteuil. *Recordings:* Orchestre National de Jazz: A plus tard, 1992; Monk, Mingus, Ellington, 1993; Bouquet final, 1994; Quoi De Neuf Docteur: A l'envers, 1995; 51 degrees below, 1996; Compilation Nato, Les films de ma ville, 1995; Ronan Robert Réunion, 1996; Odejy, Suite alpestre, 1997; Hubert Dupond, Dans le décor, 1997; Malo Vallois Quartet, Complix-cités, 1997; Aka Moon, Elohim, 1997; Jean Marc Padovani: Jazz Angkor, 1998; Minotaure Jazz Orchestra, 1998. *Honours:* First prize Composition, second prize group, Tribu, Concours de Jazz d'Etrechy, 1996; First prize, soloist, third prize for group, with Tribu, third prize composition, Concours National de La Défense, 1997. *Membership:* Union Musiciens Jazz (UMJ). *Address:* Les Denizets, 02540 Vendieres, France.

DE MESMAY Benoit; b. 10 Oct. 1961, Algeria. Composer; Musician (piano). *Education:* Licence de Droit. *Musical Education:* State diploma, professor of jazz. *Career:* European jazz festivals with Gil Evans; Orchestre National de Jazz; Elizabeth Caumont; John Scofield; Lucky Peterson. *Recordings:* 2 albums with Elizabeth Caumont; 3 albums with Laurent Cugny, Gil Evans. *Address:* 9 rue des Mortes Fontaines, 92370 Chaville, France.

DE RYCKE Herman; b. 20 Aug. 1960, Oudenaarde, Belgium. Musician (Double Bass). m. Maes Riet, 7 Jan. 1989, 2 s. *Education:* Solfège, Double

Bass. *Career:* Klepper, pop group, 1976–77; Penthouse, pop group, 1979–83; Allan Fawn and The State of the Art, pop group, 1984; Kandahar, pop group, 1983–86; The Peter Band Band, pop group, 1986; Work 4, contemporary jazz, 1987–89; Kalinka Zigeunertrio, gipsy music, 1991; TV: Villatempo (BAT), 1986. *Composition:* Blue Ballad, jazz. *Recordings:* with Penthouse: Neighbour Fool, single, LP; with Peter Pan Band: Light My Fire, single. *Honours:* Winner, Humo's Rock Rally, 1986; The Peter Pan Band, 1986; Winner, Knack Rhythm 'n Youth Trophy, 1989. *Membership:* SABAM. *Leisure interest:* Travelling. *Address:* Hoogmeers 9, 9031 Gent, Belgium.

DE SCHOOLMEESTER Beverley; b. 4 May 1962, Britain. Songwriter; Poet; Musician (bass guitar, piano); Vocalist. *Education:* National Diploma Business Studies; Student of Scientology. *Musical Education:* Pianforte to Teaching Standard; Self-taught bassist, vocalist. *Career:* Solo artist as jazz fusion singer, 1991–; Currently, bass player, backing vocalist for The Dolls, major deal pending; UK nationwide television, radio appearances also in Europe, Indonesia, Singapore, Japan, 1995; Tours: UK; France; Germany; Netherlands; Sweden; Italy; Turkey; Singapore; Indonesia; Ireland. *Recordings:* 3 EPs; Album: The Dolls: No Shame; Solo material: over 30 tracks written and demoed. *Publications:* Various poetry in magazines and local press. *Memberships:* Musicians' Union; London Academy of Music. *Leisure interests:* Badminton; Martial arts; Swimming; Horse riding; Relaxing on the beach. *Address:* 16 Battle St, Reading, Berkshire RG1 7NU, England.

DE SMET Francis; b. 3 Dec. 1962, Bruges, Belgium. Musical Supervisor; Musician (Keyboards). *Education:* Harmony and Piano, Conservatory of Bruges; Electronic Music Composition, Royal Conservatory of Brussels, Academia Chigichiana, 1992. *Career:* Musical Supervision, Transatlantic Films, Brussels, 1992–; Developing patented sound enhancer. *Compositions:* Filmtrack of The Sexual Life of the Belgians, 1993. *Membership:* AES. *Current Management:* BVBA De Smet Films, Generaal Lemanlaan 151, 8310, Bruges, Belgium.

DE SOUTEIRO Arnaldo; b. 23 June 1963, Rio de Janeiro, Brazil. Record Prod.; Journalist; Publicist; Educator. m. Ithamara Koorax, 15 April 1990. *Education:* Classical Piano, Harmony, privately with mother Pianist and Conductor Delza Agricola. *Career:* Founder and President, Jazz Station Records, 1991–; Jazz Critic, Tribune da Imprensa, 1979–; Brazilian Correspondent, Keyboard Magazine, 1986–95; Produced TV Specials for Globo and Manchete networks including Joao Gilberto and Antonio Carlos Jobim, Dizzy Gillespie, Tony Bennett, Airto, Flora Purim and Chuck Mangione. *Recordings:* As Producer, albums for Luiz Bonfá, The Bonfá Magic; Dom um Romao, Rhythm Traveller; Ithamara Koorax, Serenade in Blue; Joao Gilberto, Ao Vivo/Live in Rio; Thiago de Mello, Amazon; Deodato, Inútil Paisagem; Also produced acclaimed compilation series for Brazilian Horizons and A Trip To Brazil; Produced sessions featuring Herbie Hancock, Yana Purim, Steve Swallow, Antonio Carlos Jobim, Ron Carter, Sadao Watanabe, Larry Coryell and Gonzalo Rubalcaba. *Memberships:* Hon. Mem., International Academy of Music, 1985–; Associate Mem., International Asscn of Jazz Educators, 1991-. *Address:* Rua Miguel Lemos 99, Suite 801, 22071–000 Rio de Janeiro, RJ, Brazil.

DE VIS Alain; b. 6 Sept. 1953, Brussels, Belgium. Musician (Trumpet; Flugelhorn); Composer; Arranger. m. Nanga Marie-Jeanne, 30 June 1984, 4 s. *Education:* Mathematics and Physics; Classical, School in Nivelles, Belgium, 1971. *Career:* Small commercial bands, 1975; Jazz bands and big bands, 1979; Salsa and Brazilian bands, 1979/80–; Concerts with: Fania All Stars, 1981; Brasil Tropical, shows, in Europe; Salsa De Hoy; Dynamita Salsa. *Recordings:* Act Big Band, second album; Many studio sessions for Singers in 1980s. *Membership:* SABAM, Composer. *Current Management:* Dynamic Sounds Productions, rue G Wincqz 24, 7060 Soignies, Belgium. *Address:* Rue G Wincqz 24, 7060 Soignies, Belgium.

DE VORE David; b. 27 March 1943, Hilo, Hawaii, USA. Prod.; Engineer. m. Janine, 3 July 1976, 1 d. *Education:* 2 years college, Engineering/ Architecture. *Career:* Producer, Engineer for Fleetwood Mac; Grateful Dead; Santana; Elton John; REO Speedwagon; Ringo Starr; Russ Ballard. *Recordings include:* (as producer) Don't Let The Sun Go Down On Me; Hot Blooded; Can't Fight This Feeling. *Leisure interests:* Golf; Mountain biking; Rollerblading.

DE VRIES Marius; b. 21 Oct. 1961, London, England. Prod.; Remixer; Songwriter; Musician (keyboards); Programmer; Arranger. m. Felicity, 1 April 1989, 1 s., 1 d. *Education:* Peterhouse College, Cambridge; Music Scholarship, St Paul's Cathedral Choir School; Music Scholarship at Bedford School. *Career:* Two world tours with Blow Monkeys; Musical Director for Rick Astley's tour, 1989; Musical Director for Neneh Cherry, 1991; Television appearances include: South Banks Arts Review; Jonathon Ross; Top of The Pops; The Word; The Tube; In studio, 1991–; Music Supervisor for Warner Bros The Avengers, 1997–98. *Compositions:* Co-composer and Co-producer of score for Baz Luhrman's Romeo and Juliet, 1996. *Recordings:* Albums: with Madonna: Bedtime Stories, 1994; Ray of

Light, 1998; with Björk: Debut, 1993; Post, 1995; Homogenic, 1997; Vespertine, 2001; with Massive Attack: Protection, 1994; with Annie Lennox: Diva, 1992; Medusa, 1995; with U2: Hold Me Thrill Me Kiss Me Kill Me, 1995, Pop, 1997; with Robbie Robertson, Contact from the Underground of Red Boy, 1998; with Neil Finn, Try Whistling This, 1998; with Melanie C, Northern Star, 1999. *Publications:* Various magazine articles. *Memberships:* PRS; Musicians' Union. *Leisure interests:* Travel; Reading.

DEACON John; b. 19 Aug. 1951, Leicester, England. Musician (bass). *Education:* First class (hons) degree, Electronics. *Career:* Bass player, UK rock group, Queen, 1971–; Numerous tours include: UK; US; Australia; Japan; South America; Major concerts include: Rock In Rio Festival, Brazil, 1985; Live Aid, Wembley, 1985; Knebworth Festival, 1986; A Concert For Life, Wembley, 1992. *Recordings:* Albums include: Queen, 1973; Queen 2, 1974; Sheer Heart Attack, 1974; A Night At The Opera (No. 1, UK), 1975; A Day At The Races (No. 1, UK), 1976; Jazz, 1978; Live Killers, 1979; The Game (No. 1, UK and US), 1980; Flash Gordon (film soundtrack), 1980; Greatest Hits (No. 1, UK), 1981; Hot Space, 1982; The Works, 1984; The Complete Works, 1985; A Kind of Magic (No. 1, UK), 1986; Live Magic, 1986; The Miracle (No. 1, UK), 1989; Innuendo (No. 1, UK), 1991; Greatest Hits II (No. 1, UK) 1991; Live At Wembley '86, 1992; Made In Heaven (No. 1, UK), 1995; Queen Greatest Hits III, 1998; Small Soldiers, 1998; Surfin' Senorita, 1999; Singles include: Seven Seas of Rhye, 1974; Killer Queen, 1974; Now I'm Here, 1975; Bohemian Rhapsody (No. 1, UK), 1975; You're My Best Friend, 1976; Somebody To Love, 1977; We Are The Champions, 1977; Bicycle Race, 1978; Don't Stop Me Now, 1979; Love of My Life, 1979; Crazy Little Thing Called Love (No. 1, USA), 1979; Save Me, 1980; Play The Game, 1980; Another One Bites The Dust (No. 1, USA), 1980; Flash, 1981; Under Pressure, with David Bowie (No. 1, UK), 1981; Radio Ga Ga, 1984; I Want To Break Free, 1984; It's A Hard Life, 1984; Hammer To Fall, 1984; One Vision, 1985; A Kind of Magic, 1986; I Want It All, 1989; Breakthru, 1989; The Invisible Man, 1989; Innuendo (No. 1, UK), 1991; Headlong, 1991; The Show Must Go On, 1991; These Are The Days of Our Lives/Bohemian Rhapsody (No. 1, UK), 1991; Five Live (live EP with George Michael and Lisa Stansfield) (No. 1, UK), 1993; Heaven For Everyone, 1995; Too Much Love Will Kill You, 1995; Also contributed to recordings by: Elton John, Mick Ronson. *Honours include:* Britannia Award, 1977; Gold Ticket, Madison Square Gardens, 1978; Ivor Novello Awards: Best Selling British Record, 1976; Outstanding Contribution to British Music, 1987; Silver Clef Award, Nordoff-Robbins Music Therapy Centre, 1984; BRIT Awards: Outstanding Contribution to British Music, 1990; Best British Single, 1991. *Current Management:* c/o Jim Beach, Queen Productions, 46 Pembridge Rd, London W11 3HN, England.

DEAL Kim; b. 10 June 1961, Dayton, Ohio, USA. Musician (bass, guitar); Songwriter; Vocalist. m. John Murphy, divorced 1988. *Career:* Joined The Pixies; Early support slots to Throwing Muses; Numerous tours and festival dates; Some television appearances; Band split, 1993; Formed The Breeders; Tours and record releases; Formed The Amps, 1995. *Recordings:* With The Pixies: Singles: Gigantic, 1988; Monkey Gone to Heaven, 1989; Here Comes Your Man, 1989; Velouria, 1990; Dig for Fire, 1990; Planet of Sound, 1991; Alec Eiffel, 1991; Head On, 1991; Debaser, 1989 (charted 1997); Albums: Come on Pilgrim, 1987; Surfer Rosa, 1988; Doolittle, 1989; Bossanova, 1990; Trompe le Monde, 1991; Death To The Pixies (compilation), 1997; Live At The BBC (radio sessions), 1998; Complete B-Sides, 2001; With The Breeders: Singles: Safari, EP, 1992; Cannonball, 1993; Divine Hammer, 1993; Head To Toe, 1994; Albums: Pod, 1990; Last Splash, 1993; With The Amps singles: Tipp City, 1995; Albums: Pacer, 1995.

DEAN Elton; b. 28 Oct. 1945. Musician (saxello, alto saxophone). m. Marie-Noelle Sala, 16 Jan. 1988, 1 d. *Musical Education:* Self-taught. *Career:* Worked with: Keith Tippett Sextet; Soft Machine, Proms concert, 1970; Brotherhood of Breath; London Jazz Composer's Orchestra; Carla Bley; Leader, Just Us; EDQ; Own nine-piece group Ninesense, 1975; Elton Dean Quintet, tour of Brazil, British Council, 1986; Leader, various groups including: Unlimited Saxophone Company; In Cahoots; Equip Out; Formed quartet with Howard Riley. *Recordings:* with Julie Driscoll: Julie Driscoll; with Julie Tippetts: Sunset Glow; with Soft Machine: Third; Fourth; Fifth; with Robert Wyatt: End of An Ear; with Keith Tippett: I Am There... You Are Here; Dedicated To You... But You Weren't Listening; with Keith Tippett's Centipede: Septober Energy; with Ninesense: Oh! For The Edge; Happy Daze; with Elton Dean Quintet: Boundaries; with Elton Dean and Alan Skidmore: El Skid; with Carla Bley: European tour; with Dean, Gallivan, Wheeler: The Cheque Is In The Mail; Elton Dean's Newsense, 1998; Elton Dean Trio, Into the Nierika, 1998; Elton Dean Headless Qt, 1998; Other recordings include: Elton Dean Duos, Trios, Quartet; Elton Dean's Unlimited Saxophone Company; Elton Dean/Howard Riley Quartet; Elton Dean: The Vortex Tapes; If Dubois Only Knew, with Paul Dunmall duo, 1996; Silent Knowledge, Elton Dean Quintet, 1996; Rumours of an Incident, Quintet with Roswell Rudd, 1997; Bladik, with Mujician and Roswell Rudd, 1997; Virtually, Soft Machine, 1998; Noisette, Soft Machine,

1999; One to One, with Howard Riley, 1999; Moorsong, with Fred T Baker, 2000. *Address:* 7 Farleigh Rd, London N16 7TB, England.

DEAN Johnny; b. 12 Dec. 1971. Singer; Songwriter. *Career:* Singer, songwriter, Menswear, 1994–; Television includes: Later With... Britpop Now, 1995; Support tours with: The Charlatans, US; Pulp, Europe; Several headline British tours; Major concerts include: Heineken Festival, Leeds, 1995. *Recordings:* Albums: Nuisance, 1995; We Love You, 1996; Hay Tiempo, 1998; Singles: I'll Manage Somehow, 1995; Daydreamer, 1995; Being Brave, 1995; Sleeping In, 1995. *Address:* c/o Laurel Records, PO Box 1422, Chancellors House, Chancellors Rd, London W6 9SG, England.

DEARIE Blossom; b. 28 April 1928, East Durham, New York, USA. Singer; Songwriter; Musician (piano). *Musical Education:* Piano lessons from age 5; Studied classical music. *Career:* Joined the Blue Flames, vocal group within the Woody Herman Big Band; Member, The Blue Reys, in the Alvino Rey Band; Moved to Paris, founder member, vocal group, the Blue Stars, 1952; Returned to New York, solo artiste, New York nightclubs; Annual appearances, Ronnie Scott's Club, London, 1966–; Formed own record company, Daffodil Records, 1971; Played Carnegie Hall with Joe Williams, and jazz vocalist Anita O'Day in show the Jazz Singers, 1970s; 6 months a year, The Ballroom, Manhattan, 1983–; Appeared The Pizza On the Park, late 80s/early 90s. *Compositions include:* I Like You You're Nice; I'm Shadowing You; Hey John. *Recordings:* Albums include: My Gentleman Friend, 1961; May I Come In?, 1966; The Special Magic of Blossom Dearie, 1975; My New Celebrity Is You, 1979; Blossom Dearie Sings 1973, 1979; Blossom Dearie Sings 1975, 1979; Winchester In Apple Blossom Time, 1979; May I Come In?, 1981; Blossom Dearie, 1983; Needlepoint Magic, 1988; Featuring Bobby Jasper, 1988; Songs of Chelsea, 1988; Et Tu Bruce, 1989; Tweedledum and Tweedledee, 1991; Once Upon A Summertime, 1993; I'm Hip, 1998. *Honours:* First recipient, Mabel Mercer Foundation Award, 1985. *Current Management:* F Sharp Productions, Penthouse B, 157 W 57th St, New York, NY 10019, USA.

DEARNLEY Mark; b. 12 Aug. 1957, Barnet, England. Prod.; Engineer; Musician (keyboards). *Education:* Southampton University. *Musical Education:* Piano, Organ. *Career:* Engineer credits include: AC/DC, 3 albums; Circus of Power; The English Beat, 3 albums; Joan Armatrading; Def Leppard, remix; Paul McCartney; Producer credits include: The Dog's D'Amour, 3 albums; Steve Jones; Mother Love Bone; The Quireboys; Loudness; Bang Tango; Die Cheerleader; Owen Paul; The Wild Family; Scream 2; South Park; American Pie. *Honours:* Numerous Platinum, Gold and Silver records. *Leisure interests:* Tennis; Table Tennis. *Current Management:* Worlds End (America) Inc. *Address:* 183 N Martel Ave, Suite 270, Los Angeles, CA 90036, USA.

DEBORG Jerry Simon; b. 30 Oct. 1963, London, England. Musician (guitar); Songwriter; Singer. *Education:* Harrow College of Art. *Career:* Member of Jesus Jones, 1986–; Numerous appearances on radio and TV; Several chart hits. *Recordings:* Numerous including: Singles: Info Freako, 1989; Never Enough, 1989; Bring it On Down, 1989; Real Real Real, 1990; Right Here Right Now (No. 2, US), 1991; International Bright Young Thing, 1991; Who Where Why, 1991; The Devil You Know, 1993; The Right Decision, 1993; Zeroes and Ones, 1993; The Next Big Thing, 1997; Albums: Liquidizer, 1989; Doubt (No. 1, UK), 1991; Perverse, 1993; Already, 1997; London, 2001. *Honour:* Best New Band, MTV, 1991. *Leisure interests:* Hang gliding; Fishing; Poetry. *Current Management:* Gailforce. *Address:* c/o 30 Ives St, London SW3 2ND, England.

DEDIC Srdan; b. 13 July 1965, Zagreb, Croatia. Composer; Arranger; Musician (piano). *Musical Education:* Degree in Composition, Zagreb Academy of Music; Specialization at l'Universitè des Sciences Humaines de Strasbourg; Sweelinck Conservatorium, Amsterdam. *Career:* Participated at Gaudeamus Festival (Amsterdam); International Rostrum of Composers (Paris); Music Biennale, Zagreb; Performed solo from own compositions: Mouvement Concertante, with Zagreb Philharmonic, 9 orchestral performances; Over 50 performances in Europe, America, Australia; Writing music for television, theatres, films. *Compositions:* Snake Charmer, bass clarinet solo, 1986; Beat On, for orchestra, 1988; Canzona, cello, guitar, 1988; Calix, symphonic poem, 1990; At The Party, 1990; Concerto for cello and chamber orchestra; 12 compositions recorded for Croatian Radio; Supercussion album includes composition: At The Party. *Publications:* Composing Using Music Software (brochure). *Honours:* First Prize, UNESCO – International Rostrum of Composers, Paris, 1988; Award, student orchestral works, Music Biennale Zagreb, 1989; Winner, Composition Contest, 29th annual Contemporary Music Festival, Indiana State University, 1995. *Membership:* Croatian Composers Society. *Leisure interest:* Music software programming. *Current Management:* Dr Peter Höhn, Schanze 13, D 57392 Schmallenberg, Germany. *Address:* Srdan Dedic, Hugo de Grootplein 12, 1052 KW Amsterdam, Netherlands.

DEE Brian; b. 21 March 1936, London, England. Musician (piano). m. 28 Dec. 1966, to 1982, 1 s., 1 d. *Musical Education:* Local teacher, 6 years.

Career: Jazz pianist, late 1950s–; Session musician and accompanist; Extensive BBC radio with trio and many bands; Currently pianist with: Ted Heath Orchestra; Kenny Baker Dozen; Laurie Johnson; Performed at numerous concerts and festivals. *Compositions:* Background music. *Recordings:* Featured on approximately 12 albums in 3 years, including own albums. *Memberships:* PRS; Musicians' Union; BASCA. *Leisure interests:* Watching speedway; Football. *Address:* 130 Sheering Mill Lane, Sawbridgeworth, Hertfordshire CM21 9ND, England.

DEE Kiki, (Pauline Matthews); b. 6 March 1947, Bradford, England. Singer. *Career:* Leader, Kiki Dee band; Recording artist, 1964–; First white artist signed to Tamla-Motown; Cabaret singer, Europe and South Africa; Appearances, London musicals: Pump Boys and Dinettes, 1984; Blood Brothers, 1989; Solo acoustic tour with guitarist Carmelo Uggeri, support to Jools Holland, UK, 1995. *Recordings:* Albums: I'm Kiki Dee, 1968; Great Expectations, 1971; Loving and Free, 1973; I've Got The Music In Me, 1974; Kiki Dee, 1977; Stay With Me, 1979; Perfect Timing, 1982; Angel Eyes, 1987; Almost Naked, 1995; Singles include: I'm Gonna Run Away From You; Running Out of Fools; Amoureuse, 1973; I've Got The Music In Me, 1974; How Glad I Am, 1975; Don't Go Breaking My Heart, duet with Elton John (No. 1, UK and US), 1976; Star, 1981; True Love, duet with Elton John (No. 2, UK), 1993. *Honours:* Olivier Award Nomination, 1989.

DEFRANCO Buddy (Boniface Ferdinand Leonard); b. 17 Feb. 1923, Camden, New Jersey, USA. Musician (clarinet); Bandleader. m. Joyce Yount, 1 s. *Musical Education:* Mastbaum Music School, Philadelphia. *Career:* Clarinet/saxophone player with: Johnny Davis Band, 1939; Gene Krupa Orchestra, 1941–42; Tommy Dorsey Orchestra, 1944–48; Count Basie Septet, 1950; Bandleader, Buddy DeFranco Orchestra, 1951; Clarinettist, Jazz At The Philharmonic All-Star Tours, 1952–54; Conductor, Glenn Miller Orchestra, 1966–74; Bandleader, Buddy DeFranco Group, 1974–; Collaborations include: Fats Navarro; Charlie Barnet. *Compositions:* You Must Believe in Swing, 1997; Finegan's Walk, 1998; Skinnin' Rabbits, 1998. *Recordings:* Albums: Flying Fingers of Art Tatum and Buddy DeFranco; Cross-Country Suite (with Nelson Riddle); Mr Lucky; Mood Indigo; Chicago Fire (with Terry Gibbs); George Gershwin Song Book (with Oscar Peterson); Hark, with Oscar Peterson, 1985; Five Notes of Blues, 1992; Born To Swing, 1993; Buenos Aires Concert, 1995; You Must Believe in Swing, with Dave McKenna, 1997; Do Nothing Till You Hear From Us, with Dave McKenna, 1999; Chip Off the Old Bop. *Publications:* Buddy DeFranco on Jazz Improvisation, 1973; Modern Jazz Studies, 1973; Studies For Clarinet, 1973; Hand in Hand with Hanon. *Honours:* Voted Best Jazz Clarinettist, numerous magazine polls; Grammy Award, Cross-Country Suite, 1956; Grammy Nomination, Best Jazz Instrumental Soloist, 1998. *Memberships:* Fellow, National Asscn Jazz Educators; ASCAP; Board of Directors, ClariNetwork, 1980-. *Address:* PO Box 252, Sunnyside, FL 32461, USA.

DEGAS Jorge; b. 5 July 1953, Rio De Janeiro, Brasil. Musician (Bass). m. Stenia Degas, 4 s., 1 d. *Education:* Autodidact. *Career:* Festival of Art and Black Culture, Nigeria, 1977; Festival of Cascais, Portugal, 1978; Show, Celebration of Independance, Angola, 1979; Festival in Montreaux, Nyon, 1982; Rock in Rio, 1983; Festival in Avante, Portugal, 1984; Festival Free Jazz, Brazil, 1985; Show, Pao De Acuca, Rio, 1986; Show, Olympia de Paris, 1988; Festival, Jazz in the Garden, Berlin, 1989; Festival, Jazz in July, Berlin, 1990; Copenhagen Jazzhouse Feat, 1991; Midtfyns Festival, Denmark, 1993; Copenhagen Jazz Festival, 1994; Baixo Brasil, Bass Festival, 1996. *Compositions:* Music to Film, Paraiba Mulher Macho; Bom Burges; Dona Beija. *Recordings:* Include, M Resende and Index; Uniao; Muxima; Quarteto Negro; Ready for Changes; Violeiro; Xiame; Shadow of My Soul; Cantar a Vida. *Membership:* The Danish Music Asscn. *Leisure interests:* Family; House; Garden; Cooking. *Current Management:* Degas Skolevej 9, 5620 Glamsbjerg, Denmark.

DEGIORGIO Kirk, (As One, Future Past, Esoterik); b. 1967, London, England. Prod.; Remixer; DJ. *Career:* Worked in Reckless Records shop in London; Travelled to Detroit: Became inspired by Derrick May and Juan Atkins to make music; On return to London started producing; Founder: A.R.T.; Op-Art Records; Released tracks by artists including: Carl Craig; Black Dog; Also recorded albums for Mo' Wax and Ubiquity Records; Collaborations: Jamie Odell; Ian O'Brien; Dan Keeling; Remixed: Alien Newcleus; 4 Hero. *Membership:* PRS. *E-mail:* opart@dircon.co.uk. *Internet:* www.kirkdegiorgio.com.

DEGRYSE Fabien; b. 6 Nov. 1960, Brussels, Belgium. Guitarist; Composer; Teacher. m. Guns Colette, 1985, 2 s., 2 d. *Education:* Certificate, Berklee College of Music, Boston, USA, 2 years. *Career:* Played with Zar, 1985–87, including tour in Canada and Belgium; Played with Quadruplex, 1985–92; Concerts with PH Catherine and Toots Thielemans; Played with Panta Rhei including recording of 3 CDs and numerous concerts and festivals between 1994 and 1997, in Europe and Africa; Still plays with L'Ame Des Poetes including Recording of 2 CDs and numerous concerts and festivals and broadcasting in Europe, Africa and Canada, 1994; Tchr, Jazz Guitar, Conservatory of Brussels, Belgium.

Recordings: Quadruplex, CD, 1990; Medor Sadness, CD, 1992; Hommage á René Thomas, CD, 1997. *Publication:* L'Improvisation Jazz par les arpèges, 1999. *Current Management:* Rue E Laurent 100, 1420 Braine L'Alleud, Belgium.

DEHAVEN Penny (Charlotte); b. 17 May 1948, Winchester, Virginia, USA. Singer; Actress. *Career:* As Penny Starr: Singer on Jamboree USA; Name changed to Penny Dehaven; One of first female singers to entertain US troops in Viet Nam; Film appearances include: Country Music Story; Travelling Light; Honky Tonk Man. *Recordings:* Singles: Grain of Salt; I Feel Fine; Land Mark Tavern (with Del Reeves); We Made Memories (with Boxcar Willie); Albums: Penny DeHaven, 1972; Penny DeHaven, 1984; Film soundtrack, Bronco Billy. *Current Management:* Morningstar Public Relations, PO Box 83, Brentwood, TN 37027, USA.

DEKKER Desmond, (Desmond Dacres); b. 16 July 1941, Kingston, Jamaica. Singer. *Career:* Solo artiste, also with own group, The Aces, 1963–; Concerts and tours include: Caribbean Music Festivals, Wembley, 1969, 1970; Ethiopian Benefit Concert, London (with Smiley Culture, Lee Perry, Dennis Brown), 1985; Regular international tours. *Recordings include:* Albums: This Is Desmond Dekker, 1969; Israelites, 1969; Black and Dekker, 1980; Compass Point, 1981; King of Ska, 1991; Action!, 1994; King of Kings, 1995; Moving Out, 1996; Intensified, 1997; Writing on the Wall, 1998; Halfway To Paradise, 2000; Hit singles: 20 No. 1 recordings in Jamaica; Also: 007 (Shanty Town), 1967; The Israelites (No. 1, UK), 1969; You Can Get It If You Really Want (No. 2, UK), 1970. *Honour:* First Jamaican artiste to have UK No. 1 record, 1969. *Address:* c/o Barry Collings Entertainments, 21a Clifftown Rd, Southend-on-Sea, Essex SS1 1AB, England.

DEL FRA Riccardo; b. 20 Feb. 1956, Rome, Italy. Musician (double bass); Composer. *Education:* 3 years university, studying Sociology. *Musical Education:* Double bass, Conservatorio di Frosinone; Private studies; Self-taught guitar. *Career:* Member, RAI TV Orchestra, Rome; Played with pianist Enrico Pieranunzi; Freelance backing musician, touring with artists in Italy including: Slide Hampton; Art Farmer; Kai Winding; Played with Chet Baker, trio and quartet (9 years partnership, 12 albums, radio, television and films, tours of Europe and Japan); Freelance work with Johnny Griffin; Toots Thielemans (tours of USA and Japan); Bob Brookmeyer; Also played with Art Blakey and the Jazz Messengers; Kenny Wheeler; Paul Motian; Sonny Stitt; James Moody; Clifford Jordan; Joe Diorio (tours of Italy). *Compositions:* Silent Call (for jazz quartet and string orchestra); Inner Galaxy (for tenor sax, double bass and four cellos); Aux Fontaines Du Temple (for jazz septet, flutes, harp and string orchestra); Volo sul Lago, for symphonic orchestra and jazz septet, 1996; Many pieces for different jazz ensembles. *Recordings:* A Sip of Your Touch; 12 with Chet Baker include: Chet Sings Again; Mr B; At The Capolinea; Paris Suite, with Bob Brookmeyer; Voulouz Loar, duo with Annie Ebrel; Also recorded with Dominique Pifarely. *Honours:* Grand Prix FNAC '89, A Sip of Your Touch, 1989; 'Choc' du Monde de la Musique. *Leisure interests:* Reading; Travelling. *Current Management:* Helene Manfredi, 118 rue du Chateau, Des Rentiers, 75013 Paris, France. *Address:* 15 rue des Fontaines du Temple, 75003 Paris, France.

DELAGAYE Freddy; b. 6 June 1944, Eeklo, Belgium. Musician (trumpet); Prod.; Impressario. m. Veronica Ng, 7 March 1977, 1 s. *Education:* Economics; Languages: Dutch; French; German; English. *Musical Education:* Music Academy, piano, trumpet. *Career:* Tour with various bands: Gerry Hayes Orchestra; Bob Azzam Band, from early 60's; With own band the Freddy Delagaye Clan, late 70's–; Numerous concerts and television appearances in most European countries, Middle East, South East Asia, 1980–; MSP (Music and Show Productions), own company in Belgium for television, concerts and special events; Represents: Wall Street Crash; Helen Shapiro; Pasadena Roof Orchestra; Les Bubb. *Recordings:* Bob Azzam Band: Mustapha; C'est Ecrit Dans Le Ciel; Luna Capresse; Various studio sessions in: Benelux; Scandinavia; France; Germany; Switzerland. *Honours:* Twice winner: Euro Star Festival, representative of UK Artists: Cantabile, 1987; Fairer Sax, 1988; Award for organizing 100th day festivities, Ghent, Belgium. *Membership:* BVI (Professional Asscn Impressarios), Belgium. *Leisure interests:* Director, Big Band; Music for fun; Tennis; Holidays with family, friends. *Address:* Galgestraat 1, 9970 Kaprijke, Belgium.

DELAKIAN Michel Horen; b. 6 Nov. 1957, Saint Etienne, France. Musician (trumpet); Composer. m. Isabelle, 20 Feb. 1982, 1 s., 1 d. *Musical Education:* Ecole Nationale de Musique, St Etienne. *Career:* Member, Claude Bolling Big Band, 1982–; Also played with: Martial Solal, 1983–85; Orchestre National de Jazz, 1986–89; Michel Legrand, 1994–95; Sacha Distel et les Collegiens, 1994–95; Leads own quartet; Television: Musiques Au Coeur, France 2, 1992; Jazz A Juan, 1986; Jazz 6, 1987; Tours include: Africa, 1986; Canada, 1987; USA, 1988, 1989, 1991; Thailand; China, 1994; Mexico, 1995; Turkey, 1995. *Recordings:* Solo: Biarritz; with Orchestre National De Jazz: 1986; 1987; with Claude Bolling Big Band: Plays Ellington (Vols 1 and 2); Also recorded with

Stephane Grappelli. *Publications:* Nina, 2 compositions, included in Le Livre Du Jazz En France. *Honours:* Prix Sidney Bechet, Académie Du Jazz, 1987. *Memberships:* SACEM; ADAMI; SPEDIDAM. *Leisure interests:* Reading; Travels; Tennis; Swimming. *Current Management:* Mathilde Creixams Co-ordination Musicale. *Address:* 14 rue Giradon, 75018 Paris, France.

DELANEY Larry (Lawrence); b. 30 Aug. 1942, Eastview, Ontario, Canada. Newspaper Editor; Publisher. m. Joanne Bonell, 1 Aug. 1964, 1 s., 1 d. *Education:* College. *Career:* Co-founder, current Editor, Publisher, Country Music News, Canada's national music newspaper, established 1980, providing international exposure and profile for Canadian country music artists and industry. *Publications:* Country Music News. *Honours:* 8 times recipient, Canadian Country Music Asscn: Country Music Person of The Year; Inducted into Builders Category, Canadian Music Hall of Fame, 1989; Inducted into Canadian Country Music Hall of Honour, 1996. *Memberships:* CCMA; CMA; CPPA. *Leisure interests:* Vinyl Album Collector. *Address:* PO Box 7323 Vanier Term, Ottawa, Ont K1L 8E4, Canada.

DELANO Darlene; b. 27 Sept. 1955, Hartford, Connecticut, USA. PR Exec.; Artist Man. m. 23 June 1976 to 28 Oct. 1983, 1 d. *Education:* BA, University of Connecticut. *Career:* Publicist for: Carmine Appice; Yngwie Malmsteen; Coma; Management for: The Itch; Naked Rhythm; John Goodwin. *Honour:* Women In Business Award, 1993. *Membership:* Licensed Talent Agent, State of Florida. *Current Management:* Long Distance Entertainment. *Address:* PO Box 223907, Hollywood, FL 33023, USA.

DELGADO Junior, (Oscar Hibbert); b. 1958, Kingston, Jamaica. Reggae Singer. *Career:* School concerts and local talent contests; Singer with Time Unlimited; Solo artist, 1975–; Owner, Incredible Jux record label, Jamaica; Collaborations: Augustus Pablo; Sinead O'Connor; Yami Bolo. *Recordings:* Singles: with Time Unlimited: Reaction; The Twenty Third Psalm; Numerous solo recordings include: Rasta Dreadlocks; Skanga; Run Baldhead; Thinking; Every Natty; Tition; Devil's Throne; Love Won't Come Easy; Trickster; Armed Robbery; Away With Your Fussing and Fighting; Fisherman Row; Jah Stay; Nine Fence; Poverty; Illegal Gun; Bus I Skull; Raggamuffin Year; Forward Revolution; Hanging Tree; Riot Inna Juvenile Prison; Dubschool; We A Blood; Another Place in Time; Fearless. *Address:* c/o Rick Davey, Unit C, Imperial Works, Perren St, London NW5 7EE, England.

DELIA (Sparrow McShade); b. 14 Nov. 1969, London, England. Musician (guitar, flute, drums); Vocalist. *Musical Education:* Grade 3 flute; GCSE Music; Islington Sixth Form Centre. *Career:* Member, Mambo Taxi, 1991–95; Extensive English tours; 1 album, 3 singles; Television and radio appearances include: Chart Show, ITV; Local television; BBC Radio 1; GLR; Member, Phantom Pregnancies, 1995–; Scott Bond Commandos, 1995–; Low Down No Goods, 1995-. *Recordings:* Various split singles and compilation tracks; Latest album: Assassination City, 1995. *Publications:* But That's Downbeat and Ridiculous Shawn. *Honours:* Too Pure Awards, 1994. *Memberships:* PRS; Musicians' Union. *Address:* c/o Rough Trade Shop, 130 Talbot Rd, London W11 1JA, England.

DELP Brad; b. 12 June 1951, Boston, Massachusetts, USA. Musician (guitar); Singer. *Career:* Founder member, US rock group Boston, 1976–; One of most successful debut albums ever (17m. album sales in USA alone), 1978; British tour, 1979; US tour, 1987; Guest with Ringo Starr, 1989; Formed RTZ, 1991; Guest with Nelson, 1991. *Recordings:* Albums: Boston (No. 1, USA), 1976; Don't Look Back (No. 1, USA), 1978; Third Stage (No. 1, USA), 1986; with RTZ: Return To Zero, 1991; Hit singles: with Boston: More Than A Feeling, 1976; Long Time, 1977; Peace of Mind, 1977; Don't Look Back, 1978; Amanda (No. 1, USA), 1986; We're Ready, 1987; Cantcha Say, 1987; Also worked with: Sammy Hagar. *Current Management:* Boston, PO Box 6191, Lincoln Center, MA 01773, USA. *Address:* c/o PGE, 244 Pleasant St, Franklin, MA 02038, USA.

DELS Anita; b. 28 Dec. 1971, Amsterdam, Netherlands. Vocalist. *Career:* Singer, 2 Unlimited, 1990-. *Recordings:* Albums: Get Ready, 1992; No Limits, 1993; Real Things, 1994; Hits Unlimited, 1995; Singles: Twilight Zone, 1992; Workaholic, 1992; The Magic Friend, 1992; No Limits (No. 1, UK), 1993; Tribal Dance, 1993; Faces, 1993; Maximum Overdrive, 1993; Let The Beat Control Your Body, 1994; The Real Thing, 1994; No One, 1994; Here I Go, 1995; Do What's Good For Me, 1995. *Honours:* MTV Award Nominations: Best Dance Act; Best Song, Let The Beat Control Your Body. *Current Management:* Michel Maartens, CBA Artists, PO Box 1495, 1200 BL Hilversum, Netherlands.

DELSON Brad; b. 1 Dec. 1977, Agoura, California, USA. Musician (guitar). *Education:* University of California, Los Angeles, Communications degree. *Musical Education:* Former trumpet student; Took up guitar in sixth grade at school. *Career:* Initially in groups The Pricks and Relative Degree before forming Xero in seventh grade; Became

Hybrid Theory and signed to Warner Bros, Spring 2000; Band immediately sent to professional studio; Further name change to Linkin Park prior to first record releases; Incessant promotional activity since release of album; Live shows include: Family Values and Ozzfest tours; KROQ Acoustic Christmas Concert 2001; many international dates; TV specials include: Live At The Fillmore; Reverb. *Recordings:* Albums: Hybrid Theory, 2000; Singles: Hybrid Theory (Acoustic EP), 2000; One Step Closer, Crawling, Papercut, In The End, 2001. *Honours:* Over 10m. world-wide sales of debut album to end of 2001; Billboard Award, Best Modern Rock Artist, 2001; Rock Bear Awards: Best International Band; Best International Album, 2001; Kerrang! Award, Best International Newcomer, 2001; Rolling Stone Award, Best Hard Rock/Metal Band, 2001. *Current Management:* Andy Gould Management, 8484 Wilshire Blvd #425, Beverly Hills, CA 90211, USA. *Internet:* www.linkinpark.com.

DELVAUX Floch; b. 26 Jan. 1968, Bruxelles, Belgium. Singer; Guitarist; Songwriter. *Musical Education:* Classical music lessons, Brussels; Self-taught guitar. *Career:* Guitarist and Songwriter, Brain Damage and Depth, 1986–89; Singer and Songwriter, Brain Damage and Death, 1989–92; Singer, Guitarist and Songwriter, Goyasnada, 1990–97; Singer, Guitarist and Songwriter, K-0z Office, 1994-. *Compositions:* Several songs with Goyasnada, some released on several compilations CD; Dreamland, 1992. *Recordings:* LP with Brain Damage and Death, 1993, titled, 1986–92; CD album with K-0z Office, Rage Rage Rage, 1996; Death 2000, 1999. *Address:* c/o Delvaux Floch, 5 rue du Pacifique, 1180 Bruxelles, Belgium.

DEML Markus; b. 9 Aug. 1967, Prague, Czechoslovakia. Guitarist; Prod.; Songwriter. *Education:* Musikhochschule, Hamburg (Music University); Guitar Institute of Technologie, Los Angeles. *Career:* World-wide and European tours with Saga, John Wetton, Kingdom Come, Rödelheimhartreim – project appearances on MTV's Most Wanted Hangin Out; Rock and Ring, Montreaux Jazz Festival. *Compositions:* Earth Nation (Thoughts in Past Future); Errorhead, solo project; The Other Side, album. *Recordings:* Errorhead (The Other Side); Kingdom Come (Twilight Cruiser); Bobby Kimball (Rise Up); Earth Nation (Thoughts in Past Future); Rödelheim HP (Direkt aus Rödelheim); SNAP (Welcome to Tomorrow). *Publications:* Errorhead, The Other Side, 1998. *Memberships:* GEMA; GVL. *Leisure interests:* Sports; Music. *Address:* Alex Merch Music, Trajamstr 18, 50678, Koeln.

DEMPSEY Gaylene Katharan; b. 1 Aug. 1960, Winnipeg, Manitoba, Canada. Exec. Dir. m. David Sherman, 10 April 1993. *Education:* Creative Communications (Journalism Major); Managing and Leading in non-profit Sector Certificate, 1995. *Career:* Editor, Circuit, monthly entertainment paper, 1989–; Editor in Chief, The Insider, monthly entertainment paper, 1990–; Editor, Jazz Winnipeg Festival Programme, 1990–; Volunteer, Winnipeg Folk Festival, 1990–; Executive Director, Manitoba Audio Recording Industry Association (MARIA), 1991–; Represent the Manitoba Music Industry from songwriters to labels; Freelance work. *Publications:* SOCAN Words and Music, several articles; Grafitti Magazine, several articles. *Memberships:* FACTOR National Advisory Board; Artspace, Executive Member. *Leisure interests:* Music; Festivals; Theatre; Golf; Travel; Reading Magazines and other non-fiction. *Address:* #1–242 Spence St, Winnipeg, Manitoba, R3C 1Y4, Canada.

DEMPSEY Paul; b. 25 May 1976. Vocalist; Musician (guitar); Songwriter. *Career:* Sister is vocalist/guitarist in Melbourne group John Smith; Resides in Melbourne, Australia; Founder member: Fish of The Day group, 1994; Developed local following through pub/club gigs; Group became Something For Kate; Signed to Australian label Murmur; Instigated Scared of Horses solo side project during SFK hiatus, 1997–8; Reformed Something For Kate; Band gradually broke nationally, then internationally with first US/Japan tour, 2000; Big sell-out Australian shows including Mythology and Echo-la-la-lalia tours plus Powderfinger support slots, 2001; Occasional solo shows including Lack of Rhythm tour, 2000. *Recordings:* Albums: Elsewhere For Eight Minutes, 1997; An Empty Flight (solo as Scared of Horses), 1998; Beautiful Sharks, 1999; QandA With Dean Martin (compilation), 2000; Echolalia, 2001; Singles: The Answer To Both Your Questions (EP), Dean Martin, 1996; Intermission (EP), Captain (Million Miles An Hour), Prick, 1997; Working Against Me, Roll Credit, Harpoon/Clint, 1998; Electricity, Hallways, Whatever You Want, 1999; The Astronaut, 2000; Monsters, Three Dimensions, Twenty Years, 2001. *Honours:* Australian Music Industry Critics Awards, Album of the Year, 2000; Australian Live Music Awards, Best Live Act, 2000; Australian Record Industry Awards, 7 nominations, 2001; JJJ Listeners' Poll, Best Album, 2001. *Current Management:* Carlene Albronda, Catapult Management, Sydney, Australia. *E-mail:* carlene@presto.net.au. *Internet:* www.somethingforkate.com.

DEMUS Chaka, (John Taylor); b. 1965, West Kingston, Jamaica. Rapper. *Career:* Rapper, billed as Nicodemus Jr, on various sound systems including Supreme and Jammy's; Changed name to Chaka Demus, 1985; Solo artiste, 1985–91; Rapper, in duo Chaka Demus and Pliers, 1991-. *Recordings:* Singles: as Chaka Demus: Increase Your Knowledge; One Scotch, One Bourbon, One Beer; 2 Foot Walk; Chaka On the Move; with Chaka Demus and Pliers: Tease Me, 1993; She Don't Let Nobody, 1993; Twist and Shout (No. 1, UK), 1993; Murder She Wrote, 1994; I Wanna Be Your Man, 1994; Gal Wine, 1994; Rough this Year; Love Up the Gal; Without Love; Winning Machine; Worl' A Girls; Albums: Solo: Everybody Loves the Chaka, 1987; The Original Chaka, 1989; Unstoppable, 1996; Ruff and Tuff, 1997; with Chaka Demus and Pliers: Gal Wine, 1992; Ruff This Year, 1992; Chaka Demus and Pliers, 1992; Tease Me, 1993; Help Them Lord, 2001; with Shabba Ranks: Rough and Rugged, 1987. *Address:* c/o Free World Music Inc, 230 12th St, Suite 117, Miami Beach, FL 33139–4603, USA.

DENCH Ian; b. 7 Aug. 1964. Musician (guitar); Songwriter. *Career:* Member, EMF, 1989–96. *Recordings:* Albums: Schubert Dip, 1991; Stigma, 1992; Cha Cha Cha, 1995; Best of EMF, 2001; Singles: Unbelieveable (No. 1, USA), 1990; I Believe, 1991; Children, 1991; Lies, 1991; Unexplained (EP), 1992; They're Here, 1992; It's You, 1992; Perfect Day, 1995; I'm A Believer (with Vic Reeves and Bob Mortimer), 1995; Afro King, 1995; Guitarist on Dido, Here With Me, 2000. *Current Management:* Bedlam Management, PO Box 3074, London W4 4ZN, England.

DENIO Amy Eliott; b. 9 June 1961, Boston, Massachusetts, USA. Composer; Vocalist; Musician (Saxophones, Bass Guitar, Acoustic and Electric Guitar, Accordion). *Education:* BA, Music Composition, Performance and Improvisation, Hampshire College, Amherst, Massachusetts, 1983; Jazz India Vocal Institute, Bombay, 1997. *Career:* Solo concerts in USA, East and Central Europe, Japan, India, 1977–99; Performed in multi-instrumental duo The Entropics, performances in Canada and the USA, 1985–87; Performed in Tone Dogs, tours in USA and Europe, 1987–91; Bass on soundtrack in film Shredder Orpheus, 1988; Performed with Billy Tipton Saxophone Quartet, tours in USA and Europe, 1988–96; Composed and performed music for Sit Still, play, 1994; Performed with Nudes/Pale Nudes, in USA, Brazil and Europe, 1994–99; Performed with FoMoFlo, 1995–99; Composed music and performed for dance piece Sky Down, David Dorfman Dance Company, 1997; TV performance with Pale Nudes, 1999; Radio performances in Europe and USA, 1995–99. *Compositions include:* IandI, music for modern dance, 1990; Sax House, sax quartets and performed while dancing, 1991; Sit Still, music for theatre, 1992; Tempesta, An Urban RAPsody, with poet Luis Rodriguez, 1994; Green Fish Symphonette, for chamber orchestra, 1995; The Maids, Jean Genet play, music for ensemble soundtrack, 1997; Non Lo So, Polo, music for chamber octet and 4 voices, 1998. *Recordings include:* The Entropics, Spagga!, 1987; Tone Dogs: Ankety Low Day, 1990, Early Middle Years, 1991; Curlew with Amy Denio: A Beautiful Western Saddle, 1993; Pale Nudes: Wise to the Heat, 1997, Soul Come Home, 1998; FlMoFlo: Slug and Firearms, 1996, No 11, 1997; Greatest Hits/More Spoot, 1999; The Science Group: A Mere Coincidence, 1999; Tattoo, 2000; The Memphis Years, with George Cartwright, 2000; The Danubians, 2000; Belle Confusion, with Francisco Lopez, 2001; Kultur Shock, 2001; Amy Denio and Zu, 2001. *Honours:* Seattle Arts Commission Individual Artist Award for Composition, 1990; Artist Trust Artist Fellowship, 1996; Best Animated Film Award, New York Underground Film Festival, 1997; Bessie Award for Composition, New York Dance and Performance Award, 1997; ASCAP Special Awards 1996–2001. *Memberships:* ASCAP; Board Mem., Madrona Arts Centre. *Leisure interests:* Wilderness camping; Yoga; Language study. *Address:* Spoot Music, PO Box 85154, Seattle, WA 98145, USA.

DENNARD David Brooks; b. 5 July 1950, Dallas, Texas, USA. Record Co Exec.; Musician (bass guitar, guitar, dobro, harmonica). m. Mary Anna Austin, 4 Oct. 1980, 2 d. *Education:* Colorado College, Stanford; University of Texas-Austin. *Career:* CBS/Epic Records recording artist with: Gary Myrick and The Figures; Extensive touring, 1979–83; President, Owner, Dragon Street Records Inc, 1989–; Director of A & R, Crystal Clear Sound; Director, Steve Records, Dallas. *Recordings:* with Gary Myrick and the Figures: 2 albums, 2 singles, 7 videos, 250,000 combined sales; Recent releases by Ronnie Dawson, Gene Summers, Scott Whitaker, Buck Jones, Centromatic, Meredith Louise Miller and Pump'n Ethyl; Gene Vincert and His Blue Cape, The Lost Dallas Sessions, 1957–58; Johnny Dollar, Mr Action Packed; Groovey: Joe Poovey Greatest Grooves, various artists; The Big O Jamboree Live!, Vols 1 and 2. *Honours:* Award of Excellence, Dallas Society of Visual Communications, 1987; 2 Silver Microphone Awards, 1987; Crystal Award, 1988; Topaz Award, Best Record Company, Steve Records, 1997. *Memberships:* NARAS; Texas Music Asscn, Dallas; Cable Access of Dallas Inc; Board Mem., Documentary Arts. *Leisure interests:* Swimming; Record collecting; Dogs; Tennis; Gardening. *Address:* Dragon Street Records Inc, PO Box 670714, Dallas, TX 75367–0714, USA.

DENNEHY Timothy Christopher; b. 29 Dec. 1952, Cahersiveen, County Kerry, Ireland. National Teacher; Broadcaster; Singer. m. Máirín, 19 March 1976, 2 s. *Musical Education:* From oral tradition. *Career:* Numerous radio appearances, local, national, including own programme on Clare FM: Cuaird An Domhnaigh (Keep in Touch); Television programmes dealing with Irish traditional music; Regular performer at workshops, recitals, concerts throughout Ireland; Founded the Góilin Traditional singers club, with Donall De Barra, Dublin, 1979. *Compositions:* Many original songs. *Recordings:* A Thimbleful of Song; A Winter's Tear – Traditional and Original Songs; Farewell to Miltown Malbay, 1997. *Publication:* Working on biography of writer Sigerson Clifford. *Memberships:* IMRO; Cumann Cheoltíre Eireann. *Leisure interests:* Music; Singing; Sport; Reading; Walking. *Address:* Markham's Cross, Mullagh, Co Clare, Ireland.

DENNERLEIN Barbara; b. 25 Sept. 1964, Munich, Germany. Jazz Musician; Composer; Prod. m. Andre Baldi. *Musical Education:* Study of Music Science, Ludwig Maximilian University, Munich; Self-taught Organ Player. *Career:* Film Music, (title music), Die Partner; WDR/ARD Concerts at all Important Jazz Festivals, Den Haag, New Zealand, Montréal, Vancouver, Toronto, Edmonton, Victoria, Norway, Berlin, Frankfurt; Concerts world-wide: London, Ronnie Scott's; Tokyo, Blue Note; New York, Blue Note; Paris, Sweet Basil. *Compositions:* 100 pieces on 15 records and CDs. *Recordings:* Jazz Live, 1983; Orgelspiele, 1984; Bebab, 1985; Tribute to Charlie, 1986; Straight Ahead, 1988; B D Plays Classics, 1988; Live on Tour, 1989; B D Due, 1990; Hot Stuff, 1990; Solo, 1992; That's Me, 1992; Take Off, 1996; Junkanovo, 1997; Outhipped, 2000. *Honours:* Jazz Award for Take Off, 1995, 1997; No 1, DWR Downbeat Critics Poll, 1996; Jazz Award for Junkanoo, 1997; 3 times, Preis der Deutschen Schallplattenkritik; Outhipped, 1999. *Leisure interest:* Music. *Current Management:* Newtone Management, Tsingtauer Str 66, 81827 Munchen, Germany. *Address:* Banhofstr 9B, 85774 Unterfohring, Germany.

DENNIS Cathy; b. 25 March 1970, Norfolk, England. Vocalist; Songwriter; Prod. *Musical Education:* Self-taught. *Career:* Featured singer, D-Mob, 1989; Solo artiste, songwriter, producer, 1990–; British tour; Television appearance: Beverly Hills 90210. *Compositions include:* Natural, S Club 7, 1999; Reach, S Club 7, 2000; Never Had A Dream Come True, S Club 7 (No. 1, UK), 2000; Can't Get You Out of My Head, Kylie Minogue (No. 1, UK), 2001; Have You Ever, S Club 7 (No. 1, UK), 2001; Anything Is Possible, Will Young (No. 1, UK). *Recordings:* Solo albums: Move To This, 1991; Into The Skyline, 1992; Am I the Kinda Girl?, 1996; Singles: C'Mon and Get My Love, with D Mob, 1989; Touch Me All Night Long, 1991; Just Another Dream, 1991; Too Many Walls, 1991; Irresistible, 1992; Falling, 1993; Why, 1994; West End Pad, 1996; Waterloo Sunset, 1996; Also featured on: A Little Bit of This A Little Bit of That, D-Mob, 1989; Looking Through Patient Eyes, PM Dawn; Songs on numerous film soundtracks. *Honours:* Billboard Award, Best New Female Artist; World Music Award, Best International Newcomer; 2 BRIT Awards Nominations; Capital Radio Award, Best Female Artist; SOS Top Woman Award; SE Asia Awards, Top New Artist and Best Song of Year; 5 ASCAP Awards; Ivor Novello Award, Best Song nominee, Never Had A Dream Come True. *Membership;* ASCAP. *Leisure interests:* Sports; Racing driving. *Current Management:* Simon Fuller, 19 Management Ltd, Unit 32, Ransomes Dock, 35–37 Parkgate Rd, London SW11 4NP, England.

DENNIS Jon; b. 27 May 1965, Lewisham, London, England. Singer; Musician (guitar); Songwriter. *Education:* Leicester University. *Career:* Lead singer and guitarist with Blab Happy, 1987–93; Slinky, 1994–; Tours with Blab Happy: 'Boat' tour, UK, 1991; Support to Kingmaker, 'Eat Yourself Whole' British tour, 1992; Support to Radiohead, 'Pablo Money' British tour, 1993; with Slinky: 'Shoot Me Down' tour, 1995. *Recordings:* with Blab Happy: EPs: It's Turned Out Nice Again, 1987; Fruits of Your Labour, 1988; Mad Surge, 1991; Albums: Boat, 1991; Smothered, 1993; Singles: with Blab Happy: Down, 1991; Inside Out, 1992; Tender Hooks, 1993; with Slinky: Shoot Me Down, 1995; Producer, General MIDI, 2001. *Membership:* Musicians' Union. *Address:* 39 Nottingham Rd, Leicester LE5 3TT, England.

DENSMORE John; b. 1 Dec. 1944, Los Angeles, California, USA. Musician (drums). *Education:* Physics, Psychology. *Career:* Member, Psychedelic Rangers, 1965; Member, The Doors, 1966–72; Member, The Butts Band, 1972–; Session, solo work, 1972; Performances include: Northern California Folk-Rock Festival, 1968; Hollywood Bowl, later released as video, 1968; Toronto Rock 'n' Roll Revival Show, 1969; Isle of Wight Festival, 1970; Film documentaries: The Doors Are Open, 1968; Feast of Friends, 1969. *Recordings:* Albums: The Doors (No. 1, USA), 1967; Strange Days, 1967; Waiting For The Sun (No. 1, USA), 1968; Morrison Hotel, 1970; Absolutely Live, 1970; L A Woman, 1971; Other Voices, 1971; Weird Scenes Inside The Gold Mine, 1972; Full Circle, 1972; Live At The Hollywood Bowl, 1987; Greatest Hits, 1996; Singles: Light My Fire (No. 1, USA), 1967; Love Me Two Times, 1968; Hello I Love You (No. 1 US), 1968; Touch Me, 1969; Love Her Madly, 1971; Riders On The Storm, 1971. *Publication:* Riders On The Storm – My Life With Jim Morrison and The Doors. *Address:* Rue Lepic, 75018 Paris, France.

DENZLER Bertrand; b. 27 Oct. 1963, Geneva, Switzerland. *Education:* Studied at Zurich Conservatory, Switzerland. *Career:* Concerts, tours and recordings in Europe and South America with musicians including Barry Guy, Mark Sanders, Benoit Delbecq, Hélène Labarrière, Norbert Pfammatter, Christophe Marguet, Hasse Poulsen, Ninh Le Quan, Sophie Agnel; Festival appearances in Willisau, Cologne, Le Mans, Paris, Grenoble, Zurich, Berne, Lausanne, Neuchatel, Fribourg; Appearances at Swiss New Jazz Festival, 1998; Leader, own ensemble, Bertrand Denzler Cluster; Live or studio recordings for national broadcasting corporations throughout Europe. *Compositions:* Around 80 compositions played or recorded with various ensembles; Numerous compositions for film and theatre and for documentaries. *Recordings:* 49 Nord: Animal Language; Chamaeleo Vulgaris: Ouverture Facile; Bertrand Denzler Cluster: Y?; Denzler-Dürst-Pfammatter: Now; Denzler-Haerter Quartet: Minor Works; Burhan Öcal Group: Dervis Mustafa; Denzler-Wiesendanger: Folies. *Membership:* Swiss Musicians' Syndicate. *Address:* 18 rue Littré, 75006 Paris, France.

DEPASS Michele Karina; b. 5 Jan. 1965, Germany. Vocalist; Songwriter. *Musical Education:* 1 year MSc course, Composition, General Theory, Voice. *Career:* Lead vocals, Saxmachine, 1986–88; Lead vocals, The Happy End, 1986–87; Television, radio, British tour, with Denise Black and The Kray Sisters, 1987; Lead, backing vocals, Luddy Sams and The Deliveries, 1987–88; Lead vocals, Benjamin Zephaniah and The Union Dance Company, 1988; Soundtrack vocals, The Kitchen Child, 1988; Vocals, Haji Ackbar, Pee Wee Ellis, Maceo Parker, 1988; Vocals in Welsh, Sinaid Jones, Si Yn Y Gwnt, 1990; Soundtrack vocals, Prime Suspect, Granada TV, 1992; Backing vocals, 7 Elvis Presley tracks for karaoke, 1994; lead duet vocals, Leo sayer, 1994; Working with T-Rextasy, BV's tribute band to Marc Bolan, 1995; Television include: The Glam Rock Show, Ch4, 1995; Punt and Dennis, BBC1, 1995. *Recordings include:* Co-writer, vocals, single: Pitter Patter Biscuit, 1989. *Membership:* Musicians' Union. *Leisure interests:* Horse riding; Stained glass; Travel; Reading; Writing. *Address:* 13 Tabley Rd, Holloway, London N7 0NA, England.

DEPOLO Ozren; b. 13 March 1930, Zagreb, Croatia. Musician (saxophones, clarinet, flute); Composer. m. 29 Jan. 1959, Ljerka Polak, 2 s., 1 d. *Education:* Medical Faculty, Zagreb, 1956. *Musical Education:* Clarinet, Conservatory of Music, Zagreb, graduated 1952. *Career:* Saxophone soloist, jazz and classical music; Lead alto saxophone, Zagreb Radio-TV big band, 1952–91; Jazz Small Combos: Zagreb Jazz Quintet, Zagreb Jazz Sextet; Non Convertible International All Styars; International Festival Big Bands: Slide Hampton, Prague, 1978; Clark Terry, 1979; Jerry Mulligan, 1970; Oliver Nelson, Montreux, 1971; EBU (European RTV Union) Big Bands in Copenhagen; Barcelona; Sarajevo; Oslo; Classical Music: First performances, 3 saxophone concertos, Alto Saxophone and Symphony Orchestra: Despalji, 1964; Glazunov, 1968; Odak, 1980; Avantgarde music: Member, Acezantez group, modern music, 1966–80; Appearances on many Jazz festivals, tours, concerts. *Compositions:* Music for 53 animated (cartoon) films; 4 films; 3 short documentary films; Music, songs, 5 theatre plays; 2 TV serials; many jazz compositions; songs; Music for children; Arrangements; Orchestrations for popular music. *Recordings:* Albums: Saxophone concertos; Mistery of Blues. *Honours:* Josip Slavenski, Musical Achievement. *Memberships:* Croatian Composers Society; Croatian Musicians' Union. *Leisure interest:* Astronomy. *Address:* Ljudevita Posavskog 2, 41000 Zagreb, Croatia.

DEQUIDT Loïc; b. 1 May 1973, Arras, France. Jazz Musician (piano). *Education:* 2 years mathematics, University of Lille. *Musical Education:* Studies in Italy, with E Rava; F Dandrea; E Pieranunzi. *Career:* Played with Tommy Smith; Claus Stötter; Daniel Beaussier; Played in Paris; Rome; Brussels; Several festivals, France, Italy; Currently plays with Bruno Tommaso (Italy); Riccardo Delfra; Loïc Dequidt Trio; Radio appearances: France-Musique; France-Inter. *Honour:* Diploma, Siena Jazz Seminary, Italy. *Address:* 110 rue Lepic, 75018 Paris, France.

DERRINGER Rick, (Richard Zehringer); b. 5 Aug. 1947, Fort Recovery, Ohio, USA. Musician (guitar); Prod. *Career:* Member, The McCoys, late 1960s; Johnny Winter and Edgar Winter groups; Solo artiste, 1974–; Also leader, own group Derringer; Prolific session musician. *Recordings:* Solo albums: All American Boy, 1974; Spring Fever, 1975; Derringer, 1976; Sweet Evil, 1977; If You Weren't So Romantic, 1978; Guitars and Women, 1979; Face To Face, 1980; Rick Derringer, 1981; Good Dirty Fun, 1983; Back to the Blues, 1993; Electra Blues, 1994; Required Rocking, 1996; Blues Deluxe, 1998; Jackhammer Blues, 2000; with Edgar Winter: White Trash, 1971; Road Work, 1972; They Only Come Out At Night, 1973; Shock Treatment, 1974; Jasmine Nightdream, 1975; With Rick Derringer, 1975; with Johnny Winter: Johnny Winter and Rick Derringer, 1971; Johnny Winter Live, 1971; Still Alive and Well, 1973; Saints and Sinners, 1974; John Dawson Winter III, 1974; The Johnny Winter Story, 1980; Lead guitar solo, Eat It, Weird Al Yankovic (parody of Michael Jackson's Beat It), 1984; Also featured on albums by: Air Supply; Donald Fagen; Dan Hartman; Cyndi Lauper; Bette Midler; Meat Loaf; Mason Ruffner; Todd Rundgren; Steely Dan; Bonnie Tyler; Rosie Vela. *Current Management:* Slatus Management, 208 E 51st St, New York, NY 10022, USA.

DERUDDER Peter; Musician. *Education:* Classical, Flute, Uillean, Pipes, Bodhran, Whistles. *Career:* Group Member, The Swigshift; Dranouter

Festival, 1995, Labadoux Festival, 1997; Den Ekster, 1996–97; Paulus Festival, 1997; Sloanthe Festival, 1997; De Brakke Grond, Amsterdam, 1997; National Radio, Radio 1 De Groote Boodschap, and several regional radio and television appearances. *Compositions:* Jumpin The Fences; Dirty Wally; Friend's Sadness; Something to Fear; Shut the Pub; A Whistler's Wedding. *Recordings:* 1 CD, Tales From the Great Whiskey Book, 1996. *Honours:* Government Medal for Flute, 1986; Second place, Youth Soloist Festival, 1986; Finale, Westtalent, 1995. *Membership:* Volksmuziekfederatie, Belgium. *Leisure interest:* Music. *Current Management:* KAFT Producties, Akkerwindelaan 20, 8791 Beveren-Leie, Belgium. *Address:* Barrierestraat 49, 8940 Wervik, Belgium.

DESANDRE-NAVARRE Lavier; b. 11 Oct. 1961, Paris, France. Musician (Drums, percussion); Composer. m. Susan Mouget, 5 Sept. 1992, 1 d. *Education:* Licence in Economics. *Career:* Worked with Gil Evans, Tania Maria, Niels Lan Doky, Cbeb Mami, Orchestre National de Jazz, Les Rita Mitsouko, Michel Portal. *Composition:* Zoom. *Recordings:* Gil Evans, The Complete Recordings; Niels Lan Doky, Asian Sessions; Caccilie Norry, Queen of Bad Excuses; Solo, Zoom. *Leisure interests:* Sailing; Cooking. *Address:* 95 Ave Jean Lolive, 93500 Pantin, France.

DESEO Csaba; b. 15 Feb. 1939, Budapest, Hungary. Musician (Violin). m. Katalin Szony, 1 s. *Education:* Violin Teacher Diploma, Bartók Conservatory, Budapest, 1961. *Career:* Member, Hungarian National Philharmonic Orchestra, 1966–; Jazz Soloist, Combo Leader, 4 own LPs, 3 CDs, 1964-. *Publications:* Monthly jazz-broadcasts in Hungarian Radio; Jazz articles in Hungarian newspapers. *Memberships:* Hungarian Jazz Federation; Hungarian Composers' Union. *Address:* Bercsenyi U 36, 1117 Budapest, Hungary.

DESMARAIS Lorraine; b. 15 Aug. 1956, Montréal, Canada. Jazz Musician (Piano). *Education:* Master's Degree in Classical Piano, 1979; Jazz education in New York and Boston with Kenny Barron and Charlie Banacos. *Career:* Toured across Canada (jazz festivals) and US, in Switzerland, France, Belgium, Denmark, London, Scotland, Asia (Indonesia, Philippines); One Woman show, The History of Piano Jazz. *Compositions:* Film scores for National Filmboard of Canada; Sonata for flute and piano. *Recordings:* Trio Lorraine: Desmarais, 1985; Andiamo, 1986; Pianissimo, 1987; Vision, 1991; Lorraine Desmarais, 1995; Video: Lorraine Desmarais Quartette with Tiger Okashi, 1996; I Believe in You, with Diva, 1999; Bleu Silence, 1999; Five Play: On the Brink, 1999. *Publication:* Sonata for Flute and Piano. *Honours:* Winner, Great American Jazz Piano Competition, Jacksonville, Jazz Festival, Florida, 1986; Winner, Montréal Jazz Festival, 1984; Canada Québec Arts Council Grants; Composer's Award for Socan: Best Jazz Album: Vision, 1991. *Memberships:* SOCAN; Guilde des Musiciens du Québec. *Current Management:* Les Productions Lorraine Desmarais Inc. *Address:* 6485 Poliquin Auteuil, Laval, QC H7H 2T9, Canada.

DESMOND Denis Anthony; b. 4 July 1950, Cork, Ireland. Promoter; Band and Artist Man.; Musician (Piano and Keyboards). *Career:* Performer, RTE Radio and TV; Cork Opera House; Many other theatres and venues. *Memberships:* IFMandAP. *Leisure interests:* Reading; Walking; Shopping. *Address:* Top House, Clontarf St, Cork 1, Ireland.

DES'REE, (Des'ree Weekes); b. 30 Nov. 1968, London, England. Singer; Songwriter. *Career:* Duet with Terence Trent D'Arby on his single Delicate, 1993; Provided music to films Clockers (Spike Lee), Set It Off and Romeo and Juliet; Numerous TV appearances and live shows. *Recordings:* Singles: Feel So High, 1991; You Gotta Be, 1995; Feels So High, 1995; Life, 1998; What's Your Sign, 1998; Ain't No Sunshine, with Ladysmith Black Mambazo, 1999; You Gotta Be, 1999; Albums: Mind Adventures, 1992; I Ain't Movin', 1994; Supernatural, 1998; Endangered Species, 2000. *Honours:* Nominated, 2 MTV Music Video Awards; BMI Award; Ivor Novello Songwriting Award.

DESTAGNOL Yann; b. 14 July 1978, Paris, France. Musician (drums, keyboards); Prod.; Vocalist. *Musical Education:* Mastered flute and clarinet as a child; Studied at the American School of Modern Music, Paris. *Career:* Drummer in several rock bands prior to co-founding group Modjo and record label Modjo Music (with Romain Tranchart). *Recordings:* Album: Modjo, 2001; Singles: Lady (Hear Me Tonight), 2000; Chillin', 2001; What I Mean, 2001. *Honours:* Modjo first French group to score UK number 1 hit. *Current Management:* Modjo Music. *E-mail:* matt@modjo.com.

DETROIT Marcella, (Marcy Levy); b. 21 June 1959, Detroit, Michigan, USA. Singer; Songwriter; Musician (keyboards, guitar, harmonica). *Career:* Member, Shakespears Sister with Siobhan Fahey, 1988–93; Solo artist, 1993–; Collaborations: Elton John; Hall and Oates. *Compositions include:* Co-writer, Lay Down Sally, hit for Eric Clapton, 1977; Co-writer with Siobhan Fahey, all tracks on album Hormonally Yours, 1992. *Recordings:* Albums: Sacred Heart, 1989; Hormonally Yours, 1992; Jewel, 1994; Feeler, 1996; Abfab Songs, 1999; Dancing Madly Sideways, 2000; Singles: You're History, 1989; Goodbye Cruel World, 1991; Stay (No. 1, UK), 1992; I Don't

Care, 1992; Hello (Turn Your Radio On), 1992; My 16th Apology (EP), 1993; I Believe, 1994. *Honours:* BRIT Award, Best Video, Stay, 1993; Ivor Novello Award, Outstanding Contemporary Song Collection, Hormonally Yours, 1993. *Address:* c/o John Campbell, 55 Chiswick High Rd, London W4 2LT, England.

DEVEREUX Pete; b. 1972, Southampton, Hampshire, England. Prod.; Remixer; DJ. *Musical Education:* Brunel University, music student. *Career:* Played violin in Southampton Youth Orchestra; Formed the Artful Dodger with partner Mark Hill, 1996; Released debut album, 2001; Duo split amicably, 2001; Co-founder: Centric Records (with Hill); Solo production career, 2001–; Collaborations: Craig David; Dreem Teem; Romina Johnson; Liberty; Remixed: Sisqo; Gabrielle. *Recordings:* Albums: It's All About The Stragglers, 2001; Singles: Re-Rewind The Crowd Say Bo Selecta (with Craig David), Movin' Too Fast (with Romina Johnson), 1999; Woman Trouble (with Robbie Craig and Craig David), 2000; It Ain't Enough (with Dreem Teem), 2001. *Honours:* Ivor Novello Awards: Dance Award: Re-Rewind, 2000; Woman Trouble, 2001. *Address:* c/o London Records, Waldron House, 57–63 Old Church St, London, SW3 5BS, England.

DEVIC Lino; b. 10 May 1954, Zagreb, Croatia. Musician (fretless bass, piano). Divorced, 2 s., 1 d. *Career:* Many jazz festivals in former Yugoslavia and Germany; Studio works in France, 1976; Touring Germany with Trini Lopez; Plays with fusion trio, recorded 2 albums, 1994-. *Compositions:* 25 include: Boulevard Barbes; Blue Duck. *Recordings:* Drazen Boic Trio: Mirno Itiho (Peaceful and Quiet); LD Experience: LD Experience. *Honours:* At jazz festivals: Ingolstadt, Germany; Ljubljana; Zagreb; Maribor. *Leisure interest:* Walking with my dog. *Current Management:* A Zaie 39, Panton, Zagreb, Croatia. *Address:* N Grskovica 58, Zagreb, Croatia.

DEVINE Frank Thomas; b. 24 Nov. 1946, Dundee, Scotland. Songwriter; Musician (drums, guitar, mandolin). m. Jacqueline Harper, 12 Jan. 1968, 1 s., 1 d. *Education:* Moseley School of Art, Birmingham; Birmingham College of Art. *Musical Education:* Private drum tuition with Charles Burlison; Self-taught on stringed instruments. *Career:* Tour of England with Jimmy Cliff; Weekly appearances at the Marquee, London; Played with Blues Hounds and Mike Burney; Television appearance: Ready Steady Go (with the Alpines); Currently songwriter and plays guitar and mandolin. *Recording:* Limited edition album with Steve Winwood and Dave Mason (prior to formation of Traffic). *Membership:* Musicians' Union. *Leisure interest:* Painting. *Address:* Milford Hall Cottage, Main Rd, Milford, Staffordshire ST17 0UL, England.

DEVLIN Adam; b. 17 Sept. 1969, Hounslow, Middlesex, England. Musician (guitar). *Career:* Member, Bluetones; Released early records on own label; Obtained major label deal; Numerous tours and many TV appearances. *Recordings:* Singles: Are You Blue Or Are You Blind, 1995; Bluetonic, 1995; Slight Return, 1996; Cut Some Rug, 1996; Marblehead Johnson, 1996; Solomon Bites the Worm, 1998; Sleazy Bed Track, 1998; 4-Day Weekend, 1998; Keep The Home Fires Burning, 2000; Autophilia, 2000; Mudslide EP, 2001; Albums: Expecting to Fly (No. 1, UK), 1996; Return to the Last Chance Saloon, 1998; Science and Nature, 2000. *Honour:* Brit Award Nomination, 1997.

DEXTEXTER Even; b. 7 April 1971, Ellorio, Vizcaya, Spain. Musician (keyboards, bass, drums); Programmer. *Education:* Two years of Psychology, University. *Musical Education:* 5 years, music and piano studies, Conservatoire of Logrono, La Rioja, Spain, 1982–87. *Career:* Member, Dextexter, Nov 1994–; Tours include 2 club tours over London; 3 appearances on Basque, Spanish TV; Currently recording auto-produced and released first single. *Membership:* Musicians' Union. *Leisure interests:* Personal research in psychoacoustics; Electroacoustics discipline. *Current Management:* DDT Management. *Address:* 70 Princes Sq., London WL 4NY, England.

DI LEVA Thomas; b. 23 Oct. 1963, Gavle. Singer/Songwriter; Musician (Guitar, Keyboards). *Career:* 11 major tours 1986–97; Theatre, The City of Mahagonny by Bertolt Brecht, Gavle Folktheatre, 1987; Hamlet in Hamlet, Gavle Folktheatre, 1990; Films: Tomorrow, Tomorrow, Tomorrow, 1989; Kenny Starfighter, 1997; Several major northern TV shows and radio shows. *Compositions:* All work self-penned. *Recordings:* Prett Fat, 1985; Pussel, 1986; Vemska Jag Tro, 1987; Rymdblomma, 1989; Noll, 1991; Naked Number One, 1993; Love is the Heart, 1995; I Am You, 1997. *Honours:* Swedish Grammy, Best Artist of 1988; Gold Microphone, Best Live Artist, voted by Swedish listeners, 1997. *Leisure interests:* Meditation and yoga; Walking in nature; Travel. *Address:* AB Spaceflower, Box 6032, 10231 Stockholm, Sweden.

DI MATTEO Luis; b. 10 May 1934, Bandonfeol. Composer. m. 1 s., 1 d. *Education:* Studied composition and Bandoneon. *Career:* Bandoneon player in orchestras in Montevideo, Uruguay, and in Buenos Aires, Argentina; Astor Piazzolla's orchestra; Composer and Arranger, Bandoneonista; Regular TV appearances; First European concerts, 1983, and regular concert tours, 1983–; Cooperation with Uljanowsk Chamber Orchestra,

Russia, 1990; European concert tour with string quartet, 1997–98. *Compositions:* A Sugerencia Club, 1965; A Sugerencia del Club, 1969; Estudio Para Tres, 1971; Tango en Blue Jeans, 1975; Proceso, 1976; Monologando, 1979; Rumbo al Cenit, 1981; Latitud 55, 1983; Tango Contemporáneo, 1984; Le Dernier Tango, 1985; Tango, 1987; Mil Clores, 1987; Por Dentro De Mi, 1988; Del Nuevo Ciclo, 1991; Escribo Para Los Angeles, 1996; Um dia de mi vida, 1997; Concierto para contrabaio y orchestra, 1989. *Recordings:* Tango Contemporameo, 1984; Le Dernier Tango, 1985; Por Dentro De Mi, 1988; Del Nuevo Ciclo, 1991; Escribo Para Los Angeles, 1997; Um Dia De Mi Vida, 1998. *Publication:* First edition of compositions published with Tonos in Germany, 1998. *Membership:* AGADU, Uruguay. *Address:* Jaro Medien, Bismarckstrasse 43, 28203 Bremen, Germany.

DI MEOLA Al; b. 22 July 1954, Jersey City, New Jersey, USA. Jazz Musician (guitar); Composer. *Musical Education:* Studied with Robert Aslanian; Berklee College of Music, Boston, 1971, 1974. *Career:* Musician with Barry Miles; Member, Chick Corea's Return To Forever, 1974–76; Solo guitarist, composer, 1976–; Tours as solo artiste; Also toured with acoustic trio (with John McLaughlin and Paco de Lucia); Leader, Al DiMeola Project (musicians include Airto Moreiro), 1985–. *Recordings:* Albums include: with Return To Forever: Where Have I Known You Before, 1974; No Mystery, 1975; Romantic Warrior, 1976; Best Of, 1980; Solo albums: Land of Midnight Sun, 1976; Elegant Gypsy, 1977; Casino, 1978; Splendido Hotel, 1979; Electric Rendevous, 1982; Tour de Force Live, 1982; Scenario, 1983; Cielo e Terra, 1983; Soaring Through A Dream, 1985; Tiramu Su, 1988; World Sinfonia, 1990; Heart of The Immigrants, 1993; Kiss My Axe, 1993; Orange and Blue, 1994; The Essence of Al DiMeola, 1994; The Infinite Desire, 1998; Christmas Winter Nights, 1999; Anthology, 2000; with John McLaughlin and Paco de Lucia: Friday Night In San Francisco, 1980; Passion, Grace and Fire, 1983; with Aziza Mustafa Zadeh: Dance of Fire, 1995; with Jean-Luc Ponty, Stanley Clarke: The Rite of Strings, 1996. *Current Management:* Don't Worry Inc, 111 W 57th St, Suite 1120, New York, NY 11019, USA.

DIABATE Toumani; b. 10 Aug. 1965, Bamako, Mali. Musician (kora); Composer. *Musical Education:* Kora, self-taught. *Career:* Son of Sidiki Diabate; Recorded first ever solo kora album, Kaira; Collaborations: Kandia Kouyate; Ketama; Danny Thompson; Ballake Sissoko; Taj Mahal; Damon Albarn; Habib Koite; Keletigui Diabate; Toured Europe and US. *Recordings:* Albums include: Kaira, 1988; Songhai (with Ketama), 1989; Shake the World (including Habib Koite), 1991; Songhai 2, 1995; Djelika (with Danny Thompson and Keletigui Diabate), 1995; New Ancient Strings (with Ballake Sissoko), Kulanjan (with Taj Mahal), 1999. *Honours:* Froots, Best Album, Kulanjan, 1999.

DIAMOND Jim; b. 28 Sept. 1951, Glasgow, Scotland. Singer. *Career:* Member, bands including Jade; Bandit; PhD; Solo artiste, 1983–. *Recordings:* Solo albums: Double Crossed, 1985; Desire For Freedom, 1986; Jim Diamond, 1993; Singles include: I Won't Let You Down, PhD, 1982; Solo: I Should Have Known Better (No. 1, UK), 1984; Hi Ho Silver, theme song, UK television series Boon, 1986; Session work with: Steve Hackett; Alexis Korner; Tony Banks. *Address:* c/o LJE, 32 Willesden Lane, London NW6 7ST, England.

DIAMOND Neil Leslie; b. 24 Jan. 1941, Brooklyn, New York, USA. Singer; Composer. m. Marcia Murphey, 1975, 4 c. *Education:* Pre-med student, New York University. *Career:* Songwriter for publishing company; Formerly with Bang and MCA Records, 1973–, with Columbia; Record 20 show run at Winter Garden Theatre, 1972; Tours world-wide, include: 2 year, Love In The Round, world tour; Television and radio specials, numerous including: Christmas specials, 1992, 1993; Acted with Sir Laurence Olivier in The Jazz Singer, 1980; Set major box office records world-wide; 92m. albums sold. *Compositions include:* I'm A Believer (number 1 for Monkees); Film scores: Jonathan Livingston Seagull, 1973; Every Which Way But Loose, 1978; The Jazz Singer, 1980. *Recordings:* Albums include: The Feel of Neil Diamond, 1966; Just For You, 1967; Shilo, 1970; Velvet Gloves and Spit, 1968; Touching You Touching Me; Stones, 1971; Hot August Nights; Moods, 1972; Jonathan Livingston Seagull, 1973; Serenade, 1974; Beautiful Noise, 1976; Live At The Greek, 1977; I'm Glad You're Here Tonight, 1977; You Don't Bring Me Flowers, 1978; September Morn, 1980; Jazz Singer, 1980; Song Sung Blue, 1982; Headed For The Future, 1986; Hot August Night II, 1987; The Best Years of Our Lives, 1989; Christmas Album, 1992; Greatest Hits 1966–92, 1992; Up On the Roof – Songs From The Brill Building, 1993; Live In America, 1994; Christmas Album, Vol. II, 1994; Tennessee Moon, 1996; Live in Concert, 1997; The Movie Album, 1998; Three Chord Opera, 2001; Singles include: Sweet Caroline, 1969; Cracklin' Rosie (No. 1, USA), 1970; I Am... I Said, 1971; Song Sung Blue (No. 1, USA), 1972; Beautiful Noise, 1976; You Don't Bring Me Flowers, with Barbra Streisand (No. 1, USA), 1978; Forever In Blue Jeans, 1979; Love on the Rocks, 1980; Hello Again, 1981; Heartlight, 1982; Morning Has Broken, 1992; As Time Goes By, 1998. *Honours:* Platinum, Gold Records; Globe Awards; Grammy, 1973 for: Jonathan

Livingston Seagull. *Membership:* SESAC. *Address:* c/o Columbia Records, Media Department, 550 Madison Ave, New York, NY 1002–3211, USA.

DIBANGO Manu; b. 12 Dec. 1934, Douala, Cameroon. Musician (saxophone, piano). *Musical Education:* Classical piano. *Career:* Moved to Paris, 1949; Then Brussels, Belgium, 1956; Residency at Black Angels Club, Brussels; Joined band led by Joseph Kabsele, African Jazz, 1960; Played with African Jazz in Zaire to 1963; Returned to Cameroon, formed own band, 1963–65; Studio musician, Paris, 1965; Backed musicians including: Peter Gabriel; Sinead O'Connor; Angélique Kidjo; Geoffrey Oryema; Ray Lema; Touré Kunda; Recording artiste, 1968–. *Compositions:* Commissioned by President Ahidjo to write patriotic song for Africa Cup football match, 1971. *Recordings:* Albums: O Boso, 1971; Soma Loba, 1972; Soul Makossa, 1973; Super Kumba, 1974; Manu 76, 1976; Afrovision, 1976; Big Blow, 1976; A L'Olympia, 1977; Ceddo, 1978; Gone Clear, 1980; Ambassador, 1980; Waka Juju, 1982; Deliverence, 1983; Sweet and Soft, 1983; Melodies Africaines Vols 1 and 2, 1983; Deadline, 1984; Electric Africa, 1985; Afrijazzy, 1986; Negropolitains Vol. 2, 1993; Wakafrika, 1994; Bao Bao, 1996; Hit singles: Soul Makossa (hit in US, Europe, Africa); Wakafika; Big Blow; Sun Explosion; Abele Dance. *Publication:* Autobiography: Trois Kilos de Café, 1990. *Honours:* Gold disc, Soul Makossa; Grammy Award, Best R & B Instrumental Performance of The Year, 1973. *Membership:* President, Francophone Diffusion. *Current Management:* IPS Management, 11–13 rue Mont-Louis, 75011 Paris, France. *Address:* c/o Francophone Diffusion, 33 rue du Fbg St Antoine, 75011 Paris, France.

DICK Arthur; b. 4 Aug. 1954, Dundee, Scotland. Musician (guitar); Writer; Arranger. *Education:* BSc Hons, Liverpool University. *Musical Education:* Performing Diploma (guitar). *Career:* Numerous sessions as guitarist; Television appearances: Granada; Yorkshire; Thames; BBC; Central; Radio broadcasts: BBC; Capital; Picadilly, 1980–; MD for: Berni Flint, 1988; Susan Maughan; Recorded sessions for numerous artistes including: Cliff Richard; Paul McCartney; Cilla Black; Barbara Dickson; Formed Tracks Music for production of television and radio soundtracks, 1986; Lecturer, Goldsmith's College (London University); Guitar studies, recording, 1985–. *Publications:* Numerous for Music Sales Ltd; Works for Eric Clapton; Bon Jovi; Blues and Jazz compilations; Original guitar chord study; Guitar transcriptions of Santana; John Martyn; Robben Ford. *Memberships:* PRS; Musicians' Union. *Leisure interests:* HiFi; Walking; Swimming; Theatre; Arts; Wine.

DICKINSON (Paul) Bruce; b. 7 Aug. 1958, Worksop, Nottinghamshire, England. Singer; Author. *Education:* Degree, History, Queen Mary College, London University, 1979. *Career:* Member: Speed; Shots; Samson, 1980; Lead vocalist, UK heavy rock group Iron Maiden, 1981–93, rejoined 1999; Regular tours world-wide; Concerts include: Reading Festival, 1982; Monsters of Rock Festivals, Castle Donington, 1988, 1992; Monsters of Rock, Germany, 1988; Monsters of Rock Festival, France, 1992; Super Rock '92, Germany, 1992. *Recordings:* Albums: with Samson: Head On, 1980; Shock Tactics, 1981; with Iron Maiden: The Number of The Beast (No. 1, UK), 1982; Piece of Mind, 1983; Powerslave, 1984; Live After Death, 1985; Somewhere In Time, 1986; Seventh Son of a Seventh Son (No. 1, UK), 1988; No Prayer For The Dying, 1990; Fear of The Dark (No. 1, UK), 1992; A Real Live One, 1993; A Real Dead One, 1993; Brave New World, 2000; Solo albums: Tattooed Millionaire, 1990; Balls To Picasso, 1994; Alive In Studio A, 1995; Skunkworks, 1996; Accident of Birth, 1997; Chemical Wedding, 1998; Scream for Me Brazil, 1999; Singles include: with Iron Maiden: Run To The Hills, 1982; The Number of The Beast, 1982; Flight of Icarus, 1983; The Trooper, 1983; 2 Minutes To Midnight, 1984; Aces High, 1984; Wasted Years, 1986; Stranger In A Strange Land, 1986; Can I Play With Madness, 1988; Evil That Men Do, 1988; The Clairvoyant, 1988; Infinite Dreams, 1989; Holy Smoke, 1990; Bring Your Daughter To The Slaughter (from film A Nightmare On Elm Street 5) (No. 1, UK), 1991; Be Quick Or Be Dead, 1992; From Here To Eternity, 1992; Solo singles: Tattooed Millionaire, 1990; All The Young Dudes, 1990; Dive! Dive! Dive!, 1990; Elected (charity single for Comic Relief), 1992; Tears of The Dragon, 1994; Road to Hell. *Publications:* Novels: The Adventures of Lord Iffy Boatrace, 1990; The Missionary Position, 1992. *Leisure interest:* Fencing (once rated in UK top 10). *Current Management:* Sanctuary Music Management Ltd, First Floor Suite, The Colonnades, 82 Bishops Bridge Rd, London W2 6BB, England.

DICKSON Barbara (Ruth); b. 27 Sept. 1947, Dunfermline, Scotland. Singer; Songwriter; Musician (guitar, piano); Actress. m. Oliver Cookson, 25 Aug. 1984, 3 s. *Career:* Television appearances include: Two Ronnies; Taggart; Band of Gold; Own documentaries and most light entertainment shows; UK concert tours, 1977–; Stage performances: John Paul George Ringo and Bert, 1974–75; Blood Brothers, 1982–83, 1993; The 7 Ages of Woman, 1997–98; Friends Like This, 1998; A Slice of Saturday Night, 1999; Spend, Spend, Spend, 1999. *Recordings:* Hit singles: Answer Me, 1976; Another Suitcase, 1977; Caravans, 1980; January, February, 1980; I Know Him So Well (with Elaine Paige) (No. 1, UK), 1985; Albums include: Barbara Dickson Album, 1980; All For A Song, 1982; Tell Me It's Not True, 1983; Heartbeats, 1984; Barbara Dickson Song Book, 1985; Gold,

1985; The Right Moment, 1986; Coming Alive Again, 1989; Don't Think Twice It's Alright, 1992; Parcel of Rogues, 1994; Dark End of The Street, 1996; The 7 Ages of Woman, 1998; Greatest Hits, 2002. *Honours:* SWET Award, Blood Brothers; Platinum and Gold albums; Best Actress in Theatre, Liverpool Echo Arts and Entertainment Awards, 1997; Best Actress In A Musical, Variety Club Showbusiness Awards, 1999; Best Actress In A Musical, Laurence Olivier Awards, 2000; O.B.E., 2002. *Membership:* PRS. *Leisure interests:* Walking; Antiques; Collecting paintings; Wine. *Current Management:* Bernard Theobald. *Address:* The Coach House, Swinhope Hall, Swinhope, Lincolnshire LN8 6HT, England.

DICKSON Sean; b. 21 March 1967, Bellshill, Scotland. Singer; Songwriter; Prod.; Musician (guitar and omnichord). *Musical Education:* Self-taught. *Career:* Singer, songwriter, guitarist, producer for The Soup Dragons, 1986–94, The High Fidelity, 1995–; World-wide tours; Released 3 albums, 18 singles and 15 videos for The Soup Dragons; Member, The High Fidelity; Runs own record label, Plastique Recordings. *Recordings:* Singles: Hang-Ten!, 1987; The Majestic Head, 1988; I'm Free, 1990; Divine Thing, 1990; Mother Universe, 1990; Backwards Dog, 1990; Pleasure, 1992; Can't Take No More; with The High Fidelity; Addicted to a TV, 1998; Luv Dup, 1998; I Thank U, 2000; Unsorry, 2000; 2 Up 2 Down, 2000; Albums: with The Soup Dragons: This Is Our Art, 1988; Lovegod, 1990; Hotwired, 1992; Hydrophonic, 1994; with The High Fidelity: Demonstration, 2000. *Honours:* 2 Gold records, 1 Silver record. *Memberships:* PRS; Musicians' Union. *Leisure interests:* Making videos; Directing films; Running own label; Collecting records and junk. *Current Management:* Rick Rogers. *Address:* 132 Royal College St, Camden, London NW1 0TA, England.

DIDDLEY Bo, (Otha Bates); b. 28 Dec. 1928, McComb, Mississippi, USA. Musician (guitar); Singer. *Career:* Numerous world-wide tours with artists including Ben E King; Ron Wood (as the Gunslingers); Lightnin' Hopkins; The Clash; Major concerts include: Rock 'n' Revival, with Jerry Lee Lewis, Little Richard, John Lennon, Toronto, 1969; Hampden Scene '70, with Chuck Berry, Glasgow, 1970; Regular 1950s Rock 'n' Roll Revivals concerts, US and UK, 1971–; Jazz and Heritage Festival, New Orleans, 1990; Celebrate The Soul of American Music Festival, Los Angeles, 1991; Guitar Legends, Expo '92, Seville, Spain, 1991; Hopefest, annual charity concert for the homeless, Chicago, 1992; Television commercial for Nike, with Bo Jackson, 1989; Films: Sweet Toronto, 1969 (renamed Keep On Rockin', 1972); Let The Good Times Roll, 1973; Trading Places, 1983. *Recordings:* Albums: Bo Diddley, 1962; Bo Diddley Is A Gunslinger, 1963; Bo Diddley Rides Again, 1963; Bo Diddley's Beach Party, 1964; Two Great Guitars, with Chuck Berry, 1964; Super Blues Band, with Muddy Waters and Little Walter, 1968; Another Dimension, 1971; The London Bo Diddley Sessions, 1973; 20th Anniversary of Rock 'n' Roll, 1976; Hey Bo Diddley, 1986; Live At The Ritz, 1987; Breakin' Through The BS, 1989; Rare and Well Done, 1991; Bo's Blues, 1993; Let Me Pass, 1994; Bo Knows Bo, 1995; A Man Amongst Men, 1996; His Best, 1997; The Essential Collection, 2001; Featured on film soundtracks: La Bamba (No. 1, USA), 1987; Book of Love, with Ben E. King, 1991; Singles include: Bo Diddley (R & B No. 2, US); Who Do You Love; Say Man; Road Runner; You Can't Judge A Book By It's Over; Mona; Hey Good Lookin'; Ooh Baby. *Honours:* Inducted, Rock and Roll Hall of Fame, 1987; Handprints in Sunset Boulevard's Rock Walk, Los Angeles, 1989. *Current Management:* Margo Lewis, Talent Source, 1560 Broadway, Suite 1308, New York, NY 10036, USA.

DIDDY (Richard Dearlove); b. 22 Sept. 1966, Marston Green, Birmingham, England. Songwriter; Record Prod.; Musician (keyboards, guitar); Vocalist; Artist. *Career:* Pop, dance, singles and remixes. *Compositions:* Small World; Give Me Love, singles released as Diddy. *Recordings:* As Remixer, Producer: Blondie: Atomic, 1994; Heart of Glass, 1995; Rio and Mars: Boy I Gotta Have You; How Deep Is Love; The Tyrell Corporation: Better Days; Retro Dance Club; Now That's What I Call Music. *Membership:* Musicians' Union. *Leisure interests:* Watersports; Computers.

DIDO, (Dido Florian Cloud De Bounevialle Armstrong); b. 25 Dec. 1971, London, UK. Vocalist; Musician (piano, violin); Songwriter. *Musical Education:* Guildhall School of Music, London, from age 6. *Career:* Toured UK with classical music ensemble before joining pop groups aged 16 and touring as backing vocalist with brother Rollo's band Faithless; Discovered as solo artist by Arista Records supremo Clive Davis whilst visiting London; Album released to modest reception until track Thank You incorporated into Eminem's hit single Stan caused world-wide interest; Constant live promotion of album, 2000–01. *Recordings:* Albums: No Angel, 1999; Singles: The Highbury Fields EP, 1999; Here With Me, Thank You, Hunter, 2001; All You Want, 2002. *Honours:* World-wide album sales of over 10m. *Address:* c/o Cheeky Records, UK. *Internet:* www.didomusic.com.

DIESEL (Darren House), (Yellow Sox); b. 8 Feb. 1966, Hayes, London, England. Prod.; Remixer; DJ. *Career:* Started DJ career with partner Rocky; Formed X-Press 2 with Ashley Beedle and Rocky, 1993; Signed to Junior Boy's Own label; Member: Ballistic Brothers; Remixed: Fatboy Slim; River Ocean. *Recordings:* Albums: Ballistic Brothers vs The Eccentric Afros, 1995; London Hooligan Soul (with Ballistic Brothers), 1995; My First Acid House (with Problem Kids), 2001; Xpress-2 album forthcoming, 2002; Singles: Muzik X-Press, London X-Press, Say What, 1993; Rock 2 House, 1994; The Sound, 1995; Tranz Euro Express, 1996; Flim Flam (as Yellow Sox), 1996; Blacker (with Ballistic Brothers), 1997; AC/DC, 2000; Smoke Machine, Muzikizum, 2001. *Honours:* Muzik Awards, Best Producers, X-Press 2, 2001. *Membership:* MCPS/PRS. *Address:* c/o Skint Records, 73A Middle St, Brighton, Sussex, BN1 4BA, England.

DIF René; b. 17 October 1967, Fredriksberg, Denmark. *Career:* Formed Joyspeed; Changed name to Aqua; Obtained record deal in Denmark; Numerous TV and live appearances. *Recordings:* Singles: Itsy Blitzy, as Joyspeed; Roses Are Red; My Oh My; Barbie Girl; Doctor Jones; Lollipop; Turn Back Time; Good Morning Sunshine; Albums: Aquarium, 1997; Bubble Mix, 1998.

DIFFIE Joe Logan; b. 28 Dec. 1958, Tulsa, Oklahoma, USA. Country vocalist; Songwriter; Musician (guitar, bass guitar, drums). *Career:* Member of high school gospel group Genesis II and rock group Blitz; Later joined gospel group Higher Purpose and local bluegrass outfit Special Edition; Initial country gigs with aunt Dawn Anita and sister Monica; Earliest recorded song: Love On The Rocks by Hank Thompson; Moved to Nashville and worked for Gibson Guitars; Continued songwriting as staff writer at Forest Hills Music with occasional backing vocals and demo work for publishers; Signed by Columbia Records after vice president Bob Montgomery heard demos; Debut Billboard chart entry, 1990; Continued to chart throughout decade; Debut Opry appearance, 1990. *Compositions include:* Honky Tonk Attitude; If You Want Me To; Is It Cold In Here; New Way To Light Up An Old Flame; There Goes My Heart Again. *Recordings include:* Pick Up Man, 1994; Bigger Than The Beatles, 1995; Third Rock From The Sun, 1994; If The Devil Danced (In Empty Pockets), 1991; Home, 1990; Albums include: Regular Joe, 1992; Honky Tonk Attitude, 1993; Third Rock From The Sun, 1994. *Honours:* Billboard Award, Top Singles Artist, 1991; Cash Box, Male Artist of the Year, 1991; BMI award, There Goes My Heart Again, 1990. *Memberships:* Grand Ole Opry, 1993. *Leisure interests:* Art; Antiques; Reading; Sports; Woodwork. *Address:* c/o Buddy Lee Attractions, 38 Music Sq. E, Suite 300, Nashville, TN 37203, USA. *Internet:* www.joediffie.com.

DIFFORD Chris; b. 4 Nov. 1954, Greenwich, London, England. Vocalist; Musician (guitar); Songwriter. *Career:* Founder member, Squeeze, 1974–; Longstanding writing partnership with Glenn Tilbrook; Performances include: Reading Festival, 1978; Dalymount Festival, Dublin, 1980; US tours, 1978–; Jamaica World Music Festival, 1982; Support to Fleetwood Mac, US tour, 1990; Crystal Palace Bowl, London, 1991; Support to Bryan Adams, British tour, 1992. *Compositions include:* Songs for Labelled With Love, musical, 1983; Worked with Helen Shapiro; Paul Young; Jools Holland; Aimee Mann; Joe Cocker; Mark Knopfler; Lyricist for Marti Pellow album, Smile, 2001. *Recordings:* Albums: Squeeze, 1978; Cool For Cats, 1979; Argy Bargy, 1980; East Side Story, 1981; Sweets From A Stranger, 1982; Singles 45 and Under, 1982; Cosi Fan Tutti Frutti, 1985; Babylon and On, 1987; Frank, 1989; A Round and A Bout, 1990; Greatest Hits, 1992; Some Fantastic Piece, 1993; Ridiculous, 1995; Piccadilly Collection, 1996; Excess Moderation, 1996; Six of One, 1997; Domino, 1998; with Glenn Tilbrook: Difford and Tilbrook, 1984; Singles include: Take Me I'm Yours, 1978; Cool For Cats (No. 2, UK), 1979; Up The Junction (No. 2, UK), 1979; Slap and Tickle, 1979; Another Nail In My Heart, 1980; Pulling Mussels From A Shell, 1980; Tempted, 1981; Labelled With Love, 1981; Hourglass, 1987; This Summer, 1995; Heaven Knows, 1996. *Current Management:* Firstars, 3520 Hayden Ave, Culver City, CA 90232, USA.

DIGBY Roger; b. 19 April 1949, Colchester, Essex, England. Teacher; Musician (concertina). m. Sian Chatterton. 30 Nov. 1985, 2 s. *Education:* BA Hons, Bristol University; MA, Carlton University, Ottawa, Canada. *Career:* Leader, Anglo concertina player, Flowers and Frolics, 10 years; Venues include The Albert Hall, South Bank, Italian Alps; 7 years as co-organizer, acoustic music venue The Empress of Russia, Islington. *Recordings:* Albums: Bees On Horseback; Sold Out; Wait Till The Work Comes Round (with Bob Davenport). *Publications:* Numerous reviews. *Memberships:* Musicians' Union; EFDSS; International Concertina Asscn. *Leisure interests:* Reading; Cricket; Good beer. *Address:* 3 Wolsey Rd, London N1 4QH, England.

DIGITAL Didge; b. 18 May 1955, Shipley, West Yorkshire, England. Musician (keyboard); Programmer. 1 s. *Musical Education:* Piano lessons from age 6. *Career:* Keyboard player: FM; Tours with: Meat Loaf; Tina Turner; Bon Jovi; Gary Moore; Gerry and the Pacemakers; Status Quo; Television appearances: Pebble Mill; James Whale Show; Chart Show; Garden Party. *Recordings:* Albums: FM: Indiscreet; Tough It Out; Takin' It To The Streets; Chris Norman: Jealous Heart. *Honours:* Second Best Keyboard Player, Metal Hammer, 1987; Fourth Best Keyboard Player, International, 1987. *Leisure interests:* Swimming; Anything to do with Star Trek. *Current Management:* Flair Management and Agency. *Address:* 28 Cornmill Lane, Liversedge, Heckmondwike, Yorkshire, England.

DIGWEED John; b. 3 April, 1967, Hastings, East Sussex, England. Prod.; Remixer; DJ. *Career:* Began DJ career in Hastings at his own Bedrock events, early '90s; Formed highly successful DJ partnership with Sasha leading to a residency at Twilo in New York; Released several successful mix compilations with Sasha including: Renaissance; Northern Exposure; Founder: Bedrock Records; Member: Bedrock with production partner Nick Muir; Runs Bedrock event at London's Heaven club every month; Remixed: Sasha; Danny Tenaglia; Farley and Heller; The Orb; New Order. *Recordings:* Singles: For What You Dream Of, 1993; Set In Stone, 1997; Heaven Scent, 1999; Voices, 2000; Beautiful Strange, 2001. *Honours:* DJ Magazine, Top 100 DJs in the World, No. 1, 2001. *Membership:* MCPS/PRS. *Address:* c/o Bedrock Records, PO Box 4185, London, W1A 6XH, England.

DILLARD Doug; b. 6 March 1937, East St Louis, Illinois, USA. *Career:* Formed bluegrass group, The Dillards, with brother Rodney, 1962; Left to form Dillard and Clark with Gene Clark, 1968; Occasional sideline, Dillard-Hartford-Dillard, with brother Rodney and John Hartford. *Recordings:* Albums: With The Dillards: Back Porch Bluegrass, 1963; The Dillards Live! Almost, 1964; Pickin' and Fiddlin', 1965; with Dillard and Clark: The Fantastic Expedition of Dillard and Clark, 1968; Through The Morning, Through The Night, 1969; Solo: Dueling Banjos, 1973; You Don't Need a Reason, 1974; Heaven, 1976; with Doug Dillard Band: Jackrabbit, 1997; What's That, 1986; Heartbreak Hotel, 1989; There Is a Time, 1991.

DILLARD Rodney; b. 18 May 1942, East St Louis, Illinois, USA. Singer; Musician (guitar). *Career:* Formed bluegrass group, The Dillards, with brother Doug, 1962–; Various line-up changes, but Dillard remained leader of group; Occasional sideline, Dillard-Hartford-Dillard, with brother Doug and John Hartford. *Recordings:* Albums: Back Porch Bluegrass, 1963; The Dillards Live! Almost!, 1964; Pickin' and Fiddlin', 1965; Wheatstraw Suite, 1969; Copperfields, 1970; Roots and Branches, 1972; Tribute To The American Duck, 1973; The Dillards Versus The Incredible LA Time Machine, 1977; Mountain Rock, 1978; Decade Waltz, 1979; Homecoming and Family Reunion, 1979; I'll Fly Away, 1988; Let It Fly, 1991; Roots and Branches, 1996; First Time Live, 1999. *Current Management:* Keith Case and Associates, 59 Music Sq. W, Nashville, TN 37203, USA.

DILLON Cara; b. 1975, Dungiven, County Derry, Northern Ireland. Vocalist; Songwriter. *Career:* Member: Oige; Equation, 1995; Formed writing partnership with Sam Lakeman; Now work as a duo. *Recordings:* Live (with Oige), 1994; Interview With The Angel (with Ghostland), Cara Dillon, 2001. *Honours:* All-Ireland Traditional Singing trophy, 1989; BBC Radio 2 Folk Awards: Best Traditional Track, Black is the Colour; Horizon Award, 2002. *Address:* c/o Glass Ceiling PR. *E-mail:* promo@glassceilingpr.com.

DIMOND David; b. 23 Nov. 1964, Barking, Essex, England. Freelance Musician (saxophone, clarinet, flute); Music Teacher. *Education:* BSc Hons, Microbiology, University of Surrey. *Musical Education:* Clarinet, flute Grade 8, Royal Schools of Music; 1 year post-diploma, saxophone (Guildhall School of Music and Drama). *Career:* Mainly jazz-based, duos including Duojazz; Quartets, quintets include Jim Mullen quintet; Octets include Caliban; Big bands include: Superjazz, NYJO; Played Ronnie Scott's; Bass Clef; 606 Club; Royal Albert Hall; Festival Hall; Festivals include: Soho Jazz Festival; Edinburgh Festival; Tour with Bondera. *Compositions:* Over 50. *Recordings:* Recorded with numerous jazz set-ups as well as for library music, jingles on tenor saxophone. *Publications:* Article for international journal on acoustics. *Leisure interests:* Painting; Breeding lizards; Reading; Travel. *Address:* 18 Osborne Rd, Dagenham, Essex RM9 5BB, England.

DIO Ronnie James, (Ronald Padavona); b. 10 July 1949, New Hampshire, USA. Rock Vocalist; Musician (bass, piano, trumpet); Songwriter; Prod. m. Wendy Dio. *Career:* Member, various bands including: The Vegas Kings; Ronnie and The Rumblers; Ronnie and The Redcaps, late 1950s; Singer, musician, Ronnie Dio and The Prophets, 1961–67; Founder, Elf (formerly The Electric Elves), 1967–75; Member, Rainbow, 1975–79; Member, Black Sabbath, 1980–82; Founder member, Dio, 1983–91; Member, Black Sabbath, 1992–93; Also organizer of Hear 'N' Aid project (famine relief in Ethiopia), 1986. *Recordings:* Albums: with Ronnie Dio and The Prophets: Dio At Dominos, 1963; with Elf: Elf, 1972; Carolina County Ball, 1974; Trying To Burn The Sun, 1975; Live, 1976; with Rainbow: Ritchie Blackmore's Rainbow, 1975; Rainbow Rising, 1976; Live On Stage, 1977; Long Live Rock 'n' Roll, 1978; with Black Sabbath: Heaven and Hell, 1980; Mob Rules, 1981; Live Evil, 1982; with Dio: Holy Diver, 1983; The Last In Line, 1984; Sacred Heart, 1985; Intermission, 1986; Dream Evil, 1987; Lock Up The Wolves, 1990; Strange Highways, 1994; Angry Machines, 1996; Inferno, 1998; Magica, 2000; Other recordings: The Butterfly Ball, Roger Glover, 1975; Hear 'N' Aid, 1986; Northwinds, David Coverdale, 1978. *Current Management:* c/o Wendy Dio, Niji Management, 12334 Ventura Blvd, Studio City, CA 91604, USA.

DION Celine; b. 30 March 1968, Charlemagne, Québec, Canada. Singer. m. Rene Angelil, 17 Dec. 1994. *Career:* Began singing in father's restaurant; Recording artiste, 1979–; Winner, Eurovision Song Contest for Switzerland, 1988; Recorded in French until 1990; 35m. albums sold to date. *Recordings:* Albums: 9 albums recorded in French (including Tellement J'ai D'Amour; Dion Chante Plamondon; Incognito); Unison, 1990; Celine Dion, 1991; The Colour of My Love, 1994; D'Eux, 1995; Falling Into You, 1996; Live à Paris, 1996; Let's Talk About Love, 1997; A l'Olympia, 1998; Chansons en Or, 1998; These Are Special Times, 1998; Let's Talk About Love, 1999; All The Way – A Decade of Song, 1999; S'il Suffisait D'Aimer, 2001; Singles: Les Chemins De Ma Maison, 1984; Melanie, 1985; Une Colombe, 1985; Incognito, 1988; Where Does My Heart Beat Now, 1991; Beauty and The Beast, duet with Peabo Bryson, 1992; When I Feel [Fall] In Love, from film soundtrack Sleepless In Seattle, 1993; The Power of Love (No. 1, USA), 1994; Think Twice (No. 1, UK), 1995; Pour Que Tu M'Aimes Encore, 1995; Misled, 1995; Only One Road, 1995; Falling Into You, 1996; Because You Loved Me, from film Up Close and Personal (No. 1, USA), 1996; It's All Coming Back To Me Now, 1996; All By Myself, 1996; Call The Man, 1997; Tell Him, duet with Barbra Streisand, 1997; The Reason, 1997; My Heart Will Go On, from film soundtrack of Titanic (No. 1, UK and US), 1998; Immortality, collaboration with The Bee Gees, 1998; I'm Your Angel, duet with R Kelly (No. 1, USA), 1998; Treat Her Like a Lady, 1999; That's The Way It Is, 1999. *Honours:* Gala de L'Adisq Awards: Pop Album of Year, 1983; Best Selling Record, 1984, 1985; Best Selling Single, 1985; Pop Song of the Year, 1985, 1988; Female Artist of Year, 1983–85, 1988; Discovery of the Year, 1983; Best Québec Artist Outside Québec, 1983, 1988; JUNO Awards: Album of the Year, 1991; Single of the Year, 1993; Female Vocalist of the Year, 1991–93; Journal de Québec Trophy, 1985; Spectrel Video Award, Best Stage Performance, 1988. *Current Management:* c/o Rene Angelil, Feeling Productions Inc, 755-2540 Daniel-Johnson, Laval, QC H7T 2S3, Canada.

DIRNT Mike, (Mike Pritchard); b. 4 May 1972, Berkeley, California, USA. Musician (bass). *Career:* Formed early band Sweet Children, became Green Day; Numerous tours and TV appearance; Side projects, Pinhead Gunpowder and Screeching Weasel; Obtained major label recording contract; Provided track for film soundtrack Godzilla; Appeared in cartoon King of the Hill as The Stubborn Stains. *Recordings:* Singles: Slappy EP, 1990; Welcome to Paradise, 1992; Longview, 1994; Geek Stink Breath, 1995; Stuck With Me, 1996; Brain Stew, 1996; Hitchin' A Ride, 1998; Time of Your Life, 1998; Nice Guys Finish Last, 1999; Minority, 2000; Waiting, 2001; Albums: Kerplunk, 1992; Dookie, 1994; Insomniac, 1995; Live, 1995; Nimrod, 1997; Foot in Mouth, 1998; Warning, 2000; International Superhits (compilation), 2001.

DIRTY PIK; b. 1 Sept. 1961, Tielt, Belgium. Singer; Musician (guitar). 2 d. *Career:* The Dirty Scums, 1981. *Recordings:* with the Dirty Scums: Dirty Songs, LP, 1985; Martens, single, 1986; Full Speed Ahead!, LP, 1987; Fifth Anniversary Gig, tape (C-60), 1988; 'Rit 'n Zatte Skit 'N, single, 1988; The Booze and the Chicks, LP, 1989; The Early Years, tape (C-60), 1990; If the Barkeepers are United, the Scums will Never be Divided, tape (C-72), 1992; Really High, single, 1993; The Pils Sessions and Setting New Standards to Stupidity, CD, 1996; Santa Clauz Has Come!, CD, 1997; Proud to be a Punk and Something Else, CD, 1999; Dirtier Than You'll Ever Be, tape (C-90), 2000. *Leisure interest:* Music – parties. *Address:* The Dirty Scums, Kapelleweg 10, 8700 Tielt, Belgium.

DISCLEZ Yves; b. 22 April 1956, Brussels, Belgium. Writer; Composer; Artist. m. Carine Mairesse, 28 April 1990, 1 s., 1 d. *Musical Education:* Music Academy, Ciney, Belgium; Up With People, Tucson, Arizona, as guitar player. *Career:* 839 shows, USA, 1975–76; Up With People programme; Up With People on tour; Intermission of the Super Bowl, Miami 1976 (Television audience 250,000); Chicago Theatre, 3 days; Civic Center, Long Beach; National Television, USA, 1975–76; Belgian television: Palmares, 1983; 4 tours, Belgium, 1982–90; Appearances: RTL/TV1, 19 in 1990, 21 in 1991; All national radio. *Recordings:* Nostalgie, 1983; Compteur A Zero, 1984; J' M'en Fou, 1986; Dazibao, 1989; Conquiatador, 1990; Le Môme de la Bas, 1991; Romanc, 1994. *Publications:* Nostalgie; J'M'en Fou; Romanc. *Honours:* Prize of Belgium Artistic Promotion (PAB), 1986; First prize, French Song, Walcourt, Belgium, 1989. *Memberships:* SABAM (Belgium); Copy Right (Washington, USA). *Leisure interests:* Tennis; Friends; Good wine and good food. *Current Management:* Mr Patrick Dccam, Sony Music (Belgium). *Address:* 27, Ave de la Restauration, 5500 Falmagne (Dinant), Belgium.

DISTEL Sacha; b. 29 Jan. 1933, Paris, France. Singer; Songwriter; Musician (guitar). m. Francine Breaud, 1963, 2 s. *Career:* Professional jazz guitarist, age 16; World-wide cabaret star; Films: Les Mordus, 1960; Nous Irons A Deauville, 1962; La Bonne Soupe, 1964; Le Voyou, 1970; Sans Mobile Apparent, 1971; Television presenter, France, England, Germany; Co-star, Golden Songs of The Silver Screen tour; Producer of shows: Sacha Show; Top à Sacha Distel, 1973; Sacha's In Town, 1972; Producer, performer, La Belle Vie, 1984–85. *Recordings:* Hit singles include: Scoubidou, 1959; Raindrops Keep Falling On My Head, 1970; Albums include: Sacha Distel, 1970; Love Is All, 1976; Forever and Ever, 1978;

Golden Hour of Sacha Distel, 1978; 20 Favourite Love Songs, 1979; From Sacha With Love, 1979; The Sacha Distel Collection, 1980; Move Closer, 1985; More Than More, 1987; Dedications, 1992; Ecoute Mes Yeux, 1998; Very Best of Sacha Distel, 1998; Collaborated with UK band Dubstar on recording of Poupee De Cire Poupee De Son for TV Eurovision tribute, A Song For Eurotrash, 1998. *Honours include:* Best Guitarist, Jazz Hot Magazine, Critics Poll, 1957–59; Chevalier des Arts et des Lettres, 1987; Chevalier de la Legion D'Honneur, 1997. *Address:* c/o Prosadis, 83 rue Michel-Ange, 75016 Paris, France.

DISTLER Jed (John Edward); b. 8 Dec. 1956, Newark, New Jersey, USA. Composer; Musician (Piano); Artistic Dir of Composers Collaborative. m. Célia Cooke, 24 July 1984. *Education:* BA, Sarah Lawrence College; Composition lessons with Andrew Thomas; Piano with Stanley Lock and William Komaiko. *Career:* Artistic Director, ComposersCollaborative Inc, a non-profit presenting organization for new music; Numerous live appearances on National Public Radio and alternative music stations; Faculty Member, Sarah Lawrence College. *Compositions:* The Death of Lottie Shapiro; Calypso for Piano; Diva Demento; Landscapes for Peter Wyer; Sonata for Violin and Piano and Toy Piano; Assault on Pepper; String Quartet No 1 (Mr Softee Variations). *Recordings:* Three Landscapes for Peter Wyer; Margaret Leng Tan; Arrangements and transcriptions for Conversations with Bill Evans, Reflections on Duke Ellington, with Jean-Yves Thibaudet, pianist; Eleven Art Tatum Transcripts, with Steven Mayer, piano. *Publications:* Transcription books: Art Tatum: Jazz Master; Bill Evans 4; Contributing writer for Gramophone magazine. *Honours:* With ComposersCollaborative: Grants and Awards, Meet the Composer, The Virgil Thomson Foundation, The Aaron Copland Fund for Music, Foundation for Hellenic Culture. *Memberships:* American Federation of Musicians (Local 802); American Music Center; American Composers Forum; ASCAP. *Leisure interests:* Travel, cooking. *Current Management:* Célia Cooke, personal representative.

DITCHAM Martin Russell; b. 22 Feb. 1951, Ilford, Essex, England. Musician (percussion, drums). *Musical Education:* Studied trumpet, violin, recorder, percussion, at school. *Career:* World tours with Sade; Chris Rea; Live Aid; Everything But The Girl, US tour; British tours with The Beautiful South. *Recordings:* All four Sade albums; Last eight Chris Rea albums; Undercover, Rolling Stones; Ross, Diana Ross; Duets, Elton John; 3 albums with Talk Talk; Nik Kershaw; Mike and The Mechanics; Jimmy Nail; The Sundays; Heather Small; Tanita Tikaram; The Waterboys; International recordings with: Patricia Kaas (France); Westernhagen (Germany); Takanaka (Japan); Presuntas Implicados (Spain). *Honours:* BPI, ASCAP Awards for Sade, Sweetest Taboo (one of most played songs of year). *Memberships:* Musicians' Union; PRS. *Leisure interests:* Motor racing; Record collecting. *Current Management:* Real Life Ltd. *Address:* 10 Glyn Mansions, Hammersmith Rd, London W14 8XH, England.

DIVLJAN Vladimir; b. 10 May 1958, Belgrade, Yugoslavia. Songwriter; Musician (guitar); Singer; Film Composer; Sound Designer. *Education:* BSc, Geology, University of Belgrade, 1983; Specialist, Extension Course in Sound Design, AFTRS, Sydney, 1997; programming. *Musical Education:* Self-taught, guitar. *Career:* Songwriter, Guitarist and Singer, Belgrade based New Wave Band, Idoli (The Idols), 1980–84, National (Yugoslav) Tours, 1981, 1982, 1983; Songwriter, Solo Performer, Film and TV Composer, Yugoslavia and Australia, 1985-. *Compositions:* Composed music for features: Six Days in June, 1984; The Rise and Fall of Rock 'N' Roll, 1989; Documentaries: Across Australia, 1993; Heart of the Matter, 1995; You Might as Well Live, 1995. *Recordings:* Realised 13 albums including: Paket Aranzman, 1981; Odbrana I Poslednji Dani, 1982; Tajni Zivot A P Sandorova, 1988; Odbrana I Zastita, 1996. *Honours:* Idoli, ranked Fourth Most Promising Group by 8 leading European magazines, 1988; LP, Odbrana I Poslednji Dani, voted Best Yugoslav Rock Record of All Times, 1988; Nomination, Australian Film Institute (AFI) Award, 1997; Quantegy Award for Audio Excellence, AFTRS, 1997. *Memberships:* Australian Performers Rights Asscn; Australian Guild of Screen Composers. *Current Management:* Radio B92, Makedonska 22/V, 11000 Beograd, Yugoslavia.

DIXON Jolyon Keith; b. 6 Dec. 1973, Salisbury, Wiltshire, England. Musician (guitar); Singer; Songwriter. *Musical Education:* Self-taught guitar from age 9; Music A-Level. *Career:* Tours: Two British tours backing Toyah Wilcox; Central American tour with Toyah; 2 support tours as: Friday Forever; 2 Heineken Music Festivals; Support to Bryan Ferry, with Scarlet, UK, 1995; Joined as guitarist in Mark Owen's band, and has toured extensively with them; Sold 1m. albums world-wide with Mark Owen; First band to perform in Abbey Road studios since the Beatles; Numerous radio appearances with: Scarlet; Toyah; Television: 3 times, Top of The Pops; What's Up Doc?; Richard and Judy; Pebble Mill; Parallel Nine. *Recordings:* Toyah: Take The Leap, 1993; Scarlet: Naked, 1995; Green Man with Mark Owen, 1996; Hit single: Independent Love Song; follow-up singles; Unreleased albums: Voice of The Beehive: East/West; Judie Tzuke: Duck. *Publications:* with Mark Owen's band: Child, 1996; Clementine, 1997; I Am What I Am, 1997. *Membership:* Musicians'

Union. *Leisure interests:* Playing guitars; Squash; Producing other acts. *Current Management:* Friday's Productions. *Address:* 51A Estcourt Rd, Salisbury, Wiltshire, England.

DIYICI Senem; b. 30 March 1953, Istanbul, Turkey. Singer. m. Alain Blesing, 1989, 2 d. *Musical Education:* Istanbul Music Academy, from age of 6. *Career:* Joined children's choir in Istanbul; 3 albums in Turkey, moved to Germany; Formed several groups, produced 1 album; Arrived in France, in quest for new harmonies and musical crossover; Performs about 100 shows throughout world annually. *Recordings:* Nar Haniti, 1970; Hatimeyva, 1976; Casino No 1, 1979; Anatoliv, 1986; Takalar, 1989; Geste, 1993; Divan, 1995; Jell me Trabizan. *Memberships:* SACEM; ADATI; SPEDIDAM. *Leisure interests:* Painting; Children. *Current Management:* Equator Produkties, The Netherlands. *Address:* Essenburg Singel 198B, 3022 E N Rotterdam, The Netherlands.

DJ HOMICIDE (Craig Anthony Bullock); b. 17 Dec. 1970. Musician (drum programming; effects); DJ. *Career:* Formerly radio presenter on Los Angeles hip-hop stations, K-DAY and The Beat; Worked in studio on Sugar Ray's Lemonade and Brownies album; Joined group for live shows then became full-time member; Act built up world-wide fanbase through touring and TV appearances; Cameo in Fathers Day film, 1997. *Recordings:* Albums: Lemonade and Brownies, 1995; Floored, 1997; 14–59, 1999; Sugar Ray, 2001; Singles: Mean Machine, Iron Mic, 1995; Fly, RPM, 1997; Every Morning, Someday, 1999; Falls Apart, 2000; When It's Over, Answer The Phone, 2001. *Honours:* Second/third albums certified double/ triple platinum by RIAA respectively. *Address:* c/o PO Box 12018, Costa Mesa, CA 92627, USA. *E-mail:* management@sugarray.com. *Internet:* www.sugarray.com.

DJ JAZZY JEFF, (Jeffrey Townes); b. 22 Jan. 1965, Philadelphia, Pennsylvania, USA. *Career:* Started as DJ, 1970's; Formed duo with Will Smith, as DJ Jazzy Jeff and the Fresh Prince; Collaborated with Will Smith on Smith's solo album, Big Willie Style, 1997; guest on I Don't Know, Slum Village, 2000; Formed A Touch of Jazz Inc, collective of producers working on rap and R & B projects. *Recordings:* Singles: Girls Ain't Nothing But Trouble, 1986; Just One of Those Days; Parents Just Don't Understand; A Nightmare on Elm Street; Brand New Funk; The Groove; I Think I Can Beat Mike Tyson; Summertime; Ring My Bell; The Things That U Do; Boom! Shake the Room; I'm Looking for the One (To Be With Me); Albums: Rock the House, 1987; He's the DJ, I'm the Rapper, 1988; An In This Corner, 1989; Homebase, 1991; Code Red, 1993. *Honours:* Grammy Awards, as DJ Jazzy Jeff and the Fresh Prince, Best Rap Performance, 1988, 1991.

DJ KILMORE (Chris Kilmore); b. 21 Jan. 1973, Pittsburgh, Pennysylvania, USA. DJ. *Career:* Shortly after relocation to LA, replaced DJ Lyfe in Immortal/Epic-signed group Incubus, 1998; Built US and European following support slots on tours with Sugar Ray; Black Sabbath; Korn; Drive reached #1 on US Modern Rock Chart, 2001; First Japanese and Australian live dates, 2001. *Recordings:* Albums: Make Yourself, 1999; Morning View, 2001; Singles: Pardon Me, 1999; Stellar, When Incubus Attacks Vol. 1 EP, 2000; Drive, Wish You Were Here, 2001. *Honours:* Make Yourself album certified double platinum by RIAA; Billboard Award, Modern Rock Single of The Year, 2001. *Current Management:* Steve Rennie, REN Management, California, USA. *Internet:* www.enjoyincubus.com.

DJ LETHAL (Leor DiMant); b. 18 Dec. 1972, Latvia. DJ; Musician (rhythm/sound effects). *Career:* Member: House of Pain, 1992–96; Limp Bizkit, 1996–; Striking live shows at concerts and festivals; Group spearheaded 'nu-metal' breakthrough in Europe, 2001; Various remixes and executive production for other artists including: Sugar Ray; Rob Zombie. *Recordings:* Albums: with House of Pain: House of Pain, 1992; Same As It Ever Was, 1994; Truth Crushed To Earth Shall Rise Again, 1996; with Limp Bizkit: Three Dollar Bill, Y'All $, 1997; Significant Other, 1999; Chocolate Starfish and The Hot Dog Flavored Water, 2000; New Old Songs (remix album), 2001; Singles: with House of Pain: Jump Around, Shamrocks and Shenanigans, 1992; Top O' The Morning To Ya, Who's The Man, 1993; On Point, It Ain't A Crime, 1994; Fed Up, 1996; with Limp Bizkit: Faith, 1997; Nookie, Rearranged, 1999; Break Stuff, Take A Look Around (from Mission Impossible 2 OST), My Generation, 2000; Rollin', My Way, Boiler, 2001. *Honours:* Second and third Limp Bizkit albums both debuted at #1 on US chart; Significant Other sales in excess of 6m. *Current Management:* The Firm (Management), 9100 Wilshire Blvd, Suite 400W, Beverly Hills, CA 90212, USA. *Internet:* www.limpbizkit.com.

DJ MUGGS, (Lawrence Muggerud); b. 28 Jan. 1968, New York, USA. DJ; Prod. *Career:* Member, Cypress Hill; Numerous tours including Lollapalooza; Collaboration with Pearl Jam on the film soundtrack Judgement Night, 1993; Solo project, Muggs Presents... The Soul Assassins, 1997; Refused further touring with the band. *Recordings:* Singles: Phuncky Feel One, 1991; Hand on the Pump, 1991; Latin Lingo, 1991; Insane in the Brain, 1993; We Ain't Goin' Out Like That, 1994; Throw

Your Set in the Air, 1995; Boom Biddy Bye Bye, 1996; Unreleased and Revamped, 1996; Illusions, 1996; Tequila Sunrise, 1998; Rap Superstar, 2000; Albums: Cypress Hill, 1991; Black Sunday, 1993; Cypress Hill III – Temples of Boom, 1995; IV, 1998; Stoned Raiders, 2001.

DJ ÖTZI, (Gernot Friedle); b. 7 Jan. 1971, St Johann, Tyrol, Austria. Vocalist; DJ. m. Sonja Kein, 8 Aug. 2001. *Education:* Stams boarding school; Imst Agricultural College. *Career:* Became DJ with assistance of professional DJ father. *Recordings:* Albums: Anton – Das Album, 2000; Never Stop The Alpenpop, 2001; Love Peace and Vollgas, 2001; Singles: Anton Aus Tirol, 1999; Gemma Bier Trinken, 2000; Hey Baby (Uhh, Ahh), 2000; Do Wah Diddy, 2001; X-mas Time, 2001. German Echo Music Award, Best International Rock/Pop Single, Anton Aus Tirol, 2001. *Address:* c/o Herbert Fechter, Sieveringerstrasse 194, 1190 Wien, Austria. *E-mail:* office@fechter-management.com.

DJ PREMIER (Chris Martin), (Primo); b. Houston, Texas, USA. Prod.; DJ. *Career:* Formed Gang Starr with rapping partner Guru, 1989; Debut album No More Mr Nice Guy released on Wild Pitch Records; In-demand producer for acts including: Common; Black Eyed Peas; Collaborations: Rakim; Jay-Z; Mos Def; Jeru The Damaja. *Recordings:* Albums: No More Mr Nice Guy, 1989; Step In The Arena, 1990; Daily Operation, 1992; Hard To Earn, 1994; Moment of Truth, 1998; Singles: Jazz Thing, 1990; Lovesick, 1991; Code To The Street EP, 1994; You Know My Steez, 1997. *Address:* c/o Chrysalis Records, EMI House, 43 Brook Green, London, W6 7EF, England.

DJ SHADOW (Josh Davis); b. 1973, USA. DJ; Prod. *Career:* One of the first Hip Hop DJ's; Joined artists' collective Sole Sides; Remixed Zimbabwe Legit; Obtained record deal; Worked with Paris, DJ Krush, Depeche Mode and Massive Attack; Support slot live to Radiohead; Work on collective U.N.K.L.E. with James Lavelle and Thom Yorke of Radiohead; Provided film soundtrack to Wim Wenders's The End of Violence, 1997. *Recordings:* Singles: Asia Born, 1993; Chief Xcel; DJ Shadow and the Groove Robbers: In/Flux/Hindsight; Lost and Found, with DJ Krush; What Does Your Soul Look Like, 1996; A Whim, with DJ Krush; Midnight In a Perfect World, 1995; Stem, 1996; High Noon, 1997; Camel Bobsled Race, live mix, with Q-Bert, 1997; The Number Song; Dark Days, 2000; Albums: Endtroducing, 1996; Preemptive Strike, 1998.

DJAVAN, (Djavan Caetano Viana); b. 1949, Maceio, Alagoas, Brazil. Vocalist; Musician (guitar); Songwriter. *Career:* Started own band, LSD, playing Beatles covers in local venues, aged 16; Moved to Rio de Janeiro, 1973; Hired to sing TV soap opera themes between regular night club appearance; Composition Abertura placed second in TV Globo's festival of same name, 1975; First album released, 1976; Eponymous album brought national success, 1979; Signed to CBS and began recording in US, 1982; Returned to roots and Rio, 1986; Regular album releases ever since. *Recordings:* Albums include: A Voz E O Violao, 1976; Djavan, 1979; Alumbramento, 1980; Seduzir, 1981; Luz, 1982; Lilas, 1984; Meu Lado, 1986; Nao E Azul Mas E Mar, 1987; Oceano, 1989; Coisa De Acendar, 1992; Novena, 1994; Malasia, 1996; O Bicho Solto, 1998; Ao Vivo, 1999; Malageiro, 2001; Para Siempre, 2002. *Honours:* Latin Grammy, Best Brazilian Song, Acelerou, 2000. *Current Management:* Sony Music Brazil. *Internet:* www.djavan.com.br.

DJINDI Dilon, (Venancio de Conceicao Dilone Jinge); b. 14 Aug. 1927, Marracuene, Mozambique. Vocalist; Musician (guitar); Songwriter. *Musical Education:* Self-taught. *Career:* Started playing home-made guitar, 1939; Formed first group Estrela de Marracuene (Star of Marracuene), 1960; First recording for local radio broadcast, 1964; Member: Mabulu, 1998; First international appearance with Mabulu, 2001. *Recordings:* with Mabulu: Karimbo, 2000; Soul Marrabenta, 2001. *E-mail:* promusic@teledata.mz.

DMX (Earl Simmons), (DMX The Great, Dark Man X); b. 18 Dec. 1970, Baltimore, Maryland, USA. Rapper; Prod. *Career:* Became a DJ in the local projects; Released debut single on Columbia Records after winning Source magazine's Unsigned Hype Award, 1991; Signed to Ruff Ryders/Def Jam label, 1998; Debut album entered the Billboard chart at #1; Collaborations: Ja Rule; Jayo Felony; Ice Cube; Jay-Z; Eve; Limp Bizkit. *Recordings:* Albums: It's Dark and Hell Is Hot, Flesh of My Flesh – Blood of My Blood, 1998; And Then There Was X, 1999; The Great Depression, 2001; Singles: Get At Me Dog, I Can Feel It, 1998; Slippin', 1999; Party Up, 2000; What's My Name, 2001; Who We Be, 2002. *Honours:* Source Award, Artist of the Year, 1999. *Address:* c/o Def Jam, 825 Eighth Ave, New York, USA.

DOBES Pavel; b. 22 March 1949, Frydek-Mistek. Songwriter; Singer; Musician (Guitar). m. Ing Dana Hostinska, 3 s., 2 d. *Education:* Traditional School of Art. *Career:* Songs regularly transmitted on private and National Radio; About 100 concerts a year, at home and outside Czech Republic. *Compositions:* Jarmila; Blazek; Zapomenuty Trumf; Vite Vono Holky; Neco O Lasce; Zpatky do Trenek; Lisa z NYC. *Publications:* Still Life In A Company with Worms, Panton Records; Back To The Shorts, Monitor

Records; Something About America, Monitor EMI Records; Pilot Voyage, Monitor EMI. *Memberships:* OSA; Intergram. *Leisure interests:* Reading; Downhill Skiing; Swimming. *Current Management:* Monitor EMI, Kovarova 39, CZ 155 00 Prague 5; Pear Agency, Sekaninova 416, CZ 500 11 Hradec Kralove. *Address:* Pavel Dobes, Sekaninova 416, CZ 500 11 Hradec Kralove.

DOBRE Liudmila; b. 12 Sept. 1941, Chisinau, Moldavia. Agent; Impressario. m. Victor Dobre, 3 Feb. 1979, 1 s. *Musical Education:* 3 years supplementary music school, canto. *Career:* Worked for the state before the Revolution; Now Managing Director of own agency, with rock, folk, pop and easy listening artistes; Also worked as solo singer and in theatre in Arad, Romania. *Leisure interests:* Pictures; Tourism. *Address:* West Artistic Agency, Str Grigorescu 7, 2900 Arad, Romania.

DOC MULDOON (Wilbur); b. 24 April 1965, Walton, Wakefield, England. Musician (guitar); Vocalist. m. Jane Elaine Donali, 18 Oct. 1986, 1 s. *Education:* Hull College. *Musical Education:* Self-taught. *Career:* Lead guitarist, vocalist with Muldoon Brothers; Currently on permanent British tour; 3 tours, Southern Ireland; RTE TV (Ireland); 2 Danish visits including national TV; 1 visit to Sweden, includes Malmo Festival. *Recordings:* Album, video: Back O' The Barn; Singles: Cigarettes and Whiskey; Cotton Eyed Joe; Video album: Live At The Frontier. *Honours:* Best Country Music Newcomer Award, 1993. *Membership:* Musicians' Union. *Leisure interests:* Soccer; Squash. *Current Management:* International Artistes Music Ltd. *Address:* International Artistes Music Ltd, 2 Bond Terrace, Risworth St, Wakefield WF1 2HW, England.

DOKKEN Don; b. 29 June 1953, USA. Rock Vocalist. *Career:* Backing vocalist, Scorpions (recordings unreleased), 1982; Founder, lead singer, rock group Dokken, 1982–88; Solo artiste, 1989–; World-wide concerts. *Recordings:* Albums: with Dokken: Breaking The Chains, 1982; Tooth and Nail, 1984; Under Lock and Key, 1985; Back For The Attack, 1987; Beast From The East, 1988; Back On The Streets, 1989; Dysfunctional, 1995; One Live Night, 1995; Shadowlife, 1997; Very Best of Dokken, 1999; Erase The Slate, 1999; Live From The Sun, 2000; solo: Up From The Ashes, 1990. *Honours:* Multi-platinum discs.

DOKY Christian Minh; b. 7 Feb. 1969, Glostrup, Denmark. *Musical Education:* Self-taught. *Career:* Started on Bass, age 15 (acoustic bass, age 17); Classical piano, age 5–14; Working professionally, age 16, Copenhagen; Moved to New York City, 1988, age 19; Alumni, David Sanborn, Mike Stern, Ryuichi Sahamod; Signed with Blue Note Records, 1995. *Compositions:* Composed theme for Danish Crownprince Frederiks, 30 year Anniversary Portrait Movie. *Recordings:* Solo records: Appreciation, 1988; The Sequel, 1989; Letters, 1990; The Toronto Concort, 1990; Paris Nights, 1991; Doky Bros, 1996; Doky Bros 2, 1997; Minh, 1998. *Publication:* Tunes and Thoughts, 1998. *Honour:* Simon Spirs Award for Artist of the Year, 1991. *Current Management:* David Burrell, Tropix, New York City, USA. *Address:* c/o EMI Records, Vegnmageroade 10, Copenhagen 1120 K, Denmark.

DOKY Niels Lan; b. 3 Oct. 1963, Copenhagen, Denmark. Composer; Prod.; Jazz Musician (piano). m. Valentine Farlot, 3 June 1989, 1 s., 1 d. *Musical Education:* Degree, Berklee College of Music. *Career:* Solo artist; Co-leader of Doky Brothers Band (with brother Chris); Tours, concerts, television and radio appearances world-wide with: Randy Brecker; Joe Henderson; Charlie Haden; Jack DeJohnette; John Scofield; Producer for Verve. *Recordings:* 17 albums as Niels Lan Doky on jazz labels. *Publication:* Jazz Transcription; Compositions and Improvisations, 1996. *Honours:* Oscar Peterson Award, 1984; Simon Spies Musik Prize, 1993. *Memberships:* DJBFA; NCB; KODA. *Leisure interest:* Cooking. *Current Management:* Word of Mouth, Copenhagen. *Address:* 7 rue d'Espagne, 95470 Fosses, France.

DOLBY Ray; Engineer. *Education:* Physics, London, England. *Career:* Inventor, Dolby noise-reduction units; Opened laboratory, 1965; Dolby 'A' system sold to recordings studios; Work on noise-reduction for tape cassette and 8-track cartridge led to Dolby 'B' system, 1971; Now adopted world-wide; Adapted for cinema, 1978; Film soundtrack, Star Wars, first to be enhanced by Dolby noise reduction; Dolby systems upgraded for digital recordings, 1991.

DOLBY Thomas, (Thomas Morgan Robertson); b. 14 Oct. 1958, Cairo, Egypt. Musician (synthesizers); Singer; Songwriter; Programmer; Prod. m. Kathleen Beller. *Education:* Meteorology. *Musical Education:* Self-taught. *Career:* Built own synthesizers and PA system; Sound engineer, various groups; Co-founder, Camera Club, 1979; Musician with Lene Lovitch, 1980; Solo recording artiste, 1981–; Musician with David Bowie, Live Aid, Wembley, 1985. *Compositions include:* New Toy, Lene Lovitch; Film scores include: Howard – A New Breed of Hero. *Recordings:* Albums: The Golden Age of Wireless, 1982; The Flat Earth, 1985; Aliens Ate My Buick, 1988; Astronauts and Heretics, 1992; Gate to the Mind's Eye, 1994; Hyperactive, 1999; Singles: Urges; Europa and The Pirate Twins, 1981;

Windpower, 1982; She Blinded Me With Science, 1983; Hyperactive, 1984; Close But No Cigar, 1992; Contributor, recordings by: Foreigner; Joan Armatrading; M; Stevie Wonder; Grace Jones; Howard Jones; Herbie Hancock; Ofra Haza, Robyn Hitchcock, Belinda Carlisle, Dusty Springfield; Record producer for artists including: Joni Mitchell; Prefab Sprout. *Current Management:* Mary Coller Management. *Address:* 11288 Ventura Blvd, Suite 304B, Studio City, CA 91604, USA.

DOLENZ Mickey (George Michael Jr); b. 8 March 1945, Tarzana, Los Angeles, California, USA. Musician (drums); Singer; Actor; Prod.; Author. m. (1) Samantha Juste, 1968, divorced, (2) Trina Dow, 1977. *Education:* Architectural Design at Valley College and Los Angeles Technical Institute. *Career:* Child actor, television series, Circus Boy, 1956–58; Other acting roles in Peyton Place; Route 66; Mr Novak; As musician: Member, The One Nighters; The Missing Links; Member, The Monkees, 1966–70; 1985–91; Actor, Monkees TV series, 1966–68; Other television includes: 33 1/3 Revolutions Per Monkee TV Special, NBC; Film appearance, Head; Stage performances: Remains To Be Seen, 1970; The Point, 1978; Solo artiste, 1971–72; Broadway production of Grease, 1994; Member, Dolenz Jones Boyce and Hart, 1975–76; Also television director, producer, 1977–85; Voiceovers for: My 3 Sons; Scooby Doo; Adam 12; Devlin; Solo artiste, Rockin' Back To The 60s Tour, 1992; Monkees reunion concert, 1997. *Recordings:* Albums: The Monkees (No. 1, USA and UK), 1966; More of The Monkees (No. 1, USA and UK), 1967; Headquarters (No. 1, USA), 1967; Pisces, Aquarius, Capricorn and Jones (No. 1, UK); The Birds, The Bees and The Monkees, 1968; Head (soundtrack), 1969; The Monkees Greatest Hits, 1969; The Monkees Present, 1969; Instant Replay, 1969; Changes, 1970; Then and Now, 1986; Pool It!, 1987; Listen to the Band, 1991; Greatest Hits, 1995; Music Box, 2001; Hit singles: Last Train To Clarksville (No. 1, USA), 1966; I'm A Believer (No. 1, UK and US), 1966; I'm Not Your Steppin' Stone, 1967; A Little Bit Me, A Little Bit You, 1967; Alternate Title, 1967; Daydream Believer (No. 1, USA), 1967; Valleri, 1968; Tear Drop City, 1969. *Publication:* I'm A Beliver: My Life of Monkees, Music and Madness (autobiography), with Mark Bego. *Honours:* NARM Awards, Best Selling Group and Album, 1967; Emmy, Outstanding Comedy Series, 1967; 3 BMI Awards, 1968; Monkees Day, Atlanta, 1986; Star on Hollywood Walk of Fame, 1989. *Address:* c/o Nationwide Entertainment Services, 2756 N Green Valley Parkway, Suite 449, Las Vegas, NV 89014–2100, USA.

DOMAY Michael; b. 23 Oct. 1945, Newcastle-upon-Tyne, England. Medical Laboratory Scientist; Music teacher (guitar, bass, piano); Musician (guitar, bass). m. Stephanie Dennant, 18 April 1970, 2 s., 1 d. *Education:* Salisbury College; Bristol Polytechnic. *Musical Education:* Vocal training, church choir, 1955–59; Head soloist, 1957–59; Piano and theory training, 1955–60; Guitar (Spanish and electric), bass guitar, self-taught, 1960-. *Career:* Established rock bands: The Falcons, with Jim Cregan (Rod Stewart); Unit 4, with Greg Lake (Emerson Lake and Palmer) and John Wetton (Asia, King Crimson), 1960–69; Freelance bass guitar, guitar, in dance bands, pit orchestras, cabaret bands, 1970–; Private teacher, guitar, bass guitar, keyboards, piano; Many exam successes to date (students include Lydia Cascarino of Dear John; Richard Oakes of Suede); Examiner, Registry of Guitar Tutors. *Honour:* John-Louis Riccardi Finalist, Young Guitarist of the Year, 1998. *Memberships:* Musicians' Union; Registered teacher with Associated Board, Guild Hall, Rock School, RGT; Fellow, Institute of Biomedical Scientists; British Andrology Society; British Electrophoresis Society. *Leisure interests:* Sailing; Art; Music. *Current Management:* MD Music, Dorset. *Address:* 20 Argyll Rd, Parkstone, Dorset BH12 2DR, England.

DOMINIQUE Carl-Axel Martinelli; b. 1 Sept. 1939. m. Monica Dominique, 3 s. *Education:* Royal Academy of Music, Stockholm; Studied with Martin Canin, Juilliard School of Music, NY, 1965; Swedish Film School, 1969–70. *Career:* Concert Pianist, 1965; Soloist, All Swedish Symphony Orchestras, 1968; led jazz fusion group, Solar Plexus; Composer; Theatre Productions, Television Shows. *Compositions:* 31 Songs from Aniara; Music for Television, Film, Theatre; Songs and Orchestral Works. *Recordings:* Blinded; D Messiaen; Vingt Regards Sur L'Enfant Jesus; Complete Bird Music for Piano Solo (BIS). *Publications:* We Play Together, Co Written with Monica Dominique. *Honours:* Expressen Musical Prize, 1984. *Memberships:* Swedish Composers of Popular Music. *Leisure interests:* Mushroom Excursions. *Current Management:* The music Production Company, Dominique Musik AB. *Internet:* www.dominiquemusik.se.

DOMINIQUE Monica; b. 20 July 1940, Sweden. m. Carl-Axel Dominique, 3 s. *Education:* Royal Academy of Music, Stockholm. *Career:* Solo Piano Program, Swedish Radio; Played with Best Swedish Singers, Theatres, Concert Halls, Radio, Television; Joined Vocalgroup Gals and Pals, 1967; Cabaret Artist, Solo Singer and Actress, 1970–75; Led Jazz Fusion Group, Solar Plexus. *Compositions:* Swedish Love in Southern Bronx; Inside The Rainbow; No Man Is An Island; Oh, What a Wonderful World; ODA; Tillagnan. *Recordings:* Monica-Monica; Tillagnan; Inside the Rainbow. *Publications:* We Play Together, Co Written with C A Dominique. *Honours:* Expressen Musical Prize, 1994; The Evert Taube Award, 1994.

Memberships: Swedish Composers of Popular Music; Swedish Jazz Academy; Swedish Jazz Musicians. *Leisure interests:* Fishing; Mushroom Excursions. *Current Management:* Music Production Company, Dominique Musik AB. *Internet:* www.dominiquemusik.se.

DOMINO Fats (Antoine); b. 26 Feb. 1928, New Orleans, USA. Musician (piano); Singer; Songwriter. *Musical Education:* Piano lessons with Harrison Verrett. *Career:* Legendary R & B performer, 1949–; Regular US R & B tours, 1954–; Debut UK performance, 1967; Long-standing partnership with bandleader, arranger, writer Dave Bartholomew; Film appearances: Shake, Rattle and Roll; Jamboree; The Big Beat; The Girl Can't Help It; Any Which Way You Can; Television special, Fats Domino and Friends, 1987. *Recordings:* Numerous hit singles include: The Fat Man; Every Night About This Time; Goin' Home; Don't You Know; Goin' To The River; Please Don't Leave Me; Ain't That A Shame; You Done Me Wrong; Walking To New Orleans; I'm In Love Again; Blueberry Hill; My Girl Josephine; Valley of Tears; Blue Monday; Whole Lotta Loving; I Want To Walk You Home; Be My Guest; Albums: Carry On Rockin', 1955; Fats Domino – Rock and Rollin', 1956; This Is Fats Domino!, 1957; Here Stands Fats Domino, 1958; Fabulous Mr D, 1958; Let's Play Fats Domino, 1959; Fats Domino Sings, 1960; I Miss You So, 1961; Twistin' The Stomp, 1962; Just Domino, 1963; Here Comes Fats Domino, 1963; Fats On Fire, 1964; Fats Domino '65, 1965; Getaway With Fats Domino, 1966; Fats Domino, 1966; Stompin' Fats Domino, 1967; Trouble In Mind, Fats Is Back, 1968; Very Best Of, 1970; Sleeping On The Job, 1979; My Blue Heaven, 1990; They Call Me The Fat Man, 1991; Whole Lotta Loving, 1992; Greatest Hits: Live, 1992; Out of New Orleans, 1993; Concert Collection: Blueberry Hill, 1993; Christmas is a Special Day, 1993; The Fats Man, 1995; Fat Man Sings, 1996; You Can Call Me Fats, 1997; Gold Collection, 1998; Live at Gilley's 1999; Domino Effect, 1999; Blast From The Past, 2001. *Honours:* Inducted, Rock and Roll Hall of Fame, 1986; Grammy, Lifetime Achievement Award, 1987. *Current Management:* Al Embry International. *Address:* PO Box 23162, Nashville, TN 37202, USA.

DONALDSON John; b. 29 June 1954, London. Composer; Musician (Piano). m. Agotha Coffey, 2 s., 1 d. *Education:* Anglia University. *Career:* US Broadcasts With Eddie Henderson, Richie Cole; BBC With Septpiece, Dick Pearce Quartet; Film, Painted Lady With Helen Mirren; Festivals Include, San Francisco, San Sebastian, Bath, London, Appleby, Malta. *Compositions:* Cakes and Wine; Medjugorje; Carneo; Django's Dilemma; Mirror Image; HRD; Plain Song; Balance. *Recordings:* Septpiece; Sing The Line; Meeting In Brooklyn. *Honours:* Best Soloist, 1980; Cambridge University Press Prize for Performance, 1982. *Memberships:* PRS; Musicians Union. *Current Management:* Clever Dick Management. *Address:* 22 Albany Rd, St Leonards On Sea, E Sussex TN38 0LN.

DONALDSON Louis (Lou); b. 1 Nov. 1926, Badin, North Carolina, USA. Jazz Musician (alto saxophone). m. Maker, 1950, 2 d. *Education:* Political Science, North Carolina A & T University. *Musical Education:* Began clarinet at age 9. *Career:* Played in Navy band, 1945; Moved to New York, 1950; Played with numerous notable musicians including: Charlie Parker; Sonny Stitt; Bud Powell; Milt Jackson; Philly Joe Jones; Horace Silver; Clifford Brown; Member, Art Blakey's Jazz Messengers; Toured extensively in Europe and Japan. *Recordings:* Albums: Blues Walk, No 1 album; Alligator Boogaloo; New Faces, New Sounds; A Night at Birdland; Her 'Tis Midnight Creeper; Hot Dog; Sassy Soul Strut; Forgotten Man; Birdseed; Caracas; Sweet Papa Lou; Sentimental Journey; with Jimmy Smith: The Sermon. *Honours include:* Charlie Parker Memorial Medal; Baseball field named in his honour, Badin, North Carolina; Scholarship established in his name, North Caroline AandT University. *Current Management:* Maxine S Harvard Unlimited. *Address:* c/o Maxine S Harvard Unlimited, 7942 W Bell Rd, Suite C-5, Glendale, AZ 85308, USA.

DONEGAN Lonnie (Anthony); b. 29 April 1931, Glasgow, Scotland. Skiffle Musician (guitar, banjo). *Career:* Musician, jazz bands, 1949–53; Member, Chris Barber's Jazz band, 1954; Leader, Lonnie Donegan Skiffle Group, 1955–; Owner, publishing company, Tyler Music; Regular panelist, New Faces talent show, ITV, 1970s; Semi-retirement, 1976–; Founder, Donegan's Dancing Sunshine, 1986-. *Recordings:* Singles include: Rock Island Line, 1956; Lost John, 1956; Skiffle Session, 1956; Bring A Little Water Sylvie, 1956; Don't You Rock Me Daddy-O, 1957; Cumberland Gap (No. 1, UK), 1957; Puttin' On The Style/Gamblin' Man (No. 1, UK), 1957; My Dixie Darling, 1957; Jack O'Diamonds, 1957; Grand Coolie Dam, 1958; Sally Don't You Grieve, 1958; Tom Dooley, 1958; Does Your Chewing Gum Lose Its Flavour (On The Bedpost Overnight), 1959; Fort Worth, 1959; Battle of New Orleans, 1959; Sal's Got A Sugar Lip, 1959; San Miguel, 1959; My Old Man's A Dustman (No. 1, UK), 1960; I Wanna Go Home, 1960; Lorelei, 1960; Lively, 1960; Have A Drink On Me, 1961; Michael Row The Boat, 1961; The Comancheros, 1962; The Party's Over, 1962; Pick a Bale of Cotton, 1962; Albums: Lonnie Donegan Showcase, 1957; Putting On The Style, 1957; A Golden Age of Donegan, 1962; A Golden Age of Donegan Vol. 2, 1963; Putting On The Style, 1978; Sundown, 1979; Jubilee Concert, 1981; Golden Hour of Lonnie Donegan, 1991; Rare and Unissued, 1985; Rock Island Line, 1985; Muleskinner Blues, 1999; The Skiffle Sessions (with Van Morrison and Chris Barber), 2000. *Honour:* First UK act to enter charts at No. 1, My Old Man's A Dustman, 1960. *Current Management:* Cromwell Management, 4–5 High St, Huntingdon, Cambs PE18 6TE, England.

DONELIAN Armen; b. 1 Dec. 1950, New York, New York, USA. Musician (Piano); Composer; Bandleader; Author. *Education:* Artists' Certificate, Westchester Conservatory of Music; Bachelor of Music, Columbia University; Private study with Carl Bamberger (conducting), Ludmila Ulehla (harmonic analysis), Richard Beirach (jazz piano), Harold Seletsky (Schoenberg harmony and counterpoint). *Career:* Performed with Sonny Rolins, Chet Baker, Mongo Santamaria, Billy Harper, Lionel Hampton, Paquito D'Rivera, Joe Williams and other jazz musicians in festivals, concerts, clubs, TV and radio, world-wide, 1975-. *Compositions:* Over 40 recorded by various artists; Several published arrangements including Metropolitan Madness, Harem Girl, Stargazer. *Recordings:* Stargazer; A Reverie; Secrets; The Wayfarer; Trio '87. *Publications:* Training the Ear, 1992; Rutgers Annual Review of Jazz Studies, 1994–95; Downbeat, 1997–98; Keyboard, 1997. *Honours:* 6 Jazz Performance Fellowships, National Endowment for the Arts, 1984, 1987, 1990, 1992, 1994, 1996. *Leisure interests:* Meditation; Yoga. *Current Management:* Donelian Music, New Jersey. *Address:* 37 Overlook Ave, West Orange, NJ 07052, USA.

DONELLY Tanya; b. 14 July 1966, Newport, RI, USA. Singer; Songwriter; Musician (guitar). m. Dean Fisher, 22 Sept. 1996. *Career:* Founding Member, Throwing Muses, 1985–91; Member, The Breeders, 1989–92; Member, Belly, 1992–96; Solo career, 1996–; Appearances on David Letterman (USA); The Tonight Show (USA); Conan O'Brien (USA); The Word (England); The Later Show (England); Mark Radcliffe (England); The Black Sessions (France); Support tour to REM. *Recordings:* with Throwing Muses: Singles: Chains Changed, 1987; Dizzy, 1989; Counting Backwards, 1991; Not Too Soon, 1991; Albums: Throwing Muses, 1986; The Fat Skier, 1987; House Tornado, 1988, Hunkpapa, 1989; The Real Ramona, 1991; with The Breeders: Pod, 1990, Safari EP, 1992; With Belly: Singles: Slowdust, 1992; Gepetto, 1992; Feed The Tree, 1993; Now They'll Sleep, 1995; Seal My Fate, 1995; Albums: Star (No. 2, UK), 1993; King, 1995; Solo career: Singles: Sliding and Driving, 1996; Pretty Deep, 1997; The Bright Light, 1997; Sleepwalk, 2001; Albums: Lovesongs for Underdogs, 1997; Beauty Sleep, 2002. *Honours:* Grammy Nominations for Best Alternative Album, 1993, Best New Artist, 1993. *Current Management:* Gary Smith. *Address:* Fort Apache, One Camp St, Suite 2, Cambridge, MA 02140, USA.

DONNELLY Johnny; b. 14 Feb. 1972, Dublin, Ireland. Musician (drums). *Career:* Member, The Saw Doctors; Tours: Ireland; UK; Europe; USA; Canada; Australia; Television and radio appearances include: BBC Late Show; Documentary, Saw Doctors, RTE; Channel 4; BBC Radio 1. *Recordings:* Albums: If This Is Rock and Roll I Want My Old Job Back; All The Way From Tuam. *Honours:* Best Band; Best Live Band; Biggest selling single ever in Ireland. *Memberships:* PRS; Musicians' Union. *Leisure interests:* Running; Walking by the sea. *Current Management:* Ollie Jennings. *Address:* 13 St Mary's Terrace, Taylors Hill, Galway City, Ireland.

DONNELLY Kerr; b. 1 May 1964, Lanarkshire, Scotland. Singer; Songwriter; Entertainer; Musician (guitar). m. Lynn Fullwood, 1 s., 2 d. *Career:* Member: Legend, 1978; Tennessee Flash Cats, 1982; Crazy Wolf, 1982; Kerr Donnelly Band, 1987–; Radio Interviews: BBC Radio East Midlands; BBC Radio Scotland; CMR; World-wide radio airplay; Concerts: Americana – Country in The Park (Biggest UK open-air country music festival); Set up KDML record label. *Compositions:* over 287 songs including: Country Boy; One Burger One Coke; Thats Life; Sneakin 'n' Cheatin; Rattlesnake Rock; As The Curtain Falls, 1999; If I Knew Then What I Know Now, Homewrecker, 2000. *Recordings:* Albums: No Help Needed, 1987; EPs and Early Days, Haunted Heart, 1992; Rough Cuts, Country Rocker, 1995; The Singles and Album Picks, 1997; Guess Who?, 1998; As The Curtain Falls 20/21, 1999; That's Right, 2001. *Memberships:* International Songwriters Asscn; British Country Music Asscn. *Leisure interests:* Songwriting; Films; Reading; Writing Stories. *Current Management:* KDML Records and Publishing, 36 Sankey Rd, Blackfords Estate, Cannock, Staffs, WS11 2DT, England. *Internet:* www.kerr-donnelly.countrymusic.co.uk.

DONNER Otto; b. 16 Nov. 1939, Tampere, Finland. Composer; Musician (trumpet). *Musical Education:* Sibelius Academy, Helsinki; Studied with Ligeti. *Career:* Began jazz career, Tampere, late 1950s; Worked at Siemens electronic music studios, Germany; Co-leader, jazz quintet with Christian Schwindt; Worked with American composer Terry Riley; Founder, record label Love Records, 1966–79; Director, Finnish Radio's entertainment section, 1970–74; Leader, The Otto Donner Treatment; Performing new material with own band. *Compositions include:* Music for numerous Finnish films; Dalens Ande (The Spirit of The Valley) suite; Pieces for UMO (New Music Orchestra). *Recordings:* Album: Quintet with Christian Schwindt: Friends and Relatives; with The Otto Donner Treatment: En

Soisi Sen Päättyvän, 1970; Kuinka Myohään Valvoo Blues?, 1980. *Address:* Jomalvik, 10600 Tammisaari, Finland.

DONOHOE David; b. 22 May 1940, Ashton-Under-Lyme, Lancashire, England. Musician (trombone); Bandleader. m. Victoria Hancock, 8 Sept. 1962, 2 s., 2 d. *Education:* Regional College of Art, Manchester (part time). *Musical Education:* Private tuition, 1 year; Brass Band, 1 year. *Career:* Concert with Woody Allen (actor, clarinet player), New Orleans Festival, 1971; 6 times guest, radio chat shows; 6 television appearances; Tour of USA with International Band including: Butch Thompson, Sammy Rimmington, 1977; 10 appearances, Ascona Festa, New Orleans Music; Switzerland; 3 tours with bands from New Orleans, Switzerland. *Recordings:* 10 albums, 6 in own name. *Honours:* Ambassador of Ninove, Belgium, for services to music, 1989. *Membership:* Musicians' Union. *Leisure interests:* Running; Researching American Old West; Old films. *Current Management:* Terry Dash Management, Herts. *Address:* 5 Saddleworth Fold, Uppermill, Oldham OL3 6EQ, England.

DONOVAN (Donovan Leitch); b. 10 May 1946, Maryhill, Glasgow, Scotland. Folk Singer; Songwriter. m. Linda Lawrence, Oct. 1970, 1 s., 2 d. *Career:* Appearances include: NME Poll Winners Concert, Wembley, 1965; Newport Folk Festival, with Bob Dylan, 1965; World-wide concerts, tours include: Royal Albert Hall, 1967; National Blues Festival, Windsor, 1967; International Film Festival, Cannes, France, 1968; Woburn Music Festival, 1968; Carnegie Hall, New York, 1968; Bath Festival, 1970; Isle of Wight Festival, 1970; Tour, Australia and New Zealand, 1975; Edinburgh Festival, 1980; Support to Happy Mondays, Wembley Arena, 1990; British tour, 1992. *Compositions include:* Own recorded songs; Songs for film: If It's Tuesday It Must Be Belgium, 1969; The Pied Piper, 1971; Film score, Brother Sun, Sister Moon, 1972. *Recordings:* Singles include: Catch The Wind, 1965; Colours, 1965; Universal Soldier, 1965; Sunshine Superman, 1966; Mellow Yellow, 1966; There Is A Mountain, 1967; Jennifer Juniper, 1968; Hurdy Gurdy Man, 1968; Atlantis, 1969; Barabajagal (Love Is Hot), with the Jeff Beck Group, 1969; Albums include: What's Bin Did and What's Bin Hid, 1965; Catch The Wind, 1965; Fairy Tale, 1965; Sunshine Superman, 1966; The Real Donovan, 1966; Mellow Yellow, 1967; Universal Soldier, 1967; A Gift From A Flower To A Garden, 1968; Like It Is, Was and Evermore Shall Be, 1968; Donovan In Concert, 1968; Barabajagal, 1969; The Best of Donovan, 1969; Open Road, 1970; Donovan P Leitch, 1970; HMS Donovan, 1971; Cosmic Wheels, 1973; Essence To Essence, 1974; 7-Tease, 1974; Slow Down World, 1976; Donovan, 1977; Neutronica, 1980; Love Is The Only Feeling, 1980; Lady of The Stars, 1983; Rising, 1990; Troubadour – The Definitive Collection 1964–76, 1993; Island of Circles, 1991; Live in Concert, 1992; Originals, 1995; Sutras, 1996. *Current Management:* Monarch Productions, 8803 Mayne Street, Bellflower, CA 90706, USA.

DONOVAN Ida M; b. 6 Sept. 1948, Canada. Song Writer; Musician. m. Edwin Donovan, 1 s., 4 d. *Musical Education:* Self-taught. *Career:* Country Gospel Group. *Memberships:* Canadian County Music Asscn. *Leisure interests:* Acting; Writing. *Address:* 211 Macintyre Lane, Glace Bay, NS Canada B1A 4S1.

DONOVAN Jason; b. 1 June 1968, Melbourne, Australia. Singer; Actor. *Career:* Actor, Australian television series: Skyways, 1979; I Can Jump Puddles, 1979; Neighbours, 1985–89; Heroes, 1988; Shadows of The Heart, 1988; Stage appearances: Lead role, Joseph and The Amazing Technicolour Dreamcoat, London Palladium, 1991–92; Appeared in Rocky Horror Picture Show, West End; Concert tours, Australia; Far East; Europe. *Recordings:* Albums include: Ten Good Reasons, 1989; Between The Lines, 1990; Joseph and The Amazing Technicolour Dreamcoat, 1991; Greatest Hits, 1991 (reissued 1999); Hit singles include: Nothing Can Divide Us, 1988; Especially For You (duet with Kylie Minogue) (No. 1, UK), 1988; Too Many Broken Hearts (No. 1, UK), 1989; Sealed With A Kiss (No. 1, UK), 1989; Everyday, 1989; Hang On To Your Love, 1990; Another Night, 1990; Rhythm of The Rain, 1990; Doing Fine, 1990; Any Dream Will Do (No. 1, UK), 1991; Happy Together, 1991; Dream, 1991; RSVP, 1991; Rough Diamonds, 1994. *Honours:* Numerous show business awards. *Leisure interests:* Surfing; Biographies. *Address:* Richard East Productions Pty Ltd, Toorak Rd, South Yarra, VIC 3141, Australia.

DONY; Vocalist; Musician (bass); Songwriter; Arranger. *Career:* Member, Atlas, Bulgaria, 1987–93; Formed Dony and Momchil, 1993–; Numerous tours, Bulgaria, include Sofia National Theatre (unplugged with National Philharmony), 1995. *Recordings:* with Atlas: Doll; with Dony and Momchil: CD Albums: The Album!, 1993; The Second One, 1994. *Honours:* Best Band, Atlas, 1991; Orpheus: Best Single: The Little Prince; Best Video For Duo Or A Group.

DOONICAN Val (Michael Valentine); b. 3 Feb. 1927, Waterford, Ireland. Singer; Musician (guitar, mandolin); Presenter. *Musical Education:* Guitar, mandolin. *Career:* Member, various Irish bands; Member, vocal group The Four Ramblers; Group had radio series over 2 years, Riders of The Range, BBC, 1951; Solo artiste, late 1950s-; Television appearances: Beauty Box; Sunday Night At The London Palladium, 1964; Own show, 1964–88; Radio includes: Dreamy Afternoon; A Date With Val; Videos, Songs from My Sketchbook – Memories are Made of This; Thank You For The Music, 1993. *Recordings:* 30 albums include: Val Doonican Rocks But Gently, 1967; Song Sung Blue, 1974; Some of My Best Friends Are Songs, 1977; By Request, 1987; Love Songs, 1999; Singles include: Walk Tall, 1964; The Special Years, 1965; Elusive Butterfly, 1966; What Would I Be (No. 2, UK), 1966; Memories Are Made of This, 1967; If The Whole World Stopped Loving, 1967; If I Knew Then What I Know Now, 1968; Morning, 1971. *Publication:* Walking Tall The Special Years. *Honours:* TV Personality of the Year (3 times). *Current Management:* Bernard Lee Management. *Address:* Moorcroft Lodge, Fairleigh Common, Warlingham, Surrey CR3 9PE, England.

DORAN Brian John; b. 2 March 1965, Croydon, Surrey, England. Singer; Songwriter; Musician (guitar, flute). m. Jane Kendrick, 19 Aug. 1994. *Education:* Diploma in dispensing optics. *Musical Education:* Grade 8 theory, singing, flute; Self-taught guitar. *Career:* Lead singer, Orchid Waltz, 1983–86; Played all over England; Acoustic duo Richard III's with Lee Collinson (now popular folk artist); Solo acoustic world tour, 1990–91; Currently solo and session work. *Composition:* Song: Lady of The 80s, written for Edinburgh Festival. *Recordings:* Orchid Waltz; Trident (album not released); Solo album: Acoustics, 1991; Backing vocals, Compassion, Keith Hancock, 1993. *Membership:* Branch committee mem., Musicians' Union. *Leisure interests:* Walking; Cinema; Opera; Theatre. *Current Management:* 124 Lisbon Ave, Twickenham, Middlesex TW2 5HN, England.

DORE Michael; b. Cleethorpes, Lincolnshire, England. Singer; Musician (piano). *Musical Education:* Graduate, Guildhall School of Music and Drama, (GGSM London); Holder of Postgraduate Certificate In Education (PGCE). *Career:* Member, Swingle Singers, 1981–87; Electric Phoenix, Chameleon; Concert soloist with: BBC Radio 2; London Symphony Orchestra; Los Angeles Philharmonic; Swedish National Radio; Royal Variety Performances; Music of Andrew Lloyd Webber; Jesus Christ Superstar (Peter); Magic of The Musicals; Rogers and Hammerstein At The Barbican; Worked for Royal National Theatre, Royal Shakespeare Company; Nederlands Dans Theater; West End credits include: Cats; Starlight Express; Grease; Debuts: Carnegie Hall (New York); Royal Albert Hall Proms, 1994; One Man Show, 1995. *Recordings:* Solo Albums with BBC Concert Orchestra: West Side Story, 1993; Crazy for Gershwin; Let's Face the Music, tribute to Fred Astaire; Hits of Broadway; Love and Romance; Passion, original London cast; Wonderful Town, with Simon Rattle; as session singer: commercials, films, television; Every Song Has Its Play with Gilbert O'Sullivan (manager); Numerous with Swingle Singers; with Berio: Sinfonia, Canticum. *Memberships:* British Actors Equity; Musicians' Union. *Current Management:* c/o British Actors Equity Asscn. *Address:* Guildhouse, Upper St Martins Lane, London WC2H 9EG, England.

DORGE Pierre; b. 28 Feb. 1946, Frederiksberg, Denmark. Composer; Conductor; Musician (guitar). m. Irene Becker, 24 Aug. 1985. *Musical Education:* Music, KDAS, College of Copenhagen. *Career:* Formed own group, Copenhagen Jazz Quintet, 1960; Formed New Jungle Orchestra, 1980; Recorded with: Niels-Henning Orsted Petersen; John Tchicai; Svend Asmussen; Marilyn Mazur; Johnny Dyani; Tours: Europe; US; Canada; Indonesia; Ghana; USSR; Australasia. *Composition:* Symphony in C, 1994. *Recordings include:* with New Jungle Orchestra: Pierre Dorge and New Jungle Orchestra, 1982; Brikama, 1984; Even The Moon Is Dancing, 1985; Johnny Lives, 1987; Different Places – Different Bananas, 1989; Peer Gynt, 1989; Live in Chicago, 1991; David Murray and the Jazzpar Prize, 1992; Karawane, 1993; Polar Jungle Orchestra, 1994; Absurd Bird, 1995; Music from the Danish Jungle, 1996; China Jungle, 1997; Giraf, 1999; Swinging Europe, 1999. *Honours:* Grants, Danish Arts Council; JASA prize, 1985. *Leisure interest:* All music. *Current Management:* Copenhagen Concerts.

DORNEY Tim; b. 30 March 1965, Ascot, Berkshire, England. Musician (Keyboards). *Career:* Former member, Flowered Up; Formed Republica; Numerous TV appearances and festival dates; Contributed track Are Friends Electric for Gary Numan tribute album, 1997. *Recordings:* with Flowered Up: Singles: It's On, 1990; Phobia, 1990; Take It, 1991; Weekender, 1992; Albums: A Life With Brian, 1991; with Republica: Singles: Out of This World, 1994; Bloke, 1994; Ready to Go, 1996; Drop Dead Gorgeous, 1996; From the Rush Hour With Love, 1998; Albums: Republica, 1996; Speed Ballads, 1998.

DORONJGA Sinisa; b. 15 March 1942, Zagreb, Croatia. Musician; Singer; Entertainer; Actor. m. Bosiljka Kello, 22 March 1969, 1 s., 1 d. *Musical Education:* Secondary music school. *Career:* Singer, musician, Bijele Strijele, 1961; World tour, 1968–69; Producer, composer, songwriter, arranger, Suzy record label; Television entertainer. *Recordings:* Hit album: Domestic songs, Platinum, 1979; 7 Gold albums, 1979–95; Main songs from albums: Hrvatska Mati; Boze Dragi Sacuvaj Hrvate; Hrvatski Sinovi. *Publications:* Book, video, Dosel Je Sv Martin (St Martin)

traditional ceremony in Croatia. *Honours:* Croatian Government and Croatan Music AID Awards, Order for a lifetime of music work. *Membership:* General secretary, Croatian Musicians' Union. *Leisure interests:* Hunting; Fishing; Cooking. *Current Management:* Simpy and Friends Production and Management. *Address:* Sinisa Doronjga, Siget 18 b/v, 10020 Zagreb, Croatia.

DOROUGH Howard Dwaine, (Howie D); b. 22 Aug. 1973, Orlando, Florida, USA. Singer. *Career:* Acting roles in Cop and Parenthood films; Community Theatre; Member, Backstreet Boys; Numerous television appearances, tours and hit singles. *Recordings:* Singles: We've Got it Going On, 1995; Quit Playing Games, 1998; I'll Never Break Your Heart, 1998; Everybody, 1998; As Long As You Love Me, 1998; Anywhere for You, 1998; All I Have to Give, 1998; I Want It That Way, 1999; Albums: Backstreet Boys, 1996; Live in Concert, 1998; Backstreet's Back, 1998; Millennium, 1999. *Leisure interests:* Weightlifting; Water skiing; Dancing; Racquetball; Films.

DORSET Ray; b. 21 March 1946, Ashford, Kent, England. Musician (guitar); Vocalist. *Career:* Member, Mungo Jerry, 1970–; Appearances include: Hollywood Pop Festival, Staffordshire, 1970; Briefly member, Katmandu, with Peter Green, 1986. Compositons include: Feels Like I'm In Love, Kelly Marie (No. 1, UK), 1980. *Recordings:* Albums: Mungo Jerry, 1970; Electronically Tested, 1971; You Don't Have To Be In The Army To Fight In The War, 1971; Boot Power, 1972; Greatest Hits, 1973; Golden Hour, 1974; Long Legged Woman, 1974; Impala Saga, 1976; Lovin' In The Alleys, Fightin' In The Streets, 1977; File, 1977; Ray Dorset and Mungo Jerry, 1978; Six Aside, 1979; Together Again, 1981; The Early Years, 1992; Best of Mungo Jerry, 1998; Solo album: Cold Blue Excursion, 1972; with Katmandu: A Case For The Blues, 1986; Singles include: In The Summertime (No. 1, UK), 1970; Baby Jump (No. 1, UK), 1971; Lady Rose, 1971; You Don't Have To Be In The Army To Fight In The War, 1971; Alright Alright Alright, 1973; Longlegged Woman Dressed In Black, 1974. *Address:* c/o Hal Carter Organisation, 101 Hazelwood Lane, London N13 5HQ, England.

DORUZKA David; b. 25 Jan. 1980, Prague, Czech Republic. *Education:* Private studies with 3 Prague-based guitar teachers; Berklee College Jazz Clinic, Frydlant, Czech Republic, 1997. *Career:* Numerous performances at Prague jazz clubs with leading Czech jazz musicians; Leader of band, Eye of the Hurricane and member of Jaromir Honzak Trio; Performances at Montréal Jazz Festival, 1996, with Honzak Trio; Performances in New York City, Stockholm, Warsaw and many festivals in Czech Republic. *Compositions:* Forgotten Time, on You Know What I Mean, 1997; Was This The Last Time, on Czech Radio, 1996; 12 + 3/4, Ups and Downs, Sincerely, Czech Radio, 1998. *Recordings:* Karel Ruzicka Jr: You Know What I Mean, 1997; Several radio and TV broadcasts. *Honours:* Jazz Kaja Award, Best Talent of the Year, Czech Jazz Society, 1995; You Know What I Mean, CD of the Year, 1997. *Membership:* Czech Jazz Society. *Leisure interests:* Literature; Mountain hiking; Swimming. *Address:* Zeleny pruh 14, 14700 Prague 4, Czech Republic.

DORUZKA Lubomir; b. 18 March 1924, Prague. Jazz Writer. m. Blazena Doruzkova, 1 s. *Education:* Charles University, Prague. *Career:* Editor of Music Journals; International Copyright Manager, Supraphon Prague; Lecturer, Prague Conservatoire. *Publications:* Karel Vacek Biography; Popular Music Industry, Business, Art; Panorama of Memoirs. *Honours:* Personality of the Year, 1998. *Memberships:* International Jazz Federation. *Leisure interests:* Moutain Hiking. *Address:* 14 Zeleny Pruh, 146 00 Prague 4, Czech Republic.

DOSS Buster (Colonel); b. 4 Feb. 1925, Jefferson, Texas, USA. Entertainer; Prod.; Writer. m. Barbara Ann Solomon, 14 April 1967, 1 s., 1 d. *Education:* College. *Musical Education:* Began playing mandolin age 4, guitar, age 5, bass, age 6. *Career:* Writer, over 500 songs recorded by artists including: Billy Walker; Billy Grammer; Tex Ritter; Marty Robbins; Producer, 1949-, over 2000 albums; Manager, Grand Ole Opry acts; Owned 7 radio stations; 7 newspapers; Owner, record labels; Owner, 3 publishing companies; Co-owner, 7 publishing companies; Owner, Theme Parks: Codyland, Missouri; Six Shooter Junction, Texas; Television shows: Star of The Cactus Kid; Magic on Ed Sullivan Show, Tonight Show; Owned Country Music theatres: Missouri; Harlingen, Texas; Ashdown, Arkansas; Mt Pleasant, Athens; Georgetown, Texas; Winchester (Tennessee); Moved to Shreveport, for Louisiana Hayride, 1948, included Kitty Wells, Elvis Presley, Jim Reeves as an announcer; Numerous appearances, 1949-, Grand Ole Opry. *Publications:* Owner The Country Gazette. *Honours:* Over 1000 awards for excellence in show business, including: Pioneer Award and Living Legend, CMA of America. *Membership:* BMI. *Leisure interest:* Writing songs. *Current Management:* Colonel Buster Doss Presents. *Address:* 341 Billy Goat Hill Rd, Winchester, TN 37398, USA.

DOUCET Michael Louis; b. 14 Feb. 1951, LaFayette, Louisiana, USA. Cajun Musician (fiddle, guitar, bass, mandolin, piano). m. Sharon Lee Arms, 14 Feb. 1951, 2 s., 1 d. *Education:* BS, English Major, Louisiana

State University, 1973. *Career:* First band Coteau dissolved 1977; Formed Beausoleil, 1975; Projects with Savoy-Doucet band and solo work; Performed at Jimmy Carter's inaugural gala, 1977; World-wide tours with Beausoleil, including Carnegie Hall, New York, 1982; Great American Music Hall, San Francisco, 1988; Numerous television and radio appearances: Austin City Limits; Today Show; Conan O'Brien; Good Morning; Prairie Home Companion. *Compositions:* Danse De La Vie; Zydeco Gris Gris; L'Ouragon; Music for films: Belizaire The Cajun, 1985; The Big Easy, 1987. *Recordings:* Solo albums: Beau Solo; Cajun Fiddle; Beausoleil albums include: Bayou Boogie, 1985; Cajun Conja, 1991; Danse De La Vie, 1993; L'Echo, 1994; Mad Reel, 1994; 3 albums with Savoy-Doucet. *Honours:* Master Folk Musician, Louisiana; National Endowment for the Arts Grant, 1975; 6 Grammy Nominations with Beausoleil; First Clifton Chenier Award, 1990. *Leisure interests:* Chess; Research; French; Poetry. *Current Management:* The Rosebud Agency. *Address:* PO Box 170429, San Francisco, CA 94117, USA.

DOUDELLE Jacques; b. 4 July 1949, Paris, France. Musician (soprano and tenor saxophones); Bandleader. *Musical Education:* Self-taught. *Career:* Formed Jacques Doudelle Orchestra, Festival du Marais, Paris, 1975; Numerous appearances across France include: Casino de Paris; Marciac Jazz Festival (3 times); Sidney Bechet Night, 1993, 1994; Festivals in Italy; Belgium; Switzerland; Germany; Greece; Turkey; Television: Accords Parfaits, with Pierre Petit; Jazz 6, with Philippe Adler; Sacrée Soirée, with Jean-Pierre Foucault. *Compositions include:* T'Exagères; Moulin à Légumes; Détournement de Mineur; Coeur de Perles; Film music: Des Enfants Gâtés; Félicité. *Recordings:* 5 albums, 1978–95; Recordings with Roger Guerin; Jean Lou Longnon; Fabrice Eulry; Sidney Bechet Jr. *Honours:* Laureate, Concours National de Jazz de la Défense, 1986. *Membership:* President, Sidney Bechet Academy. *Address:* Jacques Doudelle Jazz Orchestra, 58 Ave Philippe de Girard, 93420 Villepinte, France.

DOUGLAS John Henry; b. 19 June 1920. Composer; Arranger; Conductor. m. Babs, deceased, 1 s., 1 d. *Musical Education:* Self-taught. *Career:* Pianist, Neville Hughes Sextet, 1939; Formed own RAF dance band; Arranging for many dance bands including: Bert Ambrose, Ted Heath and Edmundo Ros; Staff Arranger to George Elrick; Pianist, Arranger with the Cyril Stapleton Band; Staff Arranger, music publishers, 1948; Scoring and conducting vocal backings for Decca, 1952, first hit was Tex Ritter's High Noon; 1960: Scored and conducted 80 LPs for RCA; Composing and scoring for films; Own BBC Radio programme, Swing Song, ran for 2 years; Composed and arranged the wall-to-wall music for the American TV animation series Spiderman and His Amazing Friends, Dungeons and Dragons, The Incredible Hulk, The Transformers; Arranging, TV shows for international stars including Shirley Jones, Howard Keel, Vera Lynn, Shirley Bassey. *Recordings include:* It's Magic, CD, cassette. *Honours:* Melody Maker Jazz Jamboree Award; Gold Disc. *Address:* 39 Tadorne Rd, Tadworth, Surrey KT20 5TF, England.

DOUGLAS Leslie; b. 1 May 1914, London, England. Singer; Bandleader; Songwriter. m. Marian Cherry, 29 March 1969, 4 s., 2 d. *Musical Education:* Composition, Charles Prentice, Music Bac Percussion, Wag Abbey. *Career:* Featured singer, radio, and recording bands including: Henry Hall; Carrol Gibbons; Ambrose; Charlie Kunz; Teddy Joyce; Phil Green; Fred Hartley; Joined RAF, 1940; Organizer, director, Bomber Command Dance Band; Tours include: India, Malaysia, Germany; Later bandleader, Leslie Douglas and his Orchestra; Numerous radio broadcasts, variety concerts and ballroom functions. *Compositions:* Swing Serenade; Oh Miss Muffet; Lead; Little Miss Valentine; Le Touquet; Swinging Inbetween; Old Country; New Boots; One Man Went To Blow; Boys and Girls; Nursery Rhythm. *Recordings:* As bandleader, and with Carrol Gibbons; Ambrose; Henry Hall. *Memberships:* PRS; British Academy of Songwriters; Musicians' Union. *Leisure interests:* Gardening; Reading. *Current Management:* Able Artistes and Associates. *Address:* 32 Manor Rd, Wallington, Surrey SM6 OAA, England.

DOUGLAS Robert James Elliot; b. 13 May 1942, Gifford, East Lothian, Scotland. Musician (Guitar, Banjo). m. Margaret, 18 March 1983, 1 s. *Musical Education:* Self-taught. *Career:* Clyde Valley Stompers, 1960–61; It's All Happening, with Tommy Steele and On the Beat, Norman Wisdom; Aley Welsh Band, 1963–82; Newport Jazz Festival, 1966; Freelance, 1982–; Working with Keith Smith, Dave Shepherd, Dig By Fairweather. *Recordings:* Complete Discography with Pamra; All Aley Welsh LPs; 2 CDs with Great British Jazz Band; 2 CDs recorded in Namburg with Vaché, Brother'/Bob Haggart; Various LPs accompanying American Stars. *Honour:* British Jazz Award (Guitar), 1992. *Membership:* Musicians Union Pamra. *Leisure interests:* Golf; Cooking (3 years as Chef). *Address:* 20 Gillan Way, Houghton Regis, Dunstable, Beds, LU5 5RD, England.

DOWDING Andrew Maurice; b. 23 July 1961, Lowestoft, Suffolk, England. Musician (drums, percussion); Teacher. *Musical Education:* Self-taught. *Career:* Toured with Linda Lewis, Ben E King and extensive international tours with Suzi Quatro. *Recordings:* Played on albums for

Wayland and Suzi Quatro. *Membership:* Musicians' Union. *Leisure interests:* Eating out; Shopping; Relaxation. *Address:* 9A Ellis Rd, Clacton-on-Sea, Essex CO15 1EX, England.

DOWNES David; b. 9 June 1975, Dublin, Ireland. *Musical Education:* Currently in third year of Music degree, Trinity College, Dublin. *Career:* Live and television shows for Phil Coulter (including US tour); Eleanor McEvoy and Alan Stivell. *Compositions:* Numerous soundtracks for RTE TV; Many orchestral works and arrangements. *Recordings:* Solo albums: Saltwater, 1994; Pavilion, 1995; Rusted Wheel of Things, 1995; Also collaborated with: Maire Brennan, Clannad, Fir Na Keol, James Galway. *Membership:* Irish Musicians' Rights Organisation. *Current Management:* Real Good Management Ltd. *Address:* 17 Dame Court, Dublin 2, Ireland.

DOWNES Geoffrey; b. 25 Aug. 1952, Stockport, Manchester, England. Musician (keyboards); Songwriter; Prod. m. Suzanne Baker, 25 Sept. 1999, 1 step-s., 2 d. *Musical Education:* City of Leeds College, graduated in Modern Music Studies. *Career:* Session musician; Jingles composer; Record producer; Best known as artist with: The Buggles; Yes; Asia; First band to sell out 16 consecutive concerts at Madison Square Gardens, with Yes, 1980; First video shown MTV: Buggles, Video Killed The Radio Star, 1981; First live MTV global satellite broadcast with Asia, from Budokan, Tokyo to 25m. people, 1983; First band to play Moscow Olympic Stadium, 1990; Solo artist, with New Dance Orchestra. *Recordings:* with Buggles: Singles: Video Killed The Radio Star (No. 1, UK), 1979; The Plastic Age, 1980; Clean Clean, 1980; Elstree, 1980; Albums: Age of Plastic, 1979; Adventures In Modern Recording, 1981; with Yes: Drama, 1980; with Asia: Asia, 1982; Alpha, 1983; Astra, 1985; Then and Now, 1990; Live In Moscow, 1991; Aqua, 1992; Aria, 1994; Arena, 1995; Archiva, 1996; Anthology, 1998; Aura, 2001; with GTR: GTR, 1986; Geoff Downes with NDO: The Light Program, 1987; Vox Humana, 1993; Evolution, 1995; The World Service, 2000; Various artists: Earthquake, 1989; Kate Bush; Mike Oldfield; Thompson Twins. *Honours include:* Over 40 Silver, Gold, Platinum discs; with Buggles: Ivor Novello Award Nomination, 1980; NME Award, 1980; Deutsche Gramaphon Award, 1980; with Asia: Billboard, Cashbox and Circus Magazine awards, 1982; FM Magazine Award, 1983; 2 Grammy Nominations, 1983; Ampex Gold Reel, 1979, 1980, 1986; Keyboard Magazine Awards, 1980, 1982, 1983; ASCAP Best Rock Song, 1982, 1983. *Memberships:* PRS; Musicians' Union; ASCAP; PAMRA; MCPS. *Leisure interests:* Mountain biking; Skiing; English literature; Computers. *Current Management:* Asia Management, Plas Llecha, Llanhennock, Newport, Monmouthshire NP18 1LU, Wales.

DOWNEY Brian; b. 27 Jan. 1951, Dublin, Ireland. Musician (drums). *Career:* Founder member, drummer, rock group Thin Lizzy, 1969–83; Member, Grand Slam (with Thin Lizzy's Phil Lynott), 1984; Regular UK and international appearances with Thin Lizzy include: Reading Festival, 1974, 1975, 1983; Great British Music Festival, London, 1975; World Series of Rock, Cleveland, 1983; Monsters of Rock European tour, 1983. *Recordings:* with Thin Lizzy: Hit singles: Whiskey In The Jar, 1973; Wild One, 1975; The Boys Are Back In Town, 1976; Don't Believe A Word, 1977; Dancin' In The Moonlight, 1977; Rosalie, 1978; Waiting For An Alibi, 1979; Sarah, 1979; Killer On The Loose, 1980; Killers Live EP, 1981; Cold Sweat, 1982; Albums: Thin Lizzy, 1971; Shades of a Blue Orphanage, 1972; Vagabonds of The Western World, 1972; Nightlife, 1974; Fighting, 1975; Jailbreak, 1976; Johnny The Fox, 1976; Bad Reputation, 1977; Live and Dangerous, 1978; Black Rose (A Rock Legend), 1979; Chinatown, 1980; The Adventures of Thin Lizzy, 1981; Renegade, 1981; Thunder and Lightning, 1983; Dedication – The Very Best of Thin Lizzy, 1991; Wild One, 1996.

DOWNING Paul Scott; b. 4 March 1966, London, England. Composer; Musician (Bass Guitar). *Education:* Leeds College of Music; Guildhall School of Music and Drama. *Career:* Worked With Martha Reeves, Mark Murphy, Jimmy Ruffin, Cayenne, Coup D'Etat, Anne Clark, John Etheridge, Vile Bodies, Evalution, Victoria Newton, Eva Abraham, Peter Byrne. *Compositions:* Flight Through Sunlit Clouds; Elegy For A Lost Summer; So Quiet Here; Come In; At Midnight; Summer Night In Paris; Beetles Party. *Recordings:* The Law Is An Anagram of Wealth; Elegy For A Lost Summer; Flight Through Cloudless Skies; Live 'n' Hot At Ronnie Scotts. *Honours:* Licentiate of The Guildhall School of Music and Drama. *Memberships:* Musicians Union; PRS; MCPS; PAMRA. *Leisure interests:* Reading; Photography; Cooking; Skiing.

DOWNING Will; b. 29 Nov. 1963, Brooklyn, New York, USA. Singer; Vocalist. 1 s., 2 d. *Education:* Virginia Union University. *Compositions:* That Good Morning Love; Don't Wait For Love; I Can't Make You Love Me; Just A Game. *Recordings:* Albums: Will Downing, 1988; Come Together as One, 1989; A Dream Fulfilled, 1991; Love's the Place to Be, 1993; Moods, 1995; Invitation Only, 1997; Pleasures of the Night, 1998; All The Man You Need, 2000; Singles: Just A Game, early 1980s; Where Is the Love, Top 20, Duet with Mica Paris, 1990; Wishing on a Star, 1990; Don't Make Me Wait, 1991; I Go Crazy, 1991; I Try, 1991; There's No Living Without You, 1993; Do You Still Love Me, 1993; Break Up To Make Up, 1994; Sorry I, 1995; Pleasures of the Night, 1998; I Can't Make You Love Me, 1999.

DOWNS Jeanne; b. 6 Jan. 1967, Rustington, Sussex, England. Singer; Songwriter; Television Presenter; Actress; Prod. m. Aron Friedman, 15 May 1993. *Musical Education:* Arts Education School (Stage School). *Career:* Continually writing, recording, producing; Developing own music for Manuka, with album deal; Television appearances include: Presenter, Children's ITV, 1989–91; Disney Club; TV Weekly; Ghost Train; MotorMouth; Television commercial voiceovers: Kelloggs Honey Nut Loops; Coco Pops; Ultimate Dance; Kiss FM radio jingles. *Recordings:* as Jeanne Dee: Simple Solution, 1992; No Life Without Love, 1993. *Memberships:* Musicians' Union; Pact; PRS; Equity. *Leisure interests:* Television production; Writing; Programme ideas; Tennis. *Current Management:* Billy Budis, Kudos Management, Crown Studios, 16–18 Crown Rd, Twickenham, Middlesex TW1 3EE, England.

DOWSETT Ian David; b. 30 Sept. 1963, Chesterfield, England. Musician (fingerstyle jazz guitar). *Musical Education:* Classical guitar evening classes, De Bovoir Institute; Jazz and Pop course, Goldsmith's College. *Career:* Began in Rock and Blues bands, occasional solo gigs, Spanish guitar; Recently playing in duos: saxophone and guitar, 2 guitars; Performances: Union Chapel; Festival Hall Foyer; Conway Hall; Recording for EMI Bacer EMI Bacology project, Abbey Road Studio. *Leisure interests:* Gardening; Eastern philosophy. *Address:* 28 Westpoint, Avondale Sq., Old Kent Rd, London SE1 5NY, England.

DOY Carl William; b. 6 May 1947, Camberley, Surrey, England. Musician (piano); Arranger; Composer; Prod. m. Kathleen Mary, 1973, 2 s. *Musical Education:* Royal College of Music (Herbert Howells, Eric Harisson). *Career:* Staff arranger at TVNZ for 15 years; Resident Pianist New Zealand Today and Saturday Live; Arranged, recorded with Dame Kiri Te Kanawa; Played for Gladys Knight and The Pips; Bob Hope; B B King; Shirley Bassey. *Recordings:* Double album: Piano By Candlelight (Platinum), 1995; Moonlight Piano, USA, Australian release, 1995. *Honours:* Artistic Award World Song Festival, Los Angeles, 1984; Grand Prix, Pacific Song Contest, 1979; Winner, American Song Festival, 1981. *Membership:* APRA. *Leisure interests:* Walking; Crosswords. *Current Management:* Murray Thom. *Address:* PO Box 35–767, Browns Bay, Auckland 10, New Zealand.

DOYLE Candida; b. 25 Aug. 1963, Belfast, Northern Ireland. Musician (Keyboards). *Career:* Joined Pulp, 1984; Numerous tours, TV appearances and festival dates; Contributed track to film soundtrack for Mission Impossible, 1996. *Recordings:* Singles: Little Girl (With the Blue Eyes), 1985; My Legendary Girlfriend, 1990; O.U. (Gone, Gone), 1992; Babies, 1992; Razzmatazz, 1993; Lipgloss, 1993; Do You Remember The First Time, 1994; The Sisters EP, 1994; Common People (No. 2, UK) 1995; Mis-Shapes/Sorted for E's and Wizz (No. 2, UK), 1995; Disco 2000, 1995; Something Changed, 1996; Help the Aged, 1997; This is Hardcore, 1998; A Little Soul, 1998; Party Hard, 1998; The Trees/Sunrise, 2001; Albums: Freaks, 1987; Separations, 1992; His 'N' Hers, 1994; Masters of the Universe: Pulp on Fire 1985–86, 1995; Different Class (No. 1, UK), 1995; Countdown 1985–87, 1996; This is Hardcore (No. 1, UK), 1998; We Love Life, 2001. *Honours:* Mercury Music Prize nominations, 1994, 1996. *Internet:* www.pulppeople.demon.co.uk.

DOYLE Teresa; b. 26 Jan. 1951, Prince Edward Island, Canada. Singer. m. Brett Bunston, 1 s. *Education:* BA, University of Prince Edward Island, Canada; McGill Conservatory of Music. *Career:* Performed at festivals and concerts in Japan, Canada, the US and UK; Performed with Chieftains. *Recordings:* Prince Edward Isle, Adieu; Forerunner; Stowaway; Songs for Lute and Voice; Dance to Your Daddy; If Fish Could Sing. *Honour:* East Coast Music Award, Children's Album of the Year. *Membership:* American Federation of Musicians. *Leisure interests:* Gardening; Painting. *Current Management:* Jensen Productions, Box 3445, Charlottetown, C1A 8W5 Canada. *Address:* RR #3, Belfast, Prince Edward Island C0A 1A0, Canada.

DOZIER Lamont; b. 16 June 1941, Detroit, Michigan, USA. Composer; Record Prod. *Career:* Motown artist, 1950s-67; Member, songwriting and production team Holland/Dozier/Holland (with Eddie and Brian Holland), 1963–73; Co-founder, Invictus and Hot Wax Records, 1967; Resumed solo recording career, 1972–; Founder, own Megaphone label, 1983. *Recordings:* Solo albums: Out Here On My Own, 1973; Black Bach, 1974; Love and Beauty, 1975; Right There, 1976; Peddlin' Music On The Side, 1977; Bittersweet, 1979; Working On You, 1981; Lamont, 1982; Bigger Than Life, 1983; Inside Seduction, 1991; Going Back To My Roots, 2000; Solo singles include: Let's Talk It Over, 1960; Why Can't We Be Lovers, 1972; Tryin' To Hold On To My Woman, 1974; Fish Ain't Bitin', 1974; Let Me Start Tonite, 1974; Love in the Rain, 1991; As co-writer/producer: with Marvin Gaye: Can I Get A Witness?; Little Darling; How Sweet It Is; You're A Wonderful One; with Martha and The Vandellas: Heatwave; Quicksand; Nowhere To Run; Jimmy Mack; with the Supremes: You Can't Hurry Love; You Keep Me Hanging On; Love Is Here and Now You've Gone; Where Did Our Love Go?; Baby Love; Come See About Me; Stop! In The Name of Love; Back In My Arms Again; with the Isley Brothers: This Old Heart of Mine; Put Yourself In My Place; I Guess I'll Always Love; with the Four Tops:

Baby I Need Your Loving; I Can't Help Myself; (It's The) Same Old Song; Reach Out and I'll Be There; Bernadette; Standing In The Shadows of Love; Other recordings for artistes including: The Miracles; Kim Weston; Aretha Franklin; Al Wilson; Freda Payne. *Address:* c/o McMullen and Co, 9744 Wilshire Blvd #301, Beverly Hills, CA 90212–1828, USA.

DR DRE, (Andre Young); b. 18 Feb. 1965, Los Angeles, California, USA. Rapper; Prod. *Career:* Member, World Class Wreckin' Cru; Member, NWA; Worked with Snoop Doggy Dogg, Warren G; Co-founder, Death Row Records; Produced numerous acts including Blackstreet and Foxy Brown; Formed new record company, Aftermath; Worked with Eminem on The Slim Shady LP, 1999; The Marshall Mathers LP, 2000. *Recordings:* Singles: Deep Cover, 1992; Nuthin' But a 'G' Thang, 1993; 2, 1993; House Calls, 1993; Dre Day, 1994; Juice, 1995; Dre's Beats, 1995; Hit Hip-Hop on Hot Vinyl, 1995; Keep Their Heads Ringin', 1995; Zoom, 1998; Lil' Ghetto Boy, 1999; Albums: The Chronic, 1992; Concrete Roots, 1994; Back N Tha Day, 1996; Dr Dre Presents the Aftermath, 1996; Chronic 2001, 1999. *Honour:* Grammy Award, Best Rap Solo Performance, Let Me Ride.

DR ROBERT (Bruce Robert Howard); b. 2 May 1961, Norfolk, England. Singer. *Career:* Former footballer, Norwich City Football Club; Former pop music journalist; Member, The Blow Monkeys, 1984-. *Recordings:* Albums: Limping For A Generation, 1984; Animal Magic, 1986; She Was Only A Grocer's Daughter, 1987; Whoops There Goes The Neighbourhood, 1989; Choices, 1989; Atomic Lullabies (compilation), 2001; Singles include: Digging Your Scene, 1986; It Doesn't Have To Be This Way, 1987; (Celebrate) The Day After You (featuring Curtis Mayfield), 1987; Choice?, 1989; Slaves No More (featuring Sylvia Tella), 1989; Springtime For The World, 1990; The Coming of Grace; Contributor, You Don't Own Me, to soundtrack for film Dirty Dancing; as Dr Robert: Duet with Kym Mazelle: Wait, 1989; Solo albums: Realms of Gold, 1996; Bird's Gotta Fly, 2001; Also recorded with: Paul Weller, Beth Orton. *Address:* c/o Primary Talent, London, England.

DRAGON Daryl; b. 27 Aug. 1942, Los Angeles, California, USA. Musician (keyboards); Songwriter. m. Toni Tennille, 14 Feb. 1974. *Career:* Keyboard player, co-writer, The Beach Boys stage band; Member, Natalie Cole's Malibu Music Men; Member, duo Captain and Tennille (with Toni Tennille), 1972–80; Tour with The Beach Boys, 1972; White House Dinner, in honour of Queen Elizabeth II, 1976; The Captain and Tennille, premiere, ABC TV, 1976; Runs Rambo Rec studio, 1979-. *Recordings:* Albums: with The Captain and Tennille: Love Will Keep Us Together (No. 2, US), 1975; Song of Joy, 1976; Come In From The Rain, 1977; Captain and Tennille's Greatest Hits, 1978; Dream, 1978; Make Your Move, 1980; Twenty Years of Romance, 1995; Casablanca Records' Greatest Hits, 1996; Size 14, 1997; Tennille Sings Big Band, 1998; Incurably Romantic, 2001; Hit singles include: The Way I Want To Touch You, 1975; Love Will Keep Us Together (No. 1, USA), 1975; Lonely Night (Angel Face), 1976; Muskrat Love, 1976; Shop Around, 1976; Can't Stop Dancin', 1977; You Never Done It Like That, 1979; Do That To Me One More Time (No. 1, USA), 1980. *Honours:* Grammy Award, Record of The Year, Love Will Keep Us Together, 1976; JUNO Award, Best International Single, Love Will Keep Us Together, 1976. *Current Management:* c/o Cheri Ingram Enterprises, 2225 E Flamingo Rd, Suite 303, Las Vegas, NV 89119, USA.

DRAMINSKY HOJMARK Jakob; b. 18 Nov. 1959, Copenhagen, Denmark. Composer; Musician (Bass Clarinet; Sopranino Saxophone). *Education:* Instrumental and composition studies with Pierre Dorge, Copenhagen, Wolfgang Fuchs, Berlin and Gabriel Brncic, Barcelona; Electroacoustic workshops in DIEM, IRCAM and PHONOS. *Career:* Car-Horn Concert, concrete music event for cars and trucks in Copenhagen; Münchausen in Aarhus, with Tzarina Q Cut, 25th anniversary of National Danish Arts Foundation; Stairways performed by Frith, Cora and Fuchs; Margrethe Fjorden, Intermedia event, curated by Eric Andersen, Roskilde, Denmark; Slip 'n' Slide sonata for construction equipment; Collaborated with French toy pianist Pascal Comelade with recordings, tours, festivals in France, Spain and Germany. *Compositions:* Turandot, cabaret-like opera, 1993; Memory: song cycle for choir and piano, 1997; En Landsoldats dagbog electroacoustic, pocket opera, 64928, electroacoustic chamber opera for 3 voices, cello and electronics, 1998. *Recordings:* At the Gallery, 9 collected chamber works; Memory; En landsoldats dagbog, Dreamjingles. *Honours:* Grants from the National Danish Art Foundation. *Membership:* DJBFA. *Current Management:* Multisounds. *Address:* H C Orstedsvej 17 III, 1879 Frb C, Denmark.

DRAPER Paul; b. Chester, Cheshire, England. Singer. *Education:* Wrexham Art College. *Career:* Lead singer/songwriter, Mansun. *Recordings include:* Debut album, Attack of The Grey Lantern, 1997; Singles: Egg Shaped Fred (EP), 1996; Take It Easy Chicken (EP), 1996; Stripper Vicar (EP), 1996; Wide Open Space (EP), 1996; Taxloss, EP, 1997; Closed for Business, EP, 1998; Legacy, EP, 1998; Being A Girl, EP, 1998; Negative, EP, 1998; I Can Only Disappoint You, 2000; Electric Man, 2000; Fool, 2001; Albums: Attack of the Grey Lantern (No. 1, UK), 1997; Six,

1998; Little Kix, 2000. *Current Management:* Rock 'n' Roll Management, Studio 2, 108 Prospect Quay, Point Pleasant, London SW18 1PR, England.

DREES Michèle Marie; b. Carshalton, Surrey, England. Musician (drums, percussion). *Musical Education:* GSMD post graduate, advanced jazz course. *Career:* Marc Almond tour video, television, 1993; Member of houseband, Jonathan Ross TV Show, backing k d lang; Suzanne Vega; Mica Paris; Candy Dulfer; Hair, musical, Old Vic, 1993; Freak Power, 1993, 1994; Many jazz concerts, played with: Jean Toussaint; Dill Katz; Tim Whitehead; salsa band Candela; Seal; Eurovision Song Contest; Crystal Aquarium film, CH4, 1995; Marie-Clare D'Ubaldo. *Memberships:* Musicians' Union; Equity. *Leisure interests:* Guitar; Singing, mainly Brazilian songs. *Current Management:* Simon Harrison. *Address:* Lavender Cottage, Love Lane, Kings Langley, Hertfordshire WD4 9HN, England.

DREVER Ivan Cursiter; b. 10 June 1956, Orkney. Singer; Songwriter; Guitar. 2 s., 2 d. *Musical Education:* Self-taught. *Career:* Solo/duo work, 6 years; Joined Wolfstone, 1991; Toured America, Canada, Spain, Denmark, Germany and Far East; Networked in appearances with band. *Compositions:* Many compositions recorded. *Recordings:* with Wolfstone: Unleashed, 1991; Chase, 1992; Year of the Dog, 1994; Half Tail, 1996; Pick of the Litter, 1997; This Strange Place, 1998; 3 solo albums; 3 duo albums with Knowe O'Deil. *Honours:* 2 Gold Discs for albums, Unleashed and The Chase. *Memberships:* MCPS; PRS. *Leisure interests:* Reading; Sleeping. *Address:* 10B View Pl., Inverness, IV2 4SA.

DREW Martin; b. 11 Feb. 1944, Northampton, England. Musician (drums). m. Tessa Denise Rose, 5 Sept. 1965, 1 s., 2 d. *Musical Education:* Taught by George Fierstone. *Career:* Worked with Oscar Peterson, 1974–; Ronnie Scott, 1975–; Played world-wide with many major artists including television, radio, album appearances; Played with: George Coleman; Niels H O Pedersen; James Moody; Dizzie Gillespie; Zoot Sims; Michael Brecker. *Recordings:* Featured with: Oscar Peterson; Ronnie Scott; Arturo Sandoval; Chucho Valdes; Bill Watrous; Joe Pass; Warren Vache; Dick Morrissey; John Critchinson; Joe Temperley; Tony Lee; Freddy Hubbard; Harry Edison. *Honours:* 3 times winner, British Jazz Awards (Drums). *Memberships:* Musicians' Union; Jazz Umbrella. *Leisure interests:* Cars; Photography.

DREWETT Steve; b. 29 Oct. 1954, Islington, London, England. Singer; Songwriter; Musician (guitar). *Musical Education:* Self-taught. *Career:* John Peel Sessions, BBC Radio 1; Old Grey Whistle Test, BBC 2; Support tour with Billy Bragg. *Recordings:* Albums: Beggars Can Be Choosers, 1983; Repercussions, 1985; Kickstarting A Backfiring Nation, 1986; Is Your Washroom Breeding Bolsheviks, 1988; 45 Revolutions Per Minute, 1990. *Membership:* Musicians' Union. *Leisure interest:* Surfing the Internet. *Current Management:* No Wonder Management. *Address:* 154 Bishopsfield, Harlow, Essex, England.

D'RIVERA Paquito; b. 4 June 1948, Havana, Cuba. Musician (saxophone, clarinet); Bandleader; Composer; Arranger. *Career:* Performs with Paquito D'Rivera Ensemble and the Caribbean Jazz Project; Conducts Dizzy Gillespie's UN Orchestra; Guest soloist, jazz, classical, Latin/Caribbean music concerts; Television appearances include: CBS Sunday Morning; The David Letterman Show. *Compositions:* The New York Suite, for saxophone quartet, 1987; Aires Tropicales, for woodwind quintet, 1994; 5 Pieces for brass quintet, 1997. *Recordings:* Over 20 solo albums, bebop, classical, Latin/Caribbean music. *Publications:* Music Minus Me instructional tapes, albums; Lessons With the Greats; Jamey Aebersold, Play-along, Vol. 77; My Saxual Life, 1999. *Honours:* Lifetime Achievement Award, Contribution to Latin music, Carnegie Hall; Grammy Award, for Portraits of Cuba, 1997; Diploma h.c., Universidad de Alcalá de Henares, Spain. *Memberships:* Artistic Director, New Jersey Chamber Music Society; Board of Directors, Chamber Music America. *Current Management:* Havana-NY Music Co. *Address:* PO Box 4899, Weehawken, NJ 07087, USA.

DROGE Peter; b. 11 March 1969, Eugene, Oregon, USA. Singer; Songwriter. *Career:* Tours supporting Tom Petty; Melissa Etheridge; Sheryl Crowe; Appearance, Late Night With David Letterman; Included on soundtracks for films: Beautiful Girls; Dumb and Dumber; Tour supporting Neil Young. *Recordings:* Albums: Necktie Second, 1994; Find a Door, 1996; Spacey and Shakin', 1998; Singles: If You Don't Love Me, 1995. *Honour:* Find a Door voted Most Overlooked Album of the Year, The Rocket, 1996. *Membership:* ASCAP. *Current Management:* Curtis Management. *Address:* 417 Denny Way, Suite 200, Seattle, WA 98109, USA.

DROSSOS Petros; b. 11 June 1966, Athens, Greece. Sound Engineer; Prod. *Career:* Tape Operator, several Parisian studios, 1986; Assistant Engineer, Polysound Studios, Athens, Greece, 1987; In-house Engineer, Davout Studios, Paris, France, 1988–91; Freelance engineer, music, television, post-production, 1991-. *Recordings:* Engineer, producer: Single: with Mano Negra: King Kong Five; Albums: Raggabuzzin (French Reggae Compilation); with Rosemary's Babies: Lutte De Classe; Engineer: with Mano Negra: Live à la Cigale (TV programme tracks); with Hector Zazou and Les Polyphonies Corses, Ghetto Youth Progress (French Ragga Hip-Hop Compilation); IAM: Red, Black and Green (maxi-single). *Leisure interest:* Drinking Ouzo. *Address:* 213 Blvd Davout, 75020 Paris, France.

DRUMMIE Richard; Vocalist; Musician (guitar, keyboards); Songwriter. *Career:* Songwriting partnership with Peter Cox, ATV Music; Founder member, duo Go West, 1982-. *Compositions include:* One Way Street (for film soundtrack Rocky IV). *Recordings:* Singles: We Close Our Eyes, 1985; Call Me, 1985; Don't Look Down, 1985; The King of Wishful Thinking, 1990; What You Won't Do For Love, 1993; Albums: Go West, 1985; Bangs and Crashes, 1986; Dancing On The Couch, 1987; Cries and Whispers, 1989; Indian Summer, 1992; Session work: White Men Can't Jump, 1992; Deborah, for Deborah Gibson, 1997; Growing Pains, for Billie Myers, 1997; Moonchild, for Deborah Gibson, 2000. *Current Management:* Blueprint Management, 134 Lots Rd, London SW12 0RJ, England.

DRUMMOND Bill (William Butterworth); b. 29 April 1953, South Africa. *Career:* Former fisherman, set designer, carpenter, Scotland; Member, Big In Japan, 1977; Co-founder, Zoo Records; Manager, producer, Teardrop Explodes; Echo and The Bunnymen; A & R Executive, WEA Records, 1985; Formed KLF Communications, with Jimmy Cauty; Various recordings as: JAMS, 1987–88; Disco 200, 1987–89; Timelords, 1988; KLF, 1989–92; Justified Ancients of Mu Mu, 1991–92; 2K, 1997; DMC European Convention, Amsterdam, 1990; Own studios, Transcentral 1988; Announced departure from music business, 1992. *Recordings:* Solo albums: The Man, 1986; Bill Drummond, 1987; Albums: The White Room, KLF, 1989; Chill Out, KLF, 1990; Hit singles: Doctorin' The Tardis, The Timelords (No. 1, UK), 1988; What Time Is Love, KLF, 1990; 3am Eternal, KLF (No. 1, UK), 1991; Last Train To Trancentral, KLF, 1991; It's Grim Up North, Justified Ancients of Mu Mu, 1991; Justified and Ancient, KLF with Tammy Wynette, 1992; America – What Time Is Love?, KLF, 1992; Fuck The Millennium, 2K, 1997. *Publications:* The Manual (guide to having a hit record), 1988; Bad Wisdom, with Mark Manning, 1996; 45, 2000.. *Honours:* Gold discs: The White Room, 1991; 3am Eternal, 1991; BRIT Award, Best British Group, KLF (co-winners with Simply Red), 1992.

DRUSKY Roy Frank; b. 22 June 1930, Atlanta, Georgia, USA. DJ; Country Singer; Songwriter; Television Host. *Education:* Veterinary medicine, Emory University. *Musical Education:* Self-taught guitar. *Career:* Formed Southern Ranch Boys; Radio DJ, television announcer, 1950s; Member, Grand Ole Opry, 1958–; Concerts include: Regular British tours; Wembley Festival; Film appearances: Forty Acre Feud; The Golden Guitar; White Lightning Express; Now involved in production and publishing; Hosts own television programme. *Compositions include:* Alone With You, Faron Young (US Country No. 1), 1958. *Recordings:* Hits include: Three Hearts In A Tangle; Second Hand Rose; Yes Mr Peters, duet with Priscilla Mitchell; If The Whole World Stopped Loving; Numerous albums include: Anymore With Roy Drusky, 1961; It's My Way, 1962; Yesterday's Gone, 1964; Country Song Express, 1966; All My Hard Times, 1970; Peaceful Easy Feeling, 1974; This Life of Mine, 1976; Roy, 1981; Night Flying, 1976; English Cold, 1980; Songs of Love and Life, 1995; with Priscilla Mitchell: Love's Eternal Triangle, 1965; Together Again, 1966; We Belong Together, 1968.

DUBE Lucky; b. 3 Aug. 1964, Ermelo, Eastern Transvaal, South Africa. Vocalist; Songwriter. *Career:* Formed The Skyway Band in school; Recorded first album Mbaqanga (with The Love Brothers), 1982; First solo album Lengane Ngeyetha went gold; Recorded first ever South African reggae album, 1985; Third reggae release Slave was first ever album to sell more than 300,000 copies in South Africa; Performed at Reggae Sunsplash in 1991; Starred in and composed score for the film Getting Lucky; Also appeared in film Voice in the Dark. *Recordings:* Albums include: Slave, 1987; Prisoner, 1989; House of Exile, 1991; Victims, 1993; Trinity, 1995; Serious Reggae Business, 1996; Taxman, 1997; The Way It Is, 1999; Soul Taker, The Rough Guide to Lucky Dube, 2001. *Honours:* OKTV Award, Best Male Vocalist; Kora Award, Best African Video, The Way It Is, 2000. *Address:* c/o Gallo, PO Box 2897, Parklands 2121, South Africa. *Internet:* www.luckydube.net.

DUBFIRE (Ali Shirazinia); b. 19 April 1971, Iran. Prod.; Remixer; DJ. *Career:* Relocated to Washington DC, USA; Formed Deep Dish and founded Deep Dish/Yoshitoshi Records with partner Sharam, 1992; Released BT's A Moment of Truth, 1993; Signed to Tribal Records, 1993; Moved to Deconstruction, 1996; Collaborations: Danny Tenaglia; John Selway; Everything But The Girl; Remixed: Madonna; De'Lacy; Billie Ray Martin; Joi Cardwell; Dusted; Sven Vath; The Shamen; Eddie Amador. *Recordings:* Albums: Junk Science, 1998; Singles: A Feeling (as Moods), 1992; Sexy Dancer (as Quench), 1993; The Dream, 1994; Love Songs (as Chocolate City), Stay Gold, 1996; The Future of The Future, 1998. *Honours:* Grammy Award, Remixer of The Year, 2001. *Address:* c/o Deconstruction, Bedford House, 69–79 Fulham High St, London, SW6 3JW, England.

DUBOWSKY Jack Curtis; b. 16 Aug. 1965, Connecticut, USA. Composer; Arranger; Record Prod.; Musician (guitar, bass, piano); Vocalist. *Education:* Graduate, University of California. *Musical Education:* Tutored by mother. *Career:* Radio appearance on German radio, 1990; Recording Technician with Metallica, Live Shit box set, 1994; Actor with Sick and Twisted Players, San Francisco; Currently playing with Snopea Chamber Ensemble; Produced Glen Meadmore, Hot Horny and Born-Again, 1998, and Virgin Whore Complex, Succumb, 1998. *Compositions:* The Silver Whistle, chamber opera, 1995; Slave, chamber opera, 1997. *Recordings:* Diazepam Nights, 1989; Helot Revolt, 1992; Fallout, 1990; Duchampians, 1991; Produced Glen Meadmore's songs for film Hustler White, 1996; Voyagers, chamber opera, 1998. *Honours:* Zellerbach Family Fund Grant, 1997; Friends of the San Francisco Library grant, 1997; Meet the Composer grant, 1998. *Membership:* BMI. *Leisure interests:* Skiing; MG maintenance and repair. *Current Management:* De Stijl Records. *Address:* PO Box 170206, San Francisco, CA 94117–0206, USA.

DUCAS George; b. 1 Aug. 1966, Texas City, Texas, USA. Artist; Singer-Songwriter; Guitarist. *Education:* BA Economics, Vanderbilt University, Nashville, Tennessee. *Career:* Moved to Nashville, 1991; Began songwriting and playing local clubs; Signed with Capitol Records, 1994; Television appearances include: CBS This Morning; CNN Showbiz Today; Entertainment Tonight; Good Day New York; Sound FX; FX Breakfast Time; Live From Queens; At The Ryman. *Recordings:* Singles, videos: Teardrops; Lipstick Promises (Top 10); Hello Cruel World, 1995; Kisses Don't Lie, 1995; Every Time She Passes By, 1996; Albums: George Ducas, 1995; Where I Stand, 1997. *Memberships:* ASCAP; County Music Asscn. *Leisure interests:* Fitness; Travel; Sports. *Current Management:* Coast to Coast.

DUCHARME Annette Marie-Jeanne Thérèse; b. 23 Feb., Windsor, Ontario, Canada. Recording Artist; Singer; Songwriter; Musician (guitar, bass, piano, keyboards). *Education:* BA, Drama, English. *Musical Education:* Self-taught. *Career:* Appeared: Peter Czowski show modelling for Evelyn Roth, 1977; Sang, played keyboards, Grade 8 Concert, St Mary's Academy; As lead singer, writer, bass player, toured with Bowers/Ducharme Trio, 1980–81; Keyboards, tour with John Lee Hooker, 1982–83; Opened for Richard Marx with own band, cross-Canada tour, 1989; Own band, opening tour for Larry Gowan, 1994; Sang at Kumbaya Benefits, 1993, 1994; Sang at: Grey Cup Half-time Show, with Tom Cochrane, 1994. *Composition:* Sinking Like A Sunset, recorded by Tom Cochrane. *Recordings:* Bowers/Ducharme, 1981; Blue Girl, 1988–89; Mad Mad World, 1992; Sanctuary, 1994; Ragged Ass Road, 1995; Flowers In The Concrete, 1995; Don't Argue with Her, 1996; Mythos, 1998. *Honours:* (West Coast) Caras Award for Most Promising New Artist, 1985; Juno Nomination for Best New Female Singer, 1990; CMPA Award for number 1 Rock Song of The Year, 1993; SOCAN Award for Pop Song of the Year, 1993; Last two for: Sinking Like A Sunset. *Membership:* SOCAN. *Leisure interests:* Dancing; Reading poetry; Hiking up mountains; Loves water. *Current Management:* TKO Management. *Address:* 1669 E 13th Ave, Vancouver, BC V5N 2B7 Canada.

DUCHEMIN Philippe; b. 2 Jan. 1957, Toulouse, France. Jazz Musician (piano). *Musical Education:* Self-taught. *Career:* Played with Kenny Clarke; Lionel Hampton; Ray Brown; Joe Newman; Benny Powell; Wild Bill Davis; Frank Wess; Toured Europe with many French and American musicians, 1985–; Performed at Jazz Festivals with own trio throughout Europe, North Africa, 1990–. *Recordings:* Middle Jazz Quartet, 1980; Hommage à Count Basie, 1985; François Guin Et Les Four Bones, 1987; with Philippe Duchemin Trio: Alizés, 1990; Live!, 1992; Three Pieces, 1994; Trio with Dominque Vernhes, 1995; with Paris Barcelona: Swing Connection, 1990; Hard Swing, 1991; Wild Cat, 1992; Frank Wess Meets The Paris Barcelona, 1992; Three Colours, 1998. *Leisure interest:* Cooking. *Address:* 42 rue de la Madeleine, 72000 Le Mans, France.

DUDGEON Gus; Prod. *Education:* Haileybury and Imperial Service College, Summerhill. *Career:* Recording engineer, Decca Records, 1960s; Worked with Rolling Stones; Small Faces; Marianne Faithfull; Ten Years After; Founder, own production company, 1968; Worked with The Strawbs; Ralph McTell; Bonzo Dog Doo-Dah Band; Producer for Elton John, 1969–76, 1984–86. *Recordings:* Producer, albums: with Elton John: Elton John, 1970; Tumbleweed Connection, 1971; Madman Across The Water, 1971; Honky Chateau (No. 1, USA), 1972; Don't Shoot Me, I'm Only The Piano Player (No. 1, UK and US), 1973; Goodbye Yellow Brick Road (No. 1, UK and US), 1973; Caribou (No. 1, UK and US), 1974; Captain Fantastic and The Brown Dirt Cowboy (No. 1, USA), 1975; Rock of The Westies (No. 1, USA), 1975; Here and There, 1976; Blue Moves, 1976; Ice On Fire, 1985; Leather Jackets, 1986; with Elkie Brooks: Pearls; Pearls II; Heart Over Mind, Jennifer Rush, 1987; Nonesuch, XTC, 1992; Albums with Ralph McTell; Joan Armatrading, Ten Years After; Strawbs, The Strawbs; Singles include: Urban Spaceman, Bonzo Dog Doo-Dah Band, 1968; Space Oddity, David Bowie, 1969 (No. 1, UK, 1975); I've Got The Music In Me, Kiki Dee, 1974; Don't Go Breaking My Heart, Elton John and Kiki Dee (No. 1, UK and US), 1976; Fool If You Think It's Over, Chris Rea, 1978; The

Disappointed, XTC, 1992; Menswear, We Love You, 1996. *Honour:* Grammy nomination, 1970, 1974 (x2), 1975 (x2). *Membership:* MPG. *Current Management:* c/o Stephen Budd Management, 109B Regents Park Rd, London NW1 8UR, England.

DUDLEY Anne; Musician (keyboards); Arranger; Prod.; Composer; Songwriter. *Career:* Pianist, Playschool, BBC TV; Founder member, Art of Noise, 1984–90, 1999–; Solo artiste, composer, producer, arranger, 1990-. *Compositions include:* Television commercials: Volvo; Vauxhall Astra; Reebok; Television scores: Jeeves and Wooster; Anna Lee, Crime Traveller, Kavanagh QC. *Recordings:* Early session work includes: The Lexicon of Love, ABC, 1982; Duck Rock, Malcolm McLaren, 1983; Two Tribes, Frankie Goes To Hollywood, 1984; Albums: with The Art of Noise: Albums: (Who's Afraid Of) The Art of Noise, 1984; In Visible Silence, 1986; Daft, 1987; In No Sense? Nonsense!, 1987; The Best of The Art of Noise, 1988; The Ambient Collection, 1990; The Seduction of Claude Debussy, 1999; Solo albums: Songs From The Victorious City, with Jaz Coleman, 1990; Ancient and Modern, 1999; A Different Light, 2001; Singles: with The Art of Noise: Into Battle, 1983; Beat Box, 1984; Close To The Edit, 1985; Peter Gunn, with Duane Eddy, 1986; Paranoimia, 1986; Kiss, with Tom Jones, 1988; Art of Love, 1990; Minarets and Memories, 1990; Ziggarats of Cinnamon, 1991; Film themes and scores: include: Buster; Wilt; Say Anything; Mighty Quinn; The Crying Game; The Grotesque (with Sting); Hollow Reed; The Full Monty; Monkeybone; Also worked as arranger with: Lloyd Cole; A-Ha; Phil Collins; Rush; Boyzone; Spice Girls, Elton John, Paul McCartney, Pet Shop Boys, Pulp, The The, S Club 7. *Honours:* Grammy, Best Rock Instrumental Performance, Peter Gunn, 1987; Academy Award, Best Original Comedy Score, for The Full Monty, 1998. *Current Management:* Air Edel, 18 Rodmarton St, London W1H 3FW, England.

DUDLEY Dave, (David Darwin Pedruska); b. 3 May 1928, Spencer, Wisconsin, USA. Country vocalist; Songwriter; Musician (guitar). *Career:* Played semi-pro baseball in Wisconsin and for the Gainsville Owls in Texas until injury stopped career; DJ and singer at radio stations: WTWT Wausau, Wisconsin; KBOK, Waterloo, Iowa; KCHA, Charles City, Minnesota; Formed Dave Dudley Trio and worked throughout Midwest, 1953–60; First country chart single, Maybe I Do, on Vee Records, 1961; Signed to Mercury Records, 1963; Became especially known for records with a trucking theme including Six Days On The Road; Awarded a solid gold security card by the Truckers Union in appreciation of musical services on behalf of truckers. *Compositions include:* Comin' Down; Fly Away Again. *Recordings include:* The Pool Shark, 1970; Six Days On The Road, 1963; Truck Drivin' Son-Of-A-Gun, 1965; Cowboy Boots, 1963; What We're Fighting For, 1965; Albums: Truck Drivin' Son-Of-A-Gun, 1965; Lonelyville, 1966; Travelin' With Dave Dudley, 1964. *Address:* c/o Country Music Asscn, Nashville, TN, USA.

DUFEK Milan; b. 6 May 1944, Prague, Czech Republic. m. Dr Stana Dufkova, 2 s. *Education:* Konzervator Jaroslava Jezka, 1984–88. *Career:* Member of Group Rangers, Plavci, 1965–98; 20 Television Shows. *Compositions:* 100 Songs Including, Memories of Home; Gettin' Married; Let Say I Do; Left Hand. *Recordings:* 14 CDs; 21 Records Including, Country Our Way; On The Country Road; Country Grass Band. *Publications:* Rangers I; Rangers II; Ranger On The Road. *Honours:* Porta Festival Prize, 1968, 1969; Country Festival Prague Prize, 1970; Country Radio Prague Award, 1997, 1998. *Leisure interest:* Sport. *Address:* Pod Stadiony 5, 150 00 Prague 5, Czech Republic.

DUFFIN Graeme Ian; b. 28 Feb. 1956, Glasgow, Scotland. Musician (guitar). m. Pamela, 15 April 1978, 1 s., 1 d. *Education:* HNC, Medical Laboratory Science (Biochemistry). *Musical Education:* Piano training; Guitar self-taught. *Career:* Member, folk group New Celeste, 1977–80; Member, Wet Wet Wet, 1985–; Major tours in UK, Europe, USA, Far East and Australia; Live video recorded at Glasgow Green, Edinburgh Castle and Royal Albert Hall. *Recordings:* Albums: Popped In Souled Out 1987; The Memphis Sessions, 1988; Holding Back The River, 1989; High On The Happy Side, 1991; End of Part One (Greatest Hits), 1993; Picture This, 1995; 10, 1997; Best of British Folk Rock; Hit singles include: Wishing I Was Lucky, 1987; Sweet Little Mystery, 1987; Angel Eyes, 1987; With A Little Help From My Friends (No. 1, UK), 1988; Sweet Surrender, 1989; Goodnight Girl (No. 1, UK), 1992; Love Is All Around (No. 1, 15 weeks, UK charts); Julia Says, 1995. *Honours:* Brit Awards, Best Newcomers, 1987; Award for co-production of Love Is All Around. *Current Management:* The Precious Organisation, 14/16 Spiers Wharf, Port Dundas, Glasgow, Scotland.

DUFFY Billy; b. 12 May 1959, Manchester, England. Musician (guitar). *Career:* Guitarist, Theatre of Hate; The Cult (formerly Southern Death Cult and Death Cult), 1983–; World-wide tours; Concerts with: Bauhaus; Billy Idol; Big Country; Metallica; Guns N'Roses; Lenny Kravitz; Concerts include: Futurama Festival, Leeds, 1983; A Gathering of The Tribes, US, 1990; Cult In The Park '92 Festival, Finsbury Park, London, 1992; Guns N' Roses concert, Milton Keynes, 1993. *Recordings:* Albums: Southern Death

Cult, 1983; Dreamtime, 1984; Love, 1985; Electric, 1987; Sonic Temple, 1989; Ceremony, 1991; Pure Cult, 1993; The Cult, 1994; Ghost Dance, 1996; High Octane Cult, 1996; Forever Mod, 1998; Ten Years After, 1998; Rare Cult, 2000; Beyond Good and Evil, 2001; Singles include: Fat Man, 1983; Spiritwalker, 1984; She Sells Sanctuary, 1985; Rain, 1985; Love Removal Machine, 1987; Lil' Devil, 1987; Wild Flower, 1987; Fire Woman, 1989; Edie (Ciao Baby), 1989; Sweet Soul Sister, 1990; Wild Hearted Son, 1991.

DUFFY Keith; b. 1 Oct. 1974, Dublin, Ireland. Vocalist. *Career:* Member, Boyzone; Presenter: FBi, BBC-TV, 2000; The Race, ITV2, 2001. *Recordings:* Singles: Working My Way Back To You, 1994; Key To My Life, 1995; Love Me For A Reason, 1995; So Good, 1995; Father and Son, 1995; Coming Home Now, 1995; Words, 1996; Isn't It A Wonder, 1997; Baby Can I Hold You Tonight, 1997; Mystical Experience, 1997; Picture of You, 1997; All That I Need, 1998; I Love The Way You Love Me, 1999; When The Going Gets Tough, 1999; You Needed Me, 1999; Girl You Know It's True, with Shane Lynch, 2000; Albums: A Different Beat, 1997; Where We Belong, 1998; By Request, 1999.

DUFFY Martin; Musician (keyboards). *Career:* Member, Primal Scream; Obtained record deal with Creation; Work remixed by DJ Andrew Weatherall, and collaborations with Jah Wobble, Denise Johnston and Alex Paterson of The Orb; Other session work includes: Felt; Beth Orton; Dr John; Charlatans; Shack; Numerous tours and festival appearances; Contributed track, The Scream Team meets the Barmy Army Uptown for the Irvine Welsh film Trainspotting, 1996. *Recordings:* Singles: Loaded EP, 1990; Come Together EP, 1990; Higher Than The Sun, 1991; Don't Fight It, Feel It, 1991; Movin' On Up, 1991; (I'm Gonna) Cry Myself Blind, 1994; Jailbird, 1994; Rocks/Funky Jam, 1994; The Big Man and the Scream Team Meet the Barmy Army Uptown, 1996; Star, 1997; Burning Wheel, 1997; Kowalski, 1997; If They Move, Kill 'Em, 1998; Swastikka Eyes, 1999; Kill All Hippies, 2000; Accelerator, 2000; Albums: Sonic Flower Groove, 1987; Primal Scream, 1989; Screamadelica, 1991; Give Out But Don't Give Up, 1994; Echo Dek, 1997; Vanishing Point, 1997; XTRMNTR, 2000. *Honour:* Mercury Music Prize Winners, 1992.

DUFFY Stephen Anthony James; b. 30 May 1960, Birmingham, England. Singer; Songwriter. *Education:* Birmingham Polytechnic. *Career:* Founder member, Duran Duran, 1978; Solo artiste, under own name and as Dr Calculus, 1982–; Leader, own group Duffy, 1994–; Founder member, The Lilac Time, 1987–91. *Recordings:* Albums: Solo: The Ups and Downs, 1985; Because We Love You, 1986; Designer Beatnik (as Dr Calculus), 1986; Music In Colours, with Nigel Kennedy, 1993; with The Lilac Time: The Lilac Time, 1987; Paradise Circus, 1989; And Love For All, 1990; Astronauts, 1991; Duffy, 1995; Kiss Me, 1995; I Love My Friends, 1998; Looking for a Day in the Night, 1999; Lilac 6, 2001; Singles: Solo: Kiss Me, 1982; Hold It, 1982; Kiss Me (re-release), 1985; Icing On The Cake, 1985; London Girls, 1995; Sugar High, 1995; with The Lilac Time: Return To Yesterday, 1988; Needle Mythology; 17+3; with Me Me Me: Hanging Around, 1996; Other collaborations include: Donovan, Saint Etienne. *Address:* PO Box 2, Bromyard, Herefordshire HR7 4UU, England.

DUGMORE Geoff; Drummer; Songwriter; Prod. 1 s. *Compositions:* The Europeans, Vocabulary LP, Live LP and Recurring Dreams LP; Wildlife, Wildlife LP. *Recordings:* Played on records for: Deborah Harry; Stevie Nicks, US No 1; Killing Joke; Tina Turner, UK No 1 Foreign Affair; Jeff Beck; Gabrielle, both albums; Art of Noise; Gypsy Kings; Zoe; Rod Stewart; Joan Armatrading; Underworld; Tim Finn; Bob Geldof; Dido, Natalie Imbruglia; Heather Nova, Robbie Williams, Russell Watson; Produced records for: Wildlife; Deborah Harry; Belouis Some; Boss Beat; Sonny Roche; Jason Feddy. *Current Management:* One Management, 43 St Alban's Ave, London W4 5JS, England.

DUJMIC Ratko; b. 7 Aug. 1954, Zagreb, Croatia. Musician (piano, violin, electronic keyboards). m. Snjezana Simek-Dujmic, 2 Dec. 1990, 1 s. *Musical Education:* Music Academy, Theory of Music and Pedagogy. *Career:* Fourth and sixth places, Eurovision Song Contests, 1987, 1988; Winner, Eurovision song contest, 1989; Sold 38m. recordings; 4 solo television shows; 1 film score, much theatre music; Large number world tours include Opera House, Sydney, Australia. *Compositions:* About 800 works, many compositions for children and TV Series. *Recordings:* Around 90, audio and video, world-wide. *Honours:* All Festivals in former Yugoslavia. *Memberships:* Union Professional Musicians; Society of Composers, Croatia (DHS). *Leisure interests:* Swimming; Writing poetry. *Current Management:* Croatia Records; Avet Publishing Company. *Address:* LL Maksimirsko Naselje I/V, 41000 Zagreb, Croatia.

DUKE George; b. 12 Jan. 1946, San Rafael, California, USA. Jazz Musician (keyboards); Composer. *Musical Education:* Piano lessons at school; BMus, San Francisco Conservatory, 1967. *Career:* Keyboardist, recording artist, 1966–; Accompanist, Dizzy Gillespie, 1965–67; Jean Luc Ponty, 1969; Member, Frank Zappa's Mothers of Invention, 1970–75; Formed jazz-fusion duos with Billy Cobham and Stanley Clarke; Also played with Cannonball Adderley; Bobby Hutcherson; Airto and Flora

Purim; John Scofield; Lee Ritenour; Paulinho Da Costa; Major concerts include Nelson Mandela Tribute, Wembley. *Recordings:* Albums include: Save The Country, 1969; George Duke, 1969; The Inner Source, 1971; Inner Source, 1973; Feel, 1974; Faces In Reflection, 1975; I Love The Blues She Heard Me Cry, 1975; The Aura Will Prevail, 1975; Liberated Fantasies, 1976; Live In Europe, 1976; Solo Keyboard Album, 1976; From Me To You, 1977; Reach For It, 1977; Don't Let Go, 1978; Follow The Rainbow, 1979; Master of The Game, 1979; A Brazilian Love Affair, 1980; Dream On, 1982; Guardian of The Light, 1983; Secret Rendezvous, 1984; Thief In The Night, 1988; Night After Night, 1989; George Duke Collection, 1991; Snapshot, 1992; Muir Woods Suite, 1996; Three Originals, 1994; Illusions, 1995; Rendezvous, 1995; Is Love Enough, 1997; After Hours, 1998; Cool, 2000; Numerous albums with Stanley Clarke include: Clarke Duke Project, 1981; Clarke Duke Project 2, 1982; 3, 1990; with Jean Luc Ponty: Live In LA, 1971; with Frank Zappa: Apostrophe, 1972; Roxy and Elsewhere, 1975; with Billy Cobham: Crosswinds, 1974; Live In Europe, 1976; BC, 1979; with Miles Davis: Tutu, 1986; Also recordings by: Airto; George Benson; Billy Cobham; Aretha Franklin; Freddie Hubbard; Michael Jackson; Al Jarreau; Shalamar. *Current Management:* Herb Cohen Management. *Address:* 740 N LaBrea Ave, Los Angeles, CA 90038, USA.

DUKES Rebecca W, (Becky); b. 21 Nov. 1934, Durham, North Carolina, USA. Vocalist; Musician (Piano); Songwriter. m. Charles A Dukes Jr, 20 Dec. 1955, 2 s., 1 d. *Education:* BA, Duke University; Vocal student with Todd Duncan. *Career:* Numerous stage performances including The Kennedy Center, Normandie Farm Lounge, Dulles Holiday Inn, The Castle, Thompson's Restaurant, Ocean City, Capitol Hill Club, Post Office Pavilion; Most recent stage show as feature artist for Philharmonic sponsored concert; Performed with US Navy Band commemorating 200 years of balloon flight in America; 2 cable specials, 1990's. *Compositions:* 47 individual compositions recorded. *Recordings include:* Alive, 1992; Rainbow, 1994; Borrow the Sun, 1995; Almost Country, 1999. *Publications:* Poetry published in several editions, 1992–94. *Honours:* 5 ASCAP Awards for Pop Writing, 1994–98; Numerous Awards, Mid-Atlantic Song Contest, 1984–92; American Women Composers' Song Contest Award; Billboard Award, For the Children of the World, 1996. *Memberships:* ASCAP; NARAS; SAI; SAW; NSAI; FMMC. *Leisure interests:* Skiing; Writing poetry; Tennis; Attending concerts. *Address:* 7111 Pony Trail, Hyattsville, MD 20782, USA.

DULFER Candy; b. 19 Sept. 1969, Amsterdam, Netherlands. Musician (saxophone). *Musical Education:* Soprano saxophone from age 7. *Career:* First recording with father Hans Dulfer, aged 11; Founder, jazz-funk group Funky Stuff, aged 15; Support to Madonna, Dutch tour, 1987; Prince, Dutch tour, 1988; Also played with: Van Morrison; Aretha Franklin; Pink Floyd; Dave Stewart. *Recordings:* Albums as with Funky Stuff; Solo albums include: Saxuality, 1991; Sax-A-Go-Go, 1994; Big Girl, 1996; For the Love of You, 1997; What Does it Take, 1999; Girls Night Out, 2001; Also featured on We Too Are One, Eurythmics, 1989; Film soundtrack, De Kassiere, with Dave Stewart, 1990; Singles: with Prince: Party Man; with Dave Stewart: Lily Was Here (No. 1, Netherlands), 1990; 2 Funky, 1993; Gititon, 1997; Saxy Mood, 1998. *Address:* c/o Inge Dulfer, PC Hoofstraat 154, 1071 CG Amsterdam, Netherlands.

DUMBRECK Allan M; b. 11 March 1961, Edinburgh, Scotland. Music Lecturer; Musician (keyboards). *Education:* BSc, Electrical Engineering, Edinburgh University. *Career:* Keyboard player, Big Dish, 1986–87; Horse, 1988–89; Lecturer, Jewel and Esk Valley College, 1986–91; North Glasgow College, 1991–98; University of Westminster, 1998–99; James Watt College 1999–; Ariadne Publications, 1998–; Established HND Music, Performance and Promotion; NGM Records, 1993; NGM Publishing, 1994. *Recordings:* The Same Sky, Horse, 1990; Rifferama, Thrum, 1994. *Publication:* Music Education Directory, editor and compiler, 1996-. *Membership:* PRS. *Leisure interest:* Property Restoration. *Address:* c/o Ariadne Publications, 20 Kensington Gate, Glasgow G12 9LQ, Scotland.

DUNBAR Sly (Noel Charles); b. 10 May 1952, Kingston, Jamaica. Reggae Musician (drums); Prod. *Career:* Played with: The Upsetter; Skin Flesh and Bones; The Revolutionaries; Member, houseband, Channel One label; Member, US rhythm partnership, Sly and Robbie, with Robbie Shakespeare, 1975–; Formed own record label Taxi; Prolific session musician with numerous artistes including: Peter Tosh; Bunny Wailer; Black Uhuru; Grace Jones; Bob Dylan; Ian Dury; Joan Armatrading; Buju Banton; Beenie Man; Dennis Brown; Jimmy Cliff; Mikey Dread; Gregory Isaacs; King Tubby; The Mighty Diamonds; Sugar Minott; U-Roy; Tours with Black Uhuru. *Recordings:* Solo albums: Simple Sly Man, 1978; Sly Wicked and Slick, 1979; Sly-Go-Ville, 1982; with Sly and Robbie: Sly and Robbie Present Taxi, 1981; A Dub Extravaganza, 1984; Language Barrier, 1985; Sly and Robbie Meet King Tubby, 1985; Reggae Greats, 1985; The Sound of Taxi, Vol. 1, Vol. 2, 1986; Rhythm Killers, 1987; Taxi Fare, 1987; Uhuru In Dub, 1987; The Summit, 1988; Hardcore Dub, 1989; Silent Assassin, 1990; Remember Precious Times, 1993; Mambo Taxi, 1997; Fatigue Chic, 1999; Dub Fire, 2000; In Good Company, 2001. *Current*

Management: Starline Entertainment, 1045 Pomme de Pin Lane, New Port Richey, FL 34655, USA.

DUNCAN Charles Melville; b. 25 Dec. 1928, Eltham, London, England. Architect (retired); Semi-pro Musician (tenor saxophone). Widower, 1 d. *Musical Education:* Piano tuition, school; Private accordion tuition; Self-taught saxophone, clarinet. *Career:* Played with various local jazz bands from age 20; Later, member 2 hotel quartets, 8 years each; Leader, own 9 piece band: The Golden Era jazz Band; Convenor, Annual Jazz Extravaganza, Perth (now in fourth year). *Membership:* Musicians' Union. *Leisure interests:* Playing saxophone; Arranging for own band; Architecture; Woodwork. *Address:* 120 Burghmuir Rd, Perth PH1 1HU, Scotland.

DUNCAN Johnny (John Richard); b. 5 Oct. 1938, Dublin, Texas, USA. Country vocalist; Songwriter; Musician (guitar). *Education:* Texas Christian University, studied English. *Career:* Cousin of country singer Dan Seals and Jim Seals from pop duo Seals and Crofts; Moved to Dublin, Texas to Clovis, New Mexico, 1959; Recorded demos with Norman Petty; Unsuccessfully promoted by Petty as pop singer, visiting England to have string section added to recordings; DJ on WAGG-Franklin radio station, Tennessee, 1964; Appeared on Nashville local TV shows with Ralph Emery; Spotted and signed by Columbia Records producer Don Law, 1967; Initial recordings produced by Frank Jones; Debut country chart entry, 1967; Minor hits until run of 9 consecutive country top ten hits (including 3 #1s), 1976–79; Collaborations: June Stearns; Janie Frickie (a.k.a. Janie Fricke). *Compositions include:* I'd Rather Love You; Summer Sunday; Fools; I Ain't All Bad; She's Too Good To Be True. *Recordings include:* Thinkin' of a Rendezvous, 1976; It Couldn't Have Been Any Better, Come A Little Bit Closer (with Janie Fricke), 1977; She Can Put Her Shoes Under My Bed (Anytime), Hello Mexico (and Adios Baby To You), 1978; Albums include: The Best of Johnny Duncan, 1976; Greatest Hits, 1978; In My Dreams, Nice 'N' Easy (with Janie Fricke), 1980. *Address:* c/o The Country Music Association, Nashville, Tennessee, USA.

DUNCAN Torey Atkins; b. 5 Aug. 1961, Summerfield, North Carolina, USA. *Career:* Regular Member, father's band, Bobby Atkins and the Countrymen; Recorded with father on Old Homestead Records, 10 years; Guest Starred, The Country Side of Bobby Atkins, album. *Recordings:* Enough to Keep Me Dreaming On; Lost Below Heaven. *Address:* c/o Bobby Atkins, PO Box 251, Summerfield, NC 27358–0251, USA.

DUNCKEL Jean Benoit; b. Versailles, France. Prod.; Keyboards. *Education:* Studied at the Conservatoire, Paris. *Career:* Formed Orange with Alex Gopher; Band joined by fellow Conservatoire student Nicolas Godin; After departure of Gopher from band, formed duo Air, 1995; Released debut single, 1996; Signed to Virgin and released their debut album, 1997; Collaborations: Jean Jacques Perrey; Francoise Hardy; Alex Gopher; Gordon Tracks; Remixed: Depeche Mode; Neneh Cherry. *Recordings:* Albums: Moon Safari, 1997; The Virgin Suicides, Premieres Symptoms, 1999; 10000 Hz Legend, 2001; Singles: Modulor, Casanova 70, 1996; Sexy Boy, 1997; Kelly Watch The Stars, 1998; Playground Love, 2000; Radio No. 1, 2001. *Address:* c/o Source Records, 113–117 Farringdon Rd, London, EC1R 3BX, England.

DUNHAM Aubrey; b. Houston, Texas, USA. Singer; Blues Musician (saxophone); Writer; Arranger; Prod. *Musical Education:* BA, Musical Education, Texas Southern University. *Career:* Tours, performances with artists including: Wilton Felder; Johnny Clyde Copeland; The O'Jays; The Temptations; Roy Head; Hank Crawford; Leader, own band, Aubrey Dunham and The Party Machine; Writer, arranger, producer. *Recordings:* Album: Now I'm Singing The Blues, songs include: I Used To Be A Dog (hit single); Shot Gun; I'm Glad About My Good Time. *Membership:* Houston Blues Society. *Leisure interest:* Teaching music to youth. *Current Management:* Sirron Kyles, Samuel Rogers and Associates. *Address:* PO Box 8305, Houston, TX 77288, USA.

DUNKELMAN Stephan; b. 7 May 1956, Brussels. Composer. m. 1 s., 1 d. *Compositions:* Signallures; Rituellipses; Metharcana; Thru, Above and Between, 1998; Dreamlike Shudder In An Airstream, 1999. *Recordings:* Acousnatica; Signallures; Aquaeray; Rituellipses. *Honours:* Stockholm Electronic Arts Award, Mention, 1993; Stockholm Electronic Arts Award, for Metharcana, 1998; Ars Electronica, Special Mention. *Memberships:* SACEM; SACD; ACSR; CEC. *Address:* Loutrier St 42, B 1170 Brussels, Belgium.

DUNKLEY Craig Anthony Spencer; b. 25 March 1964, Leicester, England. Musician (percussion). *Musical Education:* Artist in Education Course at Polytechnic. *Career:* Two week tour of Russia; Interview on Russian TV; 3 Week tour of Germany; 5 Day tour of Ireland; Local Radio sessions and interviews; Video shown on C4 TV programme, D-Energy. *Recording:* Album with TYD. *Honour:* Endorsed by Premier Percussion. *Membership:* Musicians' Union. *Leisure interests:* Most sports; Travel;

Adventure. *Current Management:* Access to Music; Big Wheel. *Address:* 86 Hopefield Rd, Leicester LE3 2BL, England.

DUNLOP Andy; b. 16 March 1972, Scotland. Musician (guitar). *Career:* Member, Travis; Numerous tours and television appearances. *Recordings:* Singles: U16 Girls, 1997; All I Want To Do Is Rock, 1997; Tied to the 90s, 1997; Happy, 1997; More than Us, 1997; Writing to Reach You, 1999; Driftwood, 1999; Why Does It Always Rain on Me?, 1999; Turn, 1999; Coming Around, 2000; Sing, 2001; Side, 2001; Albums: Good Feeling, 1997; The Man Who (No. 1, UK), 1999; The Invisible Band (No. 1, UK), 2001. *Honours:* Q Magazine Award, Best Single, 1999; Select Magazine, Album of the Year, 1999; Brit Awards: Best British Group; Best British Album, 2000.

DUNMALL Paul Norman; b. 6 May 1953, London, England. Musician (saxophones, woodwind, bagpipes). *Musical Education:* Clarinet, Blackheath Conservatoire. *Career:* Tours, Europe with Marsupilami, 1970–71; USA with Blue Aquarius, 1972–74; USA/Europe tour with Johnny Guitar Watson; Tours of Europe in 1980s with: Spirit Level; Tenor Tonic; London Jazz Composers Orchestra; Danny Thompson; Mujician in Russia, 1991. *Recordings:* Ain't That A Bitch; Johnny Guitar Watson; Mice In The Wallet; Killer Bunnies; Spirit Level; Andy Sheppard; Journey; Poem About the Hero; Birdman; Industry; Bladek; Colours Fulfilled; Solo albums: Soliloquy, 1986; Bebop Starburst, 1999; East West North South, 2001. *Honour:* Best Soloist, Dunkirk Jazz Festival, 1979. *Memberships:* PRS; MCPS. *Leisure interests:* Artwork; Wood engraving; Metal detecting. *Current Management:* Nod Knowles. *Address:* Linley House, 1 Pierre Pl., Bath, Avon BA1 1JY, England.

DUNN Alan R; b. 19 Oct. 1955, Boothstown, Lancashire, England. Musician (accordion, keyboards, tinwhistles). m. Wendy Elizabeth, 6 Jan. 1984. *Career:* Musician for various projects with artistes include: Richard Thompson; Loudon Wainwright III; Bob Geldof; Rolf Harris; Vladimir Asriev; Tour with Toy Dolls, 1997–98. *Recordings:* Albums: Clannad: Magical Ring, 1983; Lyle McGuiness Band, 1983; Richard Thompson: Across a Crowded Room, 1985; Watching the Dark, 1993; Doom and Gloom, 1994; Toy Dolls, One More Megabyte; Alison Moyet, Essex, 1994; Rolf Harris, Can You Tell What It Is Yet?, 1997; John Tams, Unity, 2000. *Address:* 10 Holden House, Deptford Church St, London SE8 45Q, England.

DUNN Gary Michael; b. 7 March 1960, Sunderland, England. Musician (guitar). *Career:* Tours, Europe and USA, including Glastonbury Festival (Pyramid stage); Reading Festival; Appearances at major concert halls including Dominion Theatre; Sadlers Wells; Town and Country Club; Television and radio appearances include: Whistle Test; Jools Holland. *Recordings:* Albums with: Martin Stephenson and the Dainties: Boat To Bolivia; Gladsome Humour and Blue; Salutation Road and The Boys Heart. *Memberships:* Musicians' Union; PRS; MCPS. *Leisure interests:* Football; Photography. *Address:* 280 Fulwell Rd, Sunderland SR6 9AP, England.

DUNN Holly S; b. 22 Aug. 1957, San Antonio, Texas, USA. singer; Songwriter. *Education:* Bs, Abilene Christian University, 1979. *Career:* Today Show; Prime Time Country; Crook and Chase; Vicki Lawrence Show; Maury Povich; Hosted Morning Radio Shaw; Host of Opry Backstage on TNN; Appeared On Numerous Country Music Specials and Award Shows. *Compositions:* Daddy's Hands; You Really Had Me Going; Love Someone Like Me; Are You Ever Gonna Love Me; Only When I Love; Strangers Again. *Recordings:* Albums, Holly Dunn; Cornerstone; Across The Rio Grande; The Blue Rose of Texas; Heart Full of Love; Getting It Done; Milestones-Greatest Hits; Life and Love and All The Stages; Leave One Bridge Standing; Maybe; A Face In The Crowd. *Honours:* Academy of Country Music, New Female Country Singer, 1986; Country Music Foundation, Horizon Award; 3 Grammy Nominations; BMI Songwriter of The Year, 1988. *Memberships:* AFTRA; AFM; NARAS. *Leisure interests:* Reading; Drawing; Painting; Jet Skiing; Snow Skiing; Movies. *Current Management:* Refugee International Management. *Address:* 209 10th Ave S, Suite 347, Nashville, Tennessee 37203, USA.

DUNN Ronnie Gene; b. 1 June 1953, Coleman, Texas, USA. Country vocalist; Prod.; Songwriter. *Career:* Lead vocalist, country duo Brooks and Dunn (with Kix Brooks). *Compositions include:* Boot Scootin' Boogie; Brand New Man; Darned If I Don't – Danged If I Do; Hard Workin' Man; He's Got You; Honky Tonk Truth; I Can't Get Over You; I'll Never Forgive My Heart; A Man This Lonely; Little Miss Honky Tonk; My Next Broken Heart; Neon Moon; You'll Always Be Loved By Me; She's Not The Cheatin' Kind; She Used To Be Mine; That Ain't No Way To Go; We'll Burn That Bridge; Whiskey Under The Bridge; You're Gonna Miss Me When I'm Gone. *Recordings:* solo: It's Written All Over Your Face, 1983; She Put The Sad In All His Songs, 1984; as Brooks and Dunn: Brand New Man, 1991; My Next Broken Heart, 1991; Neon Moon, 1992; Boot Scootin' Boogie, 1992; Hard Workin' Man, 1993; We'll Burn That Bridge, 1993; She Used To Be Mine, 1993; Rock My World (Little Country Girl), 1993; That Ain't No Way To Go, 1994; She's Not The Cheatin' Kind, 1994; Little Miss Honky Tonk, 1995; You're Gonna Miss Me When I'm Gone, 1995; Whiskey Under The Bridge, 1995; My Maria, 1996; I Am That Man, 1996; A Man This Lonely,

1996; He's Got You, 1997; Honky Tonk Truth, 1997; How Long Gone, 1998; Husbands and Wives, 1998; I Can't Get Over You, 1999; You'll Always Be Loved By Me, 2000; Ain't Nothing 'Bout You, 2001; Only In America, 2001; The Long Goodbye, 2002; Albums include: Brand New Man, 1991; Hard Workin' Man, 1993; Waitin' On Sundown, 1994; Borderline, 1996; The Greatest Hits Collection, 1997; If You See Her, 1998; Tight Rope, 1999; Steers and Stripes, 2001. *Honours:* various including: CMA, Vocal Duo of the Year, 1993–98. *Internet:* www.brooks-dunn.com.

DUPONT Hubert; b. 5 May 1959, Versailles, France. Jazz Musician (contrebass); Composer. m. 13 Oct. 1990, 1 s. *Education:* Engineering diploma, INSA (Lyon). *Musical Education:* Schools; Self-taught; Master classes. *Career:* Played with: Steve Lacy; Glenn Ferris; Mathieu Michel; Harold Land; Robin Eubanks; Stefano Di Battista; Noël Akchoté; George Brown; Tommy Smith; Steve Potts; Laurent De Wilde; Le Marmite Infernale (ARFI); Mathias Rüegg; Paolo Fresu; Benoit Delbecq; Guillaume Orti. *Recordings:* Altissimo, Hubert Dupont; Pression, Kartet; A L'Envers, Quoi De Neuf Docteur. *Memberships:* Collectif HASK; UMJ (Union des Musiciens de Jazz). *Leisure interests:* Bass; Photography; Books; Travel. *Address:* 9 Ave Pasteur, 93100 Montreuil, France.

DUPREE Cornell; b. 19 Dec. 1942, Fort Worth, Texas, USA. Musician (guitar). m. Erma, 23 June 1959, 2 s., 1 d. *Education:* 1 year college. *Musical Education:* High School saxophone; Self-taught guitar. *Career:* Joined King Curtis Band, New York City, 1962, appeared with Jimi Hendrix, Chuck Rainey; Session player, more than 2500 records with artists including: Sam Cooke; Wilson Pickett; Miles Davis; Joe Cocker; Michael Bolton; Mariah Carey; Bonnie Raitt; Toured and recorded with Aretha Franklin, 1967–76; Tours with: Roberta Flack; Joe Cocker; Grover Washington Jr; Currently tours with Herbie Mann and The Deep Pocket Band; Early 70's, teamed with Richard Tee, Steve Gadd to form STUFF, house band for Saturday Night Live. *Recordings:* Albums: Teasin', 1973; Shadow Dancing, 1978; Guitar Groove, 1987; Coast to Coast, 1988; Can't Get Through, 1991; Child's Play, 1993; Bop 'n' Blues, 1994; Uncle Funky, 1998; Unstuffed, 1998; Double Clutch, 1998; Also appeared on: King Curtis: Soul Seranade; Brook Benton: Rainy Night In Georgia; Aretha Franklin: Live At Fillmore West; Joe Cocker: Sting Ray; Barbra Streisand: Guilty; Donny Hathaway: Live At the Bitter Inn; Stuff: Stuff. *Publications:* Coast To Coast; Happy Farms; Southern Comfort. *Honours:* 2 Grammy Nominations. *Memberships:* NARA; ASCAP. *Leisure interests:* Sketching; Drawing. *Current Management:* Fred Hirsch.

DURAL Stanley 'Buckwheat' Jr; b. 14 Nov. 1947, Lafayette, Louisiana, USA. Musician (zydeco, accordion). m. Bernite Dural. *Career:* Professional musician from age 9; Formed Buckwheat and the Hitchikers, 1970's; Joined 'father of zydeco' Clifton Chenier, 1978–80; Formed Buckwheat Zydeco, 1979; Signed to Island Records, 1987 (first zydeco artist on major record label). *Recordings include:* Ma 'Tit Fille; What You Gonna Do; Also recorded with artists including: Eric Clapton; Willie Nelson; Dwight Yoakam; Keith Richards. *Honours:* 4 Grammy Nominations. *Current Management:* Ted Fox. *Address:* c/o Ted Fox, PO Box 561, Rhinebeck, NY 12572, USA.

DURHAM Judith; b. 3 July 1943, Melbourne, Australia. Singer; Songwriter; Musician (piano, tambourine). m. Ron Edgeworth, 21 Nov. 1969, deceased 1994. *Education:* Secretarial Course, Royal Melbourne Institute of Technology; AMusA, Piano, with Ronald Farren Price, Melbourne University, 1961. *Career:* First international female chart-topping recording artist, 1965; Lead Vocalist, The Seekers, folk pop group; Royal Command Performance, 1966; Guinness Book of Records, for largest crowd in southern hemisphere; Highest ever rating, Australian TV show Seekers Down Under, 1967, and The World of the Seekers, 1968, shown in cinemas. *Compositions:* Australia Land of Today; Gotta Be Rainbows, musical; Colours of My Life; One World Love; Calling Me Home; It's Hard to Leave; Self-penned solo album, Let Me Find Love. *Recordings:* With The Seekers: I'll Never Find Another You (No. 1, UK), 1965; A World of Our Own, 1965; The Carnival Is Over (No. 1, UK), 1965; Someday One Day, 1966; Walk With Me, 1966; Morningtown Ride, 1966; Georgy Girl, 1967; When Will the Good Apples Fall, 1967; 7 Seekers albums including Future Road, 1997; Solo albums include: Mona Lisas, 1996; Hot Jazz Duo, 2001; Onto Your Dream, 2001; 3 solo jazz albums with husband. *Publication:* Colours of My Life: The Judith Durham Story, biography by Graham Simpson, 1994, 1998. *Honours:* Australian of the Year, 1967, jointly with The Seekers; Aria Hall of Fame, 1997; Medal of the Order of Australia. *Membership:* Patron, Motor Neurone Disease Asscn. *Leisure interests:* Vegetarian; Teetotal; Meditation; Piano. *Address:* PO Box 555, South Yarra, Victoria 3141, Australia.

DURITZ Adam; b. 1 Aug. 1964, Baltimore, Maryland, USA. Vocalist; Musician (piano). *Career:* Formed acoustic duo with David Bryson, later joined with Matt Malley, Charlie Gillingham and Steve Bowman to record a demo; Joined by Dan Vickrey and began recording as Counting Crows; Numerous live tours and TV appearances including several on MTV; Bowman left, replaced by Ben Mize. *Recordings:* Singles: Round Here, 1994; Mr Jones, 1994; Rain King, 1994; Angels of the Silence (live), 1996;

Albums: August and Everything After, 1993; Recovering the Satellites, 1996; Across a Wire: Live in New York, 1998; Long December, 1999; Daylight Fading, 1999; Appearances on: Sweet Relief: Benefit for Victoria, 1993; Nanci Griffith: Flyer, 1994; Wallflowers: Bringing Down the Horse, 1996; Dog's Eye View: Daisy, 1997; Ryan Adams: Gold, 2001.

DURRANT Bertie (Brian); b. 25 July 1945, Gloucester, England. Jazz Musician (clarinet, soprano, tenor and baritone saxophones, blues harmonica); Vocalist. m. (1) Janice Newman, 1966; m. (2) Diane Thompson, 1976, 2 s., 1 d. *Education:* Mid-Essex Technical College; University of East London. *Musical Education:* Self-taught. *Career:* Industrial and advertising photographer; Professional musician, 1983–; Founder member, City Vagabonds (prize-winning Essex trad band); Numerous other bands including Tom Collins (4 years); Currently running own name line-up; tours, Europe; North America; Played jazz festivals throughout UK. *Membership:* Asscn of British Jazz Musicians. *Leisure interests:* Collecting elderly reed instruments, clocks; Trying not to learn the banjo. *Address:* 23 Upper Moors, Great Waltham, Essex CM3 1RB, England.

DURRANT Clare Joanne Mary; b. 2 Dec. 1962, Southport, England. Musician (keyboards, percussion, violin, guitar); Vocalist. *Education:* Lancaster University; Salford University College. *Musical Education:* John Hammond; Tommy Odueso; Wadada; Clare Hogan-Taylor; Salford University College. *Career:* Keyboard player for Suns of Arqa as Ireti, 1987–; Major concerts include: Womad Festival; Phoenix Festival; Hit The North, BBC Radio session; Set up Ireti Percussion workshops; Formed Otherworld, 1992. *Recordings:* Album: with Otherworld: Messages; Also tracks licensed for Compilations; with Suns of Arqa as Ireti: Hey Jagunath; Bhoopali (track part of BBC Radio 5 session Hit The North). *Leisure interests:* Art; Designing and making clothes. *Address:* 52 Riverbank Tower, Salford M3 7JY, England.

DURRANT Richard; b. 2 Nov. 1962, Brighton, England. Musician (Guitar, Mandolin, Banjo, Double Bass, Bodhran). m. Louise, 1 d. *Education:* Royal College of Music. *Career:* Debut, Purcell Room, London, 1986; 1,200 Concerts for Yehudi Menuhins, Live Music Now; Played Lead Guitar with Sky; Prolific Concert Guitarist, UK and Europe; Busy Multi Instrumental Session Player; Composer of Concert and Television Music. *Compositions:* Acoustic Rain; A Lowland Cinderella; The Rucenitsa Quartet. *Recordings:* Guitar Latina; The Music of Mario Castelnuovo-Tedesco; The Summer EP. *Memberships:* PRS; MCPS; MU. *Current Management:* LongMan. *Address:* West House, Forthaven, Shoreham By Sea, West Sussex BN43 5HY, England.

DURST Fred (William Frederick); b. 20 Aug. 1970, Gastonia, North Carolina, USA. Vocalist. m. 1990, divorced, 1 s., 1 d. *Career:* Senior Vice-President of Interscope Records; Owner Flawless record label; Formed Limp Bizkit, 1994; Signed to Flip/Interscope on strength of demo tape; Live shows at concerts and festivals; Group spearheaded 'nu-metal' breakthrough in Europe, 2001; Preparing solo LP, 2001. *Recordings:* Albums: Three Dollar Bill, Y'All $, 1997; Significant Other, 1999; Chocolate Starfish and The Hot Dog Flavored Water, 2000; New Old Songs (remix album), 2001; Singles: Faith, 1997; Nookie, Rearranged, 1999; Break Stuff, Take A Look Around (from Mission Impossible 2 OST), My Generation, 2000; Rollin', My Way, Boiler, 2001. *Honours:* Second and third albums both debuted at #1 on US chart; Significant Other sales in excess of 6m. *Current Management:* The Firm (Management), 9100 Wilshire Blvd, Suite 400W, Beverly Hills, CA 90212, USA. *Internet:* www.limpbizkit.com.

DUTIRO Chartwell; b. 26 Dec. 1957, Bindura, Zimbabwe. Vocalist; Musician (mbira, saxophone, hosho); Songwriter. *Musical Education:* Learned mbira from family; Later saxophone; SOAS, University of London, MMus in Ethnomusicology, 1998. *Career:* Played mbira in traditional ceremonies from early teens; Member: Rhodesia Prison Band; Thomas Mapfumo's Blacks Unlimited, 1988–94; Relocated to UK; Formed Spirit Talk Mbira; Teaches mbira, singing and percussion at School of Oriental and African Studies. *Recordings:* Albums include: with Thomas Mapfumo: Zimbabwe – Mozambique, 1988; Chamunorwa, 1990; with Spirit Talk Mbira: Ndonga Mahwe – Return As Spirit, 1997; Nhimbe, 1998; Dzoro, 1999; Voices of Ancestors, 2000. *Address:* c/o Rachel Levay, Ingoma, 52 Picton St, Bristol, BS6 5QA, England. *E-mail:* rachel@ingoma.co.uk. *Internet:* www.dham.net/soe/stm.

DUTOT Pierre; b. 11 June 1946, Caen, France. Musician (trumpet); Trumpet teacher. m. Catherine Groult, 21 June 1975, 1 s., 2 d. *Education:* CAPEPS in EPS; DUEL in Psychology. *Musical Education:* Premier Prix Conservatoire National Supérieur de Musique, Paris, 1971. *Career:* Solo trumpeter, National Orchestra of Lyon; Professor CNSM Lyon and CNR Bordeaux ; Solo concert artiste; Tutor, international Master Classes; Member, numerous ensembles: Hexagone; Trompolis; Polygone; Jericho. *Recordings:* 10 albums as solo artiste; Recordings with: Hexagone; Trompolis; Polygone. *Leisure interests:* Basketball; Skiing; Tennis;

Esoterism. *Current Management:* Concept Music BPZ, 69126 Brindas-Lyon, France. *Address:* Domaine des Cerisiers, 105 Chemin du Soyard, 69126 Brindas-Lyon, France.

DUVIVIER Jérôme; b. 9 Oct. 1965, St Cloud, France. Jazz Singer. *Musical Education:* Little Singers of Paris; Lessons with Stephanie Crawford, Michelle Hendricks. *Career:* Concerts in jazz clubs, France: Le Sunset; Le Petit Journal Montparnasse. *Recordings:* Un Effet Boeuf; L'Ennui; Courtoisies; Epilogue. *Honours:* Prix de la SACEM, Crest Festival. *Membership:* Jazz on the Blocks (French Jazz Singers Asscn). *Address:* 29 rue Basfroi, 75011 Paris, France.

DVORAK Jim; b. 16 Dec. 1948, New York City, USA. Musician (trumpet); Composer; Teacher. *Musical Education:* Eastman School of Music. *Career:* Regular international jazz festivals and concert tours; Connected with South African musicians, including Brotherhood of Breath, District Six, Zila, 1970s-80s; Also played with: Dreamtime; In Cahoots; Leader, own band Bardo State Orchestra; Workshop leader with Community Music, London; Major tour of Netherlands with Bardo State Orchestra and with Tibetan Gyuto Monks, 1998. *Compositions include:* Score for jazz drama Animal Farm, 1979; Co-writer, score for Kosh Theatre Company's production, The Jago, 1983. *Recordings:* with District Six: Aguzwakale; Ingoma Yabantwana; Leave My Name At The Door; To Be Free; with Annabel Lamb: Once Bitten; The Flame; When Angels Travel; Brides; Justice; with In Cahoots: Live In Japan; Recent Discoveries; Parellel; with Research: Laws of Motion; Social Systems; with Harry Moscoe: Country Boy; Sexy Dancer; Bunny Up, Dreamtime; Innocence, Joe Gallivan; Mama, Mama Quartetto; Gland, Fonolite; Joy, Joy; Thunder In Our Hearts, Jabula; Stanislav Sojka, Stanislav Sojka; Gasoline Band, Gasoline Band; Hat Music, Katie Perks; This Isn't Sex, Eric Mingus; Newsense, Elton Dean; The Covenant, Wally Brill; Zenfish, Dreamtime. *Honours:* Young Jazz Musicians Award, Greater London Arts, 1976; Bachelor of Music. *Memberships:* Performing Right Society; Composers Guild. *Address:* 43B Mulkern Rd, London N19 3HQ, England.

DVORSKY Petr; b. 29 June 1966, Czech Republic. Musician (Doublebass). *Education:* Conservatory of Jaroslav Jezek. *Career:* Brecon Jazz Festival, 1996; Festival Pragues Spring, 1994; Festival Liege, Belgium, 1998. *Recordings:* The Four: Space and Rhythm; Stever Houben, Buhemia After Dark; Roman Pokorny, Jazz Perception. *Honours:* Nomination of Czech Jazz Society, Talent of The Year, 1996. *Memberships:* Czech Society Jazz Society. *Leisure interest:* Photography. *Address:* Veleslavinska 43, 162 00 Prague 6, Czech Republic.

DVORZAK Zlatko; b. 5 March 1939, Zagreb, Croatia. Musician (piano); Composer; Conductor; Arranger; Teacher. m. Gordana Dvorzak, Oct. 1970, 1 s., 1 d. *Musical Education:* Zagreb Musical Academy, graduated 1970. *Career:* Tours of Poland; Bulgaria; Russia; Hungary; Austria; Germany, 1961–76; Played and recorded with: Ernie Wilkins; Clark Terry; Art Farmer; Albert Mangelsdorff; Kai Winding; John Lewis; Bosco Petrovic; Stan Getz; Bud Shank; Al Porcino; Lee Harper; Sal Nistico; Gianni Basso; Ozren Depolo; Dusko Gojkovic; Johnny Griffin; Also performed music for radio and television. *Compositions include:* Revue; Amoroso; Clarinetorama; Black Street; All That Swing; Discopathia; Fender Express; Mr Hammond; Trumpet Swing; Jazz Concertino for String Quartet and Jazz Sextet; Croatian Folk Motives. *Recordings:* with BP Convention Big Band: Blue Sunset, 1975; Green Lobster Dream, 1978; Josipa Lisac and BP Convention, 1975; Croatian Big Band, 1977. *Honours:* First Prize, Contest for Young Pianists, Croatia, 1958; Best Arrangement, Belgrade Pop Festival, 1971. *Memberships:* Croatian Composers' Society; Orchestras Society; Jazz Club, Zagreb. *Leisure interests:* Painting; Table tennis. *Address:* Buconjiceva 26, 10000 Zagreb, Croatia.

DWECK Sydney Stevan; b. 28 Dec. 1926, New York City, USA. Musician. Divorced, 2 s. *Education:* AA, honours, Los Angeles Valley College, 1966; BA, honours, California State University at Northridge, 1968; PhD, University of Southern California, 1977. *Career:* Freelance drummer and percussionist, Broadway shows including Hello Dolly, fiddler on the Roof, Kismet, Pajama Game; Film soundtracks include: Double Trouble, The Swinger, Made in Paris; Percussionist, TV Specials including Bob Hope, Lucille Ball, Perry Como, Fred Astaire, Perry Mason, Liberace; Albums include Stan Kenton, Freddy Martin, Jack Jones; Musical Director, artists including Debbie Reynolds, Carol Channing, Liza Minelli, Jane Russell; Command performances for Royal Family of Monaco, England, Presidents Kennedy, Johnson, Nixon, Bush, Reagan. *Compositions:* Scores, Altoon's Dance, 1965; Danny Thomas Show. *Memberships:* American Federation of Musicians; Masonic lodge. *Address:* 1507 Seacrest Dr., Corona Del Mar, CA 92625, USA.

DYENS Roland; b. 19 Oct. 1955, Tunis, Tunisia. Musician (guitar); Composer (classic-fusion style). m. Claire Fischbein, 7 Sept. 1986, 1 s., 1 d. *Musical Education:* Concert degree, Ecole Normale de Musique de Paris. *Career:* Concert artist playing throughout world; Guitar festivals include: Nice; Cannes; Paris; Festival du Marais (Paris); Aix En Provence; Radio

France Festival, Montpellier; Midem; Printemps de Bourges; Musicora; Carrefour Mondial De La Guitare (Martinique); Liège (Belgium); Arvika (Sweden); Tichy (Poland); Estergom (Hungary); Marktoberdorf (Germany); Classical Guitar Festival of Great Britain; Tours: Middle East; Indonesia; Scandinavia; Poland; Brazil; Numerous television and radio shows; Composer and arranger; Teacher; Member of juries of international contests including Montélimar; Geneva; Fort de France; Bari. *Compositions include:* Works for guitar solo; 2 octets; Concerto Métis (for guitar and string orchestra); Concerto En Si (for guitar and ensemble of 21 guitars). *Recordings:* Heitor Villa-Lobos Preludes and Roland Dyens works; Hommage à Brassens with the Enesco Quartet and Roland Dyens works; Ao Vivo (jazz trio); Suite Populaire Brésilienne, Heitor Villa-Lobos (concerto for guitar and string orchestra); French Songs Vols 1 and 2; Concerto En Si (for guitar and ensemble of 21 guitars). *Honours:* Grand Prix du Disque, Academie Charles-Cros. *Memberships:* SACEM; ADAMI.

DYLAN Bob, (Robert Allen Zimmerman); b. 24 May 1941, Duluth, Minnesota, USA. Singer; Musician (guitar, piano, harmonica, autoharp); Poet; Composer. *Musical Education:* Self-taught. *Career:* Solo folk/rock artist, also performed with The Band; The Traveling Wilburys; Grateful Dead; Songs recorded by estimated 3000 artists, including U2, Bruce Springsteen, Rod Stewart, Jimi Hendrix, Eric Clapton, Neil Young; Numerous tours: USA, Europe, Australia, 1961–; Film appearances include: Pat Garrett and Billy The Kid; Concert For Bangladesh; Hearts of Fire. *Compositions include:* Blowin' In The Wind; Like A Rolling Stone; Mr Tambourine Man; Lay Lady Lay; Forever Young; Tangled Up In Blue; Gotta Serve Somebody; Don't Think Twice; It's Alright; A Hard Rain's Gonna Fall; The Times They Are A-Changin'; Just Like A Woman; I'll Be Your Baby Tonight; I Shall Be Released; Simple Twist of Fate; Paths of Victory; Dignity. *Recordings:* Over 40 albums include: The Freewheelin' Bob Dylan, 1964; Bringing It All Back Home, 1965; Highway 61 Revisited, 1965; Blonde On Blonde, 1966; John Wesley Harding, 1968; Nashville Skyline, 1969; Self Portrait, 1970; New Morning, 1970; Before The Flood, 1974; Hard Rain, 1976; Desire, 1976; Street Legal, 1978; Slow Train Coming, 1979; Infidels, 1983; Empire Burlesque, 1985; Knocked Out Loaded, 1986; Down In The Groove, 1988; Biograph (5 record set), 1988; Oh Mercy, 1989; Under The Red Sky, 1990; MTV Unplugged, 1995; Time Out of Mind, 1997; Love and Theft, 2001; with The Band: Planet Waves, 1974; Blood On The Tracks, 1975; with Traveling Wilburys: Traveling Wilburys, 1988; Vol. 3, 1990; with Grateful Dead, Dylan and The Dead, 1989; Singles include: One Too Many Mornings, 1965; Mr Tambourine Man, 1966; Love Sick, 1997. *Publications:* Tarantula, 1966; Writings and Drawings, 1973; The Songs of Bob Dylan 1966–75, 1976; Lyrics 1962–85, 1986. *Honours include:* Hon. D Mus, Princeton University, 1970; Inducted, Rock and Roll Hall of Fame, 1988; Grammy, 1990. *Current Management:* Jeff Rosen, PO Box 870, Cooper Station, New York, NY 10276, USA.

DYNNESEN Lise Kruuse; b. 24 Dec. 1956, Copenhagen, Denmark. Musician (piano, keyboards); Composer (church organ, piano). *Education:* University studies: Danish Literature; Music. *Musical Education:* Student, organ, Royal Danish Academy of Music, 1991-. *Career:* Freelance musician, composer, experimental, rhythmic music scene, Copenhagen, 1978–; Bands include: Primi Band with Marilyn Mazur, 1982–85; Salsanama, 1988–91. *Compositions:* Sleigh Song – Or Minea's Tale, for organ, 1994. *Honours:* Scholarships from: The Art Foundation of The Danish State; The Royal Danish Academy of Music; The Society of Danish Jazz Beat Folk Authors (DJBFA). *Membership:* DJBFA. *Leisure interests:* Skiing; Cycling. *Address:* Bregnegangen 5, 2300 Copenhagen S, Denmark.

DYSON John; b. 11 March 1948, Sheffield, England. Musician (keyboards, guitar); Music Prod.; Analytical Chemist. *Education:* Technical college. *Musical Education:* Self-taught. *Career:* Formed Wavestar (electronic music), with Dave Ward-Hunt, 1983; Concerts include: UK Electronica '85, Sheffield; Concerts throughout UK; Festivals in France; Record label folded, band split 1988; Formed UK Label Surreal to Real with current partner/director Anthony Thrasher; Played major Dutch Festival, 1990–92; Now established as UK's leading independent label for contemporary instrumental/synthesizer music. *Recordings:* with Wavestar: Mind Journey; Zenith; Moonwind; Solo: Evolution; Aquarelle; Different Values; Various others for compilation; Wavestar albums re-released on own label. *Honours:* Voted Best Newcomer, National German Radio E M Show, 1991. *Memberships:* PRS; MU. *Leisure interests:* Reading science fiction; Films; Driving; Space; Watching Sheffield Wednesday Football Club. *Current Management:* Surreal To Real. *Address:* PO Box 33 Evesham, Worcestershire WR11 6UX, England.

DZIERZANDWSKI Udo; b. 23 June 1964. Musician (Guitar). *Education:* Guitar Craft, 1987. *Career:* International Touring, Europa String Choir; CD, The Starving Moon; Appearance on John Schaeffa's New Sounds Programme, New York; Local and National Radio, England, Italy and Germany. *Recordings:* The Starving Moon, 1995; Real Promo Demo, 1998. *Leisure interests:* Computing; Drumming; Walking; Swimming; Table Tennis. *Address:* 95 Albert Rd, Parkstone, Poole, Doreset, BH12 2BX.

DZIUBINSKI Tomasz; b. 14 Sept. 1961, Katowice, Poland. Artist Man.; Promoter. m. Mariola Bractawik, 27 Dec. 1990, 2 s. *Education:* Building Engineer, Technical University. *Career:* Promoter for: Deep Purple; AC/DC; Metallica; Black Sabbath; Fish; Chris Rea; Europe; Slayer; Paradise Lost; Sepultura; Faith No More; Dr Alban; Biohazard. *Recordings:* Produced over 20 albums of best Polish heavy metal bands including: Acid Drinkers; Kat; Turbo; Flapjack; Dynamind. *Memberships:* IFPI; ILMC. *Leisure interests:* Sport; Music. *Address:* ul Szeligiewicza 8/21, 40–044 Katowice, Poland.

E

EARL SIXTEEN (Earl Daley); b. 9 May 1958, Kingston, Jamaica. Songwriter; Vocalist; Record Prod. Seperated, 2 s. *Musical Education:* Self-taught. *Career:* Producer for L. Perry; Mikey Dread; Derrick Harriott; Neil Frazer; Douglas; Soundtrack of Judge Dredd with Leftfield; Currently touring with Dreadzone Band; Major Concert, Glastonbury, 1995. *Compositions include:* Love Is A Feeling, Studio One; Release The Pressure. *Recordings:* Solo albums include: Reggae Sound, 1981; Babylon Walls, 1992; Also appears on: World War Three, Mikey Dread, 1980; Holding Back The Years (single), Simply Red, 1985; Leftism, Leftfield, 1995; Second Light, Dreadzone, 2001. *Honours:* Silver disc, Leftfield album. *Memberships:* PRS; Musicians' Union; MCPS. *Leisure interests:* Writing; Reading; Driving; Swimming. *Current Management:* Martin Poole. *Address:* 30 Jackson Rd, Holloway, London N7, England.

EARLE Steve; b. 17 Jan. 1955, Fort Monroe, Virginia, USA. Singer; Songwriter; Musician (guitar). m. Lou Anne. *Career:* Bar room musician, Nashville; Solo artiste, with own band The Dukes, 1986-. *Compositions include:* My Old Friend The Blues, recorded by Janie Frickie; The Devil's Right Hand, recorded by Waylon Jennings; The Rain Came Down, for Farm Aid II benefit concert. *Recordings:* Albums: Guitar Town, 1986; Early Tracks, 1987; Exit O, 1987; Copperhead Road, 1988; The Hard Way, 1990; Shut Up and Die Like An Aviator, 1991; Essential Steve Earle, 1993; Train A Comin', 1995; I Feel Alright, 1996; El Corazón, 1997; The Mountain, 1999; Transcendental Blues, 2000; Together At The Bluebird Cafe, 2001. *Current Management:* Asgard Management, London, England; Four Twenty Two Management, Nashville, USA. *Address:* Dan Gillis Management, 1815 Division St, Suite 205, Nashville, TN 37203, USA.

EARLY David; b. 6 April 1956, Lewisham, London, England. Musician (drums, ethnic hand, atmospheric, percussion). *Career:* Recording, performance with Mud; Dollar; National Youth Jazz Orchestra; The Nolans; Spitting Image; Sade; Andy White; Maura O'Connell; The Chieftains; Chris Rea; Van Morrison; Mary Black; Kieran Goss and Francis Black; Brian Kennedy; Carmena; Tamalin. *Recordings:* with Sade: Diamond Life; Promise; with Van Morrison: Avalon Sunset; Enlightenment; Greatest Hits Vol. 1; Hymns To The Silence; Live From The Beacon Theatre; Carrying A Torch; Tom Jones/Van Morrison; Francis Black and Kieran Goss: Gorgeous and Bright; with Mary Black: The Holy Ground; The Circus. *Membership:* The Legendary Unknowns. *Leisure interests:* Swimming; Cycling; Papier Maché; My hammock; Heading West. *Address:* Belfast, Northern Ireland.

EASTON Sheena, (Sheena Shirley Orr); b. 27 April 1959, Bellshill, Glasgow, Scotland. Singer; Actress. m. Rob Light, 15 Jan. 1985. *Education:* Speech and Drama, Royal Scottish Academy of Music and Drama. *Career:* Singer, Glasgow club circuit, 1979; Featured in television series The Big Time, BBC1, 1980; Solo recording artiste, 1980-; Concerts and tours worldwide, including: Royal Variety Show, 1980; The Big Day festival, Glasgow, 1990; Television appearances include: TV special, Sheena Easton... Act 1, NBC, 1983; Actress, Miami Vice, NBC, 1987; Stage debut, Man of La Mancha, Chicago, then Broadway, 1991-92; Launched own Seven Minute Flat Stomach fitness video. *Recordings:* Albums: Sheena Easton, 1981; You Could Have Been With Me, 1981; Madness Money and Music, 1982; Best Kept Secret, 1983; A Private Heaven, 1985; Do You, 1985; The Lover In Me, 1989; For Your Eyes Only – The Best of Sheena Easton, 1989; The Collection, 1989; What Comes Naturally, 1991; No Strings, 1993; My Cherie, 1995; Body and Soul, 1997; Freedom, 2000; Fabulous, 2000; Hit singles include: Modern Girl, 1980; Morning Train (9 To 5) (No. 1, USA), 1981; One Man Woman, 1981; When He Shines, 1981; For Your Eyes Only, theme music to James Bond film, 1981; We've Got Tonight, duet with Kenny Rogers, 1983; Telefone, 1983; Strut, 1984; Sugar Walls, 1985; U Got The Look, duet with Prince, 1987; The Lover In Me (No. 2, US), 1989; What Comes Naturally, 1991; You Can Swing It, 1991; To Anyone, 1991; Contributor, Voices That Care charity record, 1991; Givin' Up Givin' In, 2001; Contributor, film soundtracks: Santa Claus – The Movie, 1985; About Last Night, 1986; Ferngully... The Last Rainforest, 1992. *Honours include:* Grammy Awards: Best New Artist, 1982; Best Mexican/American Performance, with Luis Miguel, 1985; First artist in history to have Top 5 hits in all major US charts (Pop, R & B, Country, Dance, Adult Contemporary), 1985; Emmy Award, Sheena Easton...Act 1, 1983. *Current Management:* Harriet Wasserman Management, 15250 Ventura Blvd, Suite 1215, Sherman Oaks, CA 91403-3201, USA.

EASTWOOD Al 'Bama'; b. 26 Oct. 1943, Birmingham, England. Musician (guitar, flute, drums, harmonica); Vocalist. *Career:* Played drums, rock and roll bands; Member, backing group for Gene Vincent; Television, radio include: Thank Your Lucky Stars; Beat Club, BBC; Jazz FM; John Cirl Show; Paul Jones Show; American radio. *Recordings:* Album: Seeds; Album

and single (own compositions). *Honour:* Non-drum competitions, Birmingham. *Membership:* Musicians' Union. *Leisure interests:* Poetry; Classical music; Tai Chi. *Address:* 104 Maughn Court, Palmerston Rd, Acton, London W3, England.

EATON Christopher; b. 16 Sept. 1958, Dudley, West Midlands, England. Singer; Songwriter; Musician (keyboards). *Musical Education:* Grade 6 Piano. *Career:* Songwriter for: Cliff Richard; Janet Jackson; Amy Grant; Sheena Easton; Patti Austin; Michael Ball; CeCe Winans; Sheila Walsh; Tours with Amy Grant and Cliff Richard; Performed at Grammy's New York, 1992; Solo recording career, contemporary Christian and pop music. *Compositions include:* songs for Heat In Motion, Amy Grant (5m. copies sold); Saviours Day, Cliff Richard, (No. 1, UK), 1990. *Recordings:* Solo albums: Vision, 1986; Wonderful World, 1995; What Kind of Love, 1998. *Honours:* Christian Song of the Year, Breath of Heaven, 1993, USA. *Memberships:* Musicians' Union; Equity. *Leisure interests:* Tennis; Golf; Country walks; Indian food; Soccer. *Current Management:* Stuart Ongley, SGO Music. *Address:* The Old Brewery, Church St, Tisbury, Wilts, England.

EATON Nigel; b. 3 Jan. 1966, Southampton, Hampshire, England. Musician (hurdy-gurdy). *Musical Education:* Guildhall School of Music. *Career:* Member, Blowzabella, 1985-90; Ancient Beatbox, 1990; Whirling Pope Joan, 1993-; Robert Plant and Jimmy Page, 1995-; Also with Howard Skempton: Hurdy-gurdy Concerto; Bournemouth Sinfonietta, 1994; BBC Welsh Symphony, 1992; Aldeburgh Festival with Scottish Chamber Orchestra; Films: Aliens; Friends; Harnessing Peacocks; Mansfield Park, 1999; The Hunchback of Notre Dame, 1999; Video: Snub TV, 1989, VH1, 1995. *Recordings:* 5 albums, Blowzabella; Album: Ancient Beatbox; Spin, Whirling Pope Joan, 1994; Unledded, MTV; No Quarter, Plant and Page, 1995; Sessions for: Marc Almond, 1987; Loreena McKennitt, 1994; Scott Walker, 1995; Gary Kemp, 1995; Peter Gabriel, 1999; Loreena McKennitt, 1999; Afro-Celt Sound System, 1999; Solo: Music of The Hurdy-Gurdy, 1987. *Leisure interest:* Sound Engineer. *Address:* 15 Becondale Rd, Upper Norwood, London SE19 1QJ, England.

EBB Fred; b. 4 Aug. 1936, New York, New York, USA. Songwriter; Lyricist. *Education:* NYU graduate; Columbia University Masters. *Career:* Lyrics for: Cabaret; Flora; The Red Menace; Zorba; Happy Time; 70, Girls, 70; Woman of The Year; The Rink; Kiss of The Spider Woman; Chicago; The Act; And the World Goes Round. *Composition:* Steel Pier, 1997. *Honours:* 3 Tonys; 4 Emmys; 1 Grammy; Songwriters Hall of Fame; Peabody and Ace Awards; Kennedy Center Award, 1998. *Memberships:* BMI Dramatics Guild; AFTRA; Equity. *Leisure interest:* Collecting art. *Current Management:* Sam Cohn, ICM, 40 W 57 St, New York, USA. *Address:* 146 Central Park W, New York City, New York, USA.

EBBAGE Leonard Charles; b. 21 Aug. 1931, Gorleston-on-Sea, England. Bandleader; Musician (keyboards, accordion). m. (1) Hazel Brown 13 June 1953, 3 s.; m (2) Gwen Leach, 1 July 1981, 1 d. *Musical Education:* Piano lessons, 5 years; 20 years working in holiday camps. *Career:* Broadcast with Hughie Green and Opportunity Knocks; Over 20 full summer seasons for Pontins; Ladbrooks; Holimarine; Warners; Walk-on, BBC and ITV; Now one of the top sequence dance bands in the country, playing short break dance holidays and sequence festivals all over England. *Recordings:* Albums: Goody-Goody; 50 Years of Dancing; Dancing Time; Sequence and Party Dances; Say It With Music. *Honour:* Played for Carl Alan Awards, 1994. *Memberships:* Musicians' Union; Equity. *Leisure interests:* DIY; Gardening; Big bands. *Address:* Rosanne, Dyers End, Stambourne, nr Halstead, Essex, England.

ECCLES Albert; b. 25 June 1940, Aston, Birmingham. Musician (Bass Guitar). 3 s. *Musical Education:* Self-taught. *Career:* Ready Steady Go; Top of The Pops; 1966 Beatle Tour. *Compositions:* Decca. *Recordings:* Go Now; Easy Child; Bottom of My Heart; Everyday; This Is My House; Magnificent Moodies. *Honours:* Gold Discs. *Memberships:* Musicians Union. *Leisure interest:* Fishing. *Address:* Brian Epstein, Ridge Pride.

ECKERT John Wallace; b. 13 March 1939, New York, USA. Musician (trumpet, horns). *Musical Education:* BA, Music, University of Rochester, 1961. *Career:* Musician with Stan Kenton; Si Zentner; American Brass Quintet; Buddy Morrow; Maynard Ferguson; Ten Wheel Drive; Deodato; Simon and Garfunkel; Benny Goodman; Gerry Mulligan; Toshiko Akiyoshi Jazz Orchestra, 1984-; American Jazz Orchestra, 1988-; Buck Clayton, 1989-. *Recordings:* Albums include: Brief Replies, Ten Wheel Drive, 1970; Chris Williamson, Chris Williamson, 1971; Whirlwinds, Deodato, 1974; Concert In Central Park, Simon and Garfunkel, 1981.

ECKERT Vojtech; b. 27 Jan. 1956, Prague, Czechoslovakia. m. Iva Hanusova, 7 March 1997. *Education:* Faculty of Medicine, Charles University; Private Student of famous Czech Jazzman Karel Velebny. *Career:* Played piano, from age 4; Multiinstrumentalist, since age 15; Leader of many groups, since age 15; Established top Czech Jazz Trio in Prague, 1983. *Compositions:* CD Blues; A First Piece; Humoresque From Phillips' Hill; Hammond Intermezzo; Blues for Unknown Queen. *Recordings:* CD with CSABA DESEO, Magic Violin, 1995; LP Eva Olmerova, 1986; Radio records, 1986–; Svatopluk Kosvanec, CD, 1998. *Publications:* Regular articles from sphere of jazz criticism and education in monthly periodical, Muzikus, 1992–95. *Membership:* Czech Jazz Society. *Leisure interests:* Volleyball; Geography; History; History of Art; Architecture; Hunting; Fishing; Cooking. *Address:* MUDr Vojtech Eckert, Balbinova 5, 120 00 Prague 2, Czech Republic.

EDDIE (Jon Edwards); b. 1 April 1951, Hampstead, London, England. Musician (drums, percussion). m. Dee Dee, 3 Nov. 1989, 1 s., 1 d. *Musical Education:* Studies with Joel Rothman. *Career:* Member, The Vibrators; Member, The Inmates; Numerous television and radio appearances worldwide, including Top of the Pops. *Recordings:* Albums: 14 albums with The Vibrators include: Pure Mania; V2 (UK Top 30); Hunting For You; 25 Years of Pure Mania (compilation), 2001; 10 albums with The Inmates include: First Offence (US Top 30); Five; Fast Forward; Singles include: Dirty Water; The Walk; Also recorded with: Chris Spedding; PIL; Christophe J; Garrie Lammin. *Membership:* Musicians' Union. *Leisure interests:* Cricket; Travel. *Address:* 16 Crouch Hill, London N4 4AU, England.

EDDY Duane; b. 26 April 1938, Corning, New York, USA. Musician (guitar); Songwriter; Prod. m. Miriam Johnson, Aug. 1961. *Career:* Bandleader, The Rebels, 1958; Appearances include: British tour, with Bobby Darin, Clyde McPhatter, Emile Ford, 1960; British tour, 1967; First Rock 'n' Roll Show, London, 1968; US tour, with band including Ry Cooder, 1983; Film appearances: Because They're Young, 1960; The Savage Seven, 1967; Kona Coast, 1967. *Recordings:* Albums: Have Twangy Guitar Will Travel, 1959; Especially For You, 1959; The Twang's The Thang, 1960; Songs of Our Heritage, 1960; A Million Dollar's Worth of Twang, 1961; Girls Girls Girls, 1961; Twistin' and Twangin', 1962; Twangy Guitar – Silky Strings, 1962; Dance With The Guitar Man, 1963; Twanging Up A Storm, 1963; Lonely Guitar, 1963; Duane Eddy, 1986; Twang Twang, 1993; As producer: Star Spangled Springer, Phil Everly, 1973; Singles include: Moving 'n' Groovin', 1958; Rebel Rouser, 1958; Ramrod, 1958; Cannonball, 1959; The Lonely One, 1959; Yep!, 1959; Peter Gunn Theme, 1959; Forty Miles of Bad Road, 1959; Some Kinda Earthquake, 1959; Kommotion, 1960; Because They're Young (No. 2, UK), 1960; Bonnie Come Back, 1960; Pepe, 1961; Theme From Dixie, 1961; Ring of Fire, 1961; Caravan, 1961; The Ballad of Paladin (theme for television series Have Gun Will Travel), 1962; Dance With The Guitar Man, 1962; Boss Guitar, 1963; Play Me Like You Play Your Guitar, 1975; Peter Gunn, with Art of Noise, 1986; Other recordings include session work with: Phil Everly, Foreigner, Waylon Jennings, Kenny Rogers, Marty Stuart. *Honours:* NME Top Readers Poll Winner, World Musical Personality, 1960; Grammy, Best Rock Instrumental Performance, 1986. *Current Management:* Fat City Artists and Management, 1906 Chet Atkins Plaza, Suite 502, Nashville, TN 37205, USA.

EDE Terence Frederick (Terry); b. 4 Aug. 1935, London, England. Musician (saxophones, clarinets, flute, oboe). m. Brenda Bonner, 14 March 1959, 1 s., 1 d. *Musical Education:* Private, first tuition on piano. *Career:* Professional freelance player, 1962–; Tours include: Englebert Humperdinck; Jimmy Witherspoon; Larry Williams; Johnny Ray; Well-known teacher both at various schools and privately. *Memberships:* Musicians' Union; Asscn of British Jazz Musicians. *Leisure interests:* Music; Motorcycling. *Address:* 7 Church Farm Lane, Cheam, Surrey SM3 8PT, England.

EDER Linda; b. 3 Feb. 1961, Tucson, Arizona, USA. Vocalist. m. Frank Wildhorn. *Career:* Duo Paul and Linda, 1980–87; Work with Pianist Jeremy Roberts; Winner on TV talent show Star Search, 1987–88; Appeared in musical Jekyll and Hyde, 1990-, Svengali, 1991-. *Recordings:* Albums: Linda Eder, 1990; Highlights from Jekyll and Hyde, 1990; The Complete Work Jekyll and Hyde: The Gothic Music Thriller, 1994; And So Much More, 1994; The Scarlet Pimpernel, 1995; It's Time, 1997; It's No Secret Anymore, 1999; Christmas Stays The Same, 2000. *Leisure interests:* Animals; Tennis; Skiing. *Address:* c/o Kragen and Co, 1112 N Sherbourne Dr., Los Angeles, CA 90069, USA.

EDGE (THE) (David Evans); b. 8 Aug. 1961, Wales. Musician (guitar); Songwriter. *Career:* Founder member, guitarist, rock group U2, 1978–; Regular national and world-wide tours; Major concerts include: US Festival, 1983; The Longest Day, Milton Keynes, 1985; Live Aid, Wembley, 1985; Self Aid, Dublin, 1986; A Conspiracy of Hope (Amnesty International tour), 1986; Smile Jamaica (hurricane relief fundraiser), 1988; Very Special Arts Festival, White House, Washington, 1988; New Year's Eve Concert, Dublin (broadcast live Europe), 1989; Yankee Stadium,

New York (second ever concert there). *Compositions include:* Music to A Clockwork Orange 2004, Royal Shakespeare Company, 1990. *Recordings:* Albums: Boy, 1980; October, 1981; War (No. 1, UK), 1983; Under A Blood Red Sky, 1983; The Unforgettable Fire (No. 1, UK), 1984; Wide Awake In America, 1985; The Joshua Tree (No. 1, UK and US), 1987; Rattle and Hum, also film (No. 1, UK and US), 1988; Achtung Baby (No. 1, USA), 1991; Zooropa (No. 1, USA and UK), 1993; Passengers, film soundtrack (with Brian Eno), 1995; Pop, 1997; The Best of 1980–90 (compilation), 1998; All That You Can't Leave Behind, 2001; Hit singles include: Out of Control (No. 1, Ireland), 1979; Another Day (No. 1, Ireland), 1980; New Year's Day, 1983; Two Hearts Beat As One, 1983; Pride (In The Name of Love), 1984; With Or Without You (No. 1, USA), 1987; I Still Haven't Found What I'm Looking For (No. 1, USA), 1987; Where The Streets Have No Name, 1987; Desire (No. 1, UK), 1988; Angel of Harlem, 1988; When Love Comes To Town, with B. B. King, 1989; All I Want Is You, 1989; The Fly (No. 1, UK), 1991; Mysterious Ways, 1992; Even Better Than The Real Thing, 1992; Who's Gonna Ride Your Wild Horses, 1992; Stay, 1993; Hold Me, Thrill Me, Kiss Me (from film Batman Forever), 1995; Discotheque (No. 1, UK), 1997; Staring At The Sun, 1997; If God Will Send His Angels, 1997; The Sweetest Thing, 1998; Beautiful Day (No. 1, UK), 2000; Stuck In A Moment That You Can't Get Out Of, 2001; Walk On, 2001; Contributor, Mystery Girl, Roy Orbison, 1988; Red Hot + Blue, 1990; Pavarotti and Friends, 1996. *Honours include:* Grammy Awards: Album of The Year, 1987; Best Rock Performance, 1987, 1989; Best Rock Vocal, 1993; Record of The Year, Song of The Year, Best Rock Performance By Duo Or Group (all for Beautiful Day), 2001; BRIT Awards: Best International Act, 1988–90, 1992, 1998, 2001; Best Live Act, 1993; Outstanding Contribution To The British Music Industry, 2001; JUNO Award, 1993; World Music Award, 1993; Q Magazine Awards: Best Producer (with Flood, Brian Eno), 1993; Best Act In The World, 1990, 1992, 1993; Merit Award, 1994; Numerous magazine poll wins and awards; Gold and Platinum discs. *Current Management:* Principle Management. *Address:* 30–32 Sir John Rogersons Quay, Dublin 2, Ireland.

EDMUNDS Dave; b. 15 April 1944, Cardiff, Wales. Singer; Musician (guitar); Record Prod. *Career:* Member, bands including 99ers; The Raiders; The Image; Member, Love Sculpture, 1968–69; Solo artiste, 1969–77; Founder, Rockpile, 1977–81; Solo artiste, 1981–; Record producer, 1969–; Built own Rockfield Recording Studios, 1969; Numerous tours include: with Bad Company, US, 1977; with Nick Lowe, 1977, 1978; Elvis Costello, Mink DeVille, US, 1978; Rock 'n' Roll Revue, US tour, 1990; Concerts include: Knebworth Festival, 1978; Concert For Kampuchea, with Wings, Elvis Costello, 1979; Reading Festival, 1982; US Festival, 1982; Princes Trust Rock Gala, Wembley Arena, 1987; John Lennon Tribute Concert, Merseyside, 1990; Television includes: South Bank Show; Blue Suede Shoes, Carl Perkins special, C4; Film appearance: Stardust, 1974. *Recordings:* Albums: with Love Sculpture: Blues Helping, 1968; Forms and Feeling, 1969; with Rockpile: Tracks On Wax, 1978; Repeat When Necessary, 1979; Seconds of Pleasure, 1980; Solo: Rockpile, 1972; Subtle As A Flying Mallet, 1975; Get It, 1977; Tracks On Wax, 1978; Twangin', 1981; The Best of Dave Edmunds, 1982; DE7, 1982; Information, 1983; Riff Raff, 1984; Closer To The Flame, 1990; I Hear You Rockin', 1993; Plugged In, 1994; Musical Fantasies, 1999; A Pile of Rock (live), 2001; Singles include: with Love Sculpture: Sabre Dance, 1968; Solo: I Hear You Knocking (No. 1, UK), 1970; Baby I Love You, 1973; Born To Be With You, 1973; I Knew The Bride, 1977; Girls Talk, 1979; Queen of Hearts, 1979; Singin' The Blues, 1980; The Race Is On, 1981; Contributor, I Fell In Love, Carlene Carter, 1990; Producer for artistes including: Brinsley Schwartz; The Flamin' Groovies; Shakin' Stevens; Stray Cats; Nick Lowe, Fabulous Thunderbirds; Everly Brothers; Status Quo; k d lang; Music for film soundtracks: Porky's Revenge; Planes, Trains and Automobiles. *Current Management:* Gold Mountain Entertainment, 3575 Cahuenga Blvd W, Suite 450, Los Angeles, CA 90068, USA.

EDRISSI Tahir El; b. Morocco. Vocalist; Musician (sintir, percussion). *Career:* Left Morocco for London, 1980s; Founder member of band MoMo (Music of Moroccan Origin); Act's fusion of North African Gnawa music with western-style drum kit, samples and contemporary dance styles (including house and garage) described as 'Dar'; Popular live band; Released first album, 2001. *Recordings:* Album: The Birth of Dar, 2001. *Honours:* BBC Radio 3 Award for World Music, Boundary Crossing nominee, The Birth of Dar, 2002.

EDWARDS Bloater B; b. 2 Dec. 1971, Aldershot, Hampshire, England. Musician (guitar); Singer (drums, bass, piano). m. Lisa Janine, 29 April 1995. *Career:* Band: Big Boy Bloater and His Southside Stompers; Appearances include: Lyon Jazz Festival; Birmingham Jazz Festival; London's Forum; Hammersmith Palais; Hemsby Rock 'n' Roll Festival; Classic Cars, Channel 4 TV; Actor: Let Him Have It; Lipstick On Your Collar; Shine On Harvey Moon. *Recordings:* Album: (1 track) Haunted Highway; Jump For Joy With The Big Boy (EP), Big Boy Bloater and His Southside Stompers. *Membership:* Musicians' Union. *Leisure interests:* Writing songs; Touring; Recording. *Address:* Aldershot, Hampshire, England.

EDWARDS Dave; b. 9 Aug. 1948, Shrewsbury, England. Music Teacher; Musician (steel pan, guitar). m. Andrea, 28 Dec. 1978, 1 s. *Musical Education:* Shoreditch College of Education, Surrey; Graduate Courses, Wolverhamapton Polytechnic and Northumbria University; Qualified Special Needs Teacher; Self-taught. *Career:* Scandinavian tour with Razzle Dazzle Gatemouth Spasm String Band, 1973; Member and Musical Director, Pan L Beaters Steel Band, 1992–96; Member, Steel Spirit Steel Band, 1999–; Television: with North Tyneside Steelband: Boom, 1991; Local news, 1994, 1996; Numerous local radio broadcasts; Freelance Tutor and Workshop Leader, Musical Director for Steel Bands; Teacher, GCSE Music and Music Appreciation; Helped organize 3 national steelband festivals, 1994–96. *Compositions:* Steelband: Sunshine; Geordie Calypso; Several other steelband compositions and arrangements. *Recordings:* Some self-promoted recordings. *Publications:* Steelpan booklet, 1991. *Honours:* Blood donor (silver); Certificate of Merit, North Tyneside Steel Band, National Steelband Festival, 1991. *Memberships:* Musicians' Union; NUT. *Leisure interests:* Outdoor; Travel; Caravanning; DIY. *Address:* Aynuck's Lodge, 20 Glendale Ave, Whitley Bay, Tyne and Wear NE26 1RX, England.

EDWARDS Don; b. 20 March 1939, Boonton, New Jersey, USA. Vocalist; Songwriter; Musician (acoustic guitar, banjo, mandolin). m. Kathy Jean Davis, 7 Jan. 1978, 2 d. *Career:* Started as actor, singer, stuntman, Six Flags Over Texas, 1961; First record, 1964; Part owner, White Elephant Saloon, Fort Worth, Texas; Recognition through Cowboy Poetry Gathering, Elko; Tours USA; Canada; Britain; New Zealand; Europe; Performs solo, with cowboy band, with horse, with cowboy poet Waddie Mitchell as The Bard and The Balladeer; As The Cowboy Jubilee; Musicologist, author on Western and traditional cowboy music; Educational services to universities; Appeared with Fort Worth, Las Vegas and Colorado Springs symphony orchestras. *Recordings:* Happy Cowboy; America's Singing Cowboy; Songs of The Cowboy; Guitars and Saddle Songs; Desert Skies and Cowtown Blues; Songs of The Trail; Goin' Back to Texas; West of Yesterday; Saddle Songs; My Hero, Gene Autry; The Bard and The Balladeer (with Waddie Mitchell); Prairie Portrait, 2000; Kin To The Wind, 2001; Also recorded on: Other Voices, Other Rooms, Nanci Griffith; The Wild West (soundtrack); How The West Was Swung, Tom Morrell; Ridin' West, Vols I and II; with Buckaroo: Visions and Voices of The American Cowboy; A Christmas Tradition; with Michael Martin Murphey: Cowboy Songs; Cowboy Christmas. *Publications:* Classic Cowboy Songs; Book/tape anthologies: Songs of The Cowboy; Guitars and Saddle Songs. *Honours:* Western Heritage Wrangler Award, Outstanding Traditional Music, Cowboy Hall of Fame, 1992; Western Heritage Wrangler Awards, 1992, 1996. *Membership:* AFTRA. *Leisure interests:* Ranching; Horses; Antiques; Cowboy, Western collectibles; Vintage instruments. *Current Management:* Scott O'Malley and Associates. *Address:* PO Box 9188, Colorado Springs, CO 80932, USA.

EDWARDS Janet; b. Huddersfield, Yorkshire, England. Singer; Musician (piano). m (1), 2 s.; m (2). *Education:* College of Technology, Huddersfield. *Musical Education:* Studied piano, with Dr Michael Kruszynski. *Career:* Piano and song recitals, 1974–; Performed with artists including those from Royal Opera House, ENO soloists; Performances: Italy; France; Germany; United Kingdom including South Bank, Wigmore Hall; Devised, performed own shows: Sounds Entertaining; I Say I Play; Munich, London, other British halls; Solo work, classical, popular, theatre, jazz music, in: Europe; Scandinavia; Middle East; Accompanist, assistant musical director, Royal Gala Performance of works by Stephen Sondheim, Theatre Royal Drury Lane; Work as voice coach began Royal Academy of Music, early 1980s; Master class group sessions working with professionals and non-professionals, 1989–; Played: Anna in Girls Were Made To Love and Kiss, West End, 1994; Also runs professional seminar in auditioning techniques, workshops and seminars for the general public; Began one-woman show, 'S' Wonderful, 'S' Marvellous, in theatres and venues in the UK, 1997–; London shows including Pizza on the Park, performing own songs and recording, 1999–. *Honours:* Diploma with distinction, Huddersfield College of Technology; ARCM; LTCL Dip Ed. *Leisure interests:* Tai Chi; Tennis.

EDWARDS Terry David; b. 10 Aug. 1960, Hornchurch, Essex, England. Musician (saxophones, trumpet, guitar, piano). *Musical Education:* BA (Hons), University of East Anglia, 1979–82. *Career:* Founder member, The Higsons, 1980–86; Co-founder, with Mark Bedford, Butterfield 8, 1988–; Solo artist with and without The Scapegoats, 1991–; Session player with: Madness; Jimi Tenor; Lydia Lunch; PJ Harvey; Spleen; Jesus and Mary Chain; Lush; Julian Cope; Gallon Drunk; JJ Stone; Nick Cave; The Brood; Drugstore; Frank and Walters; Tindersticks; Billy Bragg; Robyn Hitchcock; Keziah Jones; Dopesmugglaz; Delakota; Boo Radleys; 18 Wheeler; The Creatures; Spiritualized; Scott 4; Strangelove; Anthony Moore; David Holmes; Jack; Serious Drinking; Dept S; Test Department; Moonshake; Farmers Boys; Bikini Beach. *Compositions:* Pump, for symphony orchestra, 1998; Slow Bossa/Wallflower, for cello and piano, 1997. *Recordings:* Blow, with Butterfield 8, 1988; Plays, Salutes, and Executes, 1993; No Fish is Too Weird for Her Aquarium, 1994; I Was

Dora Suarez, with Derek Raymond and James Johnston, 1994; My Wife Doesn't Understand Me, 1995; I Didn't Get Where I Am Today, 1997; Large Door, 1998; Birth of The Scapegoats, 1998; Yesterday's Zeitgeist, 1999; No Fish Is Too Weird For Her Aquarium, 2000. *Memberships:* Associate mem., PRS; MCPS; SPNM; Musicians' Union. *Address:* c/o PO Box 30608, London E1 1TS, England.

EDWINS Myron; b. 4 Jan. 1958, Washington, PA, USA. Singer; Musician; Entertainer; Prod. (Bass Guitar, Keyboards). *Career:* Solo artist from 1989–; Tours with The Edwards Generation in Switzerland, Norway, Germany, Japan and Canada; Appeared on TV specials: Mike Douglas in San Francisco, Evening Magazine and Zoom; Business Ventures: MEP; EPB Management, Music publishing; Currently lead singer and keyboardist for R & B group, Movin'. *Recordings:* Do You Love Me, 1990; Do You Like The Way I Do It, 1991; Love Is, 1993; Let Me Entertain You, 1994; The Best Thing To Do, 1994; I'll See You Again, Myron Edwins, 1995. *Leisure interests:* Video Taping; Swimming; Dancing; Films; Parks and Beaches. *Current Management:* Entertainment Agency; MEP. *Address:* Myron Edwins Productions, Box 8442, Pittsburg, CA 94565–8442, USA.

EGAN Kian John Francis; b. 29 April 1980, Sligo, Ireland. Singer. *Career:* Member, Westlife; Numerous television appearances and hit singles. *Recordings:* Singles: Swear It Again (No. 1, UK), 1999; Flying Without Wings (No. 1, UK), 1999; Seasons in the Sun/I Have a Dream(No. 1, UK) 1999; Fool Again (No. 1, UK), 2000; Against All Odds (with Mariah Carey; No. 1, UK), 2000; My Love (No. 1, UK), 2000; What Makes A Man, 2000; Uptown Girl (in aid of Comic Relief charity; No. 1, UK), 2001; Queen of My Heart (No. 1, UK), 2001; World of Our Own (No. 1, UK), 2002; Albums: Westlife, 1999; Coast To Coast (No. 1, UK), 2000; World of Our Own (No. 1, UK), 2001.

EHRENSTRALE Nan; b. 17 Sept. 1947, Malmo, Sweden. Librarian; Musician (Double Bass, Sousaphone). m. Kurt Jensen. *Career:* Plays with Jensens New Orleans Band, Copenhagen. *Recordings:* Jazz Classics and Evergreens, 1996; A Tribute to Kid Thomas, 1997. *Address:* Bogardsvej 106, 3050 Humlebaek, Denmark.

EINARSDOTTER Elise; b. 11 July 1955. Musician (piano). m. Olle Steinholtz, 1 d. *Musical Education:* Diploma of Arranging and Composition, Berklee College of Music, USA, 2 years; Royal Academy of Music, Stockholm, 2 years. *Career:* Leads, Elise Einarsdotter Ensemble, 1984–; Composes music to lyrics; Writes for choir and orchestra; Tours in Scandinavia, Italy, USA, Sweden, Norway, France, Belgium, Holland, England, Ethiopia and India. *Compositions:* My Heart; Alexandrinen; Sphinx Acre; Ljus, Dagg, Grönska; I Live in Music. *Recordings:* CDs: Sacred Hearts; Secrets of Living; Senses; Rosenäng; Sketches of Roses; Green Walk, Slow Talk, 1998. *Publication:* Rosenäng. *Honours:* Numerous grants and awards; Lo-Kulturpris, 1993; Stockholm City Award of Honor, 1998. *Membership:* Swedish Academy of Jazz; NYA IDUN. *Leisure interests:* Family and Friends; Sailing. *Current Management:* Mistral Music. *Address:* Bandyvägen 47, 129 49 Hagersten, Sweden.

EINZIGER Mike (Michael Aaron); b. 21 June 1976, Los Angeles, California, USA. Musician (guitar). *Career:* Formed group Incubus with school friends in Calabasas, California, 1991; Initially played small parties, graduating to support slots in Hollywood, California; Circulated demo tapes of Closet Cultivation and Incubus before independent album release, 1995; Group signed by Immortal/Epic; Built US and European following support slots on tours with: Sugar Ray; Black Sabbath; Korn; Drive reached #1 on US Modern Rock Chart, 2001; First Japanese and Australian live dates, 2001. *Recordings:* Albums: Fungus Amongus, 1995; S.C.I.E.N.C.E., 1997; Make Yourself, 1999; Morning View, 2001; Singles: Enjoy Incubus EP, 1997; Pardon Me, 1999; Stellar, When Incubus Attacks Vol. 1 EP, 2000; Drive, Wish You Were Here, 2001. *Honours:* Make Yourself album certified double platinum by RIAA; Billboard Award, Modern Rock Single of The Year, 2001. *Current Management:* Steve Rennie, REN Management, California, USA. *Internet:* www.enjoyincubus.com.

EISLER Fil; Musician (bass, guitar); Prod. *Recordings:* Robbie Williams; Machine; Imogen Head; Jason Feddy; Ali Thompson and Yazz; Messiah; Galliano; Denzil; Crazy Little Trees. *Current Management:* One Management Ltd, 43 St Alban's Ave, London W4 5JS, England.

EKBERG Ulf 'Buddha'; b. 6 Dec. 1970, Sweden. Prod.; Songwriter; Vocalist. *Career:* Member, Ace of Base, 1990–. *Recordings:* Albums: Happy Nation, 1993; The Bridge, 1995; Singles of The 90s (compilation), 1999; Singles: All That She Wants (No. 1, UK), 1993; Wheel of Fortune, 1993; The Sign (No. 1, USA), 1994; Don't Turn Around, 1994; Lucky Love, 1995; Life Is A Flower, 1998; Cruel Summer, 1998; Always Have Always Will, 1998; No. 1 records in UK; US; Canada; Across Europe; Australia; New Zealand; Israel; Argentina. *Honours:* Highest-ever world-wide sales for a debut album (Happy Nation, 19m.); 3 Grammy Nominations, 1994; Platinum discs world-wide. *Current Management:* Siljemark Production AB, Gårdsvägen 4, 171 52 Solna, Sweden.

ELDRITCH Andrew, (Andrew Taylor); b. 15 May 1959, England. Vocalist. *Education:* Oxford University. *Career:* Founder member, Sisters of Mercy, 1980–85; Regular international tours; Concerts include: York Rock Festival, 1984; Royal Albert Hall, London, 1985; Performed as the Sisterhood, 1986; Reforms Sisters of Mercy, 1987–; European tour, 1990; Tune In Turn On Burn Out tour, with Public Enemy, Gang of Four, Warrior Soul, 1991; Reading Festival, 1991; Support to Depeche Mode, Crystal Palace, 1993. *Recordings:* Albums: First and Last and Always, 1985; Gift (as the Sisterhood), 1986; Floodland, 1988; Vision Thing, 1990; Some Girls Wander By Mistake, 1992; Greatest Hits, Vol. 1, 1993; Slight Case of Overbombing, 1993; Go Figure, with SSV, 1997; Singles include: Temple of Love, 1983; Body and Soul, 1984; Walk Away, 1984; This Corrosion, 1987; Dominion, 1988; Lucretia My Reflection, 1988; More, 1990; Temple of Love (1992), 1992; Under The Gun, 1993. *Current Management:* Hard To Handle Management, 1133 Broadway Suite 1301, New York, NY 10010, USA.

ELFMAN Danny; b. 29 May 1954, USA. Composer; Musician (guitar); Vocalist. *Career:* Lead singer, songwriter, guitarist, band Oingo Boingo. *Compositions:* Film scores: Pee-Wee's Big Adventure; Beetlejuice; Batman; Batman Returns; Dick Tracy; Darkman; Edward Scissorhands; Sommersby; Mars Attacks!; Sleepy Hollow; Other music for films includes: Weird Science; Ghostbusters II; Something Wild; Television series score: The Simpsons. *Recordings:* Albums: with Oingo Boingo: Only A Lad, 1981; Nothing To Fear, 1982; Good For Your Soul, 1983; Dead Man's Party, 1985; Boingo, 1986; Skeletons In The Closet, 1989; Dark At The End of The Tunnel, 1990; Article 99, 1992; Batman Returns, 1992; Dolores Claiborne, 1995; Mission Impossible, 1996. *Honour:* Emmy Nomination, The Simpsons. *Current Management:* L.A. Personal Development, 950 N Kings Rd, Suite 266, West Hollywood, CA 90069, USA.

ELIS Hefin; b. 4 June 1950, Port Talbot, Wales. Composer; Arranger; Musician (piano, guitar, bass guitar). m. Marian Thomas, 25 July 1981, 2 d. *Education:* University College of Wales, Aberystwyth. *Career:* Founder member, Welsh language rock band, Edward H Dafis; Recording Engineer, Producer for Sain Records. *Composition:* I'r Gad. *Recording:* Ysbryd Y Nos. *Memberships:* PRS; Musicians' Union. *Leisure interests:* Football; Rugby; Current affairs. *Address:* Bryn Gellyg, 22 Lon Ddewi, Caernarfon, Gwynedd, Wales.

ELLIOT Sean Andrew; b. 24 Jan. 1970, London, England. Musician (guitar); Programming. *Musical Education:* Private guitar tuition; Part time musicianship, Goldsmiths College. *Career:* UK circuit tour with: Out of My Hair; TV Sky Star Search with Earthworks, 1991; Many regional radio appearances and live radio 1, GLR, 1994–95. *Recordings:* Guitar on: Out of My Hair; Debut album, 2 singles, 1994–95; Sessions for alternative mixes of Seal's Crazy. *Membership:* Musicians' Union. *Leisure interests:* Parties; Clubs; Animation and video. *Current Management:* Space Band Management. *Address:* 32B Weinster Sq. London, W2 4NQ, England.

ELLIOTT Anthony (Tony); b. 18 Dec. 1963, Liverpool, Merseyside, England. Songwriter; Musician (bass guitar, guitar, piano/keyboard). *Musical Education:* Self-taught, 1997; Qualifications in Sound Engineering. *Career:* Member: Sebastian's Men, 1982–85; Various appearances on UK regional and national radio including Radio 1 John Peel session; 16 Tambourines, 1986–90; Signed to BMG Publishing; Various British tours supporting Wet Wet Wet, Hue and Cry and Squeeze; Numerous appearances on regional/national TV and radio (including Radio 1 sessions); The Tambourines, 1990–93; Various European dates including Barcelona Olympic Festival; Numerous headlining tours, shared billing with Echo and the Bunnymen, River City People and The Real People; Catapult, 1996–99; British tour and various appearances; Partner in writing/production projects: The Elliott Davis Project, 1999–; Alto Music Productions (TV and radio advertisements), 1999–2001; Catapult Enterprises, 2001–; working on Patches Flemmings Loons and Spoons, The Somnambulists and further music for advertisements. *Recordings:* with Sebastians Men: Horizon, 1984; with 16 Tambourines: Singles: If I Should Stay; How Green Is Your Valley, 1990; Album: How Green Is Your Valley; with The Tambourines: She Blows My Mind EP; You're So Beautiful, 1992; 5 Miles Wide, featured track on Unearthed compilation, 2001; with Catapult: Everybody Gets There In The End, featured track on Transpotting compilation, 1998. *Membership:* Musicians' Union. *Address:* 210 Mather Ave, Allerton, Liverpool, Merseyside, L18 9TG, England.

ELLIOTT Chris; b. 5 Aug. 1966, Lidlington, England. Musician (piano, keyboards); Songwriter, Arranger. m. Kerry, 24 June 1995, 1 d., Georgette. *Education:* Dartington College of Arts; Goldsmiths College, London. *Career:* Played piano and keyboards with Anne Clark 1993–96; Performer, writer and arranger with Bruce Woolley and the Radio Science Orchestra, 1994–; performed with Paul McCartney, George Michael, Elvis Costello, Sinaed O'Connor, Marianne Faithful, The Pretenders, Tom Jones, Neil Finn, Johnny Marr, 1999; Anne Clark, 2000; played piano for The Pretenders, TFI Friday and Later with Jools Holland, 1999. *Recordings:* Ambient Orchestral, Chappell, 1996; Memories of the Future, Radio Science

Orchestra, 1997; Storm (from the film 'The Avengers') for Grace Jones and the Radio Science Orchestra, 1999; Reverb, Radio Science Orchestra, 1999; Different Roads, Joe Cocker, Piano, 1999; Orchestral Arrangements: I Wish You Love, (from the film 'Eye of the Beholder'); Chrissie Hynde, 1998; Storm, Grace Jones and Radio Science Orchestra, 1998; Live and Let Die, Geri Halliwell, 1999; Film and TV: Century, Nagano Olympic Theme, 1998; The Second World War in Colour, 1999; Churchill's Secret Army, 1999; Moulin Rouge (Orchestration) 2000. *Honour:* Ivor Novello Scholarship, Dartington International Summer School, 1992. *Memberships:* Musicians' Union; Performing Right Society. *Current Management:* Richard Kirstien, Zomba Music.

ELLIOTT Joe; b. 1 Aug. 1959, Sheffield, England. Vocalist. *Career:* Vocalist, UK rock group Def Leppard, 1977–; Concerts include: Tours supporting Sammy Hagar; AC/DC; Ted Nugent; Reading Rock Festival, 1980; World tour, 1983; Monsters of Rock Festival, Castle Donington; BRIT Awards, Royal Albert Hall; Freddie Mercury Tribute Concert, Wembley, 1992; Radio includes: Stand-in DJ for Simon Bates, BBC Radio 1, 1992. *Recordings:* Albums: On Through The Night, 1980; High 'n' Dry, 1981; Pyromania, 1983; Hysteria, 1987; Adrenalize, 1992; Retroactive, 1993; Vault 1980–95, 1995; Slang, 1996; Euphoria, 1999; Singles include: Hello America, 1980; Photograph, 1983; Rock of Ages, 1983; Foolin', 1983; Animal, 1987; Pour Some Sugar On Me, 1987; Hysteria, 1987; Armageddon It, 1988; Love Bites (No. 1, USA), 1988; Rocket, 1989; Let's Get Rocked (No. 2, UK), 1992; Make Love Like A Man, 1992; Have You Ever Never Needed Someone So Bad, 1992; Stand Up (Kick Love Into Motion); Heaven Is, 1993; Tonight, 1993; Two Steps Behind, featured in film The Last Action Hero, 1993; When Love and Hate Collide (No. 2, UK), 1995; All I Want Is Everything, 1996; Promises, 1999. *Honours include:* American Music Awards: Favourite Heavy Metal Album, Favourite Heavy Metal Artists, 1989; RIAA Diamond Award, 10 Million copies of Hysteria sold. *Current Management:* Q-Prime Inc, 729 Seventh Ave, 14th Floor, New York, NY 10019, USA.

ELLIOTT Missy 'Misdemeanour'; b. 1971, Portsmouth, Virginia, USA. Rapper; Prod.; Vocalist. *Career:* Joined vocal group, Sista, obtained record deal; Began collaborating with Tim Mosley on singles with Aaliyah; Guest rapper on various releases; Obtained solo record deal; Founded own company, The Gold Mind, 1996; Began releasing solo records as vocalist and rapper; Numerous successful acts signed to own company; Supervised and guest on soundtrack of film, Why Do Fools Fall in Love, 1998; Live appearances include Lilith Fair travelling festival, 1998; Started own lipstick line with Iman Bowie's cosmetics line. *Recordings:* Singles: Sock it 2 Me, 1997; Rain, 1998; Hit 'Em Wit Da Hee, 1998; Beep Me 911, 1998; She's a Bitch; I Want You Back, featuring Melanie G (No. 1, UK), 1998; All 'N My Grill, with MC Solaar, 1999; Hot Boyz, 2000; Get Ur Freak On, 2001; One Minute Man, 2001; Albums: Supa Dupa Fly, 1997; Da Real World, 1999; So Addictive, 2001.

ELLIS Bobby (Robert); b. 2 July 1932, Kingston, Jamaica. Musician (trumpet). 4 s., 3 d. *Musical Education:* At Alpha Boys School, tutor, Raymond Harper, Rueben Delgado. *Career:* Played with Tony Brown Band; Val Bennett; Luther Williams; Joined The Mighty Vikings, 1962; Played with The Soul Brothers; Lyn Taitt and The Jetts; Billy Vernon; Lance Helwell; The Wailers; Bob Marley and The Wailers (Peace Concert, Jackson 5, Stevie Wonder); Jimmy Cliff (BBC Concert); Toots and The Maytals; Brent Dowe; John Holt; Dennis Brown; The Two Ton Machine; Burning Spear (including Sunsplash Tour); Bunny Wailer (Music City Hall, Madison Square Garden). *Compositions:* Wrote with Cyrus; Sweet Meat; Up Park Camp; Stormy Weather; Rhythm for reggae hit: Diseases, Michigan and Smiley, 1983–84; Songs: Shaka; Pep-Up; Jiheje Chant; Cutlass; Sounds of Reggae; Three Finger Jack; Doreth. *Recordings:* Early records with Burning Spear; Debut solo album: Shaka; All records by Burning Spear; Other recordings by: Herbie Mann; Blazing Horns; Bobby Ellis Meets The Aggravators; Tommy McCook; Numerous singles. *Membership:* JFM. *Leisure interests:* Football; Cricket; Baseball; Basketball. *Address:* 13 Savannah Rd, Independence City, Gregory Park PO, Saint Catherine, Jamaica.

ELLIS John Stewart Maxwell; b. 22 Feb. 1945, Lower Slaughter, Gloucestershire, England. Teacher. *Musical Education:* RMSM Kneller Hall, Bretton Hall College. *Career:* Armed Forces, 1960–72; Brass Teacher, 1972–77; Founder, Director of Music, Doncaster Youth Jazz Association, 1973–, (priority, preparing young musicians for modern profession); Performance tours: Russia; Germany; Poland; Sweden; France; USA; Doncaster Jazz Orchestra first UK band to appear jazz festivals: Montreux, 1979; Nice, 1981; Royal Performance invitations to Buckingham Palace and Windsor Castle, 1991; Numerous television and radio appearances; Currently, band masterclasses and workshops; Jazz panel adjudicator (home and abroad); Head of Music Department, Northcliffe School. *Recordings:* 6 jazz albums, 1979-: Live From Montreux; France... Here Again; A Celebration; A Concert For Friends; You're Nobody Till Somebody Loves You (Second, Jazz Journal International Record of The Year, 1988); Just For Phil. *Honours:* MBE, for Services to Education, 1995; European Curriculum Award, 1992; BBC Big Band of The Year, 1994; 7 NFMY Outstanding Performance Awards, 1977–87. *Memberships:* International Asscn of Jazz Educators (IAJE); Musicians' Union; NUT. *Leisure interests:* Touring France; Reading wine labels (elected to Ordre De Compagnons De Beaujolais, 1994). *Address:* High-Holme, 25 Sandcliffe Rd, Wheatley Hills, Doncaster DN2 5NP, England.

ELLIS Katherine (Jane Margaret); b. 21 June 1965, Bromley, Kent, England. Singer; Songwriter. m. Aug. 1998. *Musical Education:* Private classical singing lessons. *Career:* Don't Dream It's Over – Less Stress featuring Katherine Wood for Boys Own, Substance, 1990–91; Regular demos for PWL Ltd (Pete Waterman) include: Loveland demos; 6 single releases, 1994–95; Hundreds of jazz, soul, R & B concerts, 1984–; Supported Rod Stewart, Elton John, Stevie Wonder; Backing singer, Belinda Carlisle, European Tour, 1995–; Album, 1995; Lawnmower Man II session on soundtrack, plays Radio 1, Sussex, Kiss, GLR, BSBF, Choice, 1995; Single, Whole Lotta Love with Goldbug, appeared live on Top of the Pops, 1996; In choir for entire Evita soundtrack; Backing vocals for Chaka Khan on National Lottery Show; 4 tracks on Speaker album, 1997; With '70's cover band, Fret Monkey, played at Peter Phillips' 21st birthday party, Windsor Castle, 1998. *Compositions:* Co-wrote Dreaming, Ruff Driverz and Arrolla, 1998. *Recordings:* Single: with Voice of Public Demand: Celebrate The World, 1995; Out of The Blue, Wood, Henshall, Phillips; Wrote and sung theme tune for International television series Dolphin Stories; With Ruff Driverz: Don't Stop; Deeper Love; Dreaming. *Memberships:* PRS; MCPS; Musicians' Union; British Music Writers Council; PAMRA; Equity. *Leisure interests:* Reading; Yoga; Movies; Theatre; Listening to music; Jazz and Blues; Walking in the country.

ELLIS Paul David; b. 27 April 1956, Manchester, England. Composer; Arranger; Prod.; Musician (keyboards); Programmer. m. Yasuko Fukuoka, 12 March 1993. *Education:* BA Hons, Fine Art, Sunderland. *Musical Education:* Self-taught. *Career:* Tours with Hot Chocolate: Germany, UK, 1983; Middle East, 1984, 1985; Australia, 1986; British tour with Alison Moyet, 1984; Tours with Billy Ocean: UK, USA, 1986, 1988; Japan, 1986; Japanese tour with Epo, 1988; Software Consultant, Yamaha R & D Centre, London, 1990-. *Recordings:* Player, arranger, 2 Top 10 albums with Koji Tamaki (Japanese artist); Producer, tours, album, Epo, 1988; Many UK sessions, 1981–90. *Membership:* Musicians' Union. *Leisure interests:* Literature; Psychology; Travel. *Current Management:* The Music Network Ltd (own company). *Address:* 55D Stapleton Hall Rd, London N4 3QF, England.

ELLIS Ron; b. 12 Sept. 1947, Southport, England. DJ; Broadcaster; Writer. m. Sue Hargreaves, 5 Aug. 1978, 2 d. *Education:* John Moores University, Liverpool. *Career:* Radio presenter, Dune FM; Promotions Manager, WEA Records; Music Historian and Biographer. *Compositions:* Hot California Nights, recorded by P J Proby. *Recordings:* Boys On The Dole (Top 10, New Wave Charts), 1979; New CD from The Johnny Ace Show, forthcoming. *Publications:* Journal of a Coffin Dodger; Murder First Glass; Snort of Kings; Playground Pets, 2000; Diary of a Discotheque; Ears of the City, Headline, 1998; Mean Streets, 1998; Framed, 1999; The Singing Dead, 2000; Last of the Lake Poets. *Honours:* Most Jobs In Britain: Daily Mail, 1976, Sun, 1989. *Membership:* Crime Writers' Asscn. *Address:* 5 Mayfield Court, Freshfield, Liverpool L37 7JL, England.

ELLIS-BEXTOR Sophie; b. May 1979. Vocalist. *Education:* Godolphin and Latimer School, Hammersmith, London. *Career:* Daughter of TV director Robin Bextor and presenter Janet Ellis; Fronted group theaudience, scoring 3 UK hit singles, 1998; Teamed up with Italian DJ Cristiano Spiller for international hit, 2000; Solo career 2001-. *Recordings:* Albums: theaudience, 1998; solo: Read My Lips, 2001; Singles: with theaudience: If You Can't Do It When You're Young When Can You Do It?, A Pessimist Is Never Disappointed, I Know Enough (I Don't Get Enough), 1998; with Spiller: Groovejet (If This Ain't Love), UK #1, 2000; solo: Take Me Home, 2001; Murder On The Dancefloor, 2001. *Address:* c/o Polydor UK, 72–80 Black Lion Lane, London, W6 9BE, United Kingdom.

ELMS Gerald; b. 18 June 1961, London, England. Prod. *Career:* Began with various up and coming bands; Became session musician (keyboards); Currently record producer. *Recordings:* Right Said Fred album; First Contact, Roger Sanchez, 2001; Singles: G-Club, 1997; The Way To Find Love, 1998. *Leisure interests:* Golf. *Address:* 57 Devereux Rd, London SW11 6JR, England.

ELSDON Alan Robert; b. 15 Oct. 1934, Chiswick, London, England. Musician; Trumpet Player; Band Leader; Jazz Panelist; Record Reviews. m. June Patricia Elsdon, 21 May 1960, 2 s. *Education:* Private tuition with Tommy McQuater; Freddie Staff and Phil Parker. *Career:* Joined CY Laurie's Band, aged 19 and Graham Stewart 7; Recorded with both groups; Moved to Terry Lightfoot's Band, 1959–61; Formed own group, 1961; Backed many visiting US Musicians including Edmond Hall, Albert Nicholas, Bud Freeman, Wingy Mannone, Warren Vache, Kenny

Daverne and Marti Grosz; Broadcasts include Easy Beat Saturday Club; Jazz Club. *Recordings:* Keepers of the Flame; Hotter Than That, Tape, CD; The Alan Elsdon All Star Jazz Band; Played guest slots over Europe and Middle East, including Germany, Belgium, Holland, Hong Kong. *Honour:* Played in Westminster Abbey at Philip Larkin's Funeral. *Leisure interest:* Golf. *Address:* 29 Dorchester Rd, Northolt, Middlesex UB5 4PA, England.

ELSNER Jürgen; b. 22 April 1932, Finsterwalde. Musicologist. *Education:* Music Theory, Musicology. *Career:* Assistant, Senior Assistant, Humboldt University, Berlin, Marx University, Leipzig, 1958–70; Lecturer, Ethnomusicology, Humboldt University, 1970; Chair Ethnomusicology, Humboldt University, 1975–96. *Publications:* Nordafrika, 1983. *Honour:* Hanns Eisler Prize, 1971. *Memberships:* ICTM; SEM. *Address:* Heinestr 97, D16341 Zepernick, Germany.

ELY Joe; b. 9 Feb. 1947, Amarillo, Texas, USA. Singer; Songwriter; Musician (guitar). m. Sharon Thompson, 17 April 1983, 1 d. *Musical Education:* Self-taught. *Career:* Concerts include: 8 European tours; David Letterman TV show; Appearances on: Country Music Awards TV; The Road ABC TV show; 3 Austin City Limits TV; Radio City Music Hall Madison Square Gardens. *Recordings:* Joe Ely, 1977; Honky Tonk Masquerade, 1978; Down On The Drag, 1979; Live Shots, 1980; Musta Notta Gotta Lotta, 1981; Hi Res, 1983; Lord of The Highway, 1987; Dig All Night, 1988; Live At Liberty Lunch, 1989; Love and Danger, 1992; Letter To Laredo, 1995; Twistin' in the Wind, 1998; Live At Antone's, 2000. *Honours include:* Rolling Stone Top 10 of 70s. *Memberships:* ASCAP; BMI; NARAS. *Leisure interests:* Billiards; Computers. *Current Management:* Fitzgerald-Hartley Co. *Address:* 34 N Palm Ave, Suite 100, Ventura, CA 93001, USA.

EMERSON Darren; b. 30 April 1971, Hornchurch, Essex, England. Prod.; Remixer; DJ. *Career:* Started as DJ around London, early 1990s; Became major figure in London's progressive house scene; Formed Underworld group with Rick Smith and Karl Hyde, 1990; Act signed to Boy's Own label; Released debut album, 1993; Left Underworld to concentrate on DJ career, 2000; Founder: Underwater Records; Remixed: Bjork; Shakespear's Sister; Slam; Massive Attack. *Recordings:* Albums: Dubnobasswithmyheadman, 1993; Second Toughest In The Infants, 1996; Beaucoup Fish, 1998; Everything Everything, 2000; Singles: Mmm Skyscraper I Love You, Rez, 1993; Dark and Long, 1994; Born Slippy, 1995; Jumbo, 1999; King of Snake, 1999; Scorchio (with Sasha), 2000. *Membership:* PRS. *Address:* c/o Underwater Records, Fulham Palace, Bishop's Ave, London, SW6 6EA, England.

EMERSON Keith; b. 2 Nov. 1944, Todmorden, West Yorkshire, England. Musician (keyboards); Composer. *Career:* Member, The T-Bones; Emerson Lake and Palmer (ELP), 1970–; Solo artiste; Also recorded as: Emerson Lake and Powell (with Cozy Powell), 1985–86; 3, 1988; Performances include: Isle of Wight Festival, 1970; Mar-Y-Sol Festival, Puerto Rico, 1972; Film, Pictures At An Exhibition, 1973. *Recordings:* Albums: Emerson Lake and Palmer, 1970; Tarkus (No. 1, UK), 1971; Pictures At An Exhibition, 1971; Trilogy, 1972; Brain Salad Surgery, 1974; Welcome Back My Friends..., 1974; Works, 1977; Works Vol. Two, 1977; Love Beach, 1978; Emerson Lake and Palmer In Concert, 1979; The Best of Emerson Lake and Palmer, 1979; Emerson Lake and Powell, 1986; To The Power of Three, 1988; Black Moon, 1992; The Atlantic Years, 1992; Live At The Royal Albert Hall, 1992; Return of The Manticore, 1993; ELP Live In Poland, 2001; Solo albums: Inferno; Nighthawks; Best Revenge; Muderock; Harmageddon, 1987; The Christmas Album, 1988; Changing States, 1995; Singles include: Fanfare For The Common Man, 1977; Solo: Honky Tonk Train Blues, 1976. *Address:* c/o Premier Talent, L3 E 54th St, 14th Floor, New York, NY 10022, USA.

EMILIO (Navaira); b. 23 Aug. 1962, San Antonio, Texas, USA. Tejano and Country Music Singer. m. Cindy Casias, 29 Nov. 1986, 2 s. *Musical Education:* Voice Scholarship, Southwest Texas State University, San Marcos. *Career:* Toured with David Lee Garza, 1985–88; Founder, own group Rio, 1989; Currently solo artiste; Major peformances include: CMA Awards show, 1995; San Antonio Livestock Show and Rodeo, 1994, 1995; Texas State Fair, Cotton Bowl, Dallas, 1995; Houston Livestock Show and Rodeo, with Selena, Houston Astrodome (set concert attendance record for the year), 1995; National Anthem at NBA All-Star Game, 1996; Suuport to Alan Jackson, US tour, 1996; Shared billing with: George Strait; Ricky Van Shelton; Pam Tillis; Vince Gill; Also performed with Dallas and San Antonio Symphony Orchestras. *Recordings:* Albums: Emilio y Rio, 1989; Sensaciones, 1990; Shoot It, 1991; Unsung Highways, 1992; Emilio Live, 1992; Southern Exposure, 1993; Sound Life, 1994; Life Is Good, 1995; Quedate, 1996; It's on the House, 1997; A Mi Gente, 1997; 10 Aniversario, 1999. *Honours include:* 2 Grammy Nominations, Best Mexican-American performance; Numerous Tejano Music Awards including: Male Vocalist of the Year, 4 times; Album of the Year, 6 times; Male Entertainer of the Year, 7 times; Listed in top 10 New Stars of 1996, County America magazine, 1996. *Membership:* Tejanos For Children Foundation. *Current*

Management: Stuart Dill, Refugee Management International. *Address:* 209 10th Ave S, Suite 347, Nashville, TN 37203, USA.

EMINEM (Marshall Bruce Mathers), (Slim Shady); b. 17 Oct. 1972, St Joseph, Missouri, USA. Rapper. m. Kim Mathers, 1999, 1 d.; divorced, 2001. *Career:* Moved to Detroit, aged 12; Dropped out of high school to join local rap groups: Basement Productions; D12; Released debut album The Infinite on independent label FBT; After releasing Slim Shady EP, made guest appearances with Kid Rock and Shabbam Shadeeq, leading to deal with Dr Dre's Aftermath Records; Collaborations: Dr Dre; Kid Rock; D12; Missy Elliott; Dido. *Recordings:* Albums: Infinite, 1997; The Slim Shady LP, 1999; The Marshall Mathers LP, 2000; Singles: The Slim Shady EP, 1998; Just Don't Give A F***, My Name Is, Guilty Conscience, 1999; The Real Slim Shady, The Way I Am, Stan 2000. *Honours:* MTV Awards: Best Album, The Marshall Mathers LP; Best Hip Hop Artist, 2000. *Address:* c/o Interscope Records, 2220 Colorado Ave, Santa Monica, California, USA.

EMMETT Rik; b. Canada. Musician (guitar); Vocalist. *Career:* Founder member, Canadian rock group Triumph, 1975–88; Later worked with Lee Aaron. *Recordings:* Albums: Triumph, 1976; Rock 'n' Roll Machine, 1977; Just A Game, 1979; Progressions of Power, 1980; Allied Forces, 1981; Never Surrender, 1982; Thunder Seven, 1984; Stages, 1985; The Sport of Kings, 1985; Surveillance, 1987; Classics, 1989; Absolutely, 1990; Spiral Notebook, 1996; Raw Quartet, 1999; Live At Berklee, 2000. *Honour:* Toronto Music Award, 1987. *Current Management:* Randon Entertainment Group, 121 Logan Ave, Toronto, ON M4M 2M9, Canada.

ENDRESEN Sidsel Margrethe; b. 19 June 1952, Trondheim, Norway. Singer; Composer; Lyricist. *Education:* University Degrees in English and Social Anthropology, University of Oslo, 1975–79. *Musical Education:* Various private teachers. *Career:* Singer, Poet, Composer, 1981–; Toured Scandinavia and Europe; Various Radio and TV Programmes in Scandinavia, BBC, Europe and USA; Composed music for various theatre and dance productions, Norway; Worked with many Norwegian and International Jazz Musicians; Fronted numerous groups. *Compositions:* Pagan Pilgrimage, commission for Molde Jazz Festival, 1993; Exile, 1994; also compositions and lyrics on all recordings. *Recordings:* Jivetalking, 1981; Polarities, 1982; City Visions, 1984; Stories, 1985; Pigs and Poetry, 1987; So I Write, 1990; Exile, 1994; Nightsong, 1994; Duplex Ride, 1998. *Honours:* Norwegian Grammy, 1981, 1985, 1998; Radka Toneff Memorial Prize, 1993; State Cultural Scholarship, 1995–98. *Memberships:* Norwegian Jazz Federation; Norwegian Popular Composers. *Current Management:* ACT Music and Vision, Germany.

ENEVOLD Per; b. 4 Aug. 1943, Copenhagen, Denmark. Choir Conductor. m. Margrete Enevold, 3 d. *Education:* Masters Degree, Music, University of Copenhagen; Diploma for Nationally Approved Music Teachers Certificate in Singing, Royal Danish Conservatoire of Music; Studied under Conductors Eric Ericson, Stockholm and Arvid Jansons, Leningrad. *Career:* Artistic Director, Chamber Choir Trinitatis Kantori, 1993–; Founder and Conductor, Copenhagen Chamber Choir, Camerata, 1965–85; Cantor, Copenhagen Cathedral, Vor Frue Kirke, 1983–90; Conductor, Copenhagen Boys' Choir, 1984–91; Conductor, Danish National Radio Choir, 1985–88; Visiting Professor, Music Department, St Olaf College, Northfield, Minnesota, USA, 1991; Cantor, Trinitatis Kirke, Copenhagen, 1997-. *Recordings:* Trinitatis Kantori; Camerata; Copenhagen Boys' Choir; Radio Choir. *Honours:* The Gladsaxe Award, 1976; First Prize, Bela Bartok Competition, Debrecen, Hungary, 1978; The Mogens Wöldike Award, 1982. *Membership:* Danish Conductors Asscn. *Address:* Strandvejen 61, 2th, 2100 Copenhagen, Denmark.

ENGDAHL Elisabeth; b. 17 Dec. 1956, Karlskrona, Sweden. Musician; Composer. m. Thomas Gustafsson, 7 April 1985, 2 d. *Education:* Degree, Afro-American Arrangement, Swedish Academy of Music, 4 years. *Career:* Orchestral Leader and Performing Musician in a small big band and lady band, 1987–93; Orchestral Leader, Performing House Band Pianist, television show, Good Morning Sweden, 1989–90; Performing Saxophonist, in charge of musical arrangement of a Swedish Talk Show, 1993–95; Concert Performances in Shanghai, China, 1994. *Compositions:* Musical Score, Kurt Olsson – The Movie About My Life As Myself, 1989; The Love Project Jazz Opera, 1996. *Recordings:* Musical Arrangements of three records with Kurt Olsson's Lady Band, 1987, 1988, 1990. *Memberships:* Swedish Popular Music Composers; Swedens Media Composers. *Leisure interest:* Family. *Address:* Landalagangen 5, 411 30 Goteborg, Sweden.

ENGEL Soren Peter Bjarne; b. 6 April 1947, Copenhagen, Denmark. Musician (guitar, bass guitar). m. Anne Grethe, 9 May 1991, 1 s. *Career:* Television appearances in France; Germany; Sweden; Finland; Norway; Denmark; European tours with Bo Diddley; Link Wray; Sonny Terry; Brownie McGee; Delta Cross Band. *Recordings:* with Delta Cross Band: No Overdubs, 1979; Rave On, 1980; Up Front, 1981; Slide, 1984; Through Times, 1991; with C V Jorgensen: Tidens Tein, 1980; Vinden Vender, 1982. *Honours:* Several Silver, Gold and Platinum records. *Memberships:* Danish

Artists' Union. *Leisure interests:* Wife; Long walks with dog. *Current Management:* Århus Musik Kontor.

ENGLAND Ty; b. 5 Dec. 1963, Oklahoma City, USA. Singer; Musician (Guitar). m. Shanna Burns England, 3 s., 1 d. *Education:* Oklahoma State University, USA, 2 years; Graduate, Central State University. *Career:* Harmony Vocalist and Acoustic Guitarist for former college room-mate Garth Brooks, 6 years; Started solo career, released 2 albums, Ty England, 1995, Two Ways to Fall, 1996. *Recordings:* Singles: Should've Asked Her Faster; Smoke In Her Eyes; Irresistible You; Too Many Highways, 1998; Albums: Ty England, 1995; Two Ways to Fall, 1996; Highways and Dancehalls, forthcoming. *Honours:* National Spokesperson for the Future Farmers, American Alumni Asscn, 1996–97; Nominee for Star of Tomorrow-Male, TNN/Music City News Awards, 1996–97; Nominee, Performance Magazine, New Country Touring Artist of the Year, 1996. *Leisure interests:* Trailbike Riding; Hunting; Waterskiing. *Current Management:* Mike Palmer, Nashville. *Address:* 1111 17th Ave S, Nashville, TN 37212, USA.

ENGLISH Michael; Singer. *Career:* Toured with The Singing Americans; Joined, The Goodmans; Joined Gospel Group with Legend Bill Gaither; Solo Artist; Signed Record Contract with Curb Records, 1994; Member, The Gaither Vocal Band, 1995; Appeared On Trinity Broadcasting Networks, Praise The Lord, 1997. *Recordings:* In Christ Alone; Michael English; Hope; Healing; Freedom; Your Love Amazes Me; I Bowed On My Knees; Heaven To Earth, 2000. *Honours:* 6 Trophies Including Artist of the Year and Best Male Vocalist, 1994 Dove Awards; Dove Award for Best Southern Gospel Recorded Song of the Year. *Address:* c/o Trifecta Ent, 209 10th Ave S, Suite 302, Nashville, TN 37203, USA.

ENGLUND Sverker; b. 26 Nov. 1968, Stockholm, Sweden. Ethnomusicologist. *Education:* BA, Major in Ethnology, Minor in Musicology; PhD Student, Department of Ethnology, Stockholm University. *Publications:* De sista ljuva åren: upptäcktsresor i oldranders musikaliska landshap, 1996; Srigfinnare i pensionarsland, 1998; Det Gemensamma Minners Melodier, in Pigga pensionärer och populärkultur, 1998. *Membership:* International Council for Traditional Music. *Leisure interests:* Music – vocals and electric guitar; Badminton; Travel; Indian classical music. *Address:* c/o M Eklund, Torkel Knutssonsg 33 IV, 11849 Stockholm, Sweden.

ENO Brian Peter George; b. 15 May 1948, Melton, Suffolk, England. Prod.; Musician (keyboards). *Recordings:* Albums as producer include: with John Cale: Fear, 1974; with Robert Calvert, Lucky Lief and The Longships, 1975; with Michael Nyman: Decay Music, 1976; with Penguin Café Orchestra: Music From The Penguin Café, 1976; with Ultravox: Ultravox, 1977; with Talking Heads: More Songs About Buildings and Food, 1978; Remain In Light, 1980; with Devo: Q- Are We Not Men? A- We Are Devo, 1978; with U2: The Unforgettable Fire, 1984; The Joshua Tree, 1987; Achtung Baby, 1991; Zooropa, 1993; Passengers (film soundtrack), 1995; All That You Can't Leave Behind, 2000; with Carmel: The Falling, 1986; with Geoffrey Oryema: Exile, 1990; with James: Laid, 1993; Wah Wah, 1994; Whiplash, 1997; Millionaires, 1999; Pleased To Meet You, 2001; with Laurie Anderson: Bright Red, 1994; Collaborations include: with Roxy Music: Virginia Plain, 1972; Roxy Music, 1972; For Your Pleasure, 1973; Pyjamarama, 1973; with David Bowie: Low, 1977; Heroes, 1977; Lodger, 1979; As guest musician: Captain Lockheed and The Starfighters, Robert Calvert, 1974; The End, Nico, 1974; The Lamb Lies Down On Broadway, Genesis, 1974; with Phil Manzanera: Diamond Head, 1975; Listen Now, 1977; with John Cale: Slow Dazzle, 1975; Helen of Troy, 1975; Rain Dances, Camel, 1977; Exposure, Robert Fripp, 1979; Yellow Rain, The Neville Brothers, 1989; Rattle and Hum, U2, 1989; Mamouna, Bryan Ferry, 1994; with Jah Wobble: Spinner, 1995; Solo albums include: Here Come The Warm Jets, 1974; Taking Tiger Mountain, 1974; Another Green World, 1975; Before and After Science, 1977; Music For Films, 1978; Ambient 1: Music For Airports, 1978; Apollo: Atmospheres and Soundtracks, 1983; Thursday Afternoon, 1987; Nerve Net, 1992; The Drop, 1997; I Dormienti, 1999; Drawn From Life, 2001; Remix productions include: Unbelieveable, EMF, 1992; I Feel You, Depeche Mode, 1993; The River, Geoffrey Oryema, 1993; I'm Only Looking, INXS, 1993; In Your Room, Depeche Mode, 1993; Brian Eno: Box I and Box II, 1993; Introducing The Band, Suede, 1994; 39 Steps, Bryan Ferry, 1994; Protection, Massive Attack, 1994. *Honours:* Dr, Technology, University of Plymouth; Ivor Novello Award; 2 Grammy Awards; BRIT Awards: Best Producer, 1994, 1996; Q Magazine Awards: Best Producer (with Flood, The Edge), 1993; Inspiration Award (with David Bowie), 1995;. *Memberships:* PRS; BASCA. *Current Management:* Anthea Norman-Taylor, Opal Ltd. *Address:* 3 Pembridge Mews, London W11 3EQ, England.

ENTHOVEN David John; b. 5 July 1944, Windsor, Berkshire, England. Co Dir; Artist Man. Twice married, 1 s., 1 step-s., 1 d., 1 step-d. *Career:* Founded EG Group of Companies, 1969; Signed: King Crimson; T Rex; Emerson Lake and Palmer; Roxy Music; Brian Ferry; Founded IE Music Ltd, 1988; Artist Manager for Robbie Williams, Horace Andy, Archive,

Jamie Catto. *Leisure interest:* Motorbikes, American Sports Cars. *Address:* IE Music Ltd, 111 Frithville Gardens, London W12 7JG, England.

ENTWISTLE John; b. 9 Oct. 1946, Chiswick, London, England. Musician (bass). *Career:* Member, UK rock group The Who, 1964–84; Appearances include: National Jazz and Blues Festival, 1965, 1966, 1969; Monterey Pop Festival, 1967; Farewell tour, 1982–83; Live Aid, Wembley, 1985; Reunion tour, 1989. *Recordings:* Albums: with The Who: My Generation, 1965; A Quick One, 1966; The Who Sell Out, 1968; Direct Hits, 1968; Tommy, 1969; Live At Leeds, 1970; Meaty Beefy and Bouncy, 1971; Who's Next, 1971; Quadrophenia, 1973; Odds and Sods, 1974; The Story of The Who, 1976; The Who By Numbers, 1975; Who Are You, 1978; The Kids Are Alright (film soundtrack), 1979; Face Dances, 1981; It's Hard, 1982; Hooligans, 1982; Rarities Vols 1 and 2, 1983; Once Upon A Time, 1983; The Singles, 1984; Who's Last, 1984; Who's Missing, 1985; Two's Missing, 1987; Who's Better Who's Best, 1988; Joined Together, 1990; 30 Years of Maximum R & B, 1994; Solo albums: Smash Your Head Against The Wall, 1971; Wistle Rymes, 1972; Rigor Mortis Sets In, 1973; Too Late The Hero, 1981; Rock, 1996; Thunderfingers, 1996; King Biscuit Flower Hour, 1997; Left for Live, 1999; Music From Van Pires, 2000; Singles include: I Can't Explain, 1965; Anyway, Anyhow, Anywhere, 1965; My Generation, 1965; Substitute, 1966; I'm A Boy, 1966; Pictures of Lily, 1967; I Can See For Miles, 1967; Pinball Wizard, 1969; See Me Feel Me, 1970; Won't Get Fooled Again, 1971; Join Together, 1972; Who Are You, 1978; You Better You Bet, 1981. *Honours include:* with The Who: Gold Ticket, Madison Square Garden, 1979; Ivor Novello Award, 1982; BRIT Award, 1988; Inducted into Rock 'n' Roll Hall of Fame, 1990. *Current Management:* Trinifold Management, 22 Harley St, Marylebone Rd, London NW1 4PR, England.

ENYA (Eithne Ni Bhraonain); b. 17 May 1961, Gweedore, County Donegal, Ireland. Singer; Musician (piano, keyboards); Composer. *Musical Education:* Clasical piano. *Career:* Member, folk group Clannad, 1980–82; Solo artiste, 1988–; 25m. albums sold to date. *Compositions:* Music for film and television scores: The Frog Prince, 1985; The Celts, BBC, 1987; LA Story, 1990; Green Card, 1990. *Recordings:* Albums: with Clannad: Crann Ull, 1980; Fuaim, 1982; Solo albums: Watermark, 1988; Shepherd's Moon, 1991; Enya, 1992; The Celts (reissued), 1992; The Book Memory of Trees, 1996; On My Way Home, 1998; Storms in Africa, 1998; A Day Without Rain, 2000; Wild Child, 2001; Singles include: Orinoco Flow (No. 1, UK), 1988; Evening Falls, 1988; Storms In Africa (Part II), 1989; Caribbean Blue, 1991; How Can I Keep From Singing, 1991; Book of Days, 1992; Anywhere Is, 1995; Only If, 1997; Oiche Chiun, 1998. *Honours:* Grammy Award, Best New Age Album, Shepherd's Moon, 1993; IRMA Award, Best Irish Female Artist, 1993. *Current Management:* Aigle Music, 6 Danieli Dr., Artane, Dublin 5, Ireland.

EPPLE Kat; b. 21 Aug. 1952, Ohio, USA. Musician (Flute); Composer. *Education:* BA, Electronic Music and Anthropology, University of South Florida; Synclavier technique, 1996. *Career:* Concerts at: Guggenheim Museum, New York City, 1997, National Gallery, Washington DC, Hollywood Palace, Guggenheim Museum, Bilbao, Spain; Concerts in Russia, China, Africa, Europe, Japan, Columbia, Brazil and Peru; Live performances with Parson's Dance Company. *Compositions:* Television soundtracks for National Geographic, PBS-Nova, Carl Sagen, Guiding Light, Another World, CNN; Musical Director, feature film Captiva Island, 1996. *Recordings:* Dragon Wings, 1978; Whispered Visions, 1979; Sound Trek, 1980; Aqua Regia, 1981; Valley of the Birds, 1982; Nocturne, 1983; Lights of the Ivory Plains, 1985; Catspaw, 1986; Dreamspun, 1988; Manatee Dreams, 1990; White Crow, 1997. *Honours:* 6 Emmy Awards for Music, 1978, 1982, 1983, 1985, 1989, 1998; Nominated, Grammy Award, 1986, Best New Age Album. *Memberships:* BMI; Board Mem., Alliance of the Arts of Lee County; Board Mem., New Arts Festival. *Leisure interests:* Collecting and playing flutes from around the world. *Address:* PO Box 3156, North Fort Myers, FL 33918, USA.

ERICSON Peter R; b. 2 July 1950, Uppsala, Sweden. Composer; Prod.; Musician (guitar); Singer. m. Nina, 1975, 2 s., 1 d. *Education:* Journalist's School; English, University; 1 year, St Martins College, Lancaster, England. *Musical Education:* 1 year, guitar; 4 years, piano. *Career:* Four albums with group, Mobben, 1970s; 6 solo albums, 1980s, 1990; Television, radio appearances and regular tours; Currently writing music for major film. *Compositions:* Music for major Swedish artists including: Monica Zetterlund; Cornelis Vreeswijk. *Recordings:* 6 solo albums; Many albums as producer. *Leisure interests:* Sailing; Motorcycle riding; Fishing; Travel. *Current Management:* Hawk Records; Taby, Stockholm, Sweden. *Address:* Hawk Records, Scandinavian Songs Music Group, Box 109, 18212 Danderyd, Sweden.

ERIKSON Duke (Doug); b. USA. Musician (Guitar, Bass, Keyboards). *Career:* Guitarist and Singer, Spooner and Firetown; Worked with Nine Inch Nails, L7, U2; Member, Garbage; Numerous TV and radio sessions; Live gigs and festival appearances. *Recordings:* Subhuman, 1995; vow, 1995; Milk, 1996; Stupid Girl, 1996; Only Happy When It Rains, 1996; Queer, 1997; I Think I'm Paranoid, 1998; Special, 1998; Push It, 1998;

When I Grow Up, 1999; Trick Is To Keep Breathing, 1999; You Look So Fine, 1999; Androgyny, 2001; Albums: Garbage, 1995; Version 2.0, 1998; Beautifulgarbage, 2001. *Honours include:* Grammy Award nomination, Best Rock Song, Special, 2000.

ERNA Sully (Salvatore Paul); b. 7 Feb. 1968, Lawrence, Massachusetts, USA. Vocalist. *Career:* Ex-drummer of Sire/Reprise act Stripmind; Joined Godsmack group as vocalist, 1995; Recorded independent debut album for $2500 over 3 days with money borrowed from friend, 1996; Heavy local airplay on Boston-based WAAF radio station led to deal with Republic/Universal, 1998; Debut LP remixed/repackaged with eponymous title; Album banned by US Wal-Mart and K-Mart stores for profane content; US and European gigs in 1999 and 2000 including: Woodstock '99; Ozzfest; MTV's Return of The Rock tour; Second album recorded in warehouse in Massachusetts, 2000; First major amphitheatre tour, 2001. *Recordings:* Albums: All Wound Up, 1997; Godsmack, 1998; Awake, 2000; Singles: Whatever, Keep Away, 1998; Voodoo, Bad Religion, 1999; Awake, 2000; Greed, Bad Magick, 2001. *Honours:* Whatever single spent record total of 33 weeks on Billboard Top 10; Boston Music Awards, Act of The Year, 2000 and 2001; Billboard Award, Rock Artist of The Year, 2001. *Address:* c/o Paul Geary, PGM, PO Box 9134, Boston, MA 02205, USA. *E-mail:* godsmack@pgmglobal.com. *Internet:* www.godsmack.com.

ESCALLE Jean-Louis; b. 3 March 1954, Aurimont, Gers, France. Jazz Musician (drums). m. Marie-Jeanne, 24 May 1982, 1 s., 2 d. *Musical Education:* Toulouse Conservatory, 6 years. *Career:* Jazz sideman, with regional and national jazz musicians, South of France. *Recordings:* 4 records with regional musicians: J M Pilc; R Calleja; Ch Brun. *Leisure interest:* Reading. *Address:* Orbessan, 32260 Sissan, France.

ESSEX David, David Albert Cook; b. 23 July 1947, Plaistow, East London, England. Singer; Musician (drums); Actor. *Career:* 20 British tours; Many world tours; Television appearances include: Top of The Pops; David Essex Specials; Cher; Johnny Carson; Grammy Awards; Subject, This Is Your Life, 1995; Stage performances: Jesus, Godspell, 1971–73; Che, Evita, 1978; Lord Byron, Childe Byron, at Young Vic; Fletcher Christian, Mutiny; Films: That'll Be The Day; Stardust; Silver Dream Racer; Wrote most of own recordings. *Recordings:* 23 UK hit singles, (2 at No. 1), including: Gonna Make You A Star; Hold Me Close; Rock On (No. 1, USA); Silver Dream Machine; Winter's Tale; Numerous albums include: Rock On, 1973; David Essex, 1974; All The Fun of The Fair, 1975; Out On The Street, 1976; Imperial Wizard, 1979; Collection, 1980; Stagestruck, 1982; The Whisper, 1983; Centre Stage, 1986; Touching The Ghost, 1989; Spotlight, 1991; Cover Shot, 1993; Back To Back, 1994; Living in England, 1995; Missing You, 1996; Here We Are All Together, 1998; Everlasting Love, 2000; Also appeared on Jeff Wayne's War of The Worlds (with Richard Burton, Justin Hayward, Phil Lynott), 1978. *Honours:* Variety Club of Great Britain, Best Newcomer, 1971; Best Performer, Evita, 1978; Ambassador, Voluntary Service Overseas. *Memberships:* American Federation Television; American Screen Actors Guild; Equity-UK. *Leisure interests:* Football; Cricket; Piloting helicopter. *Current Management:* Derek Bowman, Lamplight Music Ltd; Mel Bush Organisation. *Address:* 109 Eastbourne Mews, London W2 6LQ, England.

ESSIET Chief Udoh; b. 21 Nov. 1959, Ikot Ekpene, Nigeria. Musician (African percussion); Singer; Composer; Bandleader. m. Sherry Margolin, 1 s. *Career:* In Nigeria until 1983; Performed traditional native music, Highlife music, with Dr Victor Olaiya; Rex Williams; Rex Lawson; Juju (Sunny Ade); Performed Afrobeat music with Fela Anikulapo Kuti, 1978–83; Based in Paris, 1983–; Founded Ghetto Blaster, first part for Fela, James Brown, 1984; Mory Kante; Salif Keita; Formed Afrobeat Blaster, tours in Europe, 1989-. *Recordings:* with Ghetto Blaster: Preacher Man, 1984; People, 1986; with Salif Keita: Soro; with Sixun, Fela Anikulapo Kuti: ITT; Unknown Soldier; Coffin For Head of State; Authority Stealing; 2000 Black (with Roy Ayers); with Afrobeat Blaster: No Condition Is Permanent, 1991. *Publications:* Film: Ghetto Blaster, 1983. *Honours:* Chief of African Feeling, Amsterdam, 1986. *Memberships:* SACEM; SPEDIDAM; ADAMI. *Leisure interests:* Cooking African food; Playing with son.

ESSING John Leo Thomas; b. 15 Aug. 1964, Stockholm. Musician (guitar, synthesizer, percussion). *Musical Education:* Self-taught guitar, synthesizer, percussion. *Career:* Member, bob hund, 1991; More than 300 gigs around Scandinavia; Played at famous Roskilde, Lollipop, Ruisrock, Quartfestivalen and Hultsfred. *Compositions:* I Stället för Musik, 1996; Düsseldorf, 1996. *Recordings:* bob hund – bob hund, 1993; bob hund – Edvin Medvind, 1994; bob hund – Omslag: Martin Kann, 1996; Düsseldorf, 1996; Ett fall and en lösning, 1997; Nu är det väl revolution på gång?, 1998; Jag rear ut min själ! Allt skall bort!!!, 1998; Helgen V, 1999; Sover aldrig, 1999. *Honours:* Grammy, best live act, 1994; Grammy, best lyrics, 1996. *Memberships:* STIM; SAMI. *Leisure interests:* Music; Books; Food; Movies; Drinking. *Address:* c/o bob hunds förlag, Råsundavägen 150, 169 36 Solna, Sweden.

ESTEFAN Gloria, (Gloria Fajado); b. 1 Sept. 1957, Havana, Cuba. Singer; Songwriter. m. Emilio Estefan, 1 Sept. 1978. *Education:* BA, Psychology, Univeristy of Miami, 1978. *Career:* Singer, backed by Miami Sound Machine, 1974–; Billed as Gloria Estefan, 1989–; Appearances include: Tokyo Music Festival, Japan, 1985; World tour, 1991; The Simple Truth, benefit concert for Kurdish refugees, Wembley, 1991; White House State Dinner, for President of Brazil, 1991; South American tour, 1992; Royal Variety Performance, London, before Prince and Princess of Wales, 1992; Co-organizer, benefit concert for victims of Hurricane Andrew, Florida, 1992; 45m. albums sold to date. *Compositions include:* Anything For You; Don't Wanna Lose You; Oye Mi Canto (co-written with Jorge Casas and Clay Ostwald); Cuts Both Ways; Coming Out of The Dark (co-written with Emilio Estefan and Jon Secada); Always Tomorrow; Christmas Through Their Eyes (co-written with Dianne Warren). *Recordings:* Albums: Renacer, 1976; Eyes of Innocence, 1984; Primitive Love, 1986; Let It Loose, 1988; Anything For You (No. 1, UK), 1989; Cuts Both Ways, 1989; Exitos De Gloria Estefan, 1990; Into The Light, 1991; Greatest Hits, 1992; Mi Tierra, 1993; Christmas Through Your Eyes, 1993; Hold Me, Thrill Me, Kiss Me, 1994; Abriendo Puertas, 1995; Destiny, 1996; Gloria!, 1998; Alma Caribena, 2000; Greatest Hits Vol. 2, 2001; Also featured on: Jon Secada, Jon Secada (also co-producer), 1991; Til Their Eyes Shine (The Lullaby Album), 1992; Hit singles include: Dr Beat, 1984; Conga, 1986; Hot Summer Nights, used in film soundtrack Top Gun, 1986; Bad Boy, 1986; Words Get In The Way, 1986; Rhythm Is Gonna Get You, 1987; Can't Stay Away From You, 1988; Anything For You (No. 1, USA), 1988; 1–2–3, 1988; Oye Mi Canto (Hear My Voice), 1989; Here We Are, 1989; Don't Wanna Lose You, 1989; Get On Your Feet, 1989; Coming Out of The Dark (No. 1, USA), 1991; Remember Me With Love, 1991; Always Tomorrow, 1992; Cuts Both Ways, 1993; Go Away, 1993; Mi Tierra, 1993; Turn the Beat Around, 1994; Abrienda Puertos; Tres Deseos; Mas Alla. *Honours:* Grand Prize, Tokyo Music Festival, 1985; Numerous Billboard awards, 1986–; American Music Award, Favourite Pop/Rock Duo or Group, 1989; Crystal Globe Award, 21 Club, New York, 1990; Latin Music Award, Crossover Artist of Year, 1990; Humanitarian Award, B'Nai B'rith, 1992; Desi Entertainment Awards, Performer of Year, Song of Year, 1992; Humanitarian Award, National Music Foundation (for helping victims of Hurricane Andrew), 1993. *Address:* c/o Estefan Enterprises, 555 Jefferson Ave, Miami Beach, FL 33139, USA.

ESTER Pauline; b. 18 Dec. 1963, Toulouse, France. Singer. *Musical Education:* Private lessons; Different vocal coaches. *Career:* Tours: France; Belgium; Bulgaria; Canada, Québec; Opening act, Patrick Bruel tour, 1991; Appearances on all major television and radio shows, France, Canada, Québec. *Recordings:* Albums: Le Monde Est Fou, 1990; Je L'Autre Côté, 1992; Singles: Il Fait Chaud; Oui, Je T'Adore; Le Monde Est Fou; Une Fenêtre Ouverte. *Honours:* France Internationnal, 1991; Trophy Radio, SACEM: Best Song of Year, 1991; Best New Artist, 1992. *Membership:* SACEM, 1989. *Leisure interests:* Dance. *Current Management:* Jean-Claude Camus Production. *Address:* 6 rue Daubigny, 75017 Paris, France.

ESTRIN Mitchell Stewart; b. 23 Dec. 1956, New York, USA. Performer; Educator. m. Jane Estrin, 1 s. *Education:* BA, MMus, Juilliard School. *Career:* Clarinetist, New York Philharmonic, 1979–99; Professor of Clarinet, University of Florida, 1999–; Television Appearances, Phil Donahue Show; Live From Lincoln Center; Late Show With David Letterman. *Recordings:* The Shadows of October; New York Philharmonic; Amadeus Ensemble; Motion Picture Sountracks. *Honours:* Naumburg Scholarship; Sudler Foundation Award; Outstanding Young Men In America. *Memberships:* American Federation of Musicians; Recording Musicians of America; College Music Society. *Leisure interests:* Computers; Numismatics; Chess; Sports. *Address:* University of Florida, College of Fine Arts, School of Music, PO Box 117900, Gainesville, Florida 32611.

ETHERIDGE John M G; b. 12 Jan. 1948, London, England. Musician (guitar). 1 s., 1 d. *Education:* BA, History of Art, University of Essex. *Musical Education:* Self-taught. *Career:* Soft Machine, 1975–79; Stephane Grappelli, 1976–81; Solo tours: Australia; USA; England; 1982–84; MD, Bertice Reading, 1985–90; European tour with Birelli Lagrene, Vic Juris, 1989; European tours with Dick Hextall-Smith (saxophone); Danny Thompson's Whatever, 1989–93; Own Quartet, 1990–; Andy Summers Duo, 1993–; Nigel Kennedy Group, 1993-. *Recordings:* with Soft Machine: Soft; Alive and Well; Triple Echo; with Stephane Grappelli: At The Winery; Live At Carnegie Hall; with Stephane Grappelli and Yehudi Menuhin: Tea For Two; Strictly For The Birds; with Nigel Kennedy, Kafka, 1996; Kennedy Experience, 1999; with own quartet: Second Vision, 1981; Sweet Chorus: Tribute to Stefan Grapelli, 1999; with Vic Juris: Bohemia, 1989; with Dick Heckstall-Smith: Obsession Fees, 1990; with Danny Thompson: Elemental, 1991; with Andy Summers: Invisible Threads, 1993; with Wolf: Saturation Point, 2001; Solo albums: Ash, 1994; Sweet Chorus dedicated to Grappelli, 1998. *Publications:* The Guitar, OUP, editor, Michael Stimpson; Numerous articles for guitar magazines. *Leisure interests:* Cricket; Walking. *Current Management:* Andy Morley. *Address:* Exeter and Devon Arts Centre.

ETHERIDGE Melissa Lou; b. 29 May 1961, Leavenworth, Kansas, USA. Singer; Songwriter; Musician (guitar). *Musical Education:* Berklee College of Music, Boston. *Career:* Musician, Los Angeles bars, 5 years; Recording artiste, 1988-. *Recordings:* Albums: Melissa Etheridge, 1988; Brave and Crazy, 1989; Never Enough, 1992; Yes I Am, 1993; Your Little Secret, 1995; Breakdown, 1999; Skin, 2001; Singles: I'm the Only One, 1994; Come to My Window, 1994; If I Wanted To, 1995; Nowhere to Go, 1996; Angels Would Fall, 1999. *Honours:* Grammy Nomination, Bring Me Some Water, 1988. *Current Management:* Bill Leopold, W F Leopold Management.

EUBANKS Robin; b. 25 May 1955, Philadelphia, Pennsylvania, USA. Jazz Musician (trombone). *Career:* Played in bands on Broadway; Appeared in film: Cotton Club; Member, Duke Ellington and Cab Calloway bands; Played on Motown Television special; Played with: Art Blakey; Abdullah Ibrahim; Marvin 'Smitty' Smith; Geri Allen; Dave Holland; Wynford and Branford Marsalis; Steve Coleman; Regular tours: USA; Europe; Japan. *Recordings:* Different Perspectives, 1988; Dedications, 1989; Karma, 1990; Mental Images, 1994; Wake Up Call, 1997; 4:JJ/Slide/Curtis and Al, 1998; Get 2 It, 2001; Musician on: Art Blakey: Live At Montreux and Northsea; Not Yet; Kevin Eubanks: Guitarist; Steve Coleman: World Expansion; Sine Die; Marvin 'Smitty' Smith: Keeper of The Drums; Geri Allen: Open On All Sides; Mark Helias: The Current Set; Herb Robertson: Shades of Bud Powell; Dave Holland: The Razor's Edge; Branford Marsalis: Scenes In The City. *Address:* SESAC, 55 Music Sq. E, Nashville, TN 37203, USA.

EURIPIDES Georganopoulos; b. 12 Dec. 1961, Thessaloniki, Greece. Composer; Prod.; Musician (keyboards). m. Dr Agnes Leotsakos, 22 Feb. 1992, 1 s. *Musical Education:* ARCM, Dip RCM (Royal College of Music). *Career:* Writing music for television and video productions; Director, Optimus International Ltd (music production company); Composition, production work in UK, France, Germany, Malta, Greece, Poland. *Recordings:* Arranger, producer, Hits of The War Years (No. 4, UK Music Video Charts), 1995. *Memberships:* BASCA; Musicians' Union; PRS; MCPS. *Leisure interests:* Backgammon. *Address:* 35 Elm Rd, London SW14 7JL, England.

EVANS Dan (David Rhys); b. 26 May 1956, Middlesbrough, Cleveland, England. Folk Musician (dulcimer, guitar). m. Mary Collins, 12 May 1995. *Education:* BSc hons (Dunelm). *Career:* Performing in folk clubs, art centres, theatres in UK for 25 years; frequent radio appearances; frequent performances in USA; a leading exponent on mountain dulcimer in UK, highly respected and innovative finger-style guitarist; specialist on electro-acoustic effects. *Recordings:* Sampler, 1988; Guardian Spirit, 1993; Spirit Dancing, 1997. *Publications:* contributor to Dulcimer Players News (USA) and Nonsuch Dulcimer Newsletter (UK). *Memberships:* PRS; MCPS; PPL; MU. *Leisure interests:* Photography. *Current Management:* DanSing Music. *Address:* 61 Sillswood, Olney, Bucks MK46 5PN, England.

EVANS Faith; b. 10 June 1973, Lakeland, Florida, USA. Vocalist. m. Christopher Wallace (Notorious BIG), 4 Aug. 1994, deceased 1997. *Career:* Started as backing singer for Mary J Blige and Color Me Badd; Released debut solo single You Used To Love Me, 1995; Performed on tribute single to murdered rapper husband, I'll Be Missing You, 1997; Collaborations: Puff Daddy; Whitney Houston; Eric Benet; DMX. *Recordings:* Albums: Faith, 1995; Keep The Faith, 1998, Faithfully, 2002; Singles: You Used To Love Me, 1995; I'll Be Missing You (with Puff Daddy and 112), 1997; Love Like This, 1998; All Night Long, 1999; You Gets No Love, 2002. *Honours:* Grammy Award, Best R & B Performance By A Duo Or Group nominee, Can't Believe (with Carl Thomas), 2001; I'll Be Missing You single sold over 7m. copies world-wide, First single to debut at No. 1 on US and UK singles charts. *Address:* c/o Bad Boy Records, 1540 Broadway 33rd Floor, New York, USA.

EVANS Frank; b. 1 Oct. 1936, England. Jazz Musician (guitar); Arranger. m. Mary, 23 May 1954, 2 s. *Musical Education:* Self-taught. *Career:* Tours with bands; Television: Parkinson (solo); BBC Jazz Club, World Service; Strictly Instrumental, Composed for more than 60 television dramas, documentary films. *Recordings:* Jazz Tete-á-Tete Tubby Hayes, Tony Coe; Mark Twain Suite (77 records); Noctuary; Soiree; Ballade; Frank Evans For Little Girls; Stretching Forth. *Publications:* The Jazz Standard, 1998. *Honour:* Inclusion in The Great Jazz Guitarists. *Memberships:* PRS; MCPS; PRC. *Leisure interest:* Snooker. *Current Management:* Don Percival, Artists Promotion. *Address:* 9 Holbrook House, Paul's Cray Rd, Chislehurst, Kent BR7 60E, England.

EVANS Lee; b. 7 Jan. 1933, New York, USA. Composer; Musician (piano). *Education:* BA, NYU, 1957; MA, Columbia University, 1958; EdD, 1978. *Career:* Worked with various artists include: Tom Jones; Cat Stevens; Engelbert Humperdinck; Gilbert O'Sullivan; Professor, Five Towns College, Seaford, 1977–78; President, Piano Plus Inc, 1973–; Leader, Lee Evans Trio, 1966–73; Featured pianist, television specials, The Gershwin Years; Ed Sullivan; Merv Griffin; Performed at 2 White House Command Performances for President Lyndon B Johnson. *Publications:* Author, series of jazz keyboard books; Contributor to journals. *Memberships:*

ASCAP; AFofM; National Asscn of Jazz Educators. *Address:* Piano Plus Inc, New York, USA.

EVANS Sara; b. 2 May 1971, Booneville, Missouri, USA. Country vocalist. m. Craig Schelske. *Career:* First performed on mandolin aged 4 as part of a family act, The Evans Family Band, started by mother Pat and including seven year old Matt on banjo and nine year old Jay; Group played local PTA meetings and bluegrass festivals; Group became the Sara Evans Band; Switched to country music and played in various groups; First regular gig at the Country Stampede, Columbia, Missouri; Worked as waitress and wrote songs on first trip to Nashville, 1991; Met future husband Craig Schelske, joined a band with his two brothers and returned to Oregon; Played country club venues for next three years as Sara Evans and North Santiam; Returned to Nashville, singing demos for Tree Publishing, 1995; Introduced by RCA to Dwight Yoakam's producer Pete Anderson who eventually produced moderately successful debut album Three Chords and The Truth; Popularity increased significantly with second album and stature has grown subsequently; Hosted the British Country Music Awards, 1997; Teamed up with Martina McBride and Reba McEntire for first all-female country music tour, Country Divas, 2001. *Compositions include:* Born To Fly; No Place That Far; Three Chords and The Truth. *Recordings include:* Not That Far, 1999; Born To Fly, 2000; I Couldn't Ask For More, 2001; Albums include: Three Chords and The Truth, 1997; No Place That Far, 1998; Born To Fly, 2000. *Leisure interests:* Reading; Watching films; Listening to bluegrass music; Watching biographies of famous people. *Address:* c/o The Country Music Asscn, Nashville, Tennessee, USA. *Internet:* www.saraevans.net.

EVANS Tania; Vocalist. *Career:* Singer, German dance act Culture Beat, 1990-. *Recordings:* Singles: Erdbeermund, 1990; I Like You, 1993; Mr Vain (No. 1 throughout Europe, including UK, Germany), 1993; Anything, 1994; World In Your Hands, 1994; Prisoner of Love, 1998; Insanity, 2001. *Current Management:* Pyramid Entertainment Group, Los Angeles, USA. *Address:* c/o Epic Records, 10 Great Marlborough St, London W1V 2LP, England.

EVELYN George; b. 15 Jan. 1970, England. *Musical Education:* Drums at High School. *Career:* Promoter, club: Funky Mule and The Headz Club, Leeds; DJ, under name of E A S E (Experimental Sample Expert), Leeds; Founder member, Nightmares on Wax, with Kevin Harper. *Recordings:* Dextrous; Stating A Fact; Aftermath; EP: A Case of Funk; Set Me Free; Happiness; Alive; Finer, 1999; Albums: A Word of Science, 1991; Smokers Delight, 1996; Car Boot Soul, 1999; DJ Kicks, 2000. *Memberships:* PRS. *Leisure interests:* Squash; Swimming; Making Music. *Current Management:* Timebomb, Concorde. *Address:* 2 Authorpe Rd, Leeds LS6 4JB, England.

EVENTHAL Avril; b. 21 May 1947, Liverpool, Merseyside, England. Entertainer; Prod. (Honky Tonk piano). m. Philip Howard Eventhal, 12 Aug. 1975. *Education:* Salford Technical College, Sound Engineer. *Career:* Television appearances: The Gong Show with Frankie Howerd, CH4; My Kind of People, Michael Barrymore; Support to 3 Degrees, Hippodrome Club, London; Prepared Bad Taste Tour of England, BBC Radio, 1988. *Recordings:* Paris Is For Lovers; The Man In My Life; You're A Man (No. 10 in Buzzcharts); Yesterday's Lovers; 2 commercial videos: Sex Slaves of New Orleans. *Memberships:* PRS; BASCA; Equity; MCPS; PPL. *Leisure interests:* Choreography; Photography (modelling). *Address:* 26 Dovedale Ave, Prestwich, Manchester M25 0BU, England.

EVERARD Christopher; b. 26 May 1964, Widnes, England. Singer; Songwriter; Musician (guitar, piano). Partner: Karen Halliburton, 2 s., 2 d. *Musical Education:* Self-taught guitar, piano, songwriting. *Career:* Hundreds of small venue gigs include Mean Fiddler; Appearance, Granada TV Arts Festival, 1990; Several sessions on local radio. *Compositions:* Tracks: Just To Survive; The Hunger; Far Over The Fields; Goodnight Angel; Fat Cats. *Recording:* Debut album released 1995. *Publications:* Widnes Weekly News; Weekly World. *Membership:* Musicians' Union. *Leisure interests:* Poetry; Classical music.

EVERHART Robert; b. 16 June 1936, Nebraska, USA. Musician (12 String Guitar, Harmonica). m. Sheila Dawn Armstrong, 1 d. *Education:* College University of Nebraska, 1959–62; Iowa West BVN College, 1971; University of Oklahoma, 1990. *Career:* Associate Producer, Host, PBS National Program, Old Time Country Music; Producer, Host of Nationally Syndicated Radio Show, Old Time Music Hour; DJ, Various Stations; Curator, Owner, Pioneer Music Museum. *Compositions:* Songwriter, BMI Royal Flair Music Pub, 1964; Lets Go; Dream Angel; She Sings Sad Songs; Bad Woman Blues; Fish Pole John; Time After Time; Street Sleepers; No One Comes Near; Berlin Folksinger; I Like It Raw; Desparados Ride Again. *Recordings:* 1 Waitin For A Train; Time After Time; Everhart International; Everhart Takes The Fifth; Everhart Alive At Avoca; Keepin' It Country; Headed West; Paid Our Dues. *Publications:* Tradition Magazines; Clara Bell; Hartsbluff; Listen To The Mocking Bird; Silver Bullets; Prairie Sunrise; Snoopy Goes to Mexico; Life of Jimmie Rodgers. *Honours:* National Traditional Music Performer Award; PMECI Hall of Fame; Country Music Showcase International Hall of Fame;

Grammy Nomination for Time After Time; First Place Old Time Country Music Contests Over 10 years; Lifetime Achievement Award from World Music Events; Kentucky Col. *Memberships:* PMECI; SPBGMA; World Music Events; NTCMA; Great Plains Old Time Music Asscn. *Leisure interests:* Director of National Old Time Country Music Contest and Festival. *Current Management:* Prairie Music, PO 492, Anita, IA 50020, USA.

EVERLY Don (Isaac Donald); b. 1 Feb. 1937, Brownie, Kentucky, USA. Vocalist; Musician (guitar); Songwriter. m. Adela Everly, 22 March 1997. *Career:* Member, the Everly Brothers (with brother Phil), 1955–73; 1983–; Solo artiste, 1973–83; Performances include: Debut, Grand Ole Opry, 1957; British tour, supported by Bo Diddley, Rolling Stones, 1963; Represented US, Grand Gala Du Disque, Holland, 1965; Reunion Concert, Royal Albert Hall, 1983; British tour, 1991; US tour, 1992; Royal Albert Hall, 1993; Televison includes: Everly Brothers Show, ABC TV, 1970. *Recordings:* Albums include: The Everly Brothers – They're Off and Running!, 1958; Songs Our Daddy Taught Us, 1958; It's Everly Time!, 1960; The Fabulous Style of The Everly Brothers, 1960; A Date With The Everly Brothers, 1961; Instant Party, 1962; The Golden Hits Of, 1962; The Very Best of The Everly Brothers, 1964; Gone Gone Gone, 1965; Rock 'n' Soul, 1965; In Our Image, 1966; Two Yanks In England, 1966; The Hit Sound of The Everly Brothers, 1967; The Everly Brothers Sing, 1967; The Everly Brothers Show, 1970; The Everly Brothers Original Greatest Hits, 1970; Stories We Could Tell, 1972; Pass The Chicken and Listen, 1973; The Very Best Of, 1974; Walk Right Back With..., 1975; Living Legends, 1977; Love Hurts, 1983; The Reunion Concert, 1984; Born Yesterday, 1986; Some Hearts, 1989; Classic Everly Brothers, 1992; Heartaches and Harmonies, 1994; Craftsmen, 1995; Heroes of Country Music, 1996; Brothers in Rhythm, 1998; Devoted To You, 2000; Solo albums: Don Everly, 1971; Sunset Towers, 1974; Brother Jukebox, 1977; Singles include: Bye Bye Love; Wake Up Little Susie; All I Have To Do Is Dream (No. 1, USA), 1958; Bird Dog; Problems; (Til) I Kissed You; Let It Be Me; Cathy's Clown (No. 1, USA), 1960; When Will I Be Loved; So Sad (To Watch Good Love Go Bad); Like Strangers; Walk Right Back (No. 1, UK), 1961; Temptation (No. 1, UK), 1961; Crying In The Rain. *Honours:* Star on Hollywood Walk of Fame, 1986; Inducted into Rock 'n' Roll Hall of Fame, 1986; Inducted into Jukebox Legends Hall of Fame, 1990; Lifetime Achievement Grammy, 1997. *Current Management:* International Creative Management, 8942 Wilshire Blvd, Beverly Hills, CA 90211, USA.

EVERLY Phil; b. 19 Jan. 1939, Chicago, Illinois, USA. Vocalist; Musician (guitar); Songwriter. *Career:* Member, The Everly Brothers (with brother Don), 1955–73; 1983–; Solo artiste, 1973–83; Performances include: Debut, Grand Ole Opry, 1957; British tour, supported by Rolling Stones, 1963; Represented US, Grand Gala Du Disque, Holland, 1965; The Reunion Concert, Royal Albert Hall, 1983; British tour, 1991; US tour, 1992; Royal Albert Hall, 1993; Television includes: The Everly Brothers Show, ABC TV, 1970. *Recordings:* Albums include: The Everly Brothers – They're Off and Running!, 1958; Songs Our Daddy Taught Us, 1958; It's Everly Time, 1960; The Fabulous Style of, 1960; A Date With The Everly Brothers, 1961; Instant Party, 1962; Everly Brothers Sing Great Country Hits, 1963; The Very Best Of, 1964; Gone Gone Gone, 1965; Rock 'n' Soul, 1965; In Our Image, 1966; Two Yanks In England, 1966; The Everly Brothers Show, 1970; Stories We Could Tell, 1972; Pass The Chicken and Listen, 1973; Living Legends, 1977; The New Album, 1977; The Reunion Concert, 1984; EB 84, 1984; Some Hearts, 1989; Classic Everly Brothers, 1992; Heartaches and Harmonies, 1994; Heroes of Country Music, 1996; Brothers in Rhythm, 1998; Devoted To You, 2000; Solo albums: Star Spangled Springer, 1973; There's Nothing Too Good For My Baby, 1975; Mystic Line, 1975; Living Alone, 1982; Phil Everly, 1983; Louise, 1987; Singles include: Bye Bye Love, 1957; Wake Up Little Susie (No. 1, USA), 1957; All I Have To Do Is Dream (No. 1, USA), 1958; Bird Dog; (Til) I Kissed You; Let It Be Me; Cathy's Clown (No. 1, USA); When Will I Be Loved; So Sad (To Watch Good Love Go Bad); Like Strangers; Temptation (No. 1, USA); Crying In The Rain; Duets with: Cliff Richard, She Means Nothing To Me, 1983; Nanci Griffith, You Made This Love A Teardrop, 1989. *Honours include:* Star on Hollywood Walk of Fame, 1986; Inducted into Rock 'n' Roll Hall of Fame, 1986; Inducted into Jukebox Legends Hall of Fame, 1990. *Current Management:* International Creative Management, 8942 Wilshire Blvd, Beverly Hills, CA 90211, USA.

EVERS Jörg; b. 21 June 1950, Bayreuth, Germany. Composer; Prod.; Arranger; Musician (guitar). m. Anna Maria, 18 March 1981, 1 s., 1 d. *Musical Education:* Musical Science (Uni München); Richard Strauss Konservatorium München. *Career:* Tours in Europe with: Embryo; Amon Düül II; Peter Maffay; Pack. *Recordings:* Claudja Barry: Boogie Woogie Dancin' Shoes; Sylvie Vartan: Disco Queen; Claudja Barry: Down and Counting; Television: Herzblatt; Advertising: McDonalds; Odol; Maggi; Burger King; Löwenbräu; Wrigley's; Reebok; Esso. *Honours:* Best Composer's Award, Ninth Tokyo Music Festival, 1980; NY Clio Award, 1991; Div Platinum, Gold Records. *Membership:* GEMA. *Address:* PO Box 1122, 85765 Unterföhring, Munich, Germany.

EVORA Cesaria, (La Diva aux Pieds Nus); b. 27 Aug. 1941, Mindelo, Sao Vincento, Cape Verde. Vocalist; Songwriter. *Career:* Niece of composer B Leza; Sang in bars in Mindelo from late teens; Left the island for the first time in her forties; Travelled to Lisbon to record two tracks for a compilation of Cape Verdean singers; Later went to Paris to record first solo album; Critical acclaim for Miss Perfumado; First large-scale US tour, 1995; Continues to tour internationally. *Recordings:* Albums include: Miss Perfumado, 1992; Cesaria, 1995; Mar Azul, 1999; Café Atlantico, 1999; Sao Vincente di Longe (featuring Caetano Vaeloso, Chucho Valdes and Bonnie Raitt), 2001. *Honours:* Grammy, Best World Music Album nominee, Cesaria, 1995. *Address:* c/o Lusafrica, 13 rue Auger, 93500 Pantin, France. *Internet:* www.lusafrica.com.

EWANJE Charles; b. 19 Dec. 1937, Douala, Cameroon. Musician (Guitarist). m. Michelle Lissandre, 12 July 1973, 3 s., 5 d. *Education:* Bachelor's Degree, Economics, French Baccalaureat. *Career:* Dance Band Musician, Guitar, Flute and Arrangements, 1960–72; Classical Guitar Teacher, 1972–76; Artist, African Classical Guitar, 1977–; Participation in Cameroon and French Televisions. *Compositions:* Makala Ma Mbasi; African Strings for Luther King; Munenge Mwe o Mboa; Earth Paradise; Esok'am; Longe Lasu. *Recordings:* Munenge and Esok'am; Ewanje; Longe Lasu. *Honours:* First Prize of Composition, Guitar Word Thoroughfare, 1982; Arranger Diploma, 1991. *Leisure interests:* Billiards; Chess. *Address:* 35 rue Savier, 92240 Malakoff, France.

EWING Thomas D; b. 1 Sept. 1946, Columbus, Ohio, USA. Musician (guitar); Singer. m. (1) Margaret Avren, 10 June 1967; (2) Pamela Gwen McReynolds, 12 June 1994, 2 s., 1 d., 1 step-s., 1 step-d. *Education:* BA, Journalism, BS, Education, The Ohio State University. *Musical Education:* Self-taught. *Career:* Earl Taylor and the Stoney Mountain Boys, 1974–77; Bill Monroe and His Blue Grass Boys, 1986–96; David Davis and the Warrior River Boys, 1996–97; Jim and Jesse and the Virginia Boys, 1998; Tours: USA; Europe; Japan; Carnegie Hall, 1988; WSM Grand Ole Opry; The Nashville Network, television; Appeared in film: High Lonesome. *Recordings:* Albums: with Earl Taylor: Body and Soul, 1976; with Bill Monroe: Bluegrass '87, 1987; Southern Flavour, 1988; 50 Years at Grand Ole Opry, 1989; Cryin' Holy Unto The Lord, 1991; Solo albums: Take Me Home, 1989; Lookin' Out A Window, 1990; It's Good To Be Home, 1992. *Publications:* 30 Years Ago This Month, Bluegrass Unlimited Magazine; Editor, The Bill Monroe Reader, forthcoming. *Membership:* AFofM. *Address:* 564 Ziegler's Fort Rd, Gallatin, TN 37066, USA.

EYDMANN Stuart Anthony; b. 1 May 1953, Dunfermline, Fife, Scotland. Musician (fiddle, concertina); Ethnomusicologist. m. Mairin Downes, 27 July 1991, 1 s., 1 d. *Education:* Diploma, Glasgow School of Art, 1975; PhD, The Open University, 1995. *Career:* Performer, various Scottish traditional music groups, 1972–79; Member, Whistlebinkies, 1980–; Composer, Scottish Circus, including collaborations with John Cage; Worked with: Scottish Chamber Orchestra; Scottish Ballet; Royal Scottish National Orchestra; Yehudi Menuhin, in works by Edward McGuire; Various film scores; Edinburgh International Festival and Festival Fringe; Sessions with The Cutting Crew; Tours: Sweden; France; China; Hong Kong; Holland; Engaged in ethnomusicological research, 1985-. *Recordings:* As performer, co-writer, co-producer: The Whistlebinkies 3, 1980; The Whistlebinkies 4, 1982; The Whistlebinkies, 1985; The Whistlebinkies Anniversary, 1991; The Whistlebinkies Inner Sound, 1991; Wanton Fling, 1996; As guest: The Music of Midlothian, 1990. *Honours:* The Glenfiddich Living Scotland Award, 1984. *Memberships:* Fellow, Society of Antiquarians of Scotland; Musicians Union; Traditional Music and Song Asscn of Scotland. *Leisure interests:* Architectural Conservation; Ethnomusicology. *Current Management:* Jester Management. *Address:* 41 Hamilton Dr., Glasgow G12 8DW, Scotland.

EYRE Simon James; b. 30 Nov. 1964, Sheffield, England. Musician (Guitar, Bass, Vocals). *Career:* Concert tours with Elaine Page, The Style Council, Womack and Womack, Jimmy Ruffin; TV appearances with Randy Crawford, Jim Diamond, Sister Sledge, Second Image and Lenny Henry. *Recordings:* With Robert Palmer, Shara Nelson, and Errol Brown; Also with The Lighthouse Family, Ocean Drive album and singles Ocean Drive and Lifted. *Honours:* Quadruple Platinum Award, for Ocean Drive. *Memberships:* Musicians' Union; Associate Mem., PRS. *Address:* 4 Luffman Rd, London SE12 9SX, England.

EZEKE (Ezeke Gray); b. 26 Oct. 1943, Jamaica. Singer; Broadcaster; Entertainer; Composer; Caterer. m. Linda Lewis, 11 Oct. 1974, 1 s., 1 d. *Education:* Catering, Clarendon College of Further Education, Nottingham. *Musical Education:* Royal School of Church Music. *Career:* Television appearances include Opportunity Knocks; Search For A Star; Nationwide; Pebble Mill At One; Arena; Resident performer, Monte Carlo Sporting Club, 1979–84; Extensive Tours: Europe; Asia; Middle East; Radio Broadcaster, Radio ERI (Cork City, Eire); BBC Radio 3 Counties, 1986; BBC Radio One (Sunshine Show), 1990–93; BBC Radio One (Ones On One), 1993. *Recordings:* Sitting In The Moonlight, 1961; Righteous Festival, 1972; Rastaman A Come, 1972; Who's Grovelling Now? (with Tony Greig, England Cricket Captain), 1978; Ragga Ragga 1994; Oh Diana, 1994; Soon You'll Be Gone. *Publications:* Jakmandora (childrens stories). *Honours:* Voted Jamaica's Top Entertainer, 1970–75; Sony Awards Certificate; Stanford St Martin Religious Broadcasting, third prize, 1992, first prize, 1994. *Membership:* Musicians Union. *Leisure interests:* Golf; Swimming; Cooking. *Current Management:* Habana Productions Ltd. *Address:* 78 Stanley Gardens, London W3 7SN England.

F

FABBRI Franco; b. 7 Sept. 1949, Sao Paulo, Brazil. Musician; Musicologist. m. Monica Silvestris, 31 May 1980, 1 d. *Education:* Chemistry, State University of Milan; Composition, Conservatory Giuseppe Verdi, Milan; Musicology, University of Gothenburg, Sweden. *Career:* Member, experimental rock group, Stormy Six/Macchina Maccheronica, 1965–82; Freelance writer and lecturer, 1983–85; Consultant to musical institutions in Milan: Musica Nel Nostro Tempo; G Ricordi and Co, (publishers). *Recordings:* 9 albums with group La Chitarra Rotta; Domestic Flights, 1983; Tempo Rubato, 1983; La Casa Parlante, 1984; Various soundtracks and stage music. *Publications:* La Musica In Mano, 1978; Elettronica e Musica, 1984; La Musica Che Si Consuma, 1985; Editor, What Is Popular Music?, 1985; Compositore, 1986. *Address:* Strada Ave, Torre 1, San Felice, 20090 Segrate, Italy.

FABER Shane; b. 23 Dec. 1953, Gainesville, Florida, USA. Prod.; Songwriter; Midi Expert; Musician (guitar, keyboards). m. Elizabeth Burkland, 22 May 1994. *Musical Education:* Bachelor Music/Jazz Guitar, University of Miami, Florida, 1977. *Career:* Member, Bad Sneakers, 1979–86; Video, Caught in the Act; Moved to New York, 1986; Engineer for: De La Soul; A Tribe Called Quest; Queen Latifah; Brand Nubians; Biz Markie; Omar; China Black; Musical Supervisor, film Double Platinum, 1999. *Compositions:* Shine On; Ladies First. *Recordings:* Producer/mixer of albums: Reachin', Digable Planets; Debut album, Bass Is Base; Singles: Cool Like Dat; Turtle Power, from Teenage Mutant Ninja Turtles soundtrack; Digigal Flavor on the Sonic Frontier, by JeepJazz Project. *Honours:* Numerous Golden Reel Awards; 2 Gold albums; 1 Platinum album; 2 Gold singles. *Current Management:* Steven Scharf Entertainment, New York. *Address:* c/o JeepJazz Music, 1 Riverdale Ave No. 3, Riverdale, NY 10463, USA.

FABIANO Roberta Mary; b. 25 June 1952, New York, USA. Musician (guitar); Vocalist; Composer. *Musical Education:* BA, Composition and Arrangement, Berklee College of Music, Boston, 1975. *Career:* Guitarist, composer, Lester Lanin and Peter Duchin Orchestras, 1983–84; Doc Pomus, 1984–; Songwriter for Count Basie Band; Performed for HRH Queen Elizabeth, 1985, 1986; Also performed with: Cleo Laine; Melissa Manchester; Al B Sure!; Debbie Gibson; Carol Channing; Gloria Loring; Julia Budd. *Recordings include:* Working Girl (film soundtrack). *Honours:* American Song Festival Award, 1982; New York Songwriters Showcase Award, 1984; New York State Senate Achievement Award, 1984. *Memberships:* AFofM; Songwriters Guild; AFTRA.

FABRY Anne; b. 13 Aug. 1950, Uccle, Belgium. Musician (drums, piano, keyboards). Divorced, 2 s. *Recordings:* Drava; Vent; Deux; Trio. *Leisure interests:* Kobudo; Taichi. *Address:* 31 Av Clementine, 1060 Brussels, Belgium.

FAGAN James; b. 27 Jan. 1972, Australia. Vocalist; Musician (bouzouki, mandolin, tin whistle, clarinet, guitar, piano); Composer. *Career:* Son of Bob and Margaret Fagan, prominent participators of Sydney folk scene; Half of a duo with Nancy Kerr and also recorded and toured as part of trio with Nancy and Sandra Kerr. *Recordings:* Albums: with Nancy Kerr: Starry Gazy Pie, 1997; Steely Water, 1999; Between The Dark and The Light, 2002; features on Scalene, Sandra and Nancy Kerr, 1999; Yellow Red and Gold, Sandra Kerr, 2000. *Honours:* BBC Horizon Award, Best New Act, Nancy Kerr and James Fagan, 2000.

FAGEN Donald; b. 10 Jan. 1948, Passaic, New Jersey, USA. Vocalist; Musician (keyboards). *Career:* Member, Steely Dan, 1972–81, reunited 1990s; Solo artiste, 1981–; Tours world-wide; Organized New York Rock and Soul Revue, New York, USA, 1990, 1991; Music Editor, US film magazine Premiere, 1988. *Recordings:* Albums: with Steely Dan: Can't Buy A Thrill, 1973; Countdown To Ecstacy, 1973; Pretzel Logic, 1974; Katy Lied, 1975; The Royal Scam, 1977; Aja, 1977; Greatest Hits, 1979; Metal Leg, 1980; Gaucho, 1981; Steely Dan Gold, 1982; Reelin' In The Years, 1985; Do It Again, 1987; Remastered – The Very Best of Steely Dan, 1993; Citizen Steely Dan – 1972–80, 1993; Alive In America, 1995; Two Against Nature, 2000; Solo albums: The Nightfly, 1982; Kamakiriad, 1993; Singles include: Do It Again, 1972; Reelin' In The Years, 1973; Show Biz Kids, 1973; My Old School, 1973; Rikki Don't Lose That Number, 1974; Black Friday, 1975; Haitian Divorce, 1976; Deacon Blues, 1977; Peg, 1977; FM (No Static At All), 1978; Hey Nineteen, 1980; Time Out of Mind, 1981; Solo singles: True Companion; Century's End, used in film Bright Lights Big City, 1988; I G Y (What A Beautiful World), 1982; Tomorrow's Girls, 1993; Contributor, Zazu, Rosie Vela, 1987; The New York Rock and Soul Revue – Live At The Beacon, 1992. *Honours:* Grammy Award, Best-Engineered Non-Classical Recording, Aja, 1978; Q Inspiration Award, 1993; Inducted into Hollywood's Rock Walk, 1993; 4 Grammy Awards, including Album of

The Year, for Two Against Nature, 2001. *Current Management:* HK Management, 8900 Wilshire Blvd, Suite 300, Beverly Hills, CA 90211, USA. *Internet:* www.steelydan.com.

FAHEY Siobhan; b. 10 Sept. 1957, London, England. Singer; Songwriter. m. Dave Stewart, 1 Aug. 1987. *Career:* Press officer, Decca Records; Singer, Bananarama, 1981–88, rejoined 1998; Member, Shakespears Sister, with Marcella Detroit, 1988–93. *Recordings:* Albums: with Bananarama: Deep Sea Skiving, 1983; Bananarama, 1984; True Confessions, 1986; Wow!, 1987; with Shakespears Sister: Sacred Heart, 1989; Hormonally Yours, 1992; Also appeared on: Aerial No. 5: A Journey in Sound, 1992; Greetings from the Gutter, 1995; Divas of Pop, 1996; Singles include: with Bananarama: Really Sayin' Somethin', 1982; Shy Boy, 1982; Na Na Hey Hey Kiss Him Goodbye, 1983; Cruel Summer, 1983; Robert De Niro's Waiting, 1984; Venus (No. 1, USA), 1986; I Heard A Rumour, 1987; Love In The First Degree, 1987; with Shakespears Sister: You're History, 1989; Goodbye Cruel World, 1991; Hello (Turn Your Radio On), 1992; Stay (No. 1, UK), 1992; My 16th Apology (EP), 1993; I Can Drive, 1996; Co-writer, Young At Heart, The Bluebells, 1984 (No. 1, UK, 1993); Backing vocalist, It Ain't What You Do, It's The Way That You Do It, with Fun Boy Three, 1982; Contributor, Do They Know It's Christmas?, Band Aid (No. 1, UK), 1984; Let It Be, Ferry Aid (Zeebrugge ferry disaster relief) (No. 1, UK), 1987; Waterloo, with Bananarama, for TV special, A Song For Eurotrash, 1998. *Honours:* BRIT Award, Best Video, Stay, 1993; Ivor Novello Award, Outstanding Contemporary Song Collection, Hormonally Yours, 1993.

FAIRBAIRN Keith; b. 14 Jan. 1963, Horsham, Surrey, England. Musician (percussion). *Musical Education:* Guildhall School of Music. *Career:* Worked with: Shirley Bassey; Mike Oldfield; Lulu; Judy Tzuke; Madelaine Bell; Vic Damone; Dionne Warwick; Joe Longthorne; Madonna; Tom Jones; Numerous television shows for BBC; LWT; Granada. *Recordings:* Andrew Lloyd Webber; Jim Steinman; Nick Heyward; Shirley Bassey; Madelaine Bell; Joe Longthorne; Evita; Cats; Whistle Down the Wind; Numerous films, shows, library music. *Honours:* AGSM. *Membership:* Musicians' Union. *Address:* 11 Craydon Rd, Amptuill, Bedfordshire MK45 2CE, England.

FAIRLEY Colin; Prod.; Engineer; Musician (drums). *Career:* Former drummer; Engineer, Air Studios; Freelance record producer, engineer, 1981-. *Recordings:* As producer/engineer, albums include: with Nick Lowe: Cowboy Outfit; The Rose of England; Pinker Than Proud; for Elvis Costello: Punch The Clock; Goodbye Cruel World; Blood and Chocolate; for The Teardrop Explodes: Wilder; Everybody Wants To Shag The Teardrop Explodes; also T-Bird Rhythm, Fabulous Thunderbirds; Sisters, The Bluebells; Gentlemen Take Polaroids, Japan; Welcome To The Cruise, Judie Tzuke; Stop, Sam Brown; Titles, Mick Karn; Porcupine, Echo and The Bunnymen; Singles include: with Madness: It Must Be Love; Grey Day; Driving In My Car; also Pills and Soap, Elvis Costello; Young At Heart, The Bluebells; Quiet Life, Japan; Reward, Teardrop Explodes; Stay With Me 'Til Dawn, Judie Tzuke. *Current Management:* c/o Stephen Budd Management. *Address:* 109B Regents Park Rd, London NW1 8UR, England.

FAIRWEATHER-LOW Andy; b. 8 Aug. 1950, Ystrad Mynach, Hengoed, Wales. Singer; Musician (guitar). *Career:* Member, The Taffbeats; The Sect Maniacs; Founder member, Amen Corner, 1966–69; Performances include: Headline act, Pop Proms, Royal Albert Hall, 1969; Solo artiste; Session musician for artists including: Pink Floyd; Roger Waters; Sang with All-Star ARMS band (benefit for research into multiple sclerosis), 1987; Tour with Chris Rea, 1990; Tour with George Harrison, Eric Clapton, Japan, 1991; Member, Eric Clapton's backing band, 1990s; Film appearance, Scream and Scream Again, 1969. *Recordings:* Albums: with Amen Corner: Round Amen Corner, 1968; Explosive Company, 1969; Solo albums: Beginning From An End, 1971; Spider Jivin', 1974; La Booga Rooga, 1975; Be Bop 'N' Holla, 1976; Mega-Shebang, 1980; with Eric Clapton: Unplugged, 1992; From The Cradle, 1994; Pilgrim, 1996; Reptile, 2001; Singles include: Gin House Blues, 1967; World of Broken Hearts, 1967; Bend Me Shape Me, 1968; High In The Sky, 1968; (If Paradise Is) Half As Nice (No. 1, UK), 1969; Solo: Natural Sinner, 1970; Reggae Tune, 1974; Wide Eyed and Legless, 1975.

FAITH Adam, (Terence Nelhams); b. 23 June 1940, Acton, London, England. Singer; Actor; Prod. *Career:* Member, skiffle group The Worried Men group, 1957; Solo artiste, 1958–; Residency on Drumbeat, BBC TV, 1959; Film appearances include: Beat Girl, 1960; Never Let Go, 1960; Mix Me A Person, 1962; Stardust, 1974; Yesterday's Hero, 1979; McVicar, 1980; Television acting appearances: Budgie, 1971; Love Hurts, 1991; Alfie, 1992; Now You Know, 1996; Dosh, 1996; A Chorus Line, 1997; Theatre appearances: Billy Liar, 1967; Twelfth Night, 1967; Night Must Fall, 1967; City Sugar, 1976; Musical version, Budgie, 1988; Artist manager for Leo Sayer, 1972–; Owner, Faith Corporation, (financial advice company). *Recordings:* Singles include: What Do You Want (No. 1, UK), 1959; Poor Me (No. 1, UK), 1960; Someone Else's Baby, 1960; Made You, 1960; When Johnny Comes Marching Home, 1960; How About That, 1960; Lonely Pup, 1960; Who Am I, 1961; Don't You Know It, 1961; The Time Has Come, 1961; Lonesome, 1962; The First Time, 1963; We Are In Love, 1964; A Message To Martha, 1964; Albums: Adam, 1960; Adam Faith, 1962; Faith Alive, 1965; I Survive, 1974; 20 Golden Greats, 1981; Not Just a Memory, 1983; Midnight Postcards, 1991; Adam Faith Singles, 1999; Contributor, Scouse The Mouse (with Ringo Starr, Barbara Dickson), 1977; As producer: Daltrey, Roger Daltrey, 1973. *Current Management:* Alan Field Ltd. *Address:* 3 The Spinney, Bakers Hill, Hadley Common, Herts EN5 5QJ, England.

FAITHFULL Marianne; b. 29 Dec. 1946, Hampstead, London, England. Singer. 1 s. *Career:* Recording artist, 1964–; Tours, appearances include: British tour with Roy Orbison, 1965; US tour with Gene Pitney, 1965; Uxbridge Blues and Folk Festival, 1965; Montreux, Golden Rose Festival, 1966; Roger Water's The Wall, Berlin, 1990; Chieftains Music Festival, London, 1991; Acting roles include: I'll Never Forget Whatisname, 1967; Three Sisters, Chekkov, London, 1967; Hamlet, 1970; Kurt Weill's Seven Deadly Sins, St Ann's Cathedral, New York, 1990; Film appearance, Girl On A Motorcycle, 1968. *Recordings:* Singles include: As Tears Go By; Come and Stay With Me; This Little Bird; Summer Nights; Something Better/ Sister Morphine; The Ballad of Lucy Jordan; Dreaming My Dreams; Electra, 1999; Albums: Come My Way, 1965; Marianne Faithfull, 1965; Go Away From My World, 1966; Faithfull Forever, 1966; Marianne Faithfull's Greatest Hits, 1969; Faithless, with the Grease Band, 1978; Broken English, 1979; Dangerous Acquaintances, 1981; A Child's Adventure, 1983; Strange Weather, 1987; Blazing Away, 1990; A Secret Life, 1995; 20th Century Blues, 1997; The Seven Deadly Sins, 1998; Vagabond Ways, 1999; Stranger On Earth (compilation), 2001; Contributor, Lost In The Stars – The Music of Kurt Weill, 1984; The Bells of Dublin, The Chieftains, 1992. *Publications:* Faithfull (ghost written by David Dalton). *Honours include:* Grammy Nomination, Broken English, 1979. *Current Management:* Art Collins Management, PO Box 561, Pine Bush, NY 12566, USA.

FAKANAS Viorgos; b. 18 July 1961, Athens, Greece. Composer; Arranger; Musician (bass); Author. m. Nicoletta Pitsikali, 12 June 1992, 1 s. *Education:* Diploma, Economics (University of Athens). *Musical Education:* Classical guitar; Classical piano; Self-taught bass. *Career:* Only Greek correspondant as bass player, Europe, (European Community Youth Jazz Orchestra), 1981–84; Founder, ISKRA (major Greek jazz group), 1984–88; Numerous concerts, Greece and abroad, include: Locabettus Theatre; Herodio, Athens Concert Hall, performed own composition: Topazi, A Composition For Large Strings and Jazz Ensemble; Founder, tutor, Contemporary Music School of Athens; Numerous TV, radio appearances; Currently leader of own jazz group. *Recordings:* A New Day, 1986; Horizon, 1989; Parastasis, 1990; Amorosa, 1992; Stand-Art, 1995; Session musician, more than 200 recordings with major Greek artists. *Publications:* Educational books: For The Bass (Vol. I, II); Scales of Modern Music, Jazz Harmony, Modern Counterpoint. *Honours:* Hon. Mem., Greek Radio and TV's Jazz Orchestra. *Membership:* Mem., Hellenic Musician's Union. *Leisure interests:* Football; Theatre; Travel. *Current Management:* Nicoletta Pitsivalli. *Address:* 3 L Possidonas St, 18344 Moshato – Athens, Greece.

FALLON Peter Sean; b. 3 June 1968, Reigate, Surrey, England. Record Prod.; Songwriter. *Musical Education:* Piano from age 6. *Career:* Signed to Big One Records aged 18, 1986; UK Club Promo Tour, signed to Swanyard Records, 1990; Performed at Cesmé 91 Festival in Turkey; Top of The Pops; Pebble Mill; This Morning, ITV, 1993; BBC Radio 1 Session, 1994. *Recordings:* with Twin Beat: Let's Pick Up The Pieces, 1988; with Fallon: Get On The Move, 1990; with Technotronic: Get Up Remix, 1991; with Stevie Wonder: You Never Lose Remix, 1991; As writer, producer: with David Hasselhoff: If I Could Only Say Goodbye, 1993; Tighter and Tighter, 1993; with Dannii Minogue: Love and Affection; As writer: with Celine Dion: Don't Turn Away From Me; with Groove U: Step By Step. *Memberships:* PRS; BASCA; ASCAP. *Leisure interests:* Tennis; Rollerblading; Reading. *Current Management:* EMI Music Publishing London. *Address:* c/o Broadhill Recording Studios, Ockley Lane, Keymer, Hassocks, West Sussex BN6 8PA, England.

FÅLTSKOG Agnetha; b. 5 April 1950, Sweden. Singer; Actress. m. (1) Bjorn Ulvæus, 1971, divorced, (2) Tomas Sonnenfeld. *Career:* Solo recording artist, aged 17; Actress, Jesus Christ Superstar, Sweden; Singer, Abba, 1973–82; Appearances include: Winners, Eurovision Song Contest, 1974; Royal Performance, Stockholm, 1976; Royal Albert Hall, 1977; World-wide tours; Television: A Gift of Song – The Music For UNICEF Concert, NBC, 1979; This Is Your Life, Swedish TV, 1986; The Story of Abba, C4, 1991; Solo artiste, 1982–90; Films: Abba – The Movie, 1978; As actress:

Rakenstam, 1983. *Recordings:* Albums include: with Abba: Waterloo, 1974; Abba, 1976; Arrival, 1977; The Album, 1978; Voulez-Vous, 1979; Super Trouper, 1980; The Visitors, 1982; Various compilations, most recently: The Singles Collection, 2001; Solo: Eleven Women In One Building, 1975; Wrap Your Arms Around Me, 1983; Eyes of a Woman, 1985; I Stand Alone, 1988; My Love My Life, 1998; Hit singles include: with Abba: Ring Ring, 1973; Waterloo (No. 1, UK), 1974; Mamma Mia (No. 1, UK), 1975; Dancing Queen (No. 1, UK and USA), 1976; Fernando (No. 1, UK), 1976; Money Money Money, 1976; Knowing Me Knowing You (No. 1, UK), 1977; The Name of The Game (No. 1, UK), 1977; Take A Chance On Me (No. 1, UK), 1978; Summer Night City, 1978; Chiquitita, 1979; Does Your Mother Know?, 1979; Gimme Gimme Gimme (A Man After Midnight), 1979; The Winner Takes It All (No. 1, UK), 1980; Super Trouper (No. 1, UK), 1980; On and On and On, 1981; Lay All Your Love On Me, 1981; One of Us, 1981; The Day Before You Came, 1982; Solo: I Was So In Love (No. 1, Sweden); The Heat Is On; Can't Shake You Loose; I Wasn't The One (Who Said Goodbye). *Honours include:* Gold discs; Best selling group in pop history, Guinness Book of Records, 1979; World Music Award, Best Selling Swedish Artist of Year (with Abba), 1993.

FAME Georgie, (Clive Powell); b. 26 Sept. 1943, Leigh, Lancashire, England. Singer; Musician (keyboards). *Career:* Member, Billy Fury's backing group, The Blue Flames, 1961; Band replaced with the Tornados; London residencies, Georgie Fame and the Blue Flames, 1961–63; Tours, concerts television include: UK Tamla Motown Package Tour, 1965; National Jazz and Blues Festival, 1965, 1966; Pop From Britain concert, Royal Albert Hall, 1965; Grand Gala Du Disque, Amsterdam, 1966; Founder, Georgie Fame Band, 1966; Concerts include: International Popular Music Festival, Brazil, 1967; Royal Albert Hall, 1967, 1969; Television series with Alan Price, 1971; Concerts as leader of various groups and ensmebles; Television variety shows and commercials, 1971–; Keyboard player, Van Morrison tour, 1989; International Jazz Festival, Blackpool, 1992; Continues to play on jazz circuit. *Recordings:* Hit singles: Yeh Yeh (No. 1, UK), 1965; In The Meantime, 1965; Get Away (No. 1, UK), 1966; Sweet Things, 1966; Sunny, 1966; Sitting In The Park, 1967; Because I Love You (own composition), 1967; The Ballad of Bonnie and Clyde (No. 1, UK), 1968; Peaceful, 1969; Rosetta, with Alan Price, 1971; Albums: Rhythm and Blues At The Flamingo, 1963; Fame At Last, 1964; Sound Venture, 1966; Hall of Fame, 1967; Two Faces of Fame, 1967; The Third Face of Fame, 1968; Seventh Son, 1969; Fame and Price, Price and Fame Together, 1971; All Me Own Work, 1972; Georgie Fame, 1974; That's What Friends Are For, 1978; Georgie Fame Right Now, 1979; Closing The Gap, 1980; Hoagland, with Annie Ross, 1981; In Goodman's Land, 1983; My Favourite Songs, 1984; No Worries, 1988; Georgie Fame – The First 30 Years, 1989; Cool Cat Blues, 1991; Three Line Whip, 1995; Blues and Me, 1996; Walking Wounded, 1999; Name Droppin', 1999; Poet In New York, 2001; How Long Has This Been Going On, with Van Morrison, 1996; Contributor, Avalon Sunset, Van Morrison, 1989; Contributor, film soundtrack Glengarry Glen Ross, 1992. *Address:* The Leighton Pope Organisation, 8 Glenthorpe Mews, 115a Glenthorne Rd, Hammersmith, London W6 0LJ, England.

FANFANT Thierry; b. 27 March 1964, Paris, France. Musician (Bass Guitar). *Education:* Diploma of Audiovisual Technician. *Musical Education:* Self-taught Bass, 1976; Private lessons, 2 years, 1986–87; Course in musical centre, 1 year. *Career:* Olympia, with Michel Pugain, 1993; Casino de Paris, 1995; France Follies, La Rochelle, 1994, 1995, 1996; France Follies, Montréal; Pantemps de Bourges, 1990, 1991, 1995; Festival Jazz, Nice, 1994; Petit Journal, 1997. *Compositions:* Don d'organe; Ernest et firmin; Pausove Muen. *Recordings:* With: Enzo-Enzo; Michel Fugain; Maria Glen; Tuluo De Piscopo; Hajime Mizoguehi; Shukichi Kina; Beethova Obas; Mario Canonge; Taratata; Tery Boise. *Honour:* Success Prize of the Year, 1994. *Leisure interests:* Photography; Cinema. *Address:* 3 Allée, Claude Bernard, 93440 Dugny, France.

FANNING Bernard; b. 15 Aug. 1969. Vocalist; Musician (guitar, keyboards). *Education:* University of Queensland, Journalism student. *Career:* Joined Brisbane-based rock group Powderfinger, 1992; Steadily built reputation on many Australian tours/festival appearances; International breakthrough with Odyssey Number Five album; Constant world-wide touring throughout 2000–01 ending with New Suburban Fables 2001 Australian shows. *Recordings:* Albums: Parables For Wooden Ears, 1994; Double Allergic, 1996; Internationalist, 1998; Odyssey Number Five, 2000; Singles: Powderfinger Blue (EP), Transfusion (EP), 1993; Tail, Grave Concern, 1994; Save Your Skin, Mr Kneebone (EP), 1995; Pick You Up, D.A.F., Living Type, 1996; Take Me In, 1997; The Day You Come, Don't Wanna Be Left Out/Good-Day Ray, 1998; Already Gone, Passenger, 1999; My Happiness, 2000; Like A Dog, The Metre, 2001. *Honours:* ARIA Awards: Album of The Year; Song of The Year; Best Rock Album; Best Cover Artwork, 1999; six times platinum fourth album on Australian chart for 67 weeks by end of 2001; Only home-grown act ever to play more than 3 consecutive nights at Festival Hall, Australia. *Address:* c/o Republic Records, Australia. *Internet:* www.powderfinger.com.

FARGO Donna (Yvonne Vaughn); b. 10 Nov. 1945, Mount Airy, North Carolina, USA. Country Singer; Songwriter. m. Stan Silver. *Career:* Solo recording artist, 1969–; Numerous television and stage appearances include Country Music Festival, Wembley, 1978. *Compositions include:* Funny Face, 1972; The Happiest Girl In The Whole USA, 1972; Superman, 1973; You Were Always There, 1973; You Can't Be A Beacon (If Your Light Don't Shine), 1974; That Was Yesterday; Soldier Boy (all US Country No. 1 hits); Members Only (duet with Billy Joe Royal), 1988; Albums include: The Happiest Girl in the Whole USA, 1972; My Second Album, 1973; Shame on Me, 1977; Dark-Eyed Lady, 1978; Brotherly Love, 1981, Winners, 1986; Country Sweethearts, 1996. *Honours:* Billboard, Best New Female Country Artist, 1972; NARM Best Selling Country Artist, 1972–73; ACM Top Female Vocalist, 1972–73; Robert J Burton Award, Most performed country Song, 1972–73; C & W Record of Year on Jukeboxes, 1973; Grammy, Best Female Country Performer, for Funny Face, 1973; Gold discs world-wide. *Current Management:* c/o Stan Silver, Prima-Donna Entertainment Corpn, PO Box 150527, Nashville, TN 37215, USA.

FARLEY Terry; b. 13 June 1959, London, England. Prod.; Remixer; DJ. *Career:* Co-founder: Boy's Own fanzine (with Andrew Weatherall and Cymon Eccles), Boy's Own Records (later Junior Boy's Own, now Junior Recordings); Promoter/DJ at Boy's Own events; Remixed (with Pete Heller): Ultra Nate, Primal Scream, Janet Jackson, Happy Mondays; Member: Bocca Juniors, Fire Island, Roach Motel; Collaborations: Pete Heller, Andrew Weatherall, Rui Da Silva. *Recordings:* Singles: Raise (with Bocca Juniors), 1990; In Your Bones (with Fire Island), 1992; There But For The Grace of God (with Fire Island), 1994; Ultra Flava (with Pete Heller), 1995; The Rising Sun (with Pete Heller), 1999. *Current Management:* c/o Junior Recordings, The Saga Centre, 326 Kensal Rd, London, W10 5BZ, England.

FARNELL Thomas; b. 24 Aug. 1947, Birmingham, England. Musician (drums). m. 22 Sept. 1968, 1 s., 2 d. *Career:* Toured USA extensively with Savoy Brown; Worked with Fairport Convention; Worked with Raymond Frogatt (Top British Country singer). *Recordings:* Recorded with: Savoy Brown; Fairport Convention; Raymond Froggatt. *Honours:* Diploma Ed, Percussion. *Membership:* Musicians' Union. *Leisure interests:* Drum tuition; Session work. *Address:* 94 Leasow Dr., Edgbaston, Birmingham B15 2SW, England.

FARNHAM John Peter; b. 1 July 1949. Singer. m. April 1973, 2 s. *Career:* Singer; Entertainer; TV Host; Ld Singer, Little River Band, 1982–85; Launched Greenpeace album, Rainbow Warriors, Moscow, 1989. *Recordings include:* Uncovered, 1980; Whispering Jack, album, 1986; Age of Reason, 1988; Chain Reaction, 1990; Full House Album, 1991; Played Jesus in Jesus Christ Superstar, Jesus Christ Superstar – The Album, 1992; Romeo's Heart, album, 1996; 33 1/3, 2000; Highlights of the Main Event, live recording of concert with Olivia Newton-John and Anthony Warlow. *Honours include:* Whispering Jack, biggest selling album in Australia by Australian Artist; Australian of Year, 1988; Talk of the Town Tour largest grossing Australian tour, 1994; AO, 1996; Most Broadcast Australian Artist, Phonographic Performance Company of Australia, 1997. *Address:* c/o Talentworks Pty Ltd, Suite 1, 633 Victoria St, Abbotsford, Victoria 3067, Australia.

FARRELL Eileen; b. 13 Feb. 1920, Willimantic, Connecticut, USA. Vocalist. *Musical Education:* Studied opera. *Career:* Debuted in Cavalleria Rusticana, 1956; Although regularly performed in operas and as a concert singer, noted particularly for many forays into MOR/jazz circles. *Recordings:* I Gotta Right To Sing The Blues, 1960; Sings Harold Arlen, 1965; Sings Alec Wilder, 1985; Sings Rodgers and Hart, 1988; Sings Johnny Mercer, 1990; This Time It's Love, Sings Torch Songs, It's Over, 1991; Here, 1993; With Much Love, 1994; Love Is Letting Go, 1995; Carols For Christmas Eve, 1998. *Address:* c/o Reference Records, Charlotte, North Carolina, USA.

FARRELL Perry, (Perry Bernstein); b. 29 March 1959, New York, USA. Vocalist. *Career:* Member, Jane's Addiction, 1980's; Originator, Lollapalooza rock festival; Jane's Addiction split; Formed Porno for Pyros, 1993; Collaboration with Steven Perkins, and David Navarro and Flea from Red Hot Chili Peppers on soundtrack for Howard Stern film Private Parts, 1997; Set up Insect World record label; Contributed track Tonight (from West Side Story) for MOM2 charity album; Band split, 1998. *Recordings:* Singles with Jane's Addiction: Been Caught Stealing, 1990; Stop, 1990; Classic Girl, 1991; Then She Did, 1991; Albums: Jane's Addiction, 1987; Nothing's Shocking, 1988; Ritual do lo Habitual, 1990; Singles with Porno for Pyros: Pets, 1993; Sadness, 1994; Albums: Porno for Pyros, 1993; Good God's Urge, 1996; Solo albums: Rev, 1999; Song Yet To Be Sung, 2001.

FARRENDEN Shaun; b. 17 April 1962, Bishopstoke, England. Musician (didjeridu). *Musical Education:* Self-taught. *Career:* Concerts include: Glastonbury Festival; Glastonbury Assembly Rooms. *Recordings:* Albums: Earth Songs, 1992; Double Spiral, 1994; Yidaki, 1996; With Global: Shamanka; Gig na Gig; Guest musician, Welcome To The Cali, Ron

Kavana and the Bucks; Television music for Channel 4. *Publications:* Earth Vibrations, An Introduction To The Didjeridu. *Membership:* Musicians' Union. *Leisure interests:* Bridge; Computers; Forest walking; Making didgeridoos. *Address:* 125 Ashmore Rd, London W9 3DA, England.

FARRER Rob; b. 20 March 1974, Leicester. Percussionist. *Education:* Charles Keene College; Guildhall School of Music and Drama, 1992–96; GSMD Post Diploma Orchestral Training Course, 1996–97. *Career:* TFI Friday; Top of the Pops; Saturday Live with Lee Hurst; Glastonbury, 1998; Radio 1 Sessions. *Recordings:* Casanova; Short Album About Love; Fin De Siecle. *Leisure interests:* Football; Tennis. *Current Management:* Divine Management, Top Floor, 1 Crowcross St, London EC1M. *Address:* The Grange, 50 Main St, Hoby, Leicester LE14 3DT.

FARRINGTON Clive; b. 25 Sept. 1957, Altrincham, South Manchester, England. Vocalist; Musician (bass guitar, keyboards, programming, drums, percussion). *Education:* Civil Engineering City and Guilds. *Musical Education:* A Level Music Theory, Technology. *Career:* Vocalist, bass guitarist, When In Rome, 2 major US tours, 1985, 1986; Tours: Europe, Brazil, 1992; Remix for Diesel track Man Alive, Australia, 1994; Remix, Chill Factor track One Touch, Australia; Writer, producer, Underground Circus on tracks: Wrapped Around Your Finger; Crazy; Tree Without A Shadow; Remix for Bing Abrahams track One Touch; Currently working with John McGeoch on project Blue, as vocalist, programmer, producer. *Recordings:* Writer, producer, lead vocalist, album: When In Rome (hit in USA, Europe, South America); Single: The Promise (No. 1, USA Dance chart). *Memberships:* Musicians' Union; PRS (Associate mem.). *Leisure interests:* Driving; Moto cross; Clothes. *Current Management:* William Hunt. *Address:* 68 Neal St, Covent Garden, London WC2, England.

FARROW Andrew McGregor; b. 24 July 1964, Hamilton, Bermuda. Music Man.; A & R Consultant. *Education:* Sheffield Polytechnic. *Career:* Vocalist, Living Dead, 1980–82; Established AMF Music, 1987; Partner, Far North Music, 1988; Proprietor, (renamed) Northern Music Company. *Honours:* BA (Hons). *Leisure interest:* Cycling. *Address:* Northern Music Company, Cheapside Chambers, 43 Cheapside, Bradford BD1 4HP, England.

FASSIE Brenda; b. 1964, Cape Town, South Africa. Vocalist; Songwriter. *Musical Education:* Self-taught. *Career:* Singing for tourists by age 5; Went to Johannesburg and joined vocal trio Joy, aged 15; Moved on to group Family and recorded international hit Weekend Special; Group renamed Brenda and The Big Dudes; Welcomed Mandela at his home on release and recorded Black President in his honour; Has toured Africa and Europe. *Recordings:* Albums include: Brenda Fassie, 1990; Too Late For Mama; 1991; Amagents, 1993; Now Is The Time, Umuntu Uyashintsha, 1996; Paparazzi, 1997; Memeza, 1998; Nomakanjani, 1999; Aamadlozi, 2000; Mina Nawe, 2001. *Honours:* Memeza (Shout) album was first South African recording to go platinum on its first day of release, selling more than 500,000 units; Kora All Africa Music Award, Best Female Artist, 1999; South African Music Award, Best Selling Recording Artist, 2001.

FAST, (Brian Leiser); b. 29 March, USA. Musician (kayboards, bass, trumpet, harmonica, programming). *Career:* Founder Member, Fun Lovin' Criminals, 1993; Numerous TV appearances and live dates. *Recordings:* Singles: Scooby Snacks, 1996; The Grave and the Constant, 1996; King of New York, 1997; Sing the Fun Lovin' Criminal, 1997; I'm Not In Love, 1997; Love Unlimited, 1998; Big Night Out, 1998; Korean Bodega, 1999; Loco, 2001; Bump, 2001; Albums: Come Find Yourself, 1996; 100% Colombian, 1998; Mimosa – The Lounge Album, 1999; Loco, 2001.

FATONE Joey (Joseph Anthony, Jr); b. 28 Jan. 1977, Brooklyn, NY, USA. Vocalist. *Career:* Father sang in New York doo-wop group The Orions; Relocated to Orlando aged 12; Member of boy band *N Sync signed to BMG Ariola Munich, 1997; First headline US tour, 1998. *Recordings:* Albums: *N Sync, 1998; Home For Christmas, 1998; No Strings Attached, 2000; Celebrity, 2001; Singles include: I Want You Back, 1997; Tearin' Up My Heart, 1997; Let The Music Heal Your Soul (various artists charity single credited to Bravo All Stars), 1999; Music of My Heart (with Gloria Estefan), 1999; Bye, Bye, Bye, 2000; I'll Never Stop, 2000; It's Gonna Be Me, 2000; This I Promise You, 2000; Pop, 2001; Gone, 2001. *Honours:* *N Sync reported as music industry's biggest earners in 2000 (estimated $184m); Recognition at MTV and Billboard Awards; Presented with keys to City of Orlando, 2000. *Address:* c/o Wright Entertainment Group, PO Box 590009, Orlando, FL 32859–0009, USA. *Internet:* www.wegmusic.com.

FAWCETT David Everington; b. 27 March 1938, Watford, Hertfordshire, England. Commercial Man.; Musician (banjo). m. Gloria Ann (née Jeffrey), 1 s., 1 d. *Career:* Television: Winner, with Main Avenue Jazz band, Opportunity Knocks, 1978; Radio broadcasts, with TJ4, Sounds of Jazz, BBC Radio, 1982–85. *Recordings:* with TJS: Richard Leach's Northside Jazzband. *Membership:* Musicians' Union. *Leisure interests:* Watford Football Club; Semi-pro football supporter. *Address:* 31 Langley Rd, Watford, Herts WD1 3PR, England.

FEEHAN David; b. 9 Oct. 1948, Wellington, New Zealand. Singer; Songwriter; Prod.; Vocal Tutor. m. Shelley Catherine Melody, 3 s. *Education:* UE Accountancy Units. *Musical Education:* Classical to Grade 8, 3 years New Zealand Opera Company. *Career:* EMI Session vocalist, 1964–70; Lead singer, top New Zealand band Tapestry, 1970–78; Lead singer, Rodger Fox Big Band, 1976–88; Concerts at Ronnie Scotts, London; Montreux Jazz Festival, Switzerland; Hong Kong; Singapore; New York; Poland; Los Angeles; Sydney; Vancouver; Leader of David Feehan Band, 1988–; Appearances on all major New Zealand television shows and concerts; Played Jesus in Jesus Christ Superstar, 1983. *Recordings:* with Tapestry: It's Wrong, number 3 hit, 1973; Vocalist on Rodger Fox Big Band albums including: Montreux Live, 1980–; Montreux II Live, 1981; New York Tapes, 1980; Runner-up, Songwriters Contest, San Diego with: Still The One, 1989; 2 solo albums: Ballade, 1986; DF, 1993; Appearances on over 20 other albums. *Publications:* 2 childrens books due for publication; Writing a vocal technique book. *Honours:* Finalist, APRA and Best New Artist Awards (Composition); Best Jazz Album Award. *Membership:* Music tutor at Massey University, Wellington, New Zealand. *Leisure interests:* Photography; Writing; Squash; Rugby; Rugby League; Community work. *Current Management:* Tapestry Music Ltd. *Address:* PO Box 575 Wellington, New Zealand.

FEEHILY Mark Michael Patrick; b. 28 May 1980, Sligo, Ireland. Singer. *Career:* Member, Westlife; Numerous television appearances and hit singles. *Recordings:* Singles: Swear It Again (No. 1, UK), 1999; Flying Without Wings (No. 1, UK), 1999; Seasons in the Sun/I Have a Dream(No. 1, UK) 1999; Fool Again (No. 1, UK), 2000; Against All Odds (with Mariah Carey; No. 1, UK), 2000; My Love (No. 1, UK), 2000; What Makes A Man, 2000; Uptown Girl (in aid of Comic Relief charity; No. 1, UK), 2001; Queen of My Heart (No. 1, UK), 2001; World of Our Own (No. 1, UK), 2002; Albums: Westlife, 1999; Coast To Coast (No. 1, UK), 2000; World of Our Own (No. 1, UK), 2001. *Honours include:* Brit Award, Best Pop Act, 2001. *Internet:* www.westlife.co.uk.

FEHLING Annika; b. 25 Oct. 1962, Gothenburg, Sweden. Singer; Songwriter; Plays Guitar and Piano. *Education:* University of Lund, Sweden, 1981–82; Theatre Art School of Skara, 1982–83; State School of Theatre, Malmo, 1988. *Musical Education:* Singing and Piano lessons; Self-taught guitar, long-term course in Arranging and Composing, Stockholm, 1993. *Career:* Mére Ubu in King Ubu, musical; Solo-singer, Duke Ellingtons Sacred Concert; Participated in films, Women on the Roof, Petri Tears; Participating in the Sweden Song Contest, televised, 1998; Concerts with Visby Big Band in Norway, Poland, Rhodes. *Composition:* A Woman's Jazz. *Recordings:* Singles: Oktoberbarn (October Child), 1993; Naren Stjarna Faller (When a Star Falls), 1998; Solo Albums: Jazz Fehlings, 1996; Alskar Du? (Do You Love), 1997. *Publication:* The Real Swede, 1997. *Honours:* STIM, Swedens ASCAP Prize, 1992, 1996, 1999; State Art Prize, Art Cncl, 1993, 1994, 1999; SKAP Prize, 1997. *Memberships:* STIM; SKAP. *Current Management:* Musicano Records, c/o Arne Söderquist, Strandg 22 II, 62156 Visby, Sweden.

FEIGIN Leo; b. 1 Feb. 1938, Leningrad, USSR. m. Lora Feigin Denisenko, 1 s. *Education:* Institute of Physical Culture and Sports, Leningrad; Pedagogical Institute. *Career:* Master of Sports, USSR, 1959; Broadcaster, World Service, BBC, 1974–92; Producer, Presenter, Weekly New Music Programme, 1974–98; Proprietor, Leo Records, 1979-. *Recordings:* Over 400 LPs and CDs. *Publications:* Russian Jazz, 1985; New Music From Russia, Documentary. *Memberships:* PRS; MCPS. *Address:* Leo Records, The Cottage, 6 Anerley Hill, London SE19 2AA.

FEINSTEIN Michael Jay; b. 7 Sept. 1956, Columbus, OH, USA. Singer; Musician (piano); Actor; Musicologist. *Career:* Archivist, Ira Gershwin, 1977–83; Assistant to Harry Warren, 1979–81; Hotel residencies in US, 1984–89; Accompanist, artistes including Liza Minnelli; Estelle Reiner; Rose Marie; Jessie Matthews; Rosemary Clooney, 1991–; Numerous concerts include: George Gershwin 50th Anniversary celebration, Los Angeles, 1987; Irving Berlin 100th Anniversary celebration, Los Angeles, 1988; Royal Command Performance, London, 1988; Cole Porter 100th Birthday Concert, Carnegie Hall, New York, 1991; Michael Feinstein in Concert- Isn't It Romantic, Broadway/US tour, 1988–89; Stage: Ira Gershwin Centennial, Carnegie Hall, 1996; Television appearances include: Broadway Sings – The Music of Jule Styne, 1987; George Gershwin Remembered, 1987; Thirtysomething, 1987; Omnibus, 1989; Sing a Song of Hollywood, 1995. *Composition:* Film score and songs for Get Bruce, 1997. *Recordings:* Numerous albums include: Pure Gershwin, 1985; Live At The Algonquin, 1986; Michael Feinstein Sings Irving Berlin, 1987; Isn't It Romantic, 1987; Over There -Songs of War and Peace, 1989; The Mem Album, 1989; Burton Lane Song Book, Vol. I, 1990; Jule Styne Song Book, 1991; Pure Imagination, 1991; Jerry Herman Song Book, 1994; Hugh Martin Song Book, 1995; Such Sweet Sorrow, 1995; Nice Work If You Can Get It, 1996; Nobody But You, 1998; Big City Rhythms, 1999; Michael Feinstein With The Israel Philharmonic Orchestra, 2001. *Publications:* Editor, Ira Gershwin Song Book; Contributor, Washington Post and New York Times; Autobiography, Nice Work If You Can Get It, 1995. *Honours:* 3

Golden Laurel Awards; San Francisco Council For Entertainment; NYC Seal of Approval, 1987; Drama Desk Award, 1988; Outer Critics Circle Award, 1988; Doctorate of Fine Arts, California State University at Los Angeles, 1997; Scholarships in his honour established in New York colleges. *Membership:* ASCAP. *Address:* 648 N Robertson Blvd, Los Angeles, CA 90069, USA.

FELD Malcolm; b. 7 Sept. 1940, London, England. Theatrical Agent; Promoter. m. Georgina Maher, 17 Aug. 1989, 2 d. *Career:* Promoted artists in all major venues for 30 years; Joined Issy Bonn Organisation, 1955; Director, Slim Millar Entertainments Agency, late 1960s; Moved to MAM: Created own company: MFA Ltd, late 70's; Expanded as: MFA Casting; MFA Limousine Hire. *Leisure interest:* Snooker. *Address:* 7 The Old Quarry, Woolton, Liverpool L25 6HE, England.

FELDMAN Samuel Leon; b. 14 March 1949, Shanghai, China. Entertainment Co Exec. 1 s., 2 d. *Career:* President, S L Feldman and Associates, a Division of A & F Music Ltd, fully-integrated entertainment company, co-owned with partner Bruce Allen; Management clients include: Bryan Adams, Joni Mitchell, The Chieftains and Sissel; Partner, TMP, largest independent publisher in Canada. *Leisure interests:* Running; Snooker; Golf. *Address:* #200–1505 W Second Ave, Vancouver, British Columbia V6H 3Y4, Canada.

FELICIANO José; b. 10 Sept. 1945, Lares, Puerto Rico. Singer; Musician (guitar, bass, drums, piano, percussion). *Career:* Moved to New York as child; Performer, English and Latin music, becoming one of most popular artists in Spanish-speaking world and English pop music world; Chosen to sing The Star Spangled Banner, World series baseball, first one to ever stylise it, 1968; Recorded albums in Argentina, Mexico, Venezuela, Italy, USA, Austria; Television show throughout South America; Sang and composed theme music to TV series Chico and The Man; Recording artiste, classical guitar music, English pop, Spanish-language and jazz recordings. *Recordings include:* The Voice and Guitar of José Feliciano, 1964; A Bag Full of Soul, 1965; Feliciano!, 1967; Feliciano 10 To 23, 1969; Alive Alive-O, 1969; Souled, 1969; Fireworks, 1970; That The Spirit Needs, 1971; José Feliciano Sings, 1972; Compartments, 1973; And The Feeling's Good, 1974; Just Wanna Rock 'N' Roll, 1974; Sweet Soul Music, 1976; José Feliciano, 1980; Escenas De Amor, 1982; Romance In The Night, 1983; Los Exitos De José Feliciano, 1984; The Best of José Feliciano, 1985; Portrait, 1985; Tu Immenso Amor, 1987; I'm Never Gonna Change, 1989; Steppin' Out, 1990; Latin Street '92, 1992; A Tribute To The Beatles, 1993; Americano, 1996; On Second Thought, 1997; Senor Bolero, 1998; Noches De Bohemia, 2000; Singles: Light My Fire; Hi Heel Sneakers; The Sun Will Shine. *Honours:* Six Grammy Awards; Billboard Lifetime Achievement Award; ASCAP Golden Note Award. *Current Management:* John Regna, 297–101 Kinderkamack Rd, Oradell, NJ 07649, USA.

FELIX DA HOUSECAT (Felix Stallings), (Sharkimaxx, Thee Maddkatt Courtship, Aphrohead, Thee Maddkatt Chronicles); b. 1971, Detroit, Michigan, USA. Prod.; Remixer; DJ. *Career:* Based in Chicago; Started producing house tracks with DJ Pierre; Pierre's Phantasy Club classic Phantasy Girl released, 1986; Founder: Radikal Fear; Clashbackk; Thee Black Label; Recorded tracks for numerous labels including: Strictly Rhythm; Soma; Guerilla; FFRR; Collaborations: DJ Pierre; Miss Kittin; Mark Bell; Harrison Crump; K Alexi. *Recordings:* Albums: By Dawn's Early Light, 1994; Metropolis Present Day? – Thee Album, 1995; I Know Electrikboy, 1999; Kittins and Thee Glitz, 2001; Singles: Thee Dawn, In The Dark We Live (Thee Lite), 1993; Clashback (as Sharkimaxx), 1994; Dirty Motha (with Qwilo), 1996; My Life Muzik, 1999; Crybaby, Silver Screen/Shower Scene, 2001. *Honours:* Muzik Award, Best Album, Kittins and Thee Glitz, 2001. *Address:* c/o London Records, Waldron House, 57–63 Old Church St, London, SW3 5BS, England.

FELL Simon Howard; b. 13 Jan. 1959, Dewsbury, West Yorkshire, England. Musician (Double Bass); Composer. m. Jo Fell, 2 Oct. 1982. *Education:* Fitzwilliam College, University of Cambridge. *Musical Education:* Self-taught in composition; Double Bass with Peter Leah, 1974–78. *Compositions:* Compilation I, 1985; Compilation II, 1990; Four slices of Zappa, 1992; Music for 10(0), 1993; LeoSuite, 1996; Icons, 1997; Cubism, 1998; Composition N 30, 1998; Papers, 1998; Three Mondrians, 1999. *Recordings:* Compilation I, 1985; Compilation II, 1990; Music for 10(0), 1995; Composition No 30, 1998; Registered Firm, 1998; Pure Water Construction, 1998; Ghost Notes, 1998; Frankenstein, 1998. *Publications:* Report on the Composition of Improvised Music Nos 1–4, 1993, 1994, 1997, 1998. *Memberships:* PRS; MCPS; Musicians Union. *Current Management:* Bruce's Fingers. *Address:* c/o PO Box 57, Haverhill, Suffolk CB9 8RD, England.

FELLOUÉ Guillermo; b. 10 Feb. 1932, Havana, Cuba. Musician (bugle, trumpet). m. Rosana Felloué, 15 July 1969. *Musical Education:* Conservatory; Private teachers. *Career:* Professional from age 13; First trumpet and soloist with leading Cuban singers: Arsenio Rodriguez; Benny More; Soloist with Perez Prado, South America; Tours, Europe, Japan with

Havana Cuban Boys of Armando Oreficge; First trumpet and soloist, with the Rosana and Guil Afro-Cuban jazz show, 2 tours Japan; Arrived in Paris aged 19; Played at Moulin Rouge; Casino de Cannes; Palm Beach; First trumpet soloist, Big Band from Bourdeaux-Aquitane for radio; Casino, Sporting Club, Monte-Carlo, for 7 years; First trumpet, soloist, Bekumernis of Luc Le Masne; Television concerts, tours with singer Ellie Medeiros: Japan; New York; Canada; Co-director, Los Salseros. *Recordings:* with Arseño Rodriguez Conjunto Colonial, Cuba; 3 albums with Bekumernis de Luc Le Masne; Album and single with: Ellie Medeiros; Album: Los Salseros; Single with Pierre Vassiliu. *Leisure interest:* Chess. *Address:* 20 rue de Rungis, 75013 Paris, France.

FELTHAM Mark; b. 20 Oct. 1955, London, England. Musician (harmonica); Composer. m. Susan, 25 June 1994, 1 s. *Education:* South East London Technical School, Greenwich. *Musical Education:* Self-taught. *Career:* Founder member, Nine Below Zero, 1977–82; Harmonica player with Rory Gallagher for last 11 years; Varied studio work including: Georgie Fame, 1984; Godley and Creme (harmonica album), 1986; New Model Army; Deacon Blue, 1988; Texas, 1988; The The, 1989–91; Talk Talk, 1989–92; Joan Armatrading, 1992; Annie Lennox, 1995. *Recordings include:* Albums: with Nine Below Zero: Packed Fair and Square, 1979; Live At The Marquee, 1980; Don't Point Your Finger, 1981; with Godley and Creme: Goodbye Blue Sky, 1986; Other recordings include albums by: Rory Gallagher; Roger Daltrey; Roy Harper; Talk Talk; Paul Young; Lightning Seeds; Oasis; Annie Lennox; Joe Cocker; Michael Ball; Robbie Williams; Ocean Colour Scene; Television documentary scores, live guest appearances. *Membership:* Musicians' Union. *Leisure interests:* Reading; Sport. *Current Management:* Session Connection, London SW9, England.

FELTS Narvel; b. 11 Nov. 1938, Keiser, Arkansas, USA. Country/Rockabilly Singer; Musician (Guitar). m. Loretta Stanfield Felts, 30 April 1962, 1 s., deceased, 1 d. *Career:* High School talent contest aged 17, Bernie, Missouri; One of original rockabillies, career lasting over 43 years; One of the major country artists of the '70's. *Compositions:* Three Thousand Miles; Lonely Hours; Red Hair and Green Eyes; Four Seasons of Life; Foggy Misty Morning; When We Were Together; Away. *Recordings:* Reconsider Me; Lonely Teardrops; Drift Away; Somebody Hold Me (Until She Passes By); Funny How Time Slips Away; When Your Good Love Was Mine; Everlasting Love; My Prayer; All in the Name of Love; Honey Love. *Honours:* Single of the Year, Billboard and Cashbox, 1975; 10 ASCAP Awards, 1973, 1974, 1977, 1979; ASCAP Artist of the Year, 1977; Rockabilly Hall of Fame, 1997. *Memberships:* American Federation of Musicians; Reunion of Professional Entertainers. *Current Management:* Joe Taylor Artist Agency. *Address:* 2802 Columbine Pl., Nashville, TN 37204, USA.

FENDER Freddy, (Baldemar G Huerta); b. 4 June 1937, San Benito, Texas, USA. Singer; Musician (guitar). m. Evangelina Muniz, 10 Aug. 1957, 2 s., 1 d. *Education:* Sociology degree. *Career:* Solo Country music singer; Founder member, Texas Tornados, 1990; Film appearance: The Milagro Beanfield War, 1987. *Recordings:* Singles: Don't Be Cruel; Wasted Days Wasted Nights; Before The Next Teardrop Falls (No. 1, USA); Secret Love; Vaya Con Dios; You'll Lose A Good Thing; Albums include: Before The Next Teardrop Falls, 1975; Since I Met You Baby, 1975; Are You Ready For Freddy?, 1975; If You're Ever In Texas, 1976; Rock 'n' Country, 1976; Don't You Love Me, 1977; Swamp Gold, 1978; The Texas Balladeer, 1979; Tem-Mex, 1979; Together We Drifted Apart, 1980; El Mejor De Freddy Fender, 1986; Crazy Baby, 1987; 16 Greatest Hits, 1993; with Texas Tornados: Texas Tornados, 1990; Zone of Your Own, 1991; The Freddie Fender Collection, 1991; Canciones de Mi Barrio, 1993; Wasted Days and Wasted Nights, 1995; In His Prime, 1997; Crazy Cajun Recordings, 1999; Tell It Like It Is, 1999. *Honour:* Grammy, Outstanding Mexican-American award, 1977. *Memberships:* CMA; AFTRA; Broadcast Music Inc; AFofM. *Current Management:* Jim Halsey Co. *Address:* 3225 South Norwood, Tulsa, OK 74135, USA.

FENGER Sos; b. 2 Dec. 1961, Copenhagen, Denmark. Singer; Songwriter. 1 s. *Musical Education:* Piano, guitar and singing lessons. *Career:* Touring with Pop Band, News, early 1980's; Soulband with brother, Love Construction, 1986–89; Solo Career, 1989–; Tour with Doky Brothers and Adam Nussbaum; Recording with Toots Thielemanns and Randy Brecker; Contributor on several Scandinavian Albums. *Recordings:* Vinterdage, 1989; Sos Fenger on Holiday, 1992; Et Kys Herfra, 1994; Camouflage, 1996; Greatest Hits, 1998. *Honours:* Female Singer of the Year, 1986, 1990; Grammy Awards; Spies Fondet's Music Award, 1993. *Current Management:* Annetta Elmo, Holbergsgade 16, Kobenhavn K, Denmark. *Address:* kanslergade 7, 2100, Denmark.

FENTON Graham; b. 28 May 1949, West London, England. Singer. m. Caroline, 25 May 1991. *Career:* Various bands, 1970s; Matchbox, 1979–86; Television and radio includes over 12 appearances Top of The Pops; Hits, tours, Germany, Holland, Switzerland, Spain, Austria, Belgium, Yugoslavia; Television commercial, Japan; Tour with Gene Vincent's Blue Caps, UK and Europe, 1993; Solo tour, television and radio, Australia,

1994; Buddy Holly tribute, Clear Lake, Iowa, USA, 1994; Occasional work with original hit line-up of Matchbox as well as solo work. *Recordings:* Rockabilly Rebel, (No. 1 hit in many countries); Buzz Buzz A Diddle It; Midnite Dynamoes; When You Ask About Love (No. 4, UK charts); Over The Rainbow; Babes In The Wood; Recent compilations: Matchbox Live, 2000; Rockabilly Rebel, 2000; Films: Blue Suede Shoes; Born Too Late (biography). *Honours:* Gold, Silver, UK, Australia, Finland, Yugoslavia. *Membership:* Musicians' Union. *Leisure interests:* Record collection (jukeboxes); British motorcycles; American cars; Keeping fit. *Current Management:* Paul Barrett, Rock 'n' Roll Enterprises. *Address:* 16 Grove Pl., Penarth, South Glamorgan CF6 2LD, South Wales.

FENWICK Raymond John; b. 18 July 1946, Romford, Essex, England. Musician (guitar); Prod. *Musical Education:* Guitar lessons; Self-taught. *Career:* Member, The Sydicats, 1965; Marty Wilde, 1965; The Tee Set, 1966; After Tea, 1968; The Spencer Davis Group, 1968–72; Fancy, 1974; The Ian Gillan Band, 1977; Forcefield, 1984–92; Johnny Mars Band, 1990; Concerts include: US tours with The Spencer Davis Group, 1968–72; Fancy, 1974; Butterfly Ball, 1974; Ian Gillan Band, 1977; Japanese tour, 1977; Wizzard's Convention, 1995. *Recordings:* After Tea, 1968; Magpie, television theme music, 1970s; Bo Diddley sessions, London, 1972; with Fancy: 2 US Top 20 singles: Wild Thing, 1974; Touch Me, 1974; with The Ian Gillan Band: Albums: Live At The Budokan, 1978; Child In Time, 1976; Clear Air Turbulence, 1977; Scarubus, 1977; What I Did on My Vacation, 1986; Rockfield Mines, 1997; Live at the Rainbow, 1998; Solo album: Keep America Beautiful – Get A Haircut, 1997; Riding The Rock Machine (compilation), 1997. *Memberships:* PRS; MCPS; Repro. *Leisure interests:* Record collecting. *Current Management:* Fenwick Productions. *Address:* 4 Cassons Close, Weston Hills, Lincolnshire PE12 6DX, England.

FERGUSON David; b. 24 May 1953, London, England. Composer. 1 s. *Education:* BA Hons, School of Slavonic and East European Studies, 1971–74. *Career:* Keyboards, composer with Random Hold, 1978–82; Touring Europe and US with Peter Gabriel; XTC; Orchestral Manouevres In The Dark. *Compositions:* TV series include: Cracker (first and second series); The Gambling Man; A Fatal Inversion; TV films: Disaster At Valdez; Coded Hostile; Life After Life; Bad Girl; Hostile Waters; Touch and Go; The Woman in White; Black Box. *Recordings:* Albums: The View From Here; Burn The Buildings; Nine Ways To Win; The View From Now, 1998; Für Alle Fälle Fitz. *Memberships:* Asscn of Professional Composers; British Academy of Composers and Songwriters. *Current Management:* Music For Films. *Address:* 34 Batchelor St, London N1 0EG, England.

FERGUSON James Warner; b. 10 Dec. 1950, Missouri, USA. Musician (Bass); Vocalist. m. Antonia F Ferguson, 1 d. *Education:* MM, Jazz Performance, University of South Carolina, 1981. *Career:* Staff Bassist, The American Popular Singer, NPR; Staff Bassist, Main St Jazz Festival, PBS; Staff Singer, Country Music Association Awards. *Compositions:* Not Just Another Pretty Bass. *Recordings:* The Messiah – A Soulful Celebration; Together At Last; Great Hits of the Past; Shadowlands; Three Good Reasons; Cheek to Cheek; River of Love; First Christmas; Our Love Is Here To Stay; Not Just Another Pretty Bass. *Honours:* Music Department Aluminus of the Year, 1997. *Memberships:* Screen Actors Guild; American Federation of Television and Radio Artists; American Federation of Musicians. *Leisure interests:* Black Belt, World Tae Kwon Do; Jim Ferguson Double Bass Shop. *Current Management:* Jim Ferguson Music, 210 Mayfair Rd, Nashville, TN 37205, USA.

FERGUSON Maynard; b. 4 May 1928, Montréal, Québec, Canada. Musician (trumpet); Bandleader. *Career:* Trumpet player with Boyd Raeburn, Jimmy Dorsey, Charlie Barnet, 1940s; Trumpeter, Stan Kenton Orchestra, 1950–53; Freelance musician, 1953–56; Leader, own 13 piece orchestra, 1957–65; Leader, own sextet, 1965–; Worked with Slide Hampton; Don Sebesky; Bill Chase; Don Ellis; Bill Berry, 1950s-60s. *Recordings:* Numerous albums include: Sketches On Standards, with Stan Kenton, 1953–55; Dimensions, 1954; Maynard Ferguson Octet, 1955; Around The Horn With Maynard Ferguson, 1955; Maynard Ferguson Conducts The Birdland Dream Band, 1956; Boy With A Lot of Brass, 1957; A Message From Newport, 1958; Swingin' My Way Through College, 1958; A Message From Birdland, 1959; Plays Jazz For Dancing, 1959; Newport Suite, 1960; Let's Face The Music and Dance, 1960; Straightaway Jazz Themes, 1961; Si! Si!, M F, 1962; Message From Maynard, 1963; The New Sound Of..., 1964; Come Blow Your Horn, 1964; Color Him Wild, 1964; The Blues Roar, 1964; Sis By Sis, 1965; Ridin' High, 1966; Live At Expo '67 Montréal, 1967; M F Horn, 1970; Alive and Well In London, 1971; Magnitude, 1971; M F Horn 2, 1972; M F Horn 3, 1973; M F Horn 4 + 5, Live At Jimmy's, 1973; Chameleon, 1974; Primal Scream, 1975; New Vintage, 1977; Hot, 1977; Carnival, 1978; Uncle Joe Shannon, 1978; Conquistador, 1978; It's My Time, 1980; Hollywood, 1982; Storm, 1982; Live From San Francisco, 1983; High Voltage, 1988; Big Bop Nouveau, 1989; Footpath Cafe, 1993; Live from London, 1993; These Cats Can Swing, 1994; One More Trip to Birdland, 1996; Brass Attitude, 1998. *Honours include:* Grammy Nominations, 1978, 1984. *Address:* c/o Rogers and Cowan PR, 1888 Century Park E, Suite 500, Los Angeles, CA 90067–1709, USA.

FERGUSON Neil; b. 6 Dec. 1954, Castleford, Yorkshire, England. Prod.; Engineer; Musician (guitar, keyboards). m. Helen Mary Ferguson, 11 Dec. 1976, 1 s., 1 d. *Career:* Records produced, engineered for: Black Lace; Chumbawamba; Smokie; Credit To The Nation; Chris Norman; Nick Berry; Current member, Chumbawamba. *Recordings:* Agadoo; Teenage Sensation; Heartbeat (television theme music); Tubthumping, by Chumbawamba (No. 2, UK), 1997; Amnesia, by Chumbawamba, 1997; Tacky Love Song, by Credit To The Nation, 1998; Top of The World, by Chumbawamba, 1998; Uneasy Listening album, by Chumbawamba, 1999; backing vocals on This Is The Voice, by The Oyster Band, 1999. *Memberships:* Musicians' Union; PRS. *Address:* Frobisher House, 3 Lawns Close, Altofts, Normanton WF6 2NR, England.

FERGUSON Sheila Diana; b. 8 Oct. 1947, Philadephia, Pennsylvania, USA. Singer; Actress; Author; Presenter. m. Christopher L Robinson, 8 March 1980, two d. (twins). *Career:* Lead singer, Three Degrees, 1965–86; Solo artist; Star of Thames sitcom: Land of Hope and Gloria, 1990; Cameo roles: French Connection; Sandford and Son; Desmonds; Brookside; Presenter GMTV; BBC, LWT variety shows; Major world tours; West End debut, Always: The Musical, 1997; Grande Theatre, Blackpool, 1996; Ronnie Scott's, 1997; Performed for the armed forces in Bosnia, Germany, Falklands, Cyprus, N Ireland. *Recordings:* 28 Gold records include: Dirty Old Man; When Will I See You Again (No. 1, UK), 1974; Take Good of Yourself; T S O P; The Runner; Givin' Up Givin' In; Toast of Love; Golden Lady Movie; Also appears on: Best of the Three Degrees, 1996; Great R & B Female Groups, 1998. *Publications:* Soul food: Classic Cuisine of The American South, 1990. *Honours:* Tokyo Music Festival; 28 Gold Records; Best Book of The Year, nominated LA Times, 1991. *Memberships:* Equity Councilor; Musicians' Union; SAG; AFTRA; Founder Director, PAMRA. *Leisure interests:* Writing; Cooking; Tennis. *Current Management:* Brian Marshall (Variety); Jean Diamond, London Management (Acting). *Address:* PO Box 1400, Maidenhead Berkshire, SL6 8LX, England.

FERRER Ibrahim, (Ibrahim Ferrer Planas); b. 1927, Santiago, Cuba. Vocalist. *Career:* Sang with local bands from age 13 including: Los Jóvenes del Son; Conjunto Sorpresa; Conjunto Wilson; Pacho Alonso's Maravilla de Beltran; Hit record El Platanar de Bartolo with Orquesta Chepin-Chóven, 1955; Worked with Orquesta Ritmo Oriental and Beny Moré; Toured internationally with Los Bocucos, 1962; Retired, 1991; Made a comeback on the Buena Vista Social Club recordings; Appeared in Wim Wenders' documentary film Buena Vista Social Club; Collaborations: Ruben González; Omara Portuonda; Ry Cooder; Afro-Cuban All-Stars; Sings various Cuban song styles including: Guaracha; Son; Bolero. *Recordings:* recent Albums: Buena Vista Social Club, 1997; Buena Vista Social Club Presents Ibrahim Ferrer, 1999; appears on: Toda Cuba Le Gusta (with Afro Cuban All-Stars), 1997; Distinto Diferente (with Afro Cuban All-Stars), 1999; Chanchullo (with Ruben González), 2000; Latin Simone, Qué Pasa Contigo (with Gorillaz), 2001. *Honours:* Grammy, Best New Artist, 2000. *Address:* c/o World Circuit Ltd, First Floor, Shoreditch Stables, 138 Kingsland Rd, London, E2 8DY, England.

FERRERA Stephen; b. 26 Dec. 1959, Boston, Massachusetts, USA. Prod.; Songwriter; Musician; Record Exec. *Musical Education:* BM, New England Conservatory of Music; MM, Juilliard School of Music. *Career:* As producer, songwriter, arranger, musical director, musician, worked with: Bob Dylan; Billy Joel; Chaka Khan; Eurythmics; Suzanne Vega; Julian Cope; Shakespears Sister; Holly Cole; Shawn Colvin; Tom Jones; Mica Paris; Womack and Womack; Dave Stewart; Currently Head of A & R, The Echo Label. *Honours:* Platinum and Gold records. *Memberships:* Musicians' Union; NARAS; ASCAP. *Address:* The Echo Label, The Chrysalis Building, 13 Bramley Rd, London W10 6SP, England.

FERRIS Jim; b. 29 March 1955, Coventry, England. Musician (drums); Drum Tutor. m. Janice, 1990. *Musical Education:* Coventry School of Music. *Career:* Member, Coventry Corps of Drums, age 11–16; Appeared Albert Hall aged 15; Supported many major television artists in cabaret; Several BBC radio broadcasts, German television, West Country television; Worked in cabaret bands, theatre orchestra, rock bands. *Recordings:* 2 albums released by AJ's Big Band; Session recording work at studios in London and the Midlands. *Publications:* Mere Mortals Guide To Drumming, Levels 1–4, 1994–99. *Honours:* Described as 'a fantastic drummer', Stage and TV Today. *Membership:* Musicians' Union. *Leisure interests:* Cars; Writing tutor books, teaching. *Current Management:* Jim Ferris. *Address:* Brodick House, 31 Hereford Close, Exmouth, Devon EX8 5QT, England.

FERRONE Stephen; b. 25 April 1950, Brighton, West Sussex, England. Musician (drums). 1 s., 1 d. *Musical Education:* Nice Conservatory of Music, France. *Career:* Played with: Brian Auger; Average White Band; Eric Clapton; Duran Duran; Tom Petty and The Heartbreakers; Chaka Khan; Jeffery Osbourn; George Benson; Anita Baker; Chris Botti; David Bowie;

Sophie B Hawkins; Al Jarreau; Scritti Politti; Steve Winwood; Paul Young; Tribute To Buddy Rich. *Recordings:* with Average White Band: Cut The Cake; Soul Searching; Person To Person; Journey Man-Unplugged, Eric Clapton; I Feel For You, Chaka Khan; Secret Story, Pat Metheny; Wildflowers, Tom Petty; Stay With Me Tonight, Jeffery Osborne; I'm Your Baby Tonight, Whitney Houston. *Membership:* ASCAP. *Current Management:* Steve White (Cavaricci and White). *Address:* 120 E 56th St, Suite 1150, New York City, NY 10022, USA.

FERRY Bryan; b. 26 Sept. 1945, Washington, County Durham, England. Singer; Songwriter; Musician. 4 s. *Education:* Fine Art, Newcastle University. *Career:* Formed Roxy Music, 1971–83, reformed for concert tour 2001; Solo artiste, 1973–; Worked with: Brian Eno; Phil Manzanera; Andy Mackay; Steve Ferrone; David Williams; Robin Trower; Pino Palladino; Nile Rodgers; Carleen Anderson; Shara Nelson; Jhelisa; Numerous world-wide tours; Major concerts include: Crystal Palace, 1972; Live Aid, Wembley, 1985; Radio City, New York, 1988; Wembley, 1989; Support tours, Alice Cooper, David Bowie; Television appearances include: Subject of Without Walls documentary, 1992; Videos: New Town (live), 1990; Total Recall (documentary), 1990. *Recordings:* Singles include: Love Is The Drug, 1975; Dance Away, 1979; Angel Eyes, 1979; Over You, 1980; Jealous Guy (No. 1, UK), 1981; Slave To Love, 1985; The Right Stuff, 1987; I Put A Spell On You, 1993; Albums: Solo: These Foolish Things, 1973; Another Time Another Place, 1974; Let's Stick Together, 1976; In Your Mind, 1977; The Bride Stripped Bare, 1978; Boys and Girls (No. 1, UK), 1985; Bete Noire, 1987; The Ultimate Collection, 1988; Taxi, 1993; Mamounia, 1994; As Time Goes By, 1999; with Roxy Music: Roxy Music, 1972; For Your Pleasure, 1973; Stranded, 1973; Country Life, 1974; Siren, 1975; Viva Roxy Music, 1976; Manifesto, 1979; Flesh and Blood (No. 1, UK), 1980; Avalon, (No. 1, UK), 1982; The High Road (live mini-album), 1983; The Atlantic Years, 1983; Street Life, 1987; Recent compilations include: The Thrill of It All, 1995; More Than This – The Best of Roxy Music and Bryan Ferry, 1995; Slave To Love – Best of The Ballads, 2000; The Very Best of Roxy Music, 2001. *Honours include:* Grand Prix Du Disque, Best Album, Montreux Golden Rose Festival, 1973. *Current Management:* IE Management, 59a Chesson Rd, London W14 9QS, England_.

FEW Bobby (Robert); b. 21 Oct. 1935, Cleveland, Ohio, USA. Musician (piano); Composer. m. 7 July 1972, 1 s., 2 d. *Musical Education:* Cleveland Institute of Music; 2 private teachers. *Career:* Played vibraphone with Bob Cunningham (cousin); Played with Hyawatha Edmonson; Dick Shelton; Member, Bill Dixon's Free Jazz Workshop, 1958; Worked with Frank Wright; Booker Ervin; Formed own trio; Pianist, musical director, 3 major tours with, Brook Benton; Accompanist, Frank Foster; Roland Kirk; Formed group Center of The World; Collaboration with Alan Silva's Celestial Communication Orchestra; Member of Steve Lacy's Sextet, tours USA, 1980–; Several solo piano television appearances, Paris; Live concerts, television and radio, France, Japan, Italy, Spain, Morocco. *Recordings:* Solo albums: Few Coming Thru; More Or Less Few; Continental Jazz Express; Mysteries; With own trio: Bobby Few Trio; with Steve Lacy: The Owl; The Flame; Dreams; Prospectus; Songs; Ballets; Momentum; Brion Gysin Songs; Condor; Live At The Sweet Basil In New York; with Center of The World Group: Center of The World; Last Polka In Nancy; Solo and Duets; Uhuru Na Umoja (with Art Taylor); with Albert Ayler: Reevaluations; Music Is The Healing Force; Last album; with Archie Schepp: Coral Rock; Peachin' Can; The In-Between, Booker Erwin; Traffic, Noah Howard; Egyptian Oasis, Talib Kibwe; Indians, Sunny Murray; El Saxofon, Hans Dulfer; What Else Is New, Mike Ellis; Secrets From The Sun, Joe Lee Wilson; Diom Futa, Jo Maka; Flowers Around Cleveland, David Murray 1995; Also appears on: Vespers, 1993; Critics Picks Vol. 2, 1997. *Membership:* SACEM. *Leisure interests:* Cycling; Mountain walking. *Address:* 42 rue Deuingand, 92300 Levallois, France. *E-mail:* boobyfew@minitel.net.

FIALA Vít; b. 13 June 1943, Mladà, Boleslav. Musician (Double Bass); Composer; Arranger. m. Lidmila Hlusková 1 s., 1 d. *Education:* Charles University, Prague. *Career:* Hana Hegerová Ensemble; Eva Pilarová Ensemble; Jazzee-Czech; Jazz Festivals, Europe. *Compositions:* Mene Tekel Blues; More Note Samba; I Remember Jobim; I Remember Rogers; Super Blue Note Blues. *Recordings:* The Famous Jazz Tunes, Tea For Two; Eva Emingerová; Blue Soul; Irena Budwciscrová. *Membership:* Czech Jazz Society. *Leisure interest:* Country Cottage. *Address:* Judr Vít Fiala Spanelská 8, 120 00 Prague 2, Czech Republic.

FIDRI Ladislav; b. 30 May 1940, Osijek, Croatia. Musician (trumpet); Arranger; Conductor. m. Mia Fidri, 11 March 1961, 1 s. *Musical Education:* Pedagogue Teacher's College of Music. *Career:* Soloist, Radio-television Big Band, Zagreb, Croatia; Played most jazz festivals, Europe; Member, Gerry Mulligan's International Big Band, Europe; Also played with Clark Terry Big Band; Several times member, EBU Big Bands in Europe; Played, recorded with: Lucky Thompson; Stan Getz; Johnny Griffin; Sou Nistico; Leo Wright; Art Farmer; Albert Mangelsdorf; Kay Winding; Buddy DeFranco; Maynard Ferguson. *Publications:* Jazz Greetings From The East; Blue Sunset; Nuages. *Memberships:* HRT Big Band; Croatian

Musician Union. *Leisure interests:* Dogs (Golden Retriever); Mushrooms. *Current Management:* Raimund Frick. *Address:* Kreuzacker 5, 85049 Ingoldstadt, Germany.

FIELD Lauren Danielle; b. 15 July 1962, London, England. Singer. m. 7 June 1990, Charles Foskett, 1 s. *Education:* Drama School Diploma. *Musical Education:* Grade 5 Music Theory; Grade 6 Piano; Voice Theory; Singing. *Career:* Musical Theatre: Duke of York's; New End, Hampstead; Recording sessions for many top artists; Television appearances: Top of The Pops; Pebble Mill; Radio sessions for BBC Radio 2 and local stations; Leader, own 7-piece band; Currently playing London showcases; Opened own school and workshops for vocal coaching and tuition, 1997; Co-writer, co-producer, Joe Cocker, 1997. *Memberships:* PRS; Equity. *Leisure interest:* Songwriting. *Current Management:* Veracruz Music International. *Address:* 43 Capron Rd, Dunstable, Bedfordshire LU5 5AL, England.

FIGES Kevin John; b. 29 Aug. 1964, Portsmouth, England. Jazz, Classical Musician (saxophone); Composer. *Education:* Hons Degree, Masters Degree, Electrical and Electronic Engineering. *Musical Education:* Diploma, Classical Saxophone (Guildhall School Music). *Career:* Performed in own jazz quartet, all major venues, West Country, across UK; Appeared on Radio 2 Jazz Parade and on Radio 4; Writes own material for quartet; Performed with contemporary jazz orchestra Ultrasound. *Compositions:* Bacon Madras, 1997; HP Source, 1997. *Recordings:* Dishy; Critical Moment, with Ultrasound. *Honours:* South West touring awards, 1994; Lottery Funding for CD, 1997; Jazz Services Touring Award, 1997. *Membership:* Musicians' Union. *Leisure interests:* Walking; Films. *Address:* 64 Robertson Rd, Eastville, Bristol BS56 6JT, England.

FILAN Shane Steven; b. 5 July 1979, Sligo, Ireland. Singer. *Career:* Member, Westlife; Numerous television appearances and hit singles. *Recordings:* Singles: Swear It Again (No. 1, UK), 1999; Flying Without Wings (No. 1, UK), 1999; Seasons in the Sun/I Have a Dream(No. 1, UK) 1999; Fool Again (No. 1, UK), 2000; Against All Odds (with Mariah Carey; No. 1, UK), 2000; My Love (No. 1, UK), 2000; What Makes A Man, 2000; Uptown Girl (in aid of Comic Relief charity; No. 1, UK), 2001; Queen of My Heart (No. 1, UK), 2001; World of Our Own (No. 1, UK), 2002; Albums: Westlife, 1999; Coast To Coast (No. 1, UK), 2000; World of Our Own (No. 1, UK), 2001. *Honours include:* Brit Award, Best Pop Act, 2001. *Internet:* www.westlife.co.uk.

FILEK Michal; b. 22 April 1964, Pardubice, Czech Republic. Double Basist; Jazz/Blues Singer; Band Leader – Twin Q, Prague. m. Marie Kurova, 1985, 1 d. *Education:* Jaroslav Jezek's Conservatory, Prague; Summer courses in Frydland; General Double Bass Teachers, Frantisek Uhlir, Jaromir Honzák. *Career:* Jazz Entertainer, Bass Player, Singer, Twin Q, Prague, Metropolitan Jazz Band; Jazz-Blues Singer, Twin Q Group; Teacher, state school bass and improvisation; Accompaniment of many prominent soloists and groups. *Compositions:* Berny Blues; Everywhere is It Good, At Home is My Wife. *Recordings:* Twin Q and Elena, 1995; Metropolitan Jazz Band, 1996; Everybody's Looking for Wonders; Lenka Filipova, 1998. *Membership:* Jazz Club Sydney. *Leisure interests:* Lyrics writing; Making of musical instruments. *Current Management:* Volf Music Centre, Str Mechenická 2556/10, 141 00 Prague 4, Czech Republic. *Address:* Nevanova 1054, 16300 Prague 6, Czech Republic.

FILT Anni Martensen; b. 23 Nov. 1955, Thorsted, Denmark. Singer; Songwriter. m. Klaus Filt, 25 June 1977. *Career:* Lead singer, Anni and the Countrysun, 1989–92; Savannah Rose Band, 1992–; Television host, 1991–93. *Recordings:* Show Me The Way To Nashville, 1989; Tall Dark Stranger, 1991; Giving It All, 1993; Savannah Rose Band, 1995; Dream Catcher, 1997; Clovo Walker, 1999. *Membership:* Danish Artists Union. *Leisure interests:* Patchwork; Books; Music. *Address:* Smedevaenget 12, 8464 Galten, Denmark.

FINER Jem; b. Stoke on Trent. Musician. m. Marcia Farquhar, 12 March 1983, 2 d. *Education:* BA, Computer Science, Keele University. *Career:* Films: Straight to Hell; French Connection IV; Member, Pogues, 1981–96, played Banjo, Saxophone, Hurdy Gurdy; Experimental electronic music, film music, sound art, industrial country and western, 1994-. *Compositions:* Wall of Sound; Tilt; Longplayer; Fiesta; Fairytale of New York; Misty Morning Albert Bridge; Numerous other Pogues songs; Film and installation music. *Recordings:* Wall of Sound; Tilt; The Library; 8 Pogues albums including: Red Roses For Me, 1984; Rum, Sodomy and The Lash, 1985; If I Should Fall From Grace With God, 1988; Peace and Love, 1989; Hell's Ditch, 1990; Best of The Pogues, 1991; Rest of The Pogues, 1992; Waiting For Herb, 1993; Pogue Mahone, 1995; numerous singles including: A Pair of Brown Eyes, 1985; Sally Maclennane, 1985; Dirty Old Town, 1985; Poguetry In Motion (EP), 1986; Haunted, 1986; The Irish Rover, with the Dubliners, 1987; Fairytale of New York, with Kirsty MacColl (No. 2, UK), 1987; Fiesta, 1988; Tuesday Morning, 1993. *Publications:* 3 Essays on

Autodestruction, 1998–99; Plot, 1999. *Honour:* J F Sloane Golden Academy Award, Long Duration Music, 1990–99. *Membership:* PRS.

FINLAY Neil M; b. 25 Dec. 1955, Hamilton, New Zealand. Musician (electric and acoustic guitar, harmonica). Separated, 2 d. *Education:* Bursary photography. *Career:* Harmonica player with Brownie McGhee, tours throughout New Zealand; Special guest appearances at folk festivals throughout New Zealand; Appeared with Champion Jack Dupree, Billy Joe Shaver. *Recordings:* Solo album: Jumping The Tracks; Session work with The Topp Twins; Al Hunter; Patsy Rigger. *Membership:* Penonport Folk Club. *Leisure interest:* Photography. *Current Management:* Sun Pacific Records. *Address:* 271 Henderson Valley Rd, Auckland, New Zealand.

FINLAYSON Rhonda (Maria Valery Finlayson); b. 28 Aug. 1954, Kingston, Jamaica. Semi-professional Singer; Actress; Lyricist; Songwriter. *Education:* BA Hons, Creative Arts; Diploma in Careers Guidance and Recreational Arts for Community. *Career:* Backing singer with Little Douglas Band, 1984; Lead vocalist, Rhonda, 1985–89; Velvet Palm, 1989-. *Recordings:* Bugs On The Wire, compilation album; 1 track for Radio Lancashire; Black and Strange, Bop cassette tape with Rhonda band. *Membership:* Musicians' Union. *Leisure interests:* Watching live concerts; Dance events; Dancing; Writing lyrics; Poetry. *Address:* Flat 87, Lowton Court, Teddington Rd, Moston, Manchester M40 0DW, England.

FINN Neil; b. 27 May 1958, Te Awamutu, New Zealand. Singer; Musician (guitar); Songwriter. *Career:* Member, Split Enz, 1977–85; Founder member, Crowded House, 1985–96; Duo with brother Tim, 1995; International concerts include: A Concert For Life, Centennial Park, Sydney, 1992; WOMAD Festival, 1993; Television appearances include: Late Night With David Letterman, NBC; The Tonight Show, NBC; In Concert '91, ABC; Return To The Dome, Ch4; MTV Unplugged; Top of The Pops, BBC1. *Recordings:* Albums: with Split Enz: Frenzy, 1978; True Colours, 1979; Beginning of The Enz, 1980; Waita, 1981; Time and Tide, 1982; Conflicting Emotions, 1984; See Ya Round, 1985; History Never Repeats Itself – The Best of Split Enz, 1993; Oddz and Endz, 1993; Rear Enz, 1993; with Crowded House: Crowded House, 1986; Temple of Low Men, 1988; Woodface, 1991; Together Alone, 1993; Seductive and Emotional, 1994; Unplugged in the Byrdhouse, 1995; Recurring Dream (No. 1, UK), 1996; Originals, 1998; with Tim Finn: Finn, 1995; Solo Albums: Try Whistling This, 1998; Encore!, 1999; One Nil, 2001; Singles: with Split Enz include: I See Red, 1979; I Got You, 1980; History Never Repeats, 1981; Six Months In A Leaky Boat, 1982; with Crowded House include: Don't Dream It's Over (No. 2, US), 1987; Something So Strong, 1987; Better Be Home Soon, 1988; Chocolate Cake, 1991; Fall At Your Feet, 1991; Weather With You, 1992; Four Seasons In One Day, 1992; Distant Sun, 1993; Nails In My Feet, 1993; Instinct, 1996; Solo Singles: Sinner, 1998; She Will Have Her Way, 1998; Last One Standing, 1999; Can You Hear Us, 1999. *Honours:* Q Awards: Best Live Act (with Crowded House), 1992; Best Songwriter, 1993; OBE, for services to New Zealand, 1993. *Current Management:* Grant Thomas Management, 3 Mitchell Rd, Rose Bay, NSW 2029, Australia.

FINN Tim; b. 25 June 1952, Te Awamutu, New Zealand. Singer; Musician (piano, guitar, drums); Songwriter. *Education:* Auckland University. *Career:* Founder member, Split Enz, 1972–85; Solo artiste, 1983–86; Member, Crowded House, 1991; Solo artiste, 1992–; Member, ALT (with Andy White and Liam O'Maonlai), 1994; Duo with brother Neil, 1995; Appearances include: Tours, UK Australia, New Zealand, USA; Television include: Late Night With David Letterman, NBC; The Tonight Show, NBC; In Concert '91, ABC. *Recordings:* Solo albums: Escapade, 1983; Big Canoe, 1985; Tim Finn, 1989; Before and After, 1993; Say It Is So, 2000; Feeding The Gods, 2001; Albums: with Crowded House: Woodface, 1991; with ALT: Altitude, 1994; with Neil Finn: Finn, 1995; Solo singles: Not Even Close, 1989; Hit The Ground Running, 1993; Persuasion, 1993; How'm I Gonna Sleep, 1993; Runs in the Family, 1994; Magnificent Nose and Other Stories, 1996; Singles: with Split Enz include: I See Red, 1979; I Hope I Never, 1981; Dirty Creature, 1982; Six Months In A Leaky Boat, 1982; with Crowded House: Chocolate Cake, 1991; Weather With You, 1992; Fall At Your Feet, 1991. *Honour:* OBE, Services to New Zealand, 1993. *Current Management:* Grant Thomas Management, 3 Mitchell Rd, Rose Bay, NSW 2029, Australia.

FINNEY David Steven; b. 3 June 1963, Stoke Newington, London, England. Writer; Musician; Tutor. m. Anne Catherine, 18 Sept. 1988, 1 s., 1 d. *Musical Education:* Self-taught. *Career:* Five years, pop/indie band The Company She Keeps; Wide television and radio coverage of first single includes video starring Rick Mayall; Second single became jingle on Garry Davies Show, BBC Radio 1; Solo venture backed by Gerry Cott (formerly Boomtown Rats). *Recordings:* with The Company She Keeps: What A Girl Wants; The Men Responsible. *Publications:* Flesh. *Honours:* Single of The Week, Smash Hits/Record Mirror. *Memberships:* Musicians' Union; PRS. *Leisure interests:* Reading; Unix computer operating systems; Arsenal Football Club; Own children; Films. *Address:* 15 River Way, Loughton, Essex IG10 3LJ, England.

FIRESTAR; b. 18 Oct. 1958, Iserlohn, Germany. Musician (Harp; Flute). 1 s. *Education:* Degree in Business and Artist Management, Marketing and Public Relations; Grade 12, Royal Conservatory Diploma for Additional Theory, Composition, Copyright and Legal Graduate Courses in Canada. *Career:* Composer; Musician; 28 years of performance live on television in Canada; Various programmes, CBC composing soundtracks for film and television; Performing live on radio. *Compositions:* 2 albums published, recorded: Heavenly Angels; Crescent Moon. *Recordings:* Heavenly Angels, album; Crescent Moon, album. *Honours:* Many local performance honours, cash money won towards recordings on albums. *Memberships:* Pacific Music Industry Asscn; Society of Composers, Authors and Music Publishers of Canada. *Leisure interests:* Composing; Recording; Performing; Travelling; Camping; Swimming; Relaxing. *Current Management:* Eachdraidh Productions Inc. *Address:* 5241 S Santa Fe Dr., Littleton, CO 80120, USA. *E-mail:* music.daviefirestar.com@att.net.

FIRTH Steve; b. 1 Feb. 1968. Musician (bass). *Career:* Member, Embrace; Obtained major label deals in UK and USA, 1996; Released debut single independently; Support slot to Manic Street Preachers, 1997; Headline tours and TV appearances. *Recordings:* Singles: Fireworks, 1997; One Big Family, 1997; All You Good Good People, 1997; Come Back To What You Know, 1998; My Weakness Is None of Your Business, 1998; The Good Will Out, 1998; Hooligan, 1999; Save Me, 2000; Wonder, 2001; Albums: The Good Will Out, 1998; Drawn From Memory, 2000; If You've Never Been, 2001. *Address:* c/o PO Box 7, Brighouse, HD6 4UR. *Internet:* www.embrace.co.uk.

FISH (Derek William Dick); b. 25 April 1958, Edinburgh, Dalkeith, Scotland. Vocalist; Lyricist. *Career:* Member, Stone Dome; Lead singer, lyricist, UK progresssive rock group, Marillion, 1981–88; Regular tours, UK; Europe; US; Concerts include: Theakston Festival, 1982; Reading Festival, 1982, 1983; Nostell Priory Festival, 1982, 1984; Support to Rush, New York City Music Hall, 1983; Milton Keynes Bowl, 1984; Monsters of Rock Festival, Castle Donington, 1985; Colombian Volcano Appeal Concert, Royal Albert Hall, 1986; Solo artiste, 1988–. *Recordings:* Albums: with Marillion: Script For A Jester's Tear, 1983; Fugazi, 1984; Real To Reel, 1985; Misplaced Childhood (No. 1, UK), 1985; Brief Encounter, 1986; Clutching At Straws, 1987; B-Sides Themselves, 1988; Solo albums: Vigil In A Wilderness of Mirrors, 1990; Internal Exile, 1991; Songs From The Mirror, 1993; Yin, 1995; Yang, 1995; Sunsets on Empire, 1997; Raingods with Zippos, 1999; Fellini Days, 2001; Singles: with Marillion: Market Square Heroes, 1982; He Knows You Know, 1983; Garden Party, 1983; Punch and Judy, 1984; Kayleigh (No. 2, UK), 1985; Lavender, 1985; Heart of Lothian, 1985; Incommunicado, 1987; Sugar Mice, 1987; Warm Wet Circles, 1987; Solo singles: Shortcut To Somewhere (with Tony Banks), 1986; State of Mind, 1989; Big Wedge, 1990; A Gentleman's Excuse Me, 1990; Internal Exile, 1991; Credo, 1991; Just Good Friends (with Sam Brown), 1995; Incomplete, 1999.

FISHER Damian Robert; b. 21 Jan. 1971, Dartford, Kent, England. Musician (drums). *Musical Education:* Masterclass Studios, Bob Armstrong. *Career:* Hank Wangford tour; Only The Lonely (West End Show); The Sound of Fury (stage show); Bobby Davro Show; Concerts with: The Bert Kaempfert Orchestra; Stutz Bear Cats; Johnny Howard Band; Gerrard Kenny. *Membership:* Musicians' Union. *Leisure interests:* Drawing; Squash; Golf; Playing The Piano. *Address:* Flat 5, Duncombe Court, Wingrove Dr., Purfleet, Essex RM19 INF, England.

FISHER James Scott; b. Perth, Australia. Music Co Exec. *Career:* Television newscaster, presenter of Late Nite Line Up; First presentation as editor, BBC Radio 1 and 2; Artist Liaison, RCA; International General Manager, Motown and Jobette Music, 1976–81; Regional Director, ASCAP, 1981–94; General Secretary, International Managers Forum, 1994-. *Leisure interests:* The Arts; Food; Travel. *Address:* 14 Ashburn Gardens, London SW7 4DG, England.

FISHER Morgan; b. 1 Jan. 1950, London, England. Musician (keyboards). m. Aki Kuniyasu, 26 May 1987. *Education:* Hendon County Grammar School, 1968. *Career:* Keyboard player, rock/soul band Love Affair, 1968–70; Leader, progressive rock band Morgan, 1971–2; Keyboard player, rock band Mott The Hoople, 1973–6; Solo recording artist, producer, founder, experimental music label Pipe Records, 1977–81; Keyboard player, rock band Queen, 1982; Solo musician, composer, producer, 1984-. *Compositions include:* Electronic Music for Institute of Contemporary Art, London, 1971; Numerous film and television soundtracks. *Recordings include:* Single: Everlasting Love, Love Affair, 1968; Albums: The Hoople, Mott The Hoople, 1972; As producer: Miniatures (concept album) featuring 51 contemporary artists such as Robert Fripp, Michael Nyman, Penguin Cafe Orchestra, The Pretenders, The Damned, XTC, Gavin Bryars, Pete Seeger, George Melly, 1980; Slow Music, 1980; Echoes of Lennon, ambient versions of John Lennon songs, with guest Yoko Ono, 1990. *Publications:* Far East Tour Diary (account of a tour with a Japanese rock band), 1995. *Honours:* Two Gold discs and one Silver disc for record sales, Mott The Hoople. *Memberships:* Phonographic

Performance Limited; Performing Rights Society; National Academy of Recording Arts and Sciences; Performing Artists Media Rights Asscn. *Address:* 2–9–7 Narita-Higashi, Suginami-ku, Tokyo 167, Japan.

FISHER Reuben (Ruby); b. 20 Aug. 1923, New York, USA. Composer; Lyricist; Record Prod. m. Sheila Ratner, 11 June 1950, 2 s. *Education:* City University of New York; Manhattan School of Music. *Career:* Producer, Live at the Blazer!, for Big Band Jump, syndicated radio programme, 1997. *Compositions:* Shame, Shame, Shame (Baby Doll); Last Bicycle to Brussels; This One Day (General Hospital); Thai Silk (with Lionel Hampton); The Dolphin (with Luis Eça). *Recordings:* Bill Kenny, Star Sapphire; Ink Spots, Command Me; Dolores Gray, Tattered and Torn; Bobby Scott, Johnny River; Steve Clayton CD, At His Very Best; 3 Lew Anderson CDs: Feelin' Good, Yeah…, Fired Up, Live at the Blazer!; Swingin' for Hamp, Concord Jazz. *Honours:* US Bicentennial Composition Award, 1976; ASCAP Pop Music Award, 1998. *Memberships:* ASCAP; Songwriters Guild of America; National Academy of Recording Arts and Sciences. *Address:* Aloft Music Enterprises Inc, 1501 Broadway, Suite 1310, New York, NY 10036, USA.

FISHER Sharon Mary; b. 29 Sept. 1944, Orange, New Jersey, USA. Vocalist; Musician (Harp). m. Andrew Fisher IVth, 16 Aug. 1969. *Education:* BMusEd, Westminster Choir College, 1966; Academy of Vocal Arts, Philadelphia, Opera Scholarship, 1967; Temple University, Philadelphia. *Career:* Member, Westminster Choir, 1964–66; Vocal Music Teacher, Philadelphia Public School, 1967–69; Section Leader, Philadelphia Boys' Choir, 1969; Manhattan Light Opera, 1969–70; Soprano Soloist, St Peter's Episcopal Church, Manhattan, 1975–79; Organist, Church of the Saviour, Denville, New Jersey, 1981–84; Harpist/ Singer and Lecturer in USA, Scotland Ireland, 1986-. *Recordings:* Solo recordings: Voice and Harp Concert Memories, 1991; Ireland, Land of Harp and Song, 1998. *Honours:* Harp/Voice Trophy, O'Carolan Harp Festival Competition, Keadue, Ireland, 1988; Scots Awards, 1988, 1989; Marietta MacLeod Award, 1989. *Memberships:* American Harp Society; Clarsach Society; National Asscn of Teachers of Singing; Comhaltas Ceoltoiri Eireann. *Leisure interests:* Study of languages, medicine and music as healing. *Address:* 46 W Shore Rd, Denville, NJ 07834, USA.

FISHKIN Paul E; b. 29 April 1943, Philadelphia, Pennsylvania, USA. Record Co Exec. m. Janis Beckerman, 3 July 1982, 1 s., 1 d. *Education:* BSc Pharmacy (Phila College, Pharmacy and Science). *Career:* Co-owner, Bearsville Records, with Albert Grossman, 1971–79; Established careers of Todd Rundgren; Foghat; Paul Butterfield; Jesse Winchester; Founder, Modern Records with Danny Goldberg, 1979; Signed and established solo careers of Stevie Nicks and Natalie Cole. *Membership:* RIAA. *Leisure interests:* Vegetable gardening; Reading. *Address:* 8295 Sunset Blvd, Los Angeles, CA 90046, USA.

FISK Zebadi (Thomas William Fisk); b. 24 June 1968, Little Thorpe, County Durham, England. Performer (guitar, mandolin); Vocalist; Composer; Teacher. m. Traci Ann Firby, 4 March 1989. *Career:* Lead guitarist, The Rye until 1994; Lead guitarist, Voodoo Guru, 1994-. *Recordings:* with The Rye: Songs of Innocence and Experience, 1991; Twist, 1992; Burst, 1993; Flying High, 1994; Even As We Speak, 1994; with Voodoo Guru: Do. *Memberships:* Musicians' Union; Registry of Music Teachers. *Current Management:* Tony Davies. *Address:* PO Box 181, Darlington DL3 6YX, England.

FITZGERALD Cathleen Bernadette Maureen (Cathy); b. 1 April 1964, Kitchener, Ontario, Canada. Entertainer; Singer; Artist. *Education:* Fourth year, BA in Psychology. *Career:* Performing, 1986–; Involved, several variety/charity events; Prime time country since 1990; Won 3 consecutine championships, Canadian Open Country Singing Competition, Simcoe, Ontario; Several firsts at Ontario Open Singing Competition: Toronto; Ottowa; Many local radio and television programmes; Released 2 singles, Canada and Europe, 1992–; Currently working with producer Gary Buck out of Nashville, on first 10 song album to be released, USA, 1995; Single to be released in: USA; Canada; Europe. *Honours:* Many trophies Canadian singing competitions, nine first place victories since 1989. *Membership:* Canadian Country Music Asscn, 1991-. *Leisure interests:* Reading; Songwriting; Singing. *Current Management:* Howard Scales, Target Entertainment Group. *Address:* 100 Denlow St, Kitchener, ON N2B 3T7, Canada.

FITZGERALD Dandan; b. 14 Dec. 1955, Cork, Ireland. Recording Engineer; Prod.; Live Engineer. *Education:* Electronic Technical College. *Musical Education:* Self-taught on drums, guitar and keyboards. *Recordings:* No Frontiers, by Mary Black; A Different Shore, by Nightnoise; Horse with a Heart, by Altan; Celts Rise Again, 1990; Good People All, 1993; Best of Altan, 1997; Winter's Tale, 1998; Bastard Complex, 1999. *Membership:* AES. *Current Management:* Dennis Muirhead, Chelsea, London. *Address:* 2 Ivy Cres., Riverway, S Douglas Rd, Cork, Ireland.

FITZGIBBON Martin William; b. 11 May 1950, West Drayton, Middlesex, England. Musician (drums); Singer. m. Frances Trussell, 20 June 1981. *Musical Education:* National Youth Jazz Association, private tuition. *Career:* Appearances: Original production, The Rocky Horror Show, London, 1973; BBC radio and television; Major concerts, tours, throughout UK. *Recordings:* The Rocky Horror Show, original London cast; Moondog Man; The Dockery Boys; Zydcajun Cowboy; Do You Feel Like Dancing. *Membership:* Musicians' Union. *Leisure interests:* Sleeping; Procrastination. *Current Management:* Mike Batt Management. *Address:* c/o Nibley House, Blakeney, Goucestershire GL15 4AR, England.

FITZSIMMONS Keven Robert Mario; b. Glasgow, Scotland. Musician (keyboards, guitar) Conductor; Composer; Screenwriter; Actor; Dir. *Musical Education:* Royal Scottish Academy of Music and Drama, 1972–78; Graduated, London Royal Academy of Music, 1979. *Career:* Theatre includes: Andrew Lloyd Webber's Jesus Christ Superstar, Evita, Cats, Song and Dance; Anthony Phillips' Alice (founder member/ex of Genesis); Television includes: LWT, The South Bank Show; Own groups: The Little Concert; The 13th Guest; The Trio of Doom; Film appearances include: Indiana Jones and the Temple of Doom; Deva, 1994; Wasted Youth (also composer), 1994; The Stated Dose (co-writer, composer, actor, director), 1994; Latter three premiered, Edinburgh Film Festival, 1995; Film scores include: Hoppla (Special Commendation, Channel 4 Young Film Maker of The Year Award), 1994; Wasted Youth; The Stated Dose; Co-writer, The Enlightening One – The Life of Ho Chi Minh (forthcoming). *Recordings:* Marti Webb: Gershwin/Performance albums, 1994; Jesus Christ Superstar, 20th Anbniversary Album; K Fz – Film Music (1 and 2). *Current Management:* TDS Media/Tutti Sruti Music. *Address:* 5 E London St, Edinburgh EH7 4BN, Scotland.

FIX Michael; b. 23 Sept. 1959, Wollongong, NSW, Australia. Musician (guitar); Composer; Performer. m. Susan Jarvis, 4 s. *Education:* Diploma of Teaching. *Career:* Leading Acoustic Guitarist; Sydney Band Hat Trick, 1984–90; Working with award-winning singer/songwriter Graeme Connors, touring Australia as Lead Guitarist with Connor's Prodigal Sons band, 1991–95. *Recordings:* Tantalise, 1992; Fingerpaintings, 1993; The Heart Has Reasons, 1996; Single: Falling, 1996; Video: No Secrets!, 1997; Single: Breakup Breakdown, 1997; Promise, 1998; Walkin' the Walk, 1999; Gershwin Country, 1999. *Honours:* Winner Instrumental of the Year Category, 1999, 2000, CMAA Awards; Instrumental of the Year Finalist, 1994–2000. *Memberships:* APRA; AMCOS. *Leisure interests:* Golf; Reading. *Address:* Via PO Box 1194, Sunnybank Hills, Qld 4109, Australia.

FIXX-IT (Guam Elmzoom); b. 1 July 1970, Paramaribo, Suriname. Rapper; Dancer; Dressman; Composer. 1 s. *Education:* Private dance training and show education. *Musical Education:* Self-taught. *Career:* Founder, Twenty 4 Seven, 1988; 3 European major hits; Solo career, 1990–; Male Rapper on Cappella and Anti-Capella songs, 1994–95; Member, Anti-Cappella. *Recordings:* with Twenty 4 Seven: I Can't Stand It, 1990; with Cappella: Move On Baby (co-writer); U and Me (co-writer); Anti-Cappella: Move Your Body. *Honours:* 3 Golden singles. *Membership:* FNV Kunstenbond. *Leisure interests:* Music; Child. *Current Management:* Hans Van Pol Management. *Address:* PO Box 9010, 1006 AA Amsterdam, Netherlands.

FLACK Roberta; b. 10 Feb. 1937, Black Mountain, North Carolina, USA. Singer. m. Stephen Novosel, 1966, divorced 1972. *Education:* BA, Music Education. *Career:* Teacher, music and English literature, 1959–67; Recording artist, 1968–; Appearances include: Star, ABC TV Special, The First Time Ever, 1973. *Compositions:* (with Jesse Jackson, Joel Dorn) Go Up Moses; Television theme song Valerie. *Recordings:* Singles include: The First Time Ever I Saw Your Face, used in film Play Misty For Me, 1972; Where Is The Love, 1973; Killing Me Softly With His Song, 1973; The Closer I Get To You, 1978; Back Together Again, with Donny Hathaway, 1980; Making Love, 1982; Tonight I Celebrate My Love, with Peabo Bryson, 1983; Set The Night To Music, with Maxi Priest, 1991; Albums include: First Take, 1970; Chapter Two, 1970; Quiet Fire, 1972; Killing Me Softly, 1973; Feel Like Makin' Love, 1974; Blue Lights In The Basement, 1978; Roberta Flack, 1978; Roberta Flack Featuring Donny Hathaway, 1980; Live and More, 1981; The Best of Roberta Flack, 1981; I'm The One, 1982; Born To Love, 1983; Hits and History, 1984; Roberta Flack's Greatest Hits, 1984; Roberta Flack, 1985; Oasis, 1989; Roberta, 1995; Christmas Album, 1997; Collaborated with Quincy Jones on When You're Smiling, for film $ (sometimes called The Heist), 1971; Also contributed to albums including: Coming Around Again, Carly Simon, 1986; Les Is More, Les McCann, 1990; Peculiar Situation, Earl Klugh, 1999; Unconditional Love, Peabo Bryson, 1999. *Honours:* Gold record, First Time Ever I Saw Your Face, 1972; Grammy Awards: Best Record, 1972, 1973; Best Pop Vocal Duo, 1972; Best Female Pop Vocal, 1973; Roberta Flack Human Kindness Day, Washington DC, 1972. *Current Management:* Magic Lady, 234 Fifth Ave, Suite 504, New York, NY 10001, USA.

FLAHANT Richard; b. 12 April 1968, Ipswich, Suffolk, England. Musician (keyboards); Vocalist. *Musical Education:* Jazz studies, Chichester College of Technology, 1989–90. *Career:* The Addicts, 1985–; Venues include: 100 Club and The Marquee, 1989–90; Function bands include: Caribbean Cruise; Appearances, Big Breakfast Show, 1986–94; Recording with co-writer Matt Gray on various projects, 1993–; Signed to Albinus Records, 1994. *Recordings:* Singles: After The Fall, 1994; Meaning of Our Life, 1995. *Memberships:* Musicians' Union; PRS. *Leisure interests:* Cycling; Travel; Relaxing. *Address:* 62 Dover Rd, Walmer, Deal, Kent CT14 7JN, England.

FLAHERTY Nicholas Simon; b. 18 Feb. 1967, Brewood, Staffordshire, England. Vocalist; Songwriter. *Career:* Singer, Voodoo Sioux, 1991–; Support tours with Little Angels; Terrorvision; Rockhead; Headline concert, Milton Keynes Day of Rock, 1994; Radio appearances: Radio One session, 1993; Won Radio One Rock War, 1993; Television appearances: Noisy Mothers (interview and video), ITV, 1994; European, UK, Japanese tours, June 1995-. *Recordings:* Debut album: Skrape, Voodoo Sioux, 1995. *Memberships:* Musicians' Union; PRS; MCPS. *Leisure interests:* Songwriting; Films; Travel; Poetry; Photography. *Current Management:* c/o Bill Sneyd, White Buffalo, 2 Chillington Close, Cheslyn Hay. *Address:* 1 Victoria Court, Victoria Rd, Shifnal, Shropshire TF11 8AF, England.

FLANAGAN Kevin Edward; b. 25 Feb. 1954, Lowell, Massachusetts, USA. Musician (tenor saxophone, alto saxophone, flute, clarinet); Composer. *Musical Education:* Goldsmiths, London, England, Music degree; Anglia Polytechnic University, Cambridge, England, MA in Composition. *Career:* Worked as jazz musician around New England, USA before moving to UK with British Wife, mid 1980s; Played in London Jazz scene and did session work, late 1980s and early 1990s; Currently teaches saxophone and lectures in Jazz at Anglia Polytechnic University, Cambridge, UK; Recorded two albums with vocalist and pianist Chris Ingham, double bassist Andy Brown and drummer Russ Morgan under the name Flanagan-Ingham quartet; Band play gigs and tour regularly; An album of jazz settings of Beat poets currently under production; Recently began composing pieces that explore the cross-fertilization between contemporary composition and jazz. *Recordings:* with Flanagan/Ingham Quartet: Zanzibar, 1995; Textile Lunch, 1999; features on: Walking On Sunshine, Katrina and The Waves, 1983; The Pros and Cons of Hitch Hiking, Roger Waters, 1984; Live At Heartbreak Hotel, The Pretty Things, 1984; Eureka, The Bible, 1988; Groove Merchant, Tommy Chase, 1991. *E-mail:* kflanagan@btinternet.com. *Internet:* www.flanaganingham.f9.co.uk.

FLANAGAN Larry; b. 5 Dec. 1953, Detroit, Michigan, USA. Musician (viola, violin). *Career:* Violist with several orchestras in: Michigan; South Carolina; Ontario, Canada; Violinist/violist for various artists including Natalie Cole; Gladys Knight and the Pips; Melissa Manchester; Barry White; Geri Allen; Isaac Hayes; Sylvia Moy; Concerts include: Montreux Jazz Festival; Detroit Jazz Festival; Film appearance, as fiddler, Disney's Perfect Harmony, 1991; Lecturer, music consultant for schools in Decatur, Georgia.

FLANAGAN Mark 'Sonny'; b. 27 Oct. 1957, Liverpool, England. Musician. *Career:* Resident musician on BSkyB satellite television; 26 shows, Happening; Don't Forget Your Toothbrush, C4; Occasionally on Later With Jools Holland, BBC2; Recorded songs for film: Roadrunner, with George Harrison; Twice played live on Wogan; Numerous other television, radio, tours. *Honours:* (as band mem.) Don't Forget Your Toothbrush, Golden Rose Montreux, 1995. *Memberships:* Musicians' Union; PAMRA; PRS. *Leisure interests:* Photography; Painting; Yoga. *Current Management:* Paul Loasby, One Fifteen, Greenwich, London. *Address:* Helicon Mountain, Halstow Rd, Greenwich, London SE3 7LP, England.

FLANZER Richard; b. 30 Feb. 1951, New York, USA. Personal Man.; Television Prod.; Concert Promoter. m. Janice Rothman, 9 Feb. 1990, 2 s., 1 d. *Education:* Boston University. *Career:* Clients have included: Roger Daltrey; Manhattan Transfer; Jackson Browne; Dr John; Producer, largest two-day gross and fastest sell-out in history at Carnegie Hall, Roger Daltrey and Friends, 1994; Producer, largest festival in Florida history (115,000 audience), Florida Sunfest, 1977; Producer, A Day In The Country (first festival ever at Rose Bowl), Pasadena, California; Consultant to Jimi Hendrix Estate; Producer, National Music Critics Awards. *Memberships:* ASCAP; Chairman, National Critics Awards, 1995. *Leisure interests:* Auto racing; Travel; Tennis. *Address:* 152 W 57th St, 40th Floor, New York, NY 10019, USA.

FLASKETT Peter; b. 9 July 1950, Woking, Surrey, England. Guitar Teacher; Musician (guitar, bass guitar). m. Patsy Poley, 24 June 1983. *Musical Education:* London College of Furniture and Music, 1968–70. *Career:* Worked with: Long John Baldry; Screaming Lord Sutch; Tex Withers; Savoy Brown; Jim McCarty (of the Yardbirds); Recorded and toured extensively with: Emile Ford and The Checkmates; The Ramrods; The Flying Tigers; 30 years teaching guitar; 20 years repairing guitars. *Recordings:* Numerous recordings with Emile Ford; Extensive session work on guitar and bass guitar. *Memberships:* Institute of Musical Instrument Technology; Musicians' Union. *Current Management:* Kernow Entertainments, Falmouth, Cornwall. *Address:* 23 Bridge, St Columb Major, Cornwall.

FLAVELL Roger Barry; b. 10 Feb. 1946, Ruislip, England. Musician (bass guitar); Vocalist. m. Annie Conlon, 31 July 1971, 2 d. *Musical Education:* Self-taught. *Career:* Magic Roundabout, 1966–68; Sessions, 1969; Geno Washington's Ram Jam Band, 1970; Tommy Hunt Band, 1971–72; Christie, 1973–74; Tommy Hunt Band, 1975; Lonnie Donegan Band, Johnny Wakelin and The Kinshasha Band, 1976; Sessions, 1977–78; Band leader, top cabaret venue, 1978–88; The Byron Band, 1982; Sessions, 1989–95. *Compositions include:* Music for television: The Animates, co-written with Vic Elmes; 2 songs for From Out of The East album, 1999. *Recordings:* Albums: Judd, Kris Ife; Live At Wigan Casino, Tommy Hunt; A Sign of The Times, Tommy Hunt; On The Rocks, Byron Band; Only One, Joe Longthorne; Hold Fast, Roger Flavell; Christie: singles and album. *Memberships:* PRS; BACS. *Leisure interests:* Sport parachuting. *Address:* Marlow, Buckinghamshire, England.

FLAVOR FLAV (William Drayton); b. 16 March 1959, Roosevelt, Long Island, USA. Rapper. 3 c. *Career:* Founder member, US rap group Public Enemy, 1984–; Concerts include: Support to the Beastie Boys, US tour, 1987; Support to LL Cool J, European tour, 1987; British tour, 1990; Tour of a Black Planet, 1990; Apocalypse '91 US tour, with Anthrax, 1991; The World's Best Rap Show Ever, 1992; Greenpeace Stop Sellafield concert, with U2, Manchester, 1992; Reading Festival, 1992; Support to U2, Zooropa tour, 1992; MC, The Entourage (hip-hop venue), Long Island, New York, 1986; Solo recording artist, 1993–. *Recordings:* Yo! Bum Rush The Show, 1987; It Takes A Nation of Millions To Hold Us Back, 1988; Fear of a Black Planet, 1990; Apocalypse '91... The Enemy Strikes Back, 1991; Greatest Misses, 1992; Muse Sick 'n' Hour Mess Age, 1994; He Got Game, OST, 1998; There's A Poison Goin' On, 1999; Solo album: Flavor Flav, 1993; Singles include: Rebel Without A Pause, 1987; Bring The Noise, 1988; Don't Believe The Hype, 1988; Night of The Living Baseheads, 1988; Black Steel In The Hour of Chaos, 1988; Fight The Power, theme for film Do The Right Thing, 1989; Welcome To The Terrordome, 1990; 911 Is A Joke, 1990; Brothers Gonna Work It Out, 1990; Can't Do Nuttin' For Ya Man, 1991; Can't Truss It, 1992; Shut 'Em Down, 1992; Nighttrain, 1992; Give It Up, 1994; Do You Wanna Go Our Way??, 2000; Also guest on: Amerikka's Most Wanted, Ice Cube, 1990; Bring The Noise, Anthrax, 1991; Burning, Material, 1999. *Honours include:* Platinum discs; Rolling Stone Readers Poll, Best Rap Group, 1991; Best Rap Album, Soul Train Music Awards, 1992. *Current Management:* Malik Entertainment Management, 3 Third Pl., Roosevelt, NY 11575, USA.

FLEA (Michael Balzary); b. 16 Oct. 1962, Melbourne, Australia. Musician (bass). *Career:* First trumpet, Los Angeles Jr Philharmonic; Founder member, Red Hot Chili Peppers, 1983–; Trumpet player, Trulio Disgracias, 1988; Founder, punk band Hate, playing Hollywood clubs, 1988; International tours including US, UK, Europe, Australia, New Zealand; Major appearances include: Lollapalooza Festival tour, 1992; Hollywood Rock Festival, Rio de Janeiro, 1993; Glastonbury Festival, 1993; Television includes: Late Night With David Letterman; Rapido, BBC2; Saturday Night Live; The Word, C4 TV; Top of The Pops, BBC1; Guest host, The Ben Stiller Show, Fox TV, 1992; Actor, films The Decline of Western Civilization, 1991; Suburbia, 1991; Motorama, 1992. *Recordings:* Albums: The Red Hot Chili Peppers, 1984; Freaky Styley, 1985; The Uplift Moto Party Plan, 1987; Mother's Milk, 1989; Blood Sugar Sex Magik, 1991; What Hits?, 1992; One Hot Minute, 1995; Planet Bad, 1995; Good God's Urge, 1996; Grace of My Heart, 1996; Live on Letterman, 1997; Spirit, 1998; Californication, 1999; Singles include: Higher Ground, 1990; Taste The Pain, 1990; Under The Bridge, 1992; Breaking The Girl, 1992; Give It Away, 1994; Soul To Squeeze, from film Coneheads, 1993; Warped, 1995; My Friends, 1995; Aeroplane, 1996; Love Rollercoaster, 1997; Scar Tissue, 1999; Around The World, 1999; Californication, 2000; Road Trippin', 2001; Contributor, Peace Choir, 1991; Beavis and Butthead Experience, 1993. *Honours:* MTV Music Video Awards, 1992; Rolling Stone Readers Poll Winner, Best Bassist, 1993; Grammy, Best Hard Rock Song, Give It Away, 1993; Grammy Award, Rock Song, Scar Tissue, 2000. *Current Management:* Lindy Goetz Management, 11116 Aqua Vista #39, Studio City, CA 91602, USA.

FLECK Bela; b. New York City, USA. Musician (banjo); Singer; Composer. *Musical Education:* Graduate, New York High School of Music and Art, 1976; Studied banjo with Tony Trishka, Erik Darling, Mark Horowitz. *Career:* Banjo player, composer, 1976–; Played with: Tasty Licks, 1976–79; Spectrum, 1979–81; New Grass Revival, 1982–91; Formed Bela Fleck and the Flecktones, 1989–; Concerts include support to Bonnie Raitt, British tour, 1992; Also recorded solo albums; Studio work, Nashville, with Loretta Lynn; The Statler Brothers; Randy Travis; Television appearances: Hee Haw; Nashville Now; Lonesome Pine Specials. *Recordings include:* Crossing The Tracks, 1980; Natural Bridge, 1982; Deviation, 1984; Daybreak, 1987; Inroads, with Jerry Douglas, Mark O'Connor, 1987;

Places, 1988; Bela Fleck and The Flecktones, 1990; Flight of The Cosmic Hippo, 1992; UFO TOFU, 1993; ; Tales From The Acoustic Planet, 1994; Outbound, 2000; Perpetual Motion, 2001; Contributor, Hot House, Bruce Hornsby, 1995. *Honours:* 2 Grammy Award Nominations for instrumental solos; Frets Readers Poll Winner, Top Banjo Player, more than 6 times, 1981–. *Current Management:* Firstars, 3520 Hayden Ave, Culver City, CA 90232, USA.

FLEDELIUS Soren; b. 7 Feb. 1969, Vejle, Denmark. Singer; Songwriter; Musician. *Education:* Higher Business Degree, Horsens Business School, Denmark, 1989. *Musical Education:* Self-taught Guitar, Bass and Drums. *Career:* 'Voldvo', Denmark Tour 1991; Touring with Stonejuice, 1992–94; Studio Musician for Hege Tokle, Norway, 1995; Touring Denmark with Oktoberdrengene, 1995; Ich Bin So Geil Tour 96, with Halla Da; Halla Da USA Tour, 1996; Appeared in Starship Troopers, Live Concert, Danish National Radio, 1997; Halla Da Denmark Tour, 1997; All Major Festivals. *Compositions:* Hvorfor Fa'en Skal vi Vare Sa Brune; Von Hinten Fritz; Theme From Shotgunfire Blues. *Recordings:* Halla Da Albums: Ich Bin So Geil, 1995, Hvorfor Fa'en Skal vi Vare Sa Brune, 1996; Ultra-Brun Edition 2, 1997. *Honour:* Danish Champion of Rock, 1997. *Leisure interest:* Movie Acting. *Current Management:* Louis Fontaine, World Records. *Address:* Off-Beat Productions, West End 15, 1661 KBH V, Denmark.

FLEEMAN Jim; b. 21 June 1966, Chesterfield, England. Musician (drums, percussion). *Musical Education:* City of Leeds College of Music; Guildhall School of Music and Drama. *Career:* Tour, concerts, with Omar; Dana Bryant, CH4 television pilot; Tour, concerts with Guildhall Jazz Band; Kenny Wheeler, London concerts; Various theatrical productions; Instrumental tuition and workshops; Senior Percussion Tutor, Brunel University College; Various network and cable television and radio broadcasts; Music Consultant, various corporate clients. *Recordings:* Featured soloist, Essence, Guildhall Jazz Band, 1989; Various commercial, theatrical recordings. *Leisure interests:* Travel; Film; Theatre. *Address:* 95 Belgrave Rd, London SW1V 2BQ, England.

FLEETWOOD Mick; b. 24 June 1942, London, England. Musician (drums). m. (1) Jenny Boyd, (2) Sara Recor, 1988, 2 d. *Career:* Drummer, John Mayall, 1967; Drummer, Fleetwood Mac, 1967–; Appearances include: Tours include: USA; Scandinavia; Europe; Concerts; Fillmore East; Miami Pop Festival Fillmore West, San Francisco; Reading Festival; Tampa Stadium, Florida, with the Eagles; Madison Square Garden; Hollywood Bowl, Los Angeles; US Festival, with Jackson Browne, The Cars, The Grateful Dead, Eddie Money; The Police; Santana; Talking Heads, 1982; Forms new band, Zoo, signs to Capricorn Records, 1992; Fleetwood Mac reunion, Presidential Inauguration concert, 1993; Film appearance: The Running Man, 1987; Owner, Fleetwoods club, Los Angeles, 1991. *Recordings:* Albums: Fleetwood Mac, 1968; English Rose, 1969; Pious Bird of Good Omen, 1969; Then Play On, 1969; Blue Jams At Chess, 1969; Kiln House, 1970; Fleetwood Mac In Chicago, 1971; Black Magic Woman, 1971; Future Games, 1971; Bare Trees, 1972; Penguin, 1973; Mystery To Me, 1973; Heroes Are Hard To Find, 1974; Rumours, 1977; Tusk, 1979; Tango In The Night, 1987; Behind The Mask, 1990; Time, 1995; The Dance, 1997; The Blues Years, 2000; Also appears on: I'll Sleep When I'm Dead, 1996; Susanna Hoffs, 1996; As It All Began, 1998; Solo: The Visitor, 1981; I'm Not Me, 1983; Singles include: Black Magic Woman; Need Your Love So Bad; Albatross; Man of The World; Over My Head; Rhiannon (Will You Ever Win); Go Your Own Way; Don't Stop; Tusk; Sara; Think About Me; Hold Me; Love In Store; Big Love; Everywhere; As Long As You Follow. *Publications:* My Life and Times In Fleetwood Mac, 1990. *Honours:* Favorite Band, Duo Or Group, Pop/Rock, American Music Awards, 1978; Grammy: Album of The Year, Rumours, 1978; Gold Ticket, Madison Square Garden, 1990; Platinum, Gold discs. *Current Management:* Courage Management, 2899 Agoura Blvd, Suite 562, Westlake, CA 91361, USA.

FLEMING Kye; b. 9 Oct. 1951, Pennsacola, Florida, USA. Songwriter; Publisher. *Education:* 2 years college. *Career:* President, Publishing Companies: Dream Catcher Music; Gila Monster Music; Painted Pony Music. *Compositions:* Co-wrote: Smokey Mountain Rain; Give Me Wings; I Was Country When Country Wasn't Cool; Nobody; Some People's Lives; Years; Sleeping Single In A Double Bed; Roll On Mississippi; Walk The Line (album), Kennedy-Rose. *Recordings:* with James Galway, Wayward Wind, 1982; with Marti Jones, Used Guitars, 1988. *Honours:* 2 Grammy Nominations; 43 BMI Awards; 2 CMA Award Mominations; 3 time BMI Songwriter of the Year; NSAI Songwriter of The Year; CMA Triple Play Award. *Memberships:* NSAI; CMA; BMI. *Leisure interests:* Clay sculpting; Horses; Land sculpting. *Current Management:* Dream Catcher; Gila Monster Music. *Address:* 1109 16th Ave S, Nashville, TN 37212, USA.

FLEMING Mark; b. 6 Jan. 1962, Montréal, Canada. Music Publisher; Artist Man.; Film and Television Composer Agent. *Education:* BA in Political Science and Communications; Legal and Practical Aspects of Recording and Music Publishing, University of California, Los Angeles. *Musical Education:* Basic Theory, Piano. *Career:* Manager, Eddie Murphy for Transition Music; Developed Crash Test Dummies, BMG Music Publishing Canada Inc; Own business, MERS Music, publisher, film and television composer agent; Manager for Ian Halperin; Mandela Benefit Concert at Wembley; DJ Ray. *Recordings:* As producer: Giving You The Best That I Got, Anita Baker; As administrator for: The Bee Gees; Annie Lennox; Dave Stewart; Film soundtrack, Beverly Hills Cop. *Memberships:* AIMP; SOCAN; BMI. *Leisure interests:* Sports, especially hoops and tennis. *Address:* 1396 Ste Catherine St W, Suite 424, Montréal, QC H3G 1P8, Canada.

FLETCHER Andrew John; b. 8 July 1961, Nottingham, England. Musician (keyboards). m. Grainne Mullan, 16 Jan. 1993, 1 s., 1 d. *Career:* Founder Member, Depeche Mode, 1980-. *Recordings:* 11 Top Ten Singles including: Just Can't Get Enough, 1981; See You, 1982; Everything Counts, 1983; People Are People, 1984; Master and Servant, 1984; Enjoy the Silence, 1990; I Feel You, 1993; Condemnation, 1993; In Your Room, 1994; Barrel of a Gun, 1997; It's No Good, 1997; Dream On, 2001; 12 Top Ten Albums including: Speak and Spell, 1982; A Broken Frame, 1982; Construction Time Again, 1983; Some Great Reward, 1984; The Singles 81–85, 1985; Black Celebration, 1986; Music For the Masses, 1987; 101, 1989; Violator, 1990; Songs of Faith and Devotion, 1993; Ultra, 1997; The Singles: 86>98, 1998; Exciter, 2001. *Honours:* BPI Brit Award, Enjoy the Silence, 1991. *Leisure interests:* Football; Reading. *Current Management:* Jonathan Kessler, Baron Inc, 41 River Terrace, #3308 New York, NY 10282, USA. *Address:* First Floor, Regent House, 106 Marylebone High St, London W1M 3DB, England. *Internet:* www.depechemode.com.

FLETCHER Christopher Jeffrey; b. 1 July 1952, Berlin, Germany. Musician (percussion, drums); Vocalist. m. Kate Cochrane, 1 s., 1 d. *Career:* Percussion and backing vocals for many artists 1969-, including: Chris Rea, Road To Hell Tour, 1989–90; Christians, Couler Tour, 1990–91; Beautiful South, 0891 Tour, 1991–92; Judy Tzuke, Wonderland Tour, 1992; Mark Almond, Jaque Tour; Live apperances with: Fergal Sharkey; Roger Chapman; Dusty Springfield; Steve Williams; Cayenne; Paz; Stretch; Morrissey Mullen; The Montellas; Neucleus; Limmy and The Family Cooking; Currently running a 16 piece band of top session players. *Recordings:* Albums by: Beautiful South; Manfred Mann; Roger Chapman; Cayenne, 2 albums; Paz, 4 albums; Stretch; Morrissey Mullen, 5 albums; John Critchinson; Martin Drew; Peter Green; Molly Duncan; The Montellas; Neucleus; Alan Price. *Leisure interests:* Tennis; Snooker; Comedy; Hang-gliding. *Current Management:* Chance Management. *Address:* 106 Cleveland Gardens, London SW13 0AH, England.

FLETCHER Matt James Harry; b. 27 Feb. 1968, Lambeth, London, England. Musician (keyboards); Programmer; Engineer; Prod. *Education:* Goldsmiths College, University of London, BSc Psychology. *Career:* Keyboards for Bros' TV appearances; Numerous remixes including Shine, by Aswad; Numerous TV commercials and themes; Regular freelance work; Technical advisor to Youth; Signed as Rampage, 1994; Currently writing and producing Betty Boo's third album. *Recordings:* Top of The Pops theme, 1991–95; One Foot In The Grave, theme remixes; For Rampage: Monkees; Why; Godfather; Album: Priority One; Betty Boo's singles, 1995. *Publication:* Tuning Your Breakbeat, article, Sound On Sound, May 1993. *Honour:* D & AD Silver Award, Best TV Soundtrack, Glad, Miller-Lite, 1991. *Membership:* Musicians' Union. *Leisure interests:* BMWs; Reading; Clubs; Computer programming. *Current Management:* Jazz Summers, Big Life Management. *Address:* 15a Little Portland St, London W1N 5DE, England.

FLICK Vic; b. 14 May 1937, Worcester Park, Surrey, England. Musician (guitar); Composer. m. Judith Mary, 19 May 1960, 1 s., 1 d. *Education:* Graduate diploma. *Musical Education:* Piano and theory LRAM, guitar. *Career:* Recorded with most major recordings artistes including: Tom Jones; Nancy Sinatra; Henry Mancini; Engelbert Humperdinck; John Barry; Cilla Black; The Walker Brothers; Shirley Bassey; Sandie Shaw; Bee Gees. *Compositions:* Themes and background music for television, radio and film includes: Music scores for The Europeans; Conquest of Light, Irish Tourist Board; Commercials: Cheseboro-Ponds; Palitoy. *Honours:* Two Royal Command Performances. *Memberships:* PRS; ASCAP. *Leisure interests:* Sailing; Reading; Writing; Music. *Address:* 2021 Ocean Ave No. 225, Santa Monica, CA 90495, USA.

FLINT Keith; Vocalist. *Career:* Member, The Prodigy, 1990–; Festival appearances include: Glastonbury, 1995, 1997; V97, 1997; Lollapalooza, 1997. *Recordings:* Albums: Experience, 1992; Music for the Jilted Generation (No. 1, UK), 1994; The Fat of the Land (No. 1, UK and US), 1997; Evolution, 1998; Star Profiles, 1998; Interview, 1999; The Dirtchamber Sessions, 1999; Hit Singles: Charly, 1991; Everybody In the Place, 1991; Fire, 1992; Out of Space, 1992; Wind It Up, 1993; One Love, 1993; No Good (Start the Dance), 1994; Voodoo People, 1994; Poison, 1995; Firestarter (No. 1, UK), 1996; Breathe (No. 1, UK), 1996; Smack My Bitch Up, 1997. *Address:* c/o XL Recordings, 17–19 Alma Rd, London SW18 1AA, England.

FLOREK Jaki; b. Bradford, Yorkshire, England. Vocalist; Lyricist. 2 s., 1 d. *Education:* Cardiff College of Art. *Career:* Tours with Shattered Dolls and Adam's Family; Editor, Feedback Music magazine. *Recordings:* Singles: with Shattered Dolls: Lipstick Killer (EP); with Adam's Family: Sometimes I Wonder (EP), 1987; Frustration, 1994; Album: with Adam's Family: Disease, 1995, CD, 1997. *Publications:* Adam's Family: The Scouse Phenomenon, Vols 1 and 2; Stories in anthologies. *Memberships:* PRS; Musicians' Union. *Leisure interest:* Ceramic Artist. *Current Management:* Loose Records. *Address:* PO Box 67, Runcorn, Cheshire WA7 4NL, England.

FLORES Remedios, (Alendrina De Los Remedios Flores); b. 30 Jan. 1952, Ronda, Malaga, Spain. Flamenco Singer. m. Rodrigo Flores, 7 July 1973, 2 s., 1 d. *Musical Education:* Learned from family. *Career:* Toured for 20 years with famous guitarist Rodrigo; Under contract to Los Angeles City Schools, presenter, flamenco music; State grants to present Flamenco Song in concert atmosphere; Principle vocalist, El Cid, tablao flamenco, Hollywood (most prestigious flamenco nightclub in world). *Composition:* music to National Geographic Special, The Soul of Spain. *Recordings:* Albums: Flamenco Caravan; Remedios Flores-Gipsy Flamenco Singer; The Gipsy 4; Rumba Festival; Trio Flamenco; Passionate Flamenco Dances; La Familia Flores; Inpiraciones; Flamenco Fantastico (Live); Video: Flamenco Sounds. *Honours:* Winner, Billboard Magazine Song Contest (Latin Category): Nos Volvemos A Querer. *Membership:* National Asscn Female Executives. *Leisure interests:* Swimming; Cooking traditional gypsy/ Spanish food. *Current Management:* Sounds-Vision Music. *Address:* PO Box 3691, La Mesa, CA 91944, USA.

FLOWERS Herbie; b. 19 May 1938, London, England. Musician (bass guitar, double bass, tuba). m. Ann, 1 Aug. 1959, 1 s., 1 d. *Musical Education:* RAF School of Music. *Career:* Played tuba in Royal Air Force, 1955–63; Played double bass, Fender bass, London theatre, club, studio circuit; Joined Blue Mink, 1970; Worked for David Bowie, tour of USA, 1974; Member, T-Rex, 2 years; Played on recordings with: Elton John; David Essex; Paul McCartney; Al Kooper; Nilsson; Tom Jones; Tiny Tim; Dusty Springfield; Henry Mancini; George Harrison; Ringo Starr; Formed Sky with John Williams; Is now in demand as a jazz double bass player; Gary Potter; David Jones; Tina May; Lectures, Fun With Music, East Sussex County Council; Residential free week-long music courses, RockShops, on University campuses. *Recordings:* Albums: Transformer, Lou Reed; Diamond Dogs, David Bowie; Burn Down The Mission, Elton John; Rock On, David Essex; Broad Street, Paul McCartney; 10 albums by Sky; Recent albums include: The Business, with Mike Hatchard, 1998. *Leisure interests:* Playing double bass with his new project, Shuffle Jazz. *Address:* 15 High St, Ditchling, East Sussex BN6 8SY, England.

FLOYD Eddie; b. 25 June 1937, Montgomery, Alabama, USA. Singer; Prod.; Composer. 6 s., 2 d. *Musical Education:* Wayne School of Music, Detroit. *Career:* Founder member, The Falcons, 1954–62; Solo artist, 1962–; Guest singer, The Original Blues Brothers Band, Booker T and the MG's; World-wide tours with the above; President, Floyd Entertainment Group Inc. *Compositions:* Songs for Otis Redding, Wilson Pickett, and Sam and Dave, including 634–5789; Ninety-Nine and A Half (Just Won't Do); You Don't Know What You Mean To Me; Knock On Wood. *Recordings:* With The Falcons: You're So Fine; I Found A Love; Solo albums: Knock On Wood; I've Never Found A Girl; Rare Stamps; You've Got To Have Eddie; California Girl; Down To Earth; Baby Lay Your Head Down; Soul Street; Experience; Try Me; Flashback; Back To The Roots; All The Hits Plus More, 2001; with the Blues Brothers Band: Live In Montreux; The Red White and Blues; California Girl. *Honours:* Governors Award/Memphis Blues Foundation Inductee, Tennessee; Honourary Lieut Col, Alabama; President Bush Performance Award; Alabama Hall of Fame Inductee; NAACP BMI 1 Million Performances Award, Knock On Wood; BMI Award. *Memberships:* BMI. *Current Management:* Andy Nazer, Performance Representation. *Address:* 39 Hopton Rd, London SW16 2EH, England.

FLYNN Frank E; b. 13 April 1921, Havana City. Musician. m. Martha Francisa Montes Cobian, 1 s. *Education:* The Cuban Association for Blind People. *Compositions:* Midnight Theme; Zapateo Cubano; Sasauma; Gandinga, Mondongo y Sandunga; Rico Melao; Leungo; Reflejos Ancestrales; Fuguetta Cubana; Frank Emilio Interpreta a Ignacio Cervantes; Tribute to Ernesto Lecuona; Barbarisimo; Reflejos Ancestrales; A Tiempo de Danzon; Los Amigos. *Publications:* Notacion Musical Sistema Braille. *Honours:* Distinction a la Cultura Cubana; Medal and Reward, UNEAC; Crystal Walking Stick, Blind Asscn; Nominated, Artistic Interpretation, National Premium in Music. *Memberships:* National Asscn for Blind People; Cuban Music Institute. *Leisure interests:* Reading; Listening all Kinds of Music but Mainly Classical. *Current Management:* Institute Cubano de la Musica. *Address:* Luis Estevez #210 Entre Concejal, Veiga y Alcalde O'farrill, Santos, Suarez, 10 de Octubre, CP 10500 Cuidad le la Habana, Cuba.

FLYNN Jerome; b. 16 March 1963, Kent, England. Actor; Singer. *Career:* Actor, UK television series Soldier, Soldier, 1991–95; Ain't Misbehaving,

1996; Badger, 1999; Film appearances: Best, 2000; Singer, duo Robson and Jerome, 1995–96. *Recordings:* Albums: Robson and Jerome, 1995; Take Two, 1996; Singles: Unchained Melody/White Cliffs of Dover, 1995; I Believe/Up On The Roof, 1995; What Becomes of The Brokenhearted/Saturday Night At The Movies/You'll Never Walk Alone, 1996. *Honour:* Best selling UK single and album of the year, 1995; First act to debut at #1 with first three UK single releases, 1995–96.

FOAD Paul; b. 26 Sept. 1957, Liverpool, England. Musician (guitar); Songwriter; Guitar Teacher. m. Kim Hamilton (singer), 7 May 1994, 1 s., 4 d. *Musical Education:* Birmingham Guitar School, 3 years; Barney Kessel Workshop summer School. *Career:* With group Au Pairs: BBC TV, Old Grey Whistle Test; BBC Radio 1: 3 John Peel sessions; Janice Long; Kid Jensen session; Local radio; 3 tours, USA; 5 tours, Europe, including Pink Pop, Netherlands; Session guitar for jazz artist Andy Hamilton; Session for local artists; Solo guitar, Birmingham International Film Festival; Member, Andy Hamilton's band, Blue Notes. *Recordings:* Au Pairs: (studio albums) Playing With A Different Sex; Sense and Sensibility; (live album) Live In Berlin; 1 radio compilation CD: Equal But Different. *Publications:* One chapter on Au Pairs in: In The Facists Bathroom, by Greil Marcus; Author, The Caged Guitarist, guitar tutor book. *Honour:* Songwriters Award, New York's Village Voice, 1980. *Memberships:* MCPS; PRS; Musicians' Union. *Current Management:* EMI Publishing; RPM Records. *Address:* 41 Garfield Rd, North Chingford, London E4 7DG, England.

FOGELBERG Dan; b. 13 Aug. 1951, Peoria, Illinois, USA. Musician (guitar, piano); Songwriter. *Education:* University of Illinois. *Musical Education:* Piano from age 14. *Career:* Musician, California folk circuit, including tours with Van Morrison, 1971; Recording artiste, 1974–; Support to the Eagles, 1975. *Recordings:* Singles include: Longer, (No. 2, US), 1980; Same Auld Lang Syne, 1981; Leader of The Band, 1981; Rhythm of the Rain, 1990; Albums: Home Free, 1973; Souvenirs, 1975; Captured Angel, 1975; Netherlands, 1977; Twin Sons of Different Mothers, with Tim Weisberg, 1977; Phoenix, 1980; The Innocent Age, 1981; Windows and Walls, 1984; Greatest Hits, 1985; High Country Snows, 1985; Exiles, 1987; The Wild Places, 1990; Dan Fogelberg Live – Greetings From The West, 1991; River of Souls, 1993; No Resemblance Whatsoever, 1995; Love Songs, 1995; First Christmas Morning, 1999; Live – Something Old New Borrowed and Some Blues, 2000. *Current Management:* HK Management, 8900 Wilshire Blvd, Suite 300, Beverly Hills, CA 90211, USA.

FOGERTY John; b. 28 May 1945, Berkeley, California, USA. Singer; Composer; Songwriter; Musician (guitar). *Career:* Member, Blue Velvets, (later known as the Golliwogs), 1959–67; Group became Creedence Clearwater Revival, 1967–71; Solo artiste, 1972-. *Compositions include:* Almost Saturday Night, recorded by Dave Edmunds; Rockin' All Over The World, recorded by Status Quo. *Recordings:* Albums: with Creedence Clearwater Revival: Creedence Clearwater Revival, 1968; Bayou Country, 1969; Green River, 1969; Willie and The Poor Boys, 1969; Cosmo's Factory, 1970; Pendulum, 1970; Mardi Gras, 1972; Live In Europe, 1973; Live At The Royal Albert Hall, 1980; Creedence Clearwater Revival (box set), 2001; Solo albums: The Blue Ridge Rangers, 1973; John Fogerty, 1975; Centerfield, 1985; Eye of a Zombie, 1986; Blue Moon Swamp, 1997; Premonition, 1998; Singles: with the Golliwogs: Don't Tell Me No More Lies; Fight Fire; Walk Upon The Water; with Creedence Clearwater Revival: Suzie Q; I Put A Spell On You; Proud Mary; Green River; Bad Moon Rising; Down On The Corner; Travellin' Band; Up Around The Bend; Looking Out My Back Door; Have You Ever Seen The Rain; Solo: Bayou, 1973; Hearts of Stone, 1975; Comin' Down The Road, 1975; The Old Man Down The Road, 1985; Blueboy, 1997. *Current Management:* 15030 Ventura Blvd, Suite 777, Sherman Oaks, CA 91403, USA.

FOLEY Thomas Henry; b. 1 April 1961, London, England. Dir, React Music Ltd. *Career:* Editor of Songplugger, 1986–87; Publisher and Editor of Bandit, 1988–90; Personal Assistant to Dave Pearce at Reachin Records up to 1991; Currently, Director of React Music Ltd. *Address:* 138B West Hill, Putney, London SW15 2UE, England.

FOLLETT Marie-Claire; b. 11 May 1973, Cardiff, Wales. Singer; Songwriter; Actress; Dancer. *Education:* Brooklands College. *Musical Education:* Academy of Live and Recorded Arts. *Career:* Radio broadcasts include: Radio Warsaw, Poland; Thicker Than Water, BBC Radio 2; The Hardcore Show, Kiss FM, 1998; Television appearances include: Regis and Kathy Lee Show, ABC-TV, US; Legionnaires, 1999; Concerts in London include: Marquee; The Orange; Earls Court; Birmingham NEC; Finalist in Yamaha Music Quest; Bands include Subway; Nemesis; Fabba-Mania; The Fortune Cookies; Antisocial, 1998; Tina Turner support, 1999. *Recordings:* Spreadeagle, Sky TV; A Guide For The Divorced Child, Jann Turner (film soundtrack); Singles: Cry; Indestructable; Get Into Love, with Antisocial, 1999. *Memberships:* Musicians' Union; Equity. *Current Management:* Richard Gillinson. *Address:* 1.3 The Alaska Works, 61 Grange Rd, London SE1 3BA, England.

FONTANA Wayne (Glyn Ellis); b. 28 Oct. 1940, Manchester, Lancashire, England. *Career:* Founder member, The Jets; The Mindbenders, 1963–65; Solo artiste, 1965–; Tours include: UK, with Brenda Lee, 1964; UK, supporting Del Shannon, 1965; British Song Festival, Brighton, 1965; Tour, with Herman's Hermits, The Fortunes, Billy Fury, 1965; Swinging '66 Tour, with the Small Faces, 1966; Resident songwriter, Chappell music publishers, 1970–; English Invasion Revival US tour, 1973; Resumed recording career, 1976; Revival tour, 1979; Festival of The 10th Summer, Manchester, 1986. *Recordings:* Albums include: Wayne Fontana and The Mindbenders, 1965; Eric, Rick, Wayne and Bob, 1966; The Mindbenders, 1966; Hit singles: with The Mindbenders: Um Um Um Um Um Um, 1964; The Game of Love (No. 2, UK), 1965; Just A Little Bit Too Late; She Needs Love; Solo: Come On Home; Goodbye Bluebird; Pamela Pamela. *Address:* c/o Barry Collings Entertainments, 21a Clifftown Rd, Southend-on-Sea, Essex SS1 1AB, England.

FONTENOT Glenn Dale; b. 23 Aug. 1951, Jennings, Louisiana, USA. Vocalist; Musician (Guitar). m. Jenny Fontenot, 14 Feb. 1997, 2 d. *Education:* McNeese State University, Louisiana. *Career:* Singer and Leader of the Renegades, performing night clubs, fairs, festivals and private parties. *Compositions:* 10 songs for album, Memories, 1990. *Recording:* Memories. *Memberships:* Chamber of Commerce, Picayune; Louisiana Fair and Festival Asscn. *Leisure interest:* Fishing. *Address:* 303 Hwy 43 S No. 10, Picayune, MS 39466, USA.

FORCIONE Antonio; b. 2 May 1960, Italy. Musician (guitar); Composer. 1 d. *Education:* Visual Arts, 5 years. *Musical Education:* Private Jazz and Folk tuition in Italy; Self-taught. *Career:* World-wide tours as solo artist and with bands, Antonio Forcione Acoustic Band and Acoustic Mania, in theatres and major festivals; Numerous radio and television appearances; Performed with Barney Kessel, Martin Taylor, Birelli Lagrene, Claudio Roditi and others; Double bills with John McLaughlin, opened for Phil Collins, Barclay James Harvest, Zucchero, Jools Holland, Pino Daniele, Bobby McFerrin; Masterclasses world-wide; Composed music for TV, radio and documentaries. *Recordings:* Albums: Light and Shade, 1984; Eurotour, 1986; Celebration, 1987; Poema, 1992; Acoustic Revenge, 1993; Live Edinburgh Festival, 1993; Dedicato, 1996 Talking Hands, 1997; Meet Me in London, 1998; Ghetto Paradise, 1998. *Memberships:* Musicians' Union; PRS. *Leisure interests:* Dance; Painting; Acting. *Current Management:* Kunst Music Promotions. *Address:* 28a Devonshire Rd, London W4 2HD, England.

FORD Baby (Peter Ford), (Twig Bud, Solcyc); b. 1960, England. Prod.; Remixer; DJ. *Career:* Started recording career as part of the Acid House explosion, late 1980s; Co-founder: Trelik and Ifach Records, two of England's most respected techno labels; Collaborations: Eon; Mark Broom. *Recordings:* Albums: Fordtrax, 1988; Ooo The World of Baby Ford, 1989; BFord 9, 1992; Headphone Easyrider, 1997; Singles: Oochy Koochy, Chikki Chikki Ahh Ahh, 1988; Children of The Revolution, 1989; Beach Bump, 1990; Fetish, 1992; Treatment Feel (with Minimal Man), 1994; Normal, 1998. *Address:* c/o Ifach Records, PO Box 1797, London, England.

FORD Gerry; b. 25 May 1943, Athlone, Eire. Country Music Entertainer; DJ; Journalist; Singer; Songwriter. m. Joan, 4 April 1964, 1 s. *Career:* Qualified Baker, Confectioner; Served in Edinburgh City Police until 1976; Became professional entertainer, while broadcasting 2 country music programmes for Radio Forth, Edinburgh and performing in clubs; Joined BBC Radio Scotland, Country music presenter, 1978–93; Own series, BBC Radio 2, 1988–89. *Recordings:* 15 albums, 1977–; 7 duets with Jean Shepard. *Honours:* 3 Albums of the Year, BCMA, 1986; BCM Radio Play Album of the Year, 1991; Presenters Award, 1993; Hon. Citizen, Nashville, Tennessee; 21 appearances, Grand Ole Opry, Nashville; 33 Awards, Male Vocalist, Recording Artiste, various country music clubs and magazines. *Address:* 13 Winton Park, Edinburgh EH10 7EX, Scotland.

FORD Lita; b. 23 Sept. 1959, London, England. Singer; Musician (guitar). m. Chris Holmes, divorced. *Career:* Original member, all-girl group, The Runaways, 1976–79; Solo artiste, 1980-. *Recordings:* Albums: with the Runaways: The Runaways, 1976; Queens of Night, 1977; And Now The Runaways, 1979; Flamin' Schoolgirls, 1980; Solo albums: Out For Blood, 1983; Dancin' On The Edge, 1984; Lita, 1988; Stiletto, 1990; Dangerous Curves, 1991; Black, 1995; Singles: Hungry, 1990; Lisa, 1990; Shot of Poison, 1991; Playin' with Fire, 1992; Killin' Kind, 1995; Greatest Hits Live, 2000; Hit singles include: Kiss Me Deadly; Close My Eyes Forever (duet with Ozzy Osbourne).

FORD Marc; b. 13 April 1966, Los Angeles, California, USA. Musician (Guitar). *Career:* Joined The Black Crowes; Numerous tours world-wide; Supported the Rolling Stones on Voodoo Lounge tour, 1995. *Recordings:* Singles: Remedy; Albums: The Southern Harmony and Musical Companion, 1992; Amorica, 1994; Three Snakes and One Charm, 1996.

FORD Vince; b. 9 April 1962, Newark, Nottinghamshire, England. Singer; Songwriter; Prod.; Record Co Exec. m. Julie, 14 Sept. 1991, 1 s. *Musical Education:* None (formal). *Career:* Formed Capital Queue, 1979; Formed Temper, Temper, 1987; Formed Sheer Bravado Records, 1989. *Membership:* PRS. *Leisure interests:* Sport; Computers; Photography. *Address:* 7 Backs Close, Waddington, Lincoln LN5 9SG, England.

FORDE Brinsley; Singer; Musician (guitar). *Career:* Child actor, Here Come The Double Deckers, BBC TV, 1971; Founder member, UK reggae group Aswad, 1975–; Performances include: Cliff Richard – The Event, Wembley Stadium, 1989; Nelson Mandela International Tribute concert, Wembley, 1990; Glastonbury Festival, 1990; Reggae Sunsplash US tour, 1991; Heineken Festival, Leeds, 1995; Musician, actor, film Babylon, 1980; Please Sir, Diamonds are Forever, Leo the Last; Also featured in Bob Marley Tribute, Rapido, BBC2 TV, 1991; Presenter, Soul Vibration, VH-1. *Recordings:* Singles include: Back To Africa, 1976; Don't Turn Around (No. 1, UK), 1988; Give A Little Love, 1988; Set Them Free, 1988; Beauty's Only Skin Deep, 1989; On and On, 1989; Next To You, 1990; Smile, 1990; How Long (with Yazz), 1993; Dance Hall Mood, 1993; Shine, UK No 5; Albums: Aswad, 1976; Hulet, 1979; New Chapter, 1980; Not Satisfied, 1982; Live and Direct, 1983; Rebel Soul, 1984; To The Top, 1986; Distant Thunder, 1988; Renaissance, 1989; Too Wicked, 1990; Live, 1991; Roots Rocking, 1997; Big Up, 1997; Roots Revival, 1999. *Honours include:* Reggae Industry Award, Best Group, 1995. *Current Management:* Hit and Run Music, 30 Ives St, London SW3 2ND, England.

FORDHAM Julia; b. 10 Aug. 1962, Hampshire, England. Singer; Songwriter; Musician (guitar). *Career:* Began performances own material, folk music clubs, age 14–15; 5 years as backing vocalist; Signed solo record deal, 1987. *Recordings include:* Albums: Julia Fordham, 1988; Porcelain, 1989; Swept, 1991; Falling Forward, 1994; East West, 1997; Julia Fordham Collection, 1998; Concrete Love, 2002; Singles include: Happy Ever After, 1988; Love Moves In Mysterious Ways, 1992. *Honours:* Silver Prize, Tokyo Music Festival, 1989; 4 Gold records, Japan. *Memberships:* Musicians' Union; Equity. *Leisure interests:* Boogie boarding; Gardening. *Current Management:* JFD Management. *Address:* Unit 9, Acklam Workshops, 10 Acklam Rd, London W10 5QZ, England.

FORRESTER John; b. 16 March 1969, Pembury, Kent, England. Musician (bouzouki, bass, acoustic guitar); Vocalist. *Career:* Vocals, bass, Killing The Rose, 1986–87; Vocals, bass, The Colour Mary, 1988–92; Vocals, bass, bouzouki, Pressgang, 1992–94; Solo artiste, vocals, bouzouki, acoustic guitar, 1993–; Vocals, bass, WOB, 1993–94; Vocals, bouzouki, bass, Sunspeak, 1995; Tours: with Pressgang: England, France, Germany; with WOB: England, France, Germany, Austria, Holland; Solo: England, France, Germany; Radio: The Colour Mary Live From The Marquee, BBC Radio 1, 1990. *Recordings:* EPs: with The Colour Mary: Trash and Treasure, 1988; The World Don't Spin, 1989; Black and White, 1990; Sunspeak, 1991; Mindfield, 1992; with Pressgang: Donkey, 1993; Albums: with Pressgang: Burning Boats, 1994; with WOB: Can't Stay Long, 1995; Straight On Til Morning, 1998; Solo: Scars and Memories, 1993; Tales of Nothing, 1997; Lanterns, EP, 1998; All The Wrong Things, 2000; Ne Me Quitte Pas, songs by Brel, 1998. *Membership:* Musicians' Union. *Leisure interests:* Walking; Drinking. *Current Management:* Seaview Music. *Address:* Seaview Music, 88 Greenham Wood, Bracknell, Berkshire RG12 7WH, England.

FORRÓ Daniel; b. 19 Feb. 1958, Jihlava, Czech Republic. Composer; Musician; Musicologist; Product Specialist; Teacher; Writer; Consultant. *Education:* Jamu Janaceks Academy of Music, Brno. *Career:* Keyboards in Rock Groups, 1978–84; Own Project of EA and Computer Music, Forrotronics, since 1983; Plays with Drum Group Dama Dama; Teacher, Jamu, since 1991; Editor, Writer, Music Magazine Muzikus, since 1991; Product Specialist, Yamaha Europe, Hamburg, since 1992; Writer, Series of Expert Books on Musitronics, since 1993; Founder, Society for Micro Intervallic Music, 1995; International Master Summer Classes, Janaceks Academy of Music, since 1996; National Rock Music Courses, since 1998. *Compositions:* Over 1,100 of all Styles. *Publications:* Midi Communication In Music; Computers and Music; Home Recording; World of Midi. *Memberships:* Society for EA Music; Society for MicroIntervallic Music; Society Q. *Leisure interests:* Languages; Mathematics; History; Literature; Architecture. *Current Management:* D F, Lucní 40, 61600 Brno, Czech Republic.

FORSMAN Ingela 'Pling'; b. 26 Aug. 1950, Stockholm, Sweden. Lyricist; Record Prod.; Recording Artist. m. Lars, 1990, 1 s. *Education:* English, University of Stockholm. *Career:* Former recording artist with girl group Bambis; Tours: Sweden; Germany; Lyricist, 1971–; 12 years in record business, some as producer; Translated musicals into Swedish: Cats; Grease; Fame; Hair; Also translated songs in films, including: The Little Mermaid; Beauty and The Beast; Hymn for Swedish Hymnbook; Written over 1000 lyrics, most of them recorded. *Honours:* Swedish Song Contest (Two first places, many in Top 3); SKAP Award. *Memberships:* STIM; NCB; SKAP. *Leisure interests:* Cooking; Country life. *Address:* Pling AB, Kungsholms Hamnplan 3, 112 20 Stockholm, Sweden.

FORWARD Fast; b. 24 March 1954, Whitley Bay, England. Composer. m. Lucienne Vidah, 9 Nov. 1993. *Education:* Ashington Technical College; Jacob Kramer Art College, Leeds, 1972; BFA, Fine Arts, Newcastle upon Tyne Polytechnic, 1976; MFA, Centre for Contemporary Music, Mills College, Oakland, California, USA, 1978. *Career:* Performances and concerts include Whitney Museum of American Art, New York; National Gallery, Hamburger Bahnhof, Berlin; Museum of Modern Art, Montréal, Canada; Merkin Concert Hall, New York; Walker Art Center, Minneapolis; Shaffy Theatre, Amsterdam; Tenjin Barca Festival, Osaka, Japan; Studio 200, Tokyo; Time of Music Festival, Finland; New Music America Festival, Philadelphia; Guest Musician, Merce Cunningham Dance Company, 1994–97; Producer of his own music and also musical events; Curated The Accident, 9 evenings of performance, with Wooster Group; Composed and performed music for dance companies and theatre performances. *Compositions include:* Red Raw Steel Drum, 1985; The Dream State, 1988; Machine Guns, 1988; Rollerball, 1990; Waterball, 1990; Flip Flop, 1990; Simultaneous Music, 1995; Feeding Frenzy, 1995; 186, 1998; Questionnaire, 1999; Raw Footage, 1999; No Fly Zone, 1999. *Recordings:* Same Same; Panhandling; The Caffeine Effect; %; Rotorblade. *Honours:* New York State Council on the Arts Commissions, 1986, 1992; DAAD Fellowship, Berlin, 1988, 1998; Meet the Composer, Fellowship, New York Foundation for the Arts, 1989; Asian Cultural Council Fellowship, New York, 1997. *Membership:* ASCAP. *Leisure interests:* Cooking; Cycling; Computing. *Current Management:* Bent Out of Shape Productions. *Address:* 224 E Seventh St No. 17, New York, NY 10009, USA.

FOSKETT Charles A; b. 27 March 1949, Newcastle-upon-Tyne, England. Musician (guitar, bass); Composer; Prod. m. Lauren Daniele Field, 7 June 1990, 1 s. *Musical Education:* Self-taught. *Career:* Major tours, television and radio sessions including Andy Peebles, BBC; Tyne Tees, Chat Show; Started in Newcastle, played alongside The Animals, 1960s; Put together The Anti Heroin Project, EMI, 1985, 1986, 1987; Wrote, produced double album: It's A Live In World, featuring and bringing together hundreds of big name artists; Worked with: Kim Wilde; Ringo Starr; Precious Wilson; John Cleese; Bonnie Tyler; Elkie Brooks; Daryl Pandy; Cliff Richard; Holly Johnson; Sheila Ferguson; Robin Gibb; Nick Kershaw; Hazel O'Connor; Founder, Veracruz Music International, record production company. *Compositions:* Theme music, Strike Command, TV advertisement, 1996; Theme music, ITV six-part series, 1997; Theme music, High 5, Channel 4, 1997; New Age Jazz, ambient music for Midnight Music, film for TV, Los Angeles; Compositions for: Sarah Jory, Joe Cocker; I Wanna Be There, Prudential Mexico '97. *Recordings:* Writer/producer for artists including: Bonnie Tyler; Kim Wlde; Elkie Brooks; Ringo Starr; Holly Johnson; Cliff Richard; Jim Diamond; Sheila Ferguson; Robin Gibb; Nik Kershaw; Hazel Dean; Zak Starkey; Hazel O'Connor; Catherine Zeta-Jones; Produced: Sinitta; Edwin Star; Phil Fearon; John Parr; Mike Peters/Eddie McDonald (The Alarm); Steve Harley; Suggs (Madness); Bucks Fizz; Chas and Dave; Brinsley Forde/Drummie Zeb (Aswad); Nick Heywood; The Icicle Works; Elvis Costello; Thompson Twins; Sarah Jory; Joe Cocker. *Honour:* Royal Academy Artist. *Memberships:* PRS; Equity. *Current Management:* Veracruz Music International. *Address:* 43 Capron Rd, Dunstable, Bedfordshire LU5 5AL, England.

FOSSATI Ramon; b. 14 Sept. 1965, Barcelona, Spain. Musician (guitar, trombone); Composer; Prod. *Career:* Creator, co-leader, Paris-Barcelona Swing Connection; Played with Frank Wess; Teddy Edwards; Wild Bill Davis; Performed at Jazz Vienne (France), 1993; Jazz Festival, Birmingham, 1992–94; Terrassa, Spain, 1993–95; Frankfurt, 1995; More than 500 concerts around Europe. *Recordings:* with the Paris-Barcelona Swing Connection: Hard Swing; Live In Barcelona; with Frank Wess: Frank Wess Meets The Paris-Barcelona Swing Connection; with Wild Bill Davis: Wild Cat. *Current Management:* Foscar Society. *Address:* 41 Ave Saint Saëns, 91600 Savigny Sur Orge, France.

FOSSEN Sverre; b. 4 Oct. 1973, Trondheim, Norway. Musician (guitar). *Education:* College. *Career:* Joined Hedge Hog, 1990; Several tours, Norway; Toured Europe, 1994, 1995. *Recordings:* Erase, 1992; Surprise, 1992; Primal Gutter, 1993; Mercury Red, 1994; Mindless, 1994; The Healing EP, 1995; Thorn Cord Wonder, 1995. *Publications:* Sverre – A Voice From the Gutter, 1994. *Membership:* Norwegian Asscn of Musicians. *Leisure interests:* Painting; Football.

FOSTER Geoff; b. 5 May 1965, Wimbledon, London, England. Recording Engineer. Partner: Dawn Tait, 2 d. *Education:* Marlborough College; Brunel University; Electronics Degree. *Career:* Worked for Stones Mobile, 1985; Cold Storage Studios, 1986; Air Studios, 1987; Chief Engineer, 1994. *Recordings:* Film scores: Stargate; Restoration; Romeo and Juliet; Mighty Ducks 3; Don Juan de Marco; Last of the Dogmen; Meet Wally Sparks; Smilla's Sense of Snow; Photographing Fairies; Alien Love Triangle; Amy Foster; B. Monkey; Black Beauty; City of Angels; Cousin Bette; Dreaming of Joseph Lees; Entrapment; Great Expectations; Jack and Sarah; James and the Giant Peach; Les Visiteurs; Loss of Sexual Innocence; Lost Souls; Mickey Blue Eyes; Midsummers Night Dream; Peacemaker; Plunkett and Macleane; Pola X; Prince of Egypt; Purdita Durango; Ride with the Devil;

Robinson Crusoe; Shadows of the Empire; Summer of Sam; The Avengers; The Beach; The Bone Collector; The Gold Diggers; The Last September; The Matchmaker; The Other Conquest; The Place of Lions; The Visitor; The War Zone; Tobacco Project; Tomorrow Never Dies; The World Is Not Enough; Tropical Island Hum; Une Femme Francaise; What Dreams May Come True; Wing Commander; Wings of a Dove; When A Man Loves A Woman; Albums: George Martin; Martin Okasili; John Martyn; Crowded House; Debbie Harry; Hothouse Flowers; Jethro Tull; Grace Jones; Pulp; Roachford; Robert Palmer; Sting; The Pretenders; Paul Carrack; Radiohead; The The; Kula Shaker; David Essex; José Carreras; Vanessa-Mae; John Williams; Akin; Akira; Alishas Attick; All Saints; Baby Bird; Bjork; Blur; Bone Muffin; Cast; Cilla Black; Dario G; David Cassidy; Petula Clarke; David McCalmont; Debbie Gibson; Eliza Carthy; Elkie Brooks; Elton John; Fine Young Cannibals; Fredrick; Garbage; Gary Barlow; Gilbert O'Sullivan; Hombres G; Irene Barnes; Jimmy Nail; Joni Mitchell; Jo Hisaishi; Phil Collins; Leftfield; Lisa Stone; Madonna; Maestro Hattori; Mel C; Michael Ball; Michael Jackson; Michael Crawford; Mike Oldfield; Ofra Haza; Outfield; Paul Brady; Peter Cox; Phil Campbell; Rolph Harris; Rory McLeod; Sisters of Mercy; Stephen Duffy; Nigel Kennedy; Sugar Ray; The Pet Shop Boys; The Trash Can Sinatras; Tyrell Corporation; Virginia McNaughton; Yell; Eliza Carthy; Ute Lemper; Pulp; Sir Neville Marriner; Placido Domingo; Giselle Bendor; Jose Carreras; Kiri Te Kawana; John Adams. *Membership:* AMIEE. *Current Management:* Air Management, Lyndhurst Hall, Lyndhurst Road, London NW3 5NG, England.

FOUNTAIN Peter; b. 3 July 1930, New Orleans, LA, USA. Clarinettist. m. Beverly, 27 Oct. 1951, 2 s., 1 d. *Career:* Operator night club Pete Fountain's New Orleans; Member, Basin Street Six, 1949–54, Lawrence Walk Orchestra, 1957–60; Leader, own group; Appeared in (films), Pete Fountain Sextet, 1962, Pete's Place, 1966, The New Orleans Jazz Museum, 1967; Featured in: PBS spl, Dukes of Dixieland and Friends, 1980; Featured Guest with major orchestras throughout world; Co-author: A Closer Walk: The Pete Fountain Story, 1972; Appeared on Johnny Carson Show, 59 times; Performed for Papal visit, White House for Presidents Eisenhower, Nixon, Ford and Reagan, 1987. *Recordings:* 85 albums including: The Blues; Down on Rampart Street; Swingin' Blues, 1991; High Society, 1992; Cheek to Cheek, 1993. *Honours:* 3 Gold Albums; 1 Gold Single (A Closer Walk). *Address:* 2 Poydras St, New Orleans, LA 70130–1656, USA.

FOWLER Simon; b. 25 April 1965, Birmingham, England. Vocalist; Musician (guitar). *Career:* Formed The Fanatics with Damon Minchella; Formed Ocean Colour Scene; Gained recording deal with indie label !Phffft, taken over by Fontana; Many support slots on tours including Paul Weller's 1993 tour; Joined Paul Weller as backing vocalist, 1993; Support to Oasis tour, 1994; Major record deal, 1995; Numerous TV and radio appearances; Riverboat Song used as theme tune for TV show TFI Friday; Several headlining tours. *Recordings:* Singles: With Fanatics, Suburban Love Songs EP; Riverboat Song, 1996; The Day We Caught The Train, 1996; You've Got It Bad, 1996; The Circle, 1996; 100 Mile High City, 1997; Travellers Tune, 1997; Better Day, 1997; It's A Beautiful Thing, 1998; July/I Am The News, 2000; Up On The Downside, 2001; Albums: Ocean Colour Scene, 1992; Moseley Shoals, 1996; B-Sides, Seasides and Freerides, 1997; Marchin' Already (No. 1, UK), 1997; One From The Modern, 1999; Mechanical Wonder, 2001; Songs For The Front Row (compilation), 2001. *Internet:* www.oceancolourscene.com.

FOX Angela; b. 31 July 1960, Birkenhead, Cheshire, England. Musician (guitar, dulcimer); Singer. *Career:* Appearances most folk clubs, festivals, New Zealand; Several radio appearances includes National radio interview, during tour, 1991; Television, 1995. *Recordings:* Two solo albums: Takin' A Chance, 1990; Deceptive Love, 1992; Worked on over 50 recording projects as session vocalist, guitarist, arranger, second engineer, producer. *Honours:* Nominee, New Zealand Music Award. *Leisure interests:* Music; Art. *Address:* 193 Scenic Dr., Titirangi, Auckland, New Zealand.

FOX Donal L; b. 17 July 1952, Boston, Massachusetts, USA. Composer; Musician (Piano); Improviser, Jazz and Classical. *Education:* New England Conservatory of Music, 1962–64; Berklee College of Music, 1968; Berkshire Music Center, Tanglewood, 1969; Studied Theory and Counterpoint with Avram David, 1972–74, Composition and Harmony with T J Anderson, 1975–76, Composition and Orchestration with Gunther Schuller, 1977–82. *Career:* TV Show, Donal Fox and David Murray in Session, 1993; The Fox/Troupe Project, TV show, 1993; World premiere of Oliver Lake's Movements Turns and Switches for violin and piano, Library of Congress, Washington, piano and improviser, with Regina Carter, violin, 1993; World premiere, The Demon, International Ottawa Jazz Festival, National Gallery of Canada, 1995; World premiere of Anthony Kelley's Africamerica, for piano and orchestra, piano and improviser, 1999. *Compositions:* Dialectics for Two Grand Pianos, 1988; Variants on a Theme by Monk, for alto saxophone and piano, 1990; Jazz Sets and Tone Rows, for alto saxophone and piano, 1990; Vamping with T.T., for bass clarinet and piano, 1993; T-Cell Countdown, for voice, piano and double

bass, 1993; River Town Packin House Blues, The Old People Speak of Death, Following the North Star Boogaloo, for piano and poet, 1993; Gone City, ballet in three movements, for clarinet, piano and double bass, 1994. *Recordings:* Boston Duets, 1992; Videmus, 1992; Ugly Beauty, 1995; Donal Fox: Mellow Mood, 1996; Donal Fox: Gone City, 1997. *Honours:* Meet the Composer/Rockefeller Foundation/National Endowment for the Arts Grant, 1991; Guggenheim Fellowship in Music Composition, 1997; Bogliasco Fellowship in Music Composition, 1998; Djerassi Foundation Fellowship in Music Composition, 1999. *Memberships:* Massachusetts Cultural Council, 1984–; BMI, 1993-. *Leisure interests:* Running; Cycling; Camping. *Current Management:* Leonellis Music. *Address:* 14 Highland Park Ave, Roxbury, MA 02119, USA.

FOX George William; b. 23 March 1960, Cochrane, Alberta, Canada. Singer; Songwriter. *Career:* Over 75 TV appearances include: George Fox's New Country, CBC, 1990; Nashville Now, 1991; Newsworld, CBC, 1992; Tommy Hunter Show, 1992; All About Country, 1992; Country Gold, 1992; Canada Day – Seville, Spain, 1992; New Year's Eve Niagara, Baton Broadcasting, 1993; Crook and Chase, TNN, 1993; Sang National Anthem, World Series, Toronto, 1993; Juno Awards, 1989–94, 1996; Rita and Friends, CBC, 1994, 1995; George Fox – Time of My Life, CBC Special, 1995; Terri Clark – Coming Home, 1998; A George Fox Christmas, CBC Special, 1999. *Compositions:* Angelina, 1988; Mustang Heart, 1993; Breakfast Alone, 1993; Honest Man, 1993; No Hasta La Vista Tonight; 1994; Wear and Tear On My Heart, 1994; What's Holding Me, 1995; First Comes Love, 1995; I Give You My Word, 1997; Survivor, 1998; How Do I Get There From Her, 1999. *Recordings:* George Fox (Gold), 1988; With All My Might (Gold), 1989; Spice of Life, 1991; Mustang Heart (Gold), 1993; Time of My Life (Gold), 1995; Greatest Hits 1987–97, 1997 (Gold); Survivor, 1998; A George Fox Christmas, 1999. *Honours:* Canadian Country Music Asscn, Vista Rising Star, 1989; Country Male Vocalist, 1989–93; Juno Awards, Country Male Vocalist of Year, 1990, 1991, 1992; SOCAN Song of Year, Clearly Canadian, 1993. *Memberships:* CARAS; NARAS; CMA; CCMA; ACTRA; AFofM. *Leisure interests:* Hiking; Farming. *Address:* c/o Balmur Inc, 1105 17th Ave, Nashville, TN 37212, USA.

FOX John, (David Bell, Peter Balding); b. 30 April 1926, Sutton, Surrey, England. Composer; Arranger; Conductor; Musician (piano). m. Joy Devon, 17 May 1980, 2 s., 1 d. *Musical Education:* Royal College of Music (ARCM); Composition scholarship, Fitznells College of Music. *Career:* Pianist, arranger, numerous groups; Arranger, conductor, BBC Radio Orchestra, 1960s; Conducted Krakow Radio Symphony Orchestra, recordings, Poland; Broadcasts with John Fox Orchestra and voices; Recorded in London, Customs easy listening music for USA networks; Over 200 easy listening arrangements on the internet; Concerts: John Fox Concerts, BBC, Pebble Mill, Musical World of John Fox, Magic of John Fox (London), Numerous String Sound and Romantic Strings, broadcast sessions, 1980s; Also acapella broadcasts with John Fox Singers, Friday Night Is Music Night, BBC Radio; Conductor, arranger, for concerts with vocalist (wife) Joy Devon, Philharmonie Concert Hall, Cologne, Germany; Performed Earth and Space Suite, Huntingdon, England; Owner, publishing company, Coniston Music Publishing; The Musical World of John Fox Talks with musical illustrations at different venues throughout the UK and USA. *Compositions:* Over 1,500 published works with Sonoton Music, Amphonic Music and Sound Stage, EMI; Arrangements: well over 1,000 in BBC Music Library. *Recordings:* Memory; Unforgettable Melodies, Nos 1 and 2; Love Is A Many-Splendoured Thing; Whispers of Love; Pomp and Glory; Heartstrings; Earth and Space; Sailing By; Two's Company; Instrumental Pops (series); John Fox Presents, Vols 1–18; with J F Orchestra and Voices: Gershwin; Here There and Everywhere; with J F Singers: Fairest Isle; Animal Lovers; Listen Easy (1) 60's; Listen Easy (2) 70's (BBC World-wide); Produced (with Joy Devon) albums own material (with large symphony orchestras), Munich, Berlin, Leipzig, London, Yugoslavia, Budapest, Poland. *Honours:* STEMRA Music Award, Netherlands, for Best Film, 1993. *Memberships:* PRS; MCPS; MU; APC; BASCA. *Leisure interests:* Walking dog; Follower of cricket and rugby; Travel; Swimming. *Current Management:* Coniston Music Publishing Co, 26 Garratts Lane, Banstead, Surrey SM7 2EA, England.

FRAITURE Nikolai; b. 13 Nov. 1979, New York City, USA. Musician (bass guitar). *Career:* Member: The Strokes, 1998-. *Recordings:* Albums: Is This It, 2001; Singles: The Modern Age, Hard To Explain/New York City Cops, Last Nite/When It Started, 2001. *Honours:* Brit Award, Best International Newcomer, 2002; NME Awards: Band of The Year; Best New Act; Album of The Year, 2001. *Current Management:* Ryan Gentles, Wiz Kid Management. *Internet:* www.thestrokes.com.

FRAME Roddy; b. 29 Jan. 1964, East Kilbride, Scotland. Singer; Songwriter; Musician (guitar). *Career:* Founder member, Aztec Camera, 1980–; International appearances include: Support to Elvis Costello, US, 1983; The Ritz, New York, 1985; Royal Albert Hall, 1988; Cambridge Folk Festival, 1991; Edinburgh Festival, 1991; Support to Bob Dylan, 1993; Phoenix Festival, 1995. *Compositions include:* Composed all songs on albums. *Recordings:* Singles include: Oblivious, 1983; Walk Out To

Winter, 1983; How Men Are, 1988; Somewhere In My Heart, 1988; Working In A Goldmine, 1988; Good Morning Britain, 1990; Spanish Horses, 1992; Sun, 1995; Reasons for Living, 1998; Albums: High Land, Hard Rain, 1983; Knife, 1984; Love, 1987; Stray, 1990; Dreamland, 1993; Frestonia, 1995; North Star, 1998; The Best of Aztec Camera (compilation), 1999; Contributor to: Red Hot + Blue, 1990; Ruby Trax (duet with Andy Fairweather-Low), 1992. *Honours include:* Gold Discs: High Land Hard Rain, 1983; Knife, 1985; Platinum disc, Love, 1988. *Current Management:* Southside Management, 20 Cromwell Mews, London SW7 2JY, England.

FRAMPTON Peter; b. 22 April 1950, Beckenham, Kent, England. Musician (guitar); Singer. *Career:* Member, The Herd; Session musician, Johnny Hallyday; Member, Humble Pie, 1969–71; Solo artiste, 1971–; Performances include: Support to J Geils Band, New York, 1972; Don Kirshner's Second Annual Rock Music Awards, CBS, 1976; Madison Square Garden, New York, 1979; Guitarist, Glass Spider tour, David Bowie, 1987; Tour with Stevie Nicks, 1987; Formed new backing band, Escape, 1990; Appearance, Lynyrd Skynyrd and Friends 20th Anniversary concert, 1993; Film appearance, Sgt Pepper's Lonely Hearts Club Band, 1978. *Recordings:* Albums with Humble Pie: As Safe As Yesterday Is, 1969; Town and Country, 1969; Humble Pie, 1971; Rock On, 1971; Performance – Rockin' The Fillmore, 1972; Solo albums: Wind of Change, 1972; Frampton's Camel, 1973; Somethin's Happening, 1974; Frampton, 1974; Frampton Comes Alive, 1976; I'm In You, 1977; Where Should I Be, 1979; Breaking All The Rules, 1981; The Art of Control, 1982; Premonition, 1983; Peter Frampton Classics, 1987; New World, 1988; When All The Pieces Fit, 1989; Shine On – A Collection, 1992; Peter Frampton, 1994; Peter Frampton Comes Alive II, 1995; Love Taker, 1995; Winds of Change, 1998; A Day in the Sun, 1999; Beat the Bootleggers, 1999; Live In Detroit, 2000; Solo singles include: Show Me The Way, 1976; Baby I Love Your Way, 1976; Signed, Sealed Delivered (I'm Yours), 1977; I Can't Stand No More, 1979; The Bigger They Come, featured in film Harley Davidson and The Marlboro Man, 1991. *Honours include:* Gold Ticket, Madison Square Gardens, 1979. *Address:* Firstars, 3520 Hayden Ave, Culver City, CA 90232, USA.

FRANCE Martin Perry; b. 29 Feb. 1964, Rainham, Kent, England. Musician (drums, percussion). *Musical Education:* Music O Level; 10 year's private study. *Career:* To date Performed in 36 countries, all usually recorded for television/radio; Featured in various newspapers, music magazines; Performed with many leading jazz musicians; 1994-, working in new quartet led by Kenny Wheeler with John Taylor, Dave Holland. *Recordings:* First House: Erendira; Cantilena; Iain Bellamy: Balloon Man; All Men Amen; Cleveland Watkiss: Green Chimneys; Julian Argnelles: Phaedrus; Django Bates: Music For The Third Policeman; Summer Fruits and Unrest; Winter Truce and Homes Blaze; Django Bates; Loose Tubes: Loose Tubes Live; Human Chain: Pyrotechnics; Mark Lockheart: Clec; Perfect Houseplants; New Folk Songs, 2001; Billy Jenkins: Aural Art; Sounds Like Bromley; Summer Fest; Eddie Parker: Eddie Parker; Buckley/Batchelor: Whole and The Half; Arguelles, Swallow, Walker and France. *Current Management:* P Partnerships, 5 Dryden St, London WC2 9NW. *Address:* 2 Dewhurst Lane, Wadhurst, E Sussex, England.

FRANCE Nicolas Michael; b. 30 March 1956, Standon, Hertfordshire, England. Musician (percussion, drums, piano). m. Billie (Susan Mary) Preston, 21 Oct. 1983, 1 s., 2 d. *Musical Education:* Chorister, Ely Cathedral; G Mus Diploma (Music), CCAT, Cambridge. *Career:* Professional musician, 1980–; Worked with: Tanita Tikaram; Bill Withers; Jackie Graham; Working Week; Mose Allison; Recorded with Pete Townshend; Thomas Dolby; L Shankar; Session player with artists including: Phil Todd; Robbie Macintosh; Snake Davies; Laurence and Richard Cottle; Danny Cummings; Martin Ditcham; Played with jazz artists including: Loose Tubes; Ronnie Scott Quintet; John Taylor; Alan Holdsworth; Jim Mullen; Concerts and tours include: Tours with Loose Tubes, 1983–86; 3 European tours, 3 festivals with Working Week, 1984–87; 2 tours, UK, Europe, 1988–89; Tour, including Montreux and Nice festivals, with Heitor; 3 world tours with Tanita Tikaram, 1990–95. *Recordings:* with Loose Tubes: Loose Tubes; Delightful Precipice, 1983–85; The Way Through The Woods, Bronte Brothers, 1993; Johnson, The Fat Lady Sings, 1993; with The Working Week: Working Nights; Companeros; Fire In The Mountain; Rodrigo Bay from Absolute Beginners; Fire In The Mountain; Supergrass; Comic Strip Movie (film soundtrack), 1984–87; with Tanita Tikaram: Everybody's Angel; Eleven Kinds of Loneliness; Lovers In The City, 1990–95. *Honour:* G Mus, Music diploma. *Membership:* PRS. *Leisure interests:* Tennis; Cycling.

FRANCES Andrew; b. 17 March 1950, New York City, USA. Record Co Exec.; Prod.; Man. *Education:* Graduated New York City High School of the performing Arts; Bachelor degree, Northwestern University. *Career:* Worked for labels: MCA; RCA; Millenium; RSO; Founded own labels: Chameleon/Elektra; North South/Atlantic; Grammy Award-winning recordings on own labels; Own management company Adwater and Stir; Artists handled include: David Bowie; Wang Chung; Ruth McCartney;

Benny Mardones. *Memberships:* NARAS; CMA. *Leisure interest:* Volleyball. *Address:* 1303 16th Ave S, Nashville, TN 37212, USA.

FRANCIS Chris; b. 11 Aug. 1948, London, England. Bandleader; Jazz Musician (alto/soprano saxophone, G flute). m. Penny, 1976, 1 s. *Education:* Manchester and Chelsea Art Schools. *Musical Education:* Studied privately. *Career:* Founded Naima, band ranging from trio to fifteen piece, toured Europe, Britain; Founder member, Joy quintet; Recorded with many pop stars, toured with rock bands and folk groups. *Recordings:* Herm Island Suite, BBC Radio; (session man) Adam Ant: Goody Two Shoes; Numerous broadcasts of own compositions. *Honours:* Joint winner, GLAA: Young Jazz Musicans Award, 1976. *Memberships:* Musicians' Union; PRS; MCPS. *Leisure interests:* Painting; Photography; Sailing. *Current Management:* Art Services. *Address:* 10a Putney High St, London SW15 1SL, England.

FRANCIS Connie, (Concetta Rosa Maria Franconero); b. 12 Dec. 1938, Newark, New Jersey, USA. Singer. *Musical Education:* Began playing accordion age 4. *Career:* Professional musician, 1949–; Winner, Arthur Godfrey Talent Show; Recording artiste, 1955–; Charity work for organizations including UNICEF; Entertained US troops, Viet Nam, 1960s; Retired from public performance, 1970s; Resumed performances, 1981–; London Palladium, 1989; Las Vegas, 1989. *Recordings:* Albums include: Who's Sorry Now?, 1958; The Exciting Connie Francis, 1959; My Thanks To You, 1959; Italian Favourites, 1960; Rock 'n' Roll Million Sellers, 1960; Country and Western Golden Hits, 1960; Sings Great Jewish Favorites, 1961; Songs To A Swinging Band, 1961; Never On Sunday, 1961; Folk Song Favorites, 1961; Do The Twist, 1962; Second Hand Love and Other Hits, 1962; Country Music Connie Style, 1962; Modern Italian Hits, 1963; In The Summer of His Years, 1964; Great Country Favourites, with Hank Williams Jr, 1964; A New Kind of Connie, 1964; Connie Francis Sings For Mama, 1965; Love Italian Style, 1967; Happiness, 1967; My Heart Cries For You, 1967; Hawaii Connie, 1968; Connie and Clyde, 1968; The Wedding Cake, 1969; Connie Francis Sings Great Country Hits, Vol. 2, 1973; Sings The Big Band Hits, 1977; I'm Me Again – Silver Anniversary Album, 1981; Connie Francis and Peter Kraus, Vols 1 and 2, 1984; Country Store, 1988; Various compilations including: Star Power, 2001; UK No. 1 singles: Who's Sorry Now; Stupid Cupid; US No. 1 singles: Everybody's Somebody's Fool; My Mind Has A Heart of Its Own; Don't Break The Heart That Loves You. *Current Management:* Stan Scottland c/o JKES Services Inc. *Address:* 404 Park Ave S, 10th Floor, New York, NY 10016, USA.

FRANCIS Eddie; b. Ontario, Canada. Country Singer; Writer; Musician (Guitar). *Education:* BA; BEd. *Career:* Various Radio Appearances; Singer, Musician In Countless Shows; Actor, Singer In Various Amateur Theatres. *Composition:* Peterson Road. *Recordings:* CD Album, Hills and Valleys. *Memberships:* CCMA; OSSTF. *Leisure interests:* Operating A Small Farm; Travel. *Current Management:* Independent Associate In Commonlight Music Canada. *Address:* PO Box 186 Mill St, Combermere, ON Canada K0J 1L0.

FRANCIS Terry, (Love Panda); b. 1966, Leatherhead, Surrey, England. Prod.; Remixer; DJ. *Career:* Began DJ career at the legendary Stern's Club; Co-founder: Wiggle Records and underground house night in London with Nathan Coles; Compiler and mixer of Architecture series for Pagan Records; Resident DJ at Fabric club in London; Member: 2 Smokin' Barrels; The Delinquents; Collaborations: Nathan Coles; Housey Doingz. *Recordings:* Albums: Architecture Vols 1 and 2 (DJ-mixed compilations); Singles: Dub Town, 1997; Took From Me, 1998; Breaking The Law EP (with The Delinquents), 1998; Smokey Rooms EP, 1999; Strong Woman EP, 2001. *Honours:* Muzik Awards, Best New DJ, 1997. *Address:* c/o Wiggle Records, 2 Vanbrugh Park Rd W, Blackheath, London, SE3 7QD, England.

FRANCOMBE Mark; b. 4 Dec. 1963, Ongar, Essex, England. Musician (guitar, bass, keyboards). *Education:* Portsmouth Art College. *Career:* Numerous tours of Europe and USA with the Cranes; Also support tour with The Cure, USA and Europe, 1992; Various radio and television appearances include: 2 sessions on John Peel show, BBC Radio 1; MTV; Snub TV, BBC. *Recordings:* with The Cranes: Self Non Self; Wings of Joy; Forever Loved; Radio Oddyssey, 1996; Population 4, 1997. *Leisure interests:* Side project Eardrum; Fire walking. *Current Management:* Adrian Maddox; Agent: AMPI.

FRANKLIN Aretha; b. 25 March 1942, Memphis, Tennessee, USA. Singer; Songwriter. m. Glynn Turman, 1978. *Career:* Recording artist, 1960–; European tour, 1968; Appearances include: Inaugural Eve Gala, Jimmy Carter, Washington DC; Jamaica World Music Festival, 1982; Budweiser Superfest, 1982; Actress, film The Blues Brothers, 1980; Subject, TV specials: Aretha Franklin – The Queen of Soul, 1988; Aretha Franklin – Duets, 1993. *Recordings:* Albums include: The Great Aretha Franklin, 1960; The Electrifying Aretha Franklin, 1962; The Tender, The Moving, The Swinging, 1962; Unforgettable – A Tribute To Dinah Washington, 1964; Runnin' Out of Fools, 1965; Yeah!!!, 1965; Soul Sister, 1966; I Never Loved A Man (The Way I Loved You), 1967; Aretha Arrives,

1967; Aretha: Lady Soul, 1968; Aretha In Paris, 1968; This Girl's In Love With You, 1969; Spirit In The Dark, 1970; Aretha Live At Fillmore West, 1971; Amazing Grace, 1972; Hey Now Hey (The Other Side of The Sky), 1973; Let Me In Your Life, 1974; With Everything I Feel In Me, 1975; You, 1975; Sweet Passion, 1977; Almighty Fire, 1978; La Diva, 1979; Aretha, 1980; Love All The Hurt Away, 1981; Jump To It, 1982; Get It Right, 1983; Who's Zoomin' Who?, 1985; The First Lady of Soul, 1986; Aretha, 1987; One Lord, One Faith, One Baptism, 1988; Through The Storm, 1989; What You See Is What You Sweat, 1991; Queen of Soul, 1993; Greatest Hits 1980–94, 1994; A Rose Is Still A Rose, 1998; You Grow Closer, 1998; Love Songs, 2001; Hit singles include: I Never Loved A Man (The Way I Loved You), 1967; Respect (No. 1, USA), 1967; Baby I Love You, 1967; (You Make Me Feel Like A) Natural Woman, 1967; Chain of Fools, 1968; (Sweet Sweet Baby) Since You've Been Gone, 1968; Think, 1968; I Say A Little Prayer, 1968; Call Me, 1970; Don't Play That Song, 1970; You're All I Need To Get By, 1971; Rock Steady, 1972; Young Gifted and Black, 1972; Day Dreaming, 1972; Until You Come Back To Me, 1974; Sisters Are Doin' It For Themselves, duet with Annie Lennox, 1985; I Knew You Were Waiting For Me, duet with George Michael (No. 1, UK and US), 1987; Through The Storm, duet with Elton John, 1989; Contributor, film soundtracks including: Sparkle, 1976; Jumpin' Jack Flash, 1986; White Men Can't Jump, 1992. *Honours include:* Aretha Franklin Day, Detroit, 1967; Numerous Grammy Awards, 1968–; American Music Awards; Inducted into Rock 'n' Roll Hall of Fame, 1987; Living Legend Award, NARAS, 1990; Rhythm and Blues Foundation Lifetime Achievement Award, 1992. *Current Management:* Aretha Franklin Management, 30150 Telegraph Rd, Suite 444, Birmingham, MI 48025, USA.

FRANOLIC Drazen; b. 4 July 1961, Biograd, Croatia. Musician (Arabian lute); Composer. m. Vesna Gorse, 20 June 1992. *Career:* Member, Franolic-Gorse Duo; Gorse-Franolic Trio; Tao; Concerts: Zagreb; Belgrade; Ljubljana; Sarajevo; Rijeka; Dubrovnik; Italy; Czechoslovakia; Live album recordings, Lisinsui Concert Hall, 1992, 1995. *Recordings:* with Vesna Gorse: Waterfalls, 1986; New Era of Instrumental Music, 1990; Wonderland, 1990; Asgard Live, 1993; Just A Music, 1995. *Honours:* 2 Porin Award Nominations, Asgard Live, 1994. *Memberships:* Croatian Composers' Society; Croatian Music Union; Amnesty International. *Leisure interest:* Films. *Current Management:* Vesna Gorse. *Address:* Vankina 3/4, 41020 Zagreb, Croatia.

FRANZÉN K B V Hawkey; b. 29 March 1946, Böda, Kalmarlän, Sweden. Composer; Singer; Songwriter; Artist; Actor (Guitar, Keyboard, Accordion, Ten Sax). *Career:* Lea Riders Group, 1962–68; Jason's Fleece, 1970–71; Solo Performer, Theatremusic-composer and for radio and TV; Filmmusic, Dom Kallar Oss Mods (They Call Us Misfits). *Compositions:* LP: Visa Från Djupvik, 1969; Visa Från Gungor och Sand, 1970; Visa Från och Till, 1971; Jason's Fleece, 1970; Visa Av och Med, 1972; Smulvisor and Bitlåtar, 1981; Det Blåser På Månen, 1985; Plötsligt Skulle Vi Skiljas, 1988. *Recordings:* Lea Riders Group, 1989; Många Varv Kring Solen, CD, 1996. *Honours:* Stockholm City; Prize for Best Private Theatre Play, 1969; Konstnärsnämnden, Arts Grants Cttee Schlsps, 1971, 1975, 1985, 1986, 1989, 1990, 1992, 1993, 1996, 1997, 1998; STIM, Swedish Performing Rights Society, 1995, 1997. *Memberships:* Swedish Performing Rights Society; Swedish Society of Popular Music Composers; Swedish Artists and Musicians Interest Organisation; Svenska Teaterförbundet, Swedish Actors Equity Asscn. *Leisure interests:* Nature; Reading. *Current Management:* Linnéa Musik Produktion. *Address:* Nygatan 5 nb, 599 31 Ödeshög, Sweden.

FRASER Elizabeth; b. 29 Aug. 1963, Grangemouth, Scotland. Singer. 1 d. *Career:* Member, Cocteau Twins; Sang on collective projects with This Mortal Coil; Collaboration with pianist Harold Budd; Guest appearances with Ian McCullough on Candleland album, with Future Sound of London on Lifeforms, with Massive Attack on Teardrop single and tracks on their Mezzanine album. *Recordings:* Singles: Lullabies, 1982; Peppermint Pig, 1983; Sunburst and Snowblind, 1983; Pearly Dewdrops' Drops, 1984; Aikea-Guinea, 1985; Tiny Dynamine, 1985; Echoes in a Shallow Bay, 1985; Love's Easy Tears, 1986; Iceblink Luck, 1990; Evangeline, 1993; Frosty the Snowman, 1993; Bluebeard, 1994; Twinlights, 1995; Otherness, 1995 Tishbite, 1996; Violaine, 1996; with This Mortal Coil, Song to the Siren, 1983; Teardrop, with Massive Attack, 1998; Albums: Garlands, 1982; Head Over Heals, 1983; Treasure, 1984; The Pink Opaque, 1985; Victorialand, 1986; The Moon and the Melodies, with Harold Budd, 1986; Blue Bell Knoll, 1988; Heaven or Las Vegas, 1990; Four Calendar Café, 1993; Milk and Kisses, 1996; The BBC Sessions, 1999; Stars and Topsoil (compilation), 2000.

FRATER Josephine; b. 16 May 1963, Glasgow, Scotland. Singer; Composer; Musician (percussion). m. Stephen D Taylor, 6 Sept. 1991. *Musical Education:* Goldsmiths University; Guildhall School of Music and Drama. *Career:* Joint owner, i.2.i Records with Steve Taylor; Co-run The Runners with Steve Taylor; Appeared on cable TV; Concerts include: Ronnie Scott's; The Jazz Cafe; British tour; International tour, 1996. *Compositions:* Hours; Crooked Man; Be Yourself Tonight; Secret World; Journeying. *Recordings:* Album: Phonetic. *Honours:* Advanced Certificate

Jazz and Pop Music; Postgraduate diploma, Jazz and Studio Music. *Memberships:* PRS; Musicians' Union. *Leisure interests:* Travel; Gardening; Art; Cycling; Socialising. *Address:* PO Box 7038, London N3 2HF, England.

FRAZIER Stan (Charles Stanton); b. 23 April 1968. Musician (drums). *Career:* Played colleges and parties with local group The Tories; Group became The Shrinky Dinx; Signed to Atlantic Records following circulation of self-made demo video; Act renamed Sugar Ray owing to threat of legal action prior to record releases; Built up world-wide fanbase through touring and TV appearances; Cameo in Fathers Day film, 1997. *Recordings:* Albums: Lemonade and Brownies, 1995; Floored, 1997; 14–59, 1999; Sugar Ray, 2001; Singles: Mean Machine, Iron Mic, 1995; Fly, RPM, 1997; Every Morning, Someday, 1999; Falls Apart, 2000; When It's Over, Answer The Phone, 2001. *Honours:* Second/third albums certified double/triple platinum by RIAA respectively. *Address:* c/o PO Box 12018, Costa Mesa, CA 92627, USA. *E-mail:* management@sugarray.com. *Internet:* www.sugarray.com.

FREDERICKX Jan; b. 30 Sept. 1971, Mol, Belgium. Singer; Songwriter; Musician (Bass, Guitar). *Education:* Ancient Latin and Greek Languages; Psychology; Socio-Cultural Sciences. *Musical Education:* Classical Guitar, Music Academy, Geel, Belgium, two years; Self-taught Bass Guitar. *Career:* Played in bands including: Hellsaw; MSD; Extreem; Acoustic Grinder; Concerts with: Napalm Death; Extreme Noise Terror; The Varukers; Death; The Gathering; Doom; John Peel-Session, BRTN Session; 3 official live videos, BRTN TV. *Compositions:* Agathocles: Riek Boois, 1988; Cabbalic Gnosticism, 1988; Disgorge, 1989; Fascination of Mutilation, 1989; If This is Cruel, 1989; Violent Noise Attack, 1990; Blood, 1990; Putrid Offal, 1990; Morbid Organs Mutilation, 1990; Nasum, 1990; Agarchy, 1991; Psycho, 1991; Violent Headache, 1992; Kompost, 1993; Distrust and Abuse, 1993; Nyctophobic, 1993; Man is the Bastard, 1993; Patareni, 1993; Audiorrea, 1993; Social Genocide, 1993; No Use (Hatred), 1993; Punisher, 1994; Carcass Grinder, 1994; Plastic Grave, 1994; Back to 1987, 1994; Mincemongers in Barna, 1994; Unholy Grave, 1996; Praparation H, 1996; Krush, 1996; Excruciating Terror, 1997; Shikabane, 1997; Theatric Symbolisation of Life, 1991; Black Clouds of Determinate, 1994; Black Sharp Daggers, 1995; Thanks for Your Hostility, 1996; Humarrogance, 1997; Agathocles Tribute CD, South Africa; X-piration, 1997; Deadmocracy, 1998; Bloodsuckers, 1998; Skitliv, 1998; Unholy Grave, 1999; Grind Buto, 1999. *Honours:* BRTN, Session, 1996; John Peel, Session, 1997; Kill Your Idols, CD, Tribute to Agathocles CD. *Leisure interests:* Writing Poetry; Painting; Cooking; Workshops. *Current Management:* Agathocles, Asberg 8, 2400 Mol, Belgium.

FREDERIKSEN Lars; b. 1972. Musician (guitar); Vocalist. m. Megan, 1998. *Career:* Member, UK Subs; Joined Cajones; Formed Slip, 1992, gigged with Rancid; Joined Rancid; Numerous live shows. *Recordings:* Singles: Radio, Radio, Radio, 1994; Roots Radicals, 1995; Time Bomb, 1995; Ruby Soho, 1996; Bloodclot, 1998; Hooligans, 1998; Brad Logan, 1998; Albums: Let's Go, 1994; And Out Come the Wolves, 1995; Life Won't Wait, 1998; Rancid, 2000.

FREDRICKSSON Marie; b. 29 May 1958, Sweden. Singer. 1 d. *Career:* Solo recording artist, 1980s; Formed Roxette with Per Gessle, 1986–; 21m. albums sold, 12m. singles sold world-wide; Appearances in Europe; North America; Central and South America; Television includes: The Tonight Show, NBC TV; MTV Unplugged. *Recordings:* Albums: Pearls of Passion, 1986; Look Sharp!, 1988; Joyride, 1991; Tourism, 1992; Den Sjunde Vagen, 1993; Den Standiga Resa, 1993; Efter Stormen, 1993; Mammas Barn 1993; Crash! Boom! Bang!, 1994; Het Vind, 1995; Don't Bore Us, Get To The Chorus – Roxette's Greatest Hits, 1995; Have A Nice Day, 1999; Room Service, 2001; Singles include: The Look (US No. 1), 1989; Listen To Your Heart (No. 1, USA), 1989; Dangerous, 1989; Dressed For Success, 1989; It Must Have Been Love, featured in film Pretty Woman (No. 1, USA), 1990; Joyride (No. 1, US, Sweden, Germany, Netherlands, Australia, Canada), 1991; Fading Like A Flower (No. 2, US), 1991; The Big L, 1991; Spending My Time, 1991; Church of Your Heart, 1992; How Do You Do!, 1992; Queen of Rain, 1992; Almost Unreal, featured in film Super Mario Brothers, 1993; Sleeping In My Car, 1995. *Current Management:* Rascoff/Zysbalt Organization, 110 W 57th St, New York, NY 10019, USA.

FREELAND Adam; b. 1974 London, England. Prod.; Remixer; DJ. *Career:* Founder: Marine Parade Records, Friction club night (pioneering the Nu-Skool Breakbeat sound); World-wide DJ; Remixed: Pressure Drop, Aquasky, BT; Member: Tsunami One; Collaborations: Kevin Beb. *Recordings:* Albums (DJ-mixed compilations): Coastal Breaks #1, 1997; Coastal Breaks #2, 1998; Tectonics, 2000; On Tour, 2001; Singles: No 43 With Steamed Rice Please (with Tsunami One), 1997; Hip Hop Phenomenon (with Tsunami One), 1999. *Current Management:* c/o Marine Parade Recordings, 29 Kensington Gardens, Brighton, BN1 4AL, England.

FREEMAN John David; b. 2 Jan. 1955, Jarrow, Tyne and Wear, England. Musician (Bass Guitar); Vocalist; Songwriter; School Teacher. m. Alison Freeman, 11 Aug. 1979, 2 s. *Education:* Loughborough College of Education. *Musical Education:* Self-taught. *Career:* Bass Player, Vocalist and Co-writer of material for band, Havana Fireflies, playing at Glastonbury Festival, 1993 and 1994; Radio appearances include: Johnny Walker Show, and as unsigned band of the week on Steve Wright Show, BBC Radio 1, also airplay of album on GWR Radio; Various television appearances on HTV West shows, Spotlight and First Cut. *Recording:* Barbed Wire Prophets, by The Havana Fireflies. *Membership:* Musicians' Union. *Leisure interest:* Sport, especially cricket. *Address:* 40 High St, Dilton Marsh, Wiltshire, England.

FREEMAN Matt; b. 1966, Albany, New York, USA. Musician (bass); Vocalist. *Career:* Formed Operation Ivy with Tim Armstrong, 1987; Joined MDC, 1990; Formed Rancid with Tim Armstrong. *Recordings:* Singles: Rancid, 1993; Radio, Radio, Radio, 1994; Roots Radicals, 1994; Time Bomb, 1995; Ruby Soho, 1996; Bloodclot, 1998; Hooligans, 1998; Brad Logan, 1999; Albums: Rancid, 1993; Let's Go, 1994; And Out Come the Wolves, 1995; Life Won't Wait, 1998. *Leisure interest:* Old cars.

FREHLEY Ace (Paul); b. 22 April 1951, Bronx, New York, USA. Musician (guitar). *Career:* Member, US rock group Kiss, 1973–82; Numerous US, UK, European and world-wide tours; Left Kiss following serious car accident, 1982; Founder, guitarist, Frehley's Comet, 1987-. *Recordings:* Albums: with Kiss: Kiss, 1974; Dressed To Kill, 1975; Alive!, 1975; Destroyer, 1976; The Originals, 1976; Rock and Roll Over, 1976; Kiss Alive II, 1977; Love Gun, 1977; Double Platinum, 1978; Dynasty, 1979; Kiss Unmasked, 1980; Music From The Elder, 1981; Killers, 1982; Creatures of The Night, 1982; Solo albums: Ace Frehley, 1978; Trouble Walking, 1989; with Frehley's Comet: Frehley's Comet, 1987; Live + 1, 1988; Second Sighting, 1989; 12 Picks, 1998; Loaded Deck, 1998; Singles include: Rock 'N' Roll All Nite; Beth; Detroit Rock City; Hard Luck Woman; Calling Dr Love; I Was Made For Lovin' You; Also features on: Post Orgasmic Chill, Skunk Anansie, 1999. *Honours:* Footprints at Grauman's Chinese Theatre, Hollywood, 1976; Gold Ticket, Madison Square Garden, 1979; Gold and Platinum discs. *Current Management:* The Sewitt Group, 17 Ash Court, Highland Mills, NY 10930, USA.

FRENCH Frank; b. 19 Aug. 1952, Oakland, California, USA. Musician (piano); Composer. m. Carolyn Massonneau French, 19 Jan. 1991. *Education:* 4 years college. *Musical Education:* San Francisco Conservatory of Music; San Francisco State University; Bachelor of Music. *Career:* Performances in United States, Canada, Europe, Australia; Public radio, television appearances; American and foreign music festival appearances. *Compositions:* Original compositions featured on La Bamboula, Frontiers; Lacumbia, 1992; Womba Bomba, 1995; Toca con Clave, suite for piano, 1997. *Recordings:* The Well Tempered Clavier, 48 preludes and fugues, by Bach; Tangos of Ernesto Nazareth; La Bamboula; More American Souvenirs; Frontiers; (with David Thomas Roberts, Scott Kirby); Terra Verde, new music for piano solo with Scott Kirby and David Thomas Roberts; Creole Music, Piano duets with Scott Kirby; American Originals, music of Louis Moreau Gottschalk, for solo piano. *Memberships:* BMI; Piano Technicians Guild. *Leisure interests:* Brewing beer; Outdoor activities; Hiking and biking. *Current Management:* Artia Concerts, Sumner, Washington. *Address:* Frank French, PO Box 4034, Boulder, CO 80306, USA.

FRENGEL Mike; b. 20 Jan. 1972, Mountain View, California, USA. Composer; Musician (guitar). *Education:* BA, Music Composition, San Jose State University; MA, Electro-Acoustic Music Composition, Dartmouth College; PhD, Music Composition, City University, London, England. *Career:* Participant as composer/performer in international comtemporary music festivals, 1990–; Early internet broadcast of electro-acoustic music at ArtNet Concert, San Jose State University, 1995; Completed Polyrhythmic Modulation Studies for Masters Thesis, 1999. *Compositions:* Three Short Stories; Long Slender Heels; Rock Music; Variations on an Already Complex Theme No 1; Dropped On My Head, Upside Down; And Then, Romina…, 1999; The 3 Faces of Karen Black, 2000. *Recordings:* ICMC'97 Hong Kong; CDCM Vol. 26; Sonic Circuits VII; Luigi Russolo, 2000. *Honour:* Luigi Russolo Prize, 2000. *Memberships:* American Composer's Forum (ACF); International Computer Music Asscn (ICMA); Society for Electro-Acoustic Music in the United States (SEAMUS); Broadcast Music Inc (BMI); Electronic Arts Focus, London, founder and board mem.

FRESU Paolo; b. 10 Feb. 1961, Berchidda, Sardinia, Italy. Musician (Trumpet, Flugelhorn, Arr, Comp). *Education:* Electronics Expert, Certificate, University/DAMS, Bologna, Italy; Conservatory of Music, Cagliari, Sardinia; March Band, 1972–80; Pop Music, 1976–80; Conservatory of Music, Certificate, 1982. *Career:* Professor, Siena Jazz National Seminars, 1985–; Jazz University courses at Terni, 1987–; Winter courses, Siena and sems in Nuoro, 1989–; Guest Soloist, many innovative jazz recording projects; Artistic Director, Time in Jazz Festival in Berchidda, 1988–; Eurojazz Concorso Internazionale per Giovani Musicisti Europei' in Oristano, 1994 and Jazz Seminary in Nuoro, 1989-. *Recordings:* Ostinato, 1984; Inner Voices, 1986; Live in Montpellier, 1980; Ensalada Mistica, 1994; Mythscapes, 1995; Night on the City, 1995; Wanderlust, 1997; Angel, 1998; Metamorfosi, 1999. *Publications:* The first 63 jazz compositions, 1989; 49 compositions, 1996. *Honours:* Best Italian Musician, 1990; First Italian Young Musician, 1994; Best European Musician, 1996. *Leisure interests:* Literature; Poetry; Design; Movie. *Current Management:* Pannonica, Albani Vittorio, Bolzano, Italy. *Address:* PO Box 6, 40047, Riola, Italy.

FREY Glenn; b. 6 Nov. 1948, Detroit, Michigan, USA. Musician (guitar); Vocalist. *Career:* Member, Longbranch Pennywhistle (duo with J D Souther), 1968–71; Founder member, The Eagles, 1971-. *Recordings:* with Longbranch Pennywhistle: Longbranch Pennywhistle, 1969; with The Eagles: The Eagles, 1972; Desperado, 1973; On The Border, 1974; One of These Nights (No. 1, USA), 1975; Their Greatest Hits 1971–75 (No. 1, USA), 1976; Hotel California (No. 1, USA), 1978; The Long Run, 1979; Eagles Greatest Hits, Vol. 2, 1982; The Best of The Eagles, 1985; Hell Freezes Over, 1994; Selected Works 1972–99, 2000; Solo albums: No Fun Aloud, 1982; The Allnighter, 1984; Soul Searchin', 1992; Strange Weather, 1993; Singles include: Witchy Woman, 1972; Peaceful Easy Feeling, 1973; The Best of My Love (No. 1, USA), 1975; One of These Nights (No. 1, USA), 1975; Lyin' Eyes, 1975; Take It To The Limit, 1976; Hotel California (No. 1, USA), 1977; Heartache Tonight (No. 1, USA), 1979; The Long Run, 1980; I Can't Tell You Why, 1980; Seven Bridges Road, 1981; Solo hits: The Heat Is On (from film Beverly Hills Cop), 1985; You Belong To The City, 1986; Also contributed to recordings by: Jackson Browne; Dan Fogelberg; Don Henley; Elton John; Joni Mitchell; Randy Newman; Linda Ronstadt; Bob Seger; Carly Simon; Joe Walsh; Warren Zevon. *Honours:* Grammy Awards: Best Vocal Performance, 1976; Record of The Year, Hotel California, Best Arrangement For Voices, 1978; American Music Awards, Favourite Album, 1977. *Current Management:* Peter M Lopez, 2049 Century Park E, Suite 3180, Los Angeles, CA 90067, USA.

FRICK Bob Scott; b. 19 April 1940, Indiana, Pennsylvania, USA. Musician (guitar); Vocalist; Prod.; Publisher; Minister. m. Ruth Cornman, 13 May 1961, 2 s. *Career:* Play guitar, singer, throughout USA, Canada; Produce recordings for many artists; Publisher of hundreds of songs; Also duplicate tapes for many artists; Personal appearances are at churches, fairs; Appearances at Jerry Lewis Telethon; Grand Ole Opry (gospel); Videos on ACTS TV; Jerry Falwell and others. *Recordings:* Release Me (gospel); I Found Jesus In Nashville (tape and video); The King and I; You and Me Jesus. *Publication:* Message In Song (song book). *Memberships:* ASCAP; BMI. *Leisure interests:* Golf; Woodworking; Loves the water. *Current Management:* S & S Talent Agency. *Address:* 404 Bluegrass Ave, Madison, TN 37115, USA.

FRICKIE Janie, (Jane Fricke); b. 19 Dec. 1947, South Whitley, Indiana, USA. Country Singer. m. Randy Jackson. *Education:* University. *Career:* Session singer, Los Angeles; Member, Lea Jane Singers, Nashville; Uncredited backing voice to Johnny Duncan; Solo recording artiste; Tours with Alabama; Regular session singer; Vocalist with own group Heartache. *Recordings:* US Country No. 1 hits: Don't Worry 'Bout Me, Baby; He's A Heartache (Looking For A Place To Happen); It Ain't Easy Bein' Easy; Tell Me A Lie; Other singles include: What're You Doing Tonight? Please Help Me I'm Falling; Albums: Singer of Songs, 1978; Love Notes, 1979; From The Heart, 1980; I'll Need Someone To Hold Me When I Cry, 1981; Nice 'n' Easy, with Johnny Duncan, 1980; Sleeping With Your Memory, 1981; It Ain't Easy, 1982; Love Lines, 1983; The First Word In Memory Is Me, 1984; Someone Else's Fire, 1985; Black and White, 1986; After Midnight, 1987; Saddle The Wind, 1988; Labor of Love, 1989; Janie Fricke, 1991; Crossroads, 1992; Now and Then, 1993; Bouncin' Back, 2000; Numerous recording sessions as backing vocalist include: with Johnny Duncan: Jo and The Cowboy; Stranger; Thinkin' of a Rendevous; It Couldn't Have Been Any Better; I'll Get Over You, Crystal Gayle; My Way, Elvis Presley; (I'm A) Stand By My Woman Man, Ronnie Milsap; Here's Some Love, Tanya Tucker; I'd Love To Lay You Down, Conway Twitty; Duets include: Till The End, with Vern Gosdin; On My Knees, with Charlie Rich (US Country No. 1); A Place To Fall Apart, with Merle Haggard (US Country No. 1); All I want To Do In Life, with George Jones; The Cowboy and the Lady, Tommy Cash; From Time To Time, with Larry Gatlin; Who Cares?, with Ray Charles. *Address:* c/o Janie Frickie Concerts, PO Box 798, Lancaster, TX 75146, USA.

FRIDAY Gavin, (Fionan Hanvey); b. 1959, Dublin, Ireland. Singer; Songwriter. *Career:* Member, The Virgin Prunes; Solo artiste, 1990-. *Compositions:* Co-writer, film score: In The Name of The Father; In production: Passion of Darkly Noon; Angel Baby. *Recordings:* Virgin Prunes albums: If I Die I Die, 1982; The Hidden Lie, 1986; Sons Find Devils, 1998; Solo albums: Each Man Kills The Thing He Loves, 1990; Adam and Eve, 1992; Shag Tobacco, 1995; Film soundtrack: The Boxer (with Maurice Seezer), 1998. *Address:* c/o Island Records, 22 St Peters Sq., London W6 9NW, England.

FRIED Gerald; b. 13 Feb. 1928, New York, New York, USA. Composer; Conductor; Musician (Oboe). 3 s., 1 d. *Education:* BS, Juilliard School, 1948. *Career:* Jazz Saxophonist, New York, 1945–51; Principal Oboe, English Horn, Dallas Symphony, Pittsburgh Symphony, New York Little Orchestra, Los Aangeles Philharmonic, 1948–59; Composer, Conductor, Arranger, numerous motion pictures, TV and mini series, theatre works, operas and albums. *Compositions:* Scores for motion pictures include: Birds Do It, Bees Do It; Whatever Happened to Aunt Alice; One Spy Too Many; One of Our Spies Is Missing; The Cabinet of Dr Caligari; A Cold Wind in August; Cast A Long Shadow; Machine Gun Kelly; Paths of Glory; The Killing; Blood Money; Fear and Desire; Animation: The Great Rights; Scores for numerous mini-series and TV pilots and series including Flamingo Road; Roots; Police Woman; Star Trek; The Man from UNCLE; The Mouse That Roared; Gunsmoke; Rawhide; Symphonic suites for Roots; The Bell Jar; The Mystic Warrior; Time Travel for Oboe and Orchestra. *Recordings:* Vampire Circus; Return of Dracula; The five early Stanley Kubrick films; Star Trek Vol. 1; Roots; More Music from The Man from UNCLE; The Cabinet of Dr Caligari; The Mystic Warrior; Sounds of the Night, with Johnny Mercer. *Honours:* Academy Award nomination, 1975; Emmy Winner, 1977; Teacher of the Year Award, UCLA, 1992. *Memberships:* AMPAS; ASCAP; ATAS; SGA. *Current Management:* Soundtrack Music Asscn. *Address:* 6585 Portshead Rd, Malibu, CA 90265, USA.

FRIED Joshua; b. 8 July 1959, Los Angeles, California, USA. Composer; Performance Artist. *Education:* BA, Cornell University, 1981. *Career:* Pioneer of headphone-driven performance, and musical shoes, activated by electronics; Remixed works by They Might Be Giants, Chaka Khan and Ofra Haza; Work presented at New Music America, Israel Festival, ICC Tokyo, Café de la Danse, Lincoln Centre, Dutch Royal Palace, Knitting Factory, The Kitchen, Limelight, Irving Plaza, La MaMa Experimental Theatre; Group Sound Art Exhibition, Constriction, New York, 1996; Visiting Composer, Yale University, Bucknell University, 1997. *Recordings:* New Live Dub, 1985; Jimmy Because (My Name Is), single, 1987; Hello The Band, 1993; Insane, single, 1996. *Honours:* NEA Composers Fellowship, 1994; New York Foundation for the Arts Fellowship, 1995; American Composers Forum Commission, 1996; Rockefeller Foundation Residency, 1997; Grand prize, Danish Radio's Competition in Sound, 1997; MacDowell Colony Fellowship, 1997; Yaddo Residency, 1998. *Address:* 277 N Seventh St, Apt 4R, Brooklyn, NY 11211, USA.

FRIPP Robert; b. 16 May 1946, Wimborne, Dorset, England. Musician (guitar); Composer; Prod. m. Toyah Willcox, 16 May 1986. *Career:* Member, Ravens; The League of Gentlemen; Founder member, Giles, Giles and Fripp, which became King Crimson, 1969–84; Regular UK, Europe, US and Far East tours; Collaborations with Brian Eno; The League of Gentlemen, 1980–81; Solo recording artiste, 1979–; Founder, Guitar Craft guitar school, 1985; Reformed King Crimson, 1994-. *Recordings:* Albums: with Giles, Giles and Fripp: The Cheerful Insanity of Giles, Giles and Fripp, 1968; with King Crimson: In The Court of The Crimson King, 1969; In The Wake of Poseidon, 1970; Lizard, 1971; Earthbound, 1972; Larks' Tongues In Aspic, 1973; Starless and Bible Black, 1974; Red, 1974; USA, 1975; Discipline, 1981; Beat, 1982; Three of a Perfect Pair, 1984; Vrooom, 1995; Thrak, 1995; B'Boom, 1995; THRaKaTTak, 1996; Epitaph, 1997; The Nightwatch, 1997; Absent Lovers, 1998; Live at the Marquee, 1969, 1998; Live at Jacksonville 1972, 1998; The Beat Club Bremen 1972, 1999; Cirkus, 1999; Live at Cap D'Adge 1982, 1999; On Broadway, 1999; Live in Mexico City, 1999; No Construkction, 2000; Vrooom Vrooom, 2001; with Brian Eno: No Pussyfooting, 1975; Evening Star, 1976; with The League of Gentlemen: The League of Gentlemen, 1981; God Save The King, 1985; Solo albums: Exposure, 1979; God Save The Queen/Under Heavy Manners, 1980; Let The Power Fall, 1981; Robert Fripp and The League of Crafty Guitarists, 1986; Network, 1987; Live II, 1990; Show of Hands, 1991; The Bridge Between, 1995; Soundscapes – Live In Argentina, 1995; A Blessing of Tears, 1995; Radiophonics, 1996; That Which Passes, 1996; November Suite, 1997; The Gates of Paradise, 1997; with FFWD (Fripp, Fehlman, Weston, Dr Alex): FFWD, 1994; with Andy Summers: I Advance Masked, 1982; Bewitched, 1984; with Toyah: Kneeling At The Shrine, 1991; The Lady and The Tiger, 1987; with David Sylvian: The First Day, 1993; Damage, 1994; Contributor, albums by David Bowie; Peter Gabriel; Daryl Hall; Producer: Gabriel; Hall; Roches; several experimental jazz releases.

FRISCH Al(bert T); b. 17 March 1916, Brooklyn, New York, USA. Composer. m. Celia Hirschorn Frisch, 1 d. *Career:* Saxophonist in night clubs, ocean liners, summer resorts; Entertainer, pianist and singer; Weekly column in Music in Print, Billboard Magazine; Wrote lyrics, music, songs, instrumentals, albums and shows for TV; Worked with Roy Alfred, Buddy Bernier, Johnny Burke, Sylvia Dee, Allan Roberts, Bernard Spiro; Sid Wayne. *Compositions:* Hundreds include: I Won't Cry Anymore; Roses in the Rain; All Over the World; Monte Carlo Melody; Flowers Mean Forgiveness; The Language of Love; Late in December Starry-Eyed and Breathless; April and You; Winter in Miami; Gregory's Chant; Not So Long Ago; Io Canto; People, Places and Things; Bordello; Fiddle Rock; Song of the Raccoons; Madame Misia; Hallucination Ballet; To Please the Woman in

Me; Great Company. *Memberships:* ASCAP; American Guild of Authors and Composers; Dramatists Guild. *Leisure interests:* Reading; Travel; Entertaining. *Address:* Myra Music Co, 33F, 177 White Plains Rd, Tarrytown, NY 10591, USA.

FRISCH Albert; b. 27 March 1927, New York, USA. Composer; Pianist; Saxophonist. *Career:* Saxophonist in nightclubs, on ocean liners and summer resorts; also entertainer, pianist and singer; Writer, weekly column, Music in print, Billboard magazine; Wrote words and music, songs, instrumentals, albums, shows and TV special material; Chief Collaborators: Roy Alfred, Buddy Bernier, Johnny Burke, Sylvia Dee, Buddy Kaye, Larry Kusick, Julian More, Allan Roberts, Al Neiburg, Bernard Spiro, Charles Tobias, Sid Wayne, Fred Wise; Songs and instrumental works: This Is No Laughing Matter; Two Different Worlds; I Won't Cry Anymore; Roses in the Rain; All Over the World; That's What They Meant By the Good Old Summertime; Monte Carlo Melody; Congratulations to Someone; Flowers Mean Forgiveness; The Show Must Go On; Winner Take All; Broadway at Basin Street; What Lies Over the Hill; The Language of Love; Just Married Today; Sipping Cider By the Zuyder Zee; Let It Rain; The Best President We Ever Had (pancho Maximillian Hernandez); The Cool School; The Wonderful World of Christmas; Come On, Come In; Late in December; Starry-Eyed and Breathless; Little Miss Irish; My Mother's Lullaby; She Never Left the Table; April and You; Something for Nothing; Let's Harmonize; Go You Where Go; Tears to Burn; The Same Old Moon; Here Comes That Heartache Again; The Melancholy Minstrel; Now; Palermo; Lovin' Up a Storm The Moment of Truth; Have Have to Believe in Someone; Weep for the Boy; Winter in Miami; Music From Out of Space; If I'm Elected; Gregory's Chant; It Must Be Emily; Come Back to Rome; Idle Conversation; Always Love Me; I've Got Some Cryin' to Do; All I Get From You are Heartaches; A Chocolate Sundae on a Saturday Night; In Time; Not So Long Ago; My Need For You; He Came on a Long Long Journey; Wherefore Art Thou Romeo; Sweet Brown-Eyed Baby; What More Is There to Say; Give Me the Right; Unafraid; Four Walls, Two Windows, and One Broken Heart; He Cha Cha'd In; After the Fall; No Hard Feelings; Really O, Truly O; Mama, Teach Me to Do the Charleston; Io Canto; You Pass This Way Only Once; People, Places and Things; Fiddle Rock; The Hornet's Nest; Tunes for Muzak; TV Shows: My Love Song to You; Song of the Racoons; Bordello, Show-Queen's Theatre, London; A Place Like This; Yourself; A Country Bride; Morality; Business Tango; Simple Pleasures; Art Should Be Art; Family Life; If You Should Leave Me; Madame Misia; All the Time in the World; I Love Me; The Way I See It; The Girl in Cabin 54; What Does It Take; Can-Can Ballet; Hallucination Ballet; Show- Christy; When the Penny Poets Sing, A Somewhere Rainbow; Where's My Rainbow; To Please the Woman in Me; Grain of the Salt of the Earth; Until the Lives of You; Come Out Wherever You Are; Picture Me; The Morning After; It's a Lonesome Thing; All's Fair in Love and War; Great Company; With One Fell Swoop; Beach Ballet; The Heart's Wonder; Down the Hatch; Gallant Little Swearers' Be a Hero. *Address:* Myra Music Company, 177 White Plains Rd, 33F, Tarrytown, NY 10591, USA.

FRISCHMANN Justine Elinor; b. 16 Sept. 1969, London. Singer; Musician; Songwriter. *Career:* Rhythm guitarist for band, Suede; Formed own band, Elastica, 1993–2001; Toured extensively world-wide; Television appearances include Top of The Pops. *Compositions:* Album, Elastica; Elastica, EP. *Recordings:* Singles: Stutter, 1993; Line-Up, 1994; Connection, 1994; Waking Up, 1995; Elastica EP, 1999; Albums: Elastica (No. 1, UK), 1995; The Menace, 2000; The Radio 1 Sessions, 2001. *Honours:* Nomination for Brit Award; NME Readers Award for Best New Band. *Current Management:* CMO Management International Ltd, Unit 32, Ransomes Dock, 35–37 Parkgate Rd, London SW11 4NP.

FRISELL Bill; b. 18 March 1951, Baltimore, Maryland, USA. Musician (guitar, banjo, ukulele, bass). *Musical Education:* North Colorado University, 1969–71; Diploma, arranging, composition, Berklee College of Music, Boston, 1977. *Career:* Played with artists including: Eberhard Weber; Mike Gibbs; Jan Garbarek; Charlie Haden; Carla Bley; John Scofield; Member, Power Tools (with Ronald Shannon Jackson, Melvin Gibbs); John Zorn's Naked City; The Paul Bley Quintet (with Paul Bley, Paul Motian, John Surman); Paul Motian Trio (with Paul Motian, Joe Lovano); David Sylvian; Bono; Marianne Faithfull; Robin Holcomb; Gavin Bryars; Brian Eno; Daniel Lanois. *Recordings:* Albums: In Line, 1983; Rambler, 1985; Lookout For Hope, 1988; Before We Were Born, 1989; Is This You?, 1990; Where In The World?, 1991; Have A Little Faith, 1993; Music From The Films of Buster Keaton (comprising The High Sign/One Week and Go West), 1995; Quartet, 1996; Nashville, 1997; Gone, Just Like a Train, 1998; Songs We Know, 1998; Good Dog, Happy Man, 1999; Ghost Town, 2000; Blues Dream, 2001; Bill Frisell With Dave Holland and Elvin Jones, 2001; with Tim Berne: Theoretically, 1984; with John Zorn, George Lewis: News For Lulu, 1987; More News For Lulu, 1992; with Power Tools: Strange Meeting, 1987; with John Scofield: Grace Under Pressure, 1992; with Elvis Costello: Deep Dead Blue, Live At Meltdown, 1995; The Sweetest Punch 1999; with Ginger Baker Trio: Going Home Again, 1995. *Honours:* Harris Stanton Guitar Award; Guitarist of the Year, Downbeat

Critics' Poll, 1998; Deutsche Schallplatten Preis, 1998; Critics Award, Best Guitarist, Industry Award, Best Guitarist, Annual Jazz Awards, 1998. *Current Management:* Songline/Tone Field Productions, 1649 Hopkins St, Berkeley, CA 94707, USA.

FRISTORP Göran; b. 26 May 1948, Skara, Sweden. m. 1 July 1975, 1 d. *Education:* Conservatory of Gothenburg and Framnäs in Ojebyn. *Career:* Winner, European Song Contest, Sweden, 1973; Many television and radio appearances; 20 LPs and CDs. *Compositions:* I Belong; Lyrics: Hal David; Music: Göran Fristorp. *Recordings:* Sings Nils Ferlin; Atersken; Riktning; Psalmer; Evert Taube; Flickan Från Fjärran. *Publications:* Nils Perlin, 1975; Egna Ltar, 1974; Psalmer, 1989; Flickan Prån Fiärran, 1996. *Honours:* Evert Taube Prize, 1997; Nils Ferlin Troubadour Prizedeolith, 1998; Several Artists Prizes. *Memberships:* STIM; SKAP; GRAMO (Norway); SAMI. *Leisure interests:* Travelling; Food; Wine. *Current Management:* Stageway, Bergen Norway.

FROSCH Wolfgang; b. 2 July 1960, Knittelfeld, Austria. Musician (bass); Backing Vocalist. m. Maria, 31 March 1989, 1 s., 2 d. *Education:* Carpenter. *Musical Education:* Self-taught, left hand bassist. *Career:* Member, Blues Pumpm, 1978–; Member, Giant Blonder, 1988–94; Tours, television and radio appearances throughout Europe. *Recordings:* Albums: with Giant Blonder: Colours of Rock; with Blues Pumpm: Albums: Bluespumpm, 1979; Edlau, 1980; Village, 1981; Live With Friends, 1985; The 5th Ten Years Jubilee, 1987; Live At Utopia, 1988; Live With Friends, 1991; Birthday, 1991; Live In Vienna, 1992; The 5th, 1992; Living Loving Riding, 1994; Singles: Wolfgang Session and Song, 1980; Men From Milwaukee, 1993. *Honours:* Silbernes Ehrenzeicher, 1992; Third Best Blues Album Ö3 Rot-Weiss-Rote Critics Poll, Live In Vienna, 1992. *Memberships:* AKM; AUME; LSG. *Leisure interests:* Children; Music; Reading. *Current Management:* Peter Steinbach, RGG Management.

FROST Jenny; b. 22 Feb. 1978, Liverpool, England. Vocalist. *Career:* Represented UK in Eurovision Song Contest 1999 as part of female vocal quintet Precious; Replaced Kerry Katona in Atomic Kitten, January 2001; Group achieved pan-European breakthrough with Whole Again single; Guest at Celebrate South Africa Freedom Concert, London, 2001. *Recordings:* Albums: with Precious: Precious, 2000; with Atomic Kitten: Right Now (revised issue), 2001; Singles: with Precious: Say It Again, 1999; Rewind, 2000; It's Gonna Be My Way, 2000; New Beginning, 2000; with Atomic Kitten: Eternal Flame, 2001. *Honours:* Successes at UK Disney Channel and Smash Hits Awards 2001. *Current Management:* Innocent Records, Kensal House, 553–579 Harrow Rd, London, W10 4RH, England.

FROST Per Christian; b. 30 Oct. 1954, Aarhus, Denmark. Musician (guitar, bass guitar); Vocalist. m. Dorthe Th. Holtet, 25 July 1987, 2 s. *Education:* 1 year, Art Academy. *Musical Education:* Self-taught. *Career:* Member, Gnags, 1974–; Tours: Europe; Africa; India; Cuba; Nicaragua; Numerous television appearances; Also solo artist, guest musician. *Recordings:* with Gnags, 17 albums; Solo albums: Ned Ad Gaden, 1979; Old Friend's Back, 1990; Breakin' Ice, 1995. *Honours:* Award of Honour, Danish Musicians' Union, 1988; IFPI Prize, (Danish Grammy), 1990. *Memberships:* DMF; DJBFA; KODA. *Leisure interests:* Running; Painting. *Current Management:* Rock On International, Copenhagen, Denmark.

FROST Soren; b. 5 Feb. 1965, Aarhus, Denmark. Musician (drums, percussion). *Education:* Drummer Collective, 10 Week Certificate Program, New York City, 1988. *Career:* Played Pop Rock, Jazz and Chorus Line, Sweet Charity Jesus Christ Superstar; Worked with Lillian Boutte, Dr John, Bob Berg, Eliane Elias, Lee Konitz, Bob Brookmeyer, Thad Jones, Slide Hampton, Dee Dee Bridgewater; Many TV and radio shows and tours of Japan, 1990, USSR, 1988, Thailand, 1991, USA, 1997. *Recordings:* Lillian Boutte: The Jazz Book; The Danish Radio Orchestra: Fusion Symphony; Nikolaj Bentzon: Brotherhood; Jazzgroup 1990 with Bob Berg: Live in Denmark, My Sisters Garden. *Honours:* Grants from Danish Companies to Go to New York. *Current Management:* Blegdamsvej 84 5th, 2100 Kobenhavn O, Denmark.

FRUITBAT (Leslie Carter); b. 12 Feb. 1958. *Career:* Founder member (with Jimbob), duo, Carter The Unstoppable Sex Machine (later billed as Carter USM), 1988–; International concerts, including US, Japan. *Recordings:* Albums: 101 Damnations, 1990; 30 Something, 1991; 1992 – The Love Album (No. 1, UK), 1992; Post Historic Monsters, 1994; Worry Bomb, 1995; Straw Donkey, 1996; A World Without Dave, 1997; I Blame The Government, 1998; Live, 1999; Singles: Sheltered Life, 1988; Sherriff Fatman, 1989; Rubbish, 1990; Anytime, Anyplace, Anywhere, 1990; Bloodsports For All, 1991; After The Watershed, 1991; Only Living Boy In New Cross, 1992; Lean On Me I Won't Fall Over, 1993; Glam Rock Cops, 1994; Let's Get Tattoos, 1994; Young Offenders Mum, 1995; Born On Fifth November, 1995. *Current Management:* Adrian Boss Promotions. *Address:* c/o 3 Gunstor Rd, London N16 8HF, England.

FRUSCIANTE John; b. 5 March 1970, New York, New York, USA. Musician (guitar). *Career:* Member, Red Hot Chili Peppers; Joined band

in 1989; Left, 1993; Rejoined band, 1998. *Recordings include:* Singles: Higher Ground, 1990; Taste The Pain, 1990; Give It Away, 1991; Suck My Kiss, 1991; Under The Bridge, 1992; Scar Tissue, 1999; Behind the Sun; Around The World, 1999; Californication, 2000; Albums: Mother's Milk, 1989; BloodSugarSexMagik, 1991; Californication, 1999; Solo albums: Niandra Ladies and Usually Just A T-Shirt, 1995; Smile From The Streets You Hold, 1997; To Record Only Water For Ten Days, 2001; Other session work includes: Perry Farrell; Tricky. *Honours include:* MTV Music Video Awards, 1992; Grammy, Best Hard Rock Song, Give It Away, 1993; Grammy Award, Rock Song, Scar Tissue, 2000.

FRY Martin; b. 9 March 1958, Manchester, Lancashire, England. Vocalist; Prod. *Education:* English Literature, Sheffield University. *Career:* Launched fanzine, Modern Drugs, 1979; Lead singer, ABC, 1980–; UK and world tour, 1982; Featured in Julien Temple's film Man Trap, 1983; Subject, BBC documentary, That Was Then, This Is Now, 1990. *Recordings:* Albums with ABC: The Lexicon of Love (No. 1, UK), 1982; Beauty Stab, 1983; How To Be A Zillionaire, 1985; Alphabet City, 1987; Up, 1989; Absolutely, 1990; Abracadabra, 1991; Skyscraping, 1997; ; Hello – An Introduction To ABC, 2001; The Look of Love (The Very Best of ABC), 2001; Singles include: Tears Are Not Enough, 1981; Poison Arrow (No. 6, UK), 1982; The Look of Love (No. 4, UK), 1982; All of My Heart (No. 5, UK), 1982; That Was Then But This Is Now, 1983; Be Near Me, 1985; When Smokey Sings, 1987; The Night You Murdered Love, 1987; One Better World, 1989.

FRY Tristan Frederick Allan; b. 25 Oct. 1946, London, England. m. Dorothy E Garland, 25 Oct. 1993. *Musical Education:* Taught by Peter Allen, Royal Academy of Music and many amateur orchestras and groups, London. *Career:* Concerts with Sky in Europe; Australia; Asia; First group to play Westminster Abbey (televised concert); Concerts with Academy of St Martin In The Fields Orchestra around world. *Compositions include:* Connecting Rooms; Then and Now. *Recordings:* All Sky singles and albums; 3 recordings, Bartók's 2 piano and percussion concerto; Academy albums include award winning Amadeus; Film score albums include: James Bond, Pink Panther; Also recorded with many artists world-wide including: Kevin Ayers; Nick Drake; Keith Emerson; John Martyn. *Membership:* Royal Society of Musicians.

FUGLER Jon; Vocalist; Musician; Sound Engineer. *Career:* Founder member, Fluke, 1983–; Concerts include: British tour, 1994; Glastonbury Festival; Appearances include: Smash Hits Poll Winners Party, with Björk; MTV Awards, with Björk. *Recordings:* Albums: The Techno Rose of Blighty, 1991; Out (mini-album); Six Wheels On My Wagon; Oto, 1995; Singles: Thumper; Joni; Slid; Electric Guitar; Groovy Feeling; Bubble; Bullet; Remix, Big Time Sensuality, Björk. *Address:* c/o Circa Records, Kensal House, 553–579 Harrow Rd, London W10 4RH, England.

FUJII Naoki; b. 1 July 1960, Japan. Lutenist. *Education:* Royal Conservatory, The Hague, The Netherlands, 1979–84. *Career:* Amsterdam Concertgebouw; Radio France; NHK FM Japan; University of Coimbra, Portugal. *Recordings:* Haru No Umi. *Address:* Stuyvesantstraat 9–1, 1058 AJ Amsterdam, The Netherlands.

FULKS Robbie; b. 25 March 1963, Pennsylvania, USA. Singer; Songwriter; Musician. m. Donna, 3 s. *Education:* Columbia College, New York. *Career:* Two Mountain Stage appearances, 1997, 1998; 1 Fresh Air NPR, 1998; 3 World Cafe and 2 Acoustic Cafe Appearances, 1996–99; 1 Austin City Limits, 1998; Cast Member, Woody Guthrie's American Song, 1990–93; Staff Instructor, Old Town School of Folk Music, Chicago; Films Featuring Performances of Original Songs. *Recordings:* Country Love Songs, 1996; South Mouth, 1997; Let's Kill Saturday Night, 1998; The Very Best of Robbie Fulks, 2000; Couples In Trouble, 2000; 13 Hillbilly Giants, 2001. *Leisure interests:* Cooking; Alcholism. *Address:* PO Box 1512, Lake Villa, Illinois 60076, USA.

FULLER Parmer; b. 15 July 1949, San Francisco, California, USA. Composer; Conductor; Music Dir; Musician (Piano). m. Narcissa C Vanderlip, 14 March 1982, 1 d. *Education:* BA, cum laude, Music, Harvard University; MM, Music Composition, Indiana University; PhD, Music Composition, University of California at Los Angeles. *Career:* Composer, music for feature films including Daddy's Girl, Reflections on a Crime, Mortal Passions, Time Trackers, Spirit of the Eagle, Ulterior Motives; music for TV shows: The Morton Downey Jr Show, Distant Cousins, Easy Street, Dynasty, Family, Ronn Lucas Show, Monsters; Miscellaneous compositions for educational films, interactive CDs; Solo performances as Pianist including shows for President Reagan, George Bush, Gerald Ford and Richard Nixon; Conductor, Young Musicians' Foundation Orchestra concerts; Coached actor James Caan in conducting skills; Appeared as self in Easy Street. *Compositions include:* Concert works: Spirit of the Eagle; Twice Upon a Time; A Child's Christmas in Wales; Alpine Wanderings; Music Comedy: Director and Conductor: The Sound of Music; Singin' in the Rain; Oklahoma; Little Shop of Horrors; Guys and Dolls; Crazy For You; Into The Woods; My Fair Lady; Camelot;

Opera: Composer, Solferino; Numerous arrangements, including works for Pavarotti and Jack Lemmon. *Honours:* Frank Sinatra Prizes; Henry Mancini Award. *Memberships:* ASCAP; BMI; SCL; AFM. *Leisure interests:* Skiing; Softball; Hiking; Yodelling. *Current Management:* None. *Address:* 10374 Cheviot Dr., Los Angeles, CA 90064, USA.

FUMAROLA Martin Alejandro; b. 22 Nov. 1966, Argentina. Composer; Music Researcher; Computer Specialist. *Education:* Composition Studies with Cesar Franchisena and Ariel Martinez, National University of Cordoba. *Career:* Associate Composer, Electroacoustic Music Studio, National University of Cordoba; Concert Curator, in many International Festivals of Electroacoustic Music, pieces performed world-wide. *Compositions:* Estatismo; In Movile; Set In; Peregrinar de la Arana; Callejuelas; Shaguir; Omen. *Honours:* Scholarship, Argeninian National Endowment for the arts; Grant of the Spanish Ministry of Culture. *Memberships:* ICMA; SEAMUS; CEC; FARME. *Address:* Casilla de Correo 1145, Correo Central, Cordoba RA 5000, Argentina.

FUNKEY; b. 20 July 1961, Sint-Niklaas, Belgian. Musician (Synthesizer, Singer). *Musical Education:* Self-taught. *Career:* Gigs: debut, Keyboard player and singer, The Soap, 1992; Oortcloud, 1993; Radio: Several times on Bassta, 1995–96; TV: Prettig Gestoord, 1996. *Publications:* Oortcloud: Raindances, 1995; Colour Dot: Floating Atmospheres, 1997. *Honour:* Studio Brussels' Candidate for Debut Rock Contest. *Memberships:* SABAM; ZAMU. *Leisure interest:* Internet. *Current Management:* Higher Grow Productions, Damstraat 2, B9100 Sint-Niklaas, Belgium.

FUREY Eddie; b. 23 Dec. 1944, Tipperary, Ireland. Musician (guitar, mandola, mandolin, harmonica, fiddle, bodhran); Vocalist. m. Bibi, 5 c. *Career:* Member, duo, with brother Finbar, 1960s; Joined Clancey Brothers, US tour, 1969; Member, Tam Linn, with Davey Arthur, Paul Furey; Apperances include: Cambridge Folk Festival; Member, The Fureys and Davey Arthur, 1980. *Recordings:* Albums: The Sound of The Fureys and Davey Arthur, 1981; When You Were Sweet Sixteen, 1982; Steal Away, 1983; In Concert, 1984; Golden Days, 1984; At The End of The Perfect Day, 1985; The First Leaves of Autumn, 1986; The Fureys Finest, 1987; The Fureys Collection, 1989; The Scattering, 1989; The Very Best Of, 1991; The Winds of Change, 1992; Irish Folk Favourites, 1994; Best of Irish Folk, 1998; Essential Fureys, 2001; with Finbar Furey: The Dawning of The Day, 1970; Traditional Irish Pipe Music, 1998; Singles include: When You Were Sweet Sixteen, 1981; Green Fields of France; Red Rose Café. *Membership:* IMRO. *Leisure interest:* Golf. *Current Management:* Joe McCadden Promotions, Dublin. *Address:* 19 Stockton Green, Castleknock, Dublin 15, Ireland.

FUREY Finbar; b. 28 Sept. 1946, Dublin, Ireland. Musician (uillean pipes, banjo, whistles, flute); Vocalist. *Career:* Member, duo with Eddie Furey, 1960s; Played clubs, radio work; Joined Clancey Brothers, US tour, 1969; European tours, 1972; Joined Tam Linn, with Eddie and Paul Furey, Davey Arthur; Appeared at Cambridge Folk Festival; Later became The Fureys and Davey Arthur, 1980-. *Recordings:* Albums: The Cisco Special, 1960; Songs of Woody Guthrie, 1961; I Ain't Got No Home, 1962; The Sound of The Fureys and Davey Arthur, 1981; When You Were Sweet Sixteen, 1982; Steal Away, 1983; In Concert, 1984; Golden Days, 1984; At The End of a Perfect Day, 1985; The First Leaves of Autumn, 1986; The Fureys Finest, 1987; The Fureys Collection, 1989; The Scattering, 1989; The Very Best Of, 1991; The Winds of Change, 1992; Wind and the Rain, 1997; Traditional Irish Pipe Music, 1998; ; Essential Fureys, 2001; with Eddie Furey: The Dawning of The Day, 1972; Solo album: Love Letters, 1990; Singles include: When You Were Sweet Sixteen, 1981. *Address:* c/o Joe McCadden Promotions, 19 Stockton Green, Castleknock, Dublin 15, Ireland.

FUREY George; b. 11 June 1951, Dublin, Ireland. Vocalist; Musician (guitar, accordion, mandola, autoharp, whistles); Songwriter. m. Mary, 1971, 3 s., 3 d. *Career:* Member, The Buskers, 1972; Later became The Furey Brothers; TV appearances in the UK and Ireland. *Compositions include:* Evening Falls, 1979; Green Fields of France. *Recordings:* Albums: The Cisco Special, 1960; Songs of Woody Guthrie, 1961; I Ain't Got No Home, 1962; The Sound of The Fureys and Davey Arthur, 1981; When You Were Sweet Sixteen, 1982; Steal Away, 1983; In Concert, 1984; Golden

Days, 1984; At The End of Perfect Day, 1985; The First Leaves of Autumn, 1986; The Fureys Finest, 1987; The Fureys Collection, 1989; The Scattering, 1989; The Very Best of The Fureys and Davey Arthur, 1991; The Winds of Change, 1992; Through the Eyes of an Irishman, 1997; The Fureys: 21 Years On This Year, 1999; Essential Fureys, 2001; Singles include: When You Were Sweet Sixteen; I Will Love You (Every Time When We Are Gone); Green Fields of France; Red Rose Café. *Honours:* Playing for the Pope in Ireland, 1979; Gold Albums in Australia, South Africa, Canada, UK, USA, New Zealand and Germany. *Memberships:* IMRO; Phonographic Performance Ltd. *Leisure interest:* Golf. *Current Management:* Joe McCadden Promotions, Dublin. *Address:* 19 Stockton Green, Castleknock, Dublin 15, Ireland.

FUREY Paul; b. 6 May 1948, Dublin, Ireland. Musician (accordion, melodeon, concertina, whistles); Vocalist. m. Catherine, 1977, 3 s. *Career:* Member, The Buskers (with George Furey, Davey Arthur), 1972; Member, Tam Linn; Appeared at Cambridge Folk Festival; Member, The Fureys and Davey Arthur, 1980–; Mbr, The Furey Brothers; TV appearances in the UK and Ireland. *Recordings:* Albums: The Cisco Special, 1960; Songs of Woody Guthrie, 1961; I Ain't Got No Home, 1962; When You Were Sweet Sixteen, 1982; Steal Away, 1983; In Concert, 1984; Golden Days, 1984; At The End of a Perfect Day, 1985; The First Leaves of Autumn, 1986; The Scattering, 1989; Winds of Change, 1992; Traditional Irish Pipe Music, 1998; Various compilations including: Essential Fureys, 2001; Singles include: When You Were Sweet Sixteen, 1981; Green Fields of France; Red Rose Café. *Membership:* IMRO. *Leisure interests:* Golf; Reading. *Current Management:* Joe McCadden Promotions, Dublin. *Address:* 19 Stockton Green, Castleknock, Dublin 15, Ireland.

FURIC Stephane; b. 15 July 1965, Paris, France. Composer. m. Laurence Horvilleur, 25 July 1992, 2 s. *Musical Education:* Diploma in Professional Music, Berklee College of Music, Boston, USA; Private studies with William H Curtis, David Liebman. *Career:* Concerts including international jazz festivals, tours, radio shows, with Stephane Furic Project (also featuring Chris Cheek, Patrick Goraguer, Jim Black); Hiroshi Minami; Philippe Le Baraillec; Antonio Hart; Guillaume Orti (Europe, USA, Japan); Television shows. *Compositions:* Kishinev, 1990; Gorag' Rag, 1991; Suite of Dances, 1994; Song of the Open Road, 1994; Song of the Universal, 1994; Words, 1997. *Recordings:* Kishinev, 1991; The Twitter-Machine, 1993; Crossing Brooklyn Ferry, 1995. *Memberships:* BMI; SACEM (as writer and publisher). *Current Management:* Limbo Jazz, 505 Bow St, Elkton, MD 21921, USA. *Address:* 151 East St, South Salem, NY 10590, USA.

FURTADO Nelly Kim; b. 2 Dec. 1978, Victoria, British Columbia, Canada. Vocalist; Musician (guitar, ukelele, trombone); Songwriter. *Career:* Trombonist in various jazz/marching/concert bands while at school; Performed and recorded with trip-hop outfit Nelstar, aged 18; Discovered by current manager at Toronto talent contest; Relocated there to forge songwriting partnership with Gerald Eaton and Brian West of successful Canadian group The Philosopher Kings. *Recordings:* Albums: Whoa Nelly!, 2000; Singles: I'm Like A Bird, 2000; Turn Off The Light, 2001. Much recognition at Canadian music industry awards. *Current Management:* Chris Smith Management Inc, 21 Camden St, Toronto, ON, Canada. *Internet:* www.chrissmithmanagement.com.

FYFFE William John Angus; b. 18 Sept. 1927, Margate, Kent, England. Musician (piano); Musical Dir. m. (1) Michelle Franks, 1951, 1 s., 1 d.; (2) Sue Addams, 1968, 1 s., 1 d.; Present partner, Anthea Askey. *Education:* George Watson's College, Edinburgh. *Career:* Son of Will Fyffe, comedian, writer of song I Belong To Glasgow; Joined Rank Organisation film studios, 1948; Moved to Chappells as song plugger; A & R, Decca Records; Personal accompanist to artists including: Allan Jones, Josef Locke, Evelyn Laye, Frankie Vaughn, Petula Clark, Ronnie Hilton, 1950s-70s; Senior MD, Triumph Productions; In Concert act with Anthea Askey; Numerous appearances, television, radio and stage. *Compositions:* Music score for Glasgow Belongs To Me (working title); Songs include: My September; With A Love Like Ours. *Memberships:* PRS; BASCA. *Leisure interests:* Photography; Swimming; Travel. *Address:* Appletree Lodge, Golden Acre, Angmering On Sea, West Sussex BN16 1QP, England.

G

G Kenny (Kenneth Gorelick); b. 1959, Seattle, Washington, USA. Musician (saxophone); Composer. *Education:* Accounting, University of Washington. *Career:* European tour with Franklin High School Band, 1974; Musician with Barry White's Love Unlimited Orchestra, 1976; Backing musician, numerous artistes including: Whitney Houston; Natalie Cole; Aretha Franklin; Toni Braxton; Peabo Bryson; Member, Cold, Bold and Together; Member, jazz fusion group Jeff Lorber Fusion; Solo artiste, 1981–; Regular collaborations with Michael Bolton, including US tour, 1990. *Recordings:* Solo albums: Kenny G, 1982; G Force, 1983; Gravity, 1985; Duotones, 1986; Silhouette, 1988; Kenny G Live, 1989; Breathless, 1992; Miracles, 1994; The Moment, 1996; Classics in the Key of G, 1999; Faith, 1999; with Michael Bolton: Soul Provider, 1989; Time, Love and Tenderness, 1991. *Honours:* Multi-platinum records. *Current Management:* Turner Management Group, 3500 W Olive Ave, Suite 690, Burbank, CA 91505, USA.

GABRIEL (Gabriel J Maciocia); b. 8 Oct. 1948, Providence, Rhode Island, USA. Record Prod.; Songwriter; Playwright. *Education:* Masters Degree, RIC, 1972. *Musical Education:* Masters in arranging and composition of music. *Career:* Producer: Budweiser Girls Band (Single of Week, Cashbox Magazine); Produced 18 albums; Produced for Joey Welz of Caprice Records; Also, Four Tops, for Arista, Warner, Slack Records; Writer of play, Christmas Holiday on the Moon; Writer of music score and screen play for film, Hearts of Bounty; currently filming film on location abroad. *Compositions:* Elvis is Smiling, 1989; You Don't Own Me, 1989. *Recordings:* Sexy Lady, The Four Tops; Crying Shame, Gloria Gaynor; Elvis Is Smiling; Ice Cream, Soda Pop and Wine, Joey Welz; Wild Weekend. *Publications:* Whisper Pines (novel). *Honours:* Single of Week, Nov 1988, Cashbox Magazine; Nominated, First round of Grammy Awards, 1999. *Memberships:* BMI; ASCAP. *Leisure interest:* Snorkelling. *Current Management:* Caprice Records, Lititz PA, Joey Welz. *Address:* 108 Humbert St, North Providence, RI 02911, USA.

GABRIEL Gilles (Blacky); b. 1 Nov. 1946, Clermont Ferrand, France. Musician (drums). Divorced, 1 s., 1 d. *Musical Education:* Self-taught; Percussion, double bass, Music High School, Nancy, 1968–69. *Career:* First professional appearance, cabaret, Nancy, 1967; Member, Dance Orchestra, 1967–; Appearances include: World Circus Festival, Nancy, 1968; Casinos include: Vichy; Châtel Guyon; Cruise Ships: Massalia; Mermoz (with Isabelle Aubret, Nicole Croisille); Azur; Meridien Hotels: Dakar (with Francis Lemarque); Abu Dhabi; Accompanied Pierre Douglas, Michel Lebb, Monte Carlo (sporting), 1978; Concerts with US musicians: Hal Singer; Benny Waters; John Littleton; Mickey Backer; Stars of Faith; French musicians: Michel Hausser; Dany Doriz; Laurent Gianez; Françoise Pujol; Eddy Gaddum (Surinam); Member, big bands including Swing Orchestra; Packard Blues: First sets: Toots Thielemans (Belgium): Mint Julep (UK); Jimmy Johnson (USA); Big Wheeler (USA); Many concerts in France, Germany, Luxembourg, Belgium; Jazz festivals include: Nancy; Strasbourg; Many concerts with jazzmen in John's Place, Saarbrücken, Germany; with Eddy Gaddum (Jazz Combo) concerts in Luxembourg, Germany, Belgium; Jazz Festival, Luxemburg, 1995; Teacher, music school, private lessons; Leader, Myster Black (jazz), 1989–; Jaguars, 1995; Pat and the Blue Wizards, 1999-. *Membership:* SLAM. *Address:* 6 rue du Maréchal Oudinot, 54000 Nancy, France.

GABRIEL Juan (Alberto Aguilera Valadéz); b. 7 Jan. 1950, Parácuaro, Michoacán, Mexico. Singer; Songwriter. *Recordings:* Singles include: Perdoname (Forgive Me); Lagrimas Y LLuvia (Tears and Rain); La Costumbre (The Habit); Amor Eterno (Eternal Love); Pero Que Necesitad (But The Need); Over 50 albums including: Juan Gabriel En El Palacio De Bellas Artes; Debo Hoceria; Gracias Por Esperar; Celebrando, 25 años de Juan Gabriel, 1998. *Current Management:* Hauser Entertainment Inc. *Address:* PO Box 978, 11003 Rooks Rd, Pico Rivera, CA 90660, USA.

GABRIEL Peter; b. 13 Feb. 1950, Cobham, Surrey, England. Singer; Songwriter. *Career:* Founder member, Genesis, 1969–75; Appearances include: with Genesis: Reading Festival, 1971, 1972, 1973; UK and US tours; Solo artiste, 1975–; Solo appearances include: World-wide tours; Knebworth II, 1978; Reading Festival, 1979; Inaugurator, WOMAD Festival Bath, 1982–; Amnesty International benefit tour, 1987; Hurricane Irene Benefit, Japan, 1987; Prince's Trust Rock Gala, 1988; Nelson Mandela tribute concerts, Wembley, 1988, 1990; Senegal (with Youssou N'Dour), 1991; The Simple Truth concert for Kurdish refugees, Wembley, 1991. *Compositions include:* Co-writer: Bully For You, Tom Robinson; Listen To The Radio, Tom Robinson; Animals Have More Fun, Jimmy Pursey; Film scores: Birdy, 1985; Last Temptation of Christ, 1989; Original music for Millennium Dome show, Greenwich, London, 2000. *Recordings:* Albums with Genesis: From Genesis To Revelation, 1969;

Foxtrot, 1972; Genesis Live, 1973; Selling England By The Pound, 1973; Nursery Crime, 1974; The Lamb Lies Down On Broadway, 1974; Solo albums include: 4 albums all entitled Peter Gabriel, 1977–82 (Third album No. 1, UK, 1980); Peter Gabriel Plays Live, 1983; So (No. 1, UK), 1986; Passion, 1989; Shaking The Tree – Sixteen Golden Greats, 1990; Us, 1992; Revisited, 1992; Secret World (interactive CD), 1995; Come Home to Me Snow, 1998; Ovo, 2000; Featured on: All This and World War II, 1975; Exposure, Robert Fripp, 1979; Conspiracy of Hope (Amnesty International), 1986; Set, Youssou N'Dour, 1989; Exile, Geoffrey Oryema, 1990; It's About Time, Manu Katche, 1992; Until The End of The World, (soundtrack), 1992; Tower of Song (Leonard Cohen tribute), 1995; Compiler, Plus From Us, 1993; Singles include: Solsbury Hill, 1977; Games Without Frontiers, 1980; Biko, 1980 (live version, 1987); Shock The Monkey, 1982; Sledgehammer (No. 1, USA), 1986; In Your Eyes, 1986; Don't Give Up (duet with Kate Bush), 1986; Big Time, 1987; Red Rain, 1987; Digging In The Dirt, 1992; Steam, 1993; Blood of Eden, 1993; Kiss That Frog, 1993; Come Talk to Me, 1993; Lovetown, 1994; Snow Flake, 1994; Contributor, Sun City, Artists United Against Apartheid, 1985; Rainbow Warriors, 1989; Until The End of The World (soundtrack), 1991; Give Peace A Chance, the Peace Choir, 1991. *Honours:* Ivor Novello Awards: Outstanding Contribution To British Music, 1983; Best Song, 1987; BRIT Awards: Best British Male Artist, Best British Music Video, Sledgehammer, 1987; Best Producer, 1993; 9 Music Video Awards for Sledgehammer, and Video Vanguard Trophy, 1987; Grammy Awards: Best New Age Performance, 1990; Best Short Form Video, 1993. *Address:* c/o Real World Inc, Real World Studios, Box, Wiltshire SN13 8PL, England.

GABRIELLE (Louisa Gabrielle Bobb); b. 16 May 1970, Hackney, London, England. Singer; Songwriter. *Career:* Solo recording artiste, 1993–; US tour, 1994; British tour, 1996; Performed with Paul Weller. *Recordings:* Albums: Find Your Way, 1993; Gabrielle, 1996; Rise (No. 1, UK), 2000; Dreams Can Come True: Greatest Hits Vol. 1, 2001; Hit singles: Dreams (No. 1, UK), 1993; Going Nowhere, 1993; I Wish, 1994; Because of You, 1994; Give Me A Little More Time, 1996; Forget About The World, 1996; If You Really Cared, 1996; If You Ever, with East 17, 1996; Walk On By, 1997; Sunshine, 1999; Rise (No. 1, UK), 2000; When A Woman, 2000; Should I Stay, 2000; Out of Reach, featured in film Bridget Jones' Diary, 2001; Don't Need The Sun To Shine (To Make Me Smile), 2001. *Honours:* Brit Awards: Best Newcomer, 1994; Best British Female Solo Artist, 1997. *Current Management:* Johnny Lawes Management, 18 All Saints Rd, Unit 8, London W11 1HH, England.

GAGE Peter; b. 31 Aug. 1954, London, England. Musician (Guitar, Keyboards); Prod.; Arranger; Programmer; Engineer. m. 1) Elkie Brooks, 2) Ruby James, 15 Aug. 1996. *Education:* Eltham College, London, England; BSc, Computing, University of Westminster, London. *Musical Education:* O Level Music; Grade 5 Classical Piano. *Career:* Formed and Lead, Geno Washington and the Ram Jam Band; Formed Dada and Vinegar Joe; Featuring Robert Palmer and Elkie Brooks; 1973: Musical Director for Elkie Brooks; Commenced Production, Engineering career with Debut LP for Joan Armatrading, 1974; TVs including Best of the Old Grey Whistle Test. *Compositions:* She's Lost You, for film, Less Than Zero; Hazy Shade of Winter, Bangles; Black Smoke, Calumet, UK Top 20, 1972. *Recordings:* Back To the Night, Joan Armatrading, album, 1974; Wrecking Crew, album; Johnny Remember Me, The Meteors, 1985; Live at the Klubfoot, 1985–87. *Leisure interest:* Counting money. *Current Management:* c/o Stamina Management. *Address:* 47 Prout Grove, London NW10 1PU, England.

GAHAN David; b. 9 May 1962, Epping, England. Vocalist. m. 1) Joanne Fox, 4 Aug. 1985, 1 s., 2) Theresa Conroy, 11 April 1992, 3) Jennifer Skilas, 14 Feb. 1999, 1 d. *Career:* Founder Member, Depeche Mode, 1980–. *Recordings:* 12 Top Ten Singles include: Just Can't Get Enough, 1981; See You, 1982; Everything Counts, 1983; People Are People, 1984; Master and Servant, 1984; Enjoy the Silence, 1990; I Feel You, 1993; Condemnation, 1993; In Your Room, 1994; Barrel of a Gun, 1997; It's No Good, 1997; Dream On, 2001; 13 Top Ten Albums include: Speak and Spell, 1981; A Broken Frame, 1982; Construction Time Again, 1983; Some Great Reward, 1984; The Singles 81–85, 1985; Black Celebration, 1986; Music For the Masses, 1987; 101, 1989; Violator, 1990; Songs of Faith and Devotion, 1993; Ultra, 1997; The Singles 86>98, 1998; Dream On, 2001. *Honour:* Brit Award, Enjoy the Silence, 1991. *Leisure interest:* Painting. *Current Management:* Jonathan Kessler, Baron Inc, 41 River Terrace, #3508 New York, NY 10282, USA. *Address:* First Floor, Regent House, 106 Marylebone High St, London W1M 3DB, England.

GALANIN Sergey; b. 16 Nov. 1961, Moscow, Russia. Singer; Songwriter; Musician (Guitar, Bass). m. Olga Galanina, 5 Feb. 1982, 1 s. *Education:*

Railroad College. *Musical Education:* Music School. *Career:* Member of various bands including: Redkaya Ptitsa, Gulliver, Brigada S, Brigadiry Ser'ga; Regular tours in Russia, and appearances at festivals; Concerts in Finland, 1987; Tours of Germany and USA, 1989; Concerts in Poland and Czechoslovakia; Played at Moscow Musik Peace Festival in 1989 with Bon Jovi, Scorpions, Ozzy and others. *Recordings:* All This Is Rock 'N' Roll, by Brigada S; Rivers, by Brigada S; I Adore Jazz, by Brigada S; Dog's Waitz, by Ser'ga, 1994; Ser'ga, 1995. *Leisure interest:* Studio Work. *Current Management:* Dmitri Griosman. *Address:* 121309 Moscow, Novozavodskaya St 27, Russia.

GALLAGHER Benny; b. Largs, Ayrshire, Scotland. Singer; Songwriter; Musician (guitar). *Career:* Songwriting partnership with Graham Lyle, 1960s-; Member, McGuinness Flint, 1969–71; Folk duo, Gallagher and Lyle, 1972–79; Solo artiste, 1980-. *Compositions:* Co-writer with Graham Lyle: Mr Heartbreak's Here Instead, Dean Ford; International, Mary Hopkins; for McGuinness Flint: When I'm Dead and Gone; Malt and Barley Blues; for Gallagher and Lyle: Heart On My Sleeve; I Wanna Stay With You. *Recordings:* Albums: with Gallagher and Lyle: Gallagher and Lyle, 1972; Willie and The Lap Dog, 1973; Seeds, 1973; The Last Cowboy, 1974; Breakway, 1976; Love On The Airways, 1977; Showdown, 1978; Gone Crazy, 1979; Lonesome No More, 1979; The Best Of, 1980; Breakaway, 1981; Live In Concert, 1999; Singles: I Wanna Stay With You, 1976; Heart On My Sleeve, 1976; Also contributed to albums by: Sandy Denny, Slim Chance, Jim Diamond, Isla St Clair.

GALLAGHER Eve; b. 12 Feb. 1956, Sunderland, England. Singer. *Education:* Drama at College; Language Schools; Swiss Schools. *Musical Education:* Opera lessons. *Career:* Actress, singer, various West End musicals include: Hair; Oh Calcutta; Signed by, and co-writer with Boy George, More Protein Records. *Recordings:* Hit Dance single: Love Come Down, 1991; Love Is a Master of Disguise, 1995; The Dubs EP, 1996; Heartbreak, 1996; Album: Woman Can Have It, 1995; features on: The Unrecouped One Man Bandit, Boy George, 1999. *Honours:* Best Actress in Shakespeare aged 18: Queen Margaret in Richard III. *Leisure interests:* Opera; Biographies; Cooking; Languages. *Current Management:* Action Artist Management, Förrlibuckstrasse 66, 8005 Zurich, Switzerland. *Address:* 7 Pepys Court, 84 The Chase, London SW4, England.

GALLAGHER Liam; b. 21 Sept. 1972, Burnage, Manchester, England. Vocalist; Musician (guitar, keyboards). m. Patsy Kensit, 1 s. *Career:* Founder member, Oasis, 1991–; Support tours with Verve; Concerts include: Glastonbury Festival, 1994; US debut, Wetlands, New York; Earls Court, London (UK's largest-ever indoor concert), 1995; Glastonbury, headlining, 1995; Knebworth (largest-ever outdoor concert), 1996; Regular tours, UK, Europe, USA; Left Creation Records to set up own Big Brother label, 1999. *Recordings:* Albums: Definitely Maybe (No. 1, UK), 1994; What's The Story (Morning Glory)? (No. 1, UK), 1995; Be Here Now (No. 1, UK), 1997; Masterplan, 1998; Standing on the Shoulder of Giants (No. 1, UK), 2000; Familiar To Millions (Live), 2001; Singles: Supersonic, 1994; Shakermaker, 1994; Cigarettes and Alcohol, 1994; Live Forever, 1994; Whatever, (No. 3, UK), 1994; Some Might Say (No. 1, UK), 1995; Wonderwall (No. 2, UK), 1995; Roll With It (No. 2, UK), 1995; Don't Look Back In Anger (No. 1, UK), 1996; D'You Know What I Mean, (No. 1, UK), 1997; Stand By Me (No. 2, UK), 1997; All Around the World (No. 1, UK), 1998; Go Let It Out (No. 1, UK), 2000; Who Feels Love?, 2000; Sunday Morning Call, 2000. *Honours:* BRIT Awards: Best Newcomers, 1995; Best Album, Best Single, Best Video, Best British Group, 1996; BRIT Nominations: Best Group, Best Album; Q Awards: Best New Act, 1994; Best Live Act, 1995; 2 Multi-Platinum albums. *Current Management:* Ignition, 54 Linhope St, London NW1 6HL, England.

GALLAGHER Noel; b. 29 May 1967, Burnage, Manchester, England. Singer; Songwriter; Musician (guitar). m. Meg Matthews. *Career:* Roadie, guitar technician, Inspiral Carpets, 1990–93; Member, Oasis, 1991–; Full-time member, 1993–; Debut performance, Boardwalk, Manchester, 1991; Support tours with Verve; Concerts include: Glastonbury Festival, 1994; US debut, Wetlands, New York, 1994; Earl's Court, London (UK's largest ever indoor concert), 1995; Glastonbury, headlining, 1995; Knebworth, largest ever outdoor concert, 1996; Regular tours, UK; Europe; US. *Recordings:* Albums: Definietely Maybe (No. 1, UK), 1994; What's The Story (Morning Glory)? (No. 1, UK), 1995; Be Here Now (No. 1, UK), 1997; The Masterplan, 1998; Standing on the Shoulder of Giants (No. 1, UK), 2000; Familiar To Millions (Live), 2001; Hit singles: Supersonic, 1994; Shakermaker, 1994; Cigarettes and Alcohol, 1994; Live Forever, 1994; Whatever, (No. 3, UK), 1994; Some Might Say (No. 1, UK), 1995; Wonderwall (No. 2, UK), 1995; Roll With It (No. 2, UK), 1995; Don't Look Back In Anger (No. 1, UK), 1996; D'You Know What I Mean, (No. 1, UK), 1997; Stand By Me (No. 2, UK), 1997; All Around the World (No. 1, UK), 1998; Go Let It Out (No. 1, UK), 2000; Who Feels Love?, 2000; Sunday Morning Call, 2000; Also contributed vocals to Chemical Brothers' singles: Setting Sun (number 1, UK), 1996; Let Forever Be, 1999. *Honours:* BRIT Awards: Best Newcomers, 1995; Best British Group, Best Album, Best Single, Best Video, 1996; BRIT Nominations: Best Group; Best Album; Q

Awards: Best New Act, 1994; Best Live Act, Ivor Novello Award 1995; 2 Multi-Platinum albums; Music Week Award, Top Songwriter, 1996. *Current Management:* Ignition Management, 54 Linhope St, London NW1 6HL, England.

GALLAGHER Rob, (Rob Galliano, Earl Zinger); b. 18 Oct. 1964, London, England. Vocalist; Prod. *Career:* Founder and member of Galliano, 1988–96; Group signed to Gilles Peterson's Talkin' Loud label; Solo career, recording as Earl Zinger; Collaborations: Mick Talbot; Valerie Etienne; Ski Oakenfull. *Recordings:* Albums: In Pursuit of The 13th Note, 1991; A Joyful Noise Unto The Creator, 1992; The Plot Thickens, 1994; 4our, 1996; Put Your Phazers On Stun and Throw Your Health Food Skyward (as Earl Zinger), 2001; Singles: Frederick Lies Still, 1988; Prince of Peace, Skunk Funk, 1992; Roofing Tiles, 1996; Song 2 (as Earl Zinger), 2000. *Membership:* PRS. *Address:* c/o Red Egyptian Records, 15 Allen Rd, Stoke Newington, London, N16 8SB, England.

GAMBLE Patsy; b. 13 Sept. 1963, Stroud, Gloucestershire. Saxophonist; Teacher. *Career:* Teacher, Schools and Improvisation Workshops, 1990–; Toured with British Blues Circuit with The Little Big Horns; Worked With 90 Proof, Ray Sharpe, Eddie Martin, Steve Winwood, Gary Baldwin, Dick Heckstall-Smith. *Recordings:* Albums, Life On The Plains; Blue To The Bone; Fires and Floods. *Memberships:* Musicians Union; PAMRA. *Leisure interests:* Walking; Painting; Dogs. *Current Management:* P Gamble, Hendy, Butterrow Lane, Stroud, Gloucester, GL5 2LX.

GANC David; b. 24 May 1958, Rio De Janeiro, Brazil. Musician (flute and saxophone); Arranger. m. Monique C Aragao, 1 s. *Musical Education:* Graduate, Music, Federal University of Rio De Janeiro; BA Professor of Music, Berklee College of Music; Flute pro-art Semibars (Odette Ernest Dia), Norton Morozonicz, Federal University of Rio with C Noltzenlogel, Berklee College with Joe Viola, Gary Burton; Harmony with John Neschling. *Career:* Side musician, recording and playing with artists including: Stevie Wonder (Free Jazz Festival '95); Gal Costa; Simone; Paulo Moura; Luiz Melodia; Nivaldo Ornelas; Elba Ramalho; Geraldo Azevedo; Monique Aragao; Emílio Santiago; Recording musician at Globo TV; Special radio programme with David Ganc Quartet at Radio Mec; Played as guest saxophonist, Brazilian Symphony Orchestra; Also from Brasilia. *Recordings:* Solo album: Brazilian Ballads, 1996; Solo track at Contemporary Woodwind Brazilian Players, 1994; More than 60 CDs and records, as musician; Appears on: Visom Brazil, 1993; Antonio Carlos Sings the Music of Jorge Amado, 1997; Recorded for films, theatre, ballet soundtracks. *Leisure interests:* Literature; Cinema. *Current Management:* Zillion Prod Art LTDA. *Address:* R Miguel Couto 134–404 Rio de Janiero RJ, Brazil.

GANE Tim; b. 12 July 1964, Barking, Essex, England. Musician (guitar, keyboards, percussion, programming); Songwriter. *Career:* Member: Unkommuniti, early 1980s; McCarthy, c. 1985–90; Stereolab, 1991–; Blip; Turn-On; Son Alex with band member Laetitia Sadier; Collaborations: Ui; Brigitte Fontaine; Nurse With Wound; Herbie Mann. *Recordings:* Albums include: Peng!, 1992; Transient Random Noise Bursts With Announcements, 1993; Mars Audiac Quintet, 1994; Music For The Amorphous Body Study Center, 1995; Emperor Tomato Ketchup, 1996; Dots and Loops, 1997; Cobra and Phases Group Play Voltage In The Milky Night, 1999; The First of The Microbe Hunters, 2000; Sound-Dust, 2001. *Current Management:* Martin Pike c/o Duophonic Ultra High Frequency Disks. *Internet:* www.stereolab.co.uk.

GANLEY Allan; b. 11 March 1931, Tolworth, Surrey, England. Musician (drums); Arranger; Composer. m. June, 15 Aug. 1970, 1 d. *Musical Education:* Composing, arranging, Berklee School of Music, Boston, USA, 1970. *Career:* Started 1953, with big bands of Jack Parnell; Ambrose; Geraldo; John Dankworth; Own small band, later joined The Tubby Hayes Quintet; Accompanied many American artistes, including: Jim Hall, Stan Getz; Ronnie Scott; Clark Terry; Performed with: Al Haig; Dizzy Gillespie; Bobby Brookmeyer; George Shearing; Peggy Lee; Blossom Dearie; The Pizza Express All-Star Band; Dave Shepherd Quintet; Stephane Grappelli; Carol Kidd; Cleo Laine and John Dankworth; 10 years in Bermuda; Invited to Florida to appear in March of Jazz programme. *Compositions:* Composed, arranged and conducted for BBC Radio Orchestra; BBC Radio Big Band; Jack Sharpe Orchestra; Arrangements for Marion Montgomery; Carol Kidd; Elaine Delmar; Georgie Fame. *Recordings with:* Henry Mancini; Robert Farnon; George Shearing; Yehudi Menuhin; Stephane Grappelli; Nelson Riddle; 2 albums with Scott Hamilton; series of albums with Warren Vache and Tony Coe; Recorded in New York with Jim Hall. *Honours:* Melody Maker Poll winner, several times, 1950s-60s; British Jazz Awards, 1980s, 1990s; Best Arranger/Composer, British Jazz Awards, 1998. *Leisure interests:* Keen tennis player; Studying scores. *Address:* 5 Asher Dr., Ascot, Berkshire, England.

GANNON Oliver; b. 23 March 1943, Dublin, Ireland. Jazz Musician (guitar). m. Patty Hervey, 14 Feb. 1979, 1 s., 1 d. *Education:* 2 years, Engineering, University of Manitoba. *Musical Education:* BMus, Berklee

College of Music, Boston, USA. *Career:* Lives and performs in Vancouver area; Played at major jazz festivals world-wide including Montreux, Switzerland; Concord, USA; North Sea, Netherlands; Toronto; Québec; Montréal; Winnipeg; Vancouver; 3 Russian tours with Fraser MacPherson Quartet. *Recordings:* with Fraser MacPherson: Live At The Planetarium; Live From Montreux; I Didn't Know About You; Indian Summer; Honey and Spice; Encore; In The Tradition; with Ian MacDougall Quartet: Rio; Three; The Warmth of the Horn; also albums with George Robert Quintet; Pacific Salt; Fred Stride; Kenny Colman; Wynton Marsalis and Pearl Brown; Gary Guthman; Charles Mountford. *Honour:* JUNO Award, Best Jazz Album, I Didn't Know About You, 1982. *Memberships:* SOCAN; Musicians' Asscn. *Leisure interests:* Golf; Computer programming. *Address:* 2781 McKenzie Ave, White Rock, BC V4A 3H5, Canada.

GARBAREK Jan; b. 4 March 1947, Norway. Musician (saxophone); Songwriter; Prod. *Musical Education:* Self-taught saxophone. *Career:* Group with Jon Christensen, Arild Andersen, Terje Rypdal, 1960s; Played with: Keith Jarrett's Belonging, Ralph Towner, 1970s; Leader, own groups, featuring Bill Frisell, Eberhard Weber, Nana Vasconcelos, 1980s-; Also played with: Don Cherry; George Russell. *Recordings:* Esoteric Circle, 1969; Afric Pepperbird, 1971; Triptykon, 1972; Sart, 1972; Dis, 1977; Places, 1978; Photo With, 1979; Eventyr, 1980; Paths, Prints, 1982; Wayfarer, 1983; Works, 1984; It's OK To Listen To The Gray Voice, 1985; All Those Born With Wings, 1986; Legend of The Seven Dreams, 1988; I Took Up The Runes, 1990; Twelve Moons, 1993; Visible World, 1996; Rites, 1999; Mnemosyne, 1999; Rosensfole, 2000; with Keith Jarrett: Belonging; My Song; Luminesence; Arbour Zena; with Ralph Towner: Solstice; Sounds and Shadows; with George Russell: Othello Ballet Suite; Trip To Prillarguri; Electronic Sonata For Souls Loved By Nature; with L Shankar: Song For Everyone; Art Lande: Red Lanta, 1974; with Bobo Stenson: Witchi-Tai-To, 1974; Dansere, 1976; with Charlie Haden and Egberto Gismonti: Magico, 1980; Folk-songs, 1981; with Kjell Johnsen: Aftenland, 1980; with Agnes Buen Garnås: Rosensfole, 1991; with Ustad Fateh Ali Khan: Ragas and Sagas, 1993; with The Hilliard Ensemble: Officium, 1994; with Anouar Brahem, Madar, 1994.

GARBUTT Vin; b. South Bank, Middlesbrough, England. Folk Musician (guitar, tin-whistle); Singer; Songwriter; Humorist. *Career:* Professional musician, songwriter, 1969-; Appearances include: USA; Canada; Australia; Hong Kong; Indonesia; Europe; New Zealand; Bermuda; Festivals world-wide including: Cambridge; Edinburgh; Wath; Auckland; Fylde; Television show, Small Folk, Yorkshire TV (proceeds to Save The Children Fund). *Recordings:* Albums include: The Valley of Tees, 1972; Young Tin Whistle Pest, 1974; King Gooden, 1976; Eston California, 1978; Tossin' A Wobbler, 1978; Little Innocents, 1983; Shy Tot Pommy, 1986; When The Tide Turns, 1989; The South Banker Show, 1991; The Bypass Syndrome, 1992; Bandalised, 1994; Plugged, 1995; When The Tide Turns Again, 1998; Word of Mouth, 2001; Video: The South Banker Show, 1991; Appeared on: Street Cries, Ashley Hutchings, 2001. *Current Management:* c/o Jim McPhee, Acorn Entertainments. *Address:* Winterfold House, 46 Woodfield Rd, Kings Heath, Birmingham B13 9UJ, England.

GARCIA Dean; b. 3 May 1958, London, England. m. J P Fletcher, 1 s., 1 d. *Career:* World tours: Eurythmics; Sinead O'Connor; Tours: Bryan Ferry; Curve (own band), radio, television, world touring; Television: Ian Dury; Japan; Established multimedia internet company. *Compositions include:* Chinese Burn, for Sony Minidisc advertisement, 1998. *Recordings:* Albums: Curve: Doppleganger, 1992; Cuckoo, 1993; Public Fruit; Come Clean, 1998; Open Day At The Hate Fest, 2001; Gift, 2001; Eurythmics: Touch, 1983; Be Yourself Tonight, 1985; Mick Jagger: Primitive Cool, 1987; Lethal Weapon 1, film soundtrack; Gang of Four: Tattoo; Ultrasound: Flying Saucer; Last of England soundtrack (Derek Jarman); Recoil: Liquid, 2000; Strange Hours, 2000. *Memberships:* PRS; Musicians' Union; PAMRA. *Leisure interests:* Animation; Photography; Sampling; Sleeping; Worrying. *Current Management:* Scott Rodger Quest Management. *Address:* c/o mushimushi, PO Box 26332, London N8 9WZ, England. *Internet:* www.mushimushi.net.

GARDEUR Jacques; b. 9 Nov. 1953, Paris, France. Musician (guitar); Composer. m. 7 July 1990, 2 s. *Education:* University. *Musical Education:* Study, Music department, Paris 8 University; Master class with: Barre Philips, Charlie Haden; Jose Barrense-Dias. *Career:* Began career, 1965; Album recorded with choir school; Session man with several blues, jazz and funk music groups, 1975-; Currently plays with Gwendoline Sampe, jazz singer. *Compositions:* TV film music for Antenne 2 (France TV). *Membership:* Union des Musiciens de Jazz (UMJ). *Leisure interests:* Sport; Motor racing; Family. *Current Management:* Mezza-voce. *Address:* 1 rue de L'Emaillerie, 93200 St Denis, France.

GARDINER Bobby; b. 1939, Aughdarra, County Clare, Ireland. Musician (accordion); Teacher. *Career:* Member: Kilfenora Ceili Band; Malachy Sweeney band, 1950s; Moved to New York, 1961; Made recordings and joined US Army; Returned to Ireland, 1970s; Member: Bru Boru; Teaches at University College, Cork. *Recordings:* Albums: Memories of Clare, 1962;

Bobby Gardiner At Home, 1979; The Best of Bobby Gardiner, 1982; The Master's Choice, 1989; The Clare Shout, 1998. *Address:* c/o Bobby Gardiner, Burncourt, Cahir, County Tipperray, Ireland.

GARDINER Boris Oliver Patrick; b. 13 Jan. 1943, Kingston, Jamaica. Vocalist; Musician (bass, piano, guitar). Divorced, 2 s., 2 d. *Musical Education:* Self-taught. *Career:* Lead singer, singing group, The Rhythm Aces, 1960; Kes Chin and Souvenirs Band, 1962; Bassist, vocalist, Carlos Malcolm Afro Jamaican Rhythm Band, 1964; Formed own band, The Boris Gardiner Happening, 1968-82; Performances: USA; Canada; Central America; Caribbean Islands; Bahamas; Guyana; major concerts: Dupon Plaza, Miami; New York Hilton; Playboy Hotel, Jamaica; Sun Splash, Jamaica; The Cat and Fiddle, Nassau, Bahamas; Oslo, Norway; UK; Shared stages with: Jackie Wilson; Brook Benton; Roy Hamilton; The Stylistics; Nina Simone; The Blue Notes; Bob Marley; Radio, TV include: Top of The Pops, BBC1 TV; France; Spain; Netherlands. *Recordings:* Elizabethan Reggae, 1970; I Wanna Wake Up With You (No. 1, UK), 1986; You Are Everything To Me, 1986; Next to You, 1992; Reggae Happening, 1996; Melting Pot, 1999; Solo albums include: Is What's Happening, 1995; Studio musician, bass guitar, recordings include: Punky Reggae Party, Bob Marley; Young Gifted and Black, Bob and Marcia; Police and Thieves, Junior Marvin and The Upsetter - Lee Perry. *Honours:* Best Vocalist, Swing Magazine Awards, 1972; Canadian Reggae Music International Awards, Top Reggae Single, I Wanna Wake Up With You, 1986; Annual Hall of Fame Award, Excellence In The Arts, Jamaica. *Memberships:* MCPS; PRS. *Leisure interests:* Dominoes; Backgammon; Watching TV; Fixing Things. *Address:* 2 Solo Way, Queensborough, Kingston 19, Jamaica.

GARDNER Colin David; b. 16 Jan. 1952, Quernmore. Leader Singer; Musician (Rhythm Guitarist). m. Caroline Gardner, 2 s., 2 d. *Career:* Air play on major radio stations; Interview on Louth Meath FM. *Compositions:* Thoughts of Yesterday; Mother Natures Miracle Anew; Hands of Time; Brand New Dawn; Reasons; Honky Tonking; Missing You; Boomers Bar Blues; My Wife; Mr Blues. *Recordings:* Brand New Dawn; In The Stillness of The Night. *Membership:* PRS. *Leisure interests:* Song Writer. *Current Management:* Mike Croft, Monster Music. *Address:* 28 Glen View Cres., Heysham, Morecambe, Lancashire LA3 2QW, England.

GARDNER Jeff; b. 23 Oct. 1953, New York, USA. Musician (piano); Composer; Educator. *Education:* 2 years Harvard University. *Musical Education:* Study with Hall Overton; Nadia Boulanger; John Lewis; Jaki Byard; Don Friedman; Ivan Tcherepnin. *Career:* Played in Brazil with Wayne Shorter; Hermeto Pascoal; Pat Metheny; Helen Merrill; Helio Delmiro; Monterey Jazz Festival, with Victor Assis Brasil, Clark Terry, Slide Hampton, 1980; European tours with Steve Lacy and Eddie Harris; Concerts with Gary Peacock; Freddie Hubbard; Solo concerts for French television and radio; Piano Quartet with Martial Solal, Paul Bley, Jaki Byard, 1985; Solo concert tour, Brazil, 1992; Tour, France with Rick Margitza, 1995; Also played with Kenny Wheeler; André Ceccarelli; Paulo Moura; Charlie Mariano; Etta Cameron; Duo with Andrew Schloss, performed IRCAM, Paris; Germany; USA; Worked with soprano S'Ange Susan Belling; Concerts include: October Jazz Festival, Saint Lucia; CMAC, Martinique; Paris Jazz Festival; Madajazzcar Festival, Antananarivo; Tour of Japan, with Lisa Ono, 1996. *Recordings:* Continuum, trio with Eddie Gomez, Billy Hart; Alchemy, duo with Gary Peacock; Spirit Call; Sky Dance, with Gilberto Gil; Second Home, with Rick Margitza; California Daydream, Kenny Wheeler. *Publications:* Jazz Piano - Creative Concepts and Techniques; Co-author, Jazz Transcription, with Niels Lan Doky. *Membership:* SACEM. *Current Management:* Lena Michals, 1802 Laurel Canyon Blvd, Los Angeles, CA 90046, USA. *Address:* 44 rue Sarrette, 75014 Paris, France.

GARFUNKEL Art (Arthur); b. 5 Nov. 1941, Forest Hills, New York, USA. Singer; Actor. m. Kim Cermak, 18 Sept. 1988, 1 s. *Education:* BA, Columbia, 1965; MA, 1967. *Career:* Member of duo Simon and Garfunkel (with Paul Simon), 1966-70; Appearances with Paul Simon include: Royal Albert Hall, 1967, 1968; Monterey Pop Festival, 1967; Madison Square Garden, 1972; Central Park, New York, 400,000 audience, 1981; Several other reunion tours and benefit concerts; Solo artiste, 1972-; Concerts include: Carnegie Hall, New York, 1981; Sofia, Bulgaria, for 1.4m. people, 1990; Film appearances include: Catch 22, 1970; Carnal Knowledge, 1971; Bad Timing... A Sensual Obsession, 1980; Good To Go, 1986. *Recordings:* Albums include: with Simon and Garfunkel: Wednesday Morning 3AM, 1966; Sounds of Silence, 1966; Parsley Sage Rosemary and Thyme, 1967; Bookends (No. 1, UK and US), 1968; The Graduate (soundtrack) (No. 1, UK and US), 1968; Bridge Over Troubled Water (No. 1, UK and US), 1970; Greatest Hits, 1972; Concert in Central Park, 1982; Old Friends, 1997; Tales From New York (compilation), 2000; Solo: Angel Clare, 1973; Breakaway, 1975; Watermark, 1978; Fate For Breakfast, 1979; Scissors Cut, 1981; The Art Garfunkel Album, 1984; The Animals Christmas, 1986; Lefty, 1988; Garfunkel, 1991; Up 'Til Now, 1993; Across America, 1997; Songs from a Parent to a Child, 1997; Numerous hit singles include: with Simon and Garfunkel: The Sound of Silence (No. 1, USA), 1965; Homeward

Bound, 1966; I Am A Rock, 1966; Hazy Shade of Winter, 1966; At The Zoo/ 59th Street Bridge Song (Feelin' Groovy), 1967; Scarborough Fair, 1968; Mrs Robinson (No. 1, USA), 1968; The Boxer, 1969; Bridge Over Troubled Water (No. 1, UK and US), 1970; Cecilia, 1970; El Condor Pasa (If I Could), 1970; America, 1972; My Little Town, 1975; Solo: All I Know, 1973; I Only Have Eyes For You (No. 1, UK), 1975; Crying In My Sleep, 1977; Bright Eyes (film theme for Watership Down) (No. 1, UK), 1979; Contributed vocals to: Grateful, John Bucchino, 2000. *Honours include:* Numerous Grammy Awards, for Mrs Robinson, 1969; Bridge Over Troubled Water, 1971; Britannia Award, 1977; Inducted into Rock and Roll Hall of Fame, 1990. *Current Management:* Metropolitan Entertainment, PO Box 1566, 7 N Mountain Ave, Montclair, NJ 07042, USA.

GARIEPY Kevin; b. 7 March 1958, Montréal. Residential Counsellor. 1 d. *Education:* BA, McGill University, Psychology; Classical Guitar with Mike Nipoliano and Juan Tomas. *Career:* Part Time Musician, Multi Instrumentalist; Composer and Publisher with Ursa Major Music. *Compositions:* Drums of Change; The Rhythm King; Wonderous World. *Address:* 15713 Thrift Ave, White Rock, BC Canada, V4B 2M3.

GARLAND Hank 'Sugarfoot' (Walter Louis); b. 11 Nov. 1930, Cowpens, South Carolina, USA. Jazz and Country Musician (guitar); Songwriter. *Musical Education:* Self-taught. *Career:* Session guitarist, Nashville; Played numerous sessions with Elvis Presley, 1958–61; Concerts with Elvis include: Benefit Show, Honolulu, 1961; Moved into country-jazz; Television and radio shows include New York City and Chicago; Car accident affected playing ability, 1961. *Recordings include:* Solo albums: The Velvet Guitar of Hank Garland; Jazz Winds From A New Direction, 1961; Unforgettable Guitar; And His Sugar Footers, 1992; with Elvis Presley: Original 50 Gold Award Hits; Something For Everybody; Elvis Is Back; Elvis Aron Presley; His Hand In Mine; Other recordings include: A Legendary Performer, Jim Reeves; Original Golden Hits, Jerry Lee Lewis; Lonely Weekends, Charlie Rich; Gibson, Guitars, and Girls, Don Gibson; Country Hall of Fame, Patsy Cline; with Webb Pierce: The Best Of; Western Express; Boogie With A Bullet, Dutch Redita; The Red Foley Story, Red Foley; Also recorded with: Justin Tubb; Patti Page; Grady Martin; Owen Bradley; Autry Inman; Tommy Jackson; Hank Williams Sr; Johnny Horton; Bobby Darrin; The Nashville All-Stars; Various anthologies. *Honours:* Rock and Roll Hall of Fame; Gibson Hall of Fame; Country Music Hall of Fame. *Memberships:* BMI; ASCAP. *Current Management:* Brother Billy. *Address:* Jacksonville, Florida, USA.

GARLAND Tim, (Tim Garland-Waggett); b. 19 Oct. 1966, Ilford, Essex, England. Musician (saxophone); Composer. m. Amanda Phillipa Cooper, 28 July 1995. *Education:* West Kent College. *Musical Education:* Guildhall School of Music. *Career:* Joined Ronnie Scotts Band, aged 23; Started jazz/ folk fusion band Lammas; Several British tours; Radio appearances include: Radio 3, Lammas with strings; Circle Suite, South Bank; Dankworth Generation Band, Jason Rebello, London Jazz Orchestra; Full time member of Chick Corea's Origin sextet, 1999; CD recorded for Stretch Records, spring 2000. *Compositions include:* Dance For Human Folk, for big band (recorded by BBC Big Band). *Recordings include:* Lammas: Lammas; Lammas: This Morning; The Broken Road, 1995; Source Book, 1997; Sea Changes, 1999; Dankworth Generation Band: Nebucadnezzar; Live At Ronnies; Solo: Enter the Fire, 1996. *Honours:* BBC Soloist Award, 1988; British Jazz Awards: Best Ensemble, 1993; BBC Composition Award, 1995. *Memberships:* PRS; MCPS. *Leisure interests:* Meditation; Folk traditions. *Address:* Lammas, Flat 7, 75 West Hill, London SW15 2UL, England.

GARNIER Laurent; b. 1 Feb. 1966, Boulogne Sur Seine, France. Prod.; Remixer; DJ. *Career:* Trained as a chef; Moved to London to work in French embassy; Relocated to Manchester; DJ at the world famous Hacienda club; Co-founder: F Communications record label; Resident DJ at the Rex Club, Paris; Remixed: Reese Project; System 7. *Recordings:* Albums: A Shot In The Dark, 1994; 30, 1996; Unreasonable Behaviour, 2000; Singles: Acid Eiffel, Astral Dreams, 1994; Club Traxx EP, 1995; Crispy Bacon, Flashback, 1997; The Man With The Red Face, Greed, 2000. *Honours:* Victoire De La Musique Award, 30 (album), 1996. *Address:* c/o F Communications, 20–22 rue Richer 75009 Paris, France. *E-mail:* info@fcom.fr.

GARRETT Kenny; b. 1960, Detroit, Michigan, USA. Musician. *Career:* Joined The Duke Ellington Orchestra, 1978; Musician, The Mel Lewis Orchestra and the Dannie Richmond's Quintet, 1982; Numerous concerts world-wide; Extensive Tours. *Recordings:* Black Hope; Triology; Pursuance: The Music of John Coltrane; Song book; Amandla Dingo; Live Around The World; Miles Davis and Quincy Jones: Live at Montreux; Introducing Kenny Garrett; Prisoner of Love; African Exchange Student; Simply Said, 1999; Old Folks, 2001; Also guests on recordings by: Cindy Blackman; Art Blakey; Donald Byrd; Herbie Hancock; Jon Hassell; Freddie Hubbard; Branford Marsalis; Marcus Miller; Jon Scofield. *Honours:* Named Hot Jazz Artist, Rolling Stone, 1996; Named Alto Saxist of the Year, Down Beat Readers Poll, 1996; Grammy Nomination, Best Jazz Instrumental

Performance by a Group, 1997. *Current Management:* Burgess Management, 3225 Prytania St, New Orleans, LA 70115, USA.

GARRETT Peter; b. Australia. Singer. *Education:* BA, Australian National University; BLLB, University of New South Wales, 1977. *Career:* Member, Rock Island Line; Lead singer, Midnight Oil, 1976–; Regular tours world-wide including: Earthquake benefit concert, New South Wales (with Crowded House), 1990; Solo performance, Earth Day Sound Action benefit, Foxboro, Massachusetts (with Joan Baez, Steve Miller, The Kinks), 1992; Earth Day Sound Action Benefit, Columbia, 1993; Strong links with ecological groups; Benefit concerts for: Aboriginal Rights Association; Tibet Council; Song proceeds for Deadicated to Rainforest Action Network and Cultural Survival; Protest concert, Exxon Building (Exxon Valdez oil spill), 1990; Ran for Australian Senate, Nuclear Disarmament Party, 1984. *Recordings:* Albums: with Midnight Oil: Head Injuries, 1979; Bird Noises, 1980; Place Without A Postcard, 1981; Red Sails In The Sunset, 1982; 10 9 8 7 6 5 4 3 2 1, 1983; Diesel and Dust, 1987; Blue Sky Mining, 1990; Scream In Blue – Live Earth, Sun and Moon, 1992, 1993; Breathe, 1996; 20,000 Watt RSL – The Midnight Oil Collection, 1997; Redneck Wonderland, 1998; The Real Thing (live), 2000; Hit single: Beds Are Burning, 1989; Contributor, Artists United Against Apartheid album, 1985; Deadicated (Grateful Dead tribute album), 1991. *Honours:* 4 Australian Record Industry Assen Awards, 1991; Crystal Globe Award, Sony Music, 1991; Gold and Platinum discs. *Memberships:* Past President, Australian Conservation Foundation, 1987; Board mem., Greenpeace International. *Current Management:* Gary Morris Management, PO Box 186, Glebe, NSW 2037, Australia.

GARRETT Siedah; b. 1963, Los Angeles, California, USA. Singer; Songwriter. *Career:* Backing Singer for Quincy Jones and Michael Jackson; Joined Brand New Heavies, 1997–98; Solo career. *Recordings:* Don't Look Any Further, duet with Dennis Edwards, 1984; I Just Can't Stop Lovin' You (duet with Michael Jackson) (No. 1, UK), 1987; co-wrote Man In The Mirror, Michael Jackson (No. 1, USA), 1988; Solo: Kiss of Life, 1991; K.I.S.S.I.N.G., 1991; Refuse to Be Loose, 1991; Backing vocals: Madonna, True Blue, 1986; Michael Jackson, Bad, 1987; Sarah Vaughan, Brazilian Romance, 1987; Barbra Streisand, Till I Loved You, 1988; Aretha Franklin, Through the Storm, 1989; Curtis Stigers, Curtis Stigers, 1991; Michael Jackson, Dangerous, 1992; Mica Paris, Whisper a Prayer, 1993; Quincy Jones, Q's Jook Joint, 1994; Michael Jackson, History: Past, Present and Future, 1995; Dionne Warwick, Aquarela Do Brazil, 1995; Dumb and Dumber, film soundtrack, 1995; Brand New Heavies, Shelter, lead vocals and arrangements, 1997; Ray Charles, Ultimate Hits Collection, 1999; Quincy Jones, I'm Yours, single, 1999; Scorpions, Eye II Eye, 1999; Enrique Iglesias, Escape, 2001.

GARRICK Michael; b. Enfield, England. Composer; Pianist; Bandleader; Organist; Teacher; Lyricist. *Education:* BA Hons, London; Postgraduate Certificate in Education; Open Fellowship to Berklee College of Music, Boston, Massachusetts, USA. *Career:* BBC broadcasts, 1960–; Director, Poetry and Jazz in Concert, 1961–69; Director of Travelling Jazz Faculty, Founder, Wavendon Jazz Course; Director, Jazz Academy vacation courses and record label; Group Leader of Trio, Sextet, Big Band, ensembles; First jazz musician to give concerts on pipe organs at St Paul's Cathedral, 1968; Royal Festival Hall, 1969; Coventry Cathedral, 1973; Guest Conductor, European Community Youth Jazz Orchestra; Faculty, RAM 1985–98, Trinity College of Music, Guildhall summer school. *Compositions include:* Jazz Praises, 1967: Mr Smith's Apocalypse, 1969; Judas Kiss, 1971; The Hobbit Suite, 1973; Heavenly Bodies, 1977; Underground Streams, 1979; Faces of Love, 1980; Catechism, 1981; Zodiac of Angels, 1988 (symphony orchestra); Carioca Celebration, 1983; New Flower of Europe, 1981; The Stirring, 1982; Romance of the Rose, 1986 (Rhapsody for jazz violinist and orchestra); Hardy Country, 1990; Garrick's Jazz Characters, 1960–; The Royal Box, 1993; Bovingdon Poppies, 1993; A Diana Sonata, 1997; Asha's Ear, 1999; For Children: All God's Children; Tree of Dreams; What is Melody?; Norman Gnome and the Rhinoceros; Jazz Curries. *Recordings:* Poetry and Jazz in Concert (4 Vols); October Woman; Promises; Black Marigolds; Heart is a Lotus; Home Stretch Blues; Troppo; You've Changed; Kronos; Cold Mountain; Anthem; Jazz Praises at St Paul's, 1968; A Lady in Waiting, 1993; Meteors Close at Hand, 1994; Parting is Such, 1996; For Love of Duke... and Ronnie, 1998; Down on Your Knees, 1999. *Contributions to:* Jazz Now; Times Educational Supplement; The Stage; Piano Magazine. *Honour:* Hon. ARAM; Whittingham Award, 1997. *Memberships:* Royal Society of Musicians; Assen of British Jazz Musicians; President, Berkhamsted Jazz Society. *Leisure interests:* Sound Recording; Motorcycling. *Current Management:* Jazz Academy Resources, 12 Castle St, Berkhamsted, Hertfordshire HP4 2BQ, England.

GARRITY Freddy; b. 14 Nov. 1936, Manchester, England. Vocalist. *Career:* Member, groups The Red Sox; The John Norman Four; The Kingfishers, later changed to Freddy and The Dreamers; Performances include: Cavern Club, with the Beatles, 1962; Royal Albert Hall, 1963; British tour with Roy Orbison, 1964; Beatles Christmas Show, Hammersmith Odeon, London, 1964; Regular television appearances include: Let's Go; Beat Show; Sunday Night At The London Palladium; Shindig; Hullaballoo; Film appearances: What A Crazy World, 1963; Every Day's A Holiday, 1964; Regular club and cabaret performances with the New Dreamers, 1968–; Concerts include: The Biggest '60s Party In Town, Olympia Hall, London, 1992; Actor, stage performance, The Tempest, 1988. *Recordings:* Hit singles: If You Gotta Make A Fool of Somebody, 1963; I'm Telling You Now (No. 1, USA), 1963; You Were Made For Me, 1963; I Understand, 1964; Albums: Greatest Hits, 1998. *Address:* c/o Jason West Agency, Gables House, Saddlebow, Kings Lynn, Norfolk PE34 3AR, England.

GARTSIDE Green, (Green Strohmeyer-Gartside); b. 22 June 1956, Cardiff, Wales. Singer; Songwriter. *Education:* Leeds Art School. *Career:* Founder member, Scritti Politti, 1977–; Concerts include: British tour, support to Joy Division, 1979; Futurma Festival, Leeds, 1979; Montreux Pop Festival, 1988. *Compositions:* The Sweetest Girl, 1981 (also recorded by Madness); The Perfect Way, 1985 (also recorded by Miles Davis); Love of a Lifetime, Chaka Khan, 1986; L Is For Lover (co-written with David Gamson), Al Jarreau, 1986. *Recordings:* Albums: with Scritti Politti: Songs To Remember, 1982; Cupid and Psyche 85, 1985; Provision, 1988; Anomie and Bonhomie, 1999; Singles: The Sweetest Girl, 1981; Faithless, 1982; Asylums In Jerusalem/Jacques Derrida, 1982; Wood Beez (Pray Like Aretha Franklin), 1984; Absolute, 1984; Hypnotize, 1984; The Word Girl, 1985; The Perfect Way, 1985; Oh Patti, 1988; She's A Woman (with Shabba Ranks), 1991; Take Me In Your Arms and Love Me, 1991; Tinseltown To The Boogiedown, 1999; Contributor: Sweet Dreams (Are Made of This) album, Eurythmics, 1982; film soundtrack Who's That Girl?, 1987; Music of Quality and Distinction Vol. II, British Electric Foundation compilation album, 1991. *Current Management:* c/o Simon Hicks, PO Box 2950, London W11 3ZX, England.

GARVEY Phil; b. 14 Jan. 1965, Reading, Berkshire, England. Vocalist; Musician (guitar, percussion). *Career:* Random Music, 1985–86; Plumbers, 1986–87; Solo folk clubs to 1990; Daisy Telethon Band, 1990; Free Spirits, 1991–94; Misfits Menagerie, 1994-. *Compositions:* 93 titles include: Would She Dance For Me; Step Out Your Frame; Nobody Fights Time; Here Comes The Twist. *Recordings:* Dance With Me Daisy (comedey record), 1990; Free Spirits album: Spirited Approach, 1993. *Publications:* A Good Day To Run Away, short novel, 1994. *Membership:* Musicians' Union. *Leisure interests:* Writing; Travel; Abstract ideas; Cartoons. *Current Management:* J Cooper. *Address:* J Cooper, 44 Springhill Rd, Goring, Berkshire RG8 0DA, England.

GARZON Albert; b. 26 Feb. 1960, Newburgh, New York, USA. Record Prod.; Ragtime Musician (piano); Co Pres. *Education:* BS, Fredonia State College, New York. *Musical Education:* Studied piano; Music composition; Sound recording. *Career:* Produced over 50 albums for artists including: 10,000 Maniacs; Brenda Kahn; Hypnolovewheel; Arson Garden; Antietam; Solo Piano Rags of James Scott; President, Com Four Distribution, import/exporter of CDs and LPs. *Recordings:* Music of James Scott. *Leisure interests:* World travel, especially Russia, Africa, Mexico. *Address:* 7 Dunham Pl., Brooklyn, New York, NY 11211, USA.

GATELY Stephen; b. 17 March 1976, Dublin, Ireland. Vocalist. *Career:* Member, Boyzone; Solo career, 2000-. *Recordings:* Singles: Working My Way Back To You, 1994; Key To My Life, 1995; Love Me For A Reason, 1995; So Good, 1995; Father and Son, 1995; Coming Home Now, 1995; Words (No. 1, UK), 1996; A Different Beat (No. 1, UK), 1996; Isn't It A Wonder, 1997; Baby Can I Hold You Tonight, 1997; Musical Experience, 1997; Picture of You, 1997; All That I Need (No. 1, UK), 1998; I Love The Way You Love Me, 1998; When The Going Gets Tough (No. 1, UK), 1999; You Needed Me (No. 1, UK), 1999; Albums: A Different Beat, 1997; Where We Belong, 1998; By Request (No. 1, UK), 1999; Solo Singles: New Beginning/Bright Eyes, 2000; I Believe, 2000; Solo album: New Beginning, 2000.

GATLIN Larry Wayne; b. 2 May 1948, Seminole, Texas, USA. Singer; Songwriter. m. Janis Gail Moss, 9 Aug. 1969, 1 s., 1 d. *Career:* Country singer, songwriter, 1971–; Member, Gatlin Brothers. *Recordings:* Albums: with Gatlin Brothers: Partners; Living In The Land of Dreams; Cooking Up A Storm; Live At 8pm; Pure 'n' Simple; Solo albums include: Houston To Denver, 1984; Straight Ahead; Adiois, 1992; Moments to Remember, 1993; In My Life, 1998; 16 Biggest Hits, 2000. *Honours:* 2 BMI Songwriter Awards for Delta Dirt, 1975; Broken Lady, 1976; 3 ACM Awards, Best Album, Single, Male Vocalist, 1980. *Membership:* CMA. *Address:* c/o Gatlin Enterprises, 7003 Chadwick Dr., Suite 360, Brentwood, TN 37027, USA.

GATTO Olivier; b. 22 Jan. 1963, Manosque, France. Musician (double bass); Arranger; Composer. m. Lydia Filipovic, 11 Sept. 1993. *Education:* University of Sciences, Bordeaux, France. *Musical Education:* Berklee College of Music, Boston, USA. *Career:* Concerts with Joe Henderson Quartet; Billy Cobham Quartet; Ravi Coltrane Quartet; Roy Hargrove and Antonio Hart; Julian Joseph; Ernie Watts; Bill Evans; Benny Golson Quartet; Vincent Herring Quartet; Mark Turner; Jerry Bergonzi; European

tour with John Stubblefield, George Cables and Billy Hart; French television shows, Radio France, Voice of America. *Recordings:* Album: Here and There (featuring Billy Cobham, George Cables, John Stubblefield), 1996; Craig Bailey, Brooklyn, featuring Rufus Reid. *Leisure interests:* History; Cooking; Football; Jogging. *Current Management:* Danielle Gatto. *Address:* 2 Ave Jules Valles, 77176 Savigny le Temple, France.

GAUDETTE Claude; b. 15 Oct. 1959, Montréal, Québec, Canada. Composer; Prod.; Musician (keyboards). *Musical Education:* Montréal Conservatory of Music; Dick Grove School of Music, Los Angeles; New York Recording Workshop. *Career:* Musical Director, France Joli, Yamaha International Song Festival, 1985; Keyboards, David Foster's Super Producer '94 Tour, Japan. *Recordings:* Producer, writer, musician on albums: The Colour of My Love, Celine Dion; Belinda, Belinda Carlisle; Everlasting, Good To Be Back, Natalie Cole; Slip of The Tongue, Whitesnake; also albums by Fiona; Michael Bolton; Peter Cetera; Earth Wind and Fire; Roberta Flack; Sergio Mendes; Eddie Money; Dionne Warwick; Kenny Loggins; Five Star; Little River Band; Smokey Robinson; Martika; Barry Manilow; George Benson; The Commodores; Celine Dion; Ricky Martin; Singles: Mad About You, Belinda Carlisle; Wind Beneath My Wings, Bette Midler; Time of My Life, Bill Medley and Jennifer Warnes; Make Me Lose Control, Eric Carmen; I Live For Your Love, Pink Cadillac, Natalie Cole; Walk Away, Dionne Warwick; also singles by Sheena Easton; Kenny Loggins; Melissa Morgan; Ziggy Marley; Film soundtracks include: Pretty Woman; Three Men and A Little Lady; Raw Deal; Dirty Dancing; Beaches. *Memberships:* BMI; NARAS; SCL. *Leisure interests:* Cooking; Water Sports; Golf. *Address:* 4912 Stern Ave, Sherman Oaks, CA 91423, USA.

GAUDRY Michel-Marie-Marcel; b. 23 Sept. 1928, Eu, France. Divorced, 2 d. *Musical Education:* Piano from ages 5 to 8; Clarinet from 8 to 23, then bass. *Career:* Jazz music, singers; TV shows; Accompanied Billie Holiday; Carmen McRae; Blues singers; T Flanagan; Sweden; Madagascar; La Reunion; Les Autilles; European Jazz Orchestra (London); Europe; Russia; Japan; Africa; South America; USA; Canada; England. *Recordings:* With Duke Ellington; Louis Armstrong; Billy (Strayhorn); Barney Kessel; Bud Powell Trio; Double-Six of Paris; Records with Barbera; G Moustaki; C H Dumont. *Honours:* Representing France, Big-Band Jazz Europe, London. *Leisure interests:* Drawing; Photography; History.

GAUL Sven H; b. 11 April 1953, Flensburg, Germany. Musician (drums); Television Personality. *Education:* Degree, University of Aarhus in German Language. *Career:* Member, rockband, Taurus, 1974–80; Member, Pop/rockband, TV-2, 1980–; Host, television show, Lul, Lul, Rocken Gaar, 1989; Member, Danish Music Council, 1991-. *Recordings:* 1 live recording and numerous other releases. *Honour:* Danish Grammy, 1985. *Membership:* Danish Musician Union. *Leisure interests:* Film and Design. *Address:* Arhus Musikkontor, Mindegadelo, 8000 Aarhus, Denmark.

GAUSDEN Guy; b. 8 Aug. 1965, Bromley, Kent, England. *Career:* Member of The Beloved, until 1987; Drummed with various artists; Director, 13 Artists Agency; Manager, Element and Fanzine. *Address:* 13 Artists, 36 Langham St, London W1N 5RH, England.

GAUTHIER Marcel; b. 7 Nov. 1963, Iberville, Québec, Canada. Arranger; Publisher. 1 s., 1 d. *Education:* BAC, Musique Generale; DEC, Musique Professionel; Classical Guitar, 1977–; Jazz Piano, 1985. *Career:* Arranger and Copyist, Samedi de Rire, Demons du Midi, Country Centre-Ville, Double Etoiles, La Fureur, La Boite à Chansons, ADiSQ. *Compositions:* Il fait toujours beau quelque part, Radio theme, Radio Canada; Un pitbull chez les moules (big band); Desert (recorded by Robin Grenon); Stimulus (Robin Grenon). *Recordings:* Stimulus (with Robin Grenon, harp); Dionne (with Jean-Marie Dionne); Carmen Bonifacio (keyboards); Claude Olivier (keyboards); Secret Lake (with Christian Vanderre). *Membership:* SOCAN. *Leisure interests:* Birdwatching; Insects; Reflexology; Computers. *Current Management:* Notason. *Address:* 440 de L'Église, Verdun, QC H4G 2M4, Canada.

GAUTHIER Mary Veronica; b. Thibodaux, Louisiana, USA. Vocalist; Musician (guitar). *Education:* Louisiana State University, studied Philosophy. *Career:* Surname pronounced 'go-shay'; Sometimes bracketed as a country artist but is more in the singer-songwriter or alternative country area; After a troubled few years as an adolescent and young adult involving crime, drugs and alcohol, went to University and opened an award-winning restaurant; Now concentrates on music career and plays many of the top USA folk festivals including: Kerrville; Philadelphia; Newport. *Recordings:* Dixie Kitchen, 1997; Drag Queens In Limousines, 1999. *Honours:* GLAMA (Gay and Lesbian American Music Awards), Country Artist of the Year, 2000. *Internet:* www.marygauthier.com.

GAVIN Frankie; b. 1956, Corrandulla, County Galway, Ireland. Musician (fiddle, whistle, flute); Composer. m. Tracey Harris. *Musical Education:*

Learned music from parents. *Career:* Founder: De Danann, 1973; Performed for: President Kennedy; Prince Charles; Francois Mitterand; Collaborations: Rolling Stones; Yehudi Menuhin; Stephane Grappelli; Appeared in TV series Bringing It All Back Home, 1992; Wrote soundtrack for TV series The Irish RM. *Recordings:* Albums include: Anthem (with De Danann), 1985; Omos Do Joe Cooley (with Paul Brock), 1986; Jigs and Jazz (with Stephane Grappelli), 1993; Welcome To The Hotel Connemara (with De Danann), 2000; solo: Croch Suas E, 1983; Frankie Goes To Town, 1991; Fierce Traditional, 2001. *Honours:* Winner: All Ireland Fiddle; All Ireland Flute competitions, 1973; Gold disc, How The West Was Won, 2000; AIB, Traditional Music Award, 1996. *Internet:* home.att.net/~FrankieGavin/.

GAY Albert; b. 25 Feb. 1928, London, England. Clarinet; Soprano Sax; Tenor Sax. m. Doreen Gay, 1 Sept. 1983, 1 d. *Education:* Guildhall School of Music. *Career:* Many broadcasts with Freddy Randall, Alex Welsh, Al Gay Quartet (BBC Jazz Club); Background Music in films: Two Left Feet; L-Shaped Room; TV: Alex Welsh; Bob Wallis; Keith Smith; Harry and Laurie Gold; Jo Daniels Bands. *Compositions:* South Track for South Bank Show; Band Leader, Queen Mary, 1961. *Recordings:* CDs; Paul Jones-Elaine Delmar; Ruby Braff, Alex Welsh and Freddy Randall; The World's Greatest Jazz Band, Stockholm. *Honour:* Nominated Melody Maker and Birmingham Jazz Society. *Membership:* Musicians' Union. *Leisure interest:* Cooking. *Current Management:* Freelance. *Address:* Lanterns, North St, Winkfield, Berks, SL4 4SY, England.

GAYLE Crystal, (Brenda Gail Webb); b. 9 Jan. 1951, Paintsville, Kentucky, USA. Country Singer. m. Vassilios (Bill) Gatzimos, 1 s., 1 d. *Career:* Recording artiste with Decca Records, late 1960s; Regular appearances, Jim Ed Brown's television show, The Country Place; Played UK concerts with Kenny Rogers; Loretta Lynn (sister); Appeared at Wembley Country Music Festivals, 1971, 1977, 1979; First US country artist to perform in China, 1979; Contributor, film soundtrack, One From The Heart, 1982. *Recordings:* Hit singles include: Wrong Road Again; Beyond You; I'll Get Over You; Don't It Make My Brown Eyes Blue; Talking In Your Sleep; Your Kisses Will; Your Own Cold Shoulder; Half The Way; Cry; You and I, with Eddie Rabbitt; Making Up For Lost Time, with Gary Morris; Albums include: Crystal Gayle, 1974; Somebody Loves You, 1975; Crystal, 1976; We Must Believe In Magic, 1977; When I Dream, 1978; I've Cried The Blues Right Out of My Eyes, 1978; We Should Be Together, 1979; Miss The Mississippi, 1979; A Woman's Heart, 1980; These Days, 1980; Hollywood/Tennessee, 1981; True Love, 1982; One From The Heart, with Tom Waits, 1982; Cage The Songbird, 1983; Nobody Wants To Be Alone, 1985; Crystal Gayle, 1986; Straight To The Heart, 1986; What If We Fall In Love, 1987; Nobody's Angel, 1988; Ain't Gonna Worry, 1990; Three Good Reasons, 1992; Someday, 1995; Walk with Me, 1996; Mountain Christmas, 1996; Sings the Heart and Soul of Hoagy Carmichael, 1999; In My Arms, 2000. *Honours:* Female Vocalist of the Year, Academy of Country Music, 1976; Grammy Awards: Beat Female Country Vocal Performance, Best Country Song; Female Vocalist of The Year, CMA. *Current Management:* Gayle Enterprises Inc, 51 Music Sq. E, Nashville, TN 37203, USA.

GAYLE Michelle; b. 2 Feb. 1971, London, England. Singer; Songwriter; Actress. m. Mark Bright. *Career:* Actress, UK television series: Grange Hill; EastEnders; Solo singer, 1993–; Concerts include: Radio 1's Massive Music British tour, 1995; Starred in Beauty and the Beast, West End show, London. *Recordings:* Albums: Michelle Gayle, 1995; Sensational, 1997; Hit singles: Looking Up, 1993; Sweetness, 1994; I'll Find You, 1994; Freedom, 1995; Happy Just To Be With You, 1995; Sensational, 1997; Do You Know, 1997; Contributor, The Gift of Christmas, Child Liners, 1995; Guest vocals on In My Room, Me One, 2000. *Honours:* Smash Hits Awards; Gold Disc, Michelle Gayle. *Current Management:* Denis Ingoldsby, First Avenue Management, The Courtyard, 42 Colwith Rd, London SW6 1RU, England.

GAYNOR Gloria; b. 7 Sept. 1947, Newark, New Jersey, USA. Singer. *Career:* Singer with the Soul Satisfiers, 1960s; Solo disco music artiste, 1970s-. *Recordings:* Albums: Never Can Say Goodbye, 1975; Experience Gloria Gaynor, 1976; I've Got You, 1976; Glorious, 1977; Love Tracks, 1979; I Have A Right, 1979; Stories, 1980; I Kinda Like Me, 1981; Gloria Gaynor, 1983; I Am Gloria Gaynor, 1984; The Power of Gloria Gaynor, 1986; Best Of, 2000; The Album, 2002; Hit singles: Never Can Say Goodbye, 1974; Reach Out I'll Be There, 1975; I Will Survive (No. 1, USA and UK), 1979; I Am What I Am, 1983; Can't Take My Eyes Off of You, 1991; Love Is Just a Heartbeat Away, 1995; Mighty High, 1997; Set Me Free, 1998. *Current Management:* Cliffside Music Inc, PO Box 374, Fairview, NJ 07022, USA.

GEDDES Chris; b. 2 Oct. 1975. Musician (piano, keyboards). *Career:* Member: Belle and Sebastian, 1996–; V Twin 1999–; Golden Rodeo; Collaborations: Arab Strap; Salako; Curated Bowlie Weekend Festival with other Belle and Sebastian band members, 1999. *Recordings:* Albums: Tigermilk, If You're Feeling Sinister, 1996; The Boy With The Arab Strap 1998; Fold Your Hands Child – You Walk Like A Peasant, 2000; Singles: Dog On Wheels EP, Lazy Line Painter Jane EP, 3–6–9 Seconds of Light

EP, 1997; This Is Just A Modern Rock Song EP, 1998; Legal Man, 2000; Jonathan David, I'm Waking Up To Us, 2001. *Honours:* Brit Award, Best Newcomer, 1999. *Current Management:* Banchory Management, PO Box 25074, Glasgow G2 6YL, Scotland. *Internet:* www.belleandsebastian.co.uk.

GEERS Didier; b. 9 Sept. 1954, Ghent, Belgium. Drums; Percussion; Vocal. m. Naima Barbro Johansson, 10 Aug. 1986, 2 s., 1 d. *Education:* Ghent Music Conservatoir; Drums and percussion lessons; Vocal coaching by Richard Boone. *Career:* 32 albums as Contributor: Sammy Rimington Band, Waso Quintet, George Probert, Al Casey, Bill Dillard Earl Warren; 3 Solo Albums: Didier Geers Jazz and Blues Band, 1986–89; Touring with Eddie Burns Guitar (blues); Member of Papa Bue's Viking Jazz Band, Copenhagen-DK, 7 years; Actual, with own trio The DNA Band. *Honour:* Golden Mermaid Award, Oostende, 1971. *Leisure interests:* Music; Theatre. *Current Management:* Wim Wigt Productions, Roghorst 303, PO Box 201, 6700 AE, Wageningen, Holland. *Address:* Didier Geers, Karl Nils väg 15–17, 290 11 Linderöd, Sweden.

GEFFEN David; b. 21 Feb. 1943, Brooklyn, New York, USA. Film, Recording and Theatre Exec. *Career:* Worked at William Morris talent agency, 1964; Launched new film studio DreamWorks, with Steven Spielberg and Jeffrey Katzenberg, 1996; Co-founder (with Laura Nyro), Tunafish Music Publishing; Joined Ashley Famous Agency; Executive Vice-President, Creative Man, 1968; Co-founder (with Elliot Roberts), Asylum Records and Geffen-Roberts Manufacturing Company, 1970 (later merged with Elektra Records); Vice Chairman, Warner Brothers Pictures, 1975–76; Founder, Geffen Records, Geffen Film Company; Films produced include Little Shop of Horrors; Beetlejuice; Men Don't Leave; Defending Your Life; Co-producer, musicals: Dreamgirls; Little Shop of Horrors; Cats; Chess; Founder, DGC record label. *Address:* c/o Geffen Film Company, 9130 Sunset Blvd, Los Angeles, CA 90069, USA.

GEILS Jerome; b. 20 Feb. 1946, New York, USA. Musician (guitar). *Education:* Worcester Technical College. *Career:* Member, The Hallucinations; Founder member, guitarist, The J Geils Blues Band, 1968–85; Appearances include: Fillmore East, New York, with the Allman Brothers, Beach Boys and Mountain, 1971; Mar Y Sol Festival, Puerto Rico, 1972; Pink Pop Festival, Netherlands, 1980; Regular tours, Europe, US, UK; Group disbands, 1985; Concert as Magic Dick/J Geils Blue Time, Paradise Club, Boston, 1992; Television includes: In Concert, ABC TV, 1973; Runs vintage and sports car shop, 1992-. *Recordings:* Albums: J Geils Band, 1971; The Morning After, 1971; Live, 1971; Bloodshot, 1973; Nightmares..., 1974; Hotline, 1975; Blow Your Face Out, 1975; Monkey Island, 1977; Sanctuary, 1979; Love Stinks, 1980; Freeze Frame (No. 1, US; No. 3, UK), 1982; Showtime!, 1983; You're Getting Even While I'm Getting Odd, 1984; Flashback, 1987; The J Geils Band Anthology: A Houseparty, 1993; The Best of The J Geils Band, 1998; Singles include: Looking For Love; Give It To Me; Must've Got Lost; Centrefold (US No. 1, 6 weeks); Angel In Blue; Freeze Frame; I Do; Fright Night, title track for film Fright Night. *Honours:* Rolling Stone magazine, Most Promising New Band, 1971; Various Gold discs; Platinum disc for Freeze Frame, 1982.

GELDOF Bob; b. 5 Oct. 1954, Dublin, Eire. Vocalist; Songwriter. m. Paula Yates, divorced, 3 d. *Education:* Black Rock College. *Career:* Journalist, New Musical Express, Melody Maker; Founder member, Boomtown Rats, 1975–84; Organizer, Band Aid Trust (incorporating Live Aid, Band Aid, Sport Aid), for Ethiopian famine relief, 1984–92; Solo artiste, 1986–; International tours, including UK, Europe, US, Japan, Australia; Major concerts include: California Music Festival, 1979; Live Aid, Wembley Stadium, 1985; Freddie Mercury Tribute, Wembley Stadium, 1992; Gosport Festival, 1992; Green Belt Festival, 1992; WOMAD's 10th Birthday, 1992; Film appearances: The Wall, 1982; Number One, 1985; Organizer, Do They Know It's Christmas?, Band Aid, (No. 1, UK), 1984; Participator, We Are The World, USA For Africa, 1984; Organizer, Live Aid concerts, Wembley and Philadelphia (estimated television audience of 2 billion, raising $70m.), 1985; Total of $144m. raised by 1992; Owner, television production company, Planet 24, creators of The Word (Channel 4 UK, 1990–95), The Big Breakfast (Channel 4 UK, 1992-), Survivor (ITV UK, 2001). *Recordings:* Albums with Boomtown Rats: The Boomtown Rats, 1977; A Tonic For The Troops, 1978; The Fine Art of Surfacing, 1979; Mondo Bongo, 1981; V Deep, 1982; Solo: Deep In The Heart of Nowhere, 1986; The Vegetarians of Love, 1990; The Happy Club, 1993; Sex Age and Death, 2001; Singles include: Looking After No 1, 1977; She's So Modern, 1978; Like Clockwork, 1978; Rat Trap (No. 1, UK), 1978; I Don't Like Mondays (No. 1, UK), 1979; Diamond Smiles, 1979; Someone's Looking At You, 1980; Banana Republic, 1980; House On Fire, 1982; Solo: This Is The World Calling, 1987; Love Like a Rocket, 1987; The Great Song of Indifference, 1990; Love or Something, 1990. *Publication:* Autobiography, Is That It?, 1987. *Honours include:* KBE (Hon), 1986; 4 Ivor Novello Awards; Order of Two Niles, Sudan; Order of Leopold II, Belgium; Irish Peace Prize; UN World Hunger Award; EEC Gold Medal; MTV Video Award, Special Recognition Trophy, 1985; American Music Award, Special Award of Appreciation, 1986; Gold and Platinum discs; Hon. degrees, Kent,

London, Ghent Universities. *Current Management:* Jukes Productions, 330 Harrow Rd, London W9 2HP, England.

GENEST Francis; b. 31 Dec. 1960, Paris, France. Musician (percussion). *Education:* Translator, Interpreter, Mastership in English. *Musical Education:* Self-taught; Worked with Giovanni Hidalgo, Farafina. *Career:* Performed at many festivals throughout Europe (France, Spain, Belgium, Italy); Several concerts for Radio France and the French Speaking Public Radios Community. *Recordings:* Albums with the Cache-Cache Trio: L'Océane; Tandems. *Honour:* First prize, National Jazz Contest with Cache-Cache trio. *Membership:* Union des Musiciens de Jazz, Paris. *Address:* La Guéraudière, 37380 Nouzilly, France.

GENTELET Hugues; b. France. Tour Man.; Co-Dir. *Career:* French tour manager for: Whigfield; Reel 2 Reel; A Deva; Rozalla; Dr Alban; Imagination; Boney M; Pasadenas; Kool and The Gang; Numerous other dance acts; Commercial director, Nuits Magiques Production. *Address:* Nuits Magiques Production, 50 Ave Du President Wilson, BT 104, 93214 La Plaine St Denis CDX, France.

GENTRY Bobbie, (Roberta Lee Streeter); b. 27 July 1944, Chicasaw County, Mississippi, USA. Singer; Songwriter; Musician (guitar). m. (1) Bill Harrah, (2) Jim Stafford. *Education:* Philosophy, Music. *Career:* Recording artiste, 1967–; UK television series, The Bobby Gentry Show, 1969; Retired from performing to look after business interests. *Recordings:* Hit singles: Ode To Billie Joe (No. 1, USA), 1967; Let It Be Me, with Glen Campbell; All I Have To Do Is Dream, with Glen Campbell; I'll Never Fall In Love Again (No. 1, UK), 1969; Albums: Bobbie Gentry and Glen Campbell, 1968; Local Gentry, 1968; Touch 'Em With Love, 1969; I'll Never Fall In Love Again, 1970; Fancy, 1970; Patchwork, 1971; Sittin' Pretty/Tobacco Road, 1971; Greatest Hits, 1990; The Golden Classics, 1998; Ode To Bobbie Gentry, 2000.

GENTRY Teddy; b. 22 Jan. 1952, Fort Payne, Alabama, USA. Musician(bass); Vocalist. *Career:* Founder member, country group Wild Country, 1969; Became Alabama, 1977–; Worked with Lionel Richie, 1986. *Recordings:* Albums: Alabama, 1980; My Home's In Alabama, 1980; Feels So Right, 1981; Mountain Music, 1982; The Closer You Get, 1983; Roll On, 1984; 40 Hour Week, 1985; The Touch, 1986; Greatest Hits, 1986; Just Us, 1987; Southern Star, 1989; Pass It On Down, 1990; Greatest Hits, Vol. 2, 1991; American Pride, 1992; Gonna Have a Party, 1993; In Pictures, 1995; Dancin' on the Boulevard, 1997; For the Record, 1998; When It All Goes South, 2001; Singles include: I Want To Be With You; My Home's In Alabama; Tennessee River; Feels So Right; Love In The First Degree; Pass It On Down. *Current Management:* Dale Morris and Associates, 818 19th Ave S, Nashville, TN 37203, USA.

GEORGE Jimmy; Composer; Prod.; Record Label Owner; Publisher. *Career:* Studio guitarist, played on many No 1 hits; Produced many top recording artists; Owner, recording studio; Two vocal hits while at University; Produced Mary Kaye Trio; Performed, Night clubs in Los Angeles; Toured US with the Beach Boys; Wrote and recorded with Jackie De Shannon, Dr John; Played guitar on hits for Michael Jackson, the Jackson Five, Diana Ross, Marvin Gaye, Thelma Houston; Performer, recording producer and musician for Etta James, Little Richard, Leon Russell, Chuck Berry, Ike and Tina Turner and Kenny Rogers; Songs recorded by Carl Anderson, Nancy Sinatra, Bobby Womack, the Commodores, Smokey Robinson, Taylor Dayne, The Temptations and George Benson; Performed in many major venues world-wide with Jimi Hendrix, Sly and the Family Stone, Crosby, Stills, Nash and Young, Janis Joplin; Performed on TV commercials and programmes; Toured as guitarist/bass player with Shaun Cassidy, Leif Garrett, Gary Lewis and the Playboys. *Compositions:* Numerous including: Magic Man; Just To See Her; I Wonder Who She's Seeing Now, The Temptations; I'll Always Love You, Taylor Dayne; Real Thing; Love Remembers, George Benson; Everything Reminds Me of You, Commodores; A Night To Remember. *Honours:* Numerous Grammy Awards and nominations. *Memberships:* Musicians Union, Los Angeles; American Federation of Television and Radio Artists; National Academy of Recording Arts and Sciences; Los Angeles World Affairs Council.

GEORGE Siwsann; b. 2 April 1956, Treherbert, Rhondda, Wales. Musician (harp, concertina, guitar, spoons); Teacher; Broadcaster. m. Roger Plater, 29 June 1991, 1 s. *Education:* Graduate, Aberystwyth University; Welsh College, Music and Drama. *Musical Education:* Traditional school grounding, mainly self-taught. *Career:* Lead singer, Mabsant (Welsh roots band), 1980–; Tours: USA; Far East; Western Europe; Latvia; Hungary; British Council; As soloist: British tour with Ray Fisher and Jo Freya, 1995; Purcell Room, London, 1995; With Robin Williamson, 1996. *Recordings:* With Mabsant: over a dozen recordings; Solo: Traditional Songs of Wales, with various musicians accompanying, 1994; Several television and film scores. *Publications:* Mabsant – Book of 54 Welsh Folk Songs. *Honours:* 3 times Pan Celtic Singing Winner, 1980–90. *Memberships:* Musicians' Union; Equity; Welsh Folk-song Society. *Leisure*

interests: Walking; Yoga. *Address:* 26 Bassett St, Abercynon CF45 4SP, Wales.

GERALDO Neil; b. 29 Dec. 1955. Musician (guitar); Record Prod. m. Pat Benatar, 20 Feb. 1982. *Career:* Guitarist, Derringer; John Waite; Guitarist, record producer, Pat Benatar, 1977–. *Compositions:* many for Pat Benatar. *Recordings:* with Pat Benatar: Albums: Crimes of Passion, 1980; Precious Time, 1981; Get Nervous, 1982; Get Nervous (producer), 1982; Live From Earth, 1983; Tropico, 1984; In The Heat of The Night, 1985; Seven The Hard Way, 1985; Best Shots, 1987; True Love (producer), 1991; Gravity's Rainbow, 1993; Also appears on: Best of Steve Forbert, 1993; Rock and Roll Hoochie Coo, 1996; Yesterday Today Tomorrow, 1997; Best of Rick Springfield, 1999; Singles include: Heartbreaker; All Fired Up; Treat Me Right; Love Is A Battlefield; Hell Is For Children; Invincible; Hit Me With Your Best Shot; Sex As A Weapon; We Belong. *Current Management:* Gold Mountain Management, 3575 Cahuenga Blvd W, Suite 450, Los Angeles, CA 90068, USA.

GERIMON Paul; b. 14 Oct. 1954, Dinant, Belgium. Singer-Deep Bass. *Education:* Classic Humanities, St Paul's College and Dinant's Royal Athenee; Superior Diplomas Violin and Voice; Opera Studio Brussels; Centre de Musique Baroque, Paris. *Career:* First appearance on Belgian Television singing Spirituals, 1972; Sings Opera, Standards, Original Songs, Musicals, Baroque and Contemporary, 1974–; First part of Kid Creole, with Allez Allez, 1982; Bass Soloist, Opera Royal Wallonie, 1983–86; TV-Radio appearances on Rai, O Globo, Radio France, RTB, WDR, FR3; Regularly invited at Festival D'Aix, TRM of Brussels, Berlin Philharmonie, Barbican Centre, Brooklyn Academy, Amsterdam, Lisbon, Rome, Paris, New York; Played part of Don Juan at Theatre, 1990; Tricentenary of La Monnaie, 1995; International tour with R. Jacobs and Trisha Brown Company, 1998–99; The Phantom of the Opera, 2000. *Recordings:* M. Kolbe, 1989; DuMont, 1992; WOMA, 1992; Sodoma, 1993; L'Orfeo, 1995; Intra Muros, 1996; Allez Allez, 1997; Euridice, 1998; Don Giovanni, 1999; TV-Films: La Vida Breve, 1985; M. Kolbe, 1989; L'Orfeo, 1998; Le Dernier Chant d'Orphée, 1998. *Honours:* Orphée D'or, 1991, De L'Académie du Disque, Paris. *Membership:* Union Des Artistes, Brussels. *Leisure interest:* Cycling. *Address:* Concertbureau Arien, De Boeystraat 6, 2018 Antwerpen, Belgium.

GERRITSEN Rinus; b. 9 Aug. 1946, The Hague, Netherlands. Vocalist; Musician (bass). *Career:* Founder member, Dutch rock group, Golden Earring, 1961–; Tours, Europe; Canada; US; Support to The Who, European tour, 1972; Support to Rush, 1982. *Recordings include:* Albums: Just Earrings, 1965; Winter Harvest, 1967; Miracle Mirror, 1968; On The Double, 1969; Eight Miles High, 1970; Golden Earring, 1971; Seven Tears, 1971; Together, 1972; Moontan, 1973; Switch, 1975; To The Hilt, 1975; Rock of The Century, 1976; Contraband, 1976; Mad Love, 1977; Live, 1977; Grab It For A Second, 1978; No Promises No Debts, 1979; Prisoner of The Night, 1980; Second Live, 1981; Cut, 1982; N E W S, 1984; Something Heavy Goin' Down, 1984; The Hole, 1986; Face It, 1994; Lovesweat, 1995; Naked II, 1997; Paradise In Distress, 1999; Fully Naked, 2001; The Devil Made Us Do It, 2001; Last Blast of The Century, 2001; with Michel Van Dijk: De G V D Band, 1979; Labyrinth, 1985; Very Best Vols 1 and 2, 1988; Bloody Buccaneers, 1991; Supernatural Fairy Tales, 1996; Hit singles include: Please Go, 1965; Dong-Dong-Di-Ki-Di-Gi-Dong (No. 1, Netherlands), 1968; Radar Love (No. 1, Netherlands), 1973; Twilight Zone, 1982; When the Lady Smiles, 1984; Turn the World Around, 1989; Temporary Madness, 1991; Another 45 Miles, 1993; Angel, 1995; Burning Stuntman, 1997; The Devil Made Me Do It, 1998. *Current Management:* Rob Gerritsen, Regentessestraat 29, 2713 EM Zoetermeer, Netherlands.

GERUP Martin; b. 24 Feb. 1960, Himmelev Sogn, Denmark. Singer; Composer; Musician (keyboards). m. Dorte Schou, 13 May 1995, 1 d. *Musical Education:* Danish Conservatory of Jazz, Rock and Latin Music. *Career:* Roskilde Festival, with Dieters Lieder, 1988; Roskilde Festival, with Flying Fish, 1993; Several radio and television shows. *Recordings:* with Dieters Lieder: Jeg Ka' Lieder, 1983; Hvorflink Ka' Man Blive?, 1986; with Flying Fish: It's Almost Fairytime, 1993. *Memberships:* Danish Artists Society; Danish Jazz, Rock and Folk Authors. *Leisure interests:* Fishing; Skiing. *Address:* Danish Artist Society, Vendersgade 24, 1363, Copenhagen K, Denmark.

GESSLE Per; b. 12 Jan. 1959, Halmstad, Sweden. Musician (guitar); Vocalist: Songwriter. *Career:* Member, Gyllene Tider; Solo artist and songwriter; Formed Roxette with Marie Fredriksson, 1986–; 38m. albums and 12m. singles sold world-wide by 1999; Tours throughout Europe; US; Central and South America; Asia; Television includes: The Tonight Show, NBC TV; MTV Unplugged, 1993; Founder and owner of music publishers: Jimmy Fun Music; Hip Happy; Tom Bone Music, co-owner; Gessle Music; Happy Accident Music. *Recordings:* Albums: Pearls of Passion, 1987; Look Sharp!, 1988; Joyride, 1991; Tourism, 1992; Crash! Boom! Bang!, 1994; Don't Bore Us, Get To The Chorus – Roxette's Greatest Hits, 1995; Balades En Español, 1996; Have a Nice Day, 1999; Room Service, 2001; Singles include: The Look (No. 1, USA and 22 countries), 1989; Listen To Your

Heart (No. 1, USA), 1989; Dressed For Success, 1989; Dangerous, 1990; It Must Have Been Love, featured in film Pretty Woman (No. 1, USA), 1990; Joyride (No. 1, US, and 18 other countries), 1991; Fading Like A Flower, 1991; The Big L, 1991; Spending My Time, 1991; Church of Your Heart, 1992; How Do You Do!, 1992; Queen of Rain, 1992; Almost Unreal, featured in film Super Mario Brothers, 1993; Sleeping In My Car, 1995; You Don't Understand Me, 1996; Wish I Could Fly, 1999; Anyone, 1999; Stars, 1999. *Honours:* Platinum and Gold discs; Grammy Awards; MTV Awards. *Current Management:* D & D Management, Lilla nygatan 19, 111 28 Stockholm, Sweden.

GHIGLIONE Bill Barita Daniel; b. 5 July 1947, Nice, France. Composer; Arranger; Musical Dir; Musician (keyboards). *Education:* University Literature Diploma (second cycle). *Musical Education:* Classical piano studies. *Career:* Tours include: Eddy Mitchell, 1976–77; Claude Nougaro, 1977; Johnny Halliday, 1978–79; Michel Polnareff, Japan (musical director), 1979; Maxime Le Forestier, Europe, 1982–83; Member, Dallas; Performer, theme music, television series Dallas; Producer, composer, Lasya Victory. *Recordings:* Dallas album, 1981; with Lasya Victory: L'Age D'or, 1989; Tout Ça Nous Fait Mal, 1990; Messie Est De Retour, 1991; Tout S'Arrange, 1992; Mona, 1993; Sound Design, television series Inventions of Life 3, 1995; Léa Ivanne, A Prendre ou à Laisser, 1999; Song of the Universal Exposition 2000 (Hanovre) Pavillion de France, To Enlighten The World, by Léa Ivanne (WEA). *Honours:* Double Gold Record Award, Dallas theme, 1982; Best French Record of Year, Tout Ça Nous Fait Mal, 1990. *Memberships:* SACEM; SCPP. *Leisure interests:* Esoterism; Unity of Religions; Peace on Earth. *Address:* 15 bis rue J J Rousseau, 94200 Ivry/Seine, France.

GIANEZ Laurent, (Laurent Gilbert Gianesini); b. 13 May 1942, Moyeuvre-Grande, France. Musician (flute). *Musical Education:* Diploma, flute, Conservatory, Metz. *Career:* Member various jazz groups including Duo J M Albertucci-Gianez; Ecaroh (style of Art Blakey); Quartet Gianez (own compositions, Samba music); Annual concert with Archie Shepp and Ted Curson. *Recordings:* Album with Duo Denis Moog-Gianez: Car La Rouille N'Aura Pas Raison Du Jazz (saxophone, guitar, trumpet); Currently recording own quartet. *Membership:* SACEM (Paris). *Address:* 26 rue de l'Eglise, 57140 Saulny, France.

GIBB Barry Alan Crompton; b. 1 Sept. 1946, Douglas, Isle of Man, England. Singer; Songwriter. m. Linda Gray, 1 Sept. 1970, 4 s., 1 d. *Career:* Formed The Bee Gees, with brothers Robin and Maurice, 1958–69; Reformed group, 1971; Appeared on own weekly television show, Australia; Returned to England; Signed with NEMS Enterprises, 1967; Performed live with Barbra Streisand, One Voice Concert/Video, 1987; Compositions: Co-writer (with brothers), Saturday Night Fever soundtrack, 1977 (40m. copies sold); Producer, co-writer, albums for: Andy Gibb; Barbra Streisand: Guilty; Dionne Warwick: Heartbreaker; Diana Ross: Eaten Alive; Kenny Rogers: Eyes That See In The Dark; Second most Top Ten hits written (after Lennon and McCartney); 5 simultaneous US Top Ten hits written by the Gibb brothers, 1978; Only artists to write and produce 6 consecutive No. 1 singles, 1979; Producer, writer, Grease, for Frankie Valli; Bee Gees songs recorded by artists including: Boyzone, Take That, Steps, 911, Tina Turner, Celine Dion, Elton John, Eric Clapton, Elvis Presley, Janis Joplin, Andy Williams, Glen Campbell, Rod Stewart, Roberta Flack, Frankie Valli, Michael Bolton; Saturday Night Fever musical stage show at London Palladium, Broadway and Sydney, as well as Cologne, Germany and Japan; Sell-out stadium concerts in Dublin, Wembley Stadium, London, Buenos Aires, South Africa, 1998; Stadium concerts, New Zealand, new Olympic stadium in Sydney, 1999; Millennium Eve concert, South Florida, 1999; 6 shows in Europe planned for 2000. *Recordings:* Albums include: Bee Gees 1st, 1967; Horizontal and Idea, 1968; Odessa, 1969; Cucumber Castle, 1971; Two Years On, 1971; Trafalgar, 1972; Life In A Tin Can, 1973; Mr Natural, 1974; Main Course, 1975; Children of The World, 1976; Here At Last... Live, 1976; Saturday Night Fever, 1977; Spirits Having Flown, 1978; Living Eyes, 1980; ESP, 1988; One, 1989; The Very Best of The Bee Gees, 1990; Tales From The Brothers Gibb (A History In Song 1967–90), 1990; High Civilisation, 1991; You Wouldn't Know, 1992; Size Isn't Everything, 1993; Solo: Now Voyager, 1984; Hawks, 1988; Still Waters, 1997; One Night Only (live), 1998; This Is Where I Came In, 2000; Their Greatest Hits – The Record, 2001; Singles include: To Love Somebody, 1967; Massachusetts (No. 1, UK), 1967; World, 1967; Words, 1968; I Gotta Get A Message To You (No. 1, UK), 1968; Don't Forget To Remember, 1969; Run To Me, 1972; Jive Talkin' (No. 1, USA), 1975; You Should Be Dancing, 1976; How Deep Is Your Love (No. 1, USA), 1977; Stayin' Alive (No. 1, USA), 1978; Night Fever (No. 1, UK and US), 1978; Too Much Heaven (No. 1, USA), 1978; Tragedy (No. 1, UK and US), 1979; Love You Inside Out (No. 1, USA), 1979; Spirits Having Flown, 1979; You Win Again (No. 1, UK), 1987; Secret Love, 1991; For Whom The Bell Tolls, 1993; Alone, 1997; Immortality, with Celine Dion, 1998; This Is Where I Came In, 2001. *Honours include:* 7 Grammy Awards; Inducted into Songwriters Hall of Fame; Inducted in Rock and Roll Hall of Fame, Cleveland; Lifetime Achievement Award, Brit Awards, London; International Artist Award, American Music Awards, Los Angeles.

Memberships: Musicians' Union; Equity. *Current Management:* Left Bank Organization, 9255 Sunset Blvd, Second Floor, Los Angeles, CA 90069, USA. *Address:* c/o 1801 Bay Rd, Miami Beach, FL 33139, USA.

GIBB Maurice Ernest; b. 22 Dec. 1949, Douglas, Isle of Man, England. Singer; Songwriter. m. Yvone Spenceley, 17 Oct. 1975, 1 s., 1 d. *Career:* Formed the Bee Gees, with brothers Barry and Robin, 1958–69; Reunited 1971; Performed in Australia during 1960s; Returned to England, signed with NEMS Enterprises, 1967; First US television appearance, American Bandstand, 1967; Saturday Night Fever musical stage show opens at London Palladium, 1998, Cologne, Germany, 1999, Sydney and Japan, 2000; Sell-out stadium concerts in Dublin, Wembley Stadium, London, Buenos Aires, South Africa, 1998; Stadium concerts in New Zealand and at new Olympic Stadium in Sydney, 1999; Millennium Eve concert in South Florida, 1999; 6 more shows planned in Europe, 2000. *Compositions:* Co-writer (with brothers), Saturday Night Fever soundtrack, (sold 40m. copies), 1977; Co-writer (with brothers), albums for: Andy Gibb; Barbra Streisand: Guilty; Dionne Warwick: Heartbreaker; Diana Ross: Eaten Alive; Kenny Rogers: Eyes That See In The Dark; Co-writer, second most Top 10 hits (after Lennon and McCartney); Only artists to write and produce six consecutive No. 1 singles; As producer: Co-producer (with Robin Gibb), Sunrise, Jimmy Ruffin; Three solo albums for Robin Gibb, 1982, 1984, 1986; Runaway, Carolla (Swedish star), 1986; Writer, producer, A Breed Apart film soundtrack; Bee Gees songs recorded by: Al Green; Elvis Presley; Janis Joplin; Sarah Vaughn; Johnny Mathis; Andy Williams; Glen Campbell; Richie Havens; Jose Feliciano; Rod Stewart; Eric Burdon; Roberta Flack; Nina Simone; Frankie Valli; Michael Bolton; Boyzone; Take That; 911; Steps; Tina Turner; Eric Clapton; Elton John; Celine Dion. *Recordings:* Albums include: Bee Gees 1st, 1967; Horizontal and Idea, 1968; Odessa, 1969; Cucumber Castle, 1971; Two Years On, 1971; Trafalgar, 1972; Life In A Tin Can, 1973; Mr Natural, 1974; Main Course, 1975; Children of The World, 1976; Here At Last... Live, 1976; Saturday Night Fever, 1977; Spirits Having Flown, 1978; Greatest Hits, 1979; Living Eyes, 1980; ESP, 1988; One, 1989; The Very Best of The Bee Gees, 1990; Tales From The Brothers Gibb, A History in Song 1967–90, 1990; High Civilisation, 1991; You Wouldn't Know, 1992; Tomorrow The World, 1992; Size Isn't Everything, 1993; Still Waters, 1997; One Night Only (live), 1998; This Is Where I Came In, 2000; Their Greatest Hits – The Record, 2001; Singles include: To Love Somebody, 1967; Massachusetts (No. 1, UK), 1967; World, 1967; Words, 1968; I Gotta Get A Message To You (No. 1, UK), 1968; Don't Forget To Remember, 1969; Run To Me, 1972; Jive Talkin' (No. 1, USA), 1975; You Should Be Dancing (No. 1, USA), 1976; How Deep Is Your Love (No. 1, USA), 1977; Stayin' Alive (No. 1, USA), 1978; Night Fever (No. 1, UK and US), 1978; Too Much Heaven (No. 1, USA), 1978; Tragedy (No. 1, UK and US), 1979; Love You Inside Out (No. 1, USA), 1979; Spirits Having Flown, 1979; You Win Again (No. 1, UK), 1987; Secret Love, 1991; For Whom The Bell Tolls, 1993; Alone, 1997; Immortality, with Celine Dion, 1998; This Is Where I Came In, 2001. *Honours include:* 6 Grammy Awards; Inducted into Songwriters Hall of Fame; Inducted into Rock and Roll Hall of Fame, Cleveland; Lifetime Achievement Award, Brit Awards, London; International Artist Award, American Music Awards, Los Angeles. *Memberships:* Musicians' Union; Equity. *Current Management:* Left Bank Organization, 9255 Sunset Blvd, Second Floor, West Hollywood, CA 90069, USA. *Address:* c/o 1801 Bay Rd, Miami Beach, FL 33139, USA.

GIBB Robin Hugh; b. 22 Dec. 1949, Douglas, Isle of Man, England. Singer; Songwriter. m. Dwina Murphy, 31 July 1985, 2 s., 1 d. *Career:* Formed the Bee Gees with brothers Maurice and Barry, 1958; First single, 1963; Own weekly television show, Australia, 1960s; Moved to England, 1967; First US TV appearance, American Bandstand, 1967; Saturday Night Fever musical stage show opens at London Palladium 1998, Cologne, Germany and Broadway, 1999, Sydney and Japan, 2000; Sell-out stadium concerts in Dublin, Wembley Stadium, London, Buenos Aires, South Africa, 1998; Stadium concerts in New Zealand and at new Olympic stadium in Sydney, 1999; Millennium Eve concert, South Florida, 1999; 6 shows planned in Europe during 2000. *Compositions:* Co-writer, Saturday Night Fever soundtrack, 1977 (40m. copies sold); Co-writer, albums: Guilty, Barbra Streisand; Heartbreaker, Dionne Warwick; Eaten Alive, Diana Ross; Eyes That See In The Dark, Kenny Rogers; Second only to Lennon and McCartney for most Top 10 hits written; Five simultaneous US Top 10 hits, 1978; Six consecutive No. 1 singles, 1979; Bee Gees songs recorded by: Boyzone; Take That; Steps; 911; Tina Turner; Eric Clapton; Elton John; Celine Dion; Al Green; Elvis Presley; Janis Joplin; Sarah Vaughn; Johnny Mathis; Andy Williams; Glen Campbell; Richie Havens; Jose Feliciano; Rod Stewart; Eric Burdon; Roberta Flack; Nina Simone; Frankie Valli; Michael Bolton. Most covered songs: Massachusetts; Stayin' Alive; To Love Somebody; How Do You Mend A Broken Heart. *Recordings:* Albums: Bee Gees 1st, 1967; Horizontal and Idea, 1968; Odessa, 1969; Cucumber Castle, 1971; Two Years On, 1971; Trafalgar, 1972; To Whom It May Concern, 1972; Life In A Tin Can, 1973; Mr Natural, 1974; Main Course, 1975; Children of The World, 1976; Here At Last. Live, 1976; Saturday Night Fever, 1977; Spirits Having Flown, 1978; Greatest Hits, 1979; Living Eyes, 1980; ESP, 1988; One, 1989; The Very Best of The Bee Gees, 1990; Tales From The Brothers Gibb (A History In Song 1967–90), 1990; High

Civilisation, 1991; You Wouldn't Know, 1992; Size Isn't Everything, 1993; Still Waters, 1997; One Night Only (live), 1998; This Is Where I Came In, 2000; Their Greatest Hits – The Record, 2001; Singles include: To Love Somebody, 1967; Massachusetts (No. 1, UK), 1967; World, 1967; Words, 1968; I Gotta Get A Message To You (No. 1, UK), 1968; Don't Forget To Remember, 1969; Run To Me, 1972; Jive Talkin' (No. 1, USA), 1975; You Should Be Dancing (No. 1, USA), 1976; How Deep Is Your Love (No. 1, USA), 1977; Stayin' Alive (No. 1, USA), 1978; Night Fever (No. 1, UK and US), 1978; Too Much Heaven (No. 1, USA), 1978; Tragedy (No. 1, UK and US), 1979; Love You Inside Out (No. 1, USA), 1979; Spirits Having Flown, 1979; You Win Again (No. 1, UK), 1987; Secret Love, 1991; For Whom The Bell Tolls, 1993; Alone, 1997; Immortality, with Celine Dion, 1998; This Is Where I Came In, 2001; Solo singles: Saved By The Bell, 1969; Juliet (No. 1, many European countries), 1983. Solo albums: Robin's Reign, 1970; How Old Are You, 1982; Secret Agent, 1984; Walls Have Eyes, 1986 Singles include: Alone; Solo albums: Robin's Reign, 1970; How Old Are You, 1982; Secret Agent, 1984; Walls Have Eyes, 1986. *Honours include:* 6 Grammy Awards; Inducted into Songwriters Hall of Fame; Inducted into Rock and Roll Hall of Fame, Cleveland; Lifetime Achievement Award, Brit Awards, London; International Artist Award, American Music Awards, Los Angeles. *Memberships:* Musicians' Union; Equity. *Current Management:* Left Bank Organization, 9255 Sunset Blvd, Second Floor, West Hollywood, CA 90069, USA. *Address:* c/o 1801 Bay Rd, Miami Beach, Florida 33139, USA.

GIBBONS Beth; b. 4 Jan. 1965, Devon, England. Singer; Songwriter. *Career:* Advertising agency in Bristol; Singer, Portishead. *Recordings:* Albums: Dummy, 1994; Herd of Instinct, 1995; Portishead, 1997; PNYC, 1998; Glory Times, 1998; Singles: Numb, 1994; Sour Times, 1994; Glory Box, 1995; All Mine, 1997; Over, 1997; Only You, 1998; Duet with Tom Jones, Motherless Child, contained on his album Reload (No. 1, UK), 1999. *Honours:* Mercury Music Prize, Best Album, 1995; NME Brat Award, 1995. *Current Management:* Fruit Management, Unit 104, Saga Centre, 326 Kensal Rd, London W10 5BZ, England.

GIBBONS Ian Ronald; b. 18 July 1952, Rochford, Essex, England. Musician (keyboards, accordion). m. Amanda Gaskin, 8 June 1985. *Musical Education:* Grade 6 Piano accordion. *Career:* Worked with: The Kinks; Sweet; Roger Chapman; The Crystals; The Shirelles; Dr Feelgood; Eddie and the Hotrods; Chris Farlowe; Kursaal Flyers; The Inmates; Television includes: Top of The Pops; Saturday Night Live. *Recordings:* All Kinks albums, 1979-, also single: Come Dancing; Recent Albums with Dr Feelgood (Chess Masters, 2000) and Roger Chapman (In My Own Time, 1999). *Honour:* Rock and Roll Hall of Fame, as mem. of The Kinks. *Membership:* PRS. *Leisure interests:* Travel; Cinema; Theatre; Horse riding; Car restoration. *Current Management:* Pete Scarbrow, Pro Active Management. *Address:* Mushroom Studios, Lubards Farm, Hullbridge Rd, Rayleigh, Essex SS6 9QG, England.

GIBBONS Steve; Singer; Songwriter; Musician (guitar). *Career:* Founder, own R & B band The Steve Gibbons Band, 1971; Tours with The Who, Europe, USA; First foreign act to play in German Democratic Republic. *Compositions:* Numerous songs recorded by other artists. *Recordings:* Tulane, 1977; Other singles include: Sweetheart; Take Me Home; Eddy Vortex; Get Up and Dance; Loving Me, Loving You; Personal Problem; Albums include: Short Stories, 1971; Any Road Up, 1976; Rolling On, 1977; Caught In The Act, 1977; Down In The Bunker, 1978; Street Parade, 1980; Saints and Sinners, 1981; On The Loose, 1986; From Birmingham to Memphis, 1995; The Dylan Project, 1998; On The Loose, 2000. *Current Management:* Jim McPhee, Acorn Entertainments. *Address:* Winterfold House, 46 Woodfield Rd, Kings Heath, Birmingham B13 9UJ, England.

GIBBS Terri; b. 15 June 1954, Augusta, Georgia, USA. Singer; Musician (piano). *Career:* Gospel singer as teenager; Formed own group, Sound Dimension; Residency in Augusta restaurant, 1975; Recording artist, 1981-. *Recordings:* Singles: Somebody's Knockin'; Rich Man; Mis'ry River; Somedays It Rains All Day Long; Anybody Else's Heart But Mine; Slow Burning Fire (duet with George Jones); Albums: Somebody's Knockin', 1981; I'm A Lady, 1981; Somedays It Rains All Night, 1982; Over Easy, 1983; Hiding From Love, 1984; Old Friends, 1985; Comfort the People, 1991; The Best of Terri Gibbs, 1996; Turn Around. *Address:* c/o Richard A Barz and Associates, 25 Cobble Creek Dr., RD 1, Box 91, Tannersville, PA 18372, USA.

GIBERT Alain; b. 1 Jan. 1947, Langogne, France. Musician (trombone); Composer; Arranger. m. Nadine Faure, 26 April 1970, 3 s. *Education:* Mathematics. *Musical Education:* Self-taught. *Career:* Co-founder, ARFI (Association à la Recherche d'un Folklore Imaginaire); Member, various bands: Marvelous Band; Marmite Infernale; Apollo; Bomonstre. *Compositions:* Music for Louis Sclavis; Steve Waring. *Recordings:* L'Age Du Cuivre, Apollo; Trombonist, singer, Chariot D'Or; Pticado; As composer, arranger: Le Roi Demonte; L'Art De La Retraite Sonne. *Memberships:* SACEM; ARFI. *Current Management:* ARFI, 13 rue de l'Arbre Sec, 69001 Lyon, France. *Address:* Montmorin, 63160 Billom, France.

GIBSON Deborah; b. 31 Aug. 1970, Brooklyn, New York, USA. Singer; Songwriter; Pianist; Actress. *Musical Education:* Private piano and voice lessons. *Career:* Youngest performer to have written, performed and produced a number 1 song; Sold over 9m. records world-wide; Starred in Grease, London, West End, 1994. *Recordings:* Only In My Dreams; Shake Your Love; Out of The Blue, 1987; Foolish Beat (No. 1, USA), 1988; Lost In Your Eyes (No. 1, USA), 1989; Electric Youth, 1989; No More Rhyme; Anything Is Possible, 1990; Losin' Myself, Body Mind Soul, 1993; Think With Your Heart, 1995; Deborah, 1997; What You Want, 2000; MYOB, 2001. *Honours:* ASCAP, Writer of the Year. *Current Management:* Gibson Management, 300 Main St #201, Huntington, NY 11743, USA.

GIBSON Don; b. 3 April 1928, Shelby, North Carolina, USA. Musician (guitar); Songwriter. *Career:* Recording artist, 1949-. *Compositions include:* Sweet Dreams, recorded by Faron Young, Patsy Cline, Emmylou Harris, Roy Buchanan, Reba McIntyre, Elvis Costello; I Can't Stop Loving You, also recorded by Kitty Wells, Ray Charles, Van Morrison; (I'd Be) A Legend In My Time, recorded by Ronnie Milsap; Album of own songs, Roy Orbison Sings Don Gibson, Roy Orbison, 1967; Oh Lonesome Me; Woman (Sensuous Woman). *Recordings:* Albums include: The King of Country Soul, 1968; Dottie and Don, with Dottie West, 1969; A Perfect Mountain, 1970; Country Green, 1972; Woman (Sensuous Woman), 1972; Sample Kisses, 1972; Am I That Easy To Forget, 1973; The Two of Us Together, with Sue Thompson, 1973; Touch The Morning, 1973; Warm Love, with Sue Thompson, 1973; Just Call Me Lonesome, 1973; Snap Your Fingers, 1974; Bring Back Your Love To Me, 1974; Just One Time, 1974; Oh How Love Changes, with Sue Thompson, 1975; Don't Stop Loving Me, 1975; Starting All Over Again, 1978; Look Who's Blue, 1978; Rockin' Rollin' Gibson, Vol. 1, 1982; Vol. 2, 1982; Don Gibson and Los Indios Tabajaras, 1986; Currents, 1992; Country Spotlight, 1992; Sings Hank Williams Sr, 1992; Oh Lonesome Me, 1998; Greatest Hits, 1999; RCA Country Legends, 2001.

GIBSON Lee; b. 5 March 1950, Watford, Hertfordshire, England. Singer. m. Gerry Boyce (musician), 1 Aug. 1973, 1 d. *Education:* BA Hons, Humanities. *Musical Education:* Self-taught. *Career:* Worked all over Europe with: UMO Danish Orchestra, Helsinki; Danish Radio Band, Copenhagen; Skymasters; Metropol Orchestra, Netherlands; Television appearances in France, Belgium, Italy; Album of television concert with Sarah Vaughn and Francy Boland Band, Dusseldorf; WDR Band, Cologne; Montreux Festival; Over 1,000 BBC solo broadcasts, UK; Film, television includes: The Great Muppet Movie; Privates On Parade; Victor Victoria; Yentl; An American Tale; Willow; Benny Hill Show; Only Fools and Horses; Morecambe and Wise Show; Barrymore, 3 Royal Variety Shows; Concerts include: tours with Syd Lawrence Orchestra; Don Lusher Band; Big Band Specials, BBC Radio Band; Guest appearances with Glen Miller UK Orchestra; Herb Miller Band; Singer, The Music of Andrew Lloyd Webber, concert for Prince and Princess of Wales at Expo '92, Seville; Singer, UK jazz circuit, including: Barbican; Queen Elizabeth Hall; Festival Hall; Rotherham Arts Centre; Brecon, Southampton Jazz Festivals; Ronnie Scotts; Ruislip Jazz Club; Pizza On The Park. *Recordings:* Chorale; One World One Peace; You Can See Forever; Never Let Me Go; Also appears on: Music of Andrew Lloyd Webber, 1988; Broadway Musicals, 1991; Jesus Christ Superstar, 1992; Swing Boogie, 1999. *Publications:* Music reviews for The Musician. *Honour:* Singers Prize, Knikke Festival. *Memberships:* Musicians' Union; Equity. *Leisure interest:* Gourmet food.

GIFFORD Alex; b. 1965. Musician (saxophone, keyboards); Recording Engineer. *Career:* Musician, brass section with The Stranglers; Sound engineer for The Grid; Member of Propellerheads, with Will White. *Recordings:* Albums: with Propellerheads: Drumsanddecksandrockandroll, 1998; Extended Play, 1999; Singles: On Her Majesty's Secret Service (with David Arnold), 1997; Dive, 1997; Take California (EP), 1997; Spybreak (EP), 1997; History Repeating (with Shirley Bassey), 1997; Guest musician on Enlightenment, Van Morrison; Producer of album VIP, Jungle Brothers, 1999. *Honours:* Mercury Music Prize Nomination, 1998. *Address:* c/o Wall of Sound, Office 3, 9 Thorpe Close, London W10 5XL, England.

GIFT Roland; b. 28 May 1962, Birmingham, England. Singer; Musician (saxophone); Actor. *Career:* Musician and actor, Hull, 1980s; Singer, Fine Young Cannibals, 1984–; Regular UK and US tours; Film appearances: Group featured in Tin Men, 1987; Actor, films: Sammy and Rosie Get Laid, 1987; Scandal, 1989; Theatre: Romeo, in Romeo and Juliet, UK rep tour, 1990. *Recordings:* Hit singles: Johnny Come Home, 1985; Suspicious Minds, 1986; Ever Fallen In Love, 1987; She Drives Me Crazy (No. 1, USA), 1989; Good Thing (No. 1, USA), 1989; Don't Look Back, 1989; Albums: Fine Young Cannibals, 1985; The Raw and The Cooked (No. 1, UK and US), 1989; Beautiful Girls, 1996; Finest, 1996; Contributions to film soundtracks: Something Wild, 1986; Tin Men, 1987; Contribution, Red Hot + Blue, 1990. *Honours:* BRIT Awards, Best British Group, Best British Album, 1990.

GIGOT Raquel; b. 9 Nov. 1965, Ottignies, Belgium. Chromatic and Diatonic Accordions; Composer. *Career:* Professional Musician, 1990–; Numerous Radio and TV performances in different countries; Studio musician recording with different artists. *Compositions:* Bully Wully Jig; Blue Room; Road to Bally Heighue; Rue Des Dunes; Lesidren; Mouse in the Kitchen. *Recordings:* 1990; Blue Room; Restless Home; Leaving the World Behind; Histoires de Rue; Oceanides; About to Go. *Current Management:* VZW Worm Productions, 136 Chaussee De Wemmel, 1090 Brussels, Belgium.

GIL Gilberto, (Gilberto Passos Gil Moreira); b. 3 March 1942, Salvador, Brazil. Vocalist; Musician (guitar, accordion); Songwriter. *Education:* Federal University, Bahia, Business Administration. *Career:* Began playing accordion aged 8; Played with Os Desafina Dos whilst studying; Composed songs for Television advertisements in early 1960s; Appeared in Nos Por Exemplo, a show directed by Caetano Veloso, 1964; After moving to Sao Paulo in 1965, had first hit when Elis Regina recorded Louvação; Sang protest songs, which proved controversial with the military dictatorship, and was part of the Tropicalia movement; After imprisonment in 1968 relocated to UK; Worked with groups such as Pink Floyd, Yes, Incredible String Band and Rod Stewart's band in London Clubs; Returned to Brazil, 1972; Toured with Caetano Veloso, Gal Costa and Maria Bethania; Became involved in politics in early 1990s and was elected to office in Salvador. *Recordings include:* Singles: Sua Música, Sua Interpretação, 1963; Procissão/Roda, 1965; Oriente, 1972; No Woman, No Cry (with Jimmy Cliff) (Brazilian #1 hit), 1980; Albums: Louvação, 1967; Gilberto Gil, 1968; Gilberto Gil (recorded in London), 1971; Expresso 2222, 1972; Temporada de Verão (live with Catano Veloso and Gal Costa), 1974; Refazenda, 1975; Refavela, 1977; Nightingale, 1978; Realce, 1979; Gente Precisa Ver O Luar, 1981; Quilombo, 1984; Vamos Fugir (with The Wailers), 1984; Dia Dorim Noite Neon, 1985; Ao Vivo Em Tóquio – Live in Tokyo, 1987; O Eterno Deus Mu Dança, 1989; Parabolicamará, 1991; Tropicália 2, 1993; Acoustic – Gilberto Gil Unplugged, 1994; Luar, 1996; Indigo Blue, 1997; Quanta, 1997; Copacabana Mon Amour, 1998; Eu Tu Eles – Me You Them (Film Soundtrack), 2001; São João Vivo, 2001. *Honours:* Shell Prize, 1990. *Internet:* www.gilbertogil.com.br.

GILBERT Gillian; b. 27 Jan. 1961, Manchester, England. Musician (keyboards, guitar). *Education:* Stockport Technical College, Stockport. *Career:* Musician, all-girl punk group, The Inadequates; Member, New Order, 1980–; The Other Two, 1991–; Tours: UK; Europe; US; Far East; South America; Australia; New Zealand; Concerts include: Futurama Festival, Leeds, 1982; Glastonbury Festival, 1981, 1987; San Remo Festival, 1988; Reading Festival, 1989; Television includes: Documentary, Celebration, BBC, 1982; Rock Around The Clock, BBC, 1985. *Compositions:* (with Stephen Morris) numerous tracks for New Order; Television soundtracks: Making Out; Shooting Stars; Reportage. *Recordings:* Albums with New Order: Movement, 1981; Power Corruption and Lies, 1983; Peel Sessions, 1984, 1986; Brotherhood, 1986; Substance, 1987; Technique (No. 1, UK), 1989; BBC Radio 1 Live In Concert, 1992; Republic (No. 1, UK), 1993; Best of New Order, 1994; Rest of New Order, 1995; Blue Monday 95, 1995; Get Ready, 2001; with The Other Two: The Other Two and You, 1994; Superhighways, 1999; also appears on: Technology Alert, 1996; Singles include: with New Order: Temptation, 1982; Blue Monday, 1983; Confusion, 1983; Thieves Like Us, 1984; The Perfect Kiss, 1985; Subculture, 1985; Shellshock, 1986; Bizarre Love Triangle, 1986; True Faith, 1987; Touched By The Hand of God, 1987; Fine Time, 1988; Round and Round, 1989; World In Motion (with England World Cup Football Squad) (No. 1, UK), 1990; How Does It Feel?, 1992; Regret, 1993; Ruined In A Day, 1993; World, 1993; Spooky, 1993; 1963, 1995; Crystal, 2001; 60 Miles An Hour, 2001; with The Other Two: Tasty Fish, 1991; Selfish, 1993. *Internet:* www.newordergetready.com.

GILBERT Grant Mitchell; b. 11 Aug. 1957, London, England. Music Prod.; Artistic Dir; Creative Prod. and Co-ordinator. 1 s., 2 d. *Musical Education:* Implosion at The Roundhouse, Camden Town, 1970–72. *Career:* Co-founded Torch Song and Guerilla (Productions), with William Orbit and Laurie Mayer, 1983; Founded The Crucial Chemystry Corporation (CCC), 1988; Launched E Zee Possee and Jeremy Healy's DJ career; Set up CCC in Japan introducing British graphic designer Neville Brody and numerous House/Techno artists and DJ's; Co-producer of Glastonbury Festival Green Futures Field, 1993-. *Recordings:* Torch Song, with William Orbit and Laurie Maye; EZ Posse: Everything Starts with An E; Producer, solar-powered CD, Deep Green: Music to Wake Up, featuring Solar Quest. *Honour:* Artistic Director of Green Futures Field Gaiasphere Stage, Glastonbury, 1995. *Leisure interests:* Underground comics; Science Fiction; Vegan cooking; Eating; Developing new musical and creative talent. *Current Management:* CCC. *Address:* CCC, PO Box 10, London N1 3RJ, England.

GILBERT Paul; b. 6 Nov. 1966, Carbondale, Illinois, USA. Musician (guitar). *Career:* Guitarist, rock groups: Racer X, 1986–88; Mr Big, 1989–96. *Recordings:* Albums: with Racer X: Street Lethal, 1986; Second Heat, 1987; Extreme Volume... Live, 1988; with Mr Big: Mr Big, 1989; Lean Into It, 1991; Bump Ahead, 1993; Hey Man, 1996; Solo: King of Clubs, 1998; Flying Dog, 1999; Beehive Live, 1999; Alligator Farm, 2001; Singles include: Green-Tinted Sixties Mind; To Be With You. *Current Management:*

Herbie Herbert Management, 2501 Third St, San Francisco, CA 94107, USA.

GILBERT Simon; b. 23 May 1965. Musician (drums). *Career:* Member, Suede, 1991–; Concerts include: Glastonbury Festival, 1993; Tours, UK; Europe; America; Japan; Television appearances include: Top of The Pops, BBC1; 12th BRIT Awards, Alexandra Palace; The Beat, ITV; Later With Jools Holland, BBC2; The Tonight Show, NBC TV. *Recordings:* Albums: Suede (No. 1, UK), 1993; Dog Man Star, 1994; Sharks Patrol These Waters, 1995; Coming Up, 1996; Sci-Fi Lullabies, 1997; Head Music, 1999; Singles include: The Drowners, 1992; Metal Mickey, 1992; Animal Nitrate, 1993; So Young, 1993; Stay Together, 1994; We Are The Pigs, 1994; New Generations, 1994; The Wild Ones, 1995; Trash, 1996; The Beautiful Ones, 1996; Saturday Night, 1997; Lazy, 1997; Filmstar, 1997; Electricity, 1999; She's In Fashion, 1999; Everything Will Flow, 1999; Can't Get Enough, 1999. *Honours include:* Mercury Music Prize, 1993. *Current Management:* Interceptor Enterprises, The Greenhouse, 34–38 Provost St, London N1 7NG, England.

GILBERTO Astrud; b. 30 March 1940, Bahia, Brazil. m. Joao Gilberto. *Career:* Singer with husband Joao Gilberto (guitar) and Stan Getz (saxophone); Tours with Stan Getz. *Recordings:* Albums: The Astrud Gilberto Album, 1965; The Shadow of Your Smile, 1965; Once Upon A Summertime, 1971; Haven't Got Anything Better To Do, 1968; The Girl From Ipanema, 1977; Best Of, 1982; The Essential Astrud Gilberto, 1984; Look To The Rainbow, 1986; So and So, 1988; with James Last: Plus, 1986; Astrud Gilberto, 1996; Live in New York, 1999; Astrud Gilberto's Finest Hour, 2001; Hit single: The Girl From Ipanema, 1964. *Address:* c/o Subrena Artist Corpn, 330 W 56th St, Suite 18-M, New York, NY 10019, USA.

GILBERTO Bebel; b. 1966, New York City, New York, USA. Vocalist; Songwriter. *Career:* Daughter of Joao Gilberto and Miucha, niece of Chico Buarque; Made first appearance with mother and Stan Getz at Carnegie Hall, 1975; Appeared on children's TV in Brazil, late 1970s; Recorded vocals for various soundtracks, 1980s; Released solo EP, 1989; Returned to New York City, 1991; Became influenced by the dance club scene and started performing on the club circuit; Worked with musicians including: David Byrne; Arto Lindsay; Romero Lubambo; Co-wrote club hit Technova (with Towa Tei), 1995; Moved to London, 1997; Contributed vocals to Kenny G's recording of The Girl From Ipanema, 1999; Signed to Ziriguiboom and released first solo album, 2000. *Compositions:* Technova; Preciso Dize Que Te Amo; Tanto Tempo; August Day Song; Sem Contencao; Mais Feliz; Alguem; Lonely; Close Your Eyes. *Recordings:* Bebel Gilberto EP, 1986; Tanto Tempo, 2000; features on: Next Stop Wonderland OST; Classics In The Key of G, Kenny G. *Honours:* Primio Sharp Award, Best Single, Preciso Dize Que Te Amo, 1989. *Address:* c/o Ziriguiboom, Crammed Discs, 43 rue General Patton, Brussels, Belgium. *E-mail:* crammed@crammed.be. *Internet:* www.bebelgilberto.com.

GILBERTO João; b. 10 June 1931, Juazeiro, Bahia, Brazil. Vocalist; Musician (guitar), Songwriter. m. (1) Astrud Gilberto, (2) Miucha. *Career:* father of Bebel Gilberto; Started playing guitar, aged 14; On radio in Salvador by age 18; Joined the station's band Garotos Da Lua and moved with them to Rio de Janeiro; Left band to do live solo gigs in Porto Alegre; Signed record deal with Odeon and released Chega De Saudade, 1959; Upon success of this and 2 follow-up LPs, relocated to USA, 1961–80; Made classic bossa nova records with Stan Getz during this period; Still performing and making records, but prefers to life away from public glare. *Compositions include:* Bim Bom; Ho-Ba La La; Minha Saudade; Abraco No Bonfa. *Recordings:* Albums include: Chega De Saudade, 1959; O Amor O Sorriso E A Flor, 1960; João Gilberto, 1961; Getz/Gilberto, 1963; Getz/Gilberto #2, 1966; João Gilberto En Mexico, 1970; João Gilberto, 1973; Best of Two Worlds, 1976; Amoroso, 1977; João Gilberto Prado Pereira De Oliveira, 1980; Brasil, 1981; João Gilberto Live In Montreux, 1986; João, 1991; Eu Sei Que Vou Te Amar, 1994; João – Voz E Violao, 2000. *Address:* Universal Brasil, Rio de Janeiro, RJ, Brazil.

GILKYSON Eliza; b. 24 Aug. 1950, Hollywood, California. Singer; Musician (piano, guitar); Songwriter. m. Reavis Moore, 23 Aug. 1981, 1 s., 1 d. *Career:* Tours with Ladysmith Black Mambazo; Dan Fogelberg; Arlo Guthrie; Andreas Vollenweider; Mary Chapin Carpenter; Television appearances: Austin City Limits; Showtime Concert Special; Film appearances: Two Lane Blacktop; Eight Minutes To Midnight. *Composition:* Rosie Strike Back, recorded by Roseanne Cash. *Recordings:* Albums: Pilgrims; Legends of Rainmaker; Through The Looking Glass; Eolian Minstrel, with Andreas Vollenweider; Undressed, 1994; Redemption Road, 1997; Misfits, 2000; Hard Times In Babylon, 2000; Also appeared on albums by: Tom Paxton; Tom Russell. *Leisure interest:* Horse riding. *Current Management:* Open Door Management. *Address:* PO Box 9858, Santa Fe, NM 87504, USA.

GILL Andy; b. 1 Jan. 1957, Manchester, England. Musician (guitar); Composer. *Education:* BA Hons, Fine Art, Leeds University. *Career:* Formed Gang of Four, 1977. *Compositions include:* 8 Gang of Four albums; Solo album: Dispossession; Other recordings with: Anthony More; Louise Goffin; The Red Hot Chili Peppers; Almighty Hi Fi; Hugh Cornwell; Terri Nun, Berlin; Television includes: Zero Option, BBC1 (also arranger, producer, recording engineer); Pandora's Box, BBC1, 1992; The Westminster Programme, BBC2, 1992; Westminster Daily, BBC2, 1992; Westminster Live, BBC2, 1993; Scrutiny, BBC, 1993; Films: Karate Kid; Dogs In Space; The Last of England; Pump Up The Volume; Urgh! A Music War; Requiem Apache; Delinquent (composer, performed as Gang of Four). *Recordings:* As performer and producer: with Gang of Four: Entertainment, 1979; Solid Gold, 1981; Songs of The Free, 1982; Hard, 1983; Mall, 1991; Shrinkwrapped, 1995; At The Palace (live); Entertainment, 1995; 100 Flowers Bloom, 1998; Compilation: A Brief History of The 20th Century; As producer: with Red Hot Chili Peppers (Gold disc); What Hits? (Platinum disc); with Busta Jones: Hands Are Shaking; with The Balancing Act: Curtains; Tracks for: The Most Beautiful Girl; Downey Mildew; Addie Brik; Miracle Legion, for film A Matter of Degrees; with MCD: Tantric Sex Disco, 1995; with Inastella: What Y'Gonna Do, 1995; with The Morgans: Tell Me What You Taste EP; for Michael Hutchence: Michael Hutchence, 1999; Diversity album in production. *Membership:* PRS. *Leisure interests:* Tantric Disco; Clay Pigeon shooting. *Current Management:* Polar Union; Sanctuary Group. *Address:* The Colonnades, 82 Bishops Bridge Rd, London W2 6BB, England.

GILL Janis; b. 1 March 1955, Torrance, California, USA. Singer; Musician (guitar). m. Vince Gill, 1 d. *Musical Education:* Studied Music Theory. *Career:* Member, duo Sweethearts of The Rodeo with sister Kristine Arnold; Signed to Columbia Records; Sugar Hill Records; Winners, Wrangler Country Showcase, 1985. *Recordings:* Sweethearts of The Rodeo, 1986; Anthology, 2000; Top 20 hits include: Since I Found You; Midnight Girl/ Sunset Town; Satisfy You; Chains of Gold, 1987; Rodeo Waltz, 1993; Video: Things Will Grow. *Honours:* CMA's Vocal Duo, 9 consecutive years; Music City News, Best Vocal Duo; TNN Viewers Choice Award, Favourite Group; NAIRD Award, Best Country Album, 1994. *Current Management:* M Hitchcock Management. *Address:* PO Box 159007, Nashville, TN 37214, USA.

GILL Vince (Vincent Grant); b. 5 April 1957, Norman, Oklahoma, USA. Country Singer; Musician (guitar); Songwriter. m. Janis Oliver. *Career:* Member, Mountain Smoke (as a schoolboy); Member, Bluegrass Alliance, 1975–79; Member, Pure Prairie League, 1979–81; Member, Rodney Crowell's band, The Cherry Bombs, 1982; Solo artiste, 1983-. *Compositions include:* Never Knew Lonely; Look At Us (co-written with Max Barnes). *Recordings:* Hit singles: When I Call Your Name, duet with Patti Loveless; Pocket Full of Gold; Liza Jane; Look At Us; I Still Believe In You (US Country No. 1); Take Your Memory With You); A Little More Love; Albums: with Pure Prairie League: Can't Hold Back, 1979; Firin' Up, 1980; Something In The Night, 1981; Solo album: Turn Me Loose, 1983; The Things That Matter, 1984; Vince Gill, 1985; The Way Back Home, 1987; When I Call Your Name, 1989; Pocket Full of Gold, 1991; I Never Knew Lonely, 1992; I Still Believe In You, 1992; Let There Be Peace on Earth, 1993; When Love Finds You, 1994; The Essential, 1996; The Key, 1998; Let's Make Sure We Say Goodbye, 2000; Contributor: Patti Loveless albums; On Every Street, Dire Straits; recordings by Alison Brown; George Jones; Lyle Lovett; Reba McEntire; Mark O'Connor; Faith Hill; Trisha Yearwood. *Honours:* CMA Single of The Year, with Patti Loveless; CMA Male Vocalist of Year, 1991, 1992; Song of The Year, Look At Us, 1992. *Current Management:* Fitzgerald Hartley Co, 1212 16th Ave S, Nashville, TN 37203, USA.

GILLAN Ian; b. 19 Aug. 1945, Hounslow, London, England. Vocalist. m. Bronwen, 21 July 1984, 1 d. *Career:* Lead singer, rock bands: Episode Six; Deep Purple; Gillan; Black Sabbath; Gillan and Glover (with Roger Glover); Singer on over 20 albums, selling in excess of 100m. copies; Numerous world-wide tours, television and radio appearances; Singer, Jesus Christ Superstar. *Compositions include:* Woman From Tokyo; Smoke On The Water; Black Night; Child In Time. *Recordings:* Albums include: with Episode Six: Here There and Everywhere, 1966; with Deep Purple: In Rock, 1969; Best Of, 1970; Machine Head, 1972; Who Do We Think We Are, 1973; 24 Carat Purple, 1975; Perfect Strangers, 1984; Purpendicular, 1996; with Gillan: Child In Time, 1976; Gillan, 1978; Mr Universe, 1979; Glory Road, 1980; Future Shock, 1981; Double Trouble, 1981; Magic, 1982; with Black Sabbath: Born Again, 1983; with Gillan and Glover: Accidentally On Purpose, 1988; with Ritchie Blackmore: Rainbow; No Smoke Without Fire, 2000; with The Javelins: Sole Agency and Representations, 2001. *Current Management:* Phil Banfield, Performing Artistes Network. *Address:* No. 1 Water Lane, Camden Town, London NW1 8NZ, England.

GILLESPIE Bobby; b. 22 June 1964, Scotland. Singer. *Career:* Drummer, Jesus and Mary Chain, 1984; Singer, Primal Scream, 1984–; Performances include: Miners Benefit Trust Concert, Sheffield Arena, 1992. *Recordings:* Singles include: All Fall Down, 1985; Crystal Crescent, 1986; Ivy Ivy Ivy, 1989; Loaded, 1990; Come Together, 1990; Higher Than The Sun, 1991; Don't Fight It Feel It, 1991; Dixie-Narco (EP), 1992; Rocks/Funky Jam, 1994; Jailbird, 1994; Cry Myself Blind, 1994; Kowalski, 1997; Star, 1997;

Burning Wheel, 1997; Swastikka Eyes, 1999; Kill All Hippies, 2000; Accelerator, 2000; Albums: Psychocandy, 1985; Sonic Flower Groove, 1987; Primal Scream, 1989; Screamadelica, 1991; Give Out But Don't Give Up, 1994; Let Your Dim Lights Shine, 1995; Vanishing Point, 1997; Echo Dek, 1997; XTRMNTR, 2000; Contributor, Dope Dogs, Parliament/ Funkadelic, 1994; Surrender, The Chemical Brothers, 1999; The Contino Sessions, Death In Vegas, 1999; Bow Down To The Exit Sign, David Holmes, 2000; Get Ready, New Order, 2001. *Honour:* Mercury Music Prize, Screamadelica, 1992. *Current Management:* Scream Heights Management.

GILLESPIE Dana; b. 30 March 1949, England. Singer; Songwriter. *Recordings:* 30 albums released; Foolish Seasons, 1967; Box of Surprises, 1968; Jesus Christ Superstar, 1972; Weren't Born a Man, 1973; Ain't Gonna Play No Fiddle, mojo blues band, 1974; Blue Job, 1982; Solid Romance, 1984; Below the Belt, 1984; It Belongs to Me, 1985; Move You Body close to Me, 1986; I'm a Woman, 1986; Hot News', 1987; Amor, 1990; Blues It Up, 1990; Where Blue Begins, 1991; Boogie Woogie Nights, 1991; Big Boy, with Joachim Palden, 1992; Methods of Release, 1993; Andy Warhol, 1994; Blue One, 1994; One to One, 1995; Hot Stuff, 1995; Have I Got Blues for You, 1996; Mustique Blues Festivals, 1996; Inner View, 1996; Cherry Pie, with Big Jay McNeeley, 1997; Jan Mustique Bluesfest, 1997; Back to the Blues, 1999; Experienced, 2000. *Honours:* Voted Top British Female Blues Vocalist, 1993, 1994, 1995, 1996.

GILLEY Mickey Leroy; b. 9 March 1936, Natchez, Mississippi; Country vocalist, Musician (piano, guitar); Songwriter; Actor. *Career:* Local record success, 1960s; Country hits on labels: Playboy; Epic; Airborne Records, 1974–89; Owner of Gilley's night club, Pasadena, Texas with Sherwood Cryer, 1971–89; Club featured in film Urban Cowboy with Gilley in cameo role; Opened own theatre Branson, Missouri, early 1990s; TV appearances include: Murder She Wrote; Dukes of Hazzard; Fantasy Island; Cousin of country vocalist Jerry Lee Lewis and evangelist Rev Jimmy Swaggart. *Recordings include:* I Overlooked An Orchid, 1974; Window Up Above, 1975; She's Pulling Me Back Again, 1977; Lonely Nights, 1981; Paradise Tonight (with Charly McClain), 1983; Albums: Room Full of Roses, City Lights, 1974; Overnight Sensation, 1975; Gilley's Smokin', Gilley's Greatest Hits Vol. 1, 1976. *Address:* c/o The Mickey Gilley Theater, 3455 W Hwy 76, Branson, MO 65616, USA.

GILLINGHAM Charlie; b. 12 Jan. 1960, Torrance, California, USA. Musician (Keyboards). *Career:* Member, Counting Crows; Numerous headlining tours and TV appearances including MTV. *Recordings:* Round Here, 1994; Mr Jones, 1994; Rain King, 1994; Angels of the Silence (live), 1996; Albums: August and Everything After, 1993; Recovering the Satellites, 1996; Across a Wire: Live In New York, 1998; Long December, 1999; Daylight Fading, 1999.

GILLIS Verna; b. 14 June 1942, New York, USA. Artist Man.; Record Prod. m. Brad Graves, 1 May 1965. *Musical Education:* PhD, Ethnomusicology. *Career:* Host, Radio Programme, WBAI, 1975–83; Founder, Director, Soundscape Performance Space, New York City, 1979–85; Record Producer; Artist Manager for: Youssou N'dour, Yomo Toro, Salif Keita, Malouma Mint Maideh, Habib Faye, Ivan Rubenstein-Gillis. *Publications:* DIW, Live From Soundscape. *Honour:* Woman of the Year, 1975. *Leisure interests:* Planting; Antiques. *Current Management:* Roswell Rudd/Raquel Hithet. *Address:* 799 Greenwich St, New York, NY 10014–1843, USA.

GILMOUR David; b. 6 March 1946, Cambridge, England. Vocalist; Musician (guitar); Composer. m. Polly Samson, 1994. *Career:* Member, Pink Floyd, 1968–; Performances include: Rome International Pop Festival, 1968; Hyde Park, London, 1968; Bath Festival, 1970; Montreux Festival, Switzerland, 1971; Pink Floyd Live At Pompeii (recorded for film release), 1972; Knebworth Festival, 1975; Guitarist with Bryan Ferry, Live Aid, Wembley, 1985; Played at Colombian Volcano Appeal, Royal Albert Hall, 1986. *Recordings:* Albums: A Saucerful of Secrets, 1968; More (film soundtrack), 1969; Ummagumma, 1969; Atom Heart Mother (No. 1, UK), 1970; Relics, 1971; Meddle, 1971; Obscured By Clouds, 1972; The Dark Side of The Moon (No. 1, USA), 1973; Wish You Were Here, (No. 1, UK and US) 1975; Animals, 1977; The Wall (No. 1, USA), 1979; The Final Cut (No. 1, UK), 1983; A Momentary Lapse of Reason, 1987; The Delicate Sound of Thunder, 1988; Shine On (box set), 1992; The Division Bell (No. 1, UK and US), 1994; Pulse (No. 1, UK and US), 1995; Echoes: The Very Best of Pink Floyd, 2001; Also appears on: I'll Sleep When I'm Dead, 1996; Very Best of John Martyn, 1998; Madcap Laughs, 1999; Solo albums: David Gilmour, 1978; About Face, 1984; Discovered Kate Bush, Executive Producer for her album The Kick Inside; Played on: Bête Noire, Bryan Ferry; Slave To The Rhythm, Grace Jones; So Red The Rose, Arcadia; Tribute To Muddy Waters; Singles include: Another Brick In The Wall (No. 1, UK and US), 1979; When The Tigers Break Free, 1982; Not Now John, 1983; Learning To Fly, 1987; On The Turning Away, 1987; 1 Slip, 1988; Take It Back, 1994; High Hopes, 1994; Contributor, film soundtrack of Zabriskie Point, 1970. *Honours:* Silver Clef Award, Nordoff-Robbins Music Therapy, 1980; MTV

Music Video Award, 1988; Ivor Novello Award, Outstanding Contribution To British Music, 1992; Q Award, Best Live Act, 1994; Inducted into Rock and Roll Hall of Fame, 1996; Grammy Award, Producer in Best Instrumental Performance for Marooned. *Current Management:* Steve O'Rourke, EMKA Productions Ltd, 43 Portland Rd, Holland Park, London W11 4LJ, England.

GILTRAP Gordon; b. 6 April 1948, East Peckham, Tonbridge, Kent, England. Musician (guitar). *Career:* Played college, folk club and university circuit; Regular tours, with Ric Sanders; Solo work; Duets with John Renbourn and Juan Martin. *Compositions include:* Heartsong, theme to Holiday programme, BBC TV, 1980s; Other television music for: Wish You Were Here; The Open University; Hold The Back Page, 1985. *Recordings:* Albums: Early Days, 1968; Gordon Giltrap, 1968; Portrait, 1969; Testament of Time, 1971; Giltrap, 1973; Visionary, 1976; Perilous Journey, 1977; Fear of The Dark, 1978; Performance, 1980; The Peacock Party, 1981; Live, 1981; Airwaves, 1982; Elegy, 1987; A Midnight Clear, 1988; Gordon Giltrap – Guitarist, 1988; Mastercraftsman, 1989; One To One, with Ric Sanders, 1989; A Matter of Time, with Martin Taylor, 1991; Live at the BBC, 1995; Music for the Small Screen, 1995; Live At Oxford, 2000; Compilations: The Very Best of Gordon Giltrap, 1988; The Best of Gordon Giltrap – All The Hits Plus More, 1991. *Publications:* Contributor, Guitarist magazine. *Current Management:* NE Music Management, Priory House, 55 Lawe Rd, South Shields, Tyne and Wear NE33 2AL, England.

GIMENES Raymond François; b. 12 Dec. 1939, Fes, Morocco. Arranger; Conductor; Prod.; Musician (guitar); Composer. m. Beatrice Belthoise, 11 Sept. 1987, 2 s., 1 d. *Education:* Sciences at University. *Musical Education:* First Prize for Violin; Studied harmony, counterpoint, fuga and composition. *Career:* Backing guitarist for Petula Clark, Dean Martin, Shirley Bassey; Musical Director for Sacha Distel, Henri Salvador, Charles Aznavour; Solo guitarist for Paul Mauriat Orchestra, including US tour, 1971; Japanese tours, 1971, 1986, 1988, 1990. *Recordings:* 4 albums as leader of Guitars Unlimited; As guitarist: Wings, Michael Colombier; Slide Hampton with Jazz Big Band; Hajime Mizoguchi; Dionne Warwick In Paris. *Publication:* Orchestration for Paganini's Sonata for Viola and Symphonic Orchestra. *Honour:* Award for commercial, Radio Spot, 1989. *Memberships:* SACEM; SPEDIDAM; ADAMI. *Leisure interests:* Computers; Watching tennis. *Current Management:* Charley Marouani, 37 rue Marbeuf, 75008 Paris, France. *Address:* 185 bis rue Paul Doumer, 78510 Triel sur Seine, France.

GINAPÉ Viviane; b. 30 April 1955, Paris, France. Singer. m. Lionel Bouton, 12 Nov. 1988. *Musical Education:* CNRBB, Supérieur. *Career:* Singer with: Urban/Sax; Claude Bolling; Denis Badault; Yochk 'O Seffer; François Mechali. *Recordings:* Fraction Sur Le Temps, Urban Sax, 1989; Opéra Jazz François Mechali, L'Archipel, 1995; Café, Viviane Ginapé Quartet, 1999. *Current Management:* Charlotte Productions. *Address:* 1 rue de la Dhuis, 75020 Paris, France.

GINGER (David Walls); b. 1964, South Shields, Tyne and Wear, England. Rock Singer; Songwriter; Musician (guitar). *Career:* Member, rock groups, The Quireboys; The Throbs; Founder, The Wildhearts, 1991–; Numerous tours, UK; Europe; Ireland; Support tours with Pantera; Manic Street Preachers; The Almighty; Suicidal Tendencies; Performances include: Monsters of Rock Festival, Castle Donington, 1994; Reading Festival, 1994. *Recordings:* Albums: with The Quireboys: A Bit of What You Fancy, 1989; with The Wildhearts: Earth Vs The Wildhearts, 1993; Fishing For Luckies, 1994; P H U Q, 1995; The Best of The Wildhearts, 1996; Endless, Nameless, 1997; Singles with The Wildhearts: Mondo Akimbo A-Go-Go (EP), 1992; Don't Be Happy... Just Worry (EP), 1992; TV (EP), 1993; Suckerpunch, 1994; Caffeine Bomb, 1994; I Wanna Go Where The People Go, 1995; Geordie In Wonderland; Just In Lust, 1995; Sick of Drugs, 1996; Red Light Green Light EP, 1996; Anthem, 1997; Urge, 1997; with Clam Abuse: Stop Thinking, 1999; with Supershit 666: Supershit 666, 2000; Solo single: I'm A Lover, Not A Fighter, 2001; Solo album: Grevious Acoustic Behaviour: Live At The 12 Bar, 2001. *Current Management:* Tribal Management, 7 Vicarage Rd, Wednesbury, West Midlands WS10 9BA, England.

GINMAN Lennart Vidar; b. 2 March 1960, Copenhagen, Denmark. Composer; Musician (double bass). m. Lisbeth Maria Hansen, 31 Dec. 1987, 2 d. *Musical Education:* Private studies, Copenhagen, New York. *Career:* Began professional career around 1985; Now one of most sought after bassists in Denmark; Tours with: Kenny Werner; Harry 'Sweet' Edison; Al Foster; Lee Konitz; Cæcilie Norby. *Recordings:* 1991, Lennart Ginman/Kirk Lightsey; Blachman Introduces Standard Jazz and Rap, Thomas Blachman; Cæcilie Norby: Cæcilie Norby, 1994; My Corner of the Sky, 1997; Beatin' Bop, Page One; Jens Winther, Scorpio Dance, 1994. *Honours:* Composers Honour Award, 1992, DJBFA. *Leisure interests:* Gardening; Clothes. *Address:* C F Richsvej 80, 2000 Frederiksberg, Denmark.

GIROT Pierre; b. 11 May 1936, Neuilly, France. Jazz Musician (guitar). m. 30 June 1960, 2 d. *Musical Education:* Academie de Guitare de Paris; Student of Henri Salavador. *Career:* Accompanied Josephine Baker, Charles Trenet, Worked with jazz artists: Trio Arvanitas; Guy Lafitte; Lou Bennett; Bill Coleman; Hal Singer; International Festivals include: Antibes Juan-les-Pins; Zurich; San Sebastian; Souillac; Marciac; Montpellier; Clermont-Ferrand; French radio and television. *Compositions:* Flamenco Blues, 1996; Melancoliquement Vôtre, Mister JC, 1996; Birdy, 1996. *Recordings:* Album: Jazz and Brazilian guitar with Quatuor Galilé. *Publications:* Festival 92; Birdy; Clin d'Oeil, 1998. *Honour:* Third prize, Festival of Juan-les-Pins, 1960. *Memberships:* SACEM; SPEDIDAM. *Leisure interests:* Chess; Football. *Address:* Chemin de Fadat, 19100 Brive, France.

GIUFFRE James P (Jimmy); b. 26 April 1921, Dallas, Texas, USA. Musician (saxophones, flutes, clarinet); Composer. m. Juanita Odjenar Giuffre, 22 June 1961. *Education:* BA North Texas State. *Musical Education:* Private Studies with Dr Wesley La Violette. *Career:* Lincoln Center; Carnegie Hall; Numerous European tours; Television and filmscores (art films, 1 feature). *Compositions:* Four Brothers; Train; The River. *Recordings:* Free Fall; The Jimmy Giuffre 3. *Publications:* Jazz Phrasing and Interpretation. *Honours:* Guggenheim Fellowship, National Endowment of The Arts. *Membership:* Broadcast Music Inc. *Leisure interests:* Listening to music. *Current Management:* Thomas Stowsand, Soudades Tourneen, Austria.

GIUSSANI Claudio D C; b. 19 Sept. 1969, London, England. Musician (keyboards, percussion- djembe); Programmer; Engineer; Remixer. *Education:* BEng (Hons) University of Warwick, Coventry, UK. *Musical Education:* Mostly self-taught, lessons in percussion. *Career:* Formed band Urban Shakedown (making new breakbeat music), 1990; Formed Union Jack (trance music), 1992, 93; Regular tours, USA; Canada; Russia; Europe; PA in clubs. *Recordings:* With Urban Shakedown: Some Justice (Top 20 hit); Bass Shake; With Union Jack: Album: There Will Be No Armageddon, 2001; Single: Two Full Moons and A Trout; Productions include: Speed Limit 140 BPM, 1994; All Mixed Up, 1995; Dimensions in Ambience, 1996; Platipus Records Ultimate Dream, 1996; Journey into Ambient Groove, 1996; Quando Un Musicista, 1999. *Memberships:* PRS; MCPS; PPL. *Leisure interests:* Playing the djembe; Travel. *Current Management:* Platipus Records.

GJERSTAD Frode; b. 24 March 1948, Stavanger, Norway. Musician (saxophone). m. Judith Sorvik, 24 March 1983, 1 s., 1 d. *Career:* Worked with: John Stevens; Johnny Dyani; Kent Carter; Billy Bang; Bobby Bradford; Borah Bergman; Derrek Bailey; Paul Rutherford; Terje Isungset; Audun Kleive; Pierre Dorge; Bjorn Kjellemyr; Peter Brötzmann; William Parker; Rashid Baker; Harold Drake. *Recordings:* Backwards and Forwards, 1983; Okhela, 1984; Ness, 1987; Way It Goes, 1988; Accent, 1989; In Time Was, 1991; Less More, 1992; Enten Eller, 1993; Seeing New York From The Ear, 1995; Sunshine, 1996; Seeing New York from the Ear, 1996; Last Detail, 1996; Remember to Forget, 1998; Borcalis, 1998; Ikosa Mure, 1998; ISM, 1998; Invisible Touch, 1999; Ultima, 1999. *Honour:* Jazz Musician of the Year, Norway, 1997. *Leisure interests:* Reading; Mixing music. *Current Management:* Circulasione Totale. *Address:* Gansveien 15, 4017 Stavanger, Norway.

GLADWELL Robert; b. 16 June 1950, Colchester, England. Musician (guitar, bass); Journalist. Married, divorced, twice; 4 s., 1 d. *Musical Education:* Martin Lukins School of Music (studied guitar). *Career:* Session guitarist, clinician, worked for Gibson Guitars for 10 years; Own guitar workshop, building, customising guitars; Toured extensively with Steve Harley and Cockney Rebel; Currently touring, recording with Suzi Quatro, 1990s-. *Recordings:* with Twink: Mr Rainbow, 1990; with Steve Harley: Yes You Can, 1992; Christmas All Stars Album, 1994; with Suzi Quatro: Free The Butterfly, 1995; What Goes Around, 1996. *Publications:* Dr Robert column, guitarist magazine, 11 years; Guitar Electronics and Customising, book, 1995. *Membership:* Musicians' Union. *Leisure interests:* History; Listening to music; Instrument restoration. *Current Management:* Jive Music Management.

GLADWIN Tom; b. 1973, England. Musician (bass). *Career:* Member, Shed Seven; Obtained major label record deal; Numerous live and television appearances. *Recordings:* Singles: Mark, 1994; Dolphin, 1994; Speakeasy, 1994; Ocean Pie, 1994; Where Have You Been Tonight?, 1995; Getting Better, 1996; Going For Gold, 1996; Bully Boy, 1996; On Standby, 1996; Chasing Rainbows, 1996; She Left Me On Friday, 1998; The Heroes, 1998; The Devil in Your Shoes, 1998; Disco Down, 1999; Cry For Help, 2001; Albums: Change Giver, 1996; A Maximum High, 1996; Let It Ride, 1998; Going for Gold: The Best of Shed Seven, 1999; Truth Be Told, 2001. *Internet:* www.shedseven.com.

GLASSER Adam; b. 20 Sept. 1955, Cambridge, England. Musician (keyboards, chromatic harmonica). m. Vivien Roberts, 21 May 1994, 1 d. *Education:* BA (Hons) English and European Literature, Warwick

University. *Musical Education:* Self-taught. *Career:* MD, The Manhattan Brothers (SA Township legends); Toured, recorded with DuDu Pukwana; Tour and television with Martha Reeves and The Vandellas; Concerts with Jimmy Witherspoon; Appeared in Musicians In Exile, Ch4; SA Blues, BBC2; Performed with Joe Zawinul Syndicate; Harmonica with Eurythmics, Sting, BBC Concert Orchestra. *Recordings:* August One on Zila '86 album; Title music for Battle of The Bikes, Ch4, 1994; Talking Woods, with Thebe Lipere; Pedalmarch (for Jazz Sextet) features on continental bike racing in Cycle Sport; Filmscore, Hard Rain, played harmonica with Toots Thielemans; Film scores with London Philharmonic Orchestra: Harmonica on Chinese Coffee, 1998; EXistenZ, 1998; with Dominic Alldis: If Love Were All, 2000; with Dominic Miller: Second Nature, 2000. *Honours:* Winner, Peter Whittingham Award, Musicians' Benevolent Society, 1997. *Memberships:* Musicians' Union; Asscn Internat des Journalistes du Cyclisme. *Leisure interest:* Cycling.

GLATZL Friedrich; b. 17 March 1956, Gmünd, Austria. Musician (guitar); Backing Vocalist. m. Marianne, 3 Dec. 1982, 1 s., 1 d. *Education:* VSA; HSA; Sales Manager. *Career:* Founder member, Giant Blonder, 1972–83; Guest musician on: Blues Pumpm Live With Friends Tour, 1982; Member: Blues Pumpm, 1983–; Television, radio tours, most of Eastern Europe. *Recordings:* Albums: with Giant Blonder: Giant Blonder; Rock and Blues 2; Single: with Johannes Müller Blues Zappa and Pumpm Fritz: Der Letzte Zug; with Blues Pumpm: Albums: Live With Friends, 1985; The 5th Ten Years Jubilee, 1987; Live At Utopia, 1988; Birthday, 1991; Live In Vienna, 1992; The 5th, 1992; Living Loving Riding, 1994; Singles: Train and Quick Shoes, 1985; Men From Milwaukee, 1993. *Honours:* Silbernes Ehrenzeichen, 1992; Third Best Blues Album Ö3, Rot-Weiss-Rote Critics Poll, Live In Vienna, 1992. *Memberships:* ALM; AUME; LSG. *Leisure interests:* Music; Family. *Current Management:* RGG Management, Peter Steinbach.

GLAZER Tom (Thomas Zacariah); b. 2 Sept. 1914, Philadelphia, Pennsylvania, USA. Folksinger; Writer; Composer. m. Miriam Reed Eisenberg, 25 June 1944, divorced, 2 s. *Education:* City College of New York, 1938–41. *Career:* Recording artist, 1946–; Folksinger. *Compositions:* Melody of Love, 1956; Till We Two Are One; A Worried Man; Skokiaan; On Top of Spaghetti; Songs and Score, Film, A Face in the Crowd. *Recordings:* First artist to record Greensleeves and Twelve Days of Christmas. *Publications:* Tom Glazer's Treasury of Songs for Children, 1963; America The Beautiful, 1987; Limited edition selections of poems. *Honours:* Several Peabody Awards for Radio and TV Shows. *Memberships:* ASCAP; AFTRA; American Federation of Musicians; Screen Actors' Guild; Songwriters' Guild of America. *Leisure interests:* Tennis; Literature; French; Science; Philosophy. *Address:* PO Box 165, Scarborough, NY 10510, USA.

GLEESON David Sean; b. 3 June 1968, Newcastle, Australia. Vocalist. *Education:* Music, Higher School Certificate. *Career:* Played with local rock band Aspect, 1985; Played with The Screaming Jets, 1989–; 3 British tours, 2 US tours, 2 European tours; Toured with the Quireboys and Thunder. *Recordings:* Albums with The Screaming Jets: All For One; Tear of Thought; The Screaming Jets; Engineer on albums by: Mariah Carey; Kenny G; Michael Bolton; Celine Dion; Jennifer Lopez; Linda Ronstadt; Savage Garden; Destiny's Child, Jessica Simpson. *Leisure interests:* Golf; Surfing; Gambling; Beer. *Current Management:* c/o Aaron Chugg, Grant Thomas Management, PO Box 176, Potts Point, NSW 2011, Australia.

GLEN Alan; b. Wupperthal, Germany. Musician (harmonica). m. Jacqueline Lewis, 31 May 1995, 3 s. *Career:* with Nine Below Zero: Sting, tour of Spain, Scandinavia, 1993; Toured with and supported Eric Clapton, Scandinavia, 1993; Royal Albert Hall, 1994; ZZ Top; Joe Cocker, 1994; Alvin Lee, 1994; Played and recorded with: Alannah Myles, Canadian tour, 1994; Alvin Lee, US tour, 1994; Television, radio appearances: USA; Canada; Italy; Sweden; Switzerland; France; Hungary; Austria; Germany; Britain; Member, Little Axe, 1996–97; Member, Yardbirds, 1998–. *Compositions:* Bad Town Blues, film soundtrack for Circuitry Man II; Another Kind of Love; It's Nothing New. *Recordings:* Albums: with Nine Below Zero: Off The Hook, 1993; Best of Nine Below Zero, 1994; Hot Music For A Cold Night, 1994; Ice Station Zebro, 1995; Singles: with Nine Below Zero: Soft Touch, 1993; Workshy, 1993; with Alannah Myles: Never Loved A Man, 1994; Down By The River, 1995; with Little Axe, Slow Fuse, 1996; with Dr Feelgood, On the Road Again, 1996; with Junior Delgado, Reasons, 1999. *Memberships:* BASCA; Musicians' Union. *Current Management:* Mickey Modern, Arctic King Management. *Address:* 72 Woods Rd, London SE15 2SW, England.

GLENNIE James (Jim); b. 10 Oct. 1963, Manchester, England. Musician (Bass); Songwriter. *Career:* Formed James, 1982; Early support slots to The Smiths; Numerous tours, festival dates and television appearances. *Recordings:* Singles: Jimone, 1983; James II, 1985; Hymn from a Village, 1985; Come Home, 1989; Sit Down (No. 2, UK), 1989, reissued 1991; Sound, 1991; Born of Frustration, 1992; Sometimes (Lester Piggott), 1993; Laid, 1993; Say Something, 1994; She's A Star, 1997; Tomorrow, 1997; Destiny Calling, 1998; Sit Down '98, 1998; I Know What I'm Here For, 1999; Just

Like Fred Astaire, 1999; Getting Away With It (All Messed Up), 2001; Albums: Stutter, 1986; Strip-Mine, 1988; One Man Clapping, live, 1989; Gold Mother, 1990; Seven, 1992; Laid, 1993; Wah Wah, live, 1994; Whiplash, 1997; The Best of James (compilation), 1998; Millionaires, 1999; Pleased To Meet You, 2001. *Current Management:* Rudge Management, 1 Star St, London W2 1QD, England. *Internet:* www.jamestheband.com.

GLENNIE-SMITH Nicholas Hugh; b. 3 Oct. 1951, Kingston-On-Thames, England. Composer; Musician (keyboards); Engineer. m. Janet, 21 Dec. 1974, 2 s., 2 d. *Education:* Chorister, New College Oxford. *Musical Education:* Trinity College, London. *Career:* Tours with: David Essex; Randy Edelman; Glen Campbell; Classic Rock; Roger Waters, The Wall, Berlin. *Compositions:* Two if by Sea, 1995; The Rock, 1996; The Preacher's Wife, 1996; Fire Down Below, 1997; Home Alone 3, 1997; The Man in the Iron Mask, 1998; Lion King II: Simba's Pride, 1998; The Secret Adventures of Jules Verne, 1999. *Recordings:* Albums: with Cliff Richard: I'm No Hero, 1980; Wired For Sound, 1981; Silver, 1983; with Leo Sayer: Living In A Fantasy, 1980; Strange Day In Berlin, 1983; with Nik Kershaw: Human Racing, 1984; with Tina Turner: Private Dancer, 1984; Break Every Rule, 1986; Foreign Affair, 1989; with The Adventures: Theodore and Friends, 1985; Sea of Love, 1988; with Beltane Fire: Different Breed, 1986; Also appeared on albums by: Phil Collins; Paul McCartney; Roger Waters; Roger Daltrey; Katrina and The Waves; Five Star; Barbara Dickson; Film soundtracks: The Lion King; K2; Point of No Return; Calendar Girl; Con Air; Cool Runnings; House of The Spirits; I'll Do Anything; Monkey Trouble; Renaissance Man; Beyond Rangoon; Bad Boys; Crimson Tide; 9 Months. *Honours:* Grammy, as Musician, What's Love Got To Do With It. *Memberships:* ASCAP; PRS. *Current Management:* Kraft Benjamin Engel Management, California. *Address:* Belle Haven 275, James River Rd, Scottsville, VA 24590, USA.

GLITTER Gary, (Paul Gadd); b. 8 May 1944, Banbury, Oxfordshire, England. Singer; Entertainer; Songwriter. *Career:* Leader, skiffle group Paul Russell and the Rebels; Worked in Germany as Paul Raven; Relaunched career as glam rock singer Gary Glitter, 1971–; Considerable success in UK, 1970s–; Appearances include: London Rock 'n' Roll Festival, Wembley Stadium, 1972; British tours, 1974–; Charity concert, Theatre Royal, London, 1976; Slough Festival, 1992; Numerous television appearances include: Remember Me This Way (full length film/ documentary), 1973; Presenter, Night Network, 1988; Hyde Park Prince's Trust Concert, 1996; Performed in Quadrophenia with The Who; Toured USA in Quadrophenia with The Who, 1996. *Compositions:* Numerous hits co-written with Mike Leander. *Recordings:* Albums: Glitter, 1972; Touch Me, 1973; Remember Me This Way, 1974; Always Yours, 1975; GG, 1975; I Love You Love, 1977; Silver Star, 1978; The Leader, 1980; Boys Will Be Boys, 1984; Leader II, 1991; Numerous compilations; Hit singles include: Rock 'n' Roll Part 2 (No. 2, UK), 1972; I Didn't Know I Loved You (Till I Saw You Rock 'n' Roll), 1972; Do You Wanna Touch Me (No. 2, UK), 1973; Hello Hello I'm Back Again (No. 2, UK), 1973; I'm The Leader of The Gang, (No. 1, UK), 1973; I Love You Love Me Love, (No. 1, UK), 1973; Always Yours (No. 1, UK), 1974; Remember Me This Way, 1974; Oh Yes You're Beautiful (No. 2, UK), 1974; Love Like You and Me, 1975; Doin' Alright With The Boys, 1975; Another Rock 'n' Roll Christmas, 1984. *Publication:* Leader – The Autobiography of Gary Glitter, 1991. *Honours:* Nordoff Robins Lifetime Achievement Award, 1997; BASCA Gold Badge Award, 1997. *Current Management:* Jef Hanlon Management Ltd. *Address:* 1 York St, London W1H 1PZ, England.

GLOCKLER Nigel Ian; b. 24 Jan. 1953, Hove, Sussex, England. Musician (drums, percussion). *Education:* Brighton College. *Musical Education:* Self-taught. *Career:* Member: The Associates, 1980–82; Toyah, 1980–81; Saxon, 1981–87; GTR, 1987–88; Saxon, 1989–; Tours with Toyah, Saxon; Television and radio appearances. *Recordings:* Albums include: with Associates: The Affectionate Punch; Sulk; with Toyah: Anthem; with Saxon: The Eagle Has Landed; Power and The Glory; Crusader; Solid Ball of Rock; Dogs of War; Forever Free; Rock The Nations; Innocence Is No Excuse; Unleash the Beast; with Asia: Aqua; Japanese film soundtrack album; Archiva; with Steve Howe: Turbulenz; Guitar Speak; with Tony Martin: Back Where I Belong; with Fastway: Bad Bad Girls. *Memberships:* PRS; MCPS; Musicians' Union. *Current Management:* Blackmail Management. *Address:* 60 Cleveland Rd, New Malden, Surrey KT3 3QJ, England.

GLOJNARIC Silvestar; b. 2 Dec. 1936, Ladislavec, Croatia. m. Ana Jurisic, 7 July 1962, 1 s., 1 d. *Musical Education:* Zagreb Music Academy, Composition and Theory Department. *Career:* Tours, concerts, Zagreb Jazz Quartet, Europe; Tours with Zagreb Radio Big Band, Europe including Russia; Television, radio appearances with various orchestras as composer, arranger, conductor; Most European Jazz Festivals. *Recordings:* Zagreb Big Band with: Art Farmer; Slide Hampton; Stan Getz; J Griffin; SFB Big Band, Berlin; NDR Big Band, Hamburg; Ljubljana Big Band; John Lewis, A Mangelsdorf: Animal Dance; Buck Clayton, BJ Turner: Feel So Fine; Georgie Fame. *Membership:* Croatian Composers' Asscn. *Current*

Management: Silverstar Glojnaric. *Address:* Cujetno Naseltje 3, 41430 Samobar, Croatia.

GLOSSOP Mick; b. 18 March 1949, Nottinghamshire, England. Engineer; Mixer. m. Elva Williamson, 1 d. *Career:* Recording Engineer, various studios, UK and Canada, until 1979; Freelance record producer and engineer, 1980-. *Recordings:* Van Morrison: Wavelength; Into the Music; Inarticulate Speech; Sense of Wonder; No Guru...: Poetic Champions; Avalon Sunset; Enlightenment; Too Long in Exile; Hymns to the Silence; A Night in San Francisco; Days Like This; Frank Zappa: Joe's Garage; The Waterboys: This is the Sea; The Wonder Stuff: Never Loved Elvis; Dizzy; Numerous albums and singles including Public Image Ltd, Suede, The Ruts, The Skids, Camel, Ian Gillan, UFO, Pino Daniele; The Alarm; Magazine; Furniture; The Men They Couldn't Hang. *Honours:* Certificate of work with John Lee Hooker, National Academy of Recording Arts and Sciences. *Membership:* Music Producers Guild. *Current Management:* Stephen Budd Management. *Address:* 109B Regents Park Rd, London NW1 8UR, England.

GLOVER Corey; Vocalist; Actor. *Career:* Actor, film: Platoon, 1985; Reunion, 2001; Singer, funk rock group Living Colour, 1985–95; Tours include: Support to Cheap Trick; Robert Palmer; Anthrax; Billy Bragg; Rolling Stones, Steel Wheels North American Tour, 1989; Miracle Biscuit tour, 1990; Lollapalooza tour, 1991; Stained In The UK tour, 1993; Concerts include: Earth Day concert, Central Park; Reading Festival, 1990; Phoenix Festival, 1993. *Recordings:* Albums: Vivid, 1988; Time's Up, 1990; Biscuits, 1991; Stain, 1993; Also appears on: In from the Storm, 1995; Rhythm of the Games, 1996; Black Night, 1997; Guest on Primitive Cool, Mick Jagger, 1986; Singles include: Cult of Personality, 1989; Glamour Boys, 1989; Love Rears Its Ugly Head, 1991; Solace of You, 1991; Leave It Alone, 1993; Solo album: Hymns. *Honours:* Elvis Award, Best New Band, International Rock Awards, 1989; MTV Awards: Best New Artist, Best Group Video, Best Stage Performance, 1989; Grammy Award, Best Hard Rock Performance, Time's Up, 1991; Rolling Stone Critics Poll Winners, Best Band, 1991. *Membership:* Black Rock Coalition. *Address:* c/o Jim Grant, Suite 1C, 39A Gramercy Park N, New York, NY 10010, USA.

GLOVER Roger; b. 30 Nov. 1945, Brecon, Powys, Wales. Musician (bass); Composer; Record Prod. *Career:* Founder, The Madisons; Member, Episode Six, including 9 singles, 1966–69; Member, Deep Purple, 1970–73; Record producer, albums for: Nazareth; Status Quo; Judas Priest; Rory Gallagher; Rainbow; Elf; David Coverdale; Pretty Maids; Spencer Davis; Ian Gillan; Rupert Hine; Barbi Benton; Young and Moody; Solo recording artiste; Member, Rainbow, 1979–84; Concerts include: Monsters of Rock Festival, UK, 1980; Member, Deep Purple, 1984–; Also worked with Ian Gillan; Numerous world-wide tours with the above. *Compositions include:* The Butterfly Ball (led to book and film), 1974; Co-writer, with Ritchie Blackmore; All Night Long; Can't Happen Here. *Recordings:* Albums: with Deep Purple: Concerto For Group and Orchestra, 1970; In Rock, 1970; Fireball, 1971; Machine Head, 1972; Made In Japan, 1973; Who Do We Think We Are?, 1973; Perfect Strangers, 1984; House of Blue Light, 1987; Nobody's Perfect, 1988; Slaves and Masters, 1990; The Battle Rages On, 1993; Purpendicular, 1996; Abandon, 1998; Solo: Elements, 1978; Mask, 1984; with Gillan/Glover: Accidentally On Purpose, 1988; with Rainbow: Down To Earth, 1979; Difficult To Cure, 1981; Straight Between The Eyes, 1982; Bent Out of Shape, 1983; Finyl Vinyl, 1986; Hit singles: with Deep Purple: Black Night, 1970; Strange Kind of Woman, 1971; Smoke On The Water, 1973; Knocking At Your Back Door, 1985; with Rainbow: Since You've Been Gone, 1979; All Night Long, 1980; I Surrender, 1981; Can't Happen Here, 1981; Also performed with: Dave Cousins; Andy Mackay; Dan McCafferty. *Current Management:* Thames Talent, 45 E Putnam St, Greenwich, CT 06850, USA.

GLYNN Dominic; b. 27 Sept. 1960, Cuckfield, West Sussex, England. Composer; Prod. *Musical Education:* Self-taught. *Career:* Incidental music: BBC TV's Doctor Who; Space Vets; Various education series; Half of experimental electronic act Syzygy; Appearances London's Kiss FM. *Recordings:* Theme from Doctor Who, 1986; Numerous albums for Chappell Recorded Music Library; With Syzygy: Morphic Resonance; Terminus; With The Swarm; Forsaken – The Music, 1999; With Fluid: Digital Phunk, 2000; With Cybajaz: The Devil Is An Idiot, 2000. *Leisure interests:* Friends; Clubs; Music. *Current Management:* Cardinus Management. *Address:* 57 Farningham Rd, Caterham, Surrey, England.

GNATYUK Mikola; b. 14 Sept. 1952, Ukraine. Singer. 1 s. *Musical Education:* Music Institut, Rovno, Ukraine. *Career:* Numerous television and radio appearances: Moscow; Ukraine; Germany, including: Aein Kessel, Rund; Concerts: Prague; Warsaw; Tours: Russia; Ukraine; Germany. *Recordings:* Songs: Bazaban; Molinovoi Zvon; Belii Stavni (number 1, Ukraine), 1994; Shas Rikog Pluve; Starenki. *Honours:* First prize, Sopot Festival, Poland; Grand Prix Festival, Dresden. *Membership:* SVIATO. *Leisure interests:* Visiting son in Germany. *Current Management:* Mother in Kiev. *Address:* 252040 Kiev, Vasilkovski 2A/126, Ukraine.

GOBAC Davor; b. Karlovac, Croatia. Singer; Composer; Entertainer; Actor; Text-writer. m. Deana Pavic, 5 Feb. 1994, 1 s. *Career:* Netherlands tour, 1989; Support to Ramones, Zagreb, Ljubgjana, 1990; Russian tour, 60 concerts, 1991; Toronto, 1993; Germany, Italy, Austria; 3 clips, MTV; Marcel Vanhilt Show; Many television and radio shows, Croatia. *Recordings:* Godina Zmaja (Year of Dragon), 1988; Live In Amsterdam, 1989; Sexy Magazin, 1990; Tko Je Ubio Mickey Mousea (Who Killed Mickey Mouse), 1991; Skrebrne Svinje (Silver Pigs), 1993, 1994; Video: Brkiant Video Pop, 1989. *Honours:* Croatian Film and Video Award, Oktavijan Miletic, 1995. *Membership:* Hrvatska Glalbena Vnija (Croatian Musicians' Union). *Leisure interests:* Painting; Acting. *Address:* Sljemeuska 27, 41211 Zapresic, Croatia.

GODFREY Mary; b. 10 Sept. 1960, Chicago, Illinois, USA. Singer; Songwriter; Musician (Bass, Guitar). *Musical Education:* Organ and Bass Guitar lessons; Self-taught guitar. *Career:* Has performed for past four years at South by Southwest Music Conference, Austin, Texas. *Compositions:* Temperature Change, 1990; Hit and Run, 1990; Mine Tonight and Send Me An Angel, 1994; The Edge in the Night, 1995. *Recordings:* Faces of Emotion: Hot Love, 1987; Back to the Light, 1988; TOC Album, 1989; Solo Recordings: Mary Godfrey, 1991; Contributor: Down O'Keele, backing vocal, 1993. *Honours:* Chicago Talent Search Winner, 1990; Second Place Lead Vocalist, Chicago Rocker Awards, 1990; Second Place Mem., Dunce Category, Chicago Rocker Awards, 1990. *Memberships:* NARAS, Vice President for WIM (Chicago Outreach Committee, 1989–91); ASCAP; National Academy of Songwriters. *Leisure interests:* Freelance Writer for various magazines; Artist (Acrylic showing at the Ashwell Gallery, Beverly, USA, 1996). *Current Management:* English Cathy, Transatlantic Management, Box 2831, Tucson, AZ 85702, USA.

GODIN Nicolas; b. Versailles, France. Prod.; Musician (keyboards). *Education:* Studied at the Conservatoire, Paris. *Career:* Met Jean Benoit Dunckel at Conservatoire, Paris; Joined Dunckel's band Orange; After departure of Alex Gopher from band, formed duo Air, 1995; Released debut single, 1996; Signed to Virgin and released their debut album, 1997; Collaborations: Jean Jacques Perrey; Francoise Hardy; Alex Gopher; Gordon Tracks; Remixed: Depeche Mode; Neneh Cherry. *Recordings:* Albums: Moon Safari, 1997; The Virgin Suicides, Premieres Symptoms, 1999; 10000 Hz Legend, 2001; Singles: Modulor, Casanova 70, 1996; Sexy Boy, 1997; Kelly Watch The Stars, 1998; Playground Love, 2000; Radio No. 1, 2001. *Address:* c/o Source Records, 113–117 Farringdon Rd, London, EC1R 3BX, England.

GODINHO Sergio; b. 31 Aug. 1945, Portugal. Singer; Songwriter. *Career:* 17 CDs of original songs; Hundreds of live shows; Film score writer; Actor; Occasional script writer; Director. *Compositions:* O Primeiro Dia, Lisboa Que Amanhece. *Recordings:* Noites Passadas; Rivolitz. *Publications:* Book For Children; Play. *Honours:* Record of The Year; Artist of The Year. *Memberships:* SPA. *Current Management:* Praça Das Flores, R Da Imprensa Nacional 36, 1250 Lisboa, Portugal.

GODLEMAN Martin John; b. 6 Jan. 1958, Hammersmith, London, England. Vocalist; Writer; Musician (drums). *Musical Education:* BA Hons, Hatfield Polytechnic, 1979; MA, University of Surrey, 1991. *Career:* Bands: Faut Parler, 5 piece (Serge Gainsbourg jazz band), Mean Fiddler, 1993; Adventures of Parsley, 5 piece (vocals, percussion), Radio One, Mark Radcliff Show, 1995; Mark Lamarr Show, GLR, 1995; Comedy Cafe Anniverary Show, London, 1995; Adventures of Parsley, Leadline 5 piece (vocals); Big Breakfast TV Show, (Comedy Cafe gig highlights), Ch4, 1995; Edinburgh Fringe (Gilded Balloon), (Adventures of Parsley), 1997. *Recordings:* Singles: Magpie, Adventures of Parsley, 1995; Intoxicated Man, Faut Parler, 1996; Minder (Adventures of Parsley), 1997; Albums: Top TV Themes (Adventures of Parsley), 1997. *Publication:* Chapter in The Power of The Page, 1993. *Memberships:* FRA (Royal Academy); Collingwood Athletic Club. *Leisure interests:* Theatre; Running (to half-marathon level); Soccer commentary (with West Ham United Football Club); Songwriting; Production. *Current Management:* Norbert J Hetherington Management. *Address:* 6 Roxburgh Court, 69 Melrose Rd, London SW18 1PG, England.

GODLEY Kevin; b. 7 Oct. 1945, Manchester, Lancashire, England. Vocalist; Musician (drums); Songwriter; Prod.; Video Dir. *Career:* Founder member, drummer, 10cc, 1972–76; Appearances include: Reading Festival, 1974; Knebworth Festival, 1976; US and British tours; Producer, songwriter, duo Godley and Creme (with Lol Creme), 1976–; Television includes: One World One Voice, series of programmes, with contributions from artists including: Sting, Peter Gabriel, Lou Reed, Chrissie Hynde, Stewart Copeland; Feature film, Howling At The Moon, 1988. *Recordings:* Albums: with 10cc: Sheet Music, 1974; Original Soundtrack, 1975; Greatest Hits, 1975; How Dare You?, 1976; Meanwhile, 1992; Mirror Mirror, 1995; Greatest Hits, 1998; with Godley and Creme (mostly self-written and produced): Consequences, 1977; L, 1978; Music From Consequences, 1979; Freeze Frame, 1979; Long Distant Romancer, 1981; Ismism, 1981; Birds of Prey, 1983; The History Mix, Vol. 1, 1985; The Changing Faces of 10cc and Godley and Creme, 1987; Goodbye

Blue Sky, 1988; Singles include: with 10cc: Donna, 1972; Rubber Bullets (No. 1, UK), 1973; The Dean and I, 1973; Wall Street Shuffle, 1974; Silly Love, 1974; Life Is A Minestrone, 1975; I'm Not In Love (UK No. 1, USA No. 2), 1975; Art For Art's Sake, 1975; I'm Mandy Fly Me, 1976; with Godley and Creme: Under Your Thumb, 1981; Wedding Bells, 1981; Cry, 1985; Producer, albums including Long Distant Romancer, Mickey Jupp, 1981; One World One Voice, 1989; Director, videos including: Every Breath You Take, The Police; Rockit, Herbie Hancock; Feel The Love, 10cc; Relax, Frankie Goes To Hollywood; Two Tribes, Frankie Goes To Hollywood; Kele Le Roc; Duran Duran; Black Crowes; Sting; Charlatans; Director, TV commercials, including: Seafrance, PSEG. *Honours:* Ivor Novello Awards: Best Beat Song, Rubber Bullets, 1974; Most Performed British Song, Best Pop Song, International Hit of The Year, I'm Not In Love, 1976; 5 MTV Video Awards, Rockit, 1984; MTV Video Vanguard Award, 1985. *Membership:* Co-founder, environmental organization, ARK.

GOETHE-MCGINN Lisa; b. 31 Jan. 1965, St Louis, Missouri, USA. Musician (Flute). m. Gregg McGinn, 10 Aug. 1996. *Education:* BM, Millikin University, Decatur, Illinois, 1987; MM, University of Illinois at Urbana, 1993. *Career:* Performer and Interpreter of contemporary music and free improvisation; Performed at many festivals and music series in the USA and abroad; Committed to performing music by contemporary composers; Active member, numerous new music ensembles in Chicago; Has worked with composers including Helmut Lachenmann, Salvatore Martirano and Herbert Brün; Performed at Museum of Contemporary Art, The Arts Club of Chicago Renaissance Society and others. *Honours:* Participant, Fishoff Chamber Music Competition, 1993, Gaudeamus International Interpreters Competition, 1995, 1999. *Memberships:* American Composers Forum; National Flute Asscn; Chicago Flute Club. *Leisure interests:* Cycling; Fashion; Travelling. *Address:* 142 Harrison St No. 2, Oak Park, IL 60304, USA.

GOFFEY Danny; b. 1975, Oxford, England. Musician (drums). *Career:* Member, The Jennifers; Drummer, Supergrass, 1994–; Concerts include: Support to Blur, Alexandra Palace, 1994; British tour with Shed Seven, 1994; T In The Park Festival, Glasgow, 1995. *Recordings:* Albums: I Should Coco (No. 1, UK), 1995; In it for the Money (No. 2, UK); Supergrass, 1999; Singles: Caught by the Fuzz, 1994; Mansize Rooster, 1995; Lenny, 1995; Alright (No. 2, UK), 1995; Going Out, 1996; Richard III (No. 2, UK), 1997; Sun Hits the Sky, 1997; Late In The Day, 1997; Pumping On Your Stereo, 1999; Moving, 1999; Mary, 1999. *Honours:* Q Award, Best New Act, 1995; BRIT Award Nominations: Best British Newcomer, Best Single, Best Video, 1996. *Current Management:* Courtyard Management, 22 The Nursery, Sutton Courtenay, Abingdon, Oxon OX14 4UA, England.

GOHIL Jitesh; b. 3 April 1967, Kenya. Record Exec. *Education:* First Class Degree, Economics, Accounting, Bristol University. *Career:* Joined Multitone Records, 1988; Multitone developed into largest Asian record label in world, pioneered Bhangra genre; Multitone Records joined BMG Group, 1992; Now Managing Director, Multitone. *Address:* 1274 Uxbridge Rd, Hayes End, Middlesex UB4 8JF, England.

GOLBEY Brian James; b. 5 Feb. 1939, Pycombe, Sussex, England. Musician (guitar, fiddle); Vocalist; Journalist. m. (1) 20 Sept. 1969, divorced, 2 s.; (2) Sandi Stubbs, 3 May 1980, 1 s. *Career:* Television with Pete Stanley (partner, 27 years) includes: 3 times Blue Peter; George Hamilton IV shows, BBC2; Many local television appearances; Old Grey Whistle Test; Cajun Moon, 1975; Magpie, ITV, 1969–; Concerts, most theatres include: Wembley Festival of Country Music, several times; London Palladium; Royal Albert Hall; Recordings for Pye, 1970; Emerald/ Decca, 1973–74; Chrysalis, 1975; Waterfront Records, 1979–80s. *Publications:* Regular columnist, Country Music People, 1989–; Essay for Aspects of Elvis, 1994. *Honours:* Billboard; Record Mirror Award, Top UK artist, 1972; CMA Award, Top UK Soloist, 1972; BCMA Committee Award for long and continuing service to Country music in Britain, 1993. *Membership:* PRS. *Leisure interests:* Music; Painting; School activities. *Address:* 7 Hallcroft Beeston, Nottingham NG9 1E2, England.

GOLD Harry; b. 26 Feb. 1907, Dublin, Ireland. Musician (clarinet, all saxophones including bass). m. Margaret (Peggy), 4 Oct. 1936, deceased 2 July 1995, 4 s. *Musical Education:* London College of Music, Bachelor of Music. *Career:* Professional, 1923–; Composer, arranger, orchestrator, musical director; Founder, leader, Pieces of Eight Jazz Band; Rhapsody In Green, Radio Telefis Concert Orchestra; Television: Lowest of The Low. *Compositions:* Very numerous, about 50 compositions and arrangements published. *Publications:* Autobiography published, February 2000. *Honours:* BBC Special Award; Freeman of City of London; Derry, Northern Ireland; Blarney, Co Cork; Patron, Cork Jazz Festival. *Memberships:* Musicians' Union; British Academy of Songwriters, Composers and Authors; PRS. *Leisure interest:* Cooking. *Address:* Flat 126, 53 Foxham Rd, London N19 4RR, England.

GOLDBERG Barry; b. 25 Dec. 1942, Chicago, Illinois, USA. Musician (piano); Songwriter. m. Gail, 15 May 1971, 1 s. *Musical Education:* Self-

taught. *Career:* Appeared at Newport Folk Festival with Bob Dylan, 1965; Played at Woodstock and Monterey pop festivals; Has written the score or contributed songs for films: Forrest Gump; Ruby; Flashback; Pow-Wow Highway; Dirty Dancing; Nobody's Fool; Adventures In Babysitting; Studio sessions with: Leonard Cohen; The Byrds; Mitch Ryder; The Ramones; Charlie Musselwhite; Additional associations with: Electric Flag; Bob Crewe; Jimi Hendrix; Gerry Goffin; Neil Young; Solomon Burke; Merry Clayton; Percy Sledge. *Recordings:* I've Got To Use My Imagination, recorded by Gladys Knight, Joe Cocker and Bobby Blue Bland; It's Not The Spotlight, recorded by Rod Stewart; Sittin' In Circles, recorded by Steve Miller; Additional songs recorded by artists including: Tom Jones; B J Thomas; Manhattan Transfer; Ben E King; The Neville Brothers; Jeff Healey; The Persuasions; Carole King; Junior Walker; Sam Moore. *Honour:* Pioneer Award, BMI, USA. *Memberships:* BMI; NARAS; AFofM. *Current Management:* Christopher Nassif Agency, Joe Schneider, CNA, Century City, Los Angeles, California, USA.

GOLDIE (Clifford Price); b. 1966, Wolverhampton, England. Prod.; Actor. *Career:* Producer, Drum 'n bass/jungle music; Acting roles include UK TV soap, EastEnders, 2000. *Recordings:* Albums: Goldie Presents Metalheadz: Timeless, 1995; Saturnz Return, 1998; Incredible Sound of Drum N Bass, 2000; Singles: Inner City Life, 1995; Kemistry, 1997; Digital, 1997; Temper Temper, 1998; Ring of Saturn, 1998; Believe, 1998. *Current Management:* NUR Entertainment, Canalot Studios, Unit 218A, 222 Kensal Rd, London W10 5BN, England.

GOLDING Lynval; b. 24 July 1951, Coventry, England. Vocalist. *Career:* Member, The Specials; Early tours supporting The Clash; Established own record label, 2-Tone; Debut album produced by Elvis Costello; Numerous tours and television appearances; Left band, formed Fun Boy Three with Terry Hall and Neville Staples, split 1983. *Recordings:* with The Specials: Singles: Gangsters, 1979; A Message to You, Rudi, 1979; Too Much Too Young (Live EP) (No. 1, UK), 1980; Rat Race, 1980; Stereotype, 1980; Do Nothing, 1980; Ghost Town (No. 1, UK), 1981; Albums: The Specials, 1979; More Specials, 1980; Singles, 1991; Stereotypes (As, Bs and Rarities), 2000; With Fun Boy Three: The Lunatics Have Taken Over the Asylum, 1981; It Ain't Wha You Do, with Bananarama, 1982; Really Saying Something, with Bananarama, 1982; The Telephone Always Rings, 1982; Tunnel of Love, 1983; Our Lips Are Sealed, 1983; Albums: Fun Boy Three, 1982; Waiting, 1983.

GOLDSBORO Bobby; b. 18 Jan. 1941, Marianna, Florida, USA. Musician (guitar); Singer; Songwriter. *Career:* Guitarist, Roy Orbison, 1960; Solo artiste, 1964–; Later, country artiste, 1980s. *Recordings:* Hit singles include: See The Funny Little Clown, 1964; Whenever He Holds You; Little Things; Voodoo Woman; It's Too Late; Blue Autumn; Honey (No. 1, US; No. 2, UK), 1968; Watching Scotty Grow; Summer (The First Time); Albums include: Honey, 1968; Today, 1969; Muddy Mississippi Line, 1970; We Gotta Start Lovin', 1971; Come Back Home, 1971; Goldsboro, 1977; Roundup Saloon, 1982; Also numerous compilations; Albums: The Bobby Goldsboro Album, 1964; Honey, 1968; Easter Egg Mornin', 1993; The Best of Bobby Goldsboro, 1996; The Greatest Hits, 1999; Hello Summertime, 2001. *Current Management:* Jim Stephany Management, 1021 Preston Dr., Nashville, TN 37206, USA.

GOLDSMITH Harvey; b. 4 March 1946, London, England. CEO; Impresario. m. Diana Gorman, 1971, 1 s. *Education:* Christ's College; Brighton College of Technology. *Career:* Partner, Big O Posters, 1966–67; Organized first free open-air concert in Parliament Hill Fields with Michael Alfandary, 1968; Opened Round House, Camden Town, 1968, Crystal Palace Garden Party series of concerts, 1969–72; Merged with John Smith Entertainments, 1970; Formed Harvey Goldsmith Entertainments (rock tours promotion company), 1976; Acquired Allied Entertainments Group (rock concert promotions company), 1984; Formed Classical Productions with Mark McCormack, 1986; Promoter and Producer of pop, rock and classical musical events including: Concerts: Bruce Springsteen; The Rolling Stones; Elton John; The Who; Pink Floyd; Opera: Aïda, 1988, Carmen, 1989, Tosca, 1991, Earls Court; Pavarotti at Wembley, 1986; Pavarotti in the Park, 1991; The Three Tenors, 1996; Lord of the Dance, 1996–97; Cirque du Soleil, 1996–97; Mastercard Masters of Music, 1996; Music for Montserrat at the Royal Albert Hall, 1997; The Bee Gees, 1998; Ozzfest, 1998; Paul Weller, 1998. *Honour:* CBE, 1996. *Memberships include:* Chairman, Concert Promoters Asscn, 1986; Chairman, National Music Festival, 1991; Co-Chairman, President's Club, 1994; Vice Chairman, Prince's Trust Action Management Board, 1993; Vice President, REACT, 1989; Vice President, Music Users Council, 1994; Trustee, Band Aid, 1985; Trustee, Life Aid Foundation, 1985; Trustee, Royal Opera House, 1995; Trustee, CST, 1995; British Red Cross Communications Panel, 1992; Prague Heritage Fund, 1994; London Tourist Board, 1994. *Address:* Greenland Pl., 115–123 Bayham St, London NW1 0AG, England.

GOLDSMITH Timothy Simon; b. 1 Dec. 1962, West London, England. Musician (drums). *Career:* Tours with: Paul Brady; Tanita Tikaram; Nik Kershaw; Joan Armatrading; Jaki Graham; Television appearances include: Top of The Pops; Old Grey Whistle Test; Live radio, videos. *Recordings include:* Albums: Alf, Alison Moyet; Go West, Go West; Track Record, Joan Armatrading. *Membership:* Musicians' Union. *Leisure interests:* Fishing; Cinema. *Address:* 343a Upper Richmond Rd W, East Sheen, London SW14, England.

GOLT Debbie; b. 2 April 1952, London, England. Consultant; Music and Arts Management. 2 d. *Education:* BA Hons, History, York University; PG Diploma, Applied Youth and Community Work, Manchester Polytechnic. *Career:* Diverse career on alternative/independent circuit; Parallel career in youth work and Arts Management; Ran sound system battles and concerts with Rock Against Racism, 1977–80; Managed major UK based African Band, Taxi Pata Pata (first UK-based African band on BBC RI and Arts Council support); Director, Nyrangongo record label, 1985–90; Co-directed Half The Sky, first women's promotions group promoting female world music; Introduced Oumau Sangare to UK and top television / press coverage; Panelist for RI Sound City, In The City, Umbrella, 1991–93; Set up Eleventh Hour Arts; Co-director, Portobello Jazz; Co-manager, Frank Chickens, 1994–96; Manager of MoMo (music of Moroccan Origin), 1997–; Advisor to Frank Chickens, Gifty Naa DK, Sandira, Rose Dede Tetteh, TakiPata Pata; Co-ordinator, World Music Portobello Festival; Consultant for festivals, global music, women's music; Established Eleventh Hour. *Publications:* Contributor to several publications including Worldbeat; World Music Magazine; The Guardian; Froots; Straight No Chaser, Black Film Maker Magazine, independent catalogue; Women in Music Now; Published style magazine, Topical, 1991–93; Radio programmes on Radio 1, Radio 5, GLR and local radio; DJ and Presenter on gaialive internet radio. *Memberships:* Women In Music, chair; Sound Sense; IMF; Advisory Board of Modal. *Leisure interests:* Reading widely; Cultural activities with own children; Art galleries; Gym; Macrobiotic food; Walking in the hills; Wide range of music. *Address:* Eleventh Hour Arts, 113 Cheesemans Terrace, London W14 9XH, England.

GONZALEZ Celina; b. Jovellanos, Cuba. Singer. m. Rentilio Dominguez, Dec. 1971, 1 s. *Career:* Country singer, formerly duo with husband, now with own band Campo Alegre; Daily radio show, Radio Taino, Havana; Regular television appearances include: Palmas y Canas, Cuba; Tours throughout Cuba, Dominican Republic, Columbia; Concerts in New York, and Cali Fest, 1984. *Recordings:* Singles: Santa Barbara, 1994; La Rica Cosecha, 1997; Salsa, 1998; Celina Gonzalez, 2000. *Honours:* Distinction of National Culture; Egrem Silver disc; 6 Premios Girasoles; Most popular artist in Cuba. *Address:* c/o World Circuit Records, 106 Cleveland St, London W1P 5DP, England.

GONZALEZ Kenny, (Kenny Dope, The Bucketheads, Untouchables, Powerhouse, Swing Kids); b. 7 June 1970, Brooklyn, New York, USA. Prod.; Remixer; DJ. *Career:* Started producing for New York labels: Strictly Rhythm; Nu Groove; Formed Masters At Work with Louie Vega; Duo also recorded as Nu Yorican Soul; Co-founder: MAW Records; Collaborations: India; Marc Anthony; Jocelyn Brown; James Ingram; Stephanie Mills; Remixed: Shanice; Tito Puente; Barbara Tucker; Jamiroquai; Atmosfear; Incognito; Luther Vandross; Ce Ce Peniston; Martha Wash; Ballistic Brothers; Alex Gopher; Melanie B. *Recordings:* Albums: Nu Yorican Soul, 1997; Singles: Makin' A Livin (as Powerhouse), 1991; I Can't Get No Sleep (as Masters At Work), 1992; Deep Inside (as Hardrive), 1993; Love and Happiness (as River Ocean), 1994; The Nervous Track (as Nu-Yorican Soul), 1994; The Bomb (as The Bucketheads), 1995; I Am The Black Gold of The Sun (as Nu-Yorican Soul), 1996; What A Sensation (as Kenlou), 1996; To Be In Love, 1997; Brasilian Beat, 1998; Brazilica, 2001. *Address:* c/o Strictly Rhythm, 920 Broadway 1403, New York, USA.

GONZÁLEZ Rubén; b. April, 1919, Santa Clara, Cuba. Musician (piano). *Career:* Played with La Orquesta Paulina, Conjunto Canayo, Los Hermanos, Raúl Planas, Mongo Santamaría and Arsenio Rodríguez, 1940s; Toured Panama and South America; Back in Havana played with various bands including Conjunto Kubavana de Alberto Ruiz and Conjunto de Senen Suárez; Played with Enrique Jorrín in 1980s and took over as bandleader on Jorrín's death; Retired, late 1980s; Made comeback with the Buena Vista Social Club series of recordings; Appeared in Wim Wenders' documentary film Buena Vista Social Club. *Recordings:* recent Albums: Buena Vista Social Club, Introducing Rubén González, A Toda Cuba Le Gusta (Afro Cuban All-Stars), 1997; Buena Vista Social Club Presents Ibrahim Ferrer, 1999; Buena Vista Social Club Presents Omara Portuonda, Chanchullo, 2000; features on Distinto Diferente (with Afro Cuban All-Stars), 1999. *Address:* c/o World Circuit Ltd, First Floor, Shoreditch Stables, 138 Kingsland Rd, London, E2 8DY, England.

GOOD Larry J; Entertainer; Musician (guitar). m. Jennifer, 22 Feb. 1985. 1 d. (by previous marriage). *Musical Education:* Playing with Grand Ole Opry stars. *Career:* Shows with major artist including: Charley Pride; Waylon Jennings; Marty Robbins; Roy Acuff; Ray Price; Ernest Tubb; Television appearances: Regular on several local television shows; Ernest Tubb Midnight Jamboree. *Recordings:* Albums include: Some Old Some New; As Good As It Gets; Moving Country; Jesus is My Hero (gospel); The

Best of Larry Good; Singles include: Raise Your Glass; Long Way To Kansas City. *Honour:* Nebraska Country Music Hall of Fame. *Leisure interest:* Gardening. *Current Management:* Lari-Jon Promotions. *Address:* PO Box 216, 325 W Walnut, Rising City, NE 68658, USA.

GOODACRE Tony; b. 3 Feb. 1938, Leeds, England. Singer; Entertainer; Musician (guitar). m. (1) Cherry, 18 June 1960, 1 s., 2 d.; (2) Sylvia, 29 July 1974. *Career:* First professional engagement, 1956; First recording, 1957; Radio debut, 1958; Formed band Goodacre Country, 1969; Guest, The Arthur Smith Show, USA television, 1973; First appearance, Grand Ole Opry, Nashville, 1977; Wembley Festival, 1982, 1983; Started own Music Publishing Company: Sylvantone Music, 1983; Promoted career of Stu Page, 1984–86; Sarah Jory, 1987–88. *Recordings:* Albums: Roamin' Round In Nashville, 1974; Grandma's Feather Bed, 1975; Thanks To The Hanks, 1976; Written In Britain, 1977; The Best of Tony Goodacre, 1978; Mr Country Music, 1978; You've Made My Life Complete, 1979; Recorded Live In Ilkley, 1980; 25th Anniversary, 1981; Red Roses, 1983; Sylvantone Song Book, Vols 1 and 2, 1984–85; The Tony Goodacre Collection, 1986; Country Favourites, 1988; Something Special, 1989; Livin' On Livin', 1992; 40th Anniversary Album, 1996; The Millenium Project, 2000. *Honours:* Record Mirror Award, 1973; 3 British Country Music Asscn Awards, 1982–84; Favourite Male Vocalist in Europe, Country Gazette (Dutch Magazine), 1986; 18 Country Music Club Awards, Top Solo Artist; 3 Country Music Club Awards, Top Duo, with Sarah Jory, 1987. *Leisure interest:* Travel. *Current Management:* Sylvantone Promotions. *Address:* 17 Allerton Grange Way, Leeds LS17 6LP, England.

GOODIER David Charles Gray; b. 11 July 1954, Salisbury, England. Musician (bass guitar fretted/fretless, double bass). Partner, Lynn Thompson, 1 s., 2 d. *Education:* BEd Hons, St Luke's College, Exeter University. *Musical Education:* Self-taught, studied briefly with Peter Ind and Rufus Reid. *Career:* Interests Funk, Fusion, Salsa, Mainstream, Modern and contemporary jazz; Worked in theatre pit bands made radio broadcasts (R3, R2); Television and radio sessions; Many festival appearances: Brecon; Glastonbury; Worked with jazz musicians, including: Guy Barker; Dave De Fries; Tal Farlow; Art Farmer; Slim Gaillard; Dick Morrissey; Gerard Presencer; Don Rendell; Andy Sheppard; Norma Winstone; Often as part of the Dave Gordon Trio with Tony Orrell; Musical Director, Bristol Jazz Workshop, 1991-. *Recordings:* John Parricelli, Mark Lockheart: Matheran; The Korgis: This World's For Everyone; Brass Reality: For Real. *Leisure interests:* Squash; Badminton; Walking. *Current Management:* LDT Management.

GOODMAN Clare; b. 19 May 1966, Frimley, Surrey, England. Singer; Dancer. *Musical Education:* West Street School of Performing Arts. *Career:* Live: Joseph and The Amazing Technicolour Dreamcoat, British tour, 1994–95; Appearance with Just Music (for anti-racist alliance) Arafest '94; Films: Frankenstein (Mary Shelley's); The Muppet Christmas Carol; Video: Give Me Just A Little More Time, Kylie Minogue; I've Got A Spell On You, Bryan Ferry; Commercials: Kool-aid; Red Stripe. *Membership:* Musicians' Union. *Leisure interests:* Painting and drawing; Fashion design; Cycling; Skating; Tennis. *Current Management:* Pineapple Agency. *Address:* 29 Womersley Rd, Crouch End, Hornsey, London N8 9AP, England.

GOODRICK Mick; Jazz Musician (guitar). *Musical Education:* BM Berklee College of Music. *Career:* Former faculty member, Berklee College of Music; Faculty member, Jazz Studies, New England Conservatory of Music; Performed and recorded with: Jack DeJohnette; Gary Burton; Paul Motian; Steve Gadd; Pat Metheny; Michael Brecker; Charlie Haden. *Recordings:* In Passing, 1978; Biorhythms, 1990; Cities, 1992; Rare Birds, 1993; Sunscreams, 1993; 2 albums with Jack DeJohnette's Special Edition. *Publication:* Author, The Advancing Guitarist. *Address:* New England Conservatory of Music, 290 Huntington Ave, Boston, MA 02115, USA.

GOODRIDGE Robin; b. 10 Sept. 1966, Crawley, West Sussex, England. Musician (drums). *Career:* Former Member, Future Primitive, became Bush; Obtained major US record deal; Heavy radio airplay in USA and numerous headlining tours; UK gigs and festival appearances. *Recordings:* Singles: Little Things, 1995; Comedown, 1995; Swallowed, 1997; Greedy Fly, 1997; Cold Contagious, 1999; Chemicals Between Us, 2001; Albums: Sixteen Stone, 1994; Razorblade Suitcase, 1996; Deconstructed, 1997; The Science of Things, 1999; Golden State, 2001. *Internet:* www.bush-music.com.

GOODWIN Christopher Neil; b. 10 Aug. 1962, Oldham, England. Drummer. *Education:* Graduated from Tameside College. *Career:* Various TV appearances including a Granada TV special, High and Dry; 2 British tours and a European tour; Appeared in Leeds supporting Happy Mondays; Radio sessions on the Mark Goodier and Mark Radcliffe shows. *Recordings:* Albums: Somewhere Soon, with The High, and Hype, with The High; Singles: Tomorrow's Sunset, with Buzzcocks, and Exiles, with Buzzcocks. *Memberships:* PRS; Musicians' Union. *Leisure interest:* Football. *Current*

Management: Stuart Windsor Inc. *Address:* 27 Lausanne Rd, Withington, Manchester, England.

GOODWIN Len; b. 24 Aug. 1940, Sheffield, England. Songwriter; Author. m. Lynne Abbott, 18 Sept. 1982, 1 s., 2 d. *Musical Education:* Self-taught. *Career:* Own songs performed by various artists on Crackerjack, BBC TV; Video Entertainers, Granada Network; Starburst, Granada Network; This Morning, Granada Network; Granada Reports, Granada TV; BBC Radio 1 and 2, local and independent radio. *Compositions:* Writing credits on recordings: Good Old Coronation Street; Special Train; This Is A Record of My Love (Happy Birthday Darling); Here We Are, (England Football Song); Football Anthem; Ain't This A Funny World, If Only Women Cry; Handle Me With Care. *Publication:* The Money Making Secrets of Successful Songwriting, 1997, new edition as So You Wannabe a Songwriter, 1998. *Memberships:* PRS; MCPS; PPL. *Leisure interests:* Keep fit; Cooking. *Current Management:* Tram Promotions/Gable Records. *Address:* 16 Pendle Court, Astley Bridge, Bolton, Lancashire BL1 6PY, England.

GOODWIN Ronald Alfred; b. 17 Feb. 1925, Plymouth, Devon, England. Composer; Conductor. m. Heather Dunsden, 22 Sept. 1986, 1 s. *Musical Education:* Self-taught. *Career:* Broadcasting and recording, 1950–; Composed 61 feature film scores and many documentaries; Guest Conductor, major orchestras in UK and internationally. *Compositions include:* Battle of Britain; 633 Squadron; Frenzy; Where Eagles Dare; Those Magnificent Men in Their Flying Machines; Operation Crossbow; The Trap. *Recordings:* Many soundtrack albums; Numerous recordings as Ron Goodwin and His Orchestra. *Honours:* 3 Ivor Novello Awards, 1956, 1972, 1994; Gold Disc, 1975; Platinum Disc, 1978; Fellow, City of Leeds College of Music, 1993. *Memberships include:* Asscn of Professional Composers; Worshipful Company of Musicians; Young Persons Concert Foundation. *Leisure interests:* Chess; Walking. *Current Management:* Robert Light Agency, USA. *Address:* Blacknest Cottage, Brimpton Common, Reading, Berks RG7 4RP, England.

GORCE Partrick; b. 23 May 1962, Alger, Algeria. m. Odile, 24 April, 1 s., 1 d. *Education:* Baccalauréat, Music with Mention, 1981. *Musical Education:* First Prize, L'Ecole Superieur de Batterie, Dante Agostini, Paris. *Career:* Tours; USA; Europe; Performed Paris clubs, Zénith, Olympia, New Morning; Playued with: Ghetto Blaster; Luis Antonio; Jean-Claude Borrelli; Richard Clayderman; TV series; Teacher, Drumming and Traditional Percussion. *Compositions:* Tambours De La Paix (50 participants). *Recordings:* African Vibration, Samy Samiamam; Clypso O'Samba, Ile Axe; Percussions of Latin America; Travel and See, Nomadic Activities. *Honours:* Titualire de la Bourse 'Lavoisier', Ministry of Foreign Affairs. *Membership:* SPEDIDAM. *Address:* 21 bis rue Solferino, 94100 St Maur, France.

GORDON Noah Adrian; b. 19 Sept. 1971, Pinckneyville, Illinois, USA. Singer; Writer; Musician (guitar, drums). *Education:* 14 years; Degree in Electrical Engineering Technology. *Musical Education:* Self-taught. *Career:* Charlie Daniels Volounteer Jam, 1992; Nashville Now; Music City Tonight; Country Music Television; The Nashville Network; Nascar Country; Wal-Mart Country Music Across America Tour; TNN Wildhorse Saloon, 1994–95. *Recordings:* I Need A Break, 1995; Christmas Time In Dixie, Charlie Daniels, 1994–95. *Memberships:* AFTRA; AFofM. *Leisure interests:* Remote Control Modelling; Racquetball; Tennis. *Current Management:* Entertainment Artist Inc, 819 18th Ave S, Nashville, TN 37203, USA.

GORDON Robert; b. 4 Oct. 1966, Sheffield, England. Music Programmer. 2 d. *Career:* Recording Engineer, Producer. *Composition:* Track With No Name, The Forgemasters. *Recordings:* House Arrest, Krush, 1987; Wanted, album, Yazz, 1988; Track With No Name, The Forgemasters; Rob Gordon Projects, album, 1996; Ozooma, 1996; Produced Lost In Music and Why Are People Grudgeful (singles) and Shiftwork (album), The Fall, 1993; Remixed Pop Will Eat Itself, Art of Noise, Yellow Magic Orchestra. *Honours:* Silver Disc, Krush, 1988; Double Platinum Disc, Yazz, 1988. *Memberships:* PRS; MCPS; PEMRA; PPL; Musicians' Union. *Leisure interests:* Girls; Travelling; Hifi; Electronics; Design; Parties. *Address:* 18 Talbot Gardens, Sheffield, S2 2TE, England.

GORDON Rod; b. 6 Feb. 1934, Flatbush, Alberta, Canada. Songwriter; Recording Artist; Musician (guitar). m. Jennette Richardson, 9 May 1964, 2 s., 2 d. *Musical Education:* Self-taught. *Career:* Appeared on GERN-TV, Edmonton, Alberta and CHLT-TV, Sherbrooke, Québec; Personal radio shows across Canada; Club bookings across Canada. *Compositions:* 200 compositions including Little Girl. *Recordings:* 2 singles released. *Honour:* Certificate of Merit for Outstanding Efforts in Advancement of Country Music. *Memberships:* Canadian Country Music Asscn; Country Music Asscn of Nashville. *Leisure interests:* Fishing; Writing music. *Current Management:* 21st Century Records. *Address:* 530 Third Ave S No. 2, Nashville, TN 37210, USA.

GORDON William 'Flash'; b. 16 March 1947, Miami, Florida, USA. Vocalist; Songwriter; Musician (bass, guitar); Actor. m. Mary Ellen Jesse. *Education:* United States Army Engineering School. *Musical Education:* Miami Dade Jr College. *Career:* Played at Willie Nelson's Fourth of July Picnic, 1974, 1976; Member: David Allan Coe band; Toured with: Charlie Walker; Justin Tubb; Jan Howrard; Bobby Lewis; various Grand Ole Opry stars. *Compositions:* All You Ever Have To Do Is Touch Me, Charlie Rich; My Woman's Honky Tonkin' Me To Death, Mel Tillis; As Far As This Feeling Will Take Us, David Allan Coe; In The Arms of Cocaine, Hank Williams Jr (on gold-selling album); (She Won't Have A Thing To Do With) Nobody But Me, Alabama (on triple platinum-selling album). *Recordings:* Albums: Alternative Country, 1992; Flash II, 1995; Confessions of a Cowboy Singer, 1999. *Memberships:* BMI; Nashville Publishers Network. *Leisure interests:* Horse racing; Fishing; Farming. *Current Management:* Georgia Boy Management, Box 265, Springfield, Tennessee 37172, USA. *Address:* 4545 Mount Sharon Rd, Greenbrier, TN 37073, USA. *E-mail:* wgordon327@aol.com.

GORDY Berry Jr; b. 28 Nov. 1929, Detroit, Michigan, USA. Record Co Exec.; Songwriter. m. Grace Eaton, 17 July 1990, 6 c. *Career:* Owner, record store, Detroit, 1955; Composer and independent producer, late 1950s; Founder, Jobete Music, 1958; Tamla Records, 1959; Motown Record Corporation, 1961–88; Chairman, The Gordy Co; Executive Producer, film Lady Sings The Blues, 1972. *Recordings:* As composer / producer: Reet Petite, Jackie Wilson; Shop Around, The Miracles; Do You Love Me, The Contours; Try It Baby, Marvin Gaye; Shotgun, Junior Walker and The All-Stars; I Want You Back and ABC, The Jackson 5; Compilation: The Music, The Magic, The Memories of Motown, 1995. *Honours:* American Music Award, Outstanding Contribution to Music Industry, 1975; Inducted into Rock and Roll Hall of Fame, 1988; NARAS Trustees Award, 1991. *Address:* Gordy Co, 6255 Sunset Blvd, Los Angeles, CA 90028, USA.

GORE Lesley; b. 2 May 1946, New York, USA. Singer; Actress. *Education:* BA, English and American literature, Sarah Lawrence College, Bronxville, New York. *Career:* Appearances include: Greatest Record Show of 1963; TAMI Show (released as film Gather No Moss), with Beach Boys, Chuck Berry, Rolling Stones, 1964; Richard Nader's Rock 'n' Roll Revival, Madison Square Garden, 1975; Acting debut, The Donna Reed Show, 1966; Also appeared in Batman; Theatrical debut, Half A Sixpence, 1967; Nightclub and stage work, 1970s. *Recordings:* Albums: I'll Cry If I Want To, 1963; Lesley Gore Sings of Mixed-Up Hearts, 1964; Boys Boys Boys, 1964; Girl Talk, 1964; The Golden Hits of Lesley Gore, 1965; My Town, My Guy and Me, 1965; California Nights, 1967; Someplace Else Now, 1972; Love Me By Name, 1975; Back to Back, 1992; Lesley Gore, 1992; The Essential Collection, 2001; Singles include: It's My Party (debut sold 1m.; No. 1, UK), 1963; Judy's Turn To Cry; She's A Fool; You Don't Own Me; That's The Way The Boys Are; Maybe I Know; Sunshine Lollipops and Rainbows; My Town My Guy and Me; California Nights. *Current Management:* c/o Stan Scottland, JKE Services Inc, 404 Park Ave S, 10th Floor, New York, NY 10016, USA.

GORE Martin Lee; b. 23 June 1961, London, England. Musician (keyboards, guitar); Vocalist; Songwriter. m. Suzanne (Boisvert), 27 Aug. 1994, 2 d. *Career:* Founder Member, Depeche Mode, 1980-. *Compositions:* As Depeche Mode's Principal Songwriter since 1982, has written vast majority of songs recorded by the band. *Recordings:* 12 Top Ten Singles including: Just Can't Get Enough, 1981; See You, 1982; Everything Counts, 1983; People Are People, 1984; Master and Servant, 1984; Enjoy the Silence, 1990; I Feel You, 1993; Condemnation, 1993; In Your Room, 1994; Barrel of a Gun, 1994; It's No Good, 1997; Dream On, 2001; 13 Top Ten Albums including: Speak and Spell, 1981; A Broken Frame, 1982; Construction Time Again, 1983; Some Great Reward, 1984; The Singles 81–85, 1985; Black Celebration, 1986; Music For the Masses, 1987; 101, 1989; Violator, 1990; Songs of Faith and Devotion (No. 1, UK and US), 1993; Ultra (No. 1, UK), 1997; The Singles 86>98, 1998; Exciter, 2001; Solo album: Counterfeit, 1989. *Honour:* BPI Brit Award, Enjoy the Silence, 1991; Ivor Novello Award – International Achievement, 1999. *Leisure interests:* Reading; Computer Games. *Current Management:* Jonathan Kessler, Baron Inc, 41 River Terrace, #3308 New York, NY 10282, USA. *Address:* First Floor, Regent House, 106 Marylebone High St, London W1M 3DB, England.

GORE Simon Anthony; b. 14 Nov. 1962, Bristol, England. Musician (drums). *Education:* Technical College. *Career:* Television debut at age 14 on BBC 1; Touring and recording with Andy Sheppard including many television and radio appearances, 1986–91; Currently teaching at several schools in Bristol and The Welsh College of Music and Drama in Cardiff. *Recordings:* Andy Sheppard, 1987; Introductions In The Dark, 1988; Soft On The Inside, also on video, 1990. *Memberships:* Musicians' Union; PAMRA. *Leisure interest:* Cycling. *Address:* 133 British Rd, Bedminster, Bristol BS3 3BY, England.

GORGON James; b. 23 March 1963, Peterborough, Cambridgeshire, England. Musician (drums, percussion). *Musical Education:* Madras

College, Pipeband Solo Competitions, private percussion. *Career:* Tours in USA, Middle East, Germany; 2 festivals, France; Television: Wish You Were Here; Holidays In Scotland, Grampian Television; Appearances at various music festivals; Various radio programme on: BBC Scotland; BBC Radio 2; Local radio; Two major tours of Thailand. *Recordings:* with Albany: East West Hame's Best, 1986; Till A' Seas Gang Dry, 1993; Muirhead Accordion Band, 1991; Gathering of the Clans Tour, 1992; Ted Poletyllo, 1993; with Paul Anderson: In Full Spate, 1994; with The Cutting Edge: Turning The Tide, 1994; Badenoch. *Honours:* Various Solo Pipeband, Drumming and Drum Corps Awards. *Membership:* Musicians' Union. *Leisure interests:* Swimming; Squash. *Current Management:* Ninegates Music, Unit 48, Forum Centre, Dundee, Scotland.

GORHAM Scott; b. 17 March 1951, Santa Monica, California, USA. Rock Musician (guitar). *Career:* Guitarist, pub circuit, with Fast Buck, early 1970s; Guitarist, UK rock group Thin Lizzy, 1974–83; Founder member, 21 Guns, 1992; Appearances with Thin Lizzy include: Reading Festival, 1974, 1975, 1983; Great British Music Festival, London, 1975; World Series of Rock, Cleveland, 1979; Monsters of Rock, European tour, 1983; Reunion tribute to Phil Lynott, Self Aid concert, Dublin (with Bob Geldof), 1991. *Recordings:* with Thin Lizzy: Singles: The Boys Are Back In Town, 1976; Dancin' In The Moonlight, 1977; Rosalie, 1978; Sarah, 1979; Waiting For An Alibi, 1979; Chinatown, 1980; Killer On The Loose, 1980; Killers Live (EP), 1981; Cold Sweat, 1982; Thunder and Lightning, 1983; Albums with Thin Lizzy: Nightlife, 1974; Fighting, 1975; Jailbreak, 1976; Johnny The Fox, 1976; Bad Reputation, 1977; Live and Dangerous, 1978; Black Rose (A Rock Legend), 1979; Chinatown, 1980; Adventures of Thin Lizzy, 1981; Renegade, 1981; Thunder and Lightning, 1983; Dedication – The Very Best of Thin Lizzy, 1991; Thin Lizzy Live, 1992; Wild One, 1996; One Night Only, 2000; with 21 Guns: Salute, 1992. *Address:* 49 Oakhill Rd, Putney, London SW15, England.

GORMAN Steve; b. 17 Aug. 1967, Hopkinsville, Kentucky, USA. Musician (drums). *Career:* Member, Black Crowes; Numerous tours, TV and radio appearances. *Recordings:* Singles: She Talks to Angels, 1990; Seeing Things, 1991; Twice as Hard, 1991; Sting Me, 1992; One Mirror Too Many, 1996; Only a Fool, 1999; Albums: Shake Your Money Maker, 1990; The Southern Harmony and Musical Companion, 1992; Amorica, 1994; Three Snakes and One Charm, 1996; By Your Side, 1999; Lions, 2001. *Internet:* www.blackcrowes.com.

GORME Eydie (Edith); b. 16 Aug. 1931, New York, USA. Singer. m. Steve Lawrence, 29 Dec. 1957. *Career:* Toured with Tommy Tucker; Tex Beneke; Night club singer; Recording artiste, 1952–; Own radio show, Cita Con Eydie; Regular shows and recordings with husband Steve Lawrence, 1953–; Member, Steve Allen's Troupe, Tonight Show, 1954; Stage performances: Jerry Lewis Stage Show, Broadway, 1967; Golden Rainbow, Broadway, 1968; Numerous other US stage performances and television specials, including tributes to George Gershwin, Cole Porter, Irving Berlin; Television adaptation, Alice In Wonderland, 1987; Support to Frank Sinatra, Diamond Jubilee world tour, 1991. *Recordings:* Singles: I've Gotta Crow; Tea For Two; Fini; Too Close For Comfort; Mama Teach Me To Dance; Love Me Forever; You Need Hands; with Steve Lawrence: I Want To Stay Here; I Can't Stop Talking About You; Numerous albums include: Eydie Gorme, 1957; Eydie Swings The Blues, 1957; Eydie In Love, 1958; On Stage, 1959; Eydie Sings Showstoppers, 1959; Eydie In Dixieland, 1960; Come Sing With Me, 1961; I Feel So Spanish, 1962; Blame It On The Bossa Nova, 1963; Let The Good Times Roll, 1963; Amor, 1964; More Amor, 1965; Don't Go To Strangers, 1966; Tonight I'll Say A Prayer, 1970; Toname O Dejame, 1985; Come In From The Rain, 1985; Canta, 1987; Blanca Navidad, 1990; Muy Amigos, 1993; Personalidad, 1996; Corazon, 1998; Eres Tu, 1999; with Steve Lawrence: We Got Us, 1960; Cozy, 1961; On Broadway, 1967; What It Was, Was Love, 1969; Real True Lovin', 1969; We Can Make It Together, 1975; Our Best To You, 1977; Alone Together, 1989; Black Hole Sun, recorded for Loungeapalooza compilation, 1998. *Honours:* Grammy Awards: We Got Us, 1960; Female Vocalist of The Year, 1967; 7 Emmy Awards, Steve and Eydie Celebrate Irving Berlin. *Address:* c/o Premier Artists Services, 1401 University Dr. #305, Coral Springs, FL 33071, USA.

GORNA Jarmila Xymena; b. 26 April 1967, Lodz, Poland. Musician (Piano, Vocalist); Composer. *Musical Education:* MA, Karol Szymanowski Academy of Music. *Career:* Sovay, Television Documentary, 1989; OKF Concert, 1990; Trolley Stop, 1995–97; Radio 3FM Interview, 1996; Union Chapel, 1997; Jerusalem, Bird of Paradise Cafe, 1997; London ICA, 1998; Jazz Cafe, 1999. *Compositions:* Numerous including, Which Way?; Swansong; Always?; Dark Spell; Swallow Flight Dream; Tatra; Pebbles and Seagulls; Fairy Tale World; It's OK; Love Search. *Recordings:* Hashgacha; Furmanka. *Memberships:* Musicians Union. *Leisure interests:* Skiing; Swimming; Yoga; Aromatherapy; Philosophy; World Religion; Science. *Address:* Flat 3, 51 Clapton Common, London E5 9AA, England.

GORR Jon Carl; b. 26 Sept. 1958, Fredericksburg, Virginia, USA. Composer; Musician (keyboards). *Musical Education:* Jazz Composition,

Chatauqua Institute, 1975; BM, Jazz Composition, Berklee College of Music, 1980. *Career:* President, Massmedia, 1983–; Songwriter, Cortlem Production, 1983–88; Castle Music, 1984–87; Keyboard player for: I-Tones; Eek-A-Mouse; Mighty Diamonds; Horace Andy, 1980–88; Steve Recker, 1986–87; Bo Diddley, 1987–88; Keyboard player, Gladiators (Europe), 1988–89; Composer, television and film music; Film appearance: Day of The Dead, 1976; Television appearance: Spenser For Hire, 1987. *Recordings:* Albums: It's No Lie, 1985; Walk On By, 1985; On The Right Track, 1988. *Honours:* Boston Music Award, Best Reggae Band, 1987; Beat Magazine Readers Poll, Best Keyboard Player, 1987.

GORRIE Alan; b. 19 July 1946, Perth, Scotland. Singer; Musician (bass). *Career:* Member, The Vikings, Scotland, 1964–67; Member, Scots of St James, London, 1967–68; Member, Forever More, 1969–71; Founder, The Average White Band, 1972–83; Renaissance, 1989; Member, Daryl Hall Band and Hall and Oates, 1993–94; Currently with Average White Band; International performances include: Lincoln Festival, 1972; Support to Eric Clapton, London, 1973; US tours, 1973; The Summer of 80 Garden Party, Crystal Palace, London, with Bob Marley, Joe Jackson, 1980; Group reformed, 1989. *Compositions include:* Pick Up the Pieces, 1974; Cut the Cake, 1972, 1975; When Will You Be Mine, 1978; Lets Go Round Again, 1980; Sleepless Nights, 1984; Every Beat of My Heart, 1995. *Recordings:* Singles include: Pick Up The Pieces (No. 1, USA), 1975; Cut The Cake, 1975; Let's Go Round Again, 1980; Albums: Show Your Hand, 1973; Average White Band, 1974; Cut The Cake, 1975; Soul Searching, 1976; Person To Person, 1977; Benny and Us, 1977; Warmer Communications, 1977; Atlantic Family Live at Montreux, 1977; Feel No Fret, 1979; Shine, 1980; Vol. VIII, 1980; Cupid's In Fashion, 1982; Sleepless Nights, solo, 1985; Aftershock, 1989; Soul Alone, with Daryl Hall, 1993; Soul Tattoo, 1996; Very Best of, 1998; Played on Tommi Mischell, Tommi Mischell, 2001. *Honours:* Grammy Nominations, 1974, 1975, 1978; ASCAP R & B Awards, 1993, 1996; 14 Platinum, Gold and Silver Discs world-wide, 1975, 1976, 1977, 1978, 1980, 1992, 1993. *Memberships:* PRS; ASCAP. *Current Management:* Wm Morris Agency, 151 El Camino Dr, Beverly Hills, CA 90212, USA; Miracle Artists, 1 York St, London W1H 1PZ, England.

GORSE Vesna; b. 30 Sept. 1961, Skopje, Macedonia. Musician (alto saxophone); Composer; Writer. m. Drazen Franolic, 20 June 1992. *Career:* Gorse-Franolic duo; Gorse-Franolic trio; Group: Tao; Concerts: Vatroslav Lisinski Concert Hall, Zagreb; Ljubljana; Belgrade; Sarajevo; Dubrovnik; Rijeka; Maribor, Italy; Multi-media festival, Czechoslovakia; Live album recordings at Lisinski. *Recordings:* with Drazen Franolic: Waterfalls, 1986; New Era of Instrumental Music, 1990; Wonderland, 1990; Asgard Live, 1993; Just A Music. . ., 1995. *Honours:* 2 Nominations, Porin '94 Awards: Asgard Live. *Memberships:* Croatian Composers' Society; Croatian Music Union; Amnesty International; World SF. *Leisure interests:* Books; Films. *Current Management:* Vesna Gorse. *Address:* Vankina 3, Zagreb, Croatia.

GOSDIN Vern; b. 5 Aug. 1934, Woodland, Alabama, USA. Country Singer; Songwriter; Musician (guitars, banjo, mandolin). *Career:* Member, Gosdin Family (with brothers), radio station, Birmingham, Alabama; Nightclub owner, Chicago, 1956; Member, Golden State Boys, early 1950s; The Hillmen, with Chris Hillman; Session musician, includes Gene Clark, 1966; Owner, glass shop, Atlanta, 1967–76; Solo artiste, and as Gosdin Brothers, 1977–. *Compositions include:* Someone To Turn To, The Byrds. *Recordings:* US Country No. 1 hits: I Can Tell By The Way You Dance; Set 'Em Up Joe; Other hits: Hangin' On; Yesterday's Gone; Till The End; Albums: with The Hillmen: The Hillmen, 1969; with The Gosdin Brothers: Gene Clark With The Gosdin Brothers, 1966; Sounds of Goodbye, 1968; Solo albums: Till The End, 1977; Never My Love, 1978; You've Got Somebody, 1979; Passion, 1981; If You're Gonna Do Me Wrong, Do It Right, 1983; Today My World Slipped Away, 1983; Dream Lady, 1984; There Is A Season, 1984; If Jesus Comes Tomorrow, 1984; Time Stood Still, 1985; Chiseled In Stone, 1988; Alone, 1989; Out of My Heart, 1991; Nickels and Dimes and Love, 1993; The Gospel Album, 1995; Set 'Em Up, 1995; If You're Gonna Do Me Wrong, 1996; 24 Karat Heartache, 1997; Silver Eagle Cross Country, 1997; Time Stood Still, 1998. *Address:* c/o Kathy Gangwisch and Associates Inc, 5100 Harris Ave, Kansas City, MO 64133–2331, USA.

GOSS Kieran John; b. 18 May 1962, Newry, Northern Ireland. Songwriter; Singer. *Education:* LLB, Queen's University, Belfast. *Career:* Various TV appearances, Ireland; UK; Australia include: Late Late Show; Wogan; Kenny Live; Tours in Ireland; UK; Australia; New Zealand. *Recordings:* Brand New Star; Frances Black and Kieran Goss; New Day, 1995; Worse Than Pride, 1998; Red Letter Day, 2000. *Honours:* Platinum record, Folk Album of Year In Scotland, for New Day, 1995. *Membership:* Musicians' Union. *Leisure interests:* Football; Swimming. *Current Management:* George McCann, SMA Management. *Address:* 77 Castle St, Belfast BT1, Northern Ireland.

GOSSARD Stone; b. 20 July 1966, Seattle, Washington, USA. Rock Musician (guitar). *Career:* Member, Green River, 1987–89; Guitarist, Mother Love Bone, 1989; Member, Pearl Jam, 1990–; Member, tribute group Temple of The Dog, 1991; Formed Shame (renamed Brad), 1993;

Concerts with Pearl Jam: Support to Alice In Chains, 1991; Lollapalooza Festival tour, 1992; Group appeared in film Singles, 1992; Drop In The Park concert, Seattle, 1992; Neil Young's Bridge School Benefit, with Elton John, Sammy Hagar, James Taylor, 1992; Concert appearances with Keith Richards; Neil Young. *Recordings:* with Mother Love Bone: Shine (EP), 1989; Apple, 1990; Albums with Pearl Jam: Ten (No. 2, US), 1992; Vs. (No. 1, USA), 1993; Vitalogy, 1994; No Code, 1996; Yield, 1998; Live on Two Legs, 1998; Binaural, 2000; Live, 2000; with Temple of The Dog: Temple of The Dog, 1992; with Brad: Shame, 1993; Interiors, 1997; Singles with Pearl Jam: Alive, 1992; Even Flow, 1992; Jeremy, 1992. *Honours:* Platinum discs; American Music Awards, Favourite New Artist, Pop/Rock and Hard Rock categories, 1993; Rolling Stone Readers' Awards: Best New American Band, Best Video, 1993; 4 MTV Awards, 1993; Highest 1-week album sales total in history, Vs., 1993. *Current Management:* Curtis Management, 417 Denny Way, Suite 200, Seattle, WA 98109, USA.

GOTT Karel; b. 14 July 1939, Plzen, Czech Republic. Singer. 2 d. *Education:* Studied under Professor Karenin, Prague Conservatory. *Career:* Member, Semafor Theatre, Prague, 1963–65; Member, Apollo Theatre, Prague, 1965–67; Freelance artiste, 1967–; Numerous foreign tours; Co-operation with record companies; Founder, chairman, Interpo Foundation, 1993-. *Honours:* Numerous Golden Nightingale Trophies, annual pop singer poll, 1963–; MIDEM Prize, Cannes, 1967; Music Week, Star of The Year, 1974, 1975; Artist of Merit, 1982; Gold Aerial, BRT radio station, Belgium, 1984; National Artist, 1985; Polydor Golden Pin, Germany, 1986; Gold discs. *Address:* Nad Bertramkou 18, 15000 Prague 5, Czech Republic.

GOTT Larry; b. 24 July 1957, England. Musician (guitar). *Career:* Member, James, 1985; Numerous tours, festival dates and television appearances; Left band, 1995. *Recordings:* Singles: Come Home, 1989; Sit Down (No. 2, UK), 1989, reissued 1991; Sound, 1991; Born of Frustration, 1992; Sometimes (Lester Piggott), 1993; Laid, 1993; Say Something, 1994; Albums: Stutter, 1986; Strip-Mine, 1988; One Man Clapping, live, 1989; Gold Mother, 1990; Seven, 1992; Laid, 1993; Wah Wah, live, 1994; The Best of James (compilation), 1998. *Internet:* www.jamestheband.co.uk.

GOTT Susan (Susi); b. 4 Sept. 1962, Asheville, NC, USA. Musician (Fiddle); Singer; Songwriter. m. Christian Séguret, 30 Sept. 1990, 1 s., 1 d. *Education:* BA, Environmental Science. *Musical Education:* Self-taught Musician. *Career:* Performing, including The Smithsonian National Institute, 1977; The Kennedy Center, with Masters of Bluegrass, 1986; NPR's All Things Considered, 1982; Nashville Networks' Fire on the Mountain; The Knoxville World's Fair, 1982; Sacrée Soirée, Paris, with Hugues Aufray. *Compositions:* Bound for New Orleans; Dancing Man; Hole in the Deep Blue Sea, with Christian Séguret. *Recordings:* CMH with Eddie Adcock and Talk of the Town; Cowbell Hollow; A Video Postcard of the Blue Ridge, with David Holt; Talking Feet, with Mike Seeger; Guitars, with Christian Séguret and Thierry Massoulore. *Honours:* Champion Fiddler, Fiddler's Grove, 1978, 1984; First Place Songwriter, Chris Austin Songwriting Contest, 1996. *Memberships:* International Bluegrass Music Asscn; Women in Bluegrass; SACEM. *Leisure interests:* Poetry; Essays; Gardening; Mothering. *Current Management:* Co-Prod Music. *Address:* 1 rue du Pourtour, 45340 Auxy, France.

GOTTLIEB Gordon; b. 23 Oct. 1948, Brooklyn, New York, USA. Musician (Percussion). *Education:* BM, 1970, MS, 1971, Juilliard School of Music. *Career:* Performed with Stevie Wonder, Ray Charles, Patti LaBelle, Tony Bennett, Paula Abdul, Michael Bolton, Bette Midler, Sarah Vaughan, Quincy Jones, Al Jarreau, Paul Winter. *Compositions:* The River Speaker; Improvisations with Jay Gottlieb; Ritual Dancer; Fanfare, with Paul Winter; Various jingles. *Recordings:* History, Michael Jackson; Kingdom of the Sun, film with Sting; Bulletproof Heart, with Grace Jones; A Secret Life, with Marianne Faithfull; Romulus Hunt, My Romance, with Carly Simon; Sostice Live!, Prayer for the Wild Things, with Paul Winter; Pete, Pete Seeger; Many films and jingles; Currently recording latest album with Steely Dan. *Publications:* The Percussion of Carnival, for Modern Percussionist magazine, 1984; World Influences: Africa and South India, 1985; 3 articles on studio playing, 1985. *Honours:* Grammy Awards, Paul Winters, Prayer for the Wild Things, 1994; Pete Seeger, Pete; NARAS Most Valuable Player Award, New York Studios, 1989; Grants: Martha Baird Rockefeller Grant, 1980, Meet the Composer Grant, 1989. *Memberships:* Percussive Arts Society; NARAS; Recording Musicians Asscn. *Leisure interest:* Scuba diving. *Address:* 29 W 17th St Fl 8, New York, NY 10011, USA.

GOUGH Orlando; b. 24 Aug. 1953, Brighton, England. Composer. m. Joanna Osborne, 2 Dec. 1989, 2 s. *Career:* Member of Bands: The Lost Jockey, 1978–82; Man Jumping, 1983–87; Founded the choir The Shout, 1998. *Compositions:* Hoovering the Beach, 1979; Buzz Buzz Buzz Went the Honeybee, 1980; Secret Gardens, 1981; New Tactics, 1982; Further and Further into the Night, 1984; Mozart At Palm Springs, 1983–84; Bosendorfer Waltzes, 1985; Weighing The Heart, 1986–87; Goes Without Saying, 1988; Mathematics of a Kiss, 1989; Savage Water, 1989; Currulao,

1989; Late, 1991; Lives of the Great Poisoners, 1991; Slow Walk, Fast Talk, 1992; The Air Shouts, 1992; Earth Bound, 1993; Saeta, 1993; The Empress, 1992–93; Escape at Sea, 1994; On the Rim of the World, 1994–97; Badenheim, 1995; People's Century, 1995–97; Sleeping with Audrey, 1996; Hotel, 1996–97; Room of Cooks, 1996–97; Room of Cooks, 1997; Axaxaxas Mlo, 1997; When We Stop Talking, 1998; The Shouting Fence, 1998; Why Do You Sing?, 1998; Corona, 1999; Pierrot: A Biography, 1999; Fortune Cookies, 1999. *Recordings:* Message From the Border, 1996; The Dancing Lawn, 1999. *Publication:* The Complete A Level Maths, 1987. *Leisure interests:* Cooking; Cricket. *Current Management:* Soundtrack, 25 Ives St, London, SW3 2ND, England. *Address:* 12 Spencer Rise, London NW5 1AP, England.

GOUIRAND Doudou (Gérard); b. 28 April 1940, Menton, France. Musician (alto and soprano saxophones). m. Monica Adrian, 28 Oct. 1966, 2 s., 1 d. *Education:* University degree. *Career:* Various European festivals; Most French jazz festivals; Tours and festivals, Canada; Africa; Scandinavia; Lithuania; Algeria; Middle East; UK (including Pan-Africa Festival, London, 1984); Poland. *Recordings:* Albums: with Chris McGregor, 1981; Mouvements Naturels, with J. Dyaui/Pierre Dorge, 1982; Chanting and Dancing, with World Music Company, 1985; Forgotten Tales, with Don Cherry, 1986; Space, with Mal Waldron, 1987; La Nuit De Wounded Knee, 1990; Le Matin D'Un Fauve, with Mal Waldron, 1994; Nino Rota Fellini, W. G. Pansanel, 1995. *Leisure interests:* Music; Films; Reading; Walking; Swimming. *Current Management:* Opus Productions, Montpellier, France.

GOULD Tony; b. 21 Feb. 1940, Melbourne, Australia. Musician (Pianist); Composer; Educator. *Education:* BMus, Melbourne University; MA, Monash University; PhD, LaTrobe University. *Career:* Lecturer, University of Melbourne, 1973–83, Head, Postgraduate Department and Improvisation Department, School of Music, Victorian College of Arts, Melbourne; Chief Music Critic, Herald Sun. *Compositions:* Concerto for Percussion, Violin, Viola Piano and Saxophone; Music for Narration of Dylan Thomas's Under Milk Wood; Music for various jazz ensembles. *Recordings:* Gould Plus Gould; Best of Friends; Tony Gould Quartet; Chronicle; Lirill; Tin Roof For The Rain. *Publications:* Contributor, New Grove Dictionary of Jazz, 1988, 1999, Oxford Companion to Australian Music, 1997. *Membership:* Australia Council Music Fund. *Leisure interests:* Tennis; Swimming. *Current Management:* Ruben Zylbenspic, St Kilda, Victoria. *Address:* PO Box 605, Woodend, Vic 3442, Australia.

GOULDMAN Graham Keith; b. 10 May 1946, Manchester, England. Songwriter; Musician (guitar, bass). m. Gill, 7 Oct. 1988, 2 s., 2 d. (1 s., 1 d., by previous marriage). *Career:* Many concert tours, television and radio appearances as member of 10cc. *Compositions:* for The Yardbirds: For Your Love; Heart Full of Soul; for The Hollies: Bus Stop; Look Thru Any Window; for Herman's Hermits: No Milk Today; Co-wrote for 10cc: Rubber Bullets; Wall Street Shuffle; I'm Mandy Fly Me; Good Morning Judge; I'm Not In Love; Things We Do For Love; Dreadlock Holiday; Co-wrote for Wax: Bridge To Your Heart; Co-wrote Straight To Video, with Kirsty MacColl, for her album Tropical Brainstorm, 1999. *Recordings include:* 10cc hit singles: Donna, 1972; Rubber Bullets (No. 1, UK), 1973; The Dean and I, 1973; Wall Street Shuffle, 1974; Silly Love, 1974; Life Is A Minestrone, 1975; I'm Not In Love (No. 1, UK; No. 2, US), 1975; Art For Art's Sake, 1975; I'm Mandy Fly Me, 1976; The Things We Do For Love, 1976; Good Morning Judge, 1977; Dreadlock Holiday (No. 1, UK), 1978; solo: Graham Gouldman Thing, 1968; Animalolympics, 1980. *Honours:* Ivor Novello Awards for: Rubber Bullets; I'm Not In Love; BMI citations for most of the above songs. *Memberships:* Musicians' Union; PRS; SODS (Society of Distinguished Songwriters). *Leisure interest:* Collecting guitars. *Current Management:* Harvey Lisberg. *Address:* Harvey Lisberg Associates, 6 Highgate, St Margarets Rd, Altrincham, Cheshire WA14 2AP, England.

GOUPY Christian; b. 21 June 1962, Evreux, France. Composer; Musician (piano). *Education:* Brevet de Technician Superieur Mechanique et Automatisme. *Musical Education:* American School of Modern Music; Conservatoire International, Paris. *Career:* Concerts in France with The Footprints Quintet and The Croco Jazz Big Band; Pianist, Dagorno Restaurant, Paris; Now working with the marching band, Les Pieds Mobiles (piano, sax and drums) playing jazz, funk and groove music. *Recordings:* Escale, Footprints Quintet; Oh Happy Day, Voce Vita Gospel Group; Next To, Croco Jazz Big Band. *Publications:* Editions Combre, Paris; Quatuors de Saxs. *Leisure interests:* Tennis; Scuba diving. *Current Management:* Christian Goupy Asscn Evasion. *Address:* 18 Impasse St Sébastien, 75011 Paris, France.

GOURDIKIAN Herve; b. 31 Dec. 1966, Lyon, France. Musician (saxophones, piano). m. Olga Kroutolapova, 23 April 1992, 1 d. *Musical Education:* Two years at Berklee College of Music, Boston; French Conservatory, Lyon. *Career:* Tour, Rêve Orange (Liane Foly); Tour, Les Petites Notes (Liane Foly); Concert Place de la Concorde for Liberation of Paris (audience 500,000); TV show: Taratata; Nulle Part Ailleurs with Andoine de Camaes. *Recordings:* With Liane Foly: Reve Orange; Cameleon;

Lumières; Sweet Misery; Also with: Nilda Fernandez; HMF; Mellow Man; Brigitte Fontaine; Mario Stanchen. *Honours:* Gold record, Lumières, Liane Foly. *Leisure interest:* Crosswords. *Address:* 258 Ave Georges Clemenceau, 92000 Nanterre, France.

GOURLEY Jimmy (James Pasco Jr); b. 9 June 1926, St Louis, Missouri, USA. Musician (guitar); Singer; Composer. *Musical Education:* Self-taught. *Career:* Began in Chicago, 1944; Member, Jay Burkhart Orchestra with Sonny Stitt, Gene Ammons, Lou Levy; Member, Jackie Cain, Roy Kral Quintet; Played in Chicago with Chubby Jackson, Anita O'Day, 1951, 1954–57; Worked in Paris with Lester Young, Kenny Clarke, Stan Getz, Stéphane Grappelli, 1957–96. *Recordings:* (with) Clifford Brown; Zoot Sims; Bob Brookmeyer; Kenny Clarke; Eddy Louiss; Lou Bennett; Henri Renaud; Lee Konitz; Chubby Jackson; Lester Young; Duke Ellington; Guy Lafitte; Richard Galliano; (Own recordings) Jimmy Gourley and the Paris Heavyweights, 1972; Graffitti, 1976; Good News, 1981; Feeling Jazzy, 1983; The Jazz Trio, 1983; The Left Bank of NY, 1986; Flying The Coop (with Richard Galliano Four), 1991; The Jazz Trio, 1995; Jazz Guitar – Essential Jazz, 1995; Our Delight, 1995; with Stan Getz: Stan Getz, 1958; Live In Europe, 1958; with Stéphane Grappelli: Satin Doll, 1972; Plays Gershwin, 1973; Plays Cole Porter, 1973. *Membership:* SACEM. *Address:* 114 Ave Anatole France, 94190 Villeneuve St Georges, France.

GOURLEY Sean; b. 12 Dec. 1963, Paris, France. Jazz Musician (guitar); Singer. *Musical Education:* Classical guitar, age 6–14; Jazz harmony, USA, 1983–84; Jazz harmony, with father, Jimmy Gourley and personal coaches. *Career:* Player, singer, arranger, own band, playing bebop jazz, concerts, clubs; Plays with father Jimmy Gourley in Family Affair Band; Festivals include: Calvi, Corsica; Madagascar (US Embassy); Guitar Masters of Pau, France; Played with: Barney Wilen; Stephanie Crawford; Kim Parker; Also with arrangers Onzy Mathews; Mundell Lowe; Various French musicians. *Leisure interests:* Talking with good friends; Henry Miller's novels. *Address:* 6 rue Sauffroy, 75017 Paris, France.

GOVERT Eddy (Van Mouffaert); b. 15 Jan. 1949, Bruges, Belgium. Accordionist; Songwriter; Prod. m. Anneke Van Thorre, 12 Aug. 1991, 2 d. *Musical Education:* Muziek Conservatorium, Bruges. *Career:* Many appearances, band player, 1964–70; Singer, songwriter, as Eddy Govert, 1970–; Solo as international accordion act Le Grand Julot, 1973–; Founded Jump Records and Music, 1975; Professional singer, 1980's. *Recordings:* with Paul Severs: Ik Ben Verliefd Op Jou, 1971; Love, 1972; with Ronald and Donald: Couac Couac, 1974; with Ricky Gordon: Such A Night; with Margriet Hermans: Don Bosco; Many top 10 hits, 1975–81; as Eddy Govert: Te Kort Van Duur, 1988; Albums: International 1, 1991; International 2, 1993; Belgian Accordion Championship, 1965. *Honours:* Golden Lion Joepie, 1974; Gold Record, 1974; Cultuurprys Erpe-Mere, 1996. *Memberships:* SABAM; URADEX, Brussels; ZAMU, Brussels. *Leisure interests:* Walking; Travel; Listening to music. *Current Management:* Happy Melody VZW. *Address:* Langemunt 71, G420 Aaigem, Belgium.

GRABOWSKI Stephan A; b. 18 Dec. 1964, Copenhagen, Denmark. Musician; Singer; Composer; Prod.; Arranger. 1 d. *Musical Education:* Private Lessons by Hans Fagt, Hanne Bekow; Self-taught on Keyboards and Guitar. *Career:* Played with Lars H.U.G., 1987–93; Several national tours; Several television and radio appearances and gigs in France, Russia, Greenland; With Love Shop, Janes Rejoice, Goldfinger and special appearances with Peter Bell, Caroline Henderson, Thomas Di Leva, Elisabeth, Shirtsville, Nina Forsberg. *Compositions:* Girl in the Ghetto, 1993; Crazy Restless Summer, Who Are You?, 1996; Verden Folo Af Frugt, Gaderne Huisker, 1997. *Recordings:* Glitter Angels, 1993; Songs For Night Clubs, 1996; Underligere End Kaerlighed, 1997. *Honours:* Reward, National Arts Trust, 1994, 1996; Numerous Grammy's with Lars H.U.G., 1990–92. *Memberships:* Artisten; Danish Artist Union; DPA. *Leisure interests:* Travel; Studying Religion and Philosophy. *Address:* c/o Skriver, Guldbergsgade 12 St Tv, 22000 Kobenhavn N, Denmark.

GRACE Whyte; b. England. Composer; Musician (electronic keyboards, guitar); Singer; Poet. m. twice, single 1986-, 3 s., 1 d. *Musical Education:* Self-taught. *Career:* Toured schools, clubs libraries, playing acoustic guitar solos, reading poetry, singing folk-songs in Bedfordshire, 1970s-80s; Performer, keyboards at dinners, matinees, festivals, London, 1990s-; Show, Life's a Gas with Grace; Fundraiser for ChildLine. *Compositions:* Over 100 instrumentals and ballads; Over 100 poems for adults and children; Programme for children of music, singing, stories, poems, dancing, games, puppets; Currently compiling album of musical stories for children. *Publications:* 18 anthologies of poetry; The Londonium Bug, book of verse and cartoons, 1997. *Honours:* Poetry competition winner, 1970; Pictures exhibited; Inducted into the International Poetry Hall of Fame. *Memberships:* Musicians' Union; Designers and Artists Copyright Society (DACS); ABI; IBC. *Address:* 56 Warltersville Mansions, Warltersville Rd, London N19 3AS, England.

GRACIE Charlie (Charles); b. 14 May 1936, Philadelphia, Pennsylvania, USA. Singer; Musician (guitar). m. Joan D'Amato, 15 Feb. 1958, 1 s., 1 d.

Education: Tutored by father, Sam Gracie; Studied Guitar under professional teacher. *Career:* Youthful Guitar Prodigy, Paul Whiteman TV Teen Show; Played on radio commercials for the Sealtest, Big Top, CBS Program; Headlined, The Alan Freed Show, Brooklyn Paramount, 1957; Ed Sullivan Show; Numerous appearances on American Bandstand TV; Headlined the London Hippodrome and Palladium, 1957; Headlined Yarmouth Rock Festival, England, 1980s; Continues to tour Europe, Italy, Germany, England; Starred in Warner Brothers Rock Movie, Jamboree, 1958; opened major US shows for, and recording with, Van Morrison, 2000. *Composition:* Fabulous, included on Sir Paul McCartney's maxi CD single of 1950's rock 'n' roll classics, 1999. *Recordings:* Butterfly; Fabulous; I Love You So Much; Albums: Charlie Gracie – The Cameo, 1979; Amazing Gracie, 1982; Charlie Gracie: Live at the Stockton Globe 1957, 1996; It's Fabulous – It's Charlie Gracie (compilation), 1996; It's All Right, 2001. *Honour:* Gold Record Award, 3 Million Seller, Butterfly, 1957. *Membership:* ASCAP. *Leisure interests:* Animals; Ancient European History. *Current Management:* Paul Barrett R and R Enterprises, 16 Grove Pl., Penarth, CF64 2ND, Wales. *Address:* 820 Edmonds Ave, Drexel Hill, Pennsylvania, 19026, USA.

GRAESSER Johann Peter, (Hanno); b. 26 Dec. 1961, Wehrda, Germany. Violin Teacher; Publisher; Music Scientist. *Education:* State Exam for Violin Teachers, Music College, Dortmund, 1989; MA, Music Education, Music and Theatre Science, University of Munich, 1993; Dr Phil, Jazz Research, University of Giessen, 1995. *Publications:* Jazz Violin, 1991; Stéphane Grappellis Violintechnik, 1994; Der Jazzgeiger Stéphane Grappelli, 1996; Stéphane Grappelli und die Musik des Quintette du Hot Club de France, 1997; Electric Violins, 1998. *Membership:* International Society for Jazz Research, 1992-. *Address:* Lenzhalde 88, 73732 Esslingen, Germany.

GRAHAM Bruce Hebenton; b. 9 Nov. 1941, Dundee, Scotland. Musician (multi-instrumentalist); Composer; Author; Entertainer. m. (1) Phyllis Elizabeth McFarlane, 18 Sept. 1963, 1 (adopted) d., (2) Sharon Belinda Maxim, 7 April 1988. *Musical Education:* Private tuition; Schillinger Course of Composition; Pupil, Henry Nelmes Forbes, ABCA. *Career:* Session musician; Musical Director, London recording, television and film studios, West End Theatres; Founder, Jingles Records and Jingles Music, 1985; Featured in cabaret, Old Tyme Music Halls, one-man keyboard concerts, 1988; Worked with: Andy Williams; Rock Hudson; Juliet Prowse; Lulu; The Three Degrees; Sacha Distel; Bob Hope; Sir Harry Secombe; Faith Brown; Tommy Steele; Paul Daniels; Cleo Laine and John Dankworth; Matt Monro; Bruce Forsythe; Marti Webb; Richard Chamberlain; Vince Hill; Jimmy Shand; Jeff Wayne; Des O'Connor; Rolf Harris; Val Doonican; Anthony Newley; Helen Reddy; Wayne Sleep; David Hemmings; Michael Crawford; Lionel Blair; Gemma Craven; Tony Basil; Miss World TV Orchestra; Andrew Lloyd Webber; Phil Tate; Ray McVay; Johnny Howard; Ike Isaacs; Geoff Love; Orchestras include: Sydney Thompson's Old Tyme; National Philharmonic; London Concert; BBC Radio; Scottish Radio; Northern Dance; London Palladium; Own small groups. *Compositions include:* Two Symphonies; A Divertimenti For Strings; Reverie For Brass Band; 10 Suites for Large Jazz Orchestra; One-act Ballet; A Musical; Over 300 songs and shorter pieces. *Publications:* Magazine articles; Music and The Synthesizer, 1969. *Memberships:* Musicians' Union; Equity; British Music Writers Council. *Leisure interests:* Magic; Writing; Boating. *Address:* 25 Milton Rd, Wallington, Surrey SM6 9RP, England.

GRAHAM Irvin; b. 18 Sept. 1909, Philadelphia, Pennsylvania, USA. Composer; Lyricist. m. Lillian Gologter, 2 Sept. 1943. *Career:* Composer of numerous popular tunes; Wrote Walt Disney's The Whale Who Wanted to Sing at the Met; TV appearances: Your Show of Shows; Fred Waring; Jane Freman. *Compositions:* I Believe; You Better Go Now; With a Twist of the Wrist; In Love with a Married Man. *Recordings:* I Believe, recorded by Barbra Streisand, Elvis Presley; You Better Go Now, recorded by Billie Holliday, Chet Baker, Ben Webster, Johnny Mathis, Jeri Southern. *Honours:* Fellow of the Arts, Yaddo, Banff, Virginia, The MacDowell Colony. *Memberships:* ASCAP; WGA; SAG; AFTRA; Dramatists Guild. *Address:* 366 E 55th, New York, NY 10022, USA.

GRAHAM Mikey; b. 15 Aug. 1972, Dublin, Ireland. Vocalist. *Career:* Member, Boyzone. *Recordings:* Singles: Working My Way Back To You, 1994; Key To My Life, 1995; Love Me For A Reason, 1995; So Good, 1995; Father and Son, 1995; Coming Home Now, 1995; Words, 1996; Isn't It A Wonder, 1997; Baby Can I Hold You Tonight, 1997; Picture of You, 1997; Mystical Experience, 1997; All That I Need, 1998; No Matter What, 1999; I Love The Way You Love Me, 1999; When The Going Gets Tough, 1999; You Needed Me, 1999; Albums: A Different Beat, 1997; Where We Belong, 1998; By Request, 1999; Solo recording: You're My Angel, 2000.

GRAHAME Alan; b. Cornwall, England. Musician (percussion). m. Dulcie Sawyer, 1 s., 2 d. *Career:* Ralph Sharon Sextet, London Jazz Club groups; Jerry Allen Trio; Variety; Music Hall; Freelance studio percussionist; Major tours, UK and Europe with Tom Jones; Shirley Bassey; Perry Como;

Englebert Humperdinck; Howard Keel; Radio broadcasts: BBC Radio Orchestra; London Studio Players; Ken Moule Strings; Played with orchestras of: Alec Gould; Ronnie Aldrich; Frank Chacksfield; Cy Payne; Colin Sell; Television appearances include: Jerry Allen Trio; Lunch Box, ATV (8 years); BBC Top of The Pops Orchestra; Benny Hill; Come Dancing; Two Ronnies; Morecombe and Wise; Wogan; Parkinson; Pebble Mill; Miss World; Basil Brush; Crackerjack; Torvil and Dean; Last of The Summer Wine; Tomorrow's World; Playschool; Record Breakers; With artistes: Tom Jones; Shirley Bassey; Roy Castle; Dionne Warwick; Neil Diamond; Buddy Greco; Richard Clayderman; Demis Roussos; Stylistics; Trini Lopez; Vic Damone. *Recordings:* With: Tom Jones; Shirley Bassey; Englebert Humperdinck; Matt Monro; Love Affair; White Plains; Brotherhood of Man; Casuals; 101 Strings; Dana; Lena Zavaroni; Rolf Harris; Frank Pourcell; Jack Emblow; David Essex; Mike Batt; Les Reed; Jeff Wayne; Bee Gees; Peters and Lee; Lena Martell; contributed to albums: Festivals Blues and Saunters, 2000; Rumba, 2001. *Publications:* Articles in Percussion Press (drums, percussion). *Memberships:* ISM; Musicians' Union.

GRAILLIER Michel François; b. 18 Oct. 1946, Lens, France. Musician (piano, synthesizer). m. Micheline Pelzer, 9 July 1982. *Education:* Electronic Engineering. *Musical Education:* Private teacher for 10 years; Self-taught in jazz. *Career:* Tours with group Magma, 1972–73; Juan-les-Pins Festival, 1977–84; Japan with Chet Baker, 1986; Videos: Candy and Live At Ronnie Scott's with Chet Baker; Liege Jazz Festival, 1992; Radio: MG's trio in 1991–94. *Recordings:* As leader with: Ad Lib; Fairly; Dream Drops; Others with: Chet Baker; M & B; Al Capolinea; Candy; Chet Sings Again; At Ronnie Scott's; French Ballad; Barney Wilen: Moshi; S Glossman: Born At The Same Time. *Honour:* Django Reinhardt Prize, France, 1978. *Memberships:* SACEM; SPEDIDAM; ADAMI. *Leisure interest:* Reading. *Current Management:* Micheline Pelzer. *Address:* 1 Passage Cottin, 75018 Paris, France.

GRAMM Lou, (Louis Grammatico); b. 2 May 1950, Rochester, New York, USA. Singer; Songwriter. *Career:* Lead singer, Black Sheep, 1975; Foreigner, 1976–90, 1992–; Regular world-wide tours; Major concerts include: California Jam II, 1978; Reading Festival, 1979; New York State Fair, 1994; Also founder member, Shadow King, 1990–91; Also solo artiste. *Recordings:* Albums: with Black Sheep, Black Sheep, 1975; Encouraging Words, 1975; with Foreigner: Foreigner, 1977; Double Vision, 1978; Head Games, 1979; 4 (No. 1, USA), 1981; Records, 1983; Agent Provocateur (No. 1, UK), 1984; Inside Information, 1987; The Very Best Of, 1992; The Very Best... and Beyond, 1992; Mr Moonlight, 1994; Solo albums: Ready Or Not, 1987; Foreigner in a Strange Land, 1988; Long Hard Look, 1989; Hit singles: with Foreigner: Feels Like The First Time, 1977; Cold As Ice, 1977; Long Way From Home, 1978; Hot Blooded, 1978; Double Vision, 1978; Blue Morning Blue Day, 1979; Head Games, 1980; Urgent, 1981; Juke Box Hero, 1981; Waiting For A Girl Like You, 1981; I Want To Know What Love Is (No. 1, USA), 1985; That Was Yesterday, 1985; I Don't Want To Live Without You, 1988; Solo: Midnight Blue, 1987; Just Between You and Me, 1990; Provided backing vocals for: Drivers Eyes, Ian McDonald, 1999. *Address:* c/o Dennis Katz, 845 Third Ave, New York, NY 10022, USA.

GRANAT Endre; b. 3 Aug. 1937, Hungary. Musician (violin). m. Mimi, 21 Aug. 1993, 1 s. *Education:* University. *Musical Education:* Pupil, Joseph Gingold, Jascha Heifetz. *Career:* Tours: Europe; USA; South America; Asia; Concert master, soloist, major Hollywood films. *Honours:* Ysaye Award; Grand Prix du Disque. *Membership:* AFofM. *Leisure interests:* Piloting single engine airplanes; Tennis; Scuba diving. *Current Management:* CAMS.

GRANDE Johnny; b. Philadelphia, USA. Musician (piano). *Career:* Original member, Bill Haley's Comets, 1952–62; Leading innovator of rock 'n' roll music; First rock band to headline a film. *Recordings:* Rock Around The Clock (No. 1, UK and US), 1955; See You Later Alligator, 1956; Crazy Man Crazy; Shake Rattle and Roll, 1954; Rock The Joint, 1957; Mambo Rock, 1955; Rudy's Rock, 1956; Florida Twist; Skinny Minnie; On The Air (compilation), 2001. *Publications:* Rock Around The Clock; We're Gonna Party; Never Too Old To Rock. *Honours:* Best Vocal Group, 1954; Best Instrumental Group, 1956; Rock and Roll Hall of Fame; Gold Records. *Address:* Rock It Concerts, Bruno-Hofer Platz 1, 80937 Munich, Germany.

GRANDMASTER FLASH (Joseph Saddler); b. 1 Jan. 1958, Barbados. DJ; Rapper. *Career:* Mobile DJ, The Bronx, New York; Formed Grandmaster Flash and the 3 MCs, 1977–83; Solo artiste, 1985–; Performed, UK Fresh, Capital Music Festival, Wembley, 1986. *Recordings:* Albums: The Message, 1982; Greatest Messages, 1984; Solo albums: They Said It Couldn't Be Done, 1985; The Source, 1986; Ba Dop Boom Bang, 1987; On the Strength, 1988; Greatest Hits, 1992; Adventures On The Wheels of Steel (compilation), 1999; Singles: Freedom, 1980; The Adventures of Grandmaster Flash On The Wheels of Steel, 1981; The Message, 1982; White Lines (Don't Do It), 1983; Dance to the Beat, 1998; Solo: Sign of The Times, 1985; U Know What Time It Is?, 1987. *Address:* c/o

Richard Walters Entertainment Inc, 421 S Beverly Dr., Eighth Floor, Beverly Hills, CA 90212, USA.

GRANFELT Ben Edward; b. 16 June 1963, Helsinki, Finland. Musician (guitar); Songwriter. m. Nanna Granfelt, 14 Jan. 1997. *Musical Education:* Self-taught Guitarist, Songwriter. *Career:* Films: Leningrad Cowboys Meet Moses; Tours in Europe, Scandinavia, England, USA, Australia, Japan, with Leningrad Cowboys, Europe, USA, England; Support to Status Quo, with Gringos Locos; Leningrad Cowboys Meet the Alexandrow Red Army, chorus and ensemble, Live. *Recordings:* Ben Granfelt: The Truth; Radio Friendly Live; Guitar Slingers: I; Song and Dance; That Little Something; Leningrad Cowboys: We Cum From Brooklyn; Leningrad Cowboys Go Space; Let's Work Together; Russian Red Army Ensemble; Live in Prowinzz; Gringos Locos: Raw Deal; Punch Rock; Gringos Locos: Ego, 2000. *Honour:* Pro Musica Award, Gymnasiet Grankulla Samskola. *Leisure interests:* Martial Arts (Karate, Krava Maga, Shootfighting). *Current Management:* Sprucefield Oy Ltd, Viipurinkatu 8 B 65, 00510 Helsinki, Finland.

GRANT Amy Lee; b. 25 Nov. 1960, Augusta, Georgia, USA. Singer; Songwriter. m. Gary W Chapman, 19 June 1982, 1 s., 2 d. *Education:* Furman University; Vanderbilt University. *Career:* Contemporary Christian (later also pop) singer, songwriter; Began recording career, 1978–; Has sold 18m. records world-wide; First full tour, 1981; Longest tour, Unguarded Tour, 18 months 1985–86; Star of TV Christmas Special: Headin' Home For The Holidays, with Dennis Weaver, Art Garfunkel, Jimmy Webb, 1986. *Compositions include:* Tender Tennessee Christmas (co-writer). *Recordings include:* Amy Grant In Concert Vols I and II; Age To Age, 1982; A Christmas Album, 1983; Unguarded, 1985; Lead Me On, 1988; Heart in Motion, 1991; Home for Christmas, 1992; House of Love, 1994; Behind the Eyes, 1997; A Christmas to Remember, 1999; A Special Wish, 2001. *Publication:* Amy Grant's Heart To Heart Bible Stories, book and cassette. *Honours:* 5 Grammy Awards; 17 Dove Awards including Artist of The Year (4 times); Pax Christi, St John's University (First entertainer, third woman to receive this), 1994. *Leisure interests:* Golf; Snow skiing; Painting; Trail riding. *Current Management:* Blanton/Harrell Entertainment. *Address:* 2910 Poston Ave, Nashville, TN 37203, USA.

GRANT Eddy, (Edmond Montague Grant); b. 5 March 1948, Plaisance, Guyana. Singer; Prod.; Musician (multi-instrumental). *Career:* Member, The Equals; Founder, own production company; Solo artiste, 1977–; Founder, record label Ice Records; Own studio, The Coach House. *Recordings:* Albums: Message Man, 1977; Walking On Sunshine, 1979; Love In Exile, 1980; Can't Get Enough, 1981; Killer On The Rampage, 1982; Going For Broke, 1984; All The Hits, 1984; File Under Rock, 1988; The Best of Eddy Grant, 1989; Barefoot Soldier, 1990; Paintings of the Soul, 1992; Soca Baptism, 1993; I Don't Wanna Dance, 1997; Eddy Grant's Greatest Hits, 2001; Singles: with The Equals: Baby Come Back (No. 1, UK), 1968; Viva Bobbie Joe, 1969; Black Skin Blue Eyed Boys, 1970; Solo: Living On The Front Line, 1979; Do You Feel My Love, 1980, Can't Get Enough of You, 1981; I Don't Wanna Dance (No. 1, UK), 1982; Electric Avenue (No. 2, UK and US), 1983; Gimme Hope Joanna, 1988; Electric Avenue (remix), 2001; Walking On Sunshine (remix), 2001. *Current Management:* Metro Management, 24–7 Coda Centre, 189 Munster Rd, London SW6 6AW, England.

GRANT Ian Fraser; b. 17 Dec. 1950, Lancing, Surrey, England. Artist Management. m. 6 Nov. 1975, 1 s., 1 d. *Musical Education:* GCE and Royal Schools of Music, pianoforte. *Career:* Manager, acts include: The Stranglers, 1975–80; The Skids, 1980–81; Big Country, 1982–; The Cult, 1985–88; Hazel O'Connor, 1980–81; The Members, 1980–81; Maxi Priest, 1987–88. *Leisure interests:* Football; Cricket; Horse racing; Gardening; Camping. *Current Management:* Ian Grant Management, PO Box 107, South Godstone, Redhill, Surrey RH9 8JL, England.

GRANT Manson; b. 9 April 1951, John O'Groats, Scotland. Singer; Musician (keyboards, trumpet, accordion). *Education:* HNC, Business studies. *Musical Education:* Piano. *Career:* Television appearances include: Grampian TV; Channel 4; Holiday Programme, BBC2; Concerts include: CMA Fan Fair, Nashville, Tennessee (representing Scotland); Wembley Country Music Festival, London; Joined Dynamos Band, 1970. *Recordings:* 15 albums/cassettes; 3 CDs; 2 videos. *Honours:* More than 60 club and theatre awards. *Membership:* Musicians' Union. *Leisure interests:* Music; Computing. *Current Management:* R Cameron. *Address:* Achnaclyth, Tannach, Wick, Caithness KW1 5SF, Scotland.

GRANT Wanda L; b. 6 May 1965, Antigonish, Nova Scotia, Canada. Songwriter. *Education:* Bachelor, Religious Education. *Musical Education:* Grade 7, Royal Conservatory. *Compositions:* Christmas Musicals: I've Been Searchin', 1993; Miracle Morn, 1994; The Fisherman's Trade, Breakin' Tradition, 1996. *Honours:* Gospel Music Trailblazer Nomination, Airplay International. *Membership:* Gospel Music Asscn. *Leisure interest:* Painting. *Current Management:* W L Grant. *Address:* PO Box 305, Port Hawkesbury, Nova Scotia B0E 2V0, Canada.

GRAY Catherine; b. 28 Feb. 1946, Glasgow. Musician. 2 s. *Education:* BA, University of Edinburgh; London College of Music; The Royal Academy of Music. *Publications:* Guide To The Collection, 1987; The Guinness Encyclopedia, Music From Around The World, 1990; Womens Rights in Uganda, 1992; Patterns of Textual Recurrence in Kiganda Song, 1992; The Endongo, A Ugandan Lyre and Its Music, 1993; Compositional Techniques in Roman Catholic Church Music in Uganda, 1996; Temporalistes: Temps, Rhythmes et Musiques, 1996; Static and Dynamic Codes in Kiganda Lyre Song, 1998; Temporal Heterogeneities in Kiganda Music, 1998. *Memberships:* Society of Ethnomusicology; British Forum of Ethnomusicology; International Council for Traditional Music. *Leisure interests:* Climbing; Walking; Theatre; Opera; Reading. *Address:* 15 Jocks Hill Cresent, Linlithgow, West Lothian EH48 7BJ, Scotland.

GRAY David; b. 1970 Manchester, UK. Vocalist; Musician (multi-instrumentalist); Songwriter. m. Olivia Rooney. *Education:* Ysgol Dewi Sant, St Davids, Pembrokeshire; University of Liverpool, studied art. *Career:* Relocated to Wales with family, aged 9; Experimented in various punk bands prior to residence in London; Signed to Hut/Virgin then EMI for first 3 albums; Built up reputation through live performances; Recorded and released acclaimed fourth album on self-owned IHT label; Contributed tracks to and appeared in film This Year's Love, 1998; Major concert, festival appearances and US tour, 2000–01. *Recordings:* Albums: A Century Ends, 1993; Flesh, 1994; Sell, Sell, Sell, 1996; White Ladder, 1999; Lost Songs 95–98, 2000; Singles: Birds Without Wings, 1992; Shine, 1993; Wisdom, 1993; Babylon, 1998; This Year's Love, 1999; Please Forgive Me, 1999; Sail Away, Say Hello – Wave Goodbye, 2001. *Honours:* Ivor Novello Award, Best Song Lyrically and Musically, Babylon, 2001; Grammy Award, Best New Artist nominee, 2002. *Current Management:* c/o East-West Records, United Kingdom. *Internet:* www.davidgray.com.

GRAY Howard; Record Engineer; Prod.; Musician. *Career:* Engineer to Steve Lillywhite; Independent Producer mid 1980s; Recording artiste with Apollo 440; Numerous remixes/production credits. *Recordings:* Producer, Mixer, Recording Engineer: Terence Trent D'Arby: Introducing The Hardline; Danny Wilson: Danny Wilson; The Cure: Head On The Door; UB40: Labour of Love; OMD: Sugar Tax; Scritti Politti: Cupid and Psyche '85; Tom Verlaine: Cover; Blue Pearl: Naked; Other recordings by: Yazz; Mori Kante; Geoffrey Williams; Kirsty MacColl; Genesis; U2; Duran Duran; Youssou n'Dour; Manic Street Preachers; Skunk Anansie; Siegman; Dust Junkys; Apollo 440 Singles include: Astral America, 1994; Liquid Cool, 1994; Don't Fear The Reaper, 1995; Krupa, 1996; Ain't Talkin' Bout Dub, 1997; Raw Power, 1997; Rendezvous 98, 1998; Lost In Space, 1998; Stop The Rock, 1999; Heart Go Boom, 1999; Charlie's Angels, 2000. *Current Management:* XL. *Address:* Studio 7, 27A Pembridge Villas, London W11 3EP, England.

GRAY Les; b. 9 April 1946, Carshalton, Surrey, England. Singer. m. Carol, 16 April 1980. *Musical Education:* Self-taught. *Career:* Member, skiffle and trad jazz bands; Lead singer, Mud, 1967–; Concerts include: Search For Sound, Song Contest Winners, 1967; British tour supporting Tom Jones, 1973; British tours, 1974, 1978; Second Hemsby 70s and Glam Rock Weekender (with Glitter Band, Alvin Stardust, ShowaddyWaddy, Sweet, Rubettes, Mungo Jerry), 1991. *Recordings:* Hit singles with Mud include: Dyna-Mite, 1974; Tiger Feet, (No. 1, UK), 1974; The Cat Crept In, (No. 2, UK), 1974; Rocket, 1974; Lonely This Christmas, (No. 1, UK), 1974; The Secrets That You Keep, (No. 3, UK), 1975; Oh Boy, (No. 1, UK), 1975; L-L-Lucy, 1975; Show Me You're A Woman, 1975; Lean On Me, 1976; Albums: Mud Rock, 1974; Mud Rock Vol. 2, 1975; Mud's Greatest Hits, 1975; Use Your Imagination, 1975; Mudpack, 1978; Rock On, 1979; As You Like It, 1979; Mud, 1983; Let's Have A Party, 1991; Greatest Hits, 2000. *Memberships:* Musicians' Union; Equity; PRS; PPL; PRC. *Leisure interest:* Cooking. *Current Management:* Sharon Sly. *Address:* 99 Wood Vale, London N10 8DL, England.

GRAY Macy, (Natalie McIntyre); b. 1969, Canton, Ohio, USA. Singer; Songwriter. Divorced, 3 d. *Education:* Seven years' classical piano training; Studied, Screenwriting Programme, USC Film School. *Career:* Began as lyricist for musician friends; Began to fill in as singer; Worked as session jazz singer; Signed recording contract, 1998, released first single and album. *Recordings:* Singles: Do Something, 1999; I Try, 1999; Still, 2000; Why Didn't You Call Me, 2000; Demons, with Fatboy Slim, 2000; Sweet Baby, with Erykah Badu, 2001; Sexual Revolution, 2001; Albums: On How Life Is, 1999; The Id, 2001. *Honours include:* Brit Awards: Best International Newcomer, Best International Female Artist, 2000; Grammy Award, Female Pop Vocal Performance, I Try, 2001. *Internet:* www.macygray.com.

GRAY Tom; b. 1976, Southport, England. Musician (guitar, bass, keyboards, percussion); Vocalist. *Career:* Member, Gomez; Numerous live dates and television appearances. *Recordings:* Singles: 78 Stone Wobble, 1998; Whippin' Piccadilly, 1998; Get Myself Arrested, 1998; Bring It On, 1999; Rhythm and Blues Alibi, 1999; We Haven't Turned Around (featured on American Beauty OST), 1999; Machismo EP, 2000 Albums: Bring It On,

1998; Liquid Skin, 1999; Abandoned Shopping Trolley Hotline, 2000. *Honours:* Mercury Music Prize, Bring It On, 1998; Brit Award nominations, 1999–2000.

GREBENSCHIKOV Boris Borisovitch; b. 27 Nov. 1953, St Petersburg, Russia. Musician (guitar); Singer; Poet; Composer. m. Irina Grebenschiova, 29 May 1992, 2 d. *Education:* Leningrad University, Applied Mathematics. *Musical Education:* Self-taught. *Career:* Formed Aquarium, 1972; Started recordings (not government approved), 1980; Tapes widely circulated throughout Russia to great success; After Peristroika toured extensively in Russia; Solo album, produced by Dave Stewart, 1988–89; Subject of film: Long Way Home, Granada TV. *Recordings:* 10 cassette-only albums, 1980–86; Ravnodenstvie, 1987; Radio Silence, 1989; Russian Album, 1992; Rameses The IV Favourite Songs, 1992; Sands of St Petersburg, 1993; Kostroma Mon Amour, 1994; Navigator, 1995; Snow Lion, 1996; Hyperborea, 1997; Lilith, 1997; Refuge, 1998; Psi, 1999. *Publications:* Master Bo's Business, 1991; 14 song books, 1992; Prose, 1993; Complete Works, Vol. I-II, 1997. *Honours:* Triumph Prize, major addition to Russian culture, 1998. *Memberships:* Russian Cinematographer's Union; Cinematographers Union; PEN club, 1997. *Leisure interests:* Painting; Translation of Buddhist texts into Russian (Bardo Guidebook). *Current Management:* Aquarium Management. *Address:* Flat 3, 2 Marata St, St Petersburg 191025, Russia.

GREEN Barnaby; b. 4 Oct. 1967, Farnborough, Kent, England. *Education:* Centre for Young Musicians, Pimlico, London; BA, Music, Cambridge College of Arts and Technology; PGCE, Music, Open University. *Career:* Glastonbury Festival, Avalon Stage, with Junction, 1995; WOMAD One, World Stage, with Roots Progress, 1996; Gigs at Ronnie Scott's, the Jazz Cafe, Royal Albert Hall, Festival Hall and St Paul's Cathedral; Principal Percussionist, working with Stockhausen, British Premiere of Sternklang, Huddersfield Contemporary Music Festival; Musical Director, Composer, Viva O Carnival, Lillian Bayliss Theatre, Sadlers Wells, London; Wrote music for 2 short films, Seeing Things and Open and Shut Case; Percussion Tutor, Morley College, London. *Compositions:* I'm On My Way, with Green Pig; Spin Out, with Blunt. *Recordings:* Random Groove Movement (band); When Love Gives You Up, CD single. *Memberships:* Musicians' Union; Asscn of Teachers and Lecturers; Professional Asscn of Teachers. *Leisure interests:* Travel; Writing; Squash; The Internet; Dining out; Cinema. *Address:* 36 Middleton Rd, London E8 4BS, England.

GREEN Earl Oliver; b. 11 Feb. 1945, Kingston, Jamaica. Singer. m. Valerie Jean, 3 Oct. 1973, 1 s., 1 d. *Career:* Most major blues festivals in Europe including: Belgium Rhythm and Blues Festival; Nyon Festival; Lugano Festival, Switzerland; Diamond Awards, Antwerp; Radio broadcasts include: Paul Jones Show, BBC Radio 2; GLR; Mary Costello Show; Radio in Netherlands; Television appearances: Spain; Netherlands; Belgium; Switzerland; France; UK, McKewans The Concert, James Whale Show. *Recordings:* Always Hot, Otis Grand and The Dance Kings; Special Delivery, He Knows The Blues, Otis Grand. *Honour:* British Blues Connection Nomination, Best Blues Vocalist, 1992–93. *Memberships:* PRS; Musicians' Union. *Leisure interests:* Gardening; Photography. *Current Management:* George McFall. *Address:* 213 Staines Rd, Laleham, Middlesex TW18 2R8, England.

GREEN Edward; b. 11 Nov. 1951, Queens, New York, USA. Composer; Musician (Keyboards). *Education:* Oberlin College, 1973; Studied Aesthetic Realism with philosopher Eli Siegel, 1974–78. *Career:* Staff developer, Imagery Films, 1980-, working with director Ken Kimmelman: film scores include What Does a Person Deserve?; Musical Director, Aesthetic Realism Foundation, 1978-: productions include The Melody Presents and Ethics is a Force; Faculty, Manhattan School of Music: classes include, Songwriting, Film Composition, Non-Western Music; also faculty New York School for Commercial Music and Aesthetic Realism Foundation; Performed duet with flautist Barbara Allen (played keyboards). *Compositions:* Piano Concertino; Chamber Symphony for Guitars and Flutes; Brass Quintet; Quartet for Guitars; Shakespeare Songs; Constitutional Amendment; Overture to Aesthetic Realism Autobiographies. *Publications:* The Press Boycott of Aesthetic Realism, 1978; Over 200 articles published worlwide on music, social issues, Aesthetic Realism; Editorial Columnist, US African Eye, 1998-. *Honours:* Delius Award for Musical Composition, 1985; First Prize, Julius Albert Composers' Competition, 1996; First Prize, Zoltan Kodaly Composers' Competition, 1996. *Membership:* ASCAP. *Address:* 208 E Broadway, J1007, New York, NY 10002, USA.

GREEN Ian; b. 8 Oct. 1969. Prod.; Writer; Mixer; Musician (keyboards, bass, drums, guitar). *Career:* Various television appearances including Wogan and Pebble Mill. *Recordings:* Voices, Kenny Thomas; Wait For Me, Kenny Thomas; True Spirit, Carleen Anderson; Closer To You, Brand New Heavies; Midnight At The Oasis, Brand New Heavies; Also recordings for Nu Colours; Misty Oldman; Monie Love. *Memberships:* Musicians' Union; Performing Rights Society. *Current Management:* BAMN

Management. *Address:* c/o A and M Records, 136–144, New Kings Rd, London SW6 4LZ, England.

GREEN Ian Michael; b. 19 Nov. 1957, London, England. Musician (percussion, drums). m. Carolyn Margaret Morris, 7 May 1994. *Musical Education:* Kingsdale, 1968–74. *Career:* Musician with: Mike Oldfield, 1972–73; Druid, 1977–78; Catherine Howe; Randy Edelman; Lindsey De Paul; Sally Oldfield (Germany), 1978–79; Matt Monroe (London), 1980–81; Michael Crawford, Barnum, TV and radio; Tony Britten; Sammy Davis Jr (Monte Carlo), 1988; Jerry Lee Lewis (Monte Carlo), 1991–92. *Recordings:* with artistes including: Michael Crawford; Mike Oldfield; Sally Oldfield; Anthony Newley, produced single: What Kind of Fool Am I?; Film and television: Lace 1 and 2; Lennon The Movie; Casualty; Head Over Heels; Shows: Barnum, 1981; Guys and Dolls, 1987; She Loves Me, 1994; The Snow Queen, 1995; Fame, 1995; Singing In The Rain; Stop The World. *Memberships:* Musicians' Union; ISM. *Leisure interests:* Writing; Driving. *Address:* 223 Hayes Lane, Kenley, Surrey CR8 5HN, England.

GREEN John R; b. 8 May 1971, Roehampton, London, England. Musician (Keyboards); String Arranger; Composer. *Career:* Left college, 1989; Session artist; Co-Producer, album for Ruby Blue; Recorded with J B Horns; Sessioned, Power of Dreams; Worked with Marc Almond on albums and on tour; Joined Sleeper as keyboard player, 1996, worked on albums The It Girl and Pleased to Meet You; Played keyboards and wrote string arrangements for Manic Street Preachers on Everything Must Go, many live shows; Returned to Sleeper, 1998; Pete Wylie and the Mighty Wah; Music Director, Liz Horsman; Worked with Geneva, Feeder, Des'ree, Aztec Camera, Holly Johnson; Remixed singles for LL Cool J, Don-e and Lewis Taylor. *Recordings:* Contributions to: I Like It Like That, J B HOrns, 1993; Fantastic Star, Marc Almond, 1995; The It Girl, Sleeper, 1996; Everything Must Go, Manic Street Preachers, 1996; Further, Geneva, 1996; Pleased to Meet You, Sleeper, 1997; Heavy High, Liz Horsman, 1999; Open All Night, Marc Almond, 1999. *Leisure interests:* Fishing; Outdoor activities; Martial arts. *Current Management:* Titled Management. *Address:* 62 Ashleigh Rd, Mortlake, London SW14 8PX, England.

GREEN Robson; b. 18 Dec. 1964, Hexham, Northumberland, England. Actor; Singer. *Career:* Actor, UK television series: Soldier Soldier; Casualty; Reckless; Touching Evil; Take Me; Close and True; Blind Ambition; Singer, duo Robson and Jerome, 1995. *Recordings:* Albums: Robson and Jerome, 1995; Take Two, 1996; Singles: Unchained Melody/White Cliffs of Dover (No. 1, UK), 1995; I Believe/Up On The Roof (No. 1, UK), 1995; What Becomes of The Brokenhearted/Saturday Night At The Movies/You'll Never Walk Alone (No. 1, UK), 1996. *Honour:* Best selling UK single and album of the year, 1995; First act to debut at #1 with first three UK single releases, 1995–96.

GREEN Sam; b. 2 Jan. 1960, Melbourne, Australia. Singer; Songwriter (guitar, keyboard). *Education:* Diploma of Horological Studies. *Career:* Played live to air with Greenmoss, group, 1979; Played in streets of Europe, 1980; Played with Tome the Poet and street poets, 5 times each week, 1982–86; Players All Are We: Live to air 3 CR, 1994; Live to air Southern FM, 1995; Appeared on Asylum channel 31, 1995; Host of Local and live (7 months), 1995; Appeared new years' night channel 31; Made video played on Rage channel 2, 1996. *Compositions:* For the Ocean, 1986; Angel of the Morning, 1994. *Recordings:* live But for Love, 1986; Players All Are We, 1994; I Think Its About Time, 1997. *Memberships:* APRA; ASA, Full Mem.; AMCOS Affiliated. *Leisure interests:* Keeping time (clocks and watches). *Current Management:* B Green Management. *Address:* 242 Swan St, Richmond, Victoria 3121, Australia. *E-mail:* samgreen@bigpond.com. *Internet:* www.mrmusicman.com.

GREEN(E) Al; b. 13 April 1946, Forrest City, Arkansas, USA. Soul Singer; Songwriter. *Career:* Founder, The Creations, 1964; Singer, Al Greene and The Soul Mates; Founder, own record label, Hot Line Music Journal, 1967; Performances include: Tokyo Music Festival, Japan, 1978; Nelson Mandela's 70th Birthday Tribute, Wembley, 1988; New Orleans Jazz and Heritage Festivals, 1992; Ann Arbor Blues and Jazz Festival, 1992. *Recordings:* Albums: Al Green Gets Next To You, 1971; Let's Stay Together, 1972; I'm Still In Love With You, 1972; Green Is Blues, 1973; Call Me, 1973; Livin' For You, 1974; Al Green Explores Your Mind, 1975; Greatest Hits, 1975; Al Green Is Love, 1975; Full of Fire, 1976; Have A Good Time, 1977; Greatest Hits Vol. II, 1977; Truth 'n' Time, 1978; The Belle Album, 1978; Cream of Al Green, 1980; The Lord Will Make A Way, 1980; Higher Plane, 1982; Precious Lord, 1983; I'll Rise Again, 1983; White Christmas, 1983 Going Away, 1986; Soul Survivor, 1987; Hi-Life – The Best of Al Green, 1988; I Get Joy, 1989; Greatest Hits, 1991; Al, 1992; Love and Happiness (box set), 2001; Hit singles include: Tired of Being Alone, 1971; Let's Stay Together (No. 1, USA), 1972; Look What You've Done For Me, 1972; I'm Still In Love With You, 1972; You Ought To Be With Me, 1972; Call Me (Come Back Home), 1973; Here I Am (Come and Take Me), 1973; Sha-La-la (Make Me Happy), 1974; L-O-V-E (Love), 1974; Sailin' On The Sea of Love, duet with Shirley Caesar, 1985; Going Away, 1986; Everything's Gonna Be Alright, 1987; Put A Little Love In Your Heart,

duet with Annie Lennox, (used in film Scrooged), 1988; As Long As We're Together, 1989. *Honours include:* American Music Award, Favourite Soul/R & B Album, 1974; Grand Prize, Tokyo Music Festival, 1978; Al Green Day, Los Angeles, 1978; Soul Train, Best Gospel Recording, 1987; Numerous Grammy awards include: Best Soul Gospel Performances, 1982–85, 1988, 1990; Best Male Soul Performance, 1987. *Address:* c/o Al Green Music, 3208 Winchester, Memphis, TN 38118, USA.

GREENE Jack Henry; b. 7 Jan. 1930, Maryville, Tennessee, USA. Country vocalist; Songwriter; Musician (guitar, drums). *Career:* Known as The Jolly Green Giant; Vocalist and guitarist with the Cherokee Trio, Atlanta, 1940s; On WGAP radio, Maryville with Clyde Grubbs; Member: Clyde Grubbs and the Tennessee Valley Boys; Drummer with the Rhythm Ranch Boys, 1950; Played with Peachtree Cowboys, mid-1950s; Drummer, later vocalist, with Ernest Tubb, 1962; Formed the Jolly Green Giants, later renamed the Renegades, 1965; Signed to Decca, 1965; Debut single Ever Since My Baby Went Away; Billboard country single chart hits including duets with Jeannie Seeley until 1984; Hits included There Goes My Everything, later a pop hit for Engelbert Humperdinck, 1967. *Recordings include:* There Goes My Everything, 1966; All The Time, 1967; Statue of a Fool, 1969; Until My Dreams Come True, 1968; You Are My Treasure, 1968; Albums: There Goes My Everything, 1967; All The Time, 1967; What Locks The Door, 1967. *Honours:* various including: CMA: Single of the Year; Song of the Year; Album of the Year, There Goes My Everything; Male Vocalist of the Year, 1967; Cash Box, Most Promising Male Vocalist of the Year, 1967; Record World, Most Promising Male Vocalist of the Year, 1967; Cash Box, Most Programmed Song, All The Time, 1968. *Memberships:* Grand Ole Opry, 1967. *Address:* c/o Fat City Artists, 1226 17th Ave S, Suite 2, Nashville, TN 37212, USA.

GREENSLADE Dave; b. 18 Jan. 1943, Woking, Surrey, England. Composer; Musician (keyboards). m. Jan Greenslade, 2 d. *Career:* Keyboard player with Chris Farlowe's The Thunderbirds; Worked with Geno Washington in the Ram Jam Band; Formed Colosseum, with Jon Hiseman; Wrote and co-wrote hit album: Valentyne Suite; Colosseum disbanded 1971; Founder, Greenslade, 1972; Colosseum reformed, reunion tour of Europe and album, 1994; Wrote hit albums, also solo project: Cactus Choir; Wrote television score for BBC series: Gangsters, success led to full time composition; Reforming Greenslade with original line-up. *Compositions:* Worked on more than 35 drama series, single plays, films, stage plays; Credits include: Kinsey, BBC TV; A Very Peculiar Practice, BBC TV; Wipe Out, Granada TV; Tales of The Unexpected, Anglia TV; The Detective, BBC TV; Bratt Farrer, BBC TV; Bird of Prey, BBC TV; The Houseman's Tale, BBC TV; A Family Man, BBC TV; Films: Artemis, BBC Films; Jekyll and Hyde, BBC films; Worked with novelist Terry Pratchett on recording project based on the DiscWorld fantasy novel series; Storms Behind the Breeze; The Playground; No Pleasin'; Wherever I Go; The Other Side of the Sky. *Recordings include:* Colosseum: Daughter of Time; Live; Valentyne Suite; Albums with Greenslade (now re-issued on CD); Cactus Choir; Pentateuch, double album based on illustrations of Patrick Woodroffe; DiscWorld project, 1995; Large Afternoon, 2000; Live 1973–75, 2000. *Honours:* Premio Ondas TV Award at Barcelona Film Festival; Won Prix Italia at Palermo; Toyama Prize, Japan. *Memberships:* Musicians' Union; PRS; MCPS. *Current Management:* Soundtrack Music Management. *Address:* 16 Queens Rd, Berdhamsted, Hertfordshire HP4 3HU, England.

GREENWICH Ellie; b. 23 Oct. 1940, Brooklyn, New York, USA. Songwriter; Record Prod.; Singer. *Education:* BA, Holfstra University, 1962. *Career:* Singer, 1958–; Songwriting partnership with Jeff Barry, 1960–67; Founder member, The Raindrops, 1963; Solo artist and songwriter; Performed in revue Leader of The Pack. *Compositions:* Hit songs include: Hanky Panky, Tommy James and The Shondells; Da Doo Ron Ron, The Crystals; And Then He Kissed Me, The Crystals; Do Wah Diddy Diddy, The Exciters; Leader of The Pack, The Shangri-Las; River Deep Mountain High, Ike and Tina Turner; Baby I Love You, The Ronettes; Be My Baby, The Ronettes; Writer, producer, songs recorded by Neil Diamond; Cyndi Lauper; Bette Midler; Nona Hendryx. *Recordings:* Albums: Ellie Greenwich Composes Produces and Sings, 1968; Let It Be Written, Let It Be Sung, 1973; I Can Hear Music, 1999; Backing vocals on: Dreaming, Blondie, 1979; Girls Just Wanna Have Fun, Cyndi Lauper, 1983. *Honours:* 19 BMI Awards; Inducted into Songwriters Hall of Fame; National Academy of Popular Music Award, 1984. *Membership:* Songwriters Guild.

GREENWOOD Bernard Paul; b. 21 April 1940, Bath, England. Dr; Musician (saxophone, keyboards). *Education:* Medicine, London, Oxford; Social Anthropology, Cambridge. *Career:* Saxophone player, Chris Farlowe and the Thunderbirds; The Glands; Doctor Kitch; Alkasalsa; Joey The Lips; Jazz Posse; Dicky Pride and the Original Topics; King Cobra and the Rattlesnakes; Tour with Lindsay Kemp. *Recordings:* Buzz With The Fuzz; Treat Her Right; The Fool; Mr Pitiful (with Chris Farlowe). *Publication:* Buzz With The Fuzz. *Address:* Woodcote, Chagford, Devon TQ13 8JF, England.

GREENWOOD Colin; b. 26 June 1969, Oxford, England. Musician (bass). *Career:* Member, On A Friday, later became Radiohead; Secured major record deal, 1991; Numerous support slots on tour including REM in 1995; Many headlining tours, festival dates including Glastonbury 1996, numerous TV appearances. *Recordings include:* Singles: Anyone Can Play Guitar EP, 1993; Creep, 1993; Stop Whispering, 1994; My Iron Lung EP, 1994; Street Spirit (Fade Out), 1995; Fake Plastic Trees, 1995; Just, 1996; High and Dry, 1996; Paranoid Android, 1997; Airbag, 1997: Karma Police, 1997; How Am I Driving EP, 1998; No Surprises, 1998; Knives Out, 2001; Pyramid Song, 2001; Albums: Pablo Honey, 1993; The Bends, 1995; OK Computer (No. 1, UK and US), 1997; Kid A (No. 1, UK and US), 2000; Amnesiac, 2001; I Might Be Wrong, 2001. *Honours include:* Grammy Award, Alternative Music Performance, Kid A, 2001. *Internet:* www.radiohead.com.

GREENWOOD Jonny; b. 5 Nov. 1971, Oxford, England. Musician (guitar, keyboards). *Career:* Member, On A Friday, changed name to Radiohead; Signed major record deal with Parlophone; Support tours including REM, 1995; Many headlining tours; Helped work on Michael Stipe's film Velvet Goldmine; Numerous festival dates throughout Europe. *Recordings include:* Anyone Can Play Guitar EP, 1993; Creep, 1993; Stop Whispering, 1994; My Iron Lung EP, 1994; Street Spirit (Fade Out), 1995; Fake Plastic Trees, 1995; Just, 1996; High and Dry, 1996; Paranoid Android, 1997; Airbag, 1997: How Am I Driving EP, 1998; No Surprises, 1998; Knives Out, 2001; Pyramid Song, 2001; Albums: Pablo Honey, 1993; The Bends, 1995; OK Computer (No. 1, UK and US), 1997; Kid A (No. 1, UK and US), 2000; Amnesiac, 2001; I Might Be Wrong, 2001. *Honours include:* Grammy Award, Alternative Music Performance, Kid A, 2001. *Internet:* www.radiohead.com.

GREENWOOD Lee Melvin; b. 27 Oct. 1942, Southgate, California, USA. Country Singer. m. Melanie Cronk. *Recordings:* Singles: It Turns Me Inside Out; IOU; Ring On Her Finger, Time On Her Hands; Ain't No Trick; She's Lyin'; Going Going Gone; Fools Gold; with Barbara Mandrell: To Me; It Should Have Been Love By Now; Albums: Inside and Out, 1982; If There's Any Justice, 1983; Somebody's Gonna Love You, 1983; The Wind Beneath My Wings, 1984; You've Got a Good Love Comin', 1985; Christmas is Christmas, 1987; God Bless the USA, 1990; Holdin' a Good Hand, 1991; American Patriot, 1992; Back to Back, 1996; Wounded Heart, 1998; Same River Different Bridge, 2000; Have Yourself A Merry Little Christmas, 2001; with Barbara Mandrell: Meant For Each Other. *Honours:* CMA Male Vocalist of Year, 1983, 1984; ACM Male Vocalist of Year, 1984; Cash Box Choice Award, 1984; Music City Awards, Best Male Vocalist, 1984, 1985. *Leisure interest:* Sport. *Address:* Lee Greenwood Inc, PO Box 6537, Seiverville, TN 37864, USA.

GREGORY Colin; b. 30 Dec. 1961, Radcliffe, Manchester, England. Musician; Songwriter. *Education:* Lancaster University. *Musical Education:* Self-taught. *Career:* Tours of USA, Europe and Japan, 1992; TV and Radio appearances in USA, 1994; UK television appearances include: Snub; The Beat; Northern Routes; The Chart Show; John Craven's Newsround; Look North; Many radio sessions on John Peel, Mark Radcliffe, Janice Long, Mark Goodier and Johnny Walker shows. *Recordings:* 3 albums in the UK, 2 albums in USA and 2 albums in Japan; 10 UK singles and 8 singles internationally; Albums with One Thousand Violins: One Thousand Violins, 2001. *Memberships:* Musicians' Union; PRS. *Leisure interests:* Music; Football; Philosophy. *Current Management:* Rockmasters Management. *Address:* Brunswick Studios, 7 Westbourne Grove Mews, London W11 2RU, England.

GREGSON Clive James; b. 4 Jan. 1955, Ashton-Under-Lyne, Lancashire, England. Musician; Singer; Songwriter; Record Prod. m. Nancy Ann Kirkland, 6 Nov. 1993. *Education:* Crewe and Alsager College of Education. *Musical Education:* Mostly self-taught. *Career:* Founder, leader, Any Trouble, 1976–84; Member, duo, Clive Gregson and Christine Collister, 1985–92; Member, Richard Thompson Band, 1987–92; Solo artist, 1992-. *Recordings:* with Any Trouble: Where Are All The Nice Girls, 1980; Live At The Venue, 1980; Wheels In Motion, 1981; Any Trouble, 1983; Wrong End of The Race, 1984; Solo: Strange Persuasions, 1985; Welcome To The Workhouse, 1990; Carousel of Noise, 1994; People and Places, 1995; I Love this Town, 1996; Happy Hour, 1999; Comfort and Joy, 2001; With Gregson and Collister: Home and Away, 1986; Mischief, 1987; A Change In The Weather, 1989; Love Is A Strange Hotel, 1990; The Last Word, 1992; with Eddi Reader and Boo Hewerdine: Wonderful Lie/Last Night I Dreamt That Somebody Loved Me/Who's Your Jailer Now?, 1993. *Memberships:* PRS; BASCA; EFDSS; Musicians' Union. *Leisure interests:* Stamp collecting; Ornithology. *Current Management:* John Martin. *Address:* Gregsongs, 50 Stroud Green Rd, London N4 3EF, England.

GREINKE Arthur Joseph; b. 19 March 1963, Milwaukee, USA. PR Exec. *Education:* BA Mass Communications, Journalism, University of Wisconsin, Milwaukee. *Career:* Freelance entertainment journalist, Milwaukee, 1981–89; Program co-ordinator, The Great Circus Parade, Milwaukee, 1985–; Principal Partner, Greinke, Eiers and Associates, Milwaukee, 1985–; Director, Public relations and advertising, Eastside Compact Disc, 1988–; Cooler Music Promotions, USA, Inc, 1990–; Executive Producer (music group), Project Mix, 1985–87. *Publications:* Articles on national, regional recording industry news to college newspapers, local trades, Rolling Stone magazine; Advertising copy; Rock news scripts for Milwaukee television video show. *Memberships:* PRSA; IABC, Treasurer, 1989, President, 1990; SPJ; NARAS. *Leisure interests:* Beatles Authority; American Football; Films; Music. *Address:* 2557C N Terrace Ave, Milwaukee, WI 53211–3822, USA.

GRESSWELL Steve; b. 20 Jan. 1955, Reading, Berkshire, England. Composer; Prod.; Musician (keyboards); Programmer. m. Jacqui, 1 Oct. 1993, 1 s., 1 d. *Career:* Justin Canns, 1971–76; Scorpio, 1977–81; Steve Gresswell Band, 1981–82; Dream, 1982–84; Poiema, 1984–85; After Dark, 1985; Guardian Angel, 1985–86; Formed own label, Sumo Records, with recording studio, 1988; Video with SG Band: Just For You, 1989; Robin Wilson Productions, 1990; Coalition, 1992-. *Compositions:* Story of The Gods, Rock Oratorio. *Recordings:* with Scorpio: Taking England By Storm, 1977; with Oddjob: Express Yourself, 1977; with Dream: Just For You, 1982; with Poiema: 2 singles from play: Cross Purposes, 1984; with After Dark: Call of The Wild, 1985; Album: Masked By Midnight, 1985; with SG Band: Just For You (Official Record for Lockerbie Air Disaster Fund), 1989; Producer, single for duo, Vincent, 1989; Composer, musician, engineer, producer, album for Czech rock guitarist Karel Espandr, 1990; Producer, composer, Robin Wilson Project single (fundraising for child with Cerebral Palsy), 1990; Steve Gresswell: Spirit of Freedom, 1994; Coalition: Rise of the Coalition, 1996, 1997; Steve Cresswell: Visions, 1997; Produced and arranged Brent Morley, Burn, 1997. *Memberships:* Musicians' Union; PRS; PPL; MCPS; BASCA; BSWC; PAMRA. *Leisure interest:* Music. *Current Management:* Sumo Records. *Address:* Searles, The Chapel, 26a Munster Rd, London SW6 4EN, England.

GREY Carola; b. 5 Aug. 1968, Munich, Germany. Drummer; Composer; Prod. *Education:* Classical Piano, for 12 years; Master degree, Music and Music Education (Jazzdrums). *Career:* Performed and/or recorded with: Mike Stern, Ravi Coltrane, Benny Green, Craig Handy and others Jazzartists; Drummer for New York based all female gothic rock band, Maria Excommunikata Bandleader, 1989–; Clubs and festivals in Europe, US and Asia (Thailand International Jazz Festival, 1996; Jakarta Jazz Festival, 1995–96; Indian Music Festival Madras, 1996); TV features include: Deutsche Welle, Berlin (Germany); Star TV, (India) WDR, Cologne (Germany), Polish TV. *Recordings:* Carola Grey, Noisy Mama, 1992; Carola Grey, The Age of Illusion, 1994; Carola Grey, Girls Can't Hit, 1996; Composer, all music for band; Music for minor films and dance theatres: Vox, international cable; MC for the Zildjian Day Berlin, Germany, 1997. *Honours:* Govt Grant, for extraordinary artists, 1995; Nomination for SWF Jazzprize and Munich Jazz Prize, 1998. *Membership:* International Drum Organisation. *Leisure interest:* Kung-Fu. *Current Management:* Noisy Mama Productions, Rattenbergerstr 22, 81373, München, Germany.

GRIDLEY Andrew David; b. 3 May 1960, Maldon, Essex, England. Musician (6 and 12 string guitar, keyboards); Singer; Songwriter. *Musical Education:* Performing Arts at college. *Career:* Appearances include: Production, London Lights, Ingatestone; Chelmsford Youth Spectacular, Civic Theatre; England Entertains, Clacton, Essex; First EP released Essex Radio, Witham; Live Elvis performance, Southend-On Sea, Cliffs Pavilion; Played guitar for Dr Barnardo's Charity; Accompanied Helen Shapiro on 12 string guitar. *Compositions:* Forever, 1997; I Want You, 1997; You're Sexy, 1997; Smile on My Pinstripe, 1997. *Recordings:* Day Through To Night; Leading Lady; Green; Love and Affection; From Me To You; Lonely As A Cloud; Love Can Be; Summer Sun; Take Me; Beautiful; Wild Wild Women; Taking a Chance on Love; I'm a Fool in Love; Lost in Time (Reflections). *Publications:* Total Guitar, 1997. Contributions to: Times Education Supplement. *Honour:* Recommended, One of best guitar and music teachers, Times Educational Supplement. *Memberships:* PRS; BASCA; MCPS. *Leisure interests:* Photography; Walking; Listening to music; Socialising. *Address:* 17 Coopers Ave, Heybridge, Maldon, Essex, England.

GRIFF Ray; b. 22 April 1940, Vancouver BC, Canada. Artist; Writer; Musician (Piano, Guitar). m. Trudy Griff. *Career:* Own Television Series, Host, Goodtime Country; Ray Griff Show; Sun Parlour Country; Guest, Includes Rollin' On The River, Dean Martin Show, Kenny Rogers, Grand Ole Opry, Porter Wagoner Show, Calgary Stampede. *Compositions:* Written Over 2000 Songs, Including Baby; Step Aside; The Morning After Baby Let Me Down; Darlin'; It Couldn't Have Been Any Better; Canadian Pacific; Where Love Begins; After The Laughter; Who's Gonna Play This Old Piano; Better Move It On Home. *Recordings:* Over 550 Including, Baby; Better Move It On Home; Hold Me; Getting Back To Norma; You're Wearin' Me Down; After The Laughter; Where Love Begins; Step Aside; It Couldn't Have Been Any Better; Between This Time and The Next. *Honours:* 7 BMI Citations for Song Writing and Publishing; 87 ASCAP hit song Awards for Artist, Producer, Song Writer and Publisher; Hall of Fame Walkway, Nashville; Calgary White Hat Honour. *Memberships:* ASCAP; NSA; BMI;

CMA; CCMA. *Leisure interests:* Tennis; Reading. *Address:* Suite 193, 132–250 Shawville Blvd SE, Calgary, AB, Canada T2Y 2Z7.

GRIFFIN Ian; b. 1 June 1965, Neath, Glamorgan, Wales. Musician (keyboards, electronic organ, piano). m. Jane Elizabeth Cribb, 2 Sept. 1989, 2 d. *Musical Education:* London College of Music. *Career:* Solo and group musician, 1980–; Television appearances: Young Entertainers, heat winner, BBC1, 1978; Heno, S4C TV, 1991–; HTV Friday Live, 1996–; Radio appearances include Keyboard, ILR Swansea Sound, 1978–; Keyboard Music, ILR Two Counties, 1987–; Keyboard Magic, BBC West Midlands Radio, 1988–; The Organist Entertains, BBC Radio 2, 1988–; Played at National Keyboard Festivals, 1980–; Opened own sound recording studio, for artists backing, 1989–; Appeared at the Grand Theatre, Swansea, 1993; Formed own cabaret show band, Casual Affair, 1994; Two appearances on HTV Television with Casual Affair, 1996. *Recordings:* In The Hands of Ian Griffin, 1986; Introducing Keyklix, 1987; Just Me – Ian Griffin, 1988; Half Way To Paradise, 1995; Penny Arcade, 2000. *Honour:* Best Keyboard Player Under Age 18, Organ Player and Keyboard Review Readers, 1982; Organist of the Year, Verwood and District Organ Society, 1996. *Leisure interests:* Boats; Sailing. *Address:* The Studio, 9 Mynachlog Terrace, Pontyberem, Llanelli, Dyfed SA15 5EE, Wales.

GRIFFIN Sid (Albert Sidney); b. 18 Sept. 1955, Louisville, Kentucky, USA. Musician; Journalist; Record Co Exec. m. Kate St John, 5 May 1993. *Education:* BA, Journalism, University of South Carolina, 1977. *Career:* Played with The Frosties, 1973–77; The Unclaimed, 1979–82; The Long Ryders, 1982–87; Soloist and Leader with The Coal Porters; Released various singles, EPs and albums with these bands; Owner, Prima Records Ltd. *Recordings:* With the Long Ryders: 10–5–60 (EP), 1983; Native Sons, album, 1984; State of Our Union, 1985; Two-Fisted Tales, 1987; Metallic BO, 1988; Anthology, 1998; Others: Danny and Dusty, The Lost Weekend, 1986; Rebels Without Applause, The Coal Porters, 1992; Land of Hope and Crosby, The Coal Porters, 1994; Los London, The Coal Porters, 1995; Solo: Little Victories, 1997; Roulette (EP), 1998; The Gram Parsons Tribute Concert, 1999; The Chris Hillman Tribute Concert, The Coal Porters, 2001. *Publications:* Contributor to Q, Mojo, BAM, and Country Music International magazines. *Honour:* Hon. Mem. of Athenaeum Literary Asscn. *Memberships:* AFofM; The Paisley Underground. *Leisure interests:* Baseball; Basketball; Drinking in Scotland. *Current Management:* Prima International, London, England. *Address:* PO Box 2539, London NW3 6DF, England.

GRIFFITH Nanci; b. 6 July 1953, Seguin, Texas, USA. Singer; Songwriter; Musician (guitar). *Education:* Studied Education, University of Texas. *Career:* Professional musician, 1977–; Formed backing band, The Blue Moon Orchestra, 1986; Formed own publishing company. *Compositions include:* Love At The Five and Dime; The Wing and The Wheel; Ford Econoline; Outbound Plane (co-written with Tom Russell). *Recordings:* There's A Light Beyond These Woods, 1978; Poet In My Window, 1982; Once In A Very Blue Moon, 1984; Last of the True Believers, 1986; Lone Star State of Mind, 1987; Little Love Affairs, 1988; One Fair Summer Evening, 1988; Storms, 1989; Late Night Grand Hotel, 1991; Flyer, 1994; Blue Roses from the Moons, 1997; Revisited, 1999; The Dust Bowl Symphony, 1999; Clock Without Hands, 2001. *Current Management:* Vector Management, PO Box 128037, Nashville, TN 37212, USA.

GRIFFITHS Franny; b. 1970. Musician (keyboards); Songwriter. *Career:* Member, Space; Numerous tours and television appearances. *Recordings:* Singles: If It's Real, 1993; Money, 1995; Neighbourhood, 1996; Female of the Species, 1997; Me and You vs the World, 1997; Dark Clouds, 1997; Avenging Angels, 1997; The Ballad of Tom Jones, with Cerys Matthews, 1998; Begin Again, 1998; Bad Days, 1998; Albums: Spiders, 1996; Remixes and B-Sides, 1997; Tin Planet, 1998; Greatest Hits, 2001; Also collaborated with Tom Jones, Sunny Afternoon (on Reload album), 1999.

GRIFFITHS Matthew David; b. 6 March 1968, Cardiff, Wales. Musician (percussion); Composer. m. Sarah Fisher, 18 Sept. 1993. *Musical Education:* BA, First Class Honours in Performing Arts, specialising in Music, Leicester Polytechnic, 1989. *Career:* Solo percussion recitals, 1989–; Concerts include: St David's Hall, Cardiff; Cheltenham Town Hall; Bradford Alhambra; Phoenix Arts, Leicester; Bath Festival; Warwick Festival; Swansea Festival; Chichester Festival; Sounds Like Birmingham; Percussion '90 Festival; Television appearances include: The Clothes Show, BBC1; Heno, Channel 4/S4C; Midlands Today; Radio appearances include: Radio Wales; Radio Leicester; Radio WM; Worked with dance companies in the theatre and for various contemporary music ensembles; Gives workshops, and composer in residence projects in schools, hospitals, prisons and day centres. *Compositions:* Concerto for Percussion and Embroidery Machine, premiere at Warwick Festival, 1991; Miles Around, with Warwick Festival premiere, 1992; World of Hospitality, commissioned by Rubbermaid, premiered at Earls Court, 1994. *Publication:* The North Indian Tabla and Its Use in Modern, Western Music (dissertation), 1989. *Honours:* ABSA Award, Concerto for Percussion

and Embroidery Machine. *Memberships:* Musicians' Union; Advisor, Arts Council. *Leisure interests:* Vegetarian cooking; Tennis. *Address:* 15 Bartletts Rd, Bedminster, Bristol BS3 3PL, England.

GRIGOROV Robert (Robo); b. 25 Sept. 1964, Bratislava. Singer; Composer; Prod. 1 d. *Career:* Film: Fontana Pre Zuzanu 1, actor and singer, 1986; Music for Theatre: Eunuch, 1985; Music for Films: Obyeany Den, 1985; Most, 1993; Touring with own group, Midi, 1982-. *Compositions:* Robo and Midi, 1985; Mohy, LP, 1986; Olohy, 1984; Cierny Kon, 1989; Chcemja Najst, 1985; Espresso Orient, 1987; Unplugged, 1994; Udychni Reggae, 1995; The Best of Chodci Sveta, 1997. *Recordings:* About 13 LPs and CDs. *Publications:* Zuvacka za uchom, 1983; EDO, 1984; Monika, 1985; Dvaja, 1984; Ona Je Madona, 1993. *Honours:* Bratislavska Lira, 1984, 1985, 1986; Cena Hulobne'ho Fontu, 1985; Diskosla'vik, 1984. *Memberships:* SOZA; Slovenskyhudobny Fond; Lita. *Leisure interests:* Music (oriental, reggae, classical and ethnology). *Address:* Stredna 26, 82104 Bratislava, Slovakia.

GRILLO Alex; b. 7 March 1956, Fiume-Veneto, Italy. Musician (vibraphone). *Musical Education:* Conservatory: Percussion, harmony and Orchestration. *Career:* Jazz concert, Radio France, 1982; Nîmes Jazz Festival, 1985; Duo with Steve Lacy, 1987–88; Orchestra De Nove, Paris, New Morning, Angoulême, 1988; First underwater musician with Michel Redolfi, 1989; Nice, 1989; Brisbane, 1991; Lisbon, 1993; Duo with Terry Riley by satellite, 1993; Duo with Barre Philips, 1994. *Recordings:* A Table!, 1985; Neuf Pour Neuf, 1988; Mass For Choir and Organ; Music for theatre and ballet, 1990, 1991; Album: Vibraphone Alone, 1993; Sweet Desdemone (rock jazz oratorio), 1995. *Publication:* C'est Tout Droit (suite for xylophone). *Memberships:* SACEM; SACD; UMJ. *Address:* 182 rue de Charenton, 75012 Paris, France.

GRILLO Carmen; b. 8 Aug. 1954. Musician; Guitar; Vocalist. 1 s. *Musical Education:* Private instruction and self-taught. *Career:* with Bill Champlin, Rita Coolidge, Tower of Power. *Compositions:* One More Day (Chicago 18); Personal Possessions; Who Do You Think You Are; You, Come to a Decision; Soothe You (Tower of Power). *Recordings:* Tower of Power, What Is Hip? -The Tower of Power Anthology, 1999; with Rita Coolidge, Boz Scaggs, Smokey Robinson, Tom Scott and Helen Reddy. *Publications:* Guitar Player Magazine. *Memberships:* AFM; SAG; AFTRA. *Leisure interests:* Tennis; Cooking. *Current Management:* Airtight Management, PO Box 113, Winchester Center, CT 06094, USA.

GRIM Joy Marie Goodman; b. 19 Oct. 1948, Sharon, PA, USA. Country Gospel Vocalist; Musician (woodwind). m. Harold L Grim Jr, 1 s., 1 d. *Education:* BA from Bob Jones University (Early Childhood Education). *Musical Education:* Piano, aged 9; Flute, aged 11; Clarinet, aged 12; Oboe, aged 14; Saxophone, aged 20; Melodica, aged 35. *Career:* Appearances at Govenor's Palace Theatre, Pigeon Forge, TN; Video with James Blackwood and numerous appearances with Blackwood Quartet; Bruce, Community TV broadcast in Bruce, MS. Happy; I Stood Alone; For God So Loved; Mama; Soldiers III, Home From Kosovo. *Recordings:* Ashes To Gold; Praise His Dear Name; Album: Ashes To Gold, 2000. *Honours:* Country Gospel Music Guild Golden Harp Award, Female Horizon Artist, 2001. *Memberships:* Christian Country Music Asscn; Country Gospel Music Guild. *Leisure interests:* Collecting dolls; Driving. *Current Management:* Blackwood Management, 1106 Tramel Rd, Sevierville, TN, 37862, USA. *Internet:* www.joygrim.com.

GRIMES Ged; b. 28 March 1962, Dundee, Scotland. Musician (bass guitar, upright bass, percussion, keyboards, drum programming); Writer. m. Patricia Colette Boyle, 13 July 1991. *Education:* Duncan of Jordanstone College of Art. *Musical Education:* Self-taught. *Career:* Founder member, Danny Wilson, 1983–90; Tours: USA, UK, Japan; Toured with Eddi Reader, 1994–95; Television and radio appearances: Montreux Rock Festival; Top of The Pops; Chart Show; The Late Show; Jools Holland Show; Radio 1 sessions. *Composition:* Soundtrack for computer game Earthworm Jim 3D, 1999. *Recordings:* Hit single: Mary's Prayer, 1987; Albums: with Danny Wilson: Meet Danny Wilson, 1987; Be-Bop Mop-Top, 1988; Sweet Danny Wilson, 1991; with Gary Clark: Ten Short Songs About Love, 1993; ; contributed to: White Lillies Island, Natalie Imbruglia, 2001. *Memberships:* Musicians' Union; PRS; PPL; PAMRA. *Leisure interests:* Food and drink; Travel. *Address:* c/o Jack's Hoose Recording Studios, The Radio Tay Building, 6 N Isla St, Dundee DD3 7JQ, Scotland.

GRIP Erik; b. 2 July 1947, Nykobing, Denmark. Singer; Songwriter; Composer; Musician (guitar, piano). m. Joan Riboe, 2 s., 1 d. *Education:* Cand Arch. *Career:* Danish folk singer; General Secretary, Danish Society for Jazz, Rock and Folk Composers (DJBFA), 1976–86. *Recordings:* 15 albums released. *Address:* Stationsvej 23, 4320 Lejre, Denmark.

GRISOLIA Bill (William Francisco); b. Singer; Songwriter; Musician (Piano); Bandleader; Prod. m. Yolanda Vincenza Foley, 1 s., 1 d. *Education:* University of Valencia, Spain; University of San Francisco, California; University of Michigan at Ann Arbor; Kansas State University, Manhattan,

Kansas. *Career:* Live performances include Opening for Johnny Mathis, 1994, Dionne Warwick, 1996, Burt Bacharach, 1996; Performances in Europe, North America and Mexico, 1976–; Television work includes interviews and performances in Los Angeles; Satellite broadcast on Spanish National television, Un paso por el Tiempo, 1994; Capicua, Valencia, 2000; Radio interviews and performances in USA. *Composition:* Rosarita. *Recordings:* Blue Café, 1999; Wish Upon a Song, 2000. *Honour:* Nominated, Los Angeles Music Award. *Memberships:* National Academy of Recording Arts and Sciences; California Lawyers for the Arts. *Leisure interests:* Travel; Swimming and water sports; Onophile.

GROBER Jacques; b. 11 Feb. 1951, Paris, France. Writer; Composer; Singer. 2 d. *Education:* Baccalaureat, Licence et Maitrise de Russe. *Musical Education:* with Sarah Gorby. *Career:* Singer, traditional Yiddish and Russian songs, and own compositions; Appearances in Paris: Theatre 18, Centre Mandapa, TN Chaillot, 1989; Theatre du Tourtour, 1991–92, 1997–98; Bobigny, 1994; Maison de Radio-France, 1995; Théâtre des Songes, 1999; Other appearances include: Strasbourg, Nancy, Grenoble, Orleáns, Toulouse, Rennes (Festival Tombées de la Nuit); Out of France: Zurich; Brussels; Amsterdam; Germany; Romania. *Recordings:* Le Paon Doré; Autres Chants Yiddish; Voix du Ghetto (collection); Il faut crier toujours jusqu'a la fin du monde, collection. *Membership:* Animateur Chorale Yiddish. *Leisure interests:* Design; Writing. *Address:* 58 rue de L'Egalité, Le Verseau 31, 92130 Issy Les Moulineaux, France.

GROCOTT Stephen; b. 21 Feb. 1953, London, England. Composer; Musician (guitar, mandolin, harmonium, flowerpots); Vocalist; Teacher. *Education:* BA Hons, Literature, Kent University. *Musical Education:* Traditional music, Ireland; Carl Orff Society, England. *Career:* Television and radio appearances with: The Wise Monkeys, 1990; The Drones, BBC1, 1991; Ch4, Radio 4 and 5, 1995; The Toy Symphony premiered by The Drones at the Purcell Rooms and Norwich Festival. *Compositions:* Playing With Fire (music for bonfire, pyrotechnics, quartet), 1991; The Toy Symphony (music for toys and instruments) 1992. *Recordings:* Albums: with The Drones: The Drones, 1992; Giant Bonsai, 1994; with Rory McLeod: Angry Love, 1996; Footsteps and Heartbeats, 1996. *Memberships:* PRS (associate); Musicians' Union; Carl Orff Society. *Leisure interests:* Thinking; Gardening. *Current Management:* The Shed Studios.

GROHL Dave; b. 14 Jan. 1969. Musician (drums). *Career:* Member, Dave Bramage Band; Scream; Nirvana, 1990–94; World-wide appearances include: European tour with Sonic Youth, 1991; Reading Festivals, 1991, 1992; Transmusicales Festival, Rennes, France, 1991; Benefit concert, Washington State Music Coalition, 1992; Benefit concert, Bosnian Women's group, San Francisco, 1993; Member, Foo Fighters, 1994–; Concerts include Reading Festival, 1995. *Recordings:* Albums: with Nirvana: Nevermind (No. 1, USA), 1991; Incesticide, 1993; In Utero (No. 1, UK and US), 1993; Unplugged In New York, 1994; From the Muddy Banks, 1996; Hormoaning, 1999; with Foo Fighters: Foo Fighters, 1995; Colour and Shape, 1997; There Is Nothing Left to Lose, 1999; Singles: with Nirvana: Smells Like Teen Spirit, 1991; Come As You Are, 1992; Lithium, 1992; In Bloom, 1992; Oh, The Guilt, 1993; Heart-Shaped Box, 1993; All Apologies, 1993; Contribution to The Beavis and Butthead Experience album, 1993; with Foo Fighters: This Is A Call, 1995; I'll Stick Around, 1995; For All the Cows, 1996; Big Me, 1996; Monkey Wrench, 1997; Everlong, 1998; My Hero, 1998; Learn to Fly, 1999; Breakout, 2000; Next Year, 2000. *Honours:* 2 MTV Music Video Awards, Smells Like Teen Spirit, 1992; BRIT Award, Best International Newcomer, with Nirvana, 1993; BRIT Award Nomination, Best International Act, Best International Newcomers, with Foo Fighters, 1995; Grammy Award, Rock Album, 2001. *Address:* c/o Gold Mountain Entertainment, Suite 450, 3575 Cahunega Blvd W, Los Angeles, CA 90068, USA.

GROOM Don; b. 10 Nov. 1939, Walthamstow, London, England. Session Musician (drums). m. Lorna Heather, 16 Nov. 1963, 1 s., 2 d. *Musical Education:* Music theory, Royal Academy of Music; Drum tuition, Max Abrams, Frank King; Arranging, Berklee School of Music, Boston. *Career:* Professional musician, 1960–; Tours in Germany including Hamburg's Top Ten Club and Kaiser Keller; Drummer with: Mike Berry and the Outlaws, 1962; John Leyton; The Crickets, including tours with Bobby Vee, 1962; The Beatles, 2 tours, 1963–64; Rolling Stones tours, 1963–64; Backed Franki Valli and Four Seasons, English tour, 1964; Backed Jet Harris, NME Poll Winners Concert, Wembley. *Recordings:* with Mike Berry: Don't You Think It's Time; with John Leyton: Son This Is She; Two Sides of John Leyton (album), 1962; with Pinkerton's Assorted Colours: Mirror Mirror. *Leisure interests:* Aviation; Sport.

GROSZ Martin Oliver; b. 28 Feb. 1930, Berlin, Germany. Musician (guitar). m. Rachel Whelan, 1956, 2 s. *Education:* 2 years at college. *Musical Education:* Self-taught. *Career:* Professional musician, 1948–; Recorded under own name in 1950s; Lived in Chicago, 1954–75; Performed with: Village Stompers; Dukes of Dixieland; Bandleader, Sounds of Swing, for National public television; New York Jazz repertory

group, Soprano Summit, 1975–76. *Recordings:* Hooray For Bix, Riverside '57, 1975; Let Your Fingers Do The Walking (Guitar Duets), 1978; Swing It; Unsaturated Fats. *Publications:* Writer on Jazz Guitars and Frank Teschemacher for Time/Life magazines. *Honour:* Winner, Jazzology Guitar Poll, 1986. *Membership:* Musicians Union, New York. *Leisure interests:* Designing album and CD covers; Writing arrangements. *Current Management:* Popinjay Productions, 46 Upper Ritie St, Piermont, NY 10968, USA.

GRUNTZ George; b. 24 June 1932, Basel, Switzerland. Musician; Composer; Bandleader. *Education:* Studies, Basel, Zurich. *Career:* Member, European All-Star Band, Newport International Band, 1958; Appearances at Most Major Jazz Festivals, including: Newport/Kool/JVC, 1958, 1969, 1982, 1984, 1989, 1994, Berlin, Warsaw, Monterey, 1967, 1977, Antibes, Montreux, Pori, Northsea; Several radio and television productions; Accompanied Many US Top Jazz Artists on European Tours; Chief Musical Director, Zurich State Theatre (Schauspielhaus), 1971–87; Program Director, Producer, Berlin Jazz Festival, 1972–94. *Compositions include:* Spanish Castles; Capricci Cavallereschi; Spring Song; Perambulation I and II; Concerto Sequenzes; Steppenwolf Concorde Suite; Thundermove, for large orchestra; Cosmopolitan Greetings, jazz opera commissioned by Hamburg State Opera, 1988. *Honours:* Several First Prizes in Many Jazz Festivals; First Prize, Best Performance Award, Japanese Music Critics Asscn, 1988; German Legion of Honour (Bundessverkienstkreut, klasse 1), 1997. *Current Management:* Euromusic, Therwil, Switzerland. *Address:* Weiherweg 1, 4123 Allschwil, Switzerland. *Internet:* www.eurojazz.ch.

GRUSIN Dave; b. 26 June 1934, Littleton, Colorado, USA. Composer; Record Prod.; Musician (piano, keyboards). *Education:* University of Colorado. *Career:* Director of Music, Andy Williams Show, 1959–66; As pianist, played with Art Pepper; Spike Robinson; Terry Gibbs; Benny Goodman; Thad Jones; Carmen McRae; Sarah Vaughan; Arranger for: Phoebe Snow; Peggy Lee; Barbra Streisand; Patti Austin; The Byrds; Grover Washington Jr; Al Jarreau; Donna Summer; Co-founder, owner, GRP Records, with Larry Rosen, 1976–; Client roster includes: Grover Washington Jr, Dizzy Gillespie, Lee Ritenour; ChickCorea; Dianne Schuur; Dave Valentin; Gary Burton; Michael Brecker; Steve Gadd; David Benoit; Don Grusin; Solo pianist, also performs with brother Don Grusin, and jazz-fusion septet NY-LA Dream Band. *Compositions:* For numerous films including: Three Days of The Condor; The Graduate; Heaven Can Wait; On Golden Pond; Tootsie; Reds; The Little Drummer Girl; The Goonies; The Milago Beanfield War; The Fabulous Baker Boys; Also television themes: St Elsewhere; Roots; Numerous television films. *Recordings:* Solo albums: Candy, 1961; The Many Moods of Dave Grusin, 1962; Kaleidoscope, 1964; Discovered Again, 1976; One of a Kind, 1977; Dave Grusin and the GRP All-Stars, 1980; Out of The Shadows, 1982; Mountain Dance, 1983; The NY-LA Dream Band, 1988; Cinemagic, 1987; One of a Kind, 1988; Migration, 1989; Havana, 1990; The Dave Grusin Collection, 1991; The Gershwin Collection, 1992; Homage To Duke, 1993; The Orchestral Album, 1994; Two for the Road, 1996; Presents West Side Story, 1997; Two Worlds, 2000; with Lee Ritenour: Harlequin, 1984; with Don Grusin: Sticks and Stones, 1988; Also recorded with Billy Joel; Paul Simon; Gerry Mulligan. *Honours:* Academy Award, Original Score, The Milagro Beanfield War, 1988; 3 Academy Award Nominations. *Address:* c/o GRP Records, 555 W 57th St, New York, NY 10019, USA.

GRUZ Sergio; b. 17 Feb. 1968, Buenos Aires, Argentina. Musician (piano); Composer. *Education:* University of Buenos Aires. *Musical Education:* Jazz music and classical. *Career:* Festival Des Allumées, 1992; Festivals in France; European Jazz Competition with Sergio Gruz Trio, Germany; Concours National de Jazz à la Défense, Paris; Belgian Jazz Festival. *Recordings:* Bernardo Baraj Quintet, Argentina, 1992; Tierra del Fuego, France, 1994; Sergio Gruz Trio, France, 1995; Misanthrope, France, 1997; Point de vue, Sergio Gruz Quintet, 1998. *Address:* 12 rue du Plateau, 75019 Paris, France.

GRYTT Kajsa; b. 20 June 1961, Stockholm, Sweden. Singer; Songwriter; Musician (Guitar). 1 s. *Career:* Leader, Tant Strul, punk group. *Compositions:* Amason, Dunkar varmt, Sucka Migren, Igen, Vand Digbort, Han Sager, Om Du Kunde Semig, Som Om Himlen; Revolution; Visa Horman Alskar. *Recordings:* Tant Strul; Amason; Ojag Onskar Dig; Historier Fran En Vag; Den Andra Varuden, Kajsa Grytt, Revolution. *Publications:* Amason, 1983; Dunkar Varmt, 1983; Historier Fran En Vag, 1986; Revolution, 1994. *Honours:* Skap Stipendie, 1981; Nominated to Swedish Grammy, 1991. *Memberships:* SKAP; Svenska Musiker Föbundet. *Current Management:* Warner Chappell.

GUÉRAULT Stéphane; b. 19 Dec. 1936, Reims, France. Musician (clarinet, saxophone); Bandleader. m. Isabelle Escoffier, 19 July 1985, 2 d. *Education:* University graduate, Law. *Musical Education:* Studies with Madame Dussequier. *Career:* Bandleader; Sideman with: Bill Coleman; Wild Bill Davis; Numerous concerts throughout France; Festival appearances include: Lille; Nice; Marciac. *Recordings:* with Wild Bill

Davis; Bill Coleman; Marc Fosset. *Honour:* Sidney Bechet Award, French Musical Academy, 1993. *Membership:* SACEM. *Leisure interest:* Antique cars. *Address:* 20 rue Murillo, 75008 Paris, France.

GULBRANDSSEN Arve; b. 25 Sept. 1972, Namsois, Norway. Musician (drums). *Education:* University, 3 years. *Musical Education:* 2 years, University of Trondheim. *Career:* Played various jazz bands like: Fotveita; Smaagnagerne; Joined Hedge Hog, 1993; Toured Europe, 1994, 1995. *Recordings:* Primal Gutter, 1993; Mercury Red, 1994; Mindless, 1994; The Healing EP; Thorn Cord Wonder, 1995; Party Terror Vol. 2, 1996. *Membership:* Norwegian Asscn of Musicians.

GULLEY J K (John Kenneth); b. 11 Oct. 1954, Toronto, Ontario, Canada. Singer; Songwriter; Prod.; Musician (guitar). m. Wilma Schmidt, 1 May 1987, 2 s., 3 d. *Musical Education:* Self-taught. *Career:* 15 charted singles; Tours across Canada; USA; Europe; Scandinavia; with Glen Campbell; Billie Jo Spears; Freddie Hart; Michelle Wright; Television appearances: Ronnie Prophet Show, CTV; John Cameron, CBC; Global Easy Country, NCN; CMT Video and Songwriters Café Special. *Recordings:* Over 100 songs recorded and released, including, Dusty Road, 1978; Under Cover, 1987; Blue Jeans Boy, 1990; If She Only Knew Me, 1995. *Honours:* Juno Nomination, Country Duo of The Year, 1992; 5 Nominations, Producer of the Year, CCM; RPM Big Country Awards; Winner, Vista Rising Star Award, CCMA, 1986; SOCAN Song of the Year Award, Blue Jeans Boy, 1990. *Memberships:* CCMA; AFofM; CARAS. *Leisure interest:* Golf. *Current Management:* Steve Thompson, Backstage Productions. *Address:* #11–333 Sunnidale Rd, Barrie, ON L4N 6H5, Canada.

GULLIN Peter; b. 12 April 1959, Milani, Italy. Composer; Musician (Saxophone). *Education:* Music Conservatory of Stockholm. *Career:* Debut as Saxophonist and Composer; Written Classical Music and Big Band Stuff; Television Program, Sologram; Played In Festival Classic; Own Music With String Quartet, New Trio Forms. *Compositions:* Unital, 1986; Suite Per Chitarra e Quintetto a Fiati, 1986; Tokdårarnas Paradis, 1988; Tresma Midsummer Sagor, 1988. *Recordings:* CDs, Unita With Jazz Composers Orchestra; Ved Profetens Shaegg; Tenderness; Transformed Evergreen; Untold Story. *Publication:* Sunnanvind i Andevärlden, Collection of Short Fantasy Tales. *Honours:* Golden Record Award, 1992. *Leisure interests:* Chess; Aquarium; Nature; Books. *Address:* Jenny Linds Vag 24, 75650 Uppsala, Sweden.

GUMBLEY Christopher James; b. 22 May 1958. Musician (clarinet, saxophones, piano). 1 s. *Musical Education:* Huddersfield School of Music, 1976–79. *Career:* Classical and jazz music; Work includes television, radio, session work, classical recitals, theatre work, international exhibitions; Tours of Europe, Caribbean; Member, Saxtet, resident ensemble at Birmingham Conservatoire; Appeared at Edinburgh Festival; Television and radio: BBC Children In Need; Pebble Mill; Loose Ends, BBC Radio 4; Founded Gumbles Jazz Club, Stafford; Established annual jazz course, Stoke-on-Trent; Music workshops nationwide; Recently worked with the Pasadena Roof Orchestra in Britain, Germany and Abu Dhabi and on the touring Joseph and His Amazing Technicolour Dreamcoat show; Professor of Saxophone, Birmingham Conservatoire. *Recordings:* with Saxtet: Safer Sax. *Publications:* Cops Caps and Cadillacs (5 Jazz-rock pieces for clarinet or saxophone and piano); Game Show Addicts, duets. *Honours:* BA Hons, Music; LTCL (Clarinet Performers). *Membership:* Musicians' Union. *Leisure interests:* Squash; Aerobics; Badminton; Gardening; Composing. *Address:* 53 Peel Terrace, Stafford ST16 3HE, England.

GUNDECHA Ramakant; b. 24 Nov. 1962, Vijrin, MP, India. Musician. m. Renu Ramakant, 1 s. *Education:* MA, Music; MCom. *Career:* Performed Dhrupad Music (vocal) with brother, Umakant, all major festival of India and in Germany, Switzerland, England, France, USA, Norway and Hong Kong. *Honours:* Ustad Allauddin Khan Fellowship, 1993; Sanskriti Award, 1994. *Membership:* Multi Arts Complex, Bharat Bhavan, Bhopal, MP, India. *Address:* Sundaram, 15 Professor Colony Bhopal 462002, Madhya Pradesh, India.

GUNDECHA Umakant; b. 8 May 1959, Vijrin, MP, India. Musician. m. Aruna Umakant, 1 s., 1 d. *Education:* MA, Music; MA, Economics. *Career:* Performed Dhrupad Music (vocal) with brother, Ramakant, all major festivals of India and in Germany, Switzerland, England, France, USA, Norway and Hong Kong. *Honours:* Ustad Allauddin Khan Fellowship, 1993; Sanskriti Award, 1994. *Membership:* Multi Arts Complex, Bharat, Bhavan, Bhopal, MP, India. *Address:* Sundaram, 15 Professor Colony Bhopal, 462002, Madhya Pradesh, India.

GUNN Andrew David; b. 13 Dec. 1974, Paisley, Scotland. Musician (guitar); Songwriter. *Education:* Charleston Academy, Inverness. *Musical Education:* Mainly self-taught. *Career:* Appeared at Pointblank Blues Festival, The Borderline Club, London, 1992; Eddi Reader's Musicality TV show, No Stilletoes, on BBC Radio 1, 2 and 4, Clyde and Forth Radio; Numerous concerts in Scotland. *Compositions:* Wrote and recorded album, Shades of Blue, Jumpin' The Gunn, 1992; Many blues-based songs.

Memberships: PRS; MCPS; Musicians' Union. *Leisure interest:* Swimming. *Address:* 16A Pict Ave, Inverness IV3 6LX, Scotland.

GUO Wenjing; b. 1 Feb. 1956, Chongqing, China. Composer. 1 d. *Education:* Chongqing Song and Dance Ensemble, 1970–77; Graduated, Composition, Central Conservatory of Music, 1983. *Career:* Dean and Professor, Composition Department, Central Conservatory of Music, Beijing; Works performed at major festivals in Europe; Works performed by London Sinfonietta, New York Music Consort, Lincoln Center Chamber Music Society, Hong Kong Chinese Orchestra; Visiting Scholar, Asian Cultural Council, USA; Lectured at Swedish Royal Institute of Music, University of Cincinnati, Manhattan School of Music; Appeared in film Broked Silence; Numerous appearances on TV talk shows. *Compositions:* Wolf Cub Village, chamber opera, 1994; Night Bouquet, chamber opera, 1998. *Leisure interests:* Writing columns for newspapers; Watching football. *Address:* Central Conservatory of Music, 43 Baojia St, Beijing 100031, China.

GURD Geoffrey Robert; b. 24 Feb. 1951, Nottingham, England. Composer; Songwriter; Musician (guitar, keyboards). *Education:* Manchester University. *Musical Education:* Self-taught; Film-scoring classes, UCLA. *Career:* Guitarist, singer with Crystal, The Sadista Sisters, 1975–79; Musical Director, acts including: The Flirtations, Ritz, Love Bandit; Member, The Twentieth Century Saints, 1979–81; Member, The Flying Fratellinis, 1981–82; Chief Sound Engineer, Red Shop Studios, London, 1982–85; Member, Design For Living, 1985–86; Started own production company, 1986; Formed own publishing company, De Mix Music, 1989; Lived in Los Angeles, 1991–93; Started own record label, DiscoVery, 1994. *Compositions:* As producer: Hold On, Claudia, 1985; Library music album, music for Corporate videos, commercials including: British Airways; Legal and General; Export Financing, 1986; Writer, producer for artists including: Freddie McGregor, Lisa Stansfield, June Montana, 1986–89; Love Is A House, Force MDs, 1987; Better Be Good Tonight, Nick Kamen, 1988; Music for APV Films, Artworks, ITV; Music for Eye To Eye, BBC TV; Songs for Gina Foster, Chyna, 1989–91; Don't Be A Stranger, Dina Carroll, for So Close album, 1993. *Recordings include:* Travels Within, Richmond Gurd (duo), 1994. *Honours:* Quadruple Platinum disc, Don't Be A Stranger. *Memberships:* BASCA; PRS; Musicians' Union; BMI. *Leisure interests:* Travel; Writing; Learning languages. *Current Management:* De Mix Music Ltd. *Address:* De Mix Music Ltd, PO Box 5705, London W10 6WG, England.

GURTU Trilok; b. 30 Oct. 1951, Bombay (Mumbai), India. Vocalist; Musician (percussion); Composer; Prod. *Career:* Son of Indian classical singer, Shobha Gurtu; Father also well-known as sitar player; Played with prominent jazz musicians for many years including: John McLaughlin; Ralph Towner; Pat Metheny; Larry Coryell; Jan Garbarek; Bill Evans; Nana Vasconcelos; Joe Zawinul; Member: Don Cherry's band, 1976–78; Oregon (acoustic jazz-fusion group), 1984–88; Began making solo albums, late 1980s; More recently moved towards a fusion between Indian and African music with African Fantasy and the Beat of Love in collaboration with musicians such as: Oumou Sangare; Angelique Kidjo; Salif Keita; Zap Mama's Sabine Kabongo. *Recordings:* Albums include: Usfret, 1987; Living Magic, Similado, 1990; Crazy Saints, 1993; Believe, Bad Habits Die Hard, 1995; Glimpse, 1997; Kathak, 1998; African Fantasy, 2000; The Beat of Love, 2001; with Oregon: Ecotopia, 1987; 45th Parallel, 1988; features on: End of August, Philip Catherine, 1982; Song For Everyone, Lakshminarayana Shankar, 1984; Song For Everyone, Jan Garbarek 1985; My People, Joe Zawinul, 1992; Somethin' Else, Jack Bruce, 1993; Promise, John McLaughlin, 1995; Visible World, Jan Garbarek, 1995; Rythmagick, Ayib Dieng/Bill Laswell, 1997; O Sol De Oslo, Gilberto Gil, 1998; Tala Matrix, Tabla Beat Science, 2000; Crossing Borders, Larry Coryell, 2001. *Honours:* BBC Radio 3 Award for World Music, Asia/Pacific nominee, Beat of Love, 2002.

GURU (Keith Elam), (Bald Head Slick); b. Boston, Massachusetts, USA. Rapper; Prod. *Career:* Name stands for Gifted Unlimited Rhymes Universal; Formed Gang Starr with production partner DJ Premier, 1989; Debut album No More Mr Nice Guy released on Wild Pitch Records; Started Jazzmatazz, solo project with guest vocalists and musicians, 1993; Collaborations include: Ronny Jordan; Dee C Lee; Bilal; Craig David; Bahamadia; N'Dea Davenport; Angie Stone; Chaka Khan; Macy Gray. *Recordings:* Albums: with Gang Starr: No More Mr Nice Guy, 1989; Step In The Arena, 1990; Daily Operation, 1992; Hard To Earn, 1994; Moment of Truth, 1998; solo: Jazzmatazz Vol. 1, 1993; Jazzmatazz Vol. 2, 1995; Streetsoul – Jazzmatazz Vol. 3, 2001; Singles: with Gang Starr: Jazz Thing, 1990; Lovesick, 1991; Code To The Street EP, 1994; You Know My Steez, 1997; solo: Trust Me (with N'Dea Davenport), No Time To Play (with Dee C Lee), 1993; Watch What You Say (with Chaka Khan), Feel The Music, 1995; Livin' In This World/Lifesaver, 1996; Keep Your Worries (with Angie Stone), 2000; Supa Love (with Kelis)/Certified (with Bilal), 2001. *Address:* c/o Virgin Records, 304 Park Ave S, New York, USA.

GUSEV Nickolai; b. 12 May 1957, St Petersburg, Russia. Composer; Songwriter; Lyrics Author; Musician (Keyboards). m. Marina Guseva, 31 May 1987, 2 d. *Education:* St Petersburg Electrical Engineering Institute; History of Philosophy, St Petersburg University; Jazz Piano, Music College; Composition, St Petersburg, ongoing. *Career:* Founder and Member, alternative bands, Strannye Igry and Avia; Russian tours, international tours, with Avia; Toured UK, Germany, Netherlands, Italy, France, Belgium, Finland, 1988–93; Author, Promotional spots for FM Radio and for TV; Music for films. *Compositions:* I Don't Like You, with Avia; St Petersburg region anthem, 1997. *Recordings:* Albums with Strannye Igry: Red Wine, 1984; Keep Your Eyes Open, 1986; With Avia: Zudov, 1987; Avia for Everybody, 1989; Horray!, 1991; The Songs About Love and Nature, 1994; Solo: Zdanov, soundtrack, 1995; No Mistakes!, 1997. *Honours:* Best Keyboard Player, St Petersburg Open Rock Festivals, 1985, 1987, 1988, 1990, 1992. *Memberships:* Russian Authors Asscn; Russian Journalists Society. *Leisure interests:* Beer; Books; Bed. *Address:* Moskovsky Prospekt 204, F2, 196135 St Petesburg, Russia.

GUTHRIE Arlo; b. 10 July 1947, Coney Island, New York, USA. Folk Singer; Songwriter. *Career:* Appearances on folk circuit include Newport Folk Festival, 1967. *Compositions:* Alice's Restaurant Massacre; Highway In The Wind; Presidential Rag; Children of Abraham. *Recordings:* Albums: Alice's Restaurant, 1967; Arlo, 1968; Running Down The Road, 1969; Alice's Restaurant (soundtrack), 1969; Washington County, 1970; Hobo's Lullaby, 1972; Last of The Brooklyn Cowboys, 1973; Arlo Guthrie, 1974; Together In Concert (with Pete Seeger), 1975; Amigo, 1976; Outlasting The Blues, 1979; Power of Love, 1981; Someday, 1986; Son of the Wind, 1992; Arlo Guthrie/Pete Seeger, More Together Again, 1994; Alice's Restaurant The Massacre Revisited, 1995; Mystic Journey, 1996; Appears on: The Girls Won't Leave The Boys Alone, Cherish The Ladies, 2001. *Address:* c/o Rising Son Records, PO Box 657, Housatonic, MA 01236, USA.

GUTHRIE Colin Thomas; b. 16 April 1962, Liverpool, England. Musician (guitar). 1 d. *Musical Education:* Self-taught. *Career:* Semi-professional melodic rock guitarist; Toured Britain with various bands including Gran Torino; Stadium; Cherokee. *Compositions:* Co-writer, 3 tracks: Take My Heart Away; Somewhere; Out of The Fire, from album Customized, Gran Torino, 1988; Composer, jingles for local independent radio station. *Leisure interests:* Classical music; Interest in phenomena and the unexplained. *Address:* 55 Arley Dr., Hough Green, Widnes, Cheshire WA8 9XS, England.

GUTHRIE Robin; b. 4 Jan. 1962, Grangemouth, Scotland. Musician (guitar, keyboards); Prod. m. 1 d. (with Elizabeth Fraser). *Career:* Member, Cocteau Twins, 1980–97; Member, Violet Indiana, 1999–; Worked with 4AD collective This Mortal Coil; Collaboration with pianist Harold Budd; Producer for numerous indie acts including Lush, Ian McCulloch, Felt, Guy Chadwick; Established own label Bella Union; Contributed with band to Found Sound by Spooky, 1996. *Recordings:* with Cocteau Twins: Singles: Lullabies, 1982; Peppermint Pig, 1983; Sunburst and Snowblind, 1983; Pearly Dewdrops' Drops, 1984; Aikea-Guinea, 1985; Tiny Dynamine, 1985; Echoes in a Shallow Bay, 1985; Love's Easy Tears, 1986; Iceblink Luck, 1990; Evangeline, 1993; Frosty the Snowman, 1993; Bluebeard, 1994; Twinlights, 1995; Otherness, 1995; Tishbite, 1996; Violaine, 1996; Song to the Siren, with This Mortal Coil, 1983; Albums: Garlands, 1982; Head Over Heels, 1983; Treasure, 1984; The Pink Opaque, 1985; Victorialand, 1986; The Moon and the Melodies, with

Harold Budd, 1986; Blue Bell Knoll, 1988; Heaven or Las Vegas, 1990; Four Calendar Café, 1993; Milk and Kisses, 1996; The BBC Sessions, 1999; Stars and Topsoil (compilation), 2000; Solo album: Drifting, 1999; with Violet Indiana: Singles: Choke EP, 2000; Special EP, 2001; Killer Eyes, 2001; Album: Roulette, 2001.

GUTIERREZ Ivan; b. 17 May 1967, New York, USA. Songwriter; Singer; Guitarist. *Education:* BA, Mathematics, BA, Philosophy, SUNY, Binghamton; MA, Philosophy, University of Wisconsin, Madison. *Musical Education:* Self-taught guitar; 4 semesters of music theory, SUNY, Binghamton. *Career:* Extensive stage performances; TV and radio appearances in Czech Republic and Slovakia, 1993–; Sporadic stage performances in New York, Wisconsin, Minnesota, USA. *Compositions:* America; Jaruska; La Violencia; Siendo fuego. *Recordings:* Tres; Vera Bila and Kale, Guest Guitar. *Leisure interests:* Languages; Literature. *Address:* Zuzana Hanousková, Jugoslavskych Partyzanu 36, 160 00 Prague 6, Czech Republic.

GUTJAHR Michael; b. Mühlacker, Germany. Man.; Singer; Songwriter. m. Andrea Gutjahr, 27 April 1990, 1 s. *Education:* Management, CaroCord Gimbtt Music Company. *Musical Education:* with Stromberger (music group); Composing and Text. *Career:* ZDF Volkstumliche Hitparade; ARD Schlagerparade der Volksmusik; MDR, SWF television shows and radio interviews. *Compositions include:* As lyricist and composer: Jeden Tag Nur Sonnenschein; Das Ist Unser Land; Menschen Helfen Menschen; Frage Nicht; Flieg Vogel Flieg. *Recordings:* Mitdem Glück Per Du, Stromberger; 5 albums with Stromberger and others. *Honours:* SDR Golden 7, 1993. *Memberships:* GEMA; IFPI; GVL. *Leisure interests:* Writing; Nature. *Current Management:* CaroCord Gmbh, Music Company. *Address:* CaroCord Gmbh, Aischbühlstr 28, 75443 Ötisheim, Germany.

GUY Buddy (George); b. 30 July 1936, Lettsworth, Louisiana, USA. Blues Musician (guitar). *Career:* Played with artists including Slim Harpo; Lightnin' Slim; Member, Rufus Foreman Band; Solo artiste; Member, houseband, Chess Records, including sessions with Muddy Waters; Howlin' Wolf; Musical partnership with Junior Wells; Performances include: Support to Rolling Stones, tour, 1970; Guest, Eric Clapton's Blues Night, Royal Albert Hall, London, 1990. *Recordings:* Albums: Blues From Big Bill's Copa Cobana, 1963; A Man and The Blues, 1968; This Is Buddy Guy, 1968; Hold That Plane!, 1972; I Was Walking Through The Woods, 1974; Hot and Cool, 1978; Got To Use Your House, 1979; Dollar Done Fell, 1980; DJ Play My Blues, 1982; The Original Blues Brothers – Live, 1983; Ten Blue Fingers, 1985; Live At The Checkerboard, Chicago, 1979, 1988; Breaking Out, 1988; Damn Right I Got The Blues (with Eric Clapton, Jeff Beck, Mark Knopfler), 1991; My Time After Awhile, 1992; Feels Like Rain, 1993; American Bandstand, Vol. 2, 1993; Slippin' In, 1994; I Cry, 1995; Live! The Real Deal, 1996; As Good As It Gets, 1998; Heavy Love, 1998; Last Time Around, 1998; The Real Blues, 1999; 20th Century Masters – The Millennium Collection, 2000; with Junior Wells: Buddy and The Juniors, 1970; Buddy Guy and Junior Wells Play The Blues, 1972; Drinkin' TNT and Smokin' Dynamite, 1982; Alone and Acoustic, 1991; Alive In Montreux, 1992; Various compilations; Singles include: First Time I Met The Blues; Stone Crazy; Contributions to Junior Wells: Hoodoo Man Blues; It's My Life Baby. *Current Management:* The Cameron Organisation Inc, 2001 W Magnolia Blvd, Suite E, Burbank, CA 91506–1704, USA.

H

HACKETT Eric Dexter; b. 13 April 1956, Los Angeles, USA. Musician (keyboards). *Musical Education:* BMus, University of South California, 1977. *Career:* Keyboard player with Diana Ross and the Supremes; Talk Back, Forward Motion; Scheme Payne; The Temptations; The Four Tops; Musical Director, Curtis Mayfield, 1977–83; President, Can't Hack It Music, 1978-. *Memberships:* NARAS; AFofM.

HACKETT Steve; b. 12 Feb. 1950, London, England. Musician (guitar). *Career:* Member, Quiet World; Genesis, 1971–77; Concerts include: Reading Festivals, 1971–73; Regular UK and US tours, 1973–; Lamb World tour, 1974; Film premiere, Genesis In Concert (attended by Princess Anne), 1977; Solo artiste, 1975–; Member, GTR, 1986. *Recordings:* Albums: with Genesis: Nursery Cryme, 1971; Foxtrot, 1972; Genesis Live, 1973; Selling England By The Pound, 1973; The Lamb Lies Down On Broadway, 1974; A Trick of The Tail, 1976; Wind and Wuthering, 1977; Seconds Out, 1977; Archive Vol. 1: 1967–75, 1999; Archive Vol. 2 1976–92, 2001; Solo albums: Voyage of The Acolyte; Please Don't Touch; Spectral Mornings; Defector; Cured; Highly Strung; Bay of Kings; Till We Have Faces; Blues With A Feeling; Momentum, 1988; Time Lapse, 1992; Guitar Noir, 1993; There are Many Sides to the Night, 1995; Genesis Revisited, 1996; A Midsummer Nights Dream, 1997; Tokyo Tapes, 1999; Darktown, 1999; Sketches of Satie, 2000; Feedback 86, 2001; Live Archive, 2001; with GTR: GTR, 1986. *Honour:* Ivor Novello Award, 1979. *Current Management:* Kudos Music, Crown Studios, 16–18 Crown Rd, Twickenham, Middlesex TW1 3EE, England.

HADDAWAY Nester Alexander; b. Tobago. Singer; Dancer. *Career:* Founder, group Elegato, Germany; Solo singer, dance music, 1992-. *Recordings:* Albums: Haddaway – The Album, 1993; The Drive, 1995; Let's Do It Now, 1999; Singles: What Is Love?, 1993; I Miss You, 1994; Rock My Heart, 1994; Stir It Up, 1994; What Is Love?, 1999; All The Best (compilation), 2001. *Address:* c/o Coconut Records, Nachtigalenweg 34, 53758 Hennef, Germany.

HADJINEOPHYTOU George Constantinou; b. 28 Oct. 1965, London, England. Composer; Musician (bouzouki, saz, lyra). m. Eleni, 23 Oct. 1994. *Musical Education:* GCE O Level, Grade 5 Theory. *Career:* International Eisteddfod (Wales); BBC World Service, London Greek Radio; Mad About Music, BBC TV. *Recordings:* Psyche and Eros (animation), Channel 4; Grandmother's Hands (short film for television). *Honour:* Drama Film Festival (Greece). *Memberships:* PRS; Musicians' Union; MCPS; PRC. *Leisure interests:* Greek folk dancing; Cooking. *Address:* 41 Burlington Rise, East Barnet, Hertfordshire EN4 8NH, England.

HADJOPOULOS Sue; b. 26 June 1953, New York, USA. Musician (percussion); Vocalist. *Education:* BA, Anthropology, Columbia University, 1975. *Musical Education:* Mannes College of Music. *Career:* Professional percussionist, 1970–; Founder member, female salsa group Latin Fever; Tours include: World tours with Joe Jackson, 1982–83, 1991–; World tour with Simple Minds, 1985–86; True Colors tour with Cyndi Lauper; Support tours with The Who; The Rolling Stones; Performed and recorded as freelance musician with: Laurie Anderson; Mick Jones; Michael Monroe; Laura Nyro; Teena Marie; Percussionist for numerous commercials. *Recordings:* with Joe Jackson: Night and Day, 1982; Mike's Murder (soundtrack), 1983; Live 1980–86, 1988; Blaze of Glory, 1989; Laughter and Lust, 1991; Heaven and Hell, 1997; Night and Day II, 2000; with Simple Minds: Once Upon A Time, 1985; Live In The City of Light, 1987; also appears on: Strange Angels, Laurie Anderson, 1989; David Byrne, David Byrne, 1994; Factory Showroom, They Might Be Giants, 1996. *Publications:* One of Top Latin Percussionists, Modern Drummer Magazine Poll, 1984; Platinum discs with Joe Jackson, Simple Minds. *Memberships:* AFTRA; ASCAP; NARAS; AFofM; Percussive Arts Society; Recording Musicians Asscn.

HADLEY Tony (Anthony); b. 2 June 1960, Islington, London, England. Singer. *Career:* Member, Spandau Ballet, 1979–90; Performances include: Royal Albert Hall, 1983; Royal Festival Hall, 1983; Wembley Arena, 1984; Live Aid, Wembley, 1985. *Recordings:* Singles include: To Cut A Long Story Short, 1980; The Freeze, 1981; Musclebound, 1981; Chant No. 1 (I Don't Need This Pressure On), 1981; Instinction, 1982; Lifeline, 1982; Communication, 1983; True (No. 1, UK), 1983; Gold, 1984; Only When You Leave, 1984; I'll Fly For You, 1984; Highly Strung, 1984; Round and Round, 1984; Solo: Lost In Your Love, 1992; For Your Blue Eyes Only, 1992; The Game of Love, 1992; Absolution, 1993; Build Me Up, from the film When Saturday Comes, 1996; Save a Prayer, 1998; Dance with Me, 1998; Obsession (Live), 2000; Dance With Me, 2001; with Erikah Karst, Separate Lies, 1997; with Tin Tin Out, Dance with Me, 1997; Albums: Journey To Glory, 1981; Diamond, 1982; True, 1983; Parade, 1984; The

Singles Collection, 1985; Through The Barricades, 1986; Heart Like A Sky, 1989; The Best of Spandau Ballet, 1991; Solo album: Tony Hadley, 1997; Contributor, Do They Know It's Christmas?, Band Aid, 1984. *Honours include:* BRIT Awards, Sony Trophy For Technical Excellence, 1984.

HADWEN Julie; b. 4 Jan. 1965, Reading, Berkshire, England. Singer; Songwriter; Musician (piano, guitar). *Musical Education:* Private studies, piano, guitar, classical, blues, jazz. *Career:* Supported Kane Gang on tour, 1984; Montreux Jazz Festival, 1985; British Big Sound Authority tour, 1985; Television appearances include: The Tube; Old Grey Whistle Test; Top of The Pops; Wogan; Oxford Road Show; Live radio sessions for Bruno Brookes, Janice Long. *Recordings:* Albums: An Inward Revolution; Sanctuary; Singles: This House Is Where Your Love Stands; Bad Town; Moving Heaven and Earth; Don't Let Our Love Start A War. *Membership:* Musicians' Union. *Leisure interests:* Live music; Psychology; Film; Theatre; Comedy. *Address:* 72 Makepeace Ave, Highgate, London N6 6HB, England.

HADZO, (Davor Kodzoman); b. 27 Jan. 1967, Zagreb, Croatia. Musician (guitar, bass guitar); Songwriter; Music Writer; Singer. *Education:* Electrical Engineer. *Musical Education:* Self-taught Guitar and Bass Guitar. *Career:* Underground out of Yugoslavia, TV documentary, 1986; J Peel Show, Radio 1, played Stop the War, Bring the Noiz 7, 1992; Fiju Briju 1, 1993, 3, 1995, 4, 1996, Fiju Briju, 1997, biggest festivals in Croatia and Salata, 1997; Ecstazy, Berlin, 1990; Zoro, Leipzig, Germany, 1993. *Compositions:* Obrij mc Majko Motornom Pilom, 7, LP, CD; Fuck You All, 1993; Pataren; Sank; Nema Vise; MTV. *Publications:* Croatian Pop/Rock Encyclopedia, 1994; Patareni Tribute, 1996; Patareni Buka, We Can't Be Banned From Here, 1991. *Honour:* Porin for Best Alternative Album in 1993, Hladno Pivo Dzinovski, 1994. *Membership:* Croatian Musicians Union. *Leisure interests:* Dreaming; Listening to Music; Always being ready to help if needed. *Current Management:* Jabukaton, B Trenka 9, 10000 Zagreb, Croatia. *Address:* Davor Kodzoman, Tuskanova 26, 10000 Zagreb, Croatia.

HAFER John Richard (Dick); b. 29 May 1927, Wyomissing, Pennsylvania, USA. Musician (Tenor Saxophone, Clarinet, Flute, Oboe, English Horn). m. 1 s., 1 d. *Education:* Studied Theory and Harmony privately; Studied Saxophone, Clarinet, Flute and Oboe privately, and Oboe with Albert Golter of the New York Philharmonic. *Career:* Played with: Charlie Barnet Orchestra; Claude Thornhillock; Woody Herman Orchestra; Charles Mingod Orchestra; Bobby Hackett band; Appeared on Merv Griffin TV Show for 12 years; Appeared in Broadway shows No No Nanette, How to Succeed in Business, Fade On, Fade Out, Molly, Golden Boy Morne, They're Playing Our Song; Played with Benny Goodman Orchestra, Ruby Broff. *Recordings:* Road Band, Woody Herman; Classic Jazz, Charlie Barnet; The Black Saint and the Sinner Lady and Mingus, Mingus, Mingus, with Charlie Mingus; Prez Impressions, Dick Hafer Quartet; In A Sentimental Mood: Dick Hafer. *Membership:* AFM Life Member. *Leisure interests:* Playing oboe; Woodwing quartets; Golf. *Address:* 10500 Reseda Blvd, Northridge, CA 91326, USA.

HAGAR Sammy; b. 13 Oct. 1947, Monterey, California, USA. Rock Vocalist; Musician (guitar); Songwriter. *Career:* Singer, bands: Fabulous Castillas; Skinny; Justice Brothers; Dust Cloud; Lead singer, Montrose, 1973–75; Support to The Who, London; Solo artiste, 1975–87; Support to Kiss; Boston; Kansas; One-off project, HSAS (with Neal Schon, Kenny Aaronson and Michael Shrieve), 1984; Lead singer, US rock group Van Halen, 1987–97; Regular US and international tours including Monsters of Rock US tour, 1988; Co-host, Westwood One radio show with Michael Anthony, 1992. *Recordings:* with Montrose: Montrose, 1973; Paper Money, 1974; Solo albums: Nine On A Scale of Ten, 1976; Sammy Hagar Two, 1977; Musical Chairs, 1978; All Night Long-Live, 1978; Street Machine, 1979; Danger Zone, 1979; Loud and Clear, 1980; Standing Hampton, 1982; Rematch, 1982; Three Lock Box, 1983; Live From London To Long Beach, 1983; VOA, 1983; Voice of America, 1984; Looking Back, 1987; Sammy Hagar, 1987; Red, 1993; Unboxed, 1994; Marching to Mars, 1997; Red Voodoo, 1999; Ten Thirteen, 2000; with HSAS: Through The Fire, 1984; with Van Halen: 5150 (No. 1, USA), 1986; OU812 (No. 1, USA), 1988; For Unlawful Carnal Knowledge (No. 1, USA), 1991; Right Here Right Now, 1993; Balance, 1995; Singles include: Solo: Your Love Is Driving Me Crazy; I Can't Drive 55; Heavy Metal, film theme from film Heavy Metal; Winner Takes All, from film Over The Top; Give To Live; Eagles Fly; with Van Halen: Why Can't This Be Love, 1986; Love Walks In, 1986; Dreams, 1986; When It's Love, 1988; Finish What Ya Started, 1988; Feels So Good, 1989; Poundcake, 1991; Top of The World, 1991; Right Now, 1992. *Honours:* Numerous Platinum discs; Grammy Award, Best Hard Rock Performance, 1992; American Music Award, Favorite Album, 1992; Bay Area Music Awards, Outstanding Male Vocalist, 1992, 1993; MTV Music Video Award,

1992. *Leisure interest:* Fast cars. *Current Management:* KP Management, 24608 Varese Court, Valencia, CA 91355, USA.

HAGGARD Merle; b. 6 April 1937, Bakersfield, California, USA. Singer; Songwriter. *Career:* Accompanied Wynn Stewart, 1960; Founder, The Strangers; Successful songwriting and recording career, including 40 US Country No. 1 records. *Recordings:* Hit singles (own compositions) include: I'm A Lonesome Fugitive, 1966; Okie From Muskogee, 1969; I Take A Lot of Pride In What I Am; Silver Wings; Today I Started Loving You Again; If We Make It Through December; Poncho and Lefty, with Willie Nelson; Albums include: Just Between The Two of Us, with Bonnie Owens, 1966; Same Train A Different Time, 1969; The Land of Many Churches, with Bonnie Owens, Carter Family, 1971; My Love Affair With Trains, 1976; A Taste of Yesterday's Wine, with George Jones, 1982; Poncho and Lefty, with Willie Nelson, 1983; Heart To Heart, with Leona Williams, 1983; That's The Way Love Goes, 1983; The Epic Collection – Live, 1983; It's All In The Game, 1984; Kern River, 1985; Amber Waves of Grain, 1985; Out Among The Stars, 1986; A Friend In California, 1986; Seashores of Old Mexico, 1987; Chill Factor, 1988; 5:01 Blues, 1989; Blue Jungle, 1990; Super Hits, Vol. 2, 1994; Super Hits, Vol. 3, 1995; If I Could Only Fly, 2000; New Light Through Old Windows, 2000; Cabin In The Hills, 2001. *Publications:* Autobiography, Sing Me Back Home, with Peggy Russell. *Current Management:* Hag Inc, PO Box 536, Palo Cedro, CA 96073, USA.

HÄGGMAN Ann-Mari (Solveig); b. 19 Sept. 1941, Vasa, Finland. Music Organization Exec. m. Lars-Eric Häggman, 11 April 1964, 1 s., 1 d. *Musical Education:* PhD in Ethnomusicology. *Career:* Researcher and Head of Svenska litteratursällskapets Folkkultursarkiv; Assistant Professor, Department for Folklore, Helsinki University, 1993–95; Head of the Institute of Finland-Swedish Traditional Music, 1985-. *Publications:* Magdalena på källebro (The Ballad of Mary Magdalene's Conversion), dissertation, 1992; Numerous articles, CDs and films about folk music in Finland. *Memberships:* Word of Honour of the Finlands svenska spelmansförbund (League of Traditional Musicians); Board Mem., Swedish Literature Society; Numerous folk music organizations. *Leisure interests:* Literature; Outdoor life. *Address:* c/o Finlands svenska folkmusikinstitut, Handelsesplanaden 23A, 65100 Vasa, Finland.

HAGUE Mel (Melvyn Ian); b. 20 Jan. 1943, Whiston, South Yorkshire, England. Singer; Entertainer; Songwriter; Musician (guitar). m. Ivy Walton, 6 Aug. 1966, 1 s., 1 d. *Career:* Grew up in Canada, 1951–61; Played most UK concert venues, including Wembley Conference Centre; All UK Country music festivals; Several European tours; Appearances: Regional television stations: Country Club, BBC2; Nightride; WSM Nashville radio, television; Much regional radio; Own record label, OGB Records. *Recordings:* 15 albums (9 on own label), 1974–99. *Publication:* Music, book reviewer, Doncaster Entertainer. *Contributions to:* Traditional Music Maker; Country Music Round-Up. *Honour:* Aria Guitars/Daily Mirror Golden Guitar Award, Top Country Entertainer, 1981. *Memberships:* Performing Rights Society; Equity. *Leisure interests:* Writing reviews and stories; Cycling; Snooker and pool; Science Fiction books and films. *Address:* 37 Wroot Rd, Finningley Village, Doncaster DN9 3DR, England.

HAHN Joe (Joseph); b. 15 March 1977, Glendale, California, USA. DJ. *Education:* Studied painting at Pasadena Art College of Design. *Career:* Joined fellow college student Mike Shinoda's group Xero; Became Hybrid Theory and signed to Warner Bros, Spring 2000; Band immediately sent to professional studio; Further name change to Linkin Park prior to first record releases; Incessant promotional activity since release of album; Live shows include: Family Values and Ozzfest tours; KROQ Acoustic Christmas Concert 2001; many international dates; TV specials include: Live At The Fillmore; Reverb; Currently resides in Los Angeles, California. *Recordings:* Albums: Hybrid Theory, 2000; Singles: Hybrid Theory (Acoustic EP), 2000; One Step Closer, Crawling, Papercut, In The End, 2001. *Honours:* Over 10m. world-wide sales of debut album to end of 2001; Billboard Award, Best Modern Rock Artist, 2001; Rock Bear Awards: Best International Band; Best International Album, 2001; Kerrang! Award, Best International Newcomer, 2001; Rolling Stone Award, Best Hard Rock/Metal Band, 2001. *Current Management:* Andy Gould Management, 8484 Wilshire Blvd #425, Beverly Hills, CA 90211, USA. *Internet:* www.linkinpark.com.

HAIMOVICI Fabien-David; b. 22 April 1968, Bordeaux, France. Musician (drums). *Education:* College. *Musical Education:* 4 years in France, drum school; 1 year in Los Angeles, Musicians Institute. *Career:* Played with Bireli Lagrene; Tours all over USA, Europe, Japan; Tour with French artists Jacques Higelin; Nicole Croisille; Tours in Japan, France; Played with international artists in France including Lucky Peterson; Currently plays and records with Coke Tale (comprised of top Paris studio musicians). *Recording:* Solo rock album. *Honours:* Diploma: Outstanding Student of The Year, Musicians Institute, Los Angeles. *Leisure interests:* Wind surfing; Films. *Address:* 16 rue des cascades, 75020 Paris, France.

HAINES Luke; b. 7 Oct. 1967, Walton-on-Thames, Surrey, England. Singer; Songwriter. *Career:* Member: UK groups: The Auteurs; Black Box Recorder. *Recordings:* with The Auteurs: Singles: Showgirl, 1992; Lenny Valentino, 1993; How Could I Be Wrong, 1993; Chinese Bakery, 1994; Back With The Killer, 1995; Light Aircraft On Fire, 1996; The Rubettes, 1999; Albums: New Wave, 1993; Now I'm A Cowboy, 1994; After Murder Park, 1996; How I Learned To Love The Bootboys, 1999; with Black Box Recorder: Singles: Child Psychology, 1998; England Made Me, 1998; The Facts of Life, 2000; The Art of Driving, 2000; Albums: England Made Me, 1998; The Facts of Life, 2000; Solo albums: The Oliver Twist Manifesto, 2001; Christie Malry's Own Double-Entry (soundtrack), 2001; Also appears on: Baader Meinhof, 1997. *Honour:* Mercury Prize Nomination, 1993. *Current Management:* Tony Beard, PROD.

HAINES Margaret Ewart Blackwood; b. 28 April 1941, Detroit, Michigan, USA. m. Peter E Haines, 28 Aug. 1965, 1 s., 1 d. *Education:* BA, Elementary Education, Minor in Music, Albion College, Albion, MI, USA; Independent study in composition, theory, harmony, orchestration. *Career:* Marge and Friends, TV programme, 1980–83, 1984–85; Featured interviews with leading Christian national and local people, 1980–83. *Compositions:* Love Song: You Are the Love of My Life; Songs of Jesus, song book, vocal cassette; Cantos de Jesus, 6 Spanish scripture/Worship songs; The Revelation of Jesus Christ!, song book: Cantata to Revelation; The Revelation of Jesus Christ Song Book, 1999, and Orchestration, 1999. *Recordings:* Songs of Jesus; Are You Ready: 20 Gospel Favorites; The Revelation of Jesus Christ!; Elaine O'Neill: Favorite Hymns. *Publications:* Revelation of Jesus Christ Song Book, 1991, 1994, 1997; Orchestration, 1998; Songs of Jesus Song Book, 1996; Children's Scripture Song Book; Isiah Cantata, forthcoming. *Honours:* Phi Mu Alpha Sinfonia Music Society, 1963; Senior Piano Recital: Albion College, 1963; Grant to study effect of music in teaching retarded children, 1970–71. *Memberships:* National Religious Broadcasters; Christian Copyright Licensing International; ASCAP; American Music Center. *Leisure interests:* Music; Composition; Gardening; Piano Composition; Improvising; Arranging; Swimming. *Address:* Margaret E Haines, PO Box 66 85 Crease Rd, Budd Lake, NJ 07828, USA.

HAJDOVSKA-TLUSTA Katerina; b. 27 Feb. 1953, Prague, Czech Republic. Singer; Musician (percussion); Songwriter. m. Martin Tlusty, 30 Jan. 1982, 2 step-d. *Education:* Special Pedagogy, Prague Charles' University. *Career:* FOK, folk-rock; Foersters Choir; J Vycpálek Folklore Music; Ukrainian Folklore Music, Ignis; Prague Madrigals, Chesed, Jewish music; Ester, Jewish music; Music and Musicotherapy Teacher; Czech Radio broadcasts. *Recordings:* Albums: with Ester: To You, Jerusalem; with Alexander Hajdovsky, Ester: Shalom, Chaverim, 1998; with Chesed: Jewish Feasts in Songs; Jewish Songs Live. *Leisure interest:* Biblical Study. *Current Management:* K Hajdovská-Tlustá, Michnova 1626, 149 00 Prague 4, Czech Republic.

HAJDOVSKY-POTAPOVIC Alexandr 'Lesik'; b. 27 Feb. 1953, Prague, Czech Republic. m. Miroslava Hajdovska-Vlková, 7 Dec. 1973, 2 s. *Career:* Documentary film music; Advertisement music; Member of Czech television and radio broadcasting groups: FOK, folk rock, Svehlik, rock; Mazelé, rap; Extempore, rock/humour; Ester, Jewish traditional songs. *Recordings:* Albums: Jizák; Lesik Hajdovsky: Uz horísvíce; Lesik Hajdovsky: Manzelé; Prague: Zizkov Kuplets; Svehlík: There's No Time; Ester: Shalom Chaverim, with Katerina Hajdovska-Tlusta, 1998. *Honours:* Nomination Award Magazine, 1985, 1988; Mlady svet – Bílá Vrána; Melodie magazine award, 1991. *Membership:* OSA. *Leisure interest:* Painting pictures. *Current Management:* Katerina Hajdovská-Tlustá, Michnova 1626, 149 00 Prague 4, Czech Republic. *Address:* Brodského 1672, 149 00 Prague 4, Czech Republic.

HALE Alan Spencer; b. 31 May 1965, Morristown, Tennessee, USA. m. Michelle, 2 d. *Career:* Opened Shows, Concerts for Exile, Mel McDaniel, Marty Stuart, Confederate Railroad, Western Flyer, Highway 101, Ricochet; Opened Third Annual Forks of the River Jam; Featured Performed and Master of Ceremonies, First Night in Kingsport; Closed The Season for Bonnie Lou and Buster Smoky Mountain Hayride Show; Featured Performer for Las Vegas Producer, John Stuarts Country Music Show; FOA Network Aired 2 Television Specials; Performed at Pegeon Forge, The Music Mountain Amphia Theater, The Rainbow Theater, Tennessee Music Theater, 1993-. *Compositions:* I'll Be True; The Weight; The Band; Once In A Lifetime. *Recordings:* Ain't Man Enough; Come On In; Happiness; Forever Gone; Can't Get There; Better Or Worse; Slippin' Away; Lady Lied; Once In A Lifetime; The Weight; I'll Be True. *Honour:* Kingsport Key To City. *Leisure interests:* Old Cars; Building my house; Writing songs. *Address:* Alan Spencer Hale Fan Club, St Paul Rd, Morristown 5476 TN 37813, USA.

HALE Keith; b. 6 Nov. 1950, Hull, East Yorkshire, England. Songwriter; Musician (keyboards); Record Prod. 1 d. *Musical Education:* Dartington College of Arts, Devon. *Career:* Formed Blood Donor, 1977; Support to J J Burnel on Euroman Tour; Member, Hawkwind, 1980; Left with Ginger

Baker, formed Ginger's Nutters, toured Europe, 1981; Member, Toyah's band for Warrior Rock tour, 1982. *Composition:* It's A Mystery, 1981. *Recordings:* Producer, Toyah's first album Sheep-Farming In Barnet; Other albums include: Zones/Stonehenge, Hawkwind; Toyah On Tour, 1983; Ginger Baker In Concert, 1985; Toyah – Live and More, 1998. *Memberships:* PRS; MCPS; Musicians' Union. *Leisure interest:* Reached Scrabble quarter-finals, 1980. *Current Management:* Gems. *Address:* Firs Cottage, 5 Firs Close, London SE23 1BB, England.

HALE Simon B; b. 23 April 1964, Birmingham, England. Composer; Arranger; Prod.; Musician (keyboards). m. Claire Moore, 15 Oct. 1994, 1 s., 1 d. *Musical Education:* A Level Music, Grade VIII piano, violin; Bachelor of Music, Goldsmiths' College, University of London, 1985. *Career:* Keyboards with Seal: World tour; US Grammy Awards, 1992; Top of The Pops; Wogan; Live videos; Keyboards with: Howard New; Wendy and Lisa; Tri; Gail Ann Dorsey; Geoffrey Williams; Arranger for: Incognito; George Benson; Yo Yo Honey; Shawn Lee; Maysa Leak; Conductor, MD, concert with Incognito, Royal Festival Hall, 1995; Producer for: 2 albums, Kumiko Yamashita. *Compositions:* George Benson; British Film Institute; Nescafé; Solo album, 1992; String arranger: 100° and Rising, Incognito; String arranger, composer, George Benson; Composer, orchestrator, Tomoyasu Hotei; Solo album: East Fifteen, 1994; Seal, single, EP; BBC TV theme tune The Vote Race, 1992. *Recordings:* with Jamiroquai: Travelling without Moving, 1996; Canned Heat, 1999; Synkronized, 1999; with Duncan Sheik: Duncan Sheik, 1996; Humming, 1998; M People, 1997; Rat Bat Blue, 1997; with Incognito: No Time Like The Future, 1999; with Steps, Buzz, 2000; with Becky Taylor, A Dream Come True, 2001. *Memberships:* Musicians' Union; PRS; MCPS; Asscn of Professional Composers. *Leisure interest:* Cycling. *Current Management:* c/o IRc2 (London) Ltd. *Address:* 1 Star St, London W2 1QD, England.

HALEY Mark Jonathan; b. 2 Feb. 1961, Portsmouth, Hampshire, England. Musician (keyboards, guitar). *Musical Education:* Classical training in piano, guitar, trumpet. *Career:* Began Haley Brothers, 1976; Television appearance, Rund Pop show, East Germany, 1984; Toured with Billy Fury, 1982; Joined The Monkees comeback tours, 1986–89; Member, The Kinks, 1989–93; The Chaps, 1994–96; Current member, The Rubettes, joined January 2000; Formed Gorge, 1997; Album: On This. *Composition:* Don't Answer, on The Other Side of Hank Marvin, 1998. *Recordings:* with Haley Brothers: One Way Love Affair, 1978; with The Monkees: That Was Then, This Is Now, 1986; with The Kinks: Down All The Days, 1991; with The Chaps: The Collector, 1995; Programmer, This Is Hardcore, Pulp album, 1998. *Publication:* Journeyman, autobiography on internet, 1999. *Honour:* Ivor Novello Award Services To Music (The Kinks). *Memberships:* PRS; Executive Committee Mem., Musicians' Union; MCPS; Brit Awards Voting Academy. *Leisure interests:* Tennis; Golf; Watching West Ham United Football Club. *Current Management:* Via Management.

HALFORD Rob; b. 25 Aug. 1951, Birmingham, England. Singer. *Career:* Lead singer, UK heavy rock group Judas Priest, 1974–90; Tours include: Support to Led Zeppelin, US, 1977; Support to Kiss, 1979; Turbo – Fuel For Life tour, 1986; Painkiller tour, US, 1990; US tour, with Alice Cooper, Motörhead, 1991; Concerts, festivals include: Reading Festival, 1976; Monsters of Rock Festival, Castle Donington, 1980; Heavy Metal Sunday, San Bernadino, California, 1983; Live Aid, Philadelphia, 1985; Founder, lead singer, heavy rock group Fight, 1991–; Appearance as stand-in singer for Black Sabbath, Pacific Amphitheatre, California, 1992. *Recordings:* Albums: with Judas Priest: Rocka Rolla, 1974; Sad Wings of Destiny, 1976; Sin After Sin, 1977; Stained Class, 1978; Killing Machine, 1978; Unleashed In The East, 1979; British Steel, 1980; Point of Entry, 1981; Screaming For Vengeance, 1982; Defenders of The Faith, 1984; Turbo, 1986; Priest Live, 1987; Ram It Down, 1988; Painkiller, 1990; A Touch of Evil, 1991; Metal Works 1973–93, 1993; Best of Judas Priest, 1998; with Fight: War of Words, 1994; Mutations, 1994; A Small Deadly Space, 1995; Solo album: Resurrection, 2000; Singles include: with Judas Priest: Take On The World; Living After Midnight; Breaking The Law; You've Got Another Thing Coming. *Contributions to:* Stars, Hear 'n' Aid (charity record for Ethiopian famine relief), 1986; Singer, with Pantera, for film soundtrack Buffy The Vampire Slayer, 1992. *Current Management:* c/o John Baxter, EMAS, PO Box 55810, Phoenix, AZ 85078, USA.

HALL Brian John; b. 27 Nov. 1939, Hoylake, Wirral, England. Musician (guitar, bass). *Career:* Singer, musician with various bands; Solo performer, songwriter, recording service manager. *Composition:* Amanda, hit for Stuart Gillies, 1973. *Honours:* Golden Note Award; Winner, Opportunity Knocks with song Amanda. *Memberships:* BASCA; PRS; MCPS; Equity. *Leisure interests:* Dining out; Table tennis. *Address:* 6 Fieldway, Meols, Wirral, Merseyside L47 9SD, England.

HALL Chris; Musician (accordion, drums); Singer; Agent; Record Co Exec.; Journalist; Radio Presenter; Festival Organizer. *Career:* Accordion player, vocalist with R Cajun and The Zydeco Brothers; The Bearcats; Accordian Player with Zydecomotion; Tour organizer, US and UK agent, for Cajun and Zydeco; Writer, co-partner, Cajun Users Manual; Radio presenter, BBC

Radio 2; Club organizer, The Swamp Club; Manager, Bearcat Records; Recorded and appeared on TV with Paul McCartney; featured accordion player on McCartney's Run Devil Run album recorded at Abbey Road and also featuring Dave Gilmour (Pink Floyd), Ian Paice (Deep Purple), Mick Green (The Pirates) and Pete Wingfield. *Address:* Swamp, PO Box 94, Derby DE22 1XA, England.

HALL Daryl, (Daryl Franklin Hohl); b. 11 Oct. 1948, Pottstown, Pennsylvania, USA. Singer; Musician (guitar); Songwriter. *Education:* Temple University. *Career:* Member, Kenny Gamble and The Romeos; Gulliver; Session singer, Sigma Sounds Studios; Backing singer, The Stylistics; The Delfonics; Member, duo Hall and Oates, with John Oates, 1969–; Concerts world-wide include: Live Aid, Philadelphia, 1985; Rainforest benefit concert, Madison Square Garden, with The Grateful Dead, 1988; Earth Day, Central Park, New York, 1990; USA Harvest National Hunger Relief concert, 1991; The Simple Truth, benefit concert for Kurdish refugees, Wembley, 1991. *Compositions:* Many hit songs co-written with John Oates; Other songs include: Sara Smile; Wait For Me; Kiss On My List (co-written with Janna Allen); One On One; Did It In A Minute (co-written with Sara and Janna Allen); Foolish Pride; Everything Your Heart Desires; Swept Away, for Diana Ross; Film theme, Ruthless People (co-written with Mick Jagger and Dave Stewart). *Recordings:* Albums: with Hall and Oates: Whole Oats, 1972; Abandoned Luncheonette, 1974; War Babies, 1974; Daryl Hall and John Oates, 1975; Bigger Than Both of Us, 1976; No Goodbyes, 1977; Beauty On A Back Street, 1977; Livetime, 1978; Along The Red Edge, 1978; X-Static, 1979; Private Eyes, 1981; H2O, 1982; Big Bam Boom, 1984; Live At The Apollo With David Ruffin and Eddie Kendricks, 1985; Ooh Yeah, 1988; Change of Season, 1990; The Best Of. . ., 1991; Solo albums: Sacred Songs, 1980; Three Hearts In The Happy Ending Machine, 1986; Soul Alone, 1993; Can't Stop Dreaming, 1999; Best of The Ballads, 2000; US No. 1 singles with Hall and Oates: Rich Girl, 1977; Kiss On My List, 1981; Private Eyes, 1981; I Can't Go For That (No Can Do), 1982; Maneater, 1982; Out of Touch, 1984; Numerous other hit singles include: She's Gone, 1976; Every Time You Go Away, 1980; You've Lost That Lovin' Feelin', 1980; Family Man, 1983; Say It Ain't So, 1983; Method of Modern Love, 1985; Solo hits: Dreamtime, 1986; Stop Loving Me, Stop Loving You, 1993; Featured on: Journeyman, Eric Clapton, 1989. *Contributions to:* We Are The World, USA For Africa, 1985; Sun City, Artists Against Apartheid, 1985; The Last Temptation of Elvis, 1990; Two Rooms – Celebrating The Songs of Elton John and Bernie Taubin, 1991. *Honours include:* American Music Awards: Favourite Pop/Rock Duo or Band, 1983–85; 19 US Gold and Platinum discs (most successful duo in US recording history). *Current Management:* All Access Entertainment. *Address:* 53 W 23rd St, 11th Floor, New York, NY 10010, USA.

HALL Gary Martin; b. 29 Nov. 1964, Ormskirk, Lancashire, England. Singer; Songwriter; Musicians (guitar). *Career:* Member, The Stormtroopers, 1986–92; Television appearances: Granada TV, three times; Italian TV; Numerous appearances on radio; Tours of Europe. *Recordings:* Writer, all songs on albums: Garage Heart, 1989; Wide Open To The World, 1991; What Goes Around, 1993; Twelve Strings and Tall Stories, 1996; Return to the Flame, 1998; Also collaborated with: Townes Van Zandt; John Prine; Guy Clark. *Honours:* Rising Star Award, BCMA, 1995; Southern Radio Award Nomination, Song of The Year, 1995. *Memberships:* PRS; MCPS. *Leisure interest:* Music. *Address:* 10 Rose Terrace, Ashton, Preston, Lancashire PR2 1EB, England.

HALL G P (Graham Peter); b. 15 July 1943, Hampton Hill, England. Artist; Composer; Ambient Sound Sculptures; Musician (saxophone, bass, flamenco guitar, synthesiser, elctric guitar). m. Päivi Annikki Vilkman, 26 June 1987, 4 s., 2 d. *Musical Education:* Studied flamenco guitar. *Career:* Member, blues bands, 1960s; Toured Europe, 1962–68; Video: The Estates, 1977; Tour: Estates, 1977; Festivals: France; Germany; Spain; Holland, 1982; North Africa, 1983; Southwest England, 1992; Docklands The Space performance, 1998; Radio includes: Radio Bristol; Radio Sussex; Radio Mercury; Radio Surrey; Radio Lotus, Denmark; Radio Lux, Ukraine; Television: Wire TV; Germany; Netherlands; Queen Elizabeth Hall, London, 1996; Western Isles tour, 1997. *Composition:* Commissioned, Sea Sorrow (Isle of Lewis), 1997. *Recordings:* New Town Suite; The Estates, 1977; Manifestations; Full Moon Over Madrid, 1977; Harbinger, Colours, 1986; Imaginary Seasons, 1992; Slipstreams, Glow, 1994; Shooting Stars, 1995; Eclectic Guitars, 1996; Figments of Imagination, 1996; Mar-Del-Plata, 1997; Steel Storm and Tender Spirits, double CD, 1998; Marks on the Air, live at The Spitz, London and Phantom Theatre, Wilshire, 1998; Recorded 143 titles, all instrumental; Video: Paths of The Lonely, 1995. *Publications:* River Flow; Off The Shell; Filmtrax; Prototype; Countdown Productions. *Honour:* Mercury Music Prize Nomination, Imaginary Seasons, 1992. *Memberships:* PRS; Musicians' Union; MCPS; PAMRA. *Leisure interests:* Time with family; Relaxing. *Current Management:* Imaginary Music.

HALL Jim (James S); b. 4 Dec. 1930, Buffalo, New York, USA. Musician (guitar). m. Jane Herbert, 9 Sept. 1965, 1 d. *Musical Education:* Cleveland Institute of Music. *Career:* Musician with Chico Hamilton, Jimmy Guiffre

Trio, 1957–59; Ella Fitzgerald, 1959–60; Sonny Rollins, 1961–62; Formed Quartet with Art Farmer, 1962–64; Leader, own trio/quartet, 1962–; Concerts include: The White House; Carnegie Hall; Duke Ellington's Birthday Party; Jazz Festivals include: Berlin; Concord; Monterey; Newport; Unbria; Many club appearances in USA, Canada, England, France, Japan; Television appearances world-wide including The Sound of Jazz, CBS; The Tonight Show; Film appearance: Jazz On A Summer's Day, 1958. *Recordings:* Albums include: with Bobby Brookmeyer and Jimmy Raney: Street Swingers; with Bill Evans: Undercurrent; Intermodulation; with Sonny Rollins: The Bridge; with Art Farmer: Big Blues; with Paul Desmond: Paul Desmond and Friends; Easy Living; with Ron Carter: Alone Together; Live At The Village West; Telephone; with Michel Petrucciani's Power of Three (featuring Jim Hall and Wayne Shorter): Three; Solo, own ensembles: All Across the City; Live At Town Hall, Vols 1 and 2; Subsequently: Youkali; Something Special; Dedications and Inspirations; Other recordings with Red Mitchell; George Shearing; Tom Harrell. *Publications:* Jazz Improvisation, Transcriptions of Jim Hall Solos, 1980; Exploring Jazz Guitar, 1991; Master Sessions with Jim Hall, (instructional video), 1993; Jim Hall-Jazz Guitar Environments, 1994. *Honours include:* Downbeat Critics Poll Awards, 1963–; Downbeat Reader's Poll Winner, 1965–66; Playboy All-Star Poll Winner, 1968–71; Jazz Magazine Award, Best Performer, 1965–66; Grammy Nominations. *Current Management:* Mary Ann Topper, Jazz Tree Agency. *Address:* 648 B'way Suite 703, New York, NY 10012, USA.

HALL Keith Robert; b. 24 April 1951, Edgware, Middlesex, England. Musician (drums). *Musical Education:* Mainly self-taught; Studied with Joe Hodson; Frank King; Joe Morello. *Career:* Professional musician, 1966–; Founder member, Pickettywitch, 1969–72; Member, Gerry and The Pacemakers, 1973–77; Terry Lightfoot, 1978–84; Musicals: Hair National Tour; 1980; Godspell, 1980; Joseph and The Amazing Technicolour Dreamcoat, 1981; Freelance musician, played with: Kenny Ball; Maxine Daniels; Bertice Redding; Fiona Duncan; Jay McShan; Ellen Rucker; Ritchie Cole, 1984–; Formed jazz-rock fusion band Storm Warning, with Jill Jarman, 1987; Concerts include: Festivals throughout Europe; Toured with Engelbert Humperdinck; with June Harris, 1987–89; Also toured Scandinavia; Worked with: Tom Whittle; Januz Carmello; Al Gray; Spike Robinson; Dick Hestall-Smith, 1990; Moved to Helsinki, 1990; Regular drummer with Antti Sarpila Swing Band; Also worked with: UMO; Espoo Big Band; Pentti Lasanen; Severi Pyysalo; Karita Mattila; Appearances at most Finnish music festivals, including the Pori International Jazz Festival 1992–95, 1997–99 and on Finnish television and radio; Republic of Finland's President's Independence Day gala party in Helsinki, with the Antti Sarpila swing band, 1999. *Recordings:* with Pickettywitch: That Same Old Feeling, 1970; Sad Old Kinda Movie, 1970; Baby I Won't Let You Down, 1970; with Gerry and The Pacemakers: Lovely Lady, 1974; Albums: with Pickettywitch: Pickettywitch, 1970; Spirit Level albums include: Storm Warning, 1988; Killer Bunnies; Mice In The Wallet, On The Level; Proud Owners; with Antti Sarpila: Father, Son and Holy Swing, 1993; Chrisse Schwindt Memorial Concert, 1993; Live At Storyville, 1994; with Claus Anderson: Chrisse Schwindt Memorial Concert, 1993; with Swing Gentlemen: Swing Gentlemen's Ball, 1995. *Memberships:* Musicians' Union; Finnish Drummers Asscn; Finnish Musicians' Union; PAMRA; GAMEX. *Leisure interests:* Golf; Fishing; Photography. *Address:* Rakuunantie 17 A12, 00330 Helsinki, Finland.

HALL Martin; b. 26 April 1963, Copenhagen, Denmark. Singer; Composer; Musician (multi-instrumentalist). *Musical Education:* Academy of Piano and Music, Copenhagen; Royal Academy of Fine Arts, Copenhagen. *Career:* Singer, composer, Ballet Mécanique; Ritual, The World Music Days, Århus Musikhus, 1983; Requiem, The Taksigelses Church, Copenhagen, 1989; Inskription, The Danish National Radio, 1983; Gud Og Grammatik, Danish Academy of Fine Arts, 1984; Current Works, Danish Natonal Radio, 1995. *Recordings:* Avenues of Oblivion, 1980; The Icecold Waters of The Egocentric Calculation, 1981; For, 1982; Ritual, 1983; Apparently All The Same, 1984; Free Force Structure, 1984; Fusion, 1985; Relief, 1985; Warfare, 1985; Treatment, 1985; Cutting Through, 1986; Beat of The Drum, 1988; Presence, 1988; Surreal Thing, 1989; The Martin Hall Document, 1989; Crush-The Point of No Return Soundtrack, 1989; Prime Material, 1990; Imperfect, 1990; Dreamworld, 1990; Palladium, 1990; The Rainbow Theatre, 1990; Read Only Memory, 1991; Sweet Mystery, 1993; All The Way Down, 1993; Strange Delight, 1993; A Touch of Excellence, 1993; Angel of The Night, 1994; Phantasmagoria, 1994; Random Hold, 1996; Testcards 1989–95, 1997; Performance, 1997. *Publications:* 4 books; 5 anthologies; 28 albums, magazines, works; The World Days, 1996. *Honours:* Hon. Award, Danish Asscn of Composers, 1995; The 3 Year Major Grant, National Fund For The Endowment of the Arts, 1995; Asscn of Danish Composers (DJBFA); KODA; GRAMEX; NCB. *Leisure interests:* Music; Writing books. *Current Management:* Motor Danmark. *Address:* Motor Danmark, Linnésgade 14, 1361 Copenhagen K, Denmark.

HALL Terry; b. 19 March 1959, Coventry, Warwickshire, England. Singer. *Career:* Singer, The Special AKA (later as The Specials), 1977–81; International concerts and tours include: Concert for People of

Kampuchea, London, 1979; Founder member, Fun Boy Three, 1981–83; Founder, Colourfield, 1983–88; Member, Terry, Blair and Anouchka, 1989–90; Member, Vegas (with Dave Stewart), 1992; Also solo artiste. *Recordings:* with The Specials: Singles: Gangsters, 1979; A Message To You Rudy, 1979; Too Much Too Young (No. 1, UK), 1980; Rat Race, 1980; Stereotype, 1980; Do Nothing, 1981; Ghost Town (No. 1, UK), 1981; Albums: Specials, 1979; More Specials, 1980; Dance Craze (film soundtrack), 1981; Singles Collection, 1991; Stereotypes (compilation), 2000; with Fun Boy Three: Singles: The Lunatics Have Taken Over The Asylum, 1981; It Ain't What You Do (with Bananarama), 1981; Summertime, 1982; The Telephone Always Rings Twice, 1982; The Tunnel of Love, 1983; The More I See, 1983; Our Lips Are Sealed, 1983; Albums: Fun Boy Three, 1982; Waiting, 1983; Best Of..., 1984; with The Colour Field: Singles: Thinking of You, 1985; Castles In The Air, 1985; with Terry Blair and Anouchka: Albums: Ultra-Modern Nursery Rhymes, 1990; with Vegas: Album: Vegas, 1992; Solo: Singles: Forever J, 1994; Rainbows, 1995; Albums: Terry Hall – The Collection, 1993; Home, 1995; Laugh, 1997; Co-writer, Sense, The Lightning Seeds, 1992; Jollification, The Lightning Seeds, 1994; Guest vocals: Poems, Nearly God (collaboration with Tricky), 1996. *Current Management:* Asgard Management, 125 Parkway, London NW1 7PS, England.

HALL Thomas James; b. 19 May 1957, Longview, Washington, USA. Record Prod.; Sound Engineer. *Education:* BA, radio and television production, East Washington University, 1980. *Career:* Producer, sound engineer, Viacom Studios; Logic West Studios; London Bridge Studios; Triad Studios, 1982-. *Recordings:* As producer/sound engineer: with Queensryche: Queensryche, 1983; Mindcrime Live, 1991; with Kenny G: Kenny G Live, 1990. *Address:* Triad Studios, 4572 150th Ave NE, Redmond, WA 98052, USA.

HALL Tom T; b. 25 May 1936, Olive Hill, Kentucky, USA. Songwriter; Singer; Author. *Career:* Broadcaster, musician, WMOR radio station, Kentucky, with Kentucky Travellers, 1950s-60s; Leader, own touring band The Storytellers; Currently concentrating on novel-writing and composing children's songs. *Compositions include:* DJ For A Day, Jimmy C Newman; Goodbye Sweetheart, Hello Viet Nam, Johnny Wright; Mama Tell 'Em What We're Fighting For, Dave Dudley; Harper Valley PTA, Jeannie C Riley; I Can't Dance, Gram Parsons and Emmylou Harris; Margie's At The Lincoln Park Inn, Bobby Bare; A Week In The County Jail; Pinto The Wonder Horse Is Dead; I Miss A Lot of Trains; Old Dogs, Children and Watermelon Wine. *Recordings:* Albums include: The Storyteller, 1972; The Rhymer and Other Five and Dimers, 1973; For The People In The Last Hard Town, 1973; Country Is, 1974; Songs of Fox Hollow, 1974; Faster Horses, 1976; The Magnificent Music Machine, 1976; About Love, 1977; New Train Same Rider, 1978; Places I've Done Time, 1978; Saturday Morning Songs, 1979; Ol' T's In Town, 1979; Soldier of Fortune, 1980; The Storyteller and The Banjoman (with Earl Scruggs), 1982; In Concert, 1983; World Class Country, 1983; Everything From Jesus To Jack Daniels, 1983; Natural Dreams, 1984; Songs In A Seashell, 1985; Country Songs For Kids, 1988; Loves Lost and Found, 1995; Songs from Sopchoppy, 1996; Homegrown, 1997; A Soldier of Fortune, 1997; The Ultimate Collection, 2000; features on: Write Your Story, Scott Burnett, 2001. *Publications:* The Songwriter's Handbook; The Storyteller's Nashville; The Laughing Man of Woodmont Cove; Spring Hill (novel). *Honour:* Grammy Award, Tom T Hall's Greatest Hits. *Address:* c/o Tom T. Hall Enterprises, PO Box 1246, Franklin, TN 37065, USA.

HALLAM Nick (The Head); b. 11 June 1960, Nottingham, England. Prod.; DJ. *Career:* Founder, Gee Street Studio and Record Label; Founder Member, Stereo MCs; Remixed artists including Jungle Brothers, U2, PM Dawn, Queen Latifah, Disposable Heroes of Hiphoprisy, Monie Love, Electronic, Madonna (Frozen); Established music publisher, Spirit Songs; Numerous gigs and TV appearances with Stereo MCs. *Recordings:* Elevate My Mind, 1990; Lost in Music, 1991; Connected, 1992; Step It Up, 1993; Ground Level, 1993; Creation, 1993; Deep Down and Dirty, 2001; We Belong In This World Together, 2001; Albums: 33–45–78, 1989; Supernatural, 1990; Connected, 1992; Stereo MCs, 1993; Deep Down and Dirty, 2001. *Honours include:* Brit Awards: Best British Album; Best British Group, 1993.

HALLDORSSON Bjorgvin Helgi; b. 16 April 1951, Hafnarfjordur, Iceland. Singer. m. Ragnheidur B Reynisdottir, 9 Dec. 1977, 2 s., 1 d. *Education:* Piano with private tutor, Brauner. *Career:* Appearances, Little Shop of Horrors, 1985; Evita, 1997; Köldum klaka, 1991; Eurovision Song Contest, 1996. *Compositions:* Skyiö; Riddari Gotunnar; Vertu ekki aö plata mig I útvarpinu heyröi ég lag; Ennpá thessi asni; Undi blaum mana. *Recordings:* Bjorgvin, 1982; Kristján Johannson, 3 albums; Diddú, 3 albums; Iceland Symphony Orchestra, 3 albums. *Honours:* 28 Gold Records, 1974–98. *Memberships:* APRS; STEF of Iceland; FTT, Iceland. *Current Management:* Skifan HF, Iceland. *Address:* PO Box 520, 220 Hafnarfjordur, Iceland.

HALLIWELL Geri Estelle; b. 7 Aug. 1972, Watford, England. Singer. *Career:* Member, Spice Girls, until 1998; Started as Touch, renamed as Spice Girls; Found manager and obtained major label recording deal; Numerous television appearances, radio play and press interviews; British, European and US tours; Film: Spiceworld, 1997; Nominated United Nations Ambassador, 1998; Solo Career, 1998–; Video and book releases. *Recordings:* Singles with Spice Girls: Wannabe (No. 1, UK and US), 1996; Say You'll Be There (No. 1, UK), 1996; 2 Become 1 (No. 1, UK), 1996; Mama/Who Do You Think You Are (No. 1, UK), 1997; Spice Up Your Life (No. 1, UK), 1997; Too Much (No. 1, UK), 1997; Stop, 1998; (How Does It Feel to Be) On Top of the World, as part of England United, 1998; Move Over/Generation Next, 1998; Viva Forever, 1998; Albums: Spice (No. 1, UK), 1996; Spiceworld (No. 1, UK), 1997; Solo Singles: Look At Me (No. 2, UK), 1999; Mi Chico Latino (No. 1, UK), 1999; Lift Me Up (No. 1, UK), 1999; Bag It Up (No. 1, UK), 2000; It's Raining Men, (No. 1, UK), 2001; Scream If You Wanna Go Faster, 2001; Albums: Schizophonic, 1999; Scream If You Wanna Go Faster, 2001. *Honours:* With Spice Girls, numerous music awards in polls.

HALLYDAY Johnny, (Jean-Philippe Smet); b. 15 June 1943, Paris, France. Singer; Musician (guitar). m. Sylvie Vartan. *Musical Education:* Violin lessons. *Career:* Radio debut, 1960; Film appearance: Les Parisiennes, 1961. *Recordings:* Numerous albums include: Johnny Hallyday Sings America's Rockin' Hits, 1962; Flagrant Delit, 1975; Drole De Metier, 1986; Trift De Rattles, 1986; Les Grandssuccess De Johnny Hallyday, 1988; La Peur, 1988; La Nuit Johnny (42 CD box set), 1993; Parc De Princes, 1993; Tes Tendres Annees, 1994; Destination Vegas, 1996; Rough Town, 1996; Aimer Vivre, 1997; Retiens La Nuit, 1997; Ce Que Je Sais, 1998; Insolitudes, 1999; Derriere l'Amour, 1999; Sang Pour Sang, 2000; Singles include: T'Ai Mer Follement; Let's Twist Again (bilingual version), 1961; If I Were A Carpenter (duet with Emmylou Harris), 1985. *Address:* c/o 6 rue Daubigny, 75017 Paris, France.

HALSALL Jennie; b. 23 Jan. 1954, London, England. Media Exec.; Man.-Dir. *Education:* Kilburn Polytechnic, London. *Career:* Jacksons Advertising Agency; Cue Films Ltd; EMI Records, UK; David Geffen and Elliot Roberts Management, USA; Elektra Asylum Records, USA; Independent PR; Formed own business, Jennie Halsall Consultants (media consultants in Europe and the world outside USA), 1980-. *Honour:* PR of The Year, 1980. *Leisure interests:* Tennis; Books; Films; Eating out; Travel; Skiing. *Address:* 208A King St, London W6 0RA, England.

HAMASAKI Ayumi; b. 2 Oct. 1978, Fukuoka, Kyushu, Japan. Vocalist; Musician (piano); Songwriter. *Career:* Moved to Tokyo to act and model; Released moderately successful rap record; Relocated to New York for vocal lessons, 1997; Combines music with advertising/modelling career; Concert tours of Japan, 2000–01; Launched own range of cellphones, 2001. *Recordings:* Albums: Nothing From Nothing (as Ayumi featuring Dohzi-T and DJ Bass), 1995; A Song For XX, Love Appears, 1999; Duty, 2000; A Best, 2001; Singles: Nothing From Nothing (as Ayumi featuring Dohzi-T and DJ Bass), 1995; Poker Face, You, Trust, For My Dear…, Depend On You, 1998; Whatever, Love – Destiny, To Be, Boys and Girls, Monochrome, Appears, Kanariya, 1999; Fly High, Vogue, Far Away, Seasons, Surreal, Audience, M, 2000; Evolution, Never Ever, Endless Sorrow, Unite!, Dearest, A Song Is Born (with Keiko), 2001. *Honours:* Japan Music Award, Grandprix Award, 2001; Japan Gold Disc Award, Artist of The Year (for record sales in excess of 11m. in one year), 2001; World Music Award, Best Selling Japanese Artist, 2001. *Address:* c/o Rhythm Republic/Axex, Japan. *Internet:* www.avexnet.or.jp/ayu.

HAMBE Alf; b. 24 Jan. 1931, Sweden. Composer; Song Writer; Author; Poet; Artist; Musician. m. Ulla, 1 s., 1 d. *Musical Education:* Self-taught; Private Studies in Composition, Piano, Accordian and Guitar. *Career:* Debut, First Song Collection, Astronaut on Horseback, 1962; Full Time Writer, Composer, 1962–; Stage, television and radio appearances. *Compositions:* 15 collections of songs and poems. *Recordings:* Alf Hambe in Molom; 20 Recordings with Songs From My Collections; Song in Molom; Scandinavian Songs with Alice and Svend. *Publications:* Song in Molom; Another Song About The Forest of the Green Mist. *Honours:* Prize to the Memory of Ulf Peder Olrog, 1975; Nils Ferlin Prize, 1988; 2 Evert Taube Prizes, 1990. *Memberships:* Swedish Composers of Popular Music; Swedish Composers International Association; Swedish Authors Association. *Leisure interests:* Walking; Reading; Travel. *Address:* Alf Hambe, Steninge, 31042 Haverdal, Sweden.

HAMILL Andy; b. 25 March 1972, Glasgow, Scotland. Session Musician (Double Bass and Bass Guitars). *Career:* Gigs with American jazz singers, Mark Murphy, Annie Ross, Steve Kowalczyk and Rebecca Paris; Played with Chris Bowden at Glastonbury, 1997, and with 4 Hero at Montreux Jazz Festival, 1998; Mercury Music Awards, 1998; Currently working with singer/songwriters Rebecca Hollweg, Vanessa Freeman, Rosie Brown and Jont Whittington. *Recordings:* Chris Bowden, Time Capsule; 4 Hero, EP Earth Pioneers, CD Two Pages; Trudy Kerr, Sweet Suprise, Trudy; L T J Bukem, Mystical Realms; Flying Fish, The Storyteller; The Herbaliser,

Very Mercenary; Nitin Sayhnie, Beyond Skin; Valerie Etienne, For What It Is; Flora Purim and Airto Moreira's Fourth World, remix album. *Membership:* Musicians' Union. *Address:* 14A Emu Rd, London SW8 3PR, England.

HAMILTON Andy, (Raphael Thomas Hamilton); b. 26 March 1918, Port Maria, Jamaica. Jazz Musician (tenor saxophone). m. Mary, 4 s., 6 d. *Career:* Moved to Birmingham, 1949; Worked with Jean Toussaint; Mick Hucknall; David Murray; Steve Williamson; Andy Sheppard; Jason Rebello; Bernardo Sassetti; Son, Graeme (trumpet player); Concerts: St Lucia Jazz Festival; Co-producer with Jean Toussaint. *Recordings:* Albums: Silvershine, 1991; Jamaica By Night, 1993; with Steve Byrd: Late and Live, 1997. *Current Management:* Alan Cross, 120 Lightwoods Rd, Bearwood, Birmingham B67 5BE. *Address:* c/o World Circuit Records, 106 Cleveland St, London W1P 5DP, England.

HAMILTON Chico; b. 21 Sept. 1921, Los Angeles, California, USA. Jazz Musician (drums); Bandleader. *Career:* Drummer with: Dexter Gordon, Charles Mingus, Buddy Collette, whilst at school; Lionel Hampton, Slim Gaillard, 1940; Count Basie, Lester Young, late 1940s; Lena Horne, 1948–55; Founder, own quartet, 1955; Own bands (trio, quartet, quintet, octet) featured musicians including: Buddy Collette; Fred Katz; Ron Carter; Jim Hall; Eric Dolphy; Gabor Szabo; Larry Coryell; Eric Gayle; John Abercrombie; Film appearances: Sweet Smell of Success, 1957; Jazz On A Summer's Day, 1958; Leader, own group Euphoria, 1980s. *Recordings:* Numerous albums include: Spectacular, 1955; Sweet Smell of Success, 1957; Newport Jazz, 1958; The Three Faces of Chico, 1959; That Hamilton Man, 1959; Passin' Thru, 1962; Man From Two Worlds, 1963; Chic Chic Chico, 1965; The Dealer, 1966; The Further Adventures of El Chico, 1966; The Gamut, 1967; El Exigente, 1970; Head Hunters, 1974; Peregrinations, 1975; Chico Hamilton and The Players, 1976; Reaching For The Top, 1978; Nomad, 1979; Euphoria, 1986; Reunion, 1989; Chico The Master, 1992; Trio, 1992; My Panamanian Friend, 1992; Dancing to a Different Drummer, 1993; Timely, 1999; The Original Ellington Suite, 2000; Foreststorm, 2001. *Address:* Chico Hamilton Productions Inc, 321 E 45th St Penthouse A, New York, NY 10017, USA.

HAMILTON Frank; b. 3 Aug. 1934, New York City, USA. Musician; Singer. m. Mary Hamilton, 15 Jan. 1983. *Education:* Los Angeles City College, 1952, 1955, 1966; Roosevelt University, Chicago, 1960–61; Los Angeles Valley College, Van Nuys, 1963–64; Santa Monica City College, 1964–69; California University, Los Angeles, 1970, 1978; Santa Barbara City College, 1974; California University, Northridge, 1978; Georgia State University, 1984–87. *Career:* Co-Founder of The Old Town School of Folk Music, Chicago, 1957; House Musician, Gate of Horn, Chicago, 1958–62; Newport Folk Music Festival, 1959; With Folk Music Group, The Weavers, Carnegie Hall, Lincoln Center, Forest Hills Stadium, 1963; Concert with Pete Seeger, Abbott Hall, Marblehead, MA, 1984; Meridian Folk Trio, 1986–2000. *Compositions:* We Shall Overcome, 1956; Survival, 1965; The Surfers, 1964; Baby, What I Mean, 1965; I Feel It, 1967. *Recordings:* A Folksingers Folksinger; Frank Hamilton Sings Folk-songs; Nonsuch, with Pete Seeger; The World of Frank and Valucha; Weavers Reunion at Vanguard Carnegie Hall; Folk Festival at Newport; Long Lonesome Home, 1999; Goodnight Irene (Weavers compilation), 2000. *Publication:* Choosing a Guitar Teacher, 1981. *Honour:* Composition Award, Los Angeles Valley College, 1963. *Memberships:* Chicago Historical Society; Irish Arts of Atlanta; Founder, Hot Club of Atlanta. *Current Management:* Frank Hamilton Productions. *Address:* 852 Cinderella Court, Decatur, GA 30033, USA.

HAMILTON George IV; b. 19 July 1937, Winston-Salem, North Carolina, USA. Singer; Musician; Songwriter. m. Adelaide Peyton, 1958. Eduaction: University of North Carolina. *Career:* Recording artist, 1956–; Tours with Buddy Holly; Eddie Cochran; Gene Vincent; Broadway appearance with Louis Armstrong; Regular UK appearances include: Wembley Country Music Festival; First country artist to perform in Soviet Union; Occasionally works with son, George Hamilton V. *Recordings:* Hit singles include: A Rose and A Baby Ruth; If You Don't Know I Ain't Gonna Tell You; Why Don't They Understand; Only One Love; Now and For Always; The Teen Commandments of Love (with Paul Anka and Johnny Nash); I Know Where I'm Going; Abilene; Break My Mind; Fort Worth, Dallas Or Houston; She's A Little Bit Country; Albums include: On Campus, 1958; Mister Sincerity, 1965; By George, 1966; Canadian Pacific, 1969; Down Home In The Country (with Skeeter Davis), 1971; Heritage (with The Hillsiders), 1971; Down East Country, 1972; Bluegrass Gospel, 1974; Fine Lace and Homespun Cloth, 1977; Feel Like A Million, 1978; Forever Young, 1979; Cuttin' Across The Country, 1981; One Day At A Time, 1982; Songs For A Winter's Night, 1982; Music Man's Dream, 1984; Hymns Country Style, 1985; A Country Christmas, 1989; American Country Gothic (with the Moody Brothers), 1989; Country Classics (with George Hege Hamilton V), 1992; County Boy, 1996; George Hamilton IV, 1999; Beyond The River, 2001. *Honours:* International Ambassador of Country Music, Country Music People magazine, 1974; Trendsetter Award, Billboard magazine,

1975. *Current Management:* Blade Productions, PO Box 1556, Gainesville, FL 32602, USA.

HAMILTON Mark; b. 21 March 1977, Lisburn, Northern Ireland. Musician (bass). *Career:* Founder Member, Ash; Early indie releases, leading to record contract; Support slots to Suede, Dinosaur Jr and Elastica; Headline dates, TV appearances and festival dates; Headlining US tour. *Recordings:* Singles: Jack Names the Planets, 1994; Petrol, 1994; Uncle Pat, 1994; Kung Fu, 1995; Girl From Mars, 1995; Goldfinger, 1996; Oh Yeah, 1996; A Life Less Ordinary, 1997; Jesus Says, 1998; Sometimes, 2001; Shining Angel, 2001; Burn Baby Burn, 2001; Candy, 2001; There's A Star, 2001; Albums: Trailer, 1994; 1977, 1996; Live At The Wireless, 1997; Nu-Clear Sounds, 1998; Free All Angels, 2001.

HAMILTON Natasha Maria; b. 17 July 1982, Kensington, Liverpool, England. Vocalist. *Career:* Joined Atomic Kitten 1999; UK Support tours 1999–2000; Co-spearheaded MTV Asia Awards 2000 reaching 675m. viewers; Pan-European breakthrough with Whole Again single; Guest at Celebrate South Africa Freedom Concert, London, 2001. *Recordings:* Albums: Right Now, 2000 (revised issue 2001); Singles: Right Now, 1999; See Ya, 2000; I Want Your Love, 2000; Follow Me, 2000; Whole Again, 2001; Eternal Flame, 2001. *Honours:* Successes at UK Disney Channel and Smash Hits Awards 2000/2001. *Current Management:* Innocent Records, Kensal House, 553–579 Harrow Rd, London, W10 4RH, England.

HAMILTON Page; b. Eugene, Oregon, USA. Musician (guitar). *Education:* MA, Jazz Guitar, Manhattan School of Music, New York. *Career:* Played in Glenn Branca's Guitar Orchestra; Member, Band of Susans; Formed Helmet, 1989; Numerous live dates; Appears on: Opening Credits, Laptop, 2000. *Recordings:* Singles: Born Annoying; In the Meantime; Unsung; Primitive; Just Another Victim; Biscuits for Smut; Wolma's Rainbow, EP; Exactly What You Wanted; Albums: Strap It On, 1990; Meantime, 1992; Betty, 1994; Aftertaste, 1997.

HAMILTON Patrick; b. 16 March 1963, Bruges, Belgium. Prod.; Musician (Keyboards); Songwriter. m. Brigitte Vandewalle, 20 Nov. 1987, 2 s., 1 d. *Education:* Classical Music Degree; Organ and Piano lessons. *Career:* Played with several well known bands in Belgium; Tour with Johnny Logan, 1990s; Tour in Belgium and The Netherlands for Hammond-organs, 1980s. *Compositions:* Composed for Sandra Kim, Eurovision contest winner mid 1980s; 2 Lips; Partyzone; Monday Justice; Marisa; Confetti's. *Recordings:* The Roof, own studio. *Address:* Sint-Jorisstraat 30, 8730 Beerncm, Belgium.

HAMLISCH Marvin; b. 2 June 1944, New York, USA. Composer; Conductor; Musician (piano); Entertainer. m. Terre Blair, 29 May 1989. *Education:* Professional Children's School; Queen's College, New York. *Musical Education:* The Juilliard School, New York. *Career:* Debut as pianist, Minnesota Orchestra, 1975; Solo concert tours; Conductor of various orchestras throughout US; Principal Pops conductor for: Pittsburgh Symphony Orchestra; National Symphony Orchestra, 2000–; Musical director and conductor, Barbra Streisand tours: The Concert, 1994; And Timeless, 1999. *Compositions include:* Film scores: Frankie and Johnny, 1966; The Swimmer, 1968; Take The Money and Run, 1969; Bananas, 1971; The Way We Were, 1974; The Sting (adaptation), 1974; Same Time Next Year, 1979; Starting Over, 1979; Ordinary People, 1980; Seems Like Old Times, 1980; Sophie's Choice, 1982; Film themes for: The January Man; Three Men and A Baby; Little Nikita; The Experts; Popular songs: Sunshine Lollipops and Rainbows; Good Morning America; Nobody Does It Better; Broadway musicals: A Chorus Line, 1975; They're Playing Our Song, 1979; The Goodbye Girl, 1993; Other works: Anatomy of Peace, Symphony In One Movement, 1991; One Song, for Barcelona Olympics, 1992. *Publication:* The Way I Was (autobiography), 1992. *Honours:* 3 Academy Awards; 4 Grammy Awards; 3 Emmy Awards; 1 Tony Award; 3 Golden Globes; Pulitzer Prize, for show A Chorus Line. *Membership:* ASCAP. *Leisure interests:* Loves to travel; Baseball. *Address:* c/o Nancy Shear Arts Services, 180 West End Ave, Suite 28N-P, New York, NY 10023, USA.

HAMMARLUND Jan; b. 17 July 1951, Stockholm, Sweden. Singer; Songwriter; Guitarist; Translator. *Musical Education:* Private singing lessons, 1981–92. *Career:* Festivals: Gärdet, Stockholm; Västervik; Roskilde; Midtfyn; Hultsfred; Mariposa; Chile Crea; Tour of England, 1978; California, 1979; Denmark, 1978–86; Chile, 1991; Swedish TV Portrait, 1990. *Compositions:* Songs: Ville, 1979; Translations of Violeta Parra; Dag Vill Leva I Europa, 1981; Malvina Reynolds. *Recordings:* 12 LPs, 1972–86; Tusentals Swarnor Over Chile, 1974; Karlek Olh Sang, 1981; Among 6 CDs: Jan Hammarlund, 1972–92; Tvars Over Garn, French cabaret songs, 1995; Om Trädgårdsbevattning, songs by Brecht, 1996. *Honours:* Awards with Grants: SKAP, 1978; STIM, 1989; Konstnärsnämnden (Artists committee), 1992–96; José Martí Award, 1994. *Memberships:* STIM; Svenska Teateförbundet, SKAP; Musikcentrum. *Leisure interest:* Travel. *Address:* Skördemane AB, c/o Hammarlund, Vapengatan 22, 12652 Hagersten, Sweden.

HAMMEL Joan; b. 11 Aug., Lake Forest, Illinois, USA. Professional Vocalist. *Education:* Columbia College. *Career:* Professional Singer, performing primarily in the US; toured the Caribbean; hosted the Midday Show, on radio; numerous commercials, television and film work. *Compositions:* Learn To Fly; Love Prevails; Run Like The Wind; The Gift; Give It To Me Straight; Timeless; See Ya. *Recordings:* Oh Lady Di, Tribute To Princess Diana. *Honours:* Emmy, Best Childrens Special, 1987; ITVA Award, Best Health Care Video, 1986, 1987; National and International Vocal Competition Medals. *Memberships:* NARAS; NATAS; ACCOP. *Leisure interests:* Scubadiving; Animals; Glass Fusing. *Current Management:* Paxton Productions, PO Box 486, Grayslake, IL 60030, USA.

HAMMER (Stanley Kirk Burrell); b. 30 March 1962, Oakland, California, USA. Rapper; Dancer. *Career:* Former baseball player; Member, rap duo Holy Ghost Boys; Founder, Bustin Records; Solo artiste (originally as MC Hammer), 1987–; Concerts include: Please Hammer, Don't Hurt 'Em US tour, 1990; US tour, with Vanilla Ice and En Vogue, 1990; UK and Japan tours, 1991; The Simple Truth (benefit concert for Kurdish refugees), Wembley, 1991; Too Legit To Quit tour, with Boyz II Men, 1992; USA Harvest Hunger Relief Concert, 1992; Kiel Summer Jam, largest rap festival ever, 1992; Television includes: Lou Rawls Parade of Stars, 1990; Ray Charles, 50 Years In Music Uh-Huh, 1991; Hammer's MTV Birthday Bash, 1992; Hammer From The Heart, CBS, 1992; Hammerman Cartoon series, ABC, 1991; Founder, management, production and video company, Roll-Wit-It Entertainment, 1992. *Recordings:* Hit singles include: U Can't Touch This, 1990; Have You Seen Her?, 1990; Pray, (No. 2, US), 1990; Here Comes The Hammer, from Rocky V film soundtrack, 1991; Yo! Sweetness, 1991; Addams Groove, from Addams Family film soundtrack, 1992; 2 Legit 2 Quit, 1992; Do Not Pass Me By, 1992; It's All Too Good, 1994; Pumps and A Bump, 1994; Don't Stop, 1994; Going Up Yonder, 1995; Sultry Funk 1995; Albums: Feel My Power, 1987; Please Hammer Don't Hurt 'Em (No. 1, US, 10m. copies sold), 1990; Too Legit To Quit, 1991; The Funky Headhunter, 1994; Inside Out, 1995; Family Affair, 1998; Active Duty, 2001. *Honours:* Several American Music Awards, 1990–91; 3 Grammy Awards, 1991; People's Choice Award, 1991; BRIT Award, Best International Newcomer, 1991; MC Hammer Day declared, Fremont, California, 1991; 2 Bammy Awards, 1991; JUNO Award, International Artist of the Year, 1991; 3 Rolling Stone Readers Poll Wins, 1991; 4 Soul Train Awards, including Sammy Davis Jr Award, 1991–92; 4 NARM Awards, 1991. *Current Management:* Superstar Management, 7633 Sunkist Dr., Oakland, CA 94605, USA.

HAMMER Jan; b. 17 April 1948, Prague, Czechoslovakia. Musician (keyboards); Composer. *Musical Education:* Prague Academy of Music and Arts, 1966–68; Berklee College of Music, Boston, USA, 1968. *Career:* Moved to US, 1968; Jazz musician, 1968–71; Member, John McLaughlin's Mahavishnu Orchestra, 1971–73; Freelance musician and bandleader, 1973-. *Compositions:* Film scores: A Night In Heaven, 1983; Secret Admirer, 1985; Television series soundtrack: Miami Vice, 1984-. *Recordings:* Singles: Theme From Miami Vice (No. 1, USA), 1985; Crockett's Theme (No. 2, UK), 1987; Too Much to Lose, 1989; Solo albums: Like Children, 1974; First Seven Days, 1975; Timeless, 1975; Make Love, 1976; Oh Yeah, 1976; Melodies, 1979; Black Sheep, 1979; Escape From TV, 1987; Snapshots, 1989; Behind The Mind's Eye, 1993; Country and Eastern Music, 1993; Drive, 1994; Snapshots 1.2, 2000; with John McLaughlin: Inner Mounting Flame, 1971; Birds of Fire, 1973; Love Devotion and Surrender, 1973; with Jeff Beck: Wired, 1976; Live With The Jan Hammer Group, 1977; There and Back, 1980; Flash, 1985; with Al Di Meola: Elegant Gypsy, 1977; Splendido Hotel, 1979; Electric Rendezvous, 1982; Tour de Force, 1982; Scenario, 1983; with John Abercombie: Timeless, 1975; Five Years Later, 1982; Other recordings with: Tommy Bolin; Stanley Clarke; Billy Cobham; Steve Lukather; Santana; Jerry Goodman; Neal Schon.

HAMMER Joseph; b. 7 June 1954, San Antonio, Texas, USA. Musician (drums, fairlight); Composer. m. Jacqueline Henry, 28 Feb. 1983, 1 s. *Musical Education:* Drum Instruction, Berklee School of Music; Boston School of Electronic Music. *Career:* Studio production, 1975–85; Co-production for Daniel Balavoine; Tours, concerts, with Daniel Balavoine, France Gall, Jean-Michel Jarre. *Compositions:* Summer Dreaming; Love of a Woman. *Recordings:* Daniel Balavoine; Jean-Michel Jarre; Jon Anderson; Mick Jagger; Peter Gabriel. *Publications:* Trophee Sonor, 6–10 Drums. *Membership:* Institut de Percussions Modernes. *Leisure interest:* Fishing. *Current Management:* La Fretite Studios. *Address:* La Fretite Studios, 10 rue Jean Lefevbre, 95530 La Frette, Paris, France.

HAMMETT Barry James; b. 31 Oct. 1944, Swansea, Wales. Musician (guitar); Guitar Teacher. m. 16 March 1968 to 19 March 1978, 2 d. *Education:* Swansea Technical College. *Musical Education:* Self-taught. *Career:* Lead guitar, Johnny Kidd and Pirates, 7 years; Swansea Top Rank (resident band), 7 years; PandO Cruises, 14 months with Kiki Dee, Blood Brothers tour. *Recordings:* Numerous radio and TV sessions as featured band, backing musician. *Membership:* Musicians' Union. *Leisure interest:*

Arranging music. *Address:* 52, Ael-y-Bryn, Fforestfarch, Swansea, West Glamorgan, SA5 8JB, Wales.

HAMMETT Kirk; b. 18 Nov. 1962, USA. Musician (guitar). *Career:* Guitarist, Exodus; Joe Satriani; Member, US heavy rock group Metallica, 1983–; World-wide tours include: Masters of Puppet world tour, 1986–87; US tour, 1988; Damaged Justice British tour, 1989; World tour, 1991–; Also tours with Raven; Ozzy Osbourne; Twisted Sister; Motörhead; Major concerts include: Monsters of Rock Festival, Castle Donington, 1985, 1987, 1991; German Monster Rock festivals, 1987; Monsters of Rock, Europe and US tours, 1988, 1991; Day On The Green, Oakland, 1991. *Recordings:* Albums: Kill 'Em All, 1983; Ride The Lightning, 1984; Master of Puppets, 1986; …and Justice For All, 1988; Metallica (No. 1, USA and UK), 1991; Live Shit, 1993; Load, 1996; Reload, 1997; Mama Said, 1998; SandM, 1999; Singles: Garage Days Revisited (EP), 1987; Harvester of Sorrow, 1988; One, 1989; Enter Sandman, 1991; The Unforgiven, 1991; Nothing Else Matters, 1992; Wherever I May Roam, 1992; Sad But True, 1992; Until It Sleeps, 1996; Hero of the Day, 1996; Memory Remains, 1997; The Unforgiven, 1998; Whisky in the Jar, 1999; Die Die My Darling, 1999; I Disappear, 2000; Stone Cold Crazy, track featured on Rubáiyát (Elektra's 40th Anniversary compilation). *Honours:* Platinum and Gold discs; Grammy Awards: Best Heavy Metal Performance: One, 1989; Stone Cold Crazy, 1991; The Unforgiven 1992; Best Hard Rock Performance: Whiskey In The Jar, 2000; Rock Instrumental Performance, Call of The Ktulu, 2001; American Music Award, Favourite Heavy Metal Artist, 1993; Bay Area Music Awards: Outstanding Album, 1992; Outstanding Heavy Metal Album, Outstanding Group, Outstanding Guitarist, 1993; Rolling Stone Readers Poll Winners, Best Heavy Metal Band, 1993. *Current Management:* Q-Prime Inc. *Address:* 729 Seventh Ave, 14th Floor, New York, NY 10019, USA.

HAMMILL Peter; b. 5 Nov. 1948, London, England. Vocalist; Musician (guitar, piano). *Career:* Founder member, Van Der Graaf Generator, 1968–72, 1975–78; Also recording artiste. *Recordings:* Albums with Van Der Graaf Generator: Aerosol Grey Machine, 1968; The Least We Can Do Is Wave To Each Other, 1969; H To He Who Is The Only One, 1970; Pawn Hearts, 1971; Godbluff, 1975; Still Life, 1976; World Record, 1976; The Quiet Zone; The Pleasure Dome, 1977; Box Set 1968–78, 2001; Solo albums include: Fool's Mate, 1971; Chameleon In The Shadow of Night, 1972; The Silent Corner and The Empty Stage, 1974; In Camera, 1974; Nadir's Big Chance, 1975; Over, 1977; The Future Now, 1978; PH7, 1979; A Black Box, 1980; Sitting Targets, 1981; Enter K, 1982; Patience, 1983; The Love Songs, 1984; Skin, 1986; And Close as This, 1986; In a Foreign Town, 1986; Out of Water, 1990; The Fall of The House of Usher, 1991; Fireships, 1992; The Noise, 1993; Roaring Forties, 1994; X My Heart, 1996; Everyone You Hold, 1997; This, 1998; None of The Above, 2000; What Now, 2001. *Current Management:* Gailforce Management, 24 Ives St, London SW3 2ND, England.

HAMMOND Albert Jr; b. April 1980, Los Angeles USA. Musician (guitar). *Career:* Son of Albert Hammond; Member: The Strokes, 1998-. *Recordings:* Albums: Is This It, 2001; Singles: The Modern Age, Hard To Explain/New York City Cops, Last Nite/When It Started, 2001. *Honours:* Brit Award, Best International Newcomer, 2002; NME Awards: Band of The Year; Best New Act; Album of The Year, 2001. *Current Management:* Ryan Gentles, Wiz Kid Management. *Internet:* www.thestrokes.com.

HAMMOND John Paul; b. 13 Nov. 1942, New York, New York, USA. Blues Musician (guitar); Singer. *Career:* Began playing guitar aged 17; Recording artist, 1962–; British tours, 1960s; Worked with artists including Duane Allman; JJ Cale; John Lee Hooker; Robbie Robertson; Bill Wyman; Charles Brown; Charlie Musselwhite; Duke Robillard; Bob Dylan; Michelle Shocked; Host, performer, television documentary The Search For Robert Johnson, 1992. *Recordings:* Albums: John Hammond; Big City Blues; Country Blues; So Many Roads; Mirrors; I Can Tell; Sooner Or Later; Southern Fried; Source Point; I'm Satisfied; Triumvirate; Can't Beat The Kid; John Hammond Solo; Footwork; Hot Tracks; Mileage; Frogs For Snakes; John Hammond Live; John Hammond Live In Greece; Nobody But You; Got Love If You Want It; Trouble No More; Found True Love; Wicked Grin, 2001; Featured on film soundtracks: Little Big Man, 1971; Matewan, 1987; Long as I Have You. *Honours:* Grammy Award, Blues Explosion (with Stevie Ray Vaughan, Koko Taylor), 1985; Grammy Nominations: Got Love If You Want It, 1992; Trouble No More, 1993; Found True Love, 1997. *Current Management:* Tri Tone Management, 331 Carrera Dr., Mill Valley, CA 94941, USA.

HAMPTON Andy; b. 8 May 1958, Sheffield, England. Composer. m. Jennifer Stirling, 22 July 1994, 1 s., 1 d. *Education:* York University, BA Hons; MA, Open University. *Musical Education:* Guildhall, London; LTCL Trinity College, London. *Career:* Appearance as actor/musician, Lennon, London's West End 1985. *Compositions:* Themes for: BBC Radio 1; BBC Radio 2; Granada TV; Sky Network; Screensport. *Publications:* Jazzworks for Clarinet, Saxophone students; Unbeaten Tracks; Saxophone Basics. *Honour:* Best Music, National Student Drama Festival, 1979.

Memberships: PRS; MCPS. *Leisure interests:* Sailing; Football. *Address:* 28 Harold Rd, London N8 7DE, England.

HAMPTON Lionel Leo; b. 20 April 1908, Louisville, Kentucky, USA. Composer; Conductor; Musician. m. Gladys Riddle, 11 Nov. 1936 (deceased). *Career:* Member, Benny Goodman Quartet, 1936–40; Leader, Lionel Hampton Orchestra (first band to feature electric bass and organ), 1940–; Professor of Music, Howard University, 1981–; Appointed UN Ambassador of Music, 1985; Established Lionel Hampton Jazz Endowment Fund, 1984; Human Rights Commissioner, New York, 1984–86. *Compositions:* King David Suite (symphonic work), 1953. *Recordings:* Albums include: Sentimental Journey, 1986; Flying Home, 1991; Outrageous, 2000; Ring Dem Bells, 2001; with Chick Corea: Chick and Lionel Live At Midem, 1972. *Honours:* Established in his honour: Lionel Hampton School of Music, University of Idaho, 1987; Lionel Hampton Research Foundation, 1987; Voted into Playboy's All-Stars band, 28 years in succession; Gold Medal, City of Paris, 1985; Ebony magazine Lifetime Achievement Award, 1979; Numerous Hon. MusD and PhD Mus; Hon. Chairman, Musicians Emergency Fund, Jazz Foundation of America; Given 90th birthday party at the White House by President Clinton. *Current Management:* Philip Leshin. *Address:* 20 Vinton Ave, Box 616, Bedford, NY 10506, USA.

HAMZA Kawkab; b. 1 July 1944, Babylon, Iraq. Composer. Divorced, 1 s., 2 d. *Musical Education:* Fine Art Institute, Baghdad; 5 years, USSR High Institute. *Career:* Composed first song, 1966, Moved to Syria, 1983, wrote 4 theatre plays, 2 television series; Moved to Detroit, composed for theatre; Now refugee in Denmark, Composing for theatre; Takes part in international musical festivals. *Compositions:* 6 theatre plays; 4 documentary films; 2 television, music classes; more than 70 songs including: Songs for: Husein Naamah; Fuaad Salim; Saadun Jaber; Anwar Abd Alwahab; Albums: Nehebbkum Wallah Nehebkum; New Babylon Music; Sar Alumur Mahetat. *Membership:* Danish Society for Jazz, Rock, Folk Composers. *Leisure interest:* Music. *Address:* Tårnvej 209–2, 2610 Rodovre, Denmark.

HANCOCK Herbie; b. 12 April 1940, Chicago, Illinois, USA. Composer; Jazz Musician (piano, synthesiser). m. Gudrun Meixner, 31 Aug. 1968, 1 d. *Education:* BA, Grinnell College, Iowa. *Musical Education:* Manhattan School of Music, New York, 1 year. *Career:* Chicago Symphony Orchestra, 1952; Miles Davis Quartet, 1963–68; Television: Coast To Coast (Showtime), Host; Television Scores: Hey, Hey, Hey, It's Fat Albert – Bill Cosby Special; Film Scores: Blow Up, 1966; Death Wish, 1974; A Soldier's Story, 1974; Round Midnight, 1986; Jo Jo Dancer, Your Life Is Calling, 1986; Colors, 1988. *Recordings:* Taking Off, 1962; Maiden Voyage, 1965; Speak Like A Child, 1967; Headhunters, 1973; Thrust, 1974; Manchild, 1975; VSOP, 1977; Sunlight, 1979; Feets Don't Fail Me Now, 1979; Future Shock, 1983; Sound System, 1984; Perfect Machine, 1988; Tribute To Miles, 1994; Dis Is Da Drum, 1995; The New Standard, 1996; Future 2 Future, 2001; with Miles Davis Quartet: Miles In The Sky; Nefertiti; Sorcerer; ESP; Miles Davis In Concert (My Funny Valentine); In A Silent Way; Jack Johnson; Seven Steps To Heaven; Contributor, Colour and Light – Jazz Sketches On Sondheim, 1995. *Publications:* A Tribute to Miles, 1994; Dis is Da Drum, 1994; The New Standard, 1996; I H with Wayne Shorter, 1997; Gershwin's World, 1998. *Honours:* Jay Award, Jazz Magazine, 1963; Downbeat Award, 1967; Several Awards, Black Music Magazine, 1967–71; 5 MTV Awards, including Best Concept Video, Rock It, 1983; 3 Grammy Awards, including Best R & B Instrumental Performance, Rock It, 1983; Academy Award, Best Original Score, Round Midnight, 1986. *Memberships:* AFofM; NARAS; AFTRA; SAG; AMPAS. *Leisure interest:* Digital Technology. *Current Management:* DPE. *Address:* c/o 3 E 28th St, Sixth Floor, New York, NY 10016, USA.

HANCOCK Keith; b. 28 Oct. 1953, Manchester, England. Singer; Songwriter; Musician (diatonic accordion). m. Janet Karen Wood, 29 Sept. 1979, 2 s. *Musical Education:* Self-taught. *Career:* Progressed through English Country dance bands; Began writing, 1984; Toured: Europe; Canada; New Zealand; Hong Kong; Australia; TV Ballads, BBC2, 1995; New Band, Keith Hancock's Famous Last Words, 1996. *Compositions include:* best known song Absent Friends. *Recordings:* This World We Live In, 1985; Madhouse, 1988; Compassion, 1993; Born Blue, 1997. *Memberships:* Musicians' Union; Equity. *Leisure interests:* Music; Manchester City Football Club. *Current Management:* Janet Hancock, Spiv Promotions. *Address:* PO Box 35, SE PDO, Manchester M18 8JY, England.

HANCOCK Robin Jonathon Coventry; b. Croydon, Surrey, England. Record Prod.; Musician (guitar). *Education:* BSc Electric Engineering, Reading University. *Musical Education:* Grade 6, Classical guitar. *Recordings:* Erotica, Madonna; Cyberpunk, Billy Idol; Seal, Seal; Other recordings by Tina Turner; Simple Minds; Robert Miles. *Leisure interests:* Skiing; Snowboarding; Windsurfing; Sailing. *Current Management:* Sarm Productions. *Address:* 38 Turneville Rd, West Kensington, London W14 9PS, England.

HAND Richard; b. 27 Nov. 1960, Marsden, Yorkshire, England. Musician (guitar). *Musical Education:* Open Scholarship to Royal Academy of Music. *Career:* Member, English Guitar Quartet: Tours of Israel; Member, flute and guitar duo: The Lightfingered Gentry; Tours include: Germany; Holland; Gulf States; Egypt; Member, Hand/Dupré Guitar Duo tours: Norway; Poland; India; Bangladesh; Sri Lanka; Philippines; Malaysia; Indonesia; Singapore; Hong Kong; Television, radio appearances worldwide include: BBC Radio 2, 3, 4; Premieres of new works by: Peter Dickinson; Tim Souster; Jonathon Lloyd; David Bedford; Roger Steptoe; Michael Ball; Brian May; Judith Bingham; Wilfred Josephs. *Honours:* Julian Bream Prize; Associate of Royal Academy of Music. *Memberships:* ISM; Musicians' Union. *Address:* 61 Balcombe St, Marylebone, London NW1 6HD, England.

HANLEY Ged, (Ray Kershwin); b. 22 March 1960, Scotland. Musician (guitar, piano); Vocalist. m. Donna Marie Archibald, 25 Nov. 1994, 2 s., 1 d. *Musical Education:* Self-taught. *Career:* Tours (backing vocals) with Runrig; Wreck On The Highway; BBC appearances and recording. *Membership:* Musicians' Union. *Leisure interest:* Music. *Address:* 114 Carnethie St, Rosewall, Midlothian EH24 9AL, Scotland.

HANLON Jef; b. 5 July 1943, Blackpool, England. Artist Man.; Concert Promoter; Agent. m. Alice Welsh, 8 Dec. 1973. *Career:* Guitarist, England and Germany, 1958–64; Personal/tour manager: Wayne Fontana; Herman's Hermits; Extensive world tours, 1964–69; Partner, Billings-Hanlon Management, 1969–73; Clients: Jimmy Ruffin, Kiki Dee, The Hermits; Director, Rock Artist Management Group of Companies, 1973–76; Clients included: Gary Glitter; The Glitter Band; Bay City Rollers; Barry Blue; Hello; New Seekers; The Damned; Springfield Revival; Director, Derek Block Artists Agency and Derek Block Concert Promotions, 1976–89; Clients included: Duran Duran; UB40; The Police; Tears For Fears; Gary Glitter; The Clash; Ian Dury; Agent for William Morris Agency Inc, (USA), 1977–84; Clients included: Diana Ross; Stevie Wonder; Barry Manilow; Rod Stewart; Concert promotions include: Rod Stewart; Chuck Berry; David Brubeck; Simon and Garfunkel; Stevie Wonder; Bob Hope; Bing Crosby; Duran Duran; Gary Glitter; B B King; Johnny Mathis; The Everly Brothers; Neil Sedaka; The Temptations; Don McLean; Also major tours: Australasia; Japan; Europe; UK; Formed Jef Hanlon Management Ltd, 1990–; Major client: Gary Glitter; Also managed The Wild Swans; Promoted tours: Bob Hope; Don McLean; Juan Martin's Flamenco Dance Company (Seville); Village People; Bootleg Beatles; Joaquin Cortes; Recently promoted Dave Brubeck Quartet, Culture Club, and co-promoted B B King. *Memberships:* President, Agents' Asscn of Great Britain, 1995–97; Chairman, International Managers' Forum, 1998–; Mem., Concert Promoters' Asscn. *Address:* 1 York St, London W1H 1PZ, England.

HANNAN Neil; b. 12 Aug. 1952, Christchurch, New Zealand. Musician (bass). m. Jacqui Fitzgerald, 16 Dec. 1993, 1 d. *Musical Education:* 2 years Victoria University, Wellington, New Zealand; Various private tutors from age seven, piano, guitar. *Career:* Professional musician since age 19; Performed in New Zealand with Randy Crawford, Renee Geyer; Member, popular New Zealand bands: Hello Sailor; Coup d'Etat; Midge Marsden's Country Flyers; Numerous radio programmes and recordings; Professional work in Australia, UK, USA. *Recordings:* Solo albums: Scoop This Loop; 24 Hour Oasis. *Publication:* Working on Bass Teaching book. *Honour:* Single of Year (with Coup d'Etat), 1981. *Memberships:* Australasian Peforming Right Asscn (APRA); Recording Industry Asscn of New Zealand (RIANZ). *Leisure interests:* Swimming; Reading. *Address:* 19 Wynyard Rd, Mt Eden, Auckland, New Zealand.

HANNAN Patrick Edward Dean; b. 4 March 1966, Lymington, Hampshire, England. Musician (drums). 1 d. *Career:* Two major world tours with the Sundays. *Recordings:* Albums: with the Sundays: Reading Writing Arithmetic, 1990; Blind, 1992; Static and Silence, 1997; with Perry Rose: Bright Ring of The Day, 1995; with Arnold, Windsor Park, 1997; Hillside, 1998; with Tim Keegan, Long Distance Information, 1998; with Theaudience, Theaudience, 1998; with Robyn Hitchcock, Jewels for Sophia, 1999; Singles: with Star 69: Mama Don't Let, 1995; You Are Here, 1995. *Honours:* Gold and Silver Discs; Gold US Disc. *Membership:* Musicians' Union. *Leisure interests:* 60s Cars; Golf; Pubs.

HANNIBAL Lars; b. 15 July 1951, Risskov, Denmark. Musician (Lute, Guitar). m. Michala Petri, 2 d. *Education:* Guitar, Royal Danish Conservatory, Aarhus; Lute, with Toyohiko Satoy, The Hague. *Career:* Jazz/Rock Musician; Toured as Chamber Musician; throughout Europe, USA, Japan, 1980–; Worked with musicians such as Michala Petri, Kim Sjøgren, Palle Mikkalborg, Niels Henning, Orsted Pedersen, Svend Asmussen. *Compositions:* Du Drømmer, Vesterled, both for lute and violin. *Recordings:* 10 CDs with Duo Concertante, violin and guitar, including music by Giuliani, Paçanini, Sarasate and Lalo and contemporary music; Solo CD, Romance; 2 CDs with recorder player Michala Petri, Air and Souvenir; Golden CD winning album, Memory, with trumpeter Michael Brydenfelt, 1999; Formed duo with baritone singer

Lars Thodberg Bertelsew. *Honours:* FiF Cultural Prize, 1991; Danish Soloist Union, Anniversary Grant, 1993. *Membership:* DMF; Danish Soloist Union; Solistforeninen. *Leisure interests:* Psychology; Tennis. *Address:* Nordskraenten 3, 2980 Kokkedal, Denmark.

HANNON (Edward) Neil (Anthony); b. 7 Nov. 1970, Londonderry, Northern Ireland. Songwriter; Singer; Musician (guitar). *Career:* Member, The Divine Comedy; Released four albums and 2 mini albums; Six top forty singles; Numerous live and TV appearances including Top of the Pops, TFI Friday, Later, with Jools Holland. *Compositions:* Something for the Weekend; Songs of Love (theme to TV comedy series Father Ted); In Pursuit (Theme from Tomorrow's World). *Recordings:* Singles: Something For The Weekend, 1996; Becoming More Like Alfie, 1996; The Frog Princess, 1996; Everybody Knows, 1997; I've Been To A Marvellous Party, 1998; Generation Sex, 1998; The Certainty of Chance, 1998; National Express, 1999; The Pop Singer's Fear of The Pollen Count, 1999; Gin Soaked Boy, 1999; Bad Ambassador, 2001; Albums: Liberation, 1991; Promenade, 1995; Casanova, 1996; Fin de Siecle, 1998; Secret History (compilation), 1999; Regeneration, 2001; Vocals on: No Regrets (single), Robbie Williams, 1998; Reload, Tom Jones, 1999; Punishing Kiss, Ute Lemper, 2000. *Leisure interests:* Computer games; Drinking in pubs; Being famous. *Current Management:* Divine Management, Top Floor, 1 Cowcross St, London EC1M 6OR, England.

HANOT Pierre; b. 25 March 1952, Metz, France. Singer; Writer; Composer. Artist. m. Martine Bonici, 28 Feb. 1992, 2 d. *Education:* Modern and classical French. *Musical Education:* Guitar. *Career:* More than 700 concerts, in clubs, festivals, pubs, cultural centres, 1975–; Dates in: France; Germany; Luxemboug; Belgium; Spain. *Recordings:* Rock Derivé, 1985; En Un Instant Damnés, 1995. *Membership:* SACEM. *Leisure interests:* Dogs; Love; Collages. *Current Management:* Martine Bonici. *Address:* 8A Pl. du Temple, 57530 Courcelles Chaussy, France.

HANRAHAN Michael; b. 19 Sept. 1958, Ennis, County Clare, Ireland. Songwriter; Musician (guitar); Vocalist. m. Donna Barnes, 3 Sept. 1994. *Career:* Tours world-wide with Stockton's Wing, 1974–94; Performed with Sammy Davis Junior, Dublin; Numerous television, radio shows; Currently touring as solo artist. *Compositions:* Most successful songs: Beautiful Affair; Walk Away. *Recordings:* 7 albums with Stockton's Wing; For imminent release: Someone Like You. *Membership:* Irish Music Rights Organisation (Board mem.). *Leisure interest:* Golf. *Current Management:* Kara Hamahoe. *Address:* 29, St Fintans Villas, Deansgrange, Co Dublin, Ireland.

HANSARD Glen; b. 21 April 1970, Dublin, Ireland. Vocalist; Musician (guitar); Songwriter. *Career:* Busker on the streets of Dublin; Founder member: The Frames, late 1980s; Set up own label Plateau Records; Tours of US and Europe with The Frames and solo; Appeared as Outspan in The Commitments film. *Recordings:* Another Love Song, 1992; Fitzcarraldo, 1994; Dance the Devil, 1999; For the Birds (produced by Steve Albini), 2001. *Honours:* For the Birds album reached Irish Top 10. *E-mail:* cleadbitter@framesoffice.freeserve.co.uk.

HANSEN Hanne Wilhelm; b. 23 Jan. 1927, Copenhagen, Denmark. Theatre Agent; Artist Man. *Career:* Music publisher until 1988; Theatre and artist manager and publisher; Chairman of the Wilhelm Hansen Foundation. *Address:* Gothersgade 11, 1123 Copenhagen K, Denmark.

HANSEN Jacob; b. 9 Nov. 1970, Denmark. Guitarist; Singer. *Career:* Touring and Recording with Heavy Metal Band, Invocator, 1986–94; Released 4 Albums; Appeared three times on National Television; 2 European Tours; Freelance Producer, Engineer, 1993-. *Recordings:* Excursion Demise, 1991; Weave The Apocalypse, 1993; Early Years, 1994; Dying To Live, 1994. *Honour:* Nominated for Danish Grammy, 1992. *Memberships:* KODA; GRAMEX. *Leisure interests:* Running a Record Company; Serious Entertainment. *Address:* Kongensgade 84, 6700 Esbjerg, Denmark.

HANSEN Kai; b. Germany. Vocalist; Rock Musician (guitar). *Career:* Founder member, German rock band, Helloween, 1984; Numerous tours across Europe; Appearances include: Monsters of Rock Festival, Castle Donington, 1988; Founder, Gamma Ray, 1989; Extensive tours in Europe and Japan. *Recordings:* Albums: with Helloween: Helloween (mini-LP), 1985; Walls of Jericho, 1986; Keeper of The Seven Keys, Part I, 1987; Part II, 1988; Live In The UK 1989; with Gamma Ray: Heading For Tomorrow, 1990; Sigh No More, 1991; Insanity and Genius, 1993; Land of the Free, 1995; Somewhere out in Space, 1997; Alive '95, 1999; Power Plant, 1999; Blast From The Past, 2000; No World Order, 2001; Features on Dark Assault, Iron Saviour, 2001; Also tracks featured on: Death Metal, compilation album, 1984. *Current Management:* Sanctuary Music (Overseas). *Address:* First Floor Suite, The Colonnades, 82 Bishops Bridge Rd, London W2 6BB, England.

HANSON Lloyd A; b. 1 Nov. 1964, Fredericton, New Brunswick, Canada. Musician (bass); Record Prod.; Recording Engineer. *Musical Education:* Berklee College of Music, Boston, USA, 1986. *Career:* Recording career from 1988; Played bass in many jazz, folk, experimental ensembles at major festivals including: Mama's and Papa's, 1987; Harvest Jazz and Blues Festival, with Long John Baldry, 1992; Formed Thrash Peninsula, 1993; Producer, engineer, composer, arranger. *Recordings:* with Thrash Peninsula: A Different Drummer; A D Shade Café; Thunder God's Wife; with Brent Mason: Down To Heaven; with Ned Landry: Fiddling Champ. *Honour:* New Brunswick Arts Branch Creation Grant, 1992. *Memberships:* AFofM; Musicians' Union; SOCAN. *Leisure interests:* Walk average 7 miles a day; Reading spiritual and science; Books; Listening to music. *Address:* 741 McEvoy St, Fredericton, New Brunswick E3A 3B8, Canada.

HANSON Simon; b. 3 Feb. 1964, Grantham, Lincolnshire, England. Musician (drums). m. Kath Hanson, 3 Aug. 1994. *Musical Education:* Lincolnshire Youth Orchestra, 1977–80. *Career:* Drummer/programmer for Radio Science Orchestra; European Tour: Energy Orchard; Full time member, The Blessing; UK, European tours. *Recordings:* The Blessing: Locust and Wild Honey; Radio Science Orchestra: Arcitec; Film Soundtrack: Tall Story. *Publications:* Regular columnist, UK Rhythm Magazine, 1994-. *Membership:* Musicians' Union. *Leisure interest:* Water skiing. *Current Management:* Paul Crockford Management; Agent: Simon Harrison. *Address:* c/o 8 Kingston Rd, Ewell Village, Surrey KT17 2AA, England.

HANZICK Helene Hommel Brincker; b. 18 June 1958, Copenhagen, Denmark. Musician (Bass Guitar); Songwriter; Singer. m. Poul F Hanzick, 15 Aug. 1987. *Career:* Singer, Mayflowers band, 1980; Solo Musician, 1981–82; Formed country duo, Twins, with husband; Twins have played all over Denmark and in Norway, Sweden, Holland and Canary Islands; Moved to Sweden, 1994. *Compositions:* From Alaska to LA, 1989; No Good Full-Time-Cheating, Good-For-Nothing Son-Of-A-Gun, 1991, 1996; Ten Days Together, 1991; She'll Come Again, 1991. *Recordings:* Champagne and Bourbon, CD, 1989; Days Together, CD, 1991; I Love You/Blue Moon of Kentucky, single, 1986. *Honour:* Danish Championship in Country Music, 1989. *Membership:* Danish Musicians' Union. *Leisure interests:* Painting; Camping; Old Black Gunpowder Weapons. *Address:* PO Box 35, 28221 Tyringe, Sweden.

HANZICK Poul Fynbo; b. 22 May 1954, Mariager, Denmark. Musician (Guitar); Singer. m. Helene H B Hanzick, 15 Aug. 1987. *Career:* Played in several dance and rock bands, 1969–82; Formed the country duo, Twins, with wife Helene; Twins have played all over Denmark and in Norway, Sweden, Holland and Canary Islands; Moved to Sweden, 1994. *Recordings:* I Love You, Blue Moon of Kentucky, single, 1986; Days Together, CD, 1991; Champagne and Bourbon, CD, 1989. *Honour:* Won Danish Championship in Country Music, 1989. *Membership:* Danish Musicians' Union. *Leisure interests:* Camping; Old Black Gunpowder Weapons; Old American Cars. *Current Management:* Freelance. *Address:* PO Box 35, 28221 Tyringe, Sweden.

HAQUE Asadul; b. 1 March 1930, Pabna, Bangladesh. Retired. m. Firoza Asad, 3 June 1955, 1 s., 1 d. *Education:* Studies of Classical, Semi Classical and Folk Songs. *Career:* Researcher, National Poet Kazi Nazrul Islam and Classical Music of the Sub-Continent; Music Producer, Radio Pakistan, Karachi, 1963–65, Rawalpindi, 1969–71; Performer, Vocal Songs on Radio and Television. *Publications include:* Nazrul Sangiter Rupaker, 1990; Nazrul Saralipi, Vol. 4, 1990; Antaranga Aloke Nazrul O Pramila, 1994; Chalachitrey Nazrul, 1994; Nasruler Hindi Gan, 1995; Amar Surer Jadukar, 1996. *Contributions to:* Leading Newspapers of Bangladesh and Calcutta. *Honours:* Sanad E Khidmat, First Class, Pakistan Government, 1970; Nazrul award, Churulia Nazrul Academy, West Bengal, 1997. *Membership:* Bangla Academy, Dhaka. *Leisure interests:* Research; Writing. *Address:* 12/D Eastern Housing, Sidheswari, Dhaka 1217, Bangladesh.

HARBO Nils; b. 12 May 1956, Nyborg, Denmark. Musician; Record Prod. m. Ulla Rasmussen, 2 s. *Career:* Rock Musician, Guitar Player, 1978–90; Record Producer, var artists, 1990–; Own Projects, Jimi Bikini, Jox, Palle Pirat, A.O.; Editor, Danish Music Yearbook. *Compositions:* Fidt På Fyn, 1991; Palle Pirat, 1996; Out of Control, 1997; Cant Let Go, 1997. *Recording:* Palle Pirat. *Publications:* Improvisation, 1981; Danish Music Yearbook, 1992–98. *Memberships:* KODA; NCB; DMF; DJBFA. *Leisure interests:* Soccer; Italian Food. *Current Management:* Techpoint. *Address:* Birkebakken 8, 2500 Valby, Denmark.

HARCOURT Stephen David; b. 30 Nov. 1973, Harlow, Essex, England. Musician (guitar); Sequencing. *Musical Education:* Self-taught. *Career:* Formed Collapsed Lung, 1992; Several tours, UK and Ireland; Reading Festival; Minor stage, Phoenix Festival; Radio: In Session (Mark Goodier's), Radio 1; Television: Raw Soup, MTV; The Beat; Song, Eat my Goal, used for Coca-Cola advertising campaign; Collapsed Lung split, 1997; Now working as solo and in partnership under names Jack Slack (solo), Spoiler (with Lee

Edwards), Aerobic Christians (with Donald Cummings) and Slackwagon (solo). *Compositions:* with Slackwagon, Dirty Monkeys; Italian Jobbers; Short film scores, 1998. *Recordings:* Albums: Jackpot Goalie, 1995; with Collapsed Lung, Cooler, 1996; Singles: Thundersley Ivacar, 1993; Chainsaw Wedgie, 1993; Down With The Plaid Fad, 1994; Dis-MX, 1994; As G L Stealers, Interactive, 1995; Eat My Goal/London Tonight, 1996; Board Games, 1996. *Membership:* Musicians' Union; PRS. *Leisure interests:* Membership of Church of the Subgenius; Strange Phenomena (Forteana). *Current Management:* Bell Management. *Address:* Slackwagon Productions, 139 Pennymead, Harlow, Essex CM20 3JB, England.

HARDAKER Sam; b. 1971, London, England. Prod.; Remixer. *Career:* Started as studio engineer; Began remixing with partner Henry Binns under the name Zero 7; Produced own material as Zero 7; Released debut album, 2001; Also successful as a live act; Collaborations: Sia Furler; Sophie Barker; Remixed: Terry Callier; Radiohead; Lenny Kravitz. *Recordings:* Albums: Simple Things, 2001; Singles: EP 2, 2000; Destiny (featuring Sia and Sophie), I Have Seen, 2001. *Honours:* Mercury Music Prize nominee, Simple Things, 2001; Muzik Award, Best New Artist, 2001. *Membership:* PRS. *Address:* c/o Ultimate Dilemma Records, 1 Shorrolds Rd, London, SW6 7TR, England.

HARDCASTLE Paul; b. 10 Dec. 1957, London, England. Musician (keyboards); Composer; Mixer; Record Prod. *Compositions:* The Wizard (used as Top of The Pops theme, BBC), 1986–91; Songwriter, composer for television, including: Themes to BBC series, Supersense and Lifesense; Founder, own record label Fast Forward. *Recordings:* Singles: 19 (No. 1, UK), 1985; Just For Money, 1985; Don't Waste My Time, with Carol Kenyon, 1986; The Wizard, 1986; Rainforest 90, 1991; Can't Stop Now, 1994; Other recordings under pseudonym: Def Boys; Beeps International; Jazzmasters; Kiss The Sky (with Jaki Graham); Albums: Hardcastle, 1996; Cover to Cover, 1997; First Light, 1997; Jazzmasters III, 1999; Jazzmasters: The Greatest Hits, 2000; P.H., 2001; Producer for: LW5; Phil Lynott; Carol Kenyon; Remixed: Third World; Ian Dury.

HARDING Mike (Michael); b. 23 Oct. 1944, UK. Vocalist; Musician (english concertina, banjo guitar); Comedian; Writer; Broadcaster; Actor. *Education:* Degree in Education. *Career:* Played in skiffle and rock bands, 1960s; After a variety of jobs, took a degree in education whilst working in folk clubs; Began telling jokes to fill pauses as band tuned up during a gig with the Edison Spasm Band at Leeds University, 1967; Jokes and real-life storytelling became part of act; National exposure with UK hit single The Rochdale Cowboy, 1975; In addition to folk music, has diversified into areas including: travel writing; comedy writing; poetry; playwriting; short stories; photography; First acting role as Valdimir in Beckett's Waiting For Godot, Octagon Theatre, Bolton; Presents radio programme Folk on 2. *Recordings:* Singles: The Rochdale Cowboy, 1975; Albums: A Lancashire Lad, 1972; Mrs 'Ardin's Kid, 1975; The Rochdale Cowboy Rides Again, One Man Show, 1976; Mike Harding's Back, Old Four Eyes Is Back, 1977; Captain Paralytic and The Brown Ale Cowboys, 1978; On The Touchline, Komic Kutz, 1979; The Red Specs Album, 1981; Take Your Finger Off It, 1982; Rooted!, 1983; Bombers' Moon, 1984; Roll Over Cecil Sharp, 1985; Foo Foo Shufflewick and Her Exotic Banana, 1986. *Internet:* www.mikeharding.co.uk.

HARDING Stan (Walter Stanley); b. 11 March 1930, Islington, London, England. Musician (drums); Singer; Songwriter. m. Joyce Matthews, 5 June 1954, 2 s., 1 d. *Musical Education:* Self-taught. *Career:* Toured American Air Force Bases with Bill Kenyon Combo, 1958–62; Shared billing with Cliff Richard, 1959; Short residency at Royal Garden Hotel; Concert appearances with Jack Emblow; Singer with Billy Smart's Circus; Starred in cabaret at Pizza On The Park; Appearance on Late Night BBC. *Composition:* Costa Brava, samba for The Polka Dots, 1963, and broadcast by Billy Cotton and Edmundo Ros. *Recording:* Flying High, with Jack Emblow and Tony Compton. *Publication:* Costa Brava. *Memberships:* Musicians' Union; Equity. *Leisure interests:* DIY; Musical activities; Film acting; Countryside. *Address:* 9 Lilford Rd, Billericay, Essex CM11 1BS, England.

HARDY Françoise; b. 17 Jan. 1944, Paris, France. Singer; Author; Lyricist; Actress; Songwriter. m. Jacques Dutronc, 1981, 1 s. *Education:* Le Bruyère College. *Career:* Recording artiste, 1962–; Lyricist for artistes including: Julien Clerc; Diane Tell; Alaine Lubrano; Khalil Chanine; Also worked as model and actress. *Recordings:* Numerous since 1962–; Recent albums include: Clair Obscur, 2000; En Resume, 2000; Singles include: Tous Les Garçons Et Les Filles, 1962; All Over The World, 1965. *Publications:* Le Grande Livre De La Vierge, with B Guenin; Entre Les Lignes Entre Les Signes, with Anne-Marie Simond, 1991; Notes Secrètes, W E Dumont, 1991; Françoise Hardy Présente L'Astrologie Universelle, 1986. *Leisure interest:* Reading. *Address:* 13 rue Hallé, 75014 Paris, France.

HARJO Joy; b. 9 May 1951, Tulsa, OK, USA. 1 s., 1 d. *Education:* Institute of American-Indian Arts; University of New Mexico; University of Iowa. *Career:* Indigo Girls, Tour, 1995; Bumbleshoot Festival, 1995; Cultural Olympica, 1996; European Tour; A Map of The Next World; Reggee In The

River, 1999. *Compositions:* Letter From The End of The 20th Century; the Musician Who Became A Bear. *Recordings:* Letter From The End of The 20th Century. *Publications:* She Had Some Horses; In Mad Love and War; The Woman Who Fell From The Sky; A Map To The Next World. *Honours:* Outstanding Musical Achievement; NM Governors Award. *Membership:* National Council On The Arts. *Current Management:* Mekko Rabbit Productions Inc, 1140 D Alewa Dr., Honolulu, HI 26817, USA.

HARKET Morten; b. 14 Sept. 1959, Konigsberg, Norway. Singer; Songwriter. *Career:* Singer with various groups including: Mercy; Laelia Anceps; Souldier Blue; Formed A-Ha with Mags Furuholmen and Pal Waaktaar, 1982; Appearances include: Montreux Pop Festival, 1986; World tour, 1986; Royal Albert Hall, London, 1987; World tour, 1987; Rock In Rio II Festival, 1991; British tour, 1991; Starred in film Kamilia and The Thief, 1989; Presenter/Host, Eurovision Song Contest, 1996. *Recordings:* Albums: Hunting High and Low, 1985; Scoundrel Days, 1986; Stay On These Roads, 1988; East of The Sun, 1990; Headlines and Deadlines – The Hits of A-Ha, 1991; Memorial Beach, 1993; Minor Earth, Major Sky, 2000; Solo album: Wild Seed, 1995; Numerous hit singles include: Take On Me (No. 1, USA), 1985; The Sun Always Shines On TV (No. 1, UK), 1985; Train of Thought, 1986; Hunting High and Low, 1986; I've Been Losing You, 1986; Cry Wolf, 1986; Manhattan Skyline, 1987; The Living Daylights (theme music for James Bond film), 1987; Stay On These Roads, 1988; The Blood That Moves The Body, 1988; Touchy!, 1988; You Are The One, 1988; Crying In The Rain, 1990; I Call Your Name; Dark Is The Night; Can't Take My Eyes Off You, for film soundtrack Coneheads; Angel; Solo single: A Kind of Christmas Card (No. 1, Norway), 1995. *Honours:* 8 MTV Music Video Awards, for Take On Me and The Sun Always Shines On TV (record number of awards for one act), 1986; BMI Award, One Million Broadcast Performances, for Take On Me, 1991; World Music Award, Best Selling Norwegian Artist of The Year, 1993; Record number of awards for one artist, Norway, 1993. *Current Management:* Terry Slater. *Address:* c/o Thatched Cottage, Hollow Lane, Headley, Hampshire, England.

HARLEY Steve; b. 27 Feb. 1951, London, England. Singer. *Career:* Former journalist; Founder member, Cockney Rebel, 1973–77; 1989–; Solo artiste, 1978–88; Appearances include: Reading Festival, 1974; Support to The Kinks, US, 1975; All Is Forgiven reunion tour, UK, 1989; Heineken Music Big Top, Portsmouth, 1992; Presenter, Sounds of The 70s, BBC Radio 2, 1999-. *Recordings:* Albums: Human Menagerie, 1973; The Best Years of Lives, 1975; Timeless Flight, 1976; Love's A Prima Donna, 1976; Face To Face – A Live Recording, 1977; Hobo with a Grin, 1978; Candidate, 1979; Greatest Hits, 1988; The Best of Steve Harley and Cockney Rebel, 1992; Make Me Smile, 1996; Stripped to Bare Bones, 1999; Yes You Can, 2000; In Pursuit of Illusion, 2000; Singles: with Cockney Rebel: July Teen, 1974; Mr Soft, 1974; Make Me Smile (Come Up and See Me), 1975; Mr Raffles (Man It Was Mean), 1975; Here Comes The Sun, 1976; Solo: The Phantom of The Opera (duet with Sarah Brightman), 1986. *Contribution to:* Whatever You Believe, UK TV telethon charity single, 1988. *Address:* c/o Arctic King Music, Cambridge House, Card Hill, Forest Row RH18 5BA, England.

HARMACEK Václav; b. 6 Nov. 1952, Prague, Czech Republic. Musician (clarinet, saxes, viola); Recording Dir; Teacher. Divorced, 2 d. *Education:* Philosophical Faculty, Charles University, Prague, 1977. *Career:* Appearance in numerous jazz festivals as Member of various bands and orchestras (notably Prague Big Band, Original Prague Syncopated Orchestra, Causa Bibendi); Several TV and radio appearances in various types of programmes (notably Causa Bibendi or the Reason for a Drink, Czech TV, 1994). *Contributions to:* albums of the orchestras: Prague Big Band, 1974–78; Original Prague Syncopated Orchestra, 1979–84; Causa Bibendi – Czech Swingharmonic Orchestra, 1992; Blue World, 1996; Prague Folklore Cymbalon Orchestra, 1975–91. *Publication:* Editor and Contributor, Small Encyclopaedia of Music, 1983. *Leisure interests:* Sports; Computers; Music; Bandleader of the Causa Bibendi-Czech Swingharmonic Orchestra, The Head of the CB Art Agency. *Address:* Studentská 2, 160 00 Prague 6, Czech Republic.

HARMAN Buddy; b. 23 Dec. 1928, Nashville, Tennessee, USA. Musician (drums). *Career:* Studio musician, Nashville, 1952–; Thousands of recording sessions with Elvis Presley, records and films. *Recordings:* Hits with Elvis Presley: A Fool Such As I, 1958; A Big Hunk O'Love, 1958; Stuck On You, 1960; The Girl of My Best Friend, 1960; It's Now Or Never, 1960; Are You Lonesome Tonight, 1961; Surrender, 1961; His Latest Flame, 1961; Suspicion, 1961; Good Luck Charm, 1962; Devil In Disguise, 1963; Crying In The Chapel, 1965; Love Letters, 1966; Also worked with: Jerry Lee Lewis, Connie Francis, Doc Watson, Charlie Rich, Brenda Lee. *Honours:* NARAS Superpicker Awards, 1965–70. *Membership:* AFofM (executive board of directors, 1981).

HARMAN James Gary; b. 8 June 1946, Anniston, Alabama, USA. Bandleader; Singer; Songwriter; Prod.; Musician (harmonica). m. Ella Caroline Harman, 2 s. *Education:* Gulf Coast College, University of Florida. *Musical Education:* Self-taught. *Career:* Bandleader, Southern dance circuit, 1962–; Recording artist, 1964–; Bandleader, house band

Ash Grove Club, Los Angeles, 1970s; International tours; Numerous appearances, television, radio, festivals world-wide; Songs for films; Several songs used in TV shows; Plays in every major blues festival world-wide; Played harmonica on ZZ Top single, What's Up With That; Appeared on David Letterman Show, 1997. *Recordings:* Recent albums include: Do Not Disturb, 1991; Two Sides To Every Story, 1993; Cards On The Table, 1994; Back and White, 1995; Extra Napkins, 1997; Takin' Chances, 1998; Extra Napkins Vol. II, 1999; Mo'Na'Kins, 2000; Other recordings include: So Many Women, Invasion; Kiss of Fire, The Accused; Jump My Baby (in 3 films). *Honours:* Nominee, W C Hardy, 7 times; Alabama Music Hall of Fame. *Leisure interests:* Drag racing, hot rods; Motorcycles; Record collecting. *Current Management:* Icepick Productions. *Address:* 718 Schwarz Rd, Lawrence, KS 66049, USA.

HARNICK Sheldon Mayer; b. 30 April 1924, Chicago, Illinois, USA. Lyricist. m. (1) Mary Boatner, 1950, (2) Elaine May, 1962, (3) Margery Gray, 1965, 1 s., 1 d. *Education:* Northwestern University. *Career:* Contributor to revues: New Faces of 1952; Two's Company, 1953; John Murray Anderson's Almanac, 1954; The Shoestring Revue, 1955; The Littlest Revue, 1956; Shoestring 1957, 1957; with composer Jerry Bock: Body Beautiful, 1958; Fiorello, 1959; Tenderloin, 1960; Smiling The Boy Fell Dead (with David Baker), 1961; She Loves Me, 1963; Fiddler On The Roof, 1964; The Apple Tree, 1966; The Rothschilds, 1970; Captain Jinks of The Horse Marines (opera with Jack Beeson), 1975; Rex (with Richard Rodgers), 1976; Dr Heidegger's Fountain of Youth (opera with Jack Beeson), 1978; Gold (cantata with Joe Raposo), 1980; Translations: The Merry Widow, 1977; The Umbrellas of Cherbourg, 1979; Carmen, 1981; A Christmas Carol, 1981; Songs of The Auvergne (musical; book; lyrics), 1982; The Appeasement of Aeolus, 1990; *Contributions to:* ABC: A Tribute To Adler, Bock and Coleman, 2000. *Address:* Kraft, Haiken and Bell, 551 Fifth Ave, Ninth Floor, New York, NY 10176, USA.

HARPER Phillip Melbourne; b. 16 Nov. 1970, Islington, London, England. Musician (drums, percussion). *Musical Education:* GCSE Music, Certificate in music workshop skills. *Career:* Drummer for Pete Brown (songwriter with Cream); Phil Ryan (ex-keyboard player, Man); The Interceptors British tour, 1995; Percussionist, Ronnie Laws band, featured guest Jean Carne, Shepherd's Bush Empire; Percussionist, Akwaaba People; Live performance, GLR Radio, 1995; Performances: Ronnie Scott's, 1995; Jazz Café, 1995; Festivals: Hackney Show; Phoenix; Jazz Izz, Highbury Fields, 1995; Live TV (cable channel), 1995; Teacher, drums, percussion, Secondary schools: Highbury Grove; Parliament Hill; Acland Burghley; Islington Sixth form centre; Young Musicmakers (Independent). *Membership:* Musicians' Union. *Address:* 27 Approach Close, Spencer Grove, London N16 8UG, England.

HARPER Ray; b. 6 Jan. 1961, Copperhill, Tennessee, USA. Singer; Entertainer; Musician (guitar, fiddle, banjo). *Education:* 4 quarter management course; Other technical courses. *Career:* Hamby Mt Music Park, Baldwin, Georgia; Many guest appearances, Carl Story Radio Program, WESC, Greenville, South Carolina; Former member, Carl Story's Rambling Mountaineers; Also worked with Bill Monroe, Larry Sparks and others; Played shows, festivals across US with audiences up to 10,000; Guest appearances on Rambling Mountain Bluegrass Radio Show WESC in Greenville; Now performs as Ray Harper and Friends. *Recordings:* Ray Harper and Friends with Special Guest Carl Story, 1992; Solo: What A Wonderful Saviour Is He, 1994. *Memberships:* International Bluegrass Music Asscn; Bluegrass Music Asscn of Georgia, South Carolina, North Carolina. *Leisure interest:* Music. *Address:* 1131 Farrs Bridge Rd, Pickens, SC 29671, USA.

HARPER Roy; b. 12 June 1941, Manchester, England. Singer; Songwriter. *Career:* Busker, played across Europe; Residency, Les Cousins club, London; Solo recording artiste, 1966-. *Compositions include:* McGoohan's Blues; The White Man; Tom Tiddler's Ground; Hell's Angels; When An Old Cricketer Leaves The Crease; One of Those Days In England; Watford Gap. *Recordings:* Albums: The Sophisticated Beggar, 1966; Come Out Fighting Genghis Smith, 1967; Folkjokeopus, 1969; Flat Baroque and Berserk, 1970; Stormcock, 1971; Lifemask, 1973; Valentine, 1974; Flashes From The Archives of Oblivion, 1974; HQ (a.k.a. When An Old Cricketer Leaves The Crease), 1975; Bullinamingvase, 1977; Harper 1970–75, 1978; The Unknown Soldier, 1980; Work of Heart, 1981; Whatever Happened To Jugula, 1985; Born In Captivity, 1985; In Between Every Line, 1986; Descendents of Smith, 1988; Loony On The Bus, 1988; Once, 1990; Death Or Glory?, 1992; Return of the Sophisticated Beggar, 1997; Dream Society, 1998; The Green Man, 2001; Hats Off! (compilation), 2001; Guest vocalist, Have A Cigar, on album Wish You Were Here, Pink Floyd. *Address:* c/o Acorn Entertainments, Winterfild House, 46 Woodfield Rd, Kings Heath, Birmingham B13 9UJ, England.

HARRELL Bill (George William); b. 14 Sept. 1934, Marion, Virginia, USA. Singer; Musician (guitar, mandolin); Songwriter. m. 8 Dec. 1959, deceased 14 Dec. 1982, 2 s., 1 d. *Education:* University of Maryland. *Musical Education:* Self-taught. *Career:* Television and radio appearances: Monthly, Jimmy Dean Show, ABC Network, 1961–63; Numerous guest spots, Grande Ole Opry, Nashville, Tennessee; 6 months regularly wheeling West Virginia Jamboree; WWVA Radio; The Today Show, NBC, 1985. *Recordings:* After the Sunrise, 1994; And Friends, 1995; Blue Virginia Blue, 1997; Song for Everyone, 1997; The Cat Came Back, 1998; Ballads and Bluegrass. *Honours:* Spigma Bluegrass Singer of Year, 1985; Virginia Music Hall of Fame. *Membership:* BMI. *Leisure interests:* Fishing; Travel. *Current Management:* Attoway Music. *Address:* 938 St George Barber Rd, Davidsonville, MD 21035, USA.

HARRIGAN Katie; b. 17 Sept. 1963, Irvine, Scotland. Musician (Celtic harp). *Education:* BA Hons, French and Spanish, Heriot Watt University, UK; Diploma in European Politics, College of Europe, Bruges, Belgium. *Musical Education:* Studied Clarsach (Celtic harp) with Sanchia Pielou and studied piano. *Career:* Celtic harpist with: Flumgummery, 1981–83; Hamish Moore, including US tour, 1985–86; Ceolbeg, 1988–91; Toured Canada and USA with Vale of Atholl Pipe Band, 1988; Periodically has worked with Billy Ross; Currently, solo harpist. *Recordings:* Flumgummery One, with Flumgummery, 1982; Highland Mandolin, with Dagger Gordon, 1988; Not The Bunny Hop, with Ceolbeg, 1990; Celtic Connection, with KPM, 1994. *Honours:* Solo Clarsach Champion, National MOD, 1980 and 1982; Solo Clarsach Champion, Edinburgh Music Festival, 1981. *Membership:* Life mem. of Clarsach Society. *Address:* 9 Coleherne Rd, London SW10 9BS, England.

HARRIS Dale G; b. 25 July 1968. Musician (guitar). *Education:* Brooklands College, Weybridge, Surrey. *Musical Education:* West London Institute, Brunel University, Isleworth, Middlesex, England. *Career:* Guitarist and arranger with Pretty Blue Gun; UK radio airplay on Virgin Radio, BBC Radio 1, and GLR, 1990–93; Guitarist with The Lorne Gibson Trio, 1993-. *Recordings:* with Pretty Blue Gun: The Only Girl; Big Blue World. *Leisure interests:* English literature; Weightlifting; Animal welfare. *Current Management:* Standfast Music. *Address:* 48 Atney Rd, Putney, London SW15 2PS, England.

HARRIS Emmylou; b. 2 April 1947, Birmingham, Alabama, USA. Singer. 2 d. *Education:* UNC, Greensboro. *Career:* Toured with Fallen Angel Band; Performed across Europe, USA; Recording artist; Appeared in rock documentary, The Last Waltz. *Compositions:* Songs; Co-writer, co-producer, Ballad of Sally Rose with Paul Kennerley, 1985. *Recordings:* Singles include: Together Again, 1975; Two More Bottles of Wine, 1978; Beneath Still Waters, 1979; (Lost His Love) On Our Last date, 1982; To Know Him is to Love Him (Trio), 1987; We believe in Happy Endings (duet with Earl Thomas Conley), 1988; Wheels of Love, 1990; Never Be Anyone, 1990; High Powered Love, 1993; Albums include: Gliding Bird, 1969; Pieces of The Sky, 1975; Elite Hotel, 1976; Luxury Liner, 1977; Quarter Moon In A Ten-Cent Town, 1978; Blue Kentucky Girl, 1979; Roses in the Snow, 1980; Evangeline, 1981; Cimarron, 1981; Last Date, 1982; White Shoes, 1983; Profile: Best of Emmylou Harris, 1984; The Ballad of Sally Rose, 1985; Thirteen, 1986; Trio (with Dolly Parton, Linda Ronstadt), 1987; Angel Band, 1987; Bluebird, 1989; Brand New Dance, 1990; Duets (with Nash Ramblers), 1990; At The Ryman, 1992; Cowgirls Prayer, 1993; Wrecking Ball, 1995; Portraits, 1996; Nashville, 1996; Spyboy, 1998; Light of the Stable, 1999; Red Dirt Girl, 2000; Singing With Emmylou Vol. 1, 2000; Anthology, 2001; Assisted Gram Parsons on album GP, Grievous Angel, 1973. *Honours:* 7 Grammy Awards, 1976–95; 27 Grammy Nominations; Female Vocalist of the Year, Country Music Asscn, 1980; Academy Country Music Award, Album of the Year, 1987. *Membership:* President, Country Music Foundation, 1983. *Current Management:* Monty Hitchcock Management, PO Box 159007, Nashville, TN 37215, USA.

HARRIS Kenneth Philip (Kenny); b. 21 May 1927, London, England. Musician (drums); Author. *Education:* Brooklyn School of Modern Music, USA. *Career:* Musician on Queen Mary and Mauretania, 1950–53; Played for shows in France and Germany, 1953; Jazz Clubs in London, 1953–56; Emigrated to USA, 1956; Played in Clubs; To Bermuda, 1960; Played in Hotels and worked as Producer, Bermuda Broadcasting Company; To Canada, 1970; Worked for Capitol Records, own Record Company and Producer at Radio Stations, CKNW, CFMI, C-JAZ; Bermuda, 1983; Bermuda Broadcasting Company; Defontes Broadcasting, 1991; To Uk, 1992. *Recordings:* Ralph Sharon Sextet, 1953; Joe Wylie Trio, 1964; Gene Harris Trio, 1958; Gene Harris Trio, 1959; British Jazz Trio, 1959. *Publications:* Author, First Call Drummer Don Lamond, 1997; Geraldo's Navy, 1998. *Honour:* Juno Award, Canadian Academy of Arts and Sciences, 1981. *Membership:* Society of Composers, Authors and Publishers of Canada. *Address:* 36, The Maltings, Riverside Way, Brandon, Suffolk, IP27 0BL, England.

HARRIS Paul; b. 9 June 1964, London, England. Singer; Musician (piano); Composer. m. Alison Harris, née Dodd, 3 s. *Education:* Kingston Art College. *Musical Education:* Private tuition from age 7–16; Self-taught, 16 onwards. *Career:* Appearances: Top of The Pops, 1995; BBC1 Song For Europe, with co-written entry, Spinning Away; Live radio: Radio 1, Radio 2, London Talkback, Radio Coventry; Live gigs with own band, BFBS Radio

(world-wide); County Sound Radio; Eclipse Radio; Tours: UK; Portugal. *Compositions:* Spinning Away, with M Smith; I Don't Care, with M Smith; It Never Rains, with S Root; The Great Divide, with M Smith, S Root, S Emney. *Recordings:* Singles: Spinning Away, with Paul Harris Band, 1995; The Warning, 1996; Dream EP, 1996; Also appears on numerous other recordings by other artists, 1966–99. *Membership:* Musicians' Union. *Leisure interests:* Travel; Weights; Socialising; Giving up smoking. *Current Management:* Music Business PHD. *Address:* 21 Walton St, Walton-On-The-Hill, Tadworth, Surrey KT20 7RR, England.

HARRIS Roland Oliver; b. 6 April 1962, Havant, England. Record Prod.; Music Recording Engineer. *Education:* Queen Mary College, University of London. *Career:* PRT Studios, Recording and Maintenance Engineer; Nova Studios, Chief Engineer, 8 years; Various freelance recording, arranging, producing work with an emphasis on Sound synchronised to picture; Live sound/production includes: Rata Blanca; Spain, Mexico (Monsters of Rock, Mexico), Rupert Parker, UK and Europe. *Recordings:* Several albums with Rupert Parker; Various television, theatre recordings with Michael Nyman; 2 albums with Rata Blanca. *Membership:* Musicians' Union. *Current Management:* Mabley Street Productions Ltd. *Address:* Unit 31, Buspace Studios, Conlan St, London W10 5AP, England.

HARRIS Rolf; b. 30 March 1930, Perth, Australia. Entertainer; Singer; Musician (piano, accordion, digeridoo, wobbleboard); Artist. m. Alwen Myfanwy Wiseman Hughes, 1 March 1958, 1 d. *Education:* West Australian University. *Musical Education:* Piano Grade 1, AMEB. *Career:* International television entertainer, artist and host, Cartoon Time; Animal Hospital; Rolf On Art. *Recordings:* Numerous singles include: Tie Me Kangaroo Down Sport, 1960; Sun Arise, 1962; Jake The Peg; Two Little Boys (No. 1, UK), 1969; Stairway To Heaven, 1993; The Court of King Caractacus; Can You Tell What It Is Yet?; Albums include: King Rolf, 2001. *Publications:* 12 titles including: How To Write Your Own Pop Song. *Honours:* OBE; AM. *Membership:* Equity. *Leisure interests:* Wood Carving; Stone Polishing. *Current Management:* Jan Kennedy, Billy Marsh Associates Ltd.

HARRIS Sam; b. 4 June 1961, Cushing, Oklahoma, USA. Actor; Singer; Writer. *Education:* UCLA. *Career:* Concerts and shows include: Carnegie Hall; Universal Amphitheatre, Los Angeles; London's West End; Grease, Broadway; Joseph and The Amazing Technicolour Dreamcoat, National tour; The Life, Broadway; Television includes: Star Search; Oprah Winfrey Show; Rosie O'Donnell Show; Tonight Show; Numerous television specials and talk shows. *Compositions:* Musicals: Hurry! Hurry! Hollywood!; Hard Copy; Television sitcom, Down To Earth. *Recordings:* Sam Harris; Sam-I-Am; Standard Time; Different Stages; The Life, cast album; Grease, cast album; A Hollywood Christmas; A Gershwin Tribute; Best of the Motown Sessions; Revival, 1999; On This Night, 2000; Film: In The Weeds. *Honours:* Drama Desk nomination, Grease; Dramalogue Awards for Hard Copy and Different Hats; Drama League Award and Tony, Drama Desk and Outer Critics' Circle nominations for The Life; RIAA Gold Album status for Sam Harris and Sam-I-Am. *Leisure interests:* Gardening; Refinishing furniture. *Current Management:* Mark Sendroff, 1500 Broadway #2001, New York, NY 10036 USA. *Address:* 250 W 57th St, Suite 703, New York, NY 10107, USA.

HARRIS Sean; Singer; Songwriter. *Career:* Founder member, UK rock group Diamond Head, 1977–85; One of leading groups in New Wave of British Heavy Metal (NWOBHM), UK, 1980s; British tours, 1980, 1982; Monsters of Rock Festival, Castle Donington, 1983; Member, Notorious, with Robin George, 1990; Reformed Diamond Head, 1991–; Tours include support to Metallica. *Compositions include:* In The Heat of The Night; Am I Evil; Helpless; It's Electric. *Recordings include:* Albums with Diamond Head: Lightning To The Nations, 1980; (remixed as Behold The Beginning, 1986); Canterbury, 1983; Death and Progress, 1993; with Robin George: Notorious, 1990; Rising Up (mini-album), 1992; To Heaven from Hell, 1997; Diamond Nights, 2000; Compilation: Am I Evil, 1987.

HARRIS Simon Kenneth; b. 10 Sept. 1962, London, England. DJ; Prod. *Career:* Record Producer and Remixer with 2 Top 40 Hits; Production Credits include: Derek B, Ambassadors of Funk, Daddy Freddy; Remix Credits include: Stone Roses; James Brown; Tony Toni Tone; Real Thing; DMB; Prince; Steve Silk Hurley; Joyce Simms; Appeared on Top of the Pops, Good Morning, Big Breakfast. *Recordings:* Solo singles include: Bad On The Mike, 1987; Bass (How Low Can You Go), 1988; Here Comes That Sound, 1988; Another Monsterjam 1989; Don't Stop The Music, 1990. *Honour:* NME Rap Label of the Year, 1988–89. *Memberships:* PRS; BMI. *Leisure interests:* Disney Toys; Laser Discs; Films. *Current Management:* Chris France, Music of Life. *Address:* Liscombe Park, Soulbury, LU7 0JL, England.

HARRIS Steve; b. 12 March 1957, Leytonstone, London, England. Rock Musician (bass). *Career:* Member, pub band, Smiler; Founder member, UK heavy rock group Iron Maiden, 1976–; Regular tours world-wide; Concerts include: Reading Festival, 1980, 1982; Monsters of Rock Festival, Castle

Donington, 1988, 1992; Monsters of Rock, Germany, 1988; Monsters of Rock, France, 1992; Super Rock '92, Germany, 1992. *Recordings:* Albums: Iron Maiden, 1980; Killers, 1981; The Number of The Beast (No. 1, UK), 1982; Piece of Mind, 1983; Powerslave, 1984; Live After Death, 1985; Somewhere In Time, 1986; Seventh Son of a Seventh Son (No. 1, UK), 1988; No Prayer For The Dying, 1990; Fear of The Dark, 1992; A Real Live One, 1993; A Real Dead One, 1993; The X-Factor, 1995; Best of the Beast, 1996; Virtual XI, 1998; Ed Hunter, 1999; Brave New World, 2000; Hit singles include: Running Free, 1980; Run To The Hills, 1982; The Number of The Beast, 1982; Flight of Icarus, 1983; The Trooper, 1983; 2 Minutes To Midnight, 1984; Aces High, 1984; Wasted Years, 1986; Can I Play With Madness, 1988; Evil That Men Do, 1988; The Clairvoyant, 1988; Infinite Dreams, 1989; Holy Smoke, 1990; Bring Your Daughter To The Slaughter (No. 1, UK), 1991; Be Quick Or Be Dead, 1992; From Here To Eternity, 1992; Fear of The Dark, 1993; Hallowed Be Thy Name, 1993; Man On The Edge, 1995; Virus, 1996. *Honours include:* Grammy Award, Best Metal Performance nomination, The Wicker Man, 2001. *Address:* c/o Sanctuary Music (Overseas), First Floor Suite, The Colonnades, 82 Bishops Bridge Rd, London W2 6BB, England.

HARRISON Gavin; b. 28 May 1963, Harrow, London, England. Musician (drums, bass, keyboards); Composer. *Career:* Founder member, Dizrhythmia; Worked with: Level 42; Paul Young; Iggy Pop; Eros Ramazotti; Claudio Baglioni; Incognito. *Recordings:* Albums include: with Sam Brown: Stop, 1988; with Incognito: Inside Life; Always There; Also recorded with: Tom Robinson; Kevin Ayers; Black; Dave Stewart; Paul Young; Iggy Pop. *Publications:* Rhythmic Illusions Book; Columns for: Rhythm, Modern Drummer magazines. *Leisure interest:* Pole vaulting. *Current Management:* B and H Management. *Address:* Lavender Cottage, Love Lane, Kings Langley, Hertfordshire WD4 8EW, England.

HARRISON Oscar; b. 15 April 1965, Birmingham, England. Musician (drums, keyboards). *Career:* Member, jazz rock reggae band Echo Base; Joined The Fanatics; Band split, joined Ocean Colour Scene; Support slot on 1994 Oasis tour; Numerous TV appearances and much radio play; Riverboat Song used as theme tune to TV series TFI Friday; Several headlining tours. *Recordings:* Singles include: Riverboat Song, 1996; The Day We Caught The Train, 1996; You've Got It Bad, 1996; The Circle, 1996; 100 Mile High City, 1997; Travellers Tune, 1997; Better Day, 1997; It's A Beautiful Thing, 1998; July/I Am The News, 2000; Up On The Downside, 2001; Albums: Ocean Colour Scene, 1992; Moseley Shoals, 1996; B-Sides, Seasides and Freerides, 1997; Marchin' Already (No. 1, UK), 1997; One From The Modern, 1999; Mechanical Wonder, 2001; Songs For The Front Row (compilation), 2001. *Internet:* www.oceancolourscene.com.

HARRY Deborah Ann; b. 1 July 1945, Miami, Florida, USA. Singer; Songwriter; Actress. *Career:* Former Playboy bunny waitress; Singer, groups: Wind In The Willows; The Stilettos; Founder, Blondie, 1974–83, reformed 1998; Appearances include: New York punk club, CBGBs, 1974; Support to Iggy Pop, US, 1977; Solo recording career, 1981–; Actress, films including: Blank Generation, 1978; The Foreigner, 1978; Union City, 1979; Roadie, 1980; Videodrome; Hairspray; The Killbillies; Intimate Stranger, 1991. *Recordings:* Hit singles: with Blondie: Denis (Denee), 1978; (I'm Always Touched By Your) Presence Dear, 1978; Picture This, 1978; Hanging On The Telephone, 1978; Heart of Glass (No. 1, UK), 1979; Sunday Girl (No. 1, UK), 1979; Dreaming, 1979; Union City Blue, 1979; Call Me (No. 1, USA and UK), 1980; Atomic (No. 1, UK), 1980; The Tide Is High (No. 1, UK), 1980; Rapture (No. 1, USA), 1981; Island of Lost Souls, 1982; Maria (No. 1, UK), 1999; Solo: Backfired, 1981; French Kissin' (In The USA), 1986; I Want That Man, 1989; I Can See Clearly, 1993; Albums with Blondie: Blondie, 1976; Plastic Letters, 1978; Parallel Lines (No. 1, USA), 1978; Eat To The Beat (No. 1, UK), 1979; Autoamerican, 1980; The Best of Blondie (No. 1, UK), 1981; The Hunter, 1982; No Exit, 1999; Livid, 2000; Solo albums: Koo Koo, 1981; Rockbird, 1986; Def, Dumb and Blonde, 1989; Debravation, 1993; Compilations: Once More Into The Bleach, 1988; The Complete Picture, 1991; Blonde and Beyond, 1993. *Contributions to:* film soundtracks: American Gigolo, 1980; Roadie, 1980; Scarface; Krush Groove, 1984. *Publications:* Making Tracks – The Rise of Blondie (co-written with Chris Stein), 1982. *Memberships:* ASCAP; AFTRA; Equity; Screen Actors Guild. *Current Management:* Overland Productions, 156 W 56th St, Fifth Floor, New York, NY 10019, USA.

HART Angela Ruth; b. 8 March 1972, Adelaide, Australia. Singer; Musician. *Career:* Solo artiste; Also singer with Frente; Australian tour, 1992–93; US tour, 1994; Support to Beautiful South; Crowded House; Counting Crows; They Might Be Giants. *Recordings:* Albums: Marvin The Album, 1993; Ruby's Arm, Tom Waits Tribute, 1995; Shape, 1996; Singles: Whirled, 1991; Clunk, 1992; Accidentally Kelly Street, 1992; No Time EP, 1993; Ordinary Angels, 1994; Lonely, 1994; Labour of Love, 1994; Bizarre Love Triangle, 1994; What's Come Over Me, 1996. *Honours:* DBL Platinum album, Australia; Gold album, Canada, Indonesia, Phillipines, Malaysia, Thailand. *Leisure interests:* Stained glass; Art.

HART Freddy, (Frederick Segrest); b. 21 Dec. 1926, Loachapoka, Alabama, USA. Country vocalist; Songwriter; Musician (guitar). *Career:* Left school, aged 12; Joined marines at 15 by lying about age; Saw action in Guam and Iwo Jima; Returning to Nashville, became roadie for Hank Williams Sr, 1949; First song cut Every Little Thing Rolled Into One, George Morgan, 1949; Toured with Lefty Frizzell, 1950–53; Regular on Home Town Jubilee TV Show in Hollywood; Composition, Loose Talk, a country chart hit for Carl Smith, 1954; Song subsequently recorded by others including Patsy Cline; Signed to Columbia Records, 1959; Label debut, The Wall, was first of many Billboard chart entries until 1987; Most successful in early 1970s; Easy Loving made US Top 20 pop chart, 1971; Currently semi-retired concentrating on business interests: Trucking company Hartline; 40 acres of plum trees; Over 200 breeding bulls; Also runs school for handicapped children in Burbank, California. *Compositions include:* Bless Your Heart; Easy Loving; Got The All Overs For You; Hang In There Girl; Hank Williams' Guitar; If You Can't Feel It (It Ain't There); Loose Talk; My Hang-Up Is You; Trip To Heaven. *Recordings include:* Easy Loving, 1971; My Hang Up Is You, Got The All Overs For You (All Over Me), Bless Your Heart, 1972; Super Kind of Woman, Trip To Heaven, 1973; Albums: Easy Loving, 1971; Got The All Overs For You, My Hang-Up Is You, Bless Your Heart, 1972; Super Kind of Woman, 1973; Greatest Hits, 1975. *Honours:* Numerous including: CMA, Song of the Year, Easy Loving, 1971 and 1972; ACM: Entertainer of the Year; Top Male Vocalist; Single of the Year, Easy Loving; Album of the Year, Easy Loving, 1971. *Memberships:* Grand Ole Opry, early 1960s. *Current Management:* Richard Davis Management, 1030 North Woodland, Kansas City, MO 64118, USA.

HARTNOLL Paul; b. 19 May 1968, Dartford, Kent, England. Musician (keyboards). *Career:* Member, Orbital; Obtained indie label deal; Numerous live appearances at clubs and raves; Glastonbury Festival, 1994, and Tribal Gathering appearances along with other festivals; Royal Albert Hall Concert; Collaborations with Metallica's Kirk Hammett and composer Michael Kamen; Work on soundtracks for films Shopping, 1994, The Saint, 1996, Spawn, 1997. *Recordings:* Singles: Omen, 1990; Chime, 1992; Diversions EP, 1992; Impact, 1993; Lush, 1993; Halcyon, 1993; Times Fly, 1995; Are We Here?, 1995; The Box, 1996; Satan Live, 1996; The Saint, 1997; Style, 1999; Beached, with Angelo Badalamenti, 2000; Funny Break (One Is Enough), 2001; Albums: Orbital, 1991; Orbital 2, 1992; Snivilisation, 1994; In Sides, 1996; Middle of Nowhere, 1999; The Altogether, 2001. *Internet:* www.loopz.co.uk/orbital.

HARTNOLL Phil; b. 9 Jan. 1964, Dartford, Kent, England. Musician (keyboards). *Career:* Member, Orbital; Obtained indie label deal; Numerous live performances at clubs, raves and festivals including Glastonbury 1994 and Tribal Gathering; Royal Albert Hall show; Collaborations with Metallica's Kirk Hammett and composer Michael Kamen; Film soundtrack work for Shopping, 1994, The Saint, 1996 and Spawn, 1997. *Recordings:* Singles: Omen, 1990; Chime, 1992; Diversions EP, 1992; Impact, 1993; Lush, 1993; Halcyon, 1993; Times Fly, 1995; Are We Here?, 1995; The Box, 1996; Satan Live, 1996; The Saint, 1997; Style, 1999; Beached, with Angelo Badalamenti, 2000; Funny Break (One Is Enough), 2001; Albums: Orbital, 1991; Orbital 2, 1992; Snivilisation, 1994; In Sides, 1996; Middle of Nowhere, 1999; The Altogether, 2001. *Internet:* www.loopz.co.uk/orbital.

HARVEY Brian (Lee); b. 8 Aug. 1974, Edmonton, London, England. Singer. *Career:* Member, East 17; Numerous television and live appearances. *Recordings:* Singles include: House of Love, 1992; Deep, 1993; West End Girls, 1993; It's Alright, 1993; Around The World, 1994; Stay Another Day (No. 1, UK), 1994; Steam, 1994; Thunder, 1995; If You Ever, with Gabrielle, 1996; Hey Child, 1997; Each Time, 1998; Betcha Can't Wait, 1999; Albums: Walthamstow, 1993; Steam, 1994; Up All Night, 1996; Around the World – The Journey So Far, 1996; Resurrection, 1998; Solo: Singles: True Step Tonight, with the True Steppers and Donell Jones, 2000; Straight Up (No Bends), 2001; Loving You, with The Refugee Crew, 2002.

HARVEY Mick (Michael John); b. 29 Aug. 1958, Rochester, Australia. Musician (Guitar, Drums); Arranger; Prod. *Compositions:* The Mercy Seat; Red Right Hand. *Recordings:* The Birthday Party, entire catalogue; Nick Cave and the Bad Seeds, entire catalogue; Intoxicated Man, 1995; Pink Elephants, 1997. *Honours:* Aria Award, Best Soundtrack, To Have and To Hold, 1997; Aria Nomination, Best Adult, Contemporary Album, for Intoxicated Man, 1996. *Memberships:* APRA; PPCA; PAMRA. *Address:* 7 St Andrews St, Nth Melbourne, Vic 3051, Australia.

HARVEY9 PJ (Polly Jean); b. 9 Oct. 1969, England. Singer; Songwriter; Musician. *Career:* Television appearances include: MTV's Most Wanted; 120 Minutes; David Letterman Show; Jay Leno Show; Conan O'Brien Show; Top of The Pops; The White Room; Later With Jools Holland; Concerts include Glastonbury Festival, 1995; Tours, USA, Europe, Japan, 1995; Acting debut, Hal Hartley film, The Book of Life, 1998. *Recordings:* Albums: Dry, 1992; Rid of Me, 1993; 4 Track Demos, 1993; To Bring You My Love, 1995; Is This Desire?, 1998; Stories From The City, Stories From The

Sea, 2000; Singles: Dress, 1991; Sheila Na Gig, 1992; 50ft Queenie, 1993; Man-Size, 1993; Down by the Water, 1995; C'Mon Billy, 1995; Perfect Day Elise, 1998; Wind, 1999; Good Fortune, 2000; This Is Love, 2001; A Place Called Love, 2001; Collaborations include: John Parish; Nick Cave and The Bad Seeds. *Honours:* Mercury Music Prize, winner, 2001; Nominations for awards include: Brit Award, 1996, 2001; BRAT Award, 1996; 2 Grammy Awards, 1996; Danish Grammy, 1995. *Current Management:* Principle Management. *Address:* 30–32 Sir John Rogersons Quay, Dublin 2, Ireland.

HARVEY Tim; b. 1 Nov. 1973, Leeds, England. Musician (bass); Songwriter. *Education:* BEng, Leeds Met University. *Musical Education:* Self-taught. *Career:* Played violin in North Yorkshire Youth Orchestra, 1980–87; Took up bass guitar playing throughout North East England with various jazz and pop bands, 1990–; Studio session work leading to the formation of The Saints, indie pop band. *Recordings:* Composition and session work for A Dark Affair, 1993; Someone, Toytown, 1994; If I Was Your Father Christmas, Toytown, 1995; I Can Save You (EP), The Saints, 1995. *Leisure interests:* Football; Computer-aided designing; Art. *Address:* 1 Malpas Rd, Northallerton, North Yorkshire DL7 8TJ, England.

HARVIE Ian; b. 19 May 1962, Glasgow, Scotland. Musician (Guitar). *Career:* Member, Del Amitri; Numerous tours; Session recorded for the BBC with DJ John Peel. *Recordings:* Singles: Nothing Ever Happens; Spit in the Rain; Kiss This Thing Goodbye, 1993; When You Were Young, 1993; Just Like A Man, 1993; Be My Downfall, 1993; Roll to Me, 1995; Tell Her This, 1996; Albums: Del Amitri, 1985; Waking Hours, 1989; Change Everything, 1992; Twisted, 1995; Some Other Sucker's Parade, 1997; Hatful of Rain (Live), 1999.

HASLAM Annie; b. Bolton, England. Singer; Songwriter. m. Marc I Hoffman, 8 June 1991, divorced. *Education:* Art College. *Musical Education:* 9 months' opera training with Sybil Knight, London. *Career:* 65 tours, USA with rock band Renaissance; Tours: Canada; UK; Europe; Middle East; Performances include: Carnegie Hall (New York Philharmonic and Renaissance), 1975; Royal Albert Hall (Royal Philharmonic Orchestra and Renaissance), 1978; Tour of Japan (Annie Haslam Band), 1991; Solo guest with New York Philharmonia Virtuosi, 1986. *Recordings:* with Renaissance: Prologue, 1972; Ashes Are Burning, 1973; Turn of The Cards, 1974; Scheherazade and Other Stories, 1975; Live At Carnegie Hall, 1976; Novella, 1977; In The Beginning, 1978; Song For All Seasons, 1978; Azure d'Or, 1979; Camera, Camera, 1981; Timeline, 1983; Tales of 1001 Nights, Vols 1–2, 1990; Solo: Annie In Wonderland, 1977; Still Life (with Royal Philharmonic Orchestra), 1985; Annie Haslam, 1989; with Annie Haslam's Renaissance: Blessing In Disguise, 1994; Annie Haslam Live in Brazil, 1997; Novella, 1998; Azure d'Or, 1998; Live Under Brazilian Skies, 1998; The Dawn of Ananda, 2000; It Snows In Heaven Too, 2001; Guest on: Intergalactic Touring Band, 1977; with Mike Read: Betjeman, 1990; with Akio Dobashi: Fox, 1990; with Raphael Rudd: Skydancer, 1991; Guest on: Tales from Yesterday (Yes tribute), 1995; Suppers Ready (Genesis tribute), 1995; with Raphael Rudd, Awakenings, 1996; Renaissance Live at the Royal Albert Hall, with the Royal Philharmonic Orchestra, Vols 1 and 2; Songs from Renaissance Days: Rarities, recorded 1977, 1984. *Honours:* Silver disc for: Single Northern Lights, 1978; Fifth Top Female Singer, Melody Maker, 1978; Silver album, Song For All Seasons. *Membership:* Equity. *Leisure interests:* Vegetarian cooking; Photography; Active in animal welfare. *Current Management:* The White Dove Organisation Inc, PO Box 1157, Doylestown, PA 18901, USA.

HASLAM George; b. 22 Feb. 1939, Preston, Lancashire, England. Jazz Musician (baritone saxophone, tarogato). m. Beryl Murphy, 7 Dec. 1960, 4 s., 1 d. *Education:* PhD, Manchester University. *Musical Education:* Some private tuition but mainly self-taught. *Career:* Two albums on Spotlite, early 1980s; Extensive work in Eastern Europe; Tour of Mexico; Cervantino Festival, led first British jazz group to play in Cuba, 1986; Founded record label, SLAM, 1989; First British Jazz musician to play in Argentina, 1990; Founder, Oxford Jazz Festival, 1990; Featured in Impressions of George Haslam, BBC Radio 3, 1993; Working in Ukraine, Russia and Finland, 1996-, including first jazz concert in Odessa Opera House and first CD of improvised music released in Ukraine; Regular tours include: Argentina, Cuba, Hong Kong, Europe; Leads blues and improvisation workshops. *Recordings:* Live In Hungary, 1984; The Healing, 1986; 1989 and All That, 1989; The Holywell Concert, 1990; Level Two, 1992; Argentine Adventures, 1994; Waldron-Haslam, 1994; Two New, 1995; Early October, 1995; Argentine Adventures Part 2, 1996; SOLOS East West, 1997; DUOS East West, 1998. *Memberships:* Musicians' Union; PRS; MCPS. *Leisure interests:* Walking; Reading. *Address:* 3 Thesiger Rd, Abingdon, Oxon OX14 2DX, England. *E-mail:* georgehaslam@aol.com.

HASSELL David; b. 26 Nov. 1947, Manchester, England. Musician (drums, percussion). m. Valerie, 29 April 1967, 1 s., 2 d. *Musical Education:* Private tuition; Studies with Geoff Riley; Jim Blackley; Manik Popatkar; Tony Oxley. *Career:* Performer, almost every style of music: Jazz; Funk; Rock; Folk; Latin; Show; Cabaret; Symphonic; Session musician for television including: Coronation Street; Brideshead Revisited; Old Grey

Whistle Test; Jim'll Fix It; Sunday Night At The London Palladium; Emmerdale Farm; Musician for radio, jingles, records and films; Performed numerous sessions with top artists including: ABBA; The Three Degrees; The Drifters; Cliff Richard; Barbara Dickson; Vince Hill; The Ramones; The Platters; Harold Melvin and The Blue Notes; Les Miserables; Lilly Savage; Maddy Prior; Shirley Bassey; Gloria Gaynor; Bertice Redding; Alan Price; Kiki Dee; Happy Mondays; Sad Cafe; Lisa Stansfield; Roger Whittaker; George Hamilton IV; Mary O'Hara; Moira Anderson; Ute Lemper; Conductors include: Ronnie Hazelhurst; Michel Legrand; Alan Aynsworth; Leader, Apitos, one of UK's foremost Latin American ensembles; Lecturer, Drums and Percussion, Royal Northern College of Music; Royal Academy of Music, London; Salford College of Technology; Chethams School of Music; Royal Scottish Academy of Music and Drama; Trinity College. *Recordings:* Both Hands Free, 1976; with Stan Barker: The Gentle Touch, 1990; Also appears on: Changing Winds, Maddy Prior; Snap Crackle Bop, John Cooper-Clarke; Pauline Murray and the Invisible Girl, Pauline Murray; Morning Like This, Sandi Patti; Bummed, Happy Mondays. *Publications:* Graded Course For Drum Kit 1–2 (book and tape); Latin Grooves (book and tape), 1994. *Memberships:* Musicians' Union; NAPT; PAS. *Leisure interests:* Squash; Horse riding; Skiing. *Address:* 22 Park Rd, Timperley, Altrincham, Cheshire WA14 5AU, England.

HASSELQUIST Eric; b. 15 Sept. 1965, Stockholm, Sweden. Record Co Exec. *Education:* Master Degree in Business Economics. *Career:* Music Manager for Readers Digest Scandinavia, 1990–91; General Manager, Stockholm Records, 1991-. *Recording:* Impact (EP), Rimshot Party, 1991. *Address:* PO Box 20504, 16102 Bromma, Sweden.

HASTINGS Deborah; b. 11 May 1959, Evansville, Indiana, USA. Musician (bass guitar); Photographer. *Musical Education:* Music, University of Wisconsin. *Career:* Freelance bass player, 1975–; Photographer, 1976–81; Performed with: Ron Wood; Bo Diddley; Chuck Berry; Jerry Lee Lewis; Ben E King; Little Anthony; Performed at President George Bush Inauguration, with Billy Preston, Dr John, Carla Thomas, Sam Moore, 1979; Founder, A-Prompt Computer Teleprompting Services Inc, 1995; Performed with Johnnie Johnson; Played at President Clinton's inauguration, 1997. *Recording:* Bo Diddley, A Man Amongst Men. *Publication:* Author, Photographers Market, 1981. *Address:* c/o Talent Source, 1560 Broadway, Suite 1308, New York, NY 10036, USA.

HATCH Tony; b. 30 June 1939, England. Composer; Arranger; Musical Dir. *Musical Education:* London Choir School. *Career:* Band Coldstream Guards, 1959–61; Record Producer, Pye Records, 1961–71; Producer for Petula Clark; Jackie Trent; The Searchers; Musical Director, Carols In The Domain, (Australia) 1984–94; Television: Regular Panelist, New Faces, 1973–78; Films: Travels With My Aunt; Sweeney II. *Recordings:* Singles: Downtown; Call Me; I Know A Place; Where Are You Now; Joanna; Don't Sleep In The Subway; I Couldn't Live Without Your Love; Television theme music for Neighbours; Crossroads; Emmerdale; Musical: The Card; Compilation: Hatchback, 2001. *Publication:* So You Want To Be In The Music Business, 1975. *Honours:* Several Ivor Novello Awards; ASCAP Awards; BMI Awards. *Leisure interest:* Tennis. *Current Management:* Billy Marsh Associates. *Address:* c/o Lyric Productions Ltd, 3 Warwick Way, London SW1V 1QU, England.

HATFIELD Bobby; b. 10 Aug. 1940, Beaver Dam, Wisconsin, USA. Singer. *Career:* Member, The Variations; Formed The Righteous Brothers with Bill Medley, 1962–67; Support to the Beatles, US tour, 1964; Duo continued with Jimmy Walker, 1967–73; Reforms Righteous Brothers with Bill Medley, 1974–; Solo recording artist, 1968–; Appearance on Cheers, 1991. *Recordings:* Singles include: You've Lost That Lovin' Feelin' (No. 1, UK and US), 1964; Just Once In My Life, 1965; You Can Have Her, 1965; Justine, 1965; Unchained Melody, 1965; Ebb Tide, 1966; You're My Soul and Inspiration, 1966; Solo: Nothing Is Too Good For You, 1969; Rock 'n' Roll Heaven, 1974; Albums: You've Lost That Lovin' Feelin', 1965; Some Blue-Eyed Soul, 1965; This Is New!, 1965; Just Once In My Life, 1965; Back To Back, 1966; Soul and Inspiration, 1966; The Best of The Righteous Brothers, 1966; Go Ahead and Cry, 1966; Sayin' Somethin', 1967; Greatest Hits, 1967; One For The Road, 1968; Re-Birth, 1969; Greatest Hits, Vol. 2, 1969; Righteous Brothers Greatest Hits, 1990; The Best Of..., 1990; The Very Best Of..., 1990; Anthology (1962–74), 1990; Out of Our Souls, 2001. *Address:* c/o William Morris Agency.

HATFIELD Juliana; b. 27 July 1967, Wiscasset, Maine, USA. Singer; Songwriter. *Musical Education:* Berklee School of Music. *Career:* Member: Blake Babies, 1986–92; Juliana Hatfield Three, 1993–95; Solo career, 1995–; Recent concerts include: Reading Festival, 1995. *Recordings:* Albums: with the Blake Babies: Nicely Nicely, 1987; Slow Learner, 1989; Earwig, 1990; Sunburn, 1992; Innocence and Experience (compilation), 1993; with The Lemonheads: It's A Shame About Ray, 1992; with The Juliana Hatfield Three: Become What You Are, 1993; Only Everything, 1995; Solo albums include: Hey Babe, 1992; Forever Baby; Bed; Juliana's Pony – Total System Failure, 2000; Beautiful Creature, 2000; Singles include: Universal Heartbeat, 1995; Please Do Not Disturb. *Publication:* The Music of Juliana Hatfield. *Membership:* AFofM. *Leisure interests:* Ice Skating; Baking. *Current Management:* c/o Gary Smith, One Camp St, Suite 2, Cambridge, MA 02140, USA.

HATHERLEY Charlotte; b. 20 June 1979, London, England. Musician (Guitar). *Career:* Former Member, Night Nurse; Joined Ash, 1997; Contributed track to film A Life Less Ordinary, 1997; Headlining tours and TV appearances. *Recordings:* Singles: A Life Less Ordinary, 1997; Jesus Says, 1998; Sometimes, 2001; Shining Angel, 2001; Burn Baby Burn, 2001; Candy, 2001; There's A Star, 2001; Albums: Live At The Wireless, 1997; Nu-Clear Sounds, 1998; Free All Angels, 2001.

HAUG Ian; b. 21 Feb. 1970, Tasmania, South Australia. Musician (guitar). *Education:* Brisbane University, Architecture student. *Career:* Joined Brisbane-based rock group Powderfinger, 1992; Steadily built reputation on many Australian tours/festival appearances; International breakthrough with Odyssey Number Five album; Constant world-wide touring throughout 2000–01 ending with New Suburban Fables 2001 Australian shows; Also member of side-project group F.O.C. *Recordings:* Albums: Parables For Wooden Ears, 1994; Double Allergic, 1996; Internationalist, 1998; Odyssey Number Five, 2000; Singles: Powderfinger Blue (EP), Transfusion (EP), 1993; Tail, Grave Concern, 1994; Save Your Skin, Mr Kneebone (EP), 1995; Pick You Up, D.A.F., Living Type, 1996; Take Me In, 1997; The Day You Come, Don't Wanna Be Left Out/Good-Day Ray, 1998; Already Gone, Passenger, 1999; My Happiness, 2000; Like A Dog, The Metre, 2001. *Honours:* ARIA Awards: Album of The Year; Song of The Year; Best Rock Album; Best Cover Artwork, 1999; Six times platinum; Fourth album on Australian chart for 67 weeks by end of 2001; Only home-grown act ever to play more than 3 consecutive nights at Festival Hall, Australia. *Address:* c/o Republic Records, Australia. *Internet:* www.powderfinger.com.

HAUGEN Tom Jackie; b. 29 Sept. 1961, Telemark, Norway. Songwriter; Folksinger; Musician (Guitar). 1 d. *Career:* Television NRK, Reisen Til Sputnikland Miote Med Prestestranna Vel Vel Vel; Television 2, Go Ettermiooag Norge; Television 3, Pa Tide and Los Pa Traden; Television Norge, Sommatkveld; Radio, Norsktoppen, 10 I Skuooet, Nitimen, Sonoagsposten. *Compositions:* Gunnaer Gt; Bestefars Hevn; Veivesenet Farrsvant Me Potetakern; Terror I Dobbeltseng. *Recordings:* Haeimomkring, 1992; Bestefars Hevn, 1993; Ingrid Bergman, 1994; Rosmala Neger, 1998. *Honours:* This Years Artist, 1994; Language Prize, 1995. *Current Management:* M and P, Greveveien 9A, 3257 Larvik, Norway. *Address:* Tordalsun 52, 3750 Drangedal, Norway.

HAURAND Ali; b. 15 Nov. 1943, Viersen, Germany. Musician (double bass); Teacher. 1 d. *Musical Education:* Studied classical music, Folkwangschool, Essen, Germany. *Career:* Member, leader, founder, George Maycock Trio, 1967–79; Quintet with Philly Joe Jones, 1968–69; International Jazz Quintet with Jon Eardly, 1969–70; Third Eye, 1970; European Jazz Quintet, 1977; SOH Trio, 1978–84; The Quartet, 1982; European Jazz Ensemble, 1984; Numerous tours and festivals in Europe, USA, Canada and Australia with these and other ensembles featuring: Bobby Jones; Don Byas; Ben Webster; John Handy; Jan Akkerman; John Surman; Gerd Dudek; Joachim Kühn; Enrico Rava; Numerous television and radio appearances including: Jazz at Midnight, German television, 1991; Talking Jazz, Superchannel, 1993; Over 40 recordings with: The Quartet, European Jazz Ensemble; European Jazz Quintet, 1970–; Played at Celebration 1996 X> 20th Anniversary with European Jazz Ensemble; Presenter German TV WDR for Jazz Series Round Midnight and Fullhouse, 1992–; Played with Charlie Mariano and Daniel Humair as Mariano-Haurand-Humair, played festivals in Paris, Barcelona, Amsterdam, Geneva, 1999; Played pantomime and Jazz with Milan Sládek. *Compositions:* Pulque; Television music on three CDs. *Honours:* European Jazz Poll, Jazz Forum, 7 times. *Membership:* Jazz Union, Germany. *Leisure interests:* Languages; Paintings, Art. *Current Management:* K Adenauer Ring 10, 41747 Viersen, Germany.

HAUSER Tim; b. 1942, New Jersey, USA. Singer; Songwriter. *Career:* Founder member, singer, Manhattan Transfer, 1971–; Television includes: Mary Tyler Moore Television Special, 1975; Own television show, 1975; Star Parade, Germany; Regular US and European tours; Performed at MIDEM, Cannes, France, 1977. *Recordings:* Hit singles: Tuxedo Junction; Chanson D'Amour; Birdland; Boy From New York City; Albums include: Junkin' (Unofficial), 1971; Manhattan Transfer, 1975; Coming Out, 1976; Pastiche, 1978; Live, 1978; Extensions, 1979; Mecca For Moderns, 1981; Best of Manhattan Transfer, 1981; Bodies and Souls, 1983; Bop Doo-Wop, 1985; Vocalese, 1985; Live, 1987; Brasil, 1988; The Off-Beat of Avenues, 1991; Contributor, film soundtrack A League of Their Own, 1992. *Honours* include: German Grammy, Best New Group, 1975; Numerous Grammy Awards (Best Vocal Arrangement, Best Jazz Fusion Performance, Best Jazz Vocal Performance, Best Pop Vocal Performance, Best Contemporary Jazz Performance), 1980–, including 3 Grammy Awards and 12

Nominations, for Vocalese album, 1985. *Address:* c/o Columbia Records, 10 Great Marlborough St, London W1V 2LP, England.

HAUTA-AHO Teppo; b. 27 May 1941, Finland. Composer; Musician (bass). *Musical Education:* Diploma, Sibelius Academy, 1970; Studied with Professor Frantisek Posta. *Career:* Bassist, Helsinki Philharmonic, 1965–72; Finnish National Opera, 1975–; Played with numerous artists including: Seppo Paakkunainen, early 1960s; Juhani Vilkki; Kaj Backlund Big Band; Pekka Pöyry quartet; Tuohi Quartet; Leader, own group Kalmisto-Klang; Member, Quintet Moderne, 1980s–; Also classical and chamber musician; Performed at annual festivals, Kuhmo; Currently concentrating on composing; Duos with: singer/pianist Carita Holmström; pianist/composer Eero Ojanen; Member, Cecil taylor European quintet. *Compositions include:* Fantasy, for trumpet and orchestra; Kadenza, for contrabass, used as set piece in international bass competitions, 1990–99. *Honours:* Composer's Prize, Royal Academy, Stockholm; First prize, Reine Marie José competition, Geneva, 1986; Winner with Tuohi Quartet, EBU competition for jazz groups, Montreux, 1971. *Address:* Mechelininkatu 27 B, 00100 Helsinki, Finland.

HAVENS Richie; b. 21 Jan. 1941, Brooklyn, New York, USA. Singer. *Career:* Performances include: Tribute concert to Woody Guthrie, Carnegie Hall, New York, 1968; Miami Pop Festival, 1968; Woodstock Music and Art Fair, Bethel, New York, 1969; Isle of Wight Festival, 1970; Crystal Palace Garden Party, London, 1972; Stage debut, rock opera, Tommy, 1972; Stonehenge Free Festival, 1977; The Gold Medal Celebration, Carnegie Hall, 1987; Freedom Festival '90, 1990; Troubadours of Folk Festival, Los Angeles, 1993; Actor, Othello, in Jack Good's Catch My Soul, 1974; Film appearances: Greased Lightning, 1977; Hearts of Fire, 1987. *Recordings:* Albums include: Mixed Bag, 1967; Stonehenge, 1970; Alarm Clock, 1971; The Great Blind Degree, 1971; Richard P Havens, 1983; Sings Beatles and Dylan, 1990; Best of – The Millennium Collection, 2000. *Current Management:* ELD Productions, 123 W 44th St, Suite 11F, New York, NY 10036, USA.

HAVET Didier; b. 9 March 1964, Lille, France. Musician (tuba, bass trombone). m. 12 March 1994, 1 d. *Musical Education:* Lille Conservatory; Paris Conservatory. *Career:* Member, National Jazz Orchestra, France (ONJ), 1986–94; Worked with orchestras of: Martial Solal; Jean Loup Longnon; Ivan Jullien; Laurent Cugny; Jean Jacques Ruhlman; Luc Le Masne; Marc Steckar; Jean Marc Padovani; Bertrand Reaudin; Gerard Badini; Bass trombone player with Belmondo Big Band; Tour, Europe, with Mingus Big Band of New York, 1994; Paris and Nice Jazz Festival, 1995; Tours, Netherlands; Norway; Finland; Member, Bloc-notes Quintet, Peru and Columbia, 1995; Regular work in traditional jazz and dixieland. *Recordings:* 5 records with National Orchestra of Jazz, France; Other recordings with: Michel Legrand; Claude Bolling; Julien Clerc; Jacques Higelin; Georges Moustaki; William Sheller; Also appears on: Santander, with Laurent Cugny; Golden Hair, with Gil Evans; Danses, with Terra Nova; Cyclades, with Jean-Loup Longnon; 20 Ans de Jazz en France; Mingus Cuernavaca, with Padovani/Cormann; Montgolfiere, with Gianmaria Testa. *Address:* 3 rue Robert Lavergne, 92600 Asnières, France.

HAWKEN Dominic; b. 19 April 1967, Welwyn Garden City, Hertfordshire, England. Musician (keyboards); Songwriter; Prod.; Remixer; Multimedia and Internet Consultant. *Musical Education:* Piano, classically trained to Grade VIII. *Career:* Session keyboard player, performed with Joy Polloi, Kid Deluxe, Eric and the Good Good Feeling, late '80s-early '90s; Writer and producer, various leading artists, 1994–; Keyboard/Remix credits include: Shamen; Donna Summer; Malcolm McLaren; A Tribe Called Quest; Errol Brown; Kym Mazelle; Hammer; Mike Oldfield; Black Duck; Writing/Production credits include: North and South; Alphaville; Shiona; Right Said Fred; Babe Instinct; Rey; David Fernandez; Produced: Adam Masterson; Directorships: AL Digital Ltd (Multimedia and internet technology); Volume Records Ltd; Federation Records Ltd; Proprietor of WhiteHouse recording studios, London. *Compositions:* Co-writer East 17 tracks: Stay Another Day (Christmas No. 1, UK), Be There, Let It All Go, 1994; I Remember, Don't You Feel So Good, Someone To Love, 1995; Ant and Dec tracks: Cloud 9, Bound, 1997. *Recordings:* on keyboards: Steam (album), East 17; as writer/keyboard player: Albums: Up All Night, East 17, 1995; All Around the World, East 17, 1996–97; as writer/producer: The Cult of Ant and Dec (album), 1997; as additional producer/remixer/keyboards: Don't Call Me Baby (UK number 1 single), Madison Avenue, 2000; Prickly Heat (theme music for Sky TV), 2001. *Honours:* 2 Ivor Novello Award Nominations, Stay Another Day, 1995. *Memberships:* BASCA; PRS; Musicians' Union. *Current Management:* The Deluxe Corporation. *Address:* 13 Charnhill Cres., Bristol, BS16 9JU, England. *Internet:* www.aldigital.co.uk.

HAWLEY Richard; Musician (Guitar). *Career:* Member, The Longpigs. *Recordings:* Singles: Happy Again, 1995; She Said, 1995; Jesus Christ, 1995; Far, 1996; On and On, 1996; Lost Myself, 1996; Blue Skies, 1999; The Frank Sonata, 1999; Albums: The Sun is Often Out, 1996; Mobile Home,

1999; Solo single: Coming Home, 2001; Solo albums: Late Night Final, 2001.

HAWORTH Bryn; b. 29 July 1948, Blackburn, Lancashire, England. Musician (guitars, especially slide, mandolin); Singer. m. Sally, 22 Jan. 1973. *Musical Education:* Self-taught. *Career:* Joined Fleur De Lys, Motown/soul band, house band for Atlantic Records, late 1960s; Went to California, toured USA in bands including: Jackie Lomax Band; Wolfgang; Returned to England, 1973; Signed to Island Records; Numerous radio and television appearances include: 2 Old Grey Whistle Test; Tours, England, Europe, supporting artists including: Traffic; Bad Company; Gallagher and Lyle; Fairport Convention; Worked with musicians including: Chris De Burgh; Marianne Faithfull; John Cale; Ian Matthews; Joan Armatrading; Gerry Rafferty; Cliff Richard (toured with as member of band); Currently leader, The Bryn Haworth Band, extensive tours, UK; Notable exponent slide guitar. *Recordings:* Albums include: Let The Days Go By, 1974; Sunny Side of The Street, 1975; Grand Arrival, 1978; Keep The Ball Rolling, 1979; The Bryn Haworth Band Live; 6 Gospel albums include: Gap; Pass It On; Wings of The Morning; 12 Classics; Mountain Mover; with Gerry Rafferty: On A Wing and A Prayer; Over My Head, 1995; Slide Don't Fret, 1996; The Finer Things in Life, 1997. *Publication:* Bryn Haworth Song Book, Vol. One. *Leisure interest:* Music. *Address:* PO Box 28, Teddington, Middlesex TW11 0QU, England.

HAWTHORN Heather; b. 11 June 1936, Essex. Musician (Accordion). m. Donald, 2 s. *Career:* Full time entertainer; Sing-a-longs at Residential Homes; Talks to clubs; Playing for Folk and Ballroom Dancing; Accordion music from France, Italy and the British Isles. *Membership:* Musicians' Union. *Leisure interests:* Gardening; Theatre. *Address:* 88 Clifton Rd, Ruddington, Nottingham, NG11 6DE, England. *Internet:* www.heathermixture.co.uk.

HAWTIN Richie, (Plastikman, Fuse); b. 1970 Banbury, Oxfordshire, England. Prod.; DJ. *Career:* Co-founder Plus 8 Records (with John Aquaviva); World-wide DJ; Collaborations: Eddie Richards, Joey Beltram. *Recordings:* Albums: Dimension Intrusion (as Fuse), 1993; Sheet One (as Plastikman), 1993; Musik (as Plastikman), 1994; Consumed (as Plastikman), 1998; Decks, EFX and 909 (DJ mix album), 1999; DE9 – Closer To The Edit (DJ mix album), 2001; Singles: F.U. (as Fuse), 1991; Substance Abuse (as Fuse), 1991; Krakpot (as Plastikman), 1993; Spastik (as Plastikman), 1993; Do Da Doo (as Robotman), 1994; Sickness (as Plastikman), 1997; Minus Orange, 1999. *Current Management:* c/o Mute Records, 429 Harrow Rd, London, W10 4RE, England.

HAY Barry; b. 16 Aug. 1948, Saizabad, Netherlands. Vocalist; Musician (guitar, flute, saxophone). *Career:* Member, Dutch group, Golden Earring, 1966–; Tours, Europe; Canada; US; Support to The Who, European tour, 1972; Support to Rush, 1982. *Recordings:* Winter Harvest, 1967; Miracle Mirror, 1968; On The Double, 1969; Eight Miles High, 1970; Golden Earring, 1971; Seven Tears, 1971; Together, 1972; Moontan, 1973; Switch, 1975; To The Hilt, 1975; Rock of The Century, 1976; Contraband, 1976; Mad Love, 1977; Live, 1977; Grab It For A Second, 1978; No Promises No Debts, 1979; Prisoner of The Night, 1980; Second Live, 1981; Hole, 1986; Face It, 1995; Numerous compilation albums; Solo album: Only Parrots, Frogs and Angels, 1972; Hit singles: Dong-Dong-Di-Ki-Di-Gi-Dong (No. 1, Netherlands), 1968; Radar Love (No. 1, Netherlands), 1973; Twilight Zone, 1982; Lady Smiles. *Current Management:* c/o Rob Gerritsen, Regentessastraat 29, 2713 EM Zoetmeer, The Netherlands.

HAY Deborah Leigh; b. 30 May 1970, Middlesex, England. Musician (guitar); Singer; Composer; Teacher. m. Wayne Wiggins, 1 d. *Education:* BA Hons, Visual and Performing Arts, Brighton, 1988–91. *Musical Education:* Jr student, Trinity College of Music, London, 1982–88; MBT, The Playground, London, 1991. *Career:* Guitarist, Divas Dance Co; Arranger, El Punal Entra En El Corazón, 1991–93; Performed throughout Europe; Concerts include Queen Elizabeth Hall, 1991; Classic FM broadcast, 1993; Mute Opera, 1992–95; Composer, guitarist, Gaudette; Concerts include British tours. *Compositions include:* Gaudette, 1992. *Recordings:* Nothing But Love, 1988; El Punal Entra En El Corazón, 1992; Gaudette, 1993. *Honours:* Alliance and Leicester Award, El Punal Entra En El Corazón, 1992; Billy Mayerl Award, 1987; Cornelius Cardew Composition Award, Gaudette, shortlisted 1993; South East Arts Award, Mute Opera. *Memberships:* Musicians' Union; Brighton New Music; Brighton Guitar Orchestra. *Leisure interests:* Reading; Poetry; Painting; Swimming.

HAY Roy; b. 12 Aug. 1961, Southend-on-Sea, Essex, England. Musician (Guitar; Keyboards). *Career:* Member, Russian Bouquet; Joined Culture Club, 1981–87; reformed 1998–; Landed major recording contract, 1982; Numerous TV appearances and live tours; Various solo projects; Composer for television including: Fitz, ABC-TV, 1996–97. *Recordings:* Singles: Do You Really Want to Hurt Me (No. 1, UK), 1982 (re-released 1998); Church of the Poisoned Mind, 1983; Victims, 1983; It's a Miracle, 1983; Karma Chameleon (No. 1, UK and US), 1983; The War Song, 1984; The Medal Song, 1986; I Just Wanna Be Loved, 1998; Your Kisses are Charity, 1999;

Albums: Kissing to be Clever, 1982; Colour By Numbers, 1983; Waking Up With The House On Fire, 1984; From Luxury to Heartache, 1986; Greatest Moments (Live), 1998; Don't Mind If I Do, 1999; Also recorded with: Paul Young, Jaki Graham, The Beach Boys.

HAYDEN Joe; b. 25 Dec. 1972, Louisville, Kentucky, USA. Recording Engineer; Prod. *Education:* Conservatory of Recording Arts and Sciences, Phoenix, Arizona, USA. *Career:* Produced many acts in Nashville, Tennessee; Engineer, numerous recording sessions, music of all types including rock, country, jazz, bluegrass, latin, orchestral. *Recordings:* Engineer, Heaven'z Movie by Bizzy Bone, and for Bruce Robison, Victor Wooten, Members of Phish, Robbie Fulks; Jimmy Buffett. *Leisure interests:* Chess; Fishing; Outdoors; Flying. *Address:* 1720 Timber Ridge Rd 164, Austin, TX 78741, USA.

HAYES Darren Stanley; b. 8 May 1972, Brisbane, Australia. Vocalist; Songwriter. m. Colby Taylor, divorced. *Education:* Kelvin Grove University, Australia. *Career:* Played in Red Edge until breaking away with fellow group member Daniel Jones to form Savage Garden; Hugely successful world-wide; Live performances include closing ceremony of Olympic Games, Sydney, 2000; Band split, 2001; Solo career, 2001–; Currently resides California, USA. *Recordings:* Albums: Savage Garden, 1997; Affirmation, 1999; solo: Spin, 2002; Singles: I Want You, To The Moon and Back, 1996; Truly Madly Deeply, Break Me Shake Me, Universe, 1997; The Animal Song, I Knew I Loved You, 1999; Affirmation, Crash and Burn, Chained To You, 2000; Hold Me, 2001; solo: Insatiable, 2001. *Honours:* First LP sales of over 11m.; ARIA Awards, won a record 10 awards, 1997; APRA Award, Songwriters of The Year, 2000; Truly Madly Deeply set new record for longest stay on Billboard Adult Contemporary Airplay Chart (106 weeks), 2000. *Current Management:* Leonie Messer. *Address:* c/o Roadshow Music, Australia. *Internet:* www.darrenhayes.com.

HAYES Isaac; b. 20 Aug. 1942, Covington, Tennessee, USA. Rapper; Arranger; Musician (keyboards, organ). 11 c. *Career:* Leader, various groups; In-house keyboard player, staff songwriter (with David Porter) for Sam and Dave, Stax Records, 1964; Leader, arranger, Isaac Hayes Movement; Television actor, including Soul Survivors, BBC-TV, 1995; Rockford Files; Voice featured on South Park animation, Comedy Central, 1997–. *Compositions include:* Film scores: Shaft; Truck Turner; Tough Guys; As co-writer with David Porter: Hold On I'm Coming, Sam and Dave; Soul Man, Sam and Dave; B.A.B.Y., Carla Thomas; I Had A Dream, Johnnie Taylor. *Recordings:* Presenting Isaac Hayes, 1967; Hot Buttered Soul, 1969; The Isaac Hayes Movement, 1970; To Be Continued, 1971; Shaft, 1971; Black Moses, 1971; Joy, 1973; Live At The Sahara Tahoe, 1973; Tough Guys, 1974; Truck Turner, 1974; Chocolate Chip, 1975; Use Me, 1975; Disco Connection, 1976; Groove-A-Thon, 1976; Juicy Fruit, 1976; New Horizon, 1977; Man and A Woman, with Dionne Warwick, 1977; New Horizon, 1977; Memphis Movement, 1977; For The Sake of Love, 1978; Don't Let Go, 1978; Royal Rappin', with Millie Jackson, 1980; And Once Again, 1980; Light My Fire, 1980; A Lifetime Thing, 1981; U Turn, 1986; Isaacs Moods, 1988; Love Attack, 1988; Branded, 1995; Raw and Refined, 1995; Thanks to the Fool, 1995; Fragile, 1995; Simultaneous, 1999; The Man (compilation), 2001; Hit singles include: Walk On By, 1969; By The Time I Get To Phoenix, 1969; I Stand Accused, 1970; The Look of Love, 1971; Never Can Say Goodbye, 1971; Theme From Shaft (No. 1, USA), 1971; Do Your Thing, 1972; Theme From The Men, 1972; Joy, 1973; Wonderful, 1974; Disco Connection, 1976; Don't Let Go, 1979; Chocolate Salty Balls (No. 1, UK), 1998. *Honours:* Academy Award, Best Original Score, Shaft, 1972; Platinum disc, Hot Buttered Soul. *Current Management:* Ron Moss Management, 2635 Griffith Park Blvd, Los Angeles, CA 980039, USA.

HAYES (Tony) Wade; b. 20 April 1969, Bethel Acres, Oklahoma, USA. Country vocalist. *Career:* Began playing music, initially on mandolin but switching to guitar, age 11; Sang backing vocals in father's band Country Heritage; Dropped out of school to pursue music career, returning to Nashville; Played guitar on demos and wrote songs with producer Chick Rains, who organized audition with Columbia's A & R director Don Cook Hayes; Signed to Columbia Records and Tree publishing; Made progress throughout 1990s and into 2000s, charting regularly and touring extensively with own road band Wheel Hoss. *Compositions include:* I'm Still Dancin' With You; Old Enough To Know Better. *Recordings include:* Old Enough To Know Better, 1994; I'm Still Dancin' With You, Don't Stop, What I Meant To Say, 1995; On A Good Night, 1996; The Day That She Left Tulsa (In A Chevy), 1997; Albums: Old Enough To Know Better, 1995; On A Good Night, 1996; When The Wrong One Loves You Right, 1998; Highways and Heartaches, 2000. *Honours:* various including: ACM, Top New Male Vocalist, 1995; TNN/Music City News, Male Star of Tomorrow, 1997. *Current Management:* Mike Robertson Management, 1227 17th Ave S, Second Floor, Nashville, TN 37212, USA.

HAYMES Jerry; b. 30 Aug. 1940, Vernon, Texas, USA. Musician (drums, guitar); Vocalist; Actor; Speaker. m. (1) Brenda D, 1 Aug. 1961, 1 s., 1 d.; (2) Joan New, 1 Jan. 1987. *Education:* BSc, Abilene Christian University;

Kilgore College Police Academy. *Musical Education:* Associate Music, Southern Methodist University. *Career:* World tours; Performed with Hometown USA Show, World Trade Fair, Berlin, 1961 (first Country show to do so); Performed in Russia at Russian Embassy's request; Armed Forces Radio; Television personality, newsman; Original member, Sun Records Legends Group; Session musician, many hits, various labels. *Recordings:* Major hits: Rose Marie; Smile of a Clown; Big Big World; Marry Me; So Fine (Caroline); Let's Have A Party; Party Doll; What Then (gospel hit for Mahalia Jackson). *Publications:* Southwest Conference Baseball Umpire. *Honours:* Male vocalist, Bandleader, Video commercial, Gospel Music Asscn Songwriter Awards. *Memberships:* AFofM; President, Texas Art and Entertainment Council. *Leisure interests:* Music; Law enforcement; Sport official. *Current Management:* Umpire Entertainment Enterprises.

HAYNE Michael (Shane); 22 Nov. 1937, Plymouth, England. Vocalist. m. Heather Anne Tarry, 26 June 1971, 1 s., 1 d. *Education:* Warren's College, Plymouth. *Career:* Lead vocalist, R & B band The Betterdays, 1963–66; Television appearances: Westward TV; TSW; Radio: BBC Plymouth; BBC Radio Devon; Plymouth Sound; Tours throughout UK, 1991-. *Recordings:* Here Tis; Cracking Up; Aw Shucks; Hush Your Mouth; Don't Want That; Honey What's Wrong; (all 1964–65); EPs: Howl of The Streets, 1991; Down On The Waterfront, 1992; Here Tis, 1992; No Concessions, 1993; Also featured on compilation albums, Australia, France, USA. *Leisure interests:* 5-a-side football; Cricket; Reading; History. *Current Management:* Mike Weston. *Address:* 4 Ashburnham Rd, West Park, Plymouth PL5 2LR, England.

HAYNES Kevin; b. 5 Feb. 1965, Paddington, London, England. Musician (saxophone, percussion). 1 s. *Education:* North London College of Performing Arts, 1984–85; Theory, Kingsway College, 1986–87. *Career:* Concerts: Tours, Oshmare Brazilian Theatre and Dance Companies; Tours with: Steve Williamson, UK; Courtney Pine, UK, Israel, 1990; Own group, British tour, 1994; Radio: BBC Radio 3 and 4 (Kaleidoscope). *Recordings:* Albums: Ed Jones: The Home Coming, 1988; Steve Williamson: Waltz For Grace, 1989; with Courtney Pine: Bath Jazz Festival, 1993; Kevin Haynes Group: Eleggra, 1994; Recording track for Bacheology, 1995. *Membership:* Musicians' Union. *Current Management:* Fish Krish.

HAYNES Warren Dale; b. 6 April 1960, Ashville, North Carolina, USA. Singer; Songwriter; Musician (guitar, slide guitarist); Prod. *Musical Education:* Self-taught (with high school theory course). *Career:* David Allan Coe, 1980–84; Studio musician, 1984–87; Dickey Betts Band, 1987–89; Allman Bros Band, 1989–; Currently solo artist, member of Government Mule, 1994–; World-wide tours: Johnny Carson; Jay Lane; Conan O'Brian; David Letterman. *Compositions:* (co-writer), Two of a Kind (Workin' On A Full House) for Garth Brooks; True Gravity; A Kind of a Bird. *Recordings:* Allman Bros Band albums: Seven Turns; Shades of Two Worlds; An Evening With...; Where It All Begins; Second Set; Solo album: Tales of Ordinary Madness; Also appears on: Language, with Richard Leo Johnson, 2000. *Honours:* 2 Grammy Nominations; Allman Bros Band inducted into RandR Hall of Fame, 1995. *Memberships:* AFTRA; AFofM; BMI. *Leisure interests:* Outdoors; Travel; Musical Activities. *Current Management:* Doc Field, Creative Action Music. *Address:* 865 Bellevue Rd, Suite E-12, Nashville, TN 37221, USA.

HAYWARD (David) Justin; b. 14 Oct. 1946, Swindon, Wiltshire, England. Singer; Musician (guitar). *Career:* Member, The Offbeats; Marty Wilde trio; Singer, The Moody Blues, 1967–74; 1978–; Appearances include: Isle of Wight Festival, 1969; Royal Albert Hall, 1969; Royal Festival Hall, London, 1970; Carnegie Hall, New York, 1970; Opened own recording studio, London, 1974; Solo recording career, 1974-. *Recordings:* Singles include: (own composition) Nights In White Satin, 1968; Question (No. 2, UK), 1970; Isn't Life Strange, 1972; I'm Just A Singer (In A Rock 'n' Roll Band), 1973; Gemini Dream, 1981; The Voice, 1981; Your Wildest Dreams, 1986; Solo: Forever Autumn, 1987; It Won't Be Easy, 1987; Albums: with the Moody Blues: Days of Future Passed, 1967; In Search of The Lost Chord, 1968; On The Threshold of a Dream (No. 1, UK), 1969; To Our Children's Children's Children, 1969; Caught Live + 5, 1969; A Question of Balance (No. 1, UK), 1970; Every Good Boy Deserves Favour (No. 1, UK), 1971; Seventh Sojourn (No. 1, USA), 1972; This Is The Moody Blues, 1974; Octave, 1978; Out of This World, 1979; Long Distance Voyager (No. 1, USA), 1981; The Present, 1983; Voices In The Sky, 1985; The Other Side of Life, 1986; Sur La Mer, 1988; Keys of The Kingdom, 1991; Live At Red Rock, 1993; Strange Times, 1999; Live At The Royal Albert Hall, 2000; Journey Into Amazing Caves, 2001; Solo albums: Blue Jays, with John Lodge, 1975; Songwriter, 1977; Night Flight, 1980; Moving Mountains, 1985; Classic Blue, 1989; View from the Hill, 1996; Contributor, War of The Worlds, Jeff Wayne, 1978. *Honour:* Ivor Novello Award, Outstanding Contribution to British Music (with the Moody Blues), 1985. *Address:* c/o Bright Music Ltd, 2 Harwood Terrace, London SW6 2AB, England.

HAZELL Patrick James; b. 23 Sept. 1945, Burlington, Iowa, USA. Musician (piano, organ, harmonica, drums); Singer; Songwriter. m. Pamela Ann Cummings, 28 Oct. 1967, 3 s., 1 d. *Education:* College

Degree. *Musical Education:* College classes, recording techniques. *Career:* Professional musician, 1960–; Founder, Mother Blues Band, 1968–70; Founder, Sound Pool, 1972; Member, Rocket 88's; Reformed Mother Blues Band, 1973–83; Reformed Mother Blues Band, 1997–; Solo performer, 1983–; Music instructor, Washington High School, 1987–95; Numerous tours, Midwest US, Europe, Paraguay; Concerts supporting: Led Zeppelin; Jefferson Airplane; John Mayall; Robert Cray; Muddy Waters; John Lee Hooker; George Thorogood; Suzy Bogguss; Luther Allison; Asleep At The Wheel; Junior Walker. *Recordings:* Albums include Band Music, Vol. 1, 1975; Vol. 2, 1978; Vol. 3, 1980; Vicksburg Vol. 1, 1981; Vol. 2, 1981; Christmas Visions, 1982; Studios Solos, 1985; The New Cool, 1986; Solo Improvisations, 1986; Patrick Hazell-Live!, 1987; Blues Jam, 1988; East of Midnight, 1989; Nemo's Island, 1989; Mystery Winds, 1989; Santa Was Eating The Christmas Tree/Nicci and The Project, 1989; Tuba and Piano Jam Session, 1990; Blues on the Run, 1995; Patrick Hazell and the Mother Blues Band, 1975–80, 1996; In The Prairieland, 1996; Dreamcatcher, 1996; Blue Blood, 1997; Soundtracks, 1997; Cityscape Precipice, 1997. *Honours:* 4 Prairie Sun Awards, Best Rhythm and Blues Band. *Memberships:* Arts Midwest; Iowa Arts Council; Touring Arts Team of Iowa; Official endorsee, Hohner Harmonicas. *Leisure interest:* Music. *Address:* 220 E 17th St, Washington, IA 52353, USA.

HEALEY Jeff; b. 25 March 1966, Toronto, Ontario, Canada. Blues/Rock Musician (guitar, multi-instrumentalist); Singer; Songwriter; Actor. *Career:* Blind since age 1; Founder, Blue Direction aged 15, Toronto; Played with Albert Collins; Stevie Ray Vaughn; Founder, Jeff Healey Band, 1985; Own record label, Forte, 1985–88; World tour, 1990; Actor, singer, film Roadhouse, 1989. *Recordings:* Singles: Confidence Man, 1988; Angel Eyes, 1989; Full Circle, 1990; Cruel Little Number, 1992; Stuck In The Middle With You, 1995; Albums: See The Light, 1989; Hell To Pay, 1990; Feel This, 1992; Cover To Cover, 1995; The Very Best of Jeff Healey, 1998; The Master Hits, 1999; Featured on film soundtrack, Roadhouse, 1989. *Address:* c/o Forte Records and Productions, 320 Spadina Rd, Toronto, ON M5R 2V6, Canada.

HEALY Fran; b. 23 July 1973, Scotland. Singer; Musician (guitar). *Career:* Member, Travis, 1990–; Concert performances include support tour to Oasis, 1997; Numerous tours and television appearances. *Recordings:* Singles: U16 Girls, 1997; All I Want to Do is Rock, 1997; Tied to the 90s, 1997; Happy, 1997; More Than Us, 1997; Writing to Reach You, 1999; Driftwood, 1999; Why Does it Always Rain on Me, 1999; Turn, 1999; Coming Around, 2000; Sing, 2001; Albums: Good Feeling, 1997; The Man Who (No. 1, UK), 1999; The Invisible Band (No. 1, UK), 2001. *Honours:* Q Magazine Award, Best Single of 1999; Select Magazine, Album of the Year, 1999; BRIT Awards: Best British Group; Best British Album, 2000. *Address:* c/o Wildlife Entertainment Ltd, 21 Heathmans Rd, London SW6 4TJ, England.

HEALY Jeremy; b. 18 Jan. 1962, Woolwich, London, England. DJ; Prod. *Career:* Formed band Haysi Fantayzee with Kate Garner; 2 hits world-wide; Became scratching-mixing DJ. *Recordings:* Albums: Mixmag Live, 1995; House Collection Vol. 4, 1996; British Anthems, 1998; Ibiza The Closing Party, 1999; Singles: Stamp, 1996; Argentina, 1997; Other recordings: with Haysi Fantayzee: John Wayne Is Big Leggy, 1982, Shiny Shiny, 1983, Sabres of Paradise; Everything Starts With An 'E', E-Zee Possee, 1989. *Honours:* Gold album, Haysi Fantayzee; Silver single, John Wayne Is Big Leggy; DJ of the Year, Mixmag, 1995; Most Popular Face, 1995. *Membership:* PRS. *Leisure interest:* Travel. *Current Management:* Francesca Cutler, Selective Management. *Address:* 6 Brewer St, London W1R 3FR, England.

HEARD Paul; b. 5 Oct. 1960, London, England. Musician (keyboards, programming). *Career:* Former Member, Orange Juice; Joined M People, 1990; Numerous live dates and television appearances; Song, Search for the Hero used in TV advertisement. *Recordings:* Singles: How Can I Love You More, 1991; Colour My Life, 1991; Padlock, 1992; Excited, 1992; One Night in Heaven, 1993; Moving on Up (No. 2, UK), 1993; Don't Look Any Further, 1993; Renaissance, 1994; Sight For Sore Eyes, 1994; Open Your Heart, 1995; Search for the Hero, 1995; Love Rendezvous, 1995; Itchycoo Park, 1995; Just for You, 1997; Fantasy Island, 1997; Angel St, 1998; Testify, 1998; Dreaming, 1999; Albums: Northern Soul, 1992; Elegant Slumming, 1993; Love Rendezvous, 1995; Bizarre Fruit, 1994; Fresco, 1997. *Honours:* Brit Award, Best Dance Band, 1992; Mercury Music Prize, 1993.

HEARN Martin Peter; b. 3 Dec. 1955, London, England. Musician (drum, percussion); Teacher. m. Noelle Loyd, 16 Aug. 1986, 4 s. *Musical Education:* National Youth Jazz Association. *Career:* Worked with: The Drifters; David Soul; Joe Longthorne; Ben E King; Tommy Cooper; Cilla Black; Michael Barrymore; Bob Monkhouse; Joe Longthorne; John Paul James; National Youth Jazz Orchestra; London West End Shows: Cats; Evita; Me and My Girl; Rocky Horror Show; NYSO; North Sea Festival; Montrose Jazz Festival; Pebble Mill; Sunday Sunday; Founder of STIX School of Rhythm, Music school for the rhythm section of modern music, working bands, 1994. *Honours:* Rock and Roll Hall of Fame, with the Drifters, 1985.

Memberships: National Youth Jazz Asscn; NYSO; Musicians' Union; Chamber of Commerce and Trade. *Leisure interests:* Scuba-diving; Camping; Photography. *Current Management:* STIX School of Rhythm, Noëlle Hearn. *Address:* STIX School of Rhythm, Kings Arm Yard, Church St, Ampthill, Bedfordshire MK45 2PJ, England.

HEATH Martin; b. 12 March 1961, Sussex, England. Record Co Exec. *Education:* BA Hons. *Career:* Managing Director, UK-based indie record label Rhythm King Records, co-founded with Adele Nozedar, 1986; Founder, Renegade Software and Perfect World Programmes. *Leisure interests:* Horse riding; Sailing; Walking; Military history. *Address:* c/o Rhythm King Records, 121 Salisbury Rd, London NW6 6RG, England.

HEATH Rohan Vernon; b. 19 July 1964, Wembley, London, England. Songwriter; Musician (keyboards). *Education:* BSc, Biology; MSc, Entomology. *Musical Education:* Grade IX Piano, Victoria College of Music. *Career:* Keyboards, A Guy Called Gerald, 1990–91; Keyboards, Together, 1991–92; Keyboards, Eek A Mouse, 1992–93; Leader, Urban Cookie Collective, 1993–; Tours include: USA, Canada, Australia, Japan, Singapore, UK, Europe, Israel, Lithuania, Turkey. *Compositions:* co-wrote: Automatik, A Guy Called Gerald. *Recordings:* Urban Cookie Collective singles: The Key The Secret (No. 2, UK), 1993; Spend the Day; Feels Like Heaven; Sail Away; High On A Happy Vibe; Tales from the Magic Fountain; Bring It On Home; Reggae Summer Splash; Compilation: Very Best of The Urban Cookie Collective, 2000. *Publications:* The Phylogenetic Significance of The Ventral Nervous Chord In Carabid Beetles, Journal of Entomology. *Honours:* Platinum and Gold discs; Music Week Independent Single, 1994; Perfect 10 Award, Best Live Act, Singapore, 1994. *Leisure interests:* Travel; Music. *Address:* c/o Blitz, Edgeware Bury Farm, Edgeware Bury Lane, Edgeware HA8 8QX, England.

HEATLIE Bob; b. 20 July 1946, Edinburgh, Scotland. Musician (keyboards, saxophone, flute). m. Mary Jane Davie, 3 March 1967, 3 s. *Musical Education:* Taught by father, Thomas Heatlie. *Recordings:* Aneka: Japanese Boy, No. 1; Merry Christmas Everyone, No. 1; Cry Just A Little Bit; Many television theme tunes. *Honours:* 8 Gold discs (singles); 1 Silver and 1 Platinum (albums); 2 ASCAP Awards. *Memberships:* MCPS; PRS; BASCA. *Leisure interests:* Photography; Drawing. *Address:* 3 Victoria St, Edinburgh EH1 2HE, Scotland.

HEATON Mike; b. 18 Sept. 1968. *Career:* Member, Embrace; Obtained major label deals in UK and USA, 1996; Released debut single independently; Support slot in tour with Manic Street Preachers, 1997; Headline tours and TV appearances. *Recordings:* Singles: Fireworks, 1997; One Big Family, 1997; All You Good Good People, 1997; Come Back To What You Know, 1998; My Weakness Is None of Your Business, 1998; Hooligan, 1999; You're Not Alone, 2000; Save Me, 2000; I Wouldn't Wanna Happen To You, 2000; Wonder, 2001; Albums: The Good Will Out, 1998; Drawn From Memory, 2000; If You've Never Been, 2001.

HEATON Paul David; b. 9 May 1962, Birkenhead, Merseyside, England. Singer; Songwriter; Musician. *Career:* Lead singer, The Housemartins, 1983–88; Released 8 singles (6 Top 20 hits); 3 albums; Founder member, The Beautiful South, 1988–; Releases to date: 14 singles (11 Top 40); 5 albums (All top 5); Concerts include: T In The Park Festival, Glasgow, 1995; McAlpine Stadium, Crystal Palace Stadium, 1997. *Recordings:* Albums: with the Housemartins: London 0 Hull 4, 1986; The People Who Grinned Themselves To Death, 1987; Now That's What I Call Quite Good, 1988; with the Beautiful South: Welcome To The Beautiful South, 1989; Choke, 1990; 0898, 1992; Miaow, 1994; Carry On Up the Charts (No. 1, UK), 1994; Blue is the Colour, (No 1, UK), 1996; Quench, 1998; Painting It Red, 2000; Solid Bronze (compilation), 2001; Singles: with the Housemartins: Flag Day, 1985; Sheep, 1986; Happy Hour, 1986; Think For A Minute, 1986; Caravan of Love (No. 1, UK), 1986; Five Get Over Excited, 1987; Me and The Farmer, 1987; Build, 1987; There's Always Something There To Remind Me, 1988; with the Beautiful South: Song For Whoever, 1989; I'll Sail This Ship Alone, 1989; You Keep It All In, 1989; A Little Time (No. 1, UK), 1990; My Book, 1990; Let Love Speak Up Itself, 1991; Old Red Eyes Is Back, 1992; We Are Each Other, 1992; Bell-Bottomed Tear, 1992 Good As Gold, 1994; Everybody's Talkin', 1994; Prettiest Eyes, 1994; One Last Love Song, 1994; Pretenders To The Throne, 1995; Rotterdam, 1996; Don't Marry Her, 1996; Blackbird on the Wire, 1997; Liars Bar, 1997; Perfect 10, 1998; Dumb, 1998; How Long's A Tear Take to Dry?, 1999; The River, 2000; Solo album, as Biscuit Boy: Fat Chance, 2001. *Honours:* BPI Awards: Best Newcomers, the Housemartins, 1987; Best Video, A Little Time, The Beautiful South, 1991. *Leisure interests:* Watching and playing football; Writing. *Address:* The Beautiful South, PO Box 87, Hull, East Yorkshire HU5 2NR, England.

HECKARD Gary Davis; b. 15 March 1974, Los Angeles, USA. Composer; Improviser. *Education:* EdM, Teachers College Columbia University; Manhattan School of Music, BM, Berklee College of Music. *Career:* Composer in Residence, the Greenwich Village Orchestra; Member, Grussner Band, Toured World-wide, Radio Broadcasts on National

Radios. *Compositions include:* Triple Concerto for Jazz Orchestra, 1995; Three Months in Rotterdam, 1996; Two Pages in the New City, 1997; Continuation, 1 997; …Fore, 1998; Untitled, 1998; Recollection, 1999. *Recording:* Gary Davis Heckar – Improvisations. *Memberships:* Compose NY; The American Music Center; BMI; BMI Classical.

HECTOR Kevin Jon; b. 17 Jan. 1967, Nantwich, Cheshire, England. Prod.; Musician (guitar); Electronic artist. *Education:* Fashion, St Martins. *Musical Education:* Classical singing; Jazz/classical guitar. *Career:* Session guitarist, 1983–87; London Club DJ, 1988–; Dance producer, 1990–; Autocreation world tour, 1993; Including live broadcast on Japan TV. *Compositions:* Miscellaneous dance compositions. *Recordings:* Mettle, Autocreation. *Leisure interests:* Surfing; Writing. *Address:* PO Box 3605, London NW8 0DD, England.

HEDEGAARD Svend; b. 19 Dec. 1959, Sonderborg, Denmark. Musician; Composer. *Education:* Private studies and several seminars in composition; Guitar and piano lessons. *Career:* Guitarist, numerous rock, fusion and jazz bands, 1979–98; Composer, 15 theatre plays, 6 television productions, several major works for different classical ensembles and orchestras in Denmark, 1986–98; Wind O Four, jazz fusion quartet, 1991-. *Compositions:* Maximal/Minimal, 1991; Some Colours Remain, Some Remind, 1991; Twins Turn, 1996; Efter regnen sas…, 1996; Sangenes Sang, 1997; Via, 1998. *Recordings:* With Wind O Four, Jazz Quartet, 1995, Voices, 1997. *Honours:* Laurens Bogtman Fondens Haederslegat, 1996; DJBFA, Arbejdslegat, 1997. *Memberships:* Danish Musicians' Union; Danish Jazz, Beat and Folk Music Composers; KODA. *Leisure interests:* Painting; Nature; Music. *Address:* Romersgade 23 2 tv, 1362 Kobenhavn K, Denmark.

HEDGES Mike; Record Prod. *Career:* Engineer, Morgan Studios, late 1970s-80s; Founder, Playground Studio, 1980s; Converted Chateau Rouge Motte, Normandy, into full residential studio, 1990. *Recordings:* Producer, albums include: with Siouxie and The Banshees: Kiss In A Dreamhouse; Hyena; Peep Show; Nocturne; Through The Looking Glass; with Marc Almond: Vermine In Ermine; Stories of Johnny; A Woman's Story; Mother Fist; Virgin's Tale No. 2; with The Beautiful South: Welcome To The Beautiful South; Choke; with The Cure: Three Imaginary Boys; Seventeen Seconds; Faith; Split, Lush; with McAlmont and Butler: Yes; Sound of McAlmont and Butler; with Manic Street Preachers: Everything Must Go, 1996; This is My Truth, 1999; Know Your Enemy, 2001; Also: Baby The Stars Shine Bright, Everything But The Girl; Drop, The Shamen; Mask, Bauhaus; Songs of Strength and Heartbreak, Mighty Wah!, 2000; Also singles with Wah!; Bauhaus; The Cure; Siouxie and The Banshees; The Creatures; Marc Almond; Everything But The Girl; The Beautiful South. *Current Management:* Jessica Norbury, 3Khz Management, 54 Pentney Rd, London, SW12 0NY, England. *E-mail:* threekhz@hotmail.com.

HEIL Gail A; b. 20 Aug. 1945, St Louis, MO, USA. Musician (Fiddle, Banjo, Guitar, Autoharp); Singer. m. Bob Bovee. *Education:* University of Missouri. *Career:* Regular Tours of USA, 1981–; Iowa Public Television; River City Folk; Rural Route 3; Other Syndicated Radio Shows; Festival of American Fiddle Tunes. *Recordings:* For Old Times Sake, 1985; Behind The Times, 1986; Come All You Waddies, 1988; Come Over and See Me, 1991; Rural Route 2, 1996; Master Fiddler For Iowa State Folk Arts Apprenticeship Program and Minnesota State Folk Arts Apprenticeship Program. *Leisure interests:* Gardening; Reading. *Address:* Rt 2 Box 25, Spring Grove, MN 55974, USA.

HEINILA Kari Juhani; b. 31 Oct. 1966, Kiukainen, Finland. m. Arja Mäkelä, 2 s., 1 d. *Musical Education:* Classical Piano and Flute in Music School, Saxophone and Improvisation in Sibelius Academy's Jazz Department, 1984–88; Private composing studies, 1993–95. *Career:* Saxophonist, Umo Jazz Orchestra, 1987–93; Jazz Groups under own name, 1987–; Recordings and concerts with the top names in Finnish Jazz; Performing with such internationally respected Jazz artists as Billy Hart, Tim Hagans, Vince Mendoza, Anders Jormin and Wayne Krantz; Active Composer in contemporary jazz scene; Regular Techer, Sibelius Academy's Jazz Department, 1993-. *Compositions:* Frozen Petals; Blue in the Distance; Crossings; Wavestar. *Recordings:* Espoo Big Band: Grand Mystery; Jarmo Savolainen: Blue Dreams, True Image; Edward Vesala: Lumi; Umo Jazz Orchestra: Selected Standards; Pekka Luukka, Splash of Colors; Jukka Linkola, The Tentet; Sonny Heinla, Tribus. *Honours:* BAT-Finland Composition Prize, 1992; Pori Jazz Festival's Artist of the Year Prize, 1995. *Address:* Hannuksenkuja 4A3, 02270 Espoo, Finland.

HELFER Erwin; b. 20 Jan. 1936, Chicago, Illinois, USA. Blues and Jazz Musician (piano); Piano teacher. *Musical Education:* Mus B American Conservatory of Music; Mus M, Northeastern Illinois University. *Career:* Annual performances at Chicago Blues Festival; Annual concert tours, Europe, Rolf Schubert Concertburo, Cologne, Germany; Plays in local jazz and blues clubs, Chicago; College tours, USA; Recording artist for Flying Fish; Steeple Chase; Red Beans; CMA. *Recordings:* Erwin Helfer and Friends On The Sunny Side of The Street, 1979; Erwin Helfer Plays

Chicago Piano, 1986; Appears on: Voice of Blues, Angela Brown, 2000. *Honours:* Critics Choice Award, Maybee I'll Cry, Downbeat Magazine, 1983; Illinois Arts Council Grant, 1986; Nomination for Jazz Music Award, National Asscn for Campus Activities. *Leisure interests:* Animals; Transpersonal psychology; Comparative religion; Reading; Gardening. *Current Management:* Erwin Helfer, 2240 N Magnolia, Chicago, IL 60614, USA.

HELLER Jana Louise Greenberg; b. 18 July 1948, California, USA. Singer; Songwriter; Musician (guitar, dulcimer, piano, celestaphone). m. A Gilhooley, 1999. *Education:* Stephens College, Missouri, University of Southern California, USA; UCLA, Santa Monica City College. *Musical Education:* 8 years piano. *Career:* Solo work; Bands: AAAHS; The Phantoms; Concerts, folk, music festivals: UK; US; Poland; Radio: KPFK's Folkscene, Los Angeles, USA; Kroc, USA; Radio Poznan, Poland; BBC Radio II (We Stayed In With Jungr and Parker); GLR Radio; London Talkback Radio; BBC Radio Essex Folkscene; Kazu Radio, USA; Brian Willoughby's All Stars. *Recordings:* Mad Waltzing, 1986; Twist and Turn, 1990; Laughing In Crime, 1995. *Honours:* American Song Festival, winner lyric division. *Memberships:* Musicians' Union; PRS. *Leisure interests:* Travel; Writing and illustrating children's books; Antique clothing; Horse riding. *Current Management:* Mr Squashy Agency. *Address:* 2 Friars Close, Wilmslow, Cheshire SK9 5PP, England.

HELLER Pete, (Stylus Trouble); b. 1965, London, England. Prod.; Remixer; DJ. *Career:* Part of Boy's Own collective; Remixed (with Terry Farley): Ultra Nate, Primal Scream, Janet Jackson, Happy Mondays; Member: Bocca Juniors, Fire Island, Roach Motel; Collaborations: Terry Farley, Andrew Weatherall, Rui Da Silva. *Recordings:* Singles: Raise (with Bocca Juniors), 1990; In Your Bones (with Fire Island), 1992; There But For The Grace of God (with Fire Island), 1994; Ultra Flava, 1995; The Rising Sun (with Terry Farley), 1999; Big Love, 1999; Sputnik One (as Stylus Trouble), 2001. *Current Management:* c/o Junior Recordings, The Saga Centre, 326 Kensal Rd, London, W10 5BZ, England.

HELLQUIST Mats; b. 15 May 1964, Stockholm, Sweden. Musician (bass, guitar). 1 s., 2 d. *Musical Education:* Self-taught bass and guitar. *Career:* Member, bob hund, 1991; More than 300 gigs around Scandinavia; Played at famous Roskilde, Lollipop, Ruisrock Quartfestivalen and Hultsfred. *Compositions:* I Stället för Musik: Förvirring, 1996, Düsseldorf, 1996. *Recordings:* bob hund, 1993; Edvin medvind, 1994; I stället för musik: Förvirring, 1996; Omslag: Martin Kann, 1996; Düsseldorf, 1996; Ett fall and en lösning, 1997; Nu är det väl revolution på gång, 1998; Jag rear ut min själ Allt skall bort!!!, 1998; Helgen V, 1999; Sover aldrig, 1999. *Honours:* Grammy, best live act, 1994; Grammy, best lyrics, 1996. *Memberships:* STIM; SAMI. *Leisure interests:* Music; Books; Food; Drinking. *Address:* c/o bob hunds förlag, Råsundavägen 150, 169 36 Solna, Sweden.

HELLRIEGEL Jan; b. 2 Sept. 1967, Auckland, New Zealand. Musician (piano, guitar); Singer; Songwriter; Actor. *Education:* BA, University of Otago. *Musical Education:* Classical singing and piano; Rock guitar; University papers. *Career:* Four national solo tours, eight with band; TVNZ Music Awards Television and Film Awards, New Zealand, 1993; Big Day Out Concert, supporting Bavid Byrne, The Cure. *Recordings:* Singles: The Way I Feel; Manic Is A State of Mind; Solo albums: It's My Sin, 1993; Tremble, 1995; with Cassandras Ears Band: Private Wasteland (EP), 1990; Your Estimation, 1992 (EP); with Working With Walt: 5 Sides (EP), 1990. *Honours:* Songwriter of the Year, 1993; Most Promising Female Vocalist, 1993; Nomination, Entertainer of the Year, 1993. *Leisure interests:* Reading; Films; Social Services. *Current Management:* MGM Management, 9 Dundas Lane, Albert Park, Victoria 3206, Australia.

HELMIS Dimitrios; b. 11 Jan. 1962, Pireaus, Greece. Promoter; Agent. 1 s. *Career:* Owner, Neo Revma International Ltd, 10 years promoting and booking international and local acts in Greece and Balkan area; Hundreds of shows include: Pink Floyd; Michael Jackson; The Scorpions; Stevie Wonder; Guns 'n' Roses; Metallica; Philip Glass; Goran Bregovic; Michael Nyman; Neville Brothers. *Address:* Neo Revma International Ltd, 8 Ainanos Str 104–34, Athens, Greece.

HELMS Mickey; b. 4 Sept. 1972, California, USA. Composer. *Education:* AA, De Anza College, 1992; BM, San Jose State University, 1997. *Career:* Composer. *Compositions:* Whispering Modulations, 1996; Variations On A Theme By Chris Mann, 1996; Music For Tuba and Piano, 1998. *Recordings:* Frog Peak Collaborations Project, 1998; Music From Cream, 1998. *Memberships:* BMI; International Computer Music Association; Society of Electro-Acoustic Music in the United States; Society of Composers. *Leisure interests:* Hiking; Cycling; Movies; Music. *Current Management:* Mickey Helms. *Address:* 244 Corral Ave, Sunnyvale, CA 94086, USA.

HELSON Robert (Bob); b. 20 Aug. 1949, Bristol, England. Music (drums, percussion). *Musical Education:* Drum lessons with Geoff Smith, 1966–69. *Career:* Drummer with: Plasma, early 1970's; Bullit, 1974–90; Appearances with Bullit include: Bracknell Festival, 1986; Le Mans Jazz Festival, 1987;

Will Menter's Wind and Fingers, appearing at Bristol Arnolfini and Dunkirk Jazz Festival, 1976; Both Hands Free, 1976–82; Community, appearing at Palais de Beaux Arts, Brussels and Arnolfini, 1980–81; Out Loud, 1984–87; Keith Tippett's Canoe, 1984–85; Dance and percussion duet with dancer Beppie Blankert, Bristol Arnolfini, 1981; Broadcasts on BBC Radio 3, Jazz In Britain, with: Both Hands Free, 1979; Steve Mulligan Quartet, 1983, 1984; Out Loud, 1986; Bullit, 1987. *Recordings:* with Both Hands Free: Use From The Pocket, 1978; Solo percussion improvisations: Noise Reduction, 1979; Will Menter's Community, 1981. *Leisure interests:* Nature; Countryside; Screaming about the mess we're making of this planet. *Address:* Basement Flat, 34 Cornwallis Cres., Clifton, Bristol BS8 4PH, England.

HEMINGWAY Dave; b. 20 Sept. 1960, Hull, England. Vocalist. *Career:* Former Member, The Housemartins, 1987–88; Founder member, The Beautiful South, 1988; Numerous TV appearances and tours; Festival appearances. *Recordings:* with The Housemartins: Singles: Five Get Over Excited, 1987; Me and The Farmer, 1987; Build, 1987; There's Always Something There To Remind Me, 1988; Albums: The People Who Grinned Themselves To Death, 1987; Now That's What I Call Quite Good, 1988; with The Beautiful South: Singles: Song For Whoever, 1989; You Keep It All In, 1989; My Book EP, 1991; One Last Love Song, 1992; Prettiest Eyes, 1994; Everybody's Talking, 1994; Rotterdam (Or Anywhere) 1996; Don't Marry Her, 1996; Liar's Bar, 1997; Perfect 10, 1998; Dumb, 1999; The River, 2000; Albums: Welcome To the Beautiful South, 1989; Choke, 1990; 0898, 1992; Miaow, 1994; Carry On Up The Charts, 1994; Blue is The Colour, 1996; Quench, 1998; Painting It Red, 2000; Solid Bronze (compilation), 2001.

HEMMINGS Paul; b. 24 May 1963, Liverpool, England. Musician (guitar, lap steel, mandolin). *Education:* BA, History and Politics, North Staffs Polytechnic. *Career:* Guitarist with the La's, 1986–87; Guitarist with The Onset, The Australians, Sensurround, 1988–93; Guitarist, Lightning Seeds, 1994–; Tours: UK; Europe; USA; Various radio sessions; Television appearances include: Danny Baker Show; Music Box; What's Up Doc; Top of The Pops; German TV. *Compositions:* Co-writer: Saddest Song; Shake, Shake, Shake. *Recordings:* Albums: Pool of Life, The Onset, 1988; Timeless Melody, The La's, 1990; Electric Mothers of Invention, Neuro # Project, 1993; Pool of Life Revisited, The Onset, 1994; Other recordings: Way Out (EP), The La's, 1987; What You Say (EP), The Onset, 1990; When I Get To Heaven (single), Sensurround, 1993; Lucky You (live single), Lightning Seeds, 1994; With Lightning Seeds, What If; Here Today (live version); Three Lions 98, with Lightning Seeds, with Skinner and Baddiel; Hillsborough Justice Concert, 3 live tracks with Lightning Seeds and Holly Johnson. *Honours:* Brit Awards, 2 consecutive years. *Memberships:* Musicians' Union; PRS. *Leisure interests:* Photography; Cinema; The Arts; Sport. *Address:* Woodcroft, Beaconsfield Rd, Liverpool L25 6EJ, England.

HENDERSON Hamish Scott; b. 11 Nov. 1919, Blairgowrie, Perthshire, Scotland. Poet; Songwriter. m. Felicity Schmidt, 16 May 1959, 2 d. *Education:* Downing College, Cambridge. *Musical Education:* With traditional singers, Perthshire and Aberdeenshire. *Career:* Collection of soldiers songs in WWII, published in Ballads of World War II, 1947; Collection of North-East Scottish folk songs with Alan Lomax, 1951; Joined School of Scottish Studies, Edinburgh University, 1952; Collection of Gaelic and Lowland Scottish Songs and Tales. *Compositions:* Numerous songs popular with Scottish folk revival include: The Freedom Come-All-Ye; The 51st Highland Division's Farewell To Sicily; The Gillie More; The Men of Knoydart. *Recordings:* Album: Freedom Come-All-Ye. *Publications:* Elegies For The Dead In Cyrenaica, 1948; Alias MacAlias, essays on folklore, 1992; The Armstrong Nose, selected letters, 1996; Gramsci's Prison Letters, 1996. *Honour:* Somerset Maugham Award, 1949. *Memberships:* Hon. Mem., Saltire Society, Edinburgh; Hon. Mem., Folklore Fellows, Helsinki; Hon. Fellow, School of Scottish Studies. *Leisure interests:* Singing; Songwriting.

HENDERSON Scott; b. 26 Aug. 1954, West Palm Beach, Florida, USA. Composer; Musician (guitarist). *Education:* Florida Atlantic University, 1 year Musicians Institute. *Career:* Touring, recording, 1981–; 3 years with Jean-Luc Ponty; 1 year, Chick Corea; 4 years, Joe Zawinul; 10 years, Tribal Tech (co-led, Gary Willis). *Recordings:* Albums: with Tribal Tech: Spears; Dr Hee; Nomad; Tribal Tech; Illicit; Face First; Reality Check; Dog Party; Primal Tracks; Giddy Up Go; Tore Down House; Vital Tech Tones; Thick; with Joe Zawinul: The Immigrants; Black Water; with Chick Corea: Elektrik Band; Solo: Thick, 1999. *Publications:* The Scott Henderson Guitar Book. *Honours:* Best Jazz Guitarist, Guitar World magazine, 1990; Guitar Player magazine, 1991; Best Blues Album, Dog Party, Guitar Player magazine, 1994. *Leisure interest:* Dogs. *Address:* 6044 Buena Vista, Los Angeles, CA 90042, USA.

HENDRICKS Jon; b. 16 Sept. 1921, Newark, Ohio, USA. Vocalist; Lyricist. *Education:* Studied Law. *Career:* Sang on local radio in Toledo; After serving in military during WWII, switching to jazz playing drums and writing songs; Composition I Want You To Be My Baby recorded by Louis Jordan, 1952; Made own first recordings in 1957 with the Dave Lambert

Singers on self-penned lyric versions of classic jazz instrumentals including Four Brothers; Cloudburst; Later same year, teamed up with Lambert and Annie Ross forming vocal trio Lambert Hendricks and Ross; Toured and recorded together (Ross replaced by Yolande Bevan, 1962) until 1964; Moved to Europe, 1965; Returned as jazz critic for the San Francisco Chronicle, early 1970s; Began teaching jazz; Formed The Hendricks Family (with wife and 2 children) which continues to perform and tour. *Compositions:* Transformed instrumental solo parts of bebop jazz instrumentals by writing lyrics for classic works including: I Remember Clifford; Airgin; Centrepiece; Little Pony; Sing Joy Spring; Birdland. *Recordings:* with Lambert Hendricks and Ross: Sing A Song of Basie, 1957; The Swingers, Sing Along With Basie, 1958; The Hottest New Group In Jazz, 1959; Lambert Hendricks and Ross Sing Ellington, 1960; The Way-Out Voices of Lambert Hendricks and Ross, 1961; with Lambert Hendricks and Bevan: Live At Basin Street, At Newport '63, Havin' A Ball At The Village Gate, 1963; solo: A Good Git-Together, New York New York, 1959; Evolution of The Blues Song, 1960; Fast Livin' Blues, 1961; In Person At The Trident, Salute To Joao Gilberto, 1963; Cloudburst, 1972; Tell Me The Truth, 1975; September Songs, 1976; Love, 1981; Freddie Freeloader, 1990; In Person, 1991; Boppin' At The Blue Note, 1993; Birdmen and Birdsongs, 2000. *Current Management:* B H Hopper Management. *Internet:* www.hopper-management.com.

HENDRICKS Michele; b. 27 Sept. 1953, New York, USA. Vocalist. m. Pierre Bornard, 28 July 1992. *Education:* 2 years college. *Musical Education:* Music major at college. *Career:* Appearances at: North Sea Festival; Monterey Festival; Montréal Festival; Vienna; Pori; Marciac; Juan Les Pins; Nice; Crest; Mt Fuji; Television: Johnny Carson; Mike Douglas; various local television in Europe, Japan, USA; Has sung with: Jon Hendricks; Buddy Rich; Stan Getz; Count Basie; Bennie Golson; Slide Hampton; George Benson; Al Jarreau; Bobby McFerrin; Roland Hannah; Herbie Hancock; Freddie Hubbard. *Recordings:* Me and My Shadow; Keepin' Me Satisfied; Carryin' On; Live At Ronnie Scott's With Buddy Rich; Love with Jon Hendricks and Company; The Peacocks with Stan Getz and Jimmy Rowles; Vocal Summit; Santa's Bag; Second Impression; Boppin' At The Blue Note. *Honour:* Grammy Nomination, Best Jazz Vocal Group, Love. *Memberships:* ASCAP; Shellrose Music (ASCAP). *Leisure interests:* Cooking; Arranging. *Current Management:* Pee Bee Jazz, Pierre Bornard. *Address:* 182 rue Nationale, 75013 Paris, France.

HENDY John (Jonathan Darren); b. 26 March 1971, Barking, Essex, England. Vocalist. *Career:* Member, East 17; Numerous television and live appearances. *Recordings:* Singles include: House of Love, 1992; Deep, 1993; West End Girls, 1993; It's Alright, 1993; Around The World, 1994; Stay Another Day (No. 1, UK), 1994; Steam, 1994; Thunder, 1995; If You Ever, with Gabrielle, 1996; Hey Child, 1997; Each Time, 1998; Betcha Can't Wait, 1999; Albums: Walthamstow, 1993; Steam, 1994; Up All Night, 1996; Around the World – The Journey So Far, 1996; Resurrection, 1998.

HENLEY Don; b. 22 July 1947, Linden, Texas, USA. Musician (drums); Vocalist. *Career:* Member, The Four Speeds, 1963; Member, Shiloh, 1970; Founder member, The Eagles, 1971–; Solo artiste, 1982–; Performances include: California Jam Festival, 1974; Solo appearances: Guest drummer with Guns 'N' Roses, American Music Awards, 1989; Indian River Festival, 1991; Madison Square Garden, 1991. *Recordings:* Albums: with the Eagles: The Eagles, 1972; Desperado, 1973; On The Border, 1974; One of These Nights (No. 1, USA), 1975; Their Greatest Hits 1971–75 (No. 1, USA), 1976; Hotel California (No. 1, USA), 1977; The Long Run (No. 1, USA), 1979; Live, 1980; Eagles' Greatest Hits, Vol. 2, 1982; The Best of The Eagles, 1985; Solo albums: I Can't Stand Still, 1982; Building The Perfect Beast, 1984; The End of Innocence, 1989; Inside Job, 2000; Featured on Leap of Faith (film soundtrack), 1992; Contributor, Amused To Death, Rogers Waters, 1992; Actual Miles, 1995; Producer, title track, Tell Me The Truth, Timothy B Schmit, 1990; Singles include: The Best of My Love (No. 1, USA), 1975; One of These Nights (No. 1, USA), 1975; Lyin' Eyes, 1975; Take It To The Limit, 1976; New Kid In Town (No. 1, USA), 1977; Hotel California (No. 1, USA), 1977; Heartache Tonight (No. 1, USA), 1979; Duet with Stevie Nicks: Leather and Lace, 1982; Solo hits: Dirty Laundry, 1983; The Boys of Summer, 1985, 1999. *Honours:* Grammy Awards: Best Pop Vocal, 1976; Record of The Year, 1978; Best Rock Vocal, 1986; American Music Awards, 1977, 1981; MTV Music Video Awards, 1985, 1990; People For The American Way's Spirit of Liberty Award, 1990; Boston Music Awards, Special Recognition Award, 1992. *Current Management:* c/o Irving Azoff, Revolution, 8900 Wilshire Blvd, Suite 200, Beverly Hills, CA 90211, USA.

HENNES Peter Michael; b. 25 Feb. 1954, Great Lakes, Illinois, USA. Musician (guitar, bass); Educator. *Education:* Wayne State University, 1972; University of Michigan, 1973–74. *Musical Education:* Professional diploma, Berklee College of Music, Boston, 1978. *Career:* Musician with numerous artistes including: Frank Sinatra; Liza Minnelli; Perry Como; Anthony Newley; Marvin Hamlisch; Musician, touring stage productions including: Grease; Evita; A Chorus Line; 42nd Street; La Cage Aux Folles;

Instructor, Jazz Studies, Georgia State University School of Music, 1982–88. *Membership:* AFofM.

HENNING Ann-Marie Elisabeth; b. 2 Dec. 1952, Stockholm, Sweden. Jazz Musician; Composer; Arranger. *Education:* Royal Academy of Music, Stockholm, 5 years; Berkeley College of Music, Boston, USA, 2 years. *Career:* Tours in Sweden and Europe with Rockband NQB, 1973–74; Member, Jazzrock Group, Wave Play, 1978; Own Jazz Group, Blue Cluster, 1987; Jazz Festivals, Radio Concerts; Out of Blue Cluster, Formed Red Cluster, 1992; Pianist, Big Band Jatin Dolls, Television, Saturday Night Live Show, Theatre Shows; Accompanist to Musical Artists. *Compositions:* April Light, for Big Band; The Trees Are Listening; Waltz for Evert; The Rubber Jolly Boat. *Recordings:* Blue Cluster, 1989; Tidal Dreams, 1997. *Publication:* Co-Author, The Real Swede. *Honours:* Swedish Composers Organization Grant, 1987, 1996; Swedish Composers of Popular Music Grant, 1993. *Memberships:* Swedish Composers Organization; Swedish Composers of Popular Music; Swedish Jazz Musicians Organization. *Leisure interests:* Sailing; Nature. *Address:* Finnbodav 9B, 131 31 Nacka, Sweden.

HENOCQ Benjamin; b. 1969. Musician (drums). *Musical Education:* Private lessons, 1976–83; Conservatoire du Centre de Paris, 1983–85; Ecole Agostini, IACP, 1985–87; Private lessons with Daniel Humair; Paul Motian; Keith Copeland. *Career:* Member, PRYSM; Jean-Christophe Beney Quartet; Jean-Christophe Cholet Quartet; David Patrois Quintet; Philippe Sellam Quintet; Les Standardistes (Funk Octet); Phantastique Orchestre Modulaire; Quoi de Neuf Docteur Big Band; Numerous clubs, Paris; Festivals, France; Played with: Eric Le Lann; Stéphane Belmondo; Robin Eubanks; Glenn Ferris; Tommy Smith; Red Holloway; Rick Margitza; François Janneau; Lionel Belmondo; Sylvain Beuf; Geoffroy de Mazure; Peter Osborne; Olivier Ker-Ourio; Philip Catherine; Louis Winsberg; Harold Land; Laurent de Wilde; Franck Amsallem; Andy Emler; Denis Badault; Wayne Dockery; Henri Texier; Michel Benita; Patrice Caratini; Paul Breslin; Jean-Marc Thorès; KARTET; Teacher, IACP, 1986–88. *Recordings:* Le Retour, Quoi de Neuf Docteur Big Band, 1991; Hask, KARTET, 1992; En Attendent La Pluie, Quoi de Neuf Docteur Big Band, 1993; AL'Envers, Quoi de Neuf Docteur Big Band, 1994; Pression, KARTET, 1995; La Compil, Instant Charirés, 1995; PRYSM, PRYSM, 1995. *Honours:* First Prize, La Défense National Jazz Contest, 1994; Soloist Award, La Défense National Jazz Contest, 1994. *Address:* 55 rue Navier, 75017 Paris, France.

HENRIK Wellejus; b. 15 Dec. 1954, Frederiksberg, Copenhagen, Denmark. Composer; Musician. *Musical Education:* Private Musical Education. *Career:* Theatre Music Appearances: En Rede i Traeet, 1983; Det Umuligste Af Alt, 1986; Fra Bord Til Bord, 1987; Hvor Godtfolk Er, 1988; Orla Frösnapper, 1990; Otto Er Et Naesehorn, 1993. *Honour:* Winner, Music Contest, Young Music Magazine. *Membership:* Danish Songwriters Guild. *Leisure interests:* Television; Classical music; Reading; Bible reading. *Current Management:* Radiophelia, 928 MHZ, Box 6, 3100 Hornbaek, Denmark. *Address:* Sauntevaenget 14B, 3100 Hornbaek, Denmark.

HENRIKSON Richard Ralph; b. 27 Nov. 1948, Portland, Oregon, USA. Composer; Lyricist; Musician (violin). *Musical Education:* BS, Juilliard School of Music, 1972; MusM, 1973. *Career:* Violinist, various orchestras and chamber ensembles, 1970–; Violinist, Barnum, Broadway, 1980–82; Musical director, numerous stage productions include: Singing In The Rain; Sweet Charity; Me and My Girl; Fiddler On The Roof; Les Miserables, 1991–; Musical director, violinist, numerous artistes including: Tom Jones; Billy Ocean; George Benson; Freddie Jackson; Jeffrey Osborne; Stephanie Mills; Gregg Allman; Rick Wakeman; Paul Anka. *Recordings:* Albums with: Music Minus One; The Tango Project; Hampton String Quartet; Violinist, film soundtracks: The Wiz; Silkwood; The Cotton Club; When Harry Met Sally; Do The Right Thing; Recordings by numerous artistes including: Diana Ross; Sheena Easton; Paul Simon; Billy Cobham; John Sebastian. *Memberships:* ASCAP; AFofM; NARAS; Recording Musicians of US and Canada. *Address:* Hampton String Quartet, 344 W 72nd St, New York, NY 10023, USA.

HENRY Jay Edward; b. 17 Feb. 1950, Brooklyn, New York, USA. Record Prod.; Sound Engineer. *Education:* Broadcasting Engineering, Cabrillo College; San Francisco State University. *Career:* Producer, engineer, Visual Music, 1983–; Secret Society Records, 1986-. *Recordings:* Albums include: with LL Cool J: Bigger and Deffer, 1987; Walking With A Panther, 1989; with Heavy D: Livin' Large, 1987; with Public Enemy: It Takes A Nation of Millions, 1987; with Run DMC: Tougher Than Leather, 1988; with Defunkt: Defunkt In America, 1988; with Living Colour: Vivid, 1989; with Pet Shop Boys: Behavior, 1990; with George Michael: Five Live, 1993; with Elton John: Duets, 1993; with Deniece Williams: Love Solves It All, 1996. *Honours:* 5 Gold Reel Awards, Amplex, 1986–89; Numerous Platinum and Gold records; International Producer Award, 1990. *Memberships:* NARAS; Audio Engineering Society.

HENRY Michael Anthony; b. 10 March 1963, London, England. Singer; Composer; Musician (saxophone, clarinet); Arranger; Songwriter. *Musical Education:* Centre for Young Musicians, 1977–81; Royal College of Music, 1981–85. *Career:* Singer, writer with Buddy Curtess and The Grasshoppers, 1985–89; Singer and Songwriter with The Flying Pickets, 1991–95; Singer, songwriter, co-producer with Cut 2 Taste, 1994–; Tours include: support to Roy Orbison, 1985; Backing vocalist, Pet Shop Boys, 1989; Flying Pickets, 1991–95; Concerts: Support concerts to: Beach Boys, Wembley, 1986; Bo Diddley, Hammersmith Odeon, 1987; Dr Feelgood, 1987; Glastonbury, main stage, 1987; Television and radio appearances include: The Tube, 1987; Saturday Live, 1987; Ruby Wax, 1988; Meltdown, 1988; BBC1 and C4 Schools workshops, 1991–93; Opera performances, 1991–93; Presenter, Young Musician of The Year, 1992; Judge, Choir of The Year, 1993; Concert support, Ray Charles, 1993; Cue The Music, 1995; Support to Michael Jackson, tour, 1997. *Compositions:* Wind Quartet No. 1; Say Ave For Me, for saxophone and piano, performed on BBC Radio 3. *Recordings:* with Buddy Curtess and the Grasshoppers: Shoobey Baby; Shout; Hello Suzie; Bridge Over Troubled Water; Design For Me; Forever Young, Pretenders, 1992; Sugar Daddy, Billy Bragg, 1996; Other recordings include: Caravan, John Harle, all vocals, 1990; Rain Song, Moodswings, 1990; Real Love, Driza Bone, 1991; The Warning, Flying Pickets, 1993. *Publications:* 3 Interludes for saxophone and piano; Birdwatching, for clarinet quartet, 1998. *Honours:* Dip RCM, ARCM; Winner of composition prizes: Joseph Horowitz; Stanford; Cornelius Cardew; Time Out Magazine Best Live Act, 1986, 1987. *Memberships:* Musicians' Union; PRS; Equity; Society For Promotion of New Music (SPNM) ISM. *Leisure interests:* X-Men comics; Cryptic crosswords; Dancing; Learning languages. *Address:* 83 Lucien Rd, London SW17 8HS, England.

HENSHALL Ruthie; b. 1967, Bromley, Kent, England. Vocalist; Actor. *Musical Education:* Studied musical theatre at Laine Theatre Arts, Surrey, England. *Career:* Joined British tour of a Chorus Line followed by appearances in: Cats; Miss Saigon; Children of Eden; Spent a summer at the Chichester Festival Theatre; Returned to West End, subsequent appearances include: Les Miserables; Crazy For You; She Loves Me; Peggy Sue Got Married; Chicago; Joined New York cast of Chicago, leading to other Broadway roles including: Putting It Together; Ziegfeld Follies of 1939; The Vagina Monologues; US and UK TV credits include: Law and Order; Deadline; Mysteries of 71st Street; Get Back; Currently pursuing recording career. *Recordings:* Albums: cast recordings: Children of Eden, 1991; Crazy For You, 1993; Godspell, 1993 (studio cast); She Loves Me, 1994; Divorce Me Darling, 1997; Chicago, 1998; solo: Love Is Here To Stay, 1994; Pilgrim, 2001. *Honour:* Olivier Award, Best Actress In A Musical, She Loves Me, 1994. *Internet:* www.ruthiehenshall.co.uk.

HENSLEY Ken; b. 24 Aug. 1945, London, England. Musician (guitar, keyboards); Singer; Record Prod. *Career:* Musician, singer, Kit and The Saracens; Jimmy Brown Sound; The Gods; Musician, singer, producer, UK rock group Uriah Heep, 1969–80; US rock group Blackfoot, 1981–84; Director, artistic relations, St Louis Music Inc, 1987-. *Recordings:* Albums: with Uriah Heep: Very 'Umble, Very 'Eavy, 1970; Salisbury, 1971; Look At Yourself, 1971; Demons and Wizards, 1972; Magician's Birthday, 1972; Live, 1973; Sweet Freedom, 1973; Wonderworld, 1974; Return To Fantasy, 1975; Best Of, 1975; High and Mighty, 1976; Firefly, 1977; Innocent Victim, 1978; Fallen Angel, 1978; Conquest, 1980; Time of Revelation, 1996; Classic Heep, 1998; Rarities, 2000; Ballads, 2000; Blood On Stone, 2001; with Blackfoot: Siogo, 1983; Vertical Smile, 1984. *Honours:* Gold and Platinum discs. *Address:* St Louis Music Inc, 1400 Ferguson Ave, St Louis, MO 63133, USA.

HERMAND Charles; b. 23 June 1960, Namur, Belgium. *Career:* Brasov Festival in Romania with Boy George and James Brown, 1994; Support to Dave at Cirque Royal in Brussels, 1997. *Recordings:* Save Me Now, 1992; Les Petits Pains seventies, 1993; Vague d'Amour, 1993; Les Yeux vers le Ciel, 1994; Trop Fatigué, 1995; Rien ne nous sépare, 1999; Album: A tescôtés, 1999. *Membership:* SABAM, Belgium. *Leisure interest:* Specialist on dolphin protection world-wide. *Current Management:* Up Way Music. *Address:* Rue de Vrière 67–69, 1020 Brussels, Belgium.

HERMANS Jozef Eduard; b. 1 March 1948, Antwerp, Belgium. Psychologist; Singer; Songwriter. m. Faes Monique, 31 Jan. 1998, 1 s., 1 d. *Musical Education:* Self-taught Guitar, Banjo, Mandolin, Melodeon. *Career:* Psychologist, City of Antwerp; Member, Flemish Folkgroup, Katastroof; Radio and TV appearances, occasionally. *Compositions:* More than 100 songs on 13 albums of Katastroof; Met De Wijven Niks As Last; Het Geloof; Paterkesdans; Johnny. *Recordings:* 12 CDs with Katastroof; 3 CDs with Jos Smos: Jos Smos in het Blote Beestenbus, 1996; Smarten en Andere Lappen, 1997; Over Het Geloof, 1998. *Publication:* Book about reincarnation and regression, forthcoming. *Membership:* Sabam, Belgium. *Leisure interests:* Reincarnation Therapy; Computers; Photography. *Address:* Tweelingenstraat 15, 2018 Antwerp, Belgium.

HERMITAGE Richard; b. 20 Oct. 1955, London. Agent; Man.; Record Co Exec. *Career:* Agent, artists included: The Human League; Steel Pulse;

ABC; INXS; UB40; Psychedelic Furs; Aswad; Daf; The Art of Noise; The Residents; Agencies worked at: March Artists; TKA; Asgard; ITB; Fair Warning, 1974–85; Management, artists included: The Human League; Pale Saints; The Darling Buds; Slowdive; The Boo Radleys; Teenage Fanclub; Denim, 1986–93; Currently Manager, management company War Zones; General Manager, record company 4AD, 1994–95. *Leisure interests:* Football; Cricket; Mountaineering. *Current Management:* War Zones (management). *Address:* 33 Kersley Rd, London N16 0NT, England.

HERRING-LEIGH Judy; b. 3 Oct. 1945, Cape Girardeau, Missouri, USA. Concert Artist; Recording Artist; Songwriter; Vocal Music Teacher; Minister of Music; Children's Choir Co-ordinator. m. Jim Leigh, 1 Oct. 1994, 1 s., 1 d. *Education:* Bachelor Music Performance; Master Early Childhood Education. *Musical Education:* Private Voice, 13 years; 4 year Voice Major, Oklahoma Baptist University; Life Vocal Music Certification grades K-12; Music courses in Master's Program. *Career:* 26 years in Music Ministry; Five concert tours, England, also crusades; 6–10 US tours over past 20 years; Recorded 3 albums, 1 live performance tape, 1 gospel songs tape; Musical evangelist, public relations representative for Virginia Baptists; Morningstar album #16 on gospel music charts of Christian Broadcasting Network, April, 1977; Appeared, PTL, CBN, BBC networks, 1978–79; Sang for Governor's Prayer Breakfast, President's Prayer Breakfast, 1980; Minister of Music, 9 churches over 26 years; Music teacher; 10 concert tour, England, Scotland, 1997; Soloist, Good News Mission Trip, Odessa, Ukraine, 1997. *Compositions:* Morningstar; God's Rose; Suffer The Little Children; The Woman; Brand New Start; Arrangements: Take My Life and Let It Be; Victory In Jesus; I've Been Redeemed. *Recordings:* Albums: Morningstar; Christmas Means Thinking of Jesus; God's Rose; Tapes: Old Gospel Hymns; Live in Concert; Cherished Moments, 1997; Tribute to Fanny Crosby and George Beverly Shea. *Publications:* Reflections On God's Rose, article, New Music Magazine, 1979; Experiencing Loss With A Youth Ministry, Equipping Youth Magazine, 1985. *Honours:* Dimitri Mitropolis Award; Personalities of The South, 1979; Stylemaker of The Year, 1979. *Memberships:* SESAC; Southern Baptist Convention's Music Evangelists, USA; Gospel Music Asscn, Nashville, Tennessee. *Leisure interests:* Fishing; Water skiing; Composing music.

HERSH Kristin; b. 7 Aug. 1966, Atlanta, Georgia, USA. Musician (guitar); Singer. 3 s. *Musical Education:* Self-taught. *Career:* Singer, Musician, Throwing Muses, 1986–97; Solo Singer/Songwriter, 1994-. *Recordings:* Albums: Hips and Makers, 1994; Strings, 1994; Strange Angels, 1998; Sky Motel, 1999; Sunny Border Blue, 2001; Singles: The Holy Single, 1995; Like You, 1998; Echo, 1999; Also appears with Throwing Muses: Throwing Muses, 1986; Chains Changed, 1987; House Tornado, 1983; The Fat Skier, 1987; Hunkpapa, 1989; The Real Ramona, 1991; Red Heaven, 1992; University, 1995; Limbo, 1996. *Membership:* AFofM. *Current Management:* Throwing Music Ltd, 520 Southview Dr., Athens, GA 30605, USA.

HERZHAFT Gerard; b. 8 Nov. 1943, Meyzieu, France. m. Lise Briere de L'Isle, 27 Sept. 1967, 1 s., 1 d. *Education:* Licence of History, Sorbonne, Paris. *Career:* Numerous radio broadcasts and TV shows; Musician (blues); Concerts: Blues Passion, Cognac; Thullins Festival; Café Campus (Montréal); Parthenay Blues; Doua De Jazz; Sathonay Blues Festival. *Compositions:* It It Wasn't For Muddy Waters; Rhone River is Rising; Old Bluesman From Texas; Redneck Blues; My Blues Will; Write, Gerard, Write, 1998; A Full Bank Account, 1998. *Recordings:* Three recordings; Two CDs with Herzhaft Blues; Never Been Plugged; Two Brothers and a Pick; Bluesfans, 1999. *Publications:* 20 books incl.: Encyclopedia of the Blues; A Long Blues in a Minor; Le Blues; La Country Music; Catfish Blues; John Lee Hooker; Le dernier chant de l'Inca, 1999; Guide de la Country Music et du Folk, 1999. *Honours:* Grand Prix Littéraire de la Ville de Lyon, 1986; Prix Des Auteurs et Ecrivains Lyonnais, 1987; Prix Societe des Gens De Lettres, 1995; Prix Des Lyceens D'Ile De France, 1997. *Leisure interests:* US Films from the 40's and 50's; Travel throughout the world. *Address:* 57 rue Florian, 69100 Villeurbanne, France.

HESSION Paul; b. 19 Sept. 1956, Leeds, England. Musician (drums). m. Cecilia Jane Charnley, 23 May 1987, 1 s., 1 d. *Musical Education:* Self-taught drummer; Studied instrument technology. *Career:* Toured Mexico and Cuba with The Siger Band, 1986; Played in Derek Bailey's Company week in London (twice); Duos with Alan Wilkinson on BBC Radio 3, Mixing It; Music for radio play, BBC Radio 4 with Keith Jafrate; Sound symposium, St Johns, Newfoundland, Canada, with Hession, Wilkinson, Fell. *Recordings:* Album: The Real Case, with Hans-Peter Hiby; Albums with Hession/Wilkinson/Fell: Foom Foom; The Horrors of Darmstadt; with Mick Beck: Start Moving Earbuds; Solo: St Johns, 2000. *Honours:* Jazz bursaries from ACGB, 1986, 1991. *Membership:* Musicians' Union. *Leisure interest:* Art. *Address:* 41 Hanover Sq., Leeds L53 1BQ, England.

HESTER Paul; b. 8 Jan. 1959, Melbourne, Australia. Musician (Drums). *Career:* Member, Crowded House; Early acoustic gigs in restaurants and clubs; Numerous headlining tours, festival dates and TV and radio appearances; Left band, 1994; Rejoined for Sydney Harbour Bridge and Opera House Farewell Concert, 1996 and for new tracks on Best of compilation album; Band split. *Recordings:* Singles include: World Where You Live, 1986; Crowded House EP, 1986; Something So Strong, 1987; Don't Dream It's Over, 1987; Sister Madly, 1988; I Feel Possessed, 1989; Four Seasons In One Day, 1991; Fall at Your Feet, 1991; Weather With You, 1991; It's Only Natural, 1992; Pineapple Head, 1993; Locked Out, 1993; World Where We Live, 1993; Distant Sun, 1993; Nails in My Feet, 1994; Not the Girl You Think You Are, 1996; Everything Is Good For You, 1996; Albums: Crowded House, 1986; Temple of Low Men, 1988; Woodface, 1991; Together Alone, 1993; Recurring Dream: The Best of Crowded House, 1996.

HETFIELD James Alan; b. 3 Aug. 1963, Los Angeles, California, USA. Musician (guitar); Vocalist. *Career:* Member, Obsession; Leather Charm; Member, US heavy rock group Metallica, 1981–; World-wide tours include: Master of Puppets world tour, 1986–87; US tour, 1988; Damaged Justice tour, UK, 1989; World tour, 1991–; Also tours with Raven; Twisted Sister; Ozzy Osbourne; Motörhead; Major concerts include: Monsters of Rock Festival, Castle Donington, 1985, 1987, 1991; German Monster Rock festival, 1987; Monsters of Rock Europe, US tours, 1988, 1991; Day On The Green, Oakland, 1991; Freddie Mercury tribute, Wembley, 1992. *Recordings:* Albums: Kill 'Em All, 1983; Ride The Lightning, 1984; Master of Puppets, 1986; ...and Justice For All, 1988; Metallica (No. 1, UK and US), 1991; Live Shit, 1993; Garage Inc, 1998; SandM, 1999; Singles: Garage Days Revisited (EP), 1987; Harvester of Sorrow, 1988; One, 1989; Enter Sandman, 1991; The Unforgiven, 1991; Nothing Else Matters, 1992; Wherever I May Roam, 1992; Sad But True, 1992; Stone Cold Crazy, track featured on Rubáiyát (Elektra's 40th anniversary compilation); I Disappear, 2000. *Honours:* Platinum and Gold discs; Grammy Awards: Best Heavy Metal Performance: One, 1989; Stone Cold Crazy, 1991; The Unforgiven, 1992; Best Hard Rock Performance: Whiskey In The Jar, 2000; Rock Instrumental Performance, Call of The Ktulu, 2001; American Music Award, Favourite Heavy Metal Artist, 1993; Bay Area Music Awards: Outstanding Album, 1992; Outstanding Metal Album, Outstanding Group, 1993; Rolling Stone Readers Poll Winners, Best Heavy Metal Band, 1993. *Current Management:* Q-Prime Inc. *Address:* 729 Seventh Ave, 14th Floor, New York, NY 10019, USA.

HEURLIN Martin; b. 20 Nov. 1963, Frederiksberg, Denmark. Musician (guitar, bass, keyboards); Vocalist; Prod. 3 s. *Musical Education:* Self-taught. *Career:* Founder, rock band Sy-Daff; Member, KB Hallen, 1980; Support act to Sweet, 1982; Played at Roskilde Festival, 1983; Played club circuit in Los Angeles, 1986–88; Guitarist on Danish television for Michael Penn, John Farnham, Anders Glenmark and Tomas Ledin, 1990; Pupil Live, television and radio broadcasts, 1998. *Compositions include:* TV show theme, Set and Swet; Pupil, Frederik Jorgensen, major hit in Denmrk, 1997. *Recordings:* Soundtracks for many Danish television documentary programmes, 1990–; Albums with: Sy-Daff, 1982; Mr Man, 1987; James Thomas, 1991; Pupil, 1997; Solo album, 1995. *Publication:* Pupil: Superglasojne, 1997. *Membership:* DJFBA. *Leisure interests:* Books; Television; Running. *Current Management:* TBA, Strulasgade 14, 2300 Copenhagen S, Denmark. *Address:* Ryesgade 108B Kld, 2100 Copenhagen O, Denmark.

HEWAT Corrina Dawn; b. 21 Dec. 1970, Edinburgh, Scotland. Singer; Musician (Harp, Clarsach); Composer. *Education:* BA, one year, Performance, Royal Scottish Academy of Music and Drama; Hons Degree, Jazz, Contemporary and Popular Music, City of Leeds College of Music. *Career:* Band, Bachué, formed with David Milligan, 1995; Band, Chantan, formed 1996; Appeared on Taile A Bhaile, BBC 2, Channel 4, Radio 3 and Demo TV; Writing music for audio books, Saltire Society; Teaching, Visiting Tutor, Balnain House, Home of Highland Music, Inverness and Fettes College, Edinburgh; Working with Lammas, Carol Kidd, Eric Bibb, Seannachie; Commissions: Songs of Redshank, The Highland Festival, 1997; Making the Connection, Celtic Connections Festival 1998; Photons In Vapour, 2000; Many compositions of a traditional nature recorded. *Recordings:* Bachué Café, 1996, 1998; Primary Colours, 1997; A Certain Smile, 1999; Contributor: Something Blew, 1995; Northlins, 1995; Vol. 4 of Burns' Complete Works, 1998. *Honour:* Finalist, Young Traditional Musician of the Year, 1995. *Memberships:* Musicians' Union; Clarsach Society; UKHA; PRS; MCPS; PAMRA. *Current Management:* The Balnain Agency, 40 Huntly St, Inverness IV3 5HR, Scotland.

HEWINS Mark Jesson; b. 24 March 1955, Hertfordshire, England. Musician (guitar); Composer. m. Yvonne, 23 Sept. 1989, 1 d. *Career:* Started as professional guitarist aged 15; Tours, Europe and USA; Played with musicians including: Phil Collins; Julie Felix; Joe Lee Wilson; Long association with Casio as Midi guitarist, leading to compiled sample libraries, supplied accompaniment patterns, demonstration tunes for their keyboards; Introduced Lou Reed to Midi guitar; Midi consultant. *Compositions include:* music for guitar, strings, orchestra. *Recordings:* Featured on many albums; Solo album: The Electric Guitar; Veritable Centaur, Soft Heap. *Publications:* Markie's Little Fake

Books 1 and 2; Canterbury Tales (relating to Canterbury music scene), published extensively in various journals. *Membership:* Musicians' Union; PRS; MCPS; British Music Writers Council. *Leisure interests:* Cricket, 1900–50; Stamps; Photographs. *Current Management:* Y A Ledley, Musart Services. *Address:* c/o Musart Services, 81 Knollys Rd, London SW16 2JW, England.

HEWITT Steve; b. 22 March 1971, England. Musician (drums, percussion). *Career:* Played in early bands The Electric Crayons, with Tim Burgess of The Charlatans, Mystic Deckchairs; Joined Breed, toured Germany; Joined the Boo Radleys, worked on their debut album, and played numerous gigs; Played with K-Klass, dance outfit; Numerous contracts with session work and provided music for advertisements; Returned to tour with Breed, including tour with Nick Cave and the Bad Seeds; Joined Placebo as drummer. *Recordings:* Singles: Come Home, 1996; 36 Degrees, 1996; Teenage Angst, 1996; Nancy Boy, 1997; Bruise Pristine, 1997; Pure Morning, 1998; You Don't Care About Us, 1998; Every You Every Me, 1999; Without You I'm Nothing, featuring David Bowie, 1999; Taste In Men, 2000; Slave To The Wage, 2000; Albums: Without You I'm Nothing, 1998; Black Market Music, 2000.

HEX Andrew (Andy) Joe; b. 25 June 1966, Houston, Texas, USA. Musician (piano); Vocalist. *Education:* Sweetwater Christian School, Houston, Texas (Liberal Arts; Drama; Choir; Soccer; Track Team). *Musical Education:* Banner University, Kingwood, Texas (Evangelical Ministries; Praise and Worship Music Ministerial Studies). *Career:* Scored and producer music for Taking The Turf, 2000. *Compositions:* She Knows, 1999. *Recordings:* She Knows, 1999; God's Amazing Grace, 2001. *Memberships:* BMI; CMA; Gospel Music Asscn; Texas Accountants and Lawyers for the Arts; Dove Music Awards nomination committee. *Leisure interests:* Martial arts; Cycling. *Address:* 8723 Meadowview, Houston, TX 77037, USA.

HEYWARD Nick; b. 20 May 1961, South London, England. Singer; Musician (guitar); Songwriter. *Career:* Founder, Haircut 100, 1981–82; Solo artiste, 1983–; Major concerts include: Support to Wham!, The Final farewell concert, Wembley, 1986. *Compositions:* Most recordings self-written. *Recordings:* Albums: with Haircut 100: Pelican West (No. 2, UK) 1982; Solo albums: North of a Miracle, 1983; Postcards From Home, 1986; I Love You Avenue, 1989; The Best of Nick Heyward and Haircut 100, 1989; From Monday To Sunday, 1993; Tangled, 1995; The Apple Bed, 1996; Pizza Tears; Hit singles with Haircut 100: Favourite Shirts (Boy Meets Girl), 1981; Love Plus One, 1982; Fantastic Day, 1982; Nobody's Fool, 1982; Solo singles: Whistle Down The Wind, 1983; Take That Situation, 1983; Blue Hat For Blue Day, 1983; Rollerbalde, 1996; The Man You Used to Be, 1997; Today, 1997; Stars in Her Eyes, 1998.

HIATT John; b. 20 Aug. 1952, Indiana, USA. Singer; Songwriter; Musician (guitar). *Career:* Member, bands: Four Fifths; The White Ducks; Joe Lynch and The Hangmen; Songwriter, Tree Publishing, Nashville, early 1970s; Solo artist, 1974–; Also musician for Sonny Terry and Brownie McGhee; Leon Redbone; Tom Waits; Tours with: Leo Kottke; Southside Johnny and the Astbury Jukes; Edie Brickell; Joined Ry Cooder's backing band, 1981; Concerts include: A Black and White Night, with Roy Orbison, Los Angeles, 1987; Reading Festival, 1988; Roy Orbison Concert Tribute, Universal City, California, 1990; Formed Little Village, with Ry Cooder, Nick Lowe, Jim Keltner, 1992. *Compositions include:* Thinking of You, Tracy Nelson; As Sure As I'm Sitting Here, Three Dog Night; Bring Back Your Love To Me, Earl Thomas Conley. *Recordings:* Albums: Hangin' Round The Observatory, 1974; Overcoats, 1974; Slug Line, 1979; Two Bit Monsters, 1980; All of a Sudden, 1982; Riding With The King, 1983; Warming Up To The Ice Age, 1985; Bring The Family, 1987; Slow Turning, 1988; Stolen Moments, 1990; Love Gets Strange, 1993; Perfectly Good Guitar, 1993; Walk On, 1995; Litle Head, 1997; The Best of John Hiatt, 1998; Crossing Muddy Waters, 2000; The Tiki Bar Is Open, 2001; with Little Village: Little Village, 1992; Featured on: Borderline, Ry Cooder, 1981. *Honours:* Grammy Award, Contemporary Folk Album nominee, 2001; As songwiter: BMI Country Music Award, Bring Back Your Love To Me, Earl Thomas Conley, 1991. *Current Management:* Metropolitan Entertainment Group, 2 Penn Plaza 26th Fl, New York, NY 10121, USA.

HIBBERT Frederick (Toots); Vocalist. *Career:* Lead singer, reggae group The Maytals, later billed as Toots and the Maytals; Leading vocal group in Jamaica, 1960s and 1970s; Film appearance, The Harder They Come. *Recordings include:* The Sensational; Never Grow Old; Sweet and Dandy; From The Roots; Monkey Man; Funky Kingston; In The Dark; Slatyam Stoot; Reggae Got Soul; Toots Live; Life Could Be A Dream; Toots in Memphis; with Otis Reading: Otis! The Definitive Otis Redding, 1993; Appears on: The Good The Bad and The Funky, Tom Tom Club, 2000; Hits include: Daddy/It's You (No. 1, Jamaican charts), 1965; 54–46 That's My Number; Do The Reggay; Monkey Man. *Honours include:* Winners (with the Maytals), Jamaican Festival Song Competition, 1966, 1969 and 1972.

Address: c/o Zoe Productions, 450 Broome St, Eighth Floor, New York, NY 10013, USA.

HICKLING Anna Jo; b. 5 Sept. 1966, Stockport, Cheshire, England. Singer; Songwriter; Prod.; Partner in Record Label. *Education:* University of Bath. *Musical Education:* O-Level Music; Singing, piano, trumpet tuition; Mostly self-taught; Recording studio engineering course. *Career:* Backing vocalist for various Manchester bands: Victor Brox; The Glee Company, 1983; Local clubs include Band On The Wall; Writer, lead vocalist Inside Out, 1984; Concerts at The Boardwalk, Manchester; Lead vocalist, Touch of Spice, 1987; Played Moles Club, Bath; Womad Festival; Various universities, HTV appearance; Invited to play and record at Real World Studios; Backing vocalist, Tammy Payne, British tour; Also played at Southport Soul Weekender; The Theklar, Bristol; The Underworld, London; Ashton Court Festival. *Recordings:* Session vocals for: Smith and Mighty; Banderas remix; Startled Insects; Toop (EP); Lead vocals, band member, writing and production work on EPs with: Tommorowland; (Currently) Transport; Remix for single: I Am Free, Morgan King. *Memberships:* Musicians' Union; PRS; PAMRA. *Leisure interests:* Clothes designing; All kinds of dancing; Experimental cooking; Walking in places of natural beauty. *Address:* Revelstoke Rd, Wimbledon Park, London, England.

HICKS Hinda; b. 1977, Tunisia. Singer. *Career:* Basketball Player and Coach; Member, The Fabulous Fug Band; Began solo career; Numerous live dates including tours with Boyzone and 911; Television appearances; Collaborations: Lynden David Hall; A+;. *Recordings:* I Wanna Be Your Lady, 1997; If You Want Me, 1998; You Think You Own Me, 1998; Truly, 1998; My Remedy, 2000; Albums: Hinda, 1998; Everything To Me, 2000. *Honour:* Brit Award, Best Newcomer nominee.

HICKS Ivan; b. 6 July 1940, Upper Sackville, New Brunswick, Canada. Musician (fiddle, guitar, mandolin). m. Vivian Paulette Webb, 4 July 1970. *Education:* BA; BEd; MEd. *Career:* As teenager, formed: The Golden Valley Boys; 1964, began teaching, Salisbury, New Brunswick; Formed: danceband Marshwinds, 1969–89; Formed old time and bluegrass band: Ivan Hicks and Maritime Express, 1979–; Workshops; Teacher fiddling; Television appearances include: Up Home Tonight (ATV), 1980's, 8 years; Host, weekly radio show, CFQM Moncton, 1982–95; MC of Maritime Old-Time Fiddling Contest (CBC-TV), 1985–; Concerts: Canada, USA; Entertainer, special occasions; Organizer, promoter, concerts, tours; Retired from teaching, 1996. *Compositions include:* Apohaqui; Gram Lee's Waltz; Jim, The Fiddle Maker; Marshwinds Waltz; Purple Violet Waltz; Riverview Jig; Maritime 40; Forever Friends; Memories of Father James Smith; Fiddler's Roast; The MacDonalds of Highfield; The Fiddler From Douro; Sussex Avenue Fiddlers Two Step. *Recordings:* The Life and Music of Ivan and Vivian Hicks (video); For You; Shingle The Roof; Old Time Christmas; Fiddlingly Yours; Swinging Fiddles; Purple Violet Fiddling; Friendly Fiddling The Maritime Way; Fiddling For Fun and Friends; The Strength of God's Hand, 1997. *Publications:* Ivan Hicks Fiddle Tunes and Souvenirs; Ivan Hicks: Fifty Years of Fabulous Fiddle Music by Allison Mitcham, 1996. *Honours include:* Two-time winner, Maritime Fiddling Contest, 1979–80; Finalist: Canadian Fiddling Contest; 1985, Inducted into New Brunswick Country Music Hall of Fame; Inducted into North American Fiddlers Hall of Fame, 1990; Recipient, Governor General's Caring Canadian Award, 1999. *Memberships include:* Canadian Country Music Asscn; Director, Maritime Fiddlers Asscn; Director, National Oldtime Fiddlers Asscn; East Coast Music Asscn; President, Fiddles of the World Society; Director, New Brunswick Country Music Hall of Fame; Director, Music New Brunswick. *Leisure interests:* Promoting old-time fiddle music; Travel; Camping. *Address:* 157 Sussex Ave, Riverview, New Brunswick E1B 3A8, Canada.

HICKS Jacqueline (Jacqui); b. 7 July 1966, Pontefract, West Yorkshire, England. Vocalist; Musician (saxophone, flute, clarinet); Songwriter. m. Patrick Hartley. *Education:* Wakefield District College. *Musical Education:* City of Leeds College of Music, 1984–87; Guildhall School of Music and Drama, 1987–88. *Career:* Four years with National Youth Jazz Orchestra; Matt Bianco; Tours: Japan; Indonesia; Europe; Tour with Shakatak, South East Asia; South Africa; Japan; Also with: John Dankworth; Dick Morrisey; Harry Becket; Don Lusher; Supported George Benson, 1993; Own jazz/funk band, Jacqui Hicks Band; Tours with Shakatak in Moscow, Georgia and Lithuania. *Recordings:* Own album: Looking Forward, Looking Back, 1990; Spellbound, 1999; with Macfarlane Group: Bright Lights Big City; with NYJO: Cooking With Gas; with Matt Bianco: Another Time Another Place; Gran Via; with Matt Bianco: A Collection; with Shakatak: Let the Piano Play; View from the City; Live at Ronnie Scott's; Latin Trip, with CPD, 2001. *Address:* Hemel Hempstead, Hertfordshire, England.

HIGHAM Darrel; b. 5 Jan. 1970, Bedford, England. Musician (Lead Guitar, Double Bass); Singer; Songwriter; Prod. *Musical Education:* Self-taught. *Career:* Solo career, Singer, Guitarist with backing band, The Enforcers; Supported Chuck Berry, 1995; Played Lead Guitar for Rocky Burnette, Glen Glenn, Johnny Carroll, Vernon Taylor, Merrill E Moore,

Don and Dewey; Toured US, 1992 fronting Eddie Cochran's original backing band, The Kelly Four; Worked in Londons West End, Lead guitar and Singing, Elvis The Musical, 8 months, 1996; TV work includes appearances on Blue Peter, Theatreland; Many radio appearances; Currently tours in UK, throughout Europe and US. *Compositions:* Prolific Songwriter with over 30 compositions released world-wide. *Recordings:* 5 solo albums: Mobile Corrosion (Nervous), 1995; Let's Rock Tonight (Fury), 1995; Rockin' At the Coconut Top (Crazy Love), 1996; The Cochran Connection (Rockstar), 1997; Darrel Higham and the Barnshakers (Gaofin'), 1998; How To Dance The Bop, 2000; 2 solo EPs; 3 Albums with Bob and the Bearcats; 2 with Johnny Bach and the Moonshine Boozers; 1 with Dave Phillips; 1 with the Blue Devils as Lead Guitarist. *Membership:* Musicians' Union. *Address:* 18 Biggleswade Rd, Upper Caldecote, Beds SG18 9BL, England.

HIGHAM Mike; Programmer. *Career:* Worked with Seal on Spacejam, film soundtrack, Fly Like An Eagle; Completed work for Tina Turner, Barry White and Boyzone; Other projects include: The Art of Noise, Public Demand, Gary Barlow, Eric Clapton; Clients include: Seal: MTV Unplugged, album; Seal II, album; A Prayer For the Dying 12 remix; Bobby Brown, Every Little Step I Take 12 remix; Tina Turner, Wildest Dreams, album; Ministry of Sound, 6 albums; Whitney Houston, I'm Your Baby Tonight; Rod Stewart: Spanner in the Works; Spice Girls: Spiceworld; Eric Clapton: Pilgrim; Geri Halliwell, Scream If You Wanna Go Faster. *Address:* SARM Productions, SP2 Holdings Ltd, The Blue Building, 42/46 St Luke's Mews, London W11 1DG, England.

HILBORNE Phil; b. 20 Jan. 1959, Poole, Dorset, England. Musician (guitar); Prod.; Teacher; Journalist. m. 17 Feb. 1977, divorced, 2 s., 1 d. *Musical Education:* Classical guitar studied with Professor W Grandison, Harpsichordist D Galbraith, Trinity College; Electric guitar, self-taught. *Career:* UK, Europe and USA tours with Phil Hilborne Band and Nicko McBrain (Iron Maiden); Live demonstrations for companies including: Gibson; Ampeg; Vigier; Paiste; Sonor; Zildjian, Fender; Kitty Hawk; Marshall; PRS; Music Editor, Guitarist magazine (Playing Rock Guitar/Solo Analysis articles plus various features and interviews), 1985–95; Music/CD Editor, Guitar Techniques magazine, 1994–; Felsted Music School, Head of Guitar, 1993–99; Guitar tutorials throughout Europe including the Bath International Guitar Festival, 1999–2002; Owns and runs Essex-based WM Studios. *Recordings include:* Are You Serious?, 1992; 'Bout Time, 1993; featured solo tracks on compilations: Bath International Guitar Festival CD, 2000; Fret-King CD, 2001; 15th Anniversary Album, 2001; featured peformances include: John McEnroe and Pat Cash with the Full Metal Rackets, Rock and Roll (single), 1991; Angel Easy, Lightning Strikes, 1990; Geoff Whitehorn, Big In Gravesend, 1994; Drome, Overload, 1996; Memphis Roots, Things Can Change, 1998; Blaze Bayley, Silicon Messiah, 2000; Greg Fitch, This Is Greg Fitch, 2000; Eric Roche, Spin, 2001; various tracks for specialist guitar magazine CDs, 1994–; Collaborations include: Maria Kern; Mark Cherrie; Tony Muschamp; Frank Gambale; Productions include: Dave Kilminster and Fraser T Smith, Playing With Fire, 1996; Genelab, Anorak Lou (unplugged), 1999; numerous demos, radio/TV sessions. *Publications:* Solo, 1987; Led Zeppelin Off The Record, 1988; Editor: Reijo Hittunen's Guitar Chord Method, 1993. *Contributions to:* Jimi Hendrix Electric Gypsy, 1990; Elton John Rockscore, 1991; Instructional Video: Phil Hilborne Rock Basics, 1992. *Membership:* Musicians' Union. *Leisure interests:* Music; Golf. *Current Management:* Phil Hilborne Band Management. *Address:* Phil Hilborne Band/Widdle Music, PO Box, 1001, Basildon, Essex, SS13 1SR, England.

HILL Beau; b. 25 Sept. 1952, Dallas, Texas, USA. Record Prod.; Musician (keyboards, guitar). *Education:* BA, Music and Western European History. *Musical Education:* Classical training 1958–; Music Major, University of Colorado. *Career:* Signed as recording artist, Columbia Records, 1978; Chrysalis Records, 1981; BMI writer, 1981–; Producer for Bob Dylan: Down in the Groove; Alice Cooper: Constrictor; Ratt: Dancin' Undercover; Warrant: Cherry Pie; Winger, Winger; Europe: Prisoners in Paradise; Chaka Khan; Fiona; Roger Daltrey; John Miles; Gary Moore; Steve Stevens; Bad Brains. *Recordings:* Compilations: Europe 1982–2000, Europe, 2000; Greatest and Latest, Warrant, 2000. *Memberships:* NARAS; AES. *Leisure interests:* Scuba-diving. *Address:* c/o Stuart Silfell, 488 Madison Ave, New York, NY 10023, USA.

HILL Dave; b. 4 April 1946, Fleet Castle, Devon, England. Musician (guitar). *Career:* Member, The Vendors, Wolverhampton, 1965; Member, UK rock group Slade (formerly N'Betweens, Ambrose Slade), 1966–; Currently billed as Slade II; Concerts include: First British tour, 1972; Fanfare For Europe festival, London Palladium, 1973; Great British Music Festival, 1978; Reading Festival, 1980; Film: Flame, 1974. *Recordings:* Albums: Beginnings (as Ambrose Slade), 1969; Play It Loud, 1970; Slade Alive, 1972; Slayed, 1973; Sladest, 1973; Old New Borrowed Blue, 1974; Slade In Flame (soundtrack), 1974; Nobody's Fool, 1976; Slade Alive Vol. 2, 1978; Return To Base, 1979; Slade Smashes, 1980; Till Deaf Do Us Part, 1981; We'll Bring The House Down, 1981; Slade On Stage, 1982; The Amazing Kamikaze Syndrome, 1983; Slade's Greats, 1984; Rogue's Gallery,

1985; Crackers, 1985; You Boyz Make Big Noize, 1987; Wall of Hits, 1991; Keep On Rockin', 1996; Slade II, 2001; UK No. 1 hit singles: Coz I Luv You, 1971; Take Me Bak 'Ome, 1972; Mama Weer All Crazee Now (later recorded by Mama's Boys, Quiet Riot), 1972; Cum On Feel The Noize, 1973; Skweeze Me Pleeze Me, 1973; Merry Christmas Everybody, 1973; Other hits: Look Wot You Dun, 1972; Gudbuy T'Jane, 1972; ; My Friend Stan, 1973; Everyday, 1974; Bangin' Man, 1974; Far Far Away, 1974; Thanks For The Memory, 1975; In For A Penny, 1975; We'll Bring The House Down, 1981; My Oh My, 1983; Run Run Away, 1984; All Join Hands, 1984. *Publication:* Life story. *Current Management:* Len Tuckey. *Address:* c/o Hal Carter Organisation, London, England.

HILL Dusty (Joe Michael); b. 19 May 1949, Dallas, Texas, USA. Musician (bass); Vocalist. *Career:* Formed The Warlocks, with brother, Rocky, 1967; Renamed American Blues, 1968; Formed ZZ Top, 1970; Regular tours, 1970–; Tours include: Eliminator tour, 1984; Afterburner tour, 1985–87; Recycler tour, 1990; Rock The Bowl '91, Milton Keynes, 1991. *Recordings include:* Albums: 2 with The American Blues, 1968; with ZZ Top: ZZ Top's First Album 1970; Rio Grande Mud, 1972; Tres Hombres, 1973; Fandango, 1975; Best Of, 1978; Deguello, 1979; El Loco, 1981; Eliminator, 1983; Afterburner, 1985; Recycler, 1990; Greatest Hits, 1992; Antenna, 1994; Rhythmeen, 1996; XXX, 1999; Singles include: La Grange, 1974; Tush, 1975; Gimme All Your Lovin', 1983; Sharp Dressed Man, 1983; Legs, 1984; Sleeping Bag, 1985; Velcro Fly, 1986; Stages, 1986; Rough Boy, 1986; Doubleback, from film Back To The Future Part III, 1990; Viva Las Vegas, 1992. *Honours:* Several MTV Video Awards; ZZ Top Day, Texas, 1991; Silver Clef Award, Nordoff-Robbins Music Therapy Foundation, 1992. *Current Management:* Lone Wolf Management, PO Box 163690, Austin, TX 78716, USA.

HILL Jason; b. 28 Aug. 1948, Portsmouth, Hampshire, England. Barn Dance Caller; Musician (guitar, melodeon, autoharp). m. Gwyneth Mair Bound, 22 Feb. 1986. *Education:* University of Keele, 1967–71; Birmingham University, 1990–91. *Career:* Caller and musician with Oatcake Billy's Ideal Band, 1977–90; Alf Alfa and The Wild Oats, 1991–; Radio broadcast: Shropshire Folk Programme, 1993; Festivals: Potteries Folk Festival, 1991; Crewe and Nantwich Folk Festival, 1992. *Recordings:* with Alf Alfa: Climbing The Walls, 1995. *Memberships:* Musicians' Union; English Folk Dance and Song Society. *Current Management:* Barn Dance Agency Ltd. *Address:* 62 Beechwood Rd, South Croydon, Surrey CR2 0AA, England.

HILL Lauryn; b. 26 May 1975, South Orange, New Jersey, USA. Singer; Actor. 1 s. *Education:* Columbia University. *Career:* Joined Tranzlator Crew, with Wyclef Jean and Pras Michel; Renamed as The Fugees; Numerous television and live appearances; Minor acting roles including As The World Turns on television and in film in Sister Act II; Began solo career; Wrote, Rose is Still a Rose for Aretha Franklin. *Recordings:* With The Fugees: Singles: Boof Baf, 1993; Nappy Heads, 1994; Vocab, EP, 1994; Ready or Not (No. 1, UK), 1996; The Score, 1996; Fu-Gee-La, 1996; Killing Me Softly (No. 1, UK), 1996; Rumble in the Jungle, 1997; Albums: Blunted on Reality, 1994; The Score (No. 1, USA), 1996; Solo: Singles: Doo Wop (That Thing), 1998; Ex-Factor, 1998; Everything is Everything, 1999; Album: The Miseducation of Lauryn Hill, 1998; Lauryn Hill Story, 2000; Also contributed to recordings by: Whitney Houston; Mary J. Blige. *Honours:* Brit Award, Best International Group, 1997; Five Grammy Awards, Album of the Year, Best New Artist, Best Female R & B Vocal Performance, Best R & B Song, Best R & B Album, 1999.

HILL Mark; b. 1972, Wales, England. Prod.; Remixer; DJ. *Musical Education:* Southampton University, music student. *Career:* Played violin in Southampton Youth Orchestra; Formed the Artful Dodger with partner Pete Devereux, 1996; Released debut album, 2001; Co-founder: Centric Records (with Devereux), Duo split amicably, 2001; Continues to record and produce under Artful Dodger name; Collaborations: Craig David; Dreem Teem; Romina Johnson; Melanie Blatt; Remixed: Sisqo; Gabrielle. *Recordings:* Albums: It's All About The Stragglers, 2001; Singles: Re-Rewind The Crowd Say Bo Selecta (with Craig David), Movin' Too Fast (with Romina Johnson), 1999; Woman Trouble (with Robbie Craig and Craig David), Please Don't Turn Me On (with Lifford), 2000; It Ain't Enough (with Dreem Teem), Twentyfourseven (with Melanie Blatt), 2001. *Honours:* Ivor Novello Awards: Dance Award: Re-Rewind, 2000; Woman Trouble, 2001; Songwriters of the Year (with Craig David); Best Contemporary Song, 7 Days (co-writer), 2001. *Address:* c/o London Records, Waldron House, 57–63 Old Church St, London, SW3 5BS, England.

HILL Warren; b. Canada. Musician (alto, soprano saxophone). *Musical Education:* Berklee College of Music, Boston. *Career:* Television appearances including: Tonight Show; Arsenio Hall Show; Unforgettable tour supporting Natalie Cole; Also supported: Ray Charles; Air Supply; Four Play; Worked with: Mitch Malloy; Sheila E; Alex Acuna; Lenny Castro; Jeff Pocaro; Ricardo Silveira. *Recordings:* Albums: Kiss Under The Moon, 1982; Devotion, 1993; Truth, 1994; Shelter, 1997; Life Thru

Rose Coloured Glasses, 1998; Performed on: Restless Heart: Tell Me What You Dream (No. 1 Billboard charts); Also The Passion Theme, from Body of Evidence soundtrack; Can't Get You Out of my Mind, with Aswad and General Levy; Jazz at Midnight; Hot Summer Swing. *Current Management:* SESAC. *Address:* 55 Music Sq. E, Nashville, TN 37203, USA.

HILLERED Eva Karin Maria; b. 4 April 1958, Stockholm, Sweden. Singer; Songwriter; Singing Teacher. m. Peter Ostman, 1 d. *Musical Education:* Drama, music and psychology, University; Choir leader tuition, 1 year; Studied singing, 1 year. *Career:* Backing Singer, Bob Manning, Py Backman, Eva Dahigren, Anne-Grete Preus, Rolf Wikstrom, Marie Bergman; Toured with Rock Runt Riket, Py Backman, Anne-Grete Preus, Eva Dahlgren, Rolf Wikstrom, Riksteaterns Cornelis-show; Own shows in Stockholm. *Recordings:* Inte Varfor Utan Hur, 1988; Straets langd, 1990; Jag Vet, 1995; Oppningsskedet, 1996. *Honour:* Nominated for Grammy Award, 1989. *Memberships:* STIM; SKAP. *Leisure interests:* Travel; Films; Reading; Theatre; Cooking. *Current Management:* Diva Records, Sweden. *Address:* Tureholms Gard, 619 92 Trosa, Sweden.

HILLMAN Chris; b. 4 Dec. 1944, Los Angeles, California, USA. Musician (bass, guitar); Songwriter; Singer. *Career:* Musician, groups: Scottsville Squirrel Barkers; Golden State Boys; The Hillmen; The Byrds, 1964–68; Performances include: Beach Boys Summer Spectacular, 1966; Monterey Festival, 1967; Grand Ole Opry, 1968; Newport Pop Festival, 1968; McGuinn Clark and Hillman (with Gene Clark and Roger McGuinn); The Flying Burrito Brothers; Manassas; Souther Hillman Furay Band; Desert Rose Band. *Recordings:* Albums with the Byrds: Mr Tambourine Man, 1965; Turn! Turn! Turn!, 1965; Fifth Dimension, 1966; Younger Than Yesterday, 1967; The Notorious Byrd Brothers, 1968; Sweetheart of The Rodeo, 1968; History of The Byrds, 1973; The Byrds, 1990; with The Flying Burrito Brothers: The Gilded Palace of Sin, 1969; Burrito Deluxe, 1970; The Flying Burrito Brothers, 1971; The Last of The Red Hot Burrito Brothers, 1972; Flying Again, 1975; Airborne, 1976; Close Encounters On The West Coast, 1978; Live In Tokyo, Japan, 1978; Flying High, 1980; Back To The Sweethearts of The Rodeo, 1988; Southern Tracks, 1990; with Manassas: Manassas, 1972; Down The Road, 1973; with Souther Hillman Furay Band: Souther Hillman Furay, 1974; Trouble In Paradise, 1974; with Desert Rose Band: The Desert Rose Band, 1987; Running, 1988; Pages of Life, 1990; True Love, 1991; A Dozen Roses, 1991; Life Goes On, 1994; Solo: Slippin' Away, 1976; Sixteen Roses: Greatest Hits, 1995; Bakersfield Bound, 1996; Like a Hurricane, 1998; with Rice, Rice, Hillman and Pederson: Running Wild, 2001; Singles with the Byrds include: Mr Tambourine Man (No. 1, USA), 1965; All I Really Want To Do, 1965; Eight Miles High, 1966; So You Want To Be A Rock 'n' Roll Star, 1967. *Honour:* Inducted into Rock and Roll Hall of Fame, 1991.

HINCHLIFFE Keith Phillip; b. 4 Jan. 1951, Glossop, Derbyshire, England. Musician (guitar); Singer. *Education:* BA, English, Leicester University; Doctorate in English, Hull University. *Career:* Several years, Folk and Blues club and concert circuit; Member, Albion Band, 1991–92; Extensive tuition and workshop experience; Several appearances, BBC Radio, ITV. *Recordings:* Albums: Carolan's Dream, 1994; The Albion Band: Captured, 1994; Islands, 1999. *Publications:* Carolan's Dream, 1995; Original guitar music in Guitar International; O'Carolan for Everyone, 1999. *Memberships:* PRS; Musicians' Union; PAMRA. *Leisure interests:* Reading; Cycling; Hill-walking. *Address:* 23A Spring Hill, Sheffield S10 1ET, England.

HINCHLIFFE Roger Redman; b. 27 Dec. 1944, Springfield, Vermont, USA. Singer; Composer; Translator. m. Karen Soderberg, 30 Sept. 1995, 2 d. *Education:* BA, Bowdoin College, 1966; MBA, Cornell University, 1968; Excellence in Swedish, Stockholm University, 1974; Voice and Theoretical Studies, Glee Club. *Career:* Ten Tours of USA as solo vocalist, including 80 Concerts in 20 States, 1988–; Guest appearances on Television and Radio in the USA and Sweden. *Compositions:* Over 30 English Translations and Solo Recordings of Sweden's Greatest Popular Songs; 12 Original Compositions. *Recordings:* Cantalucha, 1979; Festival Theme, 1980; Swedens Greatest, 1988; Swedes on Love, 1992; Master Olof's Choir, 1994. *Publications:* Over 100 including: Films Translated from Swedish to English: Three Loves, 1990; Greta Garbo, 1994; Who Killed Olof Palme?, 1995; Jerusalem, 1996; Tattooed Widow, 1997. *Honours:* 10 Festival Awards for Translations, Cannes, Montreux, 1986–98. *Memberships:* American Asscn of Sweden; Compact Disc Asscn. *Leisure interests:* Tennis; Basketball; Fishing; Diving; Boating. *Current Management:* c/o RogeRecords, PO Box 414, Cedar Mt, NC 28718, USA.

HINDLEY Guy Niall; b. 5 July 1956, Manchester, England. Musician (Accordion, bass trombone). m. Aileen, 6 July 1996. *Education:* BA, Geography; MSc, Transport Technology. *Musical Education:* Piano lessons, and self-taught on accordion. *Career:* Second accordion with Carousel Ceilidh Band, 1997; Playing bass trombone. *Membership:* Musicians' Union. *Leisure interest:* Playing accordion for Morris dancers. *Address:* 32 Tuxford Rd, Ansdell, Lytham St Annes, Lancashire FY8 4BH, England.

HINE Rupert Neville; b. 21 Sept. 1947, Wimbledon, England. Record Prod.; Musician (multi-instrumentalist). m. Natasha, 1 s. *Musical Education:* Self-taught. *Career:* Songwriter for: Tina Turner; Stevie Nicks; Wilson Phillips; Robert Palmer; Dusty Springfield. *Recordings:* Albums include: with Quantum Jump: Quantum Jump, 1976; Barracuda, 1977; Solo albums: Pick up a Bone, 1971; Unfinished Picture, 1973; Immunity, 1981; Waving Not Drowning, 1982; Wildest Wish to Fly, 1983; Deep End, 1995; Producer of over 100 albums for artists including Tina Turner; Bob Geldof; Rush; The Fixx; Howard Jones; Chris De Burgh; Stevie Nicks; Duncan Sheik; Numerous film scores and television projects, including One World One Voice featuring: Peter Gabriel; Chrissie Hynde; Suzanne Vega; Lou Reed; Laurie Anderson; Dave Stewart; Sting; Also 300 other musicians from 6 continents. *Honours:* Producer, Grammy award-winning tracks; Numerous Gold discs. *Leisure interests:* Flying; Classic cars. *Current Management:* Jukes Productions Ltd. *Address:* c/o Jukes Productions Ltd, 63 Sutherland Ave, London W9 2HF, England.

HINKLER Simon Thomas; b. 13 Nov. 1959, Sheffield, England. Musician (guitar, keyboards); Prod.; Programmer. *Musical Education:* Self-taught. *Career:* Multi-instrumentalist with groups Artery and Pulp, 1980–85; Guitarist, The Mission, 1986–90; World-wide tours (first western band to play Paraguay), numerous television appearances; Programmer, producer, freelance, 1994-. *Recordings:* Albums: Oceans, 1982; Pulp-it, 1983; Artery Live In Amsterdam, 1985; The Flight Commander, 1985; God's Own Medicine, 1986; The First Chapter, 1987; Children, 1988; Carved In Sand, 1990; Room Full of This, 1993; with Pulp: Pulpintro – The Gift Recordings, 1993; Pulped (compilation), 2001; with Mission: Salad Daze, 1994. *Publication:* Names Are For Tombstones Baby, 1993. *Honours:* Gold Discs, all Mission albums. *Memberships:* Musicians' Union; PRS; PPL. *Leisure interests:* Walking; Films; Computers. *Current Management:* Curveball Management. *Address:* PO Box 899, Walkley, Sheffield S6 2YY, England.

HIRABAYASHI Makiko; b. 17 Sept. 1966, Tokyo, Japan. Musician. m. Morten Kargaard Nielsen, 24 Sept. 1990. *Education:* Music Degree, Berklee College of Music; Major, Piano, Rhythmic Conservatory, Denmark. *Career:* Performed with Morten Kargaard Group and Sisters, Copenhagen Jazz Festival, 1991–97; Japan Tour with Third Floor Jazz Quartet, 1992, 1993, 1994; Performed, Yokohama Jazz Promenade, 1993, 1994; Performed with Sisters, Stockholm Water Festival, 1996, 1997; Performed with Maravilla, Roskilde Festival, 1997. *Recordings:* Later Still, 1993; Colour of a Moment, 1996; Elk Dance, 1996; Sa Ka La Musika, 1997; A Story of Multiplicity, 1998; BIMWO Swing, 1998. *Honour:* Third Prize, Best Arrangement, Public Award, Europe Jazz Contest, Belgium, 1995. *Address:* Linnesgade 33 3tv, 1361 Copenhagen K, Denmark.

HIRD Colin; b. 21 April 1964, Sunderland, England. Musician (Bass, Chapman Stick, Keys); Prod. m. Jane Hird, 24 April 1991. *Musical Education:* HND in Music Technology; Studied Bass under Nick Beggs. *Career:* It's Crucial tour, 1985; McCallum, Left Handed Tour, 1988; TV appearance on BBC 2's Out of Our Heads, 1988, and ITV's Comedy Bites, 1995 with Morgan Le Fay. *Recordings:* Left Handed, with McCallum, 1988; Growing Up In Public, with The Flair, 1994. *Membership:* Musicians' Union. *Leisure interest:* Midi Computer Programming. *Current Management:* Major Management, Blyth, Northumberland, England. *Address:* 2 Cowpen Rd, Blyth, Northumberland NE24 5BS, England.

HIRST Clare; b. 13 Aug. 1959, Alston, Cumbria, England. Musician (saxophone); Vocalist; Composer. m. Alan Barnes, 31 July 1995, 1 s. *Musical Education:* Self-taught, some private tuition. *Career:* Member, pop band The Bellestars, 1981–86; Played on Live Aid with David Bowie; Toured with The Communards; Sandie Shaw; Iggy Pop; Hazel O'Connor; Maxi Priest; Amazulu; Quireboys; Television appearances include: Jazz 606, BBC2. *Recordings:* All Belle Stars recordings; with The Communards: Don't Leave Me This Way (No. 1, UK), 1986; with Luxuria: Unanswerable Lust, 1988; with Clare Hirst Quartet: Tough and Tender, 1995; Singles with The Belle Stars include: Iko Iko, 1982; The Clapping Song, 1982; Sign of The Times, 1982; Sweet Memory, 1983; The Entertainer, 1983. *Current Management:* c/o 33 Records, 33 Guildford St, Luton, Bedfordshire, England.

HIRST Willie; b. 2 May 1941, Barnsley, South Yorkshire, England. Bandleader; Musical Dir; Arranger; Musician (saxophone, clarinet, flute, recorder). m. Hazel Irene Rainbow, 4 April 1966, 2 s. *Musical Education:* Huddersfield College of Music; Bretton Hall College. *Career:* Musical director, Wakefield Theatre Club, for 15 years; Tours: Bobby Vee; Tony Christie; Marti Caine; Lionel Blair; Concerts: Johnny Mathis; Tony Bennett; Buddy Greco; Victor Borge; Sacha Distell; Tommy Steele; Bruce Forsythe; Matt Monro; Drifters; Des O'Connor; Bob Monkhouse; Gladys Knight and the Pips; Les Dawson; Three Two One; Television appearances: Play Guitar; Radio: Jimmy Young Show; Late Night Show; Early Breakfast Show. *Honours:* LRAM (saxophone); ARCM (clarinet); LTCL (recorder); Certificate of Education; Lecturer in Instrumental Music at Bretton Hall College and Leeds College of Music. *Membership:* Musicians' Union. *Leisure*

interests: Antiques; Cricket; Golf. *Current Management:* Partner with Hazel Hirst, Maestro Music and Entertainment Agency. *Address:* Belmont House, 32 Bell Lane, Ackworth, Pontefract, West Yorkshire WF7 7JH, England.

HITZ Michael; b. 12 Oct. 1968, Baden, Switzerland. Musician (Jazz and Pop Singer). *Musical Education:* Private Instructions, Acting, Singing, Phonetics. *Career:* Church Singing, Nightclubs, 1986; Stage Cariete Polygon, Zuerich, 1989; Radio Show, Risiko, Seeperle, DRS Kultur, 1992; Tour Switzerland and Germany, Worked with The platters, Sina, Maja Brunner, Musical Remember Me, 1994; Talk Show, Bernard Theatre Zurich, 1997–98. *Recordings:* CDs, Polygon, Clowns, Remember Me, Like A River Flows. *Memberships:* Freunde Des Leedes, SUISA. *Leisure interests:* Composing; Texting; Animals, Star Trek. *Current Management:* Daisy Entertainment. *Address:* Thurwiesenstrasse 15, CH 8037 Zurich.

HNILICKA Jaromir; b. 11 Feb. 1932, Bratislava. Composer; Musician. Divorced, 2 d. *Education:* Graduate, State Conservatory for Music. *Career:* Trumpet Soloist, Gustav Brom Big Band; Composer, Arranger, 1953-. *Compositions:* Missa Jazz, 1968, 1989. *Recordings:* Missa Jazz, 1968, 1989. *Honours:* Prize, Josef Blaha; Prize, Ludek Hulan; Prize, Composers Asscn. *Membership:* OSA. *Leisure interests:* Nature; Dogs; Skiing; Cycling; Windsurfing; Good Books. *Address:* Kupkova 22, 63800 Brno, Czech Republic.

HO Fred Wei-Han Houn; b. 10 Aug. 1957, Palo Alto, California, USA. Composer; Musician (Baritone Saxophone); Writer; Prod. *Education:* BA, Sociology, Harvard University. *Musical Education:* Self-taught musically. *Career:* Next Wave Festival, Brooklyn Academy of Music, 1997; San Francisco Jazz Festival, Herbst Theatre, 1998. *Compositions:* Warrior Sisters, opera; Night Vision, opera; Journey Beyond the West: The New Adventure of Monkey; A Chinaman's Chance, opera. *Recordings:* Warrior Sisters; Monkey: Part One and Part Two; Underground Railroad to My Heart; Tomorrow Is Now!; Turn pain Into Power!. *Publications:* Sounding Off!, Music as Subversion, 1996; Womyn Warriors Calendar. *Honours:* Duke Ellington Distinguished Artist Lifetime Achievement Award, 1988; National Endowment for the Arts Jazz Competition Fellowship, 1992. *Memberships:* ASCAP; American Composers Forum; American Music Center. *Leisure interest:* Swimming with dolphins and whales. *Current Management:* Big Red Media. *Address:* 443 12th St, Brooklyn, NY 11215, USA.

HOBBS Paul Ernest Leonard; b. 28 Dec. 1948, Burnt Oak, Edgware, Hendon, Middlesex, England. Musician (drums). m. (1) Jane Pitkin, 26 July 1975, (2) Sylvia Picton, 25 July 1987, 2 d. *Musical Education:* Self-taught with help from Buddy Rich, Phil Seaman, James Blades, Sylvia Hobbs, Diana Clement. *Career:* Member, 'Twas Brillig, 1964–65; Dr John and the Blues Preachers, 1965–67; Dream Machine, 1967–68; Mahogany, 1968–72; Roy Powell Combo, 1971–72; Hobson's Choice With Tigger, 2001; Utrecht Railway Museum Performance for Jam, Dutch TV, 1970, 1971; Late Night Line-up, with Marty Wilde, BBC TV, 1970–71; BBC Radio 1 Club. *Recordings:* Albums: Mahogany, produced by Tony Clark, 1969; Mahogany With Marty Wilde, 1970; Bring Back Rock 'n' Roll, Old Nick's Trainset, 1972; Good Rockin' Now and Then, Marty Wilde, 1973; Take It Easy, Robert Bee Blues Corporation, 1993; Kirsch, 1973; Pale Lights, 1973–76; Graunch, 1973–74; Cochise, 1980–82; T-Bone Boogie Band, 1983–84; Pink 'n' Black, 1984; The Anxious Brothers, 1987–89; W Arts and All, 1990–99; Robert Bee Blues Corporation 1992–93; Danny White and the Shadds, 1995–98; Ray Cave and Paul Hobbs Sounds and Colour, 1998–99. *Publications:* 2 books awaiting publication. *Membership:* Musicians' Union. *Leisure interests:* Model railway and all main forms of civil transport (UK). *Address:* 82 Bourne Cres., Kingsheath, Northampton, Northamptonshire NN5 7JA, England.

HOBBS Rebecca Ann (Becky); b. 24 Jan. 1950, Bartlesville, Oklahoma, USA. Singer; Songwriter. *Education:* 1 year college, Tulsa University. *Musical Education:* 6 years piano lessons. *Career:* Performed in more than 40 countries; Performed on: Hee Haw; Academy of Country Music Awards Show; Nashville Now; Prime Time Country; Pop! Goes The Country; Staler Bros Show. *Compositions:* co-wrote Angels Among Us, recorded by Alabama; Co-wrote I Want To Know You Before We Make Love, number 1 country hit for Conway Twitty; Co-wrote, recorded, Jones On The Jukebox; Other songs recorded by: George Jones, Loretta Lynn; Glen Campbell; Emmylou Harris; Helen Reddy; Shirley Bassey. *Recordings:* Albums include: From Oklahoma With Love, 1998. *Honours:* Most Promising International Act, In Country Music Round-Up, 1989; Top Female On Independent Label, 1994. *Memberships:* NSAI; AFofM; AFTRA; CMA. *Leisure interests:* Loves cats; Collects antiques; Oil-painting. *Address:* Becky Hobbs, c/o Beckaroo Music, PO Box 150272, Nashville, TN 37215, USA.

HOBROUGH Mark; b. 11 Sept. 1965, Cheshire, England. Record Co Exec.; Artist Man. *Education:* BA Hons in Archaeology, Dunelm. *Career:* Spin Promotions Ltd, 1989; Managing Director, Revolution Promotions and Lemon Records, 1991; Managing Director, Revolution Promotions and

Jealous Records; Manager of Sack and Darling Sugar Honey (Revolution Management), 1995. *Leisure interests:* Football; Cricket. *Address:* 172A Arlington Rd, Camden, London NW1 7HL, England.

HOCHMAN Larry; b. 21 Nov. 1953, New Jersey, USA. Composer; Orchestrator. m. Diane Hochman, 1 step-s., 1 step-d., 1 d. *Education:* Manhattan School of Music, 1972–75. *Career:* Co-Founder, with Larry Gates, Newfound Music Productions. *Compositions include:* Stephen Spielberg's Amazing Stories, 1986; Views of a Vanishing Frontier, 1987; Phantom of the Opera, 1990; In Memoriam, 1993; Dear America, 1993; American Portraits, 1996; The Very Last Butterfly, 1997; Music for the Movies, 1998; Hot Klezmer, 1998; Orchestrated: How Glory Goes, Audra McDonald, 2000. *Recordings:* one Man Band; In Memoriam. *Honours:* New Jersey Theatre Group Applause Award; Various CLIO Awards; ASCAP Award; Bistro Cabaret Award. *Memberships:* American Federation of Musicians; Pushcart Players. *Address:* 10 Kershner Pl., Fair Lawn, NJ 07410, USA.

HODES Paul William; b. 21 March 1951, New York, New York, USA. Attorney; Record Co Pres.; Musician; Prod. m. Margaret A Horstmann, 29 June 1979, 1 s., 1 d. *Education:* BA cum laude, Dartmouth College, 1972; JD cum laude, Boston College Law School, 1978. *Career:* Founder, Town Meeting Theatre Workshop, Vermont; Worked as Actor, Director, Producer, Film Maker, Playwright; Assistant Attorney General; Trial and Entertainment Attorney, Shaheen and Gordon PA, Concord, New Hampshire; Founding Member, Peggosus, rock group; President, Big Round Records Inc. *Recordings:* Peggosus Jubilee!, 1986; Peggosus Diggin' in the Dirt, 1991; Peggot Paul Patchwork Quilt, 1996; Peggo and Paul's Winter's Light, 2000. *Honours:* ASCAP Awards; Parents Choice Honours, 1987, 1996. *Memberships:* ASCAP; Chairman, Capitol Center for the Arts, 1990–96; Board Mem., Concord Community Music School, Children's Entertainment Asscn, New Hampshire Children's Alliance. *Leisure interests:* Sailing; Collecting vintage guitars. *Current Management:* CandM Management Group, Brentwood, Tennessee. *Address:* Shaheen and Gordon PA, Box 2703, Two Capital Plaza, Concord, NH 03302, USA.

HODGE Andrew; b. 17 Aug. 1966, Ickenham, Middlesex, England. Freelance Musician (bass guitar). m. Susan Louise Jinks (Madeleine Harvey, actress), 27 Sept. 1992. *Musical Education:* Colin Spencer, Classical Guitar Studio, Torquay. *Career:* Lorna Luft, Dave Willetts Magical World of The Musicals Tour; Jerry Playle, album promotional tour Beyond Silence; Brotherhood of Man, British tour, 1994–95; Home and Away, National Tour; That'll Be The Day, British tour, 1999–2000. *Recordings:* Albums: L and A, acoustic; Foreverly Yours; with Dangerously Big: Dangerously Big; with Innocence Lost: Love Is In. *Membership:* Musicians' Union. *Leisure interests:* Reading; Driving; Walking. *Address:* 26 The Reddings, Borehamwood, Herts WD6 4ST, England.

HODGE Philip Norman; b. 11 Sept. 1953, Aylesbury, Buckinghamshire, England. Musician (keyboards); Computer Engineer. m. Lisa Mary Jane Stacey, 18 June 1994. *Musical Education:* Piano Grade 6. *Career:* Semi-pro band: Synthesis, 1970–75; Steve Hillage Band (Virgin), British tour, 1976; American tour, support to ELO, 1977; Hyde Park concert with Queen, 1976; TV: Old Grey Whistle Test, 1976; European TV shows, concerts; Semi-pro bands: Six; As Above So Below; Radio 1, Friday Rock Show; Concert with Dave Stewart, Barbara Gaskin, as keyboard player. *Publications:* Articles, keyboard reviews, Organ Player Magazine. *Leisure interest:* Music. *Address:* 50 Corbet Ride, Linslade, Leighton Buzzard, Bedfordshire LU7 75J, England.

HODGES Chas (Charles Nicholas); b. 28 Dec. 1943, Edmonton, London, England. Musician (piano, guitar, bass); Entertainer; Songwriter. m. Joan Adeline Findley, 6 Oct. 1966, 2 d., 1 s. *Musical Education:* Self-taught. *Career:* Turned professional, 1960; Member of bands: Mike Berry and the Outlaws; Cliff Bennett and the Rebel Rousers; Heads, Hands and Feet; Cockney duo Chas and Dave (with Dave Peacock); World-wide tours; Numerous radio and television appearances; Collaborations: Billy Fury; Oliver Nelson; Bobby Graham; Gene Vincent; Albert Lee; Labi Siffre. *Compositions:* Over 300 songs; Biggest hit single Ain't No Pleasin' You, Chas and Dave, co-written with Dave Peacock (No. 2, UK), 1982; Biggest Hit Album/Video: Chas and Dave's Street Party (No. 3, UK), 1995. *Recordings include:* with Chas and Dave: Gertcha, 1979; Rabbit, 1980; Stars Over 45, 1981; Margate, 1982; Snooker Loopy, with The Matchroom Mob, 1986; Hit records with all the above artists. *Publication:* Chas Before Dave, autobiography. *Honours:* Bass Player of Year, 1962; Over 20 Gold albums and singles. *Memberships:* PRS; MCPS; Musicians' Union. *Leisure interest:* Gardening. *Current Management:* Bob England, Hurricane Entertainments.

HODGSON Lee James; b. 18 May 1961, Chelmsford, England. Musician (guitar, midi); Vocalist; Educator. m. Gloria Maria Ricardo, 20 Aug. 1984, 2 s. *Musical Education:* Self-taught. *Career:* Club concerts from age 16;

Professional, age 18; Tours with Odyssey, 1980–81; Bobby Thurston, 1980; Television and radio commercial sessions, mid-1980's; Several years with comedy showband Barley; Formed country band Memphis Roots, 1987; Concerts include: Wembley Arena; Royal Albert Hall; Festivals; Instructor, Guitar Institute, 1990's. *Recordings:* Best of Memphis Roots; Good Noise: The Best of Western Line Dancing. *Publications:* Grade pieces for Rockschool Ltd; Hot Country, guitar tutorial, 1997; Columnist, Guitar Techniques magazine; Guitarist magazine. *Memberships:* Musicians' Union; PRS. *Leisure interest:* Occasional photography. *Address:* 2 The Poplars, Pitsea, Basildon, Essex SS13 2ER, England.

HOEG Thorsten Sehested, (Dane T S Hawk); b. 6 Jan. 1957, Copenhagen, Denmark. Musician (saxophone); Composer; Writer; Entertainer. *Musical Education:* Studied with John Tchicai, 1973–78; Courses, private lessons. *Career:* Member, John Tchicai and the Festival Band, 1975–78; Formed Cockpit Music, 1978; Tours: Scandinavia; Yugoslavia; Czechoslovakia; Switzerland; France; Bandleader, Tapehead, 1981–86; Somesax, 1985–90; 18 piece big band, Dane T S Hawk and his Great Mongo Dilmuns; Solo, 1980–; Numerous appearances include: Copenhagen Jazz Festival; Roskilde Festival; Århus Festuge; Pori Jazz Festival, Finland; Gothenburg Book Fair, Sweden; Numerous television and radio appearances; Wrote text and music, 3 plays for Danish Radio. *Compositions:* Scores to Danish, French dance companies, The Royal Danish Theatre, Billedstofteatret, Denmarks Radio; My River Came Forth In A Flood, 1990; Sweet Devil On The Loose, 1994; I'm 3, 1994; Opera score: Soap Opera (libretti by poet Morti Vizki) 1994; All material for own big band Dane T S Hawk and his Great Mongo Dilmuns. *Recordings:* Cockpit Music: Transworlds of Sounds, 1981; Snow Lake City, 1982; Salute For General Wasteland, 1983; Stop/Go, 1985; Hands Up, 1988; Foss/Hoeg/ Schneidermann/Skeel: How To Play, Vol. 3, 1989; Somesax: Flapper, 1990. *Publications:* Books: Amokoma, 1982; Landskab Ruller Zone, 1983; 1/2 Så Gammel Som Tiden, 1987; Hotel Kontinental I Likvidation, 1990; Gutboy, Autumn, 1995. *Contributions to:* magazines, newspapers. *Honours:* Several awards and grants for literature and music. *Memberships:* PEN; DJBFA; DSF. *Address:* Frederiksbergalle 7, 1621 Copenhagen V, Denmark.

HOFF Jan Gunnar; b. 22 Oct. 1958, Bodo, Norway. Musician (piano); Composer. *Musical Education:* 3 year plate study, Trondelag Music Conservatory. *Career:* Debut concert, Harstad Music Festival as solo artist, 1992; Concerts with Jan Gunnar Hoff Group; Concert, Vossa Jazz, Norway, 1995; Molde International Jazzfestival, 1996; Oris London Jazz Festival, Barbican, 1996; Bergen Festival, 1996, 1998; Stavanger International Jazz Festival, 1998. *Recordings:* Syklus, 1993; Moving, 1995; Crosslands, 1998. *Honour:* The Stubö Prize, 1997. *Memberships:* NOPA (popular composers); Gramart (recording artists). *Address:* Harald Langhellesv. 16B, 8003 Bodo, Norway.

HOFFS Susannah; b. 17 Jan. 1959, Los Angeles, California, USA. Singer; Musician (guitar). *Education:* Graduate, University of California, Berkeley. *Career:* Founder member, all-female group The Bangles (originally Supersonic Bangs, then The Bangs), 1981–89; Tours and concerts include: Support to The Beat, 1982; Debut British tour, 1984; World tour, 1986; Support to Simple Minds, Milton Keynes Bowl Pop Festival, 1986; Support to Queen, Ireland, 1986; US tour, 1986; Solo recording career, 1989–; US tour, support to Don Henley, 1991; Actress, The Allnighter, 1986. *Recordings:* Albums: with The Bangles: The Bangles, 1982; All Over The Place, 1984; Different Light, 1986; Everything, 1988; Bangles' Greatest Hits, 1989; All Over the Place/Different Light, 1997; with Tom Petty: Playback, 1995; featured on Poptopia 80's Power Pop Classics, 1997; Solo albums: When You're A Boy, 1991; Susannah Hoffs, 1996; Hit singles: Manic Monday, 1986; If She Knew What She Wants, 1986; Going Down To Liverpool, 1986; Walk Like An Egyptian, (No. 1, USA), 1986; Hazy Shade of Winter (used in film soundtrack Less Than Zero), 1988; In Your Room, 1988; Eternal Flame (No. 1, UK), 1989; Be With You, 1989; Solo singles: My Side of The Bed, 1991; All I Want, 1996. *Current Management:* c/o Gold Mountain Entertainment, Suite 450, 3575 Cahuenga Blvd W, Los Angeles, CA 90068, USA.

HOFSTEIN Francis; b. 9 Oct. 1937, France. Psychoanalyst; Critic; Writer. m. Nicole Cerf, 3 s. *Education:* Docteur En Medecine; Conservatoire de Musique. *Publications:* Au Miroir Du Jazz; Oakland Blues; James Pichette Et Le Jazz; Le Rhythm and Blues; Jazz-Suite Pour Sacha; Blue Moon; Muddy Waters (biography), 1996. *Membership:* Academie Du Jazz. *Leisure interest:* Collecting Everything About Jazz. *Address:* 5 rue Ernest et Henri Rouselle, 75013 Paris, France.

HOGAN Michael; b. 29 April 1973, Maycross, Ireland. Musician (bass). *Career:* Member, The Cranberries; Set up early band, The Cranberry Saw Us; Recruited Dolores O'Riordan on vocals and changed name to The Cranberries; Obtained major label deal; Early tour of USA supporting Suede; Numerous subsequent headlining tours, festival appearances; Numerous TV and radio appearances; Played Woodstock 2 in USA. *Recordings:* Singles: Linger, 1993; Dreams, 1994; Zombie, 1994; Ode To

My Family, 1994; I Can't Be With You, 1995; Ridiculous Thoughts, 1995; Doors and Windows, 1995; Salvation, 1996; Free to Decide, 1996; Promises, 1999; Animal Instinct, 1999; Albums: Everybody Elso Is Doing It So Why Can't We, 1993; No Need to Argue, 1994; To The Faithful Departed, 1996; Bury The Hatchet, 1999; Wake Up and Smell The Coffee, 2001. *Internet:* www.cranberries.com.

HOGAN Noel; b. 25 Dec. 1971, Moycross, Ireland. Musician (Guitar). *Career:* Member, The Cranberries; Formed early band, The Cranberry Saw Us, changed name to Cranberries when Dolores O'Riordan joined as singer; Signed major label record deal; Early American tour supporting Suede; Numerous headlining live appearances, festival dates, radio and TV appearances; Played Woodstock 2 in the USA; Massive world-wide sales. *Recordings:* Singles: Linger, 1993; Dreams, 1994; Zombie, 1994; Ode To My Mother, 1994; I Can't Be With You, 1995; Ridiculous Thoughts, 1995; Doors and Windows, 1995; Salvation, 1996; Free to Decide, 1996; Promises, 1999; Animal Instinct, 1999; Albums: Everybody Else is Doing It So Why Can't We, 1993; No Need To Argue, 1994; To The Faithful Departed, 1996; Bury the Hatchet, 1999; Wake Up and Smell The Coffee, 2001. *Internet:* www.cranberries.com.

HOGARTH Steve; b. 14 May 1959, Kendal, Cumbria, England. Musician; Singer; Songwriter. m. 16 Aug. 1980, 1 s., 1 d. *Career:* Singer, groups The Europeans; How We Live; Lead singer, UK progressive rock group, Marillion, 1989–; Tours include: UK, 1991; North America, 1992; South America, 1992; Colaborations with The The, Julian Cope and Toni Childs; World tours with the Europeans; 5 world tours with Marillion. *Recordings:* Albums: with The Europeans: Vocabulary, 1982; Recurring Dreams, 1984; with Marillion: Season's End, 1989; Holidays In Eden, 1991; A Singles Collection 1982–92, 1992; Brave, 1994; Afraid of Sunlight, 1995; Made Again, 1996; This Strange Engine, 1997; Radiation, 1998; Afraid of Sunlight, 1999; Solo as H: Ice Cream Genius; Singles: Hooks In You, 1989; Uninvited Guest, 1989; Easter, 1990; Cover My Eyes (Pain and Heaven), 1991; No One Can, 1991; Dry Land, 1991; Sympathy, 1992. *Current Management:* Hit and Run Music Ltd. *Address:* 30 Ives St, London SW3 2ND, England.

HÖGLUND Kjell; b. 8 Dec. 1945, Östersund, Sweden. Songwriter; Artist; Musician (guitar). Partner, Margaretha Granström. *Education:* Bachelor of Arts. *Career:* 12 albums with own songs; Pioneer of making own records; Legend, Swedish underground music. *Compositions include:* Songs: Witch-Trial; Smooth Water; Sea of Gennesaret; One Big Strong; One Gets Accustomed; The Last Battle. *Recordings:* Albums: Wonder, 1971; Flower Season, 1972; Witch-Trial, 1973; Baskervilles Hound, 1974; The Heart Is To The Left, 1975; Dr Jekyll's Will, 1979; The Road Towards Shangri-La, 1980; Signs of The Times, 1984; Secret Love, 1986; Year of The Serpent, 1989; Höglund Forever, 1992; Incognito, 1995. *Publications:* Song book: Burnt Ships, 1987; Novels: Magnum Opus, 1991; The Sicilian Seal, 1997. *Honours:* Numerous scholarships; Nominated for Swedish Grammy Award, 1992. *Leisure interests:* Pet cat Mirre; Alchemy; Egyptology; Ark of the Covenant. *Current Management:* RMP Management, Stockholm. *Address:* Atlantis Records, Karlbergsvägen 57, 113 35 Stockholm, Sweden.

HÖH Volker; b. 24 April 1959, Altenkirchen, Pfalz, Germany. Musician (Guitar). m. Jutta Maria Höh, 20 June 1980, 2 d. *Education:* University Rheinland-Pfalz, Koblenz; Staatliche Hochschule für Musik, Westfalen-Lippe, Münster. *Career:* Recitalist and Soloist with orchestras; Radio and TV engagements; Performed in most major cities and festivals; Teacher, Guitar, University of Koblenz; Masterclasses and workshops. *Recordings:* Calliope Calls, with Christina Ascher, mezzo and percussion, CD; Triops-Botschaft, solo LP of Tilo Medek's works for guitar; solo CD, Danzas Fantasticas, dances from Spain and Latin America for guitar; Webern op 10, Shostakovich, Jazz Suites with RSO Frankfurt. *Publications:* Editor, Pedagogic and Chamber Music guitar literature; Author of articles on guitar in music periodicals. *Honours:* Stipends and Scholarships from Kultusministerium Rheinland-Pfalz, Darmstädter Ferienkurse, Richard Wagner Verband, Deutscher Musikrat. *Memberships:* EGTA; BDZ. *Leisure interests:* Reading; Jogging. *Address:* Am Nörrenpfad 30 A, 56337 Eitelborn, Germany.

HOIER Svein; b. 18 Nov. 1970, Oslo, Norway. Musician (guitar, keyboard, drummer). *Education:* 4 years, Trondheim University. *Career:* Started as drummer: Closet Queens; Joined Hedge Hog, playing guitar, keyboard, sampler, 1994; Toured Europe, 1994, 1995. *Recordings:* Closet Queens: Closet Queens, 1993; Hedge Hog: Mindless, 1994; The Healing EP, 1995; Thorn Cord Wonder, 1995. *Publications:* 2 short films released: Smoking; Svein. *Honour:* Swein, Best Film, Trondheim Film Festival, 1995. *Leisure interests:* Chess; Opera; Poetry.

HOLDER Noddy (Neville); b. 15 June 1950, Walsall, Warwickshire, England. Vocalist; Songwriter; Musician (guitar). *Career:* Guitarist, backing vocalist, Steve Brett and The Mavericks; Vocalist, guitarist, UK rock group, Slade (formerly N'Betweens, Ambrose Slade), 1966–91; Concerts include: First British tour, 1972; Fanfare For Europe festival,

London Palladium, 1973; Great British Music Festival, 1978; Reading Festival, 1980; Radio presenter, Piccadilly Radio, Manchester; Capital Gold, London; Numerous TV appearances, including: The Grimleys, ITV, 1997–2001; I Love 1973, BBC2, 2000; Film: Flame, 1974. *Compositions:* Co-writer, all Slade's Top 20 hits, with Jimmy Lea. *Recordings:* Albums: Beginnings (as Ambrose Slade), 1969; Play It Loud, 1970; Slade Alive, 1972; Slayed, 1973; Sladest, 1973; Old New Borrowed Blue, 1974; Slade In Flame (soundtrack), 1974; Nobody's Fool, 1976; Slade Alive Vol. 2, 1978; Return To Base, 1979; Slade Smashes, 1980; Till Deaf Do Us Part, 1981; We'll Bring The House Down, 1981; Slade On Stage, 1982; The Amazing Kamikaze Syndrome, 1983; Slade's Greats, 1984; Rogue's Gallery, 1985; Crackers, 1985; You Boyz Make Big Noize, 1987; Wall of Hits, 1991; UK No. 1 hit singles: Coz I Luv You, 1971; Take Me Bak 'Ome, 1972; Mama Weer All Crazee Now (later recorded by Mama's Boys, Quiet Riot), 1972; Cum On Feel The Noize, 1973; Skweeze Me Pleeze Me, 1973; Merry Christmas Everybody, 1973; Other hits: Look Wot You Dun, 1972; Gudbuy T'Jane, 1972; My Friend Stan, 1973; Everyday, 1974; Bangin' Man, 1974; Far Far Away, 1974; Thanks For The Memory, 1975; In For A Penny, 1975; We'll Bring The House Down, 1981; My Oh My, 1983; Run Run Away, 1984; All Join Hands, 1984.

HOLDSWORTH Allan; b. 6 Aug. 1948, Bradford, West Yorkshire, England. Musician (guitar). 1 s., 1 d. *Musical Education:* Self-taught. *Career:* Tours, television appearances world-wide. *Recordings:* (Solo albums) The Sixteen Men of Tain, 2000; 'Igginbottom's Wrench, 2000; Flat Tire, 2001; Recordings with: Tempest; Soft Machine; Gordon Beck; Allan Holdsworth Band: Sand; Atavachron; Secrets; IOU; Wardencliffe Tower; Hard Hat Area; Tony Williams; Bill Bruford; Donovan. *Honour:* Guitar Hall of Fame. *Leisure interests:* Cycling; Making beer. *Current Management:* Marco Polo. *Address:* 3 The Lilacs, 50 Elm Grove, Hayling Island, Hampshire PO11 9EF, England.

HOLGATE David Edward; b. 19 April 1939, Romford, Essex, England. Musician (double bass, bass guitar). m. Anne Malmström, 1 April 1962, 1 s., 1 d. *Musical Education:* Private lessons pianoforte to higher grade RSM. *Career:* Anglia TV session work for many years include: Crescendo; Miss Anglia; About Anglia; The Mid-day Show; Music Match; BBC Radio One Club; Mr and Mrs; The Seeds of Love; Beach Boys support group: The Rainbow People. *Recordings:* Singles include: The Walk'll Do You Good; Dreamtime; The Sailing Song; Rainbows. *Membership:* Musicians' Union. *Leisure interests:* Sculpture; Computers; French Language. *Address:* 18 Cow Hill, Norwich NR2 1HD, England.

HOLIDAY Doc, (Edward Wohanka); b. 29 Jan. 1943, New Jersey, USA. Record Prod.; Recording Artist; Record Co Exec. 1 s., 2 d. *Musical Education:* Degrees in Music from Juilliard School of Music; Berkeley University; University of Miami. *Career:* Television appearances include: The Tonight Show; American Bandstand; Merv Griffin Show; Joe Franklin Show; Grammy Awards Show; 76 US Country No. 1 hits as a record producer. *Recordings include:* As recording artist: Expressway To Your Heart; Just My Imagination; Walkin' In Memphis; As producer: Cajun Baby, Hank Williams Jr; Louisiana Man, Doug Kershaw; Mr Jones, Big Al Downing. *Honours include:* 36 Music Awards; 2 Grammy Awards; ICMA Producer of the Year, 1993–95. *Memberships:* BMI; ASCAP; SESAC. *Leisure interests:* Fishing; Travel. *Address:* c/o Doc Holiday Productions, 10 Luanita Lane, Newport News, VA 23606, USA.

HOLLAND Annie (Annabel); b. 26 Aug. 1965. Musician (Bass Guitarist). *Career:* Member of Elastica, 1992–95; Toured extensively world-wide. *Recordings:* Albums: Elastica (No. 1, UK), 1995; The Menace, 2000; The BBC Sessions, 2001; Singles: Stutter, 1993; Line Up, 1994; Connection, 1994; Waking Up, 1995; Elastica, EP. *Honours:* Nomination for Brit Award; NME Readers Award for Best New Band. *Current Management:* CMO Management International Ltd, Ransomes Dock, 35–37 Parkgate Rd, London SW11 4NP, England.

HOLLAND Brian; b. 15 Feb. 1941, Detroit, Michigan, USA. Composer; Record Prod. *Career:* Lead singer, the Satintones, 1950s; Member, composition and production team Holland/Dozier/Holland (with brother Eddie Holland and Lamont Dozier), 1963; Joined Motown label, 1960s; Co-founder, Invictus and Hot Wax record labels, 1967–75. *Recordings:* As co-writer, producer: with Marvin Gaye: Can I Get A Witness?, 1963; You're A Wonderful One, 1964; How Sweet It Is (To Be Loved By You), 1964; Little Darling, 1966; with Martha and The Vandellas: Heatwave; Quicksand; Nowhere To Run; Jimmy Mack; with Diana Ross and the Supremes: Where Did Our Love Go (No. 1, USA), 1964; Baby Love (No. 1, UK and US), 1964; Come See About Me (No. 1, USA), 1965; Stop! In The Name of Love (No. 1, USA), 1965; Back In My Arms Again (No. 1, USA), 1965; You Can't Hurry Love (No. 1, USA), 1966; You Keep Me Hanging On (No. 1, USA), 1966; Love Is Here and Now You're Gone (No. 1, USA), 1967; The Happening (No. 1, USA), 1967; with the Four Tops: Baby I Need Your Loving, 1965; I Can't Help Myself (No. 1, USA), 1965; (It's The) Same Old Song, 1965; Reach Out I'll Be There (No. 1, UK and US), 1966; Bernadette, 1967; Standing In The Shadows of Love, 1967; with the Miracles: Mickey's Monkey; I'm The One

You Need; with the Isley Brothers: This Old Heart of Mine, 1966; Put Yourself In My Place, 1969; I Guess I'll Always Love You, 1966; Other recordings with Aretha Franklin; Kim Weston; Freda Payne; Chairmen of The Board.

HOLLAND David; b. 5 April 1948, Northampton, England. Musician (drums). *Musical Education:* Self-taught. *Career:* Member, Pinkerton's Assorted Colours, 1966–69; Trapeze, 1969–79; Judas Priest, 1979–88; Over 20 North American and European tours; Numerous radio and television appearances with the above. *Recordings:* Albums: with Trapeze, 1970–78: Trapeze, 1970; Medusa, 1970; You Are The Music We're Just The Band, 1972; The Final Swing, 1974; Hot Wire, 1974; Trapeze, 1975; Hold On, 1978; Running, 1978; with Judas Priest 1980–88: British Steel, 1980; Point of Entry, 1980; Screaming For Vengeance; Defenders of The Faith, 1984; Turbo, 1986; Priest-Live, 1987; Ram It Down, 1998; Also featured on: Play Me Out, Glenn Hughes, 1977; Songwriter, Justin Hayward, 1977; Nightflight, Justin Hayward, 1980; Dangerous Music, Robin George, 1985. *Honours:* Over 20 Platinum, Gold, Silver albums with Judas Priest; Crystal Globe Award. *Leisure interests:* Cycling; DIY; Entertaining.

HOLLAND Dexter, (Bryan Keith Holland); b. 29 Dec. 1966, Orange County, California, USA. Vocalist; Musician (guitar). m. Kristinia Luna, 1 d. *Education:* University of Southern California, PhD graduate in molecular biology. *Musical Education:* Self-taught guitarist. *Career:* Former drummer; Formed group Manic Subsidal with fellow school cross-country team members, 1984; Group metamorphosised into The Offspring, 1985; Privately pressed single took over 2 years to sell 1000 copies, 1987; Signed to independent labels, Nemesis and Epitaph, for 1988–95 releases; Major US breakthrough following heavy MTV/radio play rotation, 1994; Accused of betraying punk roots when signing to Columbia after dispute with former label, 1996; Consolidated world-wide success by scoring UK number 1 hit single, 1999; Live shows include: Woodstock festival, 1999; KROQ Weenie Roast, 2000; European tour, 2001; Band gave lucky fan $1m. in Offspring prize draw, 2000; Co-owner: Nitro label with Offspring manager Jim Guerinot, releasing records by Guttermouth and The Vandals. *Recordings:* Albums: The Offspring, 1989; Ignition, 1992; Smash!, 1994; Ixnay On The Hombre, 1997; Americana, 1998; Conspiracy of One, 2000; Singles: I'll Be Waiting, 1987; Baghdad EP, 1988; Come Out and Play (Keep 'Em Separated), Self-Esteem, 1994; Gotta Get Away, 1995; All I Want, Gone Away, 1997; Pretty Fly (For A White Guy), 1998; Why Don't You Get A Job?, The Kids Aren't Alright, She's Got Issues, 1999; Original Prankster, 2000; Want You Bad, Million Miles Away, 2001. *Honours:* Over 9m copies of Smash album sold world-wide, best selling independent record of all time. *Current Management:* Jim Guerinot, Rebel Waltz Management, 31652 Second Ave, Laguna Beach, CA 92651, USA. *Internet:* www.offspring.com.

HOLLAND Eddie; b. 30 Oct. 1939, Detroit, Michigan, USA. Composer; Record Prod. *Career:* Member, the Fideltones; Member, songwriting and production team Holland/Dozier/Holland (with Brian Holland and Lamont Dozier); Co-writer, producer, numerous records by major Motown artists, including a dozen US number 1 hits, 1963–68; Split from Motown, 1967; Co-founder, Invictus and Hot Wax record labels, 1967–75. *Recordings:* As co-producer, writer: with Marvin Gaye: Can I Get A Witness?, 1963; You're A Wonderful One, 1964; How Sweet It Is (To Be Loved By You), 1964; Little Darling, 1966; with Martha and The Vandellas: Heatwave; Quicksand; Nowhere To Run; Jimmy Mack; with Diana Ross and the Supremes: Where Did Our Love Go (No. 1, USA), 1964; Baby Love (No. 1, UK and US), 1964; Come See About Me (No. 1, USA), 1965; Stop! In The Name of Love (No. 1, USA), 1965; Back In My Arms Again (No. 1, USA), 1965; You Can't Hurry Love (No. 1, USA), 1966; You Keep Me Hanging On (No. 1, USA), 1966; Love Is Here and Now You're Gone, 1967; The Happening (No. 1, USA), 1967; with the Four Tops: Baby I Need Your Loving, 1965; I Can't Help Myself (No. 1, USA), 1965; (It's The) Same Old Song, 1965; Reach Out I'll Be There (No. 1, UK and US), 1966; Bernadette, 1967; Standing In The Shadows of Love, 1967; with the Miracles: Mickey's Monkey; I'm The One You Need; with the Isley Brothers: This Old Heart of Mine, 1966; Put Yourself In My Place, 1969; I Guess I'll Always Love You, 1966; Other recordings with Aretha Franklin; Kim Weston; Freda Payne; Chairmen of The Board.

HOLLAND Jools (Julian); b. 24 Jan. 1958, London, England. Musician (keyboards); Broadcaster; Bandleader. 1 s., 2 d. *Career:* Founder member, pianist, Squeeze, 1974–81, 1985–90; Solo artiste and bandleader: Jools Holland and his Big Band, 1982–84; Jools Holland and his Rhythm and Blues Orchestra, 1991–; Radio presenter, BBC Radio 2, 1997–; Television presenter, music shows: The Tube, C4, 1982–87; Later With Jools Holland, BBC2, 1993–; Various other television specials, including Sunday Night, NBC, 1989; The Groovy Fellers, Channel 4, 1989; Juke Box Jury, BBC2, 1989–90; The Happening, BSB, 1990; Beat Route, BBC 2, 1998–99. *Recordings:* Albums: with Squeeze: Squeeze, 1978; Cool For Cats, 1979; Argy Bargy, 1980; Cosi Fan Tutti Frutti, 1985; Babylon and On, 1987; Frank, 1989; Solo albums: A World of His Own, 1990; The Full

Complement, 1991; A To Z of The Piano, 1992; Live Performance, 1994; Solo Piano, 1994; Sex and Jazz and Rock and Roll, 1996; Lift the Lid, 1997; The Best of Jools Holland, 1998; Sunset Over London, 1999; Hop The Wag, 2000; Small World – Big Band, 2001; Hit singles include: with Squeeze: Take Me I'm Yours, 1978; Cool For Cats, 1979; Up The Junction, 1979; Slap and Tickle, 1979; Another Nail In My Heart, 1980; Pulling Mussels From A Shell, 1980; Hourglass, 1987; 853 5937, 1988; Also contributed to numerous albums including: Soul Mining, The The, 1983; The Raw and The Cooked, Fine Young Cannibals, 1989; Sam Brown; Dr John. *Memberships:* Musicians' Union; Equity; Writer's Guild. *Leisure interests:* Jazz and R & B music; Architectural sketching. *Current Management:* c/o Paul Loasby, One Fifteen, The Gallery, 28–30 Wood Wharf, Horseferry Pl., London SE10 9BT, England.

HOLLINGWORTH Roy; b. 12 April 1949, Derby, England. Singer; Songwriter; Musician (guitar); Poet; Writer. *Education:* Nottingham University. *Career:* Feature writer, critic with Melody maker, London, 1970–74; Editor, Melody Maker, American Bureau, New York, 1973; Session musician, New York, 1973–78; Performance poet, singer, Greenwich Village, New York, 1973–80; American, Canadian tours, Germany, 1995; European Tour, 1997. *Recordings:* Albums: Guitarist, Electric Shocks, Roger Ruskin Spear, 1973; Solo album: Roy Hollingworth – In The Flesh, 1994; with Barclay James Harvest: Barclay James Harvest, 1994. *Honour:* BBC Radio One, London, Rock Writer of The Year, 1972. *Membership:* GEMA, Germany (artists and composers). *Leisure interest:* Occultist – Order of Initiates (Bardic). *Address:* 10 Genoa Ave, London SW15 6DY, England.

HOLLOWAY Laurence; b. 31 March 1938, Oldham, Lancashire. Musician (Piano); Composer; Musical Dir. m. Marion Montgomery, 16 June 1965, 2 d. *Career:* Touring Dance Band Pianist, 1950s; Cyril Stapleton Showband; Joe Daniels Hotshots, 1950s; Cunard Line, 1956–57; London Weekend Television, regular pianist, 1967–80; Musical Director, Engelbert Humperdinck, 1970–75; Played at studios in London, 1975–85; Musical Director for many top artistes such as Judy Garland. *Compositions:* Numerous TV signature tunes including Blind Date, Beadle's About. *Recordings:* Solo albums: Blue Skies; Showtime; Cumulus; About Time; Also recorded with many artists including Kiri Te Kanawa, Marion Montgomery, Robert Farnon, Rolf Harris. *Honour:* Gold Badge of Merit, BASCA. *Leisure interests:* Golf; Shooting; Gardening. *Current Management:* Ann Zahl. *Address:* Elgin, Fishery Rd, Bray, Berkshire SL6 1UP, England.

HOLLWEG Rebecca; b. 30 June 1964, London, England. Singer; Songwriter. *Education:* BA (Hons), French, German, Oxon. *Musical Education:* Guildhall School of Music and Drama, Jazz Course. *Career:* Venues include: 12-Bar Club; Royal Festival Hall foyer; 606 Club; Kashmir Klub; Borderline; Manchester Royal Exchange; Cabot Hall; Radio Broadcasts: 2 studio sessions for BBC Radio Scotland. *Recording:* The Demos, 1999. *Contributions to:* 3 songs on soundtrack of The Bitterest Pill, short drama for television, 1999; Track on Band Register CD, June Babies. *Memberships:* PRS; Musicians' Union; Equity. *Address:* 14A Emu Rd, London SW8 3PR, England.

HOLMBERG Patricia; b. 21 Oct. 1934, Montana, USA. Musician; Composer; Piano Teacher. m. Russell Holmberg, 1 s., 3 d. *Education:* BMus, University of Colorado, 1955; MM, University of Colorado, 1958. *Compositions:* Various Choral Anthems, Art Songs and Piano Pieces, 1973–; Songs For Seniors; Concerto For Jazz Piano and Concert Band. *Recordings:* Boulder Rags; Songs For Seniors; Christmas In The Rockies; Mountain Images; Hymns We All Remember. *Honour:* Grant, City of Boulder. *Memberships:* BMI; American Federation of Musicians; American Music Center; Music Teachers National Asscn. *Leisure interests:* My Friends; Sewing. *Address:* 2244 Kincaid Pl., Boulder, Colorado 80304, USA.

HOLMES David; b. 1969, Belfast, Northern Ireland. Prod.; Remixer; DJ. *Career:* Started as concert promoter in Belfast; Began to DJ at own club night Sugar Sweet, early 1990s; First recorded with Ashley Beedle as the Disco Evangelists, 1992; Offers of remix work followed; Signed to Go! Discs as artist; Produces music for film soundtracks; Collaborations: Ashley Beedle; Bobby Gillespie; Remixed: Saint Etienne; U2; Monkey Mafia; Manic Street Preachers. *Recordings:* Albums: This Film's Crap – Let's Slash The Seats, 1995; Resurrection Game OST, Let's Get Killed, 1997; Out of Sight OST, 1998; Bow Down To The Exit Sign, 2000; Ocean's Eleven OST, 2002; Singles: De Niro (with Disco Evangelists), 1992; Gone, My Mate Paul, 1996; Don't Die Just Yet, Gritty Shaker, 1997. *Membership:* PRS. *Address:* c/o Go! Discs, 72 Black Lion Lane, Hammersmith, London, W6 9BE, England.

HOLMES Ian Johnstone; b. 11 March 1935, Dumfries, Scotland. m. Margaret Bell, 6 Nov. 1958, 2 d. *Education:* Accordion lessons with Alex Carter. *Career:* Appeared on TV in White Heather Club; Recorded TV shows in Germany; Broadcast on BBC Radio Scotland, 1958-, as Soloist and Bandleader, 1962-. *Compositions:* Around 275 tunes in various styles, especially Scottish dance music, and also accordion tunes in French, Norwegian, Swedish and Swiss styles. *Recordings:* 16 albums, mostly of Scottish dance music; Recordings of music by the Beatles and Scandinavian and Swiss accordion music. *Publications:* The Dumfries Collection of Music by Ian Holmes, Vols 1, 2 and 3. *Honours:* All-Scotland Champion of Traditional Music, 1957; Honourary mem. of the Bromolla Accordion Orchestra (Sweden) in 1987. *Memberships:* MCPS; PRS; Phonographic Performance; PAMRA. *Leisure interest:* Family. *Address:* 11 Averill Cres., Rotchell, Dumfries DG2 7RY, Scotland.

HOLSKE Robin M; b. 24 July 1941. Piano Teacher; Musician (Jazz Pianist). 2 d. *Education:* Friends Academy, NY, 1959; Antioch College, OH, 1965. *Career:* Played Piano, Salsa Bands, New York; Led Numerous Jazz Groups, New Hampshire, 1974-. *Compositions:* David, Saul and Jonathan; Eleanor; Cassanova. *Recordings:* Rey Davila-Ya Era Tiempo. *Honour:* Billboard International Award. *Membership:* AFM. *Leisure interests:* Photography; Bird Watching; Cooking. *Address:* 296 Corn Hill Rd, Boscawen, NH 03303, USA.

HOLSTEIN Christina Staël von; b. 13 Aug. 1969, Lausanne, Switzerland. Singer; Musician (guitar); Lyricist; Composer. *Musical Education:* Guildhall Singing Grade 5 – Honours. *Career:* Member, bands The New Quartet; Vers La Flammes; Here Lies A Crime; Paper Fish; Guest vocalist, Wax Club; Jaded Halo; Musicals: West Side Story; Sweeney Todd, The Demon Barber of Fleet Street; The Boyfriend. *Recording:* Album: Visitations From A Universal Mind, in progress. *Memberships:* Musicians' Union; Montessori School, Balderton Street; British School of Complementary Therapists, Harley Street; The Place To Be (charity for children with learning and emotional difficulties). *Leisure interests:* Writing children's stories; Dance; Travel. *Address:* 44 Palace Gardens Terrace, London W8 4RR, England.

HOLZHAUER Rudy; b. 14 Dec. 1951, Hamburg, Germany. Music Publisher; Man. *Career:* Live engineer; Studio engineer; Music publisher; Artist manager; Owner, Musikverlag Progressive GmbH. *Memberships:* GEMA; DMV; DKV. *Leisure interests:* Graphic design; Computing. *Address:* Bramfelder Chaussee 238c, 22177 Hamburg, Germany.

HONK J (Herbert Gebetsroither); b. 5 Oct. 1957, Linz a.d. Donau, Austria. Musician (guitar, piano); Songwriter; Performing Artist; Music Publisher; Instrumental Music Teacher. *Musical Education:* Guitar, piano, voice, theory (jazz), Franz Schubert Conservatory, Vienna. *Career:* Member, US salsa and latin band Obote; Tours of Germany and Netherlands; Founder, Jivi Honk and band, 1983–; 500 live concerts in and around Austria, 1985–; Various own projects include Jivi Honk and the Funkplanet; The Honk Rock Project, Honk Instrumental Project, 1990; Concerts include: U4, Vienna; Vienna State Opera; Budapest Town Hall; Italian tour, 1989; Velden; Zürs; Television appearances include: ORF FS1; radio includes: Over 1000 appearances on German and Austrian public radio and various European stations, 1988–; Tokyo FM, 1990-. *Recordings:* Instrumentals: Lovedancer; Space Me To The Stars, 1988; Sunrider; Vienna Skyline; Moonrider; Highway of Fame; Golden Days, 1993, 1994; Albums: as Jivi Honk: Got My Style, 1990; Sunrider, 1993; Moonrider, 1993; Golden Days, 1994; Live At The Garage, 1995; Stardance, 1999. *Memberships:* AKM; Austro Mechana; LSG/Östig. *Leisure interests:* Nature; Philosophy; Reading. *Current Management:* Honk Music, Warner Chappel Group, Austria. *Address:* Hormayrgasse 3/25, 1170 Vienna, Austria.

HOOK Peter; b. 13 Feb. 1956, Salford, Lancashire, England. Musician (bass). *Career:* Member, Joy Division, 1977–80; New Order, 1980–; Revenge, 1989–96; Monaco, 1996–; Tours: UK; Europe; Australia; New Zealand; Far East; US; South America; Concerts include: Glastonbury Festival, 1981, 1987; Futurama Festival, Leeds, 1982; San Remo Festival, 1988; Reading Festival, 1989; Leader, house band, The Mrs Merton Show, Granada/BBC-TV, 1994–95. *Recordings:* Albums: with Joy Division: Unknown Pleasures, 1979; Closer, 1980; Still, 1981; The Peel Sessions, 1988; Also featured on: Short Circuit – Live At The Electric Circus, 1978; with New Order: Movement, 1981; Power Corruption and Lies, 1983; Low Life, 1985; Brotherhood, 1987; Substance, 1987; Technique (No. 1, UK), 1989; Republic (No. 1, UK), 1993; The Best of New Order, 1994; The Rest of New Order, 1995; Get Ready, 2001; with Revenge: One True Passion, 1990; with Monaco: Music For Pleasure, 1997; Singles include: with Joy Division: An Ideal For Living EP, 1978; Transmission, 1979; Atmosphere, 1980; Love Will Tear Us Apart, 1980; with New Order: Ceremony, 1981; Procession/ Everything's Gone Green, 1981; Temptation, 1982; Blue Monday, 1983, remixed 1988, 1995; Confusion, 1983; Thieves Like Us, 1984; The Perfect Kiss, 1985; Subculture, 1985; Shellshock, 1986; State of The Nation, 1986; Bizarre Love Triangle, 1986; True Faith, 1987; Touched By The Hand of God, 1987; Fine Time, 1988; Round and Round, 1989; World In Motion (with England World Cup Football Squad) (No. 1, UK), 1990; How Does It Feel?, 1992; Regret, 1993; Ruined In A Day, 1993; World, 1993; Spooky, 1993; 1963, 1995; Crystal, 2001; 60 Miles An Hour, 2001; with Revenge: Reasons, 1989; Pineapple Face, 1990; Slave, 1990; Gun World Porn, 1991; with Monaco: What Do You Want From Me?, 1997; Sweet Lips, 1997;

Shine, 1997. *Current Management:* Spark Management, 100 Wilshire Blvd, Suite 1830, Santa Monica, CA 90064, USA.

HOOKER Jake; b. 5 March 1951, New York, USA. Songwriter; Record Prod.; Musician (guitar). m. 7 Sept. 1994, 1 s., 2 d. *Musical Education:* Self-taught. *Career:* Wrote No. 1 international hit I Love Rock and Roll; Formed UK group The Arrows, 1974. *Recordings:* I Love Rock and Roll; Destination Unknown (from film soundtrack Top Gun); Sweetest Victory (from film soundtrack Rocky IV); Iron Eagle (from film soundtrack Iron Eagle); with Edgar Winter, Not a Kid Anymore, 1994; Real Deal, 1996; with Justin Trevino, Loud Music and Strong Wine, 2000. *Publication:* The Arrows Biography. *Honours:* Several Platinum and Gold records. *Memberships:* NARAS; BMI; AFofM. *Leisure interest:* Tennis. *Current Management:* HEI.

HOOKER Steve; b. 19 May 1953, Rochford, Essex. Musician (guitar) Singer; Songwriter; Prod. m. (1) 1 s., (2) Elaine, 11 Aug. 1992. *Education:* Southend Art College, Cordwainers, London. *Musical Education:* Self-taught. *Career:* The Heat, 1977; Shakers, 1982–87; Jeremy Gluck, 1987; Steve Hooker and Wilko Johnson, (recording project) 1988; Boz and the Bozmen, 1988; Steve Hooker Band, 1989–91; Rumble, 1994; Steve Hooker and the ST's, 1999; Television includes: Marquee series (Anglia TV); FR3 (France); Several radio appearances; Musical contributor to soundtrack, Burnin' Love, film noir. *Compositions include:* Elmore Stroll, on Hell for Leather, Rumble, 1996; The Raid, Captain Drugbuster, 1997. *Recordings:* with The Shakers: Temptation Walk, Catch On; Solo album: Boogie-Chal; Also featured on: Really Gone, 1984; Wild Heroine, Boz and the Bozmen; Dress in Deadmens Suits, 1988; Rockin' Ace of Spades, on Locorumble, 1998. *Publications:* Sleeve notes with journalist John Tobler. *Honour:* Diploma in design of shoe and footwear. *Membership:* Musicians' Union. *Leisure interest:* Collector of Rock 'n' Roll and 50's memorabilia.

HOOPER Nellee; Record Prod.; Arranger. *Career:* Member, The Wild Bunch Crew; Member, mixing crew Massive Attack; Joined Soul II Soul, offering sound systems services to UK dance clubs, 1985; Residency, Africa Centre, Covent Garden, London; Relocated to Fridge Club, Brixton, 1988; Opened 2 shops, London, 1988; Developed video and film company, fan club, talent agency, record company, 1990-. *Recordings include:* Albums: with Soul II Soul: Club Classics Vol. I, 1989; Vol. II, A New Decade, 1990; Vol. III – Just Right, 1992; Singles include: Keep On Movin', 1989; Back To Life (However Do You Want Me), 1989; A Dream's A Dream, 1990; Missing You, with Kym Mazelle, 1990; Joy, 1992; Just Right, 1992; Move Me No Mountain, 1992; Wish, 1993; As producer: with Massive Attack: Unfinished Sympathy; Protection; with Madonna: Bedtime Stories; with Björk: Debut; Post; Universal James, James Brown, 1993; with Madonna: Something to Remember, 1995; Special Brew: Special Brew, 1996; with All Saints, All Saints, 1997; Best of Bond... James Bond, 1999; As arranger (with Jazzie B): Nothing Compares To U, Sinead O'Connor, 1990 Contributor, Mad About The Mouse (Disney compilation), 1991. *Honours include:* Platinum discs; Top Dance Sales Artists, Billboard, 1989; 3 American Music Awards, 1990; 4 British DMC Dance Awards, 1990; Grammy Award, Best R & B Instrumental Performance, 1990; 3 Soul Train Awards, 1990; BMI College Radio Award, Back To Life, 1991; ASCAP Award, Back To Life, 1991; BRIT Award, Best Producer, 1995; BRIT Award Nominations, Best Producer, 1994, 1996.

HOPE-EVANS Peter John; b. 28 Sept. 1947, Brecon, Wales. Composer; Performer; Musician (mouth organ, mouth bow, Jews harp). m. Christine Frances Rich, 26 Oct. 1973. *Education:* MA, Romanticism and Modernism, 1991–92. *Musical Education:* Texas Slim; Maurice Blanchot; Edgar Fünf. *Career:* Played with: Medicine Head; Pete Townshend; Deep End; Ronnie Lane; The Ravishing Beauties; Films: White City, 1986; Mourning; Radio: Strange Navigations (Pirate Radio), 1993–; Embers/descendres/eschenglet, 1994; Classical: 4'33 uncaged (Fünf), 1981, 1985, 1989; Multi-media: sigh code: airilicked, 1993; Theatre: La Folie Du Jour, 1989; Manslaughter/ Woman's Laughter, 1992. *Recordings:* New Bottles Old Medicine, 1970; with Pete Townshend: Pete Townshend Live, 1999; with Tears for Fears; Seeds of Love, 1999; with Robbie McIntosh, Wide Screen, 2001; Cassette only series: Elgin Moveme(a)nts; Closer Than Breath (Itself); In The Sacred Cedars; Shadow of The Object; Theatre: Up Your Ass Solanas, 1992; The Tempest (RSC), 1995. *Publications:* Harmonica Yoga, 1990; Philosophising With A Harmonica (Back To Nietzsche), 1992. *Honours:* Prix Italia (music and arts): Strangefish (DV8) 1994. *Leisure interests:* Merdre Sans Tête (performance/study group of the Clown and the Hanged woman in Western Popular Culture). *Address:* 14 Eastbank Rd, Hampton Hill, Middlesex TW12 1RP, England.

HOPKIN Mary; b. 3 May 1950, Pontardawe, Wales. Singer. *Career:* Winner, talent show, Opportunity Knocks, 1968; Debut hit, Those Were The Days, also recorded in Spanish, French, German, Italian, Hebrew (sales exceeded 8m.); British tour, 1969; Backing vocals for various artistes, 1970s; Member, harmony trio, Sundance, 1980; Lead vocalist with Oasis (with Peter Skellern, Julian Lloyd Webber), 1984; Performances include: The Chieftains Music Festival 1991, London Palladium, 1991. *Recordings:* Albums: Post Card, 1969; Earth Song – Ocean Song, 1971; Those Were The

Days, 1972; Spirit, 1991; with Oasis: Oasis, 1984; with Dave Cousins: Bridge, 1994; with Ralph McTell: Sand in your Shoes, 1996; with Future Sound of London: My Kingdom; Dead Cities, 1996; with Brian Willoughby: Black and White, 1999; Singles include; Those Were The Days (No. 1, UK), 1968; Goodbye, 1969; Temma Harbour, 1970; Knock Knock Who's There, UK Eurovision entry, (No. 2, UK), 1970; Think About Your Children; If You Love Me. *Contributions to:* The King of Elfland's Daughter, 1977; Dylan Thomas' Under Milk Wood, 1988.

HOPKINS Philip Nicholas; b. 5 Feb. 1962, Surrey, England. Musician (percussion, chromatic harmonica). m. Barbara Mason, 17 July 1993. *Education:* MA, Oxford University. *Musical Education:* Music scholarship, King's School, Canterbury. *Career:* Sweeney Todd, National Theatre, UK/Europe Tours, 1993–94; London theatre work includes A Little Night Music, National Theatre, 1995; Concert tours, USA with: Phil Coulter; Maura O'Connell; Liam Clancy including Carnegie Hall, New York; Played harmonica for film Fanny and Elvis, and TV series Roger Roger, 1998. *Recordings:* Television, album made with: Leon Redbone; Phil Coulter; Billy Connolly; The Dubliners; Rory Gallagher; Val Doonican; Television, radio sessions include: Next of Kin; Men of The World, BBC1, 1995; Appeared on CD of Royal National Theatre's production A Little Night Music, 1996, Lady in the Dark, 1997, Oklahoma!, 1998. *Publications:* Articles in Modern Drummer, USA. *Membership:* Musicians' Union. *Leisure interests:* Swimming; Golf. *Address:* 5 Claygate Rd, Dorking, Surrey, England.

HOPPER Hugh; b. 29 April 1945, Whitstable, Kent, England. Musician (bass guitar); Composer. 2 d. *Musical Education:* Self-taught. *Career:* Wilde Flowers; Soft Machine; Isotope; Carla Bley; Robert Wyatt; Own bands. *Compositions:* Memories, Robert Wyatt and Whitney Houston; Facelift, Soft Machine; Was A Friend, Shleep, Robert Wyatt. *Recordings:* Soft Machine 2–6; Hoppertunity Box; 1984; Caveman Hughscore; Delta Flora; Cryptids, 2000; The Swimmer, 2001. *Publication:* Rock Bass Manual. *Memberships:* Musicians' Union; MCPS; PRS; PAMRA. *Leisure interests:* Cycling; Sailing; Fresh air. *Address:* 29 Castle Rd, Whitstable, Kent CT5 2DZ, England. *E-mail:* hhopp@ukonline.co.uk.

HOPPUS Mark (Markus Allen); b. 15 March 1972, Ridgecrest, California, USA. Musician (bass guitar). m. Skye Everly, 2001. *Career:* Co-founder: Blink-182, 1993; Built popularity with string of popular independent 7 singles; Signed to MCA through Cargo Music/MCA joint venture deal, 1997; Numerous TV appearances and concerts world-wide including:The Enema Strikes Back '99 tour, released on CD as The Mark Tom and Travis Show; 11-week US Summer tour, 2001; Cameo appearance with group in American Pie film, 1999. *Recordings:* Albums: Fly Swatter (mini-LP), 1993; Cheshire Cat, 1994; Buddah, 1995; Dude Ranch, 1997; Enema of The State, 1999; The Mark Tom and Travis Show (live), 2000; Take Off Your Pants and Jacket, 2001; Singles: Short Bus (split 7 with The Iconoclasts), 1996; They Came To Conquer Uranus (7 EP), Lemmings (split 7 with Swindle), Dick Lips, Dammit (Growing Up), I Won't Be Home For Christmas, 1997; Josie, 1998; What's My Age Again, All The Small Things, 1999; Adam's Song, Man Overboard, 2000; The Rock Show, Stay Together For The Kids, 2001. *Honours:* World-wide sales of 1999 album in excess of 7m. *E-mail:* mark@loserkids.com. *Internet:* www.blink182.com.

HOPWOOD Freddy; b. 22 Dec. 1948, Lichfield, England. Musician (drums, penny whistle, concertina). m. Beryl Agnes Nutt, 17 May 1974, 2 s. *Education:* Uttoxeter and Burton Technical College. *Musical Education:* Self-taught. *Career:* Member, Dr Strangely Strange, 1970–71; Television appearances, John Peel session, BBC Radio 1; Member, Sutherland Brothers Band, 1972; Support tours, Free, Mott The Hoople; David Bowie; Performance at Montreux Golden Rose Festival; Television appearances: Switzerland; Denmark; France; Numerous television and radio appearances, 1987–97; Member, R Cajun and Zydeco Bros, 1984-, Zydeco Hot Rods, 1993–; Formed Vice Bishop's Blues Band, 1997; Session work for Paul McCartney, 1998. *Recordings:* Albums/singles with Sutherland Brothers Band, 1971; Leonard and Squires, 1976; R Cajun and the Zydeco Brothers, 1984–2000; Yeah Jazz, 1992; Vice-Bishops of Uttoxeter, 1995; Big Red Kite, 1996. *Memberships:* PRS; MCPS; PAMRA. *Leisure interests:* Cycling; UFOs; Folklore; Musicology. *Current Management:* Smalltown Records. *Address:* 17 Colne Mount, Uttoxeter, Staffs ST14 7QR, England.

HORABIN Gren; b. 15 May 1939, Rainhill, Liverpool, England. Senior Lecturer (director of studies); Musician (alto and tenor saxophones, clarinet). m. Catherine Rawlinson, 28 Dec. 1968, 1 s. *Education:* Technical Teachers Certificate. *Musical Education:* Private tuition, pianoforte, saxophone clarinet; Bandsman in Royal Air Force. *Career:* Bands include: Leader, alto clarinet, Gren Horabin Combo; Alto saxophone, Band of The Royal Air Force, Bridgnorth; Leader, saxophones, clarinet, Crescendo; Currently tenor clarinet, John Shepherd Combo; Alto, tenor clarinet, Leader, 42nd Street Swing; Jazz, dance gigs, various venues in Midlands with Pete King, Mick Large, Ricky Allan; Allan Billings; various small mainstream groups; Productions include: Lady

Audley's Secret; Dirty Work At The Crossroads; Hits From The Blitz; Concert Style In Jazz (with Duncan Swift, Geraint Ellis); Creator, author, original Jazz Studies Units, BTEC National Diploma Level, Kidderminster College, Worcestershire; Senior Lecturer, Director of Studies, Creative Arts and Community Studies, Kidderminster College, retired; Currently leading own band, 42nd Street Swing; Alto, Tenor and Clarinet with John Shepherd Band. *Compositions include:* Jingle, Calypso Lipstick commercial for Prides Ltd; Classical, modern, theatre and dance. *Honours:* Skills Assessors and Verifiers Awards. *Memberships:* Musicians' Union; Assen of British Jazz Musicians. *Leisure interests:* Jazz; Music; Golf. *Address:* 9 Waterlaide Rd, Hartlebury, Worcestershire DY11 7TP, England.

HORN Shirley; b. 1 May 1934, Washington DC, USA. Vocalist; Musician (piano). 1 d. *Education:* Havard University. *Career:* Concerts include: Lincoln Center, New York, 1989; Blue Note, Tokyo, 1989. *Recordings:* Albums: Cat On A Hot Fiddle, 1959; Embers and Ashes, 1960; Live At The Village Vanguard, 1961; Loads of Love, 1963; Shirley Horn With Strings, 1963; Travelin' Light, 1965; For Love of Ivy, 1968; A Dandy In Aspic, 1968; Where Are You Going?, 1972; A Lazy Afternoon, 1979; All Night Long, 1982; Violets For Your Ears, 1983; The Sentimental Touch, 1985; I Thought About You, 1987; Softly, 1988; Close Enough For Love, 1988; Tune In Tomorrow, 1990; You Won't Forget Me, 1991; Dedicated To You – Tribute To Sarah Vaughn (with Carmen McRae), 1991; I Love You, Paris, 1992; Light Out of Darkness, 1993; The Main Ingredient; 1995; Loving You, 1997; I Remember Miles, 1998; You're My Thrill, 2001. *Current Management:* Sheila Mathis Enterprises, 200 Haven Ave, Suite 5P, New York, NY 10033, USA.

HORN Trevor; b. 15 July 1949. Record Prod.; Record Co Exec.; Vocalist; Musician (guitar). m. Jill Sinclair. *Career:* Session musician, 1970s; Founder, Buggles, 1977–80; Member, Yes, 1980 81; Member, Art of Noise, 1983–85, 1998–; Independent record producer, 1982–; Founder, ZTT Records. *Compositions include:* Theme music, television series The Tube. *Recordings:* Albums: with Buggles: The Plastic Age, 1980; with Yes: Drama, 1980; with Art of Noise: Who's Afraid of The Art of Noise, 1984; Daft, 1986; The Seduction of Claude Debussy, 1999; Singles with Buggles: Video Killed The Radio Star (No. 1, UK), 1979; The Plastic Age, 1980; Clean Clean, 1980; Elstree, 1980; I Am A Camera, 1981; Singles with Art of Noise include: Into Battle EP, 1983; Beatbox, 1983; Close (To The Edit), 1984; Moments In Love, 1985; As producer: Albums include: The Lexicon of Love, ABC, 1982; Duck Rock, Malcolm McLaren, 1983; 90125, Yes, 1983; Welcome To The Pleasure Dome, Frankie Goes To Hollywood, 1984; Seal, Seal, 1991; Tubular Bells II, Mike Oldfield, 1992; Singles include: with Dollar: Hand Held In Black and White, 1981; Mirror Mirror, 1981; Give Me Back My Heart, 1982; Videotheque, 1982; with ABC: Poison Arrow, 1982; The Look of Love, 1982; All of My Heart, 1982; with Spandau Ballet: Instinction, 1982; with Malcolm McLaren: Buffalo Gals, 1982; Double Dutch, 1983; with Yes: Owner of a Lonely Heart (No. 1, USA); with Frankie Goes To Hollywood: Relax (No. 1, UK), 1983; Two Tribes (No. 1, UK), 1984; The Power of Love (No. 1, UK), 1984; Rage Hard, 1986; with Propaganda: Dr Mabuse, 1984; with Grace Jones: Slave To The Rhythm, 1985; with Pet Shop Boys: Left To My Own Devices, 1988; It's Alright, 1989; with Simple Minds: Belfast Child (No. 1, UK), 1989; This Is Your Land, 1989; with Seal: Crazy, 1990; Killer, 1991; Kiss From A Rose, 1994; with Rod Stewart: Downtown Train, 1990; Rhythm of My Heart, 1991; with Marc Almond: Jacky, 1991; The Days of Pearly Spencer, 1992; with Tom Jones: If I Only Could, 1994; Other recordings with Tina Charles; Hans Zimmer; Tina Turner; Genesis; LeAnn Rimes; Cher. *Honours:* BRIT Awards: Best British Producer, 1985, 1992; Q Award, Best Producer, 1991. *Current Management:* Sarm Productions, The Blue Building, 42–46 St Lukes Mews, London W11 1DG, England.

HORNE Lena; b. 30 June 1917, Brooklyn, New York, USA. Singer; Actress. m. Lennie Hayton, 1947 (deceased 1971). *Career:* Chorus singer, Cotton Club, Harlem, 1934; Singer with Noble Sissle's Society Orchestra, 1935–36; Charlie Barnet, 1940–41; Film appearances: Panama Hattie, 1942; Cabin In The Sky, 1943; Stormy Weather, 1943; Thousands Cheers; I Dood It; Swing Fever; Broadway Rhythm; Two Girls and A Sailor; Ziegfield Follies; Till The Clouds Roll By; Words and Music; Duchess of Idaho; Meet Me In Las Vegas; Death of a Gunfighter; The Wiz; Television appearances include: Harry and Lena, 1970; Cosby Show; Sanford and Son; Stage appearances: Dance With Your Gods, Broadway, 1934; Blackbirds of 1939; Jamaica, Broadway, 1957; The Lady and Her Music, Broadway, 1981; Recent appearances include: JVC Jazz Festival, 1993. *Recordings:* Hits include: Stormy Weather; Deed I Do; As Long As I Live; Love Me Or Leave Me; Albums include: The Men In My Life, 1989; We'll Be Together Again, 1994; An Evening with Lena Horne, 1994; Lena Horne Christmas, 1995; Being Myself, 1998; Once in a Lifetime, 1999; Best of The War Years, 2000; Also recorded with: Cab Calloway; Artie Shaw; Teddy Wilson. *Publications:* Lena (with Richard Schickel); In Person. *Honours include:* Tony Award, Distinguished Achievement In The Theatre; Drama Desk Award; New York Drama Critics' Special Award; Handel Medallion, New York City; Emergence Award, Dance Theatre of Harlem; 2 Grammy Awards; NAACP Springarn Award; Honour For Lifetime Contributions To The

Arts, 1984; Paul Robson Award, Actor's Equity, 1985; Hon. doctorate, Harvard University, 1979. *Address:* c/o Casterbridge Ltd, 1204 Third Ave, Suite 162, New York, NY 10021, USA.

HORNSBY Bruce Randall; b. 23 Nov. 1954, Richmond, Virginia, USA. Musician (piano); Songwriter. m. Kathy Lynn Yankovich, 31 Dec. 1983, 2 s. *Musical Education:* BA, Music, University of Miami, 1977. *Career:* Played on over 100 albums for other artists including: Bob Dylan; Grateful Dead; Bonnie Raitt; Don Henley; Bob Seeger; Willie Nelson; Branford Marsalis; Chaka Khan; Squeeze; Robbie Robertson; 10 US top 40 hits (6 as an artist, 4 as a songwriter); Written songs with: Don Henley; Robbie Robertson; Leon Russell; Chaka Khan; Randy Scruggs; Tupac Shakur. *Recordings:* 5 albums: The Way It Is, 1986; Scenes From the Southside, 1988; A Night On The Town, 1990; Harbour Lights, 1993; Hot House, 1995; Spirit Trail, 1998; Here Come The Noise Makers, 2000. *Honours:* 3 Grammys; 10 Grammy Nominations; 8 times winner, Keyboard Magazine Readers Poll; Daytime Emmy Award, Outstanding Achievement in Music, 1987–88; ASCAP Song of The Year: The Way It Is, 1987; Elvis Award, International Rock Awards, 1991; Album of The Year: Downbeat Readers Poll: Harbour Lights, 1994; Platinum, Gold albums, world-wide. *Memberships:* ASCAP; AFofM. *Leisure interests:* Sports (basketball, running); Reading. *Current Management:* Q-Prime Management, New York. *Address:* PO Box 3545, Williamsburg, VA 23187, USA.

HOROWITZ Adam; b. 31 Oct. 1966, New York, USA. Rapper; Musician. *Career:* Founder member, US rap/rock group The Beastie Boys, 1983–; Appearances include: Support to Madonna, Virgin Tour, 1985; Supports to Run DMC, Raisin' Hell Tour, 1986, Co-headliners with Run DMC, Together Forever Tour, 1987; Reading Festival, 1992; Made horror film, Scared Stupid; Film apperances: Krush Groove; Run-DMC film, Tougher Than Leather. *Recordings:* Albums include: Licensed To Ill, 1986; Paul's Boutique, 1989; Check Your Head, 1992; Ill Communication, 1994; Root Down, 1995; The In Sound From Way Out, 1996; Hello Nasty, 1998; Sounds of Science (compilation), 1999; Singles include: Fight For Your Right To Party, 1987; No Sleep Till Brooklyn, 1987; She's On It, 1987; Hey Ladies, 1989; Pass the Mic, 1992; Jimmy James, 1992; Get It Together/Sabotage, 1994; Sure Shot, 1994; Intergalactic, 1998; Body Movin', 1998; Remote Control, 1999; Alive, 1999. *Current Management:* Gold Mountain Entertainment, 3575 Cahuenga Blvd W, Suite 450, Los Angeles, CA 90068, USA.

HORSLEY Richard; b. 5 Jan. 1970, Chelmsford, Essex, England. Record Co Exec.; Musician (drums); Recording Artist; Prod. *Musical Education:* 10 years drum tuition. *Career:* Underground producer, recording artist under name of Timeslip; Numerous remixes; Private commissioned work; Owner, record label, R H Records. *Recordings:* Kinky and Hypnotiq, 1996. *Memberships:* PPL; PRS; BASCA. *Leisure interests:* Tennis; Working out; Listening to music. *Address:* R H Records, Greatworth House, Greatworth, Banbury, Oxon OX17 2DR, England.

HOTATSU Nami; b. 3 Sept. 1969, Tokyo, Japan. Singer; Songwriter; Musician (piano, keyboards, synthesizer, Irish harp). *Education:* Graduated, Kunitachi College of Music, Tokyo, Japan, 1992; Classical Piano, 4 years old; Musicology, Kumitachi College of Music; Vocal lesson, Japanese Traditional Style and Pop Style. *Career:* Shu Uemura Make Up Installation, 1992; Eden in the Sky, Yellow, 1993–94; Partheno-Jenesis, Ambient Opera, Tokyo, 1995; Earth Festival, Fili Festival, 1996; Haruomi Hosono and Japanese Sea's Mongoloid, 1996; WaterScape, Nagoya, 1996; Earth Sonic, Tokyo, 1996; The World of Shakespeare, Dramatic Reading, Shakespeare Country Park, Chiba, Japan, 1997. *Compositions:* Making Sense of Jewel, 1993; Hotatsu-Nami, 1994; Luna Drifting On the Glittering Waves, 1995; Stranger Than Movies, 1997. *Recording:* Happy Birthday to Me Itaka, 1996. *Membership:* Japan Soundscape Asscn. *Leisure interests:* Movies; Books; Cooking; Ecology; Animals. *Current Management:* Macaroni Tone, #201, 1–5–4 Sakuradai, Nerima-ku, Tokyo 176, Japan. *Address:* #201, 1–5–4 Sakuradai Nerima-ku, Tokyo 176, Japan.

HOTTE Kevin Richard; b. 16 Nov. 1959, Port Colbourne, Ontario, Canada. Composer; Prod. m. 16 Oct. 1982. *Education:* Graphic Arts, Photography, Niagara College. *Musical Education:* Privately trained: drums, percussion, keyboards. *Career:* Owner, Musicom Music Productions; The Sound Kitchen Recording Studio; Creative Images Media; Creative Images, sydicated radio show about photography technique. *Compositions:* Various radio jingles, corporate video scores. *Recording:* Windows (14 song debut album). *Memberships:* SOCAN; ASCAP. *Leisure interests:* Photography; Martial arts; Motor racing. *Address:* St Catharines, Ontario, Canada.

HOUSTON Cissy, (Emily Drinkard); b. 1933, Newark, New Jersey, USA. Singer. 1 d. *Career:* Member, family gospel group Drinkard Singers; Backing singers for numerous artists including: Wilson Pickett; Solomon Burke; Vocalist, Sweet Inspirations, 1967–70; Prolific session singer. *Recordings:* Albums: Cissy Houston, 1977; Warning Danger, 1979; Step Aside For A Lady, 1980; Mama's Cooking, 1987; I'll Take Care of You, 1992;

Face to Face, 1996; He Leadeth Me, 1997; Singles: I'll Be There, 1970; Be My Baby, 1971; Think It Over, 1978; Other albums: with Whitney Houston (her daughter): Whitney Houston, 1985; Whitney, 1987; with Aretha Franklin: Let Me Into Your Life, 1974; Love All The Hurt Away, 1981; Jump To It, 1982; with Van Morrison: Moondance, 1970; No Sheets, 1974; with Diana Ross: Diana's Duets, 1982; Silk Electric, 1982; The Wiz (soundtrack), 1978; with Paul Simon: Paul Simon, 1972; Greatest Hits etc, 1977; with Luther Vandross: Never Too Much, 1981; Forever, For Always, For Love, 1982; Busy Body, 1987; The Night I Fell In Love, 1985; Give Me The Reason, 1987; Other recordings with numerous artists including: Joe Cocker; Judy Collins; Kiki Dee; Jackie De Shannon; Gregg Allman; The Drifters; J Geils Band; Chaka Khan; Don McLean; John Prine; Linda Ronstadt.

HOUSTON Thelma; b. 7 May 1943, Leland, Mississippi, USA. Singer; Actress. *Career:* Singer, gospel group the Art Reynolds Singers, late 1960s; Solo artiste, 1969–; Also recorded with Jerry Butler; Actress, films: Death Scream; Norman... Is That You?; The Seventh Dwarf. *Recordings:* Albums: Sunshower, 1969; Thelma Houston, 1973; Anyway You Like It, 1977; The Devil In Me, 1978; Ready To Roll, 1978; Ride To The Rainbow, 1979; Breakwater Cat, 1980; Never Gonna Be Another One, 1981; I've Got The Music In Me, 1981; Qualifying Heats, 1987; Throw You Down, 1990; The Best of Thelma Houston, 1991; With Jerry Butler: Thelma and Jerry, 1977; Two To One, 1978; Hit singles: Don't Leave Me This Way (No. 1, USA), 1976; If You Feel It, 1981; You Used To Hold Me So Tight, 1984. *Current Management:* Gross Management Organization, 930 Third St, Suite 102, Santa Monica, CA 90403, USA.

HOUSTON Whitney; b. 9 Aug. 1963, Newark, New Jersey, USA. Singer. m. Bobby Brown, 18 July 1992, 1 d. *Musical Education:* Singing lessons with mother, Cissy Houston. *Career:* New Hope Baptist Jr Choir, age 8; Nightclub performances with mother, 1978; Backing vocalist, Chaka Khan and Lou Rawls, 1978; Model, Glamour and Seventeen magazines; Actress, television shows, USA; Solo artiste, 1985–; First US and European tours, 1986; Montreux Rock Festival, 1987; Nelson Mandela Tribute concert, Wembley, 1988; National anthem, Super Bowl XXV, Miami, 1991; Speaker, HIV/AIDs rally, London, 1991; Television specials include: Welcome Home Heroes (return of Gulf troops), 1991; Whitney Houston – This Is My Life, ABC, 1992; Actress, film The Bodyguard, 1992; 87m. albums sold. *Recordings:* Singles include: You Give Good Love, 1985; Saving All My Love For You (No. 1, UK and US), 1985; How Will I Know (No. 1, USA), 1986; Greatest Love of All (No. 1, USA), 1986; I Wanna Dance With Somebody (No. 1, USA and UK), 1987; Didn't We Almost Have It All (No. 1, USA), 1987; So Emotional (No. 1, USA), 1987; Where Do Broken Hearts Go (No. 1, USA), 1988; Love Will Save The Day, 1988; One Moment In Time (No. 1, UK), 1988; I'm Your Baby Tonight (No. 1, USA), 1990; All The Man That I Need (No. 1, USA), 1991; Miracle, 1991; My Name Is Not Susan, 1991; I Will Always Love You (No. 1 in 11 countries), 1992; I'm Every Woman, 1993; I Have Nothing, 1993; Run To You, 1993; Queen of the Night, 1994; Something In Common, with Bobby Brown 1994; Exhale (Shoop Shoop), 1995; Count On Me, with CeCe Winans, 1996; Why Does It Hurt So Bad, 1996; Step by Step, 1997; I Believe In You and Me, 1997; When You Believe, with Mariah Carey, 1998; It's Not Right But It's Okay, 1999; My Love Is Your Love, 1999; I Learned from the Best, 1999; If I Told You That, with George Michael, 2000; Could I Have This Kiss Forever, with Enrique Iglesias, 2000; Heartbreak Hotel, with Faith Evans and Kelly Price, 2000; Albums: Whitney Houston, 1985; Whitney, 1987; I'm Your Baby Tonight, 1990; My Love Is Your Love, 1998; The Greatest Hits, 2000; Love, Whitney, 2001; Film soundtrack: The Bodyguard (No. 1 in 20 countries), 1992; Also featured on: Life's A Party, Michael Zager Band; Duet with Teddy Pendergrass, Hold Me, 1984; Duet with Aretha Franklin, It Isn't, It Wasn't, It Ain't Ever Gonna Be, 1989. *Honours include:* 3 Grammy Awards, including Grammy Award, Female R & B Vocal Performance, It's Not Right But It's Okay, 2000; 7 American Music Awards; Emmy, 1986; Songwriter's Hall of Fame, 1990; Numerous Gold and Platinum discs. *Current Management:* Nippy Inc, 2160 N Central Rd, Fort Lee, NJ 07024, USA.

HOVMAN Klavs; b. 27 Oct. 1957, Aarhus, Denmark. Musician (double bass, bass). 1 d., 1 s. *Career:* Member, Savage Rose, 1991–92; Played with numerous jazz/rock bands; Toured with: Ernie Wilkins Almost Big Band; Horace Parlan; Toots Thielemans; Lee Konitz; Svend Asmussen; Bassist with Etta Cameron's jazz and gospel groups, 1980–; Gospel concerts, Europe, 1990's; Member, Marilyn Mazur's groups Future Song and Pulse Unit. *Compositions:* Music for New Music Orchestra, Copenhagen Jazz Festival Event. *Recordings:* Album: Baraban, Peter Danemo, 1991; Månebarn, Savage Rose, 1992; Marilyn Mazur's Future Song, 1992; Echoez Of..., Harry Beckett and Pierre Dorge, 1992; Being, Lotte Anker/Mette Peterson Quintet, 1993; Savage Rose 25, Savage Rose, 1993; Gospel Concert, Etta Cameron, 1995; Circular Chant, Marilyn Mazur/Pulse Unit, 1995.

HOWARD Dominic James; b. 12 July 1977. Musician (drums). *Career:* Spent pre-teen years in Rotherham, England; Formed group Gothic Plague in adopted hometown of Teignmouth, aged 13; Group became Fixed Penalty then Rocket Baby Dolls before finally settling on name Muse; Released two 1000-copy EPs on UK independent label Dangerous; Signed to Madonna's US label Maverick following lauded UK In The City '98 and New York CMJ festival appearances; Rapid rise to fame followed; Live shows include: Ill-fated Woodstock '99 US festival; Headline slots at UK's Leeds, Reading and T In The Park festivals, 2000; European tours, 2001. *Recordings:* Albums: Showbiz, 1999; Origin of Symmetry, 2001; Singles: Muse EP, 1998; Muscle Museum EP, Uno, Cave, 1999; Sunburn, Unintended, 2000; Plug In Baby, New Born, Bliss, Hyper Music/Feeling Good, 2001. *Honours:* NME Award, Best Newcomer, 2000; Kerrang! Award, Best British Band, 2001. *Current Management:* Taste Media/SJP Management, 263 Putney Bridge Rd, London, SW15 2PU, England. *Internet:* www.muse-official.com.

HOWARD Dominic Richard Vincent; b. 3 Dec. 1965, Birmingham, England. Musician (bass guitar). m. Lorraine Rogers, 12 May 1995. *Education:* North East Surrey College of Technology. *Musical Education:* Self-taught. *Career:* Televison appearances: with Paul Harris: Top of The Pops, Song For Europe '95; with B A Robertson: Pebble Mill; Radio appearances: BBC Radio 1, 2; BBC GLR; BBC Southern Counties; BBC Radio Coventry; Mercury; BFBS World-wide Network. *Recordings:* Paul Harris: Spinning Away; Lee Collinson: Slip The Driver A Fiver. *Membership:* Musicians' Union.

HOWARD John; b. 9 April 1953, Bury, Lancashire, England. Record Co Exec.; Musician (keyboards). *Education:* Art College. *Musical Education:* Private piano tuition, age 7–16. *Career:* Songwriter; Singer; Signed to CBS Records, 1973; Moved to Ariola Records with Trevor Horn, 1977; Returned to CBS with Nicky Graham, 1980; Member of Quiz, with Steve Levine and Graham Broad, 1981–83; Label Manager, Conifer Records, 1985; A & R Manager, Pickwick Records, 1986; Strategic Marketing Manager, MCA Records, 1993; A & R Director, Carlton Records, 1995. *Recordings:* Albums: Kid In A Big World, 1975; On Reflection, 1993; Singles: with Quiz: It's You I Want; And The World; Solo: Nothing More To Say; Songs: Casting Shadows, for film Open Season; with Dave Willetts: Stages of Love; with Stephanie Lawrence: Footlights; with Des O'Connor: Blue Days; International Music Development, Reader's Digest, 1997. *Leisure interests:* Reading biographies; Music; Writing. *Address:* Reader's Digest, 11 Westferry Circus, Canary Wharf, London E14 4HE, England.

HOWARD Johnny; b. 5 Feb. 1931, Croydon, Surrey, England. Bandleader; Musician (saxophone). m. 28 Sept. 1970, 1 s., 1 d. *Musical Education:* Private tuition. *Career:* Professional big band leader, 1959–; Worked Mecca Dancehall circuit until 1967; Radio broadcasts, including 5 years on Easybeat, own lunchtime show, One O'Clock Jump; Television includes: Come Dancing, 1960s-70s; Played corporate and conference engagements, 1980s-90s. *Recordings:* More than a dozen albums and singles, 1960s-70s; Hit single: Rinky Dink (used by Radio Caroline as theme tune). *Honour:* Carl Alan Award, Britain's Best Band, 1967. *Leisure interest:* Design. *Current Management:* Fanfare 3000. *Address:* The Folly, Pinner Hill Rd, Pinner, Middlesex HA5 3YQ, England.

HOWARD (Kevin) Robert; b. 31 Oct. 1962, Huddersfield, England. Engineering Technician; Semi-Professional Musician (drums). m. Nicola Jane, 24 June 1989, 2 s. *Education:* HNC, Industrial Measurement and Control. *Musical Education:* Studied privately with Geoff Myers, Leeds, from age 13, drums. *Career:* Les Howard's Northern Dance Orchestra (NDO), 1988–94; Currently with Herb Miller Orchestra, touring Great Britain and Europe, 1996–; Radio appearances: Several on BBC Radio 2, Jazz Parade; Radio 2 Arts Programme; Appearances at many jazz festivals around Britain. *Recordings:* with Rod Mason's Concept, 1984–88; Alan Skidmore, 1993; Memphis Bell Orchestra, 1995; New Squadronairs Orchestra, 1998; played with many bands, eg Syd Lawrence Orchestra, Andy Prior Orchestra, Andy Ross Orchestra. *Membership:* Musicians' Union. *Leisure interests:* Shooting; Sea Fishing; Conservation; DIY (home and cars). *Address:* 9 Golcar Brow Rd, Meltham, Huddersfield, West Yorkshire HD7 3LD, England.

HOWARD Rex; b. 23 July 1930, Thunder Bay, Ontario, Canada. Vocalist; Musician (pedal steel guitar, dobro). m. Candice James, 12 May 1990, 1 s., 2 d. *Education:* 1 year university. *Career:* Member, Bootleg, support tour with John Anderson; Toured USA, as opening act and steel player and sideman with: Hank Williams Sr; Ernest Tubb; Dave Dudley; Performing in Western Canada with the band Saddlestone. *Recordings:* Little Peg and The Blind Man; A Heartache As Big As Texas; Roadside Ride; If Heaven's Missin' An Angel; An Old Dusty Heartache. *Honours:* Instrumentalist of The Year, SCCMA; Male Vocalist of Year, 1993. *Memberships:* SOCAN; AFofM; CIRPA. *Leisure interests:* Model ship building; Painting; Creative Art; Songwriting. *Current Management:* Silver Bow Management. *Address:* 6260–130-St, Surrey, British Columbia V3X 1R6, Canada.

HOWE Bob; b. 22 Dec. 1956. Musician (Guitars, Harmonica); Singer; Composer. m. Karen Versace, 21 Nov. 1992. *Career:* Australian Cabaret Artist and Session Musician; Musical Director for Frank Ifield, 1984–88; Guy Mitchell, 1991; Portrayed Paul McCartney, Australian Production of

Lennon – The Musical, 1986–87; Toured with Countless Australian Artists, Lucky Starr, Slim Dusty. *Compositions:* White Man's Blues; Some People Change. *Recordings:* Contributor to: John Chester Love in the Meantime; Waltzing Matilda, Diana Trask; Cross Country, Sarah Jory; The Fire Still Burns, Frank Ifield. *Publication:* Cowboys in Cyberspace, 1997. *Honour:* Most Popular Guitarist, Musician and Newcomer, Southern Hemisphere Country Music Awards, 1982. *Membership:* Music Arrangers' Guild of Australia. *Leisure interest:* Internet Web-design. *Address:* PO Box 7341, Bondi Beach, NSW 2026, Australia.

HOWE Brian; b. 22 July 1957, Portsmouth, Hampshire, England. Singer. 1 s., 1 d. *Career:* Member, Ted Nugent Band; Lead singer, rock group Bad Company, 1986–93; US Holy Water tour with Damn Yankees, 1990–91; Last Rebel Here Comes Trouble US Tour, supporting Lynyrd Skynyrd, 1993; Solo Artist, 1993–; Numerous television appearances including: MTV, VH1, Tonight Show, Letterman. *Compositions:* Co-writer and performer as lead singer on How About That, the number 11 Song of All Time in 100 year Billboard Chart Edition in Album Rock. *Recordings:* Albums: Penetrator, Ted Nugent, 1984; Fame and Fortune, 1986; Dangerous Age, 1988; Holy Water, 1990; Here Comes Trouble, 1992; Best of Bad Company Live, 1993; Solo album: Tangled in Blue, 1997; Hit Singles include: Shake It Up, 1986; Holy Water, 1990; If You Needed Somebody, 1991; Walk Through Fire, 1991; How About That, 1992; This Could Be The One, 1992. *Membership:* NARAS, Grammy Voting Member. *Leisure interests:* Boating; Football; Portsmouth Football Club supporter. *Current Management:* TopNotch Entertainment Corp, Box 1515, Sanibel Island, FL 33957–1515, USA.

HOWE Ronald; b. 7 Dec. 1957, Leatherhead, Surrey, England. Musician (tenor saxophone). m. Carolanne Edge, 6 July 1989, 1 d. *Musical Education:* Private tuition, adult education, Goldsmith's, London. *Career:* Concerts, tours with many bands; Large amount of studio work and recording; Toured and recorded with: Fools Can Dance; Worked on Cure album; Worked live with Damned; Currently with The Bucket Band; Videos; Major venues include: Hammersmith Palais; Teaching saxophone (theory, performance, improvisation); Brass/horns arrangement; Music transcription. *Recordings:* A Night Like This; The Cure; Box Office Poison; Beyond The Twilight Zone; Checkmate; Numerous others. *Memberships:* Musicians' Union; PAMRA. *Leisure interests:* Ex-powerlifter; Photography; Trees. *Address:* 7 Wentworth, Aurum Close, Horley, Surrey RH6 9BE, England.

HOWE Steve; b. 8 April 1947, London, England. Musician (guitar). *Career:* Member, The Syndicats; The In Crowd; Tomorrow; Bodast; UK progressive rock group Yes, 1970–81; Concerts included: Queen Elizabeth Hall, London; Reading Festival; Madison Square Garden; Asia, 1981–90; World-wide tours, including Asia In Asia concert, Tokyo, Japan (broadcast by MTV to audience of 20m.), 1983; Member, GTR, 1986–91; Rejoined Yes, 1991–; Concerts include: Yesshows '91 – Round The World In 80 Dates Tour, 1991. *Recordings:* Albums: with Yes: Time and A Word, 1970; The Yes Album, 1971; Fragile, 1971; Close To The Edge, 1972; Yessongs, 1973; Tales From The Topographic Ocean, 1973; Relayer, 1974; Yesterdays, 1975; Going For The One, 1977; Tormato, 1978; Yesshows, 1981; Union, 1991; Yesstory, 1991; Symphonic Music of Yes, 1993; History of The Future, 1993; Open Your Eyes, 1998; Ladder, 1999; with Asia: Asia, 1982; Alpha, 1983; Astra, 1985; Aqua, 1992; Archiva Vol. 1, 1996; Anthology, 1999; with GTR: GTR, 1986: Solo albums: Beginnings, 1975; Steve Howe Album, 1979; Turbulence, 1991; The Grand Scheme of Things, 1993; Mothballs, 1994; Not Necessarily Acoustic, 1994; Seraphim, 1995; Voyagers, 1995; Homebrew, 1996; Quantum Guitar, 1998; Pulling Strings, 1999; Portraits of Bob Dylan, 1999; With Anderson Bruford Wakeman Howe: Anderson Bruford Wakeman Howe, 1989; Singles include: with Yes: Roundabout; Wondrous Stories; Going For The One; Brother of Mine; Lift Me Up; with Asia: Heat of The Moment; Only Time Will Tell; Don't Cry; with GTR: When The Heart Rules The Mind; The Hunter; Solo albums include: Homebrew 2, 2000; Natural Timbre, 2001. *Contributions to:* Welcome To The Pleasuredome, Frankie Goes To Hollywood, 1984; A Secret Wish, Propaganda, 1985. *Honours:* Gold Ticket, Madison Square Garden, with Yes, 1978; Top New Artist, Top Album, with Asia, Billboard magazine, 1982. *Current Management:* Tiz Hay Management, 44 Oswald Close, Leatherhead, Surrey KT22 9UG, England.

HOWELL Mark; b. 11 July 1952, USA. Composer; Performer; Musician (Guitar, Trumpet). m. Stephanie Artz. *Education:* BA, University of Southern Mississippi; MA, SUNY, Stony Brook, NY. *Career:* Stop at Nothing, The Kitchen, 1987; Zero Pop, 1986–96; In Memory, 1989; Gt Schubertide, 1997. *Compositions:* History of Magic, 1990; For A Birthday, 1996; To The Heart, 1997. *Recordings:* Include, Swimman, Better Than Death Twin Tone, 1985; North America, Moers, 1986; Glows in the Dark, Zero Pop, 1992; Parts and Labour, Rough Trade, 1992; Quartets, 1994. *Publication:* Locronets: An Automatic Sketching Technique, The Improviser, 1989. *Memberships:* BMI; Society for Ethnomusicology. *Leisure interests:* Painting; Carpentry; Swimming; Yoga. *Address:* 344 E Sixth St, Apt #2D, New York, NY 10003, USA.

HOWELL-JONES Richard Mark; b. 18 April 1960, Altrincham, Cheshire, England. Actor; Musician (drums, percussion); Singer. *Education:* Manchester Polytechnic. *Musical Education:* Self-taught. *Career:* Drummer, vocalist, with R & B band Flat Hedgehog, 1981–83; Theatre performance band Celebration of Joe, 1984–85; Roy Woodward Big Band, 1985–87; R & B band The Shades, 1990–91; Television: King Lear, C4, 1983; Dear Ladies, BBC TV, 1984; Films: The Last Meeting, 1996; Currently touring Dusty Pens by Derek Martin. *Recording:* Celebration of Joe, with Brian Roberts, 1984. *Memberships:* Musicians' Union; Equity. *Leisure interests:* Aero-modelling; Reading; Philosophy; Conversation; Computer programming; Keeping fit. *Address:* 18 Wardle Rd, Sale, Cheshire M33 3DB, England.

HOWLETT Liam; Songwriter; Musician. *Career:* Member, The Prodigy, 1990–; Festival appearances include: Glastonbury, 1995, 1997; V97, 1997; Lollapalooza, 1997. *Recordings:* Albums: Experience, 1992; Music for the Jilted Generation (No. 1, UK), 1994; The Fat of the Land (No. 1, UK), 1997; The Dirtchamber Sessions, 1999; Hit Singles: Charly, 1991; Everybody In the Place, 1991; Fire, 1992; Out of Space, 1992; Wind It Up, 1993; One Love, 1993; No Good (Start the Dance), 1994; Voodoo People, 1994; Poison, 1995; Firestarter (No. 1, UK), 1996; Breathe (No. 1, UK), 1996; Smack My Bitch Up, 1997; Poison, 1997. *Honours:* Mercury Music Prize nominations, 1994, 1997; BRIT Awards, Best British Dance Act, 1997, 1998. *Current Management:* Midi Management Ltd. *Address:* The Old Barn, Jenkins Lane, Great Hallingbury, Essex CM22 7QL, England.

HOYDAL Annika; b. Tórshaun, The Faroe Islands. m. Klavs Lockwood, 25 June 1994. *Education:* Graduated, Actress, Statens Teaterskole, Copenhagen, Denmark, 1973. *Career:* Debut: The Faroe Islands, 1966; Freelance Actress and Singer, throughout Scandinavia. *Compositions include:* Mit Eget Land; Min Krop; Hjemme; Drímmen; Bekendelse; Mírket; Lammet; Aldan, Dråben; Kasper; Til Dans; Tjipp; Munnur; Á Palli; Á Havi; Morgun; Snigil; Alt; Dulcinea; Hvalspýggja; Taraloppa; Ljós; Kópagenta; Dreymahav; Inn Móti Landi; Marmennil; Farin; Sjólátin; Nú Sigla...; Tid; Find en Sten. *Recordings include:* Til Børn og Vaksin, 1975; Annika og Jógvan, 1979; Spor í Sjónum, 1983; Dulcinea, 1991; Havid/The Ocean, 1997. *Honour:* Melodi Grand Prix for Faroe Islands, Denmark, 1979. *Memberships:* Dansk Artist Forbund; Danish Jazz Beat and Folk Music Composers Organization; Dansk Solist-Forbund. *Current Management:* Arte Booking, Copenhagen. *Address:* Admiralgade 22 2 tv, 1066 Copenhagen K, Denmark. *E-mail:* hoydal@image.dk.

HRADECKY Emil; b. 25 Feb. 1953, Prague, Czech Republic. Teacher; Composer. m. Alexandra Hradecká, 10 Nov. 1978. *Education:* Prague Conservatory. *Compositions:* (classical) Love Songs, song cycle for tenor and piano; String Quartet; Meditace per flauto solo; Melancolic danza a rondo, flute quartet; Nine variations and fugue on a theme by Mozart, piano; Suite for flute and violin. *Recordings:* Omnis sermo Dei ignitus; Ne glorieris in crastinum ignorans; Principium sapientiae timor Domini, for mixed boys and male voice choir. *Publications:* Little Jazz Album; Little Jazz Pieces for 20 Fingers; Dances For The Guitar; Jazz Flute and MC; Jazz Trumpet and MC; Jazz Trombone and MC; Von Blues Bis Disco and MC; Jazz Etudes; Der Kinderkarneval; Kleine Jazz-Stücke Für 20 Finger; Zwei-Seiten Stücke; Klienes Jazz-Album; Tanz-Kompositionen Für Vier Hände; Tänze für Gitarre; Fox-Polka; Swing-Polka; Der Sonnige Rag; We Play The Piano According To The Chord Marks. *Honours:* Musical Prize, Children's Choirs, Prague, 1995, 1997. *Leisure interest:* Sport. *Address:* Konselská 11, 180 00 Prague 8, Czech Republic.

HUCKNALL Mick; b. 8 June 1960, Manchester, England. Singer; Songwriter. *Career:* Formed early band, Frantic Elevators, 1979; Formed Simply Red, essentially a solo career with changing band members; Numerous hit singles, television appearances; Numerous tours and festival dates world-wide; Founder, Blood and Fire label, dedicated to vintage reggae tracks. *Recordings:* Singles include: Money's Too Tight to Mention, 1985; Holding Back the Years (No. 1, USA), 1986; Ev'ry Time We Say Goodbye, 1987; The Right Thing, 1987; It's Only Love, 1989; If You Don't Know Me By Now (No. 1, USA), 1989; A New Flame, 1989; Something Got Me Started, 1991; Stars, 1991; For Your Babies, 1992; Thrill Me, 1992; Your Mirror, 1992; Fairground (No. 1, UK), 1995; Remembering The First Time, 1995; Never Never Love, 1996; We're In This Together, 1996; Angel, 1996; To Be Free; Night Nurse, with Sly and Robbie, 1997; Say You Love Me, 1998; The Air That I Breathe, 1998; Ghetto Girl, 1998; Ain't That A Lot of Love, 1999; Your Eyes, 2000; Albums: Picture Book, 1985; Early Years, 1987; Men and Women, 1987; A New Flame (No. 1, UK), 1989; Stars (No. 1, UK), 1991; 12ers, 1995; Life (No. 1, UK), 1995; Greatest Hits (No. 1, UK), 1996; Blue, 1998; Love and The Russian Winter, 1999; It's Only Love, 2001. *Honours include:* BRIT Awards, Best British Group; Best British Male Solo Artist, 1993. *Internet:* www.simplyred.com.

HUDSON Colin; b. 8 Dec. 1950, Tilbury. DJ; Prod. 1 d. *Education:* Private. *Career:* Audio De Luxe, 1984–92; Colin Hudson, DJ; Talis Mantra, New Band. *Compositions:* 60 Seconds; We Are Not Alone; The Damn Thing Keeps Kickin; Stones. *Recordings:* 60 Seconds; We Are Not Alone; The

Damn Thing Keep Kickin; Stones. *Honours:* Blackechoes Club DJ, 1983, 1984; Blues and Soul Club DJ, 1985, 1986. *Membership:* Musicians Union. *Leisure interests:* Books; Films. *Current Management:* Midi Management Ltd. *Address:* The Old Barn, Kenkins Lane, Gt Hallingbury, Essex CM22 7QL.

HUGGETT Mark J; b. 3 July 1961, Birmingham, England. Musician (drums). *Education:* BA Fine Art, Reading University. *Career:* Concerts: Italia '90 (official Irish rock promotion with Pepe jeans); Reading Festival, 1992; Fleadh Festival, 1992; Television and radio includes: BBC2 Taking Liberties; MTV; RTE, Ireland; Dave Fanning, Irish radio; RTI, Italy; Italian radio; Simon Mayo, BBC Radio One. *Recordings:* Albums: Red Harvest: Strange; Saved; Singles: World Won't Listen (playlisted Radio One); Dr Millar and The Cute Hoors: Romance In A Flat (number 12, Irish charts); Currently recording with Chant. *Leisure interests:* Film; Animation. *Current Management:* Johnny Rogan. *Address:* 101/103 Devonport Rd, Shepherds Bush, London W12 8PB, England.

HUGHES Christoper Merrick; b. 3 March 1953. Record Prod.; Musician (drums). m. Elizabeth, 2 s., 1 d. *Career:* Drummer, Adam and the Ants. *Compositions:* Co-Work, Everybody Wants To Rule The World. *Recordings:* Kings of The Wild Frontier; Songs From The Big Chair; Everybody Wants to Rule The World. *Honours:* Record Producer of the Year Award, 1981. *Current Management:* Isisglow Ltd, The Wool Hall, Castle Corner, Beckington, Somerset, BA3 6TA.

HUGHES David Alan; b. 25 April 1960, Birkenhead, England. Composer; Musician (keyboards); Prod. m. 25 April 1984, 1 s., 1 d. *Musical Education:* Self-taught. *Career:* World-wide tours, OMD and Thomas Lang; Founder member, electronic duo, Dalek 1; Composer, film scores with composer John Murphy; Television appearances include: The Tube; Wired; Top of The Pops; Old Grey Whistle Test. *Compositions:* Film scores: IlPaladini; CHUD; Hearts and Armour; Film scores with John Murphy: Leon The Pig Farmer; Feast At Midnight; Solitaire For Two; Welcome To The Terrordome; Beyond Bedlam; Body Memories; Dinner In Purgatory; Destroying Angels; Proteus; Giving Tongue; Clockwork Mice; For television: White Men Are Cracking Up; All The President's Women. *Recordings:* As composer, producer: 4 albums with Thomas Lang. *Memberships:* Musicians' Union; PRS; BASCA. *Leisure interests:* Football; Computing. *Current Management:* Soundtrack Music Management. *Address:* 22 Ives St, Chelsea, London SW3 2ND, England.

HUGHES David James; b. 1 June 1950, Rotherham, Yorkshire, England. Musician (guitar, cello); Composer; Arranger. *Education:* Art School, Fine Art, Sir John Cass, Goldsmiths. *Musical Education:* Self-taught guitar; Cello study with Alfia Bekova. *Career:* Channel 9 (band); Roy Hill Band; Television, radio, tours: EMI Outbar, TV Pebble Mill At One; 73 children's shows; Radio One Live. *Compositions:* Disco Eddy; Away From The Heat; When The Bad Men Come; The Lion Within; Radio One Chart Show (intro music and chart read-out underlay). *Honour:* Arts Council GLAA Award, Jazz Musician of the Year, 1980. *Address:* 7A Cleveland Rd, London N1 3ES, England.

HUGHES Garry; Prod.; Programmer. *Career:* Currently working with Trevor Horn; Recent production work includes: Tina Turner, Unfinished Sympathy (Wildest Dreams), album; Suggs: Cecilia; Camden Town; Selected programming and playing credits: Bjork, Debut Album; Gabrielle, Forget About the World; Charles and Eddie: Would I Lie To You; Duophonic (first album); Chocolate Milk (2nd album); D Mob: It's Time to Get Funky; Put Your Hands Together; The Way of the World; Come On and get My Love; Bayete and Jabu Khanyil: Africa Unite; Vitamin C: Vitamin C; Genesis: Turn It On Again; Pokemon: The First Movie. *Address:* SARM Productions, SP2 Holdings Ltd, The Blue Building, 42/46 St Luke's Mews, London W11 1DG, England.

HUGHES James William; b. 18 May 1960, Liverpool, England. Musician (drums, percussion); Backing Vocalist. 1 d. *Musical Education:* Studied with Red Carter, Liverpool. *Career:* Member, Black; Tours of Europe and Japan; Member, The Darling Buds; Tour of US; Television appearances: Top of The Pops; Wogan; Jim'll Fix It; The Chart Show; The Roxy; The Tube; Various children's programmes. *Recordings:* Albums: Wonderful Life, Black; The Darling Buds of May, two albums. *Honour:* Gold album, Wonderful Life. *Membership:* Musicians' Union. *Leisure interests:* Making video films; Making music. *Address:* 247 Fernhill Rd, Bootle, Merseyside L20 0AQ, England.

HUGO Chad, (Chase); b. Virginia, USA. Prod.; Remixer. *Career:* Formed The Neptunes production duo with school friend Pharrell Williams; One of the most successful production teams, 2000–01; Produced: Jay-Z; Kelis; Britney Spears; Mystikal; Formed recording act N.E.R.D. (Nobody Ever Really Dies), 2001; Collaborations: Kelis; Usher; Ol' Dirty Bastard; Ludacris. *Recordings:* Albums: In Search Of... (with N.E.R.D.), 2001; Singles: Lapdance (with N.E.R.D.), 2001. *Honour:* Source Award,

Producer of The Year, The Neptunes, 2001. *Address:* c/o Virgin, 304 Park Ave S, Fifth Floor, New York, USA.

HULAN Miroslav; b. 23 April 1959, Brno, Czech Republic. Guitar, Mandolin Player. m. Drahomira Spidlikova, 4 July 1981, 2 s. *Career:* Debut: With Group Poutnici, 1980; Member, Group Poutnici, 1980–; Duo with Michal Hromcik, 1995-. *Composition:* Pocta Davidovi. *Recordings:* Supraphon: Poutnici, 1987; Wayfaring Strangers, 1989; Chromi kone, 1990; The Days of Auld Lang Syne, 1991; Poutnici Live, 1991; GZ: Je to v nas, 1992; UMG: Pisne brnenskych kovboju, 1994; GZ: Co uz je pryc, 1997. *Publications:* Guitar School for Beginners, 1993; Guitar School for Advanced, 1997. *Honours:* Best Non-American Bluegrass Recordings, 1989, 1990. *Membership:* Czech Bluegrass Music Asscn. *Leisure interests:* Computers; Bikes. *Address:* Blatnicka 3, 628 00 Brno, Czech Republic.

HULJIC Tonci; b. 29 Oct. 1961, Split, Croatia. Composer; Prod. m. Vjekosava Huljic, 5 Sept. 1987, 1 s., 1 d. *Musical Education:* High School of Music, piano. *Career:* Leader, composer, most popular group in Croatia: Magazin; 15 albums (9m. copies sold); 7 major tours; Many television shows; Tours: Russia: USA; Canada; 20 Gold, Platinum, Diamond records with Magazin and other popular Croatian singers; Eurovision Song Contest, sixth place with song Nostalgia, 1995; Many Grand prix in music festivals, Croatia, 1995–96; European promotion of trilogy; Songs published in Benelux countries, Scandinavia; US; South Africa. *Honours:* Composer of The Year, 1988, 1989, 1994; Special Prize for Record Sales. *Memberships:* Croatian Music Society; President, Croatian Music Union; Croatian Composers Asscn; Rotary Club. *Current Management:* Skalind Production, Croatia; Bim, Slavia Publishing, Asse, Belgium.

HUME Alastair Martin Roderick; b. 1 Aug. 1958, London, England. Musician (flute, saxophone, keyboards); Arranger; Teacher. m. Vanessa V A Cowlard, 22 July 1989, 1 d. *Musical Education:* Guildhall School of Music and Drama; Homerton College, Cambridge. *Career:* Cambridge Footlights, 1979; De Blahdeblah Jazz Orchestra, 1979; MD, Littlehampton Community School Big Band, 1982–86; Royal Oman Symphony Orchestra Instructor, 1986–88; Backed Penny Lane and Gordon Scott; Taverners Big Band, German tour, 1983, 1996; MD, Swing Bin and The Liners, 1990–; Tours: Canada, 1991; Lake Geneva, 1994; Lake Garda/Venice, 1996; Brass Roots; Choral conductor, Gli Amici Della Musica, 1977–83; Poole Arts Centre, 10th anniversary concert, 1979. *Honours:* GGSM Hons; Cert Ed Cantab. *Membership:* Musicians' Union. *Leisure interests:* Cricket; Golf; Video; Winemaking; DIY. *Address:* 3 Donnelly Rd, Tuckton, Bournemouth, Dorset BH6 5NW, England.

HUMPERDINCK Engelbert, (Arnold George Dorsey); b. 3 May 1936, Madras, India. Singer. m. Patricia Healey, 1963, 2 s., 1 d. *Career:* Originally billed as Gerry Dorsey; Television includes: Oh Boy, 1950s; Changed name, late 1960s; Own series, The Engelbert Humperdinck Show, 1970; Regular concerts, US and UK. *Recordings:* Hit singles: Release Me (No. 1, UK), 1967; There Goes My Everything (No. 2, UK), 1967; The Last Waltz, 1967; Other hits include: Am I That Easy To Forget; The Way It Used To Be; Les Bicyclettes De Belsize; A Man Without Love; Winter World of Love; Albums include: Release Me, 1967; The Last Waltz, 1967; A Man Without Love, 1968; Engelbert, 1969; Engelbert Humperdinck, 1969; We Made It Happen, 1970; Another Time Another Place, 1971; Live At The Riviera, 1972; Greatest Hits, 1974; Getting Sentimental, 1975; Remember I Love You, 1987; The Engelbert Humperdinck Collection, 1987; Hello Out There, 1992; Golden Love; Ultimate; King of Hearts; Last of The Romantics; with Tom Jones: Back To Back, 1993; Love Unchained, 1995; Lovely Way to Spend an Evening, 1997; In the Still of the Night, 1999; The Ultimate Collection, 2000. *Honours:* Georgie Award, American Guild of Variety Artists, Best Singer, 1978; Over 50 Gold and 15 Platinum discs. *Current Management:* 3D Management, PO Box 16817, Beverly Hills, CA 90209–2817, USA.

HUNT Bill; b. 23 May 1947, Birmingham, England. Music Educator; Musician. *Musical Education:* Birmingham School of Music. *Career:* Original member, ELO; First ELO tour, Italy; Original member, Wizzard; Video and live performances with Raymond Froggatt. *Compositions:* Co-wrote songs for Slade (with Dave Hill). *Recordings:* First album and single, ELO; First album and hit singles, Wizzard; Various tracks, Slade and Slade II; Miles Hunt; Featured on ELO compilation, Flashback, 2000. *Honour:* Hon. Treasurer, Don Arden Veterans Appreciation Society. *Leisure interests:* River cruisin'; Boozin'. *Address:* Bromsgrove, Worcestershire, England.

HUNT Brian George Edward; b. 7 June 1937. Singer; Musician. 1 s. *Musical Education:* Self-taught; Clavissimo Music School, Antwerp, Belgium. *Career:* Guitarist, Group, The Blue Tones, 1960s'; International Country, Folk, Soft Rock, Ballad Music; Television and Radio in Belgium; Support Act to Steeleye Span and Frank Ifield. *Recordings:* Louisa From Louisiana; Sing This Song With Me Tonight. *Honour:* Award, Assistant in the Promotion of Country Music World-wide, 1981. *Membership:* Country Music Asscn. *Leisure interests:* Old Cars; Reading. *Address:* Karel De Preterlei 212, 2140 Borgerhout, Belgium.

HUNT Crispin; b. London, England. Musician (Guitar); Vocalist. *Career:* Member, Longpigs. *Recordings:* Singles: Happy Again; She Said; Jesus Christ; Far; On and On; Lost Myself; Blue Skies; The Frank Sonata; Albums: The Sun is Often Out; Mobile Home.

HUNT Kevin Tony; b. 17 Dec. 1962, Great Yarmouth, Norfolk, England. Musician (drums). *Musical Education:* Self-taught. *Career:* Member, group Runestaff, 1981–86; Released self-titled album and 2 singles; Extensive radio, television and live appearances; Member, Thieving Gypsies, 1991–; Recently changed name to Sliver; Debut single/album, 1996; Extensive work with Princes Trust charity, including work with Phil Collins. *Recordings:* with Runestaff: Album: Runestaff; Singles: Road To Ruin; Do-It!. *Memberships:* PRS; MCPS. *Leisure interests:* Travel; Walking; Camping; Coarse fishing. *Current Management:* John Giacobbi, Entertainment Law Associates, 9 Carnaby St, London W1V 1PG, England.

HUNTER Ian; b. 3 June 1946, Shrewsbury, Shropshire, England. *Career:* Singer, Mott The Hoople, 1969–74; Solo artiste, 1975–; Performances include: Royal Albert Hall, London, 1971; Woodstock of The West Festival, Los Angeles, 1972. *Recordings:* Hit singles include: with Mott The Hoople: All The Young Dudes, 1972; All The Way From Memphis, 1973; Roll Away The Stone, 1973; Solo: Once Bitten Twice Shy, 1975; Albums: with Mott The Hoople: Mott The Hoople, 1969; Mad Shadows, 1970; Wild Life, 1971; Brain Capers, 1971; All The Young Dudes, 1972; Rock 'n' Roll Queen, 1972; The Hoople, 1974; Mott The Hoople – Live, 1974; Solo albums: Ian Hunter, 1975; All American Alien Boy, 1976; Overnight Angels, 1977; You're Never Alone With A Schizophrenic, 1979; Shades of Ian Hunter, 1979; Ian Hunter Live/Welcome To The Club, 1980; Short Back and Sides, 1981; All The Good Ones Are Taken, 1983; YUIOrta, 1990; Dirty Laundry, 1995; Artful Dodger, 1997; Welcome to the Club, 1998; Missing In Action, 2000; Rant, 2001. *Publication:* Diary of a Rock 'n' Roll Star, Ian Hunter.

HUNTER James; b. 2 Oct. 1962, Colchester, Essex, England. Singer; Musician (guitar, harmonica); Actor. *Career:* Formerly performed as, Howlin' Wilf; Television appearances: The Tube, 01 For London, and Wide Angle; Radio guest on Andy Kershaw and Paul Jones shows; Theatre appearance in Buddy; Toured UK, Europe and USA as guest with Van Morrison R & B Revue. *Recordings:* Albums: Cry Wilf, Howlin' Wilf and The Vee-Jays; A Night In San Francisco, Van Morrison; Believe What I Say featuring Van Morrison and Doris Troy, 1996; Kick It Around, 2001; EPs and mini-albums include: Blue Men Sing The Whites; Shake Your Hips; Six By Six; Days Like This; Duet with Van Morrison. *Memberships:* Musicians' Union; PRS; Equity. *Current Management:* Frank Warren, Matters Musical. *Address:* The Loft, Rear of 8 West St, Dorking, Surrey RH4 1BL, England.

HUNTER Mark; b. 5 Nov. 1968, England. Musician (keyboards). *Career:* Member, James, 1990–; Numerous tours, festival dates and television appearances. *Recordings:* Singles: Come Home, 1990; Sit Down (No. 2, UK), 1991; Sound, 1991; Born of Frustration, 1992; Sometimes (Lester Piggott), 1993; Laid, 1993; Say Something, 1994; She's A Star, 1997; Tomorrow, 1997; Destiny Calling, 1998; Sit Down '98, 1998; I Know What I'm Here For, 1999; Just Like Fred Astaire, 1999; We're Going To Miss You, 1999; Getting Away With It (All Messed Up), 2001; Albums: Gold Mother; Seven, 1992; Laid, 1993; Wah Wah, live, 1994; Whiplash, 1997; The Best of James, 1998; Millionaires, 1999; Pleased To Meet You, 2001.

HUNTER Robert (Bob); b. 30 Oct. 1936, Corbridge, Northumberland, England. Vocalist; Musician (violin). m. Margaret, 13 Aug. 1960, 1 s., 1 d. *Musical Education:* Violin from early age; Studied voice in Royal Engineers Band. *Career:* Appeared every televised show, The Black and White Minstrels, 1959–; Also radio series with George Mitchell Singers; Now freelance, worked with many groups, radio and television including: The Two Ronnies, various Command Performances; Summer seasons in major resorts with The Black and White Minstrel Show; More recently with The Minstrel Stars; Concerts, cabaret with Original Blend and The Square Pegs, including radio programmes: Friday Night Is Music Night; Round Midnight; Among Your Souvenirs, BBC Radio 2. *Recordings:* Albums: The Black and White Minstrel Show; Around The World In Song; The Minstrel Stars; Original Blend Entertains. *Memberships:* Equity; Musicians' Union. *Leisure interests:* Tennis; Table Tennis; Stamp Collecting. *Address:* 15 Lynwood Rd, Ealing, London W5 1JQ, England.

HUNT-TAYLOR Amanda; Songwriter. *Career:* Songwriter with Warner Chappell Music, 1991; Songwriter with Bluewater Music, Nashville, 1996; Co-writer credits with: Rick Giles; Steve Bogard; John Scott Sherrill; Gene Nelson; Kent Robbins; Janis Ian; Rory Bourke; Director, AmandaRick Records, 1999-. *Compositions:* Your Love Amazes Me, recorded by John Berry; Tanya Tucker; Andy Childs; Joel Nova; All She Wants, recorded by Rena Gaile; No One Else Like You, recorded by Janis Ian; Able, recorded by Happy Goodmans; Wish I Could Wish On A Star, recorded by Mandy Barnett; A Fire In The Rain, recorded by Doug Supernaw; I Really Do Love You Lovin' Me, recorded by Lori Morgan; Wishing it all away, recorded by

Tania Tucker. *Recordings:* Backup vocalist on Janis Ian's Revenge album; vocals on Jay Turner, Celebration Day, 2001; Debut CD: Only When I Breathe, 1999. *Honours:* For Your Love Amazes Me: SESAC Songwriter of the Year, 1994; SESAC Song of the Year, 1994; Country Grammy Nomination; NSAI Achievement Award, 1995; Music City News Country Songwriters Award, Song of the Year, 1995; Song of the Year, 2nd Annual Country Radio Music Award Show, 1995; 2 NSAI Awards. *Address:* PO Box 140494, Nashville, TN 37214, USA.

HURLEY Luke; b. 31 Aug. 1957, Nyeri, Kenya. Songwriter; Musician (guitar); Performer. m. Jann, 16 May 1992, 1 s., 2 d. *Education:* 1 year university. *Musical Education:* Self-taught. *Career:* Major shows since early 1982 specialising in Houseconcerts; Support act for Michelle Shocked, Marianne Faithfull, New Zealand; Only performer to play live, Radio With Pictures television show; Touring Europe, 1998–99; Invented product for the CD industry. *Compositions:* Mona Lisa; Fait Accompli; Japanese Overdrive; Greenfields; Precious Time; Missing You; Hungry Gun Song; Information Station. *Recordings:* Albums: Policestate; Japanese Overdrive; Make Room; First Civilian; Alone in Her Field; Reha; Videos: Japanese Overdrive; Make Room; Mona Lisa.

HURLEY Steve 'Silk', (JM Silk, Jack Master Silk); b. 9 Nov. 1962, Chicago, Illinois, USA. Prod.; Remixer; DJ. *Career:* Started as a DJ in Chicago, c. 1979; Own show on local radio station WBMX; First release Music Is The Key (as JM Silk), 1985; Set up Silk Entertainment, 1997; In-demand remixer and songwriter; Collaborations: Chantay Savage; Jamie Principle; Maurice Joshua; Keith Nunnally; Remixed: Michael Jackson; Kym Sims; Ce Ce Peniston; Melanie B; Rahsaan Patterson; Madonna. *Recordings:* Albums: Hold Onto Your Dreams, 1987; Singles: Music Is The Key, Jack Your Body, 1985; Let The Music Take Control, 1987. *Honour:* Grammy Award, Best Remixer nominee (Bob Marley 'Soul Shakedown Party'), 2002. *Address:* c/o Silk Entertainment Inc, 3011 W 183rd St #302, Homewood, Illinois, USA. *E-mail:* silkentertainment@msn.com.

HUSBAND Gary; b. 14 June 1960, Leeds, Yorkshire, England. Musician (drums, piano, keyboards). *Musical Education:* Classical piano. *Career:* Allan Holdsworth; Jack Bruce Trio; Billy Cobham Band; Gary Moore; Level 42; Gary Husband Group. *Compositions:* Written for albums by Allan Holdsworth and Level 42; Diary of a Plastic Box; From The Heart, The New Gary Husband Trio; Skin Fever, album, 1998. *Recordings:* Albums include: with Allan Holdsworth: Metal Fatigue, 1985; with Level 42: Staring At The Sun, Steve Topping: Time and Distance, 1988; Focused, 1998; also with Lemon D, Dick Heckstall-Smith, Jimmy Nail, Dillinger, Geoff Keezer, Billy Cobham, Randy Brecker Group; Video: Interplay and Improvisation, 1998. *Memberships:* Musicians' Union; PRS. *Leisure interest:* Music.

HUSBANDS Simon Patrick; b. 2 Feb. 1957, Nottingham, England. Musician (keyboards, guitar, bass guitar); Songwriter; Programmer; Singer. m. Janet Johnson, 9 July 1994. *Education:* Newark-Sherwood College. *Career:* Keyboard player, bass player, singer with band Blue Train; Single All I Need Is You, used in Baywatch television show, 1991; Current solo projects include DIN and UXB. *Recordings:* Co-producer, album The Business of Dreams; Singles: All I Need Is You (13 weeks, US charts); The Hardest Thing; The Business of Dreams. *Memberships:* PRS; Musicians' Union; BMI, USA. *Leisure interests:* Computers; Cinema. *Current Management:* GOSH! Productions, UK; Gary Heller Management, 11692 Chenault St #202, Los Angeles, CA 91411, USA. *Address:* 40 Millicent Rd, West Bridgford, Nottingham NG2 7PZ, England.

HUSEIN Hasanefesic; b. 30 Jan. 1954, Banja Luka, Croatia. Musician (guitar); Songwriter. m. Viki Peric, 22 March 1980, 1 s., 1 d. *Musical Education:* 8 years music school, Zagreb. *Career:* 20 years on top with own band, Parni Valjek (Steam Roller). *Recordings:* 15 albums (most of them Platinum). *Honours:* 7 Porins (Croatian equivalent of Grammy), 1995. *Memberships:* HGU; HDS. *Leisure interests:* Tennis; Sailing. *Current Management:* HGU, HDS, Nenas Drobnjak. *Address:* Zelengaj 67, 10000 Zagreb, Croatia.

HUSKY Ferlin, (Simon Crum, Terry Preston); b. 3 Dec. 1927, Cantwell, Missouri, USA. Country vocalist; Songwriter; Musician (guitar, bass); Actor; Comedian. *Career:* DJ in Bakersfield, California, 1940s; Played bass with Big Jim DeNoone and fiddler Fred McMurray; Later with Smiley Burnette and Gene Autry in Salinas, California; Recorded guitar instrumentals as Tex Terry; Later as Terry Preston on 4 Star Records, 1949; Worked with Tennessee Ernie Ford; Signed to Capitol Records, 1951; Over 50 Billboard country chart entries, 1953–75; Early records miscredited to Ferlin Huskey; Recorded as Ferlin Husky, 1957–; Occasional releases as comedy alter ego Simon Crum; Hosted Arthur Godfrey TV and radio show, 1950s; Appearances in Kraft Television Theatre show, 1957; Toured with group The Hushpuppies, 1960s to mid-1970s; Appearances in films include: Mister Rock and Roll, 1957; Country Music Holiday, 1958; Las Vegas Hillbillys (a.k.a. Country Music USA), 1966; Hillbillys In A Haunted House, 1967; Forty Acre Feud, 1968; Swamp

Girl, 1971; That's Country, 1977; Appeared at Christy Lane's Theater, Branson, Missouri. *Compositions include:* Country Music Is Here To Stay; Timber I'm Fallin'. *Recordings include:* Dear John Letter (with Jean Shepard), 1953; Gone, Just For You, 1957; Country Music Is Here To Stay, 1958; Wings of a Dove, 1960; Albums: By Request, 1964; I Could Sing All Night, 1966; Just For You, 1968. *Honour:* Volunteer Gunner Citation, WWII. *Memberships:* Grand Ole Opry; The Order of Police; National Sherrifs Asscn. *Current Management:* Richard Davis Management, 1030 North Woodland, Kansas City, MO 64118, USA.

HUSSENOT Emmanuel; b. 29 Sept. 1951, Saint Cloud, France. Variety Artist; Jazz Musician (cornet, trumpet, saxophone, recorder). 1 d. *Musical Education:* Self-taught. *Career:* Cornet player, French traditional band, Sharkey and Co; Composer, singer, trumpet, saxophone and recorder player, Orpheon Celesta, 1980-. *Recordings:* with Sharkey and Co, 1972–78; with Orpheon Celesta: Siphonnée Symphonie; La Prehistoire du Jazz; Best Of; La vocalise en carton. *Honours:* Prix Sydney Bechet de l'Academie du Jazz, 1990; Grand Prix du Festival d'Humour de Saint Gervais, 1994; La Vocalise en carton, 1998. *Current Management:* Blue Line, Paris. *Address:* 74 rue Alexandre Guilmant, 92190 Meudon, France.

HUSSEY Wayne; b. 26 May 1959. Musician (guitar); Vocalist. *Career:* Member, groups Dead Or Alive; The Walkie Talkies; Member, Sisters of Mercy, 1983–85; Concerts include York Festival, 1984; The Mission, 1986–; Regular UK, European and world-wide tours, including concerts with The Cult and U2; Appearances include: Reading Festival, 1986, 1987, 1989; Lockerbie Air Disaster Fund benefit concert, 1989; Hillsborough football disaster benefit concert, 1989; Finsbury Park, London, 1991; Off The Street benefit concert, London, 1993. *Recordings:* Albums: with Sisters of Mercy: First and Last and Always, 1985; Possession, 1991; Slight Case of Overbombing, 1993; with The Mission: God's Own Medicine, 1986; The First Chapter, 1987; Children (No. 2, UK), 1988; Carved In Sand, 1990; Masque, 1992; Neverland, 1995; Resurrection, 1999; Singles: with Sisters of Mercy: Temple of Love, 1983; Body and Soul, 1984; Walk Away, 1984; with The Mission: Stay With Me, 1986; Wasteland, 1987; Severina, 1987; Tower of Strength, 1988; Beyond The Pale, 1988; Butterfly On A Wheel, 1989; Deliverance, 1990; Hands Across The Ocean, 1990; Like A Child Again, 1992.

HUTCHINGS Ashley Stephen; b. 26 Jan. 1945, Southgate, Middlesex, England. Musician (bass guitar); Songwriter; Prod.; Dancer; Scriptwriter. m. 6 Aug. 1971, to 1978, 1 s. *Career:* Founder member, leading folk-rock groups in England: Fairport Convention, 1967–; Steeleye Span, 1970–; Albion Band, 1972–; Music Director, National Theatre, London, 1977–81; Considered Father of Folk-Rock in Britain by media. *Recordings include:* Albums: with Fairport Convention: Fairport Convention, 1968; What We Did In Our Holidays, 1969; Unhalfbricking, 1969; Liege and Leaf, 1970; with Steeleye Span: Hark The Village Wait, 1970; Please To See The King, 1971; Ten Man Mop, 1971; with The Albion Band: Battle of The Field, 1976; Prospect Before Us, 1977; Rise Up Like The Sun, 1978; Albion River Hymns March, 1979; Light Shining Albino, 1984; The Wild Side of Town, 1987; I Got New Shoes, 1987; Give Me A Saddle I'll Trade You A Car, 1989; 1990; Acousticity, 1993; Albion Heart, 1995; Solo albums: By Gloucester Docks I Sat Down and Wept, 1987; Twangin' N' A-Traddin', 1993; Crab Wars Remembered, 1994; Sway with Me, 1996; The Guv'nor, 1999; Along The Downs, 2000; Street Cries, 2001. *Publication:* A Little Music, collection of folk-songs, tunes and dances. *Memberships:* PRS; MCPS. *Leisure interests:* Theatre; Music. *Current Management:* c/o 994 Burnage Lane, Manchester M19 1TD, England. *Address:* 994 Burnage Lane, Manchester M19 1TD, England.

HUTCHINSON Steff; b. 11 May 1964, Halton, England. Singer, Musician (Guitar). *Education:* BA, Portsmouth Polytechnic; PGCE, City of Birmingham Polytechnic. *Career:* Solo Singer, Guitarist, 1978; Various bands, 1981–90; Member of Dead After Dark, 1991–99; Current member of Firedaze; Appeared on BBC in the Midlands Radio; Live At The Y, Leicester Cable Television; Soundwaves, Colt Television. *Compositions:* Co Writer, of all Dead After Dark and Firedaze songs. *Recordings:* Album, No Time To Waste, 1996; EP, See, 1998; EP, Firedaze, 1999. *Honours:* Finalist, Radio One Battle of The Bands, 1989; Finalist, Live Television Battle of The Bands, 1996. *Membership:* Musicians' Union. *Leisure interests:* Painting; Photography. *Address:* DeAD Music, PO Box 213, Leamington Spa, Warwickshire, CV31 1ZP, England.

HUTCHISON Hamish; b. 22 July 1968, Beckenham, Kent. Record Prod.; Remixer; Mixing Engineer. *Recordings:* Producer, numerous acts including: Chesney Hawkes; Big Fun; Glen Goldsmith; Booker Newbury III; Remixer for: PJ and Duncan; China Crisis; Lucianna; Jack 'N' Chill; Chesney Hawkes. *Membership:* Musicians' Union. *Address:* c/o Time and Space, PO Box 306, Berkhamsted, Herts HP4 3EP, England.

HUTMAN Olivier; b. 12 Nov. 1954, Boulogne, France. Musician (piano); Arranger; Composer. *Education:* PhD, Ethnology on Urban Music in Ghana. *Musical Education:* 10 years study, piano, National Conservatory of Music, St Maur. *Career:* Jazz performer, accompanist for pop singers; Founder, Moravigne, 1975; Member, Chute Libre, 1975–77; Founds own trio, 1983–84; Member Eric Lelann Quartet, 1984–88; Tours, festivals include: Singapore; Bombay; Montréal; Prague; Tokyo, 1991, 1993; Newport, USA, 1993; Tahiti, 1995; Martinique, 1994, USA (Boston, San Fransisco, Los Angeles), 1995; Antibes; Nimes; La Reunion; Montreux. *Compositions:* Composer, arranger in jazz, theatre, films: jingles, music for industrial films, TV documentaries, Long Range Films include: Mon Oncle, 1985; High Speed, 1987; Printemps Perdu, 1990; Ma Soeur Chinoise, 1994; Commissioned by International Musik Fetsival, Davos, to write suite performed by members of New York Philharmonia, 1993. *Recordings:* with: Moravagine; Chute Libre; J P Debarbat; G Ferris; Eric Lelann; Christian Escoude; Toots Thielemans; C Bellonzi; C Barthelemy; P Delletrz; J P L Labador; S Marc; G Acogny; Abus; Barney Wilen, 1992; A Brunet; M Barrot Quartet; R Galliano; Stephane Grappelli; Luigi Trussardi; Solo: Six Songs, 1984; The Man With The Broken Tooth, trio with Marc Bertaux, Tony Rabeson, 1987; Creole and African music recordings. *Honours:* Prix Boris Vian, French Academy of Jazz, for Best Record of The Year, 1983; 2nd European Keyboardist in Jazz, Hot Magazine, 1987; Awards for music for films: Mon Oncle, 1986; Printemps Perdu, 1990. *Current Management:* A21 Muth Productions, 14 rue Bleue, 75009 Paris. *Address:* 36 rue de Fontanay, 94300 Vincennes, France.

HUTTON Mick; b. 5 June 1956, Chester, England. Jazz Musician (Double Bass, Piano, Cuatro). Separated, 1 s. *Musical Education:* Studied Piano, Organ and Cello at School; Self-taught on Double Bass. *Career:* Professional Musician, 1981–; Toured and recorded extensively with artists including Nigel Kennedy, Humphrey Lyttelton, John Surman, John Taylor, Kenny Wheeler, Bill Bruford, Courtney Pine, Annie Ross, Tina May, The Style Council and others; Appeared on over 30 jazz albums and over 200 radio broadcasts; Work in film, TV and with West End shows. *Recordings include:* Blue Glass, with John Taylor Trio; Busy Listening, with Steve Arguelles Band; Time Will Tell, with Tina May; Heavenly Bodies, with Bill Bruford's Earthworks; This Old Gang of Ours, with Humphrey Lyttelton; Morning Sunrise, with Barry Nathan Trio; 1 2 3, with Nick Purnell Group; Blues in the Night, with The Cast; Amazing Grace, with Martin Speake; Chris Biscoe Sextet; PyroTechnics, various artists; Triple Exposure, with Mark Edwards; From the Heart, with Gary Husband Trio. *Memberships:* Musicians' Union; PRS; PAMRA. *Leisure interest:* Photography. *Address:* 16 Birch St, Birch, Essex CO2 0NF, England.

HVASS Claus; b. 4 Feb. 1959. Composer; Prod.; Musician (guitar). m. Birgitte Rode, 14 June 1992, 1 s. *Career:* Roskilde Festival; Toured England; Concerts: California; France; Norway; Germany; Sweden; Denmark; Grand Prix, Slovenia; National and international television and radio. *Composition:* Medea. *Recordings:* with Johnny and The Cold Demons: Paraneuropa; with Walk The Walk: Walk The Walk; Feet On the Ground; Frog Dance. *Publication:* The International Discography of New Wave, Dansk Rock. *Honours:* 5 National Music Awards, 1991–95. *Membership:* DJBFA. *Leisure interest:* Sailsports. *Current Management:* Zing Zing Musicproduction and Management. *Address:* Kirkegaardsgade 3, 9000 Aalborg, Denmark.

HYDE Maria Jane; b. 23 Jan. 1969, London, England. Singer; Actress. m. Dr Uwe Bodzian, 21 July 1995. *Career:* Acted: Peppee, in Annie, Victoria Palace, 1980; Ovaltines singing group, 1982; Various TV shows, Children's Royal Variety Performance, London Palladium; Acted: Pearl, Starlight Express, London, 1985–88; Pearl, Starlight Express, Bochum, West Germany, 1989–91, 1994–95; Assistant Dance and Skate Coach, 1995. *Recordings:* Albums: Ovaltine Group Album, 1982; Heaven Sent (No. 5, German charts), 1995; Single: Heaven Sent, UK, 1994. *Membership:* Equity. *Current Management:* Edward Hyde. *Address:* Morland House, 11 Woodside Green, London SE25 5EY, England.

HYDE Roger Erik; b. 3 June 1951, Hollywood, USA. Composer; Record Prod.; Theorist. *Musical Education:* AB in Music Theory and Composition, UCLA, 1975, with special endorsements in electronic music and composition for film; Studied history of jazz with Paul Tanner (Glen Miller Band), Composition with Gerald Strang, Film scoring with David Raksin, Production with Nik Venet. *Career:* Folk Scene radio concert, 1970; Series of Los Angeles salon concerts and readings, 1975–76; Director of Washoe Records, producer for Scatman Crothers, 1980–81; Director and Producer, Blue Planet Records, 1985-. *Compositions:* Our Hearts and Our Hands, song cycle, 1979; Pittsburg; 2811; Symphony à Trois. *Recordings:* As producer, Scatman Crothers and the Hollywood Radio Hooligans. *Publications:* Novels: Famous Death, and Weighing of Secret Burdens. *Contributions to:* The Whole Earth Catalogues. *Membership:* AES. *Leisure interests:* Kite designing; Scholar. *Address:* PO Box 91922, Los Angeles, CA 90009, USA.

HYDER Ken; b. 29 June 1946, Dundee, Scotland. Musician (drums); Vocalist. *Education:* Harris Academy, Dundee. *Musical Education:* Studied with John Stevens. *Career:* Moved to London 1970; Formed

Celtic-Jazz band, Talisker; Played and recorded with Celtic musicians including Dick Gaughan, then with Tibetan monks, Russian musicians, duo with Tim Hodgkinson, South African musicians, Siberian shamans. *Recordings:* with Talisker: Dreaming of Glenisla; Land of Stone; The Last Battle; The White Light; Humanity; Under The Influence; The Big Team; Fanfare For Tomorrow, with Dick Gaughan; Shams, with Tim Hodgkinson; The Goose, with Hodgkinson, Ponomareva; Piping Hot, with Dave Brooks; The Crux of The Catalogue, with Tomas Lynch; Hot Sounds From The Arctic, with Vladimir Rezitsky; The Ultimate Gift, Bardo State Orchestra; Urban Ritual, Ntshuks Bonga's Tshisa; Stillness in the Solouki, Northern Lights; In the Stone, Ken Hyder with Maggie Nichols and Dave Brooks. *Honour:* Order of The Red Banner, Angarsk. *Membership:* London Musician Collective. *Leisure interests:* Mountain climbing; Travel. *Current Management:* Oor Wullie Presentations. *Address:* 69 Ravenslea Rd, Balham, London SW12 8SL, England.

HYLAND Brian; b. 12 Nov. 1943, New York City, USA. Singer; Musician (guitar, keyboards, bass, harmonica). m. Rosmari Dickey, July 1970, 1 s. *Musical Education:* Church Choir; Self-taught musician. *Career:* Television and radio appearances: Host, American Bandstand, 1960–70; Murray The K Show, with Jackie Wilson, 1961; Television special, Japan, 1961; Thank Your Lucky Stars; Jukebox Jury; Saturday Club, UK Radio, 1963; Top of The Pops, 1975; RandR Palace, Nashville Now, 1988; Numerous tours include: Japan, South America, USA, UK, South East Asia. *Recordings:* Itsy Bitsy... Polka Dot Bikini, 1960; Let Me Belong To You, 1961; Ginny Come Lately, 1962; Sealed With A Kiss, 1962; Warmed Over Kisses, 1962; The Joker Went Wild, Run Run Look and See, 1966; Tragedy, 1968; Gypsy Woman, 1970; Greatest Hits, 1994; Very Best of Brian Hyland, 1998. *Honours:* 3 Gold records; Gee Gee Award, Star of Tomorrow, 16 Magazine, 1961–62. *Memberships:* AFofM; AGVA; AFTRA; ASCAP. *Leisure interests:* Art; Drawing; Photography; Astronomy; Computers. *Current Management:* Stone Buffalo. *Address:* PO Box 101, Silver Lakes, CA 92342–0101, USA.

HYLAND Vic; b. 7 June 1959, Wilmington, Kent, England. Musician (guitar); Singer; Educator. m. Jane Parker, 28 May 1993, 4 d. *Musical Education:* Studies in classical guitar, Indian music under Helen Lohmueller, Kessel and Lobb. *Career:* Guitarist, various musical styles from rock and jazz to Indian music; Brief spell playing classical concerts; Worked with Geoff Moore project, mid-1980s; Established as leading guitar educator in Kent area; Formed Red Touch, late 1980s; Currently with record deal, sponsorship, radio support. *Recordings:* Grahams Garden; I Don't Care; Before I Made You Cry; Album: Walk On, forthcoming. *Publications:* Advanced Techniques and Creative Guitar; Self Improvement For Musicians. *Memberships:* Musicians' Union; Registry of Electric Guitar Tutors. *Leisure interests:* Walking; Windsurfing; Reading; Painting. *Current Management:* RTI. *Address:* 5 Pleasant Villas, Kent St, Mereworth, Kent ME18 5QN, England.

HYND Richard; b. 17 June 1965, Aberdeen, Scotland. Musician (Drums). *Career:* Member, Texas; Numerous tours and festivals; TV appearances. *Recordings:* Singles include: I Don't Want a Lover, 1989; Tired of Being Alone, 1993; Say What You Want, 1997; Halo, 1997; Put Your Arms Around Me, 1997; Black Eyed Boy, 1997; In Our Lifetime, 1999; Summer Son, 1999; When We Are Together, 1999; In Demand, 2000; Inner Smile, 2001; Albums: Southside, 1989; Mother's Heaven, 1991; Rick's Road, 1993; White on Blonde, 1997; The Hush, 1999; Greatest Hits, 2000.

HYNDE Chrissie; b. 7 Sept. 1951, Akron, Ohio, USA. Singer; Musician (guitar); Songwriter. *Education:* Kent State University. *Career:* Model, St Martin's School of Art; Writer, New Musical Express, 1973; Member of groups The Frenchies; Jack Rabbit; Berk Brothers; Founder member, singer, guitarist, The Pretenders, 1978–; World tours made include UK, USA, Far East, Australia; Concerts include: Concert For Kampuchea, London, 1979; Heatwave Festival, Toronto, Canada, 1980; Concerts in Japan, Hong Kong, Australia, 1982; US Festival, San Bernardino, California, 1983; Radio City Music Hall, 1984; Live Aid, Philadelphia, 1985; Nelson Mandela Tribute, Wembley Stadium, 1990; Bob Dylan 30th Anniversary Tribute, Madison Square Garden (USA), 1992; Rock and Roll Hall of Fame; Cleveland Municipal Stadium, 1995; Burt Bacharach Tribute, Hammerstein Ballroom, New York, 1998; Here There and Everywhere – Tribute to Linda McCartney, London, 1999. *Recordings:* Albums: Pretenders, 1980; Extended Play, 1981; Pretenders II, 1981; Learning to Crawl, 1984; Get Close, 1986; The Singles, 1987; Packed!, 1990; Last of the Independents, 1994; The Isle of View, 1995; Viva El Amor, 1999; Singles include: Stop Your Sobbing, 1979; Kid, 1979; Brass In Pocket (No. 1, UK), 1979; Talk of The Town, 1980; Message of Love, 1981; I Go To Sleep, 1981; Back On The Chain Gang, 1983; 2000 Miles, 1983; Middle of the Road, 1984; Thin Line Between Love and Hate, 1984; Don't Get Me Wrong, 1986; Hymn to Her, 1987; Night in My Veins, 1994; I'll Stand by You, 1994; Human, 1999. *Contributions to:* Tame Yourself, animal rights album, 1991; Stone Free – A Tribute to Jimi Hendrix, 1993; The Concert for the Rock and Roll Hall of Fame, 1996; The Bridge School Concerts Vol. I, 1997; Film Soundtracks: King of Comedy (Back on the Chaingang, 1983); The Living Daylights (Where Has Everybody Gone and If there was a Man,

1987); Indecent Proposal (I'm Not in Love, 1993); With Honours (Forever Young, 1994); 1969 (Windows of the World, 1988); Boys on the Side (Everyday is Like Sunday, 1995); G I Jane (Goodbye and The Homecoming, 1997); The Other Sister (Loving You is All I Know, 1999); Musical collaborations: UB40 (I Got You Babe No 1 UK, 1985 and Breakfast in Bed, 1988); Moodswings (Spiritual High, 1992); Frank Sinatra (Luck be a Lady, 1994); Emmylou Harris (She – Tribute to Gram Parsons, 1999). *Honours:* Honoured at the People For The Ethical Treatment of Animals (PETA) 10th Anniversary Humanitarian Awards Gala, 1988; International Rock Awards MUP Lead Female Singer, ASCAP pop Award, 1995, 1996; Gibson Guitar award for Best Female Rock Guitarist, 1996; Ivor Novello Award for Outstanding Contribution to British Music, 1999. *Address:* 24 Ives St, London SW3 2ND, England.

HYNDMAN Clint; Musician (drums). *Career:* Resides in Australia; Joined Fish of The Day group, 1994; Developed local following through pub/club gigs; Group became Something For Kate; Signed to Australian label Murmur; Temporary hiatus to recruit new bassist, 1997–8; Band reformed and gradually broke nationally, then internationally with first US/Japan tour, 2000; Big sell-out Australian shows including Mythology and Echo-la-la-lalia tours plus Powderfinger support slots, 2001; Group subject of JJJ radio station special, 2001. *Recordings:* Albums: Elsewhere For Eight Minutes, 1997; Beautiful Sharks, 1999; QandA With Dean Martin (compilation), 2000; Echolalia, 2001; Singles: The Answer To Both Your Questions (EP), Dean Martin, 1996; Intermission (EP), Captain (Million Miles An Hour), Prick, 1997; Working Against Me, Roll Credit, Harpoon/Clint, 1998; Electricity, Hallways, Whatever You Want, 1999; The Astronaut, 2000; Monsters, Three Dimensions, Twenty Years, 2001. *Honours:* Australian Music Industry Critics Awards, Album of the Year, 2000; Australian Live Music Awards, Best Live Act, 2000; Australian Record Industry Awards, 7 nominations, 2001; JJJ Listeners' Poll, Best Album, 2001. *Current Management:* Carlene Albronda, Catapult Management, Sydney, Australia. *E-mail:* carlene@presto.net.au. *Internet:* www.somethingforkate.com.

I

IAN Janis, (Janis Fink); b. 7 April 1951, New Jersey, USA. Singer; Songwriter; Musician (guitar, piano, French horn); Columnist; Lecturer. *Partner:* Patricia Snyder. *Musical Education:* Mainly self-taught, including conducting and orchestration. *Career:* Solo artiste, 1965–; Debut hit single, Society's Child, featured in Leonard Bernstein's television special, Inside Pop – The Rock Revolution, 1966; Performances include: Royal Festival Hall and Royal Albert Hall, London; Carnegie Hall and Philharmonic Hall, New York; Sydney Opera House; Carre, Amsterdam; Appearances on most major television shows, including 8 times on Tonight Show. *Compositions include:* Society's Child, 1966; Jesse, recorded by Roberta Flack; At Seventeen, 1976; Fly Too High (co-writer with Giorgio Moroder) for film soundtrack Foxes, 1979; Tattoo; When Angels Cry; Some People's Lives, recorded by Bette Midler; Other compositions recorded by artistes including: Mel Tormé; Dianne Schuur; Chet Atkins; Stan Getz; John Mellencamp; Hugh Masakela. *Recordings:* Albums: Janis Ian, 1967; A Song for All the Seasons of Your Mind, 1968; The Secret Life of J Eddy Fink, 1969; Who Really Cares, 1969; Present Company, 1971; Stars, 1974; Between The Lines, (No. 1, USA), 1975; Aftertones, 1976; Miracle Row, 1997; Janis Ian, 1978; Night Rains, 1979; Restless Eyes, 1981; Breaking Silence, 1993; Revenge, 1995; Hunger, 1997; The Bottom Line Encore, 1999; God and The FBI, 2000. *Publications:* Monthly columnist, The Advocate; Regular columnist, Performing Songwriter Magazine; Book of poetry, 1968. *Honours:* 2 Grammy Awards, 9 Grammy Nominations; GLCCLA Award for Creative Integrity, 1993; Fisk University Award for Creative Excellence, 1994; Multiple Platinum records world-wide, including Japan, Australia and US. *Leisure interests:* Archaeology; Snorkelling; Reading. *Current Management:* Simon Renshaw, Senior Management. *Address:* c/o Janis Ian Subscriber Service, PO Box 121797, Nashville, TN 37212, USA.

IANORA Stéphane; b. 16 Jan. 1960, Paris, France. Musician (drums). m. Motomi Ryu, 17 March 1989, 2 d. *Education:* University (Japanese Ursus); Graduated (Dev6). *Career:* Drummer, Bird X funk band, featuring Wally Badatov, 1979; Concerts with William Sheller, 1981–84; Concerts, tours, with: David Koven; Kurim Kalel; Rachid Bahri; Elli Medeiros; Jeanne Mas; World tours with Richard Clayderman, 1989–; Television shows with Vanessa Paradis. *Recordings:* with William Sheller: J'suis Pas Bien; Civic Olympia, 89; Karim Kalel: P'tite Soeur; David Koven: David Koven; Etè Torride; Marvin; Elli Medeiros: Elli; Jeanne Mas: En Concert; Sheila: Live Olympia 89; Richard Clayderman: English Pop Songs. *Leisure interests:* Tai Chi Chuan; Japanese studies (language and civilization). *Address:* 4 Allée des Tilleuls, 94220 Charenton, France.

IBOLD Mark; b. 1967, Cincinnati, Ohio, USA. Musician (Bass). *Career:* Member, Pavement; Joined band, 1992; Numerous headlining tours; Appearance on cartoon Space Ghost Coast to Coast, 1997. *Recordings:* Singles: Trigger Cut, 1992; Cut Your Hair, 1994; Gold Soundz, 1994; Range Life, 1995; Rattled by La Rush, 1995; Father to a Sister of Thought, 1995; Pacific Trim EP, 1996; Stereo, 1997; Shady Lane EP, 1997; Spit on a Stranger, 1999; Carrot Rope, 1999; Albums: Slanted and Enchanted, 1992; Crooked Rain, Crooked Rain, 1994; Wowee Zowee, 1995; Brighten the Corners, 1997; Terror Twilight, 1999.

IBRAHIM Abdullah, (Adolphe 'Dollar' Brand); b. 9 Oct. 1934, Capetown, South Africa. Musician (piano); Composer. m. Sathima Bea Benjamin, 1965. *Musical Education:* Studied piano from age 7. *Career:* Became professional musician, 1949; Member: The Jazz Epistles (with Hugh Masekela and Kippi Moeketsi); Met Duke Ellington in the Africana Club, Zurich and recorded album together, 1963; Appeared at the Newport Jazz Festival, 1965; Several appearances as Ellington's substitute with the Ellington Orchestra; Collaborations: Elvin Jones; Don Cherry; Gato Barbieri; Max Roach; Munich Radio Philharmonic Orchestra toured with arrangements of his work, 1998; 1988 album Mindif used as soundtrack for film Chocolat. *Recordings:* Albums include: Duke Ellington Presents The Dollar Brand Trio, 1963; Mindif, African Sun, Tintinyana, Blues for a Hip King, African Horns, Voice of Africa, 1988; African River, 1989; Mantra Mode, 1991; Yarona, 1995.

ICE CUBE (O'Shea Jackson); b. 15 June 1969, Los Angeles, California, USA. Rapper. *Education:* Architectural Degree, University of Phoenix, 1988. *Career:* Worked with Public Enemy; Began rapping with CIA with partner Sir Jinx; Formed N.W.A. with Dr Dre; Formed new rap posse Da Lench Mob; Began own corporation, including work by protegée YoYo which he wrote and produced; Numerous tours including Lollapalooza; Converted to Islam, 1992; Began to concentrate on film appearances including Boyz N The Hood, 1991, Trespass, 1992, Higher Learning, 1995, The Glass Shield, 1995, Friday, 1996, Dangerous Ground, with Liz Hurley, 1997, Anaconda, 1997, The Player's Club (also directed), 1997.

Recordings: Singles: AmeriKKKa's Most Wanted, 1990; Kill At Will EP, 1990; It Was A Good Day, 1993; Check Yo Self, 1993; Really Doe EP, 1994; You Know How We Do It EP, 1994; Bop Gun (One Nation) EP, 1994; My Posse, 1995; World Is Mine, 1997; Pushin' Weight, 1998; Albums: AmeriKKKa's Most Wanted, 1990; Death Certificate, 1991; The Predator, 1992; Wicked, 1992; Lethal Injection, 1993; Bootlegs and B Sides, 1994; War and Peace, 1998; War and Peace 2 – The Peace Disc, 2000; Greatest Hits, 2001.

ICE-T (Tracey Marrow); b. 14 Feb. 1959, Newark, New Jersey, USA. Rapper; Actor. *Career:* Innovator of LA Gangsta Rap; Recording artist, 1987–; Rapper, rock group Body Count, 1992; Tours: UK; Europe; US; Canada; South America; Asia; Australia; Middle East; Actor, films include New Jack City; Trespass; Breakin'; Tank Girl; Television includes: Players; Baadasss TV; Owner, Rhyme Syndicate Records; Lecturer and spokesman, major US universities; Also involved in Hands Across Watts and South Central Love, 2 youth intervention programmes. *Recordings:* Singles include: Lifestyles of Rich and Infamous, 1991; New Jack Hustler, 1991; What Really Goes On, 1998; Valuable Game, 1999; Albums: Rhyme Pays; Power; The Iceberg...; Freedom of Speech – Just Watch What You Say; O. G.- Original Gangster; Home Invasion; Ice VI-Return of The Real; with Body Count: Body Count; Born Dead; Cold as Ever; Seventh Deadly Sin; Also featured on film soundtracks: Colors; Dick Tracy. *Publication:* The Ice Opinion, 1994. *Honours:* Best Male Rapper, Rolling Stone Readers Poll, 1992; Grammy Award, Best Rap Song for Back on the Block. *Current Management:* Rhyme Syndicate Management, 4902 Coldwater Canyon Ave, Sherman Oaks, CA 91423, USA.

IDOL Billy, (Willem Wolfe Broad); b. 30 Nov. 1955, Stanmore, Middlesex, England. Singer; Musician (guitar); Composer. *Career:* Lead singer, guitarist, UK punk group Generation X, 1977–81; Solo artiste, 1981–; World-wide concerts include: Charmed Life Tour, 1990; Rock In Rio II Festival, 1991; Roskilde Festival, Denmark, 1991; Supported Bon Jovi, Milton Keynes Bowl, 1993. *Recordings:* Albums: with Generation X: Generation X, 1978; Valley of The Dolls, 1979; Kiss Me Deadly, 1981; Solo albums: Don't Stop, 1981; Billy Idol, 1982; Rebel Yell, 1984; Vital Idol, 1985; Whiplash Smile, 1986; Idol Songs, 1988; Charmed Life, 1990; Cyberpunk, 1993; L A Woman, 1993; All Summer Single, 1993; Don't Need a Gun, 1993; featured on: Punk Lost and Found, 1996; Retro 80's Vol. 1, 1998; Solo singles include: Hot In The City, 1982; White Wedding, 1983; Rebel Yell, 1984 (both re-released 1985); Eyes Without A Face, 1984; Flesh For Fantasy, 1984; Catch My Fall, 1984; To Be A Lover, 1986; Don't Need A Gun, 1987; Sweet Sixteen, 1987; Mony Mony (No. 1, USA), 1987; Cradle of Love (No. 2, US), featured in film Adventures of Ford Fairlane, 1990; LA Woman, 1990; Shock To The System, 1993. *Honour:* Double Platinum disc, Rebel Yell, 1984. *Current Management:* East End Management, 8209 Melrose Ave, 2nd Floor, Los Angeles, CA 90046, USA.

IEUAN Dafydd; b. 1 March 1969, Bangor, Wales. Musician (drums). *Career:* Member, Super Furry Animals; Early releases on small indie label, then obtained major indie label deal; Numerous tours in the UK and abroad; Many festival appearances. *Recordings:* Singles: Llanfairpwllgwyngyllgogerychwyndrobwl... EP, 1995; Moog Droog EP, 1995; God! Show Me Magic, 1996; If You Don't Want Me To Destroy You, 1996; The Man Don't Give A Fuck, 1996; Hometown Unicorn, 1996; Something 4 The Weekend, 1996; The International Language of Screaming, 1997; Hermann Loves Pauline, 1997; Demons, 1997; Play It Cool, 1997; Ice Hockey Hair, 1998; Northern Lights, 1999; Fire In My Heart, 1999; Do Or Die, 2000; Albums: Fuzzy Logic, 1996; Radiator, 1997; Outspaced, 1998; Guerrilla, 1999; Mwng, 2000; Rings Around The World, 2001.

IF Owen, (Ian Frederick Rossiter); b. 20 March 1959, Newport, Wales. Musician (Drums). *Career:* Member, Stereo MCs; Numerous club and live appearances, TV appearances and radio sessions. *Recordings:* Singles: Elevate My Mind, 1990; Lost In Music, 1991; Connected, 1992; Step It Up, 1993; Creation, 1993; Albums: Supernatural, 1990; Connected, 1992; Stereo MCs, 1993.

IG CULTURE (Ian George Grant), (Son of Scientist, Da One Way, Likwid Biskit); b. 17 June 1965, London, England. Prod.; Remixer; DJ. *Career:* Started production career as part of Dodge City Productions, 1990; Founder: Main Squeeze label, late '90s; Co-promoter: The Co-Op club night in London with 4 Hero and Phil Asher; Formed the New Sector Movements collective, debut album released 2001; Collaborations: 4 Hero; Kaidi Tatham; Frank McComb; Julie Dexter; Dodge; Ronny Jordan; Remixed: 4 Hero; Noel McKoy; Luniz. *Recordings:* Albums: Steppin' Up and Out (with Dodge City Productions), 1993; Download This (with New Sector

Movements), 2001; Singles: As Long As We're Around (with Dodge City Productions), 1992; Unleash Your Love (with Dodge City Productions), Tings A Gwan, 1993; My History (with New Sector Movements), 1997; No Tricks EP (with New Sector Movements), The Sun (with New Sector Movements), 2001. *Membership:* MCPS/PRS. *Address:* c/o Main Squeeze Records, Adela St, 326 Kensal Rd, London, W10 5BZ, England.

IGLAUER Bruce; b. 10 July 1947, Ann Arbor, Michigan, USA. Record Co Exec. m. Jo Kolanda, 5 Aug. 1995. *Education:* BA, Lawrence University, Appleton, Wisconsin. *Career:* Founder, Alligator Records, 1971; President, Alligator Records; Released over 150 contemporary blues recordings. *Recordings:* Produced almost 100 blues albums including artists: Albert Collins; Koko Taylor; Johnny Winter; Ray Buchanan; Saffire; Bob Margolin. *Publication:* Co-founder: Living Blues Magazine. *Membership:* Founder, Senior Board of Trustees mem., National Asscn of Independent Record Distributors and Manufacturers. *Address:* PO Box 60234, Chicago, IL 60660, USA.

IGLESIAS Julio, (Julio Jose Iglesias de la Cueva); b. 23 Sept. 1943, Madrid, Spain. Singer; Songwriter. m. Isabel Preisler, 20 Jan. 1971, divorced, 3 s. *Education:* Law student, Cambridge University. *Musical Education:* Learnt to sing in hospital (recovering from car crash). *Career:* Goalkeeper, Real Madrid junior team; Winner, Spanish Song Festival, Benidorm, 1968; Professional singer, songwriter, 1968–; Winner, Eurovision Song Contest, Netherlands, 1970; Major success in Latin America, 1970s; English Language releases, 1981–; Concerts and television appearances world-wide; In excess of 100m. records sold to date. *Compositions include:* La Vida Sigue Igual; Mi Amor; Yo Canto; Alguien El Alamo Al Camino; No Ilores. *Recordings:* Over 70 albums include: Soy, 1973; El Amor, 1975; A Mis 33 Anos, 1977; De Nina A Mujer, 1981; 1100 Bel Air Lace, 1984; Un Hombre Solo, 1987; Starry Night, 1990; La Carretera, 1995; Tango, 1996; Corazon Latino, 1998; Noche De Cuatro Lunas, 2000; Una Donna Puo Cambiar La Vita, 2000; Ao Meu Brasil, 2000; Also on: Duets (with Frank Sinatra), 1993; Hit singles include: Manuela, 1975; Hey, 1979; Begin The Beguine, 1981; To All The Girls I've Loved Before, duet with Willie Nelson, 1983; My Love, duet with Stevie Wonder, 1988. *Publication:* Autobiography: Entre El Cielo y El Infernierno, 1981. *Honours:* Grammy, Best Latin Pop Performance, 1987; Diamond Disc Award, Guinness Book of Records (most records in most languages), 1983; Medaille de Vermeil de la Ville de Paris, 1983; Eurovision Song Contest Winner, 1970. *Membership:* Hon. Mem., Spanish Foreign Legion. *Address:* c/o Anchor Marketing, 1177 Kane Concourse PH, Bay Harbour Island, FL 33154, USA.

IGREC Mario; b. 24 May 1959, Zagreb, Croatia. Musician (guitar); Composer; Arranger; Guitar Teacher; Backing Singer. m. Snjezana Drkulec Igrec, 22 Nov. 1986, 3 s. *Education:* Professor of Philosophy. *Musical Education:* Conservatory; Degree, jazz guitar. *Career:* Member, various groups including Zagreb Jazz Portrait; Hot Club Zagreb; Steve Klink Quartet; Mario Igrec Quintet; Pentagon; Good Day; Ritmo Loco; Jazz Big Band HGZ; Big Festival Orchestra; Live concerts and programmes for state television in Slovenia, Austria, Croatia; International jazz festivals include: Croatia; Slovenia; Germany; Hungary. *Compositions:* Vanova; A Better Tomorrow; Brimbi; Daimonion; Blues No 4; Balrog. *Recordings:* Moment Notice; Zagreb Jazz Portrait, 1984; with Ritmo Loco: Baila Como Yo, 1992; For A Love of One Woman, 1995. *Honour:* Heineken Award for Jazz Band, Croatia, 1995. *Memberships:* Croatian Music Union (HGU); Jazz Club, Zagreb. *Leisure interests:* Cycling; Table tennis. *Current Management:* Vesna Vrandecic, Zitnak 1, 41000 Zagreb, Croatia. *Address:* Mario Igrec, Ozaljska 93, 41000 Zagreb, Croatia.

IHA James; b. 26 March 1968, Elk Grove, Illinois, USA. Musician (Guitar). *Career:* Member, Smashing Pumpkins; Early support gigs for Jame's Addiction, Red Hot Chili Peppers, Pearl Jam; Lollapalooza tour, 1994; Numerous headlining tours; TV and radio appearances; Launched Stratchie Records with D'Arcy Wretzky, 1997; Contributed 2 tracks to soundtrack of film Batman and Robin. *Recordings:* Singles include: Lull EP, 1992; Today, 1994; Cherub Rock EP, 1994; Disarm, 1994; I Am One, 1994; Bullet with Butterfly Wings, 1995; Thirty Three, 1996; Tonight Tonight, 1996; End is the Beginning is the End, 1997; Perfect, 1998; Stand Inside Your Love, 2000; Try Try Try, 2000; Albums: Gish, 1991; Siamese Dream, 1993; Mellon Collie and the Infinite Sadness (No. 1, USA), 1995; Adore, 1998; MACHINA/The Machines of God, 2000; Rotten Apples, 2001.

ILLESLEY John; b. 24 June 1949, Leicester, England. Musician (Bass). *Career:* Member, Dire Straits; Obtained major label deal and subsequent management contract; Support slot on Talking Heads 1978 European tour; Numerous headlining tours and TV appearances; Prince's Trust Concert and Nelson Mandela 70th Birthday tribute concert, 1988. *Recordings:* Singles: Sultans of Swing, 1978; Romeo and Juliet, 1981; Private Investigations (No. 2, UK), 1982; Twisting By the Pool, 1983; So Far Away, 1985; Walk of Life (No. 2, UK), 1985; Money for Nothing, featuring Sting (No. 1, USA), 1985; Brothers In Arms, 1985; Your Latest Trick, 1986; Calling Elvis, 1991; Albums: Dire Straits, 1978; Communiqué, 1979;

Making Movies, 1980; Love Over Gold (No. 1, UK), 1982; Alchemy, 1984; Brothers in Arms (No. 1, UK and US), 1985; Money For Nothing (No. 1, UK), 1988; On Every Street (No. 1, UK), 1991; On the Night, 1993; Live At the BBC, 1995; Sultans of Swing – The Very Best Of, 1998.

IMBRUGLIA Natalie; b. 4 Feb. 1975, New South Wales, Australia. Singer; Songwriter; Actress. *Career:* Actress, TV series Neighbours, Australia; Moved to London, 1995; Solo recording artiste, 1997-. *Recordings:* Albums: Left of The Middle, 1997; White Lillies Island, 2001; Hit Single: Torn, 1997; Wishing I Was There, 1998; Big Mistake, 1998; Smoke, 1998. *Honours include:* BRIT Award, Best International Female, Best International Newcomer, 1999. *Address:* c/o RCA Records, Bedford House, 69–69 Fulham High St, London SW6 3JW, England.

INABA Kazuhiro; b. 12 June 1960, Osaka, Japan. Musician (5-string banjo, guitar, fiddle). m. Tomoe Mori, 4 June, 1994, 1 s. *Education:* BA, Kansai University for Foreign Studies. *Career:* Played with many artists from USA including: Butch Robbins; Larry Stephenson; The Lonesome River Band; Bill Clifton; Producer, Bluegrass concerts; Interpreter, Leon Russell, Japan Tour, 1995. *Recordings:* Albums: Shore To Shore, 1986; Hard Times Come Again No More, 1989; Goin' Across The Sea, 1993. *Publications:* Featured articles, Moonshiner magazine, Japan (Bluegrass Journal). *Honour:* Second place, Bluegrass Banjo, Galax Fiddlers Convention, 1983. *Memberships:* Musicians' Union, Japan; IBMA (International Bluegrass Music Asscn), Owensboro, Kentucky. *Current Management:* Office White Oak. *Address:* 4–2–16, Nishi-Tezukayama, Sumiyoshi, Osaka 558, Japan.

INAMDAR Jayshree S; b. 20 Sept. 1974, Kalyan, India. Tabla Player. *Education:* Diploma in Computer Management, Datapro Institute, India; Currently studying for Diploma in Hindustani Vocal Light Music, Bombay University. *Career:* TV Programme of Marathi songs, Gudi Padva festival; Radio programme, Sangli Radio Centre, Yuva Vani; Professional stage drama in Marathi, 1999. *Leisure interests:* Reading books; Writing poems. *Address:* 302 Sundar Apartment, Patharli, Naka No. 8, Dombivli, India.

INDERBERG John Pål; b. 6 Aug. 1950, Steinkjer, Norway. Musician (saxophone); Music Prof. m. Kirsten Oxaal, 23 July 1976. *Education:* University of Trondheim. *Career:* Played with J Eks; Bob Brookmeyer; Lee Konitz; Warne Marsh; Many albums and tours; EBU Musician, soloist with Symphony Orchestra; Duos with Henning Sommerro; Professor of Music, Music Conservatory, Trondheim, Norway. *Recordings:* Albums: with Warne Marsh: Sax of a Kind, 1987; For The Time Being, 1988; with Siri's Svale Band: Blackbird, 1990; with Lee Konitz: Steps Towards A Dream, 1995. *Honours:* Buddy Award, Norwegian Jazz Federation. *Membership:* Norwegian Musician's Federation. *Leisure interest:* Moosehunting. *Current Management:* Eirik Kvam Olavsfestdagene, Dronnigens Gate 1B, 7011 Trondheim, Norway. *Address:* Kjopmannsgt 12, 7013 Trondheim, Norway.

INEZ Mike; b. 14 May 1966, San Fernando, California, USA. Musician (Bass). *Career:* Joined Alice in Chains; Numerous tours and TV appearances including MTV Unplugged. *Recordings include:* Singles: Heaven Beside You, 1998; Albums: Facelift, 1990; Dirt, 1992; Sap, 1992; Jar of Flies, 1994; Alice in Chains, 1995; I Stay Away, 1995; Unplugged, 1996; Music Bank, 1999; Live, 2000.

INGEBRIGTSEN Christian; b. 25 Jan. 1977, Oslo, Norway. Vocalist; Musician (piano, guitar); Songwriter. *Musical Education:* Liverpool Institute for Performing Arts, England. *Career:* Son of Norwegian '70s pop star Stein Ingebrigtsen; Grandfather spent 17 years as violinist in the Chicago Symphony Orchestra; Joined A1 pop group; Signed recording contract, 1999; Sell-out theatre tours of South-East Asia and UK, 2000–01. *Recordings:* Albums: Here We Come, 1999; The A List, 2000; Singles: Be The First To Believe, Summertime of Our Lives, Ready Or Not/ Everytime, 1999; Like A Rose, Take On Me, Same Old Brand New You, 2000; No More, 2001; Caught In The Middle, 2002. *Honours:* Brit Award, Best Newcomer, 2001; Also honoured at MTV Mandarin Music Awards. *Current Management:* c/o Byrne Blood Ltd. *Internet:* www.a1-online.com.

INGMAR; b. 31 Dec. 1970, Antwerp, Belgium. Composer; Musician (Keyboards); Singer; Writer; Translator. *Education:* Modern Languages; Basics in Jazz, Jazz Studio, Antwerp. *Career:* Secretary/Translator, until 1998; Freelance; Several national radio appearances; Several major stage live gigs (including one for His Majesty The Former King of Belgium). *Compositions:* The Quest for Beauty and Truth Continues, 1996; Ramifying Parallels on USA Import Music, 1997. *Recordings:* Insanity; Sister Sun; Amour Fatale; Exceptional; Solitude; The Quest; Beyond the Stars; The Dream. *Publications:* The Quest on Club Excentrique, 1996; Waiting... In These Skies, poem trilogy, 1997; Ramifying Parallels and Humanity, 1997; Solitude, number 1 album, 1999; 18 Poems and a Song, an introduction, poetry book, 1999. *Honours:* Requested to write composition in honour of King of Belgium, 1991; Laureate in national New Song Contest, SABAM, 1993. *Memberships:* SABAM, International Copyright Institute;

International Writers and Artists Asscn. *Leisure interests:* Cars; Movies; Music; Literature; European football; Kick-boxing.

INGRAM Charlie Alexander; b. 24 Oct. 1972, Cheltenham, England. Musician (guitar, mandolin); Singer. *Education:* Studying for BA Hons Music Technology, Rose Bruford College. *Musical Education:* Self-taught. *Career:* with Eden Burning, touring extensively throughout UK and Europe, 1993-. *Recordings:* Mirth and Matter, 1994; You Could Be The Meadow (EP), 1994; Be An Angel, 1995; Brink, 1995. *Membership:* Musicians' Union. *Leisure interests:* Walking; Climbing; Weight training. *Address:* 9 Wildmoor Lane, Catshill, Bromsgrove B61 0NT, England.

INNES Andrew; Musician (Guitar). *Career:* Member, Primal Scream; Numerous tours and festival appearances; Collaborations with DJ Andrew Weatherall, vocalist Denise Johnson, Jah Wobble and Alex Paterson from The Orb. *Contributions to:* One Dove, Morning Dove White, 1993; title track to the film Trainspotting, co-written with Irvine Welsh, 1996. *Recordings:* Singles: Loaded EP, 1990; Come Together EP, 1990; Higher Than The Sun, 1991; Don't Fight It, Feel It, 1991; Movin' On Up, 1991; (I'm Gonna) Cry Myself Blind, 1994; Jailbird, 1994; Rocks/Funky Jam, 1994; The Big Man and the Scream Team Meet the Barmy Army Uptown, 1996; Star, 1997; Burning Wheel, 1997; Kowalski, 1997; If They Move, Kill 'Em, 1998; Swastika Eyes, 1999; Kill All Hippies, 2000; Accelerator, 2000; Albums: Sonic Flower Groove, 1987; Primal Scream, 1989; Screamadelica, 1991; Give Out But Don't Give Up, 1994; Echo Dek, 1997; Vanishing Point, 1997; XTRMNTR, 2000. *Honour:* Mercury Music Prize Winner, 1992.

IOMMI Tony; b. 19 Feb. 1948, Birmingham, England. Rock Musician (guitar); Composer. *Career:* Guitarist, UK heavy rock group Black Sabbath, 1967-; Major appearances include: Madison Square Gardens, New York, 1975; Live Aid, Philadelphia, 1985. *Recordings:* Singles include: Paranoid; Iron Man; War Pigs; Never Say Die; Albums: Black Sabbath, 1969; Paranoid, 1970; Master of Reality, 1971; Vol. 4, 1972; Sabbath Bloody Sabbath, 1973; Sabotage, 1975; Technical Ectasy, 1976; Never Say Die, 1978; Heaven and Hell, 1980; Mob Rules, 1981; Live Evil, 1983; Born Again, 1983; Seventh Star, 1983; The Eternal Idol, 1987; Headless Cross, 1990; Tyr, 1990; Dehumanizer, 1992; Forbidden, 1995; Under Wheels of Confusion, 1996; Reunion, 1998; Numerous compilations; Solo album: Iommi, 2000. *Current Management:* Gloria Butler Management, PO Box 2686, Knowle, Birmingham B94 5NQ, England.

IREDALE Simon James; b. 21 Nov. 1970, Bradford, West Yorkshire, England. Songwriter; Performer; Musician (Guitar, Keyboards). *Musical Education:* Grade V, Music and Theory at age 9. *Career:* Has been in various bands from age 6; Toured Britain with the band, Terrorize and The Love Generation; On tour with the band, Hothead; Radio appearances on Pennine Radio, BBC Radio 1, and BBC GLR programme, Unplugged with Janice Long. *Recordings:* Numerous recordings, with Hothead. *Memberships:* Musicians' Union; National Band Register. *Leisure interest:* Music. *Current Management:* Calderbank and Clarke Management. *Address:* 22 Devonshire Rd, Chorley, Lancashire, England.

IRELAND Michael E; b. 10 Feb. 1962, Kansas City, Missouri, USA. Country Singer/Songwriter; Musician (Bass). Divorced. *Education:* BA, Music Education; MA, English, University of Missouri at Columbia. *Career:* Appearance, Prime Time Country, TNN, 1998, World Cafe, WXPN radio, 1998, Acoustic Cafe, national syndicated radio, 1998. *Recording:* Learning How to Live, 1998. *Membership:* BMI. *Current Management:* Joyce Linehan Management, Boston. *Address:* 10 A Burt St, Boston, MA 02124, USA.

IRONS Jack; b. 18 July 1962, Los Angeles, California, USA. Musician (Drums). *Career:* Member, Red Hot Chili Peppers; Joined Pearl Jam, 1994; Numerous tours and TV appearances. *Recordings:* Singles: Animal, 1994; Spin the Black Circle, 1994; Merkin Ball, 1995; Not for You, 1995; Immortality, 1995; I Got Id EP, 1995; Who You Are, 1996; Albums: Vitalogy, 1994; No Code, 1996; Live on Two Legs, 1998; Yield, 1998.

ISAACS Gregory; b. 1951, Kingston, Jamaica. Reggae Singer. *Career:* Solo singer, 1970s-; Established own African Museum Shop and label, with Errol Dunkley, 1973; Extensive international tours. *Recordings:* Numerous albums include: Mr Isaacs; Extra Classic; The Early Years; Sly and Robbie Present; The Best Of, Vols 1 and 2; Cool Ruler; Soon Forward; Lonely Lover; My Number One; Red Roses For Gregory; Taxi Show Case; Night Nurse; Out Deh; Warning; Can't Stay Away, 1992; No Luck, 1993; Private Lesson, 1995; Mr Love, 1995; Memories, 1995; Mr Cool, 1996; Live at Maritime Hall, 1998; Cool Ruler, 1999; Turn Down the Lights, 1999; The Best of Gregory Isaacs Vol. 1 and 2, 1999; Private and Confidential, 2000; Dancing Floor, 2000; Reasoning With The Almighty, 2001. *Honours include:* Grammy Nomination, Reggae Album, Private and Confidential, 2001. *Address:* c/o Fantasma Tours International, 2000 S Dixie Hwy, West Palm Beach, FL 33401, USA.

ISAACS Jason; b. 30 April 1968, England. Singer; Songwriter; Guitar. m. Marion. *Career:* Dance Macabre, 1985; The Promise, 1994; Triggerfish, 1996; Solo Artist, 1996-, various radio apps; Various sessions as Backing Vocalist. *Compositions:* A Girl Called Jesus; Sigh; C-Life; Bike; Funky Chuny; Gun; Only a Northern Band; News; Hold It Down; Who Says I Can; Cornucopia. *Recordings:* Debut single released, 1997, A Girl Called Jesus, 1998. *Leisure interests:* Football; Skiing. *Current Management:* Sound Judgement Partnership, 42 Brent Moor Rd, Bramhan, Stockport, Cheshire SK7 3PT, England.

ISAAK Chris; b. 26 June 1956, Stockton, California, USA. Singer; Songwriter; Actor. *Education:* Degree, English and Communication Arts. *Career:* Singer, 1984-; Extensive international tours include: Turku Festival, Finland, 1993; Support to Tina Turner, US tour, 1993; Television appearances include: The Last Resort; The Tonight Show; Saturday Night Live; Late Show With David Letterman; Actor, films: Married To The Mob, 1988; Wild At Heart, 1989; The Silence of The Lambs, 1990; Twin Peaks – Fire Walk With Me, 1993; Little Buddha, 1993. *Compositions:* Music for films: Blue Velvet; Wild At Heart; Music for television: Days of Our Lives; The Preppie Murder; Private Eye. *Recordings:* Albums: Silvertone, 1985; Chris Isaak, 1987; Heart Shaped World, 1989; Wicked Game, 1991; San Francisco Days, 1993; Forever Blue, 1995; Baja Sessions, 1996; Speak of the Devil, 1998; Wicked Ways Anthology, 1998; Always Got Tonight, 2002; Singles include: Blue Hotel, 1987; Wicked Game, 1989; Blue Spanish Sky, 1991; Don't Make Me Dream About You, 1991; Two Hearts, 1993; Can't Do A Thing (To Stop Me), 1993; Dark Moon, 1993; Solitary Man, 1993; Go Walking Down There, 1995; Somebody's Crying, 1995; Please, 1998; Bad Thing, 1999. *Honours:* International Rock Award, Best Male Vocalist of the Year, 1991; 3 MTV Music Video Awards, Wicked Game, 1991. *Current Management:* Howard Kaufman, H K Management, 8900 Wilshire Blvd, Suite 300, Beverly Hills, CA 90211, USA.

ISHAM Mark; b. 7 Sept. 1951, NYC, NY, USA. Composer; Prod.; Sound Engineer; Jazz Musician (Trumpet). m. Donna Linson, 24 Feb. 1990. *Career:* Film scores include: Never Cry Wolf, 1983; Mrs Soffel, 1984; The Times of Harvey Milk, 1984; Country, 1984; Trouble in Mind, 1985; The Hitcher, 1986; Made in Heaven, 1987; The Moderns, 1988; The Beast, 1988; Everybody Wins, 1990; Love at Large, 1990; Reversal of Fortune, 1990; Mortal Thoughts, 1991; Crooked Hearts, 1991; Point Break, 1991; Little Man Tate, 1991; Billy Bathgate, 1991; Cool World, 1992; A Midnight Clear, 1992; Of Mice and Men, 1992; The Public Eye, 1992; A River Runs Through It, 1992; Sketch Artist, 1992; Nowhere to Run, 1993; Fire in the Sky, 1993; Made in America, 1993; Short Cuts, 1993; Romeo is Bleeding, 1994; The Getaway, 1994; Quiz Show, 1994; Mrs Parker and the Vicious Circle, 1994; Nell, 1994; Losing Isiah, 1995; The Net, 1995; Home for the Holidays, 1995; Last Dance, 1996; Gotti, 1996; Fly Away Home, 1996; Night Falls on Manhattan, 1997; Afterglow, 1997; The Education of Little Tree, 1997; TV Themes include: Chicago Hope EZ Streets: recordings include (solo) Vapor Drawings, 1983; Castalia, 1988; Tibet, 1989; Mark Isham, 1991; Education of Little Tree, 1998; Afterglow, 1998; Miles Remembered: The Silent Way Project, 1999; Blue Sun, with Charles Jankel, 1995; Deal It Out, with America, View From the Ground (with Van Morrison), Live at the Belfast Opera House; Into the Music, Inarticulate Speech of the Heart; Common One; Beautiful Vision (with Art Lande); Story of Baku; Eccentricities of Earl Dant; Rubisa Patrol; Desert Marauders; We Begin (with Group 87); Group 87; A Career In Dada Processing (with the Rolling Stones); Voodoo Lounge (with Bruce Springsteen); Human Touch (with Willie Nelson); Across the Borderline (with Toots Thielmans); Toots. *Current Management:* Ron Moss Management.

ISLAM Yusuf, (Steven Georgiou, Cat Stevens); b. 21 July 1948, London, England. Writer; Dir of Production Co. m. Fawzia Mubarik Ali, 7 Sept. 1979, 2 s., 1 deceased, 4 d. *Musical Education:* Self-taught. *Career:* Commenced with release of I Love My Dog, Oct 1966; Achieved international status with multi-platinum sales of albums Tea For The Tillerman, 1970; Teaser and The Firecat, 1971; Following extensive tours, including: Bamboozle, 1974; Majikat, 1976; Numerous television appearances; Decided to retire at summit of popularity in 1978 after embracing Islam. *Recordings include:* Hit singles: I Love My Dog, 1966; Matthew and Son (No. 2, UK), 1967; I'm Gonna Get Me A Gun, 1967; A Bad Night, 1967; Lady D'Arbanville, 1970; Moonshadow, 1971; Morning Has Broken, 1971; Can't Keep It In, 1972; Another Saturday Night, 1974; Remember The Days of The Old School Yard, 1977; Albums include: Matthew and Son, 1967; New Masters, 1968; World of Cat Stevens, 1970; Mona Bone Jakon, 1970; Tea For The Tillerman, 1971; Teaser and The Firecat, 1971; Very Young and Early Songs, US, 1971; Catch Bull At Four, 1972; Foreigner, 1973; Buddha and The Chocolate Box, 1974; View From The Top, 1974; Numbers, 1975; Greatest Hits, 1975; Iztso, 1977; Back To Earth, 1978; Cat's Cradle, 1978; Footsteps In The Dark (Comp), 1984; Classics Vol. 24 – Cat Stevens, 1989; Very Best of Cat Stevens, 1990; As Yusuf Islam: The Life of The Last Prophet(s), 1995; A Is For Allah, 2000. *Publications:* Cat Stevens-Definitive Career, Chris Charlesworth; The Boy Who Looked At The Moon, David Evans, 1995. *Memberships:* Musicians'

Union; Mem., exclusive club of artists whose composition has been performed more than 2m. times, in US alone (with Morning Has Broken). *Leisure interests:* Swimming; Riding; Reading. *Address:* c/o Cat Music, 3 Furlong Rd, London N7 8LA, England.

ISLEIFSSON Arni; b. 18 Sept. 1927, Reykjavik, Iceland. Musician. m. Kristin Axelsdottir, 1 s., 3 d. *Education:* Music School. *Career:* Television and radio appearances. *Compositions:* Children's songs, 3 records, 1960, 1961; Record, 1984. *Honours:* Invited as Jazz Music Director, Trip to New Orleans by Atlanta Airlanes and Channel 2 and Travelbureou Samvinnuferdir Landsyn. *Memberships:* Jazzclub Egilsstadir; Egilsstadir Jazz Festival. *Leisure interests:* Fly Fishing. *Current Management:* Egilsstadir Jazz Festival. *Address:* Hraunbar 122 110 Reykjavík, Iceland.

ISLEY Ernie; b. 7 March 1952, Cincinnati, Ohio, USA. Musician (guitar, drums). *Career:* Member, The Isley Brothers with brothers: Rudolph, Ronald, Marvin and cousin Chris Jasper, 1969–84; Member, Isley, Jasper, Isley (with Marvin and Chris), 1984-. *Recordings:* Albums: with The Isley Brothers: The Brothers Isley, 1969; Live At Yankee Stadium, 1969; Givin' It Back, 1971; Brother Brother Brother, 1972; The Isleys Live, 1973; The Isleys' Greatest Hits, 1973; Live It Up, 1974; The Heat Is On (No. 1, USA), 1975; Harvest For The World, 1976; Go For Your Guns, 1977; Forever Gold, 1977; Showdown, 1978; Winner Takes All, 1979; Go All The Way, 1980; Grand Slam, 1981; Inside You; 1981; The Real Deal, 1982; Between The Sheets, 1983; with Isley Jasper Isley: Broadway's Closer To Sunset Boulevard, 1985; Caravan of Love, 1985; Masterpiece, 1985; Different Drummer, 1987; Solo album: High Wire, 1990; Tracks of Life (with Marvin and Ronald), 1992; Beautiful Ballads, 1994; Funky Family, 1995; Mission to Please, 1996; It's Your Thing: The Story of the Isley Brothers, 1999; Love Songs, 2001; Eternal, 2001; Singles include: with the Isley Brothers: Love The One You're With, 1971; Spill The Wine, 1971; That Lady, 1973; Summer Breeze, 1974; Fight The Power, 1975; For The Love of You (Part 1 and 2), 1975; Who Loves You Better, 1976; Harvest For The World, 1976; It's Disco Night (Rock Don't Stop), 1979; with Isley, Jasper, Isley: Caravan of Love, 1985. *Honours:* Inducted into Rock and Roll Hall of Fame, 1992; Gold Ticket, Madison Square Garden, 1980. *Current Management:* Ron Weisner Management, 9200 Sunset Blvd, Penthouse 15, Los Angeles, CA 90069, USA.

ISLEY Marvin; b. 18 Aug. 1953, Cincinnati, Ohio, USA. Musician (bass, percussion). *Career:* Member, The Isley Brothers (with brothers, Rudolph, Ronald, Ernie and cousin Chris Jasper), 1969–84; Member, Isley, Jasper, Isley (with Ernie and Chris), 1984-. *Recordings:* Albums with the Isley Brothers include: The Brothers Isley, 1969; Brother Brother Brother, 1972; The Isleys Live, 1973; The Isleys' Greatest Hits, 1973; Live It Up, 1974; The Heat Is On (No. 1, USA), 1975; Harvest For The World, 1976; Go For Your Guns, 1977; Showdown, 1978; Winner Takes All, 1979; Go All The Way, 1980; Grand Slam, 1981; Inside You, 1981; The Real Deal, 1982; Between The Sheets, 1983; with Isley Jasper Isley: Broadway's Closer To Sunset Boulevard, 1985; Caravan of Love, 1985; Different Drummer, 1987; Tracks of Life, (with Ernie and Ronald), 1992; Beautiful Ballads, 1994; Funky Family, 1995; Mission to Please, 1996; It's Your Thing: The Story of the Isley Brothers, 1999; Love Songs, 2000; Eternal, 2001; Singles include: It's Your Thing, 1969; Love The One You're With, 1971; Spill The Wine, 1971; Lay-Away, 1972; Pop That Thang, 1972; That Lady, 1973; Summer Breeze, 1974; Highway of My Life, 1974; Fight The Power, 1975; For The Love of You, 1975; Harvest For The World, 1976; It's A Disco Night, 1979; Goodnight (It's Time For Love), 1980. *Honours:* Gold Ticket, Madison Square Garden, 1980; Inducted into Rock and Roll Hall of Fame, 1992. *Current Management:* Ron Weisner Management, 9200 Sunset Blvd, Penthouse 15, Los Angeles, CA 90069, USA.

ISLEY Ronald; b. 21 May 1941, Cincinnati, Ohio, USA. Singer. *Career:* Member, gospel group, Isley Brothers, early 1950s; Formed trio with Rudolph and O'Kelly, 1955; First British tour, 1964; Formed T-Note record label, as producer and writer, 1969; 2 further Isley brothers join, Ernie and Marvin, 1969–84; Group currently billed as The Isley Brothers Featuring Ronald Isley, 1989-. *Recordings:* Albums: Twist and Shout, 1959; This Old Heart of Mine, 1966; It's Our Thing, 1969; Givin' It Back, 1971; Brother Brother Brother, 1972; The Isleys Live, 1973; The Isleys' Greatest Hits, 1973; Live It Up, 1974; The Heat Is On (No. 1, USA), 1975; Harvest For The World, 1976; Go For Your Guns, 1977; Forever Gold, 1977; Showdown, 1978; Winner Takes All, 1978; Go All The Way, 1978; Grand Slam, 1978; Inside You, 1978; The Real Deal, 1978; Between The Sheets, 1978; Masterpiece, 1985; Smooth Sailin', 1987; Spend The Night, 1989; Tracks of Life (with Ernie and Marvin), 1983; Live, 1993; Beautiful Ballads, 1994; Funky Family, 1995; Mission to Please, 1996; It's Your Thing: The Story of the Isley Brothers, 1999; Love Songs, 2000; Eternal, 2001; Singles include: Shout, 1959; Twist and Shout, 1962; Testify, 1964; This Old Heart

of Mine, 1966; I Guess I'll Always Love You, 1966; Behind A Painted Smile, 1968; It's Your Thing, 1969; I Turned You On, 1969; Put Yourself In My Place, 1969; Love The One You're With, 1971; Spill The Wine, 1971; Pop That Thang, 1972; Work To Do, 1972; That Lady, 1973; Summer Breeze, 1974; The Highway of My Life, 1974; Fight The Power, 1975; For The Love of You, 1975; Who Loves You Better, 1976; Harvest For The World, 1976; Livin' In My Life, 1978; Goodnight (It's Time For Love), 1980; Spend The Night, 1989. *Honours:* Grammy Award, Best R & B Vocal, It's Your Thing, 1969; Inducted into Rock and Roll Hall of Fame, 1992. *Current Management:* Ron Weisner Entertainment, 9200 Sunset Blvd, Penthouse 15, Los Angeles, CA 90069, USA.

ISLEY Rudolph; b. 1 April 1939, Cincinnati, Ohio, USA. Singer. *Career:* Member, Isley Brothers, gospel group, early 1950s; Formed trio with brothers Ronald and O'Kelly, 1955–; Formed T-Neck record label, writing, producing, became vice-president, 1969; Group joined by brothers Ernie, Marvin, and cousin Chris Jasper, 1969–84. *Recordings:* Albums: Shout, 1959; Twist and Shout, 1962; This Old Heart of Mine, 1966; It's Our Thing, 1969; The Brothers, 1969; Live At Yankee Stadium, 1969; Brother Brother Brother, 1972; The Isleys Live, 1973; The Isleys' Greatest Hits, 1973; Live It Up, 1974; The Heat Is On (No. 1, USA), 1975; Harvest For The World, 1976; Go For Your Guns, 1977; Showdown, 1978; Winner Takes All, 1978; Go All The Way, 1978; Grand Slam, 1981; Inside You, 1981; The Real Deal, 1982; Between The Sheets, 1983; Smooth Sailin', 1987; The Isley Brothers Greatest Hits, 1988; Spend The Night, 1989; Love Songs, 2000; Eternal, 2001; Singles include: This Old Heart of Mine, 1966; I Guess I'll Always Love You, 1966; Behind A Painted Smile, 1968; It's Your Thing, 1969; I Turned You On, 1969; Put Yourself In My Place, 1969; Spill The Wine, 1971; Love The One You're With, 1971; That Lady, 1973; Summer Breeze, 1974; What It Comes Down To, 1974; Highway of My Life, 1974; For The Love of You (Part 1 and 2), 1975; Harvest For The World, 1976; It's Disco Night (Rock Don't Stop), 1979; Goodnight (It's Time For Love), 1980. *Honours:* Grammy Award, Best R & B Vocal Performance, 1970; Gold Ticket, Madison Square Garden, New York, 1980; Inducted into Rock and Roll Hall of Fame, 1992. *Current Management:* Ron Weisner Entertainment, 9200 Sunset Blvd, Penthouse 15, Los Angeles, CA 90069, USA.

ITAMARACÁ Lia De, (Maria Madalena Correio do Nascimento); b. 1944, Itamaracá, Brazil. Vocalist; Songwriter. *Career:* Singing cirandas (dance song set to distinctive percussive rhythm with mostly rurally-themed lyrics) since aged 11; Composed Esta Ciranda Quem Me Deu Foi Lia with Teca Calazans, aged 18; Song became well known all over Brazil; Recorded her first LP, 1977, but subsequently faded from the limelight; Continued to perform cirandas in Itamaracá and recent national interest in this folk form has revived career; Performed shows all over Brazil and recorded second album Eu Sou Lia. *Compositions:* Esta Ciranda Quem Me Deu Foi Lia. *Recordings:* Eu Sou Lia, 2000.

IVEY Lee (Carole Lee); b. Kentucky, North Carolina, USA. *Career:* Performed with Bobby Atkins; Screenwriter; The Legend of Broken Heart Creek, screenplay, 6 months, 1993; Songwriter; Currently working on script for Come Back to Broken Heart Creek. *Recordings:* Bunnie Mills and Friends, CD; It's Your Lie, 1998; Just for Old Times Sake, 1998. *Address:* 4100 N Ohenry Blvd, Lot#158 Greensboro, NC 27405, USA.

IVITSKY Conrad; b. 28 Oct. 1978, Edinburgh, Scotland. Singer; Musician (Bass). *Career:* Toured onver 30 countries with British Council, WOMAD and others; Appeared on Cuban TV alongside Fidel Castro. *Recordings:* Venus in Tweeds; A Whisky Kiss and Live with Shooglenifty; Numerous performances as session player. *Leisure interest:* Skydiving. *Address:* 23 St Leonards Bank, Edinburgh, Scotland.

IWAN Dafydd; b. 24 Aug. 1943, Glanaman, Wales. Welsh Singer-Songwriter; Record Co Dir. m. Bethan Jones, 24 Sept. 1988, 2 s. (2 s., 1 d. from previous marriage). *Education:* Brynaman, Rhydaman, Bala, University of Wales. *Career:* Regular stage performances (as solo artist, with folk group, and with own band), 1962–; Regular television appearances, 1965–; Tours: North America; Europe; Celtic countries. *Recordings:* 11 albums; Songs include: Yma O Hyd; Carlo; Pam Fod Eira'n Wyn; Ai Am Fod Haul; Hawl I Fyw; Cynnar; Caneuon Gwerin; Dal i Gredu; Can Celt. *Publications:* Several song books including: Holl Ganeuon (151 songs). *Honours:* Hon. mem., Gorsedd of Bards; Gold Disc for Services to Welsh Recording Industry, 1990; Hon. Fellow, University of Wales (Bangor and Aberystwyth), for Services to Welsh Music and Language, 1998. *Membership:* Equity. *Leisure interests:* Poetry; Sport; Art. *Current Management:* Sain. *Address:* Canolfan Sain, Llandwrog, Caernarfon, Gwynedd LL54 5TG, Wales.

J

JA RULE, (Jeff Atkins); b. 29 Feb. 1977, Queens, New York, USA. Rapper. *Career:* Began rapping at 16; First appeared on Mic Geronimo's Time To Build, 1995; Collaborations: Jay-Z; Blackstreet; So Plush; DJ Clue; Dru Hill; Jennifer Lopez. *Recordings:* Albums: Venni Vetti Vecci, 1999; Rule 3.36, 2001; Singles: Murdergram, 1990; Holla Holla, 1999; Put It On Me, Between Me and You, 2001. *Honour:* MOBO Awards, Best Hip Hop Artist nominee, 2001. *Address:* c/o Def Jam, 825 Eighth Ave, New York, 10019–7472, USA.

JACKSON Alan Eugene; b. 17 Oct. 1958, Newnan, Georgia, USA. Singer; Songwriter. m. Denise Jackson, 12 Dec. 1979, 3 d. *Education:* 2 years college. *Career:* Multi-platinum album sales, over 24m.; Performed before over 3m. fans; Appeared on numerous award shows; Television includes: The Late Show with David Letterman; The Tonight Show; Regis and Kathie Lee. *Compositions include:* Chattahoochee (No. 1, USA). *Recordings:* Albums: Here In The Real World, 1990; Don't Rock The Jukebox, 1991; A Lot About Livin', 1992; Who I Am, 1994; Greatest Hits Collection, 1995; Everything I Love, 1996; High Mileage, 1998; Under the Influence, 1999; Super Hits, 1999; When Somebody Loves You, 2000. *Honours:* Academy of Country Music Male Artist of The Year, 1995; Country Music Assn Entertainer of The Year, 1995. *Memberships:* ASCAP; NARAS; ACM; CMA. *Leisure interests:* Fishing; Collecting cars and Harley Davidson motorcycles; Boating. *Current Management:* Chip Peay Entertainment. *Address:* Alan Jackson Fanclub, PO Box 121945, Nashville, TN 37212–1945, USA.

JACKSON Bob; b. 6 Jan. 1949, Coventry, England. Musician (keyboards, guitar); Vocalist; Songwriter. m. Christine, 18 Oct. 1980, 2 s., 1 d. *Musical Education:* Self-taught. *Career:* Bands: Indian Summer; with Ross: 2 US tours, 1 supporting Eric Clapton, 1974; with Badfinger: British tour with Man, 1974; 4 US tours, 1982–85; BBC television documentary, 1986; with Dodgers: Various television and radio include: In Concert, Crackerjack, Supersonic; Scene; David Byron Band; Fortunes. *Compositions:* Various songwriting deals with Essex, Island, 16 song releases. *Recordings:* Album/single releases with all the above bands. *Memberships:* PRS; MCPS; Musicians' Union. *Current Management:* Brian Yeats. *Address:* Home Farm House, Canwell, West Midlands B75 5SH, England.

JACKSON Carl Eugene; b. 18 Sept. 1953, Louisville, Mississippi, USA. Songwriter; Musician (banjo). *Career:* Musician, Jim and Jesse; The Sullivan Family; Glen Campbell, 1972–84; Songwriter, Glen Campbell Publishing, 1984–87; Ricky Skaggs/Polygram Music Publishing, 1987–90; Famous Music Publishing, 1990–93; McSpadden Smith Music, 1993–96; Colonel Rebel Music, 1996–. *Compositions:* Letter To Home; Little Mountain Church House; Put Yourself In My Place; Breaking New Ground; Against The Grain; No Future In The Past; Fit For A King; Lonesome Dove. *Recordings:* Albums: Roll On, Alabama, 1984; 13, Emmylou Harris, 1987; Angel Band, Emmylou Harris; Trio III, Linda Ronstadt, Dolly Parton, Emmylou Harris; Sevens, Garth Brooks; Ropin' The Wind, Garth Brooks; This Time, Dwight Yorkam; Gone, Dwight Yorkam. *Honours:* IBMA Song of The Year, Little Mountain Church House, 1990; Grammy for Best Bluegrass album, Spring Training, 1991; Dove Award for Best Southern Gospel Song, Where Shadows Never Fall, 1991. *Memberships:* CMA; ACM, NARAS.

JACKSON Clarence; b. 28 Dec. 1923, Green Sea, South Carolina, USA. Recording Artist; Prod.; Musician (steel guitar, dobro). m. Carolyn W Jackson, 5 June 1949, 1 s. *Education:* Clemson College; Coyne Electrical School; Elkin's Radio School. *Career:* Radio and television personality; Tent, theatre, school and park Country shows; Toured with Western film stars: Al 'Lash' Larue; Cowboy Tex Ritter; Shows on US armed forces radio, World War II; Recorded 500 pure dobro guitar tunes (world record for dobroist); PBS radio broadcasting; Traditional music dobro man, comedian. *Recordings include:* with Sister Foye Turner: Country Gospel; Old Time Country Songs; with Roger Hopkins: Smokey Mountain Favourites; with Billie and Gordon Hamrick: Gospel Time; with Bernard Sturkie: Gene Autrey Favourites; with Mutt Poston: Favourite Waltzes; James Wall Sings 20 Carter Family Songs; Hoedowns; Hawaiian and Country; Country Get Together; Red White and Country Gospel; with Roy Rea: Dobro Honky-Tonking; with Maggie Country Singers: Country Favourites; Heart Warming Recitations, with C Band; Big John Demarcus: Jimmie Rogers Favourites; The Carolina Boys; 23 guitar instructional videos: How To Play By Ear The Clarence Jackson Way. *Publication:* Autobiography. *Honours:* US Air Force; US National Guard; US Army; Country Music Assns. *Address:* 308 Starbright Lane, Moncks Corner, SC 29461, USA.

JACKSON David Nicholas George; b. 15 April 1947, Stamford. Musician; Teacher; Consultant. m. Susan Elizabeth Jackson, 1 s., 1 d.

Education: MA, St Andrews University; PGCE, Surrey University. *Career:* Van Der Graff Generator, 1969–77; Teacher, 1978–89; Musician, Soundbeam Consultant, David Jackson's Tonewall, an interactive performance with Soundbeams, Echo-Mirrors and Jelly-bean Tree suitable for all abilities and disabilities, 1990; Radio 1 Newsbeat, Radio 3 and 4, Soundbeam Specials; Television, Tomorrows World. *Compositions:* The House That Cried; Beam Machine, Star Messenger. *Recordings:* Van Der Graff Generator; Long Hello Series; Fractal Bridge; Peter Hamill. *Publications:* Special Children; Soundbeam Artistry. *Memberships:* PRS; MCPS; Sound Sense. *Leisure interests:* Music; Walking. *Address:* 37 Carey Rd, Wokingham, Berkshire, RG40 2NP, England.

JACKSON Elizabeth Lilian Mary, (Elizabeth Hoey); b. 4 Dec. 1946, Hendon, London, England. Singer (Mezzo Soprano). m. Peter W Jackson, 16 Aug. 1969, 1 s., 3 d. *Education:* Watford College of Further Education, Hertfordshire; Watford School of Music, 1965–66; Royal College of Music, 1966–69; Birmingham School of Music (pt-time), 1969–72. *Career:* Singer, Coombe Abbey Medieval Banquets; Formed Welsh Road Warblers, 3 singers and acoustic guitar, 1987; Appearances in voluntary clubs and societies in the West Midlands; Interview, CWR, 1996; Local charity rock and light entertainment, concerts, 1998; Light-hearted music, poetry and comedy sketches. *Recordings:* Folk Seasons; Sam Richard's Evening Love Song, 1996; A Bird in the Hand; Eliz: The Drummer and Cookie, 1997. *Membership:* Music for Disabled. *Leisure interests:* Moravian Church organist; School and nursery assistant. *Current Management:* Jo Tucker, Leamington Spa. *Address:* Holly Tree House, School Lane, Priors Marston, Southam CV47 7RR, England.

JACKSON Janet; b. 16 May 1966, Los Angeles, USA. Singer; Actress. m. El DeBarge, 1984, divorced 1986. *Career:* First appearance with family singing group The Jacksons, aged 7; Television actress, 1977–81; Appeared in US television series: Good Times, CBS-TV; Diff'rent Strokes; Fame; A New Kind of Family; Solo recording artiste, 1982–; Concerts and tours include: Rhythm Nation World Tour (US, Europe, Far East), 1990; Film debut, Poetic Justice, 1993. *Recordings:* Albums: Janet Jackson, 1982; Dream Street, 1984; Control, 1986; Janet Jackson's Rhythm Nation (No. 1, USA), 1989; Janet (No. 1, UK and US), 1993; Design of a Decade 1986–96, 1995; The Velvet Rope, 1997; All For You, 2001; Hit singles include: What Have You Done For Me Lately, 1986; Nasty, 1986; When I Think of You (No. 1, USA), 1986; Control, 1987; Let's Wait Awhile, 1987; The Pleasure Principle, 1987; Miss You Much (No. 1, USA), 1989; Rhythm Nation, 1989; Come Back To Me, 1990; Escapade (No. 1, USA), 1990; Alright, 1990; Black Cat (No. 1, USA), 1990; Love Will Never Do (Without You), (No. 1, USA), 1991; The Best Things In Life Are Free, duet with Luther Vandross, from film Mo' Money, 1992; That's The Way Love Goes (No. 1, USA), 1993; If, 1993; Again (No. 1, USA), 1993; Because of Love, 1994; Any Time Any Place, 1994; You Want This, 1994; Whoops Now, 1995; Scream, with Michael Jackson, 1995; Runaway, 1995; Twenty Foreplay, 1996; When I Think of You, 1996; Got Til It's Gone, 1997; Together Again, 1997; Go Deep, 1998; Every Time, 1998; I Get Lonely, 1998; Girlfriend, 1999; What's It Gonna Be, with Busta Rhymes, 1999; Doesn't Really Matter (No. 1, USA), 2000. *Current Management:* Roger Davies Management, 15030 Ventura Blvd #772, Sherman Oaks, CA 91403, USA.

JACKSON Jermaine Lajuan; b. 11 Dec. 1954, Gary, Indiana, USA. Singer; Musician (bass); Record Prod. m. Hazel Gordy, 15 Dec. 1973. *Career:* Member, Jackson Five (later The Jacksons), US family singing group, 1969–75; Solo recording artiste, 1972–; Career development of artists including Devo; Michael Lovesmith; Syreeta; Formed own production company, and record label, WORK Records; Producer, US television series The Jacksons – An American Dream, ABC, 1992. *Recordings include:* Albums: with The Jacksons: Diana Ross Presents The Jackson 5, 1970; ABC, 1970; Third Album, 1970; Christmas Album, 1970; Maybe Tomorrow, 1971; Looking Through The Windows, 1972; Skywriter, 1973; Get It Together, 1973; Anthology, 1976; Victory, 1984; Motown Legends, 1993; Ultimate Collection, 1995; Solo albums: Jermaine, 1972; Come Into My Life, 1973; My Name Is Jermaine, 1976; Feel The Fire, 1977; Let's Get Serious, 1980; Jermaine, 1981; I Like Your Style, 1981; Let Me Tickle Your Fancy, 1982; Jermaine Jackson, 1984; Precious Moments, 1986; Don't Take It Personal, 1990; You Said, 1992; The Heritage Collection, 2000; Singles include: Daddy's Home, 1973; Let's Get Serious, 1980; Let Me Tickle Your Fancy, with Devo, 1982; What Do You Do, 1985; I Think It's Love, 1985; Do What You Do, 1993. *Contributions to:* film soundtracks: Voyage of The Rock Aliens, 1985; Perfect, 1985; As record producer: Tracks for Whitney Houston debut album, 1986.

JACKSON Joe; b. 11 Aug. 1954, Burton-Upon-Trent, Staffordshire, England. Singer; Songwriter. *Musical Education:* Violin and piano lessons; S Level, Music; Composition, orchestration, piano and percussion, Royal College of Music, London. *Career:* Played with Johnny Dankworth; Member, National Youth Jazz Orchestra; Musical director, Coffee and Cream, 1977; Singer, 1978–; Regular UK and international tours, 1978–; Concerts include: The Summer of '80 Garden Party, with Bob Marley, Average White Band, Crystal Palace, 1980. *Compositions include:* Film scores: Mike's Murder, 1983; Shijin No Ie (House of The Poet), 1985; Tucker, 1988. *Recordings:* Albums: Look Sharp!, 1979; I'm The Man, 1979; Beat Crazy, 1980; Joe Jackson's Jumpin' Jive, 1981; Night and Day, 1982; Big World, 1986; Will Power, 1987; Live 1980/86, 1988; Blaze of Glory, 1988; Laughter and Lust, 1990; Steppin' Out – The Best of Joe Jackson, 1990; Night Music, 1994; Heaven and Hell, 1997; Symphony 1, 1999; Summer In The City, 2000; Night and Day II, 2001; Hit singles include: Is She Really Going Out With Him?, 1978; It's Different For Girls, 1980; Steppin' Out, 1982, 1996, 1998. *Honour:* Grammy Nomination, film score Tucker, 1988; Grammy Award, Pop Instrumental Album, Symphony 1, 2001. *Current Management:* C Winston Simone Management, 1790 Broadway, 10th Floor, New York, NY 10019, USA.

JACKSON LaToya; b. 29 May 1956, Gary, Indiana, USA. Singer. *Career:* Began as backing vocalist for Jackson family; Turned solo artist, 1979; Backing vocals on Michael Jackson's Thriller album; Numerous TV appearances. *Recordings:* Singles: Bet'cha Gonna Need My Lovin'; Heart Don't Lie; Sexual Feel; Albums: LaToya Jackson, 1980; My Special Love, 1981; Heart Don't Lie, 1984; Imagination, 1986; LaToya, 1988; From Nashville to You, 1994; Be My Lover, 1995; Bad Girl, 1995; You're Gonna Get Rocked, 1995; Moulin Rouge, 2001.

JACKSON Michael (Joseph); b. 29 Aug. 1958, Gary, Indiana, USA. m. (1) Lisa Marie Presley, divorced, (2) Debbie Rowe, divorced, 1 s., 1 d. *Career:* Lead singer, family singing group Jackson Five (later the Jacksons), 1969–75; Solo artist, 1971–; Lengthy world tours, including Bad Tour 1987; Dangerous World Tour, 1992; Film appearances: The Wiz, 1978; Captain Eo, 1986; Moonwalker, 1988; TV: The Jacksons, 1976; Guest voice, The Simpsons (as John Jay Smith), 1991; Founder, Heal The World Foundation (children's charity); Owner, ATV Music Company (including rights for John Lennon and Paul McCartney songs); Owner, MJJ record label. *Compositions include:* Co-writer with Lionel Richie, We Are The World, USA For Africa famine relief single, 1985. *Recordings:* Albums: with Jackson Five/Jacksons include: Diana Ross Presents The Jackson Five, 1969; ABC, 1970; Third Album, 1970; Goin' Back To Indiana, 1971; Maybe Tomorrow, 1971; Looking Through The Windows, 1972; Farewell My Summer, 1973; Get It Together, 1973; Skywriter, 1973; Dancing Machine, 1974; Moving Violation, 1975; Joyful Jukebox, Music, 1976; The Jacksons, 1976; Goin' Places, 1977; Destiny, 1978; Triumph, 1980; Boogie, 1980; Live, 1981; Victory, 1984; Solo albums: Got To Be There, 1971; Ben, 1972; Music and Me, 1973; Forever Michael, 1975; The Best Of, 1975; The Wiz (film soundtrack), 1978; Off The Wall, 1979; ET – The Extra Terrestrial (film soundtrack), 1982; Thriller (No. 1 in every Western country), 1982; Bad (No. 1, UK and US), 1987; Dangerous (No. 1, USA and UK), 1991; HIStory – Past, Present and Future Book I, 1995; Invincible, 2001; Hit singles with Jackson Five/Jacksons include: I Want You Back (No. 1, USA), 1969; ABC (No. 1, USA), 1970; The Love You Save (No. 1, USA), 1970; I'll Be There (No. 1, USA), 1970; Never Can Say Goodbye, 1971; Maybe Tomorrow, 1971; Looking Through The Windows, 1972; Doctor My Eyes, 1973; Dancing Machine, 1973; Enjoy Yourself, 1976; Show You The Way To Go (No. 1, UK), 1977; Blame It On The Boogie, 1978; Shake Your Body Down To The Ground, 1979; Lovely One, 1980; Can You Feel It?, 1981; Walk Right Now, 1981; State of Shock, 1984; Numerous solo hit singles include: Got To Be There, 1971; Rockin' Robin, 1972; Ain't No Sunshine, 1972; Ben (No. 1, USA), 1972; Don't Stop Till You Get Enough (No. 1, USA), 1979; Off The Wall, 1979; Rock With You (No. 1, USA), 1980; One Day In Your Life (No. 1, UK), 1981; She's Out of My Life, 1980; The Girl Is Mine, duet with Paul McCartney (No. 1, UK), 1982; Billie Jean (No. 1, USA and UK), 1983; Beat It (No. 1, USA), 1983; Wanna Be Startin' Somethin', 1983; Human Nature, 1983; Say Say Say, duet with Paul McCartney (No. 1, USA), 1983; Thriller, 1983; PYT, 1984; Farewell My Summer Love (recorded 1973), 1984; I Can't Stop Loving You, with Siedah Garrett (No. 1, UK and US), 1987; Bad (No. 1, USA), 1987; The Way You Make Me Feel (No. 1, USA), 1988; The Man In the Mirror (No. 1, USA), 1988; Dirty Diana (No. 1, USA), 1988; Another Part of Me, 1988; Smooth Criminal, 1988; Leave Me Alone, 1989; Liberian Girl, 1989; Black and White (No. 1, UK and US), 1991; Remember The Time, 1992; In The Closet, 1992; Jam, 1992; Heal The World, 1992; Give In To Me, 1992; Scream (with Janet Jackson), 1995; You Are Not Alone (No. 1, UK), 1995; Earth Song (No. 1, UK), 1995; They Don't Care About Us, 1996; Ghosts, 1997; Stranger in Moscow, 1997; Blood on the Dance Floor, 1997 (No. 1, UK); You Rock My World, 2001; Cry, 2001. *Contributions to:* recordings by Minnie Ripperton; Carol Bayer Sager; Donna Summer; Paul McCartney. *Publications:* Moonwalk (autobiography), 1988; Dancing The Dream (poems and reflections), 1992. *Honours include:* Numerous Grammy Awards, 1980- (including 7 awards, 1984; Song of The Year, 1986; Legend Award, 1993) Numerous American Music Awards, 1980- (including 11 awards, 1984; Special Award of Achievement, 1989); BRIT Awards: Best International Artist, 1984, 1988, 1989; Artist of a Generation, 1996; Soul Train Awards, 1988–; MTV Video Vanguard Award, 1988; 2 NAACP Image Awards, 1988; Entertainer of the Decade, American Cinema Awards Foundation, 1990; First recipient, BMI Michael Jackson Award, 1990; 3 World Music Awards, 1993; Most successful album ever, Thriller (50m. copies sold world-wide); Star on Hollywood Walk of Fame, 1984; Numerous magazine poll wins and awards; Gold and Platinum records; won Artist of the Century award at American Music Awards, 2002. *Current Management:* Bob Jones, MJJ Productions. *Address:* 10960 Wilshire Blvd, 2204 Los Angeles, CA 90024, USA.

JACKSON Millie; b. 15 July 1944, Thompson, Georgia, USA. Singer. *Career:* Professional singer, 1964–; R & B singer, then Country singer; Collaborations with Isaac Hayes. *Recordings:* Ask Me What You Want; Hurts So Good, from film Cleopatra Jones; My Man A Sweet Man; Act of War, duet with Elton John; Albums: Millie Jackson, 1972; It Hurts So Good, 1973; Caught Up, 1974; Soul Believer, 1974; Still Caught Up, 1975; Best of Millie Jackson, 1976; Free and In Love, 1976; Lovingly Yours, 1977; Get It Out 'Cha System, 1978; A Moment's Pleasure, 1979; Live and Uncensored, 1980; For Men Only, 1980; Just A Lil' Bit Country, 1981; Live and Outrageous, 1982; Hard Times, 1982; ESP (Extra Sexual Persuasion), 1984; An Imitation of Love, 1986; The Tide Is Turning, 1988; Will You Love Me Tom, 1989; Back to the Shit, 1989; Young Man Older Woman, 1991; Check in the Mail, 1994; Love Quake, 1994; Rock N' Soul, 1994; It's Over, 1995; Breaking Up Somebody's Home, 1996; Did You Think I Wouldn't Cry, 1997; Not For Church Folk, 2001. *Current Management:* Keishval Enterprises, 133 Cedar Lane, Suite 208, Teaneck, NJ 07666, USA.

JACKSON Ronald Shannon; b. 12 Jan. 1940, Fort Worth, Texas, USA. Jazz Musician; Bandleader. *Career:* Musician, Charles Mingus; Betty Carter; Albert Ayler; Ornette Coleman; Cecil Taylor; Bandleader, RSJ and The Decoding Society, 1979–; Musician with Bill Laswell, Bill Frisell, 1980-. *Recordings:* 12 albums with RSJ and The Decoding Society; Over 40 albums with other artists. *Current Management:* World-wide Jazz, 1128 Broadway, Suite 425, New York, NY 10001, USA.

JACKSON Steve; Sound Engineer; Mixer. *Recordings:* Dire Straits: Brothers in Arms; Money For Nothing; Wet Wet Wet, Holding Back the River; Bryan Adams, So Far So Good; Paul Young, Simply Red, Roachford, James Taylor Quartet, Tori Amos, Sting, Deacon Blue, Capercaillie, Cast, Whipping Boy, Mark Knopfler. *Honour:* Studio Master Award for Excellence for Homelands by Steve Booker, 1990. *Leisure interest:* Sailing. *Address:* 43 St Alban's Ave, London W4 5JS, England.

JACKSON Stevie; b. 16 Jan. 1969. Vocalist; Musician (guitar); Songwriter. *Career:* Member: Belle and Sebastian, 1996–; Curated Bowlie Weekend Festival with other band members, 1999. *Recordings:* Albums: Tigermilk, If You're Feeling Sinister, 1996; The Boy With The Arab Strap 1998; Fold Your Hands Child – You Walk Like A Peasant, 2000; Singles: Dog On Wheels EP, Lazy Line Painter Jane EP, 3–6–9 Seconds of Light EP, 1997; This Is Just A Modern Rock Song EP, 1998; Legal Man, 2000; Jonathan David, I'm Waking Up To Us, 2001. *Honour:* Brit Award, Best Newcomer, 1999. *Current Management:* Banchory Management, PO Box 25074, Glasgow G2 6YL, Scotland. *Internet:* www.belleandsebastian.co.uk.

JACKSON Stonewall; b. 6 Nov. 1932, Tabor City, North Carolina, USA. Country Singer; Musician (guitar). *Musical Education:* Self-taught. *Career:* Member of Grand Ole Opry, 1956; Worked with Ernest Tubb; Recording artist, 1957-. *Compositions include:* Don't Be Angry, recorded by Daniel O'Donnell; I Washed My Face In Muddy Water; Stamp Out Loneliness. *Recordings:* Hit singles include: Life To Go, 1958; Waterloo (US Country No. 1), 1959; BJ The DJ (US Country No. 1), 1963; Me and You and A Dog Named Boo, 1971; Numerous albums include: The Dynamic Stonewall Jackson, 1959; Sadness In A Song, 1962; I Love A Song, 1963; Trouble and Me, 1965; The Exciting Stonewall Jackson, 1966; All's Fair In Love 'N' War, 1966; Help Stamp Out Loneliness, 1967; Stonewall Jackson Country, 1967; The Great Old Songs, 1968; Thoughts of a Lonely Man, 1968; Nothing Takes The Place of Loving You, 1968; I Pawned My Past Today, 1969; The Old Country Church, 1969; A Tribute To Hank Williams, 1969; The Real Thing, 1970; The Lonesome In Me, 1970; Stonewall Jackson Recorded Live At The Grand Ole Opry, 1971; Waterloo, 1971; Me and You and A Dog Named Boo, 1971; World of Stonewall Jackson, 1972; Nashville, 1974; Stonewall, 1979; My Favourite Sin, 1980; Stonewall Jackson, 1982; Solid Stonewall, 1982; Greatest Hits, 1982; Alive, 1984; Up Against The Wall, 1984; 20 Greatest Hits, 1994; All the Best, 1995; Classic Country, 1998; Stonewall Jackson, 1999. *Address:* c/o Ace Productions, PO Box 292725, Nashville, TN 37229–2725, USA.

JACKSON Tito; b. 15 Oct. 1953, Gary, Indiana, USA. Singer. *Career:* Member, The Jackson 5; Signed to Motown Records, 1969; Numerous television appearances and concerts; Later became The Jacksons. *Recordings include:* Singles: I Want You Back (No. 1, USA), 1969; ABC (No. 1, USA), 1970; The Love You Save (No. 1, USA), 1970; I'll Be There (No. 1, USA), 1970; Rockin' Robin, 1972; Mama's Pearl, 1972; Never Can

Say Goodbye, 1971; Looking Through The Windows, 1972; Doctor My Eyes, 1973; Dancing Machine, 1973; Enjoy Yourself, 1976; Show You The Way To Go (No. 1, UK), 1977; Blame It On The Boogie, 1978; Shake Your Body (Down to the Ground), 1979; Who's Lovin' You?; Heartbreak Hotel, 1980; Walk Right Now, 1981; Can You Feel It?, 1981; Nothin' That Compares 2 U, 1989; Albums: I Want You Back; Diana Ross Presents the Jackson 5; ABC; Goin' Back to Indiana; Maybe Tomorrow; Looking Through The Windows; Skywriter; Get It Together; Dancing Machine; Stand; Moving Violation; Joyful Jukebox Music; Motown Special; Goin' Places; Destiny; Zip a Dee Doo Dah; Boogie; Live; Fliphits; Victory; 2300 Jackson Street; Children of the Light; Never Can Say Goodbye.

JACKSON Trevor, (The Underdog); b. London, England. Prod.; Remixer. *Career:* Producer: The Brotherhood; Remixed: Massive Attack, Sabres of Paradise, The Pharcyde; Member: Playgroup. *Recordings:* Albums: Elementalz (with The Brotherhood), 1996; Playgroup (with Playgroup), 2001; Singles: Alphabetical Response (with The Brotherhood), 1995; One Shot (with The Brotherhood), 1996; Punk Funk (with The Brotherhood), 1996; Make It Happen (with Playgroup), 2000; Number One (with Playgroup), 2001. *Current Management:* c/o Source Records, 113–117 Farringdon Rd, London, EC1R 3BX, England.

JACKSON Wanda Lavonne; b. 20 Oct. 1937, Maud, Oklahoma, USA. Singer; Songwriter. *Career:* Toured with Hank Thompson Band; Red Foley; Recording artiste, 1956–; Began recording Christian music, 1970s. *Compositions include:* Right Or Wrong (hit for Ronnie Dove, George Strait). *Recordings:* Albums include: Wanda Jackson, 1958; Rockin' With Wanda, 1960; There's A Party Goin' On, 1961; Right Or Wrong, 1961; Lovin' Country Style, 1962; Wonderful Wanda, 1962; Love Me Forever, 1963; Two Sides of Wanda Jackson, 1964; Blues in My Heart, 1964; Sings Country Songs, 1966; Reckless Love Affair, 1967; You'll Always Have My Love, 1967; The Best Of, 1967; Cream of The Crop, 1968; The Happy Side Of, 1969; Many Moods Of, 1969; Country!, 1970; Woman Lives For Love, 1970; I've Gotta Sing, 1971; I Wouldn't Want You Any Other Way, 1972; Praise The Lord, 1972; When It's Time To Fall In Love Again, 1973; Country Keepsakes, 1973; Now I Have Everything, 1974; Rock 'N' Roll Away Your Blues, 1984; Greatest Country Hits, 1985; Early Wanda Jackson, 1986; Rockin' In The Country, 1990; Ultimate Compilation, 1996; Tears Will Be the Chaser for Your Wine, 1997; Queen of Rockabilly, 2000; Singles include: I Gotta Know; Let's Have A Party; In The Middle of a Heartache. *Honours:* Twice nominated for Grammy Award. *Address:* c/o Wanda Jackson Enterprises, PO Box 891498, Oklahoma City, OK 73189–1498, USA.

JACOBI Gina; b. 12 Dec. 1962, Hammerdal, Sweden. Composer; Singer; Keyboard Player. 3 d. *Education:* Preschool Teacher, University, 2.5 years. *Career:* Director, 5 projects including music, singing, theatre, choirs with young people; Composed music for theatres, commercial videos; 3 bigger tours after release of albums; 5 videoclips to songs; Appearances in Swedish TV, 20 times; Appearances in Kurdish Satelite. *Recordings:* Bagateller, Trifles, album, 1985; Tid and Rum, Time and Space, album, 1986; Pa jakt efter solen, Haunting, album, 1988; Ga som pa natar, Walking as Upon, album, 1989; Gare Seretaye, The Kurdish Cassette, album, 1996; Alla ar, Everybody In, album, 1996. *Honours:* Schlsp from Olof Palmes Fond; Selected as Best Female Artist in Swedish Grammis Galan. *Leisure interests:* Painting in oil and acrylic colours; Writing novels; Writing music for coming album; Working in a music project with refugees, result being recorded and released as cassette in 1998. *Address:* Gränsg 28, 852 38 Sundsvall, Sweden.

JACOBS Jon; Engineer; Mixer. *Recordings:* Engineered, Mixed, Produced: Tom Ribiero, album, 1990; The Slow Club, World of Wonders, album, 1990; Graham Parker, Burning Questions, album, 1992; Mary McLaughlin, Daughter of Lir, 1993; The Pretenders, 1992/93; Wendy James, singles, 1993; The Ya Ya's, See No Rain, single, 1993; Kenji Jammer, album mixed, 1993; Psychedelix, Psychadelix II, album mixed, 1993; Raw, 1993; Planet Claire, After the Fire, album mixed, 1993; Rynten Okazaki, album, 1994; Pacifists, album, 1994; Gota, album, 1995; Rynten Okazaki, album, soundtrack film, 1994; Psychedelix, 1995; Yuki Saito, album, 1995; Elio, Eat the Phikus, 1996; The Beatles, new singles, 1995–96; Elvis Costello, All This Useless Beauty, 1996; Paul McCartney: Flaming Pie, 1996; World Tonight, 1997; The Divine Comedy: Short Album about Love, 1997; Fin de Siecle, 1998; Certainty of chance, 1999; Secret History: Best of Divine Comedy, 1999. *Current Management:* Muirhead Management, 202 Fulham Rd, Chelsea, London SW10 9PJ, England.

JACOBS Judith (Judy) Kaye; b. 27 Sept. 1957, Lumberton, North Carolina, USA. Singer. m. James Eric Tuttle, 24 July 1993. *Education:* BA, Christian Education, Minor in Music. *Musical Education:* Production and Arrangement, with Lari Goss, Lee College, Cleveland, Tennessee. *Career:* Trinity Broadcasting, PTL; Recording artist for New Vision Records with radio airplay all over USA; Performed with Larnelle Harris; Carmen; Brooklyn Tabernacle Choir; Four Him; Major annual tours world-wide. *Recordings:* For Times Like These, 1993; Once and For All, 1995. *Honour:* Awarded Distinguished Music Performer, as special guest with Brooklyn

Tabernacle Choir. *Leisure interests:* Golf; Whitewater rafting; Raquetball. *Current Management:* Jamie Tuttle, His Song Ministries. *Address:* His Song Ministries, Inc, 233 Broad St NW, PO Box 0891, Cleveland, TN 37364, USA.

JACOBS Laurie; b. 16 April 1950, London, England. Jazz Promoter; Musician (saxophone). m. Ann Cummings, 12 Sept. 1974, 3 s. *Education:* Medical Graduate, Edinburgh University, 1974. *Musical Education:* Clarinet, saxophone, Leslie Evans. *Career:* Founded Peterborough Jazz Club, 1992; Monthly presentations, best in British and American Jazz; As musician, played Dean Street; Pizza Express; Pizza-On-The-Park; Appeared in Soho Jazz Festival. *Honour:* Peterborough City Leisure Award for Jazz Club, 1996. *Membership:* Musicians' Union. *Leisure interests:* Art; Sport. *Address:* 38 Church St, Werrington, Peterborough, Cambridgeshire PE4 6QE, England.

JACOBSEN Bo; b. 13 March 1945, Copenhagen, Denmark. Musician (drums, alto saxophone); Vocalist. 1 s., 1 d. *Education:* Architecture studies, 1966–70. *Musical Education:* Self-taught. *Career:* Member, Blue Sun, 1969–75; Osiris (with Lone Kellermann); Nada, 1977–83; Paul Ehlers Quartet, 1985–88; Crescent, 1988–89; Dream City, 1991–98; Support tours with Jimi Hendrix; Procol Harum; Dollar Brand; Memphis Slim; Numerous festivals include: Roskilde Festival; Aarhus International Jazz Festival; Midtfyn Festival; Langeland Festival; Djurs Blues Festival; Started teaching in music schools, 1996; Playing with Flower Pot Party at major concerts and festivals across Denmark, 1996–98; Chairman of Musicians' Union, Grenaa Dep, 1998; Founded own band, Bo Jacobsen World Jazz Orchestra, 1999. *Composition:* Sagarmantha Suite, electro-acoustic music CD, 1994–97. *Recordings:* with Blue Sun: Peace Be Unto You, 1970; Festival, 1970; Blue Sun, 1971; Blue Sun 73, 1973; with Nada: Nada 1, 1978; Nada 2, 1979; African Flower, 1982; with Dream City: Do The Blues, 1993; Syre, with Dream City, CD, 1996; with Bo Jacobsen's World Jazz Conspiracy: Thank You For Your Tips, 2001. *Memberships:* Danish Musicians' Union; DJFBA; KODA; Gramex; NCB; Chairman of Musicians' Union, 1998. *Leisure interests:* Chess; Country life; Mountain walks; Travel. *Current Management:* DanArtist, Overgade 41, 5100 Odense, Denmark. *Address:* Emmelev Kaervej 3, 8500 Grenaa, Denmark.

JACOBSEN Sonia Michelle; b. 5 Feb. 1967, Camden, Australia. *Education:* Jazz Degree, The New School, Mannes, New York; Musicology Degree, Grenoble and Lyon University, France; Jazz Degree, Chambery Conservatory, France. *Career:* Co-Leader, Composer, Conductor, Mosaic Orchestra; Composer, Musical Director, No Strings Attached; Leader, Melting Pot. *Compositions:* Tryzone Suite; Melting Pot. *Recordings:* Avalanche, 1995; No Strings Attached, 1997. *Membership:* American Music Center. *Current Management:* Sun Sounds, PO Box 60, Cold Spring Harbor, NY 11724, USA. *Address:* 183 Harbor Rd, Colo Spring, Harbor, NY 11724, USA.

JACOBSSON (Ruth) Ewa (Maria); b. 8 Dec. 1956, Uppsala, Sweden. Composer; Vocalist; Musician (piano). 2 s. *Education:* Konstfack, School of Arts and Handicraft (painting); Stockholm, Sweden; The Royal Academy of Fine Arts (Painting; Mixed Media, Performance); Copenhagen, Denmark. *Musical Education:* Classical piano, pianist Kerstin Åberg, Uppsala, Sweden; Classical song education, Uppsala, Sweden, Copenhagen, Denmark. *Career:* Emerald Song, 1985, Concert and television appearances, Stockholm, Sweden; Found Language, 1987, in collaboration with choreographer Jody Oberfelder-Riehm, New York; Die Menschmaschine, in collaboration with composer Morten Carlsen and theatre group Exment, Copenhagen; Voix concert, 1989, Copenhagen; Delta concert and radio appearance, 1991–92, Copenhagen; Lingua concert, 1993, Copenhagen; Guldbukar concert, 1994, Copenhagen; Interferens, Danish Radio, 1997; Ways of Red, concert, 1998; Xfelt, exhibition, Museum of Contemporary Art, Roskilde, Denmark, 1998; Contemporary Lies I, exhibition, Eindhoven, The Netherlands, 1998. *Compositions:* Voix, 1989 (tape, vocal, poem); Détour, 1990 (solo performance, vocal, tape, 8mm film, poem); Delta, choir, words by Martin Sondergaard, 1991–92; Lingua, 1993, (solo performance, tape, vocal, poem, photographic movement); Guldbukar (Golden Belly), 1994, (tape, colour-slides); Anonymous (solo performance, vocal, tape, photo and objects), 1996; LOGR (solo performance, vocal, tape, objects, waterfountain Gefjon), 1996; Kongehoved (choir, tape, photo, words by Jens Bjorneboe), 1996; Cold Dews (tape, poem), 1996; No Title (installation with tape, poem, objects, twin pictures), 1998; Ways of Red (solo performance, vocal, tape, objects), 1998; Contemporary Lies I (soundbook, tape, text, photo), 1998. *Memberships:* DJBFA; DICEM (Danish section, International Confederation for Electroacoustic Music); SKRAEP, Experimental Music Forum for Composers. *Address:* Evens Gate 7, 0655 Oslo, Norway.

JACQUEMIN André; b. 16 Jan. 1952, Hampstead, London, England. Composer; Sound Designer; Prod.; Musician (bass player); Music Programmer. m. 24 Jan. 1988, 1 d. *Musical Education:* Guitar course; APRS engineering course. *Career:* Joined recording industry aged 17 as studio runner and started engineering after 9 months to present date;

Record producer for Monty Python and produced every Python project, 1972–; Live performances include: Tis-Was; Top of The Pops; Various venues in UK and live interviews for national TV. *Compositions include:* Co-writer: Every Sperm Is Sacred (Monty Python's Meaning of Life); The Brian Song (Monty Python's Life of Brian); Six songs for Wind In The Willows, feature film; Six songs for Mumbo Jumbo, feature film; Score for The Big Freeze, Eric Sykes feature film; Score for The Hound of the Baskervilles, feature film; A Christmas Adventure; Love Potion No. 9; Ezekiel; Rubbish King of the Jumble, network cartoon series; One Foot in the Grave; Plus many commercials and incidental music compositions. *Recordings:* include: Girlschool; Classix Nouveaux; Powerhouse; Geordie; Mungo Jerry. *Publications:* Future Music; Sound On Sound; Home Studio Recording; Pro Sound News; Sound Engineer and Producer; Sound International; Radio Month; Professional; International Musician. *Honours:* BAFTA Nomination, Most Original Song in a Feature Film, Every Sperm Is Sacred; Over 80 awards for sound productions in film and television. *Membership:* Re-Pro Producers Guild of Great Britain. *Leisure interests:* Computers; Harley-Davidsons; Music; Films. *Current Management:* Old Man Jobson's.

JAFET Jean Marc; b. 8 May 1956, Nice, France. Musician (bass). *Musical Education:* Conservatoire de Musique de Nice. *Career:* Played with: Didier Lockwood; Toots Thielmans; Christian Escoude; Christian Vander (Magma); Trio Ceccarelli; Richard Galliano; Own band Agora. *Recordings:* Dolores, Agora; 3 albums with Trio Ceccarelli; 3 albums with Kalil Chahine; Brazilian Witch, Christian Escoude. *Publications:* Dolores; Hat's Snatcher; L'Arcange. *Honours:* For Hat's Snatchers, Trio Ceccarelli, Victoires Music 1994. *Membership:* SACEM. *Leisure interests:* Badminton; Football. *Current Management:* Marie Poindront. *Address:* 12 rue Seuignet, 94370 Sucy Enbrie, France.

JAFFE Jerry; b. 12 Sept. 1946, New York City, USA. Artist Man. m. Celeste Kringer, 9 Oct. 1983. *Education:* PhD Columbia University, New York City, 1972. *Career:* Manager, current artists: Joe McIntyre; Ann Marie Montade; Manager, previous artists: Jesus and Mary Chain; Catherine; Course of Empire; Joey McIntyre; Nancy Boy; Saint Etienne; co-manager with Chris Morrison: Dead Or Alive; Midge Ure; John Moore; U S Head; Creation Records, 1992–94; Formerly Senior Vice-President (Rock Division) and Vice-President Promotion and A & R, Polygram Records, USA; Promotion; Press; Artist development. *Current Management:* Management By Jaffe, 1560 Broadway, New York, NY 10036, USA.

JAGGER Mick; b. 26 July 1943, Dartford, Kent, England. Singer; Songwriter. m. Bianca Pérez Morena de Macias, 1971 (divorced 1979), 1 d., (2) Jerry Hall, 2 s., 2 d.; 1 d. by Marsha Hunt. *Education:* London School of Economics. *Career:* Member, Rolling Stones, 1962–; Numerous tours, concerts include: National Jazz and Blues Festival, Richmond, 1963; Debut British tour, 1963; Debut US tour, 1964; Free concert, Hyde Park, 1969; Free concert, Altamont Speedway, 1969; Knebworth Festival, 1976; Live Aid, Philadelphia, 1985; Solo tour including Japan, 1988; Steel Wheels North American tour, 1989; National Music Day Celebration of The Blues, with Gary Moore, 1992; Voodoo Lounge World Tour, 1994–95; Bridges to Babylon Tour, 1997–98; Films include: Ned Kelly, 1970; Performance, 1970; Freejack, 1992; Bent, 1996. *Compositions:* Co-writer for the Rolling Stones, with Keith Richards (under the psuedonym The Glimmer Twins). *Recordings:* Albums include: The Rolling Stones (No. 1, UK), 1964; The Rolling Stones No 2 (No. 1, UK), 1965; Out of Our Heads (No. 1, USA), 1965; Aftermath (No. 1, UK), 1966; Between The Buttons, 1967; Their Satanic Majesties Request, 1967; Beggar's Banquet, 1968; Let It Bleed (No. 1, UK), 1969; Get Yer Ya-Ya's Out (No. 1, UK), 1969; Sticky Fingers (No. 1, UK and US), 1971; Exile On Main Street (No. 1, UK and US), 1972; Goat's Head Soup (No. 1, UK and US), 1973; It's Only Rock and Roll (No. 1, USA), 1974; Black and Blue (No. 1, USA), 1976; Some Girls (No. 1, USA), 1978; Emotional Rescue (No. 1, UK and US), 1980; Tattoo You (No. 1, USA), 1981; Still Life, 1982; Undercover, 1983; Dirty Work, 1986; Steel Wheels, 1989; Flashpoint, 1991; Voodoo Lounge (No. 1, UK), 1994; Stripped, 1995; Bridges to Babylon, 1997; Solo albums: She's The Boss, 1985; Primitive Cool, 1987; Wandering Spirit, 1993; Goddess In The Doorway, 2001; Singles include: Come On, 1963; I Wanna Be Your Man, 1963; Not Fade Away, 1964; It's All Over Now (No. 1, UK), 1964; Little Red Rooster (No. 1, UK), 1964; The Last Time (No. 1, UK), 1965; (I Can't Get No) Satisfaction (No. 1, UK and US), 1965; Get Off of My Cloud (No. 1, UK and US), 1965; 19th Nervous Breakdown, 1966; Paint It Black (No. 1, UK), 1966; Have You Seen Your Mother Baby, Standing In The Shadow, 1966; Let's Spend The Night Together/Ruby Tuesday (No. 1, USA), 1967; We Love You, 1967; Jumping Jack Flash (No. 1, UK), 1968; Honky Tonk Women (No. 1, UK and US), 1969; Brown Sugar (No. 1, USA), 1971; Tumbling Dice, 1972; Angie (No. 1, USA), 1973; It's Only Rock N Roll, 1974; Fool To Cry, 1976; Miss You (No. 1, USA), 1978; Emotional Rescue, 1980; Start Me Up, 1981; Waiting On A Friend, 1981; Undercover of The Night, 1983; Harlem Shuffle, 1986; Mixed Emotions, 1989; Rock and A Hard Place, 1989; Highwire, 1991; Love Is Strong, 1994; Out of Tears, 1994; I Go Wild, 1995; Like A Rolling Stone, 1995; Solo singles include: Memo From Turner, 1970; State of Shock, with The Jacksons, 1984; Just Another Night, 1985; Dancing In The Street, with

David Bowie (No. 1, UK), 1985; Ruthless People, 1986; Let's Work, 1987; Sweet Thing, 1993. *Honours:* with Rolling Stones include: Grammy Lifetime Achievement Award, 1986; Inducted into Rock and Roll Hall of Fame, 1989; Q Award, Best Live Act, 1990; Ivor Novello Award, Outstanding Contribution To British Music, 1991. *Current Management:* Rupert Loewenstein, 2 King St, London SW1Y 6QL, England.

JAM Jimmy (James Harris); b. USA. Prod. *Career:* Joined Terry Lewis' band Flyte Tyme, 1972; Rejoined Flyte Tyme, renamed The Time, 1981–83; Formed (with Terry Lewis) Flyte Tyme Productions, 1982–; Built Flyte Tyme Studios, Minneapolis, 1984; Launched own label (with Terry Lewis), Perspective Records, 1991–; Helped launch new acts including Sounds of Blackness; Involved with International Association of African American Music (IAAAM), 1990-. *Recordings:* Producer (with Terry Lewis): Wild Girls, Klymaxx, 1983; Just Be Good To Me, SOS Band, 1983; Heat of The Heart, Patti Austin; Encore, Cheryl Lynn; I Didn't Mean To Turn You On, Cherelle; Saturday Love, Cherelle and Alexander O'Neal; Runaway, Janet Jackson; The Best Things In Life Are Free, Janet Jackson and Luther Vandross; Albums with Janet Jackson: Control; Rhythm Nation; Janet (all No. 1, USA); Other recordings with: Mint Condition; Low Key; George Michael; Karyn White; Boyz II Men; Johnny Gill; Fine Young Cannibals; New Edition; Mariah Carey; Shaggy; Yolanda Adams; Chante Moore; Mary J Blige; The Human League; The Isley Brothers; Film soundtrack, Mo' Money. *Honours include:* R & B Songwriting Awards, American Society of Composers and Publishers, 1989–94.

JAMAL Ahmad; b. 2 July 1930, Pittsburg, Pennsylvania, USA. Musician (piano). Divorced, 1 d. *Musical Education:* Private master classes with Mary Caldwell Dawson and James Miller. *Career:* George Hudson Orchestra, national tour, 1949; First group, The Four Strings, 1949; Accompanist to The Caldwells, 1950; Trio, The Three Strings, 1950–; Television: The Sound of Jazz, 1962; Many concert tours (including Philip Morris); Exclusive Steinway artist, 1960s-; Appeared on film soundtracks: Mash, 1970; Bridges of Madison County, 1995. *Compositions:* Comissions: 6 works for Asai Quartet, Yale University, 1994; New Rhumba; Ahmad's Blues; Night Mist Blues; Extensions; The Awakening; Excerpts From The Blues; Tranquility; Manhattan Reflections. *Recordings:* Over 50 albums include: Poinciana; But Not For Me, (including Bridges of Madison County), 1995; Olympia, 2000. *Honours:* Man of the Year, Pittsburgh Jay Cee's, 1958; NEA American Jazz Master; Duke Ellington Fellow, Yale University; Pittsburgh Mellon Jazz Festival dedication, 1994; Django D'Or Award, Paris for Essence Part 1, 1996. *Current Management:* Ellora Management. *Address:* PO Box 295, Ashley Falls, MA 01222, USA.

JAMES Alex (Stephen Alexander); b. 21 Nov. 1968, Bournemouth, Dorset, England. Musician (bass guitar). *Education:* Goldsmith's College. *Musical Education:* Violin lessons at school. *Career:* member, Blur; Television, radio, includes: Top of The Pops; Later With Jools Holland; Extensive tours include: Alexandra Palace; Reading Festival, 1993, 1999; Glastonbury Festival, 1994, 1998; Mile End, 1995; V97, 1997; All UK Arena's, 1997; Glastonbury, 1998; T In The Park, 1999; Reading/Leeds Festival, 1999. *Recordings:* Blur: Albums: Leisure, 1991; Modern Life Is Rubbish, 1993; Parklife, 1994; The Great Escape, 1995; Blur, 1997; 13, 1999; The Best of Blur, 2000; Singles: She's So High, 1990; There's No Other Way, 1991; Bang, 1991; Popscene, 1992; For Tomorrow, 1993; Chemical World, 1993; Sunday Sunday, 1993; Girls and Boys, 1994; To The End, 1994; Parklife, 1994; End of a Century, 1994; Country House (No. 1, UK), 1995; The Universal, 1995; Stereotypes, 1996; Charmless Man, 1996; Beetlebum (No. 1, UK), 1997; Song 2, 1997; On Your Own, 1997; MOR, 1997; Tender, 1999; Coffee and TV, 1999; No Distance Left To Run, 1999; Music Is My Radar, 2000; Solo recordings: Hanging Around, Me Me Me, 1996; Vindaloo, Fat Les, 1998; Naughty Christmas, Fat Les, 1998; Jerusalem, Fat Les, 2000. *Honours:* Mercury Prize Nomination; Platinum Album: Parklife; BRIT Awards, Best Single, Video, Album, Band, 1995; Q Awards, Best Album, 1994, 1995; Q Awards, Best Band, 1999; Blur, Platinum, 1999; 13, Platinum, 1999; Mercury Prize Nomination, 1999. *Current Management:* CMO Management, Unit 32, Ransome Dock, 35–37 Parkgate Rd, London SW11 4NP, England.

JAMES Etta, (Jamesetta Hawkins); b. 25 Jan. 1938, Los Angeles, USA. Singer. *Career:* Performed and recorded with Harvey Fuqua; Muscle Shoals (Chess Records houseband); Solo soul/R & B singer, 1961; Sang at opening ceremony, Los Angeles Olympics, 1988. *Recordings:* Albums: At Last!, 1961; Second Time Around, 1961; Etta James, 1962; Etta James Sings For Lovers, 1962; Etta James Top Ten, 1963; Etta James Rocks The House, 1964; Queen of Soul, 1965; Tell Mama, 1968; Etta James Sings Funk, 1970; Losers Weepers, 1971; Etta James, 1973; Peaches, 1973; Come A Little Closer, 1974; Etta Is Betta Than Evah!, 1978; Deep In The Night, 1978; Changes, 1980; Good Rockin' Mama, 1981; Chess Masters, 1981; Tuff Lover, 1983; R & B Queen, 1986; Blues In The Night, 1986; Late Show, 1986; Her Greatest Sides, Vol. I, 1987; R & B Dynamite, 1987; Chicago Golden Years, 1988; On Chess, 1988; Seven Year Itch, 1989; Stickin' To My Guns, 1990; The Right Time, 1992; Time After Time, 1995; Mystery Lady, 1995; I Just Wanna Make Love To You – The Best Of, 1996; Love's Been

Rough on Me, 1997; Hickory Dickory Dock, 1998; The Heart of a Woman, 1999; Hit singles: All I Could Do Was Cry, 1960; At Last, 1961; I Just Wanna Make Love To You, 1961 (re-released in 1996); Stop The Wedding, 1962; Pushover, 1963; Security, 1967; Tell Mama/I'd Rather Go Blind, 1967; Good Rocking Daddy, 1981. *Honour:* Grammy Nomination, Etta James, 1973. *Current Management:* De Leon Artists, 4031 Panama Court, Piedmont, CA 94611, USA.

JAMES Jessica; b. 1 Dec. 1981, Los Gatos, California, USA. Singer; Songwriter. *Career:* Signed to AandM Records, aged 13; Stage performances: Wizard of Oz; Annie; A Winter's Tale; Sang with local bands, performing with Smokey Robinson, Rodney Dangerfield; Singer, own band, America's Most Wanted Band; Television appearances: Up All Night; Channel 11 Morning News; Arsenio Hall; Subject of documentary, BBC, England; Singer, National Anthem, major US sporting events and Democratic State Convention; Numerous charity functions; Featured soloist, Gospel Choir, First African Methodist Episcopalian Church, Los Angeles. *Membership:* SAG (Screen Actors' Guild). *Leisure interests:* Rollerblading; Volleyball; Songwriting. *Current Management:* Rick Frio. *Address:* 3050 N Chandelle Rd, Los Angeles, CA 90046, USA.

JAMES Mo; b. 16 March 1951, Darlington, England. Vocalist; Musician (piano); Radio Prod.; Presenter. m. Mike Jowett, 23 July 1983, 1 s., 1 d. *Musical Education:* Northumbria Studio of Music. *Career:* Lead Singer: White Rabbit, 1968–70; Solo artist; Numerous concert appearances, including Greenbelt Festival, Knebworth; Royal Gospel Gala, Albert Hall; Television appearances: Pebble Mill; TVAM; Rock Gospel Show; Leader, Mo James Soul Band, 1984–90; Solo artiste, 1990–; Producer, presenter, regular talk shows on BBC Radio (North). *Recordings:* Debut album: More Love, 1982, (with Joe English). *Publication:* Music reviewer, Crossrhythms magazine. *Memberships:* Musicians' Union; Asscn of Christians in Local Broadcasting. *Leisure interests:* Reading; Home and children; Antique and collectors fayres. *Current Management:* Stanley Joseph, ATS Ltd. *Address:* 26 St Michael's Rd, Headingley, Leeds LS6 3AW, England.

JAMES Rick; b. 1 Feb. 1948, Buffalo, New York, USA. Performer; Prod. *Career:* Formed The Mynah Birds, with Neil Young, Bruce Palmer (Buffalo Springfield) and Goldy McJohn (Steppenwolf); Worked as Writer and Producer for Motown, with artists including The Detroit Spinners and The Marvelettes; Protegés, The Mary Jane Girls. *Recordings:* Singles: Give It To Me Baby; Super Freak (sampled by MC Hammer for U Can't Touch This); Fire and Desire (with Teena Marie); Dance Wit' Me; Cold Blooded; 17; Glow; Albums: Come and Get It; Bustin' Out of L Seven; Fire It Up; Wild and Peaceful; Garden of Love; Street Songs; Reflections of Rick; You; Glow; Rick and Friends; Urban Rhapsody; 20th Century Masters, 2000.

JAMES Ruby; b. 23 May 1957, Manchester, Jamaica. Vocalist; Session Singer. *Career:* Lead Singer, Stax; Recorded with Micky Most, Dick Lehy and other producers; Top Session Singer – George Michael, Boy George, Erasure, Spandau Ballet, Blancmange, James Last Orchestra; Cabaret and Sessions; TV Concert; Live Aid with Spandau Ballet. *Recording:* Locomotion with Ritz. *Membership:* Musicians' Union and Equity. *Current Management:* Stamina Management, 47 Prout Grove, London NW10 1PU, England.

JAMES Sian; b. 24 Dec. 1961, Wales. Folk Singer; Songwriter. m. Gwyn Jones, 2 s. *Education:* BMus, Bangor University; Harp lessons, 11 years old; Piano lessons, 6 years old; Violin lessons, 8 years old. *Career:* Various tours around folk festivals in Brittany, Galicia, Spain, Italy, America, Canada, Japan, Ireland, Wales, England, Scotland, 1980–97; Appearances in stage shows for various theatre companies in Wales, 1987–94; Leading role in major film for S4C: Tylluan Wen (White Owl); Own series on S4C. *Recordings:* Cysgodion Karma (Shadows of Karma), 1990; Distaw (Silent), 1993; Gweini Tymor (Traditional album), 1996; Di-Gwsg (Sleepless), 1997; Birdman, BBC World-wide. *Memberships:* Equity; PRS; MCPS; PAMRA. *Current Management:* Sain Records, Llandwrog, Caernarfon, Gwynedd, Wales.

JAMES Sonny, (James Loden); b. 1 May 1929, Hackleburg, Alabama, USA. Country Musician (guitar, fiddle). *Career:* Successful recording artist, 1953–; Film appearances: Second Fiddle To An Old Guitar; Nashville Rebel; Las Vegas Hillbillies; Hillbilly In A Haunted House. *Recordings:* 72 US Country chart hits; 23 US Country No. 1's include: You're The Only World I Know; Behind The Tear; Take Good Care of Her; The Minute You're Gone; A World of Our Own; I'll Never Find Another You; That's Why I Love You Like I Do; Only The Lonely; It's Just A Matter of Time; Running Bear; When The Snow Is On The Roses; Is It Wrong (For Loving You)?; Other hit singles include: That's Me Without You; She Done Give Her Heart To Me; For Rent; The Cat Came Back; Young Love; First Date, First Kiss, First Love; Numerous albums, 1957- include Young Love, 1962; Only the Lonely, 1969; Empty Arms, 1971; American Originals, 1989; Young Love: The Classic Hits, 1997; Sonny 1957, 2000; As producer: Paper Roses, Marie Osmond.

JAMES Stafford Louis; b. 24 April 1946, Evanston, Illinois, USA. Musician (double bass, piano); Composer. m. Claudine Decouttère, 17 April 1992, 1 d. *Education:* Loop College, Chicago; Chicago Conservatory College; Mannes College of Music, New York. *Career:* Member, Ukrainian National Orchestra, Limberg, 1991; International Congress of Viola D'amore, Europansches Musik Festival, Stuttgart, 1988; WDR Radio, Köln, Germany, 1989, 1992, 1994–97; European tours with Stafford James Project (trio) and Stafford James Special Project (quartet), Netherlands; France; Luxembourg; Germany; Italy; Austria; Sicily; Spain; Switzerland; European tour with Stafford James Project, Autumn 2001, France, Austria, Belgium, Germany; Television: The Days and Nights of Molly Dodd, 1987; USIA tours: India, Syria, Sudan, Egypt, Morocco, 1984; Argentina, Peru, Chile, Uruguay, Mexico, 1986; Played with: Art Blakey and The Jazz Messengers; Betty Carter; Jimmy Heath; Pharoah Sanders; Woody Shaw; Dexter Gordon; Joe Williams; Mingus Dynasty; Randy Weston; The Gounawas (from Morocco); Teacher, double bass, UN International School, New York, 5 years; New School of Social Research, New York, 2 years; Privately in Paris, France. *Compositions:* More than 150 pieces (many written for double bass as lead melodic voice) including: Les Pyrénées à la Mer; Sonatina (duet for viola d'Amore/contrabass)); That's What Dreams Are Made Of; Ethiopia Suite; Bertha Baptist; Game; Teotiuacan; Sashianova; Nighthawk; Blues in The Pockets; Des Alpes aux Carpates; Conspectus; Changing World; Muguet; Rejuvenation; Sixth Sense; Kaleidoscope; Horizon; Us Together; Conscience, Mujiza; Meissa; Morning Dew; Metamorphosis; Bouncybernaughty. *Recordings:* Music Is The Healing Force of The Universe, Albert Ayler, 1969; Homecoming, Dexter Gordon, 1976; with Woody Shaw: Little Red's Fantasy Muse, 1975; For Sure, 1980; Night Music, 1980; United, 1980; Stafford James Ensemble. *Honours include:* Grants from NEA, NYSCA; Gold Medal, Music, Karlstad, Sweden; Civitella Ranieri Foundation Fellowship, 1998. *Memberships:* SACEM; BMI; BIMC; Thomastik Infcld Sponsoree, 2000. *Leisure interests:* Fishing; Model trains; Antiques hunting. *Current Management:* STAJA Music. *Address:* 6 Quai des Célestins, 75004 Paris, France. *E-mail:* staja.music@wanadoo.fr.

JAMES Stephen; b. 6 Feb. 1956, New York City, USA. Composer; Musician (sarod, violin). m. Judith Papp, 11 April 1986. *Musical Education:* North Indian Classical Music, 1973–83; Shri Vasant Rai, Pandit Ravi Shankar, 1983. *Career:* Boston MIT; Zakir Hussain and Sitara Devi; New York, Festival of India, Empire State Building; Asia Society and Columbia University; Shri Ram Center, North Delhi India; Franz Liszt Academy, Budapest; Zurich Hallenstadion; Frankfurt Messe Halle; Milan Pallazzrussardi; Appeared at festivals in: Hungary; Italy; France; Switzerland; Germany; Bombay; Delhi Doordashan; Radio and television. *Recordings:* with Annindo Chatterjee: Raga; Tala; Makam; with Bill Laswell and Nicky Skopelitis: Axiom; with Bebo Baldan and David Torn: Earth Beat; Diving Into the World; Solo: Waiting For The Dawn, 2000. *Honours:* Bhartiya Vidya Bhavan, New York. *Membership:* Founder mem., Central Europe RIMPA (Ravi Shankar Institute For Music and Performing Arts). *Leisure interest:* Music. *Current Management:* Stress Management. *Address:* Sabrak ul. 3, 1141 Budapest, Hungary.

JAMES Steve; b. 19 Feb. 1954, London, England. Record Prod. 3 s., 1 d. *Career:* Record Producer and engineer, various projects, several years; Early production work includes albums with Toyah; Later credits include Grammy-nominated soundtrack, The Rutles; Monty Python's The Life of Brian, featuring the single Always Look On The Bright Side of Life; Worked with Angel City, Mental As Anything, The Screaming Jets in Australia, 1988–93; Returned to UK, worked with: Paul Young; Kiki Dee; Peter Skellern; Way of Thorns. *Recordings include:* Numerous as producer, co-producer, engineer including: Albums: with Toyah: Sheep Farming In Barnet, 1979; Toyah Toyah Toyah, 1982; with Peter Skellern: Astaire, 1980; The Continental, 1981; Stardust Memories, 1994; with Neil Innes: Off The Record, 1981; with Ginger Baker: Nutters, 1983; with Mental As Anything: Cyclone Raymonde, 1989; with The Screaming Jets: All For One, 1990; Tear of Thought, 1991; with The Angels: Redback Fever, 1992; with Kiki Dee: Best of Kiki Dee, 1994; with Paul Young: Acoustic tracks, 1994; Live tracks, 1995; 2 tracks, animated version of Wind In The Willows, Kirsty MacColl and Tim Finn, 1995; Singles include: In The City, The Jam, 1979; Something Else, The Sex Pistols, 1979; Rock and Roll Music, Mental As Anything, 1988; Other recordings with: Shirley Bassey, 1976; Thin Lizzy, 1977; Pat Travers, 1977; Golden Earring, 1978; Ryan Douglas, 1993; Way of Thorns, 1995; The Rutles, LP, 1996; The Screaming Jets, album, 1997; The Teletubbies, LP, 1997; Oblivia and Cold Chisel, 1998; Weta and H-Block, 2000. *Membership:* Producers' Guild. *Current Management:* Clive Banks. *Address:* c/o Clive Banks Ltd, 1 Glenthorne Mews, 115a Glenthorne Rd, London W6 0LJ, England.

JAMES (Walter) Kevin (Earl); b. 19 Aug. 1967, Greenville, Texas, USA. Country singer/songwriter. *Education:* Commerce, Texas AandM University; Private study. *Career:* Best Little Whorehouse in Texas, stage appearance; Ernest Tubb's Midnight Jamboree, Nashville, Tennessee; Mesquite Opry, stage; Oklahoma Opry, stage; Good Morning Texas, TV Show; Airplay US coast to coast and in parts of Europe; TNN appearances.

Compositions: Late to Breakfast; Generation Tex; First Sight, Second Look; Jealous; Don't Answer That. *Recordings:* Wrapped in Hope, album; True Americans, single; Generations, album. *Memberships:* BMI; Press Club of Dallas, IFCO. *Leisure interest:* Political memorabilia. *Current Management:* CQK Records, Dallas, and Dick McVey Ent, Nashville. *Address:* 2402 Beverly Dr., Greenville, TX 75402, USA.

JAMISON Jimi; b. 23 Aug. 1951, Durant, Mississippi, USA. Singer; Songwriter; Musician (guitar, piano). m. Deborah Teal, 1 May 1985, 1 s., 2 d. *Education:* University of Memphis, two years. *Musical Education:* High School Choir. *Career:* Lead singer, major tours with: Target, 1976; Cobra, 1979–82; Survivor, 1983–; Solo artist, 1990–; Numerous television appearances include Solid Gold; MTV guest VJ; American Video Awards, 1986; Empires, 1999. *Compositions:* I'm A Fighter; Vital Signs; High On You; I Can't Hold Back; Is This Love; Burning Heart (Rocky IV soundtrack); Moment of Truth (Karate Kid soundtrack); In Good Faith; When Seconds Count; Rebel Son; The Search Is Over; Too Hot To Sleep; Man Against The World; Rock Hard; When Love Comes Down; Co-writer, I'm Always Here (Baywatch TV theme). *Recordings:* with Target (2 albums); with Cobra (1 album); with Survivor (6 albums) including: Vital Signs, 1984; When Seconds Count, 1986; Too Hot To Sleep, 1988; Lead singer on all tracks; Hit recordings include: Burning Heart, Survivor, 1985; Solo albums: When Love Comes Down, 1991; Empires, 2000; Backing vocals for: ZZ Top; Jeff Healey; Fabulous Thunderbirds; George Thorogood; Colin James; Point Blank; Johnny Diesel; Krokus; De Garmo and Key; Joe Walsh; Gary Chapman; Ten Years After; Rick Vito; Michael Anderson; Empires, 1999. *Publications:* Burn Magazine, 1999; Metal Hammer, 1999. *Honours:* Voted in Top 10 Male Vocalists in World, Kasey Kasem Countdown; St Jude Special Olympics Award; Arkansas Governor's Award; Ohio Governor's Award; Tennessee Governor's Award; Numerous Gold and Platinum albums for Survivor, Rocky IV, ZZ Top, and Krokus. *Memberships:* AFTRA; SAG; NARAS; Grammy Award Committee, 1992. *Leisure interests:* Tennis; Softball; Local and National charities.

JAN Hajnal; b. 11 Dec. 1943, Kojice, Slovakia. m. Maria Hajnalova, 14 Dec. 1968, 1 d. *Musical Education:* Piano, Classical Music Degree, Elementary Music School, 10 years; Konzervatorium in Kojice, Piano and Double Bass; Self-taught Composer, with some lessons from best Slovak Composers. *Career:* Several own TV programmes as a Pianist; Numerous recordings in Slovak Radio as a Pianist, Composer, Arranger, Leader, Jazz and higher popular music; Participant of jazz festivals in Europe; Solo performance and small groups – jazz music; Piano Entertainer performance in America, Asia, Europe; Solo piano and 2 pianos perfomances (jazz) on classic music festival in Kojice, 1995. *Compositions:* Monk's Tatran Dream, 1994; Mosebacke, Early Morning, Geneiro, Home made Blues, many others. *Recordings:* Slovak Jazz Mainstream, CD, 1994; Samplers from Slovak Jazz Days with Slovak Jazz Quintet. *Publications:* Recorded in main Czechoslovak Lexikon of Popular Music, 1982-. *Honour:* First Prize, Frame of the Year, Slovak Music 1996 Competition for Composition: Monk Tatran Dream. *Memberships:* Slovak Jazz Society; Slovak Music Fond. *Leisure interest:* Music. *Current Management:* Slovak Music Fond Bratislava.

JANDA Dalibor; b. 21 March 1953, Hranice Na Morave, Czech Republic. Singer; Songwriter; Musician. m. Jirina Jandova, 3 April 1981, 1 s., 1 d. *Education:* Classical Music Degree, 4 year Guitar Studium. *Career:* Singers in various rock bands, 1969–79; First recording in radio, 1979; Professional Singer, 1981; First single, 1983; First LP, named Hurricane, 1985; Second LP, MC KDE JSI (Where Are You?), 1987; Third album, 1988. *Compositions:* Ten Fingers for Living; Take Them to Mars, 1988; Dalbiro Janda and Prototype, 1989. *Recordings:* Jen Ty Samotna A Ja (Only You and Me), 1989; Povidant Spisnickami (Talking with Singing), 1990; Cose Ma'stat (What Was Happened), 1992. *Publications:* Zlaty Vyber, Gold Best, 1994; Vlasce Nejsou Maty (There is no Maps in Cove), 1995; Krasne Silena (Pretty Crazy), 1996. *Honours:* Gold Decin Pop Festival, 1985; Gold Nightingale, 1986, 1987, 1988; 6 gold albums, 1 platinum album. *Leisure interests:* Nature; Enthomology. *Current Management:* Hurricane Records. *Address:* Hurricane Records, Kamenicka 39/303, 170 00 Prague 7, Czech Republic.

JANDA Petr; b. 2 May 1942, Prague, Czech Republic. Composer; Musician (guitar); Vocalist. m. (1) Jana, 7 Sept. 1966; (2) Martina, 7 March 1992, 1 s., 2 d. *Education:* Graduate. *Musical Education:* Conservatory Jaroslava Jezka, Prague; Conservatory Jaroslava, Jezka, Prague (composition). *Career:* Leader, famous rock group, Olympic, 32 years, 6 Golden Records. *Recordings:* Albums: Zelva; Ptak Rosom'k; Prazdniny Na Zemi; Ulice; Jasna Zprava; Okno Me Lasky. *Publications:* Encyklpedie Ceske Hydby. *Honour:* Grammy (Olympic), 1993. *Membership:* OSA. *Leisure interests:* Music; Sport. *Current Management:* Best IA, Pristavni 31, 17000 Prague 7, Czech Republic.

JANIS Conrad; b. 11 Feb. 1938, New York City, USA. Jazz Musician (trombone); Actor; Film Dir. m. Maria Grimm, 30 Nov. 1987. *Musical Education:* Private tuition, trombone, piano, violin. *Career:* As actor: Film

credits include: Airport '75; Buddy Holly Story, 1977; The Duchess and The Dirtwater Fox, 1976; Mr Saturday Night, 1992; The Feminine Touch, 1995; Television series include: Mork and Mindy; Quark; St Elsewhere; I Bonino; Over 350 starring roles include: Murder She Wrote; Golden Girls; Kojak; Happy Days; Laverne and Shirley; Talk show appearances include: 25 Tonight Shows, with Johnny Carson; 12 times, Mike Douglas; Dinah Shore; Several TV specials; As Jazz musician: Bandleader, Beverly Hills Unlisted Jazz Band; Tailgate Jazz Band; TV Specials: Jerry Lee Lewis Telethon; Bert Convey Special; American Jukebox Special; This Joint Is Jumping; That's A Plenty; Don Lane Show; Concerts include: New York Town Hall, 1962; Phil Academy of Music, 1955; Carnegie Hall, 1981; Monterey Festival, 1983–87; Victoria BC Terrivic Festival, 1989–93; LA Classic Jazz Festival, 1984–95; Worked with: Roy Eldridge; Henry Red Allen; Wild Bill Davison; Yank Lawson; Claude Hopkins; Coleman Hawkins; Panama Francis; Hot Lips Page; Herbie Hancock; Jimmy McPartland. *Recordings:* CJ and The Talegate Jazz Band, 1950–58; Jammin' At Rudi's, 1953; with Tony Parenti: A Night At Jimmy Ryan's, 1972; with Conrad Janis and The Beverly Hills Unlisted Jazz Band: Way Down Yonder In Beverly Hills, 1986; America, 1987; This Joint Is Jumpin', with Jack Lemmon, Bea Arthur, Dudley Moore, 1989; with Tom Kubis: At Last, 1992. *Honours:* Playboy Poll Nomination, 1960, 1961. *Current Management:* Maria Janis. *Address:* 1920 S Beverly Glen, Suite 306, Los Angeles, CA 90025, USA.

JANKE Daniel Jacob; b. 8 Sept. 1957, Edmonton, Alberta, Canada. Composer; Piano; Kora. m. Susan Alton, 31 Aug. 1993, 2 s., 1 d. *Musical Education:* MA, Ethnomusicology. *Career:* CBC Radio, Two New Hours; BBC, Kaleidoscope and Mixing It; Radio France, La Muse En Circuit. *Composition:* Commission, Music Canada 2000, 1999. *Recordings:* Debut, 1984; Big Dance, 1989; In A Room, 1997; Not Too Dark, Longest Night Orchestra, 1999. *Honours:* Canada Council B Grant; 1989 Casby Nomination. *Membership:* Canadian Music Centre, Associate Composer. *Leisure interest:* Wilderness Hiking. *Current Management:* David Petkovich. *Address:* PO Box 5381, Whitehorse Yukon, Canada Y1A 4Z2.

JANNAH Denise; b. 11 May 1956, Paramaribo, Suriname. Vocalist; Songwriter; Voice Teacher. *Education:* Law Studies, University of Utrecht, The Netherlands; Degree, Jazz Department, Conservatory of Hilversum, The Netherlands also Teaching Degree. *Career:* Performed with Carnegie Hall Jazz Orchestra, Dutch Jazz Orchestra, The Rosenberg Trio, Jon Hendricks, Willem Brekker Collective, Dutch Metropole Orchestra; Own Band: Denise Jannah Quintet; Musicals: A Night at the Cotton Club, 1989–90; Joe, The Musical, 1997–98; Musical Show: Ain't Misbehaving, 1998–99; Vocal Director, Theatre Plays, 1987–99; International TV: EBU Jazz Night (16 European Countries, 1994); Bet on Jazz (USA, 1996); Opening Act for Wynton Marsalis (Barbados, January 2000); Perfomance for Queen Beatrix of Holland and the President of USA, Bill Clinton and his First Lady, Hilary Clinton; Top of European Union, International Concerts, Festivals and Tours; Teacher at conservatories of Rotterdam and Utrecht, The Netherlands. *Compositions:* Alone, Never Lonely, 1995; I'll Always be Here, 1996; Your Eyes, 1996; Never Meant to Be, 1996; Different Colours, One Rainbow, 1997; If Only, 1999; Wide Awake, 1999; The Madness of Our Love, 1999. *Recordings:* All Solo Albums: Take It From the Top, 1991; A Heart Full of Music, 1993; I Was Born in Love With You, 1995; Different Colours, 1996; The Madness of Our Love, 1999; International TV: Hallo 2000, (50 countries world-wide), 1999. *Publications:* Film Documentary: Jannah, New Lady in Jazz, 1996. *Honours:* DDR: Lieder Festival, Menschen und Meer, 1989; Third Prize, International Golden Orpheus Festival, Bulgaria 1992; First Prize, Dutch Edison Award for Album, A Heart Full of Music; Edison Award Nomination, The Madness of Our Love, 2000. *Leisure interests:* Music; Theatre; Books. *Current Management:* Management for Europe, International Music Holland, Sloterweg 1254, 1066 CW Amsterdam, The Netherlands. *Address:* I B Bakker-Laan 29, 3582 VE Utrecht, The Netherlands.

JANOW Steven; b. 12 July 1973, Rhinebeck, New York, USA. Composer; Musician (Saxophone). *Education:* Liberal Arts, State University of New York; Studies at North Carolina School of the Arts; Bachelor of Music, University of Hartford. *Career:* Performances in New York City, upstate New York. *Compositions:* Piano Sonata; New Blues or Ojan; Symphony; Saxophone Orchestra; Untitled music for brass and saxophone band; Flight of the Dragon, Jazz/metal fusion; Various jazz and serious compositions. *Honours:* Ascap awards, 1998, 1999. *Membership:* ASCAP. *Address:* 69 Chestnut St, Rhinebeck, NY 12572, USA.

JANS-BROWN Andrew Michael; b. 8 May 1970, Victoria, Australia. Vocalist; Musician (guitar); Songwriter; Poet. *Education:* Studied acting at National Institute of Dramatic Arts. *Musical Education:* Studied opera with Maggie Norman; Jazz theory at Sydney Conservatorium of Music; Musical theatre with Andrew Ross and Terrence Clark whilst at NIDA. *Career:* Vocalist with band Iris; Various minor roles in film, TV and theatre. *Compositions:* Seek Beauty; Autumn; This Is Eden. *Recordings:* Distance 'Till Empty EP, 2000; You Got Me Thinking, 2001. *Address:* PO Box 3/41,

Gould St, Bondi Beach, Sydney, Australia, 2026. *E-mail:* kofad@hotmail.com. *Internet:* www.irisdaband.com.

JANSCH Bert; b. 3 Nov. 1943, Glasgow, Scotland. Vocalist; Musician. *Career:* Folk musician; Founder member, folk group, Pentangle, 1967–72; 1982–; Also solo artiste. *Recordings:* Solo albums: Bert Jansch, 1965; It Don't Bother Me, 1965; Jack Orion, 1966; Bert and John (with John Renbourn), 1966; Nicola, 1967; Birthday Blues, 1968; Lucky Thirteen, 1969; Stepping Stones (with John Renbourn), 1969; Rosemary Lane, 1971; Moonshine, 1973; LA Turnaround, 1974; Santa Barbara Honeymoon, 1975; A Rare Conundrum, 1978; Avocet, 1979; Thirteen Down, 1980; Heartbreak, 1982; From The Outside, 1985; Leather Laundrette, 1988; Bert Jansch and Jack Orion, 1993; When The Circus Comes To Town, 1995; Crimson Moon, 2000; Live In Australia, 2001; Various compilations; with Pentangle: The Pentangle, 1968; Sweet Child, 1968; Basket of Light, 1969; Cruel Sister, 1970; Reflections, 1971; History Book, 1971; Solomon's Seal, 1972; Open The Door, 1982; Pentangling, 1973; The Pentangle Collection, 1975; Anthology, 1978; The Essential Pentangle Vol. 1, 1987; The Essential Pentangle Vol. 2, 1987; In The Round, 1988; So Early In The Spring, 1989; One More Road, 1993; People On The Highway 1968–71, 1993. *Current Management:* Folklore Inc, 1671 Appian Way, Santa Monica, CA 90401, USA.

JANSEN Steve, (Stephen Batt); b. 1 Dec. 1959. Musician (drums). *Career:* Member, Japan, 1977–83; The Dolphin Brothers (with Richard Barbieri), 1987; Rain Tree Crow (with 3 members of Japan), 1991; Tours include: British tour supporting Blue Oyster Cult, 1978; Backing musician to No-Man, British tour, 1991; Abstract Day tour of Japan with Jansen, Barbieri and Karn, 1997; Mick Karn Bestial Cluster Tour, Europe, 1994; Yukhiro Takahashi tours of Japan, 1985, 1986, 1998. *Recordings:* Albums with Japan: Adolescent Sex, 1978; Obscure Alternatives, 1978; Life In Tokyo, 1979; Quiet Life, 1980; Gentlemen Take Polaroids, 1980; Assemblage, 1981; Tin Drum, 1982; Japan, 1982; Oil On Canvas, 1983; Exorcising Ghosts, 1984; with David Sylvian: Brilliant Trees, 1984; Gone to Earth, 1986; Secrets of the Beehive, 1987; Dead Bees on a Cake, 1999; with The Dolphin Brothers: Catch The Fall, 1987; with Rain Tree Crow: Rain Tree Crow, 1991; with Richard Barbieri: Stories Across Borders, 1991; Stone To Flesh, 1995; Other Worlds in a Small Room, 1996; with Richard Barbieri and Mick Karn: Beginning to Melt, 1994; Seal, 1994; with Richard Barbieri and N Takemura: Changing Hands, 1997; with Yukikieu Takahashi: Pulse, 1997; Ism, 1999; Kinoapparatom, 2001; Singles: with Japan: The Art of Parties, 1981; Quiet Life, 1981; Visions of China, 1981; Ghosts, 1982; Cantonese Boy, 1982; Life In Tokyo, 1982; Night Porter, 1982; Canton, 1983. *Address:* c/o Medium Productions, 74 St Lawrence Rd, Upminster, Essex RM14 2UW, England.

JARDINE Al; b. 3 Sept. 1942, Lima, Ohio, USA. Musician (guitar); Vocalist. *Career:* Member, the Beach Boys, 1961–62; 1963–; Numerous tours and concerts include: Beach Boys Summer Spectacular, Hollywood Bowl, 1966; London Palladium, 1968; Big Sur Folk Festival, Monterey, 1970; Carnegie Hall, 1971; Royal Festival Hall, London, 1972; Wembley Stadium, 1975, 1980; Knebwroth Festival, 1990; Independence Day concert, Washington DC, 1980; Live Aid, Philadelphia, 1985. *Recordings:* Albums: Surfer Girl, 1963; Little Deuce Coupe, 1963; Shut Down Vol. 2, 1964; All Summer Long, 1964; The Beach Boys Concert, 1964; The Beach Boys Christmas Album, 1964; The Beach Boys Today, 1965; Summer Days (and Summer Nights), 1965; Surfin' USA, 1965; Beach Boys Party, 1966; Pet Sounds, 1966; The Beach Boys Today, 1966; Smiley Smile, 1967; Wild Honey, 1968; Friends, 1968; Close-Up, 1969; Greatest Hits, 1970; Surf's Up, 1971; Carl and The Passions/So Tough, 1972; Holland, 1973; The Beach Boys In Concert, 1974; Endless Summer (No. 1, USA), 1974; Spirit of America, 1975; Good Vibrations – Best Of…, 1975; 15 Big Ones, 1976; The Beach Boys Love You, 1977; LA (Light Album), 1979; Ten Years of Harmony (1970–80), 1982; The Very Best Of…, 1983; The Beach Boys (with Stevie Wonder), 1985; Made In The USA, 1986; Still Cruisin', 1989; Summer Dreams, 1990; Summer In Paradise, 1992; Good Vibrations, 1993; Stars and Stripes Vol. 1, 1996; Ultimate Christmas, 1998; Greatest Hits, Vol. 2, 1999; Singles include: Surfin' USA, 1963; Surfer Girl, 1963; Little Deuce Coupe, 1963; Fun Fun Fun, 1964; I Get Around (No. 1, USA), 1964; When I Grow Up (To Be A Man), 1964; Dance Dance Dance, 1965; Help Me Rhonda (No. 1, USA), 1965; California Girls, 1965; The Little Girl I Once Knew, 1965; Barbara Ann, 1965; Sloop John B, 1966; God Only Knows/ Wouldn't It Be Nice, 1966; Good Vibrations (No. 1, UK and US), 1966; Heroes and Villains, 1967; Wild Honey, 1967; Darlin', 1968; Do It Again (No. 1, UK), 1968; I Can Hear Music, 1969; Breakaway, 1969; Cottonfields, 1970; Sail On Sailor, 1973; Rock and Roll Music, 1976; Here Comes The Night, 1979; Lady Lynda, 1979; Getcha Back, 1985; Kokomo (No. 1, USA), 1988; Fun Fun Fun, collaboration with Status Quo, 1996. *Honours include:* Inducted into Rock and Roll Hall of Fame, 1988; Special Award of Merit, American Music Awards, 1988. *Current Management:* Elliott Lott, 4860 San Jacinto Circle W, Fallbrook, CA 92026, USA.

JARLETT Dee; b. 28 Oct. 1951, Manchester, England. Singer; Musician (guitar); Songwriter. m. John Jarlett, 9 Oct. 1977, separated, 2 s., 1 d.

Education: DipEd, Teaching Music; RSA Diploma, Teaching Adults. *Career:* Member, folk duo Orion; British tours of folk clubs; Numerous local radio appearances; Played film music for Rosie The Great, HTV; Member, Sweet Soul Sisters; Radio appearances: Start The Week, BBC Radio 4; Woman's Hour, BBC Radio 4; BBC Radio 2 arts programme, local radio and HTV. *Recordings:* with Orion: Jack Orion, 1987; Chicken Soup, 1989; with Sweet Soul Sisters: Live and Lovin' It, 1990; Freshly Squeezed, 1995. *Current Management:* Maggie Haines, 4 Archfield Rd, Cotham, Bristol BS6 6NB, England. *Address:* 27 Narroways Rd, St Werburghs, Bristol BS2 9XB, England.

JARRE Jean-Michel; b. 24 Aug. 1948, Lyons, France. Musician (synthesizers, keyboards); Composer; Record Prod. m. Charlotte Rampling, 1977. *Musical Education:* Piano and guitar from age 5; Conservatoire de Paris, with Jeanine Reuff. *Career:* Solo debut, Paris Opera, 1971; Youngest composer to appear, Palais Garnier, 1971; Major concerts, often including lasers and fireworks, filmed for video releases include: Beijing, China, 1981; Bastille Day, Place De La Concorde, 1979; Houston, Texas (1.3m. audience), 1986; London Docklands, 1988; La Defense, Paris (2.5m. audience), 1990; Sun City, Johannesburg, South Africa, 1993; Member of jury, First International Visual Music Awards, Midem, France, 1992. *Compositions include:* Oxygène Part IV, used for several television themes; Ballet and film scores include: Des Garçons Et Des Filles, 1968; Deserted Palace, 1972; Les Granges Brûlées, 1973; La Maladie De Hambourg, 1978; Gallipoli, 1979. *Recordings:* Albums (all self-composed and produced): Deserted Palace, 1971; Oxygène, 1977; Magnetic Fields, 1981; The Concerts In China, 1982; The Essential Jean-Michel Jarre, 1983; Zoolook, 1984; Rendez-Vous, 1986; In Concert Lyons/Houston, 1987; Revelations (No. 2, UK), 1988; Jarre Live, 1989; Waiting For Cousteau, 1990; Images – The Best of Jean-Michel Jarre, 1991; Chronologie, 1993; Jaree Hong Kong, 1994; Cities in Concert, 1997; China Concert, 1999; Metamorphoses, 2000. *Honours:* Grand Prix, Academie Du Disque, Zoolook, 1985; First Western artist to play in China, 1981; Numerous Platinum and Gold discs world-wide. *Address:* c/o Dreyfus Records, 26 Ave Kléber, 75116 Paris, France.

JARRE Maurice Alexis; b. 13 Sept. 1924, Lyons, France. Composer. m. (1) France Pejot, 1946, 1 s., (2) Dany Saval, 1965, 1 d., (3) Laura Devon, 1967, (4) Khong Fui Fong, 1984. *Musical Education:* Conservatoire National Supéreur de Musique. *Career:* Musician, Radiodiffusion Française, 1946–50; Director of Music, Théatre National Populaire (TNP), 1950–63. *Compositions:* Symphonic music; Music for theatre and ballet include: Roland Petit's Notre-Dame de Paris (Paris Opera), 1966; Numerous film scores include: Lawrence of Arabia, 1963; Dr Zhivago, 1965; Ryan's Daughter, 1970; Shogun, 1980; Doctors In Love, 1982; A Passage To India, 1985; The Mosquito Coast, 1987; Tai-Pan, 1987; Gaby, 1988; Gorillas In The Mist, 1989; Ghost; Dead Poets Society, 1990; Fatal Attraction. *Recordings:* recent album: The Emotion and The Strength, 2002. *Honours:* Officer, Légion d'Honneur, Commander des Arts et Lettres; Prix Italia, 1955, 1962; Grand Prix du Disque, Academy Charles Cros, 1962; Hollywood Golden Globe, 1965, 1984; People's Choice Award, 1988. *Address:* c/o Paul Kohner Inc, 9169 Sunset Blvd, Los Angeles, CA 90069, USA.

JARREAU Al; b. 12 March 1940, Milwaukee, USA. Singer. *Education:* BS Psychology, Ripon College, 1962; MS Psychology, University of Iowa, 1964. *Career:* Solo artiste, 1975-. *Recordings:* Solo albums: We Got By, 1975; Glow, 1976; Look To The Rainbow Live, 1977; All Fly Home, 1978; This Time, 1980; Breaking Away, 1981; Jarreau, 1983; High Crime, 1984; Al Jarreau Live in London, 1985; L Is For Lover, 1986; Heart's Horizon, 1988; Heaven and Earth, 1992; Tenderness, 1994; Best of Al Jarreau, 1996; Tomorrow Today, 2000; Also appeared on: I Heard That!, Quincy Jones, 1976; The Love Connection, Freddie Hubbard, 1980; Friends, Larry Carlton, 1983; Two Eyes, Brenda Russell, 1983; Back On The Block, Quincy Jones, 1989. *Honours:* Grammy Awards: Best Jazz Vocal, Look To The Rainbow, 1977, All Fly Home, 1978, Best Pop Vocal, Breakin' Away, 1981, Best Jazz Vocal, Breakin' Away, 1981, Best R & B Vocal, Male, Heaven and Earth, 1992; Downbeat Reader's Poll Winner, 1977–79. *Current Management:* Bill Darlington, 1103 11th St, Santa Monica, CA 90403, USA.

JARRETT Anita; b. 8 Aug. 1964, London, England. Vocal; Singer; Songwriter. 1 s., 1 d. *Career:* Television and radio performances Europe; Yo Yo Honey, 1990–92; Solo mini tour, Jamaica, 1993. *Recordings:* with Yo Yo Honey: Voodoo soul album; Angel; Ghetto Blues; Rolling Stones remix: You Got Me Rocking, 1994; with Pressure Drop: Elusive, 1997; Vocal, Okenfeld Project. *Publication:* Still Waiting and Persevering To Achieve and Reach the So Called Perfection of Expression Via The Medium of Music. *Membership:* Musicians' Union. *Leisure interests:* Sports design; Swimming; Sauna; Walking; Travel; Reading; Smoking occasionally; Photography; Good food and pampering. *Current Management:* Trenton, NUR Entertainment. *Address:* Camelot Studios, Unit 218A, 222 Kensal Rd, London W10 5N, England.

JARRETT Keith; b. 8 May 1945, Allentown, Pennsylvania, USA. Musician (piano); Composer. *Career:* First solo concert, age 7, followed by professional appearances; 2 hour solo concert, own compositions, 1962; Led own trio, Boston; Worked with Roland Kirk; Tony Scott; Joined Art Blakey, 1965; Tours, Europe, with Charles Lloyd, 1966; with Miles Davis, 1970–71; Soloist, leader, own groups, 1969-. *Recordings:* Personal Mountains, 1974; Luminessence, 1974; Mysteries, 1975; Changeless, 1987; At The Blue Note – The Complete Recordings, 1994 La Scala (live), 1995; Tokyo '96 (live), 1998; The Melody at Night with You, 1999; Whisper Not, 2000; Inside Out, 2001. *Honours include:* Grammy Award nomination, Jazz Instrumental Solo, I Got It Bad and That Ain't Good, 2001. *Address:* c/o Don Lucoff, D L Media, 270 Park Ave S, Suite 5C, New York, NY 10010, USA.

JARVIS Jane; b. 31 Oct. 1915, Vincennes, Indiana, USA. Musician (piano, organ); Composer; Lyricist. 1 s., 2 d. *Education:* Bachelor Pace University, New York City, New York. *Musical Education:* Scholarships to Bush Conservatory; Chicago Conservatory; De Paul School of Music. *Career:* Staff Pianist, WJKS; Featured in High School musicals with Karl Maldin and Red Skelton; Staff musician, WJMJ, Milwaukee and WOC Davenport; Rehearsal Pianist, NBC, New York; Vice President, Muzak Corporation; Lecturer, Yale University; Performed with Clark Terry; Lionel Hampton; Chosen by Smithsonian Institute for Jazz Archives. *Compositions:* Over 300 original compositions. *Recordings:* Organ Magic; Cut Glass; LA Jazz Quartet; To Duke; Back To Basics; Statesmen of Jazz; Two-Time (musical). *Publications:* Various profiles of fellow musicians. *Honours:* Governor Kentucky for song; Governor Indiana; Made Sagamare Indian Chief; Jane Jarvis Jazz Festival, Tampa, Florida, in her honour. *Memberships:* ASCAP; NARAS, former Governor. *Leisure interest:* Reading.

JARVIS Toby J; b. 8 May 1965, London, England. Composer; Musician (piano, percussion, samplers, guitar, synthesisers). *Career:* Arranger, music for films and television; Composed music for television themes and shows, UK, USA; Composed music for over 4000 television commercials worldwide; Wrote, recorded songs for: Maxine Harvey; Hunter (The Gladiators); Georgia Lewis. *Compositions:* Numerous dance and club hits including Twink Goes Disco and Goin' Outa My Head. *Recordings:* Loved Up, BBC TV; Schofield's Quest, LWT; Outlaws, BSkyB; Beat That, Channel 4; Super Champs, Thames; British Comedy Awards, LWT; Comedy Club, LWT; Hot House People, BBC. *Honours:* EDLE Prix De Jeunesse, for Beat That. *Memberships:* SPAM; Musicians' Union; PRS; Stonewall. *Leisure interests:* Travelling world in search of musical sounds unheard before. *Current Management:* Mcasso Music Production. *Address:* 9 Carnaby St, London W1V 1PG, England.

JAY David (Dave) John; b. 13 Nov. 1971, Brentwood, Essex, England. Singer; Songwriter; Musician (guitar, keyboard). *Education:* BA, Politics. *Musical Education:* Self-taught. *Career:* Remix work with Vibe Alive Production for London Records and Atlantic Records, USA; Solo and session work for Mr Exe, Wubble-U, Acorn Arts and various independent labels. *Recordings:* After The Dance, Austin; Ain't It Rough, The Dave Jay Project; Dedicated To Love, The Journeyman (5 track EP); House of Love, East 17; Love Is Blind, Echora; Spring Box EP, Dilemma; Change the Style/ Windows…, Mighty Alliance; Spring Box Remix, Matrix vs Dilemma; Taking It Back, Stone Players featuring Soul Hooligan. *Membership:* Musicians' Union. *Leisure interests:* Jogging; Weight-training; Reading. *Address:* 8 The Meads, Cherry Trees, Ingatestone, Essex CM13 1LX, England.

JAY DEE (James Yancey); b. Detroit, Michigan, USA. Prod. *Career:* Started as part of a Tribe Called Quest's production team, The Ummah; Formed Slum Village during the '90s; Debut album finally got a release, 2000; In-demand producer for artists including: Common; D'Angelo; Erykah Badu; Bilal; Remixed: Spacek; Busta Rhymes. *Recordings:* Albums: Fantastic Vol. 2, 2000; Welcome To Detroit (solo album), 2001; Singles: Climax, 1998; I Don't Know, 2000; Raise It Up, 2001. *Address:* c/o Source Records, 113–117 Farringdon Rd, London, EC1R 3BX, England.

JAY Martin; b. 27 July 1949, London, England. Singer; Musician (guitar); Writer; Prod. m. Lorraine Jay, 6 Nov. 1985, 1 s. *Musical Education:* Self-taught. *Career:* Television appearances on Top of The Pops with 5,000 Volts and Enigma; with Cockney Rebel: Yamaha Song Festival, In Concert, LWT; Chile Song Festival. *Recordings:* with 5,000 Volts: I'm On Fire; Dr Kiss Kiss; Medleys with Enigma: Ain't No Stoppin'; I Love Music; Back To The 60's, Tight Fit; Saturday Night Fever 'Megamix'. *Memberships:* Musicians' Union; Equity. *Leisure interests:* Tennis; Cricket. *Address:* 17 Brook Way, Chigwell, Essex IG7 6AW, England.

JAY Michael, (Michael Jay Margules); b. 17 Dec. 1959, Chicago, Illinois, USA. Songwriter; Record Prod. *Education:* Lincoln College, Illinois; Illinois State University. *Career:* A & R for Curtis Mayfield, Curtom Records, Chicago, 1980; Discovered Martika, 1988. *Compositions:* Declaration of Love, 1996; Bridge of Hope, 1996. *Recordings:* Producer, Toy Soldiers, Martika; Cross My Heart, Patsy Kensit and Eighth Wonder; Hot Summer Nights, Gloria Estefan (Top Gun soundtrack); The World Still

Turns, Kylie Minogue; I Wish The Phone Would Ring, Exposé; The Slightest Touch and If I Say Yes, Five Star; Writer and producer, Shining Through, recorded by Nancy Kerrigan, Olympic Silver Medallist ice-skater; Declaration of Love, Celine Dion; Bridge of Hope, Lara Fabian. *Honours:* AMPEX Golden Reel Awards, Silk and Steel and Martika; Grammy Award Album of The Year, Falling For You, Celine Dion, 1996. *Memberships:* NARAS; BAFTA; BMI. *Leisure interests:* Horse riding; Raquetball; Photography. *Current Management:* Alan Melina. *Address:* Shankman DeBlasio Melina, 740 La Brea Ave, Hollywood, CA 90038, USA.

JAY Norman; b. London, England. DJ; Prod.; Remixer. *Career:* Co-founder: Good Times sound system (with brother Joey); Played at Notting Hill Carnival; Set up pirate radio station Kiss FM with Gordon Mac; Presented The Original Rare Groove Show; Put on some of London's first warehouse parties with partner Judge Jules as Shake and Fingerpop, mid 1980s; Resident DJ and promoter of High On Hope club, early '90s; Presents weekly Giant 45 radio show on London Live; Remixed: Azzido Da Bass; Montano vs Trumpetman. *Honours:* Blues and Soul Magazine, Club DJ of the Year, 1996–97. *Current Management:* c/o Slice PR. *E-mail:* slice@slice.co.uk.

JAY Robert; b. 15 Nov. 1967, Dieren, Netherlands. Musician (guitar); Prod.; Artist; Singer. *Education:* Higher Business Economics and Trade. *Musical Education:* Conservatory. *Career:* Schüttorf Open Air Concert; 4 television (national) shows; De 5 Uur show; Glamourland; Actor, television series; Tour manager, clients include: Emmylou Harris; Freddie Fender; Chris Beckers; Ernie Watts; Randy Bernsen; Performed in USA; Canada; Germany; Israel; Egypt; Spain; France; Artists performed with: Hans Dulfer; Candy Dulfer; Jan Akkerman; Adje Vanderberg; Jasper Van't Hof; Joe Sample; Writer for several pop journals; Organizer, music festivals. *Membership:* EMI Music/Publishing. *Leisure interests:* Cars; Sports; Football; Tennis. *Current Management:* Frisbee Management, PO Box 658, 7500 AR Enschade, Netherlands.

JAY-Z, (Shawn Carter); b. 4 Dec. 1969, Brooklyn, New York, USA. Rapper. *Career:* Co-founder of Roc-A-Fella Records; Wrote and directed semi-autobiographical film Streets Is Watching, 1998; Collaborations: Puff Daddy; Lil' Kim; Foxy Brown; Notorious BIG; Mary J Blige; Mariah Carey; Foxy Brown; Timbaland. *Recordings:* Albums: Reasonable Doubt, 1996; In My Lifetime Vol. 1, 1997; Vol. 2, Hard Knock Life, 1999; Vol. 3, Life and Times of S. Carter, 1999; The Dynasty – Roc La Familia, 2000; Blueprint, 2001; Singles: Ain't No Nigga, 1996; Can I Get A…, 1998; Hard Knock Life (Ghetto Anthem), 1998; Anything, 2000; Big Pimpin', 2000; Izzo (H.O.V.A.), 2001; Girls Girls Girls, 2002. *Honour:* MOBO Awards, Best International Hip Hop Act, 1999. *Address:* c/o Roc-A-Fella Records, 825 Eighth Ave, New York City, New York, USA, 10019 7472.

JAZZIE B (Beresford Romeo); b. 16 Jan. 1963, London, England. Musician; Prod.; Songwriter. *Career:* Founder Member, Soul II Soul, collective with Philip Daddae Harvey and producer Nellee Hooper; Joined by vocalist Caron Wheeler; Launched fashion label and clothes shops; Remixer/arranger for many artists including Sinéad O'Connor, Fine Young Cannibals and The Family Stand; Caron Wheeler left, 1990; Nellee Hooper left to become independent producer, 1993; Wheeler returns, 1993; Numerous club appearances and appearances on TV and radio. *Recordings:* Singles: Fairplay, 1988; Feel Free, 1988; Keep on Moving, 1989; Back To Life (However Do You Want Me) (No. 1, UK), 1989; Get A Life, 1989; A Dream's A Dream/Jazzie's Groove, 1990; Missing You, 1990; People, 1990; Joy, 1992; Move Me No Mountain, 1992; Just Right, 1992; Wish, 1993; Love Enuff, 1995; I Care, 1995; Pleasuredome, 1997; Represent, 1997; Albums: Club Classics Vol. I, 1989; Keep On Moving, 1989; Vol. II 1990 – A New Decade, 1990; Vol. III Just Right, 1992; I Care, 1995; Vol. V Believe, 1995; Time for Change, 1997.

JAZZY M (Michael Schiniou); b. 5 Jan. 1962, Edmonton, London, England. Prod.; Remixer; DJ. *Career:* Started as a mobile DJ in London; Worked in Spin Off Records; Landed job as a DJ on LWR Radio; Presented The Jacking Zone, responsible for introducing house music to London on the airwaves; Opened Vinyl Zone record shop on the King's Road, London; Founder: Oh Zone Records, original label of Orbital's club hit Chime; Resident DJ at Ministry of Sound club; Collaborations: Julian Jonah; Mr Fingers; Remixed: Infinity and Duane Harden; Ramsey and Fen; Double 99. *Recordings:* Singles: Soft To Hard/Boom Ah! (as Klubzone 1), Forever On (as Zoogie), 1992; Be Yourself Be Free (as Sao Paulo), 1998; Jazzin' The Way You Know, 2000. *Address:* c/o Ministry of Sound, 103 Gaunt St, London, SE1 6DP, England.

JEAN Wyclef (Jeannel); b. 17 Oct. 1972, Haiti. Vocalist; Rapper. *Career:* Formed Tranzlator Crew with Lauryn Hill and Pras Michel; Renamed The Fugees; Numerous television and live appearances; Producer, Destiny's Child; Collaboration with Bono for Drop the Debt campaign. *Recordings:* With The Fugees: Singles: Boof Baf, 1993; Nappy Heads, EP, 1994; Vocab, EP, 1994; Ready or Not (No. 1, UK), 1996; The Score, 1996; Fu-Gee-La, 1996; Killing Me Softly (No. 1, UK), 1996; Rumble in the Jungle, 1997;

Albums: Blunted on Reality, 1994; The Score, 1996; Solo: We Trying to Stay Alive, 1997; The Sweetest Thing, with Lauryn Hill, 1997; Guantanamera, 1997; Gone Till November, with Bono, 1998; Cheated, 1998; New Day, 1999; 911, with Mary J. Blige, 2000; Perfect Gentleman, 2001; Albums: The Carnival, 1997; Ecleftic: Two Sides II A Book, 2001. *Honours include:* BRIT Award, Best International Group, 1997.

JEANES Alan LLoyd; b. 22 May 1923, Penarth, South Wales. Composer; Arranger. *Musical Education:* Jazz Musicianship, Goldsmiths College, London. *Career:* Founder, former director, University of Greenwich Big Band; Tutor, Jazz Musicianship for various authorities, England and Wales; Arranger for jazz groups. *Leisure interests:* Motoring; Vintage cars; Country inns. *Address:* 4 Oldfield Rd, Bickley, Bromley, Kent BR1 2LF, England.

JEAN-MARIE Alain (Judes); b. 29 Oct. 1945, Pointe-A-Pitre, Guadaloupe. Musician (piano). *Musical Education:* Self-taught. *Career:* Prix Django Reinhardt, 1979; Concerts with: Chet Baker; Art Farmer; Johnny Griffin; Hal Singer; Slide Hampton; Clark Terry; Records with: Abbey Lincoln; Charles Tolliver. *Recordings:* Latin Alley, with Niels Henning Orsted Pedersen, 1987; The Scene Is Clean, with Aldo Romano, Henri Texier, 1996; Biguines Reflections, 1997; Serenade, 1998; Firoliu with Teca Calazan, 1999. *Honour:* Prix Django Reinhardt, Academie du Jazz, 1979. *Current Management:* Martine Palmé, 33 bis rue Doudeauville, 75018 Paris, France. *Address:* Chemin Des Cotillons, 95130 Franconville, France.

JECZALIK Jonathan Edward Stephen; b. 11 May 1955, Banbury, Oxfordshire, England. Musical Dir. m. Joanna Louise Hill, 2 d. *Education:* Hons degree, Geography. *Musical Education:* Self-taught. *Career:* Programmer, Fairlight CMI; Producer for Pet Shop Boys; Artist with Art of Noise and Art of Silence (current). *Recordings:* Singles include: with Art of Noise: Into Battle EP, 1983; Beatbox, 1983; Close To The Edit, 1984; Moments In Love, 1985; Peter Gunn (Grammy Award winner), 1986; Paranoimia, 1986; Dragnet, 1988; Kiss, collaboration with Tom Jones, 1988; Albums include: Who's Afraid of The Art of Noise, 1984; In Visible Silence, 1986; In No Sense Nonsense, 1987; Best of The Art of Noise, 1988; Below The Waste, 1989; The Ambient Collection, 1990; Producer of: Kiss Me, Stephen Tin Tin Duffy, 1985; Opportunities, Pet Shop Boys, 1985. *Honour:* Grammy Award, Best Rock Instrumental, 1986. *Membership:* Musicians' Union. *Leisure interests:* Clay shooting; Golf; Gardening; Children.

JEFFERSON Marshall; b. 19 Sept. 1959, Chicago, Illinois, USA. Prod.; Remixer; DJ. *Career:* Inspired by listening to Ron Hardy DJ at the legendary Music Box club, Chicago, started producing own tracks with other Chicago house producers including Adonis, mid 1980s; Recorded for Chicago's Trax Records; Formed group Virgo (with Vince Lawrence and Adonis); Produced Ten City's debut album; Remixed: The Pasadenas; Tom Jones; System 7; Kym Mazelle. *Recordings:* Albums: Virgo (with Virgo), 1989; Singles: I've Lost Control (with Sleazy D), Move Your Body (The House Music Anthem), 1986; Open Our Eyes (with The Truth), 1988; Do You Know Who You Are (with Virgo), 1989; Mushrooms (with Noosa Heads), 1998; Everybody Dance (Clap Your Hands) (with DJ Pierre), 2001. *Address:* c/o Milk and 2 Sugars, Broadway Studios, 28 Tooting High St, London, SW17 0RG, England.

JEFFRIES Peter John Martin; b. 1 March 1928, London, England. Composer; Arranger; Musician (piano); Musical Dir. m. Pauline Lander, 7 April 1955, 1 s., 1 d. *Musical Education:* Eastman School of Music; Private lessons. *Career:* Pianist, arranger, Phil Tate Orchestra; Arranger, musical director, Philips Records, Pye Records, Decca Records; Radio appearances include: Own broadcasting orchestra, Breakfast special, Radio 2, 1967–72; Accompanist for: Kenny Lynch; Jimmy Tarbuck; Morecambe and Wise; Anne Shelton; Vera Lynn. *Compositions:* Composer, conductor, 21 film scores, 1966–80; Co-arranger, If My Friends Could See Me Now, Cy Coleman. *Memberships:* PRS; MCPS; BASCA. *Leisure interest:* Golf. *Address:* 15 Collins Court, Lea Close, Bushey, Hertfordshire WD2 3BT, England.

JELAVIC Matko; b. 29 March 1958, Split, Croatia. Singer; Composer; Musician (drums). m. 31 July 1982, 2 s. *Education:* Dipl OECC. *Musical Education:* Music School (guitar). *Career:* Drummer, rock band Metak; Drummer in studios; More than 50 albums of different singers and groups; Singer, composer, 1988–; Very successful in Croatia and among Croatians abroad; Biggest concert in Sydney, Australia, audience 10,000 people. *Recordings:* Album: Dobra Vecer Prijatelji, 1988; (Biggest hit) Majko Stara, 1988; Ljube Ljubavi, 1989; Sretno Ti Bilo Andele, 1990; Matko Jelavic Mix, 1992; Moja Ljubavi, 1993; Pianino, 1995. *Honours:* 3 Gold albums, rest Silver; Winner, Split Festival, 1988; Most Popular Song Award In Croatia, 1988. *Memberships:* HGU (Croatian Music Union); DSH (Union of Composers). *Leisure interests:* Basketball; Other popular sports. *Current Management:* Mr Branko Paic, CBS Zagreb. *Address:* Dubrovacka 25, Split, Croatia.

JENKINS Delyth, (Delyth Evans); b. 28 May 1955, Oswestry, Shropshire, England. Musician (celtic harp). m. Nigel Jenkins, 29 June 1982, 2 d. *Education:* Hons Degree, English and French. *Musical Education:* Self-taught harpist. *Career:* Welsh Folk band Cromlech, 1978–82; Aberjaber, 1982–; Solo work; Tours: UK; Europe. *Recordings:* Gwlith Y Bore, 1980; Igam Ogam, 1982; Aberjaber, 1985; Aber-Dau-Jaber, 1988; Delta, 1991; Aberjaber – The Perfect Bucket, 1997; Ar Y Ffin, 1998. *Publication:* Del Y Delyn, 1994. *Current Management:* Elizabeth Jones Entertainments, 3 Conifer Heights, Sunningdale, Knightwick, Worcestershire WR6 5TP, England. *Address:* 124 Overland Rd, Mumbles, Swansea SA3 4EU, Wales.

JENSEN Mark Russell; b. 20 Nov. 1959, Eastbourne, England. Composer; Arranger; Conductor; Prod.; Recording Artiste. *Education:* Eastbourne College. *Musical Education:* Rodney Sadler; John Walker, MA. *Career:* Arranger, conductor, record producer for singles and albums, 1978–; Recording artiste, 1985–; Composer, arranger, conductor for film, television, theatre, 1992–; Recorded as Spritzo Scaramanga to 1993, as Mark Jensen, 1994-. *Compositions:* for film/television: The Papermen, 1993; Angleterre Underground, 1994; Caravan To Arcadia, 1995; Monk Dawson (pilot), 1995; Famine, 1998; for theatre: Romeo and Juliet, 1993; The Changeling, 1994; The Tempest, 1994; Hamlet, 1995; The Way of Danger (ballet score), 1996; Monk Dawson (feature), 1997; Maestro, 1999–2000. *Recordings:* as Spritzo Scaramanga, single, 1993; Monk Dawson, original soundtrack album, 1998; as Mark Jensen: Album, Zoom In… The Zest Zone, 1999. *Memberships:* Performing Rights Society; British Music Writers Council; Musicians' Union. *Address:* c/o Zest Zone, 44 Carew Rd, Eastbourne, East Sussex BN21 2JN, England.

JENSEN Soren Kjær; b. 1 Dec. 1961, Aarhus, Denmark. Musician (bass); Composer; Prod. m. Turid N Christensen, 22 July 1995. *Education:* University of Aarhus. *Musical Education:* Studied jazz at the New School for Social Science, New York, USA. *Career:* Teacher, Royal Conservatory of Music, Aalborg; Musik Projekt Aarhus; Space invaders production for Multimedia; Lecturer, Anthropology of Music, University of Aarhus; Musical Director and Producer; Numerous television appearances. *Compositions:* Numerous works for television, video, film, Planetaria, theme parks, CD-Roms and CD-I; Producer and co-producer: Waaberi, New Dawn, 1997; Maryam Mursal, 1998. *Recordings:* Appeared on recordings by many artists including: Maryam Mursal (The Journey), Jacob Haugaard, Evald Krog, Holger Laumanns Orkester, Extrem Normal, Nikos Veropoulos and Bonehead. *Honours:* Scholarships from: Danish Music Council; Danish Arts Council; Danish Rock Council; Queen Margrethe and Prince Henriks Foundation; European Commission, Innovation Programme; Ministry for the Interior; Danish Cultural Foundation; Awards: Best CD-ROM in Scandinavia, 1997; Industrial Design Award, 1998. *Memberships:* KODA; NCB; Danish Musicians' Union. *Leisure interests:* Reading; Travel. *Current Management:* Target Music. *Address:* Mejlgade 50, 1 tv, 8000 Aarhus C, Denmark.

JENSEN Theis Eigil; b. 5 Aug. 1938, Copenhagen, Denmark. Singer; Musician (trumpet); Graphic Designer. m. Lesley Celina Geen, 3 June 1961, divorced 1976. *Education:* Graduate, Graphic Design, Art School, 1959. *Career:* Member: Louisiana Jazzband, 1952–55; Henrik Johansen's Jazzband, 1955–56; Adrian Bentzon's Jazzband, 1956–63; Co-leader, Theis/Nyegaard Jazzband, 1963–98; Theis' Jazzband, 1998–; Tours and festivals: Europe; USA; Argentina; Brazil; Uruguay; Australia; Television and radio appearances: Scandinavia; South America. *Recordings:* Traditional Jazz, 1964; Theis/Nyegaard Concert At Gothenberg, 1969; Theis/Nyegaard Live At Montmartre, 1972; Papa Bue's Viking Jazz Band Live At Vingården, 1976; Jazztage Hanover, 1977; Jazz For Hatz-Lovers, 1979; Theis Jensen 1956–72, 1980; Mand Mand, 1980; Los Estudiantes Daneses En El Hot Club De Buenos Aires, 1980; Gamle Er Unge, Der Er Blevet Aeldre, 1981; The First 25 Years, 1988; Jorgen Svare Meets Theis Jensen, 1991; Jazz Event, 1992; Theis-Nyegaard Jazzband, Tonight Live, 1996. *Publication:* Historier Om Theis, 1992. *Honour:* Jazz Musician of the Year, 1965. *Membership:* DJBFA. *Leisure interests:* Graphic Design; Jazz Music. *Address:* Lovenborg Alle 11, 4420 Regstrup, Denmark.

JERBIC Zeljko; b. 10 Oct. 1954, Koprivnica, Croatia. Record Prod.; Teacher. *Education:* Academy of Pedagogics. *Musical Education:* High School of Music. *Recordings:* As Music and Executive Producer: Damned Die Hard, Phonebox Vandals, 1990; Foxxin, Messerschmitt, 1990; Ikona, Lola V Stain, 1990; 4 x 12, Borghesia, 1991; Mansarda, Lola V Stain, 1992; Asgard Live, Vesna Gorse and Drazen Franolic, 1993; So Shine, Don't, 1995; Ulje Je Na Vodi, Haustor, 1995; KC Rock 98, 1998. *Honours:* Porin Award Nominations, 1994, 1995. *Membership:* Croatian Musicians' Union. *Address:* Attn Mr Zeljko Jerbic, Blind Dog Records, Svilarska 34, 480 00 Koprivnica, Croatia.

JERROLF Mats; b. 28 Aug. 1951, Stockholm, Sweden. Composer; Musician. *Education:* Archaeology, Ethnology, University, 1977. *Career:* Touring in Sweden; Appearances in various Folk music programmes in radio. *Compositions:* Bekannelsen I Logen, 1991; Adjo Till Stockholms

Stad, 1993; Krakemala Namdemanlard, 1993; Förskingrarvisan, 1995. *Recordings:* Skanska Lasses Visor, 1987; Flickan Fran Bellmansro, 1988; Collage, 1990; Haveri, 1993; Namdemans Blandning, 1995. *Publications:* Birka, 1981; Historisk Malarresa, 1981. *Honours:* STIM Award, 1991, 1995, 1997; Folk Music Foundation Award, 1992; SKAP Award, 1995. *Memberships:* SKAP; SAMI. *Leisure interests:* Football; Pubs. *Address:* Reimersholmsi 8, 117 40 Stockholm, Sweden.

JERVIER Paul Joseph; b. 21 Nov. 1966, London, England. Musician (drums); Music Prod. *Recordings:* 4 UK No. 1 singles with Take That; Other recordings for artists include: Yazz; Eternal; Kaos; Gabrielle; R Kelly; Danny Rampling. *Membership:* Musicians' Union. *Leisure interests:* Writing; Sports; Holidays; DIY; Driving. *Address:* 108 Perry Rise, London SE23 2QU, England.

JESSE Graham; b. 19 Oct. 1955, Sydney, Australia. m. Peta, 24 May 1986, 1 s., 1 d. *Musical Education:* Sydney Conservatorium of Music to Study Flute; Conservatorium Jazz Course; Studied Saxophone with Dave Liebman and Musical Composition with Ludmilla Uhlehla, New York, 1981–82. *Career:* Member, Midday Show, live daily TV entertainment programme, 15 years; Toured with Daly Wilson Big Band, Peter Allen, David Atkins; Performed with Sydney Dance Company, James Morrison, Marcia Hines. *Compositions:* Reflections, CD; In the Company of Women, Sydney Dance Company. *Recordings:* Leader: Reflections, CD, 1996; In the Flow, CD, 2000; Featured Soloist: Tommy Emmanuel: Dare to Be Different; Up From Down Under; Gondwanaland; featured soloist and composer, Pamela Knowles, Boites De Jazz. *Honour:* Bicentennial Music Week Award, Most Outstanding Studio Musician, 1988. *Memberships:* Australian Musicians' Union; ARRA. *Address:* 50 Sugarloaf Cres., Castlecrag, NSW 2068, Australia. *E-mail:* grahamjesse@netscape.net.

JETT Joan; b. 22 Sept. 1960, Philadelphia, USA. Vocalist; Musician (guitar). *Career:* Member, US all-female group, The Runaways, 1976–79; Solo artiste, with own backing band, The Blackhearts, 1979-. *Recordings:* Albums: with The Runaways: The Runaways, 1976; Queens of Noise, 1977; Live In Japan, 1977; Solo/with The Blackhearts: Bad Reputation, 1980; I Love Rock 'N' Roll, 1981; Album, 1983; Glorious Results of a Misspent Youth, 1984; Up Your Alley, 1988; Good Music, 1989; Hit List, 1990; Notorious, 1991; Pure and Simple, 1994; Fetish, 1999; Fit To Be Tied, 2001; Singles: I Love Rock 'n' Roll (No. 1, USA), 1981; Don't Surrender, 1991; As I Am, 1994; Love Is All Around, 1996. *Address:* c/o Blackheart Records Group, Suite 6H, 155 E 55th St, New York, NY 10022, USA.

JEWELL Jimmy; b. 18 Feb. 1945, Bricrfield, Lancashire, England. Musician (saxophones); Composer; Arranger. m. Mary-Kay Lombardo, 9 Oct. 1983, 2 d. *Musical Education:* Largely self-taught. *Career:* Keef Hartley Band: Woodstock Festival; 4 years touring, recording with Gallagher and Lyle; Original member, Ronnie Lane's Slim Chance; McGuiness-Flint recorded with Joan Armatrading (Love and Affection solo). *Recordings:* 2 solo albums, jazz fusion, 1977, 1978; Several privately produced tapes, jazz featuring original compositions; Recently released First Phase, 2000; Almost Straight Ahead, 2001. *Memberships:* Musicians' Union; PRS; MCPS. *Leisure interests:* Homebrewing; Winemaking. *Address:* 105 Britton St, Gillingham, Kent ME7 5ES, England.

JIA-ZI Zhao; b. 30 Aug. 1934, Jiang-Su, China. Musicology. m. Xu Si-Jie, 1 s., 1 d. *Education:* Shanghai Conservatory of Music, 1956–61. *Career:* Research Scholar, Music University of New Dheli, The Indian Art Centre, Madras Ethonomusicology Research Institute, 1986–88; Head of Institute Music Research of Shanghai Conservatory of Music; Full Time Supervisor, Shanghai Conservatory of Music; Deputy Director, World Ethnomusicological Association, Oriental Music Association. *Publications:* Collection of Writings on the Music of Shen Zhi-Bai; Indian Music Around The Period of Sui and Tang Dynasty; Rabindranath Tagore and his Music; Gamelan Music in Java and Bali; A Comparative Study of Wu Dan-Qi Shen and Qi Tiao Bei. *Memberships:* Indian Musicological Society; Singapore Asscn for Asian Studies; Chinese Writers' Asscn; Chinese Musicians' Asscn. *Leisure interest:* Photography. *Address:* 6 Garden Court, The Ave, Sunny Bank Hills 4109, Brisbane, Australia.

JIMBOB (James Morrison); b. 22 Nov. 1960. Musician. *Career:* Founder member (with Fruitbat), duo Carter The Unstoppable Sex Machine (later known as Carter USM); Founder member, Jim's Super Stereoworld, 1998; International tours, US, Japan; Extensive British tour, 1999. *Recordings:* 101 Damnations, 1990; 30 Something, 1991; 1992 – The Love Album, 1992 (No. 1, UK); Post Historic Monsters, 1994; Worry Bomb, 1995; Straw Donkey, 1996; A World Without Dave, 1997; I Blame The Government, 1998; Live, 1999; Singles: Sheltered Life, 1988; Sherriff Fatman, 1989; Rubbish, 1990; Anytime, Anyplace, Anywhere, 1990; Bloodsports For All, 1991; After The Watershed, 1991; Only Living Boy In New Cross, 1992; Lean On Me I Won't Fall Over, 1993; Glam Rock Cops, 1994; Let's Get Tattoos, 1994; Young Offenders Mum, 1995; Born On 5th November, 1995; Bonkers In The Nut; Could UB The One I Waited 4; Solo album: JR.

Current Management: Adrian Boss Promotions, 3 Gunstor Rd, London N16 8HF, England.

JIMENEZ-OLARIAGA Marcos Andres; b. 25 April 1960, Madrid, Spain. Jazz Musician (piano). 1 d. *Musical Education:* Classical studies, Geneva CPM, with S Risler. *Career:* Various concerts with saxophonist M Magnoni; Television and radio shows with own band: Chris Cross; Cully Jazz Festival with singer, C Python. *Recordings:* Albums: Chris Cross; Allastor; Outland Souvenirs; Nirohda. *Publications:* Helas Moulino, edited in Le Livre du Jazz en France. *Honours:* Piano certificate with jury congratulations. *Membership:* AMR, Geneva. *Address:* 801 Chemin des Broues, 01220 Divonne, France.

JIRUCHA Jan; b. 24 June 1945, Novy Bydzov, Czech Republic. Musician (Trombone and Vocal). m. 15 Sept. 1973, 1 s., 1 d. *Musical Education:* Private elementary music school. *Career:* Numerous concert appearances. *Recordings:* Studio, traditional jazz, 1984; Echoes and Confessions, traditional jazz, 1987; Classic Jazz Collegium, 1988; Big Fat Mammah, 1991; TJS, 1994; Revival Swing, 1995; J J Jazzmen, Sunday Swing, 1997. *Leisure interest:* Gardening. *Current Management:* J J Jazzmen Band Agency. *Address:* Cestmirova 8, 140 00 Prague 4, Czech Republic.

JOAN Marianne; b. 12 March 1973, Jamestown, ND, USA. Singer. *Education:* MFA in voice, California Institute of the Arts; BA in voice, Peabody Conservatory; Studied with Sopranos Phyllis Bryn-Julson, Jacqueline Bobak and Irene Gubrud. *Career:* Voice for Brigantia, recorded score by Clay Chaplin, Canadian Choreographer Anik Bouvrette; Created new multi-media works with trio, Three Lanes Over, Los Angeles, 1999, and the Digital Improvisation Ensemble, Los Angeles, 1998; Soloist with Schola Antiqua, a medieval music ensemble. *Memberships:* AES; ICMA. *Leisure interests:* Aromatherapy; Herbal Medicine; Homeopathy; Poetry.

JOBE Badou; b. Gambia. Musician (bass guitar). *Musical Education:* Self-taught. *Career:* Started career with Foyer band, late 1950s; Joined African Jazz; Founder member: Super Eagles, 1968; Name change to Ifang Bondi, 1973; Based in Holland, 1984-. *Recordings:* with The Super Eagles: Viva Super Eagles, 1969; Senegambian Sensation; with Ifang Bondi: Saraba, 1976; Mantra, 1983; Sanjo, 1989; Daraj, 1994; Gis Gis, 1998; Ifang Bondi Live, 2001. *Honours:* EverGreen Award, Gambia, 1997; Kora Award, 1999. *E-mail:* mail@ifanbondi.demon.nl.

JOE (Joseph Thomas); b. 1972, Cuthbert, Georgia, USA. Vocalist; Prod. *Career:* Started singing in the choir of parents' Pentecostal Church, Alabama; Moved to New Jersey; Worked in a gospel music store; Played guitar at a local church; Introduced to Vincent Herbert and recorded a 3-song demo together; Signed to Jive Records as solo artist, 1997; Recordings have featured on soundtracks including: Don't Be A Menace; Booty Call; Rush Hour; Collaborations: Brandy; Jay-Z; SWV; Big Punisher; Case; Mariah Carey. *Recordings:* Albums: Everything, 1993; All That I Am, 1997; My Name Is Joe, 2000; Better Days, 2001; Singles: I'm In Luv, 1993; The One For Me, All Or Nothing, 1994; All The Things (Your Man Won't Do), 1996; Don't Wanna Be A Player, The Love Scene, 1997; No-One Else Comes Close, Still Not A Player, Faded Pictures, All That I Am, 1998; I Wanna Know 1999; Thank God I Found You (with Mariah Carey and 98°), Treat Her Like A Lady, 2000; Stutter, 2001. *Address:* c/o Jive Records, 137–139 W 25th St, New York, USA.

JOEL Billy (William Martin); b. 9 May 1949, Bronx, New York, USA. Musician (piano); Singer; Songwriter. m. Christie Brinkley, 23 March 1989, divorced 1994, 1 d. *Education:* LHD (hon), Fairfield Univesity, 1991; HMD (hon), Berklee College Music, 1993. *Career:* Popular solo recording artist, 1972-. *Compositions include:* Just The Way You Are, 1978; Honesty, 1979; We Didn't Start The Fire, 1989; The River of Dreams, 1994. *Recordings:* Hit singles include: Piano Man, 1973; The Entertainer, 1974; Just The Way You Are, 1978; Movin' Out (Anthony's Song), 1978; My LIfe, 1978; All For Leyna, 1980; It's Still Rock 'n' Roll To Me (No. 1, USA), 1980; Allentown, 1982; Tell Her About It (No. 1, USA), 1983; Uptown Girl (No. 1, UK), 1983; An Innocent Man, 1984; The Longest Time, 1984; We Didn't Start The Fire (No. 1, USA), 1989; River of Dreams, 1993; All About Soul, 1993; Albums include: Cold Spring Harbor, 1972; Piano Man, 1973; Streetlife Serenade, 1974; Turnstiles, 1976; The Stranger, 1978; 52nd Street (No. 1, USA), 1978; Glass Houses (No. 1, USA), 1980; Songs In The Attic, 1981; Nylon Curtain, 1982; An Innocent Man, 1983; Greatest Hits, Vols I and II, 1985; The Bridge, 1986; KOHUEPT-Live In Leningrad, 1987; Storm Front (No. 1, USA), 1989; River of Dreams (No. 1, USA), 1993; Greatest Hits, 1997; 2000 Years – The Millennium Concert, 2000. *Honours:* 6 Grammy Awards include: Record of Year, Song of Year, Best Male Vocal Performance, 1978; Best Album, 1979; 10 Grammy Nominations include: Best Song, Record, Producer, Male Vocal Performance of Year; American Music Award, Best Album, 1980; Grammy Legend Award, 1990; Inducted into Songwriters Hall of Fame, 1992; ASCAP Founders Award, 1997; Hon. DHL, Hofstra University, 1997. *Leisure interest:* Boating. *Address:* c/o Maritime Music Inc, 200 W 57th St, Suite 308, New York, NY 10019, USA.

JOHANSEN Per Oddvar Eide; b. 1 March 1968, Oslo, Norway. Musician (drums). *Musical Education:* Music Gymnasium, Rud High School, three years; Studied Jazz at Trondelag Music Conservatory of Music, Trondheim, three years. *Career:* Freelance drummer, mostly Jazz and improvised music; Has toured in Norway and Europe with numerous groups including: Airamero; Kenny Weeler; John Surman; Karin Krog; Nils Petter Molvaer; Jon Christensen; Tore Brunborg; Vigleik Storaas; The Source; Close Erase. *Recordings:* include: Airamero, Airamero; Olemanns Kornett, The Source; This Is You, Jacob Young; Close Erase; No. 2. *Honours:* Spellemannsprisen for Vigleile Storans trio, Bilder, 1995; Spellemannsprisen for Vigleile Storans trio, Andre Bilder, 1997. *Memberships:* Norwegian Jazz Federation; Norwegian Musical Union. *Leisure interests:* Animals; Old records and instruments; Vintage drums. *Address:* Gamleveien 122E, 1350 Lommedalen, Norway.

JOHANSSON Lars-Olof (Lasse); b. 23 Feb. 1973, Huskvarna, Sweden. Musician (Keyboards, Guitar). *Career:* Joined The Cardigans, 1993; Numerous TV and radio appearances, live tours and festival dates. *Recordings:* Singles: Sick and Tired; Carnival; Hey! Get Out of My Way; Rise and Shine; Lovefool; Been It; Your New Cuckoo; My Favourite Game; Erase and Rewind; Burning Down The House, with Tom Jones; Albums: Emmerdale; Life; First Band On The Moon; Gran Turismo. *Contributions to:* films Romeo and Juliet and A Life Less Ordinary.

JOHANSSON Markku; b. 22 March 1949, Lahti, Finland. Conductor; Arranger; Composer; Musician (trumpet, flugelhorn). m. Riita Kvitunen, June 1971, 1 s., 1 d. *Musical Education:* Music conservatory in Lahti; Sibelius Academy in Helsinki; Jazz studies in New York, with Thad Jones, Lew Soloff. *Career:* Radio, television, recording artist, as conductor, arranger, trumpet player; Conductor, UMO Jazz Orchestra, 1992–93; Conductor, Vantaa Pops Orchestra, 1988-. *Recordings:* Blue Echoes; Tenderly; Exorbitant; Vantaaa Pops Orchestra; Umo Jazz Orchestra; with Nils Lindberg: Saxes Galore, Brass Galore, 1994; with Lena Jansson: Lena Jansson, 1995; with Thad Jones: Thad Jones, Mel Lewis and Umo, 1995. *Honour:* Yrjö Award 1993 (Musician of the Year). *Current Management:* MJ-Music Oy. *Address:* Aalto 6 B 18, 02320 Espoo, Finland.

JOHN Elton (Sir), (Reginald Kenneth Dwight); b. 25 March 1947, Pinner, Middlesex, England. Singer; Songwriter; Musician (piano). m. Renate Blauer, 14 Feb. 1984, divorced 1988. *Musical Education:* Piano lessons aged 4; Royal Academy of Music, 1958. *Career:* Member, Bluesology, 1961–67; Worked at Mills Music Publishers; Solo artiste, 1968–; Long-term writing partnership with Bernie Taupin, 1967–; Partnership wrote for Dick James Music; Founder, Rocket Records, 1973; Own publishing company, Big Picture, 1974; Performances include: Wembley Stadium, 1975; First Western star to perform in Israel and USSR, 1979; Live Aid, Wembley, 1985; Wham's farewell concert, Wembley, 1985; Prince's Trust concerts, London, 1986, 1988; Farm Aid IV, 1990; AIDS Project Los Angeles – Commitment To Life VI, 1992; Film appearance, Tommy, 1975. *Recordings:* Hit singles include: Your Song, 1971; Rocket Man, 1972; Crocodile Rock (No. 1, USA), 1973; Daniel, 1973; Saturday Night's Alright For Fighting, 1973; Goodbye Yellow Brick Road, 1973; Candle In The Wind, 1974; Don't Let The Sun Go Down On Me, 1974 (live version with George Michael, No. 1, UK and US, 1991); Philadelphia Freedom (No. 1, USA), 1975; Lucy In The Sky With Diamonds (No. 1, USA), 1975; Island Girl (No. 1, USA), 1975; Pinball Wizard, from film Tommy, 1976; Don't Go Breaking My Heart, duet with Kiki Dee (No. 1, UK and US), 1976; Sorry Seems To Be The Hardest Word, 1976; Bennie and The Jets (No. 1, USA), 1976; Song For Guy, 1979; Blue Eyes, 1982; I Guess That's Why They Call It The Blues, 1983; I'm Still Standing, 1983; Kiss The Bride, 1983; Sad Songs (Say So Much), 1984; Passengers, 1984; Nikita, 1985; Sacrifice (No. 1, UK), 1989; The One, 1992; True Love (with Kiki Dee), 1993; Don't Go Breaking My Heart, with RuPaul, 1994; Ain't Nothing Like The Real Thing, with Marcella Detroit, 1994; Can You Feel The Love Tonight, 1994; Circle of Life, 1994; Made In England, 1995; Blessed, 1995; Believe, 1995; You Can Make History, 1996; Live Like Horses, 1996; Candle In The Wind 97/Something About The Way You Look Tonight (No. 1, World-wide, over 33m. copies sold), 1997; If The River Can Bend, 1998; Written in the Stars, 1999; I Want Love, 2001; This Train Don't Stop There Anymore, 2001; Contributor, That's What Friends Are For, Dionne Warwick and Friends (charity record), 1986; Albums include: Elton John, 1970; Tumbleweed Connection, 1971; Friends, 1971; 17–11–70, 1971; Madman Across The Water, 1972; Honky Chateau (No. 1, USA), 1972; Don't Shoot Me, I'm Only The Piano Player (No. 1, UK and US), 1973; Goodbye Yellow Brick Road (No. 1, UK and US), 1973; Caribou (No. 1, UK and US), 1974; Captain Fantastic and The Brown Dirt Cowboy (No. 1, USA), 1975; Rock of The Westies (No. 1, USA), 1975; Here and There, 1976; Blue Moves, 1976; A Single Man, 1978; Lady Samantha, 1980; 21 At 33, 1980; Jump Up!, 1982; Too Low For Zero, 1983; Breaking Hearts, 1984; Ice On Fire, 1985; Leather Jackets, 1986; Live In Australia, 1987; Reg Strikes Back, 1988; Sleeping With The Past (No. 1, UK), 1989; The Very Best of (No. 1, UK), 1990; The One, 1992; Made In England, 1995; Big Picture, 1997; Love Songs, 1998; Live in Australia, 1999; Songs From The West Coast, 2001. *Honours include:* First album to go straight to No. 1 in US

charts, Captain Fantastic…, 1975; Numerous Ivor Novello Awards for: Daniel, 1974; Don't Go Breaking My Heart, 1977; Song For Guy, 1979; Nikita, 1986; Sacrifice, 1991; Outstanding Contribution To British Music, 1986; Star on Hollywood Walk of Fame, 1975; Madison Square Gardens Honours: Hall of Fame, 1977; Walk of Fame (first non-athlete), 1992; American Music Awards: Favorite Male Artist, Favourite Single, 1977; Silver Clef Award, Nordoff-Robbins Music Therapy, 1979; BRIT Awards: Outstanding Contribution To British Music, 1986; Best British Male Artist, 1991; Grammy, Best Vocal Performance By A Group, 1987; MTV Special Recognition Trophy, 1987; Hitmaker Award, National Academy of Popular Music, 1989; Hon. Life President, Watford Football Club, 1989; Inducted into Songwriters Hall of Fame (with Bernie Taupin), 1992; Q Magazine Merit Award, 1993; Officer of Arts and Letters, Paris, 1993; KBE, 1998. *Current Management:* John Reid Enterprises Ltd, Singers House, 32 Galena Rd, London W6 0LT, England.

JOHN Lee; b. 23 June 1967, Hackney, London, England. Singer; Songwriter; Musician (keyboards); Record Prod.; Arranger. *Musical Education:* Hewanoma Strolling Players; Anna Scher Stage School; World-wide Productions, New York. *Career:* Lead singer, Imagination; Backing vocalist, major artists; Concerts include: Prince's Trust Concert (played to Prince and Princess of Wales), Royal Albert Hall; Concerts for: Mandela family; President of Algeria; Princess Caroline, Prince Albert of Monaco; Sellout tours with Imagination, 1982–83. *Recordings:* with Imagination: Body Talk, 1981; Flashback, 1981; In and Out of Love, 1981; Just An Illusion (No. 2, UK), 1982; Music and Lights, 1982; In The Heat of The Night, 1982; Changes, 1982; Looking At Midnight, 1983; Thank You My Love, 1984; Instinctual, 1988; Albums include: Body Talk, 1981; Scandalous, 2000; Solo: Let There Be Love (featured with Arthur Baker); The Mighty Power of Love; Your Mind Your Body Your Soul, 2000. *Honours:* Diamond Award; Gold and Platinum discs world-wide; Blues and Soul Award. *Memberships:* Musicians' Union; BASCA; PRS; PPL. *Leisure interests:* Writing; Old films; Musicals; Reading; Swimming; Running. *Current Management:* Johnny X Productions, c/o Gina Smith Management. *Address:* 22 Croftside, Vigo Village, Kent DA13 0SH, England.

JOHNSON Alastair; b. 1 July 1966, Oxford, England. Recording Engineer; Record Prod.; Programmer; Writer. *Career:* Initially live sound engineer, then house engineer, various UK studios including: Red Bus, Jacobs, Wool Hall, late 1980s; Artist manager, 2 years; Returned to studio as freelance engineer, producer. *Recordings:* Engineer, albums: First of a Million Kisses, Fairground Attraction; Extricate, The Fall; Infinity, Donovan. *Leisure interest:* Clubbing. *Current Management:* Strongroom Management. *Address:* Strongroom Studios, 120 Curtain Rd, London EC2A 3PJ, England.

JOHNSON Brian; b. 5 Oct. 1947, Newcastle. Vocalist; Lyricist. *Career:* Lead singer, UK rock band Geordie; Lead singer, heavy rock group AC/DC, 1980–; Appearances include: Monsters of Rock Festival, Castle Donington, 1981, 1984; European rock festivals, Switzerland, Hungary, Belgium, Germany, 1991; Concert, Moscow, 1991. *Recordings:* with Geordie: Hope You Like It, 1973; Don't Be Fooled By the Name, 1974; Brian Johnson and Geordie, 1981; with AC/DC: Singles include: Back In Black, 1981; You Shook Me All Night Long, 1981; Rock 'n' Roll Ain't Noise Pollution, 1981; Let's Get It Up, 1982; For Those About To Rock (We Salute You), 1982; Guns For Hire, 1983; Nervous Shakedown, 1984; Shake Your Foundations, 1985; Who Made Who, 1985; That's The Way I Wanna Rock 'n' Roll, 1988; Heatseeker, 1988; Thunderstruck, 1990; Moneytalks, 1991; Are You Ready, 1991; Big Gun (used in film The Last Action Hero), 1993; Hard As A Rock, 1995; Stiff Upper Lip, 2000; Albums: Back In Black (No. 1, UK), 1980; For Those About To Rock (We Salute You) (No. 1, USA), 1981; Flick of The Switch, 1983; Fly On The Wall, 1985; Who Made Who, 1986; Blow Up Your Video, 1988; The Razor's Edge, 1990; Live, 1992; Ballbreaker, 1995; Bonfire, 1997; Stiff Upper Lip, 2000; Also appears on: Zappa The Yellow Shark, 1993; Adventures of the OC Supertones, 1996; Chase the Sun, 1999. *Current Management:* Hard To Handle Management, 640 Lee Rd, Suite 106, Wayne, PA 19087, USA.

JOHNSON David Allen; b. 15 Dec. 1954, Indiana, USA. Songwriter; Musician (Vocals, Percussion). m. Coleen Gail Johnson. *Education:* BA, Indiana University, 1977. *Career:* Appearance on the Late Show with David Letterman. *Leisure interest:* Listening To and Collecting Classical Rock Music. *Address:* 6008 Laurel Hall Dr. Apt 4, Indianapolis, IN 46226 2455, USA.

JOHNSON David Paul; b. 8 Oct. 1957, WA, USA. Composer; Musician; Educator. 1 s., 2 d. *Education:* BA, Whitman College, 1979; MA, Music University of Oregon, 1992; PhD, Music University of Oregon, 1997. *Career:* Blue Buddha Performance at the International Computer Music Conference, 1996; Informatique Musicale, 1996; These Sins Will Not Be Forgiven. *Compositions:* Blue Buddha; These Sins Will Not Be Forgiven; Ozone; Warwords; Empathy Atrophied. *Recordings:* David Paul Johnson 5x5. *Honour:* Composer in Residence, 1992. *Memberships:* Music Educators

National Conference; International Computer Music Asscn. *Leisure interests:* Photography; Cycling. *Address:* 445 W 19th, Eugene, OR 97401, USA.

JOHNSON Derick; b. 7 June 1963, Manchester, England. Musician (bass guitar). 2 s. *Career:* Started 52nd Street, 1983–86; Played with Swing Out Sister, 1989–; 4 tours: Italy; Phillipines; Spain; UK; Japan; America; Radio One sessions, Top of The Pops, Tube, The Word, Pebble Mill. *Compositions:* That's The Way It Goes; Low Down Dirty Business; Cool As Ice. *Recordings:* Live album: Swing Out Sister; Get In Touch With Yourself; The Living Return. *Membership:* Musicians' Union. *Leisure interests:* Electronics; Lovemaking. *Address:* 66 Avebury Rd, Boguley, Wytheshowe, Manchester M23 2QE, England.

JOHNSON Henry Joseph Jr; b. 28 Jan. 1954, Chicago, Illinois, USA. Jazz Musician (guitar); Vocalist. *Education:* Indiana University. *Musical Education:* Self-taught (from jazz recordings). *Career:* Guitarist, for organist Jack McDuff, 1976; Singer, Donny Hathaway, 1977; Pianist, Ramsey Lewis, 1979–82; 1985–; Singer, Joe Williams, 1986–; Saxophonist, Stanley Turrentine, 1995–; Solo artiste, 1987–; Performances include: All jazz festivals including Playboy Jazz Festival; JVC Jazz Festival; North Seas Jazz Festival. *Recordings:* 5 as solo artiste, include: You're The One; Future Excursions; New Beginnings; 3 with jazz vocalist, Joe Williams; 6 with pianist, Ramsey Lewis. *Honours:* Downbeat: CD: You're The One, awarded 5 stars; Billboard Top 100 List, 1986, 1987, 1988. *Memberships:* Musicians' Union; AFTRA; NARAS. *Leisure interests:* Recording music; Producing music; Cooking; Reading; Basketball. *Current Management:* John Levy Enterprises. *Address:* 2810 W Charleston Blvd G-72, Las Vegas, NE 89102, USA.

JOHNSON Holly (William); b. 9 Feb. 1960, Liverpool, England. Singer; Songwriter; Author; Artist; Actor. *Career:* Member, Big In Japan; Founder Member, Frankie Goes to Hollywood, 1980–87; Appearances include: World tours; Montreux Rock Festival, MTV, in the Motion Picture Body Double, 1995, Band Aid single, Hillsborough Justice Concert, 1997; Solo Artist, 1987–; Exhibition of paintings and sculptures, The House of Holly, Cork Street Gallery, London, 1996; Owner, Pleasuredome record label. *Recordings:* Albums: with Frankie Goes to Hollywood: Welcome to the Pleasuredome, (No. 1, UK), 1984; Liverpool, 1986; Blast (No. 1, UK), 1989; Hollelujah, 1989; Dreams That Money Can't Buy, 1991; Bang! – Greatest Hits of Frankie Goes to Hollywood, 1993; Reload, 1994; Maximum Joy, 2000; Solo album: Soulstream, 1999; Singles include: Relax, (No. 1, UK), 1984; Two Tribes (No. 1, UK), 1984; The Power of Love (No. 1, UK), 1984; Welcome to the Pleasuredome, 1985; Rage Hard, 1986; Warriors of the Wasteland, 1986; Watching the Wildlife, 1986; Solo singles: Love Train, 1989; Americanos, 1989; Atomic City, 1989; The Power of Love, 1999; Soulstream, 1999. *Contributions to:* Ferry Cross The Mersey, charity single with The Christians, Paul McCartney and Gerry Marsden (No. 1, UK), 1989; Last Temptation of Elvis, compilation album, 1990. *Publication:* A Bone in My Flute, autobiography, 1994. *Honours:* Only group to have 2 Platinum singles with first 2 releases, first three singles went to No. 1, UK, 1984; Two BRIT Awards, Best British Single, Best British Newcomer, 1985; Ivor Novello Award, Best Contemporary Song, Two Tribes, 1985. *Address:* Pleasuredome, PO Box 425, London SW6 3TX, England.

JOHNSON John (J J); b. 27 Oct. 1951. Newark, Nottinghamshire, England. Musician (drums, keyboards); Vocalist; Prod. Partner, Christine Robertson, 2 s. *Musical Education:* Self-taught. *Career:* Drummer, Wayne County and The Electric Chairs, 1976–80; with Mystere Five; Drums, vocals, Flying Lizards, Thomas Dolby; Skids; Nico; GBM, drums, vocals. *Recordings:* with The Electric Chairs: The Electric Chairs (EP), 1977; Blatently Offensive (EP), 1978; Albums: The Electric Chairs, 1977; Storm The Gates of Heaven, 1978; Things Your Mother Never Told You, 1979; 8 singles include: Thunder When She Walks, 1977; Trying To Get On The Radio, 1978; Eddie and Sheena, 1978; Waiting For The Marines, 1979; Berlin, 1979; So Many Ways, 1979; with Mystere 5 singles include: Heart Rules The Head and No Message, 1980; with The Fying Lizards, album: Fourth Wall, 1981; Single: Lovers and Other Strangers; Jungle Line (EP), Thomas Dolby, 1981; Albums: Drama of Exile, Nico; Joy, The Skids, 1981; Ten Thirty On A Summer's Night, Richard Jobson, 1983; with GBM, album: Method In The Madness; with Neil Finn: One Nil, 2001; Singles: Strange News; Diction and Fiction; Whistling In The Dark, 1983–84. *Membership:* Musicians' Union. *Leisure interests:* Swimming; Camping. *Address:* GBM Productions, 41B Kingsgate Rd, London NW6 4TD, England.

JOHNSON Kelly; Musician (Guitar); Vocalist. *Career:* Joined Girlschool; Introduced to management deal by Lemmy from Motorhead, and supported Motorhead on their Overkill tour; Obtained record deal; Numerous tours, television performances and hit singles; Further collaborations with Motorhead; Tours in Canada and the USA; Album produced by Noddy Holder and Jim Lea of Slade; Left Girlschool, 1983, rejoined reformed group, 1995. *Recordings:* Singles: Emergency/Furniture Fire; Nothing to Lose; Race with the Devil; Hit and Run; Yeah Right; C'mon Let's Go; St

Valentine's Day Massacre, Hard Rock, Motorschool, with Motorhead; 20th Century Boy; Albums: Demolition, 1980; Hit and Run, 1981; Play Dirty, 1983; Girlschool, 1995; Collection, 1995; Live, 1996; Race with the Devil Live, 1998; Emergency, 1998; Can't Keep A Good Girl Down, 2000.

JOHNSON Kenny; b. 11 Dec. 1939, Halewood, Merseyside, England. Country Singer; Songwriter; Musician (guitar). 1 s., 1 d. *Musical Education:* Rock 'n' Roll clubs around Liverpool. *Career:* Leader of group Northwind; 40 years professional; Television appearances throughout UK, Europe and US; Major tours with: Marty Robbins; Billie Jo Spears; Johnny Cash; Major concerts: Rhyman Auditorium, original Grand Ole Opry tour, USA; Grand Ole Opry, Tennessee; Falklands, 3 times; Belize, twice; Euromasters Festival, Holland; Presenter, weekly radio shows, BBC Radio Merseyside, BBC Northwest; Owner, Stocks Records. *Recordings:* 16 albums include: Today: City Lights; Today; Summer Nights; Blue Rendezvous. *Honours:* 2 British Country Music Radio Awards, 1992; CMRU International Publishers Award, 1993; BCMA Award, Best British Male Performer, 1993; Gold Star Award, Netherlands; Best Male Vocalist, Variety Club of Great Britain; 2 MCM Awards. *Memberships:* Musicians' Union; PRS. *Address:* 54 Edward Rd, Whiston, Merseyside L35 5AJ, England.

JOHNSON Laurie; b. 1927, London, England. Composer. m., 1 d. *Education:* Royal College of Music. *Career:* Taught at Royal College of Music; Orchestral pieces broadcast by age 20; Composer, arranger, Ted Heath Band and all major bands and orchestras of 1950s; Entered film industry, 1955; Co-owner, film production companies including Gainsborough Pictures, 1979–; Founder, The London Big Band (25 British jazz and orchestral musicians), for concerts and recordings with international star guests, 1994. *Compositions include:* Lock Up Your Daughters, musical; Pieces of Eight, revue; The Four Musketeers, musical; Scores for over 400 cinema and television films including: Dr Strangelove; First Men In The Moon; The Avengers; The Professionals; The New Avengers; Television themes include: This Is Your Life; World In Action; Whicker's World. *Recordings:* Synthesis, symphony; The Wind In The Willows, tone poem; Suite for symphonic band (RAF commission for 50th anniversary of Battle of Britain); The Conquistadors, music for Royal occasions; Numerous albums with own studio orchestra. *Honours:* Various awards and nominations for music scores and record or film productions. *Address:* The Laurie Johnson Organisation Ltd, 10 College Rd, Harrow, Middlesex HA1 1DA, England.

JOHNSON Matt; b. 15 Aug. 1961, East London, England. Singer; Songwriter; Musician (guitar); Record Prod. *Musical Education:* Self-taught. *Career:* Member, first band Road Star, aged 11; Recording engineer, London, aged 15, 1976; Formed The The, aged 17, 1979; The The, general music collective, over 300 artists to date (including Sinead O'Connor, Jools Holland, Johnny Marr, Neneh Cherry, Zeke Manyika, Warne Livesey), 1979–; Concerts and tours include: Residency at Marquee, London (with Marc Almond, Zeke Manyika), 1983; World tours, 1989–90, 1992–93; Royal Albert Hall, 1990; Headliners, Reading Festival, 1993; Films: Infected (long-form video to accompany album), 1987; The The Versus The World, 1991; From Dusk 'Til Dawn, 1994. *Recordings:* Albums: Burning Blue Soul, 1981; Soul Mining, 1983; Infected (also film and book), 1986; Mind Bomb, 1989; Dusk, 1993; Solitude, 1994; Hanky Panky, 1995; Naked Self, 2000; with Orang: Herd of Instinct, 1995; with Shudder to Think: First Love Last Rites, 1998; Singles include: Controversial Subject, 1981; Uncertain Smile, 1982; Perfect, 1983; This Is The Day, 1983; Sweet Bird of Truth, 1986; Heartland, 1986; Infected, 1986; Slow Train To Dawn, 1987; Armageddon Days, 1989; The Beat(en) Generation, 1989; Gravitate To Me, 1989; Shades of Blue, EP, 1991; Dogs of Lust, 1993; Slow Emotion Replay, 1993; Love Is Stronger Than Death, 1993; Dis-Infected EP, 1994; I Saw The Light, 1995. *Publication:* Infected (lyrics and paintings), 1987. *Honours include:* Best Long Form Video, Montreux Film and Music Festival, Infected, 1988; Platinum, Gold or Silver records for all albums. *Leisure interests:* Film making; Photography. *Current Management:* c/o Fran Musso, REN Management, 1125 Coldwater Canyon, Beverly Hills, CA 90210, USA.

JOHNSON Mike; b. 27 Aug. 1965, Grant Pass, Oregon, USA. Musician (guitar, bass); Songwriter; Singer. m. Leslie, 21 Nov. 1994. *Education:* AA. *Career:* Solo artiste; Basssist, Dinosaur Jr, 1992–; Cameo; Appearances in Grace of My Heart. *Recordings:* Where Am I, 1994; Year of Mondays; 1996; I Feel Alright, 1998; with Dinosaur Jr: Whatever's Cool with Me, 1991; Where You Been?, 1993; Without a Sound, 1994; Hand It Over, 1997; The BBC Sessions, 2000; Ear-Bleeding Country (compilation), 2001. *Membership:* BMI. *Leisure interests:* Drinking; Smoking. *Current Management:* BYD Management. *Address:* c/o BYD, 501 N 36th #196, Seattle, WA 98103, USA.

JOHNSON Robb Jenner; b. 25 Dec. 1955, London, England. Singer; Songwriter; Musician (guitar). m. Meeta Kanabar, 22 Aug. 1992. *Education:* BA Hons, MA, English Literature. *Career:* Folk clubs, 1975–80; Band, Grubstreet, 1980–84; Agit-prop trio, Ministry of Humour, 1984–86; Solo, then duo with Pip Collings, 1989–94; Solo: Nicaragua TV,

Managua Concert for the 10th anniversary of the Revolution, 1989; CH4 documentary, Beyond The Maypole, 1991; Tour of Belgium, 1995; 25th Anniversary, Glastonbury Festival, 1995. *Recordings:* Albums: Skewed Stewed and Awkward, 1987; Small Town World, 1989; Overnight, 1991; Heart's Desire, 1993; Lack of Jolly Ploughboy, 1994; This Is The UK Talking, 1994. *Publications:* Rosa's Lovely Daughters; I Close My Eyes; Boxing Day; Herald of Free Enterprise. *Honour:* 1980 Northwest Songwriters Competition. *Memberships:* Musicians' Union; PRS. *Leisure interests:* Painting; Paris. *Address:* c/o Rhiannon Records, Freepost LON 6347, London E8 2BR, England.

JOHNSON Stanley Glen; b. 1 Sept. 1953, Hillsdale, Michigan, USA. Recording Artist; Artist Man. m. Jacalyn Joy Ware, 29 Aug. 1970, 1 s., 2 d. *Education:* Jackson Community College. *Musical Education:* Self-taught. *Career:* Radio in USA; Local church concerts and special fair programmes. *Compositions:* As songwriter: Hold On; There'll Be Hell To Pay; Not Guilty. *Publications:* The Singing News; The Gospel Voice; Gospel Music News. *Honours:* Editors Choice Awards; National Library of Poetry. *Membership:* BMI. *Leisure interests:* Songwriting; Poetry; Hunting; Fishing. *Current Management:* CER Records (USA).

JOHNSON Wilko; b. 12 July 1947, Canvey Island, Essex, England. Singer; Musician (guitar). m. Irene Knight, 6 April 1968, 2 s. *Education:* BA Hons, English. *Musical Education:* Self-taught. *Career:* Guitarist, songwriter, founder member of Dr Feelgood; Played with Ian Dury and The Blockheads, 1980–82; Extensive tours with own band, 1985-. *Compositions include:* Back in the Night; She Does It Right; Roxette. *Recordings:* Albums include: Down By the Jetty, 1975 and Stupidity, 1976 (with Dr Feelgood); Barbed Wire Blues; Don't Let Your Daddy Know; with Mick Farren: Vampires Stole My Lunch Money, 1978; with Ian Drury: Laughter, 1980; with Stranglers: Live in Concert, 1995; Solo Albums: Solid Senders, 1978; Ice on the Motorway, 1981; Bottle Up and Go, 1983; Pull the Cover, 1995; Going Back Home, 1998; Dr Feelgood compilations include: Live At The BBC 1974–75, 1999; The BBC Sessions 1973–78, 2001; Singled Out (As Bs and Rarities), 2001. *Memberships:* MCPS; PRS. *Leisure interests:* Reading; Astronomy. *Current Management:* Irene Knight.

JOHNSON Yana; b. 23 Sept. 1969, England. Singer; Songwriter. *Education:* BSc Environmental Control. *Musical Education:* Grade 1 Classical. *Career:* Writer, scripts and song material for theatrical productions; Backing vocalist, 291 Talent Show; Worked with Total Contrast; Session work with artists including: Massive Attack; Nenah Cherry; Raw Stylus; Cold Cut; British tour with Drizabone. *Recordings:* Songs: I Do, Total Contrast (on compilation album Full Swing); Believe, Cold Cut; Writer, producer, demo material, I've Found You, Troi; also written with Shola Ama on second album: That Thing; Surrender; Bring It On, album. *Membership:* Musicians' Union. *Leisure interests:* Travel; Fashion; Songwriting; Backing vocals. *Current Management:* Urban Management, c/o Nick Sellars.

JOHNSTON Jim; b. 20 Dec. 1954, Dundalk, Ireland. Singer; Songwriter; Dancer. m. Patricia, 19 June 1981, 1 s., 2 d. *Education:* Teaching Diploma, St Patrick's Training College, Drumcondra, Dublin. *Musical Education:* Tuition in Drums, CCÉ, Dundalk; Studied Traditional Fiddle with Rose O'Connor; Self-taught Guitar, Harmonica; Matthews School of Irish Dance. *Career:* Songwriter and Dancer; Toured Czechoslovakia with Dún Dealgan Cabaret, 1978; Comhaltas Tour of Britain, 1980; Toured Austria with Lá Lugh (traditional band), 1995; Irish Music Festival, Copenhagen, 1996; Appeared on RTÉ Live at 3, 1997; Sibín Tna G, 1998; Played support to Mary Coughlan, 1994, Mick Hanly, 1994, Sonny Condell, 1995, Don Baker, 1995, Freddie White, 1996; Something Happens, Drogheda, 1998. *Compositions:* Victory or Defeat; Squeeze Gut Alley Blues; Fairhill – Time Stood Still; It's The Same Sun; The Paragon Seven. *Recordings:* The Factories – They're All Closing Down, 1986; Rian An Uaignis, 1993, CD version, 1996; Guested on Orla – The Blue Note, 1998; Album, Politics of The Heart, 1999. *Publication:* Pléaráca Dhún Dealgan (The Humours of Dundalk: Collection of Folk-songs), 1985. *Honours:* Men's World Irish Dancing Champion, 1975, 1977, 1979. *Membership:* Irish Music Rights Organization. *Leisure interests:* Fishing; Reading. *Current Management:* Uaigneas Music.

JOHNSTON Timothy John; b. 12 Nov. 1963, Newcastle-Upn-Tyne, England. Musician (drums). *Musical Education:* 1 year light music course, Newcastle College. *Career:* Toured extensively with Pauline Murray and The Storm, including full tour supporting The Mission, 1985-; Television and radio appearances with The Light Programme and Swing Palace, 1987–94; Regular appearances at national jazz festivals; Toured with Deacon Jones and the Sinners, 1994; Performing in resident band, Bourbon Street, at Hilton, Park Lane, London, 1995. *Recordings:* 2 albums with The Light Programme, 1987, 1989; Album Storm Clouds, 1989, and 2 singles, This Thing Called Love and New Age, with Pauline Murray; 2 albums with Swing Palace, 1991, 1993. *Membership:* Musicians'

Union. *Leisure interests:* Football; Playing guitar. *Address:* 20 Highbury, Monkseaton, Whitley Bay, Tyne and Wear NE25 8EF, England.

JONASSON Jonas; b. 28 Aug. 1967, Angelholm, Sweden. Musician (synthesizer, vocoder, melodica). m. Malin Jonasson-Sahlstedt, 16 May 1992, 2 d. *Musical Education:* Self-taught on synthesizer. *Career:* Member, bob hund, formed in 1991; More than 300 gigs around Scandinavia; Played at famous Roskilde, Lollipop, Ruisrock, Quartfestivalen and Hultsfred. *Compositions:* I Stället för Musik: Förvirring, 1996; Düsseldorf, 1996. *Recordings:* bob hund – bob hund, 1993; bob hund – Edvin Medvind, 1994; bob hund – Omslag: Martin Kann, 1996; bob hund – Omslag: Martin Kann, 1996; bob hund, Stenaldern Kan Borja, 2001. *Honours:* Grammy, best live act, 1994; Grammy, best lyrics, 1996. *Memberships:* STIM; SAMI. *Leisure interests:* Music; Books; Food; Drinking. *Address:* c/o Bob Hunds Förlag, Råsundavägen 150, 169 36 Solna, Sweden.

JONES (John) Howard; b. 23 Feb. 1955, Southampton, Hampshire, England. Songwriter; Singer; Musician (keyboards, computer); Record Prod. m. Janet Lesley Smith, 25 Oct. 1978. *Musical Education:* Royal Northern College of Music, Manchester. *Career:* Piano teacher; Solo recording artiste, 1983–; Tours include: US tour, support to Eurythmics, 1984; British tour, 1984; Live Aid, Wembley Stadium, 1985; Tour, North America, 1992. *Recordings:* Albums: Human's Lib, 1984; The Twelve Inch Album, 1984; Dream Into Action, 1985; Action Replay, 1986; One To One, 1986; Cross That Line, 1989; The Best of Howard Jones, 1993; In The Running, 1998; Greatest Hits; Working In The Backroom; Live Acoustic America, 1996; Angels and Lovers, 1997; People, 1998; Pefawm, 2000; Singles include: New Song (No. 3, UK), 1983; What Is Love (No. 2, UK), 1984; Hide and Seek, 1984; Pearl In The Shell, 1984; Like To Get To Know You Well, 1984; Things Can Only Get Better, 1985; Look Mama, 1985; Life In One Day, 1985; No One Is To Blame, 1986; All I Want, 1986; You Know I Love You... Don't You?, 1986; Everlasting Love, 1987; The Prisoner, 1989; Lift Me Up, 1992; What Is Love, 1993; IGY, 1993; Tomorrow Is Now, 1998; Let the People Have Their Say, 1999. *Contributions to:* Live-in World (Anti-Heroin Project charity album), 1986; Rubáiyát (Elektra's 40th Anniversary album), 1990. *Memberships:* ASCAP; PRS. *Leisure interest:* Watching Formula One motor racing. *Current Management:* David Stopps, Friars Management. *Address:* 33 Alexander Rd, Aylesbury, Bucks HP20 2NR, England.

JONES Alan John; b. 2 April 1947, Rotherham, Yorkshire, England. Musician (Bass Guitar). 2 c. *Education:* Eric Guilder School of Music, London. *Career:* Appearances at London Palladium, Royal Albert Hall, Caesar's Palace, Las Vegas; Musician, film music for Live and Let Die, with George Martin and Paul McCartney, theme music for Taggart, STV, theme tune for quiz show Blockbusters, music for advertisement, Milk Tray. *Compositions:* A Shadow in Time, for Bucks Fizz; Puttin' On the Style, for Lonnie Donegan; Somewhere in England, for George Harrison; Gone Troppo, for Julio Iglesias; Libra, for Hank Marvin. *Recordings:* Appearances on The Best of Hank Marvin and the Shadows; The Freddy Mercury Album; Gilbert O'Sullivan Himself; Back to Front; I'm a Writer Not a Fighter; Greatest Hits; 20 Golden Greats, for Cliff Richard; I'm Nearly Famous. *Publication:* A Shadow in Time, 1986. *Honour:* Appearance on Royal Variety Performance with Cliff Richard and The Shadows, 1984. *Memberships:* Musicians' Union; POAMRA. *Leisure interests:* Music; Eating out in restaurants; Musical tuition. *Address:* 4A Mercury Close, Bampton, Oxon OX18 2AH, England.

JONES Bill (Belinda Helen); b. 17 Aug. 1973, Codsall, Wolverhampton, England, UK. Vocalist; Musician (accordion, piano, flute, whistle); Composer. *Musical Education:* London City University. *Career:* Folk musician; worked with Scots accordionist Phil Cunningham; BBC radio sessions for Folk on 2 and Andy Kershaw. *Recordings:* Singles: Bits and Pieces, 2001; Albums: Turn To Me, 2000; Panchpuran, 2001. *Honour:* BBC Horizon Award for New Talent, 2001. *Current Management:* Felicity Jones, 10 Meadowbank Ave, Weston, Stafford, ST18 OHE, England. *Internet:* www.brickwallmusic.com.

JONES Booker T; b. 12 Nov. 1944, Memphis, Tennessee, USA. Musician (keyboards); Songwriter; Record Prod. m. Priscilla Coolidge. *Career:* Session musician, Memphis; Leader, Booker T and The MGs (Memphis Group), 1962–71; Concerts include: Soul Sensation British tour, 1967; Monterey Pop Festival, 1967; Solo songwriter and vocalist, 1971–; Reunions with the MGs: Album, 1977; Tours of Europe, US, 1990; Backing band for Neil Young's US tour, 1993. *Compositions include:* Film score, Up Tight, 1969; Songwriter, musician with Sam and Dave; Wilson Pickett; Otis Redding; Rufus Thomas. *Recordings:* Albums: Up Tight, 1969; Booker T and Priscilla, 1972; The Runaway, 1972; Try and Love Again, 1978; with the MGs: Green Onions, 1964; Hip Hug-Her, 1967; Back To Back, 1967; Doin' Our Thing, 1968; Soul Limbo, 1968; Best Of..., 1968; The Booker T Set, 1969; McLemore Avenue, 1970; Greatest Hits, 1970; Melting Pot, 1971; Union Extended, 1976; Universal Language, 1977; As producer: Stardust, Willie Nelson, 1978; Singles include: Green Onions, 1962 (included in film soundtrack Quadrophenia); Boot-Leg, 1965; Hip Hug-

Her, 1967; Groovin', 1967; Soul Limbo, 1968; Hang 'Em High, used as film theme, 1969; Time Is Tight, from film Up Tight, 1969; Melting Pot, 1971. *Honour:* Rock and Roll Hall of Fame, Booker T and the MGs, 1992. *Address:* c/o Concerted Efforts, PO Box 99, Newtonville, MA 02169, USA.

JONES Chris; b. 10 Jan. 1963, Paris, France. Author; Composer; Writer; Prod. m. Anne Nbole, Salome Mga, Helene Betala, 4 d. *Education:* Composition; Musicology; Copyright Law Business. *Career:* Concentrated On Studio Work and Writing. *Compositions:* Include, Silent Over; Till The Middle of The Night; Call Me; Hold On Me; Boys Come and Go; Lovin' Livin' Givin'; Stay Around; Boogie Dancin' Shoes. *Recordings:* Silent Lover; Till The Middle Of The Night; Call Me; Lovin' Livin' Givin'. *Publication:* Surviving For Your Love. *Memberships:* SACEM; ASCAP. *Leisure interests:* Music; Reading; Cooking; Cinema. *Address:* PO Box 6101, Yaounde, Cameroon, Africa.

JONES Chris Alan; b. 18 Dec. 1966, Reading, England. Musician (drums, percussion). *Musical Education:* Drum lessons, 1993-. *Career:* Drummer, Mega City Four, 1987-; 6 albums; Major world tours with each release; Appeared on: Chart Show; The Word; MTV 120 Minutes; Recorded 2 sessions, John Peel Show. *Recordings:* with Mega City Four: Tranzophobia, 1989; Who Cares Wins, 1990; Terribly Sorry Bob, 1991; Sebastopol Road, 1992; Magic Bullets, 1993; 2 sessions, John Peel Show, album, 1994. *Publication:* Tall Stories and Creepy Crawlies, by Martin Roach. *Membership:* Musicians' Union. *Leisure interests:* Teaching drums; Martial arts. *Current Management:* Paul Bolton, ICM/Fair Warning. *Address:* 5 Rother Rd, Cove, Farnborough, Hampshire GU14 9LP, England.

JONES Daniel; b. 22 July 1973, Essex, England. Musician (multi-instrumentalist). *Education:* Shailer Park High, Logan City, Australia. *Career:* Relocated to Brisbane, Australia, as a child; Worked as a printer and in a supermarket; Played in Red Edge until breaking away with fellow group member Darren Hayes to form Savage Garden; Hugely successful world-wide; Live performances include closing ceremony of Olympic Games, Sydney, 2000; Band split, 2001; Move into production work, 2001-. *Recordings:* Albums: Savage Garden, 1997; Affirmation, 1999; Singles: I Want You, To The Moon and Back, 1996; Truly Madly Deeply, Break Me Shake Me, Universe, 1997; The Animal Song, I Knew I Loved You, 1999; Affirmation, Crash and Burn, Chained To You, 2000; Hold Me, 2001. *Honours:* First LP sales of over 11m.; ARIA Awards, won a record 10 awards, 1997; APRA Award, Songwriters of The Year, 2000; Truly Madly Deeply set new record for longest stay on Billboard Adult Contemporary Airplay Chart (106 weeks), 2000. *Address:* c/o Larry Tollin Entertainment, 9255 Sunset Blvd, Suite 411, Los Angeles, CA 90069, USA. *E-mail:* savage@village.com.au. *Internet:* www.savagegarden.com.

JONES Davy; b. 30 Dec. 1945, Manchester, Lancashire, England. Singer; Actor; Musician (guitar). *Career:* Member, The Monkees, 1966-70; 1986-89; Actor, The Monkees comedy television series, 1966-68; 33 1/3 Revolutions Per Monkee, TV Special, NBC; Television actor in: June Evening; Coronation Street; Z-Cars; Ben Casey; Farmers Daughter; Trainer; Stage performances include: Oliver; Pickwick; The Point; Founder, Davy Jones Presents record label, 1967; Owner, Zilch Boutique, 1967; Member, Dolenz, Jones, Boyce and Hart, 1975-76. *Recordings:* Albums: The Monkees (No. 1, USA and UK), 1966; More of The Monkees (No. 1, USA and UK), 1967; Headquarters, (No. 1, USA), 1967; Pisces, Aquarius, Capricorn and Jones Ltd, 1967; The Birds, The Bees and The Monkees, 1968; Head (soundtrack), 1969; The Monkees Greatest Hits, 1969; The Monkees Present, 1969; Instant Replay, 1969; Then and Now, 1986; Pool It, 1987; Monkees Greatest Hits, 1999; Music Box, 2001; The Definitive Monkees, 2001; with Big Foot Chester: Devil in Me, 1998; Tabernacalin', 1998; Singles: Last Train To Clarksville (No. 1, USA), 1966; I'm A Believer (No. 1, USA), 1966; (I'm Not Your) Steppin' Stone, 1967; A Little Bit Me, A Little Bit You, 1967; Alternate Title, 1967; Pleasant Valley Sunday, 1967; Daydream Believer (No. 1, USA), 1967; Valleri, 1968; Tear Drop City, 1969. *Honours:* NARM Awards, Best Selling Group, Best Album, 1967; Emmy Award, Outstanding Comedy Series, 1967; 3 BMI Awards, 1968; Monkees Day, Atlanta, 1986; Star on Hollywood Walk of Fame, 1989. *Leisure interest:* Horse-racing. *Address:* c/o Nationwide Entertainment Services, 2756 N Green Valley Parkway, Suite 449, Las Vegas, NV 89014-2100, USA.

JONES Donell; b. Chicago, Illinois, USA. Vocalist. *Career:* Influenced by gospel singer father; Noticed by Eddie F of Untouchables Entertainment at Black Radio Exclusive conference; Signed within a month to Untouchable/ LaFace Records; Debut album My Heart released, 1996; Written and produced tracks for Silk, Brownstone and Usher; Contributed vocal arrangements for Madonna's Bedtime Stories album; Collaborations: Guru; True Steppers; Lisa 'Left Eye' Lopes. *Recordings:* Albums: My Heart, 1996; Where You Wanna Be, 1999; Singles: Knocks Me Off My Feet, 1997; U Know What's Up, 1999; Shorty, 2000. *Honour:* Amercian Music Award, Favorite New Artist, 2001. *Address:* c/o LaFace Records, 3350 Peachtree Rd 1500, Atlanta, Georgia, USA.

JONES Ed (Edgar Francis); b. 8 July 1961, Amersham, Buckinghamshire, England. Musician (saxophone); Composer. *Musical Education:* BA Music, Middlesex University. *Career:* World-wide tours, television and radio with US3; Incognito; Ed Jones Quartet/Quintet; Teevision appearances include: MTV; CNN; Stations in USA; Europe; Japan; Far East. *Recordings:* Solo: The Home Coming, 1989; Pipers Tales, 1995; Featured on compilations: Mellow Mahem, 1988; Talkin' Land II, 1993; Bachology, 1995; Other recordings include: Hand On The Torch, US3, 1993; Where One Is, Dick Heckstall-Smith, 1989; New Cool, John Stevens, 1994; Sound Advice, Ron Wallen, 1993; Siren Song, Jessica Lauron, 1994; 100% and Rising, Incognito. *Memberships:* PRS; MCPS; Musicians' Union. *Leisure interests:* Cooking; The countryside; Literature. *Address:* Flat C, University House, 16 Victoria Park Sq., London E2 9PE, England.

JONES George Glenn; b. 12 Sept. 1931, Saratoga, Texas, USA. Country Singer; Musician (guitar). m. Tammy Wynette, 1969-75; Nancy Sepulveda, 1983. *Career:* Recording artist, 1953-; Worked under names of Johnny Williams, Hank Davis, Glen Patterson; Worked with The Big Bopper; Johnny Preston; Johnny Paycheck; Recorded duets with Gene Pitney; Melba Montgomery; Tammy Wynette; Elvis Costello; James Taylor; Willie Nelson. *Compositions include:* The Window Up Above, Mickey Gilley; Seasons of My Heart, Johnny Cash, Jerry Lee Lewis. *Recordings:* 150 Country hits include: Why Baby Why; White Lightning; Tender Years; She Still Thinks I Care; You Comb Her Hair; Who Shot Sam?; The Grand Tour; He Stopped Loving Her Today; Recorded over 450 albums; Recent albums include: First Time Live, 1985; Who's Gonna Fill Their Shoes, 1985; Wine Coloured Roses, 1986; Super Hits, 1987; Too Wild Too Long, 1987; One Woman Man, 1989; Hallelujah Weekend, 1990; You Oughta Be Here With Me, 1990; And Along Came Jones, 1991; Friends In High Places, 1991; Salutes Bob Wills and Hank Williams, 1992; Live At Dancetown USA, 1992; Walls Can Fall, 1992; One, 1995; I Lived to Tell It All, 1996; In a Gospel Way, 1997; It Don't Get Any Better Than This, 1998; The Cold Hard Truth, 1999; Live with the Possum, 1999; The Rock Stone Cold Country, 2001; with Tammy Wynette: We Can Go Together, 1971; Me and The First Lady, 1972; Golden Ring, 1976; Together Again, 1980. *Honours include:* Grammy Award, Male Country Vocal Performance, Choices, 2000. *Address:* c/o Nancy Jones, Jones Country, 48 Music Sq. E, Nashville, TN 37203, USA.

JONES Gordon Thomas; b. 21 Nov. 1947, Birkenhead, Merseyside, England. Musician (guitar); Record Co Exec. m. Jackie Jones, 26 May 1984, 1 s. *Education:* Art College, Edinburgh, Scotland. *Career:* Founder, Scottish folk band Silly Wizard, recording 9 albums; Founder, partner, Harbourtown Records, producing 36 albums to date including 2 MRA award winners; Toured Europe and USA over 17 years. *Recordings:* All Silly Wizard albums; Produced most Harbourtown Productions. *Honours:* 2 MRS Awards as producer; Naird Award as musician, 1986. *Memberships include:* MCPS; PRS; PPC. *Address:* PO Box 25, Ulverston, Cumbria LA12 7UN, England.

JONES Grace; b. 19 May 1952. Vocalist; Composer; Actor. *Career:* Film appearances include: Gordon's War; A View To Kill. *Recordings:* Albums: Portfolio, 1977; Fame, 1978; Muse, 1979; Warm Leatherette, 1980; Night Clubbing, 1981; Living My Life, 1982; Island Life, 1985; Slave To The Rhythm, 1985; Inside Story, 1986; Bulletproof Heart, 1990; Private Life: The Compass Point Sessions, 1998; The Dance Collection, 2000; Singles include: Private Life, 1980; Pull Up To The Bumper, 1981; The Apple Stretching/Nipple To The Bottle, 1982; My Jamaican Guy, 1983; Slave To The Rhythm, 1985; La Vie En Rose, 1986; Love Is The Drug, 1986; I'm Not Perfect, 1986; Pull Up To The Bumper, with Funkstar DeLuxe, 2000; Appearance on: The Notorious K.I.M., Lil' Kim, 2000. *Current Management:* Pyramid Entertainment Group (USA), 89 Fifth Ave, Seventh Floor, New York, NY 10003, USA.

JONES Jack (John Allen); b. 14 Jan. 1938, Los Angeles, California, USA. Singer; Actor. *Musical Education:* Studied singing at high school. *Career:* Club singer, 1957; Recording artiste, 1962-; Appearances with Jerry Lewis; Bob Hope; Actor, television: The Palace; Funny Face; Love Boat; Condominium; The Comeback; Film appearance: Juke Box Rhythm; Stage performance, Guys and Dolls, US, 1991; Regular concert tours, US and UK. *Recordings:* Albums include: Call Me Irresponsible, 1963; Wives and Lovers, 1963; Bewitched, 1964; Dear Heart, 1965; My Kind of Town, 1965; There's Love and There's Love and There's Love, 1965; For The In Crowd, 1966; The Impossible Dream, 1966; Jack Jones Sings, 1966; Lady, 1967; Our Song, 1967; Without Her, 1967; If You Ever Leave Me, 1968; Where Is Love, 1968; A Time For Us, 1969; A Song For You, 1972; Breadwinners, 1972; Together, 1973; Write Me A Love Song Charlie, 1974; Harbour, 1974; The Full Life, 1977; All To Yourself, 1977; I've Been Here All The Time, 1980; I Am a Singer, 1987; Sings Michel Legrand, 1993; Live at the Sands, 1993; New Jack Swing, 1997; Numerous compilations; Hit songs include: Lollipops and Roses, 1961; Wives and Lovers, 1963; Call Me Irresponsible, 1963; The Impossible Dream, 1966; Film music includes: A Ticklish Affair, 1963; Where Love

Has Gone, 1964; Love With A Proper Stranger, 1964; Kotch, 1967. *Honours:* Grammy Awards: Lollipops and Roses, 1962; Wives and Lovers, 1964; Cash Box Award, Most Promising Vocalist, 1962, 1963; Golden Globe Award, film theme for Kotch, 1967. *Current Management:* Roy Gerber and Associates, 515 N Rexford Dr., Beverly Hills, CA 90210, USA.

JONES John Paul (John Baldwin); b. 3 June 1946, Sidcup, Kent, England. Musician (bass); Prod.; Arranger; Composer. *Career:* Member, UK rock group Led Zeppelin, 1968–80; Also reunion concerts, Live Aid, Philadelphia, 1985; Atlantic's 40th Anniversary concert, Madison Square Gardens, 1988; Producer; Arranger; Session musician; Film score composer; Performances include: Bath Festival, 1969, 1970; Newport Jazz and Blues Festival, 1969; Montreux Jazz Festival, Switzerland, 1970; Madison Square Garden, 1970; Earls Court, 1975; Knebworth Fair, 1979; UNICEF Rock For Kampuchea, 1979; Film appearance, The Song Remains The Same, 1976; Producer for acts including: Butthole Surfers; Stefan Grossman; Ben E King; The Mission; John Renbourn; Arranger for artists including: REM; Raging Slab. *Recordings:* Albums: with Led Zeppelin: Led Zeppelin, 1969; Led Zeppelin II (No. 1, USA), 1969; Led Zeppelin III (No. 1, USA), 1970; Four Symbols (No. 1, UK), 1971; Houses of The Holy (No. 1, UK), 1973; Physical Graffiti (No. 1, USA), 1975; Presence (No. 1, USA), 1976; The Song Remains The Same (No. 1, UK), 1976; In Through The Out Door (No. 1, UK) 1979; Coda, 1982; Kingdom of Zep, 1991; Remasters, 1992; Complete Studio Recordings, 1993; Pleeease!, 1994; Solo albums: Zooma, 1999; Lovin' Up A Storm, 2000; The Thunderthief, 2001; Contributor to Comin' Atcha, Madeleine Bell, 1973; Also appears on recordings by: Jimmy Page; Paul McCartney; Brian Eno; Jeff Beck; Butthole Surfers; Singles include: Whole Lotta Love, 1970; Immigrant Song, 1971; Black Dog, 1972; Rock and Roll, 1972. *Honours include:* Ivor Novello, Outstanding Contribution To British Music, 1977. *Current Management:* c/o Hip Music Group, 326 N Western Ave, Suite 150, Los Angeles, CA 90004, USA.

JONES Kelly; b. 3 June 1974, Aberdare, Wales. Musician (guitar); Vocalist; Songwriter. *Career:* Ex-market trader and aspiring boxer; Founder member: Tragic Love Company, 1991; Name change to Stereophonics prior to joining Richard Branson's newly-formed V2 records, 1996; Toured UK, Europe and USA supporting acts include: Manic Street Preachers; Ocean Colour Scene; The Who; Aerosmith; Headlined various UK gigs and festivals including: Hillsborough Benefit Concert, 1997; Cardiff Castle, 1998; Reading Leeds and Glasgow Festivals, 2000; Donington, Chepstow, T In The Park, 2001; Undertook solo tour to promote group album release, 2001. *Recordings:* Singles: Looks Like Chaplin, 1996; Local Boy In The Photograph, More Life In A Tramp's Vest, A Thousand Trees, Traffic, 1997; The Bartender and The Thief, 1998; Just Looking, Pick A Part That's New, I Wouldn't Believe Your Radio, Hurry Up and Wait, 1999; Mama Told Me Not To Come (with Tom Jones), 2000; Mr Writer, Have A Nice Day, Step On My Old Size Nines, Handbags and Gladrags, 2001; Albums: Word Gets Around, 1997; Performance and Cocktails, 1999; Just Enough Education To Perform, 2001. *Honours:* Brit Award, Best Newcomer, 1998; Kerrang: Best New Band, 1998; Best Band, Best Album, 1999; Q Awards, Best Live Act, 1999; BAFTA Cymru, Best Music Programme, Stereophonics – Live At Morfa, 1999. *Current Management:* Marsupial Management Ltd, Unit 3, Home Farm, Welford, nr Newbury, Berkshire, RG20 8HR. *E-mail:* marsupial@btinternet.com. *Internet:* www.stereophonics.com.

JONES Mick; b. 27 Dec. 1944, London, England. Musician (guitar); Songwriter; Record Prod. m. Ann. *Career:* Musician with: Nero and The Gladiators; Johnny Hallyday; Spooky Tooth; Leslie West; Also worked with Otis Redding; Jimi Hendrix; Jimmy Page; Founder member, rock group Foreigner, 1976–; World-wide appearances include: California Jam II, 1978; Headliners, Reading Festival, 1979; North American tour, 1982; American tour, 1991; New York State Fair, 1994; World Tour, 1994–95; American tour, 1996. *Compositions:* Bad Love, recorded by Eric Clapton; Street Thunder, 1984 Olympic Marathon Theme; Numerous tracks for Foreigner, including: Feels Like The First Time; I Want to Know What Love Is; I Don't Want to Live Without You; As co-writer (with Lou Gramm): Dirty White Boy; Waiting For A Girl Like You; That Was Yesterday. *Recordings:* Albums: with Foreigner: Foreigner, 1977; Head Games, 1979; 4 (No. 1, USA), 1981; Records, 1982; Agent Provocateur (No. 1, UK), 1985; Inside Information, 1988; Unusual Heat, 1991; The Very Best Of, 1992; The Very Best... and Beyond, 1992; Mr Moonlight, 1994; Solo album: Mick Jones, 1989; As producer: 5150, Van Halen, 1986; Fame and Fortune, Bad Company, 1986; Stormfront, Billy Joel, 1989; In Deep, Tina Arena, 1997; Singles with Foreigner include: Feels Like The First Time, 1977; Cold As Ice, 1977; Long Long Way From Home, 1978; Hot Blooded, 1978; Double Vision, 1978; Blue Morning Blue Day, 1979; Dirty White Boy, 1979; Head Games, 1979; Urgent, 1981; Juke Box Hero, 1981; Waiting For A Girl Like You, 1982; I Want To Know What Love Is (No. 1, UK), 1985; That Was Yesterday, 1985; I Don't Want To Live Without You, 1988. *Honour:* Grammy Award, Bad Love, 1989. *Current Management:* Somerset Songs Publishing Inc, 214 E 70th St, New York, NY 10021, USA.

JONES Mickey Wayne; b. 10 June 1941, Houston, Texas, USA. Actor; Musician (drums). m. (1) Sandra Davis, 1976; (2) Phyllis Star, 7 June 1980, 1 s., 1 d. *Education:* North Texas State College, 1959–62. *Career:* Drummer for Trini Lopez, 1957–64; Johnny Rivers, 1964–66; Bob Dylan, 1966–67; Kenny Rogers, 1967–76; Actor, 1976–; Film appearances include: Starman; National Lampoon's Vacation; Stir Crazy; Nadine; The Couch Trip; Television appearances include: V; Mash; The Incredible Hulk; The Colbys; T J Hooker; Numerous other guest roles, commercials, theatre. *Recordings:* Albums include: with Trini Lopez: Live At P J's; with Bob Dylan: Blonde On Blonde; with Johnny Rivers: Last Boogie In Paris; Also for Jan and Dean, Kenny Rogers; Singles include: with Johnny Rivers: Maybelline; Mountain of Love; Secret Agent Man; with Kenny Rogers and The First Edition: Just Dropped In To See What Condition My Condition Was In; Ruby, Don't Take Your Love To Town. *Memberships:* AFTRA; Screen Actors Guild; AFofM; AGVA; Screen Extras Guild. *Leisure interest:* Golf.

JONES Nigel Mazlyn; b. 26 June 1950, Dudley, West Midlands, England. Performer; Songwriter; Musician (acoustic guitar, santoor). Divorced, 1 s., 1 d. *Career:* Professional performer, 1975–; Toured folk clubs, colleges; Special guest to Judy Tzuke, Renaissance, national tours; Special guest, Euro Major venue circuit with Barclay James Harvest, 1980; Also, Eurorock circuit, 1984; Glastonbury Festival, 1990; Featured solo on BBC documentary, Festival; Bob Geldof British tour, 1990; Music used on TV landscape films; Two BBC TV commissions. *Recordings:* Albums: Ship To Shore, 1976; Sentinel, 1979; Breaking Cover, 1981; Water From The Well, 1987; Video album: Beyond This Point, 1988; Mazlyn Jones, 1991; Angels Over Water, 1993; CD Album, Mazlyn Jones Live with Guy Evans and Nik Turner, 1997; BBC2 TV feature programme, Planet For Sale, 1998; CD Album, Behind The Stone, 1999. *Memberships:* Musicians' Union; PRS; MCPS. *Leisure interests:* Cliff walking; Sky gazing; Water renovation (wells/springs). *Current Management:* Isle of Light. *Address:* PO Box 1, Polzeath, Cornwall PL27 6YZ, England.

JONES Paul; b. 24 Feb. 1942, Portsmouth, Hampshire, England. Singer; Musician (harmonica); Composer; Actor; Broadcaster. m. Fiona Hendley, 16 Dec. 1984, 2 s. (previous marriage). *Education:* Edinburgh Academy; Jesus College, Oxford. *Musical Education:* Cathedral Choir; Self-taught. *Career:* Lead singer, harmonica player with Manfred Mann; Television includes: Thank Your Lucky Stars; Top of The Pops; Ready Steady Go; Solo tours of UK, Australia, New Zealand and Europe, 1966–; Theatre: Conduct Unbecoming, London and New York; The Beggar's Opera; Guys and Dolls, National Theatre; Kiss Me Kate, Royal Shakespeare Company; Vocalist, harmonica player with Blues Band, 1979–; Actor, films and television; TV presenter; Radio: Radio 2 Rhythm and Blues, 1985–; JFM radio, 1990-. *Compositions include:* 54321 (Theme for Ready Steady Go); Songs recorded by: Brian Poole and The Tremeloes; Helen Shapiro; Eric Clapton; Ten Years After; TV and film scores: Intimate Reflections; Fighting Back; The Wednesday Play. *Recordings:* All Manfred Mann albums to 1966; Blues Band albums include: Bootleg; Ready; Itchy Feet; Paul Jones Collection Vol. 1–3, 1996–98. *Contributions to:* The Independent on Sunday; Sight and Sound; Tribune. *Honours:* British Blues Connection, Male Singer, 1990, 1991; Scroll of Honour, 1993. *Memberships:* Musicians' Union; BACSA; Equity. *Leisure interests:* Reading; Walking; Theatre. *Current Management:* Chatto and Linnit.

JONES Quincy; b. 14 March 1933, Chicago, Illinois, USA. Record Prod.; Composer; Arranger; Musician (trumpet); Conductor. 5 c. *Education:* Seattle University. *Musical Education:* Berklee College of Music; Boston Conservatory. *Career:* Trumpeter, arranger, Lionel Hampton Orchestra, 1950–53; Arranger for various singers, orchestra leaders include: Count Basie; Frank Sinatra; Peggy Lee; Dinah Washington; Sarah Vaughn; Trumpeter, Dizzy Gillespie, 1956; Leader, own orchestra, concerts, television appearances, 1960–; Music Director, Mercury Records, 1961; Vice President, 1964. *Recordings:* Hit singles include: Soul Bossa Nova, 1962; Stuff Like That, 1978; Ai No Corrida, 1981; Razzmatazz, 1981; I'll Be Good To You, with Ray Charles and Chaka Khan; Solo albums include: You've Got It Bad Girl, 1973; Walking In Space, 1974; Body Heat, 1974; Mellow Madness, 1975; I Heard That!, 1976; Quintessence, 1977; Sounds and Stuff Like That, 1978; The Dude, 1981; Bossa Nova, 1983; The Q, 1984; Back On The Block, 1989; QD III Soundlab, 1991; Q – The Musical Biography of Quincy Jones, 2001; Producer, video Portrait of An Album, 1986; Q's Jook Joint, 1995; Music, television series Fresh Prince of Bel Air, 1990–; Guest musician, albums: with George Benson: Shape of Things To Come, 1976; Give Me The Night, 1980; with James Ingram: It's Your Night, 1983; Never Felt So Good, 1986; with Michael Jackson: Thriller, 1982; Bad, 1987; Singles include: Blues in the Night, 1989; Listen Up, 1991; I'm Yours, 1999; Conductor, film music includes: In The Heat of The Night, 1967; The Slender Thread, 1968; McKenna's Gold, 1968; For The Love of Ivy, 1968; Banning, 1967; The Split, 1968; Bob and Carol and Ted and Alice, 1969; The Out-Of-Towners, 1970; The Anderson Tapes, 1971; The Hot Rock, 1972; The New Centurions, 1972; The Getaway, 1972; The Wiz, 1978; The Color Purple, 1985. *Honours include:* Golden Note, ASCAP, 1982; Hon degree, Berklee College, 1983; Over 20 Grammy Awards; Lifetime

Achievement, National Academy of Songwriters, 1989; ASMAC Golden Score Award. *Address:* c/o Quincy Jones Productions, 3800 Barham Blvd #503, Los Angeles, CA 90067, USA.

JONES Richard; b. 23 May 1974, Aberdare, Wales. Musician (bass). *Career:* Ex-electrician, scaffolder and coalman; Founder member: Tragic Love Company, 1991; Name change to Stereophonics prior to joining Richard Branson's newly-formed V2 records, 1996; Toured UK, Europe and USA supporting acts including: Manic Street Preachers; Ocean Colour Scene; The Who; Aerosmith; Headlined various UK gigs and festivals including: Hillsborough Benefit Concert, 1997; Cardiff Castle, 1998; Reading Leeds and Glasgow Festivals, 2000; Donington, Chepstow, T In The Park, 2001. *Recordings:* Singles: Looks Like Chaplin, 1996; Local Boy In The Photograph, More Life In A Tramp's Vest, A Thousand Trees, Traffic, 1997; The Bartender and The Thief, 1998; Just Looking, Pick A Part That's New, I Wouldn't Believe Your Radio, Hurry Up and Wait, 1999; Mama Told Me Not To Come (with Tom Jones), 2000; Mr Writer, Have A Nice Day, Step On My Old Size Nines, Handbags and Gladrags, 2001; Albums: Word Gets Around, 1997; Performance and Cocktails, 1999; Just Enough Education To Perform, 2001. *Honours:* Brit Award, Best Newcomer, 1998; Kerrang: Best New Band, 1998; Best Band, Best Album, 1999; Q Awards, Best Live Act, 1999; BAFTA Cymru, Best Music Programme, Stereophonics – Live At Morfa, 1999. *Current Management:* Marsupial Management Ltd, Unit 3, Home Farm, Welford, nr Newbury, Berkshire, RG20 8HR. *E-mail:* marsupial@btinternet.com. *Internet:* www.stereophonics.com.

JONES Rickie Lee; b. 8 Nov. 1954, Chicago, Illinois, USA. Singer; Songwriter. *Career:* Signed to Warner Brothers (after own composition recorded by Lowell George on his album, Thanks I'll Eat Here), 1977; US tour, 1979; Appearance, Saturday Night Live, 1979; Jam session with Bruce Springsteen and Boz Scaggs at Whiskey A Go-Go club, Los Angeles, 1979; Major tour, includes Carnegie Hall, 1979; Singer of ballad for film: King of Comedy, 1983; The Magazine tour, 1984; Tours, Australia, Europe, UK, Eastern bloc concerts, 1985; Saturday Night Live, NBC TV, 1989; 2 US tours, 1990; Bread and Roses benefit, San Francisco, 1991; US tour, 1991; Appearances at Wiltern Theatre, Los Angeles, 1992; Dominion Theatre, Royal Festival Hall, London, 1992; The Tonight Show, 1993. *Compositions include:* Easy Money; The Last Chance; Texaco; Chuck E's In Love (platinum hit record, 1979). *Recordings:* Albums: Rickie Lee Jones, 1979; Pirates, 1981; Girl At Her Volcano, 1983; The Magazine, 1984; Flying Cowboys, 1989; Pop Pop, 1991; Traffic From Paradise, 1993; Naked Song, 1995; Ghostyhead, 1997; It's Like This, 2000; Features on: Duets, Rob Wasserman, 1989; The Bells of Dublin, The Chieftains, 1991; Joshua Judges Ruth, Lyle Lovett, 1992. *Honours:* Grammy: Best New Artist, 1979; Rolling Stone Awards, 1979, 1981; Grammy: Best Jazz Vocal Performance, Duo or Group, 1990. *Current Management:* Gold Mountain Entertainment, Suite 450, 3575 Cahuenga Blvd W, Los Angeles, CA 90068, USA.

JONES Simeon; b. 10 March 1964, London, England. Musician (saxophone, flute, harmonica). 2 s. *Education:* BSc English. *Career:* Tours, television with various name acts including: Gary Glitter; Take That; Bad Manners; Geno Washington; Otis Grand. *Recordings:* With acts including: Gary Glitter; Take That; Tom Jones; Edwyn Collins; Black; Sam Brown; Shampoo; Blessing. *Membership:* MU. *Address:* 105 Taybridge Rd, London SW11 5PX, England.

JONES Simon; Musician (Bass). *Career:* Founder Member, The Verve, 1990; Obtained record deal, 1991; Support slots with The Black Crowes, and live dates on Lollapalooza tour, 1994; Numerous live shows and festival dates; Band split, 1995, reforms, 1997; Headline appearance at Reading festival, 1997; Band splits again, 1999. *Recordings:* Singles: She's A Superstar, 1992; Gravity Grave, 1992; All in the Mind, 1993; Slide Away, 1993; Blue, 1993; This Is Music, 1995; On Your Own, 1995; History, 1995; Bittersweet Symphony (No. 2, UK), 1997; Lucky Man, 1997; Drugs Don't Work (No. 1, UK), 1997; Albums: A Storm in Heaven, 1993; No Come Down, 1994; A Northern Soul, 1995; Urban Hymns (No. 1, UK), 1997. *Honours:* BRIT Awards, Best British Group, Best British Album, 1998.

JONES Steve; b. 3 May 1955, London, England. Musician (guitar). *Career:* Guitarist, UK punk group, The Sex Pistols, 1975–78; Performances include: First gig, St Martins School of Art, London, 1975; Screen On The Green Midnight Special, London, 1976; 100 Club punk rock festival, 1976; Anarchy In The UK Tour, 1976; Tours: Europe, 1977; US, 1978; Winterland Ballroom, San Francisco, 1978; Films: The Great Rock 'n' Roll Swindle, 1979; The Filth and The Fury, 2000; Reunion concert, 1996. *Recordings:* Albums: Never Mind The Bollocks – Here's The Sex Pistols (No. 1, UK), 1977; The Great Rock 'n' Roll Swindle, 1979; Some Product – Carri On Sex Pistols, 1979; Flogging A Dead Horse, 1980; Kiss This, 1992; Singles: Anarchy In The UK, 1976; God Save The Queen (No. 2, UK), 1977; Pretty Vacant, 1977; Holidays In The Sun, 1977; No One Is Innocent (A Punk Prayer By Ronnie Biggs), 1978; Something Else, 1979; Silly Thing, 1978; C'mon Everybody, 1979; The Great Rock 'n' Roll Swindle,

1979; Solo Albums: Mercy, 1987; Fire and Gasoline, 1989; with Siouxsie and the Banshees: Kaleidoscope, 1980; with Generation X: Perfect Hits 1975–81, 1986; with Si Kahn: I Have Seen Freedom, 1991; with Buckcherry: Buckcherry, 1999. *Address:* c/o Eclipse Entertainment, 100 Wilshire Blvd, Suite 1830, Santa Monica, CA 90028, USA.

JONES Steven; Singer; Songwriter. *Career:* Founder/Main Member, Baby Bird; Member, theatre troupe, Dogs in Honey; Began making recordings at home; Wrote hundreds of pop songs; Obtained music publishing deal; Progressed to record deal; Formed band, numerous television appearances and live dates. *Recordings:* Singles: Goodnight, 1996; You're Gorgeous, 1996; Candy Girl, 1997; Cornershop, 1997; Bad Old Man, 1998; If You'll Be Mine, 1998; Back Together, 1999; The Word, 2000; Out of Sight, 2001; Albums: I Was Born A Man, 1995; Bad Shave, 1995; Fatherhood, 1996; The Happiest Man Alive, 1996; Ugly Beautiful, 1996; Dying Happy, 1997; Something's Going On, 1998; Bugged, 2000; Compilation: 1985–2000, 2001. *Internet:* www.babybird.co.uk.

JONES Tom, (Thomas Jones Woodward); b. 7 June 1940, Pontypridd, Wales. Entertainer. m. Melinda Trenchard, 1956, 1 s. *Career:* Former bricklayer, factory worker, construction worker; Singing debut, aged 3, later sang in clubs, dance halls, with self-formed group The Playboys; Became Tom Jones, 1963; First hit record It's Not Unusual, 1964; Appeared on radio, television; Toured US, 1965; Television show, This Is Tom Jones, 1969–71; Many international hits, albums in Top 10 charts, Europe, USA; Over 30m. discs sold by 1970; Toured continuously, television appearances, 1970s-; Score, musical play Matador; Hit single: A Boy From Nowhere, 1987; Frequent Amnesty International; Simple Truth, 1991; Rainforest Foundation, 1993; Shelter, 1993; Television series: The Right Time, 1992; Glastonbury Festival of Contemporary Performing Arts, 1992; Live stage appearance, Under Milk Wood, Prince's Trust, 1992. *Recordings:* Hits include: It's Not Unusual (No. 1, UK), 1965; What's New Pussycat, 1965; Thunderball, 1966; Green Green Grass of Home (No. 1, UK), 1966; Detroit City, 1967; Funny Familiar Forgotten Feelings, 1967; I'll Never Fall In Love Again, 1967; I'm Coming Home, 1967; Delilah, 1968; Help Yourself, 1968; Love Me Tonight, 1969; Without Love, 1969; Daughter of Darkness, 1970; I Who Have Nothing, 1970; She's A Lady, 1971; Till, 1971; The Young New Mexican Puppeteer, 1972; Can't Stop Loving You; Letter To Lucille, 1973; Something Bout You Baby I Like, 1974; Say You Stay Until Tomorrow, 1976; A Boy From Nowhere, 1987; It's Not Unusual (reissue), 1987; Kiss, with Art of Noise, 1988; All You Need Is Love, 1993; If I Only Knew, 1994; Burning Down The House, with The Cardigans, 1999; Baby It's Cold Outside, with Cerys Matthews, 1999; Mama Told Me Not To Come, with Stereophonics, 2000; Sex Bomb, with Mousse T, 2000; You Need Love Like I Do, with Heather Small, 2000; Albums include: Green Green Grass of Home, 1967; Delilah, 1968; This Is Tom Jones, 1969; Tom, 1970; I Who Have Nothing, 1970; Close Up, 1972; The Body and Soul of TJ, 1973; I'm Coming Home, 1978; At This Moment, 1989; After Dark, 1989; The Lead and How To Swing It, 1994; Reload (No. 1, UK), 1999. *Honours include:* BRIT Award, Best British Male Solo Artist, 2000. *Memberships:* SAG; AFTRA; AGVA. *Leisure interests:* Music; History. *Current Management:* Mark Woodward, Manager, William Morris Agency. *Address:* Tom Jones Enterprises, 10100 Santa Monica Blvd, Suite 205, Los Angeles, CA 90067, USA.

JONES Tommy; b. 5 Oct. 1926, Liverpool, England. Musician (drums); Bandleader; Musical Dir. m. Kathy Knight (vocalist), 26 April 1954, 3 s., 1 d. *Education:* College of North East London; Ceddo Film and Television School. *Musical Education:* Max Abrams (noted drum tutor); Trinity College of Music; London College of Music. *Career:* Played, concerts, clubs, broadcasts with bands including: Pete Pitterson Quintet; Cab Quaye Trio; Dill Jones Trio; Jack Butler (US) Band; Leslie 'Jiver' Hutchinson Band; Bertie King Band; Dave (Jazz FM) Lee Trio; Tubby Hayes Band; Jimmy Deucher All-Stars; Acker Bilk Band; Major Holly and Rose Murphy (US); Bruce Turner Band; Hutchinson/Henderson Band; Humphrey Lyttleton Band; Mike McKenzie Trio; Joe Harriot Quintet; Shake Keane Quintet; Sliderulers; Tommy Jones Trio; Tommy Eytle Trio; Just Jazz, 1950–; Venues include: Royal Festival Hall, 1953, 1954, 1956; Edinburgh Festival of Jazz, 1958; Les Ambassadeurs Club, 1960; Residency, Lunchtime Jazz, Bishopsgate, 1961; Bix's Club, San Francisco, 1989; Hollywood Savoy Restaurant, Paris, 1990; Films: Blood Orange, 1951; Rough and The Smooth, 1958; Phoelix, 1979; Television includes: TV Series, Crane, 1956; 6.5 Special, BBC TV, 1958; Episode, Danger Man, 1958; Producer, director, Cable Jazz, Cable London TV, 1992; House of Elliott, 1991; Radio includes: Carribean Carnival series, 1955; BBC Jazz Club, 1956, 1958, 1960; Commercial, Smiths Crisps, 1993; Musical Director, Clark Brothers' (US) Dancers, 1966–68. *Recordings:* Jazz At Club Basie, 1956; In My Condition, Shake Keane Quintet, 1960; With Shake Keane Quintet, 1961. *Membership:* Musicians' Union. *Leisure interests:* Film and TV Production. *Current Management:* Sue and Michael Jones. *Address:* 11 Albany Rd, London N4 4RR, England.

JONES Wizz; b. 25 April 1939, Croydon, Surrey, England. Musician (acoustic guitar); Singer. m. Sandy, 14 Sept. 1963, 3 s., 1 d. *Career:*

Began as itinerant busking skiffle/folk singer, late 1950s; Formed bluegrass duo with banjo-picker Pete Stanley, recorded single, album, played Folk Club and College circuit, 1960s; Solo artiste, 1967–; Collaborated with songwriter Alan Tunbridge, guitarist Peter Berryman; Played in group Lazy Farmer with wife Sandy; Appears festivals, tours of acoustic folk and blues circuit, 1990s. *Recordings:* 11 albums include: The Grapes of Life, 1988; The Village Thing Tapes, 1993; Late Nights and Long Days (with saxophonist son Simeon); Dazzling Stranger, (first US release), 1995; 2 tracks on Acoustic routes, from BBC TV documentary on Bert Jansch. *Memberships:* Musicians' Union; PRS. *Leisure interests:* Music and film appreciation; Maintaining old vehicles. *Current Management:* Guitar Classics. *Address:* 38 Webbs Rd, London SW11 6SF, England.

JOOLZ; b. 16 April 1966, London, England. Vocalist; Actress; Dancer; Presenter. *Musical Education:* O Level Music. *Career:* Session work with artists including: Neneh Cherry; Neil Diamond; Danny Red; Soul II Soul; Tours, world-wide with Soul II Soul, including appearances on children's shows; Member, R & B group Just Good Friends; Supported Glen Jones; H. Town; Silk; Brandy; Keith Sweat; Appeared on Count Prince Miller's Jamaican Independence television special; Cable TV special supporting Don Campbell. *Recordings:* Looking For An Answer, 1993; The More I Try, Just Good Friends. *Membership:* Musicians' Union. *Leisure interests:* Reading; Keep fit/dance; Cooking; Going to the theatre; Live shows. *Current Management:* Phat Management. *Address:* 35 Tubbs Rd, Harlesden, London NW10 4RA, England.

JORDAN Cathy; b. 1 April 1969, Roscommon, Ireland. Vocalist; Musician (bodhran). *Career:* Solo singer for 5 years, mainly based in Ireland; Joined Dervish, 1990; Tours internationally. *Recordings:* Harmony Hill, 1993; Playing With Fire, 1995; At The End of The Day, 1996; Live In Palma, 1997; Midsummer's Night, 1999; Decade, 2001. *Honours:* Hot Press magazine, Traditional Folk Album of the Year, At The End of The Day, 1996; Irish Music magazine Readers' Poll, Best Overall Traditional Folk Band of the Year, 1997; Irish Times, Best Traditional Album, Midsummer's Night, 1999; Irish Music magazine, Best Compilation Album, Decade, 2001. *Address:* c/o Dervish/Whirling Discs Ltd, Business Innovation Centre, Unit G-2001, Institute of Technology Campus, Ballinode, Sligo, Ireland. *E-mail:* whirling@oceanfree.net. *Internet:* www.dervish.ie.

JORDAN Lorraine; b. 22 Nov. 1965, Wales. Singer; Songwriter; Musician (guitar, bouzouki). *Musical Education:* Family influences in Irish music. *Career:* Singer, guitarist and bouzouki player, bands Mooncoin and Malin Head; Solo artiste, 1991–; Toured Europe and Scandinavia extensively, performing in numerous major folk festivals; Appearances on television and radio; Leader, own band or solo performer. *Recordings:* Inspiration, 1991, 1993; Crazy Guessing Games, 1994; features on: Sophistry and Illusion, Dalriada, 2001. *Membership:* Musicians' Union. *Address:* c/o Katherine Alexander, Saltire Promotions, Broadwood, Gilkerscleugh, Abington, Lanarkshire ML12 6SQ, Scotland.

JORDAN Marc Wallace; b. 6 March 1948, New York, USA. Musician (guitar, keyboards); Songwriter; Recording Artist. m. Amy Sky, 31 Jan. 1989, 1 s., 1 d. *Education:* University. *Musical Education:* private guitar and piano lessons. *Compositions include:* Songs recorded by: Diana Ross (2); Manhattan Transfer (6); Rod Stewart (2); Bette Midler (2); Joe Cocker; Chicago; Kansas; Natalie Cole; Fall From Grace, Amanda Marshal; 9 platinum in Canada. *Recordings:* 7 albums include: Blue Desert, 1979; A Hole In The Wall, 1983; Talking Through Pictures, 1987; Reckless Valentine, 1992; Taxi-taxi, Cher, 1998–9; features on: Soul and Inspiration, Barry Mann, 2000. *Honours:* Juno Award, Producer of The Year, 1993; 1 Genie Nomination; 2 Juno Nominations. *Memberships:* AFTRA; ACTRA; AFofM. *Leisure interests:* Riding; Tennis. *Current Management:* Kathleen Shea, Revolution Man, 343 Danforth Ave #2, Toronto, Canada. *Address:* 9744 Wilshire Blvd, Suite #305, Beverly Hills, CA 90212, USA.

JORDAN Montell; b. 1968, Los Angeles, California, USA. Recording Artist; Prod.; Songwriter; Musician (piano, saxophone). *Education:* BA in Organizational Communication, Pepperdine University, Malibu. *Musical Education:* Self-taught; Church/gospel background. *Career:* Budweiser Superfest tour, with Boyz II Men, TLC, Mary J Blige; Television includes: Ricki Lake Show; Rolanda Show; The Beat Winter Cooldowns; Host, MTV Jams; Film appearance, The Nutty Professor. *Recordings:* Albums: This Is How We Do It, 1995; I Am LV; More to Tell, 1996; Let's Ride, 1998; Singles include: This Is How We Do It (No. 1, USA), 1995; Daddy's Home, 1995; I Like, 1996; What's on Tonight, 1997; I Can Do That, 1998; Get It On... Tonite, 1999; Jungle Groove (used in film soundtrack Pet Detective); Nutty Professor (film soundtrack); Smooth/Ghetto Life; Other recordings include collaborations with: Kelly Price; Gina Thompson; Lil Mo; Peter Andre; Deborah Cox. *Honours:* Grammy Nomination; 3 MTV Video Award Nominations. *Membership:* ASCAP. *Leisure interests:* Snowboarding; Wave running; Gym. *Current Management:* Mad Money Management. *Address:* 8726 S Sepulveda Blvd, Suite C-161, Los Angeles, CA 90018, USA.

JORDAN Stanley; b. 31 July 1959, Chicago, Illinois, USA. Jazz Musician (guitar, piano). *Musical Education:* Self-taught guitar; Theory, electronic music and composition, Princetown University. *Career:* Member, various Chicago groups, 1970s; Regular international jazz festivals, 1976; Musician with Dizzy Gillespie; Benny Carter; Dionne Warwick; Booker T and the MG's; Mark Knopfler; Solo recording artist, 1982–; Leading exponent of hammering-on technique. *Recordings:* Albums: Touch Sensitive, 1982; Magic Touch, 1985; Standards, 1986; Cornucopia, 1990; Street Talk, 1990; Stolen Moments, 1990, Bolero, 1994; Live in New York, 1998. *Current Management:* c/o Mario Tirado, Agency for the Performing Arts, 888 Seventh Ave, Suite 200, New York, NY 10106, USA. *Internet:* www.stanleyjordan.com.

JORGENS Peter Ole; b. 20 April 1958, Sorgenfri, Denmark. Multi Instrumentalist, mostly percussion including Marimba and Vibe. m. Reneé Paaschburg, 30 May 1992. *Education:* Classical Percussion with Suzanne Ibstrup, 1970–76, Improvisation with John Tchicai, 1975–77, Percussion with Paul Motian, 1978. *Career:* John Tchikai Festival Band, 1975–78; Tchikai/Dorge Quartet, 1976–77; Cockpit Music, 1978–; Gronvirke, 1982–83; Global Guaranty Orchestra, 1983–; Clinch, 1987–89; The Wild Mans Band, 1990–; Dog God, 1992–; Sweethearts in a Drugstore, 1996; David Moss/PO Jorgens Duo, 1989–96; Ghost in the Machine, 1989–; Played solo concerts, 1995; Knitting Factory, New York and 1997 at LEM Festival Barcelona; Gefion Calls, 1996, with David Thomas (Pere Ubu), Jorgen Teler and Per Bull Acs, Two Midnight concerts in The Fountain, Gefion, Copenhagen. *Compositions include:* Soil, 1990; Metal 1–10, 1992; Digital Metal, 1994; Cambodia, 1995; Black Box, 1995; Springtime 1–15, 1996; Somfoni, 1996; The War Kitchen, 1996; The Joy of Feeding Birds, 1997; The Adventure of Hale Bob, 1997. *Recordings include:* Dog God: Dog God, 1993; Global Guaranty Orchestra, Musical Hair-Splitting in a Remote World, 1993; Wiuf/Jorgens/DeRegt: Catchuptime, 1994; Evan Parker/Ghost in the Machine, 1995; Cockpit Music, The Great Dividing Range, 1996; Dog God: God is Love, 1997; PO Jorgens: The Technology of Touch, 1997; Sweethearts in a Drugstore:, 1997. *Honours:* 3 Year Grant for Composing From, The Danish Arts Foundation, 1984; One Year Grants, nearly every year, 1982-. *Memberships:* SKREP (Danish Experimental Composers); DJBFA. *Leisure interests:* Gardening; Literature. *Current Management:* Ninth World Music. *Address:* PO Jorgens, Frydenlund, Humlebaekvej 56, 3480 Fredensborg, Denmark.

JORGENSEN Carsten Valentin; b. 9 May 1950, Lyngby, Denmark. Singer; Musician (guitar); Composer; Poet. m. Anne Marie Albrectsen, 27 Jan. 1979. *Education:* Graduate, Art School, 1975. *Career:* Founder, own band, C V Jorgensen, 1974–; Tours: Denmark, Sweden, Norway, Germany, 1976–; Roskilde Festival, 6 appearances; Television appearances: Numerous C V Jorgensen specials, 1980–94; Danish Live Aid, 1985; Dylan and The Danes, 1991; Leonard Cohen Talkshow, 1992; Performed on films: Kloden Rocker, 1978; Som Et Strejf, 1992; Lyricist/vocalist, film soundtracks: Mig and Charly, 1978; Johnny Larsen, 1979. *Recordings:* Storbyens Små Oaser, 1977; Tidens Tern, 1980; Lediggang Agogo, 1982; Vennerne and Vejen, 1985; Indian Summer, 1988; Sjaelland, 1994. *Honours:* Poetens Pris (Poets Award), 1989; 2 Grammy Awards, Songwriter of Year, Rock Album of Year, 1991; Prize of Honour, DJBFA; 2 Danish State Art Foundation Awards, 1993, 1994; 4 Grammy Nominations, 1995. *Memberships:* Nordic Copyright Bureau; KODA; Gramex; DJBFA. *Leisure interests:* Collecting Jazz and Rock Records; Reading Biographies; Wine. *Current Management:* Rock On.

JORGENSEN Per; b. 9 Sept. 1952, Bergen, Norway. Musician (trumpet, guitar, percussion); Vocalist). m. Else Vågen, 8 May 1987, 1 d. *Education:* Pre-school teacher. *Musical Education:* Self-taught. *Career:* Freelance musician, 20 years; All major Scandinavian Jazz Festivals with different groups; Tours, concerts in: India; Japan; USA; Germany; Spain; France; Austria; Numerous concerts recorded for television and radio; Jazz visit, teaching and working with Danish musicians, Copenhagen, 1997. *Recordings:* with Jokleba (trio): On and On; with Jokleba and the Magnetic North Orchestra: Further; with Anders Jormin: Jord; with Marilyn Mazur: Circular Chant; with Tamma (including Don Cherry and Ed Blackwell): Tamma; with David Murray: Jazzpar Prize, 1991; with Jon Balke: Nonsenstration, 1992; with Michael Mantler: School of Understanding, 1997; with Sjogren/Voust: The Thule Spirit, 1997. *Honours:* Vossajazz Prize, 1990; Jazz Musician of The Year in Norway, 1991. *Leisure interests:* Children; Nature; Drawing. *Address:* Lia 17, 5280 Dalekvam, Norway.

JORY Sarah Elizabeth; b. 20 Nov. 1969, Reading, Berkshire, England. Professional Entertainer; Country Singer; Songwriter. *Career:* Television appearances include: Opportunity Knocks; Pebble Mill; The South Bank Show; RTE TV Ireland; Ulster TV; Dutch and Belgian TV; Satellite TV world-wide; CBS News America; Anglia TV; East Midlands TV; Concerts: London Palladium; Toured with: Eric Clapton, Glen Campbell and Charley Pride; Broadcasts on BBC Radio 1, 2, 4 and all local radio. *Compositions:* 4 instrumentals. *Recordings:* 12 solo recordings; Two for record company: Sarah On Steel, 1984; Cross Country, 1985; The Way To Survive, 1987; No

Time At All, 1988; Deep In The Heart of Texas, 1988; Dallas City Lights, 1989; Especially For You, 1990; Sarah's Dream, 1990; New Horizons, 1992; Web of Love, 1994; Love With Attitude, 1995; Kiss My Innocence, 1998; Sarah Jory Band Live, 2000. *Honours:* 6 British Country Music Awards; 3 European Awards; Many other regional awards. *Memberships:* PRS; Musicians' Union. *Leisure interests:* Swimming; Cycling; Walking; Listening to music. *Current Management:* Arthur Jory (personal). *Address:* 10 Tennyson Rd, Balderton, Newark, Notts NG24 3QH, England. *Internet:* www.sarahjory.co.uk.

JOSEPH Julian Rapheal Nathaniel; b. 11 May 1966, London, England. Musician (piano); Composer. *Musical Education:* Classical Composition, Berklee College of Music, Boston, USA. *Career:* Julian Joseph Weekend, Barbican Centre; Julian Joseph Series, Wigmore Hall; The Proms, Royal Albert Hall, London, 1995; Montréal Jazz Festival. *Compositions include:* Film score, A Tale of a Vampire; Commissioned work, Winds of Change; Orchestral works. *Recordings:* Albums: The Language of Truth; Reality; Julian Joseph In Concert At The Wigmore Hall; Universal Traveller, 1996. *Honours:* Award to Study at Berklee College of Music; Southern Comfort Award, Best Jazz Group; John Dankworth Award. *Memberships:* PRS; MCPS; BASCA. *Current Management:* James Joseph Music Management. *Address:* 85 Cicada Rd, London SW18 2PA, England.

JOURGENSEN Al(len); b. 9 Oct. 1958, Havana, Cuba. Vocalist; Musician (Guitar). *Career:* Member, Ministry; Signed major label contract, 1983; Numerous side projects including Revolting Cocks, Lard, with Jello Biafra of Dead Kennedys, 1000 Homo DJs, with Trent Reznor of Nine Inch Nails, Pigface, with Steve Albini, Jello Biafra, Chris Connelly and Dwayne Goettell; Worked with Butthole Surfers' Gibby Haynes; Numerous tours including Lollapalooza; Contributed track to Neil Young's Bridge School Benefits album, 1998. *Recordings:* Singles: Cold Life, 1981; I Wanted To Tell Her, 1983; Revenge, 1983; Work for Love, 1983; All Day, 1985; Cold Life, 1985; Over the Shoulder, 1985; Halloween Remix, 1987; Stigmata, 1988; Burning Inside, 1989; Jesus Built My Hotrod, 1991; N.W.O., 1992; Just One Fix, 1992; The Fall, 1995; Lay Lady Lay, 1996; Bad Blood, 1995; Albums: With Sympathy, 1983; Twitch, 1985; Twelve Inch Singles 1981–84, 1987; The Land of Rape and Honey, 1988; The Mind is a Terrible Thing to Taste, 1989; In Case You Didn't Feel Like Showing Up (Live), 1990; Psalm 69: The Way To Succeed and the Way To Suck Eggs, 1992; Filth Pig, 1996; Dark Side of the Spoon, 1999; Greatest Hits (compilation), 2001; with Revolting Cocks: Beers, Steers and Queers, 1990; With Lard: Pure Chewing Satisfaction, 1997.

JOYCE, (Joyce Silveiro Palhano de Jesus); b. 31 Jan. 1948, Rio de Janeiro, Brazil. Vocalist; Musician (guitar, violin); Songwriter. *Career:* First recorded as part of vocal group, 1964; Solo debut, 1968; Dropped out of the music business until invitation by Vinicius de Moraes to join him on international tour, 1975; Moved to New York City, 1977; Signed contract with EMI, 1980; Independent releases, 1984–; 1990s brought a new audience when the 'drum 'n' bossa' style rejuvenated interest in recordings. *Recordings:* Albums include: Veu De Noiva, 1969; Nelson Angelo E Joyce, 1972; Passarinho Urbano, 1977; Aqua E Luz, 1980; Tardes Cariocas, 1981; Music Inside, 1990; Language and Love, 1991; Sings Antonio Carlos Jobim and Vinicius De Moraes, 1993; Ilha Brasil, 1996; Astronauta – Songs of Elis, 1998; Tudo Bonito, 2000; Gafieira Moderna, 2001. *Address:* c/o Far Out Records. *Internet:* www.joyce.com.

JUB; b. Oxfordshire, England. Musician (double bass); Vocalist. *Musical Education:* Guildhall School of Music, London. *Career:* Bass player, Kreisler String Orchestra; English National Opera; London Festival Ballet; London Contemporary Dance Theatre; Member, The Carnival Band, 1985–; Appearances include: Glasgow Cathedral; Birmingham Symphony Hall; Barbican Centre; Arts centres and theatres; Plays material from: Sweden; Croatia; US; Bolivia; Spain; UK; France. *Recordings:* Album with Maddy Prior: Christmas Carols. *Current Management:* c/o Jim McPhee, Acorn Entertainments. *Address:* Winterfold House, 46 Woodfield Rd, Kings Heath, Birmingham B13 9UJ, England.

JUDD Naomi Ellen; b. 1 Nov. 1946, Ashland, Kentucky, USA. Singer; Songwriter; Author; Speaker. m. Larry Strickland, 6 May 1989; 2 d. *Education:* RN degree. *Career:* Member, country music duo The Judds, with daughter Wynonna, 1984–90; Sold 15m. albums; Most successful duo

in country music history. *Recordings include:* Singles: Had A Dream For The Heart, 1983; Mama He's Crazy, 1984; Why Not Me, 1984; Girls Night Out, 1985; Rockin' With The Rhythm of The Rain, 1986; Let Me Tell You About Love, 1989; Albums: The Judds, 1984; Why Not Me?, 1985; Rockin With The Rhythm of the Rain, 1986; Heartland, 1987; Greatest Hits, 1988; River of Time, 1989; Love Can Build A Bridge, 1990; The Judds Collection, 1991; The Essential, 1996; Collection, 1997; Otherside, 1997; New Day Dawning, 2001. *Publications:* Love Can Build A Bridge. *Honours:* 7 Grammy Awards; 4 Academy Country Music Awards, Best Duet; 3 Country Music Asscn Awards, Best Vocal Duo; Undefeated, 3 major Country Music Award shows, 8 consecutive years. *Leisure interest:* Walking in nature. *Current Management:* William Morris. *Address:* The Judd House, 325 Bridge St, Franklin, TN 37064, USA.

JULES Judge, (Julius O'Riordan); b. 26 Oct. 1965, London, England. DJ; Record Prod.; Remixer; Radio Presenter; A and R. *Education:* Degree in Law, London School of Economics. *Career:* World-wide appearances in over 30 countries; Remixed and produced over 20 top 30 singles, 1994–. *Recordings include:* I Like To Move It, Reel 2 Real; Doop, Doop; Saturday Night, Tempo; High on a Happy Vibe; I Put a Spell on You; Funky Groove; Down with the Underground; Pulsating Rhythms; Albums include: Clubbed, 2001. *Contributions to:* The Face, ID, Mix Mag, and DJ Mag. *Honours:* Best Club DJ, DJ Mag, 1995; Best DJ, London Club Awards, 1995. *Membership:* Musicians' Union. *Leisure interests:* Current Affairs; Psychology; Law; Football. *Current Management:* Serious Artist Management. *Address:* PO Box 13143, London N6 5BG, England.

JUNGR Barb; b. 9 May 1954, Rochdale, England. Singer; Performer; Songwriter; Musician (mandolin, harmonica); Cabaret artist; singer. *Education:* BSc, Leeds. *Musical Education:* Master of Music, Goldsmiths College; Doctoral Research, Voice and Emotion. *Career:* Television appearances with Julian Clary in all series of Sticky Moments, Terry and Julian; Radio broadcasts: 5 series, We Stayed In With Jungr and Parker, BBC Radio 2; National tours with Alexei Sayle and Julian Clary. *Compositions:* Television themes, 1990–2000; Theatre, 1990–2000. *Recordings:* 3 Courgettes; Barb; The Stroke; Jungr and Parker; Bare, 1999; Chanson, 2000; Every Grain of Sand – Barb Jungr sings Bob Dylan, 2002. *Honours:* Perrier Award, 1987; Swansea Fringe Award, 1988. *Memberships:* PRS; PPL; MCPS; British Voice Asscn; Malawian Musicians Asscn; British Forum Ethnomusicology; Centre Performance Research; Musicians' Union; Equity; ICTM; Women In Music; Jazz Singers Network. *Leisure interest:* Aikido. *Current Management:* Sonia Beldom Brown, London.

JUNKERA Kepa, (Kepa Junquera Urraza); b. 1965, Bilbao, Spain. Musician (trikitixa); Composer. *Career:* Basque folk musician; Plays the trikitixa (Basque diatonic accordion); Performed with band Oskorri and continues to guest on their albums and tours; Collaboration with John Kirkpatrick and Riccardo Tesi (known as the Trans-Europe Diatonic project), with associated album and international tours, brought Junkera to wider European audience; Collaborations with renowned Basque musicians and international artists including: The Chieftains; Julio Pereira; Carlos Nuñez; Dulce Pontes; Andreas Vollenwaider; As composer, has combined jazz with own folk music and written pieces performed with Bilbao Symphony Orchestra. *Recordings:* Albums: with Kepa Zabaleta eta Motriku: Infernuko Auspoa, 1987; Triki Up, 1990; solo: Trikitixa Zoom, 1991; Trans-Europe Diatonic (with Riccardo Tesi and John Kirkpatrick), 1992; Kalejira Al-Buk, 1994; Lau Eskutara (with Julio Pereira), 1995; Leonen Orroak (with Ibon Koteron), 1996; Bilbao 00–00h, 1996; Maren, 2001. *Honour:* Young Contemporary Folk Musician Prize, 1990. *Internet:* www.kepajunkera.com.

JURICIC Max Wilson; b. 10 June 1958, Zagreb, Croatia. Musician (guitar); Backing Singer. m. Vanja Matujec, 11 June 1988, 1 s., 1 d. *Education:* Economist. *Career:* Member, Azra, 1977–78; Film, 1978–86; Le Cinema, 1986–88; Vjestice, 1989–99; Ziu Zao, 1995; So! Mazgoon, 1999. *Recordings:* with Film: Film 1; Live Kulusic; Zona Sumraka; Sva Cuda Svijeta; Signali U Noći; with Le Cinema: Live Kulusic; with Vjestice: Totalno Drukciji Od Drugih; Bez Tisine; Live In Schwarzwald; Djevojke U Ljetnim Haljinama Volim; Kradljivac scra; with So! Mazgoon, 1999. *Honour:* Porin 1987, for best album in alternative music. *Membership:* HGU. *Leisure interests:* Swimming; Skiing. *Address:* Auzvinkl Tomisalavov trg 19, Zagreb, Croatia.

K

K Greg, (Gregory David Kriesel); b. 20 Jan. 1965, Glendale, California, USA. Musician (bass guitar). m. Jane Costello, 1 s. *Education:* Long Beach State University, California, BA in Finance. *Career:* Privately pressed single took over 2 years to sell 1000 copies, 1987; Signed to independent labels, Nemesis and Epitaph, for 1988–95 releases; Major US breakthrough following heavy MTV/radio play rotation, 1994; Accused of betraying punk roots when signing to Columbia after dispute with former label, 1996; Consolidated world-wide success by scoring UK No. 1 hit single, 1999; Live shows include: Woodstock festival, 1999; KROQ Weenie Roast, 2000; European tour, 2001; Band gave lucky fan $1m. in Offspring prize draw, 2000. *Recordings:* Albums: The Offspring, 1989; Ignition, 1992; Smash!, 1994; Ixnay On The Hombre, 1997; Americana, 1998; Conspiracy of One, 2000; Singles: I'll Be Waiting, 1987; Baghdad EP, 1988; Come Out and Play (Keep 'Em Separated), Self-Esteem, 1994; Gotta Get Away, 1995; All I Want, Gone Away, 1997; Pretty Fly (For A White Guy), 1998; Why Don't You Get A Job?, The Kids Aren't Alright, She's Got Issues, 1999; Original Prankster, 2000; Want You Bad, Million Miles Away, 2001. *Honours:* Over 9m copies of Smash album sold world-wide, best selling independent record of all time. *Current Management:* Jim Guerinot, Rebel Waltz Management, 31652 Second Ave, Laguna Beach, CA 92651, USA. *Internet:* www.offspring.com.

KAAS Patricia; b. 5 Dec. 1966, Forbach, France. Singer. *Career:* Scène de Vie tour, 1990–91 (196 concerts, audience 750,000, 12 countries); Tour de Charme, 1993–94 (145 concerts, audience 600,000, 19 countries). *Recordings:* Mademoiselle Chante, 1988; Scène De Vie, 1990; Carnet De Scène (double live album) 1991; Je Te Dis Vous, 1993; Tour de Charme, (live album) 1994; Dans Ma Chair, 1997; Rendez-Vous, 1998; Le Mot de Passe, 1999; Live, 2000; Longbox, 2001; Les Indispensables, 2001. *Publication:* Patricia Kaas-Tour De Charme, 1994. *Honours:* 6 Victoires de la Musique; 2 World Music Awards. *Leisure interest:* Fashion. *Current Management:* Cyril Prieur, Richard Walter. *Address:* Talent Sorcier, 3 rue des Petites Écuries, 75010 Paris, France.

KAASINEN Sari Johanna; b. 15 Sept. 1967, Rääkkylä, Finland. Singer; Musician (kanteler); Record Prod. m. Heikki Kemppainen, 21 June 1991, 1 d. *Musical Education:* Master of Music, Sibelius Academy, Helsinki, 1994. *Career:* Leader, Singer, Värttinä, 1983–96; Tours, Festivals throughout Europe and US include: Kaustingen, Finland, 1985–; WOMAD, UK, 1992; Dranouter, Belgium, 1992; Glastonbury, UK, 1993; Ruisrock, Finland, 1993; Molde Jazz Festival, Norway, 1994; Owner, Producer, Mipu Music; Television appearances: Music From Karelia, Finnish documentary, 1990; Late Late Show, Dublin, 1991; Prize of Europe, 1994; Leading Sirmakka group currently; Persuing solo project; Teacher of Music, Rääkkylä. *Compositions:* Iro, 1996; Pojaton, 1996; Limoni Ennen, 1996. *Recordings:* Albums with Värttinä: Värttinä, 1987; Musta Lindu, 1989; Oi Dai, 1991; Seleniko, 1992; Aitara, 1994; Kokko, 1996; With Sirmakka, Tsihi Tsihi, 1997; with Hector Zazou: Songs From The Cold Seas, 1995. *Honours:* Emma Award, Finland, 1992; State Music Art Prize, 1992; Northern Karelian Music Art Prize, 1992. *Membership:* Finnish State Music Art Committee, 1995–97. *Current Management:* Hoedown. *Address:* Laivurinrinne 2, 00120 Helsinki, Finland.

KAERSAA Morten; b. 26 Sept. 1957, Copenhagen, Denmark. Musician (Piano); Vocalist. 1 s. *Career:* Member of band, Sneakers; Member of Moonjam. *Compositions:* 9 albums for Moonjam; All Sneakers material. *Recordings:* Moonjam: Songs for Saxophone; Saxophone Songs Vol. II; Sarai; Bag De Bla Bjerge; Osten Fur Solen. *Honours:* Platinum album for Songs for Saxophone, 1992; Platinum album for Moonjam's Greatest Hits. *Current Management:* FPH Management, Copenhagen. *Address:* Moonlab Dampfaergevej 2 CD, 2100 Copenhagen, Denmark.

KAERSAA Rasmus; b. 29 Dec. 1960, Copenhagen, Denmark. Musician (Bass). m. Annika Hueg, 25 June 1995, 1 s. *Career:* Member, Danse Orkestret; Member, Moonjam. *Compositions:* Below the Yellow Moons; National hit, Kom Tilbage Nu (Come Back Now), with Jacob Andersen. *Recordings:* Albums with Moonjam: Songs for Saxophone; Saxophone Songs Vol. II; With Danse Orkestret: Danse Orkestret. *Honours:* Platinum album, Danse Orkestret, 1986; Platinum album, Songs for Saxophone, 1992. *Current Management:* FDH Management, Copenhagen. *Address:* Moonlab Damfaergevej 2 CD, 2100 Copenhagen, Denmark.

KAGADEEV Andrei; b. 9 July 1961, Moscow, Russia. Songwriter; Musician. m. Tatiana Kagadeeva, 2 March 1985, 1 d. *Education:* Humanitarian University Courses, Technical University of St Petersburg; Guitar Lessons. *Career:* Songwriter, Composer for the NOM Band; Appearances on Western European Television Channels; Participation in Big Festivals, Les Allummees, Nantes, 1991, Sziget, Budapest, 1995;

Concert Tours in Western Europe. *Compositions:* Films: Masters of the USSR or Ape's Snout, 1994; Made In Europe, (documentary), 1996. *Recordings:* Albums: Brutto, 1989; To Hell With It, 1991; Superdisc, 1992; Senka-Mosgas, 1994; In the Name of Mind, 1996; Ultracompact, 1996; Live is Game, 1996; Gire, 1997. *Honours:* Grand Prix, Alternative Video Contest, Exotica 95, Moscow; Best Low Budget Video, Ukrblues, Midem 96 Fair, Cannes, France. *Leisure interests:* Writing Fiction; Art Design; Film Making. *Current Management:* Agency of Gerhard Busse, St Petersburg, Russia. *Address:* Bogatyrsky pr 5/1–283, St Petersburg 197348, Russia.

KAJDAN Jean-Michel; b. 16 July 1954, Paris, France. Musician; Song Writer; Singer. *Musical Education:* Self-taught, Guitar, Bass Guitar. *Career:* Sideman, Didier Lockwood, Michel Jonasz, Eddy Mitchell, Lionel Ritchie, Eddy Louiss; The Big Blue (film); Subway (film); Taratata, (television with L Ritchie); Taratata (television with D E Mitchell); Montreux Jazz Festival (with Lassy Carlton), 1997. *Compositions:* The Spy (D Lockwood Album); Spying Taranto; Song for LC. *Recordings:* Blue Scales; Blue Noise; Fasten Seat Belts; La Mouvellevie. *Memberships:* SACEM; SPEDIDAM; ADAMI; SACD. *Current Management:* Maurice Suissa, Suissa Despa Productions. *Address:* 1 rue du Général de Gaulle, 27500 Pont Audemer, France.

KALANIEMI Maria Helena; b. 27 May 1964, Espoo, Finland. Musician; Composer. m. Olli Caris. *Education:* MMus, Sibelius Academy, 1992. *Career:* Leader, Member, Various Ensembles and Side Projects, Including, Niekku, Helsinki Melodeon Ladies, Anna Kaisa Liedes Group, Ramunder, Vesa Matti Loiri Group, 1983–; Teacher, Sibelius Academy Folk Music Department; Leader, Composer of Ensemble Aldargaz, 1992–; Member of Group Accordion Tribe, 1996-. *Compositions:* Hermannin Riili, 1992; Lomasavel, 1995; Iho, 1995; Ahma, 1998; Kaamos, 1998; Kamppi, 1998; Lovina, 1998. *Recordings:* Maria Kalaniemi, 1992; Iho, 1995; Accordion Tribe, 1998; Ahma, 1999. *Honours:* Golden Accordion Competition, 1983; Prize of Finland, 1996; 3 Years Composer Grant, 1997. *Current Management:* Hoedown, Laivurinrinne 2, 00120 Helsinki, Finland. *Address:* Kellonsoittajantie 1B, 02770 Espoo, Finland.

KALASZ Juraj; b. 14 Nov. 1963, Bratislava, Czechoslovakia. m. Dr Krausova Dagmar, 15 Dec. 1990, 1 s. *Education:* Machine Engineering University, 6 years (Slovak Technological University), Dipl Ing, 1983–89; Studying Double Bass, State Conservatory in Bratislava, 1991–97. *Career:* First Prof Eng, 1987 with local (Bratislava) groups (Exprit, Bratislava Trio), 1991; Just Jazz (tours in Denmark and Czech Republic), 1993; Czechoslovak Quintet (Bratislava Jazz Days Festival); 1995 Tubu (tour in Spain); 1995 Member of Janusz Muniak, Quartet (Cracow, Poland); 1996 Member of Shawn Loescher Trio). *Compositions:* Tribute to Charlie Parker, recorded for Slovak Radio. *Recordings:* Czechoslovak Quintet, for Slovak Radio, 1993; Chamber Jazz Trio, 1996. *Publication:* Walking Double Bass, 1997. *Honour:* Prize for Outstanding Performance, Zilina Jazz Festival, 1989. *Membership:* Slovak Jazz Society. *Leisure interests:* Swimming; Books. *Address:* Rara Musica (Adrian Raiter), Fand Who 1, 81103 Bratislava, Slovakia.

KALIMOULLIN Rashid; b. 6 May 1957, Zelenodolsk City, Tatarstan, Russia. Composer. m. Rosa Kalimoullina, 7 July 1979, 1 s., 1 d. *Education:* Degree in Composition, Kazan State Conservatoire; Postgraduate Studies. *Compositions include:* Opera, Cuckoo's Cry, Libretto by I Yuziev, 1989; Symphonic Works: Concert for clarinet with orchestra, 1985; Bulgary, poem, 1986; Silence and Tranquillity, vocal symphonic poem, 1987; Chamber works: Quartet for wooden wind instruments, 1981; About Silence, poem for voice and piano, lyrics by N Arslanov, 1985; Sonato for piano no 1, 1985; Sonata for cello solo No 1, 1986; About Happiness, poem for voice and two flutes, lyrics by R Mingalimov, 1989; Forgotten Prayer, fantasy for organ, 1992; Morning in Istanbul, fantasy for piano, 1993; Quartet No 4, for two violins, viola and cello, 1994; We Are Answerable to God, for choir a capella, 1995; Fantasy for Saxophone, 1997; Head Into the Noose, for violin and percussion (one performer), 1998; Fantasy for oboe solo, 1998. *Recordings:* Rashid Kalimoullin: Chamber Music, 1989; Piano arrangements of songs by the Beatles: Hyper Beatles, 1993; Chamber Works CD, 1994; String Quartet No 4, CD, 1996. *Honours:* First Prize, K M Veber Competition, Germany, 1987; Shostakovich Award, Russia, 1998. *Membership:* Chairman, Union of Composers of Tatarstan. *Leisure interests:* Travelling; Pretty women. *Address:* 44/6, 49 Dostoevsky Str, 420043 Tatarstan, Russia.

KALLIN Ivor; b. 28 Sept. 1957, Glasgow, Scotland. Deputy Headteacher; Musician (Violin, Viola, Double Bass, Bass Guitar). m. Jenny Kallin, 26 Aug. 1979, 1 s., 2 d. *Education:* BA, Social Studies; PGCE. *Compositions:*

Mainly involved in improvised music. *Recordings:* Kneel Down Like A Saint, with London Electric Guitar Orchestra; Gorilla, CD; 13 Lumps of Theatre, CD; Relay, contribution to CD; Moonbrake, track; Unmen, track. *Membership:* London Musicians' Collective. *Address:* 13 Alconbury Rd, Clapton, London E5 8RG, England.

KALOGJERA Niko Nikica; b. 19 May 1930, Beograd, Croatia. Conductor; Composer. m. Ljupka Dimitrovska, 2 March 1978, 2 s., 1 d. *Education:* Medical University. *Musical Education:* High Music Academy. *Career:* Chief conductor, Croatian Radio-television Orchestra, International Festival Awards, 28 include: Split 1969; MIDEM, 1969; Athens, 1970; Rio, 1971; Malaga, 1971; Vina Del Mar, 1971; Tokyo, 1971; Dresden, 1972; Eurovision Song Contest, 1989. *Compositions:* Over 1000 songs on LP, MC, CD, VC (about 400 in foreign countries); Music for theatre, films; Artists: Mireille Mathieu; Claudio Villa; Raymond Lefevre; Tony Christie. *Publications:* Columnist in many music publications. *Membership:* Vice-president, Croatian Composers Asscn. *Leisure interests:* Comparative Philology; Swimming. *Current Management:* AVET, Zagreb, Croatia. *Address:* 10000 Zagreb, Tuskanac 33, Croatia.

KAMAI Allen; b. 6 Dec. 1960, Marin County, California, USA. Musician (Bass). *Musical Education:* College of Marin. *Career:* Tours with: Oleta Adams; Sheena Easton; Wendy and Lisa; The Rainbirds; Michael Penn; Jude Cole; Ronnie Montrose; Extensive television and video performances in USA; Europe; Canada; Japan. *Recordings with:* Sass Jordan; Curt Smith; Miki Howard; Jeanette Katt; Bronx-Style Bob; Pretty In Pink; The Rainbirds; Chanise Wilson; Wendy and Lisa; Kristian Vigard; Jim Chappell. *Honour:* Yamaha Soundcheck, Outstanding Bassist, 1987. *Leisure interests:* Mountain biking; Off-road 4x4 racing. *Current Management:* Doug Buttleman Management. *Address:* 14625 Dickens #207, Sherman Oaks, CA 91403, USA.

KANDA BONGO MAN; b. 1955, Inono, Democratic Republic of Congo. Vocalist; Songwriter. *Career:* Started singing in Kinshasa, 1973; Member: Orchestre Bella Mambo, 1976; Moved to Paris, 1979; Performed at WOMAD UK, 1983; International career began; Accredited with birth of kwassa kwassa dance rhythm; Later Minister of Arts and Culture in new Democratic Republic of Congo. *Recordings:* Iyole, 1981; Non Stop Non Stop, 1985; Amour Fou, 1985; Kwassa Kwassa, 1989; Zing Zong, 1991; Soukous in Central Park, 1992; Francophonix, 1995; Welcome to South Africa, 1998; Sweet, 1999; Best of Kanda Bongo Man, 1999; Balobi, 2001; Very Best of Kanda Bongo Man, 2002. *Address:* c/o Gallo Records, PO Box 2897, Parklands 2121, South Africa. *Internet:* www.gallo.co.za.

KANE Gregory; b. 11 Sept. 1966, Coatbridge, Strathclyde, Scotland. Singer; Lyricist; Composer. *Education:* Engineering student. *Career:* Formed Hue and Cry with brother Patrick; Concerts include: Royal Albert Hall; Support to Madonna, Wembley Stadium; Composer for television themes and musical scores. *Recordings:* Albums: Seduced and Abandoned, 1987; Ordinary Angel, 1988; Bitter Suite, 1989; Remote, 1989; Stars Crash Down, 1991; Labours of Love, 1993; Showtime!, 1994; Piano and Voice, 1995; Jazz Not Jazz, 1999; Next Move, 2000; Singles: Labour of Love, 1987; Violently, 1989; Looking For Linda, 1989. *Leisure interests:* Pool; Golf.

KANE Patrick; b. 10 March 1964, Coatbridge, Strathclyde, Scotland. Singer; Musician (piano, keyboards); Songwriter; Journalist. *Education:* Degree, English and Media Studies. *Career:* Formed Hue and Cry with brother Gregory; Concerts include Royal Albert Hall; Support to Madonna, Wembley Stadium; Also journalist, The Guardian; Radio presenter, Usual Suspects, BBC Radio Scotland; Broadcaster, Radio 4; Rector, Glasgow University. *Recordings:* Albums: Seduced and Abandoned, 1987; Ordinary Angel, 1988; Bitter Suite, 1989; Remote, 1989; Stars Crash Down, 1991; Labours of Love, 1993; Showtime!, 1994; Piano and Voice, 1995; Jazz Not Jazz, 1999; Next Move, 2000; Singles: Labour of Love, 1987; Violently, 1989; Looking For Linda, 1989. *Membership:* Founder, Artists For An Independent Scotland. *Address:* c/o BBC Radio Scotland, Queen Margaret Dr., Glasgow G12 8DG, Scotland.

KANE Stevie (Stephen); b. 13 April 1961. Musician (fretted and fretless bass, double bass). *Career:* Tours with The Silencers: Dance To The Holyman European tour, 1992; Seconds of Pleasure tour, 1993–94; So Be It, 1995; Other concerts include: Rock-Am-Ring, 1993; London Fleah, 1993; St Gallen, 1994; Appearances include: Radio 1 Roadshow, 1993; Free Wheels, 1993; Live Aus Dem Nachtwerk, 1993; Summit In The City, 1993. *Recordings:* with The Silencers: Seconds of Pleasure; So Be It. *Current Management:* Tartan Ghost. *Address:* 423 Merry St, Motherwell, Strathclyde ML1 4BP, Scotland.

KANNBERG Scott; b. 1967, Stockton, California, USA. Musician (Guitar); Vocalist. *Career:* Founder Member, Pavement; Released first EP on own label; Obtained bigger indie label deal; Numerous live gigs; Appearance of group in cartoon Space Ghost Coast to Coast. *Recordings:* Singles: Perfect Sound Forever EP, 1990; Watery, Domestic, EP, 1992; Trigger Cut, 1992;

Cut Your Hair, 1994; Gold Soundz, 1994; Range Life, 1995; Rattled by La Rush, 1995; Father to a Sister of Thought, 1995; Pacific Trim EP, 1996; Shady Lane/Slowly Typed, 1997; Stereo, 1997; Spit on a Stranger, 1999; Carrot Rope, 1999; Albums: Slanted and Enchanted, 1992; Crooked Rain, Crooked Rain, 1994; Wowee Zowee, 1995; Brighten the Corners, 1997; Terror Twilight, 1999; features on: Brilliant Career, Film School, 2001.

KANTARDZIJEV-MLINAC Petko; b. 21 Oct. 1945, Sofia, Bulgaria. Composer; Sound Engineer; Prod.; Musician (piano). m. Mirjana, 15 Aug. 1971, 1 d. *Education:* Faculty of Electronics, 1971. *Musical Education:* High School for Music, department, Composing and Piano, 1964. *Career:* Rock musician, 1961–69; Music editor, TV Zagreb, 1969; Rehearser, music, Comedy Theatre, Zagreb: A Man From La Mancha; Fiddler On The Roof; Promises Promises, 1969–71; Radio-television, Zagreb, 1970–89; Music Producer, Suzy Record Company, 1971–72; Sound engineer, Jugoton Record Company, 1974–76; Director, Multimedia Youth Centre, 1987–88; Pianist, 1990-. *Compositions:* Over 150 compositions and arrangements, pop, easy listening, classical, number recorded for Radio Zagreb and various records. *Recordings:* As sound engineer: More than 200 soundtracks; films; animations; documentaries; Television series; films; 100 albums include: John Luis; Clarck Terry; Sal Nistico; Art Farmer. *Honours:* First prizes, Best Soundtracks, Yugoslavia, 1982, 1984, 1985, 1986; First prizes, Festivals in: Opatija, 1968; Zagreb, 1986; Fish Eye animated film, Ottawa, 1981. *Memberships:* Croatian Composers' Asscn; Croatian Artiste's Asscn. *Leisure interests:* Playing piano; Tennis; Bridge. *Address:* Maksimirska 81, 10000 Zagreb, Croatia.

KANTNER Paul; b. 12 March 1941, San Francisco, California, USA. Musician (guitar). 1 d. *Education:* University of Santa Clara, 1959–61; San Jose State College, 1961–63. *Career:* Founder member, Jefferson Airplane, 1965–73; Renamed Jefferson Starship, 1974–84; Member, Planet Earth Rock 'n' Roll Orchestra, 1984–85; KBC (Kantner Balin Casady) Band, 1985–88; Rejoined Jefferson Airplane (later as Jefferson Starship – The Next Generation), 1989–; Appearances include: Berkeley Folk Festival, 1966; Monterey Jazz Festival, 1966; Monterey Pop Festival, 1967; Newport Pop Festival, 1968; Isle of Wight Festival, 1968; Atlantic City Festival, 1969; Woodstock Music and Art Fair, 1969; Altamont Speedway, with Rolling Stones, 1969; Bath Festival, 1970; Festival of Hope, 1972; Knebworth, 1978; Free concert, Golden Gate Park, 1989. *Recordings:* Albums: Jefferson Airplane Takes Off, 1966; Surrealistic Pillow, 1967; After Bathing At Baxter's, 1968; Crown of Creation, 1968; Bless Its Pointed Little Head, 1969; Blows Against The Empire, 1970; The Worst of Jefferson Airplane, 1971; Sunfighter, 1972; Long John Silver, 1972; 30 Seconds Over Winterland, 1973; Baron Von Tollbooth and The Chrome Nun, 1973; Dragonfly, 1974; Red Octopus, 1975; Spitfire, 1976; Flight Log (1966–76), 1977; Jefferson Starship Gold, 1979; Freedom At Point Zero, 1980; Modern Times, 1981; Winds of Change, 1983; Nuclear Furniture, 1984; Jefferson Airplane, 1989; Jefferson Airplane Loves You, 1992; A Guide Through the Chaos, 1996; Jefferson Airplane and Beyond, 1997; Windows of Heaven, 1999; Roar of Jefferson Airplane, 2001; Ignition, 2001; with KBC Band: KBC Band, 1986; Solo: The Planet Earth Rock and Roll Orchestra, 1983; Singles include: Miracles, 1975; With Your Love, 1976; Runaway, 1978; Jane, 1980. *Publication:* Author, Nicaraguan Diary, 1988. *Current Management:* Bill Thompson Management, 2051 Third St, San Francisco, CA 94107, USA.

KANTONEN Seppo; b. 13 Nov. 1963, Kivijärvi. Finland. Musician (piano, keyboards). *Musical Education:* Sibelius Academy, Helsinki, 1979. *Career:* Began career playing with Nono Söderberg and Otto Donner Treatment; Pianist with UMO (New Music Orchestra); Pianist with Eero Koivistoinen, 1980s-; Jazz soloist, accompanist, Afro-American tradition; Worked with numerous rock bands including Mustat Lasit, 1980s; Recorded as duo with Jarmo Savolainen. *Recordings:* Albums: with Jarmo Savolainen: Phases; with Eero Koivistoinen: Dialog, 1995. *Honour:* Yrjö Award, Finnish Jazz Federation, 1985. *Address:* Ruusankatu 6 A 18, 00250 Helsinki, Finland.

KAPELLE Frances; b. 21 Aug. 1956, London, England. Vocalist. m. Paul Raymond Oldridge, 26 May 1978, divorced, 1 d. *Education:* College. *Career:* Backing vocalist for singers including: Ian Shaw; Carol Grimes; Brian Kennedy; Mary Coughlan; Preproduction singer, backing vocal arranger, writer with Violet Williams, film soundtrack The Commitments. *Recordings:* Albums: Junk Puppets, An Emotional Fish (backing vocals); Why Don't They Dance, Carol Grimes. *Membership:* Musicians' Union. *Leisure interest:* Worked with exotic animals (leopards, tigers). *Address:* Brockton Farm, Egerton Rd, Charing Heath, Kent TN27 0AX, England.

KAPHAN Bruce Robert; b. 7 Jan. 1955, San Francisco, California, USA. Musician; Prod.; Composer; Engineer. m. Michele White, 12 Dec. 1987. *Musical Education:* Mostly self-taught. *Career:* Tours with American Music Club, USA, Western Europe; Television appearances with Jewel (Saturday Night Live and MTV Unplugged), 1997; European and USA tours with David Byrne, including television appearances on the Late Show with David Letterman and Sessions at W 54th St on PBS. *Recordings:* with John Lee Hooker: Chill Out; with The Black Crowes: Amorica; with Chris Isaak:

Forever Blue; with American Music Club: Everclear; Mercury; San Francisco; Black Crowes, Three Snakes and One Charm, Love and Rockets, Sweet FA; Jellyfish, Spilt Milk; Red House Painters, Songs for a Blue Guitar; Francesco di Gregori, Premiere E Lasciare; Susanna Hoffs, Susanna Hoffs; Tara MacLean, Silence; Suzanne Little, Be Here Now; Mark Eitzel, 60 Watt Silver Lining, West; Up, REM; Legacy, Jewel; Solo album: Slider – Ambient Excursions For Pedal Steel Guitar, 2001. *Honours include:* Award Winner, Northern California Film and Video Festival, 2000. *Membership:* AFofM. *Leisure interest:* Backpacking. *Address:* PO Box 2012, Fremont, CA 94536, USA.

KAPILIDIS Nick; b. 2 Jan. 1955, Zanthi, Greece. Musician (drums). m. 1973–92, 1 s., 1 d. *Musical Education:* Ethnico Conservatory, 4 years piano, 1 year flute, private lessons drums. *Career:* Jazz festivals, Patea, Athens, Thessaloniki; Live performances with J Stubblefield; D hayes; M Boyd; G Bailey; K Rampton; D Lynch; Y Fakaqnas; L Christofis; TV appearances with many famous Greek composers and singers. *Recordings:* Electric Jazz Trio, 1990; Flying To The Unknown, M Alexiou, 1995; Oramata, L Christofis, 1996; Forthcoming recording: Serious Fun, with own band. *Publications:* Book: Modern Greek Odd Rhythms. *Membership:* Greek Musicians' Union. *Leisure interests:* Music; Theatre. *Address:* Markou Botsazi 24, Galatsi 1145, Athens, Greece.

KAPSEU Jean Robert; b. 30 Sept. 1968, Bangoua. Songwriter; Composer; Musician (Guitar). 2 s., 1 d. *Career:* Musical Concerts, 1996–; Appearances, Radioscopy of a Star, 1997. *Compositions:* Let's Fight for Life, The Road Is Not A Mystery; Confirmation. *Recordings:* Union Plus; Luttons Laus La Vie; Que Faire; Travailler, La Vie N'est Pas Facile; Sida, Passera Jariais Pas Moi; L'Hymne Bangoua. *Publications:* The Age of Maturity, 1990; Let's Fight For Life, 1996; Confirmation, 1999. *Memberships:* Socinada; AA Mont. *Leisure interests:* Cinema; Football; Dancing. *Address:* PO Box 11624, Yaounde, Cameroon.

KARAKOSTOVA Rumiana; b. 12 May 1951, Sofia, Bulgaria. Musicologist. m. Lubomir Karakostov, 26 Oct., 1 d. *Education:* Pancho Vladigerov, State Music Academy, Sofia. *Career:* Dramatist, Stefan Makedonsky, State Music Theatre, Sofia; Show scripts with State Musical Theatre; Broadcasts for Bulgarian national radio; Screenplays for biographical films of Bulgarian musicians and actors; Lecturer, National Academy of Theatre and Cinema Art, Plovdiv Fine Arts Academy. *Publications:* Bulgarian Music Theatre; State Music Theatre Stefan Makedonski: Historical Development and Contemporary Problems, in Guide for Operetta Theatres Abroad, 1991; Numerous essays in musicological and music history journals. Contributions to: Bulgaria Encyclopaedia Vols IV and VI; History of Bulgarian Music. *Memberships:* Union of Bulgarian Composers; Vienna Club, Sofia. *Leisure interests:* Poetry; Drama; Literature. *Address:* 136 ap, 8ent, 131 bl, Suhodolska-1 St, Zapaden Park, Krasna Polyana, Sofia 1373, Bulgaria.

KARGES (Matthew) Murphy; b. 20 June 1967. Musician (bass guitar). *Career:* Toured USA with LA punk group The Weirdos, 1990; Joined The Shrinky Dinx; Group signed to Atlantic Records following circulation of self-made demo video; Act renamed Sugar Ray owing to threat of legal action prior to record releases; Built up world-wide fanbase through touring and TV appearances; Cameo in Fathers Day film, 1997. *Recordings:* Albums: Lemonade and Brownies, 1995; Floored, 1997; 14–59, 1999; Sugar Ray, 2001; Singles: Mean Machine, Iron Mic, 1995; Fly, RPM, 1997; Every Morning, Someday, 1999; Falls Apart, 2000; When It's Over, Answer The Phone, 2001. *Honours:* Second/third albums certified double/triple platinum by RIAA respectively. *Address:* c/o PO Box 12018, Costa Mesa, CA 92627, USA. *E-mail:* management@sugarray.com. *Internet:* www.sugarray.com.

KARN Mick, (Anthony Michaelides); b. 24 July 1958, Nicosia, Cyprus. Musician (Bass Guitar). *Career:* Member, Japan, 1977–82; Member, Dali's Car, 1984; Japan reunion, 1989; Member, Rain Tree Crow (with 3 members of Japan), 1991; Member, Polytown, 1994; Member, Jansen, Barbieri, Karn (with 2 members of Japan), 1995 Sculptor, exhibition of work, London, 1981, 1992, Japan, 1982, Italy, 1985. *Recordings:* Albums: with Japan: Adolescent Sex, 1978; Obscure Alternatives, 1978; Quiet Life, 1980; Gentlemen Take Polaroids, 1980; Assemblage, 1981; Tin Drum, 1981; Oil On Canvas, 1983; Exorcising Ghosts, 1985; Solo albums: Titles, 1982; Dreams of Reason Produce Monsters, 1987; Bestial Cluster, 1994; The Tooth Mother, 1995; with Dali's Car: The Waking Hour, 1984; with Rain Tree Crow: Rain Tree Crow, 1991; Singles include: with Japan: The Art of Parties, 1981; Quiet Life, 1981; Visions of China, 1981; Ghosts, 1982; Cantonese Boy, 1982; Life In Tokyo, 1982; Night Porter, 1982; with Dali's Car: The Judgement is the Mirror, 1984; Solo: Sensitive, Buoy, 1982; 1987; With Polytown: Polytown, 1994; With Jansen, Barbieri, Karn: Beginning to Melt, 1995; Seed, 1996; Liquid Glass, Yoshihiro Hanno, 1998; Ism, 1999; Each Eye A Path, 2001. *Current Management:* Medium Productions, 74 St Lawrence Rd, Upminster, Essex RM14 2UW, England.

KÄRTSY (Kari Hatakka); b. 17 Dec. 1967, Helsinki, Finland. Musician; Composer; Lyricist; Singer. *Career:* European tours, 1993–97; Lead singer, Finnish rock band, Waltari, 1994; Roskilde Festival, Denmark, 1994, 1995; Ethno Meets Metal tour with Angelin Tytöt, 1995; European tours, 1995, 1996, 1997. *Recordings:* Monk Punk, 1991; Torcha!, 1992; So Fine!, 1994; Big Bang, 1995; Yeah! Yeah! Die! Die! Death Metal Symphony in Deep C, 1996; Space Avenue, 1997; Decade, 1998. *Leisure interests:* Yoga; Swimming; History. *Current Management:* East Border/Jone Nuutinen. *Address:* Tallberginkata 1 D Fifth Floor, 00180 Helsinki, Finland.

KARVONEN Jartsa; b. 27 June 1955, Finland. Musician (drums). *Musical Education:* Oulunkylä Institute, 1976. *Career:* Began playing, Rovaniemi, Lapland; Played with bands: Blue Train; Jukka Syrenius Band; Tapiola Big Band, including appearance at Detroit Festival; Played with numerous artists including: Jukka Linkola; Olli Ahvenlahti; Pentti Lahti; Mircea Stan; Regular member, UMO (New Music Orchestra), 1989. *Honours:* Musician of The Year, 1989; Voted Best Drummer, Finnish Jazz Federation's magazine JazzIt Readers Poll, 1989. *Address:* Paraistentie 11 A 6, 00280 Helsinki, Finland.

KASPERSEN Jan Per Sommerfeldt; b. 22 April 1948, Copenhagen, Denmark. Musician (piano); Composer; Arranger. 1 s. *Career:* Musician, European Jazz scene, 1969–; Bandleader, trios up to quintets, using name Space and Rhythm Jazz. *Recordings:* 23 releases, including Memories of Monk; Live At Sofie's Cellar; Heavy Smoke; Ballads and Cocktails; Special Occasion Band: Live In Copenhagen Jazz-House; Space and Rhythm Jazz; Joining Forces; Jan Kaspersen and the Danish Radio Jazz Orchestra: Live in Copenhagen Jazzhouse; Out of Sight; Katuaq Concert; More Ballads and Cocktails. *Honours:* DJBFA Jazz Composer prize, 1987; JASA prize, 1988. *Memberships:* Danish Musicians' Union; Society of Danish Bandleaders. *Current Management:* Space and Rhythm Jazz, Danish Music Agency. *Address:* c/o Space and Rhythm Jazz, Copenhagen, Denmark.

KÄTKÄ Ismo (Ippe) Paavo Matias; b. 19 March 1948, Seinajoki, Finland. Composer Prod. Musician (Drums, Keyboards). Divorced, 1990, 2 s. *Musical Education:* Self-taught. *Career:* Local bands, dance, pop, rock, jazz, 1965–; Starboys, Tangopojat, Yahoos, Kari Larne Group, Woodoo, Matthews, Kirka and Islanders, Royals, Pekka Pohjola Group, Veltto and Heru, Ippe Kätkä Band, Tampere Jazz Orchestra, Juice Leskinen, Dave Lindholm, Anssi Tikanmäki Film Orchestra, Krakatau, Ismo Alanko, Galaxy (Senegal); International tours: Pekka Pohjola Group, 1980–82, A T Film Orchestra, 1989–93, Krakatau, 1993–96, Galaxy, 1993-. *Compositions:* For films, TV, radio, theatre, modern dance ranging from classics through Shakespeare to modern poetry. *Recordings:* Royals: Spring 76; Out; Live; Pekka Pohjola Group: Kätkävaaran Lohikäärme; Veltto and Heru: Tahdon; Ippe Kätkä Band: Tre Jazz Orchestra: Makumoka; Juice: Minä; Sinä; Dave: Sissi; Sillalla; A T Film Orchestra: Greed; Krakatau: Matinale; Ismo Alanko: Irti; Taiteilijaelämää; Galaxy: Nobeel. *Honours:* Several state grants, 1982–; Tampere City Creative Musician Award, 1989; Critic's Poll, Best Group and Best Album of Year, 1985, 1994; KOURA Award for the best radio programme, 1997. *Memberships:* ELVIS ry, composers and writers. *Leisure interest:* Music. *Current Management:* Global Music Centre, Mikkolantie 17, Fin 00640 Helsinki, Finland. *Address:* Tallberginkatu 1c/47, Fin 00180 Helsinki, Finland.

KATONA Kerry Jane Elizabeth; b. 6 Sept. 1980, Warrington, England. Vocalist. m. Bryan McFadden, Jan. 2002, 1 d. *Career:* Joined Atomic Kitten 1999; UK Support tours 1999–2000; Co-spearheaded MTV Asia Awards 2000 reaching 675m. viewers; Left group January 2001 owing to family commitments. *Recordings:* Albums: Right Now, 2000; Singles: Right Now, 1999; See Ya, 2000; I Want Your Love, 2000; Follow Me, 2000; Whole Again, 2001. *Honours:* Successes at UK Disney Channel and Smash Hits Awards 2000. *Current Management:* Innocent Records, Kensal House, 553–579 Harrow Rd, London, W10 4RH, England.

KATZ Simon; b. 16 May 1971, Nottingham, England. Musician (Guitar). *Career:* Member, Jamiroquai; Numerous tours and TV appearances. *Recordings:* Singles: When You Gonna Learn, 1992; Too Young To Die, 1993; Blow Your Mind, 1993; Emergency on Planet Earth, 1993; Space Cowboy EP, 1994; Half The Man, 1994; Stillness In Time, 1995; Virtual Insanity, 1996; Cosmic Girl, 1996; Light Years, 1996; Alright, 1997; Deeper Underground (No. 1, UK), 1998; High Times, 1998; Canned Heat, 1999; Supersonic, 1999; King For A Day, 1999; Little L, 2001; You Give Me Something, 2001; Albums: Emergency on Planet Earth, 1993; Travelling Without Moving, 1996; Synkronized, 1999; A Funk Odyssey, 2001. *Honours:* Numerous Gold and Platinum Albums; Many MTV Video Music Awards.

KAUKONEN Jorma; b. 23 Dec. 1940, Washington DC, USA. Musician (guitar, dobro, steel guitar). *Education:* BA, Sociology, Santa Clara University; Antioch College. *Musical Education:* Self-taught; Studied under Ian Buchanan and Rev Gary Davis. *Career:* Member, The Triumphs; Member, Jefferson Airplane, 1966–72; Member, side project Hot Tuna, 1968–78, 1992–; Jefferson Airplane Reunion, 1989–90;

Appearances include: Berkeley Folk Festival, 1966; Monterey Jazz Festival, 1966; Monterey Pop Festival, 1967; Newport Pop Festival, 1968; Isle of Wight Festival, 1968; Atlantic City Pop Festival, 1969; Woodstock Festival, 1969; Altamont Speedway, with the Rolling Stones, 1969; Bath Festival, 1970. *Recordings include:* Albums: Jefferson Airplane Takes Off, 1966; After Bathing At Baxter's, 1968; Crown of Creation, 1968; Bless It's Pointed Little Head, 1969; Volunteers, 1969; Blows Against The Empire, 1970; Long John Silver, 1972; Flight Log (1966–76), 1977; Jefferson Airplane, 1989; Jefferson Airplane Loves You, 1992; with Hot Tuna: First Pull Up Then Pull Down, 1971; Burgers, 1972; The Phosphorescent Rat, 1974; America's Choice, 1975; Yellow Fever, 1975; Hoppkorv, 1976; Double Dose, 1978; 2400 Fulton Street, 1987; Quah; Jorma; Barbeque King; Too Hot To Handle; Land of Heroes, 1995; Jorma Kaukonen Christmas, 1996; Too Many Years, 1998; Guest musician, If Only I Could Remember My Name, David Crosby, 1972. *Current Management:* Vanessa Lillian, Gabra Management, 37000 Kingsbury Rd, Pomeroy, OH 45769, USA.

KAVANAGH Niamh; b. 13 Feb. 1968, Dublin, Ireland. Vocalist; Recording Artist. *Musical Education:* Voice training, 4 years, Bel canto school. *Career:* Appearance on Grammies 1992, with Commitments, 1992; Television and radio throughout Europe, 1993–; Eurovision Song Contest, 1993. *Recordings:* Tracks on Commitments soundtracks Vols I and II; Eurovision winner: In Your Eyes, 1993; Debut solo album: Flying Blind, 1995. *Honours:* Yamaha International Award of Excellence; Grammy Nomination, with Commitments, 1992; Eurovision Song Contest Winner, In Your Eyes, 1993. *Membership:* Musicians' Union. *Leisure interests:* Reading; Films; Computers. *Current Management:* Mairead Wright. *Address:* 49 Old Shore Rd, Trooperslane, Carrickfergus, Co Antrim BT38 8PF, Northern Ireland.

KAVANAGH Ron; b. Fermoy, County Cork, Ireland. Musician; Prod.; Arranger; Songwriter; Composer. *Career:* Former session musician, producer, arranger; Worked with artists including: Charlie Watts; Richard Thompson; Paddy Moloney; The Pogues; Elvis Costello; Dr John; Clarence Henry; Doug Sahm; Big Jay McNeely; Member, various groups including: Loudest Whisper; Panama Red; Chris Farlowe Band; Identity Kit, with guitarist Ed Deane; Juice On The Loose; In-house bandleader, producer for Ace Records; Member, various bands with Alexis Korner, 1980s; Bees Make Honey; Leader, own band Alias Ron Kavana; 3 support tours with The Pogues; Other projects include: Home Fire; The Bucks; Founder, director, member of LILT (Live Irish Live Trust), non-profit making organization committed to peace in Northern Ireland; Appearances, songwriter for films including: Ryan's Daughter; Sid and Nancy; Clash of The Ash, RTE; Hidden Agenda. *Compositions include:* Co-writer with The Pogues: Young Ned of The Hill; Every Man Is A King. *Recordings:* Solo albums: Rollin' and Coasting; Home Fire; with Alias Ron Kavana: Think Like A Hero, 1989; Coming Days, 1991; Galway To Graceland, 1995; with Loudest Whisper: The Children of Lire; with Donovan, Liam Og O'Fynn, Philip Donnelly, RTE Chamber Orchestra: The Children of Lire (re-recorded), 1993; with The Bucks: Dancing To The Ceilli Band, 1995; with LILT: For The Children; Guest musician with The Pogues: Sid and Nancy (soundtrack); Fall From Grace. *Honours:* Best Live Act In The World, Folk Roots Magazine, 1989–91. *Current Management:* c/o Jim McPhee, Acorn Entertainments. *Address:* Winterfold House, 46 Woodfield Rd, Kings Heath, Birmingham B13 9UJ, England.

KAY Jason (Jay); b. 30 Dec. 1969, Manchester, England. Singer. *Career:* Member, Jamiroquai; Numerous tours and TV appearances. *Recordings:* Singles: When You Gonna Learn, 1992; Too Young To Die, 1993; Blow Your Mind, 1993; Emergency on Planet Earth, 1993; Space Cowboy EP, 1994; Half The Man, 1994; Stillness In Time, 1995; Virtual Insanity, 1996; Cosmic Girl, 1996; Light Years, 1996; Alright, 1997; Deeper Underground (No. 1, UK), 1998; High Times, 1998; Canned Heat, 1999; Supersonic, 1999; King For A Day, 1999; Little L, 2001; You Give Me Something, 2001; Albums: Emergency on Planet Earth, 1993; Travelling Without Moving, 1996; Synkronized, 1999; A Funk Odyssey, 2001. *Honours:* Several Gold Albums; Numerous MTV Video Music Awards.

KAY Simon; b. 1 May 1960, London, England. Songwriter; Prod.; Musician (keyboards). *Career:* Keyboard player, Ultramarine; US Tour, Orbital, 1992; Concerts include: Glastonbury Festival; Strawberry Fayre; Radio and television include: Radio 1; Radio 5; 5 Live sessions; MTV Live; Tours with Björk include: USA, Europe, 1993; Britronica; Russian Tour; Glastonbury Festival; Forest Fayre; Megadog, 1994; Formed Exile with partner Tim Ericson; Exile production credits include debut album by Cry. *Recordings:* with Ultramarine: Album: United Kingdom; Single: Kingdom; Happy Land; Hymn; As producer: Single: with Cry: (It's About) Time For Love. *Current Management:* MRM. *Address:* Panther House, 38 Mount Pleasant, London WC1X 0AP, England.

KAYE Carol; b. 24 March 1935, Everett, Washington, USA. Musician (Electric Bass, Guitar). 1 s., 2 d. *Career:* Professor, Guitar, 1949–; Taught Electric Bass, 1969–; On The Road, Big Band, 1954–55; Played Bebop Jazz, Black Night Clubs, 1956–61; Special Records, Studio Guitarist, 1957–66;

Studio Electric Bassist, 1963–; Invented 16th Note Bass Recording Styles. *Recordings:* credits on guitar include: Zippity Doo Dah; Birds and Bees; The Best Goes On; You've Lost That Lovin Feelin; credits on bass include: Way We Were; Feelin Alright; Good Vibrations; Wouldn't It Be Nice; Heat of Night; I Don't Need No Doctor; Little Green Apples; Baby Love; River Deep Mountain High. *Publications:* Writer, Composer of over 27 Tutorials; How To Play The Electric Bass; Jazz Improvisation For Bass; CDs, First Lady On Bass; Thumbs Up; California Creamin'. *Membership:* Musicians' Union. *Leisure interests:* Fishing; Reading; Teaching. *Address:* PO Box 2122, Canyon Country, CA 91386 2122, USA. *Internet:* www.carolkaye.com.

KAYE Hereward Hilken Swain; b. 29 June 1953, Middlesbrough, Cleveland, England. Singer; Songwriter; Composer. m. Patricia Mary Lord, 6 July 1974, 3 s. *Education:* Drama College. *Musical Education:* Self-taught. *Career:* Member, The Flying Pickets, 4 albums; International tours from Australia to Iceland. *Compositions:* Moby Dick, Cameron Mackintosh musical, Piccadilly Theatre, 1992; Arranger, musical director, Return To The Forbidden Planet; Composer, lyricist, Hell Can Be Heaven, computer game, musical, opening 1996; with Flying Pickets: Blue Money, 1996; Composer lyricist, Underworld, musical, Seattle, 1998. *Honour:* Evening Standard Musical of The Year, Are You Lonesome Tonight (as Musical Director). *Membership:* PRS. *Leisure interests:* Middlesbrough Football Club; Snooker; Cooking; Writing; Home studio; Songwriting; Partying. *Current Management:* Sacha Brooks, 55 Greek St, London W1V 5LR, England. *Address:* 4 Orchard Rd, Linthorpe, Middlesbrough, Cleveland TS5 4PW, England.

KAZAN Paul; b. 9 April 1956, Taplow, Buckinghamshire, England. Singer; Musician (piano, violin); composer; Prod. m. Montserrat Arruga, 21 Oct. 1994, 1 s. *Musical Education:* 1 year at Bristol University; Grade VIII Piano; Grade VII violin. *Career:* Classical background; Settled in Spain, 1976; Session musician, arranger until 1990; Solo artiste, 1990–; Presented first solo album in concert at Barcelona Olympic Games, 1992. *Recordings:* Albums: Stay, 1992; Miracle Street, 1996. *Membership:* Spanish Society of Authors (SGAE). *Leisure interests:* Model railways; Travel. *Current Management:* Oniria International, S L. *Address:* Alzines, 3, Sant Quirze Park, 08192 Sant Quirze Del Valles, Barcelona, Spain.

KAZASSIAN Hilda; b. 1970, Sofia, Bulgaria. Vocalist; Musician (keyboards, drums, percussion); Composer; Arranger. *Musical Education:* Graduate, Academy of Popular Music, Sofia, 1993; Studied percussion in the United Kingdom and Italy. *Career:* Hot Jazz debutant; Guest appearances at several jazz festivals; Winner of percussion competitions in Rome and London; Currently working with Acoustic Version (Bulgaria's leading jazz combo); Writes and arranges own compositions. *Recordings:* Albums: Cover Girl, 1994; Why Not, 1996. *Address:* c/o Union Media Ltd, 71 Evlogi Georgiev Blvd, Entr. A, Sofia 1142, Bulgaria.

KAZDA Jan; b. 3 Oct. 1958, Prague, Czech Republic. Musician (Bass, Guitar); Composer; Prod. m. Karen K, 1988, 1 s. *Education:* Classical Music Degrees; Artists Maturity Degree. *Career:* Tours with: Ginger Baker, Randy Brecker, Peter Brötzmann, Sonny Sharrock; with own band: Das Pferd and KAZDA, Frankfurt Jazz Festival, Sibiu Jazz Festival (Rumanian), Ruhr-Jazz Leverkusener Jazz Festival; Rockpalast TV HR/WDR TV. *Compositions:* Composer, 5 CDs with Das Pferd; 2 CDs with KAZDA, 1994–97; 4 CDs with singer Tom Mega, 1988–92. *Recordings:* Das Pferd, KAZDA, Tom Mega, 1987–97; Recorded with Ginger Baker, Harry Beckett, Randy Brecker, Marilyn Mazur, Ronnell Bey, Frank Wunsch, Nordwestdeutsche Philharmonique (classical orchestra), Therion. *Address:* Dörpfeldstr 41, 42369 Wuppertal, Germany.

KEANE Dolores; b. 1953, Caherlistrane, County Galway, Ireland. Vocalist; Musician (flute). *Musical Education:* Born into a family of sean nos singers; Sister of Sean Keane; Learned to sing from aunts Rita and Sarah Keane. *Career:* First recording for Radio Eireann, aged 5; Founding member of De Danann; Collaborations: Planxty; The Chieftains; Lead role in Dublin production of Brendan Behan's play The Hostage; Also appeared on stage, again in Dublin, in The Playboy of the Western World; Contributed to the RTE/BBC TV production Bringing It All Back Home, 1992; Continues to record and tour internationally. *Recordings:* Albums include: There Was A Maid, 1978; Sail Og Rua, 1983; Ballroom (De Danann), 1987; Dolores Keane, 1988; Lion In A Cage, 1989; Solid Ground, 1994; The Best of Dolores Keane, 1997; Night Owl, 1998; How The West Was Won (De Danann), 1999; featured on soundtrack: Dancing At Lughnasa, 1998. *Honours:* Topped Irish charts with singles, The Rambling Irishman and Lion In A Cage, and The Best of Dolores Keane album; Featured track on Ireland's biggest ever selling album, A Woman's Heart, 1992; Awarded Fiddler's Green Hall of Fame, 1995; Irish Music Magazine: Best Female Folk Performer; Best Folk CD, The Best of Dolores Keane, 1997. *Internet:* www.doloreskeane.com.

KEANE Sean; b. 24 Aug. 1961, County Galway, Ireland. Vocalist. *Musical Education:* Learned music from family; Brother of Dolores Keane, nephew of Rita and Sarah Keane. *Career:* Member: Shegui, 1970s; Reel Union,

1980s; Arcady; Turned professional, 1994. *Recordings:* Albums include: Around The World For Sport (with Shegui); There Was A Maid (with Reel Union); Atlantic Breeze (with Shaskeen); Muintir Chathain (with the Keane family); solo: All Heart No Roses (produced by John Faulkner and Arty McGlynn), 1994; Turn A Phrase, 1996; No Stranger, 1998; The Man That I Am (featuring Nanci Griffith and an arrangement by Sir George Martin), 2000; The Best of Sean Keane, 2001. *Honours:* Won 13 All-Ireland titles; Irish Music Magazine: Performer of the Year, 1997–98; Best Male Folk Singer, 1997–2001. *Address:* c/o Circin Rua. *E-mail:* virginiak@eircom.net. *Internet:* www.seankeane.com.

KEAREY Ian; b. 14 Oct. 1954, London, England. Singer; Musician (guitar, bass guitar, banjo, mandolin). m. Rebekah Zoob, 19 April 1986, 1 s., 1 d. *Education:* University of Kent, Canterbury. *Musical Education:* Self-taught. *Career:* Member, Oyster Band, 1976–88; Member, Blue Aeroplanes, 1983–; Producer for: Michelle Shocked; Bootfare; Many television appearances include: Top of The Pops; Many radio appearances include: Radio 1, Radio 2 sessions; Freelance sessions, 1986–; Member, Heaven Factory, 1990-. *Recordings include:* with Blue Aeroplanes: Bop Art, 1984; Swagger, 1990; Beatsongs, 1991; Life Model, 1993; Rough Music, 1994; Cavaliers, 2000; with Oyster Band: Liberty Hall, 1985; Step Outside, 1986; Wide Blue Yonder, 1987; Trawler, 1995; Granite Years (compilation), 2000; with Gerard Langley: Siamese Boyfriends, 1987; with Heidi Berry: Love, 1991; with Leon Rosselson: Perspectives, 1998. *Publications:* Contributor, Folk Roots Magazine, 1984-. *Honours:* Freedom of the City of Bangor, 1980; Hon. BSC, Indian Institute of Technology, 1986. *Membership:* Musicians' Union. *Leisure interests:* Cycling; Reading; Collecting music-hall ephemera. *Current Management:* E Bunbury, RFM. *Address:* 88 Roundhill Cres., Brighton, East Sussex BN2 3FR, England.

KEATING Ronan; b. 3 March 1977, Dublin, Ireland. Vocalist. *Career:* Lead Singer, Boyzone; Co-Host, Eurovision Song Contest, Ireland; Solo career. *Recordings:* Singles: Working My Way Back To You, 1994; Key To My Life, 1995; Love Me For A Reason, 1995; So Good, 1995; Father and Son; Coming Home Now, 1995; Words (No. 1, UK), 1996; A Different Beat (No. 1, UK), 1996; Isn't It A Wonder, 1997; Picture of You, 1997; Baby Can I Hold You Tonight, 1997; Mystical Experience, 1997; All That I Need (No. 1, UK), 1998; No Matter What (No. 1, UK), 1998; I Love The Way You Love Me, 1998; When The Going Gets Tough (No. 1, UK), 1999; You Needed Me (No. 1, UK), 1999; Every Day I Love You, 1999; solo: When You Say Nothing At All (No. 1, UK), 1999; Life Is A Rollercoaster (No. 1, UK), 2000; The Way You Make Me Feel, 2000; Lovin' Each Day, 2001; Albums: Different Beat, 1996; Where We Belong, 1998; By Request, 1999; solo: Ronan, 2000. *Internet:* www.ronankeating.com.

KEEL Howard, (Harold C Leek); b. 13 April 1917, Gillespie, Illinois, USA. Singer; Actor. *Career:* In-house entertainer, Douglas aircraft manufacturing company; Appeared in musicals: Carousel, 1945; Oklahoma, London; Film appearances: The Small Voice, 1948; Annie Get Your Gun, 1950; Show Boat, 1951; Kiss Me Kate, 1953; Calamity Jane, 1953; Rose Marie, 1954; Seven Brides For Seven Brothers, 1954; Kismet, 1955; Various western films; US revival tours, 1960s; Regular television appearances, US series Dallas, 1981–; Solo recording artiste, 1984–; Farewell Tour, UK, 1993. *Recordings:* And I Love You So, 1984; Reminiscing, 1985; The Collection, 1989; The Great MGM Stars, 1991; Close To My Heart, 1991; With Love for Yesterday, Today and Tomorrow, 1998; And I Love You So, 2001; Various soundtrack albums. *Address:* c/o Producers Inc, 11806 N 56th St, Suite B, Tampa, FL 33617, USA.

KEEREMAN Peter; b. 21 Aug. 1968, Brugge, Belgium. Prod.; Composer; Pianist. *Education:* Degree in Music Education, Ghent, Belgium; Graduate, Berklee, College of Music, Music Production and Engineering. *Career:* Concert tours with Belgian artists; Performances for BRT – Radio and Television. *Compositions:* Everlasting Love and Revende Hemel (Intersong Primakera); Spaceflight/Snow Flakes; Crazy Comedy Capers (Parsifal). *Membership:* SABAM Author Organisation. *Leisure interests:* Running; Swimming. *Address:* Doornstraat 47, 8200 Brugge, Belgium.

KEEZER Geoffrey Graham; b. 20 Nov. 1970, Eau Claire, Wisconsin, USA. Jazz Musician (piano); Composer; Arranger. m. Mayumi Tomokane, 23 April 1995. *Musical Education:* 1 year, Berklee College, Boston. *Career:* Pianist with Art Blakey and the Jazz Messengers, 1989–90; Pianist with Art Farmer, 1991–95; Leader of Geoff Keezer trio and quartet, 1988; Tours: Japan; England; Europe; Russia; Scandinavia; Canada; Performed: at Lincoln Center; with Carnegie Hall Jazz Orchestra; with Hollywood Bowl Orchestra. *Compositions:* Many large and small ensemble pieces. *Recordings:* As leader: Here and Now, 1991; World Music, 1992; Other Spheres, 1993; All For One, with Art Blakey; The Key Players, with The Contemporary Piano Ensemble; Color and Light – Jazz Sketches On Sondheim; Some of My Best Friends..., with Ray Brown; Turn Up The Quiet, 1998; Zero One, 2000; Live At Starbucks, 2001. *Membership:* BMI; AMRA. *Leisure interests:* Karate; Okinawan weaponry; Japanese language. *Address:* The Jazz Tree, 648 Broadway, Suite 703, New York, NY 10012, USA.

KEITA Salif; b. 1949, Djoliba, Mali (West Africa). Singer. *Career:* Japan Tour, 1993; Grande Parade du Jazz de Nice, 1992; WOMAD Festivals: Reading, 1992; Adelaide, 1993; Las Palmas, 1993; Australian tour, 1993; Annual European tour including summer festivals; Montreux Jazz Festivals, 1993, 1995; Canadian tour, 1994; US tour, 1994; African tour, including South Africa, 1994; Parkpop Festival, The Hague, Holland, 1995. *Recordings:* Soro, 1987; Koyan, 1989; Destiny of a Noble Outcast, 1991; Amen, 1991; Mansa of Mali, 1994; Folon, 1995; Rail Band, 1996; Seydou Bathili, 1997; Papa, 1999; Sosie, 2001; Compilation – 1969–80, 2001. *Publications:* Video: Noble of An Outcast. *Honours:* Chevalier of Arts and Letters, France; Chevalier of Order of The Nation, Mali; Nominated for US Music Awards: Best World Music Artist, 1992; Grammy. *Current Management:* Mad Minute Music, Paris, contact Corinne Serres. *Address:* c/o Mad Minute Music, 5–7 Paul Bert, 93400 St Ouen, France.

KEITH (John) Larry; b. 1 March 1955, Hendersonville, North Carolina, USA. Musician (guitar, bass); Vocalist. m. Denna O Nix, 23 Dec. 1988, 1 s., 2 d. *Musical Education:* Blue Ridge Community College, Hendersonville, North Carolina. *Career:* WKIT-WHKP Radio Hendersonville; The Charlie Renfro Concerts, 1980–84; Appearances with: Carl Story and The Ramblin' Mountaineers; The Boys From Indiana; Jim and Jesse and the Virginia Boys; Bill Monroe and The Bluegrass Boys; Doyle Lawson and Quicksilver; Mac Wiseman; Dolly Parton's Premiere Bluegrass Band, Pigeon Forge, Tennessee, 1984–88. *Recordings:* Albums: First Time Around; On and On; Head Over Heels; Second Time Around; The Old Country Church. *Publications:* The Bluegrass Newsletter (monthly). *Memberships:* IBMA; The Bluegrass Music Asscns of North Carolina, South Carolina, Georgia. *Leisure interests:* Gardening; Classic cars. *Current Management:* The McMinn Family Band. *Address:* PO Box 384, Tuxedo, NC 28784, USA.

KEITHLEY Joseph Edward; b. Burnaby, BC, Canada. m. Laura Susan, 2 s., 1 d. *Musical Education:* Self-taught. *Career:* 20 years in punk rock band, DOA; Solo acoustic folk act; Appeared in cult films, Terminal City; The Widower. *Compositions:* 10 albums with DOA. *Recordings:* Bloodied But Unbound; War on 45; Last Scream of the Missing Neighbours. *Publications:* Spin, 1985; High Times, 1995; Rolling Stone, 1997. *Current Management:* Laurie Mercer Management, PO Box 27070, Collingwood PP, Vancouver, BC, Canada.

KELIS (Kelis Rogers), (Thunderbitch); b. 1979, Harlem, New York, USA. Vocalist. *Education:* La Guardia High School of Music and Art and the Performing Arts, New York. *Career:* Started singing in Boys and Girls Choir of Harlem; Collaborated with the Gravediggaz before joining girl group B.L.U.; Began solo career working The Neptunes production team; Collaborations: Ol' Dirty Bastard; Busta Rhymes; Foxy Brown. *Recordings:* Albums: Kaleidoscope, 2000; Wanderland, 2001; Singles: Caught Out There, Good Stuff, Get Along With You, 2000; Young Fresh n' New, 2001. *Honour:* NME Award, Best R & B Artist, 2001. *Address:* c/o Virgin America, 304 Park Ave S, Fifth Floor, New York, USA.

KELLARD Colin Alan; b. 9 Jan. 1941, Bury St Edmunds, Suffolk, England. Insurance Claims Inspector; Musician (banjo, guitar). m. Pamela Randall, 24 Sept. 1966, 1 s., 1 d. *Musical Education:* Self-taught. *Career:* Member of Alvin Roy Saratoga Jazz Band, 1959–63; Tours of Germany, 1961 and 1962; Television appearance: Let's Go, BBC, 1961; Member of Rad Newton Jazz Friends, with various appearances at jazz festivals in UK and Holland, 1987–92; Leader, own Jazz band, 1992-. *Recordings:* Many recordings with Alvin Roy Saratoga Jazz Band; Own label recordings with Tad Newton Jazz Friends and Colin Kellard Band. *Honour:* Winner, Soho Fair Jazz Band Contest with Alvin Roy Saratoga Jazz Band, 1960. *Leisure interest:* Music. *Address:* 15 Nathaniel Walk, Tring, Hertfordshire HP23 5DQ, England.

KELLERMANN Lone; b. 20 March 1943, Copenhagen, Denmark. Singer. *Musical Education:* Self-taught. *Career:* Member of several bands; Numerous film, television, theatre and radio appearances; Many interviews, Scandinavian papers. *Recordings:* 5 solo albums; Several other recordings. *Memberships:* DJBFA; Danish Artistes' Union. *Leisure interest:* Having a good time. *Current Management:* Danish Artistes' Union. *Address:* Amagengade 11, 1423 Copenhagen, Denmark.

KELLIE Michael Alexander; b. 24 March 1947, Birmingham, England. Musician (drums). m. (1) April 1969, 1 d., (2) Elizabeth, Sept. 1997, 2 s. *Musical Education:* Self-taught. *Career:* Original member, Island Records family, 1966–76; Spooky Tooth, 1967 to end; The Only Ones, 1976–81; World tours with above; Recordings with many others; Currently involved in running Spookytooth.com; Writing a book; Working with church musicians to promote Christian music. *Recordings:* Spooky Two, Spooky Tooth; With A Little Help From My Friends, Joe Cocker; Tommy (film soundtrack), The Who; Cross Purpose, Spooky Tooth, CD, 1999. *Memberships:* Musicians' Union; PAMRA. *Leisure interests:* Farming; Songwriting. *Current Management:* Alec Sutton, Attic Music. *Address:* GEK, 22 Holly Rd, Edgbaston, Birmingham B16 9NH, England.

KELLNER Olda; b. 14 March 1948, Prague, Czech Republic. Vocalist; Musician (Guitar, Keyboards); Composer; Record Studio Owner. m. Vera Spalova, 27 March 1971, 1 d. *Education:* Conservatoire. *Career:* Member, Prague Rock Group, Blue Effect, 1981–88. *Publication:* Encyklopedie Jazzu a Moderni Popula'rni Hudby, 1990. *Memberships:* OSA Prague; Intergram Prague. *Leisure interest:* Painting pictures. *Address:* Konstantinova 10, 14900 Prague 4, Czech Republic.

KELLY Charles; b. 19 Aug. 1930, Dallas, Texas, USA. Singer; Writer; Musician (Trombone). m. Bev Kelly, 2 s. *Education:* BA, MA, Sierra University; University of California; Oklahoma University. *Career:* Wrote and Edited Numerous Policies and Procedures, Manuals, Software Manuals, Proposals, Northrop, Boeing, Hughes Aircraft Company; Group Singer; Television Performer; Numerous Commercials, 1959–76; Motion Picture Voice Tracks, 1965–70. *Publications:* Over 500 Articles and Stories; Technical Editor: Pharmacology, Biology and Clinical Applications of Anrogens; The Alchemy of Intelligence; Editor: The Book of Love and Sex; Ghostwriter: Love Making-The Psychology of Making Love; Writer: The Amazing John Holmes; Sammy; Silent Obsession; Work in progress: Memoirs of a Personal Manager-From The Glenn Miller Singers to Johnny Carson. *Memberships:* ASCAP; AFTRA; SAG. *Leisure interests:* Music; Metaphysics; Hypnosis. *Address:* 248 Laverne Ave, Long Beach, CA 90803, USA.

KELLY Jeff; Songwriter; Musician (multi-instrumentalist). m. Susanne. *Career:* Formed the Green Pajamas, 1984–; Also solo artiste. *Compositions include:* Kim The Waitress, covered by Material Issue and Sister Psychic. *Recordings:* Albums: with The Green Pajamas: Summer of Lust, 1984, 1990; Halloween, 1984; Book of Hours, 1987; November, 1988; Ghosts of Love, 1990; In A Glass Darkly, 2001; Solo: Baroquen Hearts, 1985; Coffee In Nepal, 1987, 1991; Portugal, 1990; Twenty Five, 1991; Private Electrical Storm, 1992; Ash Wednesday Rain, 1995; Melancholy Sun, 1999; Indiscretion, 2001; Featured on compilations: Monkey Business, 1986; Splat Sampler, 1988; Time Will Show The Wiser, 1989; The Fourth Adventure, 1991.

KELLY Jon; Record Prod. 3 c. *Recordings:* Produced Records for: Blue is the Colour, Beautiful South, UK No 1; Deacon Blue; Chris Rea; Kate Bush; The Damned; Jimmy Nail; The Levellers; Fish; Quench, Beautiful South, UK No 1 album; Prefab Sprout; Painting It Red, Beautiful South, 2000. *Current Management:* One Management, 43 St Alban's Ave, London, W4 5JS, England.

KELLY Juliet; b. 6 May 1970, London, England. Jazz Vocalist. *Education:* BSc (Hons), Economics; MA, Television Production. *Musical Education:* Post-graduate Jazz course, Guildhall School of Music and Drama. *Career:* Part of a cappella Group, Darker Than Blue (formerly Jazz Voices); Performed at Purcell Room, South Bank, part of London Jazz Festival, 1994; Festivals in Germany, 1995; Australia, 1996; Touring with Orphy Robinson, Phoenix Dance Company Project, across UK, including Sadlers Wells, 1995. *Membership:* Musicians' Union. *Leisure interests:* Travel; Cinema; Reading.

KELLY Laoise; b. 1973, Westport, County Mayo, Ireland. Musician (harp, fiddle). *Education:* Maynooth; University College, Cork. *Career:* Member: Ciabh Rua, age 15; Bumblebees, 1996; Harp teacher at UCC, 1993; Performed in: Bill Whelan's Seville Suite, 1993; Micheal O'Suilleabhain's Lumen, Eurovision, 1995; Charlie Lennon's Famine Suite; Toured US and Australia, 1997; Collaborations: Natalie MacMaster; The Chieftains; Tunde Jegede; Co-founder: FACE (with Steve Cooney); Teacher, DIT, Dublin; Appearances in TV series: River of Sound, 1995; Sult, 1996; Sin E E (with Liam O Maonlai); Geantrai (with Matt Molloy), 1996. *Recordings:* with Bumblebees: Bumblebees, 1996; Buzzin', 1999; solo: Just Harp, 1999. *Honours:* All-Ireland titles: 1989; 1991; 1992; Keadue O'Carolan Festival, winner, 1989; Granard harp competitions: 1989; 1990 1992; Belfast Bicentennial Harp Festival, winner, 1992. *E-mail:* laoise.kelly@face.ie.

KELLY Mark; b. 9 April 1961, Dublin, Ireland. Musician (keyboards). *Career:* Member, Chemical Alice; UK progressive rock group, Marillion, 1981–; Appearances include: Theakston Festival, 1982; Reading Festival, 1982; Nostell Priory Festival, 1982, 1984; Glastonbury Festival, 1983; Support to Rush, Radio City Music Hall, New York, 1983; Milton Keynes Bowl, 1984; Monsters of Rock Festival, Castle Donington, 1985; Nelson Mandela Birthday Party with Midge Ure, Wembley Stadium, 1987; Welcome To The Garden Party, Milton Keynes Bowl, 1986. *Recordings:* Albums: Script For A Jester's Tear, 1983; Fugazi, 1984; Real To Reel, 1984; Misplaced Childhood, 1985; Brief Encounter, 1986; Clutching at Straws, 1987; B-Sides Themselves, 1988; The Thieving Magpie, 1988; Season's End, 1989; Holidays In Eden, 1991; A Singles Collection 1982–92, 1992; Brave, 1994; Afraid of Sunlight, 1995, 1999; This Strange Engine, 1997; Radiation, 1998; Marillion.com, 1999; Anoraknophobia, 2001; Made Again Live, 2001; Singles include: Market Square Heroes, 1982; He Knows You Know, 1983; Garden Party, 1983; Punch and Judy, 1984; Assassing, 1984; Kayleigh (No. 2, UK), 1985; Lavender, 1985; Heart of Lothian, 1985; Incommunicado,

1987; Sugar Mice, 1987; Warm Wet Circles, 1987; Freaks, 1988; Hooks In You, 1989; Uninvited Guest, 1989; Easter, 1990; Cover My Eyes (Pain and Heaven), 1991; No One Can, 1991; Dry Land, 1991; Sympathy, 1992. *Current Management:* Hit and Run Music Ltd, 30 Ives St, London SW3 2ND, England.

KELLY Paul; b. 23 July 1962, England. Musician (guitar); Songwriter. *Career:* with groups: East Village; Saint Etienne; British tours, 1988–90 with East Village; Played with Saint Etienne, 1992–; Tours: UK; Europe; Japan; USA; Festivals: Glastonbury; Roskilde; Hultsfred; Television includes: Top of The Pops; The Beat; The Word; Later With Jools Holland; Glastonbury, 1994; BBC Radio 1 session with St Etienne, 1994. *Recordings:* Albums: with East Village: Drop Out; Hot Rod Hotel; with Birdie: Some Dusty, 1999; Triple Echo, 2001.

KELLY R (Robert); b. 8 Jan. 1969, Chicago, Illinois, USA. Prod.; Vocalist; Musician; Songwriter. *Career:* Began work with band Public Announcement; Wrote and produced hits for Aaliyah, Mary J. Blige, Toni Braxton, The Isley Brothers, Kelly Price and Janet Jackson; Wrote You Are Not Alone, recorded by Michael Jackson for HIStory album; Produced soundtrack for film Lifers featuring Eddie Murphy. *Recordings:* Singles include: Why You Wanna Play Me, 1990; She's Got That Vibe, 1991; Sex Me, 1993; Your Body's Callin', 1994; Bump N' Grind (No. 1, USA), 1994; Summer Bunnies, 1994; You Remind Me of Something, 1995; Down Low, 1996; I Can't Sleep, 1996; I Believe I Can Fly (No. 1, UK), 1997; Gotham City, 1997; Half on a Baby, 1998; Home Alone, 1999; I'm Your Angel, with Celine Dion (No. 1, USA), 1998; Did You Ever Think?, 1999; If I Could Turn Back The Hands of Time, 1999; Satisfy You, with Puff Daddy, 2000; Only The Loot Can Make Me Happy, 2000; I Wish, 2000; Albums: Born into the 90's, 1992; 12 Play, 1993; R Kelly, 1995; R, 1998; TP-2.com, 2000. *Honours:* Grammy Awards for Best Male R & B Vocal Performance, Best R & B Song and Best Song Written For a Motion Picture, Television or Other Visual Media.

KELLY Roger; b. 3 April 1953, Balby, Doncaster, England. Musician (guitar). m. Sabine Kirchner, divorced. *Education:* BA Hons, Business Studies. *Musical Education:* Self-taught. *Career:* Toured with Streetband (with Paul Young); Appeared Top of The Pops, 1979; Appeared Rock Palast, Germany with Starry-Eyed and Laughing; Session work with Sandy Shaw in 1980s; Teaching and transcription work, also production. *Recordings:* Albums: Streetband: London; Dilemma; Hit single: Toast (B Side of Hold On) 1979; Co-wrote, produced all album, single material with Paul Young and co-member, John Gifford. *Membership:* PRS. *Leisure interests:* Guitar playing; Reading; Cycling. *Address:* 1 Salvington Gardens, Worthing, Sussex, England.

KELSEY Peter R; b. 25 Jan. 1949, Lincoln, England. Recording Engineer; Prod. m. Catherine Deguilly, 22 Oct. 1985, 2 d. *Education:* BSc Hons, Mathematics. *Career:* Started Trident Studios, London, 1972; Chief Engineer, 1976; Freelance Engineer, 1978; Moved to USA, 1979; Freelance engineer and producer, recordings, film and television music. *Recordings:* Goodbye Yellow Brick Road, Elton John; Heat Treatment, Graham Parker; Discreet Music, Brian Eno; Dialects, Zawinul; Sans Regrets, Veronique Sanson; Outside From The Redwoods, Kenny Loggins; with Kitaro: Mandala; Heaven and Earth; 7 albums with Jean-Luc Ponty including Mystical Adventures; No Absolute Time; Television: Thirtysomething; Picket Fences; Tekwar; Films: Color of Night; Best of Best 2; Poison Ivy. *Honours:* NME Engineering Award, Cafe Jacques, 1976; Emmy Nomination, Kenny Loggins, 1994; Emmy Award, sound mixing for Ally McBeal, 1998–99. *Memberships:* NARAS; Re-Pro; ATAS. *Leisure interests:* Reading; Computers; Tennis; Tae Kwon Do. *Address:* 11022 Haskell Ave, Granada Hills, CA 91344, USA.

KEMANIS Aina; b. 15 June 1952, Berkeley, California, USA. Singer. Folk/Rock background. *Career:* Contemporary Jazz with Barre Phillips, 1979–82; Sang in Kitka, Eastern European Women's Chorus, 1987–88; Toured Europe and Scandinavia with Marilyn Mazur, 1988–99; Member Alex Cline Ensemble, 1987–99. *Recordings:* Journal Violone II, 1979; The Lamp and The Star, 1989; Future Song, 1993; Montsalvat, 1995; Small Labyrinths, 1997; Sparks Fly Upward, 1999. *Address:* 3 South Trail, Orinda, CA 94563, USA.

KEMP Gary; b. 16 Oct. 1959, Islington, London, England. Musician (guitar); Songwriter; Actor. *Career:* Founder member, Spandau Ballet (originally the Makers), 1979–90; Performances include: Royal Albert Hall, 1982; Royal Festival Hall, 1982; Wembley Arena, 1984; Live Aid, Wembley, 1985; Solo appearances: Labour Party Red Wedge Tour, 1986; Prince's Trust Rock Gala, 1987; Actor, films: The Krays (with brother Martin), 1988; The Bodyguard, 1992; Killing Zoe, 1994; Dog Eat Dog, 2001. *Compositions:* All hit singles by Spandau Ballet. *Recordings:* Singles include: To Cut A Long Story Short, 1980; The Freeze, 1981; Musclebound, 1981; Chant No. 1 (I Don't Need This Pressure On), 1981; Instinction, 1982; Lifeline, 1982; Communication, 1983; True (No. 1, UK), 1983; Gold, 1983; Only When You Leave, 1984; I'll Fly For You, 1984;

Highly Strung, 1984; Round and Round, 1984; Fight For Ourselves, 1986; Through The Barricades, 1986; Be Free With Your Love, 1989; Sample of True used as basis for Set Adrift On Memory Bliss, PM Dawn (No. 1, USA), 1991; Albums: Journeys To Glory, 1981; Diamond, 1982; True, 1983; Parade, 1984; The Singles Collection, 1985; Through The Barricades, 1986; Heart Like A Sky, 1989; The Best of Spandau Ballet, 1991; Gold, 2001; Solo album: Little Bruises, 1995. *Honours include:* BRIT Award, Sony Trophy for Technical Excellence, 1984. *Current Management:* Steve Dagger, Dagger Enterprises, 14 Lambton Pl., London W11 2SH, England.

KEMP Martin; b. 10 Oct. 1961, Islington, London, England. *Education:* Acting lessons, Anna Scher's Children's Theatre, 1970. *Career:* Member, Spandau Ballet, 1979–90; Concerts include: Royal Albert Hall, Sadlers Wells, Royal Festival Hall, London, 1983; Live Aid, Wembley, 1985; TV special, Ibiza 92, 1987; Actor, films: The Krays (with brother Gary), 1988; Waxwork II – Lost In Time, 1992; Actor, television series: Growing Rich, 1991; EastEnders, 1998-. *Recordings:* Albums: Journeys To Glory, 1981; Diamond, 1982; True, 1983; Parade, 1984; The Singles Collection, 1985; Through The Barricades, 1986; Heart Like A Sky, 1989; The Best of Spandau Ballet, 1991; Gold, 2001; Singles include: To Cut A Long Story Short, 1980; The Freeze, 1981; Musclebound, 1981; Chant No. 1 (I Don't Need This Pressure On), 1981; Paint Me Down, 1981; Instinction, 1982; Lifeline, 1982; Communication, 1983; True (No. 1, UK), 1983; Gold (used for BBC's Olympics coverage, 1984), 1983; Only When You Leave, 1984; Highly Strung, 1984; Round and Round, 1984; Fight For Ourselves, 1986; Through The Barricades, 1986; Be Free With Your Love, 1989; Contributor, Do They Know It's Christmas?, Band Aid, 1984. *Honours include:* BRIT Award, Sony Trophy For Technical Excellence, 1984. *Current Management:* AIM, 5 Denmark St, London WC2H 8LP, England.

KENDALL Tony, (The Essex Man); b. 9 May 1944, Walthamstow, Essex, England. Musician (acoustic bass, guitar, fiddle). m. Carole Anne Bailey, 18 June 1966, 1 d. *Education:* East Ham CAT, London University. *Musical Education:* Self-taught. *Career:* Collector, writer, performer, traditional and original songs, County of Essex (1000 songs in repertoire); Regular broadcaster for BBC Essex; Appeared at Royal Festival Hall, London Barbican, folk club, history societies nationwide; Musician, Chingford Morrismen, Barnet Fair Ceilidh Band; Good Easter Molly. *Recordings:* Albums: Rose of Essex; Closer To The Heartland; An Essex Terret; A Christmas Wassail; A Bicycle Ride With Vaughan Williams, 1995. *Memberships:* Musicians' Union; PRS; MCPS. *Leisure interests:* Countryside issues; Local history; Campaigner for (sufferer from) ME. *Current Management:* Stormforce Arts. *Address:* 18 Edward Ave, Chingford, London E4 9DN, England.

KENNEDY Brian; b. 12 Oct. 1966, Belfast, Northern Ireland. Vocalist; Musician (guitar); Songwriter. *Career:* Toured internationally and recorded with Van Morrison's band; Performed duet with Morrison in Belfast for President Clinton's visit, viewed by TV audience of one billion; Toured with The Corrs and Tina Turner; Appeared on film soundtracks: When A Man Loves A Woman; Moondance; Broadway debut in Riverdance, 2000; Recent collaboration with Juliet Turner. *Recordings:* Albums include: with Van Morrison: One Night In San Francisco, 1993; No Prima Donna, 1994; Days Like This, 1995; The Healing Game, 1997; Back On Top, 1999; featured on: Ronan, Ronan Keating, 2000; solo: The Great War of Words, 1990; A Better Man, 1996; Now That I Know What I Want, 1999; Get On With Your Short Life, 2001. *Honours:* A Better Man gained quadruple platinum status in Ireland; IRMA, Best Irish Male Album; Hot Press/2TV Award, Best Irish Male Artist. *Internet:* www.briankennedy.co.uk.

KENNEDY Peter Douglas; b. 18 Nov. 1922, London, England. Ethno-Musicologist. m. Beryl, 3 s., 1 d. *Education:* Architectural Association School of Architecture, London, 1940–42. *Career:* Sometimes referred to as Mr Folk; Was main catalyst in post-war Folk Revival in England; North East Area Representative, English Folk Dance and Song Society, 1947–48; Joined BBC Staff, Bristol, 1949; Started mobile recording of traditional folk singers and instrumentalists, Britain and Ireland, 1950–; Leader, own Haymakers Folk Dance band, including Village Barn Dance radio broadcasts, 1951; BBC Folk Music and Dialect Recording Scheme, with Seamus Ennis, 1952–58; EFDSS staff, London, 1958–68; Established Performers Booking Agency and first Folk-song Club in London; Co-organizer, first National Folk Festival, Keele University, 1964, and National Folk Federation, 1965; Degree Lecturer, Folk Studies, Dartington College of Arts, Totnes, Devon, 1969–79; Set up International Folk Archive, 1980; Regular radio and television broadcaster, 1950–70; As I Roved Out, 1953–57. *Recordings:* Numerous field recordings of traditional singers and players, customs, dialect and traditions, 1950–; Also recorded many well-known folk performers including Ewan McColl, Bert Lloyd, The Dubliners and the Liverpool Spinners; Recent CDs include: Sea Songs and Shanties; Songs of the Travelling People, 1994; Traditional Songs of Ireland, 1995; Bagpipes of Britain and Ireland, 1996; Traditional Dance Music of Ireland, 1997; English Customs and Traditions, 1997; World Library of Folk and Primitive Music: England and Yugoslavia, 1998. *Publications include:* The Fiddler's Tunebook, 2 Vols, 1951, 1953;

Everybody Swing, Square Dance music, 1952; Editor, UNESCO International Folk Film Directory, 1970; Editor, International Folk Directory, 1973; The Folk-songs of Britain and Ireland, 1975; Fiddler's Book of Reels, 1997; Fiddler's Book of Jigs, 1998; Fiddler's Book of Hornpipes, 1999. *Honour:* McColvin Award, Outstanding Reference Book of 1975. *Memberships:* The English Folk Dance and Song Society; The Folklore Society; The Society for Folk-Life Studies. *Address:* Folk and Blues International Archive, 16 Brunswick Sq., Gloucester GL1 1UG, England.

KENNELL Richard W (Rick); b. 8 Nov. 1952, Fort Wayne, Indiana, USA. Musician (bass guitar); Recording Artist; Record Prod. m. Leah Marie Waybright, 8 Jan. 1976. *Education:* Indiana University; James Madison University. *Recordings:* 6 albums currently available: Happy The Man; Happy The Man; Crafty Hands; Better Late; Beginnings; Retrospective; Happy The Man Live; Death's Crown; Also: Run Into The Ground. *Memberships:* ASCAP; NARAS; AES. *Leisure interests:* Basketball; Working in studio. *Current Management:* The Inner Circle. *Address:* 77 Tarrytown Rd, Suite 201, White Plains, NY 10607, USA.

KENRICK Hilgrove; b. 13 Feb. 1977, Birmingham, England. Freelance Composer; Musician (Piano, Voice, Clarinet, Tenor Saxophone). *Education:* ABRSM Grades in Theory, Piano and clarinet. *Career:* Piano Singer, West Midlands, 1994–96; Resident Pianist, Harry Ramsden's, Birmingham, 1995; Scores for Solihull School dramatic production The Right Place, 1995; Macbeth, 1996; Music Director, Handsworth Parish, 1996–97; Choirs: Birmingham Cathedral, Head Chorister, Blue Coat School, Selhell Barbershop Quartet. *Compositions:* Theatrical score, Death Threat, 1997; Film score, Witchcraft, 1998; Music for Methodist Youth Conference, NEC Birmingham, 1999. *Recordings:* Produced album, In Remembrance of Me, R-Men, 1996; Ad-Hoc, One Hot Day, 1999. *Membership:* Musicians' Union. *Leisure interests:* Skiing; Windsurfing. *Address:* 37 Richmond Hill Rd, Edgbaston, Birmingham B15 3RR, England.

KENT Jeffrey John William; b. 28 July 1951, Stoke-on-Trent, England. Musician (Vocals, Keyboards, Percussion); Writer; Lecturer. m. Rosalind Ann Downs, 14 July 1987. *Education:* BSc Econ, Hons, International Relations, University of London, 1973; Postgraduate Teaching Certificate, Crewe College of Higher Education, 1974. *Career:* Freelance Writer, 1972–; Performing Musician, 1975–; Dragon Fair, 1984; Open Air Concert, Chamberlain Square, Birmingham, 1984; Green Party Conference Concert, 1987; Artists for the Planet Concert, 1989; Appearance on BBC Midlands TV, launching new album, 1992. *Compositions:* Butcher's Tale/ Annie with the Dancing Eyes, single, 1981; Tales from the Land of the Afterglow, Part 1, Part 2, 1984; Port Vale Forever, album, 1992; Only One World, album, scheduled for release, 2000. *Recordings:* all compositions recorded. *Publication:* Port Vale Forever album song book, 1992. *Leisure interests:* Composing; Research and writing; Co-ordinator, Mercia Movement. *Address:* Cherry Tree House, 8 Nelson Cres., Cotes Heath, via Stafford ST21 6ST, England.

KENT Rolfe; b. 18 April 1963, St Albans, Hertfordshire, England. Composer; Film Composer. *Education:* BSc Hons, Psychology, Leeds University. *Career:* Film scores: Final Combination, 1993; Voices From A Locked Room, 1995; Mercy, 1995; Television scores: Big City Metro, 1989; Shalom Joan Collins, CH4, 1989; So Haunt Me, BBC, 1991; Inside Out, 1990; Musicals: Air and Opportunity, 1995. *Honour:* AICP (American Independent Commecial Producers) Award, Best Music, 1993. *Memberships:* PRS; AFofM; BMI. *Leisure interests:* Hiking; Watching Sumo wrestling; Travel. *Current Management:* David May, Santa Monica, California, USA.

KENYON Duncan; b. 10 Dec. 1961, Wembley, Middlesex, England. Rehearsal Studio Owner; Musician (bass guitar, guitar). m. 6 Sept. 1991, divorced 1993. *Musical Education:* Self-taught from age of 8 years. *Career:* With French Impression; Toured with The Cool Notes; Support to Rose Royce; Odyssey; German television Oldie Parade with Hello, performed Tell Him and New York Groove; Currently touring with Hello. *Recordings:* Singles with French Impression: Breaking Love, 1984–5; Get Up and Dance; Currently recording Hello album, and Christmas songs. *Memberships:* PRS; Musicians' Union. *Leisure interests:* All sports; Social hobbies. *Current Management:* David Blaylock. *Address:* 39 Leyton Rd, Harpenden, Herts AL5 2JB, England.

KERNON Neil Anthony; b. 13 Sept. 1953, London, England. Record Prod.; Sound Engineer. m. Kellie O'Neal, 13 July 1991. *Career:* Recording engineer, Trident Studios, UK, 1971–75; Le Chateau d'Herouville, France, 1975; Startling Studios, UK, 1976–79; Independent producer, USA, 1979-. *Recordings:* As engineer, producer: Albums with Hall and Oates: Voices, 1980; Private Eyes, 1981; H2O, 1982; Rock 'n' Soul Part 1, 1983; Sign In Please, with Autograph, 1984; with Dokken: Under Lock and Key, 1985; Back For The Attack, 1987; Singles: with Hall and Oates: Kiss On My List, 1980; Private Eyes, 1981; I Can't Go For That, 1981; Maneater, 1982. *Honours:* Platinum and Gold discs. *Leisure interests:* Sport; Travel; Films.

Current Management: Louis Levin Management, 130 W 57th St, #10B, New York, NY 10019, USA.

KERR Jim; b. 9 July 1959, Glasgow, Scotland. Singer. m. (1) Chrissie Hynde, 1984, divorced, 1 d., (2) Patsy Kensit, 1993, divorced, 1 s. *Career:* Founder, Scottish rock group Simple Minds, 1978–; World-wide tours and concerts include: WOMAD Festival, Somerset, 1982; Phoenix Park, Dublin, 1983; Support to the Pretenders, US tour, 1984; Live Aid, Philadelphia, 1985; Headliners, Milton Keynes Bowl Pop Festival, 1986; Nelson Mandela 70th Birthday Tribute, 1988; Nelson Mandela – An International Tribute concert, Wembley, 1990. *Recordings:* Albums: Life In A Day, 1979; Real To Real Cacophony, 1980; Empires and Dance, 1980; Sons and Fascinations, 1981; Sister Feelings Call, 1981; Celebration, 1982; New Gold Dream, 1982; Sparkle In The Rain (No. 1, UK), 1984; Once Upon A Time (No. 1, UK), 1985; Live In The City of Light (No. 1, UK), 1987; Street Fighting Years (No. 1, UK), 1989; Themes (4 vols), 1990; Real Life, 1991; Glittering Prize 81–92, 1992; Good News From The Next World, 1995; Neapolis, 1998, Neon Lights, 2001; Hit singles include: Promised You A Miracle, 1982; Glittering Prize, 1982; Someone Somewhere (In Summertime), 1982; Waterfront, 1983; Speed Your Love To Me, 1984; Up On The Catwalk, 1984; Don't You Forget About Me, used in film Breakfast Club (No. 1, USA), 1985; Alive and Kicking, 1985; Sanctify Yourself, 1986; All The Things She Said, 1986; Ghostdancing, 1986; Promised You A Miracle (Live), 1987; Belfast Child (No. 1, UK), 1989; This Is Your Land, 1989; Kick It In, 1989; The Amsterdam EP, 1989; Let There Be Love, 1991; See The Lights, 1991; Stand By Love, 1991; Love Song, 1992; She's A River, 1995; Hypnotized, 1995; Glitterball, 1998. *Honours include:* Q Award, Best Live Act, 1991. *Current Management:* Clive Banks, 1 Glenthorne Mews, 115A Glenthorne Rd, London W6 0LJ, England.

KERR Nancy; b. 29 July 1975, England. Vocalist; Musician (violin, viola, cello, guitar, mandolin); Composer. *Career:* Daughter of folk singer Sandra Kerr; Plays predominantly traditional material, both instrumentals and songs; Toured and recorded with Eliza Carthy and also made an album with mother before forming duo with Australian musician James Fagan. *Recordings:* Eliza Carthy and Nancy Kerr, 1993; Shape of Scrape (with Eliza Carthy), 1995; with Sandra Kerr: Neat and Complete, 1996; Scalene, 1999; with James Fagan: Starry Gazy Pie, 1997; Steely Water, 1999; Between The Dark and The Light, 2002; features on: Waterson Carthy, 1994; Yellow Red and Gold, Sandra Kerr, 2000; Mazurka Berserker, John Kirkpatrick, 2001. *Honours:* BBC Horizon Award, Best New Act, Nancy Kerr and James Fagan, 2000.

KERR Sandra, (Sandra Joan Faulkner); b. 14 Feb. 1942. Vocalist; Musician (concertina, guitar); Songwriter. *Career:* Folk singer, mother of Nancy Kerr; Recorded music for UK children's TV series Bagpuss with John Faulkner; Member of female vocal group Sisters Unlimited with Janet Russell, Rosie Davis and Peta Webb; Perform close harmony renditions of contemporary and traditional songs exploring women's issues; Recently recorded and toured with daughter and James Fagan. *Recordings:* John and Sandra, 1969; Nuclear Power, 1981; Supermum, 1984; We Were There, 1987; Neat and Complete (with Nancy Kerr), 1996; Scalene (with Nancy Kerr and James Fagan), 1999; Yellow Red and Gold, 2000; with Sisters Unlimited: No Limits, 1991; No Bed of Roses, 1995; features on: Nancy Kerr and James Fagan Albums: Starry Gazy Pie, 1997; Steely Water, 1999.

KERSHAW Martin John; b. 13 July 1944, Shipley, Yorkshire, England. Musician (guitar, banjo, bouzouki, mandolin, ukelele); Composer. Divorced, 1 d. *Musical Education:* Self-taught. *Career:* Member, number of bands including Manfred Mann; Moved to London, 1966; Played with: John Dankworth Big Band; Jack Parnell Orchestra; James Last Orchestra; Session guitarist; Guitarist on all 120 Muppet Shows; Television shows, performances include: Perry Como, Michael Jackson; Randy Crawford; Kate Bush; John Denver; Jack Jones; David Essex; David Bowie; Elton John; Buddy Rich; Johnny Cash; Ray Charles; Tom Jones; Glen Campbell; Bing Crosby; Petula Clark; Crystal Gayle; Diana Ross; Dusty Springfield; Andy Williams; Linda Ronstadt; Dizzy Gillespie; Burt Bacharach; Peggy Lee; Perry Como; Julie Andrews; Englebert Humperdinck; Playing featured in films including: Passage To India; Mad Max Thunderdome; Little Shop of Horrors; Diamonds Are Forever; Ghandi; You Only Live Twice; Live and Let Die; TV series, Riders; Began composing, 1983–; Recently toured with Sasha Distel. *Compositions include:* Film: Nightmare Weekend; Commercials include: Sainsbury's; Interflora; Persil; Dulux Paint; Unipart; Boots; TV Themes: Eurosport coverage Olympic Games, 1992; Russell Harty Show; London Programme; Incidental music includes: Prisoner Cell Block H; A Bouquet of Barbed Wire; Cagney and Lacey; Within These Walls; Promotional videos; Titles for Production Music Libraries include: Bruton; Music House; Peer; Weinberger. *Memberships:* Musicians' Union; PRS. *Leisure interests:* Fishing; Birdwatching. *Current Management:* Broadley Music. *Address:* 1 Bramley Close, Pewsey, Wilts SN9 5HB, England.

KERSHAW Nik (Nicholas David); b. 1 March 1958, Bristol, England. Singer; Musician (guitar); Songwriter. m. Sheri. *Career:* Member, jazz-funk group Fusion; Solo artiste, with backing band The Krew, 1983-. *Compositions include:* The One and Only, Chesney Hawkes (No. 1, UK), 1991. *Recordings:* Albums: Human Racing, 1984; The Riddle, 1984; Radio Musicola, 1986; The Works, 1990; The Collection, 1991; Wouldn't It Be Good, 1994; The Best of Nik Kershaw, 1998; 15 Minutes, 1999; Singles: I Won't Let The Sun Go Down On Me (No. 2, UK), 1984; Wouldn't It Be Good, 1984; Somebody Loves You, 1999; Guest musician, Nikita, Elton John, 1985.

KERSHAW Sammy, (Samuel Cashat); b. 24 Feb. 1958, Abbeville, Louisiana, USA. Country vocalist; Songwriter; Musician (guitar); Actor. *Career:* Played in local bands, including Blackwater; DJ work; Cut first singles for local labels (later collected on a 1993 MTE Records album entitled Sammy Kershaw); Recording contract with Mercury Records after performing a showcase for Harold Shedd and Buddy Cannon; First Billboard charting single Cadillac Style released, 1991; Hits continued throughout the 1990s; Appeared in the film Fall Time directed by Paul Warner, 1995. *Recordings include:* She Don't Know She's Beautiful, 1993; Love of My Life, 1997; Third Rate Romance, 1994; National Working Woman's Holiday, 1994; Cadillac Style, 1991; Albums include: Don't Go Near The Water, 1991; Haunted Heart, 1993; Feelin' Good Train, 1994; Politics, Religion and Her, 1997; Labor of Love, 1997; Maybe Not Tonight, 1999; The Hits – Chapter One, 1995; Coverin' The Hits, 2000; The Hits – Chapter Two, 2001. *Current Management:* James Dowell Management, 50 Music Sq. W, Suite 207, Nashville 37203, USA. *Internet:* www.sammykershaw.com.

KERSHAW Steve P; b. 17 March 1959, Bradford, Yorkshire, England. Musician (double bass, bass guitar). *Education:* Bristol University, BA Hons, 1978–81; PhD, 1986. *Musical Education:* Bass Institute of Technology, Hollywood, California. *Career:* Member, British Youth Symphony Orchestra, 1978–82; After Hours; False Idols; Then There Were Six; Claude Bottom and The Lion Tamers; The Honkin' Hep Cats; The Rascals of Rhythm; Stekpanna; The John Hoare 4; The Flat Back Four; Television: Out West, HTV; ITV Telethon; Film: The Clothes In The Wardrobe; Great Moments in Aviation; Radio: The Usual Suspects; Jungr and Parker At The Edinburgh Festival; Loose Ends; Mary Costello Show; Breakfast Breakout; Honkin' With The Hep Cats At The Edinburgh Festival. *Recordings:* with After Hours: All Over Town, 1980; with False Idols: Ten Seconds To Midnight, 1981; Centre of Attention, 1985; Fine Blue Line, 1987; with L'Orange, Si J'Etais Vous, 1991; with The Honkin' Hep Cats: What's The Use?, 1989; Honkin' 'n' Stompin', 1992; Rantin' Ravin' 'n' Misbehavin', 1994; with Stekpanna: Standin' Tall, 1997; with The Steve Tayton Quartet and The Rolls Royce Brass Band, Dark To Light, 1999; with Luis D'Agostino, Otros Caminos, 1999; with The Flat Back Four, Dig-Dig. *Honours:* Outstanding Vocational Honours Award, GHS, 1996, Outstanding Student of the Year Award, Fender, 1996, Musicians Institute. *Memberships:* Musicians' Union; International Society of Bassists. *Leisure interests:* Cricket; Rugby League; Malt Whisky. *Current Management:* Flat Five Management. *Address:* 5 Cardwell Cres., Headington, Oxford OX3 7QE, England.

KERWIN Michael Thomas; b. 19 Feb. 1970, Freiburg, Germany. Prod.; Engineer. *Education:* Hons in Music, Humber College, 1994. *Career:* Founder, Newmarket Multimedia Recording Studio, 1994; Co-Founder, Limit Records Inc, 1995. *Recordings:* Producer, Engineer: 30 Odd 6, 1996; Beru's Nephew, 1996; Stone Idols, 1997; Co Producer, Engineer: Woodrow, 1997; The Salads, 1997; Engineer: Sarah Sloan, 1997; Al Connelly, 1996. *Current Management:* Last Call Promotions, Unit 5, Newmarket, ON, L3Y 3E3, Canada. *Address:* 312 Maple St, Newmarket, ON L3Y 3K3, Canada.

KEVORKIAN Francois; b. 10 Jan. 1954, Rodez, France. Prod.; Remixer; DJ; Musician (drums). *Career:* Drummer with various French bands before relocation to New York in 1975; Continued to perform in nightclubs until finding work as DJ at New York New York; A & R work for disco label Prelude Records led to remix projects – firstly Musique's In the Bush; Subsequently remixed: D-Train, Yazoo, Depeche Mode, The Cure; Opened Axis Studios in New York; Founder of Wave Records; Resident DJ at Body and Soul club in New York. *Recordings:* Singles: FK EP, 1995; Time and Space, 1998. *Current Management:* c/o Wave Records, King St, New York City, New York USA.

KEYS Alicia; b. 25 Jan. 1981, Manhattan, USA. Vocalist; Musician (piano); Songwriter. *Musical Education:* Classically trained pianist; Professional Performance Arts School, Manhattan, majored in Choir Studies. *Career:* Signed to Clive Davis' new J Records label, 1999; Appeared at all-star charity telethon in aid of World Trade Center tragedy victims, 2001; Collaborations: Angie Stone; Jimmy Cozier. *Recordings:* Albums: Songs In A Minor, 2001; Singles: Girlfriend, Fallin', A Woman's Worth, 2001. *Honours:* American Music Awards, six nominations, 2002; Grammy Awards, six nominations; Billboard Awards, 8 nominations, 2001; Debut album quadruple platinum in USA. *Address:* c/o Jeff Robinson, MBK Entertainment Inc, 156 W 56th St, New York, NY 10019, USA. *Internet:* www.aliciakeys.net.

KHALADJ Madjid; b. 11 Nov. 1962, Ghazvin, Iran. Musician (percussion; tombak); Composer. *Education:* Graduate, School of Fine Arts, Paris. *Musical Education:* Graduate, Traditional Academy of Persian Art Music, Iran. *Career:* Concerts and radio appearances: Grand Palais, Paris, 1991; Barbad Symposium, Tadjikstan, with Master Shadjarian, 1991; Grande Auditorium de Radio France, with Master Alizadeh, 1992, 1994; Opéra de Lille, 1992; Los Angeles Festival, USA, J Paul Getty Museum, 1993; Théâtre de la Ville, Paris, 1993; Théâtre de la Colline and Radio France, with Master Tala'i, 1994. *Recordings:* Persian Classical Music, 1992; Persian Art Music, 1992; Iran-The Art of Tombak, 1993; Music of Iran, Vols 1 and 2, 1993; Iranian Music, Improvisations, 1994; Persian Classical Music, 1994; Los Angeles Festival, 1995; Tombak and Percussion, 1996; Anthology of Iranian Rhythms, Vol. 1, 1997; Vol. 2, 1999. *Honours:* Hon. guest, nominated professor at the Centre for Oriental Studies, Paris, Sorbonne Musicology Institute, 1984-. *Membership:* SACEM. *Current Management:* Madjid Khaladj Management, 56, rue de Sèvres, 92100 Boulogne, France.

KHALED, (Khaled Hadj Brahim, Cheb Khaled); b. 29 Feb. 1960, Wahrane, Algeria. Vocalist; musician (keyboard, accordion); Songwriter. *Career:* Member: The Five Stars; First recording, aged 14; First hit Trigue Al Lissi (The Way To School), 1975; Lyrics censored in Algeria until 1983; Relocated to Paris, 1990; First international rai hit Didi (produced by Don Was), 1992; Collaborations: Chaba Zahouania; Rachid Taha and Faudel; over 100 cassettes released. *Recordings:* Albums include: Rai King of Algeria, 1985; Fuir Mais Ou?, 1991; Khaled, 1992; N'ssi N'ssi, 1993; Sahra, 1996; Kenza, 1997; Les Monstres Sacrés du Rai; Ya Taleb (with Chaba Zahouania). *Honours:* Crowned King of Rai at the first rai festival in Oran, 1985; Cesar Award, Best Soundtrack, N'ssi N'ssi.

KHAN Ali Akbar; b. 14 April 1922, Shivpur, Bangladesh. Musician (sarode); Composer. *Career:* Musician, 1936–; Numerous tours, concerts and major festivals world-wide, 1955–; Founder, Ali Akbar College of Music, Calcutta, India, 1956; San Rafael, California, 1968; Basel, Switzerland, 1982; Collaborations with artists including: Yehudi Menuhin; Ravi Shankar; Duke Ellington; Lecture recitals, major universities, US and Canada; Owner, record company Alam Madina Music Productions; Founder, Ali Akbar Khan Foundation, 1994; MacArthur Foundation Fellowship, 1991. *Compositions:* Concerti, orchestral pieces and ragas, including Chandranadan; Gauri Manjari; Alamgiri; Medhavi. *Recordings include:* Legacy, 1996; Passing on the Tradition, 1996. *Honours:* Five Grammy Nominations, 1970, 1983, 1996–98; for films: Devi; Householder; President of India Award, 1963, 1966; Grand Prix Du Disque, 1968; Hon DLitt Rabindra Bharati University, Calcutta, 1974; Padmabhibhushan Award, 1989; Dr of Arts, California Institute of Arts, 1991; Kalidas Award, 1992; Bill Graham Lifetime Award, BAM, 1993; Meet the Composer Award, 1996; National Heritage Fellowship, National Endowment for the Arts, 1997; Asian Paints Shiromani Award – Hall of Fame, Calcutta, 1997; Governor's Award for Outstanding Achievement, NARAS, 1998; Indira Gandhi Gold Plaque, Asiatic Society, Calcutta, 1998; Swaralaya Puraskaram Award, New Dehli, 1999; Appointed Distinguished Adjunct Professor of Music, University of California at Santa Cruz, 1999. *Current Management:* Gregory Digiovine, Santana Management, 121 Jordan St, San Rafael, CA 94901, USA. *Address:* Ali Akbar College of Music, 215 West End Ave, San Rafael, CA 94901, USA.

KHAN Chaka, (Yvette Stevens); b. 23 March 1953, Great Lakes, Illinois, USA. Singer. *Career:* Member, Afro-Arts theatre, Chicago; Member, groups Shades of Black; Lock and Chain; Rufus, 1972–79; Renamed Rufus and Chaka Khan, 1978; Appearances include: Support to Elton John, Wembley, 1975; Rock 'n' Bowl, for US Special Olympics, 1977; Solo artiste, 1978–; Concerts and tours include: European tour, 1988; World tour, 1992; A Night On The Town Concert Tour, 1993; Montreux Jazz Festival, 1993; North Sea Jazz Festival, The Hague, 1993; JVC Jazz Festival, Nice, 1993. *Recordings:* Albums: with Rufus: Rufus, 1979; Rags To Rufus, 1974; Rufusized, 1975; Rufus Featuring Chaka Khan, 1976; Ask Rufus, 1977; Street Player, 1978; Numbers, 1979; Masterjam, 1980; Camouflage, 1981; Party 'Til You're Broke, 1981; Live – Stompin' At The Savoy, 1983; Life Is A Dance – The Remix Project, 1989; Sweet Things – Greatest Hits, 1993; Solo albums: Chaka, 1978; Naughty, 1980; What Cha' Gonna Do For Me, 1981; Chaka Khan, 1983; I Feel For You, 1984; Destiny, 1986; C.K., 1989; The Woman I Am, 1992; Come 2 My House, 1998; I'm Every Woman, 1999; Contributor, Echoes of An Era, Lenny White, 1982; Rock Rhythm and Blues compilation, 1989; Music of Quality and Distinction compilation, 1991; Hallelujah!, Quincy Jones, 1992; Hot House, Bruce Hornsby, 1995; Hit singles: with Rufus: Tell Me Something Good, 1974; You Got The Love, 1974; Once You Get Started, 1975; Sweet Thing, 1976; Solo singles: I'm Every Woman, 1979; Ain't Nobody, 1983; I Feel For You, 1984; This Is My Night, 1985; Eye To Eye, 1985; Own The Night (used in television series Miami Vice), 1986; Love of a Lifetime, 1986; Underground, duet with David Bowie, for film Labyrinth, 1986; Feels Like Heaven, duet with Peter Cetera, 1992; Don't Look at Me That Way, 1993; Miles Blowing, 1995; Love Me Still, 1995; Never Miss the Water, 1996; Contributor, Dreamland, Joni Mitchell, 1978;

Stuff Like That, Quincy Jones, 1978; Higher Love, Steve Winwood, 1986; I'll Be Good To You, Quincy Jones, 1990. *Honours:* Grammy Awards: Best R & B Vocal Performance, Chaka Khan, Best R & B Performance, Ain't Nobody, Best Vocal Arrangement, Be Bop Medley, 1984; Best Female R & B Vocal Performance, I Feel For You, 1985; Best R & B Performance, The Woman I Am, 1993; Gold discs. *Current Management:* The Brokaw Company, 9255 Sunset Blvd, Suite 804, Los Angeles, CA 90069, USA.

KHAN Steve Harris; b. 28 April 1947, Los Angeles, California, USA. Musician (guitar); Prod. *Musical Education:* BA, Composition, UCLA. *Career:* Solo guitarist and prolific session musician. *Recordings:* Solo albums: Tightrope, 1977; The Blue Man, 1978; Arrows, 1979; Evidence, Best Of, 1980; 1981; Blades, 1982; Eyewitness, 1983; Casa Loco, 1983; Helping Hand, 1987; Local Colour, 1988; Public Access, 1990; Let's Call This, 1991; Crossing Bridges, 1993; Got My Mental, 1996; You Are Here, 1998; Other recordings with numerous artists including: Ashford and Simpson; Patti Austin; George Benson; Michael and Randy Brecker; Billy Cobham; Judy Collins; Larry Coryell; Blood, Sweat and Tears; Luther Allison; Donald Fagen; Aretha Franklin; Billy Joel; Chaka Khan; Kenny Loggins; David Sanborn; Phoebe Snow; Steel Dan; Grover Washington; Bob James. *Publications:* Wes Montgomery Guitar Folio, 1978; Pat Martino Guitar Solos, 1991; Steve Khan Song Book, 1991. *Current Management:* Christine Martin Management. *Address:* 688 Hands Creek Rd, East Hampton, NY 11937, USA.

KHANYILE Jabu; b. 1959, Soweto, South Africa. Vocalist; Songwriter. *Musical Education:* Self-taught: Guitar; Percussion. *Career:* Earned living through busking; Member: The Editions; The Movers; Joined Bayete as drummer; Bayete disbanded, 1993; Reformed under Khanyile. *Recordings:* Albums include: Mbombela, 1987; Hareyeng Haye, 1990; Mmalo-we (world-wide release), 1994; Umkhayalo, 1995; Africa Unite, 1997; Prince Umbele 2001. *Honours:* Mmalo-We certified gold and won various South African Awards; Kora Award, Best Artist or Group from Southern Africa, 2000; SAMA Award, Best Duo or Group, 2001. *Address:* c/o Gallo Records, PO Box 2897, Parklands 2121, South Africa. *Internet:* www.gallo.co.za.

KHARISSOV Ildar; b. 21 Jan. 1972, Yelabuga, Russia. Musicologist; Ethnomusicologist. *Education:* State Conservatoire of Kazan; Free University of Berlin. *Publications:* Towards Stability and Mobility In The Melodics of The Trtar, Ozon Koj, 1998; Tartar Song In Berlin, 1999. *Membership:* International Council For Traditional Music. *Leisure interest:* Quarter Tone Techno Music. *Address:* Erich Weinert Str 21, 20 10439 Berlin, Germany.

KHOZA Valanga; b. 21 Dec. 1959, Tzaneen, South Africa. Singer; Songwriter; Musician (Kalimba, Guitar, Marimbas, Kora, Mouthharp, M'bira, flute). *Education:* University of South Africa, Pietersburg; BA, Business Accounting, Goshen University, Indiana, USA. *Career:* Solo peformance, Hemisphere, 5 piece acapella and percussion; Band Safika, 8 piece; Toured Australia extensively; Support act to Geoffrey Oryema, Lucky Dube, 1996; Lady Smith Black Mambazo, 1995; Soweto String Quartet, 1997; Major festivals all over Australia; Festival of Cultures, Sydney Opera House; Images of Africa, Festival Copenhagen, Denmark, 6 weeks tour, 1996; ABC Music Deli Program (radio); Jaslyn Halls World Music; Live to air, Australian Broadcasting Commission. *Recording:* Sebe. *Honour:* Finalist, Aria Awards World Music Category, 1996. *Leisure interests:* Running; Developing new instruments. *Current Management:* KU Promotions, Box 77, Uki, 2484, Australia.

KID COCO (Marc Diericx); b. 11 Nov. 1964, Ghent, Belgium. Singer; Composer; Musician (guitar, keyboards). *Career:* Lead vocalist, The Dinky Toys, 1981–94; Solo artiste, 1995-. *Recordings:* Albums: with The Dinky Toys: The Colour of Sex, 1992; Colourblind, 1993; Keep Hope Alive, 1994. *Honours:* Several No. 1 and Top 10 hits; Platinum album; ZAMU Award, Best Live Performer, 1994. *Membership:* SABAM/ZAMU. *Current Management:* Luc Standaert, Tempo Belgium. *Address:* Krijgslaan 61–9000 Gent, Belgium.

KID CREOLE (August Twelfth Darnell); b. 12 Aug. 1950, Bronx, New York, USA. Entertainer; Singer. 4 s., 3 d. *Education:* BA, Hofstra University. *Career:* Leader, Kid Creole and the Coconuts; World-wide tours, 15 years; Member, Dr Buzzard's Original Savannah Band, 3 years; Starred in West End Production of Oh What A Night, London. *Recordings:* Hit singles include: Me No Pop I, with Coati Mundi, 1981; I'm A Wonderful Thing, Baby, 1982; Stool Pigeon, 1982; Annie I'm Not Your Daddy (No. 2, UK), 1982; Dear Addy, 1982; There's Something Wrong In Paradise, 1983; The Lifeboat Party, 1983; The Sex of It, 1990; Albums include: Tropical Gangsters, 1982; Fresh Fruit In Foreign Places, 1982; Doppelganger, 1983; Cre-ole, 1984; Private Waters in the Great Divide, 1990; Kiss Me Before the Light Changes, 1995; To Travel Sideways, 1995; Too Cool To Conga, 2001. *Honours include:* BPI Best International Act, Kid Creole, 1982. *Memberships:* BMI; AFTRA. *Leisure interests:* Rowing; Sailing; Cycling; Antique cars.

KIDJO Angelique; b. 1960, Ouidah, Benin. Vocalist; Songwriter. m. Jean Hebrail. *Career:* Performed with mother's theatre group from age 6; Later in the Kidjo Brothers Band; One of Benin's only professional female singers by age 20; Moved to Holland, then Paris; Signed to Island Records, 1989; Collaborations: Carlos Santana; Manu Dibango; Branford Marsalis; Toured US with Dave Matthews Band, Neville Brothers and Macy Gray, 2001. *Recordings:* Albums include: Parakou, 1989; Logozo, 1991; Aye, 1994; Fifa (featuring Carlos Santana), 1996; Oremi (featuring Branford Marsalis), 1998; featured on soundtracks: Ace Ventura 2; Ma Saison Preferee. *Internet:* www.angeliquekidjo.com.

KIEDIS Anthony, (Antoine the Swann); b. 1 Sept. 1962, Grand Rapids, Michigan, USA. Vocalist. *Career:* Member, Red Hot Chili Peppers; Appeared as Sylvester Stallone's son in F.I.S.T.; Met Flea, Hillel Slovak and Jack Irons at high school; Formed Red Hot Chili Peppers and obtained deal with EMI records; Numerous line-up changes; Hillel Slovak dies and Jack Irons leaves; Joined by John Frusciante and Chad Smith; Musical contribution to The Simpsons. *Recordings:* Abbey Road EP, 1988; Higher Ground, 1989; Taste the Pain, 1989; Give It Away, 1991; Under The Bridge, 1992; Suck My Kiss, 1992; Breaking the Girl, 1993; If You Have to Ask, 1993; Soul 2 Squeese EP, 1994; My Friends, 1995; Aeroplane, 1996; Love Rollercoaster, 1997; Warped, 1998; Scar Tissue, 1999; Behind the Sun, 1999; Around The World, 1999; Otherside, 1999; Californication, 2000; Albums: Red Hot Chili Peppers, 1984; Freaky Styley, 1985; The Uplift Mofo Party Plan, 1987; Mother's Milk, 1989; BloodSugarSexMagik, 1991; Live, Rare, Remixed, 1994; Out in LA, 1994; One Hot Minute, 1995; Californication, 1999; Guest vocals, Blowback, Tricky, 2001. *Honours include:* Grammy Award, Songwriter, Rock Song, Scar Tissue, 2000.

KIENLEIN Kevin D; b. 12 July 1960, Vernon, BC, Canada. Singer; Entertainer; Songwriter; Musician (Guitar, Fiddle, Violin, Bass, Organ, Piano, Tenor Banjo); Inspirational speaker. *Career:* First performances were: organ at church, guitar, church coffeehouse; Joined The BC Oldtime Fiddlers, 1980; Joined The Velvet Rodeo Band, 1989; Solo performances; Joined String Loaded Bluegrass, 1995; at Festivals, Special Events, Benefits, Concerts, 1995–; Inspirational Speaking. *Compositions:* 16 Original Fiddle Tunes Published In 169 Brand New Oldtime Fiddle Tunes, 12 In Canadian Fiddle Music. *Recordings:* Fiddlers Rag; Heartbeats. *Memberships:* SOCAN, BC Oldtime Fiddlers; National Oldtime Fiddlers Asscn; BC Country Music Asscn; Canadian Country Music Asscn; Catgut Acoustical Society. *Leisure interests:* Amateur Ham Radio; Stamp Collecting; Darts; Billiards; Painting; Repairing Violins; Fishing. *Current Management:* Krash Productions. *Address:* 3101 18 Ave, Vernon, BC Canada V1T 1C6.

KIERAN (Donley); b. 1 Nov. 1970, Manchester, England. DJ; Record Prod.; Recording Artist. *Musical Education:* Self-taught. *Career:* Promoting Spectrum Oxford; Dance music DJ at Universe and Fantazia among many others; Recording artist as: Oxide and Hoi Polloi. *Membership:* Musicians' Union. *Leisure interests:* Walking; Squash; Dancing. *Current Management:* Adrian Hicks, Equation. *Address:* 9 Cavell Rd, Oxford, England.

KILGORE Merle; b. 8 Sept. 1934, Chickasha, OK, USA. Artist Man. m. Judy Kilgore, 1 s., 2 d. *Career:* Louisiana Hayride; Coal Muhers Daughter; Nashville; WW and The Dixie Dance Kings; Roadie; Living Proof; Willa. *Compositions:* Ring of Fire; Wolverhampton MT; More and More; Johnny Reb; Baby Rocked Her Dolly; She Went A Little Bit Farther. *Recordings:* Dear Mama; Love Has Made You Beautiful. *Honours:* SRD Manager of The Year, 1990; Louisiana Hall of Fame, 1993; Byrd High School Hall of Fame, 1993. *Memberships:* CMA; NSAI; ROPE; NSF; AFM; SAG. *Leisure interest:* Boating. *Current Management:* Merle Kilgore Management. *Address:* 2 Music Circle S, Nashville, TN 37203, USA.

KILKELLY Frank; b. 17 Sept. 1960, Republic of Ireland. Musician (acoustic guitar). *Education:* BSc, Marketing. *Musical Education:* Piano lessons, miscellaneous guitar teachers. *Career:* Regular touring in Europe, USA; Television includes: Pebble Mill At One, BBC; Anderson On The Box, BBC, Northern Ireland; Kenny Live, RTE, Ireland; Late Late Show, RTE, Ireland; Radio broadcasts: Digby Fairweather's Jazz Notes, BBC2; Anderson's Fine Tunes; Travelling Folk, BBC Scotland. *Recordings:* Luke Daniels, Tarantella, CD, 1994; Zumzeaux, Blazing Fiddles, CD, 1995; Kimbara Brothers, Now!, cassette, 1995; Kimbara Brothers, Time To Leave, CD, 1995; Power and Kilkelly, Jig Jazz, CD, 1996; Simon Mayor: New Celtic Mandolin, video, 1997; Mandolin Essentials, CD, 1997; Simon Mayor: New Celtic Mandolin, CD, 1998; Maggie Boyle Gweebarra, CD, 1998; Pierre Schryer and Dermot Byrne, CD, 1999; with The Grappelli Trio: Gipsy Swing, 2000. *Publication:* Accompanying Irish Music on Guitar, book and CD, 1999. *Leisure interests:* Music; Non-competitive sports. *Current Management:* Brass Tacks, Orchard House, Gloucester Rd, Hartpury, Gloucestershire GL19 3BG, England.

KIMBALL Bobby (Robert Toteaux); b. 29 March 1947, Vinton, Louisiana, USA. Vocalist. *Career:* Supported acts including: Jackson Browne; Aretha Franklin; Barbra Streisand; Lead vocalist, Toto,

1978–84; Solo artiste, 1984–; Member, Far Corporation. *Recordings:* Albums: with Toto: Toto, 1979; Hydra, 1979; Turn Back, 1981; Toto IV, 1982; Isolation, 1984; Past to Present, 1990; Toto XX, 1998; Mindfields, 1999; Solo: Rise Up, 1996; Singles: with Toto: Hold The Line, 1979; Georgy Porgy, 1980; 99, 1980; Rosanna, 1982; Make Believe, 1982; Africa (No. 1, USA), 1983; I Won't Hold You Back, 1984; with Far Corporation: Stairway To Heaven, 1986; Woods to Stock, 1995; Backing vocalist, albums by Boz Scaggs: Silk Degrees, 1976; Down Two Then Left, 1977. *Honours:* 6 Grammy Awards with Toto: Best Record, Best Album, Best Producer (Toto), Best Engineered Recording, Best Vocal Arrangement, Best Instrumental Arrangement, 1983. *Current Management:* Artists International Management, 9850 Sandalfoot Blvd, Suite 458, Boca Raton, FL 33428, USA.

KINCAID Jan; b. 17 May 1966, Ealing, London, England. Musician (Drums). *Career:* Founder Member, The Brand New Heavies; Obtained independent label record deal; Worked with several vocalists including Jaye Ella Ruth, N'Dea Davenport, Siedah Garrett and Carleen Anderson; Numerous television appearances and live dates. *Recordings:* Singles: Stay This Way, 1991; Never Stop, 1991; Dream Come True, 1991; Spend Some Time, 1994; Dream on Dreamer, 1994; Mind Trips, 1995; You've Got A Friend, 1997; You Are the Universe, 1997; Sometimes, 1997; Shelter, 1998; Saturday Nite, 1999; Apparently Nothing, 2000; Albums: The Brand New Heavies, 1990; The Brand New Heavies, 1992; Heavy Rhyme Experience, 1992; Brother Sister, 1994; Original Flava, 1994; Excursions, 1995; Shelter, 1997.

KING AD-ROCK (Adam Horowitz); b. 31 Oct. 1966, Manhattan, New York, USA. Rapper; Musician (guitar). *Career:* Founder member, US rap/rock group Beastie Boys, 1983–; Appearances include: Support to Madonna, Virgin Tour, 1985; Supports to Run DMC, Raisin' Hell Tour, 1986; Coheadliners with Run DMC, Together Forever Tour, 1987; Reading Festival, 1992; Film appearances: Krush Groove; Run DMC film Tougher Than Leather; Scared Stupid; Acting roles: The Equalizer, TV series; Santa Ana Project; Lost Angels; Roadside Prophets. *Recordings:* Singles: She's On It, 1987; Fight For Your Right To Party, 1987; No Sleep Till Brooklyn, 1987; Girls/She's Crafty, 1987; Hey Ladies, 1989; Pass The Mic, 1992; Get It Together/Sabotage, 1994; Sure Shot, 1994; Intergalactic, 1998; Body Movin', 1998; Remote Control, 1999; Alive, 1999; Albums: Licensed To Ill, 1986; Paul's Boutique, 1989; Check Your Head, 1992; Ill Communication, 1994; Root Down, 1995; The In Sound From Way Out, 1996; Hello Nasty (No. 1, UK and US), 1998; Sounds of Science, 1999. *Current Management:* Gold Mountain Entertainment. *Address:* 3575 Cahuenga Blvd W, Suite 450, Los Angeles, CA 90068, USA.

KING B B (Riley); b. 16 Sept. 1925, Itta Bena, Mississippi, USA. Singer; Musician (guitar). *Musical Education:* Self-taught guitar. *Career:* Performed with the Elkhorn Singers; Played with Sonny Boy Williamson, 1946; Regular broadcast slot, The Sepia Swing Show, Radio WDIA; Averaged 300 performances a year, 1950s-70s; Numerous world-wide tours with wide variety of R & B and pop artistes; Appearances include: Newport Jazz Festival, 1969, 1989; Atlantic City Pop Festival, 1969; Atlanta Pop Festival, 1970; Mar Y Sol Festival, Puerto Rico, 1972; Kool Jazz Festival, New York, 1983; Live Aid concert, Philadelphia, 1985; Benson and Hedges Blues Festival, Dallas, 1989; JVC Jazz Festival, Newport, 1990; Memphis In May Festival, 1991; Montreux Jazz Festival, 1991; San Francisco Blues Festival, 1991; Guitar Legends, Expo '92, Seville, Spain, 1991; Westbury Music Fair, New York, 1993; Pori Jazz, Finland, 1995; Opened B B King's Memphis Blues Club, Memphis, Tennessee, 1991. *Recordings:* Albums: Completely Well, 1970; The Incredible Soul of B. B. King, 1970; Indianola Mississippi Seeds, 1970; Live In Cook County Jail, 1971; Live At The Regal, 1971; B B King In London, 1971; LA Midnight, 1972; Guess Who, 1972; The Best Of.., 1973; To Know You Is To Love You, 1973; Friends, 1974; Lucille Talks Back, 1975; King Size, 1977; Midnight Believer, 1978; Take It Home, 1979; Now Appearing At Ole Miss, 1980; There Must Be A Better World Somewhere, 1982; Love Me Tender, 1982; Blues 'n' Jazz, 1984; Six Silver Strings, 1986; Live At San Quentin, 1991; Blues Summit, 1993; Lucille and Friends, 1995; Live in Japan, 1999; Makin' Love Is Good For You, 2000; A Christmas Celebration of Hope, 2001; Anthology, 2001; with Bobby Bland: Together For The First Time – Live, 1974; Together Again – Live, 1976; Hit singles include: Three O'Clock Blues; You Didn't Want Me; Please Love Me; You Upset Me Baby; Sweet Sixteen; Rock Me Baby; The B. B. Jones (used in film soundtrack For The Love of Ivy); The Thrill Is Gone; Blues Come Over Me; Also featured on: Happy Anniversary, Charlie Brown!, 1989; When Love Comes To Town, U2, 1989; Heroes and Friends, Randy Travis, 1990; The Simpsons Sing The Blues, 1990. *Honours include:* Grammy Awards: Best Male R & B Vocal Performance, 1971; Best Ethnic or Traditional Recording, 1982; Best Traditional Blues Recording, 1984, 1986, 1991, 1992; with Dr John: Pop Collaboration With Vocals, 2001; with Eric Clapton: Traditional Blues Album, Riding With The King, 2001; Inducted into Rock and Roll Hall of Fame, 1987; Lifetime Achievement Awards include: NARAS, 1988; Songwriters Hall of Fame, 1990; Gibson Guitars, 1991; Star in Hollywood Walk of Fame, 1990; MTV Video Award, with U2, 1989;

Q Inspiration Award, 1992. *Membership:* Co-chairman, Foundation For The Advancement of Inmate Rehabilitation and Recreation. *Current Management:* Sidney A. Seidenberg Inc, 1414 Sixth Ave, New York, NY 10019, USA.

KING Ben E (Benjamin Earl Nelson); b. 28 Sept. 1938, Henderson, North Carolina, USA. Singer; Songwriter. *Career:* Singer, bands including The Four Bs; The Moonglows; The Crowns; Featured vocalist, The Drifters, 1957–60; Solo artiste, 1960–; Cabaret and club circuit, 1968–73; Member, Soul Clan, 1978; Rejoins The Drifters for tours, 1978–; Appearances include: San Remo Festival, Italy, 1964; Prince's Trust Rock Gala, Wembley Arena, 1987; Glastonbury Festival, 1987; Television: UK television debut, Ready Steady Go!, 1964; David Letterman's Sixth Anniversary Special, 1988. *Compositions include:* Co-writer, There Goes My Baby; Co-writer, Don't Play That Song (also recorded by Aretha Franklin); Stand By Me, later used in: film soundtrack, Stand By Me, 1986; Levi 501 jeans commercial (No. 1, UK) 1987; How Can I Forget. *Recordings:* Albums: Supernatural, 1975; Let Me Live In Your Life, 1978; Music Trance, 1980; Street Tough, 1981; Stand By Me (The Ultimate Collection), 1987; Dancing In The Night, 1987; Save The Last Dance For Me, 1988; Anthology, 1993; Drifters, 1996; Shades of Blue, 1999; Eleven Best, 2001; Hit singles include: with The Drifters: There Goes My Baby, (No. 2, US); Dance With Me; True True Love; This Magic Moment; Save The Last Dance For Me (No. 1, US; No. 2, UK); I Count The Tears; Solo: Spanish Harlem; Stand By Me (R & B No. 1, USA); Amor; I Who Have Nothing; Seven Letters; Supernatural Thing (R & B No. 1, USA); Other recordings: with Average White Band: Benny and Us, 1977; Book of Love, with Bo Diddley, featured in film Book of Love, 1991; Guest vocalist, Coast To Coast, Paul Shaffer, 1989. *Honour:* One of BMI's Most Performed Songs 1940–90 (over 3m. plays), Stand By Me, 1990. *Current Management:* Randy Irwin Associates. *Address:* 7231 Radio Rd, Naples, FL 33942, USA.

KING Bob (Robert); b. 2 July 1955, Kilmarnock, Scotland. Musician (guitar). m. Hazel, 30 March 1974, 2 s. *Education:* Diploma of Higher Education. *Career:* Appearances most major country music festivals include: Americana, British and Irish Country Music Festival, Worthing; The Inverness Festival of Country Music. *Recordings:* Several compositions recorded by artists in Ireland. *Honours:* Sylvia Saunders Trophy Winner, 1994; Several Act of The Year Awards throughout career. *Memberships:* PRS; Equity. *Leisure interest:* All aspects of information technology (computers). *Address:* 10 Hector Rd, Longsight, Manchester M13 0QN, England.

KING BRITT, (The Force, Oba Funke); b. Philadelphia, Pennsylvania, USA. Prod.; Remixer; DJ. *Career:* Started as on-tour DJ for Philadelphia rap outfit Digable Planets; Co-founder: Ovum Records (with Josh Wink); Formed Sylk 130; Debut album released on Ruffhouse/Columbia, 1998; World-wide DJ; Residency at London's The End club; Collaborations: Josh Wink; Vikter Duplaix; Martin Fry; Alison Moyet; Remixed: 4Hero; Donna Lewis; Tori Amos; Jazzanova; Macy Gray. *Recordings:* Albums: When The Funk Hits The Fan (with Sylk 130), 1998; Re-Members Only (with Sylk 130), 2001; Singles: Tribal Confusion (as E-Culture), 1991; Strong Song (as Just King and Wink), 1992; Supernatural (as Firefly), 1995; Last Night A DJ Saved My Life (with Sylk 130), 1998. *Current Management:* Elite Music Management, PO Box 3261, Brighton, East Sussex, BN2 4WA, England. *Internet:* www.kingbritt.net.

KING Carole; b. 9 Feb. 1942. Singer; Songwriter. *Career:* Songwriter in partnership with Gerry Goffin; Worked with artists including: Eric Clapton; Crosby and Nash; Branford Marsalis; David Sanborn; Numerous concerts and tours; Actress in theatre including: Starring role, Mrs Johnstone, Broadway production, Blood Brothers, 1994; Environmental activist for natural forest preservation; Studied European traditional music. *Compositions:* Hit songs include: Will You Love Me Tomorrow; Take Good Care of My Baby; Go Away Little Girl; The Locomotion; Up On The Roof; Chains; One Fine Day; Hey Girl; I Feel The Earth Move; Natural Woman; Smackwater Jack; You've Got A Friend; Now and Forever (For film, A League of Their Own); Soundtrack, animated film, Really Rosie. *Recordings include:* Albums: The City, 1968; Writer, 1970; Tapestry, 1971; Rhymes and Reasons, 1972; Music, 1972; Fantasy, 1973; Wrap Around Joy, 1974; Thoroughbred, 1975; Really Rosie, 1975; Simple Things, 1977; Welcome Home, 1978; Greatest Hits, 1978; Touch The Sky, 1979; Pearls, 1980, 1994; One To One, 1982; Speeding Time, 1983; City Streets, 1989; For Our Children, 1991; A League of Their Own, 1992; 'Til Their Eyes Shine, 1992; Colour of Your Dreams, 1993; In Concert, 1994; Time Gone By, 1994 A Natural Woman, 1994; Carnegie Hall Concert, 1996; Goin' Back, 1998; Love Makes The World, 2001; Single: Anyone at All, 1999. *Honours include:* Inducted Songwriters' Hall of Fame, 1987; Rock and Roll Hall of Fame, 1990; National Academy of Songwriters' Lifetime Achievement Award, 1988; Grammy Awards; Multi-Platinum, Platinum and Gold albums; Academy Award Nomination, Now and Forever. *Memberships:* AFTRA; AMPAS: NARAS; NAS; SAG; AFofM. *Current Management:* Lorna Guess. *Address:* 11684, Ventura Blvd, #273, Studio City, CA 91604, USA.

KING Eileen Maria Goretti; b. 6 Aug. 1959, Bandbridge, Co Down, Northern Ireland. Singer. m. Joe Rafferty, 21 July 1987. *Education:* College. *Career:* Television apperances: BBC, UTV, RTE; Concerts include: Wembley Festival; Fanfare Grand Ole Opry, Nashville; Has recorded in Nashville, The Fireside Studios; The Porter Wagoners Studio. *Recordings:* 6 albums. *Honours:* Won numerous music awards. *Membership:* Equity. *Leisure interests:* Cinema; Sport. *Current Management:* JR Promotions. *Address:* 229 Newtownhamilton Rd, Armagh, Co Armagh, Northern Ireland.

KING Evelyn 'Champagne'; b. 1 July 1960, Bronx, New York, USA. Singer. *Career:* Soul/dance music singer, 1977-. *Recordings:* Albums: Smooth Talk, 1977; Music Box, 1979; Call On Me, 1980; I'm In Love, 1981; Get Loose, 1982; Face To Face, 1983; So Romantic, 1984; A Long Time Coming, 1985; Flirt, 1988; The Best Of, 1990; The Essential Works Of, 1992; Singles include: Shame, 1977; I Don't Know If It's Right, 1979; I'm In Love, 1981; Get Loose, 1982; Face To Face, 1983. *Address:* c/o Nationwide Entertainment Services, 2756 N Green Valley Parkway, Suite 449, Las Vegas, NV 89014–2100, USA.

KING Jonathan; b. 6 Dec. 1944, London, England. Singer; Music Journalist; Television Presenter. *Education:* English, Cambridge University. *Career:* Occasional recording artist, 1965–; Talent spotter for Decca Records (discovered Genesis, produced their first album); Launched UK Records, 1972; Newspaper and magazine columnist, radio and television presenter, including own show Entertainment USA, BBC, 1980s; Organizer, A Song For Europe (UK's Eurovision Song Contest qualification show), 1995-. *Recordings:* Solo albums: Or Then Again, 1965; King Size King, 1982; The Butterfly That Stamped, 1989; The Many Faces of Jonathan King, 1993; Singles include: As Jonathan King: Everyone's Gone To The Moon; Green Is The Grass; It's Let It All Hang Out; Una Paloma Blanca; Wild World; Involved in novelty hits including: Johnny Reggae, The Piglets'; Sugar Sugar, Sakkarin; The Same Old Song, The Weathermen; Leap Up and Down (Wave Your Knickers In The Air), St Cecilia; Producer: Genesis, 4 albums; Rocky Horror Picture Show, 1984; Kylie Minogue; Eric Felton.

KING Mark; b. 20 Oct. 1958, Isle of Wight, England. Vocalist; Musician (bass). *Career:* Founder member, Level 42, 1980–; Regular international tours, 1983–; Concerts include: Prince's Trust Rock Gala, 1986, 1987, 1989; Crystal Palace Bowl, 1991; Midem Festival, Cannes, France, 1992. *Recordings:* Albums with Level 42: Level 42, 1981; The Pursuit of Accidents, 1982; Standing In The Light, 1983; A Physical Presence, 1985; World Machine, 1985; Running In The Family, 1987; Level Best, 1989; Guaranteed, 1991; Solo: Influences, 1984; One Man, 1999; Hit singles: The Chinese Way, 1983; The Sun Goes Down (Living It Up), 1983; Hot Water, 1984; Something About You, 1985; Leaving Me Now, 1985; Lessons In Love (No. 1 in 8 European countries), 1986; Running In The Family, 1987; To Be With You Again, 1987; It's Over, 1987; Heaven In My Hands, 1988; Tracie, 1988; Guaranteed, 1991. *Honours:* Making Music magazine poll, Best Bass Player, 1987; BMI Award, 1m. US performances, Something About You, 1991. *Current Management:* Paul Crockford Management, 56–60 Islington Park St, London N1 1PX, England.

KING Michael Weston; b. 11 Nov. 1961, Derbyshire, England. Singer; Songwriter; Musician (guitar). m. Ann Carter, Aug. 1987, 2 s., 1 d. *Career:* Lead singer, songwriter, Fragile Friends, 1982–87; Solo artist, 1988; Guitarist, Gary Hall and The Stormkeepers, 1989–93; Lead singer, songwriter, The Good Sons, 1993–; UK and European tours; Television appearances on BBC, ITV and RTE, Ireland; Broadcasts on various radio stations including sessions on BBC Radio 1. *Recordings:* Albums: with Fragile Friends: For Play; with The Stormkeepers: Garageheart; Wide Open To The World; with The Good Sons: Singing The Glory Down, 1995; The King's Highway, 1996; Wines, Lines and Valentines, 1997; Angels In The End, 1998; Singles: with Fragile Friends: Paper Doll; The Novelty Wears Off; with The Stormkeepers: Where The River Meets The Sea (EP); with The Good Sons: The Good Sons (EP), 1994; The Kings Highway, 1996; Wines, Lines and Valentines, 1997; Various songs recorded by other artists: Riding The Range, Townes Van Zandt; Watch My Dreamboats Sail, Tower of Strength, Carolyn Hester; In Her Father's Bed, Arthur Brown; From These Hills, Carolyn Hester, 1996; Rear View Mirror, Townes van Zandt, 1997; Out of the Blue Vol. I, 1995, Vol. II, 1996, Vol. III, 1997. *Current Management:* CMP. *Address:* 34 Market St, Southport, Merseyside PR8 1HJ, England.

KING Morgana; b. 4 June 1930, Pleasantville, New York, USA; Vocalist; Actor. *Career:* Trained as opera singer but switched to jazz, c. 1955; Recording career began with release of For You For Me Forever More on Mercury Records, 1956; Worked the New York City club circuit, late 1950s – early 1960s; Recorded for many labels including: Mercury; United Artists; Mainstream; Reprise; Verve; Muse; Acting roles include Mama Carmella Corleone in The Godfather trilogy. *Recordings:* Albums include: For You For Me Forever More, 1956; Morgana King Sings The Blues, 1958; A Taste of Honey, 1964; It's A Quiet Thing, 1965; Cuore Di Mama, 1972; Everything

Must Change, 1978; Simply Eloquent, 1986; This Is Always, 1992; Tender Moments, 2000.

KING Peter; b. 1941. Musician (alto saxophone). *Career:* Played opening night, Ronnie Scott's, 1959; Played, recorded with numerous American artists including: Zoot Sims; Philly Joe Jones; Red Rodney; Nat Adderley; Hampton Hawes; Big bands of Maynard Ferguson, Tubby Hayes; Own quartets, quintets, 1980s; Popular in France, extensive tours; Began with Ben Watt (Everything But The Girl), 1982; Featured soloist, Count Basie Band, 1990; Berlin Jazz Festival with Tete Montoliu, 1990; Partnership with Charlie Watts, appearances include: Ronnie Scott's, London and Birmingham, England; Blue Note, New York; Spiral Hall, Tokyo; Played with Horace Parlan Quartet, 1994; Tour of Spain; Festival, Belgium, 1990; Took place of Steve Grussman in quartet at festivals: Molde, Norway; Pori, Finland, 1994; Peter King Quartet, Top of The Bill, Ronnie Scott's, 1994; with Phil Woods, Jackie McLean, Count Basie Orchestra, Berlin Jazz Festival, 1994; with Rene Urtreger, Middleheim Festival, Belgium, 1994; with George Coleman, Ronnie Scott's, 1995; Adviser, Consultant to Christies Auction House, Sale of Charlie Parkers Grafton Saxophone. *Recordings:* New Beginning, 1982; East 34th Street, 1983; Peter King Quintet; Brother Bernard, 1988; Peter King In Paris; High Fly; Crusade; Tete Montoliu featuring Peter King; Speed Trap, 1996; Also featured on four Everything But The Girl albums.

KING Stove; b. 8 Jan. 1975, Ellesmere Port, Merseyside, England. Musician (Bass). *Career:* Formed Grey Lantern with Paul Draper and Dominic Chad; Changed name to Mansun; Numerous live and TV appearances. *Recordings:* Take It Easy Chicken, 1996; Egg Shaped Fred, 1996; Stripper Vicar; Wide Open Space; Legacy, 1998; Six, 1999; Albums: Attack of the Grey Lantern, 1997; Six, 1999.

KINNAIRD Alison Margaret; b. 30 April 1949, Edinburgh, Scotland. Musician (scottish harp, clarsach). m. Robin Morton, 23 Feb. 1976, 1 s., 1 d. *Education:* MA, Edinburgh University. *Musical Education:* Studied Scottish harp with Jean Campbell. *Career:* Freelance musician, 1971–; Concerts: Edinburgh; London; New York; San Francisco; Hawaii; Tokyo; Berlin; Presenter, The Music Show, Channel 4, 1995. *Recordings:* The Harp Key, 1978; The Harper's Gallery, 1980; The Harpers Land, 1983; Music In Trust I and II, 1988; The Quiet Tradition, 1989; Mactalla, 1994; features on: Gun Sireadh Gun Larraidh, Christine Primrose, 2001. *Publications:* The Harp Key; The Small Harp Tutor; Tree of Strings (with Keith Sanger). *Honours:* MTA Music Award, 1983; Living Tradition Award, 1995; MBE for Services to Music and Art, 1997. *Membership:* Life mem., The Clarsach Society. *Leisure interests:* Glass-engraver (other career); Family. *Current Management:* Robin Morton, Shillinghill, Temple. *Address:* Shillinghill, Temple, Midlothian EH23 4SH, Scotland.

KINNEY Sean; b. 27 May 1966, Seattle, Washington, USA. Musician (Drums). *Career:* Member, Alice in Chains; Numerous tours and TV appearances including MTV Unplugged. *Recordings:* Singles: Sap EP; Would?, 1993; Them Bones, 1993; Angry Chair, 1993; Down In A Hole, 1993; Grind, 1995; Heaven Beside You, 1996; Albums: Facelift, 1990; Dirt, 1992; Sap, 1992; Jar of Flies, 1994; Alice in Chains, 1995; I Stay Away, 1995; Unplugged, 1996.

KINSEY Tony; b. 11 Oct. 1927, England. Composer; Musician (drums, piano). m. Patricia, 1 d. *Musical Education:* Studied percussion with Bill West, Cozy Cole, Jazz College, New York; Composition, orchestration, arrangement with Bill Russo, Columbia College, Chicago. *Career:* Professional musician from age 18; Joined John Dankworth, as drummer with Dankworth 7; Preferred drummer in 1960s-70s, for visiting jazz stars including: Oscar Peterson; Ella Fitzgerald; Lena Horne; Sarah Vaughn; Billie Holiday; Ben Webster; Clarke Terry; Musical director, That's Life, BBC TV, 3 years. *Compositions include:* Films: Souvenir; On The Bridge; Televison: That's Life, BBC; Castle of Adventure, TVS; The John Bird Show, BBC; The Londoners, BBC; A Tribute To Her Majesty; Colour; Four Seasons; Life At The Limit; Two's Company; Over 100 commercials including: Lloyds Bank; Kellogg's Rice Krispies; Danish Bacon; Baby Cham; Domecq; Marshall Cavendish; Raleigh Bicycles; Classical compositions: Pictures; Three Suites For String Quartet; River Thames Suite; Alice Through The Looking Glass. *Recordings include:* (own compositions) Alice Through The Looking Glass; Classical Lines 1, 2; Time Gentlemen Please; How To Succeed In Business; Jazz At The Flamingo; The Tony Kinsey Quintet; Foursome; Lougerhythms; River Thames Suite; Aspects of Jazz; Jazz Scenes; Midnight Sax; It Had To Be You. *Current Management:* Soundtrack Music Management. *Address:* 22 Ives St, Chelsea, London SW3 2ND, England.

KIPPER (Marc Eldridge); b. 19 March 1962, Frimley, Surrey, England. Prod.; Arranger; Writer; Musician (guitar, keyboards). *Musical Education:* Guitar from 9 years old, Jazz and Classical training. *Career:* Member, One Nation; Toured with: Jeff Beck; The Temptations; Ruby Turner; MD with Beijing Spring; Toured with: Curtis Stigers; Richard Marx; 3 major tours as guitarist for Gary Numan. *Recordings:* with One Nation: Strong Enough;

Big Life Big Tears; Machine and Soul; with David Essex: Back 2 Back; with Sting: Brand New Day, 2000. *Publication:* The Complete Singer, 1995. *Membership:* PRS. *Leisure interests:* Skiing; Tennis; Motorcycling. *Address:* East Manor Barn, Manor Yard, Fringford, Bicester, Oxon OX6 9DQ, England.

KIRK Nicholas Kenneth; b. 27 Dec. 1945, Bradford, West Yorkshire, England. Musician (New Orleans jazz banjo); Electronics Engineer. *Education:* BSc Hons, University of Wales; Postgraduate Diploma in Communications, Southampton University; Postgraduate Diploma in R F and Microwave, Bradford University. *Musical Education:* Self-taught. *Career:* Appearances on radio and Television Wales with Clive Evans' River City Stompers, 1966–67; Appeared at the Keswick Jazz Festival, Bude Jazz Festival, Marsden Jazz Festival, and at jazz clubs and pubs in Yorkshire, Wales and South of England, with the Dennis Browne Creole Band; Appeared at the 100 Club in London with the New Era Jazzband; Author of British Patent for apparatus for Recording and Replaying Music (The Musical Arranger and Sequencer). *Composition:* Clouds. *Recording:* Float Me Down The River, with the Dennis Browne Creole Band, cassette; City of a Million Dreams, cassette. *Memberships:* Musicians' Union; Fellow, Royal Microscopical Society. *Leisure interests:* Mountaineering; Languages. *Address:* 36 Kilpin Hill Lane, Staincliffe, Near Dewsbury, West Yorkshire WF13 4BH, England.

KIRKE Simon Frederick; b. 28 July 1949, London, England. Musician (drums, guitar, piano); Songwriter. m. Lorraine Dellal, 15 Dec. 1982, 1 s., 3 d. *Musical Education:* Self-taught. *Career:* Member, Black Cat Bones; Founder Member, Free; Founder Member, Bad Company, 1973–83; Performed at 2 Isle of Wight Festivals; Many US tours, 2 world tours; Television: Several Top of The Pops; Radio includes: John Peel. *Compositions:* Bad Company with Paul Rodgers; Several songs on Free and Bad Company albums. *Recordings:* With Champion Jack Dupree: Single: I Haven't Done No One No Harm, 1968; Album: When You Feel the Feelin' You Was Feeling, 1968; With Free: Singles: All Right Now (No. 2, UK), 1970; My Brother Jake, 1971; Little Bit of Love, 1972; Wishing Well, 1973; Albums: Tons of Sobs, 1968; Free, 1969; Fire and Water, 1970; Highway, 1971; Live, 1971; Free At Last, 1972; Heartbreaker, 1973; The Free Story, 1973; Best of Free, 1991; Walk in My Shadow: An Introduction to Free, 1998; With Amazing Blondel: Albums: Blondel, 1973; Mulgrave Street, 1974; With Bad Company: Singles: Can't Get Enough; Feel Like Makin Love; Young Blood; If You Need Somebody; Holy Water; Here Comes Trouble; Hey Hey; Hammer of Love; Albums: Bad Company, 1974; Straight Shooter, 1975; Run With The Pack, 1976; Burning Sky, 1977; Desolation Angels, 1979; Rough Diamonds, 1982; 10 From 6, 1985; Fame and Fortune, 1986; Dangerous Age, 1988; Holy Water, 1990; Here Comes Trouble, 1992; Company of Strangers, 1995; Albums: With John Wetton, Caught in the Crossfire, 1980; With Wildlife, Wildlife, 1983; With Mick Ralphs, Take This, 1983; With Jim Colpody, Let the Thunder Die; Also recorded with Jim Diamond, Snowy White, Bon Jovi, Ringo Starr; John Wetton. *Honours:* Gold Disc, All Right Now; 12 Gold and Platinum Albums with Bad Company. *Membership:* Musicians' Union. *Leisure interests:* Photography; Golf; Skiing; Motorbikes. *Address:* c/o Gremlin Productions, PO Box 148, Fincham, Norfolk PE33 9EH, England.

KIRKPATRICK Chris (Christopher Allan); b. 17 Oct. 1971, Clarion, Pennsylvania, USA. Vocalist. *Education:* Associate of Arts Degree, Valencia College, Dayton, Ohio. *Musical Education:* Dance and vocal training at Rollins College, Ohio. *Career:* Member of boy band *N Sync signed to BMG Ariola Munich, 1997; First headline US tour, 1998; Appointed spokesman for Child Watch of North America; Owner of FuMan Skeeto clothing firm. *Recordings:* Albums: *N Sync, 1998; Home For Christmas, 1998; No Strings Attached, 2000; Celebrity, 2001; Singles include: I Want You Back, 1997; Tearin' Up My Heart, 1997; Let The Music Heal Your Soul (various artists charity single credited to Bravo All Stars), 1999; Music of My Heart (with Gloria Estefan), 1999; Bye, Bye, Bye, 2000; I'll Never Stop, 2000; It's Gonna Be Me, 2000; This I Promise You, 2000; Pop, 2001; Gone, 2001. *Honours:* *N Sync reported as music industry's biggest earners in 2000 (estimated $184m); Recognition at MTV and Billboard Awards; Presented with keys to City of Orlando, 2000. *Address:* c/o Wright Entertainment Group, PO Box 590009, Orlando, FL 32859–0009, USA. *Internet:* www.wegmusic.com.

KIRKPATRICK David Gordon (Slim Dusty); b. 13 June 1927, Kempsey, New South Wales, Australia. Entertainer; Country Singer; Recording Artist. m. Joy McKean, 22 Dec. 1951, 1 s., 1 d. *Career:* Called himself Slim Dusty, 1938; Records first songs: Song for the Aussies; My Final Song, 1942; Record six titles: When the Rain Tumbles Down in July, 1946; Launches Slim Dusty Show, 1954; Showground partnership with Frankie Foster, 1956–63; The Pub With No Beer, (Australia's first Gold Record Award), 1952; Released first album: Slim Dusty Sings, 1960. *Recordings:* Albums include: Slim Dusty Sings, 1960; Walk a Country Mile, 1979; No 50 Gold Anniversary, 1981; Trucks on the Track, 1985; Beer Drinking Songs of Australia, 1986; Neon City, 1987; G'day, 1989; Coming Home, 1990; Two Singers, One Song, 1991; Live into the Nineties, video, 1992; Country Way of Life, 1995; 91 Over 50, 1996; A Time to Remember,

1997; Makin' a Mile, 1997; Looking Forward Looking Back, 2000; Down The Dusty Road, 2001. *Publications:* Walk a Country Mile, autobiog w J Lapsley, 1979; Another Day, Another Town, autobiog w Co-auth, 1996. *Honours:* MBE, 1970; AO, 1998; Australian Country Music Roll of Reknown; Australian Record Industry Asscn Hall of Fame. *Membership:* Chairman, Country Music Asscn of Aust. *Leisure interests:* Fishing, painting, leatherwork. *Address:* PO Box 115, St Ives, NSW 2075, Australia.

KIRKPATRICK John Michael; b. 8 Aug. 1947, Chiswick, London, England. Musician (melodeon, button accordion, anglo concertina). m. Sue Harris, divorced. *Career:* Joined Hammersmith Morris Men in their second week, 1959; Took up the melodeon, button accordion and, finally, the anglo concertina whilst with them; Member: Albion Country Band; Magic Lantern; The Richard Thompson Band; Umps and Dumps; Steeleye Span; Brass Monkey; Trans-Europe Diatonique; Band of Hope; Played with numerous ceilidh bands and made many albums with, then wife, Sue Harris; Collaborations include: Leon Rosselson; Roy Bailey; Martin Carthy; Ashley Hutchings; Sandy Denny; Ralph McTell; Gerry Rafferty; Founder: The Shropshire Bedlams morris team, 1975; Performed with The Albion Band for National Theatre productions of Lark Rise and Candleford; Also worked with: The Victoria Theatre (later The New Victoria Theatre), North Staffordshire; The Orchard Theatre Touring Company, Devon; As songwriter, composer, choreographer and musical director, has contributed to over sixty plays in the theatre and on radio. *Recordings:* Albums include: Jump At The Sun, 1972; The Compleat Dancing Master (with Ashley Hutchings), 1974; Plain Capers, 1976; Going Spare, 1978; Three In A Row (The English Melodeon), 1983; Blue Balloon, 1987; Sheepskins, 1988; Earthling, 1994; Welcome To Hell (John Kirkpatrick Band), 1997; One Man and His Box, 1998, Mazurka Berserker, 2001; with Sue Harris: The Rose of Britain's Isle, 1974; Among The Many Attractions At The Show Will Be A Really High Class Band, 1976; Shreds and Patches, 1977; Facing The Music, 1980; Stolen Ground, 1989; with Junkera, Tesi and Kirkpatrick: Trans-Europe Diatonic, 1993; with Brass Monkey: Brass Monkey, 1983; See How It Runs, 1986; Sound and Rumour, 1998; Going and Staying, 2001; with Steeleye Span: Storm Force Ten, Live At Last, 1978; with Albion Band: No Roses, 1971; Battle of The Field, 1976; Larkrise To Candleford, 1979; BBC Sessions, 1998; with Band of Hope: Rhythm and Reds, 1994; features on: Richard Thompson albums: Henry The Human Fly, 1972; Hand of Kindness, 1983; Amnesia, 1988; Rumour and Sigh, 1991; Sweet Talker, 1991; Mirror Blue, 1994; Richard and Linda Thompson albums: I Want To See The Bright Lights Tonight, 1974; Hokey Pokey, 1974; First Light, 1978; Sunnyvista, 1979; Martin Carthy albums: Because It's There, 1979; Out of The Cut, 1982; Right of Passage, 1988; Leon Rosselson albums: That's Not The Way It's Got To Be (Roy Bailey and Leon Rosselson), 1975; Bringing In News From Nowhere, 1986; I Didn't Mean It, 1988; other featued appearances: Young Hunting, Tony Rose, 1970; Roy Bailey, 1971; Morris On, 1972; Sandy, Sandy Denny, 1972; Rave On, 1974; Amaranth, Shirley Collins, 1976; Julie Covington, 1978; Slide Away The Screen, Ralph McTell, 1979; Night Owl, Gerry Rafferty, 1979; Still Pause, Maggie Holland, 1983; Leaves From A Tree, Roy Bailey, 1988; The Tenement Year, Pere Ubu, 1988; Jali Roll, Dembo Konte and Kausu Kuyateh, 1991; Reve De Siam, Dan Ar Braz, 1992; Fanafody, Tarika Sammy, 1992; Till The Grass O'Grew The Corn, 1997; Wassail!, 1997; The Garden of Love, Frankie Armstrong, 1999. *Internet:* johnkirkpatrick.co.uk.

KISSEL Michael Case; b. New York, USA. Musician; Composer; Lyricist; Record Prod. m. Elena Thorton, 29 June 1985. *Career:* Former bandleader, Los Amigos de Las Americas, Honduras; Musician, composer, producer, vocalist, various artists include: The Drifters; The Pointer Sisters; Gloria Gaynor; Elvin Bishop; Jocelyn Brown; Otis Rush; Ernie Isley; Toots and The Maytals. *Recordings:* Albums: Surrender, Robin Clark and David Bowie, 1985; Healing Session, Babatunde Olatungi, 1991; Peace Is The World Smiling, Babatunde Olatungi, Pat Seeger, Taj Mahal, 1989; Film soundtracks: In The Blood, 1990; Best Shots, 1990; Pumping Iron II, 1985. *Memberships:* ASCAP; NARAS; Songwriters Guild; AFofM.

KITCHEN Elizabeth Jane; b. 1 April 1959, Rochdale, England. Composer; Aranger; Musician (drums). *Musical Education:* Studied with: James Blades; Gilbert Webster RNCM. *Career:* Writes, arranges for television: Playdays; Monster Cafe; Roundabout Stop; Dot Stop; Worked on films/TV: Life and Loves of a She Devil; King of The Ghetto; Played with the Blues Band; Barbara Dickson in Blood Brothers; Works with Chickenshed company. *Recordings:* Freelanced with the Hallé Orchestra; RLPO; Northern Ballet; Opera North; Written many theatre shows: Young Vic; Battersea Arts Centre. *Honours:* Graduate: RNCM; PRNCM. *Memberships:* PRS; MCPS. *Leisure interests:* Swimming; Sport; Eating. *Address:* 1 Warwick Rd, London N11 2SA, England.

KITT Eartha Mae; b. 26 Jan. 1928, Columbia, South Carolina, USA. Actress; Singer; Entertainer. 1 s. *Education:* High School of Performing Arts, New York. *Career:* Dancer and vocalist, Katherine Dunham Dance Group, 1948; Night club singer, Europe, 1949–; Appearances world-wide; Stage performances: Dr Faust, Paris, 1951; New Faces of 1952, New York,

1952; Mrs Patterson, Broadway, 1954; Shinbone Alley; The Skin of Our Teeth; The Owl and The Pussycat; Bunny; The High Bid; Timbuktu, Broadway, 1978; Blues In The Night, 1985; Follies, London, 1988; A Night At The Cotton Club, UK revue tour; Film appearances: New Faces, 1953; Accused, 1957; St Louis Blues, 1957; Mark of The Hawk, 1958; Anna Lucasta, 1959; Saint of Devil's Island, 1961; Synanon, 1965; Up The Chastity Belt, 1971; Dragonard; Ernest Scared Stupid, 1991; Boomerang, 1992; Fatal Instinct; Numerous television appearances include: I Spy; Mission Impossible; Played the original Catwoman in Batman series; Living Single; New York Undercover; Jack's Place; Matrix; Subject, documentary All By Myself, 1982; Featured, Unzipped, 1995; International concerts in over 100 countries. *Recordings:* Numerous albums include: Down To Eartha, 1955; Thursday's Child, 1956; Revisited, 1961; Bad But Beautiful, 1976; At Her Very Best, 1982; C'est Si Bon, 1983; I Love Men, 1984; The Romantic Eartha Kitt, 1984; That Bad Eartha, 1985; In Person At The Plaza, 1988; My Way, 1988; I'm Still Here, 1989; Best of Eartha Kitt, 1990; Live In London, 1990; Thinking Jazz, 1992; Back In Business, 1994; My Greatest Songs, 1998; The Best of Eartha Kitt, 1999; Purr-Fect – Greatest Hits, 1999; Excellent and Decadent, 2001. *Publications:* Autobiographies: Thursday's Child, 1954; Alone With Me, 1976; Confessions of a Sex Kitten, 1989. *Honours:* NANM Woman of The Year, 1968; Star on Hollywood Walk of Fame; 2 Tony Award Nominations: Mrs Patterson; Timbuktu; Emmy Award Nomination, I Spy; 3 Grammy Nominations; Academy Award Nomination, Anna Lucasta. *Current Management:* c/o Stan Scottland, JKE Services Inc, 404 Park Ave S, 10th Floor, New York, NY 10016, USA.

KJAER Torben Edvard; b. 26 Oct. 1946, Gentofte, Denmark. Jazz Musician (piano); Composer; Arranger; Conductor. m. Marianne Kampmann, 28 Sept. 1968, 1 s. *Musical Education:* Theory, Composition, Conducting, Institute Music and Science, University of Copenhagen, 1966–73; Studied with George Russell, 1971; Piano degree, Copenhagen Music Conservatory, 1973. *Career:* Professional Musician, 1973–; Pianist with: Dexter Gordon; Dizzy Gillespie; Ben Webster; Clark Terry; Al Grey; Roy Eldridge; Red Mitchell; Milton Batiste; Rasheema; Founder, own jazz quartet; Conductor, Danish Radio Jazz Group, 1973–79; Danish Radio Light Orchestra, 1979–88; Danish Radio Big Band; Royal Orchestra; Orchestra Leader, TV Shows, 1986–92; Composer/Arranger for numerous groups including Tritonius (Danish Gospel Choir) and Copenhagen Music Ensemble; Arrangements include: Chamber Version, Candide; Faust, Royal Theatre, Copenhagen; Arranger, musicals including: Guys and Dolls; My Fair Lady; Chicago; Kiss Me Kate; also music for television, radio, film, theatre, cabaret, commercials. *Compositions include:* Mass of Peace, 1976; Christmas Oratory, 1981; Concerto Grosso, 1983; David and Batseba, 1985. *Recordings include:* Whalesongs, 1983; Jazz In Danish, 1988; Tower At The End of The World, 1988; Stolen Moments, Rasheema, 1995. *Honours:* Awards, Danish State Fund of Art; Best Popular Composer, 1979. *Membership:* Vice President, Danish Jazz, Beat and Folk Music Authors. *Address:* Skovvej 12, 2820 Gentofte, Denmark.

KJELLEMYR Bjorn; b. 4 Dec. 1950, Bamble, Norway. Bassist (Accoustic and Electric). m. Mette Havrewold, 2 s. *Musical Education:* Academy of Music, Oslo. *Career:* European tours mainly with Terje Rypdal, appearing at festivals and other concerts, appearing with Joe Henderson, Chet Baker, and Palle Mikkelborg. *Recordings:* Chasers, 1986; Blue, 1988; Singles Collection, 1989; If Mountains Could Sing, 1995; Heat, 1995; Electronique Noire, 1998. *Honours:* Jazz Musician of The Year, Norway, 1991; Buddy Award, 1995. *Current Management:* PJP, 5000 Bergen, Norway.

KKOSHI Chaz (The Bat); b. 3 Feb. 1962, London, England. Record Prod.; Musician (keyboards, drums); Vocalist. m. Maria Capsalis, 23 May 1993, 1 d. *Education:* Tottenham Technical College, A Level Technical Drawing. *Musical Education:* Trinity Musical College Grade 8, pianoforte. *Career:* Spartacus World Tour, 1982; Hammersmith Odeon, Double Take, Eurovision, 1986; BBC Radio 1 Roadshow, 1992, 1994, 1995; 6 O'Clock Show, LWT, 1991; The Word, 1994; Des O'Connor Show, 1994; Several appearances, Top of The Pops, 1984-. *Recordings:* Party 4 The Word, Steve Walsh; Gypsy Kings remix; Four Seasons remix; Awesome – The Singles; Supernatural Love, Alex Brown; Shadows and Elton John compilation; Culture Club Album, 1999; Numerous dance hits. *Membership:* Musicians' Union. *Leisure interests:* Going to the cinema; Spending time with daughter Sophia. *Current Management:* Pass Go Productions. *Address:* PO Box 3707, London N12 7LZ, England.

KLAKEGG Rune; b. 19 April 1955, Skien, Norway. Musician (piano); Composer. m. Kathryn Bresee, 14 Aug. 1992, 2 d. *Musical Education:* 2 years study, University of Oslo. *Career:* Freelance jazz musician, composer, since late 1970s; Appeared with groups: Cutting Edge; Out To Lunch; Soyr; Rune Klakegg Trio; All major jazz festivals; Arranger, band leader, Van Morrison, Vossajazz, 1988. *Recordings:* Cutting Edge: CE, 1982; Our Man In Paradise, 1984; Duesenberg, 1986; Out To Lunch: OTL, 1988; Kullboksrytter, 1995; Soyr: Vectors, 1988; Bussene lengter hjem, 1994; Med Kjøtt og Kjærlighet, 1997; R K Trio: Anaerobics, 1992; Fuzzy Logic: FL,

1996. *Honour:* NOPA Best Composition of the Year for Pamplemousse, 1995. *Memberships:* TONO; NOPA. *Leisure interests:* Outdoor activities; Skiing. *Address:* Ole Bullsgt 45, 0475 Oslo, Norway.

KLASTERKA Zeljen; b. 24 Jan. 1958, Zagreb, Croatia. Musician (guitar); Composer; Guitar Teacher. m. Neda Urlicic, 1 July 1995. *Education:* University graduate. *Musical Education:* 14 years, graduation, Faculty of Music University, Zagreb. *Career:* Lead guitarist with Notturno; Ritmo Loco; Patchwork; Studio musician; Classical guitar duet with Milivoj Majdak, Stanko Selak Big Band (orchestra of Music Academy); Music editor, major television show in Croatia: 7 NOC. *Recordings:* Album: Canto Latino, Patchwork video live concert of Zagreb Bienalle, 1994; Nek'ti Bude Ljubav Sva, Eurovision song contest entry, 5 video spots, Croatian Television. *Honour:* First Prize, Croatian Contest, Eurovision Song Contest. *Memberships:* HGU; ZAMP. *Leisure interests:* Sailing; Skiing. *Current Management:* Neda Urlicic-Klasterka. *Address:* Davor 3, 10000 Zagreb, Croatia.

KLEIN Harry; b. 25 Dec. 1928, London, England. Musician (baritone saxophone). *Musical Education:* Various teachers including Harry Hayes. *Career:* Tours with Stan Kenton with groups backing Tony Bennett, Ella Fitzgerald, Aretha Franklin, 1960s-80s; Now semi-retired doing various solo dates. *Recordings:* Played on Lady Madonna (No. 1, UK), Honey Pie, Savoy Truffle, The Beatles, 1968; It's Not Unusual (No. 1, UK), Tom Jones, 1965; Compilation with group The Jazz Five: The Five of Us, 2001; solo: Nemo; Big Ben. *Honours:* Poll Winner, Melody Maker Poll, 1952–58. *Membership:* Musicians' Union. *Leisure interest:* Music. *Address:* 8 Bowling Green House, Chelsea, London SW10, England.

KLEINENBERG Sander; b. 1972, The Hague, Netherlands. Prod.; Remixer; DJ. *Career:* Started to DJ in 1987; Resident DJ at The Roxy in Amsterdam; Remixed: Oliver Lieb, Junkie XL, Destiny's Child. *Recordings:* Albums: Sander Kleinenberg Presents Melk, 1998; Singles: My Lexicon, 2000; Penso Positiva, 2000; 4 Seasons, 2000. *Current Management:* c/o London Records, PO Box 1422, 72 Chancellor's Rd, London, W6 9SG, England.

KLEMMER John; b. 7 July 1956, Chicago, Illinois, USA. Musician (saxophones, flutes, clarinets, kalimba, piano, keyboards, synthesizers, percussion); Vocal composer. *Musical Education:* Interlochen National Music Camp; Private studies, age 5 to mid 20s; Studied, classical saxophone, flute, clarinet; Jazz improvisation with Joseph Daly; Studied composition, arranging, conducting; Private studies, orchestration, film scoring with Albert Harris. *Career:* Tours with: George Benson; Herbie Hancock; Miles Davis; Weather Report; others; With Don Ellis Orchestra, USA, Europe, England; State Department tour of 11 countries of French West Africa with Oliver Nelson Septet, Impulse Artists on tour; Live Performances, concerts, clubs include: Shellys Manne Hole, The Light House, all major jazz and rock clubs, concert venues, USA; Carnegie Hall; Newport Jazz Festival; Antibes Jazz Festival; Montreux Jazz Festival; Television and radio include: Voice of America shows; Midnight Special; Rock Concert; Merv Griffin Show; At One With; Dial M for Music; Live at Tanglewood PBS Special; Kitty Hawk, featuring John Klemmer solo saxophone PBS Special; WWTW presents John Klemmer; Started own record company, Touch Records, 1999. *Compositions include:* Walk In Love, recorded by Manhattan Transfer, Acker Bilk; The Old Man's Tear; Last Summer's Spell, recorded by Don Ellis; Lost In Love, recorded by Freda Payne, 1975; The Beauty of Her Soul; Touch. *Recordings include:* Blow on Gold, 1969; Touch, 1975; Barefoot Ballet, 1976; Cry, solo saxophone, 1980; Hush, solo saxophone, 1981; Life, solo saxophone, 1981; Making Love Vol. 1, 1998. *Publication:* The Jazz Styles of John Klemmer. *Honour:* Down Beat Magazine International Jazz Critics Poll, Talent Deserving Writer Recognition, 1973. *Memberships:* BMI; ASCAP; NARAS. *Leisure interests:* Psychology; Poetry; Puppeteering. *Current Management:* Borman Entertainment, Gary Borman. *Address:* Sally Poppe, 9220 Sunset Blvd, Suite 320, Hollywood, CA 90069, USA.

KLUGH Earl; b. 16 Sept. 1953, Detroit, Michigan, USA. Musician (guitar). *Career:* Member, George Benson Group; Chick Corea's Return To Forever; Solo recording artist, 1975–; Performed with numerous artists including George Shearing; Flora Purim; McCoy Tyner; Bob James; Chet Atkins. *Recordings:* Solo albums include: Earl Klugh, 1976; Living Inside Your Love, 1977; Finger Paintings, 1977; Magic In Your Eyes, 1978; Heart String, 1979; Dream Come True, 1980; Late Night Guitar, 1980; Crazy For You, 1981; Two of a Kind, 1982; Delta Lady, 1983; Low Ride, 1983; Night Songs, 1984; Wishful Thinking, 1984; Key Notes, 1985; Life Stories; Soda Fountain Shuffle; Whispers and Promises; Solo Guitar; Midnight In San Juan; Best of Earl Klugh, 1991; Sounds and Visions, 1991; Cool, 1992; Move, 1993; Sudden Burst of Energy, 1995; Peculiar Situation, 1999; with George Benson: White Rabbit; Body Talk; with Al Jarreau: This Time; with Jimmy Buffet: One Particular Harbour; with Jennifer Holliday: Say You Love Me; with McCoy Tyner: Inner Voices; with Flora Purim: Stories To Tell; with Bob James: Touchdown; One On One. *Address:* EKI, 24225 W Nine Mile Rd, Southfield, MI 48034, USA.

KNAUER Wolfram; b. 28 Jan. 1958, Germany. Musicologist; Dir. *Education:* Kiel University, 1980–89. *Career:* Director, Jazz-Institute Darmstadt; Teaching appointments at several major universities in Germany; Speaker at international conferences in Europe, USA. *Publications:* Numerous including, Zwischen Bebop Und Free Jazz; Jazz In Deutschland; Jazz In Europa; Translations from English into German; Scholarly essays; Many articles, interviews, concert, book and record reviews. *Memberships:* Hessische Jazzakademie; International Society for Jazz Research. *Address:* Jazz Institute Darmstadt, Bessunger Strase 88d, D 64285 Darmstadt, Germany.

KNEPPER James Minter (Jimmy); b. 22 Nov. 1927, Los Angeles, California, USA. Jazz Musician (trombone). m. Maxine Fields, May 1954, 1 s., 1 d. *Musical Education:* Harmony, Orchestration, LA City and State Colleges. *Career:* Played with: Charlie Spivak; Charlie Parker; Charley Barnet; Charlie Mingus; Benny Carter; Benny Goodman; Thad Jones; Gil Evans; Toshike; Stan Kenton; Woody Herman; Eric Dolphy; Miles Davis; Al Kooper; Kenny Burrell; Mose Allison; Herbie Mann, State Dept tour in Africa, 1960; Mingus Dynasty; Broadway: Funny Girl; On Your Toes (revival); Me Nobody Knows; National Jazz Ensemble; American Jazz Orchestra; Smithsonian Jazz Orchestra; George Grunz Concert Jazz Band; Tony Scott; Joe Albany; Joe Maini; Dean Benedetti. *Honours:* International Critics Poll; Readers Poll of Down Beat Magazine. *Membership:* AFofM. *Address:* 11 Bayview Pl., Staten Island, NY 10304, USA.

KNIGHT Emrys Glyn; b. 15 June 1951, South Glamorgan, Wales. Musician (lead guitar). *Musical Education:* Self-taught. *Career:* Member, Rose Among Thorns; Common Ground; Snatch It Back; Tours, UK and Europe; Numerous television and radio appearances; Concerts and albums with the above; British tours with Ralph McTell; Toured with Stone Free (Jimi Hendrix tribute band) in the UK and Europe. *Memberships:* Musicians' Union; PRS; MCPS. *Leisure interests:* Building guitar amplification; Guitar wiring. *Address:* 187 College Rd, Whitchurch, Cardiff CF14 2NT, Wales.

KNIGHT Gavin; b. 17 April 1966, Southampton, Hampshire, England. Musician (drums, percussion); Writer; Prod.; Programmer; Arranger; Remixer. *Musical Education:* Self-taught; Studied with Antony Christmas, 2 years and Albert Cooper, 2 years, Southampton. *Career:* Drummer with The Shamen, 1991–95; Extensive world tours including Europe, Scandinavia, USA, Australia and the Far East; Headlined Glastonbury Festival; Numerous TV appearances world-wide; Drummer, Maroontown, 1993–94; European shows and album recording; Urban Hype, live UK shows, 1992; The Good Strawberries, live UK shows and TV, 1994; Played for Marc Almond, major show at the Royal Albert Hall, London, TV appearances and album recording, 1995–98; with Victoria Wilson-James, European shows and TV appearances, 1996–; Russian shows with Jam and Spoon, 1997; Remixed, programmed various projects include: The Shamen; Co-writer and Producer, single release, Urban Hype, 1992; Marc Almond; Rhythm programming for album and single, Angelique Kidjo; Victoria Wilson-James; Assisted the Shamen on theme tune, The Ozone, TV programme, 1995; Worked with P J Proby, 1996; Co-Composer, TV programme for Meridian Television, 1996; Co-Member, dance production team, Universal State of Mind, 1996; Rhythm programming for commercial Release, Viva!, 1996. *Recordings:* Syncronous, Inca, 1994; Tunnel Vision, The Ticket Men, 1995; Co-writer, The Feeling, with Urban Hype, 1992 (released in Japan on compilation album); All Because of You, Universal State of Mind, 1997. *Memberships:* Musicians' Union; PAMRA. *Leisure interests:* Wining and dining; Playstation; Self-confessed Trekkie. *Address:* c/o The Cottage, 1a Bursledon Rd, Hedge End, Southampton, Hampshire SO30 0BP, England.

KNIGHT Gladys; b. 28 May 1944, Atlanta, Georgia, USA. Singer. *Career:* Singer, Gladys Knight and the Pips, 1957–89; Signed to Motown Records, 1966; Appearances include: Grand Gala Du Disque, Amsterdam, 1969; European tour, 1974; Kool Jazz Festival, San Diego, 1977; London Palladium, 1978; World Music Festival, 1982; Solo artiste, 1989–; Concerts include: Westbury Music Fair, New York, 1992; Television includes: Gladys Knight and The Pips Show, NBC, 1975; Happy New Year America, CBS, 1986; Motown 30 – What's Goin' On, 1990; Ray Charles – 50 Years In Music, Uh-Huh!, 1991; Gladys Knight's Holiday Family Reunion, ABC-TV, 1991; Actress, film Pipe Dreams, 1976; Actress, US sitcoms: Charlie and Co, 1985–86; Guest star, Out All Night, 1992. *Recordings:* Albums: Everybody Needs Love, 1967; Feelin' Bluesy, 1968; Silk 'n' Soul, 1969; Gladys Knight and The Pips' Greatest Hits, 1970; If I Were Your Woman, 1971; Standing Ovation, 1972; Neither One of Us, 1973; All I Need Is Time, 1973; Imagination, 1974; Anthology, 1974; Knight Time, 1974; Claudine, 1974; A Little Knight Music, 1975; I Feel A Song, 1975; 2nd Anniversary, 1975; The Best of Gladys Knight and The Pips, 1976; Pipe Dreams, 1976; Still Together, 1977; 30 Greatest, 1977; The One and Only, 1978; About Love, 1980; A Touch of Love, 1980; Visions, 1983; The Collection – 20 Greatest Hits, 1984; Solo: Good Woman, 1991; Just for You, 1994; Many Different Roads, 1998; At Last, 2000; Hit singles include: I

Heard It Through The Grapevine (No. 2, US), 1967; If I Were Your Woman, 1971; Help Me Make It Through The Night, 1972; The Look of Love, 1973; Neither One of Us (Wants To Be The First To Say Goodbye) (No. 2, US), 1973; Midnight Train To Georgia (No. 1, USA), 1973; I've Got To Use My Imagination, 1974; Best Thing That Ever Happened To Me, 1974; On and On, 1974; The Way We Were, 1975; Baby Don't Change Your Mind, 1977; Bourgie Bourgie, 1980; That's What Friends Are For, with Elton John, Stevie Wonder and Dionne Warwick (No. 1, USA), 1985; Licence To Kill, 1989. *Current Management:* Newman Management Inc, 2110 E Flamingo Rd, Suite 300, Las Vegas, NV 89119, USA.

KNIGHT Holly; b. 24 Sept. 1956, New York City, USA. Songwriter; Prod.; Musician (keyboards, piano). m. Michael Whitis-Knight, 24 March 1990, 2 s. *Musical Education:* Classical piano, age 4–14 years. *Career:* Member, Spider, 2 albums; Member, Device, album 1989; Have written many hits and film songs. *Compositions include:* for Pat Benatar: Love Is A Battlefield; Invincible; Sometimes The Good Guys Finish First; for Tina Turner: Better Be Good To Me; One of The Living; The Best; Ask Me How I Feel; Love Thing; Be Tender With Me Baby; You Can't Stop Me Loving You; for Heart: Never; All Eyes; There's The Girl; Tall Dark Handsome Stranger; I Love You; Love Touch, Rod Stewart; Ragdoll, Aerosmith; Change, John Waite; The Warrior, Patti Smyth; Stick To Your Guns, Bon Jovi; Space, Cheap Trick; Pleasure and Pain, the Divinyls; Soul Love, Hall and Oates: Baby Me, Chaka Khan; Just Between You and Me, Lou Gramm; Hide Your Heart, Bonnie Tyler; Turn It On, Kim Wilde; Stiletto, Lita Ford; Hide Your Heart, Kiss; Try A Little Harder, Aaron Neville; It's Over When The Phone Stops Ringing, Patsy Kensit; Wrap Your Arms Around Me, Agnetha Falkstog; Time Waits For No-One, Dusty Springfield; Between Two Fires, Jimmy Barnes; Slow Burn, Ozzy Osbourne; Tracks for: solo album; Spider; Device; A Night In Heaven film soundtrack (with Michael Desbarres). *Recordings:* Albums include: with Spider: Spider; Between The Lines; with Device: 22B3; Solo: Holly Knight, 1989; Knightworks, 1997. *Honours:* 3 Grammies, Best Rock Vocal, Better Be Good To Me; Love Is A Battlefield; One of The Living. *Memberships:* ASCAP; Songwriters Guild. *Leisure interests:* Skiing; Travel; Swimming.

KNIGHT Larry, (Fuzzy); b. 21 Oct. 1950, St Louis, Missouri, USA. Musician (bass); Singer; Songwriter. m. Aleda Trabue, 26 Oct. 1974, 1 d. *Education:* 3 years college. *Musical Education:* One year St Louis Conservatory of Music. *Career:* Played with: Albert King; Chuck Berry; Little Milton; Ike Turner, 1964–69; Tim Rose; Delaney-Bonnie and Friends; Peter Kaukenon, 1969–73; Albert Collins, Spirit, 1971–80; The Urge, 1985; Bandleader, Bassist and Lead Vocalist, Blowin' Smoke, R & B band, 1994–2000; Tours world-wide over 12 years; Appeared on many US rock shows, also Old Grey Whistle Test, England; Rock Palace, Germany; Recorded over 26 albums; 1 live Spirit album produced by Miles Copeland, Rainbow Theatre, London. *Recordings with:* Tim Rose; Delaney-Bonnie and Friends; 6 Spirit albums; Peter Kaukenon; Albert Collins; The Urge; Albert Lee; Kaptain Kopter and The Famous Twirlybirds; Randy California; Beyond The Blues Horizon, with The Blowin' Smoke Rhythm and Blues Band, CD, 1999; Deborah Gibson, 2000. *Honour:* Gold disc for Spirit. *Memberships:* NAMM; VSDA; Musicians' Union. *Leisure interests:* Music; Performing; Acting; Watching sports; Boxing; Football; Singing the blues. *Current Management:* Lawrence Weisberg, Blowin' Smoke Management and Bookings. *Address:* 7438 Shoshone Ave, Van Nuys, CA 91406–2340, USA.

KNOPFLER David; b. 27 Dec. 1952, Glasgow, Scotland. Musician (Guitar). *Career:* Former Social Worker; Member, Dire Straits; Obtained major label record deal and subsequent management contract; Support slot on tour with Talking Heads; Numerous headlining tours and TV appearances; Left band, 1980. *Recordings:* Singles: Sultans of Swing, 1978; Lady Writer, 1979; Romeo and Juliet, 1980; Making Movies, 1980; Albums: Dire Straits, 1978; Communiqué, 1979; Making Movies, 1980; Money For Nothing (compilation) (No. 1, UK), 1988; Sultans of Swing – The Best Of, 1998.

KNOPFLER Mark; b. 12 Aug. 1949, Glasgow, Scotland. Musician (guitar); Vocalist; Songwriter; Record Prod. m. Lourdes Salomone, Nov. 1983, 2 s. *Education:* English Graduate. *Career:* Former journalist, Yorkshire Evening Post; Member, Brewer's Droop; Café Racers; Founder member, Dire Straits, 1977–88, 1991–; World-wide concerts and tours, 1978–; Major concerts include: San Remo Song Festival, Italy, 1981; Live Aid, Wembley, 1985; Princes Trust Rock Gala, Wembley, 1986; Nelson Mandela 70th Birthday Tribute, 1988; Guitarist and vocalist, Eric Clapton US tour, 1988; Nordoff-Robbins charity concert, Knebworth Park, 1990. *Compositions include:* Private Dancer, Tina Turner, 1985; Setting Me Up, Waylon Jennings, 1984; Co-writer, Money For Nothing, with Sting, 1985; Water of Love, The Judds, 1989; Film music: Local Hero, 1983; Cal, 1984; The Princess Bride, 1987. *Recordings:* Albums: with Dire Straits: Dire Straits, 1978; Communiqué, 1979; Making Movies, 1980; Love Over Gold (No. 1, UK), 1982; Alchemy – Dire Straits Live, 1984; Brothers In Arms (No. 1, 20 countries), 1985; Money For Nothing (No. 1, UK), 1988; On Every Street (No. 1, UK), 1991; On The Night, 1993; with Chet Atkins: Neck and Neck,

1990; with Notting Hillbillies: Missing... Presumed Having, 1990; Solo: Local Hero (film soundtrack), 1983; Cal (film soundtrack), 1984; Golden Heart, 1996; Wag The Dog (film soundtrack), 1998; Metroland, 1999; Neck and Neck, 1999; Sailing To Philadelphia, 2000; Hit singles: with Dire Straits: Sultans of Swing, 1979; Romeo and Juliet, 1981; Tunnel of Love, 1981; Private Investigations (No. 2, UK), 1982; Twisting By The Pool, 1983; So Far Away, 1985; Money For Nothing (first video shown on MTV Europe) (No. 1, USA), 1985; Brothers In Arms (first-ever CD single), 1985; Walk of Life (No. 2, UK), 1986; Your Latest Trick, 1986; Calling Elvis, 1991; On Every Street, 1992; Solo singles: Going Home (theme from film Local Hero), 1983; Darling Pretty, 1996; Guest on albums including: Slow Train Coming, Bob Dylan, 1979; Solo In Soho, Phil Lynott, 1980; Gaucho, Steely Dan, 1980; Beautiful Vision, Van Morrison, 1982; The Phil Lynott Album, 1982; Boys and Girls, Bryan Ferry, 1985; Down In The Groove, Bob Dylan, 1988; The Shouting Stage, Joan Armatrading, 1988; Land of Dreams, Randy Newman, 1988; As producer: Infidels, Bob Dylan, 1984; Knife, Aztec Camera, 1984; Human, Rod Stewart, 2000. *Honours include:* Ivor Novello Awards: Outstanding British Lyric, 1983; Best Film Theme, 1984; Outstanding Contribution to British Music, 1989; Nordoff-Robbins Silver Clef Award, Outstanding Services To British Music, 1985; BRIT Awards: Best British Group, 1983, 1986; Best British Album, 1987; Grammy Awards: Best Rock Performance, Money For Nothing, 1986; Best Country Performance, with Chet Atkins, 1986, 1991; Hon. music doctorate, University of Newcastle Upon Tyne, 1993. *Current Management:* Ed Bicknell, Damage Management, 16 Lambton Pl., London W11 2SH, England.

KNORR Marianne; b. 3 Feb. 1949, Copenhagen, Denmark. Folksinger; Guitarist; Actress. m. Preben Friis, 13 May 1989, 2 s. *Education:* Danish State Theatre School, 4 years. *Musical Education:* Studied voice with Jens Chr Schmidt for 12 years. *Career:* Has appeared at Rimfaxe Theatre, Skagen Festival, Roskilde Festival, in Radio concerts and on Television; Concerts in Denmark, Norway, Sweden, Iceland and Greenland. *Recordings:* 4 Solo albums: Valmuer Og Jernbeton, Sa Laenge Fuglene Flyver, Sange Af Brecht, and Sommerregn. *Memberships:* Danish Actors' Asscn; Danish Society of Jazz and Beat Authors. *Address:* Strandvejen 138, 5600 Faaborg, Denmark.

KNOWLES Beyoncé; b. 4 Sept. 1981, Houston, Texas, USA. Vocalist. *Career:* Joined GirlsTyme vocal group, 1989; Group renamed Something Fresh then The Dolls before settling on Destiny's Child; Signed to Columbia Records, 1996; Numerous TV and live performances including tour with Christina Aguilera, 2000; Appeared at United We Stand concert, USA, 2001; Lead role in MTV's Hip-hopera Carmen, 2001; Forthcoming appearance as Foxy Cleopatra in film Austin Powers In Goldmember, due 2002; Solo releases planned for 2002; Managed by father Mathew Knowles. *Recordings:* Albums: Destiny's Child, 1998; The Writing's On The Wall, 1999; Survivor, 8 Days of Christmas, 2001; Singles: No No No (with Wyclef Jean), 1997; With Me (with Timbaland), She's Gone (with Matthew Marsden), 1998; Get On The Bus (from Why Do Fools Fall In Love OST), Bills Bills Bills, Bug-A-Boo, 1999; Say My Name, Jumpin' Jumpin', Independent Women (from Charlie's Angels OST), 2000; Survivor, Bootylicious, Emotion, 8 Days of Christmas, 2001. *Honours:* Countless awards world-wide including: Billboard Awards: Artist of The Year; Group of The Year; Hot 100 Singles Artist of The Year; Hot 100 Group of The Year, 2000; American Music Awards, Favourite Soul/R & B Group, 2001; Grammy Awards: Best R & B Song, Say My Name; Best R & B Performance by a Duo or Group with Vocal, Say My Name, 2001; Independent Women reached the largest audience in the USA's history of monitored airplay (over 140m. radio listeners in 1 week). *Address:* c/o Mathew Knowles, Music World Entertainment, 9898 Bissonnet, Suite 625, Houston, TX 77036, USA. *Internet:* www.destinyschild.com.

KNOX (Ian Milroy Carnochan); b. 4 Sept. 1945, London, England. Singer; Musician (guitar, keyboards). *Career:* Lead singer, songwriter, The Vibrators; Solo artiste, 1983; Singer, songwriter, The Fallen Angels; Member, Urban Dogs. *Recordings:* with The Vibrators: 11 studio albums; Solo album, 1983; with The Fallen Angels: 3 studio albums; with Urban Dogs: 2 studio albums; with Die Toten Hosen: Baby, Baby; Troops of Tomorrow. *Publication:* Writing book on The Vibrators. *Honours:* Gold disc, Baby, Baby (Germany). *Memberships:* PRS; MCPS. *Leisure interest:* Painting.

KNOX Keith; b. 1933, Belper, Derbyshire, England. Record Co Exec.; Record Prod.; Music Journalist. *Education:* Southampton University; Brighton College of Advanced Technology. *Career:* Served with Royal Air Force, 1955–57; Record producer, various recording companies including: Caprice; Storyville; Sonet; WEA; Universal Folk Sounds; Album sleeve note writer; Founder, Executive Producer, own jazz label Silkheart Records, Sweden, 1986-. *Recordings:* Artists on own label include Steve Lacy; Charles Gayle; David S Ware; Dennis Gonzalez; Matthew Shipp; Booker T Williams; Assif Tsahar; Jim Hobbs; Dennis Charles; Joel Futterman; Alvin Fielder; Rob Brown. *Publications:* Author, Jazz Amour Affair (The Lars Gullin Story); Contributor, jazz magazines including: Jazz Monthly;

Jazz Forum (International Jazz Federation magazine); Jazznews; Articles include: The Parametric Music of Terry Riley, 1967; Relax and Fully Concentrate – the music of Terry Riley; Terry Riley – This Is Our Period. *Address:* Silkheart Records, Dalagatan 33, 113 23 Stockholm, Sweden.

KNUCKLES Frankie; b. 18 Jan. 1955, South Bronx, New York City, USA. Prod.; Remixer; DJ. *Career:* DJ at The Warehouse in Chicago USA (club associated with the birth of House music); Remixed: Alison Limerick, Lisa Stansfield, Janet Jackson, Luther Vandross, Sounds of Blackness, Michael Jackson, Chaka Khan; Member of Def Mix crew (alongside David Morales and Satoshi Tomiie); Collaborations: Jamie Principle, Satoshi Tomiie. *Recordings:* Albums: Frankie Knuckles Presents, 1989; Beyond The Mix, 1991; Welcome To The Real World, 1995; Singles: Waiting On My Angel (with Jamie Principle), 1985; Your Love/Baby Wants To Ride (with Jamie Principle), 1987; Only The Strong Survive, 1988; Tears (with Satoshi Tomiie), 1989; The Whistle Song, 1991; It's Hard Sometimes, 1991; Too Many Fish (with Adeva), 1995; Keep On Movin', 2001. *Current Management:* c/o Def Mix, 928 Broadway, Suite 400, New York, USA.

KNUDSEN Hans; b. 7 Sept. 1950, Copenhagen, Denmark. Musician (piano); Singer; Songwriter. *Education:* College of Education. *Musical Education:* Guitar lessons, 1960s; Self-taught piano, 1975-. *Career:* Former teacher, Music and Biology, 1975–80; Professional musician, 1980–; Worked and toured with leading Danish jazz and blues artists, 1980–83; Member, New Orleans singer Lillian Boutté's band, 1983–90; Leader, own group Hans Knudsen Jumpband, 1990-. *Compositions include:* Music Is My Life, with Lillian Boutté. *Recordings:* with Lillian Boutté: Music Is My Life, 1984; Let Them Talk, 1986; with Hans Knudsen Jumpband: So Long John, 1995; Jump In Focus, 1997. *Address:* Kildebakkegårds Allé 92, 1 tv, 2860 Soborg, Denmark.

KNUDSEN Karl Emil; b. 16 June 1929, Copenhagen, Denmark. Record Co Owner. *Career:* Founder and Owner, Storyville Records, Sonet; Represents every genre of jazz music; Series, Masters of Jazz, The Blues Masters, The Sounds of New Orleans and recordings of the JAZZPAR Project, 1991–; Includes work of Hank Jones, Tommy Flanagan, Roy Haynes, Tony Coe, Jim Hall; Release of home videos of artists such as Louis Armstrong, Duke Ellington, Benny Goodman; TV Documentaries, The Mills Brothers Story, The Spike Jones Story; Established book publishing business, Jazz Media. *Publications:* Jazz Records, 1942–62, compiled by Jorgen Grunnet Jepsen; Discographical works on Miles Davis, Ben Webster, Chet Baker, Klaus Stratemann. *Address:* Dortheavej 39, Copenhagen, 2700, Denmark.

KNUDSEN Kenneth; b. 28 Sept. 1946, Copenhagen, Denmark. Composer; Musician (keyboard). m. Christine Heger, 22 March 1987, 1 s. *Education:* Architect, Royal Danish Academy of Fine Arts. *Musical Education:* Self-taught. *Career:* Member of jazz/fusion groups: Coronarias Dans, 1969; Secret Oyster, 1976; Anima, 1979; Heart To Heart Trio, 1986; Bombay Hotel, 1988; Special project with Jan Akkerman and Jon Hiseman, 1982; Numerous concerts and television in Scandinavia, Europe, UK, Hong Kong and Japan. *Compositions:* Film scores; Ballet music for New Danish Dance Theatre and The Royal Danish Ballet; Works for string quartet, cello, piano, choir and electronics; Prizewinning commercials for Carlsberg Breweries. *Recordings:* I Me Him, 1989; Compacked, 1989; Sounds and Silence, 1994; Appeared on more than 100 records including Garland, Svend Asmussen and L. Subramaniam; It Could Happen To You, Jan Akkerman; Entrance, Heart To Heart, with Palle Mikkelborg; Pictures and Heart To Heart with Niels Henning Orsted Pedersen; Aura, Miles Davis; Anima, Kenneth Knudsen; Music For Eyes, CD, 1998; Light and Metal, CD, 1998. *Honours:* Jazz Musician of the Year, 1973; Niels Matthiasen Memorial Grant, 1987; Danish Art Foundation Grant, 1992–94; Lifelong Grant from the Danis Art Foundation, 1998. *Membership:* Danish Composers Society. *Leisure interests:* Yachting; Visual Arts. *Address:* PO Box 51, 2840 Holte, Denmark.

KNUDSEN Marius Dahl; b. 30 June 1947, Grinsted, Denmark. Musician (Guitars; Didgeridoo). m. Lise Jelsbech Knudsen, 14 July 1979, 2 s., 1 d. *Education:* Classical Guitar, Degree in Music Teaching. *Career:* Member, Ostjydsk Musikforsyning, 20 years; Danish show-band with numerous appearances on national TV and radio; Stage: Arhus Teater: Rocky Horror Show; Return to the Forbidden Planet; Vejle Teater: Folk Og Rovere; Dansk Spildtid: Elverhoj. *Recordings:* Det Beskidte Dusin; Aarhus Syncopaterne. *Honour:* Hon. Mem., Danish Musicians' Union, Arets Revykomponist, 1996. *Membership:* Danish Musicians' Union. *Current Management:* Ostjydsk Musikforsyning, Ved Kirken 2, 8320 Marslet, Denmark. *Address:* Langballeves 44, 8320 Marslet, Denmark.

KNUDSEN Ole; b. 15 Sept. 1943, Koge, Denmark. Music Teacher; Multi-instrumentalist; Singer; Composer. *Education:* Music Teacher, Teacher training school, 1970. *Career:* Jazz drummer, 1965–70; Lead singer, guitarist, pianist, percussionist, Danish jazz-rock group: Fujara, 1970–76; Performances: Roskilde Festival, 1971–75; Leader, Arbejdersanggruppen, 1976–82; Freelance jazz-drummer, teacher, 1982-. *Recordings:* Fujara,

1973; Nattevandring, 1977; Jens Borges Fodselsdag (children's songs), 1979; Hvor Laenge Skal Vi Vente, 1980; Det Handler Om Kaerlighed, (solo) 1992. *Honours:* LO (Danish Organization of Labour) Culture Prize, Arbejdersanggruppen, 1981. *Memberships:* Danish Jazz Musicians' Organization; Danish Jazz Beat Folkmusic Authors. *Leisure interests:* Football; Tennis.

KNUTSEN Cecilie; b. 9 May 1967, Trondheim, Norway. Singer. *Education:* Conservatory of Music, Oslo, 3 years; Conservatory of Music, Arhus, Denmark, 3 years. *Career:* TV Norway, national, 1982; TV Norway, national, 1984, 1995, 1997; TV Denmark, national, 1993; Toured with Deepak Chopra, Louise Hay, Wayne Dyer and Stuart Wilde. *Recordings:* Voice of the Feminine Spirit, 1994; Violet 19, 1996. *Honour:* Gold Album, England. *Membership:* Gramart. *Current Management:* Eivind Brydoy, Artist Partner as Grini Naering Sparn 17, 1345, Osteraas, Norway.

KOITE Habib; b. 1958, Bamako, Mali. Vocalist; Musician (acoustic guitar, flute); Songwriter. *Education:* National Institute of Arts (INA), Bamako, degree (graduated first in class), 1982. *Career:* Born to a griot family; Music teacher at the INA; Sang and played on Toumani Diabate's Shake the World, 1991; Formed Bamada, 1988; Hit single Cigarette Abana; Recorded first album, 1994; Became a regular on the European festival scene; Toured US with the Voices of Mali tour, 2000. *Recordings:* Albums: Muso Ko, 1994; Ma Ya, 1998; Baro, 2001. *Honours:* Voxpole Festival in France, first prize, 1991; Radio France International Discoveries Prize, 1994; BBC Radio 3 World Music Awards, Best African artist nominee, 2001. *Address:* c/o Putumayo World Music, 324 Lafayette St, Seventh Floor, New York, NY 10012, USA. *Internet:* www.putumayo.com.

KOIVISTOINEN Eero; b. 13 Jan. 1946, Finland. Composer; Musician (tenor, soprano saxophone). *Musical Education:* Sibelius Academy, Helsinki, 1968–70, 1973–74; Berklee College of Music, Boston, US, 1971–73. *Career:* Leader, own quartet; Performed at international jazz competition, Montreux, Switzerland, 1969; Newport Festival, USA; Founder, composer, arranger for UMO (New Music Orchestra), 1975–; Leader, Dialog, 1995–; Established PRO Records Label, 1983; Teaching, 1980s. *Compositions include:* Ballet, Mother Earth, 1979; Suite, Ultima Thule, represented Finland in Nordring radio competition, 1981. *Recordings:* 16 solo albums, Later albums include Pictures In Three Colours (with John Scofield and Jack DeJohnette); Ultima Thule, UMO; Dialog, 1995. *Honours:* First recipient, Yrjö (Georgie) Award, Finnish Jazz Federation, 1967; Best Jazz Ensemble, Montreux Festival, 1969; Best Arranger, Nordring radio competition, Jersey, 1981. *Address:* Lapinlahdcnk 21 A 11, 00180 Helsinki, Finland.

KOJIMA Ian (Koko); b. 28 Dec. 1951, Toronto, Canada. Musician (saxophone, Acoustic, electric guitars, keyboards); Composer (filmscores). m. Anne Peters, 11 Nov. 1977, 1 s. *Education:* 2 years, University of Toronto, Arts. *Musical Education:* 2 years, Humber College (composition, theory, improvisation. *Career:* Saxophonist for Stampedes, Ken Tobias; Multi-instrumentalist for: Chris De Burgh; Peter Hoffman; David Hasselhoff. *Recordings:* Chris De Burgh: Live In Dublin; Man on the Line; Into the Light; High on Emotion; Filmscore: Circus On The Moon (composer, musician, actor). *Contributions to:* Canadian Music. *Honours:* 5 times Juno Award Nominee. *Memberships:* Toronto MA; British MU. *Leisure interest:* Golf. *Current Management:* Ken Thompson Management, Redhead Touring. *Address:* Thornhill, Ontario, Canada.

KOKKAS Vassilios; b. 30 Sept. 1965, Athens, Greece. Composer. *Musical Education:* Piano, Flute, Harmony, Counterpoint, Orchestration, Composition, The Hochschule Der Kunste, 1990–96. *Publication:* Navigation In Metamorphosis: Navigable Music, 1996. *Memberships:* German Society For Musical Rights; DEGEM. *Leisure interests:* Swimming; Repairing things; Poetry. *Current Management:* Institute For Research In Music and Acoustics, 105 Adrianou St, Athens. *Address:* Manteuffelstr 68, D 10999 Berlin, Germany.

KOLLOWRAT Peter; b. 5 March 1967, Vienna, Austria. Musician (Guitar). m. Birgit Kollowrat, 29 Oct. 1994. *Education:* Salzburger Musik-Schulwerk; Diploma, Master of Arts, Mozarteum, Salzburg, 1996; Studied Guitar with J Clerch and Eliot Fisk; Masterclasses with F Bungartem, L Brouwer, A Pierri and S Isbin. *Career:* Concerts in Italy, Belgium, Germany and Austria; Soloist with Halleiner Chamber Orchestra. *Recordings:* Jason und die Argonauten!!: Live in Riff-Cafe, 1996; CD with Eliot Fisk and Friends, 1999. *Honours:* Premio di Musica Cesare Grigoletto, 1997; Medal of the President of Italy, 1997. *Leisure interest:* Running marathons. *Address:* Trautmannstr 6A, 5020 Salzburg, Austria.

KOMPPA Kari; b. 5 Jan. 1939, Helsinki, Finland. Composer; Musician (tenor saxophone). *Career:* Jazz session saxophonist, band leader, television conductor/arranger, YLE/TV2, Tampere; Founder, leader, writer, member, Break Big Band, played Pori Festival, 1970, 1972, 1982, 1984; Writer for Radio (YLE) Jazz Orchestra, the UMO; Founder, leader, composer, member, Tampere Jazz Orchestra, 1981–84; Represented Finnish

Broadcasting Company (YLE), throughout Europe, including Nordring Festival, Belgium; Teacher, Big Band leader, Tampere Conservatory of Music; EBU Jazz Concert, Pori; Saxophonist, writer for Ippe Kätkä Band, 1980s; Teacher, Sibelius Academy Jazz Department, Helsinki; Currently (from the end of 1980s) withdrawn from active public performance and teaching; Still occasionally writing for UMO Jazz Orchestra and Radio (YLE); Formed Zone, (an association of forefront Finnish jazz composers), 1991; Jazz and Electronic compositions for Zone. *Compositions include:* Aldebaran, 1977; Tethys, 1981; Free Aspects, 1981; Protoscope, 1991; First Definition, 1994; Tampere Jazz Orchestra; Ippe Kätkä Band; Music for Radio Jazz Orchestra and UMO. *Recordings:* LPs: Makumoka; Ippe Kätkä Band; CDs: Nordjazz Big 5; Umo Jazz Orchestra, 1997; Zone: First Definition, 1999; Also: arranger of John Coltrane's composition, Untitled Original, on Dave Liebman CD, Joy. *Honours:* Winner (with Break Big Band), Finnish Big Band championship, 1973; Winner, EBU orchestral composition contest, Tethys, 1981; Yrjö (Georgie) Award, Finnish Jazz Federation, 1982. *Memberships:* Teosto RY; Elvis RY; Zone RY. *Address:* Martinlaaksontie 40 F 39, 01629 Vantaa, Finland.

KONTÉ Mamadou; b. June 1945, Tambacunda, Senegal. Music Dir, Concert Organizer. 1 s. *Career:* Founder, Director, Africa Fete Festival, Paris, 1979–; USA, 1993–; Dakar, Senegal, West Africa, 1993-. *Honour:* Chevalier des Arts et des Lettres, France. *Membership:* Vice President, de Zoue Franche. *Leisure interests:* Films; Music. *Address:* Africa Fete, 29 Wagane Diouf, Dakar; 29 rue Gerna'n Pilou 75010, Paris, France.

KOOPER Al; b. 5 Feb. 1944, Brooklyn, New York, USA. Musician (keyboards); Vocalist; Songwriter; Prod. *Career:* Guitarist, The Royal Teens, 1959; Session musician with artists including: Tom Rush, Peter Paul and Mary, New York; Member, The Blues Project, 1966–67; Concerts include: Monterey International Pop Festival, 1967; Founder member, Blood Sweat and Tears, 1967–68; Producer at Columbia Records; Solo artiste; Established own record label, Sounds of The Earth (acts included Lynyrd Skynyrd); Founder, Sweet Magnolia, 1970s; Recording artist, computerized soundtrack music. *Compositions:* with Bobby Brass and Irwin Levine include: This Diamond Ring, Gary Lewis and The Playboys; I Must Be Seeing Things, Gene Pitney; The Water Is Over My Head, The Rocking Berries. *Recordings:* Albums with The Blues Project: Projections, 1966; Live At Town Hall, 1967; with Blood Sweat and Tears: The Child Is Father To The Man, 1968; Solo albums: Super Session (with Mike Bloomfield and Stephen Stills), 1968; The Live Adventures of Al Kooper and Mike Bloomfield, 1969; I Stand Alone, 1969; You Never Know Who Your Friends Are, 1969; Kooper Session, 1970; Easy Does It, 1970; Landlord, 1971; New York City (You're A Woman), 1971; A Possible Projection of The Future, 1972; Naked Songs, 1973; Act Like Nothing's Wrong, 1976; Four on the Floor, 1979; Championship Wrestling, 1982; Rekooperation, 1994; Soul of a Man, 1995; Kooper Sessions, 1999; Guest musician with Bob Dylan: Highway 61 Revisited, 1965; Blonde On Blonde, 1966; New Morning, 1970; Under The Red Sky, 1990; Also featured on: Electric Ladyland, Jimi Hendrix, 1968; Let It Bleed, Rolling Stones, 1969; Producer, recordings by Nils Lofgren; Don Ellis; The Tubes; Green On Red. *Publication:* Backstage Pass, Al Kooper.

KOOYMANS George; b. 11 March 1948, The Hague, Netherlands. Vocalist; Musician (guitar). *Career:* Founder member, Dutch rock group Golden Earring, 1961–; Tours, Europe; Canada; US; Suppport to The Who, European tour, 1972; Support to Rush, 1982. *Recordings:* Albums: Just Earrings, 1965; Winter Harvest, 1967; Miracle Mirror, 1968; On The Double, 1969; Eight Miles High, 1970; Golden Earring, 1971; Seven Tears, 1971; Together, 1972; Moontan, 1973; Switch, 1975; To The Hilt, 1975; Rock of The Century, 1976; Contraband, 1976; Mad Love, 1977; Live, 1977; Grab It For A Second, 1978; No Promises, No Debts, 1979; Prisoner of The Night, 1980; Second Live, 1981; Cut, 1982; N E W S, 1984; Something Heavy Goin' Down, 1984; The Hole, 1986; Face It, 1995; Supernatural Fairy Tales, 1996; Together Alone, 1997; Nobody's Wife, 1998; Explore, 1998; Devil Made Me Do It, 2001; Solo albums: Jojo, 1971; Solo, 1987; Numerous compilation albums; Singles: Please Go, 1965; Dong-Dong-Di-Ki-Di-Gi-Dong (No. 1, Netherlands), 1968; Radar Love (No. 1, Netherlands), 1973; Twilight Zone, 1982; Lady Smiles. *Current Management:* Rob Gerritsen, Regentesstraat 29, 2713 EM Zoetmeer, The Netherlands.

KOPECKY Ladislav; b. 8 April 1944, Prague, Czech Republic. 2 d. *Education:* Economics, Faculty of International Trade, Charles University, Prague. *Career:* Musician, playing trombone, different bands; Songwriter (lyrics); More than 60 songs broadcasted by Czech TV and Radio; Cooperation with Singer and Songwriter, Petr Ulrych. *Compositions:* Pojote Dal (Hana Ulrychova); Mec A Preslice; Ententyny; Bylinky; Musical: Nikola Suhaj the robber. *Recordings:* Songs: Javory (Maple Tree); Jizda Kralu (Ride of the Kings); Trava (Grass); Kridla (Wings); Bylinky (Herbs); Kamen (Stone); Ententyny. *Honours:* Silver Prize, 1976, Golden Prize, 1980, Bratislavska Lyra Festival; Bronze Prize, 1977, Bronze Prize, 1979, Decinska Kotva Festival. *Membership:* OSA. *Leisure interests:* Music; Sport (Tennis, Ice Hockey, Ski); Climbing Mountain. *Address:* Ladislav Kopecky, Ujezd 41, 11800 Prague 1, Czech Republic.

KOPPEL Anders; b. 17 July 1947, Copenhagen, Denmark. Composer; Musician (organ, piano). m. Ulla Lemvigh-Müller, 11 Aug. 1969, 1 s., 2 d. *Musical Education:* Clarinet and piano lessons. *Career:* Child performer, piano and clarinet; Member, Savage Rose, 1967–74; Member, Bazaar, 1975–; Tours: Europe, USA. *Compositions:* Music for 10 ballets; 200 films and plays; 3 musicals; 1 opera; Piano concerto; Percussion concerto; Marimba concerto; Saxophone concerto; Bass trombone concerto; Flute/Harp concerto; Trio for saxophone, cello, piano; Trio for violin, cello, piano; Toccata for vibes, marimba and orchestra; String Quartet; Partita for chamber ensemble; Concertino for chamber ensemble; Trio for violin, horn, piano; Duo for two guitars; Portrait for sextet; Trio for three clarinets. *Recordings:* 7 solo albums. *Honours:* Wilhelm Hansen Prize; Danish State Art Foundation Lifelong Award. *Membership:* Danish Composers Asscn. *Leisure interest:* Family. *Current Management:* Wilhelm Hansen, Copenhagen. *Address:* Cæciliavej 70, 2500 Valby, Copenhagen, Denmark.

KOPPEL Annisette; b. 29 Aug. 1948, Copenhagen, Denmark. Singer; Songwriter; Writer. m. Thomas Koppel, 1971, 2 d. *Career:* Numerous tours in Europe, USA, etc; Numerous TV and radio appearances internationally; Newport Jazz Festival, 1969; Montreux Festival and numerous other festivals, 1970–97; Lead character in own musical, Bella Vita, 1997, with Thomas Koppel; Lead Singer, Savage Rose, 1968–. *Compositions:* Numerous songs recorded by Savage Rose, 1968–98; Musical Bella Vita, with Thomas Koppel, 1996–97; Lyrics for Symphonic Compositions by Thomas Koppel. *Recordings:* 19 albums with The Savage Rose; Bella Vita, 1995; Black Angel, 1996; Tameless, 1998–99. *Honours:* Nomination for the Grand Music Award of Nordic Council, 1996; Award of Honour, Danish Songwriters' Asscn; Grammy, 1996, 1999; Numerous awards from Trade Unions and Organizations. *Memberships:* Danish Artists' Union; DJBFA; KODA; Gramex. *Leisure interest:* Painting. *Current Management:* South Harbour Productions. *Address:* 2464 Lindsay Lane, Los Angeles, CA 90039, USA.

KOPPEL Thomas; b. 24 April 1944, Sweden. Musician (piano); Composer; Prod. m. Annisette Hansen, 1971, 2 s., 2 d. *Musical Education:* Soloist Diploma, Royal Danish Conservatory; Self-taught composer. *Career:* Debut concert as piano soloist, 1967; Numerous concerts and performances of symphonic works since 7 years of age; Started The Savage Rose, 1967; Numerous international tours and TV and radio appearances since 1968; Newport Festival, 1969; Numerous Scandinavian and European festivals. *Compositions:* Phrases, 1964; Visions Fugitives, 1965; Ouverture Solennelle, 1966; Opera, A Mother's Tale, Royal Theatre, 1964; Ballet, Triumph of Death, TV, Royal Theatre, 1970–73; The Moonchild's Dream, 1991; Symphony No 2, 1995; Musical, Bella Vita, 1996; Musical drama, Mass, 1995; Concerto for soprano, strings and celesta, 1999. *Recordings:* 19 albums with The Savage Rose, 1968–98; Recorder concerto, The Moonchild's Dream, 1994; Ballet, Triumph of Death; Musical drama, Mass, 1995; Bella Vita, 1995. *Honours:* Carl Nielsen Prize, 1965; First Prize, International Composers' Competition, City of Copenhagen 800 Years Anniversary, 1966; Numerous awards from trade unions and organizations; Nominated, Grand Award of the Nordic Council, 1995; H C Lumbye Award, Tivoli Gardens, 1992; Keyboard Player of the Year, 1996; Grammy, 1996. *Memberships:* Danish Composers' Asscn; Danish Artists' Union; KODA; NCB; Gramex. *Leisure interest:* Photography. *Address:* 2464 Lindsay Lane, Los Angeles, CA 90039, USA.

KORB Ron; b. 7 Sept. 1961, Scarborough, Ontario, Canada. Musician (flute, keyboards); Vocals. *Musical Education:* Music Bachelor in Performance, University of Toronto; Royal Conservatory of Music. *Recordings:* Tear of The Sun, 1990; Japanese Mysteries, 1993; Flute Traveller, 1994; Behind The Mask, 1995; Taming the Dragon, 1999; Titanic Odyssey, 1999; Persian Arabesque, 2000; Celtic Heartland, 2000. *Honour:* RTHK (radio and television, Hong Kong), Best Original Composition, 1993. *Memberships:* AFM; SOCAN. *Current Management:* Humble Dragon Entertainment. *Address:* 48 Pine Ave, Toronto, ON M4E 1M1, Canada.

KORJUS Tapio; b. 18 June 1950, Pieksamaki, Finland. Man.-Dir. m. Eija Savolainen, 7 Dec. 1984, 1 d. *Education:* Tampere University. *Career:* Founder, Rockadillo Management, 1971; Rockadillo Records and Publishing, 1982; Rockadillo Agency, 1983; Zen Master Records and Publishing, 1993; Finnish Music and Media Happening, 1989. *Recordings:* Appears on: Space Waltz, Pekka Pohjola, 1986. *Memberships:* The Finnish Rock Booking Agents' Asscn; Finnish Music Publishers Asscn. *Leisure interests:* Music; Films; Mountain biking. *Current Management:* Rockadillo. *Address:* Rockadillo, PO Box 35, 33201 Tampere, Finland.

KORN Daniel, (The Wolf); b. 23 Feb. 1958, Oak Park, Illinois, USA. Musician (Electric Guitar, Keyboards). *Education:* 4 years of private instruction; Some college training. *Career:* Musician and Lead Singer in numerous bands; Performances include Kessler's Silver Dome Ballroom. *Recordings:* Numerous songs recorded on independent labels including Mary Show Me Again; Sarah; I Bad; A Christmas Song. *Publications:* Books: How to Rock and Roll, Vols 1 and 2; I, Daniel: The Original Story of the Wolf. *Honours:* Winner of numerous talent shows. *Leisure interests:* Lawn and yard care; Collecting sheet music; Riding motorcycles. *Address:* 901 S Farwell St, 130, Eau Claire, WI 54701, USA.

KOS Lada; b. 12 Nov. 1944, Zagreb, Croatia. Singer; Writer; Composer; Arranger; Musician (Violin, Guitar, Piano). *Musical Education:* Musical Academy for Violin. *Career:* Solo concerts in Croatia, Barcelona, Paris, Milano, Berlin, Frankfurt, Wien; Tours to Russia, France, Italy, Germany, Austria and Slovenia; TV appearances on RAI, Moscow, St Petersburg, Tallin among others, also on various TV series. *Recordings include:* Zbog Ljubavi; Covjek Covjeku; Igracica Vjetrova; Music for the Theatre includes: B M Koltés, Roberto Zucco, S Sembera, Hodanje Prugom, E Kisevic, Macak u Trapericama, B Jelusic, Slava Voli Hranislava, V Parun, U Cast Darkerke Djevice Orleanske. *Honours:* 23 awards for Best Singer, Writer, Composer and Arranger. *Membership:* Croatian Composers' Society. *Leisure interests:* Fishing; Gardening. *Current Management:* Best Music, Zagreb, Croatia. *Address:* Menceticeva 26, 41000 Zagreb, Croatia.

KOSIORKIEWICZ-KSIEZCKA Jadwiga; b. 16 March 1945, Lublin, Poland. Musician (piano, guitar). m. Adam Ksiezycki (deceased 1987), 1 s. *Education:* Chemist. *Career:* Pop singer; School organist, for play in church; Composer, poetic lyrics, also sacro-poetry (150 songs, songs for children); Sings in own programme, clubs, churches, for Catholic radio, with poets. *Recordings:* (Own compositions) Christmas songs; Sacro-songs (singer). *Memberships:* Polish Authors, Composers; ZAKR; ZAJKS. *Leisure interests:* Poetic lyrics; Swimming.

KOSVANEC Svatopluk; b. 2 Jan. 1936, Usti nad Labem, Czech Republic. Musician (Trombone). m. Marie Kosvanec, 30 March 1963, 1 s., 1 d. *Musical Education:* Violin, Secondary music school; Self-taught Trombone. *Career:* Film by Vera Chutilova, Kalamita; Musical Festivals of Jazz in Denmark, Norway, 1965, Stuttgart, Germany, 1966, Switzerland, 1967, Poland, 1969, Spain, 1991; Trombone Workshop of Jazz, Prague, 1971, Italy, 1983, San Remo, 1987, Eilat, Israel, 1995. *Recordings:* Radio Big Band Prague; Old Men Play Swing; In Ironplate Pack; Jazz Cellula; Kamil Hala's Big Band; Evro Big Band, Ljubljana. *Publication:* Encyclopaedia of Jazz, Czech Republic, 1997. *Honours:* Jazz Festival, Prorov, 1966, 1967. *Memberships:* Radio Big Band; Military Band; National Theatre Big Band. *Leisure interests:* Aeronautics; Cars. *Address:* Nova 36, Strekov, Usti nad, Labem 40003, Czech Republic.

KOTEK Josef; b. 11 April 1928, Prague, Czech Republic. Musicologist. 2 s. *Education:* Charles University, Prague. *Career:* Editor, Music Journal, Music Horizon, 1957–61; Academy of Sciences, Institute for Musicology, Prague, 1962–97. *Publications:* Kronika Ceske Synkopy I/II; Dejiny Ceske Popularni Hudby a Zpevu I/II. *Honours:* Prize Czech Radio, 1993; Prize Czech Academy of Sciences, 1994. *Membership:* Asscn of Czech Musicians and Musicologists. *Address:* Severni II/3, 141 00 Prague 4, Czech Republic.

KOTRUBENKO Viktor; b. 27 Nov. 1948. Composer; Saxophonist. 1 d. *Education:* College of Technology, Electrochemical Faculty; Clarinet, School of Music, Prague. *Compositions:* Radio Productions Music: Mum, Dad, Sore Made; Film Music: Bohemian Ruby, The Light of Hope, Faul; Music for television serials: Rambles Round Bohemia and Moravia; Ecuador. *Recordings:* The Cat Crawls Through a Hole; Shadow; Virgin Eva; Virgin Bozena and a Little Dog Bobbie; Ballad About a Treefrog or When I Went Water a Little Garden; White Show; Attention Pothole; Accelerate. *Publication:* Secret of the Synthesizers. *Honours:* Prize, Saxophonist, International Jazz Festival, Prague, 1971; Silver Tablet, 1977; Appreciation for Composition, 1977; The Golden Pip, from the Asscn of the Czech Advertising Agencies for the Sound Spot Citizen. *Membership:* Asscn of Composers and Scientists. *Address:* Cerchovska 6, 120 00 Prague 2, Czech Republic.

KOUYATE Kandia; b. 1958, Kita, Mali. Vocalist; Songwriter. *Musical Education:* Learned music from parents (father balafon player, mother singer). *Career:* Born into a griot family; Member: The Apollos, in Bamako; Moved to Abidjan and recorded first cassette, 1980; Formed own band including Toumani Diabate, early 1980s. *Recordings:* Albums include: Amary Dou presents Kandia Kouyate, 1985: Project Dabia, 1987; Kita Kan (including Ousmane Kouyate), 1999.

KOVERHULT Tommy; b. 11 Dec. 1945, Stockholm, Sweden. Musician (tenor and soprano saxophone, flute). m. 17 May 1974, divorced, 4 s., 1 d. *Education:* Franz Schartau's Institute of Commerce, Stockholm. *Musical Education:* Self-taught. *Career:* Played in cellar clubs, Stockholm, 1960s; Member, Eje Thelin's Group, with festival appearances in Belgium, 1967; Played in study group with musicians from the Bernt Rosengren Quartet and Maffy Falay's SEVDA, 1967; Member, Jan Wallgren's Quintet, including tour of Germany, 1973; Founder, The Tommy Koverhult Quintet, 1980–89; Freelance musician, 1989-. *Compositions:* Several by the Tommy Koverhult Quintet. *Recordings:* with Jan Wellgren: Steel Bend Rock, 1970; Tommy Koverhult With The Jan Wallgren Quintet, 1973; with the Bernt Rosengren Quartet: Improvisations, 1969; Fly Me To The Sun,

1971; Live In Stockholm, Vols One and Two, 1974; with Lasse Werner: Saxofonsymfoni, 1972; with Maffy Falay and SAVDA: Live At Fregattan, 1973; with own Quintet: Jazz in Sweden '83, 1983; Live At Nefertiti, 1985; Various artists: Notes From Underground, 1973. *Honours:* Golden Disc Award, Orkester Journalen magazine, 1970; Winner, Orkester Journalen/ Tonfallet Readers' Poll, 1983. *Leisure interest:* Speedway. *Address:* Tjustgatan 3, 118 27 Stockholm, Sweden.

KOZLOWSKI James John, (Koz); b. 7 Sept. 1949, Hartford, Connecticut, USA. Dir Artist Development. m. Lula Shepard, 11 June 1994. *Education:* BSc, Engineering Management, Boston University, 1971; MBA, Human Behaviour, 1973. *Musical Education:* 5 years lessons, clarinet, alto, tenor saxophones. *Career:* Managed retail outlet; Started nationally syndicated radio programmes, Rock Around The World and Modern Music; Director of Purchasing, import companies, Peters International, Important Record Distributors; Held position as Label Director, Production Manager, Director Publicity, Director Creative Marketing, Director Artist Management for Relativity Records, Maze and Viceroy Music. *Recordings:* Project Co-ordinator, Surfing With The Alien, Joe Satriani; Also for all Viceroy Music acts, including Rattlesnake Guitar – The Music of Peter Green. *Publications:* Writer for Creem; Trouser Press; King Biscuit Times; Various freelance publications. *Honours:* RIAA Gold, Platinum records for Surfing With The Alien, Joe Satriani. *Leisure interests:* Wine; Food; Cooking; Photography; Sports. *Address:* 230 E 44th St #5G, New York, NY 10017, USA.

KRALL Diana; b. 16 Nov. 1966, Nanaimo, British Columbia, Canada. Vocals; Musician (piano); Composer. *Career:* Began classical piano, aged 4; First gig playing piano in local restaurant, aged 15; Won Vancouver Jazz Festival scholarship to study at Berklee College in Boston; Won Canada Arts Council grant and relocated to Los Angeles to study with Jimmy Rowles; Moved to New York City, playing the night club circuit, 1990; Recorded first album for Montréal label Justin Time Records, 1993; Signed to GRP/Impulse/Verve, 1994; Regular tours of North America, Britain, Europe and the Far East. *Recordings:* Steppin' Out, 1993; Only Trust Your Heart, 1994; All For You, 1995; Love Scenes, 1997; When I Look In Your Eyes, 1999; The Look of Love, 2001; features on soundtracks: Midnight In The Garden of Good and Evil; True Crime. *Honour:* Grammy Award, Best Jazz Vocal, When I Look In Your Eyes, 1999. *Current Management:* S L Feldman and Associates, Stephen Macklam and Sam Feldman, 1505 W Second Ave, Suite 200, Vancouver, British Columbia, V6H 3Y4, Canada. *Internet:* www.dianakrall.com.

KRAMER; b. 30 Nov. 1958, New York City, USA. Songwriter; Record Prod.; Record Label Owner; Performer. m. Shannon, 30 Aug. 1982, 1 d. *Musical Education:* Classical organ and singer; Self-taught multi-instrumentalist. *Career:* Founded/performed in: Gong, 1979; The Chadbournes, 1980–82; The Fugs, 1982–84; Shockabilly, 1982–85; Butthole Surfers, 1985; Half Japanese, 1986–88; BALL, 1987–90; Bongwater, 1987–91; Ween, 1990; Captain Howdy (with Penn Jillette), 1993–; Founder, 3 record labels: Shimmy-Disc, 1987; Kokopop, 1990; Strangelove, 1994. *Recordings:* Albums: Guilt Trip, 1992; Secret of Comedy, 1994; Let Me Explain, 1998; Songs from the Pink Death, 1998; Producer for: Palace Songs; New Radiant Storm Kings; Galaxie 500; White Zombie; King Missile; GWAR; Low; Urge Overkill, including track Girl You'll Be A Woman Soon, from Pulp Fiction soundtrack; Maureen Tucker; Daniel Johnston; Jon Spenser; Dogbowl; John Zorn. *Leisure interests:* Fishing; Films. *Current Management:* Steve Moir, Santa Monica, California.

KRAMER Billy J, (William Howard Ashton); b. 19 Aug. 1943, Bootle, Lancashire, England. Singer; Musician (guitar). *Career:* Guitarist, The Phantoms; Singer, The Coasters; Signed by manager Brian Epstein, 1963; Singer with backing group, The Dakotas, 1963–68; Regular British tours; Appearances include: Star Club, Hamburg, Germany; Mersey Beat Showcase concert, with The Beatles, Gerry and The Pacemakers, 1963; The Beatles Christmas Show, London, 1963; NME Poll Winners Concert, Wembley, with The Beatles, Cliff Richard and the Shadows, Rolling Stones, 1964; Played for HRH Queen Mother, 1964; British Song Festival, 1965; Star Scene 65 tour, with the Everlys, Cilla Black, 1965; Solo career, club tours, 1968–; Appearances include: British Re-Invasion US tour, 1973; Solid Silver Sixties Show tour, with the Searchers, Gerry and The Pacemakers, 1993. *Recordings:* Albums: Listen To Billy J Kramer, 1963; Little Children, 1964; Best of Billy J Kramer and the Dakotas, 1993; Singles include: with The Dakotas: Do You Want To Know A Secret? (No. 2, UK), 1963; Bad To Me (No. 1, UK), 1963; I'll Keep You Satisfied, 1963; Little Children (No. 1, UK), 1964; From A Window, 1964; It's Gotta Last Forever, 1965; Trains and Boats and Planes, 1965. *Honour:* Melody Maker Poll Winner, Best Newcomer, 1963. *Current Management:* Barry Collings Entertainments. *Address:* 21a Clifton Rd, Southend-on-Sea, Essex SS1 1AB, England.

KRAUSS Alison; b. 23 July 1971, Champaign, Illinois, USA. Singer; Bluegrass Musician (fiddle). *Career:* Singer, musician since age 14; Lead singer with backing band Union Station; 3 British tours. *Recordings:* 6 albums with Union Station; Solo album: Now That I've Found You, 1995; So Long So Wrong, 1997; Forget About It, 1999; New Favorite, 2001; Singles include: Baby Now That I've Found You; When You Say Nothing At All. *Honours:* Grammy Award, 1987; Country Music Television, Rising Star of 1995; 4 CMA Awards: Female Vocalist of the Year; Best New Artist; Vocal Event of the Year; Single of the Year, 1995; Great British Country Music Award: International Female Vocalist of the Year, 1996; Gavin Americana Album of the Year, So Long So Wrong, 1997; Great British Country Music Award: International Bluegrass Band of the Year, 1997–98; Dove Award, 1998; Nashville Music Award, 1998. *Address:* c/o Keith Case and Associates, 1025 17th Ave S, Nashville, TN 37203, USA.

KRAVITZ Lenny; b. 26 May 1964, New York, USA. Singer; Musician (piano, guitar); Songwriter; Record Prod. m. Lisa Bonet, divorced. *Musical Education:* Self-taught. *Career:* Actor, as teenager; Member, California Boys Choir and Metropolitan Opera; Solo artiste, 1989–; Headline tours, UK, US and world-wide, 1990–; Concerts include: Support to Bob Dylan, New York, 1990; John Lennon Tribute Shows, Tokyo, 1990; Support to the Cult, Toronto, 1991; On-stage with Prince, New York, 1993; World tour, 1993; Glastonbury Festival, 1993; Torhout and Wechter Festival, 1993; Universal Love Tour, 1993; Television includes: Tonight Show; Arsenio Hall Show; Saturday Zoo; Saturday Night Live; Late Show with David Letterman. *Recordings:* Albums: Let Love Rule, 1989; Mama Said, 1991; Are You Gonna Go My Way (No. 1, UK), 1993; Circus, 1995; 5, 1998; Greatest Hits, 2000; Lenny, 2001; Singles: It Ain't Over Till It's Over (No. 2, US), 1991; Are You Gonna Go My Way, 1993; Believe, 1993; Heaven Help, 1993; Is There Any Love In Your Heart, 1993; Rock 'n' Roll Is Dead, 1995; Get You Off, 1996; Can't Get You Off My Mind, 1996; I Belong to You, 1998; If You Can't Say No, 1998; Fly Away (No. 1, UK), 1998; American Woman, 1999; Black Velveteen, 1999; Other recordings include: Use Me, duet with Mick Jagger, Wandering Spirit album, 1993; Film soundtrack, Superfly (with Curtis Mayfield); As producer, songwriter: Be My Baby, Vanessa Paradis, 1992; Justify My Love, Madonna (No. 1, USA); Also as co-writer: Line Up, Aerosmith. *Honours include:* BRIT Award, Best International Male, 1994; Grammy Award, Male Rock Vocal Performance, American Woman, 2000; Again, 2001. *Current Management:* H K Management, 8900 Wilshire Blvd, #300, Beverly Hills, CA 90211, USA.

KRIEF Hervé; b. 3 Aug. 1965, Paris, France. Musician (guitar); Singer; Composer; Arranger. *Career:* 500 concerts, France and abroad. *Recordings:* Albums: Paris Funk, SAEP, 1988; Comme C'Est Bizarre, SAEP, 1990; Live In Paris, Hervé Krief Big Band, 1991; Barbés Blues, Hervé Krief Blues Trio, 1992; La Dolce Vita, Hervé Krief Big Band, 1994; Paris-Bruxelles, Hervé Krief Blues Trio, 1995; Strong Love Affair, 1996. *Leisure interests:* Football; Tennis; Films. *Current Management:* Gilles Ouakil, BSM Productions. *Address:* 29 rue Championnet, 75018 Paris, France.

KRIEGER Robbie; b. 8 Jan. 1948, Los Angeles, California, USA. Musician (guitar). *Career:* Member, The Doors, 1965–72; Member, The Butts Band, 1972–; Also formed Robbie Krieger and Friends; Versions; Performances include: Northern California Folk-Rock Festival, 1968; Hollywood Bowl, later released as a video, 1968; Toronto Rock 'n' Roll Revival Show, 1969; Isle of Wight Festival, 1970; Annual performances, The Love Ride, benefit for Muscular Dystrophy, 1990; Film documentaries: The Doors Are Open, 1968; Feats of Friends, 1969. *Recordings:* Albums: The Doors, 1967; Strange Days, 1967; Waiting For The Sun, 1968; Morrison Hotel, 1970; Absolutely Live, 1970; L A Woman, 1971; Other Voices, 1971; Weird Scenes Inside The Gold Mine, 1972; Full Circle, 1972; Best of The Doors, 1973; Live At The Hollywood Bowl, 1987; Solo: No Habla, 1990; RKO Live, 1995; Versions, 1996; Singles: Light My Fire (No. 1, USA), 1967; Love Me Two Times, 1968; Hello I Love You (No. 1, USA), 1968; Touch Me, 1969; Love Her Madly, 1971; Riders On The Storm, 1971.

KRISHNAMURTI Kavita, (Kavita Krishnamurhty Subramaniam); b. Delhi, India. Vocalist. m. L Subramaniam. *Education:* St Xaviers College, Bombay, Economics, honours degree. *Musical Education:* Began vocal training as a child. *Career:* Indian film playback singer; First recording for a Bengali film song was done with Lata Mangeshkar; First Hindi film under Laxmikant Pyarelal, Maang Bharo Sajna, was followed by Pyar Jhukta Nahin; Other films include: Mr India; Karma; Saudagar; Khuda Gawah; Chaalbaaz; 1942 – A Love Story; Yaarana; Mohara; Bombay; Saaz; Khamoshi; Pardesh; Bhairavi; Agnisakshi; Prem Agan; Kuch Kuch Hota Hai; Bade Miyan Chhote Miyan; Wajood; Has sung more than 1500 songs in Indian films in several languages; Has recorded and performed with internationally famous Indian Classical violinist husband on several occasions. *Recordings:* soundtracks include: Lovers, 1983; Pyaar Jhukta Nahin, 1984; Chaalbaaz, 1989; Deewana Mujhsa Nahin, Khilaaf, 1990; First Love Letter, Saudagar, 1991; Ek Ladka Ek Ladki, Khiladi, 1992; Aankhen, Boyfriend, Chandramukhi, Dalaal, Darr, Khalnayika, Phool, Sangram, Shreeman Aashique, Waqt Hamara Hai, 1993; 1942 – A Love Story, Bombay, Madhosh, Mohra, 1994; Dhanwaan, Kartavya, Milan, Nazar Ke Saamne, Tu Chor Main Sipahi, Vaarana, 1995; Agnisakshi, Chaahat, Dushmani, Jaan, Jeet, Khamoshi The Musical, Papa Kehte Hain,

Rajkumar, Tere Mere Sapne, The Great Robbery, 1996; Aar Ya Paar, Betaabi, Ishq, Judwaa, Koyla, Virasat, 1997; Dil Se.., Jeans, Keemat, Kuch Kuch Hota Hai, Prem Aggan, 1998, Dil Kya Kare, Dillagi, Hum Dil De Chuke Sanam, Hum Saath-Saath Hain, Khoobsurat, Mann, Shool, Taal, Vaastav, 1999; Badal, Dil Hi Dil Mein, Hadh Kar Di Aapne, Hera Pheri, Kya Kehna, Mela, Pukar, 2000; Daman, Dil Chahta Hai, Pyaar Ishq Aur Mohabbat, 2001; solo Albums: Koi Akela Kahan; Meera Ka Ram; Pop Time; Devotional Melodies. *Honours:* Film Fare Awards: 1942 – A Love Story, 1995; Yaarana, 1996; Khamoshi, 1997; Screen Award: Khamoshi, 1997; Sansui Viewers Choice Award, 1998; Screen Videocon Award, Hum Dil De Chuke Sanam, 1999; Lux Zee Cine Award, Hum Dil De Chuke Sanam, 1999; Stardust Millennium Award, Best Singer, 2000.

KRISTENSEN Paul; b. 21 June 1965, Oslo, Norway. Songwriter; Musician (bass guitar, drums). *Education:* Graphic Printer. *Musical Education:* Self-taught. *Career:* Formed Backstreet Girls, 1984; Tours: Norway; Sweden; Denmark; England; USA, 1987–92; Tour, Norway, with Casino Steel and The Crybabys, 1992. *Recordings:* Mental Shakedown, 1986; Boogie Till You Puke, 1988; Party On Elm Street, 1989; Coming Down Hard, 1990; Let's Have It, 1992; Live, 1993; Don't Fake It Too Long, 1995; Nykter, 1996; Hellway To High, 1999; Guest appearances with: Ziggy and The Rhythm Bulldogs; Casino Steel; Comic Messiah; A Technicolour Dream; Also several compilations. *Honours:* Norwegian Grammy Nominations, 1989, 1990. *Memberships:* TONO; GRAMO; GRAMART. *Leisure interest:* Record collecting. *Current Management:* Gram Art, Arb Samfunnets Plass 1, 0181 Oslo, Norway.

KRISTIANSEN Morten; b. 4 April 1971, Trondheim, Norway. Musician (guitar); Singer. *Education:* 2 years, University. *Career:* Started Hedge Hog, 1989; Several tours Norway; Toured Europe, 1994, 1995. *Recordings:* Erase, 1992; Surprise, 1992; Primal Gutter, 1993; Mercury Red, 1994; Mindless, 1994; The Healing EP, 1995; Thorn Cord Wonder, 1995. *Membership:* Norwegian Asscn of Musicians. *Leisure interest:* Rally Car driving.

KRISTINA Sonja; b. 14 April 1949, Brentwood, Essex. Singer; Guitar; Sax; Flute; Piano. m. Stewart Copeland, 16 July 1982, divorced 1992, 3 s. *Musical Education:* Self-taught; Extensive music performance studies. *Career:* Lead Vocalist, Curved Air, rock group; Chrissy, Original London Cast of Hair; Several Fringe Theatre Projects including Shona, directed Claire Davidson; Pentameters Hampstead, 1989. *Recordings:* Back Street LVV, single, 1971; It Happened Today, single, 1970; 8 albums with Curved Air, 1971–76; Songs From the Acid Folk; Sonja Kristina; Harmonies of Love. *Honour:* Sounds Poll, Voted Top Female Vocalist, 1971. *Memberships:* Equity; Musicians' Union; AOTOS. *Leisure interests:* Art Teaching; Singing; Theatre; Performance. *Current Management:* Mystic Records. *Address:* 226A Haverstock Hill, London NW3 2AE, England.

KRISTOFFERSON Kris; b. 22 June 1936, Brownsville, Texas, USA. Singer; Songwriter; Actor. m. (1), 1 s., 1 d., (2) Rita Coolidge, 19 Aug. 1973, divorced, 1 s.; (3) Lisa Meyers, 19 Feb. 1983, 2 s., 1 d. *Education:* PhD, Pomona College; BA, Oxford University, England. *Career:* Songwriter, 1965–; Solo recording artiste, 1969–; Numerous concerts world-wide, including: Isle of Wight Festival, 1970; Big Sur Folk Festival, 1971; New York Pop Festival, 1977; UNICEF charity concert, New York, 1978; Farm Aid II, 1987; Bob Dylan Tribute, New York, 1992; Also member of side project The Highwaymen (with Willie Nelson, Johnny Cash, Waylon Jennings), 1985–; Appeared at Farm Aid V, 1992; Actor, 1972–; Film appearances include: Cisco Pike, 1972; Pat Garret and Billy The Kid, 1973; Alice Doesn't Live Here Any More, 1974; The Sailor Who Fell From Grace With The Sea, 1976; A Star Is Born, 1976; Semi-Tough, 1977; Convoy, 1978; Heaven's Gate, 1980; Rollover, 1981; Flashpoint, 1984; Songwriter, 1984; Trouble In Mind, 1985; Big Top Pee Wee, 1988; Millenium, 1989; Christmas In Connecticut, 1992; Lone Star, 1996; Blade, 1998; Planet of The Apes, 2001; Numerous appearances, television films and mini-series. *Compositions include:* Help Me Make It Through The Night; Me and Bobby McGee, (also recorded by Janis Joplin); Why Me; For The Good Times. *Recordings:* Albums include: Kristofferson, 1970; The Silver-Tongued Devil and I, 1971; Border Lord, 1972; Jesus Was A Capricorn, 1973; Full Moon, with Rita Coolidge, 1973; Spooky Lady's Sideshow, 1974; Who's To Bless and Who's To Blame, 1975; Breakaway, with Rita Coolidge, 1975; A Star Is Born (soundtrack), 1977; Surreal Thing, 1976; Songs of Kristofferson, 1977; Easter Island, 1978; Natural Act, with Rita Coolidge, 1979; Shake Hands With The Devil, 1979; Help Me Make It Through The Night, 1980; To The Bone, 1981; The Winning Hand, 1983; Music From Songwriter, with Willie Nelson, 1984; Repossessed, 1986; Third World Warrior, 1990; A Moment of Forever, 1995; The Austin Sessions, 1999; with The Highwaymen: Highwayman, 1985; Highwaymen 2, 1992. *Honours:* CMA Song of The Year, Sunday Morning Coming Down, 1970; Grammy Awards: Best Country Song, 1972; Best Country Vocal Performance (with Coolidge), 1973, 1976; Golden Globe, Best Actor, 1976; Inducted into Songwriters Hall of Fame, 1985; with The Highwaymen: ACM Single of The Year, Highwayman, 1986; 2 American Music Awards,

1986. *Current Management:* Rothbaum and Garner, 36 Mill Plain Rd, Suite 406, Danbury, CT 06811, USA.

KRIZIC Davor; b. 29 March 1966, Zagreb, Croatia. Musician (trumpet, flugelhorn); Composer. *Musical Education:* Musical High School, Zagreb; 3 years of Jazz Music, University of Graz. *Career:* Played with: Ernie Wilkins; Ed Thighpen; Bosko Petrovic; Jimmy Woody; David Liebmon; Soloist, Croatian Radio-TV Big Band; Played at Jazz Fair, Zagreb, 1990, 1992–95; Ingolstadt Jazz Festival, 1990; Springtime Jazz Feever, 1995; Many television and radio appearances in Croatia; Greentown Jazz Band German tour. *Compositions:* Beleavin'; Some Blues; Urony. *Recordings:* Albums: with Miro Kadoic: Dry, 1994; with Mia: Ne Ne Ker Se Ne Sme, 1994; with Miljenko Prohaska: Opus 900, 1994; Leader, Boilers Jazz Quartet, Zagreb. *Honour:* Prize for Best Young Jazz Musician, Jazz Fair, Zagreb, 1990. *Memberships:* Jazz Club, Zagreb; Croatian Music Union; Croatian Artiste's Society (ZUH). *Leisure interests:* Cooking; Basketball. *Address:* Palmoticeva 25, 10000 Zagreb, Croatia.

KROEGHER Freddy; b. 23 Sept. 1967, St-Etienne, France. Singer; Composer; Musician (lead guitar, bass); Entertainer. 1 d. *Musical Education:* Studied from 17–20 at AIMRA Jazz School, Lyons, France. *Career:* Francofolies of La Rochelle, 1993; Festival of Young Creators, Tignes, 1993; National FNAC Tour, special broadcast interview in France-Inter Radio; TV clip video (Killer) 1993; Concerts; Radio appearances; TV interviews, newspapers. *Recordings:* Albums: Freddy Kroegher: Le Meilleur, 1993; Secoue Ton Seve, 1995; 3 singles; Studio session, backing guitars with: Laoassenko, 1990; Nilda Fernandez, 1991; Jimmy Oihid, 1992; Michel Nouyve, 1993; Gillo Coquard, 1994. *Honours:* Twice Best Rock Artist, Rhone-Alpes region, France, 1990, 1991. *Memberships:* RONDOR; SACEM. *Leisure interest:* Music. *Current Management:* Freddy Kroegher Production. *Address:* Route de Parisièves, 42360 Cottance, France.

KROG Karin; b. 15 May 1937, Oslo, Norway. Jazz Singer. m. Johannes Bergh, 21 Sept. 1957, 2 d. *Education:* Business School. *Musical Education:* Private study with Anne Brown, 1962–69; Ivo Knecevic, 1969–72. *Career:* Member of Kjell Karlsen Quartet, Frode Thingnaes Quintet and Egil Kapstad Trio; Leader of own groups, 1962–; Worked with Don Ellis; Clare Fischer; Mikkel Flagstad; Einar Iversen; John Surman; Bengt Hallberg; Red Mitchell; Nils Lindberg; Warne Marsh; Richard Rodney Bennett; Founder, First Chairman, Norwegian Jazz Forum, 1965–66; World-wide live, television and radio appearances include jazz festivals in Antibes, France and Norway, 1965; Warsaw and Prague, 1966; Hamburg and Berlin, 1967; Osaka, 1970; Australia, 1985; Hungary, 1989; USSR, 1990; Djakarta, 1992; Bulgaria, 1994; Umbria (Italy), Bath (England), Sardinia, 1994; Concert, Beijing, 1996; Concert, The Purcell Rooms, London, 1999; Formed Meantime Records, 1987. *Compositions include:* ballet music for Carolyn Carlson and Lario Ekson. *Recordings:* By Myself, 1964; Jazz Moments, 1966; Some Other Spring, with Dexter Gordon, 1970; Hi-Fly, with Archie Shepp, 1972; I Remember You, with Red Mitchell and Warne Marsh, 1980; Two of a Kind, with Beng Hallberg, 1981; Nordic Quartet, with John Surman, Terje Rypdal, Vigleik Storaas, 1995; Compilation: Jubilee, 30 years in recorded music, 1994; Bluesand, with John Surman, 1999. *Honours:* Buddy Award, Norwegian Jazz Foundation, 1965; Down Beat Poll Winner, Talent Deserving Wider Recognition, 1967; Spellemanns Prize, 1974; Grammy, Norway, 1974; Female Singer of the Year, European Jazz Federation, 1975; 2 Swing Journal Awards, Record of the Year, Japan, 1970 and 1978; Oslo Council Artist Award, 1981; Won the Spellemann's Prize, 1999; Awarded The Radka Toneff Memorial Prize, 1999; Several government grants and scholarships. *Memberships:* Norwegian Musicians' Federation; NOPA. *Leisure interests:* Outdoor life; Sport. *Address:* Nobelsgate 35, 0268 Oslo, Norway.

KRUST (Kirk Thompson), (DJ Krust, Gang Related, Glamour Gold); b. 1968, Bristol, Avon, England. Prod.; Remixer; DJ. *Career:* First releases on Ten Records, late '80s; Began releasing material with Roni Size on V Recordings and on Size's own Full Cycle Records; Co-founder: Reprazent (with Roni Size); Released debut solo album, 2000; Collaborations: Roni Size; DJ Die; Remixed: Bjork; Moloko; DJ Rap; Nicolette. *Recordings:* Albums: New Forms (with Reprazent), 1997; Coded Language, 2000; In The Mode (with Reprazent), 2001; Singles: Deceivers EP, 1993; Jazz Note, 1994; Quiz Show, 1995; Angles, 1996; Genetic Manipulation EP, 1997; Brown Paper Bag (with Reprazent), 1997; True Stories, 1998; Decoded EP, 2000. *Honour:* Mercury Music Prize, winner, New Forms, Roni Size/ Reprazent, 1997. *Address:* c/o Talkin' Loud Records, Chancellors House, 72 Chancellors Rd, London, W6 9QB, England.

KRZISNIK Borut; b. 7 Oct. 1961, Zagreb. Composer; Musician (Guitar). *Education:* Graduated, Psychology, Ljubljana University. *Career:* Numerous works performed including Love Song No 1, with Symphonic Orchestra of Slovenian Philharmony; Questions, Enzo Fabiani Quartet; Festival appearances with own band Data Direct: Druga Godba, 1993; Music of 20th Century, Skopje, 1994; Vorax, Vicenza, 1994. *Recordings:* Currents of Time, 1991, With Data Direct: La Dolce Vita, 1995; The Stories from Magatrea, 1999; Permanent collaboration with theatre directors Emil

Hrvatin and Julie-Anne Robinson; Music for Theatre: Camillo, at Piccolo Teatro, Milan, 1998; Yard, Bush Theatre, London, 1998; Two Gentlemen of Verona, Royal National Theatre, 1999; The New Organon, Drustvo 51, Cankarjev Dom; Music for Video, Labyrinth, 1993. *Honour:* First Prize, Napoli Danza Festival, Il Coreografo Eletronico, 1994. *Current Management:* Falcata-Galia Recordings. *Address:* Bratov Ucakar 46, 1000 Ljubljana, Slovenia.

KUBES Stanislav; b. 4 March 1952, Prague, Czech Republic. Musician (Guitar); Songwriter. m. Marcela, 28 Aug. 1973. *Musical Education:* Guitar, Public School of Art. *Career:* The Wizards, 1970; Eminence Group, 1972; Benefit Group, 1973; Respect Group, 1974–75; JIFT Schelinger Group, 1975–81; Tour of Poland with Smokie, 1977; Romance za korunu, Movie, 1975; SLS Group, 1981–85; ETC... Band, 1985–; Support for Rolling Stones, Urban Jungle Tour, Prague, 1990. *Compositions:* Jsem pry blazen jen, 1978; Vanda a Zanda, LP and TV clip, 1985; Za vodou, CD, MC, 1997; 15 titles published. *Recordings:* 35 singles, 1975–81; Hrr na ne!, LP, 1975; Nám se Líbi, 1976; SLS, LP, 1982; Coloured Dreams, LP, 1984; ETC..., 1986; ETC... 4, 1987; 20 deta duse, LP, CD, 1989; Jen se smej, CD, 1994; ETC... Band, Unplugged Live, CD, 1996; Mésto z périn, CD, 1997. *Leisure interests:* Aeronautics; Cats; Countryside. *Current Management:* Syrinx, Svornosti 8, 15000 Prague 5, Czech Republic. *Address:* Mladenovova 3231, CZ 14300 Prague 4, Czech Republic.

KUCERA Josef Simon, (Saxophone Joe); b. 8 July 1943, Prague, Czech Republic. All Saxophones; Flute. *Career:* Framus Five, soul band, Czechoslovakia, 1967–68; Musical, Hair, 1969–70; Duo: Jesse Ballard and Saxphone Joe, 1972–74; Sessions with Alexis Korner, London; Paradise Island Band, Berlin, 1976; Member, Pete 'Wyoming' Bender Band, 1980–90; Jazz Festival Karlovy Vary, Czech Republic, 1990, 1993; Japan Tour with Marta Kubisova, 1993. *Compositions:* Day Dream; Anyway; 1000 Reasons; Waltz for My Friends; Anotherway. *Recordings:* Control, 1975; Crossroads, 1982; Swindia, 1984; Balance, solo album, 1986; Triangle, Live, 1997. *Membership:* Rock and Pop Musikerverband. *Leisure interests:* Sailing; Poetry; Painting. *Current Management:* Events and Arts, H Degner, Grüntenstr 54, 12 107 Berlin, Germany. *Address:* Koloniestr 28, 13359 Berlin, Germany.

KUJAHN Lars B; b. 22 June 1958, Denmark. Drummer. *Education:* Attended Lectures in Rhythms, Istanbul Conservatory, 1988, Cairo, 1989, Casablanca, 1992, Fanoon, 1997. *Career:* Playing Jazz-Rock in Passengers, Milky Way, 1979–86; Playing Gypsy Music in Svira, 1982–87; Leader of Oriental Mood, 1991; Teacher, Oriental Percussion, 1991-. *Compositions:* Raqsa Maghzebia, 1992; Yallah Mustagbad, 1992; Maccra, 1995; Hobb Harr, 1995; Gediid, 1995; Oriential Moods, 1996; Ahman, 1997; Mapsut, 1997; 12 Ok, 1997. *Recordings:* Travels, 1994; Oriental Moods, 1996; Oriental Garden, 1996; Ax Kurdistaan, 1996; Cölbanein, 1998; Expoessive Mahala. *Memberships:* Danish Musicians Union; Danish Rhythmic Composers Organization. *Leisure interest:* Travel. *Address:* Oriental Percussion, Hane Tavsons Gade 17 4 tv, 2200 N, Denmark.

KUKKO (Jyrki) Sakari; b. 8 July 1953, Kajaani, Finland. Bandleader; Composer; Arranger; Musician (flute, saxophone, keyboards). m. Marta Cecilia Renza Villanueva, 1981, divorced 1986. *Musical Education:* Classical music, Sibelius Academy, Helsinki; Jazz with Edward Vesala. *Career:* Founder, Piirpauke, 1974–; Concerts include: Festivals in Tbilisi; Bombay; Zürich; Paris; Cannes; Barcelona; Concerts, tours with Piirpauke in 30 different countries (4 continents); Also with: Youssou N'Dour; Okay Temiz; Alameda; Aster Aweke; Television and radio appearances world-wide. *Compositions:* for the Espoo Big Band: Moonlight Caravan; Finnish Characters. *Recordings:* 20 albums with Piirpauke; 2 solo albums: Will of The Wisp, 1979; Music For Espoo Big Band, 1989; with Sensation Band Ethiopia '76: Ethiopian Groove; features on: Am Universum, Amorphis, 2001; Music for films, theatre, dance. *Honours:* Yrjö Award, Finnish Jazz Federation, 1976. *Leisure interests:* Different cultures; Yoga; Fishing; Tennis; Palindromes. *Current Management:* Tapio Korjus, Rockadillo. *Address:* Sakari Kukko, Koutaniementie 30 A, 87100 Kajaani, Finland; c/ o Rockadillo, Keskustori 7 A 11, 33100 Tampere, Finland.

KULAS Michael; Musician (Guitar, percussion, backing vocals). *Career:* Member, James, 1997–; Numerous tours, festival dates and television appearances. *Recordings:* with James: Singles: She's A Star, 1997; Tomorrow, 1997; Destiny Calling, 1998; Sit Down '98, 1998, I Know What I'm Here For, 1999; Just Like Fred Astaire, 1999; We're Going To Miss You, 1999; Getting Away With It (All Messed Up), 2001; Albums: with James: Whiplash, 1997; Millionaires, 1999; Pleased To Meet You, 2001; solo: Mosquito, 1995; Another Small Machine, 2001.

KULICK Bruce; b. 12 Dec. 1953, Brooklyn, New York, USA. Musician (guitar). *Career:* Member, various groups including: Blackjack; Goodrats; Member, US rock group Kiss, 1985–; Appearances include: US tour, with Cheap Trick, 1988; Marquee Club, 1988; US tour, 1990; Revenge '92 Tour, 1992. *Recordings:* with Kiss: Albums: Asylum, 1985; Crazy Nights, 1987; Smashes Thrashes and Hits, 1988; Hot In The Shade, 1989; Revenge, 1992;

Kiss Alive III, 1992; Carnival of Souls: The Final Session, 1997; with ESP: ESP, 1999; solo album: Audio Dog, 2001; Contributor, Hear 'N' Aid (Ethiopian famine relief charity album), 1986; Singles include: Tears Are Falling; Crazy Crazy Nights; Reason To Live; Hide Your Heart; Forever; God Gave Rock and Roll To You, featured in film: Bill and Ted's Bogus Journey, 1992. *Honours:* Inducted into Hollywood's Rock Walk, 1993; Kiss Day proclaimed, Los Angeles, 1993. *Current Management:* Entertainment Services Unlimited, Main St Plaza 1000, Suite 303, Voorhees, NJ 08043, USA.

KUPPER Eric S; b. 10 July 1962, New York, NY, USA. Prod.; Remixer; Musician; Songwriter. m. Gianna F Bavido, 1 s., 1 d. *Education:* BA, Music; BA, Theatre and Film, Hunter College, CUNY. *Career:* Top of the Pops with Frankie Knuckles; Arsenio Hall Show with Rupaul. *Compositions include:* The Whistle Song, Frankie Knuckles; Imitation of Life. *Recordings include:* P M Dawn, I'll Be Waiting; Rupaul, Supermodel, album; K-Scope, From the Deep; Instant Music;. *Memberships:* NARAS; ASCAP; AFM. *Leisure interests:* Fishing; Cigars and Pipes; AFM. *Current Management:* Seven PM.

KUSSIN Al; b. 24 Aug. 1952, Edmonton, Canada. Prod.; Musician (keyboards). *Education:* BA; MA, Economics. *Musical Education:* Grade VII Royal Conservatory, Grade II Theory. *Recordings:* Lorraine Scott: All Talk; Lorraine Scott, 1995; Party Mix: Party Mix '94; Tropirollo Vols II-VI; Celine Dion: Unison; Swing Mix, 1998; Party Mix, 1998; VIP, 1998; Code Five, 1998; Joee, 1999. *Honours:* 4 Juno nominations; 4 Platinum records. *Memberships:* SOCAN; CIRPA; AULA; CARAS. *Current Management:* Slak Productions. *Address:* 9 Hector Ave, Toronto, ON M6G 3G2, Canada.

KUTI Femi Anikulapo; b. 1963, London. Vocalist; Musician (saxophone); Songwriter. m. Funke, 1 s. *Education:* Lagos, Nigeria. *Career:* Substituted for father, Fela Kuti, in The Egypt 80 at the Hollywood Bowl, 1985; Formed the Positive Force around 1987; Signed to Motown, 1995; Later to Barclay/Polygram, 1997; Performed at WOMAD Reading, 1990. *Recordings:* Albums include: No Cause For Alarm (with the Positive Force), 1989; Wonder Wonder, 1995; Shoki Shoki, 1998; Fight To Win, 2001. *Publications:* AIDS in Africa, essay published by UNICEF in its Progress of Nations report, 2000. *Honours:* Kora Awards: Best Male Artist, Best West African Artist, 1999; World Music Award, Best Selling African Artist, 2000.

KUVEZIN Albert; b. 27 Nov. 1965, Kyzyl, Tuva, Russia. Vocalist; Musician (Marinkhur: ethnic folk string instrument). m. Natalia Toka, 16 Dec. 1990, 2 d. *Musical Education:* Kyzyl Musical College; Folk Instrument Class. *Career:* As member of Yat-Kha: Voice of Asia Festival (Brian Eno Special Prize), 1990; Sweden, 1991; Siberia Interweek, 1992–94; Berlin

Independent Days, 1993; Italy, 1993; WOMAD, 1994; US, 1995. *Recordings:* Yat-kha, 1993; Huun-Huur-Tu: Go Horses In My Herd. *Publications:* Numerous in Russian, US, Italian, Scandinavian press. *Honours:* Voice of Asia, 1990; Wales Folk Fest, 1992. *Leisure interest:* Being out in the country. *Current Management:* Etz/Artemy Troitsky. *Address:* PO Box 107, 125212 Moscow, Russia.

KWOK Aaron, (Guo Fu Cheng, Kwok Fu Shing); b. 26 Oct. 1965, Hong Kong. Vocalist; Actor. *Career:* Joined Hong Kong TVB company TV show for 3 years as professional dancer, aged 16; Transferred to TVB acting class, aged 21; Several small acting engagements before employing former college director Siu Mei as manager for professional singing/acting career; Major celebrity status in Asia following spectacular live concerts and high profile film roles including ParaPara Sakura, 2001; Records/performs in Cantonese and Mandarin languages. *Recordings:* selected Mandarin Albums: No End Love, 1990; Should I Leave Silently, Who Can Tell Me, 1991; Please Bring My Love Home, Love You, 1992; Aaron Kwok Loves You Deeply, Leave You With All My Love, Hard To Hold Back The Dreams, 1993; End of The Dream, Desire, Lover For Life, 1994; Here Is My Start, Non Stop Wind, 1995; Love Dove, 1996; Sharing Love/Who Will Remember Me, Devoted, 1997; So Afraid, 1999; Journey/Cheer, 2000; Give You All My Love, 2001; selected Cantonese Albums: Hot Beat, 1992; Without Your Love, Merry Christmas, 1993; Starting From Zero, Wild City, A Moment of Romantic II, Iron Attraction, AK-47, 1994; You're Everything, Tale of Purity, Memorandum, 1995; Most Exciting Empire, Song In The Wind, 1996; Love's Calling, Generation Next, 1997; The Best Remix, 1998; Live In Concert '98, 1999; Amazing Dream, 2000; Wu Ji vs Wei Lai (EP), Memorandum, Live On Stage In Concert (includes Mandarin), Xin Tian Di (includes Mandarin), Absolute, 2001. *Address:* c/o Warner Music, 12/F, The Peninsula Office Tower, 18 Middle Rd, TST Kowloon, Hong Kong. *Internet:* www.aaronkwokonline.com.

KYRKJEBO Sissel; b. 24 June 1969, Bergen, Norway. Singer. m. Eddie Skoller, 21 Aug. 1993. *Career:* Singer, 1985–; Sold 1.5m. discs, Norway, 1986–; World-wide tours including Scandinavian concerts with Neil Sedaka, 1991; Barcelona Cathedral; Christmas Concert in Vienna with Placido Domingo; Musical Ambassador, singer for Olympic Hymn, Winter Olympic Games, Norway, 1994; Theatre: Maria Von Trapp, Sound of Music; Solveig, Peer Gynt. *Recordings:* Albums: Sissel, 1986; Glade Jul, 1987; Soria Moria, 1989; Gift of Love, 1992; Innerst I Sjelen, 1994; All Good Things, 2001; Hit single: Fire In Your Heart (Olympic Hymn) with Placido Domingo; Vocals on the Titanic score. *Honours:* Norwegian Grammy; Artist of the Year; H C Andersen Award; Platinum disc, Innerst I Sjelen. *Membership:* GRAMO. *Current Management:* c/o Arne Svare, Stageway Impresario A/S, Skuteviksboder 11, 5035 Bergen, Norway.

L

LA PORTE-PITICCO Laurie Margaret; b. 31 Aug. 1960, Sudbury, Ontario, Canada. Singer; Songwriter; Musician (rhythm guitar). m. Steve Piticco, 1 s., 1 d. *Musical Education:* Played with musical family from age 15. *Career:* Rhythm guitarist, singer, songwriter with South Mountain; Television appearances include: Band hosted own series, 4 years, CHRO TV; Tommy Hunter Show; Canadian Country Music Awards Show; Concerts: Support to Vince Gill, Charlie Pride. *Compositions:* Co-writer: I've Got The Blues, South Mountain (Top 10 hit); Several original songs on South Mountain album: Where There's A Will. *Honour:* Vista Rising Star Award, CCMA, 1991. *Memberships:* SOCAN; Canadian Country Music Asscn. *Leisure interests:* Bible study; Time with children and friends. *Current Management:* Savannah Music Inc; Catherine Faint, Agent, Stony Plain Records. *Address:* PO Box 64, South Mountain, ON K0E 1W0, Canada.

LA SALLE Denise; b. 16 July 1941, Mississippi, USA. Vocalist; Songwriter; Publisher. m. James E Wolfe, 16 July, 1977, 1 s., 1 d. *Career:* Dick Clark; Soul Train; Rhythm and Blues Award; Blues Going On; Toured West Africa, 1972; Europe 1974–78; Co-owner, WFKX Radio Station (KIX96 FM), 1984–; Malaco World Tour, 1989; Soul Blues European Tour: France; Italy; England; Austria; Netherlands; Finland; Norway; Sweden, 1993; 5 nights at Le Meridien Hotel Lounge in Paris, 2001; Owner, Denise La Salle's Chique Boutique and Wigs; Co-owner, The Celebrity Club, Jackson, Tennessee; Own record label Ordena Records formed 1999;. *Recordings:* Trapped By A Thing Called Love; Down Home Blues; Married But Not To Each Other; The Bitch Is Bad; Lady In The Street; A Mansize Job; Now Run and Tell That; Smokin' In Bed, 1997; God's Got My Back, 1999; Down on Clinton, 1999; This Real Woman, 2000; There's No Separation, 2001. *Publications:* America's Prodigal Son, 1989; A Short Story About The Blues; How To Be A Successful Songwriter, booklet. *Honours:* Jackie Award, Chicago, 1974; BMI Award. *Memberships:* Founder: National Asscn For Preservation of Blues (NAPOB); BMI; NARAS. *Leisure interests:* Cooking; Gardening. *Current Management:* Roger Redding and Associates Maconga. *Address:* c/o Denise La Salle, Ordena Entertainment Inc, 17 Henderson Rd, Jackson, TN 38305, USA.

LABARRIERE Jacques; b. 29 Nov. 1956, Paris, France. Composer; Arranger; Musician (piano). *Musical Education:* Licence de Musicologie; Prize for harmony, counterpoint. *Career:* Shows include: Gospel; Cats; Fantasticks; 42nd Street; Trouble in Tahiti; Radio-France broadcast: ACR de France Culture; Concerts: Jazz with Joe Lee Wilson; Anette Lowman; Eric Barret; Philippe Selam; Jean-Louis Mechali; Singers: C Combe; C Magny; Perone. *Recordings:* Cats; Tie Break, Second Set; Entre 3 and 5. *Memberships:* SACEM; SACD; ADAMI; SPEDIDAM; SCAM.

LABELLE Patti, (Patricia Holt); b. 24 May 1944, Philadelphia, Pennsylvania, USA. Singer; Actress. *Career:* Founder member, The Blue Belles, 1961; Appearances include: Ready Steady Go, ITV, Thank Your Lucky Stars, ITV, British tour, 1966; Group name changed to Labelle, 1970–76; Solo artiste, 1976–; Concerts include: Live Aid, JFK Stadium, Philadelphia, 1985; Nelson Mandela International Tribute, Wembley Stadium, England, 1990; Appearance, gospel musical, Your Arm's Too Short To Box With God, Broadway, New York, 1982; Actress, film A Soldier's Story, 1984; Television appearances: Actress, Unnatural Causes, NBC, 1986; Motown 30 – What's Goin' On, CBS, 1990; Arsenio Hall Show special, devoted to Labelle, 1991; Going Home To Gospel With Patti LaBelle, 1991; Own sitcom, Out All Night, NBC, 1992. *Recordings:* Singles: with Blue Belles: I Sold My Heart To The Junkman, 1962; with LaBelle: Lady Marmalade, 1975; On My Own, duet with Michael McDonald (No. 1, USA), 1986; Oh People, 1986; Love Has Finally Come At Last, duet with Bobby Womack; Feels Like Another One, 1991; New Attitude, 1991; Somebody Loves You Baby, 1992; On My Own, 1992; The Right Kinda Love, 1994; When You Talk About Love, 1997; When You've Been Blessed, 1997; Albums: with LaBelle: LaBelle, 1971; Gonna Take A Miracle, 1971; Moonshadow, 1972; Nightbirds, 1974; Phoenix, 1975; Chameleon, 1976; Solo albums: Patti LaBelle, 1977; Tasty, 1978; It's Alright With Me, 1979; Released, 1977; The Spirit's In It, 1981; I'm In Love Again, 1984; Winner In You, 1986; Be Yourself, 1989; This Christmas, 1990; Burnin', 1991; Live!, 1992; Gems, 1994; Contributor, The Poet II, Bobby Womack, 1984; Good Woman, Gladys Knight, 1990; Hallelujah!, Quincy Jones, 1991; Am I Cool Or What?, 1992; At the Apollo, 1995; Yo Mister, 1997; Flame, 1997; Live at the Apollo, 1999; The Best of the Early Years, 1999; When A Woman Loves, 2001; Contributor, film soundtracks: Beverly Hills Cop, 1985; Outrageous Fortune, 1987; Dragnet, 1987; Licence To Kill, 1989; Leap of Faith, 1992. *Honours include:* Award of Merit, Philadelphia Art Alliance, 1986; Lifetime Achievement Award, CORE (Congress of Racial Equality), 1990; NAACP Entertainer of Year, 1992; American Music Award, Favourite Female R & B/Soul Artist, 1993; Star on Hollywood Walk of Fame, 1993. *Current*

Management: PAZ Entertainment Co. *Address:* 2041 Locust St, Philadelphia, PA 19103, USA.

LACY Steve, (Steven Lacritz); b. 23 July 1934, New York, USA. Jazz Musician (soprano saxophone). *Career:* Performed with artists including: Pee Wee Russell; Buck Clayton; Cecil Taylor; Gil Evans Orchestra, 1957; Leader, own groups; Founder, own quartet with Roswell Rudd, early 1960s; Formed sextet, Paris, 1970; Played duets with Mal Waldron, 1979-. *Recordings include:* Soprano Sax, 1957; Reflections – Steve Lacy Plays Thelonius Monk, 1958; Evidence, with Don Cherry, 1961; Paris Blues, with Gil Evans, Raps, 1977; with Steve Lacy Three: New York Capers, 1979; The Way, 1979; Ballets, 1980; Songs, 1985; Prospectus, 1986; Steve Lacy Two, Five and Six Blinks, 1986; Steve Lacy Nine: Futurities, 1986; Anthem, 1990; with Mal Waldron: Herbe de L'Oubli, 1981; Snake Out, 1981; Let's Call This, 1986; Hot House, 1991; Live at Sweet Basil, 1991; Spirit of Mingus, 1991; Actuality, 1996; Communique, 1997; Scratching the 70's/ Dreams, 1997; Sands, 1998; Cry, 1999; The Rent, 1999; Monks Dream, 2000; Snips – Live At Environ, 2000. *Honours:* Downbeat Magazine Poll winner, Best Soprano Saxophonist, several times. *Address:* 57 rue de Temple, 75004 Paris, France.

LADINSKY Gary; b. 2 May 1947, Los Angeles, California, USA. Recording Engineer. 2 s. *Education:* BA, California State University, Northridge, 1970. *Career:* Recording engineer, Record Plant, Los Angeles, 1971–75; President, Gary Ladinsky Inc/Design FX Audio, 1979-. *Recordings:* Engineer, albums by: Lynyrd Skynyrd; Van Morrison; Moody Blues; Cheap Trick; Donna Summer; George Benson; Manhattan Transfer; Mixer, film scores: Ferris Bueller's Day Off, 1987; Trains, Planes and Automoblies, 1987; Naked Gun, 1988. *Memberships:* NARAS; Audio Engineering Society; Society Professional Audio Recording Services, IATSE. *Address:* c/o Design FX Audio, PO Box 491087, Los Angeles, CA 90049, USA.

LADY BO, (Peggy Jones); b. 19 July 1940, New York City, USA. Musician (guitar); Singer; Dancer; Songwriter; Arranger; Prod.; Choreographer. m. Walter Malone, 20 Oct. 1968. *Education:* Complete Performing Arts School, New York. *Career:* First female guitarist in history of Rock and Roll, Rhythm and Blues, Soul, Pop, Jazz, Blues, 1957; First female guitarist hired, major act, 1959; First female member, original Bo Diddley recording and stage act, 1959; Principal player, protegée of Bo Diddley; The Jewels, No. 1 club band, New York, 1961–67; Backing musician: Chuck Berry, 1971; Richard Berry, 1983; Play: Thunder Knocking on the Door, San Jose Repertory Theatre, 1997; Major concerts: HIC Arena, Hawaii; Monterey Jazz Festival, 1973, 1974; Greek Theatre; Circle Star Theatre; Ventura County and Nevada State Fair; Monterey Bay Blues Festival, 1994, 1995, 1999; Tours: US, Canada, 1965–80s; Europe, 1987; NIKE Endorsement, Bo Knows, 1989; Television: The Jewels, The Mod Mecca TV Special, NYC/BBC, England, 1967; Kenny Rogers, Toronto, 1971; Donnie and Marie, Hollywood, 1976–77; Live Concert, Sweden, 1987; Arts and Entertainment Special, world-wide coverage, 1990; Lady Bo and the BC Horns, South Bay Scene, USA, 1996; Film: The Lost Boys, 1987; Video: Bo Diddley with Lady Bo and The Family Jewel: I Don't Sound Like Nobody, UK, 1992; Flashbacks: Volume One Soul Sensations, 1994; Lady Bo and The BC Horns, Say That You Love Me, 1995. *Recordings:* Albums: with Bo Diddley: Bo Diddley, 1958; Go Bo Diddley, 1959; Have Guitar, Will Travel, 1960; Bo Diddley In The Spotlight, 1961; Bo Diddley Is A Lover, 1961; Bo Diddley Is A Gunslinger, 1962; Road Runner, 1964; Bo Diddley, 16 All-Time Greatest Hits, 1964; The Mighty Bo Diddley, Ain't It Good To Be Free, USA, 1984; France, 1988; Bo Diddley – The Chess Box, 1990; Bo Diddley, The EP Collection, 1992; Bo Diddley, The Chess Years, box set, 1993; The Mighty Bo Diddley, 1994; Bo Knows Bo, 1995; Bo Diddley – His Best, 1997; with Les Cooper: Wiggle Wobble, 1962, 1988; with Fred Waring Orchestra: The Two Worlds of Fred Waring, 1966; Various artistes: Feeling Happy, 1978; The Doo Wop Era: Harlem, New York, 1987; New York R & B, Harlem Holiday, 1988; King Curtis: Soul Twist and Other Golden Classics, 1988; Lady Bo and the BC Horns, Shebo-Shebad, 2000; Singles: 19 with Bo Diddley; 8 as the Jewels; Greg and Peg; Peggy and Bob; The Bob Chords Vocal Group. *Publications:* Listed: The Great Gretsch Guitars Hall of Fame; She's A Rebel – The History of Women In Rock 'n' Roll, 1992; The Complete Bo Diddley Sessions, by George R White, 1993; Bo Diddley – Living Legend Bio, 1995; Doo Wop, The Chicago Scene, 1996; Guitar Player books, 1974, 1987, 1990; Suede News, Lady Bo, cover feature, 1997; Rolling Stone Book of Women in Rock, 1998. *Honour:* Lifetime Achievement Award, South Bay Blues Awards, 1993. *Memberships:* AFM Local #153; SheBo Shebad Music Publishing, BMI. *Current Management:* LB-BCH Productions. *Address:* 14680 Bear Creek Rd, Boulder Creek, CA 95006, USA.

LAFFY Stephen; b. 29 May 1953, London, England. Musician; Songwriter; Prod. m. Lynn Heather, 21 March 1994, 2 d. *Musical Education:* Self-taught. *Career:* Performed at Glastonbury Festival; WOMAD; Notting Hill Carnival; Overseas tours, television and radio; Formed own band Rhythm Rising. *Recordings:* When 2000 Comes, 1995; Don't Go Breaking Down; Carry On; Everybody Needs Someone. *Memberships:* Musicians' Union; PRS; MCPS. *Leisure interests:* Swimming; Gardening; Reading.

LAGERBERG Bengt Fredrik Arvid; b. 5 July 1973, Karolinska sjukhuset i Stockholm, Sweden. Musician (Drums, Bassoon, Guitar, Bass, Piano, Trumpet, Harmonica). *Career:* Joined The Cardigans, 1992; Contributed tracks to films Romeo and Juliet and A Life Less Ordinary; Numerous TV and radio appearances, tours and festival dates throughout Europe. *Recordings:* Singles: Sick and Tired; Carnival; Hey! Get Out of My Way; Rise and Shine; Lovefool; Been It; Your New Cuckoo; My Favourite Game; Erase and Rewind; Burning Down The House, with Tom Jones; Albums: Emmerdale; Life; First Band On The Moon; Gran Turismo.

LAHBIB Lahcen; b. Morocco. Vocalist; Musician (percussion). *Career:* Left Morocco for London, 1980s; Founder member of band MoMo (Music of Moroccan Origin); Act's fusion of North African Gnawa music with western-style drum kit, samples and contemporary dance styles (including house and garage) described as 'Dar'; Popular live band; Released first album, 2001. *Recordings:* Album: The Birth of Dar, 2001. *Honour:* BBC Radio 3 Award for World Music, Boundary Crossing nominee, The Birth of Dar, 2002.

LAHTI Pentti; b. 15 Aug. 1945, Finland. Musician (reeds, flutes, saxophones). *Career:* Musician with Eero Koivistoinen Octet, and Mircea Stan Quartet, early 1970s; Member, Jukka Linkola Octet, Member, UMO (New Music Orchestra); Finnish Broadcasting Company tours to Oslo, 1973; Laren Festival, Holland, 1977; Annual appearance, Pori Festival; Reed player, Wasama Quartet and Ilkka Niemeläinen's Instinct, 1980s. *Recording:* Solo album: Ben Bay; Also appears: with Edward Vesala, Nan Madol, Mau-mau; with Umo Jazz Orchestra. *Honour:* Yrjö Award, Finnish Jazz Federation, 1983. *Address:* Kärpänkuja 8, 04230 Kerava, Finland.

LAIDLAW Raymond Joseph; b. 28 May 1948, Tynemouth, England. Musician (drums). m. Lesley, 9 April 1976, 2 s. *Education:* Newcastle Art College. *Musical Education:* Club A GoGo, Newcastle. *Career:* Drummer, Lindisfarne, 1969–; Now studio owner, music publisher. *Compositions:* Joint composer: Scotch Mist instrumental (B side of Lindisfarne hit: Meet Me On the Corner). *Recordings:* Hit singles: Meet Me On The Corner, 1972; Lady Eleanor, 1972; Run For Home, 1978; Fog On The Tyne, with Paul 'Gazza' Gascoigne, 1990; Albums include: Nicely Out of Tune, 1970; Fog On The Tyne (No. 1, UK), 1971; Dingly Dell, 1972; Finest Hour, 1975; Back and Fourth, 1978; On Tap, 1994; Buried Treasure Vol. 1, 2000; Complete BBC Recordings 1971–75, 2000. *Membership:* Musicians' Union. *Leisure interests:* Walking; Talking; Eating; Drinking. *Current Management:* Lindisfarne Musical Productions. *Address:* Hi-level Recording, 18 Victoria Terrace, Whitley Bay, Tyne and Wear, England.

LAIDVEE Meelis; b. 10 Jan. 1964, Pärnu, Estonia. Musician (keyboards). m. Eve Laidlee (Lublo), 1 March 1985, 2 d. *Musical Education:* Private lessons. *Career:* Concerts, tours, 1978–; Television and radio hitlists with: Provints; Uncle Bella; The Tuberkubited, 1988-. *Recordings:* 3 abums with The Tuberkuloited. *Honours:* Radio Top 10 Award, 1994, 1995. *Address:* PO Box 2225, EE 0035, Tallinn, Estonia.

LAINE Cleo (Dame), (Clementina Dinah Dankworth); b. 28 Oct. 1927, Southall, Middlesex, England. Vocalist; Actress. m. John Dankworth, 18 March 1958, 2 s., 1 d. *Career:* Vocalist, Dankworth Orchestra, 1953–58; Lead role, Seven Deadly Sins, Edinburgh Festival and Sadlers Wells, 1961; Showboat, 1972; Colette, 1980; Also appeared in A Time To Laugh; Hedda Gabler; The Women of Troy; The Mystery of Edwin Drood, Broadway, 1986; Into The Woods, US National Tour, 1989; Numerous television appearances. *Recordings include:* Feel The Warm; I Am A Song; Live At Melbourne (Gold discs); Best Friends; Sometimes When We Touch (Platinum discs); Recent recordings: Jazz, 1993; Blue and Sentimental, 1994; Solitude, 1995; The Very Best of Cleo Laine, 1997; Live In Manhattan, 2001; Film: The Last of the Blonde Bombshells, 2000. *Publications:* Cleo, autobiography, 1994; You Can Sing If You Want To, 1997. *Honours:* DBE, 1997; OBE, 1979; Golden Feather Award, Los Angeles Times, 1973; Edison Award, 1974; Hon MA, Open University, 1975; Singer of the Year, TV Times, 1978; Hon MusD, Berklee College of Music, 1982; Grammy Award, Best Female Vocalist, 1985; Theatre World Award, 1986; NARM Lifetime Achievement Award, 1990; British Jazz Award, Best Female Vocalist, 1990; Variety Club of Great Britain Show Business Personality of Year, 1977; ISPA Distinguished Artists Award, 1999; Hon DA, Luton University, 1994; Hon MusD, York University, 1993. *Current Management:* Dankworth Management. *Address:* The Old Rectory, Wavendon, Milton Keynes MK17 8LT, England.

LAINE Frankie, (Francesco Paolo Lo Vecchio); b. 30 March 1913, Chicago, Illinois, USA. Singer; Songwriter. m. Nan Laine, 15 June 1950, deceased 1993, 2 d. *Musical Education:* Studied with Frank Teschemacher. *Career:* Singer, dance teacher, Merry Garden Ballroom; Singer, numerous dance marathons; First billed as Frankie Laine, 1938; First record deal, 1946; Sales in excess of 100m. records; Concerts world-wide include: Royal Variety Performance for Queen Elizabeth II, 1954; Film appearances include: When You're Smiling, 1950; Sunny Side of The Street, 1951; Rainbow Round My Shoulder, 1952; Bring Your Smile Along, 1955; He Laughed Last, 1956; Performed title songs, films: Gunfight At The OK Corral, 1957; Blazing Saddles, 1974; Featured in The Last Picture Show, 1971; Lemon Popsicle, 1978; Raging Bull, 1980; Television includes: Frankie Laine Time; The Frankie Laine Show; Acted in: Rawhide; Perry Mason; Burke's Law. *Compositions:* Co-writer: Put Yourself In My Place Baby (with Hoagy Carmichael); It Ain't Gonna Be Like That, with Mel Tormé; Magnificent Obsession (with Freddie Karger); Torchin' with Al Lerner; We'll Be Together Again (with Carl Fischer); Recorded by over 100 artists including Louis Armstrong; Tony Bennett; Ray Charles; Rosemary Clooney; Ella Fitzgerald; Sammy Davis Jr; Jack Jones; Frank Sinatra; Billie Holiday. *Recordings:* 80 albums and EPs, 1947–; Singles include: Jezebel, 1951; High Noon, 1952; I Believe (No. 1, 18 weeks, UK), 1953; Where The Winds Blow, 1953; Hey Joe (No. 1, UK), 1953; Answer Me (No. 1, UK), 1953; Blowing Wild, 1953; Granada, 1954; Kid's Last Fight, 1954; My Friend, 1954; Cool Water, 1955; A Woman In Love (No. 1, UK), 1956; Moonlight Gambler, 1956; Rawhide, 1959; Making Memories, 1971; Lord You Gave Me A Mountain, 1969; Albums: Memories, 1985; Mule Train, 1989; All of Me, 1993; Duets, 1994; Dynamic, 1996; Young Master, 1998; Life is Beautiful, 1998; Cocktail Hour, 2000. *Publication:* That Lucky Old Son (autobiography), co-author with Joseph Laredo. *Address:* PO Box 6910, San Diego, CA 92166, USA.

LAINE Reino; b. 11 July 1946, Finland. Musician (drums). *Career:* Played drums from age 16; Member, quartet with Pekka Pöyry, Montreux, 1968; Played with Eero Koivistoinen, winning group competition, Montreux, 1969; Also appeared at Newport Jazz Festival; Member, Seppo Paakunainen's Conjunto Baron, 1970s; Percussionist, numerous plays at Helsinki City Theatre; Played with major Finnish musicians, also artists including: Dexter Gordon; Clifford Jordan; Charlie Mariano; Appeared with Juhani Aaltonen group, The Finnish Middle-Aged All Stars, Pori Festival, 1985. *Honour:* Yrjö Award, Finnish Jazz Federation, 1981. *Memberships:* Mem. of board, Finnish Jazz Federation; Pop Musicians' Union; Mem. of government appointed organizations. *Address:* Hakaniemenranta 26 A 63, 00530 Helsinki, Finland.

LAIZEAU Francois; b. 19 Nov. 1955, Paris, France. 1 d. *Musical Education:* Agostini School, 1973–76. *Career:* Sideman for: Tania Maria; Magma; Eddy Louiss; Michel Legrand; Toots Thielemans; Louis Sclavis; Michel Portal; Dominique Pifarely; Martial Solal; Kenny Wheeler; Claus Stotter. *Recordings:* Albums with H Kaenzig and K Wheeler; Live At Fat Thursday, Michel Legrand; Eddy Louiss; Nuit Etoilée; 3 recordings with the National Jazz Orchestra; Magma, Retrospective Vol. 3, 1981; Joelle Ursull, Comme Dans Un Film December 1993, 1996; Jean-Loup Longnon, Cyclades, 1996; 20 Ans de Jazz en France, 1996. *Membership:* UMJ. *Address:* 82 rue de Rochechouat, 75009 Paris, France.

LAJOIE-DESAVBIN May-Cecile; b. 25 May 1972, Victoria Hospital, Mahe, Seychelles. Research Officer; Linguist, Ministry of Education and Culture; Singer, The Waves, band. m. Teddy Desavbin, 6 Jan. 1996, 1 s. *Career:* Music-Wise, performing in hotels every weekend with band, Waves; Performed for Miss Seychelles Beauty Pageant; Performed for Miss World, Seychelles. *Compositions:* Lavi Rezete; Only A Dream; Viktorya; Venges-Moi; Ecris-Moi; Nov Devwar; Lot Kote; Konplent Paran; Fer Mwan Oubliye. *Recordings:* Albums: Lanbeli with the Waves; Victoria, personal album, 1996. *Publication:* Lavi Rezete, song, 1995. *Honours:* Media Prizes; Best Singer Award, Radio, 1996; Best Song Award, Radio, 1996; Best Singer Award, People Magazine, 1996; Best Song Award, People Magazine, 1996; Best Band Award, Waves, 1996. *Leisure interests:* Reading; Singing; Swimming. *Address:* Anse Aux Pins, Mahé, Republic of Seychelles.

LAKE Greg; b. 10 Nov. 1948, Bournemouth, Dorset, England. Musician (bass); Vocalist. *Career:* Member, The Gods, 1968; King Crimson, 1969–70; Emerson Lake and Palmer (ELP), 1970–78; Also as Emerson Lake and Powell (with Cozy Powell), 1985–86, 1992–; Asia, 1983; Festival performances include: Isle of Wight Festival, 1970; Mar-Y-Sol Festival, Puerto Rico, 1972. *Recordings:* Albums: with King Crimson: In The Court of The Crimson King, 1969; In The Wake of Poseidon, 1970; A Beginner's Guide To... (compilation), 2000; with ELP: Emerson Lake and Palmer, 1970; Tarkus (No. 1, UK), 1971; Pictures At An Exhibition, 1971; Trilogy, 1972; Brain Salad Surgery, 1974; Welcome Back My Friends To The Show That Never Ends – Ladies and Gentlemen... Emerson Lake and Palmer, 1974; Works, Vol. Two, 1977; Love Beach, 1978; Emerson Lake and Powell, 1986; Black Moon, 1992; Live At The Royal Albert Hall, 1993; Return of The Manticore, 1993; In The Hot Seat, 1994; Isle of Wight, 1997; Live In Poland, 2001; Solo albums: Greg Lake, 1981; Manoeuvres, 1983; In Concert on the King Biscuit Flower Hour, 1996; From the Beginning – The Greg Lake Retrospective, 1997; Singles include: with ELP: Fanfare For The Common Man (No. 2, UK), 1977; Solo: I Believe In Father Christmas (No. 2, UK), 1975. *Current Management:* Booking Agent: Pilato Entertainment, 277 Alexander St, Suite 813, Rochester, NY 14607, USA. *Address:* c/o Premier Talent, 3 E 54th St, 14th Floor, New York, NY 10022, USA.

LAKE Suzanne; b. 26 June 1929, New Jersey, USA. Singer; Actress. m. George A De Vos. *Education:* Opera, Juilliard; Voice, Queena Mario, Joseph Florestano; Acting, Claudia Franck, Yul Brynner, Larry Blyden; Harmony and Theory, Mayhew Lake. *Career:* Broadway and National Tour, Tuptim, The King and I, 1951–54; Broadway and National Tour, Helen Chao, Flower Drum Song, 1961–62; Starring Acts, Desert Inn, Las Vegas, Chateau Champlain, Montréal, 1963–72; Blossom Music Festival Concerts, USA and Asia, 1970–91; Teaching, 1980–95. *Recordings:* The Soul of Chanson. *Memberships:* Agma; Actors Equity; Aftra; Agva. *Leisure interests:* Piano; Writing; Concert Going; Travel; Walking. *Address:* 2835 Morley Dr., Oakland, CA 94611, USA.

LALENDLE Luvuyo; b. 4 April 1964. Music Educationist. m. Nomahlubl Tabitta Zulu, 1 s., 2 d. *Education:* Bachelor of Pedagogics, University of Fort Hare, South Africa, majored in Music Education and Pedagogics; BEd, University of Venda, South Africa; Master in Music Education, University of Iowa, USA. *Career:* Senior Lecturer, University of Venda, South Africa; Interview with Radio South Africa, Durban, 1989; Appearance on Zimbabwe National Television, 1994. *Publications:* Music In and Out of School, Iowa Music Educators' Journal; Music Programmes in a Post-Apartheid South Africa. *Honour:* Ackerman's Scholarship, 1987; Atlas (USAID) Scholarship, 1998. *Membership:* International Council for Traditional Music, Executive Board mem., 1997-. *Leisure interests:* Tennis; Jogging. *Address:* c/o Music Department, University of Venda, P/B X5050, Thohoyandou 0970, South Africa.

LAMB Andrew John; b. 13 July 1969, North Kensington, London, England. Musician (guitar, bass). *Musical Education:* Currently studying at the Guitar Institute in London. *Career:* Member of band Slander; 2 British tours, 1992–94; Various radio appearances including: Rock Wars, BBC Radio 1; European and American radio. *Recordings:* Composed and recorded own album with Slander; Various demos with other bands as a studio session musician; Live recordings. *Membership:* Musicians' Union. *Leisure interests:* Playing guitar; Watching bands; Motorcycling. *Address:* 24 Rowsley Rd, St Annes-on-Sea, Lancashire FY8 2NS, England.

LAMB Paul; b. 9 July 1955, Blyth, Northumberland, England. Musician (harmonica). Divorced, 1 s. *Career:* Festivals, Europe and UK; Television shows include: Spender, UK; Late Late Show, Ireland; Other shows in Germany; Scandinavia; France; UK; Radio programmes: BBC Radio 2; Jazz FM; Greater London Radio; Radio stations around Europe; Concerts with Mark Knopfler; West End Show: A Slice of Saturday Night. *Recordings:* with The Blues Burglars: Breakin In; John Henry Jumps In; The Blue Album; Blues Burglars Whoopin'; with Paul Lamb and The King Snakes: Paul Lamb and the King Snakes; Shifting Into Gear; Fine Condition; She's a Killer; Harmonica Man; Compilation CDs and box sets: Cooking With The Blues; Blues Harp Boogie Music Club International; The Deluxe Blues Band, with Big Joe Louis, Otis Grand; Confessin' The Blues; Recent releases include: Take Your Time and Get It Right, 2000; Paul Lamb and The King Snakes, 2001; Session work includes: Evil, Lucky Lopez Evans. *Publication:* Blues In Britain. *Honours:* First as team in the World Harmonica Championships, Germany; Second as soloist, 1975; Voted Best UK Harmonica Player for 5 years, British and Blues Connection. *Memberships:* Musicians' Union; NHL; British Blues Connection; PRS. *Leisure interests:* Listening to old blues records; Bird watching. *Address:* 17 Pollard Rd, Whetstone, London, England.

LAMBE Rick; b. 4 Aug. 1960, Birmingham, England. Musician (slide guitar, guitars, bass, drums). m. Corinne Croucher, 29 July 1992, 1 s. *Musical Education:* Grade 5, Electric Guitar; Audio technology course, Kidderminster College, 1996–98. *Career:* Concerts include: Telford Blues Festival, 1989–90; Played 25 concerts in 1 night for Children In Need charity for BBC; Coventry Blues Festival, 1991; Appeared on BBC show celebrating 21 years of Pebble Mill programme; Appeared as Band of The Week on John Taynton Show, 1992; Live radio appearances on radio, Children In Need, and Christmas Day radio broadcast; Various sessions for BBC TV; New Year's Eve Concert with Official Receivers Soul Band, Centenary Square, Birmingham performing to over 70,000 people; Recorded an album for local folk hero Gary O'Dea; Played on Love Love, a Charlie Landsborough album; Currently teaching National Diploma in Audio Technology at Kidderminster College. *Recordings:* Two Bhangra recordings for Achanak and Ananki; Two tracks on Hazel Dean's album; Abba tribute song forthcoming; Are You Receiving Us, The Official Receivers, 1996; Loud and Clear, with Curtis Little and the Receivers, live CD, 1998; There's A Storm Comin', album, 1999. *Memberships:* Musicians' Union; PAMRA; PRS. *Leisure interests:* Songwriting; Recording; Teaching music and guitar; Photography. *Current*

Management: White Lamb. *Address:* 32 Ombersley Close, Woodrow South, Redditch, Worcestershire B98 7UU, England.

LAMBERT David; b. 3 Dec. 1965, Wye, Kent, England. Label Head, Club and Radio DJ. *Education:* BA Hons, Social Science, University of Westminster. *Career:* Helped launch Touch Magazine; Began as DJ, 1989; Performing throughout UK, Europe and Latin America; Started Positiva Dance Label at EMI with Nick Halkes, 1993; Left as Head of A & R 1998; Label Head of AM:PM Records of Universal Island Records, 1998–; Started Saturday Night radio show on ILR station TFM (Stockton-on-Tees), 1999. *Leisure interests:* Music production and remixing; Reading; Swimming; Skiing; Playing guitar; Tennis. *Address:* c/o AM:PM, 22 St Peters Sq., London W6 9NW, England.

LAMBERT Ronnie (Busker); b. 3 Oct. 1950, Newcastle, England. Singer; Musician (guitar, harmonica); Bricklayer. m. Hazel Welsh, 24 Sept. 1974, 1 s., 1 d. *Career:* Rock on the Tyne concert at Gateshead International Stadium, 1981; Appeared as singer on BBC TV 4 times, and on local ITV 4 times; Many radio appearances and interviews on BBC Radio, 1982–94; Metro Radio; Radio Magpie. *Recordings:* Singles: Home Newcastle, 1981; River Tyne EP, 1982; Goin' Up (Newcastle United official promotional song), 1984; Buildin' Site, 1990; Black and White, 1993, re-recorded 1994; Album: Pure Geordie, 1991. *Honour:* Newcastle United Football Club play his music at their home games. *Memberships:* PRS; MCPS; Musicians' Union. *Leisure interests:* Studying Bible; Painting; Songwriting; Crosswords; Newcastle United Football Club supporter. *Current Management:* QC Entertainment. *Address:* Newburn Industrial Estate, Newburn, Northumberland, England.

LAMBERTH Dag (Ebbe Olaf); b. 13 May 1923, Mjölby, Sweden. Musician (Piano); Composer; Author, Teacher. m. (1) Stina Lindblad-Rogers, (2) Marion Brechbilder-Boecher, 1 s., 2 d. *Education:* BA, MA, Musicology, Slavic Languages, Russian, Literary History, Nordic Languages, German, Universities of Stockholm and Uppsala; MA, Musicology and Piano, Conservatory of Stockholm and private masterclasses. *Career:* Early performances with Lamberth Family and also with brother (famous solo trumpeter) Arne Lamberth and Copenhagen; Radio recordings. *Compositions:* Jolly Party, for symphony band and orchestra; Love in Monte Carlo; Christine Swedish Blonde; Adaptation of poem by Per Lägerkvist for soloist and choir; Swedish translation of French waltz Pigalle. *Recordings:* Jolly Party; Love in Monte Carlo; Schwarze Ballade. *Publications:* Critical articles in Swedish newspapers and German musicological journals. *Honour:* Great Award of the Swedish State for Composers, 1968. *Memberships:* International Asscn of Swedish Composers (STIM); Swedish Composers of Popular Music (SKAP). *Leisure interests:* Family; Garden; Travels; Composing; Reading. *Address:* Bellevuevägen 43 A, 217 72 Malmö, Sweden.

LAMBRECHT Dimitri; b. 9 April 1967, Aalst, Belgium. Prod.; Composer. *Career:* First Band: PLB System, Concerts in Belgium and France, 1988, 1989; Currently on tour with Natural Born Deejays. *Compositions:* Singles: For Fun, 1991; Jump, 1992; A Good Day, 1996; Sonar Contact, 1997; Deejays Mind, 1997; Oxygen, 1998; Airplay, 1998; The Deejays Are Here, 1999. *Recordings:* Artificial Defence, 1989; A Good Day, 1996; Today, 1998. *Leisure interest:* Record collecting. *Current Management:* King International Service, Leuvensesteenweg 120 Diest 3290, Belgium.

LAMMERS MEYER Hermann; b. 7 Dec. 1952, Aschendorf, Germany. Musician (pedal steel guitar); Vocalist. m. Anke Barenborg, 21 May 1988, 1 s. *Musical Education:* Self-taught. *Career:* Worked with Clay Baker and the Texas Honky Band; Success of Texas Country Road Show in USA followed by tours of Europe, including British tour, 1981; Writes and records own songs; Tours with own band The Emsland Hillbillies, all over Europe, UK, US; Solo project: The Honky Tonk Hearts performed for Germany on Euro Country Music Masters TV Show, Netherlands. *Recordings include:* with Emsland Hillbillies: Albums: Texas Country Road Show, Vols I, 1979; Vol. II, 1981; Texas Lone Star, 1981; Solo: Singles: Moonshine Ladies/Neon Leon, 1987; Southern Comfort/You Ought To Hear Me Cry, 1989; Death of a Clown/A Song For Sarah, 1998; Waltz of The Wind, 1999; Album: Half My Heart's In Texas, 1989; Above All The Starday Session, Nashville; The End of Time; The Last Country Song; Zeitlos, 1998; I'd Like To Live It Again, with David Frizzell, Lois Johnson, Marion Möhring, 2000; Duets with: Norma Jean; Kitty Wells; Willie Nelson; Johnny Bush. *Honours:* Country Album of The Year, GACMA in Germany, 1992; European Country Music Asscn Artist of The Year; Last Country Song, Album of The Year, 1996. *Leisure interest:* Playing steel guitar. *Current Management:* Desert Kid Records/E L Hillbillies Music, Drosselweg 15 26871 Aschendorf, Germany.

LAMOND George; b. 25 Feb. 1967, Georgetown, Washington DC, USA. Recording Artist; Vocalist. m. Oct. 1994. *Education:* New York High School of Art and Design. *Musical Education:* Various keyboards and Midi courses. *Career:* Rick Dee's TV Show; CNN Showbiz Today (profile and interview); Entertainment Tonight (profile and interview); No More Games Tour, opened for New Kids On The Block; TV Show, Showtime At The Apollo

Theatre. *Recordings:* Albums: Bad of The Heart; In My Life; (Spanish) Creo Enti (2 Billboard Top 10 Latin singles); Entrega; The Hits and More; Que To Vas Remixes; GL, 2001; Singles: Bad of The Heart, Top 40, Billboard Chart; Look Into My Eyes; No Matter What; Love's Contagious; Baby, I Believe In You; It's Always You (EP); I Want You Back. *Honour:* Winter Music Conference, Best Dance 12 Award. *Membership:* NARAS. *Leisure interests:* Cooking; Paintball; Drawing; Songwriting. *Current Management:* Chris Barbosa Management.

LAMOND Mary Jane; b. 5 Nov. 1960, Kingston, Ontario, Canada. Gaelic Singer. *Education:* Degree in Celtic Studies. *Career:* Fifth Estate, 1997; Lilith Fair, 1997; Capercaillie British tour, 1997; Chieftains Canada Tour, 1997; Hanging Garden Soundtrack, 1997; Chieftains US Tour, 1998; Contributor: albums: Hi How Are You Today?; Ashley Maclsaac, 1995; Chieftains, 1997; Fire In The Kitchen, 1998; Suase!, 1998. *Recording:* Bho Thir Nan Craobh, Suas e!, 1997, Làn Dùil, 2000. *Honours:* ECMA Song, Sleepy Maggie, 1997; Much Music Global Groove Video Award, Bog a Lochain, 1997. *Memberships:* SOCAN; CARAS; ECMA. *Current Management:* Jones and Co. *Address:* 5212 Sackville St, Suite 100, Halifax, NS, B3J 1K6, Canada.

LAMONT Duncan; b. 4 July 1931, Greenock, Scotland. Musician (tenor saxophone, woodwinds); Composer. m. Bridget, 20 Feb. 1960, 2 s. *Musical Education:* Private Study, Glasgow. *Career:* Started as jazz trumpet player, aged 14; Joined Kenny Graham Afro Cubist Band, age 20; Switched from trumpet to tenor saxophone, played with many Big bands; Studio Jazz player, accompanied major stars including: Frank Sinatra; Bing Crosby; Fred Astaire; Became composer, wrote several suites, success with songs, lyrics, performed by most major singers in England, USA. *Compositions include:* Songs: Tomorrow's Standards; Best of Bossa Novas; Summer Sambas; I Told You So, recorded by Cleo Laine; Not You Again, recorded by Cleo Laine and George Shearing; Suites include: The Young Person's Guide To The Jazz Orchestra; Sherlock Holmes Suite (For City of London); The Carnival of The Animals; Cinderella; Children's television programmes: Mr Benn; King Rollo; Spot (the dog); Towser; Spot's Magical Xmas (for Disney Studios) 1995. *Publication:* Tomorrow's Standards. *Honours:* Tomorrow's Standards, The Music Retailers Asscn Annual Awards For Excellence, 1995; Best Song of Year, ASAC, USA: I Told You So, 1995. *Memberships:* PRS; ASCAP. *Current Management:* Bucks Music, 1 Farm Pl., London W8 7SX, England.

LAMPRELL Adam Charles; b. 14 June 1965, Sutton, Surrey, England. Musician (guitar). m. Penny Britchfield, 11 June 1994, 1 s. *Education:* BA Hons, Graphic Design (specializing in Photography). *Career:* Recording sessions for Michael Prophet and Ricky Tuffy; Recording sessions for Bryan Ferry; TV commercials and theme music, including BBC2 series, Nurse; Joint bandleader, The Scissormen; World-wide recording, tours, television and radio. *Recordings:* with The Scissormen: Nitwit, 1992; Mumbo Jumbo, 1995; Glee (EP), 1997; Skyscraper album, Shooters, 1998; Bryan Ferry LP, 1999; Joey Tempest, The Final Countdown; Sessions for Michael Prophet, Ricky Tuffy, album: Get Ready; Singles include: Kicks; Recording on remixes include: Chaka Demus and Pliers; Freddie McGregor. *Memberships:* Musicians' Union; PRS; MCPS. *Leisure interests:* Football; Reading. *Address:* 53 Highclere St, London SE26 4EX, England.

LANCE Dirk, (Alex Katunich); b. 18 Aug. 1976. Musician (bass guitar). *Career:* Formed group Incubus with school friends in Calabasas, California, 1991; Initially played small parties, graduating to support slots in Hollywood, California; Circulated demo tapes of Closet Cultivation and Incubus before independent album release, 1995; Group signed by Immortal/Epic; Built US and European following support slots on tours with: Sugar Ray; Black Sabbath; Korn; Drive reached No. 1 on US Modern Rock Chart, 2001; First Japanese and Australian live dates, 2001. *Recordings:* Albums: Fungus Amongus, 1995; S.C.I.E.N.C.E., 1997; Make Yourself, 1999; Morning View, 2001; Singles: Enjoy Incubus EP, 1997; Pardon Me, 1999; Stellar, When Incubus Attacks Vol. 1 EP, 2000; Drive, Wish You Were Here, 2001. *Honours:* Make Yourself album certified double platinum by RIAA; Billboard Award, Modern Rock Single of The Year, 2001. *Current Management:* Steve Rennie, REN Management, California, USA. *Internet:* www.enjoyincubus.com.

LANDA Omar; b. 30 Nov. 1970, Morelia, Michoacan, Mexico. Musician (Drums, Keyboards). *Education:* Conservatoria de Las Rosas en Morelia; Drum lessons with Abraham Calleros in Guadalajara. *Career:* Radio appearances in Mexico City, WFM Radio Station; Opening concerts for Caifanes and Maná; TV appearances playing live, Channel 2. *Compositions:* 13, 1992; Llananina, 1994; Musgosa Caja, 1994; Tierra, 1996; BaxLtTrt, 1998. *Recordings:* La Parca, 1994; BaxLtTrt, 1998; Pulso, 1999. *Honours:* Best Rock Group from Province, Nuestro Rock Awards, 1994, 1995, 1996. *Leisure interests:* Long walks; Internet; The outdoors. *Current Management:* Fatal Productions. *Address:* La Privada a Gertrudis Boconegra No. 48, Morelia, Michoacan, Mexico.

LANDER Judd; b. 1 March 1948, Liverpool, England. Session Musician; Actor; Television Prod.; Record Co Exec. m. (1) Janine de Wolfe, 3 July 1987, 2 d., (2) Danielle, (3) Sienna Tuesday. *Career:* Member, The Hideaways, 1960s; Moved to London, 1970s; Session musician, CBS Records, 1974; Numerous performances include: The Cavern, Liverpool; Kampuchea charity concert, (with Paul McCartney), 1979; Associate producer, St Lucia Jazz Festival, 1991; Floor Director, Brits Music Awards, 1994–2000; Television appearances include: Top of The Pops; The Tube; Old Grey Whistle Test; Wogan; Des O'Connor Show; MTV; Montreux Pop Festival; Later With Jools Holland; Producer, television documentary, Jerry Lee Lewis; Concerts: Wembley Stadium; Wembley Arena; Knebworth House; Reading Festival; London Palladium; Royal Albert Hall; Culture Club Tour, 1998–99. *Compositions:* Resting Rough (film score); Music for The Short Show, LWT. *Recordings:* Singles: Church of The Poisoned Mind, Karma Chameleon, Culture Club (lead harmonica lines); Say You'll Be There, Spice Girls, 1996; Albums include: Flowers In The Dirt, Paul McCartney, 1989; Medusa, Annie Lennox, 1995; Alone With Everybody, Richard Ashcroft, 2000; Session musician for Badfinger; Walker Brothers; Scaffold; Bay City Rollers; Nazareth; Madness; The The; ABC; Maxi Priest; Prefab Sprout; Communards; Mike Oldfield; Dina Caroll; Tina Turner; Kirsty MacColl; Richard Ashcroft; Numerous television commericals. *Honour:* Gold Award, The British Academy of Songwriters, Composers and Authors, 1997. *Memberships:* Musicians' Union; Equity; BASCA. *Leisure interests:* Clay pigeon shooting; Car renovation. *Current Management:* Charles Armitage, Noel Gay Artists. *Address:* 1 Albion Court, Hammersmith, London W6 0QT, England.

LANDGREN Nils Lennart; b. 15 Feb. 1956, Degerfors, Sweden. Trombone Player; Singer; Composer. m. Beatrice Jaras-Landgren, 9 July 1979. *Education:* College degree; Classical Music degree; Soloist diploma, University of Music in Arvika, Sweden. *Career:* Professional Trombone Player, age 19; Freelance work in Stockholm, Sweden; Recording and stage performance with all major Swedish artists; Star, Skål, musical, Stockholm, running 2 years; Star, Villon, musical, Stockholm. *Compositions:* Red Horn, with Bruce Swedien; Aint Nobody, recorded with Maceo Parker; Cheyenne, with Michael Ruff. *Recordings:* Planet Rock; You're My No. 1; Streetfighter; Miles From Duke, with B A Wallin; Follow You Heart; Ch 2, with Johan Norberg; CH 2 – Two; Ballads; Gotland; Live in Stockholm; Paint It Blue; Swedish Folk Moderno; Contributions (as trombonist) to: Abba, Voulez-vous; Bose Broberg, Regni, 1995; Josefin Nilsson, Shapes, 1996; Bernard Purdie, Soul to Jazz; Norrbotten Big Band, 1996. *Honours:* 2 Swedish Grammies; German Jazz Award, 1997. *Leisure interest:* Wife is my life besides music. *Current Management:* Walter Brolund Inc, Kungsv 6, 19040, Rosersberg, Sweden. *Address:* Lillkalmar vägen 100B, 18265 Djurshom, Sweden.

LANE Jamie; b. 15 Sept. 1951, Calcutta, India. Musician (drums); Record Prod.; Engineer; Programmer. m. Katerina Koumi, 8 June 1991, 1 d. *Education:* BA Hons, MA, Magdalene College, Cambridge. *Musical Education:* Self-taught. *Career:* Member, bands: The Movies, 1976–80; Sniff 'n' The Tears, 1980–82; Session drummer, 1982–; Played with: Tina Turner; Mark Knopfler; 10cc; Joan Armatrading; Agnetha; Van Morrison; Randy Newman; Ben E King; Paul Brady; Chage and Aska; Blancmange; Producer for: Microdisney; Railway Children; Pete Townshend; Paul Brady; Falco; Nick Kamen; Hot House; Jackie Quinn; Microgroove; Do Re Mi. *Composition:* Deep Water, Jackie Quinn. *Recordings:* As drummer, Living On The Ceiling, Blancmange; As producer: Don't Come To Stay, Hot House; I Promised Myself, Nick Kamen. *Membership:* Musicians' Union. *Leisure interest:* Cricket. *Current Management:* Stephen Budd Management.

LANE Rick; b. 22 April 1953, London, England. Composer; Prod.; Musician (keyboards, guitar, bass, percussion); Backing Vocalist. *Musical Education:* Guildhall Exhibition Scholar. *Career:* Founder, Rent Boys; Private Lives; 3 tours with The Edgar Broughton Band; Now produces music for film, television, radio, commercials, corporate video, station idents and multimedia. *Recordings:* with Rent Boys: 2 singles, 1 album; with Private Lives: 3 singles, 2 albums; Over 200 television, cinema, radio commercials, documentary and features for BBC, LWT, Granada, Anglia. *Honours:* N London Music Festival, Silver Medal; Highly Commended, Roland Syn/Sound, 1992; Creative Circle Nomination, 1993; D and AD Gold Pencil, 1993. *Memberships:* British Music Writers' Council; Society of Producers of Applied Music; Performing Rights Society; MCPS; BASCA; Musicians' Union; Alliance of Composer Organisations; Asscn of Professional Composers; Composers Guild of Great Britain. *Current Management:* Nim Nim Musik. *Address:* Garden Studio, 19 Venetia Rd, London W5 4JD, England.

LANE Stevens; b. 7 Nov. 1921, Hammersmith, London, England. Semi professional Musician (cornet); Bandleader. *Musical Education:* Self-taught theory; Cornet teacher, Phil Parker. *Career:* Leader, own band, The Southern Stompers, 1950–; Re-named Red Hot Peppers, 1985–; Concerts include: Poland; Czechoslovakia; France; Germany; Netherlands; Denmark; Numerous broadcasts, BBC Jazz club. *Compositions:* Songs and instrumental pieces written or arranged for the band. *Recordings:*

Albums released on VJM, Major-Minor, Stomp Off and Azure labels. *Memberships:* Musicians' Union; MCPS; PRS. *Leisure interests:* Shropshire; Medieval churches. *Address:* 32 Kenton Lane, Harrow, Middlesex HA3 8TX, England.

LANG Andy Lee; b. 26 July 1965, Vienna, Austria. Singer; Entertainer; Musician (piano). *Education:* Commercial School. *Musical Education:* Private studies with Grandfather (Music Professor and Conductor). *Career:* Piano-player of Chuck Berry, European tour, 1992–93; Concerts with: Jerry Lee Lewis; Wanda Jackson; Carl Perkins; The Magic Platters; Fats Domino; Concerts, television and radio shows in: USA; Morocco; France; Switzerland; Germany; Austria. *Recordings:* Back To Rock 'n' Roll, 1990; Rockin' Piano Man, 1991; Back In Town, 1993; That's Entertainment Live, 1994; Rockin' Christmas, 1994. *Honour:* Golden Microphone, 1991. *Membership:* Austrian Composer Asscn. *Leisure interests:* Skiing; Watching television and video. *Current Management:* Star Box, Angela Kascha. *Address:* Simmerringer Haide 6/543, 1110 Vienna, Austria.

lang k d, (Kathryn Dawn Lang); b. 2 Nov. 1961, Consort, Alberta, Canada. Singer; Composer; Actress. *Career:* Played North American clubs with own band, 1982–87; Performed at closing ceremony, Winter Olympics, Calgary, 1988; Headlining US tour, 1992; Royal Albert Hall, 1992; Earth Day benefit concert, Hollywood Bowl, 1993; Sang with Andy Bell, BRIT Awards, 1993; Television includes: Late Night With David Letterman; Wogan; The Arsenio Hall Show; The Tonight Show; Top of The Pops; Subject, South Bank Show documentary, ITV, 1995; Film appearance, Salmonberries, 1991. *Recordings:* Albums: A Truly Western Experience, 1984; Angel With A Lariat, 1986; Shadowland, 1988; Absolute Torch and Twang, 1990; Ingénue, 1992; Even Cowgirls Get The Blues (soundtrack), 1993; All You Can Eat, 1995; Drag, 1997; Invincible Summer, 2000; Live By Request, 2001; Features on soundtrack to Dick Tracy; Hit singles include: Crying (duet with Roy Orbison), 1992; Constant Craving, 1992; Mind of Love, 1993; Miss Chatelaine, 1993; Just Keep Me Moving, 1993; If I Were You, 1995; Other recordings include: Duets, with Elton John, 1993; Love Makes The World, Carole King, 2001. *Honours:* Canadian CMA Awards: Entertainer of Year, 1989; Album of Year, 1990; Grammy Awards: Best Female Country Vocal Performance, 1990; Best Pop Vocal, 1993; Album of the Year, Ingénue, 1993; American Music Award: Favourite New Artist, 1993; Songwriter of The Year, with Ben Mink, 1993; BRIT Award, Best International Female, 1995. *Internet:* www.kdlang.com.

LANG Penny; b. 15 July 1942, Montréal, Québec, Canada. Folk Singer; Songwriter; Musician (guitar). 1 s. *Education:* 1 year, Sir George Williams University, Montréal. *Musical Education:* Self-taught (musical family). *Career:* National Folk Festival, Australia; Philadelphia Folk Festival; Vancouver, Winnipeg, Mariposa Folk Festivals; The Bitter End and Gerdes Folk City, CBGB's, New York; The Riverboat, Yellow Door, Pornographic Onion Coffeehouses, Canada; Caffe Lena, New York; The Folkway, New Hampshire; The Ark, Michigan; Montréal Jazz Festival; Toronto Soul 'n' Blues Fest (Harborfront); Music for NFB documentary Marilyn Waring – Who's Counting? Sex, Lies and Global Economics; Tour of UK and France, 1998; Tönder Folk Festival, Denmark, 1998; Women's Blues Revue, Toronto, 1998. *Compositions:* Open Up Our Hearts to See; Ain't Life Sweet; Carry On Children; November Blues; Firewater; Senses of Your Leave. *Recordings:* YES!!, 1991; Live (solo), 1992; Carry On Children, 1993; Ain't Life Sweet, 1996; Penny Lang and Friends Live, 1998. *Publications:* Lyrics/music, Open Up Our Hearts To See, Sing Out magazine; Articles, reviews for: Toronto Star: Montréal Gazette; Dirty Linen. *Honours:* Several Canada Council awards for touring, writing, recording; Grant from Québec Ministère des Affaires Culturelles. *Membership:* SOCAN. *Leisure interests:* Gardening; Travel; Nature crafts; Reading.

LANGBORN Torbjorn; b. 17 May 1955, Stockholm, Sweden. Musician; Composer. 2 d. *Education:* Adolf Fredrik Music School; Musicology, Stockholm University; Piano, Pedagogic, Royal Academy of Music, Stockholm; Salsa and Latin Grove with Bebo Valdez, Sabu Martinez, Wilfredo Stephenson, Amedeo Niccoletti, Don Pancho. *Career:* Live Gigs, Radio and some Television Appearances Through Sweden, Finland, Poland, Norway; Freelance Pianist, Salsa, Tango and Jazz; Teacher, Improvisation, Afro American and Jazz Theory. *Compositions:* Sangre nueva; Maldito Primitivo; En Estocolmo no pasa nada; Sad Samba; Salsa; Oiga mi Compadre; Canciones del Alma. *Recordings:* Hot Salsa – Maldito Primitivo; Hot Salsa Meets Swedish Jazz; Torbjorn Langborn and his Feel Life Orchestra. *Memberships:* STIM; SAMI; SKAP; Musicians' Union. *Leisure interests:* Collecting Music Scores and Books; Bonsai; Vine Tests; Children. *Address:* Hjalmar Söderbergs Väg 16 D 2tr, 112 52 Stockholm, Sweden.

LANGE Barbara Rose; b. 14 Jan. 1955, Casper, New York, USA. Ethnomusicologist. *Musical Education:* PhD, Ethnomusicology, University of Washington, 1993. *Career:* Assistant Professor, Moores School of Music, University of Houston, 1996-. *Publications:* Lakadalmas

Rosk and the Rejection of Popular Culture in Post-Socialist Hungary, in Retuning Culture, 1996; Hungarian Romanian (Gypsy) Political Activism and the Development of Folkier Ensemble Music, 1997; What Was the Conquering Magic...: The Power of Discontinuity in Hungarian Gypsy Nota, in Ethnomusicology, 1997. *Honours:* IREX Exchange Fellowship, Hungary, 1990–91; Fulbright Graduate Grant, Hungary, 1990–91; Mellon Postdoctoral Fellow, Cornell University, 1995–96. *Memberships:* Society for Ethnomusicology; International Council for Traditional Music. *Address:* Moores School of Music, University of Houston, TX 77204, USA.

LARATTA David Ottavio; b. 19 April 1970, Saint Denis, France. Musician (bass, drums, trumpet). *Education:* Arts and Letters (A3). *Musical Education:* Self-taught. *Career:* Guest musician, guest Youssou N'Dour, 1990; Francopholies, La Rochelle, France, 1992; Television show, TF1, 1992; 20th Anniversary, Sony France, 1993; National Concours Jazz in Paris, La Défense, with Used 2b Bop, 1995; Numerous concerts, shows, appearances, throughout France, with various bands; Marcel Sabiani Trio; Lewis Robinson, 1997; Léa loCicero, 1997; Divan du monde, with Cheick Tidiane Seck 'Tribute to Fela', 1997; Gino Williams, 1998; Caravana, Afro Cuban, Mars, 1998. *Memberships:* SPEDIDAM; SACEM. *Leisure interests:* Drawing; Painting; Football coach (BBES II Dégré). *Address:* 4 rue de la République, 93450 L'Ile Saint Denis, France.

LARGE Graham; b. 5 May 1947, Cheshire, England. Lyricist. m. Joan, 2 s., 1 d. *Education:* London University. *Career:* Collaboration With A Number of UK Composers: Marketing Songs as Inter Active Promotions. *Memberships:* International Songwriters Asscn; Guild of International Songwriters and Composers; Director of Inter Active Promotions and Publishing. *Address:* Plas Newydd, 18 Trinity Ave, Llandudno, North Wales LL30 255.

LARSEN Jens Kjaer; b. 30 May 1964, Copenhagen, Denmark. Rapper; Singer; Songwriter. m. Camilla Palikaras, 4 Aug. 1997. *Musical Education:* Self-taught Drummer. *Career:* Member, Cut 'n' Move Band, Several Television Shows, Tours of Europe, Australia, USA and Asia. *Compositions:* Get Serious; Spread Love; Give It Up; I'm Alive; 4 Albums. *Recordings:* Get Serious; Peace Love and Harmony; The Sounds of Now; Into The Zone. *Honours:* Silver Lion, Germany; 4 Grammies, Denmark. *Leisure interest:* Performing. *Current Management:* TG Management, Denmark. *Address:* 1120 Kobenhavn K, Copenhagen, Denmark.

LARSEN Jon; b. 7 Jan. 1959, Jar, near Oslo, Norway. Musician (guitar); Composer; Record Prod. m. Barbara Jahn, 2 July 1994, 1 step-d., 2 d. *Musical Education:* High School of Music; Self-taught. *Career:* Full-time professional guitarist/composer with Hot Club de Norvege, 1979–; World-wide touring since 1990; Established Hot Club de Norvege (quartet), 1979; The Django Festival, Norway, 1980; Hot Club Records, 1982–; Norwegian Music Distribution, 1985–; The Vintage Guitar Series, 1988–; The Music Operators, 1995–; The International Gypsy Jazz Archive, 1998–; The Robert Normann Society, 1999; The Robert Normann Museum, 2000-. *Recordings:* 15 albums with Hot Club de Norvege; Produced nearly 250 albums for Hot Club Records, with Chet Baker, Ph Catherine, Stephane Grapelli, Warne Marsh, The Rosenberg Trio; Guitar on: Gipsy Swing, The Grappelli Trio, 2000. *Honour:* NOPA Composer of The Year, Norway, 1994. *Membership:* Composers' Society of Norway (NOPA); Record Producers' Society of Norway (FONO). *Leisure interests:* Painting; Mineral collecting. *Current Management:* Frost Publishing Ltd, Norway. *Address:* PO Box 5202 Majorstua, 0302 Oslo, Norway.

LARSSON Anders; b. 13 April 1958, Malmo, Sweden. Man. *Career:* Own management for Scandinavian artists, 10 years; Currently, 30 artists in pop, jazz, blues, rock; Name of company: United Stage Production AB. *Memberships:* Mem. of Board, Swedish Impressario Asscn; Swedish Publishers' Asscn. *Leisure interests:* Gardening; Food; Wine. *Current Management:* United Stage Production AB. *Address:* PO Box 9174, 200 39 Malmo, Sweden.

LASCELLES Jeremy; b. 14 Feb. 1955, London, England. Man.-Dir, Chrysalis Music. 1 s., 2 d. *Career:* Artist Management, 1972–75; Tour Management, 1975–79; A & R Consultant, 1979–80, Director of Marketing, 1980–82, Director of A & R, 1982–88, Virgin Records; Managing Director, Ten Records, 1988–92; Offside Productions and Management, 1993–94; Managing Director, Chrysalis Music, 1994–; Managing Director, The Echo Label, 1998-. *Leisure interests:* Football; Cricket; Wine; Food; Film; Travel. *Current Management:* MD Chrysalis Music. *Address:* 13 Bramley Rd, London W10 6SP, England.

LASSEN Nils; b. 10 March 1960, Denmark. Composer. m. Sisse Lassen, 1 d. *Career:* Composing for Theatre and Film, Denmark and Danish Television, including The Royal Theatre. *Compositions:* Boy of 1000 Tears, 1997; Riders of Depression, 1997; No Lilacs, No Lillies, No More, 1997. *Recordings:* Lament for Ronni, 1997; Lost in the Woods, 1997; Most of Us Prefer Not To Think, 1997; Inside/Outside, 1997. *Membership:* DJBFA.

Leisure interest: Dreaming. *Address:* Lille Istedgade 5, 1706 Copenhagen V, Denmark.

LAST James (Hans); b. 17 April 1929, Bremen, Germany. Bandleader; Arranger. *Career:* Member, Radio Bremen Dance Orchestra, 1946; Bandleader, Becker-Last Ensemble, 1948–55; Arranger, radio stations, Polydor Records, 1955; Bandleader, combination of classics, dance, pop and country music, 1965–; Worked with artistes including: Caterina Valente; Astrud Gilberto; Richard Clayderman; Over 50m. records sold world-wide. *Recordings:* Numerous albums include: Non Stop Dancing, 1965; This Is James Last, 1967; Hammond A Go Go, 1967; James Last Goes Pop, 1968; Ole, 1973; Country and Square Dance Party, 1974; Ten Years Non Stop Party Album, 1975; Make The Party Last, 1975; Christmas James Last, 1976; In London, 1978; East To West, 1978; Last The Whole Night Long, 1979; Christmas Classics, 1979; Caribbean Nights, 1980; Seduction, 1980; Classics For Dreaming, 1980; Hansimania, 1981; Roses From The South – The Music of Johan Strauss, 1981; Tango, 1983; Christmas Dancing, 1983; Greatest Songs of The Beatles, 1983; Games That Lovers Play, 1984; Rose of Tralee and Other Irish Favourites, 1984; All Aboard With Cap'n James, 1984; In Russia, 1984; In Allgau (In The Alps), 1984; In Scotland, 1985; In Holland, 1987; The Berlin Concert, 1987; Dance Dance Dance, 1987; Flute Fiesta, 1988; By Request, 1988; Plays Bach, 1988; Happy Heart, 1989; Classics By Moonlight, 1990; Together At Last, 1991; My Favourites, 1995; In Scandinavia, 1997; Macarena, 1998; Meisterstucke, 1998; Tenderly, 1998; Classics From Russia, 2000; Hammond and Trumpet, 2001; Single: The Seduction, used in film American Gigolo, 1981.

LASWELL Bill; b. 14 Feb. 1950. Musician (bass, guitar); Record Co Exec.; Record Prod. *Career:* Leader, groups: Material; Curlew; Last Exit; Founder, record labels OAO, Celluloid; Record producer for Herbie Hancock. *Recordings:* Solo albums: Baselines, 1984; Best of Bill Laswell, 1985; Point Blank, 1986; Low Life, 1987; Hear No Evil, 1988; Psychonavigation, 1994; Axiom Ambient: Lost in the Translation, 1994; Web, 1995; Cymatic Scan, 1995; Silent Recoil, 1995; Bass Terror, 1995; Dark Massive, 1996; Oscillations, 1996; Dub Meltdown, 1997; City of Light, 1997; Jazzonia, 1998; Divination: Sacrifice, 1998; Invisible Design, 1999; Imaginary Cuba, 1999; Lo Def Pressure, 2000; Radioaxiom, A Dub Transmission, 2000; Filmtracks, 2001; Points of Order, 2001; with Material: Temporary Music, 1980; Third Power; Memory Serves; One Down; with Last Exit: The Noise of Trouble; with Herbie Hancock: Future Shock; Perfect Machine, 1988; with John Zorn and Eugene Chadbourne: The Parachute Years (7-disc set), 1997; Also producer for numerous artistes including: Yoko Ono; Mick Jagger; Gil Scott-Heron; Nona Hendryx; Manu Dibango; PiL; Fela Kuti; Iggy Pop; Motörhead; Laurie Anderson; Afrika Bambaataa; Yellowman;. *Current Management:* AGM (UK), 145A Ladbrooke Grove, London W10 6HJ, England.

LATHAM Anthony John Heaton; b. 30 Oct. 1940, Wigan, England. University Lecturer. m. Dawn Catherine Farleigh, 10 Nov. 1990. *Education:* BA (Hons) Medieval and Modern History, Birmingham, 1964; PhD African Studies, Birmingham, 1970. *Musical Education:* Clarinet tuition. *Career:* Debut, Wigan Jazz Club, 1958; Penn-Latham Quintet, University of Birmingham, 1961–63; Harlech Television, 1967; Axiom Jazz Band, Swansea, 1967–68; J. J.'s Rhythm Aces, Swansea University, 1982–84; Speakeasy Jazz Band, Swansea, 1984–; John Latham's Jazztimers, 1995–; Brecon Jazz Festival, 1986–89, 1991, 1996–99; Cork Jazz Festival, 1987; Birmingham Jazz Festival, 1987, 1988; BBC Wales, 1989, 1990, 1992, 1994; Llangollen Jazz Festival, 1995–98; Bude Jazz Festival, 1998; Clubs: Fritzel's; Gazebo; Bonaparte's Retreat; In New Orleans, 1988. *Recordings:* Blanche Finlay with The Speakeasy Jazzband, 1987; John Latham's Jazztimers, Sandy's Bar, Cardiff, 1997; John Latham's Jazztimers, 1998; Sandy and Co, 1998. *Publications:* Al Fairweather Discography, 1994; Eurojazz Discographies, No 34; Stan Greig Discography, 1995; Eurojazz Discography, No 42; Sandy Brown Discography, 1997; Eurojazz Discography, No 5. Contributions to: New Orleans Music Vol. 2 No. 1, 1990; Jazz Journal International, Jan, Sept, 1993, June, 1994, May, 1996; British Jazz Times, Sept-Oct, 1994; The Jazz Rag, Mar-Apr, Nov-Dec, 1998, Jul-Aug, 1999. *Membership:* Musicians' Union; Secretary, Sandy Brown Society, 1997-. *Leisure interest:* Trout fishing.

LATTIKAS Urmas; b. 17 Aug. 1960, Tapa, Estonia. Composer; Arranger; Conductor; Musician (piano). m. Kaia, 22 Dec. 1993, 2 s. *Musical Education:* Graduated as composer, Estonian Music Academy, 1977–86; Post-graduate studies, jazz composition, piano, Berklee College of Music, Boston, USA, 1990. *Career:* Performing artist, founder, leader, own jazz group Urmas Lattikas Quintet; Arranger, jazz, pop, classical styles; Accompanist, numerous vocal and instrumental performances; Extensive club, concert appearances, numerous jazz events, Estonia and abroad; Recordings, appearances, radio and television; Urmas Lattikas Quintet represented Estonian jazz in European Jazz Night television programme; Conducted Estonian song, Eurovision Song Contest, 1994. *Compositions:* Symphonic, choral, chamber music, film scores; Music for single and album. *Recordings:*

Single: In A Twilight Room; Album: Freedom To Love, Freedom To Lose. *Honours:* First Prize, U Naissoo composition contest, 1983, 1984; Levi Jaagup Award, Keyboard Player of the Year, 1990. *Address:* Nurme 26, Tallinn EE 0016, Estonia.

LAUDET François; b. 11 Nov. 1958, Paris, France. Drummer. *Education:* Baccalaureat. *Musical Education:* Self-taught Drummer. *Career:* Best Big Band Jazz Drummer in France; Band Leader; Appearances at several Festivals and Television Shows; Replacement of Butch Miles in Count Basie Orchestra in European tour, 1997. *Composition:* Memphis Belle Blues. *Recordings:* With: Saxomania, Ellingtomania Ornicar Big Band, Super Swing Machine, Francois Laudet Big Band. *Honour:* Prix Sydney Bechet, 1994; Academie du Jazz; Nominee, Best Frence Jazz Band, Djangos D'Or, 1998. *Membership:* Union des Musiciens de Jazz. *Leisure interests:* Flying Planes; Building Plastic Models. *Current Management:* François Laudet and Corinne Bondu. *Address:* 14 rue des Carrieres, 93230 Romainville, France.

LAUDET Philippe; b. 11 Dec. 1959, Nanterre, France. Composer; Arranger; Musician (trumpet, piano). m. Catherine Laudet, 19 Dec. 1987, 1 s., 2 d. *Education:* Astrophysics, until age 28. *Musical Education:* Classical piano from age 6–16; Jazz piano from age 10; Jazz trumpet from age 15; Self-taught composer, arranger. *Career:* Leader, composer, Ornicar Big Band, 1980–95; Played all major jazz festivals in France: Paris; Nice; Salon de Provence; Marciac; Vienne; Trumpet soloist, Tuxedo Big Band, 1992–; Played in Marciac, Coutance, Spain. *Recordings:* with Ornicar Big Band: Mais où est Donc Ornicar?, 1984; Le Retour d'Ornicar, 1986; Jazz Cartoon, 1989; L'Incroyable Huck, 1991; 3 recordings with Tuxedo Big Band: Rhythm is our business, 1994; Siesta at the Fiesta, 1996; For Ella and Chick, 1998; Beautiful Love, Philippe Laudet Quartet, 1996. *Honours:* Winner, Concours National de la Defense, Paris, with Ornicar Big Band, 1982; Prizes from Academy of Jazz and Hot Club of France, with Tuxedo Big Band, 1994; Hot Club de France, for Siesta at the Fiesta, 1996. *Memberships:* SACEM; SPEDIDAM; UMJ. *Leisure interest:* Astonomy.

LAUK Tiit; b. 9 Jan. 1948, Tartu, Estonia. Musician (piano, keyboards). m. Eleonora Lauk, 22 Aug. 1952, 1 s. *Musical Education:* Estonian Academy of Music; Pianist, leader, teacher, Jazz Education at Bob Brookmeyer's. *Career:* Over 35 years as pianist and leader, 15 years, piano and jazz teacher; 3 years as Producer, Musical Programmes, Estonian TV; Director, Estonian Jazz Foundation 1991–; Debut, Gintarine Triuba Festival, Lithuania, 1968; Numerous festivals, solo concerts in former Soviet Union, Europe; Tours with famous Estonian opera singers in Sweden, Finland; Projects with Finnish, Swedish, British, Russian musicians; Numerous recordings, Estonian Radio, Estonian TV, 1972-. *Compositions:* Over 300 instrumental and vocal arrangements for jazz orchestra/band. *Recordings:* Numerous recordings since 1970 for Estonian Radio, Estonian Television; MC KohtumispaiK Jazzkaar, 1995; Pendel, 1997. *Publications:* By The Path of Estonian Light Music, Lithuania, 1987; Jazz Improvisation: Practical Course For Piano (I Bril), translation into Estonian; Several reviews in several publications in Estonia, Finland, France, Lithuania. *Honours:* Order of Nicola Rolin (France); Jazzclub du Vallage (France); Jazzclub of Tartu (Estonia). *Membership:* International Asscn of Schools of Jazz. *Leisure interests:* Riding; Travel.

LAUPER Cyndi (Cynthia Anne Stephanie); b. 22 June 1953, Queens, New York, USA. Singer; Songwriter; Actress. *Career:* Club singer, Manhattan; Lead singer, Doc West; Member, Flyer, 1974–77; Formed Blue Angel, 1978–79; Solo recording artiste, 1983–; World-wide tours; Participant, Music Speaks Louder Than Words summit, USSR, 1988; American Music Awards concerts, Tokyo, 1991; Actress, films: Vibes, 1988; Mother Goose Rock 'n' Rhyme, Disney Channel, 1990; Paradise Paved, 1990; Off and Running, 1992; Participant, The Wall by Roger Waters, Berlin, 1990. *Recordings:* Albums: with Blue Angel: Blue Angel, 1980; Solo albums: She's So Unusual, 1983; True Colors, 1986; A Night To Remember, 1989; Music Speaks Louder Than Words, 1990; Hat Full of Stars, 1993; Singles include: Girls Just Want To Have Fun, 1984; Time After Time (No. 1, USA), 1984; She Bop, 1984; All Through The Night, 1984; True Colors (No. 1, USA), 1986; Change of Heart, 1987; What's Going On, 1987; I Drove All Night, 1989; The World Is Stone, 1992; That's What I Think, 1993; Hey Now Girls, 1994; Come on Home, 1995; You Don't Know, 1997; Ballad of Cleo and Joe, 1997; Disco Inferno, 1999; Guest vocals, Blowback, Tricky, 2001; Contributor, charity records: We Are The World, USA For Africa, 1984; Give Peace A Chance, The Peace Choir, 1991; Put On Your Green Shoes, 1993. *Honours:* American Video Award, 1984; MTV Music Video Award, 1984; American Music Awards: Favourite Female Artist, Favourite Female Video Artist, 1985; Grammy Award, Best New Artist, 1985. *Current Management:* Hard To Handle Management, 640 Lee Rd, Suite 106, Wayne, PA 19087, USA.

LAURENCE Graham Richard; b. 1 April 1964, Croydon, Surrey, England. Songwriter; Musician (guitar). *Education:* City of London Polytechnic. *Musical Education:* Goldsmiths University. *Career:* Guitarist, Danielle Dax, European Tour, 1986; Guitarist/songwriter,

Queen B; Appearances: TVAM; Jonathon Ross; Box Office, Radio 1; Radio 1 News; Radio 1 Tour. *Recordings:* Red Top Hot Shot; I Love You; Satellite; Loving You. *Memberships:* Musicians' Union; Performing Rights Society. *Leisure interest:* Boxing. *Current Management:* Important Management. *Address:* Marlow, Bucks, England.

LAURENT Mark; b. 15 March 1954, Auckland, New Zealand. Singer; Songwriter; Musician (electric guitar, acoustic guitar, harmonica, Rowan lute, percussion, bass). m. (1) Adrienne Lovegrove, 5 Feb. 1977, 1 s., (2) Brenda Liddiard, 4 Aug. 1990. *Career:* Band or solo performer, playing throughout England, New Zealand and Australia, 1968–; Studio producer, 1985–; Major tours supporting Larry Norman, 1984; Barry Maguire, 1987; Larbanois Carrero, 1989; Adrian Plass, 1993; Thom Bresh, 1995; Major festivals include: Sweetwaters, 1985; Mainstage, 1987; Jackey's Marsh, Tasmania, 1990; Shelterbelt, 1993; Auckland Folk Festival, 1993–99; Parachute, 1994, 1995; Tahora, 1989–98; Wellington Folk Festival, 1999; New Spirit, 1997–99. *Recordings:* Mark Laurent, 1982; Kindness In A Strong City, 1986; Songs For Our Friends (collaboration), 1989; Trust, 1992; Heart Attack, 1996; Tahora 21, collaboration, 1997; Millenium Hippies, 1998; Songwriter, Producer, musician, other artists' albums. *Publications:* Perhaps (poetry), 1995; Various articles for music magazines. *Membership:* Australasian Performing Rights Asscn. *Leisure interests:* Creative Writing; Walking; Jamming; Films; Friends. *Current Management:* Distribution: Someone Up There Records; Digital Flower Productions. *Address:* 21 Parkfield Terrace, Grafton, Auckland, New Zealand.

LAURITSEN Joergen; b. 9 Aug. 1966, Svendborg, Denmark. Conductor; Composer; Arranger; Musician. m. Pia Boysen. *Education:* MA, Music Theory, Conducting, Royal Danish Academy of Music, 1990; MA, Piano, Composition, Rhythmic Music Conservatory, Copenhagen, 1992. *Career:* All major musicals in Denmark for the last 5 years; Chess in concert with Elaine Page, Tommy Korberg, 1997; Solo with Harolyn Blackwell, 1997; Live Symphonic with Lisa Nilsson, 1988. *Compositions:* Sarajevo Butterfly; Dance of the Clogs; Songs in the Wind; Mixed Love; Intonation For The Wizard, Danish Radio Concert Orchestra, 1998. *Recordings:* Mixed Love; Les Miserables. *Honours:* Danish Ministry of Culture, 1991; Denmark-America Foundation, 1992. *Memberships:* Danish Society of Jazz, Rock and Folk Composers; Danish Conductors Asscn. *Leisure interest:* Family Life. *Address:* Kirsten Pilsvej 10, Isal, 2920 Charlottenlund, Denmark.

LAVELLE Caroline; Musician (cello); Vocalist; Songwriter. *Career:* Leader, all-female trio Electra Strings; Group toured with Nigel Kennedy; As session musician, played with Massive Attack; Peter Gabriel; Ride; The Fall. *Recordings:* Solo albums: Spirit, 1995; Brilliant Midnight, 2001; Solo single: Moorlough Shore; Contributor: Kiss in the Dream House, Siouxsie and the Banshees; Waking Hours, Del Amitri; In Ribbons, Pale Saints; Sex and Misery, Voice of the Beehive; Expecting to Fly, Bluetones; Home of The Whale, Massive Attack, 1992; Us, Peter Gabriel, 1992; Dream Harder, The Waterboys, 1993; The Bends, Radiohead, 1995; Kafka, Nigel Kennedy, 1996; The Book of Secrets, Loreena McKennitt, 1997; Origin of Symmetry, Muse, 2001. *Internet:* www.carolinelavelle.com.

LAVELLE James, (DJ Kutmaster Lavski); b. 22 Feb. 1974, Oxford, England. Prod.; DJ. *Career:* Worked at Honest Jon's Record Shop, Ladbroke Grove; Set up Mo' Wax Records with a small loan aged 19, 1993; Co-founder: That's How It Is club night (with Gilles Peterson) at London's Bar Rumba; Formed U.N.K.L.E. with production partner DJ Shadow; Resident DJ at Fabric in London; Collaborations: DJ Shadow; Thom Yorke; Ian Brown; Slam; Remixed: The Verve; Radiohead; Breakbeat Era; Howie B. *Recordings:* Psyence Fiction, 1998; Singles: The Time Has Come, 1994; Berry Meditation, 1996; Rock On, 1997; Rabbit In Your Headlights, 1998; Be There, 1999. *Membership:* MCPS. *Address:* c/o Mo' Wax Labels Ltd, 1 Codrington Mews, London, W11 2EH, England.

LAVIS Gilson; b. 27 June 1951, Bedford, England. Musician (drums, percussion); Songwriter. m. Nicola Mercedes Keller, 10 Nov. 1993, 1 s. *Musical Education:* Self-taught. *Career:* Drummer for: The Bo Weavils; Headline News; Springfield Revival; Chris Rea; Squeeze, 1975–91; Pick up drummer, Chuck Berry, Jerry Lee Lewis; Cabaret drummer for artists including: Tommy Cooper; Bob Monkhouse; Lulu; Freddie Starr; David Frost; Engelbert Humperdinck; Currently with Jools Holland and the Rhythm and Blues Orchestra, 1991–; Concerts, tours with: Chris Rea, Europe; Chuck Berry, 2 tours, UK, Europe; Jerry Lee Lewis, British tour; Squeeze, 20 British tours, 20–25 US/Canada tours, 1 Australia tour; Jools Holland, 14 UK, 2 Ireland tours; Television includes: with Squeeze: Top of The Pops; Old Grey Whistle Test; with Jools Holland: Don't Forget Your Toothbrush, CH4, as house band drummer, working with: Jimmy Somerville, Robert Palmer, Cher, Neil Sedaka, Chaka Khan, Lulu, Roger Daltrey, Barry White, Lemmy, Vic Reeves and Bob Mortimer, Roy Wood, Kylie Minogue, Suggs, Kim Wilde, Michelle Gayle; The Happening, BSB/Sky, with artists including: Midge Ure, Mica Paris; Later With Jools Holland, BBC2, with artists including: Dusty Springfield, Sting, Stevie

Winwood, Maria Mackee; All Saints; The Corrs; BB King; Tom Jones; Dr John; House band drummer, Name That Tune, Channel 5; Drummer with the Eno and Jools Holland Rhythm and Blues Orchestra at the opening ceremony of the Millenium Dome. *Compositions:* with Jools Holland: Biggy Wiggy; Birdcage Walk. *Recordings:* Hit singles with Squeeze: Take Me I'm Yours, 1978; Cool For Cats (No. 2, UK), 1979; Up The Junction (No. 2, UK), 1979; Another Nail In My Heart, 1980; Pulling Mussels From A Shell, 1980; Labelled With Love, 1981; Tempted, 1981; Hourglass, 1987; Albums with Squeeze: Squeeze, 1978; Cool For Cats, 1979; Argy Bargy, 1980; East Side Story, 1981; Sweets From A Stranger, 1982; Babylon and On, 1987; Frank, 1989; Play, 1991; Greatest Hits, 1992; with Jools Holland: A World of His Own, 1990; The Full Compliment, 1991; The A to Z of The Piano, 1992; Live Performance, 1994; Sex and Jazz and Rock and Roll, 1996; Lift The Lid, 1997; Jools Holland The Best Of, 1998; Jools Holland's Swing Album, 2001; Small World Big Band, 2001; Solo album: Drumbaba, 1998. *Honours:* Gold, Silver, Platinum discs. *Leisure interests:* Ethnic percussion instruments; Home recording studio; Harley Davidson motorcycles. *Address:* One Fifteen Ltd, The Gallery, 28–30 Wood Wharf, Horseferry Pl., London SE10, England.

LAW Michael Charles Ewan; b. 30 March 1960, Dar Es Salaam, Tanzania. Musician (Piano); Singer; Musical Dir; Composer; Lecturer. *Education:* BA, Gonville and Caius College, Cambridge, 1979–82; Royal College of Music, 1982–86. *Career:* Musical Director, The Piccadilly Dance Orchestra, 1988–; Television Appearances Include, 4 Appearances on Pebble Mill, Daytime Live; Wogan; Sir John Mills, 92nd birthday on Channel Five; Radio Includes, Radio 2 Including Arts Programme, 3 Times and VE Day Celebration; Concerts Include, Queen Elizabeth Hall, 4 Times; Swan Theatre, Stratford Upon Avon; In Cabaret, Pizza On The Park; QE2, Royal Viking Sun, Far East Tour, 1999; Noel Coward Cabaret; Pianist, Vocalist for Noel and Gertie, for Sheridan Morley At The Mill At Sonning, Jermyn Street Theatre, 1997; Concert tour for Noel Coward Centenary with Sheridan Morley, including Far East, QEH, Purcell Room. *Compositions:* Songs Recorded Include, Play Me An Elegant Song; I'm Singin' A Swing Song Now. *Recordings:* 5 Albums with The Piccadilly Dance Orchestra, 1989, 1993, 1995, 1997, 1999. *Memberships:* PRS; MCPS. *Current Management:* Alan Bennett. *Address:* 50 Albert St, Windsor, Berks, SL4 5BU.

LAWLESS Jim (Hugh James); b. 18 Feb. 1935, Woolwich, London, England. Musician (tuned percussion). m. Carole Ann, 6 April 1968, 3 d. *Education:* HNC in Electronics. *Musical Education:* 3 years piano lessons; 35 years experience. *Career:* Became professional, joined The Eric Delaney Band on Ronnie Scott's recommendation, 1960; Worked at Hammersmith Palais, Lyceum Empire, Leicester Square, 1963–65; Freelance session player, records, television, broadcasts, films, 1965; Played jazz, Hollywood Bowl; US tour with George Shearing; US tour with Charlie Watts. *Recordings:* Recorded with: LSO; Royal Philharmonic; Ted Heath; Jack Parnell; Stéphane Grappelli; Bob Parnow; Joe Loss; BBC Big Band; George Shearing; Henry Mancini; Mel Tormé; Peggy Lee; Lene Horne; Nelson Riddle; Kiri Te Kanawa; Nearly all 60s, 70s pop stars including Lulu, The Beatles, Tom Jones. *Memberships:* Musicians' Union; PRS. *Leisure interests:* Squash; Walking dog; Practising. *Current Management:* 1 The Strand, Ferring, West Sussex BN12 5QX, England.

LAWLOR Feargal; b. 4 March 1971, Limerick, Ireland. Musician (Drums). *Career:* Member, The Cranberries; Joined early band The Cranberry Saw Us, changed name to The Cranberries; Obtained major label record deal; Early US tour supporting Suede; Numerous subsequent headlining tours and festival dates, radio and TV appearances; Played Woodstock 2 in the USA. *Recordings:* Singles: Linger, 1993; Dreams, 1994; Zombie, 1994; Ridiculous Thoughts, 1995; Doors and Windows, 1995; Free to Decide, 1996; I Can't Be With You, 1999; Promises, 1999; Albums: Everybody Else is Doing It So Why Can't We, 1993; No Need to Argue, 1994; To The Faithful Departed, 1996; Bury the Hatchet, 1999.

LAWRENCE Andrew (Andy); b. 2 Nov. 1954, Swindon, Wiltshire, England. Musician (Trumpeter, Arranger/Composer, Vocalist). 3 d. *Education:* Trumpet lessons, age 11; Brass band training. *Career:* Professional on British and US soul music scene, 1972–; 5 years touring continent, 1973–78, with Roy Pellett Jazzband; Settled West Berlin, Germany, 1976–; Freelance Studio work, Arranger, Club work, Concerts, TV (SFB, ARD, RTL) and Radio; Moved to Stuttgart, 1983; Lecturer, Instructor, Baden-Würtenberg Youth Jazz Orchestra, 1984; Numerous concert tours with Peanuts Hucko, Ben Waters, George Kelly; Lead for Joe Schwarz Orchestra (5 years); Led large and small own ensembles; Over 120 original compositions, some recorded; Authority on swing music; Currently, much in demand as arranger, soloist and vocalist. *Recordings:* 15 albums as featured Soloist – one as Leader. *Leisure interests:* Gardening; Walking; Historical literature; Cooking. *Current Management:* Andy Lawrence, Altenbergstr 32, 70180 Stuttgart, Germany. *Address:* Altenbergstr 32, 70180 Stuttgart, Germany.

LAWRENCE Denise; b. 15 Feb. 1956, Hayes, Middlesex, England. Jazz Vocalist; Bandleader. m. Tony Lawrence, 16 Aug. 1985, 2 d. *Career:* Vocalist, bandleader, The Denise Lawrence Band; Denise Lawrence and Storeyville Tickle jazz band, 15 years; Also: Denise Lawrence and Her Trio; Tony Lawrence (husband) as pianist and Musicial Director; Most major jazz clubs, festivals, UK, Europe; Compere, co-organizer, residential festivals, various holiday locations; Appears, cabaret and theatres; Particular interest, gospel music, hymns, spirituals; Regularly on radio, and television: ITV, BBC, include: Songs of Praise. *Recordings:* 10 albums; Let It Shine; Can't Help Lovin' These Men of Mine; Hangin' Around, 1997; Ain't That Good News, 1997; I Guess There's An End To Everything, 2000. *Honours:* Best vocalist, UK Jazz Travel Awards, 1994; Let It Shine, Best New Jazz Recording of Year, Der Jazzfreund, German magazine. *Membership:* Musicians' Union. *Leisure interests:* Cooking (and eating!). *Address:* 189 Loddon Bridge Rd, Woodley, Reading, Berks RG5 4BP, England.

LAWRENCE Peter Raymond; b. 29 Oct. 1957, Leamington Spa, England. Prod.; Publisher; DJ. 1 s., 1 d. *Career:* Manager, Our Price Records; Sales Manager, Making Waves Distribution; Owner, Cooking Vinyl Records; Owner, Global Headz; Founder, The Big Chill. *Recordings:* Producer: Michelle Shocked, Texas Campfire Tapes. *Address:* PO Box 7378, London N4 3RH, England.

LAWRENCE Rohn; b. New Haven, Connecticut, USA. Jazz Musician (guitar); Singer. *Musical Education:* Began playing aged 2; Building guitars aged 9; Played electric guitars aged 13. *Career:* Played in New Haven funk bands Good News; The Lift; Performed with: Marion Meadows; George Duke; Dianne Reeves; Jonathon Butler; Alex Bugñon; Freddie Jackson; Najee; Moved to Boston, 1993. *Recordings:* Hanging On A String, 1993; See Ya Around, 1998; with Pieces of a Dream: Pieces, 1997; with Will Downing, Invitation Only, 1997; with Jay Rowe: Jay Walking, 1997; Bread and Butter: Adventures of Bread and Butter, 1998; Boney James, Body Language, 1999. *Current Management:* Kim Ewing, Atlantic Jazz Publicity.

LAWRENCE Steven; b. 29 Sept. 1961, Glasgow, Scotland. Musician (bouzouki, cittern, mandola, dulcimer, percussion); Prod. *Education:* HNC in Electrical Engineering. *Musical Education:* Self-taught. *Career:* Appeared at Celtic Connections Festival, Glasgow, 1993, 1994; Member, Iron Horse; Appearances include: Poland; Eygpt; Tours of Netherlands, Germany, Brittany; Appeared at major European Festivals; National television and radio appearances in Scotland, Poland, Egypt and Sweden; Performed live with Tannas, Anna Murray, Ross Kennedy; Producing and arranging for many artists within traditional music; Composer, theme and incidental music for videos and exhibitions; Member of Canterach, 1997-. *Recordings:* Doll's House, with Marylyn Middleton Pollock, 1992; Thro' Water Earth and Stone, with Iron Horse, 1993; Five Hands High, with Iron Horse, 1994; Coineadh, with Heather Innes, 1994; Gossamer Mansion, with Arran Bede, 1994; Celtic Dawn, with Whirligig, 1995; Voice of the Land, with Iron Horse, soundtrack to BBC Documentary The Gamekeeper, 1995; Summer in Skye, with Blair Douglas, 1996; Into Indigo, with Anne Murray, 1996; Border Ballads, various artists, 1998; Fyre and Sworde, 1998; On The West Side, 1999; The White Swan, 1999; Canterach Canterach, 2000; Also appears on: Calluna, Calluna, 2000; John Wright, A Few Short Lines, 2000; Whirligig, First Frost, 2001; Bram Taylor, Fragile Peace, 2001. *Honour:* Music Retailers' Asscn Award, Best Folk Album, for Thro' Water, Earth and Stone. *Memberships:* Musicians' Union; Performing Rights Society; PAMRA; PRC. *Current Management:* KRL Records, 9 Watt Rd, Hillington, Glasgow G52, Scotland; Lee Wolfe, Canto Del Rey 28, Faro De Arriba, 33199 Oviedo, Asturias, Spain.

LAWRENCE Tracy Lee; b. 27 Jan. 1968, Atlanta, Texas, USA. Country vocalist; Songwriter; Musician (guitar). *Compositions include:* How A Cowgirl Says Goodbye; Can't Break It To My Heart; If The World Had A Front Porch; Lessons Learned; My Second Home; Stars Over Texas. *Recordings include:* Sticks and Stones, 1991; Today's Lonely Fool, 1992; Runnin' Behind, 1992; Alibis, 1993; Can't Break It To My Heart, 1993; My Second Home, 1993; If The Good Die Young, 1994; I See It Now, 1994; Any Fool Can See, 1994; Texas Tornado, 1995; If The World Had A Front Porch, 1995; If You Love Me, 1995; Time Marches On, 1996; Stars Over Texas, 1996; Is That A Time, 1996; Better Man Better Off, 1997; How A Cowgirl Says Goodbye, 1997; The Coast Is Clear, 1997; Lessons Learned, 2000; Albums include: Sticks and Stones, 1991; Alibis, 1993; I See It Now, 1994; Time Marches On, 1996; The Coast Is Clear, 1997; Lessons Learned, 2000; Tracy Lawrence, 2001. *Address:* c/o The Country Music Asscn, Nashville, Tennessee, USA. *Internet:* www.tracylawrence.com.

LAYTON Paul Martin; b. 4 Aug. 1947, Beaconsfield, Buckinghamshire, England. Entertainer; Musician (bass guitar). m. Patricia Peters, 14 June 1981, 1 s., 1 d. *Musical Education:* Hendon Music College. *Career:* Actor, films include: I Could Go On Singing, with Judy Garland; Television includes: Dixon of Dock Green; Emergency Ward 10, 1965–70; Vocalist, bass guitarist, The New Seekers, 1970–; Major world concert tours and television include: The White House for Nixon; Royal Command; Ed

Sullivan. *Compositions include:* Ride A Horse; Sweet Louise. *Recordings:* I'd Like To Teach The World To Sing; Never Ending Song of Love; Circles; You Won't Find Another Fool Like Me; I Get A Little Sentimental Over You; Look What They've Done To My Song Ma; Beg, Steal or Borrow (Eurovision 1972). *Honours:* Sun Award, Best Vocal Group; Grammy Nomination, 1972. *Memberships:* Equity; Musicians' Union. *Leisure interests:* Golf; Snooker; Horseriding. *Current Management:* Hal Carter Organisation.

LAZAREVITCH Serge; b. 18 Nov. 1957, St Germain En Laye, France. Jazz Musician (guitar); Educator. *Musical Education:* Jazz diploma, Berklee College of Music, Boston, USA. *Career:* Concerts throughout Europe with various jazz bands; Member, Orchestre National de Jazz, 1989–91; Tours, Europe, Asia; Head of Jazz Department, Perpignan Conservatory; Clinics, France; Switzerland; Belgium; Germany; Italy. *Recordings:* CDs: (as leader) Cats Are Welcome, 1987; London Baby, 1989; Walk With A Lion, 1993; Many recordings as sideman. *Honours:* Choc of The Month, Record of The Year, in Jazz Man, for Walk With A Lion. *Membership:* UMJ (Union des Musiciens de Jazz). *Leisure interests:* Films; Cooking. *Address:* 7 rue Durand, 34000 Montpellier, France.

LAZY HARRY (Mark Stephens); b. 15 June 1947. Singer; Songwriter. m. Wendy, 1 s., 1 d. *Education:* BA, Hons, Melbourne University. *Career:* Wrote and sang Proud to be Australian for Bicentenary, 1988; USA Tours, 1990–94; German Tour, 1995; Tour of Australia, 1998. *Compositions:* Proud to be Australian; Edward Kelly; Riverboats Song; Weary Dunlop; Visiting Australia. *Recordings:* Big Aussie Album; Lazy Harry Vol. II; My Country; Ned Kelly Story; Riverboats of Australia; Bound for Botany Bay. *Publications:* Lazy Harry Song Book, 1988; Video, Songs of Australia, 1998. *Membership:* Australian Performing Rights Asscn. *Leisure interests:* Gardening; Golf.

LE BON Simon; b. 27 Oct. 1958, Bushey, Hertfordshire, England. Vocalist; Lyricist. m. Yasmin Parveneh, 27 Dec. 1985, 3 d. *Education:* Birmingham University. *Career:* Vocalist, Dog Days; Lead vocalist, Duran Duran, 1980–; Arcadia, 1985–86; Performances include: British tour, supporting Hazel O'Connor, 1980; MENCAP concert, attended by HRH the Prince and Princess of Wales, 1983; Live Aid, Philadelphia, 1985; The Secret Policeman's Third Ball, 1987; An Acoustic Evening With Duran Duran, Birmingham, 1993. *Recordings:* Albums: with Duran Duran: Duran Duran, 1981; Rio, 1982; Carnival, 1982; Seven and The Ragged Tiger (No. 1, UK), 1983; Arena, 1984; Notorious, 1986; Big Thing, 1988; Decade, 1989; Liberty, 1990; Duran Duran (The Wedding Album), 1993; Thank You, 1995; Medazzaland, 1997; Greatest, 1998; Pop Trash, 2000; with Arcadia: So Red The Rose, 1985; Singles include: Planet Earth, 1981; Girls On Film, 1981; My Own Way, 1981; Hungry Like The Wolf, 1982; Save A Prayer, 1982; Rio, 1982; Is There Something I Should Know (No. 1, UK), 1983; Union of The Snake, 1983; New Moon On Monday, 1984; The Reflex (No. 1, UK and US), 1984; The Wild Boys, 1984; A View To A Kill, film theme tune (No. 1, USA), 1985; Notorious, 1986; Skin Trade, 1987; Meet El Presidente, 1987; I Don't Your Love, 1988; All She Wants, 1989; Do You Believe In Shame, used in film Tequila Sunrise, 1989; Liberty, 1990; Violence of Summer, 1990; Serious, 1990; Ordinary World, 1993; Come Undone, 1993; Too Much Information, 1993; White Lines, 1995; Singles with Arcadia: Election Day, 1985; Goodbye Is Forever, 1986; The Flame, 1986; Contributor, Do They Know It's Christmas?, Band Aid, 1984; Pavarotti and Friends (Bosnia charity record), 1996. *Honours:* Grammy Awards: Best Video and Best Album, 1984; BRIT Award, Best British Music Video, Wild Boys, 1985; Ivor Novello Award, International Hit of Year, The Reflex, 1985; Star on Hollywood Walk of Fame, 1993. *Leisure interest:* Sailing. *Current Management:* The Left Bank Organisation, 6255 Sunset Blvd #1111, Hollywood, CA 90028, USA.

LE GENDRE Dominique; b. Trinidad. Musician (guitar); Composer. *Musical Education:* Guitar tuition by Ramon de Herrera, Conservatoire Municipal de Paris XVII; Degree, Musicology, Sorbonne University; Conservatoires: Regional d'Orsay, Municipal de Pars VI; Diploma in Advanced Sound Recording; Production Techniques, Media Production Services. *Career:* Television: Body of a Poet, Channel 4; 7 Go Mad in Peru, Channel 4, 1995–96; Radio: The Darkest Eye, Hinterlands, Let Them Call it Jazz, Radio 3, 1996; Film: Sixth Happiness, directed by Waris Hussein. *Compositions:* Music for television: The Healer, BBC1; B D Women, C4; Synchro, ITV; Ragga Gyuls D'Bout, Carlton/Arts Council; Booker Prize '93, BBC2; Disabled Lives, BBC2; Kaiso For July, C4; Films: Aliki Ou La Bague Engloutie; La Petite Valse; I Is A Long Memoried Woman; Theatre music includes: Measure For Measure, London Bubble Theatre; Orinoco, National Theatre Studio; Trapped In Time, Avon Touring Theatre Company; Love At A Loss, Wild Iris Theatre; When The Bough Breaks, Theatre Centre; BBC Radio includes: A Midsummer Night Dream; The Wizard of Oz; Edward II; Dance music for: The Burial of Miss Lady, Irie! Dance Company. *Recordings:* Romeo and Juliet, King John, Twelfth Night, All's Well That Ends Well, The Merchant of Venice, A Midsummer Night's Dream, The Taming of the Shrew; In production: complete plays of Shakespeare. *Honours:* Best Performance Art Video (I Is A Long Memoried

Woman), New York, 1991; London Fringe Award Nomination, Best Music, 1994. *Memberships:* PRS; Musicians' Union. *Current Management:* Soundtrack Music Management. *Address:* 22 Ives St, Chelsea, London SW3 2ND, England.

LE MESSURIER James; b. 20 July 1958, Guernsey, Channel Islands. Musician (percussion); Arranger; Bandleader. m. Flavia Chévez De La Cruz, 23 April 1994. *Musical Education:* Bachelor of Music, Major in Professional Music, Berklee College of Music, Boston, USA. *Career:* Leader, percussionist, arranger, London based Salsa group La Clave, 1986–; Numerous appearances clubs, festivals: UK; Eire; France; Italy; Holland; Germany; Switzerland; Featured on BBC Radio One, Andy Kershaw Show, 1994; Freelance percussionist, El Sonido de Londres, Alfredo Rodriguez, Orlando Watussi, Adalberto Santiago. *Memberships:* PRS; Musicians' Union. *Address:* 38 Forestholme Close, Forest Hill, London SE23 3UQ, England.

LE Nguyên; b. 14 Jan. 1959, Paris, France. Musician (guitar, bass); Synthesizer Programmer; Composer; Arranger. *Education:* Graduate in Visual Arts; Majored in Philosophy. *Musical Education:* Self-taught. *Career:* Co-creator, multi-ethnic band Ultramarine, 1983; Member, National Jazz Orchestra, 1987; Guest soloist, WDR Big Band, with Vince Mendoza, Bob Brookmeyer, 1993; Concerts and tours throughout Europe; Martinique; Ile de la Réunion; Madagascar; Ivory Coast; USA; Canada; North Africa. *Recordings:* Miracles, 1989; Zanzibar, 1992; Init, 1993; Million Waves, 1995; Tales From Vietnam, 1996; Three Trios, 1997; with Ultramarine: Dé, 1989; Esimala, 1991. *Publications:* Isoar and Question Mark published in Real Book Vol. III. *Honours:* with Ultramarine: Best World Music Album: 1989; Telerama, 1992; Tales from Vietnam, 1996; Drapson d'Or, choice du monde de la musique; Choice of the Year, 1996 Jazzman 2nd best CD, for Jazzthing. *Current Management:* Siegfried Loch, ACT Publishing. *Address:* Gustav Freytag Strasse 10, 22085 Hamburg, Germany.

LEA Jimmy; b. 14 June 1952, Wolverhampton, England. Musician (bass, piano, violin); Songwriter; Record Prod. *Career:* Member, UK rock group Slade (formerly N'Betweens, Ambrose Slade), 1966–91; Concerts include: First British tour, 1972; Fanfare For Europe festival, London Palladium, 1973; Great British Music Festival, 1978; Reading Festival, 1980; Film appearance: Flame, 1974. *Compositions:* Co-writer, all Slade's Top 20 singles, with Noddy Holder. *Recordings:* Albums: Beginnings (as Ambrose Slade), 1969; Play It Loud, 1970; Slade Alive, 1972; Slayed, 1973; Sladest, 1973; Old New Borrowed Blue, 1974; Slade In Flame (soundtrack), 1974; Nobody's Fool, 1976; Slade Alive Vol. 2, 1978; Return To Base, 1979; Slade Smashes, 1980; Till Deaf Do Us Part, 1981; We'll Bring The House Down, 1981; Slade On Stage, 1982; The Amazing Kamikaze Syndrome, 1983; Slade's Greats, 1984; Rogue's Gallery, 1985; Crackers, 1985; You Boyz Make Big Noize, 1987; Wall of Hits, 1991; UK No. 1 singles: Coz I Luv You, 1971; Take Me Back 'Ome, 1972; Mama Weer All Crazee Now (later recorded by Mama's Boys, Quiet Riot), 1972; Cum On Feel The Noize, 1973; Skweeze Me Pleeze Me, 1973; Merry Christmas Everybody, 1973; Other hits include: Look Wot You Dun, 1972; Gudbuy T'Jane, 1972; My Friend Stan, 1973; Everyday, 1974; Bangin' Man, 1974; Far Far Away, 1974; Thanks For The Memory, 1975; In For A Penny, 1975; We'll Bring The House Down, 1981; My Oh My, 1983; Run Run Away, 1984; All Join Hands, 1984; Radio Wall of Sound, 1991; Record producer, UK rock group Chrome Molly.

LEACH Alan; b. 1970, England. Musician (Drums). *Career:* Member, Shed Seven; Numerous live dates, tours and television appearances. *Recordings:* Singles: Mark, 1994; Dolphin, 1994; Speakeasy, 1994; Ocean Pie, 1994; Where Have You Been Tonight?, 1995; Getting Better, 1996; Bully Boy, 1996; On Standby, 1996; Chasing Rainbows, 1996; She Left Me on Friday, 1998; The Heroes, 1998; The Devil in Your Shoes, 1998; Disco Down, 1999; Albums: Change Giver, 1996; A Maximum High, 1996; Let It Ride, 1998; Going for Gold: The Best of Shed Seven, 1999; Truth Be Told, 2001. *Internet:* www.shedseven.com.

LEBEUGLE Patricia; b. 19 May 1963, Le Mans, France. Jazz Musician (bass). *Musical Education:* Self-taught. *Career:* Played with Walter Bishop; Bob Mover; Bobby Porcelli; Peter Ecklund; Mark Murphy; Ted Brown; European tours with many French and American musicians, 1985–; Jazz festivals throughout Europe with Philippe Duchemin Trio, 1990–; Tour, South Africa, with pianist Jack Van Poll. *Recordings:* with Philippe Duchemin Trio: Alizés, 1990; Live!, 1992; Three Pieces, 1994; Philippe Duchemin Trio with Dominique Vernhes, 1995; Three Colors, with Philippe Duchemin, CD, 1998; with Marcel Azzola and Dany Doriz, Jazzola, 1999; Philippe Duchemin with Magali Leon, Magali chante Ella, 1999. *Leisure interest:* Horse riding. *Address:* Le Boulay, 72440 St Mars de Locquenay, France.

LECKIE John; b. 23 Oct. 1949, London, England. Prod.; Engineer. m. Christina, 1 d. *Education:* Quintin School; Ravensbourne College of Art; Rajneesh Neo-Sannyas Commune. *Career:* Tape Operator and Balance

Engineer, Abbey Road Studios, 1970; Sessions included: John Lennon; Mott The Hoople; Roy Harper; various classical; Freelance producer 1978-. *Recordings include:* Albums: Sunburst Finish, Be-Bop Deluxe, 1976; White Music, XTC, 1978; Real Life, Magazine, 1978; Empires and Dance, Simple Minds, 1980; The Stone Roses, The Stone Roses, 1989; The Bends, Radiohead, 1995; K, Kula Shaker, 1996; Showbiz, Muse, 1999; Missing You (Mi Yeewnii), Baaba Maal, 2001. *Honours:* Music Week, Best Producer, 1996; Q Magazine, Best Producer, 1996; Brit Awards, Best Producer, 1997. *Membership:* Music Producers Guild UK. *Leisure interests:* Walking the dog; Finding out about life. *Current Management:* Safia Jaffery, SJP, 1 Prince of Wales Passage, 117 Hampstead Rd, London, NW1 3EF, England. *Address:* The Well, Wainmill, Chinner, Oxon, OX39 4AB, England.

LEDIN Tomas Jonas Folke; b. 25 Feb. 1952, Östersund, Sweden. Artist; Songwriter; Prod. m. Marie Anderson, 22 May 1982, 2 s. *Education:* Art Major, 1970; Graduate, Swedish Gymnasium, 1972. *Musical Education:* Musical Science, Uppsala University, 1977. *Career:* First album released, 1972; Tours: Sweden and Scandinvia, 1980–; USA, with ABBA; Canada, Europe, 1979; Japan, 1980; Initiated Rocktrain tour, 1991; Toured with the Rocktrain, 1992–93; Appeared on all major television shows, Sweden. *Recordings:* 18 albums include: Greatest Hits, 1990; Tillfälligheternas Spel, 1990; Du Kan Lita På Mej, 1993. *Honours:* 2 Grammies, 1991; Rockbjörn Award, 1991, 1992; Mozart prize, 1991; World Music Award, 1992; Represented Sweden, Eurovision Song Contest, 1980; Platinum and Gold discs. *Membership:* SKAP (Swedish Composers Society). *Leisure interests:* Qi Gong; Skiing; Tennis; Diving. *Current Management:* Jan Beime, Desert Music.

LEE Albert; b. 21 Dec. 1943, Leominster, Hertfordshire, England. Musician (guitar). *Career:* Guitarist, Chris Farlowe and The Thunderbirds, 1960s; In-demand session musician; Also member of Country Fever; Member, Poet and The One Man Band (with Chas Hodges of Chas 'n' Dave); Group became Heads Hands and Feet; Member, the Crickets; Emmylou Harris' Hot Band; Touring bands of Eric Clapton; Jackson Browne; Jerry Lee Lewis; Dave Edmunds; Concerts include: Everly Brothers Reunion, Royal Albert Hall, 1983. *Recordings:* Solo albums: Hiding, 1979; Albert Lee, 1983; Speechless, 1986; Gagged But Not Bound, 1987; Black Claw and Country Fever, 1991; In Full Flight, 1994; Country Legend, 1998; Con Sabor Latino, 2000; Other recordings: Albums with Eric Clapton: Just One Night, 1980; Another Ticket, 1981; Money and Cigarettes, 1983; with Joe Cocker: With A Little Help From My Friends, 1969; Stingray, 1976; with The Crickets: Bubblegum, Pop, Ballads and Boogie, 1973; Remnants, 1973; with Dave Edmunds: Repeat When Necessary, 1979; DE7, 1982; with Chris Farlowe: Chris Farlowe and The Thunderbirds, 1966; Stormy Monday, 1966; Out of The Blue, 1985; with Emmylou Harris: Luxury Liner, 1977; Quarter Moon In A Ten Cent Town, 1978; Blue Kentucky Girl, 1979; Christmas Album, 1979; Roses In The Snow, 1980; Evangeline, 1981; Cimarron, 1981; Ballad of Sally Rose, 1985; with Head Hands and Feet: Head Hands and Feet, 1971; Tracks, 1972; Old Soldiers Never Die, 1973; with Jimmy Page and John Paul Jones: No Introduction Necessary, 1984; Also recorded on albums with: Chas and Dave; Bobby Bare; Gary Brooker; Teresa Brewer; Guy Clark; Rodney Crowell; Bo Diddley; Lonnie Donegan; Don Everly; Everly Brothers; Nancy Griffith; Jerry Lee Lewis; Jon Lord; Steve Morse; Juice Newton; Dolly Parton; Ricky Skaggs; Shakin' Stevens.

LEE Alvin; b. 19 Dec. 1944, Nottingham, England. Musician (guitar, vox); Songwriter. *Career:* First band: The Jailbreakers, age 13, Became The Jaybirds, then Ten Years After; Moved to London, 1966; Friday residency, Marquee Club, 1968; Fillmore East and West, Woodstock, USA, 1969; Arena dates, 28 tours in 5 years, led to band disbanding, 1976; Solo recordings, collaboration with gospel singer, Mylon Lefevre; Short reunion of Ten Years After, 1988; Returned to solo work. *Recordings include:* Albums: with Ten Years After: Ten Years After, 1967; Undead, 1968; Ssssh, 1969; Cricklewood Green, 1970; Watt, 1971; A Space In Time, 1971; Alvin Lee and Company, 1972; Rock and Roll Music To The World, 1972; Recorded Live, 1973; Positive Vibrations, 1974; Goin' Home, 1975; Hear Them Calling, 1976; The Classic Performances Of, 1977; Greatest Hits, 1979; Profile, 1980; Portfoloio, 1983; Universal, 1988; About Time, 1989; Texas International Pop Festival, 1992; Pure Blues, 1995; with Mylon Lefevre: On The Road To Freedom; Solo: In Flight, 1974; Pump Iron, 1975; Let It Rock, 1978; Rocket Fuel (and Ten Years Later), 1978; Chrysalis Classics, 1978; Ride On (and Ten Years Later), 1979; Free Fall (Alvin Lee Band), 1980; RX5, 1981; Detroit Deisel, 1986; Zoom, 1992; Nineteen-Ninety-Four, 1993; I Hear You Knockin', 1994; Pure Blues, 1995; Live in Vienna, 1996; Solid Rock, 2000; Guest artist on recordings including: The Session, Jerry Lee Lewis, 1973; Dark Horse, George Harrison, 1974; 20th Anniversary of Rock and Roll, Bo Diddley, 1976; Revue, Vol. 2, Earl Scruggs, 1976; Bull In A Ming Vase, Roy Harper, 1977; Night of The Guitar Live (1988), 1989; Under No Obligation, Roger Chapman, 1991; 38317, Peter Maffay, 1991. *Current Management:* Skarda. *Address:* Bergstrasse 13, 82069 Hohenshäftlarn, Germany.

LEE Brenda, (Brenda Lee Tarpley); b. 11 Dec. 1944, Lithonia, Georgia, USA. Singer. *Career:* Solo recording artist, 1950s-60s; Actress, film The Two Little Bears. *Recordings:* Hit singles include: Sweet Nothin's, 1960; I'm Sorry (No. 1, USA), 1960; I Want To Be Wanted (No. 1, USA), 1960; Let's Jump The Broomstick, 1961; Speak To Me Pretty, 1962; One Step At A Time; Rockin' Around The Christmas Tree, 1962; Losing You, 1963; I Wonder, 1963; As Usual, 1963; Nobody Wins; Thanks A Lot, 1965; Too Many Rivers, 1965; Albums include: Grandma, What Great Songs You Sang, 1959; Brenda Lee, 1960; This Is Brenda, 1960; Emotions, 1961; All The Way, 1961; Sincerely, 1962; Brenda, That's All, 1962; The Show For Christmas Seals, 1962; All Alone Am I, 1963; Let Me Sing, 1963; By Request, 1964; Merry Christmas From Brenda Lee, 1964; Top Teen Hits, 1965; The Versatile Brenda Lee, 1965; Too Many Rivers, 1965; Bye Bye Blues, 1966; Coming On Strong, 1966; For The First Time (with Pete Fountain), 1968; Johnny One Time, 1969; The Brenda Lee Story, 1974; LA Sessions, 1977; Even Better, 1980; Little Miss Dynamite, 1980; 25th Anniversary, 1984; The Golden Decade, 1985; The Best of Brenda Lee, 1986; Love Songs, 1986; Brenda Lee, 1991; Rockin' Around, 1995; Jingle Bell Rock, 1995; Live Dynamite, 1997; Wiedersehn Ist Wunderschon, 1997; In the Mood for Love, 1998; Miss Dynamite Live, 2000; Guest singer, Shadowland, k d lang, 1988. *Current Management:* Brenda Lee Management, 2174 Carson St, Nashville, TN 37211, USA.

LEE Christopher James; b. 24 June 1961, Cheltenham, Gloucester. Musician (Trumpet, Steel Pan). m. Lucy, 1 s., 1 d. *Career:* Founder Member, Pigbag, 1979; Toured Europe, America and Japan, 1980–83; Appeared on Top of The Pops, 1982–83; Radio sessions, John Peel, Kid Jensen, 1983–; Involved in Jazz and improvised musics, 1997-. *Compositions:* The Shell Suite; The Arrow of Time; the Magician of Riga; On The Swing of a Prayer; Jakes Dance. *Recordings:* Papas Got A Brand New Pigbag; Pigbag; The Shell Temple At Margate. *Honour:* Lottery Award Money To Make Recording With Sweet Thunder. *Memberships:* PRS; Musicians' Union; PAMRA. *Leisure interests:* Chess; Squash. *Address:* 46 Ferndale Rd, Leytonstone, E11 3DN.

LEE Crissy; b. 17 June 1943, Colchester, Essex, England. Musician (drums, percussion); Music Teacher. *Career:* Joined Ivy Benson Dance Band, aged 17, tours world-wide; Appeared with artistes including: Dinah Washington; Frank Sinatra; Fats Domino; Caterina Valente; Tom Jones; Support on The Beatles first Spanish tour; Formed the Crissy Lee Band; Worked alongside: Al Jarreau; Faith Brown; Marion Montgomery; Madeline Bell; Musical Director for guests including: Roy Castle; Ken Dodd; Bob Monkhouse; Launched and managed Koffee and Kreme duo, winners of New Faces television talent show; Other musical projects include Beauty and the Beat, backing band for acts including The Supremes, Johnny Bristol; Sam Dees; Formed The Crissy Lee and her All Female Orchestra (only 17-piece all-female band in Europe); Television appearances include: Barrymore; Wogan; Cilla Black Show; Russell Harty Show; Jack Parnell Big Band Special; Millicent Martin Show; Lady Be Good; Goldeneye; David Frost Chat Show. *Recordings:* The Beat Chics EP; The Beat Chics: Skinny Mini/Now I Know. *Memberships:* Equity; Musicians' Union; ABJM (Asscn of British Jazz Musicians). *Leisure interests:* Sports; Cars; Theatre; Reading; Animal welfare; Eating out. *Current Management:* Neil Simpson, World-wide Management. *Address:* 3 Alston Rd, Bispham, Blackpool, Lancashire FY2 0TD, England.

LEE Dave, (Joey Negro, Raven Maize, Doug Willis, Z Factor, Sessomato, Akabu, Jakatta); b. 18 June 1964, Colchester, Essex, England. Prod.; Remixer; DJ. *Career:* Founder: Republic Records (one of the first UK House labels), Z Records; First British artist to record for cult New York label Nu-Groove; Remixed: Sister Sledge, Lisa Stansfield, Pet Shop Boys, Diana Ross, M People; Member: Sunburst Band, Hed Boys; Collaborations: Mark Ryder, Taka Boom, Blaze. *Recordings:* Albums: Universe of Love (as Joey Negro), 1993; Here Come the Sunburst Band, 2000: Can't Get High Without You (Compilation), 2000; Back to the Scene of the Crime, 2001; Singles: Get Acidic (with M-D-EMM), 1988; Forever Together (as Raven Maize), 1989; Do It Believe It (as Joey Negro), 1991; Do What You Feel (as Joey Negro), 1991; One Kiss (with Pacha), 1991; Enter Your Fantasy EP (as Joey Negro), 1992; Girls and Boys (with Hed Boys), 1994; Gotta Keep Pushin' (as Z Factor), 1998; Must Be the Music (with Taka Boom), 1999; Moody (as Sessomatto), 2000; American Dream (as Jakatta), 2001; The Real Life (as Raven Maize), 2001. *Current Management:* c/o Azuli Records, 25 D'Arblay St, London, W1V 3FH, England.

LEE Eddie; b. 26 Aug. 1961, Dublin, Ireland. Musician (bass guitar, double bass); Programmer; Prod. m. Therese O'Loughlin, 17 Feb. 1996. *Education:* BSc, University College, Dublin, 1979. *Musical Education:* Self-taught. *Career:* Played or recorded with: Brian Kennedy; Maura O'Connell; Those Nervous Animals; Stockton's Wing; The Pale; Enya; Dolores Keane Band; Katell Keineg; Frances Black; Emmylou Harris (with Dolores Keane); Davy Spillane; A Woman's Heart; Garrett Wall; Speranza; Nine Wassies From Bainne (Irish avant garde group). *Recordings include:* My Friend John, Those Nervous Animals (co-writer, performer); About Time,

Speranza; Solid Ground, Dolores Keane; Tracks on A Woman's Heart (biggest selling Irish album ever); Woman's Heart 2; Producer, Assassination, Indian; Film appearance with Brian Kennedy, 1995. *Memberships:* IMRO; PRS; Musicians' Union. *Address:* Teach Mhuire, Cleveragh Rd, Sligo, Ireland.

LEE Geddy (Gary); b. 29 July 1953, Willowdale, Canada. Musician (bass); Vocalist. *Career:* Member, Canadian rock group Rush, 1969–; Sell-out tours, USA, Canada; UK; Europe; Played on bills with ZZ Top; Areosmith; Kiss; Uriah Heep. *Recordings:* Albums: Rush, 1973; Fly By Night, 1975; Caress of Steel, 1975; 2112, 1976; All The World's A Stage, 1976; A Farewell To Kings, 1977; Archives, 1978; Hemispheres, 1978; Permanent Waves, 1980; Moving Pictures, 1981; Exit... Stage Left, 1981; Great White North, 1982; Signals, 1982; Grace Under Pressure, 1984; Power Windows, 1985; A Show of Hands, 1989; Presto, 1989; Chronicles, 1990; Roll The Bones, 1991; Counterparts, 1993; Test for Echo, 1996; Retrospective, Vol. 2: 1981–87, 1997; Different Stages, 1998; My Favorite Headache, 2000; Singles include: Spirit of Radio; Tom Sawyer; Vital Signs; New World Man; Closer To The Heart; Countdown; The Big Money; Time Stand Still. *Honours:* Juno Awards: Most Promising Group, 1975; Best Group, 1978, 1979; Group named Official Ambassadors of Music, Canadian Government, 1979; Gold Ticket Award, Madison Square Garden, 1991. *Current Management:* Anthem Entertainment, 189 Carlton St, Toronto, ON M5A 2K7, Canada.

LEE Jack; b. 30 July 1929, Lakewood, Ohio, USA. Conductor; Voice Coach; Musician (Piano); Musical Dir. Divorced. *Education:* BMus, Voice and Piano, BA Drama, Baldwin-Wallace College Conservatory of Music. *Career:* Off-Broadway show: Valmouth; Broadway shows: Sweet Charity, Funny Girl, Applause, No Strings, Billy, Peter Pan, My One and Only, Grand Hotel, My Fair Lady; Movies: Postcards from the Edge, Sweet Charity. *Recordings:* My One and Only; Grand Hotel; Sweet Charity. *Honour:* Phi Mu Alpha Sinfonia. *Memberships:* The Players' Club; Tony Nominating Committee; Faculty, New York University Teaching School. *Leisure interest:* Reading. *Address:* 37 W 72nd St Apt 10 D, New York, NY 10023, USA.

LEE Jon; b. 26 April 1982, Croydon, UK. Vocalist; Actor. *Education:* Attended Sylvia Young Theatre School. *Career:* Moved to London aged 12 to star in West End production of Oliver!; Various TV acting work including soap EastEnders prior to joining S Club 7; Group quickly achieved international success following sales of TV series Miami 7 (1999), LA 7 (2000) and Hollywood 7 (2001) featuring the band's music to nearly 100 countries; Also made nature TV series S Club 7 Go Wild (2000) and various TV specials; First British tour with S Club 7, 2001. *Recordings:* Albums: S Club, 1999; 7, 2000; Sunshine, 2001; Singles: Bring It All Back, 1999; S Club Party, 1999; Two In A Million/You're My Number One, 1999; Reach, 2000; Natural, 2000; Never Had A Dream Come True, 2000; Don't Stop Movin', 2001; Have You Ever, 2001. *Honour:* Brit Award, Best British Newcomer, 2000. *Current Management:* 19 Management, Unit 32, Ransomes Dock, 35–37 Parkgate Rd, London, SW11 4NP, England.

LEE Philip Robert; b. 8 April 1943, London, England. Musician (guitar). m. Doris Anna Zingerli, 31 March 1964. *Musical Education:* Self-taught. *Career:* First bands: John Williams Big Bands, Graham Collier Septet, 1960s; Henry Lowther, Tony Coe, 1970s; Musician with singers Annie Ross; Marian Montgomery; Sylvia Sims; Norma Winstone; Member, fusion band, Gilgamesh; Played for Americans including Benny Goodman, 1980s; Member, Dardanelle, 1990s; Worked with Jessye Norman in London and Greece, 1999; Appeared in film, Eyes Wide Shut, 1999. *Recordings:* Gilgamesh, Gilgamesh; Another Fine Tune You've Got Me Into, Gilgamesh; Twice Upon A Time, Phil Lee – Jeff Clyne; Swingin' In London, Dardanelle; Meteors Close At Hand, Michael Garrick. *Memberships:* PRS; Musicians' Union. *Leisure interests:* Reading; Walking. *Address:* 7c Thurlow Rd, London NW3 5PJ, England.

LEE Robert E, (Robert Greehy); b. 30 May 1956, Leeds, England. Singer; Musician (drums, guitar, bass, keyboards). *Education:* Roundhay Grammar School, Leeds. *Musical Education:* Self-taught. *Career:* Session musician, 1975–79; Member, London Cowboys, 1980–85; Tours: Europe; Japan; USA; Scandinavia; UK; including 2 support tours, Johnny Thunders, 1981, 1982; 2 support tours, Hanoi Rocks, 1982, 1983; Producer, session musician, 1986–; World-wide television and radio appearances; Full time member of The Infidels; with The Infidels: produced debut CD, 1998; Toured England, 1998; TV and radio appearances in USA, 1998. *Compositions:* Long Time Lonely, 1998; co-wrote Faithless and Blue. *Recordings:* Albums: Animal Pleasure; Tall In The Saddle; Long Time Coming; Dead Or Alive; Singles: Centrefold; Hook, Line and Sinker; Dance Crazy; Let's Get Crazy; Street Full of Soul; Faithless and Blue, 1998; Infidels, 2000. *Publications:* Country Music International, 1998; Mojo, 1998. *Honour:* Best New British Band, Country Music International, Alternative Rock/Country Crossover. *Memberships:* PRC; PRS; MU; MCPS. *Leisure interests:* Reading; Films; Music; Travel; Arts; Photography.

LEE Sara; b. 18 Aug. 1955, Hereford, England. Musician (Bass Guitarist). *Career:* League of Gentlemen, 1980; US and European Tour, 1981–84; Moved to New York, 1984; Toured With Thompson Twins, B 52's, Joan Osborne, 1987–99; Television, Tonight Show, Lonan O'Brian, D Letterman. *Recordings:* League of Gentlemen; Robyn Hitchcock: Gang of Four; Cosmic Thing; Good Stuff; Living In Clip; Little Plastic Castle; Solo album: Make It Beautiful, 2000. *Leisure interests:* Support of Community and Agriculture Farm. *Current Management:* Peter Casperson Invasion Group. *Address:* 113 W 25 St, Fifth Floor, New York, NY 10001, USA.

LEE Tommy, (Thomas Lee Bass); b. 3 Oct. 1962, Athens, Greece. Musician (drums). m. (1) Heather Locklear, 1986; (2) Pamela Anderson, 1995, 2 s. *Career:* Member, groups Suite 19; Christmas; Founder member, US heavy rock group Mötley Crüe, 1981–; World-wide concerts include: Tours with: YandT, 1981, 1982; Kiss, 1983; Ozzy Osbourne, 1984; Iron Maiden, 1984; Cheap trick, 1986; Theatre of Pain World tour, 1985–86; World tours, 1987, 1989; Major festivals: US Festival, 1983; Monsters of Rock Festival, Castle Donington, 1984; Moscow Music Peace Festival, 1989. *Recordings:* Albums: Too Fast For Love, 1981; Shout At The Devil, 1983; Theatre of Pain, 1985; Girls, Girls, Girls (No. 2, US), 1987; Dr Feelgood (No. 1, USA), 1989; Decade of Decadence (No. 2, US), 1991; Til Death Do Us Part, 1994; Generation Swine, 1997; Greatest Hits, 1998; Supersonic and Demon Relics, 1999; Singles: Stick To Your Guns, 1981; Looks That Kill, 1984; Too Young To Fall In Love, 1984; Smokin' In The Boys Room, 1985; Home Sweet Home, 1985; You're All I Need, 1987; Dr Feelgood, 1989; Kick Start My Heart, 1990; Without You, 1990; Don't Go Away Mad, 1990; Same Old Situation, 1990; Primal Scream, 1991; Contributions to: Nine Inch Nails, Downward Spiral, 1994; Methods of Mayhem, 1999. *Publication:* The Dirt, with Mötley Crüe, 2001. *Current Management:* The Left Bank Organisation, 6255 Sunset Blvd, Suite 1111, Hollywood, CA 90028, USA.

LEES John; b. 13 Jan. 1947, Oldham, Lancashire, England. Singer; Musician (guitar). *Career:* Member, Barclay James Harvest (originally the Blues Keepers), 1967–; Regular international tours, UK and Europe, including Free concert, Berlin Wall, 1980. *Recordings include:* Albums: Barclay James Harvest, 1970; Barclay James Harvest Live, 1974; Time Honoured Ghosts, 1975; Gone To Earth, 1977; Harvest XII, 1978; Eyes of The Universe, 1980; Turn of The Tide, 1981; Concert For The People, 1981; Ring of Changes, 1981; Face To Face, 1987; Glasnost, 1988; Welcome To The Show, 1990; Alone We Fly, 1990; The Harvest Years, 1991; The Best of Barclay James Harvest, 1992; Solo album: A Major Fancy, 1977; Barclay James Harvest Through The Eyes of John Lees, featuring Wooly Wolstenhulme, 1999. *Current Management:* Handle Artists Management. *Address:* The Handle Group of Companies, Pinewood Studios, Pinewood Rd, Iver Heath, Buckinghamshire SL0 0NH, England.

LEES Simon (Buggy); b. 16 May 1970, Wolverhampton, England. Musician (guitar, drums); Singer; Songwriter; Entertainer. *Education:* BTEC ONC at Wulfrun College. *Career:* Formed Osprey, 1986; Nitebreed, 1990 (support band for The Mock Turtles); Member, The Red House Snakes, 1990; Formed Plain Jain, 1992; Member, Tantrum, 1994; Radio appearances: The Reaper Rock Show, Freedom FM, Chester; Jenny Wilkes Show, BBC Radio WM, 1999. *Recordings:* Playing Truant, recorded live at London Music Show, Wembley Conference Centre, 1994; My World, solo album, 1998. *Publication:* Guitarist magazine. *Honours:* Guitarist of The Year finalist, 1993–95, winner, 1998. *Membership:* Musicians' Union. *Leisure interests:* Cycling; Swimming; Reading. *Address:* 34 Strathmore Cres., Wombourne, Wolverhampton, Staffordshire WV5 9AS, England.

LEFTWICH Bradley Rush; b. 30 June 1953, Stillwater, Oklahoma, USA. Musician (Traditional American Fiddle, Banjo); Singer. m. Linda Higginbotham, 1 May 1982, 1 s. *Education:* BA, Anthropology, Oberlin College; MA, Anthropology, University of Chicago. *Career:* Founding Member, Plank Road, 1975–77; Toured with Linda Higginbotham as Leftwich and Higginbotham, 1981–, with the Humdingers, 1990s, and with Tom Sauber and Alice Gerrard as Tom, Brad and Alice, 1997–; Stage appearances include: The White House, Philadelphia and Winnipeg folk festivals, Piccolo Spoleto, Charleston, Bele Chere, Asheville; Radio appearances on Wheeling Jamboree, Renfro Valley Barn Dance, The Flea Market, Our Front Porch and on Danish national TV and radio. *Recordings:* Been There Still; Say, Old Man; Carrying On The Tradition; Learn to Play Old-Time Fiddle, vols 1 and 2; Rounder Fiddle; A Moment in Time; No One To Bring Home Tonight; Banging and Sawing; Buffalo Gal; Southern Clawhammer Banjo; Vocal and Instrumental Blend; Plank Road Stringband. *Publications:* Bowing Workshop, series of columns in Old-Time Herald magazine; Reflections on Southern Appalachian Fiddling, article, 1995; Clawhammer Banjo, Round Peak Style, 1999. *Honours:* Recommended LP, Buffalo Gal, Billboard Magazine, 1983; First Place, Fiddle, First Place, Band, Appalachian String Band Music Festival, 1990; Nomination, Fiddler of the Year, Society for Preservation of Bluegrass Music of America, 1984–86, Nomination, String Band of the Year, 1984–86. *Memberships:* Advisory Board, Old-Time Herald magazine; North American Folk Alliance. *Leisure interest:* Aviation.

LEGER Kenny; b. Copenhagen. Singer; Composer; Project Man. *Education:* BA, Kingston. *Career:* 10 minor television and film productions; One grand production, The African Evasion Eclipse; Various appearances on national television and radio. *Membership:* KODA. *Leisure interest:* Meditation. *Current Management:* Snedker. *Address:* 77 Hillfield Rd, Hampstead, London NW6 1QB.

LEGGETT Andy; b. 31 March 1942, Much Wenlock, England. Musician (saxophone, clarinet, guitar); Songwriter; Arranger. m. Teri Penfold, 5 Sept. 1975, 2 s., 1 d. *Education:* BA Hons, French, Hull, 1964. *Musical Education:* School Orchestra. *Career:* Member of Alligator Jug Thumpers, 1968; Pigsty Hill Light Orchestra, 1970; duo with Pete Finch, 1973; Avon Touring Theatre, 1974; Formed Sweet Substitute, 1975; Later became Musical Director, writer and arranger for them; Toured with: Midnite Follies Orchestra, Pasadena Roof Orchestra, Syd Lawrence, Bob Kerr's Whoopee Band, Temperance Seven; Playing clarinet and saxophone, Rod Mason's Hot Five, 1996-. *Compositions:* for Sweet Substitute: Tiger Blues, Dear Mr Berkeley, Sleepy Suzie, A Musical Christmas Card; for Henry's Bootblacks: Everyone's Got Horns, New Orleans Feels Like Home, Sugar Makes Your Teeth Fall Out; Co-wrote songs for the play The Godmother, directed by Mel Smith; Music for film, Betjeman Revisited, HTV, 1995. *Memberships:* Associate Mem., PRS, MCPS. *Address:* Orffstrasse 22, KAARST-Büttgen, 41564, Germany.

LEGRAND Benjamin; b. 16 Oct. 1962, Paris, France. Singer; Musician (piano, drums). m. Tita Gibert, 22 July 1994, 1 d. *Musical Education:* Piano, drums, singing lessons, Paris. *Career:* Appearances include: Television shows, Paris; Olympia Hall, Paris; Tours: Japan; Tunisia; Belgium; Switzerland; Bobino Music Hall, Paris; Concerts in, Korea; Eurodisney concerts; Cannes Jazz Festival; Calvi Jazz Festival, Corsica; Radio Shows include France Inter. *Recordings:* Album with Michel Legrand Big Band; Chansons De Paris (album of French songs); Record of Jazz Trio; Participating in album of French Songs; Album with Baden Powell and Phillipe Baden Powell. *Publications:* Letemps Qui Passe (poetry); La Pensée Universalle. *Memberships:* SPEDIDAM; SACEM. *Leisure interests:* Tennis; Long walks. *Address:* 14 Villa Molitor, 75016 Paris, France.

LEGRAND Michel; b. 24 Feb. 1932, Paris, France. Composer; Musician (piano); Conductor; Singer; Arranger. m. Isabelle, 21 Nov. 1994, 2 s., 2 d. *Musical Education:* Paris Conservatoire. *Career:* Conducted, appeared with Pittsburgh Symphony Orchestra, The National Symphony Orchestra, Minnesota Orchestra, Buffalo Philharmonic, Symphony Orchestras of Vancouver, Montréal, Atlanta, Denver, New Orleans; Collaborated with Maurice Chevalier, Miles Davis, Kiri Te Kanawa, Johnny Mathis, Neil Diamond, Sarah Vaughn, Stan Getz, Aretha Franklin, Jack Jones, James Galway, Ray Charles, Lena Horne, Barbra Streisand and numerous others; Films: (with Miles Davis) Dingo, 1990; Directed, Cinq Jours En Juin, 1989; Masque de Lune, 1991; Theatre productions, television appearances and film scores including Prêt-à-Porter, 1994. *Compositions include:* Images; I Was Born In Love With You; I Will Wait For You; Love Makes The Changes; Noelle's Theme; On My Way To You; One At A Time; Once Upon A Summertime; Little Boy Lost; The Summer Knows; Summer Me, Winter Me; Watch What Happens; The Way He Makes Me Feel; What Are You Doing The Rest of Your Life?; The Windmills of Your Mind; You Must Believe In Spring; Scored films include: The Thomas Crown Affair, 1968; Summer of '42, 1971; Yentl, 1982; Never Say Never Again, 1983; Ready To Wear, 1994; Madelaine, 1997. *Recordings include:* Erik Satie By Michel Legrand; Four Piano Blues; Michel Plays Legrand; Paris Jazz Piano, 2001. *Publication:* Michel Legrand Song Book. *Honours include:* 5 Grammy Awards, 1972–75; 3 Academy Awards, Thomas Crown Affair, 1968; Summer of '42, 1971; Yentl, 1983; Australian Film Institute Award, Dingo, 1991. *Memberships:* Songwriters' Guild; Dramatists' Guild; NARAS; Academy of Motion Arts and Sciences. *Current Management:* Jim DiGiovanni.

LEICK Vagn; b. 13 April 1939, Lydersholm, Denmark. Composer; Musician (piano). m. Jo Skovsbog, 19 April 1985, 2 s., 1 d. *Education:* PhD, Biochemistry. *Musical Education:* Private study in Jazz improvisation and composition. *Career:* Television and radio appearances in Denmark; US; France. *Recordings:* Twilight; Thing; Jazz Digit; Songscapes. *Membership:* Danish Society of Jazz, Beat and Folk Authors. *Leisure interests:* Mountain hiking; Skiing. *Current Management:* Orbit Productions. *Address:* Ved Glyptoteket 6 3th, 1575 Kobenhavn V, Denmark.

LEIGH Joy; b. 23 April 1964, Montgomery, West Virginia, USA. Country/ Southern Gospel Singer. Divorced. *Education:* Associate degree, Nursing, West Virginia Institute of Technology. *Career:* Performed on stage, Grand Ole Opry, Don Reed Talent Competition; Showcase artist, King Eagle Awards Show, Nashville, Tennessee; Headlined Fayette County, West Virginia, Fair, 1994, 1995; Performed at Boone County, West Virginia, Fair, 1994, 1995; Summerville, West Virginia's Suumerfest, 1994; Rotary Club of Montgomery, West Virginia, 1994, 1995. *Recordings:* What's In It

For Me?; Walk Away. *Honours:* Nomination, Gospel Trailblazer Award, King Eagle Awards Show; Montgomery Rotary Festival Award; United Community Services Entertainment Award. *Membership:* Gospel Music Asscn, Nashville, Tennessee. *Leisure interests:* Computers; Reading; Walks through mountains; Playing with my dogs. *Current Management:* Claudia Johnson, Johnson and Johnson Music Group, PO Box 182 Cannelton, WV 25036, USA. *Address:* Joy Leigh Enterprises, PO Box 182, Cannelton, WV 25036, USA.

LEIGHTON Brian; b. 30 June 1970, Minneapolis, Minnesota, USA. Singer; Musician (Acoustic Guitar, Harmonica). *Career:* G B Leighton Band; Movie, The Marksmen; Woman Thing Music, Phillip Morris. *Recordings:* One Time, One Life; Come Alive; Live from Pickle Park; It's All Good, 2000. *Membership:* ASCAP. *Leisure interest:* Flying kites. *Current Management:* Blue Sky Artists. *Address:* PO BOx 68124, Minneapolis, MN 55418, USA.

LEINER Boris; b. 28 Jan. 1957, Cakovec, Croatia. Musician; Singer; Drums; Percussions. Divorced, 1 d. *Education:* Study, Art Academy, Zagreb; Art University, Utrecht, Holland, 1983–86. *Career:* Drummer, Singer, Rock Band, Azra, 1977–87; Vjestice, 1987–; Naturalna Mistika, Reggae band, 1983–; Berlin's Band, Love-Sister-Hope, International Tour, 1980–92; European Tour, Vjestice, 1989–90. *Compositions:* Balkan, 1979; Lijepe Zene Prolaze Kroz Grad, 1980; Provedimo Vikend Zajedno, 1981; Uzas Je Moja Furka, 1981; Klincek Stoji Pod Oblokom, 1983; Totalno Drukciji Od Drugih, 1989. *Recordings:* Azra-Azra; Suncana Strana Ulice Azra; Ravno Do Dna-Azra Djevojke U Ljetnim Haljinama Volim, Vjestice; Kradljivci SRCA Vjestice, Totalno Drukciji Od Drugih. *Publications:* Azra I, 1980; Suncana Strana Ulice, 1981; Azra Ravno Do Dna, 1981; Krivo Srastanje, 1984; Totalno Drukciji Od Drugih, 1988; Vjestice, Kradljivci Srca, 1996. *Honours:* 3 Porin Awards, Cro Music, 1996; Kradljivci Srca, Best Alter, CD; Status Award, Best Drummer, 1996. *Memberships:* HGU, Croatian Musicians' Union; HZSU, Croatian Union of Independent Artists. *Leisure interests:* Yoga; Art Consumer. *Current Management:* Combat Rock Management, Jurici Tomislavov Trg 19, Zagreb, Croatia. *Address:* Duzice 23, 1000 Zagreb, Croatia.

LEITNER George; b. 24 Nov. 1959, Vienna, Austria. Agent, Man. m. Dr Brigitte Leitner-Friedrich, 29 Sept. 1991. *Education:* College, South Africa; University, Vienna. *Musical Education:* piano. *Career:* 1977, founded Number One Music (with Andreas Eggar); 1980, founded George Leitner Productions, representing: James Brown; Kool and the Gang; Jimmy Cliff; Blood Sweat and Tears; VSOP; The Commodores; George Clinton; others. *Publication:* Analysis of The European Music Industry (university thesis). *Honour:* Mag, Rer Soc Ök. *Leisure interests:* Horseriding; Sailing; Skiing; Tennis. *Address:* Hütteldorfstr 259, 1140 Vienna, Austria.

LEJEUNE Philippe; b. 6 Feb. 1954, Eu, France. Musician (piano). m. Irene, 5 July 1986, 2 s. *Education:* DUT, Tech de Co. *Musical Education:* Conservatoires, Rouen, Reims. *Career:* Appearances: Detroit Jazz Festival; Festival Radio France; Festival de Jazz de Montauban; Nuits Piano Jazz Lutetia, Paris; Cincinnati Queen City Blues Festival; Monterey Blues Festival. *Recordings:* Piano Duet With Memphis Slim, 1980; Live At Blue Moon, 1990; Chicago Non Stop, 1993; 100% Blues and Boogie Woogie, 1996; Piano Groove, 1999. *Memberships:* SACEM; SPEDIDAM; ADAMI. *Current Management:* Asscn Jazz Vivant. *Address:* PO Box 20, 31921 Toulouse Cedex 9, France.

LEMMY (Ian Kilminster); b. 24 Dec. 1945, Stoke-on-Trent, Staffordshire, England. Musician (bass); Vocalist. *Career:* Member, several groups including: The Rainmakers; The Motown Sect; The Rockin' Vicars; Sam Gopal's Dream; Opal Butterfly; Also road crew member, Jimi Hendrix; Member, UK rock group Hawkwind, 1971–75; Founder, UK heavy rock group Mötorhead, 1975–; Regular UK, US and international tours; Major concerts include: Heavy Metal Barn Dance, 1980; Monsters of Rock Festival, Castle Donington, 1986; Film appearance: Eat The Rich, 1987. *Recordings:* Albums: with Hawkwind: In Search of Space, 1971; Doremi Fasol Latido, 1972; Space Ritual, 1973; Hall of The Mountain Grill, 1974; Warrior On The Edge of Time, 1975; with Mötorhead: Motörhead, 1977; Overkill, 1979; Bomber, 1979; Ace of Spades, 1980; No Sleep 'Til Hammersmith, 1981; What's Words Worth, 1983; Another Perfect Day, 1983; No Remorse, 1984; Orgasmatron, 1986; Rock 'n' Roll, 1987; No Sleep At All, 1988; 1916, 1991; March Or Die, 1992; Bastards, 1993; Fistful of Aces: Best of Mötorhead, 1994; We Are Mötorhead, 2000; Solo: Best of Lemmy: Born to Lose Live to Win, 1995; Rock 'n' Roll Forever, 2000; Singles: with Hawkwind: Silver Machine, 1972; Urban Guerila, 1973; with Motörhead: Motörhead/City Kids, 1977; Louie Louie, 1978; No Class, 1979; Bomber, 1979; The Golden Years (EP), 1980; Beer Drinkers and Hell Raisers, 1980; St Valentine's Day Massacre, with Girlschool, 1981; Iron Fist, 1982; I Got Mine, 1983; Shine, 1983; Killed By Death, 1984; Deaf Forever, 1986; The One To Sing The Blues, 1991; Contributor, Hear 'N' Aid, 1987; Let It Be, Ferry Aid, 1987; The Last Temptation of Elvis, 1990. *Honours include:* Grammy Nomination, Metal Performance, Enter

Sandman, 2000. *Current Management:* Singerman Entertainment, Penthouse West, 8833 Sunset Blvd, Los Angeles, CA 90069, USA.

LENDING Kenn; b. 8 Feb. 1955, Copenhagen, Denmark. Musician (guitar); Composer; Songwriter; Vocalist. m. Karina Nevermann, 15 May 1993. *Musical Education:* Private lessons, music-writing, composing; Classical guitar lessons with Jan Ronnow, Royal Danish Academy of Music. *Career:* Member, Himmelexpressen, 1972–79; Member, Survivors, 1976–78; Member, Blues Nite, 1977–79; Formed duo with American blues pianist, singer, Champion Jack Dupree, 1979–92; Played over 1000 concerts; Formed Kenn Lending Blues Band, 1980–; Used as backing band by Jan Harrington; Louisiana Red; Jack Dupree; Luther Allison; Support tours, Fats Domino, Germany, 1987; B B King, Netherlands, 1988, Denmark, 1989; Recorded with The Band in Woodstock, 1991; Worked with Lillian Boutté Musicfriends, Spirit of Louisiana Gospel Tour, including Gospel United with Stig Rossen, 1994; Gospel United Tour with Lillian Boutté, 1995. *Recordings include:* with Kenn Lending Blues Band: Live!, 1981; I'm Coming Home, 1983; Blues For People, 1985; Steamin' Hot, 1988; Diggin' The Blues, 1990; Heartache Motel, 1993; Game of Life, 1995; with Champion Jack Dupree: An Evening With Champion Jack Dupree, 1981; Still Fighting The Blues, 1981; I Had That Dream, 1982; Blues Is Freedom To All, 1987; Back Home In New Orleans, 1990; Forever and Ever, 1991; One Last Time, 1992; After All, 1994; Live Gospel United, 1994; Louisiana Spice: 25 Years of Louisiana Music, various artists, 1995; Gospel United, People Get Ready, 1995; High on the Hog, with The Band, 1996; Portrait of Champion Jack Dupree, 2000; Also recorded with: Memphis Slim; Louisiana Red; Mickey Baker; Aron Burton; Jan Harrington; Lillian Boutté. *Honour:* Danish Blues Musician of the Year, 1995. *Memberships:* The Danish Musicians Union; DJBFA; KODA. *Leisure interests:* Birds (Parakeets); Reading (History, Philosophy, Literature). *Current Management:* Marsk Music, Farup Kirkevej 27, 6760 Ribe, Denmark. *Address:* Kenn Lending, Vendsysselvej 7, 2720 Copenhagen-Vanlose, Denmark.

LENDORPH Jorn; b. 14 June 1966, Copenhagen, Denmark. Singer; Songwriter; Prod. *Education:* Graduated, Sct Annae Music College; Copenhagen's Boys' Choir; Piano and Singing lessons. *Career:* Played in Danish TV serial, Everyone Loves Debbie, composed background music and sung title song, 1987; Leading role in film An Abyss of Freedom, wrote one song which was released as single, 1989; Composed music for various short films and songs for own album; Has sung in various TV shows, live concerts and on TV commercials; Background singer, various releases including Sound of Seduction and Shirley, Sanne Graulund. *Recordings:* Title song to Danish version of Disney's Beauty and the Beast, 1991; Loosen Up, solo album, 1996; Produced soundtrack for Danish film The Eighteenth, 1997; Produced Sanne Graulund's debut album, Better Get Some Dreams, 1998. *Membership:* Danish Artists Union. *Current Management:* Scandinavian Records. *Address:* Viktoria Gade 6 2th, 1655 Copenhagen V, Denmark.

LENGSTRAND Gert O; b. 30 May 1942, Gothenburg, Sweden. Songwriter; Publisher. m. Jeanette, 14 Aug. 1987, 1 s., 4 d. *Career:* Singer, The Streaplers, Swedish pop group, 1957–68; Songwriter, Record Producer, 1969–. *Compositions:* Hasta La Vista, Silvia, 1974; Eloise, Arvingarna, 1993. *Recordings:* Diggity Doggerty, 1963; Rockin' Robin, 1965; Mule Skinner Blues, 1964. *Honour:* Ampex Golden Reel Award, Eloise, 1993. *Leisure interests:* Sport; Music. *Current Management:* GL-Productions Ltd. *Address:* GL-Productions Ltd, PO Box 632, 44217, Kungälv, Sweden.

LENGWINAT Katrin; b. 10 Dec. 1960, Berlin, Germany. Musicologist. m. Eduardo Briceño, 16 April 1994, 1 s. *Education:* Bachelor degree; Dr phil, Musicology, Polish and German universities; Studied piano, guitar and folkharp. *Career:* Musicologist, Academy of Fine Arts, Berlin; Musicologist, Foundation of Ethnomusicology and Folklore, Caracas, Venezuela; Leader for Musicology, Free University of Berlin and Central University of Venezuela; Researcher of folk and popular music in Germany, Venezuela and Peru. *Publications:* Arpa, Maraca y Buche, 1998; Joropo Central, 1998. *Membership:* International Council for Traditional Music (ICTM). *Address:* PO Box 40.052, 1040 Caracas, Venezuela.

LENGYEL Peter M; b. 5 June 1946, New York, USA. Musician (Piano); Composer; Arranger. Divorced. *Education:* BA, Glassboro St College; MM, Theory, Indiana University, 1973. *Career:* University Teacher, 1971–85; Full time composer and arranger, 1985–; Clinician and Judge for jazz bands, marching bands, concert bands, throughout the USA; Teacher of jazz and conductor; President, P & D Jazz Publications; Head of Jazz Studies, Eastfield College, Texas, 1971–81; Performances with Don Ellis, Bill Watrous, Clark Terry, Frank Rosolino. *Compositions:* 25 large jazz ensemble pieces including performances at many major events; 4 pieces for symphonie band; Jazzamorphosis, commissioned by Army Ground Forces Band. *Honours:* Award for Teaching Excellence, University of Texas at Arlington College of Liberal Arts Music Department, 1983, 1984, 1985. *Membership:* Texas Bandmasters; Patron mem., International Asscn of

Jazz Educators. *Leisure interests:* Golf and most sports. *Address:* 4453 Wesley Way, Austell, GA 30106, USA.

LENINE (Osvaldo Lenine Macedo Pimentel); b. Pernambuco, Brazil. Vocalist; Musician (guitar); Songwriter. *Career:* Mixes North Eastern-Brazilian grooves with pop music; As Voltas Que O Mundo Dá used in major Brazilian soap opera Ana Raio e Zé Trovão; Collaborations include: Gilberto Gil; Chico César; Djavan; Elba Ramalho; Songs recorded by: Dionne Warwick; Gilberto Gil; Danilo Caymmi; Sergio Mendes. *Recordings include:* Singles: Prova De Fogo, 1981; Baque De Era, 1983; Albums: Baque Solto (with Lula Queiroga), 1983; Olha De Peixe (with Marcos Suzano), 1993; O Dia Em Que Faremos Contato, 1997; Na Pressao, 1999. *Honour:* Sharp Prize, Best Song, A Ponte (with Lula Queiroga), 1998.

LENNEVALD (John) Dhani; b. 24 July 1984, Stockholm, Sweden. Vocalist. *Education:* Gärdeskolan school, Stockholm. *Career:* Picked to be member of A*Teens group following auditions at Leslie Kühler's dance school, 1998; Continued educational studies whilst pursuing musical career; Prestigious US support tours for N*Sync and Britney Spears, 2000. *Recordings:* Albums: The Abba Generation, 1999; Teen Spirit, 2001; Singles: Mamma Mia, Super Trouper, Gimme! Gimme! Gimme!, Happy New Year, 1999; Dancing Queen, Upside Down, 2000; Halfway Around The World, Sugar Rush, 2001. *Honours:* Broke Swedish sales records with first album and single; World-wide sales of first album in excess of 3m.; Viva Music Awards, Best International Newcomer, 2000. *Address:* c/o Stockholm Records, Sweden. *Internet:* www.stockholmrecords.com.

LENNI; b. 17 April 1941, Stalybridge, Cheshire, England. Musician (saxophone); Vocalist. m. Irene Dale, March 1963, 1 s. *Musical Education:* Theory, Composition, Arrangement. *Career:* Member, Gladiators, 1959; Corvettes, 1964; St Louis Union, 1965; Tony Christie's Band, 1968–70; Sad Cafe, 1979; Norman Beaker Band, 1986; Look Twice, 1987; Supercharge, 1990; Support tours with Carlos Santana; Toto; Otis Redding; Atlantic Star; Chuck Berry; American Bluesmen: Lowell Fulson; Phil Guy; Larry Garner; Louisianna Red; Johnny Mars; Rockin' Sidney; Also played for: Jack Bruce; Dave Dee; Kiki Dee; Vince Hill; Paul Jones; Lou Rawls; Lisa Stansfield; Alvin Stardust; Herbie Goins; Claire Moore; Gavin Sutherland; Victor Brox; Carl Wayne; When In Rome. *Recordings:* Sad Cafe (8 albums); Paul Jones R & B Show (3 albums); Norman Beaker Band (3 albums); Judy Boucher (2 albums); Also albums by Cannon and Ball; Magna Carta; Gilbert O'Sullivan; Eric Stewart; 10cc; Ruby Turner; Lurrie Bell; Louisiana Red; Featured on television themes and radio commercials. *Honours:* Gold album, Facades; Silver album, Sad Cafe 4. *Memberships:* Musicians' Union; PAMRA; MENSA. *Leisure interests:* Writing; Computing; Puzzles. *Current Management:* Actual Music. *Address:* 14A Moorside Rd, Heaton Moor, Stockport, Cheshire SK4 4DT, England.

LENNON Julian; b. 8 April 1963, Liverpool, England. Singer; Songwriter; Musician. *Recordings:* Albums: Valotte, 1984; The Secret Value of Daydreaming, 1986; Mr Jordan, 1989; Help Yourself, 1991; Photograph Smile, 1998; VH1 – Behind The Music, 2001; Singles include: Valotte; Day After Day; Too Late For Goodbyes; Now You're In Heaven; Salt Water. *Address:* c/o Music From Another Room Ltd, The Penthouse, 20 Bulstrode St, London W1M 5FR, England.

LENNON Sean; b. 1976. Singer; Songwriter; Musician (Guitar). *Career:* Numerous live dates and television appearances. *Recordings:* Single: Home, 1998; Albums: Into the Sun, 1998; Half Horse Half Musician, 1999; Also appeared on: Push The Button, Money Mark, 1998; Primitive, Soulfly, 2000; Change Is Coming, Money Mark, 2001; Blueprint For A Sunrise, Yoko Ono, 2001.

LENNOX Annie; b. 25 Dec. 1954, Aberdeen, Scotland. Singer; Lyricist. m. (1) Rahda Raman, March 1984, divorced, (2) Uri Fruchtmann, 1 s., 2 d. *Musical Education:* Royal Academy of Music. *Career:* Member, with Dave Stewart, The Catch, 1977; Re-named The Tourists, 1979–80; Formed Eurythmics with Dave Stewart, 1980–89; World-wide concerts incl Nelson Mandela's 70th Birthday Tribute, Wembley, 1988; Solo artiste, 1988–; Eurythmics reformed, 1999; TV incls: Documentary, Diva, BBC2, 1992; Unplugged concert, MTV, 1992; Actress, film Revolution, 1985; 10m. albums sold to date. *Recordings:* with the Tourists: The Tourists; Reality Affect; Luminous Basement; with Eurythmics: In The Garden, 1981; Sweet Dreams (Are Made of This), 1982; Touch (No. 1, UK), 1983; 1984 (For The Love of Big Brother), 1984; Be Yourself Tonight, 1985; Revenge, 1986; Savage, 1987; We Too Are One (No. 1, UK), 1989; Eurythmics Greatest Hits (No. 1, UK), 1991; Eurythmics Live 1983–89, 1993; Peace, 1999; Solo: Diva (No. 1, UK), 1992; Medusa (No. 1, UK), 1995. *Contributions to:* Red Hot + Blue, 1990; Rock The World, 1990; Hit singles include: with the Tourists: I Only Want To Be With You, 1979; So Good To Be Back Home, 1979; with Eurythmics: Sweet Dreams (Are Made of This) (No. 1, USA), 1983; Love Is A Stranger, 1983; Who's That Girl?, 1983; Right By Your Side, 1983; Here Comes The Rain Again, 1984; Sex Crime, from film, 1984; Would I Lie To You?, 1985; There Must Be An Angel (Playing With My Heart), (No. 1, UK),

1985; Sisters Are Doing It For Themselves, duet with Aretha Franklin, 1985; It's Alright (Baby's Coming Back), 1986; When Tomorrow Comes, 1986; Thorn In My Side, 1986; Missionary Man, 1986; The Miracle of Love, 1986; Beethoven, 1987; Shame, 1987; I Need A Man, 1988; You Have Placed A Chill In My Heart, 1988; Revival, 1989; Don't Ask Me Why, 1989; The King and Queen of America, 1990; Angel, 1990; I Changed the World Today, 2000; Feels Like I'm Seventeen Again, 2000; Solo: Put A Little Love In Your Heart, with Al Green, from film soundtrack Scrooged, 1988; Why, 1992; Walking On Broken Glass, 1992; Precious, 1992; Cold, 1992; Little Bird/Love Song For A Vampire, from film Bram Stoker's Dracula, 1993; No More I Love You's, 1995; Whiter Shade of Pale, 1995; Waiting In Vain, 1995; Something So Right, 1995; Videos: Eurythmics Live; Sweet Dreams; Savage. *Honours:* Grammy Awards; BRIT Awards, including Outstanding Contribution, 1999; Ivor Novello Awards; Rolling Stone Readers Poll Winner, Best Female Singer, 1993. *Current Management:* 19 Management, Unit 32, Ransomes Dock, 35–37 Parkgate Rd, London SW11 4NP, England.

LEON Craig; b. 7 Jan. 1952, Miami, Florida, USA. Prod.; Arranger; Composer; Recording Artist. m. Cassell Webb, 10 June, 1984. *Compositions:* Izzy Album, 1998; Elysium Album, 2000. *Recordings:* 3 albums as featured artist: Nommos, 1981; Visiting, 1982; Klub Anima Theatre score, 1993; Premiered Bristol Old Vic theatre, 1993; 1 album in collaboration with Arthur Brown: Tape From Atoya, 1981; 5 albums in collaboration with Cassell Webb: Llano, 1985; Thief of Sadness, 1987; Songs of a Stranger, 1989; Conversations At Dawn, 1990; House of Dreams, 1992; Producer, Ramones, 1976; Blondie, 1977; Suicide, 1977; Richard Hell, 1977; Rodney Crowell, 1980; Sir Douglas Quintet, 1980; The Bangles, 1983; The Roches, 1983; Dr and the Medics, 1986; The Pogues, 1986; The Primitives, 1986; Adult Net, 1988; The Fall, 1989–92; Jesus Jones, 1990; New FADS, 1992; Front 242, 1993; Eugenius, 1994; Angel Corpus Christi, 1995; Martin Phillips and the Chills, 1996; Mark Owen, 1996; Cobalt 60, 1996; Psyched Up Janis, 1997; Blondie, No Exit, 1998; Izzy, 1998. *Memberships:* British Record Producers' Guild; Nominating Committee, The BRIT Awards. *Leisure interests:* Book and wine collecting. *Current Management:* Atlas Realisations Music, Trendalls Cottage, Beacons Bottom, Buckinghamshire HP14 3XF, England.

LEOPOLD Sinisa; b. 16 April 1957, Grubisno Polje, Croatia. Music Prof. m. Ljiljana Leopold (Rogic), 22 June 1985, 2 s. *Musical Education:* Academy of Music. *Career:* Chief conductor, HRT Tambura Orchestra, 1985; Lecturer, Academy of Music, University of Zagreb, 1986–; Conductor, Ferdo Livadic Tambura Orchestra, Samobor, 1985. *Recordings:* Many compositions, arrangements for Tambura Orchestras. *Publications:* Tambura School T, 1992; Tambura Among Croatians, 1995. *Honours:* Croatian Discography Award: Porin 95; Many awards at festivals. *Memberships:* Croatian Society of Composers; Croatian Folklore Society. *Leisure interests:* Bicycling; Travel. *Address:* Rapska 37A, 41000 Zagreb, Croatia.

LEPALLEC Bernard; b. 20 Dec. 1951, Paris, France. Musician (saxophone). 2 d. *Education:* Doctorate of Philosophy, Sorbonne, Paris. *Musical Education:* Self-taught. *Career:* Composer, saxophone player, improvised music; Member, jazz band Ar Jazz; Playing improvised and celtic traditional music concerts in France; Poland; Italy; Greece. *Recordings:* Album: Band Ar Jazz, Bernard Lepallec. *Membership:* SACEM. *Leisure interest:* Yachting. *Address:* 6 Chemin de Goas Meur, 22500 Paimpol, France.

LEROY Christian; b. 23 Nov. 1952. Composer; Musician (pianist). m. Nathalie Cuvelier, 2 s. *Education:* General electronic studies. *Musical Education:* Drums; Also self-taught. *Career:* Composed works for RTBF Programme 3; Works for theatre plays including Le Monde est Rond, Le Baiser de la Femme Araignée, Le Roi et le Cadavre, The Merchant of Venice; Works with Sandro Somaré, Bram Bogart, Miguel Berrocal; Lindström and others; Member of Métarythmes de l'Air musical group and Piano Kvartet, group of 4 pianists. *Compositions:* Le 37 Janvier, opera; Music for Dracula, film of Tod Browning; Music for Robert Flaherty's Nanouk the Eskimo; Images du Tarot, recorded. *Recordings:* Métarythmes de l'Air; Piano Duet with Fred Von Hove; Phagocyte; 33 Petits Tours; Le Temps Qui Passe; Les Chemins de Lumière; La Roue des Corps; Le Temps des Sabbats; The Merchant of Venice; Mystères d'un Théâtre et d'une Vie; Dracula et Nanouk l'Esquimau. *Honours:* Prix de Hainaut, 1982; Special Mention for Film Music, Caracas, 1983; Prix de la Presse, SPA Festival; Prix de la Pensée, Wallonne. *Leisure interests:* Gardens; Going for walks. *Address:* 8 rue des Berceaux, 7061 Casteau, Belgium.

LESKANICH Katrina; b. 1960, Topeka, Kansas, USA. Singer. *Career:* Lead singer, Katrina and the Waves, 1982–; Presenter, BBC Radio 2, 1999–2000. *Recordings:* Albums: Walking On Sunshine, 1983; Katrina and The Waves 2, 1984; Waves, 1985; Katrina and The Waves, 1985; Break of Hearts, 1989; Vol. 2, 1995; Anthology, 1995; Walk on Water, 1997; Hit singles: Walking On Sunshine, 1985; Going Down To Liverpool (later recorded by the Bangles), 1985; Sun Street, 1986; Love Shine A Light,

1997. *Honour:* Eurovision Song Contest, winner, Love Shine A Light, 1997. *Address:* c/o Jason West Agency, Gables House, Saddlebow, Kings Lynn, Norfolk PE34 3AR, England.

LESSARD Stefan Kahil; b. 4 June 1974, Anaheim, California, USA. Musician (bass guitar). *Musical Education:* Tandem Music School, Charlottesville, USA. *Career:* Former member of Charlottesville-Albermarle Youth Orchestra; Teamed up with Dave Matthews to assist with demo recording on recommendation of music tutor/local jazz guru John D'Earth, 1990; Became member of The Dave Matthews Band, 1991; Rapid growth of fanbase through touring; First album released on group's own Bama Rags label certified gold by RIAA; First national US tour in support of RCA debut album, 1994; Many world-wide concerts and festival appearances since including 2001 album tour; Group permits fans to tape-record shows for personal use; I Did It single officially released through Napster, 2001. *Recordings:* Albums: Remember Two Things (live), 1993; Under The Table and Dreaming, 1994; Crash, 1996; Live At Red Rocks 8–15–95, 1997; Before These Crowded Streets, 1998; Listener Supported (live), 1999; Everyday, Live In Chicago 12–19–98, 2001; Singles: Recently (EP), 1994; What Would You Say, Jimi Thing, Ants Marching, 1995; So Much To Say, Too Much, 1996; Don't Drink The Water, 1997; Satellite, Crash Into Me, Crush, 1998; I Did It, The Space Between, Everyday, 2001. *Honours:* Grammy Awards: Best Rock Performance By A Duo Or Group With Vocal, 1997; US VH-1 Awards: Favourite Group; Must Have Album; Song of The Year, 2001; Top-grossing touring band in US, 2000. *Address:* c/o Red Light Communications, 3305 Lobban Pl., Charlottesville, VA 22903, USA. *E-mail:* info@rlc.net. *Internet:* www.dmband.com.

LESTER Gregory; b. Brighton, England. Musician (guitar). *Musical Education:* Self-taught; Later, studied classical guitar. *Career:* Tours, recording and radio/television appearances with: Julia Fordham; Des'ree; Danielle Gaha; John O'Kane; Joe Roberts; Sylvia Powell; Concerts include: with John O'Kane: support to Sting, Soul Cages tour, UK/European legs; with Des'ree: Summer festivals at Wembley Stadium, Old Trafford, Gateshead International; Tour of Japan; Radio and television appearances with the above, and Kindred Spirit; 25th of May; Kim Appleby; Shania Twain;. *Recordings:* Numerous sessions include: Adam F, Aco, The Collective, Sunscream; Sandy Lam; Jimmy Somerville; Gangstarr; Pop Will Eat Itself; Des'ree; Barry Adamson; 2 Become 1, Mama, Spice Girls; Soundstation; Love City Groove; Maria Rowe; EYC; London Beat; Nightcrawlers; Freaky Realistic; Sylvia Powell; Dave Stewart; Definition of Sound; Whitney Houston; Other tracks with artistes including: Joe Roberts; Kylie Minogue; Lush Life; Azizi; Karl Keaton; Monie Love; Atlantique; Workshy; Worlds Apart; Danielle Gaha; Everything But The Girl; Adeva; Tom Robinson; Tyrell Corporation; Alison Limerick; Blade; Live long-play video: Porcelain – Live In Concert, Julia Fordham; Music for television commercials; Television music includes: My Boy, Channel 4; Theme music for The Beat; Painted Lady (Granada TV). *Honours:* BPI Awards: Platinum, 3 times, Spice Girls; Gold, Kylie Minogue, EBTG; Silver, Des'ree. *Memberships:* PRS; Musicians' Union. *Address:* 18A Southampton Rd, London NW5 4HX, England.

LETLEY Matthew; b. 29 March 1961, Gillingham, Kent, London. Musician (drums). m. Valerie Hill, 1 May 1982, 2 d. *Education:* Rochester Mathematical School, Kent. *Musical Education:* Private tuition, Graham Willard, Bob Cleall. *Career:* Tours, UK or world with: Judie Tzuke, 1983, 1985; Elkie Brooks, 1984; Kim Wilde, 1986; Bob Geldof, 1987–90; A-Ha, 1988–89; David Essex, 1990–97; Vanessa Mae, 1995–97; Hank Marvin, 1997. *Membership:* Musicians' Union. *Address:* Cone Tree House, Beckenham, Kent BR3 4DZ, England.

LEURS Lawrence; b. 9 July 1965, Bree, Belgium. Singer; Songwriter; Musician (Guitar). m. Peeters Saskia, 11 June 1994. *Education:* Licentiate in History, University of Brussels; Degree, Academy of Word and Music Maaseik, Belgium. *Recordings:* Albums: Ball and Chain, 1989; Trigger Happy, 1990; Major Panic, 1993; Be My Star, 1996; El Diablo, 1998. *Membership:* ZAMU, Union of Musical Artists Belgium. *Current Management:* Oyster Records, Setsesteenweg 222, 1081 Brussels, Belgium. *Address:* Koningin Astridlaan 37, 3680, Maaseik, Belgium.

LEVAN Christophe; b. 29 Dec. 1959, Marseilles, France. Musician (contrabass, bass guitar). 1 s. *Education:* Dental studies, Marseilles. *Musical Education:* Self-taught. *Career:* Concerts with: Michel Legrand; Michel Portal; Chet Baker; Sonny Stitt; Phil Woods; Peter King; Dee Dee Bridgewater; Nicole Croisille; Television and radio broadcasts include: Françaises Variétés et Jazz; Radio France; France Musique. *Compositions:* Minou; Libreto; Swing Gome; Merci Glop; Waltz For Theo. *Recordings:* About 20 records include: Swinging Marilyn, Gerard Badini Swing Machine; Debussy Meets Mister Swing, Gerard Badini Big Band; Chassaguite Quartet; Johnny Griffin et Hervé Sellin' Sextet; Tribute To Jazz Michel Gaucher; Cannon Blues, Hervé Meschinet Quartet. *Honours:* Django D'Or, Hervé Meshinet Quartet, 1998; Victoires de la Musique, 1998. *Membership:* Syndicate des Musiciens; Membre de la Sacem, 1998. *Leisure*

interests: Fishing; Sculpture; Drawing. *Address:* 30 rue de Musselburgh, 94500 Champigny-sur-Marne, France.

LEVANDER Jan; b. 29 March 1959, Stockholm. Composer; Musician (Saxophone, Flute, Clarinet). m. Malin Hülphers. 1, 1 d. *Education:* Stockholm Community Music Institute; Stockholm Music Conservatory. *Career:* Led, wrote music for and played in own Jazz groups, Kamel Kombo; Jan Levanders Oktett; Toured, Jazz Clubs; Festivals; Radio; Musician, Arranger, conductor in musicals and theatre music. *Compositions:* Gerlögs Runa, Opera; 12 Piece Jazzband, Festivalsvit; Big Band and String Quartet and Percussion, EBU; Jazz compositions; Chamber Music; Theatre Music. *Recordings:* Musaik; Spion För En Främmande Makt; For trio and ten piece band. *Leisure interests:* Photography; Bird Watching; Nature. *Address:* LustigKullavägen 7 5 tr, 117 66 Stockholm, Sweden.

LEVERIDGE Paul (Kermit); b. 10 Nov. 1969, Manchester, England. Vocalist. *Career:* Member, Ruthless Rap Assassins; Member: Black Grape; Numerous gigs and festival appearances including Tribal Gathering and Reading Festivals, 1997. *Recordings:* Singles: Reverend Black Grape, 1995; In The Name of The Father, 1995; Kelly's Heroes, 1995; England's Irie, 1996; Fat Neck, 1996; Get Higher, 1997; Marbles, 1998; Albums: It's Great When You're Straight... Yeah, 1995; Stupid Stupid Stupid, 1997.

LEVIEV Milcho; b. 19 Dec. 1937, Plovdiv, Bulgaria. Composer; Musician (piano); Arranger; Conductor. m. Deborah Rothschild, 19 July 1990, 1 d. *Musical Education:* Masters in Composition, Bulgarian State Conservatory, 1960. *Career:* Conductor, Bulgarian Radio and TV Pop Orchestra, 1962–66; Composer, Bulgarian Feature Film Studios, 1963–69; Arranger, Radio Frankfurt, 1970; Pianist, composer, arranger, Don Ellis Orchestra, Billy Cobham Band, Art Pepper Quartet; Music Director, Lanie Kazan Show; Co-leader, Free Flight quartet; Lecturer, University of Southern California. *Compositions:* Concerto For Jazz Combo and Strings; Music For Big Band and Symphony Orchestra; Sympho-Jazz Sketches; Orpheus Rhapsody for Piano and Orchestra; The Green House – Jazz Cantata; Film and Theatre Music. *Recordings:* Over 35 records under own name and over 50 records as a sideman; Blues For The Fisherman; Easter Parade; Live At Vartan Jazz; Anti Waltz. *Publications:* 8 Jazz Pieces, 1968; Milcho Leviev-Fake Book; 2 Songs For Jazz Choir, 1991. *Honours:* Grammy Nomination, Best Vocal Arranger, 1981; Dr h.c., Music Academy in Plovdiv, 1995; Dr h.c., New Bulgarian University, 1999. *Memberships:* AFofM; NARAS; BMI; GEMA. *Leisure interests:* Swimming; Hiking.

LEVIN Michael David; b. 29 May 1954, Syracuse, New York, USA. Musician; Composer. *Education:* BA, University of Illinois; AM, University of Chicago; PhD, University of Illinois, Institute of Communications Research. *Career:* Performed and recorded with David Bromberg, Oscar Brown Jr, Barrett Deems, Hamid Drake, The Four Tops, Fireworks Jazz, Jerry Goodman, Charlie Musselwhite, Night on Earth, Jim Post, Bernard Purdie, Claudia Schmidt, Diane Schuur, The Supremes, The Temptations, Clark Terry, The Chicago Jazz Ensemble, The Illinois Philharmonic Orchestra, The Ethos Chamber Orchestra; Appearances at numerous jazz and pop festivals. *Recordings:* Over 50 Albums. *Memberships:* Phi Kappa Phi; Phi Beta Kappa. *Address:* 1336 1/2 S Austin, Apartment D, Cicero, IL 60804, USA.

LEVITIN Daniel J; b. 27 Dec. 1957, San Francisco, CA, USA. Cognitive Psychologist; Record Prod.; Musician; Journalist. m. Caroline A Traube. *Education:* AB, Stanford University; MSc, PhD, University of Oregon; Berklee College of Music. *Career:* Television, Close To You: Remembering The Carpenters; Radio, The Sound of Musique; Music Production Editor, REP Magazine, 1989–92; Staff Writer, Billboard Magazine, 1990–93; Director, Artists and Repertoire; 415/Columbia Records, 1984–89; Assistant Professor of Psychology, McGill University, 2000-. *Compositions:* First Strike; Now That You Are Gone; I Should've Told You. *Recordings:* Heart Shaped World (Chris Isaak); Imaginoos (Blue Oyster Cult); Rockin' and Romance (Jonathan Richmond); Good News About Mental Health (The Afflicted). *Publications:* The John Fogerty Interview; Liner notes for Stevie Wonder; Music, Cognition and Computerized Sounds; The Billboard Encyclopedia of Record Producers. *Honours:* Platinum Records; Gold Medal, Venice Film Festival, Best Soundtrack, 1986. *Memberships:* NARAS; AES. *Address:* CCRMA, Deptartment of Music, Stanford University, Stanford, CA 94305, USA.

LEVY Andrew; b. 20 July 1966, Ealing, London, England. Musician (Bass). *Career:* Founder Member, The Brand New Heavies; Worked with numerous vocalists including Jaye Ella Ruth, N'Dea Davenport, Siedah Garrett and currently Carleen Anderson; Numerous television appearances and live dates, including club dates. *Recordings:* Singles: Stay This Way, 1991; Never Stop, 1991; Dream Come True, 1991; Don't Let It Go To Your Head, 1992; Spend Some Time, 1994; Dream on Dreamer, 1994; Back To Love, 1994; Midnight At The Oasis, 1994; Mind Trips, 1995; Close To You, 1995; You've Got A Friend, 1997; You Are the Universe, 1997; Sometimes, 1997; Shelter, 1998; Albums: The Brand New Heavies, 1990; The Brand

New Heavies, 1992; Heavy Rhyme Experience, 1992; Brother Sister, 1994; Original Flava, 1994; Excursions, 1995; Shelter, 1997.

LEVY Henry (Hank); b. 27 Sept. 1927, Baltimore, Maryland, USA. Teacher; Composer; Arranger. m. Gloria Hidebrand, 14 Aug. 1960. *Education:* BA, Composition. *Career:* Writer for Don Ellis Band, 1965–78; Writer for Stan Kenton Orchestra, 1968–79; Compositions found on all Kenton and Ellis recordings; Many concerts with above bands, also Jazz Ensemble for school; Taught jazz courses, Towson State University, 23 years; Clinics all over the country; Commissions to write extended works for symphony orchestra, jazz ensemble. *Publications:* All music written, orchestrated for Ellis and Kenton and schools; Over 100 pieces published. *Honour:* Professor Emeritus. *Leisure interest:* Golf. *Address:* 1504 Melton Rd, Lutherville, MD 21093, USA.

LEVY Rick; b. 1 Nov. 1949, Allentown, PA, USA. Musician (Guitar); Man.; Songwriter. Divorced, 1 s. *Education:* BA, Sociology, University of Pennsylvania, 1971; Education Degree, Moravian College, 1985; Guitar lessons, 5 years; Berklee School of Music, 1 year. *Career:* Tour US with Jay and The Techniques, 1985–; Manager, Jay and The Techniques; The Box Tops; Performed at Rock 'n' Roll Hall of Fame, September 1996; Pres: Rick Levy Management, Flying Governor Music, Luxury Records. *Composition:* Rock Roots, History of American Pop Music. *Recordings:* Love's Just Not For Sale; Ricochet Waltz; The Limits, Songs About Girls; The Main Course, Jay and The Techniques. *Honour:* Penna-Broadcasters Asscn, Rock Roots, Best Single, Children's Program, 1992. *Membership:* NARAS. *Leisure interests:* Running; Pottery. *Current Management:* Rick Levy Management, 4250 A1A S, D-11 St Augustine, FL 32084, USA.

LEWIN Giles; b. Rayleigh, Essex, England. Musician (fiddle, medieval bagpipes, recorders, shawm); Vocalist. *Education:* Music, Cambridge University. *Musical Education:* Violin, flute, viol, at school. *Career:* Member, The Dufay Collective; Plays with: The New London Consort; The Chuckerbutty Ocarina Quartet; Lost Jockey; Afterhours; Music director, The Medieval Players, tours world-wide; Student of Egyptian Fiddle styles and culture; Member, The Carnival Band, 1984–; Appearances include: Glasgow Cathedral; Birmingham Symphony Hall; Barbican Centre; Numerous Arts theatres and festivals; Plays material from: Sweden; Croatia; US; Bolivia; Spain; UK; France. *Current Management:* c/o Jim McPhee, Acorn Entertainments. *Address:* Winterfold House, 46 Woodfield Rd, Kings Heath, Birmingham B13 9UJ, England.

LEWINSON Stephen Owen Lloyd; b. 19 Feb. 1966, Coventry, England. Musician (bass). *Career:* Tours with: Phil Bent Quartet, 1989; Reggae Philharmonic Orchestra, 1990–91; Courtney Pine, 1991–92; Steve Williamson, 1992; Bomb The Bass, 1992; Tim Finn, 1992; Tom Browne, 1992; Nelson Rangell, 1992; Rebirth of The Cool, 1993; Juliet Roberts, 1993; Ronny Jordan world tour, 1993–94; Tony Remy, Mica Paris, Boy George, Orphy Robinson, Massive Attack world tour, 1995; Simply Red world tour, 1995–96; Everything But The Girl tour, 1996–97; Lisa Stansfield, 1997; Spice Girls world tour, 1997–98; Eurythmics, 1999. *Recordings:* Spice World, Spice Girls; Greatest Hits, Simply Red; Blue, Simply Red; Invisible, Five; Peace, Eurythmics; Brighter, Ronny Jordan; Tilt, Lightning Seeds; Woman In Me, Louise; Help, Massive Attack; Courtney Pine; Tony Remy; for Kylie Minogue: Light Years, 2000; Fever, 2001; for Sugababes: One Touch, 2001. *Membership:* PRS; MCPS; PAMRA; Musicians' Union. *Current Management:* Timeless Music Ltd. *Address:* 38 Coolhurst Rd, London N8, England.

LEWIS Aaron; b. 13 April 1972. Vocalist. m. Vanessa. *Career:* Played with The Geckoes; Formed Staind with Mike Mushok and others; First live gig, 1995; Released self-financed debut album, 1996; Album sold 4,000 copies; Discovered by Fred Durst, 1997; Signed to Flip/Elektra; Presented to rock cognoscenti at Limp Bizkit gold record party for Three Dollar Bill Y'All $, 1998; Major breakthrough with unscheduled smash US No. 1 radio hit Outside; Appeared on bill for Korn-founded Family Values tours, 1999, 2001; Headlined MTV's Return of the Rock tour, 2000. *Recordings:* Albums: Tormented, 1996; Dysfunction, 1999; Break The Cycle, 2001; Singles: Mudshovel, Just Go, 1999; Home, Outside, 2000; It's Been Awhile, Fade, 2001. *Honours:* Break The Cycle certified quadruple platinum by RIAA; It's Been Awhile topped Billboard Modern Rock Singles Chart for record-equalling 16 weeks; VH-1 Award, Your Song Kicked Ass But Was Played Too Damn Much prize, 2001. *Address:* c/o The Firm, Inc, 9100 Whilshire Blvd, Suite 400W, Beverly Hills, CA 90212, USA. *Internet:* www.staind.com.

LEWIS Cass (Richard Keith); b. 1 Sept. 1960, London, England. Musician (Bass). *Career:* Founding Member, Skunk Anansie; Signed to indie label One Little Indian, 1994; Numerous live tours and festival appearances; TV appearances and radio sessions. *Recordings:* Singles: Little Baby Swastikkka; Weak; Brazen (Weep), 1997; Charlie Big Potato, 1999; Albums: Paranoid and Sunburnt, 1995; Stoosh, 1996; Post Orgasmic Chill, 1999.

LEWIS David A R; b. 15 Feb. 1964, Morecambe, Lancashire, England. Songwriter; Composer; Musician (guitar). m. Andrea Lewis, 20 Sept. 1992. *Musical Education:* J L Academy. *Career:* Appearances on National and Granada TV; Single of the Week, Red Rose, Lancashire, Capital; Extensive touring throughout UK; Support to Blur at pop club; Support to Youssou N'Dour, Womad Festival, 1992. *Compositions include:* Independence Day; The Other Side; This Is England; Sunday; Revolution. *Recordings:* Jerusalem; Maralyn; Treason. *Membership:* Musicians' Union. *Leisure interests:* Skiing; Soccer. *Current Management:* Ice Factory (Management) Co Ltd. *Address:* Ice Factory (Managament) Co Ltd, c/o John Lewis, 253 Marine Rd, Morecambe, Lancashire LA4 4BJ, England.

LEWIS Huey, (Hugh Cregg III); b. 5 July 1950, New York, USA. Singer; Musician; Actor; Songwriter. *Career:* Member, Clover, 1976–79; Founder, Huey Lewis and the News, 1979–; Major concerts include: Over 30 US and Canadian tours; Notable concerts include: Madison Square Gardens, New York, Superdrome, New Orleans, attendance set at numerous venues including: Poplar Creek Amphitheatre, Illinois, Alpine Valley Amphitheatre, Wisconsin, Summerfest, Milwaukee; 7 European tours; 4 Japan Tours; 1 Australia tour; Film appearances: Back to the Future, 1985; Short Cuts, 1993; Sphere, 1998. *Recordings:* Albums: with Clover: Clover, 1977; Love on the Wire, 1977; with Huey Lewis and the News: Huey Lewis and the News, 1980; Picture This, 1982; Sports, 1983; Fore!, 1986; Small World, 1988; Hard at play, 1991; Four Chords and Several Years Ago, 1994; Time Flies (Best of), 1996; If This Is It, 1997; Only One, 1998; Plan B, 2001; Singles include: Do You Believe in Love, 1982; Workin' for a Livin', 1982; Heart and Soul, 1983; I Want a New Drug, 1983; The Heart of Rock 'n' Roll, 1984; If This Is It, 1984; Walking on a Thin Line, 1984; The Power of Love (No 1, US), 1985; Stuck With You, (No 1 US), 1986; Hip to be Square, 1986; Jacob's Ladder (No 1 US), 1987; Doing It All For My Baby, 1987; I Know What I Like, 1987; Perfect World, 1988; Small World Pt 1 and 2 (featuring Sam Getz), 1988; Give Me the Keys, 1988; Couple Days Off, 1991; It hit Me Like a Hammer, 1991; He Don't Know, 1991; It'a Alright (A capella from People Get Ready, tribute album to Curtis Mayfield), 1993; Some Kind of Wonderful, 1994; But It's Alright, 1994; Little Bitty Pretty One, 1994; Contributor to We Are the World, USA for Africa recording, 1985; Numerous film videos. *Honours:* American Music Awards: Favorite Single, 1986, Favorite Band, 1987; Academy Awards, Power of Love, Nominee, song from a film, 1986; British Music Awards, Best International Group, 1986.

LEWIS Jerry Lee; b. 29 Sept. 1935, Ferriday, Louisiana, USA. Singer; Musician (piano); Entertainer. m. 6 times. *Career:* Appeared on Louisiana Hayride, 1954; Film appearances: Jamboree, 1957; High School Confidential, 1958; Be My Guest, 1965; Concerts include: National Jazz and Blues Festival, 1968; Rock 'n' Revival Concert, Toronto, 1969; First appearance, Grand Ole Opry, 1973; Rock 'n' Roll Festival, Wembley, 1974; Numerous appearances with own Greatest Show On Earth; Subject of biographical film, Great Balls of Fire, 1989. *Recordings:* Hit singles include: Whole Lotta Shakin' Goin' On', 1957; Great Balls of Fire, 1958; Breathless, 1958; High School Confidential, 1958; What I'd Say, 1961; Good Golly Miss Molly, 1963; To Make Love Sweeter For You, 1969; There Must Be More To Love Than This, 1970; Would You Take Another Chance On Me?, 1971; Me and Bobby Gee, 1972; Chantilly Lace, 1972; Albums include: Jerry Lee Lewis, 1957; Jerry Lee's Greatest, 1961; Live At The Star Club, 1965; The Greatest Live Show On Earth, 1965; The Return of Rock, 1965; Whole Lotta Shakin' Goin' On, 1965; Country Songs For City Folks, 1965; By Request – More Greatest Live Show On Earth, 1967; Breathless, 1967; Together, with Linda Gail Lewis, 1970; Rockin' Rhythm and Blues, 1971; Sunday Down South, with Johnny Cash, 1972; The Session, with Peter Frampton, Rory Gallagher, 1973; Jerry Lee Lewis, 1979; When Two Worlds Collide, 1980; My Fingers Do The Talking, 1983; I Am What I Am, 1984; Keep Your Hands Off It, 1987; Don't Drop It, 1988; Great Balls of Fire! (film soundtrack), 1989; Rocket, 1990; Young Blood, 1995; Keep Your Eyes Off of It, 2000; By Invitation Only, 2000; Many compilations; Contributor, film soundtracks: Roadie, 1980; Dick Tracy, 1990. *Honours include:* Inducted into Rock 'n' Roll Hall of Fame, 1986; Star on Hollywood Walk of Fame, 1989. *Current Management:* Al Embry International, PO Box 23162, Nashville, TN 37202, USA. *Address:* The Lewis Ranch, Box 384, Nesbit, MS 38651, USA.

LEWIS Laurie; b. 28 Sept. 1950, Long Beach, California, USA. Musician (fiddle, guitar, bass); Vocalist; Singer; Songwriter. *Musical Education:* Traditional knowledge, skills passed on within folk/old time music community in oral tradition. *Career:* Performing, touring nationally, internationally since early 1970s; Television appearances: Music City Tonight, TNN; The Grand Ole Opry; The American Music Shop; Lonesome Pine Specials, PBS; Later with Jools, BBC; Prairie Home Companion, NPR; Mountain Stage; World Cafe. *Recordings:* Restless Rambling Heart; Love Chooses You; Singing My Troubles Away; Together (with Kathy Kallick); True Stories; The Oak and The Laurel, with Tom Rozum; Earth and Sky: Songs of Laurie Lewis; Seeing Things; Winter's Grace, with Tom Rozum, 1999; Kristin's Story, 2001. *Honours:* NAIRD Award, Best Country Album; IBMA Awards, Female Vocalist of

The Year, 1992, 1994; Song of The Year, 1994; Grammy Nomination, Traditional Folk Album, The Oak and the Laurel. *Memberships:* ASCAP; International Bluegrass Music Asscn. *Leisure interests:* Running; Riding; River rafting. *Current Management:* Cash Edwards, Under The Hat Productions. *Address:* 1121-B Bluebonnet Lane, Austin, TX 78704, USA. *Internet:* www.laurielewis.com.

LEWIS Linda; b. 27 Sept. 1953, London, England. Singer; Songwriter; Musician (guitar, piano). m. Jim Cregan, 18 March 1977 (div), 1 s. *Musical Education:* Peggy O'Farrels Stage School. *Career:* Toured with Cat Stevens, Elton John and Richie Havens, 1970s; Appeared at first Glastonbury Festival; Television appearances include: In Concert; Old Grey Whistle Test; Supersonic; Top of The Pops; Appearance with Courtney Pine; Jazz Cafe; Ronnie Scotts; numerous others. *Recordings:* Albums: Say No More; Lark; Fathoms Deep; Not A Little Girl Any More (featuring Luther Vandross, Lowell George, Deniece Williams); Woman Overboard; Second Nature, 1995; Whatever, 1998; Kiss of Life, 1999; Also appeared on: Aladdin Sane, David Bowie, 1973; Do You Think I'm Sexy, Rod Stewart, 1978; Emergency On Planet Earth, Jamiroquai, 1993; Standing On The Shoulder of Giants, Oasis, 2000; recordings by Family and Steve Harley. *Honour:* Saturday Scene British Pop Award, 1975. *Memberships:* PRS; Equity; PAMRA. *Leisure interests:* Movies; Reading (biographies, self-awareness); Walking in countryside. *Current Management:* Tenderhook Music. *Address:* c/o Ella McQuery, 175 Stafford Rd, Caterham, Surrey CR3, England.

LEWIS Monica; b. 5 May, Chicago, IL, USA. Singer. m. Jennings Lang, 1 Jan. 1956. *Musical Education:* Taught by mother (opera singer) and by father (conductor, composer, pianist). *Career:* Radio appearances, recording artist, personal appearances, TV shows and films. *Recordings:* Numerous recordings including, I Wish You Love, 1956; Albums include: My Favorite Things; Swings Jule Styne. *Honour:* First Grammy Award. *Address:* 1100 Alto Louea Rd, Los Angeles, CA 90069, USA.

LEWIS Pamela; b. 23 Nov. 1958, Rhinebeck, New York, USA. PR/Marketing Consultant; Media Exec.; Event Planning. *Education:* BA, Wells College; Practitioner, Religious Science International. *Musical Education:* Leadership Music. *Career:* CEO, founder, PLA Media, Los Angeles, Nashville; NBC Specials: This Is Garth Brooks; This Is Garth Brooks Too; 7-year career as manager to Garth Brooks, including International World Tour, 1993–94. *Publications:* Dan Rivers Poetry Anthology; American Poetry Anthology. *Honours:* Pollstar Manager of The Year, 1991, 1992; Performance Manager of Year, 1992, 1993; CMA Manager of Year, 1991. *Memberships:* Country Music Asscn; Academy of Country Music; Blair School of Music; Belmont School of Music. *Leisure interests:* Gardening; Horseback riding; Canning; Herbal vinegars; Writing; Gourmet cooking; Skiing; Travel. *Current Management:* PLA Media. *Address:* 1303 16th Ave So, Nashville, TN 37212, USA.

LEWIS Ramsey E Jr; b. 27 May 1935, Chicago, Illinois, USA. Musician (piano). m. Janet Tamillon, 10 June 1990, 5 s., 2 d. (from previous marriage). *Education:* College, 1955–57. *Musical Education:* Chicago Musical College, 1955–56. *Career:* Performed, nightclubs, concerts, festivals, in USA, Canada, Western Europe, Japan, Mexico, The Caribbean, 1957–; Also with symphony orchestras; Host, weekly syndicated radio programme; Host 1 hour weekly segment, BET's Jazz Central. *Recordings:* Over 60 albums include: The Incrowd, 1965; Sun Goddess, 1974; 3 latest recordings: Ivory Pyramid, 1992; Sky Islands, 1993; Urban Knights, 1995; Finest Hour, 2000. *Honours:* Hon. doctorates: Depaul University, 1993; University of Illinois, Chicago, 1995; White House State Dinner Performance, 1995; 3 Grammy Awards; 5 Gold records. *Membership:* Ravinia Artistic Director, Jazz Series. *Leisure interests:* Reading; Film going. *Current Management:* Andi Howard, Gardner Howard Ringe Entertainment.

LEWIS Ronald Chapman; b. 20 Aug. 1950, Louisville, Kentucky, USA. Musician (Guitar); Songwriter; Music Publisher. m. LaQuetta Wilson, June 1972, 2 s. *Education:* Associate Degree in Music, JCC University, School of Music, Louisville, 1985. *Career:* BMI Songwriter and Publisher; Show Host, Cable TV. *Compositions:* When the Spirit of the Lord; Spraggie. *Recordings:* Spraggie, Hanlon Robinson, Swindell Brothers. *Honour:* Up and Coming Songwriter's Award, Billboard Magazine. *Leisure interest:* Musical CD projects of old artists. *Current Management:* Harry Fox Agency. *Address:* Mr Wonderful Productions, 1730 Kennedy Rd, Louisville, KY 40216, USA.

LEWIS Shaznay T; b. 1977. Singer; Songwriter. *Career:* Founding member, female vocal group All Saints, 1993–2001. *Recordings:* Singles: Silver Shadow, 1994; I Know Where It's At, 1997; Never Ever (No. 1, UK), 1997; Lady Marmalade/Under The Bridge (No. 1, UK), 1998; Bootie Call (No. 1, UK), 1998; War of Nerves, 1998; Pure Shores (No. 1, UK), 2000; Black Coffee (No. 1, UK), 2000; Album: All Saints, 1997; Saints and Sinners, 2000; All Hits, 2001. *Honours include:* Brit Award, Best Single, Never Ever, 1998. *Current Management:* John Benson.

LEWIS Terry; b. USA. Record Prod. *Career:* Founder member, Flyte Time, 1972–; Joined by Jimmy Jam, become backing band for Morris Day, renamed The Time, 1981–83; Formed Flyte Tyme Productions with Jerry Jam, 1982–; Built Flyte Tyme Studios, Minneapolis, 1984–85; Founded own label (with Jerry Jam), Perspective Records, 1991; Helped launch new acts including Sounds of Blackness; Involved with International Association of African American Music (IAAAM), 1990-. *Recordings:* As co-producer with Jimmy Jam: Wild Girls, Klymaxx, 1983; Just Be Good To Me, SOS Band, 1983; Change of Heart, Change, 1984; Heat of The Heart, Patti Austin, 1984; Encore, Cheryl Lynn, 1984; I Didn't Mean To Turn You On, Cherelle, 1984 (covered by Robert Palmer, 1985); Saturday Love, Cherelle and Alexander O'Neal, 1985; The Finest, SOS Band, 1986; Human, The Human League (No. 1, USA), 1987; Keep Your Eye On Me, Herb Alpert, 1987; Criticize, Alexander O'Neal, 1987; Sensitivity, Ralph Tresvant, 1990; Optimistic, Sounds of Blackness, 1991; Co-writers and co-producers, Janet Jackson, 1986-, including: What Have You Done For Me Lately?, 1986; Nasty, 1986; When I Think of You (No. 1, USA), 1986; Let's Wait Awhile, 1987; Miss You Much (No. 1, USA), 1989; Rhythm Nation, 1989; Escapade (No. 1, USA), 1990; Alright (No. 1, USA), 1990; Love Will Never Do Without You (No. 1, USA), 1990; The Best Things In Life Are Free, with Luther Vandross, 1992; That's The Way Love Goes (No. 1, USA), 1993; If, 1993; Runaway, 1995; Doesn't Really Matter, 2001; All For You, 2001; Albums with Janet Jackson: Control, 1986; Rhythm Nation, 1989; Janet, 1993 (all No. 1, USA); Other recordings with: Mint Condition; Low Key; Sounds of Blackness; George Michael; Karyn White; Boyz II Men; Johnny Gill; New Edition; Fine Young Cannibals; Film soundtrack, Mo' Money, 1993. *Honours include:* R & B Songwriting Awards, American Society of Composers and Publishers, 1989–94. *Address:* c/o Perspective Records, 1416 N La Brea Ave, Hollywood, CA 90028, USA.

LEYERS Jan; b. 16 May 1958, Antwerp, Belgium. Vocalist; Musician (guitar, bass keyboards); Composer. *Career:* Soulsister. *Compositions:* Billboard Hot Country Chart, 1995 (No. 1); Soulsister, Repertoire; Changes, Tom Jones; The Way to Your Heart; That's As Close as I'll Get to Loving You. *Recordings:* Soulsister: It Takes Two; Heat; Simple Rule; Live Savings; Swinging Like Big Dogs; The Very Best; My Velma: Exposed. *Honours:* World Music Award, Monaco, 1990; Jozef Platteau, 1991; BMI Country Award, 1996; Golden Eye Award, 1992, 1993. *Membership:* SABAM. *Leisure interest:* Music. *Current Management:* Johan P Berckmans. *Address:* Mereldreef 3, 3140 Keerbergen, Belgium.

LIANA (Liana C Di Marco); b. 25 March 1966, Toronto, Ontario, Canada. Singer; Songwriter; Musician (guitar); Multi-media Artist. *Education:* BA Hons, Social Science. *Musical Education:* Private instruction with leading vocalists and instrumentalists. *Career:* Played viola in two local orchestras prior to 1986; Solo career as singer, songwriter, 1988–; Business ventures: LCDM Entertainments Productions, music label, and Indie Tips and The Arts, publications. *Recordings include:* Glitters and Tumbles, 1993; Songs published: Degree In Love; Sweep Me Off My Feet; By My Side; Glitters and Tumbles; You'll Never Know; Boom; Non Fa Differenza Dove Vai; Thinking of You; Country Funky. *Publications:* Indie Tips and The Arts. *Honours:* Awards in Music, Journalism, French and Cinematography. *Memberships:* CCMA; SAC; Theatre Ontario; UGA. *Leisure interests:* Ceramics; Canvas painting; Collections; Squash; Dance. *Current Management:* CAG Consultants; LCDM Entertainment.

LIBRETTI Andrea; b. 9 Nov. 1953, Italy. Musician (Trumpet, Keyboard) Music Teacher; Composer. *Education:* G Verdi Conservatory of Milan. *Career:* Muis Therapist with L M Lorenzetti, Centro di Neurologia, Milan; Member Board of Directors, Centro di Documentazione e Studio per la Musica Elettronica; Musical Consultant, Italian Commercial Television; Freelance Composer, Producer of Music for Films, Advertisments, Graphic Installations; Teacher of Electronic Music and Analysis and History of Contemporary Music, Conservatory G Verdi. *Compositions:* Anarhmoniosis; Seohento 3; Even Event; Frastagliate; Seghento 4; Frammento Da Ho. *Address:* Via Moncalvo 52/A, 20146 Milano, Italy.

LIDDIARD Brenda Christine; b. 14 Feb. 1950, Essex, England. Writer; Performer; Musician (guitar, mandolin, keyboards). m. Mark Clive Laurent, 4 Aug. 1990, 1 step-s., 1 d. *Musical Education:* Piano, to Grade 6. *Career:* Played in bands, duos, solos, 1978–; Major performances: UN Environmental Song Festival, Bangkok, 1988; Concert For The Living Earth, Auckland, 1989; QE II Arts Council, 6 week New Zealand tour, 1990; Shelterbelt Festival, 1993; Parachute Festival, 1994, 1995; Garth Hewitt, UK support, 1995; Auckland Folk Festival, 1993–95, 1999; Session player, recording, concerts. *Recordings:* Land of Plenty, Spangled Drongoes, 1985; Songs For Our Friends, with Mark Laurent, 1989; Songs of Protest and Survival, 1991; For The River, Save The Daintree, featured on award winning documetary, Earth First; Heart Attack, 1996; Millenium Hippies, 1998. *Honour:* Winner, UN Asia Pacific Environmental Song Contest, 1988. *Memberships:* NZ Composers' Foundation; APRA (Australian Performing Rights Society). *Leisure interests:* Gardening; Walking; Reading. *Current*

Management: Digital Flower Productions. *Address:* 21 Parkfield Terrace, Grafton, Auckland, New Zealand.

LIEBMAN David; b. 4 Sept. 1946, Brooklyn, New York, USA. Musician (Saxophone); Composer; Teacher. m. Caris Visentin, 30 Nov. 1986, 1 d. *Education:* BSc, New York University, USA; Studied with Joseph Allard, Lennie Tristano and Charles Lloyd. *Compositions:* 200 original compositions. *Recordings:* On the Corner, Miles Davis; Live at the Lighthouse, Elvin Jones; Lookout Farm, D Liebman; Homage To Coltrane, D Liebman; Long Distance Runner, D Liebman; West Side Story, D Liebman; New Vista, D Liebman; Water: Giver of Life; Meditation Suite; Recent releases: Time Immemorial, 2001; Liebman Plays Puccini – A Walk In The Clouds, 2001; The Unknown Jobim, 2001. *Publications:* Developing A Personal Saxophone Sound, 1989; A Chromatic Approach to Jazz, 1991; Self Portrait of a Jazz Artist, 1996; Jazz Connections, Miles Davis and David Liebman, 1996. *Honours:* Group Deserving of Wider Recognition Downbeat Magazine, 1976; Hon. Doctorate, Sibelius Academy, Helsinki, 1997; Composer Grant, National Endowment of the Arts. *Memberships:* Artistic Director and Founder, International Asscn of School of Jazz; BMI; SPEDIDAM; Gramex; Naras. *Leisure interest:* Reading. *Address:* 2206 Brislin Rd, Stroudsburg, PA 18360, USA.

LIEVEMAA Tommi Tapani; b. 10 Dec. 1966, Uusikaupunki, Finland. Musician (electric, acoustic guitar, mandolin). *Education:* Commercial School, Finland, 1982–86. *Musical Education:* Jazz, rock guitar, theory studies, Jyvaskyla School of Music, 1986–89; Jazz Course, Guildhall School of Music and Drama, London 1993–94. *Career:* Constant touring, Finland, with Ohilyönti, 1986–93; With Dixie Fred, 1987–92; Tour with Finnish pop star, Katri-Helena, 1992; National Jazz Competition, Finland, with Sale's Promotion, 1986; International Jazz Competition, Spain, Getxo, with John Crawford Group, 1994; Television appearances, Finnish TV, include: Documentary about recording process, Dixie Fried's first album, Channel 1, 1988; Pop Panel, with Dixie Fried, Channel 1, 1988; Nightline, Dixie Fried, Channel 2; Kaikki on Korassa, with Estonian Television, 1990; Haapaves: Folk Festival, Channel 2, 1991; Very many radio appearances. *Recordings:* Dixie Fried albums: Dixie Fried, 1988; Six Dicks of Dynamite, 1990; New Deal, 1991; Ohilyonti: OHOH, 1989; Himmeneuva Q, 1989; Sandels On, 1989; Markan Possu, 1990; Soita Soita, 1990; On Karhut Noussect Juhlimaan, 1992; Ankkapaallikko Anna Liisa, 1993; with R Keskinin and Co: Kapteeni, 1993; Charity album, Valaiskoon (with various Finnish stars), 1993; High Register Orchestra, Jühtü, 1993. *Honours:* First Prize, National Children's Song Contest, Finland, 1990, 1991. *Membership:* Musicians' Union, London. *Leisure interests:* Travel; Cooking; Arts. *Address:* Ylinenkatu 44 A 8, 23500 Uusikaupunki, Finland.

LIFESON Alex; b. 27 Aug. 1953, Fernie, Canada. Musician (guitar). *Career:* Guitarist, founder member, Canadian rock group Rush, 1969–; Concerts include: world-wide tours, 1974–; Sellout concerts include Madison Square Garden, New York; Maple Leaf Gardens, Toronto; Wembley Arena, London; Also member of side-project Victor, 1995-. *Recordings:* Albums: with Rush: Rush, 1969; Fly By Night, 1975; Caress of Steel, 1975; 2112, 1976; All The World's A Stage, 1976; A Farewell To Kings, 1977; Archives, 1978; Hemisphere, 1978; Permanent Waves, 1980; Moving Pictures, 1981; Exit... Stage Left, 1981; Grace Under Pressure, 1984; Power Windows, 1985; Hold Your Fire, 1987; A Show of Hands, 1989; Presto, 1989; Chronicles, 1990; Roll The Bones, 1991; with Victor: Victor, 1996; Counterparts, 1993; Test For Echo, 1996; Different Stages, 1998; Singles include: with Rush: Spirit of Radio; Tom Sawyer; New World Man; Closer To The Heart; Countdown; The Big Money; Time Stand Still; Producer: Lifer Lifer, 2001. *Honours:* JUNO Awards: Most Promising Group, 1975; Best Group, 1978–79; Group named Official Ambassadors of Music, Canadian Government, 1979; Gold Ticket Award, Madison Square Garden, 1991; Officer of The Order of Canada, Canadian Government. *Current Management:* Anthem Entertainment, 189 Carlton St, Toronto, ON M5A 2K7, Canada.

LIGGINS Len, ('The Legendary' Len Liggins); b. 9 Feb. 1957, London, England. Singer; Songwriter; Musician (guitar, violin, bass). *Education:* BA (Hons) Russian Studies, Universiy of Leeds. *Career:* Solo artist, 1984–; Lead singer, guitarist for: The Sinister Cleaners, 1984–87; Lead singer, fiddle, balalaika and sopilka player, Ukrainian line-up of: The Wedding Present, 1987–89; Lead singer, fiddle player for The Ukrainians, 1991-. *Recordings:* Solo: A Remedy For Bad Nerves, 1985; The Sinister Cleaners: Lemon Meringue Bedsit, 1985; The Wedding Present: Ukrainski Vistupi V Johna Peela, 1988; The Ukrainians: Pisni Iz The Smiths, 1993; Vorony, 1994; Kultura, 1994; Music for a Changing World, 1995. *Current Management:* c/o 23 Lushington Rd, London NW10 5UX, England.

LIGHTFOOT Gordon Meredith; b. 17 Nov. 1938, Orilla, Ontario, Canada. Singer; Songwriter. m. Elizabeth Moon. *Musical Education:* Westlake College of Music, Los Angeles, 1958. *Career:* Singer, songwriter, 1959–; Member, Swinging Singing Eight (square-dance ensemble), Canada; Folk duo Two Tones, 1960; Solo artiste, 1961–; Major concerts include:

Town Hall, New York, 1967; Royal Festival Hall, 1969; Bob Dylan's Rolling Thunder Review, 1976; Westbury Music Fair, Westbury, New York, 1989; Carnegie Hall, 1991; Television appearances include: Host, BBC series, 1963; Let's Sing Out, CTV, 1963; Film appearance: Harry Tracy, 1982. *Compositions include:* Early Morning Rain (recorded by Peter Paul and Mary); Ribbon of Darkness (No. 1, Country charts, for Marty Robbins); If You Could Read My Mind; Canadian Railroad Trilogy; Sundown; Carefree Highway; Race Among The Ruins; The Wreck of The Edmund Fitzgerald. *Recordings:* Albums: Lightfoot, 1965; The Way I Feel, 1967; Did She Mention My Name; Back Here On Earth; Sunday Concert; If You Could Read My Mind, 1971; Summer Side of Life; Classic Lightfoot, 1971; Don Quixote, 1972; Old Dan's Records, 1972; Sundown, 1974; The Very Best Of..., 1974; Cold On The Shoulder, 1975; Gord's Gold, 1976; Summertime Dream, 1976; Endless Wire, 1978; Dream Street Rose, 1980; The Best Of.., 1982; Shadows, 1982; Salute, 1985; East of Midnight, 1986; The Original Lightfoot, 1992; Waiting For You, 1993; A Painter Passing Through, 1998; Song book, box set, 1999; Singer Songwriter, 2001. *Honours:* Numerous awards include: Order of Canada, 1970; Juno Hall of Fame, 1986; Juno Gold Leaf Awards; Gold and Platinum discs; Canadian Male Artist of Decade, 1980. *Current Management:* Early Morning Productions, 1365 Yonge St, Suite 207, Toronto, ON M4T 2P7, Canada.

LIL' KIM (Kimberley Jones), (Queen Bee); b. Brooklyn, New York, USA. Rapper. *Career:* First appeared on Notorious B.I.G.'s Junior M.A.F.I.A. project; Released debut album with production by Puff Daddy, 1996; Most recent material released on Atlantic Records; Collaborations: Missy Elliott; Puff Daddy; Lil' Cease; Jay-Z; Notorious B.I.G.; Too $hort; Sisqo. *Recordings:* Albums: Conspiracy (with Junior M.A.F.I.A.), 1995; Hard Core, 1996; The Notorious KIM, 2000; Singles: Gettin' Money (with Junior M.A.F.I.A.), I Need You Tonight, 1995; No Time, 1996; Crush On You, Not Tonight, 1997; No Matter What They Say, How Many Licks, 2000. *Honours:* MTV Award, Best Female Artist, 1997. *Address:* c/o Atlantic Records, 1290 Avenue of the Americas, New York, USA.

LILLYWHITE Steve; Record Prod. *Career:* Leading international record producer, 1980–; Currently working with: Bono; Morrissey. *Recordings:* Produced: Ultravox: Ultravox; Ha Ha Ha; Siouxie and The Banshees: The Scream; XTC: Drums and Wires; Black Sea; Peter Gabriel: Peter Gabriel 3; Psychedelic Furs: Psychedelic Furs; Talk Talk Talk; Joan Armatrding: Walk Under Ladders; The Key; Sleight of Hand; Big Country: The Crossing; Steeltown; Simple Minds: Sparkle In The Rain; U2: Boy; October; War; Joshua Tree; Achtung Baby; Talking Heads; Rolling Stones: Dirty Work; Kirsty MaColl: Kite; Electric Landlady; Titanic Days; David Byrne: Rei Momo; The Pogues: If I Should Fall From Grace; Peace and Love; The La's: The La's; Red Hot + Blue (Executive Producer of 1990 AIDS Project including: U2; Annie Lennox; Sinead O'Connor; Neville Bros; Deborah Harry; Iggy Pop; Alison Moyet: Hoodoo; World Party, Bang!; Morrissey: Vauxhall and I; The Dave Matthews Band: Under The Table and Dreaming; Also: Engine; Alley; Marshall Crenshaw; The Smiths; Pretenders; Happy Mondays; David Bowie. *Current Management:* XL Talent. *Address:* Studio 7, 27A Pembridge Villas, London W11 3EP, England.

LIMERICK Alison; b. 1959, London, England. Singer. *Career:* Performer, stage musical Starlight Express; Backing Vocalist, Style Council's Our Favourite Shop, 1985; Appeared on 4AD collective Filigree and Shadow (Acid, Bitter and Sad); Worked with Peter Murphy (ex Bauhaus) on Holy Smoke, 1992; Began solo career. *Recordings:* Singles: Where Love Lives (Come On In), 1991; Come Back For Real Love, 1991; Make It On My Own, 1992; Time of Our Lives, 1994; Put Your Faith In Me, 1997; Albums: Club Classics; With A Twist; Spirit Rising, 1999. *Honour:* Best Dance Record of 1991, for Where Love Lives, Billboard Magazine, USA, 1991.

LIMIC Marin Kresimir; b. 8 Aug. 1946, Klis, Split, Croatia. Composer; Musician (piano, keyboard). m. Dubravka Zauhar, 6 Feb. 1982, 2 s. *Musical Education:* 4 semesters, Music Academy. *Career:* Over 500 television appearances including: live concerts of group Stijene, 1982–94; Television shows, 1982–83; Live concert, TV Zagreb, 1983; Tonight With You, interview, 1995; Seventh Night, HTV, 1995; Akustkoteka, unplugged concert, Fest Split, 1996, 1998–99; Voice of Asia, 1997; Cro-Turneja, 1998; Big Concert Split, 1999; International Festival, Kiev, 1999. *Compositions:* Songs: Sve Je Neobicno Ako Te Volim; Ima Jedan Svijet; Singing That Rock 'N' Roll; Balkanska Korida; Ja Sam More Ti Si Rijeka; Zaplesimo Kao Nekada; Zbogom Prva Ljubavi; Znaj, Volim Te, 1997; Jos Te Volim Kao Nekada, 1998; Caca Moj, 1998; Dodi Nam Dodi, 1999. *Recordings:* 6 singles, 1974–84; Albums: Cementna Prasina (Silver record), 1980–81; Jedanaest I Petnaest (Gold, Silver record), 1982–83; Balkanska Korida; Stijene IV, 1994; Best of Stijene, 1995; Split, 1996, 1998–99; Stijene Promo, 1997; Voice of Asia, 1997; Obecanje, 1998. *Honours:* Gold, Silver discs; Awards from festivals: Zagreb, 1980; Split, 1981, 1982, 1990; Sarajevo, 1981, 1988; First prize, Split Fest, 1996, 1998–99; Fourth prize, Voice of Asia, 1998–99. *Memberships:* HDS (Asscn of Croatian Composers); President, Split Asscn of Musicians; Vice President, Split Musicians' Sydicate; Artist-Composer, Republic of

Croatia (ZUH Zagreb); HGU (Croatian Music Union). *Leisure interests:* Artist; Painter; Sculptor; Soccer player. *Current Management:* Vladimir Mihaljek, Zagreb; House Rec, Croatia Records, Zagreb.

LINCE (John) Louis (James); b. 22 July 1941, St Helens, Lancashire, England. Musician (banjo, guitar); Bandleader. m. Gillian Everil Walker, 9 Dec. 1961, 2 d. *Career:* Member, Ken Colyer Allstars, 1976–82; Savoy Jazzmen, 1975–83; Louis Lince's New Orleans Band, 1986–; Founder member, Annie Hawkins' New Orleans Legacy, 1997; Occasional appearances with Jambalaya and Louisiana Joymakers, 1987–; Worked in New Orleans with Tuba Fats' Chosen Few, 1992–95; Lionel Ferbos, 1996, Reginald Koehler, 1996. *Recordings:* Just A Little While To Stay Here, Ken Colyer Allstars, 1978; You've Got the Right Key, 1979; Savoy Rag, 1981; Jubilee, 1983; Algiers Strut, 1985; Hot At The Dot, 1991; Backstairs Session, 1992; Yearning, 1993; Walking With The King, 1994; More Savoy Jazzmen, 1994; Louis Lince's Jelly Roll Kings, 1995; Good Morning to Heaven, 1996; Mardi Gras Parade, 1997. *Leisure interests:* Photography; Reading; Current affairs. *Current Management:* Hot Jam International. *Address:* 102A E Hill, Wandsworth, London SW18 2HF, England.

LINDEN Nick; b. 17 Nov. 1962, Woolwich, England. Musician (bass, guitar, keyboards). *Musical Education:* Music O Level. *Career:* Bass guitar, rock band Terraplane; Signed to Epic Records, 1984–89; Reading Festival, 1982; British tour supporting Meatloaf; Foreigner; ZZ Top; Various video and television appearances. *Recordings:* with Terraplane: Black and White, 1985; Moving Target, 1987; with Waterboys: Waterboys, 1983; Pagan Place, 1984; This Is The Sea, 1985; Best of the Waterboys, 1991; Secret Life of the Waterboys, 1994. *Leisure interests:* Art; Joinery. *Address:* 60 Victoria Way, Charlton, London SE7 7NQ, England.

LINDENMAIER Heinrich Lukas; b. 5 March 1946, Basel, Switzerland. Musician (Drums, Percussion, Electronics). *Education:* Academy of Arts, Munich, Germany, 1968–72; Private tuition at various workshops. *Career:* Eric Dolphy Memorial Band, 1984; John Tchicai Workshop Orchestra, 1987; Querstand, for Radio WDR and Radio RTSI; F-Orkestra, 1987–; Kxutrio, 1985–; Cecil Taylor Large Ensembles, 1988–92; Die Pilzfreunde, 1995–; Weg ins Freie, film music, 1993; Jazz Swissmade, TV film music. *Compositions:* Stage music for play Orestes, 1992; The Break Broken; Bright Pink, Yellow and Software; Die Feenfalle; Others for small ensembles or jazz orchestra. *Recordings:* Riffifi (Kxutrio); Legba Crossing (C. Taylor); Open (Stauss-Chaine-Lindenmaier); Die Pilzfreunde. *Publications:* 25 Years of Fish Horn Recording, 1982; The Man Who Never Sleeps, 1983. *Address:* Wilhelmstr 32, 79098 Freiburg, Germany.

LINDENS Traste; b. 6 May 1960, Gävile, Sweden. Singer. m. Caroline Zielfelt. *Education:* The Grafic Institut, Stockholm. *Career:* Band: Traste Linden's Kvintette; Tours: Tågtur, 1987; Never Ending Tour, 1990–93; Festivals: Hultsfred, 1988, 1991; Roskilde, 1992; Storsjeyran, 1992; Television documentary: Traste Linden's Kvintette. *Recordings:* Traste Lindens' Kvintette: Sportfiskarn, 1987; Bybor, 1989; Jolly Bob Gåriland, 1991; Gud Hjåpe, 1992; Utsålt, 1993; Som På Film, 1994; Also; Traste and Superstarana, 1980; Provins, 1985. *Honour:* Hälsinge Akademins Pris, 1992. *Current Management:* PO Box 171 80, 104 62 Stockholm, Sweden.

LINDES Hal; b. 30 June 1953, Monterey, California, USA. Composer; Musician (guitar). m. Mary Elizabeth Frampton, 2 Aug. 1979, 2 s., 1 d. *Education:* University of Maryland, USA. *Musical Education:* Self-taught. *Career:* Replaced David Knopfler in Dire Straits, 1980; Began Making Movies World Tour playing sellouts in small clubs, ended playing sold-out stadiums; Recorded, toured with band to midway through making Brothers In Arms album, 1985; Also made guest appearances with Tina Turner on release of Private Dancer album; Actor in BBC film: Drowning In The Shallow End, 1989; Began career as film and television composer. *Compositions:* Television themes include: Between The Lines, BBC; Band of Gold, Granada; Thieftakers, Carlton; The Guilty, Central; The Trial, BBC; FIA Formula 1 Grand Prix Logo Theme, FIA; Legacy – Great Civilisations of The World, Central; Into the Land of Oz, CH4; Joyriders, Granada; Drowning In The Shallow End, BBC; Born Kicking, BBC; Commercials include: Avon; Ford; Kwik Fit; Kelloggs Special K; Johnson and Johnson. *Recordings:* with Dire Straits: Singles: Private Investigations, 1982; Twisting By The Pool, 1983; Albums: Love Over Gold (No. 1, UK), 1982; Alchemy, 1984; Money For Nothing, 1988; Live at the BBC, 1995; Sultans of Swing, 1998; with Mark Knopfler: Local Hero; with Tina Turner: Private Dancer/Steel Claw; Simply the Best; with Kiki Dee: Angel Eyes; with Fish: Vigil In A Wilderness of Mirrors; Solo: Between The Lines; Senses; Best of TV Detectives; Best of German TV Themes; Game of Hearts-Rugby World Cup Theme. *Memberships:* PRS; ASCAP; British Equity. *Current Management:* Joel Roman, William Morris Agency (USA); Seifert Dench Associates; EMI (Music) Publishing Ltd (World). *Address:* c/o Seifert Dench, 24 D'Arblay St, London W1V 3FH, England.

LINDHOLM Dave (Ralf Henrik); b. 31 March 1952, Helsinki, Finland. Singer; Songwriter; Musician (guitar). m. Kirsi Koivunen, 9 Sept. 1993, 1 s.,

2 d. *Musical Education:* Taught by father and friends. *Career:* Member of bands: Ferris; Orfeus; Rock 'n' Roll Band; Pen Lee and Co; Bluesounds; 12 Bar; Dave Lindholm and Ganpaza Gypsys; Concerts in most of Europe and Texas, USA; Several blues festivals. *Recordings:* 34 albums, own music; Albums include: with Bluesounds: Black, 1980; On, 1981; Native Sons of Far Away Country, 1981; with Jonas Hellborg, 1988; Silverbuilt, 1998; Some studio sessions with various artists. *Leisure interest:* Speedway. *Current Management:* Tiina Vuorinen, Well Done. *Address:* c/o Well Done, Sorvaajarskatu 9A, 00810 Helsinki, Finland.

LINDRIDGE Nigel Paul James; b. 22 March 1950, Croydon, Surrey, England. Singer; Songwriter. m. Lynda Cauvain, 1 d., 1 step-d. *Education:* Medway College of Technology. *Career:* Lead Singer, Founder, The Menaces, 1966–68; Country Duo with John Lynott, 1970–72; Solo Act, 1972–76; Country Band, The Taverners, 1977–87; Song Writer, 1994. *Compositions:* Album, Love Is Blind; You Know Me. *Recordings:* Live Is Blind; You Know Me. *Memberships:* Musicians' Union; Performing Rights Society. *Leisure interests:* Reading; Writing. *Address:* 5 Folland Rd, Glanamman, Ammanford, Carms, SA18 2BX.

LINDSEY Mort; b. 21 March 1923, Newark, New Jersey, USA. Conductor; Composer; Orchestrator; Musician (piano). m. Betty J Bonney, 9 Oct. 1954, 2 s., 1 d. *Education:* BA, MA, EdD, Columbia University, New York City. *Musical Education:* Private study: Tibor Serly; Paul Creston. *Career:* Staff conductor, NBC; CBS and NBC Networks; Musical Director for: Judy Garland; Barbra Streisand; Merv Griffin; Pat Boone; Musical Director, Merv Griffin Show, 22 years. *Recordings:* 3 orchestra albums under own name; Film soundtrack albums; Conducted, composed, 8 major films. *Publications:* Seven Ages of Man (ballet); Popular songs: Lorna, with Johnny Mercer; Stolen Hours, with Marilyn and Allan Bergmann. *Honours:* Grammy Award: Judy Garland At Carnegie Hall; Emmy Award: Barbra Streisand in Central Park. *Membership:* ASCAP; AFofM; Sinfonia; Composers and Lyricists Guild. *Leisure interests:* Oil painting; Equestrian sports.

LINDSTROM Maria; b. 30 Aug. 1953, Stockholm, Sweden. Singer; Songwriter; Musician (Guitar). m. Kjell Andersson, 24 Aug. 1995. *Education:* Musicology, University of Lund; Music Teacher Exam, 1976. *Career:* Actress, Musician, Fringe Theatre Group, 1977–88; Freelance, 1988–; Cabaret Artiste, TV. *Compositions:* More than 100 songs including lyrics and music for stage. *Recordings:* 1 LP, 1989; 1 CD, 1995; 1 CD, songs by Birger Sjöberg, 1998. *Publications:* Produced about 15 shows. *Honour:* Swedish SKAP Prize, 1997. *Leisure interests:* Walking the dog; Cooking; Dreaming of better days. *Current Management:* Agneta Neumann, Nojesprod AB, Malmo.

LINDUP Mike; b. 17 March 1959. Musician (keyboards); Singer. *Career:* Founder member, Level 42, 1980–; Appearances include: Support to the Police, 1981; Prince's Rock Gala, Wembley Arena, 1986, 1987, 1989; Crystal Palace Bowl, 1991; Midem Festival, Cannes, France, 1992; Regular British tours. *Recordings:* Albums: with Level 42: Level 42, 1981; The Pursuit of Accidents, 1982; Standing In The Light, 1983; True Colours, 1984; A Physical Presence, 1985; World Machine, 1985; Running In The Family, 1987; Staring At The Sun, 1988; Guaranteed, 1991; Forever Now, 1994; Live at Wembley, 1996; Solo album: Changes, 1990; Hit singles: The Chinese Way, 1983; The Sun Goes Down (Living It Up), 1983; Hot Water, 1984; Something About You, 1985; Leaving Me Now, 1985; Lessons In Love (No. 1 in 8 countries), 1986; Running In The Family, 1987; To Be With You Again, 1987; It's Over, 1987; Heaven In My Hands, 1988; Tracie, 1989; Guaranteed, 1991; Keyboards on: Second Nature, Dominic Miller, 2000. *Honour:* BMI Award, 1m. US performances, Something About You, 1991. *Current Management:* Paul Crockford Management, 56–60 Islington Park St, London N1 1PX, England.

LINKA Rudy; b. 29 May 1960, Prague, Czech Republic. Musician (Jazz Guitar); Composer. m. Solveig Linka, 26 July 1985, 1 d. *Education:* People's Prague Conservatory, 2 years; Musik Institute, Stockholm; Berklee College of Music, Boston; New School, New York. *Career:* Performed with Red Mitchell, Bob Mintzer, John Abercrombie; Performed with own jazz group, at jazz clubs including Birdland, Blues Alley, Blue Note, Moods, Bimhuis. *Compositions:* Room 428; Waltz for Stephanie; To Be Named Later; The Old and New Orleans; Folk Song. *Recordings:* Rudy Linka, 1990; News from Home, 1991; Mostly Standards, 1992; Live it Up, 1993; Czech It Out, 1995; Always Double Czech, 1997. *Honours:* Jim Hall Fellowship, Berklee College of Music; Jazz Composition Grant, National Endowment for the Arts. *Memberships:* BMI; GEMA. *Current Management:* Anna Eksell Management. *Address:* 55 West End Ave 8C, New York, NY 10023, USA.

LINKOLA Jukka; b. 21 July 1955, Espoo, Finland. Composer; Musician (piano); Conductor. *Musical Education:* Sibelius Academy, Helsinki. *Career:* Has conducted Danish Radio Big Band, Bohuslän Big Band, Oslo Groove Company, UMO Big Band, Prag Radio Big Band, Ljubljana Radio Big Band, Finnish Radio Big Band, Finnish Radio Syphony Orchestra, Helsinki Philharmony, Finnish National Opera Orchestra; Musical Director,

Helsinki City Theatre, 1979–90; Currently freelance composer, Jazz, symphony, chamber and theatre music. *Compositions include:* Ronja The Robber's Daughter (ballet) for Finnish National Opera, premiered 1989; Crossings, for symphony orchestra, 1983; Two trumpet concertos, 1988, 1993; Angelika, opera, 1990; Elina, opera, 1992; String Quartet, 1996; Pegasos, for big band. *Recordings:* Albums with own octet: Protofunk; Lady In Green; Scat Suite; Ben Bay; with Eija Ahvo: Kuinka Myöhään Valvoo Blues; Crossings and Trumpet Concerto; The Tentet; EQ; Libau; Ronia the Robber's Daughter; Protofunk; Lady in Green; Sketches from Karelia. *Honours:* Yrjö Award, Finnish Jazz Federation, 1979; Finnish Broadcasting Company, Record of The Year, with singer Eija Ahvo; First Prize, LUSES competition, 1993; First Prize, Paris Opera Screen, 1993; First Prize, Midem Awards, 1994; First Prize, Concours International de Composition de la Ville du Havre, 1994; EQ; Libau, Record of the Year, 1998. *Membership:* Society of Finnish Composers. *Current Management:* Syrene Music. *Address:* c/o Syrene Music, Saarnitie 14 A, 00780 Helsinki, Finland.

LINNET Anne Kristine; b. 30 July 1953, Aarhus, Denmark. Composer; Musician; Songwriter; Singer. m. Holger Laumann, divorced, 2 s., 1 d. *Education:* Diploma, Conservatory of Music, Jutland, 1985. *Career:* Performed in group Tears, 1970; Formed own band Shit and Chanel in 1974, recording 5 albums until 1979; Formed the Anne Linnet Band with Sanne Salomonsen and Lis Soerenson, 1981, touring Scandinavia and Germany; Formed new band Marquis de Sade in 1983; Composed and recorded the musical Berlin '84, 1984; Formed own record company, Pladecompagniet in 1988; Partnership with poet and priest Johannes Moellehave composing music to his poetry; Premiere of musical Krig og Kaerlighed (War and Love) in 1990; Currently working on several major classical compositions; Participating in PaPapegoje, an album of children's songs performed by major Danish rock and pop artists; Composer of song for 1995 Eurovision Song Contest, performed by Ulla Henningsen. *Recordings:* Anne Linnet Band, 1981; Cha Cha Cha, 1982; Marquis de Sade, 1983; Hvid Magi (White Magic), 1985; En elsker, 1986; Solo: Barndommens Gade, 1986; Jeg er jo lige her (I'm Right Here), 1988; Det' saa dansk, (It is so Typical Danish), 1991; Tal til mig (Talk To Me), 1993; with Johannes Moellehave: Miri Sang (My Song), 1989. *Honours:* Recipient of numerous Gold and Platinum records. *Address:* Linnet Songs, Bohlendachvej 45, Holmen, 1437 Copenhagen K, Denmark.

LINSTEAD Johannes; b. 6 Aug. 1969, Oakville, Ontario, Canada. Composer; Guitarist; Songwriter. *Musical Education:* Private instruction on flamenco and classical guitar; Self-taught piano. *Career:* Solo performer and band leader of instrumental Latin guitar music; Theme music for television and films; Contemporary pop music written for various solo artists; Solo recording artist with Real Music, Sausalito, California. *Recordings:* Sol Luna Tierra; Cleanse; Head is Angry; Alive and Wandering. *Honour:* Jazz Band Musician of the Year, 1989. *Membership:* Society of Composers, Authors and Music Publishers, Canada. *Leisure interests:* Kung Fu; Meditation. *Current Management:* Earthscape Media. *Address:* 1312 Speers Rd, Oakville, ON L6L 2X4, Canada.

LIPA Peter; b. 30 May 1943, Presov, Slovakia. Singer; Songwriter; Bandleader. m. Norina Bobrovská, 7 Feb. 1980, 3 s., 1 d. *Education:* Technical University, Bratislava, Slovakia;. *Musical Education:* Self-taught guitar; Private lessons, violin, vocal. *Career:* Bands: Strings, Blues Five, Revival Jazz Band, Blues Band; Peter Lipa Combo; Peter Lipa and Band; Andrej Seban Band; Hundreds of TV and Radio Performances, in Slovak, Czech, German, Hungarian, Polish Radio, TV. *Recordings:* Moanin'; That's the Way It Is; Naspat Na Stromy; Spirituals; Peter Lipa; (La, La, La) Boogie Up; Cierny Peter. *Honours:* Hon. Citizen of Bratislava, 1995; Martonik Annual Jazz Prize, 1995. *Membership:* President, Slovak Jazz Society; Lions Club International. *Leisure interests:* Swimming; Music. *Current Management:* East-West Promotion Kuzmanyho 4, 81106, Bratislava, Slovakia. *Address:* Kuzmanyho 4, 81106 Bratislava, Slovakia.

LIPSON Stephen James; b. 16 March 1954, London, England. Record Prod. *Recordings:* Record producer for: Propaganda, A Secret Wish, 1985; Grace Jones, Slave To The Rhythm, 1985; Frankie Goes To Hollywood, Liverpool, 1986; Pet Shop Boys, Introspective, 1988; Simple Minds, Street Fighting Years (No. 1, UK), 1989; Annie Lennox, Diva, 1992; Prefab Sprout, If You Don't Love Me, 1992; Backstreet Boys, Drowning, 2001; Also: Paul McCartney; Gary Barlow; Boyzone; Cher; Paul Brady; Ronan Keating; S Club 7. *Honour:* Producer of the Year. *Current Management:* Zomba Management. *Address:* 165–167 High Rd, London NW10 2SG, England.

LISAK Ivan-Vanja; b. 23 Nov. 1941, Zagreb, Croatia. Composer; Musician (piano). m. Ksenija Zivkovic, 27 March 1982, 2 d. *Musical Education:* Music Academy, Teacher of Theory. *Career:* Pop festivals including: Director of oldest festival in Zagreb, 1975–79; Jazz festivals including: Bled 1983; Sofia, 1985; Prague, 1985; Moscow; Kiev; Petrograd, 1986–90; Italy, 1992–94; Tours: Concerts for Croats In Europe, Australia, The Soviet Union, USA; Numerous television and radio appearances, 1962–95. *Recordings:* Swing Party I, 1983; II, 1985; III, with Peppino Principe,

accordion, 1989; Happy Jazz I, 1991; II, 1994; Cassette: The Tree In The Yard, instrumental. *Honours:* Festival Awards, 1974, 1979, 1981, 1984. *Memberships:* Society of Musical Composers; HGU (Croatian Musical Union). *Leisure interests:* Watch collection; Swimming. *Address:* 35, Marticeva St, Zagreb 41000, Croatia.

LISBERG Harvey Brian; b. 2 March 1940, Manchester, England. Impressario; Artist Man. m. Carole Gottlieb, 5 Nov. 1969, 2 s. *Education:* Manchester University. *Musical Education:* Self-taught piano, guitar. *Career:* First in discovering: Graham Gouldman; Andrew Lloyd Webber; Tim Rice; Herman's Hermits; Tony Christie; Sad Café; Godley and Creme; 10cc; Currently representing: 10cc; Graham Gouldman; Eric Stewart; George Stiles; Anthony Drewe; Cleopatra. *Leisure interests:* Golf; Theatre; Films; Travel. *Current Management:* Harvey Lisberg Associates. *Address:* Kennedy House, 31 Stamford St, Altrincham, Cheshire WA14 1ES, England.

LITRELL Brian Thomas, (B-Rock); b. 20 Feb. 1975, USA. Singer. *Career:* Member, Backstreet Boys; Numerous television appearances, tours and hit singles. *Recordings:* Singles: We've Got It Goin' On, 1995; Quit Playing Games, 1998; I'll Never Break Your Heart, 1998; Everybody, 1998; As Long As You Love Me, 1998; Anywhere for You, 1998; All I Have to Give, 1998; I Want It That Way (No. 1, UK), 1999; Larger Than Life, 1999; Show Me The Meaning of Being Lonely, 2000; The One, 2000; Shape of My Heart, 2000; Drowning, 2001; Albums: Backstreet Boys, 1996; Live in Concert, 1998; Backstreet's Back, 1998; Millennium, 1999. *Leisure interests:* Weightlifting; Basketball; Water skiing; Listening to music.

LITTLE RICHARD (Richard Penniman); b. 5 Dec. 1935, Macon, Georgia, USA. Singer; Musician (piano). *Education:* Theological college, 1957. *Career:* R & B singer, various bands; Tours and film work with own band, The Upsetters; Gospel singer, 1960–62; World-wide tours and concerts include: Star Club, Hamburg, Germany, with Beatles, 1962; European tour, with Beatles, Rolling Stones, 1963; British tour with Everly Brothers, 1963; Rock 'n' Revival Concert, Toronto, with Chuck Berry, Fats Domino, Jerry Lee Lewis, Gene Vincent, Bo Diddley, 1969; Toronto Pop Festival, 1970; Randall Island Rock Festival, with Jimi Hendrix, Jethro Tull, 1970; Rock 'N' Roll Spectaculars, Madison Square Garden, 1972–; Muhammad Ali's 50th Birthday; Benefit For Lupus Foundation, Universal City, 1992; Westbury Music Fair, 1992; Giants of Rock 'n' Roll, Wembley Arena, 1992; Film appearances: Don't Knock The Rock, 1956; Mr Rock 'n' Roll, 1957; The Girl Can't Help It, 1957; Keep On Rockin', 1970; Down and Out In Beverly Hills, 1986; Mother Goose Rock 'n' Rhyme, Disney Channel, 1989. *Recordings:* Albums: Here's Little Richard, 1957; Little Richard Is Back, 1965; Greatest Hits, 1965; Freedom Blues, 1970; The King of Rock 'n' Roll, 1971; God's Beautiful City, 1979; Lifetime Friend, 1987; Featured on: Folkways – A Vision Shared (Woody Guthrie tribute), 1988; For Our Children, 1991; Shake It All About, 1992; Little Richard and Jimi Hendrix, 1993; Shag on Down by the Union Hall, 1996; Hit singles include: Tutti Frutti, 1956; Long Tall Sally, 1956; The Girl Can't Help It, 1957; Lucille, 1957; She's Got It, 1957; Jenny Jenny, 1957; Keep A Knockin', 1957; Good Golly Miss Molly, 1958, Baby Face, 1959; Bama Lama Bama Loo, 1964. *Honours include:* Star, Hollywood Walk of Fame, 1990; Little Richard Day, Los Angeles, 1990; Penniman Boulevard, Macon, named in his honour; Platinum Star, Lupus Foundation of America, 1992; Grammy Lifetime Achievement Award, 1993.

LITTON Martin; b. 14 May 1957, Grays, Essex, England. m. Rebekah Morley-Jones, 15 Aug. 1992. *Education:* BA Hons, Music, Colchester Institute, England, 1978. *Career:* Pieces of Eight, with Harry Gold, 1980–82; Kenny Ball and His Jazzmen, 1982–84; Tours of Middle East and Russia; Freelance work with many American Musicians, including Bob Wilber, George Masso, Peanuts Hucko, Joe Muranyi, Al Casey, Scott Hamilton; Recorded with Kenny Davern, Wild Bill Davison, Yank Lawson, Marty Grosz; Work with leading British Musicians includes recordings with Humphrey Lyttelton, Wally Fawkes and Digby Fairweather; Recent tours include Fabulous Fats, with Keith Smith; Frequent performer at London's South Bank Arts Centre; Falling Castle. *Compositions:* Forever Afternoon; Striding Down 52nd Street; Litton on the Keys; Eight Bars – Eight to the Bar; For Rebekah. *Recordings include:* Martin Litton Jazz Piano; Ring Dem Bells. *Membership:* PRS. *Leisure interests:* Reading and Painting. *Address:* 7 Bridge St, Hay-on-Wye, Herefordshire, HR3 5DE, England.

LITWIN Ralph Henry; b. 11 April 1950, Morristown, New Jersey, USA. Vocalist; Musician (5-String Banjo, Guitar, Harmonica). m. Stephanie Kraft, 26 Oct. 1981, 1 s., 1 d. *Education:* BFA, Rhode Island School of Design; Juris Dr, Rutgers Law School, Newark, New Jersey. *Career:* Host and Producer, Horses Sing None of It!, award-winning series, Manhattan, New York, Philadelphia, and cable stations in New Jersey; Music used in soundtrack for The Black West; Numerous TV and radio guest appearances including: The Today Show, The Howard Stern Show, The Uncle Floyd Show, KTV Show, Anything Goes, Jersey Beat, The Joe Franklin Show. *Compositions:* The Band with a Thousand Names; Love is Like Washing a

Potato; I'd Rather Say Goodbye to You than Give Up an Indoor Toilet. *Recordings include:* Makes My Heart Feel Happy, 1990; Wild and Lazy, 1993; Ralph Litwin and the Band with a Thousand Names, 1998. *Honours:* First Place, New Jersey Old Style Banjo Championship, twice; Cash Box Magazine Indie Album Choice; Hon. Mention, Billboard Magazine Song Contest, three times; Winner, Hometown Video Festival, three times; National Old Time Banjo Championship Finalist, 1996; First Place, Freewheelin' Style, 2nd Place, Harmonica, Uncle Dave Macon Days, Tennessee, 1996. *Memberships:* North American Folk Alliance; Folk Project; New Jersey Country Music Asscn; NE Songwriters' Alliance; New Jersey Songwriters' Circle. *Leisure interests:* Walking; Meditation; Option dialogue. *Address:* 140 Morris St, Morristown, NJ 07960, USA.

LIVESEY Warne; b. 12 Feb. 1959, London, England. Record Prod. m. Barbara, 18 May 1983. *Recordings:* Producer, albums: Diesel and Dust, Midnight Oil; Blue Sky Mining, Midnight Oil; Infected, The The; Mind Bomb, The The; When The World Knows Your Name, Deacon Blue; Perverse, Jesus Jones; Suddenly Tammy!; Prick; St Julian, Julian Cope; Babe Rainbow, House of Love; Underdogs, Matthew Good Band; Work, Lovelife, Miscellaneous, by David Devant and his Spirit Wife. *Membership:* Musicians' Union. *Leisure interest:* Photography. *Current Management:* John Reid, JPR Management Ltd. *Address:* The Power House, 70 Chiswick High Rd, London W4 1SY, England.

LL COOL J (James Todd Smith); b. 14 Jan. 1968, St Albans, Queens, New York, USA. Rapper. *Career:* Began rapping aged 9; Concerts include: Support to Run DMC, Raising Hell tour, 1986; Headliner, Def Jam '87 tour, 1987; Performed at Farm Aid IV, 1990; Budweiser Superfest, 1991; European tour, 1993; Film appearances: Krush Groove, 1985; The Hard Way, 1991; Toys, 1992; Founder, Uncle Records, 1992. *Recordings:* Singles include: I Can't Live Without My Radio, 1985; I Need Love, 1987; Goin' Back To Cali, 1988; I'm That Type of Guy, 1989; Around The Way Girl, 1991; How I'm Comin', 1993; Pink Cookies In A Plastic Bag, 1993; Stand By Your Man, 1993; Hey Lover, 1995; Loungin', 1996; Dooin' It, 1996; Ain't Nobody (No. 1, UK), 1996; Phenomenon, 1997; 4321, 1997; Candy, 1998; Father, 1998; Ripper Strikes Back, 1999; Hot Hot Hot, 1999; Say What, 1999; Albums: Radio, 1985; Bigger and Deffer, 1987; Walking With A Panther, 1989; Mama Said Knock You Out, 1990; 14 Shots To The Dome, 1993; Mr Smith, 1996; Phenomenon, 1997; The G.O.A.T. (Greatest of All Time), 2000; Contributor, King of Rock, Run DMC, 1985; Simply Mad About The Mouse, 1991. *Publication:* I Make My Own Rules, autobiography, 1997. *Honours:* Platinum discs; Soul Train Music Awards: Best Rap Album, Best Rap Single, 1988; MTV Music Video Award, Best Rap Video, 1991; Billboard Top Rap Singles Artist, 1991; Grammy Awards, Best Rap Solo Performance, Mama Said Knock You Out, 1992, Hey Lover, 1996; MTV Video Vanguard Award, 1997. *Current Management:* Rush Artist Management, 160 Varick St, New York, NY 10013, USA. *Address:* LL Cool J Inc, 186–39 Illian Ave, Jamaica, NY 11412, USA.

LLABADOR Jean-Pierre; b. 15 Dec. 1952, Nemours, Algeria. Jazz Musician (guitar); Composer. m. Annie Soulet-Pujol, 28 June 1976, 2 d. *Education:* BA, English; Degree Philosophy. *Musical Education:* Conservatoire, France; Los Angeles GIT graduate (2 special awards). *Career:* Member, various jazz, fusion and rock bands including Coincidence; Johnny Hallyday (tours, radio and television shows, recordings), 1975–85; Lead guitarist, composer, with own bands, 1985–; Many tours, Europe and Africa; International festival appearances include: Nîmes, Montpellier-Radio-France, Nancy Jazz Pulsation, Midem, Barcelona, Laseyne sur Mer, Cardiff, Bath; Numerous radio and television appearances: Radio-France, TF1, FR2, FR3, M6; Artistic Director, OJLR (Region Languedoc Jazz Orchestra). *Recordings:* Albums (mostly own compostions): French Guitar Connection, quartet (US); 5th Edition, quintet (Germany); Friendship, duo/trio (Germany); Dialogues, OJLR (France); Birds Can Fly, quintet/sextet (France). *Memberships:* Composer, improviser, SACEM; SPEDIDAM. *Leisure interests:* Family and friends; Books; Music. *Current Management:* TRIAD Diffusion. *Address:* 700 Chemin des Mendrous, 34170 Castelnau-Le-Lez, France.

LLACH Lluís; b. 7 May 1948, Girona, Catalonia, Catalan. Singer; Songwriter; Musician (piano, guitar). *Career:* Singer, songwriter since late 1960s; Pioneer, Nova Cançó (Catalan protest-song movement against General Franco); Member, El Setze Jutges, 1967; Major concerts include: Olympia, Paris, 1973, 1988; Stade de Barcelona, 1985; Edinburgh Arts Festival, 1993. *Compositions:* Arranger, songwriter on albums by: Teresa Rebull; Francesc Pi de la Serra; Dolors Lafitte; Marina Rossell; Josep Tero; Maria del Mar Bonet; Joan Americ; Carles Cases. *Recordings:* Over 25 solo albums, 1967–; Albums include: Viatge a Itaca, 1975; Campanades a Morts, 1977; El Meu Amic el Mar, 1978; Maremar, 1986; Astres, 1987; Geografia, 1988; Un Pont de Mar Blava, 1993; Porrera, 1995; Music for three films: Borrasca, 1977; La Forja de un Rebelde, 1990; El Ladrón de Niños, 1992; Numerous solo singles/EPs, including best known anthem, L'Estaca, 1974. *Publications:* Poemes i Cançons, 1979; Lluís Llach, 1979; Lluís Llach - Catalogne Vivre, 1979; Un Trobador per a un Poble, 1982; Història de les Seves Cançons Explicada a Josep Maria Espinàs, 1986; La Dáraison d'Etat,

1987; La Geografia del Cor, 1992; Lluís Llach, 1993. *Memberships:* Societat General d'Autors i Editors (SGAE); Associació de Cantants i Intérprets en Llengua Catalana (ACIC). *Current Management:* Andréas Claus. *Address:* Sepúlveda, 147–149 Principal 1a, 08011 Barcelona, Catalonia, Spain.

LLOYD Andrew Reginald, (Popman); b. 2 June 1960, Halesowen, Birmingham, England. Singer; Songwriter; Musician (guitar); Entertainer; Actor; Record Prod. *Musical Education:* Self-taught. *Career:* Bands: Mickey Mouse Revival, 1972–76; Andy Lloyd and the Wedge, 1978–79; The Bloomsbury Set, 1980–83; Popman and the Raging Bull, 1986–88; Popman and the Disciple, 1989–93; Radio sessions, Peter Powell, Radio 1, 1981–86; Tours: Judy Tzuke, 1981; Duran Duran, 1982; Various support tours, 1986–92; Headline tour, 1993; Solo acoustic US tour, 1994; Television appearances: Get It Together; Pop 77; Oxford Road Show; Track 1; Razzmatazz; TV appearances: lead guitarist for Dolly Parton on The National Lottery, 1998; Des O'Connor Show, 1998. *Recordings:* Back To School, 1978; It's Up To You, 1978; Living In America, 1979; Letters To Eva, 1979; This Year Next Year, 1981; The Other Side of You, 1981; Sweet Europeans, 1982; Hanging Around With The Big Boys, Getting Away From It All, Dress Parade, Serenade, 1983; Just Like A Woman, Casual Acquaintance, 1986; Fields In Motion, Hustling Man, 1987; New Feelings, Friends and Lovers, 1988; Pirate, 1989; Girl of My Best Friend, 1990; Little White Lies, The Same Girl, 1991; Weekend, 1992; Acoustic set, 1994; Plugs Out, 1995; Food, 1996. *Memberships:* MU; Equity; Songwriters Guild; PRS; MLPS. *Leisure interests:* Animal welfare; Gardening; Swimming; Walking; Music. *Current Management:* Nick Titchener, Don't Panic Promotions. *Address:* 74 The Archway, Ranelagh Gardens, London SW6 3UH, England.

LLOYD Gary; b. 29 Jan. 1965, Ottawa, Canada. Composer. *Education:* BA, Mathematics, University of Liverpool Chester College, England, 1986. *Career:* Ran recording studio, 1987–89; Composition and Soundtrack composer since 1989; Scored music for more than 400 productions including works for TV, film, theatre, contemporary dance, son et lumiere, art installations; First commission Neil Gaiman's Violent Cases, stageplay soundtrack, 1988. *Compositions include:* A Return To Love, for TV drama, 1994; Ignition, music for Fireworks, 1994; Land of Many Waters, for A/V show and CD release, 1995; Precis for String Orchestra, performed Cholmondeley Castle, Cheshire, England, 1996; The Ghost Tour, filmscore, 1997; Curiously England, documentary, 1997; Alien Blood, filmscore, 1998. *Recordings:* Albums: The Bridge, with Iain Banks, 1996; Brought to Light, with Alan Moore, 1998. *Leisure interests:* Skateboarding; Mathematics; Films. *Current Management:* Music for Films, 34 Batchelor St, Islington, London N1 0EG, England. *Address:* c/o Gallery Productions, PO Box 1363, Chester, CH2 3WN, England.

LLOYD Richard; b. 17 Jan. 1961, Miami Beach, Florida, USA. m. Linda Westauss, 8 June 1996. *Education:* Music School, Miami Community College; Music Major, studied with the late Cag Thaler and Charles Perry. *Career:* 20 years performing as Drummer and as Producer; Performed across country with groups such as Stevie Rae Vaughn, The Thunderbirds; ZZ Top. *Compositions:* The Answer, 1985; The Alternatives, 1985; Lady Sabre, 1987; The Sharks, 1989; The Ones, 1981; The Leap, 1983. *Recordings:* As above, plus: The Cover Doesn't Matter, 2001. *Honour:* Battle of the Bands, Houston, Texas, 1981. *Membership:* Department of Professional Regulation. *Leisure interests:* Boating; Landscape design; Real estate. *Address:* 1515 University Dr. 108A, Coral Springs, FL 33071, USA.

LLOYD WEBBER Andrew, (Baron Lloyd Webber of Sydmonton); b. 22 March 1948, London, England. Composer. m. Sarah Jane Hugill, 1971, divorced 1983, 1 s., 1 d., (2) Sarah Brightman, 1984, divorced 1990, (3) Madeleine Gurdon, 1991, 2 s., 1 d. *Education:* Magdalen College, Oxford; Royal College of Music, FRCM, 1988. *Career:* Composer and producer, musicals; Composer, film scores; Deviser, board game, and They're Off. *Compositions:* Musicals: Joseph and The Amazing Technicolour Dreamcoat (lyrics by Tim Rice), 1968; Jesus Christ Superstar (lyrics by Tim Rice), 1970; Jeeves (lyrics by Alan Ayckbourn), 1975; Evita (lyrics by Tim Rice), 1976; Tell Me On A Sunday (lyrics by Don Black), 1980; Cats (based on poems by T S Eliot), 1981; Song and Dance, 1982; Starlight Express (lyrics by Richard Stilgoe), 1984; The Phantom of The Opera (lyrics by Richard Stilgoe and Charles Hart), 1986; Aspects of Love (lyrics by Don Black and Charles Hart), 1989; Sunset Boulevard (lyrics by Don Black and Christopher Hampton), 1993; By Jeeves (lyrics by Alan Ayckbourn), 1996; Whistle Down The Wind (lyrics by Jim Steinman), 1996; The Beautiful Game (lyrics by Ben Elton), 2000; Film Scores: Gumshoe, 1971; The Odessa File, 1974; Jesus Christ Superstar, 1974; Others: Requiem, 1985; Variations On A Theme of Paganini For Orchestra, 1986; Amigos Para Siempre (official theme for 1992 Olympic Games), 1992; When Children Rule The World (official theme for the opening ceremony 1998 Winter Olympics). *Recordings:* Hit songs include: Don't Cry For Me Argentina, Julie Covington (No. 1, UK), 1976; Take That Look Off Your Face, Marti Webb, 1980; Memory, Elaine Paige, 1981; The Phantom of The Opera, Sarah Brightman and Steve Harley, 1986; All I Ask of You, Cliff Richard and Sarah Brightman, 1986; The Music of The Night, Michael Crawford,

1987; Love Changes Everything, Michael Ball, 1989; Any Dream Will Do, Jason Donovan (No. 1, UK), 1991; Amigos Para Siempre, Sarah Brightman and Jose Carreras, 1992; No Matter What, Boyzone (No. 1, UK), 1998. *Publications:* Evita (with Tim Rice), 1978; Cats: The Book of the Musical, 1981; Joseph and The Amazing Technicolour Dreamcoat (with Tim Rice), 1982; The Complete Phantom of the Opera, 1987; The Complete Aspects of Love, 1989; Sunset Boulevard: From Movie to Musical, 1993; Restaurant Columnist, the Daily Telegraph. *Honours include:* 5 Laurence Olivier Awards; 6 Tony Awards; 4 Drama Desk Awards; 3 Grammy Awards; Triple Play Award, ASCAP, 1988; Knighthood, 1992; Praemium Imperiale Award, 1995; Richard Rogers Award, 1996; Academy Award, Best Song, (with Tim Rice), 1997. *Leisure interests:* Art; Architecture; Food and wine. *Address:* 22 Tower St, London WC2H 9NS, England.

LO Cheikh N'Digel; b. 1955, Bobo Dioulasso, Burkina Faso. Vocalist; Musician (guitar); Songwriter. *Musical Education:* Self-taught: Guitar; Drums. *Career:* Member: Orchestra Volta Jazz, 1976; Moved to Dakar, 1980; Worked as a drummer for five years; Emigrated to Paris, 1985; Continued to work as a session drummer; Met Youssou N'Dour, 1989; N'Dour produced Ne La Thiass album, 1995; Appeared in the US with Africa Fete, 1998; Played at WOMAD Reading, 2001; Member and follower of the Baye Fall. *Recordings:* Albums: Ne La Thiass, 1996; Bambay Gueej (featuring Juan de Marcos Gonzalez, Oumou Sangare and Bigga Morrison), 1999. *Honours:* Kora Award, Best Newcomer, 1997; Ordre National de Merite de Leon, presented by the president of Senegal, 2001. *Address:* c/o World Circuit, 138 Kingsland Rd, London, E2 8DY, England. *Internet:* www.worldcircuit.co.uk.

LOBO Edu, (Eduardo De Goes Lobos); b. 1943, Rio De Janeiro, Brazil. Vocalist; Musician (guitar); Composer; Songwriter. *Career:* Has written songs that combine Brazilian folk music with bossa nova harmonies; Despite being born in Rio, lyrics often object to the injustice and misery of Brazil's Northeast region; Met Carlos Lyra, mid 1960s; Greatly influenced by Lyra's new bossa style, elements of northeastern music and socially conscious lyrics; First album released, 1964; Protest songs not popular with Brazilian military dictatorship in power during late 1960s, so left for the USA, 1969; Supplied four songs and played guitar on saxophonist Paul Desmond's album From The Hot Afternoon; Since return to Brazil in 1971, has mainly written music for plays, films and ballets. *Recordings:* Albums: Musica De Edu Lobo Por Edu Lobo, 1964; Reencontro, Folklore E Bossa Nova Do Brasil, 1966; Edu, 1968; Sergio Mendes Presents Lobo, 1969; Cantiga De Longe, 1971; Nissa Breve, 1973; Limite Das Aguas, 1975; Camaleão, 1978; Tom E Edu, Jogos De Danca, 1981; O Grande Circo Mistico, 1983; Edu E Bethania, 1984; Corrupião, 1993; Meia Noite, 1995; features on: From The Hot Afternoon, Paul Desmond, 1969. *Honours:* First place TV in record festival, Borandá, 1967; Gramado Film Festival, Best Soundtrack, Barra Pesada, 1979.

LOCK Eddie; b. 10 Feb. 1969, Bury St Edmunds, England. Musician; DJ; Prod. m. Maxine, 20 July 1996. *Career:* DJ, 1987; Member, Carpe Diem and SMC Project. *Compositions:* Calling My Name; Got To Get Up, 1998; La Noche Vista, 1999. *Recordings:* The Buzz; Don't Wanna Be Free; Hypnotic; Music Takes You; Snakecharmer; Space is the Place; Turkish Delight; The Phuture, 2000. *Memberships:* MCPS; BPI; PRS; Music Publishers Asscn. *Leisure interests:* Football; Drinking; Making Money. *Current Management:* Plastic Surgery/Mission Control. *Address:* The Coach House, Mansion Farm, Liverton Hill, Sandway, Maidstone, Kent ME17 2NJ, England.

LOCKETT Peter Robert; b. 8 April 1963, Portsmouth, Hampshire, England. Musician (Percussion). *Musical Education:* Self-taught; Madras Academy, 1991–93. *Career:* Live TV work, recording, touring with Kula Shaker; Live TV work and recording with Vanessa Mae; Duo concerts at Royal Festival Hall with Joji Hirota; Series on drum programming, The Mix, magazine; World percussion sample CDs for The Mix, magazine; Films: City of Angels; Plunkett and Maclean; The World Is Not Enough; The Bone Collector. *Recordings:* with Bjork; Bill Bruford; David Arnold; A R Rahman; 2 albums with top Danish guitarist, Henrik Anderson; with Natacha Atlas, Transglobal Underground; Tomorrow Never Dies, Bond film; with Mel C; Pet Shop Boys; Nitin Sawnmey; Junior Delgado; Arts Council CMN tour for Pete Lockett's Network of Sparks, featuring Bill Bruford, 2000; Taiko and Tabla, Joji Hirota/Pete Lockett. *Publications:* Drum technique articles for Modern Drummer and Rhythm Magazine. *Address:* Flat F, 26 Upper Park Rd, Belsize Park, London NW3 2UT, England.

LOCKHEART Mark; b. 31 March 1961, Hampshire, England. Musician (saxophones, clarinet, flute); Composer. m. Andrea Margo Tosic, 30 July 1985. *Musical Education:* Trinity College of Music. *Career:* Saxophone, Loose Tubes, Lysis Steve Berry Trio, 1985–91; Leader, own Perfect Houseplant Group; Co-leader, Matheran; Currently member, Django Bates' Delightful Precipice; Also bands with June Tabor, Billy Jenkins; Session work with Jah Wobble; Prefab Sprout; The High Llamas; Stereolab; Radiohead (Kid A, No. 1, UK and US, 2000). *Recordings:* with Perfect Houseplants: Perfect Houseplants, 1993; Clec, 1995; with Matheran: Mark

Lockheart-John Paracelli, 1994; with Django Bates: Summer Fruits and Unrest, 1994; with June Tabor: Some Other Time, 1989; Angel Tiger, 1992; Against The Streams, 1994; Aleyn, 1997. *Honour:* Scottish Arts Commission: Semana Santa, Multi-media Commission, 1991. *Leisure interests:* Travel; Swimming; Tennis; Cinema. *Current Management:* Eccentric Management, 29A Connaught St, London W2 2AY, England.

LOCKWOOD Didier André Paul; b. 11 Feb. 1956, Calais, France. Musician (violin); Jazz Composer. m. Casadesus, 15 Oct. 1993, 3 d. *Education:* College. *Musical Education:* Conservatoire de Calais, (violin, trumpet, piano); École Normale Supérieure de Musique, Paris. *Career:* First Prize, at Conservatory, age 16; Professional musician with French group, Magma, 1973; Worked with Stéphane Grappelli, 1978; Formed own groups, 1980–; Appearances include: Royal Albert Hall, London, 1979; Carnegie Hall, New York, 1981; 1983; Major jazz festivals; More than 2,000 concerts world-wide include Théatre des Champs Elysées, 1993; Peking, 1993. *Compositions:* Jazz and contemporary music; Violin concerto: Les Mouettes, (with symphony orchestra). *Recordings:* Recordings: Over 20 include: New World, with Antony Williams (drums), 1981; Live In Montreux, 1982; The Kid; Out of The Blue, 1986; New York Rendevouz, 1994; Storyboard, 1996; Children's Songs, 1997; Tribute To Stephane Grappelli, 2000; Om Kara, 2001. *Publications:* Violin Jazz Method book; 1 song book. *Memberships:* Blue Note Award, Newy; 2 Victoires de la Musique; Grand Prix, SACEM; Prix Charles Cross; Chevalier des Arts et des Lettres. *Leisure interests:* Painting; Tennis; Football. *Current Management:* Isoard-Sola.

LOCKWOOD Robert Jr; b. 27 March 1915, Turkeyscretch, Arkansas, USA. Musician (guitar). m. Annie Roberts, 13 Sept. 1970, 5 s., 2 d. *Career:* Belgian National Radio; Blues Festival, Peer, July 1994; Helen, Arkansas Blues Festival, Oct 1994; KFFA Radio; WCPN Radio; Lady Luck Casino; Rhythm and Blues, Lula, Mississippi. *Recordings:* Little Boy Blue; Take A Little Walk With Me, 1948; Something To Do, 1990; What's The Score?, 1990; Hanged On; Come Day Go Day, 1993; Majors Minors and Ninths, 1993; I Got To Find Me A Woman, 1999; Complete Trix Recordings, 1999; Just the Blues, 1999; Delta Crossroads, 2000. *Publications:* Vol. I Blues; Who, Who, Living, Blues. *Honours:* W C Handy, 1988; Achievement for Black History, 1994; Blues Hall of Fame, 1998; Grammy Award, Traditional Blues Album nominee, 2001. *Leisure interests:* Pool and Checkers. *Current Management:* Annie Lockwood; Agent: Concentrated Efforts Inc. *Address:* 7203 Lawnview Ave, Cleveland, OH 44103, USA.

LODDER Steve (Stephen John); b. 1951. Musician (keyboards); Composer. *Musical Education:* Cambridge (Gonville and Caius), Organ scholarship, 1969. *Career:* Before musical freelance career worked as music teacher in a comprehensive school and ran a coffee/wholefood store; Played with many artists on the London jazz scene including: Paul Nieman; Carol Grimes; Maggie Nichols; Jan Ponsford; John Etheridge; Henry Thomas; Harry Beckett, late 1970s-80s; Toured and recorded with George Russell's Living Time Orchestra, late 1980s; Also played keyboards on three Carol Grimes albums (writer/arranger on Why Don't They Dance?); Member: Brian Abrahams' District Six; Tours in Germany and UK; Musical director for Sarah Jane Morris during a six week tour supporting Simply Red, 1989; Also commenced long musical collaboration, touring and recording, with Andy Sheppard; Worked with John Harle on Duke Ellington tribute, Shadow of the Duke, 1992; Toured with John Harle (performing his Terror and Magnificence and Elvis Costello singing his Twelfth Night Settings), 1995; Worked with Paul McCartney and helped orchestrate his Standing Stones; Collaborations: Mark Ramsden; Monica Vasconcelos; Carla Bley. *Recordings:* Albums: features on: Eyes Wide Open, Carol Grimes, 1987; Why Don't They Dance?, Carol Grimes, 1989; Imgoma Yabantwana, Brian Abraham's District Six, 1989; Introductions In The Dark, Andy Sheppard, 1989; Soft On The Inside, Andy Sheppard, 1989; The London Concert, George Russell's Living Time Orchestra, 1990; In Co-Motion, Andy Sheppard, 1991; Shadow of the Duke, John Harle, 1992; Rhythm Method, Andy Sheppard, 1993; Inclassifiable, Andy Sheppard, 1994; Delivery Suite, Andy Sheppard, 1994; Terror and Magnificence, John Harle, 1996; Above The Clouds, Mark Ramsden/Steve Lodder, 1996; Moving Image, Andy Sheppard, 1996; It's About Time, George Russell's Living Time Orchestra, 1996; Nois, Monica Vasconcelos, 1997; Standing Stones, Paul McCartney, 1997; Learning To Wave, Andy Sheppard, 1998; Nois Dos, Monica Vasconcelos, 1999; Dancing Man and Woman, Andy Sheppard, 2000; The Gathering, Annie Whitehead, 2000; TV soundtracks: Ali Bongo – The Wacky Wizard; TV/radio soundtracks with Andy Sheppard: The Art Wrap; The Postman Always Rings Twice; Arena – Peter Sellers; Joseph Emidy; Syrup (short film). *E-mail:* steve@stevelodder.com. *Internet:* www.stevelodder.com.

LODGE John Charles; b. 20 July 1945, Birmingham, England. Musician (bass guitar); Vocalist. m. Kirsten, 30 Sept. 1968, 1 s., 1 d. *Education:* Birmingham College of Advanced Technology. *Musical Education:* Self-taught. *Career:* Member, El Riot and The Rebels; The Carpetbaggers; John Bullbreed; Member, Moody Blues, 1966–; Also solo artiste; Numerous tours, concerts include: Royal Albert Hall; Hollywood Bowl; Isle of Wight

Festival, 1970; Wembley Arena, 1993. *Recordings:* Albums: In Search of The Lost Chord, 1968; On The Threshold of a Dream, 1969; To Our Children's Children, 1969; A Question of Balance, 1970; Every Good Boy Deserves Favour, 1971; Days of Future Passed, 1972; Seventh Sojurn, 1972; This Is The Moody Blues, 1974; Blue Jays, 1975; Octave, 1978; Long Distance Voyager, 1981; Voices In The Sky/The Best of The Moody Blues, 1985; The Other Side of Life, 1986; Sur La Mer, 1988; Greatest Hits, 1988; Keys of The Kingdom, 1991; Live At Red Rocks, 1993; Time Traveller, 1994; Anthology, 1998; Live At The Royal Albert Hall, 2000; Solo: Natural Avenue, 1977 (re-released 1996); Singles include: Nights In White Satin, 1968; Voices in The Sky, 1968; Tuesday Afternoon, 1968; Ride My See Saw, 1968; Question (No. 2, UK), 1970; Isn't Life Strange, 1972; I'm Just A Singer (In A Rock 'n' Roll Band), 1973; Blue Guitar, duet with Justin Hayward, 1975; Gemini Dream, 1981; The Voice, 1981; Your Wildest Dreams, 1986. *Honours:* ASCAP Awards, Singer In A Rock 'n' Roll Band; Gemini Dream; 2 Ivor Novello Awards; Outstanding Contribution To British Music, Ivor Novello Awards, 1985. *Memberships:* PRS; BASCA; Songwriters Guild of America. *Leisure interests:* Music; Golf. *Current Management:* ICM (New York and Los Angeles). *Address:* c/o Threshold Records Ltd, 53 High St, Cobham, Surrey KT11 3DP, England.

LOEB Lisa; b. USA. Singer; Musician (guitar); Songwriter. *Career:* Solo artiste, billed as Lisa Loeb and Nine Stories, 1994-. *Recordings:* Albums: Tails, 1995; Firecracker, 1998; Singles: Stay (I Missed You), from film soundtrack Reality Bites, 1994; Do You Sleep?, 1995; Waiting for Wednesday, 1996; Taffy, 1996; I Do, 1997; Let's Forget About It, 1998. *Honours:* BRIT Award, Best International Newcomer, 1995. *Current Management:* Manage This!. *Address:* c/o Manage This!, 154 w 57th St # 133, New York, NY 10019, USA.

LOEFFLER Tony; b. 5 April 1947, Paterson, New Jersey, USA. Musician (guitar); Songwriter. m. 27 April 1968, 1 s., 2 d. *Education:* Psychology major. *Musical Education:* Self-taught. *Career:* Festival appearances include: Bay Shore Arts Festival, Long Island, New York, 1986; Rainbow Bash Festival, Sparta, New Jersey, 1993; Cross Rhythms Festival, Devon, UK, 1995, 1996, 1997; Sur Montreux Anniversary Jazz/Rock Festival, Switzerland, 1996, 1998; Tours throughout USA; Numerous television and radio appearances; Regular tours with Tony Loeffler and The Blue Angels. *Recordings:* 12 albums. *Publication:* Foundation (the Solid Rock Newsletter). *Memberships:* Recording Industry Asscn of America (RIAA); Gospel Music Asscn; Broadcast Music Inc. *Leisure interest:* Music. *Current Management:* Lord and Associates Music.

LOFGREN Nils; b. 21 June 1951, Chicago, Illinois, USA. Musician (guitar); Songwriter; Arranger; Singer. *Career:* Member, Grin, 1970s; Solo artiste, 1974-; Appearances with Neil Young and Crazy Horse, including Tonight's The Night tour, 1973; Trans tour, 1983; Joined Bruce Springsteen's E Street Band, 1984-; Continues as solo artist. *Recordings:* Albums: Nils Lofgren, 1975; Back It Up (official bootleg), 1976; Cry Tough, 1976; I Came To Dance, 1977; Night After Night, 1977; Nils, 1979; Night Fades Away, 1981; Wonderland, 1983; Flip, 1985; Code of The Road, 1986; Silver Lining, 1991; Crooked Lining, 1992; Everybreath, 1994; Damaged Goods, 1995; Acoustic Live, 1997; with Bruce Springsteen and the E-Street Band: Live In New York City, 2001. *Current Management:* Anson Smith Management, 3 Bethesda Metro Center, Suite 505, Bethesda, MD 20814, USA.

LOGGINS Kenny (Kenneth Clarke); b. 7 Jan. 1947, Everett, Washington, USA. Singer; Songwriter; Musician (guitar). m. Eva Ein, 31 Dec. 1976, divorced. *Musical Education:* Music, Pasadena City College. *Career:* Member, Gator Creek; Second Helping; Duo, Loggins and Messina (with Jim Messina), 1971–76; Solo artist, songwriter, 1977-. *Compositions include:* House At Pooh Corner, recorded by Nitty Gritty Dirt Band, 1971; Your Mama Don't Dance, recorded by Loggins and Messina, Elvis Presley, Poison, 1973; Danny's Song, recorded by Annne Murray; Co-writer with Michael McDonald, What A Fool Believes, recorded by Doobie Brothers (No. 1, USA), 1979; Co-writer with Melissa Manchester, Whenever I Call You Friend, 1979. *Recordings:* Hit singles include: This Is It, 1980; I'm Alright, from film Caddyshack, 1980; Don't Fight It, duet with Steve Perry, 1982; Heart To Heart, 1983; Footloose, from film Footloose (No. 1, USA), 1984; Danger Zone, from film Top Gun (No. 2, US), 1986; Meet Me Half Way, from film Over The Top, 1987; Nobody's Fool, from film Caddyshack 2, 1988; Solo: Selections from December, 1998; Albums: with Loggins and Messina: Kenny Loggins With Jim Messina Sittin' In, 1971; Loggins and Messina, 1972; Full Sail, 1973; On Stage, 1974; Mother Lode, 1974; So Fine, 1975; Native Sons, 1976; Finale, 1977; The Best of Friends, 1977; Solo albums: Celebrate Me Home, 1977; Nightwatch, 1978; Keep The Fire, 1979; Kenny Loggins:- Alive, 1980; High Adventure, 1982; Footloose, film soundtrack (No. 1, USA) 1984; Vox Humana, 1985; Top Gun, film soundtrack (No. 1, USA) 1986; Back To Avalon, 1987; Kenny Loggins On Broadway, 1988; Leap of Faith, 1991; Outside – From The Redwoods, 1993; Return to Pooh Corner, 1994; The Unimaginable Life, 1997; December, 1998; More Songs From Pooh Corner, 2000; Contributor, We Are The World, USA For Africa, 1985. *Honours:* Grammy, Song of The Year, What A

Fool Believes, 1980; Best Pop Vocal Performance, This Is It, 1981; Platinum and Gold discs. *Current Management:* Next Step, 105 Foothill Rd, Ojai, CA 93023, USA.

LOHAN Sinead; b. 21 June 1971, Cork City, Ireland. Singer; Musician. *Musical Education:* Self-taught Guitar; Piano Lessons. *Career:* Toured with Womans Heart, Support to Paul Brady, 1995, The Blue Nile, 1996, Joan Baez, 1997; Appearance at Newport Folk Festival, 1997. *Compositions include:* Who Do You Think I Am; Sailing By; Everything Around Me is Changing; Out of the Woods. *Recordings:* Albums: Who Do You Think I Am, 1995; No Mermaid, 1998; Also appears on: Womans Heart 2, 1995; Loving Time, 1997. *Honours:* Triple Platinum; Best Newcomer, Irish National Entertainment Awards. *Leisure interests:* Reading; Walking. *Current Management:* Pat Egan. *Address:* c/o Merchants Court 24, Merchants Quay, Dublin 8, Ireland.

LOHRER Eric; b. 15 Feb. 1965, Paris, France. Jazz Musician (guitar); Composer. 1 s. *Education:* Philosophy, Lycée Henri IV; La Sorbonne, Paris. *Musical Education:* Self-taught. *Career:* Bandleader for groups Eric Lohrer Trio, Open Air, 1987–93; Red Whale, 1991–95; Olympic Gramofón, solo programme based on music of Theolonius Monk, 1995–96; Tours, festivals, France; Europe; Africa; Radio appearances: France Inter; France Musique; Europe 1; Television appearances: FR3; A2. *Recordings:* Eric Lohrer Trio, 1989; Queekegg, Red Whale, 1991; Dans Le Bleu, Eric Lohrer Trio, 1992; Attitudes, Open Air, 1992; Big One, Jean-Michel Pilc, 1993; Mozol, Red Whale, 1995. *Publications:* Time and Improvisation In Jazz Music, 1986. *Honours:* First Prize, soloist and band, Vienna International Jazz Contest, 1987; 2 Band Prizes: La Défense National Jazz Contest, 1988, 1989. *Memberships:* SACEM; SPEDIDAM. *Current Management:* Supernova. *Address:* 94 rue du Mail, 95310 St Ouen L'Aumône, France.

LOKKE LARSEN Birgit; b. 11 July 1967, Fr-Vaerk, Denmark. School teacher; Musician (drums, percussion). *Education:* School teacher, Biology, Arts, 1993. *Musical Education:* Private lessons: Adam Nussbaum; Alex Riel; Participated in several drum clinics; Played at 1991 Jazz Award presentations. *Career:* Toured with: Savage Rose; Embla; The Big Bang with Palle Danielson, Lars Jansson, Han Bennink, Alex Riel; NORDICAE with Niels Petter Molvaer, Eivin Aarset, Veslemoy Solberg, Sven Ohrvik, Rune Arnsen and Edvard Askeland; ONCE with Anders Jormin, Thomas Gustafsson; SOUK with Kim Kristensen and Thomas Agergaard; April Light Orchestra (Nordic all-women big band); Member of The Ship, tour of Denmark, Norway, Sweden and Greenland, where Marilyn Mazur composed the music; Member of trio with Hugo Rasmussen and Arne Forchammer. *Composition:* Dans Under Broen; Dansen; Ballovira; music for: play, Mac and Beth, Copenhagen, 1997; play, Minotaurus, Copenhagen, 1999. *Recordings:* Moonchild, with Savage Rose, 1992; Strength of The Runes, with Veslemoy Solberg, 1996; Pulse of Time, with Kim Kristensen, 1999; Kjaerestebilder, with Veslemoy Solberg, 1999; Assimilation with Arne Forchhammer, 2000. *Honour:* Highest award, Arts examination.

LOLLIO Lou; b. 30 Dec. 1949, West Virginia, USA. Vocals; Musician (guitar, piano); Man. m. Jean Lollio, 11 Nov. 1990. *Career:* Film: A Star Is Born, 1978; Up In Smoke, 1979; Blues Brothers Movie, 1980; Fantasy Island, 1981; The Mystery Train, Nashville, 1984; Supporting act for Van Halen, 1985; Opening Act for Little Richard, 1984; Buffalo Springfield Revisited Tour, 1986. *Recordings:* Music producer, Film: LA's Lost Angels, 1969. *Publications:* Andy Warhol interview. *Memberships:* Screen Actors Guild (SAG); AFTRA; American Federation of Television and Radio Artistes; ASCAP. *Current Management:* J Lollio Management. *Address:* 264 So Lacienega Bl #327, Beverly Hills, CA 90211, USA.

LOMAS Roger David; b. 8 Oct. 1948, Coventry, England. Record Prod. m. Linda Lomas, 21 Dec. 1966, 2 s., 1 d. *Musical Education:* Self-taught. *Career:* Record producer for: The Specials; Bad Manners; The Selecter; Desmond Dekker; The Bodysnatchers; The Modettes; Special-Beat; Roy Wood. *Recordings:* 17 hit singles, 10 albums include: with Bad Manners: Can Can; Special Brew; My Girl Lollipop; Walking In The Sunshine; Lip Up Fatty; with The Selecter: On My Radio; Missing Words; Roy Wood, I Wish it Could be Christmas Everyday, live version; 18 hit singles altogether; Recent productions: for The Specials: Skinhead Girl, 2000; Conquering Role, 2001. *Honours:* Gold and Silver awards for Bad Manners and Selecter albums and singles. *Membership:* PRS. *Leisure interest:* Snooker. *Address:* 35 Dillotford Ave, Coventry, West Midlands CV3 5DR, England.

LOMAX John; b. 20 Aug. 1944. Artist Management; International Consultant; Journalist. m. Melanie Wells, 1 s., 1 d. *Education:* BA, MSLS, University of Texas, Austin. *Career:* A and R Consultant, Demon Records; Manage 3 Acts; Freelance Writer, Country Music International; Founder, President, SFL Tapes and Discs, Music City Exporters. *Recordings:* Dulcimer Deluxe; Dulcimer Player; Dulcimer Sessions. *Publications:* Nashville: Music City, USA; The Country Music Book. *Honour:* Leadership Music, 1998. *Memberships:* CMA; IMF; NARAS, Board of Governors, Nashville Chapter; NEA; CMAA. *Leisure interests:*

Reading; Photography; Travel. *Current Management:* Kasey Chambers, EMI Australia and Asylum (US/Canada).

LONGNON Jean-Loup; b. 2 Feb. 1953, Paris, France. Musician (trumpet, piano); Vocalist; Arranger; Composer; Conductor. *Musical Education:* Self-taught trumpet, jazz. *Career:* Trumpet player, various bands and big bands; Soloist or bandleader performing in concerts, recording studios, jazz clubs, master classes, festivals, tours, TV, radio, in France; Throughout Europe; Turkey; Israel; Egypt; Tunisia; Morocco; Reunion Island; Mauritius; US; Cuba (Varandero Festival); Brazil; Played with artists including: Dizzy Gillespie; Stan Getz; Clark Terry; Arturo Sandoval; Martial Solal; Stéphane Grappelli; Didier Lockwood; Michel Petrucciani; Antoine Hervé; Kenny Clarke; Chet Baker; Winton Marsalis; Michel Legrand. *Compositions:* Torride, Aquarelles, Jazz à Paris, Nathalie... Un Matin; Variations on John Coltrane themes (commissioned by National Jazz Orchestra); Suite for Orchestra on Dizzy Gillespie (commissioned by Michel Legrand for television show Grand Echiquier); Symphonic poem L'Ours (commissioned by Concert Arban brass quintet and Martin Publications); Cyclades suite for jazz soloist and symphonic orchestra (commissioned by Musique Française d'Aujourdhui). *Recordings:* include: Jean-Loup Longnon and His New York Orchestra; Bop Dreamer, CD, 1998. *Honours:* Winner, Festival de la Défense, Paris, 1977; Django Reinhardt Prize; Boris Vian Prize; European Audivisual Grand Prix; Django d'Or, 1995. *Membership:* SACEM. *Leisure interest:* Travel. *Address:* 52 Blvd Saint Germain, 75005 Paris, France.

LOPES Lisa Nicole, (Left Eye); b. 27 May 1971, Philadelphia, Pennsylvania, USA. Singer; Rapper. *Career:* Began as rapper in Philadelphia; Member, TLC; Appeared on single Not Tonight – The Remix, with Missy Elliot; Host, MTV show The Cut; Appeared on Method Man's album track Cradle Rock; Owner, record company Left Eye Productions; Owner, publishing company, U.N.I. Publishing Inc; Working on own solo album with Wyclef Jean and The Bandits. *Recordings:* Singles: Get It Up, 1993; Creep (No. 1, USA), 1994; Waterfalls (No. 1, USA), 1995; Red Light Special, 1995; Diggin On You, 1995; No Scrubs (No. 1, USA), 1999; Unpretty (No. 1, USA), 1999; Dear Lie, 1999; with Melanie C: Never Be The Same Again (No. 1, UK), 2000; Albums: Crazysexycool, 1994; Fanmail, 1999; Solo album: Supernova, 2001. *Honours:* Grammy Awards, Best R & B Performance by Duo/Group; Best R & B Album; 2 Lady of Soul Awards; 2 Billboard Music Awards; 3 Soul Train Awards; Blockbuster Entertainment Award; 4 MTV Music Video Awards, for Waterfalls; BRIT Award, Best International Group, 2000.

LOPEZ Jennifer, (J Lo); b. 24 July 1970, The Bronx, New York, USA, Vocalist; Actor; Dancer; Songwriter. m. Chris Judd. *Career:* Latin singer; Films include: Money Train; My Family; Selena; Blood and Wine; Anaconda; U Turn; Out of Sight; Antz (voiceover); The Cell; Angel Eyes; The Wedding Planner; Enough; Collaborations: Ja Rule; Big Pun; Fat Joe. *Recordings:* Albums: On The 6, 1999, J-Lo, 2001, J To Tha L-O! (remixes), 2002; Singles: If You Had My Love, Waiting For Tonight, 1999; Feelin' So Good, Love Don't Cost A Thing, 2000; Play, Ain't It Funny, I'm Real, 2001; features on: All-Star Tribute benefit single What's Going On. *Honours:* Several nominations in MTV Video Music Awards, 1999; Nominated for 2 American Music Awards, 2000; Grammy nomination, Best Dance Recording, 2000, 2001; Billboard Latin Award, Hot Latin Track of The Year, 2000; FHM Magazine, 100 Sexiest Women In The World, First place; Latin Grammy nomination; MTV Video Music Award, Best Dance Video, 2000; VH1/Vogue Fashion Awards, Versace Award, 2000; MTV Video Music Awards, 2 nominations, 2001; MTV Europe Music Award, Best Female Act, 2001; American Music Award, nomination 2002. *Internet:* www.jenniferlopez.com.

LOPEZ Orlando 'Cachaito', (Orlando Lopez Vergara); b. 1933, Havana, Cuba. Musician (double bass). *Career:* Born into a family with a long tradition of double bass virtuosity (son of Orestes López and nephew of Israel 'Cachao' López), his career has spanned popular, classical and jazz genres; Collaborations: Omara Portuondo; Ibrahim Ferrer; Rubén González; César Portillo de la Luz; Los Zafiros; Chucho Valdes; Paquito D'Rivera; Played on most of the Buena Vista Social Club series of recordings and with the Afro-Cuban All-Stars; Appeared in Wim Wenders' documentary Buena Vista Social Club; Solo album released, 2001. *Recordings:* recent Albums: Buena Vista Social Club, 1997; Cachaito, 2001; features on Introducing Santiago, Chieftains, 1996; Tibiri Tabara, Sierra Maestra, 1997; Rubén González, 1997; Toda Cuba Le Gusta (with Afro Cuban All-Stars), 1997; Buena Vista Social Club Presents Ibrahim Ferrer, 1999; Distinto Diferente (with Afro Cuban All-Stars), 1999; Buena Vista Social Club Presents Omara Portuonda, 2000; Chanchullo (with Rubén González), 2000. *Honours:* BBC World Music Album of the Year (Americas), Cachaito, 2002; BBC World Music Critics Award nominee, Cachaito, 2002. *Address:* c/o World Circuit Ltd, First Floor, Shoreditch Stables, 138 Kingsland Rd, London, E2 8DY, England.

LOPEZ Ramon; b. 6 Aug. 1961, Alicante, Spain. Musician (drums, tabla). m. Pilar Dominguez, 20 March 1992, 1 s. *Education:* Electronics specialist.

Musical Education: Self-taught, drums, 1973–; Tabla student of Krishna Govinda K C (Lucknow, India). *Career:* Teacher, Indian and modal music, Paris Conservatoire (CNSMDP); Plays with: Claude Tchamitchian; Philippe Deschepper; Enrico Rava; Howard Johnson; Jean-Marc Padovani; Yves Robert; François Cotinaud; Jean-Marie Machado; J F Jenny Clark; Glenn Ferris; Daunik Lazro; Paul Rogers; Sophia Domancich; New groups, Onj 97/2000, National Orchestra of Jazz, conducted by Didier Levallet; Many appearances, Radio France; Television: M6 Jazz 6; Cable Paris Premiere: Capitale Jazz; F3, F3 Region; RTVE (Spain); RTSR (Switzerland); RTBF (Belgium); TRI (Indonesia); WDR (Germany); Druskininkai TV, Baltic TV (Lithuania); Armenia TV. *Recordings:* Opera (with Frantois Cotinaud), 1993; Princesse, Frantois Cotinaud Quartet, 1990; Face Au Silence, Double Face, 1991; Pyramides (featuring Enrico Rava), 1992; Lousadzak, Claude Tchamitchian Septet, 1994; Portraits, Patrice Thomas Quartet, 1995; With Marc Steckar: Elephant Tuba Horde, 1987; Steckar Trinity, 1988; Tubakoustic, 1989; Jean-Marie Machado; Denis Colin Trio; Recent recordings: Eleven Drums Songs, 1998; Songs of The Spanish Civil War, 2000. *Publications:* La Region Internacional, 17 Aug 1993; Batteur Magazine, no 44, Mar 1992; Informacion de Alicante, Nov 1985; Jan 1986; July 1986; Mar 1990. *Memberships:* SACEM; SACD; SPEDIDAM; CNSMDP. *Leisure interest:* Photography. *Current Management:* Jazz Bank Ass, Ramon Lopez.

LOPEZ Trini; b. 15 May 1937, Dallas, Texas, USA. Singer; Musician (guitar). *Career:* Nightclub performer, debut appearance, 1967; Recorded for Frank Sinatra, 1963–68; World-wide entertainer, 1963–; Film roles include: Marriage On The Rocks; A Poppy Is Also A Flower; The Dirty Dozen; Antonio; Television appearances: Adam 12; The Reluctant Heroes; If I Had A Hammer. *Recordings include:* If I Had A Hammer; Trini Lopez Live At PJ's; More Trini Lopez At PJ's By Popular Demand; Trini Lopez In London; Trini Lopez Now; Trini Lopez Live At Basin Street East; Trini Lopez Greatest Hits; Trini – Transformed By Time; The Best of Trini Lopez; Hit singles include: I'm Coming Home Cindy; Michael; Lemon Tree; Kansas City; If I Had A Hammer; America; La Bamba. *Honours:* Goodwill Ambassador for US; Honoured by Congress for work in international relations; Gold disc, If I Had A Hammer. *Memberships:* AFofM; SAG. *Leisure interests:* Tennis; Golf. *Current Management:* Ray Lawrence Ltd, Studio City, CA, USA. *Address:* 1139 Abrigo, Palm Springs, CA 92262, USA.

LOPEZ-REAL Carlos Enrique; b. 25 Oct. 1969, Nairobi, Kenya. Musician (saxophone); Composer. *Education:* Psychology, Philosophy, Oxford University. *Musical Education:* Guildhall School of Music and Drama, post-graduate jazz and studio. *Career:* Leader, own quartet at festivals including Glastonbury, Oxford; Studied with Jean Toussaint; Played with Django Bates and Norma Winstone; Venues include Barbican Concert Hall; London clubs include Jazz Café, Vortex. *Compositions:* Folk Song; Para Michele; Mtengene; Soundtracks include film In Profile. *Recordings:* Dr Dig; Other sessions. *Memberships:* Musicians' Union; Clarinet and Saxophone Society. *Leisure interests:* Cooking; Film; Travel. *Address:* 38 Claverley Grove, Finchley, London N3 2DH, England.

LORD Jon; b. 9 June 1941, Leicester, England. Musician (keyboards). *Education:* Central School of Speech and Drama, London; London Drama Centre. *Career:* Member, groups including: Artwoods; Flowerpot Men; Founder member, Deep Purple, 1968–76; Member, Paice Ashton Lord, 1976–77; Member, Whitesnake, 1978–84; Also solo recording artiste; Member, Deep Purple, 1984–; World-wide tours with Deep Purple and Whitesnake; Major concerts include: with Deep Purple: USA; Japan; UK; Australia; Europe; Knebworth Festival; with Whitesnake: Reading Festival, 1979, 1980; Tours with AC/DC, Jethro Tull, USA, 1980; Monsters of Rock Festival, 1981, 1983. *Recordings:* All recordings by Deep Purple; Albums: with Ashton and Lord: First of The Big Bands, 1974; with Paice Ashton Lord: Malice In Wonderland, 1977; with Whitesnake: Trouble, 1978; Lovehunter, 1979; Ready An'Willing, 1980; Live In The Heart of The City, 1980; Come and Get It, 1981; Saints 'N' Sinners, 1982; Slide It In, 1984; Solo albums: Gemini Suite, 1970; Windows, 1974; Sarabande, 1976; Before I Forget, 1982; Country Diary of An Edwardian Lady, 1986; Pictured Within, 1997; Abandon, 1998; Anthems, 2000; Also recorded with: Tommy Bolin; Graham Bonnet; Sam Brown; David Gilmour; George Harrison; Alvin Lee; Bernie Marsden; Nazareth; Cozy Powell. *Current Management:* Thames Talent, 45 E Putnam Ave, Greenwich, CT 06830, USA. *Address:* Nr Henley-on-Thames, Oxfordshire, England.

LOREN Gina, (Gina Bellamy-Loren); b. 23 April 1957, Dallas, Texas, USA. Record Co Exec.; Record Prod.; Singer; Songwriter. *Education:* Hospital/Surgical Nursing Studies, University of Texas, 1980–82; Graduate, Degree in Geology, University of Texas, Arlington. *Musical Education:* Classical guitar, voice, music composition. *Career:* Began recording, singing career, aged 13; Duet concerts with some radio and television appearances; Stand-in actor on television series Dallas;

Organized Scootertunes Incorporated, Scooter Records, Scooter Productions and J B Quantum Music; Participated in the live radio broadcast of Willie Nelson's Farm Aid, 1994. *Recordings:* True Love Conquers All, Gina Bellamy-Loren, 1994; The Fever, The Fever (contemporary Country group), 1995; Feelings of Christmas/Santa's All Star Revue, 1996; Lavender Blue, 1997; Wild Honey, 1999; Favorites, 2000. *Memberships:* AFofM; ASCAP; BMI; NARAS. *Leisure interests:* Floral design; Gourmet cooking; Travel; Gardening; Studying foreign languages. *Current Management:* Scootertunes Inc, PO Box 610166, Dallas, TX 75261, USA. *Internet:* www.scootertunes.com.

LOTZ Rainer E; b. 27 Aug. 1937, Hamburg, Germany. Discographer; Music Historian; Engineer; Economist. m. Birgit Lotz, 1 s., 3 d. *Education:* Master, Mechanical Engineering, Karlsruhe Technical University; Doctorate in Economics, Tübingen University; Postgraduate Study in Development Policy, Berlin Institute for Development Policy. *Career:* Technical Adviser, IFCT, Bangkok, Thailand; Acting Chief of Operations, East African Development Bank, Kampala, Uganda; Head, Latin America Department, Federal German Ministry of Economic Cooperation and Development. *Recordings:* Compiler of CDs and LPs including: Harlequin anthology of the history of jazz and dance music. *Publications:* 140 articles in scholarly journals; 50 sleeve notes for CDs and LPs; Acknowledgements in 140 books by other authors; Publisher of 30 books; author of 80 monographs including Grammophonplatten aus der Ragtime-Ära, 1979; German Ragtime and Prehistory of Jazz: Vol. 1: The Sound Documents, 1985; The AFRS Jubilee Show: A Discography Vols 1 and 2, 1985; Mike Danzi: The Story of an American Musician in Berlin 1925–39, 1986; Co-editor, Under the Imperial Carpet: Essays in Black History, 1987; The Banjo on Record: A Bio-Discography, 1993; Hitler's Airwaves: The Inside Story of Nazi Radio Broadcasting and Propaganda Swing, 1997; Black People: Entertainers of African Descent in Europe and Germany, 1997; Editor of the German National Discography. *Honour:* ARSC Lifetime Achievement Award, for published recorded sound research, 1998. *Memberships:* IASA; IAJRC; ARSC. *Address:* Jean Paul Str 6, 53173 Bonn, Germany.

LOUIS Eric; b. 28 Oct. 1959, Malo Les Bains, France. Musician (trombone); Music Teacher. 1 d. *Musical Education:* Conservatoires de Perpignan, 1978; St Quentin, 1979; Ville De Paris, 1980. *Career:* Played concerts with: Diana Ross; Charles Aznavour; Jerry Lewis; Lambert Wilson; Julia Migenes-Johnson; Member, jazz groups with: Michel Legrand; Patrice Caratini; Luc Lemasne; Yanko Nilovic; Laurent Cuny; 3 tours Japan with Raymond Lefèvre; Numerous revues and shows include: Cats; 42nd Street; Cabaret; Folies Bergères; Numerous appearances on French television include 4 telethons (1988–94); Several other musical and theatrical works; Performed with Orchestre Philharmonique d'Europe, Orchestre du Luxembourg and various other orchestras; Music teacher in Guéret, 1981–82; Lucé, 1988–89; Gentilly, 1989–90; Chatou, 1991–92. *Recordings for:* Lisa Minelli; Charles Aznavour; Julia Migenes-Johnson; Pierre Perret; Georges Aperghis; Thomas Fersen; André Hoder. *Leisure interests:* Wine (Bordeaux); Horses. *Address:* 23 Ave Gütenberg, 92800 Puteaux, France.

LOUISE (Louise Redknapp), (Louise Nurding); b. 1974, London, England. Singer. m. Jamie Redknapp. *Education:* Italia Conti Stage School. *Career:* Singer, UK all-female vocal group, Eternal, 1992–95; Solo artiste, 1995-. *Recordings:* Album: with Eternal: Always and Forever, 1993; Solo Albums: Louise, 1996; Woman In Me, 1997; Elbow Beach, 2000; Best Of, 2001; Hit singles: with Eternal: Stay, 1993; Save Your Love, 1994; Just A Step From Heaven, 1994; Oh Baby I, 1994; Solo hits: Light of My Life, 1995; In Walked Love, 1996; Naked, 1996; Undivided Love, 1996; One Kiss From Heaven, 1996; Arms Around The World, 1997; Let's Go Round Again, 1997; All That Matters, 1998; 2 Faced, 2000; Beautiful Inside, 2000; Stuck In The Middle With You, 2001. *Honours:* 4 BRIT Award Nominations; Smash Hits Award. *Current Management:* First Avenue Management, The Courtyard, 42 Colwith Rd, London W6 4EY, England.

LOURAU Julien; b. 2 March 1970, Paris, France. Musician (saxophone). 1 d. *Career:* Performed at Marciac Festival; Vienna Festival; Blue Note, New York City; Hot Brass, Paris; Auditorium des Halles, Paris; Festival Banlieues Bleues; Radio-France. *Recordings:* Appears on: Scampi Fritti, 1994; Turtle's Dream, 1994; Who Used to Dance, 1996; Mad Nomad, 1997. *Publications:* A Turtle's Dream; Abbey Lincoln; Bojan Z Quartet; Julien Lourau Groove Gang. *Honour:* First prize, soloist, Concours de la Défense, 1993. *Current Management:* Carine Tedesco, Artalent. *Address:* 15 Passage de la Main D'Or, 75011 Paris, France.

LOUVIN Charlie; b. 7 July 1927, Alabama, USA. Singer. *Career:* Appearances include: Nashville Now; Ralph Emery Show; At The Ryman; Grand Ole Opry Live; Backstage At The Opry. *Recordings:* See The Big Man Cry; Will You Visit Me On Sundays? Cry Myself To Sleep; Albums: and That's The Gospel, 1991; Hoping That Your Hoping, 1992; Live in Holland, 1995; Longest Train, 1996. *Honours:* Alabama Music Hall of Fame; Songwriters Hall of Fame; Grammy Award; 4 Country Music Hall

of Fame Nominations. *Memberships:* AFofM; AFTRA. *Leisure interests:* Fishing; Golf. *Current Management:* Susie Reed, Mountain Magic Talent. *Address:* PO Box 140324, Nashville, TN 37214, USA.

LOVANO Joe; b. 29 Dec. 1952, Ohio, USA. Musician (tenor saxophone, clarinet, bass clarinet); Composer. m. Judi Silvano, 30 Sept. 1984. *Education:* Studied with father, Tony Lovano. *Musical Education:* Berklee College of Music, Boston. *Career:* Toured with: Woody Herman Big Band; Thad Jones-Mel Lewis Orchestra; John Scofield Quartet; Paul Motian Trio (with Bill Frisell); Formed own bands, tours world-wide. *Recordings:* Rush Hour; Tenor Legacy; Universal Language Sextet; Tenor Legacy, 1993; Ten Tales, 1994; Quartets: Live at the Village Vanguard, 1994; Celebrating Sinatra, 1996; Flying Colours, 1997; Trio Fascination, 1998; Friendly Fire, 1999; Unknown Voyage, 2000; 52nd Street Themes, 2000; Flights of Fancy, 2001; Recorded with Joshua Redman. *Honours:* Jazz Artist of The Year, Downbeat Magazine Critics Poll, 1995. *Membership:* AFofM. *Current Management:* The Merlin Company.

LOVE Courtney; b. 9 July 1964. Singer; Musician (guitar); Actor. m. Kurt Cobain, 24 Feb. 1992, deceased, 1 d. *Career:* Member, Faith No More, 1 year; Founder, singer/guitarist, Hole, 1991–; Tours include: Support tour to Nine Inch Nails; Reading Festival, 1994, 1995; Film appearances: Straight To Hell; Sid and Nancy; Feeling Minnesota; The People vs Larry Flynt; Man on the Moon. *Recordings:* Albums: Pretty On The Inside, 1991; Live Through This, 1994; Celebrity Skin, 1998; Singles: Doll Parts, 1994; Ask for It, 1995; Celebrity Skin, 1998; Malibu, 1998; Awful, 1999. *Current Management:* Q-Prime Inc, 729 Seventh Ave, 14th Floor, New York, NY 10019, USA.

LOVE Mike; b. 15 March 1941, Baldwin Hills, California, USA. Singer. *Career:* Member, Beach Boys, 1961–; Own band, Endless Summer, 1981; Numerous tours, concerts, include: The Beach Boys Summer Spectacular, Hollywood Bowl, 1966; UNICEF concert, Paris, 1967; Carnegie Hall, 1971; Royal Festival Hall, London, 1972; Grand Gala Du Disque, Amsterdam, 1972; Wembley Stadium, 1980; Knebworth Festival, 1980; Independence Day concerts, Washington DC, 1980s; Presidential Inaugural Gala, for President Reagan, 1985; Live Aid, Philadelphia, 1985; Tour with Chicago, 1989; Tour, supported by The Everly Brothers, 1991. *Compositions include:* Co-writer, theme for film: Almost Summer, 1978; Co-writer, song: Rock 'n' Roll To The Rescue, 1986. *Recordings:* Albums include: Surfin' Safari, 1962; Surfer Girl, 1963; Little Deuce Coupe, 1963; Shut Down Vol. 2; All Summer Long, 1964; Christmas Album, 1964; The Beach Boys Today!, 1965; Summer Days (and Summer Nights), 1965; Beach Boys Party, 1966; Pet Sounds, 1966; Smiley Smile, 1967; Wild Honey, 1968; Friends, 1968; 20/20, 1969; Sunflower, 1970; Carl and The Passions/So Tough, 1972; Holland, 1973; Endless Summer (No. 1, USA), 1974; 15 Big Ones, 1976; The Beach Boys Love You, 1977; MIU, 1978; LA (Light Album), 1980; The Beach Boys, 1985; Still Cruisin', 1989; Two Rooms, 1991; Summer In Paradise, 1992; Good Vibrations (box set), 1993; Stars and Stripes Vol. 1, 1996; Ultimate Christmas, 1998; Greatest Hits, Vol. 2, 1999; Numerous compilations; Solo album: Looking Back With Love, 1981; Singles include: Surfin' USA, 1963; Fun Fun Fun, 1964; I Get Around (No. 1, USA), 1964; When I Grow Up (To Be A Man), 1964; Dance Dance Dance, 1965; Help Me Rhonda (No. 1, USA), 1965; California Girls, 1965; The Little Girl I Once Knew, 1965; Barbara Ann, 1966; Sloop John B, 1966; God Only Knows, 1966; Good Vibrations (No. 1, UK and US), 1966; Wouldn't It Be Nice, 1966; And Then I Kissed Her, 1967; Heroes and Villains, 1967; Wild Honey, 1967; Darlin', 1967; Friends, 1968; Do It Again (No. 1, UK), 1968; Bluebirds Over The Mountain, 1968; I Can Hear Music, 1969; Break Away, 1969; Cottonfields, 1970; Sail On Sailor, 1973; California Saga, 1973; Rock and Roll Music, 1976; Here Comes The Night, 1979; Lady Lynda, 1979; Good Timin', 1979; Come Go With Me, 1982; Getcha Back, 1985; California Dreaming, 1986; Kokomo (No. 1, UK), 1988. *Honours include:* Inducted into Rock and Roll Hall of Fame, 1988; Special Award of Merit, American Music Awards, 1988. *Current Management:* Elliott Lott, 4860 San Jacinto Circle W, Fallbrook, CA 92026, USA.

LOVELESS Patty; b. 4 Jan. 1957, Pikeville, Kentucky, USA. Country Singer; Musician (guitar). m. (1) Terry Lovelace, 1976, (2) Emory Gordy Jr, 1989. *Career:* Summer job singing with the Wilburn Brothers, 1971; Singer, nightclubs and hotels, North Carolina; Moved to Nashville, 1985; Worked with Vince Gill and Emmylou Harris, including CBS' 70th Anniversary of the Grand Ole Opry; Television appearances include: The Tonight Show; Late Night With Conan O'Brian; Good Morning America; ABC In Concert Country; Music City Tonight; The Road; TNN Country News; Grand Ole Opry Live. *Recordings:* Albums: Only What I Feel, 1992; When Fallen Angels Fly, 1995; The Trouble With The Truth, 1996; Long Stretch of Lonesome, 1998; Classics, 1999; Strong Heart, 2000; Mountain Soul, 2001; Singles include: Blame It On Your Heart; Nothin' But The Wheel; You Will; How Can I Help You Can Say Goodbye; You Don't Even Know Who I Am; Halfway Down; You Can Feel Bad; You Don't Seem To Miss Me. *Honours include:* Country Music Awards, 1993, 1995; Country Music Television Award, Female Artist of the Year, 1994; Real Country Listener Award, Female Vocalist of the Year, 1995; Academy of Country Music Award, 1997;

Nominations for CMA, ACM and Grammy awards, 1994-. *Current Management:* Fitzgerald-Hartley Co, 1908 Wedgewood Ave, Nashville, TN 37212, USA.

LOVEMUSCLE Johnny; b. 3 April 1961, Hounslow, England. Record Prod.; Writer; Designer; Actor; Singer. *Education:* Design Degree. *Musical Education:* Self-taught. *Career:* Founder, The Rhythm Men, 1982; Founder, The Adventures of Johnny Lovemuscle, 1984; Formed partnership with Martin Noakes, as producers for: Gene and Jim Are Into Shakes; Afrikadelic; Little Caesar, 1988; Managed by Pete Waterman; Published by Warner Chappell. *Recordings:* Shake! (How About A Sampling Gene?); The Whole of The Moon; Piti Pata; Eez-Zee-Boo-Gie. *Honour:* BFI Nomination, Best New Act, 1988. *Memberships:* Musicians' Union; PRS; Equity. *Leisure interests:* Nightclubs; Horseracing. *Current Management:* Management To The Stars. *Address:* 28–30 Ecton Rd, Addlestone, Surrey KT15 1UE, England.

LOVERING David; b. 6 Dec. 1961, Boston, Massachusetts, USA. Musician (Drums). *Career:* Member, The Pixies; Early support slots to Throwing Muses; Numerous tours and festival appearances; Some television appearances; Band split, 1993; Formed The Martinis with Joey Santiago, 1995. *Recordings:* Singles: Gigantic, 1988; Monkey Gone to Heaven, 1989; Here Comes Your Man, 1989; Velouria, 1990; Dig for Fire, 1990; Planet of Sound, 1991 Alec Eiffel, 1991; Head On, 1991; Debaser, 1997; Albums: Come on Pilgrim, 1987; Surfer Rosa, 1988; Doolittle, 1989; Bossanova, 1990; Trompe le Monde, 1991; Death To The Pixies, 1997; Live At The BBC, 2000; Complete B-Sides, 2001.

LOVETT Lyle; b. 1 Nov. 1957, Klein, Texas, USA. Singer; Songwriter; Actor. m. Julia Roberts, 1993, divorced 1995. *Career:* Backing vocalist, Nanci Griffith, 1985; Solo singer, songwriter, 1986–; Television appearances include: Late Night With David Letterman, 1992, 1993; The Tonight Show, NBC TV, 1993; Willie Nelson – The Big Six-O, CBS TV, 1993; Regular US tours; Film appearances: The Player, 1992; Short Cuts, 1993. *Recordings:* Albums: Lyle Lovett, 1986; Pontiac, 1988; Lyle Lovett and His Large Band, 1989; Joshua Judges Ruth, 1992; Leap of Faith (soundtrack), 1992; I Love Everybody, 1994; Road to Ensenada, 1996; Step Inside This House, 1998; Live in Texas, 1999; Can't Resist It, 1999; Dr T and The Women, 2000; Backing vocalist, The Last of The True Believers, Nanci Griffith, 1985; Great Big Boy, Leo Kottke, 1991; Producer, King Tears, Walter Hyatt, 1990; Contributor, Deadicated (collection of Grateful Dead covers), 1991. *Honours include:* Grammy nomination, Male Country Vocal Performance, 2000. *Current Management:* Vector Management, PO Box 128037, Nashville, TN 37212, USA.

LOVSIN Peter; b. 27 June 1955, Ljubljana, Slovenia. Singer; Songwriter. m. Darija Lovsin, 21 Dec. 1980, 1 s., 1 d. *Education:* Faculty for Journalism. *Career:* Lead singer, punk bands: Pankrti, 1977–87; Sokoli, 1988–93; Currently solo, with support band Vitezi Om'a (The Divers). *Recordings:* 6 albums with Pankrti; 3 with Sokoli; 2 solo albums. *Publication:* Poetry: In The Service of Rock 'n' Roll. *Honour:* Croatian Youth Organisation Awards, 1980. *Leisure interests:* Football; Skiing. *Current Management:* Tales, Lovsin in Ostali. *Address:* Zadruzna 1, 61000 Ljubljana, Slovenia.

LOWE Christopher Sean; b. 4 Oct. 1959, Blackpool, Lancashire, England. *Education:* Architecture, Liverpool University. *Career:* Met Neil Tennant, founded West End, renamed Pet Shop Boys, 1981; TV special: Love Me Tender, 1987; Film: It Couldn't Happen Here, 1988; Benefit concert, Piccadilly Theatre, 1988; Television: Wogan; Top of The Pops, 1988; Tour, Hong Kong, Japan, Britain, 1988; USA: With Electronic, Dodgers Stadium; Mayan Theatre, Los Angeles; TV: Arsenio Hall Show, 1990; Performance Tour: Japan; USA; Canada; Europe; UK; Eire, 1991; 2 weeks, Simon Bates Show, Radio One, 1991, 1992; Launched own record label: Spaghetti, 1991; Concert, Heaven Nightclub, 1991; South Bank Show, 1992; Hacienda Club, Manchester, 1992; Roseland, New York, 1992; Opening, Russian MTV, 1993; Songwriter, producer, artists include: Liza Minelli; Dusty Springfield; Patsy Kensit; Boy George; Electronic; Musical: Closer To Heaven, opened London, 2001. *Recordings:* Albums: Please, 1986; Disco, 1986; Actually, 1987; Introspective, 1988; Behaviour, 1990; Discography, 1991; Very, 1993; Relentless, 1993; Seriously, 1994; Alternative, 1995; Bilingual, 1996; Nightlife, 1999; Singles: West End Girls (No. 1, UK and US), 1985; Love Comes Quickly, 1986; Suburbia, 1986; It's A Sin (No. 1, UK), 1987; with Dusty Springfield: What Have I Done To Deserve This, 1987; Rent, 1987; Always On My Mind (Christmas No. 1, UK), 1987; Heart (No. 1, UK), 1988; Domino Dancing, 1988; Left To My Own Devices, 1988; It's Alright, 1989; So Hard, 1990; Being Boring, 1990; Where The Streets Have No Name, 1991; Jealousy, 1991; DJ Culture, 1991; Was It Worth It?, 1991; Can You Forgive Her, 1993; Go West, 1993; I Wouldn't Normally Do This Kind of Thing, 1993; Yesterday When I Was Mad, 1994; Liberation, 1994; Before, 1996; Se A Vida E, 1996; Single-Bilingual, 1996; Somewhere, 1997; Red Letter Day, 1997; I Don't Know What You Want, 1999; New York City Boy, 1999; You Only Tell Me You Love Me When You're Drunk, 2000. *Publication:* Pet Shop Boys, Literally, 1990. *Honours:* Ivor Novello Awards, 1987, 1988; BPI

Award, Best Single, 1987; Best Group, 1988; Berolina, Germany, 1988. *Current Management:* Pet Shop Boys Partnership, 8 Pembridge Studios, 27a Pembridge Villas, London W11 3EP, England.

LOWE Jez; b. 14 July 1955, Sunderland, England. Singer; Songwriter; Musician. *Education:* Sunderland Polytechnic. *Career:* Professional on folk circuit, 1980–; Toured, mainly Europe, USA. *Compositions:* for Fairport Convention: London Danny; Back In Durham Jail (10 cover versions); for The Clancy Brothers: Father Mallory's Dance. *Recordings:* over 10 solo albums including: Tou A Roue, 2001; Live At The Davy Lamp, 2001; Many others as session musician and with Bad Pennies. *Publications:* Songs of Jez Lowe, 1988; Songs of Jez Lowe Vol. II. *Honour:* PRS Composers In Education Award, 1993. *Membership:* Musicians' Union. *Current Management:* Lowe Life Music (UK); Nancy Carlin Associates (US). *Address:* c/o Lowe Life Music, PO Box 25, Horden, Peterlee, County Durham SR8 3YZ, England.

LOWE Nick; b. 24 March 1949, Woodchurch, Suffolk, England. Singer; Musician (bass); Record Prod. m. Carlene Carter, 15 Aug. 1979. *Career:* Member, Brinsley Schwarz, 1969–75; Rockpile (with Dave Edmunds), 1977–81; Leader, own band Nick Lowe and The Chaps, 1981; Founder, Little Village (with Ry Cooder, John Hiatt, Jim Keltner), 1992; Appearances include: Support to Van Morrison, 1970; Knebworth Festival, 1978; Support to Blondie, US, 1979; Camridge Folk Festival, 1988, 1995; Film appearance, Stardust, 1974; Documentary, Born Fighters, UK TV, 1979. *Recordings:* Albums: with Brinsley Schwarz: Brinsley Schwarz, 1970; Despite It All, 1970; Silver Pistol, 1972; Please Don't Ever Change, 1973; Original Golden Greats, 1974; The New Favourites of Brinsley Schwartz, 1974; Solo albums: Jesus of Cool, 1978; The Abominable Snowman, 1983; Nick's Knack, 1986; Basher – The Best of Nick Lowe, 1989; Party of One, 1990; The Impossible Bird, 1994; Dig My Mood, 1998; The Convincer, 2001; with Rockpile: Labour of Lust, 1979; Seconds of Pleasure, 1980; with His Cowboy Outfit: Nick Lowe and His Cowboy Outfit, 1984; Rose of England, 1985; with Little Village: Little Village, 1992; Singles include: I Love The Sound of Breaking Glass, 1978; Crackin' Up, 1979; Cruel To Be Kind, 1979; You Inspire Me, 1998; Albums as record producer: with Elvis Costello: My Aim Is True, 1977; This Year's Model, 1978; Armed Forces, 1979; Get Happy, 1980; Blood and Chocolate, 1986; with Carlene Carter: Musical Shapes, 1980; Blue Nun, 1981; Also: Chocs Away, Kursaal Flyers, 1975; Malpractice, Dr Feelgood, 1975; Get It, Dave Edmunds, 1976; Rhythm, Fabulous Thunderbirds, 1982; Riding With The King, John Hiatt, 1984; Katydids, Katydids, 1990; Contributor, film soundtracks: Rock 'n' Roll High School, 1978; Americathon, 1980. *Address:* c/o Riviera Global Record Productions, 20 Cromwell Mews, London SW7 2JY, England.

LU WIN Annabella, (Myant Myant Aye); b. 1966, Rangoon, Burma. Singer. *Career:* Singer, Bow Wow Wow, 1980–83; Solo artiste. *Recordings:* Albums: See Jungle..., 1981; I Want Candy, 1982; When The Going Gets Tough..., 1983; The Best of Bow Wow Wow, 1989; Singles: C30, C60, C90, Go!, 1980; Chihuahua, 1981; Go Wild In The Country, 1982; I Want Candy, 1982; Louis Quatorze, 1982; Solo albums include: Fever, 1986. *Current Management:* ESP Management, 888 Seventh Ave #2904, New York, NY 10106–0001, USA.

LUBIN Jean-Claude; b. 2 Oct. 1935, Paris, France. Musician (piano); Information Scientist. *Education:* Dr in Science (Geology). *Musical Education:* Studying piano classical from 8 to 11 years. *Career:* Member, various groups, New Orleans, 1953–56; Musician, Paris, with: F Jeanneau; M Saury; A Nicholas; A Reweliotty; Also played with: B Wilen; G Laffite; L Fuentes; J L Chautemps; S Grapelly; J L Ponty; J F Jenny Clarke; A Romano; H Texier; A Lorenzi; D Humair; M Roques; J Griffin; C Baker; D Byrd; L Konitz; D Gordon; G Coleman; J McLean; D Cherry; G Barbieri. *Recording:* The Fabulous Pescara Jam Session (with C Baker), 1975. *Address:* Jean-Claude Lubin, 3 rue d'Alembert, 92130 Issy-Les-Moulineaux, France.

LUCAS David Jonathan; b. 4 Nov. 1963, Brentwood, Essex, England. Musician (electric and acoustic guitar, electric and double bass); Vocalist. *Musical Education:* Self-taught. *Career:* Double bassist with the Rhythm Doctors, 1994–; Tours of: Austria, Holland, Dutch TV, 1996; Holland, Austria, Belgium, 1997; Holland, Germany, 1998; Canada, 1999. *Recording:* Guitarist, vocalist, The Is, The Is, 1993; Various session work on guitar/bass/vocals and as producer/engineer/arranger, 1996–99; Guitar/ vocals/songwriter/co-producer, Poppy, by Field, 2000. *Membership:* Musicians' Union. *Leisure interests:* Earth mysteries; War gaming; Literature; Art; Video Games.

LUCKETT LeToya; b. 11 March 1981, Houston, Texas, USA. Vocalist; Songwriter. *Career:* Numerous print and TV commercial appearances prior to professional music career; First international solo vocal performance in Tokyo, Japan, 1990; Joined GirlsTyme vocal group, 1992; Group renamed Something Fresh then The Dolls before settling on Destiny's Child; Signed to Columbia Records, 1996; Acrimonious split from group, February 2000;

Formed new group Anjel with fellow ex-Destiny's Child member LaTavia Roberson. *Recordings:* Albums: Destiny's Child, 1998; The Writing's On The Wall, 1999; Singles: with Destiny's Child: No No No (with Wyclef Jean), 1997; With Me (with Timbaland), She's Gone (with Matthew Marsden), 1998; Get On The Bus (from Why Do Fools Fall In Love OST), Bills Bills Bills, Bug-A-Boo, 1999; Say My Name, Jumpin' Jumpin', 2000; with Anjel: 10 Things I Hate About You, 2001. *Honours:* Grammy Awards, 2 nominations for co-compositions included on The Writing's On The Wall album. *Address:* c/o 581 Records/So So Def/Columbia. *Internet:* www.sonymusic.com.

LUKA BLOOM (Barry Moore); b. 23 May 1955, Newbridge, County Kildare, Ireland. Vocalist; Musician (guitar); Songwriter. *Career:* Younger brother of Christy Moore; Performed in Dublin pubs and folk clubs around Europe, mid 1970s – mid 1980s; Brief stint as leader of rock band Red Square; Relocated to USA and changed name to Luka Bloom, 1987; Toured the country as opening act for the Pogues and Hothouse Flowers; Signed by Reprise and, later, Sony Music. *Recordings:* as Barry Moore: Treaty Stone, 1978; In Groningen, 1980; No Heroes, 1982; as Luka Bloom: Riverside, 1990; Acoustic Motorbike, 1992; Turf, 1994; Salty Heaven, 1998; Keeper of The Flame, 2000; The Barry Moore Years, 2001; Between The Mountain and The Moon, 2002. *Internet:* www.lukabloom.com.

LUKATHER Steve; b. 21 Oct. 1957, Los Angeles, California, USA. Musician (guitar). *Career:* Member, Toto, 1978-. *Compositions include:* Commissioned (with Toto) to write theme for Los Angeles Olympic Games, 1984; Co-writer (with Randy Goodrum), I'll Be Over You, 1986. *Recordings:* Albums: with Toto: Toto, 1979; Hydra, 1979; Turn Back, 1981; Toto IV, 1982; Isolation, 1984; Dune (film soundtrack), 1985; Fahrenheit, 1986; The Seventh One, 1988; Past To Present 1977–90, 1990; Kingdom of Desire, 1992; Luke, 1997; Lukather, 1998; Singles: with Toto include: Hold The Line, 1979; Georgy Porgy, 1980; 99, 1980; Rosanna, 1982; Make Believe, 1982; Africa (No. 1, USA), 1983; I Won't Hold You Back, 1983; I'll Be Over You, 1986; Without Your Love, 1987; Pamela, 1988; Contributor, We Are The World, US For Africa charity single, 1985. *Honours:* 6 Grammy Awards: Best Record, Best Album, Best Engineered Recording, Best Producer (Toto), Best Vocal Arrangement, Best Instrumental Arrangement, 1983. *Address:* c/o Fitzgerald-Hartley Co, 50 W Main St, Ventura, CA 93001, USA.

LULU (Marie MacDonald McLaughlin Lawrie); b. 3 Nov. 1948, Lennox Castle, Scotland. Singer; Entertainer. m. Maurice Gibb (divorced), (2) John Freda, 1976, 1 s. *Career:* Singer, Lulu and the Luvvers, 1963–66; Solo artiste, 1966–; British tours with: Gene Pitney, Peter and Gordon, Roy Orbison, The Beach Boys, 1965–66; Tour, Poland, with the Hollies, 1966; The Royal Variety Show, 1967, 1981; Host, own variety show, BBC1, 1968; Joint winner for UK (with France, Netherlands and Spain), Boom-Bang-A-Bang, Eurovision Song Contest, 1969; Berlin Disc Gala, 1971; Film appearance: To Sir With Love, 1966; Theatre and television includes: Guys and Dolls; Song and Dance; The Secret Diary of Adrian Mole Aged 13 3/4; New record deal and forthcoming album being recorded; Guest Presenter, Red Alert, National Lottery programme. *Recordings:* Albums: To Sir With Love, 1967; New Routes, 1970; The Most of Lulu, 1971; Take Me To Your Heart Again, 1982; Don't Take Love For Granted, 1978; Lulu, 1981; Independence, 1993; Absolutely, 1997; The Best of Lulu, 1998; Hit singles include: Shout, 1964; Leave A Little Love, 1965; Try To Understand, 1965; The Boat That I Row, 1967; Let's Pretend, 1967; To Sir With Love, 1967; Me The Peaceful Heart, 1968; I'm A Tiger, 1968; Boom-Bang-A-Bang, 1969; The Man Who Sold The World, 1974; Independence, 1993; I'm Back For More, duet with Bobby Womack, 1993; Guest vocalist, Relight My Fire, Take That (No. 1, UK), 1993; Hurt Me So Bad, 1999. *Current Management:* Running Dog Management Ltd, PO Box 225, Sunbury-on-Thames, Middlesex TW16 5RT, England.

LUMHOLDT Sara Helena; b. 25 Oct. 1984, Stockholm, Sweden. Vocalist. *Education:* Näsbydals skola, Stockholm. *Career:* Picked to be member of A*Teens group following auditions at Leslie Kühler's dance school, 1998; Continued educational studies whilst pursuing musical career; Prestigious US support tours for N*Sync and Britney Spears, 2000. *Recordings:* Albums: The Abba Generation, 1999; Teen Spirit, 2001; Singles: Mamma Mia, Super Trouper, Gimme! Gimme! Gimme!, Happy New Year, 1999; Dancing Queen, Upside Down, 2000; Halfway Around The World, Sugar Rush, 2001. *Honours:* Broke Swedish sales records with first album and single; World-wide sales of first album in excess of 3m.; Viva Music Awards, Best International Newcomer, 2000. *Address:* c/o Stockholm Records, Sweden. *Internet:* www.stockholmrecords.com.

LUNDEN Petri H; b. 29 Nov. 1963, Helsinki. Promoter; Booking Agent; Man.-Dir. 1 d. *Career:* Breaking the following acts in Scandinavia: Bjoku; Green Day; Nirvana; Offspring; Stereo MCs; Blue Oasis; Prodigy; Cranberries; Soul Asylum; Weezer; The Orb; Swedish acts worked with, world-wide: Clawfinger; Cardigans; Popsicle; Stanna Bo. *Honour:* Most Interesting Promoter of the Year, 1994. *Membership:* ECPA. *Leisure*

interests: Design; Hunting. *Address:* PO Box 53045, 40014 Goteborg, Sweden.

LUNDSTEN John; Sound Engineer. *Career:* Assistant, the Film Editor, BBC and Yorkshire TV Productions including Horizon, Omnibus, Whicker's World, 1967–69; Sound Engineer, Radio Gerinomo, Live recordings, freelance film recorder for films including Pulp with Michael Caine and O Lucky Man, recorded Glastonbury festival for album and film directed by Nic Roeg, 1969–70; Assistant Recordist for film with Peter Sellars, Daily Record film contest, 1971–74; 12 concerts for Camden Jazz Festival, Raj in Orchestra, Pakistani/Western music project, started designing and building own mixing studio, 1981; Recorded live punk album for Peter and the Test Tube Babies, Pissed and Proud, 1982; Opera and masterclass recordings of Placido Domingo, Buddy Holly memorial concert with Paul McCartney, began using digital stereo recorder, 1983; Programme of music of Count Basie with Helen Shapiro on vocals, film of band Level 42 including post-production, using digital technology, also post-production for Erasure and Status Quo, 1984; Mincing Machine tour with Julian Clary, Irish Music Festival for RTE Dublin, 2 programmes on African music for S4C, Lecturer for National Film School on Digital Auto and Stereo recording techniques, 1989; Recording and post-production for Alan Price concert, recording and sound supervision for Wet Wet Wet, recordings for numerous TV programmes on world music, started work on a sound FX database, 1990–91; Recording for documentary for Rex: The Grateful and the Dead, recording for documentary on Ute Lempe, plan for building of Alchemea College of audio engineering, 1992; Lecturer, Course Co-ordinator and Curriculum Development at Alchemea, other recording projects, 1993–95; Designed 4 studios in Chipping Norton and 2 Surround-Sound mixing rooms at Alchemea, more teaching at National Film School and other projects. *Address:* Alchemea, The Windsor Centre, Islington, London N1 8QG, England.

LUNDSTEN Ralph; b. 6 Oct. 1936, Ersnäs, Sweden. Composer; Film maker; Artist; Author; Studio owner. *Career:* Owner of Andromeda Picture and electronic music studio, including the Love Machine and other invented synthesizers, 1959–; More than 600 opus and 81 records, 12 short films, art exhibitions, a book with CD – Lustbarheter; Work for Opera House in Stockholm in Stockholm and Oslo, the Modern Museum and National Museum in Stockholm, the Louvre and the Biennale in Paris, the Triennale in Milano and the Museum of Contemporary Crafts in New York; Subject of a number of Radio and TV portraits, 1971–98; Special portrait-exhibition at the Music Museum in Stockholm, 1991–92. *Compositions include:* Nordic Nature Symphony No 1, The Water Sprite; Johannes and the Lady of the Woods; A Midwinter Saga; A Summer Saga; Bewitched; Landscape of Dreams; The Seasons; Erik XIV and Gustav III; Cosmic Love; Ourfather, Nightmare; Horrorscope; Shangri-La; Universe; Discophrenia; Alpha Ralpha Boulevard; Paradise Symphony; The New Age; Pop Age; Music for Relaxation and Meditation; Cosmic Phantazy; The Dream Master; The Gate of Time; The Ages of Man; Sea Symphony; Mindscape Music; Nordic Light; The Symphony of Joy; The Symphony of Light; The Symphony of Love; In Time and Space; Andromedian Tales; Happy Earthday; Inspiration. *Honours:* Grand Prix Biennale, Paris, France, 1967; Swedish Film Institute Prize, 1964–67; About 40 other awards for music and film making; Schwingungen Preis, Oscar of Electronic Music, 1997. *Address:* Frankenburgs väg 1, 132 42 Saltsjö-Boo, Sweden.

LUNDSTREM Oleg Leonidovisch; b. 2 April 1916, Chita, Siberia, Russia. Composer; Orchestra Leader. Widower. *Education:* High Technical Centre, Faculty of Architecture, Shanghai, 1944. *Musical Education:* Graduate, musical college, Harbin, China, 1935; Kazan Conservatory, as composer and symphony conductor, Russia, 1953. *Career:* Leader, professional jazz band, Kharbin, 1934; Leader, Concert Jazz Orchestra, Moscow, 1956; Film, A Song Without End, 1965; Many appearances on radio and television. *Compositions include:* Suite on Tatar Folklore, for Symphony Orchestra; Symphony in C Minor; Melody for Violin and Piano; Pieces for jazz big band: Interlude; Mirage; Impromptu; Together Again; Bokhara Ornament; In The Mountains of Georgia. *Recordings:* Together Again; Tribute to Jazz Masters; In Swing Time; Nowadays; In A Mellow Tone. *Honours:* People's Artist of Russia, 1984; DSc, International Academy of Sciences, San Marino, 1993; Prize of Moscow, for literature and art, 1995; Laureate of the National Musical Prize Ovation, 1996; Order, Services for the Fatherland, III degree, 1996. *Memberships:* Union of Composers, Russia; Union of Theatre Workers; International Union of Musical Workers. *Leisure interest:* Swimming. *Address:* Cherkisovskaya h 3, B J Apt 49, Moscow 107061, Russia.

LUNGHINI Elsa; b. 20 May 1973, Paris, France. Singer; Actress; Author; Composer. 1 s. *Career:* Singer: Solo artist, 1986–; European tour and Olympia, Paris, 1990; In duets with Glenn Madeiros: diamond awards, Antwerp, 1988; Actress: Festival de Cannes, for film: Le Retour de Casanova, with Alain Delon, 1991. *Recordings:* T'en Va Pas (Please Don't Go), 1986; with Glenn Madeiros: Love Always Finds A Reason, 1988; First album: Elsa, 1988; Rien Que Pour Ça, 1990; Dance Violence, 1992. *Honours:* Gold and Platinum singles and albums; Grand Prix SACEM,

1993. *Leisure interests:* Piano; Dance. *Current Management:* BMG France/ Ariola, 2 rue des quatre Fils, 75003 Paris, France (Music); Artmedia, 10 Ave Georges V, 75008 Paris, France (Films).

LUNN John Lawrence; b. 13 May 1956, Scotland. Composer; Musician. m. Sara, 1 s. *Education:* Glasgow University. *Musical Education:* Royal Scottish Academy of Music; Electronic Music, Massachusetts Institute of Technology. *Career:* Formed pop group: Earplay, 1981; Later joined avant garde music group, The Lost Jockey; Developed into: Man Jumping, mid-1980s. *Compositions:* Films: Four Weddings and A Funeral; The Cormorant, BBC2; The Gift, BBC1; After The Dance, BBC; Life of Stuff, 1998; Wisdom of Crocodiles, 1998; Get Real, 1998; Baby Mother, 1998; Other television: Finney, YTV; Hamish McBeth, BBC; The Last Machine, BBC; Beatrix, BBC; Heart of Shelley, Anglia; The Dance House, BBC2; Focal Point, BBC Scotland; Getting Hurt, 1998; Ballets: Weighing The Heart; Goes Without Saying; In Dream I Loved A Dream; Classical pieces: Le Voyage; Verve; Echoes; Leonce and Elena; Jazz Pointilliste; Strange Fruit; Black and Blue; Operas: Mathematics of a Kiss; Misper, 1998; The Maids, 1998. *Honours:* Scholarship, Scottish Arts Council; Royal Television Society, Best Drama Score for Getting Hurt, 1998. *Memberships:* Musicians' Union; PRS. *Current Management:* Sound Track Music Associates Ltd, 22 Ives St, Chelsea, London SW3 2ND, England.

LUNNY Donal; b. 1947, Newbridge, County Kildare, Ireland. Musician (guitar, bouzouki, bodhran); Prod. *Career:* Father of Cora Venus Lunny; First musician to introduce bouzouki to Irish music; Member: Rakes of Kildare (with Christy Moore); Emmett Spiceland; Planxty; The Bothy Band; Moving Hearts; Coolfin; Involved with production of first interactive CD-ROM compilation of Irish music; Collaborations: Kate Bush; Mary Black; Van Morrison; Elvis Costello; Sinead O'Connor; Involved with TV programmes: Bringing It All Back Home, 1992; A River of Sound, 1995; Presented music programme Sult, 1996; Involved in over 100 albums. *Recordings:* Albums include: Faoilean, Triona and Maighread Ni Dhomhnaill, 1975; Live Hearts, Moving Hearts, 1983; Ride On, Christy Moore, 1984; No Frontiers, Mary Black, 1989; Bringing It All Back Home, 1991; Seville Suite, Bill Whelan, 1992; Sult, 1996; Coolfin, 1998; Duiseacht, 2000; My Name Is Napoleon Bonaparte, 2001. *Honour:* The Late Late Show Special Tribute to Donal Lunny, 1996.

LUNNY Manus Bernard; b. 8 Feb. 1962, Dublin, Leinster, Republic of Ireland. Vocalist; Musician (guitar, bouzouki, bodhran). *Career:* Brother of Donal Lunny; Began career as member of The Wild Geese; Toured with Andy M Stewart and Phil Cunningham; Joined Scottish folk band Capercaillie, 1988; Group, along with original material, specialise in fusing traditional Gaelic songs with contemporary arrangements; Act had first UK top 40 single in Gaelic, Coisich A Ruin (from A Prince Among Islands EP), 1992; In-demand session musician and composer; Worked on several TV series with top folk musicians including: Tacsi; Togaidh Sinn Fonn. *Recordings:* Albums: with Capercaillie: Sidewalk, 1989; Delirium, 1991; Get Out, 1992; The Blood Is Strong, Secret People, 1993; Capercaillie, 1995; To The Moon, 1996; Beautiful Wasteland, 1997; Glenfinnan – Songs of The '45 (recorded 1995), 1998; Nàdurra, 2000; group feature on: Rob Roy OST, 1995; features solo on: Fire In The Glenn, Andy Stewart and Phil Cunningham, 1986; Dublin Lady, Andy Stewart, 1987; Donal Lunny, Donal Lunny, 1987; At It Again, Andy Stewart, 1990; Songs of Robert Burns, Andy Stewart, 1990; Somebody, Connie Dover, 1991; The Dreaming Sea, Karen Matheson, 1996; Wishing Well, Connie Dover, 1994; If I Ever Return, Connie Dover, 1997; Identities, Idir, 1999; Fused, Michael McGoldrick, 2000; Tacsi (TV series), 2000.

LUSCOMBE Stephen Alfred; b. 29 Oct. 1954, Hillingdon, Middlesex, England. Musician (keyboards); Composer; Prod. *Musical Education:* Self-taught, also pupil of John Steven's Music Workshops, 1971–72. *Career:* Member, Portsmouth Sinfonia, avant garde orchestra, 1972–74; Member, Spontaneous Music Orchestra, 1972–74; Founder, performer, Music Workshop Miru, 1973–77; Founder, with Neil Arthur, electro-pop duo Blancmange, 1979–86; Numerous tours, television and radio broadcasts, recordings; Co-founder, West India Company, with Pandit Dinesh, 1984–; With artists including: Asha Bhosle; Boy George; Apache Indian; Saeed Jaffrey; La La La Human Steps; Numerous commissions for television, radio, theatre, film productions including National Theatre, 1994; BBC Radio Drama, 1994; Lonely Planet Travel Guide (CH4), 5 programmes, 1995; Music for film Masala, starring Saeed Jaffrey and Zora Seghal, Canada, 1991; Music composition and direction for R National Theatre Production, Wicked Year, 1994. *Recordings:* with Portsmouth Sinfonia: Play The Popular Classics, 1973; Live At The Albert Hall, 1974; with Blancmange: Happy Families, 1982; Mange Tout, 1984; Believe You Me, 1985; Greatest Hits, 1990; Also 8 top 40 singles include: Living On The Ceiling; with West India Company: Ave Maria (EP), 1984; Music From New Demons, 1989; The Art of Love – Readings From The Kama Sutra, Saeed Jaffrey, 1992; Music From The Lonely Planet, with others, 1995. *Memberships:* PRS; PPL. *Leisure interests:* Cooking; Walking and climbing; Travel; Gardening. *Current Management:* Notting Hill Music Ltd. *Address:* 87 Notting Hill Gate, London W11 3JZ, England.

LUSHER Don; b. 6 Nov. 1923, Peterborough, England. Musician (trombone); Bandleader. *Career:* Member, Joe Daniels and His Hot Shots; Joined Lou Preager at Hammersmith Palais; Member, Maurice Winnick's Band, The Squadronaires and the Ted Heath Band; Extensive tours with artists including Frank Sintara, 1960s; Leader, big bands, for television and radio appearances; Educator, USA; Japan; Australia; UK. *Recordings:* Albums include: Lusher and Lusher and Lusher, 1972; Collection, 1976; Don Lusher Big Band, 1981; Don Lusher Pays Tribute To The Great Bands Vol. 2, 1988; Just Good Friends, 1993; Performance, with Marti Webb, 1994; Trippin' the Light Fantastic, with the London Starlight Orchestra, 1998; Most Beautiful Melodies of the Century, 1999. *Publication:* The Don Lusher Book. *Current Management:* Derek Boulton Management, 76 Carlisle Mansions, Carlisle Pl., London SW1P 1HZ, England.

LUSSIER Damien; b. 7 Nov. 1975, St Anne's, Manitoba, Canada. Singer; Songwriter; Musician (Guitar, Piano). 1 d. *Education:* Study in Guitar, Conservatoire du Musique de Montréal. *Career:* CBC TV Production, Télé-Relais; Boîte à Chanson II; Boîte à Chanson III; Short interviews on 2 local TV Stations; Numerous interviews on Radio Canada and local radio stations. *Compositions:* Alice; Les artistes au Rendezvous. *Recording:* D'ailleurs. *Membership:* SOCAN. *Leisure interests:* Painting; Sports. *Address:* 1067 Clarence Ave, Winnipeg, Manitoba R3T 1S5, Canada.

LUTHER Paul James; b. 1 Sept. 1974, Salisbury, England. Musician (guitar). *Musical Education:* 11 years, private tuition, classical guitar. *Career:* Two British tours backing Toyah Wilcox; Concerts for British forces, Belize; Heineken festival concerts, Gateshead, Plymouth, 1994; Member, Scarlet supporting Bryan Ferry, British tour, 1995; Further Scarlet tour supporting Wet Wet Wet, 1995; Currently pursuing career with new band, Ebb, 1998; Television: 3 appearances with Scarlet, Top of the Pops; Pebble Mill; Parallel 9; Wot's Up Doc with singer David Dixon. *Recordings:* with Toyah Wilcox: Take The Leap, 1993; with Scarlet: Naked, 1995; Unreleased: Voice of the Beehive: (as yet untitled); The Friday's Duck; Singles: with Scarlet: Independent Love Song (Top 20, UK charts); I Wanna Be Free. *Memberships:* Musicians' Union; PAMRA. *Leisure interests:* Producing local acts; Squash; Pool; Backgammon. *Address:* 295 Devizes Rd, Salisbury, Wiltshire SP2 9LU, England.

LYDON John, (Johnny Rotten); b. 31 Jan. 1956, Finsbury Park, London, England. Vocalist. *Career:* Vocalist, UK punk group the Sex Pistols, 1975–78; Founder, Public Image Ltd, 1978–; Performances include: First gig, St Martin's School of Art, London, 1975; Screen on The Green Midnight Special, Islington, London, 1986; Tour, Anarchy In The UK, 1976; Europe, 1977; USA, 1978; Last live show, Winterland Ballroom, San Francisco, 1978; Sex Pistols reunion concert, Finsbury Park, London, 1996; Phoenix Festival, 1996; Film appearances: The Great Rock 'n' Roll Swindle, 1980; The Filth and The Fury, 2000. *Recordings:* Albums: Never Mind The Bollocks – Here's The Sex Pistols (No. 1, UK), 1977; The Great Rock 'n' Roll Swindle, 1979; Some Product – Carry On Sex Pistols, 1979; Flogging A Dead Horse, 1980; Kiss This, 1992; With Public Image Ltd: Public Image, 1978; Metal Box, 1979; Paris Au Printemps, 1980; Flowers of Romance, 1981; This Is What You Want, This Is What You Get, 1984; Album, 1986; Happy?, 1987; 9, 1989; Greatest Hits So Far, 1990; That What Is Not, 1992; Plastic Box, 1999; Singles include: with The Sex Pistols: Anarchy In The UK, 1976; God Save The Queen (No. 2, UK), 1977; Pretty Vacant, 1977; Holidays In The Sun, 1977; with Public Image Ltd: Public Image, 1978; Death Disco, 1979; Flowers of Romance, 1981; This Is Not A Love Song, 1983; Rise, 1986; Seattle, 1987; Disappointed, 1989; Don't Ask Me, 1990; Cruel, 1992; Contributions to: Timezone, World Destruction, 1984; Leftfield, Open Up; In the Sun; Album: Leftism, 1995; Solo Album: Psycho's Path, 1997. *Current Management:* DMA Entertainment, 2029 Century Park E, Suite 600, Los Angeles, CA 90067, USA.

LYLE Graham; b. Largs, Ayrshire, Scotland. Singer; Songwriter; Musician (guitar). *Career:* Songwriting partnership with Benny Gallagher, 1960s; Member, McGuinness Flint, 1969–71; Folk duo, Gallagher and Lyle, 1972–79; Solo artiste, 1980-. *Compositions:* Co-writer with Benny Gallagher: Mr Heartbreak's Here Instead, Dean Ford; International, Mary Hopkins; for McGuinness Flint: When I'm Dead and Gone; Malt and Barley Blues; for Gallagher and Lyle: I Wanna Stay With You; Heart On My Sleeve; Co-writer with Terry Britten: What's Love Got To Do With It, Tina Turner; Just Good Friends, Michael Jackson. *Recordings:* Albums: with Gallagher and Lyle: Gallagher and Lyle, 1972; Willie and The Lap Dog, 1973; Seeds, 1973; The Last Cowboy, 1974; Breakaway, 1976; Love On The Airwaves, 1977; Showdown, 1978; Gone Crazy, 1979; Lonesome No More, 1979; The Best Of, 1980; Heart On My Sleeve, 1991; Singles: I Wanna Stay With You, 1976; Heart On My Sleeve, 1976.

LYNCH Colm; b. 29 April 1952, Dublin, Ireland. Musician. 1 s., 1 d. *Education:* Social Pedegog, Denmark. *Musical Education:* Drums, piano, guitar, through school; Private tutor in School of Music, Dublin. *Career:* Successful appearances on RTE (TV, Ireland): Meitheal; Saoire Samhradh; Spin Off; Jimmy Saville show, BBC; Danish radio, television. *Compositions:* Songwriter in Ireland, Singer/songwriter in UK, wrote hit singles.

Recordings: Album: Early One Morning; Hit singles: Violence Has Many Faces; Devil Among The Tailors. *Honours:* Top Selling Album, 1973; Top Irish Artist, 1973; Best Group. *Memberships:* KODA (Danish PRS); DJBFA (Danish Society, Jazz, Rock and Folk Composers). *Address:* Mejlgade 89, 8000 Aarhus C, Denmark.

LYNCH Edele Claire Christina Edwina; b. 15 Dec. 1979, Dublin, Ireland. Singer. *Career:* Member, B*Witched; Numerous tours and television appearances; Several hit singles. *Recordings:* Singles: C'est La Vie (No. 1, UK), 1998; Rollercoaster (No. 1, UK), 1998; To You I Belong (No. 1, UK), 1998; Blame it on the Weatherman (No. 1, UK), 1998; Jesse Hold On, 1999; I Shall Be There, with Ladysmith Black Mambazo, 1999; Jump Down, 2000; Albums: B*Witched, 1998; Awake and Breathe, 1999. *Internet:* www.bwitched.com.

LYNCH Ged; b. 19 July 1968, Oswaldtwistle, England. Musician (Drums). *Career:* Member, Black Grape; Numerous live gigs and festival appearances including Tribal Gathering and Reading festivals, 1997. *Recordings:* Singles: Reverend Black Grape, 1995; In The Name of The Father, 1995; Kelly's Heroes, 1995; England's Irie, 1996; Fat Neck, 1996; Get Higher, 1997; Marbles, 1998; Albums: It's Great When You're Straight... Yeah, 1995; Stupid Stupid Stupid, 1997; Also percussionist on: Michael Hutchence, Michael Hutchence, 1999; Afterglow, Dot Allison, 1999; Twisted Tenderness, Electronic, 1999; Wonderland, The Charlatans, 2001.

LYNCH Keavy-Jane Elizabeth Annie; b. 15 Dec. 1979, Dublin, Ireland. Singer; Musician (Saxophone, drums, guitar). *Career:* Member, B*Witched; Numerous tours and television appearances; Several hit singles. *Recordings:* Singles: C'est La Vie (No. 1, UK), 1998; Rollercoaster (No. 1, UK), 1998; To You I Belong (No. 1, UK), 1998; Blame it on the Weatherman (No. 1, UK), 1998; Jesse Hold On, 1999; I Shall Be There, with Ladysmith Black Mambazo, 1999; Jump Down, 2000; Albums: B*Witched, 1998; Awake and Breathe, 1999. *Internet:* www.bwitched.com.

LYNCH Shane; b. 3 July 1976, Dublin, Ireland. Vocalist. m. Easther Bennett. *Career:* Member, Boyzone. *Recordings:* Singles: Working My Way Back To You, 1994; Key To My Life, 1995; Love Me For A Reason, 1995; So Good, 1995; Father and Son, 1995; Coming Home Now, 1995; Words (No. 1, UK), 1996; A Different Beat (No. 1, UK), 1996; Isn't It A Wonder, 1997; Baby Can I Hold You Tonight, 1997; Picture of You, 1997; Mystical Experience, 1997; All That I Need (No. 1, UK), 1998; No Matter What (No. 1, UK), 1998; I Love The Way You Love Me, 1998; When The Going Gets Tough (No. 1, UK), 1999; You Needed Me (No. 1, UK), 1999; Every Day I Love You, 1999; Albums: A Different Beat, 1997; Where We Belong, 1998; By Request, 1999.

LYNGSTAD Frida (Anni-Frid); b. Narvik, Norway. Singer. m. Benny Andersson, 1978 (divorced 1981), 1 s., 1 d. (from previous relationship). *Career:* Leader, own dance band, Anni-Frid Four; Singer, Abba, 1973–82; Appearances include: Winners, Eurovision Song Contest, 1974; World-wide tours; Concerts include: Royal Performance, Stockholm, 1976; Royal Albert Hall, 1977; UNICEF concert, New York, 1979; Wembley Arena, 6 sell-out performances, 1979; Reunion with Abba, Swedish TV's This Is Your Life, 1986; The Story of Abba, C4 TV, 1991; Solo artiste, 1983–; Film: Abba – The Movie, 1977. *Recordings:* Albums: with Abba: Waterloo, 1974; Abba, 1976; Arrival, 1977; The Album, 1978; Voulez-Vous, 1979; Super Trouper, 1980; The Visitors, 1981; Abba Gold, 1992; More Abba Gold, 1993; The Singles Collection, 2001; Solo albums: Frida Alone, 1976; Something's Going On, 1982; Shine, 1983; Singles include: Ring Ring, 1973; Waterloo (No. 1, UK), 1974; Mamma Mia (No. 1, UK), 1975; Dancing Queen (No. 1, UK and US), 1976; Fernando (No. 1, UK), 1976; Money Money Money, 1976; Knowing Me Knowing You (No. 1, UK), 1977; The Name of The Game (No. 1, UK), 1977; Take A Chance On Me (No. 1, UK), 1978; Summer Night City, 1978; Chiquitita, 1979; Does Your Mother Know?, 1979; Angel Eyes/Voulez-Vous, 1979; Gimme Gimme Gimme (A Man After Midnight), 1979; I Have A Dream, 1979; The Winner Takes It All (No. 1, UK), 1980; Super Trouper (No. 1, UK), 1980; On and On and On, 1981; Lay All Your Love On Me, 1981; One of Us, 1981; When All Is Said and Done, 1982; Head Over Heels, 1982; The Day Before You Came, 1982; Under Attack, 1982; Thank You For The Music, 1983; Solo: Time (duet with B A Robertson); Albums: Djupa Andetag, 1996; Frida 1967–72, 1998; Frida: The Mixes, 1998; Svenska Popfavoriter, 1998. *Honours include:* Gold discs; Best-selling group in history of popular music, Guinness Book of Records, 1979; World Music Award, Best Selling Swedish Artist (with Abba), 1993.

LYNN Loretta, (Loretta Webb); b. 14 April 1935, Butcher Hollow, Kentucky, USA. Singer. m. Oliver Lynn, 1948, 6 c. *Career:* Sang local clubs with group The Trailblazers; Regular appearances, Grand Ole Opry; Weekly television show, with the Wilburn Brothers, Nashville; Regular duets with Ernest Tubb and Conway Twitty. *Recordings include:* 16 No. 1 singles, 60 other hits, 15 number 1 albums; Hit singles include: I'm A Honky Tonk Girl; Success; Before I'm Over You; Blue Kentucky Girl; Don't Come Home A-Drinkin' (With Lovin' On Your Mind); Coal Miner's Daughter; Pregnant Again; Albums include: Loretta Lynn Sings, 1963;

Before I'm Over You, 1964; Songs From The Heart, 1965; Blue Kentucky Girl, 1965; Hymns, 1965; I Like 'Em Country, 1966; You Ain't Woman Enough, 1966; Don't Come Home A-Drinkin', 1967; Singin' With Feelin', 1967; Fist City, 1968; Your Squaw Is On The Warpath, 1969; Woman of The World, 1969; Coal Miner's Daughter, 1971; I Want To Be Free, 1971; Alone With You, 1972; Love Is The Foundation, 1973; They Don't Make 'Em Like Our Daddy, 1974; Home, 1975; Somebody Somewhere, 1976; Out of My Head and Back In My Bed, 1978; Loretta, 1980; Lookin' Good, 1980; Makin' Love From Memory, 1982; Just A Woman, 1985; Still Country, 2000; with Ernest Tubb: Mr and Mrs Used To Be, 1965; Singin' Again, 1967; If We Put Our Heads Together, 1969; with Conway Twitty: We Only Make Believe, 1971; Lead Me On, 1971; Lousiana Woman, Misissippi Man, 1973; Country Partners, 1974; Feelin's, 1975; United Talent, 1976; Dynamic Duo, 1977; Country Partners, 1974; Honky Tonk Heroes, 1978; Diamond Duets, 1979; Two's A Party, 1981; Making Believe, 1988; Who was That Stranger, 1989; Hey Good Lookin', 1993; Country's Favourite Daughter, 1994; An Evening with Loretta Lynn, 1995. *Publication:* Coal Miner's Daughter (autobiography). *Honours include:* First woman inducted into Nashville Songwriters International Hall of Fame; First woman to be voted Country Music Asscn's Entertainer of The Year, 1972; CMA Vocal Duo of the Year (with Conway Twitty), 1972. *Current Management:* Loretta Lynn Enterprises, PO Box 120369, Nashville, TN 37212, USA.

LYNN Vera (Dame), (Margaret Lewis); b. 20 March 1917. Singer. m. Harry Lewis, 1941, 1 d. *Career:* Debut performance, 1924; Appeared with Joe Loss, Charlie Kunz, 1935; Ambrose, 1937–40; Applesauce, Palladium, London, 1941; Became known as the Forces Sweetheart, 1939–45; Radio show Sincerely Yours, 1941–47; Tour of Burma, entertaining troops, 1944; 7 Command performances; Appearances, Europe; Australia; Canada; New Zealand; Performed at 50th Anniversary of VE Day Celebrations, London, 1995; Own television shows: ITV, 1955; BBC1, 1956; BBC2, 1970; First British artist to top Hit Parade. *Recordings include:* Auf Wiederseh'n (No. 1, US; over 12m. copies sold), 1952; My Son My Son (No. 1, UK), 1954; Recent albums include: With All My Heart, 2000. *Publication:* Vocal Refrain (autobiography), 1975. *Honours:* Order of St John; LLD; MMus. *Current Management:* Anglo-American Enterprises, 806 Keyes House, Dolphin Sq., London SW1V 3NB, England.

LYNNE Jeff; b. 30 Dec. 1947, Birmingham, England. Record Prod.; Singer; Songwriter; Musician (guitar); Arranger. *Musical Education:* Self-taught. *Career:* Member, Idle Race, 1966–70; Member, The Move, 1970–72; Founder member, The Electric Light Orchestra (ELO), 1972–85; Regular international tours, 1973–; Record producer, 1983–; Formed the Traveling Wilburys (with Bob Dylan, Roy Orbison, George Harrison, Tom Petty), 1988; Also solo artiste. *Recordings:* Albums: with ELO (as singer, guitarist, writer and producer): Electric Light Orchestra, 1972; ELO II, 1973; On The Third Day, 1973; Eldorado, 1974; The Night The Light Went On In Long Beach, 1974; Face The Music, 1975; Olé ELO, 1976; A New World Record, 1976; Out of The Blue, 1977; Discovery, 1979; ELO's Greatest Hits, 1979; Xanadu (film soundtrack), 1980; Time (No. 1, UK), 1982; Secret Messages, 1983; Perfect World of Music, 1985; First Movement, 1986; Balance of Power, 1986; Afterglow, 1990; Strange Magic, 1995; Live at Wembley, 1998; Flashback, 2000; Zoom, 2001; with Traveling Wilburys (also co-writer and co-producer): Traveling Wilburys, Vol. 1, 1988; Vol. 3, 1991; Solo: Armchair Theatre, 1990; As producer: Information, Dave Edmunds, 1983; Cloud Nine, George Harrison, 1987; Mystery Girl, Roy Orbison, 1988; Full Moon Fever, Tom Petty, 1988; Singles include: with ELO: 10538 Overture, 1972; Roll Over Beethoven, 1972; Can't Get It Out of My Head, 1974; Evil Woman, 1976; Strange Magic, 1976; Livin' Thing, 1976; Telephone Line, 1977; Mr Blue Sky, 1978; Sweet Talkin' Woman, 1978; Shine A Little Love, 1979; Don't Bring Me Down, 1979; Xanadu, collaboration with Olivia Newton-John (No. 1, UK), 1980; All Over The World, 1980; Hold On Tight, 1981; Rock 'n' Roll Is King, 1983; Calling America, 1986; with the Traveling Wilburys: Handle With Care, 1988; Solo: Doin' That Crazy Thing; As producer / co-producer: You Got It, Roy Orbison, 1988; Into The Great Wide Open, Tom Petty, 1991; Free As A Bird, The Beatles, 1995; Real Love, The Beatles, 1995. *Honours:* Nationwide Music Award, Album of the Year, Out of The Blue, 1978; Ivor Novello Awards: Outstanding Contribution To British Music, 1979; Best Film Song, Xanadu, 1981; Grammy Award, Traveling Wilburys Vol. 1, 1989; Grammy Nominations: Best Producer, 1989; Best Song, Learning To Fly (with Tom Petty), 1992; Rolling Stone Award, Best Producer, 1989; BMI Songwriters Award, on broadcasts of Evil Woman, USA, 1992. *Memberships:* ASCAP; BASCA. *Leisure interests:* Computers; Tennis. *Current Management:* Craig Fruin. *Address:* PO Box 1428, Ross, CA 94957–1428, USA.

LYON Steve; Recording Engineer; Prod. *Career:* Trained under supervision of producer, Glyn Jones, West Sussex studio; Engineer, producer, Virgin Studio Group; Worked at The Townhouse; The Manor; Chief Engineer, Master Control, Los Angeles; Air Studios, London; Freelance, 1988-. *Recordings:* Albums include: with Depeche Mode: Songs of Faith and Devotion; Violator; Faith and Devotion – Live; with Wedding Present: George Best; Bizzaro; with Nitzer Ebb: Ebbhead; Other recording sessions: Dedicated, Suzanne Vega; Sowing The Seeds of Love, Tears For Fears; Rooftops (film), Dave Stewart; Flowers In The Dirt, Paul McCartney; Under Milk Wood, with George Martin; Also recorded with: Berlin; Prefab Sprout; UFO; Labi Siffre; Breathe; The Outfield; The Cure, Wild Mood Swings; The Creatures; The Dhamers; Recoil; Paradise Lost; Spookey; Ruben. *Current Management:* c/o Stephen Budd Management, 109B Regents Park Rd, London NW1 8UR, England.

LYONS Ken, (Tigger); b. 11 April 1951, Northallerton, Yorkshire, England. Musician (bass guitar); Songwriter; Composer. m. Linda Fletcher, 19 April, 1 d. *Education:* Hammersmith College of Art and Building. *Musical Education:* Self-taught. *Career:* with Flesh: Melody Maker Competition Finals, The Roundhouse, 1971; with Hustler: UK Queen Tour, 1974; Status Quo European Tour, 1975; Geordie Scene; Kid Jenson's 45; Radio 1 In Concert; with London club/pub band The Brain Surgeons, 1976–79; with LA band The Shots, 1980–83; KROQ Nick Stavross Show. *Compositions include:* for Hustler: Get Outta Me House (Get Out of My House); Little People; for Brain Surgeons: Me and My Guitar; for The Shots: Reject; Also appears on: Vineyard Sound Vol. 3, 1997. *Memberships:* MCPS; PRS. *Leisure interests:* Karate; Clay pigeon shooting; Computer animation. *Address:* Lion Music, 29 Derby Rd, Uxbridge, Middlesex UB8 2ND, England.

LYSDAL Jens; b. 12 Jan. 1960, Sweden. Vocalist; Musician (guitar, keyboards); Arranger; Record Prod. *Musical Education:* Royal Danish Music Conservatory, 1981–85. *Career:* Backing musician with Superchancen DR (Denmark's radio/television company), backing artists including Pointer Sisters; Donna Summer; Sergio Mendes, 1993; Television show, Meyerheim After 8, backing Lill Lindfors, TV2, 1994; European Song Contest as member of DR Pop-orchestra, DR, 1995; As solo singer and guitarist, Meyerheim After 8, TV 2, 1994; Bent Fabricius Bjerre's 50 year Jubilee Show, DR, 1995; Tjek Ind Hos Mygind, TV 3, 1995; Go' Morgen TV, 1998; Arranger for symphony orchestra, for Mikael Wiehe; Tamra Rosanes; Majbritte Ulrikkeholm; Peter Busborg; Kirsten Siggaard; Ulla Henningsen; Producer for Kurt Ravn and Rikke Milgaard. *Recordings:* Music for A Day In October, Kenneth Madsen film, 1990; Solo album: A Matter of Time; Music for film: The Treasure of the Forest by Nicolas Gaster; Mr Who, by Michael Brammer, 1999; Producer/arranger for Poul Dissing, Alberte, with Denmark Radio Symphony Orchestra, 2000. *Honours:* Arnold, for music to commercial, Kim's Peanuts; Winner, Golden Stag, Romania; CD of the Year, 1997. *Membership:* DJBFA. *Current Management:* Musik and Sang, Wildersgade 56, 1408 Copenhagen, Denmark. *E-mail:* j.lysdal@mobilixnet.dk.

LYTLE Marshall; b. 1933, Old Fort, North Carolina, USA. Musician (upright bass); Vocalist. Married. *Career:* Original member, Bill Hayley's Comets, 1948–55; Invented rock 'n' roll; First rock band to headline a film; Member, The Jodimans, 1955–58. *Recordings:* Rock Around The Clock; See You Later Alligator; Crazy Man Crazy; Shake Rattle and Roll; Rock The Joint; Mambo Rock; Rudy's Rock; Florida Twist; Skinny Minnie; Let's All Rock Together; Now Dig This; From the Original Master Tapes, Decca Years and More. *Publications:* Rock Around The Clock; Stage Clear; We're Gonna Party; Never Too Old To Rock. *Honours:* Rock and Roll Hall of Fame; Gold records; Best vocal group of 1953. *Address:* Rock It Concerts, Bruno Mefer Platz 1, SU937 Munchen, Germany.

LYTTELTON Humphrey Richard Adeane; b. 23 May 1921, Eton, Buckinghamshire, England. Bandleader; Jazz Musician (trumpet); Journalist; Broadcaster; Author. m. (1) Patricia Braithwaite, 1948, divorced, (2) Elizabeth Richardson, 1952, 2 s., 2 d. *Education:* Camberwell School of Art. *Musical Education:* Piano lessons; Self-taught trumpet. *Career:* Member, George Webb's Dixielanders, 1947; Bandleader, own band, 1948–; Festival appearances include: Nice; Zurich; Montreux; Warsaw; Newcastle; Edinburgh; Glasgow; Recorded and played with artistes including: Sidney Bechet; Buck Clayton; Buddy Tate; Helen Shapiro; Kenny Davern; Jimmy Rushing; Big Joe Turner; Founder, own record label, Calligraph, 1984; Owner, music publishing company Humph Music; Numerous television and radio appearances as musician and presenter; Compère, BBC radio programmes: Jazz Club; Jazz Scene; The Best of Jazz; I'm Sorry I Haven't A Clue; Freelance music journalist and critic. *Compositions:* Numerous original compositions. *Recordings:* Numerous albums include: Delving Back and Forth with Humph, 1948; Jazz at the Royal Festival Hall, 1951; Some Like it Hot, 1955; Echoes of Harlem, 1981; This Old Gang of Ours, 1985; Beano Boogie, 1989; Rock me Gently, 1991; Rent Party, 1991; At Sundown, 1992; features on: Amnesiac, Radiohead, 2001. *Publications:* I Play As I Please, 1954; Second Chorus, 1958; Take It From The Top, 1975; The Best of Jazz: Basin Street To Harlem, 1978; Humphrey Lyttelton's Jazz and Big Band Quiz, 1979; The Best of Jazz 2: Enter The Giants, 1981; Why No Beethoven?, 1984. Contributions to: Melody Maker; Harpers and Queen; Punch; High Life. *Honours:* Hon DLitt, Warwick, 1987; Loughborough, 1988; Hon DMus, Durham, 1989; Keele, 1992; Hon. Professor of Music, Keele, 1993; Sony Gold Award, radio awards, 1993; DLitt, University of Hertfordshire, 1995; Waterford Crystal Award, IEAN, 1996; DArts, De Montfort University, 1997. *Current Management:* Susan Da Costa, Bull's Head Row, The Green, Surrey, RH9 8DZ, England.

M

M K SHINE (Mark Lowe); b. England. Singer; Songwriter; Reggae Club Owner. *Education:* Certificate, Building Construction, College, Jamaica. *Musical Education:* School of Music, London. *Career:* Lead singer, founder, Destiny, with brother, 1986; Played round islands; Played Tokyo, 1989; Solo artist, using name M K Shine, 1991–; 2 week tour, Mexico, special guest at Rock Y Reggae Festival; Television, radio interviews. *Recordings:* Wild Gilbert, 1988; My Dream, 1994; Simply Magic. *Honours:* Represented Jamaica, Caribbean Broadcasting Union, 1990. *Leisure interest:* Architecture. *Current Management:* Sirron Kyles, Samuel Rogers and Associates. *Address:* PO Box 8305, Houston, TX 77288, USA.

MAAETOFT Nils; b. 17 Nov. 1950, Vejle, Denmark. Singer; Songwriter; Musician (guitar). *Career:* Singer, guitarist, main songwriter for Danish rock group The Intellectuals; Wrote, performed, under pseudonym M T Purse; 1992, formed group M T Purse. *Recordings:* with The Intellectuals: Half A-Live, 1986; Health and Happiness, 1987; as M T Purse: Cross Talk, 1992; Throwing Rocks At The Moon, 1995. *Membership:* The Danish Society for Jazz Rock Folk Composers. *Current Management:* c/o Warner/Chappell Music, Denmark. *Address:* Anker Heegaardsgade 2, 1572 Copenhagen, Denmark.

MAAL Baaba; b. 1953, Podor, Senegal. Vocalist; Musician (guitar); Songwriter. *Musical Education:* Dakar Conservatoire; Conservatoire des Beaux Arts, Paris. *Career:* Formed band Daande Lenol; Regular collaborations with Mansour Seck; Representative of United Nations Development Programme speaking out on the issue of HIV/AIDS in Africa; Involved with HIV/AIDS awareness campaign music projects: Red Hot and Gershwin; Fela Kuti tribute Red Hot and Riot. *Recordings:* Albums include: Djam Leelii, 1989; Lam Toro, 1993; Tono, 1994; Sunugal, 1995; Firin' In Fouta, 1995; Nomad Soul (produced by Simon Emmerson, Howie B and Brian Eno), 1998; Missing You – Mi Yeewnii (produced by John Leckie, featuring Mansour Seck, Kante Manfila and Kaouding Cissokho), 2001. *Honours:* Grammy, Best World Music Album nominee, Firin' in Fouta, 1995; MOBO Award, Best World Music Act nominee, 2001; Froots Critic Poll, Best New Album, Missing You – Mi Yeewnii, 2001. *Address:* c/o Palm Pictures, 8 Kensington Park Rd, London, W11 3BU, England.

MAAS Timo; b. Germany. Prod.; Remixer; DJ. *Career:* Made breakthrough as resident DJ at The Tunnel, Hamburg; Produced Die Herdplatte with fellow resident Gary D, which led to recordings with Bristol's Hope Recordings; In-demand remixer; Holds club residency at New York's Twilo; Remixed: Madonna; Azzido Da Bass; Placebo; Fatboy Slim. *Recordings:* Albums: Loud, Music For The Maases, 2001; Singles: Die Herdplatte, 1995; Mama Konda, 1998; Der Schieber, 1999; Better Make Room, 2000; Island, 2001. *Honours:* German Dance Award, Best National DJ, 2001. *Address:* c/o Perfecto Records, 1 Shorrolds Rd, London, SW6 7TR, England.

MABUS Joel Dwight; b. 13 Sept. 1953, Belleville, Illinois, USA. Singer; Songwriter; Musician (guitar, banjo, fiddle, mandolin). *Education:* Michigan State University. *Musical Education:* Self-taught. *Career:* Vancouver Folk Festival; Philadelphia Folk Festival; Winnipeg Folk Festival; Kerrville Folk Festival; Appearances on: A Prairie Home Companion, American public radio. *Recordings:* 10 solo recordings include: Promised Land; Flatpick and Clawhammer; Short Stories; Also appears on: Old Time Music on the Air, 1996. *Publications:* Big Words – The Lyrics of Joel Mabus. *Honours:* Detroit Metro Times, Instrumentalist of The Year. *Memberships:* AFofM; The Folk Alliance. *Leisure interests:* Fishing; Gardening; Reading. *Address:* c/o Fossil Records, PO Box 4754, East Lansing, MI 48826, USA.

MABY Graham Geoffrey; b. 1 Sept. 1952, Gosport, Hampshire, England. Musician (bass guitar, guitar); Vocalist. m. Mary Beth Bernard, 15 Feb. 1987, 2 s., 1 d. *Education:* 1 year technical college. *Musical Education:* Self-taught. *Career:* Performances, live, television, video, with: Joe Jackson; Marshall Crenshaw; Graham Parker; Jules Shear; Garland Jeffreys; The Silos; Freedy Johnston; Darden Smith; Chris Stamey; Peter Holsapple; Delevantes; They Might Be Giants; Henry Lee Summer; Glen Burtnik; Shania Twain; Film: Peggy Sue Got Married, 1986; Tours mainly with Joe Jackson: Europe; North America; Japan; Australia; Laughter and Lust Tour, now on Virgin Video. *Recordings:* with Joe Jackson: Look Sharp, 1978; I'm The Man, 1979; Beat Crazy, 1980; Jumpin' Jive, 1981; Night and Day, 1982; Mike's Murder, 1983; Body and Soul, 1984; Live '79–84, 1987; Blaze of Glory, 1989; Laughter and Lust, 1991; Night Music, 1994; with Marshall Crenshaw: Mary Jean and Nine Others, 1987; Good Evening, 1989; My Truck Is My Home, 1994; with Freedy Johnston: Can You Fly, 1991; This Perfect World, 1994; with Chris Stamey: It's Alright, 1987; Fireworks, 1991; with Henry Lee Summer: Henry Lee Summer, 1988; I've

Got Everything, 1989; with David Broza: A Time of Trains, 1993; Second Street, 1994; Little Victories, Darden Smith, 1993; with They Might Be Giants: John Henry, 1994; Why Does the Sun Shine, 1994; Factory Showroom, 1996; Severe Tire Damage, 1998; Also with: Patty Smyth; Graham Parker; Jules Shear; Jill Sobule; David Wilcox. *Honours:* Gold records include: Night and Day; Look Sharp; Body and Soul. *Memberships:* ASCAP; AFTRA; AFofM. *Leisure interests:* His children; Tennis; Music.

MAC DONNCHA Johnny Mháirtín Learaí; b. 9 April 1937, Galway, Ireland. Small Farmer; Craftsman; Singer. *Career:* Sean-nós singer, Specializing in traditional Irish songs, many from West Connemara; Travelled throughout Ireland as singer; Collects and teaches songs; Winner in Corn Uí Riada, Oirreachtas, Cork, 1985. *Recordings:* Bruach Na Beirtrí; Cassette, 1988; Album, 1993; Contae Mhuigheo. *Honours:* Corn Uí Riada, Winner, Cork, 1985. *Current Management:* Cló Iar-Chonnachta, Indreabhán, Co Na Gaillimhe.

MCALL Barnaby Jonathon; b. 3 Jan. 1966, Box Hill, Victoria, Australia. Jazz Pianist. *Education:* Studied Literature, Melbourne University; Graduated, Victorian College of the Arts, Bachelor of Music; Studied in New York City with Barry Harris, Mulgren Miller, Dave Kikoski, Chucho Valdez. *Career:* Toured Europe, 3 times, playing major festivals including Montreax, North Sea, 1996; Played Blue Note, Tokyo, Japan with the Groove collective; Extensive touring of Italy, Canada; Wrote music for stage show, Solstice, part of Adelaide International Festival. *Compositions:* Hindered on his way to heaven; Exit, nominated best CD, Aria Awards, 1996. *Recordings:* Exit, CD; Widening Circles, CD, featuring Billy Harper; Live At The Jazz Standard NYC, with Gary Bartz Quartet. *Honours:* Best Jazz Composition, APRA, 1993; First Prize, National Jazz Piano Competition, Solo CD Nominated CD of Year, 1996, Aria Awards in Australia. *Leisure interests:* Yoga; Reading; Being here now. *Current Management:* Martin Jackson, 16 Neave St, Hawthorn 3122, Victoria, Australia. *Address:* 97 Pembroke Rd, Mooroolbark 3138, Victoria, Australia.

MCALMONT David; Singer; Lyricist. *Career:* Singer, duo Thieves (later as McAlmont), 1993; Member, duo McAlmont and Butler (with Bernard Butler), 1994–95; Appearances include: Phoenix '95 Festival, 1995. *Recordings:* Albums: with McAlmont and Butler: The Sound of McAlmont and Butler, 1995; Solo: McAlmont, 1994; With David Arnold, Shaken and Stirred, 1997; Singles: Solo: Either, 1994; Honey, 1998; with McAlmont and Butler: Yes, 1995; You Do, 1995. *Address:* c/o MRM Productions, 9–11 Liverpool Rd, Islington, London N1 0RP, England.

MCALOON Paddy (Patrick Joseph); b. 7 June 1957, England. Musician; Singer; Songwriter. *Education:* BA, English and History, Ushaw College, Co Durham, University of Northumbria. *Career:* Singer, songwriter, Prefab Sprout; Extensive tours: UK; Europe; Japan; Numerous television appearances. *Compositions:* Songs covered by Kylie Minogue; Jimmy Nail; The Zombies; Cher; Contributed songs to television series Crocodile Shoes and Where the Heart Is. *Recordings:* Albums include: Swoon, 1984; Steve McQueen, 1985; From Langley Park To Memphis, 1988; Protest Songs, 1989; Jordan – The Comeback, 1990; Life of Surprises: Best of Prefab Sprout, 1992; Andromeda Heights, 1997. *Honours:* BRIT Award Nomination; Ivor Novello Nomination; BAFTA Nomination. *Membership:* BASCA. *Current Management:* Keith Armstrong, Kitchenware Records. *Address:* St Thomas St Stables, Newcastle Upon Tyne, England.

MACALPINE Tony; b. USA. Rock Musician (guitar, piano). *Musical Education:* Classical piano. *Career:* Solo artiste, rock guitarist, 1986–90; Formed MARS, short-lived supergroup, 1987; Founder, Squawk record label; Formed own band MacAlpine, 1990-. *Recordings:* Albums: Solo artiste: Edge of Insanity, 1986; Maximum Security, 1987; with MARS: Project Driver, 1987; with MacAlpine: Eyes of The World, 1990; Freedom to Fly, 1992; Madness, 1994; Premonition, 1994; Evolution, 1995; Master of Paradise, 1999.

MCANDREW Ian; b. 20 Oct. 1966, Sudbury, Suffolk, England. Artist Man. *Career:* Manager of artists and producers; Founded Wildlife Entertainment, 1986; Manager, Tasmin Archer; The Brand New Heavies; Bomb The Bass; Carleen Anderson; Tim Simenon; Travis; Connor Reeves. *Recordings:* 13 hits from 14 releases. *Honours:* 2 Platinum discs; 3 Gold discs; 1 Silver disc. *Membership:* Council Mem., International Managers Forum. *Leisure interests:* Old aeroplanes; Managing artists. *Address:* Wildlife Entertainment Ltd, 21 Heathmans Rd, Parsons Green, London SW6 4TJ, England.

MCATHEY Brent; b. 4 Aug. 1967, Calgary, Alberta, Canada. Singer; Songwriter. *Career:* Performs solo with prerecorded tracks or with 5 piece band in Canada; 7 piece Nashville Band in USA, Europe; Opened for: Joan Kennedy; Dick Damron; Michelle Wright; Prairie Oyster; Television: Capitol Country; Up and Coming; The Breakfast Show; Christmas Special; Radio: Canadian Super Country. *Recordings:* Brent McAthey, 9 songs composed by McAthey; Waitin' For The Sun, 1994, 3 songs by McAthey, 1 song co-written and duet with Dick Damron, 7 by Nashville Writers; Believe in Me. *Publications:* The Brent McAthey International Fan Club Newsletter. *Honours:* Nominated, Alberta Recording Asscn and Country Music Asscn of Calgary: 2 times, Most Promising New Artist; 2 times, Top Male Country artist; 2 times, Entertainer of the Year; 4 times, Top Male Recording Artist; Winner, Alberta's Male Recording Artist of the Year, Alberta Recording Industry Asscn, 1994–95. *Memberships:* Country Music Asscn of Calgary; Alberta Recording Industry Asscn; Canadian Music Asscn; CMA, Nashville; Texas Country Music Asscn; Arts Touring Alliance of Alberta; Canadian Asscn of Fairs and Exhibitions; Calgary Convention and Visitors Bureau; International Fan Club Organization. *Leisure interests:* Writing; Sports; Motorcycling. *Current Management:* PO Box 831, Black Diamond, AB T0L 0H0, Canada.

MCAULEY Jackie; b. Belfast, Northern Ireland. Musician (guitar); Songwriter. *Career:* Member, Them (with Van Morrison), aged 17; Founder member, Cult; Belfast Gypsies (with brother Pat); Trader Horn; Also solo artiste; Currently member, The Poor Mouth. *Compositions:* Dear John, recorded by Status Quo (No. 1, UK charts), 1982; 2 No. 1 recordings with the Heptones. *Current Management:* Jim McPhee, Acorn Entertainments. *Address:* Winterfold House, 46 Woodfield Rd, Kings Heath, Birmingham B13 9UJ, England.

MCAULIFFE Kim; b. England. Singer; Musician (guitar). *Career:* Founder member, UK all-girl rock band Girlschool, 1978–89; 1992–; Regular tours, including British tour with Motörhead, 1980. *Recordings:* Singles: St Valentine's Day Massacre EP, with Motörhead (as Headgirl); Please Don't Touch; Hit 'n' Run; C'mon Let's Go; I'm The Leader, with Gary Glitter; Albums: Demolition, 1980; Hit 'n' Run, 1981; Screaming Blue Murder, 1982; Play Dirty, 1983; Race With The Devil, 1986; Nightmare At Maple Cross, 1986; Take A Bite, 1988; Cheers You Lot, 1989; Girlschool, 1992; Girlschool Live, 1996; King Biscuit Flower Hour Presents, 1997.

MCBEAN Colin, (Mr G, Innersound, Mango Boy); b. London, England. Prod.; Remixer; DJ. *Career:* Started as DJ with London's KCC crew; Met Cisco Ferreira and started recording together, 1990; Formed The Advent; First release, 1994; The Advent split, 1999; Continued as solo artist, Mr G; Remixed: New Order; Lottie; Roger Sanchez; Hatiras. *Recordings:* Albums: with The Advent: Elements of Life, 1995; A New Beginning, 1997; Singles: solo: Get It Got It Good EP, Moments, Homeward Bound, 2001. *Address:* c/o Duty Free Recordings, Third Floor, 67 Farringdon Rd, London, EC1M 3JB, England.

MCBRIDE Martina; b. 29 July 1966, Medicine Lodge, Kansas, USA. Country Singer. m. John McBride, 2 d. *Career:* World-wide concert tours. *Recordings:* Albums: The Time Has Come, 1992; The Way That I Am, 1993; Wild Angels, 1995; Evolution, 1997; White Christmas, 1998; Emotion, 1999. *Honours:* CMA Video of the Year, 1994–95; CMA Song of the Year, 1995; Music Row Industry Awards Breakthrough Video; Billboard Nominations; Nammy Award, Video of the Year; Grammy Nominations, 1994; Nashville Music Awards, 1995–6; CMA Female Vocalist of the Year, 1999. *Address:* Bruce Allen Talent, #406–68 Water St, Vancouver, British Columbia V6B 1A4, Canada.

MCBRIDE Sean David; b. 7 Sept. 1953, San Francisco. Musician (Saxophone, Flute, Clarinet) Singer, Writer, Instrument teacher. m. Jean McBride, 1 s., 2 d. *Education:* BA, Essex University. *Career:* Progression of bands covering different styles of Rock Music, Soul, Reggae, Top 40 Covers, Rock 'n Roll; Performed with That'll Be The Day, 7 years; Also sessions and other media work. *Memberships:* Musicians Union; Equity; PRS. *Leisure interests:* Reading; Thinking; Living. *Address:* 9 Tidenham Way, Bristol, BS34 5LA, England.

MCBROOM Amanda; b. 9 Aug. 1947, Los Angeles, California, USA. Songwriter; Playwright; Singer; Actress. m. George Ball, 1 Dec. 1974. *Education:* BA, Drama, University of Texas. *Career:* Television: Mash; Star Trek; Hawaii 5–0; See-Saw, Broadway; Jacques Brel, Off-Broadway; Several appearances on The Tonight Show; Carnegie Hall; Rainbow and Stars; The Russian Tea Room; Greek Theatre; Great American Music Hall; Kennedy Center. *Compositions include:* The Rose. *Recordings:* Growing Up In Hollywood Town; West of Oz; Dreaming; Midnight Matinee; Amanda McBroom Live At Rainbow and Stars; Heartbeats-the cast album; Waiting Heart; Portraits: Best of Amanda McBroom. *Honours:* Grammy Nominations, The Rose, The Portrait; Golden Globe Award, Best Film Song, The Rose, 1980. *Memberships:* Actors Equity Asscn; Screen Actors Guild; NAS. *Leisure interests:* Gardening; Cooking; Animal husbandry. *Current Management:* Garry George Management.

MCCABE Nick; Musician (Guitar). *Career:* Founder Member, The Verve, 1990; Obtained record deal, 1991; Support slots to The Black Crowes in USA; Numerous live dates including Lollapalooza tour, 1994, and T in the Park festival; Band split; Rejoined, 1997; More live dates including Reading Festival, 1997; Split again, 1999. *Recordings:* Singles: She's A Superstar; Gravity Grave; All in the Mind; Slide Away; Blue; This is Music; On Your Own; History; Bittersweet Symphony; Lucky Man; Drugs Don't Work; Albums: A Storm in Heaven, 1993; No Come Down, 1994; A Northern Soul, 1995; Urban Hymns, 1997.

MCCAFFERTY Dan; Vocalist. *Career:* Founder member, Scottish rock group Nazareth, 1968–; Regular tours, UK, USA, Europe. *Recordings:* Albums: Nazareth, 1971; Exercises, 1972; Razamanaz, 1973; Loud 'N' Proud, 1974; Rampant, 1974; Hair of The Dog, 1975; Greatest Hits, 1975; Hot Tracks, 1976; Close Enough For Rock 'N' Roll, 1976; Playin' The Game, 1976; Expect No Mercy, 1977; No Mean City, 1978; Malice In Wonderland, 1980; The Fool Circle, 1981; 'Snaz, 1981; 2XS, 1982; Sound Elixir, 1983; The Catch, 1984; 20 Greatest Hits, 1985; Play The Game, 1985; Anthology – Nazareth, 1988; The Early Years, 1992; No Jive, 1992; From The Vaults, 1993; Move Me, 1995; Nazareth: Greatest Hits, 1996; Live at the Beeb, 1998; Boogaloo, 1998; Singles include: Broken Down Angel; Bad Bad Boy; This Flight Tonight; My White Bicycle; Love Hurts. *Current Management:* c/o Variety Artists International Inc, 846 Higuera St, Suite 5, San Luis Obispo, CA 93403, USA.

MCCANN Eamon; b. Creggan, Omagh, Northern Ireland. Singer; Musician (guitar). m. Margaret, 28 July 1979, 1 s., 3 d. *Education:* FTC; IRTE. *Musical Education:* Self-taught. *Career:* Television appearances include: RTE TV: Kenny Live; Live At 3; Its Bibi; Play The Game; Live From The Olympia; Lifelines; The Big Top; Summer Cabaret; Cúrsaí; Country Cool; Winning Streak; A Stretch in the Evening; Southern Nights; The Lyric Board; Anderson On The Box, Breakfast TV, PK to Right, Anderson on the Road, BBC; Kelly, UTV; Scotch 'N' Irish, Grampian Television; Radio appearances: Live on National Music Day, BBC Radio 2, 1994; RTE Radio 1; 2 FM; DTR; BBC Radio Ulster. *Compositions:* Joseph's Dream, 1998. *Recordings:* Everything That I Am; Can't Break It To My Heart; Bunch of Bright Red Roses; Gold In The Mountains; I Give You Music; I've Gone Crazy/Happy Birthday, CD single; Touch Wood, CD album; I Will Love You ('Til This Ring Turns Green); Clear Cut Country, CD Album. *Publications:* Don't Call Me; When You Come To Land; Life After You; Love Is Blind; The Gift of Love; Bunch of Bright Red Roses; Everything That I Am; More Than Two Weeks; The Love From Loneliness; Touch Wood; Exactly What I meant; Do I Really Have to Tell You That I Love You; My Home Ireland; I've Gone Crazy; Happy Birthday. *Honours:* Irish Showcase Award, Best New Male Singer, 1992; Northern Sound Radio, Best Male Singer, 1993; Donegal CMC, Best Male Singer, 1993, 1994; Rehab, Person of The Year, 1992; Ready Penny Inn, Best Male Singer of New Country, 1994, 1995; Personalities Entertainment Magazine Awards: Best Singer/Songwriter, 1995–96, Best Singer of New Country, 1995–96, Favourite Male Entertainer, 1996–97; Doubla K CMC Band of the Year, Dumfries, Scotland, 1996–97; Personalities Entertainment Magazine Awards Best Album, 1997–98; Irish World Awards Best Country Singer, 1997–98. *Memberships:* PRS; IMRO. *Leisure interests:* Gaelic football; Basketball; Squash. *Current Management:* 21st Century Promotions. *Address:* 8 Forthill Rd, Enniskillen, County Fermanagh BT74 6AW, Northern Ireland.

MCCANN Les, (Leslie Coleman); b. 23 Sept. 1935, Lexington, Kentucky, USA. Musician (piano, trumpet, keyboards). m. Charlotte Acentia Watkins, 1 s., 3 d. *Education:* LA City College. *Musical Education:* Westlake College of Music; LA City College. *Career:* White House Concert, with Aretha Franklin, 1994; Soul To Soul; African Tour and Movie; Tonight Show; Arsenio Hall Show; ROC, Fox TV; Ed Sullivan Show, CBS; Sunday Morning, CBS; Jazz Central, BET TV; Hands Across America; All major jazz festivals. *Recordings:* 84 albums; Much Les, 1968; Swiss Movement, 1969; Recent releases include: On the Soul Side, 1994; Listen Up, 1995; Pacifique, 1998; Second Movement, 1998; With Lou Rawls: Stormy Monday, 1962; with Yousef Lateef: Anthology, 1994; Featured on Atlantic Jazz Classics, 1998; Jazz for When You're Alone, 1999. *Publications:* Musican As Artist (paintings). *Honours:* First person chosen to teach at Harvard University: Artist As Performer. *Membership:* BMI; ASCAP. *Leisure interests:* Photography; Water Colour Painting; Tennis. *Current Management:* Fred Hirsch Management.

MCCANN Peter; Songwriter; Singer. *Education:* Graduate, Fairfield University, Connecticut, 1970. *Career:* Signed to Motown Records, 1971; 20th Century Fox Records, 1977 (bought by CBS, 1978); Moved to Nashville, 1985; Association with EMI music publishing; Songs recorded by: Julio Iglesias; Anne Murray; Crystal Gayle; Kenny Rogers; Oak Ridge Boys; Isaac Hayes; K T Oslin; Lynn Anderson; Ricky Nelson; Andy Williams; Paul Anka; Karen Carpenter; Lectures on songwriting for music organizations. *Recordings:* Do You Wanna Make Love?, Peter McCann, 1977; The Right Time of The Night, Jennifer Warnes, 1977; One on One, 1979; She's Single Again, Janie Fricke (No. 1); Nobody Falls Like A Fool, Earl Thomas Conley (No. 1); Treat Me Like A Stranger, Baillie and the Boys; Also sang on Whitney Houston debut album (25m. sales); What Christmas Really Means, 1995. *Honour:* Grammy for Kathy Mattea Christmas album. *Membership:* Vice-president, Nashville Songwriters Asscn, Co-chair, Legislative committee. *Current Management:* SESAC. *Address:* 55 Music Sq. E, Nashville, TN 37203, USA.

MCCARTNEY (James) Paul (Sir); b. 18 June 1942, Liverpool, England. Singer; Songwriter; Musician (bass). m. Linda Eastman, 12 March 1969, deceased April 1998, 1 s., 2 d., 1 step-d. *Musical Education:* Self-taught. *Career:* Member, The Quarrymen, 1957–59; The Beatles, 1960–70; Founder, Apple Corporation Ltd; Formed MPL Group of Companies, 1970; Founder, group Wings, 1970–81; Solo artiste, 1970–; International tours, concerts, television, radio and film appearances; Founder, Liverpool Institute of Performing Arts, 1995. *Compositions:* Co-writer, songs with John Lennon include: Love Me Do; Please Please Me; From Me To You; She Loves You; Can't Buy Me Love; I Want To Hold Your Hand; I Saw Her Standing There; Eight Days A Week; All My Loving; Help!; Ticket To Ride; I Feel Fine; A Hard Day's Night; Yesterday; Eleanor Rigby; Yellow Submarine; Penny Lane; All You Need Is Love; Lady Madonna; Hey Jude; We Can Work It Out; Day Tripper; Paperback Writer; When I'm Sixty-Four; A Day In The Life; Back In The USSR; Hello Goodbye; Get Back; Let It Be; Later compositions: Band On The Run; Mull of Kintyre; Coming Up; Ebony and Ivory; No More Lonely Nights; Pipes of Peace; Other works include: Give My Regards To Broad Street (film score), 1984; Liverpool Oratorio, conducted by Carl Davis, 1991; Standing Stone (orchestral work), commisioned for EMI Centennial celebrations, debut by LSO at Albert Hall, London, 1997. *Recordings include:* Albums: with the Beatles: Please Please Me, 1963; A Hard Day's Night, 1964; Beatles For Sale, 1964; Help!, 1965; Rubber Soul, 1965; Revolver, 1966; Sgt Pepper's Lonely Hearts Club Band, 1967; Magical Mystery Tour, 1967; The Beatles (White Album), 1968; Yellow Submarine, 1969; Abbey Road, 1969; Let It Be, 1970; with Wings include: Wildlife, 1971; Red Rose Speedway, 1973; Band On The Run, 1973; Venus and Mars, 1975; Wings At The Speed of Sound, 1976; Wings Over America, 1976; London Town, 1978; Wings Greatest Hits, 1978; Back To The Egg, 1979; Solo albums: McCartney, 1970; Ram, 1971; McCartney II, 1980; Tug of War, 1982; Pipes of Peace, 1983; Give My Regards To Broad Street, 1984; Press To Play, 1986; All The Best!, 1987; Flowers In The Dirt, 1989; Tripping The Light Fantastic, 1990; Unplugged, 1991; Choba b CCCP, 1991; Paul McCartney's Liverpool Oratorio, 1991; Off The Ground, 1993; Paul Is Live, 1993; Standing Stone (orchestral), 1997; A Garland for Linda, with 8 other composers, for a capella choir, 2000. *Honours include:* MBE, 1965; Numerous Grammy awards; 3 Ivor Novello Awards, including Special Award for International Achievement, 1980; Freeman, City of Liverpool, 1984; Doctorate, University of Sussex, 1988; Guinness Book of Records Award, most successful composer to date, 1979; Q Merit Award, 1990; Knighthood, 1997. *Address:* c/o MPL Communications, 1 Soho Sq., London W1V 6BQ, England.

MCCARTNEY Michelle; b. 5 April 1960, Paris, France. Singer; Musician (bass guitar). *Musical Education:* Self-taught bass and rhythm guitar. *Career:* Pop rock/folk singer; Major tour with Jackie Lomax (legendary blues performer); Television appearances, USA; Many radio interviews in America; Performed at major US Theatres, International Trade Shows; Tours, major US college and university circuit. *Recordings:* Singles: Everybody Wants My Man; Rocomotion; Money For Honey; Michelle; Billet-Doux; Till I Get You Back. *Publication:* The Beatles Book, UK fanzine. *Honour:* Best Dee-Jay Pop Pick in USA, for Till I Get You Back, 1993. *Membership:* ASCAP. *Leisure interests:* Karting; Songwriting; Reading comic books and biographies; Collecting vinyl records. *Current Management:* Allstar Management Incorporated. *Address:* 189 rue du Temple, 75003 Paris, France.

MCCAULEY John(ny); b. 23 April 1925, Co Derry, Northern Ireland. Songwriter; Singer; Musician (Guitar). m. Phyllis, 25 June 1949, 1 s. *Musical Education:* Weekly music education class (voluntary), St Eugene's School. *Career:* Over 70 Country and Irish songs recorded by many major artists in Ireland including many No 1 hits; Songs recorded by Daniel O'Donnell, Big Tom, Larry Cunningham, Brian Coll, Declan Nearney, Margo, Philomena Begley; Formed, Johnny McCauley Trio. *Compositions include:* Among the Wicklow Hills; My Donegal Shore; 5000 Miles from Sligo; Just Pretending; Any Tipperary Town; Pretty Girl from Omagh; Destination Donegal. *Recording:* From Ireland Country Style EP, which introduced Country 'n' Irish music. *Publication:* Skiff Rock, Beginner's Guitar Tutor, 1957. *Honours:* Honoured by Lord Mayor of Derry; 73rd birthday celebration featured many famous Irish artists; Lifetime Achievement Award, 1998. *Memberships:* MCPS; PRS; BASCA; IMRO. *Address:* 112 Preston Hill, Kenton, Harrow, Middlesex HA3 9SJ, England.

MCCLAIN Charly (Charlotte Denise); b. 26 March 1956, Jackson, Tennessee, USA. Country vocalist; Songwriter; Actor. m. Wayne Massey, July 1984. *Career:* Sang with brother in Charlotte and the Volunteers, age 9; Worked on the mid-South Jamboree 1973–75; Changed name to Charly

and modelled swimsuits, early 1970s; Toured with country singer OB McClinton; Signed to Epic, 1976; 39 Billboard country chart entries on Epic and Mercury Records until 1989; Collaborations: Johnny Rodriguez; Mickey Gilley; Wayne Massey; TV appearances include: Hart To Hart; CHIPS; Austin City Limits; Fantasy Island; Solid Gold; So You Want To Be A Star. *Recordings include:* Radio Heart, 1985; Paradise Tonight (with Mickey Gilley), 1983; Who's Cheatin' Who, 1980; Sentimental Ol' You, 1983; Dancing Your Memory Away, 1982; Albums: The Woman In Me, 1984; It Takes Believers (with Mickey Gilley), 1984; Surround Me With Love, 1981. *Honours:* Music City News, Most Promising Female Vocalist, 1981. *Address:* c/o John D Lentz, PO Box 198888, Nashville, TN 37219, USA.

MCCLARNON Liz (Elizabeth Margaret); b. 10 April 1981, Liverpool, England. Vocalist. *Career:* Joined Atomic Kitten 1999; UK Support tours 1999–2000; Co-spearheaded MTV Asia Awards 2000 reaching 675m. viewers; Pan-European breakthrough with Whole Again single; Guest at Celebrate South Africa Freedom Concert, London, 2001. *Recordings:* Albums: Right Now, 2000 (revised issue 2001); Singles: Right Now, 1999; See Ya, 2000; I Want Your Love, 2000; Follow Me, 2000; Whole Again, 2001; Eternal Flame, 2001. *Honours:* Successes at UK Disney Channel and Smash Hits Awards 2000/2001. *Current Management:* Innocent Records, Kensal House, 553–579 Harrow Rd, London, W10 4RH, England.

MCCLUSKEY Andy; b. 24 June 1959, Wirral, Cheshire, England. Vocalist. *Career:* Formed Id, 1977–78; Member, Dalek I Love You, 1978; Co-founder, singer, Orchestral Manoeuvres In The Dark (OMD), 1978–; Tours and concerts include: Tours, Europe, USA, Japan, Australia; Futurama Festival, Leeds, 1979; Supports to Talking Heads, Gary Numan, 1979; Festival of the 10th Summer, Manchester, 1986; Cities In The Park Festival, Prestwich, 1991; Support to Simple Minds, Milton Keynes Bowl, 1991. *Recordings:* Singles include: Messages, 1980; Enola Gay, 1980; Souvenir, 1981; Joan of Arc, 1981; Maid of Orleans, 1982; Genetic Engineering, 1983; Locomotion, 1984; Talking Loud and Clear, 1984; Tesla Girls, 1984; So In Love, 1985; If You Leave (used in film soundtrack Pretty In Pink), 1986; (Forever) Live and Die, 1986; Dreaming, 1988; Sailing On The Seven Seas, 1991; Pandora's Box, 1991; Stand Above Me, 1993; Dream of Me, 1993; Albums: Orchestral Manoeuvres In The Dark, 1980; Organisation, 1980; Architecture and Morality, 1981; Dazzle Ships, 1982; Junk Culture, 1984; Crush, 1985; The Pacific Age, 1986; In The Dark – The Best of OMD, 1988; Sugar Tax, 1991; Liberator, 1993; Walking on the Milky Way, 1996; Universal, 1996; Singles, 1998; Contributor, The Message of Love, Arthur Baker, 1989. *Current Management:* Direct Management Group, 947 La Cienega Blvd, Suite G, Los Angeles, CA 90069, USA.

MCCOO Marilyn; b. 30 Sept. 1944, Jersey City, New Jersey, USA. Singer. m. Billy Davis Jr, 1969. *Education:* BS in Business Administration, UCLA, 1965. *Career:* Member, the Hi-Fis; Vocalist, US harmony group Fifth Dimension (formerly the Versatiles, the Vocals), 1966–75; Appearances include: San Remo Festival, 1967; Bal Paree and Bambi Awards, Munich, Germany, 1970; Royal Albert Hall, London, 1972; Concert at the White House for President Nixon, 1973; Duo with Billy Davis Jr, 1976–80; Co-host, The Marilyn McCoo and Billy Davis Jr Show, CBS-TV, 1977; Solo artist, 1980–; Television host, Solid Gold, 1981–87; Performance before Pope John Paul II, San Antonio, Texas with Billy Davis Jr; Theatrical performances include: Man of La Mancha; Anything Goes; Showboat, Broadway, 1995; Showboat, Chicago, 1996. *Recordings:* Albums: with Fifth Dimension: Up Up and Away, 1967; The Magic Garden, 1968; Stoned Soul Picnic, 1968; Age of Aquarius, 1969; Fantastic, 1970; Portrait, 1970; The July 5th Album, 1970; Love's Lines, Angles and Rhymes, 1971; Live!, 1971; Reflections, 1971; Individually and Collectively, 1972; Greatest Hits On Earth, 1972; Living Together, Growing Together, 1973; Earthbound, 1975; Greatest Hits, 1988; with Billy Davis Jr: I Hope We Get To Love In Time, 1977; The Two of Us, 1977; Marilyn and Billy, 1978; Solo: Solid Gold, 1983; The Me Nobody Knows, 1991; Singles: with Fifth Dimension: Up Up and Away, 1967; Carpet Man, 1968; Stoned Soul Picnic, 1968; Sweet Blindness, 1968; Aquarius/Let The Sunshine In, based on musical Hair (No. 1, USA), 1969; Wedding Bell Blues (No. 1, USA), 1969; Save The Country, 1970; One Less Bell To Answer, 1970; Never My Love, 1971; Last Night I Didn't Get To Sleep At All, 1972; If I Could Reach You, 1972; with Billy Davis Jr: You Don't Have To Be A Star (No. 1, USA), 1977; Your Love, 1977. *Honours:* Grammy Awards: 4 awards, 1968; 2 awards (with Fifth Dimension), 1970; 1 award (with Billy Davis Jr), 1977; Grand Prize, Tokyo Music Festival, with Billy Davis Jr, 1977; Hon. Doctorate, Talladega University, Alabama, 1988; Star on Hollywood Walk of Fame (with Fifth Dimension), 1991. *Current Management:* The Sterling/Winters Co, 16th Floor, 1900 Avenue of the Stars, Los Angeles, CA 90067, USA.

MCCULLOCH Ian; b. 5 May 1959, Liverpool, England. Vocalist. *Career:* Founder, the Crucial Three, 1977; Group renamed Echo and The Bunnymen, 1978–88; Major appearances include: Futurama Festival, Leeds, 1979; Daze of Future Past, Leeds, 1981; WOMAD Festival, 1982;

York Rock Festival, 1984; Solo artiste, 1988–; Founder, The Prodigal Sons, 1990; US tour, 1990; Founder, McCulloch's Mysterioso Show, 1992; Formed Electrafixion, with Will Sergeant; Reformed Echo and the Bunnymen, 1999. *Recordings:* Albums with Echo and The Bunnymen: Crocodiles, 1980; Heaven Up Here, 1981; Porcupine, 1983; Ocean Rain, 1984; Songs To Learn and Sing, 1985; Echo and The Bunnymen, 1987; What Are You Going To Do With Your Life, 1999; Evergreen, 2000; Live in Concert, 2000; Solo albums: Candleland, 1989; Mysterio, 1992; With Electrafixion: Album: Burned, 1995; Singles include: with Echo and The Bunnymen: The Cutter, 1983; Never Stop, 1983; The Killing Moon, 1984; Seven Seas, 1984: Silver, 1984; Bring On The Dancing Horses, 1985; The Game, 1987; Lips Like Sugar, 1987; People Are Strange, from film The Lost Boys, 1988; Bedbugs and Ballyhoo, 1988; Pictures on my Wall, 1995; I Want To Be There When You Come, 1997; Get in the Car, 1998; Rust, 1999; Solo: September Song, 1984; Honey Drip, 1992; Lover Lover Lover, 1992; with Electrafixion: Zephyr, 1994; Never, 1995; Contributor, Last Temptation of Elvis compilation album, 1990. *Address:* c/o London Records, PO Box 1422, Chancellors House, Chancellors Rd, London W6 9SG, England.

MCCUSKER John; b. 15 May 1973, Bothwell, Scotland. Musician (fiddle, tin whistle, cittern, accordion, keyboards); Composer; Prod. m. Kate Rusby. *Musical Education:* Royal Academy, Glasgow, Scotland. *Career:* Began playing whistle aged 5, and fiddle aged 7; Played in youth orchestras; Joined a Ceilidh band, aged 12; Formed folk band Parcel O' Rogues with school friends, aged 14; Invited to join renowned Scottish folk group The Battlefield Band, aged 17; Recorded and toured internationally with The Battlefield Band; Has recorded 2 solo albums and has made guest appearances on over 100 albums; Produced albums for: Kate Rusby; Eliza Carthy; Cathie Ryan; Composed music with Kate Rusby for film Heartlands, 2002. *Recordings:* Albums: John McCusker, 1995; Yella Hoose, 2000; with Parcel O' Rogues: Parcel O' Rogues, 1987; with The Battlefield Band: After Hours, 1987; New Spring, 1991; Quiet Days, 1992; Threads, 1995; Across The Borders, 1997; Rain Hail Or Shine, 1998; Leaving Friday Harbor, 1999; Happy Daze, 2001; features on: Thirteen, Teenage Fanclub, 1993; Kate Rusby and Hathryn Roberts, 1995; Incholm, William Jackson, 1996; Easter Snow, Seamus Tansey, 1997; Donegal Rain, Andy Stewart, 1997; Eliza Carthy and The Kings of Calicutt, 1997; Hourglass, Kate Rusby, 1998; Sleepless, Kate Rusby, 1999; Little Lights, Kate Rusby, 2001; Somewhere Along The Road, Cathie Ryan, 2001. *Honours:* Glenfiddich Spirit of Scotland Award for Music, 1999. *Internet:* www.johnmccusker.demon.co.uk.

MCDANIEL Mel Houston; b. 9 Sept. 1942, Checotah, Oklahoma, USA. Country vocalist; Songwriter; Musician (guitar). *Career:* Performer from age 14; Professional debut at 15 in talent contest, Okmulgee; Worked clubs in Oklahoma, Arkansas and Kansas; Worked in King X Club, Anchorage, Arkansas, 1970–72; Debut single Lazy Me written by J J Cale; Moved to Nashville without success, 1969; Returned as staff writer and demo singer for Combine Music, 1973; Performed at the Holiday Inn lounge; Signed to Capitol Records, 1976; Over 40 Billboard country chart entries on Capitol Records until 1989; Some singles credited as Mel McDaniels; Successful songwriting career in both pop and country; Grandest Lady of Them All used to celebrate Grand Ole Opry 60th anniversary; Continues to tour an average of 200 dates per year with own band Oklahoma Wind. *Compositions include:* Goodbye Marie; Roll Your Own; Grandest Lady of Them All; Goodbye Marie; I Could Sure Use This Feeling; I Just Want To Feel The Magic; Never Say Never. *Recordings include:* Baby's Got Her Blue Jeans On, 1984; Big Ole Brew, 1982; Stand Up, 1985; Let It Roll, 1985; Louisiana Saturday Night, 1981; Albums: Let It Roll, 1985; I'm Countryfied, 1981; Stand Up, 1985. *Honours:* Grammy Award, Best Country Vocal Performance – Male, 1984. *Memberships:* Grand Old Opry, 1986. *Leisure interests:* Fishing. *Address:* c/o The Bobby Roberts Company Inc, 909 Meadowlark Lane, Goodlettsville, TN 37072, USA.

MCDILL Bob (Robert Lee); b. 5 April 1944, Beaumont, Texas, USA. Songwriter. m. Nancy Whitsett, 6 Oct. 1971, 1 s., 2 d. *Education:* Lamar University, 1962–66. *Career:* Staff writer, Jack Music, Nashville, 1969–75; Hall Clement Publications, Nashville, 1975–84; Owner, writer, Ranger Bob Music, Nashville, 1984. *Compositions:* 25 US No. 1 hits include: for Don Williams: Say It Again; She Never Knew Me; Good Ole Boys Like Me; for Ronnie Milsap; Nobody Likes Sad Songs; for Dan Seals: Everything That Glitters; for Mel McDaniel: Baby's Got Her Blue Jeans On; for Waylon Jennings: Amanda. *Honours:* Distinguished Alumnus Award University, Lamar University, 1989; Composer of Year, Cash Box magazine, 1979, 1986; Approximately 40 awards from BMI, CMA, Nashville Songwriters Asscn; 11 ASCAP Awards; 2 Grammy Awards; Top Songwriter, World Record magazine, 1977; Inducted into Nashville Songwriters Asscn Hall of Fame, 1985. *Memberships:* ASCAP; NARAS.

MACDONALD Calum; b. 12 Nov. 1953, Lochmaddy, North Uist, Scotland. Musician (songwriter, percussion, drums). *Career:* Former member, Scottish celtic rock band, Runrig; International concerts include: Canada, 1987; Berlin, 1987; Support to U2, Murrayfield Stadium, Edinburgh, 1987; Support to Genesis, 1993; Support to Rolling Stones, 1995; Concerts at:

Royal Concert Hall, Glasgow; Open-air concert, Loch Lomond. *Recordings:* Albums: Play Gaelic, 1978; Highland Connection, 1979; Recovery, 1981; Heartland, 1985; The Cutter and The Clan, 1987; Once In A Lifetime, 1988; Searchlight, 1989; The Big Wheel, 1991; Amazing Things, 1993; Transmitting Live, 1995; Mara, 1995; Long Distance, 1996; In Search of Angels, 1999. *Honours:* Amazing Things, Environmental Album of the Year, 1993. *Current Management:* Marlene Ross Management, 55 Wellington St, Aberdeen AB2 1BX, Scotland.

MCDONALD 'Country' Joe; b. 1 Jan. 1942, El Monte, California, USA. Singer; Musician (guitar). *Career:* Founder, folk group, Instant Action Jug Band, 1964; Group became Country Joe and The Fish, 1965–70; Concerts with Moby Grape, Howlin' Wolf, Led Zeppelin; Appeared at festivals: Monterey Festival, 1967; Miami Festival, 1968; Woodstock Festival, 1969; New Orleans Pop Festival, 1969; Solo artiste, 1971–; Concerts include: Bickershaw Festival, 1972; Concert with Grateful Dead, Boz Scaggs and Jefferson Starship, Vietnam Veteran's Project, 1982; Maine Arts Festival, 1989; Sporadic line-ups as The All-Star Band, Country Joe and The Fish; Also member, Energy Crisis and Barry Melton Band. *Recordings:* Albums: with Country Joe and The Fish: Electric Music For The Mind and Body, 1967; I Feel Like I'm Fixin' To Die, 1968; Together, 1968; Here We Are Again, 1969; Tonight I'm Singing For You, 1970; Solo albums: War War War, 1971; Country Joe, 1975; Paradise With An Ocean View, 1975. *Address:* c/o Tapestry Artists, 17337 Ventura Blvd, Suite 208, Encino, CA 91316–3956, USA.

MCDONALD Dave; b. 1964. Member, Portishead; Musician (Drums and Drum Machines); Prod. *Career:* Joined Portishead with Geoff Barrow, Beth Gibbons and Adrian Utley; Band signed to Go!Beat Records, 1993; Film, To Kill A Dead Man, shown in cinemas and projected on the MI5 building, London, 1995; Glastonbury Festival appearance, 1995; Live internet broadcast of New York concert, 1997. *Recordings:* Singles: Wour Times, 1994; Numb, 1994; Glory Box, 1995; All Mine, 1997; Cowboys EP, 1997; Albums: Dummy, 1994; Portishead, 1997. *Publication:* Straight Outta Bristol: Massive Attack, Portishead, Tricky and the Roots of Trip Hop, 1995. *Honour:* Mercury Music Prize, 1994.

MCDONALD J Chris; b. 25 April 1954, Millington, Tennessee, USA. Musician (trombone); Arranger; Bandleader. m. Brenda Moore, 14 Feb. 1988, 1 s. *Education:* BS, Education, University of Tennessee, 1977. *Career:* Musical director, arranger, Miss Tennessee Pageant, Jackson, 1977–; Trombonist, Nashville Jazz Machine; Leader, Contraband, 1978–; Conductor, arranger, Brenda Lee, 1982–85. *Recordings:* Arranger for artists including: Lee Greenwood; Amy Grant; BeBe and CeCe Winans; Kenny Marks; Larnelle Harris. *Memberships:* ASCAP; AFofM; NARAS.

MCDONALD Michael; b. 2 Dec. 1952, St Louis, Missouri, USA. Singer; Musician (keyboards); Songwriter. m. Amy Holland, 1 s. *Career:* Regular session singer; Member, Steely Dan, 1974; Songwriter, keyboard player, Doobie Brothers, 1975–82; Concerts include: Great American Music Fair, 1975; Day On The Green, 1976; Canada Jam, 1978; Solo artiste, 1982–; Concerts include: Roy Orbison All-Star Benefit Tribute, 1990; Special guest, Tina Turner tour, 1990; Rock 'n' Soul Revue, New York, 1991; Benefit concert for family of late Jeff Porcaro (drummer with Toto), 1993. *Compositions include:* It Keeps You Runnin', Carly Simon, 1976; Co-writer, You Belong To Me, 1978; What A Fool Believes (No. 1, USA), 1979; Minute By Minute, 1979; Real Love, 1980; Take It To Heart, 1990; Collaborations with Kenny Loggins; Michael Jackson; Brenda Russell. *Recordings:* Albums: with The Doobie Brothers: Takin' It To The Streets, 1976; Livin' On The Fault Line, 1977; Minute By Minute (No. 1, USA), 1978; One Step Closer, 1980; Solo albums: That Was Then – The Early Recordings of Michael McDonald, 1982; If That's What It Takes, 1982; No Lookin' Back, 1985; Sweet Freedom, 1986; Take It To Heart, 1990; Blink of An Eye, 1993; Blue Obsession, 1997; Other recordings (as writer and/or singer) include: Together (film soundtrack), 1979; Christopher Cross, Christopher Cross, 1979; High Adventure, Kenny Loggins, 1982; The Winner In You, LaBelle, 1986; Anywhere You Go, David Pack, 1986; Decisions, The Winans, 1987; Back of My Mind, Christopher Cross, 1988; Love At Large (film soundtrack), 1990; The Offbeat of Avenues, Manhattan Transfer, 1991; Singles include: Let Me Go Love, with Nicolette Larson; I Keep Forgettin' (Every Time You're Near), 1982; Yah Mo B There, with James Ingram, 1984; Sweet Freedom, from film soundtrack Running Scared, 1986; Tear it Up, 1990; Hey Girl, 1993; Matters of the Heart, 1994; Appeared on: Ride Like The Wind, Christopher Cross, 1979; I'll Be Over You, Toto, 1986. *Honours:* Grammy Awards: Record of the Year, Song of the Year, Best Pop Vocal Performance, Best Vocal Arrangement, 1979; Ivor Novello Award, Best Film Theme, 1987. *Current Management:* Howard Kaufman, HK Management, 8900 Wilshire Blvd, Suite 300, Beverly Hills, CA 90211, USA.

MCDONALD Richie; b. 6 Feb. 1962, Lubbock, Texas, USA. Country vocalist; Musician (guitar); Songwriter. *Career:* Began singing and writing music in school; Moved to Dallas and sang with award-winning band, Showdown; Sang on national US commercials, earning enough to move to

Nashville to pursue career; Formed Texasee with Dean Sams, Keech Rainwater, Michael Britt and John Rich, 1992; Group became resident house band at the Wildhorse Saloon, Nashville; After subsequent name change to Lonestar, came to the attention of BMG and were signed to their BNA subsidiary; Released promotional six-track live CD, recorded at the Wildhorse; First country chart entry No News/Tequila Talkin' from debut album Lonestar, 1996; Same year duetted with Mindy McCready on the country hit Maybe He'll Notice Her Now; Sole featured lead vocalist on Lonestar's second album, Crazy Nights, prompting the departure of previous joint lead singer John Rich, 1998; Single, Amazed, from third album became huge international hit and career record to date, 1999; Has written a fair share of Lonestar's output as well as material for other country artists; By early 2000s, Lonestar estimated to be the most successful country group in the world. *Compositions include:* Everything's Changed; She's Always Right; I Couldn't Dream A Love Better Than This. *Recordings include:* No News, Tequila Talkin', Maybe She'll Notice Him Now (solo with Mindy McCready), 1996; Come Cryin' To Me, You Walked In, 1997; Say When, Everything's Changed, 1998; Amazed, Smile, 1999; I'm Already There, 2002; Albums include: Lonestar, 1995; Crazy Nights, 1997; Lonely Grill, 1999; I'm Already There, 2001. *Leisure interests:* Running; Writing songs. *Address:* c/o The Country Music Asscn, Nashville, Tennessee, USA.

MACDONALD Rory; b. 27 July 1949, Dornoch, Sutherland, Scotland. Vocalist; Musician (guitar, bass). *Career:* Founder member, Scottish folk group Runrig, 1973–; International concerts include: Canada; Berlin; Support to Murrayfield Stadium, Edinburgh, 1987; Concerts at: Royal Concert Hall, Glasgow; Open-air concert, Loch Lomond. *Recordings:* Albums: Play Gaelic, 1978; Highland Connection, 1979; Recovery, 1981; Heartland, 1985; The Cutter and The Clan, 1987; Once In A Lifetime, 1988; Searchlight, 1989; The Big Wheel, 1991; Amazing Things, 1993; Transmitting Live, 1995; Troubadours of British Folk Vol. 3, 1995; Mara, 1996; The Best of British Folk Rock, 1997. *Current Management:* Marlene Ross Management, 55 Wellington St, Aberdeen AB2 1BX, Scotland.

MCELHONE Johnny; b. 21 April 1963, Glasgow, Scotland. Musician (Bass); Prod. *Career:* Member, Altered Images; Joined Hipsway; Currently, member of Texas; Numerous tours, festivals and TV appearances. *Recordings:* Singles with Altered Images: Dead Pop Stars; Happy Birthday; See Those Eyes; Pinky Blue; Hipsway: The Honey Thief; Texas: I Don't Want a Lover, 1989; Tired of Being Alone, 1993; Say What You Want; Halo; Put Your Arms Around Me; Black Eyed Boy; In Our Lifetime, 1999; Summer Son, 1999; Albums with Texas: Southside, 1989; Mother's Heaven, 1991; Rick's Road, 1993; White on Blonde, 1997; The Hush, 1999.

MCELHONE Sean; b. 4 Jan. 1970, Leeds, Yorkshire, England. Musician (guitar, keyboards). 2 d. *Musical Education:* Self-taught. *Career:* Television: ITV: Chart Show; Music Box; Radio: Radio 1, session, John Peel; Concerts: Reading Festival; Roundhay Park; Locomotive, Paris; Supported on tour: The Stone Roses; Happy Mondays; Inspiral Carpets. *Recordings:* One album; Singles: Just Good Friends; Give In; Honesty; Spirit; Don't Fear The Reaper. *Membership:* Musicians' Union. *Current Management:* Music; Art; Computers. *Address:* 37 St Alban Rd, Leeds LS9 6LA, England.

MCENTIRE Reba Nell; b. 28 March 1955, Chockie, Oklahoma, USA. Singer. m. (1) Charlie Battles, 1976, divorced; (2) Narvel Blackstock, 1989. *Career:* Singer with sister and brother as the Singing McEntires, 1972; Solo recording career (over 30m. album sales to date), 1976–; Film appearance, Tremors; 7 members of her band killed in plane crash, 1991. *Recordings:* Albums: Reba McEntire, 1977; Out of a Dream, 1979; Feel The Fire, 1980; Heart To Heart, 1981; Unlimited, 1982; Behind The Scenes, 1983; Just A Little Love, 1984; Have I Got A Deal For You, 1985; My Kind of Country, 1986; Whoever's In New England, 1986; What Am I Gonna Do About You, 1986; The Last One To Know, 1987; So So So Long, 1988; Merry Christmas To You, 1988; Reba, 1988; Sweet Sixteen, 1989; Live, 1989; Rumour Has It, 1990; For My Broken Heart, 1991; It's Your Call, 1992; Read My Mind, 1994; Starting Over, 1995; US Country No. 1 hits: Can't Even Get The Blues; You're The First Time I've Thought About Leaving; How Blue; Somebody Should Leave; Other hit singles include: (You Lift Me) Up To Heaven; Today All Over Again; For My Broken Heart; Whoever's In New England. *Current Management:* c/o Narvel Blackstock, Starstruck Entertainment, PO Box 121996, Nashville, TN 37212, USA.

MCERLAINE Ally; b. 31 Oct. 1968, Glasgow, Scotland. Musician (Guitar). *Career:* Member, Texas; Numerous tours, festivals and TV appearances. *Recordings:* Singles: I Don't Want a Lover, 1989; Tired of Being Alone, 1993; Say What You Want; Halo; Put Your Arms Around Me; Black Eyed Boy; In Our Lifetime, 1999; Summer Son, 1999; Albums: Southside, 1989; Mother's Heaven, 1991; Rick's Road, 1993; White on Blonde, 1997; The Hush, 1999.

MCEVOY Eleanor; b. 22 Jan. 1967, Dublin, Ireland. Vocalist; Musician (guitar, violin); Songwriter. *Musical Education:* BA Mod, Music, Trinity College, Dublin; Started violin lessons, aged 8. *Career:* Played with

National Symphony Orchestra of Ireland, 1988; Left to pursue solo career with major success on A Woman's Heart project; Numerous US and European tours with band; Performed for 80,000 in Dublin during US President Clinton's visit; Numerous TV appearances; Featured on soundtracks to TV series Clueless and films The Nephew and Some Mother's Son. *Compositions include:* Only A Woman's Heart, title track of album. *Recordings:* Singles: Only A Woman's Heart, 1994; Precious Little, 1996; Please Heart You're Killing Me, 1999; Albums: A Woman's Heart, 1992; Eleanor McEvoy, 1994; What's Following Me? 1996; Snapshots, 1999; Yola, 2001. *Honours:* Irish Record Industry Awards, Best Solo Artist, 1992; Irish Recorded Music Asscn, Best New Artist, 1992; Featured tracks on Ireland's best ever selling album, A Woman's Heart, 1992; Hot Press Magazine Awards: Best Solo Performer, 1992; Best Songwriter, 1993; Irish National Entertainment Award, Best New Artist, 1993. *Membership:* IMRO, board mem.; IBEC Music Industry Group. *Current Management:* Real Good Management Ltd. *Address:* 17 Dame Court, Dublin 2, Ireland. *E-mail:* eleanor@eleanormcevoy.org. *Internet:* www.eleanormcevoy.net.

MCFADDEN Brian (Bryan); b. 12 April 1980, Dublin, Ireland. Singer. m. Kerry Katona, Jan. 2002, 1 d. *Career:* Member, Westlife; Numerous television appearances and hit singles. *Recordings:* Singles: Swear It Again (No. 1, UK), 1999; Flying Without Wings (No. 1, UK), 1999; Seasons in the Sun/I Have a Dream (No. 1, UK) 1999; Fool Again (No. 1, UK), 2000; Against All Odds (with Mariah Carey; No. 1, UK), 2000; My Love (No. 1, UK), 2000; What Makes A Man, 2000; Uptown Girl (in aid of Comic Relief charity; No. 1, UK), 2001; Queen of My Heart (No. 1, UK), 2001; World of Our Own (No. 1, UK), 2002; Albums: Westlife, 1999; Coast To Coast (No. 1, UK), 2000; World of Our Own (No. 1, UK), 2001.

MACFARLANE Denis, (Dego, Tek 9); b. London, England. Prod.; Remixer; DJ. *Career:* Member: 4 Hero; Nu-Era; Jacob's Optical Stairway; Co-founder: Reinforced Records, 1990; Black Records, 2000; Collaborations: Alex Attias; Roy Ayers; IG Culture; Jill Scott; Ursula Rucker. *Recordings:* Albums: with 4 Hero: In Rough Territory, 1991; Parallel Universe, 1995; Jacob's Optical Stairway (with Jacob's Optical Stairway), 1996; It's Not What You Think It Is (as Tek 9), 1996; Two Pages, 1998; Simply (as Tek 9), 2000; Creating Patterns, 2001; Singles: with 4 Hero: Mr Kirk's Nightmare, 1991; Earth Pioneers, 1997; Escape That, 1999; Les Fleurs, 2001. *Honours:* Mercury Music Prize nominee, Two Pages, 1998. *Address:* c/o Reinforced Records, 387–389 Chapter Rd, London, NW2 5NG, England.

MACFARLANE Malcolm Douglas; b. 4 April 1961, Edinburgh, Scotland. Musician (guitar); Composer. *Musical Education:* City of Leeds College of Music, 1983–86. *Career:* Member, Barbara Thompson's Paraphernalia, 1988–; Several European tours; World tours with Shakatak, 1992–; Formed Mulford/MacFarlane group, 1994; First British tour, 1995. *Recordings:* with Barbara Thompson's Paraphernalia: Breathless; Everlasting Flame; with Mulford/MacFarlane: Jamming Frequency, 1995. *Honours:* Eric Kershaw Memorial Prize, Leeds College of Music, 1984–86. *Membership:* Performing Rights Society. *Leisure interests:* Golf; Hillwalking; Reading. *Address:* London, England.

MCGARRIGLE Anna; b. 1944, Montréal, Québec, Canada. Musician (keyboards, banjo, guitar, accordian); Vocalist. *Career:* Singer, performer in both French and English; Member, Mountain City Four, Montréal; Formed duo with sister Kate McGarrigle; Debut UK performance, 1976; Recent appearance, Cambridge Folk Festival, 1995; Barbican, 1996. *Compositions:* Songs recorded by artists including: Linda Ronstadt; Maria Muldaur; Emmylou Harris. *Recordings:* Albums include: Kate and Anna McGarrigle, 1976; Dancer With Bruised Knees, 1977; Pronto Monto, 1978; French Record, 1980; Love Over and Over, 1983; Heartbeats Accelerating, 1990; Matapedia, 1996. *Address:* c/o Concerted Efforts Inc, 59 Parsons St, West Newton, MA 02165, USA.

MCGARRIGLE Kate; b. 1944, Montréal, Québec, Canada. Musician (keyboards, guitar); Vocalist. m. Loudon Wainwright III. *Career:* Singer, performer in both French and English; Member, Mountain City Four, Montréal; Formed duo with sister Anna McGarrigle; UK debut, 1976; Recent cocnert appearance, Cambridge Folk Festival, 1995. *Compositions:* Songs recorded by artists including: Linda Ronstadt; Maria Muldaur. *Recordings:* Albums include: Kate and Anna McGarrigle, 1975; Dancer With Bruised Knees, 1977; Pronto Monto, 1978; French Record, 1980; Love Over and Over, 1983; Heartbeats Accelerating, 1990; with Anna Mcgarrigle: Matapedia, 1996; Mcgarrigle Hour, 1998; with Wainwright Loudon III: Attempted Moustache, 1973; Unrequited, 1975; History, 1992; with Emmylou Harris: Wrecking Ball, 1995; Portraits, 1996; with Linda Ronstadt: Western Wall: The Tuscon Sessions, 1999; Linda Ronstadt Box Set, 1999. *Address:* c/o Concerted Efforts Inc, 59 Parsons St, West Newton, MA 02165, USA.

MCGARRY David Graham; b. 18 Dec. 1955, Stoke-on-Trent, Staffordshire, England. Musician (keyboards). m. 9 May 1981, 2 d. *Musical Education:* Leeds College of Music. *Career:* Television appearances include: Pebble Mill At One, BBC; Nightride, BBC; ITV

Telethon; Toured with Lenny Henry and Ben E King; Musical Director at Alton Towers, 10 years. *Recordings:* Class, Linda Lewis; Style, Linda Lewis; Dreams of You, Saxtet. *Memberships:* Musicians' Union; PRS; British Music Writers Council Section of Musicians' Union. *Leisure interests:* Squash; Chess; Golf; Computers. *Address:* 8 Castleton Rd, Lightwood, Stoke-on-Trent, Staffordshire ST3 7TD, England.

MCGARVEY Patrick James; b. 2 Aug. 1971, Belfast, Northern Ireland. Musician (electric bass, guitar). *Musical Education:* Self-taught initially, basstech, grades 6 and 8 in bass. *Career:* Bassist, The Coal Porters (Sid Griffin's band), 1993–; Tours: All Europe, USA; Also live shows with Kate St John, 1995; Guitarist, bandleader, The Incredibly Strange Band; Television and radio apperances include: C4, VH1, BBC Radio 1, GLR. *Compositions:* Featured on albums: All The Colours of The World; Chasing Rainbows; Santa Mira. *Recordings:* Land of Hope and Crosby, The Coal Porters, 1994; Los London, The Coal Porters, 1995. *Membership:* Musicians' Union. *Leisure interest:* Musician. *Address:* PO Box 2539, London NW3 6DF, England.

MCGEOCH John Alexander; b. 25 Aug. 1955, Greenock, Scotland. Musician (guitar, saxophone, keyboards); Composer. m. Denise Dakin, 14 Sept. 1988, 1 d. *Education:* BA Hons. *Career:* Continuous world tours, with various bands for last 18 years; Numerous television shows. *Recordings:* Albums: with Magazine: Magazine, 1978; Second Hand Daylight, 1979; The Correct Use of Soap, 1980; with Generation X: Kiss Me Deadly, 1981; with Siouxsie and The Banshees: Kaleidoscope, 1980; Ju Ju, 1981; A Kiss In The Dreamhouse, 1982; with Public Image Ltd: Happy?, 1988; 9, 1989; That What Is Not, 1991; with Visage: Visage, 1980. *Membership:* PRS. *Leisure interests:* Clay pigeon shooting; Painting. *Current Management:* William Hunt. *Address:* 68 Neal St, Covent Garden, London WC2, England.

MCGINLEY Raymond; b. 3 Jan. 1964, Glasgow, Scotland. Vocalist; Musician (guitar). *Career:* Member, The Boy Hairdressers; Founder member, Teenage Fan Club, 1989-. *Recordings:* Albums: A Catholic Education, 1990; Bandwagonesque, 1991; Thirteen, 1993; Grand Prix, 1995; Songs from Northern Britain, 1997; Contributions to: Sharks Patrol These Waters, 1995. *Address:* c/o Creation Records, 109 Regents Park Rd, London NW1 8UR, England.

MCGOLDRICK Michael Brendan; b. 26 Nov. 1973, Manchester, England. Musician (uilleann pipes, low whistle, wooden flute); Composer. *Career:* Founder member of Manchester-based Celtic rock band Toss The Feathers; Formed Flook! with fellow flautists Brian Finnegan and Sarah Allen, 1995; Joined Scottish folk band Capercaillie, 1997; Helped form Lunasa; Collaborations: Jim Kerr; Youssou N'Dour; Alan Stivell; Kate Rusby; John McCusker; Afro-Celt Sound System; Idir; Karan Casey; Dezi Donnelly. *Recordings:* Albums: with Toss The Feathers: Live At The 32 Club, 1988; Columbus Eclipse, 1989; Awakening, 1991; TTF'94 Live, 1994; The Next Round, 1995; with Flook!: Flook! Live, 1997; with Lunasa: Lunasa, 1998; Otherworld, 1999; with Capercaillie: Beautiful Wasteland, 1997; Nadurra, 2000; solo: Champions of the North (with Dezi Donnelly), 1995; Morning Rory, 1996; Fused, 2000; At First Light (with John McSherry), 2001. *Honours:* All Ireland Championships, BBC Radio Two Young Tradition Award, 1995; BBC Radio Two Folk Awards, Best Instrumentalist, 2001. *Address:* c/o Vertical Records, 5 Newton Terrace Lane, Glasgow, G3 7PB, Scotland. *Internet:* www.verticalrecords.co.uk.

MCGOVERN Maureen; b. 27 July 1949, Youngstown, Ohio, USA. Singer; Actor; Songwriter. Divorced. *Career:* Recording Artist, concerts, stage appearances including Broadway, television and radio; Film appearances in The Towering Inferno and Airplane!; Joseph and The Cure For Boredom; Broadway debut in The Pirates of Penzance; Played Luisa in Nine; Starred with Sting in the Threepenny Opera; Mary in Brownstone; Appearances in South Pacific, The Sound of Music, Guys and Dolls, I do, I do; The Umbrellas of Cherbourne; Duet with Placido Domingo, A Love Until the End of Time, recorded with Philharmonia Virtuosi of New York; Performed, Celebrating Gershwin, 50th anniversary of his death; Revival of of Thee I Sing/Let 'Em Eat Cake, Brooklyn Academy of Music and Kennedy Center; Performed at George Gershwin Centennial Celebration, London Palladium; Television special, Maureen McGovern: Live at Wolftrap; Guest appearances with Boston Pops, PBS-Day Commemorative Concert with the National Symphony; Appeared with every US Symphony Orchestra; Host, television series, Girl's Night Out; Played Dr Berg in Pacific Blue for television. *Compositions:* (for children) The Bengal Tiger's Ball; I Want to Learn to Fly. *Recordings:* The Morning After (number 1, Academy Award-winning Gold Record); We May Never Love Like This Again (Academy Award winner); Can You Read My Mind; Another Woman In Love; State of the Heart; Naughty Baby; Christmas with Maureen McGovern; Baby I'm Yours; Out of this World: McGovern sings Arlen; Amen! A Gospel Celebration; The Music Never Ends: The Lyrics of Marilyn and Alan Bergman, The Pleasure of His Company. *Honours:* Numerous Gold Records from USA, Canada, Australia, Japan, The Philippines; Grammy Nominations, 1974 and 1999; Grand Prize, Tokyo Music Festival, 1975. *Membership:* Vice President, National Chairperson, Polymyositis/

Dermatomyositis, Muscular Dystrophy Asscn. *Address:* 8484 Wilshire Blvd 500, Beverly Hills, CA 90210, USA.

MACGOWAN Shane; b. 25 Dec. 1957, Kent, England. Musician (guitar); Singer. *Career:* Member, The Pogues, 1983–90; Support to Elvis Costello, British tour, 1984; Cambridge Folk Festival, 1985; US tours, 1986, 1988; Self Aid concert, Dublin, 1986; Glastonbury Festival, 1986; Fleadh '91, London, 1991; Chieftains Music Festival, London, 1991; Feile '91, Tipperary, Ireland, 1991; Solo artist, with backing group The Popes, 1993–; Film appearance, Straight To Hell, 1986. *Recordings:* Albums: with the Pogues: Red Roses For Me, 1984; Rum, Sodomy and The Lash, 1985; If I Should Fall From Grace With God, 1988; Peace and Lore, 1989; Hell's Ditch, 1990; The Best of The Pogues, 1991; with The Popes: The Snake, 1994; Singles include: with The Pogues: A Pair of Brown Eyes; Sally Maclennane; Dirty Old Town; Haunted, from film Sid and Nancy; Fiesta; Yeah Yeah Yeah Yeah; Misty Morning, Albert Bridge; Summer In Siam; A Fairytale of New York (with Kirsty MacColl), 1987; with The Dubliners: The Irish Rover, 1987; Jack's Heroes, 1990; with The Popes: The Church of The Holy Spook; The Woman's Got Me Drinking; Haunted, duet with Sinead O'Connor, 1995; You're The One, duet with Maire Brennan, for film soundtrack Circle of Friends, 1995; Contributor, film soundtrack Straight To Hell, 1987; The Last Temptation of Elvis, Nordoff-Robbins charity record, 1990; Red Hot + Blue, AIDS awareness record, 1990; Nick Cave: Murder Ballads, 1996; Legends of Ireland, 1998.

MCGRATH Bob (Robert Emmet); b. 13 June 1932, Ottawa, Illinois, USA. Vocalist. m. Ann L Sperry, 14 June 1958, 2 s., 3 d. *Education:* BMus, University of Michigan; Master's Degree, Manhattan School of Music. *Career:* Original host, Bob, on Sesame Street for 30 years; Tenor soloist on Sing Along With Mitch; Performed with: Robert Shaw Chorale; Fred Waring Pennsylvanians; Host for the International Children's Festival at Wolftrap for 10 years; Performed with 100 Symphony Orchestras; Has performed in over 800 concerts in the US, Canada and Japan. *Recordings:* The Baby Record; Songs and Games For Toddlers; If You're Happy and You Know It Sing Along number 1 and number 2; Bob's Favourite Street Songs; Sing Me A Story. *Publications:* I'm A Good Mommy; You're A Good Daddy; Dog Lies; The Shoveller; Me Myself; Sneakers; Uh Oh! Gotta Go; Oops! Excuse Me Please!. *Honours:* Hon. Doctorate, Medaille College; Emmanuel Cancer Foundation Tribute; Variety Club Lifetime Honourary Mem.; Parent's Choice, American Library Asscn; National Chairperson, UNICEF Day; World Children's Day Foundation, UN General Assembly; Syracuse Symphony Asscn Achievement Award for Music Education; Canadian Recording Artist Gold Record, 1992, 1993. *Current Management:* Ken Greengrass, 38 E 57th St, New York, NY 10022, USA.

MCGRATH Mark Sayers; b. 15 March 1968. Vocalist. *Education:* University of Southern California, degree in Communications. *Career:* Became band member of The Shrinky Dinx following unscheduled leap on stage at live gig; Group signed to Atlantic Records following circulation of self-made demo video; Act renamed Sugar Ray owing to threat of legal action prior to record releases; Built up world-wide fanbase through touring and TV appearances; Cameo in Fathers Day film, 1997. *Recordings:* Albums: Lemonade and Brownies, 1995; Floored, 1997; 14–59, 1999; Sugar Ray, 2001; Singles: Mean Machine, Iron Mic, 1995; Fly, RPM, 1997; Every Morning, Someday, 1999; Falls Apart, 2000; When It's Over, Answer The Phone, 2001. *Honours:* Second/third albums certified double/triple platinum by RIAA, respectively. *Address:* c/o PO Box 12018, Costa Mesa, CA 92627, USA. *E-mail:* management@sugarray.com. *Internet:* www.sugarray.com.

MCGRAW Tim, (Tim Smith); b. 1 May 1967, Delhi, Louisiana, USA. Country vocalist; Musician (guitar); Songwriter; Prod. m. Faith Hill, 6 Oct. 1996. *Education:* Northeast Louisiana University, sports scholarships. *Career:* Became involved in music when purchased guitar from a pawn-shop; Moved to Nashville and gigged around northeastern Louisiana and Jacksonville, Florida; While performing in clubs around Nashville, signed deal with Curb Records on strength of demo; Chart debut with Welcome To The Club, 1992; Released Indian Outlaw, a song using extracts of Lament of The Cherokee Reservation Indian, 1994; Track attracted criticism in USA for its alleged demeaning stereotypes of Native Americans, but received much airplay and became successful pop and country hit; Has charted consistently on both US pop and country chart, garnering many awards along the way; Produced other country artists including Jo Dee Messina. *Recordings include:* Just To See You Smile, 1997; It's Your Love (with Faith Hill), 1997; I Like It – I Love It, 1995; Don't Take The Girl, 1994, Not A Moment Too Soon, 1994; She Never Lets It Go To Her Heart, 1996; Albums include: Tim McGraw, 1994; All I Want, 1995; Everywhere, 1997; A Place In The Sun, 1999; Greatest Hits, 2000; Set This Circus Down, 2001. *Honours:* various including: CMA Award, Vocal Event of the Year, It's Your Love (with Faith Hill), 1997; Billboard: Country Artist of the Year; Male Country Artist of the Year; Country Albums Artist of the Year, Set This Circus Down; Country Album of the Year, Greatest Hits; Country Single Artist of the Year, 2001. *Current Management:* Image Management

Group, 27 Music Sq. E, Nashville, TN 37203, USA. *Internet:* www.timmcgraw.com.

MCGUIGAN Paul 'Guigsy'; b. 9 May 1971, Manchester, England. Musician (Bass). *Career:* Member, Rain; Founder Member, Oasis; Recruited Liam and Noel Gallagher; Support slots to The Milltown Brothers, BMX Bandits, The Verve, Liz Phair, The Real People, Dodgy; Obtained record deal with Creation; Numerous headline tours, television appearances and festival dates; Left band, 1999. *Recordings:* Singles: Supersonic; Whatever; Cigarettes and Alcohol; Shakermaker; Live Forever; Some Might Say; Wonderwall; Roll With It; Champagne Supernova; Don't Look Back in Anger; D'You Know What I Mean; Stand By Me; All Around the World; Albums: Definitely Maybe, 1994; What's the Story (Morning Glory), 1995; Be Here Now, 1997; The Masterplan, boxed set, 1999.

MCGUINN Roger, (James McGuinn III); b. 13 July 1942, Chicago, Illinois, USA. Vocalist; Musician (guitar). m. Camilla. *Career:* Touring musician with: The Limelighters; Chad Mitchell Trio; Judy Collins; Bobby Darin; Founder member, The Byrds, 1964–73; Solo artiste, 1973–; Also member, McGuinn Clark and Hillman (with Gene Clark and Chris Hillman), 1978–79; Performances include: The Beach Boys Summer Spectacular, 1966; Monterey Pop Festival, 1967; Grand Ole Opry, 1968; Newport Festival, 1969; Bath Festival, 1970; Tours with Bob Dylan's Rolling Thunder Revue, 1975; Roy Orbison All-Star Tribute, 1990. *Recordings:* Albums: with the Byrds: Mr Tambourine Man, 1965; Turn! Turn! Turn!, 1965; Fifth Dimension, 1966; Younger Than Yesterday, 1967; The Notorious Byrd Brothers, 1968; Sweetheart of The Rodeo, 1968; The Ballad of Easy Rider, 1970; Untitled, 1970; Byrdmaniax, 1971; Farther Along, 1972; Best of The Byrds – Greatest Hits Vol. 2, 1972; History of The Byrds, 1973; The Byrds, 1990; Solo albums: Roger McGuinn, 1973; Peace On You, 1974; Cardiff Rose, 1976; Thunderbyrd, 1977; Back From Rio, 1991; Born to Rock and Roll, 1992; Nitty Gritty Dirt Band – Roger McGuinn Live, 1994; Live from Mars; with Clark and Hillman: McGuinn Clark and Hillman, 1979; with Hillman: McGuinn/Hillman, 1979; Singles: Mr Tambourine Man (No. 1, USA), 1965; All I Really Want To Do; Eight Miles High, 1966; 5D (Fifth Dimension), 1966; So You Want To Be A Rock 'n' Roll Star, 1967; Have You Seen Her Face, 1967; I Wasn't Born To Follow. *Honour:* Inducted into Rock and Roll Hall of Fame, 1991.

MCHUGH Robert (Bob); b. 20 July 1946, Kearney, NJ, USA. Musician (Piano); Composer. m. Jane Belli, 28 June 1970, 1 s., 1 d. *Education:* BA, Music, Jersey City College; Private Study, Bill Manzi, Morris Nanton, Don Friedman, Hester Randolfi. *Career:* Performed in documentary, The Art of Worship, produced by Riverside Church, New York City, USA; Appearance on Around New York, WNYC, Concert's at Count Basic Theatre, Riverfest, New York Public Library, Lincoln Center. *Compositions:* Steamboat Rag; Rocky Ring Tune; Bus Boy Circus; Dream Street; Three Greek Dances; Baroque Piece; Buily and The Bean; Uptown; Summer Stride; Recuperation Tango, 1998. *Recordings:* Soring on Wings of Ivory and Black; Manhattan Sunrise; Interplay; MNB. *Honours:* ASCAP Popular Award, every year since 1989; Commissioned Composer for the New Jersey Music Teachers State Piano Competition, 1998–99. *Memberships:* ASCAP; NJEA; MTA. *Leisure interests:* Swimming; Walking. *Current Management:* Manduca Publications, PO Box 10550, Portland, ME 04104, USA. *Address:* 902 Lincoln Ave, Pompton Lakes, NJ 07442, USA.

MACINTOSH Adrian; b. 7 March 1942, Tadcaster, England. Jazz Musician. m. Sheila Christie, 13 April 1974. *Career:* Early work with John Taylor Trio and Norma Winstone; Alan Elsdon Band, 1970; Joined Brian Leakes' Sweet and Sour, 1978; Joined Humphrey Lyttelton's Band, 1982; Work with Helen Shapiro, 1984–; Worked with many leading jazz names including: Sonny Stitt; Teddy Edwards; Jimmy Witherspoon; Harold Ashby; Nat Pierce; Scott Hamilton; Clark Terry; Warren Vache; Kenny Davern; Al Casey. *Recordings:* Humph and Wally Fawkes, 1983; Humph and Helen Shapiro, 1984; Humph, Al Casey and Kenny Davern, 1984; Humph At The Bulls Head, 1985; Humph and Buddy Tate, 1985; Humph Gigs, 1987; Humph and Lillian Boutté, 1988; Humph At Breda Jazz Festival, 1988; Humph Beano Boogie, 1989; Ken McCarthy Quartet (featuring Dick Pearce); Produced album by Brian Leake's Sweet and Sour, 1993. *Memberships:* Musicians' Union; Chairman, Asscn of British Jazz Musicians. *Leisure interest:* Long distance walking.

MCINTOSH Bradley John; b. 8 Aug. 1981, St Thomas Hospital, London. Vocalist; Actor. *Career:* Father Steve founder member of UK reggae/soul group The Cool Notes; Band also featured mother Loraine, accomplished session vocalist; Previously in pop/R & B band Krisp; Joined S Club 7 pop ensemble while working at a pizza restaurant; Group quickly achieved international success following sales of TV series Miami 7 (1999), LA 7 (2000) and Hollywood 7 (2001) featuring the band's music to nearly 100 countries; Also made nature TV series S Club 7 Go Wild (2000) and various TV specials; First British tour with S Club 7, 2001. *Recordings:* Albums: S Club, 1999; 7, 2000; Sunshine, 2001; Singles: Bring It All Back, 1999; S Club Party, 1999; Two In A Million/You're My Number One, 1999; Reach,

2000; Natural, 2000; Never Had A Dream Come True, 2000; Don't Stop Movin', 2001; Have You Ever, 2001. *Honours:* Brit Award, Best British Newcomer, 2000. *Current Management:* 19 Management, Unit 32, Ransomes Dock, 35–37 Parkgate Rd, London SW11 4NP, England.

MACISAAC Ashley Dwayne; b. 24 Feb. 1975, Antigonish, Nova Scotia, Canada. Vocalist; Musician (violin); Composer. *Career:* Fiddle player from the Cape Breton tradition, rooted in Scottish folk music; Has great technique and, although sometimes criticised by purists for playing too fast and frenetically, flamboyant style has brought a solid fanbase; Hi How Are You Today? album was based in Cape Breton traditional music but introduced various other musical influences; Single release Sleepy Maggie (with vocals from Mary Jane Lamond) received much airplay in Canada, gaining national recognition as an artist; Follow-up album Fine Thank You Very Much is in the quintessential Cape Breton traditional style, but 2000 release Heltic Celtic explores electronic and ambient influences. *Recordings:* Single: Sleepy Maggie, 1997; Albums: Close To The Floor, 1992; Hi How Are You Today, 1995; Fine Thank You Very Much, 1998; Helter's Celtic, 2000; features on: Feelings, David Byrne, 1997; Fire In The Kitchen, The Chieftains, 1998; Suas E!, Mary Jane Lamond, 1997; Spirit Trail, Bruce Hornsby, 1998; Hanging Garden OST, 1998. *Internet:* www.ashley-macisaac.com.

MACK Bobby; b. 19 June 1954, Fort Worth, Texas, USA. Vocalist; Musician (guitar); Music Prod. m. Pat Cullen, 24 May 1994, 1 s., 1 d. *Education:* University of Texas, Austin. *Career:* Delta Blue Festival, New Orleans Jazz Festival; Tours: Former USSR; Japan; New Zealand; Australia; Scandinavia; Europe; UK. *Recordings:* Bobby Mack and Night Train Albums include: Say What; Red Hot and Humid; Honeytrap; Sugar All Night; Live at J and J Blues Bar; Highway Man; produced Mississippi Bluesman Willie Foster, My Life; produced Mark Goodwin, I Found Joy; produced Texas Guitars Vol. I – The Women. *Publications:* Writer, Texas Blue Magazine. *Leisure interest:* Rancher, Wimberley, Texas. *Current Management:* Time Train Music. *Address:* 881 Lost Creek, Wimberley, TX 78676, USA.

MACK Danny; b. 29 March 1943, Harvey, Illinois, USA. Singer; Musician (accordion, drums, trumpet, keyboards); Record Prod.; Record Co Exec. m. Caroline Panczyck, 3 Nov. 1962, 1 s., 1 d. *Education:* Criminal justice. *Musical Education:* 15 years private study music instrumental, teaching, theory. *Career:* Bandleader, 1958–; Clubs circuit until 1977; Songwriting career began with first self-penned country recording on K-Ark, 1977; Recorded Fist Full of Dollars, Nashville, Tennessee; Formed Syntony Publishing BMI and Briarhill Records, 1984; WLS TV, TCI of Indiana; Guest appearances, Sig Sakowitz radio show. *Recordings:* Jesus Is The Reason For The Season (No. 1 Christmas hit); On The Right Road Again, 1994; Old Rockers Never Die, 1994. *Publications:* Chicago Tribune; Country and Western Corner; Radio and Record News; Indie Bullet; Star Quest Magazines. *Honours:* Indie Label of The Year, Producer of The Year, CMAA, 1992, 1993, 1994; Hon. Kentucky Col; GSCMA Hall of Fame Nomination; Inspirational Record of the Year, CMA, USA, 1994; Song of Year, World Radio Network, Spain, 1994. *Memberships:* Broadcast Music Inc; NARAS; Lifetime mem., Country Music Asscns of America. *Leisure interests:* Writing music; Fishing; Vacations in Nevada. *Current Management:* The Danny Mack Music Group. *Address:* 3484 Nicolette Dr., Crete, IL 60417, USA.

MACK James Joseph; b. 12 Nov. 1971, Kensington, London, England. Musician (percussion). *Musical Education:* Guildhall School of Music and Drama; West London Institute of Higher Education. *Career:* World-wide tours and television appearances with: D:ream; Des'ree; Lonnie Liston Smith; C J Lewis; Rozalla; NYJO; Skin. *Recordings with:* D:ream (second album); Skin; NYJO; Various television commercials include: American Express; Maxwell House; John Smiths Bitter. *Honours:* Performance diploma, Guildhall School of Music and Drama. *Membership:* Musicians' Union. *Leisure interests:* Good food; Travel; Fitness. *Address:* 28 Ashburnham Mansions, Ashburnham Rd, Chelsea, London SW10 0PA, England.

MACK Warner (McPherson); b. 2 April 1938, Nashville, Tennessee, USA. Country Singer; Songwriter; Musician. *Career:* Performer, radio show, Louisiana Hayride; Successful solo career, late 1950s-; Regular tours, UK country clubs; First country artist to record national commercial for Coca-Cola. *Compositions include:* Tennessee Born, Mississippi Raised; Is It Wrong (For Loving You)? (US Country No. 1); The Bridge Washed Out. *Recordings include:* Sitting In An All Night Cafe; Talking To The Walls; How Long Will It Take?; These Crazy Thoughts; He Touched Me; Numerous albums include: The Country Touch, 1966; Drifting Apart, 1967; Love Hungry, 1970; You Make Me Feel Like A Man, 1971; Great Country, 1973; Prince of Country Blues, 1983; At Your Service, 1984; Early Years, 1998; Several compilation albums. *Current Management:* Capitol Advertising and Management, 1300 Division St #200, Nashville, TN 37203, USA.

MACKAY David; b. 11 May 1944, Sydney, Australia. Record Prod.; Composer; Musician (Keyboards). m. Brenda Anne Challis, 31 March 1973, 1 s., 1 d. *Education:* St Aloyisious College, Sydney, Australia. *Musical Education:* Conservatorium of Music, Sydney; Theory, Harmony, Arranging, Piano, Clarinet, privately studied in Melbourne; Modern Arranging, Guitar and Bass. *Career:* Producer of Records by: Blue Mink; Cliff Richard; New Seekers; Bonnie Tyler; Frankie Miller; Dusty Springfield; Johnny Hallyday; Demis Roussos. *Compositions:* Theme Punderscores for: TV Programmes: Auf Wiedersehen Pet; Bread; Blott on the Landscape. *Honours:* Ivor Novello Award for Auf Wiedersehen Pet, 1983; Nomination for BAFTAS, 1984; AKIA Award, Best Cast Album of a Musical 1990. *Memberships:* PRS; Repro; BASCA; Professional Composers Guild. *Leisure interests:* Tennis; Football; Golf. *Address:* Toftrees, Church Rd, Woldingham, Surrey CR3 7JX, England.

MACKAY Robert Andrew; b. 12 July 1973, London, England. Composer; Musician (Flute, Guitar, Bass); Singer; Actor. *Education:* BSc, Geology and Music, Keele University, 1995; MMus, Electroacoustic Composition, with Postgraduate Diploma in Music Technology and Sound Recording Techniques, Bangor University, 1997; PhD, Electroacoustic Composition, in progress. *Career:* Flute Player, Subsid, 1993; Performed in national stage production of Only Just, by Alec Davison, 1997; Session Musician, Wales, 1997–99; Composer in Residence, Radio Bratislava, Slovakia, 1998–99; Bass Player, Gyroscope, 1998; Flute and Bass Player, Tystion, 1998–99; Composer for multimedia events; Film appearance, Merlin; TV appearances: Idot; Garej; Lois, all for Channel 4 Wales; Radio appearances for BBC; Works performed in UK, France, USA and New Zealand. *Compositions:* Tempestuous Relationships, 1995; Sea Pictures, 1997; Environs, 1997; Voicewind, 1998; Postcards from the Summer, 1999. *Recordings:* ICMC '98; Shrug Off Ya Complex, Tystion; RAM JAM, BBC compilation, Gyroscope. *Honours:* Prix Residence, Bourges Synthèse Festival, France, 1997; Single of the Week, Melody Maker, with Tystion, 1998. *Memberships:* PRS; PRC; Equity; SPNM; BMIC; SAN. *Leisure interests:* Playing and writing music; Acting; Singing; Cycling; Walking; Reading; Socializing. *Address:* 239 Earlsfield Rd, Earlsfield, London SW18 3DE, England.

MCKEAN Ian; b. 9 Jan. 1958, Hertford, Hertfordshire, England. Musician (guitar). *Education:* West Surrey College of Art and Design. *Musical Education:* City Literature Institute (Music Diploma). *Career:* with Twenty Flight Rockers: Reading Festival, 1986; Numerous live and studio sessions, BBC Radio 1; with Balaam and The Angel: 2 major British tours, 1988; 4 month tour, USA and Canada, 1988; Support to Aerosmith, Belfast and Wembley, 1989. *Recordings:* Albums: Days of Madness, 1989; No More Innocence, 1991; Prime Time, 1993; Single: Little Bit of Love, 1990. *Memberships:* Musicians' Union; PRS. *Leisure interests:* Music; Art; Reading; Egyptology; General knowledge. *Address:* 63 Eton Ave, London NW3 3ET, England.

MCKEE Maria; b. 17 Aug. 1964, Los Angeles, California, USA. Singer; Songwriter. *Career:* Formed duo The Maria McKee Band with half-brother Bryan MacLean, later renamed the Brian MacLean Band; Founder member, Lone Justice; Concerts include: Support tour to U2; Solo artiste, 1987-. *Compositions include:* A Good Heart, Fergal Sharkey (UK No. 1), 1985. *Recordings:* Albums: with Lone Justice: Lone Justice, 1985; Shelter, 1987; This World Is Not My Home, 1999; Solo albums include: You Gotta Sin To Be Saved, 1993; Life Is Sweet, 1996. *Current Management:* Fabulon Management, 1 McCrone Mews, Belsize Lane, London NW3 5BG, England.

MCKENNA Mae; b. 23 Oct. 1955, Coatbridge, Scotland. Singer; Songwriter. m. James Woon, 17 Dec. 1977, 1 s. *Musical Education:* A Level Music, Diploma, Music. *Career:* Recorded and toured UK and Europe as lead singer with folk rock band Contraband, 1971–75; Sung solo gaelic air on Ultravox tour, 1983; Solo singer, 1985; Backing singer for: Scritti Politti; Blur; Madness; Jason Donovan; Cliff Richard; ABC; Wet Wet Wet; Kylie Minogue; Rick Astley; Donna Summer. *Recordings:* Solo albums: Mae McKenna; Everything That Touches Me; Walk On Water; Nightfallers; Mirage and Reality; with Contraband: Contraband. *Memberships:* Musicians' Union; Equity; PRS. *Leisure interest:* Hypnosis. *Current Management:* Keith Harris Music. *Address:* 204 Courthouse Rd, Maidenhead, Berkshire SL6 6HU, England.

MCKENNA Rafe; Record Prod.; Engineer; Mixer. *Career:* Producer, Engineer, Mixer for: David Essex; UFO; Magnum; Buggles; Elkie Brooks; Steve Hackett; Steve Howe; Wishbone Ash; Danny Wilson; Roger Daltrey; Giant; Depeche Mode; Thomas Dolby; Paul McCartney; Spandau Ballet; Gary Glitter. *Recordings:* Albums: Holy Water, Dangerous Age, Here Comes Trouble, Bad Company; Paid Vacation, Richard Marx; Popped In Souled Out, Wet Wet Wet; Unusual Heat, Foreigner; Bust A Nut, Tesla; UB44, UB40; Angels and Electricity, Eddi Reader; Cappucino Songs, Tanita Tikaram; Twisted Tenderness, Electronic; Singles: Flowers In Our Hair, All About Eve; Sweet Little Mystery, Wet Wet Wet; Broken Land, Feel The Raindrops, The Adventures; Chant, Absolute Reality, The Alarm; Here I Am, I Got Mine, UB40; Ash, A Life Less Ordinary; Hurricane, Warm

Jets; Lifted, The Corrs; also: Lewis Taylor; Liz Horsman; Big Country; Don; James Taylor Quartet; Zucchero; Sai Sai; Brian Kennedy; Mark Nevin; The Mopeds; Scream. *Honours:* Numerous Platinum and Gold albums. *Current Management:* Stephen Budd Management, 109B Regents Park Rd, London NW1 8UR, England.

MCKENNITT Loreena; b. Manitoba, Canada. Vocalist; Songwriter. *Career:* Won DuMaurier Search For Talent, 1978; Represented Canada at UNESCO in 1978 and 1985; Featured in festival productions as actor, singer and composer including: Shakespeare's The Tempest, 1982; The Two Gentlemen of Verona, 1984; Recorded debut album, 1985; Signed by Warner Music, 1991; Music featured in films: Women and Spirituality series; Jade; Highlander III; The Holy Man, Soldier; The Santa Clause; TV music for: Northern Exposure; Due South; Legacy; EZ Streets; Boston Public; Big Kelvin and Little Kelvin; Strange Luck. *Recordings:* Albums include: Elemental, 1985; To Drive The Cold Winter Away, 1987; Parallel Dreams, 1989; The Visit, 1991; The Mask and Mirror, 1994; The Book of Secrets, 1997; Live In Paris and Toronto, 1999. *Honours:* The Book of Secrets topped the Billboard World Music chart, reached number 1 on national album charts in Greece and Turkey; Juno Awards: Best Roots and Traditional Album: The Visit, 1992; The Mask and Mirror, 1995; Billboard Award: International Achievement, 1997. *Internet:* www.quinlanroad.com.

MCKENZIE Derrick; b. 27 March 1962, London, England. Musician (Drums). *Career:* Member, Jamiroquai; Numerous tours and TV appearances. *Recordings:* Singles: When You Gonna Learn, 1993; Emergency on Planet Earth, 1994; Space Cowboy EP, 1995; Cosmic Girl, 1996; Light Years, 1996; Alright, 1997; Deeper Underground, 1998; High Times, 1998; Canned Heat, 1999; Emergency on Planet Earth, 1993; Travelling Without Moving, 1996; Synkronized, 1999. *Honours:* Gold and Platinum Albums; Numerous MTV Video Music Awards.

MACKENZIE Gisèle; b. 10 Jan. 1927, Winnipeg, Manitoba, Canada. Singer; Actress. Divorced, 1 s., 1 d. *Musical Education:* Graduate Scholarship School; Royal Conservatory, Toronto, Canada. *Career:* Your Hit Parade, NBC; Jack Benny Show; Gisèle MacKenzie Show, NBC; Sid Caesar Show. *Recordings:* Single: Hard To Get (No. 1). *Honours:* 3 Television Emmy Nominations. *Memberships:* SAG; AFTRA. *Leisure interests:* Swimming; Cooking; Perfume blending. *Current Management:* Samantha Group. *Address:* 300 S Raymond, Pasadena, CA 91105, USA.

MACKENZIE Henry; b. 15 Feb. 1923, Edinburgh, Scotland. Musician (clarinet, saxophone). m. Barbara Holton, 17 Sept. 1976. *Career:* Featured soloist, clarinet, with Ted Heath, 18 years; 4 American tours including 2 at Carnegie Hall, New York, with Ted Heath; Concerts and radio appearances, Billy May and Nelson Riddle; Films with Henry Mancini; Also featured in White Mischief. *Recordings include:* Appears on: Give My Regards To Broad Street, Paul McCartney; When I'm Sixty-Four, The Beatles. *Honours:* Melody Maker Poll Winners Recording. *Leisure interests:* Bowls; Watching football. *Address:* 27 The Glade, Epsom, Surrey KT17 2HN, England.

MCKENZIE Julia Kathleen; b. 17 Feb. 1942, London, England. Actress; Singer. m. Gerald Hjert, 9 Sept. 1972. *Musical Education:* Guildhall School of Music and Drama. *Career:* Television: Fresh Fields; French Fields; Julia and Company; Maggie and Her; Numerous dramas; Stage: 5 Sondheim musicals; National Theatre; 4 Alan Ayckbourn plays; Directing: Stepping Out; Steel Magnolias; Honk The Ugly Duckling; in New York, London, Tokyo, Denmark. *Recordings:* Albums include: The Musicals' Albums; Into The Woods; Side By Side By Sondheim. *Publications:* Clothes Line. *Honours:* Swet Awards; Olivier Awards; Evening Standard Award; Emmy; Hon. Fellow of Guildhall; Dr of Letters, South Bank University. *Leisure interests:* Cooking; Gardening. *Current Management:* April Young Ltd. *Address:* April Young Ltd, 11 Woodlands Rd, London SW13 0JZ, England.

MACKENZIE Talitha; b. 3 April 1956, Oceanside, New York, USA. Vocalist; Musician (keyboards); Composer; Arranger; Actress; Dancer. m. Ian MacKenzie, 6 Sept. 1988, 2 s. *Education:* Connecticut College, 1974–76. *Musical Education:* New England Conservatory of Music, Boston, USA; Private study, Classical piano, 1960–78, Classical/Jazz Voice, 1977–80. *Career:* Concerts include: Ronnie Scott's, London; Chard Festival of Women in Music; WOMAD; Celts in Kent Festival, England; Edinburgh Festival Fringe; Celtic Connections Festival, Glasgow; Folk City, The Bottom Line, New York, USA; Vox Populi, Toronto; Cultures Canada, Ottawa; Winnipeg Folk Festival, Canada; Teatro Campoamor Oviedo; Juntos en Córdoba; WOMEX, Berlin; Melkweg, Amsterdam; Television includes: Arts and Parts, Don't Look Down, STV; Ex-S, Ainm a'Ghàidheil, Talla a'Bhaile; Sin Agad E, Brag, BBC Scotland; Global Jukebox, BSB; Radio includes: Nicky Campbell, BBC Radio 1; Mixing It, BBC Radio 3; Women's Hour, BBC Radio 4; Meridian, BBC World Service; All Things Considered, NPR, USA; The Usual Suspects, BBC Radio Scotland; Kaleidoscope, BBC Radio 4. *Compositions:* Wall of Sound (for National Museum of Scotland event, Museum of Sound), 2001.

Recordings: St James Gate, 1985; Shantyman, 1986; Mouth Music, 1990; Sòlas, 1993; Spiorad, 1996; Theatre includes: Réiteach, (Proiseact Naiseanta); Russian Ritual Wedding, Harvard University. *Publications:* The Triangle Trade: African Influences in the Anglo-American Sea Shanty Tradition, 1984; Song of the Scottish Highlands, Scot, 1985. *Honour:* Billboard Song Contest for Owen's Boat, 1994. *Memberships:* Musicians' Union; BMI; MCPS; PAMRA; British Equity. *Current Management:* Donald MacQueen, Winning Promotions, 96/1 South Gyle Wynd, Edinburgh EH12 9HJ, Scotland. *Address:* 33 Millar Cres., Edinburgh, EH10 5HQ, Scotland. *Internet:* www.sonas.swinternet.co.uk.

MCKEOWN Leslie; b. 12 Nov. 1955. Singer. *Career:* Lead singer, Bay City Rollers, 1973–78; Appearances include: British tour, 1974; Television series featuring the group, Shang-A-Lang, 1975–77; Saturday Night Variety Show, ABC, 1975; Solo artist, 1978–; Currently tours as Les McKeown's 70s Bay City Rollers. *Recordings:* with The Bay City Rollers: Hit singles include: Remember (Sha La La), 1974; Shang-A-Lang, 1974; Summerlove Sensation, 1974; All of Me Loves All of You, 1974; Bye Bye Baby (No. 1, UK), 1975; Give A Little Love (No. 1, UK), 1975; Money Honey, 1975; Saturday Night (No. 1, USA), 1976; I Only Want To Be With You, 1976; It's A Game, 1977; You Make Me Believe In Magic, 1987; Albums: Rollin' (No. 1, UK), 1974; Once Upon A Star (No. 1, UK), 1975; Wouldn't You Like It, 1975; Bay City Rollers, 1976; Rock 'N' Roll Love Letter, 1976; Dedication, 1976; It's A Game, 1977; Greatest Hits, 1978; Solo albums include: All Washed Up, 1978. *Current Management:* Brian Gannon Management, PO Box 106, Rochdale OL16 4HW, England.

MCKERRON Charlie (Charles Alastair); b. 14 June 1960, London, England. Musician (fiddle); Composer. *Career:* Member: Capercaillie, 1985–; Group, along with original material, specialises in fusing traditional Gaelic songs with contemporary arrangements; Had first UK top 40 single in Gaelic, Coisich A Ruin (from A Prince Among Islands EP), 1992; Formed Big Sky band project with John Saich and cousin Laura McKerron; Big Sky formed from the Glasgow Celtic Grooves concerts and features many top traditional and roots musicians in its mix of traditional Celtic music and contemporary electronic instrumentation. *Compositions:* Contributed to the film Rob Roy; Collaborations include: Fish; The Pearl Fishers; Fred Morrison. *Recordings:* Albums: with Capercaille: Crosswinds, 1987; Sidewalk, 1989; Delirium, 1991; Get Out, 1992; The Blood Is Strong, Secret People, 1993; Capercaillie, 1995; To The Moon, 1996; Beautiful Wasteland, 1997; Glenfinnan – Songs of The '45 (recorded 1995), 1998; Nàdurra, 2000; group feature on: Rob Roy OST, 1995; with Big Sky: Source, 2000; features solo on: Music of The Fiddle, 1981; Suilean Dubh, Tannas, 1999; Tacsi (TV series), 2000; Pray For Rain, Andrew P White, 2001. *Honours:* Daily Record Golden Fiddle award.

MACKEY Steve; b. 10 Nov. 1966, Sheffield, England. Musician (Bass). *Career:* Member, Pulp, 1987–; Numerous tours, TV appearances and festival dates; Contributed track to film soundtrack for Mission Impossible, 1996. *Recordings:* Singles: My Legendary Girlfriend, 1990; O.U. (Gone, Gone), 1992; Lipgloss, 1993; Do You Remember The First Time, 1994; The Sisters EP, 1994; Common People, 1995; Mis-Shapes / Sorted for E's and Wizz, 1995; Disco 2000, 1995; Help the Aged, 1998; This is Hardcore, 1998; Albums: Separations, 1992; His 'N' Hers, 1994; Different Class, 1995; This is Hardcore, 1998.

MACKIE, (Mackie Jayson); Musician. *Career:* Member, Cromags, Bad Brains; Joined Fun Lovin' Criminals, 1999. *Recordings:* Single: Korean Bodega, 1999; Album: Mimosa – The Lounge Album, 1999.

MACKIE Richard James; b. 6 Jan. 1960, Bolton, Lancashire, England. Composer; Artistic Dir; Musician (keyboards, saxophone). m. Christine Anne Waterhouse, 20 April 1985, 2 d. *Education:* Laban Centre For Movement and Dance. *Musical Education:* Self-taught. *Career:* Member of bands including: The Surgical Support Band; The Pharaohs; The Selecter; Extensive tours, UK and Europe; Replacement keyboard player for Madness; Apperances at Montreux Pop Festival and Saturday Night Live in New York; Theatre and radio productions, 1984–; Padmates (produced by Kate Rowland); Zeitgeist Times; Ron Koops Last Roadshow; Many compositions for dance and dance theatre. *Recordings:* Albums and single with The Selecter. *Leisure interests:* Cooking; Eating. *Address:* 44 Dallas Rd, Lancaster, Lancashire LA1 1TW, England.

MCKINNA Iain; b. 27 Jan. 1955, Kilmarnock, Scotland. Prod.; Musician (guitar, bass, keyboards); Songwriter; Recording Engineer; Programmer. 1 s. *Career:* Recording engineer, 1977–; First production released 1993; Engineer, Bay City Rollers, 1984; Own band The Harmonics; Producer, Solas, Talitha MacKenzie, 1994; Album by Mike Heron, 1996; Concerts include: Guitarist with Flying Colours, Level 42 tour, 1982; Toured with Talitha MacKenzie's band, as guitarist; Support Runrig, 1993; WOMAD '94; Womex, Berlin, 1994; Edinburgh Festival; Also played in Netherlands, Spain, Canada. *Recordings:* As producer, session musician, computer programmer: Solas, Talitha MacKenzie (No. 12, World Music Charts), 1994; Nectarine No 9; Spoonfed Hybrid. *Honour:* Best Song, Music In

Scotland Trust, with own band The Harmonics, 1993. *Memberships:* PRS; MCPS. *Leisure interest:* Fun. *Current Management:* Offbeat Scotland. *Address:* 107 High St, Royal Mile, Edinburgh EH1 15G, Scotland.

MACKINTOSH Andrew Kenneth; b. 20 May 1953, London, England. Musician (saxophone). m. Bonnie Sue 10 Jan. 1975, 1 s. *Career:* Played with: Maynard Ferguson; Buddy Rich; Quincy Jones; James Last; Currently involved in studio work in London. *Recordings:* Appeared on recordings by: Paul McCartney; Elton John; Bill Wyman; Elaine Paige; Melissa Manchester. *Memberships:* PRS; Musicians' Union. *Leisure interests:* Music; Golf. *Address:* 27 Station Rd, South Norwood, London SE25 5AH, England.

MACKINTOSH Gregor; b. 20 June 1970, Halifax, West Yorkshire, England. Musician (guitar). m. Mandy Taylor, 5 Aug. 1995, 1 d. *Musical Education:* Self-taught. *Career:* Festivals include: Rockamring; Dynamo; Roskilde; World-wide tours, television: Channel 4 Special; ITV's Chart Show; MTV; Viva TV; Noisy Mothers; Various radio, television world-wide; Soundtrack for Clarion Audio advertisements. *Recordings:* 5 albums including: Icon; Draconian Times; 3 singles including: The Last Time; Long Form video: Harmony Breaks. *Honours:* Kerrang, MTV Best video: Embers Fire, 1994. *Memberships:* PRS; Musicians' Union. *Leisure interests:* Reading; Films. *Current Management:* Northern Music, Bradford. *Address:* 43 Cheapside Chambers, Cheapside, Bradford, West Yorkshire, England.

MACKNESS Vanessa; b. Fordingbridge, Christchurch, England. Painter; Vocalist. 1 s., 1 d. *Education:* Degree, fine arts painting, Camberwell School of Art, late 1970s; Postgraduate, London University. *Musical Education:* Playing with artists including Derek Bailey; Barry Guy; Alexander Balanescu; Nishat Khan; Paul Lovens; Phil Minton. *Career:* Concert tours include: Derek Bailey's Company Week, 1990; 1991; Duo with Barry Guy, Taktlos Festival, Switzerland, 1990; Irma, opera by Tom Phillips, USA, England, 1992; 10th Anniversary Minton-Weston Makhno Project, Bern, Basel, Zürich, Taktlos Festival, Switzerland, 1993; Solo performance, Total Music Meeting, Berlin, 1993; Soloist, Reiner Korff's composition for 35 musicians, Peter Edel Festival, Berlin, 1994; Jazz and More Festival '95, Munich, with Minton/Weston's Natural Formations, 1995; Numerous interviews and recordings for radio include: Music In Our Time, Company With Derek Bailey, Radio 3, 1991; Impressions with Brian Morton, Radio 3, 1992; Trio with Butcher and Durrant, duo with John Butcher, 1996; Television includes 2 appearances Blue Peter; Duo with Phil Minton, 1991. *Recordings:* 3 CD compilations; Company '91, with Alexander Balanescu, Derek Bailey, Paul Lovens, Paul Rogers, John Zorn, Buckethead; Respirtus, duo with John Butcher. *Honours:* Awarded funding, concert tour, The Improvised Music Touring Scheme; Art Council Tour of England, with (bassist) Barry Guy, 1990. *Membership:* PRS. *Leisure interests:* Painting; Going to exhibitions; Theatre; Writing – prose, poetry, free verse; Being with family and friends. *Address:* c/o Incus Records, 14 Downs Rd, London E5 8DS, England.

MCLAREN Malcolm Robert Andrew; b. 22 Jan. 1946, London, England. *Education:* Studied Fine Art, University of London. *Career:* Opened shop on King's Road with Vivienne Westwood (known as Sex), 1972; Created The Sex Pistols, 1974–79; Managed New York Dolls, USA, 1974; Created The Damned, with Chrissie Hynde; Gave first opportunities to Siouxsie and The Banshees, The Clash; Producer for artistes: Adam and The Ants; Bow Wow Wow; Boy George; Began solo recording career, 1981; Produced rap record, Buffalo Gals; Developed idea of World Music with Duck Rock, 1982; Developed film projects with Steven Spielberg, Hollywood, 1985; Paris album with Catherine Deneuve, 1994; Writing, producing musicals for cinema, stage; Candidate, Lord Mayor of London elections, 1999. *Compositions:* Music for advertising including theme for British Airways; Screenplay: The Great Rock 'N' Roll Swindle, 1979; Television musical: The Ghosts of Oxford Street, 1991. *Recordings:* Albums: Duck Rock, 1982; Fans, 1983; Waltz Darling, 1988; Paris, 1994; Paris The Ambient Album, 1996; Buffalo Gals Back to Skool, 1998; World Famous Supreme Team Show, 1998; Singles: Buffalo Gals, 1981; Double Dutch, 1982; Madam Butterfly, 1983; Deep In Vogue, 1988; Romeo and Juliet, 1991; Revenge of the Flowers, 1995; The Bell Song, 1997; Buffalo Gals Stampede, 1998; Opera House, 1998. *Memberships:* Musicians' Union; PRS; SAG; SPAM. *Address:* 61 rue de Varenne, 75007 Paris, France.

MCLAUGHLIN David Wallace; b. 13 Feb. 1958, Washington DC, USA. Musician (guitar, piano, mandolin, violin, bass, drums, percussion, banjo). m. Marilyn Gay Harman, 1 d. *Musical Education:* Private lessons: piano, violin, classical guitar, mandolin. *Career:* Full time musician, 1978–; Carnegie Hall; Lincoln Centre; White House; Madison Square Garden; Library of Congress; Wolf Trap; Grand Ole Opry; Ambassador Auditorium; Knoxville Worlds Fair; TV appearances: TNN; PBS; CBS; Tours: USA; Canada; England; Africa; India. *Recordings:* with The Johnson Mountain Boys: Walls of Time, 1981; Working Close, 1982; Live At The Birchmere, 1983; We'll Still Sing On, 1984; Let The Whole World Talk, 1985; At The Old School House, 1988; Blue Diamond, 1990; Play Requests, 1986; with Crowe and McLaughlin: Going Back On Rounder. *Honours:* Grammy

Nominations, 1990, 1994; Awards from: IBMA; SPBGMA; WAMA. *Memberships:* IBMA; WAMA; BMI; NARAS. *Leisure interests:* Musical instrument collecting, restoration. *Current Management:* Shepherd Productions. *Address:* 18E Monmouth St, Winchester, VA 22601, USA.

MCLAUGHLIN Dermot; b. 17 Aug. 1961, Derry, County Derry, Ireland. Irish Traditional Musician (fiddle). *Education:* Graduate, Trinity College, Dublin, Early and Modern Irish Language, Literature. *Musical Education:* Largely self-taught. *Career:* National Concert Hall, Dublin; Frequent radio and television appearances in Ireland; Concert tours and performances in: Ireland; UK; Europe; Nova Scotia; Record producer for Claddagh Records, specialist Irish label. *Publications:* Strad, 1991; O Riada Lecture, University College, Cork; Claddagh and Nimbus Records. *Honours:* Foundation Scholar of Trinity College, Dublin, 1981–86. *Membership:* Music Officer for the Arts Council, Dublin. *Leisure interests:* Music; Books; Cooking; Plants. *Address:* c/o The Arts Council, 70 Merrion Sq., Dublin 2, Ireland.

MCLAUGHLIN John; b. 4 Jan. 1942, Yorkshire, England. Jazz Musician (guitar). *Musical Education:* Piano and guitar studies. *Career:* Played with Alexis Korner; Georgie Fame; Graham Bond; Gunter Hampel; Played and recorded with John Surman; Dave Holland; Member, Tony Williams' band, Lifetime, 1969–70; As solo artist, recorded with Charlie Haden; Airto Moreira; Miles Davis; Founder, Mahavishnu Orchestra (with Billy Cobham, Jerry Goodman, Jan Hammer; later with Jean-Luc Ponty, Michael Walden), 1969–; Founder, Shakti, with Indian musicians L. Shankar and Zakir Hussain; Founder, One Truth Band, 1978; Formed trio with Larry Coryell and Paco De Lucia, 1978. *Compositions include:* Mediterranean Concerto, premiered with Scottish National Orchestra, Glasgow Jazz Festival, 1990. *Recordings:* Albums include: Solo/ Mahavishnu Orchestra: Extrapolation, 1969; Devotion, 1971; My Goals Beyond, 1971; Inner Mounting Flame, 1971; When Fortune Smiles, 1972; Birds of Fire, 1973; Between Nothingness and Eternity, 1974; Apocalypse, 1974; Visions To The Emerald Beyond, 1975; Inner World, 1976; Electric Guitarist, 1978; Best Of, 1980; Belo Horizonte, 1981; Music Spoken Here, 1983; Live At The Royal Festival Hall, 1990; Greatest Hits, 1991; Que Alegria, 1992; After The Rain, 1995; The Heart of Things, 1997; Belo Horizonte, 1999; with Shakti: Shakti With John McLaughlin, 1975; Natural Elements, 1977 Remember Shakti, 1999; with Al Di Meola and Paco De Lucia: Friday Night In San Francisco, 1978; with One Truth Band: Electric Dreams, 1979; with Santana: Mclaughlin and Santana, 1994; Compilations: Compact Jazz, 1993; This is Jazz, Vol. 17, 1996.

MCLAUGHLIN John I; b. 8 Jan. 1965, Glasgow, Scotland. Songwriter; Prod. *Career:* Writer and Producer, When the Lights Go Out with Five, 1998; Contributed tracks for Billie's debut album, 1998; Contributions to 911 albums The Journey and Moving On, 1997, 1998; Contributor to Matthew Marsden's debut album; Songwriter for pop/Motown act Mero, releases forthcoming; Collaborations with Graham Lyle, Lamont Dozier, The Full Crew, Steve DuBerry, Dave James, Paul Masterson. *Compositions include:* For 911: Love Sensation; Don't Make Me Wait; Bodyshakin'; The Journey; All I Want Is You; United Forever More, for Cliff Richard. *Current Management:* Backlash Music Management, 54 Carlton Pl., Glasgow G5 9TW, Scotland.

MCLEAN Alexander James (Bone); b. 9 Jan. 1978, West Palm Beach, Florida, USA. Singer; Musician (Bass guitar). *Career:* Puppeteer, Welcome Freshmen, on Nickelodeon satellite TV; Member, Backstreet Boys; Numerous television appearances and hit singles. *Recordings:* Singles: We've Got It Goin' On, 1995; Quit Playing Games, 1998; I'll Never Break Your Heart, 1998; Everybody, 1998; As Long As You Love Me, 1998; Anywhere for You, 1998; All I Have to Give, 1998; I Want it That Way, 1999; Albums: Backstreet Boys, 1996; Live in Concert, 1998; Backstreet's Back, 1998; Millennium, 1999. *Leisure interests:* Dancing; Basketball; Golf; Bowling; Writing poetry; Pool.

MCLEAN Don; b. 2 Oct. 1945, New Rochelle, New York, USA. Vocalist; Musician (guitar, 5 string banjo); Performer. m. Patricia Shnier, 13 March 1987, 1 s., 1 d. *Education:* BBA, Iona College, 1965–68. *Musical Education:* Self-taught; Opera Bel Canto voice training, aged 12; Also learned from Josh White, Pete Seeger, Brownie McGhee. *Career:* 12 world tours, 1972–92; Concerts include Carnegie Hall, numerous times; Sydney Opera House; Sydney Entertainment Center; Royal Festival Hall; Royal Albert Hall; Hundreds of solo concerts, USA; Television appearances: The Tonight Show (Johnny Carson); The Smothers Brothers Show; Midnight Special; In Concert; The Great American Dream Machine; Sesame Street; Dinah Shore; Mike Douglas; Merv Griffin; Later, with Bob Costas; 2 BBC television specials (UK): Don McLean at the Royal Albert Hall; Don McLean and Friends; Owner, Benny Bird Co Publishing, Don McLean Music, Starry Night Music; Star of free concert for 100,000 fans, Hyde Park, 1975; Special guest, Garth Brooks Live From Central Park, 1997. *Compositions:* Headroom, 1967, 1990; Castles In The Air, 1970; Dreidle, 1972; If We Try, 1972; Prime Time, 1978; Jerusalem, 1982; Angry Words, 1995; You're My Little Darlin, 1995; This Is America (Eisenhower), 1999.

Recordings: Albums include: American Pie, 1971; Don McLean, 1972; Dominion, 1983; Headroom, 1991; River of Love, 1995; For the Memories, 1997; Favorites, 1997; Christmas Dreams, 1997; Hit singles include: Vincent (Starry Starry Night); American Pie; Castles In The Air; And I Love You So; Crying; Since I Don't Have You; Wonderful Baby; The Mountains of Mourne. *Publications:* Numerous song books. *Honours:* 5 Grammy Nominations; Israel Bonds Award, State of Israel, 1981; Over 40 Gold and Platinum records world-wide. *Memberships:* ASCAP; BMI; NARAS; AFTRA; Lotos Club; Coffee House, NYC; Groucho Club, UK. *Leisure interests:* Canoeing; Horse riding; Target shooting; Biking.

MCLEAN Jackie, (John Lenwood); b. 17 May 1932, New York City, USA. Musician (alto saxophone); Prof., African American Music. m. Clarice Simmons, 2 s., 1 d. *Education:* A & T College, Greensboro, North Carolina. *Career:* Performs regularly nationally at major concert halls; Tours Europe and Japan annually; USIS tour of South African countries: Namibia; Swaziland; Mozambique; Lesotho; South Africa (Johannesburg, Durban, Cape Town). *Compositions include:* Dig; Little Melonae; Minor March. *Recordings include:* Rhythm of The Earth; The Rites of Passage; Monuments; Contours; Jackie McLean and Co; New Soil; Dynasty; New Wine, Old Bottles; Hat Trick; Fire and Love; Nature Boy. *Honours:* Voted No. 1 alto saxophonist in Japan, Europe, America; Swing Journal Best Altoist, Downbeat Magazine Critics and Readers Poll, 1993, 1994, 1995; Awarded Officer of the Order of Arts and Letters medal by Jack Lang, Minister of Culture under Francois Mitterand. *Leisure interests:* World history; Boxing. *Current Management:* Dollie McLean. *Address:* 261 Ridgefield St, Hartford, CT 06112, USA.

MACLEOD James; b. 19 Aug. 1974, Sutton Coldfield, West Midlands, England. Musician (guitar); Singer; Composer; Lyricist; Music Teacher. *Musical Education:* ABRSM Grade 7 Theory, BTec Popular Music Course. *Career:* Bass guitarist for indie band The Cantels, 1991; Performances include Birmingham Hummingbird Club; Fronted own UK pop band She Chameleon, releasing his compositions on own label, 1992; As guitarist, performed several national BBC Radio sessions and played over 30 sets at Ronnie Scott's Club in Birmingham with Lou Dalgleish Band, 1993; Toured UK universities with Lou Dalgliesh Band and others, 1993–94; Currently teaching guitar and music theory, working on ambient film music and visuals in studio set up in 1994. *Membership:* Musicians' Union. *Leisure interests:* Various sports; Reading. *Current Management:* Pie In The Sky Management. *Address:* 8 Lincoln Croft, Shenstone, Lichfield, Staffordshire WS14 0ND, England.

MCLEOD Rory; b. 23 Jan. 1955, London, England. Singer; Songwriter; Poet; Storyteller; Musician (harmonica, guitar, trombone, percussion, tap shoes). 1 s. *Career:* Former Mexican circus clown and fire-eater; Played harmonica and guitar with Michelle Shocked; Ani Di Franco; Ali Farka Touré; Taj Mahal; Collaborated with Hassan Erraji; Kathryn Tickel; Paul Rodden; Radio and television appearances: BBC Radio 4 documentary; CH4 TV, After Image singing Farewell Welfare; Scottish Circus Physical Theatre Company as composer, musical director on Hey Big Nose, psychocomedy based on Punch and Judy. *Recordings:* Albums: Angry Love; Kicking The Sawdust; Footsteps and Heartbeats; Travelling Home; Lullabies For Big Babies, 1997; Single: I'm A Rebel Trying To Govern Myself (all self-produced, 1976–92). *Publication:* Poetry anthology: Apples and Snakes. *Honours:* Texas Harmonica Champion, 1981; Edinburgh Festival Busker of The Year. *Memberships:* Musicians' Union; PRS; MCPS. *Address:* NE Music, 55 Lawe Rd, South Shields, Tyne and Wear NE3 3AL, England. *E-mail:* talkativemusic@dial.pipex.com.

MCLINTON Delbert Ross; b. 4 Nov. 1940, Lubbock, Texas, USA. Singer; Songwriter; Musician (harmonica). m. Wendy Goldstein. *Career:* Recording artist with The Straightjackets and The Rondelles. *Compositions:* I Want To Love You; Two More Bottles of Wine; Giving It Up For Love; B Movie. *Recordings:* Albums: Victim of Life's Circumstances, 1975; Genuine Cowhide, 1976; Love Rustler, 1977; Second Wind, 1978; Keeper of The Flame, 1979; The Jealous Kind, 1980; Plain From The Heart, 1981; Live From Austin, 1989; I'm With You, 1990; Best Of..., 1991; Never Been Rocked Enough, 1992; Delbert McClinton, 1993; Let the Good Times Roll, 1995; The Great Songs – Come Together, 1995; One of the Fortunate Few, 1997; with T Graham Brown: Wine into Water, 1998; with Danny Gatton: Hot Rod Guitar, 1999; with Flying Burrito Brothers: Sons of the Golden West, 1999. *Honours:* In Top 20 Harmonica Players, Rolling Stone magazine, 1985. *Membership:* BMI. *Current Management:* Harriet Sternberg Management. *Address:* 4268 Hazeltine Ave, Sherman Oaks, CA 91423, USA.

MCMANUS John Patrick; b. Enniskillen, Northern Ireland. Vocalist; Musician (bass, low whistle, Uilleann pipes, bodhran). *Career:* First TV appearance playing whistle with Matt Molloy of The Chieftains, aged 8; All-Ulster Champion on tin whistle aged 7–12; Formed rock band Mama's Boys with brothers Pat and Tommy and toured the world twice; Numerous TV appearances: Mama's Boys disbanded owing to Tom McManus' leukaemia, 1993; Tom died 1994; Changed musical direction and formed new act

Celtus with brother Pat, 1995; Signed to Muff Winwood, Sony S2, 1996; Co-wrote Celtus' debut album; Debut performance dates for Celtus as support to Sheryl Crow at Royal Albert Hall, Wolverhampton Civic and Manchester Apollo; 2 tours followed with Paul Carrack; Played Womad Festival; Won Phil Lynott Best Album Award for Moonchild, Irish World Awards, 1998. *Recordings:* as Mama's Boys: Official Bootleg; Plug It In; Turn It Up; Mama's Boys; Power and Passion; Growing Up The Hard Way; Live Tonite; Relativity; With Celtus: Moonchild, 1997; Portrait, 1999. *Memberships:* PRS; Musicians' Union. *Leisure interests:* Shooting footage on video camera; Snooker; Strict vegetarian. *Current Management:* Lindy Benson, Shamrock Music Ltd, 9 Thornton Pl., London W1H 1FG, England.

MCMILLAN Stuart; b. 1966, Glasgow, Scotland. Prod.; Remixer; DJ. *Career:* Started career as a DJ in Glasgow; Met Orde Meikle and started putting on their own club nights, Atlantis and Slam; Formed the Slam production duo and Soma Records label; World-wide DJ; Collaborations: UNKLE; Remixed: Sunscreem; Mansun; Dave Angel; Phuture; Kym Sims; Member: Universal Principles. *Recordings:* Albums: Headstates, 1996; Alien Radio, Past Lessons – Future Theories (DJ-mixed compilation), 2001; Singles: Eterna, 1991; Positive Education, 1993; Snapshots, 1995; Dark Forces, 1996; Narco Tourists, Lifetimes, Alien Radio 2001. *Address:* c/o Soma Records, 342 Argyle St, Glasgow, G2 8LY, Scotland.

MCMURRAY Rick; b. 11 July 1975, Larne, Northern Ireland. Musician (Drums). *Career:* Joined Ash, 1992; Support slots to Suede, Dinosaur Jr and Elastica; Headlining dates, TV appearances and festival slots; US headlining tour; Contributed title track for film A Life Less Ordinary. *Recordings:* Jack Names the Planets, 1994; Petrol, 1994; Uncle Pat, 1994; Kung Fu, 1995; Girl From Mars; Goldfinger; Oh Yeah; A Life Less Ordinary, 1997; Jesus Says, 1998; Albums: Trailer, 1994; 1977, 1996; Live At The Wireless, 1997; Nu-Clear Sounds, 1998.

MCNABB Ian; b. 3 Nov. 1962. Singer; Songwriter. *Career:* Founder member, Icicle Works; Recording debut, 1981; Founder, own record label Troll Kitchen; Solo artiste, 1992-. *Recordings:* Albums: The Icicle Works, 1984; The Small Price of a Bicycle, 1985; 7 Singles Deep, 1986; If You Want To Defeat Your Enemy Sing His Song, 1987; Blind, 1987; Permanent Damage, 1990; The Best Of, 1992; Also appears: with Mike Scott, Still Burning, 1997; with the Waterboys, Whole of the Moon, 1998; with Pspyched!, 1999; Solo: Truth and Beauty, 1992; Head Like A Rock, 1994; Merseybeast; Singles include: Nirvana; Birds Fly (Whisper To a Scream); Love Is A Wonderful Colour; Hollow Horse; Understanding Jane.

MCNALLY John; b. 30 Aug. 1941, Liverpool, England. Entertainer; Musician (guitar). m. Mary Hollywood, 27 June 1964, 1 s., 1 d. *Musical Education:* Self-taught. *Career:* Member, The Searchers; Every major media appearance including: Ed Sullivan Show; Royal Variety Show; Palladium Show. *Recordings include:* Sweets For My Sweet; Needles and Pins; Walk In The Room. *Honours:* Runners-up to the Beatles in numerous 60s polls. *Leisure interest:* Sport. *Current Management:* Alan Field Ltd. *Address:* 3 The Spinney, Bakers Hill, Hadley Common EN5 5BY, England.

MCNALLY Stephen Patrick; b. 4 July 1978, Liverpool, England. Vocalist; Musician (guitar); Songwriter. *Career:* Co-founder: BBMak pop group, 1996; Signed to UK company Telstar; Gained large US popularity after licence deal with Hollywood/Disney; Performed to over 100m US viewers through group's own TV specials; Supported Britney Spears on sell-out US tour followed by 28-date first headline US tour, 2000; UK shows with The Corrs, 2001. *Recordings:* Albums: Sooner Or Later, 2000; Singles: Back Here, Still On Your Side, 2000; Ghost of You and Me, 2001. *Honours:* Debut LP sales of over 1m. copies. *Address:* c/o Diane Young. *E-mail:* DaytimeENT@aol.com. *Internet:* www.bbmak.co.uk.

MCNAMARA Danny; b. 31 Dec. 1970, Huddersfield, England. Singer; Songwriter; Musician (Guitar). *Career:* Member, Embrace; Obtained major label deals in UK and USA; Debut single released independently; Early support slots to Manic Street Preachers, 1997; Headline tours and TV appearances. *Recordings:* Singles: Fireworks; One Big Family; All You Good Good People; Come Back To What You Know; My Weakness Is None of Your Business; The Good Will Out; Hooligan; Album: The Good Will Out.

MCNAMARA Richard; b. 23 Oct. 1972, Huddersfield, England. Musician (Guitar); Backing Vocalist. *Career:* Member, Embrace; Obtained major label deals in UK and USA, 1996; Released debut single independently; Support slot to Manic Street Preachers, 1997; Headline tours and TV appearances. *Recordings:* Singles: Fireworks; One Big Family; All You Good Good People; Come Back To What You Know; My Weakness Is None of Your Business; The Good Will Out; Hooligan; Album: The Good Will Out.

MCNEAL Lutricia; b. Oklahoma, USA. Singer; Songwriter. *Career:* Teamed up with Swedish production team Rob 'n' Raz; Numerous appearances in Europe, USA and Britain. *Recordings:* Singles: Ain't That Just The Way, 1997; Someone Loves You Honey, 1998; Stranded, 1999; Albums: Ain't That Just The Way, 1998; My Side of Town, 1998.

MACNEIL Rita; b. 28 May 1944, Nova Scotia, Canada. Singer; Songwriter. 1 s., 1 d. *Career:* Host, one hour weekly CBC TV Music entertainment show; Concert tours Japan, Australia, UK, Sweden, USA, Canada. *Recordings:* Flying On Your Own, 1986; Reason To Believe, 1988; Now The Bells Ring, 1988; Rita, 1989; Home I'll Be, 1990; Thinking of You, 1992; Once Upon A Christmas, 1993; Vol. 1 – Songs From The Collection, 1994; Porch Songs, 1995; Joyful Sounds: A Seasonal Collection, 1996; Music of a Thousand Nights, 1997; with The Chieftans: Fire in the Kitchen; Celtic Colours International Festival, 1999. *Honours:* Order of Canada; 5 Hon. Doctorates; 3 JUNO Awards; 4 Canadian Country Music Awards; 3 Platinum albums; 3 Double Platinum albums; 1 Triple Platinum album; 1 Gold album; 1 Silver album. *Memberships:* SOCAN; CMA; CARAS; ACTRA; AFofM. *Current Management:* Lupins Productions. *Address:* PO Box 183, Sydney, Cape Breton, Nova Scotia B1P 6H1, Canada.

MCREADY Mike; Rock Musician (guitar). *Career:* Member, US rock group Pearl Jam, 1990–; Concerts include: Support to Alice In Chains, 1991; Lollapalooza Festival tour, 1992; Drop In The Park concert, Seattle, 1992; Bob Dylan 30th anniversary concert, Madison Square Garden, New York, 1992; Neil Young's Bridge School Benefit, with Elton John, Sammy Hagar, James Taylor, 1992; Support to Keith Richard and The Expensive Winos, New York, 1992; Concert appearances with Neil Young; Also member, tribute group Temple of The Dog, 1990; Group appears in film Singles, 1992. *Recordings:* Temple of The Dog, 1992; with Pearl Jam: Ten (No. 2, USA), 1992; Vs. (No. 1, USA), 1993; Vitalogy, 1994; No Code, 1996; Yield, 1998; Live on Two Legs, 1998; with Neil Young: Mirror Ball, 1995; with Screaming Trees: Dust, 1996; Singles: Alive, 1992; Even Flow, 1992; Jeremy, 199; Contributor, Sweet Relief benefit album, 1993; Film soundtrack, Singles, 1992. *Honours:* American Music Award, Favourite New Artist, Pop/Rock and Hard Rock categories, 1993; Rolling Stone Readers' Awards, Best New American Band, Best Video, 1993; 4 MTV Awards, 1993; Highest 1-week album sales total in history, Vs., 1993. *Current Management:* Curtis Management, 417 Denny Way, Suite 200, Seattle, WA 98109, USA.

MCREADY Mindy; b. 30 Nov. 1975. *Recordings:* Singles: Guys Do It All The Time, 1996; What If I Do, 1997; Maybe He'll Notice Her Now, 1997; You'll Never Know, 1998; One in a Million, 1999; Albums: Ten Thousand Angels, 1996; If I Don't Stay the Night, 1997; I'm Not So Tough, 1999.

MCSHERRY John; b. 1970, Belfast, Northern Ireland, UK. Musician (uilleann pipes, tin whistle, low whistle); Composer. *Career:* Formed Tamalin with brother Paul, cousin Kevin Dorris and sisters Tina and Joanne; Played in Donal Lunny's band Coolfin with Nollaig Casey, Sharon Shannon, Ray Fean and Graham Henderson; Part of Lunasa with Michael McGoldrick; Collaborations: Niamh Parsons; Nancy Griffiths; Shaun Davey; Dan Ar Braz. *Recordings:* Albums: Rhythm and Rhyme (with Tamalin), 1997; Lunasa Live, Coolfin, 1998; At First Light (with Michael McGoldrick), 2001; features on: Loosely Connected (Niamh Parsons), 1992; Each Little Thing (Sharon Shannon), 1997; Waking Ned (Soundtrack), 1998; This Is My Father (Soundtrack), 1998; Blackbirds and Thrushes (Niamh Parsons), 1999. *Honours:* All Ireland Championship, three awards by age 15; Oireachtas Piping competition, youngest ever winner at 18. *Address:* c/o Vertical Records, 5 Newton Terrace Lane, Glasgow, G3 7PB, Scotland. *Internet:* www.johnmcsherry.com.

MCTELL Ralph; b. 3 Dec. 1944, Farnborough, Kent, England. Folk Singer; Songwriter; Musician (guitar). *Career:* Folk singer, 1960s-; Appearances, UK children's television including: Alphabet Zoo, Tickle On The Tum, 1980s. *Compositions include:* Streets of London, 1969; Zimmerman Blues, 1972. *Recordings:* Albums include: Eight Frames A Second, 1968; Spiral Staircase, 1969; My Side of Your Window, 1970; Not Till Tomorrow, 1972 (re-issued 1998); Easy, 1973; Streets, 1975; Right Side Up, 1976; Ralph, Albert and Sydney, 1977 (re-issued 1997); Slide Away The Screens, 1979; Love Grows, 1982; Sighs, 1987; Stealin' Back, 1990; The Boy With The Note, 1992; The Silver Celebration, 1992; Sand in Your Shoes, 1995; Songs For Six Strings Vol. II, 1996; Hit single: Streets of London (No. 2, UK), 1974. *Current Management:* Tickety-Boo Ltd. *Address:* The Boat House, Crabtree Lane, London SW6 6TY, England.

MCVICAR Ewan Reynolds; b. 17 April 1941, Inverness, Scotland. Songwriter; Singer; Musician (guitar, banjo, autoharp); Author; Poet. m. Linda Rosemary Gammie, 30 April 1971. *Education:* Associate Member, Institute of Bankers in Scotland, 1959; Diploma in Social Work, Glasgow University, 1975; MSc (Scottish Childrens' Songs) by research, Edinburgh University, 1997–98. *Career:* Founded first folk club in Scotland, 1959; Toured and taught music in USA, 1965–67; Based in Glasgow, singing and writing, 1968–; Tour of Finland, 1980; Wrote show for the Glasgow-Nurnberg Twinning, 1985; Songmaker in Schools Project, 1991–; Mungo 200 Project with Amu Logotse, 1994–95; Scottish Arts Council, Writer in Residence, Craigmillar, Edinburgh, 1998–2000; Chair, Sangschule, Linlithgow, 1998; Co-animateur, Singers Gathering, Livingston, 1999. *Compositions:* Talking Army Blues, 1959; 20 songs commercially covered by other singers and groups; Shows written include: Salmon Spells; Church

Bells; The Fyffes Banana Boat Show; Wrote 16 songs for The Singing Kettle Shows, 1990–98. *Recordings:* Gies Peace, 1987; Produced and released album, I Was Born In Glasgow, 1989; The New Songs of Fife, 1999. *Publications:* One Singer One Song, book, 1990; Streets, Schemes and Stages, book, 1991; Cod Liver Oil and The Orange Juice, book, 1993; Pictworks, booklet of Pictish poems and songs, 1999. *Honour:* Finalist, Songsearch, 1988. *Membership:* Musicians' Union. *Leisure interest:* Music. *Current Management:* Gallus Music.

MCVIE Christine, (Christine Perfect); b. 12 July 1943, Birmingham, England. Musician (keyboards); Singer; Songwriter; Prod. m. (1) John McVie, divorced, (2) Eduardo Quintela, 18 Oct. 1986. *Career:* Member, Chicken Shack; Member, Fleetwood Mac, 1970–90; Numerous tours, concerts, television include: US Festival, San Bernadino, California; Shake The Cage tour, Europe, Australia, 1988; Wembley Stadium, with Jethro Tull, Hall and Oates, 1990; The Mask tour, 1990. *Compositions include:* Don't Stop; You Make Loving Fun. *Recordings:* Albums with Fleetwood Mac: Future Games, 1971; Bare Trees, 1972; Penguin, 1973; Mystery To Me, 1973; Heroes Are Hard To Find, 1974; Fleetwood Mac, 1975; Rumours, 1977; Tusk, 1979; Fleetwood Mac Live, 1980; Mirage, 1982; Tango In The Night, 1987; Behind The Mask, 1990; Time, 1995; Solo: Christine McVie, 1984; Film soundtrack: A Fine Mess, 1985; Contributor: Law and Order, Lindsey Buckingham, 1981; Rock, Rhythm and Blues, compilation album, 1989; Singles include: The Green Manalishi, 1970; Over My Head, 1976; Rhiannon (Will You Ever Win), 1976; Say You Love Me, 1976; Go Your Own Way, 1977; Dreams, 1977; You Make Loving Fun, 1977; Tusk, 1979; Sara, 1979; Think About Me, 1980; Hold Me, 1982; Gypsy, 1982; Oh Diane, 1983; Big Love, 1987; Little Lies, 1987; Everywhere, 1988; Solo: Got A Hold On Me, 1984; Love Will Show Us How, 1984. *Honours:* Melody Maker Female Vocalist of the Year, 1969; American Music Awards, Favourite Pop/Rock Group, Favourite Pop/Rock Album, 1978; Grammy, Album of The Year, Rumours, 1978; Star on Hollywood Walk of Fame, with Fleetwood Mac, 1979. *Current Management:* Courage Management, 2899 Agoura Blvd, Suite 562, Westlake, CA 91361, USA.

MCVIE John; b. 26 Nov. 1945, London, England. Musician (bass). m. Christine Perfect, divorced. *Career:* Member, Fleetwood Mac, 1967–; Solo artiste, 1992–; World-wide appearances include: Windsor Jazz and Blues Festival, 1967; Miami Pop Festival, 1968; Reading Festival, 1970; Bath Festival, 1970; US tour with the Eagles, 1976; US Festival, 1982; Reunion, Presidential Inaugural concert, Maryland, 1993. *Recordings include:* Albums: with Fleetwood Mac: Fleetwood Mac, 1968; English Rose, 1969; Pious Bird of Omen, 1969; Then Play On, 1969; Blues Jam At Chess, 1969; Kiln House, 1970; Fleetwood Mac In Chicago, 1971; Black Magic Woman, 1971; Future Games, 1971; Bare Trees, 1972; Penguin, 1973; Mystery To Me, 1973; Rumours, 1977; Tusk, 1979; Tango In The Night, 1987; Behind The Mask, 1990; Time, 1995; Solo album: John McVie's Gotta Band With Lola Thomas, 1992; Singles include: Black Magic Woman; Mr Wonderful; Man of The World; The Green Manalishi; Rhiannon; Go Your Own Way; Don't Stop; Dreams; You Make Loving Fun; Tusk; Hold Me; Got A Hold On Me; Everywhere; Save Me. *Honours:* American Music Awards: Favourite Band, Favourite Album, 1978; Grammy Award: Album of The Year, Rumours, 1978; Star on Hollywood Walk of Fame, 1979; Gold Ticket Award, Madison Square Garden, 1990. *Address:* c/o Ernst and Young LLP, 1999 Avenue of the Stars, Suite 2100, Los Angeles, CA 90067, USA.

MADIGAN Brian Alan; b. 27 June 1964, Enfield, Middlesex. Composer; Musician (Drummer, Flute). m. Barbara Madigan. *Education:* BA, Middlesex Polytechnic, London, 1988–91. *Career:* Composer, Performer with Hot Savoury Souffles, 1991–93; Wise Wound, 1992–96; Madigan, 1997–99; Festival appearances, 1992–99. *Compositions:* Dance Notes; Coincidence; The Fisher King. *Memberships:* SPNM; MU. *Leisure interests:* Cycling; Swimming; Walking; Painting. *Address:* 12 Bladul Buildings, Bath BA1 5LS, England.

MADLINGOZI Ringo, (Sindile Brian Madlingozi); b. 1964, Cape Town, South Africa. Vocalist; Songwriter. *Musical Education:* Self-taught. *Career:* At school, led acapella group which performed at community and youth functions; Became vocalist for the group Ikwezi, and later for Peto; Peto won national Shell Road to Fame talent competition, 1986; Prize led to the role of support act for King's Trust concert in Swaziland headlined by Eric Clapton; Moved to Johannesburg; Spent 1990s as member of Gecko Moon; Various studio session work for radio commercials, film, and album recordings including: Simply Red; The Power of One soundtrack (with Teddy Pendergrass); The Lion King soundtrack; Hugh Masekela; Caiphus Semenya; Oliver Mtukudzi; First solo album, 1996; Performs a Xhosa version of the title song of UB40's Cover Up album, 2002. *Recordings:* Vukani, 1996; Sondelani, 1997; Mamelani, Into Yam', 1999; Buyisa, 2000. *Honours:* Sondelani received double platinum sales award; FNB South African Music Awards, Best Adult Contemporary Performance (languages other than English and Afrikaans), Sondelani, 1998; Kora All-Africa Music Awards: Best Southern African Artist; Best Male Artist, 1998; Kora All Africa Music Award, Best Artist/Group in Southern Africa, 1999.

MADONNA (Madonna Louise Veronica Ciccone); b. 16 Aug. 1958, Bay City, Michigan, USA. Singer; Songwriter; Actress. m. (1) Sean Penn, 1985, divorced 1989; (2) Guy Richie, 2000; 1 d, 1 s. *Education:* University of Michigan, 1976–78. *Career:* Dancer, New York, 1979; Actress, 1980–; Solo singer, 1983–; Film appearances include: Vision Quest, 1985; Desperately Seeking Susan, 1985; Shanghai Surprise, 1986; Who's That Girl, 1987; Bloodhounds On Broadway, 1990; Dick Tracy, 1990; A League of Their Own, 1992; Numerous world-wide concerts, 1983–; Major appearances include: Live Aid, Philadelphia, 1985; Don't Bungle The Jungle, ecological awareness benefit, 1989; Television includes: In Bed With Madonna (documentary), 1991; Stage performance, Speed The Plow, Broadway, 1988; Owner, Maverick record label. *Compositions include:* Co-writer, own hits: Live To Tell; Open Your Heart; Justify My Love; Co-writer, Each Time You Break My Heart, Nick Kamen, 1986. *Recordings:* Hit singles include: Holiday, 1983; Lucky Star, 1984; Borderline, 1984; Like A Virgin (No. 1, USA), 1984; Material Girl, 1985; Crazy For You (No. 1, USA), 1985; Angel, 1985; Into The Groove (No. 1, UK), 1985; Dress You Up, 1985; Gambler, 1985; Live To Tell (No. 1, USA), 1986; Papa Don't Preach (No. 1, UK and USA), 1986; True Blue (No. 1, UK), 1986; Open Your Heart, 1986; La Isla Bonita (No. 1, UK), 1987; Who's That Girl (No. 1, USA and UK), 1987; Causin' A Commotion, 1987; The Look of Love, 1987; Like A Prayer (No. 1, UK and USA), 1989; Express Yourself, 1989; Cherish, 1989; Dear Jessie, 1989; Oh Father, 1990; Keep It Together, 1991; Vogue (No. 1, UK and USA), 1991; I'm Breathless, 1991; Hanky Panky, 1991; Justify My Love (No. 1, USA), 1991; Rescue Me, 1991; This Used To Be My Playground, 1992; Erotica, 1992; Deeper and Deeper, 1992; Bad Girl, 1993; Fever, 1993; Rain, 1993; Frozen, 1998; Ray of Light, 1998; Power of Goodbye, 1998; Nothing Really Matters, 1999; Beautiful Stranger: theme song from Austin Powers: The Spy Who Shagged Me, 1999; American Pie (No. 1, UK), 2000; Music (No. 1, UK and USA), 2000; Don't Tell Me, 2000; What It Feels Like For A Girl, 2001; Albums: Madonna, 1983; Like A Virgin, 1985; True Blue, 1986; Who's That Girl?, film soundtrack, 1987; You Can Dance, 1988; Like A Prayer, 1989; I'm Breathless, 1990; The Immaculate Collection, 1990; Dick Tracy, film soundtrack, 1990; Erotica, 1992; Bedtime Stories, 1994; Something To Remember, 1995; Evita, film soundtrack, 1996; Ray of Light (No. 1, UK), 1998; Music (No. 1, UK and USA), 2000; GHV2 (compilation), 2001. *Publications:* Sex, 1992. *Honours include:* Numerous MTV Video Awards, including Vanguard Award, 1986; American Music Awards: Favourite Female Video Artist, 1987; Favourite Dance Single, 1991; Academy Award, Best Song, 1991; Juno Award, International Song of The Year, 1991; Grammy Award, Best Longform Music Video, 1992; BRIT Awards, Best International Female, 2001; Numerous awards from Billboard, Vogue and Rolling Stone magazines. *Current Management:* Norman West Management, 9348 Civic Centre Dr., Beverly Hills, CA 90210, USA.

MADSEN Tue; b. 25 Jan. 1969, Hadsten, Denmark. Musician (Guitar); Prod. *Career:* Playing Guitar for 18 years. *Recordings:* Pixie Killers: One Size Fits All; Grope: Primates, 1994; Soul Pieces, EP, 1996; The Fury, 1996; Desert Storm, 1997. *Honour:* Danish Grammy Nominee, 1998. *Membership:* DMF. *Current Management:* Diehard, Vindegade 101, 5000 Odensec, Denmark. *Address:* Terp Skovvej 50, 8260 Vibij, Denmark.

MAEL Ronald; b. 12 Aug. 1949, California, USA. Musician (keyboards); Songwriter. *Education:* BA, Graphic Design, University of California, Los Angeles. *Musical Education:* Piano lessons, age 6–10. *Career:* Founder member, Sparks (with brother Russell); Recorded 16 albums; Concert tours: USA; UK; France; Belgium; Netherlands; Sweden; Finland; Canada; Television appearances world-wide. *Recordings:* 16 albums: Halfnelson (changed to Sparks); A Woofer In Tweeter's Clothing; Kimono My House; Propaganda; Indiscreet; Big Beat; Introducing Sparks; Number One In Heaven; Terminal Jive; Whomp That Sucker; Angst In My Pants; Sparks In Outer House; Pulling Rabbits Out of a Hat; Music That You Can Dance To; Interior Design; Gratuitous Sax and Senseless Violins; When Do I Get to Sing 'My Way'?; Now that I Own the BBC; Plagiarism; Beat the Clock; National Crime Awareness Week. *Honours:* Various Gold records. *Membership:* Sons of The Desert. *Leisure interest:* Writing songs. *Current Management:* Eric Harle, DEF Management. *Address:* 21 Premier House, 313 Kilburn Lane, London W9 3EG, England.

MAGEE Curtis; b. 12 Aug. 1965, Co. Tyrone, Northern Ireland. Country Singer; Musician. m. Lyn, 3 d. *Career:* Fronted own band for many years; Solo; Professional, 1990–; Tours include: UK; Ireland; Spain. *Compositions:* 30 Great Singalongs; 50 Xmas Hits; 20 Country Gospel; My Forever Friend; 20, Country Linde Dance; 21 Great Love Songs. *Recordings:* 13 Albums; 4 Videos. *Honours:* Numerous CMC Awards, Solo Act of the Year. *Membership;* BCMA. *Leisure interests:* English soccer, Television soaps. *Address:* 42 Greenhall Manor, Coleraine, BT51 3GN, Northern Ireland.

MAGIC Mick, (R M Lancaster); b. 21 April 1958, Wimbledon, England. Record Co Exec.; Musician (guitar, keyboards); Composer. Partner: Samantha J Taylor. *Career:* Owner, Music and Elsewhere record label, promoting new bands especially underground bands; Studio work with own band; Appearance on BBC Radio 5. *Recordings include:* with Magic

Moments At Twilight Time: Psychotron O, 1988; Zoen Nostalgia, 1989; White Hawk Atomic, 1992; Creavolution, 1996. *Publications:* The M and E Newsletter and Yearbook, United World Underground News. *Membership:* Mensa. *Leisure interests:* Cinema, especially silent films; Chess. *Current Management:* United World Underground, 6 Farm Court, Farm Rd, Frimley, Camberley, Surrey GU16 8TJ, England. *E-mail:* magic@uwunderground.fsnet.co.uk. *Internet:* music-elsewhere.hypermart.net.

MAGOOGAN Wesley; b. 11 Oct. 1951, London, England. Musician (saxophone). m. Marion Willett, 10 March 1973, 1 s., 1 d. (deceased). *Musical Education:* Royal Academy of Music. *Career:* Hazel O'Connor; The Beat (also known as The English Beat); Joan Armatrading; Elton John; Billy Ocean; Extensive world tours, 1978-. *Recordings:* Albums: with O'Connor/Magoogan: Will You; with The Beat: Special Beat Service, 1982; with Hazel O'Connor: Breaking Glass, 1980; Sons and Lovers, 1980; Cover Plus, 1981: with Joan Armatrading: Secret Secrets, 1985; Sleight of Hand, 1986; Shouting Stage, 1988; 2 albums with Billy Ocean; with Magnum: Sleepwalking, 1992. *Membership:* Royal Society of Musicians. *Leisure interests:* Reading; Painting. *Current Management:* Simon Davies. *Address:* 5 Paddington St, Marylebone, London W1M 3LA, England.

MAGUIRE Martie, (Martie Seidel); b. 12 Oct. 1969, York, Pennsylvania, USA. Musician (fiddle); Vocalist. m. Gareth Maguire, Aug. 2001. *Career:* Toured with sister Emily Erwin in teen bluegrass group Blue Night Express for six years until band broke up, 1989; Sisters joined two friends performing on Dallas sidewalks, calling the act the Dixie Chicks; Support slots for: Garth Brooks; Emmylou Harris; Loretta Lynn; Recorded three albums for local label, Crystal Clear; Signed to Sony and released debut album Wide Open Spaces; Mix of traditional bluegrass with mainstream country coupled with exuberant live stage show and quirky song material has ensured huge popularity into the 2000s. *Compositions include:* Cowboy Take Me Away; Ready To Run; You Were Mine. *Recordings include:* with the Dixie Chicks: I Can Love You Better, 1997; There's Your Trouble, 1998; Wide Open Spaces, 1998; Albums include: Wide Open Spaces, 1998, Fly, 1999. *Honours:* recent including: CMA Awards: Music Video of The Year, 1999; Single of The Year, Wide Open Spaces, 1999; Vocal Group of The Year, 1999; Entertainer of The Year, 2000; Album of The Year, Fly, 2000; Vocal Group of The Year, 2000; Music Video of The Year, Goodbye Earl, 2000; TNN Music Awards: Group/Duo of The Year, 1999; ACM Awards: Album of The Year, Fly, 1999; Favorite Duo Or Group, 1999; American Music Award, Favorite New Country Artist, 1999; Billboard Award, Favorite Country Artist, 1999; Grammy Awards: Best Country Album, Wide Open Spaces, 1998; Best Country Performance By A Duo Or Group With Vocal, 1998, 1999. *Address:* c/o The Country Music Asscn, Nashville, Tennessee, USA. *Internet:* www.dixiechicks.com.

MAHAL Taj, (Henry St Clair Fredericks); b. 17 May 1942, Massachusetts, USA. Composer; Musician. m. Inshirah Geter, 23 Jan. 1976. *Education:* BA, University Massachusetts, Amherst, 1964. *Career:* Composer, musician, 1964–; Early concerts, Boston; Tours across US; Europe; Africa; Australia; Actor in films: King of Ragtime; Sounder; Sounder II; Theatre appearance: Mule Bone. *Compositions:* Taj; Like Never Before; Film soundtracks: Sounder; Sounder II; Brothers; Television shows: Ewoks; The Man Who Broke A Thousand Chains; Brer Rabbit; The Hot Spot. *Recordings:* Albums: Taj Mahal, 1967; Natch'l Blues, 1968; Giant Step, 1969; The Real Thing, 1971; Happy Just To Be Like I Am, 1971; Recycling The Blues and Other Stuff, 1972; Sounder (film soundtrack), 1972; Ooh So Good 'n' Blues, 1973; Mo'Roots, 1974; Music Keeps Me Together, 1975; Satisfied 'n Tickled Too, 1976; Music Fuh Ya, 1977; Brothers (film soundtrack), 1977; Evolution, 1978; Taj Mahal and The International Rhythm Band, 1980; Big Blues, 1990; Mule Bone, 1991; Like Never Before, 1991; An Evening of Acoustic Music, 1995; Dancing The Blues, 1995; Phantom Blues, 1996; Señor Blues, 1997; Shakin' a Tailfeather, 1997; Taj Mahal and the Hula Blues, 1998; Sacred Island, 1998; Kulanjan, 1999; Shake it to the One you Love the Best, 1999; Big Blues: Live at Ronnie Scott's. *Honours:* Best Ethnic Music Award, Brothers, 1979; Bay Area Music Awards, Brothers, 1979. *Current Management:* Folklore Productions, 1671 Appian Way, Santa Monica, CA 90401, USA.

MAHAR Eric Frederick; b. 11 Jan. 1959, Hamilton, Ontario, Canada. Music Prod.; Music Consultant; Musician (guitar, banjo, harmonica). m. 11 June 1988. *Musical Education:* Jazz Program, Humber College; Studied classical guitar at University of Toronto. *Career:* Solo guitarist; Theatre guitarist; R & B country guitarist for The Mercey Brothers; Marie Bottrell; Joan Kennedy; Television appearances: Tommy Hunter Show; CCMA Awards Show; Sunshine Country. *Recordings:* Producer and performer for various record labels. *Membership:* Musicians' Union. *Leisure interests:* Mountain biking; Skiing; Badminton; Swimming.

MAIDMAN Ian Stuart; b. 24 Jan. 1958, Upminster, Essex, England. Record Prod.; Songwriter; Musician (multi-instrumentalist). *Musical Education:* Classical guitar; Piano; Music theory. *Career:* Producer for:

Paul Brady; Pili Pili; Murray Head; Musician, tours with: Joan Armatrading, 1983; Murray Head, 1984–; Paul Brady, 1985 ; Penguin Café Orchestra, 1985–; Boy George, 1988–89; David Sylvian, 1988; Currently with: Penguin Café Orchestra; Annie Whitehead; Paul Brady; Murray Head. *Compositions:* Songwriter, albums by Sam Brown and Boy George. *Recordings:* Extensive session work includes: Paul Brady; Gerry Rafferty; Joan Armatrading; Shakespears Sister; Boy George; Sam Brown; David Sylvian; Albums include: with Penguin Café Orchestra: When In Rome; with Paul Brady: Back To The Centre; Primitive Dance; with Shakespears Sister: Hormonally Yours. *Honour:* Back To The Centre, Best Album, Ireland, 1986–87. *Memberships:* Musicians' Union; PRS; MCPS. *Leisure interests:* Travel; Cats. *Current Management:* Positive Earth Music. *Address:* 22 Richford Rd, London E15 3PQ, England.

MAINS Natalie Louise; b. 14 Oct. 1974. Vocalist. *Education:* Texas Tech. *Musical Education:* Berklee School of Music, Boston, Massachusetts. *Career:* Father, Lloyd Maines, learned that country/bluegrass act the Dixie Chicks needed a new lead singer, 1995; Replaced Laura Lynch and signed to Sony with the band; Mix of traditional bluegrass with mainstream country coupled with exuberant live stage show and quirky song material has ensured huge popularity into the 2000s. *Compositions include:* Sin Wagon. *Recordings include:* with the Dixie Chicks: I Can Love You Better, 1997; There's Your Trouble, 1998; Wide Open Spaces, 1998; Albums include: Wide Open Spaces, 1998, Fly, 1999. *Honours:* recent including: CMA Awards: Music Video of The Year, 1999; Single of The Year, Wide Open Spaces, 1999; Vocal Group of The Year, 1999; Entertainer of The Year, 2000; Album of The Year, Fly, 2000; Vocal Group of The Year, 2000; Music Video of The Year, Goodbye Earl, 2000; TNN Music Awards: Group/Duo of The Year, 1999; ACM Awards: Album of The Year, Fly, 1999; Favorite Duo Or Group, 1999; American Music Award, Favorite New Country Artist, 1999; Billboard Award, Favorite Country Artist, 1999; Grammy Awards: Best Country Album, Wide Open Spaces, 1998; Best Country Performance By A Duo Or Group With Vocal, 1998, 1999. *Address:* c/o The Country Music Asscn, Nashville, Tennessee, USA. *Internet:* www.dixiechicks.com.

MAK Wai-Chu Clarence; b. 1959, Hong Kong. Composer; Musician (Electronics, Guitar); Educator. *Career:* Composed music for various arts groups including professional performing ensembles, dance companies and theatres; Produced concert of electronic music, computer music, contemporary music; Head of Composition and Electronic Music, Hong Kong Academy for Performing Arts; Organized projects for creative music making in Hong Kong; Radio Presenter of creative music. *Compositions:* include the works for orchestra, voice, choir, electronic means, multi-media, chambermusic, Chinese music ensemble and live computer music. *Memberships:* Hong Kong Composers Guild; Composers and Authors Society of Hong Kong; International Computer Music Asscn. *Leisure interests:* Music making, composing and perfrming; Computer programming. *Address:* School of Music, Hong Kong Academy for Performing Arts, 1 Gloucester Rd, Wan Chai, Hong Kong.

MAKAROV Jüri; b. 3 April 1959, Tallinn, Estonia. Promoter. m. Tiina Makarov, 3 July 1985, 1 s., 2 d. *Education:* Tallinn Technical University, Economy. *Musical Education:* Tallinn Music College. *Career:* Promoter, for: Jethro Tull; Steve Hackett; EMF; Bob Geldof; Procul Harum; Faith No More; The Pogues; Samantha Fox; Bonnie Tyler, 1986-. *Current Management:* A S Makarov Muusik Management. *Address:* Regati PSt 1.6 K, 0019 Tallinn, Estonia.

MAKEBA Miriam; b. 4 March 1932, Johannesburg, South Africa. Vocalist. m. (1) Hugh Masakela, (2) Stokely Carmichael. *Career:* Member, Cuban Brothers, 1950; Manhattan Brothers, 1950s; Member, touring show, African Jazz and Variety, 1957–59; Musical, King Kong; Starred in semi-documentary film, Come Back Africa; Worked on international club circuit in Europe, South America, Africa; Appearances at jazz festivals include: Montreux; Berlin; North Sea; Unofficial South African representative, Festac '77 festival, Lagos, Nigeria, 1977; Concert with Hugh Masakela, Botswana, 1982; Guest, Graceland tour with Paul Simon, 1987. *Recordings include:* Albums: The World of Miriam Makeba; Makeba, 1963; The Click Song, 1965; Pata Pata, 1972; Live At Conakry, 1975; Festac 77, 1978; Greatest Hits From Africa, 1985; Sangoma, 1989; Kilimandjaro: Live at Conakry, 1996; Malaisha, 1996; Meet Me at the River, 1996; Pata Pata: Live in Paris, 1996; Live from Paris and Conakry, 1996; Country Girl, 1997; Folk Songs from Africa, 1997; The Click Song, 1997; Myriam Makeba Live, 1997; Welele, 1997; Hit singles: Patha Patha; The Click Song; Malaika. *Publication:* Makeba, My Story (autobiography), 1989. *Honours include:* Dag Hammarskjold Peace Prize, 1986. *Current Management:* Sam Nole Management, 230 Park Ave, Suite 1512, New York, NY 10169, USA.

MAKEM Tommy; b. 4 Nov. 1932, Keady, County Armagh, Ireland. Singer; Actor. m. Mary Shanahan, 21 Sept. 1963, 3 s., 1 d. *Musical Education:* Self-taught. *Career:* Major concerts: Royal Albert Hall; Carnegie Hall; Lincoln Center; Sydney Opera House; Doothy Chandler Pavilion; Boston Symphony Hall; Tampa Performing Arts Center; Madison Square Gardens; Newport

Folkfest's Most Promising Newcomer; Television appearances: Ed Sullivan Show; Arthur Godfrey Show; Johnny Carson Tonight Show; Today Show; Merv Griffin Show; Danny Thomas Show; Entertainment Tonight; Dublin Late Show; BBC Late Show; TV series, US, England and Scotland. *Recordings:* Four Green Fields; Gentle Annie; Freedom's Sons; Rosie; Sing Me The Old Songs; The Winds Are Singing Freedom; The Winds of Morning; The Boys of Killybeg; Lord Nelson; Farewell To Carlingford; Summer Roads; Venezuela; Vancouver; Farewell To Nova Scotia; Sally O; True Love and Time; Better Times; Song Tradition. *Publications:* Tommy Makem's Ireland; The Clancy Brothers and Tommy Makem Song Book; The Tommy Makem Song Book. *Honours:* Grammy Award; Irish American Top 100 of the Year (5 years); Irish American Hall of Fame. *Leisure interests:* Irish Mythology and History; Photography; Travel. *Current Management:* Bard Enterprises. *Address:* 2 Longmeadow Rd, Dover, NH 03820, USA.

MAKHENE Blondie Keoagile Gerald; b. 16 Sept. 1955, White City Jabavu, Soweto, South Africa. Singer; Musician (guitar, piano). m. Agnes Mary, 18 Dec. 1979, 3 d. *Musical Education:* Grade 4. *Career:* Concert In The Park, 1984; Mandela Welcome Concert, Soweto South Africa, 1990; Black Radio Exclusive Conference, New Orleans, 1992; Africa For AIDS Concert, Sun City, South Africa, 1993; Panafest, Ghana, Accra, 1994. *Recordings:* Weekend Special, Brenda Fassie debut album; Amaquabane featuring Blondie Makhene, 1990; Albums: Elakho Likhona, Pure Gold; Isencane, Platform 1; Amadamara, Freddy Gwala. *Honour:* Most Outstanding Person, Voice Education Centre, South Africa. *Membership:* Dorkay House. *Leisure interest:* Swimming.

MALACH Bob; b. 23 Aug. 1954, Philadelphia, Pennsylvania, USA. Musician (saxophone, flute, clarinet). m. Janine Dreiding, 6 Jan. 1981, 1 s., 1 d. *Musical Education:* Study with: Jow Allard; Harold Bennett; Eddie Daniels; David Weber; Keith Underwood. *Career:* Ben Sidran, 1977; Stanley Clarke, 1977–79; Stevie Wonder, 1980–85; Bob Mintzer, 1983; Horace Silver, 1986; Robben Ford, 1987; Steve Miller Band, 1987; Bill Cosby Show, 1987–92; Mike Stern, 1994. *Recordings include:* Patti Labelle; Lou Rawls; The O'Jays; The Jackson 5; Soundtrack to Woman In Red (Stevie Wonder); Hoop Dreams; Miles Davis In Montreux; Solo albums: Mood Swing, 1990; The Searcher, 1997; After Hours, 1999. *Publications:* Swing Journal; Jazz Life; Ad Lib. *Memberships:* AFofM; BMI. *Leisure interests:* Darts; Tropical fish; Family life. *Current Management:* Go Jazz.

MALE Johnny; b. 10 Oct. 1963, Windsor, Berkshire, England. Musician (Guitar). *Career:* Member, Republica; Numerous TV appearances and festival dates; Contributed track, Are Friends Electric, to Gary Numan tribute album, 1997. *Recordings:* Singles: Out of This World, 1994; Bloke, 1994; Ready To Go, 1996; Drop Dead Gorgeous, 1996; From the Rush Hour With Love, 1998; Albums: Republica, 1996; Speed Ballads, 1998.

MALKMUS Stephen; b. USA. Singer; Musician (guitar). *Career:* Founder, lead singer, rock group Pavement, 1990–; Tours: USA, Europe; Japan; Australia; New Zealand; UK and Ireland including Reading Festival, 1994; Headlined Big Cat Festival Tour, Europe 1995; Lollapalooza Tour, 1995. *Recordings:* Albums: Slanted and Enchanted, 1992; Westing By Musket and Sextant, 1993; Crooked Rain, 1994; Wowee Zowee, 1995; Brighten the Corners, 1997; Terror Twilight, 1999; EPs, singles: Slay Tracks; Perfect Sound Forever; Demolition Plot; Trigger Cut; Watery Domestic; Rattled by La Rush; Father to a Sister of Thought; Pacific Trim EP; Stereo, 1997; Shady Lane EP; Spit on a Stranger. *Address:* c/o Big Cat Records, PO Box 3074, Chiswick, London W4 4ZN, England.

MALLETT Timmy; b. 18 Oct. 1955, Marple, Cheshire, England. Television Presenter; Entertainer; Singer. m. Lynda Bingham, 8 Sept. 1990, 1 s. *Education:* History Degree, Warwick University. *Career:* BBC Radio Oxford; Piccadilly Radio; BBC 3 Counties; Television presenter, Wide Awake Club; Wacaday; Utterly Brilliant; Around The World In 80 Seconds; Timmy Towers Stage Show; Headlined in pantomimes, 1991–; Director, Brilliant TV; Producer and Presenter, Timmy Towers, ITV, 1997–. *Recordings:* Singles: Itsy Bitsy Teeny Weeny Yellow Polka Dot Bikini; 7 Little Girls Sitting In The Back Seat, Bombularina (with Andrew Lloyd Webber); Albums: Huggin' and Kissin', 1990; The Bump, MC Mallett, 1991. *Publications:* How To Be Utterly Brilliant; Utterly Brilliant History of The World, 1991. *Honours:* DJ of the Year, 1984; Children's Television Personality of the Year, 1991. *Leisure interests:* Pinball; Painting; Travel; Oxford United Football Club. *Current Management:* John Miles. *Address:* Cadbury Camp Lane, Clapton in Gordano, Bristol BS20 9SB, England.

MALLEY Matt; b. 4 July 1963, USA. Musician (Bass). *Career:* Member, Counting Crows; Numerous headlining tours and TV appearances including MTV. *Recordings:* Round Here, 1994; Mr Jones, 1994; Rain King, 1994; Angels of the Silence (live), 1996; Albums: August and Everything After, 1993; Recovering the Satellites, 1996; Across a Wire: Live in New York, 1998; Long December, 1999; Daylight Fading, 1999.

MALLOZZI Charlie; b. Parma, Italy. Record Prod.; Mixer; Songwriter. *Career:* Writer, Producer with Marco Sabiu, known as Rapino Brothers;

Moved to London, 1992; Mixer, producer of Pop/Dance music; Member of groups: Tabernacle; Rapination. *Recordings:* Albums for: Take That; Kylie Minogue; Dannii Minogue; Lulu; Kym Mazelle; Rozalla; Hit singles: Could It Be Magic, Take That; Rhythm of The Night, Corona; What Is Love, Haddaway; I Know The Lord, Tabernacle; Love Me The Right Way, Rapination and Kym Mazelle; Also produced singles for: Alicia Bridges; Heaven 17; Sparks. *Honours:* BRIT Award, Single of the Year, Take That; Triple Platinum album, Take That. *Current Management:* Stephen Budd Management. *Address:* 109B Regents Park Rd, London NW1 8UR, England.

MALMI Jani; b. 1959. Jazz Musician; Record Prod. *Musical Education:* Originally self-taught; Private study with John Abercrombie and John Scofield. *Career:* Began playing with various rock bands, 1970s; Bandleader, own quartet; Leader, Jani Malmi trio (with Jorma Ojanperä and Markku Ounaskari). *Recordings include:* Graffiti, 1988; One Leg Duck, 1995; As producer: Kosketuksia, 1995.

MALMSTEEN Yngwie; b. Sweden. Rock Musician (guitar). *Career:* Played guitar from age 8; Founder, rock groups Powerhouse; Rising; Lead guitarist, Steeler, Los Angeles, 1983; Lead guitarist, Alcatrazz, 1983–84; Solo artiste, with own band, Rising Force, 1984–. *Recordings:* Albums: with Steeler: Steeler, 1983; with Alcatrazz: No Parole From Rock 'n' Roll, 1984; Live Sentence, 1984; Solo albums: Yngwie Malmsteen's Rising Force, 1984; Marching Out, 1985; Trilogy, 1986; Odyssey, 1988; Live In Leningrad, 1989; Eclipse, 1990; No Mercy, 1992; Concerto Suite for Electric Guitar, 1998; Live in Brazil, 1998; Facing the Animal, 1998; Inspiration, 1999; Alchemy, 1999. *Current Management:* James Lewis Entertainment, 14 Deerfield Lane, Greenwich, CT 06831, USA.

MALO Raul F Martinez; b. 7 Aug. 1965, Miami, Florida, USA. Vocalist, Musician (guitar, bass guitar, piano); Songwriter; Prod. *Career:* Born of Cuban parents; Began playing bass guitar in high school and joined several small bands; Made first recording with The Basics, 1987; Formed the Mavericks with high school friend, bass guitarist Robert Reynolds, late 1980s; Became band's lead vocalist and recorded eponymous debut album, 1990; Group signed to MCA, 1991, and recorded a string of successful albums; Released first solo album Today, 2001. *Recordings:* Today, 2001; with The Mavericks: Mavericks, 1990; From Hell To Paradise, 1992; What A Crying Shame, 1994; Music For All Occasions, 1995; Trampoline, It's Now It's Live, 1998; Best of The Mavericks, 2000; features on: Flaco Jimenez, 1994; Jewel of The South, Rodney Crowell, 1995; Letter To Laredo, Joe Ely, 1995; Long Stretch of Lonesome, Patty Loveless, 1997; El Cancionero – Mas Y Mas, Los Lobos, 2000; Canto, Los Super Seven, 2001. *Honours:* with The Mavericks: Grammy Award, I Don't Care If You Love Me Anymore, 1996; CMA Award, Top Vocal Group, 1995 and 1996; CMA Award, Top Vocal Group nominee, 1997 and 1998.

MALONE Tom, (Bones); b. 16 June 1947, Honolulu, Hawaii, USA. Musician; Arranger; Prod. 2 d. *Education:* BS, Psychology, North Texas State University, 1969. *Career:* As student played with: Les Elgart; The Supremes; Little Stevie Wonder; Marvin Gaye; The Temptations; Gladys Knight and The Pips; Joined Woody Herman's big band; Tours USA, Europe with: Frank Zappa, 1972; Blood Sweat and Tears, 1973; Billy Cobham, 1975; Joined Gil Evans Orchestra, 1973; Tours, Europe, Japan, Far East; Tour, USA with The Band, appeared in film: The Last Waltz, 1976; Television: Musician, arranger, Saturday Night Live, 1975–85; Musical director, above programme, 1981–85; Played with CBS Orchestra, Late Night With David Letterman, 1993–; Appeared in film The Blues Brothers; Tours with The Blues Brothers Band, 1988–90; Appearing in film, Blues Brothers 2000, 1998. *Compositions include:* Theme song, Saturday Night Live; Comedy songs for Jim Belushi, Eddie Murphy, Billy Crystal; Arrangements for films: The Blues Brothers; Sister Act; Television: Saturday Night Live; CBS Orchestra. *Recordings include:* Solo album: Standards of Living, Tom 'Bones' Malone Jazz Septet, 1991; Eastern Standard Time, 1993; Recorded with artists including: Blues Brothers; Gil Evans Orchestra; Miles Davis and Quincy Jones; Blood, Sweat and Tears; Frank Zappa; Pat Metheny; Cyndi Lauper; Sister Act; Steve Winwood; David Sanborn; James Brown; Spinners; Barry Manilow; Glen Campbell; B B King; Billy Cobham; Lou Reed; Bonnie Tyler; Diana Ross; Carla Bley; Harry Connick Jr; Pink Floyd; Buddy Rich; Woody Herman; J Geils Band; George Benson; Paul Simon; Chaka Khan; Village People; Gloria Gaynor; Carly Simon. *Leisure interests:* Softball; Golf; Homeopathic medicine. *Address:* c/o Late Show, CBS Orchestra, 1697 Broadway, New York, NY 10019, USA.

MALONE Walter (Wally); b. 20 Sept. 1946, Pittsburgh, Pennsylvania, USA. Musician (bass); Singer; Entertainer. m. Peggy Jones, 20 Oct. 1968. *Career:* Principle bassist with Bo Diddley, West Coast, 1970–94; Bassist, Lady Bo, 1969–; Backing musician for: Lightning Hopkins; Richard Berry; Chuck Berry; The Olympics; Play: Tony N' Tina's Wedding, San Jose, 1997–98; Cable Car Theatre, San Francisco, 1998–99; Concerts include: HIC Arena, 1971; Monterey Jazz Festival, 1973, 1974; Greek Theatre, 1976; Boardwalk, 1988; Monterey Blues Festival, 1994, 1995, 1999; Tours:

East Coast, 1960s; West Coast; Canada; Pacific Northwest, 1970s; Main Event European, No. 1, 1987; Bo Knows... NIKE Inc, endorsement, 1989; Television: Kenny Rogers, 1971; Donnie and Marie, 1976–77; Live concert, Sweden, 1987; Arts and Entertainment Special, world-wide coverage, 1990; Lady Bo and the BC Horns, South Bay Scene, USA, 1996. *Recordings:* Albums: The Mighty Bo Diddley: Ain't It Good To Be Free, USA, 1984; France, 1988; The Mighty Bo Diddley, Triple X Records, 1994; Lady Bo and The BC Horns, Shebo-Shebad, 2000; Video: I Don't Sound Like Nobody, Bo Diddley with Lady Bo and The Family Jewel, UK, 1992; Flashbacks: Vol. One, Soul Sensations, 1994; Say That You Love Me, Lady Bo and The BC Horns, 1997. *Publication:* Listed: The Complete Bo Diddley Sessions, by George R White, 1993. *Memberships:* President, AFM Local 153, 1996; President, RMA of Northern California; President, Professional Musicians of California. *Address:* 14680 Bear Creek Rd, Boulder Creek, CA 95006, USA.

MANCHESTER Melissa; b. 15 Feb. 1951, Bronx, New York, USA. Singer; Songwriter; Scriptwriter; Actress. *Career:* Staff writer, Chappell Music; Backing singer, Bette Midler; Solo artiste, 1973–; Actress and scriptwriter. *Recordings:* Albums: Home To Myself, 1973; Bright Eyes, 1974, 1974; Melissa, 1975; Better Days and Happy Endings, 1977; Singin', 1977; Don't Cry Out Loud, 1978; Melissa Manchester, 1979; For The Working Girl, 1980; Hey Ricky, 1982; Emergency, 1983; Mathematics, 1985; Midnight Blue, 1988; Tribute, 1989; If My Heart Had Wings, 1994; Melissa Manchester performs Pocahontas, 1995; The Colours of Christmas, 1997; Joy, 1997; The Essence of Melissa Manchester, 1997; Singles: Midnight Blue; Whenever I Call You Friend (co-written with Kenny Loggins), 1978; Dont Cry Out Loud, 1979; You Should Hear How She Talks About You, 1982. *Honours:* Grammy Award, Best Female Vocalist, 1982; NARAS Governors Award, 1997. *Current Management:* c/o Kevin DeRemer, Beacon Hill Entertainment, 5440 Carbin Ave, Tarzana, CA 91356, USA.

MANDRELL Barbara; b. 25 Dec. 1948, Houston, Texas, USA. Singer; Musician (guitar). m. Ken Dudney, 1967. *Career:* Worked with Joe Maphis, Tex Ritter, Las Vegas; Founder member, The Mandrells; Recording artist, 1966; Joined Grand Ole Opry, 1972; Television series, Barbara Mandrell and The Mandrell Sisters, 1980–82. *Recordings:* Hit singles include: Sleepin' Single In A Double Bed; Years; I Was Country When Country Wasn't Cool; (If Loving You Is Wrong) I Don't Want To Be Right; Til You're Gone; One of a Kind Pair of Fools; Albums: Treat Him Right, 1971; A Perfect Match (with David Houston), 1972; The Midnight Oil, 1973; This Time I Almost Made It, 1974; This Is Barbara Mandrell, 1976; Midnight Angel, 1976; Lovers Friends and Strangers, 1977; Love's Ups and Downs, 1978; Moods, 1978; Just For The Record, 1979; Love Is Fair, 1980; Looking Back, 1981; Live, 1981; In Black and White, 1982; He Set My Life To Music, 1982; Spun Gold, 1983; Back To Back (with David Houston), 1983; Clean Cut, 1984; Meant For Each Other (with Lee Greenwood), 1984; Christmas At Our House, 1984; Get To The Heart, 1985; Moments, 1986; Sure Feels Good, 1987; I'll Be Your Jukebox Tonight, 1988; Morning Sun, 1990; No Nonsense, 1991; Key's In The Mailbox, 1991; Standing Room Only, 1994; Entertainer of the Year, 1995; Fooled by a Feeling, 1995; It Works for Me, 1997; Branson City Limits (live), 1998; Sisters in Song, 1999. *Current Management:* Mandrell Inc, PO Box 800, Hendersonville, TN 37077, USA.

MANGESHKAR Lata; b. 1929, Indore, India. Vocalist; Actress. *Career:* Indian film playback singer; Sister of Asha Bhosle; First sang in Kiti Hasaal, 1942; Has recorded thousands of songs in 14 Indian languages and is probably the most recorded vocalist in the world. *Recordings:* Albums: soundtracks: Sargam, 1979; Darr, 1993; Hum Aapke Hain Koun...!, 1994; Dilwale Dulhania Le Jayeng, 1995; Dil To Pagal Hai, 1997; Lagaan, 2001; solo: Lata In Concert – An Era In An Evening, 1997. *Honours:* Filmfare Awards, 1958, 1962, 1965, 1969 (refused to be considered for this award after 1969 to encourage new talent); Filmfare Lifetime Achievement Award, 1993; Filmfare Special Award, 1994; National Awards, Best Female Playback Singer, 1972, 1975, 1990; Maharasthatra State Award, Best Playback Singer, 1966, 1967; Bengal Film Journalist's Award, Best Female Playback Singer, 1964, 1967, 1968, 1969, 1970, 1971, 1973, 1975, 1981, 1985; Dada Saheb Phalke Award, 1989; Videocon Screen Lifetime Achievement Award, 1996; Rajiv Gandhi Award, 1997; Lux Zee Cine Lifetime Achievement Award, 1998; IIFA London, Lifetime Achievement Award, 2000; Noorjehan Award, 2001; Maharashtra Ratna, 2001; Key of the City of Georgetown, Guyana, 1980; Hon. Citizenship of Republic of Suriname, 1980; Hon. Citizenship of Houston, Texas, USA, 1987; Hon. Doctorate, Literature from Pune University, 1990; The Government of Madya Pradesh instituted an annual national music award in 1984 named The Lata Mangeshkar Award.

MANGIONE Chuck (Charles Frank); b. 29 Nov. 1940, Rochester, New York, USA. Jazz Musician (trumpet); Composer. 2 d. *Musical Education:* MusB, Music Education, Eastman School of Music, University of Rochester, 1963. *Career:* Formed Jazz Brothers with Brother Gap, 1958–64; Director, Eastman Jazz Ensemble; Teacher, Eastman School of Music, 1968–72; Freelance musician with Maynard Ferguson and Kai Winding, 1965;

Trumpeter, Art Blakey's Jazz Messengers, 1965–67; Formed Chuck Mangione Quartet, 1968; Guest conductor, Rochester Philharmonic Orchestra, 1970; Numerous concerts world-wide include: Europe; Japan; Australia; South America; Montréal Jazz Festival, 1986; Television appearances include: PBS specials; Grammy Awards Show, 1981; Guest star, Magnum PI; Film appearance: Paradise Blues, 1984. *Compositions include:* Hill Where The Lord Hides; Land of Make Believe; Bellavia; Give It All You Got (1980 Winter Olympics theme). *Recordings:* Albums include: Chuck Mangione Quartet, 1972; Chase The Clouds Away, 1975; Main Squeeze, 1976; Feels So Good, 1977; Children of Sanchez (film soundtrack), 1978; Fun and Games, 1980; Journey To A Rainbow, 1985; Bellavia, 1986; Classics, Vol. 6, 1989; Live at the Village Gate, Vol. 2, 1995; The Feeling's Back, 1999. *Honours:* Most Promising Male Jazz Artist, Record World, 1975; Numerous Gold and Platinum records; Grammy Awards and nominations; Emmy Award, Music Composition and Direction, Give It All You Got, 1980; Numerous Magazine Poll Wins; MusD Hon, 1985; Georgie Award, Instrumental Act of Year, 1980; Regents Medal of Excellence, New York State, 1984; Jazz Music Campus Entertainment Award, NACA, 1987. *Current Management:* c/o Gates Music. *Address:* Gates Music Inc, 476 Hampton Blvd, Rochester, NY 14612, USA.

MANGRAM Myles Edwin; b. 30 July 1956, Pueblo, Colorado, USA. Personal Man.; Record Label Exec. m. Chea Rivera, 3 July 1994, 2 s. *Education:* BS, Music Science, Master, Business Administration, Entertainment, Law studies. *Musical Education:* Classical and Jazz training since age 5. *Career:* Founder, President, Tri-M Management (personal management company, consulting service); President, Black Lion Records Inc (independent record label); Professor, Music Business Studies; Professional musician and record producer with: Dizzy Gillespie; Tom Scott; Denver Symphony. *Recordings:* As producer: Alyssa Milano (Gold, Platinum discs); Anita Whitaker. *Publications:* Research reports, articles for publications include: Optic Music Magazine; Music Connection; Future Systems International. *Honours:* Outstanding Young Man of America Award; Colorado Schlars Award; Presidential Scholars Award. *Memberships:* Conference of Personal Managers; Entertainment Law Society. *Leisure interests:* Hiking; Weight training; Basketball. *Address:* Myles E Mangram, 5200 White Oak Ave, #31, Encino, CA 91316, USA.

MANGWANA Sam; b. 1945, Kinshasa, Zaire. Vocalist; Musician (guitar); Songwriter. *Musical Education:* Studied singing in the Salvation Army choir. *Career:* Member: Tabu Ley Rochereau's Africa Fiesta, c. 1962; Franco's TPOK Jazz, 1972; Formed Festival des Maquisards with Dizzy Mandjeku, 1968; Set up La Belle Sonora label; Founder: African All Stars, 1976; Based in Abidjan, toured Africa, Europe and the US; Lives in Paris. *Recordings:* Albums include: Sam and Les Maquisards, 1968; Sam and African All Stars Vols 1 and 2, 1982; Maria Tebbo, Rumba Music, 1991; Gallo Negro (featuring Papa Noel), 1998; Sam Mangwana Plays Dino Vangu, 2000. *Honours:* Sam Mangwana Plays Dino Vangu reached number 3 in the European World Music album charts, 2000. *Address:* c/o Alison Loerke, 12501 11th Ave NW, Seattle, WA 98177, USA.

MANI (Gary Mounfield); b. 16 Nov. 1962, Manchester, England. Musician (Bass). *Career:* Former member, Stone Roses; Numerous tours, TV and festival appearances; Joined Primal Scream, 1999. *Recordings:* (with Stone Roses), Singles: Made of Stone, 1989; Fool's Gold, 1989; She Bangs the Drums, 1990; One Love, 1990; I Wanna Be Adored, 1991; Waterfall, 1992; Albums: The Stone Roses, 1989; The Second Coming, 1994.

MANIFOLD Keith; b. 2 April 1947, Biggin-By-Hartington, Derbyshire, England. Musician (guitar); Vocalist; Agent; Country Music Consultant. m. Alice Nadin, 21 Nov. 1970, 2 d. *Musical Education:* Self-taught. *Career:* Television performances: Opportunity Knocks – Songwriters; Sing Country; Nationwide; Midlands; Sounds; Grampian Today; Border Today; Sons and Lovers; Radio performances: Radio 2; Local radio; Founder member, North West Promotions. *Recordings:* 20 albums include: Keith Manifold In Nashville. *Honours:* Billboard Best Solo Award '75; Nottingham Award For Special Achievement, Numerous Country Music Club Awards. *Membership:* Equity; Agents Asscn. *Leisure interests:* Gardening; Snooker. *Current Management:* Keith Manifold Entertainment Services. *Address:* Trenton House, 30 Bank Rd, Matlock, Derbyshire DE4 3NF, England.

MANIGAT Eval; b. 8 Dec. 1939, Haiti. Musician (bass, vibraphone); Composer; Arranger. Divorced, 1 s., 2 d. *Musical Education:* Self-taught. *Career:* Played with: Tropicana (Haiti); Weber Scott (Haiti); Vaccine; Karen Young Jazz Latin Band; Buzz; Chevere; Founder, band Tchaka; Fronts Many Ways (Latin-jazz ensemble); Appearances include: Montréal Jazz Festival; Ottowa Jazz Festival; Toronto Harbourfront summer festival; SOB, New York City; European tour, 1996. *Compositions include:* Contredanse, Karen Young, 1988. *Recording:* Album: Africa, 1994. *Honour:* Juno Award, Global Recording, Canada, 1994. *Leisure interests:* Computers; Reading; Yoga; Travel. *Current Management:* Louise Matte. *Address:* CP 48015, 5678 Ave du Parc, Montréal, QC H2V 4S8, Canada.

MANILOW Barry (Pinkus); b. 17 June 1946, Brooklyn, New York, USA. Singer; Musician (piano); Songwriter. *Education:* Advertising, New York City College. *Musical Education:* NY College of Music; Juilliard School of Music. *Career:* Film Editor, CBS-TV; Writer, numerous radio and television commercials; Member, cabaret duo Jeanne and Barry, 1970–72; MD, arranger, producer for Bette Midler; Solo entertainer, 1974–; Numerous world-wide tours; Major concerts include: Gala charity concert for Prince and Princess of Wales, Royal Albert Hall, 1983; Arista Records 15th Anniversary concert, Radio City Music Hall, 1990; Royal Variety performance, London, 1992; Television film Copacabana, 1985; Numerous television specials and television appearances; Broadway show, Barry Manilow At The Gershwin, 1989; West End musical, Copacabana, 1994. *Recordings:* Albums include: Barry Manilow, 1973; Barry Manilow II, 1975; Tryin' To Get The Feelin', 1976; This One's For You, 1977; Barry Manilow Live (No. 1, USA), 1977; Even Now, 1978; Manilow Magic, 1979; Greatest Hits, 1979; One Voice, 1979; Barry, 1981; If I Should Love Again, 1981; Barry Live In Britain, 1982; I Wanna Do It With You, 1982; Here Comes The Night, 1983; A Touch More Magic, 1983; Greatest Hits Vol. II, 1984; 2.00 AM Paradise Café, 1984; Barry Manilow, Grandes Exitos En Espanol, 1986; Swing Street, 1988; Songs To Make The Whole World Sing, 1989; Live On Broadway, 1990; The Songs 1975–90, 1990; Because It's Christmas, 1990; Showstoppers, 1991; The Complete Collection and Then Some, 1992; Hidden Treasures, 1993; The Platinum Collection, 1993; Singin' with the Big Bands, 1994; Another Life, 1995; Summer of '78, 1996; Manilow Sings Sinatra, 1998; Hit singles include: Mandy (No. 1, USA), 1975; Could It Be Magic, 1975; I Write The Songs (No. 1, USA), 1976; Tryin' To Get The Feelin', 1976; Weekend In New England, 1977; Looks Like We Made It (No. 1, USA), 1977; Can't Smile Without You, 1978; Copacabana (At The Copa), from film Foul Play, 1978; Somewhere In The Night, 1979; Ships, 1979; I Made It Through The Rain, 1981; Let's Hang On, 1981; Bermuda Triangle, 1981; I Wanna Do It With You, 1982. *Honours:* Grammy Awards: Song of The Year, I Write The Songs, 1977; Best Male Pop Vocal Performance, Copacabana (At The Copa), 1979; Emmy Award, The Barry Manilow Special, 1977; American Music Awards, Favourite Male Artist, 1978–80; Star on Hollywood Walk of Fame, 1980; Tony Award, Barry Manilow On Broadway show, 1976; Academy Award Nomination, Ready To Take A Chance Again, 1978; Hitmaker Award, Songwriters Hall of Fame, 1991; Platinum and Gold records. *Current Management:* Stiletto Entertainment, 5443 Beethoven St, Los Angeles, CA 90066, USA.

MANLEY Colin William; b. 16 April 1942, Liverpool, Merseyside, England. Musician (guitar). m. Sheila Jones, 17 Jan. 1972, 1 s., 1 d. *Musical Education:* Self-taught. *Career:* 1960's tours: Tommy Roe; Gene Pitney; Last Beatles tour of UK with Tommy Quickly; Recent tours with: The Swinging Blue Jeans; Gerry Marsden; The Searchers; London Palladium Orchestra, 2 years; Television appearances: Lift Off, with Remo 4; Top of The Pops; Ready Steady Go; Crackerjack. *Composition:* Lies, with Remo 4; Theme song, In The First Place, for re-release of the film Wonderwall, recorded in 1967, written and sung by self and produced by George Harrison. *Recordings:* Wonderwall album (with George Harrison); Smile In Germany, Remo 4. *Honours:* Third place in first Merseybeat Poll (behind The Beatles and Gerry Marsden); Winner, Best Instrumentalist, Beat Goes On magazine, 1996. *Membership:* Musicians' Union. *Leisure interests:* Music; Jogging. *Current Management:* Hal Carter. *Address:* c/o Hal Carter, 101 Hazelwood Lane, Palmers Green, London N13 5HQ, England.

MANN Jas (Jasbinder); b. 24 April 1970, Dudley, West Midlands, England. Singer; Musician (guitar). *Career:* Singer, The Sandkings, 1980s; Tours include: Support to Happy Mondays, Stone Roses; Lead singer, Babylon Zoo, 1994–; Concerts include: NME Brats, Midem, 1995; The Night The Earth Stood Still, London, 1995. *Recordings:* Albums: Boy With The X-Ray Eyes, 1996; King Kong Groover, 1998; Singles: Spaceman (International No. 1 hit), 1996; Animal Army, 1996; All The Money's Gone, 1998. *Honours:* Fastest selling debut single since the Beatles, with Spaceman, 1996. *Membership:* Musicians' Union. *Leisure interests:* Film; Art. *Current Management:* Clive Black, Blacklist Entertainment Ltd. *Address:* 24–25 Elysium Gate, 126–128 New Kings Rd, London SW6 4LZ, England.

MANN Manfred, (Michael Lubowitz); b. 21 Oct. 1940, Johannesburg, South Africa. Musician (keyboards); Songwriter. *Career:* Founder member, Mann-Hugg Blues Brothers, 1962; Became Manfred Mann, 1963–69; Concerts include Brighton Song Festival, 1965; Founder, Emanon, and Manfred Mann Chapter Three, 1969; Manfred Mann Earth Band, 1971–87; National and international tours with Free; Deep Purple; Savoy Brown; Blue Öyster Cult; Pink Pop Festival, Netherlands, 1977; Also taught at Goldmsith's College, London, late 1970s. *Recordings:* Albums with Manfred Mann: Five Faces of Manfred Mann, 1964; Mann Made, 1965; Mann Made Hits, 1966; As Is, 1966; Soul of Mann, 1967; Up The Junction, 1967; The Mighty Quinn, 1968; This Is Manfred Mann, 1971; Semi-Detached Suburban, 1979; The R & B Years, 1986; The Singles Plus, 1987; The EP Collection, 1989; The Collection, 1990; Ages of Mann, 1992; Two albums with Manfred Mann Chapter Three; with Manfred Mann's Earth Band: Manfred Mann's Earth Band, 1972; Get Your Rocks Off, 1973; Solar Fire, 1973; The Good Earth, 1974; Nightingales and Bombers, 1975; The Roaring Silence, 1976; The New Bronze Age, 1977; Watch, 1978; Angle Station, 1979; Chance, 1981; Somewhere In Africa, 1983; Budapest, 1983; Criminal Tango, 1986; Masque, 1987; Manfred Mann's Earth Band (13 CD box set), 1992; Solo album: Manfred Mann's Plain Music, 1991; Ages of Mann, 1995; Soft Vengence, 1996; Hit singles include: 5–4–3–2–1 (theme for ITV pop show Ready Steady Go!), 1964; Do Wah Diddy Diddy (No. 1, UK and USA), 1964; Come Tomorrow, 1965; Oh No, Not My Baby, 1965; If You Got To Go, Go Now, 1965; Pretty Flamingo (No. 1, UK), 1966; Just Like A Woman, 1966; Semi-Detached Suburban Mr James, 1966; Ha! Ha! Said The Clown, 1967; Mighty Quinn (No. 1, UK), 1968; My Name Is Jack, 1968; Fox On The Run, 1969; Ragamuffin Man, 1969; Joybringer, 1973; Blinded By The Light (No. 1, USA), 1976; Davey's On The Road Again, 1978; Runner, 1984; Contributor, film music including: What's New Pussycat?, 1965; Up The Junction, 1968.

MANN Paul Duane; b. 15 March 1972, Carmarthen, Wales. Musician (Drums, Bass Guitar). *Career:* Llanelli Schools Orchestra, 1982; School Orchestras, 1985; Royal Air Force Drum Corps and Band, 1990; The Stone Dog, alternative rock band, 1993; Power House, hard rock, 1995; Blue Desert, country, 1996; Earth Angels, gospel, USA, 1996; Borda Line, country, 1997; Freelance sessions, drumming, 1990–94; Drum Tutor and Freelance Session Drummer, 1997–; Freelance Session Electric Bass Guitar and Upright Bass Fiddle, 1999; Currently playing bass for Rattlebelly, a soul/blues band, and Cool Penguins, a gypsy jazz trio. *Membership:* Musicians' Union. *Address:* Brigadoon, Heol Ddu, Penymynydd, Llanelli, Carmarthen SA15 4RN, Wales.

MANN Steve; b. 9 Aug. 1956, London, England. Musician (guitar, keyboards); Sound Engineer; Record Prod. *Education:* 1 year university studying electronic engineering. *Musical Education:* 8 years classical piano, 1 year classical guitar. *Career:* Joined Liar, toured UK and Europe, 1977; Joined Steve Swindells, appeared on Old Grey Whistle Test, 1980; Formed Lionheart, 1981; Toured UK with Tytan, 1983; Joined MSG, played Monsters of Rock Festival, European and USA tours, 1986; Joined Sweet, 1989; Toured: USA; Canada; Australia; Europe; Russia; Producer, engineer for: Shogun; Tora Tora; MSG; Rough Silk; Letter X; Sweet; Thunderhead; Spice. *Compositions:* Co-wrote Anytime (No. 2, USA AOR charts). *Recordings:* with Liar: Set The World On Fire, 1978; with Lionheart: Hot Tonight, 1984; with Tytan: Rough Justice, 1985; with MSG: Perfect Timing, 1987; Save Yourself, 1989; with Sweet: A, 1992; Glitz, Blitz and Hits, 1995. *Memberships:* MCPS; PRS (associate mem.); Musicians' Union. *Leisure interests:* Computers; Hiking; Photography. *Address:* c/o Frida Park Studio, 30161 Hanover, Germany.

MANNING Barbara Lynne; b. 12 Dec. 1944, San Diego, California, USA. Musician; Songwriter; Singer. *Education:* 4 years college. *Musical Education:* Self-taught. *Career:* Extensive tours, USA, Europe, 1990–. *Recordings:* 28th Day, 1985; World of Pooh, 1989; One Perfect Green Blanket, B Manning, 1990; Nowhere, S F Seals, 1994; Truth Walks In Sleepy Shadows, S F Seals, 1995; Barbara Manning Sings with the Original..., 1995; 1212, 1997; In New Zealand, 1999. *Honours:* SF Goldie; SF Wammie, 1992; Bay Area Music Award, 1996. *Leisure interests:* Listening to records; Gardening. *Current Management:* Matador, 676 Broadway, New York, NY 10012. *Address:* PO Box 424762, San Francisco, CA 94142, USA.

MANNING Roger Joseph Jr; b. 27 May 1966, Inglewood, California, USA. Songwriter; Arranger; Record Prod.; Musician (keyboards). *Musical Education:* BMus, Jazz Studies, University of Southern California. *Career:* Keyboardist, Beatnik Beatch, 1987–89; Keyboardist, songwriter, arranger, Jellyfish, 1990–94; Songwriter, arranger, producer, Imperial Drag, 1995–; Keyboardist, arranger, The Moog Cookbook, 1995–; Mutations, with Beck, 1998; Playing keyboards/touring for Beck, 1999; Re-mixing other artists' work, including the French Band, Air. *Recordings:* Albums: with Beatnik Beatch: Beatnik Beatch, 1988; with Jellyfish: Bellybutton, 1990; Spilt Milk, 1993; with Imperial Drag: Imperial Drag, 1996; with The Moog Cookbook: The Moog Cookbook, 1996; The Moog Cookbook: Ye Olde Space Bande. *Honours:* Best Debut Album, with Beatnick Beatch, 1988; Jellyfish, 1990. *Membership:* ASCAP. *Leisure interests:* Collecting 60s and 70s kitsch; Vintage keyboards. *Current Management:* Sharpe Entertainment Services, 683 Palerma Ave, Pacific Palisades, CA 90272, USA.

MANOV Dragomir; Musician (guitar). *Career:* Lead guitarist, Concurent, 1986–; Numerous concerts, TV and radio appearances, Bulgaria. *Recordings:* Rock For Peace, 1988; Rock Festival In Mitchurin, 1989; The Black Sheep (rock collection), 1992; Something Wet (best-selling album, Bulgaria), 1994; The Best of Bulgarian Rock, 1995. *Honours:* First Prizes: Top Rock Band, Vidrin, 1989; Rock ring, Sofia, 1990; Top Rock Composition: The Cavalry, 1991; Group of The Year, The Darik Radio Countdown, 1994. *Address:* 40 St Stambolov Blvd, 1202 Sofia, Bulgaria.

MANSON Marilyn, (Brian Warner); b. 5 Jan. 1969, Canton, Ohio, USA. Singer; Songwriter. *Career:* Numerous television appearances, tours and videos. *Recordings:* Singles: Touniquet; Dope Show; Beautiful People; Get Your Gunn; Albums: Portrait of an American Family, 1994; Smells Like Children, 1995; Antichrist Superstar, 1996; Mechanical Animals, 1998.

MANSON Shirley; b. Scotland. Singer. *Career:* Singer, Goodbye McKenzie; Angel Fish; Lead singer, Garbage; 2 British tours. *Recordings:* Albums: with Garbage: Garbage, 1995; Version 2.0, 1997; Singles: with Garbage: Vow, 1995; Subhuman, 1995; Queer, 1995; Only Happy When It Rains, 1995; Stupid Girl, 1996; Push It; When I Grow Up; I Think I'm Paranoid; You Look So Fine; The World is Not Enough, theme from James Bond film. *Honours:* BRIT Award Nominations: Best International Group, Best International Newcomer, 1996. *Current Management:* SOS Management, 106 Cleveland St, London W1 5DP, England.

MANSOUR Ahmad; b. 7 June 1960, Tehran, Iran. Musician (guitar). *Musical Education:* Berklee College of Music, Boston, USA. *Career:* Radio and television: Boston; New York; France; Netherlands; Switzerland; Numerous tours and festivals throughout Europe. *Recordings:* 6 album releases as bandleader, featuring original compositions. *Membership:* BMI. *Current Management:* BMI. *Address:* 34 rue Maurice Braillard, 1202 Geneva, Switzerland.

MANTELS Viv; b. 31 Oct. 1964, Diest, Belgium. Actress; Dir, Theatre, Music and Film; Singer; Songwriter; Composer. *Career:* Radio (BRTN) Belgium; Film, Europe, World-wide, 1999; TV, Europe, 1998. *Compositions:* Thinking of You, with Michel Herr; All Night Through, with Mal Waldron; No More Tears, with Mal Waldron. *Recordings:* Viv Mantels and Mal Waldron Trio, 1989; Alpha and Omega, Eluca, 1984. *Memberships:* Jazz Educators, USA; National Asscn Teachers of Singing, USAS; Europe Vrouw and Musiek, Holland. *Leisure interests:* Swimming; Reading; Badminton; Walks (woods). *Current Management:* Lyons Management, Lorraine Lyons, Essex, England.

MANTLER Karen; b. 1966. *Education:* Berklee College of Music, Boston. *Career:* Child of two famous jazz musicians; Joined the Carla Bley Band (mother) on Glockenspiel, 1977, toured Europe and the USA; Carnegie Hall, 1980; Guest Musician, Jazz Composers Alliance; Formed own band, rehearsed and toured; Joined Carla Bley Band on harmonica for European Tour, 1988; Knitting Factory with own band; Played on David Sanborn's Nith Music TV show; Toured alongside The Very Big Carla Bley Band; Joined father as assistant, Watt Works, promoted to General Manager; Montréal Jazz Festival; Played Synthesizer for Steve Swallow, 1991; Played organ with Motohiko Hino; Organ player, The Very Big Carla Bley Band, 1992, played Glasgow Jazz Festival, Umbria Jazz Festival, Italy; Left Watt Works, 1993; Played again with Motohiko Hino; Glockenspiel and Harmonica, band with Terry Adams, 1994; European Tour with Carla Bley Band; Worked with drummer Michael Evans as duo, gigs and recorded material; Another tour with Carla Bley Big Band, 1996; Regular appearances at Starbuck's Coffee House, 1997; Rejoined Carla Bley Big Band, 1997, tour of England, organ player in Fancy Chamber Music with Carla Bley. *Recordings include:* My Cat Arnold; Karen Mantler and her Cat Arnold get the Flu; Farewell; Karen Mantler's Pet Project; with Carla Bley: Escalator Over the Hill; Musique Mecanique; The Very Big Carla Bley Band; Big Band Theory; The Carla Bley Big Band Goes to Church; Others: The Watt Works Family Album; Carried Away, with Robbie Dupree; Swallow, with Steve Swallow; Sailing Stone, with Motohiko Hino; Folly Seeing All This, with Michael Mantler. *Address:* c/o Watt Works, PO Box 67, Willow, NY 12495, USA.

MANZAREK Ray; b. 12 Feb. 1939, Chicago, Illinois, USA. Musician (keyboards); Prod. *Career:* Member, The Doors, 1964–72; Northern California Folk-Rock Festival, 1968; Hollywood Bowl (later released as video), 1968; Film documentary, The Doors Are Open, 1968; Documentary film, The Feast of Friends, 1969; Toronto Rock 'n' Roll Revival Show, 1969; Isle of Wight Festival, 1970. *Recordings:* Albums: The Doors, 1967; Strange Days, 1967; Waiting For The Sun, 1968; Morrison Hotel, 1970; Absolutely Live, 1970; L A Woman, 1971; Other Voices, 1971; Weird Scenes Inside The Gold Mine, 1972; Full Circle, 1972; Solo: The Golden Scarab, 1975; The Whole Thing Started With R 'n' R, 1975; Live At The Hollywood Bowl, 1987; The Doors: Myth and Reality, 1997; Singles: Light My Fire (No. 1, USA), 1967; Love Me Two Times, 1968; Hello I Love You (No. 1, USA), 1968; Touch Me, 1969; Love Her Madly, 1971; Riders On the Storm, 1971; Producer for Los Angeles band X. *Address:* c/o Goldman and Knell, CPA's LLP, 1900 Ave of the Stars, Suite 1040, Los Angeles, CA 90067, USA.

MAPFUMO Thomas; b. Oct. 1945, Marondera, Zimbabwe. Musician (mbira, guitar); Singer; Songwriter. *Career:* Known as The Lion of Zimbabwe; Important figure in local Shona music, 1970s-; Singer, local bands including the Cosmic Dots and the Springfields; Began translating American songs into Shona, early 1970s; Founder, Hallelulah Chicken Run Band, 1973; Researcher, traditional Zimbabwean folk style music; Founder, Pied Pipers Band, 1977; Founder, Acid Band, 1977–; Government banned

them from radio, Mapfumo imprisoned for subversion, 1977; Band renamed Blacks Unlimited, 1978; First tours, Britain, 1984; Europe, 1985. *Recordings:* Albums: Hokoya!, 1977; Gwindingwe, 1980; Mabesa, 1983; Congress, 1983; The Chimurenga Singles, 1983; Ndangariro, 1984; Mr Music, 1985; Chimurnega For Justice, 1986; Corruphon, 1989; Chamunorwa, 1990; Shumba, 1990; The Spirit of the Eagle, 1991; Shumba: Vital Hits of Zimbabwe, 1991; Hondo, 1994; Vanhu Vatema, 1994; Chumurenga: African Spirit Music, 1997; Gwindingwi Rine Shumba, 1997; Singles include: Morento; Ngoma Yarira. *Address:* c/o Free World Music Inc, 230 12th St, Suite 117, Miami Beach, FL 33139–4603, USA.

MARAZZI Paul Thomas Leo; b. 24 Jan. 1975, Wanstead, London, England. Vocalist; Songwriter. *Career:* Relocated to Benidorm, Spain, aged 19; Career as club dancer before brief spell modelling for Christian Dior; Joined A1 pop group; Signed recording contract, 1999; Sell-out theatre tours of South-East Asia and UK, 2000–01. *Recordings:* Albums: Here We Come, 1999; The A List, 2000; Singles: Be The First To Believe, Summertime of Our Lives, Ready Or Not/Everytime, 1999; Like A Rose, Take On Me, Same Old Brand New You, 2000; No More, 2001; Caught In The Middle, 2002. *Honours:* Brit Award, Best Newcomer, 2001; Also honoured at MTV Mandarin Music Awards. *Current Management:* c/o Byrne Blood Ltd. *Internet:* www.a1-online.com.

MARCHANT Colin; b. 27 Nov. 1937, Batley, England. Musician (drums). m. Joan Marchant, 1 s, 2 d. *Education:* Music Tuition at school. *Career:* Touring in 1960's with Gene Vincent, Danny Williams, Dusty Springfield, The Beatles and Rolling Stones; Working and living in Japan, 1968–71, 1972–; Working on Cabaret as back-up Musician. *Leisure interest:* Music.

MARGARIT Bernard; b. 19 Feb. 1956, Carcassonne, France. Musician (guitar); Composer. 1 s., 1 d. *Musical Education:* Classical guitarist, The Academie, Toulouse. *Career:* International tours with Johnny Hallyday; Television shows with: Kim Wilde; Eddy Mitchell; Johnny Hallyday; French jazz concert tours with Jean Pierre LLabador; Remy Charmasson; Philippe Petrucciani. *Recordings:* Various recordings with Johnny Hallyday; Album: Friendship (all original compositions) with jazz guitarist Jean Pierre Llabador. *Memberships:* SACEM; SPEDIDAM; ADAMI. *Leisure interests:* Sport; Yoga. *Current Management:* Edma Managements. *Address:* 13 rue du Stade, 11300 Limoux, France.

MARGOLIN Bob; b. 9 May 1949, Boston, Massachusetts, USA. Blues Musician (guitar); Writer. *Education:* Graduated Boston University, 1970. *Career:* Seven years in Muddy Waters Blues Band; Leader, own blues band, 1980-. *Recordings:* 4 solo albums; Sideman on 30 albums with other blues players, 1974–96; Albums include: with the Band: The Last Waltz, 1978; with The Nighthawks, 1979; with Muddy Waters: Live At Mr Kellys, 1971; Woodstock Album, 1975; Hard Again, 1977; I'm Ready, 1977; Mississippi Muddy Waters Live, 1977; King Bee, 1980; with Johnny Winter: Nothin' But The Blues, 1977; The Johnny Winter Story, 1980; Solo Albums: Down in the Alley, 1993; My Blues and My Guitar, 1995; Up and In, 1997; Hold Me to It, 1999. *Publications:* Senior writer, regular column for Blues Revue magazine. *Current Management:* Piedmont Talent, 1222 Kenilworth Ave, Charlotte, NC 28204, USA.

MARGUET Christophe; b. 14 May 1965, Paris, France. Musician (drums). m. Isabelle, Aug. 1992. *Musical Education:* Self-taught. *Career:* Played with: Barney Wilen; Vincent Herring; Bud Shank; Alain Jean Marie; Claude Barthélémy; Daunik Lazro; Noël Akchoté; Didier Levallet; Tours: China; Egypt; Syria; Morocco; Cameroon; Own trio with Sebastien Texier (alto sax), Olivier Sens (double bass); Played with Marc Ducret, Yves Robert, Barry Guy, Kenny Wheeler, François Jeanneau, François Corneloup, Louis Sclavis, 1997-. *Recordings:* 2 with Georges Arvanitas: Gershwin; Ellington; Altissimo, Hubert Dupont Sextet; Amazonia, Nicolas Genest; Mr Claude, Claude Barthelemy Quartet, 1997; Resistance Poetique, Christophe Marguet Trio, 1997; Strophes, Sylvain Kassap Quartet, 1998; Animal Language, 49 Nord, 1999; Ça Commence Aujourd Hui, Louis Sclavis, 1999; Les Correspondances, Christophe Marguet Quartet, 2000. *Honours:* First Prize, Orchestra, First Prize, Composition, Concours de la Défense, 1995; Django d'Or for Resistance Poetique, Best CD of Year, 1997. *Leisure interests:* Music; Painting; Photography; Theatre; Films. *Current Management:* LMD Productions, 23 rue Parmentier, 93100 Montreuil, France. *Address:* 25 rue Jeanne d'Arc, 92600 Asnieres, France.

MARINO Frank; b. Canada. Rock Musician (guitar); Vocalist. *Career:* Founder, Mahogany Rush, 1970–80; Recorded under own name, 1981–82; Major concerts include: Heavy Metal Holocaust, Port Vale, UK, 1981. *Recordings:* Albums: with Mahogany Rush: Maxoom, 1971; Child of The Novelty, 19784; Strange Universe, 1975; Mahogany Rush IV, 1976; World Anthem, 1977; Live, 1978; Tales of The Unexpected, 1979; What's Next, 1980; Solo: The Power of Rock 'n' Roll, 1981; Juggernaut, 1982; Full Circle, 1986; Double Live, 1988; Also featured on Guitar Speak Vol. 2 (compilation album), 1990; From the Hip, 1993. *Current Management:* American Famous Talent Corporation, 816 W Evergreen, Chicago, IL 60622, USA.

MARKELIUS Nike Maria; b. 29 Aug. 1962, Sweden. Songwriter; Musician; Singer. m. Rolf Markelius, 23 Aug. 1997. *Musical Education:* Self-taught Drummer; Studied Singing; Digital Audio Editing. *Career:* Drummer and vocals in Swedish Rock Groups; Usch, tours in Denmark and Sweden, 1979–81, Tant Strul, Scandinavian tours, 1981–85; Roskilde Festival, Slottsparken, Helsingfors, 1985; Songwriter, Solo Performer, Theatre Music; Smisk, tours in Sweden, 1989–97; Singer in group, Nike, tours, 1992–97. *Compositions:* Hula Hula, 1987; Fandango, 1992; Several Theatre Plays, 1992–96; Music and Lyrics for Solo Album, Nike, 1996; Creating radio programme, 1998. *Recordings:* With Groups: 3 Singles, 4 Songs on Live Album with Usch, 1979–81; 3 Albums, Amazon, 1993, Jag Önskar Dig, 1994, Samlade Singlar, 1995; Several Singles with Tant Strul, 1981–85; Studio Project, Hula Hula, 1987; Solo Album, Nike, 1996. *Honours:* Kasper Priset, 1983; Scholarship, SKAP, 1992; Konstnärsnämnden, 1992–93, 1995–96, 1998; 1999; Stockholm City Artist Grant, 1997. *Memberships:* STIM; SKAP; SAMI; SMF; Musikcentrum; DIVA. *Leisure interests:* Family; Friends; Running; Boxing; Books; Films. *Address:* Kattugglevägen 18, 123 52 Farsta, Sweden.

MARKER Steve; b. New York, USA. Musician (Guitar, Bass, Keyboards). *Career:* Co-Founder, Smart Studios; Worked with Nine Inch Nails and L7: Joined Garbage; Numerous live tours, festival appearances, TV and radio appearances. *Recordings:* Singles: Subhuman, 1995; Vow, 1995; Milk, 1996; Stupid Girl, 1996; Only Happy When It Rains, 1996; Queer, 1997; I Think I'm Paranoid, 1998; Special, 1998; Trash, 1998; Push It, 1998; When I Grow Up, 1999; Trick Is To Keep Breathing, 1999; Albums: Garbage, 1995; Version 2.0, 1998.

MARKEY Gerry, (Gerald Murphy); b. 13 Nov. 1963, Liverpool, England. Singer; Songwriter; Actor; Musician (guitar, piano, harmonica). *Education:* BA Hons, York University; PGCE, London University; AIL, Institute of Linguists. *Musical Education:* Self-taught. *Career:* Extensive tours: Europe; USA; Appeared on BBC TV performing: 95; Granada TV: St Joseph of Paradise Street; The Ballad of Dixie Dean; Talk To Me; Teacher, Art and Craft of Songwriting, Liverpool University; Currently Project Co-ordinator, The European Song Project. *Recordings:* Oh John, 1984; Sweet Liberty, 1987; Marvellous Marvin Gaye, 1993; Ballad of Dixie Dean, 1981. *Honours:* PRS, John Lennon Award, Sweet Liberty, 1987; Second place, National Music Day Songwriter of 1993, Marvellous Marvin Gaye, 1993. *Memberships:* Musicians' Union; BASCA; Sound Sense; Equity; PRS. *Leisure interests:* Photography; Modern Art; Teaching: Art and Craft of Songwriting. *Address:* The European Song Project, 12 Benson St, Liverpool L1 2ST, England.

MARKLEW Leigh (Flare); b. 10 Aug. 1968. Musician (Drums). *Career:* Formed Spoilt Bratz with Shutty, Mark Yates and Tony Wright; Renamed as Terrorvision; Secured record deal, 1991; Support slot to the Ramones; Numerous headlining tours and TV appearances. *Recordings:* My House, 1992; Oblivion, 1994; Pretend Best Friend, 1994; Alice, What's The Matter, 1994; Bad Actress, 1996; Perseverance, 1996; Easy, 1996; Moonage Daydream, 1997; Josephine, 1998; Tequila, 1999; Albums: Formaldehyde, 1993; How To Win Friends and Influence People, 1994; Regular Urban Survivors, 1996; Shaving Peaches, 1998.

MARKOVIC Milivoje; b. 20 March 1939, Zagreb, Yugoslavia. Musician (saxophone, clarinet); Composer; Conductor. *Education:* Law studies; Jazz Music Degree, Music Academy of Graz, Austria. *Career:* With Markovic-Gut Sextet performed at the Northsea Jazz Festival and toured Belgium, Germany, Soviet Union, Hungary, Romania, Italy, Turkey, Bulgaria and Cuba; Numerous TV and radio appearances. *Compositions include:* Otpisani; Ballad in Escutabile; Stemi; YuN QMM; Suze. *Recordings include:* Markovic-Gut Sextet, 1980, 1981; Clark Terry Live in Belgrade with the Markovic-Gut Sectet, 1982; Message from Belgrade, 1984; Ernie Wilkins in Belgrade with Markovic-Gut Sextet; Machito and His Salsa Big Band. *Membership:* Composers Union of Yugoslavia, President, 1987–88. *Leisure interest:* Radio amateur. *Address:* Plato Jazz Club, Student TRG, Belgrade, Yugoslavia.

MARKS Phillip; b. 22 June 1956, Manchester, England. Musician (Drums). *Education:* BA, Economics, Manchester University, 1982. *Career:* Recorded and toured England and Europe with his band Bark! (founder member); Organized, promoted, participated in numerous concerts, festivals in Manchester; Played in Grew Trio, Slip and Slant, trio; Played with musicians including Derek Bailey, Mattos, Lajonna Smith. *Recordings:* With Bark!: Celibacy, 1992; Harmfulodics, 1993; Our Traditional Values, 1994; With Grew Trio: Grew Trio, 1996. *Leisure interests:* Drawing and painting. *Address:* 47 Parvet Ave, Droylsden, Manchester M43 7SD, England.

MARKS Roger; b. 20 Feb. 1947, Tenby, Wales. Musician (trombone); Jazz Bandleader. m. (1) 1967–87, 2 s.; (2) Susan, 14 March 1998. *Musical Education:* Honiton Town Band; Later self-taught. *Career:* Television appearance: Pebble Mill At One, BBC; Southern TV; German, Dutch, Yugoslavian television; Radio broadcast: Jazz Parade, Radio 2.

Recordings: Somewhere Over The Rainbow, 1997; C'est Magnifique, 1998; Albums: with Rod Mason: Great Having You Around, 1978; After Hours, 1979; Stars Fell On Alabama, 1979; The Last Concert, 1980; Just The Five of Us, Roger Marks Quartet, 1989; Crazy Rhythm, Roger Marks Quartet and Bruce Turner, 1990; Dixie After Dark, Roger Marks Armada Jazz Band, CD 1994; Plato was a Good Parrot, 1995; Top Marks!, CD, 1996; Jazz Notes, BBC Radio 3, 1997. *Publication:* Roger Marks Discography, 1997. *Honours:* City of Plymouth Citation for Outstanding Contribution to the Arts. *Membership:* ABJM. *Leisure interest:* Ex-rugby captain.

MARKS Toby Anthony; b. 1 July 1964, London, England. Electronic Composer; Musician (guitar, keyboards, electronics, percussion); Composer. m. Sandra, 9 Sept. 1995. *Education:* University of Warwick, 1 year. *Career:* Performed in various bands and concerts in UK and Europe, 1978; Formed, Banco De Gaia (solo electronic project), performing world-wide including Europe, Russia, USA and Japan, 1989–; Appeared on John Peel Show, BBC Radio 1; MTV. *Recordings:* with Banco De Gaia: Maya, 1994; Last Train To Lhasa, 1995; Live At Glastonbury, 1996; Big Men Cry, 1997; The Magical Sounds of Banco De Gaia, 1999; Igizeh, 2000. *Honour:* Mercury Award Nomination, 1994. *Memberships:* MCPS; PRS; PPL; Musicians' Union. *Leisure interests:* Mountains; Scuba Diving; Computer Games. *Current Management:* None. *Address:* PO Box 1195, Cheddar, BS27 3YE, England.

MARLEY Ziggy, (David Robert Nesta); b. 17 Oct. 1968, Kingston, Jamaica. Singer; Musician (guitar). *Career:* Leader, Ziggy Marley and the Melody Makers. *Recordings:* Play The Game Right; Hey World; Conscious Party; One Bright Day; Jahmekya; Joy and Blues; Free Like We Want To Be; Fallen is Babylon; The Spirit of Music; The Best of Ziggy Marley and the Melody Makers. *Honours:* 2 Grammy Awards; NAACP Award; Group are UN Youth Environment Ambassadors. *Leisure interest:* Football. *Current Management:* William Morris Agency. *Address:* Ziggy Marley and the Melody Makers, 56 Hope Rd, Kingston 6, Jamaica.

MARLIN Lene, (Lene Marlin Pedersen); b. 17 Aug. 1980. Vocalist; Musician (guitar); Songwriter. *Education:* Tromsdalen Videregaende Skole, Tromsø. *Career:* Signed to Virgin, 1997; Recorded first album while still at school; Heavy European promotion schedules throughout 1999–2000; Co-wrote songs for fellow Norwegian, Sissel, 2000; Preparing second solo album, 2001. *Recordings:* Albums: Playing My Game, 1999; Singles: Unforgivable Sinner, 1998; Sitting Down Here, 1999; Where I'm Headed (from film Bad Company), 2001. *Honours:* First single fastest selling in Norwegian history; Spelleman Awards: Best Artist; New Artist; Pop Artist; Best Song, 2000; MTV-Europe Award, Best Nordic Act, 1999. *Address:* c/o Stageway Talent, Norway. *Internet:* www.lenemarlin.com.

MARLO Clair; b. New York, USA. Singer; Prod.; Arranger; Songwriter; Composer. m. Alex Baker, 1 Nov. 1995, 1 d. *Musical Education:* Berklee College of Music. *Career:* Tours: US, 1980; US, 1990; Far East, 1994; Television: Here's Johnny, The Philippines. *Recordings:* Let It Go, 1990; Behaviour Self, 1995; with Liquid Amber: Liquid Amber, 1994; Adrift, 1995; As producer: Just Ahead, Pat Coil, 1993; with Vox Mundi, 1997; with Primal Instinct, 1998; Clair Marlo, 1999. *Honours:* 10 songwriting awards; one of the top two female producers in the US, 1998; Freedom Award for film scoring, 1998. *Memberships:* ASCAP; NARAS; AIMP; CC; Musicians' Union; SCL; AES. *Leisure interests:* Skiing; Boating. *Current Management:* Mike Gormley, LA Personal Development. *Address:* 950 N Kings Rd, #266, West Hollywood, CA 90069, USA.

MARR Johnny, (John Maher); b. 31 Oct. 1963, Ardwick, Manchester, England. Musician (guitar). *Career:* Founder member, The Smiths, 1982–88; Appearance, John Peel Show, BBC Radio 1, 1983; International tours and concerts; Began playing with Billy Bragg; Brian Ferry; Paul McCartney; Talking Heads; The Pretenders; Played guitar in Midge Ure's band, Nelson Mandela's 70th Birthday Tribute, Wembley, 1988; Member, The The, 1989; Formed Electronic, with Neil Tennant, Bernard Summer, 1990; Worked with Stex, Banderas, 1990. *Recordings:* Singles include: with the Smiths: Hand In Glove; This Charming Man; What Difference Does It Make; Heaven Knows I'm Miserable Now; William It Was Really Nothing; How Soon Is it Now?, Shoplifters of The World Unite; Panic; Sheila Take A Bow; Girlfriend In A Coma; with Electronic: Getting Away With It; Get The Message; Feel Every Beat; Disappointed; Forbidden City, 1996; For You, 1996; Raise the Pressure, 1996; Second Nature, 1997; Late at Night, 1999; Albums: with the Smiths: The Smiths, 1984; Meat Is Murder, 1985; The World Won't Listen, 1986; The Queen Is Dead, 1986; Louder Than Bombs, 1987; Strangeways Here We Come, 1987; Best... I, Best... II, 1992; with Electronic: Electronic, 1990; Raise the Pressure, 1996; Guitarist, Mind Bomb, The The, 1989. *Current Management:* Ignition Management, 8A Wyndham Pl., London W1H 1PP, England.

MARS Chris; b. 30 March 1965, London, England. Singer; Musician (keyboards, piano, guitar). *Musical Education:* O-Level Music: guitar, piano. *Career:* A Flock of Seagulls, USA tour, 1986; Lead singer, The Happening, house band on Sky television, 1990–91; Live broadcast, Greater London Radio, Tim Smith Show, 1991; Solo tour, Norway, Switzerland,

Germany, 1994–95. *Recordings:* Chris Mars (debut album) release due soon. *Memberships:* Musicians' Union; PRS. *Leisure interests:* Flying aeroplanes; Making music. *Address:* Cavendish Ave, Ealing, London W13 0JW, England.

MARS Mick, (Bob Deal); b. 3 April 1955, Terre Haute, Indiana, USA. Rock Musician (guitar). m. Emi Canyn, 19 Sept. 1990. *Career:* Member, US heavy rock group Mötley Crüe, 1981–; World-wide concerts include: Tours with: Y & T, 1981, 1982; Kiss, 1983; Ozzy Osbourne, 1984; Iron Maiden, 1984; Cheap Trick, 1986; Theatre of Pain world tour, 1985–86; World tours, 1987, 1989; Major festivals: US Festival, 1983; Monsters of Rock festival, Castle Donington, 1984, 1991; Moscow Music Peace Festival, 1989. *Recordings:* Albums: Too Fast For Love, 1981; Shout At The Devil, 1983; Theatre of Pain, 1985; Girls, Girls, Girls (No. 2, USA), 1987; Dr Feelgood (No. 1, USA), 1989; Decade of Decadence (No. 2, USA), 1991; Till Death Do Us Part, 1994; Singles: Stick To Your Guns, 1981; Looks That Kill, 1984; Too Young To Fall In Love, 1984; Smokin' In The Boys Room, 1985; Home Sweet Home, 1985; You're All I Need, 1987; Dr Feelgood, 1989; Kick Start My Heart, 1990; Without You, 1990; Don't Go Away Mad, 1990; Same Old Situation, 1990; Primal Scream, 1991; Contributor, Stars, Hear 'n' Aid charity record, 1985. *Honours:* Rolling Stone Poll Winners, Best Heavy Metal Band, 1991; American Music Award, Favourite Heavy Metal Album, 1991. *Current Management:* The Left Bank Organisation, 6255 Sunset Blvd, Suite 1111, Hollywood, CA 90028, USA.

MARSALIS Branford; b. 26 Aug. 1960, New Orleans, Louisiana, USA. Jazz Musician (saxophone); Prod.; Composer; Actor. *Musical Education:* New Orleans Centre for Creative Arts; Southern University, Baton Rouge (with Alwin Bastite); Berklee School of Music, Boston. *Career:* Performed with: Art Blakey; Lionel Hampton; Clark Terry; Bu Blakey; Wynton Marsalis; Herbie Hancock; Sting; Grateful Dead; Albert Collins; Nils Lofgren; Leader of own band with Kenny Kirkland, Jeff Watts, Bob Hurst; Numerous world-wide tours; Major concerts include: Live Aid Concert, London, 1985; Nelson Mandela Concert, London, 1988; Jamaican Hurricane Relief Benefit Concert, Los Angeles, 1990; West Side Story, AIDS Project Los Angeles, 1992; Pori Jazz, Finland, 1995; Film roles: School Daze; Throw Mama From The Train; Television and radio appearances include: Bring On The Night, 1985; Host, New Visions, 1987; Story of a People, Expressions in Black, 1991; Host, Jazzset, radio series, 1992; Co-host, Best of Disney Music, 1992; Music Director, Tonight Show, 1992; Composer and performer on numerous film and television scores. *Recordings:* Scenes In The City, 1984; Romances For Saxophone, 1986; Bring On The Night, live album, 1986; Royal Garden Blues, 1986; Renaissance, 1987; Random Abstract, 1988; Trio Jeepy, 1989; Crazy People Music, 1990; Music From Mo' Better Blues, 1990; The Beautiful Ones Are Not Yet Born, 1991; I Heard You Twice The First Time, 1992; Bloomington, 1993; Buckshot Le Fonque, 1994; Dark Keys, 1996; Requiem, 1999; Also performed on albums by Wynton Marsalis and Sting. *Honours:* 3 Grammy Awards; 7 Grammy Nominations. *Current Management:* Anne Marie Wilkins, Wilkins Management.

MARSALIS Wynton; b. 18 Oct. 1961, New Orleans, Louisiana, USA. Musician (trumpet). *Musical Education:* Trained in classical music, Juilliard School, New York, USA. *Career:* Played with New Orleans Philharmonic, age 14; Joined Art Blakey and the Jazz Messengers, 1980; Tour with Herbie Hancock, 1981; Formed own group with brother Branford Marsalis on tenor saxophone, 1982; Leader, Wynton Marsalis Septet; Appearances with New York Philharmonic; Cleveland Orchestra; Los Angeles Philharmonic; London Symphony Orchestra and other major European orchestras; Conductors include: Lorin Maazel; Zubin Mehta; Leonard Slatkin; Esa-Pekka Salonen; Held Saturday Jazz for Young People, Lincoln Centre, New York; Regularly conducts masterclasses in schools and holds private tuition; Regularly holds Jazz For Young People throughout each year. *Compositions:* include: Blood on the Fields, oratorio; In This House On This Morning, for septet; (At The) Octoroon Ball, for string quartet; Jazz/Syncopated Movements; Jump Start; Sweet Release, with Judith Jamison; Citi Movement/Griot New York, with Garth Fagan; Marcial Suite, engraved in Place du Marcial, France, 1998. *Recordings include:* Joe Cool's Blues, Wynton Marsalis Septet and Ellis Marsalis Trio, 1995; In This House On This Morning, 1994; Gabriel's Garden; Jazz for Young People; Jazz/Syncopated Movements, 1997; Jump Start, forthcoming. *Honours:* Grand Prix du Disque, France; Edison Award, Netherlands; 8 Grammy Awards; Keys to many US cities; Numerous honorary Doctorates from US Universities; Named one of the USA's Most Influential People; Pulitzer Prize for Music, 1997; Concertos by Haydn, Hummel and Leopold Mozart; Grand Prix Du Disque, France; Named one of Time Magazine's Most Influential People Under 40; Grammy's in Jazz and Classical. *Current Management:* Management Ark. *Address:* c/o Shore Fire Media, 32 Court St, Brooklyn, NY 11201, USA.

MARSDEN Gerry (Gerald); b. 24 Sept. 1942, Liverpool, Merseyside, England. Singer; Musician (guitar). m. Pauline Ann, 11 Oct. 1965, 2 d. *Musical Education:* Self-taught. *Career:* 33 years in music; Gerry and the Pacemakers, 1962–; 3 No. 1 hit singles with first 3 records; Numerous

concerts and television shows world-wide; West End theatre: Charlie Girl; Pull Both Ends, (5 years). *Recordings:* Hit singles include: Ferry Cross The Mersey; I Like It; How Do You Do It; I'm The One; Don't Let The Sun Catch You Crying; You'll Never Walk Alone; Albums include: How Do You Like It, 1963; Ferry Cross The Mersey, 1964; Don't Let The Sun Catch You Crying, 1964; Girl On A Swing, 1966; Numerous compilations include: 20th Anniversary Album, 1983; Hit Singles Album, 1986; You'll Never Walk Alone, 1988; Gerry Cross the Mersey, 1995. *Publications:* I'll Never Walk Alone (autobiography). *Honours:* 2 BMI citations; Gold and Silver records; BASCA Gold Badge. *Memberships:* Musicians' Union; Equity; PRS; Songwriters' Guild. *Leisure interests:* Fishing; Shooting; Boating; Scuba diving. *Current Management:* Derek Franks Organization/PIP.

MARSDEN John Charles Stewart; b. 21 Nov. 1971, Melbourne, Australia. Vocalist; Musician (guitar); Songwriter. *Musical Education:* Guitar lessons for two years then self-taught. *Career:* Founding member of Melbourne band Wild Turkey, 1988; Nationwide tours with band; Performs in duo with drummer Kirk Syrett; Hosts Muso's Jam Nights encouraging new talent; Various minor acting roles in Australian TV and film productions. *Compositions:* Love That Kills; I Drove All Day; Burning Desire; Without You; Noon and Night; Surfin' Hearse; Mess Around Baby. *Recordings:* Albums: I Drove All Day, 1994; Love That Kills, 1997; Surfin' Hearse, 2001. *Membership:* APRA. *Leisure interests:* Collecting classic American cars and hearses. *Current Management:* Wild Turkey Management Pty Ltd, PO Box 120, Kallista, Victoria, 3791, Australia.

MARSH Barbara Lynn; b. Warwick, Rhode Island, USA. Singer; Songwriter; Musician (guitar, piano, mandolin). m. Peter Comley, Divorced 1995, 28 April 1984. *Education:* AA, Pensacola Jr College; BA, Drama, Universty of West Florida. *Musical Education:* Choral Training, Woodham High Echoes; Certificate of Jazz, Popular Musicianship (studio), Goldsmiths College, London. *Career:* The Dear Janes, 1992–; Supported the Cranberries, Royal Albert Hall, 1995; Tours: UK, Ireland, Germany, Netherlands, 1993–95; London dates with Robyn Hitchcock, 1996–97; Toured USA with Robyn Hitchcock, 1997; Radio: Woman's Hour; Kaleidoscope; Loose Ends; Johnnie Walker; GLR; Recorded: Dangerous Dangerous Nuts, BBC Screen 2, Crazy For A Kiss; Acting: 2 episodes, Broadway Stories, 1994; Solo work, London, New York (live), 1980–92; Backing vocals, Anthony Thistlethwaite. *Recordings:* With The DearJanes: Sometimes I, 1994; No Skin, 1996. *Publications:* Poetry: The Panhandler, Literary Magazine, 1981; Pensacola, Florida, USA; The Auteur, magazine, London, 1992–93. *Honours:* Third Place National Forensics (intercollegiate), Informative Speaking, 1977; Finalist, Informative Speaking, 1978. *Memberships:* PRS; Musicians' Union; MCPS; Poetry Society. *Leisure interests:* Poetry; Acting (other professions); Swimming; Water skiing. *Current Management:* Steve Weltman Management. *Address:* 10C Porchester Sq., London, W2 6AN, England.

MARSH Henry; b. 8 Dec. 1948, Bath, Somerset, England. Composer; Musician (keyboards, guitar). m. Susan Norddahl, 1 April 1970, divorced, 2 s., 1 d. *Musical Education:* O Level Viola; Otherwise self-taught. *Career:* First group, at Sherborne School (featured future actor Jeremy Irons on drums); Founder member, Sailor, 1970s; First musical, One Last Summer, opened in Atlanta; Currently writing music for television. *Recordings:* Hit singles with Sailor: Girls Girls Girls; A Glass of Champagne; Album with Sailor: Trouble – The Third Step. *Honours:* Joseph Jefferson Award, Chicago, for Best Original Music in Theatre Production, Comedy of Errors. *Memberships:* PRS; MCPS. *Leisure interests:* Transcendental meditation (for 20 years); Tennis. *Current Management:* Strawberry Hills Management. *Address:* The Red Cottage, Rood Ashton, Trowbridge, Wiltshire BA14 6BL, England.

MARSHALL Christopher William; b. 18 Sept. 1956, Calcutta, India. *Education:* BSc, Hons, Manchester. *Musical Education:* Piano studies to age 16. *Career:* Semi-pro until 26; Keyboards with bands: Biddie and Eve; The Next Step; Angie; Started record label, Rhythm Shop Records, 1994. *Compositions:* Television soundtracks: Ad Armageddon, BBC2; Zapruder Footage, BBC2; Broken Lives, BBC2; The No. 10 Show, Channel 4; Reputations: Hitchcock, BBC2, 1999; Numerous albums library music; Co-writer, Your House Or My House, Samantha Fox, 1989. *Recordings:* As producer: Tracks by: Demis Roussos; Norman Wisdom; He Ain't Heavy, He's My Brother, Jonathan Paule; Blind Fool, Insane, Make Up, Dave Pop, 1998–99; Albums: with Tight Fit: Back To The 60's Vol. II, III; with Dream On Dream: Strangeways; with Hound Dog and The Megamixers: Junior Party Megamix, 1990. *Honours:* Gold, Platinum discs: Samantha Fox. *Memberships:* APRS; Musicians' Union; MCPS; PRS; ANA; PPL. *Leisure interests:* Cricket; Films; Drinking socially. *Address:* 26 Weiss Rd, Putney, London SW15 1DH, England.

MARSHALL Jamie; b. 8 July 1955, Doncaster, Yorkshire, England. Musician (guitar, keyboards); Vocalist; Songwriter; Composer. Partner, Helen Halliday. *Education:* Hons degree, Business Studies. *Musical Education:* Self-taught (formal education to O'Level). *Career:* Over 3000 live concerts in places including: The Marquee Club; The Royal Festival

Hall; Live show, Geneva radio to estimated 2m. people; Tour, Top of The Pops appearance with Don McLean, 1991; Radio 1; Radio 5; Sky TV. *Recordings:* Album: Even The Strongest Hearts, 1988; Troubletown (EP), 1990; Third recording in progress. *Leisure interests:* Cooking; Watching sport; Live music; Cinema. *Current Management:* c/o Thump Thump Music, 1 York St, London W1H 1PZ, England. *Address:* Pound Corner, Pound Lane, Windlesham, Surrey GU20 6BP, England.

MARSHALL John Stanley; b. 28 Aug. 1941, Isleworth, Middlesex, England. Musician (drums, percussion). m. Maxi Egger. *Education:* BA (Hons) Psychology, University of Reading. *Musical Education:* Studied with Jim Marshall; Alan Ganley; Philly Joe Jones. *Career:* Freelance on London jazz scene; Played with Alexis Korner's Blues Incorporated, 1964; Graham Collier Sextet, 1965–70; Also played with John Surman; John McLaughlin; Dave Holland; Mike Westbrook; Graham Bond Organisation; Joe Harriot; Indo-Jazz Fusions; Keith Tippett's Sextet, Centipede; Alan Skidmore; Founder member, Nucleus, 1969; Montreux Festival (First Prize, 1970), Newport Festival, Village Gate, New York; Regular member, Mike Gibbs Orchestra, early 1970s; Left Nucleus to join Jack Bruce Band, 1971; Joined Soft Machine, 1972; Played with musicians including: Larry Coryell; Gary Burton; Mary Lou Williams; Ronnie Scott; Tubby Hayes; Ben Webster; Milt Jackson; Roy Eldridge; John Taylor; Norma Winstone; Volker Kriegel; Gordon Beck; Charlie Mariano; Jasper van't Hof; Philip Catherine; Joined Eberhard Weber's Colours, 1977–81; Worked with Gil Evans Orchestra; Ian Carr; Kenny Wheeler; Uli Beckerhoff; Anthony Braxton; Manfred Schoof; Joachim Kühn; Michel Portal; John Taylor; Alan Holdsworth; Norma Winstone; Gordon Beck; Jeff Clyne; Arild Anderson; John Abercrombie; John Surman Quartet; Brass Project; Teacher, Jazz Faculty of the Royal Academy of Music, London. *Recordings:* Over 60 albums include: Elastic Rock, Nucleus, 1970; Harmony Row, Jack Bruce, 1971; Bundles, Soft Machine, 1975; Stranger Than Fiction, John Surman Quartet, 1994. *Address:* 43 Combemartin Rd, London SW18 5PP, England.

MARSHALL Oren Morris; b. 14 June 1966, Geneva, Switzerland. Musician (tuba, recorder, percussion). *Musical Education:* Oboe, recorder, voice, Purcell School, 1977–79; Tuba, piano, Royal College of Music – JD, 1981–84. *Career:* Musician with every major orchestra in London, 1985; Jazz big bands include: Loose Tubes, 1984–90; Jazz Warriors, 1986; John Dankworth, 1995; Julian Joseph, 1994–95; Improvised music with: Company '92, with Derek Bailey; Say What Trio, with Steve Noble, Davey Williams, 1991–; World-wide tours, with London Brass, 1987–; Solo television appearances include: Wogan, BBC, 1987; South Bank Show, ITV, 1988; Performances with the Pan African Orchestra, UK and Ghana, 1991–94. *Recordings:* 10 albums with London Brass; other recordings include: Willcocks: Carols for Christmas, 1985; Mahler, Symphonies 9 and 10, Frankfurt Radio Orchestra, 1986; The Human Groove, Microgroove, 1988; London Brass: Christmas with the London Brass, 1990; Beyong the Groove: Contemporary Jazz, 1991; Antz Original Movie Score, 1998; Carols for Christmas Vol. 2; Solo album: Time Spent At Traffic Lights (all compositions by Oren Marshall), 1995; Noble-Marshall-Buckley, Derek Bailey Trio, 1995; Mike Gibbs Band, 1993. *Honours:* ARCM (hons), 1983; FTCL, 1984; Shell/LSO Scholarship winner, 1987; Third prize, Geneva International Music Competition, 1991. *Leisure interests:* Dancing; Swimming; Yoga; Drumming; Relaxing.

MARTENS Evert (Everardus Antonius Josephus Maria); b. 14 July 1956, Mill and St Hubert. 1 s. *Career:* Many TV and radio appearances. *Compositions:* Waltz for Rutger; La Copine; Where's My Key. *Recordings:* 4 CDs: After You're Gone; Just in Time; La Copine; Way to Go. *Honours:* First Prize, Capelino, Old Style Jazz Festival Breda, 1990. *Memberships:* NTB; VAK; SENA; BUMA; STEMRA. *Leisure interests:* Repairing all kinds of things. *Address:* Sonsbeeksingel 11, 6814 AA Arnhem, The Netherlands.

MARTENS Hervé; b. 11 June 1963, Louvain, Belgium. Keyboard Player. *Career:* Member of Soulsister; Zap Mama World Tour, 2000. *Recordings:* Producer for Bobby Womack, Gibson Brothers and Sophie and So Four. *Honour:* Best Belgium Band Monte Carlo Award, 1988. *Membership:* Sabam; Zamu. *Leisure interest:* Football. *Address:* Kerkstraat 12, 3370 Boutersem, Belgium.

MARTIN Barrie; b. 22 May 1944, London, England. Musician (baritone, tenor, alto saxophone). m. Elizabeth Gower, 5 Nov. 1976, 1 s., 2 d. *Musical Education:* 5 years with Leslie Evans (private tutor). *Career:* Member, Quotations, Walker Brothers band for 2–3 years; All concert tours except last; Solo Spot, Sunday Night at London Palladium; Also as guest of Walker Brothers on German TV from Berlin; Played with Jet Harris' band: The Jet Blacks; One Night Stand, with Pete Murray, BBC TV, 1960s; Tours with: Roy Orbison; Brenda Lee; Duane Eddy; Little Richard; Englebert Humperdinck; Geno Washington and The Ram Jam Band; Currently working with Otis Grand and the Big Blues Band. *Recordings:* Solo, on Walker Brothers EP; Walker Brothers album: Portrait; Atlantic Soul Machine album: Coast To Coast. *Membership:* Musicians' Union. *Leisure interest:* Trying to play piano. *Address:* 26 Halstow, Queens Cres., London NW5 4EH, England.

MARTIN Beranger; b. 5 May 1960, Brugge, Belgium. Jazz Musician (Guitar; 2nd Instructor Piano). m. Elsie Tuyaerts, 1988, 2 s. *Education:* Jazz School, Dworp, Belgium. *Career:* On Tour in Sweden with Waso Quartet; with own trio, Beranger Trio; Toured in France, Germany and The Netherlands; Guest Guitar Player in Australia. *Compositions:* LPs recorded with Gypsy Quintet, Piotto's; CD recorded with Big Band, Arena; Own CD for BRTN, Belgian TV. *Recordings:* Freelance Guitar Player; Swing-Jazz to Modern-Jazz and Gipsy Jazz; Guest Player on CDs. *Publication:* Cocktail, 1997. *Honour:* Jazz-Rally Hasselt, Best Solo Artist, 1990. *Leisure interests:* Music; Sports. *Current Management:* Kras Artist, Ghent Parcifal, Bruges Booking NTS, Knokke. *Address:* Sakramentstraat 8, 8300 Knokke-Reist, Belgium.

MARTIN Bill; b. 9 Nov. 1938, Glasgow, Scotland. Songwriter; Music Publisher. m. 1972, 1 s., 3 d. *Musical Education:* Royal Scottish Academy of Music. *Career:* Tours with The Drifters; Robert Parker; Winner, Eurovision Song Contest with Puppet On A String; Congratulations; All Kinds of Everything; All Bay City Roller hits including: Shang-A-Lang; Summerlove Sensation; Publisher of: Billy Connolly; Van Morrison; Sky-Songs; Writer, My Boy, for Elvis Presley; No. 1 songs world-wide. *Honours:* 20 Gold albums; 4 Platinum albums; 3 Ivor Novello Awards; 3 ASCAP Awards. *Memberships:* BASCA; PRS. *Leisure interests:* Golf; Past Captain RAC, member, St George's Hill. *Address:* 225 Kensington High St, London W8 6SA, England.

MARTIN Billie Ray; b. Germany. Singer. *Career:* Singer with Electribe 101; Now solo artiste. *Recordings:* Album: Deadline For My Memories, 1995; Singles: with Electribe 101: Talking With Myself, 1990; Solo: Your Loving Arms, 1995; running Around Town, 1995; You and I (Keep Holding On), 1996; Imitation of Life, 1996; Space Oasis, 1996; Pacemaker, 1998; Honey, 1999; Crimes and Punishment; 1999. *Honour:* International Dance Music Award, Best New Dance Solo Artist, 1996. *Address:* c/o Mark Dean, East West Records, Electric Lighting Station, 46 Kensington Court, London W8 5DP, England.

MARTIN Chris; b. 2 March 1977, Devon, England. Vocalist; Musician (guitar, piano), Songwriter. *Education:* University College, London. *Career:* Member: Coldplay, 1998-. *Recordings:* Albums: Parachutes, 2000; Singles: The Safety EP, 1998; Brothers and Sisters, The Blue Room EP, 1999; Shiver, Yellow, Trouble, 2000. *Honours:* Brit Award, Best Album, 2001; Mercury Music Prize, nominee, 2000. *Current Management:* Phil Harvey. *Internet:* www.coldplay.com.

MARTIN Claire; b. 6 Sept. 1967, Wimbledon, London. Musician (Vocalist). *Education:* Doris Holford Stage School; Studed With Marilyn Johnson, Verona Chard. *Career:* Professional Singer Predominantly Jazz; Seven Years With LINN Records; Travelled Extensively In Europe, Asia; Worked For The British Council, Pakistan, Cyprus, Indonesia. *Compositions:* Years Apart; On Thin Ice; Jack and Sarah; The Waiting Game; Victim of Circumstance. *Recordings:* The Waiting Game; Devil May Care; Old Boyfriends; Offbeat; Make This City Ours; Take My Heart. *Honours:* British Jazz Awards, Rising Star, 1994, Best Vocalist, 1996, 1997. *Memberships:* Equity; Musicians Union. *Leisure interests:* Yoga; Cycling. *Current Management:* James Taylor, Plant 3 Entertainments, PO Box 8403, Maybole, KA19 7YB. *Address:* Basement Flat, 61 Brunswick Pl., Hove, Sussex, BN3 1NE.

MARTIN Clive; b. 21 March 1963, London, England. Record Prod.; Sound Engineer. *Recordings:* As Record Producer: Albums: with Reef: Replenish; Puressence album; with Echobelly: Insomniac (EP); with Les Negresses Vertes: Mlah (double Gold disc); Famille Nombreuse (Gold disc); with Hunters and Collectors: Ghost Nation (Platinum disc); As Sound Engineer: Soundtrack, David Byrne's The Last Emperor; with Youssou N'Dour; Echobelly, Everybody's Got One, 1994; Miquel Brown, So Many Men So Little Time, 1994; Drugstore, White Magic for Lovers, 1998; Llama Farmers, Dead Letter Chorus, 1999; As Assistant Engineer: Queen; Sting; The Cure; As Assistant to Flood: Jesus and Mary Chain; Matt Johnson; Soft Cell. *Honours:* Gold and Platinum albums; Academy Award, film soundtrack The Last Emperor. *Current Management:* Caroline Ryan. *Address:* Estate House, 921A Fulham Rd, London SW6 5HU, England.

MARTIN Daniel-John; b. 25 Sept. 1965, Congleton, Cheshire, England. Jazz Musician (violin); Composer; Arranger. *Musical Education:* Schola Cantorum (superieur) American School of Music; Didier Lockwood. *Career:* Tour with the 11tet de Violon Jazz; Theatre des Champs Elysées, France, Germany; Major French radio shows; TV: Le Cercle de Minuit; First festival, Jazz Violin, with Didier Lockwood; Jazz M6, TV; with Daniel Martin Group: Sunset; Baiser Solé; Petit Journal Montparnasse; Alligators. *Recordings with:* Onxtet de Violon Jazz; Djeli Moussa (African music); Public Address (rock p-4 mati); Daniel-John Martin Group to be published. *Honours:* First Prize, Jazz Modern, Jazz Plus, Jazz Hot. *Membership:* General Secretary, Jazz and Violin Asscn. *Leisure interests:* Painting; Sculpting.

MARTIN Dey; b. 11 Sept. 1956, Los Angeles, CA, USA. Songwriter; Prod.; Musician (Guitar). *Musical Education:* Composition Degree in Music BM, University of Hawaii; MM, University of California at Irvine, USA. *Career:* Backing Guitar, Polyphemus, Lollapalloosa Tour, 1995; Producer: Woodpecker, Lung Cookie, Jalopy Kinfolk, Music West, Vancouver, 1995; Songwriter, Solo Performer, mid 1980s; Owner: Naked Jain Records. *Compositions:* String Quartet, 1978; Three Images, text by EE Cummings for classical guitar, mezzo soprano vocal and piano, 1979; Berlin Wall, 1989. *Recording:* Mr Monotony, producer. *Honour:* Young Composers, 1978–80. *Membership:* ASCAP, NAS, NARM. *Current Management:* Naked/Jain Records Inc, PO Box 4132, Palm Springs, CA 92263, USA. *Address:* 681 E Spencer Dr., Palm Springs, CA 92262, USA.

MARTIN Eric; Singer. *Career:* Founder member, Eric Martin Band; Lead singer, Mr Big, 1989–; Also member, side project Road Vultures. *Recordings:* Albums: with Eric Martin Band: Sucker For A Pretty Face, 1983; Eric Martin, 1985; with Mr Big: Mr Big, 1989; Lean Into It, 1991; Bump Ahead, 1993; Hey Man, 1996; with Working Man: Working Man, 1996; Deep House Party Vol. 4, 1996; with Sammy Hagar: Marching to Mars, 1997; with Gildas Arzel: Brazebeck, 1999; with Supersuckers: Teachers, 1999; Singles include: Green-Tinted Sixties Mind; To Be With You; I Love the Way You Love Me. *Current Management:* Herbie Herbert Management, 2501 Third St, San Francisco, CA 94107, USA.

MARTIN Juan; b. 1 Oct. 1943, Málaga, Spain. Concert Musician (guitar). m. Helen Foulds, 6 June 1973, 2 s. *Musical Education:* Self-taught. *Career:* World-wide solo tours; Tours with own Flamenco Dance Company; Played South Bank Centre, and The Barbican, London; Carnegie Hall, and the Lincoln Centre, New York; 18 date tours, including the Barbican, UK, 1993, 1995; Television includes: Wogan; Top of The Pops; Pebble Mill; Arts programmes; Radio recitals, BBC Radios 1–4; New York WNYC; Boston WGBH. *Recordings:* Exciting Sound of Flamenco, 1974; Romance, 1976; Olé Don Juan, Flamenco en Andalucia, 1977; Picasso Portraits, 1981; Serenade, 1984; Solo album, 1985; Painter In Sounds, 1986; Through The Moving Window, 1988; Andalucian Suites, 1990; Luna Negra, 1993; Musica Alhambra, 1998; Los Arte Flamenco, 1999; Through the Moving Window, 1999. *Publications:* El Arte Flamenco de la Guitarra; Fifth Edition, La Guitarra Flamenca, video series; Folios: Exciting Sound of Flamenco; 12 Solos; Andalucian Suites. *Memberships:* PRS; MCPS. *Current Management:* Flamencovision, PO Box 508, London N3 3SY, England.

MARTIN Lynne; b. 6 Nov. 1957, Bedford, England. Musician (keyboards); Arranger; Musical Dir. 1 d. *Education:* College. *Musical Education:* Sat examinations of Associated Board of Royal Schools of Music. *Career:* Television appearances: Friday People, Border TV; Look Who's Talking; Laugh-In; Musical Director for numerous summer seasons and pantomimes throughout UK; Personal Musical Director for Derek Batey for 12 years; Also MD for artistes including Max Bygraves; Moira Anderson; Frank Carson. *Composition:* Theme tune, Friday People, Border TV, 1982. *Recordings:* Numerous recording sessions. *Memberships:* Musicians' Union; Equity. *Current Management:* Ray Cornell Artistes and Productions. *Address:* Applause House, 56 St Annes Rd, Blackpool, Lancashire, England.

MARTIN Marie-Ange; b. 18 Jan. 1948, Bois Colombes, France. Jazz Musician (guitar, banjo, cello). *Musical Education:* Self-taught; 8 years cello study. *Career:* Played swing and Dixieland music with Benny Waters, Bill Coleman, 1969–76; Bebop and modern jazz, 1976–84; Guitar Institute of Technology, Los Angeles, 1985; Guitarist with own quartet; Banjo player, Hot Kings; Cellist, cello quartet Cellofans, 1986–93; Tours of Asia, Australia, Eastern Europe, with Christian Escoude and Marcel Azzola, 1993–95; Banjo and cello player, Threepenny Opera, 1996. *Recordings:* Dixieland Parade; Cello Acoustics; Also recording music of Kurt Weil. *Honours:* Outstanding Award of The Year, Guitar Institute of Technology, Los Angeles, 1985. *Leisure interests:* Knitting; Cooking; Scrabble; Computer; Gym training. *Address:* 31 rue de Fontarabie, 75020 Paris, France.

MARTIN Michael Anthony; b. 9 Nov. 1960, London, England. Musician (piano, keyboards). 2 d. *Musical Education:* Post graduate diploma; O'Level Music. *Career:* Keyboard player for Billy Paul; Aswad; Jean Carne; Cliff Richard; Television: Top of The Pops; Childrens TV; 3 world tours with Aswad; Montreux Pop Festival; International AIDS Day; Nelson Mandela at Wembley. *Compositions:* Music for BBC, State of Europe. *Recordings:* with Aswad: Don't Turn Round; Production on Heartbeat, Aswad, No. 1 Japan; Roots Rocking: The Island Anthology, 1997; Big Up, 1997; with Elementals: Waking on Each Other; with Dr Seuss: Dr Seuss Green Eggs and Ham; Solo Album: Odyssey, 1998. *Honours:* Platinum disc, for album: Rise and Shine, Aswad. *Membership:* PRS; Musicians' Union. *Leisure interests:* Music; Rollerblading.

MARTIN Millicent; b. Romford, Essex, England. Actress; Singer. m. Marc Alexander, 26 Sept. 1977. *Career:* Side By Side By Sondheim (London, Los Angeles, Broadway); 42nd Street (Broadway, Las Vegas, London); The

Boyfriend (London, Broadway); King of Hearts (Broadway); The Card (London); Shirley Valentine; Rise and Fall of Little Voice; Follies; The Rivals, England and USA; Moon Over Buffalo, USA; Television appearances: Moon and Son; Mainly Millicent; That Was The Week That Was (TW3); Downtown; LA Law; Coach; Upper Hand; Murphy Brown. *Recordings:* Side By Side; King of Hearts; Our Man Crighton; Sondheim – A Celebration. *Honours:* TV Society Medal; Variety Club Award. *Leisure interests:* Cooking; Travel; Animals. *Current Management:* Sean Diamond, London Management. *Address:* 2–4 Noel St, London WC1, England.

MARTIN Neil; b. 10 Dec. 1967, Great Britain. Musician (drums). *Musical Education:* Studied with: Paul Robinson; Ed Soph; Bob Armstrong. *Career:* Extensive sessions and television, radio appearances; Jimmy Barnes Psyclone World Tour 95 (including support to The Rolling Stones), venues from 1,000–50,000 seaters. *Compositions:* Co-writer, track Stumbling, Psyclone album, Jimmy Barnes. *Recordings:* Album: Psyclone: Jimmy Barnes. *Membership:* Musicians' Union. *Leisure interests:* Martial arts; Reading; Listening to music. *Address:* 2 Waddington Close, Enfield, Middlesex EN1 WB, England.

MARTIN Peter (Philemon Winston); b. 28 Jan. 1948, Tuitts Village, Montserrat. Musician (drums, percussion); Vocalist. 2 d. *Education:* Courses in adult education. *Musical Education:* Self-educated with evening classes. *Career:* First reggae gigs with Owen Grey, Alton Ellis, small tours of England, early 1970s; Studio musician, mid 1970s; Tours, England, Scotland, Wales, 1980s; Joined Steel and Skin, Art Company, played Danish Festival, 1983; Tour, Sweden, 1984; Recordings, gigs. tours, Europe, West Africa, Scandinavia; Tour with Dr Alban, 1992; Resident in Sweden, 1993; Taught rhythm and dance, Blå Hasten; Production of Benny The Boxer, Theatre X; Played Djembe on dance courses; Joined Afro Tiambo, West African Rhythm and dance group, 1994; Computer course, digital music recording; Sound, lighting engineer, Folkuniversitetet, theatre production, Ritten till havet; Teacher, Malmö Music High School; Television: Old Grey Whistle Test; Opportunity Works; Chinese Detective; WDR Rock Palace; MTV Live; Concerts: Ronny Lane Tour; Style Council Peace Concert, Brixton; Radio: Africa, Sweden, London; Festivals: Hultsfred; Roskilde; Tours/gigs with Jimmy Cliff; Style Council; Papa Dee; Red Mitchell; Eek-A-Mouse; Eddie Grant. Recordings include Dr Alban. *Honours:* Appearances, before Princess Margaret, London, 1978; Swedish royals, Stockholm, 1992. *Memberships:* Musicians' Union; Svenska Musik Forbondet. *Leisure interests:* Music; Documentary vidoes; Driving. *Address:* 21 Lavender Grove, Hackney, London E18 3LU, England.

MARTIN Ricky, (Enrique Martin Morales); b. 24 Dec. 1971, Puerto Rico. Singer. *Career:* Joined group Menudo, aged 13; Numerous tours and recordings; Left Menudo, 1989; Acted in Mexican soap opera Alcanzur una Estrella II; Began releasing Spanish language albums; Role as bartender in General Hospital; Won the role of Marius in Broadway production of Les Miserables; Dubbed voice in Spanish version of Disney film Hercules; Released first English Language album including a duet with Madonna; Numerous television appearances and tour dates. *Recordings:* Singles: Maria, 1996; 1 2 3 Maria, 1997; Cup of Life, 1998; La Bomba, 1999; Livin' La Vida Loca, 1999; She's All I Have Had, 1999; Albums: Ricky Martin, 1991; Me Amarás, 1993; A Medio Vivir, 1995; Vuelve, 1998; Ricky Martin, 1999. *Honour:* Grammy Award, Best Latin Pop Album, 1999.

MARTIN Roy; b. 10 July 1961, Liverpool, Merseyside, England. Musician (drums); Drum Tutor. m. Margie Yates, 20 June 1985, 2 d. *Career:* Concert tours: Played for: Modern English, 1986, 1990; Shalom Hanoch, 1987, 1988; Gavin Friday, 1992; Black, 1993; Diesel, 1993. *Recordings:* Drummer on: Jimmy Barnes: Flesh and Wood; Aretha Franklin: Jimmy Lee; Cock Robin: When Your Heart Is Weak; Black: Black; Film soundtrack (The Christians): Blame It On The Bellboy; Modern English: Pillow Lips; Joe Grushecky: Pumping Iron and Sweating Steel; Jim Hunter: Fingernail Moon (bass); Tractor: Worst Enemies; Very Best of British Dance Bands (clarinet and saxophone); Patricia Kaas: Rendez-Vous; Recorded with: Viv Stanshall; Regina Belle; Billy Brannigan; Shalom Hanoch. *Leisure interest:* Sports. *Current Management:* B and H Management, Lavender Cottage, Love Lane, Kings Langley, Hertfordshire WD4 9HN, England.

MARTIN Sarah; b. 12 Feb. 1974. Vocalist; Musician (violin, recorder). *Career:* Member: Belle and Sebastian, 1996–; Curated Bowlie Weekend Festival with other band members, 1999. *Recordings:* Albums: If You're Feeling Sinister, 1996; The Boy With The Arab Strap 1998; Fold Your Hands Child – You Walk Like A Peasant, 2000; Singles: Dog On Wheels EP, Lazy Line Painter Jane EP, 3–6–9 Seconds of Light EP, 1997; This Is Just A Modern Rock Song EP, 1998; Legal Man, 2000; Jonathan David, I'm Waking Up To Us, 2001. *Honours:* Brit Award, Best Newcomer, 1999. *Current Management:* Banchory Management, PO Box 25074, Glasgow G2 6YL, Scotland. *Internet:* www.belleandsebastian.co.uk.

MARTIN Tony; b. 19 April 1957, Birmingham, England. Singer; Songwriter. m. Mo, 18 Aug. 1990, 2 s., 1 d. *Career:* First show aged 7; Many local bands; Joined The Alliance, 1983; Signed with Warner Bros publishing, 1984; Released tracks on Bailey Bros Compilation Album; Joined Black Sabbath, 1987, 3 albums, 3 world tours; Left Black Sabbath, 1992; Signed with Polydor, 1992, solo album; Rejoined Black Sabbath, 1993, 2 albums, 2 world tours. *Recordings:* with Bailey Brothers: Vinyl Frontier; The Talisman; Forcefield II; Valley of The Kings; Blue Murder; with Black Sabbath: Eternal Idol, 1987; Headless Cross, 1989; Tyr, 1990; Cross Purposes, 1993; Forbidden, 1995; Solo: Back Where I Belong, 1992. *Leisure interest:* Life. *Current Management:* Albert Chapman. *Address:* Lethal Music UK Ltd, E9 Kenilworth Court, Hagley Rd, Birmingham B16 9NU, England.

MARTINO Al; b. 7 Oct. 1927, Philadelphia, Pennsylvania, USA. Singer; Entertainer; Actor. m. Judith Stilwell, 10 Dec. 1968, 1 s., 2 d. *Career:* Played Johnny Fontaine in The Godfather, 1972; Tours in Australia, Germany, USA and Canada; Played in Godfather I and III yearly. *Recordings:* Spanish Eyes; Here In My Heart (No. 1, UK charts); Mary In The Morning; I Love You Because; Painted, Tainted Rose; Daddy's Little Girl; The Voice to Your Heart, 1993; Volare, 1993; Spotlight on Al Martino, 1996; In Concert, 1998; There Are Such Things, 1998. *Honours:* Philadelphia Music Hall of Fame; Gold Disc, Spanish Eyes. *Leisure interest:* Cooking.

MARTUCCI Vincent; b. 21 Oct. 1954, Medford, Massachusetts, USA. Composer-Arranger; Musician (Piano); Educator. m. Elizabeth Lawrence, 21 Sept. 1981, 1 s., 1 d. *Education:* BA, Music, Colby College, Waterville, Maine; Alumnus, Berklee College of Music; Private studies with John Mehegan, Hal Galper, Dave Holland, Baikida Carroll. *Career:* Performed, synthesizer, film score, My Blue Heaven, with Steve Martin; Numerous tours, own group, Co-lead with Dan Brubeck, The Dolphins, in USA, Europe, South America, Canada; Redesign network themes, Travel Channel, Lifetime Medical Television; Showtime, children's TV series, 1989; Producer, Performer, Arranger, numerous theatrical productions with Baikida Carroll and McCarter Theatre, 1995. *Compositions:* Numerous tunes for The Dolphins; Scores for daytime drama As The World Turns, Guiding Light, Another World, 1992-. *Recordings:* Livingston Taylor, Life is Good, 1988; Dan Brubeck and the Dolphins, 3 CDs, 1989-99; Rory Black, Tornado, 1996. *Publications:* Introduction to Jazz Piano, 1997; Introduction to Blues Piano, 1997; Introduction to Rock Piano, 1997. *Honours:* 2nd Place, Billboard Song Contest, 1988; Jazz Category Finalist, Hennessey Jazz Search, 1990. *Memberships:* ASCAP; AFTRA. *Leisure interest:* Photography. *Address:* 29 Pleasant Ridge Dr., W Hurley, NY 12791, USA.

MARTY Bobby, (Etienne Martens); b. 4 Oct. 1937, Brugge (Bruges), Belgium. m. Suffys Nicole, 8 Sept. 1963, 1 s., 1 d. *Education:* Private lessons, Dirigent Pol Horna; Bass Guitar and 1 Year Piano, age of 12 years. *Career:* Andrex; Ensemble Pol Horna; The Shamrocks; Luc Rène and the Jumps; Own show with the Bobby Marty Dancers, 1980–; Radio's in Belgium and France; TV in France; Concerts with trio Tea for Three, own songs and music of the 60s, played bass, singer. *Compositions:* Houtem Mijn Dorpje; De Bruggeling; Adieu Jacques Brel; La Maison Du Bonheur; Mon Amour; Ma Guitare et Quelques Chansons; Une Belle Nuit D'Hiver; Au Rendez-Vous des Artistes. *Recordings:* 18 singles; 1 LP; 2 compilation CDs in France with other French artists; 2 solo CDs: Bobby Marty International (6 languages); Bobby Marty sings Elvis. *Publications:* Flash, own magazine, 1989-. *Honours:* Golden Record, Rose Des Neiges; Silver Record for Johnny Laat je Jodel nog eens Horen (compilation of Johnny Hoes). *Leisure interests:* All sports, especially football; Cycling; Athletics; Travel. *Address:* Molenwalstraat 8A, 8630 Houtem-Veurne, Belgium.

MARTYN John, (Iain McGeachy); b. 11 Sept. 1948, New Malden, Surrey, England. Vocalist; Musician (guitar); Lyricist. m. Beverly Kutner (divorced). *Career:* Duo with wife Beverly; Toured regularly with full-time band. *Compositions include:* Solid Air; Angeline; May You Never, recorded by Eric Clapton. *Recordings:* Albums: London Conversation, 1968; The Tumbler, 1968; Stormbringer, 1970; The Road To Ruin, 1970; Bless The Weather, 1971; Solid Air, 1973; Inside Out, 1973; Sunday's Child, 1975; Live At Leeds, 1975; One World, 1977; So Far So Good, 1977; Grace and Danger, 1980; Glorious Fool, 1981; Well Kept Secret, 1982; The Electric John Martyn, 1982; Philentrophy, 1983; Sapphire, 1984; Piece By Piece, 1986; Foundations, 1987; The Apprentice, 1990; Cooltide, 1991; BBC Radio 1 Live In Concert, 1992; Couldn't Love You More, 1992; Live, 1995; The Church With One Bell, 1998; Live, 1998; Snooo, 1999; Live at Bristol, 1999; Dirty Down and Live: Shaw Theatre, London 1990, 1999. *Address:* c/o Permanent Records, 22–23 Brook Mews, London W2 3BW, England.

MARUCCI Mathew Roger III (Mat); b. 2 July 1945, Rome, New York, USA. Musician (drums); Prod.; Writer; Author. m. Diane Marie, 25 May 1982, 1 s., 1 d. *Education:* AAS, Retail Business Management, Auburn Community College, 1965; AA, Music, Sacramento City College, 1973. *Career:* Recording artist and jazz musician; Applied Music Instructor for American River College, Sacramento; Drummer for major jazz artists including Jimmy Smith, Kenny Burrell, James Moody, Eddie Harris, Les

McCann, John Tchicai and Buddy De Franco; Appeared in feature film Uncle Joe Shannon and TV series Fantasy Island; Played on soundtracks for TV; Leader of Trio, Quartet and Quintet. *Compositions:* Festival; Ulterior Motif; Who Do Voo Doo Suite; Blue Suspension; Danse Desire; Lifeline; Quiescence. *Recordings:* Who Do Voo Doo, 1979; Lifeline, 1981; Festival, 1982; Extensity, 1982; Avant-Bop, 1983; Body and Soul, 1991; Ulterior Motif, 1998. *Publications:* Contributor of articles in magazines for Modern Drummer; Percussive Notes; Percussion News; Sticks and Mallets; Upstrokes; Drum Instructors Only. *Membership:* Percussive Arts Society; Broadcast Music Inc. *Leisure interest:* Tae Kwon Do. *Address:* Sacramento, CA, USA.

MARVIN Hank (Brian Rankin); b. 28 Oct. 1941, Newcastle-upon-Tyne, England. Musician (Guitar); Songwriter. m. Carole, 2 s. *Career:* Lead Guitarist, Cliff Richard's backing group the Drifters, 1958; Group became the Shadows, 1959-. *Recordings include:* Albums: with the Shadows: The Shadows, No. 1, UK, 1961; Out of the Shadows, No. 1, UK, 1962; The Shadows Greatest Hits, 1963; Dance with the Shadows, 1964; The Sound of the Shadows, 1965; Shadow Music, 1966; Jigsaw, 1967; Established, 1958, 1968; Shades of Rock, 1970; 20 Golden Greats, No. 1, UK, 1977; Thank You Very Much, 20th Anniversary Reunion Concert, Cliff Richard and the Shadows, 1978; String of Hits, No. 1, UK, 1980; Change of Address, 1980; Hits Right Up Your Street, 1981; XXV, 1983; Moonlight Shadows, 1986; Simply Shadows, 1987; Steppin' To the Shadows, 1989; At Their Very Best, 1989; Reflections, 1990; Themes and Dreams, 1991; Shadows in the Night, 1993; Solo albums: Hank Marvin, 1969; Words and Music, 1982; Into the Light, 1992; Heartbeat, 1993; Would You Believe It... Plus, 1994; Hank Plays Cliff, 1996; Hit singles: with the Shadows: Apache, No. 1, UK, 1960; Man of Mystery, 1960; FBI, 1961; Kon-Tiki, No. 1, UK, 1961; The Savage, 1961; Wonderful Land, No. 1, UK, 1962; Guitar Tango, 1962; Dance On, No. 1, UK, 1963; Foot Tapper, No. 1, UK, 1963; Atlantis, 1963; Shindig, 1963; Geronimo, 1963; Stingray, 1965; Don't Make My Baby Blue, 1965; Let Me Be The One, UK's Eurovision Song Contest entry, 1975; Don't Cry For Me Argentina, 1979; Cavatina (Theme From the Deerhunter), 1979; Riders in the Sky, 1980; Living Doll – charity version with Cliff Richard, No. 1, UK, 1986; Contributions to films include: Serious Charge, 1959; The Young Ones, 1961; The Boys, 1962; Summer Holiday, 1963; Wonderful Life, 1964; Finders Keepers, 1966; The Frightened City, 1961; The Deerhunter, 1979; The Third Man, 1981. *Honours include:* CBS Arbiter Award, for Services to British Music, 1977; with the Shadows: NME Record of the Year, 1960; Gold Disc, Apache, 1962; Ivor Novello Awards: Best Musical Score, 1963; Special Award for 25 Years in the Music Business, 1983; Winners, Split Song Festival, Yugoslavia, 1967. *Address:* c/o Polydor Records, 72–80 Black Lion Lane, London W6 9BE, England.

MARWICK Gavin; b. 29 Aug. 1969, Edinburgh, Scotland. Musician (fiddle). *Career:* Youngest of family of traditional/folk musicians; Involved in resurgence of Scottish music and dance, 1980s; Numerous television and radio broadcasts; Festivals and extensive tours mainly with Iron Horse, Europe, and (occasionally) USA, Africa, 1988–; Composer, television soundtracks; Recording artist and teacher; Recording sessions include: Wolfstone; Talitha MacKenzie; Old Blind Dogs; The Electrics; The Humff Family; Other projects: Twin fiddle-led trio (with members of Old Blind Dogs) Burach; Theatre music. *Recordings:* with The Iron Horse: The Iron Horse, 1991; Thro Water Earth and Stone, 1993; Five Hands High, 1994; The Gamekeeper, 1995; Demons and Lovers, 1997; with Jonny Hardie and Davy Cattanach: Up In The Air, 1995; with Burach: The Weird Set, 1995; with the Marwicks: Ceilidh Sets, 1998; with Jonny Hardie: The Blue Lamp, 1999. *Honour:* Belhaven Best New Folk Band, Burach, 1995. *Memberships:* Musicians' Union; PRS; PAMRA. *Current Management:* Peter Stott. *Address:* 11 Harling Dr., Troon, Ayrshire KA10 6NF, Scotland.

MARX Richard Noel; b. 16 Sept. 1963, Chicago, Illinois, USA. Singer; Songwriter; Record Prod. m. Cynthia Rhodes, 8 Jan. 1989, 3 s. *Career:* Backing vocalist with Lionel Richie, 1982; Solo artiste, 1986–; Extensive tours throughout USA, Europe and Asia; Major concerts include: Farm Aid V, 1992; All-star benefit concert, Pediatric AIDS Foundation, 1992; Television and radio appearances world-wide. *Compositions:* Co-writer, What About Me?, recorded by Kenny Rogers; Co-writer, album tracks with Chicago; Philip Bailey; Co-writer, co-producer, with Randy Meisner; David Cole; Fee Waybill; Vixen; Poco; Kevin Cronin. *Recordings:* Hit singles: Don't Mean Nothing, 1987; Should've Known Better, 1987; Endless Summer Nights, 1988; Hold On To The Nights (No. 1, USA) 1988; Satisfied (No. 1, USA), 1989; Right Here Waiting, (No. 1, USA), 1989; Angelia, 1990; Too Late To Say Goodbye, 1990; Children of The Night, 1990; Hard To Believe, 1991; Keep Coming Back, 1991; Hazard, 1992; Take This Heart, 1992; Chains Around My Heart, 1992; Now and Forever (No. 1, USA), 1994; The Way She Loves Me, 1994; Nothing Left Behind Us, 1994; Hazard, 1997; Until I Find You Again, 1997; Keep Coming Back, 1997; As backing singer: with Lionel Richie: All Night Long; You Are; Running With The Night; Solo albums: Richard Marx, 1987; Repeat Offender (No. 1, USA), 1989; Rush Street, 1991; Paid Vacation, 1994; Flesh and Bone, 1997; Greatest Hits, 1997. *Honours:* Grammy Nominations: Best Rock Vocal Performance, Don't Mean Nothing, 1987; Best Pop Vocal Performance,

Right Here Waiting, 1989; Billboard AC Artist of the Year, 1992; First male artist with four Top 3 hits from debut album. *Memberships:* ASCAP; SAG; AFTRA; AFofM. *Leisure interest:* Tennis. *Current Management:* The Left Bank Organization. *Address:* 9255 Sunset Blvd, Los Angeles, CA 90069, USA.

MARZEC Andrzej; b. 3 Sept. 1944, Szczytniki, Poland, Promoter. m. Ewa Olinkiewicz, 31 March 1983, 1 s., 1 d. *Education:* Law, Warsaw University. *Musical Education:* Private lessons on piano. *Career:* Since 1969, Agent for top Polish Rock and Jazz acts: Niemen; Tomasz Stanko; Michal Urbaniak; 1980-, Promoting international acts in Poland including: Kraftwerk; Tangerine Dream; Klaus Schulze; Elton John; Tina Turner; Pat Metheny; Iron Maiden; Depeche Mode; Leonard Cohen; AC/DC; Metallica; David Byrne; Iggy Pop; Bob Dylan; Chris Rea; Jack Bruce; Beastie Boys. *Leisure interests:* Travel; Cycling. *Address:* Andrzej Marzec Concerts (AMC), Mickiewicza 27/69, 01562 Warsaw, Poland.

MASAKOWSKI Steve; b. 2 Sept. 1954, New Orleans, Louisiana, USA. Jazz Musician (guitar). m. Ulrike Sprenger, 22 March 1982, 1 s., 1 d. *Education:* Berklee College of Music, Boston. *Career:* Extensive international travel with Dianne Reeves; Rick Margitza; Astral Project. *Recordings:* Direct AXEcess; What It Was; Friends; Mars; Appears on 28 albums: including Esquire Jazz Collection, 1995; Philip Manuel: Time for Love, 1995; Johnny Adams, Verdict, 1995; Astral Project: Astral Project, 1997; Jazz: Language of New Orleans, 1998. *Honour:* Voted Best Jazz Guitarist in New Orleans, Offbeat Magazine. *Current Management:* Scott Aiges, Arts International Group. *Address:* 516 S Rendon St, New Orleans, LA 70119, USA.

MASEK Jiri; b. 15 June 1970, Prague, Czech Republic. Sound Engineer. m. Zuzana, 22 May 1992, 1 s., 1 d. *Career:* Sound Engineer, 28 records including many well-known Czech pop, folk and jazz groups and singers. *Recordings:* Zalman and Spol, 4 CDs, Czech Republic; Ivan Hajnis, CD, Sweden; Happy to Meet, CD, Ireland; Wild West, CD, Czech Republic; Relief, CD, Czech Republic. *Honours:* Folk and Country Awards, 1997, 1998, 1999; Stereo and Video Award, 1998. *Leisure interest:* Old American cars. *Address:* Good Day Records, Vrsovická 74/699, Prague 10, 10000 Czech Republic.

MASEKELA Hugh Rampolo; b. 4 April 1939, Witbank, Johannesburg, South Africa. Musician (trumpet); Bandleader. m. Miriam Makeba, 1964 (divorced). *Musical Education:* Manhattan School of Music, New York. *Career:* Founder, The Merry Makers, 1955-; Joined African Jazz and Variety package tour, 1958; Joined cast of musical, King Kong, 1959; Formed the Jazz Epistles, 1959; Emigrated to USA, 1960; Formed own quartet, 1961; Signed to Motown Records, 1970; Formed Union of South Africa band, 1970; Played with Fela Kuti; Hedzollah Soundz; Herb Alpert; Major concerts include: Monterey Jazz Festival, 1967; Goin' Home concert, Lesotho, 1980; African Sounds for Mandela concert, Alexandra Palace, 1983; Graceland world tour, with Paul Simon, 1986. *Compositions include:* Music for Broadway show, Sarafina, 1989. *Recordings:* Jazz Epistles, 1959; Trumpet Africa, 1962; The Americanization of Ooga Booga, 1964; The Emancipation of Hugh Maskela, 1966; Promise of a Future, 1967; Coincidence, 1967; Maskela, 1968; Reconstruction, 1970; Home Is Where The Music Is, 1972; Your Mama Told You Not To Worry, 1974; I Am Not Afraid, 1974; The Boys Doin' It, 1975; The African Connection, 1975; Colonial Man, 1976; The Main Event, with Herb Alpert, 1978; Herb Alpert/Hugh Masekela, 1979; Home, 1982; Dollar Bill, 1983; Technobush, 1984; Waiting For The Rain, 1985; Tomorrow, 1987; Up Township, 1989; Back To The Future, 1998; Note of Life, 1999; Hugh Masakela's Latest, 1999; Hugh Masakela Is Alive and Well at the Whisky, 1999; Don't Go Lose It Baby, 1999; Lady, 1999; Colonial Man, 1999. *Current Management:* Sam Nole Management, 230 Park Ave, Suite 1512, New York, NY 10169, USA.

MASHBURN Robin Arvil (Rob); b. 5 April 1942, Andrews, North Carolina, USA. Singer; Songwriter; Musician (guitar, bass). m. Catherine Stears Mashburn, 25 Sept. 1982, 2 s. *Musical Education:* Self-taught. *Career:* Grand Ole Opry: Wolftrap; Bele Chere; Tennessee Homecoming – Museum of Appalachia; University of Chicago; Georgia Mountain Fair. *Recordings:* Albums: The Picker; Another Place Another Time; Brother of Mine; It's Me Again Lord; Misty Mountain Music; The Picker's Best, CD. *Memberships:* BMI; Bluegrass Music Asscn of North Carolina, South Carolina, Georgia. *Leisure interests:* Horseback riding; Fishing; Gardening; Musical instrument repair. *Current Management:* Catherine Mashburn. *Address:* PO Box 1318, Andrews, NC 28901, USA.

MASON Dave; b. 10 May 1947, Worcester, England. Musician (guitar). *Career:* Guitarist, The Hellions; Road manager, Spencer Davis Group; Founder member (with Steve Winwood), Traffic, 1967–68; Solo artist; Played with Eric Clapton's Derek and The Dominoes, 1970; Moved to USA, 1973; Currently recording with Fleetwood Mac. *Recordings:* Albums: with Traffic: Mr Fantasy, 1968; Solo: Alone Together, 1970; Dave Mason and Cass Elliot, 1971; Headkeeper, 1972; Dave Mason Is Alive!, 1973; It's Like You Never Left, 1973; Dave Mason, 1974; Split Coconut, 1975;

Certified Live, 1976; Let It Flow, 1977; Mariposa De Oro, 1978; Old Crest On A New Wave, 1980; Some Assembly Required, 1981; Two Hearts, 1987; Long Lost Friend: The Best of Dave Mason, 1995; Will You Still Love Me?, 1998; Ultimate Collection, 1999; The 40,000 Headmen Tour (live), 1999; with Fleetwood Mac: Time, 1995; Various compilations. *Honours include:* Gold discs.

MASON Kerry; b. 31 March 1968, Dorking, Surrey, England. Singer; Songwriter; Performer. 1 d. *Musical Education:* Singing lessons, Tona De Brett. *Career:* Singer, band Hed; Played all main festivals including: Glastonbury, Phoenix; 12 years' experience; Session singing. *Recordings:* Singles: Reigndance, 1994; Folklaw, 1995. *Membership:* Musicians' Union. *Leisure interests:* Books; Music; Parties; Friends and family. *Current Management:* Timebomb. *Address:* PO Box No. 15, 63 Camden High St, London NW1 7JL, England.

MASON Mila; b. 22 Aug. 1963, Dawson Springs, Kentucky, USA. Country vocalist. *Career:* Toured with country singer mother from an early age; Picture used by Kenner company on the Kenner toy jukebox, aged 6; Auditioned for a Bob Hope special singing I Can Feel The Earth Move, aged 8; Moved to Nashville and met songwriter Harlan Sanders (writer of hits for George Jones); Became demo singer for Sanders and other writers; Married at 19, temporarily abandoning career to raise two children, although marriage failed; Returned to Nashville to begin demo work again; Sang jingles and appeared in several music videos as well as developing own songwriting; Song co-written with Kostas came producer Blake Mevis' attention; Mevis set up showcase at a local club, 1995; This resulted in recording deal with Atlantic Records and release of debut album That's Enough of That, 1997; Appeared on the posthumous Patsy Cline duets album project singing Crazy Dreams, 1999. *Recordings include:* That's Enough of That, 1996; Dark Horse, 1997; Closer To Heaven; Albums include: That's Enough of That, 1996; The Strong One, 1998; Just A Peek, 2001. *Leisure interests:* Poetry; Kickboxing; Running; Playing basketball; Horseback riding; Gardening. *Address:* c/o Country Music Asscn, Nashville, Tennessee, USA.

MASON Nick; b. 27 Jan. 1945, Birmingham, England. Musician (drums). *Career:* Drummer, Pink Floyd, 1965–; Performances include: Rome International Pop Festival, 1968; Hyde Park, London, 1968; Bath Festival, 1970; Montreux Festival, 1971; Knebworth Festival, 1975; Films: Pink Floyd Live At Pompeii, 1972; The Wall, 1982; Autobiographical film, Life Could Be A Dream, 1985. *Recordings:* Albums: Pipers At The Gates of Dawn, 1967; A Saucerful of Secrets, 1968; More (film soundtrack), 1969; Ummagumma, 1969; Atom Heart Mother (No. 1, UK), 1970; Relics, 1971; Meddle, 1971; Obscured By Clouds, 1972; The Dark Side of The Moon (No. 1, USA), 1972; Wish You Were Here (No. 1, UK and USA), 1975; Animals, 1976; The Wall, 1979; The Final Cut, 1983; A Momentary Lapse of Reason, 1987; The Delicate Sound of Thunder, 1988; Shine On, 1992; The Division Bell, 1994; Pulse, 1995; Solo albums: Nick Mason's Ficticious Sport, 1981; Profiles, 1985; Producer, Music For Pleasure, The Damned, 1977. *Honours include:* Outstanding Contribution To British Music, 1992. *Current Management:* Steve O'Rouke, EMKA Productions Ltd, 43 Portland Rd, London W11 4LJ, England.

MASONDO David; b. KwaZulu Natal, South Africa. Vocalist; Musician (drums). *Career:* Started in church choir; Entertained guests at weddings and social functions; Joined The Groovy Boys, 1970; Drummer with The Young Brothers, 1973; Changed name to Soul Brothers after Moses Ngwenya joined the band, 1976; Various international tours; Recorded over 30 albums. *Recordings:* Albums include: Umshoza Wami, 1974; Isiphiwo, 1982; Xola, 1987; Jive Explosion, 1988; Impimpi, 1989; Isighebhezana, 1999; Induk' Enhle, 2001. *Honours:* FNB South African Music Award, Best Mbaqanga Performance; 15 gold discs, 5 platinum discs, several multiplatinum discs. *Address:* c/o Gallo, PO Box 2897, Parklands 2121, South Africa. *Internet:* www.gallo.co.za.

MASUKA Dorothy, (Aunty Dot); b. 1937, Bulawayo, Rhodesia. Vocalist; Songwriter. *Musical Education:* Self-taught. *Career:* Started performing with the African Jazz and Variety Show, a travelling road show with Miriam Makeba and Hugh Masekela, aged 12; Started recording, 1951; Exiled from South Africa, 1960; Worked as a singer throughout Europe and Africa; Returned to Zimbabwe, 1980; Performed several shows with The Golden Rhythm Crooners in Harare, 1989; Contributed to John Barry's soundtrack for Cry the Beloved Country, 1995. *Recordings:* Albums include: Hamba Notsokolo, Ingalo, 1988; Women of Africa Vol. 1, 1989; Pata Pata, 1990; Magumede, Mzilikazi, 2001. *Honours:* Pan-African Cultural Festival in Algiers, award winner, 1969.

MATHES David Wayne; b. 23 April 1933, Steubenville, Ohio, USA. Music Industry Consultant; Record Prod.; Musician (Guitar). m. (1) Pauline Sexton, 25 Sept. 1955, 1 s., 1 d., (2) DeAnna S Newman Bass, 8 Sept. 1978, 1 step-d. *Education:* Electronics I and II, VoTech, Orlando, Florida; Florida Institute of Technology, Orlando; Advanced Electronics, Tennessee State University, Nashville;. *Musical Education:* Self-taught guitar, bass, steel, mandolin; Musicianship correspondence course, Rutgers University, New Jersey; Advanced Songwriting Techniques, University of Tennessee. *Career:* On stage, country appearances with Warner Mack, Tommy Cash, Jim Ed Brown, The Rudy Sisters, Dottie West; Gospel stage appearances with the Hays Family, The Sextons, Tennessee Valley Quartet, The Frost Brothers, Jake Hess and the Imperials, The Swanee River Boys; TV appearances on Nashville Gospel, Maranatha, Sing Out America; The Music Machine; Radio appearances on Southern Gospel Hour, I Am Country Music; Sound Engineer on programmes including Johnny Cash Show, Jackie DeShannon, Ballad of the West and numerous commercials. *Compositions include:* My Love For You; Dreamers; Just A Simple Love Song; Who Can Mend A Broken Heart; Who Will Sing One Song For Me. *Recordings include:* Sounds of the Saved Soul, instrumental album; Produced: Man of the Street, Drusky; Shenandoah, The Four Guys; Just a Simple Love Song, DeAnna; Peg O My Heart, the Sgro Brothers; Golden Slippers, Smokehouse Band. *Publications:* Institute of Recording Arts and Sciences Home Study Course, 1987; Columns for Family Travel and Illinois Country Music Association, 1989; Columns for Masterpiece, 1997–98. *Honours:* Hon. Order of Kentucky Cols, 1975; Tennessee Ambassador, 1975; Hon. Lieut Col Aide de Camp, Alabama, 1986; Hon. Deputy Sheriff, Davidson County, Tennessee, 1975. *Memberships:* Audio Engineering Society; Broadcast Music Inc; Country Music Asscn; National Entertainment Journalists' Asscn; American Federation of Musicians. *Leisure interests:* Bible reading; Golf; Fishing; Gold prospecting. *Current Management:* International Promotions Ltd.

MATHESON Karen Elizabeth; b. 11 Feb. 1963, Oban, Argyll and Bute, Scotland. Vocalist. *Musical Education:* Inherited love of singing from parents; Learnt many songs from grandmother (a MacNeil from the island of Barra). *Career:* Founder member: Capercaillie; Group, along with original material, specialise in fusing traditional Gaelic songs with contemporary arrangements; Had first UK top 40 single in Gaelic, Coisich A Ruin (from A Prince Among Islands EP), 1992; Also worked on solo projects and appeared on L'Heritage de Celts, a French album with Donal Lunny and Dan Ar Braz; Project led to Matheson performing a Breton song, Que Naissant Les Enfants, with Dar An Braz and Elaine Morgan for France's entry in Eurovision Song Contest, 1996; Appeared in Rob Roy film singing an unaccompanied rendition of a Gaelic Lament; Performed on TV series Transatlantic Sessions with many well-known artists including: Emmylou Harris; The MacGarrigle Sisters; Mary Black; Collaborations with James Grant on solo albums and TV appearances. *Recordings:* Albums: with Capercaillie: Cascade, 1984; Crosswinds, 1987; Sidewaulk, 1989; Delirium, 1991; Get Out, 1992; The Blood Is Strong, Secret People, 1993; Capercaillie, 1995; To The Moon, 1996; Beautiful Wasteland, 1997; Glenfinnan – Songs of The '45 (recorded 1995), 1998; Nàdurra, 2000; group feature on: Rob Roy OST, 1995; features solo on: L'Heritage De Celts, 1994; Finisterres, Dan Ar Braz, 1997; Zenith, Dan Ar Braz, 1998; Identities, Idir, 1999; Fused, Michael McGoldrick, 2000; Dawn of a New Century, Secret Garden, 1999; On The West Side, Donnie Munroe, 2000; Searchlight, Runrig, 2000; Sawdust In My Veins, James Grant, 2000; My Thrawn Glory, James Grant, 2000; Tacsi (TV series), 2000; Dreamcatcher, Secret Garden, 2001; solo: The Dreaming Sea, 1996; Time To Fall, 2002.

MATHEWS Norman; b. 12 Sept. 1952, Rockford, Illinois, USA. Composer. *Education:* BA Hunter College, New York; MA, New York University. *Career:* Composer for Musical Theatre, Jazz, Concert Music. *Compositions:* Songs of a Poet; You Might As Well Live; Triumph of Night. *Recordings:* Songs of a Poet. *Honours:* ASCAP Standard Award, 1998, 1999. *Memberships:* ASCAP; Americian Music Center; Dramatists Guild. *Leisure interest:* Cooking. *Address:* 667 W 161st St, Apt 3H, New York, NY 10032, USA.

MATHIESEN Claus; b. 13 July 1957, Copenhagen, Denmark. Musician (clarinet, recorder). 1 s. *Musical Education:* Classical education, Copenhagen; Turkish Art Music, Istanbul Conservatory. *Career:* Musician with Ildfuglen, 1979–83; Kefir, 1983–86; Fuat Saka Band, 1986–; Wild East, 1989–93; Oriental Mood, 1993–; Chochek Brothers, 1994–; All these bands merging Western and Balkan/Middle Eastern music. *Recordings:* with Fuat Saka Band: Nebengleis, 1989; Askaroz, 1991; Sen, 1994; with Anatolia: Anatolia, 1991; with Oriental Mood: Travels, 1994; Oriental Moods, 1996; Oriental Garden, 1998; with Nazê Botan: Akh Kurdistan, 1996; Kurdistan – The Forgotten World, 1998; with Chochek Brothers: Let's Chochek!, 1998. *Publications:* Contributor, Danish National Encyclopedia. *Membership:* DJBFA. *Address:* Mariendalsvej 32C, 2000 F, Denmark.

MATHIESON Greg; b. 25 Feb. 1950, Los Angeles, California, USA. Arranger; Composer; Prod.; Musician (keyboards). m. Barbara Price, 9 July 1983, 1 s. *Career:* Tours: Al Jarreau; Larry Carlton; Abraham Laboriel. *Recordings:* Baked Potato Super Live; For My Friends; with Al Jarreau: All Fly Home; This Time; Trouble In Paradise; with Bill Champlin: Burn Down The Night; Through It All; with Laura Branigan: Gloria; with Toni Basil: Mickey; with Sheena Easton: Telefone; Strut; Almost Over You; with Donna Summer: MacArthur Park; Heaven Knows; Live and More; with

Barbra Streisand: Enough Is Enough; Songbird; Wet; with Abraham Laboriel: Dear Friends; Guidem; Frontline; Koinonia; with Manhattan Transfer: Extensions; Mecca For Moderns; Bodies and Souls; with Lee Ritenour: Banded Together; Earth Run; Collection; with Deniece Williams: When Love Comes; Hot On The Trail; Special Love; From The Beginning; with Rita Coolidge: Ann; with Rickie Lee Jones: Flying Cowboys; with Jimmy Cliff: Peace; with Steven Bishop: Bowling In Paris; with Umberto Tozzi: Gloria; Notte Rosa; Umberto Tozzi – Live; Le Une Cauzui; Equivacando; with David Hasselhoff: Crazy For You; with Helen Baylor: Live; with Tina Turner: Simply the Best; Keyboard player for: Larry Carlton; Ringo Starr; Joe Cocker; David Foster; Tom Jones; Billy Idol; Julio Iglesias; Nils Lofgren; Simple Minds; Film scores: American Flyer; Unfaithfully Yours; Midnight Express. *Honour:* One of select few producers to have top 2 singles in same week. *Current Management:* Wigwam. *Address:* 3724 Buena Park Dr., Studio City, CA 91604, USA.

MATHIESON Ken; b. 30 June 1942, Paisley, Scotland. Musician (drums, zither); Arranger; Composer. m. with 2 s., 1 d. *Musical Education:* Self-taught. *Career:* Freelance musician; 15 year residency in Black Bull Jazz Club, Milngavie, Glasgow; Working and touring with leading UK and US jazz musicians including: George Chisholm; Tommy Whittle; John McLevy; Jack Emblow; Sonny Stitt; Johnny Griffin; Tal Farlow; Played with and wrote for Fat Sam's Band (Edinburgh-based jazz group touring world-wide), 1985–96; Leader, Picante (5 piece Bop and Latin band); Jazz Écosse All-Stars (6-piece Dixieland Band featuring top Scottish players and vocalist Fionna Duncan); Jazz Celebrities (7 piece mainstream band specialising in the music of Buck Clayton and Buddy Tate); Groovebusters (8/9 piece 'wee big-band' covering Jelly Roll Morton to Benny Golson); Latest venture a trio plus vocalist Lynn O'Neill dedicated to Brazilian music of all kinds; Organized first Glasgow International Jazz Festival, 1985; Frequent broadcaster on Jazz and World Music. *Recordings:* All Fat Sam's records. *Leisure interests:* Writing music, hillwalking, languages. *Address:* 20 Kylepark Cres., Uddington, Glasgow, Scotland.

MATHIEU Jean F; b. 11 Dec. 1948, Geneva, Switzerland. Composer; Musician (Guitar, Vocals, Drums, Bass). *Career:* Musicals, Bricelet Pradise; La Dame Aux Begonins; Films, Mort In Dimanche De Plvie; Locomemory; Show, Viva La Musica; Opera, Notes Par In Opera; Theatre, Flibuste. *Compositions:* Voyage Dans In Coeur Lorulant; Herakles Ducks Again. *Recordings:* Inguitarissable; Flibuste; Notes Par Un Opera. *Honours:* Journey Through A Burning Heart, Keyboards Contest; CRPLF Contest. *Leisure interests:* Polishing My Internet Page. *Current Management:* Jay Fm Productions. *Address:* 1205 Geneva, Switzerland.

MATHIEU Mirielle; b. 24 July 1946, Avignon, France. Singer. *Career:* Television appearances include: Ed Sullivan TV Show; Andy Williams TV Show; International concerts include: Top Star Festival, 1972. *Recordings:* Albums: Mirielle Mathieu, 1968; You and I, with Paul Anka, 1979; Les Contes De Cri-Cri, 1985; Recontres De Femme, 1988; Greatest Hits, Vol. 1, 1989; Chante Piaf, 1994; L'American, 1995; Les Plus Grands Succes, Vols 1–3, 1995; Vous Lui Direz, 1995; In Meinem Traum, 1996; Rendezvous, 1997; Sings Ennio Morricone, 1999; Embrujo, 1999; Hit singles include: Mon Credo; C'Est Ton Nom; Qu'Elle Est Belle; Funambule; Les Bicyclettes De Belsize.

MATHIS Johnny (John Royce); b. 30 Sept. 1935, San Francisco, California, USA. *Education:* San Francisco State College. *Career:* Recording artist, 1964–; Tours world-wide. *Recordings include:* Singles: Wonderful! Wonderful!; Chances Are (No. 1, USA), 1957; Someone; The Twelfth of Never; It's Not For Me To Say; A Certain Smile; Misty; Winter Wonderland; There Goes My Heart; My Love For You; My One and Only Love; Let Me Love You; I'm Stone In Love With You; When A Child Is Born (No. 1, UK), 1976; Too Much, Too Little, Too Late, duet with Deniece Williams, (No. 1, USA), 1978; Other duets with Gladys Knight; Natalie Cole; Dionne Warwick; Stephanie Lawrence; Barbara Dickson; Nana Mouskouri; Albums: Johnny Mathis, 1956; Wonderful!, Wonderful!, 1957; Warm, 1957; Good Night, Dear Lord, 1958; Swing Softly, 1958; Open Fire, Two Guitars, 1959; Heavenly, 1959; Faithfully, 1960; Ride On A Rainbow, 1960; Johnny's Mood, 1960; I'll Buy You A Star, 1961; Portrait of Johnny, 1961; Live It Up, 1962; Rapture, 1962; Johnny, 1963; Romantically, 1963; I'll Search My Heart, 1964; Olé, 1965; Tender Is The Night, 1965; The Wonderful World of Make Believe, 1965; This Is Love, 1966; The Shadow of Your Smile, 1966; The Sweetheart Tree, 1967; Up, Up and Away, 1967; Johnny Mathis Sings, 1967; Love Is Blue, 1968; Those Were The Days, 1968; People, 1969; The Impossible Dream, 1969; Raindrops Keep Fallin' On My Head, 1970; The Long and Winding Road, 1970; Close To You, 1970; Love Story, 1970; You've Got A Friend, 1971; In Person, 1972; The First Time Ever I Saw Your Face, 1972; Make It Easy On Yourself, 1972; Me and Mrs Jones, 1973; Killing Me Softly With Her Song, 1973; I'm Coming Home, 1973; Song Sung Blue, 1974; The Heart of a Woman, 1974; Feelings, 1975; I Only Have Eyes For You, 1976; Sweet Surrender, 1977; When A Child Is Born, 1978; You Light Up My Life, 1978; Mathis Magic, 1979; Different Kinda Different, 1980; Friends In Love, 1982; A Special Part of Me, 1984; Right From The Heart, 1985; In the Still of The Night, 1989; How Do You

Keep The Music Playing?, 1993; Celebration: Anniversary Album, 1995; All About Love, 1996; Because You Loved Me: Songs of Diane Warren, 1998; Romeo and Juliet, 1999; Mathis Magic, 1999; In the Still of the Night, 1999; Numerous Greatest Hits, Musical and Christmas compilations. *Current Management:* Rojon Production Inc, 3500 W Olive, Suite 750, Burbank, CA 91505, USA.

MATOLU-DODE Papy-Tex; b. 28 June 1952, Kinshasa, Zaire. Singer. m. Ekofo-Wando, 21 Jan. 1989, 3 s., 8 d. *Education:* Itaga College, Kinshasa. *Career:* Singer, African Choc, 1968; Singer, African Choc (band name changed to Empire Bakuba), 1979–; Player, Etodle Filante, football team. *Compositions:* Sanda; Karibu; Sanco Yamawa; Welcome in Africa; Music Clarification. *Recordings:* Bakuba Show; Full Option; Surprise; Livre D'Or; La Belle Etoire. *Publications:* Sanda, 1973; Karibu, 1985; Bakuba Show, 1988; Full Option, 1997. *Honours:* Diplome of Performance for Development Initiative, 1995; Apid Certificate of Artistic Merit, 1987; Acknowledgement of Merit, Francophone Counsel of Songs, 1993. *Memberships:* SONECA; SACEM; SABAM; SUIZA; BURIDA. *Leisure interests:* Cinema; Football; Wrestling. *Address:* 69 rue Luapula, Commune de Kinghasa, RDC.

MATTACKS David; b. 13 March 1948, London, England. Musician (drums). m. Caron Woods, 31 Dec. 1993. *Musical Education:* Self-taught. *Career:* Apprentice piano tuner; Mecca Big Band, 3 years; Played small jazz groups; Joined Fairport Convention, 1969; 7 albums; Tours of: UK; USA; Europe; Antipodes; Japan; Freelance musician, 1974–; Combines freelance work with reformed Fairport Convention, mid 1980s–; International tours include: Europe; USA; Annual Oxfordshire Cropredy Festival; Drums and keyboards in concerts and recordings; Performed with artists including: Jethro Tull; Chris Rea; Joan Armatrading; Sandy Denny; Micky Jupp; Andy Fairweather-Low; Georgie Fame; Nick Heyward; Ashley Hutchings; Ralph McTell; The McGarrigles; The Swingles; Tours in UK, Europe, USA, with Richard Thompson Band, 1994–95; Recorded, played with: Liane Carroll; Everything But The Girl; Week's residency, Ronnie Scott's Club, London, with Liane Carroll Trio. *Compositions:* Television and film scores include: Death Wish 2; Green Ice; Give My Regards To Broadstreet; Band of Gold (ITV); Love Hurts (Barbara Dickson); Time Bandits; McVicar; Lisztomania; Hussey; Hearts of Fire; Shoestring; Fox; Leo Sayer television series; Your Cheatin' Heart. *Recordings include:* Fairport Convention: Jewel In The Crown, 1995; Also with artists including: Joan Armatrading; Barbara Dickson; Elton John; Paul McCartney; Chris Rea; The Proclaimers; Jimmy Page; Alison Moyet; XTC; Beverley Craven; Richard Thompson; Gary Brooker; Elkie Brooks; John Gorka; Cat Stevens; Roger Daltrey; Recent recordings include: with Fairport Convention: Who Knows Where Time Goes?, 1997; with Richard Thompson: Celtschmerz, 1998; with Steve Ashley: Stroll on Revisited, 1999; with Steeleye Span: Horkstow Grange, 1999; with Paul McCartney: Run Devil Run, 1999.

MATTEA Kathy; b. 21 June 1959, Cross Lane, West Virginia, USA. Country Singer; Musician (guitar). m. Jon Vezner. *Education:* University. *Career:* Member, Bluegrass group Pennsboro; Tour guide, Country Music Hall of Fame, Nashville; Singer for demos and commercials; Backing singer, Bobby Goldsboro's roadshow, 1982; Solo recording artiste, mid-80s. *Recordings:* Singles: Street Talk; Love At The Five and Dime; Goin' Gone; 18 Wheels and A Dozen Roses; Life As We Knew It; Come From The Heart; Burnin' Old Memories; Where've You Been; Ready For The Storm; Among the Missing; Albums: Kathy Mattea, 1984; From My Heart, 1985; Walk The Way The Wind Blows, 1986; Untasted Honey, 1987; Willow In The Wind, 1989; Time Passes By, 1991; Lonesome Standard Time, 1992; Good News Radio Special, 1994; Only Everything, 1995; Walking Away A Winner, 1995; Ready For The Storm – Favourite Cuts, 1995; Love Travels, 1997. *Honours:* Best Country Song of Year, Where've You Been. *Current Management:* Titley and Associates, 706 18th Ave S, Nashville, TN 37203, USA.

MATTHEWS Cerys; b. 11 April 1969, Cardiff, Wales. Singer. *Career:* Member of Catatonia; First release on Welsh Indie label Crai; Signed by Blanco y Negro. *Recordings:* Singles: Bleed/Do You Believe in Me, 1996; Mulder and Scully, 1998; Ballad of Tom Jones, with Space, 1998; Strange Glue, 1998; Road Rage; Albums: Way Beyond Blue, 1996; The Sublime Magic of Catatonia, 1996; International Velvet, 1998; Equally Cursed and Blessed, 1999.

MATTHEWS Dave (David John); b. 9 Jan. 1967, Johannesburg, South Africa. Vocalist; Musician (guitar); Songwriter. *Career:* Owner of ATO Records label; Joined band TR3; Encouraged by local studio owner Ross Hoffman to record solo, 1990; Employed musicians to first perform as The Dave Matthews Band, 1991; Rapid growth of fanbase through touring schedules; First album released on group's own Bama Rags label certified gold by RIAA; First national US tour in support of RCA debut album, 1994; Many world-wide concerts and festival appearances since including 2001 album tour; Group permits fans to tape-record shows for personal use; I Did It single officially released through Napster, 2001; Occasionally tours with

Reynolds as acoustic duo. *Recordings:* Albums: Remember Two Things (live), 1993; Under The Table and Dreaming, 1994; Crash, 1996; Live At Red Rocks 8–15–95, 1997; Before These Crowded Streets, 1998; Live At Luther College '96 (Dave Matthews and Tim Reynolds), 1999; Everyday, Live In Chicago 12–19–98, 2001; Singles: Recently (EP), 1994; What Would You Say, Jimi Thing, Ants Marching, 1995; So Much To Say, Too Much, 1996; Don't Drink The Water, 1997; Satellite, Crash Into Me, Crush, 1998; I Did It, The Space Between, Everyday, 2001. *Honours:* Grammy Awards: Best Rock Performance By A Duo Or Group With Vocal, 1997; US VH-1 Awards: Favourite Group; Must Have Album; Song of The Year, 2001; Top-grossing touring band in USA, 2000. *Address:* c/o Red Light Communications, 3305 Lobban Pl., Charlottesville, VA 22903, USA. *E-mail:* info@rlc.net. *Internet:* www.dmband.com.

MATTHEWS Donna Lorraine; b. 2 Dec. 1971, Newport, England. Musician; Songwriter. *Career:* Member of Elastica, 1992–99; Toured extensively world-wide including Reading Festival, 1994, Glastonbury, 1995, Big Day Out in Australia, 1996; Numerous television appearances including Top of The Pops; Currently working on solo projects. *Honours:* Nomination for Brit Award, 1996; NME Readers Award For Best New Band, 1994. *Current Management:* CMO Management International Ltd, Unit 32, Ransomes Dock, 35–37 Parkgate Rd, London SW11 4NP, England.

MATTHEWS Iain; b. 16 June 1946, England. Songwriter; Singer. m. Veronique, 26 Feb. 1990, 1 s., 1 d. *Career:* Bands: The Pyramid, 1965; Fairport Convention; Matthews Southern Comfort; Solo, also Plainsong, 1972; Left performing for A & R: Island Records; Windham Hill, early 1980s; Returned to performance, after success at annual Fairport Convention, late 1980s; Moved to Austin, Texas, USA; Reformed Plainsong; Started Hamilton Pool, Singing, songwriting collective, Austin Texas; Toured with Nanci Griffiths, Other Voices Too, CD, 1998. *Recordings:* with Fairport Convention: Fairport Convention, 1968; What We Did On Our Holiday, 1968; Unhalfbricking, 1968; Matthews Southern Comfort: Matthews Southern Comfort, 1969; Second Spring, 1970; Later That Same Year, 1970; Best of Matthews Southern Comfort, 1992; Solo: If You Saw Through My Eyes, 1970; Tigers Will Survive, 1971; Journeys From Gospel Oak, 1972; Valley Hi, 1973; Some Days You Eat The Bear, 1974; Go For Broke, 1976; Hit and Run, 1977; Stealin' Home, 1978; Siamese Friends, 1979; Discreet Repeat, 1980; Spot of Interference, 1980; Shook, 1983; Walking A Changing Line (The Songs of Jules Shear), 1988; Pure and Crooked, 1990; Nights In Manhattan, 1991; Orphans and Outcasts, 1991; Live Alone, 1993; Intimate Wash, 1993; The Soul of Many Places, 1993; Skeleton Keys, 1993; Best of Matthews Southern Comfort, 1997; Excerpts From Swine Lake, Iain Matthews, 1999; Orphans and Outcasts Vol. 3, 1999; Plainsong: In Search of Amelia Earhart, 1972; And That's That, 1992; Plainsong On The Air, 1992; Dark Side of The Room, 1992; Hi Fi: Demonstration Record, 1981; Moods For Mallards, 1982; The Dark Ride, 1994; Camouflage, 1995; God Looked Down, 1996; Nights in Manhattan, 1997; Voices Electric, 1994; Sister Flute, 1996; New Place Now, 1999. *Publication:* Its About Time (pictorial biography). *Membership:* NARAS. *Current Management:* Frank van den Meijden, Visserslaan 8, 4201-ZJ Copinchem, Netherlands. *Address:* PO Box 676, Buda, TX 78610, USA.

MATTHEWS Jamie (James Lindsay); b. 15 May 1951, London, England. Musician (harmonicas, ukulele, percussion, jaws harp, whistle); Vocalist. *Musical Education:* Church and school choirs; Mainly self-taught. *Career:* Extensive tours, Far East, late 1960's; Europe and North America, 1980's; Major US tour with Daily Planet, including Telluride Festival, Colorado, 1995, 1996. *Recordings:* Parlour Games, John B Spencer; Sunday Best, John B Spencer; A Month of Sundays, double album, Johnny G; Clark's Secret, Daily Planet; The Big Scoop, Daily Planet. *Honours:* Guinness All-Ireland Busking Champion as Gentleman Jamie, 1986; with Daily Planet, awarded BBMA Best Progressive Bluegrass Band, 1995. *Membership:* Musicians' Union. *Leisure interests:* Music; Crosswords. *Current Management:* Spadger Productions, Orchard House, Hartpury, Gloucester GL19 3BG, England. *Address:* 5 Cleveland Row, Bathwick, Bath BA2 6QR, England.

MATTHEWS Julie; b. 2 April 1963, Sheffield, South Yorkshire, England. Singer; Songwriter; Musician (guitar, piano). *Career:* Seven years, piano bars throughout Europe, Middle East; Member, Albion Band, 1991–92, 1994–95; Female duo with Pat Shaw; Female duo with Chris While; Toured extensively throughout Europe, Canada; Many radio appearances, sessions; Cambridge, Edmonton festivals, 1995. *Compositions include:* Song: Thorn Upon The Rose, recorded by Mary Black. *Recordings:* with Pat Shaw: Lies and Alibis; Compilation: Intuition; with Albion Band: Captured; Albion Heart; Solo album: Such Is Life, 1995; with Chris While: Blue Moon On The Rise (mini-album); with Helen Watson: Somersault, 1998. *Honours:* Nominated Rising Star, British Country Music Awards, 1995. *Memberships:* PRS; MCPS; Musicians' Union. *Leisure interests:* Cycling; Reading; Films. *Current Management:* Blue Moon Music; Circuit Music. *Address:* 130 Central Ave, Southport, Merseyside PR8 3ED, England.

MATTHEWS Roderick Newton; b. 18 May 1956, London, England. Composer; Musician (guitar); Record Prod. m. Pamela Margaret Johnson, 14 Nov. 1992, 1 d. *Education:* Balliol College, Oxford. *Musical Education:* Grade 1 piano. *Career:* Produced records for small labels, including Troggs album, 1979–84; Produced for majors, including Roland Rat, Musical Youth, chart entries in Germany, Norway, 1984–86; Remixes include Manfred Mann; Session musician, 1987–92; Writing music for television (commercials, signatures, incidentals) 1988–; MD for Lenny Henry, 1989–91; Also appeared on soundtracks: French and Saunders; Absolutely Fabulous; Alexei Sayle Shows; Lenny Henry; Rory Bremner; Harry Enfield; Girl Friday; Bad News; Blue Peter; Tracy Ullman; Newman and Baddiel; Fry and Laurie. *Compositions:* Written for 7 series of London's Burning; Newshounds (Screen Two), 1990; The Winston Pom; Funseekers (Comic Strip); Coffee Blues for Lenny Henry (in Lenny Live and Unleashed); Alexai Sayle: Shut Up; The Winjin Pom; Mary Whitehouse Experience, second series; Television commercials for Duracell; Burger King; Twix. *Recordings:* Played or sung on recordings including: Monkey, George Michael; Don't Make Me Wait, Bomb The Bass; Cross My Heart, Patsy Kensit and Eighth Wonder; ABC; Sinitta; Charles Aznavour; Rick Astley; Pepsi and Shirlee; England Football Squad; Comic Relief; John Parr, Running the Endless Mile; George Michael, Faith; Rick Astley, Hold Me in Your Arms. *Memberships:* PRS; MCPS. *Leisure interests:* Eating and drinking.

MATTHEWS Sarah; b. 22 June 1966, London, England. Singer. *Musical Education:* Self-taught. *Career:* Member, Rub Ultra; Radio 1 session; Appearance on Naked City, C4; Festivals: Glastonbury; Phoenix, 1994; 4 British tours; Played NME Brats concert; XFM concert broadcast line. *Recordings:* EPs: Combatstrength Soap, 1994; Korporate Finger Tactic, 1994; Album: Liquid Boots and Boiled Sweets, 1995. *Memberships:* Musicians' Union; PRS. *Leisure interests:* Hair renovation; Music; Concerts. *Current Management:* Nick Moore, Splash Management. *Address:* The Splash Club, 328 Gray's Inn Rd, Kings Cross, London W10, England.

MAULDIN Jermaine Dupri; b. 23 Sept. 1972, Ashville, South Carolina, USA. Prod.; Songwriter; Record Co Pres. *Recordings:* Warm It Up; Jump; Kris Kross; Understanding; Xscape: Just Kicking It; Funkdafied; Da Brat; Xscape: Feels So Good; Jermaine Dupri Presents Life in 1472, 1998; Jermaine Dupri Presents: 12 Soulful Nights; Singles include: Money Ain't a Thang, 1998; Sweetheart, 1998; Going Home with Me, 1998; Party Continues, 1998; As Producer: Da Brat: Anuthatantrum, 1996; Mase: Harlem World, 1997; Aretha Franklin: Rose is Still a Rose, 1998; TLC: Fanmail, 1999; Men in Black, 1999. *Honours:* ASCAP: Best Song of Year, 1993. *Current Management:* Michael Mauldin. *Address:* 2849 Piedmont Rd, Atlanta, GA 30305, USA.

MAULIS Zbynek; b. 24 April 1975, Kladno, Czech Republic. Musician (Bass Guitar). *Education:* Technical University, Prague, 2 years. *Career:* The Teplo, Rock and Roll group, 1992–; Brutus, Rock and Roll group, 1996–. *Composition:* Want You Go With Me, Brutus, 1996. *Recording:* Best of Brutus, 1997. *Leisure interests:* Making electrical musical instruments. *Address:* Na'm 1 Opletala 10, Kladno 4, 27204 Czech Republic.

MAUNICK Jean-Paul, (Bluey); b. 1957, Mauritius. Prod.; Musician (guitar); Songwriter. *Career:* Emigrated to London, 1967; Member: Light of The World, late '70s; Formed: Incognito with Paul 'Tubbs' Williams, 1979. *Recordings:* Albums: with Incognito: Jazz Funk, 1981; Inside Life, 1991; Tribes Vibes and Scribes, 1992; Positivity, 1993; 100° and Rising, 1995; Beneath The Surface, 1996; Blue Moods, 1997; No Time Like The Future, 1999; Life Stranger Than Fiction, 2001; Singles: Parisienne Girl, 1980; Incognito, 1981; North London Boy, 1982; Inside Life, Always There (featuring Jocelyn Brown), Crazy For You (featuring Chyna), 1991; Don't You Worry About A Thing, Change, 1992; Still A Friend of Mine, Givin' It Up, 1993; Pieces of a Dream, 1994; Everyday, I Hear Your Name, 1995; Jump To My Love, Out of The Storm, 1996; Nights Over Egypt, 1999. *Honours:* MOBO Award, Best Jazz Act, 2001. *Membership:* PRS; AURA. *Current Management:* Ricochet, 5 Old Garden House, The Lantern Bridge Lane, London, SW11 3AD, England. *Address:* c/o Talkin' Loud, Chancellor's House, 72 Chancellor's Rd, London W6 9QB, England.

MAURICE (Glynn) Mike; b. 12 Feb. 1937, London, England. Musician (piano, guitar). Record Co Exec.; Artist Man.; Promoter. 1 s., 1 d. *Career:* Artist Manager, Purple Dreams; Managing Director, M & M Records; Promoter, Merlin's Cave Nite Club, first Western club, London; Club 21, London; Hangar Lane music venue, London; Originator, Richmont Bingo clubs, Reading; Lilly Road Bingo clubs, London; Auctioneer, Petticoat Lane, 1954–62; Stage act, mind reading and telepathy, 1957–68; Toured Europe, USA, Australia, Malaysia, Japan and Israel; Lecturer and demonstrator, clairvoyance, the paranormal and healing, Arthur Findlay College, Stanstead, London, 1968–82; Proprietor, M & M Recording Studios; M & M Video Studio. *Recordings:* released through M & M Recordings; M & M Records; M & M Video Agency. *Publications:* Original publisher, free newspapers, 1969; Local Express; Spiritualist News, Vision Journals; Life (biography) due for publication 1997. *Leisure interests:* Football; Dancing; Clubbing. *Current Management:* M & M Management. *Address:* 79 Greenview Dr., Northampton NN2 7LE, England.

MAVIAN Robert A, (Gibson Case); b. 29 Oct. 1936, New York City, USA. Bluegrass Musician; Performer; Songwriter. m. Barbara Lou Pearson, 18 Aug. 1962, 1 s., 1 d. *Education:* Doctorate Degree, Veterinary Medicine and Surgery. *Career:* Sideman performer with Peter Rowan; John Herald; Hazel Dickens; The Sykes Boys; Member, duo, The Case Brothers – Martin and Gibson; Leader, founder of the Horse Country Bluegrass Band; Performed, World Original WWVA Jamboree, Wheeling West Virginia; WSM Grand Ole Opry, Ryman Auditorium, Nashville, Tennessee; Winnipeg Folk Festival, Canada; Brandy Wine Mountain Music Convention Woodstown, New Jersey; Thomas Point Bluegrass Festival, Brunswick, Maine; Waterloo Bluegrass Festival, Stanhope, New Jersey; Berkshire Mt, Bluegrass Festival, Hillsdale, New York; WKCR-NYC; WFUV-NYC; WFDM-NJ; WHUS-Storrs, CT; WOWL-TV, Florence, Alabama. *Recordings:* As The Case Brothers – Martin and Gibson, Old Time Duets With Guitar and Mandolin; The Radio Album; Also: Collectors Edition, The Berkshire Mt Bluegrass Festival; Kenneth Brewer and His Melody Kings and Queens; The Cumberland Mountain Boys, single 78 RPM's. *Memberships:* International Bluegrass Music Asscn; American Veterinary Medical Asscn; American Animal Hospital Asscn; New York State Veterinary Medical Society. *Leisure interests:* Antique cars; Horses; Fine arts and crafts. *Address:* 168 Pines Bridge Rd, Ossining, NY 10562, USA.

MAX Buddy, (Boris Max Pastuch); Recording Artist; DJ. *Career:* America's Singing Flea Market Cowboy; Manager, Singing Flea Market Cowboy, Lecanto, Florida; Kingwood Play Boys Band, performed all over New Jersey, Pennsylvania, New York; Buddy Max Radio Show, WKia, WLBE, WKFL, WINV 1560 AM, AM Radio, Florida; TV: The Buddy Max Show; Country Western Bluegrass Show, 1969–. *Recordings include:* Buddy Max, 1980; The Great Nashville Star, 1984; The Story of Freda and Bud; Cowboy Junction Stars, 1985; Tribute to Challenger's Crew of 7, 1986; With Our Friends At Cowboy Junction, 1989; Little Circle B, 1990; Together – Our Masterpiece, 1991; I Love Miss America, 1992; The Life To Fame and Fortune, 1985. *Honours:* Gold Record, 1995; Inducted into Hall of Fame, 1997; Record John F Kennedy held in Smithsonian Institute, Washington, and John F Kennedy Library, Dallas. *Memberships:* American Heart Asscn; American Lung Asscn; Girl Scouts of America; Citizens of Citrus County, Florida; Deaf Serv of Citrus County. *Leisure interests:* Farming; Singing; Playing guitar and harmonica. *Address:* Cowboy Junction Flea Market, Hwy 44, Jctn 490, Lecanto, FL 34461, USA.

MAXWELL, (Maxwell Menard); b. 23 May 1973, Brooklyn, New York, USA. Vocalist. *Career:* Started his musical career with performances at Nell's night club in New York; Demo tape reached Sony Records resulting in record deal and release of debut album in April 1996; Collaborations: Leon Ware; Stuart Matthewman. *Recordings:* Albums: Maxwell's Urban Hang Suite, 1996; MTV Unplugged, 1997; Embrya, 1998; Now, 2001; Singles: Til The Cops Come Knockin', Ascension (Don't Ever Wonder), 1996; Sumthin' Sumthin', Whenever Wherever Whatever, 1997; Fortunate, 1999; Lifetime, Gotta Let You Know, 2001. *Honours:* Soul Train Awards, Best R & B Artist, 1997. *Address:* c/o Columbia Records, 550 Madison Ave, New York, USA.

MAXWELL Thad James; b. 2 July 1945, Brooklyn, New York, USA. Musician (guitar, bass, steel guitar, drums). m. Jeanne Cornell, 1 s., 1 d. *Education:* AA, Glendale College, 1987. *Career:* Guitarist, drummer, Tarantula, 1969–70; Bassist, various artists including: Ricky Nelson; Arlo Guthrie; Linda Ronstadt; Flying Burrito Brothers, 1970–80; Steel guitarist, guitarist, Mac Davis, 1973–. *Recordings include:* with Arlo Guthrie: Hobo's Lullabye, 1972; Last of The Brooklyn Cowboys, 1973; with Tarantula: Tarantula, 1969; Other recordings include: Horizon, The Carpenters, 1975; A Little Warmth, Steve Gillette, 1979; Sweet Country Suite, Larry Murray, 1971; Sierra, Sierra, 1977; Lead Free, B W Stevenson, 1972; Swampwater, Swampwater, 1970; with Flying Burrito Brothers: Tribute to Gram Parsons, 1995. *Memberships:* AFofM; AFTRA. *Leisure interest:* Photography.

MAY Brian; b. 19 July 1947, Twickenham, London, England. Musician (guitar); Singer; Composer; Prod. *Education:* Astronomy and Physics, Imperial College, London. *Musical Education:* Self-taught guitar. *Career:* Guitarist, The Others; Smile; Guitarist, UK rock group Queen, 1970–; Numerous tours include: UK; USA; Australia; South America; Japan; Major concerts include: Rock in Rio Festival, Brazil, 1985; Live Aid, Wembley, 1985; Knebworth Festival, 1986; A Concert For Life, Wembley, 1992. *Recordings:* Albums include: Queen, 1973; Queen 2, 1974; Sheer Heart Attack, 1974; A Night At The Opera, 1975; News of The World, 1977; Jazz, 1978; Live Killers, 1979; The Game, 1980; Greatest Hits, 1981; Hot Space, 1982; The Works, 1984; The Complete Works, 1985; Live Magic, 1986; The Miracle, 1989; Innuendo, 1991; Greatest Hits II, 1991; Live At Wembley '86, 1992; Made In Heaven, 1995; Solo: Star Fleet Project, 1983; Back To The Light, 1992; Resurrection, 1994; Live at the Brixton Academy,

1994; Another World, 1998; Contributions to: Puttin' On The Style, Lonnie Donegan; All American Alien, Ian Hunter; Tribute To Muddy Waters; Singles include: Seven Seas In Rhye, 1974; Killer Queen, 1974; Bohemian Rhapsody (No. 1, UK), 1975; You're My Best Friend, 1976; Somebody To Love, 1976; We Are The Champions, 1977; Bicycle Race, 1978; Don't Stop Me Now, 1979; Love of My Life, 1979; Crazy Little Thing Called Love (No. 1, UK), 1979; Save Me, 1980; Play The Game, 1980; Another One Bites The Dust, 1980; Flash, 1981; Under Pressure (with David Bowie), 1981; Radio Ga Ga, 1984; I Want To Break Free, 1984; It's A Hard Life, 1984; One Vision, 1985; A Kind of Magic, 1986; I Want It All, 1989; Breakthru, 1989; Innuendo (No. 1, UK), 1991; The Show Must Go On, 1991; Headlong, 1991; Heaven For Everyone, 1995; Too Much Love Will Kill You, 1995; Business, 1998; Driven By You, 1998. *Honours include:* Ivor Novello Awards: Best Selling British Record, Bohemian Rhapsody, 1976; Outstanding Contribution To British Music, 1987; Gold Ticket, Madison Square Gardens, 1977; Britannia Award, Best British Pop Single 1952–77, 1977; American Music Award, Favourite Single, 1981; Silver Clef Award, Nordoff-Robbins Music Therapy Centre, 1984; BRIT Awards: Outstanding Contribution to British Music, 1990; Best British Single, 1991. *Current Management:* c/o Jim Beach, Queen Productions, 46 Pembridge Rd, London W11 3HN, England.

MAY Derrick, (Mayday, Rhythm Is Rhythim); b. 6 April 1963, Detroit, Michigan USA. Prod.; Remixer; DJ. *Career:* Founder Transmat Records; Credited with invention of techno genre as part of the Belleville Three (alongside Juan Atkins and Kevin Saunderson); World-wide DJ; Resident DJ at the Music Institute in Detroit in the early '90s; Collaborations: Juan Atkins, Kevin Saunderson, System 7, Carl Craig; Remixed: ABC, Funtopia, Yello, Inner City, DJ Rolando. *Recordings:* Albums: Innovator – Soundtrack For The Tenth Planet, 1992; Singles: Let's Go (as X-Ray), 1986; Nude Photo (as Rhythim Is Rhythim), 1987; Strings of Life (as Rhythim Is Rhythim), 1987; It Is What It Is (as Rhythim Is Rhythim), 1988; Beyond The Dance (as Rhythim Is Rhythim), 1989; The Beginning (as Rhythim Is Rhythim), 1990; Icon (as Rhythim Is Rhythim), 1993. *Current Management:* c/o Transmat Records, 1492 Gratoit Ave, Detroit, Michigan, USA.

MAY Simon; b. 15 Aug. 1944. Composer. m. Rosie, 1 s., 3 d. *Musical Education:* Choral Scholar, Degree modern languages, Cambridge University. *Career:* Taught German, French, Music, Kingston Grammar School, 8 years; Following commercial success of stage musical Smike (10,000 performances world-wide, BBC Christmas television production), became full-time composer; Songwriter, record producer, world-wide sales over 15m., include 10 UK top 20 hits; Songs recorded by: Cliff Richard; Amii Stewart; Nick Berry; The Pointer Sisters; Al Jarreau; Marti Webb; Anita Dobson; The Shadows; Richard Clayderman; Ruby Turner; Jonathan Butler; Stephanie De Sykes; Kate Robbins; Records produced for Amii Stewart include: Knock On Wood (No. 1, USA); Light My Fire. *Compositions:* Film: The Dawning; Television: EastEnders, BBC; Howard's Way, BBC; Trainer, BBC; Eldorado, BBC; The Holiday Programme, BBC; The Food and Drink Programme, BBC; Castaway 2000, BBC; Don't Try This At Home, LWT; Television Weekly, TVS; Olympic Theme, Thames; The Vet, BBC; People, BBC; Paramedics, BBC; Jobs For The Girls, BBC; The Trial of James Earl Ray, CH4; Swiss Family Robinson, 1997; Pet Rescue, 1997; Lion Country, 1997; Great Estates, CH4; Musicals: Smike; Rick Van Winkel. *Publication:* William Shatner's Twist In The Tale. *Honours:* Novello Award, Every Loser Wins, Nick Berry, 1986; 3 TRIC Awards, Best TV Theme: EastEnders; Howard's Way; Trainer. *Memberships:* PRS; Songwriters; BASCA; Equity; Musicians' Union. *Current Management:* Helstonleigh, 17 South Hill, Guildford, Surrey GU1 3SY, England.

MAY Tina; b. 30 March 1961, Gloucester, England. Singer. m. Clark Tracey, 15 June 1989, 1 s. *Education:* BA Hons, French, University of Wales. *Musical Education:* Studied singing from age 16, also at University (soprano). *Career:* Began by tours as singing actress; Then full-time singer; Broadcasts, tours of Australia, Far East, UK, Europe with own quartet. *Recordings:* Never Let Me Go; Fun; It Ain't Necessarily So; Time Will Tell; BBC Broadcast with Tina May (live); Recordings with own group; Various guest appearances on other recordings. *Honours:* Worshipful Company of Musicians: Outstanding Jazz Musician, 1993. *Memberships:* Musicians' Union; Equity; Asscn of British Jazz Music. *Current Management:* Europa Jazz Live. *Address:* 6 Belgrove, Tunbridge Wells, Kent, England.

MAYALL John; b. 29 Nov. 1933, Macclesfield, Cheshire, England. Blues Singer; Songwriter; Musician (harmonica). *Education:* Manchester Art College. *Career:* Founder, The Blues Syndicate, 1962; John Mayall's Bluesbreakers (members have included John McVie, Eric Clapton, Peter Green, Jack Bruce, Aynsley Dunbar, Mick Taylor, Mick Fleetwood), 1963–; Major concerts include: Uxbridge Festival, 1965; National Blues Festival, Windsor, 1967; Palm Springs Pop Festival, 1969; Newport Jazz Festival, 1969; Woburn Festival, 1969; Bath Festival, 1969; Regular tours, UK, USA, Australia, Europe; Launched own Crusade record label, 1969. *Recordings:* John Mayall Plays John Mayall, 1965; Blues Breakers, 1966; A Hard Road, 1967; Crusade, 1967; Diary of a Band, Vols 1 and 2, 1968; Bare Wires, 1968;

Looking Back, 1969; Blues From Laurel Canyon, 1969; The Turning Point, 1969; Empty Rooms, 1970; USA Union, 1970; John Mayall – Live In Europe, 1971; Back To The Roots, 1971; Thru The Years, 1971; Memories, 1971; Jazz Blues Fusion, 1972; Moving On, 1972; Down The Line, 1973; Ten Years Are Gone, 1973; The Latest Edition, 1974; New Year New Band New Company, 1975; Time Expired Notice To Appear, 1975; John Mayall, 1976; A Banquet of Blues, 1976; Lots of People, 1977; Blues Roots, 1978; Bottom Line, 1979; No More Interviews, 1979; Road Show Blues, 1980; Behind The Iron Curtain, 1984; The Power of The Blues, 1987; Chicago Line, 1988; A Sense of Place, 1990; Wake Up Call, 1993; Cross Country Blues, 1994; Return of tbe Bluebreakers, 1994; Spinning Coin, 1995; Blues for the Lost Days, 1997; Padlock on the Blues, 1999; Rock the Blues Tonight, 1999. *Honour:* Gold disc, The Turning Point, 1969.

MAYOR Simon; b. Sheffield, England. Musician (mandolin, mandola, mandocello, guitar, violin), Composer, Lyricist, Humourist. *Education:* Degree in Russian, Reading University. *Musical Education:* Musically self-taught. *Career:* Regular international concert touring includes: Vancouver Festival, Rudolstadt International Festival (Germany), Varazze International Mandolin Festival (Italy), Guest of Classical Mandolin Society of America Annual Conference, London's South Bank Festival, Cheltenham Literature Festival; Worked as broadcaster, BBC Radio 2, 4 and 5; Presented BBC Schools Radio music education programmes for six years; Written and performed many songs for childrens' programmes for BBC TV. *Recordings:* The Mandolin Album, 1990 (BBC Radio 2's Album of The Week); The Second Mandolin Album, 1991; Winter With Mandolins, 1992 (BBC World Service Album of The Week); The English Mandolin, 1995; Mandoliquents (The Simon Mayor Quintet), 1997; New Celtic Mandolin, 1998; Albums feature approximately 50% original compositions; Also five albums of original songs for children in the Musical Mystery Tour series. *Publications:* The New Mandolin (original compositions in music and tablature), 1993; The Mandolin Tutor (Book/CD for beginners), 1995; New Celtic Mandolin (Celtic tunes with detailed teaching notes), 1998; Musical Mystery Tour (children's song book), 1992. *Memberships:* Musicians' Union; Equity; PRS; MCPS. *Leisure interests:* Fell walking; Appalachian step-dancing. *Address:* c/o Acoustics Records, PO Box 350, Reading, Berks RG6 7DQ, England.

MAZETIER Louis; b. 17 Feb. 1960, Paris, France. Jazz Musician (piano); Composer. m. Sophie Clement, 1 s., 1 d. *Education:* MD, Radiologist, University. *Musical Education:* Self-taught. *Career:* Member, Paris Washboard; Major festivals in France: Antibes; Marciac; Bayonne; Montauban; Festivals in Europe: Breda; Dresden; Plön; Tours, New Zealand; Australia; USA (including Moodus and Santa Rosa Festivals); Argentina; Uruguay; Japan. *Recordings:* 8 with Paris Washboard; Duet with pianist Francois Rilhac; Duet with pianist Neville Dickie; Solo record; Duet with pianist Bernd Lhotzky. *Publications:* Many articles, various French Jazz Reviews, mostly about stride piano. *Honours:* Prix Sidney Bechet; Prix Bill Coleman, Academie de Jazz, 1992. *Leisure interest:* Golf. *Address:* 3 rue Larrey, 75005 Paris, France.

MAZUR Marilyn (Marie Douglas); b. 18 Jan. 1955, New York City, USA. Composer; Jazz Musician (percussion, drums, piano); Vocalist. 1 s. *Musical Education:* Degree, Teaching Percusssion, Royal Danish Music Conservatory, 1974–77. *Career:* Dancer, Creative Dance Theatre, 1971; Formed first band Zirenes, 1973; Played with Six Winds with Alex Riel; Miles Davis, 1985–88; Gil Evans Orchestra, 1986; Wayne Shorter, 1987; Jan Garbarek Group, 1991–; Leader, own projects, Future Song, Pulse Unit, Primi Band; Performed all over the world; Played with Niels Henning Orsted Pedersen; Jasper van't Hof; Andreas Vollenweider; Kenneth Knudsen; Pierre Dorge; numerous others. *Compositions:* Well of Clouds, 1982; 30 magiske omkvæd, 1986; Bydansen (City Dance), 1989; Decemberdanse, 1992; Fjellslottet, 1992. *Recordings:* Albums include: Clouds, 1982; Rhythm-a-ning (with Gil Evans, Laurent Cugny), 1986; Aura (with Miles Davis, Palle Mikkelborg), 1989; Marilyn Mazur's Future Song, 1992; Future Song, 1997; Story of Multiplicity, 1998; Jon Balke with Magnetic North Orchestra, 1994; with Pulse Unit: Circular Chant, 1995; Feature on: New Spirits in Jazz Vol. 3, 1997; with Jan Garbarek, Rites, 1999. *Honours:* Ben Webster Prize, 1983; Jasa Prize, 1989; HK-Artist of the Year, 1994. *Leisure interests:* Food; Colours; Dancing. *Current Management:* Hohensee/Bremme, Germany.

MBANDE Venacio Notico; b. 4 Oct. 1933, Chisiko, nr Zavala, Mozambique. Musician (xylophone, timbila); Composer; Performer; Master Instrument Maker. m. Alzira, 14 c. *Career:* Leading musician in Chopi xylophone and orchestration; Orchestra leader, Witwatersrand, South Africa, 1953–95; Demonstrator and lecturer in Chopi music, University of Pennsylvania, USA, 1973; Royal Conservatory of Music, The Hague, 1991, 1999; Zavala, Mozambique, 1995–; Performance in Royal Albert Hall, London with Dutch percussionists for BBC, 1995. *Compositions:* Numerous Mgodo xylophone orchestral suites. *Recordings:* Tapes held by International Library of African Music, Grahamstown, South Africa; Mozambique, Timbila Ta Venancio, CD, Germany, 1994; Musica Chope de Mozambique, Timbila ta Venancio, CD, The Netherlands, 1999.

Honours: African Arts Music Competition, Mgodo Xylophone Suite, USA, 1969; M'saho Competition, Chopie Xylophone, 1997–99, Mozambique. *Address:* PO Box No. 8, Quissico, Mozambique.

M'BANGO Charlotte; b. 16 April 1960, Douala, Cameroon. Artiste; Singer; Backing Vocalist. m. Mpacko Marcel, 4 Aug. 1984, 1 d. *Musical Education:* Solfège; Piano. *Career:* Tours: Ivory Coast; Cameroon; Gabon; Burkina Faso; Togo; USA; Spain: Barcelona, Madrid, Valencia; London; France; Radio: Africa, France; Television: France, Belgium. *Recordings:* Nakossa Nostalgie, 1987; Konkai Makossa, 1988; Maloka, 1995; Masoma, 1996; Best of Makossa Vol. 2, 1998; with Paul Simon: Rhythm of the Saints, 1990;. *Honours:* Gold Song, Palo Rabanne, 1989; Gold Lion, 1994. *Memberships:* ADAMI; SACEM; SPEDIDAM; SFA; ACOP: AMF. *Leisure interests:* Cycling; Volleyball; Relaxation. *Address:* 10 Allée d'Amblonville, 77176 Savigny Le Temple, France.

MCA (Adam Yauch); b. 15 Aug. 1967, Brooklyn, New York, USA. Rapper; Musician (bass). m. Ione Skye, 1992. *Career:* Founder member, US rap/rock group The Beastie Boys, 1983–; Appearances include: Support to Madonna, Virgin Tour, 1985; Supports to Run DMC, Raisin' Hell Tour, 1986, Co-headliners with Run DMC, Together Forever Tour, 1987; Reading Festival, 1992; Made horror film, Scared Stupid; Film apperances: Krush Groove; Run-DMC film, Tougher Than Leather. *Recordings:* Singles include: She's On It; Fight For Your Right To Party; Albums include: Licensed To Ill, 1986; Paul's Boutique, 1989; Check Your Head, 1992; Ill Communication, 1994; Root Down, 1995; The In Sound From Way Out, 1996; Hello Nasty, 1998; Singles include: Pass the Mic, 1992; Jimmy James, 1992; Hey Ladies, 1997; Intergalactic, 1998; Body Movin', 1998; Remote Control, 1999; Alive, 1999. *Current Management:* Gold Mountain Entertainment, 3575 Cahuenga Blvd W, Suite 450, Los Angeles, CA 90068, USA.

MEADE Bazil (Leonard Duncan); b. 4 May 1951, Montserrat. Musician (piano, Hammond organ). m. Andrea Encinas, 3 May 1980, 2 s., 2 d. *Musical Education:* Self-taught in Gospel and R & B. *Career:* Founder and Principal, London Community Gospel Choir, 1982; Musical Director for numerous concerts including: The London Community Gospel Choir European Tours, 1984–93; Freddie Mercury Tribute Concert, 1991; George Michael British tour, 1991; HRH Queen Elizabeth's 60th Birthday concert, Royal Opera House; Stevie Wonder, Wembley; Luther Vandross, Royal Albert Hall, 1994; Gloria Gaynor, European Tour, 1994; Also Musical Director for: Amen Corner (theatre production), 1990; Royal Variety television shows for 5 years; Hallelujah Anyhow (film); Rock Gospel (television series); Desmonds (television series); Mama I Want To Sing, 1995. *Recordings:* with Paul McCartney: Give My Regards To Broadstreet; with The London Community Gospel Choir: Live In Sweden; The London Community Gospel Choir Sings The Gospel Greats; Christmas With The London Community Gospel Choir; Hush and Listen; with Bobby Womack: No Matter How High I Get; Circle of Life (from Walt Disney's The Lion King). *Honours:* Greenbelt Award For Services To Gospel Music, 1986; Commonwealth Institute Award For Services To Gospel Music, 1986; BBC Award, Contribution To Gospel Music, 1987. *Memberships:* Musicians' Union; PRS; MCPS. *Leisure interests:* Football; Cricket; Working out; Wine tasting. *Current Management:* Choir Connexion. *Address:* 9 Greenwood Dr., London E4 9HL, England.

MEAT LOAF (Marvin Lee Aday); b. 27 Sept. 1951, Dallas, Texas, USA. Entertainer; Singer; Actor. m. Leslie Edmonds, 1975, 2 d. *Education:* University. *Career:* Appeared in films: The Rocky Horror Picture Show, 1975; Americathon, 1979; Scavenger Hunt, 1979; Roadie, 1980; Dead Ringer, 1981; The Squeeze, 1986; Out of Bounds, 1986; Motorama, 1990; Gun and Betty Lou's Handbag, 1991; Wayne's World, 1992; Leap of Faith, 1992; The Mighty, 1998; Black Dog, 1998; Fight Club, 1999; Crazy In Alabama, 1999; Outside Ozona, 1999; Plays: Hair; Rocky Horror; National Lampoon Show; More Than You Deserve; Rockabye Hamlet; Billy The Kid and Jean Harlow; As You Like It; Othello. *Recordings:* Hit singles include: Dead Ringer For Love; Bat Out of Hell; Modern Girl; Two Out of Three Ain't Bad; You Took The Words Right Out; Rock 'n' Roll Mercenaries (with John Parr); I'd Lie For You (and That's The Truth); Not A Dry Eye In The House; Albums include: Featuring Stoney and Meat Loaf, 1970; Free For All (with Ted Nugent), 1976; Bat Out of Hell, 1977; Dead Ringer, 1982; Midnight At The Lost and Found, 1983; Bad Attitude, 1984; Hits Out of Hell, 1985; Blind Before I Stop, 1986; Meat Loaf Live, 1987; Bat Out of Hell II: Back To Hell, 1993; Welcome To The Neighbourhood, 1995; Contributor, Pavarotti and Friends (Bosnia relief charity record), 1996; The Very Best Of, 1998. *Honours:* Brit Award, 1993; Grammy, 1993. *Leisure interests:* Softball; Golf. *Current Management:* The Left Bank Organization. *Address:* 9255 Sunset Blvd, 2nd Floor, W Hollywood, CA 90069, USA.

MEDLEY Bill; b. 19 Sept. 1940, Santa Ana, California, USA. Singer. *Career:* Member, The Paramours; Founder member, The Righteous Brothers (with Bobby Hatfield), 1962–67, 1974–80; Concerts include: Support to the Beatles, US tour, 1964; Television includes: Shindig!; Scene At 6.30; Ready Steady Go; Discs A Go-Go; Solo career, 1967–73, 1981–; Opened Medleys Club, Los Angeles, 1982; Appearances, Cheers,

NBC, 1990; Duet with Jennifer Warnes, for film Dirty Dancing, 1987; Returned to performing as Righteous Brothers. *Recordings:* Singles include: You've Lost That Lovin' Feelin', later used in film Top Gun (No. 1, UK and USA), 1964; Just Once In My Life, 1965; You Can Have Her, 1965; Justine, 1965; Unchained Melody (later used in film Ghost), 1965; Ebb Tide, 1966; (You're My) Soul and Inspiration, 1966; Solo: (I've Had) The Time of My Life, duet with Jennifer Warnes, for film Dirty Dancing (No. 1, USA), 1987; Albums: with the Righteous Brothers: You've Lost That Lovin' Feelin', 1965; Right Now!, 1965; Some Blue-Eyed Soul, 1965; This Is New!, 1965; Just Once In My Life, 1965; Back To Back, 1966; Go Ahead and Cry, 1966; Soul and Inspiration, 1966; The Best of The Righteous Brothers, 1966; Sayin' Something, 1967; Greatest Hits, 1967; Greatest Hits Vol. 2, 1969; Give It To The People, 1974; The Righteous Brothers Greatest Hits, 1990; The Best Of…, 1990; The Very Best Of…, 1990; Anthology (1962–74), 1990; Solo: 100%, 1968; A Song For You, 1971; Sweet Thunder, 1981; Right Here and Now, 1982; I Still Do, 1984; Someone Is Standing Outside, 1985; Still Hung Up On You, 1985; Another Beginning, 1987; The Hard Side, 1987; Blue Eyed Singer, 1991; Smile, 1991; Christmas Memories, 1996; Almost Home, 1997; Contributor, film soundtracks: Cobra; Rambo III. *Honours:* Grammy Award, Best Pop Performance, 1987. *Current Management:* DBC Management, 131 Spinnaker Court, Marina del Rey, CA 90292, USA.

MEDLEY Sue; b. 19 Aug. 1962, Nanaimo, British Columbia, Canada. Recording Artist; Singer; Songwriter. *Career:* Toured Canada with: Bob Dylan; Dwight Yoakam; Tom Cochrane (as opening act); Television, radio appearances in Canada, including; half hour special, Adrienne Clarkson presents, CBC-TV, spotlights on Much Music. *Recordings:* Albums: Sue Medley, 1990; Inside Out, 1992; Singles: Dangerous Times; Maybe The Next Time; That's Life; Love Thing; When The Stars Fall; Forget You; Jane's House; Inside Out. *Honours:* 5 West Coast Music Awards; 2 Juno Awards; 2 Songwriter Awards. *Memberships:* AFofM; CARAS; SOCAN. *Leisure interests:* Reading; Cycling; Riding. *Current Management:* Marian Donelly Artist Management.

MEIJS Norbert; b. 11 July 1952. Singer; Songwriter. m. Marianne, 2 s., 1 d. *Career:* Singer, Sophisticated Movement, 1968–71; Member of Plakband, 1973–74; Member of Teenager, 1977–78; Several Apperances as Singer, Songwriter, pseudonym Blackbyrd, 1993–99. *Compositions:* Louise; Calling Richard. *Recordings:* Baby, Hold on; Takin' My Time; Louise, recorded by the Ryes, 1999. *Memberships:* BUMA; STEMRA; PALM. *Current Management:* Longboat Management. *Address:* Keerberg 71, 6267 DB, Cadier En Keer, Netherlands.

MEIKLE Orde; b. 1964, Glasgow, Scotland. Prod.; Remixer; DJ. *Career:* Started career as a DJ in Glasgow; Met Stuart McMillan and started putting on their own club nights, Atlantis and Slam; Formed the Slam production duo and Soma Records label; World-wide DJ; Collaborations: UNKLE; Remixed: Sunscreem; Mansun; Dave Angel; Phuture; Kym Sims. *Recordings:* Albums: Headstates, 1996; Alien Radio, Past Lessons – Future Theories (DJ-mixed compilation), 2001; Singles: Eterna, 1991; Positive Education, 1993; Snapshots, 1995; Dark Forces, 1996; Narco Tourists, Lifetimes, Alien Radio 2001. *Address:* c/o Soma Records, 342 Argyle St, Glasgow, G2 8LY, Scotland.

MEIKLEJOHN Duncan Warner; b. 16 Dec. 1952, Edmonton, Alberta, Canada. Singer; Songwriter; Arranger; Prod.; Musician (keyboards, guitars). 3 s. *Musical Education:* Royal Conservatory, piano; Private vocal coach. *Career:* Concert appearances with: Michael Bolton; Sheena Easton; Dudley Moore; The Nylons; David Foster; 1994 Commonwealth Games Ceremonies. *Recordings:* Song of Songs; The Best Part (of You and Me); The Second Time Around; Paradise; Let The Spirit Live On. *Honours:* Hon. Mentions, Canadian Songwriting Contest. *Membership:* ACTRA; SOCAN. *Leisure interests:* Art (graphic, sketching); Cars; Rock Collecting; Softball; Football; Walking. *Current Management:* Brass Ring Productions, PO Box 1266 Stn A, Kelowna, British Columbia V1Y 7V8, Canada.

MEINE Klaus; b. 25 May 1948, Germany. Singer. *Career:* Lead vocalist, German heavy rock group The Scorpions, 1971–; Regular world-wide tours; Support tours to Ted Nugent; Bon Jovi; Festivals and major concerts include: World Series of Rock, Cleveland, Ohio, 1979; US Festival, 1973; Reading Rock Festival, 1973; Rock in Rio, Brazil, 1985; Monsters of Rock, Germany, 1986; First Western rock band to play former Soviet Union, Leningrad, 1989; Moscow Music Peace Festival, 1989; The Wall, with Roger Waters, Berlin, 1990; MTV New Year's Eve World Party, Berlin, 1990; Invited to meet President Gorbachev, at the Kremlin, 1991. *Recordings:* Albums: Lonesome Crow, 1972; Fly To The Rainbow, 1974; In Trance, 1975; Virgin Killer, 1976; Taken By Force, 1978; Tokyo Tapes, 1978; Lovedrive, 1979; Animal Magnetism, 1980; Blackout, 1982; Love At First Sting, 1984; World Wide Live, 1985; Savage Amusement, 1988; Best of Rockers and Ballads, 1989; Hurricane Rock, 1990; Crazy World, 1990; Live Bites, 1995; Deadly Sting: The Mercury Years, 1997; Hit singles include: There's No One Like You; Can't Live Withou You; Rock Like A Hurricane; Still Loving You; Rhythm of Love; Wind of Change; Face the Heat; Pure

Instinct; Eye II Eye. *Honours:* ASCAP Award, Wind of Change, 1993. *Current Management:* Hard To Handle Management, 1133 Broadway, Suite 1301, New York, NY 10010, USA.

MEISNER Randy; b. 8 May 1946, Scottsbluff, Nevada, USA. Musician (bass); Vocalist. *Career:* Member, The Dynamics, early 1960s; Member, Soul Survivors (later the Poor); Member, Poco, 1968–69; 1989; The Eagles, 1971–77; Solo artiste, 1977–; Member, Black Tie, 1990-. *Recordings:* Albums: with The Eagles: The Eagles, 1972; Desperado, 1973; On The Border, 1974; One of These Nights, 1975; Their Greatest Hits 1971–75 (No. 1, USA), 1976; Solo albums: One More Song, 1980; Randy Meisner, 1982; Singles include: Take It Easy, 1972; Witchy Woman, 1972; Peaceful Easy Feeling, 1973; The Best of My Love (No. 1, USA), 1975; One of These Nights (No. 1, USA), 1975; Lyin' Eyes, 1975; Take It To The Limit, 1976; New Kid In Town (No. 1, USA), 1977; Hotel California (No. 1, USA), 1977; Life In The Fast Lane, 1977. *Honours:* Grammy Award, Best Pop Vocal Performance, Lyin' Eyes, 1976; American Music Awards, Favorite Album, 1977; Album of Year, Their Greatest Hits, National Asscn of Record Merchandisers, 1977. *Address:* c/o Geoffrey Blumenauer Artists, 11846 Balboa Blvd, Suite 204, Granada Hills, CA 91344, USA.

MEISSNER Stan; b. 28 Aug. 1956, Toronto, Ontario, Canada. Songwriter. *Career:* Written songs recorded by: Celine Dion; Eddie Money; Rita Coolidge; B J Thomas; Ben Orr (from the Cars); Lee Aaron; Contributing composer for several television shows and films. *Recordings:* Albums: Dangerous Games, 1984; Windows To Light, 1986; Undertow, 1992; Metropolis, 1999. *Honours:* Gemini Award; Juno Award nomination. *Current Management:* Meissner Music Productions Inc. *Address:* 162 Wychwood Ave, Toronto, ON M6C 2T3, Canada.

MELANDER Anders; b. 7 Jan. 1948, Stockholm, Sweden. Songwriter; Composer; Musician; Prod. *Education:* Philosophy and Foreign Languages, University of Lund, Sweden. *Career:* Band Leader, Bread, 1966–68; Musical Leader, Nationalteatern, 1970–75; Score Composer, SVT, 1976–; Songwriter, various artists; Member of CUE, 1997-. *Compositions:* Score for SVT WW2 drama serial recorded by Gothenburg Symphony Orchestra, 1994; News Themes for national network TV4, 1990–; Hallå Västindien, Vikingarna, 1981; Speedy Gonzales, Magnus Uggla, 1987. *Recordings:* Bread: singles and compilations, including Rough Lover; Nationalteatern: Early albums include: Livet är en fest, 1974; Jack the Ripper; Speedy Gonzales; Bängen Trålar; Solo releases: Good Luck, 1981; Ebba and Didrik, 1990; CUE: number 1 hit single: Burnin', 3 Platinum discs, 1997–98; Crazy, 2000; Album: Cue 2000; Singles: Sway, 2000, Hello, 2000. *Honours:* SKAP Honours, 1984; Grammis Award, 1997. *Memberships:* Swedish Composers and Authors of Popular Music; Swedish Media Composers. *Leisure interest:* Linguistics. *Address:* Sprängkullsgatan 10 B, 411 23 Göteborg, Sweden.

MELANIE B (Melanie Janice Brown), (Melanie G, Scary Spice); b. 29 May 1975, Leeds, England. Vocalist. m. Jimmy Gulzar, 12 Sept. 1998, 1 d. *Career:* Member, Spice Girls; Numerous TV and radio appearances, magazine interviews; Film, Spiceworld: The Movie, 1997; World tour including dates in UK, Europe, India and USA; Parallel solo career, 1998-. *Recordings:* Singles with Spice Girls: Wannabe, 1996; Say You'll Be There, 1996; 2 Become 1, 1996; Mama/Who Do You Think You Are, 1997; Step To Me, 1997; Spice Up Your Life, 1997; Too Much, 1997; Stop, 1998; (How Does It Feel To Be) ON Top of The World, with England United, 1998; Move Over/Generation Next, 1998; Viva Forever, 1998; Solo: I Want You Back, featuring Missy 'Misdemeanour' Elliott, 1998; Word Up, 1999; Albums: Spice, 1996; Spiceworld, 1997.

MELANIE C (Melanie Jayne Chisholm), (Sporty Spice); b. 12 Jan. 1976, Liverpool, England. Vocalist. *Career:* Member, Spice Girls; Numerous TV and radio appearances, magazine interviews; Film, Spiceworld: The Movie, 1997; UK, European and US tours; Royal Command performances; Parallel solo career, 1999–; Solo world tour including festival performances including V99. *Recordings:* Singles with Spice Girls: Wannabe, 1996; Say You'll Be There, 1996; 2 Become 1, 1996; Mama/Who Do You Think You Are, 1997; Step To Me, 1997; Spice Up Your Life, 1997; Too Much, 1997; Stop, 1998; (How Does It Feel To Be) On Top of the World, with England United, 1998; Move Over/Generation Next, 1998; Viva Forever, 1998; Goodbye, 1998; Albums: Spice, 1996; Spiceworld, 1997; Solo Singles: When You're Gone, Bryan Adams featuring Melanie C, 1999; Going Down, 1999; Albums: Northern Star, 1999. *Honours:* Numerous awards in music polls.

MELDER Heinz; b. 16 Feb. 1951, Cologne, Germany. Sound Engineer; Music Prod. m. Anna Maria Melder, 20 Nov. 1976, 1 s. *Education:* Self-trained Sound Engineer, evening school education. *Career:* Manager, TMK, Musik Production, 1977-. *Recordings:* Numerous production in field of German popular music with leading artists. *Publications:* Eimol Prinz Zo Siu en Kolie Au Rhing. *Honours:* King Eagle Award, Airplay International Record Label of the Year, 1995–96. *Memberships:* VDT; IFPI; GVL; GEMA. *Leisure interests:* Music; Travelling with family. *Address:* TMK, Musik Production, Sebastian Str, 141 50735, Köln, Germany.

MELLE MEL (Melvin Glover); Rapper. *Career:* Founder member, Grandmaster Flash and The 3 MCs, 1977; Becomes Grandmaster Flash and The Furious Five, 1977–83; Founder, Grandmaster Flash, Melle Mel and The Furious Five, 1987. *Recordings:* Albums: The Message, 1982; Greatest Messages, 1984; Greatest Hits, 1992; Singles include: Freedom, 1980; The Adventures of Grandmaster Flash On The Wheels of Steel, 1981; The Message, 1982; White Lines (Don't Do It), 1983; Beat Street Breakdown Part 1, 1984; We Don't Work For Free, 1984; Sugarhill Work Party, 1984; Pump Me Up, 1985; Vice, featured on soundtrack, Miami Vice, NBC-TV, 1985; Featured on: I Feel For You, Chaka Khan, 1984.

MELLENCAMP John; b. 7 Oct. 1951, Seymour, Indiana, USA. Singer; Musician (guitar); Songwriter. m. (1) Priscilla, 1 d.; (2) Victoria, 2 c.; (3) Elaine Irwin, 1 s. *Education:* Vincennes University. *Career:* Member, Crepe Soul, 1965; Snakepit Banana Barn, 1966; Glitter-rock group Trash, 1971; Solo artiste, 1975–; Adopted name Johnny Cougar, 1976; Formed The Zone, 1977; Changed name to John Cougar Mellencamp, 1983; Major concerts include: US Festival, 1983; Organizer, inaugural Farm Aid Festival, 1985; Also appeared in Farm Aid II – V, 1986–92; Concert For The Heartland, 1993; Numerous North American tours; Film appearances: Souvenirs, 1990; Falling From Grace (own project), 1992; Exhibition of paintings, 1991. *Recordings:* Albums: Chestnut Street Incident, 1976; The Kid Inside, 1977; A Biography, 1978; John Cougar, 1979; Nothin' Matters and What If It Did, 1980; American Fool, 1982; Uh-Huh, 1983; Scarecrow, 1985; The Lonesome Jubilee, 1987; Big Daddy, 1989; Souvenirs (film soundtrack), 1990; Whenever We Wanted, 1991; Human Wheels, 1993; Dance Naked, 1994; Mr Happy Go Lucky, 1996; John Mellencamp, 1998; Dance Naked Bonus CD, 1999; Rough Harvest, 1999; Hit singles: Ain't Even Done With The Night, 1981; Jack and Diane (No. 1, USA), 1982; Hurts So Good, 1982; Hand To Hold On To, 1983; Crumblin'Down, 1983; Pink Houses, 1984; Authority Song, 1984; Lonely Ol' Night, 1985; Small Town, 1985; R O C K In The USA, 1986; Paper In Fire, 1987; Cherry Bomb, 1988; Check It Out, 1988; Pop Singer, 1989; Get A Leg Up, 1991; Again Tonight, 1992; Now More Than Ever, 1992; Wild Night, 1994; Key West Intermezzo, 1996; Just Another Day, 1997; Your Life Is Now, 1998; I'm Not Running Anymore, 1999; Contributor, A Very Special Christmas (charity album), 1987; Folkways – A Vision Shared (Woodie Guthrie tribute), 1988; Film soundtrack, Honeymoon In Vegas, 1992; As producer: Tracks for: Mitch Ryder; The Blasters; James McMurty. *Honours:* American Music Award, Favourite Male Artist (co-winner), 1983; Nordoff-Robbins Silver Clef, 1991; First US artist to have 2 Top 10 singles and No. 1 album simultaneously, 1982. *Current Management:* The Left Bank Organisation, 6255 Sunset Blvd, Suite 1111, Hollywood, CA 90028, USA.

MELLOR David; b. 23 April 1955, Middlesborough, England. *Career:* Member of Evil Twin, With Karl Blake, 1987–; Recording and Performing As The Days of The Moon, 1993-. *Recordings:* The Black Spot; The Words and Music of David Mellor; The Prince. *Address:* PO Box 671, Beaconsfield, Bucks, HP9 1AX, England.

MELLY (Alan) George (Heywood); b. 17 Aug. 1926, Liverpool, England. Jazz Singer; Critic. m. (1) Victoria Vaughn, 1955, divorced 1962, (2) Diana, 1963, 1 s., 1 step-d. *Career:* Assistant, London Gallery, 1948–50; Singer, Mick Mulligan's Jazz Band, 1949–61; Cartoon strip writer with Trog, 1956–71; As critic for The Observer: Pop Music, 1965–67; Television, 1967–71; Films, 1971–73; Film scriptwriter, Smashing Time, 1968; Take A Girl Like You, 1970; Singer, John Chilton's Feetwarmers, 1974–; Concerts include: Royal Festival Hall; Royal Albert Hall; Edinburgh Festival; Television includes: Subject, This Is Your Life. *Recordings:* 30 albums; George Melly and John Chilton's Feetwarmers: Best of Live; Anything Goes; Frankie and Johnny; Puttin' On The Ritz. *Publications:* I Flook, 1962; Owning Up, 1965; Revolt Into Style, 1970; Flook By Trog, 1970; Rum Bum and Concertina, 1977; The Media Mob (with Barry Fantoni), 1980; Tribe of One, 1981; Great Lovers, (with Walter Dorin), 1981; Mellymobile, 1982; Scouse Mouse, 1984; It's All Writ Out For You, 1986; Paris and The Surrealists (with Michael Woods), 1991; Don't Tell Sybil, 1997. *Honours:* Critic of The Year, IPC National Press Awards, 1970; Fellow, John Moores University; Dr, Middlesex and Glamorgan University; President, British Humanist Society, 1972–74; BT British Jazz Awards, 1998; Award for Lifetime Acheivement For Jazz. *Leisure interests:* Trout fishing; 1920's blues; Collecting modern paintings. *Current Management:* Jack Higgins, Pear Tree Cottage, Weymarks, Bradwell on Sea, Essex CM0 7JB, England.

MELVOIN Wendy Ann; b. 26 Jan. 1964, Los Angeles, California, USA. Musician (Guitar); Prod.; Composer. *Career:* Joined Prince's Band as Guitar Player, 1982; Toured and recorded extensively; Appearance in film Purple Rain; Part of recording duo Wendy and Lisa with Lisa Coleman; Numerous TV appearances in Europe and the USA. *Compositions:* Musical scores for films including Dangerous Minds, Soul Food, Hav Plenty. *Recordings:* Albums: Wendy and Lisa, 1987; Fuit at the Bottom, 1988; Eroica, 1990; Girl Bros, 1998; Appearances on Prince albums: 1999; Purple Rain; Around The World in a Day; Parade; Sign O' The Times; Recorded with artists including Seal, Joni Mitchell, kd lang, Sheryl Crow. *Current Management:*

Gold Mountain Entertainment. *Address:* c/o Renata Kanclerz, 2575 Cahuenga Blvd W, Suite 450, Los Angeles, CA 90068, USA.

MENEZES BASTOS Rafael José de; b. 26 Dec. 1945, Salvador, Bahia, Brazil. Anthropologist; Ethnomusicologist; Musician (Guitar). m. (2) Silvia de O Beraldo, 17 Feb. 1984, 5 s., 5 d. *Education:* AB, Music, Federal University of Bahia, School of Music, 1964; Department of Music, University of Brasilia, 1965–68; MA, Social Anthropology, University of Brasilia, 1976; PhD, Social Anthropology, University of São Paulo, 1990; Postdoctoral Studies, Massachusetts Institute of Technology, 1992–94, Smithsonian Institution, 1994. *Career:* Anthropologist, 1975–80/ Member of the Advisory Board and it's first Vice President, National Indian Foundation, 1999; Assistant Professor, Anthropology and Ethnomusicology, 1984–90, Associate Professor, 1990–; Member, Editorial Board, Federal University of Santa Catarina Press, 1991–92; Chairman, Graduate Programme, Social Anthropology, 1994–96. *Publications include:* A Musicológica Kamayura, 1978 and 1999 (2nd edition); Dioniso em Santa Catarina, editor, author of introduction and one article, 1993; Dissertations; Numerous articles in learned journals. *Memberships:* Scientific Board, Brazilian Anthropological Asscn, 1990–92, Board of Trustees, 1996–98; International Council for Traditional Music, Liason Officer in Brazil, 1993-, Executive Board, 1997–99; Advisory Board, International Encyclopaedia of the Popular Musics of the World, 1993–; Advisory Board, The World of Music, 1997-. *Address:* Departamento de Antropologia, Universidade Federal de Santa Catarina, 88.040–900 Florinópolis, SC, Brazil.

MERCÉ José, (Jose Soto Soto); b. 1955, Spain. Vocalist. *Career:* Well known singer, respected by flamenco aficionados; Appeal widened with release of Aire album, which remained within flamenco tradition but updated lyrical content to reach a contemporary audience. *Recordings:* Bandera de Andalucía, 1977; Carmen, 1983; Verde Junco, 1985; Caminos Reales Del Cante, 1987; Desnudando El Alma, 1994; Del Amanecer, 1998; Aire, 2000.

MERCEY Larry Oliver Anthony; b. 12 Dec. 1939, Hanover, Ontario, Canada. Recording Artist. m. June, 19 May 1964, 1 s., 1 d. *Musical Education:* Self-taught. *Career:* Member, The Mercey Brothers, 1957–90; Solo artist, 1990–; Appeared Grand Ole Opry, Nashville, Tennessee. *Recordings:* 17 albums, including many number 1 hits; 2 Solo albums. *Honours:* 7 Juno Awards, Top Country Vocal Group; CF Martin Life Time Achievement Award; Canadian Country Music Awards, Top Vocal Group; Inducted into Canadian Country Hall of Fame, 1990. *Leisure interests:* Golf; Gardening. *Current Management:* Larry Mercey Productions. *Address:* 590 Hunters Pl., Waterloo, ON N2K 3L1, Canada.

MERCHANT Natalie; b. 26 Oct. 1963. Singer; Songwriter; Musician (piano); Record Prod. *Education:* Jamestown Community College. *Career:* Founder, lead vocalist, 10,000 Maniacs, 1981–92; Concerts include: Tour with REM, USA, 1987; Cambridge Folk Festival, 1987, 1988; British tour, 1987; US tours, 1989, 1992; A Performance For The Planet, Maryland, 1990; Time Capsule Tour, 1990; Earth Day 1991 Concert, Massachusetts, 1991; National Earth Day, Hollywood Bowl, 1993; Television includes: Saturday Night Live; The Tonight Show; Late Night With David Letterman; MTV Drops The Ball '93; MTV's 1993 Rock 'n' Roll Inaugural Ball, Washington, 1993; Solo artiste, 1993-. *Recordings:* Albums: with 10,000 Maniacs: Secrets of The I Ching, 1983; The Wishing Chair, 1985; In My Tribe, 1987; Blind Man's Zoo, 1989; Hope Chest, 1989; Our Time In Eden, 1992; Solo albums: Tigerlily, 1995; Ophelia, 1998; Live in Concert, 1999; Singles include: with 10,000 Maniacs: Like The Weather; What's The Matter Here; These Are Days; Candy Everybody Wants; Few and Far Between; Because The Night; Solo single: Carnival, 1995; Jealousy, 1996; Carnival, 1998; Break Your Heart, 1999. *Current Management:* Jon Landau Management, 40 W Elm St, Greenwich, CT 06830, USA.

MERCIER Mel; b. 1959, Dublin, Ireland. Musician (bodhran, bones, tabla); Composer; Ethnomusicologist. *Musical Education:* University College Cork, BMus, 1989; California Institute of the Arts, MFA, 1992. *Career:* Son of Peadar Mercier; Member: The Chieftains, until 1976; Leader of Pulsus and the only Irish Gamelan ensemble; Guest lecturer at Wesleyan University, 1998; Lectured at University College, Cork; Collaborations include Liam O'Flynn; Micheál Ó Súilleabháin; De Dannan; Stockton's Wing; Donal Lunny; Nomos and Altan; John Cage; Evelyn Glennie; Appeared in Mel Mercier with Seamus Egan's Bodhrán and Bones video, 1993. *Compositions:* Medea (Abbey Theatre, 2000); Harold and Sophie (co-written with Linda Buckley, 2000); Rough Air (John Scott/Irish Modern Dance Theatre, 2001); A Midsummer Night's Dream (co-written with Linda Buckley, Corcadorca, 2001). *Recordings include:* with Pulsus: A River of Sound, 1996; with Micheál Ó Súilleabháin: The Dolphin's Way; Casadh, 1990; Gaiseadh, 1992; Templum, 2001.

MERCK Alex; b. July 1956, Germany. Publisher; Guitarist; Composer. *Education:* Economics, Mainz University, Germany; Diploma, Professional Music, Berklec College of Music, Boston; Guitar and Composition Lessons.

Career: Live tours with Raoul de Souza and as Solo Artist, 1984–86; Many TV appearances in Germany; Studio recordings, 1985–; TV-film scores, 1987-. *Compositions:* Molthe; Adios Buenos Aires. *Recordings:* Doy Days, album, 1986. *Publications:* Keyboards, Midi, Homgrecording, 1990, 1997. *Membership:* GEMA. *Leisure interests:* Surfing; Skiing; Sailing. *Address:* Trujanstr 18, 50678 Koeln, Germany.

MERCURY Daniela, (Daniela Mercuri de Almeida Póvoas); b. 28 July 1965, Salvador, Bahia, Brazil. Vocalist; Songwriter; Dancer; Choreographer. *Career:* Performs in the energetic axé style; Member of dance group Salta, early 1990s; Backing singer in Gilberto Gil band and member of Companhia Clic; Toured internationally as a solo artist. *Recordings:* Albums: Compania Clic, 1990; Daniela, 1992; O Canto Da Cidade, 1993; Musica De Ruai, 1994; Feijao Com Arroz, Swing Da Cor, 1997; Electrica, 1998; Sol da Liberdade, 2000; Sou de Qualquer Lugar, 2001; features on: Da Licenca Men Senhor, Joao Bosco, 1996; Song Book, João Donato, 1999; Ofrenda, Pedro Guerra, 2001. *Honours:* Prêmio Sharp, Daniela, 1992.

MERRILL Helen; b. 21 July 1930, New York City, New York, USA. Vocalist. *Career:* First performed, 1944; Vocalist with Reggie Childs' orchestra 1946–47; Debut album released on EmArcy, 1954; Recorded regularly with trumpeter Clifford Brown; Short spell with Atco and Metrojazz, 1959; Moved to Italy for 4 years; Returned to USA briefly, recording with pianist Dick Katz on Milestone Records, mid 1960s; Relocated to Japan to concentrated on performing, early 1970s; Returned to USA by mid '70s and resumed recording career, releasing albums on Inner City, Owl and Antilles; Currently records for Verve; Tours widely. *Recordings:* Albums include: Don't Explain, Helen Merrill With Clifford Brown, 1954; Dream of You, 1956; The Nearness of You, Merrill At Midnight, 1957; You've Got A Date With The Blues, 1959; The Feeling Is Mutual, 1965; Shade of Difference, 1969; Sposin', 1971; Chasin' The Bird, 1979; Casa Forte, 1980; Collaboration, 1987; Alone Together, 1989; Clear Out of This World, 1991; Brownie – Homage To Clifford Brown, 1995; Jelena Ana Milcactic (a.k.a. Helen Merrill), 2000. *Current Management:* Abby Hoffer. *E-mail:* webmaster@helenmerrill.com. *Internet:* www.helenmerrill.com.

MERRILL Robbie; b. 13 June 1964, Lawrence, Massachusetts, USA. Musician (bass guitar). *Career:* Spent time in various covers bands until joining Godsmack, 1995; Recorded independent debut album for $2500 over 3 days with money borrowed from friend, 1996; Heavy local airplay on Boston-based WAAF radio station led to deal with Republic/Universal, 1998; Debut LP remixed/repackaged with eponymous title; Album banned by US Wal-Mart and K-Mart stores for profane content; US and European gigs in 1999 and 2000 including: Woodstock '99; Ozzfest; MTV's Return of The Rock tour; Second album recorded in warehouse in Massachusetts, 2000; First major amphitheatre tour, 2001. *Recordings:* Albums: All Wound Up, 1997; Godsmack, 1998; Awake, 2000; Singles: Whatever, Keep Away, 1998; Voodoo, Bad Religion, 1999; Awake, 2000; Greed, Bad Magick, 2001. *Honours:* Whatever single spent record total of 33 weeks on Billboard Top 10; Boston Music Awards, Act of The Year, 2000 and 2001; Billboard Award, Rock Artist of The Year, 2001. *Address:* c/o Paul Geary, PGM, PO Box 9134, Boston, MA 02205, USA. *E-mail:* godsmack@pgmglobal.com. *Internet:* www.godsmack.com.

MERRITT Jymie, (James Raleigh); b. 3 May 1926, Philadelphia, Pennsylvania, USA. Jazz Musician (bass); Composer. m. (1) Dorothy Small, 1949 (divorced 1977), 5 s.; (2) Ave Maria Davis, 9 Sept. 1981. *Career:* Bass player with Art Blakey and The Jazz Messengers; Gregory and Maurice Hines; Max Roach; Dizzy Gillespie; Lee Morgan; Director, composer, Forerunner Jazz Organization and Orchestra, 1962-.

MERTA Vladimir; b. 20 Jan. 1946, Prague, Czech Republic. Singer; Songwriter; Film Dir; Composer; Musician (guitar, flute). m. Lucie Lucka, 2 d. *Education:* CVUT, Faculty of Architecture; FAMU – Film Faculty, Academy of Musical Arts, Prague. *Musical Education:* LSU – People's School of Arts, Prague. *Career:* Performed at: Roskilde Festival, Denmark, 1988, 1990; Japan, 1991; Vancouver Folk Festival, 1992; Edinburgh Fringe, 1993; More Than Meets The Ear, London; South Bank Centre, London, 1994; Strasbourg, Mittleeuropa; Washington Folk Life Festival; Cheltenham Litterary Festival, 1995. *Compositions include:* Five television specials, Thru The Guitar Hole; One feature script, Opera In The Wineyard; Music for 15 cartoons; 10 pieces of theatre music. *Recordings:* Ballade de Prague, 1969; Vladimir Merta Live, Vols I and II, 1989, 1990; Svatky Trpelivosti, Chtit Chytit Vitr, Biti Rublem, 1993; Jewish choir Mispaha, Vols I and II, 1993, 1995; Sefardic Songs (with Jana Lewitova), 1996. *Publications:* Advantage Server (novel), 1987; Born In The Bohemia (complete lyrics), 1993; Folk Blues Guitar and Harmonica (with 3 hour VHS cassette), 1993; Troubadour In The Age of Global Village, 1994. *Honours:* Porta, 1986. *Memberships:* OSA; INTERGRAM; SAI. *Leisure interests:* Tennis; Downhill skiing; Biking. *Current Management:* Z Agency, Zdenek Vrestal, Graficka 15, Prague 5, Czech Republic.

MESSINA Jim; b. 5 Dec. 1957, Maywood, California, USA. Musician (guitar, bass); Vocalist; Record Prod.; Engineer. *Career:* Recording engineer, member, Buffalo Springfield, 1968; Poco, 1968–70; Loggins and Messina, 1971–76; Built own studio, Gateway Studios, 1983. *Recordings:* Albums: with The Jesters: Jim Messina and The Jesters, 1967; The Dragsters, 1967; with Buffalo Springfield: Last Time Around, 1968; with Loggins and Messina: Kenny Loggins With Jim Messina Sittin' In, 1971; Loggins and Messina, 1973; Full Sail, 1973; On Stage, 1974; Mother Lode, 1974; So Fine, 1975; Native Sons, 1976; Solo albums: Finale, 1978; Oasis, 1979; Messina, 1981; One More Mile, 1981; Watching the River Run, 1996; with Poco: Legacy, 1989; Singles include: Your Mama Don't Dance, 1973; Thinking of You, 1973; My Music, 1973. *Memberships:* ASCAP; AFTRA. *Current Management:* Steve Jensen, Direct Management, 947 N La Cienega, Los Angeles, CA 90069, USA. *Address:* c/o MCO Financial Management, PO Box 176, Los Olivos CA 93441–0176, USA.

MESSINA Jo Dee Marie; b. 25 Aug. 1970, Framingham, Massachusetts, USA. Country vocalist. *Career:* Sang in country bands around New England area in teens; Performed at local talent shows, Nashville, aged 19; Brought to Curb Records by producer James Stroud; Signed to label, 1994; Debut album produced by Byron Gallimore and Tim McGraw; Debut singles Heads Carolina Tails California and You're Not In Kansas Anymore reached top ten on Billboard country singles chart, 1996; Considered quitting music business when subsequent releases were less successful; Return to chart success and popularlity, 1998-. *Recordings include:* Heads Carolina Tails California, You're Not In Kansas Anymore, 1996; I'm Alright, Bye Bye, Lesson In Leavin', 1998; Burn, 2000; Albums: Jo Dee Messina, 1996; I'm Alright, 1998; Burn, 2000. *Honours:* various including: CMA, Horizon Award, 1999; ACM, Top New Female Vocalist, 1999. *Address:* c/o The Country Music Asscn, Nashville, Tennessee, USA. *Internet:* www.jodeemessina.com.

METCALFE Andy; b. 3 March 1956, Bristol, England. Musician (bass, keyboards); Prod. m. Lilian Metcalfe, 25 July 1992, 1 s. *Education:* Sussex University. *Musical Education:* A-level, degree in Music. *Career:* 12 albums, many tours with Robyn Hitchcock, 3 of whose albums produced, 1976–94; 3 years, 2 albums with Squeeze, 1985–88; 2 series MD Vic Reeves Big Night Out Channel 4, 1990, 1991. *Recordings:* Produced: The Reivers; Edge Park; Robyn Hitchcock, 3 albums, 1976–94; Founder member, Soft Boys, 3 albums, 1976–79. *Honours:* Silver and Platinum discs with Squeeze. *Memberships:* Musicians' Union (UK); American Musicians' Union. *Leisure interests:* Reading; Crosswords; Walking. *Current Management:* Peter Jenner, Sincere Management. *Address:* c/o 421 Harrow Rd, London W10 4RD, England.

METHENY Pat (Patrick Bruce); b. 12 Aug. 1954, Lee's Summit, Missouri, USA. Musician (guitar). *Education:* University of Miami, Florida. *Career:* Music Instructor at: University of Miami; National Stage Band Camps, Florida; Berklee College Music, Boston; Guitarist with Gary Burton Quintet; Music director and guitarist, Pat Metheny Group, 1978–; Tours throughout USA; Europe; Canada; Japan; USSR; South America. *Compositions:* Film scores: The Falcon and The Snowman (with David Bowie), 1984; Twice In A Lifetime, 1985. *Recordings:* Albums include: Bright Size Life, 1976; Watercolours, 1977; Pat Metheny Group, 1978; New Chautauqua, 1979; American Garage, 1980; As Falls Wichita, So Falls Wichita Falls, 1981; Offramp, 1982; Travels, 1983; Rejoicing, 1983; Works, 1984; First Circle, 1984; Still Life (Talking), 1987; Works II, 1988; Letter From Home, 1989; Question and Answer (with Roy Haynes and Dave Holland), 1990; Song X (with Ornette Coleman); We Live Here, 1995; Quartet, 1996; Sign of Four, 1996; Imaginary Day, 1997; Passaggio Per Il Paradiso, 1998; A Map of The World, 1999; Last Train Home, 1999. *Honours include:* 5 Grammy Awards, 1982–89; 2 Grammy Nominations, 1980–81; Boston Music Awards: Outstanding Jazz Album, Outstanding Guitarist, Outstanding Jazz Fusion Group, 1986; Magazine Awards and Poll Wins: Downbeat; Jazziz; Guitar Player; Also listed in Guitar Player magazine Gallery of Greats, 1982–86. *Address:* c/o Ted Kurland Associates, 173 Brighton Ave, Boston, MA 02134, USA.

METHOD MAN (Clifford Smith), (Iron Lung, Hott Nikkels, Ticallion Stallion, Johnny Blaze); b. 1 April 1971, Staten Island, New York, USA. Prod.; Rapper. *Career:* Founder member, Wu Tang Clan; Released debut solo album, 1994; Appeared in Hype Williams' film Belly and How High (with Redman), 2002; Collaborations: Texas; LL Cool J; Redman; Notorious B.I.G.; Boyz II Men. *Recordings:* Albums: Enter The Wu-Tang Clan, 1993; Tical, 1994; Wu-Tang Forever, 1997; Tical, Judgement Day, The W, 2000; Blackout (with Redman), 2001; Singles: Release Yo' Delf, 1995; I'll Be There For You (with Mary J Blige), 1996; Break Ups To Make Ups, 1999; Da Rockwilder (with Redman), 2000; How High Part 2, 2002. *Honours:* Grammy Award, Best Rap Performance By A Duo Or Group, I'll Be There For You (with Mary J Blige), 1996. *Address:* c/o Def Jam, 825, Eighth Ave, New York, USA.

METSERS Paul; b. 27 Nov. 1945, Netherlands. Singer; Songwriter; Musician (guitar, dulcimer, mandocello). *Career:* Professional folk musician touring UK, Netherlands, Italy, Japan, Australia and New Zealand, 1980–89; Frequent radio coverage of songs and guest appearances. *Compositions include:* Farewell To The Gold, sung by various artists including Bob Dylan. *Recordings:* 5 albums. *Publications:* Song book. *Honours:* Voted in Top 10 of Best Male Folk Artists, Folk On 2 Poll; Featured in Guinness Book of Folk Music. *Memberships:* Musicians' Union; PRS; MCPS; BASCA. *Current Management:* P Brocklehurst. *Address:* Mint Cottage, Gilthwaiterigg Lane, Kendal LA9 6NT, Cumbria.

METZGER Jon Frederick; b. 30 July 1959, Washington DC, USA. Musician. m. Linda Brookshire. *Education:* BMus, 1981, MMus, 1994, North Carolina School of the Arts. *Career:* US Information Agency Arts America Program Tours of the Near East, Northern and Sub Sahara, Africa, Central America; Concert Halls, Jazz Clubs, throughout the USA, Europe, Including East Coast Jazz Festival, Lincoln Center, Kennedy Center Constitutional Hall, Smithsonian Institute, Corcoran Gallery of Art, Blues Alley, One Step Down. *Compositions include:* Spiral Passages; On Verchiels Wings; Elephant Walk; The Spinner, I'll Always Be Loving you; Time Again; Credit Line; Mixed Up; Into The Light; Out of the Dark; My Lady. *Recordings:* While We're Young; The Spinner; Into The Light; Out of The Dark; Jon Metzger, Vibes. *Publications:* The Art and Language of Jazz Vibes, 1996. *Honours:* National Endowment for the Arts Grant, 1985; American Society of Composers, Authors, Publishers Popular Award, 1985–98. *Memberships:* Artist, Clinician Musser; American Society of Composers, Authors, Publishers; International Asscn of Jazz Educators. *Leisure interests:* Tennis; Fishing; Cooking. *Current Management:* Percussion Events Registry Company, 8534 Coppertowne Lane, Dallas, TX 75243 8035, USA.

MEX Paul; b. 25 Nov. 1962, St Albans, Hertfordshire, England. Record Prod.; Musician. *Career:* Recording career producing and mixing for numerous artistes; As producer, over 500,000 record sales to credit, including Top 5 UK chart success; Business ventures: State Art; Mex One Recordings; DHE Enterprises. *Recordings:* with Poison No. 9: Lay All Your Love On Me; with United States of Europe: Free; with Son of Space: Magic Fly; with Man 2 Man: Malestripper; with Ugly As Sin: Terminal Love. *Honours:* Silver and Gold discs. *Memberships:* PRS; MCPS; Musicians' Union. *Leisure interests:* Reading; Keep-fit. *Current Management:* Mex One Recordings. *Address:* Lower Ground Floor, 3 Eaton Pl., Brighton, East Sussex BN2 1EH, England.

MEYER Patrice; b. 18 Dec. 1957, Saverne, France. Musician. *Musical Education:* Self-taught Guitar Player. *Career:* Member, Guitar Player in Hugh Hopper Band, 1989-, in Equip Out with Pip Pyle and Elton Dean; Member, Richard Sinclair's Band. *Recordings:* Patrice Meyer: Racines Croisées, 1983; Dromadaire Vicmaois, 1986; With Hugh Hopper: Mecano Pelorus, 1989; Carousel, 1994; Hooligan Romantics, 1993. *Address:* 12 Vieille Route, 77580 Voulangis, France.

MEYERS Ken; b. 20 Aug. 1965. Singer; Musician (guitar). *Education:* University of Lille III, France. *Musical Education:* Self-taught. *Career:* Support band for John Mayall, Calvin Russel, Bernard Allison, Peter Case; Numerous festivals and concerts; Appearances on: M6 (television), France; RFM (radio); Local radio stations. *Recordings:* Album: Live, CD, 1994. *Membership:* SACEM. *Leisure interests:* Making life better and the music more beautiful. *Current Management:* Ken Meyers, 117 rue Lambrecht Apt 22, 59500 Douai, France.

M'FOKO Mansiamina, (Bopol Mansiamina); b. 26 July 1949, Kinshasa, Zaire. Artiste; Composer; Musician (Guitar). *Career:* Member, Orchestre Bamboula, represented Zaire in the festival of African music in Algeria, 1969; Founder, orchestra, Rock A Mambo, 1970; Member, orchestra, Africa Fiesta Sukisa with Dr Nico, 1970; Co-founder, orchestre, Continental, began writing and composing songs, released 3 singles, 1971; Member, orchestra, Afrisa and Tabu Leye, 1973–76; Founder, Ya Toupas with Ray Lema and Manuaku, accompanied the artist M'Pongo Love, 1976; Left for West Africa, met Sam Manguana-Lokassa and Dizzy Mandjeku, joined Africa All Stars, 1978; Began solo carer, released debut album, 1979; Arrived in France, 1982; Founder, 4 Etoiles with Nyboma-Syran Mbenza and Muta Mayi, 1983; Continued with solo career; Tours in most African countries, Europe and the USA. *Recordings:* 3 single releases; Albums: Pitié, je veux la reconciliation; Mariage forcé, Manuela.

MHLONGO Busi; b. Inanda, KwaZulu Natal, South Africa. Vocalist; Songwriter. *Career:* Started singing in church and later joined choral groups; Won a Gallo Records talent contest, 1963; Appeared in stage and film productions of Alfred Herbert's African Jazz and African Follies; Lived in Portugal, America, Canada and Holland, continually performing; Collaborations: Osibisa; Ifang Bondi; Pops Mohamed; Amampondo; Brice Wassy. *Recordings:* Babemu, 1994; Urban Zulu, 1998. *Honours:* SAMA Awards: Best Female Artist; Best Adult Contemporary Album (African); Best African Pop Album, Urban Zulu, 2000; Urban Zulu also held number 1 position in European World Music Album Chart for two months.

MICENMACHER Youval; b. 18 Oct. 1949, Paris, France. Musician (percussion); Actor. m. Arnelle de Frondeville, 9 Sept. 1983, 1 s., 1 d. *Musical Education:* Self-taught from age 12. *Career:* Co-founder, jazz group, Arcane V; L'Impossible Trio, 1986; Ichthyornis (duo), 1986; Played with: Michel Godard; Philippe Deschepper; Gérard Marais; Vincent Courtois; Louis Sclavis; Mohamad Hamam; Fawzi Al-Aiedy; Djamchid Chémirani; Pierre Seghers; Michel Touraille; Jean-Marc Padovani; Claude Barthélemy; Founder, company Solos Performces; *Performances:* Peau à Peau, Festival d'Avignon, 1983; Kaddish, Montpellier, 1984; La Braraque Rouge (jazz opera), 1985; Joueurs de Jazz, Festival de Marne-La-Vallée, 1987; Très Horas de Sol (jazz and flamenco), Festival Banlieues Bleues, 1987; Psyché, Opera by Lully, Festival d'Aix En Provence, 1987; Jubal, solo, 1988; Le Rôdeur, Festival de Marne-La-Vallée, tours of France, Austria, Hungary, 1989; Opéra-Goude, with solistes de l'Ensemble Intercontemporain, 1989; Jumelles, opera, 1990; Actor, percussionist, Black Ballad (with Archie Shepp, Dee Dee Bridgewater), 1991; Sud, 1992; Echange, musical, 1992; Around About Bobby, Festival de Banlieues Bleues, 1993; Mister Cendron (jazz opera), 1993; Ma Nuit Chez Lucy, musical, 1994; Hommage à Germaine Dulac, 1994; Numerous festivals with Quartet Opera de Gérard Marais, 1995; The Voice in Upper Galilee Festival, 1995. *Recordings:* Chants Hébreux D'Orient, 1994; Fera Fera, 1994; Tres Horas De Sol; Le Rodeur; L'Impossible Trio; Nimenio; Est; Lamidbar; Turkish Songs; Global Voices, 1998; Chant Spirit in Sound, 1999; Mediterranee. *Leisure interest:* Philosophy. *Current Management:* Solos Performances. *Address:* 108 rue Gambetta, 94120 Fontenay-Sous-Bois, France.

MICHAEL George, (Georgios Kyriacos Panayiotou); b. 25 June 1963, Finchley, London, England. Singer; Songwriter; Prod. *Career:* Singer, The Executive, 1979; Singer, pop duo Wham! with Andrew Ridgeley, 1982–86; Solo artiste, 1986–; World-wide appearances include: Live Aid, with Elton John, Wembley, 1985; Prince's Trust Rock Gala, 1986; Wham's 'The Final' concert, Wembley, 1986; Nelson Mandela's 70th Birthday Tribute, 1988; Rock In Rio II Festival, Brazil, 1991; A Concert For Life, tribute to Freddie Mercury, Wembley Stadium, 1992; Elizabeth Taylor AIDS Foundation Benefit, Madison Square Garden, New York, 1992; Dispute with Epic record label, and parent company Sony Entertainment, 1992–95; Television special, Aretha Franklin: Duets, 1993. *Recordings:* Albums: with Wham!: Fantastic (No. 1, UK), 1983; Make It Big (No. 1, UK and USA), 1984; The Final, 1986; Solo albums: Faith (No. 1, USA), 1987; Listen Without Prejudice, Vol. 1, 1990; Older and Upper, 1998; Ladies and Gentlemen: The Best of George Michael, 1998; Songs from the Last Century, 1999; Contributor, Duets, Elton John, 1991; Two Rooms, 1992; Hit singles include: with Wham!: Wham Rap, 1982; Young Guns (Go For It), 1982; Bad Boys, 1983; Club Tropicana, 1983; Wake Me Up Before You Go Go (No. 1, UK), 1984; Last Christmas, 1984; Careless Whisper (No. 1, USA and UK), 1984; Everything She Wants (No. 1, USA), 1984; Freedom, 1985; I'm Your Man (No. 1, UK), 1985; The Edge of Heaven (No. 1, UK), 1986; Solo: A Different Corner (No. 1, UK), 1986; I Knew You Were Waiting For Me, duet with Aretha Franklin, (No. 1, UK), 1987; I Want Your Sex, 1987; Faith (No. 1, USA), 1987; Father Figure (No. 1, USA), 1988; One More Try (No. 1, USA), 1988; Monkey (No. 1, USA), 1988; Kissing A Fool, 1988; Praying For Time (No. 1, USA), 1990; Freedom 90, 1990; Don't Let The Sun Go Down On Me, duet with Elton John (No. 1, UK and USA); Too Funky, 1992; Five Live EP (No. 1, UK), 1993; Somebody To Love, with Queen, 1993; Jesus To A Child (No. 1, UK), 1995; Fast Love, 1996; Star People, 1997; You Have Been, 1997; Outside, 1998; Contributor, Do They Know It's Christmas?, Band Aid, 1985; Nikita, Elton John, 1985. *Publication:* Bare, with Tony Parsons (autobiography). *Honours include:* BRIT Awards: Best British Group, 1985; Outstanding Contribution to British Music, 1986; Best British Male Artist, 1988; Best British Album, 1991; Ivor Novello Awards: Songwriter of The Year, 1985, 1989; Most Performed Work (Careless Whisper), 1985; Hit of The Year (Faith), 1989; Grammy, with Aretha Franklin, 1988; Nordoff-Robbins Silver Clef Award, 1989; American Music Awards: Favourite Pop/Rock Male Artist, Soul R & B Male Artist, Favourite Album, 1989; ASCAP Golden Note Award, 1992. *Address:* c/o Connie Filipello Publicity, 17 Gosfield St, London W1P 7HE, England.

MICHAEL Richard Ewen; b. 24 July 1949, Stonehaven, Scotland. Jazz Educator. m. Morag, 12 Sept. 1972, 1 s., 2 d. *Education:* RSAMD, 1967–71. *Career:* Founder, Fife Youth Jazz Orchestra, 1976; Established Jazz Education in Fife and Scotland; Seminars giver throughout UK, Europe and in New York; One of architects of the Associate Board of Jazz Piano syllabus; Teacher, Beatit High School, Cowdenbeath, 1974-. *Compositions:* Homecoming; The Shetland Suite; Young Persons Guide to the Jazz Orchestra; Jazz Suite for Ubejo Piano. *Recordings:* Homecoming; Shetland Suite; Dedication. *Publications:* Creative Jazz Education, 1987; Small Band Jazz for the Classroom, 1996; Various Associated Board jazz pieces; Jazz Beginnings, 1996. *Honours:* Music Teacher of the Year, 1984; Jr Band Winner of BBC Big Band Competition, as Director of Fife Youth Jazz Orchestra, 1994. *Memberships:* SSTA; Musicians' Union. *Leisure interests:* Running; Malt whisky; Cricket. *Address:* 6 Dronachy Rd, Kirkcaldy, Fife KY2 5QI, Scotland.

MICHAELIS Pasquale, (Pasquale Michaux); b. 22 Oct. 1958, Auvelais. Musician (Saxophones, Clarinet, Keyboards, Hammond Piano, Electric Bass); Composer; Arranger; Vocalist. *Career:* Appearances with Deborah Brow Quartet; Art Farmer; Johnny Griffin Quartet; Kim Parker; Clark Terry Quartet; Toots, Matia Bazar; Drummin Man (P York); Adriano Celentano; D Geers; Bruce Adams/P Michaux Quintet; Hammond Swing Machine; J Halliday/T Jones/T Browne's Funk Machine. *Compositions:* My Angel's Eyes; I'll Remember You, Benny; Organology; Mild and Bourbon for Eddie Please. *Recordings:* Atmosphere; Remember Adolf Sax; Bob Lacemant Trio. *Honours:* Best Young Saxophonist, Belgium, 1979; Best Keyboards, Italy, 1985. *Memberships:* SABAM' SIAE (Author and Lyric Society). *Leisure interest:* Mechanic and collector of old cars. *Address:* 8 rue E Deroover, 1081 Brussels, Belgium.

MICHAELS Bret; b. 15 March 1963, Pittsburgh, Pennsylvania, USA. Singer. *Career:* Member, US rock groups: the Spectres; Paris; Lead vocalist, US rock group Poison, 1984–; Appearances include: Monsters of Rock Festival, Castle Donington, 1988, 1990; Solo tour, performing acoustic version of Poison material, 1991; Capitol Record's 50th anniversary gala, Hollywood, 1992; Solo participation, Lynyrd Skynyrd and Friends LYVE concert, Atlanta, 1993; The Tonight Show, NBC TV, 1993. *Recordings:* Hit singles with Poison: Talk Dirty To Me; I Won't Forget You; Nothin' But A Good Time; Fallen Angel; Your Mama Don't Dance; Unskinny Bop; Every Rose Has It's Thorn; Albums: with Poison: Look What The Cat Dragged In, 1986; Open Up and Say... Aah, 1988; Flesh and Blood, 1990; Swallow This Live, 1991; Native Tongue, 1993; Greatest Hits 1986–96, 1996; Letter from Death Row, 1998 Guest on album by comedian Sam Kinison, Leader of The Banned, 1990. *Honours include:* NARM Award, Best Selling Heavy Metal Album, Flesh and Blood, 1991. *Current Management:* H K Management, 8900 Wilshire Blvd, Suite 300, Beverly Hills, CA 90211, USA.

MICHEL Pras, (Samuel Prazakiel Michel); b. 19 Oct. 1972, Haiti. Rapper. *Career:* Member, Tranzlator Crew, with Lauryn Hill and Wyclef Jean; Renamed as The Fugees; Numerous television and live appearances; Began solo career. *Recordings:* With The Fugees: Singles: Boof Baf, 1993; Nappy Heads, EP, 1994; Vocab, EP, 1994; Ready or Not, 1996; The Score, 1996; Fu-Gee-La, 1996; Killing Me Softly, 1997; Rumble in the Jungle, 1997; Albums: Blunted on Reality, 1993; The Score, 1996; Solo: Singles: Ghetto Superstar, 1998; Another One Bites the Dust, 1998; Blue Angels, 1998; What'cha Wanna Do, 1998; Album: Ghetto Superstar, 1998.

MICHELMORE Guy; b. 27 Aug. 1957. Composer. *Education:* BA Hons, English Language, Literature, Oxford University. *Musical Education:* Studied mouth organ with Larry Adler. *Career:* Composer, film and television music including: Eyewitness; Human Animal; 341 – a film for the World Summit for Children. *Membership:* APC. *Address:* 35 Binden Rd, London W12 9RJ, England.

MICHELUTTI Andrea; b. 20 Sept. 1962, Udine, Italy. Musician (drums). m. Amerita Moretti, 2 May 1992. *Education:* Graduate, Musicology, Bologna University, Italy. *Musical Education:* Conservatory of Music (percussion), Chatou, France. *Career:* Worked with: Art Farmer; Steve Grossman; Jerry Bergonzi; Ben Sidran; Harry Sweets Edison; Hal Crook; Jimmy Owens; Roger Guerin; Michelle Hendricks; Alain Jean-Marie; Paul Bollenback; Benny Golson, Jeffery Smith; Ricky Ford; Appearances, jazz festivals, concerts: Italy; France; Switzerland; Austria; Germany; Yugoslavia. *Recordings:* Orsa Minore, L Malaguti Qintet; Tip of The Hat, La Malaguti Quintet, Sextet; L'Art d'Aimer, with Giovanni Licata Quintet; Les petits loups du Jazz, with Michelle Hendricks and Sylvain Beuf. *Address:* 33 rue Raymond Queneau, 92500 Rueil Malmaison, France.

MICHIELS Paul; b. 15 June 1948, Belgium. Musician (Lead Vocal, Guitar, Keyboards); Composer. *Career:* Soulsister. *Compositions:* Soulsister – Repertoire; Changes, Tom Jones; The Way to Your Heart. *Recordings:* Soulsister: It Takes Two; Heat; Simple Rule; Live Savings; Swinging Like Big Dogs; The Very Best of Soulsister; Paul Michiels: The Inner Child. *Honours:* Golden Eye Award, 1992, 1993; World Music Award, Monaco, 1990. *Membership:* SABAM. *Leisure interest:* Music. *Current Management:* Johan Berckmans. *Address:* Mereldreef 3, 3140 Keerbergen, Belgium.

MIDDLETON Darren; b. 4 Oct. 1972. Musician (guitar, keyboards). 1 d. *Career:* Last member to join Brisbane-based Powderfinger rock group 1992; Steadily built reputation on many Australian tours/festival appearances; International breakthrough with Odyssey Number Five album; Constant world-wide touring throughout 2000–01 ending with New Suburban Fables 2001 Australian shows; Also vocalist/guitarist in fun side-project Drag. *Recordings:* Albums: Parables For Wooden Ears, 1994; Double Allergic, 1996; Internationalist, 1998; Odyssey Number Five, 2000; Singles: Powderfinger Blue (EP), Transfusion (EP), 1993; Tail, Grave Concern, 1994; Save Your Skin, Mr Kneebone (EP), 1995; Pick You Up, D.A.F., Living Type, 1996; Take Me In, 1997; The Day You Come, Don't Wanna Be Left Out/Good-Day Ray, 1998; Already Gone, Passenger, 1999; My Happiness, 2000; Like A Dog, The Metre, 2001. *Honours:* ARIA Awards: Album of The Year; Song of The Year; Best Rock Album; Best Cover

Artwork, 1999; six times platinum fourth album on Australian chart for 67 weeks by end of 2001; Only home-grown act ever to play more than 3 consecutive nights at Festival Hall, Australia. *Address:* c/o Republic Records, Australia. *Internet:* www.powderfinger.com.

MIDDLETON Tom, (Cosmos, The Mod Wheel, Tom 'The Jedi' Middleton); b. 1971 Devon, England. Prod.; Remixer; DJ. *Musical Education:* Classically trained cellist and pianist. *Career:* Co-founder Evolution/Universal Language Records (with production partner Mark Pritchard); Protégé of Aphex Twin; Presenter of weekly Deep Step Breakbeat Show on London radio station Kiss 100 FM; Member: Global Communication, Link, Jedi Knights, The Bays; Collaborations: Mark Pritchard, Jamie Odell; Remixed: Goldfrapp, Lamb, Depeche Mode, Ian Pooley, Pulp. *Recordings:* Albums: 76–14 (with Global Communication), 1994; New School Science (with Jedi Knights), 1996; Cosmos album forthcoming, 2002; Singles: Auto Reload EP (with Global Communication), 1992; Maiden Voyage (with Global Communication), 1994; Antacid (with Link), 1995; May The Funk Be With You (with Jedi Knights), 1995; Catch The Break (with Jedi Knights), 1997; The Groove (with Global Communication), 1997; Summer In Space, 1999. *Current Management:* c/o Island Blue Records, 22 St Peter's Sq., London, W6 9NW, England.

MIDDLETON Tracey K; b. 20 Sept. 1966, Solihull, England. Musician (Accordion). *Education:* BA, Christ Church College, Canterbury; Guildhall School of Music with John Leslie; Royal School of Music, Piano, clarinet, theory with Dr Kevin Thompson. *Career:* Formed Amaryllis, accordion duo, with David Garwood, 1986; Provincial theatre work, 1986–95; Cheltenham International Music Festival, with Amaryllis, 1991; Chairman, Club Accord, Midlands UK accordion club, 1992–96; Regular performer with Amaryllis at accordion festivals such as Autumn International Accordion Festival, 1990–93, 1996–99; Various folk festivals in England with Amaryllis, 1995–99; Appearances at many folk clubs with Amaryllis, Folk dance weekly and weekend festivals; Numerous concerts at accordion clubs in England with Amaryllis; Workshops and lectures on the accordion and English and American folk dance music. *Recordings:* As Amaryllis: Here, There and Everywhere; Dance and Sing; Mendhams Maytime. *Publications:* Articles on English folk music in Accordion Times. *Memberships:* Musicians' Union; English Folk Dance and Song Society; National Accordion Organisation. *Leisure interests:* Art, mainly fabric painting; Science Fiction; Computers. *Address:* 16 Norgrave Rd, Solihull, West Midlands B92 9JH, England.

MIDLER Bette; b. 1 Dec. 1945, Paterson, New Jersey, USA. Singer; Actress; Comedienne. m. Martin von Haselberg, 1984, 1 d. *Education:* Theatre studies, University of Hawaii. *Career:* As actress: Cast member, Fiddler On The Roof, Broadway, 1966–69; Salvation, New York, 1970; Rock opera Tommy, Seattle Opera Company, 1971; Nightclub concert performer and solo artiste, 1972–; Numerous television appearances include: Ol' Red Hair Is Back, NBC, 1978; Bette Midler's Mondo Beyondo, HBO, 1988; Earth Day Special, ABC, 1990; The Tonight Show, NBC, 1991; Now, NBC, 1993; Films include: Hawaii, 1965; The Rose, 1979; Jinxed!, 1982; Down and Out In Beverly Hills, 1985; Ruthless People, 1986; Outrageous Fortune, 1987; Big Business, 1988; Beaches, 1988; Stella, 1990; Scenes From A Mall, 1990; For The Boys (also co-producer), 1991; Hocus Pocus, 1993; Own company, All Girls Productions, 1989-. *Recordings:* Albums include: The Divine Miss M, 1972; Bette Midler, 1973; Songs For The New Depression, 1976; Broken Blossom, 1977; Live At Last, 1977; Thighs and Whispers, 1979; The Rose, film soundtrack, 1979; Divine Madness, film soundtrack, 1980; No Frills, 1984; Beaches, film soundtrack, 1989; Some People's Lives, 1991; Best Of, 1993; Bette of Roses, 1995; Experience the Divine, 1997; Bathhouse Betty, 1998; From a Distance, 1998; Singles include: The Rose; Wind Beneath My Wings (No. 1, USA), from Beaches soundtrack, 1989; From A Distance, 1991. *Publications:* A View From A Broad; The Saga of Baby Divine. *Honours:* After Dark Award, Performer of The Year, 1973; Grammy Awards: Best New Artist, 1973; Best Female Pop Vocal Performance, The Rose, 1981; Record of The Year, Song of The Year, Wind Beneath My Wings, 1990; Special Tony Award, 1973; Emmy, Ol' Red Hair Is Back, 1978; Golden Globe Awards: The Rose, 1979; For The Boys, 1991; Academy Award nomination, Best Actress, The Rose, 1980; Contributor, We Are The World, USA For Africa, 1985; Oliver and Company, 1988. *Address:* c/o All Girls Productions, Animation Bldg #3B-10, 500 S Buena Vista, Burbank, CA 91521, USA.

MIGUEL Luis; b. 1970, Puerto Rico. Vocalist. *Career:* Won first Grammy aged 15 for Me Gustas Tal Como Eres (duet with Sheena Easton), 1985; Duetted with Frank Sinatra on recording of Come Fly With Me for Sinatra's Duets Vol. 2 album, 1994; One of the biggest selling Latin solo artists of all time; Continues to tour internationally. *Recordings:* Albums include: Soy Como Quiero Ser, 1986; Un Hombre Busca Una Mujer, 1988; 20 Anos, 1990; Romance, 1991; Aries, 1993; Segunda Romance, 1994; El Concierto, 1995; Romance, 1997; Amarte Es Un Placer, 1999. *Honours:* seven Grammy awards; a star in the Hollywood Walk of Fame; 1990, European Excellence Award from Spain; First Latin artist to win Best

Selling Artist award at the World Music Awards; MTV Award, Best International Video, 1992; Recognized by the Recording Industry Artists of America, 1994; sales of over 40m. records world-wide. *Internet:* www.lacasadeluismiguel.com.

MIKE D (Michael Diamond); b. 20 Nov. 1965, New York, USA. Rapper; Musician (drums). *Career:* Member, the Young and Useless, 1979; Founder, US rap/rock group the Beastie Boys, 1983–; Appearances include: Support to Madonna, Virgin Tour, 1985; Support to Run-DMC, Raisin' Hell Tour, 1986; Co-headliners with Run-DMC, Together Forever Tour, 1987; Reading Festival, 1992; Film appearances: Krush Groove; Scared Stupid; Tougher Than Leather, with Run-DMC. *Recordings:* Singles: She's On It; Fight For Your Right To Party; Albums: Licensed To Ill, 1986; Paul's Boutique, 1989; Check Your Head, 1992; Ill Communication, 1994; Root Down, 1995; The In Sound From Way Out, 1996; Also appears on: Army of Me, Bjork; Special Brew; Notorious, Pimps Playas and Hustlas; Good Will Hunting; I'm The Bad Guy, Badwayz; So... How's Your Girl?, Handsome Boy. *Current Management:* Gold Mountain Entertainment, 3575 Cahuenga Blvd W, Suite 450, Los Angeles, CA 90068, USA.

MIKKELBORG Palle; b. 6 March 1941, Copenhagen, Denmark. Musician (Trumpet); Composer; Conductor. m. Helen M Davies, 19 Aug. 1989. *Career:* Leader, Danish Radiojazz Group and Big Band, 1964–76; Riel/ Mikkelborg Quintet, 1965–70; V8, 1970–75; Entrance, 1975–88; Heart to Heart Trio, 1985–88; Palle Mikkelborg Trio, 1989–; World-wide festival, radio and TV appearances as soloist and composer/conductor. *Compositions:* Maya's Veil, 1972; Te Faru, 1979; Pictures, 1983; So Many Come, So Many Go, 1983; Aura, dedicated to Miles Davis, 1984–85; Everything Has a Purpose, 1988; Soundscape, 1995; The Noone of Night, 1997; A Moon of Light, 1998. *Recordings:* The Mysterious Corona, 1967; Tempus Incertum Remanet, 1970; Heart to Heart; Hommage; Aura; Anything But Grey; The Gerden is a Woman. *Honours:* First Prize, Montreaux, 1968; Jazz Musician of the Year, 1968; Lange-Müller Prize, 1976; 2 Grammy Awards, USA, 1990; Grammy Award, Denmark, 1993; Knight of the Order of Dannebrog, 1996; Wilhelm Hansen Composers Prize, 1997; Carl Nielsen and Anne Marie Carl Nielsen Prize of Honour, 1999. *Leisure interest:* Philosophy. *Address:* Ellegaardsvaenge 5B, 2820 Gentofte, Copenhagen, Denmark.

MILANÉS Pablo; b. 1943, Bayamo, Cuba. Vocalist; Musician (guitar); Songwriter. *Musical Education:* Amadeo Roldán Conservatory, Havana, Cuba. *Career:* Joined vocal group El Cuarteto del Rey, aged 16; Formed Los Bucaneros, 1960s; Embarked on solo career; Prominent figure in Nueva Trova (popular song) movement, late 1960s; Songs recorded by many major Cuban artists, including Omara Portuonda. *Recordings:* Versos de José Marti, 1973; Canta A Nicolás Guillén, 1975; Pablo Milanes, 1976; No Me Pidas, 1977; Aniversario, 1979; Lilia Vera Y Pablo Milanes, 1981; El Guerrero, 1983; Querido Pablo, 1985; Buenas Días América, Años Vol. 2, 1986; Comienzo Y Final De Una Verde Mañana, 1987; Proposiciones, 1988; Años Vol. 3, 1992; Orígenes, 1994; Plegaria, 1995; Despertar, 1997; Los Días de Gloria, 1994.

MILENA (Milena Slavova); b. 1966, Sofia, Bulgaria. Vocalist; Musician (guitar). Songwriter; Lyricist. m. Robert Page-Roberts. *Career:* Member, Review, Bulgaria, 1986–90; Formed own band, 1991–; Best selling female rock singer in Bulgaria; Numerous tours and concerts in Bulgaria and eastern Europe; Currently living and working in London; Writes, plays and sings own compositions with backing band; Only Bulgarian artiste to record album in the UK. *Recordings:* with Review: Review, 1989; Solo: Ha-ha, 1991; The Scandal, 1993; Sold, 1995. *Honours:* Seven-times voted First Lady of Bulgarian Rock; Best Female Voice, Bulgarian National Awards (Unison), 1994; Best Album, The Scandal. *Address:* c/o Union Media Ltd, 71 Evlogi Georgiev Blvd, Entr. A, Sofia 1142, Bulgaria.

MILES Robert, (Roberto Concina); b. 3 Nov. 1969, Fleurier, Switzerland (Italian citizen). DJ; Songwriter; Prod. *Career:* Began as DJ in club near Venice; Director of Programming at an Italian radio station; Began producing own records; Worked as producer for Italian label Metromaxx. *Recordings:* Singles: Fable, 1996; One and One, 1996; Children, 1996; Freedom, 1997; Full Moon, 1998; Albums: Dreamland, 1996; 23 AM, 1997.

MILLAR John Jhalib; b. 1 July 1951, Belfast, Northern Ireland. Musician (tabla, world percussion). 1 s., 1 d. *Musical Education:* Studied at Tabla Alla Rakha Institute of Music, Bombay, 1979-. *Career:* First studied tabla, London, 1972; Played with Steve Hillage Band, 1976; Member, Nic Turner's (Hawkwind) Sphynx; Member, Monsoon, 1982–83; Interviewed on Danish radio Copenhagen, 1980; Several compositions, contemporary percussion for major UK modern dance companies; Various sessions for television, dance scores include Chakrada, 1981; Composed with Barrington Pheloung, formed Akasa, 1988; Released 2 singles, 2 promo videos, 1 album, 1990; Guest appearance with Massive Attack, Roxy Club Bologna, Italy, 1995; Joined John Mayers Inov-Jazz Fusions, 1997. *Composition:* Sitar In The Skye, BBC1 TV series Hamish Macbeth,

1996. *Recordings:* Ever So Lonely, Monsoon, (No. 12, UK charts), 1982; with Akasa: Kama Sutra, 1989; One Night In My Life, 1990; London Contemporary Dance Theatre, Under The Same Sun, 1983; Union Dance Company, Visions of Rhythm, 1985; Sangeet Sagar (Ocean of Music), CD, 1997. *Publications:* Currently writing a tabla manual. *Honour:* Associate mem., PRS. *Memberships:* Musicians' Union; PRS; Mechanical Copyright Protection Society (MCPS). *Leisure interests:* Eastern poetry; Natural walks; Sport. *Current Management:* Clifton-Wyatt Artistes Management, 1 Poets Rd, London N5 2SL, England. *Address:* 65 Bayham St, Camden Town, London NW1 0AA, England.

MILLAR Robin; b. 18 Dec. 1951, London, England. Record Prod. 1 s., 1 d. *Education:* MA, Cambridge University. *Musical Education:* A Level Music; Grade 8 guitar. *Recordings:* As producer, arranger, musician, writer, include: with Lavine Hudson: Abraham, Martin and John, 1991; with Black: Comedy, 1991; I'm Not Afraid; with Latin Quarter and The Bhundu Boys: Radio Africa, 1991; with Patricia Kaas: Je Tu Dis Vous, 1993; Live album, 1994; with Ute Lemper: Espace Indecent, 1994; with Malcolm McLaren: Paris, 1994; with Randy Crawford: Rich and Poor; with The Christians: Ideal World; with The Bhundu Boys: True Jit; with Owen Paul: This Feeling; with Fine Young Cannibals: FYC; with The Style Council: Have You Ever Had It Blue; with Big Country: The Seer; with The Kane Gang: Big Sound Authority; with Everything But The Girl: Love Not Money; Eden; with Tom Robinson: Hope and Glory; with Bluebells: Forever Yours, Forever Mine; with Courtney Pine: Children of The Ghetto; Artists produced include: Sam Brown; Kate Bush; Wazis Djop; Herbie Hancock; Chris Rea; Juliet Roberts; Wayne Shorter; Jimmy Somerville; Additional production and mixing credits include: Elvis Costello; Wazis Djop; Peter Gabriel; Gary Kemp; Maxi Priest; Gil Scott Heron; Sting; The Special AKA; Tolu; with Sade: Diamond Life (triple Platinum album); Singles: Your Love Is King; Smooth Operator; Sweetest Taboo; When Am I Going To Make A Living (triple Platinum album); Promise; Killer Blow (Absolute Beginners soundtrack). *Membership:* Re-Pro. *Leisure interests:* Sport; Reading. *Current Management:* Dennis Muirhead, Muirhead Management, 202 Fulham Rd, Chelsea, London SW10 9PJ, England.

MILLER Andy; b. 18 Dec. 1968, London, England. Musician (Guitar). *Career:* Joined Dodgy; Debut, Dodgy Club; Frequent live shows; Formed own record label, Bostin, 1991; Signed to A & M Records, 1992. *Recordings:* Singles: Staying Out For The Summer, 1994; In A Room, 1996; Good Enough, 1997; Found You, 1997; If You're Thinking of Me, 1998; Every Single Day, 1998; Albums: The Dodgy Album, 1993; Homegrown, 1994; Free Peace Sweet, 1996; Ace A's and Killer B's, 1998.

MILLER Bill (William Scott); b. 23 Jan. 1955, Neenah, Wisconsin, USA. Entertainer; Musician (guitar, flute). m. Renee Miller, 5 Aug. 1978, 2 s., 1 d. *Education:* College. *Career:* Tori Amos tour; Television appearances: Good Morning America; Austin City Limits. *Recordings:* Native Sons; Old Dreams and New Hopes; The Art of Survival; Loon Mountain Moon; Reservation Road; The Red Road; Raven in the Snow; Ghostdance. *Leisure interests:* Camping; Hiking; Fishing. *Current Management:* Bob Burwell, William Morris Agency. *Address:* Bob Burwell, 1516 16th Ave S, Nashville, TN 37212, USA.

MILLER Dominic James; b. 21 March 1960, Buenos Aires, Argentina. Musician (guitar); Songwriter. m. 12 April 1985, 3 s., 1 d. *Musical Education:* Berklee College of Music; Guildhall School of Music. *Career:* Tours: World Party; Julia Fordham; King Swamp; Sting; Various television and radio appearances; Playing with Sting, touring and broadcasting, 1989-. *Compositions include:* Co-writer with Sting, Shape of My Heart, on Ten Summoners Tales album. *Recordings:* with The Pretenders: Packed; with Phil Collins: But Seriously; with Sting: Soul Cages; Ten Summoners Tales; Fields of Gold; with Paul Young: Other Voices. *Honours:* Guitar Album of the Year, Sunday Times, 1983; Played on Sting's and Phil Collins' Grammy Awards. *Membership:* PRS. *Leisure interests:* Sports fanatic; Family man. *Current Management:* In Between. *Address:* 5 Harley Pl., London W1 N1HB, England.

MILLER Gary Alan; b. 24 Sept. 1966, Durham, England. m. Jane, 2 July 1994. *Career:* Founded folk-rock group The Whisky Priests with twin brother Glenn, 1985; Singer/Songwriter/Guitarist, The Whisky Priests, 1985-; Over 1000 live club and festival performances throughout Europe; Numerous radio and TV appearances including The Tube (Channel 4), TV Española (Spain), Good Morning Croatia; 18 official releases on own label Whippet Records, formed with brother. *Compositions:* Alice in Wonderland; A Better Man Than You; My Ship; Song for Ewan; Side by Side; Full Circle; The Man Who Sold His Town; Success Express; When the Wind Blows; Billy Boy; Ranting Lads; The Man Who Would Be King; He's Still My Son; This Village; Forever in our Hearts; Workhorse; Halcyon Days; The Durham Light Infantry; The Hard Men; Car Boot Sale; William's Tale; Legacy of the Lionheart; Shot at Dawn; Perfect Time; The Raven; Old Man Forgotten. *Recordings:* Albums: Nee Gud Luck, 1989; The First Few Drops, 1991; Timeless Street, 1992; Bloody Well Live!, 1993; The Power and the Glory, 1994; Bleeding Sketches, 1995; Life's Tapestry, 1996; Think

Positive!, 1998; Here Come the Ranting Lads - Live!, 1999; Video: Here Come the Ranting Lads - Live!, 1999. *Memberships:* PRS; MCPS; PPL; PAMRA; Musicians' Union. *Current Management:* Whippet Promotions, PO Box 72, York YO31 1YU, England. *Address:* 46 Milton St, York YO10 3EP, England.

MILLER Glenn Thomas; b. 24 Sept. 1966, Durham, England. Musician (Accordion). m. Stephanie, 1 s. *Career:* Accordion player and songwriter with The Whisky Priests, 1985-; Over 1,000 live club and festival appearances throughout Europe; 18 official recordings released; Radio shows throughout Europe and TV appearances including Channel 4's The Tube, and shows in Spain and Germany. *Compositions:* Positive Steps; Death of the Shipyards; The Ghost of Geordie Jones; Jenny Grey; Goblins; Farewell Jobling!; Lament for the Setting Sons; Success Road; Durham; Epitaph for a Working Class Couple. *Recordings:* Albums: Nee Gud Luck, 1989; The First Few Drops, 1991; Timeless Street, 1992; Bloody Well Live!, 1993; The Power and the Glory, 1994; Bleeding Sketches, 1995; Life's Tapestry, 1996; Think Positive!, 1998; Here Come the Ranting Lads! - Live!, 1999. *Memberships:* MCPS; PRS; PPL; PAMRA; Musicians' Union. *Current Management:* Whippet Promotions, PO Box 72, York YO31 1YU, England. *Address:* 14 Springfield Close, Stockton Lane, York YO31 1LD, England.

MILLER Marcus; Jazz Musician (bass); Record Prod. *Career:* Recording artiste, worked with Joshua Redman; Lalah Hathaway; M'shell Ndege Ocello; Record producer for artists including: Miles Davis; Luther Vandross; Chaka Khan. *Recordings:* Albums: The Sun Don't Lie; Tales. *Current Management:* Patrick Rains and Associates, 1543 Seventh St, Third Floor, Santa Monica, CA 90401, USA.

MILLER Mikel; b. 13 Oct. 1949, Toronto, Ontario, Canada. Singer; Songwriter; Musician (guitar). 1 d. *Musical Education:* Self-taught Guitar. *Career:* Coffee houses, clubs and festivals throughout Canada and the USA during the 70's, 80's and 90's. *Compositions:* No More Trains, 1984; Hand In The Game, 1988; Slow Driftin' Song, 1989; The Key, 1992; Something You Never Knew, 1994; Pilgrim's Progress, 1995; The Compromise, 1998. *Recordings:* No More Trains, 1989; Another Day In Paradise, 1994; The Key, 1996; Rounder's Road, 1999; NXNE sampler, 1999; Yukon sampler RAIYA, 1999; A Norm Hacking Compilation, 1999. *Publications:* Lost Moose Catalogue, 1990; Dirty Linen Magazine, 1999. *Memberships:* Canadian Country Music Asscn; Folk Alliance; Recording Arts Industry Yukon Asscn (RAIYA). *Leisure interests:* Avid Reader; Music Collector; Mostly Folk. *Current Management:* LEA/JEN Music, Box 5073, Whitehorse, Yukon Territory, Y1A 4S3, Canada. *Address:* PO Box 5073 Whitehorse, Yukon, Y1A 4S3, Canada.

MILLER Ruth; b. 8 May 1962, Newark, Nottinghamshire, England. Songwriter; Singer; Musician (guitar). *Education:* Degree in Communications; Postgraduate Research. *Career:* Founder, Rutland Records, 1988; Member of PO!, including BBC Radio 1 session; Member of Ruth's Refrigerator, touring Europe. *Recordings:* with PO!: Little Stones, 1989; Ducks and Drakes, 1993; Not Marked on the Ordnance Map, 1996; Past Present Tense, 1997; Horse Blanket Weather, 1998; Ruth's Refrigerator: Suddenly A Disfigured Head Parachuted, 1990; A Lizard Is A Submarine On Grass, 1991. *Memberships:* PRS; MCPS; PPL; Musicians' Union. *Leisure interest:* Gardening. *Address:* c/o Rutland Records, PO Box 132, Leicester LE2 3ZF, England.

MILLER Steve; b. 5 Oct. 1943, Milwaukee, Wisconsin, USA. Vocalist; Musician (guitar); Songwriter. *Education:* Wisconsin University, 1961; Literature, Copenhagen University, Denmark. *Musical Education:* Guitar with Les Paul, 1948. *Career:* Member, Marksmen Combo, 1955; The Ardells (became Fabulous Night Train); Worked with Muddy Waters; James Cotton; Howling Wolf; Butterfield Blues Band; Member, World War Three Band (became Goldberg-Miller Blues Band); Founder, the Steve Miller Band, 1966-; Regular international appearances include: San Francisco State College Folk Festival, 1967; Monterey International Pop Festival, 1967; Northern California Folk-Rock Festival, 1968; Hollywood Music Festival, 1970; Knebworth Festival, 1975; Benefit for Texas Special Olympics, Dallas, 1990; Earth Day Sound Action benefit, 1992; All Our Colors - The Good Road benefit concert, California, 1992; Earth Day concert, Hollywood Bowl, 1992; Founder, record label Sailor Records, 1976. *Recordings:* Albums: with Steve Miller Band: Children of The Future, 1968; Sailor, 1968; Brave New World, 1969; Your Saving Grace, 1969; Number Five, 1970; Rock Love, 1971; Recall The Beginning... A Journey From Eden, 1972; Anthology, 1972; Fly Like An Eagle, 1977; Book of Dreams, 1977; Greatest Hits 1974-78, 1978; Abracadabra, 1982; The Steve Miller Band Live!, 1983; Italian X-Rays, 1984; Living In The 20th Century, 1986; Greatest Hits 1976-86, 1987; Born 2 Be Blue, 1988; The Best of Steve Miller 1968-73, 1990; Wide River, 1992; Box Set, 1994; The Very Best of Steve Miller, 1996; Greatest Hits, 1998; Singles include: The Joker (No. 1, USA), 1974; Take The Money and Run; Fly Like An Eagle; Jet Airliner; Swingtown; Abracadabra. *Honours include:* Platinum discs; Star on Hollywood Walk of Fame, 1987. *Current

Management: Scott Boorey Management, 325 Glen Arms Dr., Danville, CA 94526, USA.

MILLER Steven; b. 11 Aug. 1956. Prod.; Arranger; Engineer. *Education:* BA, Film and Music, San Francisco State University. *Career:* Vice President: Windham Hill Records; Founder: Hip Pocket Records; RCA Novus Records; Windham Hill Jazz records; Produced, engineered: Manhattan Transfer; Juliana Hatfield; Medeski Martin and Wood; Paula Cole; Michael Hedges; Will Ackermann. *Recordings:* Albums include: December, George Winston; Vapor Drawings, Mark Isham; Suzanne Vega, Suzanne Vega; Talkin' Bout You, Diane Schuur; Temporary Road, John Gorka; Mortal City, Dar Williams. *Honours:* Grammy nominations: 1984; 1988; 1989. *Memberships:* NARAS. *Leisure interests:* Wine; Food; Basketball. *Current Management:* Greg Spotts Entertainment, 1124 Fifth St, Suite 304, Santa Monica, California 90403, USA. *Address:* 35 Montell St, Oakland, CA 99611, USA.

MILLINGTON-ROBERTSON Janice Anita; b. 5 Nov. 1947, Barbados. Musician; Educator. m. Edward George Robertson, 17 April 1982, divorced, 1 s. *Education:* Queen's College, Barbados; University of the West Indies; Studied with father, James Millington, violinist, and mother, Odessa Millington, pianist; Also, piano with Gerald Hudson, and Jean Harvey; Violin with Sidney Griller and Trevor Williams; Studied at Royal Academy of Music, Berklee College of Music, Boston, Columbia University Teachers' College, Florida State University; Several masterclasses, conference presentations and workshops. *Career:* Performed for radio and TV; Own TV programme, 13 series; Recitals on violin and piano; Experimental work with piano and 2 violins including steelpan players in Trinidad; Developed calypso jazz idiom; Performed in clubs, concerts with popular and jazz musicians; Taught pop and jazz musicians for over 20 years; Author of reviews for local newspapers; Adjucator, music festivals; Freelance lecturer, cultural topics; Cultural representative for Barbados in many music education and cultural seminars. *Recordings:* Janice Millington Plays; Xmas Time with Harrison College; The Romantic Spirit (video). *Publications:* Traditional Music and Its Place in Tourism, 1991; Many articles on Barbadian and Caribbean music; Contributor, Garland Encyclopaedia of World Music. *Honours:* NOW (National Organisation of Women) Award for contribution to education in Barbados; Bureau of Women Award for Development of Barbados; Scroll of Excellence, Harrison College. *Memberships:* ARAM; GRSM; LRAM; ARCM (London) Certificate of Education, Management and Supervision (UWI); Corresponding Mem., Callaway International Resource Centre for Music Education; Advising Board Mem., Asscn of Professional Pianists and Teachers of the Americas; Barbadian Representative, International Society of Music Educators; Mem. of Incorporated Society of Musicians (UK). *Leisure interests:* Lawn tennis; Theatre; Reading; Travel. *Address:* PO Box 32W, Worthing, Christ Church, Barbados.

MILLS Crispian; b. 18 Jan. 1973, London, England. Vocalist; Musician (Guitar). *Career:* Formed Objects of Desire with Paul Winterhart and Alonza Bevan; Formed the Kays; Became Kula Shaker with Jay Darlington; Numerous TV appearances and tours; Festival appearances include Knebworth with Oasis and Glastonbury; Guest Vocals on Prodigy album The Fat of the Land, 1997; Left Kula Shaker to go solo, 1999. *Recordings:* Singles: Tattva, 1996; Hey Dude, 1996; Govinda, 1996; Hush, 1997; The Sound of Drums, 1998; Albums: K, 1996; Peasants, Pigs and Astronauts, 1999.

MILLS Jeff, (Millsart, Purpose Maker); b. Detroit, Michigan, USA. Prod.; Remixer; DJ. *Career:* Started career on Detroit pirate radio station WJLB using DJ pseudonym The Wizard before collaborating with Mike Banks as part of Underground Resistance; Relocated to New York as resident DJ at the Limelight club; Founded Axis Records in Berlin; Member: True Faith/Final Cut; Collaborations: Mike Banks; Robert Hood; Remixed: Maurizio; Lionrock; DJ Rolando. *Recordings:* Albums: Sonic Destroyer (with X101), 1991; Waveform Transmission #1, 1992; Waveform Transmission #3, 1996; Metropolis, 2001; Singles: Take Me Away (with True Faith/Final Cut), 1991; Nation 2 Nation (with Underground Resistance); World 2 World (with Underground Resistance); Tranquilizer EP (with Robert Hood), 1993; Cycle 30, 1994; Purpose Maker, 1996; Every Dog Has Its Day, 2000; Metropolis, 2001. *Address:* c/o Axis Records, Department 6277, 28 E Jackson Blvd, Chicago, Illinois, USA.

MILLS Mike; b. 17 Dec. 1958. Musician (bass). *Career:* Member, R.E.M., 1980–; International tours; Member, side project, Hindu Love Gods, 1986–90. *Recordings:* Albums: Chronic Town (mini-album), 1982; Murmur, 1983; Reckoning, 1984; Fables of The Reconstruction, 1985; Life's Rich Pageant, 1986; Dead Letter Office, 1987; Document, 1987; Eponymous, 1988; Green, 1988; Out of Time, 1991; The Best of R.E.M., 1991; Automatic For The People, 1992; Monster, 1995; Up, 1998; Star Profiles, 1999; Out of Time, 1999; with Hindu Love Gods: Hindu Love Gods, 1990; Singles: with R.E.M.: The One I Love, 1987; Stand, 1989; Orange Crush, 1989; Losing My Religion, 1991; Shiny Happy People, 1991; Near Wild Heaven, 1991; Radio Song, 1991; Drive, 1992; Man On The Moon,

1992; The Sidewinder Sleeps Tonite, 1993; Everybody Hurts, 1993; Crush With Eyeliner; What's The Frequency, Kenneth?; The Great Beyond, 2000; Nightswimming; Tracks featured on film soundtracks: Batchelor Party, 1984; Until The End of The World, 1991; Coneheads, 1993; Other recordings with: Warren Zevon; Indigo Girls; Smashing Pumpkins; Liz Phair; Contributor, albums: Tom's Album; I'm Your Fan. *Honours:* Earth Day Award, 1990; Numerous MTV Music Video Awards; Billboard Awards; Best Modern Rock Artists, Best World Album, 1991; BRIT Awards: Best International Group, 1992, 1993, 1995; Grammy Awards: Best For Performance, Alternative Music Album, Music Video, 1992; Atlanta Music Awards: Act of The Year, Rock Album, Video, 1992; IRMA, International Band of The Year, 1993; Rolling Stone Critics Awards: Best Band, Best Album; Q Awards: Best Album, 1991, 1992; Best Act In The World, 1991, 1995. *Current Management:* REM/Athens Ltd. *Address:* 250 W Clayton St, Athens, GA 30601, USA.

MILLS Richie; b. 13 Oct. 1971, Berkshire, England. Musician (Drummer). *Career:* Appeared in Short Film, When Animals Attack; Music Supplied for Major Drinks Television Commercial. *Compositions:* Freeze The Atlantic. *Recordings:* Cable; When Animals Attaack; Sub Lingual. *Honours:* Nominated Best British Band, Cable, 1997. *Membership:* Musicians Union. *Leisure interests:* Web Site Design. *Current Management:* Furtive, 29 Charlotte Rd, London EC2A, England.

MILLS Sam, (Samuel Peter Landrell-Mills); b. 15 June 1963, London, England, UK. Musician (guitar, programmer); Composer; Prod. *Career:* Member: 23 Skidoo; Tama (with Tom Diakite and Djanuno Dabo); Collaborations: Russell Mills; Paban Das Baul; Susheela Raman. *Recordings:* Singles: with 23 Skidoo: Ethics, 1979; Last Words, 1981; Tearing Up The Plans, 1982; Albums: Seven Songs (with 23 Skidoo), 1982; Real Sugar (with Paban Das Baul), 1997; Nostalgie (with Tama), 1999; Pearl and Umbra (Russell Mills and Undark), 2000; Salt Rain (Susheela Raman), 2001. *Honours:* Mercury Music Prize nominee, Salt Rain, Susheela Raman, 2001.

MILLS Vincent Delano; b. 19 April 1960, Birmingham, England. Musician (Guitarist and Electric Bassist), Composer. *Career:* Performed with bands based in Birmingham and the Midlands area, late 1970's to 1990's, soul, funk, R & B, Jazz Big Bands, The Blue Pearls and numerous session gigs for Jazz combo's; Internationally: Toured USA with chart topping reggae artist Pato Banton's backing band the Reggae Revolution, 1992; East Coast tour, Florida and Georgia, 1992; West Coast tour, with performances at The Bob Marley Day Reggae Festival, concerts in California, Washington, Arizona, Canada, Hawaii and opening for Santana in Tijuana, Mexico; Performed with top Caribbean calypso/soca bands Nu-Vybes in St Kitts, 1995 and Small Axe, St Kitts Music Festival, 1999; Performed at Birmingham, Ludlow and Keswick Jazz Festivals, Black Music Festival, London. *Recordings:* Lead and Rhythm guitar on CD, Pan In Flight, Barcelona, Jamma. *Membership:* Musicians' Union. *Leisure interests:* Music; Photography; Travel; Computing.

MILSAP Ronnie; b. Robbinsville, North Carolina, USA. Music Artist. m. Joyce. *Recordings:* Singles include: The Girl Who Waits on Tables, 1973; Please Don't Tell Me How, 1974; I'm a Stand By My Woman Man, 1976; Let My Love Be Your Pillow, 1976; Back On My Mind Again, 1978; Nobody Likes Sad Songs, 1979; Misery Loves Company, 1980; Smokey Mountain Rain, 1980; Any Day Now, 1982; Still Losing You, 1984; Only One Night of the Year, 1986; Make No Mistake, She's Mine, duet with Kenny Rogers, 1987; Button Off My Shirt, 1988; Woman in Love, 1989; Since I Don't Have You, 1991; LA to the Moon, 1992; True Believe, 1993; Albums include: Where My Heart Is, 1973; Night Things, 1975; Ronnie Milsap Live, 1976; It Was Almost Like A Song, 1977; Only One Love in My Life, 1978; Greatest Hits, Vol. 1, 1980; There's No Gettin' Over Me, 1981; Greatest Hits, Vol. 2, 1985; Lost in the Fifties Tonight, 1986; Christmas with Ronnie Milsap, 1986; Stranger Things Have Happened, 1989; Greatest Hits, Vol. 3, 1992; True Believer, 1993; Didn't We, 1996; Kentucky Woman, 1996; When It Comes To My Baby, 1996; Christmas in Dixie, 1997; Branson City Limits, 1999. *Honours include:* Grammy Awards: Best Country Male Vocal Performance, 1974, 1976, 1982, 1986, 1987, Contry Song of the Year, 1984, Best Country Duet Performance, with Kenny Rogers, 1988; Billboard Awards: Best New Male Artist, 1974, Male Singles Artist of the Year, 1976, 1980, Overall Singles Artist of the Year, 1976, Bill Williams Memorial Award, Artist of the Year, 1976, Breakthrough Award, Outstanding Achievement, 1981; CMA Awards: Male Vocalist of the Year, 1974, 1976, 1977, Album of the Year, 1975, 1977, 1978, 1986, Entertainer of the Year, 1977; Numerous others. *Current Management:* Gold Mountain Entertainment, 1514 South St, Suite 100, Nashville, TN 37212, USA.

MINCHELLA Damon; b. 1 June 1969, Liverpool, England. Musician (Bass). *Career:* Joined The Fanatics with Simon Fowler; When band split became Ocean Colour Scene; Secured indie record deal, but label taken over; Joined Paul Wellers backing band along with Fowler and Steve Cradock, while continuing with Ocean Colour Scene; Support slot to Oasis

1994 tour; Numerous TV appearances and radio play; Riverboat Song used as theme tune to TV series TFI Friday; Several headlining tours. *Recordings:* Singles: Riverboat Song; The Day We Caught The Train; 100 Mile High City; You've Got It Bad, 1996; Travellers Tune, 1997; Albums: Ocean Colour Scene, 1992; Moseley Shoals, 1996; Marchin' Already, 1997.

MINNELLI Liza May; b. 12 March 1946, Los Angeles, California, USA. Singer; Actress; Dancer. m. Peter Allen, 1967 (divorced), (2) Jack Haley Jr, 15 Sept. 1974 (divorced), (3) Mark Gero, 4 Dec. 1979. *Career:* Singer and entertainer, stage, film and television; Major appearances include: Best Foot Forward (off-Broadway), 1963; Touring productions: Carnival; The Pajama Game; The Fantasticks; Performed with mother (Judy Garland), London Palladium, 1964; Broadway debut, Flora and The Red Menace, 1965; The Act, 1977; The Rink, 1984; The Ultimate Event, international tour with Frank Sinatra, Sammy Davis Jr, 1988; Film appearances: Charlie Bubbles, 1967; The Sterile Cuckoo, 1969; Cabaret, 1972; Tell Me That You Love Me Junie Moon, 1974; Lucky Lady, 1975; A Matter of Time, 1976; Silent Movie, 1976; New York, New York, 1977; Arthur, 1981; Arthur 2 – On The Rocks, 1988; Stepping Out, 1991; Television appearances include: Liza With A 'Z', 1972; Goldie and Liza Together, 1980; Baryshnikov On Broadway, 1980; The Princess and The Pea; Showtime, 1983; A Time To Live, 1985; Sam Found Out, 1988. *Recordings:* Albums include: Liza! Liza!, 1964; It Amazes Me, 1965; There Is A Time, 1966; New Feelin', 1970; Liza With A 'Z', 1972; Liza Minnelli The Singer, 1973; Live At The Winter Garden, 1974; Lucky Lady, 1976; Tropical Nights, 1977; Live At Carnegie Hall, 1987; Live From Radio City Music Hall, 1992; Film and stage soundtracks: Best Foot Forward, 1963; Dangerous Christmas of Red Riding Hood, 1965; Flora and The Red Menace, 1965; Cabaret, 1972; with Judy Garland: Live At The London Palladium, 1964; with Pet Shop Boys: Results, 1989; Liza, 1994; Gently, 1996; Rink (oroginal Broadway cast), 1999; Single: Losing My Mind, with Pet Shop Boys, (first UK chart entry), 1989. *Honours:* Promising Personality Award, 1963; 2 Tony Awards, Best Foot Forward, 1965, The Act, 1977; Academy Award nomination, 1969; Academy Award, Best Actress, Cabaret, 1972; Emmy Award, Lisa With A 'Z', 1972; Golden Globe Award, Best Actress, A Time To Live, 1985. *Current Management:* Krost/Chapin Management, Penthouse 1, 9911 W Pico Blvd, Los Angeles, CA 90035, USA.

MINOGUE Dannii (Danielle Jane); b. 20 Oct. 1971, Melbourne, Victoria, Australia. Singer; Actress; Television Presenter. *Career:* Actress: Australian TV drama series: Skyways, 1978; The Sullivans, 1978; All The Way, 1988; Home and Away, 1989; Variety Show: Young Talent Time, Australia, 1979–88; New Generation, Australia, USA, 1988; TV Presenter: Scoop; It's Not Just Saturday; Dannii on Safari, Disney; Co-host, Big Breakfast, UK, 1993; Fan T.C., UK, 1994; Cirque du Monde, Disney, 1996; Electric Circus, UK, 1996; Disney Villans, Disney, 1997; Film appearance: Secrets, 1992; Performances: Royal Children's Variety Performance, 1991; Cesme Festival, Turkey, 1992; Gay Pride Festival, London, 1993, 1994, 1997; Promotional tours of Australia, SE Asia, USA and UK; Unleashed Tour, UK and Ireland, 1998; Sydney Gay and Lesbian Mardi Gras, Australia, 1998, 1999; Musical: Grease, The Arena Spectacular, Australia, 1998; Theatre: Journey to Macbeth, Edinburgh Festival, 1999. *Recordings:* Albums: Love and Kisses, 1991; Get Into You, 1993; Girl, 1997; Singles: 10 Top Ten singles, including: Love and Kisses, 1990; This Is It, 1993; All I Wanna Do, 1997; Major Composition: Success, 1991; Everything I Wanted, 1997; Everlasting Night, 1999; Contributor: NME Ruby Trax, British Spastic Society, 1992; The Gift of Christmas, Child Liners, 1995. *Honours:* Gold discs, UK and Australia; Young Variety Award (Australian Variety Club) 1989. *Membership:* Media, Entertainment and Arts Alliance, Australia; APRA. *Address:* c/o Jules Kulpinski, KDB Artists Pty Ltd, PO Box 26025, London SW10 9GD, England.

MINOGUE Kylie (Ann); b. 28 May 1968, Melbourne, Victoria, Australia. Singer; Actress. *Career:* Actress, Australian television dramas: Skyways, 1980; The Sullivans, 1981; The Henderson Kids, 1984–85; Neighbours, 1986–88; Film appearances: The Delinquents, 1989; Streetfighter, 1994; BioDome, 1995; Cut, 2000; Sample People, 2000; As singer, biggest selling single of decade in Australia, Locomotion, 1987; Highest UK chart entry for female artist, Locomotion, 1988; Highest debut album chart entry, Australia, UK, Kylie, 1988; First ever artist with 4 Top 3 singles from an album; First female artist with first 5 singles to recieve Silver discs; Performances include: Australian Royal Bicentennial Concert, 1988; John Lennon tribute, Liverpool, 1990; Cesne Music Festival, Turkey, 1992; Sydney Gay Mardi Gras, 1994, 1998; Prince's Trust Concert, 1994; T In The Park Festival, Glasgow, 1995; Tours of UK, Europe, Asia, and Australia. *Recordings:* Albums: Kylie, 1988; Enjoy Yourself, 1989; Rhythm of Love, 1990; Let's Get To It, 1991; Kylie – Greatest Hits, 1992; Kylie Minogue, 1994; Kylie Minogue, 1998; Intimate and Live, 1998; Singles include: Locomotion, 1987; I Should Be So Lucky, 1988; Je Ne Sais Pas Pourquoi, 1988; Especially For You, with Jason Donovan, 1988; Never Too Late, 1989; Confide In Me, 1994; Put Yourself In My Place, 1995; Where Is The Feeling, 1995; Where The Wild Roses Grow (duet with Nick Cave), 1995; Some Kind of Bliss, 1997; Did It Again, 1997; Breathe, 1998; Spinning Around (No. 1, UK), 2000; On A Night Like This, 2000; Kids, duet

with Robbie Williams, 2000; Please Stay, 2000; Can't Get You Out of My Head (No. 1, UK), 2001. *Honours:* Numerous Platinum, Gold and Silver discs; 6 Logies (Australia); 6 Music Week Awards (UK); 3 Smash Hits Awards (UK); 3 Australian Record Industry Asscn Awards; 3 Japanese Music Awards; Irish Record Industry Award; Canadian Record Industry Award; World Music Award; Australian Variety Club Award; MO Award (Australian Showbusiness); Amplex Golden Reel Award; Diamond Award, (Belgium); Woman of the Decade (UK); MTV Video of the Year, Did It Again, 1998; 25 Top Ten singles world-wide. *Current Management:* Terry Blamey Management, PO Box 13196, London SW6 4WF, England.

MINOTT Sugar (Lincoln); b. 25 May 1956, Kingston, Jamaica. Reggae Singer. *Career:* Billed as one of the African Brothers, 1970s; Success within UK reggae scene; Established own Youth Promotion/Black Roots promotion organization. *Recordings:* with the African Brothers: Collectors Item; Numerous solo albums include: Live Loving; Black Roots; Bittersweet; Ghetto-ology; Roots Lovers; Give The People; African Girl; Good Thing Going; With Lots of Extra; Herbman Hustling; Slice of The Cake; Wicked A Go Feel It; Leader of The Pack; Time Longer Than Rope; Sugar and Spice; Them Ah Wolf; Jamming In The Streets; African Soldier; Buy Off The Bar; Ghetto Youth Dem Rising; The Boss Is Back; A Touch of Class; Run Things; Breaking Free; International; Musical Murder; Easy Squeeze. *Address:* c/o Tempest Entertainment, 245 W 25th St, New York, NY 10001, USA.

MINTON Philip Watcyn; b. 2 Nov. 1940, Torquay, Devon, England. Singer; Improvisor. 1 s., 3 d. *Career:* Performed at most improvised music festivals world-wide, with hundreds of musicians from many countries. *Recordings:* Songs From A Prison Diary, with Veryan Weston; Ammo, Dadada, with Roger Turner. *Honours:* Voted Best Singer, Europe Jazz Forum Magazine, 1988. *Memberships:* LMC; Musicians' Union; PRS; MCPS. *Current Management:* Margareta Peters, Zurich, Switzerland. *E-mail:* m_peters@dplanet.ch.

MISE Marjan; b. 9 July 1952, Beograd, Croatia. Singer; Musician (drums). m. Dubravka, 22 Dec. 1973, 1 s., 1 d. *Musical Education:* Elementary Musical School. *Career:* 16 years touring former USSR; Many performances in Europe; Many international festivals include: Vilach; Bratislava; Golden Orphei; Sopot; Slovenska Popeuka; Portoroz; Split. *Recordings:* 25 singles; 7 albums; 2 CDs; 2 compilations (in English). *Honours:* Many Croatian and foreign awards. *Membership:* Croatian Musical Union. *Leisure interests:* Tennis; Football. *Current Management:* Croatian Musical Union.

MISHALLE Luc; b. 6 Jan. 1953. Musician (Saxophones). 1 s. *Education:* Licenced Law, 1976, University Antwerp. *Career:* Theatre: Musical Director of Welfare State (UK); Dog Troop (NL); Internationale Nieuwe Scene (B); Music: Marakbar; Blindman Quartet; Galileo's Left Wing. *Compositions:* Mekoue; Urbanized; Akoestische; Winterverhalen; Metropolis; Webl; Mdawa; Shark Dari. *Recordings:* Marakbar 'Live; Marockin' Antwerp; Blindman Poortenbos; Galileo's Left Wing Live; Marockin' Stories; El Adoua; Al Harmoniah. *Current Management:* VZW de Krijtkring, Timmerwerfstraat 40, 2000 Antwerp, Belgium. *Address:* 6 rue du Capitaine Linard, 1390 Grez-Doiceau, Belgium.

MÍSIA, (Susanna Alfonso); b. Oporto, Portugal. Vocalist. *Career:* Began singing Fado (Portuguese folk form) professionally, 1991. *Recordings:* Albums: Mísia, 1991; Fado, 1993; Tanto Menos Tanto Mas, 1994; Garros Dos Sentidos, 1998; Paixões Diagonais, 1999; Ritual, 2001. *Honours:* Grand Prix de L'Acadamie Charles Cross, 1997. *Current Management:* Les Visiteurs Du Soir, 40 rue del la Folie Regnault, 75011, Paris, France. *Address:* c/o WEA, The Warner Building, 28 Kensington Church St, London, W8 4EP, England. *Internet:* www.misia-online.com.

MITCHELL Alexander; b. 4 Nov. 1969, Minster, Kent, England. Musician (guitar, midi programming). *Education:* Goldsmiths College. *Career:* Guitarist with: Curve, 1991–94; Choob, 1993–95; Sparky Lightbourne, 1997–; Radio includes: John Peel Sessions for Radio 1; Concerts include: Glastonbury Festival; NME Stage; Major tours: USA; Europe; Japan; UK; Television includes The Beat; Now making Techno music, 2 EPs under name Choob. *Compositions:* with Choob: Little Girl, 1993; Choobular, 1994; as Sparky Lightbourne: EP, 1997; Sparky's Secret, 1998; Album, 1999; Chickin Lickin; Get Your Hands Off Me. *Recordings:* Albums: with Curve, 2 LPs: Doppelganger; Cuckoo; 2 EPs: Little Girl; Choobular. *Membership:* Musicians' Union; PRS; MCPS. *Leisure interests:* DJ at Teckno United Systems parties. *Current Management:* Andy Mack, Skint Records, 73a Middle St, Brighton. *Address:* 60 Crane House, Grummant Rd, Peckham, London SE15 5NG, England.

MITCHELL Dryden; b. 15 June 1976, Redondo Beach, California, USA. Vocalist; Musician (guitar); Songwriter. *Career:* Played with local bands Crossover, Out of Order, Dragonphlie; Member: Alien Ant Farm, 1996–; Self-financed independent LP released to acclaim, 1999; Signed to Papa Roach's New Noize label; Second album released in conjunction with DreamWorks label, leading to major international breakthrough, 2000–01. *Recordings:* Albums: Greatest Hits, 1999; ANThology, 2001;

Singles: $100 EP, 1996; Love Songs EP, 1998; Movies, Smooth Criminal, 2001. *Honours:* L.A. Music Award, Best Independent Album, 1999. *Address:* c/o New Noize, 2022 Cliff Dr #123, Santa Barbara, CA 93109, USA. *E-mail:* info@newnoize.com. *Internet:* www.alienantfarm.com.

MITCHELL Ian; b. 22 Aug. 1958, Downpatrick, Northern Ireland. Musician (Guitar); Vocalist. m. Wendy Antanaitis, 1992. *Career:* Began performing, aged 15; Joined Bay City Rollers, 1976, left, 1976; Founded Rosetta Stone, 1977; Formed Ian Mitchell Band, 1979; Appeared, Dinah Shore Show, Mike Douglas Show, Merv Griffin Show, Top of the Pops, all with Bay City Rollers; Own TV Programme, Fanfare, with Rosetta Stone. *Recordings:* With Bay City Rollers: Dedication, LP; With Rosetta Stone: Sunshine of Your Love; Try It On; Sheila; With the Ian Mitchell Band: Suddenly You Love Me; Hold On to Love; Boulevard LA. *Current Management:* Jeff Hubbard Productions. *Address:* PO Box 53664, Indianapolis, IN 46253, USA.

MITCHELL John Lindsay; b. 24 Aug. 1967, Manchester, England. Writer; Musician (Guitar); Singer. m. Clare Fiona Lindley. *Education:* Aberdeen College. *Career:* HM Forces, 1984–89; MOD Search and Rescue, 1990–91; Touring, Scottish Folk Festival Circuit, 1992-. *Compositions:* Leaving Carolina; Marie Celeste; Jamie Gows Farewll to Methadone; High and Low; Baroque Daydream; Squaddies Lament; Found on the Wave; The Fulmed. *Recording:* Found on the Wave, 1996. *Memberships:* PRS; PRC. *Leisure interests:* Cross Training; Hill Walking; Music. *Current Management:* Marj Mitchell, 40 Hazelhead Gardens, Aberdeen. *Address:* Cairnwell Cottage, Newtonhill, Sonehaven, Kincardineshire, England.

MITCHELL Joni, (Roberta Joan Anderson); b. 7 Nov. 1943, Fort McLeod, Alberta, Canada. Singer; Songwriter; Musician (piano, guitar, ukelele). m. (1) Chuck Mitchell, 1965 (divorced), (2) Larry Klein, 1982. *Education:* Alberta College of Art, Calgary, 1962. *Career:* Duo with Chuck Mitchell, 1965; Solo singer, songwriter, 1966-; Major concerts include: Miami Pop Festival, 1968; Carnegie Hall, New York, 1969; Isle of Wight Festival, 1970; Tours, USA, Europe, with Jackson Browne, 1971; Bob Dylan's Rolling Thunder Revue, 1975; The Last Waltz (The Band's farewell concert), 1976; Playboy Jazz Festival, Hollywood Bowl, 1979; Roger Waters' The Wall, Berlin, 1990; Troubadours of Folk Festival, 1993; Exhibition of own paintings, Canada In The City exhibition, London, 1990. *Compositions include:* Urge For Going, Tom Rush; Both Sides Now, Judy Collins; Woodstock, Crosby Still and Nash; This Flight Tonight, Nazareth. *Recordings:* Albums (own compositions): Joni Mitchell, 1968; Clouds, 1969; Ladies of The Canyon, 1970; Blue, 1971; For The Roses, 1972; Court and Spark, 1974; Miles of Aisles, 1974; The Hissing of Summer Lawns, 1976; Hejira, 1976; Don Juan's Reckless Daughter, 1978; Mingus, 1979; Shadows and Light, 1980; Wild Things Run Fast, 1982; Dog Eat Dog, 1985; Chalk Mark In A Rainstorm, 1988; Night Ride Home, 1991; Turbulent Indigo, 1994; Taming the Tiger, 1998; Both Sides Now, 2000; Singles include: Big Yellow Taxi, 1970; You Turn Me On, I'm A Radio, 1997; Help Me, 1974; Free Man In Paris, 1974; Good Friends, duet with Michael McDonald, 1986; Guest vocalist, You've Got A Friend, James Taylor (No. 1, USA), 1971. *Honours include:* Grammy Awards: Best Folk Performance, Clouds, 1970; Best Arrangement (with Tom Scott), 1975; Inducted into Juno Hall of Fame, 1981; 8 Gold discs. *Current Management:* Mind Over Management, 1505 W Second Ave, Suite 200, Vancouver, BC V6H 3Y4, Canada. *Address:* SL Feldman and Associates, 1505 W Second Ave, Suite 200, Vancouver, BC V6H 3Y4, Canada.

MITCHELL Neil; b. 8 June 1967, Helensborough, Scotland. Musician (keyboards). *Career:* Member, Wet Wet Wet, 1982-; Performances include: Greenpeace charity concert, Royal Albert Hall, 1986; Support to Lionel Richie, British tour, 1987; Prince's Trust Rock Gala, London, 1988–90; The Big Day, C4, 1990; Edinburgh Castle, 1992; Nordoff-Robbins Music Therapy Centre, Royal Albert Hall, 1992; Live At The Royal Albert Hall 1992, C4, 1993. *Recordings:* Albums: Popped In Souled Out, 1987; Sgt Pepper Knew My Father, 1988; The Memphis Sessions, 1988; Holding Back The River, 1989; High On The Happy Side, 1992; Wet Wet Wet Live At The Royal Albert Hall, 1993; Picture This, 1995; Singles include: Wishing I Was Lucky, 1987; Sweet Little Mystery, 1987; Angel Eyes (Home and Away), 1988; Temptation, 1988; With A Little Help From My Friends (No. 1, UK), 1988; Sweet Surrender, 1989; Broke Away, 1989; Hold Back The River, 1990; More Than Love, 1992; Goodnight Girl (No. 1, UK), 1992; Lip Service, 1992; Shed A Tear, 1993; Love Is All Around (No. 1, UK), 1994; She's All On My Mind, 1995; Julia Said, 1995. *Honours include:* BRIT Award, Best British Newcomer, 1988. *Current Management:* The Precious Organisation, 14–16 Spiers Wharf, Port Dundas, Glasgow, Scotland.

MITCHELL-DAVIDSON Paul; b. 29 Dec. 1946, Bristol, England. Composer; Arranger; Musician (all guitars, mandolin, banjo). *Career:* Various bands, 1960s; Monad, 1971–73; Maynard Ferguson Band, US tour, 1972; Paws For Thought, 1974; Freelance session musician, also musical director, radio and television, 1970s-; Played with many top UK and US jazz musicians; Major concert at RNCM, 1995. *Compositions:* All About Lions; Gaia; The Bestiary; Rhapsody For Duke; Solar Eclipse;

Captain Corelli; Tubafication; Work for theatre, chamber, choral, orchestral music, jazz, dance, radio, television and commercial recording sessions. *Recordings:* Out of My Head; The Joy of Paranoia, with Lol Coxhill. *Honours:* BBC Marty Paich Award, 1991–92. *Memberships:* PRS; APC; BMWC; MCPS; Musicians' Union. *Address:* 25 Bannerman Ave, Manchester M25 1DZ, England.

MITON Gilles; b. 3 July 1962, Paris, France. Musician (baritone saxophone, flute). *Musical Education:* National Conservatory, Versaille, 1980. *Career:* Television show, with Eddy Mitchell, Ray Charles, Michel Legrand; Played with: Claude Bolling; Michel Legrand; Ornical Band; Arturo Sandoval; Phil Woods; Johnny Griffin; Milky Sax; Lumiere; Laurent Cugny; Super Swing Machine, Gerard Badini; Jean-Loup Longnon; Philippe Baduoin; Antoine Hervé; Quoi de Neuf Doctor; Salena Jones; Dee Dee Bridgewater; Ray Charles; Arthur H; Charles Trenet; Michel Leeb; Le Grand Orchestre du Splendid; Manu Dibango; Sacha Distel; Eddy Mitchell. *Recordings:* Albums with: Charles Trenet; Le Grand Orchestre Du Splendid; Eddy Mitchell; Michel Legrand; Ornicar; Gerard Badini; Philippe Badouin; Quoi De Neuf Docteur; Salena Jones.

MIZE Ben; b. 2 Feb. 1971, USA. Musician (Drums). *Career:* Member, Counting Crows, 1994-; Numerous headlining tours and TV appearances. *Recordings:* Singles: Round Here, 1994; Mr Jones, 1994; Rain King, 1994; Angels of the Silence (live), 1996; Albums: August and Everything After, 1993; Recovering the Satellites, 1996; Across a Wire: Live in New York, 1998; Long December, 1999; Daylight Fading, 1999.

MIZRAKI Raf; Musician (drums, percussion, guitar, cello, dulcimer); Vocalist. *Education:* York University. *Career:* Plays with: The Dufay Collective; Arab music group, Arabesque; Soul band and various baroque orchestras; Member, The Carnival Band, 1990-; Appearances include: Glasgow Cathedral; Birmingham Symphony Hall; Barbican Centre; Arts theatres throughout UK; Plays material from: France; UK; Spain; Bolivia; USA; Croatia; Sweden. *Recordings:* Album with Maddy Prior: Christmas Carols. *Current Management:* Jim McPhee, Acorn Entertainments. *Address:* Winterfold House, 46 Woodfield Rd, Kings Heath, Birmingham B13 9UJ, England.

MOBERG Sten-Erik 'Pyret'; b. 20 Jan. 1947, Fröson, Sweden. Composer; Artist; Piano; Guitar. m. Karin Moberg-Hillmann, 2 s., 1 d. *Education:* Exam, Teachers Training College, 1972; University Studies, Social Science and Pedagogics. *Musical Education:* Piano, Guitar and Song Studies. *Career:* The Threaten, TV, Theatre, 1966; The Helper, TV, Film, 1967; Hair, Sweden, Norway, 1968–70; The Diddlers, Tours in Ireland and England, 1966–70; Appearance at Olympia, Paris, 1978; TV appearances and tours in Europe. *Compositions:* Kärleken Ar Vit (Love is White), various Swedish songs; Another Year of Music; An Irish Saga, symphony. *Recordings:* Diddlers is Good For You, 1969; Hair, 1969; Kärleken Ar Vit, 1987; Another Year of Music, 1993. *Publication:* Ett Södermalm Som Gor Dig Varm (A South Part That Makes You Warm), 1987. *Honours:* STIM Award, 1990; Authors Union, 1991. *Memberships:* SKAP; STIM; SAMI; Theatre Union. *Leisure interests:* Cinema; Theatre; Football; Pub Sessions.

MOBERLEY Gary Mark; b. Sydney, New South Wales, Australia. Musician (keyboards); Composer; Writer; Programmer. *Musical Education:* Grade 6, AMEB. *Career:* Live work/recorded with: The Sweet; John Miles Band; Terence Trent D'Arby; Prefab Sprout; Wet Wet Wet; The Damned; The Alarm; Hipsway; Jodie Watley; Girlschool; Drum Theatre; Sigue Sigue Sputnik; Little Richard; Haywoode; Nicole; Big Country (remix); Loose Ends; The Associates; Talk Talk; Kiki Dee; Band of Holy Joy; Toni Di Bart; Dangerous Grounds; Funkadelia; Steel Pulse; Trevor Horn; The JBs; ABC; Fine Young Cannibals; The Foundations; Jean Jacques Perrey; Live work with: Bee Gees; Paul Rodgers; Bonnie Tyler; Wilson Pickett; Eddie Floyd; Rufus Thomas; Ben E King; Arthur Conley; Andrew 'Junior Boy' Jones; Cookie McGhee; Texas Blues Summit; Memphis Blues Summit; 34 European tours; 9 American tours; 3 world tours; 4 albums of radio and TV themes used world-wide. *Leisure interests:* Tennis; Cars; Cycling. *Address:* Flat 4, Grove End House, 150 Grove Terrace, London NW5 1PD, England.

MOBY (Richard Hall); b. 11 Sept. 1965, New York, New York, USA. Musician (Guitar, Drums, Keyboards); Prod.; Composer; Remixer. *Education:* University Philosophy Student, University of Connecticut; Private Classical Education, 1976–83. *Career:* Production and remixes for: Metallica; Smashing Pumpkins; Michael Jackson; Depeche Mode; Soundgarden; Blur; David Bowie; Orbital; Prodigy; Freddie Mercury; Brian Eno; B-52's; Ozzy Osbourne; John Lydon; Butthole Surfers; Erasure; Aerosmith; OMD; Pet Shop Boys; Jon Spencer Blues Explosion; Tours: Lollapalooza, 1995; Red Hot Chili Peppers, 1995; Soundgarden, 1996; Big Top, 1997; Prodigy, 1993, 1995; many solo tours. *Recordings:* Albums: Moby, 1992; Underground, 1993; Move, 1994; Ambient, 1994; Everything is Wrong, 1995; Underwater, 1995; Animal Rights, 1996; Collected B-Sides, 1996; I Like to Score, 1997; The End of Everything, 1997; Play, 1999; Singles: That's When I Reach for My Revolver; Come on

Baby; Dog Heaven; Why Can't It Stop?; Fucked Up; Higher/Desperate; Into the Blue; Everytime You Touch Me; Feeling So Real; Hymn; Move; UHF; Rock the House; James Bond Theme; Go; Drug Fits the Face; Honey; Run On; Bodyrock; Next Is The E; Why Does My Heart Feel So Bad?; Natural Blues; Full film score: Double Tap, 1997; Movie soundtrack contributions: Cool World, 1993; Heat, Scream, Joe's Apartment, 1996; Tomorrow Never Dies, the Saint, The Jackal, Spawn, 1997; Gattaca, Senseless, Rounders, Species II, Ever After, Blade, The Bumblebee Flies Anyway, Dangerous Beauty, Permanent Midnight, Playing By Heart, 1998; Any Given Sunday, The Next Best Thing, The Beach, Big Daddy. *Honours:* Everything Is Wrong, Album of the Year, Spin Magazine, 1995; Top 5 Albums of the Year, Village Voice, Entertainment Weekly and Go; Live Performer in Germany, 1995, Frontpage Magazine; Nominated Grammy 2000; Nominated Brit 2000. *Memberships:* BMI; PMRS; AF of M; SAG; AFTRA. *Leisure interest:* Tennis. *Current Management:* c/o Mr Eric Harle. *Address:* c/o Mr Eric Härle, Deutsch-Englische Freundschaft Ltd, PO Box 2477, London NW6 6NQ, England.

MOFFATT Hugh; b. 3 Nov. 1948, Fort Worth, Texas, USA. Country Singer; Songwriter; Musician (guitar, trumpet). *Education:* English degree, Rice University, Houston, Texas. *Career:* Singer, songwriter, Nashville, 1970s; Recording artist, 1974–; Formed band Ratz, early 1980s. *Compositions:* Just In Case, recorded by Ronnie Milsap, 1974; Old Flames Can't Hold A Candle To You (co-writer Pebe Sebert), recorded by Joe Sun, Dolly Parton, Foster and Allen; Wild Turkey (co-writer with Pebe Sebert), recorded by Lacy J Dalton; Love Game, recorded by Jerry Lee Lewis; Praise The Lord and Send Me The Money, recorded by Bobby Bare; Why Should I Cry Over You, (co-writer Ed Penney), recorded by George Hamilton IV; Words At Twenty Paces, recorded by Alabama; Operas: King of The Clouds, with Michael Ching; Out of The Rain, with Michael Ching. *Recordings:* Putting On The Ratz (EP); Dance Me Outside, (album) duet with Katy Moffatt, 1992; Albums: Loving You, 1987; Troubadour, 1989; Live and Alone, 1991; The Wognum Sessions, 1992; The Way Love Is, 1992; The Life of a Minor Poet, 1996; Ghosts of The Music, 1998. *Address:* c/o Criterion Music, 6124 Selma Ave, Hollywood, CA 90028, USA.

MOFFATT Katherine Louella (Katy); b. 19 Nov. 1950, Fort Worth, Texas, USA. Musician (guitar); Vocalist; Songwriter. *Education:* Sophie Newcomb College, 1968; St John's College, 1969–70. *Career:* Folk singer, 1967–68; Production assistant, announcer, television stations, 1970; Musician, singer, blues band Corpus Christi, 1970; Solo artiste, 1971–; On concert bills with: Muddy Waters; Everly Brothers; Willie Nelson; Warren Zevon; Musical film roles: Billy Jack; Hard Country; The Thing Called Love; Television and radio includes: Music City Tonight; Texas Connection; Nashville Now; Bobby Bare Show; National Public Radio; E-Town; World Cafe; Mountain Stage. *Compositions:* The Magic Ring; Kansas City Morning; Gerry's Song; Take Me Back To Texas; (Waiting For) The Real Thing; Didn't We Have Love; Co-writer, Walkin' On The Moon (with Tom Russell). *Recordings:* Singles include: Take It As It Comes, 1981; Under Loved and Over Lonely, 1983; Albums: Katy; Kissin' In The California Sun; Walkin' On The Moon; The Greatest Show On Earth; A Town South of Bakersfield; Hearts Gone Wild; Child Bride; Dance Me Outside; Sleepless Nights; Midnight Radio. *Honours:* Record World Album Award, 1976; Cash Box Single Award, 1976; ACM Nomination, Best New Female Vocalist, 1985; Best Singer-Songwriter, Fort Worth Weekly, 1997. *Memberships:* AFofM; AFTRA; SAG; NARAS. *Leisure interests:* Reading; Swimming; Horse riding. *Address:* PO Box 334, O'Fallon, IL 62269, USA.

MOFFETT Johnathan Phillip; b. 17 Nov. 1954, New Orleans, Louisiana, USA. Musician (drums); Musical Dir; Songwriter. m. Rhonda Bartholomew, 26 June 1976, 1 s., 1 d. *Career:* Drummer for artists including: Patti Austin; Cameo; Lionel Richie; Madonna; Tina Marie; Jermaine Jackson; Major tours and concerts with: The Jacksons, 1979–81, Victory Tour (also as set designer), 1984; Elton John world tours, 1988–89; Madonna, Virgin and Ciao Italia tours; George Michael, Rock In Rio Festival; Musical director for concerts by Jermaine Jackson, Michael Jackson; Numerous television and video appearances with: The O'Jays; Isaac Hayes; The Kane Gang; Cameo. *Recordings:* Albums include: Silk Electric, Diana Ross, 1982; Victory, The Jacksons, 1984; One More Story, Peter Cetera, 1988; Back To Avalon, Kenny Loggins, 1988; Also recorded with Julian Lennon; Richard Marx; Jody Watley; Chico de Barge.

MOGENSEN Grethe Stitz; b. 25 May 1937, Copenhagen, Denmark. Actress; Author; Playwriter; Composer; Singer. m. Axel Busch-Jensen, 4 April 1964, 1 s., 1 d. *Education:* New Theatre Actors' School, Copenhagen. *Career:* Enlordag på Amàr, 1957; Champagnegaloppen, 1960, 1974; Farinelli, 1961; Guys and Dolls, 1992; No No Nanette, 1973; Company, 1972; Dollarprinsen, 1975; Piger tilsös, 1987; Sweeney Todd, 1988; Nitouche, 1989; Les Miserables, 1991; Cirkus Mikkelikski, 1991, 1997; Sommer i Tyrol, 1993; Mod mig på Cassiopeia, 1996; My Fair Lady, 1999; Films: Pigen i sogelyset, 1959; Bussen, 1963; Gift, 1966; Flagermusen, 1966; Tro, håb og Karlighed, 1984; Tango for tre, 1992; Singer, Denmark 1957–84; Greenland 1967; Israel, 1978; USA, 1984. *Compositions:* Cirkus Mikkelikski; Granen, Nissen sad på loftet; Okker gokkar; Hvis Katten Kunne Vrinske; Dubbing for Walt Disney.

Recordings: Enlordag på Amàr, 1959; Farinelli, 1961; En sondag på Amager, 1962; Dollarprinssen, 1964; Dyrene i Hakkebakkeskoven, 1963; Landmandsliv, 1965; Flagermusen, 1966; Shehvide, 1966; Bambi, 1970; Askepot, 1971; Pinoccio, 1971; Isyngelegeland, I-IV, 1967–87; Jul i Syngelegeland, I and II, 1971, 1979; Lidt af hvert, 1979; Cirkus Mikkelikski, 1981, 1996; Author of Teaterkattens Eventyr, 1993. *Honours:* Mogens Brandts Legat, 1960; Kiss Gregers, 1974; DPA's Haderslegat, 1991; Louis Halberstadt's Haderslegat, 1997. *Memberships:* Danish Actors League; Danish Popular Authors. *Leisure interests:* Gardening; Golf. *Address:* Engstien 4, 2791 Dragor, Denmark.

MOGENSEN Mogens Eddie; b. 31 March 1948, Odense, Denmark. Musician (Fagot/Bassoon). m. Nora Andrea Mogensen, 31 March 1972, 2 s., 1 d. *Education:* Det Fynske Musikkonservatorium, Odense, with Hagbard Knudsen. *Career:* Principal Bassoon, Royal Danish Orchestra, Copenhagen, 1972–; Teacher, Royal Danish Academy of Music, Royal Academy of Music. *Membership:* IDRS. *Address:* Landlyst Vaenge 61, 2635 Jshoj, Denmark.

MOGG Phil; b. 1951, London, England. Rock Vocalist. *Career:* Founder member, UK rock group UFO, 1969–83; Reformed twice, 1985, 1991; Regular world-wide tours. *Recordings:* Albums: UFO, 1971; UFO 2 – Flying, 1971; Live In Japan, 1972; Phenomenon, 1974; Force It, 1975; No Heavy Pettin', 1976; Lights Out, 1977; Obsession, 1978; Strangers In The Night, 1979; No Place To Run, 1980; The Wild, The Willing and The Innocent, 1981; Mechanix, 1982; Making Contact, 1982; Headstone, 1983; Misdemeanour, 1985; Ain't Misbehavin', 1988; High Stakes and Dangerous Men, 1992; Hit singles include: Doctor, Doctor; Too Hot To Handle; Lights Out; Rock Bottom; Edge of the World, 1997; Chocolate Box, 1999. *Current Management:* Singerman Entertainment, Penthouse West, 8833 Sunset Blvd, Los Angeles, CA 90069, USA.

MOHAMED Pops; b. 10 Dec. 1949, Benoni, Johannesburg, South Africa. Musician (piano-synthesizer programming, keyboards, kora, mbira, didgeridu, berimbau, marimba, percussion). Divorced, 2 s., 1 d. *Musical Education:* Studied Jazz at FUBA, 1979–84; Studied traditional instruments, 1986–93. *Career:* Lead guitarist, Les Valiants, 1969–71; Band leader: The Dynamics: El Gringoes; Society's Children; Solo albums, 1975–; Black Disco, 1975; Night Express, 1976; Black Disco 3, 1978; Movement In The City, 1979; Award as original artist for Towntalk Show, 1979; Albums: BM Movement, 1980; Innercity Funk, 1981; Recording Engineer, 1981–87; Record Producer, 1988–95; Own record label Kalamazoo Music, 1993. *Compositions:* Lolly's Song; A New Hope!, 1995; African Sketches; A New Hope. *Recordings:* When In New York, 1993. *Publications:* Kalamazoo Music. *Honours:* South African OKTV Music Awards Nominations, 1991, 1992. *Memberships:* Royal Schools and Federated Union of Black Arts. *Leisure interests:* Traditional music; Squash. *Current Management:* Kalamazoo Music Productions. *Address:* 202 Bethlen, 13th St, Orange Grove, 2192 Johannesburg, Gauteng, South Africa.

MOLDEN Nigel Charles; b. 17 Aug. 1948, Oxford, England. Music Co Dir. m. Hilary Julia Lichfield, 14 Aug. 1971, 3 s. *Education:* Bsc (Hons) London University; MSc Brunel University; PhD, Fairfax University. *Musical Education:* Piano Grade 2. *Career:* International General Manager, WEA Records, 1971–80; International Marketing Manager, Thorn EMI Video, 1980–84; Joint Chief Executive, TKO Magnum Music, 1994-. *Honours:* Freeman, City of London, 1990. *Memberships:* FRSA; FCIM; FBIM; FinstD. *Leisure interests:* Music; Writing. *Address:* Ashcombe House, Deanwood Rd, Jordans, Buckinghamshire HP9 2UU, England.

MOLKO Brian; b. 10 Dec. 1972. Singer; Musician (Guitar, Bass). *Education:* Studied Drama, Goldsmiths College, London. *Career:* Member, Placebo; Numerous television appearances; Live tours and numerous festival dates. *Recordings:* Singles: Come Home, 1996; 36 Degrees, 1996; Teenage Angst, 1996; Nancy Boy, 1997; Bruise Pristine, 1997; Pure Morning, 1998; You Don't Care About Us, 1998; Every You Every Me, 1999; Without You I'm Nothing, featuring David Bowie, 1999; Albums: Placebo, 1996; Without You I'm Nothing, 1998.

MOLLER Lars Alleso; b. 17 Sept. 1966, Copenhagen, Denmark. Musician (tenor saxophone); Composer. *Musical Education:* Lessons with David Liebman, 5 years; BFA, New School, New York, 1989; Composer workshop with Bob Brookmeyer at Rytmekons Conservatory, 1996–98; Indian classical music studies, New Delhi, 1990–94. *Career:* Own groups, with Jimmy Cobb, Niels-Henning Orsted Pedersen, Billy Hart, Mads Vinding, Alex Riel, Jukkis Outila, Thomas Clausen and John Abercrombie, 1986–91; Concerts in Canada, USA, France, Italy, Sweden, Germany, Norway and India; Television and radio broadcasts in Europe and USA; Featured soloist with Jimmy Cobb Sextet, Hermeto Pascoal Group, European Youth Big Band and European Broadcasting Union Big Band; Also played with Holmes Brothers and various Danish bands such as Sound of Choice Ensemble, with Markus Stockhausen; Played with leading artists including: Lee Konitz, Jimmy Cobb, Adam Nussbaum, Art Blakey, Roy Haynes and David Liebman; Member, Den 3 Vej (composer workshop group); Leader, 18-piece group The Orchestra Big Band, 1997–98; Beijing Music Festival, 1998. *Compositions:* Works for small jazz groups, symphony orchestra, chamber orchestra, string quartet, big band and choir. *Recordings include:* Copenhagen Groove, with Niels-Henning Orsted Pedersen, 1989; Pyramid, 1993; Cross Current, 1995; Circles, 1996; Colours, with John Abercrombie, 1997; Kaleidoscope, Nazos/Jazz, 1998; Centrifugal, 2001. *Honours:* Hon. prize from Danish Jazz Beat and Folk Authors Society (DJBFA); Grammy Award, Best Danish Jazz Release, 2000; Danish Jazzmedia (JASA) Award, 2000. *Address:* Valdemarsgade 11, 1 tn, 1665 Copenhagen V, Denmark. *Internet:* www.larsmoller.com.

MOLLISON Deborah; b. 29 May 1958, England. Composer; Musician (piano). m. Gareth Mollison, 3 May 1986. *Musical Education:* Piano and Composition, Royal Academy of Music; Master's degree, studied piano with Craig Sheppard, Lancaster University; Film Music course at UCLA; Classical composer; Tutor of Composition, Middlesex University. *Compositions:* Music for films: Stand Up The Real Glynn Vernon; Go On Make A Wish; Vampires; Television drama, The Gift of the Nile, Primetime TV; Sleeping With Mickey, BBC2; Before Your Eyes, BBC Wales; The Whistling Boy, BBC Wales; Television documentaries: Treasures At The South Pole, NBC; Thomas Cook On The Nile, Case TV; Connections 2, Discovery Channel; Given Half A Chance, Vanson Wardle Productions; Crossrail, London Transport Authority. *Honours:* Else Cross Prize, Royal Academy of Music; Song '92 UK Festival. *Memberships:* PRS; BASCA; Women In Film; Musicians' Union. *Current Management:* Soundtrack Music Management, 22 Ives St, Chelsea, London SW3 2ND, England.

MOLLOY Matt; b. 12 Jan. 1947, Ballaghadareen, County Roscommon, Ireland. Musician (flute, tin whistle). *Musical Education:* Began studying flute, aged 8. *Career:* Member: Bothy Band, c. 1974; Planxty, c. 1978; The Chieftains, 1979–; Collaborations: Paul Brady; Micheal O Suilleabhain; Donal Lunny; Irish Chamber Orchestra; Currently a publican in Westport. *Recordings:* with The Bothy Band: The First Album, 1975, Old Hag You Have Killed Me, 1976; with Planxty: After The Break, 1979, The Woman I Loved So Well, 1980; solo: Matt Molloy (featuring Donal Lunny), 1976; The Heathery Breeze, 1981; The Gathering, 1981; Contentment Is Wealth (with Sean Keane), 1985; Stony Steps, 1988; The Fire Aflame (with Liam O Flynn and Sean Keane), 1992; Music At Matt Molloy's, 1992; Voyager (with Mike Oldfield), A Irmandade Das Estrellas (with Carlos Nunez), 1996; Shadows On Stone (featuring Steve Cooney, Christy Moore and Frankie Gavin), 1997. *Honours:* All Ireland Flute championship, winner; TG4 National Traditional Award, 1999; Grammy Awards: with The Chieftains: Best Contemporary Traditional Album, An Irish Evening – Live At The Grand Opera House, 1991; Best Traditonal Album, Another Country, 1992; Best World Music Album, Santiago, 1997. *Internet:* members.shaw.ca/chieftains/index.html.

MOLONEY Paddy; b. 1938, Donnycarney, Dublin, Ireland. Folk Musician (uillean pipes, tin whistle). *Career:* Member, Ceolteoiri Chaulann Folk Orchestra, led by Sean O'Raida, 1950s; Founder member, Irish folk group, The Chieftains, 1964–; Collaborations with classical flute player, James Galway; Founding partner and executive producer of Wicklow Entertainment, 1997–; Executive producer for: The Long Journey Home, 1998; Fire In The Kitchen, 1998; Imaginary Cuba, 1999; The Message, 1999; Wingspan, 1999. *Recordings:* Albums: Chieftains 1, 1964; Chieftains 2, 1969; Chieftains 3, 1971; Chieftains 4, 1973; Chieftains 5, 1975; Women of Ireland, 1976; Bonaparte's Retreat, 1976; Chieftains Live, 1977; Chieftains 7, 1977; Chieftains 8, 1978; Vol. 9, 1979; Boil The Breakfast Early, 1980; Chieftains 10, 1981; The Chieftains In China, 1984; Ballad of The Irish Horse, 1985; Celtic Wedding, 1987; The Chieftains In Ireland (with James Galway), 1987; Year of The French, 1988; Irish Heartbeat (with Van Morrison), 1988; A Chieftains Celebration, 1989; Chieftains Collection, 1989; The Celtic Connection – James Galway and The Chieftains, 1990; Bells of Dublin, 1991; An Irish Evening, 1992; Another Country, 1992; The Celtic Harp (with Belfast Harp Orchestra), 1993; The Fire Aflame (with Sean Keane, Matt Molloy, Liam O'Flynn), 1993; Long Black Veil, 1995; Santiago, 1996; Tears of Stone, 1999. *Honours:* Doctorate of Music, Trinity College, 1988; Hon. Chief of the Oklahoma Choctaw Nation, 1995; Five times winner, Grammy Awards. *Current Management:* S L Feldman and Associates, 1505 W 2nd St, Suite 200, Vancouver, BC V6H 3Y4, Canada.

MOMCHIL; b. Bulgaria. Musician (keyboards); Vocalist; Songwriter; Arranger. *Career:* Keyboard player, new wave band Class, until 1993; Formed duo, Dony and Monchil, 1993–; Numerous tours, Bulgaria. *Recordings:* Albums: The Album!, 1993; The Second One, 1994. *Honours:* Orpheus National Music Awards: Best Single: The Little Prince; Best Video For Duo Or A Group. *Address:* c/o Union Media, 71 Evl Georgiev Blvd, Sofia 1142, Bulgaria.

MONAGHAN Brendan; b. 3 April 1958, Newtownards, County Down, Ireland. Singer; Songwriter; Musician (guitar). m. Valerie McDonnell, 6 Sept. 1980, 2 s., 1 d. *Musical Education:* Basic. *Career:* Appearances with band The Cattle Company include major country festivals, Europe;

Television and radio appearances, Ireland, Europe; USA; Cable television includes: Canada, USA. *Composition:* I'm Right, You're Wrong, I Win. *Recordings:* with Cattle Company: Hero (debut album); Love to Be Loved; Big Town After Dark, 2000; Featured on album Alive In Belfast; Solo: Sister's Lament; Johnny Got Married; Single: Let Me In, 1999. *Honours:* Top Performance Award, International Country Music Festival, Netherlands; Publishers Award, Ray Shepherd Music, Efforts In Country Music; European Country Music Asscns, Best European Group, 1995; Audio Images 2000, 1997; Best Album, North America CMA International Awards, 1999; Best International Singer, North America CMA International Awards, 1999. *Memberships:* PRS; International Songwriters Asscn; BMI, USA; United Song Makers. *Current Management:* Diamond Blue Records, 3 Pleasant View, Bridgehill, Consett, Co Durham DH8 8QY, England. *Address:* 9 Stratford Dr., Bangor, County Down BT19 6ZW, Ireland.

MONDESIR Michael Trevor Collins; b. 6 Feb. 1966, London, England. Musician (bass guitar); Composer. *Musical Education:* Self-taught. *Career:* Performed with Django Bates; Billy Cobham; Hermeto Pascoal; Pee Wee Ellis; Lenny White; Neneh Cherry; Jason Rebello; Annette Peacock; Bernard Purdie; Little Axe; Tackhead; Infinitum; Nikki Yeoh. *Recordings:* Keeping Time, Jason Rebello, 1992; Summer Fruits (and Unrest), Django Bates, 1993; The Traveller, Billy Cobham, 1994; Winter Truce (and Homes Blaze), Django Bates, 1995; Worotan, Oumou Sangare, 1996; Quiet Nights, Django Bates, 1998; Like Life, Django Bates, 1998. *Memberships:* PRS; Musicians' Union. *Leisure interests:* Cooking; Drawing; Painting; Reading. *Address:* 97A Hamlets Way, London E3 4TL, England.

MONDLOCK Buddy (Robert); b. Chicago, USA. Vocalist; Musician (guitar); Songwriter. *Career:* Has had songs recorded by: Garth Brooks; Joan Baez; Nanci Griffith; Janis Ian; David Wilcox; Maura O'Connell; Peter Paul and Mary; Performed on Chicago club scene, 1980s; Moved to Nashville after securing publishing contract with EMI, mid-1980s; Appeared on Garth Brooks album No Fences, 1990; Co-wrote Tenderness with Janis Ian and played on her Revenge album, on which song appears, 1995; Nanci Griffith recorded Coming Down In The Rain on Grammy Award-winning Other Voices Other Rooms album; Peter Paul and Mary recorded The Kid on their Lifelines album. *Recordings:* On The Line, 1987; Buddy Mondlock, 1994; Poetic Justice, 1998; features on: No Fences, Garth Brooks, 1990; Revenge, Janis Ian, 1995; Around The Campfire, Peter Paul and Mary, 1998. *Honours:* Kerrville Folk Festival Award, 1987; Kerrville Music Award, Song of the Year, The Kid, 1996. *Current Management:* Bob Doyle and Associates, 1111 17th Ave S, Nashville, TN 37212, USA. *Internet:* www.buddymondlock.com.

MONICA; b. 1980, College Park, Atlanta, Georgia, USA. Singer. *Recordings:* Singles: Before You Walk Out of My Life, 1995; Why I Love You So Much, 1996; For You I Will, 1996; First Night, 1998; The Boy is Mine, with Brandy, 1998; Street Symphony, 1999; Inside, 1999; Angel of Mine, 1999; Albums: Miss Thang, 1995; The Boy is Mine, 1998.

MONK Meredith Jane; b. 20 Nov. 1942, NY, USA. Composer; Choreographer; Dir; Singer; Filmmaker. *Education:* BA, Sarah Lawrence University, 1964; Honorary Doctorates, Bard College, 1988; University of the Arts, 1989; Juilliard School, 1998; S F Art Institute, 1999; Voice, Piano and Composition Study. *Career:* Creative Works Include, Vessel, 1971; Turtle Dreams, 1983; The Games, 1983; Book of Days, 1988; Facing North, 1990; Atlas, 1991; Three Heavens and Hells, 1992; Volcano Songs, 1994; American Archeology, 1994; The Politics of Quiet, 1996; Library of the Performing Arts Exhibition, Lincoln Center, 1996; Steppe Music, 1997; Magic Frequencies, 1997; Walker Art Center Exhibition, 1998. *Recordings:* Do You Be, 1987; Book of Days, 1990; Facing North, 1992; Atlas, An Opera In Three Parts, 1993; Monk and the Abbess, 1996; Volcano Songs, 1997. *Publications:* Art and Performance Meredith Monk, 1997. *Honours:* MacArthur Foundation Fellowship, 1995; Samuel Scripps Award, 1996; Sarah Lawrence Outstanding Allumna Award, 1996; ASCAP Award, 1996; Norton Stevens Fellow, 1993, 1994; Pentches Kritikev Preis for Best Record, 1981, 1986; Branders Creative Arts Award, 1974; Bessie Award for Sustained Achievement, 1985; National Music Theatre Award, 1986; Villager Award; Dance Magazine Award, 1993. *Memberships:* ASCAP; American Music Center. *Leisure interests:* Gardening; Horse Riding. *Current Management:* The House Foundation for the Arts Inc. *Address:* 228 W Broadway, New York, NY 10013, USA.

MONLEY Julie (Julianne Margaret); b. 1 March 1954, Denver, Colorado, USA. Musician; Singer. m. Frederic Desmoulin, 27 Feb. 1987, 2 d. *Musical Education:* Private lessons classical jazz. *Career:* Jazz Valley Festival, MJC club Dunkerque; Radio and television: France Music; Live radio: Vous En Moi; Radio shows in Denver. *Honours:* Second Prize, Tremplin Jazz, 1995; First Prize, Vocalist Jazz à Vienne, 1996. *Membership:* Jazz On The Blocks, Paris. *Leisure interest:* Painting. *Address:* 69 Blvd Barbes, 75018 Paris, France.

MONRAD Jan; b. 18 March 1951, Copenhagen, Denmark. Writer; Composer; Comedian. 1 s., 1 d. *Musical Education:* Teachers Seminarium. *Career:* Member of band Monrad and Rislund, with Saren Rislund; Several radio and television shows since 1977; Tours of Denmark and Greenland. *Compositions:* The Championship in Teddybear-Petting, 1993; The Statesman's Funeral, 1994. *Recordings:* 16 albums with Monrad and Rislund, 1976–; 1991, 1981; Jesus and Jens Vejmand, 1983; Dogstars Hospitalized, 1990; Goodbye Aage, 1994; 18 recordings and 1 video, 1976-. *Publications:* Black Sketches; Beske Barske Rimom Barn og Andre Kendisser. *Honour:* Danish Grammy Award, Entertainment Records, 1995. *Memberships:* DJBFA; Dansk Solistforbund. *Leisure interests:* Old advertisement boards; Tramways. *Address:* Toftojevej 27 B, 2720 Vanlose, Denmark.

MONTANARO Miquieù (Michel François); b. 13 Aug. 1955, Hyères, France. Composer; Musician (flutes, saxophone, accordion, piano); Actor. m. Niké Nagy, 29 April 1981, 2 s., 1 d. *Education:* Teaching diploma. *Musical Education:* Self-taught; Masters for folk music. *Career:* First concert, Edinburgh, 1973; Tours, Hungary; Bulgaria; Austria; Italy; Portugal; USA; Indonesia; Algeria; Morocco; Tunisia; West Africa; Television: Hungary; Portugal; France (France 3, Cercle de Minuit, France 2); Radio: France Inter; France Culture; France Musique; Festivals include: Bamako; St Chartier; Nantes; Budapest; Comboscuro; Plays with: B Phillips; Kiss Tamàs; Konomba Traore; A Vitous; P Aledo; G Murphy; Téka; F Frith; Vujicsics; C Tyler; Sebastyén Màrta; P Neveu; Ghymes; F Richard; J Stivin; C Brazier; D Daumas; F Kop; D Regef; C Zagaria; K Ruzicka; Szabados; F Ulihr; P Vaillant; A Gabriel; J Lyonn Lieberman; L Andrst; J N Mabelly; D Phillips; Es Soundoussia; F Gaudé; S Pesce; Hayet Ayad; Christine Wodrascka; Samia Benchikh; Senem Diyici; René Sette; Mathieu Luzi; Nena Venetsanou; Sara Alexander; Michel Bianco; Carlo Rizzo; Corou de Berra; Wayal. *Composition:* Cri, for symphonic orchestra and traditional instruments, 1997. *Recordings:* More than 40 include: Albums: Montanaro/Collage, Bonton, 1990; Mesura and Arte del Danzare, 1992; Tenson – La Nef Des Musiques, Bleu Regard, 1993; Vents d'Est/Migrations, 1993; Montanaro/Théâtre, 1994; Galoubet-Tambourin, Musiques d'Hier Et Aujourdhui, 1995; with L'Ensemble Méditerranéen P Aledo: Fusion; D'île En Ile; Tres Corpos Una Alma; Java Sampo Raharjo, 1997; Vents d'Est Ballade pour une Mer qui Chante, 1997; Maurin des Maures, 1999. *Publications:* Video K7 Noir and Blanc with Konomba Traore, CNDP, France. *Memberships:* ADAMI; SPEDIDAM; SACEM; SFA. *Leisure interests:* Walking; Skiing; Canoeing; Planting trees; Gardening. *Current Management:* Sylvie Bondier. *Address:* Grande Fontaine, 83570 Correns, France.

MONTE Marisa; b. 1967, Rio de Janeiro, Brazil. Vocalist; Musician (piano); Songwriter. *Musical Education:* Studied music theory (drums, piano) as a child; Studied opera in Rome, 1986. *Career:* Made stage debut in Veludo Azul, Rio de Janeiro, 1987; Solo shows in São Paulo, 1990; Signed with World Pacific and released live album; Subsequent albums released internationally bringing regular tours to USA, UK, Europe and throughout Latin America. *Compositions:* Beija Eu; Ainda Lembro; Eu Sei; Tudo Pela Metade; Mustapha; Na Estrada; De Mais Ninguem; Bem Leve; Equanto Isso; Amor (I Love You); Nao Va Embora; Nao E Facil; Tema De Amor; Abololo; Gentileza; Agua Tambem E Mar. *Recordings:* Marisa Monte Ao Vivo, 1990; Mais, 1991; Green Blue Yellow Rose and Charcoal, 1994; Barulhinho Bom, 1996; Memories Chronicles and Declarations of Love, 2000; Café Brasil, 2001. *Honours:* Latin Grammy Award, Best Contemporary Pop Album, Memorias Cronicas E Declaracoes De Amor, 2001. *Current Management:* Monte Criacao E Producao Ltda. *Internet:* www.marisamonte.com.br.

MONTENEGRO Oswaldo; b. 15 March 1956, Rio de Janeiro, Brazil. Composer; Singer; Author and Dir, Musical Plays; Musician (guitar, piano). 1 s. *Education:* Communication Course, University of Brazil. *Musical Education:* Musical Course, University of Rio de Janeiro. *Career:* Tours, Brazil, 1979–; TV, radio appearances, concerts, Portugal, until 1992; Shows in New Jersey; Connecticut; Boston; Miami; Orlando; Mount Vernon; Author and director, musical plays including: Veja Você Brasilia, 1981; Cristal, 1982; A Dança Dos Signos, 1983–87; Os Memestréis, 1985; Aldeia Dos Ventos, 1986; Vale Encantado, 1993; Noturno, 1993; Mayâ, 1992. *Compositions include:* Bandolins; Lua e Flor; Condor; Seo e Bia; Furtuiçào; Estrelas; Voz da Tela. *Recordings:* Trilhas, 1978; Poeta Maldito, Moleque Vadio, 1979; Oswaldo Montenegro Ao Viva, 1980; Asa De Lux, 1981; A Dança Dos Signos, 1982; Cristal, 1983; Os Menestréis, 1984; Drops De Hortelâ, 1985; Aldeia Dos Ventos, 1986; Oswaldo Montenegro, 1989; Ao Viva, 1990; Vida de Artista, 1991; Mulungo, 1992; Seu Francisco, 1993; Aos Filhos Dos Hippies, 1995. *Honours:* Third place of honour, with composition, Bandolins, TV Tupi Music Festival, 1979; First place of honour, with Agonia, TV Globo Brazilian Popular Music Festival, 1980; Gold Disc, Oswaldo Montenegro, 1989; Platinum disc, Visda de Artista, 1991. *Memberships:* UBC; SBAT; Warner-Chappell. *Leisure interests:* Movies; Sports. *Current Management:* Newton Montenegro. *Address:* R Viscondede Pirajá 51, ap 502, Ipanema, Rio de Janeiro, RJ, Brazil.

MONTGOMERY John Michael; b. 20 Jan. 1965. Country vocalist; Musician (guitar); Songwriter. *Career:* Began performing on parents' country music shows, aged 5; Performed with local country bands, aged 15; Subsequently played with father Harold and brother Eddie (later of Montgomery Gentry country duo); Played the Austin City Saloon in Lexington, Kentucky, developing local following; Signed to Atlantic Records, 1992; Continued to have hits on both pop and country charts; 1993 pop and country hit I Swear reached No. 1 in US pop chart the following year in a recording by pop/R & B act All-4-One; Song subsequently became a favourite at wedding ceremonies. *Compositions include:* I Miss You A Little. *Recordings include:* I Swear, 1993; Sold (The Grundy County Auction Incident), 1995; I Can Love You Like That, 1995; I Love The Way You Love Me, 1993; Be My Baby Tonight, 1994; If You've Got Love, 1994. *Honours:* various including: CMA, Horizon Award, 1994; AMA Country Category, Favorite Newcomer, 1994; ACM: New Artist of the Year, Single of the Year, I Swear, 1994. *Leisure interests:* Fishing; Golfing. *Address:* c/o Hallmark Direction Services, 1819, Broadway, Nashville, TN 37203, USA.

MONTREDON Jean-Claude Pierre; b. 23 Sept. 1949, Martinique. Musician (drums); Composer. *Musical Education:* Self-taught. *Career:* Member, Frères Bernard Orchestra, Tropicana Orchestra; Drums for Marius Cultier and The Surfs; Formed trio with Alain Jean Marie, Winston Berkley; Performances in Barbados, Trinidad, 1972; Bilboquet, Paris jazz club, French Radio, 1973–75; Founder, Kominkayson, with Richard Raux, Michel Alibo, 1976; Appearances include: Palais de Congrès, Paris; Cultural Center, Martinique, 1976; Played with Didier Levellet Quintet, Chris McGregor, New Morning Jazz Club, Paris, 1977–; Rock concerts with Randy Weston, Claude Sommier, Michel Alibo, 1978–81; Tours, Finland, Sweden, West Africa, with Roland Brival, 1981; Played with Liquid Rock Stonne, Paris; Appearances include France Musique, classical radio station; Sermac Dance Workshop, Martinique, 1983; Jazz Festival, Barbados; Jazz and Folk Festival, Martinique, 1985; Caribbean Jazz Workshop, Berlin; Festival of Trinidad, 1986; Barbados Festival, with West Indies Jazz Band; Caribbean Jazz Workshop, 1987; Olympia, Paris, 1988; Tours, West Indies, South Africa, 1989; Founder, The Musical Corps of Martinique, 1990–94; Currently performs with own band Kominikayson, works with Luther François. *Recordings:* Malavoi, Tropicana Orchestre; Gisèle Baka; Al Lirvart and Didier Levallet Quintet; Brotherhood of Breath; Joby Bernabe; Doudou Guirand; 2 albums with The Caribbean Ensemble; West Indies Jazz Band, 1990; 1992; Luther François, 1990. *Memberships:* SACEM; SPEDIDAM; Congés Spectacle. *Leisure interests:* Créations; Film music. *Address:* 131 rue de Rome, 75017 Paris, France.

MOODY James; b. 26 March 1925, Savannah, GA, USA. Musician (Tenor, Alto, Soprano, Saxophone, Flute). m. Linda Petersen Moody, 3 April 1989. *Education:* US Air Force Band Theory, Composition with Dizzy Gillespie, Composition and Theory with Tom McIntosh with Michael Longo. *Career:* Teachings: Cornell University, Ithaca, New York; Harvard University, Cambridge, Massachusetts; Howard University, Washington, DC; Loyola University, New Orleans, Louisiana; Stanford University, Palo Alto, California; University of Alabama; University of Florida, Gainesville, Florida; Major Performances include: Dizzy Gillespie's 70th Birthday Celebration, televised; Requently appeared in USA, Egypt, Japan, Israel, Canada, Germany including Johnny Carson's Tonight Show and The Ben Sidran Show in New York; Carneo role, Clint Eastwood's film, Midnight in The Garden of Good and Evil; Radio: Voice of America, hosted by Willis Conover, numerous times; Interviews and concerts on many stations in USA and most European countries. *Compositions:* Moody's Mood for Love; Honey's Tune, with Linda Moody; Look Into My Eyes; It's a One-Way Road; Love, Where Are You?; Never Again; Simplicity and Beauty; The Television Song; You Better Believe It; Everyone Needs It; Coffee Break; He Whispered He Loved Her; Feelin' Low; Love Was the Cause; Put Your Shoes on Baby; I Saw a Flying Saucer; Hey Herbi; Where's Alpert?; Don't Throw Your Back Out-A Whack; Diskom-blu-ba-late Me, Baby; What Do You Do; Moody's Theme; Shake, Rattle and Boogie. *Recordings:* Moody's Mood for Love, 1951; Last Train from Overbrook, 1958; Sweet and Lovely, 1989; Honey, 1991; Live at the Blue Note, 1995; Young at Heart, 1996; Moody Plays Mancini, 1997; Flute 'N the Blues, Chess; Never Again, Muse; Cookin the Blues, Cadet; Hey – Its James Moody, Argo. *Publications include:* Jazz Giants: A Visual Retrospective; The Eye of Jazz; Jazz is by Nat Hentoff; Jazz Styles: History and Analysis by Mark C Gridley; The Jazz Years: Earwitness to an Era by Leonard Feather; The Record Collector's Handbook by Alan Leibowitz. *Honours include:* James Moody Day, 1993; 1996; Jamaica Hall of Fame, 1996; New Jersey Hall of Fame, 1996; International Hall of Fame, 1996; National Endowment for the Arts Jazz Masters Award, 1998. *Memberships:* National Asscn of Recording Arts and Sciences, International Asscn of Jazz Educators; National Jazz Service Organization. *Leisure interests:* Health and Fitness; Tennis; Swimming; Books; Astronomy. *Address:* 36 Como St, Romford, Essex RM7 7DR, England.

MOOG Robert Arthur; b. 23 May 1934, Flushing, New York, USA. Music Co Exec., Musical Instrument Designer. m. Shirley Leigh, 15 June 1958, 1 s., 3 d. *Education:* BS Physics, Queens College, 1957; BSEE, Columbia University, 1957; PhD Engineering Physics, Cornell University, 1965. *Career:* President, Moog Music Inc, 1954–77; President, Big Briar Inc, 1978; Vice President, new product research, Kurzweil Music Systems, 1984–88; Designer, synthisizers, including Moog synthesizer, 1967; Mini-Moog, 1971; Polymoog, 1976; Pedal-operated Taurus system; Memory Moog; Exponents include: Walter Carlos; Keith Emerson; Jan Hammer; Rush. *Publications:* Contributor, professional journals. *Honours:* Hon. doctorates, Lycoming College, 1975; New York Polytechnic University, 1985; NARAS Trustees Award; Trendsetter Award, Billboard Magazine, 1970; Silver Medal, Audio Engineering Society, 1984; Fellow, Audio Engineering Society.

MOONEY Gordon James; b. 27 May 1951, Edinburgh, Scotland. Piper; Musician; Planner; Businessman. m. 17 Apr. 1978, 1 s., 1 d. *Education:* BSc Town Planning, Dundee University. *Musical Education:* Highland bagpipes, border pipes, Northumbrian smallpipes from age 7. *Career:* Concerts include: Edinburgh International Festival; Sanders Tagare, Harvard, Boston; Old Songs Festival, USA; Tacoma University, USA; Québec Double Reed Convention; Vermont Bagpipe Festival; Television and radio appearances: Border TV; Canadian National Radio; BBC; Radio Scotland; Radio 4; World Service. *Recordings:* O'er The Border; Global Meditation; Song For Yarrow; Leading Figure, Scottish Music Revival. *Publications:* 3 collections of music; 1 tutor book. *Honours:* Scottish Arts Council Award, 1988; Billboard Award, 1993. *Memberships:* MPRS; President of Lowland and Border Pipes Society. *Leisure interests:* Walking the high places; Archaeology; Building. *Current Management:* Traditional music.

MOONEY Tim; b. 6 Oct. 1958, Las Vegas, Nevada, USA. Musician (drums, keyboards, guitar); Songwriter. *Musical Education:* Self-taught. *Career:* Member of groups: Sleepers, 1977–79; Negative Trend, 1979–81; Toiling Midgets, 1982–92; American Music Club, 1992–95; Toured with Pearl Jam and Bob Dylan; Various BBC television appearances; Appeared at Reading and Glastonbury festivals. *Recordings:* with Sleepers: Seventh World, 1978; with Negative Trend: Beach Boulevard, Tooth and Nail, 1979; with Toiling Midgets: Sea of Unrest, 1982; Deadbeat, 1984; Son, 1992; with American Music Club: Mercury, 1993, San Francisco, 1994; with Li'l Tiger: Live, Work, Know, Growl, 1998. *Leisure interest:* Restoring and driving 'muscle cars' of the 1960s. *Current Management:* Bennett Management, 549 14th Ave, San Francisco, CA 94118, USA.

MOORE Abra; b. 8 June, Mission Bay, CA, USA. Singer; Songwriter; Musician (Guitar). *Education:* University of Hawaii. *Career:* Founding Member, Poi Dog Pondering, Solo Artist, toured with Matthew Sweet, Barenaked Ladies; Medeski, Martin and Wood, Third Eye Blind, Collective Soul, Lilith Fair and Big Head Todd and the Monsters; Appeared in feature films, Slacker and The Newton Boys; Sliding Doors, 1998; TV appearances on VH-1, E!, VH-1 (UK), CNN Showbiz Today; Live with Regis and Kathylee, Fox Live; Appearances on MTI and Westwood One Syndicated Radio. *Recordings:* Solo albums: Sing, 1995; Strangest Places, 1997; Singles: Four Leaf Clover, 1997; Don't Feel Like Cryin, 1997. *Contributions to:* national and international music magazines, newspapers and journals. *Membership:* AFTRA. *Current Management:* Tim Neece Management, 13101 Hwy 71 W, Austin, TX 78736, USA. *Address:* 13101 Hwy 71 W, Austin, TX 78736, USA.

MOORE Angelo (Christopher); b. 5 Nov. 1965, USA. Vocalist. *Career:* Member, Fishbone; Colloborations with rap artistes such as the Jungle Brothers; Numerous live appearances, including Lollapalooza in 1993. *Recordings:* Singles: Sunless Saturday, 1991; Everyday Sunshine, 1991; It's A Wonderful Life (Gonna Have A Good Time); Bonin' in the Boneyard EP; Albums: Fishbone, 1985; In Your Face, 1986; Truth and Soul, 1988; The Reality of our Surroundings, 1991; Give a Monkey a Brain and He'll..., 1993; Fishbone 101: Nuttasurusmeg, 1996; Chim Chim's Badass Revenge, 1996.

MOORE Bob Loyce; b. 30 Nov. 1932, Nashville, Tennessee, USA. Musician (bass); Record Prod. *Career:* Bassist for various artists including: Little Jimmy Dickens, 1949; Red Foley, 1950; Owen Bradley, 1951–66; Elvis Presley, 1963–71; Crystal Gayle, 1982–84; Co-owner, Monument Records, 1961–70; Record producer for Jerry Lee Lewis; George Jones; Johnny Cash; Boxcar Willie; Roy Orbison; President, K & K Productions, 1986–; President, Bob Moore Music, 1963–; Prolific studio musician, over 17,000 recording sessions for artists including: Kenny Rogers; Tammy Wynette; Don McLean; Hank Williams Jr; Tom Jones; Willie Nelson; Dolly Parton; Patsy Cline; Jim Reeves; Frank Sinatra; Simon and Garfunkel; Johnny Cash; Roy Orbison; Conway Twitty; Loretta Lynn; Brenda Lee; Ernest Tubb; Andy Williams; Connie Francis; The Statler Brothers; Clyde McFatter; Marty Robbins; Eddy Arnold; Kitty Wells. *Honours:* NARAS, Most Valuable Player Awards, 1979–82; Most

Recording Session in History; AFofM; Numerous Superpicker Awards. *Memberships:* AFofM; NARAS.

MOORE Christy; b. 7 May 1945, Dublin, Ireland. Singer; Songwriter; Musician (guitar). *Career:* Solo folk performer, club circuit, Ireland and England, 1960s; Recording artiste, 1969–; Founder member, Planxty, 1969–75, 1979–80; Involved in Anti-Nuclear Roadshow, mid 1970s; Founder, Moving Hearts, 1981; Solo artiste, 1982–. *Recordings:* Albums: Paddy On The Road (with Dominc Behan), 1969; Prosperous, 1971; Whatever Tickles Your Fancy, 1975; Christy Moore, 1976; The Iron Behind The Velvet, 1978; Live In Dublin, 1978; The Spirit of Freedom, 1983; The Time Has Come, 1983; Ride On, 1984; Ordinary Man, 1985; Nice 'N' Easy, 1986; Unfinished Revolution, 1987; Voyage, 1989; Smoke and Strong Whiskey, 1991; The Christy Moore Collection, 1991; Live At The Point, 1994; Graffiti Tongue, 1996; with Planxty: After The Break, 1979; Woman I Loved So Well, 1980. *Current Management:* Mattie Fox Management, Derynell, Ballinlee, Co Longford, Ireland.

MOORE Gary; b. 4 April 1952, Belfast, Northern Ireland. Musician (guitar). *Career:* Formed Skid Row, 1968; Formed Gary Moore Band, 1973; Guitarist with Thin Lizzy, 1974, 1977–79; Member, Colisseum II, 1975, 1977; Formed G-Force, 1979; Solo career, 1982–; Worked with various artists including: Phil Lynott; Ozzy Osbourne; Albert Collins; Albert King; B B King. *Recordings:* Singles include: Parisienne Walkways; Over The Hills and Far Away; Cold Day In Hell; Albums: with Skid Row: Skid Row, 1970; 34 Hours, 1971; with Gary Moore Band: Grinding Stone, 1973; with Thin Lizzy: Night Life, 1974; Black Rose, 1978; with Colisseum II: Strange New Flesh, 1975; Electric Savage, 1975; Wardance, 1977; with G-Force: G-Force, 1980; Solo: Back On The Streets, 1978; Corridors of Power, 1982; Victims of The Future, 1984; We Want Moore!, 1984; Run For Cover, 1985; Rockin' Every Night, 1986; Wild Frontier, 1987; After The War, 1989; Still Got The Blues, 1990; After Hours, 1992; Blues For Greeny, 1995; Desperado, 1997; Dark Days in Paradise, 1997; A Different Beat, 1999; Contributor, Tribute To Muddy Waters, 1993. *Current Management:* Part Rock Management, 53 Kings Rd, Suite 318, London SW10 0SZ, England.

MOORE John Arlington; b. 5 Oct. 1938, Kingston, Jamaica. Musician (trumpet, piano); Entertainer. 3 s., 1 d. *Musical Education:* Alpha, Jamaica Military Band; Berklee School, Boston, USA. *Career:* Played with Alpha Boy's Band; J M Band; Mapltoff Poole Band; Thaskatalites; Super Sonics; First tour, with Soul Vendors, England, 1967; with Super Sonic, 1969; Currently travelling world with Solomic Reggerstra. *Compositions:* Schooling The Duke; Something Special; Tear Up; Ringo; Swing Easy; Rockfoot Rock; Sweet Sugar Candy; Somewhere In time; Where's The Love. *Recordings:* Album: Something Special; Single: Kibir La Dims. *Memberships:* Jamaican Federation of Musicians; PRS. *Leisure interests:* Reading; Dancing; Swimming; Conversing. *Current Management:* Solomic Productions. *Address:* 173 Windward Rd Kingston 2, Jamaica.

MOORE LeRoi; b. 7 Sept. 1961, Durham, North Carolina, USA, Musician (saxophone). *Musical Education:* Classically trained; Studied tenor saxophone at James Madison University. *Career:* Member of high school bands; Spent ten years gigging in Charlottesville and Richmond, Virginia, with local jazz man John D'Earth prior to joining Dave Matthews Band, 1991; Rapid growth of fanbase through touring schedules; First album released on group's own Bama Rags label certified gold by RIAA; First national US tour in support of RCA debut album, 1994; Many world-wide concerts and festival appearances since including 2001 album tour; Group permits fans to tape-record shows for personal use; I Did It single officially released through Napster, 2001. *Recordings:* Albums: Remember Two Things (live), 1993; Under The Table and Dreaming, 1994; Crash, 1996; Live At Red Rocks 8–15–95, 1997; Before These Crowded Streets, 1998; Listener Supported (live), 1999; Everyday, Live In Chicago 12–19–98, 2001; Singles: Recently (EP), 1994; What Would You Say, Jimi Thing, Ants Marching, 1995; So Much To Say, Too Much, 1996; Don't Drink The Water, 1997; Satellite, Crash Into Me, Crush, 1998; I Did It, The Space Between, Everyday, 2001. *Honours:* Grammy Awards: Best Rock Performance By A Duo Or Group With Vocal, 1997; US VH-1 Awards: Favourite Group; Must Have Album; Song of The Year, 2001; Top-grossing touring band in USA, 2000. *Address:* c/o Red Light Communications, 3305 Lobban Pl., Charlottesville, VA 22903, USA. *E-mail:* info@rlc.net. *Internet:* www.dmband.com.

MOORE Malcolm Charles; b. 19 Jan. 1971, Chelmsford, Essex, England. Musician (bass guitar, double bassist); Singer; Songwriter. *Musical Education:* City University, London; Guildhall School of Music. *Career:* Session bass player with Steve Martland, seen on C4; BBC Symphony Orchestra; London Sinfonietta; London Philharmonic Orchestra; Tommy Chase Band; Tindersticks; Swordfish (Regular Radio 3 and Jazz FM); New rock/pop band, Felson; Elvis Costello; Spiritualized; Barry Adamson. *Recordings:* with Steve Martland: Crossing The Border; Patrol; with Tindersticks: This Way Up; Horses of Instruction; with Swordfish: Living A Life; Frank and Walters, The Russian Ship; Lost Highway Soundtrack,

Barry Adamson and David Lynch. *Membership:* Musicians' Union. *Leisure interests:* Sport (football, swimming); Comedy. *Current Management:* None. *Address:* 116 Skitts Hill, Braintree, Essex CM7 1AS, England.

MOORE Mark; b. 1965 London, England. Prod.; Remixer; DJ. *Career:* Began career as DJ at Phillip Sallon's Mud Club; Formed S-Express with Pascal Gabriel, 1988; Founder: Splish Records; Resident DJ at Chuff Chuff parties; Collaborations: William Orbit; Billie Ray Martin; Sonique; Remixed: Seal; Prince; Randy Crawford. *Recordings:* Albums: Original Soundtrack, 1990; Intercourse, 1991; Singles: Theme From S-Express, Superfly Guy, 1988; Hey Music Lover, Mantra For A State of Mind, 1989; Nothing To Lose, 1990; Find 'Em Fool 'Em Forget 'Em, 1992. *Current Management:* Ultra DJ Management, 29 City Business Centre, Lower Rd, London, SE16 2XB, England.

MOORE Nicky; b. 21 June 1952, Devon, England. Blues Singer; Musician (guitar, piano, harmonica). m. Maggie Moore, 5 Oct. 1974, 4 s., 1 d. *Musical Education:* Exeter Cathedral/RSCM. *Career:* Rock bands: Hackensack; Tiger; Samson; Mammoth; Gerry Rafferty; Blues Corporation (current and future); Films: Hearts of Fire; Just Ask For Diamond; Numerous tours, television and radio appearances. *Recordings:* Tiger: Up The Hard Way; Going Down Laughing; Test of Time; Before The Storm; Mammoth: Don't Get Mad Get Even; I Just Got Back; Holding On; Numerous singles and videos. *Membership:* Musicians' Union. *Leisure interest:* Music. *Current Management:* Julia Ficken, Steppin' Out Ltd. *Address:* PO Box 216, Sevenoaks, Kent TN14 6ZQ, England.

MOORE Sam; b. 12 Oct. 1935, Miami, Florida, USA. Singer; Entertainer. m. Joyce McRae, 26 March 1982. *Career:* Singer with Soul duo Sam and Dave; later solo artist; Television appearances include: (Solo) Best of Country; TNN Country News; Entertainment Tonight; Rhythm Country and Blues; Huey Lewis PBS Special; Roots of Country; In Concert Country; Music City Tonight; Good Morning America; Music City Today; Nashville Now; (as Sam and Dave) Ed Sullivan Show; Merv Griffin; Tonight Show; Hollywood Palace; Saturday Night Live; Midnight Special; Bandstand; Mike Douglas Show; Special appearances include: Host, The Pioneer Awards; The George Bush Rhythm and Blues Inaugural Gala; Rhythm Country and Blues, The Concert; Host, Miami Hard Rock Cafe Opening; Videos: Rainy Night In Georgia; Soul Man; Ordinary Man; Hey Joe; Films: One Trick Pony; Tapeheads; Tales of The City; Soul Man; Command performances for Queen Elizabeth II, England, and US President Jimmy Carter. *Recordings:* Hit singles include: Soul Man; Hold On I'm Coming; Soul Sister Brown Sugar; Rainy Night In Georgia, duet with Conway Twitty; I Thank You; Something Is Wrong With My Baby; Soothe Me; You Don't Know Like I Know; You Got Me Humming; Soundtracks: White Men Can't Jump; Soul Man; Tapeheads; Guest appearances on: Building The Perfect Beast, Don Henley; Human Touch, Bruce Springsteen; Soul Man, 1986; Great Outdoors, 1988; Conway Twitty Collection, 1994; Concert for the Rock and Roll Hall of Fame, 1996; Country Heartaches, 1997. *Honours:* Numerous Platinum and Gold records; Grammy, Soul Man, 1967; Rhythm and Blues Foundation Pioneer Award, 1991; Rock and Roll Hall of Fame Inductee, 1992; CMA Award Nominee (2 categories), 1994; Two Country Music Asscn Nominations, 1994; TNN Music City News Nominee, 1995. *Memberships:* NARAS. *Leisure interests:* Reading; Dogs; Pool; Snooker. *Current Management:* I'ma Da Wife Enterprises, Inc. *Address:* 7119 E Shea Blvd, Suite 109–436, Scottsdale, AZ 85254, USA.

MOORE Sean; b. 30 July 1970, Pontypool, Gwent, Wales. Musician (Drums). *Career:* Member, Manic Street Preachers. *Recordings:* Singles: New Art Riot EP, 1990; You Love Us, 1991; Motorcycle Emptiness, 1992; Theme From M.A.S.H., 1992; La Tristessa Durera, 1993; She Is Suffering, 1994; Everything Must Go, 1996; A Design for Life, 1996; If You Tolerate This Your Children Will Be Next, 1998; The Everlasting, 1998; You Stole The Sun From My Heart, 1999; Tsunami, 1999; Albums: Generation Terrorists, 1992; Gold Against The Soul, 1993; The Holy Bible, 1994; Everything Must Go, 1996; This Is My Truth, Tell My Yours, 1998.

MOORE Thurston; b. USA. Vocalist; Musician (guitar). m. Kim Gordon, 1 d. *Career:* Founder member, US rock group Sonic Youth, 1981–; Also spin-off project Ciccone Youth; Solo recording artiste, 1995–; Recent concerts include: Lollapalooza Tour (co-headliners with Hole), 1995. *Recordings:* Albums: Sonic Youth, 1982; Confusion Is Sex, 1983; Kill Yer Idols, 1983; Sonic Death, 1984; Bad Moon Rising, 1985; Evol, 1986; Sister, 1987; Daydream Nation, 1988; Ciccone Youth, 1989; Goo, 1990; Dirty, 1992; Experimental Jet Set, Trash and No Star, 1994; Washing Machine, 1995; Just Leave Me, 1996; Piece for Jetsun Dolma, 1996; Root, 1999; Promise, 1999; Singles include: Not Me, 1998; Solo album: Psychic Hearts, 1995. *Address:* c/o Gold Mountain Entertainment, Suite 450, 3575 Cahuenga Blvd W, Los Angeles, CA 90068, USA.

MOORE Tim; b. 22 May 1958, Sussex, England. Musician (keyboard player); Composer; Prod. m. Venetia, 3 Jan. 1987, 2 s. *Musical Education:* Piano since age 5, taught by father. *Career:* with Nik Kershaw: tours, television, videos; concerts include Live Aid, 1985, 1984–86; with Bee Gees:

tours, recording, television includes Royal Variety Show, 1990–93; Tours with: Johnny Hallyday, 1994–95; Saga, 1988; East 17, 1995; Television appearances with Bros; Shakespears Sister. *Recordings:* Keyboards on albums with Nik Kershaw: The Riddle, 1984; Radio Musicola, 1988; Anthology, 1995; Keyboards/programming on albums with Bee Gees: High Civilization, 1991; Size Isn't Everything, 1993; Amy Fradon, Take Me Home, 1994. *Membership:* Musicians' Union. *Leisure interests:* Pub gigs; Driving; Walking; Working out; Recording at home. *Current Management:* Debbie Haxton. *Address:* The Session Connection, 110–112 Disraeli Rd, Putney, London SW15, England.

MOORE Vinnie; Rock Musician (guitar). *Musical Education:* Jazz guitar. *Career:* Member, Vicious Rumours, 1985; Solo artiste, 1986–; Guitarist, Alice Cooper, Hey Stoopid tour, 1991. *Recordings:* Albums with Vicious Rumours: Soldiers of The Night, 1985; Solo albums: Mind's Eye, 1986; Time Odyssey, 1988; Meltdown, 1991; Out of Nowhere, 1996; Maze, 1999; Live!, 2000. *Current Management:* Frank Solomon Management, PO Box 639, Natick, MA 01760, USA.

MORALES David, (The Boss, Brooklyn Friends); b. 21 Aug. 1961, Brooklyn, New York, USA. Prod.; Remixer; DJ. *Career:* Began DJ career at the Ozone Layer in New York and was guest at the legendary Paradise Garage club; Later resident at Better Days and Red Zone in New York; Member of the Def Mix production crew (alongside Frankie Knuckles and Satoshi Tomiie); In demand remixer since early '90s; Remixed: Mariah Carey, Jody Watley, U2, Jamiroquai, Luther Vandross, Incognito, Pet Shop Boys; Collaborations: Albert Cabrera, Juliet Roberts. *Recordings:* Singles: Congo (as The Boss), 1994; Philadelphia (as Brooklyn Friends), 1995; Needin' U, 1998; Needin' U II, 2001. *Current Management:* c/o Def Mix, 928 Broadway, Suite 400, New York, USA.

MORAN Michael John; b. 18 July 1964, Birkenhead, England. Composer; Prod.; Musician (electric guitar, keyboards); Programmer. *Musical Education:* Diploma, Light Music, Sandown College, Liverpool; BA (Hons) Popular Music and Recording, University College, Salford. *Career:* Member, 16 Tambourines; Toured with: Squeeze; Hue and Cry; Wet Wet Wet; Tour Manager, 35 Summers tour with EMF; Manager, N-Trust (as Decent Exposure Management); Musical Director, Jungle Book, Redgrave Theatre, Farnham; Sgt Pepper's Magical Mystery Trip, Liverpool Playhouse. *Compositions:* Co-writer: It's Better To Love; Movies; Language of Love. *Recordings:* Album: How Green Is Your Valley, 16 Tambourines; As producer: Quiet Defiance, N-Trust; Singles: with 16 Tambourines: If I Should Stay; How Green Is Your Valley. *Memberships:* PRS; Musicians' Union; MMIA, committee member; MCPS. *Leisure interests:* Dinghy sailing; Walking; Cinema; Theatre. *Current Management:* Triple M Productions. *Address:* 93 Barrington Rd, Wavertree, Liverpool L15 3HR, England.

MORAN Mike; b. 4 March 1948, Leeds, Yorkshire, England. Composer; Musician (piano, clarinet). m. Lynda, 5 Sept. 1992, 1 d. *Musical Education:* Royal College of Music. *Career:* Musician, arranger, record producer; As musician, arranger, worked with stars including: Paul McCartney; Stevie Wonder; Kate Bush; Paul Simon; Joe Cocker; George Harrison; Gladys Knight; Robert Plant; Cliff Richard; Carly Simon; Julio Iglesias; The Four Tops; Placido Domingo; Jose Carreras; Elvin Jones; Oliver Nelson; Leo Sayer; Lulu; Dusty Springfield; Member of bands: Blue Mink; Stone The Crows; Gillan; Worked with Freddie Mercury; Took part in Wembley tribute to Freddie Mercury, 1994; Musical directorship of Rockin Robin and The Babes From Halewood, rock 'n' roll pantomime, Everyman Theatre, 1997–98. *Compositions include:* Film music: Time Bandits; The Missionary; Water; Bloodbath At The House of Death; Whoops Apocalypse; The Bitch; Top Secret; Deathwish 3; Television music includes: Taggart, STV; Harry's Game, YTV; El CID, Granada; The Contract, YTV; Bookie, STV; Killer, STV; The Racing Game, YTV; The Krypton Factor, Granada; Love Story; The Kenny Everett Show, BBC; The Consultant, BBC; Print Out; Pop Quest, YTV; The Richard and Judy Show, Granada; Commercials include: TV Times; Kentucky Fried Chicken; Halifax Building Society; British Gas; Miss Selfridge; Co-writer, song on Innuendo album, Freddie Mercury; Collaborated on album Barcelona, with Freddie Mercury and Montserrat Caballe; More than 100 songs, recorded by: Freddie Mercury; Queen; George Harrison; Ian Gillan; Maggie Bell; Oliver Nelson; John Kongos; Extreme. *Honours:* Tric Best Music Award. *Memberships:* Musicians' Union; PRS. *Current Management:* Triple M Productions. *Address:* 93 Barrington Rd, Wavertree, Liverpool L15 3HR, England.

MORAND Roger; b. 30 Sept. 1958, Nogent sur Marne, France. Musician. 1 s., 1 d. *Education:* Music School, 6 years old; Classical Accordion; Professional 16 years old. *Career:* Television, MTV, Monte Carlo, FR3, A2, TF1, Arte, M6; Radio, BBC, Radio France, France Culture; Stage, Crawfish Festival, Ugly Day, Cajun Day, Feria de Nimes Jazzavienne, Festival Country, Mirande Nuit Cajun, Playing with Nathan Abshire, John Delafose, Dewey Balfa, Denis Mcgee, Marc Savoy, Corey Harris; Leader, Morand Cajun Band; Also plays Irish and Celtic accordion and music from the centre of France (Auvergne). *Recordings:* When I'm Up, 1993; Les Blues a Bébè, 1994, Nuit Cajun, 1995, Hey Ariba, 1997. *Contributions to:* musical journals and magazines. *Honour:* European Cup, Accordion. *Membership:* SACEM. *Leisure interest:* All About Louisiana. *Address:* 3 Pl. du Doyen Gachon, 30610 Sauve, France.

MORELLO Tom; b. 1964, New York, New York, USA. Musician (Guitar). *Career:* Member, Rage Against the Machine; Member of early band Lock Up; Obtained major label deal; Support causes such as Fairness and Accuracy in Reporting, Rock for Choice and Refuse and Resist; Numerous tours including Lollapalooza; Tour with Wu Tang Clan; Collaboration with The Prodigy for soundtrack to film Spawn, 1997, and band contribution to soundtrack for Godzilla, 1998. *Recordings:* Singles: Freedom, 1994; Bombtrack Plus Live, 1994; People of the Sun EP, 1997; Albums: Rage Against the Machine, 1992; Evil Empire, 1996.

MORENO Rita, (Rosa Dolores Alverio); b. Humacao, Puerto Rico. Actress; Singer; Entertainer. m. Leonard Gordon, 1 d. *Career:* Film, stage, television, concert performer, Films include: The King and I; West Side Story, 1962; Television: Starred in own TV series, sitcom version of 9 To 5; B L Stryker, 1989–90; The Top of The Heap, Fox Network series, 1991–92; Cosby Mystery Series, 1994; Performs concerts across USA with symphony orchestras for their Pops series; Performed at President Clinton's Inauguration, 1993; White House, 1993. *Recordings include:* Rita Moreno Sings; Warm, Wonderful and Wild; Shadow of a Bull; The Electric Company Album, 1972. *Honours:* Academy Award, West Side Story, 1962; The Golden Globe Award, Golden Apple, John Jefferson Award, Best Actress, Chicago's Theatrical Season, 1968; Grammy, The Electric Company Album, 1972; Tony, The Ritz (Broadway production), 1975; Emmys, The Muppet Show, 1977; Sarah Siddons Award, 1985; Star, Hollywood Walk of Fame, 1995. *Membership:* Presidents Committee on the Arts and Humanities. *Current Management:* c/o Stan Scotland, JKE Services, 404 Park Ave S, 10th Floor, New York, NY 10016, USA.

MORETTI Fabrizio; b. 2 June 1980, Rio De Janeiro, Brazil. Musician (drums). *Education:* Dwight School, Manhattan. *Career:* Member: The Strokes, 1998-. *Recordings:* Albums: Is This It, 2001; Singles: The Modern Age, Hard To Explain/New York City Cops, Last Nite/When It Started, 2001. *Honours:* Brit Award, Best International Newcomer, 2002; NME Awards: Band of The Year; Best New Act; Album of The Year, 2001. *Current Management:* Ryan Gentles, Wiz Kid Management. *Internet:* www.thestrokes.com.

MORGAN Charlie; b. 9 Aug. 1955, Hammersmith, London, England. Musician (drums, electronic percussion). m. Daniela Francesca James, 6 Oct. 1992, 1 d. *Education:* College de Genève. *Musical Education:* Piano lessons; Classes with James Blades. *Career:* Mostly freelance, 1973–84; Toured, recorded with Tom Robinson Band, 1979; 2 albums, tours with Judi Tzuke, 1980–81; Numerous recordings for Nick Kershaw, Tracey Ullman, Kate Bush; 14 month world tour, as drummer with Elton John, 1992–93; Tour with Elton John, Billy Joel, USA, 1994–95; Currently, Elton John World Tour, May 1995-. *Compositions:* Co-wrote television theme The Bill, ITV. *Recordings:* Edge of Heaven, Wham; 2 albums with Tracey Ullman; I Am The Phoenix, Judy Tzuke; Thunderdrome (Mad Max 2), Tina Turner; Iron Man, Pete Townshend; Oasis, Oasis; Out In The Fields, Gary Moore and Phil Lynott; Who's Side Are You On?, Matt Bianco; Rock and Roll Album, Johnny Logan; Human Racing, Nik Kerhsaw; Kane Gang album; Being There, Martyn Joseph; with Elton John: Live In Sydney (with the MSO); Made In England; Silver Bird, Justin Hayward; Go West, Go West; with Chris De Burgh: Spark To A Flame; This Way Up; Magic Ring, Clannad; Golden Days, Bucks Fizz; Theodore and Friends, The Adventures; Lionheart, Kate Bush; Cabaret (Live), Tom Robinson; Linda Thompson album, 1985; Nick Heyward album, 1985; Beverley Craven album tracks, 1991; Tasmin Archer album, 1992; The Glory of Gershwin, 1994. *Memberships:* PRS; BASCA; Musicians' Union. *Leisure interest:* Motor racing, competed in British Saloons, 1984–86.

MORGAN Dennis William; b. 30 July 1952, Tracy, Minnesota, USA. Songwriter; Music Publisher. m. June Arnold, 27 July 1985. *Career:* Songwriter, Collins Music, 1969–73; Little Shop of Morgansongs, 1974-. *Compositions include:* Smoky Mountain Rain, Ronnie Milsap; I Wouldn't Have Missed It For The World, Ronnie Milsap; I Was Country When Country Wasn't Cool, Barbara Mandrell; I Knew You Were Waiting For Me, George Michael and Aretha Franklin; My Heart Can't Tell You Know, Rod Stewart; Jonny Lang, Lie to Me; Hank Thompson, Real Thing. *Honours:* 3 Grammy Nominations; Ivor Novello Award; 3 CMA Award Nominations; 43 BMI Awards. *Memberships:* CMA; Nashville Songwriters Asscn.

MORGAN Edward Lee (Ed); b. 28 April 1941, Noel, Missouri, USA. Pres., Country Breeze Productions. m. Delores Arneta Shoemake, 1 s., 1 d. *Musical Education:* Self-taught songwriter. *Career:* Many No. 1 songs on independent charts in America; Songs published by other publishing companies. *Compositions include:* Shatter Me, recorded by several artists, played world-wide, 1987. *Publications:* Publishes monthly magazine:

Midwest Newsbeat, for songwriters and artists. *Honours:* Golden Cross, for gospel label: Angel Star Records. *Memberships:* BMI; Midwest Assn of Music. *Leisure interests:* Camping; Hunting; Fishing. *Address:* 1715 Marty, Kansas City, KS 66103, USA.

MORGAN Huey (Hugh Angel Diaz); b. 8 Aug. 1968, USA. Vocalist; Lyricist; Musician (guitar). *Career:* Formed Fun Lovin' Criminals, 1993; Numerous TV appearances and live dates. *Recordings:* Singles: Scooby Snacks, 1996; The Grave and the Constant, 1996; The Fun Lovin' Criminal, 1996; King of New York, 1997; Sing the Fun Lovin' Criminal, 1997; I'm Not in Love, 1997; Love Unlimited, 1998; Big Night Out, 1998; Korean Bodega, 1999; Loco, 2001; Albums: Come Find Yourself, 1996; 100% Colombian, 1999; Mimosa – The Lounge Album, 1999; Loco, 2001.

MORGAN Jeffrey; b. 20 March 1954, Spokane, Washington, USA. Musician. *Education:* Liberal Arts, Music, Dance, Theatre, Philosophy of Aesthetics; Studied under Don Cherry, Karl Berger, Dumi Maraiere, Bert Wilson, Robert Gottlieb, Greg Steinke. *Career:* Concerts and Festivals in Europe and USA; Experimental Theatre; Workshops for Sound and Installations. *Compositions:* Quasar-Mach, 1983; Snake Eyes, 1994; Near Vhana, 1997; Bitin Thru, 1997. *Recordings:* Quasar-Mach, LP, 1983; Pokachevski Vol. I, 1990; Snake Eyes, CD, 1994; Near Vhana, CD, 1997; Bitin Thru, CD, 1997; Dial: Log-Rhythms, CD with Keith Rowe, 1998; Ensemble Works 81/95, 1999; Electroshock, 1999; Quartz and Crow Feather, 2000. *Honour:* British Arts Council Performing Arts Grant, 1992. *Membership:* GEMA. *Address:* Lübecker Str 15, 50668 Cologne, Germany.

MORGAN John Marshall; b. 3 May 1958, Clinton, Iowa, USA. Bandleader; Musician (saxophone); Composer; Teacher. m. Nancy Eichman, 15 March 1986, 2 s. *Education:* 3 Collegiate degrees, Masters. *Musical Education:* Drake University, Des Moines, Iowa, USA. *Career:* Sideman/arranger, The Russ Morgan Orchestra, The Don Hoy Orchestra; Leader, The John Morgan Band, 1984–; Saxophone guest artist with Drake Symphony Orchestra, Des Moines Municipal Band; Educator in Drake University Community School, 1986–; Des Moines School District, 1990-. *Publications:* The Instrumentalist Magazine. *Honours:* Drake Soloist Artist, 1981, 1987, WO1 Radio; Phi Kappa Lamda; Omicron Delta Kappa; Phi Mu Alpha. *Memberships:* Macusa (National Asscn of Composers). *Leisure interests:* Cartooning; Collecting 16mm films (especially Laurel and Hardy).

MORGAN Loretta Lynn; b. 27 June 1959, Nashville, Tennessee, USA. Country Singer. 1 s., 1 d. *Career:* Two years touring with George Jones; Worked at Opryland, USA aged 18; Acting debut, Proudheart, Nashville Network film; Film, The Enemy Within, ABC-TV; Television includes: Co-host, American Music Awards, 1995; CBS AM; The Ralph Emery Show; Entertainment Tonight; Late Night With David Letterman; 48 Hours; The Tonight Show; CBS 65 Years of The Grand Ole Opry; Austin City Limits; Hee Haw. *Recordings:* Albums: Leave The Light On, 1989; Something In Red, 1991; Classics, 1991; Watch Me, 1992; Trainwreck of Emotion, 1993; Merry Christmas From London, 1993; War Paint, 1994; Greatest Hits, 1995; Greater Need, 1996; Shakin' Things Up, 1997; Secret Love, 1998; Super Hits, 1998; The Essential, 1998; My Heart, 1999; Singles: We Both Walk, 1991; Back in Your Arms Again, 1995; I Didn't Know My Own Strength, 1995; Up on Santa Claus Mountain, 1995; By My Side, 1996; I Just Might Be, 1996; Go Away, 1997; I'm Not That Easy to Forget, 1998. *Honours include:* CMA Awards, Vocal Event of The Year, with Keith Whitley, 1990; Album of The Year, Common Thread, 1994; TNN/Music City News Awards: Video Collaboration of The Year, with Keith Whitley, 1991; Female Artist of The Year, 1994; CMT: Female Vocalist of The Year, 1992; CMA Nominations, 1990, 1991, 1992; TNN Nominations, 1991, 1992; 1995; ACM Nominations, 1992, 1993. *Current Management:* Susan Nadler Management. *Address:* 1313 16th Ave S, Nashville, TN 37212, USA.

MORGAN Tudur; b. 18 May 1958, Bangor, Gwynedd, Wales. Musician (acoustic guitar, bass, keyboards); Vocalist; Prod. m. Annwen Morgan, 18 Oct. 1986, 2 d. *Education:* Carmarthen Trinity College. *Musical Education:* Self-taught. *Career:* Television and radio appearances: Major television shows in Wales; BBC Pebble Mill; BBC Radio 2; Concerts throughout UK including London Albert Hall; Orkney Islands; Edinburgh Folk Festival and with Ronnie Drew of the Dubliners in Cardiff; Played with many top Welsh performers including Dafydd Iwan; Linda Healy; Plethyn; 4 Yn Y Bar; Mojo and Moniars. *Recordings:* With numerous artists including: Branwen; Dafydd Iwan; Mojo; 4 Yn Y Bar; Linda Healy; Plethyn; Moniars and Dylan Parry; World Music album for Narada Media. *Memberships:* MCPS; PRS; Musicians' Union. *Leisure interests:* Music; CDs; Rock and Roll; Cars; Travel. *Current Management:* Sblash. *Address:* c/o Sblash, 17 Perth Y Paun, Llangefni, Ynys Mon, Gwynedd LL77 7EX, Wales.

MORGAN Wayne; b. 15 Jan. 1970, Warrington, Cheshire, England. Musician (bass guitar). *Musical Education:* 2 year foundation course. *Career:* Played in: Pele, 1993–; Supports include: Wet Wet Wet; Iggy Pop;

Worked with major producers; Played bass, China Crisis tour. *Recordings:* 2 Pele albums, produced by Jon Heedy, Simon Vinestock; Various sessions include work for Gary Langan. *Membership:* Musicians' Union. *Leisure interests:* Running; Football. *Current Management:* D L Management. *Address:* No. 3 Firshaw Rd, Meals, Wirral L47 5BD, England.

MORILLO Erick 'More'; b. 26 March 1971, New York City, New York, USA. Prod.; Remixer; DJ. *Musical Education:* Center for Media Arts, Degree. *Career:* After a course in Technical Production and Engineering, released first single with reggae artist The General, 1992; Recorded for Strictly Rhythm label Reel 2 Real featuring The Mad Stuntman (Mark Quashie); Set up Subliminal Records, 1997; TV appearances include: MTV Europe's Most Wanted; Top of The Pops; The Big Breakfast; Numerous concerts and arena shows; Collaborations: Harry 'Choo Choo' Romero; Jose Nunez; Jocelyn Brown; Zig and Zag; Louie Vega; Remixed: Pete Heller; Madison Avenue; Whitney Houston. *Recordings:* Albums: Are You Ready For Some More (with Reel 2 Real), 1996; Singles: with Reel 2 Real: The New Anthem, 1993; I Like To Move It, Go On Move, Can You Feel It, Raise Your Hands, 1994; Conway, 1995; Jazz It Up, Are You Ready For Some More, 1996; Come and Take A Trip (as Smooth Touch), 1994; Reach (with Lil' Mo Yin Yang), 1995; Fun (with Da Mob), 1998; Distortion (with Pianoheadz), 1998; Believe (with Ministers De La Funk), 1999. *Honours:* International Producer of the Year, Canada, 1994; Muzik Awards: Best Remixer (with Jose Nunez and Harry Romero), 1999; Best Ibiza Club, Subliminal Sessions at Pacha, 2001. *Leisure interest:* DJ. *Current Management:* c/o Subliminal Records, 199 Hackensack Plank Rd, Weehawken, New Jersey, USA. *Address:* Positiva Records, 43 Brook St, London, W6 7EF, England. *Internet:* www.positivarecords.com.

MORISSETTE Alanis; b. 1974, Ottawa, Canada. Singer. *Career:* Solo recording artiste; Appeared on Canadian cable TV, aged 10; Concerts include: Twix Mix Jamboree, with David Bowie, Birmingham NEC, 1995; 16m. albums sold. *Recordings:* Albums: Alanis, 1991; Now Is The Time, 1992; Jagged Little Pill, 1995; Space Cakes (live), 1998; Supposed Former Infatuation Junkie, 1998; Alanis Unplugged (live), 1999; Singles: Fate Stay With Me; You Oughta Know, 1995; One Hand In My Pocket, 1995; Ironic, 1996. *Honour:* BRIT Award, Best International Newcomer, 1996. *Current Management:* Third Rail Entertainment, 9169 Sunset Blvd, Los Angeles, CA 90069, USA.

MORRICONE Ennio; b. 11 Oct. 1928, Rome, Italy. Composer. *Musical Education:* Studied trumpet and composition. *Career:* Composer for radio, television, stage and concerts; Scores for 'spaghetti' westerns. *Compositions:* Scores and arrangements for vocalist Gianni Morandi, 1950s; Arrangement, Ogni Volta, Paul Anka, 1964; Film scores include: Il Federale, 1961; A Fistful of Dollars (under pseudonym Dan Savio), 1964; Battle of Algiers, 1966; Big Birds, Little Birds, 1966; 1900, 1976; Exorcist II, 1977; Days of Heaven, 1978; The Mission, 1986; The Untouchables, 1987; Frantic, 1988; Wolf, 1994; Disclosure, 1995. *Recordings:* Albums: Moses, 1977; Film Hits, 1981; Chi Mai, 1981; The Mission, 1986; Film Music 1966–87, 1988; Chamber Music, 1988; Frantic, 1988; The Endless Game, 1989; Live In Concert, 1989; Casualties of War, 1990; The Very Best Of, 1992; Once Upon a Time in America, 1995; Queimada, 1996; Gothic Dramas 1996; Hawks and Sparrows, 1996; Secret of the Sahara, 1996; More than a Miracle, 1997; Desert of the Tartars, 1998; Corta Notte Dell Bambole Di vetro, 1998; Once Upon a Time in the West, 1999; Piume de Cristallo, 1999; Vite Strozzate, 1999; Stendhal Syndrome, 1999; Fourth King, 1999.

MORRIS Johnny; b. 30 Oct. 1935, New York, New York, USA. Musician (Piano, Vocals); Orchestral Leader. m. (1) 2 s., 1 d., (2) Jean Farrell, 3 step-s. *Education:* BS, Music Education, Piano Major, State University of New York, 1958. *Career:* Pianist, Vocalist, Orchestral Leader; Performed with Jazz greats including Buddy Rich, Ruby Braff, Scott Hamilton, Roy Eldridge; Appearances with Jimmy Ryan's All Star Dixieland Band and at Kool Jazz Festival; TV appearances on the Today Show, GI Jive, From Jumpstreet. *Recordings include:* 3 albums with Buddy Rich; Alone Together (solo cassette); East Meets West (CD, Johnny Morris Quartet). *Address:* 321 Oenoke Ridge Rd, New Canaan, CT 06840, USA.

MORRIS Lynn; b. 8 Oct. 1948, San Antonio, Texas, USA. Musician (banjo, guitar); Singer. m. Marshall Wilborn, 14 Oct. 1989. *Education:* BA, Art, Colorado College, Colorado Springs, USA. *Musical Education:* Studied classical and jazz guitar through school. *Career:* Began professionally in music, 1972; Performed in Europe; Asia; Canada; USA; Began Lynn Morris Band, 1988; Television appearances: Fire On The Mountain; Reno's Old Time Music Festival; Radio: WWVA on Wheeling Jamboree; WSM Grand Ole Opry, Nashville, Tennessee. *Recordings:* The Lynn Morris Band; The Bramble and The Rose; Mama's Hand; You'll Never Be the Sun. *Honours:* Twice, Female Vocalist (Traditional Category), Society for Preservation of Bluegrass Music in America; Twice, National Banjo Champion at Winfield, Kansas. *Memberships:* IBMA Board of Directors, 6 years; International Bluegrass Music Asscn; Folk Alliance; Society For The Preservation of Bluegrass Music in America. *Leisure interests:* Animal welfare; Wildlife

preservation; Raise cats; Listen to music. *Current Management:* Mike Drudge, Class Act Entertainment, PO Box 771, Gallatin, TN 37066, USA.

MORRIS Sarah Jane; b. 21 March 1959, Southampton, Hampshire, England. Singer; Songwriter; Actress. m. David J Coulter, 15 Aug. 1992, 1 s. *Education:* Central School of Speech and Drama for acting training. *Career:* Lead singer, The Republic, 1980–84; The Happy End, 1984–87; The Communards, 1985–87; Solo career includes 3 albums; Appearances include: Royal Albert Hall; Royal Festival Hall; Wembley Arena; Verona Arena; Venice Opera House; Support act to Simply Red, New Flame tour, 1989; Lead actress in Thin Air, BBC1; Lead Actress in film Expecting, Channel 4. *Compositions include:* I Am A Woman; Title track for television series The Mens Room, BBC, 1991–92; Music for film Expecting, C4, 1995. *Recordings:* Don't Leave Me This Way, duet with Jimmy Somerville, (No. 1, UK), 1986; Albums include: Sarah Jane Morris, 1988; Heaven, 1992; Blue Valentine, 1995; Fallen Angel, 1999. *Honours:* Freedom of the City of Verona; Best Newcomer, Italy, 1989; Nomination, Best Supporting Actress, The Beggars Opera, 1991. *Memberships:* PRS; MCPS; Equity; Musicians' Union. *Leisure interests:* Walking; Reading; Raising son Otis; Songwriting. *Current Management:* Ross Fitzsimmons, Kaliedoscope Music, 23 W Smithfield, London EC1A 9HY, England.

MORRIS Stephen; b. 28 Oct. 1957, Macclesfield, Cheshire, England. Musician (drums). *Career:* Member, Joy Division, 1977–80; New Order, 1980–; The Other Two, with Gillian Gilbert, 1991–; Tours: UK; Europe; Australia; New Zealand; Far East; USA; South America; Concerts include: Glastonbury Fayre, 1981, 1987; Futurama Festival, Leeds, 1982; San Remo Festival, 1988; Reading Festival, 1989. *Compositions include:* with Gilbert: Numerous tracks for New Order; Television soundtracks: Making Out; Shooting Stars; Reportage. *Recordings:* Albums: with Joy Division: Unknown Pleasures, 1979; Closer, 1980; Still, 1981; The Peel Sessions, 1988; Also featured on Short Circuit – Live At The Electric Circus, 1978; with New Order: Movement, 1981; Power, Corruption and Lies, 1983; Low Life, 1985; Brotherhood, 1986; Technique, 1989; BBC Radio 1 Live In Concert, 1992; Republic, 1993; with The Other Two: The Other Two and You, 1994; Singles: with Joy Division: Transmission; Love Will Tear Us Apart; with New Order: Ceremony, 1981; Temptation, 1982; Confusion, 1983; Thieves Like Us, 1984; Shellshock, 1986; True Faith, 1987; Touched By The Hand of God, 1987; Fine Time, 1988; Round and Round, 1989; World In Motion, with England World Cup Football Squad, 1990; How Does It Feel?, 1992; Regret, 1993; World; Spooky; with The Other Two: Tasty Fish.

MORRISON James; b. 11 Nov. 1962, Borrowa, NSW, Australia. Musician (Jazz Trumpet). m. Judi Morrison, 3 s. *Education:* NSW Conservatorium of Music. *Career:* Lecturer, NSW Conservatorium of Music, 1981; Formed Big Band with John, 1983; World Tour With Big Band, 1989; World Tour With Ray Charles and B B King, 1990; Performed For President Bush, Parliament House Canberra, 1992; Concert At Royal Albert Hall, London, 1994; Concert At Royal Opera House, 1995; Performed For President Clinton, Parliament House Canberra, 1996. *Recordings:* Jazz Meets The Symphony. *Honours:* Australian OPerformer of The Year; Ricky May Performer of The Year Award.

MORRISON Lindy; b. 2 Nov. 1951, Sydney, Australia. Drummer. 1 d. *Education:* BA, Social Work, 1972. *Career:* Actor, Grin and Tonic Theatre and Popular Theatre Troupe, 1976–79; Drummer, Zero, 1979; Drummer, The Go-Betweens, 1980–90; Major tours of USA, Europe and Australia, 1992–98; Musical Director, Regional Music Performances Festivals, Parades, Concerts, Theatre Shows. *Recordings:* Send Me A Lullaby; Before Hollywood; Spring Hill Fair; Liberty Belle and The Black Diamond Express; Tallullah; 16 Lovers Lane; Egg; Cleopatra's Lament. *Memberships:* Artist Director of PPCA; Music Council of Australia Board. *Leisure interests:* Tennis; Swimming; Reading. *Address:* 291 Clovelly Rd, Clovelly 2031, Sydney, Australia.

MORRISON Mark; b. Leicester, England. Soul Singer. *Career:* Solo recording artiste, 1994–; Tours include: Support to R Kelly, US tour, 1995; British tour, 1996. *Recordings:* Singles: Crazy, 1995; Let's Get Down, 1995; Return of The Mack, 1995; Moan and Groan, 1998; Best Friend, 1999; Albums: Return of The Mack (No. 1, UK), 1996; Only God Can Judge Me, 1997. *Current Management:* JLM Management, Unit 8, 18 All Saints Rd, London W11 1HH, England.

MORRISON Van (George Ivan); b. 31 Aug. 1945, Belfast, Northern Ireland. Singer; Songwriter; Composer; Musician. 1 d. *Career:* Founder, lead singer, Them, 1964–67; Solo artiste, 1967–; Appearances include: Knebworth Festival, 1974; The Last Waltz, The Band's farewell concert, 1976; Played with Bob Dylan, Wembley Stadium, 1984; Self Aid, with U2, Dublin, 1986; Glastonbury Festival, 1987; Prince's Rock Trust Gala, 1989; Performance, The Wall by Roger Waters, Berlin, 1990; Concert in Dublin, with Bono, Bob Dylan, 1993; Phoenix Festival, 1995. *Recordings:* Singles include: Gloria; Brown-Eyed Girl; Moondance; Domino; Wild Night; Albums include: Blowin' Your Mind, 1967; Astral Weeks, 1968; Moondance, 1970;

His Band and Street Choir, 1973; Tupelo Honey, 1971; St Dominic's Preview, 1972; Hard Nose The Highway, 1973; It's Too Late To Stop Now, 1974; Tb Sheets, 1974; Veedon Fleece, 1974; This Is Where I Came In, 1977; A Period of Transition, 1977; Wavelength, 1978; Into The Music, 1983; Bang Masters, 1990; Common One, 1980; Beautiful Vision, 1982; Inarticulate Speech of The Heart, 1983; Live At The Opera House Belfast, 1984; A Sense of Wonder, 1984; No Guru, No Method, No Teacher, 1986; Poetic Champions Compose, 1987; Irish Heartbeat, 1988; Best Of..., 1990; Avalon Sunset, 1989; Enlightenment, 1990; Hymns To The Silence, 1991; Too Long In Exile, 1993; Best Of..., Vol. 2, 1993; Days Like This, 1995; Songs of the Mose Allison: Tell Me Something, 1996; The Healing Game, 1997; Back on Top, 1999; The Skiffle Sessions: Live in Belfast 1998; Also recorded on albums: with The Band: Cahoots, 1971; The Last Waltz, 1978; with John Lee Hooker: Folk Blues, 1963; Mr Lucky, 1991; with Bill Wyman: Stone Alone, 1976; with Jim Capaldi: Fierce Heart, 1983; with Georgie Fame: How Long Has This Been Going On, 1996. *Honours include:* Inducted into Rock and Roll Hall of Fame, 1993; BRIT Award, Outstanding Contribution to British Music, 1994; Q Award, Best Songwriter, 1995.

MORRISON Will; b. 2 Feb. 1968, Tile Hill, Coventry, England. Musician (drums, percussion); Programmer. *Education:* Coventry University. *Musical Education:* Coventry School of Music, Drumtech, London. *Career:* Tours with Don Mescall supporting: Mary Coghlan; Davey Spillane; David Thomas; Richie Havens; The Dubliners; Festivals with Don Mescall: Phoenix; Larmer Bee; Berlin Music; Radio 1 Roadshows with Faun; Live Radio Sessions on Greater London Radio with: Philip French; Sugartrain; Don Mescall; Television includes: The Happening and Pot of Gold with Sugartrain; The Big City with Lisa Lamb Quartet. *Recordings:* State of The Arts EP; She Don't Know, Faun (featuring John Entwistle, Gordon Giltrap); Album: Here Be Dragons, Gargling With Brains. *Publications:* Working on drum tuition book: Learning To Read and Write. *Membership:* Musicians' Union. *Leisure interests:* Fitness; Art; Carpentry; Sailing; Cycling. *Current Management:* Notes For Notes. *Address:* 12 The Old Orchard, Solomon Rd, Rainham, Kent ME8 8DT, England.

MORRISS Mark; b. 18 Oct. 1971, Hounslow, Middlesex, England. Vocalist. *Career:* Member, Bluetones; Started releasing records on own label; Signed major label deal; Numerous tours and many TV appearances. *Recordings:* Are You Blue or Are You Blind?, 1995; Bluetonic, 1995; Slight Return, 1996; Cut Some Rug, 1996; Marblehead Johnson, 1996; Solomon Bites the Worm, 1998; If..., 1998; Sleazy Bed Track, 1998; 4-Day Weekend, 1998; Albums: Expecting to Fly, 1996; Return to the Last Chance Saloon, 1998.

MORRISS Scott; b. 10 Oct. 1973, Hounslow, Middlesex, England. Musician (Bass). *Career:* Member, Bluetones; Early releases on own label; Obtained major label deal; Numerous tours and many TV appearances. *Recordings:* Singles: Are You Blue Or Are You Blind, 1995; Bluetonic, 1995; Slight Return, 1996; Cut Some Rug, 1996; Marblehead Johnson, 1996; Solomon Bites the Worm, 1998; Sleazy Bed Track, 1998; 4-Day Weekend, 1998; Albums: Expecting to Fly, 1996; Return to the Last Chance Saloon, 1998.

MORRISSEY (Stephen Morrissey); b. 22 May 1959, Daryhulme, Manchester, UK. Singer. *Career:* Formed The Smiths, 1982; Appearances include: John Peel Show, Radio 1, 1983; Support to Altered Images, 1983; Solo artiste, 1987-. *Compositions include:* Co-writer (with Johnny Marr), all Smiths hits; Carrying A Torch, recorded by Tom Jones, 1991. *Recordings:* Singles include: Hand In Glove; This Charming Man; What Difference Does It Make; Heaven Knows I'm Miserable Now; William, It Was Really Nothing; The Boy With The Thorn In His Side; Big Mouth Strikes Again; Panic; Shoplifters of The World Unite; Sheila Take A Bow; Solo singles include: Everyday is Like Sunday, 1988; Suedehead, 1988 Last of The International Playboys; Ouija Board; November Spawns A Monster; Picadilly Palare; We Hate It When Our Friends Become Successful; You're The One For Me Fatty; Hold On To Your Friends; The More You Ignore Me The Closer I Get; Sunny; Dagenham Dave; Boxers; Satan Rejected My Soul; Alma Matters; Albums: with the Smiths: The Smiths, 1984; Meat Is Murder, 1993; The Queen Is Dead, 1986; The World Won't Listen, 1987; Louder Than Bombs, 1987; Strangeways Here We Come, 1987; Rank, 1988; Best 1, Best II, 1992; Solo albums: Viva Hate, 1988; Bona Drag, 1990; Kill Uncle, 1991; Your Arsenal, 1992; Beethoven Was Deaf, 1993; Vauxhall and I, 1994; Southpaw Grammar, 1995; Maladjusted, 1997; My Early Burglary Years, 1998. *Honours include:* Q Award, Best Songwriter, 1994. *Current Management:* Stiefel Phillips Entertainment, 9720 Wilshire Blvd, Suite 400, Beverly Hills, CA 90212, USA.

MORRISSEY Dick (Richard Edwin); b. 9 May 1940, Horley, England. Musician (Tenor Saxophone). *Recordings:* Albums: Up, 1977; Cape Wrath, 1979; Badness, 1981; Life on the Wire, 1982; Its About Time, 1983; After Dark, 1983; There and Back (live), 1997; Appears on numerous albums including: Georgie Fame: Sound Venture, 1966, Two Faces of Fame, 1967; J J Jackson: Greatest Little Soul Band, 1969, J J Jackson's Dilemma, 1970;

Numerous albums by If; Peter Gabriel: Peter Gabriel 1, 1977; Alexis Korner: Just Easy, 1978; Duncan Browne: Streets of Fire, 1979; Georgie Fame: That's What Friends Are For, 1979; Colin Townley: Townley, 1980; Peter Gabriel: Ein Deutsches Album, 1980, Peter Gabriel 3, 1980; Jon Anderson: Song of Seven, 1980; Roy Harper: Work of Heart, 1981; Jon and Vangelis: Friends of Mr Cairo, 1981; Shakatak: Nightbirds, 1982; Gary Numan: Warriors, 1983; Paul McCartney: Give My Regards To Broad Street, 1984; Bill Nelson: On A Blue Wing, 1986; Gary Numan: Asylum, Vols 1, 2, 3, 1994; Jazz At Ronnie Scott's, 1998.

MORROW Ian; Prod., Writer, Programmer. *Career:* Worked with Wet Wet Wet; Production work with Icelandic artist, Suala. *Recordings:* Wet Wet Wet: Holding Back the River, album, programming; High on the Happy Side, album, programming; Picture This, album, programming; Nightcrawlers, Push the Feeling On, production; Seal, Crazy, programming. *Current Management:* SARM Management. *Address:* The Blue Building, 42/46 St Luke's Mews, London W11 1DG, England.

MORTENSEN Allan; b. 27 April 1946, Aarhus, Denmark. Singer; Composer; Actor. m. Titika, March 1967, divorced, 1 d. *Education:* Lithographer. *Musical Education:* Self-taught. *Career:* Singer, rock group Midnight Sun, 1971; Stage performances include lead parts in: Jesus Christ Superstar, 1972; Hair, 1972; Two Gentlemen of Verona, 1973; Godspell, 1979; Joseph and The Amazing Technicolour Dreamcoat, 1983; Odysseus, 1983; Tom Parker's Young Messiah, 1986–87; Singer, soul group 2nd Line, 1987–89. *Compositions:* Musicals: Thor, 1989; The Concert, 1991; The Three Musketeers, 1995. *Recordings:* Midnight Sun, 1971; Love Ambulance (as singer, composer), 1976; 2nd Line Live, 1988. *Honours:* The Amber Nightingale, Poland, 1987; Helexpo, Greece, 1991. *Membership:* Danish Artist Federation. *Leisure interests:* Music; Films. *Current Management:* Danish Artist Management.

MORTIMER Tony, (Anthony Michael Mortimer); b. 21 Oct. 1970, Stepney, London, England. Singer; Songwriter; Musician (Piano). 1 d. *Career:* Began as Dancer for group Faith, Hope and Charity; Produced demo tape; Formed East 17; Signed record deal, 1992; Numerous television and live appearances; Duet with singer Gabrielle; Left band, 1996; Joined Sub Zero. *Recordings:* Singles: House of Love, 1993; Deep, 1993; West End Girls, 1993; Steam, 1994; Stay Another Day, 1994; If You Ever, with Gabrielle, 1996; Albums: Walthamstow, 1993; Steam, 1995; Up All Night, 1996; Around the World: The Journey So Far, 1996.

MORTON Eddie; Vocalist; Musician (mandolin, accordion, guitar). *Career:* Member, Sub Zero, 1983; Formed The Trick, 1984; Extensive radio play, BBC1; Hits, Europe and Australia; Worked in production, songwriting with artists including: Phil Lynott; Slade; Ruby Turner; Rozalla; Steve Lillywhite; Roy Harper; Formed own band, 1988; Tours, Europe, UK, USA; Joined The Adventure Babies, 1991; Founder member, The New Bushbury Mountain Daredevils, 1992–; Backing vocals, Slade album; Numerous television and radio performances; Producer, songwriting with dance artists. *Recordings:* Albums: with Sub Zero: Out of The Blue; with The Trick: My World; Heart of Hearts; with Rozalla: Heartbreaker; Sunny; Spirit of Africa; Perfect Kiss; as Morton: Keeper of The Light; with Adventure Babies: Adventure Babies; Laugh; Barking Mad; with Mack and The Boys: The Unknown Legends; As Eddie Morton: The Infinite Room; Way of The World; Black and Blue; with The New Bushbury Mountain Daredevils: Bushwacked; The Yellow Album; Bushbury Mountain. *Current Management:* c/o Jim McPhee, Acorn Entertainments. *Address:* Winterfold House, 46 Woodfield Rd, Kings Heath, Birmingham B13 9UJ, England.

MORTON Nigel William; b. 23 Nov. 1953, Nairobi, Kenya. Man.; Booking Agent; Consultant. m. Hilary Cooper, 26 Nov. 1977, divorced, 1 s., 1 d. *Career:* Journalist: Record Mirror; Sounds; Hi-Fi weekly; Booking agent to various acts including: Carmel; Marillion; Wishbone Ash; Jimmy Cliff; Billy Bragg; Angelic Upstarts; Donovan; The Exploited; Pentangle; The Twinkle Brothers, 1978–84; Full time manager: New Model Army, 1982–91; Co-manager: The Almighty, 1987–90; Booking Agent, Consultant, Current clients include: Bruce Cockburn; Kate and Anna McGarrigle; Hot Tuna; The Ukrainians; Porcupine Tree; Test Department, 1992–; Negotiated recording contracts for: New Model Army with: Quiet Records, 1982; Abstract Records, 1983; EMI Records, 1984; Negotiated publishing contracts for New Model Army with: Watteau Music, 1983; Warner-Chappell Music, 1986. *Leisure interests:* Reading; Writing; Music, all forms; Travel; Aircraft History; Cooking. *Address:* Forward Agency Booking, 132 Liverpool Rd, London N1 1LA, England.

MORTON Peter Michael; b. 30 July 1964, Leicester, England. Singer; Musician (guitar); Songwriter. *Musical Education:* Church choir; Busker until 1987. *Career:* Concerts throughout UK, Europe, North America; British Council Tours, Pakistan, Malaysia; Frequent guest, Folk On 2. *Compositions include:* Another Train. *Recordings:* Albums: Frivolous Love, 1987; One Big Joke, 1988; Urban Folk Vol. 1, 1989; Mad World Blues, 1992; Courage, Love, Grace, 1995; Contributions to: All Through The Year.

Honours: Most Promising Newcomer, Folk Roots Magazine, 1987. *Membership:* PRS. *Leisure interests:* Reading; Travel. *Current Management:* Small World Music. *Address:* PO Box 2259, London E17 4RD, England.

MORYKIT Dmytro; b. 3 Dec. 1956, Northampton, England. Composer; Musician (piano, keyboards). m. Elaine Morykit, 2 Nov. 1985, 1 d. *Education:* BEd, University of Leicester. *Musical Education:* Classically trained on Piano from early age to LRAM; Studied with Graham Mayo. *Career:* Member of the National Student Theatre Company, 1978–80; Composer in Residence; Session musician with various rock bands; Freelance composer and musician. *Compositions:* Many for film, theatre, dance and public performance including music for The Wasteland by T S Eliot and original music for The Lion The Witch and The Wardrobe by C S Lewis; Commissioned by Amnesty International: The Unforgiving, 1997; Prisoners of Conscience, 1998. *Recordings:* The Unforgiving; From The Dungeons To The Skies. *Publications include:* Songs For Piano, 1982; The Enchanted, 1994. *Honour:* Best Original Music, National Student Drama Festival. *Memberships:* Musicians' Union. *Leisure interests:* Music; Reading; Theatre; Cinema; Amateur Dramatics.

MOS DEF (Dante Smith), (Dante Beze); b. 11 Dec. 1973, Brooklyn, New York, USA. Rapper. *Career:* Began rapping, aged 9; Formed: Urban Thermo Dynamics with sister; Released first record, 1994; Joined the Native Tongues collective, leading to guest appearance on De La Soul's Big Brother Beat; Started recording solo material for independent label Rawkus; Formed rock group Black Jack Johnson; *Collaborations:* Jill Scott; A Tribe Called Quest; DJ Krush; Common; Talib Kweli; Scritti Politti; Ghostface Killah. *Recordings:* Albums: Mos Def and Talib Kweli Are Black Star, 1998; Black On Both Sides, 1999; Singles: The Universal Magnetic, Body Rock 1998; Umi Says, Miss Fat Booty – Part II, 2000. *Address:* c/o Rawkus Records, 676 Broadway, Fourth Floor, New York, USA.

MOSCA Sal; b. 27 April 1927, Mount Vernon, New York, USA. Musician (piano). m. Stella C Di Gregorio, 2 s., 1 d. *Musical Education:* 3 years New York College of Music and New York University; 8 years Lennie Taistano. *Career:* Alice Tulley Hall, solo recital; Carnegie Recital Hall, solo recital; Concertgebouw (Netherlands), solo recital; Solo recitals, Rotterdam, Maastricht, The Hague; Philharmonic Hall, West Berlin, with Warne Marsh, Kenny Clark, Eddie Gomez; 5 hour radio interview, WKCR. *Recordings:* 15 albums with Lee Konitz; Warne Marsh Quartet; Village Vanguard; Zinnia; 3 solo CDs: Interplay; Choice; Wave. *Honours:* ASCAP Pop Awards. *Memberships:* ASCAP; AMRA; Local AFofM. *Address:* 5 S Fifth Ave, Mount Vernon, NY 10550 3108, USA.

MOSES Jamie (James Michael); b. 30 Aug. 1955, Ipswich, Suffolk, England. Musician (guitar, bass guitar, keyboards); Singer; Musical Dir. m. Deborah Anne Webb, 30 Aug. 1983, 1 s., 1 d. *Education:* Redhill Technical College. *Musical Education:* Self-taught. *Career:* Tours with: Brian May; Bob Geldof; Eric Burdon; Broken English; S.O.S. Band; Bucks Fizz; The Hollies; Deana Carter; Stage appearances with: Paul Rodgers; Paul McCartney; Steve Lukather; Dave Stewart; Guns 'n' Roses; Fish; Chaka Khan; Curtis Stigers; Paul Young; Roger Chapman; Roger Taylor; Extreme; Kiki Dee; Television and radio with artists including: The Pretenders; Olivia Newton-John. *Recordings:* Brian May Live At Brixton Academy; Another World; The Happy Club, Bob Geldof; Comin' On Strong, Broken English; I Used To Be An Animal, Eric Burdon; Various, Paul Young; Do You Really Want Me Back, Broken English; Merlin, Merlin; Turn Unstoned?, Roger Chapman. *Memberships:* PRS; MCPS; Musicians' Union. *Leisure interests:* Video games; Tennis. *Address:* 32 William Rd, Caterham-On-The-Hill, Surrey CR3 5NN, England.

MOSES Robert (Bob); Jazz Musician (drums, keyboards); Composer; Educator. *Career:* Leader, bands: Mozamba; Drumming Birds; Founder, owner, Mozown Records, 1975–; Worked with Jack DeJohnette; Keith Jarrett; David Sanborn; Rahsaan Roland Kirk; Gary Burton. *Recordings:* Albums include: with Larry Coryell: Free Spirit, 1967; Lady Coryell, 1969; with Steve Kuhn: Playground, 1974; Non Fiction, 1978; with David Liebman: Drum Ode, 1975; with Pat Metheny: Bright Size Life, 1975; with Compost: Compost, 1971; Life Is Round, 1973; with Free Spirits: Out of Sight and Sound, 1967; Solo: Bittersweet in the Ozone, 1975; Devotion, 1979; Family, 1980; When Elephants Dream of Music, 1982; Visit with the Great Spirit, 1983; The Story of Moses, 1987; Time Stood Still, 1993; Drumming Birds, 1993.

MOSLEY Ian; b. 16 June 1953, Paddington, London, England. Musician (drums, percussion). *Musical Education:* Guildhall School of Music. *Career:* Member, Curved Air; Gordon Giltrap Band; Steve Hackett; Member, orchestras for West End musicals: Hair; Jesus Christ Superstar; Member, UK progressive rock group Marillion, 1983–; Tours, UK; Europe; USA; Major concerts include: Milton Keynes Bowl, 1984; Nostell Priory Festival, 1984; Monsters of Rock Festival, Castle Donington, 1985; Colombian Volcano Appeal Concert, Royal Albert Hall, 1986; Welcome To The

Garden Party, Milton Keynes Bowl, 1986. *Recordings:* Albums: with Gordon Giltrap: Peacock Party, 1980; Live, 1981; with Steve Hackett: Highly Strung, 1983; Till We Have Faces, 1984; with Marillion: Fugazi, 1984; Real To Real, 1984; Misplaced Childhood, 1985; Brief Encounter, 1986; Clutching At Straws, 1987; B-Sides Themselves, 1988; The Thieving Magpie, 1988; Season's End, 1989; Holidays In Eden, 1991; A Singles Collection 1982–92, 1992; Brave, 1994; Singles with Marillion include: Punch and Judy, 1984; Assassing, 1984; Kayleigh (No. 2, UK), 1985; Lavender, 1985; Heart of Lothian, 1985; Incommunicado, 1987; Sugar Mice, 1987; Warm Wet Circles, 1987; Freaks, 1988; Hooks In You, 1989; Uninvited Guest, 1989; Easter, 1990; Cover My Eyes (Pain and Heaven), 1991; No One Can, 1991; Dry Land, 1991; Sympathy, 1992; Other recordings with: Sally Oldfield; Darryl Way; Trace; Renaissance; Adrian Snell. *Current Management:* Rod Smallwood, Sanctuary Management. *Address:* Sanctuary House, 45–53 Sinclair Rd, London W14 0NS, England.

MOSS Jon; b. 11 Sept. 1957, London, England. Musician (Drums). *Career:* Session drummer, Adam and the Ants; The Damned; Joined Sex Gang Children, with Boy George and Mikey Craig; Became Culture Club; Numerous TV appearances and several tours; Band split, 1987; Various solo projects; Band reformed, 1998. *Recordings:* Singles: Do You Really Want To Hurt Me; Time (Clock of the Heart); Church of the Poisoned Mind, 1983; Victims, 1983; It's A Miracle, 1983; Karma Chameleon, 1983; The War Song, 1984; The Medal Song, 1984; I Just Wanna Be Loved, 1998; Your Kisses Are Charity, 1999; Albums: Kissing To Be Clever, 1982; Colour By Numbers, 1983; Waking Up With The House on Fire, 1984; From Luxury To Heartache, 1986; Greatest Moments (Live), 1998.

MOSS Mick (Mix); b. 25 May 1953, London, England. Prod.; A & R Consultant. *Education:* BA Hons. *Career:* Worked with: The Farm; The La's; Elvis Costello; Pete Townshend; Sonya; Racey; The Troggs; Also worked with various members of The Clash; The Christians; Flock of Seagulls; Icicle Works; Tears For Fears; Suzi Quatro band; Lightning Seeds. *Recordings:* Producer, Engineer: Singles/EPs: Bread Not Bombs, (benefit single, Campaign Against the Arms Trade), 1986; What's Happening To Our Nation?, L8 Connexion (benefit single for MTUCURC); Free, Live Transmission, 1986; Are U In Pain?, Gaynor Rose Madder, 1987; Fading, Gaynor Rose Madder, 1987; Here Comes The Floor, Benny Profane, 1987; I Love You Liverpool, Steve May, 1988; Worse Year of My Life, Wild Swans, 1989; Soldier On, Wild Swans, 1989; This Is The Age, Pupils of Parkfield School Liverpool, 1989; Post Funk War, 25th of May, 1989; Cynthia Payne, The Hoovers, 1988; MDM: 4 singles, 2 albums, include: Take What You Want, 1988–94; Awakenings, The Senses, Oh Father, Ice Factory, 1990; Disease, Adams Family, 1991; Cinemascope, Syndicate, 1994; Greytown, Syndicate, 1995. *Publications:* Various articles in music magazines. *Memberships:* PRS; MRF; IMF. *Leisure interests:* Rock 'n' Roll lifestyle; Nature; Wildlife; The Planet. *Address:* PO Box 25, Liverpool L17 8SX, England.

MOST Mickie, (Michael Peter Hayes); b. June 1938, Aldershot, Hampshire, England. Record Prod. *Career:* Toured, recorded as the Most Brothers with Alex Wharton, late 1950s; Solo artiste, South Africa, 1959–63; Producer, UK, 1964–; Head of RAK record label, 1969–; Successful RAK artists included: Hot Chocolate; Alexis Korner's CCS; Smokie; Chris Spedding; Kim Wilde; New World; Suzi Quatro; Mud; Television appearances include: Regular panelist, New Faces, UK television talent show; Presenter, television show, Revolver. *Recordings:* As producer: The Animals (7 hit singles); Lulu; Terry Reid; Jeff Beck; Donovan; Mary Hopkin; Julie Felix; Johnny Hates Jazz; Perfect Stranger; Herman's Hermits; Hot Chocolate; Brenda Lee; Also worked with Herman's Hermits; The Nashville Teens. *Address:* c/o RAK Records, 43 Brook Green, London W6 7EF, England.

MOSUMGAARD Niels Eliot; b. 20 Oct. 1961, Aarhus, Denmark. Songwriter; Musician (guitar, saxophone); Vocalist. m. Eva Baadsgaard, 18 May 1991, 2 s. *Musical Education:* Self-taught. *Career:* Songwriter, singer, Lars Liholt Band tour, 1984; Touring Denmark with own band, 1984–; Sideman, saxophone, guitar, blues, calypso and popular bands; Member, Calypsocapellet, 1984–87; Member, Sweethearts, 1989–91; Lyricist for several composers on independent scene in Danish and English; Lyricist for: Bamboo Brothers; Johnny Told Suzi, 1993 (music by Troels Skovgard); Inventor, personal mix of folk, ambient, ethnic and metal called Folkadelic; Working on album: N B Danish Lyrics, 1995.

MOTEN Frank Jr, (Tee Tah, Easy Mo'T'); b. 7 April 1967, New York, NY, USA. Prod.; Composer. *Musical Education:* Johnson C Smith University, student of Dizzy Gillespie. *Career:* TV appearances: Sesame Street, aged 4; Late Night with David Letterman; various commercials; Live performances include Carnegie Hall and The Apollo Theater; Various production projects; Recorded as Tee Tah, 1999–; Founder: OurGig.com, 2000. *Compositions:* Still Boppin/Night In Tunisia. *Recordings:* Singles: It Takes Two, Rob Base and DJ E-Z Rock, 1988; Together Forever, Lisette Melendez, 1991. *Current Management:* Prince Igor Management. *Address:*

233 E Erie St, Suite 2206, Chicago, Illinois 60611, USA. *Internet:* www.ourgig.com.

MOTIAN Stephen Paul; b. 25 March 1931, Philadelphia, Pennsylvania, USA. Musician (drums); Composer. *Education:* Private lessons; One year at Manhattan School of Music, New York. *Career:* Played with Bill Evans and with Lennie Tristano and Zoot Sims; Worked in '50s and '60s with Coleman Hawkins, Roy Eldridge, Oscar Pettiford, Thelonious Monk, Al Cohn and Zoot Sims; Formed trio with Keith Jarrett and Charlie Haden; Began releasing albums under own name; Formed Quintet with other musicians, the trio with Bill Frisell and Joe Lovano, 1980s; Formed Electric Be Bop Band 1980s, began performing and recording 1991; Toured in Europe and recorded with Trio 2000 and Trio 2000 + One, 1997; Further tours, 1998–99. *Compositions:* Over 50 compositions published and recorded. *Recordings include:* With Keith Jarrett: Eyes of the Heart; Death and the Flower; Life Between the Exit Signs; With Bill Evans: How My Heart Sings; Sunday at the Village Vanguard; New Jazz Conceptions; With Charlie Haden: The Ballad of the Fallen; Liberation Music Orchestra; With Bill Frisell: Rambler; With Paul Bley: The Paul Bley Quartet; Fragments; With Carla Bley: Tropic Appetites; Escalator Over the Hill; Other: Misterioso, 1986; Monk in Motian, 1988; Live in Tokyo, 1991; On Broadway Vol. 3, 1991; The Electric Be Bop Band, 1992; Flight of the Blue Jay, 1996; Trio 2000 + One, 1997; Electric Be Bop Band Play Monk and Powell, 1998. *Honours:* National Endowment for the Arts Grant, 1976; New York Foundation for the Arts Grant, 1987. *Current Management:* Hans Wendl, Berkeley, California, USA. *Address:* 467 Central Park W, New York, NY 10025, USA.

MOTION David; b. 23 March 1959, Hamburg, Germany. Composer. Partner, Vera Hegarty. *Musical Education:* G Gaunt; G Greed; Royal Academy of Music. *Career:* Recording engineer, 1982–84; Record producer, 1984–90; Composer. *Compositions:* Sally Potter's film Orlando; Television: Cardiac Arrest; Commercials: HSBC; Gaviscon; BMW; Ford Mondeo; Frontera; Tesco; Shell. *Recordings:* as producer: Since Yesterday, Strawberry Switchblade; Lean On Me, Red Box; Carmel; Chara; Toshihiko Takamizawa. *Honours:* D and AD Silver Award. *Leisure interests:* Food; Wine; Travel; Cycling. *Current Management:* Bob Last. *Address:* Holdings Ecosse Ltd, 9/2 Tweeddale Court, 14 High St, Edinburgh EH1 1TE, Scotland.

MOTTIRONI Adriano; b. 3 Nov. 1968, Rome, Italy. Composer; Sound Engineer. *Education:* Durham University. *Career:* Music, Sound Designing, Theatre Productions; Concert Promoter; Musical and Technical Advisor. *Compositions:* La Scoperta De L'America; Labyrinth; Romeo and Juliet; Sorry. *Leisure interests:* Sport; Nature; Photography; Animals. *Address:* Via Alla Marina 25, 00040 Lavinio, Roma, Italy.

MOUFANG David; b. 7 Sept. 1966, Heidelberg, Germany. Composer; Prod.; Musician (guitar, keyboards, percussion). *Career:* Runs two record labels with Jonas Grossmanns, Source Records, 1992-, KM 20, 1996-. *Recordings:* Earth To Infinity, 1992; Big Rooms, Deep Space Network, 1993; Intergalactic Federation, Deep Space Network and Dr Atmo, 1993; Intergalactic Federation 2, 1994; Reagenz, with Jonah Sharp, 1994; View To View, with Rob Gordon, 1994; Kunststoff, 1995; Solitaire, 1995; Koolfang with Pete Namlook, 1995; Koolgang 2, 1995; Traffic (Live '95), Deep Space Network, 1996; Cymbelin, Move D, 1996; RO70/Move D, with Roman Flügel, 1996; Exploring the Psychdelic Landscape, 1996; Lips, with Tobacco Rot, 1997; Deep Space Network Meets Higher Intelligence Agency, 1997; A Day in the Life, 1997; RO70/Move D II, with Roman Flügel, 1997; Conjoint, Berger/Hodge/Moufang/Ruit, 1997; Out to Lunch, with Dan Jordan, 1998; Lost in Music, TV documentary, 1996. *Memberships:* Sound Works Exchange (sponsored by the Goethe Institute and British Arts Council), 1995. *Current Management:* Source Records. *Address:* Kornmarkt 9, 69117 Heidelberg, Germany.

MOULD Bob; b. 1960, New York, USA. Musician (guitar); Songwriter; Record Prod. *Career:* Co-founder, lead guitarist, rock group Hüsker Dü, 1979–87; Solo artiste, 1987–92; Solo tour, 1991; Founder, guitarist, Sugar, 1992-. *Recordings:* Albums: with Hüsker Dü: Land Speed Record, 1981; Everything Falls Apart, 1982; Metal Circus, 1983; Zen Arcade, 1984; New Day Rising, 1985; Candy Apple Grey, 1986; Warehouse – Songs and Stories, 1987; Everything Falls Apart and More, 1993; Living End, 1994; Solo albums: Workbook, 1989; Black Sheets of Rain, 1990; Bob Mould, 1996; The Last Dog and Pony Show, 1998; with Sugar: Changes, 1992; Copper Blue, 1992; Good Idea, 1992; Helpless, 1992; If I Can't Change Your Mind, 1992; Beaster, 1993; FUEL (File Under Easy Listening), 1994; Your Favourite Thing, 1994; Believe What You're Saying, 1994; Gee Angel, 1994; Besides, 1995. *Current Management:* Granary Music, PO Box 4947, Austin, TX 78765, USA.

MOUNSEY Paul Fraser; b. 15 April 1959, Irvine, Scotland. Composer; Prod.; Arranger; Musician (piano). m. Dorinha Carelli, 8 July 1983. *Musical Education:* Trinity College of London: GTCL, FTCL (composition), LTCL (piano). *Career:* Part-time lecturer: Goldsmith's College, London

University, 1984–85; Songwriter, CBS (Sony) Brazil, 1986–; Producer, arranger, Sony (Brazil), EMI (Brazil) and Independents, 1987–; Musical Director, Play It Again Studios, São Paulo, Brazil, 1989–; Musical Director, Michael Nyman In Brazil, Concert, 1992; Appearances: BBC Radio Scotland, Scot FM, 1994. *Recordings:* Numerous songs; Soundtrack for mini-series: Procura-se, 1992; La Cigale Et La Fourmi, for soprano, oboe, piano, recorded and broadcast, BBC Radio 3; Nahoo, solo album, UK 1994, USA 1995; Nahoo Too, 1998. *Publications:* Articles, Brazilian newspapers; Article: Music In Brazil, Contact (British music journal), No 31, Autumn 1987. *Address:* Iona Records, 27–29 Carnoustie Pl., Scotland St, Glasgow G5 8PH, Scotland; Mesa/Bluemoon Recordings, 209 E Alameda Ave, Suite 101, Burbank, CA 91502, USA.

MOUSER Richard; b. 4 June 1962, Santa Monica, California, USA. Musician (guitar); Record Prod.; Engineer. 2 d. *Musical Education:* Theory, Classical Guitar. *Career:* Support tours with 3 Dog Night; Huey Lewis and the News; Warrant; Michael Schenker Group; Melissa Manchester; Def Leppard; Queensryche; Wrote and produced jingles for numerous commercials. *Recordings:* Producer, engineer, mixer for albums by: Green Jelly; Corrosion of Conformity; Lucy's Fur Coat; LSD; The Coup de Grace; Black Market Flowers; The Ex-Idols; Mixed album for: Imperial Tree; Mixed recordings by: Less Than Jake, Insane Clown Posse; Quickspace; Producer, The Generators, Schleprock; Engineer, Clawfinger. *Leisure interests:* Golf; Skiing. *Current Management:* Tapko Entertainment, 17337 Ventura Blvd, Suite 208, Encino, CA 91316, USA.

MOUSKOURI Nana (Joanna); b. 13 Oct. 1934, Hania, Greece. Singer; Politician. m. George Petsilas, 1 s., 1 d. *Musical Education:* Diploma in piano and singing, Athens Academy of Arts; National Conservatory, Athens. *Career:* Regular European festival performances, late 50s; Regular television appearances, UK; UNICEF Ambassador, 1993–; Member, European Parliament, 1994–; Founder and president of the Focus On Hope Foundation. *Recordings:* Numerous albums; Hit singles include: Les Enfants du Piree; Weiss Rosen Aus Then; L'Enfant Au Tambour; Parapluies De Cherbourg (duet with Michel Legrand); Guantanamera; Only Love. *Honours:* Greek Broadcasting Festival Award; Golden Tulip Award; Barcelona Festival Award; Several Gold discs, 1959–; Chevalier Des Arts Et Des Lettres; Chevalier De La Légion D'honneur, 1997. *Address:* 12 rue Gutenberg, 92100 Boulogne-Sur-Seine, France.

MOUTOUARI Pierre; b. 3 April 1950, Kimuimba. Musician. 6 d. *Career:* National and International Musician; Manager, PM Production. *Compositions:* Missengué, on Le Retour de Pierre Moutouari; Aïssa, on Tout Bouge. *Recordings:* Le Retour de Pierre Moutouari; Tout Bouge. *Honours:* Gold Medal, Tunisia, 1973; Best Composer Prize, 1982; Prize, Zaïre, 1993. *Address:* PM Production, 37 rue Archambault, Bacongo, Brazzaville, Republic of Congo.

MOWER Mike (Michael Henry); b. 9 June 1958, Bath, England. Composer; Musician (flutes, saxophones). m. Elizabeth Melia, 27 July 1994. *Musical Education:* Royal Academy of Music, London. *Career:* Mike Mower Quartet (jazz), frequent broadcasts for BBC Radio, 1980–84; Wrote arrangements for BBC Radio Orchestra Big Band, 1984–86; Formed Itchy Fingers, jazz saxophone quartet playing his music, won Jazz Sounds '86, 1986–95; Band has toured 42 countries, playing all major European jazz festivals; Currently writes commissions for soloists and ensembles specializing in jazz/classical crossover style. *Compositions:* Numerous for wind instruments. *Recordings:* Albums: Producer, writer with Itchy Fingers saxophone quartet: Quark; Teranga; Itchy Fingers Live In Europe; Full English Breakfast; with flute player Kirten Spratt): Doodle and Flight; Triligence (titles taken from jazz sonatas for flute and piano by Mike Mower); Contributions to: Björk, Debut; Brendan Power Plays the Music from Riverdance, 1997; James Galway, Unbreak My Heart, 1999. *Honours:* Hon ARAM. *Membership:* Musicians' Union. *Leisure interests:* Astronomy; Indian food. *Address:* 56 Lessar Ave, London SW4 9HQ, England.

MOYET (Genevieve) Alison (Jane); b. 18 June 1961, Billericay, Essex, England. Singer; Songwriter. 1 s., 1 d. *Musical Education:* Musical Foundation, Southend Technical College; Musical Instrument Technology. *Career:* Singer with Yazoo, 1981–83; Solo singer, 1983–. *Recordings:* Albums: with Yazoo: Upstairs At Eric's, 1982; You and Me Both, 1983; Solo albums: Alf, 1984; Raindancing, 1987; Hoodoo, 1991; Essex, 1994; Singles, 1995. *Honours:* BRITS Award, Best New Band, Yazoo, 1982; Rock and Pop Award, Best Female Artist, 1982; Brits Awards, Best Female Artist, 1984, 1987; Grammy Nomination, Best Female Rock Vocal Performance, 1992. *Leisure interest:* Following Southend United Football Club. *Current Management:* Motley Music Ltd. *Address:* 132 Liverpool Rd, London N1 1LA, England.

MOYSE Nigel Arthur; b. 26 Feb. 1952, Dublin, Ireland. Musician (electric, semi-acoustic, acoustic guitar). m. Elizabeth McColl, 15 June 1974, 1 s., 1 d. *Education:* BA, Natural Sciences, Moderator, Trinity Collge Dublin. *Musical Education:* Piano, Municipal School of Music (Dublin); Guitar, self-taught, also under Louis Stewart. *Career:* John Stevens Away and Dance Orchestra; Folkus; Freebop; Ed Speight; Nigel Moyse Quartet; Mike Stock Band; The Flirtations, backing band; Bracknell; Camden; City of London; Sheffield Festivals; Folkus, National tour, 1984; Round House; ICA; Hyde Park; 100 Club; Universities; Clubs; Jazz venues; Jazz in Britain, BBC Radio III; Visiting music teacher, Eton College, Windsor, Berkshire. *Compositions:* Co-written with Ed Speight: The Dodder Suite, 1980; Complications, 1981; Solo: Tsk Tsk; Ballad For Mick; Martin's Dilemma, 1980; (All performed live and on Jazz In Britain, 1980, 1981). *Recordings:* Away: Integration, 1980; Mutual Benefit, 1994; Dance Orchestra: Ah, 1978; Some of: Conversation Piece, 1991; A Luta Continua, 1994; Folkus: The Life of Riley, 1984. *Membership:* Musicians' Union. *Leisure interests:* Reading; Films; Gardening; Music. *Address:* Flat 1, 10 Denbeigh Rd, Ealing, London W13 8PX, England.

MR C (Richard West); b. 1964, London, England. Rapper; Vocalist; Musician (Guitar). *Career:* Joined The Shamen, 1991; Numerous TV appearances; Club gigs and dance nights; Owner, The End dance club. *Recordings:* Make It Mine, 1992; LSI (Love Sex Intelligence), 1992; Boss Drum, 1993; Phorever People, 1994; Transamazonia, 1995; Destination Eschaton, 1995; Hemp, 1996; Move Any Mountain, 1996; Universal, 1998; U Nations, 1998; Albums: Boss Drum, 1992; Different Drum, 1994; Axis Mutatis, 1995; Hempton Manor, 1996; UV, 1998.

MTUKUDZI Oliver; b. 1952, Zimbabwe. Vocalist; Musician (guitar); Songwriter. *Career:* Joined Wagon Wheels with Thomas Mapfumo, 1977; First single, Dzandimomotera, went gold; Formed Black Spirits, recording two albums a year; Sound referred to as Tuku music; Wrote and directed musical Was My Child, 1990s; Tours of Africa, Australia, America and Europe; Performed at WOMAD Reading, 1998 and 2001; Appeared in The Soul of Mbira and TV documentary Under The African Skies; Lead role in first local feature film, Jit, 1990; Appeared in and composed for film Neria; Has recorded more than 40 albums. *Recordings:* Albums include: Africa, 1980; Ziwere, 1993; Tuku Music, 1998; Paivepo, 1999; Bvuma-Tolerance, 2000. *Honours:* M-Net Award, Best Soundtrack, Neria; Zimbabwe Writers Union, honour for Was My Child; Paivepo was still in Zimbabwe's top ten albums 15 months after release; CAMA (Celebration of African Artists Ceremony) award, 2001. *Internet:* www.putumayo.com.

MUBARAK Abdel Aziz el; b. Sudan. Singer; Musician (oud). *Musical Education:* Institute of Music and Drama, Khartoum. *Career:* Popular solo artiste; Tours extensively in Africa and Arab States, including: Ethiopia; Somalia; Nigeria; Chad; Cameroon; Egypt; Kuwait; UAE; Member of trio with Abdel Gadir Salim and Mohammed Gubara; Regular television and radio appearances. *Recordings:* with Abdel Gadir Salim and Mohammed Gubara: The Sounds of Sudan, 1991. *Address:* c/o World Circuit Records, 106 Cleveland St, London W1P 5DP, England.

MUES Jan; b. 8 Feb. 1955, Leuven, Belgium. Musician (Flugelhorn; Trumpet; Composer; Arranger). m. Marie Paule Branders, 12 Nov. 1976, 1 d. *Education:* Painting, Academy Des Beaux Arts, Antwerp, Belgium. *Career:* Laureate, 11th edition, The European Jazz Contest International, 1989; Soloist, Belgian Jazz Orchestra; Jazz Festival in Milan; Several Belgian Radio and TV appearances; Jazz Middelheim Festival, Antwerp, 1995. *Compositions:* Mystic Smile; Whippy Lippy; Why Do You Skip So Tippy; Hayday; Who's Watching Who; Lullaby For the Sun; I Hope the Guys Like It; Foolish Enter; Peter's Egg. *Recording:* Mystic Smile, CD album. *Publications:* De Koning the Rijk. *Honour:* Fifth Annually Sabamprice. *Membership:* SABAM. *Leisure interest:* Painting. *Current Management:* Jan Mües, Mannenberg 70, 3270 Scherpenheuvel, Belgium.

MUGGLETON Paul Frank; b. 27 Feb. 1947, Queen Charlotte, London, England. Record Prod. Partner, Judie Tzuke, 2 s., 3 d. *Education:* Saltus Grammar School, Bermuda; University of Madrid, Faculty of Filosofia Y Letras. *Musical Education:* Classical guitar, Madrid, 18 months. *Career:* All major tours with Judie Tzuke including tour of America with Elton John; Played to 450,000, Central Park, New York (with Judie Tzuke); Television includes: Top of The Pops; many other shows; Started Big Moon Records, 1996. *Recordings:* Co-producer with Mike Paxman: All Judie Tzuke albums, 1980–92; Nick Kamen albums; Presently Scarlet. *Honours:* Song Award, Festival De Malaga, 1970. *Memberships:* PRS; Musicians' Union. *Leisure interest:* Egyptian archaeology (Armana Period). *Current Management:* Big Ocean Productions, 15–19 Cavendish Pl., London W1M 0DD, England. *Address:* Big Moon Records, PO Box 347, Weybridge, Surrey KT13 9WZ, England.

MUHL Lars; b. 14 Nov. 1950, Aarhus, Denmark. Singer; Songwriter; Musician; Author. *Musical Education:* Self-taught; Classical Piano, Jutland Conservatory of Music, 2 years. *Career:* Formed Warm Guns, released 5 Albums in Europe and Australia, 1978; Solo Career, Released 5 Albums, 1986–; Songwriting for European Artists; Author of 4 Books. *Compositions:* One More Minute; Open Up My Heart; Regnfang. *Recordings:* The Glorious Art of Breakin Little Girls Hearts and Blowin Big Boys Brains, 1984; King of Croon, 1988; When Angels Fall, 1990; Kingdom Come, 1993; Mandolina, 1997; The Best of Muhl, 1998. *Honours:* DJBFA Prize of Honour, 1990;

WCM Songwriters Million Certificate, 1996. *Memberships:* DJBFA; Danish Artists Asscn. *Address:* Warner Chappell Music, Anker Heegaardsgade 2, 1572 Copenhagen, Denmark.

MÜHLEIS Daniela; b. 27 April 1955, St Gallen, Switzerland. Singer; Musician (guitar, piano). m. Hans Georg Huber, 26 Sept. 1986, 1 adopted d. *Education:* Commercial school, commercial association, St Gallen. *Musical Education:* Music Lessons: guitar, piano. *Career:* Joined Cargo, 1979; National Country and Western Festival in Zürich, Open-Air Festival, St Gallen, 1981; Swiss finals, European Song Contest; Debut album, 1983; Band renamed, Daniela Mühleis and Band, 1984; Successful concerts, Switzerland, Italy; Country Festivals; Swiss television: Sonntagsmagazin, 1989; Holansky kapr Country Music Festival, Prague, 1989; International Country Festival, Geiselwind, 1990; German Cable TV: Offener Kanal Dortmund, 1991; PORTA Country Festival, Czech Republic, 1992; International Visagino Country Festival, Lithuania, 1993; Lithuanian television; Swiss TV: Country Roads; Video clip produced in Malta, 1994; Television: Switzerland, Malta; Own radio show in St Gallen, Country Music, 1984–97; Nominated by European Country Music Association as European Female Vocalist, 1998; Winner, International Rising Star Award, by North America Country Music Association International, 1999. *Recordings include:* Albums: Stage-fright, 1983; Die Sieger des 1 Country und Western Festivals Zürich, 1986; Far Away, 1987; Animals, 1990: Far Away, 1991; Better Life, 1993; Open Minds, 1997. *Honours:* Winner, Modern Country Music section, Swiss Country Open Air, 1985; SRI Selection, 1997. *Memberships:* CMA, USA; CMFS, Switzerland; ECMA; NACMAI, USA; ECMA, Europe. *Leisure interest:* My dog Snert. *Current Management:* DMB. *Address:* Lehnackerstrasse 9a, 9033 Untereggen, Switzerland.

MUIR Mike; Vocalist. *Career:* Member, Suicidal Tendencies; Numerous live gigs in USA; Also member, side project Infectious Grooves with Robert Trujillo, with Ozzy Osbourne guesting on debut album; Supported Blizzard of Oz No More Tears tour. *Recordings:* With Suicidal Tendencies: Suicidal Tendencies, 1983; Join the Army, 1987; How Will I Laugh Tomorrow When I Can't Even Smile Today, 1988; Controlled by Hatred, 1989; Lights, Camera, Revolution, 1990; F.N.G., compilation, 1992; The Art of Rebellion, 1992; Still Cyco After All These Years, 1993; Suicidal for Life, 1994; Prime Cuts, 1997; Friends and Family, compilation, 1998; Six the Hard Way, EP, 1998; FreeDumb, 1999; With Infectious Grooves: The Plague that Makes Your Booty Move, 1991; Sarsippius' Ark, 1993; Groove Family Cyco, 1994.

MUIRHEAD Dennis Richard; b. 7 Oct. 1941, Dubbo, New South Wales, Australia. Lawyer. m. (1) Elizabeth, Dec. 1966, 3 s., (2) Angel, 10 Dec. 1988, 1 s., 1 d. *Education:* Law, University of Adelaide, South Australia. *Career:* Consultant Lawyer, Simons, Muirhead and Burton; CEO, Dennis Muirhead Company Ltd, Muirhead Management, 1982–; Management, business, legal services to record producers, engineers, studios, artists, songwriters; Clients include producers: Hugh Padgham; Jon Jacobs; Denis Woods; Colin Richardson; Richard Bennett; R S Field; Sun Studio Entertainment, Memphis; Australian jazz pianist and composer Paul Grabowsky; Missouri rockabilly singer, songwriter Billy Swan; Council Assisting the South Australian Royal Commission into the non-medical use of drugs; Chairman of City Roads (Crisis Intervention); Chairman, Institute for the Study of Drug Dependence; Founding Chairman and council member of The Music Managers' Forum; CEO, Muirhead Music and Hugely Music Publishing; Consultant in New Media. *Memberships:* Country Music Asscn, NARAS, Nashville. *Leisure interests:* Music; Motor racing; Keeping fit; Cooking. *Address:* 202 Fulham Rd, London SW10 9PJ, England.

MULDAUR Maria, (Maria Grazia Rosa Domenica d'Avato); b. 12 Sept. 1943, Greenwich Village, New York, USA. Singer. m. Jeff Muldaur, divorced 1972. *Career:* Member, Even Dozen Jug Band (with John Sebastian, Stefan Grossman, Joshua Rifkin, Steve Katz); Jim Kweskin Jug Band; US tour, 1975; European debut, 1975. *Recordings:* Albums: Maria Muldaur, 1973; Waitress In A Donut Shop, 1974; Sweet Harmony, 1976; Southern Winds, 1978; Open Your Eyes, 1979; Gospel Nights, 1980; There Is A Love, 1982; Sweet and Slow, 1984; Transblucency, 1985; Live In London, 1987; On The Sunny Side, 1991; Louisiana Love Call, 1992; Meet Me at Midnite, 1994; Jazzabelle, 1995; Fanning the Flames, 1996; Southland of the Heart, 1998; Swingin' in the Rain, 1998; Meet Me Where They Play the Blues, 1999; Singles include: Midnight At The Oasis; I'm A Woman. *Current Management:* Piedmont Talent, 311 Oakdale Rd, Charlotte, NC 28216, USA.

MULDOON Mule (Paul Gerrard); b. 29 Oct. 1958, Huddersfield, Yorkshire, England. Musician (bass, guitar); Vocalist. m. C A Nester, 20 May 1995. *Career:* Own band, Muldoon Brothers; Appeared at many major country festivals throughout Europe; Appearances on British, Irish and Scandinavian television and radio. *Compositions:* Back O' The Barn; Following The Trail; Brandin' Time. *Recording:* Back O' The Barn, by Muldoon Brothers. *Honour:* Most Promising Country Act, 1992.

Membership: Musicians' Union. *Leisure interests:* Music; Sport; Writing. *Current Management:* International Artists Ltd. *Address:* 17 South Lane, Netherton, Wakefield, West Yorkshire WF4 4LL, England.

MULET Sergio Roberto; b. 2 Nov. 1958, Montevideo, Uruguay. Musician (drums, congas, timbales); Composer; Arranger; Music Teacher. m. Eloisa Valeria, 1 s., 2 d. *Musical Education:* AMEB sixth grade (Jazz piano, second year); Many years of study on drums, congas and percussion (various styles) with Cuban and Brazilian teachers. *Career:* Supported Gypsy Kings in Sydney, 1989; Many Australian TV appearances; Formed Sandunga (Australia's first Afro-Cuban band). *Membership:* Australian Jazz Society. *Leisure interests:* Internet; Computers; Soccer; Dancing. *Current Management:* Havana Management. *Address:* 80 King St, Manly Vale, NSW 2093, Australia.

MULLEN Larry Jr; b. 31 Oct. 1961, Dublin, Ireland. Musician (drums). *Career:* Founder member, drummer, rock group U2, 1978–; Regular national and international tours; Major concerts include: US Festival, 1983; The Longest Day, Milton Keynes, 1985; Live Aid, Wembley, 1985; Self Aid, Dublin, 1986; A Conspiracy of Hope (Amnesty International Tour), 1986; New Year's Eve concert, Dublin (broadcast live to Europe), 1989. *Recordings:* Albums: Boy, 1980; October, 1981; War (No. 1, UK), 1983; Under A Blood Red Sky, 1983; The Unforgettable Fire (No. 1, UK), 1984; Wide Awake In America, 1985; The Joshua Tree (No. 1, UK and USA), 1987; Rattle and Hum, also film (No. 1, USA) 1988; Achtung Baby (No. 1, USA), 1991; Zooropa (No. 1, UK and USA), 1993; Passengers (film soundtrack), with Brian Eno, 1995; Pop, 1997; The Best of U2 1980–90, 1998; All That You Can't Leave Behind, 2000; Hit singles include: Out of Control (No. 1, Ireland), 1979; Another Day (No. 1, Ireland), 1980; New Year's Day, 1983; Two Hearts Beat As One, 1983; Pride (In The Name of Love), 1984; The Unforgettable Fire, 1985; With Or Without You (No. 1, USA), 1987; I Still Haven't Found What I'm Looking For (No. 1, USA), 1987; Where The Streets Have No Name, 1987; Desire (No. 1, UK), 1988; Angel of Harlem, 1988; When Love Comes To Town, with B. B. King, 1989; All I Want Is You, 1989; The Fly (No. 1, UK), 1991; Mysterious Ways, 1992; Even Better Than The Real Thing, 1992; One, 1992; Who's Gonna Ride Your Wild Horses, 1992; Hold Me, Thrill Me, Kiss Me (from film Batman Forever), 1995; Theme from film soundtrack, Mission Impossible (solo with Adam Clayton), 1996; Discotheque (No. 1, UK), 1997; If God Will Send His Angels, 1997; The Sweetest Thing, 1998; Beautiful Day (No. 1, UK), 2000; Stuck In A Moment You Can't Get Out Of, 2001; Walk On, 2001. *Honours include:* Grammy Awards: Album of The Year, 1987; Best Rock Performance, 1987, 1989; Best Rock Vocal, 1989; Song of The Year, Record of The Year, Rock Performance By A Duo Or Group, 2001; BRIT Awards: Best International Group, 1988–90, 1998, 2001; Outstanding Contribution Award, 2001; Best Live Album, 1993; World Music Award, 1993; Juno Award, 1993; Q Awards: Best Act In The World, 1990; 1992; 1993; Merit Award, 1994; Gold and Platinum discs; Numerous magazine awards and poll wins. *Current Management:* Principle Management, 30–32 Sir John Rogersons Quay, Dublin 2, Ireland.

MÜLLER Anders; b. 2 Feb. 1955, Copenhagen, Denmark. Musician (piano, keyboards); Composer; Arranger. m. Anne Macholm, 6 June 1987, 2 s. *Musical Education:* Music Graduate, University of Copenhagen; Piano lessons with Ole Kock Hansen. *Career:* Leader, own jazz trio and quartets, 1975–; Member, orchestras led by Erling Kroner, Leif Johansson, Per Goldschmidt, 1979–92; Co-leader, jazz-rock group, Ariel, 1979–83; Appeared with New Music Orchestra as pianist, 1985, 1992; Conductor, 1990; Composer, 1985, 1988; Also worked with: Thad Jones; Eddie Bert; Red Rodney; Etta Cameron. *Compositions:* Tashmia; Woody's Blues, recorded by Lee Konitz. *Recordings:* with Erling Kroner; Leif Johansson; Ariel. *Honour:* First prize, Dunkerque Jazz Festival, with Soren Bogelund Quartet. *Membership:* DJBFA. *Leisure interest:* Family. *Current Management:* Mazurka Music. *Address:* Mazurka Music, Gammel Kongevej 78, 2 tv, 1850 Frederiksberg C, Denmark.

MULLIGAN Néillidh (Neil); b. 13 May 1955, Dublin, Ireland. Public Servant; Musician (Uilleann pipes). m. Sandra Ní Gharbháin, 6 Nov. 1993, 1 s., 1 d. *Musical Education:* Taught by Tom Mulligan (father) and Leo Rowsome; Self-taught. *Career:* Played and toured many parts of the world including: Europe; America; New Zealand; Concerts in major cities; Many television and radio appearances home and abroad; Represented Ireland at various International Bagpipe Festivals. *Compositions include:* Barr Na Cúille; Tom Mulligan's Hornpipe; Wings of My Soul. *Recordings:* Albums: Barr Na Cúille, 1991; The Leitrim Thrush, 1997; Guest on other albums. *Contributions to:* piping publications. *Honours:* All-Ireland Champion at various age levels. *Memberships:* Na Píobairí Uilleann; Folk Music Society of Ireland; Irish Traditional Music Archive. *Leisure interests:* Music; Sport; The Irish language and culture. *Current Management:* Darina Ní Chuinneagáin, Allegro Music Agency.

MUMBA Samantha Tamania Anne Cecilia; b. 18 Jan. 1983. Vocalist. *Musical Education:* Billie Barry Stage School, Dublin, age 3–15. *Career:* Lead role in Dublin stage musical The Hot Mikado, 1998; Various Irish TV appearances followed; Signed with manager Louis Walsh after meeting in Dublin nightclub; Made first recordings while still at school; Scored in UK with first releases; Concerted attempts to break in America, 2001. *Recordings:* Albums: Gotta Tell You, 2000; Singles: Gotta Tell You, Body II Body, 2000; Always Come Back To Your Love, Baby Come On Over, Lately, 2001. *Honours:* Smash Hits Award, Best New Female Artist, 2000. *Current Management:* Louis Walsh, Carol and Associates/WAR Management, 57 Meadowbank, Bushy Park Rd, Dublin 6, Ireland. *E-mail:* carolh@indigo.ie. *Internet:* www.samanthamumba.com.

MUNDEN David Charles; b. 2 Dec. 1943, Dagenham, Essex, England. Musician (drums); Vocalist. m. Andrée, 7 Dec. 1969, 1 s., 1 d. *Career:* Member, The Tremeloes; Toured world-wide: USA; South America; Australia; New Zealand; Iceland; South Africa; Middle East; Far East; Iceland; Germany; Eastern Bloc countries; Played with Beatles; Rolling Stones; Roy Orbison; Dusty Springfield; Television includes: Ready Steady Go; Top of The Pops; Sunday Night Live At The Palladium. *Recordings:* Twist and Shout; Do You Love Me (No. 1, UK), 1963; Someone, Someone; Candy Man; Here Comes My Baby; Silence Is Golden (No. 1, UK); Call Me Number One (No. 1, UK and world-wide); Helule Helule; Even The Bad Times Are Good; My Little Lady; Suddenly You Love Me; Me and My Life; I Shall be Released; Once on a Sunday Morning; Tremeloes played on Jeff Christie's No. 1 hit Yellow River; Albums: Shiner, 1974; As It Happened, 1983; Best of the Tremeloes, 1992. *Publications:* Guinness Book of Hit Records. *Honours:* Carl Alan Awards. *Memberships:* Musicians' Union; Equity; PRS. *Leisure interests:* Music; Driving fast cars. *Current Management:* Stephen Colyer. *Address:* 25A Cliff Parade, Leigh-On-Sea, Essex SS9 1BB, England.

MUNKGAARD Peer; b. 29 March 1965, Vejle, Denmark. Music Teacher; Freelance Musician (viola, violin). *Education:* Graduate, Esbjerg Kommunale Gymnasium, 1984; Studied viola with Gert Inge Andersson at the Music Academy in Esbjerg, 1987–93. *Career:* Danced folkdances since 1969; Played folk music (fiddle), 1973–; Danced on television show Les Lanciers, 1983; Danced in and played for numerous folkdance groups including Udöbt on their first tours in England; Danish representative on the Comhaltas Ceoltoiri Eireann European Tour, 1985; Instructor of folk dance and music at seminars, music schools and evening schools; Teacher of viola, violin, cello, chamber music, orchestras and choirs; Member of West Jutland Symphony Orchestra and the Jutland Sinfonietta; Assisted in various symphony orchestras and Esbjerg Ensemble; Also played in musicals including: The King and I, Showboat and the Phantom of the Opera. *Membership:* Danish Musicians' Union. *Leisure interests:* Kids; Cats; Cooking; Dancing; Jamming. *Current Management:* Det Klassiske Koncertbureau, Rorhaven 4, 8900 Randers, Denmark. *Address:* Peder Skrams Gade 5, II tv, 6700 Esbjerg, Denmark.

MUNRO Donnie; b. 2 Aug. 1953, Uig, Isle of Skye, Scotland. Musician (guitar); Art Teacher. m. 1980, 2 s., 1 d. *Education:* DA Hons, Dip Ed. *Career:* Member, Scottish folk group Runrig; World-wide tours; Television appearances: Own documentary; Top of The Pops; TV-AM; Pebble Mill. *Recordings:* Albums with Runrig: Play Gaelic, 1978; The Highland Connection, 1979; Recovery, 1981; Heartland, 1985; The Cutter and The Clan, 1987; Once In A Lifetime, 1988; Searchlight, 1989; The Big Wheel, 1991; Amazing Things, 1993; Townsmitting Live, 1995; Mara, 1996; Contributions to: Troubadours of British Folk, Vol. 3, 1995; Best of British Folk Rock, 1996. *Publications:* Going Home – The Runrig Story, Tony Morton. *Honours:* Rector, Edinburgh University, 1991–94; Dr h.c., 1994. *Membership:* Musicians' Union. *Current Management:* Marlene Ross Management, 55 Wellington St, Aberdeen AB2 1BX, Scotland.

MURCIA Joey; b. 21 March 1948, Brooklyn, New York, USA. Musician (guitar). 1 s. *Musical Education:* Graduate, Grove School of Music. *Career:* Session guitarist, 30 years; Major tours with: Benny Lattimore, support to James Brown, 1975; Bee Gees, Here At Last Tour, 1976, Spirits Having Flown Tour, 1979; Jay Ferguson, support to Foreigner, 1977; Andy Gibb, Shadow Dancing Tour, 1978; Performances with Ann Jillian include: Tahoe, Las Vegas, 1984; Trump Plaza, Atlantic City, 1989, 1990. *Compositions:* Cozumel, Jay Ferguson, 1978; Jennifer Slept Here, Joey Scarborough, Theme for NBC-TV series, 1985; Ann Jillian, Theme for NBC-TV series, 1990. *Recordings:* Albums: Clean Up Women, Betty Wright; Rockin Chair, Gwen McCrae; Lattimore III, Benny Lattimore; Monkey Grip Glue, Bill Wyman; Here At Last-Bee Gees Live, Bee Gees; Thunder Island, Jay Ferguson; But Seriously Folks, Joe Walsh; A Luxury You Can Afford, Joe Cocker; Grease, Frankie Valli; Saturday Night Fever, Bee Gees; Restless, Bellamy Brothers; with Andy Gibb: Flowing Rivers; Shadow Dancing; After Dark; Andy Gibb's Greatest Hits; Singles with Andy Gibb: I Just Want To Be Your Everything; Thicker Than Water; Shadow Dancing; Everlasting Love; Latimore, Straighten it Out: The Best of Latimore, 1995; Getting Down to Brass Tacks, 1995. *Honours:* 10 Gold Albums, with Bee Gees, Andy Gibb, Joe Walsh. *Membership:* AFofM, 30 years. *Current Management:* Have Mercy Music Inc. *Address:* 2080 W Hillcrest Dr., Suite # 106, Newbury Park, CA 91320, USA.

MURDOCH Stuart; b. 25 Aug. 1968, Scotland. Vocalist; Musician (guitar); Songwriter. *Career:* Member: Belle and Sebastian 1996–; Collaborations: Future Pilot AKA; Arab Strap; Hefner; Curated Bowlie Weekend Festival with other band members, 1999. *Recordings:* Albums: Tigermilk, If You're Feeling Sinister, 1996; The Boy With The Arab Strap 1998; Fold Your Hands Child – You Walk Like A Peasant, 2000; Singles: Dog On Wheels EP, Lazy Line Painter Jane EP, 3–6–9 Seconds of Light EP, 1997; This Is Just A Modern Rock Song EP, 1998; Legal Man, 2000; Jonathan David, I'm Waking Up To Us, 2001. *Honours:* Brit Award, Best Newcomer, 1999. *Current Management:* Banchory Management, PO Box 25074, Glasgow G2 6YL, Scotland. *Internet:* www.belleandsebastian.co.uk.

MURPHY Jamie; b. 1977. Musician (Guitar); Singer; Songwriter. *Career:* Founder Member, Space, 1993; Numerous television appearances and headlining tours. *Recordings:* Singles: If It's Real, 1993; Money, 1995; Neighbourhood, 1996; Female of the Species, 1997; Me and You Vs the World, 1996; Dark Clouds, 1997; Avenging Angels, 1997; The Ballad of Tom Jones, with Cerys Matthews, 1998; Begin Again, 1998; Bad Days, 1998; Albums: Spiders, 1996; Remixes and B-Sides, 1996; Tin Planet, 1998.

MURPHY John; b. 4 March 1965, Liverpool, England. Composer; Musician (guitar). *Career:* Session guitarist, worked with members of Japan, Propaganda; While working with Thomas Lang, began collaboration in composition with David Hughes. *Compositions:* with David Hughes: Films: Leon The Pig Farmer; Solitaire For 2; Clockwork Mice; Welcome To The Terrordome; Beyond Bedlam; A Feast At Midnight; Body Memories; Dinner In Purgatory; Destroying Angels; Proteus; Flame; Giving Tongue; Lock, Stock and Two Smoking Barrels; Stiff Upper Lips; The Real Howard Spitz; Television: White Men Are Cracking Up, BBC2; All The President's Women; Eunice The Gladiator, C4; Where The Bad Girls Go, Granada; Black Velvet Band, Yorkshire. *Recordings:* Lock, Stock and Two Smoking Barrels. *Memberships:* PRS; Musicians' Union. *Current Management:* Soundtrack Music Associates Ltd. *Address:* 22 Ives St, Chelsea, London SW3 2ND, England.

MURPHY Robert Joseph; b. 3 June 1936, Summit, New Jersey, USA. Musician (saxophone, percussion). m. Judith Ann Miller, 3 Aug. 1962, 2 d. *Education:* BA, Brown University, 1958; LLB, Stanford University, 1963. *Musical Education:* Jazz Studies, Deanza College, Cupertino, California, 1972–75. *Career:* European tour, 1983, 1997; 3 times guest soloist, Kobe Jazz Festival Japan, 1991–93; Ranked number 16 among soprano soloists world-wide, Jazzology Readers Poll, 1985; On faculty of Stanford Jazz Workshop. *Compositions:* Red Neck Blues, musical condemnation of racism; To the Emerald Isle. *Recordings:* 11 albums with Natural Gas Jazz Band. *Publications:* Jazz theory text for Stanford jazz workshop. *Membership:* BMI. *Leisure interest:* Music.

MURPHY Terence James; b. 3 Oct. 1948, Dublin, Ireland. Musician (mandolin, banjo, guitar); Vocalist. m. Kristina Karlsson, 26 Oct. 1991, 1 s., 1 d. *Musical Education:* Provincial High School of Music. *Career:* Tour of England, 1978; Netherlands, 1979 including television appearance; Tour of Germany with appearances on television and radio folk programmes, 1982; Touring and appearances on TV in Denmark, Sweden and Norway. *Recordings:* 4 albums with McEwan's Expotit: Hand Across The Water, 1979, McEwans, 1981, Highland Paddy, 1988, and McEwans, 1990; 3 Solo albums: Terry Murphy: A Dubliner In Denmark, 1982, Don't Bury Me 'Til I'm Dead, 1984; Jack of All Trades, 1986. *Memberships:* DJBFA; Musicians' Union; Gramex. *Leisure interests:* Aerobics; Swimming; Cycling; Writing poetry. *Address:* Humlebaekgade 7 4 tv, 2200 Copenhagen, Denmark.

MURRAY Andy; b. 31 July 1952, Isleworth, England. Composer; Songwriter; Musician (guitar, bass, keyboards). *Musical Education:* University of Sussex; Royal Academy of Music. *Career:* Top 20 hit with Piranhas, 1982; Top of The Pops; Composer, television and video soundtracks; School and college music lecturer, examiner; Advisory consultant, Music Technology in Education. *Publications:* Music Matters, Notator Software Resource Packs, 1993; The Music IT Pack, 1997; New Music Matters 11–14, CD-ROMS, 1998; Music Technology in Action, 1998; Music Technology Inspected, 1999. *Honours:* BA; LRAM; BBC Song contest winner. *Memberships:* PRS; Musicians' Union; NASUWT; ISM; NAME. *Leisure interest:* Cycling. *Address:* 69 Riley Rd, Brighton BN2 4AG, England.

MURRAY Anne; b. 20 June 1945, Springhill, Nova Scotia, Canada. Singer. m. William M Langstroth, 20 June 1975, 1 s., 1 d. *Education:* BPhys, Education, University of New Brunswick, 1966; DLitt (hon), 1978; DLitt (hon), St Mary's University, 1978. *Career:* Recording artist, 1968–; World-wide tours; Television appearances: Singer, Singalong Jubilee, CBC television network, Canada; Numerous CBS US television specials, 1970–2000; Regular guest, Glen Campbell's Goodtime Hour. *Recordings:* Hits singles: Snowbird, 1970; Danny's Song, 1973; You Needed Me, 1978; He Thinks I Still Care (No. 1, USA country chart); Just Another Woman In Love; Could I Have This Dance, from film Urban Cowboy; A Little Good News, 1983; Nobody Loves Me Like You Do, duet with Kenny Loggins (No.

1, USA country chart), 1984; Albums: What About Me, 1968; This Way is My Way, 1969; Snowbird, 1970; Anne Murray, 1971; Talk It Over In The Morning, 1971; Annie, 1972; Danny's Song, 1973; Love Song, 1974; Country, 1974; Highly Prized Possession, 1974; Together, 1975; Keeping In Touch, 1976; Let's Keep It That Way, 1978; Hippo In My Tub (children's songs), 1977; New Kind of Feeling, 1979; I'll Always Love You, 1979 Somebody's Waiting, 1980; Where Do You Go To When You Dream, 1981; The Hottest Night of The Year, 1982; A Little Good News, 1983; Heart Over Mind, 1984; Something To Talk About, 1986; Songs of The Heart, 1987; As I Am, 1988; Harmony, 1987; I Will, 1990; Yes I Do, 1991; Croonin', 1993; The Best... So far, 1994; Anne Murray, 1996; An Intimate Evening with Anne Murray, 1997; What A Wonderful World, 1999; with Glen Campbell: Anne Murray and Glen Campbell, 1973. *Honours:* Numerous JUNO Awards, Top Female Vocalist, 1970–81; Grammy, Top Female Vocalist, 1978; Star on Hollywood Walkway of Stars, 1980; Inducted into Country Music Hall of Fame; Decorated Companion Order of Canada; Inducted into the Juno Hall of Fame, 1993. *Memberships:* AFTRA; Asscn Canadian TV and Radio Artists; Executive mem., Canadian Save The Children Fund (Hon. Chairwoman, 1978–80). *Current Management:* Bruce Allen Talent, 68 Water St, Suite 406, Vancouver, BC V6B 1A4, Canada.

MURRAY Neil; b. 27 Aug. 1950, Edinburgh, Scotland. Musician (bass guitar). *Education:* London College of Printing. *Career:* Member, Gilgamesh, 1973; Hanson, 1974; Colosseum II, 1975–76; National Health, 1976–77; Whitesnake, 1978–82; Gary Moore, 1982–83; Whitesnake, 1984–86; Vow Wow, 1987–89; Black Sabbath, 1989–90; Brian May Band, 1992–93; Black Sabbath, 1994-. *Recordings:* Albums include: with Whitesnake: Trouble, 1978; Lovehunter, 1979; Ready An' Willing, 1980; Live In The Heart of The City, 1980; Come An' Get It, 1981; Saints An' Sinners, 1982; Slide It In, 1984; Whitesnake 1987, 1987; Whitesnake's Greatest Hits, 1994; with Black Sabbath: Tyr, 1990; Forbidden, 1995; Contributions to: Gary Moore, Corridors of Power, 1982; Rockin' every Night, 1983; Victims of the Future, 1983; Brian May, Back to the Light, 1993; Another World, 1998; Twang!: A Tribute to Hank Marvin, 1996. *Leisure interests:* Travel, especially in Scottish Highlands. *Current Management:* Bluefame Ltd. *Address:* 17 Hereford Mansions, Hereford Rd, London W2 5BA, England.

MURRAY Phil; b. 18 Nov. 1953, North Shields, England. Writer; Performer. m. Allison Longstaff, 15 Aug. 1980, 2 s., 1 d. *Career:* Singer, songwriter with U Boat; Member of Blackie; Actor, television programmes including: Dempsey and Makepeace; Cats Eyes; Les Dawson Show; Many theatre tours; Currently full time Personal Development Author and Presenter. *Recordings:* Album: End of My Time, U Boat; Single: Making A Bad Boy Good, U Boat; Also on albums: Talk Talk; Separate Holiday; Forever Again (love songs). *Publications:* Books: You Can Always Get What You Want; Before The Beginning Is A Thought; Empowerment, 1995; The 49 Steps to a Bright Life, 1996; Phil Murray Bites on Personal Development, 1997; You and Me Make Three, 1997; Staying Awake Forever, 1997; The Flow of Life, 1998. *Memberships:* Equity; Musicians' Union; PRS; MCPS; PPS. *Leisure interest:* Philosophy studies. *Current Management:* Perfect Words and Music. *Address:* Maderia, Hunts Rd, St Lawrence, Isle of Wight, PO38 1XT, England.

MURRELL David Evan (Dave); b. 22 Jan. 1952, London, England. Musician; College Lecturer (music); Arranger. m. Debora Anne Diamond, 5 July 1980, 2 d. *Education:* Art college. *Musical Education:* Humber College, Toronto, Canada. *Career:* Solo recordings, sessions, Transatlantic Records; Tours, Canada, USA with: Ken Tobias; Tommy Hunter; Ronnie Prophet; British artists: Psychic TV; Long John Baldry; Zoot Money; MD, arranger, World of Dance. *Recordings:* MD, Yamaha Jazz Connection; Film music: Words of Love, BBC, 1990; Long Way Home, ITV, 1991. *Membership:* Musicians' Union. *Address:* 37 Woodland Rd, Selsey, Sussex PO20 0AL, England.

MURTO Janne; b. 26 Oct. 1964. Musician (saxophone, flutes). *Musical Education:* Oulunkylä Pop/Jazz Conservatoire, 1982; Jazz Department, Sibelius Academy; Studied musical culture, Cuba. *Career:* Member, various big bands including Espoo Big Band; Big Bad Family, with Upi Sorvali; UMO Big Band; 10 years with Fiestacita (Afro-Cuban ensemble); Freelance musician for recording studios, radio and theatre; Current member, Paroni Paakunainen's Saxperiment Quartet; Kari Tenaken's Quintet.

MUSGRAVE Gerard; b. 28 Aug. 1960, Bradford, England. Musician (Bass Guitar); Composer; Songwriter. 1 s., 1 d. *Musical Education:* Private music lessons, and self-taught. *Career:* Appeared with Ruby Wax in Wax on Wheels, Channel 4 TV, 1990; Appearance, BBC2 Out of Our Heads, with Creation Roots, 1992; Appearances at Bradford Festival, Leeds Carnival, Huddersfield Carnival, Music in the Sun Reggae Festival, Sheffield Don Valley. *Recording:* Album, Troddin, 1999. *Memberships:* PRS; MCPS; Musicians' Union. *Leisure interests:* Football; Table tennis; Music; Movies. *Address:* 23 Wood End Court, West Bowling, Bradford BD5 8QL, England.

MUSHOK Mike; b. 10 April 1970, Manhasset, New York, USA. Musician (guitar). *Education:* Electrical Engineering degree. *Career:* Previously worked with HVAC Applications; Formed Staind with Aaron Lewis and others; First live gig, 1995; Released self-financed debut album, 1996; Album sold 4,000 copies; Discovered by Fred Durst, 1997; Signed to Flip/Elektra; Presented to rock cognoscenti at Limp Bizkit gold record party for Three Dollar Bill Y'All $, 1998; Major breakthrough with unscheduled smash US No. 1 radio hit Outside; Appeared on bill for Korn-founded Family Values tours, 1999 and 2001; Headlined MTV's Return of the Rock tour, 2000. *Recordings:* Albums: Tormented, 1996; Dysfunction, 1999; Break The Cycle, 2001; Singles: Mudshovel, Just Go, 1999; Home, Outside, 2000; It's Been Awhile, Fade, 2001. *Honours:* Break The Cycle certified quadruple platinum by RIAA; It's Been Awhile topped Billboard Modern Rock Singles Chart for record-equalling 16 weeks; VH-1 Award, Your Song Kicked Ass But Was Played Too Damn Much prize, 2001; Guitar World Readers Poll, Best New Talent, Mike Mushok, 2000. *Address:* c/o The Firm, Inc, 9100 Whilshire Blvd, Suite 400W, Beverly Hills, CA 90212, USA. *Internet:* www.staind.com.

MUSHROOM (Andrew Vowles); b. 10 Nov. 1967, Bristol, England. Musician (Keyboards); Prod. *Career:* Member, Massive Attack; Began as collective The Wild Bunch with Tricky, Goldie, Neneh Cherry and Nellee Hooper; Formed Massive Attack, 1986; Numerous club gigs and parties; Collaborations with Shara Nelson, Tricky, Horace Andy, Tracey Thorn of Everything But The Girl and Liz Fraser of Cocteau Twins; BRIT Award and Mercury Music Prize nominations. *Recordings:* Singles: Daydreaming, with Shara Nelson, 1990; Unfinished Sympathy, with Shara Nelson, 1991; Safe From Harm EP, 1991; Sly, 1994; Protection, with Tracey Thorn, 1995; Karmacoma, 1995; Risingson, 1997; Teardrop, with Liz Fraser, 1998; Inertia Creeps, 1998; Angel/Group Four, 1998; Albums: Blue Lines, 1991; Protection, 1994; No Protection: Massive Attack vs Mad Professor, 1995; Mezzanine, 1998.

MUSSANGO Duke; b. 6 April 1980, Yaounde, Cameroon. Drummer. *Musical Education:* Musical studies with Billy Mussango. *Compositions:* Numerous songs published. *Membership:* Socimada. *Leisure interests:* Motor sport and rallying. *Address:* c/o Billy Mussango, PO Box 8363 Yaounde, Cameroon.

MUSTAINE Dave; b. USA. Rock Vocalist; Musician (guitar); Songwriter. *Career:* Member, Metallica, 1981–83; Founder member, guitarist, songwriter, Megadeth, 1983–; World-wide tours; Concerts include: Monsters of Rock Festival, Castle Donington, 1988; Clash of The Titans Fest (with Slayer, Suicidal Tendencies, Testament), Wembley, 1990; Rock In Rio Festival, Brazil, 1991; Clash of The Titans, US tour (with Anthrax, Slayer, Alice In Chains), 1991. *Recordings:* Albums: Killing Is My Business and Business Is Good!, 1985; Peace Sells... But Who's Buying?, 1986; So Far So Good... So What?, 1988; Rust In Peace, 1990; Countdown To Extinction, 1992; Youthanasia, 1994; Hit singles: Wake Up Dead, 1987; Anarchy In The UK, 1988; No More Mister Nice Guy, 1990; Holy Wars, 1990; Hangar 18, 1991; Symphony of Destruction, 1992; Skin of My Teeth, 1992; Sweating Bullets, 1993; Other recordings: Contributor, film soundtracks: Super Mario Brothers, 1993; The Last Action Hero, 1993; Contributor, The Beavis and Butthead Experience. *Honours include:* Doris Day Music Award; Genesis Award. *Leisure interest:* Skydiving. *Current Management:* Lafitte Management, 1333 Ventura Blvd #204, Sherman Oaks, CA 91423, USA.

MYATT Charlie; b. 24 June 1965, Bristol, England. Booking Agent. *Education:* Royal Holloway and Bedford New College; Clifton College, Bristol. *Career:* Ten years as agent with: The Levellers; Radiohead; The La's; Shampoo; Compulsion; Skunk Anansie; Longpigs; Suede; Supergrass. *Address:* 13 Artists, 36 Langham St, London W1N 5RH, England.

MYCKA Katarzyna; b. 27 Oct. 1972, Leningrad, Russia. Musician (Marimba soloist). *Education:* Piano Diploma, Music School in Gdansk, Poland, 1979–85; Diploma with Distinction, 1985–91; Gdansk Academy of Music, 1991–95; Postgraduate Study, Music Academy, Stuttgart, Germany, 1993–95; Studied at Mozarteum, Salzburg, Austria, 1993–98; Soloist Class, Stuttgart Music Academy, 1995–97; Master's Degree in Music. *Career:* Winner in numerous competitions, First Prize Opole Percussion Competition, Poland, 1991; Prize, CIEM, Geneva, 1992; First Prize and Audience Prize Solo Marimba Competition, Luxembourg, 1995; First Prize First World Marimba Competition, Stuttgart, 1996; Final Round, International Percussion Competition ARD, Munich, 1997; Scholarship for Young Artists, Rotary Club, Stuttgart, 1997; Promotional Scholarship, Foundation of the Arts, Baden Wurttemberg, 1998; Festival Artist, First World Marimba Festival, Osaka, Japan, 1998; Numerous recordings for radio and TV in Germany and Poland; Masterclasses in Germany, USA, Poland, Switzerland, Luxembourg; Concerts in USA, Japan and Europe. *Recordings:* Solo CD, Katarzyna Mycka: Marimba Spirituel, 1997; Solo CD, Katarzyna Mycka: Marimba Dance, 1998. *Honour:* Ambassador of Polish Percussive Arts Society, Polish Percussive Arts Society, 1999. *Memberships:* Percussive Arts Society, USA; Percussion Creative, Germany. *Leisure*

interests: Music; Collecting percussion instruments. *Address:* Tulpenstr 50, 70180 Stuttgart, Germany.

MYERS James E; b. 26 Oct. 1919, Philadelphia, Pennsylvania, USA. Musician (drums); Bandleader; Songwriter; Arranger; Film Prod.; Actor; Publisher; Writer. *Career:* Arranger, conductor, Jimmy DeKnight and his Knights of Rhythm; Actor, over 300 films and television shows; Film producer, The Block; Owner, James E. Myers Enterprises; Chairman, Rock Around The Clock Museum; Discovered artists including: Al Alberts and the Four Aces; Al Martino. *Compositions:* Over 300 published songs, including Rock Around The Clock, Bill Haley and the Comets. *Honours include:* Grammy; Inducted, Songwriters Hall of Fame; Legendary Eagle Award, CMAA; Pioneer Award, Country Music News; Cash Box Record of The Year; Billboard Triple Crown Award; Legends Awards, Los Angeles, Nashville and Las Vegas; SONA Award; ASCAP Pop Awards; Numerous Presidential, State, City and Congressional citations; Over 100 other awards. *Memberships:* ASCAP; NMPA; Screen Actors Guild; AFTRA; CMA; SGA; EIA; VFW. *Address:* James E. Myers Enterprises, 1607 E Cheltenham Ave, Philadelphia, PA 19124, USA.

MYHRE Wenche Synnöve; b. 15 Feb. 1947. Entertainer; Singer. m. Arthur Bucharot, 3 s., 1 d. *Career:* Musical, Wizard of Oz, 1965; Cabaret, Sweden, 1968, 1969–70, 1974, 1993; Appeared, German TV and personality shows, 1974–87; Played lead in Sweet Charity, Norway, 1989–90; Appeared, 4 films, TV films; Has 650 recorded and published songs; One-woman shows, 1978–98. *Recordings:* Lameg Vaere Ung, 1964; Beiss Nicht Gleich in Jeden Apfel, 1966; Jeg Og Du Og Vi To Og Mange Fler, 1972; Vi Lever, 1982–83; Er Steht Im Tor, 1969; Love A Go Go, 1967; Albums: Wenche Myhre, 1963; Sanger Fra Dengang, 1967; Powshow, 1970; Wenche, 1976; Vi Lever, 1983; Wenches Jul, 1991; Co-Wenches Beste, 1997. *Honours:* 5 Otto Awards, Germany, 1966–70; Midem Award, 1966–67; Silver Microphone, 1967; Norwegian Grammy, 1976; Silver and Gold Discs. *Address:* Venola 22, 1315 Nesoya, Norway.

MYLES Heather; b. 31 July 1964, Riverside, California, USA. Singer; Songwriter; Musician (bass). *Education:* BA Business Administration. *Musical Education:* Self-taught. *Career:* Opened for Merle Haggard, 12 times; Charlie Daniels, 30 times; Extensive travel in Europe. *Recordings:* Albums: Untamed; Just Like Old Times; Sweet Little Dangerous (Live In London); Highways and Honky Tonks. *Honours:* Picked top 10 in Request Magazine, 1995–96. *Leisure interests:* Horse racing; Restoring cars. *Current Management:* Clyde Masters, Gehl Force Management, 1106 18th Ave S, Nashville, TN 37212, USA.

MYLLÄRI Mika; b. 17 June 1966, Kokkola, Finland. Musician (trumpet); Composer. *Musical Education:* Jazz Department, Sibelius Academy, 1986; Jazz Composition with Jukka Linkola, 1991. *Career:* Member, Espoo Big Band; Freelance musician with UMO Big Band; Formed own quintet, playing own material, 1990; Member, 10-man ensemble Zone, 1991-. *Honours:* Finnish Jazz Federation Award, Band of The Year, Mika Mylläri Quintet. *Address:* Dunckerinkatu 4 C 42, 00260 Helsinki, Finland.

MYROL Keith; b. 19 July 1950, Maple Creek, Saskatchewan, Canada. Musician (guitar). m. Trish, 22 Jan. 1972, 1 s. 1 d. *Musical Education:* Self-taught. *Career:* The Myrol Brothers; Appearances: Capital Country CFAC TV Calgary; SCMA Awards Show 1990–94; 7 Sunday In the Park concerts; Right Tracks; Gold Rush Cafe; Saskatchewan Showcase of the Arts; CBC Arts Reel; Project Discovery. *Recordings:* Albums: The Singles Collection; Raisin' The Roof; Also on: Best of the West, Vols I and II, CFAC Country Showdown. *Honours:* SCMA: Non Touring Band of The Year. *Memberships:* CCMA; SCMA Hall of Fame. *Current Management:* Agent: Cross Town Entertainment. *Address:* The Myrol Brothers, Box 969 Outlook, Saskatchewan S0L 2N0, Canada.

MYROL Myles; b. 6 March 1957, Maple Creek, Saskatchewan, Canada. Musician (bass guitar). m. Diane, 31 July 1976, 1 s., 1 d. *Musical Education:* Self-taught. *Career:* The Myrol Brothers; Appearances: Capital Country CFAC TV Calgary; SCMA Awards Show, 1990–94; 7 Sunday In The Park concerts; Right Tracks; Gold Rush Cafe; Sask Showcase of the Arts; CBC Arts Reel; Project Discovery. *Recordings:* Albums: The Singles Collection; Raisin' The Roof; Also on: Best of the West, Vols I and II, CFAC Country Showdown. *Honours:* SCMA; Non Touring Band of the Year. *Memberships:* CCMA; SCMA Hall of Fame. *Current Management:* Agent: Cross Town Entertainment. *Address:* The Myrol Brothers, Box 969 Outlook, Saskatchewan S0L 2N0, Canada.

MYROL Rick; b. 30 May 1948, Maple Creek, Saskatchewan, Canada. Musician (guitar). m. Violet, 23 Nov. 1968, 2 s. *Musical Education:* Self-taught. *Career:* The Myrol Brothers; Appearances: Capital Country CFAC TV Calgary SCMA Awards Show, 1990–94; 7 Sunday In The Park apperances; Right Tracks; Gold Rush Cafe; Saskatchewan Showcase of the Arts; CBC Arts Reel; Project Discovery. *Recordings:* Albums: The Singles Collection; Raisin' The Roof; Also on: Best of West, Vols I and II, CFAC Country Showdown. *Honours:* SCMA: Non Touring Band of The

Year. *Memberships:* CCMA; SCMA Hall of Fame. *Current Management:* Agent: Cross Town Entertainment. *Address:* The Myrol Brothers, Box 969 Outlook, Saskatchewan S0L 2N0, Canada.

MYSLIKOVJAN Ivan; b. 24 Sept. 1960, Ostrava, Czechoslovakia. Musician (alto sax, electric wind instrument). Divorced, 1 s. *Musical Education:* Graduated, Conservatory of Ostrava, Clarinet, 1982; Jazz Studio, Prague, with Karel Velebny, 1981–82. *Career:* Studio musician and soloist; Appearances at jazz festivals and clubs and rock and pop concerts; Performed with many jazz groups including Jazz Laboratory, Swing Big Band, Tabu (rock), Opavica (folk), Buty (pop); Taught: Clarinet, Bass Clarinet and Saxophone at Conservatory of Ostrava, 1982–86; Performed with Etc, 1987–89; Collaborations: Karel Ruzicka; Prague Philharmonic Orchestra; Joined Karel Gott's orchestra, 1989–92; Also worked with Milan Svoboda's Kontraband, 1990–94; Second Grass and Robert Krestan, 1990–96; Joined rock band Laura and Her Tigers, 1992, many tours; Solo projects: Blue Birds; Rhythm and Sax (with DJ Luger); Different DISCO. *Recordings include:* Tutu: Mr Jazzman; Karel Gott: Pismo Lasky; Laura and her Tigers: Sila v nás; The Classic Film Music of Bernard Herrmann; Milan Svoboda Quartet: Tonight, Tomorrow Morning; The Best of Agharta: Tutu, All or Nothing; Soundtrack of Playgirls; Lubos Malina: All You Can Eat; solo: Nice To Meet You; Information of My Soul; Christmas Inspiration; Sax and Love; Sax Art; Sax Horoscope; The 4 Sea Sons; Relax Music. *Current Management:* Viviane Management sro. *Address:* Lovosicka 768, Prague 9, 190 00, Czech Republic.

N

NABORS James Thurston (Jim); b. 12 June 1930, Tuscaloosa, Alabama, USA. Entertainer; Actor; Musician (piano). *Education:* Business Degree, University of Alabama. *Career:* The Andy Griffith Show; Gomer Pyle USMC; The Jim Nabors Variety Hour; The Jim Nabors Show (TV); Las Vegas; Reno; Atlantic City; Various personal appearances across country. *Recordings:* 28 albums, 5 Gold, 1 Platinum including: Jim Nabors by Request, 1967; 16 Most Requested songs, 1989; Jim Nabor's Christmas Album, 1990; 22 Great Hymn and Country Favorites, 2000; Featured on: The Best Little Whorehouse in Texas (Narrator), 1978. *Current Management:* William Morris Agency. *Address:* 151 El Camino, Beverly Hills, CA 91510, USA.

NAGAI Yohei; b. 5 Nov. 1938, Tokyo, Japan. Specialist in Musical Instruments Research. *Education:* Engineering Department, Tokyo University; DEA, Acoustics, Marseilles University. *Career:* 38 years in Musical Instrument Research and Design Department, Yamaha Co Ltd, 3 years General Management of Research Laboratories. *Publications:* Numerous research papers on piano, wind instruments and electronic instruments. *Memberships:* Acoustical Society of Japan; Acoustical Society of America; Acoustical Society of Europe. *Address:* 3–40–20 Sanarudai, Hamamatsu-shi, Japan.

NAIDENOV Vassil; b. 3 Sept. 1950, Sofia, Bulgaria. Singer. *Education:* Music Academy, Sofia, Bulgaria. *Musical Education:* Piano. *Career:* Pop singer, No. 1 in list of Bulgarian National TV and radio for over 10 years; Tours: Germany; Belgium; Canada; Romania; Poland; Cuba; Republics of former USSR; First success with: Adaption, 1979. *Recordings:* 5 albums; 2 singles including Seven Times; Composes most of own material. *Honours:* Second place, Eurovision, Belgium; International prizes in Cuba, 1982; USSR; Belgium; Canada; The Golden Orpheus Festival: First prize, 1981; Second prize, 1982; Silver Orpheus, 1983; Prizes for television show, Melody of The Year, 1979, 1982–84, 1986. *Membership:* Union of Bulgarian Musicians. *Leisure interests:* Antiques; Growing flowers. *Current Management:* Ivailo Manolov. *Address:* 91-A Vitosha Blvd, 1408 Sofia, Bulgaria.

NAIL Jimmy, (James Michael Aloyisius Bradford); b. 1954, Newcastle upon Tyne, England. Singer; Actor. *Career:* Actor, UK television series, Auf Wiedersehen Pet, ITV; Co-writer, actor, Spender, BBC; Actor, Crocodile Shoes, BBC; Solo recording artiste, 1992–; Own company, Big Boy Productions. *Recordings:* Singles: Love Don't Live Here Anymore; Ain't No Doubt; Crocodile Shoes; Albums: Growing Up In Public, 1992; Crocodile Shoes, 1994; Big River, 1995; Crocodile Shoes II, 1996; The Nail File: The Best of Jimmy Nail, 1997; Appeared on: Gary Moore, We Want Moore, 1984; Greatest Hits of the 90's, 1994; Now That's What I Call Music, 1995; Evita, 1996; Carnival: Rainforest Foundation, 1997; Madonna, Selections from Evita, 1997. *Honours:* Great British Country Music Awards: Best Album, Best Song, 1996. *Current Management:* Fairwarning / Wasted Talent, London, England. *Address:* c/o East West Records, Electric Lighting Station, 46 Kensington Court, London W8 5DP, England.

NAINIA Farid; b. Morocco. Vocalist; Musician (lothar, percussion). *Career:* Left Morocco for London, 1980s; Founder member of band MoMo (Music of Moroccan Origin); Act's fusion of North African Gnawa music with western-style drum kit, samples and contemporary dance styles (including house and garage) described as 'Dar'; Popular live band; Released first album, 2001. *Recordings:* Album: The Birth of Dar, 2001. *Honour:* BBC Radio 3 Award for World Music, Boundary Crossing nominee, The Birth of Dar, 2002.

NAISSOO Tonu; b. 18 March 1951, Tallinn, Estonia. Jazz Musician (piano); Composer. m. Kersti Johanson, 8 July 1977, 1 s., 1 d. *Musical Education:* Diplomas in Theory of Music, Tallinn Music School, Estonia, 1970; Composition, Tallinn State Conservatory, Estonia, 1982; Postgraduate studies, Berklee College of Music, Boston, USA (scholarship), 1989–90. *Career:* Jazz pianist, bandleader (trio, quartet), solo pianist, 1967–; Keyboardist, pop/showgroup Laine, 1972–76; As solo artiste or with Tonu Naissoo Trio/Quartet: Jazz festivals, solo concerts, former Soviet Union, 1978–89; Jazz pianist, sideman, international projects: EBU Big Band, Pori Jazz, Finland, 1985; Trio Eckert-Gaivoronski-Naissoo, Turku Jazz, Finland, 1992; Baltic Trio, Schleswig-Holstein Musik Festival, Germany, 1992; Vladimir Tarasov's Baltic Art Orchestra, Jazz Baltica, 1994; Munster Jazz Festival, Germany, 1994; Pianist, soloist, Alfred Schnittke's First Symphony, Symphony Orchestra of the USSR Ministry of Culture, 1987; Boston Symphony Orchestra, US premiere, 1988; Rotterdam Symphony Orchestra, Netherlands premiere, 1991; Pianist, entertainer, 1991-. *Compositions:* For films, television, theatre,

1969–; Jazz: First Flight, 1981; A Time There Was, 1983. *Recordings:* Tonu Naissoo Trio, 1968; Turning Point, 1980; Dedication, 1993. *Honour:* Music of The Year, Estonian Radio, 1991. *Membership:* Estonian Composers' Union, 1984. *Leisure interests:* Architecture; Aviation. *Current Management:* Jazzkaar Festival Management. *Address:* Estonian Radio, Jazzkaar, Gonsiori 21, EE 0100 Tallinn, Estonia.

NAPOLEON Marty; b. 2 June 1921, Brooklyn, New York, USA. Musician (piano). m. Marie Giordano, 15 May 1921, 1 s., 1 d. *Career:* Jazz pianist, 1941–; Played with numerous artists including: Gene Krupa; Benny Goodman; Louis Armstrong's All-Stars; Bob Crosby's Bobcats; Red Norvo; Major concerts include: Odessa Jazz Festival, Texas; Berne Jazz Festival; Carnegie Hall (with Frank Sinatra); Command Performance at the White House with Lionel Hampton Sextet; Nice Jazz Festival; North Sea Jazz Festival; Downtown Jazz Festival, Toronto; Film appearances: Glenn Miller Story; All That Jazz; Tootsie; Raging Bull. *Recordings with:* Charles Barnet; Louis Armstrong; Lionel Hampton, including Louis Armstrong, Hello Dolly, 1963. *Membership:* ASCAP.

NAS (Nasir Jones), (Nas Escobar, Nasty Nas); b. 1973, Queensbridge, New York, USA. Rapper. *Career:* Made first appearance aged 18 with Main Source on Live At The Barbecue, 1991; First solo effort Halftime appeared on Zebrahead soundtrack; Signed to Columbia with assistance of third Bass' MC Serch; Released debut album Illmatic, 1994; Collaborations: Will Smith; Puff Daddy; Missy Elliott; Notorious BIG; Mary J Blige; Allure; R Kelly. *Recordings:* Albums: Illmatic, 1994; It Was Written, 1996; I Am, 1999; Nastradamus, 2001; Singles: It Ain't Hard To Tell, 1994; If I Ruled The World, 1996; Hate Me Now, 1999; Nastradamus, 1999; Got Urself A Gun, 2002. *Address:* c/o Columbia Records, 550 Madison Ave, New York, USA.

NASH Graham; b. 2 Feb. 1942, Blackpool, Lancashire, England. Vocalist; Musician (guitar). m. Susan. *Career:* Touring musician with the Hollies; Member, Crosby Stills and Nash, 1968–; Also Crosby, Stills, Nash and Young; Also solo recording artiste; Performances include: Woodstock Festival, 1969; Altamont Speedway, with the Rolling Stones, 1969; Royal Albert Hall, 1970; Wembley Stadium, 1974; California benefit concerts with Jackson Browne, 1979; Anti-nuclear benefits, Madison Square Garden, 1979; Peace Sunday concert, Rose Bowl, California, 1982; Live Aid, Philadelphia, 1985; Madison Square Garden, New York, 1988; Amnesty International benefit concert, Chile, 1990; Television includes: Presenter, The Inside Track, interview show, cable TV, 1990. *Recordings:* Albums: with Crosby Stills and Nash: Crosby Stills and Nash, 1969; Déjà Vu, 1970; 4-Way Street, 1971; So Far, 1974; Replay, 1981; Daylight Again, 1982; Allies, 1983; Innocent Eyes, 1986; American Dream, 1989; Live It Up, 1990; Solo albums: Songs For Beginners, 1971; Wild Tales, 1974; Earth and Sky, 1980; Innocent Eyes, 1986; with David Crosby: Graham Nash/David Crosby, 1972; Wind On The Water, 1975; Whistling Down The Wire, 1976; Crosby/Nash Live, 1977; The Best Of, 1978; Singles include: Woodstock, 1970; Teach Your Children, 1970; Just A Song Before I Go, 1977; Wasted On The Way, 1982; with Neil Young, On the Beach, 1974; Zuma, 1975; with Carole King, Thoroughbred, 1976; In Concert, 1994. *Honours include:* Grammy Award, Best New Artists, 1970. *Current Management:* Management Network Inc, 346 N Larchmont Blvd, Los Angeles, CA 90004, USA.

NASH Johnny (John Lester); b. 9 Aug. 1940, Houston, Texas, USA. Singer; Actor. *Career:* Lead soprano, gospel choir; Film appearances include: Take A Giant Step, 1958; Key Witness, 1960; Singer on television variety show and as member, Teen Commandments (with Paul Anka and George Hamilton IV); Solo recording artiste, 1960s-70s; Now involved in recording and production. *Recordings:* Albums: Hold Me Tight, 1968; Let's Go Dancing, 1969; I Can See Clearly Now, 1972; My Merry-Go-Round, 1973; What A Wonderful World, 1977; Stir It Up, 1981; Johnny Nash, 1985; Here Again, 1986; Tears On My Pillow, 1987; The Very Best of Johnny Nash, 1995; The Best of Johnny Nash, 1996; Singles include: Let's Move and Groove Together, 1965; Hold Me Tight, 1969; You Got Soul, 1969; Cupid, 1969; Stir It Up (written by Bob Marley), 1971; I Can See Clearly Now, 1972; There Are More Questions Than Answers, 1972; Tears On My Pillow (No. 1, UK), 1975; Appears on: Bob Marley, Songs of Freedom, 1992; Rock to the Rock, 1998; Complete Bob Marley and the Wailers, 1998; Grosse Pointe Blank, Grosse Pointe Blank, 1997.

NASH Paul; b. 19 Feb. 1948, New York, New York, USA. Composer; Dir, Manhattan New Music Project. m. Marta Danciu, 3 Oct. 1998. *Education:* Graduate Work, Public Management, New York University, 1992; BM, Composition, Berklee College of Music, 1969; MA, Composition, Mills College, 1976; Graduate Studies, University of California at Berkeley,

1986. *Career:* JVC Jazz Festival appearance, Carnegie Hall, with Manhattan New Music Project, 1997; New York club appearances at Sweet Basil, The Fez, New School. *Compositions:* Wind Over the Lake, San Francisco Chamber Symphony, 1989; Synchronicity, Manhattan New Music Project, 1991; Intimate Structures, for two actors and electronic tape, presented by Downtown Arts Festival, 1998; Collage (flute, violin, clarinet, trumpet and cello), commissioned and performed by St Luke's Chamber Ensemble, 1999. *Recordings:* Paul Nash: A Jazz Composers Ensemble, 1979; Night Language, 1984; Musical Heritage Society, 1987; Mood Swing, 1993; Second Impression, Soul Note 1985 Reissued, 1997; Soul of Grace, 1999. *Publications:* University of Northern Colorado (UNC) Jazz Press, Advance Music (Germany); A Practical Guide to Polyrhythms, 1980. *Membership:* BMI. *Address:* 400 W 43rd St 32-A, New York, NY 10036, USA.

NASH Rob; b. 30 May 1956, Boston, Lincolnshire, England. Vocal Coach; Musician (keyboards, guitar). m. Nic Bagguley, 7 Nov. 1989, 3 s., 1 d. *Education:* Loughborough University. *Musical Education:* Ely Cathedral Chorister; Cambridge College of Arts and Technology. *Career:* Vocal coach to Michael Barrymore, for television series Barrymore; Jeremy Irons, for films The Lion King; Chorus of Disapproval; Work with Marc Almond; Simon Climie; Dion Estes; Stephanie Lawrence; Colin Blunstone; Nick Cave. *Recordings:* Work includes: Phantom of The Opera, A Touch of Music in the Night, Michael Crawford; Weather in the Heart, Carmina; Solo albums: With Love; A Touch of Music In The Night; Also forthcoming album from Carmina, producer Donal Lunny. *Honour:* Vivien Ellis Awards, 1990. *Memberships:* Equity; Musicians' Union. *Leisure interest:* Literature. *Current Management:* Bagmusic. *Address:* 31 Tyne St, St Werburgh, Bristol BS2 9UA, England.

NASTANOVICH Bob; b. 1968, Rochester, New York, USA. Musician (Drums). *Career:* Member, Pavement; Released first EP on own label, soon obtained indie label deal; Numerous headlining tours; Appeared in cartoon Space Ghost Coast to Coast, 1997. *Recordings:* Singles: Perfect Sound Forever EP, 1990; Watery, Domestic EP, 1992; Trigger Cut, 1992; Cut Your Hair, 1994; Gold Soundz, 1994; Range Life, 1995; Rattled by La Rush, 1995; Father to a Sister of Thought, 1995; Pacific Trim EP, 1996; Stereo, 1997; Shady Lane EP, 1997; Spit on a Stranger, 1999; Albums: Slanted and Enchanted, 1992; Crooked Rain, Crooked Rain, 1994; Wowee Zowee, 1995; Brighten the Corners, 1997; Terror Twilight, 1999.

NATCH (Ian Mallett); b. 28 July 1945, Birmingham, England. Songwriter; Musician (bass guitar). Divorced, 3 s., 1 d. *Musical Education:* Self-taught. *Career:* Member, group Renegades; Toured extensively in Finland, Sweden, Germany and Italy; Television appearances in several countries, including San Remo Song Festival, 1966; Currently re-launching career. *Recordings:* Cadillac, Renegades; Several albums and singles recorded, 1960s; Compilations continue to be released. *Publication:* Cracking An Ancient Code. *Memberships:* PRS; MCPS; Songwriting Guild. *Leisure interest:* Writing. *Address:* La Louisiane, 4 Tynedale, Whitby, South Wirral L65 6RB, England.

NAUMOV Julian; Musician (drums). *Career:* Member, Concurrent, 1986–; Numerous concerts, television and radio appearances. *Recordings:* Rock For Peace, 1988; Rock Festival In Mitchurin, 1989; The Black Sheep (rock collection), 1992; Something Wet (best-selling album, Bulgaria), 1994; The Best of Bulgarian Rock, 1995. *Honours:* First Prizes; Top Rock Band, Youth Festival, Vidin, 1989; Rock Ring, Sofia, 1990; Top Rock Composition: The Cavalry, 1991; Group of The Year, The Darik Radio Countdown, 1994. *Address:* 40 St Stambolov Blvd, 1202 Sofia, Bulgaria.

NAWASADIO Sylvie, (Kihanga); b. 8 Jan. 1965, Ixelles, Belgium. Member of Zap Mama, from debut until 1995; Member, Barut Trio. *Composition:* Sab Syl Ma. *Recordings:* 2 albums with Zap Mama: Zap Mama; Sab Syl Ma; Album with Barut Trio, Ndugu Yangu; Recordings with Toni Child: The Womans Boat; Sally Nyolo: Tribu; Multiculti; Beti; Kadja Nin: Free; Uinckx: I love My Job; Jaques Higelin: Au Rex; Paradis Païen; Arthur H: Bachibouzouk; H Felix Thiéfaine: Le bonheur de la tentation; Documentaries: Y-a-t'-il une femme noire dans cette ville?, 1998; La voix dans tous ses états, 2000. *Honours:* Golden Disc for Album Zap Mama, 1993; Nominated for Grammy Award, with Zap Mama, 1994; Prize, SABAM, 1997. *Address:* 37 rue de l'Avenir, 1080 Brussels, Belgium.

N'DOUR Youssou; b. 1959, Dakar, Senegal. Musician; Singer; Songwriter. *Career:* Member, Sine Dramatic, 1972; Orchestre Diamono, 1975; The Star Band (houseband, Dakar nightclub, the Miami Club), 1976–79; Founder, Etoile De Dakar, 1979; Re-formed as Super Etoile De Dakar, 1982–; International tours include support to Peter Gabriel, US tour, 1987. *Recordings:* Albums: A Abijan, 1980; Xalis, 1980; Tabaski, 1981; Thiapathioly, 1983; Absa Gueye, 1983; Immigres, 1984; Nelson Mandela, 1985; The Lion, 1989; African Editions Vols 5–14, 1990; Africa Deebeub, 1990; Jamm La Prix, 1990; Kocc Barma, 1990; Set, 1990; Eyes Open, 1992; The Best of Youssou N'Dour, 1994; The Guide, 1995; Gainde – Voices From The Heart of Africa (with Yande Codou Sene), 1996; Immigrés/Bitim Rew,

1997; Inedits 84–85, 1997; Hey You: The Essential Collection, 1988–90; Best of the 80's, 1998; Special Fin D'annee Plus Djamil, 1999; Joko, 2000; Hit single: Seven Seconds, duet with Neneh Cherry, 1995; How Come Shakin' the Tree, 1998; Recorded with: Paul Simon, Graceland, 1986; Lou Reed, Between Thought and Expression, 1992; Otis Reading, Otis! The Definitive Otis Reading, 1993; Manu Dibango, Wafrika, 1994; Cheikh Lo, Ne La Thiass, 1996; Alan Stivell, I Dour, 1998. *Current Management:* Soundscape, 799 Greenwich St, New York, NY 10014, USA.

NEDELCHEV Boyko; b. 24 April 1965, Rousse, Bulgaria. Singer; Songwriter; Composer. *Career:* Singer, songwriter and composer with brother Deyan, 1987–; Appearances: Many festivals, concerts, television and radio appearances: Bulgaria; Russia; Kazakhstan; Mongolia; Egypt; Italy; Tour of Mediterranean; Romania. *Recordings:* A Plea To The World, 1990; A Game of Love, 1991; Madly In Love, 1992; The Best of Deyan and Boyko Nedelchev, 1993; Love and Dream, 1993; La Mia Musica, 1994; Love For Love, 1994; The Hits of Deyan and Boyko Nedelchev, 1995; Atlanta, 1996; Brothers, 1996; Gently News, 1997; Grande Amore, 1998. *Honours:* Awards received from: Contest for Youth Pop Singers, 1988–89; Union of Bulgarian Writers, 1989–90, 1992, 1996; Grand Prix, Nashville, USA, 1989; Golden Orpheus International Festival, Bulgaria, 1990, 1993–96; International Festival of Melody of the Friends, Ulan-Bator, Mongolia, 1990; Step To Parnasus International Festival, Moscow, Russia, 1994; Voice of Asia International Festival, Kazakhstan, 1995; International Song Festival, Cairo, Egypt, 1995–97; Silver Eros Festival, Bulgaria, 1996; Golden Stang International Festival, Romania, 1996; Love Duets Festival, Bulgaria, 1996; Annual National Music Awards, Bulgaria, 1996–98; South Pacific International Song Contest, Australia, 1998. *Membership:* FIDOF. *Leisure interests:* Music; Sport; Cinema. *Address:* Lipnik Blvd 62, Entr G, Ap 16, 7005 Rousse, Bulgaria.

NEDELCHEV Deyan; b. 16 Jan. 1964, Rousse, Bulgaria. Singer; Songwriter; Composer. *Career:* Singer, songwriter, composer with brother Boyko, 1987–; Signed 3 year contract with Poly Gram, South Africa; Appearances: Many festivals, concerts, television appearances and radio broadcasts: Bulgaria; Russia; Kazakhstan; Mongolia; Egypt; Italy; Tour, Mediterranean; South Africa. *Recordings:* Albums: A Plea To The World, 1990; A Game of Love, 1991; Madly In Love, 1992; The Best of Deyan and Boyko Nedeltchev, 1993; Love-dream; Dedication, 1993; Love For Love, 1994; La Mia Musica, 1994; The Hits of Deyan and Boyko Nedelchev, 1995; Brothers, 1996; Atlanta, 1996; Gently News, 1997; Grande Amore, 1998. *Honours:* Awards received from: Contest for Youth Pop Singers, Bulgaria, 1988–89; Union of Bulgarian Writers, 1989–90, 1992, 1996; Grand Prix, Nashville, USA, 1989; The Golden Orpheus International Festival, Bulgaria, 1990, 1993–96; International Festival of Melody of The Friends, Ulan-Bator, Mongolia, 1990; Step To Parnasus International Festival, Moscow, Russia, 1994; Voice of Asia International Festival, Kazakhstan, 1995; International Song Festival, Cairo, Egypt, 1995–97; Silver Eros Festival, Bulgaria, 1996; Golden Stang International Festival, Romania, 1996; Love Duets Festival, Bulgaria, 1996; Annual National Music Awards, Bulgaria, 1996, 1998; South Pacific International Song Contest, Australia, 1998. *Current Management:* Poly Gram, Johannesburg, South Africa. *Address:* Lipnik Blvd 62, Entr G, Ap 16, 7005 Rousse, Bulgaria.

NEECE Timothy G; b. 2 Oct. 1946, Abilene, Texas, USA. Artist Man. m. (1) Lynda Hunnicutt, 1 d.; (2) Deborah Chaffey, 12 June 1988. *Education:* BA, Business, McMurry University. *Musical Education:* 8 years experience as musician (drums). *Career:* Manager, prior to release and through 3 albums for Christopher Cross; Bruce Hornsby and the Range; Charlie Sexton; Manager, Rickie Lee Jones during Flying Cowboys release. *Honours:* Launched careers of 2 Best New Artist Grammy Award Winners; Many Gold, Platinum awards world-wide for artists managed. *Leisure interest:* Golf.

NEFF John; b. 13 March 1951, Birmingham, Michigan, USA. Recording Engineer; Prod.; Instrumentalist; Musician. m. Nancy L B Neff, 2 s., 1 d. *Career:* Chief Engineer, David Lynch's Asymmetrical Studio; Re-Recording Mixer, The Straight Story, Mulholland Drive; Engineer, Waltor Becker Donald Faven; Morning Radio Host. *Compositions:* The Straight Story; Mulholland Drive; Lux Vivens. *Recordings:* Lux Vivens; Kamakiriad; Eleven Tracks of Wuack; Coincidences and Likely Stories; Jimmy' Road. *Honour:* Grammy Nomination, Best Album, 1993. *Memberships:* ASCAP; Audio Engineering Society. *Leisure interests:* Photography; Travel. *Current Management:* Audio Engineering Services. *Address:* PO Box 931558, Hollywood, CA 90093, USA.

NEGRAO Mario Borganovi; b. 18 Nov. 1945. Musician (Drums, Percussion, Flute). m. Sonia Dias, 2 s. *Education:* Studies with maestro Guirra Peixe. *Career:* Drummer in showa with Brazilian artists including Chico Buarque Vinicius de Moraes, Quartet em CY, Leila Pinheiro, Baden Powell; Worked with ensembles including the Brazilian Symphony Orchestra, Rio Jazz Orchestra, Bebeto (Tamba Trio), Edson Lobo and Osmar Milito; Participated in shows in Brazil with Toquinho, Vinicius and Clara Nunes, in the Sistine Theatre with Chico Buarque, Italy, in

Mexico with local orchestras, in Argentina, with Chico Buarque, Marília Barbosa, Maria Creuza, Toquinho, Vicinius and MPB4. *Compositions:* Canela de Velho; Fruta Doce; Mata Mato; Joao Mole; Orelma de Onca; Farinma Seca; Respina Fundo e Zaratudo. *Recordings:* Solo album of his own compositions; With other artists including Chico Buarque, Aresar de Voce, Calicz and Homenagem ao Malandao, Vinicius, Toquinho, Regna Très, Samba de Orly. *Honour:* Best Instrumental Recording in Originality, Critic of Panama State in Brazil, for solo album. *Address:* Rua Dois, Manga Larga, Itaipava, 92288 Petrópolis, Brazil.

NEGRIJN Thomas; b. 19 Oct. 1959, Copenhagen, Denmark. Lead Vocalist; Musician (guitar). *Education:* Art glazier 7 years. *Musical Education:* H F Music School in Copenhagen. *Career:* Own first big band, Simcess, 1985–92; Played Roskilde Festival, Denmark, 5 times; Midfyn Festival, 6 times, including 2 times on biggest stage for 30,000 – 40,000 people; Many Danish television and radio appearances; Tours: Denmark; Europe; Founder, new band Blink, 1995–; Released EP, toured Denmark, making new album. *Recordings:* with Simcess: Play With Your Life, 1988; The House, 1990; with Tam Tam Top: Secrets, 1993; with Blink: Blink, 1994. *Honour:* Title: John (Lennon) Award, Best Band, Copenhagen, 1987. *Membership:* Danish Society For Jazz Rock Folk Composers. *Leisure interests:* Sports; Football; Tennis; Basketball; Photography; Nature; Books; Listening to music; Family and friends. *Current Management:* Off Beat, Norsgade 26–28, 8000 Århus C, Denmark. *Address:* Hjort Lorenzensgade 6 4tv, 2200 Copenhagen N, Denmark.

NEIL Vince, (Vincent Neil Wharton); b. 8 Feb. 1961, Hollywood, California, USA. Singer. *Career:* Singer, Rock Candy; Member, US heavy rock group Mötley Crüe, 1981–92; World-wide concerts include: Tours with: YandT, 1981, 1982; Kiss, 1983; Ozzy Osbourne, 1984; Iron Maiden, 1984; Cheap Trick, 1986; Theatre of Pain World Tour, 1985–86; World tours, 1987, 1989; Major festivals: US festival, 1983; Monsters of Rock Festival, Castle Donington, 1984; Moscow Music Peace Festival, 1989; Actor, film The Adventures of Ford Fairlane, 1990; Solo artiste, 1992-. *Recordings:* Albums: with Mötley Crüe: Too Fast For Love, 1981; Shout At The Devil, 1983; Theatre of Pain, 1985; Girls, Girls, Girls, 1987; Dr Feelgood (No. 1, USA), 1989; Decade of Decadence, 1991; Generation Swine, 1997; Solo: Exposed, 1993; Carved In Stone, 1995; Singles: with Mötley Crüe: Stick To Your Guns, 1981; Looks That Kill, 1984; Too Young To Fall In Love, 1984; Smokin' In The Boys Room, 1985; Home Sweet Home, 1985; You're All I Need, 1987; Dr Feelgood, 1989; Kick Start My Heart, 1990; Without You, 1990; Don't Go Away Mad, 1990; Same Old Situation, 1990; Primal Scream, 1991; Solo hit: You're Invited But Your Friend Can't Come, from film Encino Man, 1992; Can't Change Me, 1993; Contributor, Stars, Hear 'n' Aid, 1985. *Honours:* Rolling Stone Readers Poll Winners, Best Heavy Metal Band, 1991; American Music Award, Favorite Heavy Metal Album, 1991. *Current Management:* Burt Stein Entertainment Co, 1514 South St, Suite 100, Nashville TN 37203, USA.

NEILL Kevin; b. 25 July 1931, Manchester, England. Musician (lead electric guitar, acoustic guitar, trombone). m. Claire Cregan, 6 April 1953, 2 d. *Career:* Johnny Ray tour, 1954; Royal Command Performance, Oh Boy, 1959; Anthony Newley Tour, 1960; Don Lang and Frantic Five; Princess Margaret's state wedding ball, with Joe Loss Orchestra, Buckingham Palace; Accompanied Vera Lynn, Frankie Vaughn; Frankie Laine; Vic Lewis Orchestra; Eric Winstone Orchestra; BBC Northern Variety Orchestra; BBC Midland Orchestra; Karl Denver Trio, 26 years; Joined John Stokes to reform The Bachelors, 1996. *Compositions:* Points North; Singin' and Swingin'. *Recordings:* Hits with Karl Denver Trio: Whimoweh; Marcheta; Mexicali Rose; Love Me With All Your Heart; Still; Sleepy Lagoon; Just A Little Love; Never Goodbye (Eurovision Song Contest entry); Harry Lime Theme; Re-recorded all The Bachelors' hits, among others: Charmaine; Diane; Ramona; I Believe. *Honours:* Examiner, electric guitar, The London College of Music; Awarded Special Achievement Award from Irish World Newspaper, 1999. *Memberships:* Vaudeville Golf Society; Variety Club Golf Society. *Leisure interest:* Golf. *Address:* 69 Polefield Rd, Blackly, Manchester M9 7EN, England.

NELSON Bonita Rae, (Bonnie Nelson); b. 4 Nov. 1949, Denver, Colorado, USA. *Career:* Ralph Emery Radio Show; Tenn Network Show; Nashville Now; German ZDE TV Special; Centecor Drug Programme; Donna Fargo Special; Girl in My Life, TV; NBC's Real People. *Recordings:* 9 albums; 16 singles; Double CD; 5 charted records nationally. *Publication:* Book, It's Not Luck, It's God, 1998. *Honour:* Entertainer and Female Vocalist, Colorado and New York, State Country Music Asscn. *Leisure interest:* Music. *Address:* PO Box 25050, Nashville, TN 37202, USA.

NELSON Matthew Edward; b. 20 March 1968, Colne, England. Singer; Songwriter. *Education:* Hotel and Catering Management, Manchester Polytechnic, 1988–89. *Career:* Lead singer with Milltown Brothers, appearing 5 times on television, touring Britain, USA, Europe and Japan, and appearing at various British Festivals. *Compositions:* Wrote songs for the BBC TV series, All Quiet On The Preston Front. *Recordings:*

Albums: Slinky; Valve; 5 Singles in UK Top 40. *Membership:* Performing Rights Society. *Leisure interests:* Golf; Cricket; Football; Rugby; Chinese and Italian cooking; Cycling. *Address:* Forest House, Forest Lane, Barrowford, Nelson, Lancashire BB9 6QL, England.

NELSON Shara; b. London, England. Singer; Songwriter. *Career:* Singer, Massive Attack; Solo artiste. *Recordings:* Album with Massive Attack: Blue Lines, 1991; Solo albums: What Silence Knows, 1993; Down That Road, 1994; Friendly Fire, 1995; Hit singles: Rough With The Smooth; I Fell; Appears on: Ref, Ref, 1994; Guru, Jazzmatazz Vol. 2, 1995; Air Cuba, Leap of Faith, 1999. *Honours:* Mercury Music Prize Nomination, What Silence Knows; BRIT Award Nominations, Best Female Singer, 1994, 1995. *Current Management:* Def Mix Productions, 938 Broadway, Suite 400, New York, NY 10010, USA.

NELSON Tracy; b. 27 Dec. 1944, Madison, Wisconsin, USA. Singer; Musician. *Education:* 2 years college. *Career:* Lead singer, Mother Earth, 1968–73; Solo artist, 1965-. *Recordings:* Albums: with Mother Earth: Living With The Animals, 1968; Make A Joyful Noise, 1969; Mother Earth Presents – Tracy Nelson Country, 1970; Satisfied, 1970; Bring Me Home, 1971; Tracy Nelson / Mother Earth, 1972; Poor Man's Paradise, 1973; Solo albums: Deep Are The Roots, 1965; Tracy Nelson, 1974; Sweet Soul Music, 1975; Time Is On My Side, 1976; Doin' It My Way, 1978; Homemade Songs, 1978; Come See About Me, 1980; In The Here and Now, 1993; I Feel So Good, 1995; Move On, 1996; Tracy Nelson Country, 1996; The Best of Tracy Nelson/Mother Earth, 1996. *Honours:* Grammy Nomination, with Willie Nelson, 1974; Nashville Music Award, Best Blues Album, 1996; 2 WC Handy Award Nominations, Best Female Vocalist. *Leisure interests:* Gardening; Animals. *Current Management:* Julie Devereux, Lucks Management, 817 18th Ave S, Nashville, TN 37203, USA; Agent: Ronnie Narmour, RNA, PO Box 19289, Austin, TX 78760, USA.

NELSON Trevor; b. 7 Jan. 1964. DJ. *Career:* Founder Member, Kiss FM Radio, London; Joined BBC Radio 1 after 10 years; Head of A & R, EMI's Cooltempo label; Club DJ sessions all over Europe; Presents Trevor Nelson's Rhythm Nation, Radio 1, 1996–; Video Jockey on MTV satellite channel. *Honour:* Best DJ, MOBO (Music of Black Origin) Awards, 1999.

NELSON Willie (Hugh); b. 30 April 1933, Abbott, Texas, USA. Country and Western Singer; Musician; Songwriter. m. Annie Marie Nelson, 3 s., 4 d. *Education:* Baylor University. *Career:* Salesman; Announcer; Host and DJ, Country music shows, Texas; Bass player, Ray Price's band; Formed own band; Appearances, Grand Ole Opry, Nashville, and throughout USA, 1964–; Tours: New Zealand; Australia; USA; Canada; Europe; Japan; Annual Fourth of July Picnics throughout USA, 1972–; Performed with: Frank Sinatra; Neil Young; Dolly Parton; Linda Ronstadt; ZZ Top; Waylon Jennings; Ray Charles; Santana; Joni Mitchell; Kris Kristofferson; Bob Dylan; Patsy Cline; Film appearances include: Electric Horseman, 1980; Honeysuckle Rose, 1980. *Compositions include:* Crazy, No. 1 for Patsy Cline; Hello Walls, No. 1 for Faron Young. *Recordings:* Albums include: The Sound In Your Mind, 1976; The Troublemaker, 1976; Willie Nelson and His Friends, 1976; To Lefty From Willie, 1977; Willie Before His Time, 1978; Wanted/The Outlaw, 1978; The Willie Way, 1978; The Best of Willie Nelson, 1978; Stardust, 1978; One For The Road, 1979; Willie and Family Live, 1979; Pretty Paper, 1979; Willie Sings Kristofferson, 1979; San Antonio Rose, 1980; Honeysuckle Rose, 1980; Family Bible, 1980; Tougher Than Leather, 1983; City of New Orleans, 1984; Me and Paul, 1985; Highwayman, 1985; The Promised Land, 1986; Partners, 1986; Island In The Sea, 1987; Seashores of Old Mexico, 1987; What A Wonderful World, 1988; A Horse Called Music, 1989; Highwayman II, 1990; Born For Trouble, 1990; Clean Shirt Waylon and Willie, 1991; Across The Borderline, 1993; Six Hours At Pedernales, 1994; Healing Hands of Time, 1994; Just One Love, 1995; Spirit, 1996; How Great Thou Art, 1996; Christmas with Willie Nelson, 1997; Hill Country Christmas, 1997; Teatro, 1998; Nashville was the Roughest, 1998; The Very Best of Willie Nelson, 1999; Night and Day, 1999; Forever Gold, 2000. *Honours:* 5 Grammy (NARAS) Awards; 8 CMA Awards; Nashville Songwriters Asscn, Hall of Fame, 1973; Playboy Hall of Fame, 1983; National Academy of Popular Music, Lifetime Achievement Award, 1983 (fourth-ever recipient); 3 ACM Awards; Tex Ritter Songwriting Award, with Kris Kristofferson, 1984; 25 Platinum and Gold albums. *Leisure interests:* Golf; Running; Swimming; Weight-lifting; Yoga. *Current Management:* Mark Rothbaum and Associates. *Address:* c/o Mark Rothbaum and Assocs Inc, PO Box 2689, Danbury, CT 06813–2689, USA.

NELSON-SMITH Simon; Musician (Guitar). *Career:* Former member, Boys Wonder; Formed Corduroy for one-off gig; Decided to continue and obtained record deal; Several UK top ten hits. *Recordings:* Singles: Something in My Eye; The Frighteners; London, England; The Joker is Wild; Overhaul; Albums: Dad Man Cat, 1992; High Havoc, 1993; Out of Here, 1994; The New You, 1997.

NERNEY Declan James; b. 20 May 1956, Drumlish, Ireland. Singer; Musician (lead guitar). *Career:* Played with Gene Stuart plus Brien Coll;

Solo artiste; Played for interval BAA Senior Football Final, Crough Park, Dublin, 1990; 3 US tours, 1995; Australian tour. *Recordings:* Picture of My World; Going Places; 3 Way Love Affair; Walking On New Grass; Lucky I Guess; Let's Dance, Album; Part of The Journey. *Honours:* 4 Gold discs; Finalist, Person of The Year, 1994; Band of The Year, Irish World Awards, 1994. *Current Management:* Frank Kilbride. *Address:* Main St, Edgeworthsown, Co Longford, Ireland.

NESBO Jo; b. Molde, Norway. Singer; Songwriter. *Education:* MBA (Master of Business Administration). *Career:* Singer, songwriter, Di Derre; 180 concerts, 1994–95. *Recordings:* Di Derre: Den Derre (Gold disc, Norway) 1992; Jenter and Sånn (Triple Platinum disc, Norway), 1994. *Current Management:* Artist Partner AS.

NESMITH (Robert) Michael; b. 30 Dec. 1942, Houston, Texas, USA. Singer; Songwriter; Musician (guitar); Actor. *Career:* Folk duo, Mike and John, with John London, 1965; Member, The Monkees, 1966–69; Actor, Monkees television series, 1966–68; 33 1/3 Revolutions Per Monkee (NBC Special); Founder, First National Band, 1970; Reformed as Second National Band, 1972; Founder, President, own Countryside and Pacific Arts Corporation, record labels, 1974; Financed and produced films Repo Man; Elephant Parts; Time Rider. *Recordings:* Albums with the Monkees: The Monkees (No. 1, USA and UK), 1966; More of The Monkees (No. 1, USA and UK), 1967; Headquarters (No. 1, USA), 1967; Pisces, Aquarius, Capricorn and Jones Ltd (No. 1, UK), 1967; The Birds, The Bees and The Monkees, 1968; Head (soundtrack), 1969; The Monkees Greatest Hits, 1969; The Monkees Present, 1969; Solo albums: The Wichita Train Whistle Sings, 1968; Magnetic South, 1970; Treason, 1972; And The Hits Just Keep On Comin', 1972; Pretty Much Your Standard Ranch Hash, 1973; The Prison, 1974; From A Radio Engine To The Photon Wing, 1977; Live At The Palais, 1978; Infinite Rider On The Big Dogma, 1979; Tropical Campfires, 1992; The Garden, 1994; Listen To The Band, 1997; Hit singles with The Monkees: Last Train To Clarksville (No. 1, USA), 1966; I'm A Believer (No. 1, USA and UK), 1966; (I'm Not Your) Steppin' Stone, 1967; A Little Bit Me, A Little Bit You, 1967; Alternate Title, 1967; Pleasant Valley Sunday, 1967; Daydream Believer (No. 1, USA), 1967; Valleri, 1968; Tear Drop City, 1969; Solo singles: Joanne, 1970; Silver Moon, 1971; Rio, 1977. *Publication:* The Prison, 1974. *Honours include:* NARM Awards, Best Selling Group, Best Album, 1967; Emmy Award, Outstanding Comedy Series, 1967; 3 BMI Awards, 1968; Grammy Award, for video Elephant Parts, 1982; Monkees Day, Atlanta, 1986; Star on Hollywood Walk of Fame, 1989.

NESTOROVIC Sascha; b. 27 Aug. 1964, Zagreb, Croatia. Musician (saxophone); Composer; Arranger. m. Vlasta Gyrura, 9 Nov. 1993. *Musical Education:* Zagreb Academy of Music. *Career:* First alto in big band, Croatian State Television; Live concerts with Zagreb Saxophone Quartet, Muscora, Paris; World Saxophone Congress, Pesaro, Italy; Tours with Zagreb Jazz Portrait: Germany; Austria; Italy; France. *Recordings:* with Zagreb Saxophone Quartet: Croatian Contemporary Music for Saxophones; Zagreb 900; with Slovenian RTV Big Band: Peter Herbolzheimer; Moments Notice, Zagreb Jazz Portrait. *Honours:* Classical awards: Darko Lukic; Milka Trnina. *Memberships:* Croatian Musicians' Union; Jazz Club Zagreb. *Leisure interests:* Chess playing; Plants. *Current Management:* Vesna Vrandecic, Zitnjak 1, 10000 Zagreb. *Address:* Sascha Nestorovic, Kustossijanska 316, 10000 Zagreb, Croatia.

NETTLETON Christopher; b. 25 Sept. 1968, Cardiff, Wales. Singer; Songwriter; Composer; Musician (guitar, keyboards). *Musical Education:* 8 years, formal piano study; Guitar, self-taught. *Career:* Played with Hollyweird, 1989–92; Played with The Nubiles, 1993–98; Toured UK, 1994–97; Supported: Blur; Elastica; Oasis; Moist; Supergrass. *Recordings:* Mindblower, album; Layabout/Mother and Father; Without Waking; Tatjana; Kunta Kinté; Layabout vs Mindblower; singles with The Nubiles, 1995–98. *Memberships:* Musicians' Union; Performing Rights Society. *Leisure interests:* Outdoor pursuits; Arts and Design; Cinema. *Current Management:* Thirst Music Management. *Address:* c/o 5 Clare Court, Lime St, Bedford MK40 1NH, England.

NEUMANN Bob; b. Chicago, Illinois, USA. Prod.; Engineer; Musician (keyboards); Electronic Music Composer; Synthesist. m. Carolyn, 28 March 1992, 1 s., 1 d. *Education:* BSc, Electronic Engineering, BSEET. *Musical Education:* General Music Theory, Organ, Piano Training. *Career:* 25 years' performance experience, Chicago area pop bands; 18 years recording, composition; Currently owns and operates Project Studio, Lemont, Illinois. *Recordings:* 3 albums, 1 dance single released on independent labels; Beatbox-D; Neu Electro; 12 dance single: Juicy. *Publications include:* Discoveries column, Keyboard Magazine; KLEM. *Honours:* Discoveries Column Alumni, State Fair, Illinois Awards. *Memberships:* EARS Society; Chicago BMI. *Leisure interests:* Electronic and dance recording; Composition; Performance; Die-cast miniature vehicle collecting; Aerobic and physical training. *Current Management:* Neu Electro Productions, USA.

NEVILL Brian Roy; b. 4 Jan. 1948, Wuppertal, Germany. Musician (drums, piano). Divorced. *Musical Education:* Royal Society of Arts School Certificate. *Career:* Played with Graham Parker; Many recording sessions including The Flying Lizards, 1975–81; Television appearances with Kirsty McColl; Founder member, Shriekback; Member, Pig Bag; Radio and television sessions with Shriekback, Pig Bag; Worked in Brussels for one year; Live work with Virginia Astley, 1982–87; Formed record label, 1989; Recorded and played with numerous blues and rock 'n' roll visiting American artists. *Recordings:* Albums: Lend An Ear, Pig Bag; The Best Of, Pig Bag; The Infinite, Shriekback; Blues and Stomps, Carl Sonny Leyland; The Panasonics; Eddie Angel's Guitar Party; Big Sixteen, Big Joe Louis and the Blueskings; Laugh It Up, Holly Golightly. *Publications:* Articles in Goldmine; Sleeve notes to album Soul Classics, The Best of Bell. *Memberships:* PRS; MCPS; Musicians' Union. *Leisure interests:* Record collecting; Reading; Travel; Films. *Address:* 6 Lancaster Lodge, 83–85 Lancaster Rd, London W11 1QH, England.

NEVILLE Alaric James; b. 28 July 1961, Derby, England. Sound Engineer; Record Prod.; Musician (guitar). *Education:* BA Hons Fine Art, Leeds University. *Career:* Sound engineer to: Oysterband; The Ukrainians; Based at Woodhouse Studios, Hall Place, Leeds. *Recordings:* Produced artists including Cud; Bridewell Taxis; The Ukrainians; Ringo's High; Ukranians, Kultura, 1996; Lazer Boy, Forget Nothing, 1996; Oyster Band, Deep Dark Ocean, 1997; Here I Stand, 1999. *Membership:* Musicians' Union. *Current Management:* Stolen Sounds. *Address:* Ivy Cottage, 36 School Lane, Chapel Allerton, Leeds L57 3PN, England.

NEVILLE Art; b. 17 Dec. 1937, New Orleans, USA. Musician (piano); Singer. *Career:* Singer, pianist: The Neville Sound, 1962–68; The Meters, 1968–77; The Neville Brothers, 1977–; with the Meters: worked with Dr John; Robert Palmer; Labelle; European tour, support to the Rolling Stones, 1975; with the Neville Brothers: Amnesty International Concert, with Joan Baez, Sting, Peter Gabriel, Bryan Adams, 1986; Glastonbury Festival, 1990; Playboy Jazz Festival, 1991; Artists Against Hunger and Homelessness benefit, New Orleans 1992; American Music Festival, 1992; Summer Stage '92 concert series, New York, 1992; Berloni Foundation leukemia benefit concert, Modena, Italy, 1992. *Recordings:* Albums with the Meters: The Meters, 1969; Look-Ka Py Py, 1970; Rejuvenation, 1974; Fire On The Bayou, 1975; New Direction, 1977; Singles include: Sophisticated Cissy; Cissy Strut; Ease Back; Chicken Strut; Hand Clapping Song; Be My Lady; Albums with The Neville Brothers: The Neville Brothers, 1978; Fiyo On The bayou, 1981; Neville-ization, 1984; Treacherous – A History of The Neville Brothers, 1987; Yellow Moon, 1989; Brother's Keeper, 1990; Family Groove, 1992; Very Best of the Neville Brothers, 1997; Solo albums: Mardi Gras Rock 'n' Roll, 1987; That Old Time Rock 'n' Roll, 1992; Art Neville – His Speciality Recordings, 1956–58, 1993; Also appears on: Red Hot + Blue: A Tribute to Cole Porter, 1991; Crescent City Soul, 1996; Gin Blossoms, Outside Lokking In, 1999; Organ-Ized, Organ-Ized, 2000. *Honours:* Best Pop Instrumental Performance, Healing Chant, 1990; Rolling Stone Critics Awards, Best Band, 1990. *Current Management:* Bill Graham Management, PO Box 42094, San Francisco, CA 94142, USA.

NEVILLE Charles; b. 28 Dec. 1938, New Orleans, USA. Musician (saxophone). *Career:* Tours South USA with various blues players, including: Jimmy Reed; Little Walter; Played with Joey Dee and The Starliters, 1962; Member, The Wild Tchoupitoulas, 1976–77; Member, The Neville Brothers, 1977–; Amnesty International Concert, with Sting, Peter Gabriel, Bryan Adams, Joan Baez, 1986; Nelson Mandela Tribute Concert, Wembley, 1990; Glastonbury Festival, 1990; Playboy Jazz Festival, Hollywood, 1991; American Music Festival, 1992; Berloni Foundation's Leukaemia benefit, Modena, Italy, 1992; Summer Stage 92 concerts, New York, 1992. *Recordings:* Wild Tchoupitoulas, 1976; The Neville Brothers, 1978; Neville-ization, 1984; Treacherous: A History of The Neville Brothers 1955–85, 1987; Yellow Moon, 1989; Brother's Keeper, 1990; Family Groove, 1992; Live on Planet Earth, 1994; Singles include: Healing Chant; Bird On The Wire; Contribution: In The Still of The Night, for album: Red Hot + Blue, 1990. *Honours:* Best Band, Rolling Stone magazine Critics awards, 1989; Grammy: Best Pop Instrumental Performance, Healing Chant, 1990; Downbeat Award, Best Blues/Soul/R & B Group, 1990. *Current Management:* Bill Graham Management, PO Box 42094, San Francisco, CA 94142, USA.

NEVILLE Cyril; b. 10 Jan. 1948, New Orleans, USA. Vocalist; Musician (percussion). *Career:* Member, The Neville Sounds, 1962–68; Soul Machine, 1968–75; The Meters, 1975; The Wild Tchouptoulas, 1976; The Neville Brothers, 1977–; Concerts include: Amnesty International Concert, with Joan Baez, Sting, Peter Gabriel, Bryan Adams, 1986; Nelson Mandela Tribute Concert, Wembley, 1990; Glastonbury Festival, 1990; Playboy Jazz Festival, Hollywood, 1991; American Music Festival, 1992; Berloni Foundation leukemia benefit concert, Modena, Italy, 1992. *Recordings:* Albums: Wild Tchoupitoulas, 1976; The Neville Brothers, 1978; Treacherous – A History of The Neville Brothers, 1987; Uptown, 1987; Yellow Moon, 1989; Brother's Keeper, 1990; Family Groove, 1992; Live on

Planet Earth, 1994; Uptown Rulin': The Best of the Neville Brothers, 1999; Singles include: Healing Chant; Bird On The Wire; In The Still of The Night; Appears on: Red Hot + Blue: A Tribute To Cole Porter, 1991. *Honours:* Grammy Award: Best Pop Instrumental Performance, Healing Chant, 1990; Rolling Stone Critics Award, Best Band, 1989. *Current Management:* Bill Graham Management, PO Box 429094, San Francisco, CA 94142, USA.

NEVIN David Charles; b. 23 Sept. 1951, London, England. Musician (multi-instumentalist); Vocalist. *Career:* Musician for: Unit 4+2; Harmony Grass; Grass; Capability Brown; Sparrow; Divine; Radio and television appearances: Radio 1; Capital Radio; New Faces; Regional Radio; Concerts: Reading Festival; European festivals; Shirley Bassey tour includes Albert Hall. *Recordings:* Voice, Capability Brown; Matthew Fisher/Strange Days, Matthew Fisher, 1996. *Publications:* Numerous. *Memberships:* PRS; Musicians' Union; BASCA. *Leisure interests:* Gardening; Cooking; Painting; Tennis. *Address:* 69 Church Lane, Walthamstow, London E17 9RN, England.

NEWBURY Mickey (Milton J Jr); b. 19 May 1940, Houston, Texas, USA. Songwriter; Recording Artist. *Compositions:* Swiss Cottage Place, recorded by Roger Miller; Here Comes The Rain Baby, Eddy Arnold and Roy Orbison; Funny Familiar Forgotten Feelings, Don Gibson and Tom Jones; How I Love Them Old Songs, Carl Smith; Sweet Memories, Willie Nelson; Just Dropped In (To See What Condition My Condition Was In), Kenny Rogers and The First Edition; She Even Woke Me Up To Say Goodbye, Jerry Lee Lewis; San Francisco Mabel Joy, John Denver, Joan Baez, Kenny Rogers; I Dont Think About Her (Him) No More, Don Williams, Tammy Wynette; American Trilogy, Elvis Presley; Makes Me Wonder If I Ever Said Goodbye, Johnny Rodriguez; Blue Sky Shinin', Marie Osmond. *Recordings:* Albums: Harlequin Melodies, 1968; Mickey Newbury Sings His Own, 1968; Looks Like Rain, 1969; 'Frisco Mabel Joy, 1971; Heaven Help The Child, 1973; Live At Montezuma, 1973; I Came To Hear The Music, 1974; Lovers, 1975; Rusty Tracks, 1977; His Eye Is On The Sparrow, 1978; The Sailor, 1979; After All These Years, 1981; In A New Age, 1988; Sweet Memories, 1988; Mickey Newbury Collection, 1998. *Honour:* Nashville Songwriters International Hall of Fame, 1980.

NEWCOMB Keith; b. 13 Oct. 1966, Yokosuka, Japan. Music Publishing Exec. *Education:* BBA, Belmont University, Nashville, Tennessee, USA, 1989. *Career:* Music Publishing Executive and Consultant, 1987–96; Worked with top songwriters including: Paul Overstreet, Robb Royer, Jimmy Griffin, Stewart Harris, Jim Weather, Dean McTaggart, Delbert McClinton and others; Investment Broker, JC Bradford and Company, 1996-.

NEWCOMER Carrie Ann; b. 25 May 1958, Dawajack, Michigan, USA. Vocalist; Musician (guitar, dulcimer); Songwriter. *Musical Education:* Learnt flute as a child. *Career:* Singer-songwriter who uses folk country, jazz and blues influences; Began playing guitar at around age 14; Played dulcimer and was lead vocalist and songwriter in the folk trio Stone Soup (with guitarist Larry Smeyak and percussionist Dennis Leas), 1981–87; Released first solo album, 1991; Toured regularly and made appearances at events such as Newport folk festival; The Age of Possibility is one of the top ten best selling albums on Rounder Records. *Recordings:* with Stone Soup: Long Fields, 1984; October Nights, 1987; solo: Visions and Dreams, 1991; An Angel At My Shoulder, 1994; The Bird On The Wing, 1995; My Father's Only Son, 1996; My True Name, 1998; The Age of Possibility, 2000. *Internet:* www.carrienewcomer.com.

NEWELL Norman; b. 25 Jan. 1919, London, England. Lyricist; Former Record Prod. *Career:* Combined record production and songwriting until 1990; Currently songwriter. *Compositions include:* More, from film Mondo Cane (over 5m. performances in USA and world hit, over 1,000 recordings); Portrait of My Love, (world hit). *Publications:* Many songs. *Honours:* Academy Nomination for More; Several BMI Awards; Golden Globe Award. *Memberships:* PRS; BMI; BASCA; MCPS. *Leisure interest:* Theatre. *Current Management:* Noel Gay Organisation (Charles Armitage). *Address:* 1 Albion Court, Galena Rd, Hammersmith, London W6 0QT, England.

NEWMAN Randy; b. 28 Nov. 1943, New Orleans, Louisiana, USA. Singer; Songwriter; Musician (piano); Arranger. m. Gretchen Newman, 1 d. *Musical Education:* Music Composition, UCLA. *Career:* Staff songwriter, Metric Music, 1962; Became staff arranger, producer, Warner Bros Records, 1967; Concerts include: Farm Aid, 1985; American Music Festival, Colorado, 1992. *Compositions include:* They Tell Me It's Summer, The Fleetwoods; I Don't Want To Hear It Anymore, Jerry Butler; I've Been Wrong Before, Cilla Black; Simon Smith and His Amazing Dancing Bear, Alan Price; Nobody Needs Your Love and Just One Smile, Gene Pitney; Mama Told Me (Not To Come), Three Dog Night (No. 1, USA); I Think It's Going To Rain Today (also recorded by UB40); I Love L.A. (used to promote 1984 Olympic Games); Songs also recorded by artists including Judy Collins; Harry Nilsson; Manfred Mann; Frankie

Laine; Jackie DeShannon; Walker Brothers; As arranger: Is That All There Is?, Peggy Lee; Film scores: Ragtime, 1982; The Natural, 1984; The Three Amigos, 1986; Awakenings, 1990; Television series Cop Rock, ABC-TV, 1991; Also contributions to soundtracks: Performance; Cold Turkey; Her Alibi; Major League. *Recordings:* Albums: The Randy Newman Orchestra Plays Music From The Hit Television Series Peyton Place, 1966; Randy Newman, 1968; Twelve Songs, 1970; Randy Newman Live, 1971; Good Old Boys, 1974; Little Criminals, 1978; Born Again, 1979; Trouble In Paradise, 1983; Lonely At The Top, 1987; Land of Dreams, 1988; Music From The Motion Picture The Paper, 1994; Faust, 1995; Bad Love, 1999; Singles include: Short People (No. 2, US), 1978; The Blues, duet with Paul Simon, 1983; Contributor, The Simpsons Sing The Blues, 1990; Film scores: Avalon, 1990; Maverick, 1994; Toy Story, 1995; Michael, 1996; James and the Giant Peach, 1996; Toy Story 2, 1999; Producer: Classic Disney Vol. IV, 1997; The Bugs Life, 1998; 2 stage productions of Faust, La Jolla Playhouse, 1995, Goodman Theatre, Chicago, 1996. *Honours:* Academy Award nomination, Best Original Song, 1982; Grammy, Best Instrumental Composition, 1984; Emmy, music for Cop Rock, 1991. *Current Management:* Cathy Kerr, for Pam Artist Management; California, USA.

NEWSTED Jason; b. 4 March 1963, Battle Creek, Michigan, USA. Rock Musician (bass). *Musical Education:* Self-taught. *Career:* Member, US heavy rock groups: Flotsam and Jetsam; Metallica, 1986–; 750 live appearances with Metallica, 1986–; Concerts include: Freddie Mercury AIDS Tribute, Wembley, 1992; Moscow Monsters of Rock Festival, 1991; Numerous world-wide tours, television and radio appearances. *Recordings:* with Flotsam and Jetsam: Flotsam and Jetsam, 1986; with Metallica: Garage Days Re-visited; Justice For All; Metallica; Metallica VI; Load; Reload; Phobos; Garage Inc; SandM. *Honours:* Grammy Awards, 1990–92; AMAs, 1992; MTV Award, 1992. *Memberships:* AFofM San Francisco; ASCAP. *Leisure interests:* Mountain biking; Basketball. *Current Management:* c/o Q-Prime Inc, 729 Seventh Ave, 14th Floor, New York, NY 10019, USA.

NEWTON (Carson) Wayne; b. 4 March 1942, Norfolk, Virginia, USA. Entertainer; Singer; Musician; Actor; Author. m. Kathleen McCrone, 9 April 1994, 1 d. *Musical Education:* Self-taught to play 11 instruments (trumpet; piano; guitar; violin; drums; steel guitar; bass; 12 string guitar; valve trombone; dobro guitar, electric guitar). *Career:* Performances include: Personal television specials; Fourth of July concert at Washington monument; USA tours; Total of 2000 television shows and films including: The Lucy Show; Jackie Gleason; Roseanne; Full House. *Recordings:* Danke Schoen; Red Roses For A Blue Lady; The Letter; Daddy Don't You Walk So Fast; 131 albums released; 300 singles. *Publications:* Autobiography – Once Before I Go. *Honours:* Entertainer of The Year (9 years); Presidential Awards; Ten Outstanding Men of America. *Memberships:* AFTRA; SAG; AFofM. *Leisure interests:* Arabian horse breeder; Car collector; Jet pilot. *Address:* 3422 Happy Lane, Las Vegas, NV 89120, USA.

NEWTON Allen; b. 30 Aug. 1950, Fort Worth, Texas, USA. Music Promoter. m. Frances, April 1983, 2 d. *Education:* Business degree. *Career:* 15 years in radio and television; Worked as: DJ; Music and programme director; Station manager; Newscaster; Sales manager; Programme producer; Owner, seven independent record labels and two publishing companies. *Honour:* Nomination, Promoter of The Year, MIRL, 1991. *Memberships:* BMI; ASCAP. *Leisure interests:* Ham and shortwave radio. *Address:* RT 1, Box 187-A, Whitney, TX 76692, USA.

NEWTON Tad (Robert Arthur William); b. 25 June 1946, Marlborough, Wiltshire, England. Jazz Musician (trombone); Vocalist. m. Anne Marie Newton, 2 Aug. 1969, 2 s., 2 d. *Education:* BA Hons, University of Southampton. *Career:* Bandleader, trombonist and vocalist, Tad Newton's Jazzfriends (7-piece dixieland and mainstream jazz band); Concert appearances include: Barbican Centre, Derngate Theatre, Royal Festival Hall, Wembley Conference Centre, major festivals; Also Jazz Promoter and Organizer. *Recordings:* Basin St To Harlem, 1988; Drivin', 1989; Jumpin' For Joy, 1991; Journey Thru' Jazz, 1994. *Membership:* Musicians' Union. *Leisure interests:* Jazz; Football; Cinema; Fell walking. *Current Management:* TNJF Management. *Address:* 23 Windmill Ave, Blisworth, Northamptonshire NN7 3EQ, England.

NEWTON-JOHN Olivia; b. 26 Sept. 1948, Cambridge, England. Singer; Actress. m. Matt Lattanzi, 1985, 1 d. *Career:* Moved to Australia, aged 5; Singer in folk group as teenager; Local television performer with Pat Carroll; Winner, National Talent Contest, 1964; Singer, actress, 1965–; Represented UK in Eurovision Song Contest, 1974; Music For UNICEF Concert, New York, 1979; Film appearances include: Grease, 1978; Xanadu, 1980; Two of a Kind, 1983; Own clothing business, Koala Blue, 1984-. *Recordings:* Albums: If Not For You, 1971; Let Me Be There, 1974; Music Makes My Day, 1974; Long Live Love, 1974; If You Love Me Let Me Know (No. 1, USA), 1974; Have You Ever Been Mellow, 1975; Clearly Love, 1975; Come On Over, 1976; Don't Stop Believin', 1976; Making A Good Thing Better, 1977; Greatest Hits, 1978; Grease (film soundtrack), 1978;

Totally Hot, 1979; Xanadu (film soundtrack), 1980; Physical, 1981; 20 Greatest Hits, 1982; Olivia's Greatest Hits Vol. 2, 1983; Two of a Kind, 1984; Soul Kiss, 1986; The Rumour, 1988; Warm and Tender, 1990; Back To Basics: The Essential Collection 1971–92, 1992; Gaia – One Woman's Journey, 1995; More than Physical, 1995; Greatest Hits, 1996; Olivia, 1998; Back with a Heart, 1998; Highlights from the Main Event, 1999; Greatest Hits: First Impressions, 1999; Country Girl, 1999; Best of Olivia Newton John, 1999; Love Songs: A Collection: Hit singles include: If Not For You, 1971; What Is Life, 1972; Take Me Home Country Roads, 1973; Let Me Be There, 1974; Long Live Love, 1974; If You Love Me (Let Me Know), 1974; I Honestly Love You (No. 1, UK), 1974; Have You Never Been Mellow (No. 1, USA), 1975; Please Mr Please, 1975; Something Better To Do, 1975; Fly Away, duet with John Denver, 1976; Sam, 1977; You're The One That I Want, duet with John Travolta (No. 1, USA and UK, third-best selling single in UK), 1978; Summer Nights, duet with John Travolta (UK No. 1, 9 weeks), 1978; Hopelessly Devoted To You (No. 2, UK), 1978; A Little More Love, 1979; Deeper Than The Night, 1979; I Cant Help It, duet with Andy Gibb, 1980; Xanadu, with ELO (No. 1, UK), 1980; Magic (No. 1, USA), 1980; Physical (US No. 1, 10 weeks), 1981; Make A Move On Me, 1982; Heart Attack, 1982; Twist of Fate, from film soundtrack Two of a Kind, 1983; Back with a Heart, 1998; Grease (Remix), 1998; I Honestly Love You, 1998; Physical Remix 1999, 1999. *Honours include:* OBE; Grammy Awards: Record of the Year, 1974; Best Country Vocal Performance, 1974; Best Pop Vocal Performance, 1975; Numerous American Music Awards, 1975–77, 1983; CMA Award, Female Vocalist of Year (first UK recipient), 1975; Star on Hollywood Walk of Fame, 1981; Numerous other awards from Record World; Billboard; People's Choice; AGVA; NARM; Goodwill Ambassador, UN Environment Programme, 1989. *Current Management:* Bill Sammeth Organisation, PO Box 960, Beverly Hills, CA 90213, USA.

NGUYA-TRASA Papy; b. 6 March 1973, Bas-Congo, Africa. Musician (Guitar); Singer. *Musical Education:* Musical interpretation, College of Arts. *Career:* Appearances at Musical Festival of Africa, 1996; Musical research performance, 1997; Festival of Jazz, 1999. *Compositions:* many performed but yet to be recorded. *Recordings:* Owala, 1994; Gaby Kwambamba, 1995; Let Them Say, 1996. *Honour:* Medal of Flying Musician of China, 1997. *Membership:* Asscns of Research Music. *Address:* Eglise Lagos-Rhema, 37/59 Av du 24 Novembre, Commune da la Ngombe, Kinshasa, Lingwala, Africa.

NGWENYA Moses; b. Soweto, South Africa. Musician (keyboards, guitar, drums). *Musical Education:* Self-taught. *Career:* Drummer with The Crocodiles; Later worked with Intombi Zesi Manje Manje; Joined The Young Brothers, 1976; Act became Soul Brothers; Involved in production with own Black Moses Productions. *Recordings:* Albums include: Umshoza Wami, 1974; Isiphiwo, 1982; Xola, 1987; Jive Explosion, 1988; Impimpi, 1989; Isighebhezana, 1999; Induk' Enhle, 2001. *Honours:* FNB South African Music Award, Best Mbaqanga Performance; 15 gold discs, 5 platinum discs, several multiplatinum discs. *Address:* c/o Gallo, PO Box 2897, Parklands 2121, South Africa. *Internet:* www.gallo.co.za.

NI MHAONAIGH Mairead; b. 1959 Gaoth Dobhair, County Donegal, Ireland. Vocalist; Musician (fiddle). m. (1) Frankie Kennedy, (2) Dermot Byrne. *Career:* Daughter of Prionsias O Maonaigh; Formed Ragairne with Frankie Kennedy; Recorded for RTE and performed at the Belfast Folk Festival; Played in US with Kennedy, 1984–85; Turned professional; Formed Altan, c. 1987; First Irish traditional group to sign to a major label, Virgin Records, 1996; Presented traditional music radio show The Long Note and TV series The Pure Drop. *Recordings:* Albums include: Ceol Aduaidh, 1983; Horse With A Heart, 1989; The Red Crow, 1990; Harvest Storm, 1992; Island Angel, 1993; Blackwater, 1996; Runaway Sunday, 1997; Another Sky, 2000. *Address:* c/o Tom Sherlock, 71 Carysfort Ave, Blackrock, County Dublin, Ireland.

NI RIAIN Nóirín; b. 12 June 1951, Limerick, Ireland. Singer; Musician (various Indian drones). m. Mícheál ó Súilleabháin, 27 June 1974, 2 s. *Education:* Dip Phil NuI. *Musical Education:* MA, BMus, Dip, CMSM. *Career:* Performed UN Conferences in Costa Rica; Rio De Janeiro; Copenhagen; Poland; India; Beijing, China, 1995; Worked with John Cage; Numerous world-wide television and radio appearances; Works extensively in Cathedral of St John the Divine, New York; Artist in residence, County of Laois, Ireland, 1999–2000. *Recordings:* Caoineadh Na Maighdine; Good People All; Vox De Nube; Soundings; Ple Hse Change; Gregorian Chant Experience. *Publications:* Im Bim Baboro; Stór Amhrán; Gregorian Chant Classics. *Honours:* MA Hons. *Leisure interests:* Walking; Tennis. *Current Management:* Personally managed. *Address:* Dromore House, Newport, Co Tipperary, Ireland.

NICHOLAS James Hayden; b. 7 May 1956, Hobbs, New Mexico, USA. Musician (guitar); Songwriter. *Education:* University of Houston, 1975–76. *Career:* Guitarist, various bands, 1975–86; Lead guitarist, songwriter, Clint Black, 1987–; Guitar technician at: Dale Mullins Studios, Houston, 1977–81; Heck Music Co, 1981–82; Appearances with Clint Black include: Grand Ole Opry; CMA Awards Show; Tonight Show; Arsenio

Hall. *Compositions include:* Better Man; Killing Time; Music City News. *Recordings:* Albums: with Clint Black include: Killing Time, 1989; Put Yourself In My Shoes, 1990. *Honours:* CMA Nomination, Song of The Year, Better Man, 1990; 2 ACM Nominations, Song of The Year: Better Man, 1990; Killing Time, 1990.

NICHOLAS Julian Conan; b. 13 Jan. 1965, London, England. Musician (Saxophone); Composer. m. 1 d. *Education:* Hons Degree, York, 1986. *Career:* Saxophonist with Loose Tubes, 1989–91; Own group, Mountain People, 1989–98; Toured Europe extensively, 1989–98; BAFTA Nominee film score, Fools Gold, Brinksmat Robbery, LWT, 1992; Lecturer and Educationist, Bishop Otter College, West Sussex, 1993–96; Access to Music, 1992–98. *Compositions:* with W Woolf: A Thousand Ships; Mountain People; Food of Love; A Dawning; Madam, I'm Adam; Dear John. *Recordings:* Mountain People; RS001; Square Groove; Food of Love; Transformations; Everything You Do To Me. *Honours:* Twice Winner, Brighton Festival, Zap Award for Jazz, 1989, 1991. *Memberships:* Musicians' Union; Performing Rights Society. *Leisure interests:* Philosophy; Cooking; Swimming. *Current Management:* Aardvark, 1 Montague Pl., Brighton BN2 1JE, England. *Address:* 8A Powis Sq., Brighton, BN1 3HH, England.

NICHOLLS Al (Alan Charles); b. 27 Feb. 1957, Wrexham, Wales. Musician (saxophone); Arranger. *Musical Education:* City of Leeds College of Music. *Career:* Four years, Big Town Playboys, 1987–91; Numerous European tours; 2 US tours; Television includes: Jools Holland Happening; Pat Savak Show, USA; 3 years, King Pleasure and The Biscuit Boys, 1991–94; Elvis: The Musical, Prince of Wales Theatre, West End, 1996; Led own band, Blue Harlem, 1996–; Television includes: What's The Noise; Blue Peter; Ray Gelato Giants, 1994–; Freelance musician; Expanding career as solo jazz performer: clubs such as Shepperton Jazz Club, 100 Club, London Cheltenham Jazz Club; Festivals: Coventry, Soho, Llangollen; Returned to Big Town Playboys, 1999-. *Recordings:* Albums: Now Appearing, Big Town Playboys; Don't Mess With The Boogieman, Big Joe Duskin; Live At The Burnley Blues Festival, Champion Jack Dupree; The Full Flavour, Ray Gelato and The Giants; with King Pleasure and The Biscuit Boys: Live At Ronnie Scott's; Blues and Rhythm Revue; Hot News, Blue Harlem, CD, 1998; Ready To Rock, Big 6; We The Boys Will Rock Ya, Big 6; Get Off It and Rock It, Big 6; Just Can't Afford It, Mike Sanchez. *Honour:* Best Dep of The Year Award, for Hot News International, 1999. *Memberships:* Musicians' Union; British Music Writers Council. *Leisure interests:* Gastronomy; Hill walking in Wales. *Address:* 23 University Mansions, Putney, London SW15 1EP, England.

NICHOLLS Billy (William Morris); b. 15 Febrary 1949, London, England. Singer; Songwriter; Prod. m. Anne Dupée, 2 s., 1 d. *Career:* Musical director for The Who: Roger Daltrey tour; Pete Townshend Psychoderelict tour; Own solo albums. *Compositions:* Can't Stop Loving You, Leo Sayer; Without Your Love, Roger Daltrey; Fake It, Pete Townshend; Music for the McVicar film. *Recordings:* Solo albums: White Horse; Love Songs; Under One Banner; with Pete Townshend: Who Came First, 1927; Rough Mix, 1977; Iron Man: a Musical, 1989; with Roger Daltrey: Celebration: The Music of the Who, 1994; McVicar, 1996; Martyrs and Madmen, 1997. *Honour:* Ivor Novello Award Nomination. *Leisure interests:* Cooking; Poetry. *Address:* 16 Park Rd, E Twickenham, Middlesex TW1 2PX, England.

NICHOLLS Jonathan Charles; b. 11 Dec. 1948, Northampton, England. Bandleader; Compere; Musician (bass guitar). m. Linda Joyce Singleton, 5 April 1969, 1 s. *Musical Education:* Self-taught. *Career:* Bandleader, top UK showband Mixed Feelings; Performed at leading international venues: New York Hilton; Bahrain Hilton; Gleneagles; Radio interview, The Tunnels of Arras 1917; Radio performance of play: Voices of The Fallen, BBC Radio 4. *Publications:* Cheerful Sacrifice – The Battle of Arras, 1917, 1992; Play: Voices of The Fallen, London, 1992–94. *Membership:* Musicians' Union. *Leisure interests:* History; Rugby Football; Music; France. *Address:* 64 Wootton Dr., Hemel Hempstead, Herts HP2 6LB, England.

NICHOLS Keith Charles; b. 13 Feb. 1945, London, England. Musician (Piano, Trombone); Arranger. m. Eve Nichols, 10 April 1976. *Education:* Guildhall School of Music. *Career:* Toured, 7 years, with jazz-comedy band, Levity Lancers, playing piano, trombone and tuba; Regular ragtime concerts, South Bank, as soloist and small ensembles; Member, Richard Sudhalter's New Paul Whiteman Orchestra, appearances in Philadelphia and Carnegie Hall, New York; Formed Midnite Follies Orchestra with Alan Cohen, 1977; Freeleance, performing throughout UK, Europe and USA; Piano player, part of Hoagy Carmichael, in feature film soundtrack Bix; Lecturer, Jazz History, Royal Academy of Music; Performed music of Benny Goodman's 1938 Carnegie Hall Concert with Royal Academy Big Band; Recent tours of France, Scandinavia, Germany, Switzerland, Ireland, Egypt; Performed with Cotton Club at Royal Festival Hall, London. *Compositions:* Arrangements and transcriptions in 20s and 30s styles. *Recordings:* Numerous solo albums; Collaboration with Bing Crosby; Many albums as bandleader and sideman; CD, recreated music of Fletcher

Henderson; Album of rare Duke Ellington and Fats Waller pieces. *Honours:* Great British Jr Champion, Accordion, 1960; GGSM, 1967; Hon. Associateship, Royal Academy of Music, 1998. *Address:* 33 Rosemary Dr., Ilford, Essex IG4 5JD, England.

NICKELL Ylonda; b. 27 Sept. 1958, Napa, California, USA. Alto Saxophonist. m. Richie Cole, 1981, 1 d. *Career:* Performed with: Sonny Stitt, Freddie Hubbard, Mose Allison, Manhattan Transfer, Robert Cray and Willie Nelson; Performed at: Monterey Jazz Festival, Russian River Jazz Festival, Cotati Jazz Festival, Concerts-by-the-Sea, The Jazz Workshop, Roland's, Great American Music Hall, Yoshi's. *Recordings:* Alto Lady; Minnesota Sax. *Current Management:* Karen Kindig. *Address:* Karen Kindig, c/o The Blue Cat Agency, PO Box 399, Novato, CA 94948, USA.

NICKS Stevie (Stephanie); b. 26 May 1948, Phoenix, Arizona, USA. Singer; Songwriter. m. Kim Anderson, 29 Jan. 1983, divorced 1984. *Career:* Member, Fritz (with Lindsey Buckingham); Member, duo Buckingham and Nicks; Member, Fleetwood Mac, 1975–90; Solo artiste, 1981–; World-wide tours and concerts include: US tour with the Eagles, 1976; US Festival, San Bernardino, California, 1982; Shake The Cage tour, Europe, Australia, 1988; Mask tour, 1990. *Compositions include:* Rhiannon (Will You Ever Win); Dreams; Sara; Gypsy; Leather and Lace; Edge of Seventeen; I Can't Wait; The Other Side of The Mirror; Co-writer with Sandy Stewart: Seven Wonders; If Anyone Falls; Co-writer with Prince: Stand Back. *Recordings:* Albums: with Lindsey Buckingham: Buckingham Nicks, 1974; with Fleetwood Mac: Fleetwood Mac (No. 1, USA), 1975; Rumours (No. 1, UK and US; 15m. sales), 1977; Tusk (No. 1, UK), 1978; Fleetwood Mac Live, 1980; Mirage (No. 1, USA), 1982; Tango In The Night (No. 1, UK), 1987; Greatest Hits, 1988; Behind The Mask (No. 1, UK), 1990; Solo albums: Bella Donna, 1981; The Wild Heart, 1983; Rock A Little, 1985; The Other Side of The Mirror, 1989; Timespace – The Best of Stevie Nicks, 1991; Street Angel, 1994; Maybe Love Will Change Your Mind, 1994; Enchanted: The Works of Stevie Nicks, 1998; Numerous hit singles include: with Fleetwood Mac: Rhiannon (Will You Ever Win), 1976; Say You Love Me, 1976; Go Your Own Way, 1977; Don't Stop, 1977; Dreams (No. 1, USA); You Make Loving Fun, 1977; Tusk, 1979; Sara, 1980; Hold Me, 1984; Oh Diane, 1983; Big Love, 1987; Little Lies, 1987; Everywhere, 1988; Solo: Stop Draggin' My Heart Around, with Tom Petty, 1981; Leather and Lace, duet with Don Henley, 1982; Edge of Seventeen, 1982; After The Glitter Fades, 1982; Stand Back, 1982; If Anyone Falls, 1983; Talk To Me, 1986; I Can't Wait, 1986; Rooms On Fire, 1989; Hard Game, 1994; Blue Denim, 1994; Also recorded with Kenny Loggins; Richie Vito; Tom Petty. *Honours:* American Music Awards: Favorite Pop/Rock Group, Favorite Pop/Rock Album, 1978; Grammy: Album of the Year, Rumours, 1978; Billboard Awards: Album of the Year, Group of the Year, 1977; Star on Hollywood Hall of Fame, with Fleetwood Mac, 1979; Gold Ticket, Madison Square Garden, 1990.

NICOL Ken (Kenneth Stephen); b. 27 May 1951, Preston, Lancashire, England. Musician (guitar); Singer; Writer. *Musical Education:* Self-taught. *Career:* Signed to CBS Records, 1974; Polydor until 1979; Played lead guitar and recorded with Al Stewart; Appeared live in USA, 1980–88; Currently member, Albion Band; Television appearances include: New Faces; This Morning; Pebble Mill; The Big Breakfast. *Recordings:* Easy Street, by Nicol and Marsh, 1974, 1976; Under The Glass, 1977; Nicol and Marsh, 1978; Living In A Spanish Town, 1993; Happy Accident, The Albion Band, 1998. *Memberships:* Musicians' Union; PRS. *Leisure interest:* Fly-fishing. *Current Management:* Ess'ntial Productions. *Address:* 298 Tag Lane, Ingol, Preston, Lancashire PR2 3UY, England.

NICOL Simon; b. 13 Oct. 1950, Muswell Hill, London, England. Folk Musician (guitar, keyboards). *Career:* Guitarist, founder member, Fairport Convention, 1967–71, 1977–; Founder, guitarist, Albion Country Band, 1971; Appearances include: Royal Albert Hall, 1969; London Palladium, 1970; Tours, festivals, annual Fairport Convention reunion concerts, 1980-. *Recordings:* Albums: with Fairport Convention: Fairport Convention, 1968; What We Did On Our Holidays, 1969; Unhalfbricking, 1969; Liege and Lief, 1970; Full House, 1970; Angel Delight, 1971; Babbacombe Lee, 1971; A Bonny Band of Roses, 1977; Moat On The Ledge, 1982; The Best Of..., 1988; Red and Gold, 1989; Fairport Convention, 1990; Them Five Seasons, 1991; Jewel In The Crown, 1995; Old-New-Borrowed-Blue, 1996; Who Knows Where the Time Goes?, 1997; Encore, Encore, 1997; Fiddlestix 1970–84: The Best of Fairport Convention, 1998; with Albion Country Band: Battle of The Field, 1976; Prospect Before Us, 1977; Rise Up Like The Sun, 1978; Albion River Hymn March, 1979; Light Shining Albino, 1984; Shuffle Off, 1984; Recordings with artist including, John Martyn, Cat Stevens, Al Stewart, Shirley Collins, Richard Thompson, Sandy Denny.

NICOLAS Clovis; b. 13 March 1973, Abidjan, Ivory Coast. Musician (acoustic bass). *Education:* DEVG Philosophy. *Musical Education:* Jazz and classical music, Conservatory of Music, Marseilles, 1993. *Career:* Played with Ted Curson; Peter King; Bobby Porcelli; Sandy Patton and

Sara Lazarus, 1994; Plays with many French jazzmen including Jean-Pierre Arnaud; Philippe Renault; Pierre Drevet; Live in Paris, 1996; Played with Brad Mehldau, Belmondo Quintet, Stefano di Batista Quintet, Vincent Herring, Aldo Romano, Laurent de Wilde, Christian Escoude. *Composition:* Groovy Globy, 1996; Li-Li Smiles Again, 1996; A Romance for JB, 1996. *Recordings:* Featured on album: Le Collectif Artistique du Cri du Port (Marseilles), 1995; Jean Christope Beney Quartet, 1997; Tenor Joke, JC Beney Quartet, 1997; Infinity, Belmondo Quintet, 1999; Le Douze, Temime Quartet, 1999. *Honours:* First prize, International competition, Jazz Orchestras, Vienne, France, 1995; First Prize, Jazz Class Conservatoire de Marseille, 1996. *Leisure interest:* Listening to music. *Address:* 9 rue Eugène Varlin, 75010 Paris, France.

NICOLS Maggie; b. 24 Feb. 1948, Edinburgh, Scotland. Musician (Voice, Piano, Keyboards); Performer; Teacher; Composer. 1 d. *Education:* Apprenticeships to Dennis Rose and John Stevens. *Career:* dancer, Windmill Theatre; sang with Great Bebop Pianist, Dennis Rose; joined innovator John Steven's Spontaneous Music Ensemble; pioneer of Vocal and Instrumental Music Workshops, Oval House Theatre, 1970–; joined Keith Tippett's Centipede, formed duo with Julie Tippetts; co-founded Feminist Improvising Group; performed internationally at Major Festivals, Moers Music Festival, Berlin Jazz Festival, Bath and Bracknell Jazz Festivals; Radio appearances include Jazz In Britain; Television appearances in Germany, Italy, France and Switzerland. *Compositions:* Numerous. *Recordings:* Nearly 50 including Sweet and S'ours; Les Diaboliques; Nevergreens; Cats Cradle. *Publications:* Many Interviews. *Honour:* A sixty piece orchestra playing my composition Evolution Revolution. *Memberships:* Musicians' Union; Equity; PRS; BASCA; PAMRA. *Leisure interests:* Yoga; Community Politics; Reading; Walking in the country; Dancing; Herbalism; Astrology; Tarot. *Address:* 23 Nottingham House, Shorts Gardens, London WC2H 9AX.

NIEBLA Salvador; b. 28 Dec. 1960, Ceuta, Spain. Drummer; Prod.; Composer. *Education:* Conservatory Isaac Albeniz, Gerona; Berklee College of Music, Boston; Drummers Collective, New York; Berkley School of Music, Gerona. *Career:* Olympic Games, Barcelona, 1992; TV 1, Big Band; TV3, Big Band; Tours with: Orquesta Mondragon; La Trinca; Max Suwer Tigo; Salvador Niebla Natural Energy; Amargos-Benavent Group; Atila; Orquesta Mirasol. *Compositions:* J Manuel Serrat; Dyango; Moncho; La Barberia; Carlos Benavent; Sabandenos; J Albert Amargos; J Has Ikitflus; Alameda; Orquesta Mirasol. *Publications:* Guide for Pop and Rock Drums, 1998; The Virtual Drummer, 1999. *Honours:* Hon. Mem., Cuban Drummers Society, Percuba, 1997; Nominated for the following publications: El Pais, Jazz-Quartica, Popular 1, as one of the best Spanish Drummers. *Memberships:* SGAE; AIE; APE; AEMA; AMSC; Drummers Collective. *Current Management:* Odisea Productions. *Address:* c/ Roselló, 217 2 1a, Barcelona, 08008, Spain.

NIELSEN Ib Lund; b. 9 Oct. 1941, Vamdrup, Jylland, Denmark. Musician. m. Inge Holten Nielsen, 19 Dec. 1964, 2 s. *Education:* Bass Lessons with John Nielsen; Dr-Radio Symphonic Orchestra, 1967–70. *Career:* Bass Player in Orchestra with Niels Husum Severel Radio AP; With Quartet, Quintet, Sextet, with the Nielshusum Septet; Bass Player in Leonardo Pedersens Jazz Kapel, 11 Piece Swing Band, 1970-. *Compositions:* Hic with Stormy's Quartet, 1960; Bass Relief, 1980. *Recordings:* Lockjaw, Sweets, 1976; Bass Relief, 1980; I Want A Roof, 1994. *Honour:* With Stormy's Quartet, Winner, Jazz Competition, Denmark, 1960. *Memberships:* DMF; NDJ. *Leisure interests:* Music; Reading; Theatre. *Address:* Hvidager 42, 2620 Albertslund, Denmark.

NIELSEN Jens G; b. 1 Aug. 1951, Denmark. Musician (drums); Record Prod.; Record Co Exec. *Career:* Member, Gnags; World-wide tours; Co-founder, Genlyd record label (bought by BMG); A & R Director, BMG, Denmark. *Recordings:* 20 Gnags albums; Producer, albums for various artists. *Honour:* Danish Grammy, Mr Swing King, 1990. *Current Management:* Rock On, Denmark. *Address:* Rådhusstræde 4a, 1466 Copenhagen K, Denmark.

NIELSEN Peter A G; b. 17 Dec. 1952, Skjern, Denmark. Singer; Composer. m. Katrine Nyholm, May 1923, 1 s., 1 d. *Education:* Danish Literature, Aarhus University. *Career:* Founder, singer, songwriter, Gnags, 1966-. *Recordings:* Gnags, 20 albums. *Honour:* Grammy Award, Mr Swing King, 1990. *Leisure interests:* Watching; Listening; Tasting; Touching. *Current Management:* Rock On, Rådhusstræde 4 A, 1466 Copenhagen, Denmark. *Address:* Haraldsgade 23, 8260 Viby J, Denmark.

NIELSEN Rick; b. 22 Dec. 1946, Rockford, Illinois, USA. Musician (guitar); Vocalist. *Career:* Member, various bands including Fuse; Sick Man of Europe; Founder member, US rock group Cheap Trick, 1969–; Appearances include: Concert, Tokyo, 1978; California Music Festival, Los Angeles, 1979; Reading Festival, 1979; British tour, 1980; Montreux Rock Festival, 1988; US tour with Robert Plant, 1988; US tour with Kiss, 1988; US tour with Heart, 1990; Solo performance, Concerto For Electric Guitar and Orchestra, Michael Kamen, with Rockford Symphony Orchestra, 1993.

Recordings: Albums: Cheap Trick, 1977; Heaven Tonight, 1978; Cheap Trick At Budokan, 1979; Dream Police, 1979; Found All The Parts, 1980; All Shook Up, 1980; One On One, 1982; Next Position Please, 1983; The Doctor, 1986; Lap of Luxury, 1988; Busted, 1990; The Greatest Hits, 1991; Singles include: I Want You To Want Me, 1979; Ain't That A Shame, 1979; Dream Police, 1979; Voices, 1980; Everything Works If You Let It, 1980; If You Want My Love, 1982; Tonight It's You, 1985; Mighty Wings, used in film soundtrack Top Gun, 1986; Ghost Town, 1988; I Can't Stop Falling Into Love, 1990; Recordings with artists including: Alice Cooper, Hall and Oates, John Lennon. *Leisure interest:* Collecting rare and unusual guitars. *Current Management:* Silent Partner Management, Carnegie Hall, 154 W 57th St, Suite 828, New York, NY 10019, USA.

NIEMELÄINEN Ilkka; b. 9 March 1956, Finland. Musician (guitar); Composer. *Musical Education:* Guitar, musical theory, Helsinki Conservatory. *Career:* Writer, performer, electronic music with Otto Romanowski, Esa Kotilainen, 1970s; Founder, composer, musical director, Wasama Quartet, 1976–85; Concerts included: Ylioppilastalo, Tampere, Finland; Detroit Kool Jazz Festival; Founder, composer, musical director Instinct, 1985–; Represented Finland at EBU Festival, Kristianstad; Numerous concerts in Finland; Founder, trio IN2á3, with Pentti Lahti, Jukka Wasama, 1990. *Recordings:* Arranger, classical album for saxophonist Pentti Lahti. *Address:* Haukilahdenrata 21 D, 02170 Espoo, Finland.

NIEWOOD Gerry (Gerard Joseph); b. 6 April 1943, Rochester, New York, USA. Musician (woodwind). m. Gurly Hulbert, 2 March 1972, 1 s., 1 d. *Musical Education:* BM, Eastman School of Music, 1970. *Career:* Woodwind player with Chuck Mangione Quartet, 1968–76; Judy Collins, 1977–80; Simon and Garfunkel, 1982–83; Alto saxophonist, Radio City Music Hall, New York, 1979–; Saxophonist with Gerry Mulligan, 1980–; Liza Minnelli, 1984–; Freelance musician, 1986–; Concerts include: Simon and Garfunkel in Central Park, 1982; The Ultimate Event, with Frank Sinatra, Liza Minnelli, Sammy Davis Jr, 1989. *Compositions:* Floating, 1972; Joy, 1976. *Recordings:* Slow Hot Wind, 1975; Gerry Niewood and Timepiece, 1977; Share My Dream, 1986; Gerry Niewood/Alone, 1988; Recorded with artists including: Liza Minelli, Liza Minelli at Carnegie Hall, 1981; Simon and Garfunkle, Concert in Central Park, 1982; Peggy Lee, Moments Like This, 1992; Randy Sandke, Awakening, 1998; Mark Murphy, Mark Murphy Sings Nat King Cole, 1999. *Honour:* Talent Deserving Wider Recognition, Downbeat Magazine, 1975, 1976. *Current Management:* Con Sona Music Inc. *Address:* 228 Bay Ave, Glen Ridge, NJ 07028, USA.

NIGAM Sonu; b. Faridabad, Haryana, India. Vocalist; Actor. *Career:* Successful as both film playback singer and pop star; Spent childhood in Delhi, often singing at functions with father; Went to Mumbai to try and break into films, aged 18; Began by taking acting roles whilst attempting to become a playback singer; First found fame with song Achha Sila Diya Tune Mere Pyaar Ka from the film Bewafa Sanam; Other film offers followed along with the chance to record pop albums; Host of TV music show TVS Sa Re Ga Ma. *Recordings:* Albums: Sapnon Ki Baat, Deewana, Kismat, Yaad, 2001; features on soundtracks: Jeet, Papa Kehte Hain, 1996; Border, Tamanna, 1997; China-Gate, Dil Se..., Dulhe Raja, Jab Pyaar Kisise Hota Hai, Jeans, Keemat, 1998; Dillagi, Hum Saath-Saath Hain, Jaanwar, Mast, Shool, Taal, Vaastav, 1999; Chori Chori Chupke Chupke, Dhadkan, Fiza, Hadh Kar Di Aapne, Har Dil Jo Pyar Karega, Jungle, Kahin Pyar Na Ho Jaaye, Kurukshetra, Kya Kehna, Mela, Phir Bhi Dil Hai Hindustani, Pukar, Refugee, Tera Jadoo Chal Gayaa, 2000; Dil Chahta Hai, One 2 Ka 4, Pyaar Ishq Aur Mohabbat, Pyaar Tune Kya Kiya.., Yaadein, 2001.

NIGHTINGALE Annie; b. 1 April, London, England. DJ. Divorced, 1 s. *Career:* Journalist, several newspapers including London Daily Express and Cosmopolitan; TV Presenter, BBC's Old Grey Whistle Test, 1978–82; Worked as Radio 1 DJ, 1970s–; Worked with nearly every major act and promoted acts such as The Police, U2, Duran Duran, Sex Pistols, Oasis, Portishead, Tricky and The Orb; Presenter, Sunday Night Request Show, 1982–94; Work for BBC World Service, Radio 4, Radio 5, British Forces Broadcasting; Presenter, Live Aid, Philadelphia, 1985; Presenter, Chill Out Zone; Produced and presented numerous music documentaries world-wide. *Publication:* Chase the Fad, autobiography, 1981. *Honour:* First female DJ, BBC. *Membership:* Ambassador, The Prince's Trust.

NILES Richard; b. 28 May 1951, Hollywood, California, USA. Composer; Prod.; Arranger; Journalist; Broadcaster; Recording Artist. *Musical Education:* B Mus, Berklee College of Music, Boston. *Career:* Arranger for: Paul McCartney; Cher; Take That; Boyzone; Tears For Fears; Kiri Te Kanawa; Producer for: Pet Shop Boys; Hue and Cry; Dusty Springfield; Pat Metheny; The Troggs; Musical Director for TV series: David Essex; Leo Sayer; Michael Ball; Ruby Wax; Composer of numerous TV commercials; Broadcaster: Writer and presenter of New Jazz Standards, BBC Radio 2; Recording Artist: Santa Rita, Black Box Records. *Compositions:* Recorded by: Ray Charles; Tina Turner; Hue and Cry; Bobby Womack; Deniece Williams; Spike Milligan. *Contributions to:* Making Music Magazine,

London. *Honours:* Golden Rose of Montreux, Score for The Strike (Comic Strip). *Memberships:* Musicians' Union; PRS; BMI; MPG. *Leisure interests:* Horticulture. *Address:* Niles Productions, 34 Beaumont Rd, London W4 5AP, England.

NIMMERSJÖ Conny; b. 20 March 1967, Angelholm, Sweden. Musician (guitar). 1 d. *Career:* Founder member, Bob Hund, 1991–; Performed more than 300 concerts around Scandinavia; Played at festivals including Roskilde, Lollipop, Ruisrock, Quartfestivalen and Hultsfred. *Compositions:* I Stället för Musik: Förvirring, 1996; Düsseldorf, 1996. *Recordings:* with Bob Hund: Bob Hund, 1993, 1994; Edvin Medvind, 1994; I Stället för Musik: Förvirring, 1996; Omslag: Martin Kann, 1996. *Honours:* Grammy Awards: Best Live Act, 1994, Best Lyrics, 1996. *Memberships:* STIM; SAMI. *Leisure interests:* Music; Books; Movies; Late night talking; Food; Drinking. *Address:* c/o Bob Hund Förlag, Råsundavägen 150, 169 36 Solna, Sweden.

NINO Harold Michael; b. 29 Nov. 1950, New York, New York, USA. Musician (Guitar); Vocalist (Blues). m. Julie Hebner, 1 s. *Education:* Major in Music, Manhattan Community College; Studied at New School for Social Research; Private lessons with Robert Yelin and Ted Meckler. *Career:* Studio Musician, New York, 1977–82; Travelling road musician, 1978–; Appeared as regular on The Music Art Show, Huntsville, Alabama, 1978–79; Recorded 30 second commercial for Villa Esperanza; Appeared as extra in the film They Want To Know Too!. *Composition:* You're Never Going to Understand, recorded by Oysters Rockefeller, 1996. *Recordings:* Past and Present, and Oysters Rockefeller, as member of blues band Oysters Rockefeller. *Honour:* Addy Award, for Villa Esperanza commercial, 1979. *Memberships:* American Federation of Musicians, local branches; Blues Music Asscn; BMI. *Leisure interests:* Cooking; Hi Fi audio. *Current Management:* O S Artists. *Address:* PO Box 6485, Springfield, IL 62708, USA.

NJIKENYA Landry; b. 3 June 1970, Douala, Cameroon. Musician (Percussion). 1 child. *Musical Education:* Musical studies with Billy Mussango. *Compositions:* 45 published songs. *Membership:* Socimada. *Leisure interests:* Football; Tennis. *Address:* c/o Billy Mussango, PO Box 8363 Yaounde, Cameroon.

NOBES Roger Michael; b. 26 Dec. 1939, Abbots Langley, Hertfordshire, England. Musician (vibraphone, piano, drums); Arranger. m. Maureen Payne, 1 June 1987, 1 d. *Musical Education:* Central School of Music. *Career:* Numerous national and international tours with The Alex Welsh Band, The Dave Shepherd Quintet; Numerous tours with American artists; Concert performers include: Festival Hall; Barbican Centre; Many radio and television appearances. *Recordings:* Recorded extensively with many bands and orchestras including The Roger Nobes Quartet. *Membership:* Musicians' Union. *Leisure interests:* Director of North Hertfordshire Youth Big Band; Cricket. *Current Management:* Roma Enterprises. *Address:* 41 Manton Rd, Hitchin, Hertfordshire SG4 9NP, England.

NOBLE Douglas; b. 9 July 1964, Edinburgh, Scotland. Guitar Instructor; Freelance Music Journalist. *Education:* BSc Psychology, Edinburgh University, 1985. *Musical Education:* ALCM, Classical guitar, London College of Music, 1986; LLCM (TD), Classical guitar, London College of Music, 1987. *Career:* Freelance music journalist, regular contributor to the Guitar Magazine (UK); Occasional contributor to Guitar Player (US); Bass Player (US); Contributions to several books on the electric guitar; Sleeve notes for several albums; Music Director for Univibes, international Jimi Hendrix magazine; Examiner, Rock School, Trinity College of Music. *Publications:* Instant Hendrix, book, 1988; Instant Peter Green, book, 1990. *Leisure interests:* Swimming; Tennis; Zen Buddhism. *Address:* 2F4 99 St Leonard's St, Edinburgh EH8 9QY, Scotland.

NOBLE Stephen Francis Paterson; b. 26 March 1960, Wallingford, Oxfordshire, England. Musician (drums, percussion,. musical saw, bugle). *Musical Education:* Self-taught, still learning. *Career:* Contemporary Music Network Tour, with Alex Maguire, 1994; Festivals: Glasgow Jazz, 1989–94; New Music America, New York, 1989; Sitges International Dance, 1991; Taklos (Swizz), 1990–92; London Jazz, 1993–94; Television and radio: Featured in On The Edge (series about improvisation), CH4; Live recording from Adrian Boult Hall, Birmingham, broadcast on Radio 3 (Impressions and Midnight Oil), with pianist Alex Maguire; Live broadcasts throughout Europe with various groups. *Compositions:* Commissioned by South Bank Centre, London to compose music for collaboration with Spanish Dance Company Mal Pelo, 1993. *Recordings:* Duo with Alex Maguire: Live At Oscar's; (voted one of top jazz albums of 1980s); Once, recordings from Derek Bailey's Company Week, featuring Bailey and Lee Konitz, 1987; The Shakedown Club. *Memberships:* Musicians' Union; PRS. *Current Management:* Ping Pong Productions. *Address:* 13 Calthorpe St, London WC1X OJP, England.

NOGALSKI Rick; b. 15 Aug. 1964, Bolton, Lancashire, England. Musician (Guitar). *Education:* BSc, Electrical and Electronic Engineering, North

Staffordshire Polytechnic; Guitar Institute, London, 1988–89. *Career:* Member, London Electric Guitar Orchestra, 1996-. *Recordings:* Kneel Down Like a Saint Gorilla and Stop; 17 Lumps of Cheese, Go!. *Address:* 37 Fulbourne Rd, Walthamstow, London E17 4AX, England.

NOLAN J William (Bill); b. 13 Nov. 1940, Derby, Connecticut, USA. Civil Rights Activist; Musicologist. m. Joan M Owens, 1962, 1 s. *Career:* Volunteer Radio Broadcaster for WPKN-FM, 1969–; Founder and Executive Director of The Rhythm and Blues Rock 'N Roll Society Inc, 1974; Founder of American Blues Movement, 1975; Volunteer helping Black African-American artists and sustaining music heritage. *Address:* c/o Rhythm and Blues Rock 'N Roll Society Inc, PO Box 1949, New Haven, CT 06510, USA.

NOLLI Giorgio; b. 5 Feb. 1965, Merano, Italy. Musician, (percussion, congas, timbales). *Musical Education:* Self-taught; Participated in various workshops in the UK. *Career:* Italian tour, pop band China Boy Hi, 1992; European tour, garage band Nicolette, 1993; Television appearance, James Whale Show, UK, 1993; Japanese tour, jungle group UK Tribe, 1995; Jonathan Ross's Big Big Talent Show, ITV, 1996; The Carmen Miranda Story, Jermyn Street Theatre, 1997. *Recordings:* Singles: I Want To Be Everything, China Boy Hi, 1992; There Isn't Any Way, China Boy Hi, 1993; Junglites, UK Tribe, 1995; Album: Jungle Soul, UK Tribe, 1995. *Membership:* Musicians' Union. *Leisure interests:* Travel; Languages; Yoga; Sci-fi. *Address:* 29 Buckingham Rd, Harlesden, London NW10 4RP, England.

NOODLES (Kevin Wasserman); b. 4 Feb. 1963, Los Angeles, California, USA. Musician (guitar). m. Jackie Wasserman, 1998, 1 d. *Career:* Resides in Tustin, Orange County, California; Member: Clowns of Death; Dirty Dot; Joined The Offspring, 1985; Privately pressed single took over 2 years to sell 1000 copies, 1987; Signed to independent labels, Nemesis and Epitaph, for 1988–95 releases; Major US breakthrough following heavy MTV/radio play rotation, 1994; Accused of betraying punk roots when signing to Columbia after dispute with former label, 1996; Consolidated world-wide success by scoring UK No. 1 hit single, 1999; Live shows include: Woodstock festival, 1999; KROQ Weenie Roast, 2000; European tour, 2001; Band gave lucky fan $1m. in Offspring prize draw, 2000; Member of side-project group Circus Penis. *Recordings:* Albums: The Offspring, 1989; Ignition, 1992; Smash!, 1994; Ixnay On The Hombre, 1997; Americana, 1998; Conspiracy of One, 2000; Singles: I'll Be Waiting, 1987; Baghdad EP, 1988; Come Out and Play (Keep 'Em Separated), Self-Esteem, 1994; Gotta Get Away, 1995; All I Want, Gone Away, 1997; Pretty Fly (For A White Guy), 1998; Why Don't You Get A Job?, The Kids Aren't Alright, She's Got Issues, 1999; Original Prankster, 2000; Want You Bad, Million Miles Away, 2001. *Honours:* Over 9m copies of Smash album sold world-wide, best selling independent record of all time. *Current Management:* Jim Guerinot, Rebel Waltz Management, 31652 Second Ave, Laguna Beach, CA 92651, USA. *Internet:* www.offspring.com.

NOONE Peter; b. 5 Nov. 1947, Davyhulme, Manchester, England. Vocalist. m. Mireille Strasser. *Musical Education:* Manchester School of Music and Drama. *Career:* Lead vocalist, Herman's Hermits, 1963–71; Solo artist, 1971–; US tour, 1965; North American tour with The Who, 1967; Madison Square Garden, 1973; Member, The Tremblers, 1980; Actor, film: Mrs Brown You've Got A Lovely Daughter, 1968; Performed, play: The Canterville Ghost, US TV, 1966; Pinocchio, 1968; Business partnership with Graham Gouldman, studio production work, New York boutique, Zoo, 1968; Performed in Pirates of Penzance, Broadway and London, 1982–83; Video jockey, US Cable TV, 1990s. *Recordings:* Introducing Herman's Hermits, 1965; Herman's Hermits on Tour, 1965; The Best of Herman's Hermits, 1965; Hold On!, 1966; Both Sides of Herman's Hermits, 1966; Vol. III, 1968; Mrs Brown You've Got A Lovely Daughter, 1965; Wonderful World, 1965; I'm Henry VIII, I Am, 1965; Just a Little Better, 1965; A Must To Avoid, 1966; No Milk Today, 1966; Dandy, 1966; There's A Kind of Hush (All Over The World), 1967; Sleepy Joe, 1968; Sunshine Girl, 1968; Something's Happening, 1969; Years May Come Years May Go, 1970; Solo: Oh You Pretty Thing, 1971; One of the Glory Boys, 1982; Pirates of Penzance, 1986; I'm into Something Good, 1989. *Current Management:* DeLauro Management, Suite 1980, 875 Avenue of the Americas, New York, NY 10001, USA.

NORBY Caecilie; b. 9 Sept. 1964, Frederiksberg, Denmark. Singer. *Education:* SKT Annae Gymnasium Music School, 1973–80; Music Theatre School, 1 year; Several Music Courses; Private Lessons in Singing and Piano. *Career:* Different Performing Groups, 1980–81; Lead Singer in the Funk Rock Band, Street Beat, 1981–84; Lead Singer in the recording band, Frontline, 1987; Lead Singer in One Two, together with colleague Nina Forsberg, 1993. *Compositions:* Several. *Recordings:* Frontline, 1985; Frontlife, 1986; One Two, 1986; My Corner of the Sky, 1996; Hvide Loegne, 1989; Getting Better, 1993; Caecilie Norby, 1995; Featured on Blue Box Vol. 2 Finest Jazz Vocal, 1998. *Honours:* Ben Webster Prize, 1987; Simon Spies Soloist Prize, 1995; 7 Grammy Nominations in Denmark. *Memberships:* Danish Artist Society; DJBFA.

Current Management: PDH Management, Copenhagen, Denmark. *Address:* Absalonsgade 7A 1Tv, 1658 Copenhagen V, Denmark.

NORCROSS Rick (Richard Charles); b. 23 March 1945, Waltham, Massachusetts, USA. Singer; Songwriter; Entertainer; Musician (guitar). *Education:* BA, Mass Communications, University of South Florida, Tampa, Florida, USA. *Career:* Solo artiste, 1963–80; 3 tours of England, 1965–75; Lead singer, Rick Norcross and The Nashfull Ramblers Western Swing Band, 1980–; Tours: Central Florida; New England Fair; Festival Circuit; Producer, 35 festivals and special events, 1974-. *Recordings:* Albums: Nashfull, 1980; Fairly Live, 1983; Tour du Jour, 1989; You Can't Get There From Here, 1991; Can't Catch A Rambler, 1994; The Legend of Scratch Leroux, 1995. *Publication:* Entertainment Editor, The Tampa Times, 1969–74. *Honour:* Vice President, Yankee Festivals and Events Asscn. *Membership:* AFofM. *Current Management:* Airflyte Productions. *Address:* 216 Battery St, Burlington, VT 05401, USA.

NORMAN Chris (Christopher); b. 25 Oct. 1950, Redcar, Yorkshire, England. Singer; Songwriter; Musician (guitar); Record Prod. m. Linda Heddle, 16 March 1970, 4 s., 2 d. *Career:* Lead singer, Kindness, Backing group to Peter Noone (ex Herman's Hermits), 1960s; Group later became Smokie, 1970s; Solo artist, 1980's-; Produced number of records. *Recordings:* Hit singles: If You Think You Know How To Love Me; Living Next Door To Alice; Lay Back In Your Arms; Don't Play Your Rock and Roll To Me; Stumblin' In; Midnight Lady; This Time (We'll Get It Right); Recorded 16 albums. *Honours:* 3 Bravo Awards, 1976–86; Golden Europa, 1986; CMT Europe, 1994. *Memberships:* PRS; MCPS; BASCA. *Leisure interests:* Music; Family. *Current Management:* Bill Tuckey Music. *Address:* 20 Tor Bryan, Ingatestone, Essex, England.

NORMAN David; b. 19 May 1962, London, England. Tour/Production Man.; Sound Engineer. m. Suzanne Feit, 18 Oct. 1992. *Career:* Television and live credits include: The Arsenio Hall Show; Late Night with David Letterman Show; The Jon Stewart Show; MTV Beach House; Top of The Pops; Showtime at the Apollo; Kenny G 'Breathless' Tour; MTV Japan; The Far East Network; Woodstock, 1994; WOMAD Tour, 1994; Lowlands Festival. *Recordings:* Engineer on albums: Through The Fire, Peabo Bryson; Zingalamundi, Arrested Development; E'ssential, Bare E'ssentials. *Leisure interests:* Reading; Bowling; Computers; Animals. *Address:* 639 Gardenwalk Blvd, Suite 1632, College Park, GA 30349, USA.

NORMAN Michael; b. 16 June 1970, Canada. Musician (Keyboards, Saxophones, Guitar, Vocals); Prod.; Songwriter. *Education:* Jazz Diploma, Malaspina College, Canada. *Career:* Canadian Country Music Award shows with Lisa Brokop, 1993; Patricia Conroy, 1995, 1999; Patricia Conroy: Wild As The Wind, 1999. *Compositions:* Too Late; Bring It On; Put A Little Distance. *Recordings:* Girls Will Be Girls; Living Beyond Our Dreams; The Message. *Honour:* BCCMA Keyboard Player of the Year, 1999. *Memberships:* AFM; CCMA. *Address:* #102A 301 Maude Rd, Port Moody, BC Canada.

NORREEN Claus; b. 5 June 1970, Charlottenlund, Denmark. Musician (keyboards, drum machines). *Career:* Worked with Soeren Rasted on film, Fraekke Frida; Formed Joyspeed; Changed name to Aqua; Obtained major record deal in Denmark Numerous TV and live appearances. *Recordings:* Singles: Itsy Blitzy, as Joyspeed; Roses Are Red; My Oh My; Barbie Girl; Doctor Jones; Lollipop; Turn Back Time (theme from film Sliding Doors); Good Morning Sunshine; Albums: Aquarium; Bubble Mix.

NORREMOLLE Jens; b. 12 Aug. 1956, Vejle, Denmark. Composer; Prod.; Musician (keyboards). 1 s. *Education:* Teacher. *Musical Education:* Self-taught. *Career:* Various bands until 1987–; Composer, singer, keyboard player for Singing Zoo; Record producer for Anne Dorte Michelsen and Venter På Far, 1987–95. *Recordings:* with Anne Dorte Michelsen: Elskerindens Have; Den Ordlose Time; Min Karriere Som Kvinde (producer, arranger, musician); Also albums with Singing Zoo and Venter På Far. *Honours:* Best Band, 1988; Musikcafé Prize with Singing Zoo. *Membership:* DMF; DJBFA. *Leisure interest:* Son. *Current Management:* Warner Chappell, Denmark. *Address:* Blågårdsgade 17 IV left, 2200 Copenhagen N, Denmark.

NORRIS Richard; b. 23 June 1965, London, England. Musician (keyboards, saxophone, drums); Prod.; Remixer. *Education:* Liverpool University. *Career:* Member musical duo, The Grid; Met partner Dave Ball, recording Jack The Tab compilation, 1988; Recorded 4 albums, 11 singles; Tours, UK, 1991–; Japan, Thailand, Singapore, New Zealand, Australia, 1995; Producer, remixer, artists including: Pet Shop Boys, Boy George, Marc Almond, Brian Eno, Happy Mondays, 1990–95; Director of Areeba Records; A & R Manager for Creation Records. *Recordings:* Albums: Floatation, Electric Head, 1990; Evolver, Texas Cowboys, 1990; Rollercoaster, Swamp Thing, 1994; Music For Dancing, Diablo, 1995; Recorded with Joe Strummer for Grosse Point Blank film soundtrack, 1997; Bigg Buddha, Be Here Now, 12. *Honours:* Silver disc, Swamp Thing, 1994; Platinum disc (Australia), Swamp Thing, 1994; Silver disc, Evolver,

LP, 1995. *Memberships:* PRS; PPL; Musicians' Union. *Address:* Unit 204, Canalot Studios, 222 Kensal Rd, London W10, England.

NORRIS Richard T; b. 9 Feb. 1966, Epping, Essex, England. Music Programmer; Writer; Recording Engineer. *Career:* Programmer, engineer for Bryan Ferry, including albums Taxi, Mamouna, 1990–95; Co-writer with Little Annie, 1989–94; Currently co-writing with Guy Pratt (Pink Floyd) under joint name Deep Cover. *Recordings:* Albums: Taxi, Bryan Ferry, 1993; Deboravation, Deborah Harry, 1993; Mix-ism, Mad Capsule Markets, 1994; Mamouna, Bryan Ferry, 1994; Grand Central, Deep Cover, from Hackers film soundtrack, 1995. *Current Management:* This Much Talent, 117 Church Rd, Barens, London SW13 9HL, England.

NORRIS Russell Anthony; b. 6 Aug. 1971, Walthamstow, London, England. Writer; Prod.; Remixer; Musician (keyboards); Insurance Broker. *Musical Education:* Self-taught. *Career:* Toured many English dance clubs, 1990–93; Scottish Club Tour, 1992; Appearances on ITV's BPM and Chart Show, and on MTV and Kiss FM. *Recordings:* Free, X-Static, 1991; The X-Static EP, X-Static, 1992; Global Vibe, X-Static, 1993. *Membership:* Musicians' Union. *Leisure interests:* Playing and watching football. *Current Management:* X-Treme Dance. *Address:* 1 Herbert Gardens, Willesden, London NW10, England.

NORVELL Loring L; b. 20 Jan. 1948, Norfolk, Virginia, USA. Composer; Arranger; Conductor. *Education:* Old Dominion University, 1974–78; MA, Radford University, 1979–80; DMA, Arizona State University, 1984–88. *Career:* Conductor, US Coast Guard Bands, Cape May, NJ and Governors Island, 1970–73; Conductor, Norfolk Savoyards, 1981–84; Conductor, Phoenix Pro-Musica Orchestra, 1985–93; Singer, Yesterdays Supper Club, 1985–99; Freelance Composer, Arranger, 1985-. *Compositions:* Festival Entrada; Oedipus Rex Ballet; Symphony For The Victims of War; 3 Woodwind Sonatas. *Honours:* Frequent Guest Conductor, Las Vegas Philharmonic, Flagstaff Symphony. *Memberships:* American Music Center; American Composers' Forum. *Leisure interests:* Movies; Cooking; Record Collecting. *Current Management:* Woody Norvell Music, 3728 E Joan De Arc, Phoenix, AZ 85032, USA.

NOTLEY Wendy; b. 28 Oct. 1957, Australia. Singer; Songwriter; Musician (guitar); Teacher. *Education:* Diploma in Early Childhood Education. *Career:* Early childhood Teacher and Director, Yinbilliko School, Sydney, Australia; Teaching, Murawina Aboriginal multi-purpose Education Centre in Redfern, Sydney, for 4 years; Singer, songwriter, guitarist, co-producer, Growin' Up Strong, by Aunty Wendy's Mob; Author, 4 children's books, Teacher's Resource Book and Education Kit. *Compositions:* Growin' Up Strong; Indigenous; We're Koori Kids; The Wheels On The Holden; Red, Black and Yellow; Wiradjuri and Bundjalung; Until The Fire Is Out; Dreamtime; There Was A Man; Stand Up; Noongar In The Bush; Melaleua; Round The Campfire Tonight; We're Bininj kids. *Recording:* Growin' Up Strong, Aunty Wendy's Mob. *Honour:* APRA Award Nomination, children's category, 1996. *Membership:* Society of Authors. *Address:* 5/355 Glebe Point Rd, Glebe, Sydney, NSW 2037, Australia.

NOVA Aldo; b. Canada. Rock Musician (guitar); Singer. *Career:* Solo recording artiste, 1980-. *Recordings:* Albums: Aldo Nova, 1982; Subject, 1984; Twitch, 1985; Blood On The Bricks, 1991; Nova's Dream, 1997; Also featured musician on albums: Bon Jovi, Bon Jovi, 1984; Blaze of Glory, Jon Bon Jovi, 1991; Falling into You, Celine Dion, 1996; Power Chords Vol. 3, 1997; Jon Bon Jovi, Destination Anywhere, 1998.

NOVOSELIC Kris; b. 16 May 1965, Croatia. Musician (bass). *Career:* Member, Nirvana, 1987–94; World-wide tours; Concerts include: Reading Festival, 1991, 1992; Transmusicales Festival, Rennes, France, 1991; Benefit concert, Washington State Music Coalition, 1992; Benefit concert, Tresnjevka Women's Group, Cow Palace, San Francisco, 1993; Founder, Sweet 75, 1995. *Recordings:* Albums: Bleach, 1989; Nevermind (No. 1, USA), 1991; Incesticide, 1993; In Utero (No. 1, UK and US), 1993; Unplugged In New York, 1994; Singles, 1996; In Utero, 1998; Box, 1998; Singles include: Smells Like Teen Spirit, 1991; Come As You Are, 1992; Lithium, 1992; In Bloom, 1992; Oh, The Guilt, 1993; Heart-Shaped Box, 1993; All Apologies, 1993; Track, I Hate Myself and Wanna Die, featured on Beavis and Butthead Experience, 1993. *Publication:* Come As You Are, Nirvana biography by Michael Azerrad. *Honours:* Platinum disc, Nevermind; Best Alternative Music Video, Best New Artist Video, Smells Like Teen Spirit, MTV Music Video Awards, 1992; Best International Newcomer, BRIT Awards, 1993.

NOWELS Rick; Songwriter; Record Prod.; Musician. *Musical Education:* Music Major, University of California at Berkeley. *Compositions:* Madonna, The Power of Good-bye, To Have and Not to Hold, Little Star; Celine Dion, Falling Into You; Robert Miles, One and One; Des'ree, Time, Get a Life; Anita Baker, Body and Soul; Belinda Carlisle, Heaven is a Place on Earth, Circle in the Sand, Leave a Light On, Live Your Life Be Free, In Too Deep, We Want the Same Thing, La Lune, Runaway Horses, Vision of You, Do You Feel Like I Feel?; Stevie Nicks, I Can't Wait, Rooms on Fire, Maybe

Love Will Change Your Mind; Roachford, Naked Without You; The Corrs, Intimacy; Maria Nayler, Naked and Sacred; New Radicals, You Get What You Give; kd lang, Anywhere But Here; Mel C, Northern Star; Enrique Iglesias, I Have Always Loved You; As a Producer: Falling Into You, Celine Dion; Heaven on Earth, Runaway Horses, Live Your Life Be Free, Belinda Carlisle; Stevie Nicks, Rock A Little; Big Area; Des'ree; The Corrs. *Honours:* Grammy Nomination, Best R & B Song, Anita Baker, 1996; ASCAP Awards; Grammy Award, Album of the Year, Falling Into You by Celine Dion, 1997. *Membership:* ASCAP. *Current Management:* Stephen Budd. *Address:* c/o 109 B Regents Park Rd, London NW1 8UR, England.

NOYCE Jonathan; b. 15 July 1971, Sutton Coldfield, England. Musician (bass guitar); Composer. m. Sara Joanna King, 15 July 1995. *Musical Education:* North Herts College, Royal Academy of Music. *Career:* with Ian Anderson (Jethro Tull): Tours, USA, Canada, Europe; VH-1 radio broadcast, Secret Life; Television: Pebble Mill; What's Up Doc?; Videos; with C J Lewis: The White Room; with David Palmer: Concerts in Venezuela; Belgium; Estonia; Romania; Germany; Various concerts and recordings. *Recordings:* with Take That: Relight My Fire, 1993; with Al Green: Keep On Pushing Love, 1994; with Sister Sledge: Thinking of You (remix), 1993; with Diana Ross: Love Hangover (remix), 1994; with Joey Negro: Universe of Love, 1993; with David Palmer: Sgt Pepper. *Honours:* LRAM, Professional Certificate of Royal Academy of Music. *Membership:* Musicians' Union. *Leisure interests:* Cooking; Camel baiting. *Address:* 1 Marcus Terrace, Wandsworth, London SW18 2JW, England.

NOYES Cameron George Albert; b. 27 Feb. 1965, Edmonton, Alberta, Canada. m. Velveeta Krisp, 1 d. *Career:* Worked in musical or industry capacities with 800 artists including: Faith No More; King Sunny Ade; The Wailers; John Cale; Donovan; SNFU; Dead Kennedys. *Recordings:* Cable; Don't Care, Didn't Care; Yuppie Flux. *Honour:* IMBH, Award of Excellence, 1992. *Memberships:* ARIA; PMIA; OTO. *Leisure interests:* Equestrian; Books; Wine collecting. *Current Management:* Phantom Product Canada. *Address:* #104–1540 E Fourth Ave, Vancouver, British Colmubia, Canada.

NOZEDAR Adele; b. 7 Aug. 1966, Yorkshire, England. Record Co Exec.; Musician (piano, harp). m. Adam Fuest, 1 Aug. 1993. *Musical Education:* Grade B Musical Theory. *Career:* Managing Director of Rhythm King Records, independent UK label founded in 1986 with Martin Heath; Co-founder of Renegade Software. *Honour:* Leslie Perrin Award for Public Relations in 1992. *Memberships:* Musicians' Union; PRS. *Leisure interests:* Stained glass making; Designing; Gilding. *Address:* c/o Rhythm King Records, 121 Salisbury Rd, London NW6 6RG, England.

N-TRANCE (Dale Longworth); b. 19 June 1966, Middleton, Manchester, England. Musician (keyboards). *Musical Education:* Degree, Sound Recording. *Career:* Sound engineer, leading PA company, most aspects of live sound (rock and roll, musicals, classical, television); Signed to PWL while working on the Hitman and Her. *Recordings:* Album: Happy Hour, 1999; Singles: Back To The Bass (unreleased); Set You Free; Turn Up The Power; Set You Free (re-released No. 2, UK); Tears in the Rain, 1999; DA YA Think I'm Sexy?, 1999; Paradise City, 1999; As producer: 200% Energy, 1995; N Trance, Stayin' Alive, 1995; Now Dance '95, 1995; Dance '96 Supermix, 1996; goodtime disco Dance Hits, 1997; Euromix Vol. 3, 1997; Night at the Roxbury, 1998; House of Boogie, 1998. *Honours:* Best UK Dance Record, 1994; Platinum Disc, 1994; (both for Set You Free). *Membership:* Musicians' Union. *Leisure interests:* Football (Manchester United); Collecting old MGs. *Current Management:* All Around The World. *Address:* All Around The World, 9–13 Penny St, Blackburn BB1 6HJ, England.

NUGENT Ted; b. 13 Dec. 1949, Detroit, Michigan, USA. Rock Musician (guitar); Singer. *Career:* Founder, guitarist, The Amboy Dukes, 1966–75; Solo artiste, 1975–89; Formed Damn Yankees, 1989–; Appearances include: Reading Festival (UK debut), 1976; California Jam II Festival, Los Angeles, 1978; California Music Festival, with Van Halen, Cheap Trick, Aerosmith, 1979; World Series of Rock, Cleveland, with Aerosmith, Journey, Thin Lizzy, 1979; Whiplash Bash, Detroit, 1988; Volunteer Jam XIV, Nashville, 1991; Television includes: Miami Vice, NBC TV, 1984; Late Night With David Letterman, NBC TV, 1991. *Recordings:* Albums: with The Amboy Dukes: Call of The Wild, 1973; Tooth Fang and Claw, 1974; Solo albums: Ted Nugent, 1975; Free For All, 1976; Cat Scratch Fever, 1977; Double Live Gonzo, 1978; Weekend Warriors, 1978; State of Shock, 1979; Scream Dream, 1980; Great Gonzos – The Best of Ted Nugent, 1981; Intensities In Ten Cities, 1981; Nugent, 1982; Penetrator, 1984; Little Miss Dangerous, 1986; Anthology, 1986; If You Can't Lick 'Em, Lick 'Em!, 1988; Spirit of The Wild, 1995; with Damn Yankees: Damn Yankees, 1990. *Honours:* Gold and Platinum discs. *Current Management:* Madhouse Management. *Address:* PO Box 15108, Ann Arbor, MI 48106, USA.

NUMAN Gary, (Gary Webb); b. 8 March 1958, Hammersmith, London, England. Singer; Songwriter. *Career:* Singer, Tubeway Army, 1978–79; Billed as solo artiste, 1979–; Own record label, Numa Records, 1984–87; Extensive tours include: World tour, 1980; Annual British tours; Regular television appearances. *Recordings:* Albums: Replicas (No. 1, UK), 1979; The Pleasure Principle (No. 1, UK), 1979; Telekon (No. 1, UK), 1980; Living Ornaments 1979–80, 1981; Dance, 1981; I Assassin, 1982; New Man Numan – The Best of Gary Numan, 1982; The Plan, 1984; White Noise Live, 1985; Strange Charm, 1986; Exhibition, 1987; Metal Rhythm, 1988; Skin Mechanic, 1989; Outland, 1991; Machine + Soul, 1992; Best of 1979–83, 1993; Dream Corrosion, 1994; Exile, 1997; Contributor, Clues, Robert Palmer, 1980; White Noise, 1998; Black Heart, 1998; My Dying Machine, 1998; Hit singles include: Are Friends Electric? (No. 1, UK), 1979; Cars (No. 1, UK), 1979; Complex, 1979; We Are Glass, 1980; I Die You Die, 1980; This Wreckage, 1981; She's Got Claws, 1981; Music For Chameleons, 1982; We Take Mystery (To Bed), 1982; White Boys and Heroes, 1982; Warriors, 1983; This Is Love; I Can't Stop; I Still Remember; Cars (E Reg Mix); with Bill Sharpe (Shakatak): Change Your Mind, 1985; New Thing From London Town, 1986.

NÚÑEZ Carlos, (Carlos Núñez Muñoz); b. Spain. Musician (gaita, recorder, tin whistle); Composer. *Musical Education:* Royal Conservatory, Madrid, studied Baroque Music. *Career:* Began playing the gaita (Galician bagpipes), aged 8; Invited to play as soloist with Lorient Symphony Orchestra, Britanny, aged 13; Studied at the Royal Conservatory of Music in Madrid, Received highest ever marks achieved for Baroque recorder; Brought new life to neglected Galician folk tradition by studying the style of Irish and Scottish pipers and bringing ornamentation into the playing of the pipes; Reached wider audience by collaborating with other Celtic musicians including: Chieftains; Dan Ar Braz. *Recordings:* Albums: A Irmandade Das Estrellas (Brotherhood of Stars), 1996; Os Amores Libres, Mayo Longo, 2000; features on: Treasure Island OST, 1989; The Long Black Veil, The Chieftains, 1995; Santiago, The Chieftains, 1996; Finisterres, Dan Ar Braz, 1997; Zenith, Dan Ar Braz, 1998; Silent Night – A Christmas In Rome, Paddy Moloney, 1998; Caminhos, Dulce Pontes, 1998; Bilbao Oh, Kepa Junkera, 1999. *Honour:* Folkest 2001, Special Award, Rome.

NUNN Charles David; b. 14 Sept. 1954, Stellenbosch, South Africa. Pastor; Musician (pan flute); Singer. m. 8 Jan. 1982, 1 s., 2 d. *Career:* Performer, preacher, gospel music, and the Gospel of Jesus Christ; Star of the Week, Afrikaans Stereo; Several radio chat shows. *Recordings:* 2 albums of pan flute music; 1 album as vocalist. *Membership:* ASAMI. *Leisure interests:* Photography; Flying; Music. *Current Management:* Studio Nunn Ministries. *Address:* PO Box 4292, Secunda 2302, South Africa.

NYE Cheryl; b. Montréal, Québec, Canada. Singer; Songwriter; Model; Musician (keyboards). *Musical Education:* BFA Music, Voice Major, Concordia University. *Career:* Sung anthems at: Toronto Skydome; Montréal Forum; Olympic Stadium; Lansdowne Park; Television: CBC; CFCF; Videotron; Télé-Métropole; RDS; CHRO; Radio-Québec; CFCL-CITO; CHNB-CKNY. *Recordings:* Singles: Never Give Up On A Dream, 1982; Heartbeat, 1986; Album: Loving You, 1993. *Honour:* B100 Pepsi Entertainer Award (USA). *Memberships:* ACTRA; CCMA; SOCAN; CMA. *Leisure interests:* Music; Dancing; Sports. *Current Management:* WE Communications. *Address:* 455 Ballantyne N Montréal W, QC H4X 2C8, Canada.

NYS (Magthea) Sandy; b. 30 July 1959, Mechelen, Belgium. Graphic Designer. *Education:* Graphic Design, Art School. *Musical Education:* School for Electronic Music: SEM by Joris De Laet, Conservatorium Antwerpen. *Career:* Tours, Europe, with bands including: Klinik, Hybryds, 1983–; World-wide radio broadcast, in independent charts. *Recordings:* Music For Rituals – An Ongoing Musical Spiritual Quest; More than 10 album releases, more than 100 hours music registered at SABAM. *Publications:* More than 100 pages, official and underground press. *Honour:* Soundtrack for Aquaria of Antwerp Zoo. *Membership:* SABAM, Belgian copyright organization. *Leisure interest:* Trying to survive. *Current Management:* 3riort Vzw. *Address:* Julian Dillenstr 22, 2018 Antwerp, Belgium.

NYSTROM Lene G; b. 2 Oct. 1973, Tonsberg, Norway. Singer. *Career:* Joined Joyspeed; Changed name to Aqua; Secured record deal in Denmark; Numerous TV and live appearances in Scandinavia and UK. *Recordings:* Itsy Blitzy, as Joyspeed, 1989; Roses are Red; My Oh My; Barbie Girl; Doctor Jones; Lollipop; Turn Back Time (from film Sliding Doors); Good Morning Sunshine; Albums: Aquarium, 1997; Bubble Mix, 1998.

O

O CONGHAILE Micheál; b. 14 March 1962, Galway, Ireland. Writer; Man.-Dir; Record Co Exec. *Education:* BA; MA; H Dip In Ed. *Musical Education:* No formal, expert on Sean-nós (Irish language unaccompanied singing). *Career:* Author on 10 books in Irish language; Former college lecturer; Founder of Cló Iar-Chonnachta, Ireland's fastest growing traditional music label, 1985; Many national literary awards. *Publications:* Song collections: Croch Suas é; Up Seanamhach!. *Honour:* Elected member of Aosdána for outstanding contribution to the arts in Ireland. *Memberships:* PRS; IMRO. *Leisure interests:* Reading; Sports; The Arts; Travel. *Address:* Cló Iar-Chonnachta, Indreabhán, Conamara, Co Galway, Ireland.

Ó CONLUAIN Proinsias; b. 17 Aug. 1919, Benburb, County Tyrone, Ireland. Radio Prod. m. Sheila Murphy, 2 Sept. 1947, 1 d. *Education:* Scholarship, Queen's University, Belfast. *Career:* Scriptwriter, Producer, Radio Éireann, 1947–60; Producer, RTÉ Radio, 1960–83; Numerous radio programmes, popular, folk, traditional music; Series included: The Ballad Tree; The Singer and The Song; Between The Jigs and The Reels; Gold-Dust On The Fiddle; Features, documentaries on traditional singers, musicians, collectors, including: Bunting; Hardebeck; Francis O Neill (The Captain from Chicago); Sam Henry (Coleraine); John Rea the Dulcimer Man (Glenarm); John Maguire (The Rosslea Pad); Robert Cinnamond (Glenavy); Mrs Eileen Keaney (Glenelly and Belfast). *Recordings:* Robert Cinnamond: You Rambling Boys of Pleasure, sleeve notes, 1975; Róise na nAmhrán, Songs of a Donegal Woman, 1994: Songs recorded Arranmore Island, Co Donegal, 1953; Introductions to Song Translations/Transcriptions. *Publications:* Articles on traditional music, musicians, in journals including: Irish Folk Music Studies; Dál gCais: The Journal of Clare, 1986; Dúiche Néill: The Journal of the O Neill Country Historical Society (founder/editor). *Honours:* Jacob's Award, radio, 1979; Gradam Sean-Nós Cois Life, 1998. *Memberships:* Founder mem., Irish Folk Music Society; Board mem., Irish Traditional Music Archive, 1993–95. *Leisure interests:* Reading; Research; Local History. *Address:* 75 Blackheath Park, Clontarf, Dublin 3, Ireland.

O CONNOR Martin (Mairtin); b. 28 March 1955, Galway, Ireland. Musician (accordion). m. Sietske Van Minnen, 28 Dec. 1983, 1 s., 3 d. *Education:* Engineering. *Musical Education:* Self-taught traditional musician. *Career:* Tours: America; Europe; Middle East; Hong Kong; Soloist, Bill Whelan's Seville Suite, with RTE Concert Orchestra, World Expo, Seville, 1993; Soloist in Riverdance; Featured in television documentaries: Bringing It All Back Home; River of Sound. *Compositions:* Music for 2 short films, many local theatre productions. *Recordings:* Solo albums: The Connachtman's Rambles; Perpetual Motion; Chatterbox (featuring own compositions); Featured as accordion player on: Riverdance, Bill Whelan, 1996; Golden Heart, Mark Knopfler, 1996; Eileen Ivers, So Far: The collection, 1979–95; Legends of Ireland, 1998; Ellen Cranitch, Karst, 1998; Maire Brennan, Whisper to the Wild Water, 1999; Retrospective, Mark O'Connor, 1999. *Honour:* AIB (Allied Irish Bank) Traditional Musician of The Year, 1995. *Memberships:* IMRO; Musicians' Union. *Leisure interests:* Bee-keeping; Golf. *Current Management:* Annagh Music. *Address:* Annaghdown Pier, Annaghdown, Co Galway, Ireland.

O DOCHARTAIGH Seoirse; b. 17 June 1946, Belfast, Northern Ireland. Teacher; Painter; Musician. *Education:* BA, Fine Arts. *Musical Education:* MA by thesis, University College, Cork. *Career:* Born into musical family, began with singing, later, guitar and tin whistle; Public performances increased 1970s, including television appearances and radio broadcasts; Tours: Germany; France; Netherlands; Ireland; UK; USA; Musical and artistic director of own band, Dúlamán, 1995-. *Recordings:* Slán Agus Beannacht, 1988; Seoirse O Dochartaigh-Live, 1989; Bláth Buí, 1992; Amhráin agus Bodhráin, 1994; Oíche Go Maidin, 1994; Seachrán Chearbhaill, 2000. *Publications:* Over 80 songs and instrumental pieces. *Honours:* Music prizes in the Oireachtas. *Memberships:* FED; PRS; IMRO; PPI; MCPS. *Leisure interests:* Travel; Musical research. *Current Management:* H Ponting, Auld of Clunie Farmhouse, Blairgowrie, Perthshire PH10 6RH, Scotland. *Address:* Teach an tSrutháin, Ráth an Aonaigh Thiar, An Lathaigh, Co Dhún na nGall, Éire.

Ó FARACHÁIN Antaine; b. 6 Feb. 1959, Dublin, Ireland. Traditional Singer; Musician. *Education:* BEd. *Career:* Organizer, Sean-Nós Cois Life Festival; Guest at various music and vocal festivals including Sidmouth Folk Festival, Inishowen Singers Festival, Ennistymon Singers Festival, Willie Clancy Summer School, Milwaukee Irish Fest; Numerous radio and television appearances: The Pure Drop, Mountain Lark, Fleádh, Tinteán, Late Late Show, Síbín, Eurovision Song Contest, 1995. *Compositions:* Various songs in traditional style, in both Engish and Irish language. *Recordings:* Seachrán Sí, CD. *Honours:* Various prizes at Oireachtas na Gaeilge (Irish

Cultural Festival). *Leisure interests:* Produces radio and television programmes on traditional music; Singing; Folklore. *Address:* 13 Bóthar Emmet, Cill Mhaighneann, Baile Átha Cliath 8, Dublin, Ireland.

Ó LIONÁIRD Iarla; b. 1964, Cúil Aodha, County Cork, Ireland. Vocalist. *Education:* University College Dublin, studied Literature. *Career:* First performance, aged 5; First radio recording, aged 7; Member: Coir Cuil Aodha; Worked as teacher and, later, singing tutor at University College, Cork; Presenter of TV series The Pure Drop, 1989; Collaborations include: Peadar O Riada; Matt Molloy; Afro Celt Sound System; Shaun Davey. *Recordings:* Aislingi Ceoil (with Tony MacMahon and Noel Hill), 1993; Seven Steps To Mercy, 1997; I Could Read the Sky (featuring Sinead O Connor and Martin Hayes), 2000; features on Afro Celt Sound System Albums: Vol. 1 – Sound Magic, 1996; Vol. 2 – Release, 1999; Vol. 3 – Further In Time, 2001. *Address:* c/o Realworld Records. *E-mail:* records@realworld.on.net.

O MAONLAI Liam; b. Dublin, Ireland. Singer; Musician (piano). *Career:* Member, punk group Congress (later became My Bloody Valentine), Dublin; Busker, duo Incomparable Benzini Brothers (with Fiachna O'Brainain), 1985; Founder member, Hothouse Flowers, 1986-. *Recordings:* Albums: with Hothouse Flowers: People (No. 2, UK), 1988; Home, 1990; Songs From The Rain, 1993; with Def Leppard, Retro Active, 1993; with Sharon Shannon, Sharon Shannon, 1993; with Liam O'Flynn, Out to the Other Side, 1993; with the Rankin Family, North country, 1994; with ALT, Altitude, 1995; with Altan, Best of Altan, 1997; with Sharon Shannon, Spellbound: The Best of Sharon Shannon, 1999; with Maire Breatnach, Angels Candles, 1999; Singles: Don't Go; I Can See Clearly Now; Give It Up; Movies. *Honour:* Street Entertainers of The Year Award, 1985. *Current Management:* Chris O'Donnell. *Address:* c/o London Records, PO Box 1422, Chancellors House, Chancellors Rd, London W6 9SG, England.

Ó SÚILLEABHÁIN Micheál; b. County Waterford, Ireland. Musician (piano); Composer; Conductor; Prod. m. Noirin Ni Riain. *Education:* University College Cork, Ireland, undergraduate degree; Queen's University Belfast, PhD. *Career:* Produced albums for artists including: Noirin Ni Riain; Liam O'Flynn; Paddy Glackin; Lecturer at University College Cork, 1975–; Established course in traditional music; Head of music department, 1994; Founder: Irish World Music centre at University of Limerick; Visiting professor to Boston College, 1990; Produced a fiddle festival and founded archive for traditional music; Founder member of world music group Hiberno-Jazz; Contributed to RTE/BBC TV series Bringing It All Back Home, 1992; Wrote and presented TV series A River of Sound, 1995. *Compositions:* Lumen, interval entertainment at Eurovision Song Contest, 1995; Maranata, vocal composition, commissioned by Cork International Choral Festival, premiered in 2000. *Recordings:* Albums include: Oro Damhnaigh, 1977; Cry of the Mountain, 1982; The Dolphin's Way (featuring Matt Molloy and Colm Murphy), 1987; Oilean (featuring Tony McMahon and Matt Molloy), 1989; Casadh (featuring Mel Mercier), 1990; Gaiseadh (with the Irish Chamber Orchestra), 1992; Becoming, 1998; Templum (featuring Mel Mercier), 2001. *Address:* c/o Irish World Music Centre, University of Limerick, Limerick, Ireland.

OAKENFOLD Paul; b. 1964, London, England. DJ; Remixer; Recording Artist. *Career:* Former chef; Began as DJ, Covent Garden, London, 1982; Resident, Heaven Club; Member, Steve Hillage's collective System 7, 1990s; Concerts include support to U2, Naples football stadium, Italy, 1993. *Recordings include:* JD15 – Paul Oakenfold In the Mix; Fantazia Presents the House Collection, 1997; Cream Anthems 97, 1997; Global Underground: Live in Oslo, 1997; Tranceport, 1998; Paul Oakenfold in New York, 1998; Global Underground, New York, 1999; Resident: Two Years of Oakenfold at Cream, 1999; Remixer, albums on Perfecto label; Produced and remixed for artists including: Boy George, U2, Happy Mondays, Olive, Cure, Insider. *Honours include:* Q Award, Best Producer, 1990. *Current Management:* 140dB, 1 McCrone Mews, Belsize Lane, London NW3 5BG, England.

OAKES Richard; b. 10 Oct. 1976, Perivale, Middlesex, England. Musician (Guitar); Songwriter. *Career:* Joined Suede to replace Bernard Butler as guitarist, 1995; Numerous tours, festival dates and TV appearances. *Recordings:* Singles: Trash, 1996; Filmstar, 1996; Lazy, 1996; Electricity, 1999; She's In Fashion, 1999; Everything Will Flow, 1999; Albums: Coming Up, 1996; Sci-Fi Lullabies, 1997; Head Music, 1999.

OAKEY Philip; b. 2 Oct. 1955, Sheffield, South Yorkshire, England. Singer; Musician (synthesizer). *Career:* Former hospital porter; Lead singer, Human League, 1978–; Concerts include: Support To Siouxsie and The Banshees, British tour, 1979; Support to Iggy Pop, European tour, 1980; Headline tours, UK, world-wide, 1980-. *Recordings:* Hit singles include: Sound of The Crowd, 1981; Love Action, 1981; Open Your Heart, 1981; Don't You Want Me (No. 1, UK and US), 1981; Being Boiled, 1982; Mirror Man, 1982; (Keep Feeling) Fascination, 1983; The Lebanon, 1984; Life On Your Own, 1984; Louise, 1984; Human (No. 1, USA), 1986; Only Human, 1994; with Giorgio Moroder: Together In Electric Dreams, for film Electric Dreams, 1984; Albums: Reproduction, 1979; Travelogue, 1980; Dare! (No. 1, UK), 1981; Love and Dancing (remixed mini-album), 1982; Hysteria, 1984; Crash, 1986; Greatest Hits, 1988; Romantic?, 1990; Octopus, 1994. *Honour:* BRIT Award, Best Newcomer, 1982. *Current Management:* Huge and Jolly Management, 56–60 Islington Park St, London N1 1PX, England.

OAKLEY Pete; b. 29 June 1962, Burton-on-Trent, Staffordshire, England. Musician (guitar); Singer; Songwriter. m. 12 April 1986. *Musical Education:* Self-taught. *Career:* Folk/blues guitarist; Many radio and television appearances including: BBC Radio 1, 2 and 5, World Service and European radio stations; Recordings for many local US and Australian radio stations; Tours, 1989–; Owner, 2 music shops, Pete Oakley Music. *Recordings:* Back Porch Blues; Old Guitars Never Lie; Ghost In The City. *Publications:* Various magazine contributions. *Memberships:* British Actors Equity; PRS. *Leisure interests:* Sports cars; Vintage guitars; Fly fishing. *Current Management:* Pete Oakley Music. *Address:* 81 Horninglow Rd, Burton-on-Trent, Staffordshire DE14 2PT, England.

OANA Augustin; b. 26 July 1942, Cabesti-Hunedoara, Romania. Folk Singer. m. 28 May 1972, 2 s. *Musical Education:* Professional school in composition; Hunedoara Musical Assembly. *Career:* Several television and radio appearances, including Bucharest radio; Major concerts throughout Romania, and tours of Turkey and Austria; Adapted poems for folk music of region; Participated in many shows and television appearances in Bucharest Radio Orchestra. *Recordings:* Record of popular music. *Address:* Str Izvorul Muresului, Nr2 Block A-9, sc-E et4 ap73, Sector 4, Bucharest, Romania.

OATES John; b. 7 April 1949, New York, USA. Singer; Songwriter; Musician (guitar). *Education:* Temple University. *Career:* Member, The Masters; Gulliver; Member, duo Hall and Oates, with Daryl Hall, 1969–; Appearances world-wide include: Live Aid, Philadelphia, 1985; Rainforest benefit concert, with Grateful Dead, Madison Square Garden, 1988; Earth Day, Central Park, New York, 1990; USA Harvest National Hunger Relief concert, 1991; The Simple Truth, benefit concert for Kurdish refugees, Wembley, 1991. *Compositions include:* Numerous hit songs co-written with Daryl Hall; Film soundtrack, Outlaw Blues, 1979; Co-writer, Electric Blue, Icehouse, 1988. *Recordings:* Albums: with Hall and Oates: Whole Oats, 1972; Abandoned Luncheonette, 1974; War Babies, 1974; Daryl Hall and John Oates, 1975; Bigger Than Both of Us, 1976; No Goodbyes, 1977; Beauty On A Back Street, 1977; Livetime, 1978; X-Static, 1979; Voices, 1980; Private Eyes, 1981; H2O, 1982; Rock 'n' Soul (Part 1), 1983; Big Bam Boom, 1984; Live At The Apollo, 1985; Ooh Yeah, 1988; Change of Season, 1990; Looking Back – The Best Of…, 1991; Atlantic Collection, 1996; Marigold Sky, 1997; Back to Back, 1998; with Keith Martin, It's Long Overdue, 1995; with Icehouse, Man of the Colours/Code Blue, 1996; Pop in the 80's Vol. 1, 1999; US No. 1 singles include: Rich Girl, 1977; Kiss On My List, 1981; Private Eyes, 1981; I Can't Go For That (No Can Do), 1982; Maneater, 1982; Out of Touch, 1984; Numerous other hit singles; Contributor: We Are The World, USA For Africa, 1985; Sun City, Artists Against Apartheid, 1985; The Last Temptation of Elvis, 1990; Two Rooms – Celebrating The Songs of Elton John and Bernie Taupin, 1991. *Honours include:* American Music Awards: Favourite Duo or Band, 1983–85; 19 US Gold and Platinum discs (most successful duo in US recording history). *Current Management:* All Access Entertainment, 53 W 23rd St, 11th Floor, New York, NY 10010, USA.

OBERG Rolf Thomas; b. 15 March 1967, Helsingborg, Sweden. Vocalist; Musician (melodica, synthesizer). *Career:* Member, bob hund, 1991–; More than 300 concerts throughout Scandinavia; Played at festivals including Roskilde, Lollipop, Ruisrock, Quartfestivalen and Hultsfred; Member with Magnus Boman of electric and electronic duo, Instant Life. *Compositions:* I Stället för Musik: Förvirring, 1996; Düsseldorf, 1996. *Recordings:* with bob hund: bob hund, 1993, 1994; Edvin Medvind, 1994; I Stället för Musik: Förvirring, 1996; Omslag: Martin Kann, 1996; with Instant Life: I Turned My Best Friends into Slaves, CD, 1993; I Made Arrangements for World Peace, 1994. *Honours:* Grammy Awards: Best Live Act, 1994, Best Lyrics, 1996. *Memberships:* STIM; SAMI. *Leisure interests:* Music; Books; Food; Drinking. *Current Management:* Bob Hunds Förlag, Råsundavägen 150, 169 36 Solna, Sweden.

OBI Ben; b. 7 Oct. 1965, London, England. Prod. *Education:* College and University of Minnesota. *Career:* Producer, Alexander O'Neal, 1996; Produced, The Sunset Music Band and A Large Percentage of New Talent Emerging From Minneapolis. *Recordings:* Loversagain; Sex On

The Beach; Sunset Celebration. *Membership:* ASCAP. *Current Management:* Savannah Street Music, 2325 Endiocott St #202, St Paul, MN 55114, USA.

O'BRIAN Sean Timothy; b. 28 April, Minesota, USA. Musician. m. Janis Kimble O'Brian, 1 d. *Career:* Concert performances, Fan Fair, Nashville, Fan Fest and Star Fest, Los Angeles, Six Flags Fiesta Texas; Television appearances include, The Crook and Chase Show, Extra, 48 Hours, Hard Copy, American Gladiators; Radio; demo and master recordings; Film commercial and stage acting; Still photography and modeling. *Recordings:* CD and Video, 1998. *Memberships:* Country Music Asscn; Academy of Country Music; Broadcast Music Inc. *Leisure interests:* Gymnastics; Swimming; Diving; Boxing; Weight Training; Horseback Riding; Water and Snow Skiing. *Current Management:* TGC of San Antonio, Texas. *Address:* PO Box 216, Karnes City, Texas 78118, USA.

O'BRIEN Ed; b. 15 April 1968, Oxford, England. Musician (Bass). *Career:* Member, On A Friday, became Radiohead; Secured record deal, 1991; Numerous live appearances and support dates including REM, 1995; Festival dates and TV appearances. *Recordings:* Singles: Anyone Can Play Guitar EP, 1993; Creep, 1993; Stop Whispering, 1994; My Iron Lung EP, 1994; Street Spirit (Fade Out), 1995; Fake Plastic Trees, 1996; Just, 1996; High and Dry, 1996; Paranoid Android, 1998; Airbag: How Am I Driving EP, 1998; No Surprises, 1998; Karma Police, 1998; Pablo Honey, 1993; The Bends, 1995; OK Computer, 1997.

O'BRIEN Steve; Musician. *Career:* Member, Fun Lovin' Criminals; Numerous TV appearances and live dates; Left band, 1999. *Recordings:* Singles: Scooby Snacks, 1996; The Grave and the Constant, 1997; King of New York, 1997; Sing the Fun Lovin' Criminal, 1997; I'm Not In Love, 1997; Love Unlimited, 1998; Big Night Out, 1998; Albums: Come Find Yourself, 1996; 100% Colombian, 1998.

O'BRIEN-OLUYEMI Rebecca Jane; b. 4 Jan. 1966, Caerphilly, Wales. Vocalist. m. Emmanuel Valentine Oluyemi, 1 Dec. 1992. *Education:* Newham Community College, 1993–94; London Central St Martins School of Art and Design, 1994–97. *Musical Education:* Private lessons; Piano theory, 1995; Vocal training course and exam, with John Campbell. *Career:* Concerts with Thomas The Voice: The Africa Centre; The Bull and Bush; Camden Palace; Backing vocals with Sandra Tavernier. *Recordings:* Backing vocals, Tell Me Where; Nothing Compares To U; Backing vocals, Time Will Tell, Footsie Drummond; She Move Thru' The Fair, with Thomas The Voice. *Membership:* Musicians' Union. *Leisure interests:* Music; Art and Design; Dance. *Address:* 57 Talbot Walk, Church Rd, London NW10 9HU, England.

O'CARROLL Sinéad Maria; b. 14 May 1978, Dublin, Ireland. Singer. *Career:* Member, B*Witched; Numerous tours and television appearances; Several hit singles. *Recordings:* Singles: C'est La Vie, 1998; Rollercoaster, 1998; To You I Belong, 1998; Blame it on the Weatherman, 1998; Jesse Hold On, 1999; Albums: B*Witched, 1998; Awake and Breathe, 1999.

OCASEK Ric (Richard); b. 23 March 1949, Baltimore, Maryland, USA. Singer; Songwriter; Musician (guitar); Record Prod. m. Paulina Porizkova, 23 Aug. 1989. *Career:* Founder, singer, guitarist, The Cars, 1976–88; Appearances with the Cars include: Residency, The Rat club, Boston, 1977; European tour, 1978; Concert to 500,000 audience, Central Park, New York, 1979; US Festival, 1982; Founded Synchro Sound recording studio, Boston, 1981; Solo artiste, 1990–; Appearances include Earth Day, Central Park, New York, 1990. *Recordings:* Albums with The Cars: The Cars, 1979; Candy-O, 1979; Panorama, 1980; Shake It Up, 1982; Heartbeat City, 1984; The Cars' Greatest Hits, 1985; Door To Door, 1987; Solo albums: Beatitude, 1983; This Side of Paradise, 1986; Fireball Zone, 1991; Negative Theater, 1993; Quick Change World, 1993; Getchertikitz, 1996; Troublizing, 1997; Hit singles: with the Cars: Just What I Needed, 1978; My Best Friend's Girl, 1978; Good Times Roll, 1979; Touch and Go, 1980; Shake It Up, 1982; Since You're Gone, 1982; You Might Think, 1984; Magic, 1984; Drive, 1984; Hello Again, 1984; Why Can't I Have You?, 1985; Tonight She Comes, 1986; I'm Not The One, 1986; You Are The Girl, 1987; Solo singles: Emotion In Motion, 1986; The Next Right Moment, 1997; Record producer, artists including: Bad Brains; Black 47. *Honours:* Rolling Stone Best New Band of the Year, 1979; Grammy Award Nomination, Best New Artist, 1979; MTV Award, You Might Think, 1984. *Current Management:* Lookout Management, 2644 30th St, First Floor, Santa Monica, CA 90405, USA.

OCEAN Billy, (Leslie Charles); b. 21 Jan. 1950, Trinidad. Singer; Songwriter. *Career:* Recording artiste, 1975–; International concerts include: Live Aid, Philadelphia, 1985. *Compositions include:* Co-writer, own hits: Loverboy; There'll Be Sad Songs; Get Outta My Dreams. *Recordings:* Albums: Nights (I Feel Like Getting Down), 1981; Inner Feeling, 1982; Suddenly, 1984; Love Zone, 1986; Tear Down These Walls, 1988; Greatest Hits, 1989; Time To Move On, 1993; L.I.F.E.; Hit singles include: Love Really Hurts Without You, 1976; Stop Me If You've Heard It

Before, 1976; Red Light Spells Danger, 1977; Caribbean Queen (No More Love On The Run), also released as European Queen and African Queen (No. 1, USA), 1984; Loverboy, 1985; Suddenly, 1985; When The Going Gets Tough The Tough Get Going, used in film soundtrack The Jewel of The Nile (No. 1, UK), 1986; There'll Be Sad Songs (To Make You Cry), (No. 1, USA), 1986; Love Zone, 1987; Get Outta My Dreams (Get Into My Car) (No. 1, USA), 1988. *Honours:* Grammy Award, Best R & B Performance, 1985; Grammy Nomination, 1986; American Music Awards: Favorite Male Video Artist, Favorite Single, 1988; ASCAP Award for Caribbean Queen, Most Played Song in USA, 1996. *Current Management:* LJE, 32 Willesden Lane, London NW6 7ST, England.

O'CONNELL Carl; b. 24 Feb. 1965, Watford, Hertfordshire, England. Musician (keyboards); Programmer. *Musical Education:* Grade II guitar; Formal jazz tuition. *Recordings:* Album: Is Nothing Sacred, Love Republic; Several Dox music albums; Production Assistant, several Mute Records remixes; Charity appearance with East 17. *Memberships:* Musicians' Union; PAMRA. *Current Management:* Archangel Music, Ilford. *Address:* 16 Fortis Green, East Finchley, London N2 9EL, England.

O'CONNOR Gerry; b. 20 July 1960, Tipperary, Ireland. Composer; Musician (banjo, guitar, violin). m. Marie, 13 May 1980, 1 s., 1 d. *Education:* Third level, UCD, Dublin. *Musical Education:* Self-taught. *Career:* Solo albums; Member, 4 Men and A Dog; Performances, television, radio: Britain; Europe; Scandinavia; Canada; USA; Australia; Workshop; Festivals; Tutor publications, book, cassette, video. *Recordings:* Time To Time; Trad At Heart; Funk The Cajun Blues; 4 Men and A Dog: Shifting Gravel; Dr A's Secret Remedies; Niamh Parsons: Loosen Up; Gordon Duncan: Circular Breath; Gaelic roots; Mighty Session; Mists of Morning; Moving Cloud: Foxglove. *Publications:* 50 Solos For Tenor Banjo; Tenor Banjo Techniques. *Honours:* International Radio Festival: Bratislava, 1989; Folk Album of the Year, 1991, (4 Men and A Dog). *Memberships:* IMRO; PRS; MCPS. *Leisure interests:* Golf; Reading; Athletics. *Current Management:* Marie O'Connor, 46 Blarney Park, Kimmage, Dublin 12, Ireland; Jim Heaney CBM, 18 Dillons Ave, Whiteabbey, Co Antrim BT37 0SX, Northern Ireland.

O'CONNOR Mark; b. Seattle, Washington, USA. Musician (violin, guitar, bass, mandolin). *Career:* Leader, own group, Nashville Strings; Musician with artistes including: Paul Simon; James Taylor; Dolly Parton; Willie Nelson; Chet Atkins; Randy Travis; Michael Brecker; Concerts include: Barbican Hall (with Yo-Yo Ma); Montreux Jazz Festival; Carnegie Hall, New York. *Recordings include:* Heroes, 1991; Johnny Appleseed (children's album with Garrison Keillor), 1995; Fiddle Concerto for violin and orchestra, 1995. *Honours:* Winner, classical guitar competition, aged 11; Country Music Assen's Musician of The Year, 4 times; Grammy Award, New Nashville Cats; Grammy Nomination, Johnny Appleseed. *Membership:* CMA.

O'CONNOR Sinead; b. 12 Dec. 1966, Glenageary, Ireland. Singer; Songwriter; Actress. m. John Reynolds, March 1989, 1 s. *Musical Education:* Dublin College of Music; Singing lessons with Frank Merriman, Parnell School of Music, 1992. *Career:* Solo artiste, Dublin, 1985; Singer, Ton Ton Macoute, 1985; Solo artiste, 1986–; Concerts include: Tours, UK, Europe, USA, 1988; Year of The Horse World Tour, 1990; Glastonbury Festival, 1990; The Wall Benefit, Berlin, 1990; Amnesty International Benefit, Chile (duet with Peter Gabriel), 1990; Simple Truth Concert (for Kurdish refugees), Wembley, 1991; Bob Dylan 30th Anniversary; As actress: Hush-A-Bye-Baby, C4, Dublin Film Festival, 1990; Ghost of Oxford Street, C4, 1991; Television documentary: Sinead O'Connor – Coffee and Cigarettes, BBC TV, 1992. *Recordings:* Singles: Heroine, 1986; Troy, 1987; Mandinka, 1988; Jump In The River, 1988; Nothing Compares To U, 1990; The Emperor's New Clothes, 1990; Three Babies, 1990; My Special Child, 1991; Thief of Your Heart, 1993; Fire On Babylon, 1994; Thank You For Hearing Me, 1994; Gospel Oak EP, 1997; This is a Rebel Song, 1997; This is to Mother You, 1997 Albums: The Lion and The Cobra, 1988; I Do Not Want What I Haven't Got, 1990; Am I Not Your Girl, 1992; Universal Mother, 1994; So Far... The Best of Sinead O'Connor, 1997; Also featured on: Mind Bomb, The The, 1989; Red Hot + Blue, 1990; Two Rooms – The Songs of Elton John and Bernie Taupin, 1992; Rising Above Bedlam, Jah Wobble, 1992; Be Still, 1993; Across The Borderline, Willie Nelson, 1993; Long Black Veil, Chieftans, 1995; Long Journey Home, 1998. *Honours include:* Grammy Award, 1991; Grammy Nomination, 1989; Numerous Music and Video Awards, 1990; 3 MTV Awards, 1990; Billboard Music Award, 1990; BRIT Award, 1991. *Current Management:* Principle Management, 30–32 Sir John Rogersons Quay, Dublin 2, Ireland.

O'DAY Anita Belle Colton; b. 18 Oct. 1919, Chicago, Illinois, USA. Singer. *Career:* Nightclub entertainer, Chicago, 1939–41; Singer, Gene Krupa's Orchestra, 1941–45; Stan Kenton, 1944; Woody Herman, 1946; Solo artiste, 1947–; Film appearances include: Gene Krupa Story, 1959; Jazz On A Summer's Day, 1960; Zigzag, 1970; Outfit, 1974; Concerts include: 50th Anniversary Concert, Carnegie Hall, 1985. *Recordings:* Solo albums include: Anita Sings; Pick Yourself Up; An Evening With Anita O'Day; Anita Sings The Winners; Lady Is A Tramp; Travellin' Light; At Mr Kelly's; Let Me Off Uptown; Live in Concert Tokyo 1976; Singin' and Swingin'; The Night Has a Thousand Eyes; Many compilation albums; Other recordings with Gene Krupa; Stan Kenton; Count Basie; Duke Ellington. *Publication:* Author: High Times, Hard Times, 1981. *Memberships:* AFTRA; BMI; Screen Actors Guild.

ODDE SORENSEN Knud; b. 25 Jan. 1955, Fröslev, Denmark. Musician (electric bass); Painter; Theatre Designer; Composer; Text Writer. *Education:* General Certificate of Education, Research Librarian. *Career:* Member, The Sods, 1977; Name changed to Sort Sol, 1980; Toured: USA, 1982; Russia, 1988; Music, scenography and costumes for Danish Royal Ballet production of Hamlet, 1996; Solo Exhibition of paintings, DCA Gallery, New York, 1999. *Recordings:* Minutes To Go, 1979; Under En Sort Sol, 1980; Dagger and Guitar, 1983; Everything That Rises Must Converge, 1987; Flow My Firetear, 1990; Glamourpuss, 1993; Unspoiled Monsters, 1996; Blackbox, 1997. *Publications:* Biography: Knud Odde by Henrik Wivel, 1994; Erich Von Stroheim, by Knud Odde, 1994. *Honours:* 3 (local) Grammies, 1991; 5 Grammies in 1994, with Sort Sol. *Current Management:* Rock On, Vesterbrogade 26, 1620 Copenhagen V, Denmark. *Address:* PO Box 613, Borups Alle 123, Copenhagen, Denmark.

ODELL Ann Mary; b. 18 April 1947, London, England. Musician (keyboards); Vocalist; Arranger. m. Stephen R Spurling, 17 June 1980, divorced 28 Nov. 1994, 2 s. *Musical Education:* Royal Academy of Music, 1964–66, LRAM Diploma. *Career:* Ivy Benson Orchestra; QE2 Maiden Voyage, Anna Dell Trio, 1969; Session musician and arranger, 1972–81; Bryan Ferry World Tour, 1977; BBC Broadcasts, R2 Nightride and Roundabout own band Blue Mink, 1992–94; Television: Top of The Pops; Les Dawson Show; Little and Large; Currently, running Watermill Jazz Club, Dorking, Surrey; Agency, MIDI recording studio, Take Note Ltd. *Recordings:* with Blue Mink: Fruity; Blue Mink; with Bryan Ferry: Another Time, Another Place; In Your Mind; Bride Stripped Bare; Solo: Ann Odell; A Little Taste; Grand Slam, Chopyn; Original Evita album, Jesus Christ Superstar film soundtrack; Beatles, Beatles Tapes; London Symphony Orchestra, Silk Road Suit; Yvonne Elliman, The Best of Yvonne Elliman; John Gustafson, Goose Grease. *Honours:* 5 Gold discs; Platinum disc; K-Tel Classic Rock Series with LSO. *Memberships:* PRS; Musicians' Union; Assen of British Jazz Musicians. *Leisure interests:* Reading; Collecting jazz recordings; Walks; Travel. *Current Management:* Take Note Ltd. *Address:* 24 Dodds Park, Brockham, Betchworth, Surrey RH3 7LD, England.

ODELL Roger Keith; b. 7 Dec. 1941, Epping, Essex, England. Musician (drums, percussion); Songwriter. m. Larraine, 18 Nov. 1968, 1 s., 1 d. *Musical Education:* Private studies, leading to Grade 8, Guildhall School of Music, Honours. *Career:* Toured throughout the world in concert, with numerous appearances on television and radio. *Compositions:* Contributed to over 20 recordings by Shakatak, as drummer and songwriter; Co-writer, several top 20 UK hits including: Night Birds; Down On The Street; Recent releases include: with Shakatak: Live at Ronnie Scott's, 1998; Shinin On, 1998; Magic, 1999; Invitations, 1999; Christmas Dreams, 1999; with Martini Grooves: Martini Grooves, 1999; Welcome to the Jazz Cafe, 1999. *Honour:* Tokyo International Song Festival, Silver Prize. *Memberships:* PRS; International Percussion Society; Professional mem., BASCA. *Leisure interest:* Music. *Current Management:* Les McCutcheon, Skratch Music Ltd. *Address:* 81, Crabtree Lane, London SW6 6LW, England.

ODGERS Brian Norman, (Badger); b. 9 Feb. 1942, Forest Gate, London, England. Musician (bass, bass guitar); Teacher of Life, Yoga. m. Jahnet McIlwain, 12 Dec. 1976, 4 d. (3 by previous marriage). *Musical Education:* Self-taught. *Career:* Played with: Herbie Hancock; Chick Corea; Freddie Hubbard; Larry Carlton; Van Morrison; Georgie Fame on Herbie's 50th birthday; Television special in Los Angeles; Tours: 2 years Van Morrison; 6 months Andy Williams; 26 years Georgie Fame; 3 years Winifred Atwel; Television, radio appearances over 30 years with most UK and World stars, include: Tom Jones; Englebert Humperdinck; Elton John; Eric Clapton; Cliff Richard; Sarah Vaughn; Shirley Bassey; Neil Diamond; Tony Bennett; Abba; Andre Previn. *Recordings:* John McLaughlin: Extrapolation; Van Morrison: Enlightenment; Orginal Evita recording with Andrew Lloyd Webber; Roger Daltrey: White Horse; Jimmy Webb: Land's End; Georgie Fame: That's What Friends Are For; Marc Bolan: Cat Black; Roger Daltrey, Martyrs and Madmen; Sweet Thursday; Session musician for 20 years; Recorded with almost every artist from rock through jazz to light classical. *Honours:* Flavour of The Month Award, 3 times. *Membership:* Musicians' Union. *Leisure interests:* Sex and drugs and rock 'n' roll; All the avenues of the esoteric. *Address:* c/o Ronnie Scotts Club, Frith St, London W1, England.

O'DONNELL Daniel; b. 12 Dec. 1961, Kincasslagh, County Donegal, Ireland. Singer. *Career:* Backing vocalist for sister Margo O'Donnell, early 1980s; Tours, UK and Ireland, 1985–; Concerts include: Carnegie Hall, New York, 1991, 1997, Opera House, Sydney, 1996; Point Theatre, Dublin, NEC, Birmingham, 1997; Own television series, Ireland.

Recordings: Albums: Two Sides of Daniel O'Donnell, 1985; I Need You, 1986; Don't Forget To Remember, 1987; The Boy From Donegal, 1987; From The Heart, 1988; Thoughts of Home, 1989; Favourites, 1990; The Last Waltz, 1990; The Very Best Of..., 1991; Follow Your Dream, 1992; Christmas With Daniel, 1994; Especially For You, 1994; The Classic Collection, 1995; Irish Collection, 1996; Timeless (with Mary Duff), 1996; Songs of Inspiration, 1996; I Believe, 1997; Love Songs, 1998; Greatest Hits, 1999; Live Laugh Love, 2001; Singles: I Just Want To Dance With You, 1992; Whatever Happened To Old Fashioned Love, 1993; Singing The Blues, 1994; Secret Love, 1995; Timeless, 1996; Footsteps, 1996; Give A Little Love, 1998; The Magic Is There, 1998; Uno Mas, 1999; The Way Dreams Are, 1999; Christmas Kiss, 1999; Light A Candle, 2000; 10 UK Country No. 1 hits; Videos include: Daniel O'Donnell Live In Concert, 1988; Thoughts of Home, 1989; TV Show Favourites, 1990; An Evening With Daniel O'Donnell, 1990; Follow Your Dream, 1992; Daniel and Friends Live, 1993; Just For You, 1994; The Classic Concert, 1995; Christmas with Daniel, 1996; The Gospel Show, Live at the Point, 1997; Give A Little Love, 1998; Peaceful Waters, 1999. *Honour:* MBE, 2002. *Address:* c/o Rosette Records, 103/105 Greenford Rd, Harrow, Middlesex, England.

O'FLYNN Liam; b. 1945, County Kildare, Ireland. Musician (uillean pipes). *Career:* Born into family of traditional musicians; Founding member: Planxty; One of the first musicians to bring classical and traditional music together as soloist in Shaun Davey's The Brendan Voyage; Appeared on film soundtracks: Cal, 1992; The Field, 1990; A River Runs Through It, 1992; Collaborations: Mark Knopfler; Kate Bush; Enya; Sinead O'Connor; International tours; Performed at the first BBC Proms night of Irish music, 1999; Recorded over 50 albums. *Recordings:* Albums include: The Brendan Voyage, 1980; The Fine Art of Piping, 1989; Out To An Other Side, 1993; The Given Note, 1995; The Piper's Call, 1998. *Honour:* Golden Insignia of the University of La Coruna, Spain, 2000. *Address:* c/o Tom Sherlock, 71 Carysfort Ave, Blackrock, County Dublin, Ireland.

O'GRADY Jenny; b. 30 Jan. 1949, Loughborough, Leicestershire, England. Singer; Vocal Coach. m. Robert Jolley, 1 s. *Musical Education:* Royal College of Music, London. *Career:* Freelance singer, radio, television, film soundtracks, wide variety recordings from Royal Opera House to pop; Also established as leading vocal coach to actors, actresses, musical theatre in London's West End, tours, shows including: Phantom of The Opera; Cats; Les Miserables; Starlight Express; Joseph; Vocal contractor: West Side Story; Michael Ball recording; Albums: Sparks, Plagiarism, 1997; Message in a Bottle, Mesage in a Bottle, 1999; Messenger: The Story of Joan of Arc, 1999; As Director or Choirmaster: Michael Card, Unveiled Hope, 1997; City of Angels (original Soundtrack), 1998; Craig Armstrong, Plunkett and Macleane, 1999; Elton John, Muse, 1999; Pet Shop Boys, Nightlife, 1999; Any Given Sunday, Any Given Sunday, 2000. *Honours:* ARCM; LRAM. *Memberships:* Equity; Musicians' Union. *Leisure interest:* Tennis. *Address:* 2 Queens Rd, Barnet, Hertfordshire ENS 4DG, England.

O'GRUAMA Aindrías; b. 9 May 1957, Dun Laoighaire, Ireland. Musician (guitar). *Career:* Guitar player with The Fatima Mansions; Many BBC radio and television sessions; Support to U2, Zoo TV tour; Tours of USA; MTV appearances. *Recordings:* Albums: Zerra (produced by Todd Rundgren); My Baby's Arm; Viva Dead Ponies; Valhalla Avenue; Lost In The Former West. *Honour:* Album of The Year, Hot Press Critics Poll, 1990. *Membership:* Musicians' Union. *Leisure interests:* Reading history and philosophy. *Current Management:* Arthog Music Productions. *Address:* 49 Chartham Court, Brixton, London Sw9 7PT, England.

O'HIGGINS David Charles; b. 1 Sept. 1964, Birmingham, England. Musician (saxophones); Composer. *Musical Education:* Trumpet, drums, piano, at school; Self-taught saxophone; Studied music, City University, London. *Career:* Regular working groups: National Youth Jazz Orchestra, 1983–86; Leader, Dave O'Higgins Quartet/Quintet, 1983–; Mezzoforte, 1986–89; Co-leader, Roadside Picnic, 1986–90; Leader, The Gang of Three, 1987–89; Leader, Dave O'Higgins and The Oblivion Brothers, 1989–91; Cleo Laine and The John Dankworth Quintet; Sax Appeal; Pizza Express Modern Jazz Sextet; Jason Rebello; Jim Mullen Quartet; Itchy Fingers; Clark Tracey Sextet; Martin Taylor's Spirit of Django; Tours include: Europe, Japan; Cuba; South Africa and Namibia; Tunisia; Sri Lanka; Bangladesh; Venues include: Montreux Jazz Festival, 1989; Havana Jazz Festival, 1993; Several residencies, Ronnie Scott's; New York's Visionez; Television includes: Wogan; Pebble Mill; Jonathon Ross Show; Appearance as busker, Mr Bean; Judge, YTV Young Jazz Musician of The Year; Many radio broadcasts. *Recordings:* with NYJO: Full Score; Concrete Cows; With An Open Mind; with Mezzoforte: No Limits; with Roadside Picnic: Roadside Picnic; For Madmen Only; with Jim Mullen: Soundbites; Rule of Thumb; with Jason Rebello: A Clearer View; with Sax Appeal: Flat Out; Let's Go; with Dave Higgins: All Good Things; Beats Working For A Living; with Clark Tracey: Full Speed Sideways; with Itchy Fingers: Full English Breakfast; with Martin Taylor: Spirit of Django; with John Dankworth: Live At Ronnie Scott's; with Matt Bianco: Another Time Another Place; with Simon Hale: East Fifteen; with Ray Charles: Strong

Love Affair; with Stephane Grappelli: Celebrating Grappelli; with Colosseum: Breads and Circuses; with James Galway: Un-Break My Heart. *Honours:* Best New Band, British Jazz Awards, 1988, 1989; Cleo Laine Personal Award, 1990; BT British Jazz Awards, Best Tenor Sax, and Rising Star, 1995.

OILING Matti; b. 20 Nov. 1942, Finland. Musician (drums). *Musical Education:* State scholarship, to study Latin-American rhythms, 1976. *Career:* Formed the Happy Jazz Band, 1969; Now playing as Oiling Boiling; Played with brass band Rempsetti, 1980s; Also plays with UHO-Trio; Regular session player; Founded Samba School, Helsinki; Founded own drumming school, 1980; Concerts include: Australia, 1986; California and Hawaii with Richie Cole, 1987; First ever Jazz festival, Jakarta, Indonesia, 1989; Palm Springs, 1989; Opened the Oiling Boiling Jazz and Blues Club, Tallinn, Estonia, 1990. *Publications:* The Drummer's ABC (first drum tutor in Finnish language), 1969; Vol. II, 1975. *Honour:* Helsinki Medal, 1989. *Address:* Ristiniementie 40 A 7, 02320 Espoo, Finland.

OJANEN Eero; b. 3 Jan. 1943, Finland. Musician (piano); Composer. *Career:* Played with: Juhani Vilkki's sextet, 1960s; Otto Donner Treatment, 1960s; Pianist, Pekka Pöyry, Montreux Festival, 1968; Concentrated on theatre and film work, 1970s; Currently playing improvised music with Jouni Kesti projects; Accompanist to numerous singers; Member, duo with bass player Teppo Hauta-Aho. *Compositions:* Väinämöinen's Music (cantata based on epic Kalevala), Pori Jazz Festival, 1974; Ballet, based on Aleksis Kivi's Seitsemän Veljestä (The Seven Brothers), 1980. *Honour:* Yrjö Award, Finnish Jazz Federation, 1968. *Address:* Mechelininkatu 16 A 7, 00100 Helsinki, Finland.

OJANPERÄ Jorma; b. 24 March 1961, Alahärmä, Finland. Musician (bass). *Musical Education:* Studied jazz, Oulunkylä Institute; Helsinki University music department; Sibelius Academy, Helsinki. *Career:* Performances with The National Theatre and symphony orchestras; Member, Pori Big Band, 1983; Regular bassist, Helsinki clubs: Groovy; Jumo; Orfeus; Played Bengt Hallberg's music, directed by Hannu Hoivula, 1989; Regular appearances at Pori Jazz Festival; Recently member of: The Seppo Kantonene Trio; Markku Johansson Quintet; Also plays with saxophonist Ion Muniz. *Address:* Rike 24 B, 07700 Koskenkylän Saha, Finland.

OKIN Earl; b. 31 Jan. 1947, Carshalton, Surrey, England. Singer; Songwriter; Musician (guitar, piano, vocal trumpet); Comedian. *Education:* BA (Philosophy, English Literature), University of Kent, Canterbury. *Career:* Various television appearances world-wide including Belgium, Germany, Australia, UK; First UK television appearance, 1959; Edinburgh Festival, 1983–; Opening act with Paul McCartney and Wings, Van Morrison, Stéphane Grappelli; Tours of Brazil as Bossa Nova singer/songwriter. *Compositions:* Over 100 various songs; Classical pieces include a string quartet. *Recordings:* Singles include: Stop! and You Will Become Aware, 1969; Albums include: Bossa Britanica. *Publications:* Various articles, liner notes on opera and jazz. *Memberships:* PRS; Musicians' Union; British Equity. *Leisure interest:* Collecting 78s. *Current Management:* Spats Music Ltd. *Address:* 248 Portobello Rd, London W11 1LL, England. *E-mail:* spats@spats.demon.co.uk. *Internet:* www.spats.demon.co.uk.

OL' DIRTY BASTARD (Russell Tyrone Jones), (ODB, Big Baby Jesus); b. 15 Nov. 1968, Brooklyn, New York, USA. Rapper. *Career:* Founder member of Wu Tang Clan, 1992; Collaborations: Mariah Carey; GZA; Pras; Mya; Blackstreet; Kelis. *Recordings:* Albums: Enter The Wu-Tang Clan (36 Chambers) (with Wu-Tang Clan), 1993; Return To The 36 Chambers, 1995; Wu-Tang Forever (with Wu-Tang Clan), 1997; Nigga Please, 1999; The W (with Wu-Tang Clan), 2001; Singles: Protect Ya Neck (with Wu-Tang Clan), 1993; Shimmy Shimmy Ya, 1995; Triumph (with Wu-Tang Clan), 1997; Got Your Money (with Kelis), 1999; Gravel Pit (with Wu-Tang Clan), 2000. *Address:* c/o Elektra Entertainment, 75 Rockefeller Plaza, New York, USA.

OLDFIELD Michael Gordon; b. 15 May 1953, Reading, Berkshire, England. Musician (multi-instrumentalist); Composer. 3 s., 2 d. *Musical Education:* Self-taught. *Career:* Two world tours, 10 European tours, numerous world-wide television and radio appearances, including premiere concert of Tubular Bells II, Edinburgh Castle, 1992. *Recordings:* Albums: Tubular Bells, 1973; Hergest Ridge, 1974; Ommadawn, 1975; Incantations, 1978; Platinum, 1979; QE2, 1980; Five Miles Out, 1982; Crises, 1983; Discovery, 1984; Islands, 1987; Earthmoving, 1989; Amarok, 1990; Heaven's Open, 1991; Tubular Bells II, 1992; Elements, 1994; The Songs of Distant Earth, 1996; Voyager, 1996; XXV The Essential, 1997; Tubular Bells III, 1998; Guitars, 1999; Millenium Bell (album), 1999; Film score: The Killing Fields. *Honours:* Grammy Award, Tubular Bells; Ivor Novello Nomination, Moonlight Shadow; BAFTA Nomination, The Killing Fields. *Leisure interests:* Squash; Guinness; Eating out.

OLIVA Stéphan; b. 7 Jan. 1959, Montmorency, France. Jazz Musician (piano); Composer. m. Cathy Frantz, 14 Oct. 1982, 1 s. *Musical Education:* Classical training, Ecole Normale De Musique De Paris. *Career:* Teacher, performer, Jah, Grim, Ajmi, Roy Hart Theatre (France); Concerts in jazz festivals with trios (with drums, bass, violin, saxophone); Selected to Biennale Des Jeunes Createurs D'Europe De La Mediterranée, 1990; Selected to Jeunes Affiches '94, SACEM, 1994; Conferences: History of Jazz Piano, 1995; Trio Jade Visions, tribute to Bill Evans, 1995. *Recordings:* with trio: Novembre, 1991; Jade Visions, 1996; Piano solo: Clair Obscur, 1994. *Honour:* Django D'Or, 1992. *Membership:* Archipel Mozaïque (Montpellier). *Leisure interests:* Table tennis; Chess; Drawing. *Current Management:* Michel Lecomte. *Address:* 2 rue du Levant, 93100 Montreuil, France.

OLIVER Tim; b. 6 Sept. 1959, England. Prod.; Engineer. *Education:* BSc, Hons, Geology. *Musical Education:* Self-taught guitar and bass guitar. *Career:* Freelance Engineer, 1981–; Sound Engineering, 1985–; Producer, 1990–. *Recordings:* Temper Temper, Temper Temper; Northern Soul, M People; Delightful, Happy Mondays; Definition of Sound, Definition of Sound; Superhighways, The Other Two; Gospel Oak, Sinead O'Connor; Live, New Order; Gene; Indigo Girls. *Publications:* Regular contributor, Future Music, The Mix and Computer Music magazines. *Membership:* Musician's Union. *Leisure interests:* Photography; Photoshop. *Current Management:* Helium. *Address:* Carol Davies, 33 Salisbury Rd, Bath BA1 6QZ, England.

OLIVOR Jane; b. 1947, Brooklyn, New York City, New York, USA. Vocalist. *Career:* Began in night clubs in New York City, early 1970s; Signed to Columbia Records, 1976; Cover of Some Enchanted Evening charted just prior to the release of second album, which became a best seller; Played major venues across America; Took long career break owing to husband's illness, and subsequent death in 1986; Returned to live performing, early 1990s; Resumed recording career by signing to Varese Sarabande label, 2000; Continues to tour extensively. *Recordings:* First Night, 1976; Chasing Rainbows, 1977; Stay The Night, 1978; The Best Side of Goodbye, 1980; In Concert, 1982; Love Decides, 2000; Songs of The Season, 2001. *Current Management:* Ed Keane Associates, 32 St Edward Rd, Boston, MA 02128, USA. *E-mail:* missjaneo@aol.com. *Internet:* www.members.com/missjaneo.

OLOMIDE Koffi (Antoine); b. 13 Aug. 1956, Kisangani, Democratic Republic of Congo. Vocalist; Musician (guitar); Songwriter. *Education:* Degree in Commercial Science, Bordeaux; University of Paris, MA in Mathematics. *Career:* Began composing while a student; Composed for: Papa Wemba; Viva La Musica; Zaiko Langa Langa; Defao; Joined Viva La Musica as backing singer, late 1970s; Formed Quartier Latin, 1986; Invented Tcha Tcho style. *Recordings:* Albums include: Kiki Ewing, 1987; Henriquet, 1988; Elle Et Moi, 1989; Tcha Tcho, 1990; Pas De Faux Pas, Diva, 1992; Noblesse Oblige, 1993; Magie, 1994; V12, 1995; Wake Up, 1996; Loi, 1997; Ngounda, Ba La Joie, 1998; Droit De Veto, 1999; Live A Bercy, Force De Frappe, 2000. *Honours:* Best Singer award in Abidjan, 1998; Kora award, Best African Artist, 1998.

OLSDAL Stefan; b. 31 March 1974, Sweden. Musician (Guitar, Bass, Keyboards). *Career:* Played drums in school orchestra, 1987; Formed Ashtray Heart, with Brian Molko; Formed Placebo with Brian and Robert Schultzberg; Signed record deal, 1996; Numerous television appearances; Live tours and numerous major festival dates. *Recordings:* Singles: Come Home, 1996; 36 Degrees, 1996; Teenage Angst, 1996; Nancy Boy, 1997; Bruise Pristine, 1997; Pure Morning, 1998; You Don't Care About Us, 1998; Every You Every Me, 1999; Without You I'm Nothing, featuring David Bowie, 1999; Albums: Placebo, 1996; Without You I'm Nothing, 1998.

OLSEN Allan; b. 18 March 1956, Frederikshavn, Denmark. Singer; Songwriter. *Career:* Intensive touring, from mid-seventies; First, solo; 1988-, with own band; All major festivals, Denmark; Touring clubs all: Denmark; Germany; Iceland; All national television programmes in Q' and special portrait features. *Recordings:* Norlan, 1989; Gaio, 1991; Pindsvin I Pigsko, 1992; Dalton (with colleagues Johnny Madsen and Lars Liholt), 1994: Dubble Live-Rygter Fra Randområderne. *Honours:* 1 Grammy, 1994; Denmark Labour Union Great Award of Culture. *Memberships:* Danish Musicians' Union; DJFBA. *Leisure interest:* Bonsai. *Current Management:* Keiser/Winther Management. *Address:* Mollevej 35, 9520 Skorping, Denmark.

OLSEN Jørgen; b. 15 March 1950, Odense, Denmark. Vocalist; Musician (guitar); Songwriter. *Career:* Moved to Copenhagen, aged 12; Formed beat group The Kids, aged 15 with brother Noller; Released 3 singles; Supported The Kinks; Group became Olsen, 1970; Starred in Danish production of musical Hair, 1970; Scandinavian pop idol in the 1970s; Worked in education, 1990–94. *Recordings:* Albums (with Noller Olsen): Olsen, 1972; For What We Are, 1973; For The Children of The World (in conjunction with UNICEF), 1973; Back On The Tracks, 1976; You're The One, 1977;

San Francisco, 1978; Dans – Dans – Dans, 1979; Rockstalgi, 1987; Greatest and Latest, 1994; Angelina, 1999; Wings of Love, 2000; The Story of The Olsen Brothers, 2000; Rockstalgi, 2001; Neon Madonna, 2001; Walk Right Back, 2001; solo: Det Stille Ocean, 1990; numerous Olsen Brothers singles. *Honour:* Eurovision Song Contest winner, Fly On The Wings of Love, 2000. *Current Management:* Steen Wittrock, International Personal Management, Store Kongenskade 46, 1264, Copenhagen K, Denmark. *E-mail:* ipm-fib@mail.tele.dk.

OLSEN Noller (Niels); b. 13 April 1954, Odense, Denmark. Vocalist; Musician (guitar); Songwriter. *Career:* Moved to Copenhagen, aged 8; Formed beat group The Kids, aged 11 with brother Jørgen; Released 3 singles; Supported The Kinks; Group became Olsen, 1970; Appeared in Danish production of musical Hair, 1970; Scandinavian pop idol in the 1970s; Worked in education, 1990–94. *Recordings:* Albums (with Jørgen Olsen): Olsen, 1972; For What We Are, 1973; For The Children of The World (in conjunction with UNICEF), 1973; Back On The Tracks, 1976; You're The One, 1977; San Francisco, 1978; Dans – Dans – Dans, 1979; Rockstalgi, 1987; Greatest and Latest, 1994; Angelina, 1999; Wings of Love, 2000; The Story of The Olsen Brothers, 2000; Rockstalgi, 2001; Neon Madonna, 2001; Walk Right Back, 2001; numerous Olsen Brothers singles. *Honour:* Eurovision Song Contest winner, Fly On The Wings of Love, 2000. *Current Management:* Steen Wittrock, International Personal Management, Store Kongenskade 46, 1264, Copenhagen K, Denmark. *E-mail:* ipm-fib@mail.tele.dk.

OLSON Carla Beth; b. 3 July 1952, Austin, Texas, USA. Musician (guitar); Singer; Songwriter. m. Saul Davis, 7 June 1987. *Musical Education:* Self-taught. *Career:* Worked with Ry Cooder; Don Henley; Barry Goldberg; Gene Clark; Phil Seymour; Appearances include: Radio City Music Hall, New York; Tours, Europe, Japan; Film soundtrack contributions include: Real Genius; Blue City; Sylvester; Saturday Night Special; A Tiger's Tale. *Compositions:* Why Did You Stop (recorded by Percy Sledge); Number One Is To Survive (recorded with Gene Clark); Trail of Tears (co-writer with Eric Johnson); Midnight Mission (recorded with The Textones); Albums: So Rebellious a Lover, 1986; Too Hot for Snakes, 1991; Live, 1991; Within an Ace, 1993; Reap the Whirlwind, 1994. *Memberships:* AFTRA; NARAS; BMI. *Leisure interests:* Foreign languages (Japanese, Italian, French). *Current Management:* Saul Davis Management, 11684 Ventura Blvd #583, Studio City, CA 91604, USA.

OLSSON Mats Fredrik; b. 3 Nov. 1929, Stockholm, Sweden. Arranger; Composer; Conductor; Prod. m. Maj-Britt Elisabeth, 19 Aug. 1950, 2 s., 2 d. *Education:* BA, University of Stockholm, 1953; Cantors Exam, Uppsala Cathedral, 1948; Royal Academy of Music, Stockholm, 1949–51; Private studies, Counterpoint, Instrumentation, Composing and Conducting, 1950–55. *Career:* Professional Musician, Pianist, 1949–57; Arranger, Conductor, Radio Sweden, Swedish TV and record companies, 1957–; Musical Director, Stockholms Stadteater, 1963–65; Conductor, Eurovision Song Contest, 1966–72; Director, A & R, CBS Records, Sweden, 1970–77; Managing Director, Planet Records and Music, 1977–94; Arranger and composer for TV series, Notknäckarna, 1981–90. *Compositions:* Suite for Orchestra; Riksväg 13; Tunnel banepolka; Lappland; Ballet music; Film music; Pop songs; Adaptions of Swedish folk songs. *Recordings:* With Love From Sweden; LPs and CDs of Swedish pop and light music; Big band recordings; Arranger, Conductor, Producer for recordings by Swedish vocal artists. *Honours:* SKAP Scholarship, 1959; Fred Winter Scholarship, 1986; Thore Ehrling Scholarship, 1991. *Memberships:* STIM; SKAP; SAMI. *Leisure interests:* Tennis; Reading; Video filming. *Address:* Gryningsvägen 28, 163 51 Spånga, Sweden.

O'MEARA Joanne V; b 29 April 1979 Essex, UK. Vocalist; Actor. *Career:* Sang in local clubs in Romford, UK before scoring minor European hit with group 2–4 Family; Also in pre-fame incarnation of Solid Harmonie; Joined S Club 7 when spotted performing at a country and western bar; Group quickly achieved international success following sales of TV series Miami 7 (1999), LA 7 (2000) and Hollywood 7 (2001) featuring the band's music to nearly 100 countries; Also made nature TV series S Club 7 Go Wild (2000) and various TV specials; First British tour with S Club 7, 2001. *Recordings:* Albums: S Club, 1999; 7, 2000; Sunshine, 2001; Singles: Bring It All Back, 1999; S Club Party, 1999; Two In A Million/You're My Number One, 1999; Reach, 2000; Natural, 2000; Never Had A Dream Come True, 2000; Don't Stop Movin', 2001; Have You Ever, 2001. *Honour:* Brit Award, Best British Newcomer, 2000. *Current Management:* 19 Management, Unit 32, Ransomes Dock, 35–37 Parkgate Rd, London, SW11 4NP, England.

ONDREICKA Karol Michal; b. 3 Nov. 1935, Bratislava, Slovakia. Composer; Arranger; Musician. Divorced, 1 s. *Education:* Master, Philosophy, Faculty of Arts, Comenius University, Bratislava. *Musical Education:* Self-taught guitar. *Career:* Leader, Combo 4, 1961–66, West Coast Jazz Quintet U5, 1975; Colaborated with Quartet pianist Ladislav Gerhardt, 1970–; Tours of Germany, Austria, Netherlands, Luxembourg, Poland, Switzerland and Greece; Performances at International Jazz Festivals in Prague, Bratislava and Athens; Appearances in clubs and festivals with: B Rosengreen, H Sachs, H Beckmann, H Koller, L Harper, K Wheeler, C Mariano, W Lackerschmid and T Küppers. *Compositions:* The Musical Rabbit, 1974; Music for television series, Boy As Any Other One, 1976; 5-Part Suite From Our Mountains, 1979; Daddy, Mummy and Me, 1979. *Recordings:* with Combo 4: Jazz On The Stage, 1962; with the SP Karol Ondreicka Quartet: Reflections, 1965; with the Karol Ondreicka Trio: Slovak Jazz Mainstream, 1994; with Ladislav Gerhardt Quartet: A Sentimental Trumpet, 1970; Bratislava Jazz Days, 1976–82; Why Did We Get Married?, 1978, We Won't Marry Anymore, 1981. *Honours:* 3 Prizes, Czech Radio Bratislava for Arrangement, 1974, 1975, 1976; Prize, Lifelong Work and Jazz Promotion, Slovak Music Fund, 1990. *Memberships:* Council, Music Fund, 1990–; Vice President, Slovak Jazz Society, 1990-. *Leisure interest:* Science Fiction. *Current Management:* MIC, Medena 29, 811 02 Bratislava, Slovakia. *Address:* Azalkova 4, 821 01 Bratislava, Slovakia.

O'NEAL Alexander; b. 14 Nov. 1954, Natchez, Mississippi, USA. Singer. *Career:* Singer, 1972–; Member, Flyte Time; Solo artiste, 1984–; Major concerts world-wide include: Prince's Trust Rock Gala, Birmingham, 1989; Simple Truth, Kurdish refugee benefit concert, Wembley Arena, 1991; World Song-Stylist Live Series, Tokyo, 1991. *Recordings:* Alexander O'Neal, 1985; Hearsay, 1987; My Gift To You, 1988; Hearsay All Mixed Up, 1988; All True Man (No. 2, UK), 1991; This Thing Called Love – Greatest Hits, 1992; Loves Makes No Sense, 1993; Lovers Again, 1997; Appeared on Affair, Cherrelle, 1988; Singles include: If You Were Here Tonight, 1985; A Broken Heart Can Mend, 1985; Saturday Love, 1986; Fake (R & B No. 1, USA), 1987; Criticize, 1987; The Lovers, 1988; What Can I Say To Make You Love Me, 1988; Christmas Song, 1988; Hitmix, 1989; All True Man, 1990; Sunshine, 1989; What Is This Thing Called Love, 1991; Shame On Me, 1991; Sentimental, 1992; Love Makes No Sense, 1992; In The Middle, 1993; All That Matters To Me, 1993; Grind, 1998; Criticize '98, 1998; Criticize '99, 1999; Duets with Cherrelle: Innocent, 1985; Never Knew Love Like This, 1987. *Honour:* Platinum disc, Hearsay, 1987. *Current Management:* Kuenstlermarketing GmbH, Hutteldorferstrasse 259/14, 1140 Vienna, Austria.

O'NEILL Bernard Anthony; b. 4 Sept. 1961, Dublin, Ireland. Musician (double bass, cello, bass guitar, keyboards). *Musical Education:* Associate of Royal Irish Academy of Music and Royal College of Music. *Career:* Teacher, composer, performer; Musical Director for numerous acts including: Rolf Harris; Viv Stanshall; Jon Spencer; Flower Sermon; Aqua Rhythms; Ether; Zumzeaux; Kimbara Brothers; Silly Sisters. *Recordings include:* with Zumzeaux: Wolf At Your Door, Live In Edinburgh; with Silly Sisters: No More To The Dance; with Andrew Cronshaw: The Language of Snakes; with Jon Spencer Band: Parlour Games. *Leisure interests:* Photography; Cooking. *Current Management:* Anne Pomerantz, Aqua Rhythms. *Address:* 5009 Riviera, Tampa, FL 33609, USA.

O'NEILL John; b. 25 Feb. 1955, Romford, Essex, England. Musician (all saxophones, clarinet, flute, piano). m. Sylvie Sims, 26 July 1986, 1 s., 1 d. *Education:* BA Hons, Modern Languages (French, German), Trinity College, Oxford, 1976. *Musical Education:* PGCE University of Reading, 1984. *Career:* with group Crosscurrents: BBC Radio 2, 1981; Bracknell Jazz Festival, 1983, 1984; Tour, Germany, Blueprint Jazz Orchestra, 1992; Musical director, arranger, saxophonist, Carlton TV series Shine On Harvey Moon, 1995. *Recordings:* Albums: The Jazz Method For Saxophone; The Jazz Method For Clarinet; The Jazz Method For Flute; The Jazz Method For Trumpet. *Publications:* The Jazz Method For Saxophone, 1992; The Jazz Method For Clarinet, 1993; The Jazz Method For Flute, 1994; The Jazz Method For Trumpet (with Steve Waterman), 1995. *Memberships:* Musicians' Union; Equity. *Leisure interest:* Cricket. *Current Management:* Helen Stafford Management, 14 Park Ave, Bush Hill Park, Enfield, Middlesex EN1 2HP, England. *Address:* 103 South View Rd, Hornsey, London N8 7LX, England.

O'NEILL Keith; b. 18 Feb. 1969, Liverpool, England. Musician (Drums). *Career:* Member, Cast; Early gigs supporting Elvis Costello and Oasis; Many headlining tours and festival appearances; Numerous TV appearances and radio sessions. *Recordings:* Singles: Finetime, 1995; Alright, 1995; Live the Dream, 1998; Guiding Star, 1998; Sandstorm, 1998; Walkaway, 1998; Albums: All Change, 1995; Mother Nature Calls, 1997.

ONGALA Remmy, (Ramazani Mtoro Ongala-Mungamba); b. 1947, Kivu, Congo. Vocalist; Musician (guitar); Songwriter. *Musical Education:* Self-taught. *Career:* Drummer and vocalist with Bantu Success; Later worked with Zairian bands: Success Mwachame; Mickey Jazz; Grand Mike Jazz; Joined Orchestra Makassy in Dar-Es-Salaam, 1978; Joined Orchestre Matimila, renaming it Orchestra Super Matimila; Joined WOMAD tour, 1988; Involved with Spirit of Africa AIDS relief project. *Recordings:* Nalilia Mwana, 1988; Songs For The Poor Man, 1989; Mambo, 1992; The Kershaw Sessions, 1994; Sema, 1996. *Honour:* Zanzibar Film Festival, Golden Dhow Award, Lifetime Achievement in Music.

ONO Yoko; b. 18 Feb. 1933, Tokyo, Japan. Singer; Prod.; Actress; Songwriter. m. John Lennon, 20 March 1969, deceased, 1 s. *Career:* Co-host, with John Lennon, Mike Douglas Show, 1972; Producer, film soundtrack, Imagine, 1988. *Recordings:* Albums with John Lennon/Plastic Ono Band include: Two Virgins, 1968; Life With The Lions, 1969; Wedding Album, 1969; Live Peace In Toronto, 1969; Sometime In New York City, 1972; Double Fantasy, 1980; Collection, 1982; Milk and Honey, 1984; Heart Play – Unfinished Dialogue, 1984; Reflections and Poetry, 1984; Solo albums: Fly, 1971; Feeling The Space, 1973; Approximately Infinite Universe, 1973; Seasons of Glass, 1981; It's Alright, 1982; Starpeace, 1985; New York Rock (original cast), 1995; Rising, 1996; A Story, 1997. *Address:* c/o The Agency Group Ltd, 1775 Broadway, Suite 433, New York, NY 10019, USA.

ORBIT William, (William Wainwright); b. 1 Oct. 1956, England. Prod.; Remixer. *Career:* Member, Torch Song, 1980s; Remixer for artists including Madonna, Prince, Human League, Erasure and Belinda Carlisle; Recorded own material under name Strange Cargo, and Bass-o-Matic; Founder, O Records; Worked with Madonna on Ray of Light hit album, 1997. *Recordings:* As remixer and producer: S Express, Hey Music Lover, 1989; Jimmy Somerville, You Make Me Feel Mighty Real, 1989; The Cure, In Between Days, 1990; Oleta Adams, Circle of One, 1990; Kraftwerk, Radioactivity, 1991; Seal, Killer, Crazy, 1991; The Shamen, Hyperreal, 1991; Madonna, Justify My Love, Erotica, 1992; Peter Gabriel, Us, 1992; One Dove, Breakdown, 1993; Kiss that Frog, 1993, Blood of Eden, 1993; Depeche Mode, Walking in My Shoes, 1993; 18 wheeler, The Hours and the Times, 1997; Dreadzone, Earth Angel, 1997; Blur, Bustin' and Dronin', 1998; Madonna, Ray of Light (album), Frozen, Ray of Light, The Power of Goodbye, 1998; Melanie C, Northern Star, 1999; Sasha, Global Underground, 1999; With Torch Song: Singles: Prepare to Energise, 1983; Don't Look Now, 1984; Ode to Billy Joe, 1985; Can't Find My Way Home, 1986; Albums: Wish Thing, 1984; Ecstasy, 1986; Toward the Unknown Region, 1995; With Bass-o-Matic: Singles: In the Realm of the Senses, 1990; Fascinating Rhythm, 1990; Ease on By, 1990; Funky Love Vibrations, 1991; Science and Melody, 1991; Go Getta Nutha Man, 1992; Albums: Set the Controls for the Heart of the Bass, 1990; Science and Melody, 1991; With Strange Cargo: Singles: Water from a Vine Leaf, 1993; Million Town, 1995; Albums: Strange Cargo, 1987, II, 1990, III, 1993; Strange Cargo Hinterland, 1995; Solo: Love My Way, single, 1987; Feel Like Jumping, single, 1987; Orbit, album, 1987; Scream, single, 1997; Pieces in a Modern Style, album, 2000.

ORCHIN Mark Alan; b. 3 Oct. 1957, London, England. Semi-professional Musician (guitar). m. Valerie Orchin, 6 Oct. 1979, 1 s., 1 d. *Career:* Lead guitar, late 70s band Possum and various pub, club bands; Currently playing folk/rock, guitar, mandolin with Touchstone; Playing for festivals, theatres, BBC Southern Counties; Recently played at Buddy Guy's, Chicago, USA; Duo with singer Bonnie Burden. *Recordings:* Albums: with Touchstone: The Night The Snow Came Down, 1995; One The Rum, 1995; Silently Calling, 1998; Principal writer of all 3 albums. *Membership:* Musicians' Union. *Leisure interests:* Tennis; Fishing; Cycling. *Current Management:* Allwood Music. *Address:* PO Box 348, Haywards Heath, West Sussex RH17 7RB, England.

ORFORD Tim; b. 10 March 1964, Cambridge, England. Sound Engineer; Programmer. *Education:* BSc Electronic Engineering. *Recordings:* Dina Carroll; EYC; Young Disciples; Carleen Anderson; Billie Curry; West End; Outlaw Posse; Watergates; Brand New Heavies; S'Express; PJ and Duncan; Sandals; Mary Kiani; Kym Mazelle; Marshall Jefferson; Alex Party; Mike; Rebecca Ryan; Grace; Kicks Like A Mule; Greatest 90's Dance Hits, 1996; Massive Dance Mix '96, 1996; Glen Scott, Without Vertigo, 1999. *Address:* The Flat, Thornton, Kingston Hill, Kingston Upon Thames, Surrey KT2 7JX, England.

ORIGJANSKI; b. 13 Nov. 1963, Skopje, Macedonia. m. Magda Origjanska, 1 d. *Career:* Member, band Anastasia; Recorded 4 albums; Numerous concerts; Work on film Before The Rain. *Recordings:* Albums: Ikon; Mansarda; Before The Rain; Melourgia. *Honour:* Golden Lion Award, Venice, 1994. *Leisure interest:* Walking in the mountains. *Current Management:* Ivo Jankoski.

O'RIORDAN Dolores; b. 1972, Limerick, Ireland. Singer; Songwriter. m. Don Burton, July 1994. *Career:* Singer, songwriter, The Cranberries, 1990–; Tours with: Moose; The The; Suede; Duran Duran. *Recordings:* Albums: Everybody Else Is Doing It, Why Can't We?, 1993; No Need To Argue, 1995; Doors and Windows, 1995; To The Faithful Departed, 1996; with Jah Wobble, Sun Does Rise, 1994; Devil's Own, Devil's Own, 1997; Amazing grace, Amazing Grace, 1997; Legacy: A Tribute to Fleetwood Mac, 1998; Singles: Linger; Zombie; Ode To My Family; I Can't Be With You; Salvation. *Current Management:* The Left Bank Organisation, 6255 Sunset Blvd, Suite 1111, Hollywood, CA 90028, USA.

ORLANDO Tony, (Michael Anthony Orlando Cassivitis); b. 3 April 1944, Manhattan, New York, USA. Singer. *Career:* Demo singer, 1960;

Worked for music publishers, 1963–70; Lead singer, trio Dawn (later billed as Tony Orlando and Dawn), 1970–77; Own television series, CBS, 1974–75; Solo artiste, 1977–; Actor, television film: Three Hundred Miles For Stephanie, 1979; Lead role, musical, Barnum, 1981; Dawn reunion, 1990. *Recordings:* Hit singles with Dawn include: Candida, 1970; Knock Three Times (No. 1, USA and UK), 1971; What Are You Doing Sunday, 1971; Tie A Yellow Ribbon Round The Old Oak Tree (No. 1, UK and US), 1973; Say Has Anybody Seen My Sweet Gipsy Rose, 1973; Steppin' Out (Gonna Boogie Tonight), 1974; He Don't Love You (Like I Love You) (No. 1, USA), 1975; Look In My Eyes Pretty Woman, 1975; Mornin' Beautiful, 1975; Cupid, 1976; Albums: Candida, 1970; Dawn Featuring Tony Orlando, 1971; Tuneweaving, 1973; Dawn's New Ragtime Follies, 1973; Golden Ribbons, 1974; Prime Time, 1974; Tony Orlando and Dawn II, 1975; He Don't Love You (Like I Love You), 1975; Greatest Hits, 1975; Skybird, 1975; To Be With You, 1976; Bless You and 17 Other Great Hits, 1997; Knock Three Times: Greatest Hits, 1997; Definitive Collection, 1998; Knock Three Times: Encore Collection. *Honours:* American Music Awards: Favourite Single, 1974; Favorite Pop/Rock Group, 1976; Tie A Yellow Ribbon Round The Old Oak Tree named one of BMI's Most Performed Songs, 1940–90, 1990. *Address:* c/o William Morris Agency, 1350 Avenue of the Americas, New York, NY 10019, USA.

OROZCO Richard Gomez; b. 5 March 1973, San Antonio, Texas, USA. Singer; Songwriter; Musician. *Education:* Nuclear Medicine, Biology, Belmont University. *Musical Education:* Self-taught Guitar. *Career:* Music City Tonight, 1995; Austin City Limits, 1995. *Compositions:* Life Is Good; I Wish He Wouldn't Treat Her That Way. *Recordings:* Buscando Una Estrella, 1996; Don't Try To Find Me, 1998. *Leisure interests:* Basketball; Golf; Cards; Dancing. *Current Management:* Refugee Management Inc. *Address:* c/o 209 10th Ave S, Cummins Station, Suite 347, Nashville, TN 37203, USA.

ORR EWING Alastair; b. 28 Nov. 1964, Netheravon, England. Musician (harmonica); Teacher. *Education:* Aberdeen University, 1983–86. *Musical Education:* Studied under David Michelson, also known as Dr Midnight. *Career:* Rasp, Rebel Yell, National Student band Final, The Powerhaus, Islington, London, 1993; Glastonbury Cabaret Stage, harmonica duo 'et al', theatre stage with Midnight Specials harmonica band, June 1994. *Honours:* Runner-up, British Harmonica Championships, 1994; Accredited teacher, National Harmonica League. *Membership:* Musicians' Union. *Leisure interests:* Travel; Sports. *Address:* 20 Santley St, London SW4 7BQ, England.

ORRALL Robert Ellis; b. 4 May 1955, Winthrop, USA. Songwriter; Prod.; Singer; Musician. *Career:* Artist, RCA, 1980–84, 1991–93, Giant, 1993–94; Songwriter, Warner Brothers, 1980–84, Zomba, 1987–88, BMG, 1989–91, EMI, 1991–; Producer, Flying Colors, 1991, Orrall and Wright, 1993, Michael Peterson, 1997. *Compositions:* Next To You, Next To Me, 1990; What's It To You, 1994, 1997; From Here to Eternity, 1997. *Recordings:* Sweet Nothing, 1979; Fixation, 1981; Special Pain, 1982; Contain Yourself, 1984; Flying Colors, 1991; Orrall and Wright, 1993; Mistakes, 1998; with Michael Peterson: Michael Peterson, 1997; Drink, Swear, Steal and Lie, 1997; Being Human, 1999; with Wedding Day Music, Wedding Day Music, 1998; with Yankee Grey, All Things Considered, 1999; Untamed, 1999. *Honours:* ASCAP Country Awards, 1990, 1993, 1994; CMA Number One Awards, 1990, 1993, 1997; CMA Vocal Duo of the Year Finalist, 1994; World Festival Charleston Grand Award, Best Music Video, 1994; ASCAP Pop Award, 1995. *Memberships:* ASCAP; AFTRA; CMA. *Current Management:* Alison Averbach Public Relations, 1229 17th Ave S, Nashville, TN 37212, USA. *Address:* 35 Music Sq. E, Nashville, TN 37203, USA.

ORTI Guillaume; b. 8 Dec. 1969, Nyons, France. Musician (alto, soprano saxophone). *Career:* Member, Kartet; Urban Mood; Paintings; Altissimo; Frequent work with theatre and dance companies; Played with Steve Argüelles; Marc Ducret; Aldo Romano; Steve Lacy; Dominique Pifarely; Thierry Madiot; Noël Akchoté; Benoît Delbecq. *Recordings:* 22 include: Altissimo; With Kartet: Hask; Pression. *Membership:* Collectif HASK. *Address:* 4 rue Bretonneau, 75020 Paris, France.

ORTMANN Carsten; b. 4 Aug. 1965, Copenhagen, Denmark. Television Prod.; Musician (drums); Singer. *Education:* MA, Aesthetics and Culture, University of Aarhus; Singing, drumming and piano lessons; Institute of Music, University of Aarhus, three years. *Career:* Drummer in Picnic, 1986–96; Drums and percussion, Hunk Ai, 1986–89; Founder, drummer and singer, Fullface Storband, 1987–89; Drums, percussion and backing vocals, Shirtsville, 1989–91; Percussion and backing vocals, Tintin og HårtGirrerne, 1993–95; Singer, Guttermændene, 1989-. *Recordings:* with Hunk Ai: Hunk Ai, 1986; Alene Hjemme, 1989; with Picnic: Barking Up the Wrong Tree, 1987; Meat King, 1990; Reverse Ahead, 1992; Lemming Nation, 1995; with Shirtsville: Secrets 3, 1990; Girls Deserve the Best, 1991; with Tintin og Hårtgirrerne: Dance Crazy, 1994; Mad Guppies Fighting the Food Chain, 1995. *Leisure interests:* Karate; Sailing. *Address:* Nirreallé 30, 2 tv, 8000 Aarhus C, Denmark.

ORTON Beth; b. Dec. 1970, Norwich, England. Singer/Songwriter; Musician (Guitar). *Career:* Member of Duo, Spill; Appeared with group, Red Snapper; Worked with Chemical Brothers; Formed backing band with Ali Friend on double bass, Ted Barnes on guitar, Lee Spencer on keyboards and Wildcat Will on drums; Began to release own records; Worked with Terry Callier; Numerous live appearances and appearances at festivals including Cambridge Folk Festival with own band. *Recordings:* Singles: She Cries Your Name, 1997; Touch Me With Your Love, 1997; Someone's Daughter, 1997; Stolen Car, 1999; Albums: Trailer Park, 1996; Central Reservation, 1999; Guest Vocalist: Strange Cargo, Water From a Vine Leaf EP, William Orbit, 1994; Exit Planet Dust, Chemical Brothers, 1995; Hinterland, Strange Cargo, 1995; Plastic Compilation Vol. 2, 1998.

ORTON Kenneth; b. 26 March 1934, Bedworth, Warwickshire, England. Musician (all saxophones, woodwind); Teacher; Arranger; Writer. m. Jean Finlay, 1 June 1960, deceased 7 Dec. 1996, 1 d. *Education:* Technical College CandG; Dip Hons, London Art College. *Musical Education:* LLCM TD, London College of Music. *Career:* Qualified Electrical Engineer, 1955; Army Band, 1955–58; Performed with name Big Bands including: Syd Dean; Ken Turner; Geraldo; Soul Bands include: Ray King; Tours with name artists, 1960s; Formed Don Ellis Connection Big Band, only band dedicated to the late Jazz Star; Retired from teaching, 1998; Reformed Don Ellis Connection Orchestra, 1999. *Compositions:* 2 songs, recorded by Ray King; Major work reconstructing Don Ellis scores; Rearrange and set to lyrics (SATB choir) certain Ellis material, establish Don Ellis library in UK, personal interviews with jazz stars; Reconstructed all Ellis 1960s vocal arrangements for Karin Krog, and presented concert for Karin Krog, 1994. *Publications:* Don Ellis' Jazz Journal; Encyclopaedia of Pop Music; Who's Who In Jazz; Album liner notes; Biography in progress: In Search of Don Ellis. *Leisure interests:* Siamese cats; Art (painting); Travel in France, USA. *Address:* 46 Coventry Rd, Bedworth, Warwickshire CV12 8NN, England.

ORZABAL Roland; b. 22 Aug. 1961, Portsmouth, Hampshire, England. Vocalist; Songwriter; Musician (guitar, keyboards); Record Prod. *Career:* Member, ska group The Graduate; Founder member, Tears For Fears (with Curt Smith), 1981–; International tours include: Support to Thompson Twins, UK, 1982; British tour, 1985; US tour, 1990. *Compositions include:* Everybody Wants To Run The World (amended from hit single), theme for Sport Aid famine relief, 1986; Writer, producer (with Smith), Oleta Adams' album, Circle of One, 1990. *Recordings:* Albums: The Hurting, 1983; Songs From The Big Chair, 1985; The Seeds of Love (No. 1, UK), 1989; Tears Roll Down – Greatest Hits 82–92, 1992; Elemental, 1993; Raoul and The Kings of Spain, 1995; Saturnine, Martial and Lunatic, 1996; Songs from Big Chair, 1999; Hurting, 1999; Seeds of Love, 1999; with Oleta Adams, The Very Best of Oleta Adams, 1998; Singles include: Pale Shelter, 1982; Mad World, 1982; Change, 1983; Mother's Talk, 1984; Shout (No. 1, USA), 1985; Everybody Wants To Rule The World (No. 1, USA), 1985; Head Over Heels, 1985; Sowing The Seeds of Love, 1989; Woman In Chains (featuring Oleta Adams), 1989; Laid So Low, 1992; Breakdown, 1993; Break It Down Again, 1993; Raoul and The Kings of Spain, 1995; Secrets, 1996. *Honours:* Smash Hits Award, Most Promising New Act, 1982; BRIT Award, Best British Single, 1985; Ivor Novello Award, Songwriter of The Year, 1986; BMI Performance awards, Head Over Heels, 1991. *Current Management:* Debrah Baum, Whirlwind Entertainment, 15025 Greenleaf St, Sherman Oaks, CA 91403, USA.

OSBORN Kassidy; b. Magna, Utah. Country vocalist. *Career:* Member, country group SheDaisy (with sisters Kristyn and Kelsi). *Recordings include:* Little Good-Byes, 1999; Albums include: The Whole Shebang, 1999; Brand New Year, 2001. *Address:* c/o PO Box 150638, Nashville, TN 37215–0638, USA. *Internet:* www.shedaisy.com.

OSBORN Kelsi; b. Magna, Utah, USA. Country vocalist. *Career:* Member, country group SheDaisy (with sisters Kassidy and Kristyn). *Recordings include:* Little Good-Byes, 1999; Albums include: The Whole Shebang, 1999; Brand New Year, 2001. *Address:* c/o PO Box 150638, Nashville, TN 37215–0638, USA. *Internet:* www.shedaisy.com.

OSBORN Kristyn; b. Magna, Utah, USA. Country vocalist; Songwriter. *Career:* Member and lead vocalist, country group SheDaisy (with sisters Kassidy and Kelsi). *Recordings include:* Little Good-Byes, 1999; Albums include: The Whole Shebang, 1999; Brand New Year, 2001. *Address:* c/o PO Box 150638, Nashville, TN 37215–0638, USA. *Internet:* www.shedaisy.com.

OSBORNE Jeffrey; b. 9 March 1948, Providence, Rhode Island, USA. Singer; Prod.; Songwriter. *Career:* Singer, LTD (Love Togetherness and Devotion), 1970–82; Solo artiste, 1982-. *Recordings:* Albums: Jeffrey Osborne, 1982; Stay With Me Tonight, 1983; Don't Stop, 1984; Emotional, 1986; One Love One Dream, 1988; Only Human, 1991; Something Warm for Christmas, 1997; Ultimate Collection, 1999; That's for Sure, 2000; Can't Go Back on a Promise, 2000; Hit singles include: On The Wings of Love, 1982; You Should Be Mine, 1986; Love Power (duet with Dionne Warwick), 1990; As singer and producer: Looking For Trouble,

Joyce Kennedy, 1984. *Current Management:* Jack Nelson and Associates, PO Box 3718, Los Angeles, CA 90078–3718, USA.

OSBORNE Joan; b. Anchorage, Kentucky, USA. Singer; Songwriter. *Career:* Performer, New York blues circuit, 1988; Solo recording artiste; Concerts include: Earth Day Concert with Midnight Oil, New York; Own record label, Womanly Hips Music. *Recordings:* Debut album: Relish, 1995; Appeared with artists including: Blues Traveller, 1990; Cracker, 1996; Spearhead, 1997; Randy Scruggs, 1998; Indigo Girls, 1999; Single: One of Us, 1995. *Address:* c/o DAS Communications, 83 Riverside, New York, NY 10024, USA.

OSBORNE John Michael; b. 28 Sept. 1960, London, England. Agent; Record Co Owner. *Education:* Royal College of Art. *Career:* Owner, Slate Records; Own Management Company, John Osborne Management, looking after many top radio DJs. *Honours:* BEDA DJ of The Year, 1992; Disco International, 1992. *Leisure interests:* Driving; Football; Eating; Theatre. *Current Management:* John Osborne Management. *Address:* PO Box 173, New Malden, Surrey KT3 3YR, England.

OSBORNE Pete; b. 15 Sept. 1957, London, England. Musician (saxophones: alto, soprano, clarinet) Composer. m. Sally Bowring, 2 April 1983. *Musical Education:* Studied with Professor Malcolm Ellingworth, classical, jazz, clarinet, saxophone. *Career:* Worked in: England; USA; Denmark; Belgium; Germany; Sweden; Italy; France; Concerts with: Herb Jeffries; Andy Sheppard; John Taylor, 1980; Georgie Fame; Andy Sheppard; Spirit Level, 1985; Bobby Shew; Mark Murphy, 1986; Radio broadcasts: with Rhythm Machine, Nightride, BBC Radio 2, 1987; with Lars Sjosten Trio, Radio Stockholm, 1989; Moved to Paris, concert with Liz McComb, 1991; 2 television shows: Taratata; Cercle De Minuit; 1 radio show, Billy Paul (Me and Mrs Jones), 1994; Concert, Elton John (MCM TV), Paris, 1995. *Compositions:* Jazz suite for Paris, and 50 original compositions (to be released) for jazz sextet. *Recordings:* with Billy Joel: Just The Way You Are, 1979; with James Brown: Album and video, 1991; Vanessa Paradis, 1992; Mc Solaar (Caroline Re-mix), 1993; with Cat Stevens: album, 1994; with Abbey Lincoln Trio: title film track, Tom Est Tout Seul, 1994. *Honours:* Best Saxophone Player, SW England, Bath Evening Chronicle, 1985, 1986, 1987. *Memberships:* Musicians' Union, London; SACEM, France; SPEDIDAM. *Leisure interests:* Cinema; Swimming; Walking; Chess; Good food; Wine. *Current Management:* Guy Fletcher. *Address:* 10 Margaret St, London W1N 7LF, England.

OSBOURNE Ozzy (John); b. 3 Dec. 1948, Aston, Warwickshire, England. Vocalist. m. Sharon Arden, 4 July 1982. *Career:* Vocalist, Black Sabbath (formerly Earth), 1967–79; Numerous concerts world-wide include: Madison Square Garden, New York, 1975; Reunion concerts include: Live Aid, Philadelphia, 1985; Solo artiste, with own backing band Blizzard of Ozz, 1979–; US Festival, 1983; Rock In Rio festival, 1984; Monsters of Rock Festival, Castle Donington, 1986; Moscow Music Peace Festival, 1989; No More Tears world tour, 1992; Created highly successful yearly touring festival, Ozz Fest, 1996; Has recorded with artists including: Alice Cooper, Mötörhead, Ringo Starr, Rick Wakeman. *Recordings:* Hit singles: with Black Sabbath include: Paranoid; Iron Man; War Pigs; Never Say Die; Solo/ with Blizzard of Ozz: Mr Crowley, 1980; Crazy Train, 1980; Bark At The Moon, 1983; So Tired, 1984; Shot In The Dark, 1986; The Ultimate Sin, 1986; Close My Eyes Forever, duet with Lita Ford, 1989; No More Tears, 1991; Perry Mason, 1995; Albums: with Black Sabbath: Black Sabbath, 1969; Paranoid, 1970; Sabbath Bloody Sabbath, 1973; Sabotage, 1975; Technical Ecstasy, 1976; Never Say Die, 1978; Numerous compilations; with Blizzard of Ozz/solo: Blizzards of Ozz, 1980; Diary of a Madman, 1981; Talk of The Devil, 1982; Bark At The Moon, 1983; The Ultimate Sin, 1986; Tribute, 1987; No Rest For The Wicked, 1988; Just Say Ozzy, 1990; No More Tears, 1991; Live and Loud, 1993; Ozzmosis, 1995; The Ozzman Cometh, 1997; OzzFest Vol. 1: Live, 1997; Diary of a Madman/Bark at the Moon/Ultimate, 1998. *Honour:* Grammy Award, 1994. *Current Management:* Sharon Osbourne Management, PO Box 15397, Beverly Hills, CA 90209, USA.

OSLIN K T (Kay Toinette); b. Crossett, Arkansas, USA. Country Music Singer; Songwriter; Actress. *Education:* Theatre Studies, Lon Morris College, Texas. *Career:* College drama; Folk singer in Houston; Touring and Broadway productions of: Hello Dolly; Promises, Promises; West Side Story; Began songwriting, 1978; Backing singer for Guy Clark; Signed Elektra Records, 1981; RCA Records, 1986; Fastest selling, highest charting country music debut album by woman (80's Ladies); Television appearances: Johnny Carson; Joan Rivers; Arsenio Hall; Oprah Winfrey; Own television specials; Television acting roles: Paradise; Evening Shade; Poisoned By Love; Film acting: The Thing Called Love; Host of Country Music Aids; Several Television commercials; Benefit concerts, 1993, 1994. *Compositions:* Songs: Do Ya?; Round The Clock Lovin'; Where Is A Woman To Go; 80's Ladies; Hold Me; Come Next Monday; Younger Men. *Recordings:* Albums include: 80's Ladies, 1988; This Woman, 1989; Love In A Small Town, 1990 (all sold 1m.); My Roots are Showing, 1996; Super Hits, 1997; At Her Best, 1998; Single: Hold Me, 1999. *Honours:* 3 Grammy

Awards; Best Female Vocalist, CMA, 1988; Song of The Year, CMA 1988; Best Female Country Vocalist, ACM, 1989. *Current Management:* Moress-Nanas Management, 1102 18th Ave S, Nashville, TN 37212, USA.

OSMAN Mat; b. 9 Oct. 1967. Musician (bass). *Career:* Member, Geoff, 1985; Suave and Elegant, 1989; Suede, 1990–; Concerts include: Glastonbury Festival; Tours, UK, Europe; America; Japan; Television appearances include: Top of The Pops, BBC1; Later With Jools Holland, BBC2; The Beat, ITV; The Tonight Show, NBC-TV; 12th BRIT Awards, Alexandra Palace, London. *Recordings:* Suede (No. 1, UK), 1993; Dog Man Star, 1994; Beautiful Ones, 1996; Trash Pt 2, 1996; Coming Up, 1996; Film Star Pt 1, 1997; Film Star Pt 2, 1997; Lazy Pt 1, 1997; Lazy Pt 2, 1997; Saturday Night Pt 1, 1997; Saturday Night Pt 2, 1997; Sci-Fi Lullabies, 1997; Head Music, 1999; Singles include: the Drowners; Metal Mickey; Animal Nitrate; Stay Together; Electricity; Everything Must Flow; She's in Fashion; Can't get Enough. *Honours include:* Mercury Music Prize, 1993. *Current Management:* Interceptor Enterprises, The Greenhouse, 34–38 Provost St, London N1 7NG, England.

OSMOND Donny (Donald Clark); b. 9 Dec. 1957, Ogden, Utah, USA. Singer. m. Debra Glenn, 8 May 1978, 3 c. *Education:* Brigham Young University. *Career:* Singer with The Osmonds, from age 4, 1963–80; Solo singer, 1971–78, 1988–; Duo with sister Marie; Television includes: Co-star, Donny and Marie TV show, 1976–79; Osmonds Family show, 1980; Film appearance with Marie: Goin' Coconuts, 1978; Head of own television production company Night Star, 1980s; Also satellite television entrepreneur; Stage role, Joseph and His Amazing Technicolour Dreamcoat, Toronto, 1992–93. *Recordings include:* Singles: with The Osmonds: You Are My Sunshine; One Bad Apple (No. 1, USA); Yo-Yo; Down By The Lazy River; Crazy Horses; Goin' Home; Love Me For A Reason (No. 1, UK); Solo: Sweet and Innocent; Go Away Little Girl (No. 1, USA); Hey Girl; Puppy Love (No. 1, UK); Too Young; Why; Young Love (No. 1, UK); The Twelfth of Never (No. 1, UK); I'm In It For Love; Soldier of Love (No. 2, US); with Marie Osmond: Make The World Go Away; I'm Leaving It All Up To You; Morning Side of The Mountain; with Dweezil Zappa: Staying Alive, 1991; Albums: Numerous albums with The Osmonds; Solo albums: The Donny Osmond Album, 1971; Too Young, 1972; Portrait of Donny, 1972; My Best To You, 1972; Alone Together, 1973; A Time For Us, 1973; Love Me For A Reason, 1974; Donny, 1974; Discotrain, 1976; Donald Clark Osmond, 1977; Eyes Don't Lie, 1990; Christmas at Home, 1998; with Marie Osmond: I'm Leaving It All Up To You, 1974; Make The World Go Away, 1975; Donny and Marie – Featuring Songs From Their Television Show, 1976; Deep Purple, 1976; Donny and Marie: New Season, 1998; Goin' Coconuts, 1998; Contributor, Voice That Cares, American Red Cross charity record. *Honour:* Georgie Award, Best Vocal Team, with Marie Osmond, 1978; Numerous Gold discs. *Current Management:* Jill Willis, Renaissance Management, 1571 Lake Lucy Rd, Excelsior, MN 55331, USA.

OSMOND Jimmy; b. 16 April 1963, Canoga Park, California, USA. Singer; Businessman. *Career:* Major UK hit with Long-Haired Lover From Liverpool, 1972; Rock impressario and restaurateur; Owner, Oz-Art advertising and design company; Promoter, Prince's Far East Tour; Assistant, Michael Jackson's Bad world tour; Owner, Osmond's family film and video centre, Utah, 1988-. *Recordings:* Singles: Long-Haired Lover From Liverpool (UK No. 1, 5 weeks), 1972; Tweedle Dee (No. 4, UK), 1973; I'm Gonna Knock On Your Door, 1974; Album: Killer Joe, 1973; Little Arrows, 1975. *Honour:* Youngest solo artiste (age 9) to top UK chart, 1972.

OSMOND Marie; b. 13 Oct. 1959, Ogden, Utah, USA. Singer. m. (1) Stephen Craig, 1982 (divorced); (2) Brian Blosil, 28 Oct. 1986, 1 s., 2 d. *Career:* Member, family singing group The Osmonds, 1966–73; Also solo artiste, 1973–; Member, duo with brother Donny Osmond; Numerous television appearances include: Donny and Marie Show, 1976–79; Osmond Family Show, 1980; Marie, NBC, 1980; Several Osmonds Christmas specials; Film appearance with Donny, Goin' Coconuts, 1978. *Recordings:* Singles with Donny Osmond: I'm Leaving It All Up To You (No. 2, UK); Morning Side of The Mountain; Make The World Go Away; Ain't Nothing Like The Real Thing; (You're My) Soul and Inspiration; Solo singles include: Paper Roses (No. 2, UK); Let Me In (No. 2, UK); You're Still New To Me; What Kind of Man; Albums with Donny Osmond: I'm Leaving It Up To You, 1974; Make The World Go Away, 1975; Donny and Marie – Songs From Their Television Show, 1976; Deep Purple, 1976; Donny and Marie – A New Season, 1977; Winning Combination, 1978; Solo albums include: Paper Roses, 1974; In My Little Corner of The World, 1974; Who's Sorry Now, 1975; This Is The Way That I Feel, 1977; I Only Wanted You, 1987; 25 Hits Special Collection, 1995. *Honours:* American Music Award, Best Country Band, Duo or Group, with Donny Osmond, 1976; Georgie Award, Best Vocal Team, with Donny Osmond, 1978; Best Country Duo of Year, with Dan Seals, 1986; Roy Acuff Community Service Award, 1988. *Current Management:* United Management, Suite 150, 3325 N University Ave, Provo, UT 84604, USA.

OSTERMANN Flemming; b. 2 June 1947, Aarhus, Denmark. Musician (guitar); Singer; Prod. m. Annette Stenbjoern, 15 Aug. 1988, 2 s., 1 d.

Education: Associate Professor, Rhythmic Music Conservatory, Copenhagen. *Career:* Tours with: Savage Rose, 1969–70; Cox Orange, 1972–76; Anne Linnet Band, 1977–80; Billy Cross and All Stars, 1980–95. *Recordings:* with Savage Rose; Cox Orange; Anne Linnet; Pia Raug; Billy Cross; Jens Rugsted. *Publication:* Rhythmic Guitar For Beginners, 1995. *Memberships:* Danish Music Society; DJBFA. *Address:* Brumleby 25, 2100 Copenhagen Ö, Denmark.

O'SULLIVAN Gilbert (Raymond); b. 1 Dec. 1946, Waterford, Ireland. Singer; Musician (piano). *Education:* Art College, England. *Career:* Solo recording artiste, 1970-. *Recordings:* Albums: Himself, 1971; Back To Front, 1972; I'm A Writer Not A Fighter, 1973; Stranger In My Own Backyard, 1974; Greatest Hits, 1976; Southpaw, 1977; Odd Centre, 1980; 20 Golden Hits, 1981; 20 of The Very Best, 1981; Life and Rhymes, 1982; 20 Golden Pieces of Gilbert O'Sullivan, 1985; 16 Golden Classics, 1986; Frobisher Drive, 1988; Sounds of The Loop, 1993; Every Song Has Its Play, 1995; Live In Japan, 1993; By Larry, 1994; Singer Sowing Machine, 1998; Singles include: Nothing Rhymed; We Will; No Matter How I Try; Alone Again (Naturally), (No. 1, USA); Clair (No. 1, UK), 1972; Get Down (No. 1, UK), 1972; Ooh Baby; Happiness Is Me and You; Christmas Song; I Don't Love You But I Think I Like You; What's In A Kiss?. *Address:* c/o Park Promotions, PO Box 651k, Oxford OX2 9RB, England.

OTIS Johnny (John Veliotes); b. 28 Dec. 1921, Vallejo, California, USA. Musician (drums, piano, vibes); Bandleader; Record Co Owner; Songwriter; Promoter; Radio DJ; Talent Scout; Author. m. Phyllis Otis, 1941, 5 s., 3 d. *Career:* Drummer, Count Otis Matthew's West Oakland House Rockers, 1939; Member, Harlan Leonard's Kansas City Rockers, 1943; Founder, Barrelhouse R & B nightclub, Los Angeles (with Bardu Ali), 1948; Founder, California Rhythm and Blues Caravan group; DJ, central Californian radio stations KPFA, KPFB and KFCF, 1950s-; Host, television series, Johnny Otis Show, 8 years; Discovered artists as talent scout including: Esther Phillips; Willie Mae (Big Mama) Thornton; Etta James; Hank Ballard; Jackie Wilson; The Robins (later The Coasters); Owner, D16 Records and Blues Spectrum record label; Played with Big Joe Turner; Louis Jordan; Charles Brown; Joe Liggins; Roy Milton; Lester Young; Illinois Jacquet; Count Basie Orchestra. *Compositions include:* Every Beat of My Heart; Mistreatin' Blues; Willie and The Hand Jive; So Fine; Dance With Me Henry (The Wallflower); Double Crossin' Blues; Cupid's Boogie; Deceivin' Blues; Gee Baby. *Recordings:* Harlem Nocturne, 1945; Double Crossing Blues, 1950; Mistreatin' Blues, 1950; Ma, He's Making Eyes At Me, 1957; Willie and The Hand Jive, 1958; Country Girl, 1968; Spirit of The Black Territory Bands, 1994; Producer, recordings with Big Mama Thornton, Johnny Ace and Little Richard. *Publications:* Author: Listen To The Lambs, 1968; Upside Your Head! Rhythm and Blues On Central Avenue, 1993; Colours and Chords – The Art of Johnny, 1995; Johnny Otis – Red Beans and Rice and Other Rock and Roll Recipies, 1997. *Honours:* Grammy Award Nomination, for Spirit of the Black Territory Bands, 1994; Inducted into Rhythm and Blues Hall of Fame and Rock and Roll Hall of Fame. *Leisure interests:* Fishing; Growing organic apples (for own brand of fruit juice). *Current Management:* Terry Gould, 4141 Shook Rd, Sebastopol, CA 94572, USA.

O'TOOLE Gary (Gerald William John); b. 27 Sept. 1958, London, England. Musician (drums); Vocalist. *Musical Education:* On stage, age 4, with parents, playing bass, drums. *Career:* played with China Crisis; Bucks Fizz; LW5; Papa D; Monroes (Norwegian tours); Orphy Robinson; 25th of May; Jean Aldebambo; Delfins (Portuguese band); Teaching at drum tech and writing part of curriculum (private lessons, degree level). *Recordings:* Roland tutorial video for TD7 (electronic kit); with Delfins: Ser Maior (1 track written on album); LW5: with Ripe For The Picking album. *Membership:* Musicians' Union. *Leisure interest:* Mu Gen Do (kick-boxing) Instructor. *Address:* 302 Essex Rd, Islington, London N1 3AU, England.

O'TOOLE Steve; b. 4 April 1969, Chesterfield, England. Musician (Guitar). *Career:* Member of Slaughterhouse 5 and Enormous. *Compositions:* Pathetic; Things She Did; Wide Open; Cigerette Machine From God; My Type. *Membership:* Musicians' Union. *Leisure interests:* Football; Drinking. *Current Management:* Beatific Management. *Address:* 31A Bishop St, Mansfield, Nottinhgam, NG18 1HJ.

OTTEWELL Ben; b. 1975, Chesterfield, England. Musician (Guitar, Bass); Vocalist. *Career:* Member, Gomez; Numerous live dates and television appearances. *Recordings:* Singles: 78 Stone Wobble, 1998; Whippin' Piccadilly, 1998; Get Myself Arrested, EP, 1998; Bring It On, 1999; Rhythm and Blues, 1999; Albums: Bring It On, 1998; Liquid Skin, 1999.

OTTO John; b. Jacksonville, Florida, USA. Musician (drums). *Musical Education:* Learnt jazz drumming, age 17. *Career:* Played in jazz band until recruited for Limp Bizkit, 1994; Signed to Flip/Interscope on strength of demo tape; Live shows at concerts and festivals; Group spearheaded 'nu-metal' breakthrough in Europe, 2001. *Recordings:* Albums: Three Dollar Bill, Y'All $, 1997; Significant Other, 1999; Chocolate Starfish and The Hot Dog Flavored Water, 2000; New Old Songs (remix album), 2001; Singles:

Faith, 1997; Nookie, Rearranged, 1999; Break Stuff, Take A Look Around (from Mission Impossible 2 OST), My Generation, 2000; Rollin', My Way, Boiler, 2001. *Honours:* Second and third albums both debuted at No. 1 on US chart; Significant Other sales in excess of 6m. *Current Management:* The Firm (Management), 9100 Wilshire Blvd, Suite 400W, Beverly Hills, CA 90212, USA. *Internet:* www.limpbizkit.com.

OTWAY John; Singer. *Career:* Began touring folk circuit with partner, Wild Willy Barrett, 1970–82; Numerous reunions and splits since; 25 years continuous touring; Television includes: Old Grey Whistle Test; Television commercials for R Whites Lemonade; Danepack Bacon; Radio credits include being banned by Radio 1 for inciting violence, 1981; Concerts include: Reading Festival, 1988; 2000th concert, London Astoria. *Recordings:* Albums: with Willy Barrett: John Otway and Wild Willy Barrett, 1977; Deep and Meaningless, 1978; Way and Bat, 1980; All Balls and No Willy, 1983; Singles include: with Willy Barrett: Really Free, 1977; Solo: Green Green Grass of Home, 1980; Headbutts, 1981; Premature Adulation, 1995. *Publication:* Cor Baby That's Really Me (memoirs), 1990. *Current Management:* Matters Musical Ltd. *Address:* The Loft, Rear of 8 West St, Dorking, Surrey RH4 1BL, England.

OUZOUNOFF Alexandre; b. 15 Nov. 1955, Suresnes, France. Musician (bassoon); Composer. m. 28 Aug. 1993, 1 d. *Musical Education:* Student of Maurice Allard. *Career:* Trio Ozi (with C Villevielle, L Aubert), Festivals: France, Europe, Africa, South Korea; Brazil; Middle East; Russia, 1976–96; Contemporary repertory Constitution; Solo bassoon recitals: Radio France; Centre Pompidou; IRCAM; Festival d'Automne à Paris; INA-GRM; MANCA (Strasbourg); GMEB (Bourges); GRAMW (Lyon); Germany; USA; Italy; Poland, 1979–87; Member, Blue Ensemble, contemporary jazz group (with T Gubitsch, J F Jenny-Clarck, J Schwartz), 1991–94; Appearances, festivals include: De La Butte Montmarte; Festival de Paris; Hyères; Presences 93/Radio France; La Rochelle; Aix En Musique; Heures Musicales de Chatres; Futurs Musiques; D'Automne; Prague; Presence 95/Radio France; Uzès; Breme; Théatre du Châtelet; Moscow-Idaho; Contemporary bassoon masterclasses, France and abroad, 1985–95. *Recordings include:* Jazz: Palissander's Night, 1988; Sokoa Tanz, 1991; with KOQ Trio: Made In Nigeria, 1993; Contemporary: with Jean Schwartz: Assolutamente, 1990; Canto, 1993; Destroy, 1990; with François Bousch: Espace-Temps, 1992; Classical: Heitor Villa Lobos, Trio d'Anches, 1989; Francis Poulenc, Trio d'Anches, 1991; Etienne Ozi, Trio d'Anches Ozi, 1991; André Caplet/Alberic Magnard, Trio d'Anches Ozi, 1994. *Publication:* Actually The Bassoon. *Honours:* First Prize, Music History, CNSM, Paris; Certificate, International Chamber Music Competition, Martigny (Switzerland). *Membership:* IDRS (International Double Reed Society). *Leisure interest:* Cooking. *Address:* 7 Pl. Victor Hugo, 94270 Kremlin Bicetre, France.

OVERETT Kelly; b. England. Singer; Dancer. *Career:* Dancer, SL2; Singer, dance music group, Cappella, 1993–95. *Recordings:* Debut album: U Got To Know, 1994; Remixes, 1994 Singles with Cappella: U Got 2 Know, 1993; U Got To Let The Music (No. 2, UK), 1993; Move On Baby, 1994; Take Me Away, 1994; Move It Up, 1994; Tell Me the Way, 1995. *Address:* c/o Media, 5–7 Mandeville Pl., London W1M 5LB, England.

OVERON Geoff(rey John); b. 26 Nov. 1953, Leicester, England. Musician (electric and acoustic guitar, bass guitar); Vocalist; Songwriter. *Education:* De Montfort University. *Musical Education:* Primarily self-taught with some private tuition. *Career:* Turned professional in 1978; Played with: Eric Clapton, Muddy Waters' sideman, Ric Grech, backed Jimmy Witherspoon, jammed with the Van Morrison Band, played at Robert Cray's wedding; Currently, composing, recording and touring with the Geoff Overon Band; Session player, producer and impresario. *Compositions:* Loving With A Loaded Dice, with Ric Grech; If It Don't Come Easy, with Anthony Thistlethwaite (Waterboys/Saw Doctors). *Recordings:* Sessions for BBC and Central TV. *Honour:* Life President, Leicester Rhythm and Blues Society. *Memberships:* British Music Writers Council; Musicians' Union teacher and Registry of Electric Guitar tutors. *Leisure interests:* Classic guitar collecting; Progressive, Blues and Jazz Records. *Current Management:* GO Productions and Promotions. *Address:* 12 Somerville Rd, Leicester LE3 2ET, England.

OVERWATER Tony; b. 24 March 1965, Rotterdam, The Netherlands. Musician (Acoustic Bass; Contrabass). 1 child. *Education:* Graduated with Hons, Royal Conservatory, The Hague, The Netherlands, 1990. *Career:* Played at Ronnie Scott's, London, with David Murray; North Sea Jazz Festival with Yuri Honing Trio; Montréal Jazz Festival; Solo TV appearance in Reiziger in Muziek; Wrote music for documentary. *Compositions:* Le Petit Prince for double bass and mezzo soprano; Eter/ Ether, for dancer/choreographer Anouk van Dijk. *Recordings:* Tony Overwater Up Close; Motion Music; Treya Quartet Plays; Gabriel Faure; Yuri Honing Trio: Sequel; Star Tracks. *Honour:* Podium Prize, Most Promising Musician of the Year, 1989. *Membership:* BIM. *Leisure interests:* Sailing; Surfing; Horse riding. *Address:* 1e Molenweg 20, 1261 TD Blaricum, The Netherlands.

OWEN Huw Dylan; b. 20 May 1971, Nantwich, Cheshire, England. Social Worker. *Education:* Polytechnic of Wales; University of Glamorgan; All Wales Occupational Therapy Programme. *Career:* Lead singer with Y Celtiaid Anhysbus, 1987–89; Singer and mandolin player with folk rock group Gwerinos, 1988–95; Regular appearances on Welsh TV and Radio, 1988–; Lead singer and guitarist with folk punk group Defaid, 1989–92. *Compositions:* Composed 7 songs on the album Tocio Mogia, Defaid, 1992; Dolgellau, 1992; Hydref, 1992; 100,000,000, 1992; Llanfair Bryn Meurig, 1992; Gobaith, 1992; Fy Allwedd I Afallon, 1994. *Recordings:* Tocio Mogia, Defaid, 1992; Di-Didlan, Gwerinos, 1994. *Publication:* Editor of Welsh language magazine Sothach!, 1991–94. *Leisure interests:* Supporter of Wrexham Football Club; Festival Organizer. *Current Management:* Adloniant Alffa Entertainment. *Address:* Maesbrith, Dolgellau, Gwynedd LL40 1LF, North Wales.

OWEN Randy; b. 13 Dec. 1949, Fort Payne, Alabama, USA. Musician (bass); Vocalist. *Career:* Founder member, country music group Wild Country, 1969; Changed name to Alabama, 1977–; Worked with Lionel Richie, 1986. *Recordings:* Albums: Alabama, 1980; My Home's In Alabama, 1980; Feels So Right, 1981; Mountain Music, 1982; The Closer You Get, 1983; Roll On, 1984; 40 Hour Week, 1985; The Touch, 1986; Greatest Hits, 1986; Just Us, 1987; Southern Star, 1989; Pass It Down, 1990; Greatest Hits Vol. 2, 1991; American Pride, 1992; Gonna Have a Party, 1993; Cheap Seats, 1993; Christmas Vol. 2, 1996; Dancin' on the Boulevard, 1997; Season of Hope: Benefit, 1997; For the Record, 1998; Country Cares for Kids Vol. 2, 2000; Singles: I Want To Be With You; My Home's In Alabama; Tennessee River; Feels So Right; Love In The First Degree; Pass It On Down. *Current Management:* Dale Morris and Associates, 818 19th Ave S, Nashville, TN 37203, USA.

OWENS Buck (Alvis Edgar Jr); b. 12 Aug. 1929, Sherman, Texas, USA. Country Singer; Songwriter; Musician (guitar). m. Bonnie Campbell, 1 s. *Career:* Musician, own radio programme with Ray Britten, 1946; Member, Mac's Skillet Lickers; Orange Blossom Playboys; Founder, own band the Schoolhouse Playboys; Session guitarist with artistes including: Sonny James; Wanda Jackson; Gene Vincent; Singer, musician with Tommy Collins; Recording artiste as Buck Owens, 1955–; Co-host, country music variety show Hee Haw, 1969; Retired from performing to run business interests, mid-1970s; Returned to recording and touring, 1988. *Compositions include:* Together Again, Emmylou Harris; Crying Time, Ray Charles. *Recordings:* US Country No. 1 hits include: Act Naturally, 1963; Love's Gonna Live Here, 1963; My Heart Skips A Beat, 1964; Together Again, 1964; I've Got A Tiger By The Tail, 1965; Before You Go, 1965; Waitin' In Your Welfare Line, 1966; Think of Me, 1966; Open Up Your Heart, 1966; Johnny B Goode, 1969; Streets of Bakersfield, 1988; Over 100 albums include: Under Your Spell Again, 1961; The Instrumental Hits of Buck Owens and The Buckaroos, 1965; I've Got A Tiger By The Tail, 1965; Carnegie Hall Concert, 1966; Buck Owens In London, 1969; Big In

Vegas, 1970; I Wouldn't Live In New York City, 1971; The Songs of Merle Haggard, 1972; Hot Dog, 1988; Act Naturally, 1989; Duets: Half a Buck, 1996; In Japan (live), 1997; Tender Loving Care, 1997; Greatest Hits Vols 1 and 2, 1998, 40 Greatest Hits, 1999. *Address:* c/o McFadden Artists, 818 18th Ave S, Nashville, TN 37203, USA.

OWENS Ginny (Virginia Lee); b. 22 April 1975, Jackson Mississippi, USA. Vocalist; Musician (piano). *Musical Education:* Bachelor of Music Education, Belmont University. *Career:* Performances at Lilith Fair and Sundance Film Festival; TV and radio appearances: Live With Regis and Kathie Lee; Ainsley Harriott Show; CNN Worldbeat; National Public Radio special; songs featured in TV series: Felicity; Charmed; Roswell. *Recordings:* Without Condition, 1999; Something More, 2002. *Honours:* Lilith Fair Talent Search, Nashville Winner, 1999; Dove Awards: New Artist of the Year, 2000; Best Enhanced CD, Without Condition, 2000; Inspirational Recorded Song of the Year, Blessed, 2001. *Current Management:* Rocketown Management, PO Box 1405, Franklin, Tennessee 37065, USA. *Address:* 404 Bridge St, Franklin, TN 37064, USA. *E-mail:* ginny@rocketownrecords.com. *Internet:* www.ginnyowens.com.

OWENS Jimmy (James Robert) Jr; b. 9 Dec. 1943, New York, USA. Jazz Musician (trumpet); Composer; Arranger. m. Lola Mae Brown, 18 March 1965. *Musical Education:* MEd, University of Massachusetts, 1975. *Career:* Musician with Lionel Hampton, 1963–64; Slide Hampton, 1963; Hank Crawford, 1964–65; Charlie Mingus, 1964–65; Thad Jones/Mel Lewis Jazz Orchestra, 1965–66; Duke Ellington, 1968; Count Basie, 1968; Billy Taylor Quintet, David Frost, 1969–72; World-wide appearances as Jimmy Owens Plus; Panelist, New York State Council of Arts, 1978–81; Director, Jazzmobile Inc, jazz workshops, 1974–90; Blackarts, National Diaspora (board member), 1986–; Faculty member, SUNY, 1981–86; Panelist, National Endowment for Arts, 1972–76; 1990–; Panelist, Ohio Arts Council, 1981–82. *Recordings include:* Impressions of The Middle East, Herbie Mann, 1967; Coming At You, Junior Wells, 1968; Zawinul, Joe Zawinul, 1971; Spectrum, Billy Cobham, 1973; Cosmic Vortex, Weldon Irvine, 1974; Sound of a Drum, Ralph MacDonald, 1976; Inner Conflicts, Billy Cobham, 1978; Anthology, Yusef Lateef, 1994; Things to Come, Dizzy Gillespie, 1996; Pure Be-Bop, 1998; Autumn Jazz, 1999; The Best of Duke Ellington, 1999. *Honours:* Drumbeat Award, Talent deserving wider recognition, 1967; Fellow, National Endowment Arts, 1980; Award for Excellence in Arts, Manhattan Borough, 1986. *Memberships:* AFofM; BMI; National Jazz Service Organization; Jazz Foundation of America.

OXAAL Adrian; Musician (Guitar). *Career:* Member, James, 1996–; Numerous tours, festival dates and television appearances. *Recordings:* Singles: Sit Down '98; She's A Star; Tomorrow; Destiny Calling; I Know What I'm Here For; Just Like Fred Astaire; Album: Whiplash, 1997.

P

PAAKKUNAINEN Seppo Toivo Juhani 'Baron'; b. 24 Oct. 1943, Tuusula, Finland. Jazz/Folk Composer; Arranger; Musician (flute, saxophone). m. Ritva Marjatta Ikävalko, 1 s., 1 d. *Musical Education:* Sibelius Academy, Helsinki; Berklee College of Music, Boston, USA. *Career:* Member, jazz groups: Pori Jazz; Soulset; Tuohi Quartet; George Gruntz Concert Jazz Band; Braxtonia Project (with Anthony Braxton); Karelia; World-wide tours, including Norway Winter Olympics, Lillehammer, 1993–94 with artists Nils-Aslak Valkeapää and Juhan Anders Dær; Played with: Most top Finnish Jazz musicians; Charlie Mariano; Mal Waldron; Palle Mikkelborg; First Finnish Jazz musician to play Carnegie Hall, New York. *Compositions:* Mysterium Sacrum (opera), 1993–94; Amazon, 1994; Numerous works for orchestras, choirs and big bands. *Recordings:* Albums include: Plastic Maailma, 1971; with Edward Vesala: Nan Madol, 1974; Unisono, 1975; No Comments, 1975; Kissapa Uu, 1977; Baron Disco-Go, 1978; Kanteletar, 1980; Sami Luondu Gollerisku with Nils-Aslak Valkeapää, 1980; with Karelia: Nunnu, 1971; Tuohihuilu, 1981; Hyvää Joulua, 1981; Maanitus, 1983; with George Gruntz: Theatre, 1983; Karelia, 1986; Best of Karelia, 1990; Sápmi Lottázan with Nils-Aslak Valkeapää and Ingor Anette Ailu Gaup, 1992; with George Gruntz: George Gruntz Concert Jazz Band, 1981; Theatre, 1984; Dálveleaikkat Wintergames with Nils-Aslak Valkeapää, 1994; Saxperiment, 1997; 2 Compositions (Järvenpää), with Anthony Buxton and Ensemble Braxtonia, 1996. *Honours:* Gold Medal, Student Youth Festival, 1968; Best Ensemble, Montreux Jazz Competition (with Tuohi Quartet), 1971; Yrjö Award, Finnish Jazz Federation, 1973; Jazz Composer of Year, Helsinki Festival, 1981; Arrangers Prize, Nordring Competition, 1982; Prix Future, West Berlin Festival, 1989. *Memberships:* Suomen Säveltäjät; ELVIS; Musicians' Union. *Leisure interests:* Finnish Folk Instrument Making; Golf; Books. *Address:* Katrillipolku 4 A, 04420 Järvenpää, Finland.

PACKHAM Blair James; b. 23 April 1959, North Bay, Ontario, Canada. Singer; Songwriter; Composer; Musician (guitar). *Education:* BA with distinction in English, University of Toronto, Canada. *Career:* Leader, The Jitters, rock 'n' roll group, 1980s; Engineer, live recordings of Bryan Adams, Stevie Ray Vaughn; Television music composer. *Compositions:* Destiny Ridge; NHL Tonight, World Cup Soccer '94 television series. *Recordings:* The Jitters; Louder Than Words. *Memberships:* AFofM; Guild of Canadian Film Composers; Society of Canadian Composers Authors and Publishers. *Leisure interest:* Long-distance cycling. *Address:* 260 Adelaide St E, Suite 131, Toronto, ON M5A 1N1, Canada.

PACZYNSKI Georges; b. 30 March 1943, Grenoble, France. Musician (drums). m. Sophie Tret, 24 April 1995, 1 d. *Musical Education:* Self-taught. *Career:* Represented France, Festival of Montreux, Festival of Zurich, 1968; Broadcasts, France Culture, with Black and Blue, 1981, 1998—; Founded trio with Jean-Christophe Levinson and Jean-François Jenny-Clark, 1984; Une Histoire De La Batterie De Jazz, broadcast, France Culture, 1993; Professor, Conservatoire National de Cergy-Pontoise; Founded new trio with Philippe Macé and Ricardo del Fra, 1996. *Compositions:* 22 pieces for percussion and piano, Paris, Zurfluh, 1985–2000. *Recordings:* Eight Years Old, 1992; Levin's Song, 1994. *Publications:* Thesis: Baudelaire Et La Musique, 1973; La Genèse Du Rythme Et L'Anthropologie Gestuelle, 1984; Book: Rythme Et Geste, Les Racines Du Rythme Musical, 1988; Une Histoire De La Batterie, Vol. 1, 1997; Une Histoire De La Batterie, Vol. 2, 2000. *Honours:* Medal of the Society of Encouragement For Progress, 1989; Charge de Corps sur le jazz et le rythme au Conservatoire National Superieur de Lyon. *Leisure interest:* Chess. *Address:* Georges Paczynski, 89 rue Nationale, 95000 Cergy-Village, France.

PADEN Jyrica; b. 3 Feb. 1955, Zagreb, Croatia. Composer; Musician (guitar); Singer. *Education:* University. *Musical Education:* 6 years classical guitar in music school. *Career:* 1,000 concerts in various groups, Croatia; 100 television appearances; Tour of former CCCP; Concerts in Netherlands, Germany. *Recordings:* About 30 albums; 10 hit singles with own group. *Honours:* Silver and Gold records; First Prize Arena-Fest, Pula. *Memberships:* HGY (Croatian Music Union); DHS (Composers Union of Croatia). *Leisure interests:* Full-contact sports; Skiing. *Current Management:* Music Time, Zagreb. *Address:* Vidriceva 31, 91000 Zagreb, Croatia.

PADEN Tom (Thomas) C; b. 13 Oct. 1956, Chattanooga, Tennessee, USA. Songwriter; Publisher; Musician (piano). m. Grace Michele Paden, 20 Nov. 1993. *Education:* BS in Business Management, University of Tennessee. *Musical Education:* Self-taught. *Career:* Staff writer for Starstruck Writer's Group, Reba McEntire's publishing company. *Compositions:* Numerous songs include: Same Time Each Year, national theme song for Ducko Unlimited. *Recordings:* Songs recorded by numerous artists including:

Aaron Neville; Tammy Wynette; Restless Heart; Kenny Rogers; Lee Greenwood. *Memberships:* NARAS; Country Music Asscn; NSAI. *Leisure interests:* Fishing; Hunting; Photography. *Address:* 3803 Bedford Ave, Nashville, TN 37215, USA.

PADGHAM Hugh Charles; b. 15 Feb. 1955, London, England. Record Prod.; Engineer. *Recordings:* As producer, engineer, mixer include: with Split Enz: Conflicting Emotions; Time and Tide; with The Police: Synchronicity; Ghost In The Machine; with Phil Collins: Face Value; Hello I Must Be Going; No Jacket Required; But Seriously; with Genesis: Genesis; Invisible Touch; with Sting: Ten Summoner's Tales; The Soul Cages; Fields of Gold-The Best of Sting; with Julia Fordham: Porcelain; Swept; with Melissa Etheridge: Yes I Am; Your Little Secret; No One Is To Blame, Howard Jones; Hysteria, Human League; English Settlement, XTC; Between Two Fires, Paul Young: Press To Play, Paul McCartney; Tonight, David Bowie; Two Rooms, Elton John and Bernie Taupin; Walkaway Joe (single), Trisha Yearwood; Clannad, 1996; Beth Hart Band, 1996; Bee Gees: Still Waters, 1997; Phil Collins: Hits, 1998; Julia Fordham: Collection, 1999; Engineering/mixing credits include: tracks from World Outside, Psychedelic Furs; Where's The Light, Toni Childs; Just Like Us, Robbie Neville; Nothing Like The Sun, Sting; Love and Affection, Joan Armatrading; Days of Open Hand, Suzanne Vega; Shakin' The Tree, Youssou N'Dour; The Scattering, Cutting Crew; My Nation Underground, Julian Cope; In The Air Tonight (88 Remix), Phil Collins; Abacab, Genesis; The Third, Peter Gabriel; Black Sea Drums and Wires, XTC; with Hall and Oates: Starting All Over Again; H2O; Dead Man on Campus; Happy Texas; Yes. *Honours:* 4 Grammys; Grammy Nominations; Brit Awards; BPI Award Nominations; Music Week Award; TEC Award For Outstanding Creative Achievement. *Membership:* Re-Pro. *Leisure interest:* Motor Racing. *Current Management:* Dennis Muirhead, Muirhead Management, 202 Fulham Rd, Chelsea, London SW10 9PJ, England.

PADILLA José; b. 1955, Spain. Prod.; Remixer; DJ. *Career:* Began DJ career in Ibiza, 1975; Became resident DJ at the island's Café Del Mar; Compiled first Vol. of Café Del Mar CD series and several further editions; Collaborations: A Man Called Adam; Phil Mison; Seal; N'Dea Davenport. *Recordings:* Albums: Souvenir, 1998; Navigator, 2001; Singles: Who Do You Love (with Angela John), 1998; Adiós Ayer, 2001. *Address:* c/o East West Records, Electric Lighting Station, 46 Kensington Court, London, W8 5DP, England.

PADOVANI Jean-Marc; b. 2 Feb. 1956, Villeneuve les Avignon, France. Musician (saxophone); Composer. m. Françoise Piotelat, 9 March 1987, 2 s. *Education:* Philosophy. *Musical Education:* Conservatoire. *Career:* First part, Miles Davis, 1984; Many tours with his quartet including: France; India; South America; East Europe, 1989–91; Flamenco /Jazz show, Tres Horas de Sol. *Recordings:* Tres Horas de Sol, 1988; One For Pablo, 1989; Nîmeño, 1990; Mingus, Cuernavaca, 1991, 1996; Nocturne, 1994; Sud, 1995. *Current Management:* Didier Vuillecot, Le Jardin des Délices. *Address:* 208 rue de la Convention, 75015 Paris, France.

PAEFFGEN Gilbert; b. 21 Jan. 1958, Würzburg, Germany. Musician (Drums, Hammered Dulcimer); Composer. m. Bettina Paeffgen Hehl, 16 Feb. 1990, 1 s., 1 d. *Career:* Member, Aventure Dupont, 1983–93, over 500 performances; ExpoSevilla, Pabellón de la Suiza; Member, The Treya Quartet, 1997–; Numerous TV appearances. *Compositions:* Where are the Mountains in this Country; Seamen Without Sea; Golden Wings; Lena; Evening Train. *Recordings:* The Treya Quartet Plays Gabriel Fauré; Songs of Seas and Ferries; Ode; Cohabitation, Aventure Dupont; Evening Train, Dei Terro. *Honour:* Mentor, Swiss New Jazz Festival, 1997. *Membership:* Cimbalon Asscn. *Address:* Mattenstutz 2, 3053 Münchenbuchsee, Germany.

PAGE Jimmy (James Patrick); b. 9 Jan. 1944, Heston, Middlesex, England. Musician (guitar); Songwriter. *Career:* Member, Neil Christian and the Crusaders, 1959; The Yardbirds, 1966–68; Concerts include: Dick Clark's Caravan of Stars, US tour, 1966; Rolling Stones '66 tour, 1966; Australia/Far East tour, 1967; Appearance in film Blow-Up, 1967; US and Japan tour, 1968; Founder, The New Yardbirds, 1968; Group becomes Led Zeppelin, 1968–80; Tours and concerts include: Royal Albert Hall, 1969, 1971; Madison Square Garden, 1970, 1976; Wembley Arena, 1971; Formed Led Zeppelin's own record label, Swan Song, 1974; Guitarist, Honeydrippers (with Robert Plant, Nile Rodgers, Jeff Beck), 1984–85; Guitarist, Coverdale/Page, with former Whitesnake singer David Coverdale, 1993; Guitarist, Page/Plant, with former Led Zeppelin singer, Robert Plant, 1994-. *Recordings:* Albums: with the Yardbirds: Over Under Sideways Down, 1966; Little Games, 1967; with Led Zeppelin (over 60m. copies sold): Led Zeppelin, 1969; Led Zeppelin II, 1970; Led Zeppelin III,

1970; Led Zeppelin IV, 1971; Houses of The Holy, 1973; Physical Graffiti, 1975; The Song Remains The Same, 1976; In Through The Out Door, 1979, with Coverdale/Page: Coverdale/Page, 1993; with Page/Plant: No Quarter, 1994; Walking Into Clarksdale, 1998; Masters, 1998; Before the Balloon Went Up, 1998 with The Honeydrippers: Honeydrippers Vol. 1, 1985; Contributor, Suicide Sal, Maggie Bell, 1973; Now and Zen, Robert Plant, 1988; As session musician: Here Comes The Night, Them; Shout, Lulu; I Can't Explain, The Who; The Crying Game, Dave Berry; Is It True, Brenda Lee; Crosby Stills and Nash; Knebworth: The Album; Joe Cocker, Anthology. *Honours include:* Outstanding Contribution to British Music, 1977; Q Magazine Merit Award (with Led Zeppelin), 1992. *Current Management:* Trinifold Management, 22 Harley House, Marylebone Rd, London NW1 4PR, England.

PAGE Patti, (Clara Ann Fowler); b. 8 Nov. 1927, Claremore, Oklahoma, USA. Singer. m. Jerry Filiciotto, 12 May 1990, 2 s., 3 d. *Career:* Discovered by Jack Rael, 1946; Signed to Mercury Records, 1947; Signed to Columbia Records, 1963; Only female artist with hits over 5 decades; Best-selling female artist of all time; 100m. record sales to date. *Recordings:* 100 albums; 160 singles, including Tennessee Waltz (10m. copies sold, second best selling single ever); Christmas with Patti Page; Songs That Made Her Famous; The Patti Page Collection; Live at Carnegie Hall; Hush Hush Sweet Charlotte/ Gentle on My Mind; Television appearances: Patti Page Oldsmobile Show, NBC; The Big Record, CBS; Patti Page Show, ABC (only musical performer with own series on all 3 US television networks); Actress, Elmer Gantry; Dondi; Boy's Night Out; Stage performances include Annie Get Your Gun. *Honours:* 14 Gold discs; Hollywood Walk of Fame; Country Music Walkway; Pioneer Award, ACM, 1980; Oklahoma Hall of Fame. *Membership:* Board of Directors, Academy of Country Music. *Leisure interests:* Tennis; Bridge. *Current Management:* Jack Rael.

PAGE Stuart; b. 12 May 1954, Leeds, West Yorkshire, England. Musician (guitar); Singer; Songwriter. 2 s.; 1 d. *Musical Education:* Self-taught. *Career:* Live appearance, Royal Albert Hall; BBC 2 Concert; Radio 2 airplay; Toured with many US country artists, Europe, UK, for last 11 years, including: Billie Jo Spears; James House; Albert Lee. *Recordings:* Wrote and performed music to ITV series A Brush With Ashley; New album due for release: Can't Sing The Blues. *Honours:* British Country Music Asscn, Band of the Year, 3 times. *Memberships:* PRS; Royal Guild of Songwriters. *Leisure interests:* Motor vehicles; The outdoors. *Current Management:* Milltown. *Address:* 26 East Parade, Bedford BD1 5HD, England.

PAICE Ian Anderson; b. 29 June 1948, Nottingham, England. Rock Musician (drums); Writer. m. Jacky, 25 May 1976, 1 s., 2 d. *Education:* Technical College. *Musical Education:* Self-taught, with father's help. *Career:* Founder, current member Deep Purple; Major concert headlining California Jam, 1973, to 350,000 people; Also played with Whitesnake and Gary Moore. *Recordings:* Albums include: Machine Head, 1972; Made In Japan, 1973; Deep Purple In Rock, 1970; Perfect Strangers, 1984; Purpendicular, 1996; Hit singles: include Smoke On The Water; Hush; Highway Star; Child In Time; Perfect Strangers. *Honours:* Biggest Selling Record Artist in USA, 1973. *Leisure interests:* Fishing; Beer; Football; Cricket; Horse racing. *Current Management:* Thames Talent, 45 E Putnam Ave, Suite 116, Greenwich, CT 06830, USA.

PAICH David; b. 25 June 1954, Los Angeles, California, USA. Vocalist; Musician (keyboards). *Career:* Member, Rural Still Life; Support to artists including: Jackson Browne; Aretha Franklin; Barbra Streisand; Member, Toto, 1978-. *Compositions include:* Commissioned (with Toto) to write theme for Los Angeles Olympic Games, 1986; Songs include: Africa, co-written with Jeff Porcaro, 1983; Without You Love, 1987. *Recordings:* Albums: Toto, 1979; Hydra, 1979; Turn Back, 1981; Toto IV, 1982; Isolation, 1984; Dune (film soundtrack), 1985; Fahrenheit, 1986; The Seventh One, 1988; Past To Present 1977-90, 1990; Kingdom of Desire, 1992; Tambu, 1995; Sax for Lovers, 1996; Toto XX, 1977-97, 1998; Mindfields, 1999; Singles include: Hold The Line, 1979; Georgy Porgy, 1980; 99, 1980; Rosanna, 1982; Make Believe, 1982; Africa (No. 1, USA), 1983; I Won't Hold You Back, 1983; I'll Be Over You, 1986; Without Your Love, 1987; Pamela, 1988; Contributor, We Are The World, USA For Africa charity single, 1985; Backing musician, albums by Boz Scaggs: Silk Degrees, 1976; Down Two Then Left, 1977. *Honours:* 6 Grammy Awards: Best Record, Best Album, Best Vocal Arrangement, Best Instrumental Arrangement, Best Engineered Recording, Best Producer (Toto) 1983. *Address:* c/o Fitzgerald-Hartley Co, 50 W Main St, Ventura, CA 93001, USA.

PAIGE Elaine; b. Barnet, England. Singer; Actress. *Education:* Ada Foster Stage School. *Career:* Stage appearances include: Hair, West End, London, 1968; Jesus Christ Superstar, 1973; Grease, 1973; Billy, 1974; Lead role of Eva Peron, Evita, 1978; Cats, 1981; Abbacadabra, London, 1983; Chess, 1986; Anything Goes, 1989; Piaf, 1993-94; Sunset Boulevard, 1995. *Recordings:* Solo albums include: Elaine Paige, 1982; Stages, 1983, 1998; Cinema, 1984; Love Hurts, 1985; Christmas, 1986; Memories – The Best of

Elaine Paige, 1987; The Queen Album, 1988; Romance and the Stage, 1994; Encore, 1996; From a Distance, 1998; Sings the Music of Edith Piaf, 1998; Appears on Tim Rice Collection: Stage and Screen Classics, 1996; Christmas with the Stars Vol. 2, 1999. *Honours:* Platinum and Gold albums; Society of West End Theatre Award, Best Actress In A Musical, Evita, 1978; Variety Club Awards: Showbusiness Personality of the Year, Recording Artist of Year, 1986; BASCA Award, 1993. *Address:* c/o D & J Arlon Enterprises Ltd, Pinewood Studios, Pinewood Rd, Iver, Bucks SL10 0NH, England.

PAINE Ed; b. 26 March 1949, Chatham, Kent, England. Musician (pedal steel guitar, dobro); Teacher. m. Beverley Paine, 24 May 1980. *Musical Education:* Formal Music Theory; Self-taught on pedal steel guitar and dobro. *Career:* Club, pub, college, theatre and festival appearances; Live and recorded local radio appearances and regional television appearances; Many recording sessions; Member of Country Cousins; Ned Porridge Band; Pan For Gold; Struck It Rich. *Compositions include:* The Tear In Daddy's Eye. *Recordings:* Sessions with many country bands including: Ned Porridge Band; Reg Haynes Outfit; Steve Scott Band; Memphis Roots; Pan For Gold. *Membership:* Musicians' Union. *Leisure interests:* Listening to music; Gardening; Photography. *Address:* Sundown, Lower Hartlip Rd, Hartlip, Sittingbourne, Kent ME9 7ST, England.

PAIVINEN Pertti 'Pepa'; b. 2 June 1955, Vantaa, Finland. Musician (saxophone, multi-instrumentalist). m. Marit Paivinen, 31 Jan. 1978, 2 s., 1 d. *Education:* Flute Study, Vantaa Music Institute, 1967–73; Theory and saxophone, Oulunkyla Pop-Jazz Conservatory, 1975–78. *Career:* Toured in Europe with Jukka Tolonen Band, 1979–80; Freelance work, television, theatre and teaching, 1980–85; Touring with Edward Vesala Sound and Fury, 1985–; UMO Big Band, 1985–; Saxophone quartet Saxperiment, 1989–; Tour with Anthony Braxton, 1988; Touring with own trio, 1998-. *Composition:* Saxophobia. *Recordings:* with Jukka Tolonen: Just Those Boys, 1980; with Edward Vesala: Death of Jazz, 1990; Invisible Storm, 1992; Nordic Gallery, 1995; with UMO: UMO Plays the Music of Muhal Abrams, 1986; Selected Standards, 1993; Green and Yellow, 1994; Umo Jazz Orchestra, 1998; with Anthony Braxton: 2 Compositions, 1988; with Saxperiment: Saxperiment, 1997; Pepa Päivinen: Saxigon, 1998; UMO, Electrifying Miles, 1998; Pepa Päivinen Trio, Umpsukkelisk, 1999. *Honour:* Pekka Poyry Reward, 1984; Award from Finnish government for artistic working, 1998–2000; Finnish State Grant, 1998–2000. *Memberships:* Finish Saxophone Society. *Address:* Kitarakuja 2, 01390 Vantaa, Finland.

PALLADINO Pino; b. 17 Oct. 1957, Cardiff, Wales. Musician (electric bass guitar). m. Marilyn Roberts, 13 Oct. 1992, 1 s., 2 d. *Musical Education:* 1 year classical guitar lessons, age 14. *Career:* Bass guitar for Paul Young, 1982–87; Recording sessions for artists including: Don Henley; Eric Clapton; Phil Collins; Elton John; Chaka Khan; Jeff Beck; Pete Townshend; Michael McDonald; John McLaughlin; Joan Armatrading. *Recordings:* No Parlez, Paul Young; Journeyman, Eric Clapton; But Seriously, Phil Collins; Building The Perfect Beast, Don Henley; Sowing The Seeds of Love, Tears For Fears; Who Else, Jeff Beck; Pilgrim, Eric Clapton; Breakdown, Melissa Etheridge; Emotional Blends, Robbie McIntosh; Oltre, Claudio Baglioni; Naked Flame, Tony OMalley. *Publications:* Standing In The Shadows of Motown. *Current Management:* Keryn Kaplan, Principle Management. *Address:* 250 W 57th St, Suite 1502, New York, NY 10019, USA.

PALMER Carl; b. 20 March 1950, Handsworth Wood, Birmingham, England. Musician (drums, percussion). m. Maureen Fraser, 4 March 1985, 1 d. *Musical Education:* James Blades, Royal Academy; Gilbert Webster, Guildhall. *Career:* Founder member, Emerson Lake and Palmer (with Keith Emerson, Greg Lake), 1970–81; Founder member, Asia, 1982–86; Numerous world-wide concerts, television, radio appearances; ELP sold 30m. albums to date. *Recordings:* ELP: Emerson Lake and Palmer, 1970; Tarkus, 1971; Pictures At An Exhibition, 1971; Trilogy, 1972; Brain Salad Surgery, 1973; Welcome My Friends (3 disc set), 1974; Works, 1974; Works Vol. II, 1977; Love Beach, 1978; In Concert, 1979; Best Of, 1980; Asia: Asia, 1982; Alpha, 1983; Astra, 1985; Albums with: Atomic Rooster; Arthur Brown; Roger Daltrey; Chris Farlowe; Mike Oldfield; PM; Three; Solo: Percussion Concerto, 1995. *Publications:* Applied Rhythms, Carl Palmer. *Honours:* Playboy Magazine Award, 1977; Hall of Fame, Modern Drummer Magazine, 1989. *Leisure interests:* Fencing; Indoor bowling. *Current Management:* Stewart Young, Part Rock Management.

PALMER Dave, (Yorkie); Musician (Bass); Backing Vocalist; Songwriter. *Career:* Member, Space, 1997–; Numerous world-wide tours and television appearances. *Recordings:* Singles: Dark Clouds, 1997; Avenging Angels, 1997; The Ballad of Tom Jones, with Cerys Matthews, 1998; Begin Again, 1998; Bad Days, 1998; Album: Tin Planet, 1998.

PALMER Florrie; b. 14 Nov. 1947, Broxted, Essex, England. Songwriter; Singer; Musician (Keyboards). 1 s., 1 d. *Musical Education:* Self-taught keyboard player. *Compositions:* Single: I Get Lonely; Nine to Five, Sheena Easton; The Heat is On, Agnetha Faltskog, ex-Abba singer; When He

Shines, Sheena Easton; Various album tracks including: Halfway There; The Last One to Leave; I Want to Marry You. *Recording:* I Get Lonely; The Mellen Bird, as Susie Mellen, 1973; Hi-fi Love. *Publication:* Never Final Till It's Vinyl, 1994. *Honours:* 9 to 5, Platinum Disc; Ivor Novello Award, Best Lyric of the Year, When He Shines. *Membership:* PRS. *Current Management:* Giles Hargreave, Hargreave Music Management, 15–16 Brooks Mews, London, W1Y 1LF, England. *Address:* 28 Frogge St, Ickleton, Saffron Walden, CB10 1SH, England.

PALMER Ian; b. 3 March 1976, Birmingham, England. Musician (drums). *Career:* Tours: Russia, 1990; USA, 1991; Numerous radio, television sessions; Youngest endorser in world for Yamaha Corporation Sabian Cymbals, Vic Firth drumsticks; Clinic tours for Yamaha Drums and Sabian Cymbals, drums, 1993, 1994, 1995. *Publications:* Practice Techniques. *Honours:* BBC Radio Big Band Drummer of Year, 1992. *Memberships:* Musicians Union; Percussionists Society. *Leisure interests:* Fitness; Reading. *Current Management:* Ian Palmer Music. *Address:* 11A Hartopp Rd, Sutton Coldfield, West Midlands, B74 2RQ, England.

PALMER Robert (Alan); b. 19 Jan. 1949, Batley, West Yorkshire, England. Singer; Songwriter. *Career:* Member, Alan Bown Set; DaDa; Founder, Vinegar Joe, 1971–74; Solo artiste, 1974–; Member, Power Station, 1985; Regular UK, Europe and US tours; Television appearances include: Arsenio Hall Show; Des O'Connor Tonight; The Tonight Show. *Compositions include:* Film soundtrack, Sweet Lies, 1987. *Recordings:* Albums: with Vinegar Joe: Vinegar Joe; Rock 'n' Roll Gypsies; Six-Star General; Solo albums: Sneakin' Sally Through The Alley, 1974; Pressure Drop, 1975; Some People Can Do What They Like, 1976; Double Fun, 1978; Secrets, 1979; Clues, 1980; Maybe It's Live, 1982; Riptide, 1985; Heavy Nova, 1988; Addictions Vol. 1, 1989; Don't Explain, 1990; Addictions Vol. 2, 1992; Ridin' High, 1992; Honey, 1994; The Very Best Of, 1995; Don't Explain, 1999; Rythm and Blues, 1999; Disturbing Behaviour, 1999; Nova, 1999; with Power Station: The Power Station, 1985; Hit singles include: Every Kinda People, 1978; Bad Case of Loving You, 1979; Some Guys Have All The Luck, 1982; Addicted To Love (No. 1, USA), 1986; Hyperactive, 1986; I Didn't Mean To Turn You On (No. 2, US), 1986; Simply Irresistible (No. 2, US), 1988; She Makes My Day, 1988; Early In The Morning, 1988; I'll Be Your Baby Tonight, with UB40, 1990; Mercy Mercy Me/I Want You, 1991; Know Me By Now, 1994; with Power Station: Some Like It Hot, 1985; Get It On, 1985; Contributor, film soundtrack, Pretty Woman, 1990; A Matter of Feel, Brent Bourgeois, 1992. *Honours:* MTV Music Video Award, Addicted To Love, 1986; Grammy Awards: Best Male Rock Vocal Performance, Addicted To Love, 1987; Simply Irresistible, 1989. *Current Management:* David Harper, What Management, 12B South Bar, First Floor, Banbury, Oxon OX16 9AA, England.

PALMER Tim; b. 4 Oct. 1962, North Shields, England. Record Prod.; Mixer. m. Nadine Marsh, 31 July 1995, 2 d. *Career:* Assistant, Utopia Studios; Engineer, Producer in England and USA for: Texas; David Bowie; Robert Plant; Pearl Jam; Tears For Fears; numerous others. *Recordings:* Now and Zen, Shaken and Stirred, Robert Plant; Tin Machine, Tin Machine 2, David Bowie; Elemental, Tears For Fears; Southside, Texas; Carved In Sand, The Mission; Ten, Pearl Jam; Reel Big Fish, Why Do They Rock so Hard; Michael Hutchence; American Pie; Gene Loves Jezebel, Voodoo Dollies: The Best of Gene Loves Jezebel; Legal Reins, Please, the Pleasure. *Membership:* Director, Re-Pro (British Record Producers Guild). *Leisure interest:* Music. *Current Management:* Sandy Roberton, Worlds End Management Inc. *Address:* 183 N Martel Ave, Suite 270, Los Angeles, CA 90036, USA.

PALMIERI Edward (Eddie); b. 15 Dec. 1936, Spanish Harlem, New York, USA. Musician (piano, percussion); Composer. m. 1 July 1955, 1 s., 4 d. *Musical Education:* Piano studies from age 8. *Career:* Started playing timbales in Chino y Sus Almas Tropicales band, aged 13; Switched to piano, 1951, and formed group with singer Joe Quijano; Became pianist in Johnny Segui's band, 1955; Joined Tito Rodriguez's Mambo Ochestra, 1958; Formed La Perfecta, 1961–68; Collaborations 1966–73 include: Tico All Stars; Fania All Stars; Harlem Drive; Cheo Feliciano; Went to Puerto Rico, 1980s; Formed Eddie Palmieri Orchestra; Returned to New York, late 1980s; Credited with creating the modern salsa; Played in numerous festivals including: North Sea Jazz Festival; Montréal Jazz Festival; Nice Jazz Festival; New Orleans; JVC Festival, New York; Muneca featured in film Carlito's Way, 1993; Puerto Rico on Spike Lee's Crooklyn soundtrack, 1994; Contributed to HIV and AIDS video Breaking Silence, 1994. *Recordings:* Albums: La Perfecta; El Molestoso; Lo Que Traigo Es Sabroso; Enchando Pa'lante; Azucar Pa'Ti; Mambo Con Conga Es Mozambique; Palmiere and Tjader: El Sonido Nuevo; Molasses; Palmiere and Tjader: Bamboleate; Champagne; Justicia; Superimposition; Vamonos Pa'l Monte; Harlem River Drive; Live At Sing Sing, Vols 1 and 2; Sentido; Live At The University of Puerto Rico; The Sun of Latin Music; Unfinished Masterpiece; Lucumi Macumba Voodoo; Eddie Palmieri; Palo Pa'Rumba; Solito; La Verdad; Sueno; Llego La India Via Eddie Palmieri; Palmas; Arete; Vortex; Jazz Latino Vol. I; El Rumbero del Piano; Live; Verdad: The Truth; Eddie's Concerto; Music Man; Salsa-Jazz-Descarga: Exploration.

Honours: various including: Grammy Awards: Best Latin Album, 1975 and 1976; Best Tropical Latin Performance, 1984 1985 and 1987; Best Salsa Album, Masterpiece (with Tito Puente), 2001. *Membership:* Board of Governors, New York, National Asscn of Recording Arts and Sciences. *Leisure interests:* Stickball; Cooking. *Current Management:* Edward Palmieri II Music Management, 1908 Parker St, Berkeley, CA 94704, USA.

PANIO John; b. 21 Feb. 1941, Ituna, Sask, Canada. Musician (Guitar, Keyboards, Vocalist). m. Angeline R Panio, 1 s., 2 d. *Education:* Ba; MMus. *Career:* CKOS Television; CJGX Radio; Cable Regina; CKRM Radio; CKCK Television. *Compositions:* The Priest and The Cantor; Angeline; Pumpkin Kolomeyka; In The Spring; Playing Across Canada. *Recordings:* Dance With The Piano Birds; Songs of Sentiment; Songs of Joy; Celebrate Saskatchewan. *Honours:* Saskatchewan Music Educators Award. *Memberships:* Canadian Country Music Asscn. *Leisure interest:* Musicology. *Current Management:* Panio Bros Band.

PANZU-NIOSI Papy; b. 21 Jan. 1975, Kinshasa, Democratic Republic of Congo. Musician (Guitar, Piano). *Musical Education:* Studied composition and musical writing. *Career:* TV and radio appearances, 1999. *Compositions:* Heritage; Testimony; Marriage; The Richness; Alleluia; Charity; Alienation; Lamb's Glory. *Honour:* Academic competition, 1997. *Membership:* Arts National Institute. *Leisure interests:* Music; Sport. *Address:* 114, Mayulu 114, Kinsangani II, Kinshasa, Democratic Republic of Congo.

PAPA DEE (Daniel David Christopher Wahlgren); b. 13 July 1966, Gothenburg, Sweden. Vocalist; Singer; Reggae MC. *Musical Education:* Church Choirs, Sweden. *Career:* Tours of Scandinavia with The Stonefunkers, 1987–89; Support to Steel Pulse Tour, USA, 1990; Support act for Ziggy Marley, London, 1991; Roskilde Festival with Papa Levi, 1991; Tour with backing band Protein Bubblers, Scandinavia, Europe, 1992–95. *Recordings:* Albums: Lettin' Off Steam, 1990; One Step Ahead, 1993; Original Master, 1994; Singles: Let The Music Play, 1988; Competition Is None, 1988; Microphone Poet, 1989; Ain't No Stopping Us, 1990; Beautiful Woman, 1990; Take It Easy, 1991; Ain't No Substitute, 1992; Runaround Girl, 1993; Mr Taxi Driver, 1993; I'd Rather Be With You, 1994; The First Cut Is The Deepest, 1995; Featured on recordings: Tribute To Martin Luther King, 1991; with The Stonefunkers: Hard As Kryptonite, 1990; Harder Than Kryptonite, 1991; No Problem '94, 1993; with Dayeene: Big Bad World; with 25th of May: Go Wild, 1992; with Timebomb Posse: Girls, 1992; with Brooklyn Funk Essentials: Single: The Creator Has A Master Plan, 1994; Album: Cool and Steady and Easy, 1994; with Leftfield: Leftism, 1995; Best of Acid Jazz, 1996; Brooklyn Funk Essential, In the Buzz Bag, 1998; TITIYO: After The Rain, 1991/92; L O V E, 1991/92; My Body Says Yes, 1991/92;. *Honours:* Swedish Dance Music Awards, Hip Hop Album of The Year, Best Male Vocalist, 1991; Grammy Nomination, 1991; Best Male Vocalist, Best Pop Album, 1995. *Membership:* Swedish Musicians' Union. *Current Management:* William Derella, Track Management, NYC. *Address:* Entertainment Resource Group Ltd, 323 Park Ave S, Third Floor, New York, NY 10010, USA.

PAPA GEORGE (George Papanicola); b. 9 May 1953, London, England. Songwriter; Blues Musician (guitar). *Musical Education:* Self-taught since 1964, also live work. *Career:* Opening act for Tina Turner, Hammersmith Apollo, 1983; Tours: Europe, Texas, Columbia; Appearances and interviews, UA TV (wire cable), 1995; Live radio GLR, local radio Wey-Valley 102–101 6FM. *Compositions include:* Co-writer with Ian Hunt: Heading South, title track, Ian Hunt; Guilty, for Paul Williams, 1995. *Recording:* Papa George Live album, 1995. *Memberships:* Musicians' Union; PRS. *Leisure interests:* Snooker; Cycling; Meditating.

PAPA NOEL, (Antoine Nedule Monswet); b. 25 Dec. 1940, Kinshasa, Democratic Republic of Congo. Vocalist; Musician (guitar); Songwriter. *Musical Education:* Self-taught: Guitar. *Career:* First recording, 1957; Member: Rock-a-Mambo; Les Bantous de la Capitale; Orchestre African Jazz; TPOK Jazz until 1989; Kekele project, 2001; Collaborations: Sam Mangwana; Mose Fan Fan; Adan Pedroso; International tours as part of Kekele with with Adan Pedroso including WOMAD Reading, 2000. *Recordings:* Bon Samaritain, 1984; Allegria, 1986; Heritage de Luambo (reunion with ex-members of TPOK Jazz), 1991; Haute Tension, 1994; Bel Ami, 2000; Rumba Congo, 2001, as part of Kekele: Mosala Makasi (with Adan Pedroso), 2001.

PAPA WEMBA, (Jules Shungu Wembadio Pene Kikumba); b. 14 June 1949, Kasai, Democratic Republic of Congo. Vocalist; Songwriter. *Career:* Began singing in church choir, 1966; Co-founder: Zaiko Langa Langa, 1969; Left to form Isife Lokole, 1974; Formed Viva La Musica with Ringo Starr, 1977; Worked with Koffi Olomide; Collaboration with Rochereau Tabu Ley's orchestra, Afrisa International, 1979. *Recordings include:* Zaiko Langa Langa Hits Inoubliables Vol. VIII, 1970–73; Yoka Lokole Dans Matembele Bangi, 1975–76; Papa Wemba and Koffi Olomide, 1978–79; Evenement, 1981–82; Papa Wemba – Destiny Ya Moto, 1985; Papa Wemba, 1988; Le Voyageur, 1991; The Kershaw Sessions, 1994; Emotion, 1995;

Molokai, 1998. *Honours:* Kinshasa newspaper Elima, Best Vocalist; Best Song of the Year, Mere Superiere, 1977. *Internet:* www.papawemba.net.

PARAMOR Susan Marie; b. 9 July 1950, Torquay, England. Songwriter; Singer; Actress. m. Graham John Paramor, 1 s., 1 d. *Education:* 6 Years Community Theatre, Salisbury College of Arts; Head of Cathedral Choir, Cyprus. *Career:* Radio, Spire FM, 1996; BBC Radio, 1995–99; Stage Lead Soloist, Super Tramp; The Bill; EastEnders; The River; Dancing In The Dark; Maria Marten; The Spice of Life; Nelson. *Compositions:* Titanic, Street of Tears; Yours Truly Jack; Souls In Pain; Sisters of the Abyss; The Bridge of Hope; Call Me; Through The Window. *Honours:* Best Musical Director, SDA, 1996. *Memberships:* Musicians' Union; British Actors Equity Asscn. *Leisure interest:* Recording Studio. *Current Management:* Parody Productions, The Stable Studio, Tinkers Cottage, Burcombe, Salisbury, Wiltshire SP2 0EN, England.

PARDESI Silinder; b. 1 Sept. 1957, Kenya. Lead Vocalist. m. R K Bhooal, 1 s., 2 d. *Education:* BSc, MISTC; Classical Training in Vocals. *Career:* Formed 'Pardesi', 1982; Television broadcasts include, The Clothes Show, Motor Mouth, Def II; Recorded live sessions BBC's Network East, What's That Noise; Performed live in Finland, France, Switzerland, Belgium, Denmark and Italy; International Music Festivals. *Recordings include:* Albums, Shabad Gurbani and Geet Guran De; Pump Up The Bhangra; Full Badmashi; Planet Earth; No To Nasha; Bollywood Seduction; On A Dance Trip; Pump n' Up Again; Seduction 2. *Honours:* Winner, Asian Song Contest, 1986; Best Album of 1990; Best Track of 1990; Top Selling Album of 1990; Best Live Band of 1990; Outstanding Singing Achievement, 1995; Award for Achievement For Enhanced CD-ROM by His Excellency High Commissioner of India Lalit Mann Singh. *Memberships:* MISTC; Musicians' Union. *Leisure interests:* Music; Hockey; Reading. *Address:* 32 Ashdown Close, Ernestford Grange, Coventry CV3 2PT, England.

PARDY Richard Alan; b. 17 April 1966, Grimsby, Lincolnshire, England. Musician (all saxophones, clarinet, flute, piano); Composer; Arranger; MD. m. 23 June 1993, 2 s. *Musical Education:* Grade 8 clarinet, piano, theory; Studied clarinet with Jack Brymer and saxophone with Al Wood; 3 year Jazz/Pop degree course, Leeds, GCLCM; PGCE. *Career:* Tours include Ben E King, Marty Wilde, Cao Quin, Martha Reeves and the Vandellas, Drifters; Tributes to Carpenters, Steely Dan/Donald Fagen, Burt Bacharach, Big Bands/Jazz Combos; Pardy Quintet (appeared at South Bank International Jazz Festival); West End shows and touring shows in UK, Europe and World-wide; TV and radio: BBC Radio 1 and 2; Jazz/ Capital FM; Pebble Mill; NZ TV; Film: Eyes Wide Shut (Cruise and Kidman), 1997. *Recordings:* Under the Orange Tree, CD; Session player on advertisement and film music; Featured soloist: Song for the United Nations; Just Can't Give It Up, Nirvana Remix-Hustler's Convention; Blue Lagoon; Living Planet, Lennon. *Publication:* Development/Evolution of the Big Bands, 1987. *Honours:* Most improved and promising woodwind student, 1980, 1982. *Memberships:* CASS; MU. *Leisure interests:* Travel; DIY; Cars; Cycling. *Current Management:* Richard Pardy Music.

PARFITT Rick, (Rick Harrison); b. 12 Oct. 1948, Woking, Surrey, England. Musician (guitar); Vocalist. *Career:* Member, the Highlights; Member, UK rock group Status Quo (originally the Spectres), 1967–; Extensive tours world-wide; Concerts and festivals include: Reading Rock Festival, 1972, 1978, 1987; NEC Birmingham, before Prince and Princess of Wales (televised by BBC), 1982; Milton Keynes Bowl, 1984; Live Aid, Wembley, 1985; Support to Queen, Wembley Stadium, 1986; Knebworth Festival, 1986; Played 4 venues in 12 hours, entered in Guinness Book of Records, 1991. *Recordings:* Albums: Picturesque Matchstickable Messages, 1968; Spare Parts, 1969; Ma Kelly's Greasy Spoon, 1970; Dog of Two Heads, 1971; Piledriver, 1973; Hello, 1973; Quo, 1974; On The Level, 1975; Blue For You, 1976; Status Quo Live!, 1977; Rockin' All Over The World, 1977; If You Can't Stand The Heat, 1978; Whatever You Want, 1979; Just Supposin', 1980; Never Too Late, 1981; 1+9+8+2, 1982; To Be Or Not To Be, 1983; Back To Back, 1983; In The Army Now, 1986; Ain't Complaining, 1988; Rock 'Til You Drop, 1991; Live Alive Quo, 1992; Don't Stop, 1996; Whatever You Want, 1997; Under The Influence, 1999; Numerous compilations; Hit singles include: Pictures of Matchstick Men, 1968; Paper Plane, 1973; Caroline, 1973; Break The Rules, 1974; Down Down, 1975; Roll Over Lay Down, 1975; Rain, 1976; Mystery Song, 1976; Wild Side of Life, 1977; Rockin' All Over The World, 1977; Again and Again, 1978; Whatever You Want, 1979; Living On An Island, 1979; What You're Proposing, 1980; Lies, 1981; Something 'Bout You Baby I Like, 1981; Rock 'n' Roll, 1981; Dear John, 1982; Ol' Rag Blues, 1983; A Mess of The Blues, 1983; Marguerita Time, 1984; Rollin' Home, 1986; In The Army Now, 1986; Burning Bridges, 1989; Anniversary Waltz, 1990. *Honours:* Silver Clef Award, Nordoff-Robbins Music Therapy Centre, 1981; BRIT Award, Outstanding Contribution To British Music Industry, 1991. *Current Management:* The Handle Group of Companies, Pinewood Studios, Pinewood Rd, Iver Heath, Buckinghamshire SL0 0NH, England.

PARIS Mica, (Michelle Warren); b. 1969, London, England. Singer. *Career:* Singer in church choir, early 1980s; Session singer, notably with Shakatak; Member, gospel group Spirit of Watts; Hollywood Beyond; Solo artiste, 1988–. *Recordings:* Singles: My One Temptation, 1988; Like Dreamers Do, 1988; Breathe Life Into Me, 1988; Where Is The Love, duet with Will Downing, 1988; Whisper a Prayer, 1993; Stay, 1998; Carefree, 1998; Albums: So Good, 1988; *Contribution,* 1990; Whisper A Prayer, 1993; Black Angel, 1998; Appears on: Stereo MCs, Connected, 1992; Courtney Pine, To the Eyes of Creation, 1992; Brenda Russell, Soul Talkin', 1993; Omar, For Pleasure, 1995; Guru Jazzmatazz, Vol. 2: The New Reality, 1995.

PARISH Alan Victor; b. 22 Oct. 1951, Edmonton, London, England. Musician (drums). Divorced, 2 s. *Education:* College. *Musical Education:* Self-taught, some lessons. *Career:* Television and radio jingles; Played with Top 40 bands; Currently member of The Hamsters, 8 years; Numerous concerts, television and radio appearances; Toured UK and Europe. *Recordings:* On all Hamsters albums and video. *Leisure interest:* Watching motor racing. *Address:* 8 Lillyville Walk, Rayleigh, Essex SS6 8UN, England.

PARISH John (Scott Tracey); b. 11 April 1959, Yeovil, Somerset, England. Record Prod.; Composer; Musician (guitar, drums, percussion); Vocalist. *Career:* Joined New Wave group Thieves Like Us, 1979; Group disbanded 1981; Founder, singer, guitarist, The Headless Horsemen, under pseudonym Scott Tracey; Frontperson, principal songwriter with experimental West Country band Automatic Dlamini, 1983–92 (with Polly Harvey and Robert Ellis); Began production career specialising in independent guitar groups; Associate lecturer, rock music and recording techniques, Yeovil College, 1991–94; Played in every PJ Harvey touring line-up, 1995–99. *Compositions:* Two original scores for theatre productions; Music for Dance Hall at Louse Point, with lyrics by PJ Harvey, used for contemporary dance piece, toured Europe 1997; Original score for Rosie, Belgian film directed by Patrice Toye, 1998. *Recordings:* Producer, composer, performer with Automatic Dlamini, The D is for Drum, 1988; From a Diva to a Diver, 1992; Producer, composer, performer with PJ Harvey, Dance Hall at Louse Point, 1996; Producer: Kettle, The Chesterfields, 1986; Myth, Becketts, 1991; To Bring You My Love, PJ Harvey, 1995; Orbit, The Harvest Ministers, 1996; Low Estate, 16 Horsepower, 1997; United States, Elliot Green, 1997; Original soundtrack, Rosie, 1999; Special Appreciation Prize for Rosie score at Bonn International Film Music Biennale, 1999. *Memberships:* PRS; Musicians' Union. *Current Management:* Sincere Management, 6B Bravington Rd, London W9 3AH, England.

PARIZO Lisa; b. 20 May 1964, Lewiston, Maine, USA. Songwriter; Musician (Guitar). *Education:* AS, Computer Technology. *Career:* Performed for Private Parties, 1990–98. *Compositions:* Life Should Be More, 1996; Anytime, Everytime, 1996. *Honour:* Certificate of Achievement, Between Now and Yesterday, 1997. *Membership:* Nashville Songwriters Asscn. *Leisure interests:* Fishing; Camping. *Address:* 2350 Shelter Creek Lane, San Bruno, CA 94066, USA.

PARK Graeme; b. 4 Aug. 1963, Aberdeen, Scotland. DJ; Remixer; Musician. m. Anne-Marie Curtis. *Career:* DJ, Garage, Nottingham, 1982; Started Hacienda, Manchester, 1988; Saturday Night resident, Hacienda, 1988–; DJ world-wide including: Australia; South America; USA; Yugoslavia; Iceland. *Recordings:* Remixed acts including: Brand New Heavies; Inner City; New Order; ABC; Jan Hammer; Eric B; Ace Remix Vol. 16. *Honours:* Dance-Aid DJ of Year, 1991, 1992, 1993. *Membership:* Musicians' Union. *Leisure interests:* Travel; Photography; Reading; Cooking. *Current Management:* Cream (DJ); Diesel (remixes, production).

PARKER Alan; b. 26 Aug. 1944, England. Composer; Musician (guitar). m. Stephanie, 1 s., 1 d. *Musical Education:* Studied classical guitar with Julian Bream, composition, orchestration, Royal Academy of Music, London. *Career:* Began as session guitarist, London's leading player, 1960s-70s; Artists worked with included: Stevie Wonder; Frank Sinatra; Elton John; Dusty Springfield; Andy Williams; Tony Bennett; Mick Jagger; David Bowie; Paul McCartney; John Lennon; Jimi Hendrix; John Denver; Johnny Cash; Dame Kiri Te Kanawa; Placido Domingo; Founder member, songwriter, Blue Mink; The Congregation. *Compositions:* Songs recorded by: Blue Mink; The Congregation; The Walker Brothers; Dusty Springfield; CCS; Arrangements for: Neil Diamond; John Denver; Dusty Springfield; The Walker Brothers; 21 films, 75 television productions include: What's Eating Gilbert Grape; Rhodes, BBC; Up on the Roof, Granada Films; Red Fox, LWT; Jaws 3; To Be The Best; Voice of The Heart; American Gothic; The Glory Boys; Dempsey and Makepeace; Firm Friends; Van Der Valk, Thames TV; Minder, Thames TV; Wild Justice; The Danedyke Mystery, Granada; Mirage; Philby Burgess and McClean; Moody and Peg; Mixed Doubles; Pop Quest, YTV; Children's ITV; Thames News; River Journeys, BBC TV; Oktober, ITV; Unknown Soldier, Carlton; Round Tower, ITV; Colour Blind, ITV; Nancherrow, BBC; Commercial jingles include: Kellogg's; Wrangler Jeans; Levi's Jeans; Volkswagen; Heinz;

Citroën; Tuborg Lager; Mass performed at the Vatican, 1993; Work for music libraries. *Recordings:* Hits with Blue Mink and The Congregation; Session guitarist, soundtracks for composers: John Barry; John Williams; Jerry Goldsmith; Lalo Schiffrin. *Honour:* Ivor Novello. *Memberships:* PRS; Musicians' Union. *Address:* Soundtrack Music Associates Ltd, 25 Ives St, Chelsea, London SW3 2ND, England.

PARKER Ed; b. 16 July 1929, Goose Creek (now Baytown), Texas, USA. Country Singer; Musician (Guitar). m. Carey Ruth Parker, 21 June 1962. *Education:* BS, MD, FBI National Academy. *Career:* Recording Artist; Live appearances, Bluegrass festivals, and guitar conventions; Film, Tomboy and the Champ. *Recordings:* Ed Parker Sings Just For You; From My Heart; I'd Like to Live It Again; One Ole Texan, Vol. 1; Still a Lot of Good Miles Left in Me. *Publication:* Policemen's Wives: Are They Important?, Texas Police Journal. *Honours:* Personality of the South; Country Music Asscn of America Hall of Fame; Airplay International Trailblazer Award, Leadership Award; International Star Music Award for Special Achievement. *Memberships:* CMA; ACM; ROPE; CMOA. *Leisure interests:* Former professional rodeo cowboy; Leather craftsman. *Address:* PO Box 1032, Orange, TX 77631, USA.

PARKER Graham; b. 18 Nov. 1950, London, England. Vocalist; Songwriter. *Career:* Member, R & B groups: The Black Rockers; Deep Cut; Vocalist, Graham Parker and The Rumour, 1975–80; Solo artiste, 1980–; Concerts include: British tour, support to Thin Lizzy, 1976; Support to Bob Dylan, 1978; US tour, support to Cheap Trick, 1979; Reading Festival, 1986; Rock 'n' roll revue US tour, 1989. *Recordings:* Albums: with Graham Parker and The Rumour: Howlin' Wind, 1976; Heat Treatment, 1976; Stick To Me, 1977; The Parkerilla, 1978; Squeezing Out Sparks, 1979; The Up Escalator, 1980; The Best of Graham Parker and The Rumour, 1980; Solo albums: Another Grey Area, 1982; The Real McCaw, 1983; Steady Nerves, 1985; Mona Lisa's Sister, 1988; Human Soul, 1989; Live! Alone In America, 1989; Struck By Lightning, 1991; Burning Questions, 1992; Passion Word – The Graham Parker Anthology 1976–91, 1993; Live on the Test, 1995; Squeezing Out Sparks/Live Sparks, 1996; The Last Rock and Roll Tour, 1997; Loose Monkeys, Spare Tracks and Lost Demos, 1999; Parkerilla, 1999; Master Hits: Graham Parker; Singles include: with the Rumour: Silly Thing, 1976; The Pink Parker EP, 1977; Hey Lord Don't Ask Me Questions, 1978; Solo: Temporary Beauty, 1982; Wake Up (Next To You); The Mona Lisa's Sister, 1988; Here It Comes Again, 1992; Christmas Cracker, 1994; 12 Haunted Episodes, 1995. *Address:* c/o RCA Records, Bedford House, 69–79 Fulham High St, London SW6 3JW, England.

PARKER Mick; b. 12 June 1952, London, England. Musician (piano, keyboards, accordion); Composer. m. Angelika Helm, 25 July 1992, 1 s. *Education:* To degree level. *Musical Education:* All piano academy grades 1–8. *Career:* Toured with: Joan Armatrading, 1976–79; Billy Ocean, 1979–80; Linda Lewis, 1980–82; Television with all the above; Touring and recording for Gilbert O'Sullivan as MD, 1991–; Toured Japan with Linda Lewis, 1997. *Compositions:* Many jingles and film music, includes Merchant Ivory film Heat and Dust, 1985; Soundtrack for Thieftakers, ITV, 1996. *Recordings:* As producer: Single: So Macho, Sinitta, 1986; As arranger: Album: Aqaba Beach, Mory Kante, 1986; As musician: Album: Este Mundo, Gipsy Kings, 1992; with Gilbert O'Sullivan: Sounds of The Loop, 1992; Live In Japan, 1993; Singer Sewing Machine, Gilbert O'Sullivan, 1996. *Honours:* Ampex Golden Reel Awards, Sinitta; Azucar Moreno. *Memberships:* PRS; MCPS; Musicians' Union.

PARKER Peter Paul; b. 31 Aug. 1964, Kingston, Surrey, England. Musician (bass); Songwriter. *Musical Education:* Basstech College, Acton; Intermediate, Advanced Course. *Career:* Bassist, Heaven Can Wait, 1982–86; Recorded album, played Hammersmith Palais; Played with Thin Lizzy, Wolverhampton, Phil Lynott Tribute, 1994. *Compositions:* Album, Out of the Blue by Emily's Sister, written, recorded and produced, 1996; EP, One of a Kind/Special Friend by Emily's Sister, written, recorded and produced, 1998. *Recordings:* Garden of Hope (EP), Afterlife, 1995; Out of the Blue, 1996. *Membership:* Musicians' Union; Guild of Master Songwriters. *Leisure interests:* Eating; Drinking; Golf; Football; Rugby. *Current Management:* Metro Music. *Address:* Metro Music Ltd, PO Box 75, Shepperton, Middlesex TW17 9NA, England.

PARKER Ray Jr; b. 1 May 1954, Detroit, Michigan, USA. Musician (guitar). *Career:* Member, houseband, 20 Grand Club, late 1960s; Toured with Detroit Spinners; Studio musician for Invicta Wax; Formed Raydio, 1977–; Solo artiste, 1982–. *Recordings:* Albums: as Raydio: Raydio, 1977; Rock On, 1979; as Ray Parker Jr and Raydio: Two Places At The Same Time, 1980; A Woman Needs Love, 1981; Solo albums: The Other Woman, 1982; Greatest Hits, 1982; Woman Out of Control, 1983; Chartbusters, 1984; Sex and The Single Man, 1985; After Dark, 1987; I Love You Like You Are, 1991; Musician, albums by Stevie Wonder: Talking Book; Innervisions; Marvin Gaye, Master, 1961–84; Diana Ross, Greatest Hits The RCA Years; Boz Scaggs, My Time the Anthology 1969–97; Nona Hendryx, Transformation; Herbie Hancock, VSOP; Singles include: Jack

and Jill; A Woman Needs Love (Just Like You Do), 1981; The Other Woman, 1982; Ghostbusters (film theme), 1984; She Needs to Get Some, 1991; The Other Woman, 1993. *Honour:* Grammy Award, Best Pop Instrumental Performance, 1984. *Current Management:* Joseph Ruffalo Entertainment, 1728 Monte Cielo Court, Beverly Hills, CA 90210, USA.

PARKINSON Bill; b. 28 Nov. 1941, Lancaster, England. Musician (guitar); Songwriter; Prod. m. Jennifer, 4 Dec. 1965, 2 d. *Musical Education:* Mostly self-taught. *Career:* The Fourmost; P J Proby; Screaming Lord Sutch; The Savages; Tom Jones backing group: The Squires (3 years); Chuck Berry; Across The Universe-The Beatles; Sammy Davis Jr; Shirley Bassey; Bobby Vee; Petula Clark; Vic Damone; Englebert Humperdink; Ted Heath Orchestra; Freddy Starr. *Compositions:* Neil Reid: Mother of Mine; Jimmy Osmond; Deep Purple: Theme to Mandrake Root. *Memberships:* PRS; MCPS; Musicians' Union. *Leisure interests:* Water colours and oils (several one-man exhibitions). *Address:* 2 Beech Pl., Epping, Essex CM16 5EJ, England.

PARLETT Michael John; b. 19 July 1963, Bexleyheath, Kent, England. Musician (alto, soprano, tenor, saxophones, flute, percussion, windsynth - WX7); Prod. *Musical Education:* B Mus, Goldsmiths College, London; PGCE, Middlesex University. *Career:* Broadcasts on Radio 2, 1994; Tours with: Iona; Gail Thompson's Jazz Africa; Appeared on: Dave Taylor, Rock 'n' roll Show, Finland; Top of The Pops; European TV, Netherlands. *Recordings:* Sessions with: Lulu; Take That; Mica Paris; Eternal; Gabrielle; Yazz; Clive Griffin; Olu; David Grant; The Jones Girls; 911; M People; Geno Washington; Currently working on solo album. *Honours:* Nomination, Arts Foundation Award for Jazz Composition. *Membership:* Musicians' Union. *Leisure interests:* Practicing; Sport; Running own big band. *Current Management:* 61 Howland Way, Surrey Quays, London SW16 1HW, England.

PARNELL Jack; b. 6 Aug. 1923, London, England. Jazz Musician (drums); Bandleader; Musical Dir. *Career:* Member, Radio Rhythm Club Sextet; Partnership with Vic Lewis as Lewis-Parnell Jazzmen, 1944–46; Member, Ted Heath's Big Band, 7 years; Musical Director, ATV, including Sunday Night At The London Palladium, 1960s; Musical Director, The Muppet Show; Bandleader, UK jazz circuit; Backing musician with touring US musicians, 1970s-. *Recordings:* Recent albums include: Big Band Show, 1976; Jack Parnell Plays Music of The Giants, 1975; Braziliana, 1977; 50 Big Band Favourites, 1984; Joe Williams, Here's to Life, 1993; Dick Sudhalter, After a While, 1994; Ted Heath, Very Best of Ted Heath, 1998; Ted Heath, Listen to my Music Vol. 3, 1999.

PARNELL Lee Roy; b. 21 Dec. 1956, Abilene, Texas, USA. Country Musician (slide guitar). 1 s., 1 d. *Musical Education:* Self-taught. *Career:* Ten Feet Tall and Bulletproof tour, with Travis Tritt and Joe Diffie, 1994; Late Show With David Letterman; The Tonight Show; Live With Regis and Kathie Lee; Music City Tonight; Happy New Year America from the House of Blues; Miller Genuine Draft radio commercial; CocaCola Radio commercial; Theme song for 'The Road' radio and television programme. *Recordings:* We All Get Lucky Sometimes; On The Road; Love Without Mercy; Lee Roy Parnell; Every Night's a Saturday Night; Hits and Highways Ahead; Singles: Lucky Me Lucky You; You Can't Get There from Here. *Honours:* CMA Nominations: Horizon Award, 1994; Collaboration, 1995; Grammy Nomination, Best Country Instrumental with Flaco Jiminez, 1996-. *Memberships:* BMI; ACM; CMA. *Leisure interests:* Songwriting; Working out; Going to pawn shops for collectable guitars. *Current Management:* Mike Robertson Management. *Address:* PO Box 120073, Nashville, TN 37212, USA.

PARR John; b. 19 Nov. 1957, Nr. Sherwood Forest, Nottinghamshire, England. Singer; Songwriter; Prod. m. Sharon, 29 Aug. 1980, 2 s. *Musical Education:* Guitar lessons. *Career:* Tours, 1985-, including tours with: Tina Turner; Bryan Adams; Toto; Heart; Beach Boys. *Recordings:* Hit singles: Naughty Naughty; St Elmo's Fire (world-wide No. 1); Rock 'N' Roll Mercenaries (with Meatloaf); Paris (with LSO and Philarmonic Choir); Miami Vice; Movie soundtracks: 3 Men and A Baby; Quicksilver; American Anthem; The Running Man; St Elmo's Fire, 1985; Near Dark, 1987; Spruce Goose, 1986; Covers with: Tom Jones; The Monkees; Meatloaf; Roger Daltrey. *Honours:* Grammy Nomination; ASCAP Award, Most Performed Song; MIDEM Award. *Memberships:* PRS; MCPS; ASCAP; AFTRA; Equity; Musicians' Union. *Leisure interests:* Tennis; Football; Martial Arts. *Current Management:* Lou Howson, Bernie Fischbach. *Address:* Fischbach, 1925 Century Park E, Suite 1260, Los Angeles, CA 90067, USA.

PARRISH Man; b. 6 May 1958, Brooklyn, New York, USA. Prod.; Musician (keyboards); Man. *Education:* Dramatic Studies, American Academy of Dramatic Arts, New York, 1971. *Musical Education:* Self-taught. *Career:* 17 years in music business; Owner, production company, Man Made Productions, 1983–; Partner, Artist Management Company; Manager, Village People, 1988–93; Member of group Man 2 Man. *Recordings:* Singles: Hip Hop Be Bop, Man Parrish; Male Stripper, Man 2 Man; I Am What I Am, Gloria Gaynor (keyboards); Solo albums: Man

Parrish, 1983; 2, 1996; Hip Hop Bee Bop (Don't Stop), 1996; The Best of Man Parrish: Heartstroke, 1996; Dream Man, 1998; Producer/writer, approximately 50 recordings, including: Village People; Michael Jackson; Boy George; Gloria Gaynor; Omar; Santana; Klaus Nomi. *Honours:* Billboard Award, Dance Artist; Bessie Smith Award. *Memberships:* ASCAP; National Music Publishers; Harry Fox Agency. *Leisure interests:* Music; Internet. *Current Management:* AM:PM Entertainment. *Address:* 415 63rd St, Brooklyn, NY 11220, USA.

PARRY J Chris; b. 7 Jan. 1949, Wellington, New Zealand. Record Co Exec.; Record Prod. Divorced, 1 s., 2 d. *Education:* HND Business Studies, 1974. *Career:* Professional drummer, 1968–71; A & R Manager, Polydor Records, 1974–78; Owner, Fiction Records, 1978–; Managing Director, Fiction Records, Fiction Songs; Managing Director, XFM Radio. *Recordings:* Albums: In The City, Modern World, All Mod Cons, The Jam; Various recordings, The Cure (as co-producer); Three Imaginary Boys, The Cure (as producer). *Memberships:* BPI; Institute of Marketing. *Leisure interests:* Sailing; Skiing; Horse riding; Scuba-diving. *Address:* 97 Charlotte St, London W1 1LB, England.

PARSONS Alan; b. 1948. Musician; Record Prod.; Engineer. *Career:* Former recording engineer, EMI Records; Founder, Alan Parsons Project, 1975–; The Alan Parsons Live Project have toured 19 different countries around the world since 1994. *Recordings:* Albums: with Alan Parsons Project: Tales of Mystery and Imagination, 1976; I Robot, 1977; Pyramid, 1978; Eve, 1979; The Turn of a Friendly Card, 1980; Eye In The Sky, 1981; Ammonia Avenue, 1983; Vulture Culture, 1984; Stereotomy, 1985; Gaudi, 1987; Instrumental Works – Best of Alan Parsons Project, 1983; Limelight – Best of (Vol. II), 1988; Try Anything Once, 1992; On Air, 1996; Definitive Collection, 1997; Recording engineer, artistes including: The Beatles; Wings; Pilot; Cockney Rebel; Al Stewart; Pink Floyd. *Address:* c/o The Agency, 370 City Rd, London EC1V 2QA, England.

PARSONS David John; b. 30 Aug. 1962, Colchester, Essex, England. Record Co Exec.; Artist Man.; Performer. m. Stephanie Bowyer, 5 Sept. 1992, 1 s. *Education:* BA Hons; Currently pursuing PhD. *Career:* Lead vocalist, Splat!, 1981–83; Owner, Ron Johnson Records, 1983–90; Director, Submission Records Ltd, 1987–90; Owner, Zung Records, 1994; Director, Too Pye Ahh Records, 1995; Lead vocalist, Chod, 1995. *Recordings:* 1936, The Ex; Mud On A Colon, Stump; Two Kan Guru, Big Flame; I Am John's Pancreas, A Witness; Dudley Dorite Wristwatch, Chod; Debut album, Wholesome Fish. *Honour:* Ron Johnson Records, Independent Label of The Year, 1986. *Memberships:* PRS; MCPS; PPL. *Leisure interest:* Aikido. *Current Management:* Purple Skunk Management, The Basement, 19 Victoria Parade, Broadstairs, Kent CT10 1QL, England.

PARSONS David Richard; b. 12 April 1959, Woking, England. Musician (Guitar, violin); Songwriter. 1 s. *Musical Education:* Violin tuition, Music O Level. *Career:* Member, Sham 69; Member, The Wanderers, with Stiv Bators on vocals; Arena, TV special with Sham 69. *Recordings:* With Sham 69: Albums: Tell Us The Truth; That's Life; Hersham Boys; The Game; Volunteer; Information Libre; Soapy Water and Mr Marmalade; All the singles; With The Wanderers: Only Lovers Left Alive, 1981; Solo Album: Reconcile. *Memberships:* PRS; MCPS; Musicians' Union. *Leisure interest:* Tai Chi. *Address:* 30 Bois Hall Rd, Addlestone, Surrey KT 15 2JL, England.

PARSONS Niamh; b. 1958, Dublin, Ireland. Vocalist. *Musical Education:* Learned singing from father. *Career:* First sang with band Killera; Formed The Loose Connections with Dee Moore; Joined Arcady, 1992; Sang for President Clinton in 1999; Lecturer at the Ballyfermot School of Music. *Recordings:* Albums include: Loosely Connected, 1992; Loosen Up, Holding Up Half The Sky, 1997; Celtic Love Songs, 1998; Blackbirds and Thrushes, 1999; In My Prime, 2000. *Honours:* AIFM award nominees: Blackbirds and Thrushes; In My Prime; appeared on Grammy-nominated album Journey to the Sun 2001; BBC Radio 2 Folk Awards: Best Album nominee, In My Prime; Folksinger of the Year nominee, 2001. *Internet:* www.niamhparsons.com.

PARTIS Lee Valentine; b. 22 Feb. 1954, Romford, Essex, England. Musician (drums); Vocalist; Actor. 1 s. *Musical Education:* Self-taught. *Career:* Played with many bands including: Kirsty MacColl; Jah Wobble; Oysterband. *Recordings:* Numerous albums include: with Oysterband: Deserters, 1992; Holy Bandits, 1993; Trawler, 1994; with Kirsty Macoll: Desperate Character, 1981. *Leisure interests:* Cricket; Tai Chi. *Current Management:* Forward Management. *Address:* 132 Liverpool Rd, London N1 1LA, England.

PARTON Dolly; b. 19 Jan. 1946, Locust Ridge, Tennessee, USA. Country Singer; Actress. m. Carl Dean, 30 May 1966. *Career:* Singer, local radio, as child; Apperances include: Grand Ole Opry, Nashville, 1968–; Regular on Porter Wagoner Show; Regular recordings with Wagoner, 1967–74; Solo artist, 1969–; Actress, films: 9 To 5, 1980; Best Little Whorehouse In Texas, 1982; Rhinestone, 1984; Steel Magnolias, 1990; Wild Texas Wind, NBC, 1990; Straight Talk, 1992; Host, own television shows, Dolly, 1976, 1987;

TV special, Dolly Parton Christmas At Home, ABC, 1990; Owner, Dollywood entertainment complex. *Compositions include:* I Will Always Love You (also recorded by Whitney Houston, for film The Bodyguard 1992). *Recordings:* Numerous US Country No. 1 hits include: Joshua, 1970; Jolene, 1974; I Will Always Love You, 1974 (also in 1982); Baby I'm Burnin', 1979; 9 To 5, 1981; Islands In The Stream, with Kenny Rogers, 1983; Think About Love, 1986; To Know Him Is To Love Him, 1987; Yellow Roses, 1989; Albums include: with Porter Wagoner: Just The Two of Us, 1969; Always, Always, 1969; Porter Wayne and Dolly Rebecca, 1970; Once More, 1970; Two of a Kind, 1971; Solo albums: My Blue Ridge Mountain Boy, 1969; Joshua, 1973; New Harvest... First Gathering, 1977; Here You Come Again, 1978; Great Balls of Fire, 1979; Dolly Dolly Dolly, 1980; 9 To 5 and Odd Jobs, 1980; Heartbreak Express, 1982; Best Little Whorehouse In Texas (soundtrack), 1982; Burlap and Satin, 1983; The Great Pretender, 1984; Rhinestone (soundtrack), 1984; Once Upon A Christmas, 1984; Greatest Hits, 1985; Trio (with Linda Ronstadt and Emmylou Harris), 1987; Rainbow, 1988; White Limozeen, 1989; Eagle When She Flies, 1991; Straight Talk (soundtrack), 1992; Slow Dancing With The Moon, 1993; Honky Tonk Angels (with Loretta Lynn and Tammy Wynette), 1993; Heartsongs: Live from Home, 1994; Something Special, 1995; Treasures, 1996; The Essential Dolly Parton, Vol. I; Hungry Again, 1998; Walking on Sunshine, 1999; The Grass is Blue, 1999; Super Hits, 1999 Contributor, Heroes and Friends, Randy Travis, 1991. *Honours include:* CMA Awards: Female Vocalist of the Year, 1975, 1976; American Music Awards: Favourite Country Album, 1978; Favourite Country Single, 1984, 1985; Grammy Awards: Best Female Country Artist, 1979; Best Country Vocal Performance, 1982; Top Country Album, 1981; Best Country Vocal, Duo or Group (with Ronstadt and Harris), 1988; ACM Record of the Year, 1983; AMA Best Country Single, 1983. *Current Management:* Maureen O'Connor, Rogers and Cowan, 10000 Santa Monica Blvd, Los Angeles, CA 90067, USA.

PARTON Stella; b. 4 May 1949, Locust Ridge, Tennessee, USA. Country Singer. *Career:* Radio debut with sister Dolly Parton, 1955; Featured on soundtrack of Dolly Parton's film Rhinestone; Actress, stage version, The Best Little Whorehouse In Texas. *Recordings:* Hit singles: I Want To Hold You In My Dreams Tonight; Standard Lie No. 1; Four Little Letters; Albums: I Want To Hold You In My Arms Tonight, 1975; Country Sweet, 1977; Stella Parton, 1978; Love Ya, 1979; So Far... So Good, 1982; Anthology, 1998. *Address:* c/o Joe Taylor Artist Agency, 2802 Columbine Pl., Nashville, TN 37204, USA.

PARTRIDGE Andy; b. 11 Nov. 1953, Malta. Musician (guitar); Singer; Songwriter; Record Prod. *Career:* Guitarist, vocalist, XTC, 1977–; Appearances include: US, Venezuela, SE Asia, Australia; Record as send-up 60s group, The Dukes of Stratosphear, 1985; XTC work as studio band only, 1982–; Producer, other bands, 1983-. *Recordings:* Hit singles: with XTC: Making Plans For Nigel, 1979; Sgt Rock (Is Going To Help Me), 1981; Senses Working Overtime, 1982; Albums as XTC: White Music, 1978; Go 2, 1978; Drums and Wires, 1979; Black Sea, 1980; English Settlement, 1982; Waxworks – Some Singles, (1977–82), 1982; Mummer, 1983; The Big Express, 1984; The Compact XTC, 1986; Skylarking, 1986; Chips From The Chocolate Fireball, 1987; Oranges and Lemons, 1989; Nonsuch, 1992; Fossil Fuel, 1996; Solo albums: Takeaway/The Lure of Salvage, 1980; as The Dukes of Stratosphear: 25 O'Clock, 1985; Psonic Psunspot, 1987; Transistor Blast, 1998; Apple Venus Vol. I, 1999; Homespun, 1999; Wasp Star (Apple Venus Vol. 2), 2000; with Martin Newell: The Greatest Living Englishman, 1993; Through the Hill, with Harold Budd, 1994; As producer: tracks by The Mission; The Lilac Time; Peter Blegvad; Wallflowers; Woodentops. *Honours:* Edison Award, 1982; Grammy Nominee, 1992; Novello Award Nominee, 1992. *Current Management:* c/o Idea, St Annes, Foxhill, Wanborough, Nr Swindon, Wiltshire SN4 0DS, England.

PASCOAL Hermeto; b. 22 June 1936, Lagoa da Canoa, Brazil. Multi-instrumentalist; Arranger; Composer. m. Ilza da Silva Pascoal, 30 July 1955, 3 s., 3 d. *Musical Education:* Self-taught. *Career:* Accordion, flute, with Quarteto Novo to 1969; Solo artist, 1970–; Concerts with Hermeto Pascoal Group include Montreux Jazz Festival, 1978; With the Danish Radio Concert Orchestra, Copenhagen, 1989; With Symphonic, Berlin, 1989; Radio Big Band, 1992; with Special Big Band, 1992; Tours, Europe, USA; Television, radio: Brazilian TV; Sinfonia do Alto da Ribeira; Sound of Aura with: President Fernando Collor de Melo; Papa Joao Paulo II; Jo Soares; Clovodil; French TV with The Tubes. *Recordings:* Quarteto Novo, 1967; Hermeto, 1979; A Musica Livre De Hermeto Pascoal, 1973; Slaves Mass, 1976; Zabumbe-bum-a, 1978; Montreux ao Vivo, 1978; Cerebro Magnetico, 1980; Hermeto Pascoal and Grupo, 1982; Lagoa da Canoa Municipalo de Arapiraca, 1984; Brasil Universo, 1986; So Nao Toca Quem Nao Quer, 1987; Por Diferentes Caminhos/Piano solo, 1988; Festa Dos Deuses, 1992; Hermeta Pascoal E Grupo, 1992. *Honours:* Best Soloist, Associacao Paulista de Criticos de Arte, Brazil, 1972; Best Group, Brazil, 1988; Best Cover and Best Tune: Pixitotina, Brazil, 1989; Concert of Year and Decade, Guardian, Q Magazine, 1994. *Membership:* SACEM, France. *Leisure interests:* Playing, making music; Listening to radio (news, football). *Address:* Rua Victor Guisard 333, Jabour, Rio de Janeiro, RJ, Brazil.

PASCU Ioan Gyuri; b. 31 Aug. 1961, Agnita, Romania. Teacher; Songwriter; Entertainer; Actor; Musician (guitar, drums); Writer; Radio, television producer. m. Daniela Marin, 15 Aug. 1993. *Education:* University of Cluj, Faculty of Philology. *Musical Education:* Private piano lessons; Self-taught. *Career:* Member, Divertis Group (humour, political satire shows) since 1990; Many radio and television shows, 1989–92; Soloist, 1991–; Established the Ioan Gyuri Pascu and The Blues Workers Band; International Jazz and Blues Festivals: Brasov, 1992; Bucharest, 1992; Russe, 1992; Brasov, 1993, 1994; International Rock Festivals: Bucharest, 1993; Dracula, Brasov, 1993; Skip Rock, Bucharest, 1994; International Pop Festival, Golden Stag, Brasov (record debut contest), 1993; Opened the Romanian tours of Beats International, 1993, Asia, 1994; Acted in Unforgettable Summer, by Lucian Pintilie (offically selected for Cannes film festival); TV specials: Stars Duel, 1993; VIP, 1993; Many Divertis Group shows, soloist in musical shows. *Compositions:* Over 30 songs; Original music for television film: Teapa, 1993; Stars School, 1995. *Recordings:* It Could Be, 1992; Mixed Grill, 1993; The Machine With Jazzoline, 1994; Video: Divertis Group, 1995. *Publications:* Short stories in Apostrof (literature magazine), 1990; Cuvantul magazine (serial). Showman of The Year: Pop Rock and Show magazine; Major Personality of the Year, 1993; The Song of the Year, The Songwriter of the Year, Radio Contact, 1994; Record of the Year, Vox, Pop, Rock magazine. *Membership:* Divertis Cultural Asscn. *Leisure interests:* Football; Handball; Tennis; Fishing; Watching action films.

PASILLAS José Antonio II; b. 26 April 1976. Musician (drums). *Career:* Started drumming in 1990; Formed group Incubus with school friends in Calabasas, California, 1991; Initially played small parties, graduating to support slots in Hollywood, California; Circulated demo tapes of Closet Cultivation and Incubus before independent album release, 1995; Group signed by Immortal/Epic; Built US and European following support slots on tours with: Sugar Ray; Black Sabbath; Korn; Drive reached #1 on US Modern Rock Chart, 2001; First Japanese and Australian live dates, 2001. *Recordings:* Albums: Fungus Amongus, 1995; S.C.I.E.N.C.E., 1997; Make Yourself, 1999; Morning View, 2001; Singles: Enjoy Incubus EP, 1997; Pardon Me, 1999; Stellar, When Incubus Attacks Vol. 1 EP, 2000; Drive, Wish You Were Here, 2001. *Honours:* Make Yourself album certified double platinum by RIAA; Billboard Award, Modern Rock Single of The Year, 2001. *Current Management:* Steve Rennie, REN Management, California, USA. *Internet:* www.enjoyincubus.com.

PASKIN Layo; b. London, England. Prod.; Remixer; DJ. *Career:* Opened London's The End nightclub with partner Mr C, 1995; Co-founder: End Recordings; Member: Killer Loop (with Mr C); Layo and Bushwacka (with Matthew B). *Recordings:* Albums: Lowlife (with Bushwacka!), 1999; Singles: as Usual Suspects: Split Personality, 1997; Nightstalkin', 1998; with Bushwacka: Deep South, 1999; with Killer Loop: Someone, 1996; Broken, 1998; The Blue Hour, 2000; Organism, 2001. *Address:* c/o End Recordings, 18 W Central St, London, WC1A 1JJ, England.

PASS Liz (Elizabeth Ann); b. Mutare, Zimbabwe. Contemporary Gospel Artist. m. Rev Dr David B Pass, 1 Sept. 1973. *Musical Education:* Bachelor of Music, Voice Performance; BA, Theatre, Communications. *Career:* Appeared on International TV with song: God Bless Africa; Tours, concerts, television appearances all over Africa, Europe, USA, South America. *Recordings:* God Bless Africa; Heart Cry For The Earth; Hymns For Africa; Christmas In Africa; African Collection; Under African Skies; Reach For Your Dreams; A Millenium Dream. *Publications:* Two song books. *Honours:* Top voice student, Biola University, 1980. *Memberships:* ASAMI; SAMRO; SARREL. *Leisure interests:* Wildlife; Conservation; Reading.

PATTON Mike; b. 27 Jan. 1968, Eureka, California, USA. Rock Singer. *Career:* Member, Mr Bungle; Lead singer, US rock group Faith No More, 1988–98; Regular international concerts include: Reading Festival, 1990; Support to Robert Plant, 1990; Monsters of Rock European Festivals, 1990; Rock In Rio II, Brazil, 1991; Day On The Green, San Francisco, 1991; Phoenix Festival, 1993, 1995. *Recordings:* Hit singles include: From Out of Nowhere, 1990; Epic, 1990; Falling To Pieces, 1990; Midlife Crisis, 1992; A Small Victory, 1992; Everything's Ruined, 1992; I'm Easy, 1993; Albums: The Real Thing, 1989; Live At Brixton Academy, 1991; Angel Dust, 1992; King For A Day, Fool For A Lifetime, 1995; Adult Themes for Voice, 1996; Pranzo Oltranzis, 1997; Album of the Year, 1997; Faith No More, Greatest Hits, 1998; with Jerry Hunt, Song Drapes, 1999. *Honours:* Grammy Nomination, Best Heavy Metal Performance, 1990; Bammy Awards: Outstanding Group, Male Vocalist, 1991. *Current Management:* Warren Entner Management, 5550 Wilshire Blvd, Suite 302, Los Angeles, CA 90036, USA.

PATTULLO Gordon James; b. 8 Sept. 1961, Dundee, Scotland. Musician (accordion). m. June Elspeth McLaren, 17 Oct. 1984, 2 s., 1 d. *Musical Education:* Dundee Accordion School of Music. *Career:* Concert tours world-wide with Andy Stewart Show, 1977–; Television appearances: 2 series for Andy's Party, Grampian TV; Thingummyjig, STV; Various Hogmanay

shows for BBC TV, Grampian and Scottish TV. *Compositions include:* The Furrows End. *Recordings:* A Gordon For You; The Northlands; Scotland's Favourite; Here's Tae A Gordon; Accordion Favourites; Scotch On The Box; All The Best; Fair Play; Scottish Accordion Hits; Golden Sound of Scottish Music; A Scottish Celebration; Ceilidh Dance Party. *Honour:* Jr Accordion Champion of Scotland, 1974. *Membership:* Musicians' Union. *Leisure interest:* Restoring vintage tractors. *Address:* Tullybaccart Farmhouse, Coupar Angus, Blairgowrie, Perthshire PH13 9LA, Scotland.

PAUL Amit Sebastian; b. 29 Oct. 1983, Boden, Sweden. Vocalist. *Education:* Kungsholmens school, Stockholm. *Career:* Picked to be member of A*Teens group following auditions at Leslie Kühler's dance school, 1998; Continued educational studies whilst pursuing musical career; Prestigious US support tours for N*Sync and Britney Spears, 2000. *Recordings:* Albums: The Abba Generation, 1999; Teen Spirit, 2001; Singles: Mamma Mia, Super Trouper, Gimme! Gimme! Gimme!, Happy New Year, 1999; Dancing Queen, Upside Down, 2000; Halfway Around The World, Sugar Rush, 2001. *Honours:* Broke Swedish sales records with first album and single; World-wide sales of first album in excess of 3m.; Viva Music Awards, Best International Newcomer, 2000. *Address:* c/o Stockholm Records, Sweden. *Internet:* www.stockholmrecords.com.

PAUL Les, (Lester Polfus); b. 9 June 1915, Waukesha, Wisconsin, USA. Inventor; Musician (guitar). m. Mary Ford (deceased 1977), 3 s., 2 d. *Career:* Musician, numerous radio appearances, 1920s-30s; Formed Les Paul Trio, 1936; Recordings and television show with Mary Ford, 1950s; Chet Atkins, 1970s; Television includes: First television broadcast with orchestra, NBC, 1939; Documentary, The Wizard of Waukesha, 1980; Concerts include: Jazz At The Philharmonic concert with Nat 'King' Cole, 1944; Guitar Legends, Seville, Spain, 1992; Pioneer, multi-track tape recording; Inventor, first 8-track tape recorder; Inventor, sound-on-sound recording; Inventor, designer, Les Paul solid body electric guitar, for Gibson Guitars; Consultant, Gibson Guitar Corporation, Nashville. *Recordings include:* Lover, 1948; Brazil, 1948; Nola, 1949; Goofus, 1950; Tennessee Waltz, 1950; Little Rock Getaway, 1950; Mockin' Bird Hill, 1951; How High The Moon (No. 1, USA), 1951; Smoke Rings, 1952; Tiger Rag, 1953; Vaya Con Dios (No. 1, USA), 1954; Albums include: with Mary Ford: New Sound Vols I and II; Les and Mary; Bye Bye Blues; The Hitmakers; Time To Dream; Lover's Luau; Warm and Wonderful; Bouquet of Roses; Swingin' South; with Chet Atkins: Chester and Lester, 1977; Guitar Masters, 1978; Multi Trakin', 1979; Tiger Rag, 1984; All Time Greatest Hits, 1994; Love Songs by Les Paul and Mary Ford, 1997; A Class Act, 1998; The World is Waiting, 1999; Early Les Paul, 1999; Other recordings with Bing Crosby; Andrews Sisters; Patti Smith. *Honours:* Grammy, Chester and Lester, 1977; Grammy Nomination, Guitar Masters, 1978; Hall of Fame Award, 1979.

PAULIK Dalibor; b. 22 Dec. 1953, Zagreb, Croatia. Composer; Musician (piano); Theatre Critic. m. Vesna Paulik, 7 June 1980, 1 s. *Education:* MSc, Theatrology; Professor, Music theatre. *Musical Education:* Secondary music school, private music seminars. *Career:* Croatian and international festivals of popular music; 500 concerts with popular Croatian singers; Music for theatre and television; Festivals in: Ireland; Latin America; Finland; Los Angeles; Croatia (Zagreb, Krapina, Split); Sarjevo; Songs for organizations: Stars of Hope (Sweden); World For Two (UK). *Compositions:* Over 200 include: Your Face In My Mirror; Goodbye Is Not For You; Love Is A Game; Never In My Life; Memories; The Violin Song; Stars of Hope; Today I'm Sad My Love; Together Forever; Dancing With The Moonlight. *Publications:* Scientific publications of HAZU; Who Is Who In Croatia; Directory of Croatian Composers Society. *Honours:* 20 at Croatian festivals; 1 in Ireland. *Membership:* Croatian Composers Society (FIDOF). *Leisure interests:* Table tennis; Fishing; Collecting theatre publications.

PAULSEN Michael Harbo; b. 23 March 1964, Jylland, Abenra, Denmark. Musician (Drums). *Education:* With Classical Music Professor Bent Lylloff, Billyhart, Idriss Muhammed. *Recordings:* Sun Quartet; Two Bass Hit; Erik Brum Spreckelsen: I'll See You Soon. *Address:* Jakob Dannefaerdsvej 14 7th, 1973, FDB C, Denmark.

PAXTON Tom; b. 31 Oct. 1937, Chicago, Illinois, USA. Folk Singer; Songwriter; Author. m. Margaret Ann Cummings, 5 Aug. 1963, 3 d. *Education:* BFA, University of Oklahoma, 1959. *Career:* Folk recording artist, 1962–; Early concerts on Greenwich Village circuit; World-wide tours and concerts, 1960–; Board of directors, Kerrville Folk Festival, 1990. *Compositions include:* Lyndon Johnson Told The Nation; Talkin' Vietnam Pot Luck Blues; Leaving London; The Hostage (also recorded by Judy Collins). *Recordings:* Albums include: Ramblin' Boy, 1964; Ain't That News, 1965; Outward Bound, 1968; Morning Again, 1968; The Things I Notice Now, 1969; Tom Paxton 6, 1970; The Compleat Tom Paxton, 1971; How Come The Sun, 1971; Peace Will Come 1972; New Songs Old Friends, 1973; Something In My Life, 1975; Saturday Night, 1976; Heroes, 1978; Up and Up, 1980; The Paxton Report, 1981; In The Orchard, 1985; One Million Lawyers and Other Disasters, 1985; Even A Gray Day, 1986; And Loving You, 1988; Politics – Live, 1989; Storyteller, 1989; Suzy is a Rocker, 1992; Goin' to the Zoo, 1997; I Can't Help Wonder Where I'm Bound, 1999;

Appears on : Tribute to Woody Guthrie, 1972; Newport Folk Festival, 1991; Where Have All the Flowers Gone, 1998. *Publications:* Ramblin' Boy and Other Songs, 1965; Tom Paxton Anthology, 1971; Politics, 1989; The Authentic Guitar of Tom Paxton, 1989; The Tom Paxton Children's Song Book, 1990; Author, children's books: Jennifer's Rabbit, 1988; Belling The Cat, 1990; Englebert The Elephant, 1990; Aesop's Fables Retold In Verse, 1988; Androcles and The Lion, 1991. *Memberships:* ASCAP; AFTRA; AFofM; Screen Actors Guild; World Folk Music Asscn (Hon. Chairman of Board). *Current Management:* c/o Susan Martinez, Martinez Management and Media, PO Box 14901, University Station, Minneapolis, MN 55414, USA.

PAYCHECK Johnny, (Donald Eugene Lytle); b. 31 May 1938, Ohio, USA. Singer; Musician (guitar). m. Sharon, 23 Dec. 1971, 1 s. *Musical Education:* Self-taught. *Career:* Joined George Jones, as bass, steel guitar player, for 6 years, mid-1950s; Worked with country artists including: Faron Young; Ray Price; Porter Wagoner; Hits began 1965; Major success with: Take This Job and Shove It; Concerts, performances include: Carnegie Hall; Wembley Festival, England; Las Vegas; Lone Star, New York City; Television includes: David Letterman Show; Music City Tonight; Nashville Now; Mike Douglas Show; Solid Gold; Major role in film; Member, Grand Ole Opry, 1997. *Compositions include:* Apartment #9, Tammy Wynette; Touch My Heart, Ray Price. *Recordings:* 67 albums; Hit songs include: Don't Take Her She's All I've Got; Someone To Give My Love To; Mr Lovemaker; For A Minute There; A-11; Memory of a Memory; Outlaw's Prayer; I'm The Only Hell My Mama Ever Raised; Slide Off Your Satin Sheets; Song and Dance Man; Colorado Kool Aid; Old Violin; 11 Months and 29 Days; Don't Monkey With Another Monkey's Monkey; Take This Job and Shove It; Me and The IRS. *Honours include:* 6 Gold albums, 1 Platinum, 1 double Platinum; Grammy Nominations include: Don't Take Her, She's All I've Got, 1970; Take This Job and Shove It; Lifetime Achievement, BMI; Entertainer of The Year, Independent Record Labels, 1991. *Memberships:* AFofM; CMA; ACM. *Leisure interests:* Golf; Fishing. *Current Management:* Marty Martel, Midnight Special Productions Inc.

PAYNE Dougie; b. 14 Nov. 1972, Scotland. Musician (Bass). *Career:* Member, Travis; Numerous tours and television appearances. *Recordings:* Singles: U16 Girls, 1997; All I Want To Do Is Rock, 1997; Tied to the 90s, 1997; Happy, 1997; More than Us, 1997; Writing to Reach You, 1999; Driftwood, 1999; Why Does It Always Rain on Me?, 1999; Turn, 1999; Albums: Good Feeling, 1997; The Man Who, 1999. *Honours:* Q Magazine Award, Best Single, 1999; Select Magazine, Album of the Year, 1999.

PAYNE Freda; b. 19 Sept. 1945, Detroit, Michigan, USA. Singer; Actress. m. Gregory Abbott, 1 Dec. 1976, 1 s. *Education:* Studied acting with Al Mancini. *Musical Education:* Detroit Institute of Musical Arts; Piano and Voice tuition. *Career:* Began singing career at age 17; Toured with Quincy Jones at such theatres as the Apollo in New York City and Regal Theatre in Chicago; Acting debut in the musical Hallelujah Baby, then as Linda in Lost in The Stars, in The Book of Numbers, Daddy Goodness, Ain't Misbehavin' and Sophisticated Ladies; Starred in the television special Freda Payne and The Stylistics, appeared in HBO's The Legendary Ladies of Rock and in the video Soul No 2 America's Music; Hosted her own TV talk show, Today's Black Woman; Has toured in UK, Germany and Japan; Starred in musical, Blues in the Night, 1990–91, and in the musical drama, Jelly's Last Jam by George C Wolf. *Recordings include:* Albums: Stares and Whispers; Supernatural High; Red Hot; Payne and Pleasure; Out of Payne Comes Love; I Hate Barney; An Evening with Freda Payne: Live; Live in Concert; Greatest Hits; Greatest Hits Live in Concert; Singles: Band of Gold; Bring The Boys Home; Deeper and Deeper; Cherish What's Dear To You; You Brought The Joy. *Honours:* Two Gold Singles; Best Ensemble Performance for Blues In The Night, Drama-Logue Award, 1990; Dame of Malta, Knights of Malta – The Sovereign Military and Hospital Order of St John of Jerusalem, 1994. *Leisure interests:* Tennis; Fishing; Skiing; Yoga; Healthy Living. *Address:* Embassy Artists/Full Circle Entertainment, 23500 Michigan Ave, Dearborn, MI 48124, USA.

PAYNE John Devereux; b. 16 Dec. 1945, Virginia, USA. Musician; Music Teacher. m. Francine Rota, 3 s. *Education:* BA, Harvard University, 1972. *Career:* Played and recorded with Van Morrison, 1968; Bonnie Raitt, 1972–78; Led own Jazz Band, 1973–77; Toured with Dave Bromberg, 1973–74; Phoebe Snow, 1977; Toured with Michael Franks, 1978, 1979–; Directing, My Music School; Playing local Boston area jazz clubs. *Compositions:* Scenes From A Journey; Rush; Reaching. *Recordings:* with Van Morrison, Astral Weeks; with Bonnie Raitt, Give It Up; Bedtime Stories; John Paynes First Album; Razors Edge. *Honours:* Nominated Best Clarinetist, Playboy Jazz Poll, 1973; Named Best of Boston Jazz Bands, 1970's. *Current Management:* John Payne Music Center, 9A Station St, Brookline, MA 02443, USA.

PAYNE Les Alexander; b. 22 Aug. 1943, Newport, Isle of Wight, England. Singer; Songwriter; Musician (guitar, keyboards). m. (1) Brigitte Jean Wilson, 1965, divorced, 1971, 1 s., (2) Rosalind Jean Butler, 1974, divorced 1993, 2 s., (3) Pennie Hawkes, 1994, 1 step-s., 1 step-d. *Musical*

Education: Music, choir at school. *Career:* Concerts supporting artists including: Genesis; Nazareth; Rory Gallagher; Mott The Hoople; 40 date tour with Leo Sayer; Gary Moore; Radio includes: Record of the Week, Radio 1, 1974; Album and single of the week, Capitol; Power Play Luxembourg, 1979; Television includes: Sky; BBC; All ITV regions; Australian documentaries. *Recordings:* Who Am I?, 1971; I Can't Help To Feel The Love, 1974; Don't Say Goodbye, 1975; Who Do You Love, 1978; By Yourside, 1979; No Money, 1979; Exposure album, 1979; Who Will Be The Winner, (single in Japan), 1982; Single: Can't Cry For You, 1990; Album: 47 Summers. *Honour:* The Harp Beat Rock Plaque. *Memberships:* PRS; Musicians' Union. *Leisure interests:* Keeping scrap books; Painting; Swimming. *Address:* High Wycombe, Buckinghamshire, England.

PAYTON Nicholas Edward; b. 14 Feb. 1972, Birmingham, England. Jazz Musician (saxophone, clarinet). *Musical Education:* Graduated from Leeds College of Music; Studied with Bob Huber. *Career:* Lead alto saxophone with the Charleston Chasers; Major concerts at the Southbank Centre, London (International Jazz Orchestra), and The Colston Hall, Bristol; Major jazz festivals in England and Europe include: Edinburgh Festival; The Cork Jazz Festival, Ireland; Also toured USA; Numerous appearances on television and radio; Performed with Bob Huber, Kenny Davern, Spike Robinson, Martyn Grost, Muriel Shane; Co-runs the band Swing Syndicate. *Recordings include:* Crazy Rhythm, 1988; I'll See You In My Dreams, 1992; Those Charleston Days, 1994; Henderson Stomp, 1994; Pleasure Mad, 1994. *Membership:* Musicians' Union. *Leisure interests:* Cooking; Study of The Works of Duke Ellington. *Address:* Halfway House, Grafton Mews, Chipping Campden, Gloucestershire GL55 6BW, England.

PAZ Ania; b. 18 June 1966, Lima, Peru. Musician (Piano); Composer. *Education:* Bachelor of Music, University of Detmold, Germany; Master of Music, University of the Arts, Philadelphia, USA. *Career:* Performances at festivals including International Jazz Festival, Lima, 1996, Jazz Astwood Festivals, 1995, 1997, 1998, San Jose Jazz Festival, 1998; Numerous television appearances. *Compositions:* San Pedro de Macorrs; Classic Night; San Francisco. *Recording:* Meta Arará. *Honours:* ASCAP Special award; Hon. Mention, USA Songwriting Contest, 1998; Plaque of Recognition, University of Missouri ALARA Conference. *Membership:* ASCAP. *Address:* c/o Blue Cat Agency, PO Box 399, Novato, CA 94948, USA.

PEACOCK Olly; b. 1974, England. Musician (Guitar, Percussion, Piano). *Career:* Member, Gomez; Numerous live dates and television appearances. *Recordings:* Singles: 78 Stone Wobble, 1998; Whippin' Piccadilly, 1998; Get Myself Arrested, 1998; Bring It On, 1999; Rhythm and Blues, 1999; Albums: Bring It On, 1999; Liquid Skin, 1999.

PEARCE Dave; b. 14 June. DJ. *Career:* Began as DJ on pirate radio, and in clubs; DJ, Radio Jackie, South London; Worked behind the scenes, BBC Radio London, late night show; Created BBC's first hip hop show; Helped create BBC's first dance show, Behind the Beat; Presenter, BBC GLR nightly dance show; A & R Director, Polydor Records; Established own label, Reachin Records; Joined Kiss FM at its establishment; Presented drivetime show with Gordon Mac, then presented The Dangerous Breakfast; Presenter, weekly music video guide on ITV networked Video View; Joined Radio 1, 1995, hosting Early Breakfast Show; Weekend Breakfast Presenter, 1997-. *Recordings:* Compiler, Dance Anthems Vols 1 and 2.

PEARSON John; b. 5 Oct. 1948, Liverpool, England. Musician (6 and 12 string guitar); Singer. *Career:* Television appearances: The Happening, 1991; National radio broadcasts: Paul Jones Blues Show, sessions, 1989, 1992; Major concerts include: Sonny Terry and Brownie McGhee; Alexis Korner; Louisianna Red; Davey Graham; Woody Mann; Jo Anne Kelly; Cephas and Wiggins. *Recordings:* Solo albums: Drive My Blues Away, 1989; Streamline Train, 1990; Busy Bootin', 1992 (with Roger Hubbard); Grasshoppers In My Pillow, 1995; John Pearson's Blue and Beyond Rhythm Oil, 2000. *Honours:* British Blues Connection Readers Poll, Best Blues Album Nomination, Busy Bootin', 1993. *Current Management:* Last Days Recording. *Address:* PO Box 128, Dover, Kent CT16 2SX, England.

PEART Neil; b. 12 Sept. 1952, Hamilton, Ontario, Canada. Musician (drums). *Career:* Member, Canadian rock group Rush, 1974–; Sell-out tours, US; Canada; UK; Europe. *Recordings:* Albums: Fly By Night, 1975; Caress of Steel, 1975; 2112, 1976; All The World's A Stage, 1976; A Farewell To Kings, 1977; Archives, 1978; Hemispheres, 1978; Permanent Waves, 1980; Moving Pictures, 1981; Exit... Stage Left, 1981; Great White North, 1982; Signals, 1982; Grace Under Pressure, 1984; Power Windows, 1985; Hold Your Fire, 1987; A Show of Hands, 1988; Presto, 1989; Chronicles, 1990; Roll The Bones, 1991; Counterparts, 1993; Solo: Burning For Buddy, 1995; Test for Echo, 1996; Retrospective Vol. II, 1997; with Jeff Berlin, Crossroads, 1998; Singles include: Spirit of Radio; Tom Sawyer; Closer To The Heart; New World Man; The Big Money; Countdown; Time Stand Still. *Honours:* Platinum discs; Juno Awards: Most Promising Group, 1975; Best Group, 1978, 1979; Group named Official Ambassadors of Music, Canadian

Government, 1979; Gold Ticket, Madison Square Garden, New York, 1991. *Current Management:* Anthem Entertainment, 189 Carlton St, Toronto, ON M5A 2K7, Canada.

PEDERSEN Karl-Erik; b. 17 Nov. 1960, Hobro, Jutland, Denmark. Singer; Songwriter; Musician (guitar, bass); Music Teacher. m. Anne Iben Hansen. *Education:* University. *Career:* Member, band Yellow Moon; Played concerts in: Denmark; Sweden; Finland; Iceland; Live concerts, national radio; Touring festivals, with Tears For Jeanie, 1998; Touring as a solo artist, 1998. *Compositions:* Songwriter for: Nikolaj and Piloterne, 1989; Björn Afzelius (Sweden), 1994; Kim C (Denmark), 1994; Music for films, documentaries with director Ole Henning Hansen; Albums: Tears For Jeanie, 1997; Fishjoint, 1997. *Recordings:* Album with Yellow Moon; Det Kinesiske Hav, 1989; Nitton År, 1994; Out There, 1997; You Gotta Believe It, 1997; Days, 1997; Crawling To You, 1998. *Memberships:* KODA; Danish Jazz Beat and Folk Authors; Danish Musicians' Union. *Leisure interest:* Football. *Current Management:* Warner/Chappell, Anker Heegårdsgade, 2 st.tv 1572 V, Denmark. *Address:* Terp Skovvej 46, 8260 Viby J, Denmark.

PEDERSEN Leonardo; b. Copenhagen, Denmark. Musician (saxophone, clarinet, flute); Songwriter. m. Annelise Pedersen, 15 Dec. 1972, 1 s., 1 d. *Musical Education:* Self-taught. *Career:* Formed first jazz band in 1958, becoming Leonardo Pedersen's Jazzkapel; Tours of Germany, Scandinavia, Eastern Europe, England, Italy, Scotland; Performed with numerous leading jazz artists including: Albert Nicolas, Ben Webster, Benny Waters, Al Grey, Bennie Bailey, Harry 'Sweets' Edison and Eddie 'Lockjaw' Davis; Appearances on national and international television and radio; Also played with: Barbarossa, 1978–88; Van Dango, 1986–89; The Original Danish Polcalypso Orchestra. *Recordings:* with Leonardo Pedersen's Jazzkapel: Danish Traditional Jazz, 1963; Leonardo Pedersen's Jazzkapel with Harry 'Sweets' Eddison, Eddie 'Lockjaw' Davis and Richard Boone, 1977; I Want A Roof, 1994; with Polcalypso: Karlekammeret, 1989; Polcalypso II, 1991; with Hans Knudsen Jumpband: So Long John, 1994; Jump In Focus, 1997; The Original Danish Polcalypso Orchestra featuring James 'Jamesie' Brewster, Live, 1996. *Current Management:* EPC Management, Ornevej 12, 2 th, 2400 Copenhagen NV, Denmark.

PEEL John, (John Robert Parker Ravenscroft); b. 30 Aug. 1939, Heswall, Cheshire, England. Radio Presenter; DJ. m. Sheila, 4 c. *Career:* Radio broadcaster, Texas, Oklahoma and California, 1960s; Broadcaster, own show Perfumed Garden, on pirate radio station, Radio London; Broadcaster, BBC Radio One; Known for promoting new and experimental music; Columnist, Radio Times; Presenter, Home Truths, Radio 4. *Recordings:* Various Peel Sessions recordings taken from own Radio One show, including: Before The Fall; Winters of Discontent; The New Breed; Too Pure. *Honours:* Sony Award, Broadcaster of the Year, 1993; New Musical Express BRAT Award, 1994. *Address:* c/o BBC Radio One, Broadcasting House, London W1A 1AA, England.

PEGG David; b. 2 Nov. 1947, Birmingham, England. Musician (Bass Guitar, Guitar, Mandolin). m. Christine, 12 Dec. 1966, 1 s., 1 d. *Musical Education:* Six months piano lessons, then self-taught. *Career:* Member, various Birmingham bands playing R & B; Double Bass, Ian Campbell Folk Group; Member, Fairport Convention, 1969-, Jethro Tull, 1979–96; Sessions, 1970's, with many folk artists including Nick Drake, John Martyn, Sandy Denny, Ralph McTell; Co-organizer, Cropredy Festival with Christine Pegg; Runs Woodworm Studios. *Compositions:* Various with Fairport Convention. *Recordings:* All Fairport Convention recordings, 1969–; Recordings with Jethro Tull, 1979–96; Numerous session appearances; Recent recordings include: Philip Picket, Bones of All Men, 1998; Fairport Convention, Woodworm Years, 1998; Allan Taylor, Sometimes/Lady, 1998; Steve Ashley, Stroll On Revisited, 1999; Jethro Tull, The Best of Jethro Tull, 1999; Fallen Angels, Happy Ever After, 1999. *Honours:* Midland Beat Bassist of the Year, 1967; Grammy Award for Crest of a Knave, with Jethro Tull, 1988. *Memberships:* Musicians' Union; MCPS; PAMRA. *Leisure interests:* Sailing; Tennis; Skiing; Watersports. *Current Management:* Woodworm Records.

PELLEN Jacques; b. April 1957, Brest, France. Musician (guitar). *Education:* University. *Musical Education:* Classical. *Career:* European tours, 1980–95; Celtic Procession (guest Kenny Wheeler), 1991; Europe Jazz Festival, Le Mans, 1994; Festival Quimper (guest Didier Lockwood); Zénith Paris, with Dan Ar Bras, 1995. *Recordings:* Celtic Progression; Sorserez (with Riccardo Del Fra); Condaghès, trio with Jacques Pellen, Paolo Fresu and Erik Marchand, 1998. *Address:* Bertrand Dupond, Ton All, 3 rue des Milad, 56630 Langonned, France.

PELLOW Marti, (Mark McLoughlin); b. 23 March 1966, Clydebank, Scotland. Singer. *Career:* Lead singer, Wet Wet Wet, 1982–97; Performances include: Royal Albert Hall, Greenpeace charity concert, 1986; Prince's Trust Rock Gala, Royal Albert Hall, London, 1988–90; Nelson Mandela's 70th Birthday Tribute, Wembley, 1988; John Lennon Tribute Concert, Merseyside, 1990; Children In Need, BBC, 1991;

Edinburgh Castle, 1992; Nordoff-Robbins Music Therapy Centre benefit, Royal Albert Hall, London, 1992; Live At The Royal Albert Hall 1992, C4, 1993. *Recordings:* Albums: Popped In Souled Out, 1987; Sgt Pepper Knew My Father, 1988; The Memphis Sessions, 1988; Holding Back The River, 1989; High On The Happy Side, 1992; Wet Wet Wet Live At The Royal Albert Hall, 1993; End of Part One (Their Greatest Hits), 1993; Picture This, 1995; 10, 1997; Singles include: Wishing I Was Lucky, 1987; Sweet Little Mystery, 1987; Angel Eyes (Home and Away), 1988; Temptation, 1988; With A Little Help From My Friends (No. 1, UK), 1988; Sweet Surrender, 1989; Broke Away, 1989; Hold Back The River, 1990; Stay With Me Heartache, 1990; Make It Tonight, 1991; Goodnight Girl (No. 1, UK), 1992; More Than Love, 1992; Lip Sevice, 1992; Shed A Tear, 1993; Love Is All Around (No. 1, UK), 1994; Goodnight Girl, 1994; She's All On My Mind, 1995; Julia Said, 1995. *Honours:* BRIT Award, Best British Newcomer, 1988. *Current Management:* The Precious Organisation, 14–16 Spiers Wharf, Port Dundas, Glasgow, Scotland.

PEMELTON Bret; m. Diana Pemelton, 2 s. *Career:* Member, Christian pop group Dream of Eden; 2 major tours, USA; Television: CCM-TV, real videos (TBN); Explosion '95 (TBN); Numerous radio appearances. *Recordings:* 2 No. 1 singles: Wonderful Thing, 1993; Into The Here and Now, 1995. *Membership:* Gospel Music Asscn. *Current Management:* Brian A Mays, BMP Artists Management.

PENAVA Pista (Pishta) Gordan; b. 29 Oct. 1967, Zagreb, Croatia. Singer; Musician (guitar); Songwriter; Television Host; Radio DJ; Journalist. *Education:* Faculty of Political Science, Journalism. *Career:* Singer, guitar player, Hard Time; Tours: Croatia; Slovenia; France; Appearances on MTV's Headbangers Ball. *Recordings:* Single cassette, 1992; Albums: Kiss My Ass and Go To Hell, 1992; Kad Poludim..., 1996; Compilation: Bijeli Put (1 song), 1993; Compilation: Cro Fest '94, Pop rock hit, 1994. *Honours:* Best Hard Rock Band of Croatia, Hard Time, 1992; Best Video Clip, Hit and Run, 1993. *Membership:* HGU (Croatian Musician Union); Zamp. *Address:* Aleja Pomoraca 11, 41000 Zagreb, Croatia.

PENDER Mike, (Michael John Prendergast); b. 3 March 1942, Liverpool, England. Musician (guitar). *Career:* Member, lead guitarist, lead vocalist, The Searchers, early 1960s-85; Numerous tours and concerts; Left The Searchers to form Mike Pender's Searchers, 1985; Performing regularly all over UK, including Japan, South Africa and Australia; Active Fan Club providing quarterly magazine and merchandise. *Recordings:* UK No. 1 Hits: Sweets For My Sweet; Needles and Pins; Don't Throw Your Love Away; Other Hits include: When You Walk In The Room; Sugar and Spice; Farmer John; Some Day We're Gonna Love Again; Goodbye My Love; Love Potion No. 9; Numerous LPs and CDs including: Meet The Searchers, 1963; Sugar and Spice, 1963; It's The Searchers, 1964; Sounds Like Searchers, 1965; Take Me For What I'm Worth, 1965; Needles and Pins, 1974; The Searchers, 1979; Play For Today, 1981; 100 Minutes of The Searchers, 1982; The Searchers Hit Collection, 1987; The EP Collection, Vol. 1, 1989; 30th Anniversary Collection, 1992; The EP Collection, Vol. 2, 1992. *Current Management:* Tony Sherwood Ltd, 5 Castleton Ave, Carlton, Nottingham NG4 3NZ, England.

PENDERGRASS Teddy (Theodore); b. 26 March 1950, Philadelphia, Pennsylvania, USA. Singer; Musician (drums). m. Karen Still, 20 June 1987. *Career:* Member, Harold Melvin and The Blue Notes, 1969–76; Solo artiste, 1976–; Major appearances include: British tours, 1981, 1982; Live Aid, JFK Stadium, Philadelphia, 1985; Film debut, Soup For One, 1982. *Recordings:* Albums: with Harold Melvin: Harold Melvin and The Blue Notes, 1971; Black and Blue, 1975; Wake Up Everybody, 1976; All Their Greatest Hits, 1976; Solo: Teddy Pendergrass, 1977; Life Is A Song Worth Singing, 1978; Teddy, 1979; Teddy Live! (Coast To Coast), 1979; T P, 1980; It's Time For Love, 1981; This One's For You, 1982; Heaven Only Knows, 1983; Love Language, 1984; Workin' It Back, 1985; Greatest Hits, 1987; Joy, 1988; Teddy Pendergrass, 1989; Truly Blessed, 1991; Singles include: with Harold Melvin: I Miss You; If You Don't Know Me By Now; Solo: The Whole Town's Laughing At Me; Close The Door; Turn Off The Lights; Love TKO; Hold Me, duet with Whitney Houston; Love 4 2; Joy; Dream Girl, from film soundtrack Soup For One, 1982; Duet with Lisa Fisher, Glad To Be Alive, from film soundtrack: The Adventures of Ford Fairlane, 1990; Contributor, Rubáiyát (Elektra's 40th Anniversary compilation), 1990. *Honours:* Platinum and Gold discs; American Music Award, Favourite Male Soul/R & B Artist, 1979. *Current Management:* Dream Street Management, 1460 Fourth St, Suite 205, Santa Monica, CA 90401, USA.

PENDLEBURY Andrew Scott; b. 30 Nov. 1951, Melbourne, Australia. Musician (guitar). *Musical Education:* Self-taught Guitar. *Career:* Major Australian Band, The Sports; Recorded 8 albums; Toured England twice; First major tour, Graham Parker and The Rumour; Finished 3 nights at Hammersmith Odeon, London, England. *Compositions:* Who Listens to the Radio, 1979. *Recordings:* 8 sports albums including: Don't Throw Stones, 1979; 4 solo albums; with Peter Lawler, King Rooster, 1998. *Leisure interest:* Makin' a Livin'. *Current Management:* Mushroom Records, ABC

Music. *Address:* 34 Wellington St, Richmond 3121, Melbourne, Victoria, Australia.

PENISTON Cece; b. Dayton, Ohio, USA. Singer; Songwriter. *Education:* Phoenix College. *Musical Education:* Vocal lessons with Seth Riggs. *Career:* Crowned Miss Black Arizona as a student; Guest vocalist with rapper Overweight Pooch; Solo artiste, 1991–; International concerts, Philippines, Japan, USA, UK, Europe; Tours with: Joe Public; R Kelly; Levert. *Recordings:* Albums: Finally, 1992; Thought 'Ya Knew, 1994; I'm Movin' On, 1996; Singles: Finally; We Got A Love Thing; Inside That I Cried; Crazy Love; Keep On Walkin'; I'm In The Mood; Keep Givin' Me Your Love, 1995; Movin' On, 1996; Somebody Else's Guy, 1998; Nobody Else, 1998; He Loves Me 2, 1999; We Got a Love Thang, 1999; Guest vocalist, Female Preacher, Overweight Pooch. *Honours:* Gold discs, Finally, 1992. *Current Management:* Devour Management, 4840 Hollow Corner Rd #421, Culver City, CA 90230, USA.

PENN Thomas Howard; b. 21 Nov. 1954, Cleveland, Ohio, USA. Artist Man.; Concert Promoter. *Career:* Commenced under name Good Time Productions, 1974; Started out throwing keg parties; Dances and school promotions, progressed to national acts, 1974–; Acts include: Tower of Power; Ronnie Laws and Pressure; George Benson; Side Effect; Karma; Donald Byrd and the Black Byrds; Steel Breeze; Taxi; Curtis Salgado and the Stilletos; Pleasure; U-Krew; Seawind; Shock; Maya; Earth Wind and Fire; Vail Johnson; Alliance with T:T Promotions Inc, Portland, Oregon, 1978–; El Chicano; Tierra; Bruce Conte.

PENNEY John; b. 17 Sept. 1968, Birmingham, England. Vocalist; Lyricist. *Career:* Vocalist, Ned's Atomic Dustbin, 1987–; Various large festivals world-wide include: Reading, 1990, 1991, 1993; Glastonbury, 1992; Phoenix, 1994; Tours: UK (15); Scandinavia (1); Europe (3); USA (9); Australia (3); Japan (3); Television: Top of The Pops (3 times); The Word (2); The Beat (5); Big Breakfast; Radio sessions: John Peel; Mark Goodyear; Johnnie Walker. *Recordings:* God Fodder, 1991; Are You Normal?, 1992; 5.22, 1994; Brainbloodvolume, 1995; Long form videos: Nothing Is Cool, 1991; Lunatic Magnets, 1993; Singles: Saturday Night, 1993; Until You Find Out, 1993; Not Sleeping Around, 1993. *Publications:* Available For Panto, by Martin Roach, 1994. *Honours:* No. 1 US Modern Rock Single for Not Sleeping Around, 1993. *Membership:* Musicians' Union. *Leisure interest:* Football. *Current Management:* Tank Gilks. *Address:* Floor 4, Sony Music UK, 10 Great Marlborough St, London, England.

PEÓN Mercedes, (Mercedes Peón Mosteiro); b. 1967, La Coruña, Spain. Vocalist; Musician (gaita, percussion); Composer. *Career:* Collects tunes, researches, teaches, lectures around the world to help preserve Galician folk tradition; Runs Discotrompo record label promoting Galician folk and traditional music; Organized several festivals including Federation of European Cultural Associations traditional music festival and Galicia Terra Unica; Previously member of Arjú before releasing solo material; Collaborations: Carlos Nunes; Xosé Manuel Budino; Manu Chao; Composed theme for Galician TV soap opera Mareas Vivas. *Recordings:* Single: Mareas Vivas; Albums: Isué, 2000; features on: Naciones Celtas II (Celtic Nations). *Honours:* Cídade Vella festival in Santiago de Compostela, special Jury Award; Santiago de Compostela Folk Days, Best Performer of Voice and Bagpipes; Lorient's Festival Interceltique, Macallan Award for Galician Pipers. *Internet:* www.mercedespeon.com.

PERCIVAL John Graham; b. 7 March 1938, Northampton, England. Musician (clarinet, saxophone, musical saw). m. Jane Allsop, 25 Aug. 1960, 3 d. *Musical Education:* Self-taught. *Career:* Appeared on television programmes Opportunity Knocks and Rising Stars, BBC TV; Ran own jazzband, Horace M Smith, 1971–87; Member, Bob Kerr Whoopee Band; Television appearances in Germany, Netherlands, France, Switzerland, Belgium, Sweden, Denmark, Russia. *Recordings:* as Horace M Smith: Hold That Tiger; with Bob Kerr Whoopee Band: Molotov Cocktails; Happy Daze; Videos: Live At The Half Moon; From Russia With Laughs; Films with Bob Godfrey: French Revolution; Happy Birthday Switzerland. *Membership:* Musicians' Union. *Leisure interests:* Drawing; Painting; Magic; Old-time radio; Variety. *Address:* 20 Stoke Rd, Blisworth, Northamptonshire NN7 3BZ, England.

PERCIVAL Lynne; b. 24 Nov. 1954, Altrincham, Cheshire, England. Teacher; Singer; Musician (guitar, mandolin). *Education:* Masters Degree in Social Science. *Career:* Semi-professional singer, guitarist and mandolin player; Member, The Fluence Band, 1988–; Specialising in Irish traditional dance music and song, performing regularly in Northern England, local residencies and ceilidhs; Support to various artists including Dick Gaughan, Maria Tolly and Meliantu; Tours in Brittany, Berlin, Canada, Denmark, Hungary, Scotland and the Isle of Mull; Co-ordinator of Irish music promotions, Club Cheoil, Manchester. *Recordings:* Early singer and songwriter tapes; Goodwill (album of Polish tour), with Wild Bill Flatpick and The Bindle Stiffs, 1987; Children In Need Compilation, 1987; Guesting on various artists recordings, 1991–93. *Honour:* Voted second folk group in local poll, 1994. *Memberships:* PRS; Musicians' Union. *Leisure interests:*

Travel; Football; Music. *Address:* 20 Alderfield Rd, Manchester M21 9JX, England.

PERCL Ivica; b. 1 Jan. 1945, Zagreb, Croatia. Musician (guitar, harmonica). m. Mirjana, 8 Jan. 1972, 2 d. *Musical Education:* Music secondary school. *Career:* Bass guitarist with groups: Mladi tehnicari, 1962; Kristali, 1963–64; Roboti, 1964–66; First Croatian protest singer, 1966; Festival of Shansone, Zagreb, 1967–71; Concerts include: Bulgaria; Russia; Finland, 1968–71; Playing protest songs, recording for Croatian radio station, Croatian television; Concerts, Boom Festival, 1972–74; Solo, 1979; Concerts on Days of Croatian Music; Advances in theatre, television as musician. *Compositions:* Over 200 include: 1966; Postovani profesore; Godine ratne, godine mirne; Izemedu tebe i mene; Kad zatvoris vrata iza sebe. *Recordings:* 7 singles; Albums: Stari Pjer, 1967–75; 30 Godina Starog Pjera, CD, 1998. *Honours:* Diploma of Soci 69, Russia, 1969; Katom, 1970; Labin, 1970. *Memberships:* Croatian Asscn of Composers; Croatian Music Unit; Professional Asscn of Composers; Croatian Music Unit. *Leisure interest:* Painting. *Address:* Vinogradska 17, 10 000 Zagreb, Croatia.

PEREIRA Francis Martin Purcell; b. 1 May 1950, Singapore. Prod.; Arranger; Musician (Guitar). m. Ann Toh Swee Hua, 1 Jan. 1985. *Musical Education:* Royal School of Music; Singapore Armed Forces Band (Trombone); Gateway School of Audio Engineering; Self-taught Guitar. *Career:* Arranger, EMI, Singapore, 1975–83; Television Brunei; Played for Sultan of Brunei, 1985–87; Played for Cilla Black, local acts; First Asean Festival of Songs, 1986; Director, Shekinah Music Trading, 1992-. *Compositions:* Local acts; Film Compositions: Eye of the Tiger. *Recordings:* Guitar Indigo Series; Guitar Latino Series; Guitar Memories; Different Class Harmonica Series; Sax with Love; Dijazz Series; Contemporary Saxophone, Vols I and II; Todos Latino; Guitarra Series, Hymns, Asia. *Honours:* Dr of Administration and Management Service; Conferred and Awarded by Golden Gates University; Affiliated Mem., Ferrum University, Virginia, USA; Ethnic Best Song Composition, 1982. *Leisure interest:* Fishing. *Current Management:* Shekinah Music Trading. *Address:* Blk 30 #07–17 Kallang Pl., Singapore 339159.

PERES Vivian; b. France. Musician (drums). *Musical Education:* Self-taught. *Career:* Participated in first Francofolies de la Rochelle; Leader, own group Traction Ailleurs; Worked at Béziers Conservatoire with René Nan; Founder member, La Compagnie du Jazz; Member, quartet Golem; Salsa group with Juan Quintana; Accompanist with numerous singers; Member, Slax; Mezcal Jazz Unit, European tour, 1994; Jazz Festival, Lithuania, 1994; Also performs with groups: Swing; Planete Jazz. *Honour:* Agfa Song Contest Winner, with group Traction Ailleurs, 1986.

PEREZ Ivan; b. 11 Nov. 1964, Orange, France. Musician (guitar); Composer. *Education:* BPA Floriculture. *Musical Education:* Conservatoire de Music; Studied improvised music with bassist B Santacruz and saxophonist Andre Jaume. *Career:* Jazz Festivals: Avignon; Sorgues; Carpentras; Music for Florence Saul contemporary dance company; Member, duo with Frederic Duvivier; Trio with Colin McKellar and Tox Drohead; Trio with Simon Fayolle and Lionel Villard. *Address:* 80 rue Henri Durant, 84100 Orange, France.

PEREZ Michel; b. 2 Jan. 1946, St Priest, France. Musician (guitar). m. Patricia Van Ginneken, 31 Dec. 1977, 1 s., 2 d. *Musical Education:* Self-taught. *Career:* Concert first part of Miles Davis, Vienne Festival, 1984; Nice Jazz Festival, 1984; Casino de Paris, 1989; Film in concert, Lyon, 1986; Around Midnight (Bertrand Taverner) with Herbie Hancock, Tony Williams, Wayne Shorter; Concert, first part of Zawinul Syndicate, 1992. *Recordings:* 2 with Spheroe: Spheroe, 1976; Primadonna, 1979; Kaleidoscope, 1982; Virgile, 1986; Orange, 1991; Toujours, Ron Carter, 1992; Film: Around Midnight, 1986. *Publications:* 3 compositions to be published in: Le Livre Du Jazz En France. *Address:* 19 rue de la Hacquière Pavillon, No. 68, 91440 Bures Sur Yvette, France.

PERKINS John Sinclair; b. 3 Aug. 1945. Hindustani Recitalist on sitar. Divorced, 2 d. *Education:* Christ College, Finchley, London; Rycotewood College, Thame, Oxon; Leicester College of Art; Visva Bharati University, Bengal. *Musical Education:* Private Clarinet Lessons. *Career:* Television Appearances, BBC 1, BBC2, LWT, Childrens Channel, Munich and Devon Educational Television; Local Radio, BBC Cornwall, Devon, Milton Keynes, Leicester; Concert Appearances, London School of Contemporary Dance, Accompanist to Suriya Kumari; Tour of South Africa, Indian Academy of Durban; South West Arts Tour; Tour of West Midlands Schools and Hospitals; Huddersfield Contemporary Music Festival; Barbican, London with BBC Scottish Symphony Orchestra, 1998; Festivals, Glastonbury; Somerfield Folk. *Recordings:* Suns of Arqa. *Membership:* Musicians Union. *Address:* 3 Ashleigh Villas, Plymouth Rd, Totnes, Devon TQ9 5PG, England.

PERKINS Walter; b. Feb. 1932, Chicago, Illinois, USA. Musician (drums). m. Barbara J Henderson, 6 d. *Musical Education:* Cosmopolitan School of Music, Chicago. *Career:* Worked in Chicago, Illinois with musicians including Ahmad Jamal; Dinah Washington; Muddy Waters; Memphis Slim; Sara Vaughn; Leader, own group, recorded under name MJT+3; Moved to New York City; Played, toured extensively with Carmen McRae; Played with major artists including: Billie Holiday; Della Resse; Art Farmer; Ernie Wilkins; Roland Kirk; Sonny Rollins; J J Johnson; Sonny Stitt; Teddy Wilson; Billy Taylor; Charles Mingus; Illinois Jacquet; Jimmy Rowe; George Duviver; Errol Garner; Played for King and Queen of England, Palladium, London, England; Numerous teaching jobs include: Public schools, New York; State Hospital; Federal funded, high schools, New York Board of Education system; Currently playing and teaching for Music for Young Audiences; Shared in co-op group with Shaw, Perkins, Holgate, featuring Marilyn Johnson; Performances include: Americana Hotel chain, USA, Caribbean; 2 Club Med resorts (Guadaloupe, Bahamas). *Recordings:* 40 albums with artists including: Ahmad Jamal; MJT+3; J J Johnson; Sonny Stitt; Sonny Rollins; Lucky Thompson; Art Farmer; Carol Sloan; Carmen McRae; Freda Payne; Josh White; Sunra; Booker Ervin; Yusef Lateef; Ray Bryant; Jaki Byard; Leo Wright; Gigi Gryce; Michael O'Bryant; Richard Williams; Hylton Ruiz; Clark Terry; George Terry; George Shearing; Milt Hinton; Ben Webster; Lightning Hopkins; Latest recordings include: Legends of Acid Jazz, 1998; with Ahmad Jamal, Priceless Jazz, 1998; Ballads for Trumpet, 1998; Impulsively Ellington: A Tribute, 1999; Great Jazz Artists Play Composition, 1999. *Honours:* US Army, Special Service, Germany; One Hundred Black Businessmens' Award. *Leisure interest:* Basketball. *Address:* 115–21 167th St, Jamaica, NY 11434, USA.

PERKIÖMÄKI Jari; b. 13 April 1961, Finland. Musician (alto saxophone, reeds, flutes). *Musical Education:* MA, Jazz programme, Sibelius Academy, 1989. *Career:* Joined Pori Big Band, aged 15; Represented Finland, EBU Big Band, 1981; Conductor, Pori Big Band; Own quartet, appearances included: Tampere Jazz Happening; Pori Jazz Festival; Debrecen Festival, Hungary; Member, Mika Mylläri; As soloist, tours, Sweden and Norway, 1987; As part of Jazz in Joiku project, including Kaamosjazz, Kalottijazz festivals, 1989; Conductor big band, Norway, on Nordic exchange programme, 1990. *Compositions include:* Music for 2 plays by Ilpo Tuomarila. *Honours:* Pekka Pöyry Award, 1985; Musician of The Year, RYTMI magazine, 1985; Thalia Award, for music to play Exit, 1988. *Address:* Reiherintie 1 H 103, 00870 Helsinki, Finland.

PERKO Jukka; b. 18 Feb. 1968, Huittinen, Finland. Musician (alto and soprano saxophone). *Musical Education:* Saxophone from 1982; Sibelius Academy, 1988. *Career:* Played Pori Jazz Festival, 1985; Played in Dizzy Gillespie 70th Anniversary Big Band, 1987; Tour with Dizzy Gillespie, 1988; Regular member, UMO (New Music Orchestra), 1989; Formed Jukka Perko Quartet; Finnish Jazz Federation Tour, 1990; Played with Horace Tapscott, Ultra Music Meeting workshop, Pori, 1990; Member, Perko-Pyysalo Poppoo, with Severi Pyysalo. *Recording:* Albums: Portrait By Heart, Jukka Perko Quartet, 1990; Uuno Kailas, Perko-Pyysalo Poppoo, 1995. *Honour:* Yrjö Award, Finnish Jazz Federation, 1989. *Address:* Minna Canthinkatu 9 A 4, 00250 Helsinki, Finland.

PERONA-WRIGHT Hilary Mary; b. 22 Dec. 1947, Godalming, Surrey, England. Musician (guitar, early musical instruments); Vocalist. m. Nigel Perona-Wright, 2 July 1975, 1 s., 1 d. *Education:* Epsom College of Art and Design (qualified with LSIA). *Career:* Started singing, songwriting at art college; Founder member, Spinning Wheel Folk Group, 1972–82; Founder member, Dragonsfire, 1982; Currently singer, instrumentalist with Dragonsfire, with special responsibility for group's presentation, publicity, costume. *Recordings:* with Dragonsfire: A Royal Array, 1989; Crossing The Borders, 1992; A Present From The Past, 1994. *Membership:* Musicians' Union. *Leisure interest:* Book illustration. *Current Management:* Dragonsfire. *Address:* 9 Hillside Rd, Ashtead, Surrey KT21 1RZ, England.

PERONA-WRIGHT Nigel Guy; b. 31 Aug. 1953, Emsworth, Havant, Hampshire, England. Musician (flute, multi-instrument woodwind); Bass Singer; Arranger; Composer. m. Hilary Mary Perona-Wright, 2 July 1975, 1 s., 1 d. *Education:* Choirboy, Westminster Abbey, 1963–67; Whitgift School, Croydon, 1967–72. *Musical Education:* LRAM; LTCL; LLCM (TD); Royal Academy of Music, 1972–75; Flute with Gareth Morris; Recorder with Christopher Taylor; Singing, privately with Michael Langdon. *Career:* Bass in choir, Royal Hospital Chapel, Chelsea, 1972–90; Peripatetic flute teacher, East Sussex Council, 1972–80; Croydon Council, 1975–79; Conductor, Sutton Chamber choir, 1977–82; Appointed flute/recorder teacher at City of London Freemen's School, Ashtead (present position), 1979–; Also choirmaster, St George's Church, Ashtead; Member, Spinning Wheel folk group, 1970–82; Founder member, director, Dragonsfire, 1982-. *Recordings:* With Dragonsfire: A Royal Array; Crossing The Borders; A Present From The Past. *Memberships:* Royal Society of Musicians; Performing Rights Society. *Leisure interests:* Music; Collecting first day cover stamps and Ashtead pottery; Theatre. *Current Management:* Dragonsfire. *Address:* 9 Hillside Rd, Ashtead, Surrey KT21 1RZ, England.

PERREAU Guy Jocelyn; b. 4 June 1950, Mauritius. m. Michol René, 18 May 1974, 1 s., 1 d. *Career:* Appeared in film Paul Et Virginie, filmed in Mauritius in late 1960s; Mimed One Sega Song; Many TV and radio appearances in Mauritius, Reunion and also Seychelles; Newspaper appearances. *Compositions:* Released 2 singles, 1977; Released 7 cassettes, 1991; Released CD 16 songs. *Recordings:* Released second album, 16 songs; Released third album, 1997; Best of Jocelyn Perreau Vol. I, 1999. *Honour:* Award for Best Entertainer for Radio and TV, Mauritius Broadcasting Corporation, 1974; Hon. Consul for Mauritius, 1986–96. *Memberships:* SACEM, France; MASA, Mauritius. *Leisure interests:* Swimming; Jogging; Walking. *Address:* Anse Aux Pins, Mahé, Seychelles, Indian Ocean.

PERRIN Roland; b. 18 Jan. 1959, New York, New York, USA. Musician (Piano); Composer; Arranger; Teacher. *Education:* BA Hons, Music, University of York, England. *Career:* Played in professional jazz/blues bands from age 15; Plays wide variety of music, specialising often in Afro-Cuban, Brazilian and South African Music; Played Mandela 70th birthday concert with Jonas Gwangwa, Wembley Stadium; Tours, sessions; Own band, Evidence, 1987–94; new band, The Blue Planet Orchestra, 1999. *Compositions:* With Evidence: Later; Kinacho; Golden Road; Salsa Diferente; Sleeping City; With South African Friends: DP; With Beaujolais Band: The New World; El Monte; Sister Grace. *Recordings:* Evidence, See You Later; It's A Triple Earth, Westway; Mark Ramsden, Above the Clouds; The Beaujolais Band, Mind How You Go; Talk, Talk and More Talk; Aster Aneke, Kaby; Dudu Pukwana, Cosmics '90; Brotherhood of Breath, In Memorium; Tumbaito, Otros Tiempos; Introducing The Blue Planet Orchestra, 1999. *Publications:* 3 piano pieces for First Associated Board Jazz Piano Exams. *Address:* Basement Flat, 47A Waldram Park Rd, London SE23 2PW, England.

PERRO Juan (Santiago Auseron); b. 25 July 1954, Zaragoza, Spain. Songwriter; Singer. m. Catherine François, 17 Nov. 1979. *Education:* Advanced studies, Philosophy, Madrid, 1972–77, Paris, 1977–78. *Career:* Songwriter, singer, Radio Futura, 1980–92; Frequent travels to Cuba, seeking roots of Afro-hispanic sound, 1984–; Released historic compilation of traditions Semilla del Son, 1992; Began touring as Juan Perro, with flamenco, jazz, rock musicians, 1993–94; First Juan Perro album, Havana, 1994. *Recordings:* (as Santiago Auseron) with Radio Futura: La Ley del Desierto, La Ley del Mar, 1984; De Un Pais En Llamas, 1985; La Cancion de Juan Perro, 1987; Escueladecalor, 1989; Veneno En La Piel, 1990; Tierra Para Bailar, 1992; as Juan Perro: Raices Al Viento (including Spanish, Cuban, British musicians), 1995; Serrat Eres Unico (producer), 1996. *Publications:* Articles on music, art and philosophy, to newspapers and magazines. *Honours:* Radio Futura acclaimed as Best Spanish Rock Band of the 1980's (voted by radio stations, rock magazines). *Memberships:* Spanish Asscn of Interpreters and Authors; Mem., Independent Production Office, Animal Tour. *Current Management:* Animal Tour. *Address:* Corazón de Maria, No. 2, Ap 230, 28002 Madrid, Spain.

PERRONE Marc; b. 8 Oct. 1951, Villejuif (Paris), France. Musician (diatonic accordion). m. Marie Odile Chantran, 27 June 1995. *Musical Education:* Self-taught. *Career:* Montparnasse, 1994; Olympia, Paris, 1995; Carnaval de Venise; Numerous foreign tours include: Africa; USA; Canada; South America; Asia; Japan, 1995; Films: La Trace, 1984; Un Dimanche à La Campagne, 1985; Maine Océan, 1986; La Vie Et Rien d'Autre, 1989; L-627, 1992. *Recordings:* Gabriel Valse, 1974; Perlinpinpin, 1974; Rondeaux Et Autres Danses Gasconnes à Samatan, 1976; Accordéons Diatoniques, 1979; Country Dances (Les Lendemains Qui Dansent), 1980; La Forcelle, 1983; La Trace (film score), 1984; Un Dimanche à La Campagne (film score), 1985; Velverde, 1988; Paris Musette, 1990; Cinéma Mémoire, 1993; Paris Musette Living It (Vol. 2), 1993; Jacaranda, 1995. *Honours:* Prix de l'Academie Charles Cros for: La Forcelle. *Membership:* Administration Council of ADAMI. *Address:* 6 Ave Parmentier, 75011 Paris, France.

PERRY André; b. 12 Feb. 1937, Verdun, Québec, Canada. Record Co Exec.; Record Prod. Divorced, 2 c. *Career:* Founder, André Perry Productions, 1968–70; Son Québec, 1970–73; Founder, President, Groupe André Perry Inc, 1974–; André Perry Video, 1980–; Founder, on board of directors, Québec Assoc Record and Entertainment Industry; Independent Record Producers Association of Canada; Founder, Le Studio (recording studios); Music co-ordinator, Montréal Olympic Games, 1976; Record producer for: John Lennon; Charles Aznavour; Wilson Pickett; Numerous Canadian artistes. *Memberships:* Audio Engineering Society; Pro-Can; Composers, Authors and Publishers Asscn of Canada; Canadian Recording Industry Asscn; Societe d'Auteurs, Compositeurs et Editeurs de Musique.

PERRY Barney (Blair); b. 2 Nov. 1953, Buffalo, New York, USA. Composer; Musician (Guitar); Singer; Teacher; Minister. m. Ethlene Perry, 2 May 1982, 2 s., 2 d. *Education:* Education Administration, Buffalo State College; Business Management and Accounting, Howard University; Lay Pastor, Ministry, Canada Christian College; Music Composition and Performance education, Howard University and Washington DC; Advanced Instrumental Techniques, Classical Guitar,

University of Buffalo; Electronic Music, Catholic University; Jazz Guitar with George Benson; Classical Guitar with Bill Harris and Oswald Rentucci; Symphonic Music with Russell Wollen and William Penn. *Career:* Activist for intellectual property rights, state courts and federal courts, New York and California; TV, Blair, Invitation to Dance Show; Numerous radio shows; Concerts and performances as soloist, quartet; Band and show with Herbie Hancock, Lenny Williams; Co-founder, Blackbyrds; Backing Guitarist, Donald Byrd, Phyllis Hyman, Vivian Reed, Jack McDuff. *Compositions:* Walking in Rhythm; Nightlife; A Hot Day Today; Virgo Princess; Who is Blair. *Recordings:* Blair: Nightlife; Live at Lafayette Square; Flying Start; Hit the Open Man; Blackbyrds. *Honours:* Outstanding Citation of Achievement, BMI; Million Plus Performance Composer; Grammy Award Nominee, Best Composer; Pop Music Award, BMI. *Memberships:* BTF; UTLA; Musicians Local; NRA; Blessed Trinity Holy Name Society. *Leisure interests:* Camping; Movies; Concerts. *Current Management:* Enterprise Management, New York.

PERRY Joe; b. 10 Sept. 1950, Boston, Massachusetts, USA. Musician (guitar). *Career:* Lead guitarist, US rock band Aerosmith, 1970–79, 1984–; Leader, Joe Perry Project, 1980–83; Concerts include: Support to the Kinks, Mott The Hoople, 1974; Schaefer Music Festival, Central Park, 1975; Reading Rock Festival, 1977; California Jam II Festival, 1978; Texas World Music Festival, 1978; Appearance in film: Sgt Pepper's Lonely Hearts Club Band, as the Future Villain Band, 1978; California Music Festival, with Van Halen, Cheap Trick, Ted Nugent, 1979; World Series of Rock, with Journey, Ted Nugent, Thin Lizzy, 1979 Monsters of Rock Festival, Castle Donington, 1990. *Recordings:* Albums: Aerosmith: 1973; Toys In The Attic, 1975; Get Your Wings, 1975; Rocks, 1976; Draw The Lion, 1977; Greatest Hits, 1981; Done With Mirrors, 1985; Classic Live!, 1986; Permanent Vacation, 1987; Retrospective Gems, 1988; Pump, 1989; Pandora's Box, 1992; Get A Grip, 1993; Big Ones, 1994; Nine Lives; Little South of Sanity, 1998; with Joe Perry Project: Let The Music Do The Talking, 1980; I've Got The Rock 'n' Roll Again, 1981; Once A Rocker, Always A Rocker, 1983; The Best of the Joe Perry Project, 1999; Singles include: Dream On; Draw The Line; Dude (Looks Like A Lady); Love In An Elevator; Janie's Got A Gun; What It Takes; Livin' On The Edge; Eat The Rich; Cryin'; Amazing. *Honours include:* Grammy Award, 1991; American Music Awards, 1991. *Current Management:* Magus Entertainment, 584 Broadway, Suite 1009, New York, NY 10012, USA.

PERRY Lee 'Scratch', (Rainford Hugh Perry); b. 1936, Hanover, Jamaica. Recording Artist; Record Prod. *Career:* Also billed as Scratch and the Upsetter; Record scout, 1950s and 1960s; Producer and songwriter for Delroy Wilson, 1963; Debut recording, 1963–; Formed own label, Upsetter, 1968–. *Recordings:* Albums include: The Upsetter, 1969; Many Moods of The Upsetter, 1970; Scratch The Upsetter Again, 1970; Prisoner of Love – Dave Barker Meets The Upsetters, 1970; Africa's Blood, 1972; Battle Axe, 1972; Cloak and Dagger, 1972; Double Seven, 1973; Rhythm Shower, 1973; Blackboard Jungle, 1974; Kung Fu Meets The Dragon, 1974; DIP Presents The Upsetter, 1974; Revolution Dub, 1975; Scratch The Upper Ape, 1976; Jah Lion – Columbia Colly, 1976; Return of The Super Ape, 1977; Roast Fish, Collie Weed and Corn Bread, 1978; Scratch On The Wire, 1979; Scratch and Company – Chapter 1, 1980; Return of Pipecock Jackson, 1981; Heart of The Ark, Vol. 1, 1982; Vol. 2, 1983; Megaton Dub, 1983; Megaton Dub 2, 1983; History Mystery and Prophecy, 1984; Black Ark In Dub, 1985; Battle of Armagideon – Millionaire Liquidator, 1986; Time Boom X De Devil Dead, 1987; Satan Kicked The Bucket, 1988; Scratch Attack, 1988; Chicken Scratch, 1989; Build The Ark, 1990; Meets Bullwackie- Satan's Dub, 1990; Meets The Mad Professor, 1990; The Upsetter and The Beat, 1992; Soundz From The Hot Line, 1993; Black Art in Dub, 1993; Larks from the Ark, 1995; Experryments at the Grassroots of Dub, 1995; Voodooism, 1996; Technomajikal, 1997; Dub Fire, 1998; Lick Shot, 1999; Lost Treasures of the Ark, 2000; As producer includes: Hurt So Good, Susan Cadogan; Police and Thieves, Junior Marvin; Punky Reggae Party, Bob Marley and The Wailers; Also with Massive Attack; The Clash; The Heptones; Max Romeo; Junior Marvin; David Isaacs; The Untouchables; Junior Byles.

PERRY Steve; b. 22 Jan. 1953, Hanford, California, USA. Vocalist. *Career:* Member, Alien Project; Lead singer, Journey, 1977–87; Solo artiste, 1987–; Concerts include: Regular tours, US, Japan and Europe; World Series of Rock, Cleveland, 1979; Mountain Aire Festival, 1981. *Recordings:* Albums: with Journey: Journey, 1975; Look Into The Future, 1976; Next, 1977; Infinity, 1978; Evolution, 1979; In The Beginning, 1979; Departure, 1980; Dream After Dream, 1980; Captured, 1981; Escape (No. 1, USA), 1981; Frontiers (No. 2, US), 1983; Raised On Radio, 1986; Greatest Hits, 1988; Time 3, 1992; Solo albums: Street Talk, 1984; For the Love of Strange Medicine, 1994; Greatest Hits + Five Unreleased, 1998; with Laidlaw, The First Big Picnic, 1999; Hit singles: Lovin' Touchin' Squeezin', 1979; Don't Stop Believin', 1981; Who's Crying Now, 1981; Open Arms (No. 2, US), 1982; Separate Ways (World's Apart), 1983; Faithfully, 1983; Send Her My Love, 1983; Only The Young, 1985; Be Good To Yourself, 1986; Tracks for film soundtracks Tron; Vision Quest; Solo singles: Oh Sherrie, 1984; Foolish Heart, 1985; You Better Wait, 1994; Missing You, 1994; When

You're in Love (For the First Time), 1998; Duet with Kenny Loggins: Don't Fight It, 1982; Contributor, We Are The World, USA For Africa, 1985. *Honours:* Bay Area Music Awards, Best Vocalist, Best Group, 1987; Numerous Platinum and Gold discs. *Current Management:* Third Rail Entertainment. *Address:* 10202 Washington Blvd, Tri-Star Bldg 26, Culver City, CA 90203, USA.

PERSSON Nina; b. 1975, Malmo, Sweden. Singer. *Career:* Singer, The Cardigans; Concerts include: Support to Blur, British tour, 1995. *Recordings:* Albums: Emmerdale, 1994; Life, 1995; First Band on the Moon, 1996; Other Side of the Moon, 1998; Gran Tourismo, 1998; Singles: Sick and Tired, 1995; Carnival, 1995; Been It, 1997; My Favorite Game, 1998; Erase/Rewind Pt I and Pt II, 1999; Hanging Around, Pt I and II, 1999; Gran Turismo Overdrive, 2000. *Honours:* Swedish Grammy Nomination, Best Group, 1994; Slitz Magazine, Best Band, 1994. *Address:* Motor SE, Box 53045, 400 14 Gothenburg, Sweden.

PESCE Serge; b. 7 Sept. 1959, Nice, France. Musician (guitar); Composer. *Musical Education:* Self-taught. *Career:* Performed with: Alan Vitous, Barre Phillips, Miquel Montanaro, Yves Rousguisto, Patrick Vaillant, Alex Grillo, Jean-Louis Ruf; Festival appearances at: Nantes, Toulon, Confolens, Uzeste, Avignon, Parthenay, St Chartier Miskols, Szeged, Hungary. *Composition:* L'odore del caffe, guitar solo. *Recordings:* Guitare Attitude; Couples; Le Gaboulet, Tambourin – Ocora Radio France; Ballade Pour Une Mer Qui Chante, Vols 2 and 3; L'odore Del Caffè; Jazzd'aià; Tenson, with Alan Vitous and Miqueu Montanaro; Silence de faune, with Yves Rousguisto; Amb la doçor, Aguillera, Zagaria. *Publications:* Yes Bomb'ai. *Memberships:* SACEM; SPEDIDAM; SACD; SFA. *Address:* Serge Pesce, Palais Théodore, 27 rue Théodore de Banville, 06100 Nice, France.

PETEJ Peco Petar; b. 18 March 1949, Split, Croatia. Musician (drums, piano). m. Nada Vicic, 12 July 1973, 2 s. *Education:* College degree. *Musical Education:* Academy for Jazz Music and Theatre Arts, Graz, Austria. *Career:* Delfini, Split, 1972; Played with leading jazz musicians with Hans Koller Free Sound; Member, rock band Time, 1973–79; Moved to Britain, 1974; Played with Jackie McAuley Throat, 1975; The Foundations vocalist Collin Young; Zagreb Jazz scene, TV Big Band, 1979; Returned to London blues scene, 1990; Back to Croatia, war humanitarian work, 1991; Indexi Sarajevo, 1994. *Recordings:* 2100 recorded minutes for TV Big Band; Recorded over 150 albums with various artists; Original music, theatre play, Hamlet and Tarzan. *Honours:* Numerous Pop and Rock Festival Awards, jazz fairs, Zagreb, Slovenia, Germany; Original Music Theatre Award, 1994. *Memberships:* Musicians' Union (UK); Croatian Music Union; Croatian Asscn of Orchestral Musicians. *Leisure interests:* Cycling; Sailing. *Current Management:* Vladimir Mihaljek, Croatian Music Art.

PETERS Mike; b. 25 Feb. 1963, St Asaph, Wales. Musician (guitar); Vocalist. *Musical Education:* School Bands, Stripey. *Career:* Lead singer, The Alarm; 6 critically acclaimed world-wide albums; 14 Top 50 singles; Concerts include: Spirit of '86 (audience of 26,000), University of California, Los Angeles, world-wide broadcast on MTV. *Recordings:* Where Were You Hiding When The Storm Broke?; 68 Guns; A New South Wales; Rain In The Summertime. *Publications:* The Words and Music of The Alarm. *Memberships:* Musicians' Union; PRS. *Leisure interests:* Music; Manchester United Football Club. *Current Management:* Track Artist Management, UK/USA. *Address:* 7B Holland Rd, London W14 8HJ, England.

PETERS Rob; b. 4 Oct. 1954, Birmingham, England. Musician, (Guitar, Drums, Percussion); Songwriter; Performer; Prod. *Education:* University of Exeter; Open University. *Career:* Songwriter, 1973–; Formed Dangerous Girls, 1978; Drummer with Here and Now, 1982–83; Drummer, Everything But The Girl, 1985–87; Session Drummer with Ruby Blue, 1987; Tour Manager, 1988–90; Percussionist with Boo Hewerdine, 1991–; Guitarist, 1996-. *Compositions:* Step Out; Man In The Glass; Dangerous Girls; Long Ride Home; Georgie's Back in Town. *Recordings:* Include, Fantasy Shift; Baby The Stars Shine Bright; Ignorance; Zinc. *Memberships:* Musicians' Union; PRS; MCPS; PPL. *Leisure interests:* Music; Cinema; Reading; Cricket; Motor Racing. *Address:* PO Box 81, Birmingham B30 2LF, England.

PETERSEN Erik; b. 25 Jan. 1953, Uppsala, Sweden. Musician; Composer; Actor. 2 s., 1 d. *Education:* Sämus Malmö, Musikhögskolan, Stockholm. *Career:* Skottes Musikteater, Gävle, 1983–86; Den goda människan i Sezvan, Gävle, Drottningens Juvelsmycke, Dramaten, Den Perfekta Kyssen, Angered, Det Susar i Säven, Stockholm, Oliver Twist, Turteatern, Kärlekens himmelska helvete, Film. *Compositions:* Skrotsymfoni, 1999. *Recordings:* Den passionerade hästen, 1986; Propeller, 1997. *Membership:* SKAP. *Address:* Byfogdevägen 10, 141 39 Huddinge, Sweden.

PETERSON Gilles; b. 28 Sept. 1964, Switzerland. DJ. *Career:* Began DJ career aged 18, Jazz Rooms, Electric Ballroom, Camden, London; Regularly ran Sunday afternoon session at Dingwalls, Camden; Worked on Acid Jazz label, Talkin Loud label; DJ's at Bar Rumba and Atmapuri, Eve Club; Presenter, Radio 1.

PETERSON Oscar Emmanuel; b. 15 Aug. 1925, Montréal, Québec, Canada. Jazz Musician (piano). 3 s., 4 d. *Musical Education:* Studied with Paul de Markey. *Career:* Weekly radio show; Johnny Holmes Orchestra, Canada, 1944–49; Appeared with Jazz at the Philarmonic, Carnegie Hall, 1949; World-wide tours 1950–; Leader of own trio, with Ray Brown, Irving Ashby, 1947–; Later with Barney Kessel, Herb Ellis, Ed Thigpen, Sam Jones, Louie Hayes; Concert appearances with Ella Fitzgerald, UK, 1955; Stratford (Ontario) Shakespeare Festival; Newport Jazz Festival. *Compositions:* Canadiana Suite; Hymn To Freedom; Fields of Endless Day; City Lights (with Norman McLaren); Begone Dull Care; Salute to Johann Sebastian Bach; Music for films: Big North; Silent Partner. *Recordings:* with Billie Holiday; Fred Astaire; Benny Carter; Count Basie; Roy Eldridge; Lester Young; Ella Fitzgerald; Joe Pass; Niels Henning; Orsted Peterson; Dizzy Gillespie; Harry Edison; Clark Terry; Recent releases include: Oscar and Benny, 1998; Summer Night in Munich, 1999; Paris Jazz Concert, 1999; Live at the Blue Note, 1999. *Publications:* Jazz Exercises and Pieces; Oscar Peterson New Piano Solos. *Honours:* Numerous, including 11 Hon. degrees, 1973–94; Edison Award, 1962; Officer, Order of Canada, 1972; Award of Merit, City of Toronto (twice); Companion, Order of Canada, 1984; American Jazz Hall of Fame, 1989; 7 Grammy Awards; 11 Grammy Nominations; Hall of Fame Awards: JUNO, 1982, Contemporary Keyboard, 1983, University of California, Berkeley, 1983; Best Jazz Pianist Award winner: Keyboard (5 times), Playboy (12 times), Downbeat (13 times), Contemporary Keyboard (5 times); Carnegie Hall Anniversary Medal; Charlie Parker Bronze Medal; Ville de Salon de Provence Medal. *Leisure interests:* Fly-fishing; Astronomy; Photography. *Address:* Regal Recordings, 2421 Hammond Rd, Mississauga, ON L5K 1T3, Canada.

PETIT Philippe; b. 23 Nov. 1954, Marmande, France. Jazz Musician (guitar); Composer. *Musical Education:* Bordeaux Conservatory of Music. *Career:* Tours with Philip Catherine; Tal Farlow; Barney Wilen; Miroslav Vitous; Eliot Zigmund; With own group including: Michel Graillier; Alain Jean Marie; Riccardo Del Fra; Al Levitt; Aldo Romano; J F Jenny-Clark. *Compositions:* Sigmanialogie 21, for jazz quartet and symphony orchestra, 1985. *Recordings:* Parfums, 1977; For All The Life, 1979; La Note Bleue, with Barney Wilen, 1986; Impressions of Paris, with Miroslav Vitous, 1989; Solo: Guitar Reflections, 1991; Standards Recital, with Tal Farlow, 1993; Guitar Attitude, 1996. *Membership:* SACEM. *Leisure interest:* Poetry. *Address:* 16 rue Jacquemont, 75017 Paris, France.

PETROV Petar; Musician (bass). *Career:* Member, Concurent, 1986–; numerous concerts, TV, radio appearances, Bulgaria. *Recordings:* Rock For Peace, 1988; Rock Festival In Mitcurin, 1989; The Black Sheep (rock collection), 1992; Something Wet (best-selling album, Bulgaria), 1994; The Best of Bulgarian Rock, 1995. *Honours:* First Prizes: Top Rock Band, Vidin, 1989; Rock Ring, Sofia, 1990; Top Rock Composition: The Cavalry, 1991; Group of The Year, The Darik Radio Countdown, 1994. *Address:* 40 St Stambolov Blvd, 1202 Sofia, Bulgaria.

PETROV Vadim; b. 24 May 1932, Prague, Czech Republic. Composer; Prof. of Composition. m. Marta Votápková, 26 June 1954, 1 s., 2 d. *Education:* Graduate, Department of Composition, Academy of Fine Arts, Prague, Czech Republic, 1956. *Career:* The Giant Mountains Fairy Tales; There Are Some Limits; The Romance of Water Spirit; The Good Old Band; Sonets Chi Seled in Stone; Pax Rerum Optima; The Swans' Lament; The Nightingale and Rose; The Twelve; Johan Doctor Faust Nocturno in G; Burlesque; The Valessian Intermezzo; Song of the Night; The Ditty. *Compositions:* Melancholical Waltz; Tango Habanero; Scherzo Poetico; Riva Dei Pini; Romans; The Silver Serenade; Russian Evangelium; Song for Jane Eyre; The Autumn Memory; Night Tango; Song of Hoping and Belief. *Recordings:* The Maple Violin; Lucy and Miracles; Anna Snegina; Don Quigxot; Don Jean and others. *Publications:* Czech and Slovak Composer, 1980; Film and Time, 1983; The Little Czechoslovak Encyclopedia, 1986. *Honours:* Award of The Asscn of Czechoslovak Composers; Czech Television, 1997; Svobodné Slovo, Prague, 1997. *Leisure interest:* Tourism. *Address:* Karasovská 833/6, 160 00 Prague 6, Czech Republic.

PETROV Vassil; b. 1964, Sofia, Bulgaria. Musician; Singer. *Musical Education:* Graduate, Academy of Popular Music, Sofia, 1990. *Career:* Best-selling Bulgarian pop and jazz star; Numerous jazz, popular music festivals; Best-selling recording artist, Bulgaria; Performances: Helsinki; Oslo; Stockholm; Belgrade; Winter Olympics, Lillehammer, Norway; Currently working with Villi Kazassyan's Big Band; Acoustic Version (Bulgaria's leading jazz group); Successful concerts with Pleven's Philharmonic Orchestra; Working on albums with composer Vassil Parmakov, lyricist Terry Kaliski; Plays and sings own compositions. *Recordings:* Only Bulgarian performer to release 3 albums in 1 year: The Other One; Castrol Presents: Vassil Petrov; Duet album with pianist

Rumen Toskov; Petrov Sings Parmakoff, 1994. *Honours:* Number One Male Voice, Bulgaria, First Bulgarian National Music Awards; Orpheus: Best Male Vocalist; Best Hit of the Year; Best Album of the Year: The Other One.

PETROVIC Bosko; b. 18 Feb. 1935, Bjelovar, Croatia. Musician (vibraphone); Composer; Record Prod.; Author. Divorced, 1 s. *Musical Education:* Self-taught. *Career:* Zagreb Jazz Quartet, BP Convention; BP Club All Stars; Over 30 radio and television serials on jazz as author and MC; Over 80 albums as musician or producer; All major jazz festivals. *Compositions:* With Pain I Was Born, 1960; Keka Kolo, 1962; Green Mood, 1962; Sigurd's Garden, 1970; Green Lobster Dream, 1972; Valse for Jazz Mama, 1988; Fin de Siècle, 1998. *Recordings:* With Pain I Was Born, 1965; Swinging East, 1971; Mistery of Blues, 1974; Stabilisation Blues, with Clark Terry, 1982; Tiffany Girl, 1985; From Moscow To LA, 1986; What's New, with Joe Pass, 1989; Meet Us At The Bar, 1991; Bosko Petrovic Meets James Newton, 1993; Green Mood, 1995; Jazz Gala, with John Lewis, 1996; The Very Beginning, with Jerome Richardson, 1998. *Honours:* Annual Award For Music, J Slavenski, 1980; Town of Zagreb Award, 1989; Croatian Grammy Award Pórin, 1995; Government decoration, Danica of Croatia, 1996. *Membership:* Composers Asscn of Croatia. *Leisure interests:* Good company; Good books; Lovely wines. *Current Management:* Jazzette Records.

PETRUCIANNI Louis; b. France. Musician (contrabass). *Musical Education:* Studies with Chuck Israël, US, 1980. *Career:* Played with Barre Phillips, 1975–80; European tour with brother Michel Petrucianni; Also played with Lenny White; Trio with brother Michel; Quartet with brother Philippe. *Recordings:* Solo albums: Loi's Blues; The Librarian; MisterLight; with Tony Petrucianni: Nuages; with Orchestre de Jazz du Languedoc-Rousillon: Dialogues; Recordings with numerous artists including: Bernard Lubat; Lee Konitz; Alain Jean-Marie; Philippe Petit.

PETTAN Svanibor Hubert; b. 11 Feb. 1960, Zagreb, Croatia. Ethnomusicologist. m. Albinca Pesek, 20 Nov. 1992. *Education:* BA, University of Zagreb, 1983; MA, University of Ljubljana, 1988; PhD, University of Maryland, USA, 1992. *Career:* Music Editor, Radio Zagreb, 1984–88; Research Scholar, Institute of Ethnology and Folklore Research, Zagreb, 1988–98; Adjunct Staff, Universities of Zagreb, 1993-, and Maribor, 1995–; Assistant Professor, University of Ljubljana, 1995–; Visiting Scholar, Norway, 1994, 1996, and USA, 1998; Frequent guest lectures and conference participations. *Recordings:* Folk Songs and Dances of Banija, selection and sleeve notes, Croatia, Vols 2 and 3, 1988; Croatia: Traditional Music of Today selection and sleeve notes, 1998; Folk Revival in Slovenia, sleeve notes, 1998. *Publications:* Lambada in Kosovo: A Profile of Gypsy Creativity, 1992; Selling Music: Rom Musicians and the Music Market in Kosovo, 1996; Making the Refugee Experience Different: Azra and the Bosnians in Norway, 1996; Music, Politics and War: Views from Croatia, editor, 1998. *Memberships:* IASPM; Liaison Officer for Slovenia, ICTM; SEM; ISME; Slovenian Musicological Society; Croatian Musicological Society. *Leisure interest:* Playing musical instruments. *Address:* University of Ljubljana, Music Academy, Stari Trg 34, 1000 Ljubljana, Slovenia.

PETTERS John David; b. 13 April 1953, Stratford, London, England. Traditional and Swing Jazz Musician (drums); Bandleader. m. Teresa Mellerick, 26 April 1980, 2 s. *Musical Education:* Self-taught. *Career:* Formed New Dixie Syncopators, 1976; Worked with John Gill and Ronn Weatherburn, 1977; Joined Ken Sims Dixie Kings, 1979; Formed John Petters Swing Band, 1982; Opened Jazz Club, The Square, Harlow, Essex; American soloists include: Wild Bill Davison; Art Hodes; Kenny Davern; George Masso; Yank Lawson; Slim Gaillard; Al Casey; Billy Butterfield; British stars include: Georgie Fame; Ken Colyer; Monty Sunshine; Humphrey Lyttelton; Cy Laurie; Maxine Daniels; George Chisholm; Stage shows and concerts include: Queens of The Blues, 1986; Roarin' 20's Show, 1987; Concerts with Lonnie Donegan; George Chisholm; Yank Lawson; Legends of American Dixieland, 1988; Swinging Down Memory Lane, 1989; Legends of British Trad, 1991; This Joint Is Jumpin', 1993; Special Magic of Benny Goodman, 1994; Boogie Woogie and All That Jazz, 1994; Ran Honky Tonk Train, Severn Valley Railway, 1995; Formed National Traditional Mailing List; Director, Mundesley Jazz Weekend Festival, 1995; Drum Crazy show and workshops, 1996; Director, This Joint Is Jumping, Blackpool, 1996; Director, first Prestatyn Jazz 'n' Swing Forum, 1997; This Is Jazz, festival, Torquay, 1997; Now You Has Jazz Jazz Jazz, Pontins; Toured UK theatres with S'Wonderful, Gershwin centenary show, 1998; Toured with Hoagy – Old Music Master, Hoagy Carmichael centenary show, 1999. *Recordings include:* Live and Swinging, with Kenny Dalvern, 1985; Mixed Salad, with Wally Fawkes, 1986; Together Again, with Art Hodes and Wild Bill Davison, 1988; Swinging Down Memory Lane, with George Chisholm OBE and Maxine Daniels, 1989; Rags Boogie and Swing, with Simon Holliday, 1989; The Legends of British Trad, 1991; Blowin' A Storm, 1991; This Joint Is Jumping, 1992; Walking With The King, 1994; Boogie Woogie and All That Jazz, with Duncan Swift, 1995; Makin' Whoopee, with John Petters Dixielanders; Swing Band, with Yank

Lawson and Kenny Davern, 1996; Bechet Centenary Band, Blame It On The Blues, with Trevor Whiting, John Wurr, Martin Litson, Dave Green, 1997; It's Me, O Lord, 1998; Shades of Jazz, with John Cherry; It's Alright With Me, with Nick Dawson; S'Wonderful, John Petters Broadway Melodists, 1998; Hoagy – The Old Music Master, John Petters and His Music Masters, 1999; Goin' Bananas, John Petters Jazz 'n' Swing Band. *Publications:* History of Jazz Drumming, Jazz Journal, 1985. *Leisure interest:* Amateur radio. *Current Management:* John Petters Entertainments. *Address:* PO Box 42, Wisbech, Cambridgeshire PE13 5RJ, England.

PETTY Tom; b. 20 Oct. 1953, Gainesville, Florida, USA. Singer; Musician (guitar); Songwriter. *Career:* Guitarist, with local groups Sundowners; Epics; Mudcrutch, 1971–; Founder, Tom Petty and The Heartbreakers, 1975–; Member, The Traveling Wilburys, with Bob Dylan, George Harrison, Roy Orbison, Jeff Lynne, 1988–; Film appearance: FM, 1978; Regular US and international tours; Concerts include: Knebworth Festival, 1978; Musicians United For Safe Energy (MUSE), Madison Square Garden, 1979; Peace Sunday (Anti-nuclear concert), Pasadena, 1982; US Festival, San Bernardino, 1982; Live Aid, Philadelphia, 1985; Farm Aid, 1985; Tours, Australia, New Zealand, Japan, supporting Bob Dylan, 1986; Amnesty International Concert, 1986; True Confesions Tour with Bob Dylan, 1986; Rock 'n' Roll Caravan tour, with Georgia Satellites, 1987; Bob Dylan 30th Anniversary Tribute, 1992. *Compositions include:* Never Be You, Roseanna Cash (No. 1, USA Country chart), 1986. *Recordings:* Albums: with the Heartbreakers: Tom Petty and The Heartbreakers, 1976; You Gonna Get It!, 1978; Damn The Torpedoes, 1979; Hard Promises, 1981; Long After Dark, 1982; Southern Accents, 1985; Pack Up The Plantation, 1986; Let Me Up (I've Had Enough), 1987; Full Moon Fever, 1989; Into The Great Wide Open, 1991; Greatest Hits, 1993; Take The Highway, 1994; She's the One (film soundtrack), 1996; Echo, 1999; with The Traveling Wilburys: Traveling Wilburys, 1988; Vol. 2, 1989; Vol. 3, 1990; Solo: Wildflowers, 1994; Hit singles include: Breakdown, 1978; Don't Do Me Like That, 1980; Refugee, 1980; Insider, 1981; You Got Lucky, 1983; Change of Heart, 1983; Don't Come Around Here No More, 1985; Jammin' Me, 1987; I Won't Back Down, 1989; Runnin' Down A Dream, 1989; Free Fallin', 1989; Learning To Fly, 1991; Too Good To Be True, 1992; You Don't Know How It Feels, 1994; It's Good to be King, 1995; Walls, 1996; Also featured on: Stop Draggin' My Heart Around, Stevie Nicks, 1981; Give Peace A Chance, Peace Choir, 1991; Film theme, Band of The Hand, with Bob Dylan, 1986; Time Takes Time, Ringo Starr; 30th Anniversary Concert, Bob Dylan, 1993; 30 Years of Randy Newman, Randy Newman, 1998. *Honours:* Gold discs; MTV Music Video Award, Don't Come Around Here No More, 1985. *Current Management:* East End Management, 8209 Melrose Ave, 2nd Floor, Los Angeles, CA 90046, USA.

PEWNY Michael; b. 11 Nov. 1963, Vienna, Austria. Boogie Woogie and Blues Musician (piano). *Education:* Master of Business Administration. *Musical Education:* Private classical education on piano, started playing age 7. *Career:* First concert, Vienna, 1981; Several radio and television appearances, ORF, Austria; 3 US tours; Festivals include: Blues Spring Festival, Belgium, 1992; Le Nuits Jazz and Boogie Festival, Paris, 1993, 1994. *Recordings:* Left Hand Roller, featuring Dana Gillespie, 1990; Boogie On My Mind, featuring Sabine Ruzicka, 1992; Vienna Boogie Woogie, featuring Torsten Zwingenberger, 1994; Crazy Bout Boogie, 1996; Movin' To Chicago; 20th Anniversary, 2000. *Current Management:* Susy Records, Stefaniegasse, 10 + 14/12, Kaltenleutgeben, Austria.

PHILLIPPS Martin John James; b. 2 July 1963, Wellington, New Zealand. Songwriter; Performer; Musician (guitar); Vocalist. *Musical Education:* Self-taught. *Career:* Member, bands: The Same, 1978–80; The Chills, 1980–92; Tours: Australasia; Europe; USA, late 1980s-early 1990s; Also played with The Clean (reformed); Snapper; Pop Art Toasters; April Fools; Relaunched as Martin Phillipps and The Chills, 1995-. *Recordings:* The Dunedin Double EP, 1982; The Lost EP, 1984; Albums: Kaleidoscope World (compilation), 1986; Brave Words, 1987; Submarine Bells, 1990; Love to Hate You, Erasure, 1991; Soft Bomb, 1992; Pop Art Toasters (EP), 1994; Heavenly Pop Hits (Best of...), 1994; Album: Sunburnt, 1996. *Honours:* New Zealand Music Awards: Top Group, 1987; Top Group, Album, Single, Songwriter, 1990. *Leisure interests:* Record and comic collecting; Film and video watching; The works of Gerry Anderson. *Address:* PO Box 705, Dunedin Central, New Zealand.

PHILLIPS (Holly) Michelle; b. 4 June 1944, Long Beach, California, USA. Singer; Actress. m. (1) John Phillips, 31 Dec. 1962, divorced, 2 s., 1 d., (2) Dennis Hopper, 1970, divorced. *Musical Education:* Voice lessons. *Career:* Member of The Mamas and the Papas; 2 US tours; Films: Dillinger; Valentino; Bloodline; Let It Ride; Television appearances include: Knots Landing (6 years); Beverly Hills 90210; Lois and Clark; The New Adventures of Superman; Murder She Wrote. *Compositions:* Co-wrote California Dreamin'; Creque Alley. *Recordings:* If You Can Believe Your Eyes and Ears; The Mamas and the Papas; Deliver – The Mamas and the Papas; with Belinda Carlisle, Heaven on Earth, 1988. *Publications:* California Dreamin'. *Honours:* 4 Gold albums; 1 Grammy; Golden Globe

nomination, 1974. *Memberships:* NARAS; ACOMPAS. *Leisure interests:* Cooking; Travelling.

PHILLIPS Bill; b. 29 Aug. 1951, Taplow, Berkshire, England. Musician (bass). Divorced, 1 d. *Career:* Many European tours with Glitter; Television: Jools Holland; MTV; The Beat; Raw Soup; Reeves and Mortimer; British tour with: Alvin Stardust; Mud; Glitter Band, 1994–95. *Recordings:* Denim album: Back In Denim; First single: Shampoo. *Membership:* Musicians' Union. *Leisure interest:* Fishing. *Current Management:* Hal Carter. *Address:* 29 Egremont Gardens, Slough, Berkshire, England.

PHILLIPS Dudley; b. 9 June 1960, Maidenhead, Berkshire, England. Musician (electric bass, bass); Composer. *Musical Education:* Self-taught. *Career:* Early experience with soul bands; World tour with Womack and Womack, Bill Withers, Mica Paris; Jazz touring with Annie Whitehead; Andy Sheppard; Orphy Robinson; Perfect Houseplants; Jazz festivals include: Montreux; North Sea; Montréal; Berlin; Numerous television and radio appearances; Projects include: Balanescu Quartet; London Sinfonietta; Orlando Consort; Ernestine Anderson; Ronny Jordan; Dave Valentin; Najma. *Compositions include:* Sextet for Vanessa Smith, for string quartet, electric bass and drums; Arrangement of early vocal music for Orlando Consort plus Perfect Houseplants; Writing for own jazz sextet. *Recordings:* 4 albums with Perfect Houseplants; Andy Sheppard's Moving Image; 2 with Orphy Robinson; 3 with Colin Town's Mask; 3 with June Tabor; Also albums with: Annie Whitehead; John Etheridge; Tim Whitehead; Permission; Huw Warren, Barrel Organ; Mark Lockheart band; Peter Sellars film with Andy Sheppard. *Honours:* First Perfect Houseplant's album voted Best Jazz Album of The Year. *Leisure interests:* Archbishop Makarios; Lizards; Indian food; Funghi. *Address:* 64 Weston Park, London N8 9TD, England.

PHILLIPS John Keith Andrew; b. 9 June 1961, Darlinghurst, Sydney, Australia. Composer; Prod.; Musician (guitar, bass). m. Emily Humphries, 1 s., 1 d. *Education:* Latrobe University, Melbourne, Australia. *Musical Education:* Self-taught, Guitar, Bass, Programming. *Career:* Founding Member, Easter, 1983–85; Not Drowning, Waving, 1984–95; Major Film Scores: Body Work, 1988; Proof, 1991; Say A Little Prayer, 1993; Greenkeeping, 1993; That Eye The Sky, 1994; What I Have Written, 1995; River St, 1996; Idiot Box, 1996; The Myth of Finger Prints, 1997; Contributor: Malcolm, 1985. *Recordings:* Another Pond; Little Desert; Cold and the Crackle; Claim; Tabaran; Circus; Stylin Up, by Christine Anu; Telek, by Telek; World Turning, by Yothu Yindi; Contributor recordings include Archie Roach, Monique Brumby, Hugo Race, Snog, Bloom, Big Bag, Solid. *Honours:* Aria Award, Proof, film soundtrack CD; Aria Award, Telek, album, 1997; Aria nominations for Not Drowing, Waving. *Current Management:* Loud and Clear Management, PO Box 276, Albert Park, 2306, Australia.

PHILLIPS Josh; b. 12 Dec. 1962. Musician (keyboards). *Musical Education:* Grade 7 piano, Guildhall School of Music syllabus, 1977. *Career:* Turned professional, 1982; Tours: Diamond Head, 1983–85; Heatwave, world tour, 1986–88; Big Country, Russia, Estonia, Europe, UK, 1988–90; Midge Ure, Europe, UK, 1991, 1992; Procul Harum, Europe, 1993–94; Steve Roux Band, UK and Europe, 1993–94; Moody Marsden Band, Europe, 1994–95; Gary Brooker All-Star Band Annual Charity Christmas Show, 1990–; Videos: Diamond Head Live; Big Country Live-Russia; Big Country East Berlin; Cliff Richard; Midge Ure; Heatwave; Moody Marsden; Procul Harum; Helen Hofner; Television appearances include: Wogan; Top of the Pops; Wired; Meltdown; Smash Hits Awards; Telethon with Sam Brown, Midge Ure; Various European pop and music shows; Currently recording with Mark Brzezicki, Tony Butler, Steve Roux. *Compositions:* Incidental television music; Meltdown ITV Rock Music Show; Comment; Music for various commercials. *Recordings:* Albums with Diamond Head; Heatwave; Big Country; Midge Ure; Pete Townshend; Tim Renwick; Bernie Marsden; Moody Marsden Band; The Hamsters. *Current Management:* Judy Totton Publicity. *Address:* EBC House, 1A Ranelagh Gardens, London SW6 3PA, England.

PHILLIPS Martyn John Courtenay; b. 24 Nov. 1960, UK. Record Prod.; Recording Engineer; Musician (Guitar, Keyboards, Viola). *Education:* BA, Hons, Engineering Science, Oxford University; Trained on viola, piano and guitar. *Career:* Recording Engineer, London, 1982; Synthesizer Programmer, 1983–; Record Producer, 1989-. *Compositions:* Dolphin Stories/Out of the Blue, music for TV series; Living with the Enemy, Title music; Songs for Lindy Layton, Akasa, Signs of Life, Deep. *Recordings:* Productions: The Beloved: Happiness, album, The Sun Rising, Hello, Time After Time, singles, Erasure: Chorus, album, single, Am I Right, single, Love to Hate You, single, Breath of Life, single; London Beat: In the Blood, album, Harmony, album, I've Been Thinking About You, single, A Better Love, single, You Bring On the Sun, single, Loved You Send Me Colours, single; Roachford: Only to Be with You, single, This Generation, single, Feel, album, How Can I? (Insecurity), single; Jesus Jones: Right Here, Right Now, single, Already, album, The Next Big Thing, single; The Christians: What's In A Word, single; Lindy Layton: Silly

Games, single, Echo My Love, single; Programmer/Engineer, Soul II Soul: 1990: A New Decade, album; Was (Not Was): What's Up Dog, album, Spy in the House of Love, single, Walk the Dinosaur, single; Swing Out Sister: It's Better To Travel, album, Kaleidoscope World, album, Breakout, single, Surrender, single. *Address:* 12 Saville Rd, London W4 5NQ, England.

PHILLIPS P J; b. 24 July 1964, London, England. Musician (bass guitar); Vocalist. *Musical Education:* Self-taught. *Career:* World-wide tours include: World tour with Nina Hagen, 1980; Television and radio apperances include: with Taylor Dayne: This Morning, Granada TV; Wogan, BBC TV, 1990; with Curtis Stigers: Wogan; Top of The Pops, BBC TV (3 times), 1992; with Michael Ball: Top of The Pops, 1992; with Nina Hagen: Chameleon Varieté TV show, 1993; with Tom Jones: Top of The Pops, BBC TV, 1994; Vetton Bass, ZDF TV, 1995. *Memberships:* Equity; Musicians' Union; PRS; BASCA. *Current Management:* Debbie Haxton, The Session Connection. *Address:* 110/112 Disraeli Rd, London SW15 2DX, England.

PHILLIPS Roy; b. 5 May 1941, Parkstone, Poole, England. Musician (keyboards); Singer. *Musical Education:* Piano lessons (5–10 years). *Career:* Had own band (trio): The Peddlars, 15 years; Worked Las Vegas, 15 seasons; 12 world tours; Regular television and radio world-wide; Ed Sullivan Show; BBC, ATV (England regularly). *Compositions:* Wrote complete album: Suite London; Heavy On The Light Side. *Recordings:* 15 albums; 83 singles; 2 No. 1 hits: Birth; Girlie; Appears on: Ollie Mitchell, Blast off, 1983; Groovy, 1997. *Honours:* No 1 Keyboards, England, 1971, 1972. *Memberships:* PRS; Screen Writers Guild; Songwriters Guild. *Leisure interests:* Art; Golf. *Address:* PO Box 10, Paihia, Bay of Islands, New Zealand.

PHILLIPS Shawn; b. 2 March 1943, Fort Worth, Texas, USA. Musician (guitar, keyboards, sitar). 1 d. *Career:* Film appearance, Run With The Wind; Lead singer, Broadway musical, Jesus Christ Superstar; Tours include: South Africa; Québec; Television includes: 4 appearances Midnight Special, CBS-TV ; In Concert, NBC-TV. *Compositions include:* Co-writer, Sunshine Superman album, with Donovan. *Recordings:* Albums: Contribution, 1970; Second Contribution, 1971; Collaboration, 1972; Faces, 1973; Furthermore, 1974; Bright White, 1975; Do You Wonder, 1976; Rumplestiltskin's Resolve, 1977; Spaced, 1978; Transcendence, 1980; Best of Shawn Phillips, 1986; Beyond Here Be Dragons, 1988; The Truth If It Kills, 1994; Another Contribution, 1995. *Honours:* Yamaha World Popular Song Festival; 3 Platinum discs for album Second Contribution. *Memberships:* SOCAN; BMI. *Leisure interest:* Firefighter. *Current Management:* Arlo Henning, Lodestone Management. *Address:* 10920 Irwin Ave S, Bloomington, MN 55437, USA.

PHILLIPS Steve (Nicholas Stephen); b. 18 Feb. 1948, London, England. Singer; Musician (guitar). 2 d. *Musical Education:* Self-taught. *Career:* Semi-professional musician, 1961–86; Professional solo artist, 1986–; Also duo with Brendan Croker; Also, member, Notting Hillbillies, 1990; Own band, Steve Phillips and The Rough Diamonds. *Recordings:* The Best of Steve Phillips, 1987; Steel Rail Blues, 1989; with Notting Hillbillies: Missing Presumed Having A Good Time, 1990; Been A Long Time Gone, 1995; Just Pickin', 1996. *Memberships:* PRS, PAMRA. *Leisure interest:* Landscape painting. *Current Management:* GTA, Wisteria House, 14 Glamorgan Rd, Hampton Wick, Surrey KT1 4HB, England.

PHIMISTER Glen; b. 15 Sept. 1953, London. Recording Engineer. m. Hortensze. *Education:* Ealing Mead Academy, London. *Career:* Engineer, Unity Gain Studio and freelance; Previously with: Studios 301, Sydney; Air Studios, London; Trident Studios, London; Worked on various pop, rock, jazz and orchestral recordings, mid 1970s-; Worked on Sydney Olympics, 2000; TV work includes: Home and Away; The Farm. *Recordings:* Olivia Newton-John; INXS; Pseudo Echo; Prague Symphony Orchestra; Split Enz; Slim Dusty; David Campbell; Iota; Jazz Police. *Address:* 294a Livingstone Rd, Marrickville, New South Wales 2204, Australia.

PHOENIX (David Michael Farrell); b. 8 Feb. 1977, Plymouth, Massachusetts, USA. Musician (bass guitar). *Musical Education:* Taught guitar by mother. *Career:* Played guitar in high school group The Snax; Joined room-mate Brad Delson's California-based group Xero as bassist; Left band after completion of college course; Rejoined Delson's group, now Linkin Park, following release of group's debut Warner Bros album; Live shows include: Family Values and Ozzfest tours; KROQ Acoustic Christmas Concert 2001; many international dates; TV specials include: Live At The Fillmore; Reverb; Co-writing forthcoming album with group. *Recordings:* DVD: Frat Party At The Pankake Festival, 2001. *Honours:* Group awards: Billboard Award, Best Modern Rock Artist, 2001; Rock Bear Awards: Best International Band; Best International Album, 2001; Kerrang! Award, Best International Newcomer, 2001; Rolling Stone Award, Best Hard Rock/Metal Band, 2001. *Current Management:* Andy Gould Management, 8484 Wilshire Blvd #425, Beverly Hills, CA 90211, USA. *Internet:* www.linkinpark.com.

PIATKOWSKI Dionizy; b. 1954, Poznan, Poland. Critic; Jazz Historian; Journalist; DJ; Prod. m. Irena, 1 s., 2 d. *Education:* Postgraduate Studies, Journalism, 1984. *Musical Education:* MA, Ethnology, specialization in Music Folklore, Poznan University, 1978. *Career:* Music Journalist, Jazz Forum, Express Poznanski, Glos Wielkopolski, Wprost, Jazz a Go Go, Jazz Magazine; Freelance journalist for several jazz magazines in Europe and the USA; Leading jazz and music publicist, producer and organizer in Poland; Lecturer on Jazz, Black Music and Folklore, University of Graz, Austria, Poznan University, Pittsburgh University, USA; DJ and Producer, Polish radio stations, shows include Jazz Academy and Let's Play Folklore; Producer, Director and A&R, jazz festivals and concerts including Dave Brubeck, Stefan Grapelli, B. B. King, Jan Garharek and Kronos Quartet; Man. Dir, Poznan Jazz Festival; Founder, Programme and Music Director, first Polish music radio station, Radio 88.4 Jazz/FM. *Publications:* Not Only Music; Fan Club Special; Komeda's Time; Jazz Giants; Blues, Punk, Disco; Encyclopaedia of Popular Music – Jazz; Numerous articles in Polish and international journals. *Memberships:* International Asscn for Jazz Research, Austria; Friends of Polish Music, USA; International Jazz Hall of Fame, Pittsburgh University, USA. *Address:* Strzelecka 37, 62–050 Mosina, Poland.

PICKERING Mike; b. Manchester, England. Musician (saxophone); Vocalist; Composer; DJ. *Career:* DJ, Manchester clubs; Singer, saxophonist, Quando Quango; Founder member, musician, songwriter, UK dance group M People, 1991–; Major concerts include: Glastonbury Festival, 1994. *Recordings:* Albums: Northern Soul, 1992; Elegant Slumming, 1993; Bizarre Fruit, 1994; Bizarre Fruit II, 1995; Hit singles: How Can I Love You More, 1991; One Night In Heaven, 1993; Movin' On Up, 1993; Sight For Sore Eyes, 1994; Itchycoo Park, 1995; Search For The Hero, 1995; Open Your Heart, 1995; Love Rendezvous, 1995. *Honours:* Mercury Prize, Best Album, Elegant Slumming, 1994; BRIT Awards, Best Dance Act, 1994, 1995. *Current Management:* RD World Wide Management. *Address:* 37 Limerston St, London SW10 0BQ, England.

PICKERING Phil; b. 27 June 1960, Pembury, Kent, England. Musician (bass guitar, didgeridoo, synthesizer). 3 s., 1 d. *Musical Education:* Guitar tuition as teenager. *Career:* Webcore; Goat; Tribal Drift; Fun-Da-Mental; Lights In A Fat City; Zuvuya. *Recordings include:* Vane: Glamorous Boys, 1981; 2 Webcore albums: Webcore, 1987; Webcore Webcore, 1988; 1 Goat album: Goat; Tribal Drift: Like This!, 1992; Medicine Hat, 1992; 2 Zuvuya albums with Terence McKenna: DMT, 1994; Shamania, 1994; Zuvuya: The Goat Faced Girl, 1994; Driving The Monkey Insane, 1994; Moose Jaw, 1994; Away The Crow Road, 1994; The Trance End of Dreaming, 1994; Turn Around, 1994; Third Zuvuya album, 1997; Quadruped, Quadruped, 1995; Fun-Da-Mental: Seize the Time, 1995; Erotic Terrorism, 1998. *Memberships:* PRS; Musicians' Union. *Leisure interest:* Alien abductions. *Current Management:* M.E.L.T. Music, Lescrow Farm, Fowey, Cornwall PL23 1JS. *Address:* Delerium Records, PO Box 1288, Gerrards Cross, Bucks SL9 9YB, England.

PICKETT Wilson; b. 18 March 1941, Prattville, Alabama, USA. Singer; Musician (guitar). *Career:* Gospel singer; Lead singer, the Falcons, 1961; Solo artist, 1963–; Recent appearances include: Pori Jazz, Finland, 1995; Sardinia Blues and Jazz, Italy, 1997; Rock and Roll Hall of Fame and Museum, USA, 1998; Star Festival, Belgium, 1998; Blues Brothers 2000, 1998. *Recordings:* Albums: In The Midnight Hour, 1965; The Exciting Wilson Pickett, 1967; The Sound of Wilson Pickett, 1967; The Best of Wilson Pickett, 1967; I'm In Love, 1968; The Midnight Mover, 1968; Hey Jude, 1969; Wilson Pickett In Philadelphia, 1970; The Best of Wilson Pickett Vol. II, 1971; Mr Magic Man, 1973; Pickett In The Pockett, 1973; A Funky Situation, 1978; I Want You, 1979; The Right Track, 1981; American Soul Man, 1988; Hit singles include: In The Midnight Hour, 1965; Don't Fight It, 1965; 634–5789, 1966; Land of 1,000 Dances, 1966; Mustang Sally, 1966; Everybody Needs Somebody To Love, 1967; I Found A Love, 1967; Funky Broadway, 1967; Stag-O-Lee, 1967; She's Lookin' Good, 1968; I'm A Midnight Mover, 1968; Hey Jude, 1969; Sugar Sugar, 1970; (Get Me Back On Time) Engine Number Nine, 1970; Don't Let The Green Grass Fool You, 1971; Don't Knock My Love, 1971; It's Harder Now, 1999. *Honours:* Inducted into Rock and Roll Hall of Fame, 1991. *Current Management:* Talent Source, 1560 Broadway, Suite 1308, New York, NY 10036, USA.

PICKFORD Andrew Cliffe; b. 22 Oct. 1965, Kegworth, Nottinghamshire, England. Musician (electronic keyboards). *Musical Education:* Self-taught. *Career:* Solo artist, Electronic music; Concerts include: Derby Cathedral, Derby Assembly Rooms and Guildhall (several times); Radio and television: Interviews and broadcasts on BBC local radio; BBC Radio 1 including John Peel show; Formed Electronic Music and Musicians Association. *Recordings:* Albums: Replicant, 1993; Terraformer, 1994; Maelstrom, 1995 (all No. 1, Electronic music charts); 2 EPs: Dystopia, 1996; Works Vol. 1, Works Vol. 2 (both live at Derby), 1997. *Memberships:* PRS; Past Secretary, EMMA. *Leisure interests:* Esoteric philosophy; Gardening. *Current Management:* David Shoesmith, Centaur Discs Ltd, 40–42 Brantwood Ave, Dundee DD3 6EW, Scotland. *Address:* The Bryans, 89 Dundee Rd, West Ferry, Dundee DD5 3LZ, Scotland.

PIERCE Jason; b. 19 Nov. 1965, Rugby, England. Musician (Guitar); Vocalist. *Career:* Member, Spacemen 3; Formed Spiritualized; Worked with Dr John and Spring Heeled Jack; Numerous live dates including world tour; Concerts at Royal Albert Hall, London, and CN Tower, Toronto. *Recordings:* Singles: Run, 1991; Anyway That You Want Me, 1991; Let It Flow, 1995; Electricity, 1997; I Think I'm In Love, 1998; Come Together, 1998; Abbey Road EP, 1998; Albums: Lazer Guided Melodies, 1992; Fucked Up Inside (live), 1993; Pure Phase, 1995; Ladies and Gentlemen We Are Floating In Space, 1997; Royal Albert Hall 10 October 1997 (live), 1998.

PIERSON Kate; b. 27 April 1948, Weehawken, New Jersey, USA. Singer; Musician (organ). *Career:* Singer, musician, B-52's, 1976-. *Recordings:* Albums: B-52's, 1979; Wild Planet, 1980; Mesopotamia, 1982; Whammy!, 1983; Bouncing Off The Satellites, 1986; Cosmic Thing, 1989; Best of The B-52's – Dance This Mess Around, 1990; Good Stuff, 1992; B Fifty Two's, Time Capsule, Greatest Hits, 1998; Associate, Associate, 1996; Singles include: Rock Lobster, 1980; Love Shack, 1989. *Current Management:* Direct Management Group, 947 N La Cienga Blvd, Los Angeles, CA 90069, USA.

PILC Jean-Michel; b. 19 Oct. 1960, Paris, France. Musician (piano, keyboards); Composer. m. *Musical Education:* Self-taught. *Career:* Played in numerous concerts, festivals, tours to over 40 countries including Africa, Asia, Europe; Sideman with artists including: Roy Haynes Quartet; Jean Toussaint (including Royal Festival Hall, London); Daniel Humair and Jean-François Jenny-Clarke; Michel Portal; Martial Solal; Aldo Romano; André Ceccarelli; Christian Escoude; Rick Margitza; Peter King; George Brown; Dave Liebman; Greg Hutchinson; Harry Belafonte; Michael Brecker; John Abercrombie; Adam Nussbaum; Omar Hakim; Jeff Watts; Dennis Irwin; Essie Essiet; Alvester Garnett; Leader with: Enrico Rava (trumpet), Marc Ducret (guitar), Mark Mondesir (drums); Composer, leader, arranger playing solo, in duo, trio and big band; Recent European tour, Germany, Switzerland, France; Moves to New York City, 1995; Plays in Sweet Basil, New York City, with his trio, 1999. *Compositions:* Music played throughout Europe, covered by many other artists; Many film scores. *Recordings:* Electrochoc, 1987; Funambule, 1989; Big One, 1993; For Edith Piaf and Charles Trenet, with Eric Le Lann/Martial Solal, 1989; Prosodie, Aldo Romano, 1995; Life I Want, Jean Toussaint, 1995; From The Heart, André Ceccarelli, 1995; Richard Bona, 1999; Elisabeth Kontomanou, 1999; Other recordings with: Elizabeth Kontomanou; Eric Le Lann; J-Loup Longnon. *Leisure interests:* Jogging; Trekking. *Current Management:* Jon Waxman Associates, 302 W 12th St, Suite 10B, New York, NY 10014, USA. *Address:* 262 Bergen St #2R, Brooklyn, NY11217, USA.

PILGREM Rennie, (Thursday Club, New Electro Sound of London, Tribal Underground); b. 15 Jan. 1961, London, England. Prod.; Remixer; DJ. *Career:* Formed: Rhythm Section (with Ellis Dee), early 1990s; Duo were big live success on Rave scene; Founder: Thursday Club Recordings; Major figure in Nu Skool Breakz scene, late 1990s; Co-promoter: Friction night in London (alongside Adam Freeland); Collaborations: Ellis Dee; Arthur Baker; Will South; B.L.I.M.; Uberzone; Remixed: BT; Quivver; Kosheen. *Recordings:* Philadelphia Bluntz (with Philadelphia Bluntz), 1998; Selected Werks (compilation), 2000; Singles: Feel The Rhythm (with Rhythm Section), Check Out The Bass (with Rhythm Section), 1991; A Place Called Acid (as Thursday Club), 1996; Sister Sister (with Philadelphia Bluntz), Like No Other (with Arthur Baker), 1998; Eskimo (with B.L.I.M.), 2001. *Address:* c/o Thursday Club Recordings, 310 King St, London, W6 0RR, England.

PILKINGTON Stephen Roy; b. 5 Oct. 1946, Bakewell, Derbyshire, England. Music Dir; Musician (piano, organ). m. Patricia Anne Wall, 18 July 1970, 1 s., 1 d. *Musical Education:* Royal Manchester College of Music, GRSM; ARMCM; LRAM; ARCO. *Career:* Music Director, many top star shows including: Royal Shows for Princess Royal, Princess Margaret, 1975–; Music Director for television series; Keyboard backing for television signature tunes and plays; Pianist for Welsh musical programmes. *Recordings:* Romance, solo piano ballads and orchestra accompaniment; Stephen Pilkington Organ Collection; Backing many Welsh recordings. *Membership:* Musicians' Union. *Leisure interest:* Watching motor racing. *Address:* Glandwr Onest, Blaenffos, Boncath, Pembrokeshire SA37 0JB, Wales.

PINE Courtney; b. 18 March 1964, London, England. Jazz Musician (saxophone). 1 s., 3 d. *Career:* International tours, with own reggae and acoustic jazz bands; Trio (with Cameron Pierre, Talvin Singh) opened for Elton John and Ray Cooper, The Zenith, Paris and Royal Albert Hall, London, European Tour, 1994; Teacher's Jazz European tour, 1996; Support to Cassandra Wilson, US and Canada, 1996; Tours, Japan, South Africa and UK, 1996; Festivals in Europe, Japan, Thailand, 1996; Television appearances: Regular guest, Later With Jools Holland; Black Christmas, Channel 4; The White Room, 1996; Featured Artist on BBC's Perfect Day recording. *Recordings include:* Albums: Journey To The Urge Within, 1987; Destiny's Song, 1988; The Vision's Tale, 1989; Closer To Home, 1990; Within The Realms of Our Dreams; To The Eyes of Creation; Modern Day Jazz Stories', 1996; Underground, 1997; Another Story, 1998;

Featured guest on: Wandering Spirit, Mick Jagger; Jazzmatazz, Guru; Jazzmatazz II – The New Reality, Guru; Summertime, track on The Glory of Gershwin (Larry Adler tribute album). *Honours:* Mercury Music Prize, one of Albums of the Year, 1996; Best Jazz Act, MOBO, 1996, 1997. *Current Management:* c/o Nikki Neave, Tickety-Boo, The Boathouse, Crabtree Lane, London SW6 6TY, England.

PINK, (Alicia Moore); b. 8 Sept. 1979, USA. Vocalist; Songwriter. *Career:* Started singing and dancing in local bands, aged 13; Spotted at Philadelphia club Fever by MCA Records talent scout; After unsuccessful stints with manufactured groups Basic Instinct and Choice teamed up with producers LA Reid and Babyface. *Recordings:* Albums: Can't Take Me Home, 2000; M!ssundaztood, 2001; Singles: There You Go, 2000; Most Girls, 2000; You Make Me Sick, 2001; Lady Marmalade (with Christina Aguilera, Lil' Kim and Mya), 2001; Get The Party Started, 2001. *Honours:* MTV Video Award, Best New Artist. *Current Management:* Wrightstuff Management, USA.

PINKSTON Steven Ray; b. 12 Dec. 1960, Columbus, Ohio, USA. Record Prod.; Engineer; Songwriter. m. Angie Akin, 30 Oct. 1993. *Education:* Belmont University, Nashville, Tennessee. *Career:* Concert tours: Linda Ronstadt; Steven Curtis Chapman; Shelley West; The Commodores; Geoff Moore and The Distance; ABC; Amy Grant. *Compositions:* Cleansing Rain, Kelli Reisen (No. 3, CCM hit); 50 albums include: 4Him; Commissioned; Angelo and Veronica; Brian White; J J Cale; Graham Maw; Videos: 4Him; Commissioned; Harvest; Brian White; Wellington Boone; Grace Lazenby; Becky Tirabassi. *Recordings include:* Natural Encounters, 1998; Mark Baldwin, In the pocket, 1999; Contemporary Christian Hits, 1999; Four Him, Basics of Life, 1999. *Memberships:* GMA; NARAS. *Address:* PO Box 40784, Nashville, TN 37204, USA.

PITCH Harry; b. 9 May 1925, Hull, Yorkshire, England. Musician (harmonica, trumpet). m. Ruby, 10 June 1946, 1 s., 1 d. *Musical Education:* Self-taught. *Career:* Session musician; Featured soloist at Sadlers Wells; Royal Festival Hall, with Hans Werner Henze; Barbican Centre with Carl Davis; Television includes: Playing for Last of Summer Wine, 25 years, Many radio series; Films with: Ron Goodwin; Laurie Johnson; James Horner; Geoff Love; One of the only harmonica players to move successfully from classical to jazz music; Many broadcasts with various groups include Rhythm and Reeds, with Jack Emblow. *Compositions:* Recorded library music. *Recordings:* Hits with various artists, throughout 1960s-80s; Solo albums. *Membership:* Musicians' Union (Gold Card mem.). *Leisure interest:* Boating. *Address:* Hunters Moon, Islet Rd, Maidenhead, Berks SL6 8HT, England.

PITCHFORD Dean; b. 29 July 1951, Honolulu, Hawaii, USA. Songwriter; Screenwriter; Dir. *Education:* Yale University, 1972. *Career:* Actor, singer: Godspell, 1971–72; Pippin, 1972–75; The Umbrellas of Cherbourg, 1978; Songwriter, screenwriter, films: Fame, 1980; Footloose, 1984; Sing, 1988; Chances Are, 1989. *Compositions:* Songs: Fame; Footloose; Let's Hear It For The Boy; You Should Hear How She Talks About You; After All; Almost Paradise; Holding Out For A Hero; All The Man That I Need; Footloose, on Broadway, 1998. *Honours:* Academy Award, Fame; Golden Globe Award, Fame; 3 Academy Award Nominations; 2 Tony Award nominations. *Memberships:* BMI; NAS; NARAS. *Leisure interest:* Yoga.

PITICCO Steve; b. 6 July 1961, Toronto, Ontario, Canada. Musician (lead guitar). m. Laurie Laporte, 25 April 1983, 1 s., 1 d. *Musical Education:* Self-taught, started country music age 15, full time, Grade 9. *Career:* Performs professionally with Fender Telecaster guitars; Formed own band, South Mountain, 1989; Toured with: Sweethearts of The Rodeo; Marty Stuart; Conway Twitty; Charlie Pride; Played shows supporting: Vince Gill; George Jones; Johnny Cash; Ricky Skaggs; Mid-Canada Television network, with South Mountain, 4 years; Picker, various bands, including South Mountain, on Canadian Country Music Awards' Annual Telecast, 1984–94; Tours in Canada and Europe, 1995. *Recordings:* 8 albums with South Mountain; Session player on recordings by: Patricia Conroy; Tracy Prescott; Don Neilson. *Honours:* 7 CCMA Instrumentalist of Year Awards, 1985–94; CCMA Rising Star Awards, 1991; CCMA Guitar Player of The Year, 1990–93. *Leisure interests:* Computers; Practising golf shots from own backyard. *Current Management:* Cathy Faint Entertainment Inc, 430 Signet Dr., Suite C, North York, ON M9L 2T6, Canada. *Address:* PO Box 64, Lot 7, County Rd 1, South Mountain, ON K0E 1W0, Canada.

PITMAN Toby John; b. 27 Sept. 1971, Crawley, West Sussex, England. Musician (guitar). *Musical Education:* Graduate Diploma, Guitar Institute of Technology, USA. *Career:* Appearances on television and radio include: Capital Radio programme, How Do They Do That, BBC, Glam Metal Detectives; Current member, funk/rock band Radio Jim. *Recording:* Rock Guitar Album. *Membership:* Musicians' Union. *Leisure interests:* Playing guitar; Live bands; Music; Cooking. *Address:* c/o E L Seeberg, Acremead, Framfield Rd, Blackboys, East Sussex TN22 5LR, England.

PITNEY Gene; b. 17 Feb. 1941, Hartford, Connecticut, USA. Singer; Songwriter. m. Lynne, 21 Jan. 1967, 3 s. *Career:* Recording artiste, 1959–; Recorded albums in Italian and Spanish; Regular international tours. *Compositions:* Songs include: Loneliness, The Kalin Twins; Today's Teardrops, Roy Orbison; Rubber Ball, Bobby Vee; Hello Mary Lou, Ricky Nelson; He's A Rebel, The Crystals; Recorded with the Rolling Stones in 1964; Nessuno Mi Puo Guidicare, second place at San Remo Song Festival, 1966. *Recordings:* Albums: The Many Sides of Gene Pitney, 1962; Only Love Can Break A Heart, 1963; Pitney Sings Just For You, 1963; Blue Gene, 1964; Gene Pitney Meets The Fair Young Ladies of Folkland, 1964; I'm Gonna Be Strong, 1965; George Jones and Gene Pitney, 1965; The Great Songs of our Time, 1965; Nobody Needs Your Love, 1966; Young Warm and Wonderful, 1967; Just One Smile, 1967; Pitney Today, 1968; Pitney '75, 1975; Walkin' In The Sun, 1979; Various compilations; Singles include: I Wanna Love My Life Away, 1961; Town Without Pity; The Man Who Shot Liberty Valance; Twenty Four Hours From Tulsa; That Girl Belongs To Yesterday; I'm Gonna Be Strong, 1964; I Must Be Seeing Things, 1965; Looking Through The Eyes of Love, 1965; Princess In Rags, 1965; Backstage, 1966; Nobody Needs Your Love, 1966; Just One Smile, 1966; Something's Gotten Hold of My Heart, 1967; Somewhere In The Country; Maria Elena, 1969; Shady Lady, 1970; Blue Angel, 1974; Pitney Espagñol, 1982; Love My Life Away, 1982; Half Heaven Half Heartache, 1983; Gene Pitney, 1984; Something's Gotten Hold of My Heart, with Marc Almond, 1988; The Definitive Collection, 1999. *Honours:* ASCAP, BMI. *Leisure interests:* Songwriting; Computers. *Current Management:* Pitney Music, c/o David P McGrath. *Address:* 6201 39th Ave, Kenosha, WI 53142, USA.

PIZZARELLI John 'Bucky'; b. 9 Jan. 1926, USA. Jazz Musician (guitar). m. Ruth Litchult Pizzarelli, 9 Jan. 1954, 2 s., 2 d. *Musical Education:* Studied with Peter and Robert Domenick. *Career:* Member, Vaughn Monroe Orchestra; White House concerts with Benny Goodman, Frank Sinatra; Staff musician with NBC; ABC; Skitch Henderson; Doc Severinson; Mitch Miller; Concerts and tours with artistes including: George Barnes and Les Paul; Stéphane Grappelli; Skitch Henderson; Bobby Short; Benny Goodman; Zoot Sims; Peter Appleyard; Barney Kessel and Charlie Byrd; Howard Alden; Festivals include: Umbria Jazz Festival; Newport Jazz Festival; Melon Jazz; Dick Gibson's Jazz Parties throughout US; Faculty Member Emeritus, William Paterson College, Wayne, New Jersey. *Recordings:* Albums include: Green Guitar Blues; Buck Plays Bix; Bucky's Bunch; Cafe Pierre Trio; Love Songs; Solo Flight; One Morning In May, Sonatina, 2000; with Stéphane Grappelli: All Stars, 1978; Passion Guitars, April Kisses, 1999; Also recorded with: George Barnes; Zoot Sims; Eddie Daniels; Benny Goodman; Joe Venuti. *Address:* 214 West Saddle River Rd, Saddle River, NJ 07458–2620, USA.

PLA Roberto Enrique; b. Barranquilla, Colombia. Musician (percussion, timbales, bongos, congas, drums); Bandleader. m. Dominique Roome, 3 Oct. 1992. *Musical Education:* Studied percussion with Pompelio Rodríguez; National University in Bogotá, 1964–. *Career:* Session musician with artists including Los Ocho De Colombia; Drummer with Orquesto Lucho Bermudez, 1968–78; Tours include Latin America and US; Weekly television appearances, Colombian television; Moved to New York, 1978; Salsa session percussionist, bands including Orquesta La Inspiracion; Moved to London, 1979; Member, jazz-fusion band Cayenne; Founder member, bands including Valdez; Sondido De Londres (co-founder); Roberto Pla Latin Ensemble (12-piece all-star band); Numerous European festivals and television appearances, 1988; Concerts include: Boney M, World tour, 1982; Joe Strummer; Gonzalez, World tour; Arrow, US tour; Radio Futura; Slim Gaillard, Japan and Far East tour, 1987; Alfredo Rodriguez, North African tour; Sonny Southon, Europe, US tours, 1991–92; US3, Europe, Far East tours, 1993; Film apperances include: I Hired A Contract Killer (with Joe Strummer); Eat The Rich (with Motörhead). *Recordings:* Numerous albums include: Cumbia Dominique, 1990; Recordings with artists including: Kate Bush; M People. *Current Management:* Salsa Boogie Productions. *Address:* 153 Shrewsbury Rd, London E7 8QA, England.

PLANKA Pavel; b. 29 May 1962, Pilsn, Czech Republic. Musician. *Musical Education:* Self-taught Drums; Public School of Arts; Prague Conservatoire. *Career:* Performances with Several Top Czech Ensembles, Jazz, Rock, Pop, Classical, Folk; Support of Rolling Stones, Voodoo Lounge; Numerous Orchestral Music. *Recordings:* Nerez, Ke zdi, 1990; Tutu, Mr Jazz Man, 1991; Zuzana Navarova, Caribe, 1992; Vitacit, Mate se hnout; Hot line, Still Callin', 1993; Merinsky-Lewitova, Sefardske pisne; Dan Barta Alice, Usta hromu, 1994; Lucie, Cerny kocky mokry zaby; Janek Ledecky, Jenom tak; Michal Pavlicek, Na kloboucku II, 1995; Tresnak-Korman-Koller, Kolaz; Roman Dragoun, Stin my krve; Veleband All Stars Big-Band, 1996; Jarek Nohavica, Divne stoleti; Musical, Hair, 1997. *Honour:* Prize, Authors Competition, Porta, 1986. *Leisure interests:* Water skiing; Mountain biking; Riding water scooters; Diving. *Address:* Nahorni 507/3, 182 00 Prague 8, Czech Republic.

PLANT Robert Anthony; b. 20 Aug. 1948, West Bromwich, Warwickshire, England. Singer; Songwriter. m. Maureen, 1 s. (deceased), 1 d. *Career:* Member, various R & B groups, including Listen; Band of Joy; Lead singer, UK heavy rock group Led Zeppelin (formerly the New Yardbirds), 1968–80; Appearances include: Carnegie Hall, 1969; Royal Albert Hall, 1969, 1971; Madison Square Gardens, 1970; Knebworth Festival, 1979; Sell-out tours, concerts, world-wide; Rock for Kampuchea concert, London, 1979; Reunion for Live Aid, Philadelphia, 1985; Formed Led Zeppelin's own label Swan Song, 1974; Film: The Song Remains The Same, 1976; Solo artiste, 1980–; Member, The Honeydrippers (with Jimmy Page, Nile Rodgers, Jeff Beck), 1984–85; Currently member of Page/Plant, with Jimmy Page (former Led Zeppelin guitarist), 1994-. *Recordings:* Albums with Led Zeppelin (over 60m. copies of albums sold): Led Zeppelin I, 1969; Led Zeppelin II, 1969; Led Zeppelin III, 1970; Led Zeppelin IV, 1971; Houses of The Holy, 1973; Physical Graffiti, 1975; Presence, 1976; The Song Remains The Same, 1976; In Through The Out Door, 1979; Coda, 1983; Remasters, 1993; Solo albums: Pictures At Eleven, 1982; The Principle of Moments, 1983; Solo albums: Now and Zen, 1988; Manic Nirvana, 1990; Fate of nations, 1993; with the Honeydrippers: The Honeydrippers Vol. 1, 1984; with Page/Plant: No Quarter, 1994; Walking Into Clarksdale, 1998; More Oar, 1999; Singles: Little By Little, 1985; Tall Cool One, 1989; Hurting kind, 1990; I Believe, 1993; 29 Palms/Whole Lotta Love, 1994; Contributor: Outrider, Jimmy Page, 1988; Last Temptation of Elvis (compilation), 1990. *Honours include:* Ivor Novello Awards, Outstanding Contribution To British Music, 1977; Silver Clef Award, Nordoff-Robbins Music Therapy Foundation, 1990; Q Merit Award (with Led Zeppelin), 1992. *Current Management:* Trinifold Management, 22 Harley House, Marylebone Rd, London NW1 4PR, England.

PLATT Ted (Edward Stephen); b. 7 Oct. 1945, West Yorkshire, England. Musician (guitar, bass); Vocalist; Arranger. 1 d. *Musical Education:* Music College, 1 year; Piano and Guitar Lessons; Arranging Techniques. *Career:* Tour with Jet Harris, 1963; Contrasts, 1965; Residencies in London, 1966; Resident guitarist and vocalist, Batley Variety Club, 1972–; Musical Director for Freddie Starr for 10 years and for Gene Pitney for 3 years; Rock and Roll Singer with tours of Australia. *Recordings:* Can't Get You Off of My Mind; Call Me; Ma He's Making Eyes At Me, by Lena Zavaroni. *Memberships:* PRS; MCPS; BASCA; Songwriters' Guild. *Leisure interests:* Painting; Reading; Metaphysics; Theology. *Current Management:* KSP (Leisure) Associates. *Address:* 19 Hyrst Garth, Batley, West Yorkshire WF1Y 7AD, England.

PLATT Tony; b. 21 Jan. 1952, Yorkshire, England. Record Prod.; Engineer. m. Jacqueline, 30 April 1974, 1 s., 1 d. *Career:* Trident Studios, London, England; Assistant Engineer, Island Studios, Basing Street, 1969–70; Recording Engineer for Bob Marley, Toots, Free, etc; Freelance, 1975–; Mutt Lange's Engineer on Highway to Hell, Backin Black, ACDC and Foreigner 4. *Recordings include:* Producer, Engineer, Marche ou Creve, Trust, 1981; Producer, Engineer, Shock Tactics, Samson, 1981; Producer, Engineer, One Vice at a Time, Krokus, 1982; Producer, Engineer, Another Perfect Day, Motorhead, 1983; Engineer, Co-Producer, Flick of the Switch, AC/DC, 1983; Remix, Producer, All Men Play on Ten, Manowar, 1984; Producer, Engineer, We Want More, Gary Moore, 1984; Producer, Engineer, Equator, Uriah Heep, 1984–85; Producer, Engineer, Brave the Storm, Shy, 1985; Producer, Engineer, Nightless City, VowWow, 1985; Producer, Engineer, Live and Dangerous, Krokus, 1986; Producer, Engineer, The Doctor, Cheap Trick, 1986; Producer, Engineer, Wired, Jeff Paris, 1986–87; Producer, BBC-Late Night in Concert, The Cult, 1987; Producer, Engineer, Cold Lake, Celtic Frost, 1988; Producer, Engineer, Love and War, Lillian Axe, 1988–89; Co-Producer, Engineer, Never Turn Your Back on the Blues, Moody Marsden Band, 1991; Producer, Engineer, The Ritual, Testament, 1992; Co-Producer, Engineer, Live in Hell, Moody Marsden Band, 1994; Co-Producer, Engineer, Green and Blues, Bernie Marsden, 1995; Producer, Engineer, Eternity, Anathema, 1996; Producer, Engineer, Ten, 1997; Producer, Engineer, Mau Mau, 1997; Producer, Mixer, Huge Baby, 1997–98. *Publications:* Contributor, Music Industry Management and Promotion, by Chris Kemp. *Memberships:* Re-Pro; PAMRA. *Leisure interests:* Walking; Motor Racing. *Current Management:* NDM (UK), 2 Bloomsbury St, London WC1B 3ST, England, and, CMI (USA), 201 E 87th St, New York, 10128, USA. *Address:* Inch House, Lower St, Pury End, Towcester, Northants, NN12 7NS, England.

PLAYFORD Robert; b. 25 March 1968, Ware, Hertfordshire, England. Record Prod.; Engineer; Programmer; Record Co Exec. *Musical Education:* Self-taught. *Career:* Formed Moving Shadow Music, 1990, pioneering and establishing Jungle music; Concerts: Orlando, Los Angeles, New York, 1992; Paris, 1994; Tokyo, US tour, Glastonbury Festival, 1995; Television and radio apperances: The Word; Interviews on Radio 1 (UK); Mars FM (Los Angeles); Radio Nova (Paris). *Recordings include:* Timeless; Metalheads; New Metalheads album, 1995; Remixes: Hand of The Dead Body, Ice-Cube and Scarface; Crazy Bald Heads, Sly and Robbie; Bee Charmer, Ingrid Schroeder; The Shadow, 1997. *Membership:* Musicians' Union. *Leisure interests:* Work; Racing driving; Net-surfing. *Address:* 55 Conifer Walk, Stevenage, Herts SG2 7QS, England.

PLIERS (Everton Banner); b. 1965, Kingston, Jamaica. DJ; Recording Artist. *Career:* Recording with Black Scorpio; Recorded for numerous lables including: Pickout; Pioneer Musik; Jammys, Harry J and Studio One; Partner, in duo Chaka Demus and Pliers, 1991-. *Recordings:* Albums: with Chaka Demus and Pliers: Gal Wine, 1992; Ruff This Year, 1992; Chaka Demus and Pliers, 1992; Tease Me, 1993; She Don't Let Nobody, 1995; For Every Kinda People, 1997; Singles: Them a Watch Me, 1992; When I'm with You, 1993. *Address:* c/o Free World Music Inc, 230 12th St, Suite 117, Miami Beach, FL 33139–4603, USA.

PLOTNIKOFF Mike; *Career:* Audio Engineer, started at Vancouver's Little Mountain Sound; Sought after by the international music community; Worked with producers including Bruce Faibairn, Bob Rock, Chris Thomas; Mix credits include, How Do I Deal; Melos Modos; Elegantly Wasted; Balance; Day and Night; All For Love; Live Pay Per View For MTV and MUCH Music; Remixes for Sons of Freedom; Taste of Joy; Ginger; Rose Chronicles; Martina McBride; Delirium; The Devlins; Anne Murray; Sandbox; Econoline Crush; Wide Mouth Mason; Bloomsday. Recording Engineer. *Honours:* Monitor Awards finalist for Best Audio Production in Tape Originated Television Specials, 1996. *Address:* c/o Bruce Allen Talent, 406–68 Water St, Vancouver BC, Canada V6B 1A4.

POE David; b. 20 July 1969, Ann Arbor, Michigan, USA. Songwriter; Recording Artist; Singer; Guitarist. m. *Education:* BS, Mass Communications, Miami University, Oxford. *Career:* Solo Performer, 1990–; Support Act for: Bob Dylan, Lisa Loeb, Ron Sexsmith, Jonathon Richman; Produced Debut Recording for Melissa Sheehan, Jenifer Jackson. *Compositions:* Blue Glass Fall; Moon; Reunion, from forthcoming solo debut; Blind Man, co-written with T-Bone Burnett. *Recordings:* David Poe, 1997; Glass Suit, 1996. *Current Management:* Pati DeVries, DeVries Entertainment 179 Franklin St, Fifth Floor, New York, N 10013, USA.

POHJOLA Jussi Pekka; b. 13 Jan. 1952, Helsinki, Finland. Musician (bass); Composer. 3 s. *Musical Education:* Studies in violin and piano, Sibelius Academy, Helsinki. *Career:* Member of Wigwam; Jukka Tolonen Band; Made In Sweden; UMO; Mike Oldfield, including European tour, 1979; Tours with Pori Big Band, 1980; Founder of several own bands; Tours throughout Scandinavia; Europe; USA; Japan. *Compositions:* Film music; Theatre music; Arrangements for different artists; One symphony, Sinfonia, 1989. *Recordings:* 12 solo albums, including Bialoipoikku The Magpie; Urban Tango; Jokamies; Space Waltz; Flight of The Angel; Heavy Jazz; Changing Waters; Numerous recordings with other artists. *Honours:* 2 Awards, Best Record of the Year, Finnish Broadcasting Company; Several state artist-grants including 15 year artist-grant. *Leisure interests:* Tennis; Swimming; Golf; Snooker. *Current Management:* Tapio Korjus, Rockadillo, Keskutori 7 A 11, 33100 Tampere, Finland. *Address:* Pisanniitty 4 B 14, 02280 Espoo, Finland.

POHJOLA Mika (Antero); b. 1 Dec. 1971, Helsinki, Finland. Musician (Jazz Piano); Composer. *Education:* Classical Piano Degree, Vantaa Conservatory, 1987; Jazz Ed Degree, Swedish Royal Academy, 1992; BM, Berklee College of Music, 1994. *Career:* Tours of Europe, USA, Canada and Japan, 1993–; Performances in major New York clubs, 1995–; Blue Note debut, 1996; Radio Feature, Jazz Matazz, BBC World Service; TV appearances in Finland, Sweden, Estonia, UK, USA, Canada, Ukraine and Japan. *Compositions:* All original music on own releases. *Recordings:* Myths and Beliefs, 1996; On the Move, 1997; Announcement, 1998; Sound of Village, 1999; Live at the Blue Note, 1999; Hur man räddar kärleken and annat, 1999. *Honours:* The Downbeat Magazine Award, 1994; American-Scandinavian Society Award, 1996; Swedish Cultural Endowment, 1998. *Memberships:* STIM, Sweden; TEOSTO, Finland. *Leisure interests:* Recording; Engineering; Cycling. *Current Management:* MikaMusik. *Address:* 333 E 14th St, Ninth Floor, New York, NY 10003, USA.

POINTER Anita; b. 23 Jan. 1948, East Oakland, California, USA. Singer. *Career:* Singer, Pointers (with sisters), San Francisco, 1969–71; Founded as session singers with Boz Scaggs, Elvin Bishop, Taj Mahal, Dave Mason; Member, US female vocal quartet The Pointer Sisters, 1972–78; Continued as trio, 1978–; Concerts include: Midem Festival, 1974, 1993; Grand Ole Opry, 1974; Television includes: 25th Anniversary of American Bandstand, 1977; Welcome Home America! (Gulf forces tribute), 1991. *Recordings:* Best of Elvin Bishop: Tulsa Shuffle, 1969; The Pointer Sisters, 1973; Live At The Opera House, 1974; Steppin', 1975; Best Of, 1976; Having A Party, 1978; Energy, 1979; Priority, 1979; Special Things, 1980; Black and White, 1981; Jump – The Best Of, 1989; Right Rhythm, 1990; Only Sisters Can Do That, 1993; Solo album: Love For What It Is, 1987; Singles: Yes We Can Can, 1973; Fairytale, 1974; How Long, 1975; Fire, 1979; He's So Shy, 1980; Slow Hand, 1981; I'm So Excited, 1982; Automatic, 1984; Jump (For My Love), 1984; Neutron Dance (used in film Beverly Hills Cop), 1985; Dare Me, 1985; Be There (used in film Beverly Hills Cop II), 1987; Solo: Duet with Earl Thomas Conley: Too Many Times, 1986; Recordings with other artists include: Rockets; Ron Wood, Kenny Loggins; Earl Thomas Conley; Working Girl; Taj Mahal; Contributions to: A Very Special Christmas, 1987; Rock Rhythm and Blues, 1989; Am I Cool Or What?, 1991; Charity singles: We

Are The World, 1984; Voices That Care, 1991. *Honours:* Grammy Awards: Best Country Vocal Performance, 1974; Best Performance By Group, Best Vocal Arrangement, 1985; Billboard Awards: Top Dance Single and Album, 1984; American Music Awards: Favourite Soul/R & B Band, 1985; Favourite Soul/ R & B Video, 1985, 1986. *Address:* c/o The Sterling/ Winters Co, Suite 1640, 1900 Ave of the Stars, Los Angeles, CA 90067, USA.

POINTER June; b. 30 Nov. 1953, East Oakland, California, USA. Singer. *Career:* Singer, Pointers (with sisters), San Francisco, 1969–71; Recorded as session vocalists for Boz Scaggs; Taj Mahal; Dave Mason; Elvin Bishop; Kenny Loggins; Ray Charles, Bruce Willis; Robert Foreman; Member, US female vocal quartet The Pointer Sisters, 1972–78; Continued as trio, 1978–; Concerts include: Midem Festival, 1974, 1993; Television includes: 25th Anniversary of American Bandstand, 1977; Welcome Home America! (Gulf forces tribute), 1991. *Recordings:* Albums: The Pointer Sisters, 1973; Live At The Opera House, 1974; Steppin', 1975; Best Of, 1976; Having A Party, 1978; Energy, 1979; Priority, 1979; Special Things, 1980; Black and White, 1981; Greatest Hits, 1982; So Excited, 1982; Break Out, 1984; Contact, 1985; Hot Together, 1986; Serious Slammin', 1988; Jump – The Best Of, 1989; Right Rhythm, 1990; Only Sisters Can Do That, 1993; Great R & B Female Groups, 1998; Solo album: Baby Sitter, 1983; Singles: with the Pointer Sisters: Yes We Can, 1973; Fairytale, 1974; How Long, 1975; Fire, 1979; Jump (For My Love), 1984; Neutron Dance (used in film Beverly Hills Cop), 1985; Dare Me, 1985; Be There (used in film Beverly Cop II), 1987; Contributions to: A Very Special Christmas, 1987; Rock Rhythm and Blues, 1989; Am I Cool Or What?, 1991; Charity singles: We Are The World, 1984; Voices That Care, 1991. *Honours:* Grammy Awards: Best Country Vocal Performance, 1974; Best Performance by Group, Best Vocal Arrangement, 1985; Billboard Awards: Top Dance Single and Album, 1984; American Music Awards: Favourite Soul/R & B Band, 1985; Favourite Soul/R & B Video, 1985, 1986. *Address:* c/o The Sterling/ Winters Co, Suite 1640, 1900 Avenue of the Stars, Los Angeles, CA 90067, USA.

POINTER Ruth; b. 19 March 1946, Oakland, California, USA. Singer. m. Michael Sayles, 8 Sept. 1990. *Career:* Member, US female vocal quartet The Pointer Sisters, 1972–78; Continued as trio, 1978–; Recorded as a session vocalist for Bill Wyman, Oliver and Company, Rockets, Kenny Loggins, Iron Eagle 2; Celine Dion; Taj Mahal; Concerts include: Midem Festival, 1974, 1993; Grand Ole Opry, 1974; Television includes: 25th Anniversary of American Bandstand, 1977; Welcome Home America! (Gulf forces tribute), 1991. *Recordings:* Albums: The Pointer Sisters, 1973; Live At The Opera House, 1974; Steppin', 1975; Best Of, 1976; Having A Party, 1978; Energy, 1979; Priority, 1979; Special Things, 1980; Black and White, 1981; Greatest Hits, 1982; So Excited, 1982; Break Out, 1984; Contact, 1985; Hot Together, 1986; Serious Slammin', 1988; Jump – The Best Of, 1989; Right Rhythm, 1990; Only Sisters Can Do That, 1993; Great R & B Female Groups: The 70's, 1998; Hit singles: Yes We Can, 1973; Fairytale, 1974; How Long, 1975; Fire, 1979; He's So Shy, 1980; Slow Hand, 1981; I'm So Excited, 1982; Automatic, 1984; Jump (For My Love), 1984; Neutron Dance (used in film Beverly Hills Cop), 1985; Dare Me, 1985; Be There (used in Beverly Cop II), 1987; Contributor: A Very Special Christmas, 1987; Rock Rhythm and Blues, 1989; Am I Cool Or What?, 1991; Charity singles: We Are The World, 1984; Voices That Care, 1991. *Honours:* Grammy Awards: Best Country Vocal Performance, 1974; Best Performance By Group, Best Vocal Arrangement, 1985; Billboard Awards: Top Dance Single and Album, 1984; American Music Awards: Favourite Soul/R & B Band, 1985; Favourite Soul/R & B Video, 1985, 1986. *Address:* c/o The Sterling/Winters Co, Suite 1640, 1900 Avenue of the Stars, Los Angeles, CA 90067, USA.

POINTON Mike; b. 25 April 1941, London, England. Musician; Vocalist; Writer; Broadcaster. *Education:* Elmwood School and Rose Bruford College of Speech and Drama, 1953–57. *Musical Education:* Private Piano Lessons; Self-taught Trombone. *Career:* Founded own band, 1950s; Worked with many European New Orleans style groups and American jazzmen and toured many countries; Documentaries for BBC Radio, including Swingtime For Hitler, 1987, Bunk and Bill, 1992, Preservation Hall, 1998; Up A Lazy River, with George Melly, 1998; Echoes of Harlem, with George Melly, 1999. *Recordings:* Barry Martyn's Band, 1961; Mezz Mezzrow/Cotton City Jazz Band, 1964; Young Olympia Brass Band, 1965; Eagle Brass Band, 1966; European Classic Jazz Band, 1983; British All-Stars, 1993; With Apex Jazzband of Northern Ireland, 1997; With Sammy Rimington and John Petters All Stars, 1999. *Membership:* Musicians' Union. *Leisure interests:* Films; Theatre; Literature; Music. *Address:* 11 Kings Court, Kings Rd, Wimbledon, London SW19 8QP, England.

POLAND Chris; b. Dunkirk, New York, USA. Rock Musician (guitar, bass). *Career:* World tours as member of Megadeth; Tours of USA, Mexico, and Canada as member of Circle Jerks; World tour as member of Damn The Machine; Also worked with Ice T and Industrial Light and Sound. *Recordings:* Killing Is My Business..., Megadeth; Peace Sells But Who's Buying?, Megadeth; Return To Metalopolis, Chris Poland; Damn The

Machine (self-titled); Ice T. *Honours:* Platinum disc, Peace Sells But Who's Buying?; Gold disc, Killing Is My Business. *Memberships:* AFTRA; ASCAP; AFofM. *Leisure interests:* Music; Guitars. *Current Management:* Andy Somers, ICM; Jane Hoffman, Speed of Sound. *Address:* Speed of Sound, 626 Santa Monica Blvd #119, Santa Monica, CA 90401, USA.

POLCER Ed (Edward Joseph); b. 10 Feb. 1937, Paterson, New Jersey, USA. Jazz Musician (cornet); Bandleader. m. Judy Kurtz, 9 May 1976, 3 s., 1 d. *Education:* BSE, Engineering, Princeton University. *Musical Education:* Professor James V Dittamo, Prospect Park, New Jersey. *Career:* Cornettist, Stan Rubin's Tigertown Five; concerts include: Carnegie Hall, Europe, Prince Rainier, Grace Kelly wedding, 1955–56; Benny Goodman Sextet, 1973; Solo artist, band leader, international Jazz Festival circuit, 1975–; Owner, manager, bandleader, Eddie Condon's NY, 1975–85; Bandleader, 8 major US tours for Columbia Artists, several European tours, 1992–97; Congressional Ball, White House, by Presidential invitation, 1995; Business ventures: BlewZ Manor Productions, concerts, festivals, recordings. *Recordings:* Albums include: Ed Polcer-Live In Concert, 1988; with Ed Polcer's All Stars: Coast To Coast-Swinging Jazz, 1990; Some Sunny Day, 1991; Barbara Lea, 1992; A Night At Eddie Condon's, 1992; The Magic of Swing Street, 1993; A Salute To Eddie Condon, 1993; Jammin' A La Condon, 1994; At The Ball, with Jim Galloway, CD, 1998. *Publications:* Co-editor, Carmina Princetonia – The Song Book of Princeton University Centennial Edition, 1968. *Membership:* President, International Art of Jazz, 1982–89. *Leisure interests:* Family; Tennis; Marathon walking. *Current Management:* BlewZ Manor Productions Inc.

POLCHENKO Yuri; b. 10 Oct. 1959, Kyiv, Ukraine. Singer; Songwriter; Prod.; Musician (Guitar); Artist; Poet. 1 s. *Education:* Kyiv Polytechinc Institute; Kyiv Jazz School. *Career:* Yunost Night Show, 1990; Promin, 1991; U Ozera, Television Show, 1996–97; Rock Existentia Festival, 1997; Resheto, Television Show, 1998; Music For Night Saxophone, Film, 1997, Ukrainian and Russian Versions Music Video; Chas Ide, 1999; Musical Clip. *Compositions:* Out of The Time, 1997; Chas Ide, 1998; Chekai, 1998. *Recordings:* Celestial Mine; Mist of Dance; Angels Sleep. *Leisure interests:* Painting, Web design. *Address:* V Pika 10, Kv 46, Kyiv 252111, Ukraine.

POLNAREFF Michel; b. 3 July 1944, Nerac, France. Vocalist; Musician (piano, guitar); Songwriter. *Musical Education:* Accomplished piano student during youth. *Career:* Signed to AZ Disques; Chose to work with UK musicians for highly acclaimed first recordings; Signed new US contract with Atlantic, scoring hit single, 1975; Sporadic but always well-received releases/performances since then; Wrote anthem for Modern Pentathlon Tournament of Monaco at request of Monaco's Principality, 2001. *Compositions:* theatre show scores: Rebelais, 1968; La Folie Des Grandeurs, 1971; film scores: L'Indiscret, 1969; Ça N'Arrive Qu'Aux Autres, 1971; Lipstick, 1976; La Vengeance Du Serpent À Plumes, 1985. *Recordings:* Albums include: Love Me Please Love Me, 1966; Le Bal Des Laze, 1968; Polnareff's, 1971; Tibilli, 1974; USA, 1975; Coucou Me Revoilou, 1978; Bulles, 1981; Télé 82, 1982; Incognito, 1985; Kama Sutra, 1990; Live At The Roxy, 1996; Nos Mots D'Amour (compilation), 1999. *E-mail:* michel@polnaweb.com. *Internet:* www.polnaweb.com.

PONCHO Ildefonso; b. 30 Oct. 1954, Laredo, Texas, USA. Congas Vocalist. m. Stella Martinez, 15 July 1973, 2 s. *Musical Education:* Self-taught. *Career:* Klon; Monterey Jazz Festival; Long Beach Jazz Festival; Playboy Jazz Festival; Jazz Central B E T (58); Japan tour; Europe tour. *Recordings:* 13 CDs released. *Publications:* Concord Jazz Picante. *Honours:* Many awards in USA. *Leisure interests:* Fishing; Music. *Current Management:* Berkeley Agency, Poncho Sanchez Latin Jazz Band. *Address:* PO Box 59236 Norwalk, CA 90652, USA.

PONOMAREVA Valentina; b. 10 July 1939, Moscow, Russia. m. Konstantin Gogunskiy, 7 Sept. 1985, 1 s. *Education:* Classical Music Degree, Khabarovsk Institute of Arts, vocal and piano. *Career:* Soloist-Vocalist, Tula Jazz big band conducted by A Kroll, 1967–70; Actress, Singer, Dancer, Moscow Gypsy Theatre Romen, 1971–78; Soloist-vocalist, Trio Romen, 1973–84; International concerts with Trio Romen, 1974–84; Metropolitan Opera, New York, 1976; Midem-76 Festival, Cannes, 1976; Edinburgh International Festival, 1977; National TV and Radio for all channels in major programmes, 1973–; Solo Performer, Russia and international concerts and tours, 1978–; Soviet Avantgarde Jazz Festival in Zurich, 1989; International workshop of free improvised music, Tokyo, Osaka, 1989; Huddersfield Contemporary Music Festival, UK, 1990; Voice Over Festival, London, 1990; International Music Festival in Davos, 1991; Europa Festival Jazz, Italy, 1991; Jazz Summer, 1991; Bolzano, 1991; USA Seven Month Tour: Los Angeles, San Francisco, Chicago, Boston, New York, 1992; Musique Action Nancy, France, 1993; Fringe 99, International Festival, Edinburgh, 1999; Festival des Arts et du Cinema Russe, Cannes, 1999;. *Recordings:* 35 issued recording albums and 25 film sound-tracks include: Solo: Fortune-teller, 1985; Intrusion, 1988; At Parting I Say, 1989; Temptation, 1989; Don't Rise My Recollection, 1990; Terra Incognita, 1990; Live in Japan, 1991; The Romances of the Friends of Mine, 1992; Dve

gitary, 1994; At Parting I Say, 1996; We Strangely Happen to Meet, 1997; Forte, 1999. *Membership:* Performing Right Society. *Current Management:* Valentina Ponomareva Musical Theatre. *Address:* PO Box 45, Moscow 103104, Russia.

PONOMARYOV Olexander; b. 9 Aug. 1973, Khmelnitsky, Ukraine. Singer; Musician (piano). *Musical Education:* Student, Third course, State Music Academy. *Career:* Joint concert with Patricia Kaas; Festivals: All-Ukrainian Chervona Ruta, first grant, 1993; International Festival, Slavonic Bazaar, second grant, 1994. *Recordings:* Album: My Love Has Grey Eyes; Song (same title) nominated for: Best Song of 1994. *Publications:* Articles on music items, Republican press. *Honours:* Grants: All Ukrainian Festival, 1993, International Festival, 1994; Best Newcomer, 1993; Best Ukrainian Singer in Popular Music, 1993–94. *Leisure interests:* Dogs; Tennis. *Current Management:* Oleg Stupka, Kiev, Ukraine. *Address:* Zarichanska Str 14/1a Ap 35, 280017 Ukraine Khmelnitsky, Ukraine.

PONTIEUX Loic; b. 10 June 1967, Harfleur, France. Musician (drums). m. 5 Jan. 1994. *Musical Education:* Conservatoire, 5 years. *Career:* Drummer with many artists including: Michel Jonasz; Claude Nougaro; Didier Lockwood; Birelli Lagrene; Al Jarreau; Pascal Obispo; Veronique Sanson; Francis Cabrel; Mauranne; Maxime Le Forestier and Bernard Cavilliers. *Recordings:* Many with various artists including: Didier Lockwood; Bernard Cavilliers; Claude Nougaro; Birelli Lagrene; Solensi; Jean Michel Kajdan; Pascal Obispo; Idrissa Diop; Jean Jacques Milteau; Babik Reihardt. *Leisure interests:* Cinema; Roller skating; Skin diving; Body building; Tennis. *Address:* 4 bis, rue André Chénier, 92130 Issy les Moulineaux, France.

PONTY Jean-Luc; b. 29 Sept. 1942, Avranches, France. Musician (jazz violin, synthesizers); Composer; Bandleader. m. Claudia Bosco, 6 Sept. 1966, 2 d. *Musical Education:* Premier Prix (First Prize), violin, Conservatoire National de Musique, Paris. *Career:* Classical violinist to 1964; Jazz violinist, Europe, 1964–69; Night clubs, music festivals, in collaboration with the George Duke Trio, USA, 1969; Toured with own group, Europe, 1970–72; Moved to USA, 1973; Pioneer electric violin, jazz innovator; Headlined international concerts with own group, 1975–; Music festivals in US include: Meadowbrook; Artpark; Wolf Trap; in Europe: Montreux; North Sea Festival; Paris Jazz Festival; Guest soloist, Montréal Symphony Orchestra, 1984; Toronto Symphony Orchestra, 1986; New Japan Philharmonic, 1987; New York Radio City Orchestra; 1990; Oklahoma Symphony Orchestra, 1995; Television includes: Soundstage; The Tonight Show; Solid Gold; Rock Concert; Fiddlers Three; Appearances in: Europe; Brazil; Chile; Venezuela. *Recordings:* (own productions) Albums include: Upon The Wings of Music; Aurora; Imaginary Voyage; Enigmatic Ocean; Cosmic Messenger; Jean-Luc Ponty – Live; Civilised Evil; A Taste For Passion; Mystical Adventures; Individual Choice; Open Mind; Fables; The Gift of Time; Storytelling; Tchokola (with African musicians); No Absolute Time; The Rite of Strings (with Stanley Clarke, Al DiMeola); Jean-Luc Ponty with the George Duke Trio; With Kurt Edelhagen and His Orchestra; Live at Chene Park; Sonata Erotica; As; Far from the Beaten Paths; Also recorded with: Elton John; Honky Chateau, 1972; Frank Zappa and the Mothers of Invention, 1973; Mahavishnu Orchestra, 1974–75; Stephane Grapelli, 1996. *Current Management:* (USA) Mario Tirado, APA, 888 Seventh Ave, Suite 602, New York, NY 10106, USA; (Europe) Pascal Bernardin, Encore Productions, 6 rue du Mont Thabor, 75001 Paris, France.

POOK Jocelyn; b. 14 Feb. 1960, Birmingham, England. Musician (viola, violin); Composer. *Education:* Performers Diploma, Guildhall School of Music and Drama; Postgraduate Year, GSMD in Orchestral and Early Music Studies. *Career:* Toured, played live with: The Communards, 1986–89; Lyle Lovett, 1994; The Cranberries, Meatloaf, 1995; Mark Knopfler, 1996; Laurie Anderson, Ryûichi Sakamoto; The Stranglers; Spiritualized, Michael Nyman, 1997; Recordings include: Peter Gabriel; PJ Harvey; Nick Cave; Paul Weller; This Mortal Coil; Eddie Reader; Co-Founder, Electra Strings; Performed in several theatre productions, Derek Jarman's Edward II, Midland Bank advertisement and regularly with Electra Strings on Later with Jools. *Compositions:* Composed extensively for theatre, dance and film; Dance productions include: Strange Fish, 1993; MSM, 1994; DV8 Physical Theatre; Deluge, 1995; Overtigo Danse; Blight; Blow The Wind Southerly, selected for Orange mobile network advertising campaign; Score for Stanley Kubrick's film, Eyes Wide Shut; In A Land of Plenty, BBC TV series, 2001. *Recordings:* Blow the Wind – Pie Jesu, 1996–97; Deluge, 1997; solo Albums: Flood, 1999; Untold Things, 2001. *Honours:* Prix Italia, Strange Fish, film, 1994; Golden Globe, Best Original Score nominee, Eyes Wide Shut, 1999. *Memberships:* Musicians' Union; Equity; PRS; MCPS. *Current Management:* Don Mousseau, 78 Greencroft Gardens, London, NW6 3JQ, England. *Internet:* www.jocelynpook.co.uk.

POOLE Brian; b. 2 Nov. 1941, Barking, Essex, England. Singer. *Career:* Lead singer, Brian Poole and the Tremeloes, 1961–66; Appearances include: Tours with artists including: Roy Orbison; The Searchers; Freddie and The Dreamers; Dusty Springfield; PJ Proby; Gerry and The Pacemakers; NME Poll Winners Concert, Wembley, with the Beatles, Cliff

Richard, 1964; Solo tour, Scandinavia, 1966; Formed new backing group, The Seychelles, 1969; Left music scene, 1969–88; Reunion with the Tremeloes, 1988; Member, The Corporation, with Reg Presley, Mike Pender, 1989; Appeared at Biggest 60's Party in Town, Olympia, London, 1991; Currently lead singer with Electrix. *Recordings:* Albums: Twist and Shout, 1963; Brian Poole and the Tremeloes, 1964; It's About Time, 1965; Brian Poole is here, 1966; Silence is Golden, 1995; Time is on My Side, 1995; Twenty Miles, 1995; Hit singles include: Twist and Shout, 1963; Do You Love Me? (No. 1, UK), 1963; I Can Dance, 1963; Candy Man, 1964; Someone Someone, 1964; Twelve Steps To Love, 1964; The Three Bells, 1965; I Want Candy, 1965; Good Lovin', 1965. *Current Management:* Brian Gannon Management, PO Box 106, Rochdale, Lancashire OL16 4HW, England.

POOLE Chris; b. 23 June 1952, New York, USA. Musician (flutes, tenor saxophone); Composer. *Musical Education:* BA, Berklee College of Music, Boston; First woman to complete Berklee's applied music programme; Studied with Gary Burton; Andy McGee; Joe Viola; James Newton. *Career:* Moved to Denmark from USA, 1975; Performed in jazz and latin bands; Numerous television and radio appearances; Solo performances, 1988–; Writer for theatre, film and modern dance including score for Troll, Norwegian film. *Recordings:* Chris Poole-Solo Flute, 1990; To The Powers That Be, with Pia Rasmussen, 1993; In Search of Solace, 1998. *Honours:* Bay Area Critics Award, Best Musical Score For A Drama, The Lady From The Sea, Berkeley Repertory Theater, USA, 1993. *Memberships:* Danish Musicians' Union; Danish Asscn of Jazz and Rock Composers; Women In Music. *Address:* Tullinsgade 5, St, th., 1618 Copenhagen V, Denmark.

POOLEY Ian, (Ian Pinnekamp, Ansicht); b. Mainz, Germany. Prod.; Remixer; DJ. *Career:* Started producing tracks while still a student in Mainz; First releases were collaborations with DJ Tonka; Has released tracks on: Transmat; Plink Plonk; Definitive; Currently records for V2; Remixed: DJ Sneak; Daft Punk; Yello; Sven Vath; Modjo. *Recordings:* Albums: Meridian, 1998; Since Then, 2000; Singles: Rollerskate Disco, 1995; Chord Memory, 1996; What's Your Number, 1998; Coracao Tambor, 2000; Balmes (A Better Life), 2001. *Address:* c/o V2 Music Ltd, 131–133 Holland Park Ave, London, W11 4UT, England.

POP Iggy, (James Jewel Osterburg); b. 21 April 1947, Ypsilanti, Michigan, USA. Singer; Musician (guitar); Actor. *Education:* University of Michigan. *Career:* Formed Iguanas, High School band, 1962; Prime Movers, 1966; Concerts in Michigan, Detroit and Chicago; Formed The Stooges (originally the Pyschedelic Stooges), 1967; 3 albums, 1969–73; Solo artiste, 1976–; Collaborations with David Bowie, 1972–; Numerous tours and television appearances; Actor, films including: Sid and Nancy; The Color of Money; Hardware; Actor, television series, Miami Vice. *Compositions include:* Co-writer, China Girl, David Bowie. *Recordings:* Albums: with The Stooges: The Stooges, 1969; Jesus Loves The Stooges, 1977; I'm Sick of You, 1977; Solo albums: Fun House, 1970; Raw Power, 1973; Metallic KO, 1976; The Idiot, 1977; Lust For Life, 1977; TV Eye Live, 1978; Kill City, 1978; New Values, 1979; Soldier, 1980; Party, 1981; I'm Sick of You, 1981; Zombie Birdhouse, 1982; I Got The Right, 1983; Blah Blah Blah, 1986; Rubber Legs, 1987; Live At The Whiskey A Go Go, 1988; Death Trip, 1988; Raw Stooges, 1988; Raw Stooges 2, 1988; The Stooges Box Set, 1988; Instinct, 1988; Brick By Brick, 1990; American Caesar, 1994; Naughty Little Doggie, 1996; Heroin Hates You, 1997; King Biscuit Flower Hour, 1997; Your Pretty Face is Going to Hell, 1998; Sister Midnight, 1999; Avenue B, 1999; Iggy Pop, 1999; Hippodrome Paris '77 (live), 1999; Singles: Beside You, 1993; Wild America, 1993; Corruption, 1999; Appears on: Rock at the Edge, 1977; Low, David Bowie, 1977; Trainspotting, 1996; Death in Vegas, Contino Sessions, 1999; Contributor, Red Hot + Blue AIDs charity record. *Publication:* Autobiography, I Need More. *Leisure interests:* Garden; Wife; Pets; Music. *Current Management:* Art Collins Management, PO Box 561, Pine Bush, NY 12566, USA.

PORCARO Steve; b. 2 Sept. 1957, Hartford, Connecticut, USA. Vocalist; Musician (keyboards). *Career:* Support musician to artists including: Jackson Browne; Aretha Franklin; Barbra Streisand; Member, Toto, 1978–87. *Composition:* Commissioned (with Toto) to write theme for Los Angeles Olympic Games, 1984. *Recordings:* Albums: with Toto: Toto, 1979; Hydra, 1979; Turn Back, 1981; Toto IV, 1982; Isolation, 1985; Dune (film soundtrack), 1985; Singles include: Hold The Line, 1979; Georgy Porgy, 1979; 99, 1980; Rosanna, 1982; Make Believe, 1982; Africa (No. 1, USA), 1983; I Won't Hold You Back, 1983; I'll Be Over You, 1986; Without Your Love, 1987; Contributor, We Are The World, USA For Africa charity single, 1985; Backing group, albums by Boz Scaggs: Silk Degrees, 1976; Down Two, 1977; Earth Wind and Fire, Elements of Love, 1990; Celine Dion, Let's Talk About Love, 1997; Ray Charles, Ultimate Hits Selection, 1999; Take Six, Greatest Hits, 1999. *Honours:* Grammy Awards: Record of the Year, Album of the Year, Best Vocal Arrangement, Best Instrumental Arrangement, Best Producer (Toto), Best Engineered Recording, 1983. *Address:* c/o Fitzgerald-Hartley Co, 50 W Main St, Ventura, CA 93001, USA.

PORTASS Nigel John; b. 23 Jan. 1943, Wisbech, Cambridgeshire, England. Musician (keyboards, saxophone, drums); Teacher. m. Dorothy Ann, 17 July 1965, 2 s. *Musical Education:* Member, backing groups for visiting artistes including Chuck Berry; Gene Vincent; Georgie Fame; Van Morrison; Ronnie Scott; Matt Monro; Music tutor and lecturer at Boston College, 1964. *Membership:* Music Teachers Asscn. *Leisure interests:* Travel; Jazz. *Address:* c/o Portass and Carter Music Shop, 26 Bridge Rd, Sutton Bridge, Spalding, Lincolnshire PE12 9UA, England.

PORTEJOIE Philippe René Paul; b. 28 Dec. 1956, Niort, France. Musician (saxophone). m. Frederique Lagarde, 15 Sept. 1990, 1 s. *Musical Education:* First Prize, CNSM, Paris. *Career:* Member duo Portejoie-Lagarde; 2 albums; 100 concerts; France; Italy; Belgium; Norway; Radio: Radio France (France Inter; France Musique); Premier alto saxophone, Big Band with Claude de Bolling. *Recordings:* 20 recordings include Musique Francaise Du XXe Siècle; Stéphane Grappelli; Strictly Classical; Saxomania Et Clark Terry; with Tsf: Ca Va Ca Va, 1996; with Claude Bolling: First Class 1991; Black Brown and Beige, 1993; Victory Concert, 1994; Cinema Dreams, 1996; Drum is a Woman, 1996; Tone Parallel to Harlem, 1999. *Honours:* Premier Prix d'Honneur à l'Unanité (Concours de Musique d'Ensemble de l'UFAM); Meilleur Formation Française (Musique de Chambre de Paris). *Memberships:* Yehudi Menuhin Foundation; Professor, Conservatoire Superieur de Paris (CNR). *Address:* 48 Blvd Mission Marchand, 92400 Courbevoie, France.

PORTELLI Rose-Marie; b. Toulon, France. Singer; Composer. *Musical Education:* British and Irish folk music; American Jazz and Blues; Italian Gospel. *Career:* Appeared at Festival of Traditional Music, Birmingham, England, 1991, Olympia in 1994, Congrés Mondial Acadien, Canada, 1994, Fête de la Musique at American Center in Paris, 1995, Francofolies de la Rochelle, 1995, Disneyland in Paris, 1995; Tour of USA and Canada, 1995. *Recordings:* Marine Marine, 1993. *Publication:* Biography of Canadian singer, Fabienne Thibeau. *Honour:* First Prize for Interpretation, SACEM, 1992. *Membership:* SACEM. *Leisure interests:* Surfing; Swimming; Sailing. *Current Management:* Natasha Grandval, Dolphin Dreams Productions. *Address:* c/o Dolphin Dreams Productions, 98 Blvd Poniatowski, 75012 Paris, France.

PORTEOUS Michael Lindsay; b. 2 Feb. 1948, The Mytertoun Menstrie, Clackmannanshire, Scotland. Ethnomusicologist: Jew's Harp Champion. *Musical Education:* Self-taught in Ethnomusicology, over 30 years playing with Folk Musicians and groups from around the world. *Career:* Several television appearances for various companies, and radio including several of own on folk instruments. *Compositions:* Dunblane, lament cassette; Farewell to Lizziewells. *Recordings:* Recordings with Heritage, 1978–93; Tell Tae Me, 1993; Greentrax, 1988; Tracks on various CD samplers, 1987–97; Cassettes. *Publication:* How to Play and Have Fun with the Jew's-Harp, 1990. *Honours:* Competition Certificates, Traditional Music Song Asscn, Scotland, 1976–97; Edinburgh Folk Festival, One Man Band Champion, 1982, 1983, 1984. *Memberships:* MU; The Traditional Music and Song Asscn of Scotland. *Leisure interest:* Making and playing traditional folk instruments. *Address:* Lindsay Porteous, Tron House, Culross, Fife, KY12 8JG, Scotland.

PORTER Christopher; b. 4 May 1954, Southampton, Hampshire, England. Record Prod. m. Virginia Guarlez, 7 April 1977, 2 d. *Education:* Art College. *Career:* Began as engineer at Good Earth Studios under Tony Visconti, 1980; Early engineering success with Lynx and Junior Giscombe; Long-standing collaboration with George Michael; Co-producer with Tim Simenon for Whycliffe and Zan Jam. *Recordings:* Producer, Engineer: Singles/tracks include: Take That: Back For Good (No. 1, UK), 1995; Babe; George Michael: tracks for Red Hot and Dance; Elton John: Don't Let The Sun Go Down On Me; Some Other World; Aswad: On and On; Don't Turn Around; Beauty's Only Skin Deep; Wham: Wham Rap; Pet Shop Boys: Se A Vida É; Diana Princess of Wales: Tribute; Robbie Nevill: Wot's It to Ya; Music of the Heart; Albums: George Michael: Faith; Listen Without Prejudice, Part 1; Wham!: The Final; Make It Big; Hazel O'Connor, Breaking Glass film soundtrack; Recordings for: Living In A Box; Robbie Nevill; Hall and Oates; Debbie Gibson; Diana Ross; Omar; Breathe; Gary Moore; The Christians; The Alarm; Simple Minds; David Bowie; Dexy's Midnight Runners; Junior Giscombe; Boomtown Rats; Thin Lizzy; A Flock of Seagulls. *Leisure interests:* Flying; Shooting. *Current Management:* The Producers. *Address:* 45–53 Sinclair Rd, London W14 0NS, England.

PORTER Henry L (Dr), (Bishop Henry Porter); b. 2 Jan. 1948, Sarasota, Florida, USA. Vocalist; Musician (piano, organ); Lecturer. m. Cynthia E Porter (Dr), 3 s., 1 d. *Education:* A&M University, Tallahassee, Florida; Yale University, New Haven. *Career:* TV appearances in series Reflection and as host of HLP Love Campaign. *Compositions:* City of Judah; Shout. *Recordings:* I Still Care; Just Good; Keep Making Tracks; The More I Travel This Road; The Love Campaign (TLC). *Memberships:* American Asscn of University Professors; Yale Club; Ivy League Club.

Current Management: Marie Watkins Music, Jewelstone Records, PO Box 49004, Sarasota 34230–6004, USA. *Internet:* www.jewelstonerecords.com.

PORTER K C; b. 27 June 1962, Encino, CA, USA. Record Prod.; Musician (Keyboards). m. Aimée Porter, 1 d. *Education:* Music Study, CSUN University, 5 years. *Career:* Producer for Santana, Ricky Martin, Selena, Patti Labelle, Ednita Nazario, Los Fabulosos Cadillacs. *Compositions:* Donde quiera que estés, 1992; Maria, 1995; La Bomba, 1997; El Farol, 1998. *Recordings for:* Boyz II Men; Toni Braxton; Sting; Bon Jovi; Brian McKnight; Geri Halliwell; Montell Jordan; Lara Fabian; India; Az Yet (Producer of Spanish Crossover Versions). *Honours:* Many Gold/Platinum Awards; ASCAP/SESAC Writer Awards, 1994; Grammy Awards, 1998–99; Gold and Platinum Awards, BMI, Song of The Year, 1997–98. *Memberships:* SAG; AFTRA; ASCAP; BMI; SESAC; NARAS; LARAS. *Leisure interests:* Tennis; Swimming; Family Time. *Current Management:* Tim McDaniels, c/o Lippman Entertainment. *Address:* 22315 Mulholland Hwy, Calabasas, CA 91302, USA.

PORTER Lisa Jean; b. 4 June 1960, New Orleans, LA, USA. *Education:* Cornish Music Institute. *Career:* TV commercials; Opening act on major stages for nationals including: BB King, Kenny G, Elvin Bishop; Voice Overs, Radio, locally. *Compositions:* CD – Rollercoaster; Land of Lie and Learn and Luv Ya, 2 song demo. *Recordings:* CD intitled Rollercoaster. *Leisure interests:* Bowling; Swimming. *Current Management:* Transatlantic Management. *Address:* 11522 Northup Way, Bellevue, WA 98004, USA.

PORTNOW Neil; b. New York, New York, USA. *Career:* Professional Musician, played with various bands; Studio Sideman, playing bass and guitar; President, Portnow-Miller Company Inc, own company, 1971; Manager, Talent Acquisition and Development, Screen Gems Publishing Group, 1972; Staff Producer, RCA Records, promoted to Executive Producer, 1977; Senior Vice President, 20th Century Fox Records, 1979; Vice President, Artists and Repertoire, EMI America Records, 1985; Senior Vice President, West Coast Operations for Zomba Group of Companies including: Jive Records; Silvertone Records; Zomba Music Publishing; Zomba Management; Segue Music; Zomba Music Clearance, Music Supervision, Wired, motion picture, 1988; Music Supervisor for Frank Mancuso Jr's production of Permanent Record, Paramount Pictures, 1987. *Memberships:* National Trustee, former National Vice President, Board of Trustees, Recording Academy; former mem. and Treasurer, Board of Governors, Los Angeles Chapter, National Academy of Recording Arts and Sciences; Advisory Board, Songwriters Resources and Services; Team Captain, Los Angeles City of Hope Music Chapter. *Address:* Zomba, 9000 Sunset Blvd #300, Los Angeles, CA 90069 5803, USA.

PORTUONDO Omara; b. Oct. 1930, Havana, Cuba. Vocalist; Dancer. *Career:* Joined her sister Haydee as a cabaret dancer at the Tropicana, 1945; Sang with sister in Loquibambla Swing with Cesar Portillode la Luz, Jose Antonio Mendez and Frank Emilio Flynn; Became known as The Fiancée of Filin (La novia del filin) after the Cuban music form combining bossa nova with American jazz influences known as feeling or filin; Founder member of Cuarteto Las D'Aida, 1952; Sang with Orquesta Aragón, 1970s; Appeared in the Wim Wenders documentary film Buena Vista Social Club; Collaborations: Ry Cooder; Ibrahim Ferrer; Afro-Cuban All-Stars. *Recordings:* recent Albums: Buena Vista Social Club, 1997; Buena Vista Social Club Presents Omara Portuondo, 2000; appears on Buena Vista Social Club Presents Ibrahim Ferrer, 1999; Distinto Diferente (with Afro Cuban All-Stars), 1999. *Address:* c/o World Circuit Ltd, First Floor, Shoreditch Stables, 138 Kingsland Rd, London, E2 8DY, England.

POST Mike; b. San Fernando Valley, California, USA. Composer; Musician (guitar); Prod.; Arranger. *Career:* Founder, Wellingbrook Singers; First Edition; Guitarist with Dick and Dee; Sammy Davis Jr; Dean Martin; Sonny and Cher; Musical Director, Andy Williams Show; Producer, Mac Davis Show. *Compositions:* Music scores and theme music for numerous television shows including: Rockford Files; LA Law; Hill Street Blues; The A-Team; Magnum PI; Doogie Howser, MD; Quantum Leap; Hardcastle and McCormick; Riptide; NYPD Blue; Law and Order; Silk Stalkings; Wiseguy; Hunter; News Radio; The Commish; Blossom; Hooperman; White Shadow; Renegade. *Recordings include:* As producer and/or arranger: Photograph, Mason Williams; Various albums by Ray Charles; Nine To Five, Dolly Parton; I Could've Been A Sailor, Peter Allen; Greatest American Hero, Joey Scarbury (also as musician and writer), 1981; As musician: All I Really Want To Do, Cher, 1965; Sandman, Herb Pedersen, 1977; Compilations: Television Theme Songs, 1982; Music From LA Law and Otherwise. *Honours:* Numerous Grammy Awards for: Rockford Files; LA Law; Hill Street Blues; Greatest American Hero; Murder 1, 1995–6.

POTTER (Allen) Dale; b. 28 April 1929, Puxico, Missouri, USA. Country Musician (fiddle). 1 s., 1 d. *Musical Education:* Few lessons, fiddle, aged 12. *Career:* Radio appearances, Poplar Bluff, Missouri, and Blytheville, Arkansas; Played on Grand Ole Opry, 1948–62; Tours with Carl Smith; Webb Pierce; Cowboy Copas; Red Sovine; George Jones; Roger Miller;

Played on Phillip Morris country Music Show, with Little Jimmy Dickens, George Morgan; Played throughout Eastern, Western and Southern US; Led 5 piece band, Honolulu, Hawaii, 1970s; Now retired. *Compositions:* Fiddlesticks Boogie, 1954; Fiddle Patch, 1954; Arrangements: Faded Love; Maidens Prayer; Orange Blossom Special, 1979–80. *Recordings:* 8 albums; Recorded with Chet Atkins and Country All Stars; Bill Monroe; Ernest Tubb; Hank Williams Sr; Webb Pierce; Red Foley; Carl Smith; Mac Wiseman; Fiddlesticks Boogie and Fiddle Patch, with Chet Atkins and Country All Stars; Everly Brothers; Marty Robbins; Charline Arthur. *Honours:* Award, Grand Ole Opry, for Outstanding Contribution To Country Music; Inducted into Western Swing Society Hall of Fame, 1988. *Memberships:* Musicians' Union; ROPE. *Leisure interests:* Horse riding; Motorcycles. *Address:* PO Box 351, Puxico, MO 63960, USA.

POUGET Nelly; b. 19 May 1955, Dijon, France. Musician (saxophone); Composer. *Education:* Classique Conservatoire; School of Art, Beaune. *Musical Education:* Conservatoire, Dijon. *Career:* Festival de Jazz de Dudelange; AMR Geneve; Festival Frankfurt; Festival du Mans; International tours; Television and radio appereances: FR3 TV Bourgogne Franche Comte; RFI Radio Interview; RTL Luxembourg; Radio Monte Carlo, Interview, Los Angeles Trilogy. *Recordings:* Albums (own compositions): Le Dire, 1991; Le Vivre, 1993; Vidéomusic, Nelly Pouget Quartet Live, 1996; Le Voir, 1997; Fraîcheur Cuivrée, solo record, in CD and Vidéomusic, 1999. *Publications:* Le Monde; The Wire; Liberation. *Honours:* Le Dire, four key Review, Telerama. *Membership:* SACEM France. *Leisure interests:* All Arts; Sculpture; Painting; Cinema; Dance. *Current Management:* Minuit Regards.

POULIOT George Stephen; b. 12 June 1954, North Hollywood, California, USA. Record Prod.; Sound Engineer; Composer. m. Erica Gardner, 7 May 1989. *Education:* Sherwood Oaks College. *Career:* Recording engineer, Steve Pouliot Music, 1979–; Sound engineer for Rita Coolidge and Dwight Yoakam. *Compositions:* Songwriter for: Micky Martin; Billy Burnett. *Recordings:* As engineer: Behind The Mask, Fleetwood Mac, 1990; As producer: Rick Vito, 1991; The Honest, 1991. *Honours:* Grammy, 1978; Gold and Platinum discs. *Membership:* BMI.

POUSSI Moussa; b. 5 May 1962, Niamey, Niger. Singer; Songwriter; Dancer. m. Adama Tahirou, 29 Dec. 1988, 2 s., 3 d. *Musical Education:* Four years musical training as vocalist, arranger, orchestrator, Centre de Formation et de Promotion Musicales, Hadj Taya. *Career:* Solderer; Comic actor; Musician; Began as entertainment singer in night clubs; Became leader of many orchestras in Niamey; Concerts in Nigeria, Ivory Coast, Burkina Faso and Mali; Leader, Le Degara-Band, Niamey. *Compositions:* Over thirty compositions including Adama; Tchirey; Nafissa; Kokaina; Waimo; Sibo; Toro. *Recordings:* Three compilation albums, Vols I, II and III, 1988; Toro, 1991, CD, 1994. *Honour:* First Prize, Concours de Musique Nigerienne Moderne, 1987. *Membership:* Nigerian Asscn of Musicians. *Address:* PO Box 11203, Niamey, CFPM, Niger.

POWELL Claire-Louise; b. Norfolk, England. Singer; Actress; Prod. *Career:* Lead singer, Pentangle; Lead singer, Sugar Mice; Cabaret at La Parisien; Ma Kindley's Musical Extravaganza; Extensive musicals, film, television, radio and opera Don Giovanni; Director, Osiris Productions; Director, Chucklefactory; Production Executive, Sound Pound; Casting Consultant, Good Vibrations. *Recordings:* Cabaret Cage; Poison Dwarf; Sacred Songs of Scotland; Rock Opera 1; Soul Sounds, Mellow Yellow. *Honours:* Le Sarlation, Most Outstanding Female Vocalist, 3 years running. *Leisure interests:* Theatre; Horse riding; Sailing; Tennis. *Current Management:* Bill Richards Personal Management.

POWELL Don; b. 10 Sept. 1950, Bilston, Warwickshire, England. Musician (drums). *Career:* Member, UK rock group Slade (formerly N'Betweens, Ambrose Slade), 1966–; Concerts include: First British tour, 1972; Fanfare For Europe festival, London Palladium, 1973; Great British Music Festival, 1978; Reading Festival, 1980; Film appearance: Flame, 1974. *Recordings:* Albums: Beginnings (as Ambrose Slade), 1969; Play It Loud, 1970; Slade Alive, 1972; Slayed, 1973; Sladest, 1973; Old New Borrowed Blue, 1974; Slade In Flame (soundtrack), 1974; Nobody's Fool, 1976; Slade Alive Vol. 2, 1978; Return To Base, 1979; Slade Smashes, 1980; Till Deaf Do Us Part, 1981; We'll Bring The House Down, 1981; Slade On Stage, 1982; The Amazing Kamikaze Syndrome, 1983; Slade's Greats, 1984; Rogue's Gallery, 1985; Crackers, 1985; You Boyz Make Big Noize, 1987; Wall of Hits, 1991; Keep On Rockin', 1996; Fantastic World of Spaghetti Westerns, 1999; Digital Transfers include: Original Rock and Roll Classics, 1996; Jerry Lee Lewis, Great Balls of Fire, 1997; Jennie C Riley, Harper Valley PTA, 1997; As Producer, Merry Soulful Christmas, 1996; Heartthrob Hits, 1998; UK No. 1 singles: Coz I Luv You, 1971; Take Me Back 'Ome, 1972; Mama Weer All Crazee Now (later recorded by Mama's Boys, Quiet Riot), 1972; Cum On Feel The Noize, 1973; Merry Christmas Everybody, 1973; Other hits: Look Wot You Dun, 1972; Gudbuy T'Jane, 1972; Skweeze Me Pleeze Me, 1973; My Friend Stan, 1973; Everyday, 1974; Bangin' Man, 1974; Far Far Away, 1974; Thanks For

The Memory, 1975; In For A Penny, 1975; We'll Bring The House Down, 1981; My Oh My, 1983; Run Run Away, 1984; All Join Hands, 1984.

POWELL James Michael; b. 25 March 1973, London. Musician (Drummer). *Education:* Tuition from John Parish. *Career:* Numerous Tours with Georgie Fame; Stephen Duffy; Alan Price; Van Morrison; Lloyd Cole; Orchestra for Whistle Down The Wind and Mamma Mia. *Membership:* Musicians Union. *Address:* 4 Thornbury Rd, London SW2 4DH.

POWELL Owen; b. 9 July 1967, Cambridge, England. Musician (Guitar). Member, Catatonia. *Recordings:* Singles: Bleed/Do You Believe In Me, 1996; Mulder and Scully, 1998; Road Rage, 1998; Strange Glue, 1998; Londinium, 1999; Albums: Way Beyond Blue, 1996; The Sublime Magic of Catatonia, 1996; International Velvet, 1998; Equally Cursed and Blessed, 1999.

POWELLS Jimmy; b. 18 March 1947, Arbroath, Scotland. Admin.; Accountant. 2 s. *Career:* Mandolin and guitar player, singer, folk groups: Town Choice; Carterbar; Television appearance: Live French TV with Town Choice; Inventor of Tees-on-Hand golf accessory. *Recording:* Romantic Mandolin/Mandolin Moments, solo mandolin instrumental album. *Honours:* Album of the Week, Great North Radio and Great Yorkshire Radio. *Membership:* Musicians' Union. *Leisure interests:* Inventor of Pro-Tactics Professional Football Coaching Board, and Soccer Logic (football board game). *Address:* 55 Langdale Dr., Cramlington, Northumberland NE23 8EL, England.

POWER Brendan; b. 20 Feb. 1956, Mombasa, Kenya. Musician (chromatic and diatonic harmonica). m. Lorraine Power, 26 June 1991. *Education:* BA, English, Religious Studies; MA, Religious Studies. *Musical Education:* Self-taught. *Career:* Top New Zealand session harmonica player; Came to Britain, 1992; In band for Riverdance; Irish TV series: A River of Sound. *Compositions:* Jig Jazz; The Real Blues Reel. *Recordings:* State of The Harp; Harmonica Nights; Digging In; Harmonica After Hours; New Irish Harmonica; Played on Sting album: Ten Summoners Tales. *Publications:* Harping On, articles on harmonica playing. *Honour:* All-Ireland Champion, 1993. *Membership:* Musicians' Union (UK).

POWER John (Timothy); b. 14 Sept. 1967, Liverpool, England. Singer; Songwriter; Musician (Guitar). m. Belinda Stone, 21 Sept. 1996, 2 c. *Career:* Bassist with the LA's; Singer/Songwriter, Guitarist, Cast. *Compositions:* All tracks on album All Change including Promised Land, Sandstorm, Fine Time, Walk Away. *Recording:* All Change. *Honour:* Nominated, Best Newcomer, Brit Awards, 1995. *Memberships:* PPL; PRS; Musicians' Union. *Leisure interests:* Football (Liverpool FC); Reading. *Current Management:* Rock 'n' Roll Management. *Address:* Studio 2, 108 Prospect Quay Point, London SW18 1PR, England.

POWER Niall; b. 14 Nov. 1957, Ireland. Musician (drums). m. Michelle, 4 Feb. 1991, 1 s. *Musical Education:* Self-taught drums; 3 years music theory in school. *Career:* 20 years, professional drummer with various Irish groups, solo artists; Tours with Bob Geldof and The Vegetarians of Love, 1990–; Hazel O'Connor, live album and tour, 1994; Also: Marianne Faithfull; Johnny Logan; Stepaside. *Recordings:* with Bob Geldof: Les Enfants Touche, 1985; Happy Club, 1994; with Hazel O'Connor: live album, 1994; Various singles, television themes, jingles. *Membership:* Musicians' Union. *Leisure interests:* Swimming; Countryside. *Current Management:* MDO Productions. *Address:* Northwood Lane, Bewdley, Worcestershire DY12 1AS, England.

POWERS Stephen H; b. 22 Aug. 1951, Rockford, Illinois, USA. Record Prod.; Entrepeneur. *Education:* Massachusetts Institute of Technology. *Musical Education:* Private tutors. *Career:* Founder, Manager, Charlotte's Web Performing Arts Center, Rockford, Illinois, 1992–; Founder, President, Mountain Railroad Records Inc, 1974; Producer, over 50 folk, blues, rock, reggae albums; Director of Entertainment, Los Angeles Olympics, 1984; Director, A & R, Capitol Records, Hollywood, 1984–87; Worked with artists including: The Beach Boys; Duran Duran; Duane Eddy; The Eurythmics; Bryan Ferry; Tina Turner; Founder, President, Chameleon Music Group, 1987–92; Co-founder, CEO, Drive Entertainment Inc, 1993–. *Recordings:* Producer, Singer In The Storm, Holly Near; 9 1/2 Weeks (soundtrack); Executive Producer, Mad Max III (soundtrack); The Healer, John Lee Hooker (Grammy Award winner), 1991. *Honours:* Producer of The Year, Wisconsin Music Awards, 1982; Independent Executive of The Year, Los Angles Music Council, 1991. *Membership:* NARAS; National Academy of Songwriters (Board of Directors); Country Music Asscn; NAIRD; NARM. *Leisure interests:* Running marathons; Cycling; Basketball; Gardening; Playing guitar. *Address:* c/o Drive Entertainment Inc, 10351 Santa Monica Blvd, Suite 404, Los Angeles, CA 90025, USA.

POZGAJEC Branko; b. 23 July 1950, Zagreb, Croatia. Vocalist; Musician (flute). m. Margita Pozgajec, 16 April 1983, 1 s., 1 d. *Education:* Graduate, Economics, university. *Musical Education:* High School of Music. *Career:* 29

years, professional singing, playing; 24 years leading Drugi Nacin, famous Croatian rock group; More than 1,800 concerts in Croatia and abroad; Numerous TV shows and radio appearances. *Compositions include:* The Right Words (Prave Rijeci); Dilemmas (Dileme); Again (Opet); Promise Me Springtime (Obecaj Mi Proljece); I'd Like To Get Back (Htio Bih Vratiti). *Recordings:* 5 singles, 4 albums with Drugi Nacin. *Memberships:* Croatian Composers Union; Croatian Artists Union; Croatian Musicians Union (vice president 1998-). *Leisure interests:* Football; Biking; Recreative running.

PRATT Guy Adam; b. 3 Jan. 1962, London, England. Musician (bass guitar); Record Prod.; Songwriter. *Musical Education:* Self-taught. *Career:* Tours and television appearances with: Icehouse; Bryan Ferry; Scritti Politti; Pink Floyd; Coverdale/Page; Womack and Womack; Bobby Womack and Jeff Beck; Currently writing stage musical with Gary Kemp. *Recordings:* with Madonna: Like A Virgin; Hanky Panky; with Robert Palmer: Riptide; Don't Explain; with Bryan Ferry: Bête Noire; Mamounia; with Pink Floyd: The Division Bell; Delicate Sound of Thunder; Pulse; Ain't No Doubt, Jimmy Nail; Storyville, Robbie Robertson; Power Station, Power Station; History, Michael Jackson; The Orb, The Orb; Communion, Debbie Harry; Toy Matinee, Third Matinee; Dream Academy; Junior Reid, Long Road; Last Action Hero; Pink Floyd, Division Bell; Ted Hawkins, Ted Hawkins Story; In Dreams, In Dreams. *Honour:* Ivor Novello Award Nomination, 1993. *Memberships:* PRS; Musicians' Union. *Leisure interests:* Art; Cinema; Sailing. *Current Management:* Paul Toogood. *Address:* Lancaster House, 14–16 St Marks Rd, London W11 1QU, England.

PREISS-HARRIS Patricia Ellen; b. 19 May 1950, New York, USA. Musician (Piano); Composer; Educator. m. William Harlow Harris. *Education:* BA, MA, Harvard University, Cambridge; New England Conservatory, 1970–71; California Institute of The Arts, 1987; Private Studies With Vera Appleton, Charlie Banacos, Dave Holland; Creative Music Studio. *Career:* Pianist Regularly Appearing At Hyam Regency Hotel and Private Functions, 190–99; Appearances At Colleges and Night Clubs Throughout The USA and Europe; Solo and Ensemble Performances; Educator, Private Piano Teacher. *Compositions:* Messages; Invocations; Complete Enlightenment For Chamber Ensemble and Speaker; Dozens of Jazz Tunes; Love Remembered. *Recordings:* Jamaica's Album; Trust In Love; Massachusetts. *Publications:* Frontiers of Improvisation. *Honours:* Music Merit Scholarship, 1985–86; Artists Grantee, Northern Berkshire Council On The Arts, 1983; Performance Grantee, Cambridge Arts Council. *Memberships:* ASCAP; The Schubert Club. *Leisure interests:* Cooking; Cycling.

PRESCOTT Peter James; b. 20 Oct. 1956, Erith, Kent, England. Singer. m. Wendy Patricia Lewsley, 22 April 1978, 2 d. *Musical Education:* Self-taught. *Career:* Singer for 23 years; 6 albums; Further 7 compilation albums; Appearances on 6 television shows in Europe; Several major festivals, Switzerland and Austria. *Recordings:* Album with Forcefield (with Cozy Powell, Neil Murray, Ray Fenwick); 2 albums with Paul Sinden; 3 albums with Swiss band Sergeant; Time Stands Still, album with band Passion Play. *Publications:* Over 70 songs published. *Memberships:* Musicians' Union; PRS; MCPS. *Leisure interests:* Running; Sailing; Reading. *Address:* 157 Bulverhythe Rd, St Leonards on Sea, East Sussex TN38 8AF, England.

PRESENCER Gerard; b. 12 Sept. 1972, London, England. Musician (trumpet, piano); Composer. *Career:* Jazz musician and session player; Played trumpet from age 10, first performing with National Youth Jazz Orchestra, aged 11; Performed and recorded with many jazz artists and ensembles including: Roadside Picnic; Clark Tracey; Pizza Express Modern Jazz Sextet; Charlie Watts Quintet; Dankworth Generation Band; Pete King; Gail Thompson's Gail Force; Stan Tracey; Tina May; Martin Taylor; Tim Garland; Ian Barnes; Don Weller; Made a number of solo albums and led own Quartet; Regular session work, both as an individual and as a member of the Horny Horns (with Denis Rollins and Michael Smith); Appearances on a wide range of artists' recordings including: The Brand New Heavies; Tina Turner; Tindersticks; Gabrielle; Beverley Knight; Incognito; Joni Mitchell. *Recordings:* Albums: Platypus, 1998; The Optimist, 2000; Dreams (with Tony Coe), 2001; features on: Brand New Heavies albums: The Brand New Heavies, 1990; Brother Sister, 1994; Shelter, 1997; Alec and John Dankworth Generation Band albums: Nebuchadnezzar, 1994; Rhythm Changes, 1995; Martin Taylor albums: Years Apart (Martin Taylor's Spirit of Django), 1996; Gold, 1997; Celebrating Grapelli, 1998; Tim Garland albums: Enter The Fire, 1997; Made By Walking, 2000; Pete King Quartet albums: Speed Trap, 1996; Lush Life, 1999; From One Charlie, Charlie Watts, 1991; Hand On The Torch, US3, 1993; Fun, Tina May, 1993; Live At The QEH, Stan Tracey, 1994; 100 Degrees and Rising, Incognito, 1995; For Heaven's Sake, New Stan Tracey Quartet, 1996; Wildest Dreams, Tina Turner, 1996; Young Mind – Old Hands, Alan Barnes and Brian Lemon, 1997; 10, Wet Wet Wet, 1997; Curtains, Tindersticks, 1997; A Dotty Blues, Alan Barnes, 1998; Prodigal Sista, Beverley Knight, 1998; Peasants Pigs and Astronauts, Kula

Shaker, 1999; Rise, Gabrielle, 2000; Still, Field of Blue, 2000; Both Sides Now, Joni Mitchell, 2000.

PRESLEY Reg, (Reginald Ball); b. 12 June 1943, Andover, Hampshire, England. Vocalist; Songwriter. *Career:* Lead singer, The Troggs (formerly The Troglodytes), 1964; Tours, concerts include: Star Scene 66, with Walker Brothers, Dave Dee Dozy Beaky Mick and Tich, 1966; Regular live work, US, UK; Concert for Hillsborough soccer disaster fund, Sheffield, 1989. *Compositions include:* I Can't Control Myself; With A Girl Like You; Give It To Me. *Recordings:* Albums: From Nowhere... The Troggs, 1966; Trogglodynamite, 1967; Best of The Troggs, 1967; Love Is All Around, 1968; The Troggs Tapes, 1972; Vintage Years, 1976; Live At Max's Kansas City, 1980; Athens Andover, 1991; Archeology (1966–76), 1992; Best of the Troggs, 1994; Athens, Georgia and Beyond, 1996; Singles include: Wild Thing (No. 1, USA) (later used for Lion Bar commercial; ITV show Gladiators; theme for film Major League), 1966; With A Girl Like You, 1966; I Can't Control Myself, 1966; Any Way That You Want Me, 1967; Give It To Me, 1967; Night of The Long Grass, 1967; Hi Hi Hazel, 1967; Love Is All Around (No. 1 hit for Wet Wet Wet, used in film 4 Weddings and A Funeral, 1994), 1967; Little Girl, 1968. *Current Management:* Stan Green Management, PO Box 4, Dartmouth, Devon TQ6 0YD, England.

PRESTON Billy; b. 9 Sept. 1946, Houston, Texas, USA. Musician (keyboards); Vocalist. *Career:* Solo singer, keyboard player, 1962–; Keyboard player, Plastic Ono Band (with John Lennon), 1969–71; Backing musician for numerous artists including: The Beatles; Ray Charles; Little Richard; Aretha Franklin; Sam Cooke; Mahalia Jackson; Martha Reeves; Luther Vandross; Stephen Stills; George Harrison; Ringo Starr; The Crusaders; Delaney and Bonnie. *Recordings:* Singles include: That's The Way (God Planned It), 1969; Will It Go Round In Circles, 1973; Nothing For Nothing, 1974; with The Beatles: Get Back, 1969; Let It Be, 1970; Solo Albums include: Whole New Thing, 1977; Behold, 1979; Fastbreak, 1979; Late At Night, 1979; Billy and Syreeta, 1980; The Way I Am, 1981; Universal Love, 1980; Pressin' On, 1982; The Best of Billy Preston, 1988; Minister of Music, 1995; Words and Music, 1996; Universal Love, 1997; Featured on other albums including: No Reason To Cry, Eric Clapton; Mad Dogs and Englishmen, Joe Cocker; Blood On The Tracks, Bob Dylan; Beat and Soul, Everly Brothers; I Heard That!, Quincy Jones; Sometime In New York City, John Lennon and Yoko Ono; Exile on Main Street, Rolling Stones; Songs from a Parent to a Child, Art Garfunkel. *Address:* c/o Embassy Artists/Full Circle Entertainment, 23500 Michigan Ave, Dearborn, MI 48124, USA.

PRICE Adrian; b. 11 March 1967, Colchester, Essex, England. Musician (drums). m. Joanna Snelling, 17 June 1995. *Musical Education:* Trinity College of Music, London. *Career:* Drummer, Scissormen; Live concerts, UK, Europe; Singles promoted on BBC Radio 1, Greater London Radio (GLR); German, French, Eastern European radio; Videos shown on British television and MTV. *Recordings:* Single: Burst/Sever, Scissormen; Glee (EP), Scissormen; Album: Mumbo Jumbo, Scissormen. *Membership:* Musicians' Union; PRS. *Leisure interests:* Travel; Literature; Watersports. *Current Management:* Diversity, 34B Haven Green, London W5 2NX. *Address:* c/o Welwyn House, 28 Wash Lane, Clacton, Essex CO15 1DB, England.

PRICE Alan; b. Fatfield, County Durham, England. *Career:* Formed Alan Price Combo, 1958; Formed the Animals, 1963; Left the Animals, 1965; Formed Alan Price Set, 1965; Formed Alan Price and Friends, 1968–69; Teamed up with Georgie Fame, many television appearances, 1971–74; Acted in Alfie Darling, 1975; 2 British tours, 1976; Director, Fulham Football Club, 1978; British tour, 1979; Series of shows, BBC2, 1980; Formed own record label Key Records, 1981; Appeared in Andy Capp, Manchester, London, 1982; Reformed Animals, 1983; Tour: Canada; USA; Hawaii; Japan; France; UK; 2 concerts, Royal Albert Hall; Wembley, with The Police, New Year's Eve, 1983; 21st Anniversary Tour, 1986; Travelling Man Tour, 1987; Liberty Tour, 1990–91; Greatest Hits Tour, 1992–93; Current band, Alan Price and the Electric Blues Company. *Compositions:* include: The House That Jack Built; Jarrow Song; Just For You; Composer, film scores, theatre music, and commercials; Film scores include: O Lucky Man, 1973; The Plague Dogs, 1982; Britannia Hospital, 1982; Whales of August, 1988; Theatre music: Home, 1970; Early Days, 1980; Musical: Andy Capp, 1982; Television appearances: Turtles' Progress; World's End; Fame Is The Spur; A Night On The Tyne; The Chalk Face. *Recordings:* Hit singles include: with The Animals: House of The Rising Sun, 1964; Don't Let Me Be Misunderstood; Gotta Get Out of This Place; with Alan Price Set: I Put A Spell On You; Hi-Lili Hi-Lo; The House That Jack Built; Don't Stop The Carnival; Simon Smith and His Amazing Dancing Bear; Jarrow Song; Goodnight Irene; Baby of Mine; Just For You; Albums: Metropolitan Man; Performing Price; Shouts Across The Street; Travelling Man; Liberty; Covers; A Gigster's Life For Me. *Honours include:* BAFTA Award, 1973; Academy Award nomination, 1973; Inducted into American Rock and Roll Hall of Fame, 1994. *Current Management:* Cromwell Management, 4–5 High St, Huntingdon, Cambs PE18 6TE, England.

PRICE James; b. 20 Nov. 1959, Copenhagen, Denmark. Composer; Orchestrator; Conductor. m. Kirsten, 14 Nov. 1992, 1 s. *Musical Education:* Composition, Royal Danish Academy of Music, 1979–84. *Career:* Debut, 1979; Musical Director, Arranger and Pianist; Revues, Vaudevilles, Musicals including Nitouche, Sound of Music, HMS Pinafore, Annie Get Your Gun, Cabaret, Annie; Host in television show; Around a Piano; Compositions for theatre, radio, television, film. *Compositions:* Ved Frokosten (Opera-Monologue, Royal Theatre, 1983); Underscore for TV Serials: Two People in Love; Karrusel; Musicals: Tordenskiold; Livsens Ondskab. *Recording:* Tordenskiold, 1994. *Honours:* Wilhelm Hansens Grant, 1992; Revue Composer of the Year, 1983, 1996. *Memberships:* Danish Songwriters' Guild; Danish Conductors' Society. *Leisure interests:* Cooking; Golf; Fishing. *Current Management:* Nordiska Strakosch Teater-Förlaget, Gothersgade 11, 4 1123 KBH Copenhagen K, Denmark.

PRICE Kelly; b. Queens, New York, USA. Vocalist. *Career:* Received musical foundation in church; Began as backing vocalist and moved into vocal arranging and writing; Signed deal as an artist in own right with Island Black Music, 1997–; Collaborations: Puff Daddy; Faith Evans; Whitney Houston; Brian McKnight. *Recordings:* Albums: Soul of a Woman, 1997; Mirror Mirror, 2000; One Family, 2001; Singles: Friend of Mine, 1997; Secret Love, 1999; You Should've Told Me, Love Sets You Free, 2000. *Honours:* Grammy Award, Best Female R & B Vocal Performance nominee, 2001. *Address:* c/o Island/Def Jam, 825 Eighth Ave, New York, USA.

PRICE Mark; b. 10 Aug. 1959, Nelson, Lancashire, England. Musician (drums); Writer; Programmer. m. Lise Regan, 26 Jan. 1989, 1 s. *Education:* BA Hons, Graphic Design. *Musical Education:* Self-taught. *Career:* Producer/Programmer; Nik Kershaw, 3 world tours; Numerous television appearances and Live Aid; Bryan Ferry; All About Eve: 4 albums and tours; The Cure: album tracks; Julianne Regan: album; Peter Murphy: American tours; Joined Del Amitri, 1997. *Compositions:* Co-writer, musician, 4 albums: All About Eve; Co-writer album: Never Swallow Stars; Jingles and commercials. *Recordings:* All About Eve albums: All About Eve; Scarlet and Other Stories; Touched By Jesus; Ultraviolet; Appears on: Amy Grant, Amy Grant, 1977; Tin Huey, Contents Dislodged During Shipment, 1979; Feelabeelia, East to West, 1985; Archers of Loaf, Icky Mettle, 1994; Cure, Wide Mood Swings, 1996; Pere Ubu Datapanik in the Year Zero, 1996; Del Amitri, Hatful of Rain, 1999. *Memberships:* Musicians' Union; PRS. *Leisure interest:* Football. *Current Management:* Lise.

PRICE P J; b. 8 July 1964, Houston, Texas, USA. Singer; Songwriter; Musician (guitar, keyboards). 2 s. *Career:* Various radio releases; Television appearances; Solo artiste on Entertainment Unlimited; Owner, Priceless Records; Owner, Taste of Texas Music. *Recordings:* Album: P J Price, 1994; Singles: Runnin' On Love; What's A Heart Like Yours. *Honours:* Star of Tomorrow, Airplay International, 1993–94; Best Female Indie and Album of The Year, World Country Music Network, 1994; No. 1, GSCMA European Chart, 1995. *Memberships:* GSCMA; NCMO. *Leisure interests:* Fishing; Photography; Tennis; Writing. *Current Management:* Priceless Promotions. *Address:* 111 Pine Valley, Huntsville, TX 77340, USA.

PRICE Ray Noble; b. 12 Jan. 1926, Perryville, Texas, USA. Country Singer; Musician (guitar). *Career:* Appeared as the Cherokee Cowboy, local radio station; Joined the Big D Jamboree, 1949; Member, Grand Ole Opry; Formed own band, The Cherokee Cowboys; Toured extensively, appeared on all major network radio and television shows; Appeared with artists including, Oscar Peterson, Barbara Mandrell, Patsy Cline, Kris Kristofferson; Hank Williams; Semi-retired, 1973–78; Returned to recording until 1980s; Film appearance, Honkytonk Man. *Recordings:* Over 100 hit singles; US Country No. 1 hits include: Crazy Arms; My Shoes Keep Walking Back To You; For The Good Times; Release Me (later recorded by Englebert Humperdinck); Other hits: Talk To Your Heart; Don't Let The Stars Get In Your Eyes; Faded Love (duet with Willie Nelson); Numerous albums include: Heart Songs, 1957; Faith, 1960; Night Life, 1964; Born To Lose, 1967; For The Good Times, 1970; This Time Lord, 1974; Help Me, 1977; San Antonio Rose (with Willie Nelson), 1980; Ray Price, 1981; Town and Country, 1981; Tribute to Willie and Kris, 1981; Diamonds In The Stars, 1981; Loving You, 1982; Somewhere In Texas, 1982; Master of The Art, 1983; Portrait of a Singer, 1985; Welcome To The Country, 1985; A Revival of Old Time Singing, 1987; The Heart of Country Music, 1987; Just Enough Love, 1988; Sometimes A Rose, 1992; Memories That Last (with Faron Young), 1992; The Old Rugged Cross, 1993; Christmas Gift for You, 1993; Release Me, 1995; Sings a tribute to the Great Bob Wills, 1996 Various compilations. *Honour:* Country Music Hall of Fame, 1996. *Current Management:* James R Doran, Original Artists Agency. *Address:* 1031 E Battlefield, Springfield, MO 65807, USA.

PRICE Rick; Singer; Songwriter. *Recordings:* Heaven Knows, 1992; Tambourine Mountain, 1995; Another Place, album, 1999. *Honours:* Apra Award, Song of Year, Heaven Knows, 1992; Australian Music Awards, Song of Year, Walk Away Renee, 1993; Album of Year, Heaven Knows, 1993;

Advance Australia Foundation, 1993; Australia Export Award, 1993; Singapore Music Award, Song of Year, Heaven Knows, 1993. *Address:* c/o RCM International, Lennox House, 229 Lennox St, Richmond, Victoria 3121, Australia.

PRIDE Charley Frank; b. 18 March 1938, Sledge, Mississippi, USA. Musician (guitar); Singer. *Career:* Former baseball player; Recording artiste, 1965–; First appeared at Grand Ole Opry, 1967. *Recordings:* 29 US Country No. 1 hits; Singles: The Snakes Crawl At Night; Just Between You and Me; Is Anybody Goin' To San Antone?; Crystal Chandelier; Kiss An Angel Good Mornin'; Albums include: Country Charley Pride, 1966; Songs of Pride… Charley That Is, 1968; I'm Just Me, 1971; Pride of America, 1974; Charley, 1975; The Happiness of Having You, 1975; Sunday Morning With Charley Pride, 1976; She's Just An Old Love Turned Memory, 1977; Someone Loves You Honey, 1978; Burgers and Fries, 1978; You're My Jamaica, 1979; There's A Little Bit of Hank In Me, 1980; Roll On Mississippi, 1981; Charley Sings Everybody's Choice, 1982; Live, 1982; Night Games, 1983; The Power of Love, 1984; After All This Time, 1987; I'm Gonna Love Her On The Radio, 1988; In Person (Special Music), 1989; Moody Woman, 1989; Amy's Eyes, 1990; Classics With Pride, 1991; My Six Latest and Six Greatest, 1994; Branson City Limits (live), 1998; Various compilations include: 36 All Time Greatest Hits, 1996; The Essential Charley Pride, 1997; 30 Years of Pride, 1999; Special Collectors Edition, 3 Vols, 1999. *Honours include:* Grammy, Best Country Record (Male), Just Between You and Me. *Current Management:* Cecca Productions Inc, 3198 Royal Lane #200, Dallas, TX 75229, USA.

PRIEST Mathew; b. 3 April 1970, Birmingham, England. Musician (Drums). *Career:* Formed Dodgy with Nigel Clarke (left band, 1998); Joined by Andy Miller; Frequent live shows and festival appearances; Formed own record label, Bostin, 1991; Signed to A & M records, 1992. *Recordings:* Singles: Staying Out For The Summer, 1994; In A Room, 1996; Good Enough, 1996; Found You, 1997; If You're Thinking of Me, 1998; Every Single Day, 1998; Albums: The Dodgy Album, 1993; Homegrown, 1994; Free Peace Sweet, 1996; Ace A's and Killer B's, 1998.

PRIEST Maxi, (Max Elliot); b. London, England. Reggae Singer. *Career:* Former carpenter, builder of sound systems; Tour with UK reggae group Saxon International Sound System; DJ; Solo artiste; Appeared with artists including Aswad, Roberta Flack, Shabba Ranks, Dennis Brown, Pieces of a Dream. *Recordings:* Albums: You're Safe, 1985; Intentions, 1986; Maxi, 1987; Bona Fide, 1990; The Best of Me, 1991; Man with the Fun, 1996; Live in Concert, 1996; CombiNation, 1999; Singles: Strollin' On; In The Springtime; Crazy Love; Some Guys Have All The Luck; Wild World; Close To You; Space in My Heart; Groovin' in the Midnight; Waiting in Vain; Dreaming; One More Chance; That Girl; Watching the World Go By.

PRIESTLEY Brian; b. 10 July 1946, Manchester, England. Writer; Musician. *Education:* BA, Hon, French; Diploma of Education, Leeds University. *Publications:* Mingus, A Critical Biography, 1982; Jazz Piano, 6 Vols, 1983–90; Charlie Parker, 1984; John Coltrane, 1987; Jazz – The Essential Companion (with Ian Carr and Digby Fairweather), 1987; Jazz on Record, A History, 1988; Jazz – The Rough Guide (with Ian Carr and Digby Fairweather), 1995. Contributions to: Reviews and articles; The Gramophone; New Grove Encyclopedia of Jazz; The Cambridge Companion to the Piano; The International Directory of Black Composers; Liner notes for recordings by artist including: Charlie Parker, Charles Mingus, Thelonius Monk, Ben Webster, Duke Ellington, Ella Fitzgerald, Lionel Hampton. Literary Agent: Barbara Levy. *Address:* 120A Farningham Rd, Caterham, Surrey CR3 6LJ, England.

PRIESTLEY Mark; b. 13 July 1963, Kabwe, Zambia. Musician (saxophone, guitar); Singer; Songwriter. 1 s. *Education:* BA; MA. *Musical Education:* Self-taught. *Career:* Various studio session work; Member of Jon Strong Band, From The Underworld, Bassa Bassa, and Dr Fray; Concert appearances include: Glastonbury Festival, 1990; WOMAD Festival, 1990; Edinburgh Fringe Festival, 1991; Live radio sessions on Radio 1. *Recordings:* with Cassandra Complex, The Word and Kay Field; as Producer: Bassa Bassa album; Not In My Back Yard. *Membership:* Musicians' Union. *Current Management:* Bassa Bassa Collective. *Address:* PO Box 10, Christ Church Mount, Leeds LS12 3NH, England.

PRIESTMAN Henry; b. 21 July 1958, Liverpool, England. Vocalist; Songwriter. *Career:* Member, The Christians, 1984–; Appearances include: Liver Aid Ethiopian Famine benefit, Liverpool, 1985; Support to Fleetwood Mac, British tour, 1988; John Lennon Tribute Concert, Merseyside, 1990; Regular UK and European tours. *Compositions:* Songs recorded by the Christians. *Recordings:* Albums: The Christians, 1987; Colour (No. 1, UK), 1990; Happy In Hell, 1992; The Best of The Christians, 1993; with the Yachts: Yachts, 1979; Yachts without Radar, 1989; with Echo and the Bunnymen, Echo and the Bunnymen, 1987; 1988 Summer Olympic Album; with Lightning Seeds, Cloudcuckooland, 1989; with Mike Peters, Feel Free, 1996; Singles include: Forgotten Town, 1987; Hooverville (They Promised Us The World), 1987; When The Fingers Point, 1987; Ideal

World, 1988; Born Again, 1988; Harvest For The World, 1988; Words, 1989; The Bottle, 1993; Contributor, Ferry 'Cross The Mersey, Hillsborough football disaster benefit, 1989. *Current Management:* Eternal Management, 55 Lark Lane, Liverpool L17 8UW, England.

PRIMORAC Vanja; b. 1 Jan. 1966, Zagreb, Croatia. Promoter; Man.; Booking Agent; Prod. 1 s. *Education:* University of Theatre and Film Art, Political Science. *Musical Education:* Mid-school, piano. *Career:* Columnist, musical critic, promotional work, 1985–; Manager, several highly-rated Croatian, Slovenian, American/English artists; producer, manager, first Yugoslavian alternative music festival: Offestum; Work with Siouxie and The Banshees, Laurie Anderson, Tuxedomoon, The Young Gods; First private promoter in ex-Yugoslavia. *Honours:* Japan Award for Festival Design. *Memberships:* Croatian (HGU, HGS). *Leisure interests:* Sea-sports; Yachting; Skiing; Books. *Current Management:* Media Nova Promotions, N L Jain. *Address:* Via Delle Murina 19, 50053 Empoli (Florence), Italy; Podvrsje 2, Zagreb 41000, Croatia.

PRIMROSE Neil; b. 20 Feb. 1972, Scotland. Musician (Drums). *Career:* Member, Travis; Numerous tours and television appearances. *Recordings:* Singles: U16 Girls, 1997; All I Want To Do Is Rock, 1997; Tied to the 90s, 1997; Happy, 1997; More than Us, 1997; Writing to Reach You, 1999; Driftwood, 1999; Why Does It Always Rain on Me?, 1999; Turn, 1999; Albums: Good Feeling, 1997; The Man Who, 1999. *Honours:* Q Magazine Award, Best Single, 1999; Select Magazine Album of the Year, 1999.

PRINCE Anna Lou; Composer; Music Publisher; Recording Artist; Construction Co Exec. 3 c. *Education:* Diploma, Carolina School of Broadcasting, 1966; Zion Diploma, Israel Bible School, Jerusalem, 1970; Diploma, SW Technical College, 1970; MusD, London Institute of Applied Research, 1991; Diplomatic Diploma, Academy Argentina de Diplomacia, 1993. *Career:* Songwriter, Hank Locklin Music Co, Nashville, 1963–70; Entertainer, World's Fair, Knoxville, Tennessee, 1982; Partner, Owner, Prince wholesale Bait Co, Canton, North Carolina, 1976–82; Prince TV Co, 1986–94; Music Publisher, Broadcast Music Inc, Nashville, 1982–; Member, Production Staff, Talent Co-ordinator, TV Series Down Home, Down Under, 1989–90; Over 20 songs recorded; Appeared, Grand Ole Opry; Executive Producer, Host, Music show and TV talk show, Real Heroes of Country Music, 1996–; Candidate for County Commissioner, Macon County, 1984. *Recordings:* I Feel A Cry Coming On, 1965; Best Part of Loving You, 1969; Anna, 1969; I'm In Love with You, 1995; We're Making Memories, 2000. *Honours:* Order of Knight of Templars (Dame); Lofsensic Order (Dame); Maison Internationales des Intellectuals; Hon. Doctorates. *Memberships:* BMI; Nashville Songwriters Asscn; Country Music Asscn; Songwriters Guild of America. *Address:* 313 Gallatin Rd S, Madison, TN 37115, USA. *Internet:* futureheroesofcountrymusic.com.

PRINCE PICHO (Emmanuel Volel); b. 24 April 1942, Port-au-Prince, Haiti. Singer; Actor; Musician (guitar, keyboards). 1 s., 2 d. *Education:* College, Hotel Management. *Musical Education:* Music studies, New-Sewell Music Conservatory, Washington DC. *Career:* Appearances include: Cable TV channel 45; Cable TV channel 33; Annual guest at Marvin Gaye Festival, African festival, Washington DC; Performed at benefit for homeless. *Recordings:* Numerous albums for Henri Debs record company, Guadaloupe, FWI; Also for Marc Recors, New York, USA. *Publications:* Numerous articles, Montgomery Journal, La Nación. *Honours:* Masons of Washington DC Award. *Membership:* New Sewell Music Conservatory. *Leisure interests:* Football; Tae-Kwon-Do; Jogging. *Current Management:* Edwardo Semperegui, Espectaculor Productions.

PRINE John; b. 10 Oct. 1946, Maywood, Illinois, USA. Singer; Songwriter. *Career:* Began writing folk songs as teenager; Regular on Chicago club circuit, 1970; Recording artiste, 1972–; Founder, president, Oh Boy record label, 1980; US tour supporting Bonnie Raitt, 1991; Summer Stage '92 concert, Central Park, New York, 1992; Cambridge Folk Festival, 1992; Cameo film appearance, Falling From Grace, 1992; Appearances with artists including: Steve Goodman, Bonnie Raitt, Nancy Griffith, David Olney, Randy Scruggs. *Compositions include:* Love Is On A Roll, Don Williams (US Country No. 1), 1980. *Recordings:* Singles include: Take A Look At My Heart, 1992; Albums: John Prine, 1972; Diamonds In The Rough, 1972; Sweet Revenge, 1973; Common Sense, 1975; Prime Prine – The Best Of, 1977; Bruised Orange, 1978; Pink Cadillac, 1979; Storm Windows, 1980; Aimless Love, 1984; German Afternoons, 1986; John Prine Live, 1988; The Missing Years, 1991; A John Prine Christmas, 1993; The John Prine Anthology – Great Days, 1993; Lost Dogs and Mixed Blessings, 1995; Live on Tour, 1997; In Spite of Ourselves, 1999. *Honours include:* Grammy Award, Best Contemporary Folk Album, The Missing Years, 1991. *Current Management:* Al Bunetta Management, 33 Music Sq. W, Suite 102A, Nashville, TN 37203, USA.

PRIOR Maddy; b. Blackpool, England. Folk Singer; Songwriter. m. Rick Kemp, 2 c. *Career:* Founder member, lead singer, folk group, Steeleye Span, 1970–; Member, The Carnival Band; Solo artiste, 1978–; Collaborations with Tim Hart, guitarist, and Nick Holland, keyboard player. *Recordings:*

Solo albums: Woman In The Wings, 1978; Changing Winds, 1978; Hooked On Winning, 1982; Going For Glory, 1983; Happy Families, 1991; Sing Lustily and with Good Cheer, 1994; Year, 1994; Hang Up Sorrow and Care, 1996; Flesh and Blood, 1998; All albums recorded by Steeleye Span; 4 albums with Tim Hart; Guest vocalist on numerous albums including: Albion River Hymn March, Albion Band, 1979; Shearwater, Martin Carthy, 1972; Too Old To Rock and Roll, Jethro Tull, 1976; Streets, Ralph McTell, 1975; Incantations, Mike Oldfield, 1978; Silly Sisters, June Tabor, 1976; First Light, Richard and Linda Thompson, 1978; Troubadours of British Folk, 3 Vols, 1995. *Current Management:* Jim McPhee, Acorn Entertainments. *Address:* Winterfold House, 46 Woodfield Rd, Kings Heath, Birmingham B13 9UJ, England.

PRITCHARD Peter Andrew; b. 13 Aug. 1955, London, England. Musician (bass guitar, double bass). m. Chrystella Maria Nicholas, 6 Oct. 1978, 1 s., 1 d. *Musical Education:* Private tuition, Trinity College of Music. *Career:* Member of Flying Saucers with numerous appearances on German, Dutch and British television and radio; Tours with Chuck Berry, Bill Haley, Scotty Moore, D J Fontana, and The Jordonaires; Film, Blue Suede Shoes. *Compositions:* 10 compositions. *Recordings:* Several singles and albums with Flying Saucers; Albums and singles with Avengers; CD with the Jordonaires. *Membership:* Musicians' Union. *Leisure interests:* Football; Art. *Address:* 56 King Edwards Rd, Edmonton, London N9 7RP, England.

PROBY P J, (James Marcus Smith); b. 6 Nov. 1938, Houston, Texas, USA. Singer; Songwriter. *Career:* Founder, The Moondogs, 1958; Work as demo singer, recording under names: Jett Powers, Orville Wood; Appeared on Beatles TV Special, London, 1964; British tours, 1965, 1966; Stage performances include: Catch My Soul (rock version of Othello), West End, 1970; Elvis (musical), 1977; Cabaret circuit and recording career continued to 1991. *Recordings include:* Hold Me, 1964; Together, 1964; Somewhere, 1965; I Apologise, 1965; Let The Water Run Down, 1965; That Means A Lot, 1965; Maria, 1965; You've Come Back, 1966; Niki Hoeky, 1967; Albums include: I Am PJ Proby, 1965; Three week hero, 1969; Elvis, 1978; I am P. J. Proby/P. J. Proby, 1996; Legend, 1997; Heroes, 1998; Phenomenon/Believe It or Not, 1998. *Honour:* Best Musical of the Year, Elvis, 1977.

PROCHAZKA Jiri; b. 23 May 1969, Prague, Czech Republic. Guitar; Keyboards; Drums; Computers; Music Teacher. m. Vladimira Prochazkova, 3 July 1990, 1 d. *Education:* Musical Psychology. *Career:* Tramp Po Cesku 1–8, video; Unlimited Warriors, videogame. *Recording:* Unlimited Warriors, videogame. *Publication:* Unlimited Warriors, videogame. *Leisure interests:* Music; Computers; Swimming; Body building. *Address:* Jiri Prochazka, Olbramovicka 715/2, 142 00, Prague 4, Czech Republic.

PROFESSOR GRIFF, (Richard Griffin); Rapper. *Career:* Member, US rap group Public Enemy, 1984–89; Concerts include: Support to the Beastie Boys, US tour, 1987; Support to LL Cool J, European tour, 1987; Brixton Academy, London, 1990; Solo artiste, 1989-. *Recordings:* Albums: with Public Enemy: Yo! Bum Rush The Show, 1987; It Takes A Nation of Millions To Hold Us Back, 1988; There's a Poison Goin' On, 1999; with Two Live Crew, Back at Your Ass for the Nine-4; Solo albums: Pawns In The Game, 1990; Kao's II Wiz-7-Dome, 1991; Disturb N Tha Peace, 1992; Blood of the Profit, 1998; Singles: Rebel Without A Pause; Bring The Noise; Don't Believe The Hype; Night of The Living Baseheads; Black Steel In The Hour of Chaos; Fight The Power, theme for film Do The Right Thing, 1989; Welcome To The Terrordrome; Jail Sale, 1991; Verdict, 1991; Verbal Intercourse, 1992; Sista Sista, 1992; Ole Bitch U Worryz, 1998.

PROKOP Michal; b. 13 Aug. 1946, Prague, Czech Republic. Singer; Composer; Musician (Guitar, Harmonica). m. Nina, 1972, 1 s., 1 d. *Education:* High School of Economics, 1968; Faculty of Philosophy, Charles University, Prague, 1992. *Career:* Rock Singer, 1967–90; Member of Parliament, 1990–92; Deputy Minister of Culture, 1992–95; Member of Parliament, 1996–98; TV Talk Show Host, I Mean It Well, 1998–; Director, European City of Culture (Prague) initiative, 2000. *Recordings:* Albums: Blues in Soul; Mesto Er; Holubi Dante; Kolej Yesterday; Nic Ve Zlým; Nic v Dobrým; Snad Nam Naše Deti Prominou; Až Si Pro Mne Prijdou; Cerný Ovce (Black Sheep). *Honours:* Melodia Award, Czechoslovakia, 1988; L'Ordre des Arts et des Lettres, France, 1995. *Address:* Na Hanspaulce 3, 160 00 Prague, Czech Republic.

PROPHET Ronnie; b. 26 Dec. 1928, Hawksbury, Ontario, Canada. Entertainer; Musician (guitar); Singer. m. Glory-Anne, 26 April 1986, 2 s. *Career:* Duo with wife, Glory-Anne; Ronnie Prophet World Tour; USO tour, England; Germany; Netherlands; Tours with Kenny Rogers; Johnny Cash; Emmylou Harris; Tammy Wynette; Janie Fricke; Appearances include: Calgary Stampede; Wembley Country Music Festival (7 years); Caesar's Palace, Sands Hotel, Las Vegas; Television appearances include: Johnny Carson Show; Co-host, Canadian Country Music Awards, 1988–90; Host, Rocky Mountain Inn; Host, Grand Ole Country (6 years); Host, Ronnie Prophet Show; Host, Music Hall America; Host, Ronnie Prophet Entertains. *Recordings:* 32 albums; The Phantom; No Holiday In LA; Ronnie Prophet, 1977; I'm Gonna Love Him out of You, 1983; Sure

Thing, 1987. *Honours:* CCMA, 1976, 1980, 1984; Juno Awards, 1977, 1978; TV Country Show of The Year, Canada, 1977–80; Angel Award, St Jude Children's Research Hospital; ASCAP Awards for 3 songs as chart records for more than 10 weeks each. *Memberships:* AFofM; ACTRA; ROPE. *Leisure interests:* Golfing; Fishing; Reading; Films. *Current Management:* Prophet Productions.

PROWSE Ian; b. 10 Jan. 1967, Ellesmere Port, England. Musician; Songwriter. *Career:* Seven full headline tours as lead singer, songwriter with: Pele; Support tours with: Del Amitri and the Pogues; Numerous television and live radio appearances; 3 Radio 1 playlists; Composed all three Pele albums. *Recordings:* Albums: Pele: Fireworks; The Sport of Kings; Alive, Alive-O. *Memberships:* PRS; Musicians' Union. *Leisure interests:* Football; Drinking. *Current Management:* Target Management, London; D L Management, Liverpool. *Address:* 2 Forge Rd, Little Sutton, Wirral, Cheshire L66 3SQ, England.

PRYCE Guto; b. 4 Sept. 1972, Cardiff, Wales. Musician (Bass). *Career:* Member, Super Furry Animals; Early releases on small indie label before obtaining major indie label deal; Numerous tours in the UK and internationally; Many festival appearances. *Recordings:* Singles: Llanfairpwllgwyngyllchwyndrobwl... EP, 1995; Moog Droog EP, 1995; God! Show Me Magic, 1996; If You Don't Want Me To Destroy You, 1996; The Man Don't Give A Fuck, 1996; Hometown Unicorn, 1996; Something 4 The Weekend, 1996; The International Language of Screaming, 1997; Hermann Loves Pauline, 1997; Demons, 1997; Play It Cool, 1997; Ice Hockey Hair, 1998; Albums: Fuzzy Logic, 1996; Radiator, 1997; Guerrilla, 1999.

PRZYGODDA Johannes Pit; b. 2 June 1968, Luthe, Germany. Musician; Composer; Textwriter. *Career:* Some Pieces For Film and Music In Germany, 1980's; Working In Hamburg, With Band, Go Plus, 1990–; Experimental Music, Together With Burkhard Beins, Rudi Mahall, Michal Griener; Making Film Music. *Compositions:* Schwerelos; Definitiv; Song For Brian; Superfreunde. *Recordings:* Go Plus; La Montanara; Largo. *Leisure interest:* Nature. *Current Management:* Kitty Yo, Torstrasse 172, 10115 Berlin. *Address:* Oelmuehle 2, 20357 Hamburg, Germany.

PUEYRREDON César; b. 7 July 1952, Buenos Aires, Argentina. Singer; Composer; Musician (keyboards). m. Cecilia Garcia Laborde, 27 Nov. 1979, 1 s., 1 d. *Education:* University. *Musical Education:* Composition, UCA (Universidad Catolica Argentina). *Career:* Member, group Banana, tours, Argentina, Uruguay, Chile, Paraguay, 1969–84; Tour, Central America, 1977; Solo artiste (as César 'Banana' Pueyrredon), tours, Argentina, Uruguay, Paraguay, Chile, Colombia, 1984–; 12 concerts, Teatro Opera, 1989; Opened for Sting, Uruguay, 1990. *Recordings include:* with Banana: Negra No Te Vayas De Mi Lado, 1971; Conociendote, 1973; Aun Es Tiempo De Soñar, 1979; Solo albums: Asi De Simple, 1984; Solo Un Poco Mas, 1985; Esta En Vivo, 1986; Mas Cerca De La Vida, 1987; Ser Uno Mismo, 1988; Tarde O Temprano, 1990; Zo Anos, 1991; Armonia, 1992; De La Ternura A La Pasión, 1993. *Honour:* 2 nominations, Premio Prensario, Best TV Musical, for Martin Fierro, 1989; Premio, Santa Clara de Asis. *Membership:* SADAIC (composers' society). *Leisure interests:* Golf; Football. *Current Management:* Abraxas Producciones Internacionales.

PULLEN Doug; b. 9 April 1957, Loring, Maine, USA. Pop Music Writer. m. Teresa, 1 s. *Education:* Bachelor in Journalism, Texas Technical University, 1975. *Career:* Journalist, El Paso Times; El Paso Herald and Post; Kalamazoo Gazette; Metro Times, Detroit; Flint Journal; MusicHound, rock, country, blues; R & B album guides. *Membership:* National Music Critics Asscn. *Leisure interests:* Softball; Volleyball; Rotisserie Baseball; Basketball. *Address:* Flint Journal, 200 E First St, Flint, MI 48502, USA.

PULSFORD Nigel; b. 11 April 1965, Newport, Gwent, Wales. Musician (Guitar). *Career:* Former Member, Future Primitive, changed name to Bush; Obtained major US record deal; Numerous US tours and lots of radio play; UK gigs and festival dates. *Recordings:* Singles: Little Things, 1995; Comedown, 1995; Swallowed, 1997; Greedy Fly, 1997; Cold Contagious, 1999; Albums: Sixteen Stone, 1994; Razorblade Suitcase, 1996; Deconstructed, 1997.

PUOLIS Rolandas; b. 20 Nov. 1969, Lithuania. Artist Man.; Broadcaster. *Education:* Vilnius Technical University. *Career:* Lithuanian radio and television DJ, 1987–92; Manager, rock group BIX, 1991-. *Recordings:* Blind Soldiers, Best Record in Lithuania, 1991; Labomba, 1992; Doozgle, Best CD, Lithuania, 1994. *Honours:* Band of The Year, 1991, 1992, 1994. *Leisure interest:* Hunting. *Address:* PO Box 552, 2024 Vilnius, Lithuania.

PURIM Flora; b. 6 March 1942, Rio De Janeiro, Brazil. m. (1), 1 d., (2) Airto Moreira, 19 March 1972, 1 d. *Education:* University of California, Long Beach; Graduate, California State University. *Recordings:* As composer/lyricist with Airto Moreira: Seeds On The Ground, 1970; Natural Feelings, 1969; Free, 1971; Fingers, 1972; Identity, 1975;

Promises of The Sun, 1976; Solo albums: Virgin Land, 1972; Butterfly Dreams, 1973; Stories To Tell, 1974; Open Your Eyes You Can Fly, 1976; 500 Miles High In Montreux, 1976; Encounter, 1977; Nothing Will Be As It Was Tomorrow, 1977; Queen of the Night, 1992; Milestone Memories, 1994; Now Go Ahead and Open Your Eyes, 1994; Speed of Light, 1995; with Chick Corea: Return To Forever, 1972; Light As A Feather, 1973; with Carlos Santana: Welcome, 1973; Borboletta, 1974; with Airto Moreira, Neville Potter: San Francisco River, 1972; with McCoy Tyner: Search for Peace, 1974; with George Duke: Love Reborn, 1973; Feel, 1974; with Airto Moreira: Alue, 1969; with Hermeto Pascoal: We Love, 1970; A Brazilian Love Affair; with Ernie Hood: Mountain Train, 1974; with Duke Pearson: How Insensitive, 1969; It Could Only Happen With You, 1970; with Airto and Deodato: Deodato/Airto In Concert, 1973; That's What She Said, Everyday Every Night, Humble People, 1985; The Magicians; The Sun Is Out, 1987; Producer, with Moreira: I'm Fine How Are You, 1977. *Honours include:* Downbeat Critics Poll, Established Singer, 1974–76, 1978; Record World, Top Female Jazz Artist, 1974, 1976; Cash Box Award, Top New Female Jazz Artist, 1974; 2 Grammy Nominations, Humble People, 1985; The Magicians. *Current Management:* A Train Management, PO Box 29242, Oakland, CA 94604, USA.

Q

Q-TIP (John William Davis), (The Lone Ranger); b. Nov. 20, 1970, Brooklyn, New York City, USA. Rapper. *Career:* Founded A Tribe Called Quest, 1988; Part of the Native Tongues collective with De La Soul and Queen Latifah; Collaborations: Lucy Pearl; Slick Rick; Mos Def; Jay-Z; Janet Jackson; Deee-Lite. *Recordings:* Albums: with A Tribe Called Quest: People's Instinctive Travels and The Paths of Rhythm, 1990; The Low End Theory, 1991; Midnight Marauders, 1993; Beats Rhymes and Life, 1996; The Love Movement, 1998; solo: Amplified, 1999; Singles: with A Tribe Called Quest: Description of a Fool, 1989; Bonita Applebum, 1990; Can I Kick It?, 1990; Scenario, 1992; Award Tour, 1993; 1nce Again, 1996; Find A Way, 1998; Stressed Out, 1998; solo: Vibrant Thing, 1999; Breathe and Stop, 1999. *Address:* c/o Arista Records, Cavendish House, 423 New King's Rd, London, SW6 4RN, England.

QUATRO Suzi, (Susan Kay); b. 3 June 1950, Detroit, Michigan, USA. Vocalist; Songwriter; Musician (bass, drums, piano); Actor; Presenter. m. (1) Len Tuckey; (2) Rainer Haas, 22 Oct. 1992, 1 s., 1 d. *Career:* Over 30 years as entertainer, 1964–; Numerous world-wide concert tours and stage appearances; Various acting, presenting and voiceover work on radio and TV including: Chat show, ITV; Happy Days; Annie Get Your Gun (West End); Author and star of stage musical about Tallulah Bankhead, Tallulah Who; Presenter, Rockin' With Suzi Q, BBC Radio 2, 1998–; Subject of This Is Your Life, 1999. *Recordings:* 16 hit singles include: Can The Can (No. 1, UK), 1973; 48 Crash, 1973; Daytona Demon, 1973; Devil Gate Drive (No. 1, UK), 1974; The Wild One, 1974; If You Can't Give Me Love, 1978; Stumblin' In, with Chris Norman, 1978; She's In Love With You, 1979; Albums include: Suzi Quatro, 1973; Quatro, 1974; Your Mama Won't Like Me, 1975; Aggro Phobia, 1977; If You Knew Suzi, 1978; Suzi and Other 4 Letter Words, 1979; Rock Hard, 1980; Greatest Hits, 1980; Main Attraction, 1982; The Wild One, 1990; Oh Suzi Q, 1990; The Latest and Greatest, 1992; Unreleased Emotion, 1998; The Best of Suzi Quatro, 1998; Original Hits, 2000; Naked Under Leather, 2001. *Honours:* Numerous Best Female Artist Awards, UK, Europe, Australia, Japan. *Leisure interests:* Swimming; Most sports.

QUAYE Finlay; b. 1974, Edinburgh, Scotland. Singer. *Education:* BTEC in Music Production, Manchester. *Career:* Worked with: A Guy Called Gerald; Graham Massey; Rainbow Tribe; Solo artiste, 1996–. *Recordings:* Album: Maverick A Strike, 1997; Singles: Ultra Stimulation (EP), 1997; Sunday Shining (EP), 1997; Even After All, 1997. *Honour:* Brit Award, Best Male Solo Artist, 1998. *Address:* c/o Epic Records, 10 Great Marlborough St, London W1V 2LP, England.

QUEEN LATIFAH (Dana Owens); b. 18 March 1970, East Orange, New Jersey, USA. Rap Vocalist. *Career:* Worked for Burger King; Worked with female rap act Ladies Fresh; Recorded with producers Dady-O, KRS-1, DJ Mark the 45 King and members of De La Soul; Moved to Motown Records; Bagan acting career with film Living Single; Other film appearances include Juice, Jungle Fever and House Party 2; Established own label and management company, Flavor Unit; Guest appearance on Shabba Ranks's single Watcha Gonna Do; Other recording collaborations with De La Soul and Monie Love. *Recordings:* Singles: Wrath of My Madness, 1990; How Do I Love Thee, 1990; Ladies First, 1990; Mama Gave Birth to the Soul Children, 1990; Come Into My House, 1993; U.N.I.T.Y., EP, 1994; Just Another Day, EP, 1994; Mr Big Stuff, 1997; It's Alright, 1997; Albums: All Hail the Queen, 1989; Latifah's Had It Up 2 Here, 1989; Nature of a Sista, 1991; Black Reign, 1993; Queen Latifah and Original Flava Unit, 1996; Order in the Court, 1998.

QUERALT Stephen Paul; b. 4 Feb. 1968, Oxford, England. Musician (bass guitar). 1 s. *Career:* Bass guitarist, rock band Ride; Concerts include: Main support act, Reading Festival, 1992; Television: 3 appearances, Top of The Pops, BBC; Recorded 2 Top 10 albums and 1 Top 20 album. *Recordings:* Albums: with Ride: Nowhere, 1991; Going Blank Again, Ride, 1992; Carnival of Light, Ride, 1994; Live Light, 1995; Tarantula, 1996; Poptopia! 90's Power Pop Classics, 1997; with Sharks Patrol These Waters: Sharks Patrol These Waters, 1995. *Current Management:* Ben Winchester, Primary Talent. *Address:* OMC, Suite 1, 2nd Floor, 65 George St, Oxford OX1 2BE, England.

QUIBEL Robert Henri Maurice; b. 12 Oct. 1930, Le Havre, France. Musician (double bass); Arranger; Dir. m. Madeleine Saumon, 23 March 1955, 1 s., 1 d. *Musical Education:* Petit Séminaire de Rouen. *Career:* Bass player with Berny Bennett; Jacques Helian; Claude Bolling, 1961–63; Backing for various French artistes including: Maurice Fanon; Jacques Martin; Musical director, director of house band on Dimanche-Matin, weekly French TV programme (France 2), 1980–. *Recordings:* The Flight of The Ox-Pecker, Claude Bolling, 1963; Various recordings for children

include: Le Petit Ménestral, Lucien Adès; Various title songs and jingles for Dimanche-Matin. *Honours:* Grand Prix de la Chanson Comique, Les Cuisses de Grenouille by Fernand Raynaud, 1965. *Memberships:* SACEM; SDRM; SACD. *Leisure interests:* Chess; Bridge; Travel. *Address:* 2 rue Ronsard, 95560 Baillet-En-France, France.

QUILLEY Denis Clifford; b. 26 Dec. 1927, Islington, London, England. Actor; Singer. m. Stella Chapman, 27 Aug. 1949, 1 s., 2 d. *Musical Education:* Studied singing with Ernst Urbach. *Career:* Candide, West End Production; The Boys from Syracuse; Privates on Parade, Piccadilly Theatre; La Cage aux Folles, Palladium; Non-musical work includes: Many seasons at National Theatre; Peter Hall season at The Old vic; National Theatre Season; Films: Masada; Evil Under the Sun; Murder on the Orient Express; Privates on Parade. *Recordings:* Grab Me A Gondola; Boys from Syracuse; High Spirits; Mark and Mabel in Concert at Drury Lane; Showboat; Shows Collection; BBC's Tribute to Jerry Herman. *Honour:* SWET Award for Comedy Performance of the Year for Privates on Parade. *Leisure interests:* Walking; Reading; Playing the flute. *Current Management:* Bernard Hunter. *Address:* 22 Willow Rd, Hampstead, London NW3 1TL, England.

QUILLIVIC Jean; b. 10 Jan. 1960, Rabat, Morocco. Composer; Musician (saxophone). m. Josiame Robakowski, 2 s., 2 d. *Education:* BA, Sciences, Brest. *Musical Education:* MA, BA, Musicology, Paris. *Career:* CIM School of Jazz, Paris, 1985; First alto saxophone in Pierre Sellin Big Band, 1985–; Formed group Oxyde de Cuivre, 1987; Formed own group Jean Quillivic Quartet, 1988; Concerts in festivals, summer tours, 1989–. *Recordings:* Prise de Bec, Zap, 1989; La Femme à La Valise, Jean Quillivic Quartet, 1990; En Public Au Fourneau 95, Oxyde de Cuivre, 1995. *Membership:* SACEM. *Current Management:* Promoart. *Address:* B P 27, 29470 Plougastel, Dadulas, France.

QUIN Andrew James; b. 12 Aug. 1960, London, England. Composer; Musician (keyboards, percussion); Music Lecturer. m. Anne Perrett, 20 Aug. 1983, 1 s., 1 d. *Education:* BA Hons Music, Electronics, Keele University, 1982. *Musical Education:* Private. *Career:* 25 albums for Dewolfe, 1984–; Freelance lecturer, Music Technology, universities and conservatories throughout UK; Currently Manchester Metropolitan University; Regular jazz performer in Midlands; Broadcasts in 36 countries, all continents; Television documentary, Quest, 1985. *Recordings:* Albums: Mirage, 1985; The Cutting Edge, 1987; Four Minus One, 1988; The Corporate Net, 1995; Television themes: Something To Treasure, 1988; Central Weekend, 1985; Scandal, 1988; Commercials: Fairy Snow, 1989; Canderel, 1990; Webster's Bitter, 1991; Lynx Deodorant, 1992. *Memberships:* Musicians' Union; PRS; APC. *Leisure interests:* Aviation sports; Badminton; Jazz piano. *Current Management:* De Wolfe Ltd. *Address:* De Wolfe Ltd, 80–88 Wardour St, London W1V 3LF, England.

QUINCY Dave; b. 13 Sept. 1939, Battle, Sussex, England. Musician (saxophone); Composer; Music Publisher. m. Patricia Ann (Patti) Quincy, 1 d. with second wife (3 marriages). *Musical Education:* Self-taught. *Career:* First tour, Little Richard, Sam Cooke, 1962; British tour as member of Jet Harris' group (ex-Shadows); Extensive tours with rock and jazz groups, 1960s; Began recording with band IF, 1969; Material now to be released in compilation album, 1995; Work, tours, recordings, many Jazz Fusion projects. *Compositions:* Material in IF compilation, 1995. *Recordings:* IF, Vols 1–4, 1969–72. *Memberships:* PRS; BASCA; MCPS; Musicians' Union; Jazz Umbrella. *Leisure interests:* Watching cricket; Doing crosswords.

QUINN Edwin Henry; b. 17 July 1963, Portsmouth, Hampshire, England. Musician (drums). 1 s., 1 d. *Musical Education:* School lessons, orchestras and bands. *Career:* Member of Dakinis, with various session work; Drummer, indie band Blow Up, 1990–92; Tours of UK and Paris showcase concerts; Video for single, World, filmed for Music Box, MTV Europe. *Recordings:* Album: Amazon Eyegasm, 1991; Single: World. *Current Management:* Sarah Heyworth Independent PR. *Address:* 67 Cobden Rd, Brighton, East Sussex BN2 2TJ, England.

QUINN Eimear; b. 18 Dec. 1972, Dublin, Ireland. Vocalist. *Education:* Degrees in Town Planning and Music; Piano Lessons; Degree in Music Studies. *Career:* Lead Voice with Anuna Vocal Group; Vocalist with Anuna, Irish Mediaeval Vocal Group; Sang Lead in London with Riverdance The Show; Toured Australia and Scandinavia as solo act. *Recordings:* The Voice, Eurovision Winner, 1996; Winter, Fire and Snow, EP, 1996; Caccini's Ave Maria. *Honour:* Eurovision Song Contest Winner, Oslo, 1996. *Current Management:* 24 Merchants Quay, Dublin 8, Ireland.

QUINN Mick; Musician (bass guitar). *Career:* Member, Supergrass, 1994–; Concerts include: Support to Blur, Alexandra Palace; British tour, with Shed Seven, 1994; T In The Park Festival, Glasgow, 1995. *Recordings:* Album: I Should Coco (No. 1, UK), 1995; In It For The Money (reached No 2), 1997; Supergrass, 1999; B-Side Trax, 2000; Singles: Caught By The Fuzz, 1994; Mansize Rooster, 1995; Lenny, 1995; Alright, 1995; Going Out, 1996; Sun Hits The Sky, 1997; Pumping on Your Stereo, 1999; Moving, 1999; Mary, 2000. *Honours:* Q Award, Best New Act, 1995; BRIT Award Nominations: Best British Newcomer, Best Single, Best Video, 1996. *Current Management:* Courtyard Management, 22 The Nursery, Sutton Courtenay, Abingdon, Oxon OX14 4UA, England.

R

RABIN Trevor; b. 13 Jan. 1954, Johannesburg, South Africa. Musician (guitar, keyboards); Songwriter; Record Prod. m. Shelley May, 17 Aug. 1979, 1 s. *Musical Education:* Orchestration with Walter Mony; 8 years of piano studies. *Career:* Formed band, Rabbitt, age 14; Several tours, film and television appearances; Moved to England, 1977; Solo artiste, tours and television, 1977–; Member, progressive rock group Yes, 1982–; International concerts include: US tour, 1987; Yesshows tour, 1991; Wembley Arena, 1991. *Compositions include:* Owner of a Lonely Heart, Yes (world-wide No. 1 hit); Composer, music for Fair Game. *Recordings:* Albums: Solo: Trevor Rabin, 1978; Face To Face, 1979; Wolf, 1981; Can't Look Away, 1989; 2 albums with Rabbitt; with Yes: 90125, 1983; 9012 Live – The Solos, 1986; The Big Generator, 1987; Union, 1991; Yesstory, 1991; Hit singles with Yes: Owner of a Lonely Heart; Leave It; It Can Happen; Rhythm of Love; Lift Me Up. *Publications:* Instructional guitar video. *Honour:* Grammy Award, Best Instrumental Performance, Cinema, 1985. *Memberships:* AFTRA; Musicians' Union. *Current Management:* Tony Dimitriades, East End Management. *Address:* 8209 Melrose Ave, 2nd Floor, Los Angeles, CA 90046, USA.

RABINOWITZ Harry; b. 26 March 1916, South Africa. Conductor; Composer; Musical Dir. m. Lorna Thurlow Anderson, 1 s., 2 d. *Education:* Guildhall School of Music, London. *Career:* Corporal, SA Forces, 1942–43; Conductor, BBC Radio, 1953–60; Head of Music, BBC Television Light Entertainment, 1960–68; LWT, 1968–77; Freelance Conductor, Composer, Hollywood Bowl, 1983–84; Boston Pops, 1985–92; London Symphony Orchestra, Royal Philharmonic Orchestra, 1996; Conductor for Films including: Chariots of Fire, Manhattan Project, Heat and Dust, The Bostonians, Time Bandits, Camille Claudel, Howard's End, The Remains of The Day, Shirley Valentine, Business Affair, Le Petit Garçon, La Fille de d'Artagnan, Death and The Maiden, Nelly and Mr Arnauld, Secret Agent, La Belle Verte, Surviving Picasso, The English Patient, Amour Sorcier, City of Angels, A Soldier's Daughter Never Crys; Message In A Bottle; Cotton Mary; The Talented Mr Ripley; Television, New Faces, 1987–88, Paul Nicholas Special, 1987–88; Julia MacKenzie Special, 1986, Nicholas Nickleby, Drummonds, the Insurance Man, Absent Friends, Simon Wiesenthal Story, Marti Caine Special, Alien Empire, Battle of the Sexes; Theatre Conductor. *Compositions:* Sign of Four; Reily Ace of Spies; The Agatha Christie Hour; Thomas and Sarah; Crocodile Bird. *Honours:* MBE; Basca Gold Award, 1986; Radio and Television Industries Award, 1984; Freeman City of London, 1996. *Memberships:* Composers Guild; British Academy of Composers and Songwriters. *Leisure interests:* Wine tasting; Gathering edible fungi. *Address:* 11 Mead Rd, Cranleigh, Surrey, GU6 7BG.

RADCLIFFE Mark; b. 1958, Bolton, Lancashire, England. DJ; Presenter. m. 1 c. *Education:* English and American Studies, Classic Civilization, Manchester University. *Career:* Jr Asst Prod., Piccadilly Radio, Manchester, 1979; Producer, Radio 1, Saturday Live and John Peel session, 1983; Head of Music, Piccadilly Radio, 1985; Began DJ work; Popular Music Producer, BBC North, including Martin Kelner on Radio 2 and In Concert series for Radio 1; Presenter, Hit the North evening programme, Radio 5, 1990; Out on Blue Six, indie show, 1991; Returned to Radio 1, 4 evenings weekly show, 1993; Stand-in, Radio 1 Breakfast Show with Lard, 1996; Breakfast Show presenter, 1997; Afternoon show, Radio 1, 1998–. *Honour:* Sony Radio Award, Best Specialist Music Programme, 1992.

RADLEY Kate; b. 19 Feb. 1965. Musician (Keyboards). m. Richard Ashcroft. *Career:* Member, Spiritualized; Numerous live dates including world tour; Concerts at Royal Albert Hall, London and CN Tower, Toronto, Canada; Left band, 1999; Worked on Richard Ashcroft's solo album, 1999. *Recordings:* Singles: Anyway That You Want Me, 1991; Run, 1991; Let It Flow, 1995; Electricity, 1997; I Think I'm In Love, 1998; Abbey Road EP, 1998.

RAE Dashiell; b. 10 Jan. 1956, New Jersey, USA. Composer; Musician (flute, piano); Vocalist. *Musical Education:* Eastman School of Music, New York. *Career:* Orchestral musician, principal flautist, soloist, New York; Moved to London, 1985; Worked with Julia Fordham (keyboards, flute, backing vocals), 1989–; Worked with: Level 42; The Style Council; Womack and Womack; Midge Ure; Aztec Camera; Paul Young; Became composer film and television music, 1992. *Compositions include:* Film: Keys; The Queen's House; The Docket Box; Tea and Bullets; Television: Hidden Hands; Art and The CIA, CH4; The Dream, BBC Wales; Childrens' Ward, Granada; Last Days At Forchwen, BBC Wales; Touch, BBC Wales; Commercials: Onken Yogurt, 1994; Various: Sky Sport, 1993; Anglia, Survival, 1994; Channel Islands TV News Theme, 1994–; Promos for BBC, ITV; Classical compositions: La Chasse (piano duet); Misere (string

orchestra). *Recordings include:* Solo piano album: Songs Without Words, 1985; Also appears on: Rattled, with Rattlers, 1985; Swept, with Julia Fordham, 1991; Wings of the Dove, 1997. *Memberships:* Musicians' Union; PRS; Equity (UK); AFTRA; ASCAP; Women in Film and TV (UK). *Current Management:* Soundtrack Music Management, 22 Ives St, London SW3 2ND, England.

RAESIDE Diane Lesley Cameron; b. Scarborough, Ontario, Canada. Country-Blues Singer. *Musical Education:* Canadian Academy For The Performing Arts, Ian Garrett. *Career:* Professional singer from age 18; Concert appearances throughout Ontario, and Zevenbergen Festival, Netherlands, 1995; Television appearance: Be A Star, Nashville Network. *Recordings:* Album: Crazy Infatuation, 1992; Since You Went Away, 1995; Singles: Turning Into Strangers; Half A Heart; I'll Cry About That Tomorrow; Run For Your Money; Just Another Day; Take Me In Your Arms Tonight; Love Is Where The Good Times Are; Crazy Infatuation; Last Date; Some Rivers Run Dry; Slow Dance; This Time of Year, Singing Songs of Love (All-star charity single). *Honours:* Labatts-Guinness Travel Bursary; Numerous Song Contests; RPM Big Country Award, Outstanding New Artist, 1992. *Memberships:* Songwriters Asscn; Canadian Country Music Asscn. *Leisure interests:* Showdogs; Swimming; Hiking. *Address:* 23 Timgren Dr., Scarborough, ON M1R 3R4, Canada.

RAFFERTY Gerry; b. 16 April 1947, Paisley, Scotland. Singer; Songwriter; Musician (guitar). *Career:* Member, The Humblebums, 1968–70; Founder member, Stealers Wheel, 1972–75; Solo artist, 1978–. *Recordings:* Albums: with The Humblebums: The New Humblebums, 1969; Open Up The Door, 1970; with Stealers Wheel: Stealers Wheel, 1973; Solo albums: Can I Have My Money Back?, 1971; City To City, 1978; Night Owl, 1979; Snakes and Ladders, 1980; Sleepwalking, 1982; North and South, 1988; Right Down The Line – The Best of Gerry Rafferty, 1990; A Wing and A Prayer, 1993; Over My Head, 1995; Clowns to the Left, Jokers to the Right, 1997; Baker Street, 1999; Singles: with Stealers Wheel: Stuck In The Middle With You, 1973; Solo: Baker Street (No. 2, US), 1978; Right Down The Line, 1978; Home and Dry, 1979; Night Owl, 1980; Days Gone Down (Still Got The Light In Your Eyes), 1980; Get It Right Next Time, 1980; Contributor, film soundtrack Local Hero, with Mark Knopfler, 1983; Producer, Letter From America, The Proclaimers, 1987. *Honours:* 2 Ivor Novello Awards, Best Song, Best Pop Song, 1979. *Address:* c/o Asgard Agency, 125 Parkway, London NW1 7PS, England.

RAFFIT Jean-Paul; b. 2 Aug. 1964, Patiers, France. Musician (guitar). *Education:* First year university. *Musical Education:* 3 years with private guitar teacher. *Career:* Jazz festivals: Montréal with B Sandoval; Kalamata (Greece) with B Sandoval; Dortmund; Bonn; Frankfurt; Petit Journal; Passage Nordouest; Cartou Cherie; Television: Nulle Part Ailleurs (Canal+) with Eric Lareine; Cercle de Minuit (France 2). *Recordings:* Albums: with B Sandoval: Camino del Alba, 1992; Caracola, 1993; Vida, 1994; Album with S Lopez, 1993; All The Generics, 1994–95; Graffiti (with 9 original compositions), 1995; Antenne Ouverte A La Conscience (video). *Publications:* Jean-Paul Raffit, Un Amour de Guitare, 1995; Flash, 1995. *Honours:* ffff (telerada) for Vida (album with B Sandoval). *Memberships:* SACEM; SPEDIDAM. *Leisure interests:* Caving; Excursions; Philosophy. *Current Management:* Michel Guilhem. *Address:* Plaisance, 09100 Madiere, France.

RAFIATOU Fifi, (Rafiatou Bellow-Adjani); b. 2 Oct. 1963, Atakpame, Togo. Singer; Composer. 1 s., 1 d. *Career:* Backing singer in Togo; Member, National Presbyterian Choir; International concerts with Papa Wemba; Alpha Blondy; Ossibissa; Miriam Makeba; Masa; Performed at St Martin Black Festival. *Compositions:* Ibama; Ahe; Ile; Wawa; Ikoule. *Publications:* Priere Pour La Paix, 1980; Nwassa, 1985; Djofe, 1990; Motus, 1997. *Honours:* Pan-African Fair of Art and Music Award, 1990; Fisrt Prize, Afrovision, 1991; Spring Festival of Dion-Yang. *Memberships:* SACEM; ADAMI. *Leisure interests:* Films; Cooking. *Current Management:* c/o Georges Konila Figah, Discorama Production, PO Box 12629 Lomé, Togo.

RAHMAN A R (Allah Rakha), (A S Dileep Kumar); b. 6 Jan. 1966, Madras, India. Vocalist; Musician (keyboards); Composer. *Musical Education:* Trinity College of Music, Oxford University, England, Music Degree. *Career:* Son of well-known film music director K A Sekar; Converted to Islam, adopting the name A R Rahman, 1988; Performed with Illaiyaraja's troupe, aged 11; Later with the orchestra of M. S. Vishwanathan and Ramesh Naidu; Accompanied Zakir Hussain and Kunnakudi Vaidanathan on world tours; Scholarship to Trinity College of Music, Oxford; Obtained a degree in Western Classical Music; Returned to India and began career in advertising; Composed more than 300 jingles winning many awards; Also won award for the theme music to Madras

Telegu Academy's Spirit of Unity Concerts; Built a studio, Panchathan Record Inn, 1989; Developed into one of India's most advanced recording studios; First film score for Tamil film Roja, 1992; Film was a huge success and won many awards; Subsequent soundtracks for blockbuster Indian films include: Pudhiya Mugaml; Gentleman; Kizhaku Seemaiyilae; Duet; May Maadham; Kadhal Desam; Dil Se..; Mani Ratham; Taal; Collaborations include: Nusrat Fateh Aki Kahn; Apache Indian; L Shankar; Zakir Hussain; Kunnakudi Vaidyanathan; Kadri Gopalnath; Vikku Vinayakram; David Byrne; Talvin Singh. *Recordings:* Albums include: Deen Isai Malai, 1988; Set Me Free, 1992; Vande Mataram, 1997; Jana Gana Mana, Live In Dubai, 2000; soundtracks include: Roja, Vaishnavar, 1992; Uzhavan, Thiruda, Thiruda, Pudhiya Mugam, Kizhaku Cheemayilae, Nippu Ravva, Mawaali Raj, Gentleman, Ashokan, 1993; Duet, Kadhalan, Karuthamma, May Maadham, Pavithra, Super Police, Vandicholai Chinraasu, 1994; Bombay, Gang Master, Indira, Muthu, Rangeela, 1995; Anthimandaari, Fire, Indhiyan, Love Birds, Mr Romeo, 1996; Daud, Iddaru, Iruvar, Kabhi Na Kabhi, Minsaara Kanavu, Ratchakan, 1997; 1947/Earth, Dil Se..., Doli Saja Ke Rakhna, Jeans, 1998; En Swasa Kaatre, Kadhalar Dhinam, Muthalvan, Padaiyappa, Pukar, Sangamam, Taal, Thakshak, 1999; Alai Payuthey, Kandukondain Kandukondain, Rhythm, Thenaali, Zubeidaa, 2000; Alli Arjuna, Lagaan, One 2 Ka 4, Parthale Paravasam, Star, 2001. *Honours:* various include: SuMu Music Award, R D Burman Award, 1993; R D Burman Award for New Musical Talent, Roja (Hindi), 1995; National Awards: Roja, 1993; Minsara Kanavu 1998; Filmfare Awards: Roja, 1993; Gentleman, 1994; Kadhalan, 1995; Rangeela, Bombay, 1996; Kadhal Desam, 1997; Minsara Kanavu, 1998; Dil Se..., Jeans, 1999; Taal, Mudhalvan, Alai Payuthey, 2000; Screen-Videocon Awards: Kadhal Desam, 1997; Minsara Kanavu, Vande Mataram, 1998; Taal, 2000; Cinema Express Awarda: Roja, 1993; Gentleman, 1994; Kadhalan, 1995; Kadhal Desam, 1997; Jeans, 1999; Zee Awards: Zee Sangeet Award, Dil Se..., 1999; Zee Cine Award, Taal, 2000; Zee Gold Bollywood Award, Taal, 2000; MTV-VMA Award, Dil Se Re (from Dil Se..), 1999; International India Film Award, Taal, 2000; Screen Award, nominees: Best Background Score; Best Music, Lagaan, 2001. *Internet:* www.arrahman.com.

RAIMON (Raimon Pelegero Sanchis); b. 2 Dec. 1940, Xàtiva, Spain. Singer; Songwriter. m. Annalisa Corti, 22 Aug. 1966. *Education:* University Graduate, Contemporary History. *Musical Education:* Elemental studies. *Career:* Tours: France, Mexico; USA; Argentina; Japan; Concerts include: Olympia Theatre, Paris, 1966, 1969, 1974; Teatro Español, Madrid, 1988; Many appearances, Barcelona, Valencia; Television includes: Especial Raimon, TVE, 1984; Raimon previously banned during Franco Dictatorship to 1977; Live broadcast, Festival of La Mercè, Barcelona, 1987; Live recital, Raimon, 30 Anys d'al Vent, Barcelona, TV3, TVE2, 1993. *Compositions include:* Al Vent; Diguem No; Jo Vinc d'un Silenci; Com Un Puny. *Recordings include:* Raimon, 1963, 1964; A L'Olympia, 1966; Diguem No, 1971; Catalonian Protest Songs, 1971; T'Adones Amic, 1974; Raimon, 1977; Quan L'Aigua Es Queixa, 1980; Entre La Nota I El So, 1984; Canta Ausiàs March, 1989; Cançons, 1993; Integral, 1993; Spain, 1994; Cancons, 1996; Anthology of 120 Songs, 1996. *Publications:* Canzoni Contro, 1971; Poemes I Cançons, 1973; Poemas y Canciones, 1976; Les Hores Guanyades, 1983; D'Aquest Viure Insistent, 1986; Les Paraules Del Meu Cant, 1993. *Honours include:* Grand Prix Francis Carco, Académie Du Disque, Paris, 1967; City of Barcelona Prize, 1982; Fundació Jaume Primer, Barcelona, 1987; Aportació Musical, Valencia, 1993; The Best Show of The Year, Barcelona, 1994; Premi Nacional De Música, 1993; Grand Prix, Nouvelle Academie Du Disque, Integral Raimon, France, 1994. *Current Management:* Annalisa Corti. *Address:* Plaça Bonsuccès, 7 atc 2a, 08001, Barcelona, Spain.

RAINEY Ron Paul; b. 3 Feb. 1946, East Stroudsburg, Pennsylvania, USA. Artist Man. *Career:* Concert agent, International Famous Agency (now International Creative Management), New York City, 1969–71; Vice President, concert department, Agency For The Performing Arts, New York City and Los Angeles, 1971–73; Chairman, chief executive officer, Magna Artists Corporation, Los Angeles, 1974–81; President, chief executive officer, Ron Rainey Management Inc, Beverly Hills, California, 1981-. *Leisure interests:* Collecting baseball cards; Fine wines; Antique books; Music memorabilia. *Address:* 315 S Beverly Dr., Suite 206, Beverly Hills, CA 90212, USA.

RAINWATER Keech; b. 24 Jan. 1963, Plano, Texas, USA. Country musician (drummer, banjo, percussion). *Career:* Had minor hits on independent label 16th Avenue as member of Canyon, 1988–90; Formed Texasee with Dean Sams, Richie McDonald, Michael Britt and John Rich, 1992; Group became resident house band at the Wildhorse Saloon, Nashville; After subsequent name change to Lonestar, came to the attention of BMG and were signed to their BNA subsidiary; Released promotional six-track live CD, recorded at the Wildhorse; First country chart entry No News/Tequila Talkin' from debut album Lonestar, 1996; Single, Amazed, from third album became huge international hit and career record to date, 1999; By early 2000s, Lonestar estimated to be the most successful country group in the world. *Recordings include:* No News,

Tequila Talkin', 1996; Come Cryin' To Me, You Walked In, 1997; Say When, Everything's Changed, 1998; Amazed, Smile, 1999; I'm Already There, 2002; Albums include: Lonestar, 1995; Crazy Nights, 1997; Lonely Grill, 1999; I'm Already There, 2001. *Leisure interests:* Rock climbing; Kayaking; Video production; Building gadgets; Riding motorized scooter. *Address:* c/o Country Music Asscn, Nashville, TN.

RAITT Bonnie; b. 8 Nov. 1949, Burbank, California, USA. Musician (guitar, piano). *Education:* Radcliffe College. *Career:* Performer, blues clubs, US East Coast; Concerts include: MUSE concert, Madison Square Garden with Bruce Springsteen, Jackson Browne, Carly Simon, The Doobie Brothers, 1979; Roy Orbison Tribute Concert with artists including: Whoopi Goldberg; kd lang; Bob Dylan; B B King, 1990; Performances with artists including: Stevie Wonder, Bruce Springsteen, Aretha Franklin, Willie Nelson, Elton John. *Recordings:* Albums include: Bonnie Raitt, 1971; Give It Up, 1972; Takin' My Time, 1973; Streetlights, 1974; Home Plate, 1975; Sweet Forgiveness, 1977; The Glow, 1979; Green Light, 1982; Nine Lives, 1986; Nick of Time, 1989; The Bonnie Raitt Collection, 1990; Luck of The Draw, 1991; Road Tested, 1995; Fundamental, 1998; Singles include: Something to Talk About, 1991; Not the Only One, 1992; Burning Down the House, 1996. *Honours include:* 4 Grammy Awards: Album of Year; Best Rock Vocal Performance; Best Female Pop Vocal Performance; Best Traditional Blues Performance (with John Lee Hooker), and numerous nominations. *Current Management:* Gold Mountain Entertainment. *Address:* 3575 Cahuenga Blvd W, Suite 450, Los Angeles, CA 90068, USA.

RAITT John Emmet; b. 29 Jan. 1917, Santa Ana, California, USA. Actor; Singer. m. Rosemary Kraemer, 2 s., 1 d. *Education:* BA University of Redlands, California. *Musical Education:* Private. *Career:* Oklahoma; Carousel; 3 Wishes For Jamie; Magdelena; Carnival In Flanders; Pajama Game (Broadway and film); Annie Get Your Gun; Zorba; On A Clear Day; Summer Chevy Show; Bell Telephone Hour; 25 Years of Summer Stock; Concerts: A Joyful Noise – Musical Jubilee. *Recordings:* Oklahoma; Carousel 1945, 1965; Showboat; Highlights of Broadway; The Best of John Raitt; Broadway Legend; Under Open Skies; Mediterranean Magic; 3 Wishes For Jamie; Annie Get Your Gun. *Honours:* Hon Dr, University of Redlands and Pepperdine and Boston Conservatory; Theater Hall of Fame, New York; Hollywood Walk of Fame. *Leisure interest:* Golf. *Current Management:* James Fitzgerald Ent. *Address:* 4300 Prominade Way #121 P, Marina Del Rey, CA90292, USA.

RAKSIN David; b. 4 Aug. 1912, Philadelphia, Pennsylvania, USA. Composer; Conductor; Author; Prof. m. Joanne Kaiser, 19 Sept. 1959, divorced, 2 s., 1 d. *Education:* University of Pennsylvania. *Musical Education:* William Happich; Harl McDonald; Isador Freed; Arnold Schoenberg. *Career:* Went to Hollywood, worked with Charlie Chaplin, music for Modern Times, 1935; Scored over 100 films, including: Laura; The Bad and The Beautiful; Several hundred radio shows; Approximately 400 television programmes; Conducted major orchestras. *Compositions:* Music from films: Laura; Forever Amber; The Bad and The Beautiful; Composed text and music, conducted premiere of Oedipus Memneitai (Coolidge Commission from Library of Congress). *Publications:* 7 articles published by Library of Congress; Book of Songs, 1996. *Honours:* Career achievement awards from: ASCAP; Composers and Lyricists Guild. *Memberships:* President, Composers and Lyricists Guild of America; Board of Directors, ASCAP; President, Society for Preservation of Film Music (appointed by the Librarian at Congress to the National Film Preservation Board). *Leisure interest:* Researching CD/ROM project Pictures At An Exhibition.

RALPH Mark; b. 2 May 1974, Stoke-on-Trent, Staffordshire, England. Musician (guitar). *Career:* Long term member of Max The Sax, 12-piece jazz funk band; Featured on We Are Family by Sister Sledge, 1993 remixes; Worked with Sure Is Pure, on further dance remixes. *Recordings:* We Are Family, Sister Sledge; Lost In Music, Sister Sledge; Manha De Brasil, Max The Sax. *Leisure interests:* Swimming; Squash. *Current Management:* Nigel Woodcock. *Address:* 73 Rothesay Ave, Newcastle-under-Lyme, Staffordshire ST5 2LQ, England.

RALPHES Paul Stuart; b. 23 Feb. 1962, Shrewsbury, England. Record Prod.; Songwriter; Musician (bass, guitar). m. Rosana Ferrao, 7 Dec. 1991. *Education:* BA in Film, University of Warwick, 1984. *Musical Education:* Self-taught. *Career:* Producer, songwriter, musician, Bliss, 1987–92; Tours with: Van Morrison; Paul Simon; Gipsy Kings; Chris Isaak; Worked with: Rupert Hine; Jon Kelly; John Shaw; Hugh Jones; Currently producer, writer, Duke Baysee. *Recordings:* As producer, writer, musician: Loveprayer, Bliss, 1989; Change In The Weather, Bliss, 1991; Sugar Sugar, Duke Baysee, 1994; Do You Love Me?, Duke Baysee, 1995; Siderado, Skank, 1999. *Honours:* Best International Act, Bliss, Italy, Brazil, 1989. *Memberships:* PRS; Musicians' Union. *Leisure interests:* Film; Liverpool Football Club; Travel. *Current Management:* Pulso Productions. *Address:* Rua Sao Felan 94, Jardim Marapendi, Barra Da Tijuca, 22630–170 Rio de Janeiro, RJ, Brazil.

RALPHS Mick; b. 31 March 1944, Hereford, England. Musician (guitar); Songwriter. 2 s., 1 d. *Career:* Founder member, Mott The Hoople, 1969–73; Founder member, Bad Company, 1973–83; Toured world-wide; Tour with Dave Gilmour (Pink Floyd), 1984; Solo recording artiste, 1983; Reformed Bad Company, 1986-. *Compositions include:* Can't Get Enough; Movin' On; Feel Like Makin' Love (co-writer with Paul Rodgers). *Recordings:* Singles with Mott the Hoople: Rock 'n' Roll Queen, 1972; All the Young Dudes, 1972; Honaloochie Boogie, 1973; All the Way from Memphis, 1973; Roll Away the Stone, 1973; Albums: Mott the Hoople, 1969; Mad Shadows, 1970; Wild Life, 1971; Brain Capers, 1971; All the Young Dudes, 1972; Mott, 1973; Greatest Hits, 1976; Mott Anthology, 1998; All the Way From Stockholm, live in 1971, 1999; Albums with Amazing Blondell: Blondell, 1973; Mulgrave Street, 1974; Singles with Bad Company: Can't Get Enough; Feel Like Makin' Love; If You Need Somebody; Holy Water; Here Comes Trouble; Hey Hey; Hammer of Love; Albums: Bad Company, 1974; Straight Shooter, 1975; Run With The Pack, 1976; Burnin' Sky, 1977; Desolation Angels, 1979; Rough Diamonds, 1982; 10 from 6, 1985; Fame and Fortune, 1986; Dangerous Age, 1988; Holy Water, 1990; Here Comes Trouble, 1992; The Best of Bad Company Live – What You Hear Is What You Get, 1993; Company of Strangers, 1995; The Original Bad Co Anthology, 1999; Solo: Take This, 1983. *Honours:* Gold and Platinum albums with Bad Company; Grammy Award, 1975; Hon. Col of Louisiana, with Bad Company. *Memberships:* Musicians' Union; PRS. *Leisure interests:* Painting; Motorcross; Vintage guitars. *Current Management:* Gremlin Productions. *Address:* PO Box 148, Fincham, Norfolk PE33 9EH, England.

RAMAGE Andrew; b. 24 Sept. 1949, Edinburgh, Scotland. Musician (guitar, bass: contra). m. Anita, 11 April 1975. *Education:* Diploma British Display Society, Telford College. *Musical Education:* Self-taught, traditional Scots/Irish folk music. *Career:* BBC TV; RME TV; STV; Grampian TV; Tours: Bermuda; Bangladesh; Iceland; Norway; Denmark; Netherlands; Switzerland; Morocco; Ireland; Radio BBC Scotland; Radio Tay; Radio Forth; Radio Moray Firth; Radio Heartland; Radio Clyde. *Recordings:* Golden Bird Vols 1 and 2, 1968; Bitter Withy Sampler, 1973; Bridging The Gap, 1983; Two For The Road, 1986; Silver Darlings, 1988; Dancing On A Wave, 1989; Naturally, 1991; Family Ties, 1993; Scotland The Brave, 1995. *Honours:* RBI, 1970; Glenfarg Quaich, 1980. *Membership:* Musicians' Union. *Leisure interests:* Wine making; Golf; Bon-Viveur. *Address:* Sunnyside House, Drunzie, Glenfarg, Perthshire PH2 9PE, Scotland.

RAMAN Susheela; b. 20 July 1973, London, England. Vocalist. *Career:* Tamil parents from South India; Moved to Australia at an early age; Learnt and gave recitals of South Indian classical music; Branched out into blues based music as a teenager; Went to India to study with Shruti Sadolikar, 1995; Returned to England, 1997; Recorded with Sam Mills, 2000. *Recordings:* Salt Rain, 2001. *Honours:* Mercury Music Prize nominee, Salt Rain, 2001; BBC Radio 3 Awards for World Music, Best Newcomer, 2002.

RAMAZZOTTI Eros; b. 28 Oct. 1963, Rome, Italy. Vocalist; Musician (guitar); Songwriter. *Career:* Participated in Castrocaro Music Festival, 1981; Led to signing first record deal and relocation to Milan; Released first single, 1982; Won Best Young Artist award at San Remo Festival, 1984; First album release, 1985, a major success throughout Europe; Achieved instant cult status in Italy; Musica E album reached an international audience, 1988; Promoted album In Ogni Senso with European / American tour culminating with world-wide broadcast of Barcelona concert, 1991; Created own management company, Radiorama, 1993; Signed new contract with BMG International. *Recordings:* Cuori Agitati, 1985; Nuovi Eroi, 1986; In Certi Momenti, 1987; Musica E, 1988; In Ogni Senso, 1990; Eros In Concert, 1991; Tutte Storie, 1993; Dove C'e Musica, 1996; Eros, 1997; Eros Live, 1998; Stile Libero, 2000. *Honours:* MTV Music Award, Best Italian Singer, 1996; Echo Award, Germany, Best International Singer, 1997; Dove C'e Musica album sales over 6m. world-wide. *Current Management:* c/o Radiorama, Milan, Italy. *Internet:* www.erosramazzotti.net.

RAMIREZ Humberto; b. 31 Jan. 1963, San Juan, Puerto Rico. Musician (trumpet); Composer; Prod.; Arranger. m. Ivette Maritza Negron, 16 Jan. 1988, 1 s., 1 d. *Education:* Escuela Libre de Musica, San Juan, Puerto Rico. *Musical Education:* Berklee College of Music, Boston, MA, Bachelor of Music. *Career:* Concerts played at Madison Square Garden; Hollywood Bowl; Miami Arena; Blue Note Jazz Club; Blues Alley; Tours: Spain, Mexico City, USA, Canada and Europe. *Recordings:* Jazz Project; Aspects; Portrait of a Stranger; Canciones de Amor. *Honours:* 5 Gold records; 4 Platinum records; Diplo Award Best Jazz Recording, 1992; TU Musica Award, Best Jazz Recording, 1994, 1995, 1996; 8 Gold and 6 Platinum Records. *Memberships:* NARAS; ASCAP. *Leisure interest:* Sports. *Current Management:* Nilpo Music Inc. *Address:* PO Box 9020924, San Juan, 00902–0924 Puerto Rico.

RAMIREZ Juan; b. 17 Oct. 1947, London, England. Flamenco Musician (guitar); Songwriter. m. Marsha, 15 April 1972. *Musical Education:* Studied flamenco guitar, dance accompaniment, Spain and London. *Career:* Full time 1974–; Formed internationally renowned Viva Flamenco Dance Company, 1976; Performed at Royal Albert Hall; Barbican; Royal Festival Hall, London; Film appearance: The Curse of The Pink Panther, 1983; World's largest production of Carmen, 1992; Numerous television appearances. *Compositions include:* Just Love. *Recordings:* with Marc Almond: The Desperate Hours; with Gary Barlow, Stronger. *Membership:* Musicians' Union. *Leisure interests:* Football; Antiques; Art; All types of music. *Address:* 122B Wood Vale, London SE23 3EB, England.

RAMIREZ Karen; b. 1972, Islington, London, England. Singer. *Career:* Began work as vocalist for producers, Souled Out, worked on their album; Began work on debut solo album. *Recordings:* Singles: Looking for Love; Troubled Girl; Album: Distant Dreams.

RAMONE Phil; b. 5 Jan. 1939, New York, USA. Record Prod.; Musician (violin). m. April 1984, 3 s. *Musical Education:* Juilliard School of Music, New York; Doctor Musicology, Berklee College of Music, Boston; Doctor Musicology, Five Towns College, New York. *Career:* Founded own studio, A & R Recording, New York, 1961; Theatre credits include: Chicago; Hair; Little Shop of Horrors; Starlight Express; The Wiz; Film credits include: A Star Is Born; Flashdance; Ghostbusters; Midnight Cowboy; Reds; Yentl; Shampoo; Television credits include: Liza With A Z; Raffi On Broadway; Extreme; Liza Live From Radio Music Hall; The Jim Henson Hour; The Academy Awards; The Grammy Awards; Simon and Garfunkel Concert, Central Park; Show Business. *Recordings include:* As producer: The Stranger, 52nd Street, Glass Houses, Songs From The Attic, Innocent Man, Billy Joel; Flashdance (soundtrack); A Star Is Born, Yentl, Barbra Streisand; One Trick Pony, Still Crazy After All These Years, 50 Ways To Leave Your Lover, Slip Slidin' Away, Paul Simon; Too Late For Goodbyes, Valotte, Julian Lennon; Send In The Clowns, Judy Collins; Alice's Restaurant, Arlo Guthrie; The Look of Love, Dusty Springfield; Leaving On A Jet Plane, Peter Paul and Mary; Duets I and II, Frank Sinatra; also producer for Elton John; Gloria Estefan; Sinead O'Connor; Barry Manilow; Jon Secada; Paul McCartney; Dionne Warwick; Art Garfunkel; Chicago; Stephen Sondheim; Burt Bacharach; George Michael; Michael Bolton. *Honours:* 8 Grammy Awards; 15 Grammy Nominations; 1 Emmy; Numerous Platinum and Gold albums and singles; TEC Hall of Fame, 1992; 3M Visionary Award, 1994; Eyes On NY Award, 1994; Rock Walk Award, 1994; Songwriters Hall of Fame. *Memberships:* Former President, New York Chapter, NARAS; NATAS; AFTRA; AFofM; ASCAP; BMI; SESAC; SAG. *Leisure interests:* Travel; Reading; Computers; Art collecting; Wine. *Current Management:* Peter Asher Management. *Address:* 644 N Doheny Dr., Los Angeles, CA 90069, USA.

RAMPLING Danny; b. 15 July 1961, London, England. DJ; Radio Presenter; Record Prod.; Remixer. *Career:* Broadcaster, BBC Radio 1; Club DJ; Record producer for the Millionaire Hippies. *Compositions:* Community of The Spirit, 1999. *Honours:* Best Radio DJ South, DMC 94, UK No 1 DJ magazine, 1994; Music Magazine, Contribution To Dance Music, 1998. *Leisure interests:* Travel; Restaurants; Gym training; Cooking. *Current Management:* Cosmack, 10 Great Marlborough St, London W1. *Address:* c/o BBC Radio 1, Broadcasting House, London W1A 1AA, England.

RANADE Ashok Da; b. 25 Oct. 1937, India. m. Hamida Ebrahim. *Education:* LLB, MA, English Literature, MA, Marathi Literature, University of Bombay; Hindustani Vocal Classical Training with Pt Gajanauruo Joshi and others. *Career:* All India Radio, Bombay; Lecturer, English and Marathi, Siddharth College of Commerce and Economics; First Director of University Music Centre, Bombay, 1968–83; Associate Director, Archives and Research Centre, Ethnomusicology, American Institute of Indian Studies, 1983–84; Deputy Director, Theatre Research and Ethnomusicology, National Centre for Performing Arts, Bombay, 1984–94; Conducts many workshops and courses in voire culture singing, music appreciation and ethnomusicology; Numerous seminars. *Compositions:* Composed music for Akar, International Exhibition of Calligraphy, New Delhi, 1988; Discovery of India, Nehru Centre, Bombay, 1989; Composed music for plays and films; Composed and compered many thematical music presentations. *Recordings:* Cassettes: Baithakchi Lavani, 1989; Devgani, 1991. *Publications include:* Lok Sangget Shastra, 1975; On Music and Musicians of Hindustan, 1984; Marathi Stage Music, 1986; Keywords and Concepts: Hindustani Classical Music, 1990; Music and Drama in India, 1991; Essays in Indian Ethnomusicology, 1998. *Honours:* Appointed National Lecturer in Music, University Grants Commission, New Delhi, 1990–91; Appointed, Tagore Chair, M S University of Baroda, 1994–95; Awarded Master Krishnarao Phulambrikar Puraskar, Maharashtra Sahitya Parishad, 1998; Award for Music Research, Music Forum, Mumbai, 1998. *Address:* 7 Dnyanadevi, Sahitya Sahawas, Kalanagar, Kalelkar Marg, Mumbai 400051, India.

RANALDO Lee; b. 3 Feb. 1956, Glen Cove, New York, USA. Artist; Writer; Musician (bass). *Education:* BFA SUNY Binghampton: Painting, Cinema, Philosophy. *Career:* Soloist, performer with Glenn Branca and Rhys

Chatham; Founding member, Sonic Youth; Duo performances: spoken word/film/music called Drift, with filmmaker Leah Singer. *Recordings:* Sonic Youth, 1984; East Jesus; Broken Circle/Spiral Hill; Bad Moon Rising, 1985; Evol, 1986; Sister, 1987; Daydream Nation, 1988; Goo, 1991; Envisioning, 1995; Scriptures of the Golden Eternity, 1995; Broken Circle, 1996. *Publications:* Road movies; Bookstore. *Membership:* AFofM. *Current Management:* ICM. *Address:* PO Box 6179, Hoboken, NJ 07030, USA.

RANDALL Alan; b. 10 June 1934, Bedworth, England. Entertainer. m. Mary Laird, 1 s., 1 d. *Career:* Wrote script, starred in, musical play, Turned Out Nice Again; World entertainer; Royal Variety Shows; Guest artist, Rolling Stones; World cruises; Radio and television appearances worldwide; Featured in Beatles video, Free As A Bird, 1995. *Compositions:* Where Does Father Xmas Hang His Stocking; Mr Banjo Man; Football, Football; Lottery Millionaire. *Recordings:* Albums, The Vibraphone Entertainer World of Alan Randall; I Remember George; Songs From World War 2; Who Do You Think You A Kidding My Hitler. *Publications:* George Formby Biography, 1974. *Honours:* Top Commercial Award, 1982. *Memberships:* Variety Club of Great Britain; Grand Order of Water Rats. *Leisure interest:* Golf. *Current Management:* United Kingdom Entertainment. *Address:* 104 Hickley Rd, Nuneaton, CV11 6LS.

RANDAZZO Teddy; b. 13 May 1935, New York City, USA. Composer; Musician; Actor. m. Rosemary Randazzo, 4 s., 3 d. *Musical Education:* Private studies. *Career:* Appeared on Ed Sullivan TV show 7 times, and in 4 films, Rock Rock Rock, The Girl Can't Help It, Mister Rock and Roll, and, Hey, Let's Twist; Appearances at various clubs including: Copa Cabana, Blaisdell Arena, Hawaii, and Araneta Colosseum, Philippines. *Recordings:* Goin' Out of My Head; Hurt So Bad; Pretty Blue Eyes; It's Gonna Take A Miracle; I'm On The Outside Looking In; Have You Looked Into Your Heart; Big Wide World; You're So Right For What's Wrong. *Membership:* BINI. *Leisure interest:* Music. *Address:* 5254 Oak Island Rd, Orlando, FL 32809, USA.

RANDOLPH 'Boots' (Homer Louis); b. 3 June 1927, Paducah, Kentucky, USA. Musician (tenor saxophone). m. Dee Barber, 17 Sept. 1947, 1 s., 1 d. *Musical Education:* High School and Army Band. *Career:* Concerts all over USA and Canada; Most variety television shows, including: Ed Sullivan; Jimmy Dean; Jackie Gleason; Boston Pops with Arthur Feedler: TNN-Nashville Network. *Recordings:* Yakety Sax, as composer and musician; Recorded 43 albums. *Honours:* 8 years Playboy All Star Jazz Poll. *Memberships:* AFofM; AFTRA. *Leisure interests:* Golf; Snow skiing. *Current Management:* Gerard W Purcell, New York, New York. *Address:* 964 Second Ave, New York, NY 10022–6304, USA.

RANEY Sue; b. 18 June 1939, McPhearson, Kansas, USA. Singer. m. Carmen Fanzone, 14 Dec. 1985. *Career:* Child star, recording debut aged 16; Performed world-wide, with stars including Don Rickles; Dean Martin; Bob Hope; Henry Mancini; Michel Legrand; Guest faculty member, Dick Grove School of Music. *Recordings:* Over a dozen albums; When Your Lover Has Gone; Songs For a Raney Day; Ridin' High; In Good Compnay; Flight of Fancy (Lyrics of Alan and Marilyn Bergman); Dreamsville (The Music of Henry Mancini); Autumn In The Air, 1998. *Honours:* Grammy nominations for 3 albums. *Membership:* Society of Singers. *Leisure interests:* Painting; Gardening. *Current Management:* Jim DiGiovanni, F Sharp Productions Ltd, 157 W 57th St, New York, NY, USA.

RANKIN Dusty; b. 8 Feb. 1924, Birchip, Victoria, Australia. Singer; Songwriter; Musician (guitar). m. Mary, 14 May 1957, deceased 1993, 2 d. *Musical Education:* Self-taught. *Career:* Worked in TV, Melbourne, 1950's; Recorded for Hadley, 1964; Recorded for Selection Records, 1980; Own show, Starnite, throughout Victoria; Toured with Skuthorpe's and Queensland Wild West Rodeos around Australia, 3 times; Toured with Athol McKoy Show, 1962; First Recordings for Columbia EMI Records, 1948. *Compositions:* Songs released on 13 compilation albums; 2 song albums (books). *Recordings:* 4 albums: Family Bible; The Country I Love; A Portrait of Dusty Rankin; Sunset Valley Calling; 5 EPs – Red Wing Smooth 'N Country; Dusty Rankin and Bernadette; Intimate Style of Dusty Rankin; Family Bible; 1 cassette, Best of Dusty Rankin; 20 of The Best – Dusty Rankin, 1999; After 50 Years, with Val Phelan. *Honours:* Won Australian Amateur Hour, 1946; Inducted into Hands of Fame, Tamworth, NSW, 1980; Inducted into Avenue of Honour Bamera, SA, 1985; Golden Guitar, Tambourine Mountain, Queensland, 1988; Inducted into Roll of Renown, Tamworth, NSW, 1996. *Membership:* Australian Performing Rights Asscn. *Leisure interests:* Golf; Fishing. *Address:* PO Box 113, Birchip, Vic 3483, Australia.

RANKIN Mark; b. Glasgow, Scotland. Vocalist. *Career:* Vocalist, Scottish rock group Gun, 1989–; Concerts include: Support to Rolling Stones, Urban Jungle Tour, Europe, 1990; Support to Simple Minds, 1990; Support to Def Leppard, UK, 1993; International tours as headline act. *Recordings:* Albums: Taking On The World, 1989; Gallus, 1992; Swagger, 1994; Singles: Better Days, 1989; Shame On You, 1989; Money, 1989; Inside

Out, 1990; Word Up, 1994; Don't Say It's Over, 1994. *Current Management:* G R Management, 974 Pollockshaw Rd, Glasgow G41 2HA, Scotland.

RANKS Shabba, (Rexton Gordon); b. 17 Jan. 1966, Sturgetown, Jamaica. Reggae / Ragga Singer. *Career:* Club artiste as DJ Don, early 1980s; Solo artiste, mid-1980s; Prolific local recording artiste, Caribbean; Support to Bobby Brown, US, 1992. *Recordings:* As Raw As Ever, 1991; Rough and Ready Vol. 1, 1992; Xtra Naked, 1992; Mr Maximum, 1992; Love Punanny Bad, 1993; No Competition, 1993; A Mi Shabba, 1995; Shine Eye Gal, 1995; Holding On, 1998; King of Dancehall, 1998; Get Up Stand Up, 1998; Loverman, 1999; Shabba Ranks and Friends, 1999; Hit singles: She's A Woman (with Scritti Politti), 1991; Housecall (with Maxi Priest), 1991; Mr Loverman, used in film soundtrack Deep Cover, 1993; Slow and Sexy, 1992; What'cha Gonna Do? (with Queen Latifah), 1993; Family Affair, used in film soundtrack Addams Family, 1993. *Honours:* Grammy Awards: Best Reggae Album, As Raw As Ever, 1992; Xtra Naked, 1993; 2 Caribbean Music Awards, 1992; 6 International Reggae Awards, 1992. *Current Management:* Shang Artist Management, 850 Seventh Ave, Suite 500, New York, NY 10019, USA.

RANSOME Steve; b. 24 Aug. 1961, London, England. Musician (keyboards); Composer; Record Prod. m. Shirley Peterson, 8 April 1994. *Musical Education:* Advanced Jazz tuition, Grangewood School in London; Qualified Yamaha Music Teacher. *Career:* ATV Production Assistant, 1977–78; Played keyboards in various bands at Wembley, Peterborough and Glasgow Festivals; Toured UK, Ireland, Europe and America; Appeared on BBC TV, ITV, MTV, Channel 4 TV and Cable TV; Yamaha demonstration concerts given; Played at Bahai Festivals, the University circuits in Scotland and on most radio stations; Owns recording studio. *Compositions include:* About 12 television themes and soundtracks; Arranger for 1988 special Olympics theme. *Recordings:* Single: Peace Moves, world-wide release; Many major artists as production assistant. *Publications:* Peace Moves; Storming The Gates; Bahai Song Book Vol. 1. *Memberships:* PRS; MCPS; Musicians' Union. *Address:* Donfield House, Backmill by Turriff, Aberdeenshire AB53 8ET, Scotland.

RAPHAEL (Rafael Martos); b. Jaén, Spain. Singer. m. Natalia Figueroa, 1972, 2 s., 1 d. *Career:* First prize, Salzburg Festival (children's singing competition) age 9; Winner, numerous subsequent competitions; Professional debut, Madrid, 1960; Represented Spain, Eurovision Song Contest, 1966, 1967; International concerts, US (including Broadway debut, 1974); USSR; Japan; Australia; Concerts include: 25th Anniversary open air concert, Bernabé Stadium, Madrid, 1985; Film appearances: Cuando Tú no Estás; The Hobo. *Recordings:* Over 200m. records sold; First major recording: Los Hombres Lloran También, 1964. *Honours include:* First Prize, Salzburg Singing Competition; Numerous Platinum and Gold discs. *Address:* c/o Arie Kaduri Agency Inc, 16125 NE 18th Ave, North Miami Beach, FL 33162, USA.

RASE Bill; b. 25 Oct. 1926, Long Beach, California, USA. Orchestra Leader. m. Shirley Bishop, 24 Aug. 1952, 2 d. *Education:* Sacramento State College. *Musical Education:* General music courses. *Career:* Vocalist, Eddie Halter Orchestra, 1946–48; Orchestra leader, Bill Rase Orchestra, 1948–; Over 8000 engagements, backed Bob Hope, Cab Calloway shows; DJ, KCRA Radio-Sacramento: The Bill Rase Show, 1952–64; Producer, host, The Bill Rase Show (talent show), KCRA TV, Channel 3, 9 years, over 500 shows; Children's show host, Bosun Bill and Popeye Show, 4 years, over 2,600 shows; Impersonated Bing Crosby, Network Eddie Cantor Show, 1962; Opened recording video production studio, Bill Rase Productions Inc, 1965–; Vocalist, Rainbow Records, Era Records, Esar Records. *Membership:* Sacramento Musicians Asscn. *Leisure interests:* Music; Art. *Address:* 955 Venture Ct, Sacramento, CA 95825, USA.

RASMUSSEN Pia; b. 10 Nov. 1954, Aarhus, Denmark. Musician (piano); Composer; Music Teacher. *Education:* Cand Phil, Musicology, Copenhagen University. *Career:* Pianist and composer, all-woman groups Sosterrock and Lilith, 1976–83; Composer for documentaries, films and theatre; Solo concerts, piano, synthesizers, 1991–; Duo with flautist Chris Poole, 1992–; Teacher, Department of Musicology, Århus University. *Recordings:* Album: To The Powers That Be; Theme song, Nordic Women's Conference, Oslo, 1988. *Publications:* Blues For Klaver, Vols 1 and 2 (educational books on blues piano). *Memberships:* DJBFA; Danish Musicians' Union; Women In Music. *Address:* Skolesvinget 8, 8240 Risskov, Denmark.

RASOANAIVO Hanitra; b. 1 Oct. 1964, Antananarivo, Madagascar. Vocalist; Dancer, Musician (percussion); Songwriter. m. Ian Anderson. *Career:* Lead singer and founding member of Tarika, 1994; Band toured US and Europe; Performed with: Weave; Gogmagogs; Women of Africa collaboration (with Oumou Sangare, Sally Nyolo and Sibongile Khumalo), performing on tour, 1998; Working on project to build an arts centre in Antananarivo. *Recordings:* Albums include: Bibiango, 1994; Avelo, 1997; Son Egal (produced by Simon Emmerson), 1997; D, 1998; Soul Makassar, 2001. *Honours:* Kora Award nominee, 1997; Indie Award, US, 1998; Tarika voted one of the ten best bands in the world by Time Magazine, October

2001. *Current Management:* Rogue Productions, PO Box 337, London, N4 1TW, England.

RASTED Peter; b. 28 July 1958, Copenhagen, Denmark. Musician (Trumpet, Flugelhorn); Arranger; Conductor. m. Annette Frandsen, 2 s. *Education:* Royal Academy of Music, Copenhagen. *Career:* Several big bands: Kluvers Big Band, Blast, The Franks, Cordero and Los Gran Daneses; Theatre appearances in Aalborg and Aarhus; Danish Television Show, Showbisserne; Studio sessions. *Recordings:* With Blast: All recordings except Blast; SKO/Torp: I Ain't Got Too Many Problems; Cordero and Los Gran Daneses: Del Norte Y Tropical. *Address:* Sandogade 4, 8200 Aarhus N, Denmark.

RASTED Soeren; b. 13 June 1969, Blovstrod, Denmark. Musician (keyboards, drum machines). *Career:* Worked with Claus Norreen on film Fraekke Frida; Formed Joyspeed; Changed name to Aqua; Obtained major label deal in Denmark; Numerous TV and live appearances. *Recordings:* Singles: Itsy Blitzy, as Joyspeed; Roses Are Red; My Oh My; Barbie Girl; Doctor Jones; Lollipop; Turn Back Time (theme from film Sliding Doors); Good Morning Sunshine; Albums: Aquarium, 1997; Bubble Mix, 1998.

RATCLIFFE Simon; b. England. DJ; Prod. *Career:* Member, Basement Jaxx; Formed Atlantic Jaxx records, 1994; Worked with vocalist Corrina Josephs; Remixes include Pet Shop Boys, Roger Sanchez, Lil' Mo Yin Yang; Numerous gigs and television appearances. *Recordings:* Singles: Samba Magic; Fly Life; Same Old Show/Automatic; Red Alert; Rendez-vu; Jump 'n' Shout; Albums: Atlantic Jaxx: Compilation, 1997; Remedy, 1999.

RATHBOURNE Andie; b. 8 Sept. 1972, Blacon, Chester, England. Musician (Drums). *Career:* Joined Mansun, 1996; Numerous TV appearances and live gigs; Appearance at Glastonbury Festival, 1997. *Recordings:* Singles: Egg Shaped Fred, 1996; Stripper Vicar; Wide Open Space; Legacy, 1998; Six, 1999; Albums: Attack of the Grey Lantern, 1997; Six, 1999.

RATZER Karl; b. 4 July 1950, Vienna, Austria. Musician (guitar); Composer; Singer. *Career:* Member, C Department, 1969; Gipsy Love, 1970; High Voltage (later known as Rufus and Chaka Khan), USA; Based in USA, 1972–81; Worked with: Chet Baker; Eddie Gomez; Joe Chambers; Steve Gadd; Joe Farrell; Sal Nistico; Bob Mintzer; Johnny Griffin; Clark Terry; Art Farmer; Fritz Baver; Lee Konitz; James Moody; Chaka Khan; Formed band project, Beat The Heat, 1991; Recordings, tours, Europe; Festivals include: Indianapolis; Tampa; Birmingham; Chicago; New York; New Orleans; Atlanta; Played Seventh Avenue Club, New York. *Recordings:* Live In Paris (I and II), Chet Baker; with Ray Mantilla: Nightbird; Conception; Tune Up; Rainforest, Jeremy Steig; Land of Dreams, Eddie Lockjaw Davis; Solo albums: In Search of The Ghost; Street-Talk; Fingerprints; Serenade; Happy Floating; Electric Finger; Dancing On A String; Fool For Your Sake; That's Jazz; Gitarre; Gitarrenfever; Gumbo Dive; Waltz For Ann; Bayou; Coasting; Saturn Returning. *Current Management:* Mr Kiss, Agency For Music and Art. *Address:* Vienna Hilton, Top 1719–1721, Landstrasser Hauptstrasse, 1030 Vienna, Austria.

RAULIN Francois; b. 17 March 1956, Annecy, France. Musician (piano); Composer. 3 s. *Education:* Mathematics. *Musical Education:* Piano lessons from age 9; Self-taught jazz since age 14. *Career:* Founder, Association Grenoble Espace Musical (AGEM), 1981; Duo, with pianist Pascal Lloret, tour, France, 1981; Studied African music, 1980–83; Pianist, La Marmite Infernale, 1982; Tours, France; Festivals include: Paris; Le Mans; Nancy; Milan, 1982; Zürich, 1984; Moers, 1984; Hofheim, 1985; Nickelsdorf, 1986; Tours: Algeria; Germany; Switzerland; Italy; Austria; Member, Louis Sclavis Group, 1985; Festivals world-wide include: All over Europe; Canada; Japan; India; Turkey; Algeria; Mexico; Festival appearances with Claude Barthelemy, Jean-Marc Padovani, 1986; Antoine Herve, 1988; Philippe Deschepper, 1992; Solo performances at festivals including: Grenoble; Lausanne; Geneva; Cologne, 1992–; Tours with trio and quartet. *Compositions include:* Quelque Chose Du Sud, with Maurice Merle; Battleship Potemkin (film music); with Louis Sclavis: Chamber Music, 1988; Clarinettes; Indigène, 1989; Duke On The Air, 1990; Face Nord, with Mathilde Monnier's Dance Company, 1991; Vue Sur Tower Bridge (Travelling) (co-writer), 1992; Work for 5 Pianos, 1993; Hit Parada, Jean Mereu, 1993; Les Violences de Rameau, 1993; Music for theatre, film and dance, with Louis Sclavis, J Mereux, A Gibert. *Recordings include:* Chine; Rouge; First Flush; Duke on The Air. *Honours:* Winner, Biennale, Barcelona (with Louis Scalvis Quartet), 1988. *Current Management:* Marion Piras, Montpellier, France. *Address:* 686 Ave Saint Jean, 38360 Noyarey, France.

RAUX Richard; b. 17 July 1995, Perigaux, France. Musician (saxophone, flute); Composer; Bandleader. m. Helena, 25 May 1970, 1 s., 1 d. *Education:* Bac Philo; 2 years university. *Musical Education:* Saxophone, Phil Woods; Flute, Caratgt; Composition, G Russell. *Career:* Played, recorded with Eddy Louis; Magma; Luther Allisson; Kenny Clarke; Mal Waldron; Charlie

Haden; Memphis Slim; Dizzy Gillespie; Festivals, concerts, clubs, Telé France; Nice, 1991, 93; London; Berlin; Jazz teacher, saxophone, flute. *Recordings:* Feel Good At Last, Richard Raux Quartet; S Murray; Eddy Louis; Under The Magnolias, Richard Raux Quartet, 1989; Live At The Dreyer, Roy Burrowes, Mal Waldron; Won't Rain in California, Sonny Rhodes, 1996; House Rent Party, 1998. *Leisure interests:* Movies; Football. *Address:* 2 Chemin du Mopulin, 95550 Bessancourt, Nr Paris, France.

RAVEN Eddy, (Edward Garvin Futch); b. 19 Aug. 1944, Lafayette, Louisiana, USA. Musician; Singer; Songwriter. 2 s. *Education:* College. *Career:* Staff writer, La Louisiane, Lafayette; Worked with: Hank Williams Jr; Alabama; Tracy Lawrence; George Strait; Reba McEntire; Alan Jackson; Charlie Daniels; Stevie Ray Vaughn; The Judds; George Jones; Conway Twitty; Merle Haggard; Dolly Parton; Roy Acuff; Barbara Mandrell; Marty Robbins; Television appearances: Co-host, Yesteryear, TNN; Founder, own publishing company; Staff writer on: La Louisianne, 1963–69; Acriff Rose, 1970–83. *Compositions:* Country Green, Don Gibson; Touch The Morning, Don Gibson; Good Morning Country Rain, Jeannie C Riley; Thank God For Kids, Oak Ridge Boys. *Recordings:* Hit Singles: Bayou Boys; I Got Mexico; Shine Shine Shine; I'm Gonna Get You; Joe Knows How To Live; 'Til You Cry; In A Letter To You; Albums: That Cajun Country Sound, 1969; This Is Eddy Raven, 1969; Desperate Dreams, 1981; Thank God For Kids, 1984; I Could Use Another You, 1984; Love and Other Hard Times, 1985; Right Hand Man, 1986; Temporary Sanity, 1989; Greatest Country Hits, 1990; Right For Flight, 1991; Wild Eyed and Crazy, 1994; 4 Best Of/Greatest Hits compilation albums; 4 Christmas compilation albums; Live At Billy Bob's, 1998. *Memberships:* ASCAP; BMI; AFTRA; AFofM; Lifetime mem., Songwriters Asscn; Tennessee Film and Entertainment Commission. *Leisure interests:* Fishing; Cooking; Baseball. *Address:* PO Box 2476, Hendersonville, TN 37077, USA.

RAWLINGS David Todd; Vocalist; Musician (guitar). m. Gillian Welch. *Musical Education:* Berklee School of Music, Boston, Massachusetts. *Career:* Met Gillian Welch whilst both students at Berklee; T-Bone Burnett heard performance in Nashville and produced Revival album, release solely under Welch's name, 1996; Appeared solo on many film soundtracks including: O Brother Where Art Thou?; Down From The Mountain; Songcatcher; The Horse Whisperer; Appearances on Dwight Yoakam and Gram Parsons tribute albums; Guested on albums by: Mark Knopfler; Ryan Adams; Steve Earle; Songs, may co-written with Welch, recorded by acts including: Ryan Adams; Christine Collister; Nitty Gritty Dirt Band; Laurie Lewis; Alison Krauss and Union Station. *Recordings:* Albums: Revival, Hell Among The Yearlings, 1996; Time (The Revelator), 2001; features on: Horse Whisperer OST, 1998; Beneath My Wheels, Kevin Welch, 1999; Mountain, Steve Earle and Del McCoury, 1999; Swing Set, Ani DiFranco, 2000; O Brother Where Art Thou? OST, 2000; Sailing To Philadelphia, Mark Knopfler, 2000; Rich From The Journey, Kimmie Rhodes, 2000; Sebastapol, Jay Farrar, 2001; Down From The Mountain OST, 2001.

RAWLS Lou; b. 1 Dec. 1935, Chicago, Illinois, USA. Singer. *Career:* Briefly member, gospel group, the Pilgrim Travellers; Solo artiste, 1958–; Also actor; Voiceovers, Budweiser beer commercials. *Recordings:* Albums: Lou Rawls Sings, 1962; Black and Blue, 1963; Tobacco Road, 1963; Nobody But Lou Rawls, 1965; Lou Rawls and Strings, 1965; Live!, 1966; Soulin', 1966; Merry Christmas Ho! Ho! Ho!, 1967; Feeling Good, 1968; You're Good For Me, 1968; The Way It Was- The Way It Is, 1969; Your Good Thing, 1969; You Made Me So Very Happy, 1970; Bring It On Home To Me, 1970; Natural Man, 1971; Silk and Soul, 1972; All Things In Time, 1976; Unmistakably Lou, 1977; When You Hear Lou, You've Heard It All, 1977; Live, 1978; Let Me Be Good To You, 1979; Sit Down and Talk To Me, 1980; Shades of Blue, 1981; Now Is The Time, 1982; When The Night Comes, 1983; Close Company, 1984; Love All Your Blues Away, 1986; At Last, 1989; Portrait of The Blues, 1992; Greatest Hits In Concert, 1993; Seasons 4 U, 1998. *Current Management:* The Brokaw Co. *Address:* 9255 Sunset Blvd, Suite 804, Los Angeles, CA 90069, USA.

RAYE Collin, (Floyd E Wray); b. 22 Aug. 1960, De Queen, Arkansas, USA. Singer. *Musical Education:* Self-taught guitar and bass. *Career:* Television appearances include: 3 Tonight Shows; Street Justice, television series; 3 Regis and Kathy; Kathy Lee Xmas special. *Recordings:* Albums: All I Can Be, 1990; In This Life, 1992; Extremes, 1994; I Think About You, 1995; Christmas The Gift, 1996; The Walls Came Down, 1998; Counting Sheep, 2000; Singles: That's My Story, 1993; Man of My Word, 1994; My Kind of Girl, 1994; One Boy One Girl, 1995; Not That Different, 1995; Someone You Used to Know, 1998; On The Verge, 1999; Couldn't Last A Moment, 2000. *Memberships:* SAG; AFTRA. *Leisure interest:* Boxing. *Current Management:* Scott Dean Management, 612 Humboldt St, Reno, NV 89509-1606, USA; William Morris Agency, 2100 West End Ave, Suite 1000, Nashville, TN 37203, USA.

RAYMONDE Simon; b. 3 April 1963, London, England. Musician (Bass, Keyboards). m. 1 c. *Career:* Joined Cocteau Twins, 1983; Collaboration with

4AD collective This Mortal Coil; Collaboration with pianist Harold Budd; Band collaborated on Spooky's Found Sound, 1996; Began singing with own band, 1997. *Recordings:* Lullabies, 1982; Peppermint Pig, 1983; Sunburst and Snowblind, 1983; Pearly Dewdrops' Drops, 1984; Aikea-Guinea, 1985; Tiny Dynamite, 1985; Echoes in a Shallow Bay, 1985; Love's Easy Tears, 1986; Iceblink Luck, 1990; Evangeline, 1993; Frosty the Snowman, 1983; Bluebeard, 1994; Twinlights, 1995; Otherness, 1995; Tishbite, 1996; Violaine, 1996; Albums: Treasure, 1984; The Pink Opaque, 1985; The Moon and the Melodies, 1986; Blue Bell Knoll, 1988; Heaven or Las Vegas, 1990; Four Calendar Café, 1993; Milk and Kisses, 1996; Solo: Blame Someone Else, 1997.

REA Chris; b. 4 March 1951, Middlesbrough, Cleveland, England. Singer; Songwriter; Musician (guitar). m. Joan, 1980. *Career:* Member, Magdelene, 1973–75; Name changed to The Beautiful Losers, 1975–76; Solo artist, 1977–; Appearances include: Great British Music Festival, Wembley, 1978; Regular UK and European tours. *Compositions include:* Film score, Soft Top Hard Shoulder, 1993. *Recordings:* Albums (self-written): Whatever Happened To Benny Santini?, 1978; Deltics, 1979; Tennis, 1980; Chris Rea, 1982; Water Sign, 1983; Wired To The Moon, 1984; Shamrock Diaries, 1985; On The Beach, 1986; Dancing With Strangers (No. 2, UK), 1987; The Best of Chris Rea – New Light From Old Windows, 1988; The Road To Hell (No. 1, UK), 1989; Auberge (No. 1, UK), 1991; God's Great Banana Skin, 1992; Expresso Logic, 1993; The Very Best Of, 1994; Contributor, Hank Marvin Guitar Syndicate, Hank Marvin, 1977; Duets, Elton John, 1993; La Passione, 1996; The Blue Café, 1998; Working on It, 1998; Dancing Shoes, 1998; Hit singles include: Fool (If You Think It's Over), 1979; I Can Hear Your Heartbeat, 1983; Stainsby Girls, 1985; On The Beach, 1986; Let's Dance, 1987; Driving Home For Christmas, 1988; The Road To Hell (Part 2), 1989; Tell Me There's A Heaven, 1990; Auberge, 1991; Winter Song, 1991; Nothing To Fear, 1992; Julia, 1993; Featured on Do They Know It's Christmas, Band Aid II (No. 1, UK), 1989. *Honours:* Grammy Nomination, Fool (If You Think It's Over), 1979; Melody Maker Award, Best Newcomers, with the Beautiful Losers, 1975. *Current Management:* Real Life Ltd, 122 Holland Park Ave, London W11 4UA, England.

READ Mark Daniel; b. 7 Nov. 1978, Kingston, Surrey, England. Vocalist; Musician (piano, drums); Songwriter. *Career:* Toured world-wide performing cover versions with parents' group throughout youth; Won Best Young Performer award whilst representing England at Romanian Song Festival; Cruise ship entertainer and small acting roles prior to joining A1 pop group; Signed recording contract, 1999; Sell-out theatre tours of South-East Asia and UK, 2000–01. *Recordings:* Albums: Here We Come, 1999; The A List, 2000; Singles: Be The First To Believe, Summertime of Our Lives, Ready Or Not/Everytime, 1999; Like A Rose, Take On Me, Same Old Brand New You, 2000; No More, 2001; Caught In The Middle, 2002. *Honours:* Brit Award, Best Newcomer, 2001; Also honoured at MTV Mandarin Music Awards. *Current Management:* c/o Byrne Blood Ltd. *Internet:* www.a1-online.com.

READER Eddi; b. 29 Aug. 1959, Glasgow, Scotland. Singer. 2 s. *Career:* Lead singer, Fairground Attraction; Later, solo artiste; Tours: UK; Europe; America; Japan; Television appearances include: Top of The Pops; Later With Jools Holland. *Recordings:* Albums: with Fairground Attraction: First of a Million Kisses; A Fond Kiss; Solo albums: Mirmama; Eddi Reader; Candyfloss and Medicine, 1996; Angels and Electricity, 1999; Singles include: Perfect, with Fairground Attraction; Nobody Lives Without Love, 1995. *Honours:* BRIT Awards: Best Single, Best Band, Best British Female Artist. *Memberships:* Equity; Musicians' Union. *Current Management:* Douglas Kean, Interface Management. *Address:* 37 Oxford Gardens, London W4 3BN, England.

READER Mark; b. 21 March 1960, Liverpool, England. Musician (guitar); Singer. 1 s. *Musical Education:* Classical guitar, classical piano. *Career:* Television with Bill Le Sage, Alec Dankworth, Alan Ganley in Body Talk; Composed music for: Bitsa; We Are The Champions; Is That A Fact; Words and Pictures; Guitarist, Liverpool Empire with P J Proby; Now fronting guitarist, singer, Strider. *Compositions:* for Bitsa: Hurry Up; For We Are The Champions: Hang On Steve, Uphill Champs; for Strider: She's The One; The Loser; Spare Me The Pain; Finding A Way; Seasons With You; UFO. *Memberships:* Musicians' Union; Equity; PRS (associate mem.). *Leisure interests:* Advanced motorcyclist; Archery; Martial arts. *Address:* 7 Thorndale Rd, Waterloo, Liverpool L22 9QP, England.

REBELLO Jason Matthew; b. 29 March 1969, Carshalton, Surrey, England. Jazz Musician (piano). *Musical Education:* Degree, Guildhall School of Music and Drama. *Career:* Concerts with Halle Orchestra; Played with Wayne Shorter, Freddie Jackson and Mica Paris; Television presenter, Artrageous. *Recordings:* Albums: A Clearer View, 1990; Keeping Time, 1993; Make It Real, 1995; Last Dance. *Honours:* The Wire Jazz Album of the Year; Perrier British Jazz Pianist of the Year. *Membership:* Freemason. *Leisure interests:* Reading; Tennis; Computer games. *Current Management:* Alex Hardee, Concorde International Artists. *Address:* 101 Shepherds Bush Rd, Hammersmith, London W6 7LP, England.

REBERT Jeph(rey) L; b. 10 June 1959, Carlisle, Pennsylvania, USA. Musician (drums, percussion); Vocalist; Senior Transportation Planner. *Education:* Pennsylvania State University, 1982; Continuing Education courses, 1987-. *Musical Education:* Private instruction: Piano; Snare Drum; Kit Drums; Class instruction: Percussion, West York Area High School music programme. *Career:* Percussionist, West York Area High School: Symphonic Band; Jazz Ensemble; Pit Orchestra; Drill Team; White Rose Drum and Bugle Corps; York City Concert Band; Pennsylvania State University Blue Band; Phi Mu Alpha Sinfonia Ensembles; Kit drummer, various local rock and lounge acts, 1975–85; Kit drummer and percussionist, 35 local and regional bands, 1989–; Percussionist, Pit Orchestra, The Actors Company of Pennysylvania, 1993; Performances: Bethlehem PA Music Festival (with Namaste), 1997; Lancaster PA Celebration of Cultures Festival (with Namaste), 1996–2000. *Recordings:* Loose Cannons, Peace of Mind, producer and musician, 1995; Single, Symptoms of Depression (compilation), 1995; Namaste, Colonial Pagoda, musician, 1997; features on compilations: Zigarettes, 1998; Breakfast With NPR, 1999. *Memberships:* National Asscn of Rudimental Drummers, 1976–80; Percussive Arts Society, 1980–83; Phi Mu Alpha Sinfonia, alumni mem.; Penn State Blue Band, alumni mem. *Address:* 59 N Lehman St, York, PA 17403, USA.

REDBONE Leon; Vocalist; Musician (guitar). 2 d. *Career:* Performer world-wide, 1973–; Numerous television, film and radio performances, 1976-. *Recordings:* Albums: On The Track, 1975; Double Time, 1977; Champagne Charlie, 1978; From Branch To Branch, 1981; Red To Blue, 1986; No Regrets, 1988; Christmas Island, 1988, (re-released 1989–91); Sugar, 1990; Up A Lazy River, 1992; Whistling In The Wind, 1994; So Relax, track used in British Rail commercials. *Honours:* Gold disc, On the Track, 1975; Silver Lion, 1989; London International Advertising Award, 1989. *Memberships:* AFofM; SAG; AFTRA; Equity. *Current Management:* Beryl Handler. *Address:* 2169 Aquetong Rd, New Hope, PA 18938–2169 USA.

REDDING Noel David; b. 25 Dec. 1945, Folkestone, Kent, England. Musician (bass, rhythm guitar); Vocalist. *Education:* Harvey Grammar School, Folkestone, Kent; Folkestone Art College. *Musical Education:* Violin lessons at school; Later self-taught. *Career:* Professional musician aged 17; Guitarist, The Burnettes, The Loving Kind; Bass player, The Jimi Hendrix Experience, 1966–69; Own band, Fat Mattress, 1969–70; Member, Road, 1971; Solo artiste, session musician, 1974-. *Recordings:* Albums with Jimi Hendrix Experience: Are You Experienced, 1967; Electric Ladyland, 1968; Axis Bold As Love, 1967; Songs include: Little Miss Strange; She's So Fine; Hey Joe; Voodoo Chile; Crosstown Traffic; Foxy Lady; Wind Cries Mary; All Along The Watchtower; with Fat Mattress: Fat Mattress, 1969; Fat Mattress 2, 1970; Road, Road, 1971; with Noel Redding Band: Clonakilty Cowboys, 1975; Blowin', 1976. *Publications:* Noel Redding's Bass Method Book (tutor); Are You Experienced? (co-author with the late Carol Appleby). *Honours:* Rock 'n' Roll Hall of Fame Inductee, 1992; Numerous others. *Memberships:* ASCAP; Equity. *Leisure interests:* Writing; Reading; Television; Restaurants. *Current Management:* Ms Deborah McNaughton, c/o Ardfield PO, Clonakilty, Co Cork, Ireland.

REDDOG Jeff Higgins; b. 28 Feb. 1954, Alexandria VA, USA. Musician (Guitar, Vocals). *Career:* Blues Player, Southeast US. *Compositions:* Four CDs Released. *Honours:* Nominated Best Blues Band Twice, New South Music Awards. *Leisure interests:* Martial Arts; Motorcycles. *Address:* PO Box 7032, Marietta GA 30065, USA.

REDDY Helen; b. 25 October 1942, Melbourne, Victoria, Australia. Singer; Actress. m. (1) Jeff Wald, (2) Milton Robert Ruth, 1 s., 1 d. *Education:* UCLA Extension College. *Career:* Singer, 1966–; Numerous concerts world-wide; Actress, films: Airport, 1975; Pete's Dragon, 1977; Television host, Midnight Special, 1970s; Campaign work for women's political movement and women in prison. *Recordings:* Albums: I Don't Know How To Love Him, 1971; Helen Reddy, 1971; I Am Woman, 1972; Long Hard Climb, 1973; Love Song For Jeffrey, 1974; Free and Easy, 1974; No Way To Treat A Lady, 1975; Greatest Hits, 1975; Music Music, 1976; Ear Candy, 1977; We'll Sing In The Sunshine, 1978; Live In London, 1979; Reddy, 1979; Take What You Find, 1980; Play Me Out, 1981; Imagination, 1983; Take It Home, 1984; Very Best Of, 1993; When I Dream, 1996; Center Stage, 1998; Hit singles: I Don't Know How To Love Him, 1971; I Am Woman, 1972; Delta Dawn, 1973; Angie Baby, 1974; I Can't Hear You No More, 1976. *Honours:* Numerous Gold and Platinum records; LA Times, Woman of The Year, 1975; NAACP Image Award, 1974; Maggie Award, 1976; Humanitarian Award, B'nai B'rith, 1975. *Address:* Helen Reddy Inc, 820 Stanford St, Santa Monica, CA 90403, USA.

REDMAN (Reggie Noble), (Dr Trevis, Funk Docta Spock); b. Newark, New Jersey, USA. Rapper. *Career:* First appeared on friend Erick Sermon's group EPMD's Hardcore and Headbanger; Signed to Def Jam on the strength of those performances; Released debut album, 1992; Starred in How High film with Method Man, 2002; Collaborations: LL Cool J; Adam F; Lil' Cease; Dave Hollister; D'Angelo; De La Soul. *Recordings:* Albums:

Whut? Thee Album, 1992; Dare Iz A Darkside, 1994; Muddy Waters, 1997; Doc's Da Name, 1998; Blackout (with Method Man), 2000; Malpractice, 2001; Singles: Blow Your Mind, 1992; Tonight's Da Night, 1994; Whateva Man, 1997; I'll Bee Dat, 1999; Da Rockwilder (with Method Man), 2000; Smash Sumthin' (with Adam F), 2001. *Address:* c/o Def Jam, 825, Eighth Ave, New York, USA.

REDMOND Melaine; b. 25 Oct. 1962, Putney, London. Session Singer. m. Brian Tench, 2 s. *Career:* World Tours With Duran Duran, Bill Wyman and The Rythym Kings, Bob Geldof; Recordings With, Duran Duran, Bill Wyman and The Rythym Kings, Boy George, Apche Indian; Television Work With Duran Duran, Bill Wyman, Dolly Parton, Sting, Dana Int; Varied Gigs With Adam Ant, Patsy Kensit, Johnny Marr; Jingles Include, Set of 5 Ads For Mazda Car Co. *Recordings:* 3 Albums including, Struttin Our Stuff; Any Way The Wind Blows. *Membership:* Musicians Union. *Leisure interests:* Clay Pigeon Shooting; Decoupage; Keep Fit. *Current Management:* Session Connection and Hobsons Agencies. *Address:* 61 Dysart Ave, Kingston, Surrey KT2 5RA.

REECE Alex; b. 18 Feb. 1970, London, England. Jungle DJ and Prod. *Career:* Early releases on Goldie's Metalheadz label; Additional recordings as Jazz Juice, Lunar Funk and Original Playboy. *Recordings:* Basic Principles, 1995; I Want You, 1995; Chill Pill; Detroit; Jazz Juice; A Nu Era; Touch Me; Pulp Fiction; Ibiza; Jazz Master; UR; Rough Cut; Atlantic Drama; Out of Time; Others; Album: So Far, 1996; Singles: Feel the Sunshine; Candles; I Want You/B-Boy Flavour, 1995; Acid Lab, 1996; Candles, 1996; As Producer: Platinum Breakz, 1996; Rawworks, for Laurent Garnier, 1996; Jungle Jazz, 1996; In Flux (remixing), 1997; Incredible Sound of Drum 'n' Bass, with Goldie, 1999. *Honour:* Best Jungle Single, Pulp Fiction, Dance Awards, Kiss FM, 1995. *Memberships:* PRS; Musicians' Union. *Leisure interests:* Driving; Golf; Snooker computer games; Smoking and drinking; Food. *Address:* c/o Island Records, 825 Eighth Ave, 24th Floor, New York, NY 10019, USA.

REECE Damon; b. 16 Feb. 1967. Musician (Drums). *Career:* Member, Spiritualized; Numerous live dates including world tour; Concerts at London Royal Albert Hall and CN Tower, Toronto. *Recordings:* Singles: Anyway That You Want Me, 1991; Run, 1991; Let It Flow, 1995; Electricity, 1997; I Think I'm In Love, 1998; Abbey Road EP, 1998; Albums: Lazer Guided Melodies, 1992; Fucked Up Inside (live), 1993; Pure Phase, 1995; Ladies and Gentlemen We Are Floating In Space, 1997; Royal Albert Hall October 10 1997 (live), 1998.

REED Brett; b. 1972. Musician (drums). *Career:* Joined Rancid; Numerous live shows. *Recordings:* Singles: Rancid, 1993; Radio, Radio, Radio, 1994; Roots Radicals, 1995; Time Bomb, 1995; Ruby Soho, 1996; Bloodclot, 1998; Hooligans, 1998; Brad Logan, 1998; Albums: Rancid, 1993; Let's Go, 1994; And Out Come the Wolves, 1995; Life Won't Wait, 1998. *Leisure interests:* Skateboarding; Collecting records; Collecting hot rods.

REED Jerry, (Jerry Hubbard); b. 20 March 1937, Atlanta, Georgia, USA. Country Musician (guitar); Singer; Composer; Actor. *Career:* Session guitarist, Nashville; Solo country artiste, 1967–; Duets with Chet Atkins, 1970s; Regular television appearances with Glen Campbell, 1970s; Film appearances include: W W and The Dixie Dance Kings, 1975; Gator, 1976; Smokey and the Bandit, 1977. *Compositions include:* Crazy Legs, Gene Vincent; Misery Loves Company, Porter Wagoner; A Thing Called Love, Johnny Cash; Guitar Man, Elvis Presley; Hits include: Amos Moses; When You're Hot, You're Hot; Lord Mr Ford; She Got The Goldmine (I Got The Shaft); Albums include: Tupelo Mississippi Flash, 1967; Alabama Wild Man, 1969; Cookin', 1970; Georgia Sunshine, 1971; When You're Hot, You're Hot, 1971; Ko Ko Joe, 1972; Jerry Reed, 1972; Hot A Mighty, 1973; Lord Mr Ford, 1973; Half and Half, 1974; Red Hot Picker, 1975; Uptown Poker Club, 1975; Smell The Flowers, 1975; Me and Chet, 1976; Eastbound and Down, 1977; Both Barrels, 1978; In Concert, 1980; Guitar Man, 1997; Pickin, 1999. *Address:* Jerry Reed Enterprises, PO Box 3586, Brentwood, TN 37024, USA.

REED Leslie David; b. 24 July 1935, Westfield, Woking, Surrey, England. Composer; Arranger; Conductor; Musician (piano). m. June Williams, 21 May 1960, 1 d. *Musical Education:* Personal tutor, age 5; London College of Music exams. *Career:* Joined John Barry Seven, 1958; Wembley Concerts; Television appearances include: Drumbeat; Oh Boy; Six Five Special; Ready Steady Go (conductor); Gadzooks; Rolf Harris Show; International Pop Proms; New Faces (panellist); Juke Box Jury. *Compositions include:* It's Not Unusual; The Last Waltz; Delilah; There's A Kind of a Hush; Love Is All; Tell Me When; Here It Comes Again; I'm Coming Home; Les Bicyclettes De Belsize; 24 Sycamore; Everybody Knows; I Pretend. *Recordings include:* As arranger, conductor: Green Green Grass of Home, Tom Jones; You've Got Your Troubles, The Fortunes; Hits recorded by Dave Clark Five; P J Proby; Sammy Davis Jr; Connie Francis; Film soundtrack CDs: Mars Attacks; Little Voice; Parting Shots. *Honours include:* Jimmy Kennedy Award, 1993; Freedom of City of London, 1994; 110 Gold discs; 10 Ivor Novello awards; OBE, 1998. *Memberships:* PRS; Vice President,

BASCA; Ambassador, FIDOF. *Leisure interests:* Study of the paranormal; Golf. *Current Management:* Donna L Ford, Rebecca Music Co Ltd. *Address:* Terwick Pl., Rogate, Nr Petersfield, Hampshire GU31 5BY, England.

REED Lou, (Louis Firbank); b. 2 March 1943, Freeport, Long Island, New York, USA. Singer; Songwriter; Musician (guitar); Poet; Journalist. m. Sylvia Morales, 14 Feb. 1980. *Career:* Founder member, lead singer, songwriter, Velvet Underground, 1964–70, 1993–; Tours as part of Andy Warhol's Exploding Plastic Inevitable show; Solo artiste, 1971–93; Appearances include: Montréal World Fair, 1967; Crystal Palace Garden Party, 1973; Reading Festival, 1975; Nelson Mandela – An International Tribute, Wembley Stadium, 1990; John Lennon Tribute Concert, Liverpool, 1990; Glastonbury Festival, 1992; Bob Dylan 30th Anniversary Concert, New York, 1992. *Recordings:* Albums: with the Velvet Underground: The Velvet Underground and Nico, 1967; White Light, White Heat, 1968; The Velvet Underground, 1969; Loaded, 1970; Solo albums: Lou Reed, 1972; Transformer, 1973; Berlin, 1973; Rock 'n' Roll Animal, 1974; Sally Can't Dance, 1974; Lou Reed Live, 1975; Metal Machine Music, 1975; Coney Island Baby, 1976; Rock and Roll Heart, 1976; Walk On The Wild Side – The Best of Lou Reed, 1977; Street Hassle, 1978; Take No Prisoners, 1979; The Bells, 1979; Vicious, 1979; Growing Up In Public, 1980; Rock and Roll Diary, 1980; The Blue Mask, 1982; Transformer, 1982; Legendary Hearts, 1983; Rock Galaxy, 1983; New Sensations, 1984; Mistrial, 1986; Retro, 1989; New York, 1989; Songs For Drella – A Fiction (with John Cale), 1990; Magic and Loss, 1992; Set The Twilight Reeling, 1996; Also appears on: Sun City single, Artists Against Apartheid, 1985; Soul Man (with Sam Moore), theme for film Soul Man, 1987; Duets album, Rob Wasserman, 1988; Victoria Williams benefit album, 1993; Set the Twilight Reeling, 1996; Live, in Concert, 1997. *Publications include:* Between Thought and Expression (poetry), 1992. *Honours:* Q Magazine Merit Award, 1991; Knight of the Order of Arts and Letters, France, 1992; Inducted into Rock 'n' Roll Hall of Fame (with Velvet Underground), 1996. *Memberships:* AFofM; Screen Actors Guild. *Current Management:* Sister Ray Enterprises, 584 Broadway, Suite 609, New York, NY 10012, USA.

REESE Della, (Deloreese Patricia Early); b. 6 July 1931, Detroit, Michigan, USA. Gospel Singer. m. (1) Vermont Adolphus Bon Taliaferro (divorced), (2) Leroy Basil Gray (divorced), (3) Franklin Thomas Lett Jr. *Education:* Wayne University. *Career:* Choir singer, 1938–; Singer with Mahalia Jackson, 1945–49; Clara Ward; Lead singer, Meditation Singers; Erskine Hawkins Orchestra, 1956; Solo artist, 1957–; Organized gospel group at Wayne University; Numerous television appearances include: Jackie Gleason; Ed Sullivan; McCloud; The Love Boat; The A-Team; Charlie and Co; Crazy Like A Fox; MacGyver; Guest host, The Royal Family, 1991; The Tonight Show; Della; Nightmare In Badham County; Ain't Misbehavin'; Blues In The Night; The Last Minstrel Show. *Recordings:* Singles: and That Reminds Me; In The Still of The Night; Don't You Know; Not One Minute More; Someday (You'll Want Me To Want You); Bill Bailey; Albums include: Special Delivery, 1961; The Classic Della, 1962; Waltz With Me Della, 1964; Let Me Into Your Life, 1975; The Classical Della, 1980; Della By Starlight, 1982; I Like It Like That, 1984; Sure Like Lovin' You, 1985; And Brilliance, 1990; Voice of an Angel, 1996; My Soul Feels Better Right Now, 1998. *Honours:* Voted Most Promising Singer of Year, 1957; Emmy Nomination, Nightmare In Badham County; Grammy Nomination, 1987. *Current Management:* William Morris Agency, 151 El Camino Dr., Beverly Hills, CA 90212, USA.

REES-JONES John; b. 9 Nov. 1948, Cardiff, Wales. Musician (Double Bass, Electric Upright Bass, Bass Guitar). *Career:* Toured and recorded with Keith Tippett's Centipede, including many other top jazz and rock musicians; Appeared with numerous artists including Yehudi Menuhin, Vilhem Tausky and Roger Norrington; Since 1970s, has worked in theatre, cabaret, studio and in jazz fields; Deputised in many West End Shows including Me and My Girl, Crazy for You, Miss Saigon and Guys and Dolls at the National Theatre; Worked in concert and in cabaret with Richard Stilgoe, Peter Skellern, Vera Lynn, Benny Green, Roy Castle, Helen Shapiro and Anita Harris; Performed on TV's South Bank Show with Petula Clark, the Noel Edmonds Show and on Soldier Soldier; Numerous other TV and radio appearances in the UK and abroad; Toured with the Inkspots, 1988–89, and with the Glenn Miller Orchestra UK; Visiting teacher, Bass Guitar and Jazz Double Bass, Eton College; Worked with many top jazz musicians including Slim Gaillard, Herb Ellis, Barney Kessell, Charlie Byrd, Scott Hamilton, Harry 'Sweets' Edison; Toured, recorded and appeared on TV as part of Giants of Jazz, including Kenny Ball and Acker Bilk, 1993; Member, 100 Club All Stars; Deputiser, Humphrey Lyttelton Band; Worked in most European countries, Hong Kong, Pakistan, Argentina and Uruguay. *Address:* May Cottage, 39 Slough Rd, Datchet, Berkshire SL3 9AL, England.

REEVES Del (Franklin Delano); b. 14 July 1933, Sparta, North Carolina, USA. Country Singer; Songwriter; Musician (multi-instrumentalist); Artist Man. *Career:* Own radio show, aged 12; Own TV show, California, 1950s; Solo recording artiste, 1961–; Regular appearances at Grand Ole Opry, 1958–; Host, numerous TV shows; Film appearances include: Second Fiddle To An Old Guitar; Artist Manager, 1992–; Discovered Billy Ray Cyrus. *Recordings:* Over 50 country hits include: Girl On A Billboard; Looking At The World Through A Windshield; Good Time Charlies; The Philadelphia Phillies; Duet with Penny DeHaven, Bobby Goldsboro, Billie Jo Spears; Albums include: Girl On A Billboard, 1965; Mr Country Music, 1966; Our Way of Life, with Bobby Goldsboro, 1967; Running Wild, 1968; Big Daddy Del, 1970; Friends and Neighbours, 1971; Truckers Paradise, 1973; With Strings and Things, 1975; By Request, with Billie Jo Spears, 1976; Del Reeves, 1979; Baby I Love You, 1988; Greatest Hits, 1994; Gospel, 1996; 20 Golden Good Time, 1996. *Address:* Joe Taylor Artist Agency, Nashville, TN, USA.

REEVES Martha; b. 18 July 1941, Eufaula, Alabama, USA. Singer; Musician (piano, tambourine). Divorced, 1 s. *Education:* 12th Grade graduate, Motown University; Lee Strassberg's Theatre Institute. *Career:* Professional Entertainer; Began as Martha LaVaille, Blues singer; Lead singer, Martha Reeves and The Vandellas; Recent appearances include: Leeza; Dick Clark Specials; Beverly Sills Special; Motown 25 Special; Dusty Springfield Specials; Ed Sullivan; K T Oslin Show; Dinah Shore; Merv Griffin; Mike Douglas; American Bandstand; Saturday Night Live; Dick Cavett; Flip Wilson; The Legendary Ladies of Rock and Roll; Music featured in films including: Thelma and Louise; Good Morning Vietnam; Carrie; Tours of USA, other countries; Performances for Charitable organizations include: Arthritis Foundation; Make A Wish Foundation; March of Dimes; Easter Seals Telethon; Detroit Music Hall; Pat Boone's Telethon; Jerry Lewis' Telethon. *Compositions:* Love Is Like A Heatwave; Nowhere To Run; Dancing In The Street. *Recordings include:* Come and Get These Memories, 1963; Love Is Like A Heat Wave, 1963; A Love Like Yours, 1963; Quicksand, 1963; Live Wire, 1964; In My Lonely Room, 1964; Dancing In The Street (No. 1), 1964; Wild One, 1964; Nowhere To Run, 1965; Love (Makes Me Do Foolish Things), 1965; You've Been In Love Too Long, 1965; My Baby Loves Me, 1966; I'm Ready For Love, 1966; Jimmy Mack, 1967; Third Finger, Left Hand, 1967; Honey Chile, 1967; Live Wire!: The Singles 1962–72, 1993; Dancing in the Street: Their Greatest Hits, 1995; Motown Milestones, 1995. *Publications:* Autobiography, Dancing In The Street (Confessions of a Motown Diva); Martha Reeves Exclusive Newsletter. *Honours:* Grammy nomination, for Love Is Like A Heatwave, 1964; Dick Clark, Soul of America Award, 1992; Rhythm and Blues Foundation Pioneer Award, 1993; Black Women In Publishing Award, 1994; Rock and Roll Hall of Fame, 1995; Alabama Music Hall of Fame, 1995; Superbowl halftime, 1998; performed for President Clinton, Christmas Tree Lighting, 1998. *Membership:* AFTRA; Screen Actors Guild, spokesperson for Rite-Aid; Breast Cancer Foundation. *Current Management:* Ace Lichtenstein, Ideal Entertainment Inc, Suite 1908, 875 Avenue of the Americas, New York, NY 10001, USA.

REEVES Thomas W Jr (Tom); b. 14 Feb. 1953, Boston, Massachusetts, USA. Sound Engineer; Mobile DJ; Musician (Electric Bass). m. Carol Reeves, 23 Jan. 1998, 1 s., 1 d. *Education:* ATI Technical Institute; School of Contemporary Music, Brookline, Massachusetts; Cabrillo College, California. *Career:* Owner, Cat's Voice Productions; Assistant Manager, Vibrations, 1988; DJ, Encore Entertainment, Newbury, Massachusetts, 1989–; Producer, Sound Block Studios, Salem, New Hampshire, 1990–; Owner, Engineer, Cat's Voice Productions, Massachusetts, 1990–; Owner, Reel Adventures II Recording Studio; Representative, Market America Inc; Manager, Member, Protex Blues Band, 1991; Marketing Agent, Tennie Komar, Fine and Devine. *Recordings:* Producer, M C Chill, 1990; Clean Shot, 1988–; One Groove At A Time, 1991; The Mangled Ducklings, 1993; Hot, Moist, Pink and Stinky, 1993; Paul Wilcox, Signature, 1996. *Memberships:* American Federation of Musicians; ASCAP; DJs of America; Brotherhood of Electrical Workers; National Asscn of Independent Record Distributors; National Asscn of Music Merchants. *Address:* 114 Kennebunk Pond Rd, Lyman, ME 04002-7719, USA.

REFOY Mark Gerard; b. 3 July 1962, Windsor, Berkshire, England. Songwriter; Musician (guitar). *Career:* Played guitar, Spacemen 3, 1989; Played guitar, Spiritualized, 1990–94; Musician, singer, songwriter, own band Slipstream. *Recordings:* Albums as guitarist: Recurring, Spacemen 3; with Spiritualized: Lazer Guided Melodies, 1992; Pure Phase, 1995; Slipstream, 1995; Be Groovy or Leave, 1997. *Memberships:* Musicians' Union; PRS. *Address:* c/o Slipstream – Che Trading, PO Box 653, London E18 2NX, England.

REGAN Julianne; b. England. Singer; Musician (bass). *Career:* Former music journalist; Backing singer, The Mission; Bass player, Gene Loves Jezebel; Lead singer, All About Eve, 1986-. *Recordings:* with All About Eve: Albums: All About Eve, 1987; Scarlet and Other Stories, 1989; Touched By Jesus, 1991; Circle Dance, 1991; Ultraviolet, 1992; Winter Words, Hits and Rarities, 1992; Singles: Our Summer, 1987; Flowers In Our Hair, 1987; Martha's Harbour, 1988. *Address:* c/o Polar Union, 45–53 Sinclair Rd, London W14 0NS, England.

REICHMANN Silke; b. 1 March 1966, Frankfurt, Germany. Musician (world music, hurdy-gurdy). *Education:* University Kassel, Germany; Tution in Hurdy-gurdy and Flute; Cornet at Conservatory Frankfurt; Hurdy-gurdy Master Class with Valentin Clastrier, Improvisation with Helmut Eisel. *Career:* Musician, Folk Dance Coach with Die Hummel, 1982–86; Teacher, Workshops in Germany, Netherlands, France, 1983–; Musician in Folk and World Music Band, Trio Grande, 1984–; with Paul Engel, World Premiere in Philharmonic Hall, Munich, 1987; solo Radio Broadcasts, Berlin, 1994; special concert for the visit of Germany's President Dr Roman Herzog, 1996; Member of EU World Music Project, Kaleidoscop, touring in Sweden, Norway and Finland, 1998; concert at Reception of Minister of Women's Affairs, International Women's Day, 1999; Teacher for Hurdy-gurdy, Music School, Berlin, 1999-. *Compositions:* Mazurka des amis; Laisser tomber!; Symbati; Zwei Lieben; Ghostdance; Vielfaches Fuer Aspe. *Recordings:* with Trio Grande: Nabucodonosor, 1990; Bagage, 1994; PiloPao, 1998; with Madre: Ghostdance on Mesmerismo; 1997. *Honour:* First prize at the Hurdy Gurdy Duo Competition, St Chartier France, 1991. *Memberships:* ProFolk; GEMA; GVL. *Leisure interests:* Chinese and Afro Brasilian Martial Arts; International Dancing. *Current Management:* World Music, Valentin Reinbold, Gorrisstrasse 9, 50674 Koeln, Germany. *Address:* Pasteurstrasse 4, 10407 Berlin, Germany.

REID Charlie; Singer; Songwriter. *Career:* Formed The Proclaimers, with twin brother Craig, 1983; Played pubs, Edinburgh, Inverness; British tour with The Housemartins; Television debut, The Tube, 1987; Signed to Chrysalis Records, 1987; First single No. 3 in charts; 145 performances, 18 countries, 1988–89; Recorded in Nashville, 1991; Song, I'm Gonna Be (500 miles), theme song to film Benny and Joon, 1993; Tour, USA, included Madison Square Gardens, 1993; Tour: Venezuela; Costa Rica; Brazil; Malaysia; Slovakia; Austria; Canada; Germany; Netherlands; Norway. *Recordings:* (own compositions) Albums: Sunshine On Leith, 1988; This Is The Story, 1994; Hit The Highway, 1994; Singles: Throw The R Away, 1987; Letter From America, 1987; Make My Heart Fly, 1988; I'm Gonna Be (500 Miles), 1988; Sunshine On Leith, 1988; King of The Road, 1990; Let's Get Married, 1994; What Makes You Cry, 1994; These Arms of Mine, 1994. *Honours:* Platinum disc, Sunshine On Leith. *Current Management:* Braw Music Management. *Address:* 78 Pentland Terrace, Edinburgh EH10 6HF, Scotland.

REID Craig; Singer; Songwriter. *Career:* Formed The Proclaimers, with twin brother Charlie, 1983; Played pubs, Edinburgh, Inverness; British tour with The Housemartins; Television debut, The Tube, 1987; Signed to Chrysalis Records, 1987; First single No. 3 in charts; 145 performances, 18 countries, 1988–89; Recorded in Nashville, 1991; Song, I'm Gonna Be (500 miles), theme song to film Benny and Joon, 1993; Tour, USA, included Madison Square Gardens, 1993; Tour: Venezuela; Costa Rica; Brazil; Malaysia; Slovakia; Austria; Canada; Germany; Netherlands; Norway. *Recordings:* (own compositions) Albums: Sunshine On Leith, 1988; This Is The Story, 1994; Hit The Highway, 1994; Singles: Throw The R Away, 1987; Letter From America, 1987; Make My Heart Fly, 1988; I'm Gonna Be (500 Miles), 1988; Sunshine On Leith, 1988; King of The Road, 1990; Let's Get Married, 1994; What Makes You Cry, 1994; These Arms of Mine, 1994. *Honours:* Platinum disc, Sunshine On Leith. *Current Management:* Braw Music Management. *Address:* 78 Pentland Terrace, Edinburgh EH10 6HF, Scotland.

REID DICK William F; b. 19 July 1952, London, England. Audio Prod.; Engineer. m. Lorna Hewitt, 5 June 1982. *Career:* CBS Studios, Whitfield Street, West Indies, 1972–73; Ramport Studios, London, 1973–83; Freelance, 1983–95. *Recordings:* with Thin Lizzy: Jailbreak; Johnny The Fox; Live and Dangerous; with Saxon: Wheels of Steel; Strong Arm of The Law; Motörhead: Iron Fist. *Honours:* 2 Platinum, 5 Gold, 6 Silver albums; Ampex Gold Reel Award. *Memberships:* Re-Pro; PRS. *Leisure interests:* Tennis; Computers. *Address:* No. 1, 35 Wemyss Rd, Blackheath, London SE3 0TG, England.

REID Junior (Delroy); b. 1965, Kingston, Jamaica. Reggae Singer; Record Prod. *Career:* First recording, aged 13; Member, Voice of Progress group; Solo recording artist, early 1980s, and 1989–; Singer, Black Uhuru, 1985–88; Founder, own record label JR Productions and own recording studio; Record producer, leading artists including: Junior Demus, Ninjaman, Dennis Brown and Gregory Isaacs. *Recordings:* Albums include: with Voice of Progress: Mini-Bus Driver; with Black Uhuru: Brutal, 1986; Positive; Solo albums: Boom Shack A Lack; Back To Back; Original Foreign Mind; Visa, 1994; Junior Reid and the Bloods, 1995; Listen to the Voices, 1996; Big Timer, 2000; Also appears on: Lovegod, Soup Dragons; Two for One, Ninjaman; Nothing Like This, Dennis Brown; Not a One Man Thing, Gregory Isaacs; Rass Portraits, Gregory Isaacs; Singles include: Jailhouse; Sister Dawn; Pallaving Street; Give Thanks and Praise; Boom Shack A Lack; Stop This Crazy Thing (with Coldcut); I'm Free (with the Soup Dragons); One Blood, 1990; Actions Speak Louder than Words, 1991; Rappa Pam Pam, 1993. *Honours include:* Grammy Nomination, for

Black Uhuru album Brutal. *Address:* c/o Zoe Productions, 450 Broome St, Eighth Floor, New York, NY 10013, USA.

REID Terry (Terrance James); b. 13 Nov. 1949, Huntingdon, Cambridgeshire, England. Vocalist; Musician (guitar, piano). 2 d. *Musical Education:* Self-taught. *Career:* Toured with: The Rolling Stones; The Hollies; Scott Walker; The Small Faces; Paul Jones; Cream; The Beach Boys; Jethro Tull; Del Shannon; Television includes: Whistle Test; Lulu; David Frost. *Compositions:* Recorded by: Crosby Stills and Nash; Cheap Trick; The Hollies; Arrival. *Membership:* PRS. *Leisure interests:* Fishing; Music. *Address:* Hollyoaks, 1a Rectory Rd, Bluntisham, Huntingdon, Cambs PE17 3LN, England.

REID Vernon; b. England. Musician (guitar). m. Mia McLeod, 6 April 1991. *Musical Education:* Ted Dunbar; Rodney Jones; Manhattan Community College, 2 years. *Career:* Musician with Defunk; Decoding Society; Founder member, funk rock group Living Colour, 1985–; Tours include: with Rolling Stones, North America, 1989; Miracle Biscuit Tour, US, 1990; Lollapalooza Tour, 1991; Stained In The UK tour, 1993; Concerts include: Host, benefit concert, Black Rock Coalition, Los Angeles, 1989; Earth Day, Central Park, 1990; Reading Festival, 1990; Phoenix Festival, 1993; Photography exhibition, Once Upon A Time, Called Now, Chicago, 1991. *Compositions include:* Writer, producer, tracks for B B King, 1990. *Recordings:* Albums: Vivid, 1988; Time's Up, 1991; Biscuits, 1991; Stain, 1993; Super Hits, 1998; Contributions to: Primitive Cool, Mick Jagger, 1986; Talk Is Cheap, Keith Richard, 1988; Funk of Ages, Bernie Worrell, 1988; Singles include: Cult of Personality, 1989; Glamour Boys, 1989; Love Rears Its Ugly Head, 1991; Solace of You, 1991; Leave It Alone, 1993. *Honours:* Elvis Award, Best New Band, International Rock Awards, 1989; MTV Awards, Best New Artist, Best Group Video, Best Stage Performance, 1989; Grammy Award, Best Hard Rock Performance, 1990; Rolling Stone Critics Poll Winners, Best Band, 1991. *Membership:* Black Rock Coalition. *Current Management:* Jim Grant, JGM, Suite 1C, 39A Gramercy Park N, New York, NY 10010, USA.

REID Wilson; b. 28 Feb. 1961, Accra, Ghana. Singer; Musician (guitar). *Education:* Qualified teacher. *Career:* Lead singer, songwriter, Death Bang Party, 1986–94; 2 major UK college tours; Headlined London Town and Country Club, 2 times, 1993; Headlined Marquee Club several times; 2 successful runs, Edinburgh Fringe Festival, 1993, 1994; Appeared on Julian Clary's Best of the Fest, CH4, 1993; Singer and Guitarist with The Tarantinos, completing two nationwide tours. *Publication:* Thrills, Pills and Backache: The Hank Williams Story, 1995. *Honours:* Nominated Best Newcomer, Daily Mail, for Edinburgh Fringe, 1993. *Memberships:* Musicians' Union; Equity. *Leisure interests:* Canoeing; Scuba diving; Salsa dancing. *Current Management:* DBP Productions. *Address:* 842 Garratt Lane, London SW17 0NA, England.

REIFF Soren, (Reiff Jr); b. 22 Oct. 1962, Butterup, Denmark. Musician (guitar, keyboard, bass); Prod. *Education:* Music College, Holstebro, 1982. *Career:* Toured Europe and USA with different artists and as a solo artist, 1989–98; Guitarist in TV houseband appearing in around 200 talkshows, Meyerheim and Co, 1991–94; Played with Robert Palmer, Randy Crawford, Paul Young, Toots Thielemanns, Jamie Walters, Curtis Stigers, Bonnie Tyler, Robin Beck and Suzi Q, 1991–98; Played in houseband on TV show Don't Forget Your Toothbrush, Denmark, 1995; Played in houseband on Safari TV show, 1996; Musical Director of houseband on It's Saturday Night, Denmark, 1997; Appeared on 199 shows with Danish trio, Linie 3, 1997–98. *Recordings:* Numerous recordings with Tower of Power, Michael Brecker and Madness 4 Real and artists from the UK, Scandinavia, Japan, India and Mexico; Guitar sample CD, 1998. *Membership:* Board Mem., Music Highschool of Jyderup, Denmark, 1998. *Current Management:* Ballroom.

REIMERS-WESSBERG Marianne; b. 6 Aug. 1957, Stockholm, Sweden. Music Publisher. m. H G Wessberg, 1 s., 2 d. *Education:* BA, Musicology, German, Economics. *Career:* Editor, Music Teachers Magazine, Musik Kultur, 1983–88; Managing Director, Reimers AB, 1990-. *Publications:* Lyssna ar Silver, Spela ar Guld, (To Listen Is Silver – To Play Is Gold), 1991. *Memberships:* Music Publishers Asscn; STIM; Swedish Music Information Center. *Address:* PO Box 15030, S 16115 Bromma, Sweden.

REINHART Randy; b. 16 Jan. 1953, NJ, USA. Musician (Trumpet, Trombone). *Education:* BA, Music Kean University. *Career:* Eddie Condons, NYC. *Membership:* Local 802 AEW. *Leisure interest:* Golf. *Address:* 14 Kensington Rd, Madison, NJ 07940, USA.

REISIG Bernd; b. 10 March 1963, Frankfurt, Germany. Media Man. *Education:* Engine Fitter; Children's Male Nurse. *Career:* Founded concert agency; Artists: Purple Schulz; Bruce Cockburn; Extrabeit, 1984; Founded music publishing agency, 1985; Founded management agency, 1987; Represent artists: Nena; Badesalz; Thomas Koschwitz; Matthias Beltz; Christian Kahrman; Founded RMG Merchandising and RMG Music Entertainment, 1993; Represent artists: Nena; The Stroke; Mellow D;

McDowell-Tarr; Dan; Several dance projects; Share in radio station, Radio 01, 1994; Share in advertising agency Koschwitz-Kommunikation; Share in television production company Feedback. *Honours:* Several Gold records, Grimme-Preis. *Memberships:* IFPI; GEMA. *Leisure interest:* Football. *Address:* Reisig Media GmbH, Lersnerstrasse 23, 60322 Frankfurt/Main, Germany.

REISSIG Heiko Christian; b. 19 Feb. 1966, Wittenberge, Germany. Singer (Tenor); Actor; Dir. *Education:* Diplomas, University of Music and Theatre, Leipzig, Berlin and Munich, 1990–97; Diploma of Teaching in Voice. *Career:* Opera Singer and Actor, Komische Oper, Berlin; Oper Leipzig; Theater Hof, Görlitz and other venues in Germany; Actor, film and TV; Singer, numerous festivals and concert tours abroad including Japan, Mexico and Austria. *Memberships:* International Yehudi Menuhin Society, London, 1997–; President of the International Society Supporting Young Stage Artists (ISSA), BühnenReif, Germany, 1997-. *Leisure interests:* Swimming; Nature; Sports; Opera; Cinema; Travel. *Address:* Richard-Sorge Strasse 11, 10249 Berlin, Germany.

RENAUD Norman Joseph; b. 11 Aug. 1938, Durban, South Africa. Author; Composer; Musician (acoustic, electric guitar, casiotone keyboards, piano, percussion); Singer; Songwriter. 3 s., 3 d. *Education:* Technical College. *Musical Education:* City University; The music industry. *Career:* Radio and television performances, in UK and world-wide; Vocalist and orchestral musician. *Recordings:* Ballads; Standards, Popular styles, Rock 'n' Roll; Soul; Dance; Country and Western styles, Popular styles, Jazz, Motown song styles. *Publications:* Currently compiling own songs and music. *Membership:* Musicians' Union. *Leisure interests:* Music; Dancing; Television and radio; Films; World of Sport; Songwriting and composing. *Current Management:* Renaud. *Address:* No. 17 Corbiere House, Fifth Floor, De Beauvoir Estate, Balmes Rd, London N1 5SR, England.

RENAULT Nathalie; b. 26 Nov. 1966, Paris, France. Musician (banjo and trumpet). *Education:* Fine Arts: National Superior Beaux-Arts School of Paris and University of Arts, Paris. *Musical Education:* Conservatory of Music, Clamart, Hauts-de-Seine. *Career:* Concerts: International Music Festival, Riga, Latvia; Centre Cuturel Francais, Skopje, Macedonia; Jazz Festival, Corinth, Greece; Malmö Festival, Sweden; Cromwell Festival, Upton Upon Severn, UK; Oude Stijl Jazz Festival, Breda, Netherlands; 12 tage Jazz, Frankfurt, Germany; Dixie Jazz Festival, Sargans, Switzerland; Jazz Festival, Vannes; Jazz Band Ball, Paris, France; Nice Jazz Festival, Nice, France. *Recordings:* with female jazz (old style) band Certains L'Aiment Chaud (Some Like It Hot): 1 cassette, 1985; 1 cassette, 1991; Album: J'ai Deux Amours, 1995. *Honours:* Sidney Bechet Prize, Jazz Academy, Paris, France, 1992. *Leisure interest:* Sculpture exhibitions, France (mainly Paris). *Address:* 113 Ave Victor Hugo, 92140 Clamart, France.

RENBOURN John; b. 8 Aug. 1944, Marylebone, London, England. Musician (guitar). *Education:* Kingston Art School. *Musical Education:* Dartington College, Devon. *Career:* Collaborations with: Bert Jansch; Stefan Groossman; Robin Williamson; Founder, groups Pentangle; John Renbourn Group; Ship of Fools; Played at Carnegie Hall; New York Town Hall; Central Park Concert; Sydney Opera House; Royal Albert Hall; Festival Hall; Les Cousins. *Recordings:* Sir Johnalot; Lady and The Unicorn; Black Balloon; Nine Maidens; Wheel of Fortune; Live in America. *Publications:* Guitar Pieces; Guitar Styles; Medieval Renaissance Anthology. *Honours:* 2 Grammy Award Nominations. *Membership:* The Galpin Society. *Current Management:* Folklore Inc, 1671 Appian Way, Santa Monica, CA 90401, USA.

RENDELL Don; b. 4 March 1926, Plymouth, England. Musician (saxophone, flute, clarinet). m. Joan Ruth Yoxall, 27 March 1948, 1 d. *Musical Education:* Self-taught (in musical family). *Career:* Oscar Rabin Band, 1948–49; Founder member, John Dankworth Seven, 1950–53; Ted Heath Orchestra, 1955–56; Stan Kenton, 1956; Own Quartet, Quintet, Sextet, 1957–; Woody Herman Anglo-American Herd, 1959; Recordings with all the above; International jazz festivals: Antibes, 1968; BBC2 TV, Greenwich, 1979; Brecon, 1991; Villeneuve, 1992; Professor, Jazz Saxophone, Guildhall School Music and Drama. *Compositions:* 100 include: On The Way; Antibes; Euphrates; Calavinas. *Recordings:* 5 albums as Rendell/Carr 5; Solo albums: Space Walk, 1971; Earth Music, 1979; Don Rendell Big 8: If I Should Lose You, 1992. *Publications:* Flute Method; Saxophone Selection; Sax Skills (video). *Memberships:* Founder mem., Clarinet and Saxophone Society (CASS); Asscn of British Jazz Musicians. *Leisure interest:* Bible study and teaching. *Address:* 23 Weir Hall Gardens, Edmonton, London N18 1BH, England.

RENE Tawamba; b. 27 July 1962, Bangasson. Author; Composer; Singer. m. Fozen Brigitte, 1 s., 1 d. *Career:* Dancer, Johny Tezano, 1987–91; Many Television and Radio Programs; Festivals. *Compositions include:* Bibi Kitoko, Palauce Sonkouss; Bjamena; Sambara Reko; Kibindo Lauce; Tika Kolela. *Recordings:* Bibi Kotoko; Confiance Perdue; Palauce Sonkouss; Bjamena; Sambara Perko; Kibindo Lauce; Tika Kolela. *Leisure interests:*

Football; Cinema; Music. *Current Management:* Jack Palance, Tawamba Rene S/C Aamont PO Box 4562, Yaoundé, Cameroon.

RENLIDEN Ivan; b. 27 Sept. 1936, Sweden. m. Sonja, 27 Oct. 1956, 1 s., 1 d. *Education:* Student, 1956; Academy of Music, Stockholm, Musical Teacher, 1964, Diploma of Piano, 1964. *Career:* Musical Leader, Arranger and Pianist, major stages in Stockholm; Almost 1000 Radio and TV Programs, lots of recordings with popular Swedish artists. *Recordings:* Svenska Melodier; Ivan Renliden Spelar Ivan Renliden; Ain't Misbehavin; Spectrum; Ivan Renliden Spelar Chopin. *Honour:* Cultural Prize of Stockholm, 1975. *Memberships:* STIM; SAMI. *Leisure interest:* Golf. *Address:* Ullerudsb 79, 12373 Farsta, Sweden.

RENO Mike; b. Canada. Vocalist; Songwriter. *Career:* Member, Moxy; Founder member, Canadian rock group, Loverboy, 1980–89; Extensive tours, USA, Canada; Support to Def Leppard, European tour, 1988. *Compositions:* Co-writer, with Bryan Adams, Jon Bon Jovi, Richie Sambora, for Loverboy tracks. *Recordings:* Albums: Loverboy, 1980; Get Lucky, 1981; Keep It Up, 1983; Lovin' Every Minute of It, 1985; Wildside, 1987; Big Ones (compilation), 1989; Six, 1997; Singles: Turn Me Loose; The Kid Is Hot Tonite; Working For The Weekend; Hot Girls In Love; Lovin' Every Minute of It. *Honours:* Multi-platinum records for all 5 studio albums; JUNO Awards: Album of the Year, Loverboy, 1981; Get Lucky, 1982; Single of the Year, Turn Me Loose, 1981; Group of Year, 1981; 1982; Composer of the Year (with Paul Dean), 1981; Tribute To West Coast Music Awards: Best Group, 1981; 1982; Best Album: 1981, 1982; Song of the Year, The Kid Is Hot Tonite, 1981; Most Promising Act, 1981; International Achievement Award, 1984; Rock Band of Year, 1981. *Current Management:* Lou Blair Management Inc. *Address:* No. 407–68 Water St, Vancouver, British Columbia V6B 1A4, Canada.

RESCALA Tim (Luiz Augusto); b. 21 Nov. 1961, Rio de Janeiro, Brazil. Composer; Arranger; Musician (piano). m. Claudia Mele, 24 June 1995, 1 d. *Musical Education:* Piano with Maria Yêda Cadah; Composition with Hans-Joachim Koellreutter, Master's degree at University of Rio de Janeiro. *Career:* Works with serious music and pop music; Musical producer at TV Globo since 1988. *Compositions:* Scores for over 50 stage productions; Compositions played in Brazil; France; Canada; Belgium; USA; United Kingdom; Music for films with director Eduardo Coutinho; Music for Berimbuu and Tape, Cliché Music; Salve O Brasil!, Ponto, Linha E Plano. *Recordings:* Cliché Music (with popular songs and a suite for instruments); Album, Estudio da Glória (electroacoustic music). *Honours:* First Prize in Villa-Lobos Competition; Mambembe Prize (theatre), 1983, 1993; Prize of Rio de Janeiro Municipality to write an opera. *Membership:* Estudió da Glória (co-founder). *Leisure interest:* Cooking. *Address:* Estúdio da Gloria, Rua Candido Mendes 53/104, Glória Cep 20.241 Rio de Janeiro, RJ, Brazil.

REUBEN Cyril; b. 30 April 1930, Bangor, North Wales. Musician (woodwind); Music Shop Retailer. m. Sylvia, 22 Dec. 1958, deceased, 1 s., 1 d. *Musical Education:* University College of North Wales. *Career:* Member, orchestras of: Geraldo; Squadronaires; Jack Parnell; Concerts, tours include: Frank Sinatra; Liza Minelli; Shirley MacLaine; Johnny Mathis; Bing Crosby; Sarah Vaughan; Liberace. *Recordings:* Records with: The Beatles; The Carpenters; Music for television series include: Thunderbirds; Stingray; Captain Scarlett; Films include: Jesus of Nazareth; Fall of The Roman Empire; In Hannibals Footsteps. *Membership:* Musicians' Union. *Leisure interests:* Travel; Driving; Good food. *Address:* Woodwind, Derek Rd, Maidenhead, Berkshire SL6 8NT, England.

REVERE Paul; b. 7 Jan. 1938, Caldwell, Idaho, USA. Musician; Comic; Businessman. m. Sydney Revere, 1980, 1 s., 1 d. *Career:* Formed Paul Revere and The Raiders, 1960; Television, hosted: Where The Action Is, with Dick Clark, 1965–66; Happening, 1968–69; 2 appearances, Ed Sullivan Show. *Recordings:* Kicks; Indian Reservation; Just Like Me; Good Thing; Louie Louie; Hungry; Ups and Downs; Him Or Me; Just Like Us. *Honours:* Northwest Music Awards; Hall of Fame; Numerous Gold Records. *Current Management:* Robert Norman/Fred Lawrence at International Management. *Address:* 8942 Wilshire Blvd, Beverly Hills, CA 90211, USA.

REYES Fernando; b. 4 Feb. 1939, Conil De La Frontera, Cádiz, Spain. Flamenco Singer; Flamenco Musician (guitar). m. Gillian Carol Hamling, 29 March 1975, 1 s., 1 d. *Musical Education:* Private musical tuition, Spain. *Career:* Performed throughout: Spain; Europe; Canada; USA; Asia; Played for Antonio and Paco Romero and The King and Queen of Belgium; Toured with: Los Paraguayos; Performances include: Madison Square Gardens; Palais De Beaux Arts; Royal Albert Hall; Royal Festival Hall; Sadlers Wells; Covent Garden; Queen Elizabeth Hall; Fairfield Hall; Purcell Room; Numerous provincial theatres; Sang in opera Carmen in UK and Germany; Television includes: Opportunity Knocks; Blue Peter; Barrymore; Good Stuff; Collector's Lot; Live musical soundtrack for film, Pain Is..., 1998; also various film scores; Broadcast on Virgin Radio. *Compositions:* Words

and music various songs. *Recordings:* Albums: Spanish, South American music; Flamenco Songs; Spanish Popular Songs; CDs: Encuentros; Flamenco; Flamenco Gypsy. *Honours:* Various medals, trophies, awards, flamenco competitions in Spain. *Membership:* Musicians' Union. *Leisure interest:* Gardening. *Current Management:* Gillian Reyes. *Address:* 19 Fairmount Rd, London SW2 2BJ, England.

REYNOLDS (Lee) Allen; b. North Little Rock, Arkansas, USA. Country record producer; Songwriter; Music publisher. *Education:* Rhodes College, Memphis, English student. *Career:* Began songwriting partnership with long-term collaborator and friend Dickey Lee at college; Moved to Texas; Joint composition I Saw Linda Yesterday became US hit for Lee, 1962; Composition about day job in a bank, Five O'Clock World, subsequently a Top 5 US pop hit for the Vogues; Moved to Nashville and began production work, including Don Williams' recording of I Recall A Gypsy Woman; Purchased Jack's Tracks Recording Studio in Nashville, 1976; Set up self-contained recording and publishing operation; Own recording career, 1978; Productions include: Kathy Mattea; O'Kanes; Bobby Bare; George Hamilton IV; Daniel O'Donnell; Randy VanWarmer; Hal Ketchum; Emmylou Harris; all of Garth Brooks' country albums; Songs recorded by artists including: Waylon Jennings; Johnny Russell; Marianne Faithfull. *Compositions include:* Catfish John; Everybody's Reaching Out For Someone; Five O'Clock World; I Saw Linda Yesterday; Ready For The Times To Get Better; Somebody Loves You; We Should Be Together. *Honours:* Sales of albums produced for Garth Brooks surpass the 100m. mark; BMI 'Millionair' Award for over 1m. radio performances of compositions Ready For The Times To Get Better and Five O'Clock World; Inducted into Nashville Songwriters Asscn Inc (NSAI) Hall of Fame with long time associate and friend Dickey Lee, 2000. *Address:* c/o Jack's Tracks Recording Studio, 1308 16th Ave S, Nashville 37212, USA.

REYNOLDS Debbie (Mary Frances); b. 1 April 1932, El Paso, Texas, USA. Actress; Singer; Entertainer. m. (1) Eddie Fisher, 26 Sept. 1955, divorced, 1959, 1 d.; m. (2) Harry Karl, 25 Nov. 1960, divorced 1973; m. (3) Richard R Hamlett, 1985. *Career:* Nightclub act, mid 1960s-; Headlines casino circuit, including Reno, Tahoe, Las Vegas, Atlantic City; London Palladium; Tours average 42 weeks a year; Over 30 films include: Three Little Words; Two Weeks With Love; Singin' In The Rain; The Unsinkable Molly Brown; The Tender Trap; Divorce American Style; Theatre includes: Irene, 1973; Annie Get Your Gun; Woman of The Year, 1983; National tour, The Unsinkable Molly Brown, 1989; Founded Debbie Reynolds Professional Rehearsal Studios, North Hollywood, late 1970s; Currently establishing Hollywood Motion Picture and Television Museum, in the Debbie Reynolds Hollywood Hotel and Casino. *Recordings:* Abba Dabba Honeymoon (from Two Weeks With Love); Tammy; 5 videos Debbie/Am I That Easy to Forget?, 1996; Post sessions producer: Baltimore Consort: Tunes from the Attic, 1997. *Publication:* Debbie My Life (co-written with David Patrick Colombia), 1987. *Honours include:* National Hon. Presented by Girl Scouts USA, 1966–69; Academy Award nomination, The Unsinkable Molly Brown; National Film Award, Humanitarian Award, National Film Society; Celebrity Hall of Fame Award, National Asscn for Mental Health; Hollywood Hall of Fame, Hollywood Historic Trust and Chamber of Commerce. *Memberships:* Supporter, fund raiser, Girl Scouts; Founder-president of the Thalians. *Address:* c/o Stan Scotland, JKE Services, 404 Park Ave S, 10th Floor, New York, NY 10016, USA.

REZNOR Trent; b. 17 May 1965, Mercer, PA, USA. Rock Musician; Singer. *Career:* Founder member, lead vocalist, US rock group Nine Inch Nails, 1989-. *Recordings:* Albums: Pretty Hate Machine, 1990; Broken (mini-album), 1992; Fixed, 1992; Downward Spiral, 1994; Children of the Night, 1996; Perfect Drug, 1997; Fragile, 1999; Singles include: Head Like A Hole, 1990; Compiler, film soundtrack Natural Born Killers, 1994. *Current Management:* John Malm, Conservative Management, 2337 W 11th St, Suite 7, Cleveland, OH 44113, USA.

RHYS Gruff; b. 18 July 1970, Haverfordwest, Wales. Vocalist. *Career:* Member, Super Furry Animals; Recorded 2 EPs on indie label, then obtained major indie label deal; Numerous tours in the UK and abroad; Began as techno outfit but became more psychedelic and progressive rock; Appeared at numerous festivals. *Recordings:* Singles: Llanfairpwllgwyngyllgogerychwyndrobwl... EP, 1995; Moog Droog, 1995; God! Show Me Magic, 1996; If You Don't Want Me To Destroy You, 1996; The Man Don't Give a Fuck, 1996; Hometown Unicorn, 1996; Something 4 The Weekend, 1996; The International Language of Screaming, 1997; Hermann Loves Pauline, 1997; Demons, 1997; Play it Cool, 1997; Ice Hockey Hair, 1998; Albums: Fuzzy Logic, 1996; Radiator, 1997; Guerrilla, 1999.

RHYS-JONES Merlin; b. 15 June 1958, Brighton, Sussex, England. Musician (guitar); Songwriter; Arranger. *Musical Education:* Self-taught. *Career:* Recorded with Lipservice; Toured with Ian Dury and The Music Students, 1983; Ian Dury and The Blockheads, 1992, 1994–95; Ellis, Beggs and Howard, 1989; Television includes: The Tube with Ian Dury; Sight and Sound; Martin Dobson's Main Course, Capital Radio. *Recordings:* Albums with Ian Dury: 4000 Weeks Holiday; Apples; Bus-Drivers Prayer and Other Stories (includes some co-writes); Warts and Audience (Live Blockheads at Brixton Academy); Several sessions for television shows; Currently teaching at Musicians Institute, Wapping. *Memberships:* Publishing agreement with Mute Song; Musicians' Union; PRS. *Leisure interests:* Fishing; Theatre. *Address:* Flat 21, 318 Hornsey Rd, London N7 7HE, England.

RIBOT Marc; b. 21 May 1954, Newark, New Jersey, USA. Musician (guitar). *Musical Education:* Studied with Frantz Casseus. *Career:* Moved to New York, 1978; Member, Realtones/Uptown Horns Band, 1979–83; Member, John Lurie's Lounge Lizards, 1984–89; Freelance musician, 1989–; Played with Jack MacDuff; Wilson Pickett; Chuck Berry; Solomon Burke; Tom Waits; Elvis Costello. *Recordings:* Albums: with Tom Waits: Rain Dogs; Big Time; Frank's Wild Years; with John Zorn: Cynical Hysterical Tour; Kristellnacht; with Elvis Costello: Spike; Mighty Like A Rose; Kojak Variety; Numerous solo albums include: Rootless Cosmopolitans, 1990; Shrek, 1994; Don't Blame Me, 1995; Shoe String Symphonettes, 1997; Prosthetic Cubans, 1998; A Yo I Killed Your God, 1999; Also recordings with: The Lounge Lizards; John Lurie; Evan Lurie; Solomon Burke; The Jazz Passengers; David Sanborn; Caetano Veloso; Marianne Faithfull; Laurie Anderson; T-Bone Burnett; Sam Philips. *Current Management:* Ribot Productions. *Address:* 151 First Ave #88, New York, NY 10003, USA.

RICE Melanie Ailene; b. 4 Nov. 1957, Philadelphia, Pennsylvania, USA. Singer; Musical Contractor. *Musical Education:* Rowan College; BA, Music, University of Delaware. *Career:* Tours: Opening act for: Joan Rivers; Smokey Robinson; Shecky Greene; David Brenner; Susan Anton; George Kirby; Bobby Vinton; Backing vocalist for: Grover Washington; James Darren; Joe Piscopo; Bobby Rydell; Various Casino Hotel appearances as solo act. *Honours:* John Phillip Sousa Award. *Membership:* NACE. *Leisure interest:* Golf. *Current Management:* Melanie Rice Entertainment, Inc. *Address:* 2511 Huntingdon Pike, Huntingdon Valley, PA 19006, USA.

RICE Tim (Sir), (Miles Bindon); b. 10 Nov. 1944, Amersham, Buckinghamshire, England. Writer; Broadcaster. m. Jane Arterata McIntosh, 1974, divorced 1990, 1 s., 1 d. *Education:* Lancing College. *Career:* EMI Records, 1966–68; Norrie Paramor Organisation, 1968–69; Founder, Director, GRRR Books Ltd, 1978-, Pavilion Books Ltd, 1981–97; Appearances on TV and radio including Just A Minute, Radio 4; Creative Works: Lyrics for stage musicals (with Andrew Lloyd Webber): Joseph and the Amazing Technicolour Dreamcoat, 1968; Jesus Christ Superstar, 1970; Evita, 1976; Cricket, 1986; Other musicals: Blondel, with Stephen Oliver, 1983; Chess, with Benny Andersson and Bjorn Ulvaeus, 1984; Tycoon, with Michel Berger, 1992; Selection of songs, Beauty and the Beast, with Alan Menken, 1994; Heathcliff, with John Farrar, 1996; King David, with Alan Menken, 1997; Aida, with Elton John, 1998; Lyrics for musical films: Aladdin, with Alan Menken, 1992; The Lion King, with Elton John, 1994, theatre version, 1997; Lyrics for songs with other compsers including Paul McCartney, Mike Batt, Freddie Mercury, Graham Gouldman, Marvin Hamlisch, Rick Wakeman, John Barry. *Publications:* Song books from musicals; Guinness Book of Hit Albums, co-auth; Guinness Books of British Hit Singles, co-author; Fill Your Soul, 1994; Cricket Writer, National Newspapers and Cricket Magazines. *Honours:* Academy Award, Golden Globe, Best New Song, A Whole New World, 1992 for Can You Feel The Love Tonight, with Elton John, 1994, and for You Must Love Me with Andrew Lloyd Webber, 1996; Gold and platinum records in numerous countries; 11 Ivor Novello Awds; 2 Tony Awards; 5 Grammy Awards; Kt, 1994. *Memberships:* Chairman, Stars Organisation for Spastics, 1983–85; Shaftesbury Avenue Centenary Committee, 1984–86; President, Lords Taverners, 1988–90; Dramatists' Saints and Sinners, Chairman, 1990; Cricket Writers; Foundation for Sport and the Arts, 1991–; Garrick Club; Groucho Club; MCC. *Leisure interests:* Cricket; History of Popular Music; Poultry. *Address:* 31 The Terrace, Barnes, London SW13 0NR, England.

RICH John; b. 7 Jan. 1974, Amarillo, Texas, USA. Country vocalist; Musician (pedal steel guitar, bass guitar). *Career:* Began career as singer and performer in the bluegrass field; Formed Texasee with Dean Sams, Keech Rainwater, Michael Britt and Richie McDonald, 1992; Originally shared lead vocal duties in band with McDonald; Group became resident house band at the Wildhorse Saloon, Nashville; After subsequent name change to Lonestar, came to the attention of BMG and were signed to their BNA subsidiary; Released promotional six-track live CD, recorded at the Wildhorse; First country chart entry No News/Tequila Talkin' from debut album Lonestar, 1996; By the time of group's second album release, Crazy Nights, effectively sidelined as Richie McDonald became Lonestar's sole featured lead vocalist, despite previously shared duties and penning band successes Come Cryin' To Me and Say When; Left band to pursue solo career, 1998; Continued association with BNA label and first solo album, produced by friend and veteran songwriter Sharon Vaughan, Underneath The Same Moon contained debut single I Pray For You. *Recordings include:* with Lonestar: No News, Tequila Talkin', 1996; Come Cryin' To Me, 1997;

solo: I Pray For You; Albums: Underneath The Same Moon. *Address:* c/o The Country Music Asscn, Nashville, Tennessee, USA.

RICHARD Cliff (Sir), (Harry Webb); b. 14 Oct. 1940, Lucknow, India. Singer. *Career:* Leader, Cliff Richard and the Shadows; Later, solo artist; Regular international concert tours, 1958–; Films include: The Young Ones; Expresso Bongo; Summer Holiday; Wonderful Life; Own television show; Frequent television and radio appearances. *Recordings:* First single, Move It, 1958; Over 120 singles to date; Over 50 albums include: 21 Today, 1961; The Young Ones, 1961; Summer Holiday, 1963; 40 Golden Greats, 1977; Love Songs, 1981; Private Collection, 1988; The Album, 1993 (all No. 1 in UK charts). *Publications:* Which One's Cliff; Jesus, Me and You; You, Me and Jesus; Mine Forever; Mine To Share; Single-Minded. *Honours:* OBE, 1980; Knighted, 1995; Numerous music awards. *Membership:* Equity. *Leisure interests:* Tennis; Gardening. *Current Management:* Cliff Richard Organisation. *Address:* c/o PO Box 46c, Esher, Surrey KT10 0RB, England.

RICHARD Marc; b. 22 Nov. 1946, Neuilly-Sur-Seine, France. Jazz Musician (saxophone, clarinet); Composer; Arranger. *Musical Education:* Self-taught musician; 3 years of courses for arrangement. *Career:* Played cornet with Haricots Rouges, 1963; Played saxophone and clarinet with many different bands including: Irakli; François Biensan; Founder, Anachronic Jazz Band, 1976; Played as sideman in Paris for many years with prominent jazzmen, including: Cab Calloway; Dee Dee Bridgewater; Harry Edison; Teacher, Jazz History, various schools. *Recordings:* Anachronic Jazz Band, Vol. 1, 1977; Vol. 2, 1980; Also appears on: Duke Ellington Complete Edition Vol. 1; Accident, John Greaves, 1982; Bix Beiderbecke, Vols 2, 4, 5, 7, 8, 1994–96; Solo recording: After You've Gone. *Leisure interests:* Golf; Cooking. *Address:* 21 Allée de Fontainebleau, 75019 Paris, France.

RICHARD Zachary; b. 8 Sept. 1950. Singer; Songwriter; Poet; Musician (Guitar, Piano, Cajun Accordion, Harmonica). m. Claude Thomas, 11 Jan. 1992. *Education:* BA, summa cum laude, Tulane University, 1972. *Career:* Innovator, Cajun and Zydeco Musical Styles. *Recordings:* Albums: Bayou des Mystères, 1976; Mardi Gras, 1977; Migration, 1978; Allons Danser, 1978; Live in Montréal, 1979; Vent D'Été, 1980; Zack Attack, 1984; Zack's Bon Ton, 1986; Mardi Gras Mambo, 1988; Women in the Room, 1990; Snake Bite Love, 1992; Cap Enragé, 1996; Who Stole My Monkey; Come on Sheila; Cap Enragé; La Ballade de Jean Batailleur. *Publications:* Poetry: Voyage de Nuit, 1986; Faire Récolte, 1997; Anthology: Travailler C'est Trop Dur, 1999. *Honours:* Prix de la Jeune Chanson Francaise, 1980; Prix Miroir de Québec, 1996; Officier de l'Ordre des Arts et Lettres, 1996; 2 Certified Gold Canadian Awards, 1978; Felix de l'ADISQ, 1997–98; Certified Platinum Canadian, 1997; Prix Littéraire Champlain, 1998. *Current Management:* Claude Thomas, PO Box 305, Scott La 70583, 318, 2699926, USA. *Address:* PO Box 456, Scott, LA 70583, USA.

RICHARDS Aled; b. 5 July 1969, Camarthen, Wales. Musician (Drums). *Career:* Member, Catatonia; Numerous festival appearances and live gigs; Many appearances on music shows on TV and radio. *Recordings:* Singles: Bleed/ Do You Believe In Me, 1996; Mulder and Scully, 1998; Road Rage, 1998; Strange Glue, 1998; Londinium, 1999; Albums: Way Beyond Blue, 1996; The Sublime Magic of Catatonia, 1996; International Velvet, 1998; Equally Cursed and Blessed, 1999.

RICHARDS Andy; Prod.; Programmer; Musician (keyboards). *Career:* As Programmer and Keyboard Player has worked with Trevor Horn and Stephen Lipson on many projects including: Frankie Goes to Hollywood, Propaganda, Grace Jones; Other Artists include: George Michael, The Pet Shop Boys, Chris De Burgh, Def Leppard, Wet Wet Wet, Cher, Annie Lennox and Tina Turner; As Producer and Programmer clients include: Alphaville; Prefab Sprout; The Pet Shop Boys; Fuzzbox; OMD; T'Pau; Dusty Springfield; Boyzone; Seal; Orchestral Manoeuvers in the Dark; Art of Noise; Genesis. *Current Management:* SARM Management, The Blue Building, 42/46 St Luke's Mews, London W11 1DG, England.

RICHARDS Dick, (Richard Boccelli); b. Philadelphia, Pennsylvania, USA. Musician (drums); Vocalist. *Career:* Original member, Bill Haley's Comets, 1954–55; Influential in early development of rock 'n' roll; First rock band to headline a film; Theatre and film actor (as Richard Boccelli). *Recordings:* Rock Around The Clock; See You Later Alligator; Crazy Man Crazy; Shake Rattle and Roll; Rock The Joint; Mambo Rock; Rudy's Rock; Florida Twist; Shimmie Minnie; with Bill Haley: From the Original Master Tapes, 1985; Decca Years and More, 1991. *Publications:* Rock Around The Clock; Stage Clear; We're Gonna Party; Never Too Old To Rock; Let's All Rock Together; Now Dig This. *Honours:* Best Vocal group of 1953 Rock and Roll Hall of Fame; Gold records. *Address:* Rock It Concerts, Bruno Mefer Platz 1, 80937 Munich, Germany.

RICHARDS Eddie, (Jolly Roger); b. Amersham, Buckinghamshire, England. Prod.; Remixer; DJ. *Career:* Started as a DJ at the Camden Palace in London; Instrumental in introducing House music to the UK as resident DJ at the Clink Street parties, 1988; Founder: Dy-na-mix DJ agency; Lunar Records; Collaborations: Mr C; Richie Hawtin; Kid Bachelor; Remixed: The Shamen; Orbital. *Recordings:* Singles: as Jolly Roger: Acid Man, 1988; Why Can't We Live Together, 1989; as Eddie Richards: Love Is/ House, 2001. *Current Management:* Dy-na-mix.com. *E-mail:* eddierichards@dy-na-mix.com.

RICHARDS Eric (Thomas); b. 21 July 1953, Alnwick, England. Musician (bass guitar, piano, guitar). 2 d. *Musical Education:* City of Leeds College of Music; BA, Durham University; Jazz and Light Music, Newcastle College of Arts and Technology. *Career:* with Gloria Gaynor: British tour, live television; with Dudu Pukwana's Zila: Tours, television and radio: UK, Europe, Africa; UK radio with Lloyd Ryan; Rhythm on Two, with Tony Evans Orchestra. *Recordings:* with Dudu Pukwana: Live At The 100 Club, 1981; Life In Bracknell and Willisau, 1983; Zila, 1986; Cosmics Chapter 90, 1990; with Lloyd Ryan: Circular Storm, 1989; Four Songs... From Under Mount Nephim, 1997; Smilin Samba, with Selma Garcia, 1998. *Publications:* The Music Factory (bass guitar instrumental workbooks). *Honours:* LTCL (flute). *Address:* Rastenburger Str 17, 44369 Dortmund, Germany.

RICHARDS Keith, (Keith Richard); b. 18 Dec. 1943, Dartford, Kent, England. Musician (guitar); Vocalist; Songwriter. m. (1) Anita Pallenberg, 1 s., 1 d.; (2) Patti Hansen, 1983, 2 d. *Education:* Sidcup Art School. *Career:* Member, The Rolling Stones, 1962–; Co-writer with Mick Jagger, numerous songs (often under psuedonym The Glimmer Twins); Appearances include: First British tour, 1963; Debut US tour, 1964; Free concert, Hyde Park, 1969; Free concert, Altamont Speedway, 1969; Knebworth Festival, 1976; Played with Chuck Berry, Chicago Blues Festival, 1986; Steel Wheels North American tour, 1989. *Recordings:* Albums include: The Rolling Stones, 1964; The Rolling Stones No 2, 1965; Out of Our Heads, 1965; Aftermath, 1966; Between The Buttons, 1967; Their Satanic Majesties Request, 1967; Beggar's Banquet, 1968; Let It Bleed, 1969; Get Yer Ya-Ya's Out, 1969; Sticky Fingers, 1971; Exile On Main Street, 1972; Goat's Head Soup, 1973; It's Only Rock 'n' Roll, 1974; Black and Blue, 1976; Some Girls, 1978; Emotional Rescue, 1980; Still Life, 1982; Steel Wheels, 1989; Flashpoint, 1991; Stripped, 1, 1995; Bridges to Babylon, 1997; No Security, 1999; Also: Hail Hail Rock 'n' Roll (with Chuck Berry), 1987; Talk is Cheap, 1988; Main Offender, 1992; Live at the Hollywood Palladium with the Expensive Winos, 1991; Singles include: It's All Over Now; Little Red Rooster; (I Can't Get No) Satisfaction; Jumping Jack Flash; Honky Tonk Women; Harlem Shuffle; Start Me Up; Paint It Black; Angie; Going To A Go-Go; It's Only Rock 'n' Roll; Let's Spend The Night Together; Brown Sugar; Miss You; Emotional Rescue; She's So Cold; Undercover of The Night. *Honours:* with Rolling Stones include: Grammy, Lifetime Achievement Award, 1986; Inducted into Rock and Roll Hall of Fame, 1989; Q Award, Best Live Act, 1990; Ivor Novello Award, Outstanding Contribution To British Music, 1991; Songwriters Hall of Fame, 1993. *Current Management:* Jane Rose, 1776 Broadway Suite 507, New York, NY 10019, USA.

RICHARDS Red (Charles); b. 19 Oct. 1912, Brooklyn, New York, USA. Jazz Musician (piano); Vocalist. m. Dorothy, 6 Aug. 1942. *Musical Education:* Studied Classics, 6 years. *Career:* Played at Savoy Ballroom with Tab Smith, 4 years; Co-leader, Saints and Sinners with Vic Dickenson; Tours as solo artist, trio, quartet: USA; Canada; Europe; Australia; Played with: Sidney Bechet; Muggsy Spanier; Mezz Mezzrow; Frank Sinatra; Wild Bill Davison; Jimmy McPartland. *Recordings include:* Big Reunion, Fletcher Henderson; Stanley Dances series with Buster Bailey; Dreamy; My Romance; Guest musician, Marion McPartland's Piano Jazz series, No. 11; Featured on All Star Jazz, 1995; ladies Sing the Blues 1945–57, 1997; Swingville All Stars: Memphis Blues, 1997; Muggsy Spanier: Live at the Hangover Club in San Francisco, 1997; Stuyvesant Stompers: Dr Jazz, 1997; Dinah Washington: Slick Chick: On the Mellow Side, 1997. *Honours:* Grand Pris Disque de Jazz, Hot Club de France, 1994. *Membership:* AFofM. *Leisure interests:* Reading; Football; Baseball; Basketball. *Current Management:* Russ Dantzler, 328 W 44th St, New York, NY 10036, USA. *Address:* 3944 Paulding Ave, Bronx, New York, NY 10466, USA.

RICHARDSON Garth John; b. 23 July 1958, Toronto, Ontario, Canada. Record Prod. m. Jennifer Quinn, 7 Oct. 1989, 2 d. *Musical Education:* Fanshawe Music College. *Career:* Engineer, Canada; Producer, USA; Producer for: Rage Against The Machine; L7; The Melvins; Ugly Kid Joe; POL; Houdini; Chase the Sun; State; Engineer for: Red Hot Chili Peppers; Ozzy Osbourne; Kiss; Mötley Crüe; Alice Cooper; American Man; Bulletboys. *Honours:* Grammy Nomination, Rage Against The Machine; Judge, JUNO Awards. *Leisure interests:* Hockey; Golf. *Current Management:* Tap/KO Entertainment.

RICHARDSON Kevin Scott; b. 3 Oct. 1972, Lexington, New York, USA. Singer. *Career:* Qualified ballroom instructor; Member, Backstreet Boys; Numerous television appearances, tours and hit singles. *Recordings:* Singles: We've Got It Goin' On, 1995; Quit Playing Games, 1998; I'll Never Break Your Heart, 1998; Everybody, 1998; As Long As You Love Me, 1998; Anywhere for You, 1998; All I Have to Give, 1998; I Want It That

Way, 1999; Albums: Backstreet Boys, 1996; Live in Concert, 1998; Backstreet's Back, 1998; Millennium, 1999. *Leisure interests:* Keyboards; Water skiing; Swimming; Surfing; Basketball; Hockey.

RICHARDSON Mark; b. 28 May 1970, Leeds, England. Musician (Drums). *Career:* Founder Member, Skunk Anansie; Signed to indie label One Little Indian, 1994; Numerous live gigs and festival appearances; TV appearances and radio sessions. *Recordings:* Singles: Little Baby Swastikkka; Weak; Brazen (Weep), 1997; Charlie Big Potato, 1999; Albums: Paranoid and Sunburnt, 1995; Stoosh, 1996; Post Orgasmic Chill, 1999.

RICHEY David Andrew; b. 21 Sept. 1965, Edgbaston, Birmingham, England. Musician (guitar); Composer; Actor; Playwright. m. Gillian MacKenzie, 4 June 1988, 1 d. *Career:* Lead guitarist, vocalist with many bands including YZI; Founder member, Aquila; Wayzgoose; Lyra and The Fianna; Created Dave Richey Music, Media Music Production company, 1993; Appeared numerous stage plays, pantomimes; Writer, plays include: The Thorn In The Rose; Directed several plays, wrote and starred in The Parkie; Writer, composer, numerous songs and instrumentals. *Memberships:* Musicians' Union; SPAM. *Leisure interests:* Computers; Fishing; Walking; Windsurfing; Gardening; Conservation. *Current Management:* Gill MacKenzie. *Address:* Sonas, Calgary, Isle of Mull, Scotland.

RICHIE Lionel; b. 20 June 1949, Tuskegee, Alabama, USA. Singer; Songwriter; Musician (piano); Actor; Record Prod. m. Diane Alexander, 1996. *Education:* BS, Econs, Tuskegee University, 1971. *Career:* Member, the Commodores, 1968–82; Support tours with The Jackson 5, 1973; The Rolling Stones, 1975; The O'Jays, 1976; Numerous other concerts; Solo artiste, 1982–; Concerts include: Closing ceremony, Olympic Games, Los Angeles, 1984; Live Aid, Philadelphia, 1985. *Compositions:* Hits songs with the Commodores: Sweet Love, 1975; Just To Be Close To You, 1976; Easy, 1977; Three Times A Lady (No. 1, USA and UK), 1979; Sail On, 1980; Still (No. 1, USA), 1980; Oh No, 1981; for Kenny Rogers: Lady (No. 1, USA), 1981; for Diana Ross: Missing You, 1984; Solo hits: Endless Love, film theme duet with Diana Ross (No. 1, USA), 1981; Truly (No. 1, USA), 1982; All Night Long (No. 1, USA), 1983; Running With The Night, 1984; Hello (No. 1, USA and UK), 1984; Stuck On You, 1984; Penny Lover (co-writer with Brenda Harvey), 1984; Say You Say Me (No. 1, USA), 1986; Dancing On The Ceiling, 1987; Love Will Conquer All, 1987; Ballerina Girl, 1987; My Destiny, 1992; Don't Wanna Lose You, 1996; Contributor, We Are The World (co-writer with Michael Jackson), USA For Africa (No. 1 world-wide), 1985. *Recordings:* Albums with the Commodores: Machine Gun, 1974; Caught In The Act, 1975; Movin' On, 1975; Hot On The Tracks, 1976; Commodores, 1977; Commodores Live!, 1977; Natural High 1978; Greatest Hits, 1978; Midnight Magic, 1979; Heroes, 1980; In The Pocket, 1981; Solo albums: Lionel Richie, 1982; Can't Slow Down, 1983; Dancing On The Ceiling, 1986; Back To Front, 1992; Louder Than Words, 1996; Time, 1998; Solo singles: All Night Long, 1985; Do It To Me, 1992; My Destiny, 1992; Ordinary Girl, 1996; Don't Wanna Lose You, 1996. *Honours include:* ASCAP Songwriter Awards, 1979, 1984–96; Numerous American Music Awards, 1979–; Grammy Awards: Best Pop Vocal Performance, 1982; Album of The Year, 1985; Producer of The Year (shared), 1986; Lionel Richie Day, Los Angeles, 1983; 2 NAACP Image Awards, 1983; NAACP Entertainer of the Year, 1987; Academy Award, Best Song, 1986; Golden Globe, Best Song, 1986. *Current Management:* John Reid. *Address:* 505 S Beverly Dr., Suite 1192, Beverly Hills, CA 90212, USA.

RICHMAN Guy Charles; b. 3 June 1965, Rush Green, England. Musician (drums). m. Alison Murray, 20 June 1994. *Musical Education:* Taught by Maz Abrams and Bobby Armstrong. *Career:* Concert dates with Kylie Minogue, 1995; World tours and television appearances with: Black; Patricia Kaas; British tours with: Joe Longthorne (including television); Sister Sledge; Odyssey; Harold Melvyn. *Recordings with:* Black; Boy George; Bucks Fizz; Patricia Kaas; Joe Longthorne; Two People; Sister Sledge; Odyssey. *Membership:* Musicians' Union. *Leisure interest:* Badminton. *Address:* 53 St Marys Lane, Upminster, Essex RM14 2QU, England.

RICHMOND Kim; b. 24 July 1940, Champaign, Illinois, USA. Musician; Composer; Arranger. m. Chris Zambon, 5 April 1989. *Education:* Graduate, University of Illinois, 1963; BA, Music Education; BM, Music Compilation. *Career:* Written and conducted original musical scores for several television series including: Kojak; Harry O; ABC-TV Movie of the Week; Composed new works for concert stage (mostly jazz); Arranger and music director for singers including: Ann Jillian, Buddy Greco, Helen Reddy and Johnnie Ray; Arranged for many acts including Pat Boone, Dianhann Carroll, Thelma Houston, Jaye P Morgan, Kaye Ballard; Written for jazz groups of Stan Kenton, Buddy Rich, Louis Bellson, Stan Getz; Toured with Percy Faith Orchestra in Japan and Australia, several years; Freelance studio work, TV shows, theatre orchestras, concerts and other musical activities in Los Angeles; Artist-in-residence, Australia's University of Sydney Music Conservatorium Jazz Studies programme; Occasional jazz radio host;

Writes articles and reviews for jazz magazines. *Compositions include:* (for large concert jazz ensemble) Augustana, Trump Card I; Trump Card II; Viridian; Range; Variations; All Together; Back A Tad; Bhakti; Big Mama Louise; The Big Sur; Brain Trouble; Chester's Way; Chic-a-brac; City of LA; Clear Command; Continued Obscurity; Fantasia For Alto Sax and Jazz Orchestra (3 movements); Firebush (3 movements); Flapjacks and Maple Syrup; Franz; Gems; Image; Blues and Likeness; Mayo; Melon Bells; Nicé; Old Acquaintances; Osage Autumn; Passages; Planos; Realization for guitar and jazz orchestra (3 movements); Soft Feelings; Sojourn; 3 Refractions; Tributaries; White Tornado; Wind Chimes; Wind-up; Trains; (for small jazz ensemble) Range; Tracks; Cal 20; Common Denominator; Data Bank; Trains; Corrective Measures; (Classical compositions) Centunia for symphony orchestra; Movements for brass quintet, strings and percussion; Mixtures for brass quintet and others. *Recordings:* (as a leader): Look At The Time; Range; Passage; Looking In Looking Out; many others for other leaders. *Memberships:* AFofM; ASCAP; ASMAC; NARAS; RMA; Pacific Composers Forum; Chamber Music Society. *Leisure interests:* Computers; Tennis; Hiking; Canoeing; Sailing. *Address:* 6248 Rogerton Dr., Hollywood, CA 90068, USA.

RICHRATH Gary; b. 18 Oct. 1949, Peoria, Illinois, USA. Musician (guitar); Songwriter. *Career:* Guitarist, songwriter, US rock group REO Speedwagon, 1971–92; Richrath, 1992–; Live concert, Denver (first stereo concert broadcast), 1981; Anti-drug concert Users Are Losers, Miami, Florida, 1990. *Recordings:* Albums: with REO Speedwagon: REO Speedwagon, 1971; R.E.O. T.W.O., 1972; Ridin' The Storm Out, 1973; Lost In A Dream, 1974; This Time We Mean It, 1975; R.E.O., 1976; REO Speedwagon Live/You Get What You Play For, 1977; You Can Tune A Piano But You Can't Tuna Fish, 1978; Nine Lives, 1979; A Decade of Rock 'N' Roll 1970–80, 1980; Hi Infidelity, 1981; Good Trouble, 1982; Wheels Are Turning, 1984; Best Foot Forward, 1985; Life As We Know It, 1987; The Hits, 1988; A Second Decade of Rock 'N' Roll 1981–91, 1991; Ballads, 1999; with Richrath: Only The Strong Survive, 1992; Hit singles include: Time For Me To Fly, 1978; Take It On The Run, 1981; Keep On Loving You, 1981; Don't Let Him Go, 1981; Keep The Fire Burnin', 1982; Can't Fight This Feeling (No. 1, USA), 1985; That Ain't Love, 1987; In My Dreams, 1987. *Honours:* Gold, Platinum discs. *Current Management:* Baruck-Consolo Management, 15003 Greenleaf St, Sherman Oaks, CA 91403, USA.

RICKFORS Mikael; b. 4 Dec. 1948, Sweden. Singer; Musician (guitar, piano); Songwriter. m. Mia, 2 s., 1 d. *Career:* Concert tours; Television (Europe, USA). *Compositions:* Yeah Yeah, recorded by Cyndi Lauper; Blue Night, Percy Sledge; Daughter of The Night, Carlos Santana; The Last Wind, Touch, Carla Olson; Recorded by the Hollies: Don't Leave The Child Alone; They Don't Realise I'm Down. *Recordings:* with the Hollies: Romany, 1972; Out on The Road, 1972; Mikael Rickfors, 1975; The Wheel, 1976; Kickin' a Dream, 1979; Tender Turns Tuff, 1981; Rickfors Live, 1981; Blue Fun, 1983; Hearthunters, 1985; Rickfors, 1986; Vingar, 1988; Judas River, 1991; Happy Man Don't Kill, 1997; Greatest Hits, 1999. *Address:* c/o Polygram Records, Stockholm, Sweden.

RIDGELEY Andrew; b. 26 Jan. 1963, Windlesham, Surrey, England. Singer; Musician (guitar). m. Keren Woodward, 1 s. *Career:* Member, The Executive, 1979–80; Member duo, Wham! with George Michael, 1982–86; Most successful English pop group of 1980s; World-wide tours and concerts include: Club Fantastic Tour, 1983; World tour, 1984; US tour, 1985; First western pop band to play in China, 1985; Farewell concert, 'The Final' concert, Wembley, 1986; Solo artiste, actor and racing driver, 1986–; Performed at Rock in Rio II, with George Michael, 1991. *Recordings:* Albums: with Wham!: Fantastic (No. 1, UK), 1983; Make It Big (No. 1, UK and US), 1984; The Final, 1986; Solo album: Son of Albert, 1990; Singles include: Young Guns (Go For It), 1982; Wham Rap!, 1982; Bad Boys, 1983; Club Tropicana, 1983; Wake Me Up Before You Go Go (No. 1, UK), 1984; Careless Whisper (No. 1, UK and US); Last Christmas, 1984; Everything She Wants (No. 1, USA), 1985; Freedom, 1985; I'm Your Man (UK number 1), 1985; The Edge of Heaven (No. 1, UK), 1986; Solo single: Shake, 1990. *Honours include:* BRIT Awards: Best British Group, 1985; Outstanding Contribution To British Music, 1986.

RIDGWAY Stanard; b. 5 April 1956, Los Angeles, California, USA. Singer; Songwriter; Composer. m. Pietra Wexstun, 17 May 1981, 1 s. *Education:* College. *Career:* Singer, Wall of Voodoo; Television appearances include: The Tube, Top of The Pops. *Compositions:* Songs include: Camouflage; The Big Heat; Mexican Radio; Calling Out To Carol. *Recordings:* with Wall of Voodoo: Wall of Voodoo, 1979; Dark Continent, 1980; Call of The West, 1981; Solo recordings: The Big Heat, 1985; Mosquitos, 1990; Party Ball, 1991; Songs That Made This Country Great, 1992. *Membership:* BMI. *Current Management:* S.R. Dis-Information. *Address:* PO Box 9524, Los Angeles, CA 90295–1924, USA.

RIDING Jules; b. 22 May 1949, Cheltenham, Gloucestershire, England. Christian Musician; Singer. m. Lynn Gousmett, 11 May 1980, 2 s., 2 d. *Education:* First year university, Auckland, New Zealand. *Musical Education:* Self-taught. *Career:* Full-time professional, 1988–; Founder,

Elkanah School of Music Ministry, 1995. *Recordings:* Albums: On This Night, 1984; Heartstrings, 1987; Revelation, 1991; Homecoming, 1992; The Fisherman, 1994; Kids Time, 1997; Amazing Sacrifice, 1998. *Publications:* Don't Let Poor Nellie Starve, poetry, 1975; New Zealand Lamb, poetry, 1981. *Honours:* New Zealand Music Awards, Gospel Album of The Year, 1984, 1987. *Membership:* APRA, New Zealand. *Leisure interests:* Photography; Running.

RIDLEY Larry (Laurence Howard II); b. 3 Sept. 1937, Indianapolis, Indiana, USA. Musician; Music Educator. m. Magdalena Ridley, 1 d. *Education:* BS, Music Education, Indiana University, 1955–59; New York University, 1971; MA, State University of New York, 1993. *Career:* Associate Professor of Music, Livingston College of Rutgers University, New Jersey, 1971–; Chairman, Department of Music, Rutgers University, 1972–80; Professor Emeritus, Rutgers University, 1999; Artist-in-residence, colleges in USA and South Africa; Bandleader, Jazz Legacy Ensemble; Recordings and international performances with numerous leading musicians including: Dizzy Gillespie; Duke Ellington; Art Farmer; Thelonious Monk; Dinah Washington; Benny Goodman; Dexter Gordon; Benny Carter; Herbie Hancock; Freddie Hubbard; Mercer Ellington; Sonny Rollins, Philly Joe Jones; Jazz Artist-in-Residence, Schomburg Centre/New York Public Library since 1993. *Honours:* Grammy Nominations, 1983, 1984 with Dameronia; Chairman, Jazz Panel, National Endowment Arts, 1976–78; National co-ordinator, NEA Jazz Artists in School pilot programme, 1978–82; Mem., National Asscn Jazz Educators (advisory board, 1981-); Mid Atlantic Arts Foundation Living Legacy Jazz Award, 1997; Inducted into the International Asscn of Jazz Educators Hall of Fame, 1998; Downbeat Magazine, Jazz Education Hall of Fame, 1999. *Address:* 3 Stuyvesant Oval, Suite 9B, New York, NY 10009, USA.

RIDLEY Tim; b. 5 Aug. 1967, Portsmouth, Hampshire, England. Teacher; Musician (keyboards, drums, percussion). *Musical Education:* Royal Academy of Music. *Career:* Keyboard player, Brotherhood of Man, 1989–; Teacher, drums and percussion, 1989–96, Assistant Master, teaching music and music technology, 1996-, Marlborough College, Wiltshire; Keyboard player, The Sounds of The Supremes Show, 1993–; Keyboard player, composer, Mentaur. *Compositions:* Daedalus (musical), 1988; Ongoing film commission; Requiem Mass, 1988. *Recordings:* Darkness Before Dawn, Mentaur, 1995; Live In Germany, The Sounds of The Supremes, 1995. *Honours:* LRAM, 1984; GRSM, 1985. *Membership:* Rollercoaster Club of Great Britain. *Leisure interests:* Flying (PPL); Music technology; Film and television. *Current Management:* Videoscope Productions. *Address:* Marlborough College, Marlborough, Wiltshire SN8 1PA, England.

RIEL Alex; b. 13 Sept. 1940, Copenhagen, Denmark. Musician (drums). *Musical Education:* Private lessons with Borge Ritz; 1 semester with Allan Dawson, Berklee School of Music, Boston, USA. *Career:* Founder, Alex Riel Trio; Member, Niels Lan Doky Trio; Freelance solo musician; Television appearances with: Nancy Wilson; Manhattan Transfer; Stan Getz; Bill Evans; Eddie Gomez; Toots Thielemans; Gerry Mulligan; Roland Kirk; Niels Henning Orsted Petersen; Played concerts with: John Scofield; Michel Petrucianni; Dizzy Gillespie; Wayne Shorter; Dollar Brand; Archie Shepp; Don Cherry; Videos: Bill Evans Trio In Oslo, 1967; Niels Lan Doky Trio, Close Encounter, 1992. *Recordings include:* In A Way, Alex Riel Trio, 1966; Emerge, Alex Riel Trio, 1993; Recorded as guest musician with numerous artistes including: Dexter Gordon; Ben Webster; Gary Burton; Thomas Clausen; Palle Mikkelborg; Karin Krog; Archie Shepp; Toots Thielmans; Jean Luc Ponty; Eddie Lockjaw Davis; Marilyn Mazur; Stéphane Grappelli. *Honours:* Danish Jazz Musician of Year, 1965; Palace Jazz Award, 1991. *Membership:* Dansk Musiker Forbund. *Leisure interest:* Dogs.

RIENIETS Andrea; b. Feb. 1963, Shepparton, Victoria, Australia. Singer; Songwriter; Composer. *Musical Education:* BA, Communications; Theatre, Opera Singing, Choir Studies, Jazz Drumming; Self-taught Guitar. *Career:* 17 scores for stage; Founder/Director of Before You Were Blonde choir, 1991–96; Guest Director, Sing It Up BIG, Indigenous Australian Choir, 1997–98; WOMAD, 1997. *Compositions:* Wooden Child, 1995; Love of a Lifetime, 1995; Something So Simple, 1998. *Recordings:* Fluently Helvetica, 1995; Something So Simple, 1998. *Current Management:* Gorgeous Girl Records. *Address:* PO Box 10059, Adelaide BC Eighth, Australia 5000.

RIGBY Paul Julian; b. 21 Dec. 1968, Blackburn, Lancashire, England. Musician (drums, piano); Bandleader. *Musical Education:* Studied at Salford University, Bretton Hall and University of North Texas, Higher Diploma in Popular Music with Recording, and BA Honours in Popular Music; PGCE. *Career:* Played with Georgie Fame; Kenny Baker; Mark Nightingale; Bobby Shew; Maynard Ferguson; Appeared in shows and musicals; Toured extensively with Wigan Youth Jazz Orchestra and Northern Jazz Orchestra; Tutor for Lancashire School Jazz Orchestra; Lecturer of Popular Music. *Recordings:* with Northern Jazz Orchestra; Good News; with Wigan Youth Jazz Orchestra: Aim For The Heart; One

More Time; Check It Out. *Membership:* Musicians' Union. *Leisure interests:* Badminton; Squash; Football. *Address:* Clairville, Manor Rd, Darwen, Lancashire BB3 2SN, England.

RILEY Howard; b. 16 Feb. 1943, Huddersfield, Yorkshire, England. Musician (Piano); Composer. *Education:* BA, 1964, MA, 1966, University of Wales; MMus, Indiana University, USA, 1967. *Career:* Festival, Club, TV, Radio appearances as Pianist (solo and group), throughout Europe and USA, 1967-. *Recordings:* 40 LPs, CDs under own name. *Publication:* The Contemporary Piano Folio, 1982. *Honour:* UK/USA Bicentennial Arts Fellowship, 1976. *Leisure interests:* Walking; Reading. *Address:* Flat 2, 53 Tweedy Rd, Bromley, Kent BR1 3NH, England.

RILEY Jeannie C, (Jeannie Carolyn Stephenson); b. 19 Oct. 1944, Anson, Texas, USA. Singer. m. Mickey Riley, 1 d. *Recordings:* Hit singles: Harper Valley PTA (No. 1, USA), 1969; The Girl Most Likely; There Never Was A Time; The Back Side of Dallas; The Rib; Good Enough To Be Your Wife; When Love Has Gone Away; Return To Harper Valley; Albums: Yearbooks and Yesterdays, 1968; Things Go Better With Love, 1969; Songs of Jeannie C Riley, 1969; Country Girl, 1970; Generation Gap, 1970; Jeannie, 1972; Down to Earth, 1973; Jeannie C Riley and Fancy Friends, 1977; From Harper Valley to the Mountain Top, 1981; Here's Jeannie C, 1991; Praise Him, 1995. *Honours:* Grammy Award, 1968; CMA Record of Year, 1969; Music Operators of America Award, 1969; Gold disc, Harper Valley PTA (6m. copies sold), 1969. *Current Management:* Morningstar Public Relations, PO Box 83, Brentwood, TN 37027, USA.

RILEY Marc, (Lard); b. 10 July 1961, Manchester, England. Musician (Guitar, Bass, Keyboards); Prod.; Presenter. m. 2 d. *Career:* Member, The Fall; Left band, formed The Creepers; PR for labels such as 4AD and Factory; Guest, Hit the North, with Mark Radcliffe, Radio 5; Researcher and Producer for Radio; Joined Mark Radcliffe on Radio 1 evening slot, 1993, stand-in on the breakfast show, 1996, permanent presenter on Breakfast Show, 1997, afternoon show, 1998-.

RILEY Teddy; b. 1967. Musician (multi-instrumentalist); Record Prod. *Career:* Considered pioneer of 'New Jack Swing'; Member, groups: Guy; Blackstreet; Musician for various artists including: Kool Moe Dee; Heavy D; Michael Jackson; Roy Brown; Own recording studio, Future Records. *Recordings:* Over 30 Platinum albums as producer; Albums include: with Michael Jackson, Dangerous, Blood on the Dance Floor; Don't Be Cruel, Bobby Brown; with Wreckx 'N' Effects, Hard or Smooth, Rap's New Generation; Make It Last Forever, Keith Sweat; Personal, Men of Vision; Another Level, Blackstreet; Get on the Bus; Ill Na Na, Foxy Brown; Make It Reign; G-Funk Classics, Nate Dogg; Hurricane; Other recordings for: Heavy D; James Ingram; Jazzy Jeff and The Fresh Prince; As musician: U Blow My Mind, Blackstreet, 1995. *Current Management:* ICM, 40 W 57th St, New York, NY 10019, USA.

RIMES (Margaret) LeAnn; b. 28 Aug. 1982, Jackson Mississippi, USA. Country vocalist. m. Dean Sheremet, 23 Feb. 2002. *Career:* Encouraged by father, part-time guitarist Wilbur Rimes, was singing and tap dancing at age 2 and winning talent shows, aged 5; Parents recorded an album to sell at gigs, aged 7; Released first commercial album on Nor Va Jack label, recorded at legendary producer Norman Petty's studio in Clovis, New Mexico, aged 11; One of album tracks Blue, written by Texas DJ and country artist Bill Mack, and very much in the style of Patsy Cline came to the attention of record executive Mike Curb, resulting in immediately signing to his Curb label; Blue re-recorded with a 50s retro feel and appeared on the album of the same name, 1996; Album reached #1 on US country chart and #3 on pop charts; Singles and album sales to date over 20m., on both pop and country charts; How Do I Live from the film Con Air became most successful US single of all time, completing 69 straight weeks on Billboard pop chart, 1997-98; Single also stayed in UK Top 40 for 30 weeks; More recent material has tended to be aimed more at the pop/AOR market with artist no longer desiring to be regarded as a country act; Has garnered many major music awards and appeared as self in films: Holiday In Your Heart, 1997; Dill Scallion, 1999; Coyote Ugly, containing UK chart-topping theme Can't Fight The Moonlight, 2000; Started litigation against Curb Records, 2000; Case eventually resolved; Filed lawsuit against father and his partner alleging they stole $7m. of earnings, 2000. *Recordings include:* One Way Ticket (Because I Can), Unchained Melody, Blue, 1996; How Do I Live, On The Side of Angels, 1997; Written In The Stars (with Elton John), 1999; I Need You, Can't Fight The Moonlight, 2000; Albums include: Blue, 1996; You Light Up My Life – Inspirational Songs, 1997; Sittin' On Top of The World, 1998; LeAnn Rimes, 1999; I Need You, God Bless America, 2001. *Address:* c/o The Country Music Asscn, Nashville, Tennessee, USA. *Internet:* www.rimestimes.com.

RINGO Sheena; b. 15 Nov. 1978, Fukuoka, Japan. Vocalist; Musician (piano, bass guitar); Songwriter. m. Junji Yayoshi, 2001. *Musical Education:* Trained as classical pianist and ballerina. *Career:* Member of various semi-professional groups including The Marvelous Marbles before

signing as solo artist to Toshiba-EMI; First live tour of Japan, 2000; Temporary career break owing to pregnancy, 2001. *Recordings:* Albums: Muzai Moratorium, 1999; Shoso Strip, 2000; Singles: Kofukuron, Kabukicho No Jyoou, 1998; Kokode Kiss Shite, Honnou, 1999; Gips, Tsumi To Batsu, 2000; Mayonaka Wa Jyunketsu, 2001. *Honours:* Annual Music Quest, Award of Excellence, 1996. *Address:* c/o Solid Bond Corp/Toshiba-EMI Ltd. *Internet:* www.toshiba-emi.co.jp/ringo/english.

RINTOUL Laura Jane; b. 3 Oct. 1950, Perth, Scotland. Singer; Musician (accordion, recorder). *Education:* HNC, Napier College, Edinburgh, Scotland. *Career:* Medical Scientist, then trained in Glasgow from 1985; Concert tour of Japan in 1989; First broadcast on BBC Radio Scotland, 1988 appearing regularly since then; Presenter, local radio, Festival of Remembrance, Perth, 1992; Appeared on Grampian TV, 1994. *Recordings:* As guest artist on: A Ceilidh From Aberfeldy, and Gather, from the Clan MacGregor Celebration Concerts. *Honours:* Silver Pendant, Edinburgh Gaelic MOD, 1987; Gold Medal, Arbroath Music Festival, 1991, Glasgow, 1992; Scots Songs Silver Medal, Perth, 1993. *Memberships:* Musicians' Union; Perthshire Musical (Competition) Festival Asscn. *Leisure interests:* Swimming; Charity Work; Scottish Country Dancing; Travel. *Address:* 18 Low Rd, Cherrybank, Perth PH2 0NF, Scotland.

RISDON Ronald Valentine; b. 14 Feb. 1950, Dorking, Surrey, England. Artist Man.; Television and Film Prod. m. Jane Risdon, 15 June 1972, 1 s. *Musical Education:* Self-taught guitar, bass, keyboards. *Career:* Bassist, then guitarist, with Marjorine, including UK, Europe tours, 1968–; Renamed Jungle Jim, 1972; Tours, North Africa, UK and Europe; Television and radio: Europe, UK, Channel Islands; Manager of various acts including: Tag, Ignorance, Heat featuring T J Felton, Treana, Craig Thomson, actor, Lucy, Gita, Blackout; Co-owner, production company Everyday Productions. *Recordings:* Singles: I Live, 1968; Big Fat Orangoman, (Top 20, UK, No. 1, France, Germany); Manager, recording artists 1980–; Released: Tag, USA; Ignorance, USA; Treana, USA; Rain; Manages record producers: G Young and K Holland; Manages Songwriters: Young/Morris, A Hayman, Holland/Palmer/Wilcocks. *Memberships:* PRS; BASCA. *Leisure interests:* Music; Films; Reading; Travel. *Current Management:* Showcase Management International, 33 Mandarin Pl., Grove, Oxfordshire OX12 0QH, England. *Address:* SMI, 3217 Overland Ave, Suite 7115, Los Angeles, CA 90034, USA. *E-mail:* selectevents@mediaone.net.

RITCHIE Billy (Darrell Jr); b. 11 Sept. 1986, High Point, North Carolina, USA. Singer; Songwriter. m. Michelle Ritchie, 6 Sept. 1990, 1 d. *Education:* BA, Communications, Gardner-Webb College, 1990. *Musical Education:* Minor in Music, Gardner-Webb College, 1990. *Career:* Full time concert artist; Songwriter; Over 500 concerts, 1991-. *Recordings:* Albums: Stand and Believe, 1992; No Turning Back, 1993; Big Time, 1995. *Memberships:* Gospel Music Asscn; BMI. *Leisure interests:* Reading; Writing. *Current Management:* Darrell Ritchie Concerts. *Address:* 1071 Colgan Court, Lawrenceville, GA 30244, USA.

RITENOUR Lee; b. 11 Jan. 1952, Los Angeles, California, USA. Jazz Musician (guitar). *Career:* Session guitarist, as Captain Fingers, mid 1970s; Also jazz fusion solo artiste; Played with Herbie Hancock; Steely Dan; Stanley Clarke; Member, Friendship (with Don Grusin). *Recordings:* Albums: First Course, 1974; Guitar Player, 1975; Captain Fingers, 1975; The Captain's Journey, 1978; Gentle Thoughts, 1978; Sugarloaf Express, 1978; Feel The Night, 1979; Friendship, 1979; Rit, 1981; Rio, 1982; Rit 2, 1983; Banded Together, 1983; On The Line, 1984; Harlequin, with Dave Grusin, 1985; American Flyers, 1986; Earth Run, 1986; Portrait, 1987; Festival, 1988; Wes Bound, 1993; Larry and Lee, with Larry Carlton, 1995; Alive in LA, 1997; This is Love, 1998. *Address:* c/o GRP Records, 33 Broadwick St, London W1V 1FR, England.

RIVERA Sandy; b. San Diego, California, USA. Prod.; Remixer; DJ. *Career:* Founder: Blackwiz Records, 1992; Deep Vision Records; Remixed: Moloko Eddie Amador; Ladysmith Black Mambazo; Member: Kings of Tomorrow; Soul Vision; Collaborations: Everything But The Girl; Jose Burgos; Julie McKnight. *Recordings:* Albums: It's In The Lifestyle (with Kings of Tomorrow), 2000; Singles: with Kings of Tomorrow: Fade II Black, 1997; Tear It Up, 2000; Finally, 2001; Tracey In My Room (as Soul Vision with EBTG), 2001. *Address:* c/o Defected Records, 14–15 D'arblay St, London, W1F 8DY, England.

RIVERS Johnny; b. 7 Nov. 1942, New York, NY, USA. Musician; Singer; Songwriter. *Musical Education:* Father a musician; Some private lessons; Watched and listened to older professionals. *Career:* President, top record and publishing company, singer and songwriter by age 25; Started American discotheque craze at Whiskey A Go Go, Los Angeles, 1963; Appeared La Riviera, with Nancy Wilson, 1966; First rock and roll act to play Copa Cabana, New York; Formed record company, Soul City Records; Currently owner, manager, Rivers Music; Influenced the careers of The Mamas and Papas; Lou Adler; Glen Campbell; Al Wilson; Wolfman Jack; Brought together Hal Blaine, Joe Osborn, Larry Knectel, creators of 1960s-

70s West Coast Sound; Special guest on Memphis Horns 25th Anniversary Concert, 1992. *Recordings:* Hits include: Memphis; Maybelline; Mountain of Love; Seventh Son; Midnight Special; Secret Agent Man; Poor Side of Town; Baby, I Need Your Lovin'; Tracks of My Tears; Summer Rain; Look To Your Soul; Rockin' Pneumonia and The Boogie Woogie Flu; Sea Cruise; Blue Suede Shoes; Help Me Rhonda; Swayin' To The Music (Slow Dancin'); Curious Mind (Um Um Um Um Um Um); Last Train to Memphis; As Producer: Jimmy Webb and The Fifth Dimension: Up, Up and Away. *Honours:* 2 Grammys; BMI Awards. *Memberships:* BMI; ASCAP; AFTRA; AFofM. *Leisure interests:* Motorcycles; Horses; Songwriting. *Current Management:* American Concert and Touring Company, Nashville, Tennessee; Variety Artists, San Luis Obispo, California. *Address:* Soul City Records Inc, 12358 Ventura Blvd # 342, Studio City, CA 91604, USA.

RIVERS Sam; b. Jacksonville, Florida, USA. Musician (bass guitar). m. Kinter, Feb. 2001. *Education:* Arlington Middle School, Jacksonville; Douglas Anderson School of The Arts. *Musical Education:* Learnt tuba at Middle School. *Career:* Joined Limp Bizkit, 1994; Signed to Flip/Interscope on strength of demo tape; Striking live shows at concerts and festivals; Group spearheaded 'nu-metal' breakthrough in Europe, 2001. *Recordings:* Albums: Three Dollar Bill, Y'All $, 1997; Significant Other, 1999; Chocolate Starfish and The Hot Dog Flavored Water, 2000; New Old Songs (remix album), 2001; Singles: Faith, 1997; Nookie, Rearranged, 1999; Break Stuff, Take A Look Around (from Mission Impossible 2 OST), My Generation, 2000; Rollin', My Way, Boiler, 2001. *Honours:* Orville H. Gibson Guitar Award, Best Rock Bass Player, 2000; Second and third albums both debuted at #1 on US chart; Significant Other sales in excess of 6m. *Current Management:* The Firm (Management), 9100 Wilshire Blvd, Suite 400W, Beverly Hills, CA 90212, USA. *Internet:* www.limpbizkit.com.

RIX (Leon) Luther; b. 11 Feb. 1942, Lansing, Michigan, USA. Musician (percussion, drums); Composer. m. Ellen Garrett, 14 May 1973, 1 s. *Musical Education:* MusB, Indiana University, 1963; Postgraduate, Jordan Conservatory of Music, Indianapolis, 1964–65. *Career:* Percussionist with Indianapolis Symphony Orchestra, 1965–67; Winter Consort, 1968; Doc Severinsen, 1970; Drummer with Bette Midler, 1971–72; Manhattan Transfer, 1974–75; Mary Travers, 1975–76; Bob Dylan, 1975–76; Leonard Cohen, Laura Branigan, 1976; Peter, Paul and Mary, 1978; Freelance musician, 1979–; Drummer with Rosenhontz, 1986–; Richard Reiter Swing band, 1987–; Crossing Point, 1990–; Musician, shows include: The Wiz; Grease; Barnum; Little Shop of Horrors. *Compositions:* Boogaloother, 1972; Like A Beautiful Song, 1980; Tightrope (also arranger), 1969; Compositions recorded by Genya Raven; Buzzy Lindhart; Kaleidoscope. *Recordings include:* with Loudon Wainwright III: Fame and Wealth, 1983; Tommy (original Broadway cast), 1993; with Bob Dylan: Greatest Hits Vol. 3, 1994; With Labelle: Something Silver, 1997. *Memberships:* ASCAP; AFTRA; BMI; AFofM.

RIZZO Carmen; b. 8 April 1964, Akron, Ohio, USA. Record Prod.; Engineer. m. 11 Dec. 1993. *Career:* Engineer, mixer, co-writer, programmer, for latest Seal album. *Recordings:* Albums for: Seal; Prince; Ray Charles; Chris Connelly (Ministry); Wendy and Lisa. *Honour:* Grammy Nomination. *Memberships:* ASCAP; NARAS. *Current Management:* Greg Spotts Management (USA); Worlds End Ltd (England). *Address:* 421 Hudson St, Suite #216, New York, NY 10014, USA.

ROACH Archie; b. Australia. Singer; Songwriter. Partner, Ruby Hunter, 5 c. *Career:* Singer, songwriter; Performed extensively across Australia; Appeared at 3 WOMADelaide festivals, with Paul Kelly; Frente; Jimmy Barnes; Weddings Parties Anything; Crowded House; Numerous Aboriginal cultural festivals including: Sydney's Survival Day Concerts; Nambundah, New South Wales; Bogong Moth; Brunswick Koori Arts, Victoria; Oyster Cove, Tasmania; Cape York, Queensland; US tour, support to Joan Armatrading and Bob Dylan, 1992; Guest (with Ruby Hunter), Corrobee Festival Festival, Southbank Centre, London, 1993; British tour, 1993; UK visit with Robin Hitchcock and The Egyptians, 1994; Berlin Independence Festival, 1994; Support to Suzanne Vega, Australia, 1994; Other appearances include AFL Grand Final, 1994; Performed before Prime Minister Paul Keating, football game, Alice Springs. *Recordings:* Albums: Charcoal Lane, 1990; Jamu Dreaming, 1994; Looking for Butter Boy, 1997. *Publications:* Anthology of lyrics: You Have The Power, 1994. *Current Management:* Julie Hickson. *Address:* 25 Overend St, Brunswick, VIC 3056, Australia.

ROACH Max(well Lemuel); b. 10 Jan. 1924, Elizabeth City, North Carolina, USA. Jazz Musician (percussion). m. (1) Mildred Wilkinson, 14 Jan. 1949 (divorced), 1 s., 1 d., (2) Abbey Lincoln, 3 March 1963 (divorced). *Musical Education:* Manhattan School of Music, New York City; MusD (hon), New England Conservatory of Music, 1982. *Career:* Jazz percussionist with Charlie Parker, 1946–48; Also played with Thelonious Monk; Bud Powell; Dizzy Gillespie; Sonny Rollins; Eric Dolphy; Co-leader, Max Roach-Clifford Brown Quintet; Appearances include: Paris Jazz Festival, 1949; Newport Jazz Festival, 1972; Producer; Director; Choreographer; Professor of Music, University of Massachusetts, 1973-.

Composition: Freedom Now suite. *Recordings:* Albums include: Percussion Bitter Sweet; It's Time; Drums Unlimited; Speak Brother Speak; The Loadstar; Conservations; Long As Your Living; Survivors; The Long March; Jazz In 3/4 Time; Scott Free; To The Max!, 1991; Max and Dizzy (with Dizzy Gillespie), 1989 Mop Mop, 1995; Festive Journey, 1996; Bejing Trio, 1998; Max roach trio, 1999; Les Incontournables, 2000. *Honours:* Down Beat Awards: Best Record of The Year, 1956; Down Beat Poll Winner, 1955, 1957–60, 1984; Metronome Poll Winner, 1951–54. *Membership:* Organizer, Jazz Artists Guild Inc; Officier des Arts et des Lettres; Hon. Mem., American Academy. *Current Management:* Max Roach Productions. *Address:* Suite 14-E, 415 Central Park W, New York, NY 10025, USA.

ROACHFORD Andrew; Vocalist; Musician (keyboards, percussion). *Career:* Performer, Soho jazz clubs, London, aged 14; Founder, own band Roachford, 1987–; Toured with Terence Trent D'Arby, The Christians, 1988;. *Recordings:* Albums: Roachford, 1988; Get Ready!, 1991; Feel, 1997; Singles include: Cuddly Toy, 1989; Family Man, 1989; Beckology, with Jeff Beck, 1991. *Current Management:* Pure Management, 6 Chingford Rd, London E17 4PJ, England.

ROADHOUSE JOHNNY; b. 13 Jan. 1921, Sheffield, Yorkshire, England. Musician (saxophone, woodwind). Divorced, 2 s., 2 d. *Musical Education:* Self-taught. *Career:* 35 years BBC Staff Musician (Principal); Freelance Syphony Orchestras: Halle; Liverpool Philharmonic; 30 years in orchestra accompanying television series: Good Old Days; Many tours with top international artists including: Tony Bennett, Vic Damone; Recordings, radio series with Nigel Ogden (Organist Entertains series). *Membership:* Musicians' Union. *Leisure interests:* Running, organising music shops; Work. *Address:* 262 Brantingham Rd, Manchester M21 0Q2, England.

ROAR Finn; b. 21 July 1937, Kolding, Denmark. Composer; Educator; Musician (piano, saxophone); Singer. m. Gisela Moberg, 8 April 1960, 3 s., 1 d. *Education:* MA, Music, French. *Musical Education:* Studies with Professor Arne Skjold Rasmussen. *Career:* Bandleader (FR 5) for radio programmes; Leader and composer, fusion group Beaver Service, 1974–; Television appearances: Denmark, SF; Many concert tours to primary schools (More Jazz To The Children); First director, Danish Conservatory of Jazz, Latin, Rock Music, 1985–88; Festivals in Denmark and France; Co-founder, Radio Jazz; Member of presidency, Rhythmic Folk College. *Recordings:* Ants In My Ears, 1981; More Jazz To The Children, 1985; U-Spring (concerto for big band), 1990; Black Messiah (oratorio), 1994; Once There Was A Carnival (opera), 1995. *Publications:* Actual Music, 1975; Have You Heard, 1975; Beaver Service, 1976; From Gregorian Chant To Rock, Western Music History, Blue Book, 1981. *Memberships:* DJBFA; IAJE. *Leisure interest:* Fishing. *Current Management:* Beaver Records, Copenhagen, Denmark. *Address:* Udbakken 21, 2750 Ballerup, Denmark.

ROBBINS Dennis Anthony; b. Hazelwood, North Carolina, USA. Musician (guitar). m. Helen Hughs, 2 d. *Career:* US Marines, toured Viet Nam, 1968; Joined the Rockets, 1976; Moved to Nashville, record deal on MCA Records, first country album released, 1985; Signed to Warner Brothers with new band, Billy Hill, 1988; First artist signed to Giant Records, 1992; Writer, performer for Warner/Chappell, 1994-. *Compositions include:* Do You Love Me, Just Say Yes, Highway 101 (No. 1) 1987; Church On Cumberland Road, Shenandoah; Two of a Kind, Working On A Full House, Garth Brooks; Finally Friday, by both Earl Thomas Connelly, George Jones; Paris Tennessee, Tracy Lawrence; I'm Just A Rebel, by both Confederate Railroad, Joy Lynn White; Home Sweet Home, Dennis Robbins; Film soundtracks: Rolling Dice (used in Pink Cadillac); Looking For A Thing Called Love (used in A Thing Called Love); I Can't Help Myself (used in My Blue Heaven). *Recordings:* Albums: The First of Me, 1986; I Am Just a Rebel, 1989; Man with a Plan, 1992; Born Ready, 1994; Singles: Mona Lisa on Cruise Control, 1993; Travelin' Music, 1994; Also appears: with Rockets: Love Transfusion, 1977; Rockets, 1979; No Ballads, 1980; Back Talk, 1981.

ROBERSON LaTavia; b. 1 Nov. 1981, Houston, Texas, USA. Vocalist; Songwriter. *Career:* First TV appearance on Ed McMann's Star Search, aged 9; Package model for Pro-Line Hair Corporation 1989–98; Various other national TV and print advertising work; Joined GirlsTyme vocal group, 1992; Group renamed Something Fresh then The Dolls before settling on Destiny's Child; Signed to Columbia Records, 1996; Acrimonious split from group, February 2000; Formed new group Anjel with fellow ex-Destiny's Child member LaToya Luckett. *Recordings:* Albums: Destiny's Child, 1998; The Writing's On The Wall, 1999; Singles: with Destiny's Child: No No No (with Wyclef Jean), 1997; With Me (with Timbaland), She's Gone (with Matthew Marsden), 1998; Get On The Bus (from Why Do Fools Fall In Love OST), Bills Bills Bills, Bug-A-Boo, 1999; Say My Name, Jumpin' Jumpin', 2000; with Anjel: 10 Things I Hate About You, 2001. Grammy Awards, 2 nominations for co-compositions included on Writing's On The Wall album. *Address:* c/o 581 Records/So So Def/ Columbia, USA. *Internet:* www.sonymusic.com.

ROBERT George (Paul); b. 15 Sept. 1960, Geneva, Switzerland. Musician (Alto and soprano sax, clarinet, piano). m. Joan Yap, May 1991. *Education:* 9 years classical clarinet studies, Conservatory, Geneva; Bachelor of Arts, Jazz Composition and Arranging, cum laude, Berklee College of Music, 1985; Master of Music, Manhattan School of Music, 1987. *Career:* Toured Europe with own quartet, 1983, performed at Montreux Jazz Festival; Lead alto sax, MSM Big Band; Formed George Robert/Tom Harrell Quintet, 1987, toured throughout USA, Canada and Europe; Freelance musician with many groups including Lionel Hampton and Toshiko Akiyoshi Jazz Orchestras, Buster Williams, Ray Drummond, Ron McClure; First Swiss jazz musician to lead successful career in USA; Formed George Robert Quartet, worked with Clark Terry, numerous tours including 16-week world tour in top jazz clubs with Clark Terry; Continued freelance work; Teacher and Jazz Clinician, USA, Canada and Europe; George Robert/Tom Harrell Quintet performed at IAJE Conference, Washington DC, 1991; Performed in numerous top clubs as leader; Director, Swiss Jazz School, Berne, 1995; Organized USA tour for SJS Big Band, 1998; Also performed at Cully Jazz Festival; Toured with own big band, 18 concerts throughout Europe, 1998; Teacher, Interlaken Jazz Workshop teaching and performing with leading names including Billy Hart, Phil Woods, Lionel Hampton, Tony Bennett, Benny Green, 1999. *Recordings include:* With George Robert Quartet: First Encounter, with Ron McClure, 1985; Looking Ahead, 1989; Live at the Q-4, with Clark Terry, 1991; Jazz on the Mountain, with Clark Terry, 1992; The Good Things in Life, with Clark Terry, 1994; Voyage, 1995; With George Robert/Tom Harrell Quintet: Sun Dance, 1988; Lonely Eyes, 1989; Live in Switzerland, 1990; Visions, 1991; Cape Verde, 1993; George Robert with the Metropole Orchestra, 1995; The Summit, with Phil Woods, Kenny Barron, Ray Drummond and Bill Goodwin, 1999. *Honours:* Down Beat Awards, Outstanding Performance, 1983, Best College Band, 1987. *Memberships:* ASCAP; SUISA; American Federation of Musicians. *Leisure interests:* Cycling; Swimming. *Address:* Wiesengrundweig 11, 3047 Bremgarten, Switzerland.

ROBERTS Austin; Songwriter; Artist; Prod.; Publisher. *Career:* Approximately 60 hits world-wide including No. 1's (7 in USA); Songs featured, films and television series; Wrote and sang many of the Scooby-Doo songs; Wrote musicals: Damon's Song; Rachinoff; Formed Hot House Music, 1992; Two Top 10 singles as recording artist. *Compositions:* Hits include: When You Put Your Heart In It; Honor Bound; Strong Heart; IOV; My Night To Howl; Desesperados; You Lie; Songs recorded by: Reba McEntire; Kenny Rogers; Crystal Gayle; Michelle Wright; Lee Greenwood; Oak Ridge Boys; Charley Pride; Lulu; Julio Iglesias; Glen Campbell; Tanya Tucker; Sonny and Cher; Dan Seals; Englebert Humperdinck; Vicky Carr; Loverboy; Billy Crash Craddock; The Osmonds. *Honours:* 1 Grammy; 3 Grammy Nominations; 3 CMA Nominations; Academy Award Nomination; Golden Globe Nomination; Music City News Award; NSAI Award; ACM Nomination; Numerous ASCAP Airplay Awards; 1 German Grammy; 4 JUNO Awards; SESAC Airplay Award. *Current Management:* Scramblers Knob Studio. *Address:* 1000 Scramblers Knob, Franklin, TN 37064, USA.

ROBERTS Graham Andrew; b. 3 Feb. 1964, Northampton, England. *Musical Education:* Royal Academy of Music. *Career:* Numerous concerts, television, radio, for BBC, ITV, various European stations; Tours, USA, Europe, Far East. *Recordings:* with Grahamphones: Let's Do It Again, 1990; with Pasadena Roof Orchestra: Breakaway, 1991; with Swing Sisters: Swing, 1992; Take Me Back, 1994; with Tetra Guitar Quartet: By Arrangement, 1993; Pasadena, 1994. *Honours:* Winner, Julian Bream Guitar Competition, 1988. *Current Management:* Hothouse Entertainments. *Address:* 7 Wychwood Close, New Duston, Northampton, England.

ROBERTS J Patricia; b. 17 Feb. 1954, Aberdeen, Scotland. Singer; Musician (clarsach, Celtic harp, guitar). *Education:* Hamilton Academy, 1966–72; BSc, (Biology) DipEd, Stirling University, 1977. *Musical Education:* Mainly self-taught, though studied clarsach briefly with Sanchia Pielou. *Career:* Teacher and Guidance Counsellor in high school, 1977–94; Appeared at Lorient Folk Festival, 1982–84; Member, folk group Chapter Four, appearing throughout Scotland, 1984–87; Solo artist, 1987–; Radio interviews, Radio Forth; Radio Bretagne; Television appearance: Carols For Christmas, BBC TV, 1994; Currently appearing in castles, stately homes and major hotels in Scotland including Gleneagles, Turnberry and Old Course. *Recording:* Just As I Am, (mainly traditional Scottish songs with clarsach and guitar accompaniment), 1993; Currently producing CD featuring traditonal and modern music and songs, 1999. *Honours:* Academic and Counselling Awards. *Membership:* Musicians' Union. *Leisure interests:* Mountaineering; Hillwalking; Gardening; Fishing; Photography; Crafts. *Address:* 113 Lothian Cres., Causewayhead, Stirling FK9 5SE, Scotland.

ROBERTS Mark; b. 3 Nov. 1969, Colwyn Bay, Wales. Musician (Guitar). *Career:* Founder Member, Catatonia, 1993–; Signed to Blanco y Negro; Numerous tours and festival appearances; Many TV appearances.

Recordings: Singles: Bleed/Do You Believe In Me, 1996; Mulder and Scully, 1998; Road Rage, 1998; Strange Glue, 1998; Londinium, 1999; Albums: Way Beyond Blue, 1996; The Sublime Magic of Catatonia, 1996; International Velvet, 1998; Equally Cursed and Blessed, 1999.

ROBERTS Rudy; b. 9 April 1966, Nantes, France. Rock Musician (guitar). *Musical Education:* American School of Modern Music, Paris. *Career:* Squealer, 1991; French support tour with UDO; Member, Starmania/ Tycoon, 1993–95; Solo artist, 1991–; Numerous concerts, France, Belgium, Switzerland, Canada, played to over 1m. people; Played with: Stuart Hamm; Jonathon Mover; Electric guitar teacher, Vitré Conservatory of Music; Demonstrator for Jackson guitars; Hughes and Kettner amplifiers. *Recordings:* with Squealer: This Is What The World Is About, 1991; with Starmania: Starmania; Solo albums: Passion Colors, 1993; Rudy Roberts Live, 1994. *Publications:* Instruction video, Plans and Techniques Hard Rock. *Honours:* Guinness World Record Holder, Non-stop guitar playing (50 hours); Ninth Victoires de la Musique Award, Best Live Show, Starmania, 1994. *Membership:* SACEM; SPEDIDAM. *Current Management:* Pierrick Morin, Move On Productions. *Address:* 7 rue Baudrairie, 35500 Vitré, France.

ROBERTS Stephen; b. 27 March 1958, London, England. Musician (drums). m. Philippa Jane, 26 May 1991. *Career:* In 1980 formed legendary New Wave of British Heavy Metal group: Silverwing, with brother Dave; Toured with Diamond Head and Phil Lynott, split 1983; Formed Pet Hate; released 2 albums; Toured USA and Canada; Appeared on C4's ECT; Formed Wild Ones, 1989; Released 1 album; Session musician with Belinda Carlisle and Rick Astley, including appearances on Wogan and at San Remo Festival, 1990; Currently with No Fit State. *Recordings:* with Silverwing: Rock and Roll Are Four Letter Words, 1980; Sittin' Pretty, 1981; Alive and Kicking, 1982; with Pet Hate: The Bride Wore Red, 1984; Bad Publicity, 1985: with Wild Ones: Writing On The Wall, 1991; with No Fit State: Welcome To..., 1995. *Membership:* Musicians' Union. *Leisure interest:* Gardening. *Current Management:* Triumphant Productions. *Address:* 1 Waterloo St, Stockport SK1 3DB, England.

ROBERTSON Brian; b. 12 Sept. 1956, Glasgow, Scotland. Rock Musician (guitar). *Career:* Guitarist, UK rock group Thin Lizzy, 1974–78; Concerts include: Regular UK and European tours; Reading Festival, 1974, 1975, 1977; US tour, supporting Bachman-Turner Overdrive, 1976; Briefly with Graham Parker and The Rumour, 1977; Founder, Wild Horses, 1978–81; Guitarist, UK heavy metal group Motörhead, 1982. *Recordings:* Albums: with Thin Lizzy: Nightlife, 1974; Fighting, 1975; Jailbreak, 1976; Johnny The Fox, 1976; Bad Reputation, 1977; Live and Dangerous (No. 2, UK), 1978; Japanese Compilation, 1980; Adventures of Thin Lizzy, 1981; Life, 1983; Dedication, 1991; with Motörhead: Another Perfect Day, 1983; Singles: with Thin Lizzy: Still In Love With You, 1975; The Boys Are Back In Town, 1976; Jailbreak, 1976; Cowboy Song, 1976; Don't Believe A Word, 1977; Dancin' In The Moonlight, 1977; Rosalie, 1978; with Motörhead: I Got Mine, 1983; Shine, 1983. *Honour:* Gold disc, Jailbreak, 1976.

ROBERTSON Donald Irwin; b. 5 Dec. 1922, Beijing, China. Composer; Musician (piano); Singer. m. (1) Ella Lucille Dinning, 2 Aug. 1946, divorced, 1 s. (deceased), 1 d., (2) Irene Symsk, 1 Jan. 1962, 2 s. *Education:* AA, University of Chicago, 1943. *Career:* Moved to US, 1927; Freelance songwriter, musician, singer, 1944-. *Recordings:* Featured on albums by numerous artists including: Elvis Presley; Bob Dylan; Willie Nelson; Dinah Shore; Nat King Cole; Waylon Jennings; Dolly Parton; Perry Como; Eddy Arnold; Roy Clark; Loretta Clark. *Honours:* Inducted, Walkway of Stars, Country Music Hall of Fame, 1967; 2 BMI Awards, 1954; Billboard Award, 1964; 17 ASCAP Awards, 1955–84; Nashville Songwriters Asscn International Hall of Fame, 1972. *Memberships:* AFTRA; ASCAP; AFofM; NARAS; NSAI; Songwriters Guild of America.

ROBERTSON Robbie (Jaime); b. 5 July 1944, Toronto, Ontario, Canada. Musician (guitar); Vocalist. *Career:* Guitarist, singer with The Band (formerly the Hawks), 1964–78; Long association with Bob Dylan; As backing band for Bob Dylan, appearances include: Don't Look Back British tour, 1965; Royal Albert Hall, 1966; Isle of Wight Festival, 1969; US tour, 1974; Performances as The Band include: Watkins Glen Festival, with the Grateful Dead, Allman Brothers, 1973; Producer, film The Last Waltz, film of final Band concert, 1977; Film appearance, Solo career, 1978-. *Compositions:* Much of Band's material including: 4% Pantomime (co-written with Van Morrison). *Recordings:* Singles: with the Band: The Weight, used in film Easy Rider, 1968; Up On Cripple Creek, 1970; Don't Do It, 1972; Solo singles include: Somewhere Down That Crazy River, 1988; Albums: with The Band: The Basement Tapes (with Bob Dylan), 1967; Music From Big Pink, 1968; The Band, 1969; Stage Fright, 1970; Cahoots, 1971; Rock of Ages, 1972; Moondog Matinee, 1973; Before The Flood (with Bob Dylan), 1974; Northern Lights Southern Cross, 1976; Best Of..., 1976; Islands, 1977; The Last Waltz, 1978; Solo albums: Robbie Robertson, 1987; Storyville, 1991; Music For The Native Americans, 1994; Contact from the Underworld of Red Boy, 1998; Producer, Beautiful Noise, Neil Diamond,

1976; Contributor, Planet Waves, Bob Dylan, 1974; Beauty, Ryûichi Sakamoto, 1989; Rainbow Warriors, Greenpeace charity album, 1979; Contributor, film soundtracks: Raging Bull; King of Comedy; The Color of Money. *Honours include:* The Band, inducted into Canadian Hall of Fame, 1989. *Current Management:* Addis Wechsler and Associates, 955 S Camillo Dr., Third Floor, Los Angeles, CA 90048, USA.

ROBIN Thierry (Titi); b. 26 Aug. 1957, France. Composer; Musician (guitar; ud – oriental lute, bouzouq). *Career:* French National Scenes including: Théatre de la Ville de Paris; Arabic World Institute; UNESCO; Most European festivals including: Transmusicales; WOMAD; Angoulême; WOMEX; Tours: Japan; Africa; Indian Ocean; Europe; USA; Canada; North Africa; Middle East; Appearances include European TV: Arte Megamix, FR3; TVS; France Inter; France Musique; Europe 1. *Recordings:* Luth et Tablá, 1985; An Henchoû Treùz, 1990; Trio Erik Marchand, 1991; Gitans, 1993; Regard Nu, 1996; Payo Michto, 1997; Kali Gadji, 1998. *Honours:* Grand Prix de l'Academie Charles Cros, 1990. *Membership:* SACEM. *Current Management:* Guillaume Dubois.

ROBINS Reed W; b. 4 June 1957. Prod.; Engineer; Musician (Piano, Guitar, Bass, Vocals); Composer. m. Sevgi Ercan. *Education:* BA, Virginia Commonwealth University. *Career:* Television Performances, Commercial With Ray Charles, Richard Tucker Galas, Pavarotti; Many Performances In Carnegie Hall including The American Premiere of Paul McCartney's Liverpool Oratorio at Carnegie. *Compositions:* Tommys; Jack and The North West Wind; The Painter. *Recordings:* Songs of Jimi Hendrix For Solo Jazz Piano; Music For Film and Theatre Vol. I; My Happiness. *Memberships:* ASCAP; American Music Center. *Current Management:* Changing Tones Corporation, 874 Broadway Suite 901, New York, NY 10003–1222, USA.

ROBINSON Barry; b. 10 Sept. 1963, Bushey, Watford, Hertfordshire, England. Musical Dir; Composer; Conductor; Arranger; Musician (piano, keyboards). *Musical Education:* Honours Graduate, Composition and arranging, Grove School of Music, Los Angeles. *Career:* Music for Television includes: Big Stage Indie Awards; Come Dancing; Variety Club Awards; Children In Need; The Accountant; Tours with: The Three Degrees; Rose Royce; The Supremes; Kiki Dee; Joe Longthorne; Helen Shapiro; West End Shows: Saturday Night Fever; Smokey Joe's Cafe; Fame; musical supervisor, Jesus Christ Superstar; Kat and The Kings. *Compositions:* Composer, arranger, Midas Touch, game show, Central Television. *Membership:* PRS. *Leisure interests:* Football; Tennis. *Current Management:* Emma Darrell, Roger Hancock Ltd. *Address:* 4 Water Lane, London NW1 8NZ, England.

ROBINSON Chris; b. 20 Dec. 1966, Atlanta, Georgia, USA. Rock Singer; Songwriter. *Education:* Georgia State University. *Career:* Singer, US rock group The Black Crowes (originally Mr Crowe's Garden), 1989–; Major concerts include: Support tours to Heart, 1990; Robert Plant, 1990; ZZ Top, 1991; Memphis In May Festival, 1991; Monsters of Rock Festival, Castle Donington, 1991; Glastonbury Festival, 1993; Phoenix Festival, 1993. *Recordings:* Albums: Shake Your Money Maker, 1990; Southern Harmony and Musical Companion, 1992; Amorica, 1995; Sho' Nuff, 1998; By Your Side, 1999; Singles include: Jealous Again; Hard To Handle; Twice As Hard; She Talks To Angels; Seeing Things; Remedy; Sting Me. *Honours:* Grammy Nomination, Best New Artists, 1991; Rolling Stone magazine, Best New American Band, Best Male New Singer, 1991. *Current Management:* Angelus Entertainment, 9016 Wilshire Blvd, Suite 3461, Beverly Hills, CA 90211, USA.

ROBINSON Orphy; b. 13 Oct. 1960, London, England. Jazz Musician (vibraphone, drums, percussion, keyboards); Composer. 1 s. *Education:* Hackney College. *Musical Education:* Hackney and Islington Youth Band. *Career:* Played with Savanna; Courtney Pine; Andy Sheppard; Balanescu String Quartet; Mica Paris; David Murray; Jazz Warriors; Lead soloist, Shivanova, 1990–; Solo artiste, 1990-. *Recordings:* I Can't Turn Away, Savanna; In and Out of Love, Imagination; Journey To The Urge Within, Courtney Pine; Out of Many One People, Jazz Warriors; When Tomorrow Comes, The Vibes Describes, Orphy Robinson; Introductions In The Dark, Andy Sheppard; Suite de Lorenzo, Ensemble Bash; Film soundtracks: Men of The Month; Bloodrights. *Honours:* British Jazz Awards, Most Promising Newcomer, 1989; Best Miscellaneous Instrumentalist, 1993. *Memberships:* PRS; Musicians' Union. *Leisure interests:* Cricket; Football; Judo. *Address:* c/o Coalition Music and Media, Devonshire House, 12 Barley Mow Passage, London W4 4PH, England.

ROBINSON Pat; b. 7 April 1948, USA. Songwriter; Singer; Musician (guitar, piano). 2 d. *Compositions:* You Got Away With Love, recorded by Percy Sledge; Civilised Man, Joe Cocker; No Promise No Guarantee, Laura Branigan; Jokers Are Wild, Gene Clark. *Recordings:* Contributions to: Wave of the Hand: The Best of Carla Olson, 1995; Textones, Cedar Creek, 1998; Revenge of the Nerds, 1998. *Membership:* BMI. *Current Management:* Saul Davis. *Address:* c/o Saul Davis, 11864 Ventura Blvd, #583, Studio City, CA 91604, USA.

ROBINSON Richard; b. 24 May 1969, Atlanta, Georgia, USA. Musician (Guitar). *Career:* Formed Black Crowes with brother Chris; Numerous tours and radio appearances. *Recordings:* Singles: She Talks to Angels, 1990; Seeing Things, 1991; Twice as Hard, 1991; Sting Me, 1992; One Mirror Too Many, 1996; Only a Fool, 1999; Albums: Shake Your Money Maker, 1990; The Southern Harmony and Musical Companion, 1992; Amorica, 1994; Three Snakes and One Charm, 1996; By Your Side, 1999.

ROBINSON Smokey (William); b. 19 Feb. 1940, Detroit, Michigan, USA. R & B Soul Singer; Songwriter; Prod. m. Claudette, 7 Nov. 1959, 2 c. *Career:* Singer with The Matadors; Singer with The Miracles, 1954–72; Also billed as Smokey Robinson and The Miracles, 1967–72; Solo artiste, 1973–; Executive producer, composer, film Big Time, 1977; Appearances on television specials: Smokey Robinson 25th Anniversary Special, ABC-TV, 1981; Motown 25th Anniversary special, NBC-TV, 1983; Motown 30 – What's Goin' On, 1990; Aretha Franklin – Duets, 1993. *Compositions include:* Most recordings with the Miracles until 1968; Other hits include: The Way You Do The Things You Do, The Temptations, 1964; Co-writer, My Guy, Mary Wells (No. 1, USA), 1964; My Girl, Temptations (No. 1, USA), 1965. *Recordings:* Albums: The Fabulous Miracles, 1963; The Miracles On Stage, 1963; Doin' Mickey's Monkey, 1964; Going To A Go-Go, 1966; Make It Happen, 1967; Special Occasion, 1968; Time Out For..., 1969; What Love Has Joined Together, 1970; A Pocketful of Miracles, 1970; One Dozen Roses, 1971; Flying High Together, 1972; Solo albums: Smokey, 1973; Pure Smokey, 1974; Smokey's Family Robinson, 1976; Deep In My Soul, 1977; Love Breeze, 1978; Smokin', 1979; Where There's Smoke, 1979; Being With You, 1981; Smoke Signals, 1986; One Heartbeat, 1987; Love Songs, 1988; Love, Smokey, 1990; Double Good Everything, 1991; Ballads, 1995; Our Very Best Christmas, 1999; Intimate, 1999; Singles include: with the Miracles: Shop Around, 1961; You've Really Got A Hold On Me, 1963; The Tracks of My Tears, 1965; Going To A Go-Go, 1966; I Second That Emotion, 1967; If You Can Wait, 1968; Baby Baby Don't Cry, 1969; The Tears of a Clown (No. 1, USA), 1970; Solo: Cruisin', 1980; Being With You (No. 1, UK), 1981; Just To See Her, 1987; Contributor, We Are The World, USA For Africa, 1985; Recorded duets with Barbara Mandrell; Kenny G; Dolly Parton; Rick James. *Honours include:* Inducted into Rock and Roll Hall of Fame, 1987; Grammy Award, Best R & B Vocal Performance, 1988; Grammy Living Legend Award, 1989; Inducted into Songwriters Hall of Fame, 1990; Soul Train Heritage Award, 1991; Motor City Music Award for Lifetime Achievement, 1992. *Current Management:* Jeff Wald Entertainment, Suite 840, 12424 Wilshire Blvd, Los Angeles, CA 90025, USA.

ROBINSON Tom; b. 1 June 1950, Cambridge, England. Songwriter. 1 s. *Career:* Joined first band Café Society, London, 1973; Album produced by Ray Davies of The Kinks, 1975; Left Café Society, formed Tom Robinson Band (TRB), 1976; Chart success, concerts for Rock Against Racism, world tours, 1977–78; Formed Sector 27, 1979; US tour with Police, 1981; Lived and worked in East Germany, 1982; Further chart success, 1983–84; Tours of USA, Australia, 1985; Purchased recording studio, 1985; Tours of Japan, Italy, UK 1987; IIit show Private View, Edinburgh Fringe, 1987; Presenter, BBC World Service, Radio 1, 1988; Reformed Tom Robinson Band, 1989; Tours throughout UK, Europe, Canada, USA, Australia, 1991–95; Presenter, BBC Radio 4 series, The Locker Room, 1992–95; Heineken Festival, Leeds, 1995. *Compositions include:* Co-writer with Peter Gabriel: Bully For You; Merrily Up On High, 1979; Atmospherics- Listen To The Radio, 1983; Co-writer with Elton John: Sartorial Eloquence; Elton's Song; Never Gonna Fall In Love Again, 1979–80; Composed music for: More Lives Than One, BBC2 TV, 1985; with Jakko Jakszyk: Hard Cases, Central TV, 1988; Lyrics for It's About Time, Manu Katché, 1991. *Recordings:* Singles include: 2–4–6–8 Motorway, 1977; Glad To Be Gay, 1978; War Baby, 1983; Atmospherics-Listen To The Radio, 1983; Hard, 1994; Albums include: Café Society, 1975; Power In The Darkness, 1978; TRB Two, 1979; Sector 27, 1981; North By Northwest, 1982; Cabaret 79, 1982; Hope and Glory, 1984; Still Loving You, 1986; We Never Had It So Good (with Jakko Jakszyk) 1990; Living In A Boom Time, 1992; Love Over Rage, 1994; Having It Both Ways, 1996; Holidays in the Sun, 1997. *Honours:* Gold Winner with You've Got to Hide Your Love Away, UK Sony Awards, 1997. *Leisure interests:* Parenthood; Swimming; Languages; Computers. *Address:* PO Box 3185, London SW18 3JG, England.

ROBISON Emily Burns, (Emily Erwin); b. 16 Aug. 1972, Pittsfield, Massachusetts, USA. Musician (guitar, dobro, fiddle, mandolin, keyboards); Vocalist. m. Charlie Robison, 1 May 1999. *Career:* Toured with sister Martie Seidel in teen bluegrass group Blue Night Express for six years until band broke up, 1989; Sisters joined two friends performing on Dallas sidewalks, calling the act the Dixie Chicks; Support slots for: Garth Brooks; Emmylou Harris; Loretta Lynn; Recorded three albums for local label, Crystal Clear; Signed to Sony and released debut album Wide Open Spaces; Mix of traditional bluegrass with mainstream country coupled with exuberant live stage show and quirky song material has ensured huge popularity into the 2000s. *Compositions include:* You Were Mine. *Recordings include:* with the Dixie Chicks: I Can Love You Better, 1997; There's Your Trouble, 1998; Wide Open Spaces, 1998; Albums include:

Wide Open Spaces, 1998, Fly, 1999. *Honours:* recent including: CMA Awards: Music Video of The Year, 1999; Single of The Year, Wide Open Spaces, 1999; Vocal Group of The Year, 1999; Entertainer of The Year, 2000; Album of The Year, Fly, 2000; Vocal Group of The Year, 2000; Music Video of The Year, Goodbye Earl, 2000; TNN Music Awards: Group/Duo of The Year, 1999; ACM Awards: Album of The Year, Fly, 1999; Favorite Duo Or Group, 1999; American Music Award, Favorite New Country Artist, 1999; Billboard Award, Favorite Country Artist, 1999; Grammy Awards: Best Country Album, Wide Open Spaces, 1998; Best Country Performance By A Duo Or Group With Vocal, 1998, 1999. *Address:* c/o The Country Music Asscn, Nashville, Tennessee, USA. *Internet:* www.dixiechicks.com.

ROCHEMAN Manuel David; b. 23 July 1964, Paris, France. Musician (piano); Composer. m. Beatriz España, 15 April 1991, 1 s., 1 d. *Musical Education:* Piano, with Alberto Neuman (CNR de Paris); Jazz with Martial Solal. *Career:* Appearances with own trio: Radio-France, 1984; Festival de Jazz Paris, 1984, 1986; Montpellier, 1986; Antibes-Juan-Les Pins, 1988; Grande Parade Du Jazz, Nice, 1992; JVC Halle That Jazz, 1992; Auditorium Du Châtelet, 1993; Festival Cervantino and Palacio de Bellas Artes (Mexico), 1993, 1994; Tours: Belgium; Switzerland; East European countries, 1993–95; Jazz Festivals: Cannes, 1996; Malta, 1996; Montréal, 1996; Copenhagen, 1997; Aarhus, 1997; New Morning in Paris, with George Mraz and Al Foster, 1998; Also played with Jean-Luc Ponty; Anthony Ortega; Johnny Griffin. *Compositions:* Concerto for piano and orchestra, 1988; San Felipe, for jazz band and philharmonic orchestra, 1995; Concerto For Piano and Orchestra, 1999. *Recordings:* Albums: Trio Urbain, 1989; White Keys, 1992; Tropic City, 1995; Come Shine, with George Mraz and Al Foster, 1998; I'm Old Fashioned, 2000. *Honours:* Prix Boris Vian, 1991; Django D'Or, 1992; Prix Django Reinhardt, 1998. *Memberships:* SACEM; SPEDIDAM; ADAMI. *Address:* 14 rue Camille Pelletan, 93600 Aulnay-Sous-Bois, France.

ROCK Bob; Prod. *Career:* Played In Punk Band, The Payolas, In 1987 changed name to Rock and Hyde; Worked alongside producer Bruce Fairbairn; Producer, secured gigs with Blue Murder, Loverboy, The Cult, Motley Crue, David Lee Roth, Cher; Teamed up with Metallica, 1991. *Recordings include:* Sonic Temple; A Little Ain't Enough; Bitter, Sweet and Twisted; Keep The Faith; The Cult; Subhuman Race; Load; Eight Arms To Hold You; Tal Bachman; On A Day Like Today; Load; Reload; Garage Inc. *Address:* c/o Bruce Allen Talent, 406–68 Water St, Vancouver BC, Canada V6B 1A4.

ROCKY (Darren Rock); b. 25 Sept. 1967, Hayes, London, England. Prod.; Remixer; DJ. *Career:* Started DJ career with partner Diesel; Formed X-Press 2 with Ashley Beedle and Diesel, 1993; Signed to Junior Boy's Own label; Co-founder: Low Pressings Records; Member: Ballistic Brothers; Problem Kids; Remixed: Cevin Fisher; Fatboy Slim; River Ocean. *Recordings:* Albums: Ballistic Brothers vs The Eccentric Afro's, 1995; London Hooligan Soul (with Ballistic Brothers), 1995; My First Acid House (with Problem Kids), 2001; Xpress-2 album forthcoming, 2002; Singles: Muzik X-Press, London X-Press, Say What, 1993; Rock 2 House, 1994; The Sound, 1995; Tranz Euro Express, 1996; Blacker (with Ballistic Brothers), 1997; AC/DC, 2000; Smoke Machine, Muzikizum, 2001. *Honours:* Muzik Awards, Best Producers, X-Press 2, 2001. *Membership:* MCPS/PRS. *Address:* c/o Skint Records, 73A Middle St, Brighton, Sussex, BN1 4BA, England.

RODE Birgitte; b. 26 Feb. 1956, Copenhagen, Denmark. Vocalist; Musician (keyboards). m. Claus Hvass, 14 June 1992, 1 s. *Musical Education:* Academy of Music, Aalborg, Denmark. *Career:* Roskilde Festival; Tours: UK; California, USA; France; Norway; Germany; Sweden; Denmark; Television appearances: Live Aid; Grand Prix-Slovenia; National and international television and radio. *Compositions:* Sculptural Music. *Recordings:* with Johnnny Og De Kolde Dæmoner: Paraneuropa; with Walk The Walk: Walk The Walk; Feet On The Ground; Frog Dance. *Publications:* The International Discography of New Wave; Dansk Rock. *Honours:* 4 National Music Council Awards, 1991–94. *Memberships:* National Musicians Society; DJBFA. *Leisure interests:* Visual Art and Culture; Sociology. *Current Management:* Zing Zing Musicproduction and Management.

RODGERS Nile; b. 19 Sept. 1952, New York, USA. Musician (guitar); Record Prod. *Career:* Member, New World Rising, 1960s; Founder member, Big Apple Band, 1972–76; Became Chic, 1977–; Also solo artiste and record producer; Member, The Honeydrippers, with Robert Plant, Jimmy Page, Jeff Beck; Leader, own trio, Outloud; Co-founder, Ear Candy record label, 1989. *Recordings:* Albums: with Chic: C'Est Chic, 1978; Risqué, 1979; The Best of Chic, 1980; Real People, 1982; Take It Off, 1982; Tongue In Chic, 1982; Believer, 1983; Freak Out, 1987; Chic-Ism, 1992; Solo albums: Adventures In The Land of The Good Groove, 1983; B-Movie Matinee, 1985; Singles include: Dance Dance Dance, 1978; Everybody Dance; I Want Your Love, 1979; Good Times (No. 1, USA); My Forbidden Lover; My Feet Keep Dancing, 1980; Soup For One, 1982; Jack Le Freak, 1987; Chic Mystique, 1992; As writer, producer with Bernard Edwards: Norma Jean,

Norma Jean Wright, 1977; He's The Greatest Dancer, Sister Sledge, 1979; We Are Family, Sister Sledge, 1979; Love Somebody Today, Sister Sledge, 1979; Upside Down, Diana Ross, 1980; Diana, Diana Ross, 1982; Why, Carly Simon, 1982; Record producer for artists including: David Bowie; Madonna; Duran Duran; Aretha Franklin; Jeff Beck; Mick Jagger; Al Jarreau; Grace Jones; Johnny Mathis.

RODGERS Paul; b. 17 Dec. 1949, Middlesborough, Cleveland, England. Singer; Songwriter; Musician (guitar and piano). 1 s., 2 d. *Career:* Singer, with Roadrunners; Brown Sugar; Founder member, Free, 1968–73; Concerts include: US tour, 1969, 1971–73; Hollywood Music Festival, Staffordshire, 1970; Isle of Wight Festival, 1970; Tours of UK and Japan, 1972; Formed Peace, 1971; Founder member, singer, Bad Company, 1973–83; Toured UK, Europe, USA, Japan and Australia; Played with Eric Clapton, Jimmy Page and Jeff Beck on The Ronnie Lane ARMS appeal concert tour, 1983; Founder member, singer, The Firm, 1984–86; Toured Europe and USA 1985–86; Founder member, singer, The LAW, 1991; Miscellaneous Concerts include: Atlantic Records 40th anniversary party, 1988; Guitar Legends, Expo '92, Seville, Spain, 1992; Gibson Night of 100 Guitars, Wembley, London, 1994; Elvis Tribute, Memphis, 1994; Woodstock '94, USA; Began solo career; Formed new bands, Paul Rodgers, 1993–; Toured Europe, USA and Japan. *Recordings include:* With Free: Albums: Tons of Sobs, 1968; Free, 1969; Fire and Water, 1970; Highway, 1971; Free Live, 1971; Free at Last, 1972; Heartbreaker, 1973; The Free Story, 1973; Best of Free, 1991; Walk In My Shadow – An Introduction To Free, 1998; Singles: All Right Now; My Brother Jake; Little Bit of Love; Wishing Well; With Bad Company: Albums: Bad Co, 1974; Straight Shooter, 1975; Run With the Pack, 1976; Burnin' Sky, 1977; Desolation Angels, 1979; Rough Diamonds, 1982; 10 From 6, 1985; The Original Bad Co Anthology, 1999; Singles: Can't Get Enough; Feel Like Making Love; Young Blood; Movin' On; Hey Hey; Hammer of Love; With The Firm: Albums: The Firm, 1985; Mean Business, 1986; Singles: Radioactive; All The King's Horses; With The Law: Album: The Law, 1991; Single: Laying Down the Law; As Solo Artist: Cut Loose, 1983; Muddy Waters Blues, 1993; The Hendrix Set, 1993; Live (The Loreley Tapes), 1995; Now, 1997 (also released as double album Now and Live); Electric, 1999; Hit single, Soul of Love, 1997; Various contributions to compilation albums. *Honours:* With Free: ASCAP Award for 1m. radio plays; Gold Disc: Single: All Right Now; With Bad Company: Grammy Award, 1975; Gold/Platinum albums with Bad Company; Hon. Col of Louisiana 1977; Solo: UK Silver Disc: Album: Muddy Water Blues. *Memberships:* Musicians' Union; PRS; MCPS. *Leisure interests:* Scuba diving; Horse riding; Working out; Motorbikes. *Address:* c/o Gremlin Productions, PO Box 216, Diss, Norfolk PE22 2TY, England.

RODNEY Godfrey Winston; b. 1 March 1945, St Ann's Bay, Jamaica. Singer; Songwriter. m. Sonia Marlene Thompson, 13 Sept. 1981, 1 s., 3 d. *Career:* Singer, songwriter, reggae group Burning Spear; Career began recording for Studio One label, 1969; Releases for Island Records, 1970s; Toured with bands including: UB40; Talking Heads; The Clash; Tour US from East to West coast; TV appearance Bet, Rockers; Many radio appearances world-wide; Rendered Estimated Prophet on Dedicated, Grateful Dead tribute album, 1991. *Recordings:* 20 albums include: Burning Spear; Rocking Time; Marcus Garvey; Man In The Hills; Garvey's Ghost; Hail H I M, 1981; Farover, 1982; Resistance, 1984; Mek We Dweet, 1990; Jah Kingdom, 1992; The World Should Know, 1993; Rasta Business, 1995. *Honours:* 5 Grammy Nominations for Reggae Album of the Year; Musicians Merit Award, Album of the Year, 1990; Martin's International Reggae Award for Most Educational Entertainer of the 1980s, 1991; Album of the Year, Best Arranger (reggae), Caribbean Music Awards; Best Reggae Album, NAIRD Indie Awards, 1992; 4 IRMA Awards, including Best Music Video, 1995; Bob Marley Award Entertainer of The Year; International Reggae Hall of Fame; Marcus Garvey Humanitarian Award. *Memberships:* PRS; ASCAP. *Leisure interests:* Football; Jogging. *Current Management:* Burning Music Production. *Address:* 130–34 231th St, Laurelton, NY 11413, USA.

RODRIGUEZ Arabella Sabina; b. Norfolk, England. Recording and Mixing Engineer. 1 s., 1 d. *Education:* Piano, Harmony, Violin, Flute. *Career:* Sound Engineer, 1986-. *Recordings:* Credits as Engineer include: Motorhead; Scritti Politti; Soul II Soul; Black Rain; Caron Wheeler; Manu Dibango; Angelique Kidjo; D-Influence; East 17; Sinead O'Connor; Natacha Atlas; Tama. *Memberships:* Repro; PRS; MCPS. *Current Management:* Stephen Budd Management, 109 B Regent's Park Rd, London, NW1 8UR, England. *Address:* 106 Albion Rd, London, N16 9AD, England.

RODRIGUEZ Johnny (Juan Raoul Davis); b. 10 Dec. 1951, Sabibal, Texas, USA. Country vocalist; Songwriter; Musician (guitar). *Career:* Performed with high school rock band The Spocks, late 1960s; Discovered by Tom T Hall and Bobby Bare while performing at Alamo Village Amusement Park, Brackettville, Texas, 1971; Moved to Nashville; Worked as guitarist with Tom T Hall's band; Signed to Mercury Records; First chart appearance, 1972; Most successful Chicano country singer of all time, recording in both English and Spanish; peak period early to mid-

1970s but continued to chart until 1989; Appeared in TV show Adam -12, 1974; Movies include: Rio Diablo; Nashville Girl (a.k.a. Country Music Daughter/New Girl In Town), 1976; La Bamba Party; The Runaway Barge (a.k.a. River Bandits, 1975; Charity work includes helping underprivileged Mexican-American children through the Life Enrichment Center. *Compositions include:* Dance With Me (Just One More Time); Down On The Rio Grande; Ridin' My Thumb To Mexico. *Recordings include:* Pass Me By (If You're Only Passing Through), 1972; That's The Way Love Goes, 1973; Just Get Up and Close The Door, 1975; You Always Come Back (To Hurting Me), 1973; Love Put A Song In My Heart, 1975; I Just Can't Get Her Out My Mind, 1975; Albums: Introducing Johnny Rodriguez, 1973; All I Ever Meant To Do Was Sing, 1973; Greatest Hits. *Honours:* various including: ACM, Most Promising Male Vocalist, 1972; Cash Box, New Male Vocalist, Singles and Albums, 1973; Music City News, Most Promising Male Vocalist, 1973 and 1974; Billboard, Trendsetter Award, 1973; Cash Box, Upcoming Male Award, 1973; Record Review, Most Promising Male Vocalist, Album Charts and Singles Chart, 1973. *Address:* c/o Fat City Artists, 1226 17th Ave S, Suite 2, Nashville 37212, USA.

ROE Tommy; b. 9 May 1942, Atlanta, Georgia, USA. Entertainer; Musician (guitar); Songwriter; Music Publisher. *Musical Education:* Self-taught. *Career:* Performances and concerts world-wide; Appearances, all major television and radio shows in 1960's; Sold 40m. records. *Recordings:* Hit Singles: Sheila; Sweet Pea; Dizzy; Everybody (all Gold discs); Hooray For Hazel; It's Now Winter's Day; Jam Up; Jelly Tight; Albums include: 12 in a Roe; Tommy Roe's Greatest Hits; Dizzy: The Best of Tommy Roe. *Honours:* 4 Gold Singles; Georgy Award; BMI Awards. *Memberships:* Society of Singers; Academy of Country Music. *Leisure interest:* Golf. *Current Management:* Dave Hoffman. *Address:* PO Box 26037, Minneapolis, MN 55426, USA.

ROEL (Anne) Charlotte; b. 3 Dec. 1964, Copenhagen, Denmark. Vocalist. m. Floyd Adams III, 21 July 1990. *Musical Education:* Manhattan School of Music, New York City. *Career:* Solo performer, 1992–; Concerts: Copenhagen Gospel Rock Festival; Opstand Festival; Glumsö Gospel Festival; Västervik Gospel Festival, Sweden; Performed; Montmartre; Copenhagen Jazz House; Huset; KB Hallen; Radio: Strax, Denmarks National Radio; More Than Music; Tjek Listen; Danish local radio; NIK Kolding; Radio Roskilde; Naestved Radio; Copenhagen FM; Radio Ballerup; Swedish radio; KFUM Sweden; Television: KKR/TV Charlotte Roel – A Musical Portrait; Norwegian TV; Hello Norden; Hostess, producer, The Five Blind Boys of Alabama. *Recordings:* Single: Perfect Love (No. 1, Denmark), 1994; Debut album, 1995. *Membership:* DAF (Danish Artist Society). *Leisure interests:* Jazz and Funk Dance; Tennis; Music. *Current Management:* William B Proven Productions. *Address:* Nörre Sögade 33 A 1, 1370 Copenhagen K, Denmark.

ROESER Donald (Buck Dharma); b. 12 Nov. 1947. Musician (guitar); Vocalist. *Career:* Lead guitarist, vocalist, US rock group Blue Öyster Cult, 1971–; Concerts: US tours, including support to Alice Cooper, 1972; World tour, 1978 Monsters of Rock Festival, Castle Donington, 1981; British tour, 1989. *Recordings:* Singles include: (Don't Fear) The Reaper, 1976; Albums: Blue Öyster Cult, 1972; Tyranny and Mutation, 1973; Live On Your Feet Or On Your Knees, 1975; Agents of Fortune, 1976; Spectres, 1978; Some Enchanted Evening, 1978; Mirrors, 1979; Cultosaurus Erectus, 1980; Fire of Unknown Origin, 1981; ETL (Extra-Terrestrial Live), 1982; Club Ninja, 1986; Imaginos, 1988; Career of Evil- The Metal Years, 1990; Live 1976, 1994; Cult Classic, 1994; Soundtrack, horror film Bad Channels, 1992; Solo album (as Buck Dharma): Flat Out; with Blotto, Collected Words, 1994; with Summerdaze, Summerdaze, 1997. *Honour:* Platinum disc, (Don't Fear) The Reaper. *Current Management:* Steve Schenck.

ROGERS David; b. 3 Jan. 1963, Dartford, Kent, England. Composer (keyboards); Programmer; Prod. m. Sue Ward, 21 Nov. 1992, 2 s. *Education:* Hons, Comparative Physiology, London University. *Musical Education:* Mrs Hoban; Also self-taught. *Career:* Founder member, Daybreak Productions, 1987; Numerous television, radio appearances including: BBC Radio 1; TV AM; Pebble Mill; Top of The Pops; Kent Rocks; Noel's House Party; Live and Kicking. *Compositions:* 346 works published by 1995; Works include: Mr Blobby; Light of Summer; Peanuts; Steady; Blobby – The Album; The Dream; Boing; Probe. *Honours:* Ivor Novello, Best Selling Song, Mr Blobby, 1993. *Memberships:* Musicians' Union; PRS. *Leisure interests:* Wildlife; Scuba diving; Travel; Ethnic music. *Address:* Carlin Music/Destiny Music, Iron Bridge House, Bridge Approach, London NW1 8BD, England.

ROGERS Kenny (Kenneth David); b. 21 Aug. 1938, Houston, Texas, USA. Country Singer; Songwriter. m. Wanda Miller. *Career:* Member, The Scholars, 1955; Founder, Ken-Lee record label (with brother Lelan); Jolly Rogers record label; Bass player, Bobby Doyle Three, 1962; Member, New Christy Minstrels, 1967; Founder member, First Edition, 1967–74; Featured in television films: The Gambler; The Gambler II; The Gambler Returns; Documentary, Kenny Rogers and The American Cowboy; Established Dreamcatcher Entertainment, 1998; European Concert Tour,

1999; AandE's Live By Request, TV concert, 1999. *Compositions include:* Sweet Music Man, recorded by Billie Jo Spears, Anne Murray, Tammy Wynette, Dolly Parton, Millie Jackson. *Recordings:* Albums: with First Edition: The First Edition, 1967; The First Editions Second, 1968; The First Edition '69, 1969; Ruby, Don't Take Your Love To Town, 1969; Something's Burning, 1970; Fools (film soundtrack), 1970; Tell It All Brother, 1971; Transition, 1971; The Ballad of Calico, 1972; Backroads, 1972; Monumental, 1973; Rollin', 1974; Solo albums include: Kenny Rogers, 1976; Love Lifted Me, 1976; Daytime Friends, 1977; Every Time Two Fools Collide (with Dottie West), 1978; Love Or Something Like It, 1978; The Gambler, 1978; Kenny, 1978; Gideon, 1980; Share Your Love, 1981; Love Will Turn You Around, 1982; We've Got Tonight, 1983; Eyes That See In The Dark, 1983; What About Me?, 1984; The Heart of The Matter, 1985; Short Stories, 1986; I Prefer The Moonlight, 1987; Something Inside So Strong, 1989; Some Prisons Don't Have Walls, 1991; Back Home Again, 1992; She Rides Wild Horses, 1999; After Dark, 1999; Albums with The First Edition include: Ruby, Don't Take Your Love To Town, 1969; Something's Burning, 1970; Fools (soundtrack), 1970; Hit singles include: Ruby Don't Take Your Love To Town; Something's Burning; Lucille (No. 1, UK); She Believes Me; You Decorated My Life; Coward of The County (No. 1, UK); Lady (No. 1, USA); I Don't Need You; Morning Desire (US Country No. 1); Tomb of The Unknown Love (US Country No. 1); Duets include: Don't Fall In Love With A Dreamer, with Kim Carnes; What About Me, with James Ingram and Kim Carnes; Make No Mistake She's Mine, with Ronnie Milsap; We've Got Tonight, with Sheena Easton; Islands In The Stream, with Dolly Parton; Contributor, We Are The World, USA For Africa, 1985. *Publication:* Making It In Music (co-author with Len Epland). *Honours:* 4 Grammys; 11 People's Choice Awards; 8 Academy of Country Music Awards; 11 Platinum Albums; 1 Platinum Single; numerous Gold Albums and Singles; Sammy Cahn Lifetime Achievement Award, 1999; Diamond Award, RIAA, 1999; LeRoy Neiman Award For Artistic Excellence, 1999. *Current Management:* Kragen and Co, 1112 N Sherbourne Dr., Los Angeles, CA 90069, USA.

ROGERS Robert; b. 27 Jan. 1926, London, England. Bandleader; Musician (guitar); Vocalist. m. Olive, 23 Sept. 1950, 1 s. *Musical Education:* Self-taught. *Career:* Over 200 TV Tonight shows with Ted Taylor Four; Don Lang's Frantic Five; 6.5 Special; Saturday Club and Country Club on radio; Hundreds of radio shows as Sounds Bob Rogers; Own series, The Towncriers; Things are Swinging; Skinnerette in the Frank Skinner TV Shows. *Recordings:* 11 albums; Session guitarist with artists including: John Barry Seven; Adam Faith; Freddy and The Dreamers; Les Reed; Banjo player with artistes including: Mike Daniels Delta Jazzmen; Sid Phillips; Joe Henderson. *Leisure interest:* Close harmony vocal groups. *Address:* 11 Darwin Close, Farnborough Village, Orpington, Kent BR6 7EP, England.

ROGERS Roy; b. 28 July 1950, Redding, California, USA. Prod.; Musician (slide guitar). m. Gaynell Toler Rogers, 28 April 1984, 1 s., 1 d. *Education:* BA, History, Hayward State University, California. *Musical Education:* Primarily self-taught. *Career:* Member, Delta Rhythm Kings; Producer/musician, John Lee Hooker, 1989–; World-wide tours, major jazz festivals; Numerous television and radio shows including John Lee Hooker special, Rock Steady Late Show, UK; Performed with: Carlos Santana; Miles Davis; Albert Collins; B. B. King; Bonnie Raitt; Robert Cray. *Composition:* The Healer, with John Lee Hooker. *Recordings:* Solo albums: Chops Not Chaps; Slidewinder; Blues On The Range; Slide Zone; Slide of Hand; Slide Zones; with Norton Buffalo: R & B; Travelin' Tracks; Rhythm and Groove, 1996; Soundtracks: The Hot Spot; One Flew Over The Cuckoo's Nest. *Honours:* 2 W C Handy Award Nominations; Best Emerging Blues Artist, Jazz Times Critics Poll, 1990; 2 Grammy Nominations; NARAS Award of Recognition. *Memberships:* AFofM; NARAS; BMI. *Leisure interest:* Collecting 78 rpm records. *Current Management:* Blue Muse Inc. *Address:* PO Box 598, Novato, CA 94948, USA.

ROKER Ron; b. 23 Jan. 1941, Lincoln, England. Composer; Songwriter; Record Prod.; Publisher. m. Karol Roker, 7 Sept. 1977, 1 s., 1 d. *Musical Education:* Self-taught, keyboards. *Career:* Founder, lead vocalist, own group, 1960's (with guitarist Albert Lee); Toured, worked with various headliners; Turned to writing and producing; Co-writers include: Gerry Shury; Barry Blue; Lynsey De Paul; Roger Greenaway; Howard Greenfield; Formed own publishing and producing company, Karon Productions. *Recordings:* Top 10 hits include: Rupert, Jackie Lee; Storm In A Teacup, The Fortunes; Do You Wanna Dance, Barry Blue; Dance Little Lady Dance, Tina Charles; Guilty, The Pearls; US Top 20 hits: Guilty, First Choice; Up In A Puff of Smoke, Polly Brown; Devils Gun, CJ and Co; Funk Theory, Rokotto and BT Express; Do You Believe In Love At First Sight, Dionne Warwick; Honey Honey, Sweet Dreams. *Honours:* Composer, Never Giving Up, performed by Sweet Dreams, 1983 Eurovision Song Contest (placed sixth). *Memberships:* IPA; Term, BASCA Council. *Leisure interests:* Computers; Reading; Football; Cricket. *Current Management:* Karon Productions. *Address:* c/o Karon Productions, 20 Radstone Court, Hill View Rd, Woking, Surrey GU22 7NB, England.

ROLLINS (Theodore) Sonny; b. 7 Sept. 1930, New York, USA. Jazz Musician (saxophone): Composer. m. Lucille Rollins, 7 Sept. 1957. *Musical Education:* Private music teachers. *Career:* Modern Jazz innovator; Numerous television appearances including solo saxophone on Tonite Show; Annual concert tours of Europe, Japan, USA by Sonny Rollins and Concert Orchestra, 1973-. *Compositions:* include Oleo; Doxy; Duke of Iron; Way Out West; Concerto For Tenor Sax and Orchestra; Soundtrack: Alfie. *Publications:* Sonny Rollins: Journey of a Jazzman; Open Sky: Sonny Rollins and His World of Improvisation by Eric Nisenson, 2000. *Honours:* Hon. Dr of Arts, Bard College; Guggenheim Fellow, 1972; Inducted, several Halls of Fame; Tufts University Lifetime Achievement Award, 1996; Hon. Doctorate of Music, Long Island University, 1998; Hon. Doctorate of Arts, Wesleyan University, 1998; Hon. Doctorate of Fine Arts, Duke University, 1999. *Current Management:* Ted Kurland Associates; Lucille Rollins. *Address:* Route 9 G, Germantown, NY 12526, USA.

ROLLINS Henry; b. 13 Feb. 1961, Washington DC, USA. *Education:* American University. *Career:* Singer, punk rock group, Black Flag, 1981–86; Concerts include: Support tours to The Exploited; The Damned; Christmas On Earth Festival, Leeds; Leader, Henry Rollins Band, 1986–; Regular tours and concerts include: World tour, 1991; Publisher, 1984–; Actor in films including The Chase, 1994 and Johnny Mnemonic, 1995. *Compositions include:* End To End, 1985; Hallucination of Grandeur, 1986; Works, 1988; Knife Street, 1989; One From None, 1991; Now Watch Him Die, 1993; Get Him In The Van: On the Road with Black Flag, 1994. *Recordings:* Albums include: with Black Flag: Everything Went Black, 1982; Damaged, 1982; Slip It In, 1984; Loose Nut, 1985; The Process of Weeding Out, 1985; In My Head, 1985; Who's Got The Ten, 1986; with Henry Rollins Band: Hot Animal Machine; Drive By Shooting, 1987; Life Time, 1988; Do It, 1989; Hard Volume, 1989; Turned On, 1990; The End of Silence, 1992; Electro Convulsive Therapy, 1993; The Weight, 1994; Everything, 1996; Black Coffee Blues, 1997; Think Tank, 1998; Live in Australia, 1999; Spoken works include: Short Walk On A Long Pier, 1987; Live At McCabe's, 1992; Deep Throat, 1992; The Boxed Life, 1993. *Contributions to:* Details; Face; Interview; Melody Maker; Sounds; Village Voice. *Honour:* Grammy Award Nomination, Best Metal Performance, 1995. *Current Management:* 3 Artist Management, 2550 Laurel Pass Ave, Los Angeles, CA 90046, USA.

ROLLO; Prod. *Career:* Pre-eminent producer of British house music; Established own label Cheeky Records, 1991; Produced Felix's Don't You Want Me, 1992; Began remixing numerous artists including Pet Shop Boys, Gabrielle, M People, Wonderstuff, Ian Wright; Produced hit singles for Out Tribe and High on Love; Formed Faithless, 1995. *Recordings:* As Remixer and Producer: Pet Shop Boys: Absolutely Fabulous, Disco 2, Can You Forgive Her, remixer; Black Grape, Get Higher, remixer; Olive, You're Not Alone, Producer and remixer; Sliding Doors, soundtrack; With Faithless: Singles: Insomnia; Salva Mea; If Lovin' You is Wrong; Take the Long Way Home; God is a DJ; Why Go?; Albums: Reverence, 1996; Sunday 8pm, 1998; Testimony, Chapter 1, 1999.

ROMAN-SMITH Lu Lu; b. 6 May 1946, Pilot Point, Texas, USA. Singer; Songwriter. Divorced, 2 s. *Career:* Gospel and Country music and contemporary Christian singer; Appearances include: Grand Ole Opry (21 years); One Woman Show, Branson, Missouri, for 3 years; Cast member, television show, Hee-Haw, 1968–; Presidential Inaugural Event for Ronald Reagan, 1980; Featured artist, Bob Hope Charity Benefits, 1988–91; Pat Boone Celebrity Spectacular, 1991; Television includes: The Love Boat; The Tony Orlando Show; The Mike Douglas Show; Sally Jesse Raphael; Nashville Now; The 700 Club; Music City Tonite; Ralph Emory Show; Featured headliner, numerous state fairs. *Recordings:* Now Let Me Sing, 1974; One Day At A Time, 1975; Love Coming Down, 1976; Lulu's Testimony, 1978; Sing For My Friends, 1979; You Were Loving Me, 1984; Take Me There, 1986; Hymns That Light The Way, 1987; Joy, 1988; Key To The Kingdom, 1990; Best Friend, 1991; King of Whom I Am; Two More Hands; Contributions to: King's Gold, 1992; Operation Angel Wings, 1993. *Honours:* Dove Award, Best Album By A Secular Artist, You Were Loving Me, 1985. *Memberships:* CCMA; GMA. *Leisure interest:* Making jewellery. *Current Management:* Century II Promotions, PO Box 40707, Nashville, TN 37204–0707, USA. *Address:* Rainey Steele, 1300 Division St, Suite 206, Nashville, TN 37203, USA.

ROMBOLA Tony; b. 24 Nov. 1964, Norwood, Massachusetts, USA. Musician (guitar). m. Sue, 3 c. *Career:* Formerly in The Crushed Tomatoes; Joined Godsmack group, 1995; Recorded independent debut album for $2,500 over 3 days with money borrowed from friend, 1996; Heavy local airplay on Boston-based WAAF radio station led to deal with Republic/Universal, 1998; Debut LP remixed/repackaged with eponymous title; Album banned by US Wal-Mart and K-Mart stores for profane content; US and European gigs in 1999 and 2000 including: Woodstock '99; Ozzfest; MTV's Return of The Rock tour; Second album recorded in warehouse in Massachusetts, 2000; First major amphitheatre tour, 2001. *Recordings:* Albums: All Wound Up, 1997; Godsmack, 1998; Awake, 2000; Singles: Whatever, Keep Away, 1998; Voodoo, Bad Religion, 1999; Awake,

2000; Greed, Bad Magick, 2001. *Honours:* Whatever single spent record total of 33 weeks on Billboard Top 10; Boston Music Awards, Act of The Year, 2000 and 2001; Billboard Award, Rock Artist of The Year, 2001. *Address:* c/o Paul Geary, PGM, PO Box 9134, Boston, MA 02205, USA. *E-mail:* godsmack@pgmglobal.com. *Internet:* www.godsmack.com.

ROMCESCU Mircea; b. 5 Feb. 1957, Bucharest, Romania. Musician (violin, piano, guitar); Songwriter; Vocalist. m. Olimpia Panciu Romcescu, 20 Nov. 1986. *Musical Education:* Special School of Music 'George Enesco', 1964–76; Academy of Music 'Ciprian Porumbesco', 1976–80. *Career:* Concerts, tours, television, radio, with own group Academica; Big Band arranging, directing; Film music; Studio musician, producer; Owner, 16 track digital studio; Violin soloist, Academy's Symphony Orchestra, 1980. *Recordings:* Albums: Academica, 1980; Music Is My Life, 1981; Olimpia, 1983; Words Against Words, 1989; Free, 1993. *Honours:* Composer of The Year, 1982; Billboard Song Contest, 3 times. *Memberships:* Danish Composer's Union; Romanian Composer's Union. *Leisure interest:* Sound designing. *Current Management:* Claes Cornelius, Mega Records. *Address:* Hyttemestervej 16, Fensmark, 4700 Naestved, Denmark.

ROMER Hanne; b. 29 July 1949, Copenhagen, Denmark. Composer; Conductor; Musician (guitar, saxophone). 2 d. *Musical Education:* Composing, arranging, conducting, Dick Grove School of Music, Los Angeles, 1983. *Career:* Founder, singer, guitarist, all-woman rock group, Hos Anna, 1975–81; Hexethyl Big Band, 1978–81; Duo with pianist Marietta Wandell; Conductor, several choirs and big bands; Leader, Nordic All-Women Big Band, 1994–; Tours throughout Denmark and Finland. *Compositions:* Piano feature, for Danish Radio Light Music Orchestra, 1985; Saxophone Concert, 1987; Several Symphonic poems; Music for string orchestras, choirs, big bands and jazz ensembles. *Recordings:* 4 albums with Hos Anna; with Marietta Wandall: Akijava, 1990; Ametyst, 1994; with the Nordic All-Women Big Band: Somewhere In Time, 1994; with the Hanne Romer Quartet: Come Rain Or Come Shine, 1994. *Address:* Amanda Music, Kirkepladsen 8 B, 6200 Aabenraa, Denmark.

ROMMEL Bernd; b. 10 June 1967, Waiblingen, Germany. Musician (drums). m. Monika, 1 d. *Musical Education:* Music High School (MHS, Graz, Austria) with jazz diploma. *Career:* Several R & B projects throughout Germany including: White Bread; Paddy Corn Band; Member, Lizl, 1990; Member, The Solutions, 1991; Member, Blues Pumpm, 1992. *Recordings:* with Lizl: Talk About Jobsharing; All Blues Pumpm productions, (1993-) including: Single: Men From Milwaukee, 1993; Album: Living Loving Riding, 1994. *Honours:* Winner, Bigband Contest Festival with High School Big Band, Graz, Austria. *Memberships:* AKM; Austromecha; LSG. *Leisure interests:* Eating; Sleeping; Snare drums. *Current Management:* Peter Steinbach, RGG Music, Favoritenstr 53/2/6/18, 1100 Vienna, Austria.

ROMO Olle; b. 3 July 1958, Stockholm, Sweden. Programmer; Engineer; Musician (drums). m. Mary Beth Romo, 11 Oct. 1991, 1 d. *Musical Education:* Stockholm Music Conservatory. *Career:* Two Eurythmics world tours as drummer; Recording career as drummer, programmer, engineer. *Recordings:* Contributions (as drummer/programmer): Feargal Sharkey, 1985; Eurythmics, Savage, 1987; Shakespear's Sister, Sacred Heart, 1989; Eurythmics, We Too Are One, 1989; Neville Brothers, Brother's Keeper, 1990; Pulp, Different Class, 1996; Alisha's Attic, Alisha Rules the World, 1996; Shania Twain, Come On Over, 1997; Bryan Adams, MTV Unplugged, 1997; Pulp, This is Hardcore, 1998; Celine Dion, These Are Special Times, 1998; Grammy Nominees, 1999. *Membership:* Musicians' Union. *Current Management:* Tony Quinn, 7 Hz Productions.

RONCHETTI Francesco; b. 18 Feb. 1962, Florence, Italy. Vocalist; Composer; Performer. m. Lyall Forsyth Harris, 1 Oct. 1998. *Education:* University, Master degree. *Musical Education:* DMus, DAMS, University of Bologna, Italy. *Career:* Member of vocal trio, Trinovox; Appearances on German television and radio, 1994; Concerts in Germany, Switzerland, Austria (Berlin, Lübeck, Stuttgart, Basel, Vienna, Innsbruck), Finland, Italy, 1994–97; Soundtrack for radio play, Bavarian State Radio, 1995; Voice specialist, teacher; Speaker at many international conferences in the field; Collaborations with established American and Italian singers, composers, musical producers; Frequent broadcast of music by Trinovox on Italian National Radio; Founded acoustic improvisational duo, The Dedications, 1999; Several North Californian tours; Founded artistic company, Ars Una. *Recordings:* Albums: with Trinovox: Incanto, 1994; Voices, (Trinovox, Sarband, The Bulgarian Voices), 1994; Earborn, Trinovox and Various Artists, 1994; Mediterranea, 1997. *Publications:* Articles: Pop-Rock Singing, in Suonare Uno Strumento, 1989; Tell Me How He Sings..., in Imparerock, 1994; The Sound of Colors, book and CD of poetry, paintings and original music. *Honours:* with Trinovox: Premio Quartetto Cetra, Italian National Award for Vocal Artists, 1994. *Memberships:* SIAE; GEMA; SIEM; Contemporary A Cappella Society of America. *Leisure interests:* Trekking; Swimming; Rowing; Reading;

Writing. *Current Management:* Ulrich Balss, Jaro Records, Bismarckstr 43, 28203 Bremen 1, Germany.

RÖNNBLOM Anders F; b. 9 May 1946, Stockholm, Sweden. Singer; Songwriter; Musician (guitar); Designer. *Education:* Graduate from College, 1966; Art and Design School, 1972. *Musical Education:* Self-taught. *Career:* First recording in 1959; Played with numerous bands in the 1960's with recordings, 1963–66; Debut album under own name in 1971; Currently 20 albums released. *Recordings include:* Jag Kysste Henne Våldsamt; Europa Brinner; Det Är Inte Snön Som Faller. *Publication:* Publishing own magazine, Mac Art and Design. *Current Management:* Studio Matchbox. *Address:* c/o Studio Matchbox, Roslagsgatan 11, 11355 Stockholm, Sweden.

RONSTADT Linda; b. 15 July 1946, Tucson, Arizona, USA. Singer. *Education:* Arizona State University. *Career:* Sang with sisters in the Three Ronstadts; Founder member, the Stone Poneys; Solo career, 1968–; Performed in operas: The Pirates of Penzance; La Boheme. *Recordings:* Hit singles: You're No Good (No. 1, USA); I Can't Help It; Somewhere Out There, duet with James Ingram (film theme to An American Tail), 1987; Don't Know Much, duet with Aaron Neville (No. 2, US), 1989; Albums: Hand Sown, Home Grown, 1969; Silk Purse, 1970; Linda Ronstadt, 1971; Don't Cry Now, 1973; Heart Like A Wheel, 1974; Prisoner In Disguise, 1975; Hasten Down The Wind, 1976; Simple Dreams, 1977; Living In The USA, 1978; Mad Love, 1980; Pirates of Penzance, 1981; Get Closer, 1982; What's New, 1983; Lush Life, 1984; For Sentimental Reasons, 1986; Trio (with Emmylou Harris and Dolly Parton), 1987; Canciones De Mi Padre, 1987; Cry Like A Rainstorm, Howl Like The Wind, 1989; Winter Light, 1994; Feels Like Home, 1995; Dedicated to the One I Love, 1996; We Ran, 1998; Compilations include: 5 Stone Poney tracks on Different Drum, 1974. *Honours:* Grammy Award, Best Female Country Vocal, I Can't Help It. *Current Management:* Peter Asher Management, 644 N Doheny Dr., Los Angeles, CA 90069, USA.

ROSE David Richard; b. Chatham, Ontario, Canada. Promoter; Musician (drums). 3 d. *Education:* 3 years study in Electronics. *Career:* Agent for 3 years; Promoter for 4 years; Owner of promotion company, Rose Concert Productions Inc, producing many concerts including Blue Rodeo, Jefferson Starship, Procol Harum, 54–40; Rusty; King, Cobb Steelie; Change of Heart; Big Sugar; Nazareth. *Memberships:* CCMA; CARAS; CAE; SOCAN. *Leisure interests:* Live racing; Travel. *Address:* Rose Concert Productions Inc, Box 23053, London, ON N6A 5N9, Canada.

ROSE Dennis Peter; b. 9 Feb. 1947, Brooklyn, New York, USA. Musician (guitar, bass, harmonica); Recording Engineer; Prod. *Musical Education:* Self-taught. *Career:* Session musician for Phil Spector, 1962, on: Bob B Sox and The Blue Jeans; Zip A Dee Do Dah; Albums with: Surf Band: The Centurions; Del-fi: Surfers Pajama Party; Shepard Records: Surf War; Other Surf compilation records; Radio KFWB Surf Battle at Deaville Castle Club, Santa Monica; No. 4, West Coast Battle of the bands, Pismo Beach, California; Second annual Teen-Age Fair, Hollywood Paladium; Backed up: Sonny and Cher; Jimmy Reed; John Lee Hooker; at the Pavilion, Huntington Beach and Marina Palace, Seal Beach; Solo Blues Album Project; Cowabunga! The Surf Box; Produced, recorded many R & B, Rock, Gospel, Jazz acts at own studio: Golden Goose Recording; Blues Album Project, studio in Costa Mesa, California. *Honours:* Platinum record: Bullwinkle P11, used for Academy Award winning: Pulp Fiction. *Membership:* ASCAP. *Leisure interests:* Oil painting; Reading; Guitar. *Address:* Golden Goose Productions, 2074 Pomona Ave, Costa Mesa, CA 92627, USA.

ROSE Michael 'Bammie'; b. 28 Sept. 1942, Jamaica. Musician (flute, tenor, alto, soprano saxophones). m. Cynthia, 1 s., 2 d. *Musical Education:* Self-taught. *Career:* Cymande, 1973; Paul Simon, 1987; Budely, 1989; Five Guys, 1993; Aswad Jazz Warriors; Jazz Jamaica; Soul II Soul. *Recordings:* Aswad; Soul II Soul; Jazz Jamaica. *Address:* 26 Blincoe Close, London SW19 5PP, England.

ROSE W Axl, (William Bailey); b. 6 Feb. 1962, Lafayette, Indiana, USA. Singer. m. Erin Everly, 28 April 1990 (annulled 1991). *Career:* Member, US heavy rock group Guns 'N' Roses, 1985–; Regular international tours include: Support to Iron Maiden, US, 1987, 1988; Mötley Crüe, US, 1987; The Cult, US, 1987; British tour, 1988; Support to Aerosmith, US, 1988; Get In The Ring tour, with Skid Row, 1991; World tour, 1992; Major concerts include: Monsters of Rock, Castle Donington, 1988; Farm Aid IV, 1990; Rock In Rio, Brazil, 1991; A Concert For Life (Freddie Mercury Tribute), Wembley, 1992; National Bowl, Milton Keynes, 1993. *Recordings:* Albums: Appetite For Destruction, 1987; G 'N' R Lies (mini-album), 1988; Use Your Illusion I and II (No. 1 and 2, US and UK), 1991; The Spaghetti Incident, 1993; Hit singles: Welcome To The Jungle, 1987; Sweet Child O'Mine (No. 1, USA), 1988; Night Train, 1989; Paradise City, 1989; Patience, 1989; Knockin' On Heaven's Door, used in film soundtrack Days of Thunder, 1990; You Could Be Mine, used in film soundtrack Terminator 2, 1991; Don't Cry, 1991; Live and Let Die, 1991; November

Rain, 1992; Yesterdays, 1992; Ain't It Fun, 1993; Live Era, 1999. *Honours include:* American Music Awards: Favourite Heavy Metal Single, 1989; Favourite Heavy Metal Artists and Album, 1989; Favourite Heavy Metal Artists, 1992; Several MTV Awards; World Music Award, Best Selling Hard Rock Artists of The Year, 1993; Rolling Stone and Billboard magazine awards. *Current Management:* Big FD Management, 510 S Coast Hwy, Laguna Beach, CA 92651–2406, USA.

ROSENTHAL David Michael; b. 1 Jan. 1961, New York, USA. Musician (keyboards); Prod.; Orchestrator; Composer; Synthesizer Programmer. m. Michelle Christo, 11 Sept. 1999. *Musical Education:* BA in Professional Music, Berklee College of Music, Boston, 1981. *Career:* World Tours: Rainbow: Straight Between The Eyes, 1982–83; Bent Out of Shape, 1983–84; Little Steven, Voice of America; Robert Palmer, Heavy Nova; Cyndi Lauper: Japan Tour, 1991; True Colors, 1986–87; Enrique Iglesias, Vivir, 1997; Billy Joel and Elton John, Face To Face, 1994–95, 1998; Billy Joel: River of Dreams, 1993–95; Greatest Hits World Tour, 1998–99; Two Thousand Years Tour, 1999–2000; Numerous TV and video appearances. *Compositions:* Producer and songwriter for Red Dawn, Never Say Surrender; Orchestrator for Yngwie Malmsteen's Millenium Concerto Suite. *Recordings:* Albums: Billy Joel: The Complete Hits Collection, 1997; Greatest Hits Vol. III, 1997; A Voyage On The River of Dreams, 1994; Yngwie Malmsteen: Millenium Concerto Suite, 1998; Inspiration, 1997; Niji-Densetsu, Legends of Rainbow, 1998; Departure: Open Your Mind, 1999; Departure, 1998; Good Rats, Tasty Seconds, 1996; Dream Theater, A Change of Seasons, 1995; Red Dawn, Never Say Surrender, 1993; Deborah Blando, A Different Story, 1991; Steve Vai, Passion and Warfare, 1990; Whitesnake, Slip of The Tongue, 1989; Nicole McCloud: Jam Packed, 1989; Love Town, 1998; Donna Allen, Heaven Goodwin, 1988; Stacy Lattisaw: Very Best of Stacy Lattisaw, 1998; Personal Attention, 1987; Rainbow: The Very Best of Rainbow, 1997; Finyl Vinyl, 1986; Bent Out of Shape, 1983; Straight Between The Eyes, 1982; Roger Glover, Mask, 1984; Hit Singles: Billy Joel, Hey Girl; Will To Power, Baby I Love Your Way/Freebird Medley; Stacy Lattisaw, Let Me Take You Down; Donna Allen, Joy and Pain; Rainbow: Stone Cold; Street of Dreams; Can't Let You Go. *Publications:* Multi-Keyboard Master Class with David Rosenthal; Macintosh, MIDI and Music: The Open Door; Columnist for Keyboard Magazine and Electronic Musician. *Honours:* Grammy Nominations, 1990, 1993; Keyboard Magazine Reader's Poll Winner, 1993; Berklee College of Music, Distinguished Alumnus Award, 1994. *Memberships:* BMI; American Federation of Musicians. *Leisure interests:* Computers and Technology. *Current Management:* Nocturnal Productions Inc.

ROSENTHAL Phil; b. 30 Sept. 1948, New Haven, Connecticut, USA. m. Elizabeth Sommers, 4 Sept. 1977, 1 s., 1 d. *Education:* BA, English Literature, University of Chicago, 1970. *Musical Education:* Self-taught. *Career:* Lead singer, guitarist, bluegrass band The Seldom Scene, including concerts: The White House; The Kennedy Centre; Philadelphia Folk Festival; Prairie Home Companion radio; Many television, radio appearances, 1977–86; Singer, guitarist, banjo player, The Sommers Rosenthal Family Band, 1993–; Founder, President, American Melody Records, 1986-. *Recordings:* 7 albums, The Seldom Scene, 1977–86; Producer, engineer, 17 albums, 1985–; Solo recordings: Indian Summer, 1978; A Matter of Time, 1981; Turkey In The Straw, 1985; The Paw Paw Patch, 1987; Chickens In The Garden, 1991; Comin' Round The Mountain, 1994; The Green Grass All Around, 1995; Animal Songs, 1996; This Land Is Your Land, 1999. *Honours:* Official Connecticut State Troubadour, 1994; 4 Parents' Choice Awards; 3 American Library Asscn Awards for solo children's music recordings, 1985-. *Membership:* International Bluegrass Music Asscn. *Current Management:* American Melody. *Address:* PO Box 270, Guildford, CT 06437, USA.

ROSKO Emperor, (Mike Pasternak); b. 26 Dec. 1942, Los Angeles, California, USA. DJ; Broadcaster. *Education:* 1 year college. *Career:* Radio Monte Carlo; Europe No 1; Radio Caroline; Radio Luxembourg, France and 208 UK; Radio 1 BBC; Virgin Radio; Nostalgie FM and many others. *Honours:* Best DJ (UK), Billboard; Top DJ, RandR. *Leisure interest:* Cooking. *Current Management:* Brian Jones (USA); Tim Jibson, International Marketing (UK).

ROSNELL Esko 'Raisin'; b. 23 June 1943, Pori, Finland. Musician (drums). *Career:* Drummer with Leo Kähkönen's dance band, 1964; Tour of Soviet Union with band; Played in groups led by: Otto Donner; Pekka Pöyry; Eero Koivistoinen; Played first Montreux Jazz Festival with Esa Pethmen's Quintet, 1967; Appearances with Heikki Sarmanto in: Scandinavia; Yugoslavia; Poland; Czechoslovakia; USA; 2 visits to Cuba in Government's cultural exchange programme; 2 visits to England with UMO (New Music Orchestra); Member, UMO, 1975–; Work in radio, television, theatre, recording studios. *Recordings include:* To A Finland Station, Dizzy Gillespie; Other recordings with UMO and own quartet. *Honour:* Best drum solo, Montreux Jazz Festival, 1967. *Address:* Gyldenintie 14 B, 00200 Helsinki, Finland.

ROSS Andrew David; b. 24 Feb. 1960, Bromley, Kent, England. Prod.; Songwriter; Musician (guitar). m. Dina Burnstock, 18 Sept. 1994. *Education:* Art School. *Musical Education:* From father, Ronnie Ross (jazz musician). *Career:* Formed band Immaculate Fools; Television appearances and tours of UK, Europe, USA; Tours and television appearances with: Howard Jones; Tom Robinson; Basia; Other television broadcasts with: Nik Kershaw; Robert Palmer. *Recordings:* with Immaculate Fools: Immaculate Fools; Tragic Comedy; Dumb Poet; Another Man's World; The Toy Shop; with Miguel Bosé: The Sign of Cain; with Howard Jones: Igy; Working In The Back Room; with Tori Amos: Crucify. *Memberships:* Musicians' Union; PRS; MCPS. *Leisure interest:* Flying (anything without an engine). *Address:* 4 Wellfield Ave, London N10 2EA, England.

ROSS Brian; b. 13 Feb. 1943, Chicago, Illinois, USA. Record Prod.; Financier; Musician (keyboards). 2 s. *Education:* UCLA (USC Law School). *Musical Education:* 25 years classical training. *Career:* Chairman, CEO, Starborn Records and International Music Commission; Placing talent in over 50 countries world-wide for 30 years; Licensing of masters and music publishing rights to labels and music firms, US and other countries; Produced records for: CBS/Sony; Phonogram; Warner Bros; RCA/BMG; AandM and MCA Record labels. *Recordings:* Producer, publisher, Music Machine, Talk Talk, 1966; Released childrens' version of We Are The World, written by Michael Jackson, Lionel Richie; Publisher, I'm On Fire, Barry White; Licensed La Bamba, Ritchie Valens. *Honours:* Gold record, Barry White, The Message Is Love; Grammy Nomination, We Are The World, USA For Africa. *Memberships:* National Academy Recording Arts and Sciences; AFTRA; Musicians' Union; Japan America Society; Asian Business League. *Leisure interests:* Tennis; Archery (world class archer, Mens Compound Freestyle). *Address:* 3884 Franklin Ave, Los Angeles, CA 90027–4661, USA.

ROSS Diana; b. 26 March 1944, Detroit, Michigan, USA. Singer; Entertainer; Actress; Fashion Designer. m. (1) Robert Ellis Silberstein, 1971, 3 d.; (2) Arne Ness, 23 Oct. 1985, 1 s. *Career:* Backing singer, the Temptations, Marvin Gaye, Mary Wells; Lead singer, Diana Ross and The Supremes; Solo artiste, 1969–; Appearances include: Opening ceremonies, Football World Cup, USA, 1994; Rugby World Cup, South Africa, 1995; Film appearances: Lady Sings The Blues, 1972; Mahogany, 1975; The Wiz, 1978; Television specials: An Evening With Diana Ross, 1977; Diana, 1980; Christmas In Vienna, 1992; Business ventures: Diana Ross Enterprises Inc; Anaid Film Productions; RTM Management Corp; Chondee Inc. *Recordings:* Albums include: Diana Ross, 1970; Lady Sings The Blues, 1972; Touch Me In The Morning, 1973; The Boss, 1979; Why Do Fools Fall In Love?, 1981; Eaten Alive, 1984; Silk Electric, 1982; Chain Reaction, 1986; Ain't No Mountain High Enough, 1989; The Force Behind The Power, 1991; Motown's Greatest Hits, 1992; Live... Stolen Moments, 1993; One Woman – The Ultimate Collection, 1993; The Remixes, 1994; Take Me Higher, 1995; Very Special Christmas, 1998; Every Day is a New Day, 1999. *Publication:* Secrets of a Sparrow (autobiography), 1993. *Honours include:* Citations: Vice-President Humphrey; Mrs Martin Luther King, Rev Abernathy; Billboard award: Record World award, World's Outstanding Singer; Grammy Award, 1970; Female Entertainer of The Year, NAACP, 1970; Golden Globe, 1972; Antoinette Perry Award, 1977; Nominated Rock and Roll Hall of Fame, 1988. *Current Management:* RTC Management, PO Box 1683, New York, NY 10185, USA.

ROSS Ricky; b. 22 Dec. 1957, Dundee, Tayside, Scotland. Singer; Songwriter. *Career:* Founder member, Deacon Blue, 1985–94; Concerts include: Reading Festival, 1988; John Lennon Tribute Concert, Liverpool, 1990; The Big Day Festival, Glasgow, 1990; Glastonbury Festival, 1990; Currently solo recording artiste. *Recordings:* Albums: with Deacon Blue: Raintown, 1987; When the World Knows Your Name (No. 1, UK), 1989; Ooh Las Vegas, 1990; Fellow Hoodlums, 1991; Whatever You Say, Say Nothing, 1993; Walking Back Home, 1999; Singles include: with Deacon Blue: Dignity, 1987; When Will You Make My Telephone Ring, 1988; Chocolate Girl, 1988; Real Gone Kid, 1988; Wages Day, 1989; Fergus Sings the Blues, 1989; I'll Never Fall in Love Again, 1990; Your Town, 1992; Solo single: Radio On, 1996; Compiler: The Tree and The Fish and The Bird and The Bell (tribute by Glaswegian bands to photographer Oscar Marzaroki), 1991; Solo albums: What You Are, 1996; New Recording, 1997. *Current Management:* CEC Management. *Address:* 4 Warren Mews, London W1P 5DJ, England.

ROSSDALE Gavin; b. 30 Oct. 1967, London, England. Vocalist; Musician (Guitar). *Career:* Former Member, Future Primitive, changed name to Bush; Obtained US record deal; Much US radio play and numerous US headlining tours; British tours and festivals. *Recordings:* Singles: Little Things, 1995; Comedown, 1995; Swallowed, 1997; Greedy Fly, 1997; Cold Contagious, 1999; Albums: Sixteen Stone, 1994; Razorblade Suitcase, 1996 Deconstructed, 1997.

ROSSELL Marina; b. 17 Jan. 1954, Barcelona, Spain. Singer. *Musical Education:* Guitar, Solfege. *Career:* Professional singer, 1970–;

Appearances include: Concerts: Theatre de la Ville, Paris, 1981–87; Festival Tenco, San Remo, Italy, 1982; Moscow, 1985; Bogotá, 1988; Festival Utono Musicale, Como, Italy, 1989; Cuban International Festival, 1994; Concert For Peace, San Sebastian, 1995; International tour, Mexico, Paris, Lisbon, Netherlands, Cuba, Canary Isles, Malaga, Pamplona, Barcelona, Sitges, 1994; Bolivian Pro-Native Concert, 1995; Television includes: TVE (Spanish National TV), 1981; Concert, TVE, 1992; Film: El Vicari d'Olot, 1981; Collaborations with composers including: Georges Moustaki; Tomatito; Antoni Ros Marbà; Manzanita; Maria del Mar Bonet; Joan Bibloni; Pau Riba. *Recordings include:* Llegendes de Catalunya, 1975; Si Volieu Escolatar, 1977; Penyora, Premio Fotogramas, Vol. 1, 1978; Festival Internacional, Vol. 1, 1979; Cos Meu Recorda, 1982; Victoria (Banda Sonora Pelicula), 1983; Maremar – Lluis Llach, 1985; Barca del Temps, Disco de Oro, 1986; Les Millors Cançons de Marina Rossell, 1990; Cinema Blau, 1990; Marina, 1993; Gracies (Recopilaciones), 1994; Cinema Blau + La Gavina, 1994. *Honours:* Silver Shot Award, 1979; Award, Best Catalan record of the Year, R-4, 1981; Best Catalan Record of The Year R-4, for Rosa De Foc (Fire Rose), 1989. *Leisure interests:* Literature; Movies. *Current Management:* Josep Sanz, JSB Management. *Address:* Calle Llauder, 161–3er. 2a., 08302 Mataró, Barcelona, Spain.

ROSSELSON Leon; b. 22 June 1934, London, England. Songwriter; Singer; Musician (guitar). m. Rina Picciotto, 27 Sept. 1959, 2 d. *Education:* BA Hon Cantab (English Literature). *Musical Education:* Grade VI Piano. *Career:* Member, Galliards Folk Group, 1959–61; BBC radio Easy Beat and Saturday Club, solo performer, 1961–; Folk clubs; Arts centres; Universities; Concert halls, including Festival Hall, Royal Albert Hall; Tours: Belgium; Netherlands; Australia; Canada; US; Songs for television programme That Was The Week That Was; Songs for stage production of They Shoot Horses Don't They?, 1973; Television includes: All You Need Is Love; The Oxford Road Show; World Turned Upside Down, singles charts, Billy Bragg, 1985; Ballad of a Spycatcher, Indie singles charts, 1987. *Recordings:* Solo albums: Songs For Sceptical Circles, 1967; A Laugh A Song and A Handgrenade, 1968; Hugga Mugga, 1971; That's Not The Way It's Got To Be, 1974; Palaces of Gold, 1975; Love Loneliness and Laundry, 1976; If I Knew Who The Enemy Was, 1979; For The Good of The Nation, 1981; Temporary Loss of Vision, 1984; Bringing The News From Nowhere, 1986; I Didn't Mean It, 1988; Rosselsongs, 1989; Wo Sind Die Elefanten?, 1991; The Happiness Counter, 1992; Intruders, 1995; Perspectives, CD, 1997; Harry's Gone Fishing, 1999. *Publications:* Bringing The News From Nowhere, 125 selected songs, 1993. *Memberships:* MCPS; PRS; Musicians' Union; Writers' Guild. *Leisure interests:* Theatre; Cinema; Walking; Tennis. *Address:* 28 Park Chase, Wembley Park, Middlesex HA9 8EH, England.

ROSSI Francis (Mike); b. 29 May 1949, Peckham, London, England. Musician (guitar); Vocalist. *Career:* Founder member, UK rock group Status Quo, 1967–; Extensive tours world-wide; Concerts, festivals include: British Great Western Festival; Reading Festival, 1972, 1978, 1987; NEC Birmingham, before Prince and Princess of Wales, (televised by BBC); Milton Keynes Bowl, 1984; Live Aid, Wembley Stadium, 1985; Support to Queen, Wembley Stadium, 1986; Played 4 venues in 12 hours, entered in Guinness Book of Records, 1991. *Recordings:* Albums: Picturesque Matchstickable Messages, 1968; Spare Parts, 1969; Ma Kelly's Greasy Spoon, 1970; Dog of Two Heads, 1971; Piledriver, 1973; Hello, 1973; Quo, 1974; On The Level, 1975; Blue For You, 1976; Status Quo Live!, 1977; Rockin' All Over The World, 1977; If You Can't Stand The Heat, 1978; Whatever You Want, 1979; Just Supposin', 1980; Never Too Late, 1981; 1+9+8+2, 1982; To Be Or Not To Be, 1983; Back To Back, 1983; In The Army Now, 1986; Ain't Complaining, 1988; Rock 'Til You Drop, 1991; Live Alive Quo, 1992; Don't Stop, 1996; Whatever You Want, 1997; Under The Influence, 1999; Numerous compilations; Hit singles include: Pictures of Matchstick Men, 1968; Ice In The Sun, 1969; Paper Plane, 1973; Caroline, 1973; Break The Rules, 1974; Down Down, 1975; Roll Over Lay Down, 1975; Rain, 1976; Mystery Song, 1976; Wild Side of Life, 1977; Rockin' All Over The World, 1977; Again and Again, 1978; Whatever You Want, 1979; Living On An Island, 1979; What You're Proposing, 1980; Lies, 1981; Rock 'n' Roll, 1981; Something 'Bout You Baby I Like, 1981; Dear John, 1982; Ol' Rag Blues, 1983; A Mess of The Blues, 1983; Marguerita Time, 1984; Rollin' Home, 1986; In The Army Now, 1986; Burning Bridges, 1989; Anniversary Waltz, 1990; Contributor, Do They Know It's Christmas?, Band Aid, 1984. *Honours include:* Silver Clef Award, Nordoff-Robbins Music Therapy Centre, 1981; BRIT Award, Outstanding Contribution To The British Music Industry, 1991; World Music Award, Outstanding Contribution To Music, 1991. *Current Management:* The Handle Group of Companies, Pinewood Studios, Pinewood Rd, Iver Heath, Buckinghamshire SL0 0NH, England.

ROSSINGTON Gary; b. 4 Dec. 1951, Jacksonville, Florida, USA. Musician (guitar); Songwriter. *Career:* Musician, US rock group, Lynyrd Skynyrd, 1970–77, 1987–; Rossington-Collins Band (with Allen Collins) later The Rossington Band, 1979–88; US tour, support to The Who, 1976; Knebworth Festival, 1976; Serious injuries in plane crash, 1977; Volunteer Jam Reunion, 1987; Farm Aid V, 1991; 20th Anniversary, Lynyrd Skynyrd and Friends LYVE (pronounced Live), cable TV pay-per-view performance, 1993; Inaugural Freebird Festival, 1993. *Recordings:* Albums with Lynyrd Skynyrd: Pronounced Leh-nerd Skin-Nerd, 1973; Second Helping, 1974; Nuthin' Fancy, 1975; Gimme Back My Bullets, 1976; One More For The Road, 1976; Street Survivors, 1977; Skynyrd's First and Last, 1978; Gold and Platinum, 1980; Best of The Rest, 1985; Legend, 1987; Southern By The Grace of God/Lynyrd Skynyrd Tribute Tour, 1988; Lynyrd Skynyrd, 1991, 1991; The Last Rebel, 1993; Endangered Species, 1994; Freebird, 1996; Lyve, 1998; Edge of Forever, 1999; with the Rossington-Collins Band; Anytime Anyplace Anywhere, 1980; This Is The Way, 1981; Love Your Man, 1988; Singles include: Sweet Home Alabama, 1974; Free Bird, 1975; What's Your Name, 1978. *Address:* c/o Alliance Artists Ltd, 6025 The Corners Parkway, Suite 202, Norcross, GA 30092, USA.

ROTH David Lee; b. 10 Oct. 1955, Bloomington, Indiana, USA. Rock Vocalist. *Career:* Singer, Red Ball Jets; Founder member, US rock group Van Halen, 1975–85; Support tours with UFO; Santana; Black Sabbath; Regular headlining US and world-wide tours; Major concerts include: California Music Festival, 1979; US Festival, 1982, 1983; Monsters of Rock Festival, Castle Donington, 1984; Solo artiste, 1985–; US tour, 1986; British tour, 1988; World tour, 1991. *Recordings:* Albums: with Van Halen: Van Halen, 1978; Women and Children First, 1980; Fair Warning, 1981; Diver Down, 1982; 1984, 1983; Solo albums: Eat 'Em and Smile, 1986; Skyscraper, 1988; A Little Ain't Enough, 1991; Your Filthy Little Mouth, 1994; DLR Band, 1998; Singles with Van Halen include: You Really Got Me, 1978; Running With The Devil, 1978; Dance The Night Away, 1979; And The Cradle Will Rock, 1980; (Oh) Pretty Woman, 1982; Dancing In The Street, 1982; Jump (No. 1, USA), 1984; Panama, 1984; I'll Wait, 1984; Hot For Teacher, 1984; Solo singles: California Girls, 1985; Just A Gigolo/I Ain't Got Nobody, 1985; Yankee Rose, 1986; Goin' Crazy, 1986; Just Like Paradise, 1988; Stand Up, 1988; A Lil' Ain't Enough, 1991; Sensible Shoes, 1991; Slam Dunk, 1998. *Honours:* Numerous Platinum discs; MTV Music Video Award, 1984. *Leisure interest:* Mountaineering. *Current Management:* Diamond Dave Enterprises. *Address:* c/o Eddie Anderson, 11288 Ventura Blvd, Suite 430, Studio City, CA 91606, USA.

ROTHERAY Dave; b. 9 Feb. 1963, Hull, England. Musician (Guitar). *Career:* Member, The Beautiful South; Numerous TV appearances and live gigs; Numerous appearances at festivals. *Recordings:* Singles: Song For Whoever, 1989; One Last Love Song, 1992; Prettiest Eyes, 1994; Everybody's Talkin', 1994; Rotterdam (Or Anywhere); Don't Marry Her; Liar's Bar, 1997; Perfect 10, 1998; Dumb, 1999; Albums: Welcome To The Beautiful South, 1989; Choke, 1990; Miaow, 1994; Carry On Up The Charts: The Best of The Beautiful South, 1995; Blue Is The Colour, 1996; Quench, 1998.

ROTHERY Steve; b. 25 Nov. 1959, Brampton, South Yorkshire, England. Musician (guitar). *Career:* Member, UK progressive rock band, Marillion, 1980–; Tours, UK; Europe; North America; Major concerts include: Theakston Festival, 1982; Reading Festival, 1982, 1983; Nostell Priory Festival, 1982, 1984; Glastonbury Festival, 1984; Support to Rush, Radio City Music Hall, New York, 1983; Monsters of Rock Festival, Castle Donington, 1985; Welcome To The Garden Party, Milton Keynes Bowl, 1986. *Recordings:* Albums: Script For A Jester's Tear, 1983; Fugazi, 1984; Real To Reel, 1984; Misplaced Childhood, 1985; Brief Encounter, 1986; Clutching At Straws, 1987; B-Sides Themselves, 1988; The Thieving Magpie, 1988; Season's End, 1989; Holidays In Eden, 1991; A Singles Collection 1982–92, 1992; Brave, 1994; Afraid of Sunlight, 1995; Blueprint of the World, 1995; Made Again, 1996; This Strange Engine, 1997; Radiation, 1998; Clutching at Straws, 1999; Singles include: Market Square Heroes, 1982; He Knows You Know, 1983; Garden Party, 1983; Punch and Judy, 1984; Assassing, 1984; Kayleigh (No. 2, UK), 1985; Lavender, 1985; Heart of Lothian, 1985; Incommunicado, 1987; Sugar Mice, 1987; Warm Wet Circles, 1987; Freaks, 1988; Hooks In You, 1989; Uninvited Guest, 1989; Easter, 1990; Cover My Eyes (Pain and Heaven), 1991; No One Can, 1991; Dry Land, 1991; Sympathy, 1992. *Current Management:* Hit and Run Music Ltd. *Address:* 30 Ives St, London SW3 2ND, England.

ROUCAN Jean-Yves; b. 2 June 1962, Neuilly Sur Seine, France. Musician (drums). 1 s., 1 d. *Musical Education:* CIM, Paris; Berklee School of Music, Boston, USA. *Career:* Jazz drummer, Triode, 1986–87; Formed own trio with M Bismut and B Paillard, 1987–; Concerts include: Nîmes Festival, 1988; Béziers Festival, 1989; Radio France Festival, 1991; Radio: France Inter, France Musique, other FM stations, 1992; Television: 4 regional shows, France 3, 1991–92; Worked with: R Beirach; D Liebman's Quest; P Motian; D Holland; B Frisell; J Lovano; D Humair; Currently, freelance jazz drummer, Plays with Passage (big band); Plays with Interplay Collectif, Switzerland. *Recordings include:* Triode Jazz Quartet; Socco, Trio Paillard-Bismut-Roucan, 1992; With Interplay Collectif: S Duner Project. *Honour:* First Prize, Concours International de Vienne, France. *Leisure interest:* Gastronomy; Wine. *Address:* 56 rue Saint Sebastien, 75011 Paris, France.

ROUGVIE Jeff James; b. 4 March 1963, Quincy, Massachusetts, USA. Dir of A & R and Special Projects. *Education:* Art School; Hartford Art School, 1984. *Career:* Signings: Sugar; Golden Smog; Alejandro Escovedo; Martin Zellar; Morphine; Resposible for catalogue development: Badfinger; Big Star; David Bowie; Elvis Costello. *Recordings:* As Producer: Ned Kelly, 1970; Jimmy Buffett, Rancho Deluxe, 1975; Born to Choose, 1993; Chitty Chitty Bang Bang, 1997; Across 10th Street, 1997. *Leisure interests:* Collecting antique toys, comic books. *Address:* Rykodisc A & R, Shetland Park, 27 Congress St, Salem, MA 01970, USA.

ROUNDS James; b. 16 Oct. 1951, Tokyo, Japan. Musician (Guitar); Songwriter. *Education:* BA, English, Dickinson College, Carlisle, PA, USA, 1973. *Musical Education:* Self-taught. *Career:* Played on stage with John Lee Hooker, Charlie Gracie and others. *Compositions:* Go Man Go, Charlie Gracie, with the Jordanaires, 1988; Where Everybody Stays, in the film, Liars Club, 1991. *Recordings:* The Metropolitans, LP, 1996. *Honours:* Help Heal LA Award, 1992; Music City (Nashville) Award for R & B Category, 1988. *Membership:* ASCAP Writer and Publisher. *Leisure interests:* Tennis; Surfing. *Current Management:* Bristol Music. *Address:* 515 Rosedale Ave, Nashville, TN 37211, USA.

ROUNDS Michelle; Singer; Songwriter. *Career:* Sydney, Australia, 1989–93; Suva, Fiji, 1993–96; Auckland Area, Aotearoa, 1996–99. *Recordings:* Never Been In Love Before, 1992; Draw Blood, 1994; Contrasts, 1996; Culture Cross, 1998; Era Bini Tu, 1998. *Honours:* Vakalutuivoce Award for Best Female Artist and Best Album; Award from Mai Time. *Current Management:* Polyphony Entertainment, Australia. *Address:* PO Box 172, Hunters Hill, 2110 Sydney, Australia.

ROUSSIN Didier Jean; b. 1 Nov. 1949, St Mandé, France. Musician (classical, electric and acoustic guitars, banjo, dobro, percussion); Writer; Artistic Advisor; Artistic Dir; Guitar Teacher. *Musical Education:* Conservatoire d'Ivry Sur Seine; Brevet d'Enseignement, Ecole Normale de Musique de Paris. *Career:* Played, recorded with singers: Renaud; Monique Morelli; Gérard Pierron; Backed American jazz accordionists: Art Van Damme, Frank Marocco; Guitarist for Jo Privat, last 13 years; Duo, with jazz accordionist Daniel Colin; Member, several groups including: Denécheau Jâse Musette; Paris-Musette; Les Primitifs du Futur; Robert Santiago's Latino-Américain; Played or recorded with jazzmen and bluesmen: Georges Arvanitas; Marcel Azzola; Steve Lacy; Bernard Lubat; Jean-Claude Fohrenbach; Pierre Michelot; Jean-Jacques Milteau; Bobby Rangell; Benny Waters; Dominique Pifarely; Co-author, French television documentary Le Blues du Musette (La Sept). *Recordings:* Juju Doudou, Dominique Cravic; Night and Day Rue de Lappe, with Jo Privat; Jazz Experience; Quel Temps Fait-il à Paris, with Daniel Colin; Denécheau Jâse Musette à Paris, with Daniel Denécheau, Robert Santiago; with Paris Musette: Vent d'Automne Vol. 3. *Publications:* CD booklets for Musette re-releases; Articles about Musette and jazz accordion in several magazines: Jazz Swing Journal; Modal; Trad Mag; Journal de la Cité de la Musique; Accordéon Magazine; Guitare et Claviers. Co-author, book L'Argot des Musiciens. *Honours:* Grand Prix du Disque de l'Académie Charles Cros, for Paris Musette Vol. I (musician, artistic advisor); Grand Prix de la Littérature Musicale de l'Académie Charles Cros, for Histoires de l'Accordéon, with François Billard. *Current Management:* Madeleine Juteau, 20, Route de Sorel, 28500 Montreux, France.

ROWBOTTOM Simon; b. Wallasey, England. Singer. *Career:* Vocalist, Boo Radleys, 1989-. *Recordings:* Albums: Ichabod and I, 1989; Everything's Alright Forever, 1992; Giant Steps, 1993; Learning To Walk, 1994; Wake Up, 1995; C'mon Kids, 1996; Solo albums under name of Eggman: First Fruits; Kingsize, 1998. *Honours:* Select and NME magazines, Album of the Year, 1993. *Current Management:* CEC Management, 4 Warren Mews, London W1P 5DJ, England.

ROWLAND Broz (Henry Cottrell); b. 30 July 1949, Dallas, Texas, USA. Prod.; Songwriter; Musician (guitar, bass, keyboards, drums). *Education:* BA, Communication in the Audio Visual Arts, University of Colorado, 1978. *Musical Education:* Self-taught. *Career:* Member, Blue Pearl band, 1978; Formed Alpha Wave, 1980; Member, Modern Kids, 1982; Producer, co-songwriter, Bodyhouse album with Allen Ginsberg, 1986; Formed The Pilots, 1990; Joined Flying Perfect, 1994. *Recordings:* You Know It's Coming (single and album), Alpha Wave, 1980; Album with Modern Kids, 1982; Co-mixer, Lonnie Hill single, You Got Me Runnin', 1986; Writer, producer, Dreams, Visions and Nightmares, The Pilots, 1992; Producer, co-writer, debut album by Flying Perfect, 1995; Producer, debut solo album, John Guillot (former partner in The Pilots), 1995; with Rowland Brothers, No Sleep for the Dreamers, 1998. *Honours:* Quarter Finalist, American Song Festival, 1980; KBCO Eighth Boulder Music Invitational, 1984; Houston International Film Festival, 1986. *Membership:* ASCAP. *Leisure interests:* Swimming; Snorkeling; Skiing; Trekking; Travel. *Address:* High Kite Productions, 1245 Elizabeth St, Denver, CO 80206, USA.

ROWLAND Kelly (Kelendria); b. 11 Feb. 1981, Atlanta, Georgia, USA. Vocalist. *Career:* Joined GirlsTyme vocal group, 1989; Group renamed

Something Fresh then The Dolls before settling on Destiny's Child; Signed to Columbia Records, 1996; Numerous TV and live performances including tour with Christina Aguilera, 2000; Appeared at United We Stand concert, USA, 2001; Acting roles planned including guest appearance on TV sitcom Taina. *Recordings:* Albums: Destiny's Child, 1998; The Writing's On The Wall, 1999; Survivor, 8 Days of Christmas, 2001; Singles: No No No (with Wyclef Jean), 1997; With Me (with Timbaland), She's Gone (with Matthew Marsden), 1998; Get On The Bus (from Why Do Fools Fall In Love OST), Bills Bills Bills, Bug-A-Boo, 1999; Say My Name, Jumpin' Jumpin', Independent Women (from Charlie's Angels OST), 2000; Survivor, Bootylicious, Emotion, 8 Days of Christmas, 2001. *Honours:* Countless awards world-wide including: Billboard Awards: Artist of The Year; Group of The Year; Hot 100 Singles Artist of The Year; Hot 100 Group of The Year, 2000; American Music Awards, Favourite Soul/R & B Group, 2001; Grammy Awards: Best R & B Song, Say My Name; Best R & B Performance by a Duo or Group with Vocal, Say My Name, 2001; Independent Women reached the largest audience in the USA's history of monitored airplay (over 140m. radio listeners in 1 week). *Address:* c/o Mathew Knowles, Music World Entertainment, 9898 Bissonnet, Suite 625, Houston, TX 77036, USA. *Internet:* www.destinyschild.com.

ROWLAND Kevin; b. 17 Aug. 1953, Wolverhampton, West Midlands, England. Vocalist; Musician (guitar). *Career:* Member, Lacy and The Lovers; The Killjoys; Lead singer, Dexy's Midnight Runners, 1978–; Solo artiste, 1988-. *Recordings:* Albums: with Dexy's Midnight Runners: Searching For The Young Soul Rebels, 1980; Too-Rye-Ay, 1982; Geno, 1983; Don't Stand Me Down, 1985; The Very Best of Dexy's Midnight Runners, 1991; Solo album: The Wanderer, 1988; My Beauty, 1999; Singles: with Dexy's Midnight Runners: Dance Stance; Geno (No. 1, UK), 1980; There There My Dear; Show Me; Come On Eileen (No. 1, UK); Jackie Wilson Said; Let's Get This Straight From The Start; The Celtic Soul Brothers; Because of You (television theme, Brush Strokes, BBC TV), 1986; Solo: Walk Away, 1988.

ROWLANDS Tom; b. 11 Jan. 1971, England. Musician. *Education:* Manchester University. *Career:* Formed First Band, Ariel; Formed, The Dust Brothers with Ed Simons; Member, Chemical Brothers. *Compositions:* All recorded: Exit Planet Dust, album; Dig Your Own Hole, album (No 1 UK); Block Rockin Beats; Setting Sun; Leave Home. *Recordings:* Song to the Siren, 1993; 14th Century Sky (EP), 1994; My Mercury Mouth (EP), 1994; Life is Sweet, 1995; Loops of Fury (EP), 1996; Setting Sun, (No 1 UK), 1997; Block Rockin Beats (No. 1, UK), 1997; Electronic Battle Weapons, 1997; Elektrobank, 1997; Melting Pot, 1998; Action, 1999. *Honours:* Twice Nominated for Brit Awards; Nomination for Mercury Prize, 1997; Grammy Award, 1997. *Current Management:* Robert Linney. *Address:* 1 Cowcross St, London EC1M 6DR, England.

ROWLES Greg; b. 6 Sept. 1965, Fredericksburg, Virginia, USA. Entertainer; Musician (guitar, bass guitar, pedal-steel guitar). m. Brandee Ann Courtney, 31 Dec. 1992, 1 d. *Education:* Gemanna College Graduate (Business Administration). *Career:* Performances include: Ed McMahon's Star Search Male Vocalist Champion; Grand Ole Opry Live; Music City Tonight; TNN Country News; Opryland Showpark, 1992–94; Tours, shows with Sammy Kershaw, Martina McBride, 1994-. *Compositions:* Professional songwriter signed with Music For The Future, 1995-. *Honour:* Spokesperson in Tennessee for child abuse prevention. *Membership:* Nashville Union. *Leisure interests:* Golf; Fishing; Camping. *Current Management:* (Agent) Buddy-Lee Attractions. *Address:* Williams Bell and Associates, Inc, 707 18th Ave S, Nashville, TN 37203, USA.

ROWLES Stacy Amanda; b. 11 Sept. 1955, Hollywood, California, USA. Musician (horns). *Career:* Major concerts: Monterey Jazz Festival, 1973; Wichita Jazz Festival, with Clark Terry All-Star Band, 1975; All-Women's Quintet, US tour, 1985; Charlie Hayden Liberation Orchestra, 1986; Performed at Woody Herman 50th Anniversary Tribute Concert, Hollywood, 1986; Freelance musician, 1987–; Member, Maiden Voyage, all-female jazz orchestra; Performed at Nice Jazz Festival, 1989. *Recordings with:* Nels Cline; Ray Brown; Donald Bailey; Jimmy Rowles; Sweets Edison; Albums: Tell It Like It Is, 1984; Me and the Moon, 1993. *Honours:* Best Flugelhorn Soloist, Orange Coast College Jazz Festival, 1973, 1974.

ROWNTREE Dave, (David Alexander De Horne); b. 8 May 1964, Colchester, Essex, England. Musician (drums). m. 16 June 1994. *Education:* HND Computer Science, Woolwich. *Musical Education:* Lessons in bagpipes, drums. *Career:* Formed Idle Vice; Played in clubs for 2 years, France; Member, Blur; Extensive television, radio includes: Top of The Pops; Later With Jools Holland; Concerts include Alexandra Palace; Reading Festival, 1993, 1999; Glastonbury Festival, 1994, 1998; Mile End, 1995; V97, 1997; All UK arenas, 1997; T In The Park, 1999; Leeds Festival, 1999. *Recordings:* Blur: Albums: Leisure, 1991; Modern Life Is Rubbish, 1993; Parklife, 1994; The Great Escape, 1995; Blur, 1997; 13, 1999; The Best of Blur, 2000; Singles: She's So High, 1990; There's No Other Way, 1991; Bang, 1991; Popscene, 1992; For Tomorrow, 1993; Chemical World,

1993; Sunday Sunday, 1993; Girls and Boys, 1994; To The End, 1994; Parklife, 1994; End of a Century, 1994; Country House (No. 1, UK), 1995; The Universal, 1995; Stereotypes, 1996; Charmless Man, 1996; Beetlebum (No. 1, UK), 1997; Song 2, 1997; On Your Own, 1997; MOR, 1997; Tender, 1999; Coffee and TV, 1999; No Distance Left To Run, 1999; Music Is My Radar, 2000. *Honours:* Mercury Prize Nomination; 4 Platinum Albums, Parklife; 3 Platinum Albums, The Great Escape; Platinum Album, Blur; BRIT Awards: Best Single, Album, Video, Band, 1995; Q Awards, Best Album, 1994, 1995; Q Awards, 1999; Platinum Album, 13. *Current Management:* CMO Management, Unit 32, Ransomes Dock, 35–37 Parkgate Rd, London SW11 4NP, England.

ROY Stephane; b. 2 July 1959, Québec, Canada. Composer. m. Claudine Jomphe, 1 s., 1 d. *Education:* BA, 1988, MA, 1990, Doctorate, 1994, University of Montréal. *Career:* Professor, Queens University, Kingston, Canada, 1993–94; Guest Composer, son Mu 95 Concert, Paris, 1995; Guest Composer, Los Andes University, Colombia, 1995; Guest Lecturer, Conservatoire Superieur de Mons, Belgium, 1996; Professor, University of Montréal, 1993–97; Guest Composer, FIMAV, 1998. *Compositions:* Paysages Interieurs; Mimetismo; Crystal Music; Inaccessible Azur; Trois Petites Histoires Concretes. *Recordings:* Crystal Music; Mimetismo; Paysages Intérieurs; Ondes Arborescences; Resonances D'Arabesques. *Publications include:* Functional and Implicative Analysis of Ombres Blaches of Francois Bayle; La Serie Schonberg; Form and Referential Citation in a Work By Francis Dhomont. *Honours:* Hon. Mention, International Computer Music Competition Ars Electronica; First Prize, 14th Luigi Russolo International Competition; First Prize, 1993 Noroit Prize; Nominated Eighth Annual International Computer Music Asscn. *Memberships:* Canadian Music Centre; International Computer Music Assocation; Canadian Electroacoustic Community. *Leisure interests:* Cooking; Reading; Gardening. *Address:* 8627 Joseph, Brentwood, MO 63114, Missouri, USA.

ROYAL Billy Joe; b. 3 April 1942, Valdosta, Georgia, USA. Singer. *Career:* Nightclub singer, Savannah, Georgia; Recording artiste, 1962-. *Recordings:* Hits include: Down In The Boondocks; I Knew You When; Cherry Hill Park; Burned Like A Rocket; I'll Pin A Note On Your Pillow; I Miss You Already; Members Only, duet with Donna Fargo; Albums: Down In The Boondocks, 1965; Billie Joe Royal, 1965; Hush, 1967; Cherry Hill Park, 1969; Looking Ahead, 1987; The Royal Treatment, 1987; Tell It Like It Is, 1989; Out of The Shadows, 1990; The Best of Billy Joe Royal, 1995; Golden Hits, 1996; Stay Close to Home, 1998.

ROZALLA (Rozalla Sandra Miller); b. 18 March 1964, Ndola, Zambia. Singer. *Career:* Support act, Michael Jackson; Support act, Alexander O'Neal; Numerous UK/US television appearances including: Wogan; Big Breakfast; Arsenio Hall. *Recordings:* Albums: Everybody's Free; Look No Further; Feelin' Good, 1998; Singles: Everybody's Free; You Gotta Have Faith; Don't Go Lose It Baby. *Honours:* Best African Artiste; Diamond Award, Best 12 Single; Silver album, Silver single. *Membership:* Musicians' Union. *Current Management:* DMA. *Address:* c/o Concorde International Artistes, Concorde House, 101 Shepherds Bush Rd, London W6 7LP, England.

RUBEL Mark; b. 1 May 1958. Musician (Bass Guitar); Record Prod.; Engineer; Studio Owner; Recording Instructor. *Career:* Freelance and Studio Musician, 1978–; Bassist, Captain Rat and the Blind Rivets, 1980; Bassist, J B Hutto and the Hawks, 1980; Has produced and recorded numerous artists, including Hum, Poster Children, Menthol, Alison Krauss, Adrian Belew, Mojo Nixon. *Current Management:* Gary Taylor Management, Canada. *Address:* Pogo Studio, 35 Taylor St, Champaign, IL 61820, USA.

RUBIE Stephen Mark; b. 14 Oct. 1952, Marlow, Buckinghamshire, England. Musician (flute, saxophone); Jazz Club Proprietor. *Education:* University College Hospital, Dental School, London. *Musical Education:* Flutes with William Bartlett, Principal with BBC Concert Orchestra, Trinity College, London; Jazz theory, harmony, with Peter Ind. *Career:* Professional freelance, 1974–; Toured Italy, 1975; Peripatetic teacher, 1978–85; Proprietor, 606 Jazz Club, 1976–; Leader, 606 Club Big Band, 1985–90; Bandleader, Jazz/Latin sextet, Samara, 1974–; Featured flute player, Julian Joseph Big Band, BBC Prom, live broadcast, 1995; African band, Amabutho, live television in Germany, 1995; Appeared on BBC2 TV series, Jazz 606, 1998. *Memberships:* Musicians' Union; Equity. *Leisure interest:* Chess. *Address:* 10A Stadium St, London SW10 0PT, England.

RUBIN Joel; b. 17 Oct. 1955, Los Angeles, USA. Musician (Clarinet); Ethnomusicologist. *Education:* California Institute of the Arts, 1973–75; BA, State University of New York, 1978; PhD, City University, London, 1995-. *Career:* Including Film, Television and Radio Appearances; Gewandhaus Leipzig, 1993; Berlin Philharmonic, 1994; Tonhalle Zurich, 1996; Cité de la Musique Paris, 1996; Co Author, Musical and Research Consultant, A Tickle in the Heart, 1996. *Recordings:* Bessarabian Symphony, 1994; Zeydes un Eyniklekh, 1995; Beregovskis Khasene,

1997; Hungry Hearts, 1998. *Publications:* Kol Rino, The Voice of Jubilation; Mazltov: Jewish American Wedding Music for Clarinet; Klezmer-Musik. *Honours:* State University of NY, Most Outstanding Student, 1978; German Record Critics Prize, 1992, 1995; Artur Brauner Prize, 1996; Prix Europa, 1996; 18th Bavarian Film Prize, 1996. *Memberships:* Society for Ethnomusicology; International Council for Traditional Music; American Folklore Society; College Music Society; International Clarinet Society. *Current Management:* Jewish Cultural Programming and Research. *Address:* Bernburger Str 18, D 10963 Berlin, Germany.

RUBIN Rick; b. 10 March 1963, Long Beach, New York, USA. Record Prod.; Record Co Exec. *Education:* BFA, New York University, 1985. *Career:* Owner, founding president, Def Jam Recordings, 1984–88; Def American Recordings, 1988–; Director, co-producer, film Tougher Than Leather, 1987. *Recordings include:* As producer: Radio, LL Cool J, 1985; License To Ill, Beastie Boys, 1986; Raising Hell, Run DMC, 1986; It Takes A Nation, Public Enemy, 1986; Electric, The Cult, 1987; Blood Sugar Sex Magic, Red Hot Chili Peppers, 1992; Tom Petty, Wildflowers, 1994; One Hot Minute, Red Hot Chili Peppers, 1995; South Park: Chef Aid, The South Park Album, 1998; Rancid, Brad Logan, 1998; Black Crowes, Sho' Nuff, 1998; Sheryl Crow, Globe Sessions, 1998; Sweet Child O' Mine, 1999; Kula Shaker, Peasants, Pigs and Astronauts, 1999; Red Hot Chilli Peppers, Californication, 1999; Melanie C, Northern Star, 1999; Beastie Boys, Sounds of Science, 1999. *Honours:* Numerous Gold and Platinum discs as producer; Rolling Stone Award, Hot Producer of Year, 1988; Joel Weber Award, New Music Seminar, 1990. *Address:* c/o American Recordings, 3500 W Olive Ave, Suite 1550, Burbank, CA 91505, USA.

RUBINI Michel; b. 3 Dec. 1942, Los Angeles, California, USA. Musical Dir; Composer; Musician; Record Prod. *Career:* Musical director for: Johnny Mathis, 1968; Nancy Wilson, 1969–70; Producer, arranger for Sonny and Cher, 1971–73; Artist, producer, Motown Records, 1975–78; Worked with numerous artists including: Elvis Presley; John Lennon; Diana Ross; Linda Ronstadt. *Compositions:* Numerous television and film soundtracks. *Recordings:* Solo albums: Secret Dreams, 1988; Secret Dreams: Improvisations I-VII, 1995; The Hunger, original soundtrack, 1995; Theme from Joe's Death, 1995; As record producer: Stoney End, Barbra Streisand; California Dreamin', Johnny Mathis; All I Never Need Is You, Sonny and Cher; Country Class, Jerry Lee Lewis; So Fine, Loggins and Messina. *Honour:* BMI Writers Award, 1985. *Memberships:* BMI; Composers and Lyricists Guild.

RUBIO Paulina; b. 1970, Mexico. Vocalist, Actress. *Career:* Began singing career in children's dancing and singing group Timbiriche, formed by producers for the Mexican TV network Televisa, 1981; Began acting in soap operas and TV series, 1998; Left Timbiriche and recorded first solo album, 1992; Continues to combine singing and acting careers, appearing in the popular soap Pobre Niña Rica and the film Bésame en la Boca. *Recordings:* Albums: La Chica Dorada, 1992; 24 Kilates, 1993; Tiempo Es Oro, 1995; Planeta Paulina, 1996; Paulina, 2000.

RUDD Raphael; Musician; Composer; Songwriter; Arranger. *Education:* BM, MM, Manhattan School of Music. *Career:* Orchestrated Final Scene of the Score to the Who Film, Quadrophenia, 1979; Arranged Horns on Pete Townshend's Hit Single, Rough Boys, 1980; Touring Member, Renaissance and Annie Haslam Band as Keyboardist, 1982–92. *Recordings:* R Rudd: Reflections, 1983; R Rudd: Skydancer, 1991; Raphael Rudd: The Awakening, with Pete Townshend, Phil Collins and Annie Haslam, 1997; Joyfest, 1998. *Honours:* Artist of the Year, Oakside/Bloomfield Cultural Center, New Jersey, 1996. *Membership:* American Harp Society. *Leisure interests:* Movies; Classical Music. *Current Management:* Rob Findlay, Headfirst Management.

RUFFIN Bruce; b. 17 Feb. 1952, St Catherine, Jamaica. Musician (guitar, piano). 3 d. *Education:* Studied for LLB (Law), England. *Musical Education:* Grade 3 piano. *Career:* Discovered in Vere John's Talent Contest, Jamaica; Member, The Techniques; Songs inspired by Duke Reid, owner Treasure Isle Label; Formed The Shades, 1969; Joined Inner Circle Band; Concerts include: Support to Stevie Wonder, Carib Theatre, 1969; UK and European tours; Guest of Czechoslovakian Government at Bratislav Song Festival, 1973; Hit single as solo artist; Television appearance: Top of The Pops, 1971; Formed Chain Reaction, 1977; Signed to RCA Records, 1979–81; Formed Slick Records and Smash Music, 1980–; Working with: Record, Publishing and Management Company, 1982–; Managing Director, Jeunesse Cosmetics Ltd; Yak Yak Babywear Company. *Compositions:* Hits include: with The Techniques: Love Is Not A Gamble; My Girl; It's You I Love; Run Come Celebrate; Man of My Word; There Comes A Time; Find Yourself A Fool; Solo: Dry Up Your Tears; Bitterness of Life; Mad About You; Long About Now; Free The People; with Chain Reaction: Never Lose and Never Win. *Recordings:* Other hit singles include: as solo artiste: Rain; Candida; with The Techniques: Queen Majesty; You Don't Care; Contributions to: King Kong Compilation, 1981; Techniques, Run Come Celebrate: Their Greatest Hits, 1993; as publisher, Smash Music: Holding On To Love; Fuchi.

Memberships: PRS; BASCA; ASCAP; MCPS. *Leisure interests:* Martial arts; Chi Kwang Do. *Current Management:* BRM Music Consultancy Ltd; BRM Music Publishing Ltd; Genius Management Agency Ltd. *Address:* 89a High Rd, Wood Green, London N22 6BB, England.

RUFFIN Jimmy; b. 7 May 1939, Collinsville, Mississippi, USA. Singer. *Career:* Session singer, early 1960s; Commercial breakthrough, major US, UK hit, What Becomes of The Broken-Hearted, 1966. *Recordings:* Albums: Top Ten, 1967; Ruff 'n' Ready, 1969; The Groove Governor, 1970; I Am My Brother's Keeper (with David Ruffin), 1970; Jimmy Ruffin, 1973; Love Is All We Need, 1975; Sunrise, 1980; Best of ERC Records, 1995; Singles include: What Becomes of The Broken-Hearted, 1966; I'll Say Forever My Love; It's Wonderful; Hold On To My Love, 1980; Turn To Me (duet with Maxine Nightingale), 1982; There Will Never Be Another You, 1985. *Address:* c/o Barry Collings Entertainments, 21a Clifftown Rd, Southend-on-Sea, Essex SS1 1AB, England.

RUFFNER Mason; b. 29 Nov. 1952, USA. Musician (guitar); Vocalist. *Career:* Support tours with: U2; Jimmy Page; Ringo Starr; Crosby Stills and Nash. *Recordings:* Solo albums: Mason Ruffner; Gypsy Blood; Evolution; You Can't Win; Other recordings include: Oh Mercy, Bob Dylan; Acadie, Daniel Lanois; Moonshine Cherrys. *Leisure interest:* Motorcycles. *Current Management:* Davis McLarty. *Address:* Rt 2 Box 592, Wimberley, TX 78676, USA.

RUFFY (Glen) David; b. 23 March 1952, York, England. Musician (drums); Programmer; Composer. m. Jennifer, 24 June 1995, 2 d. *Career:* Major tours: Sinead O'Connor; Adam Ant; Aztec Camera; Ruts; Edwyn Collins; Yazz; WaterBoys; World Party; Martin Stephenson; Concerts with Mica Paris; Kirsty MacColl; Prefab Sprout. *Recordings include:* with Ruts: Babylons Burning; In A Rut; West One; Jahwar; Rude Boys; The Crack; Grin and Bear It; Animal Now; Rhythm Collision Remixes; with Sinead O'Connor: My Special Child; Damn Your Eyes; Year of The Horse (video); Three Babies; with Kirsty MacColl: Titanic Days; What Do Pretty Girls Do?; with Aztec Camera: High Land Hard Rain; Knife; with Pigeonhead: Flash Bulb Emergency; It's Like the Man Said. *Memberships:* PRS; MCPS; Musicians' Union. *Leisure interests:* Relaxing; Swimming; Motor Rallying. *Current Management:* Southside Management; Agent: Grip. *Address:* 20 Cromwell Mews, London SW7, England.

RUHLMANN Jean-Jacques; b. 18 May 1952, Nogent-le-Rotrou, France. Musician (saxophone, clarinet); Composer. *Education:* CAPES Musicologie at the Sorbonne. *Musical Education:* C A Jazz. *Career:* Played with musicians including: J Thollot; F Jeanneau; J Gilson; E Watson; A Mangelsdorf; A Hervé; Michael O'Neil; B Renaudin; F Moerman; J F Jenny-Clark; Performed at many festivals in France; Belgium; Netherlands; Germany; Colombia; Tunisia; Spain. *Recordings:* Albums: Evensong, Michael O'Neil; Valses Manouches, with F A Moerman; Ciel De Traine (as a sideman); Windows, J J Ruhlmann Big Band. *Current Management:* M T Ruhlmann. *Address:* 3 rue des Poupardieres, 28400 Nogent le Rotrou, France.

RUNDGREN Todd; b. 2 June 1948, Philadelphia, Pennsylvania, USA. Singer; Songwriter; Musician (guitar); Record Prod. *Career:* Member, Woody's Truck Stop; Founder member, The Nazz, 1967–70; Solo recording artiste, 1970–; Formed progressive rock group Utopia, 1974–. *Recordings:* Albums: with The Nazz: Nazz, 1968; Nazz Nazz, 1969; Nazz III, 1970; with Utopia: Todd Rundgren's Utopia, 1974; Another Live, 1975; Ra, 1977; Oops! Wrong Planet, 1977; Adventures In Utopia, 1980; Deface The Music, 1980; Swing To The Right, 1982; Utopia, 1982; Oblivion, 1984; Solo albums: Runt, 1970; The Ballad of Todd Rundgren, 1971; Something / Anything?, 1972; A Wizard, A True Star, 1973; Todd, 1974; Initiation, 1975; Faithful, 1976; Hermit of Mink Hollow, 1978; Back To The Bars, 1978; Healing, 1981; The Ever Popular Tortured Artist Effect, 1983; A Cappella, 1985; POV, 1985; Anthology – Todd Rundgren, 1989; Nearly Human, 1989; Second Wind, 1991; No World Order, 1993; No World Order Lite, 1994; The Individualist, 1995; With a Twist, 1997; Up Against It, 1998; Live in Chicago 1991, 1999; Singles, 1995; Record producer, Bat Out of Hell, Meat Loaf, 1977; Also producer/engineer, recordings by New York Dolls; Grand Funk Railroad; Hall and Oates; XTC; The Band. *Current Management:* Panacea Entertainment Management. *Address:* 2705 Glendower Ave, Los Angeles, CA 90027, USA.

RUNGE Jens (Christian); b. 28 Nov. 1961, Malaysia. Guitarist, singer. *Career:* Toured Scandinavia with Hanne Boel, 1989, 1993, 1994, 1996, 1997, 1998; Sanne Salomonsen, 1990, 1991, 1992, 1995; Kasper Winding, 1987, 1988, 1989, 1990; Anne Linnet, 1988, 1989, 1991, 1992; Toured Europe with Hanne Boel, 1995; Played at Roskilde Festival with Hanne Boel, 1989, 1993, 1998, Sanne Salomonsen, 1992, 1995, Anne Linnet, 1989. *Recordings:* Hanne Boel: Dark Passion, 1990; Misty Paradise, 1994; Silent Violence, 1996; Need, 1998; Kasper Winding: No 5, 1989; Blue Isis: Kalder Pa Tiden, 1989; Paris Paris: Paris Paris, 1986; Love Construction: Caught in the Act, 1988. *Membership:* The Danish Artist Union. *Leisure interest:*

Travelling the world. *Address:* Ahlefeldtsgade 22 3 sal, 1359 Copenhagen K, Denmark.

RUOCCO Joanne; b. 26 May 1961, New Jersey, USA. Musician (drums, percussion). m. Douglas Newbery, 30 Sept. 1989. *Education:* Graduate, New Jersey. *Musical Education:* BA, Music, Fine Art, Farleigh Dickenson University, New Jersey. *Recordings with:* Duke Ellington Orchestra (Mercer Ellington); Chuck Berry; Bobby Womack; J Geils Band; Ron Wood; Hollywood Beyond; Jellybean; Mick Hucknell (Simply Red); The Style Council (Paul Weller). *Memberships:* Musicians' Union; AFofM. *Leisure interests:* Skiing; Hiking; Swimming; Photography; Travel. *Current Management:* Independent. *Address:* 7 Linwood Rd, Harpenden, Hertfordshire AL5 1RR, England.

RUPIC Hrvoje; b. 2 March 1970, Zagreb, Croatia. Musician (percussion). *Musical Education:* Latin Percussion, Drum Teaching Studios, London. *Career:* Founder and leader of latin-jazz group, Cubismo; Over 50 recorded CDs in jazz, rock, pop, latin and other music; Collaboration, concerts and recordings with Toots Thielemans, Philippe Catherine, Bob Mover, Gianni Basso, Yolanda Duke, Mind Games; Workshops for hand-drumming and Afro-Cuban rhythms; Teacher for hand-drumming at Classical Academy, Zagreb. *Recordings:* Cubismo: Cubismo; Viva La Habana; Csaba Deseo, The Swinging Violin; Mind Games, Pretty Fonky; Bob Mover, Yesterdays; Soul Fingers, Live In BP Club. *Honours:* STATUS (Croatian Musicians Union Award), 1996–97; Porin (Croatian Discography Award); 7 awards with Cubismo for numerous recordings. *Memberships:* HGU, Croatian Musicians Union; HUOKU, Croation Asscn of Orchestral and Chamber Musicians; HZSU, Croation Asscn of Freelance Artists. *Address:* Petrova 51, 10000 Zagreb, Croatia.

RUSBY Kate Anna; b. 4 Dec. 1973. Vocalist; Musician (guitar, piano, fiddle); Songwriter. m. John McCusker. *Career:* Spent some time with all-female folk group The Poozies; As solo artist performs traditional songs and own folk-influenced material. *Recordings:* Singles: Cowsong, 1998; Albums: Kate Rusby and Kathryn Roberts, 1995; Hourglass, 1997; Sleepless, 1999; Little Lights, 2001; with The Poozies: Come Raise Your Head, 1997; Infinite Blue, 1998; features on: Yella Hoose (with John McCusker), 2000; Evolving Tradition, 1995; Evolving Tradition #2, 1996. *Honours:* Mercury Music Prize nominee, Sleepless, 1999; BBC Folk Album of the Year, Sleepless, 1999. *Address:* c/o Pure Records, PO Box 174, Penistone, West Yorkshire, S30 6P, England. *Internet:* www.katerusby.com.

RUSCHKOWSKI André; b. 25 March 1959, Berlin, Germany. Composer. *Education:* PhD, Musicology, Humboldt University, Berlin, 1993. *Career:* Composer in Residence, several studios for electronic music including Berlin, Budapest, Paris, Vienna; Lecturer, Electronic Music and Music of the 20th Century, Music University Mozarteum Salzburg, Austria, 1992-, Technische Universität Berlin, University of Cologne; Professor for Electronic Music, Director, Electronic Music Studio, Composition Department. *Compositions:* Zeichen, for tape, 1989; Nasca, for tape, 1993; Succubus Quartet, for tape, 1994; Salzburgtrum, for flute, violin and percussion and tape, 1995–98; Four Short Studies, for tape, 1995; Sonama, for flute, violin and percussion, 1996; Karabontara, for piano and tape, 1996; Arara and Araku, for percussion and tape, 1997; Trakl Cycle (In blauem Kristall, Weisser Scheaf, Dunkle Stunde, Unter steinernen Bogen, 1997) for soprano, flute, clarinet, violin, cello, piano and tape, Les pas intérieurs, for female dancer, percussion and tape, 1997; Arion, Dione, Cento, Boreas, for tape, 1998; Doxa, for female dancer, video, percussion and tape, 1999. *Recordings:* Numerous. *Publications:* Soundscapes, 1990; Electronic sound synthesis and musical discoverings, 1998. *Honours include:* Prize of the City of Varese, Italy, 1990, Bourges, France, 1985, 1989; International Competition for Audio Art, Paris, 1997; Prize, Composition Competition for Computer Music, Braunschweig, 1998; Sonic Circuits, American Composers Forum, 1998. *Memberships:* Vice President, Austrian Society for Electroacoustic Music; International Computer Music Asscn. *Address:* Strauss Str 3, 83457 Bayerisch Gmain, Germany.

RUSKIN Tommy; b. 15 July 1942, Kansas City, Missouri, USA. Musician (drums). m. 11 Feb. 1963, 1 s. *Musical Education:* School band and orchestra. *Career:* Played with: Roy Johnson; Marilyn Maye; Sammy Tucker; Gary Foster; Mike Metheny; Pat Metheny; Julie Turner (wife); Clark Terry; Zoot Sims; Herb Ellis; Carl Fontana; Scott Hamilton; Bill Watrous; Warren Vaché; Jack Sheldon; Jay McShann. *Recordings:* Mike Methany: Day in Nightout; Gary Foster: Kansas City Connections; Marilyn Maye: The Second of Maye; Jay McShann: Warm. *Membership:* Musicians' Union. *Leisure interests:* Swimming; Walking. *Address:* 7225 Outlook, Overland Park, KS 66204, USA.

RUSSELL Brenda, (Brenda Gordon); b. 8 April 1949, Brooklyn, New York, USA. Singer; Songwriter; Musician; Prod. m. Brian Russell, 14 Sept. 1974, divorced, 1 d. *Musical Education:* Self-taught. *Career:* Toured with: David Sanborn; Billy Ocean; Jeffrey Osborne; Television appearances: Good Morning America; Today Show; Arsenio Hall; Late Show; British

Music Shows, Germany, Sweden; Pat Sajek Show, USA; Toured as singer (pre-solo career) with Mac Davis; Elton John; Television background work: Sonny and Cher Show. *Compositions:* Songs recorded by: Herb Alpert; Ray Charles; Joe Cocker; Rita Coolidge; Earth Wind and Fire; Roberta Flack; Chaka Khan; Johnny Mathis; Diana Ross; Donna Summer; Dionne Warwick; Oleta Adams; Regina Belle; Peabo Bryson; Alex Bugnon; Don Grusin; Layla Hathaway; George Howard; Bunny Hull; Jermaine Jackson; Walter Jackson; Al Jarreau; Koinonea; Ivan Lins; Byron Miller; Ann Murray; Phil Perry; Anita Pointer; Rufus; Patrice Rushen; Tom Scott; Marilyn Scott; Tavares; Luther Vandross; Tata Vega; Sudao Watanabe; Kirk Whalum; David Williams; Pauline Wilson; Phillipe Wynne. *Recordings:* Albums: Brenda Russell, 1979; Two Eyes, 1983; Love Life, 1980; Get Here, 1988; Kiss Me With The Wind, 1990; Soul Talkin', 1993; Singles include: So Good So Right; Piano In The Dark. *Honours:* 3 Grammy Nominations, for Piano In The Dark: Best Pop Female Vocalist, Best Duo or Group, Song of the Year. *Leisure interests:* Artist (charcoal portraits); Making clothes. *Current Management:* Turner Management Group. *Address:* 3500 W Olive Suite 770, Burbank, CA 91505, USA.

RUSSELL George Allen; b. 23 June 1923, Cincinnati, Ohio, USA. Composer; Theoritician; Bandleader; Musician (piano). m. Alice Norbury, 4 Aug. 1981, 1 s. *Education:* Wilberforce University High School. *Musical Education:* Private Study with Stephan Wolpe. *Career:* Performances with large and small ensembles world-wide, including Tokyo; Paris; London; Scandinavia; Italy; Germany; Portugal; United States; Radio and television: Broadcasts for BBC; Broadcasts in Sweden; Norway; Denmark; Japan; Finland; Germany; Italy; Commissions from National Endowments for the Arts; Massachusetts State Council on the Arts; Swedish Radio; The British Council; Cité de la Musique; Glasgow International Festival; Rocella Ionica; New England Presentors; Relache New Music; Norwegian Cultural Fund; BMI; Bradeis University; Member of faculty, New England Conservatory of Music, 1969–; Seminars and lectures world-wide. *Recordings include:* African Game; Living Time; Vertical Form VI; All About Rosie; Ezz-Thetic; Stratusphunk; Cubano Be-Cubano Bop; A Bird in Igor's Yard; Uncommon Ground; Listen to the Silence; Time Spiral; Electronic Sonata for Souls Loved by Nature; It's About Time. *Honours:* MacArthur Foundation Fellow; Guggenheim Fellow; National Endowment for the Arts American Jazz Master; Guardian Milestone Award. *Memberships:* Mem. International Society of Contemporary Music; American Federation of Musicians; Foreign Mem., Swedish Royal Academy of Music. *Current Management:* Serious Speakout, Windsor House, Fourth Floor, 83 Kingsway, London, WC2B 6SD. *Address:* c/o Concept Inc, #182, 1770 Massachusetts Ave, Cambridge, MA 02140, USA.

RUSSELL Graham Cyril; b. 11 June 1950, Nottingham, England. Singer; Musician (piano, guitar); Composer. m. Jodi Varble, 7 June 1986, 1 s., 1 d. *Musical Education:* Self-taught. *Career:* Singer, Co-founder group, Air Supply, (most successful Australian group); World-wide tours, 1975-, including China, 1995; World-wide television and radio appearances. *Recordings:* 17 albums released; 9 Top 5 songs, US charts; 25m. albums sold to date. *Honours:* Song of Year, 1980; American Music Awards, Artist of Year, 1980. *Memberships:* BMI; 2 Million Plays Club. *Leisure interests:* Outdoor Activities; Wildlife. *Current Management:* Barry Siegel. *Address:* 10345 W Olympic Blvd, Suite 200, Los Angeles, CA 90064, USA.

RUSSELL Jack Patrick; b. 5 Dec. 1960, Montebello, California, USA. Vocalist. m. Jana Whisenant, 19 Sept. 1991, 1 s. *Musical Education:* Self-taught. *Career:* Vocalist with rock group Great White; Support tours with: Whitesnake, UK, 1984; Judas Priest, USA, 1984; Dokken, USA, 1986; Night Ranger, 1987; Ratt, 1987; Twisted Sister, 1987; Whitesnake, 1987–88; Kiss, 1991; Co-headline tour with Tesla, 1989–90; Headline tours USA, 1992–95. *Recordings:* Albums: Great White, 1984; Shot In The Dark, 1986; Once Bitten, 1987; Recovery Live, 1987; Twice Shy, 1989; Hooked, 1990; Psycho City, 1992; Best of Great White, 1994; Sail Away, 1994; various live recordings. *Honours:* Grammy Nomination, Best Hard Rock Performance, 1989. *Leisure interests:* Scuba diving; Fishing; Boating. *Current Management:* Premier Talent Agency; Wildcat Management. *Address:* c/o Siegl, Feldstein, Duffin and Vuylstehe, Inc, 10345 W Olympic Blvd, Los Angeles, CA 90064–2524, USA.

RUSSELL John William Edward; b. 19 Dec. 1954, London, England. Improvising Musician (guitar). *Musical Education:* Private and self-taught. *Career:* Crossing Bridges, TV, radio include: Channel 4; Radio 3; Radio 4; Local radio; Concerts, festivals, tours include: East, West Europe, North America. *Composition:* QuaQua. *Recordings:* 20 albums and CDs. *Publications:* Essays, interviews in: Musics; Rubberneck; The Wire. *Honours:* Arts Council development bursary. *Membership:* London Musicians' Collective. *Leisure interests:* Reading; Gardening. *Current Management:* Mopomoso. *Address:* 23B Charteris Rd, London N4 3AA, England.

RUSSELL Leon, (Hank Wilson); b. Lawton, Oklahoma, USA. Musician (guitar, piano, trumpet); Singer. m. Mary McCreary, Jan. 1976, 1 s., 1 d.

Career: Multi-instrumental session musician; Regular member, Phil Spector's Wall of Sound session crew, 1962; Pianist, television series Shindig!, NBC TV; Built own recording studio, 1967; Appeared in film Mad Dogs and Englishmen, 1970; Played with Bob Dylan; Rolling Stones; Eric Clapton; Major concerts include: Concert For Bangladesh, Madison Square Garden, 1971; New Orleans Jazz and Heritage Festival, 1991; American Music Festival, with Neville Brothers, Randy Newman and Warren Zevon, 1992; Owner, video production company. *Compositions include:* Co-writer, singer, theme to Flesh and Blood, NBC TV; Delta Lady, recorded by Joe Cocker; A Song For You, recorded by The Carpenters, Donny Hathaway; This Masquerade, recorded by George Benson; Co-writer, Superstar, recorded by The Carpenters. *Recordings:* Albums: Asylum Choir, 1968; Leon Russell, 1970; Leon Russell and The Shelter People, 1971; Asylum Choir II, 1972; Carney, 1972; Leon Live, 1973; Hank Wilson's Back, 1973; Stop All That Jazz, 1974; Will O'The Wisp, 1975; The Wedding Album, 1976; Make Love To The Music, 1977; Americana, 1978; Willie and Leon (with Willie Nelson), 1979; The Live Album, 1981; Hank Wilson Vol. II, 1984; Anything Can Happen, 1992; Hank Wilson Vol. 3, 1998; Face in the Crowd, 1999; Blues: Same Old Song, 1999; Life and Love, 1999; Singles include: Tight Rope; Bluebird; Lady Blue; Back To The Island; As session musician: A Taste of Honey, Herb Alpert; Mr Tambourine Man, The Byrds. *Honours:* Grammy, Record of the Year, This Masquerade, 1976; Several Gold discs.

RUSSELL Mark J; Composer. m. Joanne Whitworth, 10 May 1997. *Education:* Hons Degree, Film Music and Composition. *Career:* Joined BBC Television's music department for three years, then left to start own recording studio; As Musican and arranger has worked with Tanita Tikaram, Julia Fordham and acclaimed Chinese flautist Guo Yue, with whom he appeared in concerts throughout Europe and Australia; Writer and presenter of BBC Radio 3's music programme Mixing It which covers jazz through to world music and experimental techno, drum and bass. *Compositions include:* For Film: Saving Grace (director Nigel Cole: Fineline); For television: The Prince of Atlantis (BBC/Canal+ Ravensburger); The Peter Principle (Hat Trick/BBC, director, Nick Woods); A Horse's World (Wall To Wall/Channel Four, director, Steve Ruggi); Barnados Children (BBC, director Michael Davies); For Whom The Bull Tolls (Tiger Aspect/Channel Four); Fragile Earth (Channel Four); Love Me Love Me Not (TVS); Comic Relief (BBC, director, Michael Davies); Crimestoppers (Carlton Television); Poets News (BBC, director, Michael Davies); Granada on Sunday (Granada Television); Dispatches: The Marchioness Tragedy, Dispatches: Lorries, Dispatches: Child Prostitution, Dispatches: Privateers, (Channel Four, director Alex Sutherland); Kingdoms of Survival (Anglia Television); Network First: Going to Chelsea (Hartswood/Carlton, director Michael Davies); Wildlife Showcase (BBC, director Tania Dorrity); Lifeline (BBC); It Happened Next Year (BBC); Style Challenge (BBC); Cold Feet (Three series, Granada); The Red Baron (BBC); Officers and Gentlemen (BBC); Passion Killers (Granada); Wonderful You (Hartswood); Playing the Field (Tiger/Aspect); For BBC Radio: Superman I, Batman, Spiderman, Independence Day, Superman II (all directed by Dirk Maggs, first four recorded and released). *Address:* c/o Soundtrack Music Associates Ltd, 25 Ives St, Chelsea, London SW3 2ND, England.

RUSSELL Paul Stuart Rupert; b. 13 Feb. 1934, Nuthall, Nottingham, England. Musician (drums, New Orleans style). m. June Vivian Hill, 25 Jan. 1958, 3 s., 1 d. *Education:* Leicester School of Architecture. *Musical Education:* Study of drumming in New Orleans, casual basis. *Career:* Member, Mercia Jazz Band (Nottingham), 1954–58; Then musician with various bands: Mike Casimir; Chris Blount; Chris Burke; Spirits of Rhythm (own band); Oriole Brass Band (own band); Dave Donohoe; Louisiana Joymakers; Worked with Sammy Rimington, accompanied many visiting Americans including: Alton Purnell; Kid Thomas; Louis Nelson; Benny Waters; Herb Hall; Sam Lee; Captain John Handy; Played at Jazz Festivals in New Orleans; Nice; Ascona; Lugano; Milan; Breda; Cork; Gent; Currently with The Teddy Fullick Quintet and the Frank Brooker New Orleans Swingtet. *Recordings:* With Dave Donahoe, Jimmy Noone Jr. *Memberships:* Musicians' Union; ARCUK. *Leisure interests:* Walking; Cycling; DIY; Reconstructing old drums. *Address:* 105 Kimberley Rd, Nuthall, Nottingham NG16 1DD, England.

RUSSO William; *Career:* Composer, Trombonist, Stan Kenton Orchestra; Composer In Residence, City and County of San Francisco; Chairman, Music Department, Columbia College Chicago; Founder, Conductor, Chicago Jazz Ensemble; Performed a tour of Sardinia and mainland Italy, 1998; Montréal Jazz Festival; Chicago Jazz Festival; Symphony Center, Chicago; Ravinia; Lower Mississippi Basin Tour, 1998; Written Operas and Film Scores; Conducted Several Orchestras In America. *Compositions:* Chicago Suite Nos 1 and 2; The Golden Bird; Listen Beneath; Dubrovsky. *Publications:* Composing Music: A New Approach, 1988. *Honours:* Life Time Achievement Award, NARAS; Koussevitsky Award. *Address:* 824 S Laffin St, Chicago, IL 60607, USA.

RUTHERFORD Mike; b. 2 Oct. 1950, Guildford, Surrey, England. Musician (guitar, bass); Record Prod. *Career:* Musician, Genesis, 1970–; Also solo artiste, 1980–; Founder, producer, Mike and the Mechanics, 1986–; Numerous world-wide tours and major concerts including: Philharmonic Hall, New York; Madison Square Gardens, New York; Giants Stadium, New York; LA Forum. *Recordings:* Albums: with Genesis: Foxtrot, 1972; Selling England By The Pound, 1973; Genesis Live, 1973; The Lamb Lies Down On Broadway, 1974; Trick of The Tail, 1976; Wind and Wuthering, 1977; Seconds Out, 1977; And Then There Were Three, 1978; Duke, 1980; Abacab, 1981; Three Sides Live, 1982; Genesis, 1983; Invisible Touch, 1986; We Can't Dance, 1991; Calling All Stations, 1997; Not About Us, 1997; Turn it On Again: The Hits, 1999; with Mike and The Mechanics: Mike and The Mechanics, 1986; The Living Years, 1988; Word of Mouth, 1991; Beggar On A Beach of Gold, 1995; Hits, 1996; Solo albums: Small Creep's Day, 1980; Acting Very Strange, 1982; Singles: with Genesis: Abacab; Follow You Follow Me; Mama; Illegal Alien; Invisible Touch; Land of Confusion; Tonight Tonight Tonight; That's All; Turn It On Again; with Mike and The Mechanics: Silent Running; All I Need Is A Miracle; The Living Years; Over My Shoulder; Also recorded on: Voyage of The Acolyte, Steve Hackett, 1975; with John Verity: Interrupted Journey, 1983; Truth of The Matter, 1985. *Honours:* Golden Ticket, Madison Square Gardens, 1986; First group, 5 Top 5 US singles from 1 album, 1986; Band of the Year, Rolling Stone Readers Poll, 1987. *Current Management:* Hit and Run Music, 30 Ives St, London SW3 2ND, England.

RUTHERFORD Paul William; b. 29 Feb. 1940, Greenwich, London, England. Musician (trombone, euphonium). *Musical Education:* RAF Musical Services; Guildhall School of Music Services. *Career:* Five years, RAF Music Services; Leading member, avant garde jazz in UK; Numerous festivals in UK; International television, radio. *Recordings:* Solo albums: Sequences 72 and 73, 1972; Gentle Harm of the Bourgeoisie, 1974; Rogues, 1988; Rottor, 1998; Played with the Tony Oxley Sextet; Mike Westbrook Bands; Spontaneous Music Ensemble; Globe Unity Orchestra; London Jazz Composers Orchestra. *Honours:* Melody Maker Poll, 3 years consecutively. *Membership:* Musicians' Union. *Leisure interests:* Reading; Politics; Art. *Address:* Flat 2, 67A Shooters Hill Rd, Blackheath, London SE3 7HS, England.

RUTKOWSKI Louise; b. 15 March 1964, Paisley, Scotland. Vocalist. *Musical Education:* Self-managed. *Career:* Worked with: Sunset Gun; This Mortal Coil; The Kindness of Strangers; Nellee Hooper; Dave Stewart. *Recordings:* 1 album and 3 singles with Sunset Gun, 1984–86; 2 albums with This Mortal Coil, 1984–86; 1 album with The Kindness of Strangers, 1990–93; 1 album with The Hope Blister, 1998; Currently performing Short Stories, the songs of Randy Newman. *Membership:* PRS. *Address:* c/o Arts Council of England, Music Department, 14 Great Peter St, London SW1P 8NQ, England.

RUTTEN Leo; b. 25 Dec. 1957, Tongeren, Belgium. Engineer (Playing 2 Row, 3 Row, Melodeon, Bagpipes, Hurdy Gurdy, Flutes, Sax). m. Lieve Veulemans, 9 July 1988, 2 s., 2 d. *Education:* Industrial Engineer Degree, Khlim Diepenbeek. *Musical Education:* Self-taught Melodeon; Summer course with Wilfrid Moonen, Riccardo Tesi, Hurdy-Gurdy with Evelyne Girardon. *Career:* Former Hurdy-Gurdy and Melodeon Player with Limburgs Dansorkest, 1984–93; TV Program 'De Milieu-Karavaan', 1987; Concert Zoo Leipzich DDR, 1988; Concert Brin Radio 3, 1993; Concert Festival St Chartier, 1993, France; Former Member, SLEMP; Current Member, Peper and playing with Poescafe, Concert Poescafe Ancienne Belgique, Brussels, 1998. *Compositions:* Biesenwals; Wals Voor Mathilde; De Groene Wants; De Gebroken Duimlus; Alvers in De Lucht. *Recordings:* Volksmuziek, 1985; Limburgsdans Orkest, 1990; Folk Music from Belgium, 1997; Poescafe, 1997. *Membership:* Belgian Bagpipe Player Asscn. *Leisure interests:* Travelling; Sailing. *Address:* Rooierheide Straat 11, B3530 Diepenbeek, Belgium.

RYAN Barbara; b. 29 May 1950, Colombo, Sri Lanka. Celtic Musician (Lead Vocals, Guitar, Bouzouki, Bodhran). m. David B Ryan, 2 s. *Education:* BA, George Washington University, 1971; Studied Voice With Lida Brodenova, Jane White, Rilla Mervine. *Career:* Founder, Traditional Celtic Music Group, Iona, 1986; Performed At Major Celtic Festivals Throughout The US; Solo Work Includes Broadcasts On The Voice of America; Singing For The National Geographic Explorer Special Series; Vocal Coach, 1988–; Founder, Potomac Celtic Festival, 1994. *Recordings:* Back To Our Roots, 1992; Holding Our Own, 1994; Nutmeg and Ginger, 1996; The Sound of Iona, 1998; Compilations: Celtic Festival, Live, 1996; The Takoma Park Folk Festival, 1997. *Memberships:* Folk Alliance; Celtic Women International; Washington Area Music Asscn. *Current Management:* Barnaby Productions Inc, PO Box 11160, Burke, VA 22009 1160, USA.

RYDELL Bobby, (Robert Ridarelli); b. 26 April 1942, Philadelphia, Pennsylvania, USA. Singer; Musician (drums). *Career:* Drummer, Teen Club television show, 3 years; Duo with Frankie Avalon, 1954; Member, Rocco and the Saints; Solo artiste, 18 Top 40 hits, 1959–63; Film appearance, Bye Bye Birdy; Cabaret and club singer. *Recordings:* Albums include: Rydell At The Copa, 1961; Bobby Rydell/Chubby Checker, 1961; Bobby's Biggest Hits, 1961; All The Hits, 1962; Top Hits of 1963, 1964; Forget Him, 1964; The Best of Bobby Rydell, 2000; Bobby's Biggest Hits, 1999; Singles include: Fatty Fatty; Kissin' Time; Wild One; Sway; Volare; Forget Him. *Current Management:* Fox Entertainment, 1650 Broadway, Suite 503, New York, NY 10019, USA.

RYDER Shaun; b. 23 Aug. 1962, Little Hulton, Lancashire, England. Singer. 1 d. *Career:* Singer, Happy Mondays, 1985–93; Tours, UK, Europe and US; Support tours to: New Order, UK, 1987; Jane's Addiction, US, 1990; Concerts include: Glastonbury Festival, 1990; Great British Music Weekend, Wembley, 1990; Feile Festival, Tipperary, 1990; Cities In The Park Festival, Prestwich, 1990; Featured in film The Ghost of Oxford Street, C4, 1990; Band disbanded, 1992; Founder member, Black Grape, 1993–; Black Grape disbanded, 1998; Reformed Happy Mondays, 1999; Concerts include: T In The Park Festival, Glasgow, 1995; Numerous television and radio appearances. *Recordings:* Albums: with Happy Mondays: Squirrel and G Men; 24 Hour Party People; Plastic Face Carnt Smile (White Out), 1986; Bummed, 1988; Pills 'N' Thrills and Bellyache, 1990; Live, 1991; Yes Please!, 1992; with Black Grape: It's Great When You're Straight... Yeah!, 1995; Stupid, Stupid, Stupid, 1997; Singles: with Happy Mondays: 24 Hour Party People; WFL; Step On, 1990; Kinky Afro, 1990; Judge Fudge, 1991; with Black Grape: Reverend Black Grape, 1995; In The Name of The Father, 1995; Kelly's Heroes, 1995; England's Irie, 1996; Fat Neck, 1996; Get Higher, 1997; Marbles, 1998. *Honours:* Best Indie Act, DMC World DJ Awards, 1991; BRIT Award Nominations: Best Newcomer, with Happy Mondays, 1991; with Black Grape, 1996. *Address:* c/o Fairwarning/Wasted Talent, The Plaza, 535 Kings Road, London SW10 0SZ, England.

RYGERT Göran T; b. 1 May 1935, Tranås, Sweden. m. (1) 2 s., (2) Janet A Rybka, 19 Sept. 1997. *Education:* Master of Architecture, Chalmers University of Technology, Göteborg, Sweden; Private, with Torsten Rygert (father), Music Director and Composer. *Career:* Arranger and Composer, field of song – ballad and folk music; String Bass Musician, Swedish song – ballad artists, in many folk music orchestras, Sweden and USA; Appearances in Swedish, American and Russian Radio and TV; many song festivals; Producer, many song books, Freelance Editor, Warner/ Chappell Music Scandinavia AB, Sweden. *Compositions:* A number of songs with words by Swedish Poets and Writers. *Publications:* Ölands Folkliga Visor och Melodier Genom Tiderna, 1987; Visor Kring Bordet, 1993; Festvisor, 1994; many other song-books, 1994–97. *Honours:* Royal Gustav Adolf's Academy Prize, 1991; Kalmar County Council Cultural Award, 1997. *Memberships:* Hon. Mem., Visans Vänner; Swedish Composers of Popular Music; Georgia Music Industry Asscn; Balalaika and Domra Asscn of America. *Leisure interest:* Composing and arranging. *Address:* 4390 Ivywood NE, Marietta, Ga 30062, USA.

RYPDAL Terje; b. 23 Aug. 1947, Oslo, Norway. Musician (piano, guitar); Composer. m. Elin Kristin Rypdal, 15 June 1988, 3 s., 1 d. *Education:* Grunnfag in Music, University of Oslo. *Musical Education:* Composition Studies with Finn Mortensen. *Career:* Musician with The Vanguards, 1962–67; The Dream, 1967–69; Jan Garbarek Group, 1969–71; Leader, own groups, 1971-. *Compositions:* 6 symphonies, 2 operas. *Recordings:* Albums include: Bleak House, 1968; Ved Sorevatn (on album of Baden Baden Free Jazz Meeting), 1969; Terje Rypdal, 1971; What Comes After, 1974; Whenever I Seem To Be Far Away, 1974; Odyssey, 1975; After The Rain, 1976; Waves, 1978; Descendre, 1980; To Be Continued, 1981; Eos, 1984; Chaser, 1986; Works, 1989; Undisonus, 1990; QED, 1993; If Mountains Could Sing, 1995; Nordic Quartet (with John Surman, Karin Krog, Vigleik Storaas), 1995; Skywards, 1997; Double Concerto/Fifth Symphony, 2000. *Honours:* Deutscher Schallplattenpreis. *Membership:* Norwegian Composers Guild. *Leisure interest:* Horses. *Address:* 6380 Tresfjord, Norway.

S

SAADIQ Raphael, (Raphael Wiggins); b. 14 May 1966, Oakland, California, USA. Vocalist; Prod. *Career:* Formed vocal trio Tony! Toni! Toné! with brother Dwayne and cousin Timothy Christian, 1988; Founder: Pookie Records; Formed Lucy Pearl with Dawn Robinson (En Vogue) and Ali Shaheed Muhammad (A Tribe Called Quest), 2001; Joi replaced Robinson, 2001; Collaborations: Q-Tip; Snoop Doggy Dogg; Willie Max; Vanessa Williams; D'Angelo; Bilal; Whitney Houston; Angie Stone. *Recordings:* Albums: with Tony! Toni! Toné!: Who?, 1988; The Revival, 1990; Sons of Soul, 1993; House of Music, 1996; with Lucy Pearl: Lucy Pearl, 2000; Singles: with Tony! Toni! Toné!: Little Walter, 1988; The Blues, Oakland Stroke, Feels Good, It Never Rains (In Southern California), 1990; Whatever You Want, House Party II, 1991; If I Had Not Loot, Anniversary, My Ex-Girlfriend, 1993; Lay Your Head On My Pillow, Leavin', 1994; Let's Get Down, 1996; Thinking of You, 1997; solo: Ask of You, 1995; Get Involved (with Q-Tip), 1999; with Lucy Pearl: Dance Tonight, Don't Mess With My Man, 2000. *Address:* c/o Virgin Records, 304 Park Ave, New York, USA.

SABER Danny; b. 22 Dec. 1966, New York, New York, USA. Prod.; Musician (Bass). *Career:* Producer; Bass Guitarist and Writer, Black Grape; Numerous live tours and festival appearances including Tribal Gathering and Reading festivals, 1997. *Recordings:* Singles: Reverend Black Grape, 1995; England's Irie, 1996; Fat Neck, 1996; Get Higher, 1997; Marbles, 1998; Albums: It's Great When You're Straight... Yeah, 1995; Stupid, Stupid, Stupid, 1997.

SABINA Leslie Michael; b. 21 Sept. 1958, Nebraska, USA. Prof. of Music. m. Evelyn May Rennie, 1 s., 1 d. *Education:* BMus, University of Toronto, 1981; BEd, University of Windsor, 1986; MM, University of Miami, 1984; PhD, Michigan State University, 1992. *Career:* Music Professor, University of Windsor, 1988–90; St Bonaventure University, 1991–; Honorary Visiting Fellow, University of York, 1998; Jazz Performances With Dizzy Gillespie, J C Heard, Joe Williams, Billy Eckstine, Della Reese, The Temptations. *Compositions:* 47 Jazz Compositions. *Recordings:* JC Heard Jazz Orchestra; Joe Coughlin. *Honours:* PROCAN Jazz Composers Award, 1986, 1988; PROCAN Jazz Composer of The Year, 1988; ASCAP Composition Award, 1995–99. *Memberships:* ASCAP; IAJE; College Music Society; North American Saxophone Alliance. *Leisure interests:* Reading; Golf. *Address:* St Bonaventure University, St Bonaventure, NY 14778, USA.

SABIU Marco; b. Forlì, Italy. Record Prod.; Mixer; Songwriter. *Career:* Writer, Producer with Charlie Mallozzi, known as Rapino Brothers; Moved to London, 1992; Classically trained pianist; Programmer, mixer, producer of Pop/Dance music; Member of groups: Tabernacle; Rapination. *Recordings:* Albums for: Take That; Kylie Minogue; Dannii Minogue; Lulu; Kym Mazelle; Rozalla; Hit singles: Could It Be Magic, Take That; Rhythm of The Night, Corona; What Is Love, Haddaway; I Know The Lord, Tabernacle; Love Me The Right Way, Rapination and Kym Mazelle; I Love My Radio, Taffy; T'pau, Red; Also singles for: Alicia Bridges; Heaven 17; Sparks. *Honours:* Brit Award, Single of Year, Take That; Triple Platinum album, Take That. *Current Management:* Stephen Budd Management. *Address:* 109B Regents Park Rd, London NW1 8UR, England.

SADASHIGE Yuzuru; b. 12 May 1966, Chiba, Japan. Composer. m. Wendy Griffiths, 4 Sept. 1998. *Education:* Bachelor of Law, Tokyo University, Japan, 1989; Bachelor of Music, Composition, Berklee College of Music, Boston, USA, 1993; Master of Music, Composition, Manhattan School of Music, New York, USA, 1995; Masterclasses with Ned Rorem, Lucal Foss, Robert Starer. *Career:* Co-Founder, Co-Artistic Director, NeWorks, contemporary music group; Composer In Residence, American Chamber Music Festival at Edsvik, Sweden, 1999; Assistant Conductor, Pianist, Golden Fleece Chamber Opera, 1995; US Premiere of Maurice Ohana's Three Stories of Honorable Flower, 1996; Pianist for ballet classes, Rehearsal Pianist for Musical Theatre; Pianist, Scott Wolson's Folk-Rock CD, Anything Left to Say; Jazz/Pop Pianist/Keyboardist, Arranger for bands, sessions and parties. *Compositions:* Third Tribe, for flute, djembe drums and piano, 1992; Electric Ice Dream, for clarinet quartet, 1996; Fractured Skies, 1998; eX-s-Tet, for clarinet, 2 violins, viola, cello, piano, 1999; Concert music performed throughout USA and Mexico by Civic Orchestra of Chicago; ONIX New Music Ensemble; The New York Clarinet Quintet; NewEar Ensemble of Kansas City; Synchronia of St Louis; Numerous commissions; Theatre scores, Dance scores; Film score for ANA: Portrait in Days, 1995. *Honours:* Hon. mention, Percussive Arts Society, 1992; Hon. mention, Vienna Modern Masters, 1993; Brian M Israel Award, Society for New Music, 1996. *Memberships:* ASCAP; American Music Center; Actors' Company Theatre. *Leisure interest:* Graphic arts (computer and manual). *Address:* 364 14th St, No. 2, Brooklyn, NY 11215, USA.

SADE (Helen Folasade Adu); b. 16 Jan. 1959, Ibadan, Nigeria. Singer; Songwriter. *Education:* St Martin's School of Art, London. *Career:* Member, Arriva; Member, Pride; Singer, founder, own band, Sade, 1983; Appearances include: Montreux Jazz Festival, 1984; Live Aid, Wembley Stadium, 1985; Film appearance: Absolute Beginners, 1987. *Recordings:* Singles: with Sade include: Your Love Is King, 1984; Smooth Operator (co-writer), 1984; The Sweetest Taboo, 1986; Never As Good As The First Time, 1986; Love Is Stronger Than Pride, 1988; Paradise, 1988; No Ordinary Love (use in film Indecent Proposal), 1993; Albums: Diamond Life, 1984; Promise, 1985; Stronger Than Pride, 1988; Love Deluxe, 1992; Best Of, 1994; Contributor, film soundtrack Absolute Beginners, 1987. *Honours:* BRIT Awards: Best British Album, Diamond Life, 1985; Best New Artist, 1986; Black Music Award, 1992; O.B.E., 2002. *Current Management:* Roger Davies Management, 15030 Ventura Blvd, Suite 772, Sherman Oaks, CA 91403, USA.

SADIER Laetitia; b. 6 May 1968, Paris, France. Vocalist; Musician (keyboards, guitar, trombone); Songwriter. *Career:* Member: Stereolab, 1991–; Monade; Son Alex with band member Tim Gane; Collaborations: High Llamas; Mouse On Mars; Ui; Brigitte Fontaine; Luna; Blur; Herbie Mann. *Recordings:* Albums include: Peng!, 1992; Transient Random Noise Bursts With Announcements, 1993; Mars Audiac Quintet, 1994; Music For The Amorphous Body Study Center, 1995; Emperor Tomato Ketchup, 1996; Dots and Loops, 1997; Cobra and Phases Group Play Voltage In The Milky Night, 1999; The First of The Microbe Hunters, 2000; Sound-Dust, 2001. *Current Management:* Martin Pike c/o Duophonic Ultra High Frequency Disks. *Internet:* www.stereolab.co.uk.

SAFARI Jean Bosco, (Jean Vijdt); b. 10 May 1954, Rwanda. Singer; Songwriter. 1 s., 1 d. *Career:* Band member of a O; Solo artist, originally as Kid Safari; Billed as Jean Bosco Safari, 1995-. *Recordings:* Wow, 1991; Romantic Heroes, 1993; Little Boy Blue, 1995. *Honour:* Gold album: Romantic Heroes. *Memberships:* SABAM; ZAMU. *Current Management:* Tempo Belgium, Time Lecompte. *Address:* Krijslaan 61, 9000 Ghent, Belgium.

SAFFRON; b. 1969, Nigeria. Vocalist. *Career:* Former ballet dancer; Lead singer, N-Joi; Lead singer, Republica, 1994-. *Recordings include:* with Republica: Album: Republica, 1997; Speed Ballads, 1998; Hit singles: Ready To Go, 1997; Drop Dead Gorgeous, 1997; From Rush Hour With Love, 1998. *Current Management:* Rise Management Ltd, PO Box 9788, London W10 5WN, England.

SAGER Carole Bayer; b. 1946, New York City, USA. Songwriter; Singer. m. Burt Bacharach. *Musical Education:* High School of Music and Art, New York. *Career:* Songwriter, 1960s; Recording artiste, 1972-. *Compositions:* Groovy Kind of Love (recorded by Patti Labelle, The Mindbenders, Phil Collins); That's What Friends Are For (raised $1m. for AIDS charity, recorded by Dionne Warwick and Friends); Co-writer, Midnight Blue (recorded by Melissa Manchester; When I Need You (recorded by Leo Sayer); They're Playing Our Song, with Marvin Hamlisch; Arthur's Theme, with Burt Bacharach (recorded by Christopher Cross); Nobody Does It Better, Carly Simon (James Bond theme); On My Own, Patti Labelle, Michael McDonald. *Recordings:* Albums: Carol Bayer Sager, 1977; Too, 1978; Sometimes Late at Night, 1981; Singles: You're Moving Out Today; Stronger Than Before (co-written with Bette Midler). *Honour:* Academy Award, Arthur's Theme.

SAGOV Margo Leona; b. 22 Dec. 1952, Cape Town, South Africa. Musician (guitar); Singer; Songwriter; Prod.; Studio Designer. *Education:* Registered architect; Studied Architectural Association, London. *Career:* Founder member, group Amazulu; Guitarist, backing vocalist, 1982–86; Signed to Towerbell Records, 1983; Island Records, 1984–86; Desert Songs, ATV Music Publishing, 1984–89; Toured extensively, UK, Europe; Television appearances include: Top of the Pops; The Young Ones; Tube; Radio sessions: John Peel; Annie Nightingale; David Jensen. *Recordings:* with Amazulu: Cairo; Smiley Stylee; Excitable; Moonlight Romance; Don't You Just Know It; Too Good To Be Forgotten; with Clicking The Mouse: I Must Be Dreaming; Numerous sessions include: The Beloved; Zeke Manyika. *Memberships:* Musicians' Union; Equity; ACTT as sound recordist; ARCUK. *Leisure interests:* Photography; Travel; Cinema; Walking. *Address:* 10 Brookfield Mansions, Highgate West Hill, London N6 6AS, England.

SAINSBURY Roy; b. 12 April 1942, Birmingham, England. Musician (guitar). m. Wendy Sainsbury, 2 s., 1 d. *Musical Education:* Studied guitar with Reg Bishop and Jack Toogood. *Career:* Appeared on BBC Radio 2, Night Ride, Jazz Parade; Played with BBC Midland Radio Orchestra and

New Millionaires Band; Solo appearances: BBC Radio 2 Arts Programme; Television in Netherlands and Malta. *Compositions:* Love and Sunshine; Crieff Melody; Wendy's Blues. *Recording:* Album: Gentle Guitar. *Membership:* Musicians' Union. *Leisure interests:* Kart racing; Walking; Travel. *Current Management:* Norman Phillips Agency, Birmingham, England. *Address:* 185 Birches Rd, Codsall, Wolverhampton WV8 2JW, England.

SAINTE-MARIE Buffy; b. 20 Feb. 1941, Saskatchewan, Canada. Singer; Songwriter; Musician (keyboards, guitar, mouthbow, computer). 1 s. *Education:* PhD, Fine Arts, University of Massachusetts (undergraduate, Philosophy). *Musical Education:* Self-taught. *Career:* Solo concerts world-wide, 1963–; Symphony concerts with: Calgary Symphony; National Arts Centre Orchestra; Vancouver Opera Symphony; Toured with various bands major cities, hundreds of Indian reservations, indigenous area world-wide. *Recordings:* 19 albums include: Sweet America, 1976; Coincidence and Likely Stories, 1992; Up Where We Belong, 1996. *Honours:* Academy Award as songwriter, Up Where We Belong, from film An Officer and A Gentleman; Billboard Best New Artist, 1964; Premico Award, Italy, 1972; Queen Elizabeth Jubilee Medal; Academy Award, 1981; Charles De Gaulle Grand Prix, Best International Artist, 1994; Saskatchewan Lifetime Achievement Award, 1994; Canada JUNO Hall of Fame, 1995. *Memberships:* ASCAP; AFofM. *Leisure interests:* Digital music; Digital painting. *Current Management:* Jack Lentz, Einstein Brothers. *Address:* 20 Duncan St, Toronto, ON M5H 3G8, Canada.

SAKAMOTO Ryûichi; b. 17 Jan. 1952, Tokyo, Japan. Musician; Composer; Actor. m. Akiko Yano, 1979. *Musical Education:* Composition and electronic music, Tokyo College of Arts; Masters degree, 1976. *Career:* Founder, Yellow Magic Orchestra, 1978; Worked with David Sylvian, 1982–83; Solo recording artist, composer, 1982–; Actor, films including Merry Christmas Mr Lawrence, 1983; Worked with leading musicians including Adrian Belew; Andy Partridge; Iggy Pop; Brian Wilson; Thomas Dolby; Robbie Robertson; Conductor, arranger, music for Olympic Games opening ceremony, Barcelona, Spain, 1992. *Recordings:* Albums: B-2 Unit, 1980; Hidariudeno (A Dream of the Left Arm), 1981; Merry Christmas Mr Lawrence (film soundtrack), 1983; Coda, 1983; Ongaku Zukan (A Picture Book of Music), 1984; Esperanto, 1985; Miraiha Yarô (A Futurist Chap), 1986; Media Bahn Live, 1986; Oneamisno Tsubasa (The Wings of Oneamis), 1986; Illustrated Musical Encyclopedia, 1986; Neo Geo, 1987; The Last Emperor (film soundtrack), with David Byrne, Cong Su, 1987; Playing The Orchestra, 1988; Tokyo Joe, 1988; Sakamoto Plays Sakamoto, 1989; Grupppo Musicale, 1989; Beauty, 1989; Heartbeat, 1991; Neo Geo, with Iggy Pop, 1992; Sweet Revenge, 1994; Soundbites, 1994; Hard to Get, 1995; 1996, 1996; Music for Yohji Yamamoto, 1997; Smoochy, 1997; Discord, 1998; Love Is The Devil, 1998; Raw Life, 1999; Intimate, 1999; Space, 1999; BTTB, 1999; Complete Index of Gut, 1999; Cinemage, 2000; Singles include: Bamboo Houses, with David Sylvian, 1982; Forbidden Colours, with David Sylvian, 1983; Field Work, with Thomas Dolby, 1986; Risky, 1988; We Love You, 1991; Moving On, 1994; Prayer/Salvation, 1998; Anger, 1998. *Publications:* Otowo Miru, Tokiwo Kiku (Seeing Sound and Hearing Time), with Shôzo Omori; Seldom-Illegal; Contributor, Album, Public Image Limited; Esperanto, Arto Lindsey. *Honours:* Academy Award, The Last Emperor, 1987. *Current Management:* David Rubinson Management, PO Box 411197, San Francisco, CA 94141, USA.

SALIM Abdel Gadir; b. Kordofan Province, Sudan. Singer; Musician (oud); Teacher. *Musical Education:* Institute for Music and Drama, Khartoum. *Career:* Headmaster in Chad; Regular national television and radio appearances popularizing traditional folk music; British tour with Abdel Aziz el Mubarak and Mohammed Gubara, 1986. *Recordings:* with Mubarak and Gubara: The Sounds of Sudan, 1991. *Address:* c/o World Circuit Records, 106 Cleveland St, London W1P 5DP, England.

SALISBURY Peter; Musician (Drums). *Career:* Founder Member, The Verve, 1990; Obtained record deal, 1991; Support dates to The Black Crowes; Played 1994 Lollapalooza tour; Band splits, 1995, then reforms; Numerous live dates including 1997 Reading Festival; Band splits again, 1999. *Recordings:* Singles: She's A Superstar; Gravity Grave; All in the Mind; Slide Away; Blue; This is Music; On Your Own; History; Bittersweet Symphony; Lucky Man; Drug's Don't Work; Albums: A Storm in Heaven, 1993; No Come Down, 1994; A Northern Soul, 1995; Urban Hymns, 1997.

SALLEY Jerry; b. Tennessee, USA. Singer; Songwriter; Prod. m. 3 d. *Career:* Regular performer, Nashville Showcase Circuit; 5 appearances, Grand Ole Oprey; Regular television appearances; Over 100 songs commercially recorded; Staff writer, Warner Chappell; Instructor, music business, Belmont University; Frequent panelist in music industry forums. *Compositions:* I Fell In The Water, John Anderson (Top 5); Breakin' New Ground, Wild Rose (Top 10); His Strength Is Perfect, Real Life Conversations, Stephen Curtis Chapman; Tracy Byrd; Roger Brown and Swing City; Songs for: Patty Loveless; The Hutchins; Woody Lee; Rhonda Vincent. *Honours:* Dove Award, for His Strength Is Perfect, 1990; Four Dove Award Nominations; 4 SESAC National Performance Activity

Awards. *Memberships:* Gospel Music Asscn; Country Music Asscn; Nashville Songwriter's Asscn; SESAC. *Current Management:* SESAC. *Address:* 55 Music Sq. E, Nashville, TN 37203, USA.

SALMINEN Simo; b. 16 Dec. 1956, Finland. Musician (trumpet, flugelhorn). *Career:* Played with: Tapiola Big Band; Paradise (dance orchestra); UMO (New Music Orchestra); Went to US, 1978; Played with Thad Jones/Mel Lewis band; Buddy Rich; Machito; Eddie Palmieri; Gladys Knight and The Pips; 1 year in Broadway show; Returned to Finland, 1983; Teacher, Oulunkylä Jazz and Pop Institute; Played in UMO; Led UMO in performance of music of Bob Moses, 1984; Leader, Arctic Big Band, 1987-. *Recordings:* Albums with: Espoo Big Band; UMO; Mel Lewis; Buddy Rich. *Address:* Hämeentie 72 A 7, 00550 Helsinki, Finland.

SALMINEN Teemu Tapio; b. 5 June 1953, Helsinki. Musician (Saxophones, Clarinet, Flutes). m. Eija Salminen. *Education:* Sibelius Academy. *Career:* Played in UMO Jazz Orchestra, 1976–; Played in several small groups; Teemu Salminen Quartet, Jukka Linkolas Octet, Quintet, Quartet, Jarmo Savolainen Nonet, Edward Vesala Group, Jukkis Uotila Quartet; Teacher, Sibelius Academy, Music Education, Jazz Department. *Compositions:* Mystery; Yes, Please; Gaudi. *Recordings:* 16 with The UMO Jazz Orchestra including, Selected Standards; Day Dreamin; Lady In Green; Green and Yellow; Electrifying Miles. *Memberships:* Musicians' Union; Flute Players Asscn; Jazz Players Asscn. *Leisure interest:* Cooking. *Address:* Tollinpolku 1B 20, 00410 Helsinki, Finland.

SALT Jack (John Robert); b. 30 Jan. 1920, Stafford, England. Musician (alto, baritone saxophones, clarinet, violin, viola). m. Katherine Barbara Barnard, 19 Aug. 1948, 4 s. *Musical Education:* Private tuition. *Career:* Sandy Powell Road Show, 1941; Alan Green, 1942; Waldini Gypsy Band, including Ensa overseas tour of War Zones: North Africa; Middle East; Far East; Europe, 1943–49; Wally Fry, 1949; Don Rico, 1952; Benny Freedman, 1953–63; Model Railways specialist, 1957–94; Television and radio broadcasts: BBC; All India Radio; Radio Solent; Radio Victory; Southern TV; Currently, Havant Symphony Orchestra. *Publications:* Featured in Frontline Theatre, Waldini; Mentioned in Life and Death of Peter Sellars, Evans. *Honours:* Italy Star; Burma Star; 1939/45 War and Victory Medals. *Memberships:* Musicians' Union; National Federation of Musical Societies. *Leisure interest:* Chamber Music. *Address:* 171 Fratton Rd, Portsmouth, Hampshire PO1 5ET, England.

SALUT Christian 'Ton-Ton'; b. 2 Feb. 1953, Montauban, France. Jazz Musician (drums, percussion). 2 d. *Education:* Literature, University of Toulouse. *Musical Education:* Certificate of Completion, Drummers Collective, New York City. *Career:* Founder, Ton-Ton Quartet, 1980–84; Accompanist for soloists including: Sonny Stitt; Siegfried Kessler; Guy Lafitte; Michel Roques; Founder, Drumpact, 1986–; Tours: Germany; Switzerland; Austria; Netherlands; Denmark; Spain; Africa (Cameroon, Nigeria); Festivals with Drumpact include: Hyères; Madrid; Berlin; Marciac; Visits and concerts, Boston, New York; Tour with Drumpact and Ballet-Theatre Le Baobab, of Yaoundé; Freelance musician with Christian Escoudé; Jack Walrath; Glenn Ferris; Hein Van de Geyn; Also played with: Magali Piétri; Yéko-Lé-Bop; Black 'n' Blue; Big Band 31 (including festivals: Vienna, Nice, Ramatuelle, Tarbes); Concerts, tours with: Christian Escoudé; Lou Bennett; Tony Pagnao; Jay Cameron; Daniel Huck; Peter King; Ted Curson; Eric Lelann; Andrew White; Turk Mauro; Jazz teacher, Conservatoire National de Région de Toulouse; Festival of Saint-Louis, Senegal, 1997–98. *Composition:* Creation for a Double Trio, in festival, Jazz sur Son 31, 1997; Ali Aba, 1994; Train Fou, 1997. *Recordings:* with Drumpact: Journey Into The World; Percussion Unlimited; New Music; with Big Band 31: Big Band; Billie; Nobody Knows, with Magali Pietri; Mauresaca, Jazz Time Big Band; Samantha's Dance, Steve Mabry, 1993; Ali-Aba, 1993; Abdu Salim Quintet, 1995; Street Music, Sonny Simmons, 1997; Don't Stop the Carnival, Hip Jazz Trio, 1997; Be Hip Be Bop, 2001. *Honour:* Nominated to: Victoires de la Musique (Jazz). *Membership:* UMJ (Union of Jazz Musicians). *Leisure interest:* Literature. *Current Management:* Jazz Unit. *Address:* 8 rue Lakanal, 31000 Toulouse, France.

SALUZZI Dino; b. Campo Tanta, Argentina. Musician (Bandoneon, Flute); Composer. *Career:* Several European, US and South American Tours including with George Gruntz, Mark Egan, Charlie Haden, Palle Mikkelbourg, Bob Moses and Enrico Rava. *Recordings:* Kultrum; Once Upon a Time; Volver; Andina. *Current Management:* Karen Kindig, c/o Blue Cat Agency, PO Box 399, Novato, CA 94948, USA.

SAMBORA Richie; b. 1 July 1959. Musician (guitar); Singer; Songwriter. *Career:* Guitarist, US rock group Bon Jovi, 1983–; Appearances include: Regular world-wide tours; Donington Monsters of Rock Festival, 1987; Moscow Music Peace Festival, 1989; Solo US tour, 1991; Solo appearance, Late Night With David Letterman, 1991; Solo performance, KISS Radio's 13th Anniversary Concert, Massachusetts, 1992; Numerous hit compositions with Jon Bon Jovi and Desmond Child. *Recordings:* Singles include: with Bon Jovi: You Give Love A Bad Name; Livin' On A Prayer; Wanted Dead Or Alive; Bad Medicine; Born To Be My Baby; I'll Be There For You; Miracle; Bed of Roses; In These Arms; I'll Sleep When I'm Dead; I Believe; These Days; Solo: The Wind Cries Mary (featured in film The Adventures of Ford Fairlane); Ballad of Youth; Albums with Bon Jovi: Bon Jovi, 1984; 7800° Fahrenheit, 1985; Slippery When Wet, 1986; New Jersey, 1988; Keep The Faith, 1992; Crossroads, 1994; These Days, 1995; Solo albums: Stranger In This Town, 1991; Undiscovered Soul, 1999; Contributor to Tribute To Muddy Waters album, 1993; Undiscovered Soul, 1998. *Honours include:* Best Stage Performance, MTV Music Video awards, 1987; All Bon Jovi albums Gold or Platinum status. *Current Management:* c/o Bon Jovi Mgmt, 248 W 17th St Apt 501, New York, NY 10011–5330.

SAMKOPF Kjell; b. 6 April 1952, Baerum, Norway. Composer; Percussionist. m. Mona Walderhaug, 23 July 1994, 2 s. *Education:* Diploma in Composition, 1977, Degree in Percussion, 1978, Norwegian State Academy of Music; Studied jazz vibraphone at the Berklee College of Music, Boston, Massachusetts, 1979. *Career:* Timpanist, Trondheim Symphony Orchestra, Norway, 1974–75; Freelance Percussionist with the Norwegian Opera Orchestra and the Oslo Philharmonic Orchestra, 1975–82; Teacher of Percussion, East Norway Conservatory, 1979–85; Head of Percussion Department, 1988-, currently Professor, Norwegian State Academy of Music. *Compositions:* Associations, for large orchestra with live electronics and 4-channel tape, 1984; Invention No 5, for solo percussion and electronics, 1981; Aqua, for tape and two percussionists, 1986; Tide, for 5 tapes, 1990; Harstad, for symphonic band and percussion solist, 1991; Did You Sing This For Grieg?, electroacoustic, 1993; Mårådalen Walk, electroacoustic, 1994; Bergen, for woodwind quintet and two percussion players, 1996. *Recordings:* Invention No 5; On The Way; Because of GH; Intention, solo percussion with electronics; Asphyxy; Positive Frustrations; Waltz Around The Circle; Intention; Blues Extract (with Sandvika Storband); Aqua (with Rob Waring Duo); Did You Sing This For Grieg?, electroacoustic; Self-Portrait; Invention No 3, solo piece for snare drum; Tokke Kraftverk; Mårådalen Walk, electroacoustic; Mountain Listening, 1998. *Publications:* Practical Drum Method, Vols 1a, 1b, 2, 1981. *Honours:* Concours International de Composition de la Ville du Havre, Special Mention of the Jury for Harstad. *Memberships:* Vice-President, Society of Norwegian Composers, 1988–90; President of the Board, Norwegian Music Information Centre, 1994–95. *Address:* Rudshagen 8, 3430 Spikkestad, Norway.

SAMS Dean; b. 3 Aug. 1966, Garland, Texas, USA. Country vocalist; Musician (keyboards, harmonica); Songwriter. *Education:* Southwest Texas State University. *Career:* Attended college for three years before moving to Nashville to pursue a career in country music, late 1980s; Secured a job at Opryland Theme Park singing in Country Music USA show; Had 16-track recording studio, engineered and produced demos for self and others; Formed Texasee with Richie McDonald, Keech Rainwater, Michael Britt and John Rich, 1992; Group became resident house band at the Wildhorse Saloon, Nashville; After subsequent name change to Lonestar, came to the attention of BMG and were signed to their BNA subsidiary; Released promotional six-track live CD, recorded at the Wildhorse; First country chart entry No News/Tequila Talkin' from debut album Lonestar, 1996; Single, Amazed, from third album became huge international hit and career record to date, 1999; By early 2000s, Lonestar estimated to be the most successful country group in the world; Developed parallel career outside of Lonestar; Co-wrote I'm Willing To Try from Joe Diffie's Life's So Funny album, 1995; Regular collaborations with other Nashville writers; Appeared in the film New Horizons directed by Tony Tarantino, 2001. *Compositions include:* I'm Willing To Try. *Recordings include:* No News, Tequila Talkin', 1996; Come Cryin' To Me, You Walked In, 1997; Say When, Everything's Changed, 1998; Amazed, Smile, 1999; I'm Already There, 2002; Albums include: Lonestar, 1995; Crazy Nights, 1997; Lonely Grill, 1999; I'm Already There, 2001. *Leisure interests:* Time with family; Working at home recording studio; Sports, particularly motor racing; Sony Playstation. *Address:* c/o Country Music Asscn, Nashville, Tennessee, USA.

SAMSING Freddy; b. 29 June 1946, Copenhagen, Denmark. Musician (Cathedral Organ). m. Anita Hyldgård Samsing, 11 Oct. 1997, 1 s., 2 d. *Education:* Royal Danish Academy of Music, Copenhagen, studied conducting. *Career:* International concert player, Northern Europe; Solo appearances on TV and Radio; Solo appearances with almost all Danish Symphony Orchestras. *Recordings:* As Soloist/Accompanist: Works by Albinoni, Bach, Vivaldi, Monteverdi; Trio with two outstanding trumpet players, Hovaldt and Son; Solo trumpet by the Royal Danish Orchestra. *Honour:* Jury Mem., International Organ Competition, Odense, Denmark. *Membership:* DOKS. *Leisure interest:* Astronomy. *Address:* Fangel Bygade 34, Fangel 5260, Odense 5, Denmark.

SAMUEL Julie; b. 15 May 1949, London, England. Music Man. Widow, 1 d. *Musical Education:* Italia Conti Stage School, London. *Career:* Began as actress, singer, 1962; Appeared in over 100 television shows, 10 films,

numerous stage plays; Started Music Management, 1980; Now Artist manager for rock group Mexico 70; Sarah Cracknell (vocalist with Saint Etienne); Janey Lee Grace (recording artist, television presenter, DJ for Virgin Radio); Donna Air, Janey Hoy, Vicky Taylor (vocal act from Byker Grove). *Honours:* Silver discs, So Tough; Fox Base Alpha; Platinum album, Smash Hits '91. *Leisure interests:* Swimming; Films; Travel. *Current Management:* Diamond Sounds Music Management, The Fox and Punchbowl, Burfield, Old Windsor, Berks Sl4 2RD, England.

SAMUELS Elaine Mary; b. 17 Sept. 1962, Hampton, Middlesex, England. Singer; Songwriter; Folk Blues and Bluegrass Musician (guitar, banjo, cittern, dulcimer, bodhran). m. Michael Paul Samuels, 23 July 1982, 1 s. *Education:* Electrical Engineering Degree. *Career:* Featured on HTV singing own songs; Appearances: Wire TV; BBC radio stations: Kent; Cambridge; Essex; Oxford; Suffolk; Kingston FM; Wey Valley Radio; Atlantis Radio, Belgium; Played at: Barbican; Marquee; Weavers; Half Moon; Mean Fiddler; Tour throughout UK, including Glastonbury, 1995. *Recordings:* Albums: Solo: Obsession; Reach Out For Me; Blue Skies; Dragonfire; with Now and Then: New Country; Best of British Bluegrass, Vol. 1. *Honours:* Second place, Leicester's Live At The Y (song competition). *Membership:* Musicians' Union. *Leisure interests:* Canoeing; Art; Sport; Youth work. *Address:* 55C Sheen Rd, Richmond, Surrey TW9 1YH, England.

SANBORN David; b. 30 July 1945, Tampa, Florida, USA. Musician (alto saxophone). *Career:* Member, Paul Butterfield group; Leading session player with artists including: David Bowie; James Taylor; Stevie Wonder; Albert King; Solo recording artiste, 1975-. *Recordings:* Albums: Taking Off, 1975; David Sanborn, 1976; Promise Me The Moon, 1977; Heart To Heart, 1978; Hideaway, 1980; Voyeur, 1981; As We Speak, 1982; Backstreet, 1983; Straight To The Heart, 1984; Double Vision (with Bob James), 1986; A Change of Heart, 1987; Close Up, 1988; Another Hand, 1991; Upfront, 1992; Hearsay, 1994; Pearls, 1995; Songs From The Night Before, 1996; Inside, 1999; Love and Happiness, 1999; Camel Island, 1999; I Told U So, 1999; Recent Singles: Got to Give it, 1994; Everything Must Change, 1995. *Honour:* Grammy Award, Voyeur, 1982. *Address:* c/o Patrick Rains and Associates, 1543 Seventh St, Third Floor, Santa Monica, CA 90401, USA.

SANBOWER Jack Douglas; b. 14 Sept. 1960, Waynesboro, Pennsylvania, USA. Bluegrass Musician (banjo, guitar, bass). m. Albina Marie, 19 Feb. 1983, 1 s., 1 d. *Education:* AA Degree Data Processing. *Musical Education:* Self-taught. *Career:* Performed at Bluegrass festivals, USA, include: Gettysburg, Pennsylvania; Bass Mountain, North Carolina; Lazy River, New York; Wind Gap, Pennsylvania; Wellsboro, Pennsylvania; Leader, No Leeway Band. *Recordings:* Four Leaf Clover Breakdown, 1983; Before The Weekend's Over, 1986; Jack In the Box, 1989; Traveling Down This Lonesome Road, 1991; Just Monkeyin' Around, 1990; Throwing Caution To The Wind, 1991; Finger Pickin' For Supper, 1992; Let Loose, 1993; Thinking of Old Memories, 1994. *Memberships:* International Bluegrass Music Asscn; Tri-State Bluegrass Asscn. *Leisure interests:* Computers; Fishing; Couch potato. *Address:* 14461 Edgemont Rd, Smithsburg, MD 21783, USA.

SANCHEZ David, (Jose David Sanchez DeLeon); b. 3 Sept. 1968, Hato Rey, Puerto Rico. Jazz Musician (tenor/soprano saxophones). *Education:* Psychology, University of Puerto Rico. *Musical Education:* Rutgers University. *Career:* Dizzy Gillespie and The United Nation Orchestra, 1991–92; An Evening with Dizzy Gillespie and Miriam Makeba, 1992; Dizzy Gillespie Diamond Jubilee Tribute Concerts, 1992; Phillip Morris Superband Tour, 1992; Member, Slide Hampton and The Jazzmasters, 1993–95; Leader, David Sanchez Quintet, 1994–99; Leader, David Sanchez Sextet, 1999-. *Recordings:* With Dizzy Gillespie: To Bird With Love, 1992; Bird Songs, recorded 1992, released 1997; With Slide Hampton and The Jazzmasters, To Diz With Love, 1993; With Roy Hargrove's Crisol, Habana, 1997; With Roy Haynes, Praise, 1998; As leader: The Departure, 1994; Sketches of Dreams, 1995; Street Scenes, 1996; Obsession, 1998. *Memberships:* AFofM; BMI. *Leisure interests:* Films; Multicultural music research. *Current Management:* Charismic Productions, 2604 Mozart Pl. W, Washington, DC 20009, USA.

SANCHEZ Paco; b. 7 June 1956, Murcia, Spain. Musician (drums). *Education:* University of Human Sciences. *Musical Education:* Paris VII Conservatory. *Career:* Played with the International Orchestra of Tchicai John in Denmark and Morocco; Played in West Africa; Benin; Festival of Brazzville, Bangui; Trio Soledad, France. *Recordings:* Soledad, with Carlos Acciari and Michel Fernandez; Narvalo, Gypsy Flamenco Music, 1998; Danza Fuego, Flamenco Poetry, 1998; Adam Del Monte, Heart and Soul: Romantic Dedications, 1999. *Honours:* First Excellency Prize. *Membership:* SACEM. *Current Management:* RDC Records. *Address:* 16 rue du Transvaal, 75020 Paris, France.

SANCHEZ Roger, (The S-Man, Roger S, Funk Junkeez, The Neanderthal); b. 1 June 1967, New York City, New York, USA. Prod.; Remixer; DJ. *Career:* Began as a New York club DJ; Progressed to producing, recording for Strictly Rhythm in New York; Founder: R-Senal Records; Presents weekly radio show on London radio station Kiss 100 FM; Collaborations: Armand Van Helden; Todd Terry; Judy Cheeks; Kathy Sledge; Remixed: Juliet Roberts; Incognito; Brand New Heavies; Michael Jackson. *Recordings:* Albums: First Contact, 2001; Singles: Luv Dancin' (as Underground Solution), 1991; Time 2 Stop (as The S-Man), 1994; Got Funk (as Funk Junkeez), 1997; I Never Knew (with Cooly's Hot Box), 1999; Another Chance, 2001. *Address:* c/o Defected Records, 14–15 D'arblay St, London, W1F 8DY, England.

SANDERS Kevin Bruce; b. 22 May 1962, Torquay, Devon, England. Freelance Musician (double bass, bass guitar); Arranger. m. 6 June 1987, 1 d. *Education:* College. *Musical Education:* Private classical double bass tuition. *Career:* Started with Dennis Rowland Trio; Later joined Lawrie Dixon Trio; Since worked with: Mornington Lockett; Kathy Stobart; Don Weller; Michael Hashim; Tony Lee; Stan Grieg; Worked with Dave Thompson Quartet, 1992–94; Lectured in bass studies at Dartington College of Arts; Runs successful 7-piece soul and blues review Rhythm Machine and contemporary jazz ensemble. *Recordings:* Rayas Pictures, 1992. *Honours:* Musicians' Union Award, Most Promising Bass Player, 1984. *Membership:* Musicians' Union. *Leisure interests:* Cooking; Motorcycling. *Current Management:* Music à la Carte Ent. Services; Bette Holman (For Rhythm Machine). *Address:* 30 Elm Park, Paignton, Devon TQ3 3QH, England.

SANDERS Tim Bryan; b. 16 April 1962, Stoke-on-Trent, Staffordshire, England. Vocalist; Songwriter. m. Jynine James, 1 May 1993, 3 s. *Education:* Music and Law Studies at Cauldon College. *Musical Education:* Guitar tuition; Private tuition for music reading, Cauldon College. *Career:* Formed the City Zones in 1979; Re-formed in 1992; Appeared in BBC Radio live sessions; Appeared on television with Toyah; Supported many early 1980s artists; Actor, Joy Swift's original Murder Weekends, German Satellite TV and BBC TV, 1990–91; Movie soundtrack co-written and recorded by Legendary Lonnie, 1994–95. *Compositions:* Don't Stop Me Now, co-written with Muchin/Ainsworth/O'Dowd, 1996. *Recordings:* La Maison De L'Amour, The City Zones, 1992; Live At The BBC, The City Zones, 1992; Born To Win; Knock Me Down Pick Me Up; Pain of Love; When I Dream; Spoils of Humanity; Past Shadows; Knock Me Down Pick Me Up, Legendary Lonnie, 1994; Sexual Affection, Stacy Grant, 2001. *Publications:* Collections of works. *Honours:* Presentation Disc for sales of La Maison De l'Amour and Pain of Love (released by Jynine James and Peter Frampton), Mr and Mrs Music Publishing, 1992, 1993. *Memberships:* PAMRA; PRS; MCPS. *Leisure interests:* Badminton; Listening to music. *Current Management:* Fast Tracks Records; Mr and Mrs Music Publishing; Djamus Ltd. *Address:* c/o Fast Tracks Records, 11 Maen Gwyn, Tan-y-Gopa Parc, Abergele, Clwyd, LL72 7BZ, Wales.

SANDIRA; b. 27 Aug. 1958, Opotiki, New Zealand. Musician (percussion); Vocalist; Programmer. *Musical Education:* Musical tuition with Nemoi Aquam (Speedy). *Career:* Tours of UK, Europe, with: The Shamen; Loop Guru; Counterfeit Stones; Denise Black and the Kray Sisters; Television and radio with above; Played Phoenix Festival as Sandira; Festivals include: Glastonbury; WOMAD; Reading; Phoenix. *Recordings:* Singles: Solo: Ishmar Du Bach; Single by Loop Guru, 1995; Also featured on albums by Labi Siffre; Loop Guru. *Membership:* Musicians' Union. *Leisure interests:* Diving; Gardening; Travel. *Current Management:* None. *Address:* 14 Drayton Rd, London NW10 4EL, England.

SANDKE Randy; b. 23 May 1949, Chicago, Illinois, USA. Composer; Arranger; Musician (Trumpet). m. Karen Kelly, 15 Sept. 1990. *Education:* University of Chicago Lab School; Indiana University; Studied TPT with Renold Shilke, Vince Penzerella; Arranging with Oliver Nelson; Composing with Henry Brant and Easley Blackwood. *Career:* TPT with Benny Goodman, 1985–86, with Buck Clayton, 1986–90; Concord Recording Artist, 1993–; Written several suites for Carnegie Hall Jazz Band; Performed on soundtracks of 3 Woody Allen films. *Compositions:* Orphic Mystery, 1997; Overture For the Year 2000, 1997. *Recordings:* NY Stories, 1986; I Hear Music, 1993; Get Happy, 1994; The Chase, 1995; Calling All Cats, 1996; Awakening, 1997; Count Basie Remembered, 1998. *Publications:* Introduction to Metatonal Music, 1997; Bix Beiderbecke From a Musician's Perspective, 1998; Annual Review of Jazz Studies. *Memberships:* NARAS; IAJRC; Musicians' Union Local 802. *Address:* 213 1/2 Bergen St, Brooklyn, New York, 11217, USA.

SANDOVAL Arturo; b. 6 Nov. 1949, Artemisia, Cuba. Musician (trumpet); Prof. m. Marianela, 17 Oct. 1975, 1 s. *Musical Education:* National Music Institute, Havana, Cuba. *Career:* Full Professor (tenure), Florida International University; Musician; Appearances: with Irakere, 1972–81; World tours, 1980–; United Nations Band; Sandoval Group, 1981; Dizzy Gillespie, 1987–91; Television includes: Super Bowl Halftime Event, 1995; King Orange Disney New Year's show, 1995; Tonight Show; David Letterman; Arsenio Hall; HBO; CNN; Summit of The Americas, Grammy Awards; Academy Awards with Celine Dion. *Recordings:* Live At Royal Festival Hall, Dizzy Gillespie; Danzón; Flight To Freedom; Dream Come

True; I Remember Clifford; Latin Train; The Classical Album; Swinging; Sandoval's Hot House; Perez Family soundtrack; Mambo Kings Soundtrack. *Publications:* Hal Leonard 4 Trumpet Method Books. *Honours:* Grammy, Best Latin Album, Irakere II; Danzón; 11 Grammy Nominations; 2 Billboard International Jazz, Jazz Central Station Best Latin Jazz Artist Award; Disney Music Hall of Fame, 1994; 4 Scholarships given in his name at various USA universities. *Memberships:* ITG; IAJE; NARAS. *Leisure interest:* Baseball. *Current Management:* Carl Valldejuli, Turi's Music Ent Inc. *Address:* 103 Westward Dr., Miami Springs, FL 33166, USA.

SANDREN Heikki; b. 1 June 1960, Finland. Musician (drums). *Musical Education:* Clarinet and drums; Sibelius Acadmey, Helsinki. *Career:* Began in music shop, early 1980s; Became professional musician; Member, Pekka Toivanen quartet; Played for Severi Pyysalo's No Hope Band; Stayed with Pyysalo's reformed band The Front; Played on tour with leading Finnish trumpeter Markku Johansson. *Address:* Lönnrotinkatu 23 B 31, 00120 Helsinki, Finland.

SANDRESKY Eleanor; b. 5 Oct. 1957, NC, USA. Composer; Musician (Piano). m. Dan Russell Dryden. *Education:* North Carolina School of Arts; Wisconsin Conservatory of Music; Eastman School of Music; Yale University School of Music. *Career:* Performed with Philip Glass Ensemble, 1991–; Co Artistic Director, Producer, Music at the Anthology, NY; Freelance Composer, Pianist, NY. *Compositions:* Mathematically Inclined; Its Come Undone; Regarding Women; My Goddess. *Recordings:* La Belle et le Bete; Complete Works of William Russell. *Honours:* Ascap Special Award, 1998, 1999; Grants from Meet the Composer Jerome Foundation and NYSCA; Most Promising Composer Award, from Yale School of Music. *Memberships:* American Music Centre; American Composers Forum; ASCAP. *Address:* 81 Warren St, New York, NY 10007, USA.

SANDS Colum; b. 26 May 1951, Newry, Ireland. Singer; Songwriter; Musician. m. Barbara Wendel, 3 May 1978, 3 s., 1 d. *Career:* Tours with Sands Family, 1972-, USA (including Carnegie Hall), Canada, Ireland, England, Germany, Belgium, France, Spain, Portugal, Netherlands, Switzerland, Austria, Italy, Poland, Luxembourg. *Compositions:* Solo albums: Unapproved Road, 1981; March Ditch, 1989; All My Winding Journeys, 1996; Songs include: Whatever You Say, Say Nothing; Almost Every Circumstance; The Man with the Cap; Looking the Loan of a Spade. *Publications:* Between the Earth and the Sky, song book, 2001. *Honour:* Living Tradition Award, Glasgow, 1996. *Memberships:* PRS; MCPS. *Current Management:* Spring Records. *Address:* 50 Shore Rd, Rostrevor, County Down, BT34 3EW, Ireland.

SANDS Tommy; b. 19 Dec. 1945, Mayobridge, Co Down, Northern Ireland. Singer; Songwriter; Musician (Guitar, Whistle, Banjo, Bodhran). m. Katrine Bescond, 1 s., 1 d. *Education:* Latin, Philosophy, Newry St Colman's College, St Patrick's Carlow. *Career:* Began playing with Sands Family, first album, 1968; Concerts, Carnegie Hall, New York, USA, 1972; Federick Palast, Berlin, 1974; Moscow Olympic Stadium, solo; Numerous world tours including appearances with Miriam Makeba; Harry Belafonte; Pete Seeger; Mikis Theodorakis. *Compositions:* There Were Roses; Daughters and Sons; Dresden; Music of Healing, with Pete Seeger; Sudako and 1000 Paper Cranes; Sarajevo, with Vedran Smailovic and Joan Baez. *Recordings:* 5 solo albums: Singing of the Times, 1985; Beyond the Shadows, 1992; Down By Bendys Lane, 1993; Hedges of County Down, 1994; The Hearts A Wonder, 1995; 20 albums with the Sands Family. *Publication:* Tommy Sands Song Book, 1986. *Honours:* Best Irish Single of the Year, There Were Roses, 1986; Living Tradition Award, 1995. *Memberships:* PRS; MCPS; MIMA. *Leisure interests:* Sport; Community Work. *Current Management:* Katrine Bescond, Spring Records.

SANGARE Oumou; b. 1968, Bamako, Mali. Singer; Songwriter. m. Ousmane Haidara, 1 c. *Career:* Began singing age 5; First performance, Stade des Omnisports, age 6; Member, National Ensemble of Mali; Djioliba percussion, 1986–89; Solo artiste, with own backing group, 1989–; Concerts: Regular tours, West Africa; Europe; First US concert, 1994; Radio includes: BBC Radio 1 session, Andy Kershaw; Television includes: The Late Show, BBC2; Campaigner, Women's Rights, Mali. *Recordings:* Moussolou (Women), 1990; Ko Sira (Marriage Today), 1993; Worotan, 1996; Appears on: African Blues, 1998; Beloved, 1998; Also recording with Ali Farka Touré. *Honours:* Best Selling African Album of Year, Moussolou, 1990; European World Music Album of the Year, Ko Sira, 1993; Performance of the Year, 1993; Numerous African Music Awards. *Current Management:* Wim Westerweldt. *Address:* c/o World Circuit Records, 106 Cleveland St, London W1P 5DP, England.

SANLUCAR Manolo; b. 24 Nov. 1943, Sanlucar De Barrameda, Cádiz, Spain. Composer; Musician (Flamenco Guitar). *Education:* Learnt to play guitar with father (famous Flamenco Guitarist). *Career:* Musical Director, Sevillanas A Carlos Saura, film; La Gallarda, Rafael Alberti. *Compositions:* Medea, composed for Ballet Nacional De España; Tauromagia; Solea.

Honours: Prize Spanish Guitarist, Record World, USA, 1978; First Prize, Mundial Competition of Guitar, Italy, 1972. *Current Management:* Intercambio De Cultura Y Arte. *Address:* c/Carretas, 14–5 I-5, 28012 Madrid, Spain.

SANSOM Frank Roger Charles; b. 3 Dec. 1946, London, England. Co Dir. m. Frances Sansom, 27 March 1976, 2 s., 1 d. *Education:* Christopher Wren, Gloucestershire and Wimbledon College of Art. *Musical Education:* Jack Jackson: Ready Steady Go; 6 5 Special. *Career:* Art Director, BandC Records, 1971; Marketing Director, Charisma Records, 1973–78; Management, 1979–81; Set up First Bill Ltd (First Independent Tele-Sales Team), 1981; First Strike, 1985; Sold companies to Stylus Music, 1987; TV Marketing Consultant, 1987–90; Managing Director, shareholder, Pulse Records launched 1990–95. *Membership:* BPI. *Leisure interests:* Swimming; Horse racing; Football; Rugby. *Address:* 53A Hereford Rd, Bayswater, London, W2 5BB, England.

SANTAMARIA Mongo (Ramón); b. 7 April 1927, Havana, Cuba. Bandleader. *Career:* Played with first charanga band, led by Gilberto Valdés; Also played with Pérez Prado; Tito Puente, 1951–57; Formed own charanga and Latin fusion groups; Hired and developed artists including Chick Corea; La Lupe; Herbert Laws; Marty Sheller. *Recordings:* Albums include: Changó, 1955; Yambú, 1958; Concert On The Campus, 1960; Our Man In Havana, 1960; Live and Direct, 1960; Más Sabroso, 1962; Viva Mongo!, 1962; Go, Mongo!, 1962; Mongo Introduces La Lupe, 1963; Mongo At The Village Gate, 1963; Mongo Explodes, 1964; El Pussy Cat, 1965; La Bamba, 1965; Hey! Let's Party, 1966; El Bravo!, 1966; Mongo Santamaria, Explodes At The Village Gate, 1967; Soul Bag, 1968; Stone Soul, 1969; Workin' On A Groovy Thing, 1969; Feelin' Alright, 1970; Mongo '70, 1970; Mongo At Montreux, 1971; At Yankee Stadium, 1974; Dawn (Amanecer), 1977; Red Hot, 1979; Mambo Show, 1990; Live At Jazz Alley, 1990; Other recordings with: Tito Puente; Cal Tjader; Joe Loco; Bob James and Charlie Palmieri; Toots Thielemans and Dizzy Gillespie; Justo Betancourt; The Fania All Stars. *Honours:* Grammy Award, Dawn (Amanecer), 1977. *Current Management:* Jack Hooke, 568 Broadway, Suite 806, New York, NY 10012, USA.

SANTANA Carlos; b. 20 July 1947, Autlan de Navarro, Mexico. Musician (guitar); Vocalist. m. Deborah, April 1973. *Career:* Played Tijuana nightclubs; Recorded with Mike Bloomfield and Al Kooper; Founder, Santana Blues Band, 1966; Played club circuit, San Francisco; Major concerts include: Woodstock, 1969; Texas International Pop Festival, 1969; Bath Festival, 1970; Crystal Palace Garden Party, 1977; California Jam II, audience of 250,000, 1978; US Festival, 1982; Support to Bob Dylan, Europe, 1983; Live Aid, Philadelphia, 1985; Peace Concert, Moscow, 1987; Freedom World Tour, 1987; Rock In Rio II Festival, Brazil, 1991; Laughter, Love and Music memorial concert, San Francisco, 1991; Performed/recorded with: Buddy Miles; McCoy Tyner; Jose Feliciano; Herbie Hancock; Wayne Shorter and Alice Coltrane; Aretha Franklin; Producer, music for La Bamba, 1986; Founder, own record company Guts and Grace, 1989. *Recordings:* Albums include: Santana, 1969; Abraxas, 1971; Santana III, 1971; Carlos Santana and Buddy Miles, Live!, 1972; Caravanserai, 1972; Love Devotion Surrender, with Mahavishnu John McLaughlin, 1973; Welcome, 1973; Santana's Greatest Hits, 1974; Illuminations, with Alice Coltrane, 1974; Borboletta, 1974; Amigos, 1976; Festival, 1977; Moonflower, 1977; Inner Secrets, 1978; Orness/Silver Dreams – Golden Reality, 1979; Marathon, 1980; Zebop!, 1981; Havana Moon, 1983; Beyond Appearances, 1985; Blues For Salvador, 1987; Viva Santana, 1988; Spirits Dancing In The Flesh, 1990; Milagro, 1992; Sacred Fire, 1993; Brothers, 1994; Dance Of The Rainbow Serpent (box set), 1995; Evolution: Original Recordings, 1995; Live at Fillmore 1968, 1997; Supernatural, 1999; Acapulco Sunrise, 1999; Contributor, The Live Adventures of Al Kooper and Mike Bloomfield, 1969; Featured on: The Healer, John Lee Hooker, 1989; Tribute To Muddy Waters, 1993; Singles include: Evil Ways, 1970; Black Magic Woman, 1971; Oye Como Va, 1971; Everybody's Everything, 1971; She's Not There, 1977; Stormy, 1979; Winning, 1981; Hold On, 1982; Smooth (no. 1, USA), 2000; María María (No. 1, USA), 2000. *Honours:* Grammy Award, Best Rock Instrumental Performance, 1989; Bay Area Music Awards: Outstanding Guitarist, 1992; Musician of The Year, 1993; Legend Award, Nosotros Golden Eagle Awards, 1992; Gold Medal Award, 1977; Numerous Gold discs; Grammy Awards, 2000, including Song Of The Year, Record Of The Year, Pop Performance Of The Year, Rock Performance Of The Year, Rock Instrumental Performance, Rock Album. *Current Management:* Santana Management. *Address:* PO Box 10348, San Rafael, CA 94912–0348, USA.

SANTIAGO Joey; b. 10 June 1965, Manila, Philippines. Musician (Guitar). *Career:* Formed The Pixies with Frank Black; Early support slots to Throwing Muses; Numerous tours and festival dates; Some television appearances; Band split, 1993; Worked with Frank Black on his solo material; Formed The Martinis, with David Lovering, 1995. *Recordings:* Singles: Gigantic; Monkey Gone to Heaven; Here Comes Your Man; Velouria; Dig for Fire; Planet of Sound; Head On; Debaser; Albums: Come on Pilgrim; Surfer Rosa; Doolittle; Bossanova; Trompe le Monde.

SAPUNDZIJEV Mary; b. 16 Feb. 1965, Melbourne, Victoria, Australia. Musicologist; Musician (piano). *Musical Education:* BA (Music Major), 1986, BA Hons (Music), 1988, PhD (Music), 1997, Monash University. *Career:* Pianist, Accompanist, Musicologist, Dancer and Choreographer; Artistic Director, Folk dance company, 1984–92; Film appearance, The John Sullivan Story, 1979; Stage appearances, Sale of the Century, 1983–86; Production Assistant, ethnic radio, Victoria; Dancer and Co-organizer of cultural festivals throughout Australia, including Multicultural Arts festival, Victoria, and Miss Yugoslav of Australia. *Publications:* Politics in Music – Music of Politics: The Choral Miniature Repertoire of First Generation Macedonian Composers, forthcoming. *Honours:* Shared Ernst Morawetz Prize for Music, Monash University Music Department, 1987; Australian Postgraduate Research Award, 1988–91; Various certificates, tokens and awards from ethnic artistic associations throughout Australia. *Memberships:* Australian Music Centre; Australian Musicological Society; International Council for Traditional Music; International Musicological Society; Board Mem., Multicultural Arts Vic, 1984–89; Artistic Director, Yugoslav Cultural Artistic Asscn, Melbourne, 1984–92. *Leisure interests:* Composition; Songwriting; Arranging. *Address:* 11 Anne St, North Blackburn, Victoria 3130, Australia.

SARA K; b. 16 May 1956, Dallas, Texas, USA. Singer; Songwriter; Musician (4 string guitar). 1 d. *Musical Education:* Art, music studies. *Career:* Chesky recording artist; PBS Radio Australia; Mountain Stage; US and international airplay. *Recordings:* Gypsy Alley; Closer Than They Appear; Play On Words; Tell Me I'm Not Dreamin', 1995; Hobo; 1997; No Cover, 1999; with Glad I'm a Girl: Glad I'm a Girl, 1997; Postman (music from the motion picture), 1997. *Honours:* Gypsy Alley, received 8 awards from New Mexico Music Industry Coalition including Best Album, 1990; Audio-Ohr award, Grammy, Play On Words album, 1994. *Leisure interests:* Hiking; Skiing; Windsurfing; Painting; Being mom. *Current Management:* Chesky Records, New York, New York. *Address:* PO Box 696, Ruidoso, NM 88345, USA.

SARIC Stanko; b. 26 June 1960, Stitar, Croatia. Musician (tambura – national instrument). m. Verca Saric (Salopek), 10 Nov. 1984, 1 s., 1 d. *Education:* Engineer of Architecture. *Musical Education:* Self-taught. *Career:* Appearances with group: Zlatni Dukati (Golden Coins), in biggest concert halls in Croatia; Tours all around the world: USA; Canada; Australia; Western Europe. *Recordings:* Patriotic songs: Don't Touch My Fields; Croatia In Me; Singing The Song About Croatia; Other popular songs: Crying Because of You; Tena; Marijana; High Road; Anica; To Whom Could I Give My Young Years; 13 albums; Christmas Songs; Classical Music. *Honours:* 10 Golden Records, many other awards. *Membership:* Croatian Musical Union. *Leisure interest:* Horse riding. *Current Management:* Josip Ivanovic. *Address:* Zlatni Dukati, Zatisje 8E, 41000, Zagreb, Croatia.

SARJEANT Derek; b. 7 June 1930, Chatham, Kent, England. Folk Singer; Musician (concertina, guitar, trumpet). m. (1) Diane Doherty, 23, Sept. 1966, 2 s., (2) Hazel King, 10 Sept. 1977, 1 s., 1 d. *Education:* Kingston College. *Career:* Member, jazz bands, leader, Golden Gate Jazzmen, 1950s; Pioneer, British Folk revival, 1960s; Organizer, one of Britain's largest Folk clubs, Surbiton and Kingston for 14 years; Assisted with Organisation of English Folk Dance and Songs Society's First Folk Festival, 1965; Radio and television, all British stations including: Hootenanny Show; Folk In Focus; Television commercials on all British independent channels, also USA; Tours solo, also with wife, Hazel: Folk clubs, concerts, festivals in UK, Europe, America; Work as session musician; Teaches Folk guitar at Adult Education Centre. *Recordings:* 24 albums, British and German labels. *Publications:* Books with records: How Do You Do, stages 1–5 (English Folk-songs For German Schools). *Honours:* First English Folk singer booked in Dublin Folkclub, 1962; Melody Maker Folk Medal of Year, Best First Record, Derek Sarjeant Sings English Folk-songs, 1962; Represented Britain, British Week, Stockholm, Sweden, 1968. *Membership:* Musicians' Union. *Leisure interests:* Collecting old musical instruments; Photography. *Current Management:* Assembly Artistes. *Address:* 4 Coneygar House, Coneygar Park, Bridport, Dorset DT6 3BA, England.

SARJEANT Hazel; b. 11 Oct. 1948, London, England. Folk Singer; Musician (guitar, concertina). m. Derek Sarjeant, 10 Sept. 1977, 1 s., 1 d. *Education:* Wimbledon College of Art; St Martin's College of Art; BA (Fine Arts). *Musical Education:* Trained in various choirs. *Career:* Resident singer, Surbiton Folkclub, 6 years; Frequent tours, concerts, festivals, folkclubs, UK, Europe and US; National radio and television; Film music for US. *Recordings:* 14 albums, cassettes, UK and German labels. *Honour:* BA Fine Arts; Winner, National Folk and Beat Final, Hammersmith Town Hall, 1967. *Memberships:* Musicians' Union; Royal College of Church Music. *Leisure interests:* Painting; Pottery; Travel. *Current Management:* Assembly Artists. *Address:* 4 Coneygar House, Coneygar Park, Bridport, Dorset DT6 3BA, England.

SARMANTO Heikki; b. 22 June 1939, Finland. Composer; Musician (piano). *Musical Education:* Music and language, Helsinki University and Sibelius Academy, 1962–64; Lessons with Margaret Chaloff, Berklee College of Music, Boston, US, 1968–71. *Career:* Regular visits to East Coast of US; Own ensemble became UMO (New Music Orchestra); Played Jazz Mass, Newport Festival, 1979. *Compositions include:* New Hope Jazz Mass (premiered in New York); Jazz Mass; Jazz opera; Songs to words by Finnish poets including: Edith Södergran; Laura Vita; Eino Leino; 3 suites for solists: Maija Hapuoja; Juhani Aaltonen; Pekka Sarmanto; Suomi, suite for jazz ensemble and strings; Passions of Man, ballet suite; Music for radio stories by Robert Shure: Man With A Sax; Felix The Great; Hearts (commissioned by WHO), 1995. *Honours include:* First prize, Jazz composition contest, Minneapolis, 1961; Yrjö Award, Finnish Jazz Federation, 1970. *Address:* Kankurinkatu 8 B 14, 00150 Helsinki, Finland.

SARMANTO Pekka; b. 15 Feb. 1945, Finland. Musician (bass). *Musical Education:* Sibelius Academy. *Career:* One of Finland's most recorded artists; Played with: Eero Koivisoinen, 1965–; Long term partnership playing with brother Heikki Sarmanto; Played at The Groovy Club, with artists including: Benny Carter; Toots Thielmans; Clifford Jordan; Joe Newman; Bob Berg; Tom Harrell; Member of UMO (New Music Orchestra), 1975–; Accompanist to numerous visiting foreign musicians; Festival appearances include: Warsaw; London; Paris; Newport; Montréal; Soloist, performance Heikki Sarmanto's suite, Song For My Brother, 1982; Duo with Juhani Aaltonen, 1980s. *Recordings include:* To A Finland Station, with Dizzy Gillespie and Arturo Sandoval, 1982; with Umo Jazz Orchestra: Umo Jazz Orchestra, 1998; with Thad Jones: That Jones Mel Lewis and Umo, 1998. *Honour:* Yrjö Award, Finnish Jazz Federation, 1978. *Address:* Albertinkatu 5 B 27, 00150 Helsinki, Finland.

SÁROSI Bálint; b. 1 Jan. 1925, Csikrákos, Harghita, Romania. Ethnomusicologist. m. Benkö Jolán, 18 Oct. 1952, 2 d. *Education:* PhD, University; Composition and Musicology, Liszt Ferenc High School of Music, Budapest, Hungary. *Career:* Research Fellow, Institute for Musicology, Budapest, 1956–, Director, Ethnomusicological Section, 1974–, retired, 1988; Lectures on folk music, Hungarian Radio, weekly programme, 1969–87; Guest Professor, University of Innsbruck, 1985–86, University of Göttingen, 1989, 1994; Invited Lecturer, most countries of Europe and USA, Japan, Armenia and Samarkand, Jerusalem. *Recordings:* Hungarian Instrumental Folk Music, 3 discs, 1980; Anthology of Hungarian Folk Music V and VI, 1993, 1995. *Publications:* Die Volksmusikinstrumente Ungarus, 1967; Gypsy Music, 1978; Folk Music, 1986; Sackpfeifer Zigeunermusikanten, 1999. *Honours:* Erkel Prize, 1976; Order of Labour, Golden Degree, 1988; Middle Cross of the Order of Hungarian Republic, 1995; Presidential Gold Medal, 2000. *Membership:* Executive Board, International Council for Traditional Music, 1978–91. *Address:* Aldás u 11, 1025 Budapest, Hungary.

SARPILA Antti Juhani; b. 11 June 1964, Helsinki, Finland. Musician (Clarinet, Saxophones). m. Minna Niemela, 23 April 1994, 3 s. *Education:* Private studies with Bob Wilber, USA, 1981–83. *Career:* Freelance Jazz Musician; Performances as soloist with different jazz orchestras world-wide including Tribute to Benny Goodman Concert at the Carnegie Hall, New York and Royal Ellington Concert at Royal Festival Hall, London. *Compositions:* Around 100 published compositions and arrangements, mostly recorded. *Recordings:* Numerous recordings under own name and around 50 recordings as guest musician. *Honour:* George Award, Finnish Jazz Federation, 1997. *Membership:* Finnish Composers and Authors Society. *Leisure interests:* Watercolour painting; Ornithology. *Address:* Museokatu 26 A 14, 00100 Helsinki, Finland.

SARSTEDT Peter; Folk Singer; Songwriter. m. Joanna. *Recordings:* Albums: Peter Sarstedt, 1969; PS..., 1979; Up Date, 1981; Asia Minor, 1987; Never Say Goodbye, 1987; with Eden Kane and Robin Sarstedt: Worlds Apart Together, 1973; Singles: I Am A Cathedral; Where Do You Go To My Lovely (No. 1, UK), 1969; Frozen Orange Juice, 1969; Beirut; Love Among The Ruins, 1982; Appears on: Acoustic Highway Collection, 1996. *Address:* c/o Jason West Agency, Kings Lynn, Norfolk, England.

SARTORIUS Paula; b. 18 Feb., New York, USA. Artist Man. *Education:* BA, Fordham University. *Career:* Artist Manager, Side One Management, for: Los Lobos; Luscious Jackson.

SASH! (Sascha Lappessen); b. 1971, Wuppertal, Germany. DJ; Prod. *Career:* Electrical Engineer; Started as DJ; Began producing as Sash!, with Thomas Lüdke and Ralf Kappmeier; Numerous gigs, television appearances and hit singles throughout Europe; Remixer for Jean-Michel Jarre and Dr Alban. *Recordings:* Singles: It's My Life, 1996; Ecuador, 1997; Erotmania 97, 1997; Stay, 1997; Encore Une Fois, 1997; La Primavera, 1998; Mysterious Times, 1998; Ma Baker, 1998; Colour the World, 1998; Adelante, 1999; Albums: It's My Life, 1997; Life Goes On, 1998.

SASHA (Alexander Coe); b. 4 Sept. 1969, Bangor, Wales. Prod.; Remixer; DJ. *Career:* Began DJ career at the Hacienda in Manchester, then Shelly's

in Stoke; World-wide DJ; Various mix compilations for Renaissance and Global Underground labels; Collaborations: Brian Transeau; Maria Nayler; Charlie May; Remixed: Urban Soul; M People; Mr Fingers; Madonna; Seal. *Recordings:* Singles: Appolonia (as BMEX), 1992; Arkham Asylum, 1996; Be As One (with Maria Nayler), 1996; Xpander, 1999; Scorchio (with Darren Emerson), 2000. *Honours:* Muzik Awards, Best DJ, 2001. *Address:* c/o Deconstruction, Bedford House, 69–79 Fulham High St, London, SW6 3JW, England.

SASSETTI Bernardo; b. 24 June 1970, Lisbon, Portugal. Musician (piano); Jazz Composer. *Musical Education:* Graduate, Lisbon Academy of Music. *Career:* Played with major jazz names including: John Stubblefield; Andy Sheppard; Frank Lacy; Al Grey; Art Farmer; Kenny Wheeler; Freddie Hubbard; Paquito d'Rivera; Benny Golson; Eddie Henderson; The United Nation Orchestra; Concerts in France; Spain; Italy; USA; South Africa; UK, including Ronnie Scott's, London. *Recordings:* Album: Salssetti, 1995; Andy Hamilton, Jamaica By Night, 1994; Carlos Martins, Passagem, 1997. *Honours:* Various local awards. *Membership:* Mem., Professor, Jazz School of HCP, Lisbon. *Current Management:* Paulo Santos Gil. *Address:* Rua Das Pracas, 66–1-DRT-1200, Lisbon, Portugal.

SATRIANI Joe; b. Long Island, New York, USA. Musician (guitar, banjo, harmonica); Educator. *Career:* Founder member, The Squares; Member, Greg Kihn Band; Solo artiste, 1984–; British tour, 1995; Guitar tutor to rock musicians Steve Vai, Kirk Hammett. *Recordings:* with Greg Kihn Band: Love and Rock 'N' Roll, 1986; Solo: Joe Satriani (EP), 1984; Not of This Earth, 1986; Surfing With The Alien, 1987; Dreaming II, 1988; Flying In A Blue Dream, 1990; Joe Satriani, 1995; Crystal Planet, 1998. *Honours:* Several Grammy Awards. *Current Management:* Bill Graham Management. *Address:* PO Box 429094, San Francisco, CA 94142–9094, USA.

SAUMAIWAI Chris Thompson; b. 14 Aug. 1943, Cleveland, Ohio, USA. Businesswoman; Ethnomusicologist; Composer; Poet. m. 2 s., 1 d. *Education:* Cleveland Baldwin Wallace College; Cleveland Institute of Music; Private composition student of Donald ERB, 1958–61; George F Strickling, CHHS Choir, 1959–63; Voice, Carmela Caffarelli, 1959–63; Oboe, Harvey McGuire, 1961–63; Music theory and composition, Baldwin Wallace Conservatory of Music, 1961–65; Music theory and composition, Cleveland Institute of Music, 1963–65. *Career:* Various hotels in Fiji, Hawaii and New Zealand as part of Counterstroke EWI benefit concerts including Suva Travelodge, Centra Suva, Wellington Park Royal Hotel, New Zealand; Also sang at Trigger Prince Kuhio Hotel, Honolulu. *Compositions:* Haiko Spring, Song Cycle; Sonnet II, Prayer of St Francis; The Waking; The Pasture; Supper Stew Blues; Could I Have Loved You More; Not Me Baby; Settler's Blues. *Publications:* Groves Dictionary of Music Vol. 12 Melanesia, Fiji; Music of Sem Conference, 1981; Fijian Lullabies and Games, Honolulu; Fiji Society, 1966; Music and Dance of Fiji Musical; Urban Fijian Musical Attitudes and Ideals (Music Cultures in Contact), 1993, Melbourne. *Memberships:* Muphi Epsilon Soroptimist International; Society for Ethnomusicology (Life Member). *Leisure interests:* Secretary, Counterstroke Fiji; Photography; Travel; Crafts; Musical Promotion. *Address:* PO Box 1206, Suva, Fiji.

SAUNDERS Cameron; b. 18 Feb. 1973, Cuxhaven, England. m. Louise Latham, 22 May 1994. *Education:* BA (Hons), Social Anthropology, King's College, Cambridge. *Career:* New Atlantic (1989–93); Extensive tours, UK, especially Scotland; Television: Hitman and Her, 1992; Top of The Pops, 1992; Radio: BBC Radio 1; Capital Radio; World Service; Interviews; Debut broadcast, Radio Berlin International (club of). *Recordings:* I Know; Into The Future; Take Off Some Time. *Honours:* Scottish Clubscene 1992: Best Newcomer, Runner-up best dance band. *Memberships:* Musicians' Union; PRS. *Leisure interests:* DJ; Clubbing; Reading. *Address:* 16 Shirdley Cres., Ainsdale, Southport PR8 3RR, England.

SAUNDERS Eddie (Edward John); b. 6 July 1965, London, England. Lead Vocalist; Composer; Lyricist; Musician (percussion, various other instruments). *Musical Education:* Self-taught. *Career:* Founder member, lead vocalist, Push; Lead and back-up vocals, Groove Nation; Extensive live appearances UK, Europe; Live work with the above, also: Reuben Wilson (Push was his UK pick-up band); Omar; Leon Ware; Jo Cang; Boogie Back All Stars; Support to Curtis Mayfield; Airto and Flora Purim; Maceo Parker; Average White Band. *Recordings:* Traffic, track on Acid Jazz and Other Illicit Grooves compilation (first ever Acid Jazz record), 1988; Further recordings with Push; Talbot/White; Jo Cang; Galliano; Groove Nation; Steve Beresford, Cue Sheets. *Memberships:* PRS; Musicians' Union; MCPS. *Leisure interests:* Sunshine; Travel; Languages; Food and Wine; Philosophy; Fitness; Annoying People. *Current Management:* Represented by Alexis Grower, McGrath and Co. *Address:* 18 Dartmouth Park Ave, London NW5 1JN, England.

SAUNDERS Gerry (Gerald Ivor Ewart); b. 3 Nov. 1929, Plymouth, Devon, England. Musician (percussion); Radio Presenter; Writer. *Career:*

ENSA, 1943–45; Theatre Pit, 1945–47; RAF, 1947–49; Big band/Orchestra tours, 1949–55; Magazine proprietor, broadcasting, writing, 1955–65; Jazz club proprietor (6 clubs), music/stage producer, jazz tours, 1965–80; Musical/stage tours, writing, band management, broadcasting, 1980–93; National Executive, South East District Council; Chairman Bournemouth Branch, Musicians' Union; Radio presenter; Writer; Jazz tours, 1980-. *Publications:* Playtime Entertainment Newspaper; Editor and Publisher, Secretary, Editor, Video Record. *Membership:* National Executive Musicians' Union; Chairman, British Citizens Band Confederation; Chief Executive, National Citizens Band Confederation; Chairman, Bournemouth Branch, Musicians' Union; Director, Coastal Radio, community radio station. *Leisure interests:* Leader, Just Jazz orchestra; Ham radio; Video photography; Neighbourhood Watch co-ordinator; Dorset Watch Liaison Group; Radio historian; After Dinner speaker; Jazz lecturer; Local charities support. *Address:* 12 Lincoln Ave, Springbourne, Bournemouth, Dorset BH1 4QS, England.

SAUNDERS Mark; b. 20 March 1959, Basingstoke, Hampshire, England. Mixing Engineer; Record Prod. *Recordings:* Albums: Raw Like Sushi, Neneh Cherry; Wild, Erasure; Maxinquaye, Tricky; Singles: with The Cure: Lullaby; Lovesong; with The Farm: Groovy Train; with Lisa Stansfield: This Is The Right Time; Erasure: Little Respect; Drama (remix); Wild!; Blue Savannah; Star; Buffalo Stance, Neneh Cherry; Rapture, Siouxsie and the Banshees; Madder Rose, Tragic Magic; David Byrne, Feelings; John Lydon, Psycho's Path; Depeche Mode, Strangelove (remix). *Address:* The Smoothside Organisation, Ashbank, Heyford Rd, Middleton Stoney, Oxfordshire OX6 8SH, England.

SAUNDERS Roger; b. 9 March 1947, Barking, Essex, England. Musician (guitar, piano). *Musical Education:* Self-taught. *Career:* Television includes: Top of The Pops; Jonathon Ross; Concerts include: Wembley Stadium; Wembley Arena; Tours throughout US, including Madison Square Gardens, New York; Middle East including Dubai, Bahrain; Europe including Germany, France, Italy, Spain, Norway, Denmark, Sweden, Finland; Concerts with: Medicine Head; Gary Glitter; Peter Skelton; Duane Eddy; Chicken Shack; Numerous recordings; Over 600 songs published. *Memberships:* PRS; MCPS; Songwriters Guild; Musicians' Union. *Leisure interest:* Music. *Address:* Barking, Essex, England.

SAUNDERSON Kevin, (Reese, E-Dancer); b. 5 Sept. 1964, Brooklyn, New York, USA. Prod.; Remixer; DJ. *Career:* Formed the Belleville Three with Juan Atkins and Derrick May; Founder: KMS Records; Member: Inner City; The Reese Project; Collaborations: Santonio Echols; Juan Atkins; Paris Grey; Remixed: Pet Shop Boys; Paula Abdul; New Order. *Recordings:* Albums: with Inner City: Paradise, 1989; Fire, 1990; Praise, 1992; with The Reese Project: Faith, Hope and Clarity, 1993; as E-Dancer: Heavenly, 1998; Singles: as Reese: Just Another Chance, 1987; Rock To The Beat, 1987; The Groove That Won't Stop, 1988; with Inner City: Big Fun, 1988; Good Life, 1988; Pennies From Heaven, 1992; Ahnonghay, 1994; Buena Vida (Good Life), 1998; Good Love, 2001; with The Reese Project: Direct Me, 1991; as E-Dancer: Heavenly, 1998. *Address:* c/o Play It Again Sam, 338A Ladbroke Grove, London, W10 5AH, England.

SAVAGE Rick; b. 2 Dec. 1960, Sheffield, England. Rock Musician (bass); Vocalist. *Career:* Bass player, UK rock group Def Leppard, 1977–; International concerts include: Support tours with Sammy Hagar; AC/DC; Ted Nugent; Reading Rock Festival, 1980; World tour, 1983; Monsters of Rock Festival, Castle Donington, 1986; World tour, 1988; Freddie Mercury Tribute Concert, Wembley, 1992. *Recordings:* Albums: On Through The Night, 1980; High 'n' Dry, 1981; Pyromania, 1983; Hysteria, 1987; Adrenalize, 1992; Retroactive, 1993; Vault 1980–95, 1995; Slang, 1996; Getcha Rocks Off, 1997; With others: Wild One: The Best of Thin Lizzy, 1996; Deseo de Oir Tu Voz, 1996; Europe, 1997; Singles include: Photograph; Rock of Ages; Foolin'; Animal; Pour Some Sugar On Me; Love Bites; Rocket; Make Love Like A Man; Let's Get Rocked; Stand Up (Kick Love Into Motion); Heaven Is; Two Steps Behind, featured in film soundtrack The Last Action Hero; When Love and Hate Collide. *Honours include:* American Music Awards: Favourite Heavy Metal Album, Favourite Heavy Metal Artists, 1989. *Current Management:* Q-Prime Inc. *Address:* 729 Seventh Ave, 14th Floor, New York, NY 10019, USA.

SAVANNAH Jonn; b. 13 Jan. 1957, Nairobi, Kenya. Musician. m. Marie. *Education:* 1 year college. *Musical Education:* Grade 4 piano. *Career:* Toured with: Tina Turner; Squeeze; Van Morrison; Session work; No. 3 hit, Germany, 1984; Signed publishing deal with EMI UK, 1994. *Recordings:* The Catch: 25 Years (No. 3, Germany). *Memberships:* PAMRA; Musicians' Union; MCPS. *Leisure interests:* Motorbikes; Gardening. *Address:* Little Barn, Plaistow Rd, Loxwood, West Sussex RH14 0SX, England.

SAVOLAINEN Jarmo Tapio; b. 24 May 1961, Iisalmi, Finland. Composer; Musician (piano, keyboards). m. Helena Haaranen, 1 d. *Musical Education:* Jazz and composition studies, Berklee College of Music, Boston, USA. *Career:* Member, various groups including:

Finnforest; Blue Train; Formed own nine-piece ensemble and quartet; Duos with Make Lievonen, 1988; Seppo Kantonen, 1990; Major jazz festivals world-wide, including Jukkis Uotila Quintet, Paris, 1984; EBU Big Band, Pori Jazz, 1985; Kalott Jazz and Blues Festival, 1995; Television appearances on many European national networks. *Compositions:* Music for big bands, theatre and films. *Recordings:* Blue Dreams, 1987; Songs For Solo Piano, 1990; First Sight, 1992; True Image, 1995; with Klaus Suonsaari: Something in Common, 1998; with Snow Queen: Grand Style, 2000. *Honour:* Jazz Musician of The Year, Finland, 1994. *Membership:* Finnish Light Music Composers. *Leisure interests:* Food; Cooking. *Address:* Porvoonkatu 17 B 25, 00510 Helsinki, Finland.

SAWHNEY Nitin; b. 1964, Kent, England. Musician (keyboards, guitar); Remixer; Prod.; Composer. *Education:* Liverpool University, Law. *Career:* Solo recordings feature influences of many cultures, including Indian, Flamenco, Jazz, Dance; Also composed for commercials, TV and film soundtracks; Produced and remixed other artists' work; Worked in comedy as part of Secret Asians double act; Original member Goodness Gracious Me team on radio and TV; Toured with the James Taylor Quartet; Formed own band The Jazztones; Worked with Talvin Singh in the Tihai Trio; Musical Director at Theatre Royal (Stratford East), London; Provided music for the National Theatre; Composed music for documentary series The Sikhs; Written for films: The Dance of Shiva; Split Wide Open; Written and produced for Amar and Aya; Songs recorded by Sinead O'Connor and Shara Nelson; Remixed: Mandalay; Khaled; Mondo Gross; Worked on Sir Paul McCartney's project The Fireman; Urban Prophecies, a commission for the Proms, premiered on at the Albert Hall, conducted by Cameron Sinclair, featuring Joanne MacGreggor (piano) and Aref Durvesh (tabla), July 18th 2000. *Recordings:* Albums: Spirit Dance, 1993; Migration, 1995; Displacing The Priest, 1996; Beyond Skin, 1999; Prophesy, 2001; features on: Drum The Bass, Shri, 1997; Intro, Mandalay, 2000; Ayeshteni, Natacha Atlas, 2001; Dallali, Cheb Mami, 2001. *Honours:* The South Bank Show Award for Popular Music, 2000; Technics Mercury Music Prize, nominee, Beyond Skin, 2000; BBC Radio 3 Award for World Music, Boundary Crossing, 2002. *E-mail:* spiritdancetour@aol.com. *Internet:* www.nitinsawhney.com.

SAWTELL Paul; b. 1 May 1959, Stourbridge, West Midlands, England. Arranger; Composer; MD; Musician (Piano). *Musical Education:* Classical Training; Contemporary Self-taught. *Career:* Numerous BBC Radio Sessions; Television Shows with Tom Jones; Shirley Bassey; Neil Sedaka; Worked with Peter King; Dick Morrisey; Jim Mullen; Norma Whinstone. *Compositions:* Over 200 Pieces. *Recordings:* 10 CDs. *Leisure interests:* Playing Bridge; Amateur Chef; Psychology. *Address:* 20 Seymour Rd, Stourbridge, West Midlands, DY9 8TB, England.

SAYER Ron James; b. 24 Oct. 1970, Wisbech, Lincolnshire, England. Musician (guitar, bass); Vocalist; Songwriter; Teacher. *Education:* BA Hons in Music; Grade 8 Electric Guitar, Grade 8 Bass Guitar. *Career:* Bassist, composer with: Monster; Spider Murphy; Played live concert broadcast on Friday Rock Show, Radio 1; Sound City 1992; Toured supporting: Quireboys; Skin; Mr Big; L7; Mini-tour with Monster and Supercircus, including Royal Standard, London; Currently guitarist with Purple Ronnie. *Recordings:* Radio broadcast concert included: So Here It Is; Innocence; What Would U Do; My Mind's Treasure; released on Rock The Canary album. *Honours:* Guitarist of The Year, 1996–97. *Memberships:* Musicians' Union; PRS; Guild of International Songwriters and Composers (GISC). *Leisure interest:* Performing live with Purple Ronnie. *Address:* 27 Morris Rd, North Walsham, Norfolk NR28 0EJ, England.

SCABIES Rat, (Chris Miller); b. 30 July 1957, Kingston Upon Thames, Surrey, England. Musician (drums). *Career:* Member, groups Rat; London SS; Member, UK punk rock group, The Damned, 1976–77; Appearances include: Mont de Marsan punk festival, France, 1976; Support to Sex Pistols, Anarchy In The UK Tour, 1976; First UK punk band to play US, 1977; Member, the White Cats, 1978; Rejoined the Damned, 1979–89; Regular international concerts include: Christmas On Earth Festival, Leeds, 1981; Farewell tour UK, 1989; UK reunion tour, 1991; Member, side project Naz and the Nomads, 1988. *Recordings:* Albums with the Damned: Damned, Damned, Damned, 1977; Music For Pleasure, 1977; Machine Gun Etiquette, 1979; The Black Album, 1980; The Best Of, 1981; Strawberries, 1982; Phantasmagoria, 1985; Anything, 1986; Light At The End of The Tunnel, 1987 Not of this Earth, 1996; Boxed Set, 1999; Eternal Damnation Live, 1999; with Naz and the Nomads: Give Daddy The Knife, Cindy, 1988; Singles with The Damned: Love Song, 1979; Smash It Up, 1979; Grimly Fiendish, 1985; The Shadow of Love, 1985; Is It A Dream, 1985; Eloise, 1986; Gigolo, 1987; Alone Again Or, 1987.

SCAGGS Boz; b. 8 June 1944, Ohio, USA. Musician (guitar); Singer. *Career:* Member, groups The Marksmen; The Ardells; Formed R & B group, The Wigs; Folk-singer in Europe, successful in Sweden; Joined Steve Miller Band, 1967; Solo artiste, 1968-. *Recordings:* Albums: Boz, 1966; Boz Scaggs, 19069; Moments, 1971; Boz Scaggs and Band, 1971; My Time, 1972; Slow Dancer, 1974; Silk Degrees, 1976; Two Down Then Left, 1977; Middle Man,

1980; Hits!, 1980; Other Roads, 1988; Some Change, 1994; Come on Home, 1997; Fade into Light (Japan bonus track), 1999; Hit singles include: Lowdown (No. 3, US); What Can I Say?; Lido Shuffle; I'll be the One. *Current Management:* HK Management, 8900 Wilshire Blvd, Suite 300, Beverly Hills, CA 90211, USA.

SCARTH Andrew; Record Prod. *Recordings:* Recordings for: Levellers; Heather Nova; Blameless; Skunk Anansie; Killing Joke; Mundy; Credit to the Nation; Addict; Underworld; Mainstream; Diamond Head; Bad Company; As Engineer: Howard Jones: Dream Into Action; Cross That Line; Prefab Sprout, Two Wheels Good; Tina Turner, Foreign Affair; Tesla, Time's Makin' Changes: The Best of Tesla; Drain STH, Freaks of Nature. *Current Management:* One Management Ltd, 43 St Alban's Ave, London W4 5JS, England.

SCAVONE Sam John; b. 12 July 1926, New York, USA. Musician (trumpet). m. (1) Esther Scavone, divorced 1961, 1 s., 1 d., (2) Marion Scavone, 1965, divorced 1973, 1 s., 1 d. *Musical Education:* Hartnet School of Music, 1948–50. *Career:* Trumpeter, jazz groups, 1943–; Played with numerous artists including: Buddy Morrow; Woody Herman; Tito Puente; Xavier Cugat; Sammy Kaye; Tex Beneke; Charlie Spivak; Les Elgart.

SCHACK Michael E K; b. 11 May 1966, St Miklaas, Belgium. Musician (Drummer); Songwriter. *Education:* Economics, Degree in Marketing. *Musical Education:* Self-taught Drummer. *Career:* Blue Blot, 1987; Drummer, with Clouseau, 1995–97; Roland Demoband, 1992; Blue Blot Tour, 1992–94; Groovemania and Clouseau, 1995; Demonstrator, Sabian – Vic Firth Endorser – Slingerland Clinician, 1997. *Compositions:* Blue Blot: Pretty Good; New Blunk; Groovemania: Posativity; Mich van Hautem, Jacky; Beasone. *Recordings:* Blue Blot Albums, 1990–94; Orphan; September Rain; De 7 Drumzonden; Live for Life, 1993; Drum Editor, Meetmusic, 1992–97. *Honour:* Drumvideo of the Year, 1996. *Membership:* SABAM, Uradex, Zamu, Belgium. *Current Management:* King IS, Leuvensesteemweg 120A, 3290 Diest, Belgium. *Address:* Eikstraat 49, 1981 Hofstade, Belgium.

SCHAFFER Jan E T; b. 24 Sept. 1945, Stockholm, Sweden. Musician. *Education:* University. *Career:* Professional from 1970–; Played on records with Abba (27 numbers); 10 solo albums (1 with Toto); Many television programmes. *Compositions:* About 120. *Recordings:* Hallmans Affair; Bersellii; Park and Electric Banana Band; Leif Strand: Year; Zodiac. *Publications:* Play Guitar, with R Gustavsson. *Memberships:* STIM; SAMI. *Leisure interests:* Skiing; Diving. *Address:* Dr Abrahamsu 43, 16152 Bromma, Sweden.

SCHECHTMAN Saul; b. 4 Sept. 1924, Winchester, Connecticut, USA. Conductor; Composer. m. Carolyn Raney, 31 July 1952, 2 d. *Education:* BA, Brooklyn College, New York, 1947; Piano and French Horn, Greenwich House Music School; Theory, Brooklyn College; Orchestral Conducting, Juilliard School of Music. *Career:* Music Director, Bronx Symphony Orchestra, 1953–56, Bergen Philharmonic, New Jersey, 1956–60; Omnibus Programme, 1954–57; Original Cast, Carnival, 1961–63; Hello, Dolly, New York, 1966–70; How To Succeed, Paris, 1964; Orchestra Piccola, Baltimore, 1976–80. *Compositions:* Diaspora Variations for Orchestra; Incidental music for Auntie Mame, original play and film. *Recordings:* Carnival; Hello, Dolly, cast album; How to Succeed in Business, French production cast album. *Publications:* Recreations for Piano, 1967; Capriccio for Organ, 1968; Diaspora Variations for Orchestra, 1994. *Honour:* Juilliard Fellowship in Orchestral Conducting, 1949–51. *Membership:* ASCAP. *Leisure interests:* Tennis; Chess. *Address:* 134 Cathedral Ave, Hempstead, NY 11550, USA.

SCHENKER Michael; b. 10 Jan. 1955, Savstedt, Germany. Musician (guitar). *Career:* Founder, German heavy rock group The Scorpions, 1971–; Member, UFO, 1973–78; Rejoined Scorpions, 1979; Formed own band, The Michael Schenker Group, later called MSG, 1979–; Contributor, Contraband recording project (with members of Shark Island, Vixen, Ratt, LA Guns), 1991. *Recordings:* Albums: with the Scorpions: Lonesome Crow, 1972; Lovedrive, 1979; with UFO: Phenomenon, 1974; Force It, 1975; No Heavy Pettin', 1976; Lights Out, 1977; Strangers In The Night, 1977; Obsession, 1978; Deadly Sting : The Mercury Years, 1997; with MSG: The Michael Schenker Group, 1980; MSG, 1981; One Night At Budokan, 1982; Assault Attack, 1982; Built To Destroy, 1983; Rock Will Never Die, 1984; Perfect Timing, 1987; Save Yourself, 1989; Never Ending Nightmare, 1992; The Michael Schenker Life Story, 1997; Unforgiven, 1999; Written in Sand, 1999; The Unforgiven World Tour: Live, 1999; Unplugged (live), 1999; Adventures of the Imagination, 2000; with Contraband: Contraband, 1991.

SCHENKER Rudolph; b. 31 Aug. 1948, Germany. Musician (guitar); Songwriter. *Career:* Founder member, German heavy rock group The Scorpions, 1971–; World-wide tours; Concerts include: Support to Ted Nugent, US, 1979; World tour, 1982; Support to Bon Jovi, US, 1984; Leningrad, Russia, 1989; Festivals include: World Series of Rock, Cleveland, Ohio, 1979; Reading Rock Festival, 1983; US Festival, 1983;

Rock In Rio, Brazil, 1985; Moscow Music Peace Festival, 1989; Roger Waters' The Wall spectacular, Berlin, 1990; Invited to meet President Gorbachev at the Kremlin, 1991. *Recordings:* Albums: Lonesome Crow, 1972; Fly To The Rainbow, 1974; In Trance, 1975; Virgin Killer, 1976; Taken By Force, 1978; Tokyo Tapes, 1978; Lovedrive, 1979; Animal Magnetism, 1980; Blackout, 1982; Love At First Sting, 1984; World Wide Live, 1985; Savage Amusement, 1988; Best of Rockers and Ballads, 1989; Hurricane Rock, 1990; Crazy World, 1990; Face The Heat, 1993; Live Bites, 1995; Deadly Sting: The mercury Years, 1997; Singles include: Can't Live Without You; No One Like You; Still Loving You; Rhythm of Love; Wind of Change, Eye II Eye, 1999. *Current Management:* McGhee Entertainment, 8730 Sunset Blvd, STE 175, Los Angeles, CA 90069, USA.

SCHICK Ignaz; b. 9 Sept. 1972, Germany. Musician (Saxophone, Electronics, Experimental Music). *Education:* Academy of Fine Arts, Munich; Studied With Josef Anton Riedl. *Career:* Toured, Played Concerts and Festivals of Experimental Music, 1989–; Festivals Include, Bonner Herbst, Donaueschingen, Autumn Concerts Graz/Austria, FEAM Berlin; Radio Broadcasts With Swiss Radio DRS, Bavarian Radio BR2; Collaboration With Mathias Bauer, Tony Buck, Jason Kahn, Tarwater, Kalle Laar. *Compositions:* Che; Die Wueste Bleibt Leer; Liebe Macht Blind; Koerper Im Abseits; Tools and Tales Against Radio Agents; Puppy Love; Perm; Vononoch. *Recordings:* Albums, Kratzen, 1990; Kaeseplatte, 1991; Donaueschingen, 1995, 1996; Lonely Woman, 1997; Tales and Tools Against Radio Agents, 1997; Nuts, 1998; Singles, Perlon, 2000. *Honours:* Foerderstipendium fur Musik, 1994. *Memberships:* GEMA; GVL; JIM. *Current Management:* Zangi Music, Weserstr 22, D10247 Berlin, Germany.

SCHIFRIN Lalo; b. 21 June 1932, Buenos Aires, Argentina. Musician (piano, keyboards); Composer; Educator; Arranger. *Education:* Sociology, Law, University. *Musical Education:* Classical piano; Studied with Olivier Messiaen, Paris Conservatoire. *Career:* Represented Argentina, Paris International Jazz Festival, 1955; Founded Argentina's first big band; Played with Dizzy Gillespie, including European tour with Jazz At The Philharmonic Ensemble, 1960–62; Also played with Quincy Jones; Jimmy Smith; Tutor, Composition, University of California, Los Angeles, 1968–71. *Compositions:* 2 suites for Dizzy Gillespie: Gillespiana; New Continent; Film music includes: The Cincinnati Kid, 1965; Bullitt, 1968; Dirty Harry, 1971. *Recordings:* Albums include: New Fantasy, 1966; Towering Toccata, 1977; Black Widow, 1976; Free Rides, 1979; Guitar Concerto, 1985; Anno Domini, 1986; Mission – Anthology, 1994; Gillespiana, 1996; Masters of Mayham, 1997; Rush Hour, 1998; Cantos Aztecas, 1999; Mannix, 1999; with Jimmy Smith: Verve Jazz, 1972; The Cat Strikes Again, 1980; with Eddie Harris: Bossa Nova, 1962; with Quincy Jones: Plays Hip Hits, 1963; with Paul Horn: Dream Machine, 1978. *Address:* c/o Ted kurland, 173 Brighton Ave, Boston, MA 02134, USA.

SCHMIDT Bjarne Gregers; b. 3 Nov. 1957, Copenhagen, Denmark. Tenor Banjo; Irish Bouzouki; Guitar. *Musical Education:* Piano lessons; Sound Engineering Course, 1996; Musical Studies, Ireland. *Career:* Foxhunters, band, Skagen Festival, 1986; Live appearance, Danish Radio, 1987, 1989, 1991, 1992, 1996, 1997; Scandinavian Tour with Irish top acts, Mary Bergin and Mick Conneely Gin Whistle and Fiddle, 1991; Live at TV-Stop, 1993, Telemark Festival Norway, 1997. *Compositions:* The Moth in the Lampshade; Happy Days, 1997. *Recordings:* Same Old Story, contributor, 1990; Folk music in Denmark 1, 1992; Folk music in Denmark 2, 1993; Trad Lads, Happy Days, 1997; Eck D'Ville, Contributor, 1997; Folk music of Denmark, 1997. *Publications:* Trad Lads, Happy Days, 1997; Eck D'Ville, 1997. *Leisure interests:* Reading; Travel. *Current Management:* Martin O'Hare, Selvedje Allé 19, 2500 Valby, Denmark.

SCHMIT Timothy B; b. 30 Oct. 1947, Sacramento, California, USA. *Career:* Member, folk trio, Tim, Tom and Ron, 1962; Member, groups: The Contenders; New Breed; Glad; Member, Poco, 1970–77; Member, The Eagles, 1977–. *Recordings:* Albums: with Poco: Poco, 1970; Deliverin', 1971; From The Inside, 1971; A Good Feelin' To Know, 1973; Crazy Eyes, 1973; Seven, 1974; Cantamos, 1974; Head Over Heels, 1975; The Very Best of Poco, 1975; Poco Live, 1976; Rose of Cimarron, 1976; Indian Summer, 1977; With The Eagles: The Long Run (No. 1, USA), 1979; Live, 1980; Eagles Greatest Hits, 1982; The Best of The Eagles, 1985; Solo albums: Playin' It Cool, 1981; Timothy B, 1987; Singles include: Heartache Tonight (No. 1, USA), 1979; I Can't Tell You Why, 1980; Seven Bridges Road, 1981. *Honours:* Grammy Award, Best Rock Vocal Performance, Heartache Tonight, 1980; American Music Awards, Favourite Band, Favourite Album, 1981. *Address:* c/o William Morris Agency, 1350 Avenue of the Americas, New York, NY 10019, USA.

SCHNEIDER John; b. 8 April 1954, Mount Kisco, New York, USA. Singer; Actor. *Career:* Performed in musicals since age 14; Actor, television series The Dukes of Hazzard, 1979–85; Country artiste, 1981–89; Actor, television series, Grand Slam, 1990-. *Recordings:* Hits: US Country No. 1 hits include: I've Been Around Enough To Know; Country Girls; What's A Memory Like You (Doing In A Love Like This)?; You're The Last Thing I Needed Tonight; Albums: Now Or Never, 1981; Dukes of

Hazzard cast album, 1982; Quiet Man, 1982; If You Believe, with Jill Michaels, 1983; Too Good To Stop Now, 1984; Trying To Outrun The Wind, 1985; A Memory Like You, 1986; Take The Long Way Home, 1986; You Ain't Seen The Last of Me, 1987; Biggest Hits for the Highway, producer, 1997. *Current Management:* Lee S. Mimms and Associates, 2644 E Chevy Chase Dr., Glendale, CA 91206, USA.

SCHNEIDER Maria; b. 27 Nov. 1960, Windom, Minnesota, USA. *Education:* BM, Theory and Composition, University of Minnesota; Studied, University of Miami; Master in Jazz and Contemporary Media, Eastman School of Music. *Career:* Led own orchestra, Maria Schneider Jazz Orchestra, New York, 1993-, performing weekly; Conducted jazz orchestras throughout Sweden, Norway, Finland, Germany, Denmark, Holland, France, Spain and Italy. *Compositions:* El Viento, Carnegie Hall Jazz Orchestra, 1994; Scenes from Childhood, Monterey Jazz Festival, 1995. *Recordings:* Evanescence; Coming About; Manhattan School of Music, Live at Montreux 1997; Dejan Terzic, Four of One. *Honours:* Evanescence, Nominated for 2 Grammy Awards, 1995, 1997; Jazztimes and Downbeat Critics, Nominated for Copenhagen's Jazzpar Prize, 1995. *Address:* 50W 72nd St #510, New York, NY 10023, USA.

SCHOELINCK Roland; b. 3 Jan. 1951, Anderlues, Hainaut, Belgium. m. Lefevre Chantal, 2 s., 1 d. *Musical Education:* Self-educated composer. *Career:* Director, private music school; Composer, Arranger and Performer, jazz, classical and popular music and studio work; Works: Ballet music, Arranger and Composer for Gerard Corbiau's film, L'année de l'éveil. *Compositions:* Toots Concerto, harmonica and symphony orchestra; Safety First, official safety hymn; Complicity, flute, piano (jazzy); 1 Symphony; 1 Symphony Poem; 1 String Quartet; 1 Wind Quintet; Pieces for Solo Piano; Dr Theodore, for symphony orchestra, 1998; Lions Ceremony; Bouglione Parade; Concerto Pur Cor et Orchestre. *Recordings:* Safety First; Dolphin Tears; Complicity; Toots Concerto. *Publications:* Sur La Voie de l'improvisation, 1996; Easy to Write, 1997; Petit Livre de Jazz, 1 and 2, 1997; Complicity, 1997; 26 Airs de Gilles, piano. *Memberships:* Belgian Composers Union; SABAM. *Address:* 6 Chemin Brulotte, B7063, Neufvilles, Belgium.

SCHOLZ Drazen; b. 25 June 1961, Zagreb, Croatia. Musician (drums). m. 28 June 1986, 1 d. *Career:* Promise of Spring; Parliament; Film: Some Like It Hot; Le Cinema; Parni Valjak (Steam Roller). *Recordings:* with Parni Valjak: Live In ZKM (Unplugged); Parni Valjak – All 15 Years (3 LPs live), 1990; Dream Hunters, 1990; Awakenings, 1994. *Honours:* 7 Porin Awards (Croatian equivalent of Grammy) with Parni Valjak. *Membership:* HGU (Croatian Music Union). *Leisure interest:* Films. *Current Management:* Nenad Drobnjak, Miramarska 15b, Zagreb, Croatia. *Address:* Laginjina 9, 41000 Zagreb, Croatia.

SCHOLZ Tom; b. 10 March 1947, Toledo, Ohio, USA. Singer; Musician. *Education:* Masters, Mechanical Engineering, Massachusetts Institute of Technology. *Career:* Founder, rock group Boston, 1976; British tour, 1979; Seven-year absence from recording; US tour, 1987. *Recordings:* Albums: Boston (No. 1, USA), 1976; Don't Look Back (No. 1, USA), 1978; Third Stage (No. 1, USA), 1986; Walk On, 1994; Greatest Hits, 1997; Singles include: More Than A Feeling, 1976; Long Time, 1977; Peace of Mind, 1977; Don't Look Back, 1978; Amanda (No. 1, USA), 1986; We're Ready, 1987; Can'tcha Say, 1987; with Arcwelder: Entropy, 1996. *Honours:* Platinum and Gold discs; Best-selling debut album all-time, 16m. copies. *Leisure interests:* Aviation; Inventing (holds numerous patents), including Rockman mini-amplifier. *Address:* c/o Boston, PO Box 6191, Lincoln Center, MA 01773, USA.

SCHON Neal; b. 27 Feb. 1954, San Mateo, California, USA. Musician (guitar); Vocalist. *Career:* Guitarist with Carlos Santana; Founder, Azteca; Founder member, US rock group Journey, 1973–87; Member, HSAS, 1984; Bad English, 1988–91; Hardline, 1992–; Partnership with Jan Hammer, 1981–82. *Recordings:* with Santana: Santana, 1972; Santana/Abraxas/Santana, 1997; Santana/Abraxas/Santana, 1998; with HSAS: Through The Fire, 1984; with Jan Hammer: Untold Passion, 1981; Here To Stay, 1982; with Bad English, Bad English, 1989; Backlash, 1991; Solo: Beyond The Thunder, 1995; Electric World, 1997; Piranha Blues, 1999; Hit singles include: with Journey: Who's Crying Now; Don't Stop Believin'; Open Arms; Separate Ways (Worlds Apart); After The Fall; Send Her My Love; Suzanne; Be Good To Yourself; Albums: Evolution, 1979; Escape, 1981; Frontiers, 1983; Greatest Hits, 1988; Escape/Frontiers/Infinity, 1998; with Bad English: When I See You Smile (No. 1, USA), 1990; Straight To The Heart, 1991. *Current Management:* Bill Thompson Management. *Address:* 2051 Third St, San Francisco, CA 94107, USA.

SCHÖNBERG Claude-Michel; b. 6 July 1944, France. Composer. m. Béatrice Szabo, 1979, 1 s., 1 d. *Career:* Record Producer for EMI France; Composer, songs and musicals, 1967-. *Compositions:* Musicals include: La Révolutions Française, 1973; Les Misérables, 1980–84; Miss Saigon, 1985–86. *Recordings:* Producer: Les Misérables, London cast recording; Miss Saigon, London cast recording; Martin Guerre, London cast recording. *Honours:* Tony Awards; Grammy Awards; Evening Standard Awards.

SCHREURS Dirk; b. 23 May 1966, Neerpelt, Belgium. Prof. of Jazz/Popular Music; Prof. Pianist, The Brussels Royal Conservatory. m. Vera Kerckhoven, 28 July 1990. *Education:* Master Degree in Arts and Humanities, University of Louvain; Master Degree in Teaching; Assistant, Faculty of Arts, University of Louvain; Master Classes with John Abercrombie and Dave Kikoski, Trilok Gurtu. *Career:* Keyboardist with Real Deal, DSWB 4, Jan Mues Quartet, Jive Talk, Marco Ruggiero Band; Appearances on Belgian Radio and TV. *Compositions:* Over 200 compositions and arrangements in various styles. *Recordings:* Flexibility, 1992; Beyond Ballads, 1993; From Blues to Funk, 1995; The Joy of Rhythm 'N Jazz, 1996. *Publications:* Author, Jazzics; A Book on Jazz Theory, Analysis and Improvisation, 1993. *Honours:* Touch Down, composition selected for publication, 1994–95. *Memberships:* SABAM; ZAMU; Zavelhof Cultural Society. *Leisure interests:* Playing Rhodes; Hammond Organ. *Current Management:* Dirk Schreurs, Don Boscostraat 98, 3940, Hechtel, Belgium.

SCHULTZ Debra Kay; b. 30 Oct. 1955, Holden, West Virginia, USA. Gospel Singer. m. Robert A Schultz, 13 Dec. 1974, 2 s. *Musical Education:* Vocal lessons, Robert Turner; Several years of piano. *Career:* Appearances, gospel concerts, Gospel TV stations, throughout USA; Radio stations internationally. *Recordings:* Radio singles: Lord You're My Strength, 1991; Don't Lift The Anchor, 1992; I Just Found Jesus, 1993. *Honours:* King Eagle Award, Christian Female Artist of the Year, Airplay International, 1994–95. *Membership:* Gospel Music Asscn (GMA). *Leisure interests:* Making crafts; Writing; Travel. *Address:* PO Box 88 Rt 17, Sharples, WV 25183, USA.

SCHULTZ Eric; b. 11 Sept. 1960, Los Angeles, California, USA. Musician (guitar, electric bass); Composer; Arranger; Teacher. *Education:* BA, Humanities, California State University, Northridge, USA. *Musical Education:* Composition, California State University, Northridge; Guitar studies with Ralph Towner; Joe Diorio; John Abercrombie; Ron Escheté. *Career:* Professional jazz player, 1982; Resident Paris, 1986–; Worked regularly with some of greatest drummers in jazz: Oliver Johnson; Barry Altschul; Sunny Murray; Frank Butler; Alan Jones; Peter Perfido; ESP with Paul Carman, 1984–85; Onzy Matthews Quartet, Peter Perfido/Andy Laster Group; Eric Schultz Trio (with Oliver Johnson, Jack Gregg), 1991–; Eric Schultz Nonet; Jean Michel Couchet/Eric Schultz Quartet, 1993–; Eric Schultz Space and Time Ensemble, 1995; Viviane Ginapé/Eric Schultz duo. *Recording:* Eric Schultz Space and Time Ensemble, 1995. *Membership:* SACEM. *Current Management:* Space and Time Productions. *Address:* 8 rue de la Pompe, 94410 St Maurice, France.

SCHULTZ Irma; b. 1 Oct. 1965, Stockholm, Sweden. Singer; Songwriter; Actress. *Education:* Special Music School, 6 years; Drama School, 4 years. *Career:* Tours of Sweden and Many Television Shows; Background Vocals on 40 Albums in Sweden; Actress in The Black Rider by Waits, Wilson and Bourroughs at the Royal Dramatic Theatre; 10 Television Productions, Leading Role in Kvällspressen, 1992; 3 Movies for Cinema. *Compositions:* Stureplan; Precis som du; Andas Fritt. *Recordings:* Da Staden Vaknat, 1989; Irma, 1991; Tröst för Stygga Barn, 1993; Andas Fritt, 1995; A Bird That Whistles, Songs of Joni Mitchell, 1996. *Honour:* Scholarships, STIM, SKAP; Grammy Award, Best Female Artist in Sweden, 1989. *Current Management:* Sony Music AB, Box 20037, 16102 Bromma, Sweden. *Address:* Erstagatan 20, 116 36 Stockholm, Sweden.

SCHULZE Erich; b. 1 Feb. 1913, Berlin, Germany. *Career:* Editor; Chairman. *Publications:* Include, Collection of Case Law Reports On Copyright, With Comments; Commentary On German Copyright Law With Regard to International Law and Community Law In The EU Member States; Commentary On Social Security For Self Employed Artists Act; Germany Copyright In Works of Music and The Development of Mechanical Music; Music and Poetry, 50 Years of The German Copyright Society; Music and Law – The Composers Royalties; Collection of Forms for Protection of Industrial and Intellectual Property. *Honours:* Cross of Knight Commander of Papal Order of Silvester, 1962; Hon. Cross of Republic of Austria, 1965; Officers Cross of Order of Merit, 1967; Bavarian Order of Merit, 1971; Commanders Cross of The Order of Merit, 1978; Bela Bartok Medal, 1980; Cross of Knight Commander of The Papal Order of Gregorius With Star, 1986; Supreme Order of Merit, 1988; Richard Strausse Medal, 1989; Gold Medal Confederation Internationale Des Societes d'Auteurs et Compositeurs, 1990; Agustin Lara Award, 1991; Golden Score of The Forderkreis, 1995. *Address:* Dr Hans Staub Strasse 3, 82031 Grunwald, Germany.

SCHUUR Diane; Singer. m. Dave Schuur. *Career:* Performances include: White House; Monterey Jazz Festival; Hollywood Bowl; Tours: Europe; Japan; Far East; South America. *Recordings:* Albums: Pilot of My Destiny, 1982; Schuur Thing, 1985; Timeless, 1986; Diane Schuur and The Count Basie Orchestra, 1987; Talkin' About You, 1988; Pure Schuur (No. 1,

Billboard contemporary jazz chart), 1991; Blues For Schuur, 1997; The Best of Diane Schuur, 1997; Music Is My Life, 1999. *Honours:* 2 Grammy Awards, 1987–88; Manhattan Asscn of Cabarets and Clubs Award, 1997; Bagley Wright Award, 1997; First Annual Ella Fitzgerald Award from the Montréal International Jazz Festival, 1999. *Current Management:* Paul Cantor Enterprises, 33042 Ocean Ridge, Dana Point, CA 92629–1708, USA.

SCHWISBERG Arnold; b. 17 Nov. 1961, Montréal, Québec, Canada. m. Kathrine Brodie, 2 s. *Education:* BA, BSc, LLB, Queens Faculty of Law, Kingston, Ontario, Canada. *Career:* Founder and Owner, President, Jazz Inspiration Records. *Address:* 2001 Sheppard Ave, Suite 808, Toronto, ON, Canada.

SCHWISBERG David; b. 20 July 1966, Montréal, Québec, Canada. *Education:* Economics and Marketing. *Career:* Co-Owner, Vice President, Jazz Inspiration Records, independent jazz label. *Address:* 5510 Robinson Ave, Suite 206, Montréal, QC, Canada.

SCOCCO Mauro; b. 11 Sept. 1962, Stockholm, Sweden. Artist; Composer. *Career:* Sales in Scandinavia: 600,000 albums; 4 Swedish Grammies; numerous other awards. *Recordings:* Sarah, single, topped every list in Sweden. *Leisure interest:* Harley Davidson Motorcycles. *Current Management:* Diesel Music. *Address:* Diesel Music, Blasieholmsg 2a, 1148 Stockholm, Sweden.

SCOFIELD John; b. 26 Dec. 1951, Ohio, USA. Jazz Musician (guitar); Composer. *Musical Education:* Berklee College of Music, Boston. *Career:* Began playing in local R & B groups; Solo artiste, 1970s–; Played with Billy Cobham; Gary Burton; Dave Liebman; Charlie Haden; Jack DeJohnette; McCoy Tyner; Marc Johnson; French National Orchestra; Mike Gibbs Orchestra; Member, Miles Davis' group, 1983–85. *Recordings:* Albums include: John Scofield Live, 1977; Rough House, 1978; Who's Who, 1979; Bar Talk, 1980; Shinola, 1981; Out Like A Light, 1981; Electric Outlet, 1984; Still Warm, 1987; Blue Matter, 1987; Loud Jazz, 1987; Flat Out, 1989; Pick Hits Live, 1989; Time On My Hands, 1990; Slo Sco, 1990; Meant To Be, 1991; Blue Matter, 1991; Grace Under Pressure, 1992; What We Do, 1993; with Miles Davis: Decoy, 1984; You're Under Arrest, 1985; Star People, 1989; Groove Elation, 1996; with Herbie Hancock: The New Standard, 1996; Also recorded with Gerry Mulligan; Chet Baker; John Abercrombie. *Current Management:* Ted Kurland Associates, 173 Brighton Ave, Boston, MA 02134, USA.

SCOTT Al; Record Prod. *Career:* Musician, Recording, session work; Live Sound for: The Jam; Little Feat; Fleetwood Mac; Composer and arranger; Record producer, with close links with Vinyl Solution. *Recordings:* Albums: The Levellers: Levelling The Land; Cud: Slip Away; Dogs D'Amour: Uncharted Heights of Disgrace; Oyster Band: Holy Bandits; Tom Robinson: Love Over Rage; Cherry Bombz: Live; Derek B: Bullet From A Gun; Bomb The Bass: Love So True; Betty Boo: Where Are You Baby; Eddie Grant: Gimme Hope Joanna; Eric B and Rakim: Paid In Full; Mad For It; Fruit Cocktail; Best Album in the World Ever; Ted Hawkins: The Ted Hawkins Story; Other artists including: Mae; Suicide Twins; Bizarre Inc; Gunshot; War; Catch My Soul. *Current Management:* XL Talent. *Address:* Studio 7, 27A Pembridge Villas, London W11 3EP, England.

SCOTT Clive Kenneth; b. 24 Feb. 1945, Coventry, England. Musician (keyboards); Prod.; Writer. m. Ann Constance, 18 June 1994, 1 s. *Musical Education:* Church choir to pop groups. *Career:* Keyboard player, co-writer for Jigsaw, 1968–81; Independent writer producer. *Recordings:* with Apollo 100: Joy; with Candlewick Green and St Etienne: Who Do You Think You Are; with Jigsaw: Sky High; The Very Best of Jigsaw; with Bad Boys Inc: Walking On Air; Disco Remix Project, Vols 5 and 6, 1997. *Publications:* Music for video and film includes Shape Challenge fitness videos. *Honours:* Gold discs, Sky High; Ivor Novello Certificate of Honour. *Memberships:* Songwriters Guild; PRS. *Leisure interest:* House renovation. *Current Management:* Chas Peate, Belsize Music. *Address:* 29 Manor House, Marylebone Rd, London NW1 5NP, England.

SCOTT David Andrew; b. 20 Aug. 1964, Falkirk, Scotland. Songwriter; Musician (guitar; keyboards); Vocalist. m. Julie Parker, 19 Aug. 1989. *Education:* Graphics, Falkirk College; Glasgow School of Art. *Career:* Appeared on Indie compilation, 1984; Other recordings as Chewy Raccoon and Hearts and Minds; Film and television commissions; Founder, My Dark Star record label to release records by The Pearlfishers, 1991–; Major concert appearances include: Scottish Fleadh, 1992; T In The Park, Glasgow, 1994; Celtic Connections, Royal Concert Hall, 1995. *Recordings:* Sacred (EP), The Pearlfishers, 1991; Hurt (EP), The Pearlfishers, 1991; Za Za's Garden, The Pearlfishers, 1994. *Memberships:* PRS; Musicians' Union. *Leisure interests:* Painting; Cooking. *Current Management:* My Dark Star Records. *Address:* PO Box 1, Glasgow G3 6TZ, England.

SCOTT Don E; b. 12 Feb. 1937, Canada. Singer; Songwriter; Musician (Guitar, Steel guitar, Mandolin, Harmonica, Dobro, Drums). m. Marie, 1 s.,

2 d. *Education:* Diplomas in Real Property Management, Public Relations, Interpersonal Skills, Economics and Social Philosophy. *Career:* Television, Radio, Video and Stage Performances; Businessman and Consultant. *Compositions:* Over 600 Songs. *Recordings:* The Real Deal; Beginnings; Room In My Heart. *Honours:* Numerous Awards and Prizes in Songwriting and Singing; also numerous honours for community services. *Membership:* Songwriters Asscn of Canada. *Leisure interests:* Ice Hockey; Downhill (Alpine) Skiing. *Current Management:* The Management Centre, 13808, 110A Ave, Edmonton, AB, Canada T5M 2M9.

SCOTT Hammond; b. 15 May 1950, Alexandria, Louisiana, USA. Record producer; Attorney. *Education:* Dr of Law. *Career:* Co-owner, Black Top Records Inc (internationally distributed and recognized blues, R & B and roots label); Produced over 100 albums; Served as personal manager of blues artist Clarence 'Gatemouth' Brown, 1970's; Former writer, Living Blues Magazine; Hosted radio show on WWOZ FM, New Orleans, for 5 years; Produced recordings by R & B artists including: Solomon Burke; Maria Muldaur; Earl King; Snooks Eaglin; Bobby Parker; Neville Brothers; Anson Funderburgh and the Rockets, Former Prosecutor, District Attorney's Office of Harry Connick Sr; Neville Brothers; Bobby Radcliff; Bobby Parker; Robert Ward; Ronnie Earl; Earl Gaines. *Honours:* Numerous W C Handy Awards, Grammy Award nominations. *Leisure interests:* Vintage arts collector and restorer; Vintage watch collector. *Address:* 5340 Camp St, New Orleans, LA 70115, USA.

SCOTT Jill; b. Philadelphia, USA. Vocalist; Poet. *Career:* Started career reading poetry until spotted by local hip hop outfit The Roots; Wrote lyrics for their Grammy Award-winning first single You Got Me; Performed with Canadian cast of stage musical Rent; Collaborations: Eric Benet; Will Smith; Common; 4 Hero. *Recordings:* Albums: Who Is Jill Scott? Words and Sounds Vol. 1, 2000; Experience, 2001; Singles: Gettin' In The Way, 2000; A Long Walk, The Way, Thickness, 2001. *Address:* c/o Hidden Beach Recordings, 3030 Nebraska Ave Penthouse Suite, Santa Monica CA 9404, USA. *Internet:* www.hiddenbeach.com.

SCOTT Lydia; b. 9 Aug. 1953, Montréal, Québec, Canada. Country Recording Artist; Musician (Guitar). *Education:* Montréal University. *Career:* Six Top 30 Chart Singles nationally. *Compositions:* The Moon She Knows; True Love; I Could Love You; As Good As You Look. *Recordings:* Isn't It Always Love; You Can Crash Here. *Honours:* Talent Contest Winner, 1989; Nominated 1990–99 In BC Awards For Country Music; Nominated Best New Artist, 1994; Winner BC Female Vocalist of The Year, 1999. *Leisure interests:* Swimming; Outdoor Activity; Travel; Tennis. *Current Management:* Publicity: Jodi Smith. *Address:* #704 2121 W 44th Ave, Vancouver BC, Canada V6M 2G5.

SCOTT Malcolm; b. 20 Aug. 1964, San Francisco, California, USA. Musician (drums, percussion, guitar); Songwriter; Singer. m. Dominique Atkins, 26 Aug. 1994. *Musical Education:* Berkshire Centre Performing Arts; Musicians Institute, London. *Career:* Musician for: The Cure; Pretenders; Belinda Carlisle; Buddy Curtiss; McAlmont; Jimmy Nail; Vanessa Mae; Skunk Anansie; Take That; Michelle Gayle; Grace. *Recordings:* Lovesongs End, Grace. *Membership:* Musicians' Union. *Leisure interests:* Football; Television; Family and friends. *Current Management:* Mickey Curbishley; Agent: Session Connection. *Address:* 16 Lynfield Court, 161 Devonshire Rd, London SE23 3ND, England.

SCOTT Matthew James; b. 11 Oct. 1967, London, England. Musician (piano); Composer. *Musical Education:* Self-taught. *Career:* Resident pianist, The Vortex, 1994–95; Regular appearances on London jazz/pop circuit, London jazz festivals, 1994–95; Clubs include: The 606; The Orange; The King's Head, Upper Street; Chat's Palace. *Compositions:* L'Esquisse, film soundtrack, 1995; Trio for strings, 1995. *Recordings:* Album: Improvisations For Solo Piano, 1995; Standards, 1995; Contributions to: Wonderful Town, London cast recording, 1986; Snoopy, original London cast recording, 1998. *Leisure interests:* Hedonism; Lunacy. *Current Management:* Paddy French. *Address:* 249 Goswell Rd, London EC1V 7JD, England.

SCOTT Mike; b. 14 Dec. 1958, Edinburgh, Scotland. Singer; Songwriter; Musician (guitar). *Musical Education:* Self-taught. *Career:* Lead singer, groups: Another Pretty Face, 1979–81; The Red and The Black, 1982; The Waterboys, 1983–93; Solo artiste, 1994–; Tours, UK, US and Japan, 1995; Glastonbury Festival, 1995; UK, Europe, Japan, 1997. *Recordings:* Albums: with The Waterboys: A Pagan Place, 1984; This Is The Sea, 1985; Fisherman's Blues, 1988; Room To Roam, 1990; The Best of The Waterboys, 1991; Dream Harder, 1993; Secret Life of the Waterboys, 1994; Solo albums: Bring 'Em All In, 1995; Still Burning, 1997; Whole of the Moon, 1998; with Characters: Characters, 1997; with Angel Grant: Album, 1998. *Publications:* Jungleland, 1977–80. *Honours:* Ivor Novello Award for composition, The Whole of The Moon, 1992. *Current Management:* Strawberry Management Ltd, 112 Maxwell Ave, Glasgow G61 H11, Scotland. *Internet:* www.mikescottmusic.com.

SCOTT Rick; b. 14 July 1948, New Jersey, USA. Singer; Songwriter; Actor; Musician (dulcimer, whimmydiddle, guitar, trombone, tuba, Japanese flute). *Musical Education:* Self-taught. *Career:* Pied Pumkin String Ensemble, 1975–76; Pied Pear, 1976–83; Rick Scott Band, 1985–86; Concert tours throughout Canada, USA, Australia, Asia as solo family performer; Starred in numerous stage plays, musicals including: Barnum (title role); The Late Blumer and Angry Housewives. *Recordings:* 10 recordings including 3 albums for children; The Electric Snowshoe, 1989; Rick Around the Rock, 1992; Philharmonic Fool, 1995. *Honours:* Juno Award nominee, 1996; Pacific Music Industry Award, Best Children's Album, 1997. *Memberships:* AFofM; SOCAN; ACTRA; Canadian Actors Equity. *Current Management:* Ms Valley Hennell, Manager. *Address:* 2736 W 13 Ave, Vancouver, BC V6K 2T4, Canada.

SCOTT Tommy; b. 18 Feb. 1966. Vocalist; Songwriter. *Career:* Founder Member, Space; Original bass player, until 1997; Numerous television appearances and live dates. *Recordings:* Singles: If It's Real, 1993; Money, 1995; Neighbourhood, 1996; Female of the Species, 1997; Me and You vs The World, 1997; Dark Clouds, 1997; Avenging Angels, 1997; The Ballad of Tom Jones, with Cerys Matthews, 1998; Begin Again, 1998; Bad Days, 1998; Albums: Spiders, 1996; Remixes and B-Sides, 1996; Tin Planet, 1998.

SCOTT Toni Lee; b. 15 Jan. 1933, San Francisco, California, USA. Singer. m. Angelo Ligi, 26 Dec. 1989. *Career:* Professional singer, from age 14; Member, Bob Scobey's Band; Bob Crosby's Band; Television shows: This Is Your Life; Johnny Carson; Steve Allen; Tennessee Ernie Ford; Mike Douglas; Radio shows across the country; Clubs include: Stardust, Las Vegas; Riviera, Las Vegas; Roundtable, New York; Mr Kelly's, Chicago; Sherman House, Chicago; Mr T's, Chicago; Pigalle, Chicago; Cafe Continental, Chicago; Memory Lane, Los Angeles; Purple Onion, San Francisco; Other appearances include: Chicago Tribune Music Festival, Chicago; Codac Benefit, Phoenix. *Recordings:* Albums: San Francisco; Goody Goody; Something's Always Happening On The River, 1959; Volume Lonely, 1963; Songs of My Friends, 1996. *Publications:* A Kind of Loving, (autobiography). *Honours:* Fade To Gold Award, Entertainer of The Year – Cerebral Palsy; Woman of The Year, Heart Asscn. *Memberships:* Society of Singers; Women In Music Business. *Leisure interests:* Swimming; Cooking. *Current Management:* Terri Tilton Management; Agent: Prince SF Productions. *Address:* 6 Haverhill Court, Novato, CA 94947, USA.

SCOTT Tony; b. 3 Oct. 1973, Paramaribo, Suriname. Rapper; Dancer; Singer; Composer. *Musical Education:* Self-taught. *Career:* First hit and recording, 1987; 10 Top 10 hits; Working with Candy Dulfer. *Recordings:* Pick Up The Pieces, 1987; Top 10 hit singles: The Chief, 1988; That's How I'm Living, 1988; Gangster Boogie, 1989; Get Into It, 1990; Greenhouse Effect, 1991; The Bigband, 1992; Love and Let Love, 1992. *Honours:* Dance Artist Award, 1989, 1990; 5 Gold singles. *Membership:* FNV Kunstenbond. *Leisure interest:* Music. *Current Management:* Hans Van Pol Management. *Address:* PO Box 9010, 1006 AA Amsterdam, Netherlands.

SCOTT-HERON Gil; b. 1 April 1949, Chicago, Illinois, USA. Singer; Songwriter. *Education:* Lincoln University, Pennsylvania, USA. *Career:* Co-founder, The Midnight Band, 1972–; Major concerts include: Phoenix Festival, 1995. *Compositions include:* The Revolution Will Not Be Televised, Labelle; Home Is Where The Hatred Is, Esther Phillips. *Recordings:* Albums: Small Talk At 125th and Lenox, 1970; Pieces of a Man, 1971; Free Will, 1972; Winter In America, 1974; The Revolution Will Not Be Televised, 1974; The First Minute of a New Day, 1975; From South Africa To South Carolina, 1975; It's Your World, 1976; Bridges, 1977; Secrets, 1978; The Mind of Gil Scott-Heron, 1979; 1980, 1980; Real Eyes, 1980; Reflections, 1981; Moving Target, 1982; The Best of Gil Scott-Heron, 1984; Amnesia Express, 1990; Spirits, 1994; Minister of Information, 1994; Singles include: The Bottle, 1973; Johannesburg, 1976; B-Movie, 1982; Fast Lane, 1982; No Exit, 1982; Re-Ron, 1984. *Publications:* Author, novels: The Vulture; The Nigger Factory; Book of poetry.

SCREECHY Jah (Elton Loye Sinclair); b. 9 Feb. 1958, Jamaica. Vocalist; DJ. *Education:* College diploma; City and Guilds. *Career:* Mechanical Engineering; Television appearances: Top of The Pops; Radio 1 Road Show, Margate; Ritzy Night Club, Streatham; Stage shows and personal appearances, England, France and Germany. *Recordings:* Walk and Skank, 1984; Shadow Move, Hop Scotch, 1985; On A Ragga Tip, 1992. *Memberships:* Musicians' Union; PRS. *Leisure interests:* Weight training; Martial arts. *Current Management:* James Augustus (Jessus). *Address:* Oxford House Studio, Oxford House, Derbyshire St, Bethnal Green, London E2, England.

SCRUGGS Earl; b. 6 Jan. 1924, Cleveland County, North Carolina, USA. Country Musician (banjo). *Career:* Member, Bill Monroe's Bluegrass Boys, 1944–48; Co-founder, Flatt and Scruggs show with Lester Flatt, 1948; Regular radio and television appearances include: Folk Sound USA; Concerts include: Newport Folk Festival, 1960; Leader, Earl Scruggs Revue, 1969–; Concerts include: Wembley Country Music Festival, 1972. *Composition:* Foggy Mountain Breakdown. *Recordings include:* Foggy Mountain Breakdown, from film Bonnie and Clyde; The Ballad of Jed Clampett, theme for television series The Beverly Hillbillies; Albums: with Earl Scruggs Revue: include: Duelling Banjos, 1973; Family and Friends, 1972; Anniversary Special Vol. I, 1975; Family Portrait, 1976; Bold and New, 1978; Today and Forever, 1979; Top of The World, 1983; Can You feel it in Your Soul, 1999; Several collections of Flatt and Scruggs; WithBill Monroe: 16 Gems, 1996; Early Years, 1998. *Publications:* Author, Earl Scruggs and The 5-String Banjo. *Honours include:* Artist of the Year, Hi-Fi Institute, 1975; Citation of Merit Country Music Asscn nomination, Best Country Instrument Group, 1975; Best Country Instrumental Group, Billboard Magazine, 1975; Certificate of Appreciation, Governor of Tennessee, 1978; Earl Scruggs Day, for contribution to American Music, 1980; Gibson Hall of Fame, 1981; Country Music Asscn Hall of Fame, 1985; Hon. Mem., Lieutenant Governors Staff, State of Tennessee, 1987; Order of the Long Leaf Pine Award, Governor of North Carolina, 1988; Hall of Honour, International Bluegrass Music Asscn, 1991; National Medal of Arts, presented by George Bush, 1992. *Memberships:* Country Music Asscn. *Current Management:* Louise Scruggs, PO Box 66, Madison, TN 37116, USA.

SEAL (Henry Samuel); b. 19 Feb. 1963, Paddington, London, England. Singer; Songwriter. *Career:* Singer, Adamski, 1990; Solo artiste, 1991–; Concerts and tours: Red Hot and Dance, AIDS benefit concert, London, 1991; Amnesty International's Big 30, 1991; Freddie Mercury Tribute, A Concert For Life, Wembley, 1992; Support to Rolling Stones, 1994. *Recordings:* Solo albums: Seal (No. 1, UK), 1991; Seal, 1994; Human Being, 1998; Seal, 1999; Singles: Killer, with Adamski (No. 1, UK), 1990; Solo singles: Crazy (No. 2, UK), 1991; Future Love Paradise, 1991; The Beginning, 1991; Prayer For The Dying, 1994; Kiss From A Rose, 1995; If I Could, 1995; I'm Alive, 1995; Don't Cry, 1996; Fly like an Eagle, 1997; Human Beings, 1998; Lost my Faith, 1999; Killer, 1999; Featured on film soundtracks: Toys, 1991; Indecent Proposal, 1993. *Honours:* Ivor Novello Award, Best Contemporary Song, Killer, 1991; Q Award, Best New Act, 1991; Variety Club of Great Britain's Recording Artist of 1991; BRIT Awards: Best Male Artist, Best British Album, Best British Video, 1992; 4 Grammy Awards, including Best Record, Best Song, 1996; Grammy Nominations, 1992, 1995; Ivor Novello Awards: Best Contemporary Song, International Hit of The Year, Crazy, 1992. *Current Management:* Third Rail Entertainment, 9169 Sunset Blvd, Los Angeles, CA 90069, USA.

SEALS Dan; b. 8 Feb. 1950, McCamey, Texas, USA. Country Singer; Songwriter. *Career:* Partnership with John Ford Coley, 1967–80; Originally billed as Southwest FOB, then as England Dan and John Ford Coley; Solo artiste, 1980-. *Recordings:* As England Dan and John Ford Coley: Hit singles include: I'd Really Love To See You Tonight; Nights Are Forever Without You; Albums: Smell of Incense (as Southwest FOB), 1968; England Dan and John Ford Coley, 1971; Fables, 1971; I Hear The Music, 1976; Nights Are Forever, 1976; Dowdy Ferry Road, 1977; Some Things Don't Come Easy, 1978; Dr Heckle and Mr Jive, 1978; Just Tell Me If You Love Me, 1980; Solo hits include: Meet Me In Montana, with Marie Osmond (US Country No. 1), 1985; Bop; Everything That Glitters (Is Not Gold); You Still Move Me; I Will Be There; Three Time Loser; One Friend; Addicted; Big Wheels In The Moonlight; Love Thing; Fired Up; Albums: Stones, 1980; Harbinger, 1982; Rebel Heart, 1983; San Antone, 1984; Won't Be Blue Anymore, 1985; On The Front Line, 1986; Rage On, 1988; On Arrival, 1990; Walking The Wire, 1992; The Songwriter, 1992; My Baby's Got Good Timing, 1994; Fired Up, 1994; In a Quiet Room, 1995; In a Quiet Room II, 1998. *Current Management:* Morningstar Management, PO Box 1770, Hendersonville, TN 37077, USA.

SEALS Troy; b. 16 Nov. 1938, Big Hill, Kentucky, USA. Songwriter; Musician (guitar). m. Jo Ann Campbell. *Career:* Guitarist, club bands, Ohio, 1960s; Formed duo with Jo Ann Campbell; Moved to Nashville as songwriter; Session guitarist and solo artiste. *Compositions:* There's A Honky Tonk Angel (Who'll Take Me Back In), recorded by Elvis Presley, Conway Twitty (US Country No. 1); Pieces of My Life, recorded by Elvis Presley; We Had It All (co-written with Donnie Fritts), recorded by Rita Coolidge, Brenda Lee, Scott Walker, Waylon Jennings; Feeling (co-written with Will Jennings and Don Goodman), recorded by Loretta Lynn and Conway Twitty (US Country No. 1); Storms (co-written with Max Barnes), recorded by Randy Travis; Seven Spanish Angels (co-written with Eddie Setser), recorded by Willie Nelson and Ray Charles (US Country No. 1). *Recordings:* Solo albums include: Now Presenting Troy Seals, 1973; Troy Seals, 1976; Contributions to: James Brown's Original Funky Divas, 1998; Lonnie Mack, Road Houses and Dance Halls; Con Hunley, I Don't Want to Lose You; Bob Ruzicka, Soft Rocker.

SEALY Denice; b. 25 Nov. 1964, London, England. Backing Vocalist. *Musical Education:* Vocal Studies, University of East London. *Career:* Greenbelt Christian Festival, with Bryan Powell, 1989–91; Hammersmith Odeon, with Jennifer Holliday, 1993; EMI Music Conference, with Kenny Thomas, 1993; Wembley Arena, with Dina Carroll, 1994; with Carleen Anderson, British tour, 1993; Motor Traders Awards, 1995; with D C Lee, UK promo tour, 1995; Television: The Beat; The Late Show, 1993; Virgin

Records Music Anniversary, 1994; Pebble Mill, 1995; Backing vocals, World (Pentecostal Conference), Jerusalem, Israel, 1995. *Recordings:* Albums: I Think of You, Bryan Powell, 1992; Michelle Gayle, 1993; Nu Inspirational Album, Soul Stirrings. *Membership:* Musicians' Union. *Leisure interests:* Tap dancing; Theatre; Gospel concerts; Tennis. *Current Management:* c/o Mixed Music Ltd. *Address:* 2 The Spinney, Dyke Rd Ave, Hove, Sussex BN3 6QT, England.

SEAMONE Joyce Evelyn; b. 21 May 1946, Bridgewater, Nova Scotia, Canada. Singer; Songwriter; Entertainer. m. Gerald Ivan Seamone, 12 Sept. 1964, 3 d. *Career:* Toured Canada, early 1970's; Television appearances, Countrytime, Canadian National TV show; Headliner, exhibitions and clubs in Eastern Canada; Currently performing in Eastern Canada. *Recordings:* Testing 1–2–3, 1972; Merry Christmas From Joyce Seamone, 1972; Stand By For A Special Announcement, 1973; I Can See It In His Eyes, 1976; The Other Side of Me, 1994; Instructional Line, Dance video, 1995. *Honours:* Gold Record, Testing 1–2–3, 1973; CHFX-FM, Country Music Hall of Fame, Halifax, Nova Scotia, Canada. *Memberships:* CCMA; SOCAN; ECMA; MIANS; SAC. *Leisure interest:* Reading. *Current Management:* Gerald Seamone. *Address:* RR2 New Germany, Nova Scotia B0R 1E0, Canada.

SEARLE Richard; Musician (Bass). *Career:* Former Member, Doctor and the Medics; Several television appearances; Formed Corduroy for one-off gig; Decided to continue and obtained record deal; Several UK top ten hits. *Recordings:* Singles: with Doctor and the Medics: Spirit in the Sky (UK number 1); Burn; with Corduroy: Something in My Eye; The Frighteners; London, England; The Joker is Wild; Overhaul; Albums: Dad Man Cat, 1992; High Havoc, 1993; Out of Here, 1994; The New You, 1997.

SEBASTIAN John; b. 17 March 1944, New York, USA. Singer; Musician (guitar, harmonica, autoharp). *Career:* Founder member, The Lovin' Spoonful, 1965–68; Appearances include: British tour, 1966; Beach Boys Summer Spectacular, Anaheim, 1966; State Fairs tour, 1966; Solo artiste, 1969–; Appearances include: Woodstock Festival, 1969; Isle of Wight Festival, 1970; Tours as one-man show, 1970s; Session musician for artistes including: Stephen Stills; Rita Coolidge; Everly Brothers; Host, The Golden Age of Rock 'N' Roll, AandE cable channel, 1991; Actor, episode, Married With Children, Fox TV, 1992. *Compositions include:* Music for television and films: Welcome Back, for Welcome Back, Kotter, ABC TV, 1976; The Care Bears; Strawberry Shortcake; The Jerk II, NBC TV. *Recordings:* Albums: with The Lovin' Spoonful: Do You Believe In Magic, 1965; Daydream, 1966; What's Shakin', 1966; Hums of The Lovin' Spoonful, 1966; The Best of The Lovin' Spoonful, 1967; Everything Playing, 1968; The Best of The Lovin' Spoonful Vol. 2, 1968; Very Best of Lovin' Spoonful, 1998; Solo albums: John B Sebastian, 1970; John Sebastian Live, 1970; Cheapo Cheapo Productions Present, 1971; The Four of Us, 1971; The Tarzana Kid, 1974; Welcome Back, 1976; Tar Beach, 1993; John Sebastian, 1995; I Want My Roots, 1996; King Biscuit Flower Hour Live, 1996; Chasin' Gus' Ghost, 1999; with Doors: Greatest Hits, 1996; with Peter Paul and mary: Around the Campfire, 1998; with Secret Sessions: Secret Sessions, 1999; Hit singles include: with Lovin' Spoonful: Do You Believe In Magic, 1965; You Didn't Have To Be So Nice, 1966; Daydream, 1966; Did You Ever Have To Make Up Your Mind, 1966; Summer In The City (No. 1, USA), 1966; Rain On The Roof, 1966; Nashville Cats, 1967; Darling Be Home Soon, 1967; Six O'Clock, 1967; She's Still A Mystery, 1967; Money, 1968. *Current Management:* c/o David Bendett, 2431 Briar Crest Rd, Beverly Hills, CA 90210, USA.

SEBASTIAN Mark Douglas; b. 20 Feb. 1951, New York City, USA. Performer; Songwriter; Screenwriter; Film Prod.; Musician (guitar, bass, keyboards). *Education:* Kim Stanley Drama Study. *Musical Education:* Piano study, New York. *Career:* Performances: New York clubs: Gaslight; Wetlands; Lone Star; Theatre Music: La Mama; Television; Solid Gold; Cheers; Wizards and Warriors; Los Angeles clubs: The Strand; Wadsworth Theatre; Also performing member, Second City Emperor (Santa Monica group). *Compositions:* Summer In The City (Lovin' Spoonful, 1966), song co-written with (brother) John Sebastian and Steve Boone, used in film Die Hard – With A Vengeance, 1996. *Honours:* 3 Gold records. *Memberships:* BMI; ASCAP; SAG; AFTRA. *Address:* c/o BMI, Los Angeles, California, USA.

SEBESTYÉN Márta; b. 1961, Budapest, Hungary. Vocalist; Musician (recorder); Songwriter. *Career:* Sings, researches and promotes roots music of Hungary and Transylvania; Grew up surrounded by folk music, mother had studied with composer Zoltan Kodaly and collected folk songs; Started singing at Budapest 'dance houses' while still at school; Joined Sebö Halmos group, 1975; Became part of Hungary's leading folk group Muzsikás, 1980; Also sang with renowned group Vujicsics; Appeared in musical based on the life of King Stephen, 1984; Toured internationally with Muzsikás. *Recordings:* Albums: Transylvanian Portraits, 1993; Kismet, 1996; with Karoly Cserepes: Hungarian Christmas Songs, 1984; Lovercord, 1985; Emigration, 1986; with Muzsikás: The Prisoner's Song, 1986; Muzsikás, 1987; Blues For Transylvania, 1991; Maramaros – The Lost Jewish Music of Transylvania, 1993; The Bartok Album, 1999; with

Vujicsics: Serbian Music From Southern Hungary, 1988; features on: East Wind, Andy Irvine and Davy Spillane, 1992; Boheme, Deep Forest, 1995; Coolfin, Donal Lunny, 1998; The English Patient OST, 1996; Flirt OST, 1996; American Rhapsody, 2001. *Honours:* Hungarian Female Singer of The Year, 1984; Liszt Award, 1991.

SECADA Jon; b. 10 April 1961, Havana, Cuba. Vocalist; Songwriter; Prod. *Musical Education:* Master's degree, Jazz Vocal Performance, University of Miami. *Career:* Central and South America Tour, 1994; US Tour, 1995; World Cup, 1994; X-Mas in Washington, 1994; National Anthem World Series, 1992; Grease, Broadway, 1995; Lifebeat concert, 1994. *Recordings:* Albums: Jon Secada, 1992; Heart Soul and A Voice, 1994; Si Te Vas, 1994; Frank Sinatra Duets II: The Best Is Yet To Come, 1994; Heart Soul and Voice, 1994; Amor, 1995; Secada, 1997; Singles include: Mental Picture, 1995; Where do I Go from You?, 1995; Whipped, 1995; If I Never Knew You, 1995; Too Late too Soon, 1997. *Honours:* Grammy: Best Latin Pop Album: Otro Dia Mas Sin Verte, 1992; Alumnus of Distinction, University of Miami. *Membership:* National Academy of Recording Arts and Sciences. *Leisure interests:* Exercising; Playing tennis; Watching sports. *Current Management:* William Morris Agency, 151 El Camino Dr., Beverly Hills, CA 90212, USA; Estefan Enterprises, 6205 Bird Rd, Miami, FL 33155, USA.

SECK Cheick Amadou Tidiane; b. 11 Dec. 1953, Segou, Mali. Musician (keyboards, African percussion); Vocalist. 1 s. *Education:* BEPC, Diplome Institut National des Arts. *Musical Education:* Lear Organ and Solfege in church. *Career:* Concert with Jimmy Cliff, 1977; African and European tours with The Ambassadors of Mali and Salif Keita; World Tour with Amina, 1992–93; Printemps de Bourges Festival; Television Show: Taratata; Cercle De Minuit; Nulle Part Ailleurs, France. *Recordings:* Salif Keita: Soro; Amen; Graham Haynes: The Griots Footstep; Joe Zawinul: Next; Hank Jones, Cheick Tidiane Seck: My People; The Madenkas; with Toure Kunda: Mouslai, 1996; Ceci N'Est Pas Une Compilation, 1998; with Tama: Nostalgie, 1999. *Honours:* Emission: Pollen by Jean Louis Foulquier; Articles: Liberation/Bingo. *Memberships:* SACEM; SPEDIDAM. *Leisure interests:* Table tennis; Football; Films; Painting. *Current Management:* Jacques Sajuan, Polygram Music, 20 rue des Fosses St Jacques, 75005 Paris, France.

SEDAKA Neil; b. 13 March 1939. Singer; Songwriter. m. Leba Margaret Strassberg, 11 Sept. 1962, 1 s., 1 d. *Musical Education:* Graduate, Juilliard School of Music. *Career:* Solo performer, world-wide, 1959–; Television appearances include: NBC-TV Special, 1976. *Compositions include:* Breaking Up Is Hard To Do; Stupid Cupid; Calendar Girl; Oh! Carol; Stairway To Heaven; Happy Birthday Sweet Sixteen; Laughter In The Rain; Bad Blood; Love Will Keep Us Together; Solitaire; The Hungry Years; Lonely Night (Angel Face). *Recordings:* Albums include: In The Pocket; Sedaka's Back; The Hungry Years; Steppin' Out; A Song; All You Need Is The Music; Come See About Me; Greatest Hits, 1988; Oh! Carol and Other Hits, 1990; Timeless, 1992; Calendar Girl, 1993; Tuneweaver, 1995; The Immaculate, 1997; Tales of Love, 1999. *Honours:* Songwriters' Hall of Fame, 1980; Platinum album, Timeless, 1992; Numerous Gold records; Various industry awards. *Memberships:* AGVA; AFofM; AFTRA. *Address:* c/o Neil Sedaka Music, 201 E 66th St, Suite 3N, New York, NY 10021, USA.

SEDGWICK Amanda; b. 7 Oct. 1970, Stockholm, Sweden. Musician; Songwriter; Composer. *Education:* Royal Swedish University College of Music, Stockholm. *Career:* Toured Sweden; Appeared on Swedish Television and Radio, including Live Broadcasts. *Compositions:* Volt, 3 movement suite for jazz group, string quartet and woodwinds. *Recordings:* Volt, 1996; Contributor to So Many Stars, 1996 and Kalabra, 1997. *Honours:* Debut of the Year, Swedish National Radio. *Memberships:* Swedish Society of Popular Music Composers; Swedish Performing Rights Society. *Address:* Stromkarlsvagen 74, 167 62 Bromma, Sweden.

SEEGER Michael; b. 15 Aug. 1933, New York, New York, USA. Singer; Musician; Folklorist. m. (1) Marjorie L Ostrow, 20 Dec. 1960, divorced, 3 c., (2) Alice L Gerrard, 16 Aug. 1970, divorced, (3) Alexia Smith, 27 Aug. 1995. *Career:* Founder member, New Lost City Ramblers, 1958–; Strange Creek Singers, 1968–76; Bent Mountain Band, 1981; Guest lecturer, English department, University of California, Fresno, 1974; Performs Appalachian vocal and instrumental music in variety of styles, radio, TV, USA and abroad; Numerous record albums and documentary recordings from traditional folk musicians and dancers. *Recordings:* Old Time Country Music, 1991; Southern Banjo Sounds, 1998. *Honours:* First prize, banjo, Galax Virginia Old Time Fiddlers Convention, 1958; National Endowment for the Arts grantee, 4 times; Visiting scholar, Smithsonian Institute, 1983, Guggenheim Fellow, 1984; 6 Grammy Nominations, Best Traditional Folk Album, 1986, 1991, 1994, 1997, 1998, 2000; Ralph J Gleason Memorial Award Rex Foundation, 1994. *Current Management:* Folklore Productions, 1671 Appian Way, Santa Monica, CA 90401–3293, USA. *Address:* PO Box 1592, Lexington, VA 24450–1592, USA.

SEEGER Peggy; b. 17 June 1935, New York, USA. Singer; Songmaker; Musician (guitar, piano, 5-string banjo, autoharp, Appalachian dulcimer, English concertina). m. Ewan MacColl, 25 Jan. 1978, 2 s., 1 d. *Musical Education:* Radclyffe College. *Career:* Concerts include: (in USA) Boston Orchestra Hall; Carnegie Hall; Australia; New Zealand; Canada; UK; Sweden; Soviet Union; France; Belgium; Netherlands; China; Many television and radio appearances; Tours since 1955. *Compositions:* Ballad of Springhill; Gonna Be An Engineer. *Recordings:* 19 solo albums; Major participation in over 100 other albums. *Publications:*; with Ewan MacColl: Travellers' Songs of England and Ireland; Doomsday In The Afternoon; Solo: Peggy Seeger Song Book: Forty Years of Songmaking; The Essential Ewan Macoll Song Book. *Honours:* Italia Prize for participation in BBC Radio Ballad: Singing The Fishing. *Memberships:* Musicians' Union; USA and UK. *Leisure interests:* Travel; Environmental work; Reading; Sports. *Current Management:* Josh Dunson.

SEEGER Pete; b. 3 May 1919, New York, USA. Folk Musician (banjo, guitar); Composer. m. Toshi, 20 July 1943, 1 s., 2 d. *Education:* Harvard College, 1936–38. *Career:* Folk singer/musician for 56 years; World-wide tours across 35 countries; Collaborated on anti-Facist and labour songs; National Director, People's Songs Inc, 1945; Formed the Weavers, 1948; appeared, until blacklisted from, on national radio and television networks; Assisted Newport Folk Festivals; Produced educational short films, Folklore Research Films; TV and film appearances: To Hear My Banjo Play, 1946; Rainbow Quest, 1965; Tell Me That You Love Me, Junie Moon, 1970. *Compositions include:* Turn, Turn, Turn; Where Have All The Flowers Gone; If I Had A Hammer (with Lee Hays); Kisses Sweeter Than Wine (with the Weavers); Also popularized Guantanamera, We Shall Overcome. *Recordings include:* Abiyoyo, 1967; Rainbow Race, 1971; The World of Pete Seeger, 1973; Live at Newport, 1993; Kisses Sweeter than Wine, 1996; Link in the Chain, 1996; God Bless the Grass, 1998; American Favorite Ballads, Vols 1, 2, 3, 4, 5; If I had a Hammer: Songs of Hope and Struggle, 1998; Pioneer of Folk, 1999; Pete Seegers Greatest Hits, 2000. *Publications:* American Folk Ballads, 1961; The Bells of Rhymney, 1964; How To Play The Five String Banjo, Henscratches and Flyspecks, 1973; The Incompleat Folksinger (with Charles Seeger), 1973; The Foolish Frog, 1973; Where Have All The Flowers Gone (autobiography), 1993; Co-writer with Robert Reiser: Abiyoyo, 1983; Carry It On, 1986; Everybody Says Freedom, 1990. *Honours:* Westchester People's Action Committee, Peace and Justice Award to Toshi and Peter Seeger, 1990; NEA National Medal of Arts, 1994; Kennedy Center Honours, 1994. *Membership:* AFofM. *Leisure interest:* Axe chopping. *Current Management:* Harold Leventhal. *Address:* Room 1218, 250 W 57th St, New York, NY 10107, USA.

SEGER Bob; b. 6 May 1945, Dearborn, Missouri, USA. Singer; Songwriter; Musician (keyboards). *Career:* Member, The Town Criers; Doug Brown and The Omens, 1965–66; Leader of own bands: The Last Heard, 1966–67; The Bob Seger System, 1967–70; The Silver Bullet Band, 1976–; Regular US tours. *Recordings:* Albums: Ramblin' Gamblin' Man, 1969; Noah, 1970; Mongrel, 1970; Brand New Morning, 1971; Smokin' OP's, 1972; Back In '72, 1973; Seven/Contrasts, 1974; Beautiful Loser, 1975; Live Bullet, 1976; Night Moves, 1977; Stranger In Town, 1978; Against The Wind (No. 1, USA), 1980; Nine Tonight, 1981; The Distance, 1983; Like A Rock, 1986; The Fire Inside, 1991; Greatest Hits, 1995; It's A Mystery, 1995; Singles include: Ramblin' Gamblin Man, 1969; Katmandu, 1975; Night Moves, 1977; Mainstreet, 1977; Still The Same, 1978; Hollywood Nights, 1978; We've Got Tonight, 1979; Fire Lake, 1980; Against The Wind, 1980; You'll Accomp'ny Me, 1980; Tryin' To Live My Life Without You, 1981; Shame On The Moon (No. 2, US), 1983; Even Now, 1983; Roll Me Away, 1983; American Storm, 1986; Like A Rock, 1986; Shakedown (No. 1, USA), from film soundtrack Beverley Hills Cop II, 1987; The Real Love, 1991; It's A Mystery, 1995; Turn the Page, 1995; Night Moves, 1997; Also contributor to: Risky Business, 1983; Teachers, 1984; Miami, for television series Miami Vice, 1986; A Very Special Christmas benefit album, 1987; Let It Roll, Little Feat, 1988; Armageddon, 1998; Guilty: 30 Years of Randy Newman, 1998. *Honours:* Numerous Platinum discs; Grammy Award, Best Rock Performance, 1981; Star on Hollywood Walk of Fame, 1988; Governors Award, NARAS, 1992; Motor City Music Awards, Musician of the Year, Outstanding National Rock 'n' Pop Album, 1992. *Current Management:* Punch Enterprises, 567 Purdy, Birmingham, MI 48009, USA.

SEGLEM Karl; b. 8 July 1961, Ardalstangen, Norway. Musician (tenor saxophone); Composer; Arranger. *Musical Education:* Private lessons. *Career:* Toured Norway and abroad with jazz and folk bands, 1985–; Now one of foremost saxophone players, Norway; Working with own music based on Norwegian folk music; Numerous television and radio appearances; Concert tours: USA; Japan; UK; Germany. *Recordings:* with Isglem: To Steg, Null G; with Utla: Juv; Brodd; Dans; Solo album: Rit: Tya; And Spir. *Honours:* Edvard Prize, 1998. *Memberships:* TONO; NOPA; GRAMO; Norwegian Musician Asscn. *Leisure interests:* Food; Nature. *Address:* Hammerstads gt 48, 0363 Oslo, Norway.

SEGUNDO Compay, (Maximo Francisco Repilado Muñoz); b. 18 Nov. 1907, Siboney, Oriente, Cuba. Vocalist; Musician (guitar, armónico, clarinet). *Career:* Invented seven-stringed guitar called an armónico; Collaborations: Quinteto Cuban Stars; Cuarteto Hatuey; Miguel Matamoros; Los Compadres (with Lorenzo Hierrezuelo); Name originated from his part as second voice in the duo Los Compadres – compay being a diminutive of compadre and segundo meaning second (or harmony) voice against Hierrezuelo's lead vocal (Compay Primero); Retired, 1970s; Began performing again with Cuarteto Patria in the 1980s; Performed and recorded in Spain, mid-1990s, before working on the Buena Vista Social Club album; Appeared in Wim Wenders' documentary film Buena Vista Social Club. *Recordings:* recent Albums: Antología, 1995; Buena Vista Social Club, 1997; Calle Salud, 1999; Las Flores de la Vida, 2000; Yo Vengo Aquí, 2001. *Current Management:* International Music Network, 278 Main St, Gloucester, MA 01930, USA. *Internet:* www.imnworld.com.

SEINE Johannes Hendricus; b. 30 March 1946, Amsterdam, Netherlands. Man.-Dir; Artist Man.; Agent. m. Annette Washington, 17 Dec. 1971, 2 s. *Career:* Manager, Amsterdam bands, 1964; Producer Dutch radio 3 Vara Drive-in show, 1969; Producer, Radio Northsea Mobile Show, 1972; Managing Director, Europop; Manager, agent for: American Gipsy; Lois Lane; Boney M; Doop; Tours organized with: Divine; Inner Circle; Latoya Jackson; Tower of Power; Capella; Prodigy. *Leisure interests:* Tennis; Football. *Current Management:* Europop. *Address:* Gaelstraat 1b, 2013 CE Haarlem, Netherlands.

SELIGMAN Matthew; b. 14 July 1955, Cyprus. Musician (bass guitar). *Career:* The Soft Boys, 1979–80; The Thompson Twins, 1981–82; Thomas Dolby, 1982–84; Toured USA, Europe, with Thomas Dolby, 1984; Performed at Live Aid with David Bowie, 1985; Session bassist, London, 1986–94; Radio Science Orchestra, 1994–98. *Compositions:* Co-writer of: The Brightest Star; Now and Forever; Motorcycle; Neon Sisters; Slipping You The Midnight Fish; Daddy; Stabbed In The Heart Again. *Recordings:* English Garden, Bruce Woolley and The Camera Club, 1979; Drip Dry Zone, SW9, 1980; with The Soft Boys: Underwater Moonlight, 1980; Lope At The Hive, 1981; Invisible Hits, 1983; The Soft Boys 1979–81, 1994; Black Snake Diamond Rock, Robyn Hitchcock, 1981; In The Name of Love, The Thompson Twins, 1982; Magic's Wand, Whodini, 1982; with Thomas Dolby: Blinded By Science, 1982; The Flat Earth, 1983; Retrospectacle, 1994; A Moral Tale, Sophie Cherie, 1983; Absolute Beginners, David Bowie, 1985; Dancing In The Street, David Bowie and Mick Jagger, 1985; Be My Enemy, The Waterboys, 1986; with Transvision Vamp: Tell That Girl To Shut Up, 1988; Baby I Don't Care, 1989; with Morrissey: Yes I Am Blind, 1989; East West, 1989; Build It Up, June Mitchell, 1989; April Moon, Sam Brown, 1990; with Sinead O'Connor: The Value of Ignorance, 1989; Fire On Babylon, 1994; God Must Live In New York City, 1998; China, Tori Amos, 1991; with The Stereo MCs: Elevate My Mind, 1990; All Night Long, 1992; The End, 1992; Nan Vernon: Manta Ray, 1994; with The Radio Science Orchestra: Theme From The Electronic City; The Architect; Beachcombing Man; The Brightest Star, 1995; with Ghostland: Blue, 1998; Free, 1998; with Moog Poets: Space Galleon; with Grace Jones and the Radio Science Orchestra: Strange Weather; As Producer: Crazy, The Pop Guns, 1991. *Membership:* Musicians' Union. *Leisure interests:* Writing; Fulham Football Club; The night sky. *Address:* 39 Essex St, London WC2R 3AT, England.

SELLAM Philippe; b. 24 Oct. 1960, Algeria. Musician (saxophone). *Musical Education:* Self-taught. *Career:* Concerts with: John Scofield; Gil Evans; European Union Radio Big Band; Michel Portal; Many tours, Africa. *Recordings:* with Gil Evans; French National Jazz Orchestra; Michel Legrand; 3 records with own band African Project. *Honour:* Best Soloist, Concours National De Jazz De Paris La Defense, 1987. *Leisure interest:* Sport.

SELLAR Gordon Maxwell; b. 13 June 1947, Glasgow, Scotland. Musican (bass guitar, guitar). m. Julie, 22 March 1975, 1 s., 1 d. *Career:* Band member: Beggars Opera; The Alex Harvey Band; The Denny Laine Band; Jackie Lynton Band; The Freddie Starr Band. *Compositions:* Featured on 2 Gordon Neville albums. *Recordings include:* Joseph and His Amazing Technicolour Dreamcoat; Evita; Robson and Jerome, 1995. *Membership:* Musicians' Union. *Address:* 2 Clewer Court Rd, Clewer Village, Windsor, Berks SL4 5JD, England.

SELLERS Joey Elton; b. 5 May 1962, Phoenix, Arizona, USA. Musician (trombone); Composer. *Education:* BS, Music Education, State University, Arizona. *Musical Education:* Studied improvisation with Warne Marsh; Chuck Mahronic; Bobby Shew; Gary Foster. *Career:* Merv Griffin with Side Street Strutters, 1984; US Presidents dinner, 1986; Numerous radio broadcasts; Brass quintets, I and II, St Louis Brass; Trombone with California Arts Trombone Quartet. *Recordings:* Joey Sellers Jazz Aggregation: Something For Nothing; Pastels, Ashes; Malby/Sellers Quartet: Cosas; Kim Richmond/Clay Jenkins Ensemble: Range; Commission for Gil Evans Fellowship: Seeds; Trumpet Summit for Summit Records featuring: Bobby Shew; Alan Vizzetti; Vince D'Marino.

Honours: Gil Evans Fellowship in Jazz Composition. *Memberships:* BMI; AFofM. *Leisure interests:* Marathon running; Basketball; Philosophy. *Current Management:* Walrus Publishing; Balquidder Music. *Address:* 4243 E Fifth St, 1, Long Beach, CA 90814, USA.

SELWAY Phil; b. 23 May 1967, Hemingford Grey, Cambridgeshire, England. Musician (Drums). *Career:* Member, On A Friday, became Radiohead; Secured major label record deal, 1991; Numerous support gigs including REM, 1995; Many headlining tours, festival appearances and TV appearances. *Recordings include:* Singles: Anyone Can Play Guitar EP, 1993; Creep, 1993; Stop Whispering, 1994; My Iron Lung EP, 1994; Street Spirit (Fade Out), 1995; Fake Plastic Trees, 1995; Just, 1996; High and Dry, 1996; Paranoid Android, 1997; Airbag: How Am I Driving EP, 1998; No Surprises, 1998; Karma Police, 1998; Albums: Pablo Honey, 1993; The Bends, 1995; OK Computer, 1997.

SELWYN Esmond Wayne; b. 19 Feb. 1948, London, England. Musician (guitar). m. Veronica, 27 July 1975, 3 s. *Education:* BA Hons, Kings, London, German with French. *Musical Education:* Personal tuition from master musicians: Ivor Mairants; Tal Farlow. *Career:* Professional musician from age 12; Varied career especially in Jazz includes: Private party, Frank Sinatra, Savoy Hotel, 1975; Malta Jazz Festival, opposite Chick Corea and Elvin Jones, 1993; Tour with Salena Jones, Thailand, 1994. *Recordings:* Matt Bianco: Tequila; Melanie Marshall: Cocktail; Robin Jones Quartet: Eye of The Hurricane; Don Rendell. *Publications:* Jake Lee Arrives; The Jakes Progress; Included in Guildhall Guitar Syllabus. *Membership:* Musicians' Union. *Leisure interest:* Tai Chi (qualified instructor). *Address:* Min Y Dyffryn, The Green, Gresford, Wrexham, Clwyd LL11 7BB, Wales.

SEMENOFF Sasha; b. 20 Sept. 1924, Riga, Latvia. Orchestra Leader, Violinist. m. Sylvia, 2 s. *Education:* Handel Music Conservatory, Munich. *Career:* Music Contractor, Las Vegas, since 1959; Romantic Strings, Merv Griffin Show, 1972; Television film, Pleasure Palace; Movies, Vegas Vacation, Casino and Honeymoon in Vegas. *Compositions:* The Song I Wrote For You, 1974; Remember; Sasha Nova; Just One More Time; Bat-Yam. *Recordings:* Live Album with Elvis Presley, International Hotel, Las Vegas, 1969–70. *Memberships:* American Federation of Musicians; Screen Actors Guild. *Leisure interest:* Tennis. *Address:* 2125 Michael Way, Las Vegas, NV 89108 3171, USA.

SEN DOG (Senen Reyes); b. 20 Nov. 1965, Cuba. Vocalist. *Career:* Member, Cypress Hill; Numerous tours including Lollapalooza; Collaboration with Pearl Jam on the film soundtrack Judgement Night, 1993; Left band, 1995. *Recordings:* Singles: Phuncky Feel One, 1991; Hand on the Pump, 1991; Latin Lingo, 1991; Insane the Brain, 1993; We Ain't Goin' Out Like That EP, 1994; Throw Your Set in the Air, 1995; Albums: Cypress Hill, 1991; Black Sunday, 1993; Cypress Hill III: Temples of Boom, 1995.

SENATOR Ronald; b. 17 April 1926, London, England. Composer; Author. m. Miriam Brickman. *Education:* Marlborough College, Oxford University; London University; Trinity College of Music. *Career:* Film Work, Music for Peter Greenaways Lightning; Incidental Music for Stage. *Compositions:* Include, Trotsky; Insects. *Honours:* Pulitzer Prize, 1991. *Memberships:* PRS; ASCAP; BASCA; BMI. *Leisure interests:* Nuclear Physics; Poetry; Walking. *Address:* 81 Hillcrest Ave, Yonkers, NY 10705, USA.

SENFLUK Jerry (Jaromir); b. 17 March 1946, Prague, Czechoslovakia. Jazz Musician (Clarinet). m. Jirina, 7 June 1973, 1 s. *Education:* Piano and Elementary Theory of Music, 1952–60; Clarinet, by Mr Karel Dlouhy, 1969–61; Intonation, 1959–61; Conservatoire in Prague, 1961–67. *Career:* Frequent bookings in West Germany, worked with a band accompanying Freddie Kohlman, and with Savoy Gang, swing quartet, 1975–77; Founded Hallmark Swingtet, Berlin, 1979–84; West End venues and composing, London, England, 1985–90; With pianist Mick Pyne, guitarist Nils Solberg, double bassist John Rees-Jones and drummer Rex Bennett, formed Capital Swing, 1991; Yves 'Little Fats' Guyot and Eric Luter, residencies at Hotel Ermitage Golf near Gstaad, Switzerland, 1991–94; Radio Appearances: BBC2, Jazz Parade, 1993; BBC 2, Jazz Notes, 1994. *Compositions:* Pas De Chat; Air Condition Breakdown. *Recordings:* From East to West, 1974; We Swing – Take It From Me, 1995; Swing Express, 1997. *Memberships:* Musicians' Union; Asscn of British Jazz Musicians. *Leisure interests:* Civil Air Transport; Fauna and Flora; Chess; Literature; History. *Address:* 280 Lordship Lane, Dulwich, London SE22 8LY, England.

SENIOR Russell; b. 18 May 1961, Sheffield, England. Musician (Guitar). *Career:* Member, Pulp; Early Radio 1 session for John Peel; Numerous tours, TV appearances and festival appearances; Contributed track to film Mission Impossible soundtrack, Left band, 1996-. *Recordings:* Singles: Little Girl (With the Blue Eyes), 1985; My Legendary Girlfriend, 1990; O.U. (Gone, Gone), 1992; Lipgloss, 1993; Do You Remember The First Time, 1994; The Sisters EP, 1994; Common People, 1995; Mis-Shapes/

Sorted for E's and Wizz, 1995; Disco 2000, 1995; Albums: Freaks, 1987; Separations, 1992; His 'N' Hers, 1994; Masters of the Universe: Pulp on Fire 1985–86, 1995; Different Class, 1995; Countdown 1985–87, 1996; This is Hardcore, 1998.

SEPE Daniele; b. 17 April 1960, Naples, Italy. Musician (wind instruments). *Musical Education:* Graduated, flute, Conservatorio Sanpietro A Masella, Naples. *Career:* Formed group, Gruppo Operaio 'E Zezi Di Pomigliano; Appeared festivals: Rennes; Martigues; Bonn, 1976; Played at festivals including: Les Allummes, Nanates; Vignola; Atina; Ravenna; Horizontal Radio Linz; Rai Stereonette; Audio Box; DOC; Radiotresuite. *Compositions include:* Arrangements for groups including: Little Italy; Bisca; Walhalla; Degrado; Music for theatre, ballet, cinema. *Recordings:* Malamusica, 1983; L'Uscita dei Gladiatori, 1991; Plays Standards and More, 1991; Vite Perdite, 1993; Spiritus Mundi, 1995; Contribututions to: Roberto Murolo, Tu Si Na Cosa Grande, 1995. *Publications:* L'Italia Del Rock; Encyclopedia Del Rock. *Honour:* Academia International Del Tango. *Leisure interests:* Good music; Good eating. *Current Management:* Roberto Balassoue. *Address:* Daniele Sepe, Via Manzoni 191, 80123 Naples, Italy.

SERGENT Carole; b. 22 Jan. 1962, Montargis, Loiret, France. Singer; Entertainer; Author; Composer; Actress. 1 d. *Musical Education:* CIM; ARIAM. *Career:* Festivals: Jacques Brel; Jazz Amiens; Jazz Montlouis; Printemps Bourges; Choralies; Jazz Paris; Tourtour Paris; Jazz Sous Les Pommiers; Estival; France Television 2; MCM Telsat; 1988–; 673rd concert, 1997. *Recordings:* Albums: Chant Du Corps, 1994; Cherche Passion, 1997. *Honours:* Ellipse d'Or Canal, 1992. *Membership:* SACEM. *Leisure interests:* Fashion; Skiing; Champagne. *Current Management:* J Fallot. *Address:* 45 rue Jussieu, 78150 Le Chesnay, France.

SERMILÄ Jarmo Kalevi; b. 16 Aug. 1939, Hämeenlinna, Finland. Composer; Musician (trumpet, flugelhorn). m. Ritva, 6 Nov. 1962. *Education:* Studied with Frantisek Kovaricek, Prague; Master's degree, University of Helsinki, 1975. *Musical Education:* Composer's diploma, Sibelius Academy, 1975. *Career:* Worked for Finnish Broadcasting Company (YLE); Director, YLE Experimental Studio, 1973–79; Jazz improvising on trumpet, 1970s-; Played with Czech artists, Emil Vicklicky, Rudolf Dasek; Artistic Director, Time of Music Festival, late 1988–99. *Compositions:* Avant-garde, electro-acoustic music; Music for chamber groups; Ballets and orchestral works. *Recordings:* Quattro Rilievi; At Bizarre Exits; Random Infinities. *Honours:* Janacek Medal, 1978; Music Reward of the City of Hämeenlinna, 1981; Smetana Medal, 1984; State Grant for Composing, 1990-. *Membership:* Finnish Composers' Society. *Address:* Niittykatu 7 A 7, 13100 Hämeenlinna, Finland.

SERNEHOLT Marie Eleonor; b. 11 July 1983, Stockholm, Sweden. Vocalist. *Education:* Rytmus school, Stockholm. *Career:* Picked to be member of A*Teens group following auditions at Leslie Kühler's dance school, 1998; Continued educational studies whilst pursuing musical career; Prestigious US support tours for N*Sync and Britney Spears, 2000. *Recordings:* Albums: The Abba Generation, 1999; Teen Spirit, 2001; Singles: Mamma Mia, Super Trouper, Gimme! Gimme! Gimme!, Happy New Year, 1999; Dancing Queen, Upside Down, 2000; Halfway Around The World, Sugar Rush, 2001. *Honours:* Broke Swedish sales records with first album and single; World-wide sales of first album in excess of 3m.; Viva Music Awards, Best International Newcomer, 2000. *Address:* c/o Stockholm Records, Sweden. *Internet:* www.stockholmrecords.com.

SERVI Jo; b. 17 May 1970, Aylesbury, Buckinghamshire, England. Vocalist; Actor. *Career:* Session singer, 1988–; Steel pan player, singer, Radcliffe Rollers Steel Band; Television: Saturday Superstore, 1986; Barrymore, 1993; Performed Tommy, Marquee, with the Who, 1993; Backing vocalist, duo, Sister-Brother; Lead singer, keyboards, The Bizz, 1993; Wind Parade, 1994; Joined Southlanders vocal quartet, 1995. *Memberships:* Musicians' Union; Equity. *Current Management:* Richard Starnowski Casting; Jackie Palmer Agency. *Address:* 2 Bateman Dr., Brookhurst, Aylesbury, Buckinghamshire WP21 8AF, England.

SEVERINSEN Doc (Carl H); b. 7 July 1927, Arlington, Oregon, USA. Musician; Music Dir. m. Emily Marshall, 1980, 2 s., 3 d. *Career:* Musician with: Ted Fio Rito, 1945; Charlie Barnet, 1947–49; Also with Tommy Dorsey; Benny Goodman; House band, Steve Allen Show, NBC, 1954–55; NBC Orchestra for Tonight Show, 1962–; MD, 1967–; Partner, Severinsen-Akwright Co. *Recordings:* Albums include: Brass Roots, 1971; Facets, 1988; Night Journey; Doc Severinsen and Friends; Ja-Da; Two Sides of Doc Severinsen; Brass on Ivory; Skyliner; Doc Severinsen and Xebron; Doc Severinsen with Strings; The Very Best of Doc Severinsen. *Current Management:* Brentwood Management Group, 11812 San Vicente Blvd #200, Los Angeles, CA 90049, USA.

SEVERSON Paul Thomas; b. 18 Aug. 1928, Fargo, North Dakota, USA. Composer; Arranger; Musician (piano, trombone). Educator. m. (1) Marie Proft, (2) Shirley Jean Thompson, divorced, 1 s., 1 d., (3) Karen Louise

Schwankel, 1 s. *Education:* BMus, 1950, MusM, 1951, Northwestern University, Evanston, Illinois, USA. *Career:* Performed with various orchestras including Stan Kenton Orchestra, Hal McIntyre Orchestra, Chicago Theatre Orchestra and Chicago Civic Symphony, 1951–54; Performed with artists including Stan Getz, Dizzy Gillespie, Louis Armstrong, Zoot Simms, Art Van Damme, Ella Fitzgerald and Al Hirt; Solo trombonist and arranger, CBS Studios, 1954–62; Composer, arranger, producer, Dick Marx Associates, 1962–73; President, Severson Enterprises, 1975–84; Director, Musical Industry programme, Moorhead (Minnesota) State University, 1984–91; Leader, Great American Ballroom Band, 1980–91; Music Director, Red River Dance and Performing Co, 1980–96; Leader, Paul Severson and Friends Jazz Quintet, 1995–; Leader, composer, arranger, Pianist, Mood Indigo orchestra, 1996–; Composer/arranger with the Jazz Arts Group Big Band. Compostions: Over 3000 compositions and arrangements in the broadcast and publishing media; Music for commercials including Chevrolet, McDonalds, Kelloggs, Sears and Wrigley; 4 network television themes; 22 music scores for films; Portrait of Stan Kenton, 1994. *Recordings:* Albums: with Paul Severson Quintet and Septet; And That's That, Jazz Arts Big Band; 3 arrangements and Portrait of Stan Kenton. *Publication:* Co-author, Brass/Wind Artistry – Know Your Instrument, Know Your Mind. *Honours:* Hollywood Advertising Club Grand Slam Award, 1965; Silver medal, Advertising Federation, 1988; 15 Clio Awards; Outstanding Advisor Award, Moorhead State University. *Leisure interests:* Fishing; Hiking; Playing bridge; Tennis. *Address:* PO Box 535, Ranier, MN 56668–0535, USA.

SEXTON Charlie; b. 11 Aug. 1968, San Antonio, Texas, USA. Singer; Songwriter; Musician (Guitar). *Career:* Toured with David Bowie, numerous appearances with Letterman, Conan O'Brien; Acted in Thelma and Louise; Last Ride, with Mickey Rourke and Lori Singer; Recorded with Steve Earle. *Compositions:* Contributed to film soundtracks: Thelma and Louise, True Romance, Beverly Hills Cop II, Air America. *Recordings:* Solo Artist: Pictures for Pleasure, 1985; Charlie Sexton, 1989; Arc Angels, 1992; Under the Wishing Tree, 1995; Contributions on albums, as Member of the band, by Bob Dylan, Don Henley, Keith Richards, Ron Wood. *Current Management:* Tim Neece Management, 13101 Hwy 71 W, Austin, TX 78736, USA. *Address:* 13101 Hwy 71 W, Austin, TX 78736, USA.

SEXTON Will; b. 10 Aug. 1970. Guitarist. *Career:* Bassist for WC Clark Bires Band, performed and recorded with Stevie Ray Vaughan, Speedy Spaks, Joe Ely, Stephen Stills, Waylon Jennings, Steve Earle; Frontman for the Kill; Member of the Sexton Sextet. *Current Management:* Tim Neece Management, 13101 Hwy 71 W, Austin, TX 78736, USA. *Address:* 13101 Hwy 71 W, Austin, TX 78736, USA.

SEYMOUR Nick; b. 9 Dec. 1958, Benalla, Victoria, Australia. Musician (Bass). *Career:* Member, Crowded House; Numerous early acoustic gigs in restaurants and clubs; Numrous headlining tours, festival dates and TV and radio appearances; Farewell gig at Sydney Harbour Bridge and Opera House, 1996; Band split. *Recordings:* Singles include: World Where You Live, 1986; Crowded House EP, 1986; Something So Strong, 1987; Don't Dream It's Over, 1987; Sister Madly, 1988; It's Only Natural, 1991; Fall At Your Feet, 1991; Weather With You, 1991; Four Seasons In One Day, 1992; Pineapple Head, 1993; Locked Out, 1993; Distant Sun, 1993; Nails in My Feet, 1994; Instinct, 1996; Not The Girl You Think You Are, 1996; Everything is Good For You, 1996; Albums: Crowded House, 1986; Temple of Low Men, 1988; Woodface, 1991; Together Alone, 1993; Recurring Dream: The Best of Crowded House, 1996.

SEYMOUR Patrick; b. 11 Dec. 1958, Reading, Berkshire, England. Composer; Musician (keyboard); Prod. *Musical Education:* BA Music, Oxford University. *Career:* Film composer, songwriter; World tours with The Eurythmics, 1986, 1989. *Compositions:* Film scores: The Feast of All Saints; Tricks; The End of Summer; Northern Lights; Co-writer: Revival, When Tomorrow Comes, Eurythmics; You're History, Shakespears Sister. *Recordings:* Keyboard player on albums with Eurythmics: Revenge; We Too Are One; with The Pretenders: Get Close; Other albums by: Mick Jagger; Bob Dylan. *Current Management:* Anxious Music Ltd. *Address:* 147 Crouch Hill, London N8 9QH, England.

SFECI Paolo; b. 15 May 1955, Zagreb, Croatia. Musician (drums). m. Gordana Farkas, 2 d. *Career:* Groups: Aerodrom; Parni Valjak; Boa. *Recordings:* 1 album with Aerodrom; 14 albums with Parni Valjak; 4 albums with Boa. *Honours:* President, Croatian Musicians' Union. *Memberships:* EC, Croatian Performers Rights Collecting Society); EC, Porin Music Awards; Croatian Musicians' Union. *Address:* Al V Ruzdjaka 37, 10000 Zagreb, Croatia.

SHABALALA Joseph; b. 28 Aug. 1940, Ladysmith, South Africa. Vocalist; Dancer; Songwriter. *Career:* Founding member and leader: Ladysmith Black Mambazo; First recording contract, 1970; Released 28 albums since; Performed at Nobel Peace Prize ceremony at the request of Nelson Mandela and FW de Klerk, 1993; Performed at Mandela's presidential inauguration, 1994; Associate professor of ethnomusicology, University of Natal; Part-time lecturer, University of California, Los Angeles; Recordings featured in TV advertisements: Heinz Beans; IBM; 7Up. *Recordings:* Albums include: Journey of Dreams, 1988; Two Worlds One Heart, 1990; Gift of The Tortoise, 1993; Thuthukani Ngoxolo, 1996; Heavenly (including Dolly Parton and Bonnie Raitt), 1997; The Star and The Wise Man (including Paul Simon and Dolly Parton), 1998; featured on soundtracks: The Lion King Part 3; Coming To America; A Dry White Season; Moonwalker; Cry the Beloved Country; featured appearances include: Graceland, Paul Simon, 1986; Conversation Peace, Stevie Wonder, 1995; Treasures, Dolly Parton, 1996. *Honours:* Grammy Award, Best Traditional Folk Recording, Shaka Zulu, 1987; six further Grammy nominations; Tony Awards, six nominations for stage production The Song of Jacob Zulu; JEFF Award, Best Original Musical Score, Nomathemba stage production; Kora Award, Special Judges Award for Contribution to African Music, 2000; SAMA Award, Best Zulu Album, Lihl'lxhiba Likagogo, 2001. *Address:* c/o Gallo, PO Box 2897, Parklands 2121, South Africa. *Internet:* www.mambazo.com.

SHACKLETON Danny J; b. 7 April 1966, Wegberg, Germany. Engineer; Prod.; Programmer; Writer; Musician (keyboards). *Education:* 4 years art college. *Musical Education:* Self-taught. *Career:* Freelance engineer, producer, studios throughout UK, for several years; Programmed for various projects including specialist jazz ventures, library music; Taught Music Technology to A Level; Various chart entries for albums, singles; Major jazz pieces due completion, July, 1995; Various dance projects, 1995. *Membership:* Musicians' Union. *Current Management:* Fairview Music. *Address:* c/o Fairview Studio, Willerby, Hull HU10 6DP, England.

SHAFRANOV Vladimir 'Vova'; b. 1948, Leningrad, Russia. Musician (piano). *Musical Education:* Piano, violin lessons from age 4; Piano diploma, Rimsky-Korsakov Conservatory, 1962. *Career:* Played with various bands throughout USSR; Became Israeli citizen, 1973; Became Finnish citizen, 1980–; Worked in Finnish jazz trios with Eero Koivistoinen; Represented Finland at Middleheim Festivals, Belgium, 1978; Ljubljana, 1979; Lived and worked in New York, 1983–; Performed duos, trios in local clubs with American jazz artists including : Ron Carter; Eddie Gomez; Mark Johnson; Al Foster; Mel Lewis. *Recording:* Album with Al Foster and George Moraz.

SHAGGY (Orville Richard Burrell); b. 22 Oct. 1968, Kingston, Jamaica. Vocalist; Songwriter. *Career:* Left Jamaica to live with mother in Brooklyn, New York, USA, aged 18; Former Gulf War veteran with US Marines; Scored New York reggae/dancehall hits with independent label releases: Mampie; Big Up; Period in military followed by world-wide #1 hit Oh Carolina after track licensed to UK label Greensleeves; Signed record-breaking deal with Virgin UK lasting to 1997; New contract with MCA after hit soundtrack duet with Janet Jackson, 1998; Opening act for Backstreet Boys' US tour, 2001; Co-owner: Big Yard record label (with manager Robert Livingston and others); Collaborations: Rayvon; Ricardo 'RikRok' Ducent; Grand Puba; Wayne Wonder. *Recordings:* Albums: Pure Pleasure, 1993; Original Doberman, 1994; Boombastic, 1995; Midnite Lover, 1997; Ultimate Shaggy Collection, 1999; Hotshot, 2000; Singles: Mampie; Big Up; Oh Carolina, Soon Be Done, 1993; In The Summertime, Boombastic, 1995; Why You Treat Me So Bad, Something Different/The Train Is Coming, That Girl (with Maxi Priest), 1996; Piece of My Heart, 1997; Luv Me, Luv Me (with Janet Jackson, from How Stella Got Her Groove Back OST), 1998; Hope (from For Love of The Game OST), 1999; Dance and Shout, It Wasn't Me, Angel, Freaky Girl, 2001. *Honours:* Grammy Award, Best Reggae Album, 1996; Billboard Music Awards: Male Artist of The Year; Male Albums Artist of The Year, 2001; Best-Selling Album 2001, Hotshot, 6 times platinum certification by RIAA. *Current Management:* Robert Livingston, Livingston Management, PO Box 231 Rockville Center, New York, NY 11571, USA. *Internet:* www.shaggyonline.com.

SHAKESPEARE Robbie; b. 27 Sept. 1953, Kingston, Jamaica. Reggae Musician (bass); Prod. *Career:* Member, US rhythm partnership, Sly and Robbie, with Sly Dunbar, 1975–; Prolific session musician with artists including: Peter Tosh; Bunny Wailer; Black Uhuru; Grace Jones; Bob Dylan; Ian Dury; Joan Armatrading; Formed own label, Taxi; Tours with Black Uhuru. *Recordings:* Sly and Robbie Present Taxi, 1981; A Dub Extravaganza, 1984; Language Barrier, 1985; Sly and Robbie Meet King Tubby, 1985; Reggae Greats, 1985; The Sound of Taxi, Vol. 1, 1986; Vol. 2, 1986; Rhythm Killers, 1987; Taxi Fare, 1987; Uhuru In Dub, 1987; The Summit, 1988; Hardcore Dub, 1989; Silent Assassin, 1990; Remember Precious Times, 1993; Dubmission, 1996; Honorary Citizen, Peter Tosh, 1997; Raw: The Best of Lady Saw, 1998; Doin' it Right, Freddie McKay, 1999; Story of Jamaican Music, 2000. *Current Management:* Starline Entertainment, 1045 Pomme de Pin Lane, New Port Richey, FL 34655, USA.

SHAKIRA (Shakira Isabel Mebarak Ripoll); b. 2 Feb. 1977, Barranquilla, Colombia. *Career:* Signed recording contract with Sony Music Colombia in 1990, when 13 years old; Released first album Magia, 1991; Subsequent albums won her success in Latin America and Spain;

Appeared for three years in Colombian television drama, El Oasis; First album in English, Laundry Service, was released in 2002. *Recordings:* Albums: Magia, 1991; Peligro, 1993; Pies Descalzos, 1996; ¿Dónde están los ladrones?, 1998; Laundry Service, 2002. Grammy for Best Female Vocal Performance, 2000. *Current Management:* Sony Music. *Internet:* www.shakira.com.

SHALIT Jonathan Sigmund; b. 17 April 1962, London, England. *Career:* Saatchi and Saatchi; Shalit Entertainment. *Recordings:* Devised and presented Charlotte Church; The Glory of Gershwin, featuring Larry Adler, produced by George Martin, guest performances include: Peter Gabriel; Sting; Elton John; Carly Simon; Elvis Costello; Cher; Kate Bush; Jane McDonald; Ruthie Henshall; Leo Sayer; Claire Sweeney; Royal National Theatre. *Publications:* Me and My Big Mouth, Larry Adler; Walking On Air, Trevor Jones. *Memberships:* Music Manager's Forum; Queen's Club. *Leisure interests:* Triathlon; Sailing. *Current Management:* Shalit Entertainment and Management. *Address:* c/o Cambridge Theatre, Seven Dials, Covent Garden, London WC2H 9HU, England.

SHAMBORGUER Naima; b. 18 April 1943, Detroit, MI, USA. Song Stylist. m. George Shamborguer, 3 s., 2 d. *Education:* Wayne State University. *Career:* Performs Professionally, Night Clubs, Festivals, Playhouses, Concerts, Privately and Publicly; Conducted Vocal Workshops in Technique and Song. *Honours:* Voted Number One Jazz Vocalist in The Detroit Area, 1989; Spirit of Detroit Award, 1994. *Current Management:* George Lee, 19760 Hartwell, Detroit, Michigan 48235, USA.

SHANK Bud (Clifford); b. 27 May 1926, Dayton, Ohio, USA. Musician (alto saxophone). m. Linda Alexander Shank, 14 May 1994. *Education:* 3 years, University of North Carolina. *Musical Education:* UNC; Private studies, New York, Los Angeles. *Career:* Played in big bands of Charlie Barnet, late 1940s, Stan Kenton, late 1950s; with Howard Rumsey's Lighthouse All Stars, also trumpet ace Shorty Rogers, 1950s; Club, university, festival apppearances, North and South America, Europe, Japan, studio work, 1960s-70s; Formed world renowned LA Four, with Ray Brown, Jeff Hamilton, Laurindo Almeida, recordings, tours, 1970s-80s; Performed with orchestras including: Royal Philharmonic; New American Jazz; Gerald Wilson Big Band; Stan Kenton's Neophonic; Duke Ellington; Created multi-media jazz performance The Lost Cathedral; Expanded Bud Shank Jazz Workshop and festival in Port Townsend, Washington; Works with sextet and quartet world-wide; Collaborated with koto player Kimio Eto and sitar player Ravi Shankar. *Recordings:* 126 as leader or co-leader, many others as sideman/featured artist; Also classical works by: Bach; Faure; Debussy; Ravel; Scriabin; Several scores for films and television. *Publications:* Autobiography in progress; Quarterly newsletter, Budnotes. *Honours:* Multiple Playboy Poll; NARAS; Theme International. *Memberships:* ASCAP; IAJE. *Leisure interests:* F1 and Indy racing; Vintage car racing; Reading; Dining out. *Current Management:* Linda Alexander Shank.

SHANKAR Ravi; b. 7 April 1920, Varansi, India. Musician (sitar). m. Sukanya, 23 Jan. 1989, 1 s., 2 d. *Musical Education:* Studied under Ustad Allaudin Khan of Maihar. *Career:* International career as solo sitarist; Former director of music, All-India Radio; Founded National Orchestra, All India Radio; Founder, Director, Kinnara School of Music, Bombay, 1962, Los Angeles, 1967; Concerts world-wide (except East and South Africa); Major festivals include: Edinburgh; Woodstock; Monterey. *Compositions include:* 2 Concertos, sitar and orchestra, 1971, 1981; Film scores: Pather Panchali; Charlie; Chappaqua; Ghandhi; Music for television production, Alice In Wonderland; Opera-ballet, Ghanashayam, 1989. *Recordings:* Over 50 albums include: Concertos 1 and 2 for Sitar and Orchestra, Raga Jageshwari, 1981; Homage To Mahatma Ghandhi, 1981; West Meets East (with Yehudi Menuhin and others). *Publications:* My Music My Life (autobiography), 1968; From India, 1997; Mantram: Chant of India, 1997; Raga Jogeshwari, 1998; In London [live], 1999l; Concerto for Sitar and Orchestra, 1999. *Honours:* Fellow, Sangeet Natak Academy, 1976; Padma Vibushan, 1981; Elected to Rajya Sabha (Indian Upper House), 1986; Magisaysay; Grand Prize, Fukuoka, Japan; 12 honorary doctorates world-wide; KBE (awarded by HM The Queen), 2001. *Leisure interest:* Reading. *Address:* c/o Sulivan Sweetland, 28 Albion St, London, W2 2AX, England.

SHANNON Sharon; b. 1968, Corofin, County Clare, Ireland. Traditional Musician. *Education:* German and Irish, Cork University. *Career:* Musician with the Waterboys, Room To Roam tour and album; Also played with Adam Clayton; Van Morrison; Sinead O'Connor; Dennis Bovell; Solo recording artiste, 1991–; Regular festival appearances including Glastonbury, Cambridge and Isle of Wight; Tours of US, Europe, Australia, New Zealand, Hong Kong, Japan. *Recordings:* Albums: Sharon Shannon, 1991; Out The Gap, 1994; Each Little Thing, 1997; Appears on: Her Infinite Variety: Celtic Woman, 1998; Coolfin, 1998; Finisterres, 1999; Moods Box Set, 1999. *Current Management:* Top Floor Management, 7–9 Sweetman's Ave, Blackrock, County Dublin, Ireland.

SHAPER Harold David (Hal); b. 18 July 1931, Cape Town, South Africa. Author; Composer; Music Publisher. m. Pippa Marsh, 1 s., 3 d. *Education:* Attorney-at-Law, Cape Bar, 1955. *Career:* Founder, Sparta Florida Music Group and Prestige Records Ltd, London; Writer of many Hollywood film songs. *Compositions include:* Softly as I Leave You (Frank Sinatra and Elvis Presley); Adaptation and libretto of opera La Bohème: Noir. *Publications:* A Prince of Liars, poetry; Book and lyrics of musical opera Cyrano, 1996; Wrote poetic epitaph on Enoch Sontonga's National Monument; Contributed to President Mandela's Heritage Day tribute Speech. *Honours:* British Academy Awards for musicals Treasure Island and Great Expectations; Freedom of the City of London, 1989; Lord of Stoke Bruerne. *Memberships:* Queens Club; Hurlingham; Chelsea Arts; Memorial Society; British Academy of Songwriters, Composers and Authors. *Leisure interests:* Songwriter memorabilia; Golf; Tennis; Chess; Poker. *Address:* Waterlane House, Wynberg Park, Cape Town, South Africa.

SHAPIRO Helen; b. 28 Sept. 1946, Bethnal Green, London. Singer. *Musical Education:* Vocal lessons, Maurice Berman Singing Academy, London. *Career:* Solo recording artiste, aged 14; Numerous radio and television appearances by age 15; Tours world-wide including: UK, supported by the Beatles, 1963; UK/Ireland, with The Beach Boys, 1967; Far East, 1964; Poland, 1965; Concerts include: Concerts with own band, 1963–98; British Song Festival, Brighton, 1966; Gospel concert with Cliff Richard, Royal Albert Hall, 1991; Humph 'n' Helen Show with Humphrey Lyttelton, 1984–98; Solid Silver Sixties Tour with The Searchers and Swinging Blue Jeans, 1998; Gospel concerts in UK and Europe; Television includes: Sunday Night At The London Palladium; Thank Your Lucky Stars; Subject of This Is Your Life, ITV, 1995; Film appearance: It's Trad Dad, 1962; Play It Cool, 1962; Theatre includes: I'll Get My Man, 1967; West End musicals: The French Have A Song For It; Oliver; Theatre: Cabaret, 1982; Goose Pimples, 1982; Ello Ello Ello, 1982; One For The Road, 1985; Sccsaw, 1987; Numerous pantomimes as principal boy. *Recordings:* Albums: Tops With Me, 1962; It's Trad, Dad (film soundtrack), 1962; Helen's Sixteen, 1963; Helen Hits Out, 1964; All for the Love of Music, 1978; Straighten Up and Fly Right, 1983; Echoes of the Duke, 1985; Humph 'n' Helen, 1990; The Pearl, 1990; Helen Shapiro 25th Anniversary Album, 1991; Kadosh, 1992; Nothing But The Best, 1995; The Essential Helen Shapiro, 1997; Enter Into His Gates, 1997; The Best of the 80's, 1997; Helen Shapiro, 1997; At Abbey Road [live], 1998; Humph 'n' Helen Mark II, 1998; Helen Shapiro at Abbey Road, 1998; Contributor, Echoes of The Duke, with Humphrey Lyttelton, 1985; Hit singles include: Don't Treat Me Like A Child, 1961; You Don't Know (No. 1, UK), 1961; Walkin' Back To Happiness (No. 1, UK), 1961; Tell Me What He Said (No. 2, UK), 1962; Little Miss Lonely, 1962. *Publication:* Walking Back to Happiness, autobiograpby, 1993. *Honour:* NME Reader's Poll Winner, Best British Female Singer, 1961; 1 Gold Disc, 3 Silver Discs; BASCA Gold Badge of Merit, 1991. *Current Management:* John Robert Williams Productions. *Address:* PO Box 423, Chislehurst, Kent BR7 5TU, England.

SHARAM (Sharam Tayebi); b. 12 Aug. 1970, Iran. Prod.; Remixer; DJ. *Career:* Relocated to Washington DC, USA; Formed Deep Dish and founded Deep Dish/Yoshitoshi Records with partner Dubfire, 1992; Released BT's A Moment of Truth, 1993; Signed to Tribal Records, 1993; Moved to Deconstruction, 1996; Collaborations: Danny Tenaglia; John Selway; Everything But The Girl; Remixed: Madonna; De'Lacy; Billie Ray Martin; Joi Cardwell; Dusted; Sven Vath; The Shamen; Eddie Amador. *Recordings:* Albums: Junk Science, 1998; Singles: A Feeling (as Moods), 1992; Sexy Dancer (as Quench), 1993; The Dream, 1994; Love Songs (as Chocolate City), Stay Gold, 1996; The Future of The Future, 1998. *Honours:* Grammy Award, Remixer of The Year, 2001. *Address:* c/o Deconstruction, Bedford House, 69–79 Fulham High St, London, SW6 3JW, England.

SHARDA Anju; b. 17 March 1969, Perivale, Middlesex, England. Singer; Songwriter. *Education:* BA Hons, Communication Studies. *Musical Education:* A level Music; Grade 8 violin. *Career:* Member, Cardiff-based trio Banana Cat (later Glorious), 1991; Television: Band appeared on Rough Mix, 1992; Dance Energy, BBC2, 1993; Left Glorious, 1993; Co-writing deal with Simon and Diamond Dougal, 1994; Co-writing deal with Jon Moss (ex-Culture Club), 1995. *Recordings:* Backing vocals, album: The Lick, Definition of Sound, 1992. *Memberships:* Musicians' Union; PRS. *Leisure interests:* Swimming; Cooking; Drinking. *Current Management:* Sue Carling. *Address:* 13 Elvendon Rd, London N13 4SJ, England.

SHARKEY Feargal; b. 13 Aug. 1958, Londonderry, Northern Ireland. Singer. *Career:* Member, The Undertones; Numerous hit singles and live appearances, television and radio appearances; Band split, 1983; Worked with Vince Clarke (of Erasure) on project The Assembly, 1983; Began solo career with numerous TV appearances; A & R man. *Recordings:* With The Undertones: Singles: Teenage Kicks; Jimmy Jimmy; My Perfect Cousin; It's Going to Happen; Crisis of Mine; You're Welcome; Albums: Teenage Kicks, 1978; Undertones, 1979; Hypnotised, 1980; Positive Touch, 1981; The Sin of Pride, 1983; Peel Sessions, 1986; The Very Best of The Undertones, 1994; With The Assembly: Single: Never Never, 1983; Solo: Singles: A Good

Heart; You Little Thief; Albums: Feargal Sharkey, 1985; Wish, 1988; Song from the Mardi Gras, 1991.

SHAW Donald Patrick; b. 6 May 1967, Ketton, Leicestershire, England. Musician (keyboards, accordion); Composer. *Career:* Founder member: Capercaillie; Group, along with original material, specialise in fusing traditional Gaelic songs with contemporary arrangements; Had first UK top 40 single in Gaelic, Coisich A Ruin (from A Prince Among Islands EP), 1992; Produced and performed on fellow Capercaillie members' solo albums: Karen Matheson, The Dreaming Sea, 1996; Michael McGoldrick, Fused, 2000; Written music for television documentaries, dramas and the feature film Rob Roy. *Recordings:* Albums: with Capercaillie: Cascade, 1984; Crosswinds, 1987; Sidewalk, 1989; Delirium, 1991; Get Out, 1992; The Blood Is Strong, Secret People, 1993; Capercaillie, 1995; To The Moon, 1996; Beautiful Wasteland, 1997; Glenfinnan – Songs of The '45 (recorded 1995), 1998; Nàdurra, 2000; group feature on: Rob Roy OST, 1995; features solo on: L'Heritage De Celts, 1994; The Dreaming Sea, Karen Matheson, 1996; Finisterres, Dan Ar Braz, 1997; Zenith, Dan Ar Braz, 1998; Identities, Idir, 1999; Suilean Dubh, Tannas, 1999; Ru-Ra, Tannas, 2000; Sawdust In My Veins, James Grant, 2000; My Thrawn Glory, James Grant, 2000; Fused, Michael McGoldrick, 2000; Source, Big Sky, 2000; Magaid A Phipir, Rory Campbell, 2000; Tacsi (TV series), 2000. *Honours:* All Britain Accordion Champion, 1984.

SHAW Ian; b. 2 June 1962, North Wales. Jazz Singer; Musician (piano, trumpet). *Musical Education:* 8 piano grades (Trinity College of Music); BMus, King's College, London. *Career:* Plays regularly Ronnie Scott's London; Tours, UK, Europe; Worked with Kenny Wheeler; John Taylor; Carol Grimes; Ruby Turner; Mari Wilson; TV includes Top of the Pops; Pebble Mill; Jools Holland's The Happening; The Jack Dee Show; The Late Show; Radio: Kaleidoscope; Nicky Campbell (Radio One); Major US Tour, 1997. *Recordings:* Lazy Blues Eyes, album of jazz love songs with Carol Grimes, 1990; Ghostsongs, Live at Ronnie Scott's, 1992; Zebra, guest singer with Yello, 1994; Taking It To Hart, a tribute to Rodgers and Hart, 1995; Famous Rainy Day, 1996; The Echo of a Song, 1996; In A New York Minute, 1999; Soho Stories, 2001. *Publications:* Making It In The Music Business, 1993. *Honours:* Perrier Award, Edinburgh, 1991; Nominated 5 times Best Jazz Singer, British Jazz Awards; British Jazz Awards nominee, 1997. *Membership:* Equity. *Leisure interests:* Cooking; Animals; Drawing; Reading. *Current Management:* Dr Darren Crowdy, 42 Elsham Rd, London, W14 8HB, England.

SHAW Paul John; b. 20 Feb. 1962, Dartford, Kent, England. Composer; Musician (keyboards, guitar); Programmer; Prod. m. Jacqueline Ives (Shaw), 2 July 1994. *Musical Education:* Self-taught. *Career:* Started business, Daybreak Productions, with David Rogers, 1987; Success with library music ever since; Regular CD-I and CD-Rom work; Conferences, television and radio including: Mr Blobby; BBC Radio; BBC Pebble Mill; Top of The Pops; Live and Kicking; House Party. *Compositions:* 345 published works co-written with David Rogers; Mostly library music (production): Peanut Vendor, 1987; Mr Blobby, 1995; Light of Summer, 1995; Mr Blobby, The Album, 1995–96. *Publications:* Various interviews in industry publications; PRS yearbooks. *Honours:* Ivor Novello, Best Selling Song, 1993; Various corporate awards for Mr Blobby. *Memberships:* Musicians' Union; PRS. *Leisure interests:* Wildlife; Sport; Motor racing. *Address:* Carlin Music/Destiny Music, Iron Bridge House, Bridge Approach, London NW1 8BD, England.

SHAW Sandie, (Sandra Goodrich); b. 1947, Dagenham, Essex, England. Singer; Songwriter; Record Prod. m. (1) Jeff Banks; (2) Nik Powell. *Education:* Pschychodynamic Psychology, university. *Career:* International recording artist, singer, composer and producer; numerous hit singles, over 30 years; Winner, Eurovision Song Contest, 1967; Semi-retirement during 1970s; Relaunched music career with Morrissey, 1984; Numerous concerts, television and radio appearances world-wide; Founder, Arts Clinic, psychological counsellor, writer and lecturer. *Compositions:* Numerous collaborations with Chris Andrews. *Recordings:* Hit singles include: (There's) Always Something There To Remind Me; Long Live Love; Message Understood; Girl Don't Come; Tomorrow; Nothing Comes Easy; Puppet On A String; Monsieur Dupont; Hand In Glove (with Morrissey and The Smiths); Most 1960s hits self-produced; Recent Albums: Choose Life, 1983; Sandie/ Me Sandie Shaw, 1996; Appears on: Docudrama, 1996 (Star Pimp); Kill the Lights, 1997 (Lowercase). *Publications:* The World At My Feet (partly autobiographical); Stress in Rock Musicians: The Phenomena of Fame and its Psychological Effect on the Developmental Processes of Artists. *Honours:* Eurovision Song Contest Winner, Puppet On A String, 1967; International Ambassador for Women Aid, United Nations, 1985; Professor of Music, Royal Society of Musicians, 1998. *Membership:* Royal Society of Musicians. *Leisure interests:* Painting; Jigsaw puzzles; Collecting faerie and angel images; Devout Buddhist. *Address:* c/o Negus-Fancey Co, 78 Portland Rd, London W11 4LQ, England.

SHAW Tommy; Musician (guitar); Singer; Songwriter. *Career:* Guitarist, Styx, 1975–89; Damn Yankees, 1989–; Also member of side project Shaw Blades (with Jack Blades), 1995; World-wide tours and concerts. *Recordings:* Albums: with Styx: Crystal Ball, 1976; The Grand Illusion, 1977; Pieces of Eight, 1978; Cornerstone, 1979; Paradise Theater (No. 1, USA), 1980; Kilroy Was Here, 1983; Caught In The Act, 1984; with Damn Yankees: Damn Yankees, 1990; Don't Tread, 1992; with Shaw Blades: Hallucination, 1995; Singles: with Styx: Sail Away; Babe (No. 1, USA); The Best of Times; Too Much Time On My Hands; with Damn Yankees: Coming of Age; High Enough; Come Again; Where You Goin' Now; Silence Is Broken, from film Nowhere To Run, 1993. *Honours:* Motor City Music Award, Outstanding National Rock/Pop Single, 1992. *Current Management:* Madhouse Management, PO Box 15108, Ann Arbor, MI 48106, USA.

SHEA George Beverly; b. 1 Feb. 1909, Ontario, Canada. Soloist. m. Karlene Aceto, 1 s., 1 d. *Education:* Annesley College, Ottawa; Houghton College, Houghton. *Career:* Radio Broadcasting, Singing on WMCA and WHN, 1929–38; Clerk, Mutual of New York Insurance Co, 1929–38; Announcer, Staff Soloist, WMBI Chicago, 1938–44; Soloist, ABC's Club Time, 1944–52; Soloist, Billy Graham Evangelistic Association, 1947–; Soloist, Hour of Decision, Radio Broadcast, 1950–; Recording Artist, RCA and Word Records, 1951-. *Compositions:* Then Sings My Soul, 1968; Songs That Lift The Heart, 1972; Then Sings My Soul, 1984. *Honours:* Grammy Award, National Academy of Recording Arts and Sciences, 1965; Elected Gospel Music Asscn Hall of Fame, 1978; Elected Religious Broadcasting Hall of Fame, 1996. *Leisure interest:* Boating. *Address:* c/o Media Relations, PO Box 9313, Minneapolis, Minnesota 55440, USA.

SHEA Pat; b. 7 Dec. 1957, Buffalo, New York, USA. Singer/Songwriter; Musician (Guitar, Piano). *Career:* Grand Prize Winner, TNN's Be A Star Talent Show, 1991; Appearances on Nashville Now, with Ralph Emery; Made Video Special at Billy Bobs in Texas for TNN's On Stage Show; Opening Act for Holly Dunn, Emmylou Harris, Tanya Tucker, Lee Greenwood, Sawyer Brown, John Berry. *Composition:* The Lord May Take Me. *Recordings:* The Lord May Take Me, single; The Road Less Travelled, album. *Honour:* Grand Prize Winner, Be A Star Talent Show, 1991. *Membership:* ASCAP. *Leisure interests:* Golf; Reading. *Address:* PO Box 991, Orchard Park, NY 14127, USA.

SHEARING George Albert; b. 13 Aug. 1919, London, England. Musician (piano); Composer. m. Beatrice Bayes, 1 May 1941 (divorced), 1 d., (2) Eleanor Geffert. *Education:* Linden Lodge School for the Blind, London. *Career:* Musician with Harry Parry; Stéphane Grappelli; Leader, own quintet, with members including Gary Burton, Joe Pass, Cal Tjader; Later played in trio, duo and as solo artiste; Played with Marian McPartland; Hank Jones; Peggy Lee; Carmen McRae; Frequent collaborations with Mel Tormé; Appearances at: London Symphony Pops Concerts, 1986, 1987; London Palladium, 1987; Concord Jazz Festival, Japan, 1987; Vice President, Shearing Music Corporation. *Compositions:* Numerous popular songs including Lullaby of Birdland. *Recordings:* Singles: September In The Rain; Lullaby of Birdland; Let Their Be Love (with Nat 'King' Cole); Numerous albums include: Latin Escapade, 1956; Velvet Carpet, 1956; Black Satin, 1957; Burnished Brass, 1957; White Satin, 1960; The Shearing Touch, 1960; Satin Affair, 1961; Jazz Concert, 1963; My Ship, 1974; The Way We Are, 1974; Continental Experience, 1975; 500 Miles High, 1977; On Target, 1979; On A Clear Day, 1980; Bright Dimensions, 1984; Grand Piano, 1985; More Grand Piano, 1986; Breakin' Out, 1987; Piano, 1989; Paper Moon: Songs of Nat King Cole, 1995; Christmas with the George Shearing Quintet, 1998; with Peggy Lee: Americana Hotel, 1959; with Stéphane Grappelli: The Reunion, 1976; with Carmen McRae: Two For The Road, 1980; with Marian McPartland: Alone Together, 1981; with Mel Tormé: An Evening With Mel Tormé and George Shearing, 1982; Top Drawer, 1983; An Elegant Evening, 1986; with Barry Tuckwell: George Shearing and Barry Treadwell Play The Music of Cole Porter, 1986; with Hank Jones: The Spirit of 1761, 1989. *Honours:* Voted Top English Pianist, 1941–47; Winner, All-American Jazz polls; American Academy of Achievement, Golden Plate Award, 1968. *Memberships:* BMI; Board directors, Guide Dogs For The Blind, San Rafael, Hadley School for the Blind, Winnetka, Illinois. *Current Management:* Joan Shulman. *Address:* 103 Avenue Rd, Suite 301, Toronto, ON M5R 2G9, Canada.

SHEEHAN Billy; b. Musician (bass). *Career:* Founder member, rock group Talas, 1980–83; Bass player, David Lee Roth, 1985–88; Founder member, Mr Big, 1989-. *Recordings:* Albums: with Talas: Talas, 1980; Sink Your Teeth Into That, 1982; Live Speed On Ice, 1983; The Talas Years, 1990; with David Lee Roth: Eat 'Em and Smile, 1986; Skyscraper, 1988; with Mr Big: Mr Big, 1989; Lean Into It, 1991; Singles include: with Dave Lee Roth: Yankee Rose; Goin' Crazy; Just Like Paradise; with Mr Big: Green-Tinted Sixties Mind; To Be With You. *Current Management:* Herbie Herbert Management, 2501 Third St, San Francisco, CA 94107, USA.

SHEHAN Steve; b. 18 Jan. 1957, Fort Eustis, Virginia, USA. Composer; Musician (percussion, bass). *Education:* Swedish Teaching Certificates. *Musical Education:* Kenny Clarke School; Classical piano, Balinese gamelan. *Career:* Concerts and recordings with: John McLaughlin, 1981; Yves Montand, 1982; Alan Stivell, 1982; Magma, 1984; Michael Jonasz, Veronique Samson, 1984; Kim Wilde, 1984; Richard Horowitz, 1985–92; Gipsy Kings, 1987–89; Amina, 1987; Leonard Bernstein, Carnegie Hall, 1989; Peter Gabriel's band and Akiro Inoué, 1989; Les Polyphonies Corses, 1989–90; Paco de Lucia's band, 1991; David Sylvian, Jon Hassel, John Cage, Manu Dibango, 1991–92; Film music with: Elliot Goldenthal, 1991; Gabriel Yared (L'Amant); Several fashion shows, as composer and performer; Own publishing and production and record label: Safar Production Inc. *Compositions:* Ballet music for Ismaël Ivo, 1998, 1999, 2000; Ballet Jazz Art; 1998. *Recordings:* Impressions de Voyages, 1984; Arrows, 1989; Assouf, with Baly Otmani Touareg, 1994; Figaro Si!, with D Figaro, 1995; Indigo Dreams, 1995; Safar – A Journey, 1995; Bye Bye, original film score, 1995; Wasts Diop, 1997; Zazie, 1997; Paul Simon, 1998, 1999, 2001; Bob Dylan, 2000; Producing and arranging Omar Farouk Tekbilek with Natacha Atlas, 2000; Recordings in: Amazonia; Indonesia; Ethiopia; Egypt; North Africa; Senegal; Spain. *Publications:* Arrows, 1990; Assouf, 1994; Indigo Dreams, 1995; Safar, 1997; Ikewan, 1997; Assarouf, 1997; Versecrêt, 1997; Awham, 1998; Amok, 1998; Plenitude, 1998;. *Membership:* SACEM. *Leisure interests:* Private pilot (multi and single engined); Ethno travelling; Recording. *Current Management:* c/o Safar. *Address:* 11 rue des Dahlias, 45300 Dossainville, France. *E-mail:* shehansteve@aol.com.

SHELDON Kenny; b. 1 May 1923, Berlin, Germany. Orchestra Leader; Conductor; Master of Ceremonies; Musician (trumpet, piano, drums, vibraphone). m. Rita Sheldon, 21 Feb. 1961. *Education:* College, New York City; New York University; Columbia University and CCNY. *Musical Education:* Private study, Berlin; Manhattan School of Music, New York; Juilliard, New York. *Career:* Entertainer in nightclubs, resorts, country clubs, colleges, hotels; World-wide tours with Dance Orchestra and Swing Jazz band; Starred, Stars and Styles, New York City; Television: Quantum Leap; Peaceable Kingdom; Composer, arranger, for own Ballroom Dance Orchestra. *Recordings:* Album: Dance Around the World with Kenny Sheldon Orchestra; Producer: Theme From Love Story, with Andy Williams. *Honours:* Plaques from various Mayors and City Councils, USA. *Memberships:* AFofM; Beverly Hills Chamber of Commerce. *Leisure interests:* Electronic engineering; Ballroom dancing; Volleyball; Tennis. *Current Management:* Kenny Sheldon Orchestras and Entertainment. *Address:* 1420 N Fuller Ave, Suite 304, Los Angeles, CA 90046, USA.

SHELTON Ricky Van; b. 12 Jan. 1952, Grit, Virginia, USA. Country Singer; Songwriter. m. Bettye Witt, 4 Aug. 1986. *Career:* Previous employment includes: Pipefitter; Plumber; Car salesman; Country singer, 1985-. *Recordings:* Hits include: US Country No. 1s include: Somebody Lied, 1987; Life Turned Her That Way, 1987; Don't We All Have The Right, 1987; I'll Leave This World Loving You; From A Jack To A King; Living Proof; Rockin' Years, with Dolly Parton, 1991; Albums: Wild-Eyed Dream, 1987; Loving Proof, 1988; Ricky Van Shelton Sings Christmas, 1989; Ricky Van Shelton III, 1990; Backroads, 1991; Don't Overlook Salvation, 1992; Greatest Hits Plus, 1992; Love and Honor, 1994; Ultimately Fine, 1994; Making Plans, 1998. *Honours:* CMA Awards: Horizon Award, 1988; Male Vocalist of Year, 1989; Nashville Network Viewer's Choice: Male Vocalist of Year, Album of Year, 1989. *Memberships:* Country Music Asscn; Academy of Country Music. *Leisure interests:* Farming; Fishing. *Current Management:* Michael Campbell and Associates, 6424 Bresslyn Rd, Nashville, TN 37205–3047, USA.

SHEPHERD Ben; b. 20 Sept. 1968, Okinawa, Japan. Musician (Bass). *Career:* Former Member, March of Crimes; Joined Soundgarden, 1990; Numerous tours and festival appearances. *Recordings:* Singles include: Rusty Cage; Spoonman; The Day I Tried To Live; Black Hole Sun; Fell on Black Days; Pretty Noose; Burden in My Hand; Blow Up The Outside World; Ty Cobb; Bleed Together; Albums: Badmotorfinger, 1991; Superunknown, 1994; Down on the Upside, 1996; A-Sides, 1997.

SHEPHERD Jean (Ollie Imogene); b. 21 Nov. 1933, Paul's Valley, Oklahoma, USA. Country vocalist; Songwriter; Musician (bass). m. Hawkshaw Hawkins, deceased 1963. *Career:* Formed all-girl band, the Melody Ranch Girls, late 1940s; Debut single Help penned by Hank Thompson who discovered group, 1948; Worked with Red Foley's Ozark Jubilee, 1955–57; Husband died in same plane crash as fellow country stars Patsy Cline and Cowboy Copas, 5 March 1963; Debut country hit A Dear John Letter (with Ferlin Huskey), #1 country, #4 pop, 1953; Forty five country chart entries mostly on Capitol and United Artists, until 1978. *Recordings include:* A Dear John Letter (with Ferlin Huskey), 1953; Slippin' Away, 1973; A Satisfied Mind, 1955; Beautiful Lies, 1955; Forgive Me John (with Ferlin Huskey), 1953; Albums: Heart We Did All That We Could, 1967; Many Happy Hangovers, 1966; I'll Take The Dog (with Ray Pillow), 1966. *Honours:* Cash Box, Top Female Singer, 1959. *Memberships:* Grand Ole Opry, 1955. *Address:* c/o Jim Chase, Ace Productions, PO Box 292725, Nashville, TN 37229, USA.

SHEPHERDSON Paul; b. 23 June 1941, Hull, England. Musician (drums); Drama Teacher, Dir, Drama and Stage Musicals. m. Sandra Nicholl, 13 July 1963, 1 s., 1 d. *Musical Education:* Self-taught drums. *Career:* Member, Mike Peters Florida Jazz Band; Supporting Kenny Ball Band; Roy Williams; Terry Lightfoot Band; Backing residental musician to most cabaret acts including: Marti Caine; The Nolans; Norman Collier; Faith Brown; Currently, own band with Martin Jones. *Compositions:* Co-writer, various musicals for local performance. *Membership:* Musicians' Union. *Leisure interest:* Greek holidays. *Address:* 73 The Wolds, Castle Park, Cottingham, Nr Hull HU16 5LQ, England.

SHEPPARD Andy; b. 20 Jan. 1957, Bristol, Avon, England. Jazz Musician (soprano saxophone). *Musical Education:* Clarinet, saxophone, flute and guitar. *Career:* Musician with: Sphere; Klaunstance; Lumiere (French Big Band); Urban Sax; Paul Dunmall; Keith Tippett; Leader, own band, 1987; Founder, Soft On The Inside Big Band, 1990; Founder, Co-motion, 1991-. *Recordings:* Albums: Andy Sheppard, 1987; Introductions In The Dark, 1989; Soft On The Inside, 1990; 66 Shades of Lipstick (with Keith Tippett), 1990; In Co-Motion, 1991; Inclassifiable (with Nana Vasconcelos and Steve Lodder), 1995; Songs With Legs (with Carla Bley), 1995; Dancing Man and Woman, 2000; with Sphere: Spere, 1988; Present Tense, 1988; Guest musician with Judy Tzuke: Ritmo, 1983; Turning Stones, 1989. *Current Management:* Serious Speakout, 42 Old Compton St, London W1V 5PB, England.

SHEPPARD Rodney Charles; b. 25 Nov. 1967. Musician (guitar). m. Gretchen, 1 s. *Career:* Played colleges and parties with local group The Tories; Group became The Shrinky Dinx; Signed to Atlantic Records following circulation of self-made demo video; Act renamed Sugar Ray owing to threat of legal action prior to record releases; Built up world-wide fanbase through touring and TV appearances; Cameo in Fathers Day film, 1997. *Recordings:* Albums: Lemonade and Brownies, 1995; Floored, 1997; 14–59, 1999; Sugar Ray, 2001; Singles: Mean Machine, Iron Mic, 1995; Fly, RPM, 1997; Every Morning, Someday, 1999; Falls Apart, 2000; When It's Over, Answer The Phone, 2001. *Honours:* Second/third albums certified double/triple platinum by RIAA respectively. *Address:* c/o PO Box 12018, Costa Mesa, CA 92627, USA. *E-mail:* management@sugarray.com. *Internet:* www.sugarray.com.

SHEPPARD T G, (William Neal Browder); b. 20 July 1944, Humboldt, Tennessee, USA. Country vocalist; Songwriter, Musician (guitar, saxophone, piano). *Career:* Moved to Memphis, 1960; Worked as backup singer with Travis Wammack's band; Recorded High School Days as Brian Stacey for Atlantic, 1966; Brief stint as record promoter for Stax label; First charted on pop and country chart with Devil In The Bottle for Motown's country subsidiary, Melodyland, 1974; Collaborations: Karen Brooks; Clint Eastwood; Judy Collins; Hits (including 14 #1s) continued on Warner/Curb and Columbia until 1991; Currently tours with band named after hit recording Slow Burn. *Compositions include:* Tryin' To Beat The Morning Home. *Recordings include:* Tryin' To Beat The Morning Home, 1975; Last Cheater's Waltz, I'll Be Coming Back For More, 1979; Party Time, I Loved 'Em Every One, 1981; Albums: 3/4 Lonely, 1979; Finally!, 1982; Greatest Hits, 1983. *Current Management:* R J Kaltenbach Personal Management, 641 Lindsay Ct, Dundee, IL 60118, USA.

SHERMAN Richard S; b. New York, USA. Record and Video Co Exec. m. Linda Jordan, 1 s., 1 d. *Education:* BS, 1948; LLB, 1950; LLM, 1951. *Career:* National Sales Manager, Product Manager, Mercury Records Corporation, Chicago, 1962–67; National Sales Manager, Warner Bros Records, Los Angeles, 1967–761; Product Manager, Sales Manager, Motown Record Corporation, Los Angeles, 1971–74; Executive Vice President, Sales Hollywood, California, 1981–85; Director, West Coast Ops, Bell Records, Los Angeles, 1974–75; Senior Vice President, Sales, Distribution Executive, Casablanca Records, 1975–81; Senior Vice President, Sales, Distribution, Marketing, Motown Records, 1981–85; Senior Vice President, Sales, Distribution, JCI, Agoura Hills, California, 1985–87; President, August Moon Productions, 1987-. *Memberships:* NARAS. *Address:* 6461 Zuma View Pl., Malibu, CA 90265 4470, USA.

SHERMAN Sandy; b. 7 March, New York, USA. Songwriter; Lyricist. m. Michael Sherman, 1 c. *Education:* BA, Brooklyn College, City University of New York; Master of Science, Major in Education, minor in Music. *Career:* Composed songs for many films and TV shows including Police Academy 4, Ghost Fever, The Substitute, Walker Texas Ranger, X Files, In the Line of Duty; Writer of children's songs for Disney, and for Shari Lewis's Lamb Chop Play Along; Lyricist, The Little Witch of Wichita. *Compositions:* He Delivers; Fast Asleep; Nighty Night; Dancing Arms; The Good News Is…; Dancin' Up a Storm, for Stacy Lattisaw; Big Rig Christmas Tree for Truckers Christmas; Cast A Stone Upon the Water; E.S.P.; When You Go Dancin'. *Honours:* Contribution to album, certified Gold by RIAA; Songwriter of the Year Award, Tennessee Songwriters' Asscn; The Little Witch of Wichita, Winner of the City of Los Angeles Cultural Affairs Department Theater Competition, 1995. *Memberships:* ASCAP; Society of

Composers and Lyricists. *Address:* PO Box 4445, Palos Verdes, CA 90274, USA.

SHERRY Rachel Patricia; b. 16 March 1960, Nottingham, England. Musician (harp); Vocalist. m. John Byron, 25 Sept. 1993. *Musical Education:* Birmingham University; Royal Academy of Music. *Career:* Appearances at Purcell Room and Queen Elizabeth Hall; Concert tours to France, Italy, Spain and throughout UK; Numerous television appearances as actress, singer and harpist; 4 programmes of music for harp and voice for BBC Radio and numerous broadcasts with BBC Singers. *Recording:* Rachel Sherry – Voice and Harp; New album due for release, 1996. *Publications:* Folk-songs For Voice and Harp, in preparation. *Memberships:* Musicians' Union; Equity. *Current Management:* Alexander Personal Management. *Address:* 16 Roughdown Ave, Hemel Hempstead, Hertfordshire HP3 9BN, England.

SHERWOOD John Torrance; b. South Africa. Composer; Prod.; Musician (guitar); Engineer. *Education:* Architectural Association of Architecture. *Musical Education:* Studied classical guitar with Patrick Bashford and Hector Quine. *Compositions:* Soundtracks: Rumours of Rain, CH4, 1992; Spoilt For Choice, BBC2, 1993; Trouble, CH4, 1993. *Recordings:* Albums: As guitarist with Haysi Fantaysee: Battle Hymns For Children Singing; As engineer with P M Dawn: of The Heart of The Soul and of The Cross; Single: Set Adrift On Memory Bliss; As engineer: Project One and Irresistible Force: Outlaw Posse: My Afro's On Fire. *Honours:* Gold records for PM Dawn: Set Adrift On Memory Bliss; Of The Heart of The Soul and of The Cross. *Memberships:* Musicians' Union; PRS. *Current Management:* Paradox Productions. *Address:* PO Box 3083, London N1 8NZ, England.

SHIJI (Awoyinka); b. 23 Oct. 1969, London, England. Singer; Songwriter; Musician (keyboards, percussion). *Education:* BEng (hons), Mechanical Engineering; MSc, Product Design. *Career:* Finalist, Sony Dance Music Search, 1993; Concerts: Ronnie Scotts, 1995; Orange, 1995; WKD, 1995. *Recordings:* Facets (Debut EP); My Lover's Embrace, 1997. *Memberships:* MCPS; PRS; Musicians' Union. *Leisure interests:* Singing; Collecting jazz records. *Current Management:* Ivy Records. *Address:* 15 Reynardsons Court, High Rd, London N17 9HX, England.

SHILKLOPER Arkady; b. 17 Oct. 1956, Moscow, Russia. Musician (horn). m. Olga Goloborodko, 22 July 1981, 1 s., 1 d. *Education:* Moscow Gnesin Institut, 1976–81. *Career:* Bolshoi Theatre Orchestra, 1978–85; Moscow Philharmonic Orchestra, 1985–89; Freelance Musician (Jazz, Classical, Folk), since 1990; Hornplayer (also Alphorn, Corno du Caccio); Jazz Podium; Jazz Time; Jazz Kwadrat. *Recordings:* with Pago Libre: Titles, 1996; Wake Up Call, 1998; Sheffield Jazz Experience, 1996; with Karl Berger: No Man is an Island, 1996; with Misha Alperin: North Story, 1998. *Memberships:* International Horn Society. *Address:* Osennij Blvd 6–526, Moscow, 121609, Russia.

SHINKARUK Irina Volodimirivna; b. 31 July 1979, Fastiv, Kiev, Ukraine. Singer. *Education:* Musical College, Zhitomyr-city, Ukraine, 1995–97; Zhitomir State Pedagogical Institute, 1995-. *Career:* Film: Cheremhove Vihola, 1993; Tours of Ukraine, 1994; Concert of The Prizewinners, at International Competition: The Voice of Asia, 1994; Tours: France; Germany; Hungary, other countries, 1994; Television show: Ukraine, Spring, Slavutich (commemorating Chernobyl), 1995. *Compositions:* Mermaid's Week, 1993; I'm Like a Bird, 1996. *Recordings:* I'm Like a Bird (14 Songs of the Period), 1993; The Fifth Season of The Year (The Season of Love), 1995; Step Towards the Summer, 1996; Best composition: The Moon Talisman (Misyachniy Oberig). *Publications:* The Stars of Chervona Ruta Academy, 1993. *Honours:* First Prize: Chervona Ruta, 1993; Grand Prize, International Festival, Bilostotsky Malvi, Poland, 1993; Diploma FIDOF vth International Festival, The Voice of Asia, 1994; The Best Singer, nominated to Magic Rock, Festival of New Stars of The Old Year, 1994. *Membership:* FIDOF. *Leisure interest:* Ukrainian folklore, especially Ukrainian legends, ancient Christian and BC rituals. *Current Management:* Vlodimir Shinkaruk. *Address:* 102 B Ten Str, Apt 65, Zhitomir 262024, Ukraine.

SHINODA Mike Kenji; b. 11 Feb. 1977, Agoura, California, USA. Vocalist. *Education:* Pasadena Art College of Design, Illustration graduate. *Career:* Half-Japanese, half-American; Temporarily worked in graphic design; Played piano for 10 years but lost interest; Formed group Xero with guitarist Brad Delson in seventh grade at high school; Became Hybrid Theory and signed to Warner Bros, Spring 2000; Band immediately sent to professional studio; Further name change to Linkin Park prior to first record releases; Incessant promotional activity since release of album; Live shows include: Family Values and Ozzfest tours; KROQ Acoustic Christmas Concert 2001; many international dates; TV specials include: Live At The Fillmore; Reverb; Currently lives in Los Angeles, California. *Recordings:* Albums: Hybrid Theory, 2000; Singles: Hybrid Theory (Acoustic EP), 2000; One Step Closer, Crawling, Papercut, In The End, 2001. *Honours:* Over 10m. world-wide sales of debut album to end of 2001;

Billboard Award, Best Modern Rock Artist, 2001; Rock Bear Awards: Best International Band; Best International Album, 2001; Kerrang! Award, Best International Newcomer, 2001; Rolling Stone Award, Best Hard Rock/ Metal Band, 2001. *Current Management:* Andy Gould Management, 8484 Wilshire Blvd #425, Beverly Hills, CA 90211, USA. *Internet:* www.linkinpark.com.

SHIPSTON Roy; b. 25 Aug. 1951, London, England. Musician (keyboards); Vocalist; Composer; Arranger; Record Prod. m. Julia Diane Twigg, 23 Nov. 1968, divorced 1994, 1 s., 1 d. *Musical Education:* ABRSM Finals: Theory of Music, Pianoforte. *Career:* Music journalist, Disc and Music Echo, 1969–71; Musician, 1971–; Member, Formerly Fat Harry; Leader, own bands: Rococo; The Legendary Brats; Future; Performed on more than 30 albums; Sessions with Peter Green; Carl Palmer (ELP); Mike Harrison (Spooky Tooth); Chris Thompson; Peter Cox (Go West); Jake Sollo (Osibisa); Biddu; Jim Diamond; Now member, First Light; Co-owner, The Mill Recording Studios, Cookham, Berkshire; 1989–94; Clients included: Elton John; George Harrison; Chris Rea; Clannad. *Honours:* 2 BASF/Studio Master Awards; Music Week Top European Engineer Award; 3M Award. *Memberships:* PRS; Musicians' Union. *Current Management:* Rococo Productions. *Address:* 2 Selwyn Court, Church Rd, Richmond, Surrey TW10 6LR, England.

SHIPWAY Nigel Howard; b. 29 March 1953, Reading, Berkshire, England. Musician (percussion, timpani, mallets). *Musical Education:* Studied percussion, composition with James Blades, Royal Academy of Music; Reg Barker, principal percussionist, Royal Opera House; Studied with Bobby Christian, USA. *Career:* Film appearances: Hunchback; The Wall; Return To Oz; Musical performances: Principal percussionist, National Symphony Orchestra, for 21 years; Academy of St Martins in the Fields; English Chamber Orchestra; Cats, New London Theatre, 13 years; Played on film scores: The Far Pavilions; Knight's Move; The Tall Guy; Morons From Outer Space; The Honorary Consul; The Killing Fields; Appearances with: The Moody Blues; Pink Floyd; Bob Geldof; Gene Pitney; Dionne Warwick; Bob Hoskins; José Carreras; Kiri Te Kanawa; Placido Domingo; Frankie Laine; The Pointer Sisters; Billy Daniels. *Compositions:* 44 studies for timpani; Style Studies For Xylophone; Concert Marimba Etude. *Recordings:* Over 1000 listings with: National Symphony Orchestra; English Chamber Orchestra; Royal Opera House Orchestra; Alyn Ainsworth Orchestra; Ron Goodwin Orchestra. *Publications:* Articles: Talking Drums; Percussive Notes. *Honours:* President (UK Chapter), Percussive Arts Society; Royal Society of Musicians. *Memberships:* Bonsai growing; Reading; Cookery; DIY; Photography; Historical research. *Current Management:* MAS. *Address:* Masters Yard, 180A South St, Dorking, Surrey RH4 2ES, England.

SHIRE David Lee; b. 3 July 1937, Buffalo, New York, USA. Composer. m. (1)Talia Rose Coppola, 29 March 1970, divorced, 1 s., (2) Didi Conn, 11 Feb. 1984, 1 s. *Education:* BA, Yale University, 1959. *Compositions:* Film scores include: The Conversation, 1973; The Taking of Pelham 1–2–3, 1974; Farewell, My Lovely, 1975; All the President's Men, 1977; Saturday Night Fever, 1977; Norma Rae, 1979; Return To Oz, 1985; TV scores include: Raid on Entebbe, 1977; The Kennedy's of Massachusetts; Sarah Plain and Tall, 1991; Rear Window, 1999; Theatre scores include: Starting Here, Starting Now, 1975; Baby, 1983; Closer Than Ever, 1989; Big, 1996. *Recordings:* Recorded songs include: What About Today?, 1965; The Promise, 1978; It Goes Like It Goes, 1979; With You I'm Born Again, 1979; Albums include: Saturday Night Fever, 1977; Starting Here, Starting Now, 1975; Baby, 1984; Return to Oz, 1985; Closer Than Ever, 1989; David Shire at the Movies, 1991; Big, 1996. *Honours:* Numerous awards, Tony nominations; Academy and Grammy Awards. *Memberships:* Composers and Lyricists Guild of America; Academy of Motion Picture Arts and Sciences; National Academy of Television Arts and Sciences; Dramatists Guild of America, council mem. *Address:* 19 Ludlow Lane, Palisades, NY 10964, USA.

SHOCKED Michelle; b. 24 Feb. 1962, Dallas, Texas, USA. Singer; Songwriter; Musician (guitar). m. 4 July 1992. *Education:* BSc, University of Texas, Austin. *Career:* World-wide tours, 1987–; Concerts include: Heineken Festival, Leeds, 1995. *Recordings:* Short Sharp Shocked, 1988; Captain Swing, 1989; Arkansas Traveller, 1992; Kind Hearted Woman, 1994; Mercury Poise, 1996; Artists Make Lousy Slaves, 1996; Good News, 1998. *Honours:* Grammy Nominations, 1988, 1992; Brit Award Nomination, 1988. *Membership:* NARAS; Rhythm and Blues Foundation. *Leisure interests:* Politics; Community Activities. *Current Management:* Janine Natter, Codikow Carroll Guido and Groffman, New York. *Address:* 828 Royal St #520, New Orleans, LA 70116, USA.

SHORROCK Glenn; b. 30 July 1944, Rochester, Kent, England. Vocalist. *Career:* Vocalist with The Twilights, Axiom, then Esperanto before international success with Little River Band (formerly Mississippi), 1975–83; 1988–; Also solo career. *Compositions:* Help Is On Its Way, 1976; Home On Monday, 1977; Cool Change, 1979. *Recordings:* Albums: Little River Band, 1975; After Hours, 1976; Diamantina Cocktail, 1977;

Sleeper Catcher, 1978; First Under The Wire, 1979; Backstage Pass, 1980; Time Exposure, 1981; Greatest Hits, 1982; Monsoon, 1988; Too Late To Load, 1989; Get Lucky, 1990; Reminiscing – The 20th Anniversary Concert, 1995; solo: Villain of The Peace, 1983; The First 20 Years, 1985; with The Twilights: '64-'69; with Axiom: '69-'71. *Honours:* ARIA, Hall of Fame, 1991. *Memberships:* APRA; board mem. 1980–98. *Current Management:* Talentworks Pty Ltd, Suite 1a, 663 Victoria St, Abbotsford, VIC 3067, Australia.

SHORTER Wayne; b. 25 Aug. 1933, Newark, New Jersey, USA. Musician (saxophone). *Education:* BA, New York University, 1956. *Career:* Saxophonist with: Art Blakey, 1959–63; Miles Davis, 1964–70; Weather Report, 1970–86; Solo artiste, 1962–; Recent appearances include: London Jazz Festival, 1995. *Recordings:* Solo albums: Freeform, 1962; Search For a New Land, 1964; Night Dreamer, 1964; Some Other Stuff, 1964; Ju Ju, 1987; Speak No Evil, 1965; All Seeing Eye, 1966; Adam's Apple, 1967; Schizophrenia, 1968; Odyssey of Iska, 1970; Super Nova, 1970; Shorter Moments, 1972; Wayne Shorter, 1974; Moto Grosso Felo, 1975; Native Dancer, 1975; The Soothsayer, 1980; Etcetera, 1981; Wayning Moments, 1984; Second Genesis (reissue) 1984; Atlantis, 1985; Best Of..., 1988; Introducing...; Phantom Navigator, 1987; Joy Ryder, 1988; High Life, 1994; with Weather Report: Weather Report, 1971; I Sing The Body Electric, 1972; Sweetnighter, 1973; Mysterious Traveller, 1974; Tail Spinnin', 1975; Black Market, 1976; Black Market/Heavy Weather, 1978; Mr Gone, 1978; 8.30, 1979; Night Passage, 1980; Weather Report, 1982; Procession, 1983; Domino Theory, 1984; Sportin' Life, 1985; This Is This!, 1986; Greatest Hits, 1991; with Miles Davis: In Berlin, 1964; ESP, 1965; Miles Smiles, 1967; The Sorcerer, 1967; Nefertiti, 1968; Miles In The Sky, 1968; Filles De Kilimanjaro, 1968; In a Silent Way, 1969; Bitches Brew, 1970; Live Evil, 1972; Big Fun, 1974; Water Babies, 1977; Circle In The Round, 1979; with Joni Mitchell: Don Juan's Reckless Daughter, 1977; Mingus, 1979; Wild Things Run Fast, 1982; Dog Eat Dog, 1985; Chalk Mark In a Rain Storm, 1988; Night Ride Home, 1991; Panthalassa: The Music of Miles Davis, 1998; Sketches of Spain/ Kind of Blue, 1998; Also featured on recordings by: Airto; Stanley Clarke; Don Henley; Herbie Hancock; Freddie Hubbard; Jaco Pastorius; Rolling Stones; Sanatana; Steely Dan; Joe Zawinul. *Address:* c/o The Jazz Tree, 648 Broadway, Suite 703, New York, NY 10012, USA.

SHOVELL (Andrew Lovell); b. 11 Feb. 1969, Jamaica. Musician (Percussion). *Career:* Member, M People; Numerous live dates and television appearances; Song, Search for the Hero used in TV advertisement. *Recordings:* Singles: Colour of My Life; Padlock; One Night in Heaven; Excited; Moving on Up; Open Your Heart; Search for the Hero; Just for You; Fantasy Island; Angel St; Testify; Albums: Elegant Slumming, 1994; Northern Soul, 1995; Love Rendezvous, 1995; Bizarre Fruit, 1995; Fresco, 1997. *Honours:* Brit Award, Best Dance Band, 1992; Mercury Music Prize, 1993.

SHPORTKO Victor; b. 30 Oct. 1944, Dniepropetrovsk, Ukraine. Singer. m. Natalia Biezko, 29 Oct. 1977, 1 s., 1 d. *Education:* Kiev Institute of Culture. *Musical Education:* Dniepropetrovsk Music Institute. *Career:* Tours: Canada; USA; Belgium; Poland; Czechoslovakia; Germany; Greece; Appears regularly on Ukrainian television and radio. *Recordings:* 3 Ukrainian cassettes. *Honours:* Singer Laureate International Competitions. *Membership:* Ukrainian Musical Societies. *Leisure interest:* Travel. *Current Management:* Nicholas Tarasinko, 3A Horkogo St, Kiev, Ukraine. *Address:* 125A Horogo St, Apartment 109, Kiev 252006, Ukraine.

SHREEVE Mark; b. 2 June 1957, Great Yarmouth, Norfolk, England. Composer; Musician (keyboards, synthesizers, guitar). *Education:* Studied architecture. *Musical Education:* Self-taught. *Career:* UK Electronica Festival, 1983, 1984, 1990; EMMA Festival, 1994; KLEM Festival, Netherlands, 1995. *Compositions:* Songs include: Touch Me, 1986; I Surrender, 1987; True Devotion, 1988 (all recorded by Samantha Fox). *Recordings:* Albums: Assassin, 1983; Legion, 1985; Crash Head, 1988; Nocturne, 1995; Soundtracks include: Turnaround, 1986; Buy and Cell, 1988; Honor Bound, 1989. *Honours:* Gold, Silver discs, UK, USA; ASCAP Awards, various songs. *Membership:* PRS. *Leisure interests:* Motorcycles; Tennis; Films. *Current Management:* Virtual World Ltd. *Address:* 155 Prince George Ave, Southgate, London N14 4TD, England.

SHRIEVE Michael; b. 6 July 1949, San Francisco, California, USA. Musician (drums). m. Cindy Weintraub, 1 May 1982, 1 s. *Education:* BA, San Mateo Jr College. *Musical Education:* BA studies with Anthony Cirome. *Career:* Long involvement as drummer/percussionist with Santana; Recorded with artists such as: The Rolling Stones; Steve Winwood; David Crosby; Also with experimental jazz musicians: Stomu Yamashta; Klaus Schulze; John McLaughlin; Bill Frisell; One of first to experiment with electronic drums, 1973-. *Compositions include:* (for film and television) The Tempest; The Bedroom Window. *Recordings:* with Santana: Santana; Abraxas; Woodstock; Santana III; Caravansérail; Welcome; Lotus; Barboletta; with Steve Winwood: Automatic Man; with Stomu Yamashta: Go; with David Crosby: If Only I Could Remember My

Name; with John McLaughlin: Love Devotion and Surrender; with The Rolling Stones: Emotional Rescue; Tattoo You; with Bill Frisell: Fascination; Solo: Two Doors. *Honours:* Melody Maker; Modern Drummer; Grammy Nomination. *Memberships:* BMI; NARAS; Percussive Arts Society. *Leisure interests:* Books; Film; Computers. *Current Management:* CMP Records. *Address:* 4756 University Village Pl. NE #288, Seattle, WA 98105, USA.

SHUMAN Earl Stanley; b. 2 Aug. 1923, Boston, Massachusetts, USA. Songwriter (lyrics); Music Publisher. m. Margaret Stein, 25 Nov. 1956, 2 s., 1 d. *Education:* BA, Yale College, 1945. *Career:* Appeared with George Gibbs on The Perry Como Show, 1953, Jackie Gleson Show, 1953, Red Buttons Show, 1953. *Compositions:* Seven Lonely Days; Banjo's Back in Town; I Am; Left, Right, Out of Your Heart; Theme For a Dream; Starry-Eyed; Most People Get Married; Caterina; Hotel Happiness; Hey There Lonely Boy (Girl); The River; My Shy Violet; Young New Mexican Puppeteer; Clinging Vine; Close to Cathy; I've Been Here; Time, Time; Leaves are the Tears of Autumn; Off-Broadway Production, Secret Life of Walter Mitty, 1964; Movie Title Songs: Disorderly Orderly; Carpetbaggers; Judith; Dondi; Situation Hopeless But Not Serious. *Publications:* Bat Out of Hell, Meatloaf, 1977. *Honours:* Gold Record, Hey There Lonely Girl, 1970; Country Music Award, Leaves Are The Tears of Autumn, 1970; Platinum Record, Bat Out of Hell, 1978. *Memberships:* ASCAP; NARAS; SGA. *Leisure interests:* Working to publish new singer-songwriters; Watching baseball games. *Current Management:* Music Sales Publishing Inc. *Address:* Earl/Peg Music Co, 111 E 88th St, Apt 3 B, New York, NY 10128, USA.

SHUTTLEWORTH David, (Shutty); b. 20 March 1967, Keighley, Yorkshire, England. Musician (Drums). *Career:* Formed Spoilt Bratz with Tony Wright, Mark Yates and Leigh Marklew; Became Terrorvision; Secured record deal, 1991; Support slot to the Ramones; Numerous headlining tours and TV appearances. *Recordings:* Singles: My House, 1993; Oblivion, 1994; Pretend Best Friend, 1994; Alice, What's The Matter, 1994; Bad Actress, 1996; Perseverance, 1996; Easy, 1996; Moonage Daydream, 1997; Josephine, 1998; Tequila, 1999; Albums: Formaldehyde, 1993; How To Win Friends and Influence People, 1994; Regular Urban Survivors, 1996; Shaving Peaches, 1998.

SHVEDOVA Irina; b. 28 April 1959, Kishivev, Moldova. Singer. Divorced, 1 d. *Education:* Kiev State Institute of Theatre Art; Music School, Kiev. *Career:* Lead role, children's radio play, 1968; Ukrainian pop concert, 1986; Diploma, Song of the Year, 1990, 1991; Hit '93, Russian competition; 10 Years on stage live, 1996. *Compositions:* America Separating, 1990; The White Waltz, 1991; Jordano, 1991; The Witch, 1992; Stay Cool, 1994; Faeton, 1998. *Recordings:* The Witch, 1993, 1994, CD, 1995; We'll Meet Again, 1996; Faeton, forthcoming. *Membership:* Theatre Artists Union, Ukraine. *Leisure interest:* Toy dolls collection. *Current Management:* Anton Klimov. *Address:* Frumenskaya na 6, 27/1, ap 50, 119196 Moscow, Russia.

SIBERIL Soïg; b. 1 Feb. 1955, France. Musician (Celtic guitar). 1 s. *Musical Education:* Self-taught. *Career:* Guitarist, 20 years; Member: Sked, 1975; Kornog, 1980; Gwerz, 1980; Pennou Skoulm, 1989; Kemia, 1989; Orion, 1992; La Rouchta, 1992; Numerous concerts and festivals all over Europe and America. *Recordings:* 1 solo album: Digor, 1993; 15 albums with other bands, including 5 with Kornog, 3 with Gwerz. *Honours:* Prix Academie du Disque Charles Cros: Gwertz, 1987, Le Sours Du Scorff, 1995. *Leisure interest:* Gardening.

SIBERRY Jane; b. 12 Oct. 1955, Toronto, Ontario, Canada. Singer; Songwriter; Musician (piano, guitar). *Education:* BSc Hons, University of Guelph (Ontario). *Musical Education:* Self-taught. *Career:* Guest at Peter Gabriel's Real World recording week, 1994; Co-wrote and performed closing title track in film: The Crow; 5 world tours; Contributing artist on Hector Zazoo's project, Songs From The Cold North Seas; Wrote, performed Calling All Angels, for Wim Wender's film Until The End of The World. *Recordings:* Albums: Jane Siberry, 1981; No Borders Here, 1983; The Speckless Sky, 1985; The Walking, 1987; Bound By The Beauty, 1989; When I Was a Boy, 1993; Maria, 1995; Teenager, 1997; Child: Music for the Christmas Season [live], 1997; Lips: Music For Saying It, 1999; Tree: Music for Films and Forests, 1999; Singles: Temple, 1993; Lovin' Cup, 1995. *Honours:* Casby (Canadian People's Choice Award); Album and Producer of the Year, 1986; Now Magazine Songwriter of The Year, 1995. *Current Management:* Bob Blumer Management. *Address:* 2700 Rutherford Dr., Los Angeles, CA, USA.

SIDDIQUI Khalid; b. 14 Feb. 1970, Oxford, England. Vocalist; Musician (guitar, lap steel, mandolin). *Education:* University of East London. *Career:* Founded Doleboy Cowboy record label, 1990; Releases own material, other bands' material, and re-issues; British tour, 1993; Television: Kilroy; Radio: GLR; Mark Radcliffe, BBC Radio 1; Working/production with other bands; Currently tours London only. *Recordings:* City of Circles; Spend Monday Evening With; Angry Young Women Don'tcha Just Love 'Em; God's Outlaw; Man With Cock; Background Music On Paper; Various other bands / productions include: Tribute To Johan Penson, Yupe Yeah. *Publications:* Contributor: Alcohol and Actors – Their Uses and Abuses; Surviving Performance Poetry Vol. III: Modernists; Various fanzines. *Honours:* Best Soundtrack (University of Westminster) Musical accompaniment (Jackson Comedy com). *Membership:* Pub-Orientation Rock National Organ. *Leisure interests:* Paranormal Arbitrator; Legal Advice; B-Movies. *Current Management:* Doleboy Cowboy Music. *Address:* 14 Westbury Rd, Feltham, Middlesex TW13 5HQ, England.

SIEBINGER Manfred; b. 6 Dec. 1956, Salzburg, Austria. Concert Promoter. *Education:* Press-distribution; Advertising Agency; High School of Music. *Career:* Promoter, with local acts, 1984; Jazz/folk groups; Singer, songwriter; Acts produced by Broadway Musical Company, New York; Promoter, Lucio Dalla; Donovan; Gilbert Becaud; Stéphane Grappelli; Golden Gate Quartet; Paco De Lucia; Canadian Brass; Jaco Pastorius; The Dubliners; Dave Brubeck; Kris Kristofferson; Golden Earring; Blues Pumpm; Chris Barber; Pasadena Roof Orchestra; Flying Pickets, 1986–94. *Leisure interests:* World travel; Cultures; Music; Modern art; Painting. *Current Management:* PO Box 165, 5024 Salzburg, Austria.

SIFFRE Labi; b. Bayswater, London, England. Singer; Musician (guitar). *Musical Education:* Studied music harmonics. *Career:* Member, various soul bands in Cannes, France; Solo artiste, late 1960s-. *Recordings:* Albums: Labi Siffre, 1970; Singer and The Song, 1971; Crying, Laughing, Loving, Lying, 1972; So Strong, 1988; Make My Day, 1989; Singles: It Must Be Love (later recorded by Madness), 1971; Crying, Laughing, Loving, Lying, 1971; Watch Me, 1972; (Something Inside) So Strong, 1987. *Current Management:* Mismanagement, 754 Fulham Rd, London SW6 5SH, England.

SIIKASAARI Eerik; b. 8 Oct. 1957, Kotka, Finland. Musician (bass). *Musical Education:* Piano, electric and acoustic bass; Oulunkylä; Diploma, Sibelius Academy. *Career:* Appeared with Jukkis Uotila Quartet, Middelheim Festival, Belgium, 1978; Association with Seppo Paakkunainen's Karelia, 1980–; Plays regularly with bands: Jukka Perko Quartet; Trio Töykeät; Espoo Big Band; Jukka Linkola Quintet; Perko-Pyysalo Poppoo; Concerts with Karelia and big bands in France, Switzerland, Germany, UK, US. *Honours:* First prize, with Trio Töykeät, Belgian jazz contest, 1988; Yrjö Award, Finnish Jazz Federation, 1995. *Address:* Apollonkatu 23 B 55, 00100 Helsinki, Finland.

SILAG Marc; b. 22 May 1953, New York, USA. Tour Production Man.; Artist Man. m. Susan Brown. *Education:* College. *Career:* General Manager, Bitter End, New York, 1974; Stage Manager, Bottom Line Theatre, New York, 1975–77; Tour, Artist Manager, 1977–; Production Manager for: Michael Urbaniak; John McLaughlin; David Sanborn; Herb Alpert; Patti Labelle; Pat Metheny Group; Paul Simon; Simon and Garfunkel; Personal Manager for: Ladysmith Black Mambazo; Chris Botti; Musical contractor, The Capeman, Broadway. *Recordings:* Co-ordinator: Graceland, Paul Simon (New York only); Rhythm of The Saints, Paul Simon; Various recordings with: David Sanborn; Ladysmith Black Mambazo; Chris Botti. *Publications:* Musician Magazine; Record Engineer and Producer. *Memberships:* AFM; AFTRA. *Leisure interest:* Fly-fishing. *Current Management:* Right Side Management. *Address:* 1674 Broadway #4C, New York, NY 10019, USA.

SILSON Alan; b. 21 June 1951, Bradford, West Yorkshire, England. Musician (lead guitar); Vocalist. m. Angela, 11 July 1986, 1 d. *Musical Education:* Self-taught. *Career:* Founder member, Smokie; Television: Top of The Pops; Old Grey Whistle Test; Television and radio appearances in Germany; Norway; Denmark; Sweden; Ireland; Australia. *Compositions include:* Boulevard of Broken Dreams (number 1 album, Scandinavia, 6 weeks). *Recordings:* Numerous albums including: Pass It Round, 1975; Midnight Cafe, 1976; Bright Lights and Back Alleys, 1977; The Other Side of The Road, 1979; Strangers In Paradise, 1982; Boulevard of Broken Dreams, 1990; 20 top 20 hits, including If You Think You Know How To Love Me, 1975; Living Next Door To Alice, 1976; Lay Back In The Arms of Someone, 1977. *Honours:* Silver, Gold, Platinum discs world-wide. *Memberships:* Musicians' Union; PRS; MCPS; PPL; BASCA. *Leisure interests:* Recording; Swimming; DIY.

SILVANO Judi; b. 8 May 1951, Philadelphia, Pennsylvania, USA. Vocalist; Composer. m. Joe Lovano, 30 Sept. 1984. *Education:* Pennsylvania Ballet School; Murray Louis/Alwin Nikolais Dance Theatre School; Graduated, cum laude, Temple University College of Music, 1974; BMI Composers Workshop; Private study with Anne Marie Moss (voice), Mark Murphy (voice), Kirk Nurock (theory), Yolanda Picucci Radlowski (flute). *Career:* Member, Group Motion Dance Troupe, Residency, Berlin Arts Festival, 1975; First European Tour and live recording at Amiens, France, with Joe Lovano, Worlds, 1989; Montréal Jazz Festival, European Tours, Montreux, Switzerland, Scandinavia, Italy, Paris, Festivals, 1991–98; BET Jazz Showcase, Judi Silvano Vocalise Band, 1997; Concerts at Carnegie Hall, Lincoln Center, Chicago Symphony Hall, Canadian Jazz Festivals with Joe Lovano Ensembles; Faculty, Rutgers

University and BANFF Jazz Workshop, 1999. *Compositions:* Bass Space and Left Behind with Joe Lovano; Ecstasy, Isadora, 23rd St, Calypso, on Dancing Voices CD; Heuchera Americana, It's So Amazing, At Home, Bass Space on Vocalise; Nature of Life, American Festival of American Composers. *Recordings:* As Leader: Vocalise, CD; Dancing Voices; Songs I Wrote or Wish I Did; With Joe Lovano: Universal Language; Celebrating Sinatra; Rush Hour; Worlds; With Kenny Werner: Paintings. *Honour:* Top 10 Vocalist, Down Beat magazine, 1995. *Memberships:* AFTRA; Internatiohal Asscn of Women Composers, New York; Composers Concordance. *Leisure interests:* Gardening; Drawing. *Address:* PO Box 218, Salisbury Mills, NY 12557, USA.

SILVER Ken(neth M); b. 23 March 1948, Philadelphia, Pennsylvania, USA. Musician (Saxophone, Clarinet); Bandleader. m. Judith Lipkin, 2 Nov. 1978, 2 s. *Education:* BSEd, 1969, MEd, 1971, Temple University; Studied clarinet with Ronald Reuben and Harold Karabell. *Career:* Performed at over 4000 Charity Balls, galas, corporate and social events since 1970; Performed a local, state and national inaugurals. *Honours:* Played for President Clinton and also for mayors, governors. *Leisure interests:* Skiing; Golf; Tennis. *Current Management:* Entertainment Solutions Inc. *Address:* Suite 525, Fox Pavilion, Jenkintown, PA 19046, USA.

SILVERLIGHT Terry; b. 15 Jan. 1957, Newark, New Jersey, USA. Composer; Prod.; Musician (Drums); Arranger. m. Judy, 7 Sept. 1995. *Education:* Princeton University; Piano with Olga Von Til; Percussion with Morris Lang. *Career:* Songs aired on TV Shows Melrose Place, Pacific Palisades, Beverly Hills 90210, The Guiding Light, CNN Lifestyles, Jag, Clueless, Seventh Heaven, The Sopranos; TV appearances as drummer with Roberta Flack and Marvin Hamlish at the White House, Peabo Bryson, Natalie Merchant on the Rosie O'Donnell Show, Sheena Easton, Barry Miles, Al DiMeola, Steven Stills. *Compositions:* All That Matters, Louise; Chasin' a Dream, Nancy Wilson; All I Wanna Do, Carl Anderson; Love's The Key, Maria Amada; Take My Love For Real, Yasuko Agawa and Philip Ingram. *Recordings:* Played drums on records for Billy Ocean, Mel Tormé, Laura Nyro, Anne Murray, Tom Jones, Barry Miles, Phil Woods, Stephanie Mills, George Benson, David Matthews, Don Johnson, Freddie Jackson, Eric Kloss, Jonathan Butler, Melba Moore, David Sancious. *Publication:* The Featured Drummer, instruction book, 1981. *Honours:* Platinum Disc for All That Matters; Numerous Gold and Platinum Discs as Drummer. *Membership:* ASCAP.

SIMARD Bernard; b. 27 Aug. 1959, Valleyfield, Québec, Canada. Musician (guitar); Singer. m. 8 July 1994, 1 s., 1 d. *Musical Education:* Self-taught. *Career:* Member: La Bottine Souriante; Gwazigan, 1996; Tours include USA, Canada, Europe, 1984–87; Member, Manigance; Tours of France, 1988–90; Current member, Cabestan; First part of Raymond Léveque, 1994; Television includes: Ad Lib (Québec), BBC (UK). *Recordings include:* with La Bottine Souriante: La Traversée de l'Atlantique, 1986; Nouvelle Manigance, 1991; Tracks also featured on Down Home, Vols I and II, 1986; with Cabestan: Tempête Pour Sortir; St Laurent-Sur-Oust, 1995; with Christian Maes: Coup de Vent, 1998; with Gwazigan: Dessus La Fougère; Y'Avait Du Monde. *Membership:* SOCAN. *Leisure interests:* Sciences; Poetry. *Current Management:* Micmac Musik, 24 Quai De La Fosse, 44000Nantes, France.

SIMINS Russell; b. 1964, Long Island, New York, USA. Musician (drums). *Career:* Member, Jon Spencer Blues Explosion. *Recordings:* Singles: The Sound of the Future is Here Today, 1992; Son of Sam, 1992; Big Yule Log Boogie, 1992; Train 3, 1993; Bellbottoms, 1995; Get With It, 1996; 2 Kindsa Love, 1996; Wail, 1997; Rocketship, 1997; Talk About the Blues, 1998; Albums: The Jon Spencer Blues Explosion, 1992; Crypt-Style, 1992; Extra Width, 1993; Mo' Width, 1994; Orange, 1994; Experimental Remixes, 1995; Now I Got Worry, 1996; Controversial Negro, 1997; Rocketship, 1997; ACME, 1998.

SIMMONS Gene (Chaim Witz); b. 25 Aug. 1949, Haifa, Israel. Musician (bass guitar); Singer; Actor; Songwriter. *Education:* ABA, Sulllivan College, SUNY, 1970; BA, Richmond College, CUNY, 1972. *Career:* Founder, Wicked Lester, 1972; Founder member, US rock group Kiss, 1973–; Regular UK, US, European and world-wide tours; Actor, films: The Runaway, 1984; Never Too Young To Die, 1986; Trick Or Treat (with Ozzy Osbourne); Dead Or Alive, 1986; Kiss Attack of The Phantom; Inventor, Axe bass guitar, 1980; Established Simmons record label, 1988- . *Compositions:* Many for Kiss. *Recordings:* Albums: Kiss, 1974; Hotter Than Hell, 1974; Dressed To Kill, 1975; Alive!, 1975; Destroyer, 1976; The Originals, 1976; Rock and Roll Over, 1976; Kiss Alive II, 1977; Love Gun, 1977; Double Platinum, 1978; Dynasty, 1979; Kiss Unmasked, 1980; Music From The Elder, 1981; Creatures of The Night, 1982; Lick It Up, 1983; Animalize, 1984; Asylum, 1985; Crazy Nights, 1987; Smashes, Thrashes and Hits, 1988; Hot In The Shade, 1989; Revenge, 1992; Kiss Alive III, 1993; Unplugged, 1996; Greatest Kiss, 1997; Carnival of Souls: The Final Sessions, 1997; Kiss, The Second Coming I and II, 1998; Psycho Circus, 1999; First Kiss, Last Licks, 1999; Solo album: Gene Simmons, 1978;

Singles include: Rock 'N' Roll All Nite; Beth; Detroit City; I Was Made For Lovin' You; I Love It Loud; Lick It Up; Tears Are Falling; Heaven's On Fire; Crazy Crazy Nights; Reason To Live; Hide Your Heart; Forever; God Gave Rock and Roll To You, featured in film Bill and Ted's Bogus Journey, 1992; Contribution, Runaway, to album Hear 'N' Aid (charity project for Ethiopian famine relief), 1986. *Honours include:* Footprints at Grauman's Chinese Theater, Hollywood, 1976; Gold Ticket, Madison Square Garden, 1979; Inducted into Hollywood's Rock Walk; Kiss Day proclaimed, Los Angeles, 1993; Numerous Gold and Platinum records. *Current Management:* Entertainment Services Unlimited, Main St Plaza 1000, Suite 303, Voorhees, NJ 08043, USA. *Address:* c/o Doc McGhee, McGhee Entertainment, 8730 Sunset Blvd, Suite 175, Los Angeles, CA 90069, USA.

SIMON Carly; b. 25 April 1945, New York, New York, USA. Composer; Singer; Musician (piano, guitar). m. (1) James Taylor, 3 Nov. 1971, divorced 1983, 1 s., 1 d., (2) James Hart, 23 Dec. 1987. *Education:* Sarah Lawrence College, 2 years. *Musical Education:* Studied with Peter Seeger. *Career:* Singer, composer, recording artist, 1971–; Appeared in film No Nukes, 1980; Television appearances include: Carly In Concert – My Romance, 1990. *Compositions:* Opera, Romulus Hunt; Film scores: Working Girl; Heartburn; This Is My Life; Postcards From The Edge. *Recordings:* Albums include: Carly Simon, 1971; Anticipation, 1972; No Secrets, 1973; Hotcakes, 1974; Playing Possum, 1975; The Best of Carly Simon, 1975; Another Passenger, 1976; Boys In The Trees, 1978; Spy, 1979; Come Upstairs, 1980; Torch, 1981; Hello Big Man, 1983; Spoiled Girl, 1985; Coming Round Again, 1987; Greatest Hits Live, 1988; My Romance, 1990; Have You Seen Me Lately?, 1991; Letters Never Sent, 1994; Clouds In My Coffee 1965–95, 1996; Film Noir, 1997; The Bedroom Tapes, 2000; Also appeared on albums by James Taylor; Lee Clayton; Mick Jones; Nils Lofgren; Tom Rush; Jesse Colin Young; Hit singles: Nobody Does It Better; Let The River Run; You're So Vain; Coming Round Again; Anticipation; Recorded with numerous artists including Paul McCartney; Luther Vandross; Mick Jagger; Linda Ronstadt; Michael McDonald; John Forte; Janet Jackson. *Publications:* Children's books: Amy The Dancing Bear, 1988; The Boy of The Bells, 1990; The Fisherman's Song, 1991; The Nighttime Chauffer, 1993; Midnight Farm, 1997. *Honours:* Grammy, Best New Artist, 1971; Academy Award, Let The River Run, 1989; Golden Globe. *Membership:* Songwriters Hall of Fame. *Leisure interests:* Painting; Decorating houses; Arguing. *Current Management:* c/o Lee Phillips, Monat Phelps and Phillips, 11355 W Olympic Blvd, Los Angeles, CA 90064, USA.

SIMON Edward; b. 27 July 1969, Comunidad Cardom, Falcon State, Venezuela. Jazz Musician (piano). m. Maria A Simon, 19 Feb. 1994. *Musical Education:* The University of the Arts, music performance, classical piano (not completed); The Manhattan School of Music, music performance, jazz piano (not completed). *Career:* Member, Bobby Watson's Horizon, 1988–92; Played with Greg Osby; Kevin Eubanks; Paquito D'Rivera; Herbie Mann; Charlie Sepulveda; Jerry Gonzalez; Currently member, The Terence Blanchard Quartet. *Recordings:* Albums: Solo: Beauty Within, 1994; Edward Simon, 1994; La Bikina, 1998; with Kevin Eubanks: The Searcher, 1989; Promise of Tomorrow, 1990; with Greg Osby: Mind Games, 1988; Season of Renewal, 1989; Man-Talk, 1990; with Bobby Watson: The Inventor, 1990; Post Motown Bop, 1991; Present Tense, 1992; Midwest and Shuffle, 1993; with Herbie Mann: Caminho de Casa, 1990; with Dave Binney: Point Game, 1990; with Victor Lewis: Family Portrait, 1992; Know It Today, Know It Tomorrow, 1993; with Claudio Roditi: Two of Swords, 1991; with Craig Handy: Split Second Timing, 1992; with Charlie Sepulveda: Algo Nuestro, 1993; with Terence Blanchard: Romantic Defiance, 1995; The Heart Speaks, 1996; with Carl Allen: The Pursuer, 1994; with Terell Stafford: Time To Let Go, 1995. *Honours:* Third Finalist, The Thelonious Monk International Jazz (Piano) Competition. *Memberships:* NARAS; BMI. *Leisure interests:* Weight lifting; Reading. *Current Management:* c/o Timothy Patterson, Split Second Timing. *Address:* 104 W 70th St #11-C, New York, NY 10023, USA.

SIMON Paul; b. 13 Oct. 1941, Newark, New Jersey, USA. Singer; Composer. m. (1) Peggy Harper (divorced), 1 s., (2) Carrie Fisher (divorced), (3) Edie Brickell, 30 May 1992, 2 s., 1 d. *Education:* BA, Queens College; Postgraduate, Brooklyn Law School. *Career:* Duo, Simon and Garfunkel, with Art Garfunkel, 1964–71; Appearances with Garfunkel include: Monterey Festival, 1967; Royal Albert Hall, 1968; Reunion concerts: Central Park, New York, 1981; US, European tours; Solo artiste, 1972–; Appearances include: Anti-war Festival, Shea Stadium, New York, 1970; Farm Aid V, 1992; Hurricane Relief concert, Miami, 1992; Born At The Right Time Tour; Tour, Europe and Russia; Television includes: Paul Simon Special, 1977; Paul Simon's Graceland – The African Concert, 1987; Paul Simon – Born At The Right Time, 1992; Film appearances: Monterey Pop, 1968; Annie Hall, 1977; All You Need Is Cash, 1978; One Trick Pony, 1980; Steve Martin Live, 1985. *Compositions include:* The Sound of Silence; Homeward Bound; I Am a Rock; Mrs Robinson; The Boxer; Bridge Over Troubled Water; Cecilia; Slip Slidin' Away; Late In The Evening; You Can Call Me Al; The Boy In The Bubble; Graceland; Paul Simon, Songs From The Capeman, 1997. *Recordings:* Albums: with Art Garfunkel: Wednesday Morning 3AM, 1964; Sounds of

Silence, 1965; Parsley Sage Rosemary and Thyme, 1967; The Graduate (film soundtrack), 1967; Bookends, 1968; Bridge Over Troubled Water, 1970; Simon and Garfunkel's Greatest Hits, 1972; Breakaway, 1975; Watermark, 1978; Collected Works, 1981; The Concert In Central Park, 1982; Various compilation albums; Solo albums: Paul Simon, 1972; There Goes Rhymin' Simon, 1973; Live Rhymin': Paul Simon In Concert, 1974; Still Crazy After All These Years, 1975; Greatest Hits Etc, 1977; One-Trick Pony, 1980; Hearts and Bones, 1983; Graceland, 1986; Negotiations and Love Songs, 1988; Rhythm of The Saints, 1990; Paul Simon's Concert In The Park, 1991; Paul Simon 1964–93, 1993; Paul Simon – Songs From The Capeman, 1997. *Publications:* The Songs of Paul Simon, 1972; New Songs, 1975; One-Trick Pony (screenplay), 1980; At The Zoo (for children), 1991. *Honours include:* Grammy awards: two for The Graduate soundtrack, 1968, six for Bridge Over Troubled Water, 1970, two for Still Crazy After All These Years, 1986, one for Graceland, 1987; Emmy Award, Paul Simon Special, NBC-TV, 1977; Inducted into Rock and Roll Hall of Fame, with Art Garfunkel, 1990; Antoinette Perry Award, The Capeman, Best Original Score Written For The Theatre 1997–98; Doctorate of Music, Berklee College of Music, 1986; Doctorate of Music, Queens College, 1995; Doctorate of Music, Yale University, 1996. *Address:* Paul Simon Music, 1619 Broadway, Suite 500, New York, NY 10019, USA.

SIMONE Nina, (Eunice Waymon); b. 21 Feb. 1933, Tyron, North Carolina, USA. Singer. *Musical Education:* Juilliard School of Music, New York. *Career:* Singer, clubs, Philadelphia; Recording artist, 1959–; Active in civil rights movement, early 1960s; Presenter, BBC Radio 2, 2000. *Recordings:* Albums: Little Girl Blue, 1950; Nina Simone At The Town Hall, 1959; At Newport, 1960; Forbidden Fruit, 1961; Nina Simone At The Village Gate, 1961; Sings Ellington, 1962; Nina's Choice, 1963; Nina Simone At Carnegie Hall, 1963; Folksy Nina, 1964; In Concert, 1964; Broadway... Blues... Ballads, 1964; I Put a Spell On You, 1965; Tell Me More, 1965; Pastel Blues, 1965; Let It All Out, 1966; Wild Is The Wind, 1966; Nina With Strings, 1966; This Is, 1966; Nina Simone Sings The Blues, 1966; High Priestess of Soul, 1967; Sweet 'N' Swinging, 1967; Silk and Soul, 1967; 'Nuff Said, 1968; And Piano, 1969; To Love Somebody, 1969; Black Gold, 1970; Here Comes The Sun, 1971; Heart and Soul, 1971; Emergency Ward, 1972; It Is Finished, 1972; Gifted and Black, 1974; I Loves You Porgy, 1977; Baltimore, 1978; Cry Before I Go, 1980; Nina Simone, 1982; Fodder On My Wings, 1982; Live At Vine Street, 1987; Live At Ronnie Scott's, 1988; Nina's Back, 1989; In Concert, 1992; A Single Woman, 1993; After Hours, 1995; In Concert, 1996; Saga of the Good Life and Hard Times, 1997; At Newport, 1998; Various compilations; Singles include: I Loves You Porgy; Gin House Blues; Forbidden Fruit; Don't Let Me Be Misunderstood; I Put a Spell On You; Ain't Got No – I Got Life; To Love Somebody; To Be Young Gifted and Black; My Baby Just Cares For Me.

SIMONS Ed; b. 9 June 1970, England. Musician. *Education:* Medieval History, Manchester University. *Career:* Member, The Dust Brothers with Tom Rowlands; Member, Chemical Brothers. *Compositions:* All recorded: Exit Planet Dust, album; Dig Your Own Hole, album (No 1 UK); Block Rockin Beats; Setting Sun; Leave Home. *Recordings:* Song to the Siren, 1993; 14th Century Sky, EP, 1994; My Mercury Mouth, EP, 1994; Life is Sweet, 1995; Loops of Fury, EP, 1996; Night Shift, 1996; Special Brew, 1996; Setting Sun (No 1 UK), 1997; Block Rockin Beats (No 1 UK), 1997; Electronic Battle Weapons, 1997; Elektrobank, 1997; Action with Liquid Todd (producer), 1999. *Honours:* Twice nomminated for Brit Awards; Nomination for Mercury Prize, 1997; Grammy Award, 1997. *Current Management:* Robert Linney. *Address:* 1 Cowcross St, London EC1M 6DR, England.

SIMPSON Jim; b. 27 Jan. 1938, Westminster, London, England. Music Co Exec.; Record Prod.; Journalist; Musician (trumpet). 1 s. *Musical Education:* Self-taught; Tuition with Dougie Roberts; Dennis Darlowe. *Career:* Played with Locomotive, 1964–69; Managed Black Sabbath, 1969–71; Recorded and toured with American Bluesmen: Lightnin' Slim; Homesick James; Doctor Ross; Snooky Pryor, through 1970s; Began Birmingham International Jazz Festival, 1985; BT British Jazz Awards, 1987; Bruce Adams/Alan Barnes Quintet, 1995; Managing Director, Big Bear Music Group. *Recordings:* with Locomotive: Rudi's In Love; 5 albums with King Pleasure and The Biscuit Boys; with Black Sabbath: Black Sabbath; Paranoid; with The Quads: There Must Be Thousands. *Publications:* Launched jazz national magazine The Jazz Rag, 1986. *Honours:* British Jazz Award, Jazz CD of The Year, 1994. *Leisure interests:* Non-League football; Belgian beers; Jazz. *Current Management:* Big Bear Music. *Address:* PO Box 944, Edgbaston, Birmingham B16 8UT, England.

SIMPSON Kerri; b. 15 Nov. 1960, Melbourne, Australia. *Musical Education:* Self-taught. *Career:* Performed, toured, nationally and internationally in New Orleans, Chicago, London, Barcelona, Blues, Gospel, Alternative Dance; Regular House Artist, ABC TV's Big Gig, 1989–91; International supports for Kylie Minogue, 1991; Charlie Musselwhite, 1991; The Church, 1995. *Compositions:* Veve; Ah Jole;

Higher; Jaguar; I Wonder; Very Popular; Shed; Billy Cowboys; Cry Mercy. *Recordings:* Veve, 1992; Veve (remix by Ollie Olsen); Albums: The Arousing, 1995; Speak, 1996; Higher; Turkey Necklasso, 1996; Psy Harmonica, Vol. 1; Confessin' The Blues, 1998; Vodou – Songs of The Spirits, 2001. *Honours:* 2 ARIA Nominations, 1995; Featured Artist, Fritz Radio Berlin, 1991. *Memberships:* MU; Australian Performing Rights Asscn. *Current Management:* Maverick Arts Management. *Address:* PO Box 780, Brunswick Lower, VIC 3058, Australia.

SIMPSON Martin Stewart; b. 5 May 1953, Scunthorpe, Lincolnshire, England. Vocalist; Musician (guitar, banjo); Composer; Songwriter. m. Jessica Ruby Radcliffe, 1985. *Career:* Folk musician; Started playing guitar, aged 12, and banjo soon after; Performed professionally from age 15; Recorded first album, Golden Vanity, at 22 and toured supporting Steeleye Span; Worked with June Tabor for over a decade and recorded 3 albums together; Relocating to the US with American wife; Worked with many folk greats including: Martin Carthy; Dave Mattacks; Ashley Hutchings; Simon Nicol; Richard Thompson; Also performed more recently with musicians from diverse backgrounds including: Wu Man (Chinese pipa player); Bob Brozman; Debashish Bhattacharya; Cool and Unusual album draws on Celtic, American and Afro-American music, featuring David Lindley, Joe Phelps and members of Tarika; Acclaimed album Bramble Briar concentrates on English folk material. *Recordings:* Golden Vanity, 1976; Special Agent, A Cut Above (with June Tabor), 1981; Grinning In Your Face, 1983; Nobody's Fault But Mine, 1985; True Dare Or Promise (with Jessica Simpson), 1987; Leaves of Life, 1989; When I Was On Horseback, 1991; A Closer Walk With Thee, 1994; Smoke and Mirrors, Red Roses, 1995; Band of Angels, Music For The Motherless Child, 1996; Live, Cool and Unusual, 1997; The Bramble Briar, 2001; features on: Larkrise To Candleford, 1980; Aqaba, June Tabor, 1988; Abyssinians, 1989. *Honours:* BBC Radio 2 Folk Awards: Best Instrumentalist; Best Album, Bramble Briar, 2002. *Current Management:* Herschel Freeman Agency Inc, 7684 Apahon Lane, Germantown, TN 38138, USA. *E-mail:* hfreeman@ixlmemphis.com. *Internet:* www.martinsimpson.com.

SIMPSON Valerie; b. 26 Aug. 1946, Bronx, New York, USA. Singer; Songwriter. m. Nickolas Ashford, 1974. *Career:* Performing and songwriting duo, with husband Nickolas Ashford; Worked with Marvin Gaye singing on recordings in place of Tammi Terrell; Solo artiste, 1971–73. *Compositions:* Co-writer with Nickolas Ashford: Never Had It So Good, Ronnie Milsap; One Step At a Time, Maxine Brown, The Shirelles; Let's Go Get Stoned, Ray Charles; Songs include: Ain't No Mountain High Enough; You're All I Need To Get By; Reach Out and Touch Somebody's Hand; Remember Me; Solid. *Recordings:* Solo albums: Exposed!, 1971; Valerie Simpson, 1972; with Nickolas Ashford: Keep It Comin', 1973; Gimme Something Real, 1973; I Wanna Be Selfish, 1974; Come As You Are, 1976; So So Satisfied, 1977; Send It, 1977; Is It Still Good To Ya?, 1978; Stay Free, 1979; A Musical Affair, 1980; Performance, 1981; Street Opera, 1982; High-Rise, 1983; Solid, 1984; Real Love, 1986; Love Or Physical, 1989; As producer: The Boss, Diana Ross, 1979; The Touch, Gladys Knight, 1981; Gladys Knight, Ultimate Collection, 1997; Supremes: Ultimate Collection, 1997; Motown 40 Forever, 1998; Martha and the Vandellas, Ultimate Collection, 1998; Marvelettes Ultimate collection, 1998. *Current Management:* Hopsack and Silk Productions, 254 W 72nd St, Suite 1A, New York, NY 10023, USA.

SINATRA Nancy; b. 8 June 1940, Jersey City, New Jersey, USA. Singer; Writer. *Musical Education:* Lessons in music, dance, drama. *Career:* Appearances include: Sinatra/Elvis Presley television special, 1959; Recording debut, 1961; 10 appearances, Ed Sullivan Show; Numerous TV specials including Movin' With Nancy, 1967; Sold over 8m. records world-wide; Film appearances include: Wild Angels; Speedway (with Elvis Presley), 1968. *Recordings:* Albums: Boots, 1966; How Does That Grab You Darlin', 1966; Nancy In London, 1966; Sugar, 1967; Country My Way, 1967; Movin' With Nancy, 1968; Nancy and Lee (with Lee Hazlewood), 1968; Nancy, 1969; Woman, 1970; Nancy's Greatest Hits, 1970; This Is Nancy Sinatra, 1971; Did You Ever (with Lee Hazlewood), 1972; All-Time Hits, 1988; Lightning's Girl – The Very Best of Nancy Sinatra, 1988; One More Time, 1995; Sheet Music: Collection of her Favorite Love Songs, 1998; Singles include: These Boots Are Made For Walkin' (International No. 1 hit); How Does That Grab You Darlin'; Sugar Town; Something Stupid, with father Frank Sinatra (No. 1, UK); You Only Live Twice (theme to James Bond film); Jackson (with Lee Hazlewood); Did You Ever (with Lee Hazlewood); For My Dad. *Publications:* Frank Sinatra My Father, 1985; Frank Sinatra – An American Legend, 1995. *Current Management:* John Dubuque, Dublen Entertainment Group, 330 Merwin Ave, Unit # F1, Milford, CT 06460, USA. *Address:* c/o Delsener/Saleter, 27 E 67th St, New York, NY 10021, USA.

SINCLAIR Cynthia; b. 17 Nov. 1951, Philadelphia, Pennsylvania, USA. Musician; Record Co Exec. *Education:* BA, Boston University, 1973; BMus, Berklee College of Music, 1983; Postgraduate, Santa Monica College, 1998–. *Career:* Founder, Myoho Records, Boston, 1984–; Assistant Cameraperson, Young Musicians' Foundation, Beverly Hills, California, 1996; Singer/

Songwriter, Red Hot to Icy Blue, No Exit, The Blues Make Good Lovers, Black in Back in Style; Member, Joe Vento Big Band Jazz Orchestra, currently touring college stadiums. *Compositions:* Composer/Arranger, Outside You; Singer/Arranger, Good Morning Heartache; Prelude to a Kiss; Composer/Lyricist, over 50 published songs. *Memberships:* Group Leader, Womens Issues, Soka Gakkai International, Boston, 1986–88; ASCAP; NARAS; American Society of Musicians, Composers and Arrangers; Mensa. *Leisure interest:* Films. *Address:* PO Box 462, Santa Monica, CA 90406, USA.

SINFIELD Peter John; b. 27 Dec. 1943, Fulham, London, England. Divorced. *Musical Education:* Self-taught. *Career:* King Crimson, writer, producer, 1969–72; Roxy Music, Producer, 1973; Solo album, 1974; Greg Lake, Co-writer, co-producer, 1974–80; Songwriting with Andy Hill, Albert Hammond, Bill Livsey and others, 1981-. *Compositions:* King Crimson: In the Court of the Crimson King; 21st Century Schizoid Man; I Talk to the Wind; Emerson Lake and Palmer: Karnevil 9; Pirates; Greg Lake: C'est La Vie; I Believe in Father Xmas; The Land of Make Believe, for Bucks Fizz; Rain or Shine, for Five Star; Don't Walk Away; Have You Ever Been in Love, for Leo Sayer; Keep Each Other Warm, for Barry Manilow; Peace in Our Time, for Cliff Richard; Waiting in the Wings, for Diana Ross; As Dreams Go By, for Bette Midler; Think Twice; Call the Man, for Celine Dion. *Honours:* Ivor Novello Awards for Best Song, Have You Ever Been in Love, 1981, Think Twice, 1992; Call The Man, 30m. album sales. *Membership:* PRS; BASCA Council, Chair of IT Committee. *Leisure interests:* Cooking; Book collecting; Herbal medicine; Politics. *Current Management:* David Ravden, MGR Ltd, 55 Loudoun Rd, St Johns Wood, London, NW8 0DL, England.

SINGER Ray; b. 4 July 1946, Tonbridge, Kent, England. Record Prod.; Film Music Supervisor; Musician (percussion). m. Janine Turkie, 20 Sept. 1987, 1 s., 2 d. *Education:* London Film School. *Career:* Singer: Television appearances: Juke Box Jury; Thank Your Lucky Stars; Gadzooks!; As percussionist toured with David Knopfler, Germany, 1992; Tours with Cinema, guest appearance on EastEnders; As film music supervisor: Another Country; Civvies; A Perfect Spy. *Recordings:* Producer: Peter Sarstedt: Where Do You Go To My Lovely; Frozen Orange Juice; Child: It's Only Make Believe; Japan: Assemblage; Robin Sarstedt: My Resistance Is Low; Produced music to over 100 TV commercials. *Honours:* Gold records; Ivor Novello Award, Best TV Series Music for Civvies. *Memberships:* PRS; Musicians' Union; Equity. *Leisure interests:* Swimming; Music; Photography. *Current Management:* Soundtrack Music Management, 22 Ives St, Chelsea, London SW3 2ND, England.

SINGH Gary; b. 31 Jan. 1969, California, USA. Composer; Media Artist; Author. m. K Yamaguchi. *Education:* BA, San Jose State University. *Career:* Musica Works Broadcast and Performed in Asia, South America, Europe, USA; Published Short Fiction; Mail Art Displays, World-wide. *Publication:* Cyberthuggee and the Ridiculous World Over, 1996. *Honours:* American College Theater Festival Meritorious Achievement for Sound. *Membership:* International Computer Music Asscn. *Leisure interests:* Ham Radio; Fly Fishing; Ice Skating. *Address:* 5580 Copeland Lane, San Jose, CA 95124, USA.

SINGH Talvin; b. 1970, London, England. *Career:* Head of Omni Records; Tabla Player; Composer and Arranger; Worked with artists including Björk, Sun Ra and Future Sound of London; Worked on projects with numerous other Asian artists, including Osmani Soundz, Amar and Milky Bar Kid; Host at Anokha club, and at Blue Note Club; Began solo career, 1997; Producer, One World One Drum percussion album; Played on Björk's world tour. *Recordings:* Singles: Anokha Sampler, 1997; O.K., mixes, 1998; Traveller, 1998; Albums: Anokha: Soundz of the Asian Underground, 1997; O.K., 1998. *Honour:* Winner, Mercury Music Prize, 1999.

SINGH Tjinder; Singer; Songwriter; Musician (guitar). *Career:* Musician and singer, Cornershop. *Recordings include:* Albums: Elvis Sex Change, 1993; Hold On It Hurts, 1994; Woman's Gotta Have It, 1995; I Was Born For The Seventh Time, 1997; Good Ships, 1998; Brimful of Asha, 1998; Sleep on the Left Side, 1998; Hit single: Brimful of Asha (No. 1, UK), 1998. *Address:* c/o Oasis Productions, 36 W 20th St, New York, NY 10011, USA.

SIOUX Siouxsie, (Susan Dallion); b. 27 May 1957, Bromley, Kent, England. Singer. *Career:* Singer, Siouxie and the Banshees, 1976–; Film appearances: Punk Rock Movie (with The Clash, Sex Pistols, Generation X), 1978; Out of Bounds, 1986; Tours, UK, Europe, US; Concerts include: Royal Albert Hall, 1983; Lollapalooza US tour, 1991; The Ritz, New York, 1992; Heineken Festival, Leeds, 1995; Also formed The Creatures, 1981. *Recordings:* Singles: with the Banshees: Hong Kong Garden, 1978; The Staircase (Mystery), 1979; Playground Twist, 1979; Happy House, 1980; Christine, 1980; Spellbound, 1981; Fire Works, 1982; Dear Prudence, 1983; Swimming Horses, 1984; Cities In Dust, 1985; This Wheel's On Fire, 1987; Peek a Boo, 1988; Kiss Them For Me, 1991; Face To Face, 1992; with the Creatures: Mad Eyed Screamers, 1981; Miss Then Girl, 1983; Right Now, 1983; Albums: with the Banshees: The Scream, 1978; Join Hands, 1979;

Kaleidoscope, 1980; Once Upon a Time, 1981; A Kiss In The Dreamhouse, 1982; Nocturne, 1983; Hyena, 1984; Tinderbox, 1986; Through The Looking Glass, 1987; Peepshow, 1988; Superstition, 1992; Twice Upon a Time – The Singles, 1992; The Rapture, 1995; with the Creatures: Feast, 1983; Second Floor, 1998; Sad Cunt, 1998; Exterminating Angel, 1998; Bestiary Of... The Creatures, 1998; Eraser Cut, 1998; Say Pt 1, 1999; Say Pt 2, 1999; Say, 1999. *Current Management:* Mission Impossible Management, 102A Western Rd, Hove, East Sussex BN3 1FA, England.

SIRACUSA Gérard; b. 6 Oct. 1957, Tunis, Tunisia. Musician (drums, percussion); Composer. m. Sophie Schneider, 28 Sept. 1984, 1 s., 1 d. *Education:* Higher level studies in Science. *Musical Education:* Gold Medal, Percussion, National Conservatory, Rueil-Malmaison, France. *Career:* Goah, 1974; G S Duo with André Jaume, 1975; Trios with Raymond Boni and Michel Redolfi, 1976; Blaguebolle (musical theatre), 1974–78; Groupe de Recherche et d'Improvisation Musicales de Marseille (GRIM), 1978–84; Molto Mobile, 1980; Touchers (percussion quartet), 1981–83; Solo percussionist, 1981–86; G S Quartet, 1985; G S Alma Ata Quintet, formed for Banlieues Bleues Festival, 1986–87; Ensemble Musique Vivante, 1982–87; Un Drame Musical Instantané, 1982–84; 1991–94; Solibrius, solo percussion, 1986–; Claude Barthélémy – G S Quintet/ Nonet, formed for Vandoeuvre-les-Nancy Festival, 1988–91; Collectif Incidences, 1990–94; G S Trio, 1991; Pied de Poule, 1991–93; Bûcher des Silences, formed for Moers Festival, 1991–; Trio Bal(l)ade, 1993–95; Duo with Valentin Clastrier, 1995; Radio: L'Heure Bleue, by Philippe Carles, France Musique, Radio France, 1992; Transversales, by Xavier Prévost, France Musique, Radio France, 1997; Musiques nouvelles: profils de passeurs, by Frédéric Deval, Radio Suisse Romande, 1998; Television: Megamix, with Valentin Clastrier, ARTE, 1994; Fête de la Musique, ARTE, 1995. *Compositions:* Jardins de Paille, 1982; Titchak, 1985; Kaling, 1990; Pas Oui C'Est Non, 1993; M'Arco Polo, 1989; Ballade Sur Une Autoroute Et Ses Sept Bretelles, with Jean-Marie Maddeddu, 1994; Diptères, with Daniel Petitjean, 1993; Les Matins De Blanche, 1993; Les Petits Endroits Du Corps, 1994; 3 Minutes De Gloire, 1994; Le Dîner Percutant, 1993; Special Percussion, 1997; Discontinuo, 1997; Music for Radio France Culture: Les Chiennes, 1987; Nationalité Française, Special Percussion 1988; Executeur 14, 1989; L'Argent, 1994; Le long voyage vers le jour, 1997; Les demeurés, 1997; Ah, Vous Dirai-je..., 1998; Les histoires du Prince Oreille au Salon du livre Jeunesse de Montreux, 1998. *Recordings:* Musique Pour 8 – L'Oc, with André Jaume, 1982; Anna S Et Autres Histoires, with Trio MRS, 1983; Jardins De Paille, 1982; Terra, Michel Doneda, 1985; Slumberland, 1986; Kind Lieder, 1991; What a Time, Michael Riessler, 1991; Hérésie, Valentin Clastrier, 1992; Crasse Tignasse, 1993; Héloïse, 1993; Jamais Tranquille, 1993; Le Bûcher Des Silences, 1994; Les Tentations d'Abelard, 1995; Stations Avant L'oubli, 1998; La Jardinière De Légumes, 1999. *Honour:* First Prize, Academie Charles Cros, for Le Bûcher Des Silences, 1995. *Memberships:* SACEM; SPEDIDAM; ADAMI; SACD. *Current Management:* En L'Air Asscn. *Address:* 27 rue des Papillons, 93100 Montreuil, France.

SISQÓ (Mark Andrews), (Sisqo The Golden Child, Dru Nasty); b. 1977, Baltimore, Maryland, USA. Vocalist. *Career:* Originally worked as a dancer; Formed group Dru Hill with college friends, named after Druid Hill Park in Baltimore; First release Tell Me from the soundtrack of film Eddie; After two hit albums, group decided to pursue solo projects; Successful solo career 1999–; Starring alongside Will Smith in Wild Wild West; Collaborations: Foxy Brown; Mya; Kelly Price. *Recordings:* Albums: with Dru Hill: Dru Hill, 1997; Enter The Dru, 1999; solo: Unleash The Dragon, 1999; Return of Dragon 2001; Singles: with Dru Hill: In My Bed, 1997; How Deep Is Your Love, 1998; solo: Got To Get It, 1999; The Thong Song, Incomplete, Unleash The Dragon, 2000; Dance For Me, 2001. *Honours:* Billboard Award, Male Artist of the Year, 2000. *Address:* c/o Def Jam, 825 Eighth Ave, New York, USA. *Internet:* www.sisqo.com.

SISSAY Lemn; b. 1967, Billinge, Manchester. Poet. *Career:* BBC Radio 4, Pick of the Week, 1994; Various appearances on BBC, Channel 4 and other British Stations. *Compositions:* Tape recordings: Blackwise, 1988; Homeland, including 2 poems, 1988. *Recordings:* The Flag, 1996; Are You Listening, 1992; Move On, 1993; Earth Flower, 1993; Advice For The Living, 2000. *Publications:* Books: Perceptions of the Pen, 1985; Tender Finger in a Clenched List, 1988; Elevator, 1999; Records: The Flag, 1996. *Current Management:* Lounge Records, Oberhafenstr 1, 3 OG, 20097 Hamburg, Germany.

SISTER BLISS, (Ayalah Bentovim); b. 1970, London, England. Musician (keyboards); Remixer; DJ. *Musical Education:* Classically trained pianist. *Career:* Began to DJ at London's Bar Industria club; Formed recording act Faithless with Rollo Armstrong, 1995. *Recordings:* Albums: Reverence, 1996; Sunday 8PM, 1998; Saturday 3AM, 1999; Outrospective, 2001; Singles: Salva Mea, Insomnia, 1995; Don't Leave, 1996; Reverence, 1997; Take The Long Way Home, God Is A DJ, 1998; Sister Sister (solo release), 2000; Muhammad Ali, 2001; We Come 1, 2001. *Membership:* MCPS/PRS. *Address:* c/o Cheeky Records, 181 High St, London, NW10 4TE, England.

SITBON Franck; b. 15 May 1957, Paris, France. Musician (keyboards); Singer. m. Brigitte Silverio, 3 July 1982, 2 s. *Musical Education:* Private piano lessons, from age 6–15. *Career:* Tour, West Coast of United States, 1979–81; Returned to Paris, Played at Casino De Paris with Nicole Croiselle; Tour with Bernard Lavilliers, 1986; With Jacques Higelin, 1989; Played Italy with Pino Danielle; Tours, Tahiti, New Caledonia, with Patrick Bruel, 1992; Bercy, with Patrick Bruel, 1994. *Recordings:* Serge Guirao: Enchanteur, 1988; Nicole Croiselle: Black and Blanche, 1990; Joelle Ursule: Comme Dans Un Film, 1993. *Publications:* Method Up Clavies, 1991. *Memberships:* SACEM; SPEDIDAM. *Leisure interests:* Writing; Taking care of sons. *Address:* 34 rue des Bordes, 94490 Ormesson, France.

SIXX Nikki, (Frank Carlton Serafino Ferrano); b. 11 Dec. 1958, San Jose, California, USA. Musician (bass); Songwriter. *Career:* Member, groups: London; Christmas; Founder member, US heavy rock group Mötley Crüe, 1981–; World-wide concerts include: Tours with: YandT, 1981, 1982; Kiss, 1983; Ozzy Osbourne, 1984; Iron Maiden, 1984; Cheap Trick, 1986; Theatre of Pain World Tour, 1985–86; World tours, 1987, 1989; Major concerts: US festival, 1983; Monsters of Rock Festival, Castle Donington, 1984; Moscow Music Peace Festival, 1989. *Recordings:* Albums: Too Fast For Love, 1981; Shout At The Devil, 1983; Theatre of Pain, 1985; Girls Girls Girls (No. 2, US), 1987; Dr Feelgood (No. 1, USA), 1989; Decade of Decadence (No. 2, US), 1991; Til Death Do Us Part, 1994; Generation Swine, 1997; Live: Entertainment or Death, 1999; Singles: Stick To Your Gun, 1981; Looks That Kill, 1984; Too Young To Fall In Love, 1984; Smokin' In The Boys Room, 1985; Home Sweet Home, 1985; You're All I Need, 1987; Dr Feelgood, 1989; Kick Start My Heart, 1990; Without You, 1990; Don't Go Away Mad, 1990; Same Old Situation, 1990; Primal Scream, 1991; Hooligan's Holiday, 1994; Misunderstood, 1994. *Honours:* Rolling Stone Readers Poll Winners, Best Heavy Metal Band, 1991; American Music Award, Favourite Heavy Metal Album, 1991. *Current Management:* The Left Bank Organisation, 9255 Sunset Blvd, Suite 1111, Hollywood, CA 90069–3309, USA.

SIXX-SCHMULEWITZ Aaron; b. 4 Aug. 1947, Feldafing, Germany. Record Co Man.-Dir. m. Lynda M Jones, 18 Aug. 1977, 1 s., 1 d. *Education:* Bachelor of Arts, University of California at Los Angeles (UCLA). *Career:* Record Executive with: 1973–74, United Artists Records, European A & R Director; 1975–77, Arista Records, Director, International Operations; 1978-, Aura Records, Music and Entertainment, Managing Director. *Address:* 1 Liverpool Rd, London W5 5NZ, England.

SIZE Roni; Musician (keyboards, drums, programming); Prod. 1 s. *Career:* Began as DJ in clubs; Formed label Full Cycle, 1993; Creative leader of Bristol-based collective Reprazent, with record deal on Talkin' Loud; Reprazent performed live at concert venues and festivals world-wide, summer 1997, 1998. *Recordings:* With DJ Die, Music Box; Agility; Solo: Jazz Thing; With Reprazent: Reasons for Sharing, limited edition EP, 1996; New Forms, 1997; Share the Fall, single, with remixes from Way Out West and Grooverider; New Forms/Share the Fall, featuring Bahamadia; Watching Windows, 1998; Brown Paper Bag, 1998; 26 Bass Snapshot, 1999. *Honour:* Winner, Mercury Music Prize, for album New Forms, 1997. *Address:* c/o Kas Mercer, Talkin' Loud, Chancellors House, Chancellors Rd, London W6 9QB, England.

SJOBLOM Titti; b. 29 Aug. 1949, Stockholm, Sweden. Singer. m. Ehrling Eliasson, 2 s. *Education:* Private Singing Lessons; Musicology. *Career:* Played, Maria Magdalena in Jesus Christ Superstar, 1976–79; Own Children Shows, 1980's on Television; Tours Every Year, Entertainment Parks, Restaurants, Churches; Entertained UN Troops. *Compositions:* Trumman; Det Tanker; Dar Utanfor. *Recordings:* Sjung Med Oss Mamma; 10 LPs; 4 CDs; For Sjal Olh Hjarta. *Honours:* Expressens Best Television Entertainment for Children, 1964; Perne Paddock Award, 1994. *Memberships:* Forsvarets Faltartist Forening. *Current Management:* Own Company and Label, Seaflower Music. *Address:* Seaflower Music, Box 7, 87032 Ullanger, Sweden.

SJOSTEN Lars; b. 7 May 1941, Oskarshamn, Sweden. Jazz Pianist; Composer; Arranger. m. Lilly, 24 April 1976. *Education:* Piano and Harmony privately. *Career:* Played with Dexter Gordon, Chet Baker, Lee Konitz and many more legendary jazz musicians; Played with Lars Gullin, 1960–76; Led own groups, numerous records and radio/television programmes; Tours and festivals in Scandinavia and Europe; Composing and Arranging Commissions for Big Band. *Compositions:* In Confidence; Denile; Thorgeirs Sang; The Inner Voice; Tidigt; Gasoline My Beloved; From Reliable Sources; The Comeback of a Tradesman; Tale of Two Trees. *Recordings:* Select Notes, 1981; Bells, Blues and Brotherhood, 1983; Dedicated to Lee, w Lee Konitz, 1983, 1995; Roots and Relations, 1989; Lars Sjosten Quartet in Moscow, 1990; In Confidence, 1990; I Love You So, with Rolf Ericson, 1997. *Honours:* Jan Johansson, 1969; Two Golden Disques, 1981, 1989; Income Guarantee, 1990; Lars Gullin Prize, 1997. *Memberships:* Musician's Union; Asscn of Swedish Jazz Musicians; Musikcentrum. *Leisure interests:* Computing; Reading; Walks; Movies.

Current Management: Musikcentrum, Chapmansgatan 4, 11236 Stockholm, Sweden. *Address:* Filipstadsbacken 70, 123 43 Farsta, Sweden.

SKAGGS Ricky Lee; b. 18 July 1954, Cordell, Kentucky, USA. Recording Artist; Musician (guitar, banjo, mandolin, fiddle, telecaster, mandocaster). m. Sharon White, 4 Aug. 1981, 2 s., 2 d. *Career:* Member of Ralph Stanley and the Clinch Mountain Boys, 1970; Country Gentlemen, 1974; Formed own band Boone Creek, 1975; Emmylou Harris' Hot Band, 1977; Whites, 1980; Solo artist 1981–; Host of own radio series, Simple Life With Ricky Skaggs; Television appearances include: Host, TNN Nashville Now; Co-host, TNN Viewer's Choice Awards. *Recordings:* 12 US No. 1 singles, 1981–89; Albums: Waitin' For The Sun To Shine, 1981; Highways and Heartaches, 1982; Don't Cheat In Our Hometown, 1983; Country Boy, 1984; Favourite Country Songs, 1985; Live In London, 1985; Love's Gonna Get Ya!, 1986; Comin' Home To Stay, 1988; Kentucky Thunder, 1989; My Father's Son, 1991; Ricky Skaggs Portrait, 1992; Super Hits, 1993; Solid Ground, 1995; Bluegrass Rules, 1997; Ancient Tones, 1999; Soldier of the Cross, 2000. *Honours include:* Ralph Stanley Dove Award, 1982; 7 Grammy Awards, 1984–99; 8 Academy of Country Music Awards including Best Touring Band, 1983–87; Edison Award, Netherlands, 1987; 8 Country Music Asscn Awards; 6 Music City News Awards; Artist of The Decade, BBC Radio 2, UK; Best Country Guitarist, Guitar Player Readers Poll, 1987–89; Best Country Instrumentalist, Playboy Readers Poll (twice); Gospel Voice Diamond Award, 1993; Bluegrass Instrumentalist Group of the Year, with Kentucky Thunder, 1998 and 1999. *Memberships:* AFTRA; AFofM. *Leisure interests:* Fishing; Photography; Vintage Clothing Stores. *Current Management:* RS Entertainment Inc. *Address:* 320 Rockland Rd, Hendersonville, TN 37075, USA.

SKARBEK Sacha J; b. Epsom, Surrey, England. Prod.; Musician (keyboards); Songwriter. *Musical Education:* BA Hons, Music, Oxford. *Career:* Tours: Europe, with Double Vision; UK with Jamiroquai, Original Son; UK with Sister Sledge, Fekisha; BBC Interview, with Innocent Lies; Tour, USA, What The Funk; Various concerts with Dana Brown. *Recordings:* Keyboard player: Seven Seconds, Youssou N'Dour and Neneh Cherry; Keyboard player: Let It Last, Carleen Anderson; Producer, writer: Desire and Somewhere, Pauline Henry; Keyboard player, writer: Album: Original Son. *Leisure interests:* Martial arts; Tennis. *Current Management:* Alan Edwards; Clem Chan. *Address:* Poole Edwards, Charlotte St, London W1, England.

SKELLERN Peter; b. 14 March 1947, Bury, Lancashire, England. Musician (piano); Singer; Songwriter. *Musical Education:* Honours graduate, Guildhall School of Music, 1968. *Career:* Member, March Hare (recorded as Harlan County), 1971; Wrote and performed 6 autobiographical programmes for BBC TV; Series of musical plays, Happy Endings; Host, chat show, Private Lives, 1983; Formed Oasis with Julian Lloyd Webber, Mary Hopkin, Bill Lovelady, 1984, 1996. *Recordings:* Peter Skellern With Harlan County, 1971; Peter Skellern, 1972; Not Without a Friend, 1973; Holding My Own, 1974; Hold On To Love, 1975; Hard Times, 1976; Skellern, 1978; Astaire, 1979; Still Magic, 1980; Happy Endings, 1981; Introducing Right From The Start, 1981; A String of Pearls, 1982; Best of Peter Skellern, 1985; Love Light, 1987; Sentimentally Yours, 1996; Singles include: You're a Lady; Love Is The Sweetest Thing, with the Grimethorpe Colliery Band. *Honours include:* Best MOR Album, Music Trades Asscn, 1979.

SKI (Dominic Oakenfull); b. 28 Jan. 1971, Sevenoaks, Kent, England. Musician (keyboards, zither); Prod.; Writer. *Education:* City University, London. *Musical Education:* Keith Rusling, Kent; K B Wizard, London. *Career:* Keyboard player, writer, producer for the K-Creative, 1991–93; Raw Stylus, 1993; Palm Skin Productions, 1993; Thats How It Is, 1994; Galliano, 1994, 1995; Solo artiste as Ski, 1993–; Writer, jingles for various radio commercials; Television appearances include Gimme 5; Top of The Pops; Later With Jools Holland; The Beat. *Recordings:* Albums: QED, K-Creative, 1992; The Plot Thickens, Galliano, 1994; Marla Glen (second album), 1995; Pushing, Raw Stylus, 1995; Galliano (fourth album), 1996; Singles: Justify, Ski featuring Chesere, 1994; Realise Your True, Ski with Ife, 1994; Theme from Millennium Falcon, 1994. *Publications:* Fender Rhodes, A Brief History, 1994. *Leisure interests:* Sport. *Current Management:* Guy Tresize, GT Management, Unit B7, 8/9 Hoxton Sq., London, England.

SKIFS Björn Nils Olof; b. 20 April 1947, Vansbro, Sweden. Singer; Performer; Composer. m. Pernilla, 20 May 1988, 2 s. *Education:* College. *Career:* Major concert tours and television shows, 1970–; Eurovision Song Festival, 1978 and 1981; Musicals and 3 major films (screenplay, leading role): Strul, 1986; Joker, 1989; Drömåken, 1993. *Recordings:* 13 albums, 1967–87, including: Hooked On a Feeling (No. 1, USA, 1974); Never My Love (Top 10, USA, 1974); Michaelangelo (No. 1, Scandinavia, 1975–76). *Current Management:* Desert AB, Box 103, 70142 Orebro, Sweden.

SKILLINGS Muzz, (Manuel Skillings); b. 6 Jan. 1960, New York, USA. Musician (Bass). *Career:* Member, Living Colour; Backed Mick Jagger on Primitive Cool album, 1986; Mick Jagger produced demo, which obtained them record deal; Support slots live to Rolling Stones; Left band, 1993. *Recordings:* Singles: Cult of Personality, 1988; Glamour Boys, 1988; Type, 1990; Love Rears Its Ugly Head, 1990; Solace of You, 1991; Talkin' Loud and Saying' Nothing, 1991; Albums: Vivid, 1988; Time's Up, 1990; Biscuits, 1991.

SKIN (Deborah Ann Dyer); b. 3 Aug. 1967, London, England. Singer. *Career:* Founder Member, Skunk Anansie, 1994; Signed to indie label One Little Indian, 1994; Numerous headlining tours, festival appearances, TV and radio shows. *Recordings:* Singles: Little Baby Swastikkka; Weak; Brazen (Weep), 1997; Charlie Big Potato; Albums: Paranoid and Sunburnt, 1995; Stoosh, 1996; Post Orgasmic Chill, 1999.

SKINNER Harry; b. 30 April 1958, Barking, Essex, England. Musician (guitar); Singer; Composer; Songwriter. m. Elizabeth Vango, 4 May 1991, 1 s., 1 d. *Education:* Southampton University, 1995–97. *Musical Education:* RMSM, Kneller Hall, Twickenham; Bournemouth and Poole College, Poole. *Career:* Oboist with Rhine Staff Band RTR, 1976–81; Formed band, Manitou, touring UK, Gemany and Japan; Formed band The Producers; Appeared at Colne Blues Festival, Burnley Blues Festival, Monighan, Templebar, Shepton Mallet and at festivals throughout Europe; Live radio session, BBC Radio 2, 1994; Tours of UK, Germany, France, Belgium and Ireland. *Recordings:* Single: Tasmania, 1984; Albums: with Manitou: Manitou At The Electric Drum I and II, 1987; Looking For The Lost, 1991; with The Producers: Escape From Muswell Hell, 1991; Ain't No Love In The World, 1993; For This Night Only, 1994; Nearly Wired, 1996; Really Wired, 1996. *Honour:* Nominated Best British Blues Album, Ain't No Love In The World, 1993. *Memberships:* Musicians' Union; Associate Mem., PRS; MCPS. *Leisure interest:* Reading. *Current Management:* Dave Saunders, Mojo Management / Mojo Records UK. *Address:* 77 Haviland Rd, Boscombe, Bournemouth, Dorset BH7 6HJ, England.

SKIPPER Svend; b. 22 April 1947, Naestved, Denmark. Musician (piano); Conductor; Composer; Arranger. m. Ghita Noerby, 15 July 1984. *Musical Education:* Studied piano, solfeggio, conducting, Royal Danish Conservatory, 1970–77. *Career:* Musical Director, all Danish theatres, Directed musicals: The Peanuts; No No Nanette; Promises Promises; Showboat; Pal Joey; Oliver; They're Playing Our Song; Chicago; My Fair Lady; Orpheus In The Underworld; Parisian Life; Beggar's Opera (Weill); Jesus Christ Superstar; Teenage Love (Finn Savery); Starting Here Starting Now; Sunday In The Park With George; Sweeney Todd; Side By Side By Sondheim; A Little Night Music; En Spurv I Tranedans (Danish vaudeville, 1880); I'm Getting My Act Together; Les Miserables, Odense and Copenhagen; Conducted all Danish symphony orchestras; Also Danish Light Music Orchestra playing jazz, rock, musicals, Indian, classical repertoire; Concerts, television and radio appearances in Denmark and Sweden; Performed with instrumentalists and singers including: Birgit Nilsson; Elizabeth Soderstroem; Anne Sofie von Otter; Indian violinist, Supramaniam; Hubert Laws; Ben Webster; Harry 'Sweets' Edison; Bob Rockwell; Doug Rayney; Touring Europe with pioneer jazz/classical Skipper-Lund-Simonsen Trio (piano, flute, bass); Own recording studio, The Holtewood Studio; Song coach for Danish version of Prince of Egypt; Conductor, Evita, recorded with Bournemouth Sinphonietta (conducting), The Little Mermaid, drama theatre, 1998. *Compositions:* Composer for Danish films, television series, songs, signatures, 8 minute comic opera, Bread; Arranger: orchestra, theatre, live and recorded music. *Recordings:* More than 100, including musicals: The Peanuts; Starting Here Starting Now; Oliver; Les Miserables, Danish cast, Spanish cast; Miss Saigon, Danish cast. *Membership:* Danish Conductors Society; DJBFA. *Leisure interests:* Films; Afghan dogs. *Address:* Pindehuggervang 19, 2840 Holte, Denmark.

SKIRVING Mark Antony; b. 13 March 1966, Wednesday, West Midlands, USA. Vocalist; Musician (Saxophone). 1 s. *Career:* 40 television appearances world-wide; Played with: B. B. King; Cab Calloway; Slim Gaillard; Matt (Guitar) Murphy; Steve Cropper; Donald Dunn; Eddie Floyd; Several small film appearances. *Recordings:* 5 albums: King Pleasure and the Biscuit Boys; This Is It; Better Beware; King Pleasure and the Biscuit Boys Live at Ronnie Scotts; Blues and Rhythm Revue, Vol. 1. *Memberships:* Birmingham Jazz Festival Board; British Jazz Awards Committee. *Leisure interest:* Acting. *Current Management:* Jim Simpson, Big Bear Music. *Address:* Big Bear Music, PO Box 944, Edgbaston, Birmingham B16 8UT, England.

SKOLNICK Alex; b. 29 Sept. 1968, Berkeley, California, USA. Rock Musician (guitar). *Musical Education:* Studied with Joe Satriani. *Career:* Toured and recorded with US heavy rock group Testament; Toured with Stu Hamm; Recorded with Michael Manring. *Recordings:* Albums with Testament: The Legacy, 1987; The New Order, 1988; Practice What You Preach; Souls of Black; The Ritual, 1992; Signs of Chaos: The Best of Testament, 1997; with Michael Manring: Thank; with Savatage: Handful of Rain, 1994; with Attention Deficit: Attention Deficit, 1998; Compilations: Guitars That Rule The World; Guitars Practicing Musicians. *Publications:*

Columnist for magazines: Guitar; Guitar Player; Guitar World. *Membership:* ASCAP. *Leisure interests:* Reading; Writing, especially fiction. *Current Management:* Marcy Straw, CMA (Creative Music Alternatives). *Address:* Alex Skolnick, c/o CMA, 2608 Ninth St, Berkeley, CA 94710, USA.

SKOVBYE Kim Lind; b. 10 Jan. 1955, Copenhagen, Denmark. Musician (harp, guitar, violin, bouzouki, mandolin, recorder); Composer; Songwriter. Partner, Anne Ostrup, 2 s., 2 d. *Musical Education:* Private lessons from age 9; 3 years study at Danish Music Academy. *Career:* 10 years teaching children; 7 years, teaching music and drama, adult training college; 10 years as street musician with the juggler and singer Heramn; Several television and radio shows; Two big concerts at the Tivoli; Several shows and tours with keyboard player, Klaus Schonning, Denmark, Germany and Netherlands. *Compositions:* Skygge Boxer (songs), 1986; Barsebeck (songs), 1987; Scandinavia (instrumental), 1990; Heartland (instrumental), 1992; Aftermath (instrumental), 1993; Ask and Riana (children), 1994; Mountains of Fire (song), 1995; Coming Albums: Wayfarer, 1995; Lord of The Rings, Part 1, 1996; Film music: Holografi, 1988; Landscapes of Childhood, 1992; The Glassheart, 1989; Song of a Tiger, 1989. *Honours:* Awards from Danish Jazz Beat Folk Society. *Leisure interest:* Staying with children in summer residence in Sweden. *Current Management:* The New Agency. *Address:* Strandvejen 324, 3060 Espergaerde, Denmark.

SLABAK Jan; b. 24 March 1941, Kelcany, Kyjova, Czechoslovakia. Musician (Trumpet); Composer; Conductor; Band Master. m. (1) Jitka Janowskova, 18 Nov. 1960, (2) Ivana Soutalova, 22 July 1976, 1 s., 1 d. *Education:* State Conservatoire (Academy of Music), Brno; Janacek's Academy of Music Arts, Brno. *Career:* State Philharmonic Orchestra, Brno; Moravanta of Jan Slabak; Many film, TV, radio appearances. *Compositions:* 210 compositions for brass band, published and recorded on LPs, MCs, and CDs. *Publications:* Hundreds of reviews and contributions, Kaoje Kdo, 1991–92; Mijosua ic Moravanka, 1997. *Honours:* TV Prize, 1973; Ministry of Culture, 1975; Golden Key, Cleveland, USA, 1978; 3 times Golden Disc, 1980, 1985, 1991; 1 Platinum Disc, 1995; 1 Diamond Disc, 1996. *Memberships:* OSA; Chair, Competition juries. *Leisure interests:* Nature; Cottage; Garden; Dog; Small animals. *Address:* Sosnova 18, Brno 63700, Czech Republic.

SLASH (Saul Hudson); b. 23 July 1965, Stoke-On-Trent, Staffordshire, England. m. Renee Suran, 10 Sept. 1992. *Career:* Member, US heavy rock group Guns 'N' Roses, 1985–; International tours include: Supports to Iron Maiden, US, 1987, 1988; Mötley Crüe, US, 1987; The Cult, US, 1987; British tour, 1988; Support to Aerosmith, US, 1988; Get In The Ring tour, with Skid Row, 1991; World tour, 1992; Major concerts include: Monsters of Rock, Castle Donington, 1988; Farm Aid IV, 1990; Rock In Rio II, Brazil, 1991; A Concert For Life (Freddie Mercury Tribute), Wembley, 1992; National Bowl, Milton Keynes, 1993; Leader, Slash's Snakepit, 1994-. *Recordings:* Albums: with Guns 'N' Roses: Appetite For Destruction, 1987; G'N' R Lies (mini-album), 1988; Use Your Illusion I and II (No. 1 and 2, UK and US), 1991; The Spaghetti Incident, 1993; Live Era '87 -'93, (Clean), 1999; with Slash's Snakepit: It's 5 O'Clock Somewhere, 1994; Hit singles: with Guns 'N' Roses: Welcome To The Jungle, 1987; Sweet Child O'Mine (No. 1, USA), 1988; Night Train, 1989; Paradise City, 1989; Patience, 1989; Knockin' On Heaven's Door, used in film Days of Thunder, 1990; You Could Be Mine, used in film Terminator 2, 1991; Don't Cry, 1991; Live and Let Die, 1991; November Rain, 1992; Yesterdays, 1992; Ain't It Fun, 1993; Sympathy For The Devil, used in film Interview With a Vampire, 1994; Contributor, Nobody's Child (Romanian Angel appeal), 1990; Contributor as guest musician: Black and White, Michael Jackson, 1991; Brick By Brick, Iggy Pop, 1990; Dangerous, Michael Jackson, 1991; Coneheads (film soundtrack), 1993; Tribute To Muddy Waters, 1993; Believe In Me, Duff McKagan, 1993. *Honours:* American Music Awards: Favourite Heavy Metal Single 1989; Favourite Heavy Metal Artist and Album, 1989; Favourite Heavy Metal Artist, 1992; Several MTV Awards; World Music Award, Best Selling Artist of The Year, 1993; Rolling Stone and Billboard Magazine Awards. *Current Management:* Big FD Entertainment, 510 South Coast Hwy, Laguna Beach, CA, 92651–2406, USA.

SLATER John; b. 12 Jan. 1957, London, England. Artist Man.; Tour Man. *Education:* 1 year Electronics at Essex University. *Career:* Stage Manager at Edinburgh Playhouse, 1976–77; Sound Engineer, 1977–80, Radio Presenter, BRMB Radio Birmingham, hosting and producing Indie and Rock evening show, 1980–91, with 1500 interviews, 200 sessions and 50 concert recordings; Compered Donington Monsters of Rock Festival in 1991; Currently in partnership with Danny Kenny managing various bands. *Honour:* Nominated for Best UK Pop Show, Sony Radio Awards, 1987. *Leisure interest:* Formula 1 Grand Prix Racing. *Address:* PNG World-wide, Westminster Court, 10 Park Rd N, Birmingham B6 5UJ, England.

SLATER Luke, (Offset, Clementine, Morganistic, Planetary Assault Systems, The 7th Plain); b. Reading, Berkshire, England. Prod.; Remixer; DJ. *Career:* Started to DJ at London's Troll club, 1988; Worked in Jelly Jam

Records shop in Brighton, East Sussex; First recordings appeared on shop's own label; Subsequently recorded for labels including: Djax; Peacefrog; GPR; Currently signed to Novamute; Remixed: Madonna; Depeche Mode; Ballistic Brothers; Slam. *Recordings:* Albums: Fluids Amniotic (as Morganistic), 1994; Freek Funk, 1997; Wireless, 1999; as 7th Plain: My Yellow Wise Rug, The Four Cornered Room, 1994; as Planetary Assault Systems: The Drone Sector, 1998; Atomic Funkster, 2001; Singles: as Planetary Assault Systems: In From The Night, Booster, 1995; solo: Love, 1997; All Exhale, 1999; Body Freefall, Electronic Inform, 2000. *Address:* c/o Mute Records, 429 Harrow Rd, London, W10 4RE, England.

SLEDGE Percy; b. 25 Nov. 1941, Leighton, Alabama, USA. Soul Singer. *Career:* Singer, The Esquires Combo; Solo recording artiste. *Recordings:* Albums include: When a Man Loves a Woman, 1966; Warm and Tender Soul, 1966; The Percy Sledge Soul, 1967; Take Time To Know Her, 1968; I'll Be Your Everything, 1974; If Loving You Is Wrong, 1986; Percy, 1987; Wanted Again, 1987; Blue Night, 1994; Percy Sledge, 1994; Wanted Again, 1998; Singles: When a Man Loves a Woman, 1966; It Tears Me Up, 1967; Out of Left Field, 1967; Take Time To Know Her, 1968. *Honours include:* Blues Foundation Soul/Blues Album of the Year, for Blue Night, 1996; Grammy Nomination, Blue Night, 1996. *Current Management:* Artists International Management, 9850 Sandalfoot Blvd #458, Boca Raton, FL 33428, USA.

SLEEN Harm van; b. 31 Dec. 1965, Utrecht, The Netherlands. Bass. m. Kerstin Lucia Venhuizen, 16 Aug. 1995, 1 d. *Education:* Bass, Hilversums Conservatory, 1989. *Career:* Played with various pop groups, 1980–89; Recorded single with Burt and the Brand New Lifestyle, 1989; Played with Jaap Dekker's Jazz and Boogie Set, 1989–93; Playing with Capelino and with Mr Boogie Woogie and the Fire Sweep Blues Band. *Compositions:* Take Me To Swine Lane; Goodbye; Gossip; Bad Day; If You Went Away; Trouble; Lovin On My Mind; Holy Boogie; Young Boys and Girls (On the Old Side of Town). *Recordings:* Relite! Revelation, 1993; Capelino, Way To Go, 1997; Mr Boogie Woogie and The Fire Sweep Blues Band, Live At the Pub, 1997. *Publication:* Mag Die Radio War Harder?!!, 1993. *Leisure interests:* Tape Collecting; Family. *Address:* Glanerschans 28, 3432 ES Nieuwegein, The Netherlands.

SLICK Grace; b. 30 Oct. 1939, Evanstown, Illinois, USA. Singer; Songwriter; Entertainer. m. (1) Gerald Robert Slick, 26 Aug. 1961 (div), 1 d.; (2) Skip Johnson, 25 Nov. 1976. *Education:* Finch College, 1957–58. *Career:* Singer of Great Society, 1965–66; Jefferson Airplane, 1966–72; Jefferson Starship (later known as Starship), 1972–; Major concerts including Woodstock and Altamont; Most television shows, including Ed Sullivan and Johnny Carson. *Recordings:* Solo albums: Manhole; Dreams; Welcome To The Wrecking Ball; Software; Albums with Jefferson Airplane/ Starship include: Surrealistic Pillow; Earth; Modern Times; Winds of Change; Blows Against The Empire; Dragon Fly; Freedom At Point Zero; Nuclear Furniture; Red Octopus; Singles include White Rabbit; Somebody To Love; We Built This City On Rock 'n' Roll; Nothing's Going To Stop Us Now. *Publications:* Grace Slick, biography by Barbara Rosa, 1978. *Honours:* 4 Bay Area Music Awards, Best Singer. *Membership:* AFofM. *Leisure interest:* Anti-vivisection. *Current Management:* Trudy Green, HK Management. *Address:* 8900 Wilshire Blvd #300, Beverly Hills, CA 90211–1906, USA.

SLIGER Robert Earl; b. 31 Oct. 1962, Detroit, Michigan, USA. Vocalist; Songwriter; Composer; Prod.; Educator; Musician (guitar, piano, keyboards, drums). *Education:* Community College of the Air Force, USA. *Musical Education:* USAF Chorale with Martha Daige (Dir), Denver, Colorado, 1980; Voice instruction with: Bill White and Sid Wright, Austin, Texas, 1981; Tom Prebble, Torejon, Spain, 1982; Gene Nice, Pensacola Civic Opera, Florida, 1985; Vaccai, Italian Opera (English); Chris Beatty, Tennessee, 1991; Thomas Appell, California, 1997. *Career:* Tenor/MC, USAF Air Force Chorale, 1980–81; Lead singer, background, with Star Fire, 1982; Tenor, Gospel Quartet, W Germany, 1983; Lead singer, background, with Angel Band, 1990–92; Producer, lead and background singer, with Liberty-N-Justice, 1991–93; Lost In Eden tour, with Liberty-N-Justice, 1993; Filmed 2 music videos with Liberty-N-Justice: All Your Love, 1992; We Are Family, 1993; Solo career, 1993–; Radio interview, WQFL, WGSL, Rockford, Illinois, 1995; Tenor, Mendelssohn's Elijah, Bradley Community Chorus and Chamber Orchestra, Bradley University, IL, 1996; Lead vocalist, with Marvin Lee Zilch, 1997–98. *Compositions:* Songs: Christ You Share, 1991; Through The Night, 1992; You're Not Alone, 1992; LORD Jesus Christ, 1993; In Your Arms, 1993; Dr Werking's Office, 1993; Your Open Door, with Marvin Zilch, 1994; When You're Needing a Friend, with Marvin Zilch, 1994; Show The Way, 1995; Majestic, instrumental, 1995; When I Walk With You (Road to Emmaus), 1997. *Recordings:* with Liberty-N-Justice: Armed With The Cross, 1992; Big Guns, 1994; with Angel Band: Down To Earth, 1992; Down To Earth (remastered), 1993; solo: EP, The Practices, 1998; The Aunt Gloria Project, 1999; with Marvin Zilch: LOVE, 1999. *Publications:* How To Read The Holy Bible – The Basics, 1988. *Honours:* Weigel Music Award Scholarship, Tennessee Temple University, 1986. *Memberships:* Gospel

Music Asscn; ASCAP. *Leisure interests:* Golf; Tennis; Running; Cycling; Reading; Studying. *Current Management:* CandR Productions. *Address:* PO Box 10763 Austin, Texas 78766, USA.

SLIJNGAARD Ray; Rapper; Songwriter. *Career:* Rapper, Belgian dance music group 2 Unlimited, 1991-. *Recordings:* Albums: No Limits, 1993; Real Things, 1994; Hits Unlimited, 1995; Singles: Get Ready For This; No Limits; Tribal Dance; Let The Beat Control Your Body; The Real Thing; No One. *Honours:* MTV Award Nominations: Best Dance Act; Best Song, Let The Beat Control Your Body. *Address:* c/o Michel Maartens, CBA Artists, PO Box 1495, 1200 BL Hilversum, The Netherlands.

SLOANE Carol; b. 5 March 1937, Providence, Rhode Island, USA. Jazz Singer. m. Edward 'Buck' Spurr, 30 Nov. 1986. *Education:* Business College. *Career:* Professional singer from age 14, with Ed Drew's Dance Band; Tours with Larry Elgart Orchestra, 1958–60; Singer with Hendricks (Dave) Lambert and Ross Trio, 1960; Shared bills with Bill Cosby, Woody Allen, Lenny Bruce, Richard Pryor, 1960s; Singer with Tonight Show Band, Johnny Carson's Tonight Show; Supper club work, regular public radio show, North Carolina, 1981–85; Moved to Boston, 1986; DJ, WGBH, 1986–95; Played Starlight Roof, Boston, 1985; Signed with Concord Jazz, 1991; Featured artist, Pre-Fujitsu/Concord Jazz Festival party, honouring Carl Jefferson (president, Concord Jazz), 1993; 10 consecutive appearances festival season, Japan; DJ, National Public Radio Station, WICN in Worcester Massachusetts, 2000-. *Recordings include:* Albums: A Night of Ballads (duets with Don Abney), 1984; But Not For Me (with Tommy Flanagan, George Mraz, Al Foster, Frank Wess), 1986; Love You Madly, (with Richard Rodney Bennett, Kenny Barron, Kenny Burrell), 1988; The Real Thing (with Phil Woods, Grady Tate, Mike Renzi, Rufus Reid), 1989; Heart's Desire (Stef Scaggiari, John Lockwood, Colin Bailey), 1990; Concord All Stars On Cape Cod, (Scott Hamilton and Dave McKenna), 1991; Sweet and Slow (with Frank Wess, Tenor Sax), 1992; Concord Christmas (Mel Torme, Rosemary Clooney, Various Artists), 1993; When I Look In Your Eyes (with Bill Charlap, Steve Gilmore, Ron Vincent), 1994; The Songs Carmen Sang (with Phil Woods, Bill Charlap, Michael Moore, Ron Vincent), 1995; The Songs Ella and Louis Sang with Clark Terry, 1996; Romantic Ellington with Benny Golson, DRG, 1999. *Leisure interests:* Cooking; Photography; Reading. *Current Management:* Buck Spurr. *Address:* Spurr Marketing Group, 215 Salem St, Woburn, MA 01801, USA.

SLUIJS Ben; b. 6 March 1967, Antwerp, Belgium. Musician (Jazz Saxophone). 2 d. *Education:* 5 years classical saxophone education; Antwerp Jazz Studio with John Ruocco, 5 years; Brussels Conservatory with Steve Houben, 1 year. *Career:* Played with Big Bands, BRT, BB, Yellow City Big Band, Act Big Band, Brussels Jazz Orchestra; Philip Catherine Trio; Represented Belgium, EBU Big Band in Slovenia; Knitting Factory, New York; Montréal Jazz Festival with Actium, 1997. *Recordings:* Till Next Time with the Ben Sluijs Quintet, 1991; Reminiscense, with the Miriam Alter Quintet, 1994, Chromatic History, with Octurn, 1994; Silent Walk, with the Miriam Alter Quintet, 1996; Ocean, with Octurn, 1996; Hamp Digs Ham, with the François Descamps octet, 1997; Food for Free, with the Ben Sluijs kwartet, 1997; Candy Century with the Ben Sluijs kwartet, 1999; Paolo Radini Live, 1999. *Honour:* Jack Van Poll Award, 1991. *Address:* Antoon Van Dyckstraat 14, 2018 Antwerp, Belgium.

SLUSHER Michael Dennis; b. 13 Nov. 1949, Oliver Springs, Tennessee, USA. Musician (trombone); Arranger; Prod. *Education:* Brevard Community College, 1967–69; BS, North Texas State University, 1975. *Career:* Musician, Elvis Presley, 1977–79; Resident musician, venues in Las Vegas, 1977–82; Producer, arranger, Take Cover Enterprises, Beverly Hills, 1983–86; Associate Producer, television and radio commercials, 1984–86; Independent producer, arranger, Seattle, 1986–; Musician with artistes including: Frank Sinatra; Sammy Davis Jr; Tony Bennett; Righteous Brothers; Tom Jones; Glen Campbell; Paul Anka; Pearl Bailey; Also played for orchestras with: Tommy Dorsey; Si Zentner; Tex Beneke; Thad Jones; Mel Lewis.

SMALE Joanne R Muroff; b. 20 June 1949, Brooklyn, New York, USA. Production, Publicity, Promotion Exec. *Education:* BA Psychology, University of Miami. *Career:* President: Joanne Smale Productions Ltd, 1980–; Vice-President, Dark Light Music Ltd; Owner, Listening House Booking Agency, 1974–80; Publicist, numerous theatre productions; music industry events; Charity and benefit events include: Rekindle The Light Festival, 1988; Arts Against Apartheid, Toronto, 1990; Industry and media organizations include: True North Records; Sam The Record Man; Began Canadian representation for events including: New Music Seminar (New York); The International Music and Media Conference (Montreux, Switzerland); American Video Conference and Awards (Los Angeles); Publicist: Road Movies, CBCTV; In The Key of Oscar, documentary, CBCTV; Co-producer, with National Film Board, The Un-Canadians. *Honours:* 6 Gold, 2 Platinum albums for work with: Rough Trade; Murray McLauchlan; Bruce Cockburn. *Memberships:* Videofact; Vice-President, Canadian Independent Recording Producers Asscn (CIRPA); Canadian Independent Film Caucus (CIFC); Canadian Women In Radio

and Television (CWRT). *Address:* Joanne Smale Productions Ltd, 51 Bulwer St, Toronto, ON M5T 1A1, Canada.

SMALL Heather; Vocalist. *Career:* Singer, soul group, Hothouse; Lead singer, UK dance group M People, 1991–; Major concerts include: Glastonbury Festival, 1994. *Recordings:* Albums: Northern Soul, 1992, 1995; Elegant Slumming, 1993; Bizarre Fruit, 1994; Bizarre Fruit II, 1995; Fresco, 1997; Testify, 1999; Hit singles: How Can I Love You More, 1991; One Night In Heaven, 1993; Movin' On Up, 1993; Sight For Sore Eyes, 1994; Itchycoo Park, 1995; Search For The Hero, 1995; Open Your Heart, 1995; Love Rendezvous, 1995. *Honours include:* Mercury Prize, Best Album, Elegant Slumming, 1994; BRIT Awards: Best Dance Act, 1994, 1995. *Current Management:* RD World-wide Management, 37 Limerston St, London SW10 0BQ, England.

SMALL Mina; b. 14 March 1958, San Francisco, California, USA. Singer; Composer; Musician (violin, voice, piano). *Musical Education:* Classical and jazz. *Career:* Concerts, entertainment, classical jazz, 1982–; Singer with pianists, jazz groups, 1984–95; Theatre production, 1989; Records for children. *Compositions:* 50 for jazz, folk groups, 1989–95. *Recordings:* Background vocalist, O Jamai; Solo cassette, 1995; Waiting, CD, 1998. *Honours:* Prix de la SACEM, CREST (France), 1995. *Memberships:* SACEM; SACD; SPEDIDAM. *Leisure interest:* Dance. *Address:* 20 rue Freycinet, 26000 Valence, France.

SMIETANA Jarek Zdzislaw; b. 29 March 1951, Krakow, Poland. Musician (Guitar). m. Anna Smietana, 21 July 1978, 1 d. *Education:* Studied Class Composition and Arranging, Academy of Music, Katowice, Poland. *Career:* One of the major jazz musicians in Poland; First Band, Extra Ball, formed 1974; One of the most successful European jazz groups. *Compositions:* A Few Warm Words; Follow the Fellow; Flowers in Mind; Children of Time; Sounds and Colours. *Recordings:* Ballads and Other Songs, 1996; Jarek Smietana Quintet Live, 1996; Phone Consultations, 1997; Songs and Other Ballads, 1998; Art Farmer Plays Standards, 1998; Speak Easy, 1999. *Publication:* Jazz Songs by Smietana. *Honours:* No 1 Jazz Guitarist in Poland, prizes every year since 1983; Fryderyk, Polish Music Award, 1998. *Membership:* Polish Jazz Society. *Leisure interest:* Collecting records. *Address:* c/o Sound Music, Os 2 Pulku Loniczego 13/118, 31867 Krakow, Poland.

SMITH Brian; b. 13 July 1936, Thornton Heath, Surrey, England. Musician (guitar, bass, banjo, mandolin, cornet). 1 d. *Musical Education:* Self-taught. *Career:* Member, Johnny Howard Orchestra, 1959; Musician, Cunard liner Queen Elizabeth I, 1961; Leader, Jazz/blues group Wes Minster Five, 1962–66; Support tours to: Sonny Boy Williamson; Memphis Slim; John Lee Hooker; Rufus Thomas; Television appearances include: Ready Steady Go; Saturday Club; Musician, Andy Ross Band and cabaret musician, 1966–; Musician for: Danny Williams; Kenny Lynch; Faith Brown; Janet Brown; Vince Hill; Bruce Forsyth; Gary Wilmott; Anita Harris; Des O'Connor; Also played with Rod Stewart; Shows (pit musician), session and film work, 1970s; Currently teacher, occasional jazz performances. *Recordings:* Film and session work with major artists; Numerous compositions with Wes Minster Five, including Shaking The Blues. *Honours:* Appointed to ILEA Panel. *Membership:* Musicians' Union. *Leisure interest:* Collecting old London buses. *Address:* 6 Selcroft Rd, Purley, Surrey CR8 1AD, England.

SMITH Bryan Christopher; b. 21 Dec. 1954, St Albans, Hertfordshire, England. Recording Engineer; Prod.; Programmer; Musician (guitar, keyboards). m. Denise, 6 July 1974, 1 s., 1 d. *Career:* Red Bus Records, 1980–82; Member, French Impression, 1984–86; Member, The Big Push, 1992–; Founded Farm Factory Studios, 1990; Support tours: Jools Holland; Cool Notes; Member, Hello, 1993. *Recordings:* Musician, engineer, programmer for: Move Your Skin; And Why Not; Amazing Colossal Men: Buddy's Song; Chesney Hawkes; Also recorded Jon Anderson/Frances Dunnery, 1991; Steve Harley demos, 1994. *Honours:* Gold disc, Chesney Hawkes: The One and Only (hit single from Buddy's Song). *Membership:* PRS. *Leisure interests:* Golf; Football. *Current Management:* Paul Loasby, One Fifteen Management. *Address:* The Gallery, 28/30 Wood Wharf, Horseferry Pl., London SE10 9BT, England.

SMITH Carl; b. 15 March 1927, Maynardsville, Tennessee, USA. Country vocalist; Songwriter; Musician (guitar); Actor. m. (1) June Carter (Cash), 1952, divorced; (2) Goldie Hill, 1957, 1 d. *Career:* Entered talent contest age 13, 1944; Early radio experience at WROL, Knoxville; Bass player and occasional vocalist with Skeets Williamson Band, 1949; Sang with Archie Campbell's band on WROL radio showsl Audition for Peer International Music led to spot on Grand Ole Opry as a guest of Hank Williams, March 1950; Signed to Columbia Records, 1950; Charted 93 times on Billboard country chart singles, 1951–78; Later hits Hickory/MGM and ABC/Hickory labels; Feature film appearances include: The Badge of Marshal Brennan, 1957; Buffalo Gun, 1961); From Nashville With Music, 1969; That's Country, 1977; Hosted TV series: Four Star Jubilee, late '50s; Carl Smith's Country TV Show, 1960s; Semi-retired to raise prize-winning quarter horses on a 500-acre farm in Franklin, TN, 1977; Father of Carlene Carter; Nicknamed 'The Country Gentleman'. *Compositions include:* I Overlooked An Orchid; Ten Thousand Drums; Mr Moon. *Recordings include:* Let Old Mother Nature Have Her Way, 1951; (When You Feel Like You're In Love) Don't Just Stand There, Are You Teasing Me, 1952; Hey Joe!, 1953; Loose Talk, 1954; Your Name Is Beautiful, 1958; Ten Thousand Drums, 1959; Albums: There Stands The Glass, The Tall Tall Gentleman, 1964; Man With A Plan, 1966; Satisfaction Guaranteed (compilation), 1996. *Address:* c/o Country Music Asscn, Nashville.

SMITH Chad; Musician (drums). *Career:* Member, Red Hot Chili Peppers, 1988–; International concerts include: Lollapalooza Festival tour, 1992; Hollywood Rock Festival, Rio De Janeiro, 1993; Glastonbury Festival, 1993; Television appearances include: Late Night With David Letterman, NBC TV; Rapido, BBC2; The Word, C4 TV; Saturday Night Live, NBC TV; Top of The Pops, BBC1; Also member of Honeymoon Stitch. *Recordings:* Albums: Mother's Milk, 1989; Blood Sugar Sex Magik, 1992; What Hits?, 1992; One Hot Minute, 1995; with John Fogerty, Blue Moon Swamp, 1997; with Private Parts: Private Parts, 1997; with Leah Andreone: Alchemy, 1998; Contributor, The Beavis and Butthead Experience, 1993; Singles include: Give It Away; Under The Bridge; Soul To Squeeze, for film Coneheads, 1993. *Honours:* MTV Music Video Awards, 1992; Grammy, Best Hard Rock Song, Give It Away, 1993. *Current Management:* Lindy Goetz Management. *Address:* 11116 Aqua Vista #39, Studio City, CA 91602, USA.

SMITH Connie, (Constance June Meador); b. 14 Aug. 1941, Elkhart, Indiana, USA. Country vocalist; Songwriter; Musician (guitar, piano). m. (1) Jerry Smith, (2) Marty Stuart, 8 July 1997. *Career:* Early appearances with Floyd Miller's Square Dance Band as a teenager; Weekly appearances on West Virginia local TV: Saturday Night Jamboree, WSAZ TV Huntington; Big Red Jubilee, Parkersburg; Discovered by country writer-performer Bill Anderson, 1963; Signed by RCA; Billboard country chart debut with Once A Day, 1964; No other solo female country artist has spent longer than the eight weeks at #1 this release achieved; Followed by nearly 50 entries, mostly for RCA; Movies appearances: Second Fiddle To A Steel Guitar, 1965; The Las Vegas Hillbillys, 1966; The Road To Nashville, 1967; Hell On Wheels, 1967; The Hi-Lo Country, 1998; Became Christian and recorded gospel material as well as country, early 1970s. *Compositions include:* I'll Come Running. *Recordings include:* Once A Day, 1964; Ain't Had No Lovin', 1966; Just One Time, 1971; The Hurtin's All Over, 1966; Cincinnati Ohio, 1967; Albums: Connie Smith, 1965; Cute 'n' Country, 1965; Miss Smith Goes To Nashville, 1966; Downtown Country, 1967; Born To Sing, 1966. *Honours:* CMA, Song of The Year, Once A Day, 1971. *Membership:* Grand Ole Opry, 1971. *Address:* c/o Fat City Artists, 1226 17th Ave S, Suite 2, Nashville 37212, USA.

SMITH Curt; b. 24 June 1961, Bath, Avon, England. Musician (bass guitar); Singer. *Education:* College. *Career:* Professional musician since age 18; Member, Graduate, 1979; Member of duo Tears For Fears, 1981–90; Solo artiste, 1991–; Concert band Mayfield, first album Mayfield, 1998. *Recordings:* Acting Your Age, Graduate, 1979; with Tears For Fears: The Hurting, 1982; Songs From The Big Chair, 1985; Seeds of Love, 1989; Songs from the big Chair (UK bonus tracks), 1999; Hurting (UK bonus tracks), 1999; Seeds of Love (UK bonus tracks), 1999; Solo album: Soul On Board, 1993; Singles include: Shout; Everybody Wants To Rule The World; Mad World; Change; Pale Shelter; I Believe; Head Over Heels. *Memberships:* in UK: Musicians' Union; PRS; in US: AFTRA; BMI.

SMITH Geoff; b. 11 May 1966, Tynemouth, England. Songwriter; Musician (Piano). m. Nicola Walker Smith, 16 Sept. 1989, 2 s. *Musical Education:* BA, Hons, Nottingham University, 1987; MPhil, Oxford University, 1989; PhD, Huddersfield University, 1996. *Recordings:* Albums: Gas Food Lodging, 1993; Fifteen Wild Decembers, 1994; Black Flowers, 1997; with Mono: Formica Blues, 1997; with Gap Mangione: Planet Gap: Big Band, 1998; with Burning Bush: Klezmer and Hassidic Music, 1998. *Publications:* Co-author, American Originals, 1994; Interviews with Harold Rudd, Philip Glass, Steve Reich. *Honours:* Debut album selected as Top 40 Album of the Year, BBC Music Magazine; Youngest Composer to be signed by Sony Classical in the history of the label. *Leisure interest:* Music. *Current Management:* Keith Armstrong. *Address:* Kitchenware, St Thomas' St Stables, Newcastle Upon Tyne, NE1 4LE, England.

SMITH James Edward; b. 2 Aug. 1952. Musician (Jazz Guitarist). m. Gloria C Smith, 2 s., 2 d. *Education:* BA, University of New Mexico, 1974; MM, Wisconsin Conservatory of Music, 1980. *Career:* Chairman, Fine and Performing Arts, Central St University; Adjunct, Associate Professor of Jazz Guitar, University of Cincinnati College, Conservatory of Music, 1984–; Four National Public Radio Broadcasts, 1992. *Composition:* Song For Om, 1992. *Recordings:* Cincinnati Seven. *Publications:* Jazz Guitar: Theory and Technique, 1982; Bebop Riffs, 1990; Guitarists Guide To Technique, 1992; Chord Thesaurus For Jazz Guitar, 1994. *Honours:* Outstanding Service To Jazz Education, 1988, 1997. *Memberships:* IAJE;

AAUP. *Current Management:* Smith Management, 4189 Sugar Leaf, Dayton, OH 45440, USA.

SMITH Josh; b. 10 July 1979, Middletown, Connecticut, USA. Blues Musician (guitar). *Musical Education:* Private study, 9 years. *Career:* Member, band, the Rhinocats, 1993–; Opened for bands including Buddy Guy; The Fabulous T-Birds; Allman Brothers Band. *Recordings:* CD: Born Under a Blue Sign, 1995; Woodsheddin, 1996; With High Karate: High Karate, 1998; with One Eighty: Crackerjack, 1998. *Honours:* Best Blues Band, State of Florida, Florida Jam Magazine, Jammy Awards, 1994. *Membership:* ASCAD. *Leisure interests:* Music; Guitar. *Current Management:* Dan Cohen, Musicians Exchange. *Address:* 8920 N W 14th St, Pembroke Pines, FL 33024, USA.

SMITH Karen M; b. 23 July 1958, Chicago, Illinois, USA. Artist Development; Record Co Exec. m. A J Smith, 5 May 1994. *Education:* 2 years college. *Career:* Currently owner, Glow In The Dark Rehearsals, (rehearsal space in Chicago); Owner, record company TOW Records, Chicago; Consultant for Ex-Idols; PO! Executive Producer for: Wait For Light; S Is For Space. *Honour:* Gottlieb Award, Best Rehearsal Studio, 1994. *Memberships:* NAMM; NARAS. *Leisure interests:* Yoga; Cinema. *Address:* PO Box 740, Oak Park, IL 60303, USA.

SMITH Keely; b. 9 March 1932, Norfolk, Virginia, USA. Vocalist; Actor. m. Louis Prima, 1953, divorced 1961. *Career:* Joined Louis Prima's band aged 16, 1948; Married Prima at 21 and settled in Las Vegas and virtually invented the 'lounge act'; After Decca contract expired, signed to Capitol as a solo artist at the insistance of Prima, securing position as a major vocalist, 1956; Appeared in films: Thunder Road (with Robert Mitchum), 1958; Senior Prom, 1958, Hey Boy Hey Girl, 1959, both with Prima; Prior to divorce, signed with Dot (again recording own albums alongside those with Prima); Joined Reprise in 1964 before semi-retirement; Re-emerged with Fantasy Records album, 1985; Currently signed to Concord Jazz; Occasional live performances in Las Vegas. *Recordings:* I Wish You Love, 1957; Politely, 1958; Swingin' Pretty, 1959; Because You're Mine, 1959; Be My Love, 1960; Swing You Lovers, 1960; Dearly Beloved, 1961; What Kind of Fool Am I, 1961; Cherokeely Swings, 1962; Keely Smith Wishes You A Merry Christmas, 1963; Little Girl Blue Little Girl New, 1964; Keely Smith Sings The Lennon and McCartney Song Book, 1965; That Old Black Magic, 1965; I'm In Love Again, 1985; Swing Swing Swing, 2000; Keely Sings Sinatra, 2001. *Current Management:* Suzy Frank. *Address:* c/o Concord Records, PO Box 845, Concord, California, 94522, USA. *Internet:* www.keelysmith.com.

SMITH Laura; b. 18 March 1952, Ontario, Canada. Singer; Songwriter; Musician (Guitar). *Career:* Contributor: albums, Chieftains, 1997; Far Cry From Leaving, Terry Kelly, 1996; Fire In The Kitchen, 1998. *Recordings:* Between the Earth and My Soul; It's a Personal Thing. *Honours:* ECMA Female Artist, 1996; ECMA Album, 1996; Gemini Award for Best Performance, 1997; Vanity Pressed: A Collection, 1998. *Memberships:* SOCAN; CARAS; ECMA; AVLA. *Current Management:* Jones and Co. *Address:* 5212 Sackville St, Suite 100, Halifax, NS, B3J 1K6, Canada.

SMITH Mark 'Hitman'; b. 20 Oct. 1972, Doncaster, Yorkshire, England. Freelance Prod. and Remixer; Programmer; Musician (keyboards). *Education:* High Melton College, Doncaster. *Musical Education:* Piano, Royal School of Music. *Career:* Producer, remixer, for Music Factory Records; Commercial DJ. *Recordings:* Mixes include: Rock 'N' Roll Dance Party; Jive Bunny; Nolans Hitmix; Hot Chocolate Hitmix; Remixes include: Kylie Minogue; 2 Unlimited; Kelly Marie. *Publications:* Contributor, Mixology Magazine. *Membership:* Musicians' Union. *Current Management:* Saint Productions, PO Box 1295, New Rossington, Doncaster DN11 0GF. *Address:* 5/7 Fitzwilliam St, Parkgate, Rotherham, South Yorkshire S62 5EP, England.

SMITH Mark E(dward); b. 5 March 1957, Salford, Manchester, England. Singer; Songwriter; Musician (guitar). m. Brix (Laura Elise Smith), divorced 1990. *Career:* Founder, The Fall, 1977-. *Recordings:* Live At The Witch Trials, 1979; Dragnet, 1979; Totale's Turns (It's Now Or Never), 1980; Grotesque (After The Gramme), 1980; Slates, 1981; Hex Enduction Hour, 1982; Room To Love, 1982; Perverted By Language, 1983; The Wonderful and Frightening World Of..., 1984; This Nation's Saving Grace, 1985; Bend Sinister, 1986; The Frenz Experiment, 1988; I Am Kurious Oranji, 1988; Seminal Live, 1989; Extricate, 1990; 458489, 1990; 458489-B Sides, 1990; Shiftwork, 1991; Code Selfish, 1992; The Infotainment Scan, 1993; Sinister Waltz, 1996; Singles: Fiery Jack; How I Wrote Elastic Man; Totally Wired; There's a Ghost In My House; Victoria. *Publication:* Play: Hey! Luciani. *Address:* c/o Permanent Records, 22–23 Brook Mews, London W2 3BW, England.

SMITH Michael; b. 19 Jan. 1967, Bridport, Dorset, England. Musician (saxophone). *Musical Education:* City of Leeds College of Music; Guildhall School of Music and Drama, London. *Career:* Saxophonist, Brand New Heavies, 1990–93; Saxophone and flute, Jamiroquai; Extensive recording, world-wide touring with above acts; Television appearances include: Top of The Pops; The Word; The Beat; MTV's Most Wanted; In-house arranger, Acid Jazz Records. *Recordings:* Arranger for: Corduroy; Mother Earth; James Taylor Quartet; Solo album: The Whole Thing, 1993; Recorded every release with The Brand New Heavies; Album: with Jamiroquai: Space Cowboy. *Memberships:* PRS; MCPS. *Leisure interests:* Coastal walking; Backgammon. *Current Management:* Richard H Smith. *Address:* 14D Wilde St, London WC2B 4AG, England.

SMITH Mike; b. 6 Dec. 1943, London, England. Record Prod.; Songwriter; Singer; Musician (keyboards). *Musical Education:* Trinity College, London. *Career:* Lead singer, keyboard player with: Dave Clark 5; Writer all songs; Writer, producer, television commercials and themes; Record producer, 2 Top 5 albums with Michael Ball. *Recordings:* with Michael Ball: Michael Ball; Always; One Careful Owner. *Memberships:* PRS; BASCA. *Leisure interests:* Music and more music. *Current Management:* Graham Carpenter, Pachuco Management, Priestlands, Letchmore Heath, Herts WD2 8EW, England.

SMITH Mike (Michael John); b. 16 Nov. 1946, Edgware, Middlesex, England. Artist Man.; Music Publisher; Television and Film Production Co Owner. m. Sally James, 22 July 1978, 3 s. *Career:* Producer, Assistant Head Light Entertainment, LWT, 1968–76; Head of A & R, Decca Records, 1976–78; General Manager, Vice President, GTO Records, 1978–80; Own companies: Yellow Balloon Productions Ltd; Mike Music Ltd; Yellow Balloon Music; Yellow Balloon Records; Universal Media Management Ltd; Unitapes UK Ltd; Unismart Ltd; Junior League Ltd. *Recordings:* As manager or producer: Rick Wakeman; Bruce Foxton; Adam and The Ants; Billy Ocean; The Moody Blues; The Smurfs; The Dooleys; Rolf Harris; Hazel O'Connor. *Honours:* Tokyo Music Festival Award; Award Winning Producer of London Bridge television programme; 30 Gold and Silver discs as producer, manager of established acts. *Memberships:* Musicians' Union; ACCA; PRS. *Leisure interests:* Clay pigeon shooting; Classic cars; Travel; Family. *Address:* Freshwater House, Outdowns, Effingham, Surrey KT24 5QR, England.

SMITH Patti; b. 30 Dec. 1946, Chicago, Illinois, USA. Vocalist; Songwriter; Musician (guitar); Poet; Author. m. Fred 'Sonic' Smith, 1 March 1980, 2 s. *Career:* Journalist, Rock magazine, 1970; Creem magazine, 1971; Solo artiste, 1972–; Concerts include: Support to New York Dolls, 1972; Formed Patti Smith Group, 1974; UK debut, 1976; European tour, 1976; Away from music business, 8 years, sporadic appearances, 1988–; Poetry performance, New Year's Day Extravaganza, New York, with Yoko Ono, 1975. *Recordings:* Co-writer (with Bruce Springsteen), Because The Night, 1978; Other singles include: Gloria; Hey Joe; So You Want To Be a Rock and Roll Star; Dancing Barefoot; Because the Night; Albums include: Horses, 1975; Radio Ethiopia, 1976; Easter, 1978; Wave, 1979; Dream of Life, 1988; Peace and Noise, 1997; Gung Ho, 2000; Guest vocalist on albums: Secret Treaties, Blue Oyster Cult, 1974; Agents of Fortune, Blue Oyster Cult, 1976; The Whole Thing Started With Rock 'N' Roll, Ray Manzarek, 1975; Nervous Night, The Hooters, 1985; Contributor, film soundtrack Until The End of The World, 1991. *Publications:* Poetry: Seventh Heaven, 1971; Kodak, 1972; Witt, 1973; Feb Babel, 1979; Co-author, play Cowboy Mouth (with Sam Shepherd), 1972; Woolgathering (short stories), 1993. *Current Management:* Rascoff/Zysblat Organization Inc, 110 W 57th St, Third Floor, New York, NY 10019–3319, USA.

SMITH Rob(ert Kevin); b. 17 Dec. 1960, West Yorkshire, England. Musician (saxophone, keyboards, percussion). m. Sarah Stone, 12 May 1990, 2 d. *Musical Education:* Nottingham University; King's College, London. *Career:* with Four Quartets: Appeared on HTV, 1987; Appeared at 'Outside In' jazz festivals in 1988 and 1993; Brecon Jazz Festival, 1984–; 2 Arctic songs with London Sinfonietta Voices, 1994; Lecturer, composition, Bath Spa University College; Musical Director, Wonderbrass, Community Jazz Orchestra. *Compositions:* Anonymous Twentieth Century, 1998; Toccata Lachrymal Tenebrae, 2001. *Recordings:* with Heavy Quartet: Poum, 1988; A Screaming Tradition, 1989; Short Stories, 1991; with The Diggers, 1993: Imbolc; Musicals: Race, 1989; Starcross'd, 1991; Dangerous Acquintances, 1997; Carnivore, Heavy Quartet, 1995; Film scores: The Knowledge, 1996; The Confectioner, 1997; Minim, 1999. *Publications:* 2 articles on trip to Gambia, Taplas, 1992. *Memberships:* PRS; Society for Promotion of New Music. *Leisure interests:* Listening to music; Walking; Food, wine and beer; Rugby. *Current Management:* HQ Enterprises, Cardiff, Wales. *Address:* 26 Burlington Terrace, Llandaf, Cardiff CF5 1GG, Wales.

SMITH Robert; b. 8 Nov. 1960, Cheshire, England. Percussionist. m. Tina, 1 s., 1 d. *Career:* Played with Bad Habits pop group; Made several television and radio recordings; Theatre work. *Recordings:* With Fodens Motor Works Band. *Honours:* Best Percussionist, Buxton Music Festival, 1984, 1985, 1986. *Membership:* Musicians' Union. *Leisure interests:* Sport; Family. *Address:* 17 Christleton Ave, Crewe, Cheshire, CW2 8TD, England.

SMITH Ruthie Elaine Foster; b. Manchester, England. Musician (saxophones); Singer; Composer. *Musical Education:* BA English/Music Honours, York University. *Career:* Member, Stepney Sisters, one of first feminist rock bands, 1974–76; Founder member, all women's jazz band The Guest Stars; World tours, jazz festivals, clubs including Ronnie Scott's; Also played with Mervyn Africa and Bryan Abrahams in South African band District Six; Toot Sweet with Jim Dvorak; Jazz in Britain, television, tours financed by The British Council; Served on Greater London Arts Council panel, 2 years. *Recordings:* 3 albums with The Guest Stars; 2 recordings with District Six; Live recordings for BBC; Currently working with Toot Sweet Jazz Band, featuring Frances Knight and Julia Doyle. *Honours:* Jazz Bursary, Arts Council of Great Britain, to compose and perform a jazz suite. *Membership:* Musicians' Union. *Leisure interests:* Gardening; Colour therapy; Astrology. *Address:* 2a Banning St, Greenwich, London SE10 9PH, England.

SMITH Spencer John; b. 8 Feb. 1967, City of London, England. Musician (drums). *Career:* Member, North of Cornwallis; Concerts include support to Nico; Member, East Village, 1986–90; Recorded 4 singles; Member, Saint Etienne, 1992; Tours include: UK; Japan; Canada; USA; Europe; Television includes: Top of the Pops (4 times); Later With Jools Holland; The Word (2 times); Festivals include: Glastonbury; Sweden; Denmark; Radio includes: Evening session, BBC Radio 1. *Recordings:* with East Village: 4 singles; Albums: Dropout; Hotrod Hotel; with St Etienne: 4 singles; 1 track on album Tiger Bay. *Honours:* Silver Disc, So Tough; Gold Disc, Too Young To Die, 1997. *Memberships:* Musicians' Union; PRS. *Current Management:* Heavenly Management, 47 Frith St, London W1V 5TE, England.

SMITH Stephen Bowden; b. 17 Oct. 1946, Oxford, England. Musician (electric, string bass). *Musical Education:* Studied electric bass with Joe Hubbard (theory and practice). *Career:* Cruise ships orchestra with Geraldo's Navy, 1969–70; PandO ships Orsova, Oriana (own trio), 1972; Michel Heuser Trio, Gstaad, Switzerland, 1972; Tour with Hindukush, Switzerland, 1974; Tommy Hawkins Band, Hammersmith Palais, 1977; John Burch Trio, London Playboy Club, 1977–78; Season and USA concerts with Matt Munro, 1978; Concerts with Vera Lynn, 1980; Accompanying jazz musicians including: Red Rodney; Tal Farlow; Slim Gaillard; Red Holloway; Harold Land; Ray Alexander; Spike Robinson; Oliver Jones; Dick Morissey; Radio, recordings, European tours, with Stutz Bear Cats, 1984; Concerts, Spanish television with Iris Williams, 1987; Tours, television, concerts, with Vince Hill, 1988; Jazz clubs, festivals, with Butchers Brew, 1993; Tour of USA with Vince Hill, 1995–96; Cruise on flagship Oriana with the Groove Company, 1997. *Compositions:* Severn Borsa Nova; Purple Parrot Road; Jive For The Cider Insid 'er (Inside); The Mango Tango; Rio Yeo Samba. *Recording:* The Session, Whisky Time, with Diana Jarrett-Harris Trio. *Leisure interests:* Skiing; Windsurfing. *Current Management:* Smith. *Address:* 23 Westbury Cres., Oxford OX4 3RZ, England.

SMITH Toby; b. 29 Oct. 1970, London, England. Musician (Keyboards). *Career:* Member, Jamiroquai; Numerous tours and TV appearances. *Recordings:* Singles: When You Gonna Learn, 1993; Emergency on Planet Earth, 1994; Space Cowboy EP, 1995; Cosmic Girl, 1996; Light Years, 1996; Alright, 1997; Deeper Underground, 1998; High Times, 1998; Canned Heat, 1999; Albums: Emergency on Planet Earth, 1993; Travelling Without Moving, 1996; Synkronized, 1999. *Honours:* Gold and Platinum Albums; Several MTV Video Music Awards.

SMITH Tommy; b. 27 April 1967, Edinburgh, Scotland. Musician (Tenor Saxophone). *Education:* Berklee College of Music, Boston, USA, 1984–86. *Career:* Hired as sideman to Gary Burton, 1986; Record deal, 1989 Began recording under own name with guest musicians; Returned to Scotland, mid-1990s; Recorded with James Talley, Gary Burton, Red Krayola; Songs performed by Garth Brooks, Marty Brown, Engelbert Humperdinck, Tracy Lawrence, Josh Logan. *Recordings:* Albums: Forward Motion: The Berklee Tapes, 1984; Step By Step, 1988; Peeping Tom, 1990; Standards, 1991; Misty Morning and No Time, 1994; Reminiscence, 1994; Beasts of Scotland, 1996; Azure, 1997; Sound of Love, 1999.

SMITH Wendy; b. 31 May 1963, Middlesbrough, Cleveland, England. Vocalist; Musician; Voice Movement Therapist. *Career:* Member, Prefab Sprout, 1982–; Extensive tours: Europe; UK; Japan; Numerous television appearances; Practitioner of Voice Movement Therapy, trained with Paul Newham, founder of Voice Movement Therapy. *Recordings:* Albums: Swoon, 1984; Steve McQueen, 1985; From Langley Park To Memphis, 1987; Protest Songs, 1988; Jordan-The Comeback, 1990; Life of Surprises: The Best of Prefab Sprout, 1992; with Bryan Savage: Cat Food, 1996; with James Bignon: What a Mighty God We Serve, 1996; with Special Delivery: This is Special Delivery, 1996; Numerous hit singles. *Honours:* 6 Gold Albums; BRIT Award Nomination. *Membership:* International Network of Voice Movement Therapy Associates. *Current Management:* Keith Armstrong, Kitchenware Records. *Address:* 7 The Stables, St Thomas St, Newcastle Upon Tyne NE41 8DU, England.

SMITH Will (Willard C II); b. 25 Sept. 1968, Philadelphia, Pennsylvania, USA. Singer; Rap Artist; Actor. m. (1) Sheree Zampino, 1 s., (2) Jada Pinkett, 1997, 1 s. *Career:* Formed duo, DJ Jazzy Jeff and the Fresh Prince; Star of TV sitcom, The Fresh Prince of Bel Air; Film appearances, Six Degrees of Separation, 1993, Bad Boys, 1995, Independence Day, 1996, Men in Black, 1997, Enemy of the State, 1999. *Recordings:* With DJ Jazzy Jeff: Singles: Parents Just Don't Understand; I Think I Could Beat Mike Tyson; Summertime, 1991; Boom! Shake the Room, 1993; Albums: Rock the House, 1997; He's the DJ, I'm the Rapper, 1988; And In This Corner..., 1989; Homebase, 1991; Code Red, 1993; Greatest Hits, 1998; Solo: Singles: Just Cruisin', 1997; Men in Black, 1997; Gettin' Jiggy With It, 1998; Miami, 1998; Wild Wild West, 1999; Albums: Big Willie Style, 1997; Willennium, 1999. *Honours:* Grammy Awards, with DJ Jazzy Jeff, Best Rap Performance, 1988, 1991; Grammy Award, Best Rap Solo Performance, 1998; MTV Music Video Awards, Best Male Video, Best Rap Video, 1998; American Music Awards, Favorite Male Artist, Favorite Album, Favorite Male Soul/R & B Artist, 1999.

SMYTH Jimmy (James Patrick); b. 22 April 1958, Navan, Ireland. Musician (guitar, keyboards); Vocalist; Prod. m. Jenny Newman, 22 March 1994. *Musical Education:* Father (music teacher, RIAM, Dublin). *Career:* Toured with: The Kinks; Thin Lizzy; Bob Dylan; Rory Gallagher; Bon Jovi; Played guitar with: Bogey Boys; Toni Childs (all world tours); Van Morrison; Paul Brady; Don Baker; Numerous television appearances world-wide, including performance at Grammy Awards Ceremony, 1989. *Compositions:* Co-wrote 6 songs on Toni Child's album The Woman's Boat; Many songs covered. *Recordings:* 2 albums as singer, guitarist with The Bogey Boys; Played on over 150 major release albums including Daniel O'Donnell: Love Hope and Faith, 1998; Winter's Tale: Winter's Tale, 1998. *Honour:* Twice voted in Top 5 guitarists in Ireland, Hot Press magazine. *Memberships:* Musicians' Union; ASCAP; IMRO; MCPS. *Leisure interests:* Reading; Swimming; Working out. *Current Management:* Bob Brimson, 2 Tynings Terrace, Bath, Avon, England. *Address:* Thatched Cottage East, Upper Stand, Malahide, Co Dublin, Ireland.

SNIDER Dee; b. New York, USA. Rock Vocalist; Lyricist. *Career:* Founder, vocalist, US rock group Twisted Sister; Sold over 8m. albums world-wide, 1983–87; Numerous world-wide tours; Major concerts include Monsters of Rock Festival, Castle Donington; Founder member, vocalist, Desperado, with Bernie Torme; Founder member, Widowmaker, 1991–; Television includes: Host, Heavy Metal Mania, MTV (now known as Headbangers Ball); Radio includes: Host, Dee Snider's Metal Nation, WRCN; Defendant for rock music and lyrics, US Senate hearings, 1985. *Recordings:* Albums: with Twisted Sister: Under The Blade, 1982; You Can't Stop Rock and Roll, 1983; Stay Hungry, 1984; Come Out and Play, 1985; Love Is For Suckers, 1987; Big Hits and Nasty Cuts: The Best of Twisted Sister; Live at Hammersmith, 1994; Early Works, 1999; with Widowmaker: Blood and Bullets, 1992; Stand By For Pain, 1994; Thunderbolt: A tribute to AC/DC, 1998; with Strangeland (executive producer): Strangeland, 1998; with Bernie Torme: White Trash Guitar, 1999; Singles: with Twisted Sister: I Am; I Wanna Rock; The Kids Are Back; Leader of The Pack; We're Not Gonna Take It; You Can't Stop Rock 'N' Roll; You Want What We Got. *Current Management:* c/o Music For Nations Records, 333 Latimer Rd, London W10 6RA, England.

SNOOP DOGG (Calvin Broadus), (Snoop Doggy Dogg); b. 20 Oct. 1972, Long Beach, California, USA. Rapper. *Career:* Worked with Warren G and Domino; Began collaboration with Dr Dre; Numerous live appearances including Lollapalooza in 1997; EP with Rage Against the Machine; Worked with K-Ci and JoJo on You Lift Me Up; Contributed to soundtrack for film Men in Black; Movie cameo roles in The Show, 1995, Half Baked, 1998, Ride, 1998, Caught Up, 1998. *Recordings:* Singles: What's My Name, 1993; Gin and Juice, 1994; We Just Wanna Party With You, 1997; The Dogfather, 1998; Da Game Is To Be Sold Not To Be Told, EP, 1998; Still a 'G' Thang, 1998; The Baller Doggy Dogg, 1999; Doggy Dogg World, 1999; Woof, 1999; Albums: Doggystyle, 1993; Tha Doggfather, 1996; Da Game Is To Be Sold Not To Be Told, 1998; Top Dogg, 1999.

SNOW Phoebe (Laub); b. 17 July 1952, New York City, USA. Singer. *Musical Education:* Piano studies, guitar. *Career:* Performer, New York clubs, 1970s; Solo recording artist, 1974–; Tours with Paul Simon; Played and recorded with Stan Getz, Donald Fagen and Michael McDonald. *Recordings:* Albums include: Phoebe Snow, 1974; Second Childhood, 1976; It Looks Like Snow, 1976; Never Letting Go, 1977; Against The Grain, 1978; Best of 1981; Rock Away, 1981; Something Real, 1989; I Can't Complain, 1998. *Address:* c/o The Agency Group, 1775 Broadway, Suite 433, New York, NY 10019, USA.

SNOWBOY (Mark Cotgrove); b. 3 July 1961, Hadleigh, Essex, England. Musician (Latin percussion); Recording Artist. *Education:* Graphics, Southend-On-Sea Technical College. *Musical Education:* Private lessons (initially with Robin Jones). *Career:* Television appearances: A13-The Road To Somewhere (documentary on self and two other Essex musicans); Festival of Brighton; Sampled Here and Now, documentary; The Pier;

Pebble Mill; Tours: Japan, 1991, 1993; Europe, 1994; World tours with: Lisa Stansfield, including Rock In Rio, Brazil 1993; Basia; James Taylor Quartet; Producer, various bands, sessions, remixes. *Recordings:* Albums: with Snowboy and the Latin Section: Ritmo Snowbo, 1989; Descarga Mambito, 1992, 1996; Something's Coming, 1994, 1996; Best Of..., 1995; The World Of..., 1995; Mambo Rage, 1998; Singles include: Casa Forte, 1999; Theme tune, Artrageous, BBC2, 1993. *Memberships:* Musicians' Union; PRS; MCPS; BPI. *Leisure interests:* Record collecting; Vintage British comedy; Music Hall. *Current Management:* Alex Hardee, Concorde Artists. *Address:* Concorde House, 101 Shepherds Bush Rd, London W6 7LP, England.

SNOWDEN John Robert; b. 17 Feb. 1968, Darlington, County Durham, England. Musician (jazz specialist guitar, bass). *Musical Education:* Salford College of Technology; Graduate diploma in band musicianship (performance passed with distinction). *Career:* Various jazz combos, Salford College Big Band, 1989; Adaptation (cruiseship MV La Palma), 1990; National Youth Jazz Orchestra, 1991; Summer season, world cruise on board QE2, backing Neil Sedaka; Vic Damone; Iris Wlliams; Doug Cameron; Jimmy Tarbuck; with Rob Charles Orchestra; London Pops Orchestra; One Hundred Years of the Great British Musical, introduced by David Jacobs, recorded by BBC Radio 2; The Sound and Style of James Last, national tour, 1994; Mike James Sound, including a Tribute To Nat King Cole, Birmingham Town Hall, 1994; Summer season and winter season on QE2, backing top artists; John Oliver Sound summer season, 1994; Ray McVay Orchestra, Blackpool Tower Ballroom, 1995; Teaching, Wigan, Bolton Education Authorities, 1994–95; Self-employed guitar/keyboard teacher. *Membership:* Musicians' Union. *Address:* 2 St Margarets Grove, Acklam, Middlesborough, England.

SNYMAN Neil (Jean Corneille); b. 3 Nov. 1956, Bellville, South Africa. Prod.; Engineer. m. 17 Dec. 1977, 1 s., 1 d. *Education:* Higher National Diploma for Technicians, Electrical Engineering. *Musical Education:* Informally trained; Multi-instrumentalist. *Career:* Specialist in Zulu ethnic recordings; Four featured documentaries on activities, all filmed, broadcast on South African television, 1994-. *Recordings:* Recorded Ladysmith Black Mambazo for Rugby World Cup, 1995; For album Anthems: Swing Low; Sosholoza; World In Union. *Honours:* SABC Artes Awards, for traditional music. *Memberships:* ASAMI; SAMRO. *Leisure interests:* Beach; Sea sport; Camping. *Current Management:* Direct.

SOARES João Paulo; b. 24 July 1969, Beira, Mozambique. Singer; Graphic Designer; Writer. *Education:* 12 years, legal education. *Career:* Solo artiste as Johnny, 1990; Lead singer, composer, Selva Urbana, 1994-. *Recordings:* Lovers (Amor Sem Fim), 1991; Island Girl (Rapariga Da Ilha), 1991; My Dreams (Meus Sonhos), 1992; Lime Light (Sonhar Bem Alto), 1993; Street Boys (Putos Da Rua), 1994; Wonderful Tonight (Esta Noire Foi Maravilhosa), 1994; Urban Jungle (Selva Urbana), 1994. *Publications:* World Music (Musica Do Mundo), 1993. *Membership:* SPA (Portuguese Authors Society). *Current Management:* JPP Productions. *Address:* Av Paulo Vi-Lote 60–2-Fte, PO Box 59–2041 Rio Maior, Portugal.

SOARES-PEIXOTO Rogerio; b. 9 May 1954, Rio de Janeiro, Brazil. Musician (Guitar, Percussion); Singer. 2 c. *Career:* Concerts on stage; Radio reports on local stations; Festivals and open-air appearances. *Recordings:* With band, Rogerio Soares-e Sveiro Azul, CDs: Rogerio Soares-e-Saveiro Azul; Sentindo a caricia do vento. *Membership:* GEMA. *Leisure interest:* Football. *Address:* Bromeis str 4a, 34125 Kassel, Germany.

SOENEN Geert; b. 25 April 1963, Wervik, Belgium. Piano Teacher; Conductor. m. Elly Deflo, 8 Oct. 1988. *Education:* Higher Degree for Chamber Music, Conservatory of Gent, Belgium; Orchestral Conducting Degree, Conservatory of Den Haag, The Netherlands. *Career:* Soloist, played on trumpet and piano, classical, popular and chamber music; Conductor, Accademia Amanti Dell'Arte, The Symphony Orchestra of Flanders, The Prague Philharmonic Chamber Orchestra; Conductor of Symphonic Youth and Music Orchestra East of Flanders. *Compositions:* Arrangements for Pitti Polak, Raymond Van Het Groenewoud, for proms with symphony orchestra. *Address:* Mispelbilk 14, 9030 Mariakerke-Gent, Belgium.

SOERENSEN Kim Hougaard; b. 21 May 1956, Haldum, Denmark. Composer; Lyricist; Journalist; Music Theatre Critic. *Education:* Journalism, Danish University, 1981. *Musical Education:* Self-taught, private lessons by Danish composers. *Career:* Keyboard player, numerous Danish pop and rockbands, 1980–90; Composer, lyricist, Danish National Concert musical, The Egtved Chronicle, tour, 1993. *Recording:* The Egtved Chronicle, 1993. *Publications:* Songs From The Egtved Chronicle, 1993. *Honours:* The Cultural Award, 1993; The VAF Foundation Award, 1993. *Memberships:* Danish Jazz, Folk and Rock Composers; Danish Board of Journalists.

SOIRAT Philippe; b. 11 March 1961, Menton, France. Jazz Musician (drums). *Musical Education:* Jazz Academy, Monaco; Centre Musical

Contemporain, Nice. *Career:* Concerts with: J R Monterose; Warren Bernhardt; Barney Wilen; John Stubbelfield; Duke Jordan; Ray Brown; Walter Bishop Jr; Bob Mover; Alain Jean-Marie; Jacky Terrasson; Georges Cables; LaVelle; James Moddy; Lou Donaldson; Horace Parlan; Emmanuel Bex; Jimmy Gourley; Dee Dee Bridgewater; Larry Schneider; Andy Laverne; Enrico Rava; Eric Lelann; Tours: Turkey (Armen Donelian Trio), 1990; France (Lee Konitz Quartet), 1992; Viet Nam, Thailand, Malaysia, Singapore (Laurent de Wilde, Ira Coleman, Eric Barret), 1993; Australia, New Zealand (Laurent de Wilde Quartet), 1995; Portugal (Carlos Barretto Quintet); Canada (Yannick Rieu Quartet); Singapore, Brunei, Poland (Laurent de Wilde Trio), 1995; Africa (Belmondo Quintet), 1996. *Recordings include:* What Is The Color of Love?, Yannick Rieu Quartet; Passione, Barney Wilen Quintet; Alone Together, Georges Cables Trio; Going Up, Carlos Barretto Quintet.

SOLEM Phil; Singer; Songwriter; Musician. *Musical Education:* Self-taught. *Career:* Member, Great Buildings since late 1970s; Member, The Rembrandts, 1991-. *Recordings:* The Tremblers, with Peter Noone, 1980; With Great Buildings: Apart from the Crowd, 1981; Gone, with Dwight Yoakum, 1995; Testimonial Dinner, with XTC, 1995; Compilation, Friends, 1995; Disney's Music from The Park, 1996; Oneman, with Dex Dickerson, 1997; Albums with the Rembrandts: The Rembrandts, 1991; Untitled, 1992; LP, 1995; Poptopia! 80's Power Pop Clasics, 1997; Poptopia! 90's Power Pop Classics, 1997; with Mango Jam: Preserves, 1998; Singles: That's Just The Way It Is Baby; Johnny Have You Seen Her; I'll Be There For You (theme for television series Friends), 1995; This House is not a Home, 1995. *Honours:* Grammy nomination, 1995; ASCAP and BMI Awards, 1995–97; LA Music Award. *Memberships:* ASCAP; SAG. *Current Management:* Under discussion. *Address:* 9744 Wilshire Blvd, Suite 305, Beverly Hills, CA 90212, USA.

SOLIS Marco Antonio; b. Michoacan, Mexico. Vocalist; Songwriter. m. Beatriz, divorced. *Career:* First group, Los Hermanitos Solis, aged 12; Formed Los Bukis, 1970s; Songwriter for singers including ex-wife and Marisela; Wrote for Mexican soap operas Amor en Silencio and El Alma no Tiene Color; Compositions recorded by singers including: Lucero; Enrique Iglesias; Solo career, 1995-. *Recordings:* Albums include: En Pleno Vuelo, 1996; Marco, 1997; Romantico Instrumental, Trozos De Mi Alma, 1999; Mas De Mi Alma, En Concierto Vol. 1, 2001. *Honour:* Pride of SESAC award, 2000. *Internet:* www.marcomusic.com.

SOLO Sal; b. Hatfield, England. Singer; Songwriter; Broadcaster. *Career:* Lead singer, Classix Nouveaux, 1979–85; Major tours, numerous hit singles in approximately 30 countries; Lead Singer, Rockets, Italy, 1984–92; Solo career, 1984–; Host, radio shows, 1988-. *Recordings:* Guilty, Night People, 1981; Is It a Dream, La Verité, 1982; Secret, Imperception, Under The Sun, 1983; San Damiano, Heart and Soul, 1985; Look At Christ, 1991; Another Future, 1992; Through Ancient Eyes, 1994; Producer: Living in Oblivion: Living in Oblivion Vol. 1, 1993; Hardest Hits Vol. 4, 1994; Our Friends Electric, Our Friends Electric, 1996. *Publications:* For God's Sake, 1993. *Honours:* Various Gold and Silver discs; CACLB Radio Award, 1990. *Membership:* Christian Music Asscn. *Leisure interest:* Work for Christian Church. *Current Management:* Falcon Stuart, 59 Moore Park Rd, London SW6 2HH, England.

SOMACH Denny; b. 30 Sept. 1952, Allentown, Pennsylvania, USA. Prod.; Record Co Exec. m. Kathy Levinsky Somach, 25 May 1995, 2 s., 1 d. *Education:* BA, Moravian College. *Career:* Radio announcer, Station WSAN, Allentown, 1971–75; Program director, 1975; Announcer, music director, Station WYSP-FM, Philadelphia, 1975–81; Record producer; Television producer: Hot Spots; USA Network, 1982–84; Rock 'n' Roll Show, CBS-TV, 1982; John Debella Show, 1990; Radio producer, Psychedelic Snack, 1985–; Ticket To Ride, 1985–; Legends of Rock, 1985–; Don Kirshner's History of Rock 'n' Roll, 1990; Producer, president, Denny Somach Productions, 1979–; President, Cinema Records, 1986–; President, founder, Musicom International, 1992. *Recordings:* Albums produced for: Dave Mason, 1987; Patrick Moraz, 1987; Johnny Winter, 1988; Eric Johnson, 1990; Barbara Mandrell, It Works for Me, 1997; Alan Parsons, Definitive Collection, 1997. *Publications:* Ticket To Ride, 1989. *Honours:* Grammy, Best Rock Instrumentalist, Eric Johnson, Cliffs of Dover. *Membership:* NARAS. *Leisure interests:* Travel; Music; Art. *Address:* 812 W Darby Rd, Havertown, PA 19083, USA.

SOMERS Lynn Marie; b. 15 April 1961, Jeanette, Pennsylvania, USA. Contemporary Christian Vocalist; Puppeteer. m. Frederick A Somers, 25 May 1984, 1 d. *Education:* BA, Psychology, Asbury College, 1983; 2 Masters degrees from United Seminary, Dayton, Ohio, 1986, 1988. *Musical Education:* Private vocal instruction, High School, college, seminary; Piano, guitar lessons as child, youth; MA, Theological Studies, Vocal performance emphasis. *Career:* Television appearance, Crosslink (United Theological Seminary), 1985; Radio interviews: Canada, 1989; WAMN, Princeton, West Virginia, 1995, Off the Cuff show on WSNJ, Bridgeton, New Jersey, 1996; Programmes in churches, prisons, community and retirement homes; TV appearances: 60 Live Show with WBPH,

Bethlehem, Pennsylvania, 1997; Edited version of Genesis video aired on WGCB, Red Lion, Pennsylvania and ACTV, Reading, Pennsylvania, 1997; Various tours through 28 states over 13 years. *Recordings:* We Are The Reason, 1986; God's House/Our House, 1992; The Gift of a Child, 1997. *Publications:* Video: Bible Stories From Genesis, for children; Puppets and Music, 1992; Dear Jesus, I wanna talk to you... My Home is Broken, story colouring book, 1996; Lynn Somers and Friends Character Coloring Book, 1996; Hand of the Master, puppet scriptbook, 1996; Various articles in publications, including Quarter Notes. *Honours:* Gospel Music Trailblazer Nomination, Airplay International, 1995. *Memberships:* Gospel Music Asscn; Fellowship of Christian Puppeteers; Christian Educators Fellowship. *Leisure interests:* Puppetry; Creative writing; Stories and scripts; Swimming; Bible study; Theatre. *Current Management:* Hand of The Master Ministries Inc (own non-profit ministry). *Address:* Lynn Somers and Friends, 103 Glen Court, Ephrata, PA 17522, USA.

SOMERVILLE Jimmy; b. 22 June 1961, Glasgow, Scotland. Singer; Songwriter. *Career:* Founder member, Bronski Beat, 1984–85; Formed The Communards, with Richard Coles, 1985–89; Tours include: UK Wedge tour, with Paul Weller and Billy Bragg, 1986; European tour, 1986; Solo artiste, 1989–; Concerts include: Red Hot and Dance AIDS benefit concert, 1991. *Recordings:* Albums with Bronski Beat: The Age of Consent, 1984; Hundreds and Thousands, 1985; with the Communards: Communards, 1986; Red, 1987; Solo albums: Read My Lips, 1990; The Singles Collection, 1984–90, 1991; Dare To Love, 1995; Manage the Damage, 1999; Hit singles: with Bronski Beat: Smalltown Boy, 1984; Why?, 1984; I Feel Love, 1985; with the Communards: You Are My World, 1985; Disenchanted, 1986; Don't Leave Me This Way, (No. 1, UK), 1986; So Cold The Night, 1986; Tomorrow, 1987; Never Can Say Goodbye, 1987; For a Friend, 1988; There's More To Love, 1988; Solo singles: Comment Te Dire Adieu, 1989; You Make Me Feel, 1990; Read My Lips, 1990; To Love Somebody, 1990; Run From Love, 1991; Hurts So Good, 1995; Heartbeat, 1995; By Your Side, 1995; Safe, 1997; Dark Sky, 1997; Something to Live For, 1999; Other recordings include: Track on Red Hot + Blue, AIDS benefit compilation, 1990; Gimme Shelter, Voice of The Beehive (for Putting Our House In Order charity), 1993. *Current Management:* Solar Management, 42–48 Charlbert St, London NW8 7BU, England.

SONDHEIM Stephen Joshua; b. 22 March 1930, New York, New York, USA. Composer; Lyricist. *Education:* BA, Williams College, 1950. *Compositions:* Incidental Music: The Girls of Summer, 1956; Invitation to a March, 1961; Twigs, 1971; Lyrics: West Side Story, 1957; Gypsy, 1959; Do I Hear a Waltz?, 1965; Candide, (additional lyrics) 1973; Music and Lyrics: A Funny Thing Happened on the Way to the Forum, 1962; Anyone Can Whistle, 1964; Evening Primrose, 1966; Company, 1970; Follies, 1971; A Little Night Music, 1973; The Frogs, 1974; Pacific Overtures, 1976; Sweeney Todd, 1979; Merrily We Roll Along, 1981, 1997; Sunday in the Park With George, 1984; Into the Woods, 1987; Assassins, 1991; Passion, 1994; Anthologies: Side by Side by Sondheim, 1976; Marry Me a Little, 1980; You're Gonna Love Tomorrow, 1983; Putting It Together, 1992; Film: Stravinsky, 1974; Reds, 1981; Dick Tracy, 1990. *Memberships:* President, Dramatists Guild, 1973–81; American Academy and Institute of Arts and Letters. *Address:* c/o Sarah Douglas, 393 W 49th St, New York, NY 10019, USA.

SONIQUE (Sonia Clarke); b. 21 June 1965, London. Vocalist; Prod.; DJ. *Career:* Vocalist with S-Express; Started as a DJ in the '90s, singing over the records; Resident DJ for Manumission in Ibiza; Solo recording career 1998-. *Recordings:* Albums: Hear My Cry, 2000; Serious Sounds of Sonique (Mixed multi-artist compilation), 2000; Singles: I Put A Spell On You, 1998; It Feels So Good, 1998; Sky, 2000. *Honours:* Brit Award, Best British Female Artist, 2001. *Membership:* MCPS/PRS. *Address:* c/o Serious Records Ltd, First Floor, Tudor House, Llanvanol Rd, Finchley Rd, London, NW2 2AQ, England.

SONNEBORN Daniel Atesh; b. 31 Oct. 1949, Illinois, USA. Composer; Prod.; Musician; Musical Dir. m. Patrizia Pallaro, 2 s. *Education:* BA, 1982, MA, 1984, University of California; PhD, UCLA, 1995. *Career:* Consultant, Educator, 1975; Project Director, Drumming at the Edge of Magic, 1988–92; Co Producer, Remembrance, 1991; Theatre, Opera, Film Composer, US and Europe, 1970–; Executive Co Producer, Available Sound, 1995. *Recordings:* Jumping Over The Fence: XA:A Viet Nam Primer; Delta Prime. *Publications:* Co Author, Planet Drum; Sufi Music. *Honours:* Best Show of the Year, 1973; La Drama Critics Circle, 1971, 1972; International Herald Tribune; Department of Music Fellowship, 1984, 1985; Presidents Fellowship. *Memberships:* Society for Ethnomusicology; International Council for Traditional Music. *Address:* 2386 I St, Petaluma, CA 94952, USA.

SORRELL Jonathan Lindsay; b. 19 Oct. 1961, Salisbury, Wiltshire, England. Composer; Record Prod.; Musician (keyboards); Programmer. m. Miriam Grech, 24 June 1994. *Musical Education:* Piano Diploma, 1976; A Level Music, 1978; BMus Degree, 1984. *Career:* Chorister, St Paul's

Cathedral, 1970–75; Keyboard player for Trevor Horn, 1984–85; Keyboard player, arranger for David Dundas, 1988–95; Freelance session musician, 1985–95; Composer, television and film commercials, 1986–95. *Compositions:* Chart Show theme, ITV; You Bet theme, LWT; Survival logo, Anglia; Star Test, CH4; Starchamber Titles; Commercials for: American Airlines; Commerical Union; BMW Cars. *Recordings:* Albums with artistes including: Frankie Goes To Hollywood; Tears For Fears; Def Leppard; Film music: Little Shop of Horrors; The Bear; Lord of The Flies; Music Box; Freddie As F.R.O.T.; Television music: ITV, LWT, CH4 television logos; BBC World News; Dark City; Sleepers; White Goods. *Memberships:* PRS; BASCA. *Leisure interests:* Tennis; Cooking; Films. *Current Management:* Jeff Wayne Music Ltd. *Address:* The Cottage, 26 High St, Prestwood, Nr Great Missenden, Bucks HP16 9ED, England.

SOSSIN Stephen Mark; b. 28 Sept. 1956, Hartford, Connecticut, USA. Music Prod.; Musician (guitar, bass, keyboards, violin). *Education:* Business, Computers, Manchester College. *Musical Education:* Heil/ Sound Engineering; Studied with Al DiMeola and Mike Ruff; Pursuing advanced degree; Special Major Programme, California University, 1997. *Career:* Early performing career with artists including: Mike Ruff (keyboards, songwriter, Grammy nomination), 1986; Tom Chapin (saxophone, horns), 1971–76; Established songwriter in original music scene, New England, 1975–; Founder, Vizion productions studio, world class digital recording facility, photo, video services; Began artist development programme, 1983–; Works mainly with emerging artist, custom writing for individual's voice; Founder-Producer, New Vizion Studios. *Composition:* Thats Why I Ran, Dianne Glynn, 1996. *Recordings:* with Bonnie Lynn: Embrace of My Heart, 1993; with Dianne Glynn: I Can't Find The Words, 1995; Thats Why I Ran, 1996; Take My Hand, 1996. *Publications:* Listed in Mixmaster Directory; Northeast Mix Plus; Recording Industry Sourcebook; Instage; Songwriters Market. *Honours:* Knight Chevalier Medal; National Patriotism Medal; AFP; Capitol Records Promotional Awards. *Memberships:* Independent Producer's Guild; NE; United States Naval Institute. *Leisure interests:* Donates time to youth groups; Outdoor hiking; Reading. *Current Management:* John Carpino; Agent: Caroline Hayes.

SOUQUES Laurent; b. 27 Oct. 1963, Paris, France. Musician (double bass); Composer. *Musical Education:* Conservatoire National Supérieur de Musiques et de Dance, Paris. *Career:* Jazz Festival, Franche Comté, 1986, 1987, 1989; Jazz Festival Suedine Bleue (Dijon), 1986; Jazz Festival Aiguillon, 1990; Jazz clubs in Paris, 1991–95; Jazz Festival Banlieue Bleue, with G Russell, Living Time Orchestra, 1993; Banlieue Bleue, G Russell, Cité de la Musique, 1995; JUC Halle That Jazz, Paris, 1995. *Compositions:* Film music; Syndrome de l'Espion – Zooleil, N Joyeux; Paris des Freres Tenebres, Muriel Mazieres. *Recordings:* Just Back From New Orleans, 1989; G Russell for Radio France, 1993, 1995; Fire Beat, Ralph Thomas Sextet, 1996; Un Charivari Entre Chien Et Loup Skymninsgslandet, 1998. *Leisure interests:* Sailing; Swimming. *Address:* 10 rue Saint Jean, 75017 Paris, France. *E-mail:* loso@free.fr.

SOUSA (Duane) 'Beans'; b. 22 July 1951. Musician (bass); Vocalist. m. Barbara Runnion, 8 April 1989, 1 s. *Career:* Bassist for major country and rock artists: Lacy J Dalton; Phoebe Snow; Larry Hosford; Studio work for major recording companies including CBS, MCA, Capitol and Shelter Records. *Recordings include:* Dream Baby, Lacy J Dalton; Solo album: You Don't Know. *Membership:* AFofM. *Leisure interests:* Golf; Fishing; Camping. *Address:* 906 30th Ave, Santa Cruz, CA 95062, USA.

SOUTH Joe, (Joe Souter); b. 28 Feb. 1940, Atlanta, Georgia, USA. Musician (guitar); Singer; Songwriter. *Career:* Session guitarist, Nashville, 1960s; Recording sessions include: Aretha Franklin; Wilson Pickett; Marty Robbins; Eddy Arnold; Bob Dylan; Simon and Garfunkel; Solo artiste, 1962-. *Compositions include:* Games People Play, Billy Joe Royal and Boots Randolph; Untie Me, The Tams; Down In The Boondocks, Billy Joe Royal; I Knew You When, Billy Joe Royal; These Are Not My People, Freddy Weller; Birds of a Feather, Paul Revere and The Raiders; Hush, Deep Purple. *Recordings:* Albums include: Introspect, 1968; Don't It Make You Want To Go Home, 1969; Walkin' Shoes, 1970; So The Seeds Are Growing, 1971; Midnight Rainbows, 1975; Look Inside, 1976; Other recordings include: Blonde On Blonde, Bob Dylan, 1966; Sound of Silence, Simon and Garfunkel, 1966; Aretha Arrives, Aretha Franklin, 1967; Lady Soul, Aretha Franklin, 1968; Dan Baird, Buffalo Nickel, 1996; Jazz Singers, 1919–94, 1998; Rock Classics of the 60s, 1998.

SPACEY-FOOTE Gary Martin; b. 15 Dec. 1961, Weybridge, Surrey, England. Musician (saxophone, flute, percussion, drums). m. Carrie Spacey-Foote, 17 Aug. 1991. *Musical Education:* Self-taught saxophone and flute; Percussion, self-taught, with some tutorage with Danny Cummings. *Career:* Two world tours, Joan Armatrading; Television appearances with Bee Gees; Tom Jones; Recording, touring, with Nightrains; The Hipjoints; Maroon Town; House of Rhythm; Jamiroquai; Kiss of Life; Espiritu; Lionel Moyst. *Recordings:* with The Hipjoints: Rock Hopper; Chillin'; with Lionel Moyst Sextet: Chillin; Contributions to:

Martini Grooves, 1998; Duboniks, On the Vibe, 1998; Chris Bangs, Dazzle, 1999. *Memberships:* Musicans' Union; PRS. *Leisure interests:* Keeping fit; Comedy; Black and white British films; Reading. *Current Management:* c/o Carrie Spacey-Foote, 34 Hampden Rd, Kingston on Thames, Surrey KT1 3HG, England.

SPANG-HANSSEN Simon Cato; b. 13 April 1955, Hellerup, Denmark. Musician (saxophonist); Composer. m. Mariane Bitran, 23 Jan. 1987, 1 s. *Musical Education:* Mainly self-taught. *Career:* Tours with: John Tchicai and Strange Brothers, Scandinavia, Germany, Italy; Andy Emler's Mega-Octet, Europe; French National Jazz Orchestra, 1991–94, Europe; Leader of Quartet, Muluankh; Duo with Denis Badault, France, Denmark, Central Africa. *Recordings:* Darktown Highlights; Ten By Two; Because Forever; Mardi Gras, Chez Toi; Instant Blue, 1998; Wondering, 1999; Identified, 1999. *Honours:* Ben Webster Prize, 1978. *Membership:* Union de Musicians de Jazz (Paris). *Leisure interests:* Travel; Discovery; Food; History; Painting; Swimming. *Current Management:* Blue Line Productions, Mr Bourgaut, Mr Vautrot. *Address:* 5 rue Leon Giraud, 75019 Paris, France.

SPARROW Edwin Harold James; b. 28 Jan. 1943, Harrogate, Yorkshire, England. Musician (drums, timpani, percussion, Latin percussion). *Musical Education:* Piano with Miss Evelyn Gunnar; ARCM; LTCL; LLCM; Timpani with Lewis Pocock, Trinity College. *Career:* Many years in France, worked with top light entertainment artistes including: Johnny Hallyday; Sylvie Vartan; Charles Aznavour; Appeared in film Les Jeunes Loups, directed by Marcel Carné; Appeared with Kevin Ayers; Mike Oldfield; Nico and others connected with The Velvet Underground; Gerry Rafferty, 1970s; Closely connected with Ballet Rambert; London Contemporary Dance Theatre; Contemporary Dance and Therapy in UK; Featured on: June The 1st, 1974; Bannamour, Kevin Ayres. *Leisure interest:* Photography (pictures published in Guitar Magazine, and on album cover to Requiem For a Hick, Adrian Legg). *Address:* Harrogate, North Yorkshire, England.

SPARROW Willy; b. 29 Aug. 1960, Buenos Aires, Argentina. Musician. *Education:* Walter Malosseti Jazz School; Berklee School. *Career:* Chacarita Festival; DSPS Festival; Other Festivals in Madrid, Barcelonia, Hamburg, Lyon, Amsterdam, Brighton. *Recordings:* Magic Band; The Impossibles; Missing Band; Stalking; Cobble Stones; Jazz Allcovers; Toko; Niks; Horizon Meeting. *Memberships:* Argentinians Musicians Union; Dutch Musicians Union. *Leisure interests:* Computers; Cycling; Travel; Football. *Current Management:* Siza Records. *Address:* Makassarstraat 38–1, Amsterdam, Netherlands.

SPEAKE Martin John; b. 3 April 1958, Barnet, Hertfordshire, England. Musician (alto saxophone); Jazz Educator; Composer. m. Rachel Cutler, 6 Jan. 1990, 1 d. *Musical Education:* A Level Music; Classical saxophone, Trinity College of Music, LTCL, FTCL diplomas. *Career:* Tours of West Africa, Latin America, Europe, with saxophone quartet Itchy Fingers; Tours of Indonesia, Philippines, Croatia, UK, with 7-piece Fever Pitch, own quartet, and duo with guitarist Phil Lee; Various radio and television appearances. *Recordings:* Albums: with Itchy Fingers: Quark; Teranga; In Our Time, Martin Speake Group; Entertainment USA, Billy Jenkins; Midnight Sun, Flora Purim and Airto Moreira. *Honours:* Schlitz Young Jazz Musicians Winner, with Itchy Fingers, 1986. *Membership:* Musicians' Union. *Leisure interest:* Tai Chi. *Address:* 1 Mawson House, Baldwins Gardens, London EC1N 7SD, England.

SPEARE Paul; b. 10 Dec. 1955, Romford, Essex, England. Musician (saxophone, flute); Arranger; Prod.; Lecturer. m. Paula Davies, 27 July 1985, 1 d. *Musical Education:* London College of Music; Birmingham Polytechnic. *Career:* Member, Dexy's Midnight Runners, 1980–82; Q-Tips British tour, 1982; Elvis Costello, US, UK, and European tours, 1983; Manager, Expresso Bongo Studios, Tamworth, 1985–94; Leader, Expresso Bongo Orchestra, 1988–94; Lecturer, Popular Music, Lewisham College, London, 1995-. *Recordings:* Singles: Come On Eileen, Too-Rye-Ay, Dexy's Midnight Runners, 1982; Punch The Clock, Elvis Costello, 1983; Free Nelson Mandela, Special AKA, 1984; Keep Moving, Madness, 1984; Hold Back The Night, KWS/The Tramps, 1992; Nick Lowe and his Cowboy Outfit, 1984; Terminal Power Company, Run Silent, Run Deep, 1992. *Membership:* Musicians' Union. *Current Management:* Mr R Speare. *Address:* 314 Upminster Rd N, Rainham, Essex RM13 9RY, England.

SPEARRITT Hannah Louise; b. 1 April 1981, Great Yarmouth, UK. Vocalist; Actor. *Education:* Joined National Youth Music Theatre. *Career:* Moved to London aged 16 to appear in West End production of Bugsy Malone; Various TV acting work including The Cater Street Hangman prior to joining S Club 7; Group quickly achieved international success following sales of TV series Miami 7 (1999), LA 7 (2000) and Hollywood 7 (2001) featuring the band's music to nearly 100 countries; Also made nature TV series S Club 7 Go Wild (2000) and various TV specials; First British tour with S Club 7, 2001. *Recordings:* Albums: S Club, 1999; 7, 2000; Sunshine, 2001; Singles: Bring It All Back, 1999; S Club Party, 1999; Two In A Million/You're My Number One, 1999; Reach, 2000; Natural,

2000; Never Had A Dream Come True, 2000; Don't Stop Movin', 2001; Have You Ever, 2001. *Honours:* Brit Award, Best British Newcomer, 2000. *Current Management:* 19 Management, Unit 32, Ransomes Dock, 35–37 Parkgate Rd, London, SW11 4NP, England.

SPEARS Billie Jo; b. 14 Jan. 1937, Beaumont, Texas, USA. Country Singer. *Career:* Country singer, 1952–; Regular recording artiste, 1964–; Television includes: Louisiana Hayride; Leader, own band, Owlkatraz. *Recordings:* Hits include: Blanket On The Ground; Mr Walker, It's All Over; What I've Got In Mind; Sing Me An Old-Fashioned Song; Misty Blue; I Will Survive; Numerous albums include: The Voice of Billie Jo Spears, 1968; Mr Walker It's All Over, 1969; Miss Sincerity, 1969; With Love, 1970; Country Girl, 1970; Just Singin', 1972; Blanket On The Ground, 1974; Billie Jo, 1975; What I've Got In Mind, 1976; By Request (with Del Reeves), 1976; If You Want Me, 1977; Everytime I Sing a Love Song, 1977; Lonely Hearts Club, 1978; Love Ain't Gonna Wait For Us, 1978; I Will Survive, 1979; Standing Tall, 1980; Special Songs, 1981; Del and Billie Jo (with Del Reeves), 1982; BJ – Billie Jo Spears Today, 1983; We Just Came Apart At The Dreams, 1984; Unmistakeably, 1992; with Guy Clark: Craftsmen, 1995. *Address:* c/o Joe Taylor Artist Agency, 2802 Columbine Pl., Nashville, TN 37204, USA.

SPEARS Britney (Jeau); b. 2 Dec. 1981, Kentwood, Louisiana, USA. Singer. *Recordings:* Singles: Baby One More Time (No. 1, UK and USA), 1999; Sometimes, 1999; (You Drive Me) Crazy, 1999; Born To Make You Happy (No. 1, UK), 2000; From The Bottom Of My Broken Heart, 2000; Oops! I Did It Again (No. 1, UK), 2000; Lucky, 2000; Stronger, 2000; Don't Let Me Be The Last To Know, 2001; I'm A Slave For You, 2001; Overprotected, 2002; I'm Not A Girl Not Yet A Woman, 2002; Albums: Baby One More Time, 1999; Oops! I Did It Again, 2000; Britney, 2001. *Honours:* Several MTV Video Music Awards, 1999; Grammy Award Nomination, New Artist; Female Pop Vocal Performance, 2000. *Address:* The Official Britney Spears International Fan Club, CS 9712, Bellingham, WA 98227, USA. *Internet:* britneyspears.com.

SPECTOR Phil (Harvey Phillip); b. 26 Dec. 1940, Bronx, New York, USA. Record Prod.; Composer; Musician. m. Ronnie Spector (divorced). *Career:* Member, The Teddy Bears; The Spectors Three; Formed Philles Records, 1961–66; Produced albums for Beatles' Apple label; Formed Phil Spector International. *Compositions:* Co-writer, with Ben E King, Spanish Harlem; Young Boy Blues. *Recordings:* As producer for artists including: LaVern Baker; Ruth Brown; Billy Storm; Twist and Shout, The Top Notes; Corrina Corrina, Ray Petersen, 1960; Pretty Little Angel Eyes, Curtis Lee; I Love How You Love Me, Paris Sisters; Work with the Crystals and the Ronettes includes: He's a Rebel, 1962; Then He Kissed Me, 1963; Be My Baby, 1963; Baby I Love You, 1963; River Deep Mountain High, 1966; Black Pearl, Sonny Charles and The Checkmates; Albums by: John Lennon; The Plastic Ono Band; Imagine; Sometime In New York City; George Harrison: All Things Must Pass; Concert For Bangladesh; Leonard Cohen: Death of a Ladies Man, 1977; Ramones: End of The Century, 1980; Compilations: A Christmas Gift To You, 1963; Phil Spector Wall of Sound, Vol. 1: The Ronettes, 1975; Vol. 2: Bob B Soxx and The Blue Jeans, 1975; Vol. 3: The Crystals, 1975; Vol. 4: Yesterday's Hits Today, 1976; Vol. 5: Rare Masters, 1976; Vol. 6: Rare Masters, Vol. 2, 1976; The Phil Spector Story, 1976; Echoes of The Sixties, 1977; Phil Spector 1974–79, 1979; Wall of Sound, 1981; The Early Productions, 1958–61; Twist and Shout: Twelve Atlantic Tracks Produced By Phil Spector, 1989; John Lennon, Anthology, 1998; All Time Greatest Movie Songs, 1998; Gene Pitney, All-Time Greatest Hits, 1999; Ramones, Hey! Ho! Let's Go: The Anthology, 1999.

SPECTOR Ronnie, (Veronica Bennett Spector Greenfield); b. 10 Aug. 1943, New York, USA. Singer. m. (1) Harvey Phillip (Phil) Spector, (2) Jonathan Greenfield, 16 Jan. 1982, 5 c. *Career:* Dancer, New York, 1962–63; Lead singer, choreographer, dancer, The Ronettes (originally Ronnie and The Relatives), 1962–67; Appearances include: Group Scene '64 Tour, support to The Rolling Stones, 1964; Solo artiste, 1969–; Writer, 1988–90. *Recordings:* Albums: with the Ronettes: Presenting The Fabulous Ronettes, 1965; Solo albums: Siren, 1981; Unfinished Business, 1987; Dangerous, 1996; Hit singles: with The Ronettes: Be My Baby, 1963; Baby I Love You, 1964; The Best Part of Breaking Up, 1964; Do I Love You, 1964; Walking In The Rain, 1964; She Talks to Rainbows, 1999; Contributor, A Christmas Gift For You compilation album, 1963. *Publications:* Be My Baby (autobiography), with Vince Waldron, 1990. *Honours:* Gee-Gee Awards, 16 Magazine, 1963, 1964; Inducted into New York Music Hall of Fame, 1982; Gold discs, 1963–65; Music Awards Nominations, 1987, 1988; Grammy Award, Walking In The Rain, 1964; Grammy Nomination, 1986. *Current Management:* GreenSpec Properties, Suite 233, 39B Mill Plain Rd, Danbury, CT 06811, USA.

SPEDDING Paul Brian; b. 28 Sept. 1945, Birmingham, England. Musician (Drums). *Career:* Various Jazz Festivals Throught UK and Europe; Stage, Royal Festival Hall with Fats Domino Band; Capital Radio Jazz Festival; Worked with Olympia Brass Band, Tuxedo BB. *Recordings:* The John Handy Memorial; Dan Pawson's Buddies. *Honours:*

Musical Prize Breda, Holland. *Membership:* Musicians Union. *Leisure interest:* Steam Railways. *Address:* 34 Old Tannery Court, Severnside South, Bewdley, Worcestershire DY12 2DS.

SPEECH (Todd Thomas); b. 1968, Milwaukee, Wisconsin, USA. Singer; Lyricist. *Education:* Art Institute of Atlanta. *Career:* Originally kmown as DJ Peech; Formed gangsta rap act DLR (Disciples of a Lyrical Rebellion), renamed Secret Society; Evolved into hip-hop act Arrested Development, 1988–; Performances include: MTV Drops The Ball '93, 1992; MTV Unplugged, 1992; Lollapalooza '93 US Tour, 1993. *Recordings:* Singles include: Tennessee, 1992; People Everyday, 1992; Revolution (used in film soundtrack Malcolm X), 1993; Mr Wendal, 1993; Albums: 3 Years, 5 Months and 2 Days In The Life Of. . ., 1993; Unplugged, 1993; Hoopla, 1999; Producer, Dropping H20 On The Fiber, Gumbo, 1993. *Honours include:* Grammy Awards: Best New Artist, Best Rap Group, 1993; Soul Train Award, Best Rap Album, 1993; 7 Atlanta Music Awards, 1993. *Current Management:* Entertainment Resources International Inc, 9380 SW 72nd St, #B-220, Miami, FL 33173, USA.

SPEIDEL Paul; b. 15 Feb. 1965, Kenmare, North Dakota, USA. Jazz and Blues Musician (guitar); High School Jazz Programme Dir. m. Adlin Quiles, 1 June 1991. *Education:* BA, Augustana College, 1986. *Musical Education:* Master of Music, University of Northern Colorado, 1990. *Career:* Freelance guitarist, bassist in Chicago, Denver, Boston; Vocal performances with Grammy nominated University of Northern Colorado Vocal Jazz I; Performances with Patti Page; Gerry Beaudoin; Jeff Benedict; Terry Cooke; Ted Pilzecker; Numerous musical shows; 3 tours, Latin and Central America with the Latin Continental Singers as Instrumental Director; Currently guitarist with the Monique Weiss Quartet; Guiarist, vocalist with the Paul Speidel Band. *Publications:* CD reviewer in bi-monthly No Name Jazz News. *Honours:* Illinois State Scholar, Colorado National Scholar. *Memberships:* International Asscn of Jazz Educators; Boston Jazz Society; Boston Blues Society; Gospel Music Asscn; Music Educators National Conference. *Leisure interest:* Reading classic and contemporary poetry and fiction. *Current Management:* PSB Management. *Address:* 130 Academy Ave, Providence, RI 02908, USA.

SPEIRS Fraser; b. 4 Oct. 1949, Glasgow, Scotland. Singer; Musician (harmonica). *Education:* Medical Illustrator, University of Glasgow. *Career:* Concert appearances with: Love and Money; Tam White; Carla Laula Band; Rab Noakes; Radio credits: Radio Clyde; Radio 2 Nightride, with David Pringle Band; Television credits: All Kinds of Country, STV. *Recordings:* Album with: Del Amitri; Fish; The Soup Dragons; Carol Kidd; Lloyd Cole and The Commotions; Love and Money; Carol Laula; Humpff Family; King Ilash; Kindness of Strangers; Theme tune to Your Cheatin' Heart. *Membership:* Musicians' Union. *Leisure interests:* Hockey; Skiing; Travel. *Address:* 53 Marywood Sq., Glasgow G41 2BN, Scotland.

SPENCER John B; b. 5 June 1944, West London, England. Singer; Musician (guitar); Bandleader; Record Prod.; Novelist. m. Lou, 26 Feb. 1966, 3 s. *Career:* Pubs, clubs, concert halls, festivals, throughout Europe, 1976–; Featured, interviewed, CH4 documentary: Living With The Blues, 1990; Radio broadcasts: Andy Kershaw Show, Radio 1, several occasions; Member: John Spencer's Louts; Spencer's Alternative; John B Spencer Band; Parlour Games; The Goods; Also worked with: Martin Simpson's Flash Company; Home Service; Toured with Fairport Convention. *Compositions:* One More Whiskey, Will This House Be Blessed, Forgotten The Blues, covered and recorded by many folk artists; Cruisin' On a Saturday Night, hit in Sweden for Jerry Williams; Outside The Wall and Bluebird recorded by Norma Waterson, 1998–99; Stockholm Sick Blues, The YoYos, 2000. *Recordings:* The Last LP, 1978; Out With a Bang, 1986; Break and Entry, 1989; Parlour Games, 1990; Sunday Best, 1992; Left Hand of Love, 1998; Appeared on: True Dare Or Promise, 1988; Blues Brittanica, 1993; The Wish and The Way, 1993. *Publications:* Novels: The Electronic Meat Market, 1975; A Case For Charley, 1984; Charley Gets The Picture, 1985; Quake City, 1995; Perhaps She'll Die, 1997; Tooth and Nail, 1998; Stitch!, 1999; Grief!, 2001. *Memberships:* Musicians' Union; PRS; MCPS. *Leisure interests:* Crime fiction; Vegetable growing. *Current Management:* Jim Driver. *Address:* PO Box 4215, London SE23 2QD, England.

SPENCER Jon; b. 1966, Hanover, New Hampshire, USA. Musician (guitar). m. Cristina Martinez. *Career:* Member, Boss Hog and Pussy Galore; Founder Member, Jon Spencer Blues Explosion. *Recordings:* Singles: The Sound of the Future is Here Today, 1992; Shirt-jac, 1992; Son of Sam, 1992; Big Yule Log Boogie, 1992; Train 3, 1993; Bellbottoms, 1995; Get With It, 1996; 2 Kindsa Love, 1996; Wail, 1997; Rocketship, 1997; Talk About the Blues, 1998; Albums: The Jon Spencer Blues Explosion, 1992; Crypt-Style, 1992; Extra Width, 1993; Mo' Width, 1994; Orange, 1994; Experimental Remixes, 1995; Now I Got Worry, 1996; Controversial Negro, 1997; Rocketship, 1997; Acme, 1998; With Boss Hog: Girl Positive EP, 1993; Albums: Drinkin', Lechin' and Lyin', 1989; Cold Hands, 1990; Boss Hog, 1995.

SPIDER JOHNSON (Etienne); b. 5 Oct. 1963, London, England. Musician (drums, bass, guitar); Vocalist. 1 d. *Musical Education:* Disc cutting course with LTS, Denmark Street, London; Electronics at Hackney College. *Career:* with Potato 5: World tour, 1989; Extensive television coverage; with The Deltones: European tour, 1991; with Nutty Boys (Madness): Crunch European tour, 1991; British tour, 1992; with Humble Souls: European tour and television coverage, 1993–94; Humble Souls and Night Trains World tour, 1994. *Recordings:* Do The Jerk, Potato 5, 1989; Five Alive, Potato 5, 1990; Silent River, Deltones, 1991; Crunch, Nutty Boys, 1991; Gone He's Gone, Stop Playing Around, Wendy Walker, 1991; Thoughts and Sound Paintings, 1993–94; Sleazeball, Night Trains, 1994. *Honours:* BPI International Reggae Award, 1992; Best Newcomer, for Wendy Walker. *Memberships:* MCPS; PRS. *Leisure interests:* Sports; Films; Concerts; Travel; Reading. *Current Management:* Concorde International. *Address:* Concorde House, Shepherds Bush Rd, London W12, England.

SPILLANE Davy; b. 1959, Dublin, Ireland. Musician (uillean pipes, whistle). *Career:* Began playing pipes, aged 13; Founder member of Moving Hearts; Released several solo albums on Tara; Formed the Davy Spillane Band; Signed to Sony, 1993; Launched label, Burrenstone Records, 2000; Soloist in Riverdance; Currently an instrument maker; Collaborations: Elvis Costello; Bryan Adams; Kate Bush; Van Morrison; Tim Finn; Baba Maal; Afro Celt Sound System; Starred in film Traveller; Featured on film soundtracks: Lamb; Wuthering Heights; Eat the Peach; Rob Roy; Michael Collins. *Recordings:* Out of The Air (featuring Rory Gallagher), Atlantic Bridge, 1988; The Storm (with Moving Hearts), 1989; Shadow Hunter, 1990; Pipedreams, A Place Among The Stones, 1994; Sea of Dreams, 1998. *Honours:* Grammy Award, Best New Age Album, Celtic Solstice, Paul Winter and Friends, 2000. *Internet:* www.davyspillane.com.

SPILLANE John; b. 1961, Cork, Ireland. Vocalist; Songwriter. *Career:* Former member of traditional band Nomos; Songs recorded by artists including: Sinead Lohan; Karen Casey; Christy Moore; Has toured France, Italy, Ireland and the US. *Recordings:* with Nomos: I Won't Be Afraid Anymore, 1995; Set You Free, 1997; solo: The Wells of The World, 1997; Will We Be Brilliant Or What?, 2002. *Honours:* Realta Irish song contest, winner (with Louis de Paor), 2001. *Current Management:* Verge Management, Henry A Crosbie Business Centre, Ossory Rd, Dublin 1, Republic of Ireland. *Internet:* www.johnspillane.ie.

SPINELLI Philip Antony; b. 30 March 1950, Newcastle-upon-Tyne, England. Musician (drums, keyboards); Vocalist. m. Biliana Mancheva, 19 Oct. 1994, 1 s. *Musical Education:* Berklee College, Boston, USA; Masterclass with Bob Armstrong, PIT, London. *Career:* Founder member, Brand X; Tours with Atomic Rooster; Edwin Starr; Rick Kenton (Roxy Music); Session work with: Chris Wood (Traffic); Pino Palladino; Several UK television appearances; Performed for HM The Queen and Royal Family, Buckingham Palace. *Recordings:* Albums: Brand X: First album (with Phil Collins); Locust: Alpha Waves; Singles with Atomic Rooster. *Membership:* Performing Rights Society. *Current Management:* Data Sound. *Address:* 19 Wharfdale, Hemel Hempstead, Herts HP2 5TQ, England.

SPINETTI Henry Anthony George; b. 31 March 1951, Cwm, South Wales. Musician (drums). Divorced, 2 s. *Career:* Tours, concerts include: Eric Clapton, 1979–82, 1993, 1995; Tina Turner, 1984, 1985, 1990; Joan Armatrading, 1972, 1990; Neil Sedaka, 1974; Andy Fairweather-Low, 1970–76; Procol Harum, 1994; Bill Wyman, 1993, 1994; Television appearances include: Top of The Pops; Radio includes: Wembley Concert with Tina Turner, 1990. *Recordings:* Albums include: with Joan Armatrading: Show Some Emotion, 1977; To The Limit, 1978; Rough Mix, Townsend and Lane, 1977; City To City, Gerry Rafferty, 1978; with Eric Clapton: Just One Night, 1979; Another Ticket, 1981; All The Best, Paul McCartney; Gone Troppo, George Harrison, 1982; Willie and The Poor Boys, 1985; Best of Dark Horse, 1989; All Day Thumbsucker Revisited, 1995; Blue, with Eric Clapton, 1999; Film soundtracks include: Lethal Weapon; Color of Money. *Membership:* Musicians' Union. *Leisure interests:* Model aircraft; Tennis.

SPITERI Sharleen Eugenie; b. 7 Nov. 1967, Glasgow, Scotland. Vocalist; Musician (guitar, piano, organ, harmonica). *Musical Education:* Self-taught. *Career:* Formed Texas with John McElhone, 1988. *Compositions:* Albums: Southside, 1989; Mothers Heaven, 1991; Ricks Road, 1993; White On Blonde, 1997; The Hush, 1999. *Recordings:* Singles: I Don't Want a Lover, 1989; Everyday Now, 1989; Alone With You, 1992; Tired of Being Alone, 1992; So Called Friend, 1993; You Owe It All To Me, 1993; So In Love With You, 1994; Say What You Want, 1997; Halo, 1997; Black Eyed Boy, 1997; Put Your Arms Around Me, 1997; Insane/Say What You Want, with Wu Tang Clan, 1998; In Our Lifetime, 1999; Summer Son, 1999; When We Are Together, 1999; In Demand, 2000; Inner Smile, 2001; Albums: Southside, 1989; Mothers Heaven, 1991; Ricks Road, 1993; White On Blonde, 1997; The Hush, 1999; The Greatest Hits, 2000; Guest vocals on: Bad Time, The Jayhawks, 1995. *Honours:* Capital Radio, Best Female

Vocal; Malta Music Prize, Best Intl. *Leisure interests:* Climbing; Snowboarding. *Current Management:* G R Management, 974 Pollokshaw Rd, Shawlands, Glasgow G41 2HA, Scotland.

SPIZZ Julian, (Spizzman); b. 17 Sept. 1968, Florence, Italy. Vocalist; Composer; Performer. *Musical Education:* Studies in field of experimental singing. *Career:* Member, Trinovox; Appearances in major German televison and radio programmes, 1994; Concerts in major German, Swiss, Austrian towns (Berlin, Bremen, Lübeck, Stuttgart, Basel, Vienna, Innsbruck), 1994–95; Soundtrack, radio play, Bavarian State radio, 1995. *Recordings:* Albums: Incanto, Trinovox, 1994; Voices, Trinovox; Sarband, The Bulgarian Voices, 1994; Earborn, Trinovox and Various Artists, 1995. *Honours:* Italian National Award, vocal artists: Quartetto Cetra (with Trinovox), 1994. *Memberships:* SIAE; GEMA. *Leisure interests:* Free climbing; Motorcycling. *Address:* c/o Ulrich Balss, Jaro Records, Bismarck 43, 28203 Bremen 1, Germany.

SPRINGER Scott; b. 1 April 1959, Birmingham, Alabama, USA. Singer; Musician (guitar, bass guitar). m. Helen C Akin, 2 Aug. 1980, 2 s., 1 d. *Career:* Tour with band Halo, USA, Canada, 1989–93; Jesus Music, 1990; 6 Christian Radio No. 1 songs, USA. *Recordings:* Halo; Heaven Calling; Hello Forever. *Publications:* CCM; Release. *Membership:* BMI. *Leisure interests:* Fishing; Basketball. *Current Management:* Halo Productions Inc. *Address:* 311 Cherokee Dr., Clanton, AL 35046, USA.

SPRINGFIELD Rick, (Richard Springthorpe); b. 23 Aug. 1949, Sydney, Australia. Singer; Musician (guitar, piano); Actor. *Career:* Member, Jordy Boys; Rock House; MPD Band; Zoot; Solo artiste, 1972–; Also television actor; Guest appearances include: The Rockford Files; Wonder Woman; The Six Million Dollar Man; Leading role, General Hospital; Actor, film, Hard To Hold, 1984. *Recordings:* Albums include: Beginnings, 1972; Comic Book, 1974; Heroes, 1974; Wait For The Night, 1976; Working Class Dog, 1981; Success Hasn't Spoiled Me Yet, 1982; Living In Oz, 1983; Tao, 1985; Rock of Life, 1988; Karma, 1998; Singles include: Human Touch; Speak To The Sky; Jessie's Girl; I've Done Everything For You; Don't Talk To Strangers; Love Somebody, used in film Hard To Hold; Bruce. *Current Management:* Ron Weisner Entertainment, PO Box 261640, Encino, CA 91426, USA.

SPRINGSTEEN Bruce; b. 23 Sept. 1949, New Jersey, USA. Singer; Songwriter; Musician (guitar). m. (1) Julianne Phillips (divorced), (2) Patti Scialfa, 1 s., 1 d. *Career:* Recording artist, 1972–; Formed own band, The E-Street Band, 1974; Numerous national and world-wide tours, include: MUSE No-Nukes Concerts, 1979; The River tour, 1980; Born In The USA tour, 1984; Tunnel of Love Express tour, 1988; Amnesty International Human Rights Now! tour, 1988; North American tour, 1992; Numerous benefit and charity concerts. *Compositions:* Numerous songs include: Born To Run; Blinded By The Light (also recorded by Manfred Mann); Fire (recorded by the Pointer Sisters); Because The Night (recorded by Patti Smith); Badlands; Hungry Heart; Dancing In The Dark; Born In The USA; I'm On Fire; I'm Goin' Down; Fire; Pink Cadillac; Cover Me; 57 Channels and Nothin' On; Better Days; Glory Days. *Recordings:* Albums: Greetings From Asbury Park, 1973; The Wild The Innocent and The E Street Shuffle, 1973; Born To Run, 1975; Darkness On The Edge of Town, 1978; The River (No. 1, USA), 1980; Nebraska, 1982; Born In The USA (No. 1, USA and UK), 1984; Live 1975–85 (No. 1, USA), 1986; Tunnel of Love (No. 1, USA and UK), 1987; Human Touch (No. 1, UK), 1992; Lucky Town, 1992; In Concert – MTV Plugged, 1993; Greatest Hits, 1995; The Ghost of Tom Joad, 1995; Contributor, We Are The World, USA For Africa, 1985; Sun City, Artists Against Apartheid, 1986; Singles include: Chimes of Freedom, 1988; 57 Channels, 1992; Streets of Philadelphia, 1994; Secret Garden, 1995; My Hometown, 1998; Tougher Than the Rest, 1999. *Honours include:* 2 Grammy Awards: Best Male Rock Vocalist, 1984, 1987; BRIT Award, Best International Solo Artist, 1986; Inducted, Rock 'n' Roll Hall of Fame, 1988; Numerous Platinum and Gold discs; Academy Award, Best Original Song In a Movie, Streets of Philadelphia, 1994. *Current Management:* Jon Landau Management, 40 W Elm St, Greenwich, CT 06830, USA.

SPRUNG Roger; b. 29 Aug. 1930, New York, USA. Folk Singer; Musician (5-string banjo); Teacher; Entertainer. m. Nancy, 24 May 1990, 2 d. *Career:* Tour with Kay Starr; Jimmy Dean TV Show; An American Experience TV Show; Dean Martin TV Show; Garry Moore Show; Appearances include: Philadelphia Folk Festival; Lincoln Center, New York; Carnegie Hall, New York. *Recordings:* 46 including: Bluegrass Gold, Vols 1–2, 1976; The Philadelphia Folk Festival, 1977; 44th Annual Galax Fiddler's Convention, 1980; Pound Ridge Fiddler's Celebration, 1981; Irish Grass, 1983; The Irish Bluegrass Connection, 1983; Southwest Winds, 1983; Let's Pick, 1988; Thyme and Beyond, 1989; Stompin' Stuff, 1990; Recordings in the Library of Congress and Smithsonian/Folkway. *Honour:* World Champion 5 string banjo player. *Leisure interests:* Music; Art; Stamps; Pets. *Current Management:* Sprung Enterprises. *Address:* 7 Papoose Hill Rd, Newtown, CT 06470, USA.

SPRY Bro, (Crispin Luke Robinson); b. 3 Nov. 1966, London, England. Musician (congas, shakers, djembs, drumkit, percussion). Separated, 2 d. *Education:* City and East London College; Kent University. *Musical Education:* Studied with Bobby Sanabria, USA; John Amira, USA; Bob Armstrong, UK; Robin Jones, UK. *Career:* First recordings with: Manassah; Soul II Soul; Yazz; Youth; Young Disciples; Signed to Polygram as part of Galliano, 1991–; Live work: Tours with Galliano include: Europe; Japan; Australia; USA; Hong Kong; Scandinavia; Marvin Gaye Tribute Concert (feauring: Al Jarreau; George Duke; Pointer Sisters; Chaka Khan; Leon Ware; Wah Wah Watson; Chuck Rainey; James Gadson), 1992; Roy Ayers, 1995; Straight No Chaser Jazz Festival, Bheki Mselku. *Recordings:* First and second albums: Soul II Soul; 3 albums with Galliano, include various compositions. *Membership:* Musicians' Union. *Leisure interests:* Afro-diasporan culture; Skateboarding; Snowballing; Busting Chalwah. *Current Management:* Steve Baker, Worldchief Management, 132 Liverpool Rd, London N1, England.

SQUIRE Chris; b. 4 March 1948, London, England. Musician (bass). *Career:* Founder member, UK progressive rock group Yes, 1968–; Concerts include: Support to Cream, farewell concert, Royal Albert Hall, 1968; Support to Janis Joplin, Royal Albert Hall, 1969; Montreux TV Festival, 1969; Support to The Nice, Royal Festival Hall, 1970; Reading Festival, 1975; Yesshows '91 – Round The World In 80 Dates Tour, 1991. *Recordings:* Albums: Yes, 1969; Time and a Word, 1970; The Yes Album, 1971; Fragile, 1971; Close To The Edge, 1972; Yessongs, 1973; Tales From Topographic Oceans, 1973; Relayer, 1974; Yesterdays, 1975; Going For The One, 1977; Tormato, 1978; Drama, 1980; Classic Yes, 1982; 90125, 1983; 9012 Live – The Solos, 1986; The Big Generator, 1987; Union, 1991; Yesstory, 1991; Keys to Ascension, 1996; Open Your Eyes, 1998; Ladder, 1999; Solo album: Fish Out of Water, 1975; Singles with Yes include: Roundabout; Wonderous Stories, Going For The One; Owner of a Lonely Heart; Leave It; It Can Happen; Love Will Find a Way; Rhythm of Love; Lift Me Up. *Honours:* Gold Ticket, Madison Square Garden, 1978; Grammy Award, Best Rock Instrumental Performance, Cinema, 1985. *Current Management:* Big Bear Management, 9 Hillgate St, London W8 7SP, England.

ST CLAIR Frank Creel; b. 17 Nov. 1936, Jacksonville, Texas, USA. Publisher; Writer; Recording Artist; Musician (Guitar). m. Barbara Mae Young, 29 Oct. 1963, 4 s., 3 d. *Education:* Fine Arts, Kilgore College, 1968–70; Graphic Arts, Texas State Technical Institute, Waco, 1970–72; Commercial Art, Tyler College, 1978–80; Understudied with Jack Rhodes, Curly Putman and others. *Career:* Third Army Special Services, Touring Southeast US; KLIV, Tyler, Texas; WFLB TV, Fayetteville, North Carolina; Major TV Stations in Deep South, 1955–70; Performed as singer in night clubs and stage shows throughout Texas, 1957-. *Compositions:* My Heart and Mind are at War, 1964; Portrait of a Fool, 1964; Guitar Bum, 1966; Mr Blues, 1966; Night Bird, 1969; This Is Life, 1969; I Hope My Guilt Don't Show, 1970; Pollution of the Mind, 1980; Good Times Are Fleeting Things, 1982. *Memberships:* BMI; Country Music Asscn; MCPS, London. *Leisure interest:* Ranching cattle. *Address:* Rr 5 Box 1635, Henderson, TX 75652, USA.

ST JAMES Rebecca; b. 26 July 1977, Sydney, Australia. Christian Recording Artist. *Musical Education:* High school music group; Coaching by Norris Brannstrom. *Career:* Carman's Revival In The Land Tour, 1991; Bryan Duncan's Slow Revival Tour, 1995; Dove Awards, Family TV Network, 1995; Side By Side Tour, 1995. *Recordings:* Refresh My Heart, 1991; Rebecca St James, 1994; Remix Album, 1995; One Way (Forefront compilation), 1995. *Publications:* Cover stories: Brio Magazine; Campus Life. *Honours:* Dove Award Nomination, New Artist of Year. *Memberships:* BMI; GMA. *Leisure interests:* Bike riding; Swimming; Bible-reading; Family games; Travel. *Current Management:* Ambassador Agency; David Smallbone Management. *Address:* PO Box 1741, Brentwood, TN 37024, USA.

ST JOHN Kate Elinor Margaret; b. 2 Oct. 1957, London, England. Musician (oboe, saxophone); Singer; Composer; Arranger. m. Sid Griffin, 28 July 1993. *Musical Education:* BSc Music, City University; Oboe at Guildhall. *Career:* Member, Ravishing Beauties, 1981–82; Member, Dream Academy, 1983–91; Oboe/saxophone session player in many bands; Member, Channel Light Vessel, 1994; Member, Van Morrison's live and recording band, 1991–95; Toured with Nigel Kennedy, 1998. *Compositions include:* For television: Harry Enfield's Television Show; Harry Enfield and Chums. *Recordings:* Albums: with Dream Academy: The Dream Academy; Remembrance Days; A Different Kind of Weather; with Channel Light Vessel: Automatic, 1994, Excellent Spirits, 1996; Solo albums: Indescribable Night, 1995; Second Sight, 1997; Hit single: Life In a Northern Town, Dream Academy; Singer with Roger Eno: The Familiar, 1993; Co-producer, Russian artist Boris Grebenschikov, 1995. *Memberships:* Musicians' Union; PRS; MCPS. *Leisure interests:* Reading; Films. *Current Management:* Mark Vernon, Firebrand. *Address:* 12 Rickett St, London SW6 1RU, England.

STAF Bernt Lennart; b. 14 Oct. 1945, Stockholm, Sweden. Singer; Songwriter. m. 2 d. *Education:* Chemist, Royal Pharmaceutical Institute, Stockholm, Sweden, 1965. *Musical Education:* Trumpet in different school orchestras; Self-taught guitar. *Career:* Writer of theatre play, Fångspel for stage and TV, 1969; Radio and TV. *Compositions:* Text and music for 10 LP and CD albums; Nar dimman lättar, 1970; Vingslag, 1971; Live, 1972. *Recordings:* Valhall, 1974; Vår, om du vill, 1976; Hycklarnas Paradis, 1981; Hammenhög Airport, 1983; Bernt Staf's Bästa, 1995; Klockor, 1997; Familjelycka och andra Guldkorn, 2000. *Publications:* Låt almatna leva, with Cornelis Vreeswijk and Fred Åkerström, 1971. *Honour:* Grammy, 1971. *Memberships:* SKAP; STIM; YTF. *Current Management:* Amigo Records; Warner. *Address:* Vågens Gata 439 III, 13661 Haninge, Sweden.

STAFF Bryan Alastair; b. 16 May 1950, Christchurch, New Zealand. DJ; Rock Music Journalist; Photographer. *Education:* BA Linguistics, Auckland University. *Musical Education:* Commercial radio. *Career:* Became an announcer, age 19, commercial radio; Specialised in local music, largely ignored on radio otherwise; Formed punk label, Ripper Records, 1979–83; In Auckland continued as rock writer, reviewer, photographer to date; Ran Ripper Records which began with New Zealand's first punk album: AK79, 1979; Ripper produced 5 albums, 20 singles over next 5 years. *Publications:* Co-author with Sheran Ashley: The Record Years, a history of New Zealand record labels. *Membership:* Recording Industry Asscn of New Zealand. *Leisure interests:* Photography; Writing. *Address:* PO Box 5154, Wellesley St, Auckland, New Zealand.

STAFFORD Jo; b. 12 Nov. 1920, Coalinga, California, USA. Singer. m. Paul Weston. *Career:* Member, country music act, with sisters; Freelance singer on radio with vocal group, The Pied Pipers; Appeared, radio with Tommy Dorsey, 1939–42; Solo recording artiste, 1940s-60s; Recorded spoof albums with husband as Jonathan and Darlene Edwards; Retired from public performance, 1959; Founder, own Corinthian record label. *Recordings include:* Singles: Little Man With a Candy Cigar; Manhattan Serenade; For You; Yes Indeed (duet with Sly Oliver); Candy (with Johnny Mercer); That's For Me; Serenade of The Bells; Some Enchanted Evening; Tennessee Waltz; My Darling My Darling (with Gordon McRae); Whispering Hope (with Gordon McRae); Make Love To Me; Shrimp Boats; Keep It a Secret; Jambalaya; You Belong To Me; Spotlight on Jo Stafford; Numerous albums, 1953-, including several with Gordon McRae.

STAFFORD Simon; b. Sheffield, England. Musician (Bass). *Career:* Member, The Longpigs. *Recordings:* Singles: Happy Again; She Said; Jesus Christ; Far; On and On; Lost Myself; Blue Skies; The Frank Sonata; Albums: The Sun is Often Out; Mobile Home.

STAGG Mark Jeffrey; b. 26 May 1961, Sheffield, Yorkshire, England. Prod.; Engineer; Programmer; Remixer. *Musical Education:* Manchester School of Sound Recording. *Career:* Member of bands: Lionrock; Pro-Gress; Much studio work includes: Production: Eskimos and Egypt; Sparks; Pro-Gress; MC Tunes; Engineering: K-Klass; Lionrock; The Grio; Björk; TC 1992; Erasure; Remixing: Nitzer Ebb; The Shamen; Supreme Love Gods; Sweet Mercy. *Recordings:* Co-writer and engineer, Rhythm is a Mystery, K-Klass (Top 3 Hit UK). *Memberships:* Musicians' Union; PRS. *Leisure interest:* Ufology. *Current Management:* DEF. *Address:* 21 Premier House, 313 Kilburn Lane, London W9 3EG, England.

STAINTON Christopher Robert; b. 22 March 1944, Sheffield, Yorkshire, England. Musician (bass, piano). m. Gail Ellyn Travi, 25 June 1970, 1 d. *Career:* Tours and recordings with: Joe Cocker, 1966–72, 1988–92; Concerts include: Woodstock; Tours and recordings with Eric Clapton, 1979–85, 1993-. *Recordings:* Albums include: with Joe Cocker: With a Little Help From My Friends, 1968; Joe Cocker, 1969; Mad Dogs and Englishmen, 1971; Something To Say, 1973; with Eric Clapton: Just One Night, 1980; Money and Cigarettes, 1983; with The Who: Quadrophenia, film soundtrack, 1979; Other recordings with: Alvin Lee; Maddy Prior; Leon Russell; Spooky Tooth; Marianne Faithfull; Ian Hunter; Jim Capaldi; Gary Brooker; Bryn Haworth; Stephen Bishop. *Membership:* PRS. *Leisure interests:* Computers. *Current Management:* Roger Forrester Management. *Address:* 18 Harley House, Regent's Park, London NW1 5HE, England.

STAKENAS Virgis; b. 10 Aug. 1953, Lithuania. Country Singer; Songwriter; Musician; Prod. m. Ramute Stakeniene, 1 d. *Education:* Siauliai University; Siauliai Music School. *Career:* Produced Country Music Festivals In Lithuania; Played In More Than 40 Big Country, Bluegrass, Pop Music Festivals in USA, Canada, Holland, Germany, Denmark, Sweden, Czechoslovakia, Poland, Russia, Latvia, Estonia, Lithuania. *Compositions:* More Than 250 Songs, 1973–98. *Recordings:* Life; The Evening; Here Is Your Home; Siauliai; Song-Book; Jumbo; 615. *Publications:* Balades, 1995. *Honours:* Too Numerous. *Memberships:* International Bluegrass Music Asscn. *Leisure interests:* Journalism; Crawfishing; Swimming; Collecting of Recordings. *Address:* Musos 7, Vijoliu k, LT 5400, Siauliu r, Lithuania.

STALEY Layne Thomas; b. 22 Aug. 1967, Bellevue, Washington, USA. Rock Vocalist. *Career:* Lead singer, US rock groups: Alice In Chains; Mad Season; Appearances with Alice In Chains: Clash of The Titans, 1991; Support tour, Van Halen, 1991; Support tour, Ozzy Osbourne, 1992; Brazil, 1993; Lollapalooza, 1993. *Recordings:* Albums: with Alice In Chains: Facelift, 1990; Sap, 1991; Dirt, 1992; Jar of Flies, 1994; Alice In Chains, 1995; Unplugged, 1996; with Mad Season: Above, 1995; Also appears on: Working Class Hero, 1995; Another Brick in the Wall, 1995; Faculty, 1998. *Honours:* MTV Award, Would. *Leisure interests:* Drawing; Painting; Photography; Computers. *Current Management:* Susan Silver Management, 207 First Ave S, Third Floor, Seattle, WA 98104, USA.

STAMPLEY Joe Ronald; b. 6 June 1943, Springhill, Louisiana, USA. Country vocalist Musician (guitar, piano, ukulele); Songwriter. *Career:* First recorded for Imperial Records, 1957; Lead vocalist and member of pop/rock group the Cutups, 1960; Later known as the Uniques, 1963; US hit with Not Too Long Ago, 1965; Solo, early 1970s; Staff writer for Gallico Music; Many country hits mostly on Epic Records, occasionally with Moe Bandy, 1971–89; Moe and Joe collaborations included controversial parody of Boy George, Where's The Dress, 1984; Continues to perform with band Double Shots. *Compositions include:* Bring It On Home To Your Woman; How Lucky Can One Man Be; If You Touch Me. *Recordings include:* Soul Song; All These Things; Just Good Ol' Boys (with Moe Bandy); Roll On Big Mama; I'm Still Loving You; Albums: Soul Song, 1973; Take Me Home To Somewhere, I'm Still Loving You, 1974; All These Things, 1976; Just Good Ol' Boys (with Moe Bandy), 1979. *Honours:* CMA, Vocal Duo of the Year (with Moe Bandy), 1980. *Leisure interests:* Golf; Fishing. *Address:* c/o PO Box 150006, Nashville, TN 37215, USA.

STAN Mircea; b. 2 Oct. 1943, Romania. Musician (trombone). *Musical Education:* 11 years study at Music High School and Conservatory in Bucharest, 1958–69; Self-taught jazz musician. *Career:* Moved to Finland, 1970s; Formed own quartet, 1972; Ran several groups including: Sextet formed for Pori Festival, 1978; Trombone quartet, toured Finland, 1980s; Played in UMO (New Music Orchestra); Also in bands run by: Heikki Sarmanto; Edward Vesala; Seppo Paakunainen; Taught trombone at Sibelius Academy; Coaches amateur jazz bands. *Recordings:* Album: Para Los Trombones, with own sextet, late 1980s; Also appears on: Mau-mau, Edward Vesala, 1982; Thad Jones, Mel Lewis and UMO. *Address:* Käsityöläisenkatu 25 E, 00750 Helsinki, Finland.

STAN Ollie; b. 28 May 1969, Kronstadt, Germany. Composer; Arranger; Musician (keyboards); Prod. *Musical Education:* Over 10 years lessons: piano, rhythm/percussion. *Career:* Tour with group: Bang!, Germany, with Dr Alban; 2 Unlimited; DJ Bobo, Mega Dance Festival, 1994. *Recordings:* Papa Winnie: You Are My Sunshine, 1994; Go: Your Body My Body, 1994; Bang! You Know I Know, 1994; Slavik/Kemmler: Indian Spirits (Dance Mixes), 1994; Powersound and Lori Glori: Freedom Forever, 1995. *Honours:* Gold, prospective Platinum for: Papa Winnie. *Leisure interests:* Beach; Cinema; Animals; Restaurants; Sports. *Address:* c/o Advance Music, Ovelgönnerweg 13, 21335 Luneburg, Germany.

STANCHEV Georgi; b. 1 June 1951, Sofia, Bulgaria. Composer; Arranger; Lyricist; Prod. m. Tsvetanca Georgieva, 3 Dec. 1976, 1 s., 2 d. *Career:* Solo vocalist, guitarist, Diana Express, 1979–81; Festivals, television; Tours: USSR, Cuba, Germany, 1984; Hungary, 1987; USSR, Romania, Israel, 1988; USSR, 1989; Worked with Hungarian group The Times, recording and performing, 1986; President, Gorgia-Venice Music House; Executive Musical Director, Peak Music Record Company. *Compositions include:* Soul; Whisper. *Recordings:* First single, 1980; Whisper, 1982; Third single, 1982; Albums: Lovers, 1983; A Handful of Sands, 1985; Be a Star Up To The End, 1991; Venice, 1995. *Honours:* Best Song of Year, Soul, 1980; Prizes, Bulgarian Television, Knoque Festival, Belgium, 1982; Prize, Dresden Festival, 1983; Best Singer, Caven, Ireland, 1984; Performer's Prize, Valletta, Malta, 1984; Grand Prize, Composer, Siofok, Hungary, 1986; Best Singer, Best Album of Year, 1991. *Address:* Suhodolska str, 2 bl, 122 vh A, ap4, 1373 Sofia, Bulgaria.

STANDAERT Luc; b. 17 Jan. 1958, Ghent, Belgium. Music Publisher; Artist Man. m. Tine Lecompte, 3 April 1981. *Education:* Architecture; Scenography. *Career:* Scenographer, 1979–82; Show Director, Tour Manager, 1982–88; Music Publisher, Artist Manager, 1988–; Business ventures: Tempo BVBA; Tempo Media Nv; Yellow House BVBA; Taste My Music. *Compositions:* Publisher of songs performed by: Arno; Dinky Toys; Francis Goya; Viktor Lazlo; Jack Radics; Jean Bosco Safari; Music for films includes: Koko Flanel; Daens; Marie. *Publications:* Vrije Radio In Vlaanderen, 1986. *Honours:* Academy Award nomination, Daens, 1993. *Memberships:* SABAM; URBEM; BVBI. *Address:* Krijgslaan 61, 9000 Gent, Belgium.

STANGER William John Nigel; b. 16 Jan. 1943, Newcastle-upon-Tyne, England. Architect; Developer; Musician (saxophone, keyboards). 2 d. *Education:* Oxford University, Newcastle University, MA (Oxon), BA, BArch. *Musical Education:* Piano, 1947–; Saxophone, 1959–; School education and self-taught. *Career:* Performed with various bands in London including: Alexis Korner, John Mayall Bluesbreakers, Alan Price Set, Herbie Goins, Night Timers, 1963–66; Performed with Newcastle Big Band (with Sting), East Side Torpedoes, Little Mo, 1996–; Currently with Crosbys; Various television and radio broadcasts. *Recordings:* with John Mayall: Live At Klooks Kleek; with Alan Price: Any Day Now; Album with Newcastle Big Band. *Memberships:* ARCUK; Musicians' Union; Equity. *Leisure interests:* Chess; Real tennis; Keep fit. *Address:* 51 Brandling Pl. S, Jesmond, Newcastle-Upon-Tyne NE2 4RU, England.

STANLEY Bob; b. 25 Dec. 1965, Horsham, Sussex, England. Musician (Keyboards, Programming). *Career:* Member, Saint Etienne; Early singles with guest vocalists; Joined by Sarah Cracknell, 1991; Released single with Charlatans' Tim Burgess; Toured with Oasis as support act; Worked with Etienne Daho, 1995; Work remixed by Aphex Twin and Chemical Brothers; Launched own label Emidisc. *Recordings include:* Singles: Only Love Can Break Your Heart, 1990; Kiss and Make Up, 1990; Nothing Can Stop Us, 1991; Filthy, 1991; Fingertips, 1991; Heartspin, 1991; Journey To The Centre of Love, 1991; He Is Cola, 1991; Join Our Club, 1992; Blade's Love Machine, 1992; Avenue, 1992; You're In a Bad Way, 1993; I Was Born On Christmas Day, with Tim Burgess, 1993; Pale Movie, 1994; Like a Motorway, 1994; Hug My Soul, 1994; Reserection, 1995; He's On The Phone, 1995; Gone, 1996; Anymore, 1996; Angel/Burnt Out Car, 1996; Goldie, 1997; Sylvie, 1998; Albums: Foxbase Alpha, 1991; So Tough, 1993; You Need a Mess of Help To Stand Alone, compilation album, 1993; Tiger Bay, 1994; Fairytales from Saint Etienne, compilation album, 1995; Too Young To Die, singles compilation album, 1995; Casino Classics, remix album, 1996; Lipslide, 1997; Good Humor, 1998.

STANLEY Damian Mark; b. 18 Aug. 1967, Nottingham, England. Prod.; Writer; Engineer; Musician (keyboards). *Career:* Recording artist with Mad; Overview; The Deadbeats; Owner, Spacehopper Recordings and Ill Communications; Remixes: Moodswings; Whycliffe; Turntable Orchestra; Ashley Beadle; Jimi Polo; Alabama 3 (DIY Dub); Humdrum (soundtrack to film Hackers); Chrissie Hynde; Sly and Love Child; Chumbawamba; Mind the Gap and Leena Conquest; Recording artist as MAD; Overview, The Deadbeats; DIY, DEA, Love Brothers; Owner, Spacehopper Records and DIY Communications. *Memberships:* PRS; MCPS. *Leisure interests:* DJ, The Garage (Nottingham); DJ, Beatroot. *Address:* Spacehopper, PO Box 350, Nottingham NG3 6DF, England.

STANLEY Ian Charles; b. 28 Feb. 1957. Record Prod.; Musician (Keyboards). *Career:* Keyboard Player, Tears For Fears Produced Tracks for Tori Amos; Mozaic; Jimmy Nail; Rialto; The Aloof and Ultra; Worked with Republica. *Compositions:* Everybody Wants To Rule The World. *Recordings:* Shout; Everybody Wants To Rule The World; Into The Fire. *Current Management:* Isisglow Ltd, The Wool Hall, Castle Corner, Beckington, Sumerset, BA3 6TA.

STANLEY Paul (Paul Eisen); b. 20 Jan. 1950, Queens, New York, USA. Singer; Musician (guitar). *Career:* Member, guitarist, US rock group Kiss, 1973–; Appearances include: Debut, Academy of Music, New York, 1973; Numerous tours include UK, 1976; US Dynasty Tour, 1979; Palladium, New York, 1980; US tour, with Cheap Trick, 1988; Marquee Club, 1988; US tour, 1990; Revenge '92 Tour, 1992; Concert, Palace of Auburn Hills, Missouri, recorded for video, album, Kiss Alive III, 1992. *Compositions:* Many for Kiss. *Recordings:* Albums: Kiss, 1974; Hotter Than Hell, 1974; Dressed To Kill, 1975; Destroyer, 1976; The Originals, 1976; Rock and Roll Over, 1976; Kiss Alive II, 1977; Double Platinum, 1978; Dynasty, 19779; Kiss Unmasked, 1980; Music From The Elder, 1981; Creatures of The Night, 1982; Lick It Up, 1983; Animalize, 1984; Asylum, 1985; Crazy Nights, 1987; Smashes Thrashes and Hits, 1988; Hot In The Shade, 1989; Revenge, 1992; Kiss Alive III, 1993; Unplugged, 1996; Psycho Circus, 1998; Solo album: Paul Stanley, 1978; Contributor, Hear 'N' Aid, charity project for Ethiopian famine relief, 1986; Numerous singles include: Rock 'N' Roll All Nite; Beth; Detroit Rock City; I Was Made For Lovin' You; I Love It Loud; Lick It Up; Heaven's On Fire; Tears Are Falling; Crazy Crazy Nights; Reason To Live; Hide Your Heart; Forever; God Gave Rock and Roll To You, used in film Bill and Ted's Bogus Adventure, 1992. *Honours:* Footprints at Grauman's Chinese Theatre, 1976; Gold Ticket, Madison Square Garden, 1979; Inducted into Hollywood's Rock Walk, 1993; Kiss Day proclaimed in Los Angeles, 1993; Numerous Gold and Platinum discs. *Current Management:* Entertainment Services Unlimited, Main St Plaza 100, Suite 303, Voorhees, NJ 08043, USA. *Address:* c/o Doc McGhee, McGhee Entertainment, 8730 Sunset Blvd, Suite 175, Los Angeles, CA 90069, USA.

STANNERS Malcolm James; b. 27 Dec. 1965, Derby, England. Sound Engineer; Programmer; Prod. *Musical Education:* Self-taught Guitar; Higher Diploma, Musical Instrument Technology. *Career:* Sound Engineer, Programmer, Paradise Studios, London, England, 1988–89, Clients include: Boy George, Bill Wyman, Errol Brown; Films: Madame Suzatska; Incredibly Strange Picture Show; Studio Owner, 4 Real Studios, 1989–; Dance Music Producer and Artist; Co-Founder, Salt Tank, London

Records. *Recordings include:* Singles: Ease the Pressure, 1991; Ethereal EP, 1992; 4 EPs, 1993–94; Peel Session EP, 1994; Eugina, 1996; Swell, 1996; Album: Science and Nature, 1996; Wavebreaks, 1998; Compilation Albums: Cafe Del Mar 2; Ministry of Sound; Cream; In the Mix 96; Horizons; Chill Out 2; Trance Europe Express; Essential Mix 2; Remixes: Sueño Latino; Chakra; Paul Van Dyke; Orbital; Chicane; Man With No Name; Hawkwind; TV Incidental Music: Grandstand, Euro 1996; Home Front; EastEnders; Hollyoaks; Wish You Were Here; Tomorrow's World. *Honours:* Reached Top 5, twice, Indie Singles Chart; Top 10, Indie Album Chart; Top 40, UK Singles Chart. *Memberships:* MCPS; PRS. *Current Management:* Doug Smith Associates, London.

STANSFIELD Lisa; b. 11 April 1966, Rochdale, Lancashire, England. Singer. *Career:* Television presenter, Razzamatazz, ITV, 1986; Formed Blue Zone, 1984; Singer, Coldcut, 1989; Solo singer, 1989–; Tours and concerts include: All Around The World Tour, 1990; Arista Records 15th Anniversary concert, 1990; Prince's Trust Rock Gala, Wembley Arena, 1990; Rock In Rio II, Brazil, 1991; Simple Truth benefit concert for Kurdish Refugees, Wembley Arena, 1991; Red Hot and Dance AIDS benefit concert, London, 1991; Amnesty International's Big 30 Concert, ITV, 1991; Dance Energy Christmas House Party, BBC2, 1992. *Compositions:* Tracks on own albums co-written and produced. *Recordings:* Albums: Affection (No. 2, UK), 1989; Real Love, 1992; So Natural, 1993; Lisa Stansfield, 1997; Swing, 1999; Never, Never Gonna Give You Up, 1999; Singles include: with Coldcut: People Hold On, 1989; Solo: This Is The Right Time, 1989; All Around The World (No. 1, UK; R & B No. 1, USA), 1989; Live Together, 1990; What Did I Do To You, 1990; You Can't Deny It, 1990; This Is The Right Time, 1990; Change, 1991; All Woman, 1992; Time To Make You Mine, 1992; Set Your Loving Free, 1992; Someday (I'm Coming Back), from film The Bodyguard, 1993; In All The Right Places, 1993; So Natural, 1993; Make It Right, 1994; Real Thing, 1997; Lisa Stansfield, EP, 1998; Remixes, 1998; Featured vocalist, Do They Know It's Christmas (reworked), Band Aid II, 1990; Contributor, Red Hot and Blue AIDS benefit record, 1990. *Honours:* Variety Club of Great Britain, Recording Artist of 1989, 1990; BRIT Awards: Best Newcomer, 1990; Best Female Artist, 1992; Ivor Novello Awards: Best Contemporary Song Award, 1990; International Hit of The Year, 1991; Nordoff-Robbins Music Therapy Charity, Best Newcomer, 1990; Rolling Stone Critics Poll Winner, Best British Female Singer, 1990; ASCAP Award, All Around The World, 1991. *Current Management:* Big Life Management. *Address:* 15 Little Portland St, London W1N 5DE, England.

STANTON Ian; b. 28 Oct. 1950, Manchester, England. Singer; Songwriter. m. Audrey Savage, 14 Feb. 1994, 1 step-s. *Career:* Lead singer, Hard Lines, 1982–85; Major concerts: Queen's Festival, Dublin, 1991; Vancouver Folk Festival, 1992; Glastonbury Festival, 1992; Edinburgh Festival, 1993; Numerous television and radio appearances include Link Biography. *Recordings:* Shrinking Man (self-produced tape), 1990; Freewheelin' (self-produced tape), 1992; Rollin' Thunder, 1995. *Memberships:* PRS; MCPS. *Leisure interests:* Writing; Computers; Board and card games. *Current Management:* Audrey Stanton. *Address:* GMCDP, Carisbrooke, Wenlock Way, Gorton, Manchester, England.

STAPLES Neville; Vocalist; Musician (Percussion). *Career:* Member, The Special AKA; Numerous tours and television appearances; Debut album produced by Elvis Costello; Established own record label, 2-Tone; Left Band, formed Fun Boy Three. *Recordings:* Singles: Gangsters; A Message to You Rudi; Too Much Too Young; Rat Race; Do Nothing; Ghost Town; Albums: The Specials, 1979; More Specials, 1980; With Fun Boy Three: Singles: The Lunatics Have Taken Over the Asylum; It Ain't What You Do, with Bananarama.

STAPLEY Jay; b. 13 April 1957. Musician (guitar); Prod.; Writer. m. 5 June 1990, 2 d. *Musical Education:* Self-taught. *Career:* Session and live work, London, 1979–; 2 world tours and albums with Roger Waters (formerly of Pink Floyd); Tubular Bells II tours with Mike Oldfield; Tours and albums with Westernhagen. *Recordings:* 4 solo albums; Also appears on: When the Wind Blows, with Roger Waters, 1987; Kiss My Soul, with Roger Chapman, 1996; Phoenix, with Toyah, 1997; Schwarz Oder Weiss, with Klaus Schulze, 1998; Just Good Stuff, Just Good Stuff, 1998. *Publications:* Articles on technical subjects in trade press. *Memberships:* PRS; MCPS. *Leisure interest:* Sailing. *Address:* 11 Glenthorne Rd, Friern Barnet, London N11 3HU, England.

STAPP Petra Rebecca; b. 29 Nov. 1964, Castleford, England. Singer; Songwriter; Musician (Acoustic Guitar). m. Timothy Alan Bigelow. *Career:* Singer, Songwriter, Carbolic Smokeball Company; Partnership with C Cahill, Wrote Songs, Performed; Record Deal with Round Tower of Dublin, 1995; Support to Nils Lofgren, Paul Carrack, Martin Carthy, Ric Sanders, Vikki Clayton. *Compositions:* I Hope It Will Be You. *Recordings:* Album, Remedy. *Memberships:* PRS; MCPS. *Leisure interests:* Crystal healing; reading; films; watching other bands. *Current Management:* Claire Hudson Management. *Address:* 25 Spa Rd, Gloucester, Gloucestershire GL1 1UY, England.

STARDUST Alvin, (Bernard William Jewry); b. 27 Sept. 1942, London, England. Singer. *Career:* Solo singer, as Shane Fenton, early 1960s; Comeback as Alvin Stardust, 1973; Chart success, 1970s-80s; Presenter, performer, BBC TV. *Recordings:* Albums: It's All Happening, 1963; Good Rockin' Tonight, 1974; Greatest Hits: Alvin Stardust, 1977; I'm a Moody Guy, 1982; I Feel Like... Alvin Stardust, 1984; 20 of The Best, 1987; Singles include: My Coo-Ca-Choo (No. 2, UK); Jealous Mind; Red Dress; You You You; Tell Me Why; Good Love Can Never Die; Pretend; I Feel Like Buddy Holly; I Won't Run Away; So Near Christmas. *Current Management:* Roy Massey Management. *Address:* 40 Salisbury Dr., Cannock, Staffs, WS12 5YP, England.

STARR Edwin, (Charles Hatcher); b. 21 Jan. 1942, Nashville, Tennessee, USA. Singer. *Career:* Formed vocal group Future Tones, 1957; Member, Bill Doggett Combo, Solo artist, 1965–; Motown recording artist, 1967–75; Based in UK, 1980s; Collaborations with the Style Council; Worked with Ian Levine's Motor City Records, 1989–91. *Recordings:* Singles include: Contact; Agent Double-O-Soul; War, Stop Her On Sight (SOS); 25 Miles; Stop The War Now; Funky Music Sho Nuff Turns Me On; Albums: Soul Master, 1968; 25 Miles, 1969; Just We Two, with Blinky, 1969; War and Peace, 1970; Involved, 1971; Hell Up In Harlem, 1974; Free To Be Myself, 1975; Edwin Starr, 1977; Afternoon Sunshine, 1977; Clean, 1978; HAPPY Radio, 1979; Stronger Than You Think I Am, 1980; 20 Greatest Motown Hits, 1986; Where Is The Sound, 1991; Timeless Energy, 1996. *Current Management:* Lilian Kyle. *Address:* 118 Derby Rd, Bramcote, Nottinghamshire NG9 3HP, England.

STARR Lucille; b. St Boniface, Manitoba, Canada. Entertainer; Singer; Musician (guitar, bass). m. (1) Bob Reagan, 19 Sept. 1955, divorced, 1 s.; (2) Bryan Cunningham, 16 April 1978, 1 step-s., 1 step-d. *Musical Education:* Studied classical (voice). *Career:* First Grand Ole Opry Tour with Hank Snow, 1961; 4 television shows in Los Angeles; Yodelling for Cousin Pearl on Beverly Hillbillies. *Recordings:* Hits include: The French Song; Jolie Jacqueline; Colinda; Yours; Crazy Arms; Pepères Mill; First Time I've Ever Been In Love; Freight Train; Leaving It Up To You; Send Me No Roses. *Honours:* Several Platinum and Gold records; First lady inducted in Hall of Honour (Canada); Hall of Fame, Canada; Street named Lucille Starr Drive in Vancouver, BC, Canada; Inducted into Walkway of Stars, Hall of Fame, Nashville, Tennessee, 1997. *Memberships:* AFTRA; Television Screen Actors Guild; Musicians' Union; Canadian Country Music Asscn. *Leisure interest:* Needlepoint. *Current Management:* Cardinal Records.

STARR Ringo, (Richard Starkey); b. 7 July 1940, Dingle, Liverpool, England. Musician (drums). m. (1) Maureen Cox, 1965, divorced, 2 s., 1 d.; m. (2) Barbara Bach, 1981. *Career:* Member, Rory Storm and The Hurricanes, Liverpool; Member, The Beatles, 1962–70; Appearances, Hamburg, 1962; World-wide tours, 1963–; Attended Transcendental Meditation Course, Maharishi's Academy, Rishkesh, India, 1968; Co-founder, Apple Corps Ltd, 1968; Solo artiste, 1969–; Narrator, childrens television series, Thomas The Tank Engine; Film appearances include: A Hard Day's Night; Help!; Candy; The Magic Christian. *Recordings:* Albums include: with The Beatles: Please Please Me, 1963; With The Beatles, 1963; A Hard Day's Night, 1964; Beatles For Sale, 1965; Help!, 1965; Rubber Soul, 1966; Revolver, 1966; Sgt Pepper's Lonely Hearts Club Band, 1967; The Beatles (White Album), 1968; Yellow Submarine, 1969; Abbey Road, 1969; Let It Be, 1970; Solo albums: Sentimental Journey, 1969; Beaucoups of Blue, 1970; Ringo, 1973; Goodnight Vienna, 1974; Blasts From Your Past, 1975; Ringo's Rotogravure, 1976; Ringo The Fourth, 1977; Bad Boy, 1977; Stop and Smell The Roses, 1981; Old Wave, 1985; StarrStruck – Ringo's Best (1976–83), 1989; Time Takes Time, 1992; Solo singles include: It Don't Come Easy; Back Off Boogaloo; Photograph; You're Sixteen; Oh My My; Snookeroo; Only You. *Honours include:* (with the Beatles) BPI Awards: Best British Album (Sgt Pepper's Lonely Hearts Club Band), Best British Group, 1952–77, 1977; Inducted into Rock and Roll Hall of Fame, 1980. *Current Management:* David Fishof Presents, 252 W 71st St, New York, NY 10023, USA.

STATHAM Robert; b. 4 April 1959, Bournemouth, Dorset, England. Musician (fretless bass guitar). *Musical Education:* Certificate of Advanced Studies, Jazz/Rock, Guildhall School of Music. *Career:* Played with John Etheridge; Dick Heckstall-Smith; Ed Jones; Paz – Keith Emerson; Theo Travis; Radio broadcasts with Paz; Ed Jones; Theo Travis; Tours with Ed Jones; Theo Travis. *Compositions:* Featured on Ed Jones album; also Ed Jones radio broadcasts, Jazz Today, 1989. *Recordings with:* Ed Jones; Paz; Kelvin Christiane; Theo Travis; Totally Wired compilation (acid jazz). *Memberships:* Musicians' Union; PRS. *Address:* 90 Bridge Lane, Golders Green, London NW11 0EL, England.

STAVNSTRUP Jens Peter Fjeder; b. 18 Oct. 1963, Naestved, Denmark. Singer/Songwriter. 1 d. *Compositions:* Power Flower; Rain; Love Junkie. *Recordings:* Velvet Revolution, The Savage Affair; Shiner, Shiner. *Leisure interest:* Soccer. *Address:* Kinavej 11 I, 2300 Copehegen S, Denmark.

STEAD Dave; b. 15 Oct. 1966, Huddersfield, Yorkshire, England. Musician (Drums). *Career:* Member, The Beautiful South. *Recordings:* Singles: Song For Whoever, 1989; My Book EP, 1991; One Last Love Song, 1992; Prettiest Eyes, 1994; Everybody's Talkin', 1994; Rotterdam (Or Anywhere); Don't Marry Her; Liar's Bar, 1997; Perfect 10, 1998; Dumb, 1999; Albums: Welcome To The Beautiful South, 1989; Choke, 1990' 0898, 1992; Miaow, 1994; Carry On Up The Charts: The Best of The Beautiful South, 1994; Blue Is The Colour, 1996; Quench, 1998.

STEELE Kevin; b. Cleveland, Ohio, USA. Singer; Songwriter; Musician (harmonica). *Musical Education:* Self-taught. *Career:* Lead singer, US rock group Roxx Gang; Performances include: Things You've Never Done Before World Tour, 1990; US Tour, 1991; The Voodoo You Love, US Tour, 1996–97; Television and radio apperances include: Various videos, MTV; BBC TV; Z-Rock coast to coast radio broadcast. *Compositions:* Soundtrack to Playboys, Girls of South Beach, 1997. *Recordings:* Things You've Never Done Before; Love 'Em and Leave 'Em; The Voodoo You Love, 1996; Mojo Gurus, 1997; Roxx Gang: Old, New, Borrowed and Blue, 1998. *Leisure interest:* Record collecting. *Current Management:* Brett Steele, Steele Management. *Address:* 7002 124th Terrace N, Largo, FL 33773, USA.

STEELE Tommy, (Thomas Hicks); b. 17 Dec. 1936, Bermondsey, London, England. Actor; Singer. m. Ann Donoghue, 1960, 1 d. *Career:* First stage appearance, Empire Theatre, Sunderland, 1956; First London appearance, Dominion Theatre, 1957; Major roles include: Buttons, Rodgers and Hammerstein's Cinderella, Coliseum, 1958; Tony Lumpkin, She Stoops To Conquer, Old Vic, 1960; Arthur Kipps, Half a Sixpence, Cambridge Theatre, 1963–64; The same, Broadhurst Theatre, New York, 1965; Truffaldino, The Servant of Two Masters, Queen's, 1969; Dick Whittington, London Palladium, 1969; Meet Me In London, Adelphi, 1971; Jack Point, The Yeoman of The Guard, City of London Festival, 1978; The Tommy Steele Show, London Palladium, 1973; Hans Andersen, 1974, 1977; One-man show, Prince of Wales, 1979; Singing In The Rain (also director), 1983; Some Like It Hot, 1992; What a Show, Prince of Wales Theatre, 1995; Film appearances: Kill Me Tomorrow, 1956; The Tommy Steele Story; The Duke Wore Jeans; Tommy The Toreador; Light Up The Sky; It's All Happening; The Happiest Millionaire; Half a Sixpence; Finian's Rainbow; Where's Jack?; Television: Writer, actor, Quincy's Quest, 1979. *Compositions:* Composed, recorded, My Life My Song, 1974; A Portrait of Pablo, 1985. *Publications:* Quincy, 1981; The Final Run, 1983; Rock Suite – An Elderly Person's Guide To Rock, 1987. *Honour:* OBE, 1979. *Leisure interests:* Squash; Sculpture. *Current Management:* James Kelly, International Artistes Ltd, 235 Regent St, London W1R 8AX, England.

STEEVES Paulette; b. 25 Nov. 1955, Whitehorse, Yukon Territories, British Columbia, Canada. Songwriter; Musician (guitar); Vocalist. Divorced. 2 s., 1 d. *Musical Education:* 1 year Canadian Academy vocal music (grant from Native American Foundation). *Career:* Formed The Mother and Child Band, with son Jesse (banjo, washboard, singer), son Dustin (harmonica, Indian hand drums), daughter Marina (tub base, spoons, tambourine, singer); Appearances: Hamilton Festival of Friends, 1992; Klienburg Binder Twine Festival, 1993; Festival of The Islands, 1993, Gananoque; Ridgetown Fair, 1993; Own Honeysuckle Records label; Workshops for making home made recycled instruments. *Recordings:* Heart For Sale; Cotton Fields. *Memberships:* SOCAN; NSWA; CAIIA. *Leisure interests:* Hiking; Camping; Nature; Horse riding. *Address:* The Mother and Child Band, Box 442, Johnson, AR 72741, USA.

STEFANI Gwen; Vocalist. *Career:* Lead singer, US group No Doubt. *Recordings include:* Albums: No Doubt, 1993; Tragic Kingdom, 1995; Good, with Gameface, 1997; Dirty Boogie, with Brian Setzer, 1998; Greatest Hits, with Sublime, 1999; Hit single: Just a Girl, 1995; Ex-Girlfriend, 2000. *Current Management:* Spark Management, 100 Wilshire Blvd Suite 1830, Santa Monica, CA 90405, USA.

STEINCKE Viggo; b. 15 Nov. 1951, Viborg, Denmark. Musician (guitar, bass); Composer. *Career:* Several live performances on Danish radio. *Recordings:* with Coma: Financial Tycoon, 1977; Amoc, 1980; Love and Madness, 1986; with Colours of Blue: Colours of Blue, 1989; Workshop, 1994. *Honours:* North Jutland Country Music Award, 1991. *Memberships:* KODA; Danish Music Foundation. *Leisure interests:* Dancing; Lying in bed; Archery. *Current Management:* Honor Agency. *Address:* Schleppegrellsgade 11, 9000 Aalborg, Denmark.

STEINER Fred(erick); b. 24 Feb. 1923, New York, New York, USA. Composer; Conductor; Musicologist. m. Shirley Laura Steiner, 2 d. *Musical Education:* Institute of Musical Art, New York City; BM, Oberlin Conservatory of Music, Ohio, 1943; PhD, Musicology, University of Southern California, 1981. *Career:* Composer, Conductor, radio in New York City; Music Director, radio programme This Is Your FBI; To Los Angeles, 1947; Many other radio programmes; First TV work, Columbia Broadcasting System, 1950; First film work, 1950; Major TV credits include Andy Griffith, Danny Thomas, Gunsmoke, Have Gun Will Travel, Hogan's Heroes, Rocky and Bullwinkle Show, Movie of the Week, Rawhide, Star

Trek, Twilight Zone, Hawaii Five-O, Dynasty, Amazing Stories, Tinytoons; Major film credits include: Della, First To Fight, Hercules, The Man From Del Rio, Run For The Sun, St Valentine's Day Massacre, Time Limit, Shipwreck, The Color Purple; Lecturer, History and Art of Film Music, University of Southern California, 1984–89, College of Santa Fe, 1990–93. *Compositions:* Perry Mason Theme; Navy Log March; Dudley Doright Theme; Five Pieces for String Trio; Tower Music for Brass and percussion; Pezzo Italiano for cello and piano; Act Without Words, for percussion ensemble; Indian Music for Viola and Piano; Transcriptions and pieces for TV and film. *Recordings:* King Kong, conductor, motion picture score by Max Steiner; Great American Film scores; Music from the Paramount TV Series Star Trek. *Publications:* Foreword, in Music on Demand (by R R Faulkner), 1983; Music for Star Trek, in Wonderful Inventions (by Iris Newsom), 1985; Fred Steiner on Film Music, in Film Score (by Tony Thomas), 1991; Interlude, in Hollywood Holyland (by Ken Darby), 1992. Contributions to: Journal of the Arnold Schoenberg Institute; Film Music Notebook; Quarterly Journal of the Library of Congress; New Grove Dictionary of American Music; Dictionary of American Biography; New Grove Dictionary of Music and Musicians; Record Album Notes. *Honours include:* Academy Award Nomination, 1986; City of Los Angeles Special Recognition Certificate; Award of Merit, Film Music Society. *Memberships include:* Academy of Motion Picture Arts and Sciences; American Musicological Society; AFofM; ASCAP; Society of Composers and Lyricists; Board of Advisors, Film Music Society. *Address:* 1086 Mansion Ridge Rd, Santa Fe, NM 87501, USA.

STEINKE Gord; b. 11 July 1959, North Battleford, Saskatchewan, Canada. Musician (bass guitar, acoustic guitar); Songwriter. m. Deb, 7 June 1985, 1 c. *Education:* BA in Journalism and Communications. *Career:* Appeared on numerous television shows in Canada with own band Hidden Agenda; Major concerts include Classic Rock Weekend with Deep Purple, George Thorogood, Rick Derringer and Nazareth, 1997. *Recordings:* Larger Than Life, Inner City, 1982; Something Wrong, Gord Steinke, 1997. *Honour:* Recognition award, International Songwriting Competition. *Memberships:* ACTRA; SOCAN; ARIA. *Leisure interests:* Motorcycles; Camping. *Address:* PO Box 57217, 2010A Sherwood Dr., Sherwood Park, AB T8A 5L7, Canada.

STEINMETZ Hugh; b. 15 Feb. 1943, Copenhagen. Composer; Conductor; Musician (Trumpet). m. Anna Lise Malmros, 1 s. *Education:* MA, University of Copenhagen. *Career:* Trumpet Player, Composer, Conductor, 1959–60; Composer, Soloist, The Danish Radio Jazz Group, The Contemporary Jazz Quinter, Cadentia Nova Danica; Latest Groups, Hugh Steinmetz Octet and Communio Musica. *Compositions:* Include Fujiama; Gizzy; Sound Like Arnoldi; Nisshinbo; Afrodisiaca; Stars and Mirrors; Mandra; Magic Waters; Relief; Traffic War Victims; Memory of a Face; Opus Statium; Electric Dancer; Flower Power; Global Community; Many Faces; Ah-Wah-Pah. *Recordings:* include, Action; Nu; Afrodisiaca; City Music; Gate of Changes. *Honours:* Danish Jazz Musician of the Year, 1966; Legacies From Danish State Art Foundation, 1967, 1997, 1998, 1999. *Memberships:* Danish Musicians Union; KODA; DJBFA. *Leisure interests:* Painting; Gardening. *Current Management:* Anna Lise Malmros. *Address:* Hyldegärdsvej 7, 1 tv, 2920 Charlottenlund, Copenhagen, Denmark.

STEINVIG Peter; b. 20 July 1955, Ronne, Denmark. Organist; Music Dir. m. Anette, 2 s., 3 d. *Education:* Ba, University of Copenhagen; MA, Royal Danish Music Conservatory; Duke University. *Career:* Music Director, Organist, Karlslunde Strandkirke; Gospel Choirleader and Clinician; Founder, KEFAS, 1975–; Originator, Copenhagen Gospel Festival, 1992–; Performances With Edwin Hawkins, Andrae Crouch, Richard Smallwood; Touring USA, 1994, England, 1996, 1998. *Recordings:* Blessed Be The Rock; Copenhagen Gospel Festival Live, 1997–99. *Publications:* 88 Salmer and Sange, Hymnbook; Dig Til Aere, Song Book. *Memberships:* Danish Guild of Organists; DOKS. *Address:* Toftenholmen 18, 2690 Karlslunde, Denmark.

STEPHENSON Larry Lee; b. 24 Oct. 1956, Harrisonburg, Virginia, USA. Musician (mandolin, guitar). *Career:* Four years with Bill Harrell and The Virginians; Five years with The Bluegrass Cardinals; Six years with The Larry Stephenson Band; Tours: The Middle East; Europe; Japan; Travelled USA, Canada; Appearances: Nashville Network; Grand Ole Opry; Many Bluegrass Festivals world-wide. *Recordings:* Albums: 5 with Bill Harrell; 3 with The Bluegrass Cardinals; 8 with The Larry Stephenson Band; including: Everytime I Sing a Love Song, 1988; Far Away in Tennessee, 1995; On Fire, 1998; Featured musician on about 25 other Bluegrass albums. *Memberships:* International Bluegrass Music Asscn; BMI, Writer and Publisher; Musicians' Union. *Leisure interests:* Movies; Boating; Doing nothing.

STEPHENSON Robert; b. 30 June 1953, Dublin, Ireland. Music Promoter; Artist Man.; Agent. *Education:* Belvedere College; Roscrea College; Blackrock College; Psychology, Trinity College, Dublin, Ireland. *Career:* Sense of Ireland Festival, London, 1980; Organizer of Irish rock festivals in London, 1986–90; Paris, 1992; Manager of bands, tour organizer, agent and promoter; Managing Director of Treasure Island

Promotions, Media, Music, Discs; Acts on record label: Dr Millar; Ruby Horse. *Leisure interests:* Music; Photography; Winter and water sports; Conversation. *Address:* Bartra Lodge, Harbour Rd, Dalkey, Co Dublin, Ireland.

STEPHENSON Wilfredo; b. 27 Feb. 1948, Lima, Peru. m. Maria, 21 June 1988, 3 s., 2 d. *Education:* BA, Econ, Howard University, USA; Graduate Economic Studies, Stockholm University; Computer Education, NM School, Stockholm, Sweden. *Musical Education:* Piano Lessons, Lima Musical Conservatory; Self-taught Percussionist and Bass Player; Private Lessons, Diverse Known Percussionists; Sabu Martinez, Pello Elafrokan, Anga, Tata Guiness. *Career:* Reader, Hot Salsa, Swedish Salsa Group, toured Scandinavia, Europe and US, 1979–95; Percussionist with Aston Reymers Riivaler, 1981–86; Co-owner, Rub a Dub Records and Studios, 1988–97; Co-Producer, Rub a Dub Catalogue (19 productions with Salsa, Afro, Flamenco and World Music), 1997. *Compositions:* Lana Turkaleza, 1997. *Recordings:* Ensemble of Salsa Percussion, solo LP, 1981; Hot Salsa, 1979; Maldito Primitivo, 1985; Hot Salsa Meets Swedish Jazz, 1988; Lamowosbacuba, 1989; Ilusiones, 1992; With Friends for Friends, 1995; First Summer, 1998. *Honours:* Swedish Grammy for Per Mernberg. *Memberships:* STIM; SAMI; SKAP; Swedish Socs for Musicians. *Leisure interests:* Football; Computers. *Address:* Alkallevagen 2, 13933 Varmdo, Sweden.

STERIAN Valeriu; b. 21 Sept. 1952, Rímnicu Sárat, Romania. Singer; Musician (guitar, drums). m. Lucia Sterian, 4 Aug. 1976, 1 s. *Education:* Psychologist. *Musical Education:* Music School. *Career:* Folk-rock group, Vali and Carmen, 1973; Lead singer, guitar, rock group, 1975–; Valeriu Sterian and Compania de Sunet; Tours: Romania; Bulgaria; Hungary; Poland; Russia; Norway; Germany; France; England. *Recordings:* Albums: Folk, 1977; Antirazbolnica, 1979; Veac XX, 1982; Nimic Fara Oameni, 1989; Noati in Norway, 1990; Vino Doamne, 1991; S-A Votat Codul Penal, 1993; Evenimentul Zilei, 1994. *Publications:* Vox Pop Rock, Romania. *Leisure interest:* Billiards. *Current Management:* Valerian Sterian Studio, B'inisor, Compania de Sunet SRL. *Address:* Str Ion Címpineanu-27, Ap 75, Sect L, Bucharest, Romania.

STES Walter; b. 24 Jan. 1950, Heist-Aan-Zee, Belgian. Musician (Bass). *Education:* Law Studies, 2 years; Oriental Philology, 2 years; Classical Education, Double Bass. *Career:* Musical Director, Theatre Arena, Ghent, 1975–85; Musical Director, Royal Ballet of Flanders, 1985–90; Leader, Blues band, Red Rooster. *Recordings:* Straight From the Heart, full CD; Bluesin' Up, full CD; On the Move, full CD. *Address:* St Anna Straat 60, 9820 Bottelare, Belgium.

STEVENS Craig Ronald; b. 30 Sept. 1959, Syracuse, New York, USA. Singer. m. Mary L Sinclair, 30 Aug. 1986. *Education:* MS. *Musical Education:* BA; AAS. *Career:* Touring artist, session musician, RCA Canada and Wurlitzer; Contract artist, keyboardist for Thrill of a Lifetime, Canada, 1982. *Recordings:* Just Another Night, 1980, 1981; Live At The Grand, 1983; Terminal Barber Shop, 1984; Risin' Child, 1994. *Publications:* Poems On The Road, 1983. *Honours:* Excellence In Music Education, 1992. *Memberships:* GMA; ASCAP; CAPAC (SOCAN). *Current Management:* Capitol Management. *Address:* Division St, #1300, Suite 200, Nashville, TN 37203, USA.

STEVENS Dane; b. 31 July 1942, Colchester, Essex, England. Country Singer; Songwriter; Musician (guitar). m. Kathleen Marian, 9 April 1985, 3 s., 1 d. (previous marriage). *Musical Education:* Self-taught. *Career:* 20 years, working professional; Solo ariste, working in country music clubs, major country festivals; Local radio interviews; Radio plays; Tours nationwide. *Compositions:* Original songs for albums; Songs recorded by The Haleys; Jolene and Barry. *Recordings:* Albums: TBL: New Country; Across The Miles. *Honours:* Best Act, Country Music Club. *Membership:* PRS. *Current Management:* Contact Direct. *Address:* 139 Harwich Rd, Colchester, Essex CO4 3DB, England.

STEVENS Michael Jefry; b. 13 March 1951, New York, USA. Musician (piano); Composer; Educator. *Education:* Masters degree, Queens College, NYC. *Musical Education:* Masters degree, Jazz Performance. *Career:* Extensive tours, Italy, Spain, Germany, Denmark, with Stevens Siegel and Ferguson trio and the Lily White Band; Various other tours including David Clayton Thomas Band; Worked with: Cecil Bridgewater; Dakota Staton; Charnott Moffett; Mark Whitfield; Ira Sullivan; Harold Vick; Ralph Lalama; Billy Drewes; Mark Feldman; Pheeroan Aklaff; Leo Smith; Gerry Hemingway; Phil Haynes; Perry Robinson; Ed Schuller; Thomas Chapin; Herb Robertson; Mark Whitecage; Billy Martin; Dave Douglas; Blood Sweat and Tears; The Platters; Carlos Patato Valdez; Jeff Andrews; Frank Gambale; Jaco Pastorius; Suzanne Vega; Head, keyboard department, National Guitar Summer Workshop; Musical Director, Music Theatre Ensemble, Barnard College, 1980–84. *Compositions:* Music for vocal and instrumental ensembles, dance, music-theatre, film. *Recordings:* with Mark Whitecage and Liquid Time: Liquid Time; Live At Brandeis; with Jim Finn: Jim Finn; Talking With Angels; with Tim Ferguson Trio:

Habitat; Dedication; Vagabond Blues; with The Lily White Band: Somewhere Between Truth and Fiction; with Phil Haynes/Michael Stevens: Music For Percussion and Piano; with The Mosaic Sextet: Today This Moment; Live At Brandeis; with Stevens/Siegel/Ferguson: One of a Kind; with Mark Whitecage/Michael Jefry Stevens: Duo Improvisations; Live At Greenwich House: Haiku, 1995; Points of View, 1996; Short Stories, 1998. *Honours:* BMI Composers Workshop; Eurie Blake Scholar. *Memberships:* BMI; Minnesota Composers Forum. *Leisure interests:* Swimming; Tennis.

STEVENS Michael William; b. 26 Jan. 1957, Wisbech, Cambridgeshire, England. Artist; Musician (saxophone, keyboards). *Musical Education:* Birmingham School of Music, 1975–79. *Career:* MD, Take That; Bill Withers; Member, LA mix; Toured as support act with: The Temptations; Dionne Warwick; Freddie Jackson. *Recordings:* 2 solo albums: Light Up The Night, 1988; Set The Spirit Free, 1990; Soloist on hits by: Cathy Dennis; Glen Goldsmith; Tom Jones; Eternal. *Honours:* ARCM; ABSM. *Memberships:* PPL, PRS, MU. *Leisure interests:* Music; Golf. *Current Management:* Sue Carling, Mike Stevens Music. *Address:* 13 Elvendon Rd, London N13 4SJ, England.

STEVENS Mike; b. 9 Oct. 1957, Sarnia, Ontario, Canada. Musician (harmonica). m. Jane Gosselin, 8 Nov. 1986, 1 s. *Education:* Electrical Instrumentation at college. *Career:* First played The Grand Ole Opry, guest of Jim and Jesse, 1989; Guested over 100 times since; Tours: Canada; USA; Japan; Bahamas; Mexico. *Recordings:* Harmonica, 1990; Blowing Up a Storm, 1992; Life's Railway To Heaven, 1994; Joy, 1998. *Publications:* Mike Stevens Harmonica Techniques For Bluegrass and Beyond. *Honours:* Recording of the Year, Central Canada, Bluegrass, 1990; 5 times Entertainer of The Year, Central Canada, Bluegrass; Best Selling Album, PRC, 1992; Made a Kentucky Col, 1994. *Memberships:* SOCAN; CMRAA; HFA; AFofM; NARAS; CARAS. *Leisure interest:* Physical fitness. *Current Management:* Jim McReynolds, 560 Zieglers Rd, TN 37066, USA. *Address:* 1595 Blackwell Rd, Sarnia, ON N7X 1A4, Canada.

STEVENS Paul; b. 30 June 1969, Hammersmith, London, England. Musician (guitars: electric, acoustic, classical); Electronics and Sound Engineer. *Education:* Chelmsford College of Further Education, Anglia Polytechnic. *Musical Education:* Colchester Music College, 1980–85; Martin Smith LLCM, 1985–94. *Career:* Parallel careers as musician and electronics/sound engineer; Sessions in London, Essex and Suffolk; Many live performances with bands including: Real Lives (early version of Blur); Hot Wired; Customs Men; Colours; Dream Age; Empathy; Product Design and Engineering Manager for Trace Elliot, designed several ranges of guitar and bass amplifiers for Trace Elliot, 1994-, Orange and Gibson, 1998-. *Recordings:* Produced solo work of guitar instrumentals, 1991; Session for U2: I Can't Help Falling In Love (remix at SARM West), 1992; Producer for: Empathy, Universal (EP), 1995. *Honours:* HNC Electronic Engineering, 1990; Trinity School of Music, Grade 8 guitar, 1994; Several nominations for Best Amplifier in various trade and retail awards ceremonies. *Memberships:* Musicians' Union; Institute of Incorporated Engineers. *Leisure interests:* Music; Electronics; British history; Reading. *Current Management:* Trace Elliot Ltd. *Address:* Blackwater Trading Estate, Maldon, Essex CM9 4GG, England.

STEVENS Rachel Lauren; b. 9 April 1978, North London, England. Vocalist; Actor. *Education:* Attended drama college whilst at school; Studied at London School of Fashion. *Career:* Worked in fashion PR directly before joining S Club 7; Group quickly achieved international success following sales of TV series Miami 7 (1999), LA 7 (2000) and Hollywood 7 (2001) featuring the band's music to nearly 100 countries; Also made nature TV series S Club 7 Go Wild (2000) and various TV specials; First British tour with S Club 7, 2001. *Recordings:* Albums: S Club, 1999; 7, 2000; Sunshine, 2001; Singles: Bring It All Back, 1999; S Club Party, 1999; Two In A Million/You're My Number One, 1999; Reach, 2000; Natural, 2000; Never Had A Dream Come True, 2000; Don't Stop Movin', 2001; Have You Ever, 2001. *Honours:* Brit Award, Best British Newcomer, 2000. *Current Management:* 19 Management, Unit 32, Ransomes Dock, 35–37 Parkgate Rd, London, SW11 4NP, England.

STEVENS Richard William; b. 17 Aug. 1962, Wegberg, Germany. Musician (drums). *Musical Education:* Private jazz tuition, Tommy Chase, John Stevens. *Career:* Performed with: Dennis Bovell; Lynton Kwesi Johnson; George Clinton; Own group: Well Red; Own project: Drumhead. *Recordings with:* Simply Red; Joan Armatrading; Oleta Adams; Boy George. *Current Management:* Copasetic Records. *Address:* 102 Ulleswater Rd, London N14 7BT, England.

STEVENS Shakin', (Michael Barratt); b. 4 March 1948, Ely, Cardiff, South Wales. Singer; Songwriter. *Career:* Enjoyed much success touring for many years with his band, the Sunsets; Starred in the multi-award-winning West End musical, Elvis, which ran for 19 months from 1977; Signed as solo artist with Epic Records world-wide in 1978; First UK Top 30 single, Hot Dog, charted in 1980; First European chart entry, Marie

Marie, in 1980; First UK No. 1, later a major international hit, This Ole House, 1981; 38 hit singles, 36 of which were consecutive, throughout the 1980s and 1990s; UK hits: Four No. 1 hits, three No. 2 hits, 12 Top 5 hits, 15 Top 10 hits, 25 Top 20 hits, 30 Top 30 hits and 32 Top 40 hits; Musical collaborations include Bonnie Tyler, Roger Taylor, Hank Marvin and Albert Lee; Tours, personal appearances and television performances world-wide; Most successful hit-maker of the 1980s in the UK, with more weeks in the charts (254 in the 80's alone) than any other international recording artist; His work has been covered by many artists including Eddy Raven (A Letter To You) and Sylvia (Cry Just a Little Bit), No 1 and No 9 in the Nashville charts, and Barry Manilow (Oh Julie), US hit in 1982. *Recordings:* Hit singles, albums and songs have sold millions of copies, earning numerous honours and awards, including many Gold and Platinum discs world-wide; Hit albums include (UK): Shakin' Stevens Take One!; Shakin' Stevens; Shaky; Give Me Your Heart Tonight; The Bop Won't Stop; Greatest Hits; Lipstick, Powder and Paint; Let's Boogie; A Whole Lotta Shaky; There's Two Kinds of Music – Rock 'n' Roll; The Epic Years; UK hit singles include: Hot Dog; Marie Marie; This Ole House; You Drive Me Crazy; Green Door; It's Raining; Oh Julie; Shirley; I'll Be Satisfied; The Shakin' Stevens EP; It's Late; Cry Just a Little Bit; A Rockin' Good Way (To Mess Around and Fall In Love), duet with Bonnie Tyler; A Love Worth Waiting For; A Letter To You; Teardrops; Breakin' Up My Heart; Lipstick Powder and Paint; Merry Christmas Everyone; Turning Away; Because I Love You; A Little Boogie Woogie (In The Back of My Mind); What Do You Want To Make Those Eyes At Me For?; Love Attack; I Might; The Best Christmas of Them All; Radio. *Honours include:* 30 Top 30 hits in a decade, unsurpassed by any other artist; Best Musical of 1977; Best singer/ performer, MIDEM; Chartmaker Award for 4 simultaneous singles in the German chart; Gold and Platinum discs world-wide; First double platinum single ever to an international artist, Sweden; Shares with the Beatles and Elton John the distinction of being the most successful British chart performer of a decade; Awarded Gold Badge Award by the British Academy of Composers and Songwriters, for contribution to the music industry, 2000. *Current Management:* Sue Davies, The HEC Organisation, PO Box 184, West End, Woking, Surrey GU24 9YY, England.

STEVENS Steve; b. New York, USA. Musician (guitar). *Career:* Lead guitarist, Billy Idol, 1981–88; Solo artiste, and leader of own group Atomic Playboys; Also worked with Michael Jackson; Ric Ocasek; Steve Lukather; Thompson Twins. *Recordings:* with Billy Idol: Don't Stop, 1981; Billy Idol, 1982; Rebel Yell, 1983; Whiplash Smile, 1986; Vital Idol, 1987; Idol Songs – 11 of The Best, 1988; Solo: Steve Steve's Atomic Playboys, 1989; Other recordings include: Bad, Michael Jackson, 1987; Lukather, Steve Lukather, 1989; Chalk Mark in a Rain Storm, Joni Mitchell, 1988; Don't Explain, Robert Palmer, 1990; Hit singles with Billy Idol include: Hot In The City; White Wedding; Without a Face; Rebel Yell; To Be a Lover; Don't Need a Gun; Sweet Sixteen; Money Money Live; Hot In The City; Other singles include: Dirty Diana, Michael Jackson. *Address:* c/o Weidenbaum Ryder and Co, 720 Palisade Ave, Englewood Cliffs, NJ 07632, USA.

STEVENSON Jeffrey; b. 14 Jan. 1947, Leeds, Yorkshire, England. Musician (guitar, piano); Singer; Songwriter. m. Cecile Louise McDonald, 30 Aug. 1969, 2 d. *Musical Education:* Self-taught. *Career:* Played role of Woof, Canadian production of musical, Hair, 1970; Singer, guitarist, co-writer, television series Spider, BBC; Support to Labi Siffre in concert; Staff writer for programme Watch, BBC TV; Numerous and television radio gigs. *Compositions:* Over 80 titles published / recorded. *Recordings:* Spider; Recorded with Marty Wilde. *Memberships:* Musicians' Union; Songwriters Guild; PRS; MCPS. *Leisure interests:* Supporting Leeds United Football Club; Committed Christian; Reading. *Address:* 30 Chiswick Village, London W4 3BY, England.

STEWART Al; b. 5 Sept. 1945, Glasgow, Scotland. Singer; Songwriter; Musician (guitar). m. Kristine Russell, 18 May 1991, 1 d. *Musical Education:* Self-taught. *Career:* Solo artist, 1967–; Appearances include: Royal Festival Hall, 1967; US tour, 1974; Cambridge Folk Festival, 1989. *Recordings:* Singles include: Midnight Rocks; License To Steal; Albums: Bedsitter Images, 1967; Love Chronicles (featuring Jimmy Page), 1969; Zero She Flies, 1970; Orange, 1972; Past Present and Future, 1974; Modern Times, 1975; Year of The Cat, 1976; Time Passages, 1978; Carrots, 1980; Live/Indian Summer, 1981; Russians and Americans, 1984; Last Days of The Century, 1988; Rock The World, 1990; Rhymes In Rooms – Al Stewart Live Featuring Peter White, 1993; Between The Wars (with Laurence Juber), 1995; Seemed Like a Good Idea, 1996; Live at the Roxy, 1997; Acoustic Evening, 1998. *Leisure interests:* Wine collecting; Reading history. *Current Management:* c/o Steve Chapman, Chapman and Co, PO Box 5549, Santa Monica, CA 90409, USA.

STEWART Dave; b. 9 Sept. 1952, Sunderland, Tyne and Wear, England. Musician (guitar, keyboards); Songwriter; Composer. m. Siobhan Fahey, 1 Aug. 1987, divorced, 1 s. *Career:* Musician, Harrison and Stewart (with Brian Harrison); Longdancer; The Catch, 1977; Renamed The Tourists, 1979–80; Formed Eurythmics with Annie Lennox, 1980–89; World-wide concerts include Nelson Mandela's 70th Birthday Tribute, Wembley, 1988;

As solo artiste: Nelson Mandela Tribute concert, Wembley, 1990; Amnesty International Big 30 concert, 1991; Founder, Spiritual Cowboys, 1990–92; Vegas, with Terry Hall, 1992–93; Founder, own record label Anxious Records, 1988; Owner, The Church recording studio, 1992; Producer, session musician, for artistes including Bob Dylan; Mick Jagger; Tom Petty; Daryl Hall; Bob Geldof; Boris Grebenshikov. *Compositions:* All Eurythmics songs co-written with Lennox; Theme for Jute City, BBC1; Co-writer, film score Motorcycle Mystics; Co-writer with Gerry Anderson, music for children's series GFI, 1992. *Recordings:* Albums: with The Tourists: The Tourists; Reality Affect; Luminous Basement; with Eurythmics: In The Garden, 1982; Sweet Dreams (Are Made of This), 1983; Touch (No. 1, UK), 1984; 1984 (For The Love of Big Brother), film soundtrack, 1984; Be Yourself Tonight, 1985; Revenge, 1986; Savage, 1988; We Too Are One (No. 1, UK), 1989; Eurythmics Greatest Hits (No. 1, UK), 1991; Eurythmics Live 1983–89, 1992; with the Spiritual Cowboys: Dave Stewart and The Spiritual Cowboys, 1990; with Vegas: Vegas, 1992; Solo: Greetings From The Gutter, 1994; Film soundtrack: De Kassiere, with Candy Dulfer, 1990; Hit singles include: with the Tourists: I Only Want To Be With You, 1979; So Good To Be Back Home, 1979; with Eurythmics: Sweet Dreams (Are Made of This) (No. 1, USA), 1983; Love is a Stranger, 1983; Who's That Girl?, 1983; Right By Your Side, 1983; Here Comes The Rain Again, 1984; Sex Crime (1984), 1984; Would I Lie To You?, 1985; There Must Be An Angel (Playing With My Heart), 1985; It's Alright (Baby's Coming Back), 1986; When Tomorrow Comes, 1986; Thorn In My Side, 1986; Missionary Man, 1986; You Have Placed a Chill In My Heart, 1988; Love Is a Stranger, 1991; Sweet Dreams, 1991; I Saved the World, 1999; 17 Again, 1999; Solo: Lily Was Here, with Candy Dulfer, 1990; Contributor, Rock The World, 1990; Give Peace a Chance, Peace Choir, 1991; Videos: Eurythmics Live; Sweet Dreams; Savage. *Honours:* MTV Music Awards, Best New Artist Video, Sweet Dreams, 1984; BRIT Awards: Best Producer, 1986, 1987, 1990; Grammy, Best Rock Performance, Missionary Man, 1987; Ivor Novello Awards: Songwriters of the Year (with Annie Lennox), 1984, 1987; Best Song, It's Alright, 1987. *Current Management:* Miss Management, 16101 Ventura Blvd, Suite 301, Encino, CA 91436, USA. *Address:* c/o East West Records, Electric Lighting Station, 46 Kensington Court, London W8 5DP, England.

STEWART Don(ald George); b. 8 Jan. 1935, Sterling, Illinois, USA. Musician; Music Industry Exec.; Composer. m. Susan Ann Trainer, 13 June 1963, divorced 1979, 1 d. *Education:* MusB, Indianana University, 1960; Postgraduate Studies, Manhattan School, 1960–62; School of Jazz, 1958–60; Studied with Ray Harris, Bernhard Heiden, Gunther Schuller. *Career:* Second Clarinet, Birmingham Symphony Orchestra, Alabama, 1954–56; Florida Symphony, Orlando, 1963; Played with numerous jazz ensembles including Ornette Coleman, David Baker, Sammy Davis, 1957–65; Woodwind, orchestras, New York, 1967–72; Founder, Boehm Quintette, New York City, 1968–88; Music Assistant, New York State Council on the Arts, 1972–75; Freelance Copyist, 1958–88; Founder, President, Trillenium Music Co, 1986–; President, Opera North, Norwich, Vermont, 1987–89; Founder, Treasurer, Chamber Music America, New York, 1977–81; Panellist, Vermont Council on the Arts, 1976–78. *Compositions:* Piccolo Concerto, 1973; August Lions, for youth orchestra, 1978; Song of Arion, 1985; First Blue Symphony, 1988; Book of Sliding Things, 1989; Green Mountain Christmas Card, opera, 1995; Never Seek To Tell Thy Love, for voice and ensemble, 1998; Transcriber, composer, arranger. *Recordings:* Numerous on several labels. *Memberships:* ASCAP; American Federation of Musicians; American Society of Music Copyists, Board of Directors 1970–87, Treasurer, 1984–87; American Music Centre; Music Publisher's Asscn; Retail Print Music Dealers Asscn, 1995-. *Address:* Trillenium Music, PO Box 88, Tunbridge, VT 05077, USA.

STEWART Jimmy (James Otto); b. 8 Sept. 1935, San Francisco, California, USA. Musician (guitar); Prod.; Composer; Writer. m. Terri Tilton, 22 April 1988. *Education:* AA, College of San Mateo, 1957. *Musical Education:* BA, Chicago School of Music, 1960; Certificate, Berklee School of Music, 1964; Private studies. *Career:* Featured soloist with: Los Angeles Philharmonic; Dallas Symphony Orchestra; St Louis Symphony Orchestra; San Francisco Light Opera; Guitarist with artists including: Ray Charles, Stan Getz, David Grisman, Dave Grusin, Michael Jackson, Quincy Jones, Herbie Mann, Shelly Manne, Gary McFarland, Carlos Santana, Sonny Stitt, Gabor Szabo; Musical director for: Lainie Kazan; Chita Rivera; Andy Williams; Vocal coach for: Linda Ronstadt; Juice Newton; Lee Ritenour; Master class tutor at: Dick Grove School of Music; Musicians Institute of Technology; Audio/Video Institute of Technology, Hollywood; University of Southern California. *Compositions include:* classical pieces, music for commercials, television, films. *Recordings:* Solo albums include: Fire Flower, 1977; The Touch, 1986; Blues Trax, 1992; The Art, History and Style of Jazz Guitar, 1993; The Complete Jazz Guitarist, 1994; Tribute To Classical Guitar, 1995; Also recorded with artists including: Gabor Szabo (7 albums); Burt Bacharach; James Brown; Sammy Davis Jr; Neil Diamond; Barbra Streisand; Everly Brothers; Maurice Jarre; Dusty Springfield; Featured on 1,200 recordings; Memorabilia, 1998. *Publications:* 21 guitar books include: Mode Mania, 1992; Heavy Metal Guitar, 1992; The Art History and Style of Jazz Guitar,

1993; The Complete Jazz Guitarist, 1994; Tribute To Classical Guitar, 1995; Numerous song books; contributor to Guitar Player, Recording Engineer and Producer magazine; Wes Montgomery Jazz Guitar Method, 1968. *Honours:* Alabama Jazz Hall of Fame; Decade of Service, Guitar Player Magazine; Communicator Award, Crystal Award of Excellence, 1998. *Memberships:* ASCAP; NARAS; IAJE; AFM. *Leisure interest:* Golf.

STEWART Jon Randall; b. 14 Feb. 1949. Vocalist; Musician (guitar, mandolin). *Career:* Lead guitar, harmony, vocals for Emmylou Harris with The Nash Ramblers, 1990–95; Opening act for Mary Chapin Carpenter, 1995; Signed with Asylum Records, 1998. *Composition:* Just Like You. *Recordings:* Albums: What You Don't Know, 1995; Emmylou Harris and The Nash Ramblers of The Ryman; Cold Coffee Morning, 1999. *Honours:* Grammy Award, Emmylou Harris and The Nash Ramblers, 1992. *Leisure interests:* Fishing; Racing. *Current Management:* M Hitchcock Management. *Address:* PO Box 159007, Nashville, TN 37215, USA.

STEWART Rod (Roderick David); b. 10 Jan. 1945, Highgate, North London, England. Singer. m. (1) Alana Collins, 1970; (2) Rachel Hunter, 1990, 1 s., 2 d. *Career:* Singer with: Steampacket; Shotgun Express; Jeff Beck Group, 1967–69; Concerts include: British tour with Roy Orbison, 1967; US tours, 1967, 1968; The Faces, 1969–75; Appearances include: Reading Festival, 1972; UK, US tours, 1972; Solo artiste, 1971–; Solo appearances include: Rock In Rio, Brazil, 1985; Vagabond Heart Tour, 1991–92. *Recordings:* Singles include: Reason To Believe; Maggie May; (I Know) I'm Losing You; Handbags and Gladrags; You Wear It Well; Angel; Farewell; Sailing; This Old Heart of Mine; Tonight's The Night (Gonna Be All Right); The Killing of Georgie (Parts 1 and 2); Get Back; The First Cut Is The Deepest; I Don't Want To Talk About It; You're In My Heart; Hot Legs; D'Ya Think I'm Sexy?; Passion; Young Turks; Tonight I'm Yours; Baby Jane; What Am I Gonna Do; Infatuation; Some Guys Have All The Luck; Love Touch; Every Beat of My Heart; Downtown Train; Rhythm of My Heart; This Old Heart of Mine; Have I Told You Lately; Reason To Believe; Ruby Tuesday; You're The Star; Albums include: 2 with Jeff Beck; 4 with the Faces; Solo albums: Every Picture Tells a Story, 1971; Never a Dull Moment, 1972; Atlantic Crossing, 1975; A Night On The Town, 1976; Foot Lose and Fancy Free, 1977; Blondes Have More Fun, 1978; Foolish Behaviour, 1980; Tonight I'm Yours, 1981; Camouflage, 1984; Love Touch, 1986; Out of Order, 1988; The Best Of, 1989; Downtown Train, 1990; Vagabond Heart, 1991; Lead Vocalist, 1992; Unplugged... and Seated, 1993; A Spanner In The Works, 1995; When We Were the New Boys, 1998; Numerous compilations. *Honours include:* BRIT Awards, Lifetime Achievement Award, 1993; First artist to top US and UK singles and album charts simultaneously, 1971. *Address:* c/o Stiefel Phillips Entertainment, 9720 Wilshire Blvd, Suite 400, Beverly Hills, CA 90212, USA.

STEWART Tommy; b. 26 May 1966, Flint, Michigan, USA. Musician (drums). *Career:* Previously in Lillian Axe and various covers groups; Joined Boston-based band Godsmack for short period, 1995; Returned, replacing Joe Darko, 1997; Group secured deal with Republic/Universal following heavy airplay of first single on local WAAF-FM station, 1998; US and European gigs in 1999 and 2000 including: Woodstock '99; Ozzfest; MTV's Return of The Rock tour; Second album recorded in warehouse in Massachusetts, 2000; First major amphitheatre tour, 2001. *Recordings:* Albums: Godsmack, 1998; Awake, 2000; Singles: Whatever, 1998; Awake, 2000; Greed, Bad Magick, 2001. *Honours:* Whatever single spent record total of 33 weeks on Billboard Top 10; Boston Music Awards, Act of The Year, 2000 and 2001; Billboard Award, Rock Artist of The Year, 2001. *Address:* c/o Paul Geary, PGM, PO Box 9134, Boston, MA 02205, USA. *E-mail:* godsmack@pgmglobal.com. *Internet:* www.godsmack.com.

STIEF Bo; b. 15 Oct. 1946, Copenhagen, Denmark. Musician (bass guitar, double bass); Composer; Bandleader; Teacher. 1 s., 2 d. *Career:* Bass player, 1963–; Began as bass player for touring soloists including: Dexter Gordon; Chet Baker; John Scofield; Don Cherry; Stan Getz; Dizzy Gillespie; Member of: Entrance; Midnight Sun; Leader, own band Chasing Dreams, 1980–; Major tours, festivals throughout Europe; Also played with: Miles Davis; Toots Thielmans; Joe Henderson; Larry Coryell; Alex Riel; Clark Terry; Archie Shepp; Yusef Lateef; Gato Barbieri; Art Farmer; Terje Rypdal; Jan Garbarek; George Russell; Astrid Gilberto; Zoot Sims; Carla Bley; AMO; Recent collaborations with: Just Friends; Palle Mikkelborg; Barbara Thompson; Ernie Watts; Jasper van't Hof Quartet. *Compositions:* Simple Song; Miss Julie, used for UN educational film. *Recordings:* Albums: with Bo Stief Chasing Dreams: Hidden Frontiers; 1987; Chasing Dreams, 1994; Also played on over 500 albums including: Aura, Miles Davis, Palle Mikkelborg, 1985; Anything But Grey, Palle Mikkelborg, 1992; Ernie Watts, Jasper van't Hof Quartet, 1993. *Honours:* Jazz Musician of the Year, 1988; Composers Award of Honour, DJBFA, 1990. *Address:* Kaermindevej 11, 2820 Gentofte, Denmark.

STIGERS Curtis; b. 1968, Boise, Idaho, USA. Singer; Musician (clarinet, saxophone). *Musical Education:* Classical training in clarinet. *Career:* Member, local punk and blues bands; Later played in blues groups, New York; Discovered in jazz trio; Currently solo artiste. *Recordings:* Album: Curtis Stigers, 1992; Time Was, 1995; Brighter Days, 1999; Singles include: Never Saw a Miracle; To Be Loved; Contributor, Tapestry Revisited – A Tribute To Carole King, 1996. *Current Management:* C. Winston Simone, 1790 Broadway, 10th Floor, New York, NY 10019, USA.

STILLS Stephen; b. 3 Jan. 1945, Dallas, Texas, USA. Vocalist; Musician (guitar). m. Veronique Sanson, Jan. 1971. *Career:* Member, Au Go Go Singers; Buffalo Springfield, 1966–68; Crosby Stills and Nash, 1968–; (also as Crosby Stills Nash and Young); Manassas, 1971–74; Performances include: with Buffalo Springfield: Monterey Festival, 1967; with Crosby Stills and Nash: Woodstock, 1969; Royal Albert Hall, 1970; Festival of Hope, New York, 1972; Wembley Stadium, 1974; Night of The Hurricane 2 benefit concert, Texas, 1976; Last Waltz concert, San Francisco, with The Band, 1976; US tour, 1979; Anti-nuclear benefits, Madison Square Garden, 1979; No Nukes benefit concert, Hollywood Bowl, 1980; Film, No Nukes, 1980; Live Aid, Philadelphia, 1985; Amnesty International benefit, Chile, 1990; Hurricane Andrew benefit, Miami, 1992; Royal Albert Hall, 1992; Imua Hawaii, 1992. *Recordings:* with Buffalo Springfield: Buffalo Springfield, 1967; Stampede, 1967; Buffalo Springfield Again, 1967; with Crosby Still and Nash: Crosby Stills and Nash, 1969; Déjà Vu, 1970; 4-Way Street, 1971; So Far, 1974; Daylight Again, 1982; What Goes Around, 1983; Allies, 1983; American Dream, 1989; Live It Up, 1990; Looking Forward, 1999; Solo albums: Stephen Stills, 1970; Stephen Stills 2, 1971; Stills, 1975; Stephen Stills – Live On Atlantic, 1976; Illegal Stills, 1976; Still Stills – The Best of Stephen Stills, 1977; Thoroughfare Gap, 1978; with Manassas: Manassas, 1972; Down The Road, 1973; with Stills/Young: Long May You Run, 1976; Singles include: with Buffalo Springfield: For What It's Worth, 1967; Bluebird, 1967; Rock 'n' Roll Woman, 1967; with Crosby Stills and Nash: Suite – Judy Blue Eyes, 1969; Woodstock, 1970; Ohio, 1970; Just a Song Before I Go, 1977; Wasted On The Way, 1982; Southern Cross, 1982; Solo: Love The One You're With, 1971. *Honours include:* Grammy Award, Best New Artist, Crosby Stills and Nash, 1970; Best International Group, Melody Maker Poll, 1971. *Current Management:* Management Network, 14930 Ventura Blvd #205, Sherman Oaks, CA 91403, USA.

STING (Gordon Matthew Sumner); b. 2 Oct. 1951, Wallsend, Newcastle-Upon-Tyne, England. Singer; Musician (bass); Actor. m. (1) Frances Tomelty, 1 May 1976, divorced 1984, 1 s., 1 d.; (2) Trudie Styler, 20th Aug. 1992, 2 s., 2 d. *Career:* School teacher, Newcastle, 1975–77; Singer, songwriter, bass player, The Police, 1977–86; Solo artiste, 1985–; Numerous world-wide tours, television and radio, with the Police and solo; actor in films: Quadrophenia, 1980; Secret Policeman's Other Ball, 1982; Brimstone and Treacle, 1982; Dune, 1984; The Bride, 1985; Plenty, 1985; Julia and Julia, 1988; Stormy Monday, 1988; The Adventures of Baron Munchausen, 1989; Broadway Performance, Threepenny Opera, 1989. *Recordings:* Hit singles include: Walking On The Moon; Message In a Bottle; So Lonely; Roxanne; De Do Do Do, De Da Da Da; Every Little Thing She Does; Every Breath You Take; Invisible Sun; Can't Stand Losing You; Don't Stand So Close To Me; If You Love Somebody; Englishman In New York; If I Ever Lose My Faith In You; Fields of Gold; Love Is Stronger Than Justice; Cowboy Song (with Pato Banton); Let The Soul Be Your Pilot; Roxanne 97; Brand New Day; Albums: with the Police: Outlandos D'Amour, 1977; Regatta De Blanc, 1979; Zenyatta Mondatta, 1980; Ghost In The Machine, 1981; Synchronicity, 1983; Bring On The Night, 1986; Solo albums: The Dream of The Blue Turtles, 1985; Nothing Like The Sun, 1987; The Soul Cages, 1991; Ten Summoner's Tales, 1994; Mercury Falling, 1996; Brand New Day, 1999; Contributor, Tower of Song (Leonard Cohen tribute), 1995. *Honours include:* 10 Grammy Awards (with Police and solo); Q Award, Best Album, 1994; BRIT Award, Best Male Artist, 1994. *Membership:* PRS. *Current Management:* Firstars, 1 Water Lane, Camden Town, London NW1 8NZ, England.

STIPE (John) Michael; b. 4 Jan. 1960, Decatur, Georgia, USA. Singer; Songwriter; Record Prod. *Career:* Member, R.E.M., 1980–; International concerts include: Earth Day Concert, Maryland, 1989; Green World tour, 1989; A Performance For The Planet concert, 1990; European tour, 1992; Own film and video company C-OO; Own vegetarian restaurant, The Grit, Athens, Georgia. *Recordings:* Chronic Town (mini-album), 1982; Murmur, 1983; Reckoning, 1984; Fables of The Reconstruction, 1985; Life's Rich Pageant, 1986; Dead Letter Office, 1987; Document, 1987; Eponymous, 1988; Green, 1988; Out of Time, 1991; Monster, 1995; Up, 1998; Star Profiles, 1999; Out of Time, 1999; Singles: The One I Love, 1987; Stand, 1989; Orange Crush, 1989; Losing My Religion, 1991; Shiny Happy People, 1991; Near Wild Heaven, 1991; Radio Song, 1991; Drive, 1992; Man On The Moon, 1992; The Sidewinder Sleeps Tonite, 1993; Everybody Hurts, 1993; Nightswimming; Crush With Eyeliner; What's The Frequency Kenneth?, 1994; The Great Beyond, 2000; Tracks featured on film soundtracks: Batchelor Party, 1984; Until The End of The World, 1991; Coneheads, 1993; Recordings with: Indigo Girls, 1988; Syd Straw, 1989; Billy Bragg, 1991; Neneh Cherry, 1991; Contributor, Disney compilation, Stay Awake, with Natalie Merchant, 1988; Tom's Album, 1991; I'm Your Fan (Leonard Cohen tribute), 1991; Producer, artistes including: Swell; Chickasaw Muddpuppies; Opal Fox Society; Co-producer, film Desperation Angels, with Oliver Stone. *Honours:* Earth Day Award, 1990; Numerous MTV Music Video Awards, Billboard Awards, 1991; BRIT Awards: Best International Group, 1992, 1993, 1995; Grammy Awards: Best Pop Performance, Alternative Music Album, Music Video, 1992; Atlanta Music Awards, 1992; IRMA Band of the Year, 1993; Rolling Stone Critics Awards, 1993; Q Awards: Best Album, 1991, 1992; Best Act In The World, 1991, 1995. *Current Management:* REM/Athens, 250 W Clayton St, Athens, GA 30601, USA.

STOCK Michael; b. 3 Dec. 1951, Margate, Kent, England. Songwriter; Record Prod.; Musician. m. Frances Roberta, Dec. 1975, 2 s., 1 d. *Education:* University of Hull. *Career:* Signed first publishing deal, 1970; Member of bands: Mirage, 1976–84; Nightwork, 1981–84; Founder, partner, writing/production team Stock Aitken Waterman, 1984–93; Relocated to new studios, started new production company and Love This Records, 1994. *Recordings:* As writer/producer, artists include: Princess; Hazell Dean; Dead or Alive; Bananarama; Mel and Kim; Rick Astley; Kylie Minogue; Jason Donovan; Donna Summer; Cliff Richard; Sybil; Kym Mazelle; Jocelyn Brown; Nicki French; Power Rangers; Robson and Jerome; Scooch. *Honours:* BPI Best Producer, 1988; IVN Songwriter of Year 3 times; BMI Award, 4 times. *Memberships:* PRS; BASCA. *Leisure interest:* Sport. *Address:* c/o Love This International, Hundred House, 100 Union St, London SE1 0NL, England.

STOCKLEY Miriam; b. Johannesburg, South Africa. Singer. *Musical Education:* Self-taught, sight reading, harmony and vocal arrangement. *Career:* Solo recording artiste; Backing vocalist for top recording stars: Kylie Minogue; Jason Donovan; Brian May; Deniece Williams; Cliff Richard; Chaka Khan; Ronan Keating; Freddie Mercury; Robert Plant; Paul Young; Dina Carroll; B*Witched; Tina Turner; Appeared on tribute to Freddie Mercury, Brian May tour; Worked extensively with Stock, Aitken and Waterman; Television includes: Spitting Image; Kenny Everett; Beatrix Potter's Peter Rabbit theme song; Perfect Day. *Compositions:* Solo album, Miriam, 1999. *Recordings:* As Praise: Only You, used in Fiat commercial (No. 3, UK), 1991; 4 albums as Adiemus, with Karl Jenkins: First album: Songs of Sanctuary (No. 3, classical charts, Spain; Gold record Germany, Holland, Japan, UK), 1995–2000; Solo album, Miriam, 1999. *Honours:* Sarie Award for Best South African Recording Artiste. *Memberships:* PRS; MCPS; GVL; PAMRA. *Current Management:* David Stopps, Friars Management Ltd. *Address:* 33 Alexander Rd, Aylesbury, Buckinghamshire HP20 2NR, England.

STOICA Laura; b. 10 Oct. 1967, Alba-Iulia, Romania. Singer; Entertainer; Actress. m. Florin Ionescu, 31 Oct. 1992. *Education:* Baccalaureat, Electrical Engineering. *Musical Education:* 5 year course, Diploma in Performing Arts (theatre, musical, pop music); Diploma, Performing Classical Music; Licence, Professional Music Interpretation. *Career:* Lead singer, Riff, Semnal M. to 1988; Solo artiste, 1987–; Lead singer, Laura Stoica Band, 1993–; Over 40 live appearances, national, international, television and radio; TV specials include: 5 O'Clock Tea, 1991, 1993–95; Bucharest International, 1990, 1993; Talk Show with Laura Stoica, 1993–95; Mamaia, 1991–95; Charity for Romanian children with AIDS and orphans, 1993, 1994; Radio specials include: Talk shows, 1991–95; Laura Stoica Live, 1992–95; Unplugged, 1995; Founder, President, Laura Stoica Charity Trust, 1993. *Recordings include:* Single: An Actor In My Life, 1992; Album: The Fire, 1994. *Honours include:* City Song Trophy, 1988; Mamaia Trophy, 1990, 91; Bucharest International Award, 1990; Golden Stag International Record Trophy, 1992; Pop, Rock and Show Award, 1991, 92, 93; Radio Contact Award, 1992; Bregenz International Pop Music Award, 1992. *Membership:* Romanian Guild of Songwriters and Composers. *Leisure interests:* Literature; Athletics; Tennis; Watching films; Theatre; Foreign languages (English, French, Italian).

STOIKOV Dimitar; b. 22 March 1931, Varna, Bulgaria. Musician (Accordion). m. Stanka Stoikova, 25 Aug. 1955, 2 s. *Education:* College of Harmony and Composition, Varna. *Career:* Film profile on Bulgarian TV; Participation in radio programmes; Concerts in Macedonia, Serbia, Turkey, Slovenia, Czech Republic, Russia, Germany. *Compositions:* Over 900 folk compositions. *Recordings:* Over 150 records including 7 albums, 8 singles, 8 cassettes and 1 CD, Imperishable Gleeds, 1999. *Honours:* SS Cyril and Methodius Order; Gold medals, prizes at folk festivals. *Membership:* Musicauter Sofia, Bulgaria. *Leisure interest:* Fishing. *Address:* 13a Sv Dimitar Salounski St, Vinitsa, 9022 Varna, Bulgaria.

STOIKOV Youri; b. 1 March 1962, Varna, Bulgaria. Composer; Musician (Keyboards). m. Savina Stoikova, 9 July 1994. *Education:* Higher Humanitarian Education, St Kliment Ochridski State University, Sofia, Bulgaria; Varna College of Musical Harmony and Composition, with Petke Mechkev. *Career:* First and Second Festivals of Electronic Music, Getse Delchev, Bulgaria, shown on national TV; Member, Jury, Diskovery 1994–1996 Festival, Varna. *Recordings:* Window to the Soul, cassette, 1988; Things, cassette, 1990; Transfiguration, CD, 1992; The Legends, CD, 1996. *Publications:* Series of articles on electronic music, 1988–89, Varna. *Honours:* First Prize for Song dedicated to the Sea, Competition of

Maritime Navigation, Bulgaria, 1992; Jury's Prize, Badalona, Spain. *Membership:* Musicautor, Sofia. *Leisure interest:* Computers. *Address:* Ap 28, Bl 43 b Chaika, Varna 9005, Bulgaria.

STOKER Richard; b. 8 Nov. 1938, Castleford, Yorkshire, England. Composer; Author; Painter; Poet. m. Dr Gillian Patricia Watson, 10 July 1986. *Education:* Huddersfield School of Music and School of Art, 1953–58; Royal Academy of Music, with Lennox Berkeley, 1958–62; Composition with Nadia Boulanger, Paris, 1962–63; Mendelssohn Scholarship, 1962–63; Also private study with Britten, Benjamin, Fenby and Truscott; Professor of Composition, RAM, 1963–87. *Career:* Composition Teacher to Paul Patterson, Joe Jackson, Malcolm Singer, the late Paul Reade and others; Performing pianist, BBC radio, television and CDs. *Compositions include:* Song lyrics and music, orchestral, choral, 3 overtures, chamber music, jazz preludes, operas; Films and theatre music; Tribute to Hoagy Carmichael, with Fazarro and Earl Okin, South Bank, 1981. *Recordings include:* Album with Susan Fazarro, Chandos; 2 CD Tribute to Hoagy Carmichael; Complete piano works, Eric Parkin; Complete guitar music, Martin Vishnick, 1999; Priory, vocal and duo piano works, 1999–2000; ASC Records Ltd, 3 CD songs: Royal, JJ, Saydisc. *Publications:* Open Window-Open Door, autobiography; Regency 'Words without Music' (outposts); Between the Lines; Portrait of a Town, filmed 1983); Tanglewood, 1994; Diva – A Novel, 1995; Collected Short Stories, 1997; 3 plays; Numerous lyrics and numerous poems in more than 30 anthologies; Numerous stories in anthologies. Contributions to: magazines and journals; Editor, Composer Magazine, 1969–80. *Honours:* Mendelssohn Scholarship, 1962; Dove Prize RAM, 1962; Associate Royal College of Music, 1962; Associate, RAM, 1965, Fellow, 1971, Royal Academy of Music; Justice of the Peace, 1995–; Twice nominated Man of the Year, American Biographical Institute; 3 Editor's Awards, National Society of Poetry, USA. *Memberships:* Executive Committee, Composers' Guild, 1969–74, 1974–80; Asscn of Professional Composers, 1977–99, Promotions Committee, 1995–; BASCA, Professional Mem., 1979–95; Executive committee, British Academy of Composers and Songwriters, 1999–; PRS, 1962–; MCPS, 1970; Founder Mem., RAM Guild, 1986-, Executive Committee, 1994–, Hon Treasurer, 1995–; Magistrates' Asscn, 1995; U3A, 1993–; Founder Mem., Atlantic Council of the UK, 1994; Euro-Atlantic Group, 1994–; PEN International; English PEN, 1996–; Royal Society of Literature, 1997-. *Current Management:* Ricordi and Co Ltd. *Address:* c/o Ricordi and Co Ltd, BMG, 210 New Kings Rd, London SW6 4NZ, England.

STOKES Mary Teresa; b. 25 Aug. 1962, Dublin, Ireland. Singer. m. Brian Palm, 14 Feb. 1994. *Education:* BA, Psychology; MA by Research. *Musical Education:* 10 years classical singing; to Grade 5. *Career:* Formed blues band The Mary Stokes Band, 1988 (now 5-piece); Performed concerts in Ireland, Europe, USA; Backed: John Lee Hooker; Fats Domino; Carey Bell; Lowell Fulson; B B King; Radio and television appearances: Ireland; BBC; UTV; Began composing, 1993. *Recordings:* 3 albums; 3 singles. *Honours:* Smithwicks Hot Press Best Newcomer Award, 1989. *Leisure interests:* Film; Literature; Current affairs.

STOKKEBYE Peter; b. 22 Aug. 1975, Copenhagen, Denmark. Musician. *Education:* Drum School, Music School, Copenhagen. *Career:* Played with Blink on a Tour to Seoul in South Korea; Concert with 50,000 People on Live Television; Several Radio Programs and Television Shows. *Recordings:* Prunes, 1996–97; Secret Garden; Standing on the Hill; Get High, 1998. *Honours:* Gold Record, Korea, 1997. *Membership:* Danish Musicians Union. *Current Management:* Sundance Records. *Address:* Nivaavaenge 196, 2990 Nivaa, Denmark.

STOLTING Arnold Hugo; b. 12 Aug. 1969, Georgetown, Guyana. Singer; Songwriter; Prod. *Education:* National Institute of Broadcasting, Toronto. *Career:* Productions aired on Radio World-wide; Producer for Songwriter demo tapes; Produces professional Recording Artists and involved with development of new talent; President, CEO, Canadance Music Records/Productions/Publishing. *Compositions:* Numerous compositions in styles of Dance, R & B, Pop, Reggae, HipHop, Rap. *Recordings:* Think I'm In Love, Hugo; Hey Pretty Boy, Crystal; Give It To Me Baby, Azz; In the Distance, Sona; Summatime, Blakborough. *Memberships:* SOCAN; CMRRA. *Leisure interest:* Helping others. *Current Management:* Canadance Music. *Address:* 36–3430 Finch Ave E, Toronto, On M1W 2R5, Canada.

STONE Angie; b. Columbia, South Carolina, USA. Vocalist; Songwriter. *Musical Education:* Self-taught: Keyboards. *Career:* Daughter of a gospel singer, started singing in church choir with father; Member of rap trio The Sequence on Sugarhill records; Reached the attention of Prince protégé Jill Jones and was recruited to work on her album; Formed vocal trio Vertical Hold; Solo career 1999–; Collaborations: Mantronix; Lenny Kravitz; D'Angelo; Omar; Mary J Blige; Guru; Alicia Keys; Prince; Gerry DeVeaux. *Recordings:* A Matter of Time (with Vertical Hold), 1993; Head First (with Vertical Hold), 1995; Black Diamond, 1999; Mahogany Soul, 2001; Singles: with The Sequence: Funk You Up, 1980; Funky Sound (Tear The Roof Off), 1981; I Don't Need Your Love, 1982; with Vertical Hold: Summertime, 1988; Seems You're Much Too Busy, ASAP, 1993; Love

Today, 1995; solo: Everyday, 1997; No More Rain (In This Cloud), Life Story, 1999; Keep Your Worries (with Guru), 2000; Brotha, 2001. *Honours:* Soul Train Award, Best R & B/Soul New Artist, 2000. *Address:* c/o Arista Records, 6 W 57th St, New York, USA. *Internet:* www.angiestoneonline.com.

STONE Brian; b. 28 Aug. 1949, Lewisham, England. Drummer; Percussionist. m. Christine Ann Stone, 1 s., 3 d. *Education:* Guildhall with Gilbert Webster, Trevor Tompkins; Trinity College with Michael Skinner. *Career:* Varied Freelance Work; Some Summer Seasons at Pontins, Various West End Clubs; Big Band and Group Work; Percussion Teacher; Guildhall Examiner and London College Examiner. *Compositions:* Independance Day, 1985; Circus Rush, 1985. *Honours:* National Award Ballroom Dancing, 1965; National Award Latin American Dancing, 1968; LTCL, 1979. *Memberships:* Musicians' Union; National Asscn of Percussion Teachers; NASUWT. *Leisure interests:* Script Writing; DIY. *Address:* 9 Church St, Ellesmere, Shropshire SY12 0HD, England.

STONE Doug; b. 19 June, Nashville, Tennessee, USA. Musician (Piano, Electric Guitar, Acoustic Guitar, Bass, Mandolin, Drums). *Career:* Mechanic by Day, Musician at Night; Eight Year Tenure with Sony Nashville; Signed with Atlantic Records; Currently Preparing His Debut Atlantic Album. *Recordings:* Numerous Including, (I'd Be Better Off)In a Pine Box; Fourteen Mintues Old; In a Different Light; Too Busy Being in Love; Why Didn't I Think of That; Make Up In Love; These Lips Don't Know How To Say Goodbye; Come In Out of The Pain. *Honours:* Grammy Award; Best Male Vocal Performance; Horizon Award; Academy of Country Music Awards; TNN Music City News Awards; Platinum and Gold Records. *Current Management:* Atlantic Records. *Address:* c/o Trifecta Eng, 209 10th Ave S, Suite 302, Nashville, TN 37203, USA.

STONE Ronald William; b. 27 March 1959, Merseyside, England. Record Prod.; Engineer; Programmer; Musician (guitar); Songwriter. *Education:* Art College. *Career:* Member, Afraid of Mice, 1978; Backing musician for China Crisis, 1982; Formed Freeze Frame, 1984 (hits in Europe, Japan, Australia); Producer/Engineer for: Easterhouse; Throwing Muses; The Pixies; Oceanic; River City People; Audioweb; Pete Wylie; Shack; Sarah Cracknell; Mansun; Christians; Live sound: Easterhouse; Jason Donovan; WOMAD 1996, 1997; Connie Lush; Sian James; Lotus Eaters; Producer/ soundtracks for TV/cinema commercials: Gas; Electricity; Tea; Yves St Laurent; Consultant A & R for major record labels; Music for BBC TV series, Birdman, 1999. *Compositions:* Numerous songs published. *Recordings:* Producer/engineer for Say Something Good, River City People; All works by Oceanic, 1991–93; Singles and album, Attack of the Grey Lantern, by Mansun (Gold Disc). *Honours:* 6 Nominations for Top Advertisement Soundtracks; Gold and Silver discs as producer, engineer. *Current Management:* Area 51 Management. *Address:* TMW House, 12 Princess Terrace, Balls Rd, Birkenhead, Merseyside L43 5RB, England.

STONE Tony (Anthony George); b. 21 Dec. 1930, Weston-Super-Mare, England. Musician (multi-instrumentalist); Music Teacher. m. Shirley Winifred Parker, 31 Aug. 1955, 3 s. *Education:* Private tuition. *Career:* Solo keyboard player; Saxophonist with dance bands, big bands, jazz bands, orchestras, pit orchestras; Bandleader, arranger, composer, teacher; Appearances on BBC Radio and commercial television; Currently leader of New Parkway Showband, 1985–. *Compositions:* The Comet; Dancing; Moonrise; Freeway; Life Goes On; My Special Xmas Wish; Chocolate Cha-Cha; Eileen; Continuation Waltz; Encounters; Easy Walk; Coleford Jaunt; Marguerite; Loneliness. *Membership:* Musicians' Union. *Leisure interests:* Science; Miscellaneous repairs. *Address:* Horfield School of Music, 22 Wellington Hill, Horfield, Bristol BS7 8SR, England.

STONEBRIDGE; b. Stockholm, Sweden. Record Prod.; Songwriter. *Career:* DJ at own club, Stockholm; Formed Swemix, DJ service and production company, late 1980s; Formed BTB record label, 1992; Increasing success as producer and songwriter; DJ; Formed Swemix, 1986; Success as producer and songwriter. *Compositions:* Jacey John's Freestyle Dub, 1990; Back It Up, 1994; Satisfy My Love, 1996; Earthbeat, 1996; Boy You Knock Me Out, 1997. *Recordings include:* All Night Long, 1999; Enough is Enough, 1999; As producer: Make My Love, Shawn Christopher; Satisfy My Love, Sabrina Johnson; I Believe, 3rd Nation; Boy You Knock Me Out, Tatyana Ali and Will Smith; Show Me Love, Robin S; Make My Love, Shawn Christopher; Numerous remix credits include: Break The Chain, Motiv 8; Right Kind of Lover, Patti Labelle; Goodbye Baby, Lulu; Show Me Love, Robin S. *Honours:* Best Remixer, Swedish Dance Awards, 1991, 1993, 1994, 1996; Best 12, Winter Music Conference, 1994. *Memberships:* STIM; ASCAP. *Current Management:* Big Management, New York. *Address:* Stonebridge Productions, Eremitvagen 6, 11264 Stockholm, Sweden.

STONER Joel; b. 13 Jan. 1964, Sewickley, Pennsylvania, USA. Recording Engineer; Prod. m. Clare B McDonald, 10 Feb. 1991, 1 s. *Musical Education:* Berklee College of Music, Boston. *Career:* Recording and mixing multi-platinum albums; Music for film, television and commericals in all styles for major record labels and film companies.

Contributions to: professional magazines including Billboard and Mix. *Leisure interests:* Computers; Cooking; Family. *Address:* 1567 Fair Ave, Simi Valley, CA 93063, USA.

STORAAS Vigleik; b. 9 Feb. 1963, Bergen, Norway. Musician (piano, synthesizer). m. Astrid Vasseljen, 3 June 1994, 1 s., 1 d. *Education:* College. *Musical Education:* Jazz Department, Conservatory. *Career:* Festival appearances with Karin Krog, John Surman and Terje Rypdal in England and Italy. *Compositions:* Co-wrote many compositions including Nordic Quartet. *Recordings:* Nordic Quartet (with John Surman, Karin Krog, Terje Rypdal), 1995; Other albums with artists including: Bjorn Alterhaug; Soyr; Norma Winstone. *Memberships:* Norsk Musikforbund; NJF; FNJ, Norway. *Leisure interest:* Family. *Address:* Bromstadekrh 21C, 7046 Trondheim, Norway.

STOREY Michael Andrew; b. 26 Oct. 1936, Wakefield, Yorkshire, England. Entertainment Agent. m. Margaret Storey, 7 June 1965, 1 s., 1 d. *Career:* RAF Travel Agent; Entertainment Agent, 1971–; 20 years as broadcaster, BBC Radio Leeds; Vice Chairman of British Country Music Association. *Memberships:* British Country Music Asscn; Entertainment Agents Asscn. *Leisure interests:* Music; Reading; Travel. *Address:* Mike and Margaret Storey Entertainment, 59 Knowl Rd, Golcar, Huddersfield, West Yorkshire HD7 4AN, England.

STORRY Richard; b. 8 Sept. 1965, Ontario, Canada. Composer; Musician (guitar, keyboards). *Musical Education:* Royal Academy of Music. *Career:* Television appearances: Motormouth; Heno; S4C; Telethon; Sky; Radio broadcasts: Radio 2; Classic FM; GLR; Performed at: Coliseum; St James' Palace; Riverside Studios; Tours throughout UK with the Tetra Guitar Quartet including South Bank Centre; West End; Accompanist for West End singers and Recreation Theatre Company's The Rivals; Music Consultant and tutor for Uncle Vanya; Adjudicator, public speaker. *Compositions:* Musicals: A Musical Term; Arthur; Spellbyte; Kennedy. *Recordings:* Tetra By Arrangement; Tetra play Vivaldi's Four Seasons. *Honours:* GRSM (Hons); LRAM; DipRAM; Julian Bream Prize; Lady Holland Award. *Memberships:* PRS; BASCA; MCPS; PAMRA. *Leisure interests:* Theatre; Long walks; Board games; Eating out. *Current Management:* LA Management International. *Address:* 52 Junction Rd, Gillingham, Kent ME7 4EQ, England.

STOTZEM Jacques; b. 17 July 1959, Verviers, Belgium. Musician (acoustic guitar). 1 s. *Musical Education:* Self-taught. *Career:* Major concerts include: Guitar Festival of Liege, 1983, 1985; Inner Circle Concert, Los Angeles, USA, 1994; International Guitar Tour, Germany, 1994; Belga Jazz Festival, 1994; Clinics for: Fishman Transducers and Lowden Guitars, in Europe; Direction, Fingerstyle Workshops in Europe; Concerts during the Namm Show, Los Angeles, 1996, 1997; International Jazz Festival of Montréal, Québec, 1997; International Guitar Festival of Birkenhead, England, 1997; International Acoustic Guitar Night, Germany, 1997; Japan Tour, 1998. *Recordings:* Last Thought Before Sleeping, 1982; Training, 1985; Words From The Heart, 1988; Clear Night, 1991; Straight On, 1993; Two Bridges, 1995; Different Ways, 1996; Fingerprint, 1997; Connections, 2000. *Publications:* Selections from Two Bridges, Straight On and Clear Night, 1996. *Membership:* ASIA (Asscn of Stringed Instrument Artisans). *Leisure interest:* Cooking. *Address:* Jacques Stotzem, 24 rue Francval, 4800 Lambermont, Belgium.

STOVEY Martin Trevor; b. 27 Feb. 1871, Bushey, Hertfordshire, England. Musician (keyboards); Songwriter; Arranger. *Education:* HNC Civil Engineering. *Career:* Kings College, Cambridge, 1990–92; Flavour of the Month at Borderline, 1993; Lindsey Wesker Show (Kiss FM). *Recordings:* Driftings; Oh La La; Love Season; Chosen Child; Populus. *Membership:* Musicians' Union. *Leisure interest:* Aviation. *Address:* 66 Milton Dr., Borehamwood, Hertfordshire WD6 2BB, England.

STRACHAN Matthew James; b. 11 Dec. 1970, London, England. Composer; Musician (piano). *Musical Education:* Dartington College of Arts, Devon. *Career:* Musical Director of stage shows: Flora The Red Menace; Godspell; You don't Have To Say You Love Me. *Compositions include:* Music written or arranged for television: The Detectives; The Hypnotic World of Paul McKenna; The Jasper Carrott Trial; The Ward; What's Cooking?; Scratchy and Co; Compositions for Theatre: Simpleton of the Unexpected Isles; The Good Woman of Setzuan; The Fly. *Membership:* PRS; FRS; MCPS. *Leisure interests:* Songwriting; Films. *Current Management:* Blaze Music. *Address:* Upper Flat, 162 George Lane, London E18 1AY, England.

STRADLIN Izzy (Jeffrey Isbell); b. Lafayette, Indiana, USA. Rock Musician (guitar). *Career:* Member, US heavy rock group, Guns 'N' Roses, 1985–91; Regular national/international tours include: US support tours, Iron Maiden; Mötley Crüe; The Cult; Aerosmith; Get In The Ring tour, with Skid Row, 1991; Major concerts include: Monsters of Rock, Castle Donington, 1988; Farm Aid IV, 1990; Rock In Rio II, Brazil, 1991; Founder, Izzy Stradlin and The Juju Hounds, 1992-. *Recordings:* Albums:

Appetite For Destruction (No. 1, USA), 1987; G 'N' R Lies (mini-album), 1988; Use Your Illusion I and II (No. 1 and 2, US and UK), 1991; with The Ju-Ju Hounds: Izzy Stradlin and the Ju-Ju Hounds, 1992; 117°, 1998; Hit singles: with Guns 'N' Roses: Welcome To The Jungle, 1987; Sweet Child O'Mine (No. 1, USA), 1988; Night Train, 1989; Paradise City, 1989; Patience, 1989; Knockin' On Heaven's Door used in film Days of Thunder, 1990; You Could Be Mine used in film Terminator 2, 1991; Don't Cry, 1991; with Ju-Ju Hounds: Pressure Drop, 1992. *Honours:* American Music Awards: Favourite Heavy Metal Single, 1989; Favourite Heavy Metal Artist and Album, 1989; Rolling Stone and Billboard magazine awards. *Address:* c/o Geffen Records, 9130 Sunset Blvd, Los Angeles, CA 90069–6197, USA.

STRAHAN Derek William; b. 28 May 1935, Penang, Malaysia. Composer; Writer; Actor; Singer; Dir; Prod. Divorced, 1 s., 1 d. *Education:* BA, Cantab Modern Languages, Cambridge University. *Career:* Singer, Songwriter, topical songs, TV appearances ABCTV, This Day Tonight, ATN7 Breakfast Show, 1970; Actor, Number 96, 1974; Actor Feature Film, Fantasy, 1990; Actor, leading role, Inspector Shanahan Mysteries (Cult of Diana), 1992; Radio Presenter, Words and Music, Eastside Radio FM, 1984-. *Compositions:* Concert Music: String Quartet No 1, The Key, 1981; Clarinet Quintet No 1 in D, The Princess 1981; Rose of the Bay, song cycle, 1987; String Trio No 1 in F, 1987; Escorts Trio, 1989; China Spring Cello/ Piano, 1989; Atlantis, Flute/Piano, 1990; Solo Cello Suite No 1, 1991; Solo Cello Suite No 2, 1992; Voodoo Fire, Trio, 1994; Eden in Atlantis, Soprano/ Flute/Piano, 1995; Clarinet Concerto No 1, 2001. *Recordings:* Film music: 30 documentaries including: Shell's Australia, 13 part, 1969–73; Aliens Among Us and Garden Jungle, 1974; Artisans of Australia, 4 part, 1985; Feature films, Leonora, 1985; Fantasy, 1990; Cult of Diana, 1992. *Memberships:* Australian Music Centre, represented composer; APRA; Music Arrangers Guild of Australia; Australian Writers Guild; Media Entertainment and Arts Alliance. *Current Management:* Revolve Pty Ltd. *Address:* PO Box 1003, Marrickville, NSW 2204, Australia. *E-mail:* dstrahan@revolve.com.au. *Internet:* www.revolve.com.au.

STRAIT George; b. 18 May 1952, Poteet, Texas, USA. Country Singer. m. Norma, 1 d. *Education:* Agriculture, SW Texas State University. *Career:* Solo singer, and with own band, Ace In The Hole, formed at college; Recording artist, Nashville, 1981–; Film appearance, The Soldier. *Recordings:* 31 US Country Singles include: Fool Hearted Memory, 1982; Amarillo By Morning, 1983; You Look So Good In Love, 1984; Does Fort Worth Ever Cross Your Mind, 1985; Nobody In His Right Mind Would've Left Her, 1986; Am I Blue, 1987; Famous Last Words of a Fool, 1988; Baby's Gotten Good At Goodbye, 1989; Ace In The Hole, 1989; Love Without End, 1990; I've Come To Expect It From You, 1990; Drinking Champagne, 1991; When Did You Stop Loving Me, 1993; Easy Come, 1993; I'd Like to Have That One Back, 1993; Lovebug, 1994; Man in Love with You, 1994; Big One, 1994; You Can't Make a Heart Love, 1994; Albums include: Strait Country, 1981; Strait From Your Heart, 1982; Right Or Wrong, 1983; Does Fort Worth Ever Cross Your Mind?, 1984; Something Special, 1985; Merry Christmas Strait To You, 1986; No 7, 1987; Ocean Front Property, 1987; If You Ain't Lovin' (You Ain't Livin), 1988; Beyond The Blue Neon, 1989; Livin' It Up, 1990; Chill of An Early Fall, 1991; Holding My Own, 1992; Pure Country, 1992; Lead On, 1995; Strait Out of The Box, 1996; Blue Clear Sky, 1996; Carrying Your Love with Me, 1997; One Step at a Time, 1998; Always Never the Same, 1999; Merry Christmas Wherever You Are, 1999. *Honours:* CMA Awards: Entertainer of The Year, 1989, 1990; Male Vocalist of The Year, 1985, 1986; Album of The Year, 1985; ACM Awards: Entertainer of The Year, 1990; Male Vocalist of The Year, 1984, 1985, 1989; American Music Award: Top Country Vocalist, 1991; SRO Touring Artist of Year, 1990. *Memberships:* ACM; CMA. *Current Management:* Erv Woolsey Compnay, 1000 18th Ave S, Nashville, TN 37212, USA.

STRAND Arthur John Philip; b. 8 Oct. 1948, Finchampstead, Berkshire, England. Musician (fretboards, lute, flamenco); Composer. *Education:* SE Berks College. *Musical Education:* Private cornet tuition; Then self-taught. *Career:* Six Minus Two; Sketch; Misty; Concerts, deps, sessions; BBC radio and TV (sound only); US Forces Europe tours and residencies; Songwriting, composing; Studio installation, promotion; Own record label; Folk Session Singarounds, Acoustic. *Compositions:* 151 songs, 1964–94; 150 instrumental melodies; 4 fusion longer works, 1985; Supplied sequence for Figure of Eight on Flowers in the Dirt album, Paul McCartney. *Recordings:* As bassist: If Not For You, Olivia Newton-John. *Publication:* Poem, Time Itself Imploded, Poetry Now, 1996; Editor, Escutcheon Magazine, 1997-. *Memberships:* ABJM; BAC & S; Musicians' Union; GISC; F/MBF; PPL; Lute Society; Peña Flamenca; MCPS; PRS; PAMRA; ISA; ASCAP; MU. *Leisure interests:* Cricket (Finchampstead CC); Berkshire County Scorer; ACUS and Berks ACUS; Umpire. *Current Management:* Escusson Deux. *Address:* Escutcheon Media, 7 Grove Close, Nine Mile Ride, Wokingham, Berkshire, England.

STRANDBERG Orjan; b. 22 Aug. 1956, Stockholm, Sweden. Composer; Lyricist; Musician (Guitar). m. Carina Strandberg, 3 July 1981, 1 d. *Musical Education:* Self-taught. *Career:* Musician, TV, 1970; Dice,

progressive rock group, 1974; Dice, first album, 1978; Touring in Sweden and Denmark, until 1980; Signed by Peer Music as Songwriter; JetSet, new group, 2 singles released; Fulltime Composer, commercials and industry, 1980–; Responsible for Swedish script and lyrics for Walt Disney's World on Ice, 1989-. *Compositions:* Commercials and industrial assignments. *Recordings:* with Dice: Dice, album, CD, 1978; The Four Riders of the Apocalypse, album, CD, 1992; Live Dice, album, CD, 1993; with JetSet: Rock 'n' Roller Skates, single, 1980; Diamonds for My Hands, single, 1980; Producer, Arranger, All Up to You, by World Youth Choir, single, 1989. *Publications:* Grönsakernas Hemliga Liv (The Secret Life of Vegetables), 1986; several papers on music and copyright between 1990 and today. *Honours:* Several awards; Silver Screen Award, 1985. *Memberships:* Board Mem., Swedish Society of Popular Music Composers; Board Mem., Swedish Performing Rights Society; Chairman, Swedish Society of Media Composers; Swedish Artists' and Musicians Organisation. *Leisure interests:* Spending time with the family; Drawing; Computing. *Current Management:* Vision and Sound AB.

STRANDBERG Paul Bocciolone; b. 21 July 1949, Malmö, Sweden. Musician. *Career:* Guitar and Cornet player; Formed Scaniazz ensemble, regular performances in Malmö and throughout Sweden; Festival appearances throughout Europe, 1975–77; Tours of Holland, Belgium, Germany, England; Played in pop and folk group playing guitar and banjo, many appearances on radio and TV; Started Absalon Orchestra, '20's style dance music band, played Breda festival, 1987; Played New Orleans Jazz and Heritage festival with Scaniazz, 1982; Band disbanded, 1987; Played cornet, Peruna Jazzmen, tours of Holland and Germany, 1983; Teacher, Jazz Institute of Malmö; Participated in events organized by Malmö College of Music; Board Member of new jazz club; Founded Paul and his Gang, 1990; Tours of Hungary and Czech Republic and at European jazz festivals including International Dixieland Festival in Dresden, Germany, 1997; Chicago, US and Toronto, Canada, 2000; Regular tours in Europe with Hot House Jazzmen and also Original Jazzmakers; Sousaphone with Swing Kings quartet. *Recordings include:* With Scaniazz: Some Like it Hot, 1977; Messin' Around, 1980; Sunset Café Stomp, 1982; In New Orleans, 1982; Jazzfestival Dresden, 1985–86; With Absalon Orchestra: Reaching for Someone, 1985; Stardust, 1986; Paul and His Gang: Jazzfestival Breda, 1982; Futuristic Rhythm, 1994; Hot House Jazzmen: Storyville's Sensation, 1994; Anthology; Hot House Jubilee, 1999. *Publications:* Essays and reviews of classical jazz in periodicals. *Honours:* Certificate of Merit, City of New Orleans, 1982; Cultural Award, Malmö, 1989; Grant, Arts Council of Sweden, 1991, 1994; Winner, Competition for Jazz Bands in Breda, Holland, 1992. *Address:* Aengelholmsgatan 10B, 214 22 Malmö, Sweden.

STRAND-HOLM Klaus; b. 6 May 1951, Praestoe, Denmark. Musician. m. Karin Maud Mortensen, 7 April 1985. *Musical Education:* Self-taught. *Career:* Released 25 Albums and 40 Singles, Many in Danish Charts, 1969–; Appearances on Television. *Recordings:* Den Bedste Pige; Lad mig Vaere den; Der' Rock, Der' Pop; 60'er musik; Herstedvester; Bank 3 gange; Oresund; Herlig Herlig; Ring Ring; Ska'det vaere os to; 25 Rode Roser; Vi Maa Passe Bedre Paa Vor Jord, with Klaus and Servants, 1999. *Memberships:* Dansk Musiker Forbund; KODA; NCB; DPA. *Address:* Stadionvej 15, 4720 Praestoe, Denmark.

STRAVATO William; b. 1 June 1968, Fondi, Italy. Musician (Guitar). *Education:* Degree in English and Spanish Language and Literature; Graduated, Guitar Institute of Technology, Hollywood, USA. *Career:* Studio and live session work for Italian pop singers; Columnist, Axe guitar magazine. *Recording:* Debut solo album, Survivor. *Address:* Viale Europa 29, 00042 Anzio, Rome, Italy.

STRAYBLOVA Blanka; b. 1952, Prague, Czech Republic. Musician; Composer; Singer. *Career:* Played In Several Important Alternative Rock Groups; Member of The Rock and Joces Extempore Band, 1978–; Innumerable Concerts; Toured London, Hungary; Founder, MCH Band. *Recordings:* Include The Extempere Band-9 Albums; MCH Band-7 Cassettes. *Address:* Romek Hanzlik Via Unijazz, Jindrisska 5, 110 00 Prague 1, Czech Republic.

STREET Karen Jane; b. 13 Dec. 1959, Burton-On-Trent, England. Musician (saxophone, accordion, clarinet, flute). *Musical Education:* Bath College of Higher Education; Welsh College of Music and Drama. *Career:* Member, The Fairer Sax; Member, Saxtet (saxophone quintet); Member, Mike Westbrook Orchestra; Extensive tours; Television and radio appearances include: Wogan; Jim'll Fix It; Blue Peter; Forty Minutes; Radio 3; Nightride; Woman's Hour. *Recordings:* Diversions; Saxpressions; Comparing Notes; Safer Sax. *Publications:* Streetwise; Easy Street; Dizzy Duets; Fairer Sax Album 1 and 2; Streetbeats; All Because of You. *Leisure interests:* Swimming; Tennis. *Address:* 14 Janice Grove, Yardley Wood, Birmingham B14 4DP, England.

STREET Stephen; b. 29 March 1960, London, England. Record Prod. m. Sarah, 14 Aug. 1987, 2 s., 1 d. *Musical Education:* Self-taught Guitar, Bass,

Keyboards. *Career:* Recording Engineer, Island Records, 1980s; Freelance, after working with The Smiths on 3 albums, 1980s; Co-wrote and Produced Morrissey's First Solo LP, Viva Hate, 1988; Pursued Production career, Indie Music Genre including: Blur, Sleeper, The Cranberries, Psychedelic Furs, Triffids, The Pretenders; Shed Seven. *Compositions:* with Morrissey: Viva Hate, album; Suedehead; Singles: Everyday Is Like Sunday; Last of the Famous International Playboys; Interesting Drug. *Recordings:* The Smiths: The Queen is Dead; Strangeways Here We come; Morrissey, Viva Hate; The Cranberries, Everybody Else is Doing It; No Need to Argue; Sleeper, The It Girl; Pleased To Meet You; Blur, Leisure; Modern Life Is Rubbish; Parklife; The Great Escape; Blur; The Pretenders, Last of the Independents, The Isle of View; Viva El Amor; Shed Seven, Let It Ride. *Honours:* Q Magazine, Best Producer, 1995; Brit Awards Nominee, 1995, 1996, 1998. *Membership:* Re-Pro. *Leisure interests:* Football; Snow Skiing. *Current Management:* Gailforce Management, 24 Ives St, London, SW3 2ND, England.

STREISAND Barbra Joan; b. 24 April 1942, Brooklyn, New York, USA. Singer; Actress; Dir; Prod.; Writer; Composer; Philanthropist. m. Elliot Gould, 1963 (divorced 1971), 1 s. *Career:* Actress since age 15; Recording artist, 1962–; Concerts include: Support to Liberace, Hollywood Bowl, 1963; Madison Square Garden (as part of first tour for 27 years), recorded for later release, 1994; Stage performances include: Nightclub debut, Greenwich Village, 1961; New York theatre debut, Another Evening With Harry Stoones, 1961; I Can Get It For You Wholesale, 1962; Funny Girl, New York 1964, London, 1966; Film appearances: Funny Girl, 1968; Hello Dolly!, 1969; On a Clear Day You Can See Forever, 1970; The Owl and The Pussycat, 1971; What's Up Doc?, 1972; Up The Sandbox, 1972; The Way We Were, 1973; For Pete's Sake, 1974; Funny Lady, 1975; A Star Is Born (also producer), 1976; The Main Event (also producer), 1979; All Night Long, 1981; Yentl (also writer, director, producer), 1984; Nuts (also producer, composer), 1987; The Prince of Tides (also director, producer), 1990; Television specials: My Name Is Barbra, 1965; Color Me Barbra, 1966; Belle of 14th Street, 1967; A Happening in Central Park, 1968; And Other Musical Instruments, 1973; One Voice, 1976; Barbra Streisand – The Concert (also producer, co-director), HBO, 1994; Executive producer, Silence: The Margarete Cammermeyer Story, NBC, 1995. *Recordings:* Hits include: You Don't Bring Me Flowers, duet with Neil Diamond, 1978; Enough Is Enough, duet with Donna Summer; Albums include: The Barbra Streisand Album, 1963; The Second Barbra Streisand Album, 1963; The Third Album, 1964; My Name Is Barbra, 1965; People, 1965; Color Me Barbra, 1966; Je M'Appelle Barbra, 1967; Barbra Streisand: A Happening In Central Park, 1968; What About Me?, 1969; Stoney End, 1970; Barbra Joan Streisand, 1972; Classical Barbra, 1974; The Way We Were, 1974; Lazy Afternoon, 1975; A Star Is Born, 1976; Superman, 1977; Songbird, 1978; Wet, 1979; Guilty (with Barry Gibb), 1980; Memories, 1981; Emotion, 1984; The Broadway Album, 1986; One Voice, 1986; Til I Loved You, 1989; Just For The Record, 1991; Butterfly, 1992; Back To Broadway, 1993; Barbra Streisand – The Concert (album and video), 1994; The Concert – Highlights, 1995; Mirror Has Two Faces, 1996; Higher Ground, 1997; A Love Like Ours, 1999; Timeless, 2000; Soundtracks include: Yentl, 1983; Nuts, 1987; The Prince of Tides, 1991. *Honours:* NY Critics Award, Best Supporting Actress, for I Can Get It For You Wholesale, 1962; Variety Poll Award, Best Foreign Actress, for Funny Girl, UK, 1966; Academy Awards: Best Actress, Funny Girl, 1968; Best Composition (joint winner), Evergreen, 1976; Special Tony Award, for Funny Girl, 1970; Golden Globe Awards: Best Actress, Funny Girl, 1968; Best Picture and Best Director, Yentl, 1984; 5 Emmy Awards, My Name Is Barbra, 1966; 5 Emmy Awards, 3 Cable Ace Awards, Barbra Streisand: The Concert, 1994; Peabody Awards: My Name Is Barbra, 1966; Barbra Streisand: The Concert, 1994; Grammy Awards: Best Female Vocalist, 1963, 1964, 1965, 1977, 1986; Best Songwriter (with Paul Williams), 1977; Awarded 37 Gold and 21 Platinum albums; Only artist to have US No. 1 albums over 4 decades. *Address:* c/o Barwood Productions, 433 N Camden Dr., Suite 500, Beverly Hills, CA 90210, USA.

STRUMMER Joe, (John Mellors); b. 21 Aug. 1952, Ankara, Turkey. Musician (guitar); Singer. *Career:* Founder member, the 101ers, 1974–76; Member, UK punk group The Clash, 1976–86; Appearances include: Support to Sex Pistols, Anarchy In The UK tour, 1976; White Riot British tour, 1977; European Punk Festival, 1977; Anti-Nazi League Carnival, London, 1978; Kampuchea benefit concert, London, 1979; Support to The Who, farewell US tour, US, 1982; Jamaican World Music Festival, 1982; US '83 Festival, 1983; Roskilde Festival, Denmark, 1985; Regular international tours; Actor, film Straight To Hell, 1986. *Compositions include:* Film scores: Walker; Permanent Record; Tours with own band, the Latino Rockabilly War, 1988; Actor, Lost In Space, 1989. *Recordings:* Singles include: Tommy Gun, 1979; I Fought The Law, 1980; London Calling, 1980; Train In Vain (Stand By Me), 1980; Bankrobber, 1980; Should I Stay Or Should I Go?, 1982, reiussed (No. 1, UK), 1991; Rock The Casbah, 1983; Guitarist on: Down In The Groove, Bob Dylan; Vocalist, A Rainy Night In Soho, The Pogues; Albums: The Clash, 1977; Give 'Em Enough the Rope, 1978; London Calling, 1979; Black Market Clash, 1980; Sandinista!, 1980; Combat Rock, 1982; Cut The Crap,

1986; The Story of The Clash Vol. 1, 1991; The Singles Collection, 1991; Solo album: Earthquake Weather, 1990; Rock Art and the X-Ray Style, 1999; Contributor, Down In The Groove, Bob Dylan, 1988.

STUART Gareth Ian; b. 26 March 1963, Bracknell, Berkshire, England. Recording Engineer; Lecturer; Musician (clarinet, saxophone, guitar). m. Amanda Jane, 23 Sept. 1989, 1 s. *Musical Education:* Guildhall School of Music (part time), CCAT, Surrey University. *Career:* Recording studio owner, engineer, 1986–; Partner, Zigzag Music Productions, 1992–; Sound projectionist for Tim Souster (Equalisation and trumpet concerto); Equale Brass, Chelmsford Festival, Philharmonia, Queen Elizabeth Hall; Sinetone Generator Operator for Stockhausen 'Mixtur' with BBC Symphony Orchestra, Barbican. *Recordings:* Sin Ti Por El Alma Adentro, for album Culture Electroniques, Julio D'Escrivan; Lady of The Grave, Faith; Hard 2 Get, Interlude; My Guitar, Bongo Blister; Hold On Tight, Bob and The Bearcats. *Publications:* Articles on recording equipment, Sound On Sound, 1987–89. *Honours:* Clarinet (Grade 8); Alto Saxophone (Grade 8); Piano (Grade 6); GMus, Distinction; PG Dip (Tonmeister), Surrey University. *Memberships:* Associate APRS; Musicians' Union; MCPS. *Leisure interests:* Recording; Songwriting; Skiing. *Address:* Zigzag Music Productions, Croeso, Church Lane, Hilton, Huntingdon, Cambs PE18 9NH, England.

STUART George K; b. 25 Jan. 1951, Edinburgh, Scotland. Musician (drums, percussion). 1 s. *Musical Education:* Self-taught. *Career:* Tour with band Scottie, 1975; Support to Showaddywaddy, Shakin' Stevens, and Hello; German tour of American airbases, 1974 and 1976; Television appearance: Arrows, Granada TV, (with Scottie), 1976; Radio appearances with Scottie; Member, Distraction, 1993-. *Recordings:* with Scottie: Happy Together, 1975; Sweet Rock 'N' Roll, 1976; The Time Has Come, 1976; with West Side Strut: Nothing I Can Do, 1978. *Membership:* Musicians' Union. *Leisure interests:* Music; Computers; Sport. *Address:* 9 Victoria Rd, Victoria Park, Newton Grange, Edinburgh EH22 4NN, Scotland.

STUART Glenn Douglas; b. 8 May 1932, Elmira, New York, USA. Musician (lead trumpet). m. Laverne, 4 Nov. 1981, 1 s., 2 d. *Musical Education:* BS, Ithaca College; MA New York University. *Career:* Played trumpet with orchestras: Tony Pastor; Richard Hayman; Noro Morales; Ralph Marterie; Vaughn Monroe; Les and Larry Elgart; Tommy Tucker; Hank Levy; Jimmy Dorsey; Stan Kenton, Don Ellis, 1965–; Tours: Canada; Bermuda; Japan; Hawaii; Europe, with Don Ellis, 1969, 1977; Jazz Festivals include: Monterey; New Port; North Sea; Montreux; Pacific; Antibes; Television, films includes: Emmy Awards Banquet; Ed Sullivan Show; Shirley Maclaine Special; Mission Impossible; French Connection I and II; Soupy Sales Special, California; Played with artists including: The Supremes; Frankie Avalon; Joe Williams; Jack Jones; Franki Valli; Chubby Checker; Cleo Laine; Johnny Mathis; Jose Feliciano; Steve Lawrence; Phyllis Diller; Pat Boone; Louis Armstrong; Paul Anka; Teaches trumpet, schools, colleges, California; Lecturer, Clinics, universities, colleges. *Recordings include:* Featured on album: Autumn, Don Ellis; Single: Child of Ecstasy, Don Ellis. *Publications:* The Art of Playing Lead Trumpet. *Honours:* Featured soloist at International Trumpet Guild, 1977. *Membership:* NA of Jazz Educators. *Leisure interest:* Boating, mainly sailing 30' sloop. *Address:* 21682 Ocean Vista Dr., Laguna Beach, CA 92651, USA.

STUART James Hamish; b. 8 Oct. 1949, Glasgow, Scotland. Singer; Musician (guitar, bass); Writer. m. Lyn, 2 May, 1 s., 2 d. *Musical Education:* 3 grades piano; Self-taught guitar, bass. *Career:* Began recording with Dream Police, 1969; Average White Band, 1972–82; Numerous tours, television shows, 1972–82; Tours with Chaka Khan, David Sanborn, numerous writing, production credits, 1982–87; 2 world tours, 5 albums with Paul McCartney. *Recordings:* Pick Up The Pieces, Person To Person, A Love of Your Own; Queen of My Soul; Schoolboy Crush, on 8 Average White Band albums; Flowers In The Dirt; Off The Ground; Paul Is Live; Tripping The Light Fantastic; Unplugged; Albums with Paul McCartney; Atlantic Starr: If Your Heart Isn't In It; Chaka Khan: Whatcha Gonna Do For Me; David Sanborn: Love and Happiness. *Honours:* 3 Grammy nominations; Many Gold, Platinum records with: Average White Band; Chaka Khan; Paul McCartney. *Memberships:* ASCAP; AFTRA; PRS. *Leisure interests:* Painting; Football; Food. *Current Management:* Ramon Hervey. *Address:* New York, Los Angeles, USA.

STUART Marty; b. 30 Sept. 1958, Philadelphia, Pennsylvania, USA. Singer; Musician (guitar, mandolin). *Career:* Concerts include No Hats Tour, 1992; Television: Marty Party, TNN, 4 shows; The Music of The Wild West, TNN Special, 1993. *Recordings:* Hillbilly Rock, 1989; Little Things; Tempted, 1991; Burn Me Down; Till I Found You; Western Girls (all Top 10); Once Upon a Time, 1992; This One's Gonna Hurt You, 1992; Love and Luck, 1994; Marty Party Hit Pack, 1995; Honky Tonkin's What I Do Best, 1996; Singles: Hey Baby, 1993; Kiss Me I'm Gone, 1994; That's What Love's About, 1994; Sweet Love, 1997. *Honours:* CMA Award, Vocal Event, with Travis Tritt, 1992; Grammy Awards: Best Vocal Collaboration, with Travis Tritt, 1993; Best Country Instrumental, with Bob Wills, 1994. *Membership:*

Inducted into Grand Ole Opry, 1992. *Leisure interests:* Photography; Collectables. *Current Management:* Rothbaum and Garner. *Address:* 119 17th Ave S, Nashville, TN 37203, USA.

STUBER William Charles; b. 25 Sept. 1951, Rochester, NY, USA. Prod.; Engineer; Percussionist; Arranger. m. Irene Stuber, 1 s. *Education:* Recording Institute of America; Stonybrook University; Cleveland Institute of electronics. *Career:* KONP; KCTS; NZOK; KZAM; ISIW; KZFM; KBPI; King Television; KIRO Television. *Compositions:* Devotion; Love's Heavenly Dream. *Recordings:* Include, Hall and Oates; Rachael Sweet; Nitty Gritty; Supersonics; Ted Nugent; The Hooters; Heart; Jesse Colin Young; Sammy Hagar; Judas Priest; London Ballet; Moscow Ballet. *Publications:* Love's Heavenly Dream, 1995; Devotion, 1996; Ultimate Love, 1997; Gems of The Seven Color Rays, 2000. *Honours:* Seattle's Best Recordings, 1979. *Membership:* RIAA. *Leisure interests:* Poetry; Healing; Photography; Watercolor. *Address:* 2076 Taylor Cutoff Rd, Sequim, WA 98382, USA.

SUGAR (Zacharia Hajishacalli); b. 8 July 1954, London, England. Musician (bouzouki, Cypriot flute); Prod. m. Androulla, 24 July 1977, 2 d. *Education:* BTec, Electronics. *Musical Education:* Master classes, bouzouki, Greece. *Career:* Toured with Boy George's Jesus Loves You Band; Concerts include: Town and Country; Ronnie Scott's; Royal Festival Hall; Television and radio appearances: The Word; BSB; Birds of a Feather, BBC; Rhythms of The World, BBC; The Green Line, CH4; Andy Kershaw Show, BBC Radio 1; Les Nuils, French TV; Cyprus TV and radio performances. *Recordings:* Produced and recorded 4 Greek albums for ARC Music; Bouzouki player on Mathilda May album; Yamaha instruments for sampling bouzouki for new synth; Bouzouki player on 4 tracks for Boy George; Composer, producer, Cypriot Flute of Sugar. *Publications:* Cypriot Flute of Sugar; Haji-Mike album. *Memberships:* Musicians' Union; PRS; MCPS. *Leisure interests:* Music; Philosophy; Star Trek; Reading; Family. *Address:* 7 Bulwer Rd, Edmonton, London N18 1QL, England.

SUGGS (Graham McPherson); b. 13 Jan. 1961, Hastings, Sussex, England. Singer. m. Bette Bright, 1982. *Career:* Singer, Madness, 1977–88; Appearances include: 2-Tone Tour, UK, 1979; Twelve Days of Madness Tour, 1980; Far East Tour 1981; Prince' Trust Royal Gala, 1982; Greenpeace benefit, London, 1983; Solo artiste, 1988–; Regular comedy host, Mean Fiddler Club, North London; Manager, The Farm; Presenter, Night Fever, TV Quiz, Channel 5; Film appearances: Dance Craze, 1981; Take It Or Leave It, 1981; Madstock – The Movie, 1992. *Recordings:* Singles: with Madness include: The Prince, 1979; One Step Beyond, 1979; My Girl, 1980; Night Boat To Cairo, 1980; Baggy Trousers, 1980; Embarrassment, 1980; Return of The Los Palmas Seven, 1981; Grey Day, 1981; Shut Up, 1981; It Must Be Love, 1982; Cardiac Arrest, 1982; House of Fun (No. 1, UK), 1982; Driving In My Car, 1982; Our House, 1982; Tomorrow's (Just Another Day), 1982; Wings of a Dove, 1983; The Sun and The Rain, 1983; Michael Caine, 1984; One Better Day, 1984; Yesterday's Men, 1985; Waiting For The Ghost, 1986; Lovestruck, 1999; Johnny the Horse, 1999; Solo singles: I'm Only Sleeping, 1995; Camden Town, 1995; Cecilia, 1996; Guest vocalist, Piccadilly Place, Morrissey, 1988; Albums with Madness: One Step Beyond, 1979; Absolutely, 1980 Seven, 1981; Complete Madness, 1982; The Rise and Fall, 1982; Madness, 1983; Keep Moving, 1984; Mad Not Mad, 1985; Utter Madness, 1986; Divine Madness, 1992; Madstock!, 1992; Wonderful, 1999; Solo album: The Lone Ranger, 1995. *Honours:* Singles Artists of The Year, NME, 1980; Ivor Novello Award, Best Pop Song, 1983.

SUGIYAMA Kazonori; b. 18 Aug. 1950, Tokyo, Japan. Prod. m. Emi Fukui, 11 Aug. 1981. *Education:* BS, Waseda University, Tokyo, also postgraduate study; MA, Boston University, Massachusetts, USA, 1977. *Musical Education:* Self-taught recording engineering. *Career:* New York Representative, Jazz Division, Toshiba EMI, 1990–93; US Representative, Executive Producer, DIW/Avant Records, 1991–; Executive Producer, Tzadik Records, 1995–; Advisory Board, New Grove Dictionary of Jazz, 1997. *Recordings:* Bud and Bird/Gil Evans, Engineer, 1988; V/Ralph Peterson Jr, Producer, 1990; Big Band and Quartet, David Murray, Producer, 1992. *Publication:* Autobiography of Miles Davis, Japanese Translator, 1989. *Honours:* Grammy Award, 1988; Jazz Album of the Year (producer), 1990; Album of the Year in Japan, Best Production, 1992. *Membership:* NARAS. *Leisure interest:* Travel. *Address:* 93 Mercer St 3W, New York, NY 10012, USA.

SULTON Kasim Anthony; b. 08 Dec. 1955, New York, USA. Musician (Bass Guitar, Guitar, Keyboards); Vocalist. m. Laurie Rampulla, 1 s., 2 d. *Career:* Joined Band, Jtopia as Bassist and Vocalist, 1976; Bassist With Joan Jett, 1986; Bassist With Hall and Oates, 1990; Guitarist With Meat Loaf, 1993; Bassist, Musical Director, Meat Loaf, 1998. *Compositions:* Set Me Free; Love Is The Answer; Mated. *Recordings:* 10 Utopia Albums, 1976–86; Meat Loaf, Bat Out of Hell, 1 and 2; Joan Jett, I Hate Myself For Loving You; Celine Dion, Falling Into You; Kasim Sulton, Kasim. *Honours:* Grammy Nomination, 1988; Best Video and Grammy Award, 1995, 1996. *Memberships:* American Federation of Musicians; American Federation

Radio and Television Artists. *Leisure interests:* Cigar aficionado; Guitar Collecting. *Address:* PO Box 060 106, Staten Island, New York 10306, USA.

SUMMER Donna, (Donna Adrian Gaines); b. 31 Dec. 1948, Boston, Massachusetts, USA. Singer; Songwriter; Actor; Artist. m. (1) Helmut Sommer, 1971, divorced, 1 d., (2) Bruce Sudano, 1980, divorced, 2 d. *Career:* Singer, various groups, Boston; Appeared in musicals, Munich, Germany, 1968–74; Also worked as model and backing singer; Solo singer, 1975–; Major appearances include: Music For UNICEF Concert, New York, 1979; 50th American Presidential Gala, 1985; American Music Awards Concert Series, Yokohama, Japan, 1991; Actress, film Thank God It's Friday, 1978; Playwrite; As artist: exhibition of paintings and lithographs, New York, Miami, Chicago, and has sold close to $1m. worth of art. *Recordings:* Albums: Love To Love You Baby, 1976; A Love Trilogy, 1976; Four Seasons of Love, 1976; I Remember Yesterday, 1977; Once Upon a Time, 1978; Greatest Hits, 1978; Live and More, 1978; Bad Girls, 1979; On The Radio, 1980; The Wanderer, 1980; Donna Summer, 1982; She Works Hard For The Money, 1983; Cats Without Claws, 1984; All Systems Go, 1987; Another Place and Time, 1989; Best of Donna Summer, 1990; The Donna Summer Anthology, 1993; Hit singles include: Love To Love You Baby, 1976; I Feel Love (No. 1, UK), 1977; Deep Down Inside, from film The Deep, 1977; I Love You, 1978; Love's Unkind, 1978; Last Dance, 1978; MacArthur Park (No. 1, USA), 1977; Heaven Knows, 1979; Hot Stuff (No. 1, USA), 1979; Bad Girls (No. 1, USA), 1979; Dim All The Lights, 1979; No More Tears (Enough Is Enough), duet with Barbra Streisand (No. 1, USA), 1979; On The Radio, from film Foxes, 1980; The Wanderer, 1980; Love Is In Control (Finger On The Trigger), 1982; She Works Hard For The Money, 1983; Dinner With Gershwin, 1987; This Time I Know It's For Real, 1989; I Don't Want To Get Hurt, 1989; State of Independence, 1995; The Donna Summer Anthology, 1993; Donna Summer Christmas Spirit, 1994. *Honours:* Academy Award, Best Original Song, Heaven Knows, 1979; Grammy Awards: Best Rhythm and Blues Vocal Performance, 1979; Best Rock Vocal Performance, 1980; Best Inspirational Performance, 1984, 1985; American Music Awards: Favourite Female Disco Artist, Disco Single, Disco Album, 1979; Favourite Female Pop/Rock Artist, Favourite Pop/Rock Single, Favourite Female Soul/R & B Artist, 1980; Star on Hollywood Walk of Fame, 1992; Hon. Doctorate of Fine Arts, University of Massachusetts, 1997; Best Dance Recording, Carry On, 1997; Hon. mem. of The Golden Key National Honor Society, University of Massachusetts, 1997; Guest speaker at American Medical Womens Asscn, 1999. *Current Management:* Moress/Nanas Entertainment; 1102 18th Ave S, Nashville, TN 37212, USA.

SUMMER Henry Lee; b. 7 May 1960, Evansville, Indiana, USA. Singer; Songwriter; Record Prod.; Musician (multi-instrumentalist). *Education:* Western Wyoming University. *Musical Education:* Self-taught. *Career:* National support tours with: Stevie Ray Vaughan; Don Henley; Eddie Money; Richard Marx; .38 Special; Chicago; Cheap Trick; The Doobie Brothers; The Allman Brothers; REO Speedwagon; Also played Indiana State Fair, with John Mellencamp, 1988; Farm Aid IV, with John Mellencamp, Willie Nelson, Guns 'N' Roses, Neil Young, Bonnie Raitt, Indiana, 1990; Television appearances: David Letterman; Arsenio Hall; Charlie Rose; Guest VJ-MTV, Rock Line. *Recordings:* Albums: Stay With Me, 1984; Time For Big Fun, 1986; Henry Lee Summer, 1988; I've Got Everything, 1989; Way Past Midnight, 1991; Slam Drunk, 1993; Tracks for various film soundtracks including Iron Eagle II and Twins. *Publications:* Song book collections. *Honours:* BMI Award, Hey Baby, 1991. *Memberships:* BMI; AFTRA; AFofM. *Leisure interest:* Basketball. *Current Management:* James Bogard Associates. *Address:* 7608 Teel Way, Indianapolis, IN 46256, USA.

SUMMERS Al; b. 9 Sept. 1957, Somerset, England. Musician; Composer. m. Gillian Rosemary Summers, 26 Sept. 1992, 1 step-s. *Education:* Dartington College. *Career:* Composition, Teaching; Various Theatre, Some Radio. *Compositions:* Several Hundred Compositions for Community Projects; Early Works Mostly Chamber Ensembles and Unusual Combinations of Instruments. *Memberships:* Musicians' Union; RGT. *Leisure interests:* Gardening; Walking. *Current Management:* Ian Grant, Action Sales, Westbury Trading Estate, Wiltshire, England. *Address:* 61 Bratton Rd, Westbury, Wiltshire BA13 3ES, England.

SUMMERS Andy, (Andrew Somers); b. 31 Dec. 1942, Poulton-Le-Fylde, Lancashire, England. Musician (guitar); Singer. *Career:* Guitarist, vocalist, The Police, 1977–86; Numerous world-wide tours, television, radio appearances with the Police; Began solo recording career, 1987–; Live Music director, The Dennis Miller Show, US television, 1992; Writer, film scores: Weekend At Bernie's; 2010. *Recordings:* Hit singles with The Police: Walking On The Moon; Message In a Bottle; So Lonely; Roxanne; De Do Do Do De Da Da Da; Every Little Thing She Does; Every Breath You Take; Invisible Sun; Can't Stand Losing You; Don't Stand So Close To Me; Spirits In The Material World; Sychronicity; Albums: with The Police: Outlandos D'Amour, 1977; Regatta De Blanc, 1979; Zenyatta Mondatta, 1980; Ghost In The Machine, 1981; Synchronicity, 1983; Solo albums: I Advance Masked, with Robert Fripp, 1982; XYZ, 1987; Mysterious Barricades, 1988; Golden Wire, 1989; Charming Snakes, 1990; World Gone Strange,

1991; Synaesthesia, 1995; The Last Dance of Mr X, 1998; Strings of Desire, 1998; Green Chimneys, 1999. *Honours include:* Grammy Awards, with the Police. *Current Management:* Firstars/Talent Bank Management, Bugle House, 21A Noel St, London W1V 3PD, England.

SUMNER Bernard; b. 4 Jan. 1956, Salford, Lancashire, England. Musician (guitar). *Career:* Member, Joy Division, 1977–80; Futurama Festival, Leeds, 1979; European tour, 1980; Member, New Order, 1980–; World-wide tours including Australia; New Zealand; Far East; US; South America; Concerts include: Glastonbury Festival, 1981, 1987; Futurama Festival, 1982; San Remo Festival, 1988; Monsters of Art tour, with PIL and Sugarcubes, 1989; Reading Festival, 1989; Electronic, 1989; Support to Depeche Mode, Los Angeles Dodgers Stadium, 1990; Cities In The Park Festival, 1991. *Recordings:* Albums: with Joy Division: Unknown Pleasures, 1979; Closer, 1980; Still, 1981; The Peel Sessions, 1988; Also featured on Short Circuit – Live At The Electric Circus, 1978; with New Order: Movement, 1981; Power Corruption and Lies, 1983; Low Life, 1985; Brotherhood, 1986; Substance, 1987; Technique, 1989; BBC Radio 1 Live In Concert, 1992; Republic, 1993; with Electronic: Electronic, 1991; Raise the Pressure, 1996; Singles: with Joy Division: Love Will Tear Us Apart, 1980; with New Order include: Ceremony, 1981; Temptation, 1982; Confusion, 1983; Blue Monday, 1983; Thieves Like Us, 1984; Shellshock, from film soundtrack Pretty In Pink, 1986; True Faith, 1987; Touched By The Hand of God, 1987; Fine Time, 1988; Round and Round, 1989; World In Motion, with England Football Squad (No. 1, UK), 1990; How Does It Feel?, 1992; Regret, 1993; World (The Price of Love), 1993; Spooky, 1993; with Electronic includes: Getting Away With It, featuring Neil Tennant, 1989; Get the Message, 1991; Feel Every Beat, 1991; Disappointed, 1992; Forbidden City, 1996; For You, 1996. *Current Management:* Rebecca Boulton, Prime Management, Ducie House, Ducie St, Manchester, England.

SUMRONGTHONG Bussakorn; b. 29 Nov. 1962, Thailand. Asst Prof. *Education:* BA, Chulalongham University; MPhil, DPhil, University of York. *Career:* Guest Lecturer; Presentations On Television; Chairman, Secretary, Chulalongkorn University; Judge, Thai Musical Ensemble Competition, The Golden Television Awards, Drawing Competition; Lecturer, Assistant Professor, Chulalongkorn University. *Compositions:* Hudan Mus-Javanese Piece On Thai Xylophone; Homnong Sakura: Composition for the New Millenium; The Thai and European Perspective Concert. *Recordings:* Manmongkol. *Honours:* First Prize, Best Thai Xylophone Player, 1984. *Memberships:* International Council of Traditional Music. *Address:* Faculty of Fine and Applied Arts, Chulalongkorn University, Bangkok 10330, Thailand.

SUN Hongjun; b. 6 Dec. 1934, Liaoyang District, Liaoning Province, China. Musician (Accordion). m. Cui Min, 1 Oct. 1957, 2 s., 2 d. *Musical Education:* ShenYang Musical College. *Career:* Attended PLA China, Liaoning Military Organization, 1956; Attended Fu Shun song and dance ensemble, assigned as accordion player, 1959; Chief, Main Editor, Fushun Office, Chinese National Music, 1979; Programmed Russian Red Army Song and dance ensemble, many others. *Compositions:* North East Drum and Wind Music, 1986; Chao Xian Folk Songs, 1991. *Recordings:* 100 Man Folk Songs of China; Xi Bo Music; Chaoxian Folk Songs; North East Drum and Wind Music. *Publication:* National Folk Musician essay, 1995. *Honour:* Man Musical Essay, First Festival of Asian Pacific Society for Ethnomusicology. *Memberships:* Cui Min; Sun Like; S Dongke; Sun Qiuke; Xiake. *Leisure interests:* Culture and travel; Discussion and study. *Address:* 5 E Sixth Rd, Xinfu District, Fushun, Liaoning Province 7677423, China.

SUN Joe; b. 25 Sept. 1943, Rochester, Minnesota, USA. Musician; Songwriter. m. Inka Sun Paulsen, 10 Oct. 1965. *Education:* Brown School of Broadcasting, Minneapolis, 1967. *Career:* National promotions director, Ovation Records, Nashville, 1976–78; Recording artist, 1978–82; Touring musician, songwriter, 1987–; Actor, film Marie – A True Story, 1986. *Honour:* Most Promising New Country Artist, Billboard, 1979.

SUND John; b. 6 Jan. 1957, Copenhagen, Denmark. Musician (guitar); Composer. *Musical Education:* Self-taught. *Career:* Debut at age 18 as soloist with the Danish Radio Big Band, 1976; Member of Creme Fraiche Big Band, broadcasting in radio and television, 1978; Permanent member of Danish Radio Jazzgroup, including appearances at Montmartre, 1976–80; Member and Contributor to Danish Radio Workshop/Palle Mikkelborg, 1978–80; Formed own band, John Sund Group, with others including American trumpet player Tim Hagans, 1977–79; Own trio, Trigon, broadcast on DR television, 1982; Played with Bo Stief, Thomas Clausen, Alex Real, Mads Vinding, Debbie Cameron, among others; Currently leading jazz/ethnic-fusion ensemble Special Venture. *Compositions:* Fusion Symphony, extended suite of 8 compositions, 1993. *Recordings:* with the Neumann Bros 3 x Neumann: Song Hits from 1920–70, 1977; with Creme Fraiche Big Band: Creme Fraiche, 1978; with Richard Boone and Debbie Cameron: Brief Encounter, 1978; Solo album: John Sund and the Danish Radio Big Band: Fusion Symphony, 1995; with

Special Venture: Special Venture, 1999. *Honour:* First jazz artist to receive Jacob Gades Grant, 1977. *Membership:* Society of Danish Jazz, Rock and Folk Composers (DJBFA). *Current Management:* Special Venture Booking, Wesselsgade 18, 4tv, 2200 Copenhagen, Denmark.

SUNDING Per Gunnar; b. 23 Nov. 1967, Lund, Sweden. Singer; Songwriter; Prod.; Musician (bass). *Musical Education:* Self-taught guitar and bass. *Career:* Formed Eggstone with Maurits Carlsson and Patrik Bartosch in 1986; Eggstone founded Tambourine Studios with Tore Johansson and Anders Nordgren in 1991; Studios used by St Etienne and the Cardigans; Founded Vibrafon Records in 1995. *Recordings:* with Eggstone: Albums: In San Diego, 1992; Somersault, 1994; Vive La Difference, 1997; with Wannadies: The Wannadies, 1990; Aquanautic, 1992; Be a Girl, 1995; Bagsy Me, 1997; Yeah, 2000; Producer: 3 Bob Hund albums; 1 Ray Wonder album; Co-producer and co-lyricist on Wannadies album Bagsy Me. *Membership:* SKAP. *Current Management:* Marcantonio Management. *Address:* Tambourine Studios, Sofielundsv. 57, 214 34 Malmö, Sweden.

SUONSAARI Klaus; b. 7 Nov. 1959, Finland. Musician (drums); Composer. *Musical Education:* Piano lessons from age 6; Drums from age 14; Studied at Lahti Conservatory; Eastman School of Music, Rochester, US; Berklee College of Music, Boston, USA; Private studies with: Billy Higgins; Jeff Hamilton; Alan Dawson; Kauko Saari; Jorma Alanne. *Career:* Living, working in New York, 1985–; Played with musicians including: Bob Berg; Niels-Henning Orsted-Pedersen; Ray Drummond; Tom Harrell; Mike Mainieri; Niels Lan Doky; Muhal Richard Abrams; International appearances in US; Canada; UK; Scandinavia; Central Europe; Performances with: Jerry Bergonzi; Randy Brecker; Geri Allen; Joe Henderson; Toots Thielemans; David Sanborn. *Recordings include:* Inside Out, 1995; Something In Common, 1998; With Every Breath I Take, 1999. *Honours:* Buddy Rich Jazz Masters Award, 1983; Quincy Jones Jazz Masters Award, 1984; Artist of The Year Award, Finland, 1992. *Memberships:* Local 802; AFofM; AFL; CIO; Associated Musicians of Greater New York. *Current Management:* Charlie Elliott Talent Group 7 Fourth St, Suite 43, Petaluma, CA 94952, USA. *Address:* 652 Blvd E, Weehawken, NJ 07087–6811, USA.

SURNOCK Richard William; b. 19 Oct. 1932, Chicago, Illinois, USA. Musician. m. Lynn Margaret Kennaugh, 16 May 1964, 1 s., 2 d. *Education:* Los Angeles City College. *Career:* Musician with: Buddy Rich, 1956; Mort Sahl and Joanie Sommers, 1958; Murry Arnold, 1960; Jim McDonald Trio, 1965–; Billy Daniels, 1970; Peggy Lee, 1980; Mickey Rooney Show, 1988; Page Cavanaugh, 1990; Palisades Symphony, 1990-.

SUTCLIFFE Jess (Jeremy); b. 25 Nov. 1958, London, England. Recording Engineer; Prod. m. Shari Lee Inoue, 25 July 1987, 1 s., 1 d. *Career:* Tape Operator and Assistant Engineer, London Recording Studios, 1977; Independent First Engineer, 1979; Engineer for Vangelis, 1982–86; Recording Engineer for films, records, and TV commercials; Freelance Engineer and Producer, 1987; Moved to Los Angeles, 1988. *Recordings:* Artists include: Vangelis; Toto; Aretha Franklin; Jon and Vangelis; Carlene Carter; Sheila E; Quincy Jones; Patti LaBelle; Willie Nelson; Patti Austin; Gary Numan; Elvis Costello; Sheena Easton; Wall of Voodoo; The Fall; Handel's Messiah; Meat Loaf; Toto; Film scores include: The Bounty; Boyz 'n the Hood. *Honours:* Platinum records; Grammy Winning Records. *Membership:* NARAS. *Current Management:* Belgravia Music. *Address:* Belgravia Music, 22647 Ventura Blvd, Suite 301, Woodland Hills, CA 91364, USA.

SUTTON Chris; b. 25 Dec. 1960, Essex, England. Vocalist; Songwriter; Musician (piano, keyboards). m. Elaine Sutton, 1 d. *Career:* First solo album with 22, produced by Motown producer Dennis Lambert; Support to James Brown, Wembley Arena, London; 2 Top 100 singles, Germany airplay. *Compositions:* That's Her Way, 1994; However Long It Takes, 1994; Miracle, 1994. *Recordings:* That's Her Way; However Long It Takes; Album: Songs Into The Light; Recorded with Paul McCartney, George Michael and Mark Knopfler; Singer, Knee Deep in the Hoopla album, Starship. *Membership:* PRS. *Leisure interest:* Sport. *Address:* c/o BME Records, Postbox 450224, 50877 Cologne, Germany.

SUTTON Graham Paul; b. 1 April 1972, Stratford, London, England. Songwriter; Singer; Prod.; Multi-instrumentalist. *Career:* Formed Bark Psychosis, 1987; Left school and home to pursue music at 16; Recorded several independently released and critically acclaimed EPs; Signed to Circa Records; Worked with: Lee Harris, Paul Webb of Talk Talk under name Orang; Also records under name Boymerang. *Recordings:* Albums: Bark Psychosis: Hex, 1994; Independency, 1994; Game Over, 1997; also appears on: White Squall; Fields and Waves; Inventing the Abbotts; Balance of the Force; Event Horizon. *Memberships:* Musicians' Union; PRS; MCPS. *Leisure interests:* Graphic design; Alcohol. *Current Management:* Mike Collins. *Address:* 40 Abbotsford Gardens, Woodford Green, Essex IG8 9HW, England.

SVARE Jorgen Christian; b. 28 Dec. 1935, Copenhagen, Denmark. Musician. 2 s., 1 d. *Musical Education:* Self-taught. *Career:* Clarinet Player, Local Bands, 1950's; Founder Member, Papa Bue's Viking Jazz Band, 1956; Played and Toured World-wide, 30 years; Own quartet, 1986–95; Club Owner, Jazz Club, Slukefter Jazzhus, Tivoli Gardens, Copenhagen, 1994–97; Co-leader of Stolle and Svare Jazz Quintet, 1995-. *Composition:* Slukefter Blues. *Recordings:* Over 60 Albums with Papa Bue; 6 albums with quartet; 1 album with Stolle and Svare Jazz Quintet, 1998. *Honour:* Sorens Penge, Denmark, 1996. *Membership:* Danish Society of Band Leaders. *Address:* Peder Hvitfeldts Straede 11, 1173 Copenhagen K, Denmark.

SVENINGSSON (Johan) Magnus; b. 4 April 1972, Falköping, Sweden. Musician (Bass); Songwriter. *Career:* Member, The Cardigans; Formed the Cardigans with Peter Svensson, 1992; Tracks contributed to films Romeo and Juliet and A Life Less Ordinary; Numerous TV and radio appearances, tours and festival appearances. *Recordings:* Singles: Sick and Tired; Carnival; Hey! Get Out of My Way; Lovefool; Been It; You New Cuckoo; My Favourite Game; Erase and Rewind; Burning Down The House, with Tom Jones; Albums: Emmerdale; Life; First Band On The Moon; Gran Turismo.

SVENNINGSSON Uno; b. 1 July 1959, Jönköping, Småland, Sweden. Singer; Songwriter. m. Carina Bihli, 11 Sept. 1993, 1 s. *Career:* Singer, songwriter, rock group Freda, 1983–93; Solo artist, 1994–; Numerous tours, television and radio appearances, major Swedish programmes. *Recordings:* En Människa, 1984; Välkommen Hero, 1986; Tusen Eldar, 1988; Undan För Undan, 1990; Alla Behöver, 1993; Freda Samling, 1993; Uno, 1994. *Honours:* Swedish Grammy Award, Best Rock Group, 1991; RockBjörnen Award, Best Male Artist, 1994; The Mozart Prize, Best Male Artist, 1994. *Leisure interests:* Reading; Films; Music. *Current Management:* The Record Station. *Address:* The Record Station, BMG Ariola, PO Box 1026, 17221 Sundbyberg, Sweden.

SVENSSON Anders Peter; b. 18 Oct. 1974, Sweden. Musician (Guitar). *Musical Education:* Music College, Jonkoping, 1991–93. *Compositions:* Gran Turismo; First Band On The Moon; Life; Emmerdale; Paus. *Honours:* Swedish Government Export Prize, 1997; Best Composer, 1998; BMI Best Song, 1997; Best Album, 1998; Best Group, 1996, 1998. *Membership:* Society for Swedish Composers of Pop Music. *Leisure interests:* Music; Art; Films. *Current Management:* Motor, PO Box 53045, S 400 14 Gothenburg, Sweden.

SWALLOW Steve; b. 1940, New York, New York, USA. Musician. *Musical Education:* Studied piano with Howard Kasschau, and trumpet; Composition, Yale University. *Career:* Tours and recordings with Paul Bley, Jimmy Giuffre Trio and George Russell Sextet, 1960; Performances with other noted jazz musicians; Joined Art Farmer Quartet, 1964; Toured with Stan Getz Quartet, 1965–67; Joined Gary Burton Quartet, 1968; Took up electric bass; Teacher, Berklee College of Music, 1974–76; Performed with Dizzy Gillespie, George Benson, Herbie Hancock and played on numerous recordings with other musicians; Joined Carla Bley Band, 1978, numerous recordings and tours; Toured and recorded with John Scofield, 1980–84, and produced many recordings; Production for numerous artists including Andy Sheppard, Karen Mantler, Lew Soloff; Numerous tours with Paul Bley, Ernie Watts, Allen Ginsberg; Reunited with Jimmy Giuffre and Paul Bley, 1989, numerous tours; Contributions to numerous recordings, 1993; Many concert appearances with Carla Bley, Jimmy Giuffre, Andy Sheppard, 1994; Numerous tours with many artists, 1994–98; Played with Harvard University Jazz Band. *Recordings include:* Deconstructed; Real Book; Go Together; Swallow; Duets; Carla; Home; Hotel Hello; With Carla Bley: Night-Glo; Sextet; With John Scofield: Shinola; Out Like a Light. *Honours:* National Endowment for the Arts Grant, 1976; First Place, Downbeat International Critics' Poll, Electric Bass, 1983–; Readers' Poll, 1985–; Winner, Jazz Times Poll, Electric Bass, several times; Nominee, Danish Jazzpar, 1999. *Address:* c/o Watt Works, PO Box 67, Willow, NY 12495, USA.

SWAN Billy; b. 12 May 1942, Cape Giardeau, Missouri, Canada. Singer; Songwriter; Musician (Guitar, Bass, Keyboards). m. Marlu, 2 d. *Career:* Musical Director, Filmography: A Thing Called Love, coached River Phoenix; Wild At Heart, acted and sang; Songwriter, Willie Nelson and Kris Kristofferson; Assistant Music Director, Great Balls of Fire; As You Like It, Scored and played singing minstrel; Toured with: T Bone Burnett; Kinky Friedman and The Texas Jewboys; Billy Joe Shaver; Black Tie; Harry Dean Stanton and Kris Kristofferson. *Recordings:* Albums: I Can Help; Rock 'n' Roll; Billy Swan; Four; You're OK, I'm OK; I'm Into Lovin' You; Black Tie; Recent Releases: Billy Swan's Best, 1993; Vinyl Junkie Country, Undying Love, 1995; The Sun Studio Story: Rockabilly B; Lonely Weekends, 1995; Bop To Be, 1995; Billy Swan Live, 1996; Billy Swan, Choice Cuts, 1997; The Best of Billy Swan, 1997; Billy Swan – collectibles, 1997; I Can Help/Rock 'n' Roll Moon and Billy Swan/Four – See For Miles, 1997. *Current Management:* Dennis Muirhead, Muirhead Management,

202 Fulham Rd, Chelsea, London SW10 9PJ, England. *Address:* Chelsea, London, SW10 9PJ, England.

SWAN Ren; Mix Engineer; Engineer. *Career:* Engineering work for Jon Douglas on: Salt 'N' Pepa, Champagne 7; Michelle Gayle, Do You Know, Sensational; Remix of Clementine for Mark Owen with Grant Mitchell (3 UK charts); Working on Gary Barlow's forthcoming album with Grant and Gary; Remixed, Above the Law, The Evil That Men Do; Working on Dee Ellington (RCA) Album; Engineering and mixing credits include: George Michael, Older; Eternal, including: Stay, Oh Baby I, Good Thing; Michael Jackson, Wanna Be Starting Something mix; De La Soul, Ring Ring; Aswad, Close to You, 7 and 12 remix; Pet Shop Boys, Where The Streets Have No Name 7. *Address:* SARM Productions, SP2 Holdings Ltd, The Blue Building, 42/46 St Luke's Mews, London W11 1DG, England.

SWANSON David James; b. 15 Aug. 1951, Edinburgh, Scotland. Musician (percussion). 1 d. *Musical Education:* Studied with James Catherwood privately; 1 year music course at college. *Career:* Played with many jazz stars including: Joe Temperley; Roy Williams; Kenny Davern; Buddy DeFranco; Tal Farlow; Louis Stewart; Tour of Middle East with Demis Roussos; Television appearances with: Tam White; Benny Waters; Healing Force; Craig McMurdo; Radio with George Chisholm; Recent tour with Herb Geller; Featured in Edinburgh Jazzfest with Alex Shaw Trio, 1997; Tutor with Fyjo and Nyjos; Member, Jack Duff Quintet; Member, Freddy King Quintet; Member, Edinburgh Light Orchestra. *Membership:* Chairman, Edinburgh Branch, Musician's Union. *Leisure interests:* Music; Snooker; Cooking. *Address:* c/o Musician's Union, 1 Seafield Rd E, Edinburgh, Scotland.

SWINFIELD Raymond; b. 14 Dec. 1939, Sydney, Australia. Musician (saxophone, clarinet, flutes). m. Rosemarie, Sept. 1970, divorced 1991. *Career:* Played on recordings by: Quincy Jones; Robert Farnon; Henry Mancini; Pat Williams; Ella Fitzgerald; The Beatles; Phil Woods; Michel Legrand; Kiri Te Kanawa; Stéphane Grappelli; Johnny Mercer; J J Johnson. *Compositions:* Sydney Suite; Rain Curtain; Caroline; Thinking On It. *Recordings:* Albums: Rain Curtain; The Winged Cliff; Angel Eyes. *Honours:* Own albums listed amongst jazz records of the Year in Gramophone Jazz Journal magazines. *Memberships:* PRS; British Jazz Musicians. *Address:* c/o Musicians' Union, National Office, 60/62 Clapham Rd, London SW9 0JJ, England.

SYKES John; b. 29 July 1959. Rock Musician (guitar); Songwriter. *Career:* Guitarist, UK rock groups Streetfighters; Tygers of Pan Tang, 1980–81; Thin Lizzy, 1982–83; Concerts include: British tour, 1982; Tours, Europe, Japan, 1983; Reading Festival, 1983; Monsters of Rock European tour, 1983; Guitarist, Whitesnake, 1984–86; Tours, UK, Europe, 1984; US tours with Dio and Quiet Riot, 1984; Rock In Rio (largest ever rock festival), 1985. *Compositions:* Co-writer with David Coverdale: Still of The Night; Is This Love?. *Recordings:* Albums: with Tygers of Pan Tang: Spellbound, 1981; Crazy Nights, 1981; with Thin Lizzy: Thunder and Lightning, 1983; with Whitesnake: Slide It In, 1984; Whitesnake, (No. 2, US), 1987; Solo: Loveland, 1997; Best of John Sykes, 1998; Please Don't Leave Me, 1999; Chapter One, 2000; Singles: with Thin Lizzy: Hollywood; Cold Sweat; Thunder and Lightning; The Sun Goes Down; with Whitesnake: Give Me More Time; Standing In The Shadow; Love Ain't No Stranger. *Honours:* Platinum and Gold discs. *Current Management:* Music Group Management. *Address:* 3500 W Olive, Suite 950, Burbank, CA 91505, USA.

SYLVAIN Dominique; b. 17 Nov. 1959, New York, USA. Haitian Singer; Author; Composer. 1 d. *Education:* DEA, degree in Anthropology. *Musical Education:* Piano, guitar, percussion, voice. *Career:* Concerts include: L'Espace Julien (Marseilles), 1993; Pollen France Inter, 1994; L'Opus Café (Paris); Festival d'Été de Besançon, 1995; 2 broadcasts for France Inter radio; Television appearances: Antenne 2; RFO. *Recordings:* Reconnais, 1994. *Honour:* First Prize, Choreography and Interpretation, FFD, 1990. *Memberships:* SACEM; ADAMI; SACED. *Current Management:* Myriam Willis. *Address:* Axile 37 rue Doudeauville, 75018 Paris, France.

SYLVESTRE Frédéric; b. Angouleme, France. Musician (guitar, synthesizer guitar). *Career:* Played with artists including: Eddy Louiss; Martial Solal; Christian Escoudé; Marcel Azzola; Michel Graillier; Bernard Lubat; Alain Jean-Marie; Pepper Adams; Albi Cullaz; Tania Maria; Claude Cagnasso; Aldo Romano; Marc Bertaux; Jacques Vidal; Eric Le Lann; Gérard Marais; Jean-Louis Chautemps; Sacha Distel; Philip Catherine; Didier Levallet; Marcel Azzola; Jimmy Gourley; Georges Arvanitas; Luigi Trussardi. *Recordings:* Five Compact, Claude Cagnasso Big Band; with the Dolphin Orchestra: Prologue; Olympia Live; Rencontre; with Jacques Vidal: Premier Grand Cru; 2+; Hommages; Trio Live; Capricorne; with Martial Solal Big Band: Martial Solal Big Band Joue André Hodeir; Big Bande de Guitares de Gerard Marais, Gerard Marais; Music Band, Teddy Lasry; Dolores, Jean-Marc Jafet; Gipsy Waltz, Christian Escoudé Octet; Salena Jones Sings Cole Porter; Holidays, Christian Escoudé; News of Bop, Jacques Vidal Quintet; Trio Sur Seine, with Marcel Azzola. *Leisure interest:* Tennis. *Address:* 31 rue de Fontarabie, 75020 Paris, France.

SYLVIAN David, (David Batt); b. 23 Feb. 1958, Beckenham, Kent, England. Singer; Musician (guitar). *Career:* Singer, guitarist, Japan, 1977–82; Solo artiste, 1982–; Member, Rain Tree Crow (with 3 members of Japan), 1991. *Recordings:* Albums: with Japan: Adolescent Sex, 1978; Obscure Alternatives, 1978; Quiet Life, 1980; Gentlemen Take Polaroids, 1980; Assemblage, 1981; Tin Drum, 1981; Oil On Canvas, 1983; Exorcising Ghosts, 1984; Solo albums: Brilliant Trees, 1984; Alchemy, An Index of Possibilities, 1985; Gone To Earth, 1986; Secrets of The Beehive, 1987; Plight and Premonition, with Holger Czukay, 1988; Flux and Mutability (with Holger Czukay), 1989; Weather Box, 1989; Ember Glance, The Permanence Memory (with Russell Mills), 1991; with Rain Tree Crow: Rain Tree Crow, 1991; with Robert Fripp: The First Day, 1993; Damage, (with Robert Fripp) 1994; Guest singer, Dreams of Reason Produce Monsters, Mick Karn, 1987; Dead Bees on a Cake, 2000; Approaching Silence; Singles include: with Japan: Life in Tokyo, 1979; The Art of Parties, 1981; Quiet Life, 1981; Ghosts, 1982; Cantonese Boy, 1982; Night Porter, 1982; Canton, 1983; Solo: Red Guitar, 1984; The Ink In The Well, 1984; Pulling Punches, 1984; Taking The Veil, 1986; Let The Happiness In, 1987; I Surrender; Godman; with Ryûichi Sakamoto: Forbidden Colours, from film Merry Christmas Mr Lawrence, 1983. *Current Management:* Opium (Arts) Ltd, 49 Portland Rd, London W11 4LJ, England.

SZABO Richard Wayne; b. 16 March 1956, Newark, New Jersey, USA. Musician (trumpet); Bandleader. *Education:* BA, Music Education, Fairleigh Dickinson University, Madison, New Jersey, USA. *Career:* Played in bands of Maynard Ferguson; Buddy Rich; Ray Anthony; Sammy Kaye; Guy Lombardo; Tito Puente; Billy May; Xavier Cugat; Frank Sinatra Jr; Appeared or recorded with: Melissa Manchester; The Grass Roots; Mel Torme; Johnny Desmond; Margaret Whiting; Helen Forrest; Regis Philbin; The Four Tops; The Four Lads; The Four Aces; The Chordettes; Author (screenplay): College Inc, 1984; Traffic Vigilante, 1986; Music director, Station WPCN-AM Radio, Pennsylvania, 1988. *Recordings:* Manhattan At Dusk; Best of Both Worlds; Big Bands 80s, Various Artists Vols 3 and 4; Jumpin' On The Bandstand. *Honours:* Listed in Who's Who in Entertainment. *Memberships:* Songwriters Hall of Fame; NARAS; AFofM; AFTRA; IJAE. *Leisure interests:* Golf; Fishing; Photography. *Current Management:* Al Bauman, Fame Management, 939 Kimball St, Phildelphia, PA 19147, USA.

SZAWLOWSKI William Stephen; b. 24 March 1955, Montréal, Québec, Canada. Record Prod.; Engineer; Arranger; Writer. m. Margaret Lilliane Boutet, 6 Sept. 1975, 2 s. *Career:* Assistant recording engineer, 1974–75; Recording engineer, 1976–83; President, SCI Productions, Record Producer, 1984–90; Independent Record Producer, Engineer, Arranger, 1991-. *Recordings:* Producer for: Marjo; Marie-Carmen; Ray Lyell; Engineer for: April Wine; Aldo Nova; Frank Marino; Robbie Robertson; Helix; Luba; Teaze; Murray Head; Walter Rossi; Cirque du Soleil; Diane DuFresne; Kashtin; Pagliaro; Nanette Workman. *Honours:* 27 Gold and Platinum discs; ADISQ Award, Best Engineer, 1987. *Membership:* SOCAN. *Leisure interests:* Home renovation; Cooking; Computers. *Address:* 7195 Mauriac St, Brossard, QC J4Y 1T8, Canada.

SZCZESNIAK Mieczyslaw Wojciech; b. 9 July 1964, Kalisz, Poland. Vocalist. *Musical Education:* Academy of Music, Katowice. *Career:* Many television and radio appearances, concerts and recitals, Poland and abroad; Pop and jazz festivals include: Jazz Jamboree, Warsaw; Gospel festivals. *Recordings include:* Debut: Niby Nowy, 1990. *Honours:* Sopot Festival, 1989; Bresenz Intertalent, 1989; Golden Orpheus, 1990; Cesmè Festival, 1990; Golden Record of Nashville (FIDOF) 1990. *Memberships:* STOMUR (Polish Society of Pop Musicians); PSJ (Polish Society of Jazz). *Leisure interests:* Painting; Gardening; Travelling; Film; Books; Theatre; Music. *Address:* Plac Wolnica 11/11, 31–060 Krakow, Poland.

SZE Jean Yi-Ching; b. 14 May 1956, Shanghai, China. Composer; Zheng Performer. m. Ming Xiao, 26 Nov. 1994. *Education:* Graduate, Shanghai Conservatory of Music, 1984; Bachelor, College of St Elizabeth, USA, 1988; Master, Virginia Tech, USA, 1992. *Career:* Composer and Zheng Performer; Organic Chemist. *Compositions:* Shi, string quartet; Mountain, electric violin, zheng, bamboo flute; Autumn, string orchestra, with bamboo flute; Flute Solo; Eastern View and Tradition Suite, violin and zheng; A Spring Morning at Miao Mountain, bamboo flute and zheng; Three Poems of Tang Dynasty, soprano, bamboo flute, yang qing, zheng, ban hu and pipa; The Sword and the Silk, 2000; The Pearl and the Thread, 2001. *Honour:* Second Prize, Shanghai National Music Competition, 1983. *Memberships:* American Music Center; American Society of Composers, Authors and Publishers; American Chemical Society. *Leisure interests:* Ping pong; Cooking; Crafts. *Address:* 13 Joann Court, Monmouth Junction, NJ 08852, USA.

SZE Kwan Leung; b. 11 Dec. 1938, China. Musician. m. Chi Wan Sze Siu, 1 s. *Education:* Tianjin Conservatory of Music, China. *Career:* The Choir of Hong Kong, Professional Teacher, Conductor; Radio Television Hong Kong; Hong Kong Chinese Folk Song Group; Recital, 1982, 1983; Professor, Tsing Hua College Music Department. *Publications:* Chorus and Chorus Conductor; The Great Singers In Record. *Memberships:* Hong Kong Ethnomusicology Society. *Address:* Flat A, Kam Fai Building, 20 Watcrloo Rd, Kowloon, Hong Kong.

T

TABOR June; b. 31 Dec. 1947, Warwick, Warwickshire, England. Folk Singer. *Career:* Singer of contemporary and traditional songs; Various collaborations with: Martin Simpson; Maddy Prior (as the Silly Sisters); The Oyster Band; Hugh Warren; Nic Jones; Martin Carthy; Peter Bellamy; The Albion Band; Fairport Convention. *Recordings:* Albums: Airs and Graces, 1976; Ashes and Diamonds, 1977; Bees On Horseback, 1977; A Cut Above, with Martin Simpson, 1980; Abyssinians, 1983; Theme From Spy Ship, 1983; The Peel Sessions, 1986; Silly Sisters, with Maddy Prior, 1986; Aqaba, 1988; Some Other Time, 1989; No More To The Dance, with Maddy Prior, 1990; Aspects, 1990; Angel Tiger, 1992; Against the Streams, 1994; Singing the Storm, 1996; Aleyn, 1997; A Quiet Eye, 2000. *Current Management:* NE Music Management, Priory House, 55 Lawe Rd, South Shields, Tyne and Wear NE33 2AL, England.

TACUMA Jamaaladeen, (Rudy MacDaniel); b. 11 June 1956, Hempstead, New York, USA. Musician (double bass); Composer. *Musical Education:* Double bass from age 13. *Career:* Session musician, 1977–; Played with Charles Earland; Ornette Coleman's band Prime Time; Jeff Beck; Jayne Cortez (poet); Solo recording artiste, 1983–; Founder, own dance band Cosmetic, 1983–; Founder member, Golden Palominos; Concerts include: Recital with the Ebony String Quartet, Carnegie Hall, 1985. *Recordings:* Albums: Solo: Showstopper, 1983; Renaissance Man, 1984; Music World, 1987; Juke Box, 1989; Boss of The Bass, 1993; Sound Symphony, 1994; Intense, 1995; Journey into Gemini Territory, 1996; Dreamscape, 1998; Live in Cologne, 1998; with Cosmetic: So Tranquilizin', 1984; with Ornette Coleman/Prime Time: Dancing In Your Head, 1977; Body Meta, 1978; Of Human Feelings, 1979; Opening At The Caravan of Dreams, 1985; In All Languages, 1987; with James Blood Ulmer: Tales of Captain Black, 1978; As producer: (I Want To) Squeeze You Hold You, Willy De Ville, 1983. *Honour:* Downbeat Poll, Talent Deserving Wider Recognition (most votes ever), 1981.

TADMAN Tad (Paul); b. 19 Oct. 1969, Sutton, Surrey, England. Musician (bass guitar). *Education:* Wimbledon School of Art. *Musical Education:* Mainly self-taught. *Career:* Member, Nutty Boys; Television appearances: TXT, ITV; The Big E, ITV; 100% programme, BBC; Radio sessions on BBC and GLR. *Recordings include:* It's OK I'm a Policeman, Nutty Boys (EP and video), 1992. *Membership:* Musicians' Union. *Leisure interests:* Photography; Classic Cars. *Current Management:* Universal, Railton Rd, London SE24, England. *Address:* c/o PO Box 3087, London NW5 3DZ, England.

TAFJORD Stein Erik; b. 2 Nov. 1953, Langevag, Norway. Musician (tuba). m. 1 Sept. 1973–93, 3 d. *Musical Education:* Norwegian State Academy of Music. *Career:* Norwegian Radio Symphony Orchestra; Carla Bley Scandinavian Orchestra; Lester Bowie; David Murrey's Jazz Baltica Ensemble; The Brazz Brothers; Soloist, several TV-radio productions in Europe, USA. *Recordings:* Participated on approximately 120 recordings, 16 with own band. *Honours:* Jazz Musician of the Year, Norway, 1991. *Membership:* Norwegian Musicians' Union.

TAHA Rachid; b. 1958, Oran, Algeria. Vocalist; Songwriter. *Musical Education:* Self-taught. *Career:* Family emigrated to France, 1968; Met future members of Carte de Séjour, 1981; Recorded first single, 1982; Debut album, 1983; Successful single, Douce France, from second album led to European tour; Group split, 1989; Solo career, 1991–; Extensive tour of France, 1998; Various live performances and festival appearances include: Egypt; Lebanon; US; Canada. *Recordings:* Albums include: with Carte De Séjour: Rhoromanie, 1983; Deux Et Demi, 1986; solo: Barbes, 1991; Rachid Taha, 1993; Ole Ole, 1996; Carte Blanche, 1997; Diwan, 1998; 1 2 3 Soleil (with Khaled and Faudel), Ach Adani, Made In Medina, 2001. *Internet:* www.rachidtaha.com.

TALBOT Jamie Robert; b. 23 April 1960, London, England. Musician (saxophone, clarinet, flute). m. Clare, 4 Nov. 1988, 1 s. *Musical Education:* Centre for Young Musicians, RCM (briefly). *Career:* Worked with: Stan Tracy; John Dankworth; Cleo Laine; Gil Evans; Ella Fitzgerald; Nelson Riddle; Frank Sinatra; Shorty Rogers; Natalie Cole. *Recordings:* Altitude, Jamie Talbot Sextet; Live At Ronnie Scott's, Stan Tracey; Genesis, Stan Tracey; Suddenly Last Tuesday, Clark Tracey. *Address:* 34 Elmers End Rd, Anerley, London SE20 7SN, England.

TALBOT Joby; b. 25 Aug. 1971, Wimbledon, London. Composer; Arranger; Musician (Piano, Oboe); Conductor. m. Claire Burbridge. *Education:* Guildhall School of Music and Drama; University of London. *Career:* Composer of Concert Music for Goups, London Sinfonietta; RRC Philharmonic; Britten Sinfonia Crouch End Festival Chorus; Keyboard Player, Arranger with The Divine Comedy, 1993–; Composer of Television

and Film Music for BBC, 1996-. *Compositions:* Incandescence; Luminescence; Young Musician of The Year Theme; Tomorrow's World Theme; League of Gentlemen Theme. *Recordings:* The Divine Comedy; Casanova; Fin De Siecle; Something For The Weekend; Becoming More Like Alfie; The Frog Princess; Everbody Knows, Except You; The Certainty of Chance; National Express. *Honours:* BBC Young Composer of The Year, 1996; BMus and MMus With Distinction. *Memberships:* Musicians' Union; PRS. *Leisure interest:* Experiences. *Current Management:* Amos Barr Music Management, 10 Huntley Close, High Wycombe, HP13 5PQ, England. *Address:* 16 Denman Rd, Peckham, London SE15 5NP, England.

TAMINIAUX Eric; b. 13 March 1963, La Hestre, Belgium. *Education:* Germanic Languages College, 1981–84. *Musical Education:* Three years, Music School; Self-taught Guitarist. *Career:* First Band, 17 years old; Singer, Guitarist, Halloween, support act for various Belgian bands, 1983–94; Singer, Guitarist, Check Point Charlie, support act for French band Miossec, 1994–. *Compositions:* With Halloween: Somebody Else Is You, 1991; Nameless People's Hotel, 1993; With Check Point Charlie, 12 Tracks Recorded. *Membership:* Belgian Society of Authors, Composers and Publishers. *Leisure interest:* Fishing. *Current Management:* Keylight. *Address:* c/o Keylight, rue Amerique 79, 6120 Ham Sur Heure, Belgium.

TAMPIER Karel; b. 24 June 1946, Ceské Budejovice, Czech Republic. Composer; Songwriter. Divorced, 3 d. *Musical Education:* Piano lessons, 9 years; Self-taught Guitar, Mandolin, Keyboards. *Career:* Leader, Guitar, Mandolin Player, Bluegrass Group, Bobri, 1970–84; Leader, Piano, Zridlo (The Source), 1979–85; Countryfuga, family group with wife and 3 daughters, 1989–93; Concerts in clubs and festivals in Czechoslovakia; About 100 songs recorded in Czech radio; 10 performances in Czech and Slovak TV; Music for Theatre; New music group, De Tampier, 1999; Music for TV films. *Compositions:* Proc Jsem Mrtev? (Why Do I Death?); Postel (The Bed) – Song and Musical. *Recordings:* Bobri, 1977–80, 1994; De Tampier, 1999. *Honours:* Czech Country and Folk Festival, Porta: Main prizes for interpretation, 1978, 1979, 1980; Main prize for songwriter, 1984. *Leisure interests:* Literature; Hiking. *Address:* Karel Tampier, Staromestská 9, 37004 Ceské Budejovice, Czech Republic.

TAMS John Murray; b. 16 Feb. 1949. Vocalist; Musician (guitar, melodeon, fiddle, banjo, harmonica); Actor; Songwriter; Prod. *Career:* Regular on the British folk scene for many years before recording first solo album, 2000; Played trumpet in a brass band as a child but is known in folk circles as vocalist/guitarist; Member: Ashley Hutching's Albion Band, 1976–87; Leader: Home Service (folk rock band); Musical Director for the National Theatre production of the Mysteries; Launched record label No Masters Co-operative with Jim Boyes; Actor and theatrical producer; Associate Director of Crucible Theatre, Sheffield; Produced radio dramas; Appeared in and composed music for TV series Sharpe. *Recordings:* Unity, 2000; with Albion Band: The Prospect Before Us, 1977; Rise Up Like The Sun, 1978; Larkrise To Candleford, 1980; 1990, 1990; with Home Service: Home Service, The Mysteries, 1985; Alright Jack, 1986; features on: Son of Morris On, 1976; Raggedy Rawney OST, 1988. *Honours:* Radio 2 Folk Award, Album of the Year, Unity, 2001; Froots Magazine Critics Poll, Album of the Year, third place, Unity, 2000.

TAÑÓN Olga; b. 13 April 1967, Santurce, Puerto Rico. Vocalist. *Career:* First sang with Orchestra Las Nenas de Ringo Y Jossie; Joined Chantelle; First solo album, 1992; Sales of over 2.5m. records; Tours internationally. *Recordings:* Sola, 1992; Mujer De Fuego, 1993; Siente El Amor, 1994; Exitos Y Mas, 1995; Nuevos Senderos, 1996; Llevame Contigo, 1997; Te Acordaras De Mi, 1998; Olga Viva – Viva Olga, 1999; Yo Por Ti, 2001. *Honours:* various including: Asscn of Entertainment Critics of New York, Ace Award, 1994; ASCAP award, 1993; Billboard International Latin Music Awards, Female Album of the Year, 1998; Grammy Awards, Best Merengue Album, 2000 and 2001. *Internet:* www.olgatanon.com.

TANT Jean-Christophe; b. 12 Feb. 1962, Lille, France. Singer; Composer; Musician (guitar). *Education:* Degree, Plastic Arts. *Musical Education:* Academy of Music, Lille. *Career:* Performed at festivals including: Montréal; Munchen-Gladbach; Edinburgh; Lille; Jelena Gora; Jazz Valley, Paris; Singapore; Television appearances: France: FR3, M6, A2; Poland, Channel 1; Radio appearances: France Inter, Europe 2, Frequence Nord. *Honour:* Golden Nono (Wazemmes), France. *Membership:* SACEM. *Current Management:* Lyse Bochner.

TAPIO Jorma Ilmari; b. 6 Aug. 1957, Mikkeli, Finland. Musician (alto saxophone, bass clarinet, flutes, percussion). *Musical Education:* Piano, private lessons, aged 6; Violin, flutes and saxophone at music school; Lessons from Pekka Pöyry, Juhani Aaltonen and Edward Vesala. *Career:*

Member, trio Lavantairyhmä, 1980–82; Member, traditional tango band, rock groups and big bands; Own tapes for radio, television documentaries, theatre, film pieces and dance performances; Numerous tours with Krakatau; Tours, recordings, television appearances and two documentary films with Edward Vesala; Founder, own group Rolling Thunder, 1995–97; Also solo appearances. *Recordings:* with Krakatau: Ritual, 1988; with Edward Vesala's Sound and Fury: Lumi, 1985; Ode To The Death of Jazz, 1989; Invisible Storm, 1991; Nordic Gallery, 1994. *Address:* Agricolankuja 2 C 96, 00530 Helsinki, Finland.

TARDLEY Ken; b. 5 Oct. 1949, Rotherham, Yorkshire, England. Musician (Dobro); Bandleader; University Lecturer. m. Lorretta Tardley, 12 Aug. 1982, 1 d. *Education:* BSc Hons, Chemistry, MSC, Systems Analysis, PGCE. *Musical Education:* Elkins College, West Virginia, 1990, 1995. *Career:* Member, US band, Muleskinner, 1990–92; Member, Sound In Mind, 1985–93; Member, Generation Gap, 1992–94; Toured USA, 1994; DJ, WTHO radio, Thompson, Georgia, USA; Curator, Dalebilly Museum, Airdale Drive, Howarth. *Recordings:* Riding Down The Canyon, Sound In Mind, 1989; Muleskinner, 1990. *Publications:* Staff writer, British Bluegrass News. *Honours:* King of The Dalebilly Dobro Players, 1995. *Membership:* Founder mem., British Bluegrass Music Asscn. *Leisure interests:* Management Cybernetics; Real Ale. *Current Management:* Loretta Tardley. *Address:* 65 Gledholt Bank, Huddersfield, West Yorkshire HD1 4HE, England.

TARKAN (Tarkan Tevetoglu); b. 17 Oct. 1972, Alzey, nr Frankfurt, Germany. Vocalist. *Musical Education:* Karamürsel Music High School, studied Turkish classical music; Continued music studies in Istanbul, Turkey. *Career:* Moved to Turkey with family, aged 14; Hugely popular in Turkey, 1993–95; Rest period followed owing to pressure of celebrity status; Commenced studies at Baruch College, New York, 1995; Returned to recording, 1997; European breakthrough with Simarik single, 1999; National military service followed by short tour of Latin America, 2000; Fronted Pepsi TV commercial, 2001; Concerts in Turkey, 2001; Now resides Manhattan, New York. *Recordings:* Albums: Yine Sensiz, 1993; A-Acayipsin, 1995; Ölürüm Sana, 1997; Tarkan, 1999; Karma, 2001; Singles (international releases): Simarik, Sikidim, Bu Gece, 1999; Kuzu Kuzu, 2001. *Honours:* World Music Awards, Best Selling Turkish Act, 1999; Asscn of Turkish Journalists, Most Successful Turkish Artist; Turkish album sales estimated to be in excess of 10m. *Address:* c/o Mehmet Sögütoglu, Istanbul Plak, Turkey. *Internet:* www.bvtarkan.com.

TASHIAN Barry M; b. 5 Aug. 1945, Oak Park, Illinois, USA. Singer; Musician (Guitar); Songwriter. m. Holly Paige Kimball, 2 s. *Education:* Boston University: Private lessons in guitar, piano and voice. *Career:* Founder, 60's Rock Band, Barry and The Remains; Appeared Ed Sullivan Christmas Show, CBS Television, 1965; Hullabaloo, NBC, 1966; Epic Recording Artists; Travelled with The Beatles as opening act, summer tour of USA, 1966; Regional chart single hits in the Boston, New England area. *Compositions:* Why Do I Cry; Two Ways To Fall; Ooh Las Vegas; Spinning Straw Into Gold; Heaven With You; Long Train of Fools. *Recordings:* The Remains; 10 Albums with Emmy Lou Harris; 5 Albums with wife, as Barry and Holly Tashian. *Publications:* Ticket To Ride: The Extraordinary Diary of The Beatles Last Tour. *Honours:* Boston Music Award, 1990; Indie Album of The Year, 1996. *Memberships:* AFM; BMI; IBMA. *Current Management:* Tashian Music, PO Box 150921 Nashville, TN 37215, USA.

TASHIAN Holly P; b. 8 Jan. 1946, New York, USA. Singer; Songwriter; Musician (guitar). m. Barry Tashian, 1 Nov. 1972, 2 s. *Education:* BA Psychology, 1 year graduate. *Musical Education:* Private lessons, violin, piano, voice. *Career:* As act Barry and Holly Tashian; Television: Grand Ole Opry Live; American Music Shop; Backstage Opry; Radio: Grand Ole Opry; Prairie Home Companion. *Compositions:* Songs recorded by Nashville Bluegrass Band and Ty England; Daniel O'Donnell; Roland White; Jody Stecher; Kate Brislin. *Recordings:* Albums: Trust In Me; Live In Holland; Ready For Love; Straw Into Gold; Harmony; Recordings with: Nanci Griffith; Delia Bell. *Honours:* NAIRD (National Asscn of Independent Record Distributors); Country Album of the Year, Straw Into Gold, 1995. *Memberships:* ASCAP; AFofM; IBMA; NARAS; Folk Alliance. *Leisure interests:* Dogs; Cooking. *Current Management:* Tashian Music. *Address:* Tashian Music, PO Box 150921, Nashville, TN 37215, USA.

TATE Geoff; Vocalist. *Career:* Lead singer, US rock group Queensrÿche, 1981-. *Recordings:* Albums: Queen of The Reich (EP), 1983; The Warning, 1984; Rage For Order, 1985; Operation – Mindcrime, 1988; Empire, 1990; Promised Land, 1994; Hear in the Now Frontier, 1997; Operation: Mindcrime, 1999; Singles include: Silent Lucidity; Best I Can; Jet City Woman. *Current Management:* Q-Prime Inc, 729 Seventh Ave, 14th Floor, New York, NY 10019, USA.

TATTERSALL Norman; b. 13 Oct. 1924, Burnley, Lancashire, England. Singer (Baritone); Teacher; Lecturer; Adjudicator. *Education:* Post Graduate Certificate (Adjudication) FRSA, 1999. *Musical Education:*

Birmingham University; Royal Academy of Music. *Career:* Freelance opera singer; Appeared with Flagstad as Sailor in Dido and Aeneas, 1953; Oratorio and recitals world-wide; Adjudicator and Judge in Canada, USA and UK; Sang Sid in Albert Herring conducted by Benjamin Britten, 1957; St Matthew Passion, conducted by Ralph Vaughan Williams, 1954; Wigmore Recital with Gerald Moore, 1955. *Publications:* Singing in a Nutshell: A Dozen Do's and Don'ts, 1988; Autobiography forthcoming, 2000. *Honours:* LRAM, 1951; ARAM, 1955; FRAM, 1981; 7 Prizes from Royal Academy of Music including Betjeman Prize, 1949, and Boise Award, 1954. *Memberships:* Association of Teachers of Singing; Founder and Chairman, RAM Guild; Mem. of the General Council British Federation of Young Choirs (First Levenhume Fellow, 1983); Mem. of the Board of the British Federation of Festivals for Music, Dance and Speech. *Leisure interests:* Theatre; Cooking; Travel. *Address:* The Sideways House, 146 Greenstead Rd, Colchester, Essex CO1 2SN, England.

TAUPIN Bernie; b. 22 May 1950, Lincolnshire, England. Songwriter. *Career:* Long-term songwriting partnership with Elton John, 1967-. *Compositions:* As co-writer with Elton John: Albums with Elton John: All albums, 1969–77; Too Low For Zero, 1983; Sleeping With The Past, 1989; Two Rooms – Celebrating The Songs of Elton John and Bernie Taupin, 1992; Solo: Bernie Taupin, 1970; Taupin, 1971; He Who Rides The Tiger, 1980; Tribe, 1987; Numerous hits include: Don't Let The Sun Go Down On Me; Crocodile Rock; Rocket Man; Sacrifice; Sorry Seems To Be The Hardest Word; Daniel; Saturday Night's Alright For Fighting; Other co-compositions: Skyline Pigeon, Roger Cook, 1968; I Can't Go On Living Without You, 1969; Snookeroo, 1975. *Honours:* Ivor Novello Awards: Best Song, Daniel, 1974; Sacrifice, 1991; MTV Award, Special Recognition Trophy, 1987; Inducted into Songwriters Hall of Fame, 1992. *Current Management:* Lippman Entertainment, 8900 Wilshire Blvd, Suite 340, Beverly Hills, CA 90211, USA.

TAVERNER Tony; b. 20 Sept. 1951, London, England. Prod.; Engineer. m. Ruth, 4 c. *Career:* Engineered Duran Duran's US No 1 single, Ordinary World and The Wedding Album, and Thank You, albums; Co-Produced and Engineered, Warren Cuccurullo's solo album project; Engineered and Produced 2 chart topping albums in Spain with Duncan Dhu; Worked with Mikel Erentxum and Diego Vasallo; Senior Engineer, Maison Rouge Studios in London, 1977–88; Engineer, various albums, with Jeff Beck, 1973–99; Teamed-up with songwriter, producer, Simon Ellis (Spice Girls, S Club 7). *Recordings:* Sound mixing on 2 Spice Girl videos; Sex Chips and Rock N Roll; TV series: Taggart; The Turnaround. *Honours:* Numerous Gold and Platinum album awards. *Current Management:* Film and TV: Soundtrack Music Associates Ltd, 25 Ives St, Chelsea, London SW3 2ND, England; Records: Pachuco Management, The Blue Building, 42–46 St Lukes Mews, London W11 1DG, England.

TAYLER Stephen William; b. 20 Sept. 1953, High Wycombe, Buckinghamshire, England. Recording and Mixing Engineer; Prod.; Programmer; Musician (various). *Musical Education:* New College School (Choir); Shrewsbury School (Music Scholarship); Royal College of Music (ARCH). *Career:* Trident Studios: House Engineer, 1974–80; Freelance engineer, musician, producer, programmer, 1980–; Worked on over 120 album projects. *Recordings:* Engineer / mixer for: Tina Turner; Stevie Nicks; Peter Gabriel; Bob Geldof; Rush; Howard Jones; The Fixx; Others. *Honours:* Numerous include: Ampex Golden Reel; 2 BASF/Studio Awards for Excellence. *Memberships:* Re-pro; Musicians' Union. *Leisure interests:* Eating; Sleeping. *Address:* c/o Chimera Records, 41 Rosebank, Holyport Rd, London SW6 6LQ, England.

TAYLOR (Nigel) John; b. 20 June 1960, Birmingham, Warwickshire, England. Musician (bass, guitar); Songwriter. 1 d. *Career:* Founder member, Duran Duran, 1978–; Member, Power Station, 1985; Performances include: Edinburgh Festival, 1980; British tour, supporting Hazel O'Connor, 1980; British tour, 1981; MENCAP charity concert, attended by HRH the Prince and Princess of Wales, 1983; Live Aid, Philadelphia, 1985; Guest appearance, Miami Vice, NBC, 1985; The Secret Policeman's Third Ball, London, 1987; An Acoustic Evening With Duran Duran, Birmingham Symphony Hall, 1993. *Recordings:* Albums: with Duran Duran: Duran Duran, 1981; Carnival, 1982; Seven and The Ragged Tiger, 1983; Arena, 1984; So Red The Rose, 1985; Notorious, 1987; Big Thing, 1988; Decade, 1990; Duran Duran (The Wedding Album), 1993; Thank You, 1995; Medazzaland, 1997; with Power Station: The Power Station, 1985; Solo: Feelings Are Good and Other Lies, 1997; Singles: with Duran Duran: Planet Earth, 1981; Girls On Film, 1981; My Own Way, 1981; Save A Prayer, 1982; Hungry Like The Wolf, 1982; Is There Something I Should Know (No. 1, UK), 1983; Rio, 1983; Union of The Snake, 1983; New Moon On Monday, 1984; The Reflex (No. 1, UK and US), 1984; The Wild Boys, 1984; A View To A Kill, theme from Bond film (No. 1, USA), 1985; Notorious, 1986; Meet El Presidente, 1987; I Don't Want Your Love, 1988; All She Wants, 1989; Do You Believe In Shame, featured in film Tequila Sunrise, 1989; Violence of Summer (Love's Taking Over), 1990; Serious, 1990; Ordinary World, 1993; Come Undone, 1993; Too Much

Information, 1993; Electric Barbarella, 1997; with Power Station: Some Like It Hot, 1985; Communication, 1985; Solo: I Do What I Do, theme from film 9 1/2 Weeks, 1986; Contributor, Do They Know It's Christmas?, Band Aid, 1984. *Honours:* BRIT Award, Best British Music Video, 1985; Ivor Novello Award, International Hit of The Year, 1985; Star on Hollywood Walk of Fame, 1993. *Current Management:* The Left Bank Organisation, 9255 W Sunset Blvd, Second Floor, Los Angeles, CA 90069, USA.

TAYLOR Andy; b. 16 Feb. 1961, Tynemouth, England. Musician (guitar). m. Tracey Wilson, 29 July 1982. *Career:* Guitarist, Duran Duran, 1979–86; Guitarist, Power Station, 1985; Solo artiste, 1986; Concerts include: Uk tour, support to Hazel O'Connor, 1980; Edinburgh Festival, 1980; US tour, support to Blondie, 1982; MENCAP charity, concert, attended by HRH the Prince and Princess of Wales, 1983; Live Aid, Philadelphia, 1985; Television appearance, Miami Vice, NBC, 1985. *Recordings:* with Duran Duran: Duran Duran, 1981; Carnival, 1982; Seven and The Ragged Tiger, 1983; with Power Station: The Power Station, 1985; Solo: Thunder, 1987; Singles with Duran Duran include: Planet Earth, 1981; Girls On Film, 1981; My Own Way, 1981; Hungry Like The Wolf, 1982; Save a Prayer, 1982; Is There Something I Should Know (No. 1, UK), 1983; Rio, 1984; Union of The Snake, 1984; New Moon On Monday, 1984; The Wild Boys, 1984; A View To A Kill, Bond film theme (No. 1, USA), 1985; with Power Station: Some Like It Hot, 1985; Get It On, 1985; Communication, 1985; Solo: Take It Easy, 1986; When The Rain Comes Down, 1986; Lola, 1990; Contributions to: Anne Runolfsson, At Sea, 1997; By Jeeves, original cast recording, 1997; Engineer, Songs of Rodgers and Hammerstein, 1999. *Honours include:* Best Group, Daily Mirror/BBC TV Nationwide/Radio 1 Awards, 1983; Grammy Awards, Best Video Short and Album, 1984; BRIT Award, Best British Music Video, Wild Boys, 1985; Ivor Novello, International Hit of The Year, 1985; Star on Hollywood Walk of Fame, 1993.

TAYLOR Caroline; b. 25 March 1965, Auborn, New York, USA. Musician; Composer. *Career:* Performed with Nikki Yeoh, Chris Lineham's Popcorn Club. *Compositions:* CT Blues; Deep Blue Sea; Mum's Cove; Chickenbutt; Blues for Sarah; Groovin' Low; For The Moment. *Recordings:* For The Moment. *Current Management:* Mike Curtis, 17 Havelock Rd, Tonbridge, Kent TN9 1JE, England. *Address:* 4B Younge Park, London N4 3NT.

TAYLOR Christopher Gordon; b. 24 Nov. 1966, Birmingham, England. Musician (keyboards, drums); Composer; Arranger. *Career:* Musical Director for Central Television: Central Weekend; Keyboards, MD, Ruby Turner, 1988–95; MD, Accompanist, many top UK cabaret artists; Musical Director for Sheila Ferguson, 1996; Musical Director for the Three Degrees and The Supremes, 1997; Oh What a Night, The Musical, Opera House, 1997; Worked with: Rose Royce; Heatwave; Jools Holland; Gloria Gaynor; Leo Sayer; Boyzone; Peter Andre; And many top UK cabaret artists. *Compositions:* Gardener's World, BBC, 1990; Central Weekend, Central TV, 1993; Home Run, Central TV, 1993; Sunday Supplement, Central TV, 1993; Millionaires, 1995; Wednesday Night Live, 1998; Many video soundtracks. *Recordings:* Producer/Musician on album, Responsible, Ruby Turner. *Memberships:* Musicians' Union; British Music Writers Council; PRS; MCPS; PAMRA. *Leisure interests:* Jazz; Sports Cars. *Current Management:* Grosvenor Records. *Address:* 16 Grosvenor Rd, Handsworth Wood, Birmingham B20 3NP, England.

TAYLOR Crispin Luke; b. 1 July 1961, London, England. Musician (drums, percussion). m. Rosamond Howe, 26 March 1994, 2 d. *Musical Education:* Self-taught. *Career:* Concerts include: Montreux Jazz Festival (twice); Nice Jazz Festival, twice; Glastonbury Festival, four times; Television appearances: The Word and Pebble Mill, with Seal; Top of The Pops, with Galliano; Dance Energy and Motormouth, with Definition of Sound. *Recordings:* with Galliano: The Plot Thickens; Joyful Noise Unto The Creator; with Urban Species: Spiritual Love; Listen; with Oui 3: Oui Love You; Tracks/singles: Wear Your Love Like Heaven, Definition of Sound (No. 12, UK charts); Let It Last, Carleen Anderson; Mathar, Indian Vibes; As co-writer, producer: Scratchmo, 1988; Same Feeling, Mica Paris, 1988. *Honours:* 2 Silver discs. *Membership:* PRS. *Leisure interest:* Piano. *Current Management:* Pump Music. *Address:* 9A Yerbury Rd, London N19 4RN, England.

TAYLOR Gary A (Anthony); b. 18 Jan. 1951, Los Angeles, California, USA. Singer; Songwriter; Musician (keyboards). 2 s., 1 d. *Education:* 5 years college (Psychology major). *Musical Education:* Self-taught piano. *Career:* Working in studios; Began songwriting early 80's; Signed to A & M Records, 1983; Virgin Records, 1988; Written, produced records for numerous artists; Radio and television commercials; solo artist, 1988-. *Compositions:* Good Love (Anita Baker); I'm Coming Back (Lalah Hathaway); Square One (Ray Parker Jr); One Day At A Time (Vanessa Williams); Songs also recorded by: Grover Washington Jr; Vesta Williams; Chico Debarge; Joyce Kennedy; The Whispers; Mac Band; Jennifer Holliday; Stephanie Mills. *Recordings:* Albums: Compassion, 1988; Take Control, 1990; Square One, 1993; The Mood of Midnight, 1995; Love Dance, 1998; Singles: Eye to Eye, 1993; Hold Me Accountable, 1994; In and Out of

Love, 1994; Restless, 1994; Special, 1995. *Leisure interests:* Gym training; People watching. *Current Management:* Steven Ivory.

TAYLOR Graeme David; b. 2 Feb. 1954, Stockwell, London, England. Musician (guitar, mandolin, banjo, piano). m. Sue Meldon, 20 July 1974, 1 d. *Musical Education:* Music O'Level, Piano lessons to Grade 4. *Career:* Tours with Gryphon, Europe, USA, supporting Yes, 1971–; Many television appearances include: Jim'll Fix It; Magpie; All BBC radio channels in 1 week; Tours in Albion Band with: Billy Connolly; Julie Covington; Theatre work: National Theatre productions, Lark Rise To Candleford; The Mysteries; Other theatre include: Cats; Joseph and The Technicolour Dreamcoat; Television includes: This Is Your Life with Rolf Harris. *Recordings:* Albums include: with Gryphon: Gryphon, 1973; Red Queen to Gryphon Three, 1974; Midnight Mushrumps, 1974; Raindance, 1975; with Albion Band: Prospect Before Us, 1977; Rise Up Like The Sun, 1978; Larkrise to Candleford, 1980; with Home Service: Mysteries, 1998; Alright Jack, 1998; Many of own compositions on these recordings. *Memberships:* Musicians' Union; PRS. *Leisure interests:* Cooking; Brewing; Gardening; Cycling. *Current Management:* London Musicians. *Address:* 15 Eastway, Morden, SurreySM4 4HW, England.

TAYLOR James; b. 12 March 1948, Boston, Massachusetts, USA. Singer; Songwriter. m. Kathryn Walker, 1985. *Career:* First album, produced by Peter Asher, Apple Records, London, 1968; Signed to Warner Brothers Records; Moved to California, with Peter Asher, 1969; Films: Two Lane Blacktop, 1971; No-Nukes, 1980; Tours, USA: 1971, 1974–77, 1979–87, 1990–92, 1994; Tours: Far East, Australia, 1981; Italy, 1985; Australia, Europe, Brazil, 1986; Australia, New Zealand, 1988; Europe, 1992; Far East, Australia, 1995; Concerts include: Carnegie Hall, 1975; No-Nukes Concerts, 1979; Rock In Rio, Rio De Janeiro, 1985; Festivals, Munich, Nurburgring, Berlin, Germany, 1986; Phoenix Festival, 1995; Television includes: Live In Concert, Atlanta, 1981; Working, PBS-TV, 1981. *Recordings:* Albums: James Taylor, 1968; Sweet Baby James, 1970; Mud Slide Slim, 1971; One Man Dog, 1972; Walking Man, 1974; Gorilla, 1975; In The Pocket, 1976; Greatest Hits, 1976; JT, 1977; Flag, 1979; Dad Loves His Work, 1981; That's Why I'm Here, 1985; Never Die Young, 1988; New Moon Shine, 1991; James Taylor (Live), 1993; In The Hands of The Inevitable, 1995; Original Flying Machine, 1996; Hour Glass, 1997; Live at the Beacon Theatre, 1998; Singles include: Carolina In My Mind, 1969; Something's Wrong, 1969; Sweet Baby James, 1970; Fire and Rain, 1970; Country Road, 1971; You've Got A Friend (by Carole King), 1971; Long Ago and Far Away (with Joni Mitchell), 1971; Don't Let Me Be Lonely Tonight, 1972; One Man Parade, 1973; Mockingbird (with Carly Simon), 1974; Walking Man, 1974; Mexico, 1975; Rainy Day Man, 1975; You Make It Easy, 1976; Stop Thinkin Bout That, 1992; Copperline, 1995; Line 'Em Up, 1997; Jump Up Behind Me, 1998; Appeared on No-Nukes album, 6 tracks, 1979; In Harmony, Sesame Street album, 1980; Producer, guitarist, singer, (sister) Kate Taylor's single, 1977, album, 1988. *Honours include:* Grammy Awards, 1972, 1978. *Current Management:* Peter Asher Management, 644 N Doheny Dr., Los Angeles, CA 90069, USA.

TAYLOR Jeremy; b. Newbury, Berkshire, England. Singer; Composer; Entertainer. *Education:* French, Italian, Oxford University. *Career:* Taught at Eton College; Taught in South Africa; Wrote hit show, Wait A Minim, West End (two years) and Broadway; Worked with Sydney Carter, Spike Milligan; One man shows throughout South Africa. *Recordings include:* Ag Please Daddy (No. 1, South Africa), now unofficial national anthem. *Current Management:* Jim McPhee, Acorn Entertainments. *Address:* Winterfold House, 46 Woodfield Rd, Kings Heath, Birmingham B13 9UJ, England.

TAYLOR John Michael; b. 24 March 1934, Retford, Nottinghamshire, England. Musician (trumpet, piano, keyboards, organ). *Musical Education:* Piano lessons, 1 year, aged 9; Trumpet lessons, 1 year, aged 12. *Career:* Mike Taylor Jazzmen, 1956–59; Micky Askman Ragtime Jazzband, 1959–63; Appearances: Morecombe and Wise Show; 2 appearances: Thank Your Lucky Stars; Kent Walton Show; BBC Jazz Club; Midland Allstars, 1964–66; Second City Jazzmen, 1969–75; Accompanied various American stars including: Billy Butterfield; Wild Bill Davidson; Eddie Miller; Bud Freeman; Art Hodes; Earl Warren; Kenny Daverne; Jim Handy; Derby Big Band, 1976–79; Burton MU Big Band, 1977–80; All That Jazz Parade band, 1984–89; Festivals: Tilburg; Giethoorn; Breda; Kassel; 2 times Ascona Jazz Festival; 3 times Upton Jazz Festival; 2 times Bude; Keswick; Edinburgh; Duke Ellington Conference, Harlem, 1985–94; German tour; Several London Night at the Cotton Club shows with: Doc Cheetham; Benny Waters; Adelade Hall; Bertice Reading; Herb Jeffries; Juanita Brooks; Hi-Life Parade Band, 1989–; Ascona Festival; 3 times Cork Jazz Festival; 2 times Bude Festival; Keswick Festival; Freelance musician, on piano, trumpet, with numerous groups. *Membership:* Musicians' Union. *Leisure interest:* Sailing. *Address:* 1 Redblock Field, Lichfield, Staffordshire WS14 0AB, England.

TAYLOR Jon T-Bone; b. 29 Aug. 1963, London, England. Blues and Jazz Musician (guitar). *Musical Education:* Guildhall School of Music. *Career:*

Leader of Bop Brothers, 1986–; Guitarist with Tim Richards' bands Roogalator and Grooveyard; Daniel Smith Blues Band and Duo, 2000–; Toured with Charlie Sayles; Champion Jack Dupree; Mojo Buford; Lefty Dizz; Dick Heckstall-Smith. *Recordings:* Strange News, Bop Brothers, 1995; Bop Brothers... and Sisters, with Earl Green, Dana Gillespie and Ruby Turner, 1998; Bop Brothers... and Sisters, with Deitra Farr, Taka Boom and Connie Lush, 2000. *Membership:* Musicians' Union. *Current Management:* Abacabe Ltd. *Address:* 10 Messaline Ave, London W3 6JX, England.

TAYLOR Linda Christina; b. 27 July 1950, Cleveland, England. Singer; Songwriter; Impressionist. m. Jeff Taylor, 28 Oct. 1968, 1 s. *Musical Education:* Piano, Professor Larman, Bedford; Voice, Jean Knight, London. *Career:* Backing vocals, albums: Chris Rea; Tom Jones; Celine Dion; Gary Moore; Kylie Minogue; Doctor John; Mike and The Mechanics; Julien Clerc; ABC; Paul Young; Jimmy Nail; Sting; Johnny Hallyday; Zucchero; Fish Tree Water Blues; Tours with: Go West; Art of Noise; Jocelyn Brown; Marvin Gaye; EPO (Japan); Chris Rea; Impressions: Spitting Image; Prime Suspect III; Crazy Horse, Paris; Television Commercials. *Compositions:* Angel; Everybody Knows; Taylor Made, (solo album, 1981); Morrisey/Mullen, 1981; Cayenne, Gary Numan, Bill Sharp; Every Waking Hour; You and Me Just Started, 1981. *Honours:* Platinum disc, Angel, 1990; Gold discs: Chris Rea, Breathe. *Memberships:* Equity; Musicians' Union; PAMRA; PRS. *Leisure interests:* Water colour painting; Fitness; Psychotherapy study. *Current Management:* Isobel Griffiths; Hobsons Singers. *Address:* 61 Sutherland Ave, Maida Vale, London W9 2HF, England.

TAYLOR Martin; b. 20 Oct. 1956, Harlow Essex, England. Musician (guitar, banjo, flute); Composer. *Career:* Son of guitarist and double bassist Will 'Buck' Taylor; Played guitar from age 4 and gigged with father's dance band in early teens; Performed with Sonny Dee's All Stars, aged 15; Various stints at Pontin's Holiday camp and various cruise liners followed; Played with Alan Elsdon, Dave Shepherd, Bob Bryan and led own quartet, mid 1970s; Began long musical association with Stéphane Grappelli, involving many world-wide tours, 1979; Worked with Ike Isaacs; Louis Stewart; Peter Ind; Dave Newton; David Grisman; Led own trio and quartet, early 1990s; Made Django Reinhardt-influenced Spirit of Django album, 1994; Subsequently toured and recorded with band named Spirit of Django; Recorded Nitelife album in Nashville with musicians including: Kirk Whalum; Jim Horn; Chester Thompson; Viktor Krauss, 2001. *Recordings:* Skye Boat, 1981; Sarabanda, 1987; Don't Fret, 1990; Change of Heart, 1991; Artistry, 1993; Spirit of Django, 1994; Portraits, 1995; Years Apart, 1996; Gypsy, 1998; Two's Company, 1999; Nitelife, 2001; features on Stéphane Grappelli albums: At The Winery, 1981; Jealousy and Other Great Standards, 1988; Menuhin and Grappelli Play..., 1991; Reunion, 1993. *Internet:* www.martintaylor.com.

TAYLOR Mick; b. Hemstead, England. Musician (guitar). *Career:* Guitarist, John Mayall's Bluesbreakers, 1960s; Played National Jazz and Blues Festival, 1968; Lead guitarist, Rolling Stones, 1969–75; Film: Gimme Shelter (including Altamont Concert), 1969; Recorded, toured with Bob Dylan; Currently, session player, solo artist. *Recordings:* Bare Wires, John Mayall's Bluesbreakers, 1968; Albums with the Rolling Stones: Let It Bleed; Get Yer Ya Ya's Out; Sticky Fingers; Exile On Main Street; Goat's Head Soup; It's Only Rock and Roll; with Bob Dylan: Infidels; Empire Burlesque; Solo: Mick Taylor, 1979; Stranger In This Town, 1990; Too Hot for Snakes, 1991; Coastin' Home, 1995; Live at 14 Below, 1995; A Stone's Throw, 2000; Also appears with: John Mayall; Carla Olson; Knights of the Blues Table; Video with John Mayall and The Bluesbreakers, Blues Alive, 1983. *Honours:* Rock and Roll Hall of Fame (with Rolling Stones); Numerous domestic and international Gold, Platinum records. *Address:* 156 Fifth Ave, Suite 434, New York, NY 10010, USA.

TAYLOR Robin; b. 17 May 1956, Copenhagen, Denmark. Composer; Multi-Instrumentalist; Prod. *Education:* Academy for Free and Commercial Art, Copenhagen. *Musical Education:* Self-taught Guitar, Bass, Keyboard, Percussion. *Career:* Member of several local rock groups, 1970s; First radio appearance, 1978; In collaboration with keyboard player Jan Marsfeldt, 1988–98; Record debut, 1991; Composer, film music; Founder: experimental jazz/rock fusion group, Taylor's Universe, 1993; Taylor's Free Universe, 2000; Member, Avant-garde Big Band Communio Musica, led by Hugh Steinmetz, 1996–97. *Recordings:* Solo albums: Essay, 1991; Cloze Test Terror, 1992; Heart Disc, 1999; The Bándbix Tapes, 2000; Edge of Darkness, 2000; Taylor's Universe: Taylor's Universe, 1994; Pork, 1996; Experimental Health, (with Karsten Vogel), 1998; Communio Musica: Special Alloy, 2000. *Membership:* Danish Musicians' Union. *Leisure interests:* Bulldogs; Weird Music. *Current Management:* Marvel of Beauty Records, Listedvej 40, 3 MF, 2770 Kastrup, Denmark.

TAYLOR Roger, (Roger Meddows-Taylor); b. 26 July 1949, Kings Lynn, Norfolk, England. Musician (drums); Singer; Prod. *Education:* Biology. *Career:* Drummer, Smile; Drummer, UK rock group Queen, 1970–; Founder, The Cross, 1987–; Numerous tours include: UK; US;

Australia; South America; Japan; Major concerts include: Rock In Rio, Brazil, 1985; Live Aid, Wembley, 1985; Knebworth Festival, 1986; Concert For Life, Wembley, 1985. *Recordings:* Albums include: Queen, 1973; Queen 2, 1974; Sheer Heart Attack, 1974; A Night At The Opera, 1975; A Day At The Races, 1977; Jazz, 1978; Live Killers, 1979; The Game, 1980; Flash Gordon (soundtrack), 1981; Greatest Hits, 1981; Hot Space, 1982; The Works, 1984; The Complete Works, 1985; A Kind of Magic, 1986; The Miracle, 1989; Innuendo, 1991; Live At Wembley '86, 1992; Made In Heaven, 1995; with the Cross: Shove It!, 1988; Solo: Fun In Space, 1981; Strange Frontier, 1984; Happiness?, 1994; Electric Fire, 1998; Singles include: Seven Seas of Rye, 1974; Killer Queen, 1974; Bohemian Rhapsody (No. 1, UK), 1975; Now I'm Here, 1975; You're My Best Friend, 1976; Somebody To Love, 1976; We Are The Champions, 1977; Bicycle Race, 1978; Don't Stop Me Now, 1979; Love of My Life, 1979; Crazy Little Thing Called Love, 1979; Play The Game, 1980; Save Me, 1980; Another One Bites The Dust (No. 1, USA), 1980; Flash, 1981; Under Pressure, with David Bowie (No. 1, UK), 1981; Radio Ga Ga, 1984; I Want To Break Free, 1984; It's A Hard Life, 1984; Hammer To Fall, 1984; One Vision, 1985; A Kind of Magic, 1986; Friends Will Be Friends, 1986; I Want It All, 1989; Breakthru, 1989; Innuendo (No. 1, UK), 1991; Headlong, 1991; Too Much Love Will Kill You, 1995; Heaven For Everyone, 1995; Pressure On, 1998. *Honours include:* Britannia Award, 1976; Gold Ticket, Madison Square Gardens, 1977; American Music Award, 1981; Silver Clef Award, Nordoff-Robbins Music Therapy Centre, 1984; Ivor Novello Award, Outstanding Contribution to British Music, 1987; BRIT Awards: Outstanding Contribution to British Music, 1990; Best British Single, 1991. *Current Management:* c/o Jim Beach, Queen Productions, 46 Pembridge Rd, London W11 3HN, England.

TAYLOR Steve; b. 9 Dec. 1957, Brawley, California, USA. Recording Artist; Songwriter; Prod.; Film maker. m. Debbie L Taylor, 16 March 1985. *Education:* BA Music, Colorado University, Boulder, USA. *Career:* Recording artist; Producer, Co-writer for Newsboys. *Recordings:* I Want To Be A Clone, 1983; Meltdown, 1984; On The Fritz, 1985; I Predict 1990, 1987; Chagall Guevara, 1991; Squint, 1993; Liver, 1995; Video: Squint: Movies From The Soundtrack, 1994; Producer, Co-writer, The Newsboys: Not Ashamed, 1992; Going Public, 1994; Take Me To Your Leader, 1996; Producer, Guardian: Buzz, 1995; Producer, Sixpence None the Richer, 1997. *Honours:* 2 Grammy Nominations; 19 Dove Award Nominations; 3 Dove Awards; 2 Billboard Music Video Awards (as artist and director); CCM Magazine, Producer of The Year, 1994; 1995. *Current Management:* Proper Management, PO Box 23069, Nashville, TN 37202, USA.

TAYLOR Steven Vernard; b. 24 Dec. 1950, Norton, Virginia, USA. Prod.; Dir A & R, RCM Recordings. *Musical Education:* Bachelor Music (opera), University of Tennessee, Complete Recording Workshop, Los Angeles Valley College. *Career:* 16 years touring as vocalist, musician; Engineered for Jimmy Buffett, Michael McDonald, Jeff Berlin; Assistant to director on Grammy winner: Boys of Summer (Don Henley); Musical consultant for television shows: Gimme A Break; Facts of Life; Diff'rent Strokes; One Day At A Time. *Recordings:* Unknown Soul (producer); Sugar Jones; Argument Clinic (producer). *Honours:* Commendation by Texas Governor Ann Richards for internationally aired song: Dear Mr President, Dear Mr Gorbachev (producer/promoter). *Leisure interests:* Hiking; Swimming; Making studio magic. *Address:* PO Box 4735 Austin, TX 78765–4735, USA.

TAYLOR Tot; b. 15 July 1957, Cambridgeshire, England. Prod.; Composer; Songwriter. *Career:* Founder, own Compact Organization record label; Songwriter, Producer for Mari Wilson, Virna Lindt, early 1980's. *Compositions:* Music for Absolute Beginners, 1986; Started Poppy Records, 1996; Picasso's Women, for the Royal National Theatre. *Recordings:* Producer: Just What I Always Wanted, Mari Wilson, 1982; World of Leather, 1995; Producer, Bachology, 1995; Released six albums under own name, 1981–95; Waterland, soundtrack, 1997; Macbeth, soundtrack, 1997; Music For The Left Handed, 1998; Whipsnade, 1999; Film soundtrack, The Shatterer, 1999; Pop Folk Jazz, 2000; The Remainder of Honey Weeks, 2000; Film soundtrack, Dream, 2001. *Honours:* DandAD Award, Best Sound Design, 2000. *Leisure interest:* Music. *Current Management:* LPA. *Address:* PO Box 562, London N10 3LJ, England.

TAYLOR Will; b. 30 Nov. 1968, DeKalb, Illinois, USA. Composer; Arranger; Musician (Jazz Violin and Viola). m. Julie A Noble, 4 April 1992, 1 s., 1 d. *Education:* University of Texas at Austin. *Career:* Arranger, Musician, Ian Moore, Eddie Harris, 8 1/2 Souvenirs, Sara Hickman, Toni Price, Betty Elders; Toured with the Turtle Island String Quartet, 1991. *Compositions:* Raga; Blues for Fritz; Tigris. *Recordings:* Reel Life, 1993; Simple Gifts, 1994; Live from Austin, 1996. *Memberships:* ASCAP; AFM. *Leisure interest:* Backpacking. *Address:* 613 Fletcher, Austin, TX 78704, USA.

TAYLOR-GOOD Karen; b. El Paso, Texas, USA. Singer; Songwriter. *Career:* Began as folk singer: Austin, Texas; Europe; Radio, television commercials: United Airlines; McDonalds; Heinz; Backing singer for: Willie Nelson; Merle Haggard; Randy Travis; Roy Rogers; George Jones; Now Solo artist on Mesa Records; Songwriter for Warner Chappell; Represented US, Musical Peace Mission to Soviet Union, 1988. *Compositions:* Songs written for: Laura Branigan; Patty Loveless; Melanie; Nana Mouskouri; Diamond Rio. *Recordings:* Sang on soundtracks: Best Little Whorehouse In Texas; Smokey and the Bandit; Main solo success with: How Can I Help You Say Goodbye. *Honours:* Best New Female, ACM; New Folk Winner, Kerrville Festival, 1992; Songwriter of Year, SESAC, 1994; Nominated for Grammy: Best Country Song, 2 CMA Awards (all for How I Can I Help You Say Goodbye); Music Video Awards, SESAC and Music Row Magazine. *Membership:* Founding mem., Planet Earth Project. *Current Management:* SESAC. *Address:* 55 Music Sq. E, Nashville, TN 37203, USA.

TCHANDO (Salvador Embalo); b. 22 March 1957, Bafata, Guinea-Bissau. Composer; Musician (guitar); Singer. *Education:* Second level, Economics, Superior Economic Institute of Lisbon. *Career:* Guitarist, backing singer for N'kassa Kobra; Issabari; Hanne Boel; Kaba Mane; Lead singer for Zebra; Continental Heat; Kilimandjaro; Solo artiste, 1991–; Television apperances: Afrika Musika and MCM (Paris); Special 'Tchando', TVE (Bissau); Radio appearances: RFT; RDN; Africa No 1. *Compositions:* Music for theatre in Denmark. *Recordings:* Albums: Solo album: Naton; with Kabe Mane: Chefo Mae Mae; Kungha; with Hanne Boel: Dark Passion. *Memberships:* Danish Musicians and Composers Union; Koda. *Leisure interests:* Films; Sports. *Address:* Bispeengen 11, 2 th, 2000 Frederiksberg, Denmark.

TE Carlos; Composer; Lyricist; Musician (Guitar). m. Olga Fortes, 1 s., 1 d. *Education:* Degree, Philosophy, Oporto University. *Career:* Worked with Rui VeLoso, writing and producing records, 1979–; Collaborations with Trovante, 1983, Gabriela Schaff, 1983, Jáfumega, 1982, 1983, CLÃ, writing and producing, 1995, Mãozinha, 1997, Santos and Pecadores, 1999. *Compositions:* Chico Fininho; Porto Covo; Porto Sentido; Nao há Estrelas no Céu; A Paixão; Lado Lunar; GTI; Novas Babilónias. *Recordings:* Mingos and Os Samurais; Auto da Pimenta; Kazoo; Lado Lunar; Avenidas. *Publications:* Ar de Rock, 1980; Rui VeLoso, 1987; Mingos and Os Samurais, 1990; Auto da Pimenta, 1991; Avenidas, 1998. *Honours:* Best Album of the Year, 1980; Best Song of the Year, Caras magazine and Nove Gente magazine, 1998. *Membership:* SPA. *Leisure interests:* Reading; Football. *Current Management:* EMI Publishing, Portugal. *Address:* Praceta Joao Moreira Bastos 468, 4400 Vila Nova de Gaia, Portugal.

TEE-BIRDD Jamaka, (Richard Anthony Johnson); b. 15 Sept. 1952, Kingston, Jamaica. Musician (keyboards, guitar, percussion); Publisher. m. Celia Caiz. *Education:* Kingston College, 1967–71; College of Art, Science and Technology, 1972–73. *Career:* Member, bands: Bare Essentials; Zap-Pow; In-Crowd; Soul Syndicate; Burning Spear; Judy Mowatt; Bunny Wailer; Boris Gardiner; Top Notch; Roots Radics; Home T; Performed on Reggae Sunsplash I-V, X, XI, reggae Sunsplash Pay Per View, 1991; Tours: USA; Europe; Africa; South America; Japan; Israel. *Composition:* Jamdown Rock, song used on radio and TV to advertise The First Reggae Sunsplash. *Recordings:* Albums: with Zap-Pow: Now; LoveHits; ZapPow; with Soul Syndicate: Harvest Uptown-Famine Downtown; Was Is and Always; Friends of Soul Syndicate; FM, Freddie McGregor; with In-Crowd: His Majesty Is Coming; Man From New Guinea; Best of In-Crowd; with Burning Spear: Far Over; Fittest of The Fittest; Resistance; People of The World; Live In Paris; Jah Kingdom; with Israel Vibration: Forever; Vibes Alive; IV; Free to Love; On the Rock; Dub-the-Rock; Live Again; IV Dub; Cry Blood, Charlie Chaplin; Party, Yellowman; World Peace Three, Radically Radics, Roots Radics; with Bare Essentials: Back-a-Yard; No Loafin'; Soca With You; with various artistes: Reggae For Kids; RORXX (Reggae On The Rocks X), Tee-Bird Showcase; Heart Monitor. *Publications:* Jamaka comic magazines, Jamaka serial cartoon in the Star daily newspaper. *Honours:* Co-arranger of The Jamaica Festival Song Competition's first and only female performed winning song Mek Wi Put Things Right. *Memberships:* PRS; JFM; Musicians' Union (UK). *Leisure interests:* Badminton; Football; Amiga computing; Drawing cartoons and comics. *Current Management:* RAS Records. *Address:* 2447 Linden Lane, Silverspring, MD 20910, USA.

TEMIZ Okay; b. 11 Feb. 1939, Ankara, Turkey. Musician (percussion). 1 s. *Musical Education:* Conservatory. *Career:* World tours: USA, Europe, India, with Don Cherry, Karnata Ka College of Percussions, Oriental Wind, Okay Temiz Magnetic Band. *Recordings:* Music For Axaba, 1974; Oriental Wind; 12 records, 1947–86; Fis Fis Tziganes, 1992; Fish Market, 1993; Don Cherry/Bobo Stainson/Okay Temiz, 1993; Ranarop, Gjallarhorn, 1998; Peregrina World, 1999. *Honours:* Year of The Musician, Istanbul, 1971. *Membership:* Swedish and Finnish Jazz Organization. *Current Management:* Denis Leblond, 99 Ave de Clichy, 75017 Paris, France; Orane Senly, Artalene, 15 Passage de la Main d'Or, 75001, Paris, France; Werner Oberender, PO Box 1926, 5450 Neuvied 1, Germany.

TEMPEST Joey; b. 19 Aug. 1963, Stockholm, Sweden. Singer; Songwriter. *Career:* Co-founder, rock group Force, 1982; Won national rock talent contest, Sweden; Recorded two albums for Swedish market; Renamed Europe, 1985–92; Solo artist, 1993–; International tours. *Recordings:*

Albums: with Europe: Wings of Tomorrow, 1985; The Final Countdown, 1986; Out of This World, 1988; Prisoners In Paradise, 1991; Solo: A Place To Call Home, 1995; Azalea Place, 1999; Hit singles include: with Europe: Carrie; The Final Countdown (No. 1, UK), 1986; Rock The Night; Cherokee; Superstitious. *Current Management:* Rascoff/Zysblat Organisation, 110 W 57th St, New York, NY 10019, USA.

TEMPLETON David J; b. 18 June 1960, Chicago, Illinois, USA. Composer; Performer; Musician (Piano, Guitar). *Education:* University of Washington; Studied jazz improvisation under Bill Smith; studied film scoring under Hummie Mann. *Career:* Concerts, Seattle Paramount Theatre, 1985; Columbia River Grand Coulee, 1993; Chateau Saint Michelle, 1997, 1998, 1999. *Compositions:* Promise; Elisha; Only With You. *Recordings:* Albums, Time Alone; Promise; The Deepest Water; Change. *Honours:* Nominated for Recording of the Year, 1992. *Memberships:* ASCAP; NARAS. *Leisure interests:* Skiing; Antiques; Gardening. *Address:* Mason Ridge Records, PO Box 942, Seahurst, WA 98062 0942, USA.

TEMPLIN Ray; b. 27 Jan. 1947, Chicago, Illinois, USA. Musician; Actor; Writer. m. Trish, 19 May 1968, 1 s., 1 d. *Musical Education:* 2 years, University of Illinois. *Career:* 30 years professional musician, bandleader specializing in stride piano; Major jazz festivals in USA, concerts, guest artist appearances; 20 years voice-over, acting, including cartoon and television voice; 5 seasons as piano playing proprietor of Ray Templin's Bar, on Matlock (NBC). *Compositions:* Jam '38 A Theatrical Experience, theatrical production. *Recordings:* Ray Templin – Piano Man; Ray Templin – Swingology; Crazy 'Bout Fats, Ray Templin's Chicagoans; Dueling Banjomania, 1997; Calling All Jitterbugs, 1998. *Memberships:* AFM; SAG; AFTRA: ASCAP. *Leisure interests:* Stereo photography; Cooking; Travel. *Current Management:* The Bigley Agency.

TEMS Michael James Anthony (Mick); b. 3 Jan. 1950, London, England. Singer; Musician. *Career:* Member, Welsh traditional group Swansea Jack, 1973–78; Member, Welsh traditional group Calennig, 1978–; Television includes: The Folk Club, BBC Wales, 1975; Torth y Fara, 1982; Folk On The Move, HTV, 1983; Trade Winds, BBC Wales, 1985; Fastest to Frisco, BBC Wales, 1986; Evening News, Dunedin, New Zealand, 1990; Celtic Magic, HTV, 1990; Gwerin, S4C, 1995. *Recordings:* Solo: Gowerton Fair, 1977; with Swansea Jack, The Seven Wonders, 1978; with Calennig: Songs and Tunes From Wales, 1980; You Can Take a White Horse Anywhere, 1983; Dyddiau Gwynion Ionawr, 1985; Dwr Glan, 1990; Trade Winds, 1994; A Gower Garland, 2000; Numerous compilations. *Memberships:* Equity; Musicians' Union; MCPS; PAMRA; NUJ; CDdWC; COTC. *Leisure interests:* Music; Writing; Travel; Welsh studies. *Address:* 1 Ty Clwyta Cottages, Cross Inn, Llantrisant, Rhondda Cynon Taf CF72 8AZ, Wales.

TENAGLIA Danny, (Soul Boy); b. New York, USA. Prod.; Remixer; DJ. *Career:* Began as a DJ in New York; relocation to Miami during the '80s led to production work; Returned to New York, 1990; Resident DJ at Vinyl in New York; Collaborations: Peter Daou; Liz Torres; Celeda; Remixed: Deep Dish; East 17; D*Note; Pet Shop Boys; Faithless; Kings of Tomorrow; Depeche Mode. *Recordings:* Albums: Hard and Soul, 1995; Tourism, 1998; Singles: Harmonica Track (as Soul Boy), 1991; Bottom Heavy, 1994; Look Ahead (with Carol Sylvan), 1995; Music Is The Answer (Dancin' and Prancin'), 1998; B (with Datar), 2000; Fever Rising (with Cass and Slide), 2001. *Internet:* www.dtenaglia.com.

TENKANEN Kari; b. 20 Feb. 1963, Finland. Musician (alto, soprano saxophone, clarinet). *Musical Education:* Mainly self-taught; Clarinet lessons age 6–10; Jazz, summer camp held by Oulunkylä Pop/Jazz Conservatoire, 1980. *Career:* Member, Espoo Big Band, 10 years; Small ensembles include Jani Malmi Quartet, 5 years; Founder, own quintet. *Address:* Mechelininkatu 15 A 15, 00100 Helsinki, Finland.

TENNANT Neil Francis; b. 10 July 1954, North Shields, Northumberland, England. *Education:* Degree, History, North London Polytechnic. *Career:* Group: Dust, 1970–71; Publishing, 1975–; Met Christopher Lowe, began writing together, founded West End, renamed Pet Shop Boys, 1981; Granada TV special: Love Me Tender, 1987; Film: It Couldn't Happen Here, 1988; Piccadilly Theatre, TV: Wogan, Top of The Pops, 1988; Tour, Hong Kong, Japan, UK, 1989; USA: with Electronic, Dodgers Stadium; Mayan Theatre, Los Angeles; Arsenio Hall Show, TV, 1990; Performance Tour, Japan; USA; Canada; Europe, UK, Ireland, 1991; 2 weeks, Simon Bates Show, Radio One, 1991, 1992; Launched own record label: Spaghetti, 1991; Concert, Heaven nightclub, 1991; South Bank Show, 1992; Hacienda Club, Manchester, 1992; Roseland, New York, 1992; Opening Russian MTV, 1993; Producer, songwriter, artists include: Dusty Springfield, Patsy Kensit; Liza Minnelli; Boy George; Electronic. *Recordings:* West End Girls (No. 1), 1985; Love Comes Quickly, 1986; Suburbia, 1986; with Dusty Springfield: What Have I Done To Deserve This?, 1987; Rent, 1987; Always On My Mind (No. 1), 1987; Heart, 1988; Domino Dancing, 1988; Left To My Own Devices, 1988; It's Alright, 1989;

So Hard, 1990; Being Boring, 1990; Where The Streets Have No Name, 1991; Jealousy, 1991; DJ Culture, 1991; Was It Worth It?, 1991; Can You Forgive Her?, 1993; Go West, 1993; I Wouldn't Normally..., 1994; Liberation, 1994; Se A Vida É, 1996; Red Letter Day, 1997; New York City Boy, 1999; You Only Tell Me You Love Me..., 2000; Albums: Please, 1991; Disco, 1986; Actually, 1987; Introspective, 1988; Behaviour, 1990; Discography, 1991; Very, 1993; Relentless, 1993; Seriously, 1994; Bilingual, 1996; Nightlife, 1999; Writer, singer, Electronic: Disappointed, 1991. *Honours:* Ivor Novello, 1987, 1988; BPI, 1987, 1988; Berolina, 1988. *Address:* Pet Shop Boys Partnership, 8 Pembridge Studios, 27a Pembroke Villas, London W11 3EP, England.

TENNILLE Toni; b. 8 May 1943, Montgomery, Alabama, USA. Singer. m. Daryl Dragon, 14 Feb. 1974. *Career:* Co-writer and performer, musical Mother Earth, San Francisco, 1972; Formed duo, The Captain and Tennille, with Daryl Dragon, 1972–80; Tour with Beach Boys, 1972; Performed at White House dinner, in honour of Queen Elizabeth II, 1976; Musical variety show, The Captain and Tennille, ABC TV, 1976; Solo artiste, 1980–; Appeared in Broadway show, Stardust, 1991; Nevada Ambassador for the Arts, 1998; Stage performance in The Rainmaker. *Recordings:* Albums: with The Captain and Tennille: Love Will Keep Us Together, 1975; Song of Joy, 1976; Come In From The Rain, 1977; Captain and Tennille's Greatest Hits, 1978; Dream, 1978; Make Your Move, 1980; Twenty Years of Romance, 1995; Solo albums: More Than You Know, 1984; Moonglow, 1986; All of Me, 1987; Never Let Me Go, 1992; Things Are Swingin', 1994; Tennille Sings Big Band, 1998; Hit singles include: Love Will Keep Us Together (No. 1, USA), 1975; The Way I Want To Touch You, 1975; Lonely Night (Angel Face), 1976; Shop Around, 1976; Muskrat Love, 1976; Can't Stop Dancin', 1977; You Never Done It Like That, 1978; Do That To Me One More Time (No. 1, USA), 1980. *Honours:* Grammy Award, Record of The Year, Love Will Keep Us Together, 1976; Juno Awards, Best International Single, Love Will Keep Us Together, Canada, 1976. *Current Management:* Cheri Ingram Co, 3575 Cahuenga Blvd, Suite 600, Los Angeles, CA 90068, USA.

TERMINATOR X (Norman Rogers); DJ; Rapper. *Career:* Member, US rap group Public Enemy, 1984–90; Concerts include: Support to the Beastie Boys, US, 1987; Support to LL Cool J, European tour, 1987; Tour of a Black Planet, 1990; Solo artiste, 1990–; Manager, The Entourage (hip-hop club), Long Island, New York, 1986. *Recordings:* Albums with Public Enemy: Yo! Bum Rush The Show, 1987; It Takes A Nation of Millions To Hold Us Back, 1988; Fear of a Black Planet, 1990; Muse Sick 'n' Hour Mess Age, 1994; Solo: Terminator X and The Valley of The Jeep Beets, 1991; Singles: Rebel Without A Pause; Bring The Noise; Don't Believe The Hype; Night of The Living Baseheads; Black Steel In The Hour of Chaos; Fight The Power, theme song for film Do The Right Thing; Welcome To The Terrordome; 911 Is A Joke; Brothers Gonna Work It Out; Want To Be Dancin'; Homey Don't Play That; Juvenile Delinquentz; It All Comes Down to Money; Under The Sun. *Current Management:* Malik Entertainment Management, PO Box 310, Roosevelt, NY 11575, USA.

TERRY Todd, (Swan Lake, Royal House, Gypsymen); b. 18 April 1967, Brooklyn, New York, USA. Prod.; Remixer; DJ. *Career:* Originally part of Masters At Work with Kenny Dope before achieving legendary house music producer status in his own right using various pseudonyms; Founder: Freeze Records; Sound Design Records; Collaborations: Kenny Dope; Roland Clark; T La Rock; Remixed: Martha Wash; Janet Jackson; Jamiroquai; Everything But The Girl; Michael Jackson; Kylie Minogue; The Corrs. *Recordings:* Albums: To The Batmobile – Let's Go, 1988; Resolutions, 1999; Singles: Can You Party (as Royal House), 1988; Bango – To The Batmobile (as Todd Terry Project), 1988; Dreams of Santa Anna (as Orange Lemon), 1989; Jumpin', 1993; Bounce To The Beat, 1995; Keep On Jumpin', 1996; Something Goin' On, 1997; Let It Ride, 1999; Babarabatiri (as Gypsymen), 2001; Raining, 2001. *Address:* In House/Sound Design Records, c/o Ministry of Sound, 103 Gaunt St, London, SE1 6DP, England.

TETTEH-LARTEY Benny; b. 29 Sept. 1965, Mayfield, Dalkieth, Scotland. Singer-Songwriter; Musician. m. Lesley Moss, 15 Sept. 1999, 1 s., 2 d. *Career:* Began 1987, several different bands; Uses 8-string acoustic guitar; Solo career; Appeared unofficially at T in the Park festival, and was asked to return; Numerous live sessions and interviews on BBC Radio Scotland's Ghetto Blasting, The Usual Suspects, Radio Forth, Scot FM; Played alongside Nick Harper at 12 Bar Club in London, 1999. *Compositions:* Head in the Sand, 1998; Injustice, 1997; Song to Papa, 1996; In the Same Boat, 1987. *Recordings:* Single: Roses Are Red, 1998; Album: Don't Be Sad, 1998; Rough Cut, 2001. *Honour:* BBC Scotland Tympanali Award (songwriter showcase), for Injustice, 1998. *Memberships:* MCPS; PRS; Musicians' Union. *Leisure interests:* Crafts; Swimming; Running; Art and design. *Current Management:* BTL Management. *Address:* 50 Paradykes Ave, Loanhead, Midlothian EH20 9LD, Scotland.

THAIN Laurie Anne; b. 18 Feb. 1955, New Westminster, British Columbia, Canada. Singer; Songwriter; Musician (guitar). *Education:* BA,

Physical Education and Theatre. *Musical Education:* Self-taught. *Career:* Concert artist specialising in the intimate singer/songwriter approach; Writer and producer of numerous custom entertainment shows and corporate events; Concerts, opening shows for Lee Greenwood; Gary Morris; Rita MacNeil; Pam Tillis; World-wide tours. *Recordings:* Hopeless Romantic, 1984; Matters of The Heart, 1987; Stages, 1992; 5 song EP, Preview, of album No 4, 1997. *Honours:* Winner, Canadian National, Du Maurier Search For Stars. *Memberships:* Canadian Country Music Asscn; AFofM. *Leisure interests:* Walking; Biking; Golf. *Address:* #205, 6359 198th St, Langley, BC V2Y 2ES, British Columbia, Canada.

THANGER Hakan; b. 23 Oct. 1943, Boo, Stockholm, Sweden. Musician (electric bass and guitar); Vocalist. Divorced. *Career:* Contributor, Swedish Eurovision Song Contest; Played and written songs and arrangements for many artists from Sweden including: Lill Babs, Jerry Williams, Family Four and others. *Composition:* Dagar Jag Ner I Min Källare. *Recordings:* More than 500 studio recordings. *Memberships:* STIM; SAMI; SKAP; TSO. *Leisure interest:* Music. *Address:* Sverkersgatan 6, 3tr, 126 51 Stockholm, Sweden.

THAYIL Kim; b. 4 Sept. 1960, Seattle, Washington, USA. Musician (Guitar). *Education:* Philosophy Degree, University of Washington. *Career:* Member, Soundgarden; Numerous live tours and festival appearances. *Recordings:* Singles: Nothing to Say; Flower; Loud Love; Hands All Over; Get on the Snake; Jesus Christ Pose; Outshined; Rusty Cage; Spoonman; The Day I Tried to Live; Black Hole Sun; Fell on Black Days; Pretty Noose; Burden in My Hand; Blow Up the Outside World; Ty Cobb; Bleed Together; Albums: Ultramega OK, 1988; Louder than Love, 1989; Badmotorfinger, 1991; Superunknown, 1994; Down on the Upside, 1996; A-Sides, 1997.

THEMIS John; b. 13 Oct. 1954. Prod.; Musician (guitar); Writer; Musical Dir. m. Anne Lawrence, 14 Jan. 1981, 1 s., 2 d. *Education:* BSc Marketing, Management. *Musical Education:* Self-taught. *Career:* UK television appearances include: Aspel; Jonathan Ross; Terry Wogan; The Big E; The Word; The Chart Show; Pebble Mill; BPM; Top of The Pops; Jools Holland Show; Brian Conley Show; Lily Savage Show; The Box; MTV Live; US apperances include: Tonite With Jay Leno; The Ru Paul Show; The John and Lisa Show; French appearances include: Le Nuils; Tarata; Couscous; C'est Nous; Also television in Germany; Belgium; Argentina; Russia; Chile; Japan; Concerts include: Hammersmith Odeon; Festival Hall; Ronnie Scott's; Pride Festival, Brockwell Park, 250,000 people; International concerts include: Canada, Romania, Japan; Musical director, songwriting partner, guitarist with Boy George, for 4 years; Played with Chris De Burgh, on Room In This Heart, BBC TV; Also worked with: Dannii Minogue; Lavine Hudson; Paul Young; Wendy and Lisa; Tim Rice; Nigel Kennedy; Jason Donavon; Kim Wilde; Ray Simson; London Chamber Orchestra. *Compositions include:* What Took You So Long (Emma Bunton); Please Stay (Kylie Minogue). *Recordings:* Albums; Sirens; Ulysses and The Cyclops; English Renaissance; As musician, producer: with Boy George; Chris de Burgh; Suggs; Blair; Cher; Evolution; Simon Climie; Lippy Lou; Malcolm MacLaren; The Grid; Billy Ray Martin; Eve Gallagher; Elton John; Pet Shop Boys; George Michael; The Beloved; Garry Kemp; Barry Manilow; Orchestral Manoeuvres In The Dark; Bad Boys Inc; Spice Girls; Gary Barlow; Boyzone; Eternal; Sophie Ellis-Bextor; Dido; Boyzone; Gabrielle; Charlotte Church; Bond; Emma Bunton; S Club 7; Five; Producer, Voices (single), Junior Reid. *Honours:* Grammy Award nominee, When Will You Learn, 1999; Ulysses, Album of the Month, British Guitarist Magazine;. *Leisure interest:* Music. *Address:* 46 The Limes Ave, London N11 1RH, England.

THERRIEN Lucie; b. 21 Aug. 1945, Newport, VT, USA. Musician (Voice, Piano, Guitar, Ethnic Instruments). *Education:* MA, UNH; Ecole Des Beaux Arts. *Career:* PBS Television, PBS Radio, Good Day Show, Radio Québec and France; Television 5 International, Radio Canada; Television and Radio in Québec; Cultural Exchanges and Performances Over 4 Continents. *Compositions:* Cousins; Memere. *Recordings:* Noel c'est l'amour; Cousins; Pot Pourri Folklorique; Un Tresor. *Memberships:* Le Conseil Francophone de la Chanson; NH Council Of The Arts; NH Humanities Council. *Leisure interests:* Travel; Languages; Swimming; Reading; People. *Current Management:* French American Music Ent, PO Box 4721, Portsmouth, NH 03802 4721, USA.

THIGPEN Edmund Leonard; b. 28 Dec. 1930, Chicago, IL, USA. Musician. Widower, 1 s., 1 d. *Education:* Los Angeles City College. *Career:* Joined The Cootie Williams Band, 1951; Worked With Dinah Washington, Johnny Hiodges Band, Avant-Garde Group of Gil Melle, Trois of Bud Powell, Jutta Hipp, Billy Taylor, 1954–58; Joined Oscar Peterson Trio, 1959–65; Travelled World-wide; Founded, The Advanced School of Contemporary Music, Toronto, Canada; Worked in Recording Studios, Making Jingles, Performing on Television and Movie Sound Tracks, 1967; Founded His Own Group, Action-Reaction; Worked As Teacher and Clinician. *Recordings:* More Than 50 Albums. *Publications:* 5 Books, Ed Thigpen Talking Drums; Rhythm Analysis and Basic Co-

Ordination; Rhythm Brought To Life; Ed Thigpen On Jazz Drumming; The Essence of Brushes. *Honours:* Thomas Jefferson High School, Music Award. *Memberships:* The Percussive Arts Society; International Asscn of Jazz Educators. *Address:* Bagerstraede 3, Second Floor, 1617 Copenhagen, Denmark.

THISTLETHWAITE Anthony Silvester; b. 31 Aug. 1955, Leicester, England. Musician (saxophone, multi-instrumentalist). *Career:* Busking, Paris, 1979–80; Member, The Waterboys, 1982–91; The Saw Doctors, 1993–95; Moved to St Petersburg, Russia, 1995; Currently working with top Russian bands Aquarium and DDT. *Recordings:* with The Waterboys: The Waterboys, 1983; A Pagan Place, 1984; This Is The Sea, 1986; Fisherman's Blues, 1989; Room To Roam, 1990; Solo albums: Aesop Wrote A Fable, 1993; Cartwheel, 1995; Other recordings with Bob Dylan; Donovan; Johnny Thunders; Psychedelic Furs; World Party; Mission; Fairground Attraction: Sharon Shannon; Eddi Reader; Solo: Cartwheel, 1995; Crawfish and Caviar, 1997. *Membership:* Musicians' Union. *Leisure interests:* Dancing; Swimming; Eating. *Address:* c/o Purpleteeth Productions, PO Box 2666, London W14 0ZT, England.

THOMAS B J (Billie Joe); b. 7 Aug. 1942, Hugo, Oklahoma, USA. Singer; Songwriter; Entertainer. m. Gloria Richardson, 9 Dec. 1968, 3 d. *Career:* Lead singer, The Triumphs; Opened for acts including Roy Orbison; The Dave Clark Five; the Four Tops; Solo artiste; Toured with Dick Clark Caravan of Stars; Regular appearances Ed Sullivan Show, nightclubs, concert halls; Became 60th member, Grand Ole Opry; B J Thomas Celebrity Theater, Tennessee Smoky Mountains. *Recordings:* Albums include: Peace In The Valley; Love Shines; Great American Dream; Shining; All Is Calm, All Is Bright; Throwin' Rocks At The Moon; Nightlife; Midnite Minute; I Believe; Singles include: I'm So Lonesome I Could Cry; Mama; The Eyes of a New York Woman; Hooked On A Feeling; Raindrops Keep Fallin' On My Head (from Butch Cassidy and the Sundance Kid soundtrack); It's Only Love; I Just Can't Help Believin'; No Love At All; Rock and Roll Lullabye; As Long As We Got Each Other (theme from series Growing Pains); Somebody Done Somebody Wrong; Broken Toys (adopted as theme tune by child abuse agencies); What Ever Happened To Old Fashioned Love; New Looks From an Old Lover; The Whole World's In Love When You're Lonely. *Publications:* Home Where I Belong; In Tune. *Honours:* 5 Grammy Awards; 2 Dove Awards; 5 Platinum, 11 Gold albums: Lifetime Achievement Award, U C Berkeley; Academy Award, 1970; Country Song of the Year, 1975. *Memberships:* AFTRA; SAG; Grand Ole Opry; AFofM; CMA; NARAS; National Songwriters' Asscn. *Leisure interest:* Golf. *Current Management:* Michael Goldstein, Goldwest, 9125 Otto St, Downey, CA 90240, USA; Agent: Lee Farmer, Marathon Attractions.

THOMAS Daniel; b. 11 Jan. 1970, London, England. Musician (keyboards); Singer; Songwriter. *Career:* Backing vocals for: Luther Vandross; Elton John; Carleen Anderson; Deuce; Eternal; Erasure; David Essex; Jools Holland; Played keyboards for: Sir Harry Secombe (Crystal Rose Show); IDMC; Bryan Powell; Ricky Grundy; Music Director for London Community Gospel Choir and Choir Director; Also teacher of vocal techniques. *Memberships:* Musicians' Union; Black Gospel Asscn. *Leisure interests:* Reading; Theatre; Dining; Writing Music. *Current Management:* Basil Meade, Choir Connexion. *Address:* 9 Greenwood Dr., Highams Park, London E4 9HL, England.

THOMAS Irma (Lee); b. 18 Feb. 1941, Pontchatoula, Louisiana, USA. Singer. *Career:* R & B singer known as The Soul Queen of New Orleans. *Recordings:* Albums: Wish Somone Would Care, 1964; Take A Look, 1968; In Between Tears, 1973; Live, 1977; Soul Queen of New Orleans, 1978; Safe With Me, 1979; Hip Shakin' Mama, 1981; The New Rules, 1986; The Way I Feel, 1988; Simply The Best, 1991; True Believer, 1992; Turn My World Around, 1993; Walk Around Heaven, 1993; The Story of My Life, 1997. *Address:* c/o Emile Jackson, PO Box 26126, New Orleans, LA 70186, USA.

THOMAS Patrice; b. 17 March 1961, Besancon, France. Musician (guitar). *Musical Education:* Diplome d'Etat Jazz. *Career:* Performed at festivals: Montpellier; Mulhouse; Calvi; Milan; Nancy; Concerts at Maison de Radio France, Paris; Radio and TV: TF1; Fr3; France Musique; France Culture; France Inter. *Recordings:* CDs: Isis; Portraits. *Honours:* Soloist, first prize, Ninth Jazz Challenge, Paris (Défense). *Membership:* UMJ; Teacher, Ecole de Musique, Montbeliard. *Address:* Refranche, 25330 Amancey, France.

THOMAS Patrick; b. 27 July 1960, Oxford, England. Musician; Composer; Prod. *Education:* BA, hons, Psychology, Open University; Private Classical Piano Lessons; Studied with Mary Howell-Pryce, St Edmund Campion School, Oxford. *Career:* Paris with Chuck Berry, Continental Drift, 1989; London with Derek Bailey, Eugene Chadbourne, Keith Rowe, 1990; London with John Zorn, Bucket Head, Paul Lovens, 1991; Germany with Tony Oxley, Sirone, Larry Stabbins, Manfred Schoof, 1992; Glasgow with Lol Coxhill, 1993; Berlin Jazz Festival with Bill Dixon, 1994; London Jazz Cafe with Thurston Moore, Lee Renaldo, 1996; Solo, Copenhagen, 1997; Austria

Graz Music Protocol, with And, 1997; CMN Tour, with Butch Morris; London Sky Scraper; Vancouver Jazz Festival, with Eugene Chadborne and Alex Ward, 1998; Cologne, Germany with Celebration Orchestra, 1998; Uncool Festival, Switzerland, with Scatter, 1999. *Compositions:* Ensemble WX7e Turntables Dialogue (with interruptions); Pulse, for drum machine and two percussionists; Reflex, for ensemble and computers. *Recordings:* With Tony Oxley Quartet, Incus, 1992; Lol Coxhill, Halim Nato, 1993; One Night in Glasgow, Scatter, 1994; Company 91, 3 Vols, 1994; Mike Cooper Island Songs, 1995; Celebration Orchestra, The Enchanted Messenger, 1996; Tones of Life, Guidance, 1997; Solo Album, Remembering, 1998; Total Tuesday, Hellington Country, 1998; And, Intakt, 1998; Hard Edge, with Rhys Chatham, 1999; Powerfield, EEE, 1999. *Publications:* Islam's Contribution to Jazz and Improvised Music, 1993; Upside Down (The Myth of Jazz History), 1998. *Honours:* Arts Council of Great Britain Jazz Bursary for 3 Electro-accoustic Compositions. *Memberships:* Performing Rights Society; London Musicians Collective. *Leisure interests:* Watching Cricket; History. *Address:* 5 Saint Omer Rd, Cowley, Oxford OX4 3HB, England.

THOMAS Rhozonda, (Chilli); b. 27 Feb. 1971, Atlanta, Georgia, USA. Singer; Choreographer. 1 s. *Career:* Professional Dancer, Damian Dame; Member, TLC; Appeared in film Have Plenty; Started own publishing company, T-Ron Music. *Recordings:* Singles: Get It Up, 1993; Creep, 1994; Waterfalls, 1995; Red Light Special, 1995; Diggin on You, 1995; No Scrubs, 1999; Unpretty, 1999; Albums: Crazysexycool, 1994; Fan Mail, 1999. *Honours:* One of 50 Most Beautiful People, People Magazine, 1996; Grammy Awards, Best R & B Performance by a Duo/Group, Best R & B Album, for Crazysexycool; 2 Lady of Soul Awards; 2 Billboard Music Awards; 3 Soul Train Awards; Blockbuster Entertainment Award; 4 MTV Music Video Awards, for Waterfalls.

THOMPSON Christopher Hamlet; b. 9 March 1947, Hertford, Hertfordshire, England. Musician. m. Maggie, 4 Jan. 1995, 1 s. *Education:* BSoc Science, Teaching Certificate. *Career:* Professional musician, 1972–; Joined Manfred Mann's Earth Band, 1975–86; Formed own band Night, 1979; Extensive tours throughout USA, Europe: With Manfred Mann's Earth Band, 1975–86; With Night, 1979–83; Working in Europe, under own name, 1986–; with The Alan Parsons Project; Singer, TV product campaigns: Rank Xerox; Mandate; De Beers; ADT; Bayer; Tennents Pilsner; Twix; Kelloggs Cornflakes; The Daily Mail; Peugeot 205; Abbey National; Budweiser. *Recordings:* with Manfred Mann's Earth Band: The Roaring Silence, 1976; Watch, 1978; Angel Station, 1979; Chance, 1980; Somewhere In Africa, 1982; Live In Budapest, 1983; Criminal Tango, 1986; Singles: Blinded By The Light; Davy's On The Road Again; Solo albums: Radio Voices, 1983; High Cost of Living, 1986; Beat of Love, 1989; Hits in Germany with: The Challenge, 1989; The Joker, 1991; Florida Lady, 1994; Songs and vocals to albums by: The Doobie Brothers; Tina Turner; Elton John; Roger Daltrey; Jefferson Starship; Brian May; Barbara Dickson; Ozzy Osbourne. *Memberships:* PRS; SAG; Equity. *Current Management:* Horst Zwipp, Feedback Music.

THOMPSON Danny Henry; b. 4 April 1939, Teignmouth, S Devon, England. Musician (Double Bass, Trombone). m. Sylvia Thompson, 2 step-s., 1 s. *Education:* Salesian College Grammar. *Musical Education:* Self-taught. *Career:* Alexis Korner, 1964–67; Roy Orbison Tour, 1964; Recording sessions, 1960s including Marianne Faithfull; Incredible String Band; Nick Drake; Donovan; Co-Founded Pentangle, 1968; Own trio with John McLaughlin, 1966; Tubby Hayes Quartet, Phil Seamen Quartet, Studio Work including Rod Stewart, Kate Bush, Talk Talk, 1970s, 1980s; Formed own band, Whatever, 1989, toured, 1992–97. *Compositions:* Take 3 Girls Theme, Light Flight; Musing Mingus; Til Minne Au Jan; Children of the Dark; Pitfalls; New Rhythms; No Love is Sorrow; Passion to Protect, film; Swedish Dance; Fair Isle Friends. *Recordings:* Sweet Child Basket of Light; Whatever; Whatever Next; Elemental; Whatever's Best; Dizrhythmia; Songhai; Solid Air; Live at Leeds, with John Martyn; The Pentangle; Industry. *Publications:* Video Basically Speaking. *Honour:* Hugo, Chicago International Film Festival; Ivor Novello Award, theme for Take 3 Girls (BBC), 1969. *Leisure interests:* Tennis; Swimming; Golf; Cricket; Snooker; Diving; Abseiling. *Address:* 43 Mount View, Rickmansworth, Herts WD3 2BB, England.

THOMPSON Gail; b. 15 June 1958, London, England. Musician (saxophone, clarinet); Composer; Conductor. m. Tim May, 10 May 1994. *Musical Education:* Studied at school; Self-taught composition, conducting. *Career:* Tenor saxophone, West End hit show Bubbling Brown Sugar, 1977; Music teacher, South East London Technical College, 1977; Manageress, Macari's Music Shop, Charing Cross Rd, 1980; Formed Jazz Funk band The Gail Thompson Approach, featured Camden Jazz Week, 1980; Founded Women In Music, 1986; Established Sax Council tuition school; Created Gail Force, 1986; Founded the Jazz Warriors, with Courtney Pine, 1986; Played regularly with Charlie Watts Big Band, Art Blakey's Jazz Messengers; Founded Music Work Resource Centre, music school, 3,000 members; Joined Greater London Arts, The Arts Council of Great Britain advisory panels, 1987; Presented, judged Schlitz Beer, Virgin Records competition; Television: Presented jazz programmes with Russell Davis,

BBC2, 1878; Sang solo with Reggae Philharmonic Orchestra, Highway, ITV, 1990–91; Travelled Africa, studying African music, 1988; Set up Frontline Productions to promote Jazz music; MC, various major jazz festivals; Reggae Philharmonic Orchestra, on Highway, ITV, 1990–91; Vocalist, panellist, The Music Game Show, Channel 4, 1992; Films: Tell Me That You Love Me, BBC1, 1991; Close My Eyes (cinema and video release), 1991; Administrator, Britain's first National Music Day with Harvey Goldsmith, 1992; Director, Jazz Services, 1992; Freelance Consultant, music schools, projects, 1992; Chairman, Arts Council Jazz Committee; ACGTS Music Panellist, 1993; Founder and Chief Executive, Turnaround Project for music media and film for the disabled; Jazz Africa appearances at Berlin Jazz Festival; Recorded live album, 1997. *Compositions:* Commissioned by BBC2, composition for Midland Big Band, featuring Courtney Pine, performed, televised, Royal Albert Hall; Various compositions commissioned include: Royal Opera House Covent Garden, featuring Stan Tracey, Andy Sheppard, 1989; Jazz Africa (suite), by Apples and Snakes, 1991; TV themes for Carlton TV. *Recordings:* Album: Gail Force Big Band; Jazz Africa Big Band; Jadu, 2001. *Memberships:* Chairperson, Arts Council Jazz Review; Started Jazz in Women Festival, 1997. *Leisure interests:* Running; Squash; Steam trains. *Address:* 5 St Faiths Rd, West Dulwich, London SE21 8JD, England.

THOMPSON Hank (Henry William); b. 3 Sept. 1925, Waco, Texas, USA. Country Singer; Songwriter; Musician (guitar, harmonica). m. Ann. *Career:* Own radio series, Hank – The Hired Hand, 1942; Founder member, the Brazos Valley Boys, 1946; Recording artiste, 1949–; First country artist recording in stereo, 1959; Tutor, School of Country Music, Claremore, Oklahoma, 1973. *Recordings:* Country hits include: (I've Got) A Humpty Dumpty Heart; Whoa Sailor; The Wild Side of Life (US Country No. 1); Waiting In The Lobby of Your Heart; Rub-A-Dub-Dub; Breakin' The Rules; Honky Tonk Girl; The Blackboard of My Heart; Breakin' In Another Heart; She's Just A Whole Lot Like You; Oklahoma Hills; Where Is The Circus?; The Older The Violin The Sweeter The Music; Mr Honky Tonk The King of Western Swing; Numerous albums include: Songs of The Brazos Valley, 1953; Hank!, 1957; Songs For Rounders, 1959; Live At The Golden Nugget (first live-in-concert country album), 1961; A Six Pack To Go, 1961; Just An Old Flame, 1967; Cab Driver – A Salute To The Mills Brothers, 1972; Movin' On, 1974; Brand New Hank, 1978; Take Me Back To Texas, 1980; Hank Thompson, 1986; Here's To Country Music, 1988; Various compilation albums; Hank Thompson and Friends, 1997. *Honours:* Inducted into Country Music Hall of Fame, 1989; Inducted into Nashville Songwriter's Hall of Fame, 1997. *Current Management:* D D Bray Management. *Address:* c/o Hank Thompson Enterprises, 5 Rushing Creek Court, Roanoke, TX 76262, USA.

THOMPSON John Alexander; b. 15 Aug. 1942, Philadelphia, Pennsylvania, USA. Reverend; Gospel Singer; Choir Leader; Songwriter. *Career:* Founder: Sunlight Jubilee Juniors, 1955; Johnny Thompson Singers, 1965; Pennsylavania District F B H Choir, 1970; Sanctificaton, 1983; Member, Philadelphia Mass Choir and Gospel Music Preservation Alliance Choir; Johnny Thompson Singers, numerous tours, Europe and Africa, including: First Gospel act to play Montreux Festival, with Bessie Griffin, 1972; First Black Gospel act to produce own video, 1980; First Gospel act behind Iron Curtain, Poland, 1981; First Black American Gospel act to play Russia, Bulgaria and Egypt; Countless television and radio appearances, Europe; Performed with numerous Gospel acts including: Marion Wlliams; Bessie Griffin; Dorthy Love-Coates; Reverend James Cleveland; Evangelist Shirley Caesar; Dorothy Norwood. *Compositions include:* The Creation; Stranger On The Road; Get Up My Brother; If I Perish; Hold Out; Happy On My Way; There Must Be A Reason; If You Gonna Pray; Wrote several Gospel plays. *Recordings:* Albums with The Johnny Thompson Singers: I'm On My Way To Zion, 1972; Philadelphia, 1975; Live At Montreux, 1977; Lord I Belong To You, 1982; Gospel At The Opera, 1985; Gospel Christmas, 1986; Spirit of Gospel, 1987; Swing Low Sweet Chariot, 1988; Oh Happy Day!, 1990; 25 Years, 1990; Hand In Hand, 1993; Glory Glory Hallelujah, 1995; with The Pennsylvania District F B H Choir: Look Over Your Shoulders, 1974; Live At Lausanne, 1977. *Honours:* Prix Mahalia Jackson, Philadelphia, 1975. *Memberships:* National Convention of Gospel Choirs and Choruses; Gospel Minister, Gospel Music Workshop of America; Choral Director, Wynnefield Academy, Philadelphia. *Current Management:* Freddy J Angstmann. *Address:* Fronhof 100, 8260 Stein am Rhein, Switzerland.

THOMPSON Keith; b. 29 Jan. 1956, Worcester, England. Blues and Rock Musician (electric and acoustic guitar, harmonica, piano, bass). m. Janette Kathleen Thompson, 26 June 1982, 1 s., 2 d. *Musical Education:* Self-taught. *Career:* Tours include: Netherlands, 1989; Denmark, 1990; UK, 1992, 1993, 1994 including appearances at The Mean Fiddler, London; The Standard, London; Greenbelt Festival, Bedfordshire; Crossrhythms Festival, Devon; Crossfire Festival, Liverpool; Road Dreams music for Tortworth TV shown on Channel 4, 1991, 1992. *Recordings:* Against The Odds, 1991; Young Hearts, 1992; Voice From Heaven, 1994; Reputation, 1996; Strange Brew, 1998. *Honour:* Songwriter of The Year, 6 Counties Festival, 1990. *Memberships:* Musicians' Union; PRS; MCPS. *Leisure*

interests: Family; Walking; Swimming; Films; Television. *Address:* 46 Libertus Rd, Cheltenham, Gloucestershire GL51 7EP, England.

THOMPSON Linda, (Linda Peters); Singer; Songwriter. m. Richard Thompson, divorced. *Career:* British tour as member of folk group Albion Band, 1972; Duo with Richard Thompson, 1972–82; Appearances include: Reading Festival, 1975; Regular British tours; Co-writer, appeared in The Mysteries, 1975. *Compositions include:* Co-writer (with Betsy Cook): Telling Me Lies (recorded by Emmylou Harris; Linda Ronstadt; Reba McEntire). *Recordings:* Albums with Richard Thompson: Henry The Human Fly, 1972; I Want To See The Bright Lights Tonight, 1974; Hokey Pokey, 1975; Pour Like Silver, 1975; First Light, 1978; Sunnyvista, 1979; Shoot Out The Lights, 1982; Solo album: One Clear Moment, 1985; Contributions to: Ashley Hutchings, Guv'nor, Vol. 3, 1999; David Thomas, Mirror Man, 1999; Cathal McConnell, Long Expectant Comes Last, 1999.

THOMPSON Richard; b. 3 April 1949, London, England. Singer; Songwriter; Musician (guitar). m. Linda Peters, divorced. *Career:* Co-founder, guitarist, folk group Fairport Convention, 1968–71; Concerts include: Folk Meets Pop, Royal Albert Hall, 1969; Royal Festival Hall, with Joni Mitchell, 1969; Bath Festival of Blues and Progressive Music, 1970; London Palladium, 1970; Partnership with wife, 1972–82; Concerts include: Reading Festival, 1975; Fairport Convention reunion concert, 1980; South Yorkshire Folk Festival, 1982; Also appeared together in groups Albion Country Band; Hokey Pokey; Sour Grapes; Solo artiste, 1982–; Regular world-wide appearances include: Guitar Legends, Seville, Spain, 1992; Cropredy Festival, 1992, 1995. *Recordings:* Albums: with Fairport Convention: Fairport Convention, 1968; What We Did On Our Holidays, 1969; Unhalfbricking, 1969; Liege and Lief, 1970; Full House, 1970; with Linda Thompson: I Want To See The Bright Lights Tonight, 1974; Hokey Pokey, 1975; Pour Like Silver, 1975; First Light, 1978; Sunnyvista, 1979; Shoot Out The Lights, 1982; Small Town Romance, 1982; Solo albums: Henry The Human Fly, 1972; Guitar Vocal, 1976; Strict Tempo, 1981; Hand of Kindness, 1983; Across A Crowded Room, 1985; Daring Adventures, 1986; The Marksman (soundtrack to BBC drama series), 1987; Live, Love, Larf and Loaf, 1987; Amnesia, 1988; Rumour and Sigh, 1991; Sweet Talker, 1992; Watching The Dark – The History of Richard Thompson, 1993; You? Me? Us?, 1996; Industry, 1997; Mock Tudor, 1999; Also featured on: Love Chronicles, Al Stewart, 1969; Drunk With Passion, The Golden Palominos, 1991; The Hunter, Jennifer Warnes, 1992; 99.9°F, Suzanne Vega, 1992. *Honours include:* New Music Awards: Solo Artist, Songwriter of Year, Life Achievement Trophy, 1991; Q Award, Best Songwriter, 1991. *Current Management:* Gary Stamler, Suite 2400, 1801 Century Park E, Los Angeles, CA 90067, USA.

THOMPSON Richard E 'Butch'; b. 28 Nov. 1943, Stillwater, Minnesota, USA. Musician (piano, clarinet). m. Mary Ellen Niedenfuer, 20 July 1991. *Education:* BA, University of Minnesota. *Career:* Clarinetist, Hall Brothers Jazz Band, 1962–94; Pianist, leader, Butch Thompson Trio in residency, National Public Radio, 1974–86; World Tours as pianist include Cairo, Egypt, 1994; 1997, 1998; European festivals, appearances with orchestras include: Hartford Symphony; Minnesota Orchestra; St Louis Symphony and many more; National tour of off-Broadway show, Jelly Roll, 1994–97; Major US jazz festivals, 1968-. *Compositions include:* Ecuadorean Memories; Yancey On My Mind; Eduadorean Suite, for piano and orchestra, premiered with Minnesota Orchestra in 1998. *Recordings include:* 10 solo CDs, including Thompson Plays Joplin, 1998; Over 100 other recordings, 25 as leader or soloist. *Honours:* Pianist on Grammy winning Verve CD, Doc Cheatham and Nicholas Payton, 1997. *Membership:* American Federation of Musicians, local 30–73. *Current Management:* Zajonc/Valenti Management. *Address:* PO Box 7023, Ann Arbor, MI 48107, USA.

THOMPSON Robert Scott; b. 17 Feb. 1959, California, USA. Recording Artist; Engineer; Prod.; Musician (Keyboards, Guitar, Vocals, Computer Music). m. Debra Mobley. *Education:* Campbell College; University of Oregon; University of California; Compostion and Computer Music With Bernard Rands, Roger Reynolds, Joji Yuasa and F Richard Moore. *Recordings:* Deeper In The Dreamtime; The Strong Eye; Ginnungagap; Shadow Gazing; Air Friction; The Silent Shore; Frontier; Fountainhead, Cloud Cover; Elemental Folklore; Summer Evening; Blue Day. *Publications:* The Stronge Eye; Shadow Gazing; The Silent Shore; Frontier. *Honours:* Bourges Electro Acoustic, 1984; Fulbright Scholar, 1991; Luiy Russolo, 1994; Irino Prize, 1996. *Current Management:* Aucourant Records. *Address:* PO Box 2231, Roswell, GA 30075, USA.

THOMPSON Teddy; b. 1976. Vocalist; Musician (guitar); Songwriter. *Career:* Son of British folk-rockers Richard and Linda Thompson; First recording singing backing vocals on father's You? Me? Us? album, 1996; Support slot on subsequent promotional tour; Debut album containing 10 self-penned songs released on Virgin, 2000. *Recordings:* solo: Teddy Thompson, 2000; on Richard Thompson albums: You? Me? Us?, 1996; Celtschmertz, 1998; Mock Tudor, 1999; features on: Psycho soundtrack,

1998; Poses, Rufus Wainwright, 2001. *Current Management:* c/o Chris Blake, Blake and Bradford, London, England.

THOMPSON Wayne; b. 28 July 1947, Toronto, Ontario, Canada. Artist Man.; Theatrical Prod. m. Wendy Cochrane, 24 July 1971, 2 s. *Education:* BA, University of Toronto, Political Science, Economics. *Career:* Manager for several major artists; Currently manager for: The Barra MacNeils, Sydney, Nova Scotia. *Membership:* Director, Pacific Music Industry Asscn.

THOMSON Colin; b. 6 July 1937. University Teacher; Researcher; Musician (all saxophones, piano, drums). m. Maureen Margaret Green, 1 Sept. 1962, 2 s., 2 d. *Education:* BSc, PhD, Chemistry, Leeds University. *Career:* Member, Eric Thomson Band, 1953–65; Colin Thomson Big Band, 1974–; Colin Thomson Jazz Quartet; Co-Director, Fife Youth Jazz Orchestra, 1975–80; Director, St Andrews Music Centre Big Band, 1992-. *Publications:* 130 Scientific publications. *Honours:* Chairman, Asscn for International Cancer Research. *Membership:* Musicians' Union. *Leisure interests:* Music Education and Jazz Courses in St Andrews. *Address:* 12 Drumcarrow Rd, St Andrews KY16 8SE, Scotland.

THOMSON Kenny; b. 18 March 1944, Irvine, Scotland. Musician (accordion). m. Cathy Rowan, 3 Oct. 1970, 2 s. *Musical Education:* Studied for 3 years with Robert McF Adamson, Cumnock. *Career:* Played with small local bands from age 10; Started radio broadcasting with BBC Radio Scotland, 1976; Currently, leader of The Wardlaw Scottish Dance Band. *Recordings:* 3 recordings of Scottish Country Dances for the Royal Scottish Country Dance Society. *Membership:* Musicians' Union. *Leisure interests:* Car maintenance; Hill walking. *Address:* 20 Walker Court, Cumnock, Ayrshire KA18 1TF, Scotland.

THORDARSON Gunnar; b. 4 Jan. 1945, Holmavík, Iceland. Composer; Prod. m. Sigrun Toby Herman, 2 s., 3 d. *Musical Education:* Mostly self-taught; Counterpoint lessons. *Career:* Record producer and writer, 1966–; Member, group Hljomar, 1963–69; Member, Trubrot, 1969–73; Record producer, over 100 records; Written hundreds of television commercials, music for 3 Icelandic films and scores for two musicals. *Compositions:* 440 songs as songwriter; Songs recorded by various artists; Work performed by Icelandic Symphony Orchestra. *Recordings:* Himinn Og Jörd, 1981; Borgar Bragur, 1986; Islensk Alpydulög, 1980; Reykjavikurflugur, 1986; I Loftinu, 1987; Ungir Mennà Uppleid, 1997. *Publications:* Film music: Pitt Fyrsta, 1994; Agnes, 1996. *Honours:* Hon. Prize for Service in Icelandic Music, 1997; Arts Grant from Government, 1997. *Memberships:* STEF, Iceland; FIH, Iceland. *Leisure interests:* Horses; Reading; Films. *Address:* Aegisgata 10, Reykjavik 101, Iceland.

THORDSEN Hanne; b. 6 Dec. 1954, Copenhagen, Denmark. Singer; Composer; Writer; Actress. m. (1) Keld Jakobsen, (2) Lasse Aagaard Nielsen, 1988, 2 d. *Education:* As social worker and Kindergarten teacher. *Musical Education:* Self-taught. *Career:* Singer with group Knap and Nap, (mainly Irish and Scottish Folk music and some Blues); Formed folk-rock group Freja; Performed at festivals including: Roskilde, Skagen and Tonder; Television appearance in 1984 and some radio broadcasting, 1993; Appeared as Salene in musical Atlantis at Östre Gasvark. *Recordings:* Kom Nu, Freja, 1988; Participant on the album Folkemusik Til Oerne; Atlantis (album of the musical), 1995. *Membership:* DJBFA. *Leisure interests:* Music; Painting; Family. *Current Management:* Morten Grunwald, Östre Gasvark Theatre, Denmark. *Address:* Gl Mejerivej 14 D, 3050 Humlebaek, Denmark.

THORHALLSSON Olafur Gaukur; b. 11 Aug. 1930, Iceland. Musician (guitar); Composer; Conductor; Prod.; Teacher. m. (1) 1 s., 4 d., (2) Svanhildur Jakobsdottir, 8 June 1963, 1 s., 1 d. *Musical Education:* Classical guitar lessons; Self-taught jazz guitar; Studied composition, Music Academy of Reykjavik, 1985; Composition, 1984, Composition for films and video, 1988, Grove School of Music, Los Angeles, USA; Guitar Institute, Hollywood, 1993. *Career:* Musician, Bandleader, Composer and Arranger on numerous shows, stage, television and radio; Own TV show, Icelandic State Television, 1968–71; Concerts with international vocal groups include The Mills Brothers, The Platters, The Delta Rhythm Boys; Arrangements for different kinds of groups, orchestras and artists including Björk; Head of own music school (mainly guitar), 1975–; Participated on over 100 albums as composer, lyricist, arranger, conductor, producer, musician. *Compositions:* Music for Icelandic feature films; Documentaries, TV shows and plays; Popular songs over 30 years. *Recordings:* 11 albums with own band or orchestra, 1968–94. *Publications:* Author of educational material including books and cassettes, mainly for guitar students. *Memberships:* Icelandic Musicians' Union; Performing Rights Society of Iceland; Jazzvakning. *Address:* Sidumula 17, 108 Reykjavik, Iceland.

THORHALLSSON Robert; b. 12 Aug. 1971, Husavik, Thingeyjarsysla, Iceland. Musician (trumpet, saxophone, drums, double bass, electric bass). *Musical Education:* Jazz Music Graduate on electric bass; Self-taught drums and double bass; Tuition on double bass, trumpet and saxophone.

Career: Played in shows staged in Iceland, Superstar 95–96; World premiere of Jim Cartwright's Stone Free; The Beatles' Sergeant Pepper's Lonely Hearts Club Band staged by the Icelandic Symphony, 1997. *Recordings:* Crougie dou là, 1995; Merman, 1996; Superstar, 1995; Stone Free, music from a play, 1996; Love, live recordings from Stone Free, 1996. *Publications:* Superstar, 1995; Stone Free, 1996; Merman, 1996. *Honours:* Gold Albums, 1996, 1997; Platinum album, 1997. *Membership:* Icelandic Musicians' Asscn (FIH). *Leisure interest:* Sport. *Address:* Sigluvogur 15, 104 Reykjavik, Iceland.

THORN Tracey; b. 26 Sept. 1962. Singer; Songwriter. *Education:* Hull University. *Career:* Member, trio, Marine Girls; Forms duo Everything But The Girl with musician Ben Watt, 1983–; Appearances include: Regular British tours, 1984–; World Tour, 1990, including Japan; Friends of the Earth Benefit Concerts, 1990; Red Hot and Dance AIDS Benefit Concert, 1991; UK and US Tours, 1993–95; World tour, 1996–97 including Japan and Australasia. *Compositions:* Writer, co-writer with Ben Watt, and Massive Attack, of own material for trio, duo and solo work. *Recordings:* Albums: Solo album: A Distant Shore, 1982; with Marine Girls: Beach Party, 1980; Lazy Ways, 1983; with Everything But The Girl: Eden, 1984; Everything But The Girl (US only), 1984; Love Not Money, 1985; Baby, The Stars Shine Bright, 1986; Idlewild, 1988; The Language of Life, 1990; World-wide, 1991; Essence and Rare (Japan only), 1992; Acoustic, 1992 (US only); Home Movies – Best of Everything But The Girl, 1993; Amplified Heart, 1994; Walking Wounded, 1996; Temperamental, 1999; with Massive Attack: Protection, 1995; Guest singer, albums by Style Council; Go Betweens; Lloyd Cole; Adam F; Deep Dish; Singles include: with Everything But The Girl: Each and Every One, 1984; Come On Home, 1986; I Don't Want To Talk About It, 1988; Missing, 1995; Walking Wounded, 1996; Wrong, 1996; Missing, 1999; Blame, 2000; Contributor with Massive Attack, film soundtrack for Batman Forever, 1995. *Current Management:* JFD Management, 106 Dalling Rd, London W6 0JA, England.

THORNTON Billy Bob; b. 4 Aug. 1955, Hot Springs, Arkansas, USA. Vocalist; Musician (drums); Songwriter; Actor. m. Pietra Dawn Thornton, Toni Lawrence, Cynda Williams, Melissa Ross, Angelina Jolie. *Career:* Primarily known as an actor but also has musical background; After playing drums and singing at high school, joined local soul group Blue and The Velvets; Later formed own soul group named after the Allman Brothers' song Hot 'Lanta; Formed Nothin' Doin' with Mike and Nick Ship, playing drums and sharing lead vocals, 1974; Scott Weiss suggested tour as a ZZ Top tribute band, resulting in new name, Tres Hombres; Toured extensively and opened for many established acts; Quit music business and moved to Hollywood to pursue acting career, 1981; Got together some old friends to perform a jam session for the crew of Slingblade film in Arkansas, 1995; Began playing more impromptu sessions and began to put together a collection of songs in Nashville; This led to eventual recording of idiosyncratic, alternative country album Private Radio. *Recordings:* Private Radio, 2001; features on: Earl Scruggs and Friends, 2001.

THOROGOOD George; b. 31 Dec. 1952, Wilmington, Delaware, USA. Blues Musician (guitar). *Career:* Former baseball player; Formed own group the Destroyers, 1973–; Opened for the Rolling Stones, 1981; Appeared at Live Aid with Albert Collins, 1985. *Recordings:* Albums: George Thorogood and The Destroyers, 1978; Move It On Over, 1978; Better Than The Rest, 1979; More George Thorogood and The Destroyers, 1980; Bad To The Bone, 1982; Maverick, 1985; Live, 1986; Born To Be Bad, 1988; Let's Work Together, 1995; Rockin' My Life Away, 1997; Half a Boy Half a Man, 1999; Live in 1999. *Current Management:* Mike Donahue Management, PO Box 807, Lewisburg, WV 24901, USA.

THORPE Anthony John; b. 20 July 1945, London, England. Musician (guitar); Writer; Singer; Actor. m. Shirley Atherton, 14 Feb. 1968, 1 s. *Education:* St Ignatius' College, London. *Career:* Guitarist, arranger, Wee Willie Harris; Tommy Steele (including West End); Guitarist, singer, Rubettes, 1970's; Guitarist, singer, The Firm, 1980's; Writer, actor, Cooger and Dark two-man show, Edinburgh Fringe; Blues Band Gas Company, John Caira Band; Also worked with Tony Crombie, Gary Boyle, Mike Walker, Tal Farlow, Jimmy Smith and Denny Laine. *Recordings:* 7 albums with The Rubettes; Lead vocals on two hit singles; with The Firm: Arthur Daley; Solo album: Illusions and Dangerous Prayer. *Publications:* Concert reviews, The Guardian, 1980s. *Memberships:* Musicians' Union; PRS. *Leisure interests:* Music; Spiritual philosophy. *Address:* 143 Marsden Rd, Burnley, Lancashire BB10 2QW, England.

THORUP Jesper; b. 9 June 1952, Copenhagen, Denmark. Composer; Singer; Musician (drums). *Musical Education:* Alex Riel; Hans Fülling; Ed Thigpen. *Career:* Dana Gillespie (UK); The Rustics (USA); Mal Waldren Trio (USA); Benny Waters (USA); Peter Thorup and Jesper Band; Paul Millins (UK); Sam Mitchel Blue Vikings (UK/Denmark); Dexter Gordon; Jackie McLean; Danish Grand Prix; Danish Radio Jazzgroup. *Compositions:* Composed and recorded with: Annegrete: Hvem Sir;

Duggen Falder: Drops: Koernes Sang; Aorta: Havnerfunk. *Honours:* First prize, Best Soloist, Dunquerque International Jazz Festival, France, 1975. *Memberships:* DMF; DJFBA. *Leisure interests:* Painting; Art. *Address:* Fabritius Alle 16, 2930 Klampenborg, Denmark. *Internet:* www.jesperthorup.dk.

THOUMIRE Simon John; b. 11 July 1970, Edinburgh, Scotland. Musician (concertina); Composer. *Musical Education:* Self-taught. *Career:* Started at 16 years old with Seannachie, 1989; Formed duo with Ian Carr; Television performance on Aly Bain's Shetland Session; First tour USA, 1990; Formed Simon Thoumire Three, 1992; Television: Aly Bains Transatlantic Sessions, 1995; Formed duo with Fergus McKenzie. *Recordings:* with Seannachie: Take Note, 1987; Devil's Delight, 1992; Hootz, Simon Thoumire and Ian Carr, 1990; Waltzes For Playboys, Simon Thoumire Three, 1994; Exhibit A, Simon Thoumire and Fergus MacKenzie, 1995. *Honours:* BBC Radio 2 Young Tradition Award, 1989; Folk Roots, Most Innovative Performance, 1989. *Membership:* Musicians' Union. *Leisure interests:* Walking; Running; Music. *Current Management:* Hootz! Productions. *Address:* 17 Redford Dr., Edinburgh EH13 0BL, Scotland.

THRALE Carlos Heinrich; b. 3 Aug. 1962, London, England. Musician (guitar). *Education:* BA Hons, Nottingham Trent University. *Musical Education:* ARCM, Royal College of Music. *Career:* Session musician for: Mica Paris; Freeze; Dr Egg; Sugar Bullet; Radio and television commercials; Also lecturer, Course co-ordinator, Popular Music. *Publications:* Guitar Theory and Technique, video and book, EMI, 1985. *Membership:* Musicians' Union. *Current Management:* Spencer Wells. *Address:* 12 Grove Rd, Bingham, Nottinghamshire NG13 8DY, England.

THROB (Robert Young); Musician (Guitar). *Career:* Member, Primal Scream; Numerous tours and festival appearances; Collaborations with DJ Andrew Weatherall, vocalist Denise Johnson, Jah Wobble and Alex Paterson of The Orb; Contributed track to the film Trainspotting, co-written by Irvine Welsh, 1996. *Recordings:* Singles: Loaded EP, 1990; Come Together EP, 1990; Don't Fight It, Feel It, 1991; Movin' On Up, 1991; (I'm Gonna) Cry Myself Blind, 1994; Jailbird, 1994; Rocks/Funky Jam, 1994; Rocks Off, 1994; The Big Man and the Scream Team Meet the Barmy Army Uptown (from Trainspotting), 1996; Star, 1997; Burning Wheel, 1997; Kowalski, 1997; If They Move, Kill 'Em, 1998; Albums: Sonic Flower Groove, 1987; Primal Scream, 1989; Screamadelica, 1991; Give Out But Don't Give Up, 1994; Echo Dek, 1997; Vanishing Point, 1997. *Honour:* Mercury Music Prize Winner, 1992.

TICKELL Kathryn Derran; b. 8 June 1967, Northumberland, England. Musician (northumbrian pipes, fiddle); Composer. *Career:* Plays traditional folk material from the North-East of England and composes own tunes; Started playing Northumbrian Smallpipes aged 9; Recorded The Long Tradition TV documentary, 1987; Performed on the Sting hit Fields of Gold; Performed with Jimmy Nail at City Hall, Newcastle; Composed, performed and recorded Music For A New Crossing with jazz saxophonist Andy Sheppard (commissioned for the opening of the Gateshead Millennium Bridge), broadcast live on the Last Night of the Proms, 2001. *Recordings:* Albums: On Kielderside, 1984; Borderlands, 1986; Common Ground, 1988; The Kathryn Tickell Band, 1991; Signs, 1993; The Gathering, 1997; The Northumberland Collection, 1998; Debateable Lands, 1999; Kathryn Tickell and Ensemble Mystical, 2000; Music For A New Crossing, 2001. *Current Management:* Karen McWilliams, PO Box 130, Morpeth, Northumberland, NE65 7WD, England. *Internet:* www.kathryntickell.com.

TIELENS Louis, (Country Lewis); b. 2 Aug. 1942, Beringen, Belgium. Broadcaster. m. Germa Baelen, 6 Aug. 1984, 1 s., 1 d. *Education:* College. *Career:* DJ 'Country Lewis'; Retired manager, Radio Animo; Retired Station Manager, Radio Loksbergen; Producer, syndicated country music programmes, De Bazuin non-profit organisation; With wife, producer, gospel programme Good News. *Membership:* Executive Committee, Country and Western Asscn, Belgium. *Leisure interest:* Reading. *Address:* Pauwenlaan 23, 3583 Paal-Beringen, Belgium.

TIERS Wharton; b. 11 Feb. 1953, Philadelphia, Pennsylvania, USA. Prod.; Musician (drums, keyboards, guitar); Songwriter; Engineer. *Education:* BA, English, Villanova University, Pennsylvania. *Career:* Producer, engineer, Indie records, 1980s-90s; Over 120 records produced; Member, Laurie Anderson's Band; Glenn Branca's Band; Played with: Theatrical Girls; Glorious Strangers; Played on US network. *Recordings:* Albums as producer: 6 albums with Sonic Youth; with Dinosaur Jr: Just Like Heaven; You're Living All Over Me; with Gumball: Special Kiss; Unsane; Urban Discipline, Biohazard; In The Meantime, Helmet; God Knows It's True, Teenage Fan Club; Anaesthesia, Dean Wareham; Primitive Origins, Prong; Headkick Facsimile, Cop Shoot Cop; Pussy Gold 5000, Pussy Galore; Brighter then Life, 1996; Twilight of the Computer Age, 1999. *Leisure interests:* Writing; Hiking; Electronic design. *Current Management:* Susan Sidel Management.

TIGER Flower; b. 29 Sept. 1934, Baojing County, Hunan Province, China. Composer. m. Zhang Xiangming, 20 Oct. 1968, 2 s. *Education:* Graduated, Minzu Normal school of Jishou City, studied under Professor of Music Liu Tianlin; Graduated, Composition, Shanghai Conservatory, studied with He Luding, Sha Hankun, Liu Zhuang, Deng Erjing. *Career:* Professional Composer, ensembles at central, provincial and prefectural levels; Over 100 published; Many televised or broadcast by stations at central and local levels. *Compositions:* Beautiful Peacock, Please Fly Back Soon; The Charming Moonlight of Tujia Home Villages; many other ethnic minority folk songs. *Recordings:* Hunting in Wuling Mountains; Grand Chorus in Praise of National Unity; Wind and Percussion Concerto; Miao Music Dance; Polyphonic Piano Suite for Chinese Folk Songs; The Drum of Blood. *Publications:* Beacon fire in Miao Borders, 1988; A New Song Anthology of National Art, 1990. *Honours:* Expert, with special subsidies from the government, 1993–; 2 Medals from the USA, while lecturing; 2 National Music Prizes, 1983, 1988. *Memberships:* Chinese Musicians' Asscn; Vice President, China Minorities Music Society. *Leisure interests:* Film; Literature; Opera; Singing. *Address:* 11 Wenyi Rd, Jishou City, Hunan Province, 416000 China.

TIJSSENS Michael Warren; b. 27 March 1961, Amersfoort, Netherlands. Lyricist; Screenwriter; Playwright. m. Dyna Justin, 26 Sept. 1987, 2 s. *Education:* Royal Academy of Dramatic Art; Sorbonne University. *Musical Education:* Self-taught. *Career:* Numerous roles as actor, singer, writer, director, dramatist and producer; Now writing for artists in music business; Has worked with: Bob Geldof; Rick Smith; Karl Hyde. *Recordings:* Joint Venture; Tropical Corridor; Blanc Nègre; Sens Unique Show; Destination Tomorrow. *Publications:* Rendez-Vous; Cahiers de Prospero; Theatre Public. *Honours:* Prix d'Honneur, Institut Radiodiffusion Suisse. *Memberships:* SACEM; SACD; ATLF. *Current Management:* Media Writers and Translators. *Address:* 13 Blvd de la Marne, 77420 Champs-Sur-Marne, France.

TIKARAM Tanita; b. 12 Aug. 1969, Münster, Germany. Singer; Songwriter; Musician (guitar). *Career:* Moved to UK, 1982; Songwriter, 1987–; Support tour, Warren Zevon, 1988; Major international tours, 1989, 1992. *Recordings:* Albums: Ancient Heart, 1988; The Sweet Keeper, 1990; Everybody's Angel, 1991; Eleven Kinds of Loneliness, 1992; Lovers In The City, 1995; Singles: Good Tradition, 1988; Twist In My Sobriety, 1988; Only The Ones We Love, 1991; I Might Be Crying, 1995; The Cappuccino Songs, 1998. *Current Management:* Stephen Budd Management, 109B Regents Park Rd, London NW1 8UR, England.

TIKHONOV Dimitri; b. 6 Aug. 1964, Vladivostok, Russia. Keyboard; Vocal; Composer. m. Juliette Alix, 12 Aug. 1994, 1 s. *Education:* Jazz School, St Petersburg, Russia. *Career:* Composer, Keyboarder and Singer of the group, Nom, St Petersburg, 1987–94; Tours over Western Europe, Italy, Czechoslovakia, France, Germany, Switzerland and Hungary; Nom video demonstrated on BBC2, MTV, M6, MCM, TV channels; Solo career as composer and bass, Geneva Opera's Choir, 1995-. *Compositions:* Nom, Masters of the USSR; Ape's Snout, 1995; Nom, Made in Europe, 1997. *Recordings:* Brutto, Nom, LP, CD, 1989; To Hell With It, LP, Super Disc, 1990; Senka – Mosgaz, LP, CD, 1992, 1994; Live is Game, CD, Ultracompact, 1995; In the Name of Mind, CD, 1995, 1996; Les Sons De Carton, solo, 1997; Some Original Melodies, 1998; The Songs of Cartoon, 1999; Jban D – soundtrack from the film of NOM, 2000; What's a Wonderful Liver, 2000. *Honours:* Skotinorap, Best Alternative Video of Russia, 1993; Nina-2, Grand Prix Exotica, 1994; Ukr Blues, Best Low Budget Video, 1996. *Address:* Tikhonov Dimitri, 9 rue du Mont-Blanc, 74100 Ville-La-Grande, France.

TILBROOK Glenn; b. 31 Aug. 1957, London, England. Vocalist; Musician (guitar); Songwriter. *Career:* Founder member, Squeeze, 1974–; Longstanding writing partnership with Chris Difford; Performances include: US tours, 1978–; Reading Rock Festival, 1978; Dalymount Festival, Dublin, 1980; Jamaica World Music Festival, 1982; Support to Fleetwood Mac, US tour, 1990; Crystal Palace Bowl, 1991; Support to Bryan Adams, British tour, 1992. *Compositions include:* Co-writer, with Elvis Costello, From A Whisper To A Scream, 1981; Songs for musical, Labelled With Love, 1983. *Recordings:* Albums: Squeeze, 1978; Cool For Cats, 1979; Argy Bargy, 1980; East Side Story, 1981; Sweets From A Stranger, 1982; Singles 45's and Under, 1982; Cosi Fan Tutti Frutti, 1985; Babylon and On, 1987; Frank, 1989; A Round and A Bout, 1990; Greatest Hits, 1992; Some Fantastic Place, 1993; Ridiculous, 1995; Six of One, 1997; Domino, 1998; Live at Royal Albert Hall, 1999; Singles include: Take Me I'm Yours, 1978; Cool For Cats, 1979; Up The Junction, 1979; Another Nail In My Heart, 1980; Pulling Mussels From A Shell, 1980; Hourglass, 1987. *Current Management:* Firstars, 3520 Hayden Ave, Culver City, CA 90232, USA.

TILBURY John; b. 1 Feb. 1936, London, England. Musician (Piano). 1 s., 2 d. *Education:* Royal College of Music, and privately with James Gibb; Warsaw Conservatory with Zbigniew Drzewecki. *Recordings:* Cage: Sonatas and Interludes; Feldman: Complete solo piano music; Stempton:

Solo piano music; Many recordings as member of AMM Free Improvisation group. *Address:* 158 Middle St, Deal, Kent CT14 6LW, England.

TILLIS Mel (Lonnie Melvin); b. 8 Aug. 1932, Tampa, Florida, USA. Country Singer; Songwriter; Musician (guitar, fiddle). *Education:* University of Florida. *Career:* Began performing, recording, 1956–57; Toured extensively with The Statesiders, 1960s-70s; Numerous tours and television appearances; Recorded duets with Glen Campbell and Nancy Sinatra; Film apperances: WW and The Dixie Dance Kings; Smokey and The Bandit 2; Murder In Music City; Uphill All The Way; Owned several publishing companies; Also cattle breeder. *Compositions include:* I'm Tired; Tupelo County Jail; I Ain't Never (all hits for Webb Peirce); Lonely Island Pearl, Johnny and Jack; Heart Over Mind, Ray Price; Ten Thousand Drums, Carl Smith; Detroit City (co-written with Danny Dill) Bobby Bare, 1963; The Snakes Crawl At Night, Charley Pride, 1966; Ruby Don't Take Your Love To Town, Johnny Darrell, 1967 (Also hit for Kenny Rogers and The First Edition, 1969). *Recordings:* US Country No. 1 hits: I Ain't Never; Good Woman Blues; Heart Healer; I Believe In You; Coca Cola Cowboy; Southern Rains; Other hits include: Life Turned Her That Way; Stateside; These Lonely Hands of Mine; Send Me Down To Tucson, featured in film Every Which Way But Loose; Take My Hand; Numerous albums include: Heart Over Mind, 1961; Stateside, 1966; Mr Mel, 1967; One More Time, 1970; Mel Tillis, 1972; Sawmill, 1973; M-M-Mel and The Statesiders, 1975; Are You Sincere, 1979; The Great Mel Tillis, 1979; Southern Rain, 1980; M-M-Mel Live, 1980; It's A Long Way To Daytona, 1982; After All This Time, 1983; New Patches, 1984; California Road, 1985; Four Legends (with Jerry Lee Lewis, Webb Pierce, Faron Young), 1985; Branson City Limits (live); Brand New Mister Me; I Believe in You; M-M-Mel Live; Also recorded with: Glen Campbell; Nancy Sinatra; Sherry Bryce. *Publications:* Stutterin' Boy, The Autobiography of Mel Tillis (with Walter Wager). *Honours:* Inducted into Nashville Songwriters International Hall of Fame; 1976; CMA Entertainer of The Year, 1976. *Address:* c/o Mel Tillis Enterprises, PO Box 1626, Branson, MO 65615, USA.

TILLIS Pam (Pamela Yvonne); b. 24 July 1957, Plant City, Florida, USA. Country vocalist; Musician (guitar, piano); Songwriter; Actor. m. Bob DiPiero. *Education:* University of Tennessee. *Musical Education:* Studied classical piano. *Career:* Member of group Billy Hill; Debut appearance with father, country vocalist Mel Tillis, and family on stage of the Grand Ole Opry singing Tom Dooley, aged 8; Bought first guitar, aged 12; Performed solo at Nashville's Exit/In during teens; At 16, car crash shattered face in 30 places requiring five years of surgery; Formed first band High Country Swing Band at University, also appearing in duo with Ashley Cleveland; After college, worked for father's publishing company, Sawgrass Music, achieving first cut I'll Meet You On The Other Side of The Morning for Barbara Fairchild; Left for San Francisco and formed the Pam Tillis Band; Returned to Nashville singing backing vocals in father's band, 1978; Achieved another cut, When I Get Around To It by Gloria Gaynor; Debut album for Warner Brothers: Beyond The Doll of Cutey, 1983; Brief spell of three months in England before returning to Nashville to continue songwriting; Debut single on Billboard country chart Goodbye Highway, 1984; Subsequent Warners singles struggled sales-wise; Signed to Tree Publishing, cuts on Chaka Khan So Close and the Forester Sisters Drawn To The Fire; Signed to Arista Records, 1989; Career took off following year Don't Tell Me What To Do reaching country chart top 5; Continued to be highly successful throughout 1990s with hit albums and singles and a clutch of awards; Appearances in TV series: LA Law, 1986; Hot Country Nights, 1991; Diagnosis Murder, 1993; Promised Land, 1996; Also appeared in The Thing Called Love film, 1993, and TV films: XXXs and OOOs, 1994; The Best of Country, 1995. *Compositions include:* Cleopatra – Queen of Denial; Spilled Perfume; Mi Vida Loca; Put Yourself In My Place; Someone Else's Trouble Now. *Recordings include:* Don't Tell Me What To Do, 1990; One of Those Things, Maybe It Was Memphis, 1991; Shake The Sugar Tree, 1992; Mi Vida Loca, When You Walk In The Room, Spilled Perfume, 1994; In Between Dances, 1995; All The Good Ones Are Gone, Land of The Living, 1997; Albums include: Put Yourself In My Place, 1991; Sweetheart's Dance, 1994; Greatest Hits, 1997; Thunder and Roses, 2001. *Honours:* CMA, Female Vocalist of the Year, 1994. *Address:* c/o The Country Music Asscn, Nashville, Tennessee, USA. *Internet:* www.pamtillis.com.

TILLMAN Floyd; b. 8 Dec. 1914, Ryan, Oklahoma, USA. Country Singer; Songwriter; Musician (mandolin, banjo, guitar). *Career:* Performed as member of Adolph Hofner; Mack Clark; Blue Ridge Playboys, 1930s; Solo artiste, 1939–60; One of first country artists to use electric guitar; Now semi-retired. *Compositions:* It Makes No Difference Now, hit for Bing Crosby, Gene Autry; Slippin' Around, recorded by numerous artists including Ernest Tubb, Jimmy Wakeley. *Recordings:* Hits include: They Took The Stars Out of Heaven (US Country No. 1); GI Blues; Drivin' Nails In My Coffin; I Love You So Much It Hurts; Albums include: Let's Make Memories, 1962; Country, 1967; Dream On, 1968; I'll Still Be Loving You, 1969; Floyd Tillman and Friends, with Willie Nelson and Merle Haggard, 1982. *Honours:* Inducted into Nashville Songwriters Asscn Hall of Fame,

1970; Inducted into Country Music Hall of Fame, 1984; Crazy Cajun Recordings, 1999; Best of Floyd Tillman, 1999.

TILLOTSON Paul; b. 18 Dec. 1964, Boise, Idaho, USA. Musician (Piano); Composer. *Education:* AAS, Edmonds CC, 1985; University of Miami, 1986; Bachelor of Music, William Patterson, 1989. *Career:* North Sea Jazz Festival; Montreux Jazz Festival; Gene Harris Jazz Festival. *Compositions:* Simple Pleasures; Tulips; Big Valley; Tidbits; Tebadadeda. *Recordings:* The Paul Tillotson Trio: Tulips; Live At The Lock; Tidbits; Sweet Mystery; Tasty Morsels. *Membership:* Local 802. *Leisure interests:* Downhill skiing; Scuba diving; Mountain biking. *Address:* 316 E Sixth St # B1, New York, NY 10003, USA.

TILSTON Stephen Thomas Gregory; b. 26 March 1950, Liverpool, England. Musician (guitar); Songwriter. m. Maggie Boyle, 27 Jan. 1984, 1 s., 3 d. *Education:* Trained as graphic artist. *Musical Education:* Self-taught. *Career:* Solo, also duo with Maggie Boyle; Member, Ship of Fools, with John Renbourn; Guitarist, Ballet Rambert. *Recordings:* Acoustic Confusion, 1971; Collection, 1973; Songs From The Dress Rehearsal, 1977, In For A Penny, 1983; Life By Misadventure, 1987; Swans At Goole, 1990; Of Moor and Mesa, 1992; And So It Goes, 1995; All Under the Sun, 1996. *Membership:* British Longbow Society. *Leisure interest:* Archery. *Current Management:* Alan King. *Address:* 78 Sydenham Park, London SE26 4DP, England.

TILTON Martha Ellen; b. 14 Nov. 1915, Corpus Christi, Texas, USA. Singer. m. James L Brooks, 3 May 1953, 2 s., 1 d. *Musical Education:* Piano. *Career:* Carnegie Hall Concert, Benny Goodman, 1937; Philco Radio Hall of Fame programme; Radio, with Paul Whiteman Orchestra, 4 years, mid 1940's; Alka Seltzer Program CBS, 8 years; Martha Tilton, Count Maskey Show, National Broadcasting Company, 6 years; Capitol Records; Decca Records; Two overseas tours with Jack Benny, Larry Adler; Ingrid Bergman, during World War II: South Pacific, 1943; Germany, 1944. *Honours:* Academy of Television Arts and Sciences: Most Outstanding Female Personality, 1959–60, 1960–61; For Dedication and Service to the City, City Council Los Angeles, 1983; National Academy of Arts and Sciences, Hall of Fame Award, 1987. *Memberships:* American Federation Television and Radio Artists; American Guild of Variety Artists. *Leisure interest:* Needlepoint. *Address:* 2257 Mandeville Canyon Rd, Los Angeles, CA 90049, USA.

TIMBALAND (Timothy Mosley); b. Norfolk, Virginia, USA. Prod.; Remixer; Songwriter. *Career:* Came to prominence as a writer on Aaliyah's One In A Million album; Went on to work with Missy Elliott, producing her debut album Supa Dupa Fly, 1997; One of the most in-demand producers in Hip Hop and R & B; Production credits include: Destiny's Child; Jay-Z; Usher; The Lox; Collaborations: Missy Elliott; Ginuwine; Magoo; Bubba Sparxx. *Recordings:* Albums: Welcome To Our World (with Magoo), 1997; Tim's Bio, 1998; We At It Again (with Magoo), 2000; Singles: Clock Strikes (with Magoo), 1998; Lobster and Shrimp (with Jay-Z), 1998; Here We Come, 1999. *Honours:* MOBO Awards, Best Producer nominee, 2001. *Address:* c/o Virgin Records, Kensal House, 553–579 Harrow Rd, London, W10 4RH, England.

TIMBERLAKE Justin Randall; b. 31 Jan. 1981, Memphis, TN, USA. Vocalist; Songwriter; Actor. *Career:* Started vocal training aged 8; Guest appearance at Grand Ole Opry, 1991; Early TV appearances: Star Search, 1992; The Mickey Mouse Club, 1993–94; Member of boy band *N Sync signed to BMG Ariola Munich, 1997; First headline US tour, 1998; Acting roles: Model Behavior, 2000; various TV films. *Recordings:* Albums: *N Sync, 1998; Home For Christmas, 1998; No Strings Attached, 2000; Celebrity, 2001; Singles include: I Want You Back, 1997; Tearin' Up My Heart, 1997; Let The Music Heal Your Soul (various artists charity single credited to Bravo All Stars), 1999; Music of My Heart (with Gloria Estefan), 1999; Bye, Bye, Bye, 2000; I'll Never Stop, 2000; It's Gonna Be Me, 2000; This I Promise You, 2000; Pop, 2001; Gone, 2001. *Honours:* *N Sync reported as music industry's biggest earners in 2000 (estimated $184m); Recognition at MTV and Billboard Awards; Presented with keys to City of Orlando, 2000. *Address:* c/o Wright Entertainment Group, PO Box 590009, Orlando, Florida 32859–0009, USA. *Internet:* www.wegmusic.com.

TIMMY C (Tim Commerford); Musician (Bass). *Career:* Member, Rage Against the Machine; Obtained major label record deal; Involvement in various causes such as Fairness and Accuracy in Reporting, Rock for Choice and Refuse and Resist; Numerous tours including Lollapalooza; Tour with Wu Tang Clan; Contributed to soundtrack for film Godzilla, 1998. *Recordings:* Singles: Freedom, 1994; Bombtrack Plus Live, 1994; People of the Sun EP, 1997; Albums: Rage Against the Machine, 1992; Evil Empire, 1996.

TINETA (Tineta Michelle Couturier); b. 24 Aug. 1972, Red Deer, Alberta, Canada. Singer; Songwriter; Musician (guitar, piano, drums). *Musical Education:* Self-taught. *Career:* Solo artist, 1989–; Support act for Steve Wariner, Pam Tillis; Major concerts: Grand Ole Opry, 1989; Big

Valley Jamboree, Craven, Saskatchewan; Big Valley Jamboree, Camrose, Alberta. *Compositions:* Slippin Away; Love On The Line; Let's Make Up; It's Rainin'; Too Bad So Sad; Walkin' That Line; That's What Love's About. *Recordings:* Albums: Love On The Line; Drawn To The Fire. *Honours:* 3 People's Choice Nominations, Single of Year, Writer of Year, Most Promising Artist, 1991; Vista Rising Star Nomination; Album of Year Nomination; Video of Year Nomination. *Memberships:* CCMA; SOCAN; CMN; CARAS; ARIA. *Leisure interests:* Horse riding; Water activities; Songwriting. *Current Management:* Keith and Dawnalyn Couturier. *Address:* PO Box 5039, Drayton Valley, AB T7A 1R3, Canada.

TINSLEY Boyd Calvin; b. 16 May 1964. Musician (violin). *Education:* Walker Middle School, Charlottesville; University of Virginia, History graduate. *Musical Education:* Tutored by Isador Saslav, concertmaster of Baltimore Symphony Orchestra. *Career:* Part-time model including work for: JanSport; Tommy Hilfiger; Gucci; As teenager helped found the Charlottesville-Albermarle Youth Orchestra; Formed duo Down Boy Down, 1987; Changed name to The Boyd Tinsley Band when augmented by other musicians; Became permanent member of The Dave Matthews Band following regular guest appearances, around 1992; Rapid growth of fanbase through touring; First album released on group's own Bama Rags label certified gold by RIAA; First national US tour in support of RCA debut album, 1994; Many world-wide concerts and festival appearances, including 2001 album tour; I Did It single officially released through Napster, 2001. *Recordings:* Albums: Remember Two Things (live), 1993; Under The Table and Dreaming, 1994; Crash, 1996; Live At Red Rocks 8–15–95, 1997; Before These Crowded Streets, 1998; Listener Supported (live), 1999; Everyday, Live In Chicago 12–19–98, 2001; Singles: Recently (EP), 1994; What Would You Say, Jimi Thing, Ants Marching, 1995; So Much To Say, Too Much, 1996; Don't Drink The Water, 1997; Satellite, Crash Into Me, Crush, 1998; I Did It, The Space Between, Everyday, 2001. *Honours:* Grammy Awards: Best Rock Performance By A Duo Or Group With Vocal, 1997; US VH-1 Awards: Favourite Group; Must Have Album; Song of The Year, 2001; Top-grossing touring band in US, 2000. *Address:* c/o Red Light Communications, 3305 Lobban Pl., Charlottesville, VA 22903, USA. *E-mail:* info@rlc.net. *Internet:* www.dmband.com.

TIPLER Paul; Record Prod.; Engineer. *Recordings:* As producer, co-producer, albums include: Mars Audiac Quintet, Stereolab; Dream of 100 Nations, TransGlobal Underground; Weird's Bar and Grill, Pop Will Eat Itself; Duniya, Loop Guru; In Love With, Mambo Taxi; Chocolate Revenge, Voodoo Queens; As engineer: Eat Yourself Whole, Kingmaker; Suspira, Miranda Sex Garden; Peggy Suicide, Julian Cope; Elastica, Elastica; Stereolab, Fluorescences; Cybele's Reverie; TransGlobal Underground, Psychic Karaoke; Vibrators, We Vibrate; Primo, Dr Feelgood; Singles with: Kingmaker; Shriek; Fun-Da-Mental; Pop Will Eat Itself; Back To The Planet; Jah Wobble; New Fast Automatic Daffodils. *Current Management:* Stephen Budd Management, 109B Regents Park Rd, London NW1 8UR, England.

TISO Wagner; b. Tres Pontas, Minas Gerais, Brazil. Musician (piano, keyboards); Composer; Arranger; Conductor; Musical Dir. m. Giselle de Andrade Goldoni, 2 d. *Musical Education:* Self-taught. *Career:* Soundtracks: O Guarani, Norma Bengell, 1995; A Ostra e o Vento, Walter Lima Jr, 1997; Television: Meu Marido, Walter Lima Jr, TV Globo; O Sorriso do Lagarto, Roberto Talma, TV Globo; Suites: Suite Tom Jobim, 1995; Cenas Brasileiras, 1995; Stage apperances: Soloist, Rhapsody In Blue, 1997; Encontro de Violoncellos, 1997; Numerous concert and festival appearances include: Montreux Jazz Festival, with Flora Purim, Airto Moreira and Ron Carter (1974), and in 1982; Festival de Música Latina, Cuba, 1983, and Paris, 1986; Festival de Música Brasileira, Rome, 1984; Jazz festivals in São Paulo, Berlin, Montmartre and Rio de Janiero. *Compositions include:* Coraçao de Estudante, for film Jango; Chorata, suite for piano and orchestra; Lenda Ao Boto; Choro de Mae; Cafezais Sem Fim. *Recordings include:* Wagner Tiso, 1978; Baobab, 1990; O Livro de Jó, 1993; Brazilian Scenes, 1997; Crooner, 1999. *Publications:* Wagner Tiso Ao Vivo na Europa, 1982; Giselle, 1986; A Floresta Amazônica (Villa Lobos), 1987; Cine Brasil (original soundtracks), 1989; Wagner Tiso Ao Vivo, with Rio Cello Ensemble, 1995. *Honours:* Best Arranger, for Sentinela, Milton Nascimento, 1981; Best Instrumental recording, Todas as Teclas, with Cesar Camargo Mariano, 1983; Best Soundtracks: Jango, 1984, Chico Rei, 1987. *Memberships:* AMAR; OMB. *Leisure interests:* Games; Reading. *Current Management:* Giselle de Andrade Goldoni, Tres Mineiro Produçoes Artisticas Ltda. *Address:* Rua Cesário Alvim 55/107 Bla, Humaitá, 22261–030 Rio de Janiero, RJ, Brazil.

TISSENDIER Claude; b. 1 Oct. 1952, Toulouse, France. Musician (saxophones, clarinet). *Musical Education:* 6 years Conservatoire. *Career:* All major jazz festivals in France; Member, Claude Bolling Band, 22 years; Leader, own band, Saxomania, 12 years. *Recordings with:* Benny Carter, 1988; Spike Robinson, 1989; Phil Woods, 1991; Guy Lafitte, 1993; Marlene Verplanck, 1994; Clark Terry, 1995; 20 albums with Claude Bolling, 1978–95. *Honours:* Sidney Bechet Prize, 1987; Best Jazz Recording Prize,

1986, 1988; Bill Coleman Prize, 1989; Django d'Or, 1996. *Leisure interest:* Cinema. *Address:* 5 rue Gracieuse, 75005 Paris, France.

TITELMAN Russ; b. 16 Aug. 1944, Los Angeles, California, USA. Record Co Exec.; Record Prod. m. Carol Wikarska, 10 May 1978. *Career:* Vice-President, A & R Department, and record producer, Warner Brothers Records, New York, 1971-. *Recordings include:* As producer: with Randy Newman: Sail Away, 1972; Good Old Boys, 1974; Little Criminals, 1977; with Ry Cooder: Paradise and Lunch, 1973; with James Taylor: Gorilla, 1975; In The Pocket, 1976; with Rickie Lee Jones: Rickie Lee Jones, 1979; Pirates, 1981; with Paul Simon: Heart and Bones, 1983; with George Benson: 20/20, 1985; with Steve Winwood: Back In The High Life, 1986; Higher Love, 1986; with Miriam Makeba: Sangoma, 1988; with Eric Clapton: Journeyman, 1989; Monkees, Anthology, 1998; Love Shouldn't Hurt, 1998; Very Best of Meatloaf, 1998; Clapton Chronicles, 1999; Also featured on recordings by: Rufus and Chaka Khan; Ladysmith Black Mambazo; Little Feat; George Harrison. *Honours:* Numerous Grammy Awards with: Rickie Lee Jones; Rufus and Chaka Khan; Steve Winwood; Eric Clapton. *Address:* c/o Warner Brothers Records, 75 Rockefeller Plaza, New York, NY 10019, USA.

TIVEY Caroline (Cara); b. 19 Feb. 1959, Wellingborough, Northamptonshire, England. Musician (piano); Backing Vocalist. m. Micky Harris, 10 Oct. 1988. *Musical Education:* Grade 8 piano, Birmingham School of Speech and Drama. *Career:* Worked with: Fine Young Cannibals; Everything But The Girl; Fuzzbox; Billy Bragg; The Lilac Time; Blur; Michael Stipe (REM); Steven Duffy; Numerous world-wide tours; Television appearances include: Top of The Pops; The Tube; The Word; Hootenanny; Letterman; The Late Show; MTV. *Recordings:* with Everything But The Girl: Baby The Stars Shine Bright; with The Lilac Time: and Love For All; The Astronauts; The Laundry; with Billy Bragg: Workers Playtime; Don't Try This At Home; William Bloke; Reaching to the Converted; The Internationale; with Ted Chippington: She Loves You; Man In A Suitcase. *Honours:* No. 1 charity single with Billy Bragg, She's Leaving Home, 1988. *Membership:* Musicians' Union. *Leisure interests:* Hillwalking; Swimming; Playing bridge. *Address:* Flat 1, 48 Somers Rd, Malvern Link, Worcestershire WR14 1JB, England.

TOBIN Karen; b. Drexel Hill, Pennsylvania, USA. Singer; Songwriter; Musician (guitar). m. Tim Boyle, divorced, 2 d. *Education:* College degree in Applied Science Education. *Musical Education:* Vocals, Bryn Mawr Conservatory of Music. *Career:* Recording artist with Arista; Atlantic Records; Nashville; Video; CMT; TNN. *Compositions:* Co-writer, Holdin' Back The Tears, L A Cowboys; Don't Want To Give Up On Love, Sam Harris. *Recordings:* Album: Carolina Smokey Man; Contributions to: Bellevue Cadillac, Prozac Nation; Boston Pops Orchestra, Dash of Pops. *Honours:* Nomination, Country Vocalist and Music Connection, 1992; Nomination, Vocalist of the Year, CCMA, 1995. *Memberships:* AFTRA; SAG; CMA. *Leisure interests:* Bike riding; Hiking; Reading; Cooking; Travel; Snorkeling. *Current Management:* Les Oreck, Weisberg and Associates Management. *Address:* 4451 Canoga Dr., Woodland Hills, CA 91403, USA.

TOCANNE Bruno; b. 19 March 1955, Paris, France. Jazz Musician (drums); Bandleader. 2 s. *Education:* Primary School Teacher studies, University. *Musical Education:* Private lessons with jazz drummers; Workshops with Steve Lacy. *Career:* Bandleader, Bruno Tocanne Réunion; Appearances include: Montréal Jazz Festival; Zagreb Jazz Festival, 1985; Belgrade Jazz Festival, 1985; Tour, Poland, 1992; TF1-France 2, France 3, 1993; Festival Radio-France, 1995; France-Musique (radio), 1995. *Recordings:* Albums: Hors-Sèrie, B Tocanne, S Domancich, Philippe Sellah, Michel Saulvier, 1992; Odessa, Bruno Tocanne Réunion, S Domacich, P Rogers, Erci d'Enfert; Funérals, Sophia Domanisch Trio and Paul Rogers, John Greaves, 1994. *Membership:* Vice-President, UMJ (Union of Jazz Musicians), 1993-. *Current Management:* Asscn Jazzland. *Address:* 80 rue de Stalingrad, 78800 Houilles, France.

TOD A; b. New York, USA. Vocalist; Musician (bass). *Career:* Vocalist, musician, Cop Shoot Cop, 1988–; Several international tours, Japan; Europe; US; Appearances at Reading Festival, 1992, 1994; World tour, 1993; Recorded radio session for John Peel, BBC Radio 1, 1992. *Recordings:* Albums: Consumer Revolt, 1990; White Noise; Ask Questions Later; Release, 1994; EPs: Headkick Facsimile; Piece Man; Suck City; Contributions to: Teleconned: We Want the Air; Firewater, Ponzi Scheme; Clay Pigeons. *Address:* c/o Big Cat Records, PO Box 3074, Chiswick, London W4 4ZN, England.

TODOROV Dimo; Musician (guitar). *Career:* Member, Concurent, 1986–; Numerous concerts, TV and radio appearances, Bulgaria. *Recordings:* Rock For Peace, 1988; Rock Festival In Mitchurin, 1989; The Black Sheep (rock collection), 1992; Something Wet (best-selling album, Bulgaria), 1994; The Best of Bulgarian Rock, 1995. *Honours:* First Prizes: Top Rock Band, Youth Festival, Vidin, 1989; Rock ring, Sofia, 1990; Top Rock Composition: The

Cavalry, 1991; Group of The Year, The Darik Radio Countdown, 1994. *Address:* 40 St Stambolov Blvd, 1202 Sofia, Bulgaria.

TOIVANEN Pekka; b. 27 Sept. 1961, Finland. Musician (tenor saxophone). *Musical Education:* Piano from age 10; Clarinet lessons from age 12. *Career:* Concerts with Kulttis Big Band; Brushane Big Band; Joined jazz department, Sibelius Academy, Helsinki, 1983; Formed own quartet, 1987. *Compositions:* Works for big bands, include Breakfast, commissioned by UMO, 1990. *Honours:* Winners, Finnish Jazz Federation band competition, 1987; Second place, Karlovy Vary contest, 1988. *Address:* Agricolankatu 7 D 94, 00530 Helsinki, Finland.

TOLJA Davor; b. 31 May 1957, Rijeka, Croatia. Singer; Musician (keyboards); Songwriter; Arranger. *Education:* 4 years technical study, Rijeka University. *Musical Education:* 6 years piano, musical school. *Career:* Keyboard player, group: Vrijeme Zemlja; Leader, author, player, singer, group Denis and Denis; Currently solo singer, composer, arranger, musician, producer; Owner, small recording studio. *Recordings:* with Vrijeme I Zemlja: Vrijeme I Zemlja, 1979; with Denis and Denis: Cuvaj Se, 1984; Ja Sam Lazljiva, 1985; Budi Tu, 1988; Solo: Stari Macak, 1990. *Honours:* Gold discs for albums: Cuvaj Se; Ja Sam Lazljiva; Best Pop Album of the Year, Rock (music magazine), Cuvaj Se, former Yugoslavia, 1984; Many pop festival awards for songs and arrangements; As a Composer participated in Eurosong, Dublin, Ireland with song Probudi Me by Group ENI, 1997. *Membership:* CMU (Croatian Music Union). *Leisure interest:* Animal protection. *Address:* Strossmayerova 11, 51000 Rijeka, Croatia.

TOLLY Maria; b. 10 Feb. 1933, Islington, London, England. Composer; Writer. m. Valeriano Rocca, 1 March 1958, divorced 1980, 3 s., 1 d. *Education:* Degree Modern Languages, 1954. *Musical Education:* Computer Music, Electronics, Music Courses, Dartington College, 1991–95. *Career:* Mezzo-soprano touring Mauritius with Rae Woodland, John Lawrenson, Paul Ferris, 1977; Lead singer, Ballet Rambert's Cruel Garden (Christopher Bruce, Lindsay Kemp), 1979, 1980; Composer, performer, Theatre, 1983–89; Singer, songwriter, guitarist, tours Belgium; Netherlands; USSR; Germany; Cuba; Yugoslavia, Italy, Czechoslovakia, 1985–90; Performer, composer, Compact Theatre, 1990–92; Performer, composer, Electro-acoustic concerts, 1992–95; Festivals in London and Sheffield, 1993–97; Composed electro-acoustic music for new ballet Women Unbound, performed by Conundrum Dance Company, premiered at The Place, followed by tour of the UK, 1997; Songwriter, Musical Director for Banner Theatre's new production Redemption Song, premiered in Birmingham followed by tour of the UK, 1997; Musical Director, Telling Tales new production Rise and Run touring UK, 1998; Composed music for small children's dance classes, 1999–2000; Performed own songs at Central Hall Westminster and Hackney Empire with dance interpretations by Lisa Grivello and Suzette Rocca. *Compositions:* Music for the under 5s to be used in schools. *Recordings:* 3 albums, original songs: Gonna Get Up, Voices, Up To Here, 1985–88; Dance drama: About Time, 1991; Musical play: Mrs Columbus Speaks Out, 1992; New works performed, Dartington Summer School; Morley College, 1993–95. *Publications:* Article in Women Live, used in syllabus of Women's Studies, 1989; Chapter, songwriting, Taking Reality By Surprise, Women's Press Ltd, 1990. *Honour:* Winner, GLC Songwriting Competition, Victor Jara Song Competition, 1983; Winner, competition for the composition, Dreams, 1998. *Memberships:* Equity; Writers Guild of Great Britain; Raindance; Screenwriters Workshop. *Leisure interests:* Cinema; Travel; Reading. *Address:* 91 Percival Rd, Enfield, Middlesex, EN1 1QT, England.

TOLONEN Jukka Jorma; b. 16 April 1952, Helsinki, Finland. Musician (guitar, piano); Composer. m. Liisa-Elina, 17 July 1992, 3 s., 1 d. *Musical Education:* Piano lessons from age 8; Sibelius Academy, 1971–72. *Career:* Member, Tasavallan Presidentti, 1967–74; Formed Jukka Tolonen Band, 1976; Also worked with: Bill's Boogie Band (with Bill Öhström); Piirpauke; Christian Sievert and Gilberto Moreira; Several concert tours: Germany; Switzerland; England; Scandinavia; Concerts: Moscow; Estonia; Georgia; Tatarstan; Festivals include: Montreux Jazz Festival; Reading Rock Festival; Roskilde Rock Festival; Television shows, Scandinavia and Germany; Old Grey Whistle Test, England. *Recordings:* 9 solo albums; 8 band albums; 4 acoustic guitar duo albums. *Honours:* Yrjö Award, Finnish Jazz Federation, 1972. *Membership:* Musicians' Union (Sweden). *Leisure interest:* Skiing, once a year.

TOMATITO (José Fernández Torres); b. 1958, Almeria, Andalucía, Spain. Musician (guitar); Composer. *Career:* Flamenco Guitarist; Began musical career in Málaga playing in Tablaos (Flamenco nightclubs); Accompanied Camarón De La Isla for many years; Collaborations: Paco De Lucia; Jose Mercé; Pansequito; Enrique Morente; Carmen Linares; Appeared on numerous flamenco albums; Participated in several film scores and composed music for the German film Bin Ich Schoen; Movie appearances: Sevillanas, 1992; Flamenco (De Carlos Saura), 1995; Vengo, 2000. *Recordings:* Albums: Rosas De Amor, 1987; Barrio Negro, 1991;

Guitarra Gitana, 1996; Spain (with Michel Camilo), 2000; Paseo De Los Castaños, 2001.

TOMICH Michael Robert; b. 24 Feb. 1948, Chiswick, London, England. Musician (bass guitar). m. Anita Kaarinä Viero, 15 Dec. 1971. *Education:* Nescot College, Ewell, Surrey; Stafford College, Kensington. *Musical Education:* Acoustic guitar, Harrow School of Music. *Career:* Played with more than 150 different acts, 1966–83; Constant tours of UK, Europe and USA; Numerous television appearances and radio broadcasts; Acts include: Clyde McPhatter; The Isley Brothers; Bonzo Dog Doo Dah Band; The Skatalites; Joan Armatrading; Peter Banks; Bill Bruford; Heron; Karl Wallinger; Atomic Rooster; Pickettywitch; The Gods; If; The Fantastics. *Recordings:* Early records with: Pickettywitch; Album: Diamond of Dreams, Heron; Many session recordings. *Honours:* Wycombe Radio Personality, 1994. *Memberships:* Musicians' Union; TV DJ Asscn. *Leisure interests:* Hospital radio and mobile DJ. *Address:* 10 Sandford Gardens, High Wycombe, Bucks HP11 1QT, England.

TOMIIE Satoshi, (Loop 7, Black Shells); b. 1966, Tokyo, Japan. Prod.; Remixer; DJ. *Career:* Formed first band in Tokyo, early 1980s; Met Frankie Knuckles at a fashion party and joined the Def Mix crew; Collaborations: Frankie Knuckles; Robert Owens; Diane Charlemagne; Remixed: Madonna; Simply Red; Janet Jackson; Michael Jackson; Gabrielle. *Recordings:* Albums: Full Lick, 2001; Singles: Tears (with Frankie Knuckles), 1989; And I Loved You (with Arnold Jarvis), 1990; The Anthem (as Black Shells), 1994; Darkness, 1998; Inspired, 2000; Love In Traffic, Up In Flames, 2001. *Address:* c/o Sony Music, 550 Madison Ave, New York, USA.

TOMMEY Glenn; b. 27 Aug. 1951, Ross-On-Wye, Herefordshire, England. Recording Engineer; Prod.; Composer; Arranger; Musician (guitar, keyboards, drums). m. Carolyn Jane Kellett, 1 Aug. 1981, 3 s. *Education:* Newton Park College, Bath. *Musical Education:* Newton Park College, Bath; University of Bristol, Certificate in Education (Music). *Career:* Resident Engineer, Crescent Studios, Bath, 1974–87; Freelance Engineer, 1987–; Projects for CBS/Sony, Tokyo; Toshiba/EMI, Tokyo; Peter Gabriel IV; XTC; Big Express; Stranglers; Rupert Holmes; Korgis; Icehouse; Currently, lecturer in music dedicated micro-technology at Bath College of Higher Education. *Honours:* Best Recorded Album of the Year, Precious, Hajime Mizoguchi, 1990. *Membership:* Musicians' Union. *Leisure interests:* Multi-media authoring; Swimming; Electronic construction; Gigging. *Address:* 99 Fairfield Park Rd, Fairfield Park, Bath, Avon BA1 6JR, England.

TOMPKINS David Mark; b. 12 Aug. 1963, Lincoln, England. Musician (double bass, bass guitar). *Education:* First Class Mathematics Degree, 1984; Jazz studies, 1987–90. *Musical Education:* Self-taught. *Career:* Performed with rock band Niadem's Ghost, 1984–86; Concerts include headlining at The Marquee Club, London; Studied Jazz, 1987–90; Member of D'semble, 1990–; Played with Martin Taylor in 1993. *Recordings:* In Sheltered Winds, Niadem's Ghost, 1985; D'Semble, D'Semble, 1992. *Honour:* Featured in Best New Band Reader's Poll with Niadem's Ghost, 'Sounds' magazine, 1986. *Membership:* Musicians' Union. *Leisure interests:* Cinema; Chess; Reading. *Address:* 2 Dawlish Rd, Chorlton, Manchester M21 8XR, England.

TONG Des; b. 30 April 1951, Woking, Surrey, England. Music Prod.; Musician (bass guitar). 1 s., 1 d. *Career:* Played bass guitar with Sad Café; Producer, Time Warp for Damian; Worked with: Real Thing; Lisa Stansfield; Joe Cocker; Alvin Stardust; Cissy Stone; Ruby Turner; Engelbert Humperdinck; Inez and Charlie Foxx; The Jacksons; Music Producer for US Gold. *Recordings include:* Sad Café, The Politics of Exissting; Producer, Ultimate Party Animal Album. *Honour:* Siver disc, Time Warp. *Membership:* PRS. *Leisure interests:* Cooking; Gardening. *Current Management:* Cissy Stone. *Address:* 108 Kingsbury Rd, Erdington, Birmingham B24 8QU, England.

TONG Pete; b. 30 July 1960, Dartford, England. DJ; A & R Exec. *Career:* Became DJ aged 15; Freelance DJ on leaving school; Worked at Blues and Soul and Black Music, 1979–83; Radio broadcaster, Radio Invicta, Capital Radio and Radio London; Radio 1; Originally on Peter Powell show, now DJ with own dance music show; Head of A & R, London/Ffrr Records. *Recordings:* Albums include: Dance Nation; Essential Mix; Ministry of Sound; Pete Tong's Essential Collection, 1997; Essential Millennium, 1999. *Leisure interests:* Travel; Tennis; Swimming; Family. *Address:* c/o London Records, PO Box 1422, Chancellors House, Chancellors Rd, London W6 9SG, England.

TONG Simon; Musician (Guitar, Keyboards). *Career:* Joined The Verve, 1996; Numerous live dates including headlining slot at Reading Festival, 1997; Band split, 1999. *Recordings:* Singles: Bittersweet Symphony; Lucky Man; Drugs Don't Work; Album: Urban Hymns, 1997.

TONTOH Frank; b. 22 May 1964, Kumasi, Ghana. Musician (drums); Writer; Composer. *Musical Education:* 2 years study, piano, Trinity College of Music. *Career:* Member, Osibisa, for 4 years; Aztec Camera, 4 years; Tanita Tikaram, 8 months; Also played with: Tasmin Archer; Level 42; Omar; Mica Paris; Zucchero; Roachford; Courtney Pine; Jason Rebello; Edwyn Collins; Misty Oldland. *Recordings:* Aztec Camera: Stray; Misty Oldland: Supernatural; Kimiko Yamashita: Love and Hate; Tony Remy: 2 albums; Theme to Wired, TV programme; Kiko Veneno: 2 albums (Gold); Bachology: 1 album; Gang of Four: 100 Flowers Bloom, 1998; Jarabe de Palo: Depende, 1998. *Leisure interests:* Cinema; Restaurants; Football and other sports.

TOPAZ Rona Lisa; b. 4 Sept. 1965, New York, USA. Vocalist; Actress; Songwriter; Musician (keyboards). m. 19 Feb. 1988, separated, 1992. *Education:* Associate Applied Sciences Degree, Performing Arts, Five Towns College; City and Guilds, Theatre Skills. *Career:* Recording sessions for Lloyd Clarke; Gary Louca; Sebastian; No Go Productions; Friction; District Six; Kezi O'Neal; Leighton Carter; Musicals include: Destiny; Say Why; Ensemble, Un Ballo In Maschera, for Capital Opera Company; Lead vocalist, solo artist for over 100 events including: Edinburgh Festival Fringe; Highbury Festival; Glasgow Big Day Festival, 1991; Supported 4 Men and A Dog, Glasgow Mayfest, 1992; Shape Arts Festival; International Jazz Day; Fitzrovia Festival; Television includes: Highway, ITV; Kazukos Karaoke Klub, Channel 4; Plays, films. *Compositions include:* Lyricist, No Second Chances, recorded 1991. *Recordings:* Lead vocals, Visualize, 1992. *Publications:* Lyrics: The Divisions Are Fine, London Voices Anthology. *Honours:* Second Prize, Croydon Music Festival; Hon. Mention, Brixton Songwriting Competition. *Memberships:* Musicians' Union; Women In Music. *Leisure interests:* Cooking; Reading; Writing. *Current Management:* Solomon Artists Management International. *Address:* c/o 30 Clarence Rd, Southend-on-Sea, Essex SS1 1BD, England.

TORK Peter, (Peter Halsten Thorkelson); b. 13 Feb. 1944, Washington DC, USA. Musician (bass, guitar, keyboards); Singer; Actor. *Career:* Folk musician with Au Go Go Singers, Los Angeles; Member, The Monkees, 1966–68; 1986–89; Actor, Monkees comedy television series, 1966–68; 33 1/3 Revolutions Per Monkee, TV Special, NBC; Monkees film, Head, premiere 1968; Founder, own groups: Release, 1969; The New Monks, 1981; High school teacher, Santa Monica, early 1970s; Rejoined Monkees, 1986–89. *Recordings:* Albums: The Monkees (No. 1, USA and UK), 1966; More of The Monkees (No. 1, USA and UK), 1967; Headquarters (No. 1, USA), 1967; Pisces, Aquarius, Capricorn and Jones Ltd (No. 1, UK), 1967; The Birds, The Bees and The Monkees, 1968; Then and Now, 1986; Pool It, 1987; Anthology, 1998; Greatest Hits, 1999; Hit singles: Last Train To Clarksville (No. 1, USA), 1966; I'm A Believer (No. 1, USA), 1966; (I'm Not Your) Steppin' Stone, 1967; A Little Bit Me, A Little Bit You, 1967; Alternate Title, 1967; Pleasant Valley Sunday, 1967; Daydream Believer (No. 1, USA), 1967; Valleri, 1968. *Honours:* NARM Awards, Best Selling Group, Best Album, 1967; Emmy, Outstanding Comedy Series, 1967; 3 BMI Awards, 1968; Monkees Day, Atlanta, 1986; Star on Hollywood Walk of Fame, 1989. *Address:* c/o Nationwide Entertainment Services, 2756 N Green Valley Parkway, Suite 449, Las Vegas, NV 89014–2100, USA.

TORRENCE Dean; b. 10 March 1940, Los Angeles, California, USA. Singer. *Education:* Graphics Degree. *Career:* Member, duo Jan and Dean (with Jan Berry), 1957–66; 1973–; Solo artiste, 1966–; Performances include: Dick Clark's Stage Show, Michigan State Fair, 1959; American Bandstand, 1959; New York, with The Animals, Chuck Berry, Del Shannon, 1964; Launched Kittyhawk Graphics, 1967; Member, Legendary Masked Surfers, 1972; California Surfer's Stomp Festival, 1973; Subject of biopic, Dead Man's Curve, 1978. *Recordings:* Albums: with Jan and Dean: Jan and Dean Take Linda Surfin', 1963; Surf City and Other Swingin' Cities, 1963; Drag City, 1964; Dead Man's Curve/The New Girl In School, 1964; The Little Old Lady From Pasadena, 1964; Ride The Wild Surf, 1964; Command Performance/Live In Person, 1965; Jan and Dean Meet Batman, 1966; One Summer Night – Live, 1982; Solo album: Save For A Rainy Day, 1967; Singles: with Jan and Dean include: Linda, 1963; Surf City (No. 1, USA), 1963; Drag City, 1964; Dead Man's Curve, 1964; The New Girl In School, 1964; The Little Old Lady (From Pasadena), 1964; Ride The Wild Surf, 1964; Catch A Wave, 1964; Popsicle, 1966; Contributions to: Hard Rock Café: Surf, 1998. *Current Management:* Bill Hollingshead Productions, 1720 N Ross St, Santa Ana, CA 92706, USA.

TORREZ Juan Pablo; b. 17 Aug. 1946, Cuba. Musician (trombone). m. Elsa Torres, 30 Dec. 1988, 1 s. *Career:* Member, Cuban Orchestra of Modern Music, with Paquito d'Rivera, Artuo Sandoval, Chuco Valdes, 1970s; Played with: Dizzie Gillespie; Don Cherry; Gato Barbieri; Mongo Santamaria; Slide Hampton; Astor Piazolla; Steve Gadd; Paquito D'Rivera; Arturo Sandoval; Hilton Ruiz; Cachao; Nestor Torres; Chocolate Armentaros; Giovanni Hidalgo; Travels throughout Spain; Portugal; France; Switzerland; Italy; Germany; Poland; Mexico; USA; Canada; Currently resident in Miami, USA. *Recordings:* Over 20 include: Trombone Man; From John To Johnny; For Elsa; Banana Split; Foot Tapping. *Honours:* CD trombone, prenominado, Grammy. *Memberships:* ITA; National Academy Recording. *Leisure interest:* Fishing. *Current Management:* Elsa Torres. *Address:* 635 SW 36 Ave, Miami, FlL 33135, USA.

TORU Mitsui; b. 31 March 1940, Saga, Japan. Prof. of Music and English. *Career:* Lecturer, Aichi University, 1964–68; Lecturer, 1969–71, Associate Professor, 1971–83, Professor, 1983–, Kanazawa University. *Publications:* Karaoke Around The World; Global Technology, Local Singing. *Memberships:* The International Musicological Society; International Asscn For The Study of Popular Music. *Address:* Graduate Program In Music, Kanazawa University, Kanazawa, Ishikawa 920–1164, Japan.

TOUNKARA Djelimady; b. 1947, Kita, Mali. Musician (guitar); Songwriter. *Career:* Born into a griot family; Member: Orchestre Misira; Orchestre National A; Pioneer Jazz (first modern dance bands in Mali); Super Rail Band, early 1970s; Later played with acoustic trio Bajourou; Director and conductor with Super Rail Band. *Recordings:* Albums include: Djali Madi Tounkara and Rail Band, 1983; Mansa (with Rail Band), 1995; In Griot Time (compilation), 2000; Sigui, 2001. *Publications:* One of the subjects of Banning Eyre's book In Griot Time. *Honours:* BBC Radio 3 Awards for World Music Award, Best African Artist, 2002. *Address:* c/o Alison Loerke, 12501 11th Ave NW, Seattle, WA 98177, USA.

TOURE Ali Farka; b. 1939, Gourmararusse, Mali. Musician (guitar, n'jurkel, njarka); Farmer. *Musical Education:* Self-taught. *Career:* Formerly, river ambulanceman, Mali; Member, Niafunke District Troupe (music and dance group), 1960s; Sound engineer, Radio Mali, late 1960s; Professional solo artiste, 1974–; Regular tours: UK; Europe; USA; Africa; Major concerts include: US tour with Ry Cooder, 1994; West Africa, Europe, USA, 1995; Womad Festival, Reading, 1995; New Orleans Jazz Festival; London Jazz Festival; Major role against music piracy in Mali; Part-ownership, EMI Mali and Bamako recording studio. *Recordings:* 6 albums, France, 1980s; 4 albums on World Circuit: Ali Farka Toure, 1988; The River, 1990; The Source, 1992; Talking Timbuktu, with Ry Cooder (No. 1, Billboard World Music Charts), 1994; Radio Mali sessions 1970–80, 1996; Niafunké, 1999; As producer: Album for Lobi Traore (Album of Year, Le Monde), 1994; Also appears on: African Blues, 1998; Alkibar, Afel Bocoum, 1999. *Honours:* Grammy, Talking Timbuktu, 1994; European World Music Album of Year, Talking Timbuktu, 1994. *Address:* c/o World Circuit Records, 106 Cleveland St, London W1P 5DP, England.

TOURNAS Kostas; b. 23 Sept. 1949, Tripolis, Greece. Musician (guitar); Singer; Composer; Lyricist; Prod.; Recording Studio Owner. m. Maria, 4 Dec. 1977. *Musical Education:* Harmony; Synthesis; Guitar. *Career:* many tours, Greece and Cyprus; Club appearances; Host or guest, radio and television talk shows; Owner, City Studios, Athens. *Compositions:* More than 500 titles released since 1971. *Recordings:* Aperanta Horafia (Endless Fields); Kiries Kai Kirioi (Ladies and Gentlemen) Duets; Poll/Anthrope (Man). *Publications:* Kostas Tournas' Songs (sheet music and lyrics of his best). *Honours:* Gold, Platinum records; Lyric awards; Forhis offer in Music Award. *Memberships:* AEPI Greece; ETE Greece; FIA. *Leisure interests:* Equipment for music making; Studio work; Multimedia. *Address:* 133 Kafkassou St, Kipseli, Athens, 11364, Greece.

TOUSSAINT Jean-Baptiste Nazaire; b. 27 July 1960, Aruba, Netherlands Antilles. Jazz Musician (tenor and soprano saxophone). *Musical Education:* Saxophone at Miami State, with Charles Cox; Associate degree, Berklee College of Music, Boston, USA. *Career:* Member, Art Blakey's Jazz Messengers, 1982–86; Concerts world-wide include: Jazz Mobile, New York, 1982; Residency, Ronnie Scott's, 1985; Concerts with John Dankworth Band, UK, 1983; Camden Jazz Festival, 1986; Teacher, Guildhall School of Music, 1987–; Formed own bands Jean Toussaint Quartet, 1987; Nazaire, 1992; Tours of Europe and Middle East with Max Roach, 1989; Member, Julian Joseph's band, 1992–94; Also worked with Jason Rebello; Bheki Mseleku; Lenny White, UK, Europe and US, 1995; Numerous world-wide television and radio appearances, 1982-. *Recordings:* Albums: with Art Blakey's Jazz Messengers: The New York Scene, 1984; Live At Kimballs, 1985; Blue Night, 1985; Solo albums: Impressions of Coltrane, 1987; What Goes Around, 1991; Life I Want (co-produced with Jason Rebello), 1995; with Nazaire: Whose Blues, 1992; with Andy Hamilton: Silvershine, 1990; Jamaica By Night (as producer), 1994; with Julian Joseph: The Language of Truth, 1991; Reality, 1993; Also appears on: Back to Back, 1998; Metropolis, 1998. *Memberships:* MCPS; PRS; Broadcast Music Inc. *Leisure interests:* Art; Films (video and cinema); DIY. *Current Management:* Agent: Fish Krish. *Address:* c/o Fish Krish, 6 Carlton House, 319 West End Lane, London NW6 1RN, England.

TOWNEND Richard James Patrick; b. 4 July 1948, London, England. Musician (banjo, guitar, fiddle). *Musical Education:* Self-taught. *Career:* Formed first school bluegrass group in UK; Played at: Royal Albert Hall; Hammersmith Odeon; Cambridge Folk Festival; Appeared on BBC Radio and television Folk and Country music programmes; Also on Kaleidoscope, BBC Radio 4; Partner in Wadhurst Bluegrass Day Venture. *Recordings:* Make The Old Times New, with Rosie Davis, 1995; The Echo Mountain

Band, 1975, (reissued 1995); Fraces on the Frets, 1997. *Memberships:* Musicians' Union; British Bluegrass Music Asscn. *Leisure interest:* Natural History. *Address:* 2 Fairview Cottages, Balaclava Lane, Wadhurst, East Sussex TN5 6EQ, England.

TOWNSHEND Peter Dennis Blandford; b. 19 May 1945, Isleworth, London, England. Musician (guitar) Composer; Publisher; Author. m. Karen Astley, 1968, 1 s., 2 d. *Education:* Ealing Art College. *Career:* Member, UK rock group The Who, 1964–84; Solo artiste, 1979–; Appearances include: National Jazz and Blues festival, 1965, 1966, 1969; Monterey Pop Festival, 1967; Rock At The Oval, 1972; Farewell tour, 1982–83; Live Aid, Wembley, 1985; Reunion tour, 1989; Films include: Tommy; Quadrophenia; The Kids Are Alright; Owner Eel Pie Recording Ltd, 1972–; Established Eel Pie (bookshops and publishing), 1972–; Established Meher Baba Oceanic (UK archival library), 1976–81; Editor, Faber and Faber, 1983-. *Compositions include:* rock operas, Tommy, 1969; Quadrophenia, 1973; Numerous songs for The Who. *Recordings:* Albums: with The Who: My Generation, 1965; A Quick One, 1966; The Who Sell Out, 1968; Direct Hits, 1968; Tommy, 1969; Live At Leeds, 1970; Who's Next, 1971; Meaty Beefy Big and Bouncy, 1971; Quadrophenia, 1973; Odds and Sods, 1974; The Who By Numbers, 1975; The Story of The Who, 1976; Who Are You, 1978; The Kids Are Alright (film soundtrack), 1979; Face Dances, 1981; Hooligans, 1982; It's Hard, 1982; Rarities Vols 1 and 2, 1983; The Singles, 1984; Who's Last, 1984; Who's Missing, 1987; Who's Better Who's Best, 1988; Joined Together, 1990; 30 Years of Maximum R & B, 1994; Solo albums: Who Came First, 1972; Rough Mix, 1977; Empty Glass, 1980; All The Best Cowboys Have Chinese Eyes, 1982; Scoop, 1983; White City, 1985; Another Scoop, 1987; The Iron Man, 1989; Psychoderelict, 1993; The Best of Pete Townshend, 1996; Pete Townshend Live, 1999; Hit singles include: with The Who: I Can't Explain, 1965; Anyway Anyhow Anywhere, 1965; My Generation, 1965; Substitute, 1966; I'm A Boy, 1966; Happy Jack, 1967; Pictures of Lily, 1967; I Can See For Miles, 1967; Pinball Wizard, 1969; See Me Feel Me, 1970; Won't Get Fooled Again, 1970; Join Together, 1972; Who Are You, 1978; You Better You Bet, 1981; Contributor, Sun City, Artists Against Apartheid, 1985. *Publication:* Horse's Neck, 1986. *Honours include:* BRIT Lifetime Achievement Award, 1983; Living Legend Award, International Rock Awards, 1991; with The Who: Gold Ticket, Madison Square Garden, 1979; Ivor Novello Award, Contribution to British Music, 1982; British Phonographic Industry Award, 1983; BRIT Award, Contribution to British Music, 1988; Inducted into Rock 'n' Roll Hall of Fame, 1990; Tony Award for Tommy score, 1993; Grammy Award for original cast recording Tommy, 1993; Dora Mavor Moore Award for Tommy in Toronto, 1994; Olivier Award, Tommy, London, 1997; Q Lifetime Achievement Award for The Who. *Address:* PO Box 305, Twickenham TW1 1TT, England.

TOWNSHEND Simon John; b. 10 Oct. 1960, Ealing, London, England. Songwriter; Musician (guitar, piano); Vocalist. m. Janie Harris, 15 July 1978, 2 s., 1 d. *Career:* First record contract, Warner Bros, age 14; Founder member, On The Air, with Mark Brzezicki, Tony Butler (Big Country), 1980; Solo artiste, Polygram US; Founder member, Animal Soup, with Zak Starkey; Sung part of Newsboy in Tommy, The Who; Singer, Rise, Rise on Smash The Mirror. *Compositions include:* Until Tomorrow; The Way It Is; Girl In New York; Ecstasy Heaven. *Recordings:* Solo: When I'm A Man, 1974; Janie, 1975; Turn It On, 1976; Ready For Action, 1980; I'm The Answer, 1984; Barriers, 1986; Albums: Sweet Sound, 1984 (produced by brother Pete Townshend); Moving Target, 1986; Among Us, 1997; Contributions to: Who's Serious: The Symphonic Music; British Rock Symphony. *Memberships:* Musicians' Union; ASCAP; PRS; PARMA. *Leisure interest:* Keen golfer (7 handicap). *Current Management:* Stir Management. *Address:* 20 Woodgrange Ave, Ealing Common, London W5 3NY, England.

TRAASDAHL Jan Ole; b. 21 Aug. 1958, Odense, Denmark. Assoc. Prof.; Pianist; Composer; Educator. m. Hanne Mulvad, 21 Nov. 1981. *Education:* MA, Musicology, University of Aarhus, Denmark; Studies, Berklee College of Music, Boston, 1981. *Career:* Performed and Recorded with many international Jazz Soloists including Thad Jones, Richard Boone and Bent Jaedig; Conducted Big Bands and Musicals; Composed Music for Big Bands, Vocal Choirs and Theatre. *Recordings:* Panta Rei, 1984; Stig Moller, 1994; Musam Big Band, 1995; Video, TVE Rio de Janeiro, 1995. *Publication:* Rhythmic Music Education, 1996; Music Education In A Multicultural Society, 1999. *Membership:* Vice President, Musicians' Union, Copenhagen, 1996. *Address:* Oster Farimagsgade 45A, 2100 Kobenhavn K, Denmark.

TRACEY Clark; b. 5 Feb. 1961, London, England. Musician (drums); Composer; Arranger. m. Tina May, 15 June 1989, 1 s. *Musical Education:* Largely self-taught. *Career:* Toured with Stan Tracey: USA; India; Australia; Middle East; Europe; 1978–; Own group to Far East; Many television and radio appearances; Solely jazz concerts; Own group toured Far East and Europe. *Compositions:* Stiperstones Suite, for own quintet, 1988; Current original album: Full Speed Sideways, for own sextet; Playing In The Yard, with Charlie Rouse and Stan Tracey; Suite for Quintet at

Finnish Festival, 1997. *Honours:* British Jazz Award, Best Drummer Category; Best Drummer Category, British Jazz Awards, 1997. *Memberships:* PRS; MCPS; PPL; Musicians' Union. *Leisure interests:* Relaxing; Doing nothing. *Current Management:* Bernard Lyons, 73 Eglantine Ave, Belfast BT9 7EU, Northern Ireland; David E Jacobs, 6 Belgrove, Tunbridge Wells, Kent, England. *Address:* 8 Oliver Rd, Hemel Hempstead, Hertfordshire HP3 9PY, England.

TRAERUP Birthe; b. 9 Oct. 1930, Kolding, Denmark. Assoc. Prof.; Musicologist. m. Erik Elias, 1966, 1 s. *Education:* MA, Musicology, Serbocroatian Linguistics and Literature, University of Copenhagen, 1959; Short-stay studies, Yugoslavia, Bulgaria, Albania, Greece, Poland, Czechoslovakia, Hungary, 1963-. *Musical Education:* Ethnomusicological studies in Yugoslavia, 1954–55, 1959–61. *Career:* Research Associate, Danish Folklore Archives, Department of Ethnomusicology, Copenhagen, 1961–64, 1967–68; Consultant, South Slavic Linguistics and Literature, Royal Library of Copenhagen, 1967–86; Adjunct Professor, 1968–72, Associate Professor, Ethnomusicology, 1972–97, Institute of Musicology, University of Copenhagen; Radio programmes and lectures on music of the Balkans, Denmark and other European countries; Research projects on songs, instrumental music in the Muslim community, Gora, Kosovo, folk music of Albanian population, studies on Karol Szymanowski and Denmark. *Publications include:* East Macedonian Folk Songs, 1970; Makedonske folkesange, 1983; Numerous contributions to musicological journals; Video productions. *Honours:* Study Scholarships, 1954–55, 1959–61; Order of Merit, Jugoslavia Esperanto-Ligo, 1964; Hon. Mem., Udruzenje Folklorista Srbije, 1972; Interval Signal Prize, Radio Denmark, 1972; Order of Merit, Ministry for Culture and Art, Poland, 1983. *Address:* Birkevang 158, 3250, Gilleleje, Denmark.

TRAMP Mike; b. Denmark. Vocalist; Singer. *Career:* Vocalist, Danish rock group Mabel; Vocalist, songwriter, White Lion, 1985–92; Vocalist, songwriter, Freak of Nature, 1992–; Numerous tours: UK; Europe; US. *Recordings:* Albums: with White Lion: Fight To Survive, 1985; Pride, 1987; Big Game, 1989; Mane Attraction, 1991; Capricorn, 1998; with Freak of Nature: Freak of Nature, 1993; Gathering of Freaks, 1994; Also featured on Sahara, House of Lords, 1990. *Current Management:* Wyatt Management World-wide. *Address:* 10797 Onyx Circle, Fountain Valley, CA 92708, USA.

TRANCHART Romain; b. 9 June 1976, Paris, France. Musician (piano, guitar); Prod. *Musical Education:* Studied guitar at the American School of Modern Music, Paris, France. *Career:* Lived in Mexico, Algeria and Brazil before relocating to Paris aged 16; Temporarily with rock band Seven Tracks before releasing underground hit single as Funk Legacy; Co-founder of group Modjo, record label Modjo Music (with Yann Destagnol). *Recordings:* Album: Modjo, 2001; Singles: Lady (Hear Me Tonight), 2000; Chillin', 2001; What I Mean, 2001. *Honours:* Modjo first French group to score UK number 1 hit. *Current Management:* Modjo Music. *E-mail:* matt@modjo.com.

TRANS-X (Pascal Leguirand); b. Paris, France. Composer; Lyricist; Vocalist. *Recordings:* New Age albums: Minos; De Harmonia; Gregorian Waves; As Incanta: Ishtar; Voice of The Cybicle; Dance albums: Trans-X; Living On Video/Vivre Sur Video (2m. copies sold world-wide); On My Own. *Honours:* Best Dance Artist, Adisq-Québec; Platinum record, Living On Video. *Membership:* SGAE (Spain). *Current Management:* Michel Huygen (Onira International).

TRAORE Boubacar; b. 1942, Kayes, Mali. Vocalist; Musician (guitar); Songwriter. *Musical Education:* Self-taught; Learned guitar from brother. *Career:* Began composing at an early age; Acted in theatre, 1957–58; Started Les Pionniers Jazz, early 1960s; Also appeared on radio show Les Auditeurs du Dimanche; Earned a living as a tailor, shop keeper and agricultural agent, training orchestras at night; After 20 years absence, invited to perform on Mali TV, 1987; Relocated to France after wife's death, 1989; Discovered by Sterns, recorded 2 CDs and toured Europe and America; Collaborations include: Ali Farka Toure; Toumani Diabate; Keletigui Diabate; Habib Koite; Returned to settle in Bamako, 1991. *Recordings:* Albums include: Mariama, 1990; Kar Kar, 1992; Les Enfants De Pierrette, 1995; Sa Golo, 1996; Maciré, 1999. *Address:* c/o Alison Loerke, 12501 11th Ave NW, Seattle, WA 98177, USA. *E-mail:* loerkeali@aol.com.

TRAORE Koniba; b. 1958, Koutiala, Mali. m. Kone Kadia, 1 s., 3 d. *Education:* Music classes with others at local, regional and national level. *Career:* Orchestral music, 1978–; Biennial competitions and national level, song and dance, 1982, 1984, 1986; Numerous TV appearances and on national radio; Participant, various festivals, including Moscow and Paris. *Compositions:* Ni bè joro, 1996; Balani, 1998. *Honours:* Biennial Artistic Prize, Bamako, 1984; Talabé Prize, Bamako, 1997. *Leisure interests:* Listening to and practising traditional African music; Football. *Address:* s/c A Diabate, PO Box 86, Koutiala, Mali.

TRAORE Rokia; b. 26 Jan. 1974, Bamako, Mali. Vocalist; Musician (guitar); Songwriter. *Career:* Received support from Ali Farka Toure,

1997; Appeared in concert with Habib Koite and Oumou Sangare and recorded first album; Toured US and Europe, 2000; UK TV appearance on Later With Jools Holland, 2001. *Recordings:* Albums: Mouneissa, 1998: Wanita, 2000. *Honours:* Mouneissa sold 40,000 copies in Europe; Radio France Internationale, African Discovery award, 1997; Kora Award, Most Promising Female, 2001; BBC Radio 3 Awards for World Music, Best African Artist nominee, 2001.

TRAVERS Pat; b. Canada. Musician (guitar); Songwriter; Singer. *Career:* Member, The Band; Founder, Pat Travers Band, London, 1976–; Concerts include: Reading Rock Festival, 1976; Worked with Nicko McBain; Scott Gorham; Pat Thrall; Tommy Aldridge; Michael Shrieve. *Recordings:* Albums: Pat Travers, 1976; Makin' Magic, 1976; Putting It Straight, 1977; Heat In The Street, 1978; Go For What You Know – Live, 1979; Crash and Burn, 1980; Radio Active, 1981; Black Pearl, 1982; Hot Shot, 1984; School of Hard Knocks, 1990; Blues Tracks, 1992; Just A Touch, 1993; Blues Magnet, 1994; Halfway to Somewhere, 1995; Lookin' Up, 1996; King Biscuit Live, 1997; Summerdaze '97, compilation, 1997; Whiskey Blues, 1997; Blues Tracks, 1998; Born Under a Bad Sign, 1998. *Current Management:* Don Barnard Management, PO Box 300023, Fern Park, FL 32730, USA.

TRAVIS Randy, (Randy Bruce Traywick); b. 4 May 1959, Marshville, North Carolina, USA. Country Singer; Songwriter; Musician (guitar). m. Lib Hatcher (Mary Elizabeth Robertson), 1991. *Career:* Played local clubs with brothers; Resident, Charlotte nightclub owned by Lib Hatcher, 1977; Early recordings as Randy Traywick; Resident singer, as Randy Ray, Nashville Palace, 1992; Name changed to Randy Travis, 1985–; Joined Grand Ole Opry, 1986. *Recordings:* US Country No. 1 hits: On The Other Hand; Diggin' Up Bones; Forever and Ever, Amen; I Won't Need You Anymore (Always and Forever); Gone Too Long; I Told You So; Honky Tonk Moon; Deeper Than The Holler; Is It Still Over; It's Just A Matter of Time; Hard Rock Bottom of Your Heart; Forever Together; Look Heart No Hands; This Is Me; Whisper My Name; Before You Kill Us All; Out of My Bones; Hole; Albums: Randy Ray Live At The Nashville Palace, 1982; Storms of Life, 1986; Always and Forever, 1987; Old 8 X 10, 1988; An Old Time Christmas, 1989; No Holdin' Back, 1989; Heroes and Friends (duets with Merle Haggard, George Jones, Loretta Lynn, Dolly Parton, Tammy Wynette and B B King), 1990; High Lonesome, 1991; Greatest Hits Vols 1 and 2, 1992; This Is Me, 1994; Full Circle, 1996; You and You Alone, 1998; A Man Ain't Made of Stone, 1999. *Honours include:* Grammy Award, Best Country Newcomer, 1986; Male Vocalist of the Year, Country Music Asscn, 1988. *Current Management:* Lib Hatcher-Travis Management, 1610 16th Ave S, Nashville, TN 37212, USA.

TRAVIS Theo (Theodore John); b. 7 July 1964, Birmingham, England. Musician (tenor and soprano saxophones and flute); Composer. m. Madelyn J Cohen, 24 May 1992. *Education:* BMus (Hons), Manchester University. *Musical Education:* Grade 8 flute; Saxophone to BMus Final recital standard. *Career:* Toured Spain with NYJO, 1985; Leader, Theo Travis Band; Also performed with: John Etheridge; Jim Mullen; John Marshall; Slim Gaillard; Radio includes: Jazz Parade, BBC Radio 2, playing original compositions, 1993; Interview, WKCR-FM, New York; Toured Japan with Mick Karn, 1997; Arts Council Tour for improvising trio with John Marshall (drums) and Mark Wood (guitar), 1998. *Compositions:* Broad Street Changes Suite for jazz septet, commissioned by West Midlands Arts; Commissioned by Derby Metro Cinema to write with Dave Sturt new music for Hitchcock silent film, The Lodger. *Recordings:* Solo: 2 AM, 1993; View From The Edge, 1994; with The Other Side: Dangerous Days, 1995; Secret Island, 1996; with Marshall Travis Wood, Bodywork, 1998; Guest appearances: Porcupine Tree, Mick Karn and Dick Heckstall-Smith. *Honours:* Financial Times Best Newcomer, 1993; Best British CD, View From The Edge, 1994; Brit Jazz Awards Nomination, Rising Star, 1995, 1996. *Memberships:* Musicians' Union; PRS; Equity. *Leisure interests:* Walking in Scottish Highlands; Cinema; Listening to music. *Address:* 20 Strathmore Gardens, Finchley, London N3, England.

TRENT Tammy; b. 11 April 1968, Grand Rapids, Michigan, USA. Musician (drums, percussion). m. Trent Lenderink, 18 Aug. 1990. *Education:* 1 year college. *Career:* Signed to Rex Music, Brentwood, Tennessee. *Recordings:* Debut album, 1995; First radio single: Your Love Is 4 Always (No. 1, Christian Hits Radio charts); Albums: Tammy Trent, 1996; You Have My Heart, 1997. *Membership:* BMI. *Leisure interests:* Basketball; Volleyball; Softball; Weightlifting; Dancing; Singing. *Current Management:* Lenderink Management. *Address:* 1271 House Rd, Belmont, MI 49306, USA.

TRETOW Michael Bo; b. 20 Aug. 1944. Recording Engineer. m. Lilian B, 1 s., 1 d. *Education:* Degree, Electronic Engineering, 1966. *Career:* Recording Engineer, around 40 Gold Records for early work; Engineer, all ABBA albums; Independent Engineer and Producer, 1980–; Composer, music for film and video, and commercials. *Composition:* Swedish TV Station Call. *Recordings:* Hubba Hubba Zoot Zoot, 1981; Den Makalösa Manicken, 1986. *Honours:* Gold Camera Award, 1988; International TV,

Cinema and Radio Award, 1988; Monaco Radio Contest, 1989. *Membership:* SSES. *Leisure interest:* Old recording equipment. *Address:* Virvelvindsvagen 8, 161 28 Bromma, Sweden.

TRETTINE Caroline Anne Halcrow; b. 4 Sept. 1958, Kingston-on-Thames, Surrey, England. Singer; Songwriter; Musician (guitar); Systems Analyst. *Education:* BA Hons, Bristol University, English with French. *Musical Education:* Self-taught songwriting, guitar. *Career:* Singer, writer, guitarist with Blue Aeroplanes, 1984–85; Solo artiste, tours with: Billy Bragg; Christy Moore; Radio 1 sessions for Richard Skinner; Bob Harris, 1985–95; Member, Library of Love, 1995. *Compositions include:* Sleep With Me; Guilty; Hope. *Recordings:* with Blue Aeroplanes: Action Painting EP: Le Petit Cadeau de Don Juan, 1985; Be A Devil EP, 1990. *Memberships:* PRS; Musicians' Union. *Leisure interests:* Cinema; Tennis; Comedy writing. *Current Management:* Sincere Management, 421 Harrow Rd, London W9, England.

TREVISAN Luciano (Fricchetti); b. 25 Sept. 1959, Venice, Italy. Musical Man.; Promoter; Publisher. *Musical Education:* DAMS, Bologna University. *Career:* Involved in Cultural Association, ARCI Manager; Record Distributors until 1986; Partner in record company, Materiali Sonori; Promoter, live events; Artist manager, 1989–; Partner, Ossigeno, Music Publishing Company, 1993–; Partner, Evolution Music, 1995; Alma Music, 2000-. *Publications:* Compra O Muori (book). *Honours:* Gold and Platinum records for album: Na Bruta Banda by Pitura Freska; Gold Record, Gran Calma, Pitura Freska. *Memberships:* Publisher Mem., SIAE. *Leisure interests:* Travel; Video. *Current Management:* Pitura Freska; Skardy; Farenheit 451; Fabio Furian. *Address:* Via Marovich, 5–30030 Mestre Venezia, Italy.

TREWAVAS Peter; b. 15 Jan. 1959, Middlesbrough, Cleveland, England. Musician (bass). *Career:* Member, The Metros; Bassist, UK progressive rock group Marillion, 1982–; Tours, UK; Europe; North America; Concerts include: Theakston Festival, 1982; Reading Festival, 1982, 1983; Nostell Priory Festival, 1982, 1984; Glastonbury Festival, 1983; Support to Rush, New York's Radio City Music Hall, 1983; Milton Keynes Bowl, 1984; Monsters of Rock Festival, Castle Donington, 1985; Colombian Volcano Appeal Concert, 1986; Welcome To The Garden Party, 1986. *Recordings:* Albums: Script For A Jester's Tear, 1983; Fugazi, 1984; Real To Reel, 1984; Misplaced Childhood, 1985; Brief Encounter, 1986; Clutching At Straws, 1987; B-Sides Themselves, 1988; The Thieving Magpie, 1988; Holidays In Eden, 1991; A Singles Collection 1982–92, 1992; Brave, 1994; Afraid of Sunlight, 1995; Made Again, 1996; This Strange Engine, 1997; Radiation, 1998; with Transatlantic: Smpte, 2000; Singles include: Market Square Heroes, 1982; He Knows You Know, 1983; Garden Party, 1983; Punch and Judy, 1984; Assassing, 1984; Kayleigh (No. 2, UK), 1985; Lavender, 1985; Heart of Lothian, 1985; Incommunicado, 1987; Sugar Mice, 1987; Warm Wet Circles, 1987; Freaks, 1988; Hooks In You, 1989; Uninvited Guest, 1989; Easter, 1990; Cover My Eyes (Pain and Heaven), 1991; No One Can, 1991; Dry Land, 1991; Sympathy, 1992. *Current Management:* Hit and Run Music Ltd, 30 Ives St, London SW3 2ND, England.

TRIBBLE (Brian Evans); b. 20 March 1953, Coventry, England. Musician (Bass, Keyboards, Guitar); Singer. Divorced, 5 s., 1 d. *Career:* Partner, Horizon Recording Studios; Extensive session work, touring with rock bands in Europe and the USA; Member, rock, reggae and jazz outfits in West Indies; Recording for numerous labels; Advertising and video soundtrack work; Member, Chainsaw; Rumrunners; The Trial; Owner/ Manager, STI/Pro-Audio; Graphic design work, arrangements, session work; Playing, programming and production of samples for dance producers; Promoter for new artists; Audio producer. *Compositions include:* The Last Great Bank Raid; The Hellpits of Nightfang; City Life; Accident Victim; Rock 'n' Roll Gambler; Werewolf; And many more as co-composer with other musicians. *Recordings include:* Police and Politicians; Devil's Daughter; Bolt From The Black; Pissed Again; Twisted and Dysfunktional; And many more with other artists/compilations. *Leisure interests:* Photography; Computer graphics; Swimming; Travel; Electronics.

TRICKY (Adrian Thaws); b. Bristol, England. Rapper; Songwriter. *Career:* Rapper, Wild Bunch; Solo artiste with singer Martina; Regular collaborations as singer/writer with Massive Attack; Leader, recording project Nearly God (duets with Björk, Alison Moyet, Terry Hall, Neneh Cherry), 1996; Concerts include: T In The Park Festival, Glasgow, 1995; Reading Festival, 1995. *Recordings:* Single: Overcome, Wild Bunch; Solo singles: Overcome, 1995; Black Steel, 1995; The Hell EP, 1995; Pumpkin, 1995; Grassroots, 1996; Poems, 1996; Makes Me Wanna Die, 1997; 6 Minutes, 1998; For Real, 1999; Albums: with Massive Attack: Blues Lines, 1991; Protection, 1995; Solo albums: Maxinquaye (No. 1, UK), 1995; Nearly God, 1996; Pre-Millenium Tension, 1996; Angels with Dirty Faces, 1998; Juxtapose, 1999. *Honours:* Face Magazine, Best Album of the Year, Blues Lines, 1991; BRIT Award Nominations: Best Album of Year, with Massive Attack, 1991; Best Male Artist, Best Dance Act, Best Newcomer, 1996; Gold record, Maxinquaye, 1995; Nomination, Mercury Music Prize; Q Award, Best Producer, 1995. *Current Management:* Fruit

Management. *Address:* Unit 104, Saga Centre, 326 Kensal Rd, London W10 5BZ, England.

TRITT Travis; b. 9 Feb. 1963, Maretta, Georgia, USA. Country Singer; Songwriter. m. Theresa, 12 April 1997. *Career:* Recording artiste, 1990–; Recorded, toured with Marty Stuart, included No-Hats Tour. *Compositions include:* Here's A Quarter (Call Someone Who Cares); Help Me Hold On, 1990; Anymore, 1991; Tell Me I Was Dreaming, 1994; Ten Feet Tall and Bulletproof, 1994; More Than You'll Ever Know, 1995. *Recordings include:* Anymore; Lord Have Mercy On The Working Man; Albums: Country Club, 1990; It's All About To Change, 1991; T-R-O-U-B-L-E, 1992; A Travis Tritt Christmas: Loving Time of Year, 1992; Rhythm, Country and Blues; The Restless Kind; Greatest Hits – From The Beginning, 1995; No More Looking Over My Shoulder, 1998. *Publication:* Ten Feet Tall and Bulletproof, autobiography, 1992. *Honours:* CMA Horizon Award, 1991; Grammy Award, 1992. *Current Management:* Falcon Goodman Management. *Address:* 1012 16th Ave S, Nashville, TN 37212, USA.

TROCMÉ Elisa Andréa; b. 21 Aug. 1955, Pennsylvania, USA. Musician (counter-bass, Bb clarinets, other winds). 2 s., 1 d. *Education:* History, French popular arts and traditions, EHESS, Paris. *Musical Education:* Private lessons, workshops with B Vitet; Tamia; Steve Lacy; Michel Fano; George Benjamin; Robert Aitken; Georges Aperghis; Toru Takemitsu; Barre Phillips. *Career:* Instrument making with B Vitet; Music Education Program with P Maretan, Paris, 1978; Irving Plaza/BCBG, New York, 1980; Le Grand Rex; New Morning; Centre Georges Pompidou; Musée d'Art Moderne; Grand Palais dance, music, plastic arts creations; Improvised music and dance encounters, Toulouse, 1992–; Art Wars, La Mama, Theater, New York, 1980; Cinema de Minuit, directed by Patricia Bardon, ProdA2, Paris, 1984; The Weapons of The Spirits, directed by Pierre Sauvage (prize-winning documentary, Cannes, 1987; 666, Julie West video-dance production, S Rougier, Paris, 1985. *Publications:* Clarinette magazine; Translations for Télérama; L'Evenement du Jeudi; L'Humanité; Melody Maker. *Honour:* Oscar de Mécémat (P Mariétam). *Membership:* ESEM (Euro Semionar of Ethnomusicology). *Leisure interests:* Life; People; Democracy; Cinema; Travel. *Current Management:* Christianne Bories. *Address:* 282 Route de Seysses, 31100 Toulouse, France.

TROTT Milton; b. 4 Nov. 1958, Adelaide, South Australia. Screen Composer Film/TV (Keyboards); Creative Consultant. *Education:* Classical Piano, Violin, Cello, Guitar, Drums, Flute. *Career:* Keyboard Player/Songwriter/Producer; Numerous local bands session too; Member, Prestigious Arts Education, 1982; Team (SA Govt), Music/Multi Media, 1985; Winner, Pot Luck, TV Talent Quest, 1989; Mr Music, Theatrespots, 1986; Musician, Magick Circus, Soundtracks TV Documentaries, 1988. *Compositions:* Sugar is Sweet, 1982; The Greens, 1984; H20, 1983. *Recordings:* Music CD, Aurora Australis, 1995. *Honour:* Young Composers Award, 1983. *Memberships:* Australian Screen Composers Asscn; Australian Performing Right Asscn. *Leisure interests:* Loosely scripted home videos, parties, World music. *Address:* Post Office Aldgate, South Australia 5154.

TROUT Walter Cooper; b. 6 March 1951, Atlantic City, New Jersey, USA. Muscian (guitar, harmonica, trumpet). m. Marie Braendgaard, 2 s. *Education:* College, 1 year. *Musical Education:* Classical trumpet, 7 years; Self-taught, guitar, harmonica. *Career:* Played with John Lee Hooker, Big Mama Thornton, Joe Tex, Pee Wee Crayton, 1979–80; Lead guitarist, harmonica, Canned Heat, 1984–89; Lead guitar, John Mayall's Bluesbreakers, 1984–89; Formed the Walter Trout Band, 1989; Name change to Walter Trout and the Radicals, 1998. *Recordings:* With Canned Heat: The Boogie Assault, 1981; Heat Brothers '84, 1984; John Mayall's Bluesbreakers: Behind The Iron Curtain, 1985; The Power of The Blues, 1987; Chicago Line, 1988; Life In The Jungle, 1992; Walter Trout Band: Life In The Jungle, 1989; Prisoner of a Dream, 1990; The Love That We Once Knew, 1990; No More Fish-Jokes Live, 1992; Radio Records, 1992; Transistion, 1992; Motivation of Love, 1992; No More Fish-Jokes Live, 1992; Tremble, 1994; Still Got The Blues, 1994; Tellin' Stories, 1994; Breaking The Rules, 1995; Where Blues Meets Rock, 1995; Jeffology (tribute to Jeff Beck), 1995; Tribute To Stevie (tribute to Stevie Ray Vaughn), 1996; Walter Trout, 1998; Livin' Everyday, 1999; Go The Distance, 2001. Blues Revue, cover story, October 2000. *Honour:* BBC Listeners' Poll, All Time Greatest Guitarists, '93, voted # 6 of 20. *Membership:* ASCAP. *Leisure interests:* Composing music; Time with family. *Current Management:* Fish-Net Productions Inc, 4933 W Craig Rd, Suite 228, Las Vegas, NV 89130, USA. *Address:* PO Box 246, Huntington Beach, CA 92648, USA.

TROW Zane Roderick; b. 25 Jan. 1956, London, England. Composer; Preformer; Artistic Dir. *Musical Education:* Self-taught. *Career:* Composer in Residence, Civilian Theatre; Composer, Performer, Common Stock Theatre Company; Artistic director, Nextwave Festival; Chairman, Contemporary Music Events Company. *Compositions:* The Wolves; Hot Time; Dream Mamma. *Recordings:* Big River. *Honours:* Numerous Grants, Australian Council for the Arts. *Memberships:* Actors Equity; PRS. *Leisure*

interests: Travel; Journalism. *Address:* Lot 15, Clifton Dr., North Maclean, Queensland 4280, Austrlia.

TROWER Robin; b. 9 March 1945, Southend, Essex, England. Musician (guitar). *Career:* Founder member, The Paramounts, 1962–66; Founder member, Procul Harum, 1967–71; Solo artiste, 1971–; Formed Jude; Miami Founder, Robin Trower Band; Founder, band BLT, 1981; Pop Festival, 1968; Palm Springs Pop Festival, 1969; Toronto Rock Festival, 1969; Atlantic City Pop Festival, 1969; Isle of Wight Festival, 1970. *Recordings:* Albums with Procul Harum: Procul Harum, 1967; Shine On Brightly, 1968; A Salty Dog, 1969; Home, 1970; Solo: Twice Removed From Yesterday, 1973; Bridge of Sighs, 1974; For Earth Below, 1975; Robin Trower Live, 1976; Long Misty Days, 1976; In City Dreams, 1977; Caravan To Midnight, 1978; Victims of The Fury, 1980; Back It Up, 1983; Beyond The Mist, 1985; Passion, 1987; Portfolio, 1987; Take What You Need, 1988; No Stopping Anytime, 1989; In the Line of Fire, 1990; 20th Century Blues, 1994; New Haven 1977; King Biscuit Flower Hour, 1996; Someday Blues, 1997. *Current Management:* Stardust Management, 4600 Franklin Ave, Los Angeles, CA 90027, USA.

TRUBETSKY Tonu (Prince); b. 24 April 1963, Revala, Tallinn, Estonia. Singer; Composer; Poet; Writer; Actor; Video Dir. m. Anu Trubetsky, 28 May 1988, 1 s., 2 d. *Education:* Diver, Engineer forces. *Musical Education:* Rock 'n' Roll High School. *Career:* Lead singer, Vennaskond, 1984–; Lead singer, Felis Ultramarinus, 1986; Prince Trubetsky and JMKE, 1986; The Un Concern, 1988; Solo artist, 1993; Business venture: Vennaskond Ltd; Films: Soda (War), 1987; Hysteria (Hysterics), 1993; Videos with Vennaskond: Elagu Proudhon! (Long Live Proudhon!), 1994; Riga My Love, 1995. *Recordings:* with Vennaskond: Ltn Schmidt'i Pojad (The Sons of Lieutenant Schmidt), 1991; Girl In Black, 1991; Rockpiraadid (The Rock Pirates), 1992; Usk. Lootus. Armastus (Faith. Hope. Love), 1993; Vaenlane Ei Maga (The Enemy Is Not Sleeping), 1995; Voluri Tagasitulek (Return of The Wizard), 1994; Inglid Ja Kangelased (Angels and Heroes), 1995. *Publications:* Books: Pogo, 1989; Inglid Ja Kanglased (Angels and Heroes), 1992; Anarhia (Anarchy), 1994; Daam Sinises (Lady In Blue), 1994. *Honours:* Levijaagup, 1990; 2 Gold records, 1993. *Leisure interests:* Ethnography; History. *Address:* Vennaskond, PO Box 2225, 0035 Tallinn, Estonia.

TRUE Roger; b. 2 June, Greensboro, NC, USA. Country Singer; Musician (Guitar). *Career:* City Stage Celebration; The Lexington Barbecue Festival; Summerfield Founder's Day Celebration; Clubs: The Blind Tiger; Kilroy's; Playing, Piedmont Triad; International Country Music Fan Fair, Nashville; Starred and Sang in motion picture, The Dam. *Recordings:* Crazy Arms; There Stands the Glass; Your Cheatin' Heart; Walk Through This World With Me; Tonight the Bottle Let Me Down; El Paso; Before the Next Teardrop Falls; Good Hearted Woman; Take This Job and Shove It; Don't Rock the Jukebox; We'll Burn that Bridge; Friends in Low Places, many more. *Honours:* Most Promising Vocal of Tomorrow Third Place, North Carolina Country Music Assocation, 1993; NCCMA Award Winner. *Memberships:* BMI; ASCAP. *Current Management:* Webb Pierce Enterprises, 1521 Clayton Ave, Nashville, TN 37217, USA.

TRUESDALE Tommy; b. 17 Nov. 1937, Annbank, Ayr, Scotland. Vocalist; Entertainer; Actor; Radio Presenter. m. Marjory, 9 Feb. 1972. *Musical Education:* Self-taught. *Career:* Television appearances: One Night Stand, Scottish TV, 1965; The Best Disco In Town, Scottish TV, 1979; The Singer and The Song, BBC, 1981; Various television and radio interviews; British headliner, Great Scottish Country Music Festival, Wonderwestworld, Ayr, 1994. *Recordings:* Albums: C'mon Everybody, 1979; Sings Country, 1985; The Best of T T Album, 1990; A Tree In The Meadow, 1993; Tommy Truesdale Favourites, 2000; Single: The United Men of Ayr, 2000. *Publications:* Columnist, Country Music News and Roots Magazine. *Honours:* Scottish Country Music Fellowship Award, Top Male Vocalist, 1989, 1990. *Membership:* British Country Music Asscn. *Leisure interests:* Walking the dog; Watching boxing, football; Listening to all types of music. *Address:* 3 McColgan Pl., Ayr KA8 9PU, Scotland.

TRUJILLO Robert; Musician (Bass). *Career:* Member, Suicidal Tendencies; Numerous live dates in US; Member, side project, Infectious Grooves, with Mike Muir and other guest musicians; Ozzy Osbourne featured as guest on debut album; Support slot to Blizzard of Oz No More Tears tour. *Recordings:* With Suicidal Tendencies: Suicidal Tendencies, 1983; Join the Army, 1987; How Will I Laugh Tomorrow When I Can't Even Smile Today, 1988; Controlled by Hatred, 1989; Lights, Camera, Revolution, 1990; F.N.G., compilation, 1992; The Art of Rebellion, 1992; Still Cyco After All These Years, 1993; Suicidal for Life, 1994; Prime Cuts, 1997; Friends and Family, compilation, 1998; Six the Hard Way, EP, 1998; FreeDumb, 1999; With Infectious Grooves: The Plague that Makes Your Booty Move, 1991; Sarsippius' Ark, 1993; Groove Family Cyco, 1994.

TRUSSARDI Louis; b. 6 June 1938, Clichy, France. Musician (contrebass). m. Martine Teyssier, 31 Jan. 1972, 3 s. *Musical Education:* 2 years, Conservatory de Versailles. *Career:* Played with: Chet Baker;

Kenny Clarke; Dizzy Gillespie; Stéphane Grappelli; 'Philly' Joe Jones; Art Taylor; Louis Hayse; Richie Cole; Teddy Edwards; Frank Morgan; Milt Jackson; Art Simmons; Dusco Boy Kovic. *Recordings:* Solo album: Vendredi 14; Also recorded with: Maurice Vander; 'Philly' Joe Jones; Kenny Clarke; Stéphane Grappelli; Chet Baker. *Membership:* SACEM. *Leisure interests:* Piccolo bass; Classical guitar. *Address:* 3 rue d'Ablis, 78660 Prunay en Yvelines, France.

TSE Nicholas, (Nicholas Tse Ting Fung); b. 29 Aug. 1980, Hong Kong. Vocalist; Actor. *Musical Education:* Professional vocal training in Japan, 1996. *Career:* Son of famous actor parents Patrick Tse Yin and Deborah Lai; Moved with family to Vancouver, Canada, aged 7; Teen-pop star and high profile actor; Film roles include: Young and Dangerous – The Prequel, 1998; Gen-X Cops, 1999; Time and Tide, 2000; Master Q, 2001; Co-directed: Heroes In Love, 2001; Records in Mandarin and Cantonese languages. *Recordings:* Albums: My Attitude, Fun, 1997; Horizons, Music Video Karaoke, 1998; Believe, Grateful For Your Love, Most Wanted, 1999; Zero Distance, Understand, 20 Twenty, Viva, Viva Live, 2000; Senses, Jade Butterfly, 2001. *Honours:* Hong Kong Film Award, Best New Actor, 1999; Numerous local awards for music. *Address:* c/o Fitto Entertainment Co Ltd, 28/F Emperor Group Centre, 288 Hennessy Rd, Wanchai, Hong Kong.

TSENOVA Julia; b. 30 July 1948, Sofia, Bulgaria. Composer; Pianist. m. Stefan Sandulov, 1 d. *Musical Education:* Piano, Musical Academy in Sofia, 1972; Composition, 1974; Associated Professor Dean, Department of Pop and Jazz Music, 1997. *Career:* Pianist and Composer. *Compositions:* Symphony; Movement for Orchestra; Cantus Firmus a Due; That Means all Gods. *Honours:* Many awards for chamber, choir and children's music. *Memberships:* Union of Bulgarian Composers; International Society for Contemporary Music. *Address:* Vassil Levski 4, 1000 Sofia, Bulgaria.

TSHMALA Mufubela; b. 11 March 1957, Ilebok Kasai Occidental, Congo. Researcher; Musician (Flute, Guitar); Singer; Composer. m. Petronie Mbombo Malumba, 1988, 4 s., 3 d. *Education:* Graduated, Administration and Management of Cultural Enterprises. *Career:* Composed music for film, La Pipe, 1983; Composed jingles for African Radio, 1983; Numerous TV and radio appearances, and work as Producer; Puppeteer and drag artist; Played in nightclubs and hotels, Kinshasa; Flautist; Teacher of Music; Researcher into traditional and modern mixing techniques; Guitarist, Flautist and Singer in group, Msumuenu. *Compositions:* Music for Le Refuge; Music for Le Crapeaud Chez Ses Beaux Parents; Revue Noire à Kinshasa No 21, 1996. *Recordings:* Naza Balado Te, 1982; Many contributions with various groups. *Publication:* La Vie de Robert le Diable, lyric drama, Colmar, France, 1984. *Honours:* First Prize, Orchestration, Festival of Central African Music, 1982; Festpam, 1996; Brazzaville Festijazz, Kinshasa, 1999. *Membership:* Asscn des Musiques de Recherche du Congo. *Leisure interests:* Sport; Tourism and travelling. *Address:* PO Box 14110, Kinshasa, Africa.

TSISKARIDZE Kakha; b. 4 June 1976, Batumi, Republic of Georgia. Musician (Drummer, Pianist, Singer, Percussionist). *Musical Education:* Batumi Musical College. *Career:* Several Concerts with S Pavliashvili on the major stages of Georgia, Russia, Miami, USA. *Compositions:* Several, Jazz, Soul, Funk, AC Jazz. *Recording:* debut album, Is Erti (The One), 1999. *Honours:* The Best Drummer of the Jazz Music Festival, Batumi, 1992; Drummer of the Year, Margarette Festival, 1996; Best Drummer of the Year (Georgia), 1996. *Memberships:* Dianaland Club, Batumi. *Leisure interests:* Soccer; Basketball; Reading; Fashion. *Address:* Gincharadzo St N 14, 384515 Batumi, Republic of Georgia.

TSUI Trix Ko-Chuan; b. 20 Oct. 1953, Taipei, Taiwan. Musician (guitar) Concert Promoter; DJ. m. Farie Hsiu-Ching Le, 1 Dec. 1979, 1 d. *Education:* Graduate, World College of Journalism and Communication. *Musical Education:* Self-taught. *Career:* Concert Promoter, Stage Manager: Chick Corea's Acoustic and Electric Band; Lee Ritnour; Brecker Brothers; Peabo Bryson and Patti Austin; Stage Manager: INXS; B B King; Hard Rock Cafe, Taipei, 1992–94; Leader, guitarist: Rock City Band, 1971–80; Diplomats, 1980–93; Now house band of Hard Rock Cafe, Taipei, Name changed back to Rock City Band, 1994–95; Radio DJ, BBC, TBC; Technical Director, Gibson and Digitech; Musical Cosultant, Taipei Communicating Arts (from the system of MIT). *Recordings:* Producer debut album by Miss Jade Lee: Hermits; Blindman Pop Group: Eden; Welfare Foundation's tribute single and collection of: International Family Years. *Publications:* Columnist for: Non-Classical Music Magazine; Audio and CD Shopper; Liberty Time newspaper. *Membership:* Musical Mountain Communication. *Leisure interest:* Collecting guitars. *Address:* 3F No. 16, Alley 88, Sec 2, Pao-Fu Rd, Yung-Ho, Taipei, Taiwan.

TUBRIDY Michael; b. 6 Aug. 1935, County Clare, Ireland. Civil Engineer. m. Céline Kelly, 25 Sept. 1961, 2 d. *Education:* University level, UCD, Dublin. *Musical Education:* Self-taught. *Career:* Longtime member, Ceoltóirí Cualann, Castle Céilí Band, The Chieftains, including various concerts, television, radio appearances. *Recordings:* Various recordings with

groups; Solo album: The Eagle's Whistle. *Publications:* Compiler of music for Irish Traditional Music, 1995; Irish Traditional Music, Book 2, 1998; A Selection of Irish Traditional Step Dances, 1998. *Membership:* IMRO. *Leisure interests:* Folk dancing; Astronomy. *Address:* 42 Woodlawn Park, Dundrum, Dublin 14, Ireland.

TUCKER David; b. 23 July 1960, Manchester. Musician. *Education:* General Music Theory, Composing and Synchronising music for film and video. *Career:* Guitarist, New Wave Pop Groups; Improvising Guitarist, Allan Tomlinson Trio, Scatter, The Guided Muscle; Radio Appearances; Principal Conductor for the London Improvisers Orchestra. *Recordings:* Mellatron; The Fall. *Leisure interests:* Experimental Film Maker; Writer.

TUCKER Maureen; b. 1945, New Jersey, USA. Musician (drums). *Career:* Musician, Velvet Underground, 1965–71; Solo artiste, 1982–; Residency, Café Bizarre; House band, Andy Warhol's Factory arts collective, New York; Member, Warhol's multi-media show, The Exploding Plastic Inevitable, 1966; Concerts include: Montréal World Fair, Canada, 1967; Reunions with Velvet Underground, France, 1990; Wembley, London, 1993. *Recordings:* with The Velvet Underground: The Velvet Underground and Nico, 1967; White Light, White Heat, 1968; The Velvet Underground, 1969; Loaded, 1970; Various compilations and collections; Solo albums: Playing Possum, 1982; Moejadkatebarry, 1987; Life In Exile After Abdication, 1989; I Spent A Week There The Other Night, 1991; Dogs Under Stress, 1994. *Honour:* Inducted into Rock 'n' Roll Hall of Fame (with Velvet Underground), 1996.

TUCKER Paul; b. 1969, Cambridge, England. Musician; Songwriter. *Education:* Newcastle University. *Career:* Member, The Lighthouse Family, 1994–; Television includes: Top of The Pops. *Recordings:* Album: Ocean Drive, 1995; Postcards from Heaven, 1997; Singles: Lifted, 1995; Ocean Drive (used for film soundtrack Jack and Sarah), 1995. *Current Management:* Kitchenware, 7 The Stables, St Thomas St, Newcastle-Upon-Tyne, Tyne and Wear NE1 4LE, England.

TUCKER Tanya; b. 10 Oct. 1958, Seminole, Texas, USA. Country Singer. *Career:* Singing at country fairs as a teenager; Recording artist, 1972–; Regular concerts include Grand Ole Opry; Film appearance: Jeremiah Johnson (with Robert Redford). *Compositions include:* Save Me; Leave Them Boys Alone (co-writer with Hank Williams Jr). *Recordings:* Hits include: Delta Dawn; Jamestown Ferry; What's Your Mama's Name?; Lizzie and The Rainman; San Antonio Stroll; Here's Some Love; I Won't Take Less Than Your Love (with Paul Davis and Paul Overstreet); Strong Enough To Bend; If It Didn't Come Easy; Dream Lover (duet with Glen Campbell); Albums: Delta Dawn, 1972; What's Your Mama's Name?, 1973; Would You Lay With Me, 1974; Lovin' and Learnin', 1975; Tanya Tucker, 1975; Here's Some Love, 1976; You Are So Beautiful, 1977; Ridin' Rainbows, 1977; TNT, 1978; Tear Me Apart, 1979; Dreamlovers, 1980; Should I Do It?, 1981; Changes, 1982; Live, 1982; Love Me Like You Used To, 1987; Strong Enough To Bend, 1988; Tennessee Woman, 1990; Greatest Hits – Encore, 1990; What Do I Do With Me, 1991; Lizzie and The Rainman, 1992; Hits, 1992; Can't Run From Yourself, 1992; Fire To Fire, 1995 Complicated, 1997; featured on Biggest Country Duets of the 80's, 1998; Paul Davis: Sweet Life His Greatest Hit Single, 1999. *Honours:* CMA Female Vocalist of Year, 1991. *Address:* c/o Tanya Tucker Inc, 109 Westpark Dr., Suite 400, Brentwood, TN 37027–5032, USA.

TUDOR-POLE Edward; b. 6 Dec. 1956, London, England. 1 s. *Education:* Yardley Court Tonbridge, KESW, RADA. *Career:* Touring and recording with own band, Ten Pole Tudor; Acting Career: Films include: the Great Rock and Roll Swindle; Absolute Beginners; Sid and Nancy; Kull the Conqueror; Theatre: The Admirable Crichton; The Rocky Horror Show; The Deep Blue Sea; TV: Top of the Pops; presented The Crystal Maze. *Compositions:* Recorded: Who Killed Bambi (Sex Pistols); Swords of 1000 Men; Throwing the Baby Out with the Bathwater; Wunderbar; Three Bells in a Row; Ted Aint Dead. *Honour:* Silver disc for Swords of 1000 Men, 1981. *Leisure interests:* Running; Reading; Riding (horses and bikes). *Address:* 37 Springdale Rd, London N16 9NS, England.

TULLY Nigel; b. 22 July 1943, Barnsley, Yorkshire, England. Bandleader; Singer; Musician (guitar, saxophone). m. Prue Lyell, 29 Sept. 1978, 1 s., 1 d. *Education:* MA Hons, Oxon. *Musical Education:* Private tuition specially with Pat Crumly, saxophone. *Career:* Bandleader, The Dark Blues, 1962–; Completed 3,500 live concerts, 1995; Highlights include 21st and 40th birthday parties for HRH Prince Charles at Buckingham Palace. *Recordings:* Overdue, 1983; Live At Ashdown, 1985; 25 and Going For Gold, 1988; Midsummer Dance, 1992. *Memberships:* Fellow, British Computer Society; Liveryman, Worshipful Company of Musicians. *Leisure interests:* Gardening, specially rose growing; Farming (Hertfordshire); Visiting my 1000-year-old farmhouse in Tuscany. *Current Management:* Dark Blues Management Ltd. *Address:* 30 Stamford Brook Rd, London W6 0XH, England.

TUREK Jan; b. 19 Oct. 1957, Most, Czech Republic. Composer. m. Hana Pegrímková, 26 June 1982, 1 s., 1 d. *Education:* University of Economics; Private study of classical guitar. *Career:* More than 40 scenic music compositions for drama and puppet shows including realization. *Compositions:* There Was a Town in Prairie, 1994; The House with 7 Circles, 1995; The Royal Seconds, 1996; Kiss the Aunt, 1999; The Tiger, 1999; Absurd Person Singular, 2000. *Recordings:* Fairy Tales of Mr Fairy-Tale, 1995; Dilia, Prague. *Leisure interests:* Economics; Playing guitar in a rock band. *Current Management:* F Agency, Zizkova 1616, 434 01 Most, Czech Republic. *Address:* Vtelno 147, 434 01 Most, Czech Republic.

TURNER Carl; b. 2 June 1969, Wolverhampton, England. Writer; Prod.; Musician (keyboards). *Education:* 2 years OND, Graphic Design, Stafford College; 2 years HND, Wolverhampton College. *Musical Education:* Self-taught. *Career:* Three major British tours; Two major US tours; One major European tour; Six appearances, Top of the Pops; Other television appearances: Hangar 17; The Big Breakfast; The Beat; The Chart Show. *Recordings:* Such A Feeling, 1991; Playing With Knives (No. 4, UK); 1992; I'm Gonna Get You (No. 3, UK), 1992; Took My Love, 1993; Southern Harmoneers, He'll Make a Way, 1995. *Honours:* Music Week Award, Top Dance Single, 1991. *Membership:* Musicians' Union; PRS. *Leisure interests:* Historic rallying; Snowboarding. *Current Management:* Antony Johnson. *Address:* BGA, Unit 1B, Hollins Business Centre, Rowley St, Stafford ST16 3RH, England.

TURNER Geraldine Gail; b. 23 June 1950, Brisbane, Australia. Actress; Singer. m. Brian Castles-Onion, 31 Dec. 1993. *Education:* Diploma in Education, Queensland. *Musical Education:* Singing, Queensland Conservatoire, two years; Classical ballet training, ten years. *Career:* Internationally renowned in cabaret and as Sondheim interpreter; Performed in Australia, England, Canada, USA and Africa; Starred in musicals: Oliver!; Chicago; Anything Goes; Company; Sweeney Todd; A Little Night Music; Into The Woods; Ned Kelly; Guys and Dolls; Plays: Don's Party; Present Laughter; Summer of The Seventeenth Doll; Operas and operettas: La Belle Helénè; HMS Pinafore; The Mikado; Film appearances: Careful He Might Hear You; Summerfield; Numerous television appearances. *Recordings:* The Stephen Sondheim Song Book; Torch Songs – and Some Not So Tortous; Once In A Blue Moon; Gala Night; One Life To Live; When We Met; Cast albums include: Anything Goes; Chicago. *Honours:* Order of Australia (OAM), 1988; Green Room Awards, for Oliver!, 1984, and Anything Goes, 1989; Mo Awards, for Sweeney Todd, 1988, and Anything Goes, 1989. *Memberships:* Federal President, Australian Actors' Equity, four years. *Leisure interests:* Rose gardening; Painting. *Current Management:* Robyn Gardiner Management, 397 Riley St, Surry Hills, NSW 2010, Australia.

TURNER Howard; b. 24 Feb. 1959, Thornage, Holt, England. Prod.; Engineer; Musician (guitar, vocals); Songwriter; Studio Designer. *Education:* BA Hons, UEA, Norwich; PGCE, UEA, Norwich. *Career:* Began Raven Recording as recording studio, 1984; Producer, Engineer for Pete DeFreitas (Echo and The Bunnymen) on Sex Gods project; Developed reputation as freelance Indie/Rock producer and engineer; Sold studios, 1991; Acquired interest in Swamp Studios, 1992; Created Raven Recording Services and Studio Wizard Organization (studio design company); Major studio installations include: GWBB (London); The Cutting Rooms (Manchester); The Temple (Malta); Numerous television and radio appearances; Sold Swamp Studios, 1998; New studios under construction; Extending into corporate training and consultancy (studio technique and design). *Recordings:* 4 albums as musician under name The Nivens; As producer/engineer, includes albums by: Jacob's Mouse; Red Harvest; Jazz Butcher; Perfect Disaster; The Pollen; Bad Manners; Close Lobsters; Girlschool; Eden; Green On Red; Other recordings for Captain Sensible and The Damned; New artists: Crome Yellow; New album, Nivens. *Memberships:* APRS; MPG; PRS; MCPS. *Current Management:* Studio Wizard, County School, Dereham NR20 5LE, Norfolk, England.

TURNER Ike (Izear) Jr; b. 5 Nov. 1931, Clarksdale, Mississippi, USA. Singer; Songwriter; Musician (guitar). m. Tina Turner (Annie Mae Bullock), 1958, divorced 1978. *Career:* Founder, Kings of Rhythm band; Session guitarist, on recordings by B. B. King; Howlin' Wolf; Johnny Ace; Duo, Ike and Tina Turner, 1960–78; One of most popular acts on R & B tour circuit, 1960s; Concerts include: with Rolling Stones, 1966; Newport 69 Festival, 1969; Support to Rolling Stones, US tour, 1969; Built Bolic Sound Recording Studio, 1970. *Recordings:* Albums: with Ike and Tina Turner: Live! The Ike and Tina Turner Show, 1965; River Deep, Mountain High, 1966; In Person, 1969; Outa Season, 1969; The Hunter, 1969; Come Together, 1970; Workin' Together, 1971; Live At Carnegie Hall, 1971; 'Nuff Said, 1970; Feel Good, 1972; Nutbush City Limits, 1974; Solo: My Confessions, 1988; My Blues Country, 1997; Singles include: with Kings of Rhythm: Rocket 88, 1951; with Ike and Tina Turner: It's Going To Work Out Fine, 1961; River Deep Mountain High, 1966; A Love Like Yours, 1966; I Want To Take You Higher, 1970; Proud Mary, 1971; Nutbush City Limits, 1973; Baby Get It On, 1975. *Honours:* Rocket 88 widely credited as first rock 'n' roll record; Rock and Roll Hall of Fame, with Tina Turner, 1991.

TURNER Joe Lynn; b. USA. Singer. *Career:* Vocalist, rock groups: Fandango, 1977–80; Last Kiss, 1979; One Night Stand, 1979; Cadillac, 1980; Rainbow, 1980–85; Yngwie Malmsteen, 1987–89; Deep Purple, 1990–91; Also solo recording artiste. *Recordings:* Albums: 4 albums with Fandango, 1977–80; with Rainbow: Difficult To Cure, 1981; Best Of, 1981; Straight Between The Eyes, 1982; Bent Out of Shape, 1983; Finyl Vinyl, 1986; Solo albums: Fandango, 1982; Rescue You, 1985; Nothing Changes, 1995; Under Cover, 1997; Hurry Up and Wait, 1999; with Yngwie Malmsteen: Odyssey, 1988; Live In Leningrad, 1989; Heaven Tonight, 1999; with Deep Purple: Slaves and Masters, 1990. *Address:* c/o American Talent Group, 221 W 57th St, Eighth Floor, New York, NY 10019, USA.

TURNER Juliet; b. 16 July 1973, Tummery, County Tyrone, Northern Ireland. Vocalist; Musician (guitar); Songwriter. *Education:* Trinity College, Dublin. *Career:* Began performing at university; Recorded first album in Scotland, 1996; Led to support slots for acts including: Tracy Chapman; Natalie Merchant; U2; Brian Kennedy; Second album sold 40,000 copies in Ireland; Collaboration with John Spillane on single Will We Be Brilliant Or What?; Signed to EastWest, 2000. *Recordings:* Let's Hear It For Pizza, 1996; Burn The Black Suit, 2000. *Current Management:* Nally Management, Derek Nally, 39, Silverstream Ave, Stameen, Drogheda, Co Louth, Ireland. *E-mail:* dereknally@oceanfree.net. *Internet:* www.julietturner.com.

TURNER Lee; b. Jacksonville, Florida, USA. Musician (piano); Composer; Arranger; Music Publisher. m. Dianne Gross, 3 s. *Education:* University of Florida; Southern Baptist Theological Seminary. *Career:* Professional pianist since high school; Studio work, Nashville and Jacksonville; Regular television and radio appearances, dances, shows and concerts; Accompanist and soloist; Appeared with The Dream Weavers, Ed Sullivan Show; Minister of music, 29 years; Director, choirs and groups, religious and secular; Owner, publishing company, TurnerSong, 1981-. *Compositions include:* Into The Night, The Dream Weavers. *Recordings include:* It's Almost Tomorrow, The Dream Weavers; Rhapsody in Stained Glass, solo piano; There's a Meetin' Here Tonight, musical; Make Every Day a Good Day!. *Honours:* Annual ASCAP Award, 1974-. *Memberships:* ASCAP; AFofM. *Address:* 4263 San Jose Blvd, Jacksonville, FL 32207, USA. *Internet:* www.turnersong.com.

TURNER Nik; b. 26 Aug. 1940, Oxford, England. Musician (saxophone, flute); Vocalist; Composer; Arranger; Teacher. *Musical Education:* Self-taught. *Career:* Formed Hawkwind, 1969; Television and radio appearances: Top of The Pops, 1972; BBC Live John Peel at Paris Theatre, 1972; Tours of Europe, 1972–76; Left Hawkwind 1976; Formed Inner City Unit/Sphynx, 1976; Nik Turner's Fantastic All Stars, 1988; Nik Turner's Space Ritual, 1994; US tours 1994, 1995; Numerous radio appearances. *Recordings:* with Hawkwind: 8 albums; Numerous samplers; 6 singles include: Silver Machine (No. 1, UK), 1972; with Inner City Unit: 6 albums, 3 singles; with Sphynx: 1 album, 1978; with Nik Turner's Space Ritual: 5 albums, USA, video, 1994/95; with Nik Turner's Fantastic All Stars: Kubano Kickasso. *Membership:* Musicians' Union. *Leisure interests:* Reading; Swimming; Cinema; Apiary; Writing. *Current Management:* Money Talks Management. *Address:* Cadillac Ranch, Pencraig Uchaf, Cwm Bach, Whitland, Dyfed SA34 0DT, Wales.

TURNER Roger; b. 3 Feb. 1946, Whitstable, Kent, England. Musician (drums, percussion). m. Sara Ljungberg, 24 July 1992, divorced, 1 d. *Education:* BA, English Literature, Philosophy, University of Sussex. *Musical Education:* Self-taught. *Career:* Tours: USA; Canada; Australia; Europe; Festival concerts from the Berlin Jazz Fest to Macao; BBC Midnight Oil; Television in Australia, France, UK. *Recordings:* I Have No Feelings, Annette Peacock; Ammo, Phil Minton; The Recedents; Solo: Blur Between; Mouth Full of Ecstasy, Phil Minton Quartet; Birthdays, with John Russell; In the Tradition, with Alan Silva and Johannes Bauer. *Honours:* Arts Council of Great Britain, Bursary Awards, 1980–83. *Membership:* London Musicians' Collective. *Current Management:* Fabe/Koschik. *Address:* 34 Lancaster Rd, London W11 1QR, England.

TURNER Scott; b. 23 Aug. 1931, Sydney, Nova Scotia, Canada. Prod.; Writer; Publisher. Divorced, 1 s., 1 d. *Education:* BA, BSc, University of Dubuque, 1955; 1 year Graduate School, Texas Tech University. *Career:* Lead guitarist, writer for Tommy Sands and the Raiders, 1957–60; Guy Mitchell, 1960–61; Eddie Fisher, 1961–63; Joined Writer and producer, A & M Records, 1963; General Manager, Central Songs, Hollywood; Executive Producer, Country division, Liberty and Imperial Records, 1964; Independent Producer for Slim Whitman, Del Reeves and Jimmy Clanton, 1976; Composer of over 350 recorded songs including co-written songs with many leading artists; Music Director for numerous television shows; Composer of many background tracks and songs in films. *Recordings:* Numerous songs recorded by various artists including: Roy Clark; Nilsson; Herb Alpert; Dean Martin; Tammy Wynette; Jimmy Dean; The Del Vikings; Skeets MacDonald; Gene Vincent, including: Shutters and Boards; Please Mr Music Man; Does He Love You Like I Do; She's My Baby. *Address:* 524 Doral Country Dr., Nashville, TN 37221, USA.

TURNER Tina, (Annie Mae Bullock); b. 26 Nov. 1939, Brownsville, Tennessee, USA. Singer. Songwriter. m. Ike Turner, 1958, divorced 1978. *Career:* Member, Ike and Tina Turner, 1958–78; World-wide tours include: Support to Rolling Stones, British tour, 1966, US tour, 1969; European tour, 1971; Newport Festival, 1969; Solo artiste, 1978–; US tour, 1981; Support to Lionel Richie, British tour, 1984; Rock In Rio Festival, Brazil, 1985; Live Aid, Philadelphia, 1985; European tour, 1985; Prince's Trust Gala, London, 1986; World tours, 1987, 1990; Record 182,000 audience attend concert, Rio De Janeiro, 1988; First woman to play Palace of Versailles, France, 1990; Film appearances: Tommy, 1974; Mad Max – Beyond Thunderdome, 1985; Life story documented in film What's Love Got To Do With It?, 1992. *Compositions include:* Nutbush City Limits. *Recordings:* Albums with Ike Turner: Live! The Ike and Tina Turner Show, 1965; River Deep, Mountain High, 1966; Outa Season, 1969; The Hunter, 1969; Come Together, 1970; Workin' Together, 1971; Live At Carnegie Hall, 1971; 'Nuff Said, 1971; Feel Good, 1972; Nutbush City Limits, 1974; Solo albums: The Acid Queen, 1975; Private Dancer, 1984; Mad Max – Beyond The Thunderdome, 1985; Break Every Rule (No. 1 in nine countries), 1986; Live In Europe, 1988; Foreign Affair (No. 1, UK), 1989; Simply The Best, 1991; What's Love Got To With It (film soundtrack), 1993; Wildest Dreams, 1996; Dues Paid, 1999; Twenty Four Seven, 1999; Hit singles include: with Ike Turner: It's Gonna Work Out Fine, 1961; Poor Fool, 1962; River Deep, Mountain High, 1966; I Want To Take You Higher, 1970; Proud Mary, 1971; Nutbush City Limits, 1973; Solo: Let's Stay Together, 1983; What's Love Got To Do With It? (No. 1, USA), 1984; Better Be Good To Me, 1984; Private Dancer, 1984; We Don't Need Another Hero, theme for film Thunderdome (No. 2, US), 1985; One of The Living, 1985; It's Only Love, with Bryan Adams, 1985; Typical Male (No. 2, US), 1986; The Best, 1989; I Don't Wanna Lose You, 1989; Be Tender With Me Baby, 1990; It Takes Two, duet with Rod Stewart, 1990; Way of The World, 1991; I Don't Wanna Fight, 1993; Goldeneye (film theme), 1995; Missing You, 1996; In Your Wildest Dreams, 1996; When the Heartache is Over, 1999; Whatever You Need, 2000; Contributor, We Are The World, USA For Africa, 1985. *Publications:* I Tina (autobiography). *Honours include:* Grammy Awards: Record of the Year; Song of the Year; Best Female Vocal Performance; Best Female Rock Vocal, 1985; American Music Awards: Favourite Soul/R & B Female Artist, and Video Artist, 1985; Best Female Pop/Rock Artist, 1986; MTV Music Video award, 1985; Star on Hollywood Walk of Fame, 1986; Rock and Roll Hall of Fame, with Ike Turner, 1991; World Music Award, Outstanding Contribution To The Music Industry, 1993. *Current Management:* Roger Davies Management, 15030 Ventura Blvd, Suite 772, Sherman Oaks, CA 91403, USA.

TUTUNJIAN Nancy M; b. 7 Dec. 1959, Needham, Massachusetts, USA. Singer; Songwriter; Actress. *Education:* Associated degree in Business. *Musical Education:* 2 years college to learn to read music. *Career:* Regional theatre; Series of concerts sponsored by WNGN-FM, New York; Numerous festival, concert appearances all over USA; Guest on Jericho cable show; Power Hour cable show; Numerous phoned radio interviews, USA; Own record company, Paraclete Records. *Compositions include:* Numerous contemporary Christian songs (lyrics and music); Three one-act Biblical theatre pieces (book, lyrics and music). *Recordings include:* Songs For The Bridegroom, 1992; Christmas Glow, 1994. *Honours:* Trailblazers Award, International Airplay Asscn; Hon. Mention Certificate; Billboard Songwriting Contest. *Membership:* BMI as songwriter, publisher. *Leisure interests:* Painting; Drawing; Cooking; Hiking; Biking; Roller-blading. *Current Management:* Paraclete Music Ministries. *Address:* PO Box 473, Watertown, MA 02272–0473, USA.

TWAIN Shania; b. 28 Aug. 1965, Timmins, Ontario, Canada. Country Singer; Songwriter. m. Robert 'Mutt' Lange. *Career:* Regular television performances on CMT and TNN. *Compositions:* Songwriting partnership with Mutt Lange (husband). *Recordings:* Albums: Shania Twain, 1993; The Woman In Me, 1995; Come On Over, 1997; On The Way, 1999; Wild and Wicked, 2000; Singles: Any Man of Mine, 1995; You're Still The One, 1998; That Don't Impress Me Much, 1998; Man I Feel Like A Woman, 1999; Don't Be Stupid, 2000. *Honours:* CMT Europe, Rising Video Star of The Year, 1993; Grammy Award for Best Female Country Vocal Performance, 2000; Grammy Award for Best Country Song, 2000. *Current Management:* Jon Landau Management, 40 W Elm St, Greenwich, CT 06830, USA;.

TWEED Karen; b. 27 May 1963, London. Musician (Accordion); Composer. *Education:* BA, Leeds Polytechnic, 1985; Studied Under Lawry Eady and John Whelan. *Career:* Kathryn Tickell Band, until 1993; All Female Folk Band, The Poozies and Anglo Swedish Ensemble, Swap. *Compositions:* Walking up in Wonderful Wark. *Recordings:* Chantoozies, 1993; Dansoozies, 1995; Infinite Blue, 1998; Fyace, 1997; Swap, 1997.

Memberships: MU; PAMRA; PRS. *Leisure interests:* Printmaking; Knitting. *Current Management:* Brass Tacks Agency, PO Box 1162, Sheffield, S8 0JY.

TYAS Michael; b. 21 June 1957, Durham City, England. Musician (bass, guitar, mandolin, dulcimer); Vocalist. m. Margaret Tyas, 26 Sept. 1992, 1 d. *Musical Education:* Self-taught. *Career:* Worked in amateur folk groups in North East England; Professional musician, 1991–; Joined the Whisky Priests, 1989–95; Formed: The Wickermen, 1998; Solo career within folk roots music, 2000–; Toured 14 European countries; Appeared on Anglia and Tyne Tees TV, BBC Radio 1 and 2, and on national radio in Belgium, Holland and Germany. *Compositions:* Geronimo's Blues; The Scissorman; Leap of Faith; England My England. *Recordings:* 5 albums with The Whisky Priests including 1 live album;. *Leisure interests:* Photography; Hill walking. *Address:* Chilton, County Durham, England.

TYLER Bonnie; b. 8 June 1951, Skewen, Wales. Singer. m. Robert Sullivan, 14 July 1973. *Career:* Lead vocalist, local bands; Solo artiste, 1976–; First solo female artist to enter UK album charts at No. 1. *Recordings:* Lost In France, 1976; It's A Heartache, 1978; Natural Force, 1978; Faster Than The Speed of Night, 1983; Total Eclipse of The Heart, 1983; Holding Out For A Hero, 1985; Secret Dreams, 1986; Hide Your Heart, 1987; Bitterblue, 1991; The Best Of, 1993; Free Spirit, 1996; All In One Voice, 1988. *Honours:* Winner, Yamaha World Song Contest, 1978; BRIT Award Nominations, Best Female Vocalist, 1984–86; Grammy Nomination, Best Female Vocalist, 1984; Winner, Best Female Vocalist, Echo, 1994; Variety Club of Great Britain, 1984. *Current Management:* David Aspden Management. *E-mail:* d.aspden@virgin.net.

TYLER Stephen, (Stephen Tallarico); b. 26 March 1948, New York, USA. Singer; Musician (harmonica). *Career:* Singer, US rock band Aerosmith, 1970–; Concerts include: Support to the Kinks, Mott The Hoople, 1974; Schaefer Music Festival, New York, 1975; Reading Rock Festival, 1977; California Jam Festival II, 1978; Texas World Music Festival, 1978; Appearance as the Future Villain Band in film Sgt Pepper's Lonely Hearts Club Band, 1978; California Music Festival, with Van Halen, Cheap Trick, Ted Nugent, 1979; World Series of Rock with Journey, Ted Nugent, Thin Lizzy, 1979; Monsters of Rock Festival, Castle Donington, 1990; Television includes: MTV 10 anniverary special, ABC-TV, 1991; Saturday Night Live, NBC TV, 1993. *Recordings:* Albums: Aerosmith, 1973; Toys In The Attic, 1975; Get Your Wings, 1975; Rocks, 1976; Draw The Line, 1978; Night In The Ruts, 1980; Greatest Hits, 1981; Rock In A Hard Place, 1982; Classic Live!, 1986; Done With Mirrors, 1986; Permanent Vacation, 1987; Pump, 1990; Pandora's Box, 1992; Get A Grip, 1993; Singles include: Dream On; Last Child; Walk This Way; Dude (Looks Like A Lady); Angel; Rag Doll; Love In An Elevator; Janie's Got A Gun; What It Takes; Livin' On The Edge; Eat The Rich; Cryin'; Amazing. *Honours include:* Inducted into Hollywood's Rock Walk, 1990; 3 Boston SKC Music Awards, 1990; American Music Awards, 1991; Grammy, Best Rock Performance, 1991; Rolling Stone and Billboard magazine awards; Platinum discs. *Current Management:* Magus Entertainment, 584 Broadway, Suite 1009, New York, NY 10012, USA.

TYRRELL John William; b. 14 March 1961, Melbourne, Australia. Drums; Man. *Career:* Manager and Drummer, Abba Tribute Band, Björn Again, 1988–; Band formed in Melbourne with partner Rod Woolley, appeared on most TV and radio shows. *Recordings:* A Little Respect/Stop; Santa Claus Is Coming to Town; So You Win Again; Flashdance – What a Feeling. *Membership:* UK Music Union. *Address:* 48 Fernhead Rd, Maida Vale, London W9 3EW, England.

TYSON Liam, (Skin); b. 7 Sept. 1969, Liverpool, England. Musician (Guitar). *Career:* Member, Cast; Support gigs with Elvis Costello and Oasis; Record deal with Polydor. *Recordings:* Singles: Finetime, 1995; Alright, 1995; Live the Dream, 1998; Guiding Star, 1998; Sandstorm, 1998; Walkaway, 1998; Albums: All Change, 1995; Mother Nature Calls, 1997.

TZUKE Judie; b. 1955, London, England. Singer; Songwriter. *Education:* Drama. *Career:* Solo artiste; Songwriting partnership with Mike Paxman, 1975. *Compositions include:* These Are The Laws, with Mike Paxman; Give Me The Love, recorded by Elton John. *Recordings:* Albums: Welcome To The Cruise, 1979; Sports Car, 1980; I Am The Phoenix, 1981; Road Noise, 1982; Shoot The Moon, 1983; Ritmo, 1983; Judie Tzuke, 1985; The Cat Is Out, 1985; Turning Stones, 1989; Left Hand Talking, 1991; BBC Live in Concert, 1995; Wonderland, 1996; Under the Angels, 1997.

U

UI CHEALLAIGH Aine; b. 29 Oct. 1959, Belfast, Northern Ireland. Singer; Musician (violin); Teacher. 2 s. *Education:* Degree, diploma, University College Dublin. *Musical Education:* City of Belfast School of Music. *Career:* Many broadcasts on RTE Radio and Television; BBC Radio; Solo singer, Riverdance-The Show, by Bill Whelan; Teacher, English, Irish and Music. *Recordings:* Solo album: In Two Minds, 1992. *Honours:* Oireachtas Gold Medal, 1990, 1992. *Leisure interests:* Singing; Traditional fiddle. *Address:* Ring, Co Waterford, Ireland.

UKIC Zoran; b. 31 May 1962, Split, Croatia. Musician (drums); Record Prod.; Man. m. Vesna, 30 June 1984, 1 s., 1 d. *Career:* with Daleka Obala: Faraway Coast tours, 1990, 1993–95; Zagreb Salata, D Dvornik, N Belan, Daleka Obala, 1992; Television show 7 Noc. *Recordings:* with Daleka Obala: Faraway Coast, 1990; Ludi Mornari Dolaze U Grad (Crazy Sailors Come On The Town); MRL, E (Dirty), 1993; Morski Pas (Shark), 1994. *Publications:* Blue and Green, Croatian Rock Encyclopedia. *Honour:* The Best Debutant, Split Festival, 1990. *Membership:* Croatian Musicians' Union. *Leisure interest:* Jogging. *Address:* Zoran Ukic, Teutina 15, 5800 Split, Croatia.

ULRICH Lars; b. 26 Dec. 1955, Copenhagen, Denmark. Musician (drums). *Career:* Former tennis player; Compiler, New Wave of British Heavy Metal album with Geoff Barton, 1979; British tour with Diamond Head; Member, US heavy rock group Metallica, 1981–; World-wide tours include: Masters of Puppets world tour, 1986–87; US tour, 1988; Damaged Justice British tour, 1989; World tours, 1991–; Also tours with Raven; Ozzy Osbourne; Twisted Sister; Motörhead; Major concerts include: Monsters of Rock Festival, Castle Donington, 1985, 1987, 1991; German Monster of Rock festivals, 1987; Monsters of Rock, Europe and US tours, 1988, 1991; Day On The Green, Oakland, 1991. *Recordings:* Albums: Kill 'Em All, 1983; Ride The Lightning, 1984; Master of Puppets, 1986; …and Justice For All, 1988; Metallica (No. 1, UK and US), 1991; Live Shit, 1993; Singles: Garage Days Revisited (EP), 1987; Harvester of Sorrow, 1988; One, 1989; Enter Sandman, 1991; The Unforgiven, 1991; Nothing Else Matters, 1992; Wherever I May Roam, 1992; Sad But True, 1992; Stone Cold Crazy, track featured on Rubáiyát (Elektra's 40th anniversary compilation). *Honours:* Platinum and Gold discs; Grammy Awards: Best Heavy Metal Performance: One, 1989; Stone Cold Crazy, 1991; The Unforgiven, 1992; American Music Award, Favourite Heavy Metal Artist, 1993; Bay Area Music Awards: Outstanding Album, 1992; Outstanding Metal Album, Outstanding Group, Outstanding Drummer, 1993; Rolling Stone Readers Poll Winners, Best Heavy Metal Band, 1993. *Current Management:* Q-Prime Inc. *Address:* 729 Seventh Ave, 16th Floor, New York, NY 10019, USA.

ULRICH Shari; b. 17 Oct. 1951, Marin County, California, USA. Composer; Musician (violin, mandolin, piano, guitar); Singer; Television Host. m. 29 April 1989, 1 d. *Education:* 1 year college. *Musical Education:* Violin training, grade 3–13, otherwise self-taught. *Career:* Member, Pied Pumpkin String Ensemble, 1972–76; Hometown Band, 1976–78; UHF (Ulrich, Bill Henderson, Roy Forbes), 1989–; Solo artist, 1978–; Composer: theme music, several Canadian television series, documentaries; Pieces for Sesame Street; Host Future Scan 1984, 1985; Host, Inside Trax, 1989–94. *Recordings:* Two albums with Pied Pumpkin, 1974, 1975; Hometown Band: Flying, 1976; Hometown Band 1977; Raffi: Bananaphone, 1994; Solo albums: Long Nights, 1978; One Step Ahead, 1980; Talk Around Town, 1982; Every Road, 1989; with UHF: UHF, 1990; UHF II, 1994. *Honours:* Juno Awards, 1977, 1981. *Memberships:* Vice-president, Songwriters' Asscn of Canada, AFofM; ACTRA; SOCAN. *Leisure interests:* Photography; Cycling. *Address:* PO Box 152, Bowen Island, British Columbia V0N 1G0, Canada.

ULRIK Hans (Jensen); b. 28 Sept. 1965, Copenhagen, Denmark. Musician (saxophone, flute). *Musical Education:* 2 years, Berklee College of Music, Boston, USA, 1984–86. *Career:* Founder, own band Hans Ulrik Quartet; Member, Marilyn Mazur Future Song; Tours: Europe, mostly Scandinavia; Numerous television and radio appearances. *Recordings:* Day After Day (with Gary Peacock, Adam Nussbaum, John Abercrombie); Strange World (with Marilyn Mazur). *Honours:* Best Soloist, Leverkusen International Jazz Competition, Germany, 1988. *Leisure interest:* Sports. *Current Management:* The Danish Jazz League. *Address:* Den Danske Jazzkreds, Kjeld Langes Gade 4 A, 1367 Copenhagen K, Denmark.

ULSTRUP Thomas Videro; b. 31 Aug. 1968, Frederiksberg, Denmark. Musician (moog synthesizers, keyboards, modified piano); Composer; Agent; Teacher. *Education:* Teacher's Academy of Art, Music and Multimedia; High Schools of Jazz and Rock; Private tuition. *Career:* Member of various experimental groups in Copenhagen, 1984–92; Solo

key performances; Co-founder with Las Nissen of Gone Fishin', 1989–96; Solo, duo and trio member and recording artist; Founder of Native Music Denmark, 1997; Radio Host, Copenhagen radio-jazz show Alternative Music; Toured with The Sun Mountain Experience in the Caribbean, 1998. *Compositions:* 10 x Cai, 1988; Jack Daniels, 1994; Meditations, 1998. *Recordings:* with Gone Fishin': Gone Fishin', 1994; Adventure: Once Upon a Time…, 1998; Alternative music: Sound Environment, 1998. *Publications:* Native Music Compilation Vols I and II, 1998; Alternative Music – Soundenvironment. *Honours:* Gold Talent Prize, Berlingske Tidende, 1988. *Memberships:* Gramex; Danish Jazz and Folk Authors (DOBFA); Composers in Denmark (KODA). *Leisure interest:* Soundscapes. *Current Management:* Native Music. *Address:* H/F Grænsen 8, Finsensvej 263, 2720 Vaniose, Denmark.

ULVÆUS Bjorn; b. 25 April 1945, Gothenburg, Sweden. Songwriter; Musician (guitar); Vocalist. m. Agnetha Fältskog, 1971 (divorced 1979). *Career:* Songwriter with Benny Andersson, 1966–; Duo with Andersson as The Hootennanny Singers; Partner in production with Andersson at Polar Music, 1971; Founder member, Swedish pop group Abba, 1973–82; Winners, Eurovision Song Contest, 1974; Regular international tours and concerts include: Royal Performance, Stockholm, 1976; Royal Albert Hall, London, 1977; Film appearance: Abba – The Movie, 1978; Continued writing and producing with Andersson, 1982–; Reunion Abba appearance, Swedish TV, 1986; Produced music for West End play with Benny Andersson, Mamma Mia. *Compositions include:* Abba songs (with Benny Andersson): Ring Ring; Waterloo; Honey Honey; I Do I Do I Do I Do I Do; Mamma Mia; Dancing Queen; Fernando; Money Money Money; Knowing Me Knowing You; The Name of The Game; Take A Chance On Me; Summer Night City; Chiquitita; Does Your Mother Know?; Gimme Gimme Gimme (A Man After Midnight); The Winner Takes It All; Super Trouper; On and On and On; Lay All Your Love On Me; One of Us; Thank You For The Music; Musical: Chess (with Tim Rice's lyrics), 1983; I Know Him So Well; One Night In Bangkok; Musical: The Immigrants, 1994. *Recordings:* Albums include: with Andersson: Happiness, 1971; with Abba: Waterloo, 1974; ABBA, 1976; Arrival, 1977; The Album, 1978; Voulez-Vous, 1979; Super Trouper, 1980; Various compilations. *Honours include:* Gold discs; Listed as biggest-selling group in pop history, Guinness Book of Records, 1979; Best Selling Swedish Artist of The Year, World Music Awards, Monte Carlo, 1993. *Address:* Södra Brobänken 41A, Skeppsholmen, 111 49 Stockholm, Sweden.

ULVESETH Sigurd; b. 13 July 1953, Bergen, Norway. Musician (acoustic bass). m. Eli, 13 March 1981, 2 s., 1 d. *Musical Education:* Mainly self-taught. *Career:* Many tours, different jazz groups; Appearances, radio and television shows; Own quartet featuring Adam Nussbaum, drums. *Recordings:* Sigurd Ulveseth Quartet: To Wisdom The Prize (with Adam Nussbaum, Knut Rüsmas; Dug Arnesen); Played on 13 other albums. *Honours:* Jade Prize, 1990. *Membership:* Norwegian Jazz Society. *Current Management:* Vaakleivbrotet 7, 5062 Bones, Norway.

UNCLE KRACKER (Matthew Lynford Shafer); b. 6 June 1974, Mount Clemens, Michigan, USA. DJ; Vocalist; Songwriter. m. Melanie, 2 d. *Career:* Owns Mount Clemens tyre store run by father, and Sunny's Tavern bar in suburban Detroit; Befriended Kid Rock, 1987; Recruited to Kid Rock's Twisted Brown Trucker touring group as DJ following release of Rock's album Grits Sandwiches For Breakfast, 1991; Became Rock's co-producer/ co-songwriter; Achieved success with solo side project recorded whilst on tour; Many solo TV and live appearances backed by Twisted Brown Trucker group, 2001. *Recordings:* Albums: Double Wide, 2000; Singles: Follow Me, Yeah Yeah Yeah, 2001. *Honours:* Debut solo album sales of around 2m. *Address:* c/o Top Dog/Lava/Atlantic Records, USA. *Internet:* www.unclekracker.com.

UNDERWOOD Charles Jeremy; b. 14 Aug. 1956, Leicester, England. Musician (saxophone). *Education:* BA Hons, Fine Art. *Musical Education:* Associated Board exams (Grade 8 clarinet). *Career:* Professional musician, 1984–; Member, John Martyn Band, 1991–; Tours: UK; Europe; USA; Glastonbury Festival; Edinburgh Festival; Bath Festival; Member, British jazz group Spirit Level, 1989–; Member, Andy Sheppard's Big-Comotion Band, also Carla Bley's Very Big Band. *Recordings:* with John Martyn: Couldn't Love You More, 1992; No Little Boy, 1993; with Andy Sheppard: Rhythm Method, 1993; Delivery Suite, 1994. *Memberships:* PRS; MCPS. *Leisure interest:* Mountaineering. *Address:* 9 Lucas House, Argyle Walk, Kings Cross, London WC1, England.

UOTILA Jukkis; b. 23 Aug. 1960, Finland. Musician (drums); Composer. *Career:* Jazz concerts, 1976–; Played and recorded with artists including: Gil Evans; McCoy Tyner; Joe Henderson; Chet Baker; Moved to New York,

1980; Worked with artists including: Randy Brecker; Eliane Elias; Ted Curson; Mike Stern; Dave Samuels; Returned to Finland; Bandleader, Jukkis Uotila Band; Performed world-wide, including festivals at Montreux, Detroit, Paris; Head of Jazz Department, Sibelius Academy, Helsinki, 1986–; Bandleader, with band featuring: Mike Stern, Bob Berg, Lars Jansson, Lasse Danielsson; Tours of Scandinavia and Germany. *Recordings:* with Bob Rockwell: No Rush, 1985; On the Natch, 1985; with Chet Baker: When Sunny Gets Blue, 1986; with Joe Bonner; Lost Melody, 1987; with Doug Raney Quintet, 1988; with Stockholm Jazz Orchestra: Soundbites, 1997; Tango, 1999. *Address:* Laivurinkatu 35 B 35, 00150 Helsinki, Finland.

UPTON Eddie; b. 4 Oct. 1944, Brighton, Sussex, England. Folk Singer; Musician (concertina, harmonica, percussion). *Education:* BA (Hons) Politics, Sussex University. *Career:* Full time folk performer, 1980–, specialising in traditional English songs, music and dance; Former member, Albion Dance Band and Etchingham Steam Band, both with Ashley Hutchings; Co-founder, artistic director, Folk South West, the folk development society for South West of England. *Composition:* Suite of song arrangements celebrating Somerset's River Parrett, 1997. *Recordings include:* The Prospect Before Us, Albion Dance Band; A Tale of Ale, Various Artists; Music For Christopher Columbus and His Crew, St Georges Canlona; Prospect Before Us, with Albion Band; Guv'nor, Vol. 2, 1996; Solo album: First Orders; where the Parrett Winds Peaceful, 1997. *Publications:* Caedmon Capers – A Collection of New Folk Dances and Folk Dance Tunes. *Memberships:* Folklore Society; English Folk Dance and Song Society; Equity; Musicians' Union; Performing Rights Society, 1997. *Leisure interests:* Walking; Working. *Address:* 2 Hayes Cottages, Stocklinch, Ilminster, Somerset TA19 9JG, England.

URBAN Stan; b. 10 Jan. 1944, Dundee, Scotland. Musician (piano); Singer. m. (1) Erika Kuhnert, 3 Sept. 1963, divorced 1984, 2 s., (2) Annette Wetterberg, 29 March 1986, deceased 1987, 1 adopted s., (3) Evelyn Jetzschmann, 15 April 1996. *Musical Education:* Self-taught. *Career:* Rock 'n' roll pianist; Formed own band of German musicians, following tour of Germany with Long John Baldry, 1962; Lived and played in Ibiza, late 60s to 1984; Scandinavia recommended by Robert Plant; Tours of Scandinavia, 1981–. *Recordings:* Single: Little Queenie, 1982; Albums: Rock 'N' Roll Cocktail, 1982; M'Roccan Rollers, 1986; Live, 1988; Through My Door, 1992; Can't Hold On Can't Let Go, 1995; The Devil Made the Boogie, 1997. *Leisure interests:* Classical music; Water skiing; Parachuting. *Address:* Skaering Sandager 18, 8250 Egå, Denmark.

URE Midge (James); b. 10 Oct. 1953, Glasgow, Scotland. Singer; Songwriter; Prod.; Dir. 4 d. *Career:* Member of bands: Slik; Rich Kids; Thin Lizzy (US tour only); Visage; Formed Ultravox; Also solo artist; Trustee of Live Aid; Musical Director, Prince's Trust, 1987–88; Musical Director, special 40 minute set, Nelson Mandela Concert; Directed video Monument for televison special; Director of videos for: Ultravox; Visage; Fun Boy Three; Bananarama; Phil Lynott; Monsoon; Midge Ure/Mick Karn; Midge Ure; Martha Ladley; Truth; Andrew Strong. *Compositions include:* Levis advertisements music, with Christopher Cross, 1983; Writer/co-writer, many hit songs; Film music: Max Headroom; Turnaround; Playboy Late Night Theme; October 22 AKG; Went To Lonely Island. *Recordings include:* Albums: with Visage: Visage, 1980; Anvil, 1982; with Ultravox: Vienna, 1980; Rage In Eden, 1981; Quartet, 1982; Lament, 1984; The Collection, 1984; U-Vox, 1986; Solo albums: The Gift, 1985; Answers, 1988; Pure, 1991; Breathe, 1996; Move Me, 2001; Singles include: with Ultravox: Sleepwalk, 1980; Vienna, 1981; All Stood Still, 1981; The Thin Wall, 1981; The Voice, 1981; Reap The Wild Wind, 1982; Hymn, 1982; Visions In Blue, 1983; We Came To Dance, 1983; Dancing With Tears In My Eyes, 1984; Lament, 1984; Love's Great Adventure, 1984; All Fall Down; Contributor, producer, co-writer (with Bob Geldof), Do They Know It's Christmas?, Band Aid (No. 1, UK), 1984; Also singles with: Slik, Rich Kids, Visage and as solo artist; Produced records for: Antrix; Ronny; Cold Fish; Phil Lynott; Pete Godwyn; Modern Man; Fatal Charm; Steve Harley; Strasse; The Messengers; Rodeo; Visage; Ultravox; Michel Van Dyke; Countermine. *Honours:* Winner of Ivor Novello and Grammy Awards. *Current Management:* Richard Beck, CMO Management, Unit 32, Ransomes Dock, 35–37 Parkgate Rd, London SW11 4NP, England.

URTREGER René; b. 6 July 1934, Paris, France. Musician (piano); Bandleader; Composer. m. Jacqueline Fornari, 1 s., 1 d. from previous marriage. *Musical Education:* Studied classical music from age 6; Serious study after war from age 11; Promoted Charlie Parker's music from age 13. *Career:* Concerts and festivals throughout the world, 1953–; Starts working at 19 with Don Byas-Buck Clayton Band, 1953; Worked with: Dexter Gordon; Zoot Sims; Stéphane Grappelli; Allen Eager; Stan Getz; Dizzy Gillespie; J. J. Johnson; Double Six; Current trio with Pierre Michelot and Kenny Clarke; House pianist for (Nicole) Barclay Records, France,

1954–65; European tours as pianist within Miles Davis Quartet, 1956; Miles Davis Quintet, 1957; Break from jazz music, 1967–77, touring with Sacha Distel and Claude Francois; Returned to jazz ensembles, 1977; Pianist with Sonny Stitt's French tour, 1982; Concerts with Peter King, 1993. *Recordings:* Numerous recordings include albums with: Lionel Hampton; Chet Baker; Bobby Jaspar; Hubert Fol; Maurice Meunier; Lester Young; Kenny Clarke; Michael Hausser; Stéphane Grappelli and Stuff Smith; Film music: Ascenseur Pour L'Echafaud, within Miles Davis Quintet; Le Poulet (Oscar short film, 1965); Other albums include: Recidive, 1978; Urtreger/Michelot/Humair Trio, 1979; Collection Privée, 1981; En Direct Du Festival D'Antibes, 1981; Jazzman, 1985; Masters, 1987; Avec Chet Baker, 1989; Serena, 1990; Chet Baker in Paris, 1998; Claude François À L'Olympia 69, 1998; Pat Metheny, All the Things You Are, 1999; Film: René Urtreger/Homme De Jazz, 1991; Saint Germains Des Presents, Telefilm by J. Ch. Averty, 1993. *Honours:* Winner, National Jazz Tournament, 1953; Prix Django Reinhardt, L'Academie Du Jazz, 1961; Prix Boris Vian, L'Academie Du Jazz, for album Jazzman, 1985; L'Ordre Des Arts and Lettres, 1988; Grand Prix, SACEM, 1993. *Leisure interests:* Chess; Football (amateur). *Current Management:* Jeanne De Mirbeck, Carlyne Music. *Address:* c/o Carlyne Music, La Prairie, 92410 Ville D'Avray, France.

USHER (Usher Raymond); b. 1978, Chattanooga, Tennessee, USA. Singer. *Career:* Appearances include Oprah Winfrey Show (TV) and the American Music Awards as part of Black Men United. *Recordings:* Can U Get Wit It, 1994; Think of You, 1995; The Many Ways, 1995; Comin For X-Mas, 1995; My Way, 1997; Nice and Slow, 1998.

USSING Joachim; b. 9 Oct. 1952, Copenhagen, Denmark. Musician (bass player); Composer. m. Henriette Rolffes Becker, 13 Feb. 1989, 1 s., 1 d. *Musical Education:* Self-taught. *Career:* Toured Scandinavia, television appearances with: Moirana; Phantom Band; Lone Kellermann and Rockband; Jomfru Ane; Doraz; Small Talk; Big Talk; Anne Grete; Peter Abrahamsen; Peter Viskinde, from 1974–95. *Recordings:* First album: Terje, Jesper, Joachim, 1970 (released 1991). *Honours:* Platinum disc, Natten Blir Til Dag, Lone Kellermann and Rockband. *Memberships:* DMF; DJBFA; KODA; GRAMEX; NCB. *Current Management:* DMA. *Address:* Vendersgade 23, 1363 Copenhagen, Denmark.

UTADA Hikaru; b. 19 Jan. 1983, New York, USA. Vocalist; Songwriter. *Education:* American School, Tokyo; Columbia University, New York, 2001. *Career:* Daughter of record producer Teruzane Utada and early '70s Japanese pop/enka vocalist Keiko Fuji; Recorded demos in downtime at father's studio, releasing them in US under alias Cubic U; First Japan releases as Hikaru Utada, 1999 while continuing education in Tokyo; Simultaneously maintained US and Japanese careers under respective names; Hosted own radio shows in Japan including Tres Bien Bohemian. *Recordings:* Albums: Precious (as Cubic U), 1998; First Love, 1999; U3*Star (live), 2000; Distance, 2001; Singles: Close To You (as Cubic U), 1998; Moving On Without You, First Love, Automatic/Time Will Tell, Addicted To You, 1999; Wait and See, For You/Time Limit, 2000; Can You Keep A Secret, Final Distance, Traveling, 2001. *Honours:* First Love album sales in excess of a record 9.5m. copies in Japan; World Music Award, Best Selling Asian Artist, 2000. *Address:* c/o Toshiba-EMI, 3-taku, Room 2–2–17, Akasaka Minato-Ku, Tokyo 107-8510, Japan. *Internet:* www.toshiba-emi.co.jp/hikki.

UTLEY Adrian; b. 1958. Member, Portishead; Musician (Guitar). *Career:* Former Member, Big John Patton; Jazz Messengers; Joined with Geoff Barrow, Beth Gibbons and Dave McDonald to form Portishead; Signed to Go!Beat Records, 1993; Film, To Kill A Dead Man, shown in cinema and projected onto the MI5 building, London, 1995; Glastonbury Festival appearance, 1995; Live internet broadcast of New York concert, 1997. *Recordings:* Singles: Sour Times, 1994; Numb, 1994; Glory Box, 1995; All Mine, 1997; Cowboys EP, 1997; Over, 1997; Albums: Dummy, 1994; Portishead, 1997. *Publication:* Straight Outta Bristol: Massive Attack, Portishead, Tricky and the Roots of Trip Hop, Phil Johnson, 1995. *Honour:* Mercury Music Prize, 1994.

UTTERBACK Joe; b. 8 Oct. 1944, Hutchinson, Kansas. *Education:* DMA, University of Kansas. *Career:* Gigs in the Jazz Centers of Kansas City, St Louis, New York City, San Francisco; Solo Jazz Piano Concerts, US. *Compositions:* Tuxedo Blues; Three Spirituals For Organ in Jazz Styles; Three Spirituals For Piano; Dr Jams Long Ragtime Special. *Recordings:* Blues and Ballads at the Movies; Christmas on the Mountain; Night and Day, Gershwin: Porgy and Bess Jazz Suite; Night Train. *Publications:* Knockin at your Door; Voluntaries; Jazz Piano Starter Set; Beautiful Night. *Honours:* Annual ASCAP Award. *Membership:* ASCAP; AGO, College Music Society. *Leisure interests:* Body building; Philosophy. *Current Management:* Jazzmuze Inc. *Address:* 50 Crooked Trail, Rowayton, CT 06853, USA.

V

VACHÉ Warren Webster; b. 27 Nov. 1914, Brooklyn, New York, USA. Musician (string bass); Bandleader. m. 18 Sept. 1948, 2 s. *Musical Education:* Self-taught. *Career:* Worked, played with: Bobby Hackett; Wild Bill Davison; Pee Wee Russell; Max Kaminsky; Sons are both jazz musicians: Warren Jr, cornet; Allan, clarinet; Leader, own 7-piece jazzband, The Celebratin' Seven; *Tours:* Germany; Switzerland; Netherlands; France; Also US and international jazz festivals. *Recordings:* Jazzology; Swingin' and Singin'; The Music of Harry Barris; The Music of Isham Jones, 1998. *Publications:* This Horn For Hire, biography of Pee Wee Erwin; Crazy Fingers, biography of Claude Hopkins; Back Beats and Rim Shots, Biography of Johnny Blowers, 1997: Jazz Gentry (anthology jazz articles), 1999; The Unsung Songwriters, 2000; Editor, Jersey Jazz (monthly publication, New Jersey Jazz Society), 18 years. *Memberships:* Life mem., American Federation Musicians; Life and founding mem., New Jersey Jazz Society; Founder, American Jazz Hall of Fame; Co-founder, American Federation of Jazz Societies. *Leisure interests:* Jazz record collecting; Stamps; Coins; Antiques. *Address:* 836 W Inman Ave, Rahway, NJ 07065, USA.

VAERNES Knut; b. 1 April 1954, Trondheim, Norway. Musician (guitar); Composer; Bandleader; Record Co Exec. 1 s. *Education:* Master of Arts. *Musical Education:* Master of Music. *Career:* 15 years as professional musician; Concerts include: All national jazz festivals; Tours in Europe; British tour with Cutting Edge, including Ronnie Scott's, 1983; Numerous television appearances; Extensive touring; Played with Jan Garbarek, Jon Christenson, Oslo, 1982; Head of jazz record label Curling Legs. *Recordings:* Albums: with Cutting Edge: Cutting Edge; Our Man In Paradise; Duesenberg; Solo albums: Admisson For Guitars and Basses, 1992; Roneo, 1993; Trio, 1995; Film music, with Jan Garbarek, 1981. *Membership:* Musicians' Union. *Leisure interest:* Tennis. *Address:* Vidarsgt. 9A, 0452 Oslo, Norway.

VAI Steve; b. 6 June 1960, Long Island, New York, USA. Musician (guitar). *Musical Education:* Tutored by Joe Satriani; Jazz and Classical music, Berklee College of Music, Boston. *Career:* Lead guitarist, Frank Zappa, 1979–84; Built own recording studio, 1984; Lead guitarist with Alcatrazz, 1985; David Lee Roth, 1986–89; Whitesnake, 1989–90; Also solo artiste; World-wide concerts and television/radio appearances with the above include: World Series of Rock, US; Monsters of Rock, UK; Super Rock, Germany; Film appearance: Crossroads. *Recordings:* Albums include: with Frank Zappa: Tinseltown Rebellion, 1981; You Are What You Is, 1981; Shut Up and Play Yer Guitar, 1981; Ship Arriving Too Late, 1982; The Man From Utopia, 1983; Thing Fish, 1984; Jazz From Hell, 1986; Guitar, 1988; You Can't Do That On Stage Anymore, 1988; with Alcatrazz: Disturbing The Peace, 1985; with David Lee Roth: Eat 'Em and Smile, 1986; Skyscraper, 1988; with Whitesnake: Slip of The Tongue, 1989; Solo albums: Flex-able, 1984; Passion and Warfare, 1990; Sex and Religion, 1993; Alien Love Secrets, 1995; Fire Garden, 1996; Flex-Able Leftovers, 1998; The Ultra Zone, 1999. *Current Management:* C Winston Simone Management, 1790 Broadway, New York, NY 10019, USA.

VAIL Frederick Scott; b. 24 March 1944, San Francisco, California, USA. Recording Studio Exec. m. Brenda Joyce Howard, 18 June 1972, divorced 1977. *Education:* California State University, 1962–64; Industrial College of the Armed Forces, 1963; Voluntary State Community College, Nashville, 1980–81. *Career:* Radio announcer, Sacramento, 1958–62; Frederick Vail Productions, 1962–66; Producer, sales manager, Teen-age Fair Inc, 1966–69; Artist manager, Beach Boys, 1969–71; Promotion Manager, Capitol Records, 1972–73; President, Frederick Vail and Associates, 1974–80; President, General Manager, Treasure Isle Recording Studios, 1980–; Consultant, Promotion and Marketing: Waylon Jennings, 1974–75; GRT Records, 1976–78; RSO Records, 1978–79; Lecturer, numerous colleges and universities; Event producer for: Beach Boys; Glen Campbell; Righteous Brothers; Four Seasons; Dave Clark Five; The Crickets. *Recordings:* Producer for: BB King; Isaac Hayes; Billy Preston; Carla Thomas; Lee Atwater; Red Hot + Blue compilation. *Publications:* Contributing author: Beach Boys – The California Myth, 1978; Beach Boys – Heroes and Villains, 1987; Contributor to Mix Magazine. *Honours:* 7 Gold, 2 Platinum discs. *Memberships:* NARAS, Board of Governors, 1981–83; CMA. *Address:* Treasure Isle Recording Studios, Nashville, Tennessee, USA.

VALDES Chucho; b. 9 Oct. 1941, Quivican, Cuba. Musician (piano, keyboards); Bandleader. *Career:* Son of Bebo Valdes; Began playing piano, aged 3; Leader of own group by age 16; Formed: Orquesta Cubana de Música Moderna, 1967; Founder: Irakare, the top Cuban jazz orchestra, 1973; Collaborations include Cesoria Evora. *Recordings:* Albums include: with Irakere: Felicidad, 1991; Live At Ronnie Scott's, 1993; Exuberancia,

1994; with Arturo Sandoval and Chucho Valdes Quartet: Straight Ahead, 1994; solo: Solo Piano, 1993; Grandes Momentos De La Música Cubana, 1994; Briyumba Palo Congo, 1999; Live At The Village Vanguard, 2000.

VALDY Paul Valdemar Horsdal; b. 1 Sept. 1945, Ottawa, Canada. Singer; Songwriter; Musician (guitar); Prod. m. Kathleen Mary Fraser, 13 Aug. 1986, 2 s. *Education:* Usgar Collegiate, St Pat's College. *Musical Education:* Piano lessons; Choir; Glee club; Victoria School of Music. *Career:* Appearances: International Pop Song Festival, Sopot, Poland, 1975; CBC TV Super Special Simulcast, Valdy and The Hometown Band, 1976; Expo '86, Vancouver; Festival Cervantino, Mexico, 1987; Olympic Arts Festival, Calgary, '88; World's Fair, Seville, Expo '92; Royal Gala, Melbourne Music Festival, Australia, 1995. *Recordings:* Albums: Country Man, 1971; Landscapes, 1972; Family Gathering, 1974; Valdy and The Home Town Band, 1976; Hot Rocks, 1978; 1001, 1979; Valdy's Kid Record, 1981; Notes From Places, 1986; Heart At Work, 1993. *Publication:* The Best of Valdy. *Honours:* 2 Juno Awards; BMI Song of The Year, Landscapes, 1974. *Membership:* AFofM, local 247; NSAI; SAC; FEPRA; CARAS; CIRPA. *Leisure interests:* Wood-butcher; Sailing; Scuba diving; Skiing; Watercolours; Golf; Billiards. *Current Management:* Paquin Entertainment Group. *Address:* 1067 Sherwin Rd, Winnipeg, Manitoba R3H 0T8, Canada.

VALENSI Nick; b. 16 Jan. 1981, New York City, USA. Musician (guitar). *Education:* Dwight School, Manhattan. *Career:* Member: The Strokes, 1998-. *Recordings:* Albums: Is This It, 2001; Singles: The Modern Age, Hard To Explain/New York City Cops, Last Nite/When It Started, 2001. *Honours:* Brit Award, Best International Newcomer, 2002; NME Awards: Band of The Year; Best New Act; Album of The Year, 2001. *Current Management:* Ryan Gentles, Wiz Kid Management. *Internet:* www.thestrokes.com.

VALENTIN David Peter; b. 29 April 1952, USA. Recording Artist; Musician (flute). *Musical Education:* High School Music and Art; One year Bronx Community College. *Career:* First artist on GRP Records; 17 albums recorded. *Compositions:* Over 30 compositions; Film soundtracks; Ghost music, Bill Cosby Show; Title track, album with Arturo Sandoval (Grammy award-winning album). *Honours:* Voted Best Flute, 6 years consecutively, Jazz Iz Magazine; Grammy Nomination, Best R & B Instrumental Performance, 1985; Entertainer of Year, NHAMAS, 1993; Vista 2000 Excellence In The Arts, 1995. *Leisure interests:* Practising the flute; Love. *Current Management:* Carl Valldejuli, Turi's Music Inc, 193 Westward Dr., Miami Springs, FL 33168, USA. *Address:* 154 Harding Park, Bronx, NY 10473, USA.

VALLANCE Jim; b. 31 May 1952. Songwriter. m. Rachel Paiement, 1 s. *Musical Education:* Private study, piano, cello. *Compositions:* for Aerosmith: Other Side; Ragdoll; Eat The Rich; for Bryan Adams: Heaven; Run To You; Summer of '69; Cuts Like A Knife; for Heart: What About Love; for Joe Cocker: When The Night Comes; for Tina Turner: It's Only Love; Back Where You Started; for Glass Tiger: Don't Forget Me When I'm Gone; for Bonnie Raitt, No Way To Treat A Lady; for Roger Daltrey, Rebel; for Ozzy Osbourne: Just Want You. *Honours:* 4 Juno Awards, Composer of the Year, (Canadian equivalent of Grammy); 3 BMI Awards (USA); More than 50 Gold and Platinum album awards (USA, Canada, Japan, UK, Germany). *Memberships:* SOCAN (Canada); ASCAP (USA); Board of Directors, PROCAN, 1987–90; Advisory Board, Songwriters Asscn of Canada, 1990–; Director of Canadian Society of Composers, Authors and Publishers, 1996–98, 2000-. *Current Management:* Rondor Music. *Address:* c/o Barbara Vander Linde, Rondor Music, 360 N La Cienega Blvd, Los Angeles, CA 90048, USA.

VALLDEJULI Carl Cats; b. 9 March 1962. Recording Artist Man. *Education:* Marine Biochemist, BS, MS. *Musical Education:* Piano; Music Theory. *Career:* Produced, co-ordinated world-wide concert tours. *Recordings:* Assistant and executive producer on over 10 albums including: Arturo Sandoval; Dave Valentin; Ed Calle. *Honours:* IAJE; NARAS; World Relief; Billboard; Grammy. *Membership:* Trustee NARAS. *Leisure interests:* Skiing; Golf. *Address:* Quiet Storm Inc, 2830 SW Lejeune Rd, Coral Gables, FL 33134–6602, USA.

VALLEJO Ramón M; b. 20 June 1963, Honduras. Singer; Musician (trombone, percussion). *Musical Education:* Musicianship at Cit Lit; Brass at Kensington and Chelsea College of Private Tutors. *Career:* Band leader, 2 Latin bands; Tours, Europe; Radio shows on news radio GLR, Jazz FM; Backing vocals for Matt Bianco; Own show in London, played with major world famous Latin players. *Compositions:* Numerous, all salsa, rumba, merengue rhythms. *Recordings:* 1 album: Shango. *Memberships:*

Musicians' Union; PRS. *Leisure interests:* Tennis; Amateur radio; Country walks. *Current Management:* RVR Promotions. *Address:* Mid Basement, 32 Queen's Gate Gardens, London SW7 5RR, England.

VALLI Frankie, (Frank Castelluccio); b. 3 May 1937, Newark, New Jersey, USA. Singer. *Career:* Member, Four Seasons, 1954–77; 1980s; Solo artiste, 1958-. *Recordings:* Albums: with the Four Seasons: Sherry and 11 Others, 1962; Ain't That A Shame and 11 Others, 1963; The 4 Seasons Greetings, 1963; Born To Wander, 1964; Dawn and 11 Other Great Songs, 1964; Rag Doll, 1964; Entertain You, 1965; The Four Seasons Sing Big Hits By Bacharach, David and Dylan, 1966; Working My Way Back To You, 1966; Lookin' Back, 1967; Christmas Album, 1967; Genuine Imitation Life Gazette, 1969; Edizione D'Oro, 1969; Chameleon, 1972; Streetfighter, 1975; Inside You, 1976; Who Loves You, 1976; Helicon, 1977; Reunited Live, 1981; Solo, 1967; Timeless, 1968; Inside You, 1975; Close Up, 1975; Story, 1976; Frankie Valli Is The Word, 1978; The Best of Frankie Valli, 1980; Heaven Above Me, 1981; Singles include: with the Four Seasons: Spanish Lace; Sherry; Big Girls Don't Cry (used in film soundtrack Dirty Dancing); Walk Like A Man; Dawn (Go Away); Rag Doll; The Night; Who Loves You; December 1963 (Oh What A Night), (No. 1, USA and UK), 1976; East Meets West (with the Beach Boys), 1984; Solo singles include: (You're Gonna) Hurt Yourself; Can't Take My Eyes Off You; I Make A Fool of Myself; To Give (The Reason I Live); You're Ready Now; My Eyes Adored You; Swearin' To God; Our Day Will Come; Fancy Dancer; Where Did We Go Wrong (with Chris Forde); Walk Like a Man, 1999. *Current Management:* International Creative Management, 8942 Wilshire Blvd, Beverly Hills, CA 90211, USA.

VAN BAVEL Boudewijn; b. 9 Jan. 1952, Breda, Netherlands. Prod.; Composer. 1 s. *Education:* Rotterdam. *Musical Education:* Music High, Rotterdam, 1975; Sound Engineering, 1989. *Career:* Producer, composer, Black Lee, Breda, Netherlands, 1973–79; Managing Director, Bo Easy Studios, Breda, 1980–89; Managing Director, Artists and Business, Rotterdam, 1990; Managing Director, Sky Trance International (studios and Theatre), Hilversum, Netherlands, and Antwerp, Belgium, 1990-. *Recordings:* California Fried Scene, Black Lee, 1979; I Got To Spend More Time, Bo Easy, 1983. *Leisure interests:* Films; Football. *Current Management:* Sky Trance International, Hilversum. *Address:* PO Box 64, 1200 AB Hilversum, Netherlands.

VAN BEST Peter; b. 15 Oct. 1951, Kaatsheuvel, Netherlands. Music Publisher; Organizer; Songwriter; Singer. *Musical Education:* School of Music (singing, piano). *Career:* Castlebar International Song Contest 1986 (RTE); Cavan International Song Contest 1988; Artemare Italy 1992; Europa Song France 1992 (Radio France); Europa Song Brussels 1993; Top Artist Show Italy, 1993; Midem Showcase 1994; Invited guest 70th anniversary in Paris of Peter Ustinov, 1991. *Compositions:* 25 years songwriting; own compositions published world-wide. *Honours:* Fidof (Festival Federation) Awards, 1988, 1990. *Memberships:* BUMA/Stemra, BASCA, FIDOF; SENA. *Leisure interests:* Jogging; Geography; Reading; Travel; Design; Languages. *Current Management:* Best Music. *Address:* Crispijnstraat 9, 5171 CH Kaatsheuvel, Netherlands.

VAN DORT Elizabeth (Liz); b. 3 March 1968, Melbourne, Australia. Singer; Composer. *Education:* Bachelor of Arts, Social Anthropology, University of Melbourne; HSC, Classical Singing; AMEB, Classical Singing Grade 7; Numerous choral and madrigal groups; piano lessons. *Career:* Vocalist/Composer, Far From the Madding Crowd, Glastonbury Festival and others; World Voices, solo show, Australia; Backing Vocalist, Invisible Opera Company Australia; What the Funk. *Recordings:* Faraway: Far From the Madding Crowd, CD; Sting and the Radio Actors, Nuclear Waste; Daevid Allen, 12 Selves, backing vocals. *Memberships:* APRA; MCPS. *Leisure interests:* Reading; Yoga. *Current Management:* Evolving Management, PO Box 2237, St Kilda, West Victoria, 3182, Australia.

VAN DYKE Leroy Frank; b. 4 Oct. 1929, Pettis County, Missouri, USA. Country Music Performer. m. Gladys Marie Daniels, 25 June 1980, 3 s., 1 d. *Education:* Graduate, Journalism, Animal Science, University of Missouri; Graduate, Reppert's School of Autioneeering. *Career:* Support for show by Marilyn Monroe; Tours regularly, USA and abroad; Played Las Vegas; Plays various venues, especially agricultural events (fairs, rodeos, livestock events); Television includes: Regular member, Red Foley's Ozark Jubilee, ABC-TV; Host, Leroy Van Dyke Show; Star, film, What Am I Bid?; Radio: Co-host, Country Crossroads. *Recordings include:* Auctioneer; Walk On By. *Honours:* Billboard magazine, Biggest Ever Country Hit, Walk On By, 1994. *Memberships:* CMA; ACM; NATD; IEBA; IAFE. *Leisure interest:* Raising mules from registered Arabian mares and mammoth jacks. *Current Management:* Leroy Van Dyke Enterprises, Gladys Van Dyke. *Address:* 29000 Hwy V, Smithton, MO 65350, USA.

VAN HALEN Alex; b. 8 May 1955, Nijmegen, Netherlands. Musician (drums). *Career:* Formed US rock group Van Halen, with brother Eddie, 1974–; Support tours with UFO; Santana; Black Sabbath; Regular headlining tours, US and world-wide; Major appearances include: First

US tour, 1978; California Music Festival, 1979; US Festival, 1982, 1983; Monsters of Rock, Castle Donington, 1984; Monsters of Rock US tour (with Metallica, Scorpions), 1988; Texas Jam, 1988. *Recordings:* Albums: Van Halen, 1978; Van Halen II, 1979; Women and Children First, 1980; Fair Warning, 1981; Diver Down, 1982; 1984, 1983; 5150 (No. 1, USA), 1986; OU812 (No. 1, USA), 1988; For Unlawful Carnal Knowledge (No. 1, USA), 1991; Right Here Right Now, 1993; Balance, 1995; Twister, 1996; Best of Van Halen, 1996; Van Halen 3, 1998; Singles include: You Really Got Me, 1978; Runnin' With The Devil, 1978; Dance The Night Away, 1979; And The Cradle Will Rock, 1980; (Oh) Pretty Woman, 1982; Dancing In The Street, 1982; Jump (No. 1, USA), 1984; Panama, 1984; I'll Wait, 1984; Hot For Teacher, 1984; Why Can't This Be Love, 1986; Love Walks In, 1986; Dreams, 1986; When It's Love, 1988; Finish What Ya Started, 1988; Feels So Good, 1989; Poundcake, 1991; Top of The World, 1991; Right Now, 1992. *Honours:* Numerous Platinum discs; Grammy Award, Best Hard Rock Performance, 1992; American Music Award, Favourite Hard Rock Album, 1992; Band awarded Gold Ticket, Madison Square Gardens, 1988; Inducted into Hollywood Rock Walk, 1991; MTV Video Awards, 1984, 1992. *Current Management:* SRO Management Inc, 189 Carlton St, Toronto, ON M5A 2K7, Canada.

VAN HALEN Eddie; b. 26 Jan. 1957, Nijmegen, Netherlands. Rock Musician (guitar). m. 11 April 1981, Valerie Bertinelli, 1 s. *Musical Education:* Piano lessons, Pasadena City College. *Career:* Founded US rock group Van Halen, with brother Alex 1974–; Support tours to UFO; Santana; Black Sabbath; Regular headlining tours, US and world-wide; Major appearances include: First US tour, 1978; California Music Festival, 1979; US Festival, 1982, 1983; Monsters of Rock Festival, Castle Donington, 1984; Monsters of Rock US tour (with Metallica, Scorpions), 1988; Texas Jam, 1988. *Recordings:* Albums: Van Halen, 1978; Van Halen II, 1979; Women and Children First, 1980; Fair Warning, 1981; Diver Down, 1982; 1984, 1984; 5150 (No. 1, USA), 1986; OU812 (No. 1, USA), 1988; For Unlawful Carnal Knowledge (No. 1, USA), 1991; Right Here Right Now, 1993; Balance, 1995; Twister, 1996; Best of Van Halen, 1996; Van Halen 3, 1998; Also appears on: Legend of 1900; Private Life; Wild Life; Singles include: You Really Got Me, 1978; Running With The Devil, 1978; Dance The Night Away, 1979; And The Cradle Will Rock, 1980; (Oh) Pretty Woman, 1982; Jump (No. 1, USA), 1984; Panama, 1984; I'll Wait, 1984; Hot For Teacher, 1984; Why Can't This Be Love, 1986; Dreams, 1986; Love Walks In, 1986; When It's Love, 1988; Finish What Ya Started, 1988; Feels So Good, 1989; Poundcake, 1991; Top of The World, 1991; Right Now, 1992; Contributor, Beat It, Michael Jackson (No. 1, USA), 1983. *Honours:* Numerous Platinum discs; Grammy Award, Best Hard Rock Performance, 1992; American Music Award, Favourite Hard Rock Album, 1992; MTV Music Video Awards, 1984, 1992; Band awarded Gold Ticket, Madison Square Gardens, 1988. *Current Management:* SRO Management Inc, 189 Carlton St, Toronto, ON M5A 2K7, Canada.

VAN HELDEN Armand; b. 1972, Boston, Massachusetts, USA. DJ; Remixer/Prod. *Career:* Member, X-Mix Productions, Boston; Began remixing many Euro-pop acts; Began parallel solo career; Now remixes numerous top acts as well as releasing own records. *Recordings include:* Singles: Witch Doktor, 1994; Armand Van Helden, 1994; Psychic Bounty Killas, 1996; The Funk Phenomena, 1996; Ain't Armand, 1997; Ultrafunkula/Reservoir Dogs, 1997; Old School Junkies, 1997; Welcome to the Meat Market, 1997; Ghetto House Groove, 1998; 2 Future 4 U EP, 1998; You Don't Know Me, 1999; Flowerz, 1999; Albums: Old School Junkies, 1996; Da Club Phenomena, 1997; Enter the Meatmarket, 1997; Armand Van Helden Phenomenon, 1999; 2 Future 4 U, 1999; As Remixer/ Producer: Latin Thang: Latin Thang, 1994; This Is Strictly Rhythm Vol. 4, 1994; Rest of New Order, 1995; Jimmy Somerville: Heartbeat, 1995; This Is Strictly Rhythm, Vol. 5, 1995; Mega Dance Party, 1995; Platinum On Black Vol. 2, 1996; Digitized, 1996; C J Bolland: Analogue Theatre, 1996; Tori Amos: Professional Widow, 1996; Best Girl Power Album Ever, 1997; Decade of Ibiza, 1997; DJ Icey: Funky Breaks, 1997; Jocelyn Brown: It's Alright I Feel It, 1997; Sneaker Pimps: Spin Spin Sugar, 1997; Apollo Four Forty: Ain't Talkin' 'Bout Dub, 1997; Henry Street Bombs Vol. 2, 1998; Tuff and Jam: Speed Garage Underground, 1998.

VAN HOVE Fred; b. 19 Feb. 1937, Antwerp, Belgium. Musician (Piano, Church Organ, Accordion). m. (2) Mie Van Cakenberghe, 2 April 1986, 3 s. *Education:* Piano, Theory, Harmony, Music Academy. *Career:* Free improvised music: Concerts, radio, TV; Festivals: Europe, Japan, USA, Canada, China, South Africa, Morocco. *Compositions:* for mixed instrument groups and improvising soloists; for Big Band and own groups: MLB III, Piano Kwartet, Nonet. *Recordings:* More than 60: Lust; Pyp; Suite for B-City; Flux; Passing Waves. *Honours:* Cultural Ambassador of Flanders, 1996, 1997. *Memberships:* Wim wzw, Asscn for Improvised Music, Antwerp, Chairman. *Current Management:* Mie, St Vincentiusstr 61, B2018 Antwerp, Belgium.

VAN OLDEREN Martin; b. 3 Jan. 1931, Netherlands. Blues Promoter; Record Prod.; Radio Broadcaster. m. Carolien Van Der Kamp, 13 March 1957, 1 s., 1 d. *Career:* Organized concert featuring Memphis Slim, Little

Brother Montgomery, Lightning Slim, Whispering Smith, 1971; Started Chicago Blues Festival, 1970–; Organized Blues Estafette, Utrecht, 1979–81; Amsterdam Blues Festival, Meervaart, annual event; Established Oldie Blues, own blues record label reproducing 78s, 1970; Compiled archive on blues music, including 15000 photos; Writes texts for CD covers; Broadcaster, own radio programme Bluesnachten (Blues Nights), VRPO, 1972–; Personal agent for blues artists playing in Holland including: Bo Diddley; Muddy Waters; Sonny Terry; Doctor Ross; BB King. *Publications:* Boogie Woogie and Blues Collector. *Membership:* President, Dutch Blues and Boogie Organisation. *Leisure interests:* Record collecting; Walking; Swimming. *Current Management:* Martin Van Olderen Blues Promotions. *Address:* Maasdrielhof 175, 1106 NG Amsterdam, Zuidoost, Netherlands.

VAN POL Hans; b. 6 Aug. 1955, Amsterdam, Netherlands. Personal Man.; Talent Scout. *Education:* Literature and Law, University of Amsterdam. *Musical Education:* Private singing and dancing lessons for 4 years. *Career:* First Gold recording as solo singer with children's choir, 1964; Singer with various rock, wave and ska bands, 1973–78; Member of Small Talk, touring through Europe, 1978–80; Member of Dutch band, Vulcano, 1980–85; Now Manager, 1985-. *Recordings:* 5 albums and 15 singles. *Honours:* 2 Gold albums; Popularity Award, 1983. *Membership:* Dutch Music Manager Asscn. *Leisure interests:* Sailing; Biking. *Address:* PO Box 9010, 1006 AA Amsterdam, Netherlands.

VANCEUNEBROUCK-WERTH Richard; b. 1952, Seattle, Washington, USA. Prod.; Composer; Musician (keyboards, percussion). *Musical Education:* Studied under electronic music pioneer Vladimir Ussachevsky, University of Utah. *Career:* Performed internationally with touring groups, 1970–77; Tangerine Dream's first North American tour, 1977; First performance, Seattle Symphony Orchestra, 1982; Composes film and special event soundtracks, 1980–; First commissioned work, IBM, Paramount, Disney, 1981; National broadcasts include CTV (Canada), ABC TV; First commissioned operatic work, Seattle's Floating Opera, 1987; Produced AFFINITY Project, release new Beethoven music 1989; Producer, composer, St Elmo's Choir; Tangerine Dream, 1989-. *Recordings:* with Tangerine Dream: Music from the 21st Century; with RV-Werth and S Chatelaine: AFFINITY; with Seattle Opera's Floating Opera: Seraphim Suite; with St Elmo's Choir: Syrenes; White Stocking Day; with R Kotta: Alive, Alive-O; And many others. *Honours:* NAMA, Best New Age Group, 1989; Commissions: Seattle Opera; National Endowment For The Arts, Seattle, Tacoma, Vancouver BC, Edmonton, Canada Arts Commissions; Longest Requested Airplay in Soviet Union, 1991-. *Memberships:* ASCAP; BMI; NAMA; International Producer's Guild. *Leisure interests:* Pioneer laser/light artist performing internationally since 1976; Film-making. *Current Management:* Omega Organisation International. *Address:* PO Box 33623-WWIM, Seattle, WA 98133–0623, USA.

VANDENBROUCQE Gérard; b. 15 May 1961, France. Musician (violin). *Musical Education:* Lessons with Pierre Cuuaz; J L Pino; Didier Lockwood. *Career:* Television: Antenne 2; M6; Europe 1; Appearances at: Montréal Festival, 1993; SOPS, New York; Radio France Inter. *Recordings:* Tango, Violin Onztet. *Membership:* Asscn Jazz et Violon. *Current Management:* c/o JMS, 12 rue Bouchut, 75015 Paris, France. *Address:* 12 rue Lazare Carnot, 92140 Clamart, France.

VANDENDRIESSCHE Johan; b. 30 May 1958, Leuven, Belgium, Musician (Saxophones, Flutes, Bass Clarinet, Drums, Bass Guitar, Keyboards); Teacher of Jazz History and Harmony (Conservatorium GENT) and Woodwinds. m. Hilde Pollet, 8 Dec. 1991, 1 s., 1 d. *Education:* Degree of Excellence, Conservatorium of Leuven; Private lessons, Jazz; Musicology, KUL, Leuven. *Career:* Appearances with Belgium Radio and TV orchestras; BRT Big Band; BRT Jazzorkest/ Philharmonic Orchestra; Euro/Jazz Orchestra; Own Band, Milkshake Banana, played in jazz festivals in Atlanta, USA, Montreux, Switzerland, Aarhus, Denmark; Concerts with Randy Crawford and John Miles as a soloist in Belgium and Holland; WDR Big Band, Cologne, Germany, with Clare Fisher; Own bands Jive Talk and The Demagogue Reacts. *Compositions:* Move; Nathalie; Cool Bird; ISIRO. *Recordings:* With Milkshake Banana, ACT Bigband, Caude Maurane, Soulsister, Claude Nougaro, Indochine, Johan Verminnen. *Publications:* Articles on jazz in KNACK magazine, 1981–82. *Honour:* First Prize, International Jazz Contest, Hoeilaart, 1979. *Leisure interests:* Literature; Monty Python; Blackadder; Hammond C3; Walking. *Current Management:* BVBA VDDR. *Address:* Groenstraat 33, 3110 Rotselaar, Belgium, 0032/161447001.

VANDROSS Luther; b. 20 April 1951, New York, USA. Singer; Songwriter; Arranger; Prod. *Career:* Member, Listen My Brother (musical theatre workshop), Harlem, 1973; Session singer (recordings and commercials), arranger, 1974–80; Leader, own group, Luther, 1976–77; Solo artiste, 1980–; Regular international concerts. *Compositions include:* Fascination, David Bowie; You Stopped Lovin' Me, Roberta Flack. *Recordings:* Albums: Luther, 1976; This Close To You, 1977; Solo albums: Never Too Much, 1981; Forever For Always For Love, 1982; Busy Body,

1984; Give Me The Reason, 1986; Any Love, 1988; The Best of Luther Vandross, 1989; Power of Love, 1991; Never Let Me Go, 1993; Songs, 1994; This is Christmas, 1995; Your Secret Love, 1996; I Know, 1998; Hit singles include: The Night I Fell In Love, 1985; Give Me The Reason, from film Ruthless People, 1986; Stop To Love, 1987; There's Nothing Better Than Love, duet with Gregory Hines, 1987; Any Love, 1989; She Won't Talk To Me, 1989; Here and Now, 1990; Power of Love/Love Power, 1991; Don't Want To Be A Fool, 1991; The Best Things In Life Are Free, duet with Janet Jackson, from film Mo' Money, 1992; Love The One You're With, 1995; Going in Circles, 1995; I Can Make It Better, 1996; Are You Using Me?, 1998; Heart of a Hero, 1999; Sessions as backing singer include: Young Americans, David Bowie, 1974; Songs For The New Depression, Bette Midler, 1975; Sounds and Stuff Like That, Quincy Jones, 1978; Le Freak, Chic, 1978; We Are Family, Sister Sledge, 1978; Other sessions for Ringo Starr; Carly Simon; Chaka Khan; Average White Band; Vocal arranger, No More Tears, Donna Summer and Barbra Streisand, 1979; Producer, recordings by Aretha Franklin; Dionne Warwick; Diana Ross; Whitney Houston; Contributor, Voices That Care (Red Cross charity record), 1991; The Heart of a Hero (AIDS research benefit record), 1992. *Honours include:* MVP Background Singer, 1977–80; Grammy Awards: Best R & B Vocal Performance, 1991, 1992; Best R & B Song, 1992; Grammy Nomination, Best R & B Vocal, 1987; Soul Train Music Awards: Best Male R & B Album, 1987, 1992; Best Male R & B Single, 1990; American Music Awards: Favourite Soul/R & B Male Artist, 1988, 1990, 1992; Favourite Soul/R & B Album, 1992; NAACP Image Awards: Best Male Artist, 1990; Best Male Vocalist, Best Album, 1992; Luther Vandross Day, Los Angeles, 1991. *Current Management:* The Left Bank Organization. *Address:* 6255 Sunset Blvd, Suite 1111, Hollywood, CA 90028, USA.

VANGELIS (Evangelos Papathanassiou); b. 29 March 1943, Volos, Greece. Musician (keyboards); Composer. *Education:* Academy of Fine Arts, Athens. *Musical Education:* Studied Classical music with Aristotelis Coudourof. *Career:* Member, Formynx, 1960s; Member, Aphrodite's Child, with Demis Roussos; Composer, Paris, 1972; Built Nemo recording studio, London, 1974; Partnership with Jon Anderson as Jon and Vangelis, 1980–84. *Compositions:* Music scores for French wildlife films, 1972; Heaven and Hell, Third Movement, theme for Carl Sagan's TV series Cosmos, BBC1, 1981; Film scores: Chariots of Fire; Blade Runner; Missing; Mutiny On The Bounty; City; 1492 – Conquest of Paradise; All tracks on solo albums self-composed, played and produced. *Recordings:* Albums: with Aphrodite's Child: 666; Solo albums: L'Apocalypse Des Animaux, 1972; Heaven and Hell, 1976; Albedo 0.39, 1976; Spiral, 1977; Beauborg, 1978; China, 1979; Film soundtrack, Chariots of Fire, 1981; Soil Activities, 1984; Mask, 1985; Opera Sauvage, 1987; Direct, 1988; Themes, 1989; 1492 – Conquest of Paradise, 1992; Voices, 1995; El Greco, 1995; Oceanic, 1997; Spiral, 1997; As Jon and Vangelis: Short Stories, 1980; The Friends of Mr Cairo, 1981; Private Collection, 1983; The Best of Jon and Vangelis, 1984; Page of Life, 1991; Singles include: with Aphrodite's Child: Rain and Tears; Solo: Heaven and Hell, Third Movement, 1981; Chariots of Fire (No. 1, USA), 1982; with Jon Anderson: I Hear You Know, 1980; I'll Find My Way Home, 1982; Also featured on Polar Shift charity album, 1991. *Honour:* Academy Award, Best Original Score, Chariots of Fire, 1982.

VANIAN Dave, (David Letts); b. 12 Oct. 1956. Singer. *Career:* Former grave digger; Vocalist, UK punk rock group, The Damned, 1976–77; Appearances include: Mont de Marsan punk festival, France, 1976; Support to the Sex Pistols, Anarchy In The UK Tour, 1976; First UK punk group to play US dates, 1977; Member, Doctors of Madness, 1978; The Damned reformed, 1978–89; International concerts include: Christmas On Earth festival, Leeds, 1981; Member, side projects: Naz and the Nomads, 1988; Dave Vanian and the Phantom Chords, 1990, 1995; The Damned reunion tour, 1991. *Recordings:* Albums: with the Damned: Damned Damned Damned, 1977; Music For Pleasure, 1977; Machine Gun Etiquette, 1979; The Black Album, 1980; The Best Of, 1981; Strawberries, 1982; Phantasmagoria, 1985; Anything, 1986; Light At The End of Tunnel, 1987; Peel Sessions, 1990; Not of This Earth, 1996; Eternal Damnation Live, 1999; with Naz and the Nomads: Give Daddy The Knife, Cindy, 1988; Singles include: with The Damned: Love Song, 1979; Smash It Up, 1979; Grimly Fiendish, 1985; The Shadow of Love, 1985; Is It A Dream, 1985; Anything, 1986; Eloise (No. 3, UK), 1986; Alone Again Or, 1987.

VANNELLI Joseph Anthony; b. 28 Dec. 1950, Montréal, Québec, Canada. Prod.; Arranger; Musician (keyboards). *Education:* 3 years university. *Musical Education:* Private. *Career:* Worked with: Gino Vannelli; Gary Morris; David Meece; Kudasai; Marilyn Scott; Jimmy Haslip; Don Sebesky and The Royal Philharmonic Orchestra; Gregory Hines; Co-producer, commercials including Pontiac; Honda; Owner, recording studio; Concerts include Gino Vannelli's World Tour, 1990–92; Television includes: Arsenio Hall Show, European television; Juno Award Show, Canada; Dick Clark Night Time; Documentary on rain forests of Costa Rica. *Recordings:* Crazy Life, 1973; Powerful People, 1974; Storm At Sunup, 1975; The Gist of The Gemini, 1976; Brother To Brother, 1978; Nightwalker, 1981; Black Cars, 1985; Big Dreamers Never Sleep, 1987;

Inconsolable Man, 1991; Gino Vannelli Live In Montréal, 1992; Yonder Tree, 1995; Man in the Moon, 1996; Sexogroove, 1998; Voices in Harmony, 1998; Never Knew, 1998; Sweetest Day of May, 1999. *Publications:* REP Magazine; Midi Magazine; Keyboard Magazine, Japan. *Current Management:* Diane Ricci. *Address:* 28205 Agoura Rd, Agoura Hills, CA 91301, USA.

VANROBAEYS Filip; Musician. *Musical Education:* Self-taught, Fiddle, Harp, Guitar, Whistles, Badhan. *Career:* Member, Group The Swigshift; Dranouter Festival, 1995; Den Ekster, 1996, 1997; Labadoux Festival, 1997; Paulus Festival, 1997; Sloanthe Festival, 1997; Gooik Festival 2002, 1997; De Brakke Grond, Amsterdam, 1997; Foleys Irish Pub, Ghent; Radio 1, De Groote Boodschap; Several Regional Radio and Television Appearances. *Compositions:* Jumpin The Fences; Dirty Wally; Friends Sadness; Something to Fear; Shut the Pub; A Whistler's Wedding. *Recordings:* Tales From the Great Whiskey Book, 1996. *Honours:* Government Medal, Flute, 1986; Second Place, Youth Soloist Festival, 1986; Finale, Westtalent, 1995. *Membership:* Volksmuziekfederatie, Belgium. *Leisure interest:* Music. *Current Management:* KAFT Productions, Akkerwindelaan 20, 8791 Beveren-Leie, Belgium. *Address:* c/o Barrierestraat 49, 8940 Wervik, Belgium.

VARIS Francis; b. 4 Feb. 1957, Clamart, France. Musician (accordion). m. Françoise Niay. *Musical Education:* Musicological License, Paris VIII University. *Career:* Tours and European jazz festivals with: American guitarist Tal Farlow, 1983; Brazilian singer Nazaré Pereira, 1985–; Saxophone player Lee Konitz, 1986–89; The Paris-Musette, Tokyo, Montréal, 1991–; Own group Bolovaris. *Recordings:* Cordes Et Lames, 1983; Medium Rare, with Lee Konitz, 1986; Accordion Madness, with accordionist Kenny Kotwitz, 1989; Paris-Musette 1 and 2, 1991, 1993; Bolovaris, 1994; Ombre, with Romane, 1998; Identities, with Idir, 1999; Ivory Port, with Jacques Bolognesi, 1999. *Honours:* Grand Prix du Disque de l'Academie Charles Cros. *Current Management:* Alain Brisemontier. *Address:* Le Moulin, 49800 Sarrigné, France.

VARSANYI Juraj; b. 14 May 1961, Bratislava, Slovakia. Drums; Percussion; Cimbalom. *Musical Education:* People's Conservatory, Bratislava. *Career:* International tours; Many TV and radio shows with: Vus-Orchestra, Gravis, Knock-Out, Jully's Orchestra, Just Jazz, Bratislava Jazz Days, 1991; Burg Mautendorf Jazzkettbewerd-Aut; Hajnal Quintet, 1987; Varsanyi Habsburg-Wedding, 1993. *Recordings:* Vus LP, 1983; Gombitova and Gravis LP, 1986; Knock Out, LP, 1987; Gravis, LP, 1989; Varsanyi, LP, 1991; La Rubia, CD, 1995; Slovak Jazz Anthology, CD, 1992. *Honours:* Gorizia, International Festival Contest, 1986; Second Prize, Slovak Jazz Festival, 1995. *Membership:* Slovak Jazz Society, 1989/90-. *Current Management:* Slovak Jazz Society, Jaku Bouonalm 12, Bratislava, Slovakia. *Address:* Varsanyi Juraj, Hlavna 20, 90044 Tomasov, Slovakia.

VARTAN Sylvie; b. 15 Aug. 1944, Iskretz, Bulgaria. m. (1) Johnny Hallyday, 1965, divorced, 1980, 1 s., (2) Tony Scotti, 1984, 1 d. *Education:* Lycée Hélène-Boucher, Paris. *Career:* Singing debut in duet with Frankie Jordan (panne d'essence), national tours, 1961–; international tours, 1965–, including Paris Olympia, 1961, 1962, 1963, 1964 (with The Beatles), 1967, 1968, 1970, 1972, 1996, 1999; Palais des Congres, Paris, 1975–76, 1977–78, 1983; Palais des Sports, Paris, 1981, 1991; Casino de Paris, 1995, Las Vegas, USA, 1982, Los Angeles, USA, 1983, Atlantic City, USA, 1984 and Sofia, Bulgaria, 1990; Songs include: Tous mes copains, En ecoutant la pluie, I'm Watching, Si je chante, La plus belle pour aller danser, Quand tu es la, Par amour par pitié, 2'35 de bonheur, Le Kid, Comme un garçon, La Maritza, La chasse a l'homme, Loup, Dilindam, L'heure la plus douce de ma vie, Pour lui je reviens, Mon père, J'ai un problème (with Johnny Hallyday), Toi le garçon, Bye bye Leroy Brown, la drole de fin, Qu'est-ce qui fait pleurer les blondes?; Le temps du swing, Petit rainbow, I don't want the night to end, Nicolas, Merveilleusement desenchantee, L'amour c'est comme une cigarette, Aimer, Des heures de desir, Double exposure, Virage, Femme sous influence, C'est fatal, Qui tu es, Je n'aime encore que toi, Sensible; TV appearances include: Show Smet, 1965; Jolie poupee, 1968; Doppia coppia, 1969; Sacha Sylvie Show, 1969; Sylvissima, 1970; Top a Sylvie Vartan, 1972, 1972; Top a Sylvie et Johnny, 1973; Je chante pour Swanee, 1974; Sylvie, 1975; Punto e Basta, 1975; Dancing Star, 1977; La Maritza, 1990; Sylvie sa vie, 1994; Irrésistiblement... Sylvie, 1998; Qu'est-ce qui fait rêver Sylvie?, 2000; Films: Un clair de lune a Maubeuge, 1962; D'ou viens-tu Johnny?, 1963; Cherchez l'idole, 1964; Patate, 1964; Les poneyttes, 1967; Malpertuis, 1971; Mon amie Sylvie, 1972; L'ange noir, 1994. *Publications:* Si je chante, 1981; Beauty Book, 1985. *Honours:* Triomphe des variétés award, 1970; Chevalier des Arts et des Lettres, 1985; Chevalier de l'ordre national du mérite, 1987; Chevalier de l'ordre du Cavalier de Madara, Bulgaria, 1996; Chevalier dans l'ordre de la legion d'Honneur, 1998. *Address:* c/o Charley Marouani, 37 rue Marbeuf, 75008, Paris, France.

VASCONCELLOS Joe; b. 9 March 1959, Santiago, Chile. Musician (percussion); Vocalist; Composer. m. Irene Gonzalez Peña, 1 March 1985. *Education:* College (Brazil, Ecuador, Japan, Italy). *Musical Education:*

Conservatorio Musicale Nicolo Paganini, Genoa, Italy. *Career:* with Maria Creuza, Musician (percussion): Tours throughout Brazil; Argentina; Uruguay; Spain; USA; As Joe Vasconcellos (Singer with own band): all national territory Chile; TV appearances: Sabado Gigante, Chile. *Recordings:* As vocalist of Congreso: Viaje Por La Cresta del Mundo; Ha Llegado Carta; Joe Vasconcellos: Esto Es Solo Una Canción; Verde Cerca; Toque, 1995; Major composition: Hijo Del Sol Luminoso. *Honours:* with Congreso: Best Group (Chile); As Joe Vasconcellos: Nominated Verde Cerca Best Record. *Membership:* Sociedad Chilena Del Derecho De Autor. *Leisure interests:* Swimming; Cycling; Walking. *Current Management:* Galo Producciones S A. *Address:* Hernando De Aguirre 944 – Providencia, Santiago, Chile.

VASCONCELOS Monica; b. 13 Nov. 1966, São Paulo, Brazil. Musician; Singer; Lyricist. *Education:* São Paulo University, Brazil. *Career:* Started Singing At 17; Bars, Parties, Backing Vocals for Record Producers; Joined Vocal, Drama Group, Beijo, 1987; Toured Brazil, Sang on Television and Radio; Recorded With Musicians in London, Roland Perrin, Ashley Slater, John O'Neall; Sang with Tim Garland, Christine Tobin, Jacqui Dankworth; Own Band, Toured England; Supported Gilberto Gil, Barbican Hall. *Compositions:* Sabonete Do Mato; Mudanca Oragao; Ivan Da Caverna; Vestidinho; Guizim; Xotemo; Bossa Zangada; Outono; Maracatu Do Pomso; Samba Da Ponte; Atabaque. *Recordings:* Beijo; Nois; Nois Dois. *Membership:* Musicians' Union.

VASIK Cassandra; b. Chatham, Ontario, Canada. Musician (acoustic guitar); Entertainer. *Musical Education:* 3 year diploma, Fanshawe College, London, Ontario. *Career:* Member, Little Egypt; Moved to Toronto; Receptionist, independent record label; Member, Lost, acoustic trio; Television: Christmas With The Troops, performing to United Nations Peace Keeping Troops, Europe and Middle East, 1992; Ear To The Ground; Canada Day; Spotlight; Winterlude '93; Friday Night With Ralph Benmergui; Video, Sadly Mistaken, No. 1, Outlaws and Heroes, Much Music: Tours with: Randy Travis; The Nitty Gritty Dirt Band; Clint Black; Steve Wariner; Vince Gill; Van Shelton; Marty Stewart. *Recordings:* Albums: Wildflowers; Feels Like Home; Singles: It Comes Back To You; Which Face Should I Put On Tonight; Those Stars; Wildflowers; Sadly Mistaken; Fortune Smiled; Roll Like A Wheel; Almost Like You Cared. *Honours:* 2 JUNO Awards, Country Female Vocalist, 1991, 1993; Vista Rising Star Award, CCMA, 1992; CCMA Award, Vocal Collaboration (with Russell de Carle), 1993; Commemorative Medal for the 125th Anniversary, Confederation of Canada, 1993. *Memberships:* CARAS; SOCAN; CCMA; ACTRA. *Leisure interests:* Cycling; Horse riding; Reading; Listening to music. *Current Management:* John W. Edwards, Renaissance Music and Entertainment.

VAUGHN Danny; b. New York, USA. Vocalist; Lyricist. *Career:* Singer, rock group Waysted, 1987; Tours include Europe, supporting Iron Maiden, 1987; Singer, lyricist, rock group Tyketto, 1988–; Concerts include: L'Amour, Brooklyn; NYC Cat Club, supporting Skid Row; Numerous US State Fairs; Tours and festivals, Europe, USA, 1991-. *Recordings:* Albums: with Waysted: Save Your Prayers, 1987; with Tyketto: Don't Come Easy, 1990; Strength In Numbers, 1994; Inishmore, 1998; Also featured on Union, Yes, 1991. *Address:* c/o Music For Nations Records, 333 Latimer Rd, London W10 6RA, England.

VAZQUEZ Roland; b. 4 July 1951, Pasadena, California, USA. m. Susan Botti, 1988, 1 d. *Education:* MM, Manhattan School of Music, 1985; Member, Manhattan School of Music Jazz Faculty, Ensembles and Composition. *Career:* Leader and Sideman, numerous recordings, on US and international jazz radio, 1979–; Appearances as Composer/Leader at major jazz festivals and venues throughout the USA, and in Canada, Scandinavia and Central America. *Compositions:* 57 compositions recorded and published for jazz quintet, octet, tentet, big band, and chamber group. *Recordings:* Albums as Composer/Leader: Urban Ensemble: The Music of Roland Vazquez, 1979; Feel Your Dream, 1982; The Tides of Time, 1988; No Separate Love, 1991; Best of the LA Jazz Ensemble, 1994; Further Dance, 1997. *Honours:* National Endowment for the Arts grant, 1977; Meet the Composer, 1986, 1997; Arts International, 1997. *Memberships:* ASCAP; NARAS; IAJE; AFIM. *Address:* 924 West End Ave No. 1, New York, NY 10025, USA.

VEAR Anthony Craigy 'Watts'; b. 4 Dec. 1970, Middlesbrough, England. Musician (drums, percussion). *Career:* At 14, 3 years' working mens' clubs; Theatre premieres of: Assassins; Stephen Sondheim; Manchester; Little Shop of Horrors; 5 tours with Cholmondelys Dance Company; World tours with: Renegade Soundwave, 1994; The Wolfgang Press, 1995; Concerts in Los Angeles with Tom Jones, 1994. *Recordings:* Albums include: Funky Little Demons, 1993–94; Tom Jones: The Lead and How To Swing It, 1994. *Honours:* Included in exhibition at New Rock and Roll Museum, Cleveland, USA. *Memberships:* Musicians' Union; LMC; SAL, UK. *Leisure interest:* Composition. *Address:* Basement Flat, 5 Gilmore Rd, London SE13 5AD, England.

VEDDER Eddie (Edward Mueller); b. 23 Dec. 1966, Evanston, Illinois, USA. Vocalist. *Career:* Lead singer, US rock group Pearl Jam, 1991–; Concerts include: Support tour, Alice In Chains, 1991; Lollapalooza Festival tour, 1992; Drop In The Park concert, Seattle, 1992; European tour, 1992; Bob Dylan 30th anniversary concert, Madison Square Garden, 1992; Band appears in film Singles, 1992; Support to Keith Richards and The Expensive Winos, 1992; Rock For Choice benefit concert, Los Angeles, 1993; Concert appearances with Neil Young. *Recordings:* Albums: with Pearl Jam: Ten, 1992; Vs. (No. 1, USA), 1993; Vitalogy, 1994; Merkin Ball, 1995; No Code, 1996; Yield, 1998; Live on Two Legs, 1998; Singles include: Alive, 1992; Even Flow, 1992; Jeremy, 1992; Contributor, Singles film soundtrack, 1992; Sweet Relief album, 1993; Dead Man Walking, film soundtrack, 1996; Tibetan Freedom Concert, 1997. *Honours:* American Music Award, Favourite New Artist, Pop/Rock and Hard Rock categories, 1993; Rolling Stone Readers Awards: Best Male Singer, Best New American Band, Best Video, 1993; 4 MTV Video Awards; Highest 1-week album sales total in history, Vs., 1993. *Current Management:* Curtis Management, 417 Denny Way, Suite 200, Seattle, WA 98109, USA.

VEE Bobby, (Robert Velline); b. 30 April 1943, Fargo, North Dakota, USA. Singer. *Career:* Founder, US group The Shadows, 1958; Solo singer, 1960–; World-wide appearances include: Hollywood Bowl, with Jerry Lee Lewis, Brenda Lee, The Shirelles, 1961; British tour with The Crickets, 1962; Dick Clark's Caravan of Stars US tour, 1963; British tour with Dusty Springfield, The Searchers, 1964; British tour, with Dusty Springfield, The Searchers, The Zombies, 1965; British tour, with Del Shannon and Brian Hyland, 1988; Annual appearances, Buddy Holly Memorial Concerts; Giants of Rock 'n' Roll, Wembley Arena, with Little Richard, Duane Eddy, 1992; Film appearances: Play It Cool, 1962; Just For Fun, 1963. *Recordings:* Albums: Bobby Vee, 1961; Bobby Vee Sings Hits of The Rockin' 50s, 1961; Take Good Care of My Baby, 1962; Bobby Vee Meets The Crickets, 1962; A Bobby Vee Recording Session, 1962; Golden Greats, 1962; Merry Christmas From..., 1962; The Night Has A Thousand Eyes, 1963; Bobby Vee Meets The Ventures, 1963; Bobby Vee Sings The New Sound From England, 1964; Come Back When You Grow Up, 1967; Just Today, 1968; Nothing Like A Sunny Day, 1972; The Bobby Vee Singles Album, 1980; Favorites, 1997; Down the Line, 1999; Hit singles include: Devil Or Angel, 1960; Rubber Ball, 1961; More Than I Can Say, 1961; Take Good Care of My Baby (No. 1, USA), 1961; How Many Tears, 1961; Run To Him, 1961; Sharing You, 1962; A Forever Kind of Love, 1962; The Night Has A Thousand Eyes, from film Just For Fun, 1963; Charms, 1963; Come Back When You're Grown Up, 1967. *Current Management:* DHM – Dave Hoffman Management. *Address:* PO Box 26037, Minneapolis, MN 55447, USA.

VEGA Louie, (Little Louie Vega, Groovebox); b. 12 June 1965, New York, USA. Prod.; Remixer; DJ. *Career:* Began as a DJ in New York, 1980's; Starting doing mixes for artists including The Cover Girls; Worked with Todd Terry before teaming up with Kenny 'Dope' Gonzalez as Masters At Work; Duo also recorded as Nu Yorican Soul; Co-founder: MAW Records; Collaborations: India; Marc Anthony; Jocelyn Brown; James Ingram; Stephanie Mills; Remixed: Debbie Gibson; St Etienne; Shanice; Tito Puente; Barbara Tucker; Jamiroquai; Atmosfear; Incognito; Luther Vandross; Ce Ce Peniston; Martha Wash; Ballistic Brothers. *Recordings:* Albums: Nu Yorican Soul, 1997; Singles: Ride On The Rhythm (with Marc Anthony), 1991; I Can't Get No Sleep (as Masters At Work), 1992; Deep Inside (as Hardrive), 1993; Love and Happiness (as River Ocean), 1994; The Nervous Track (as Nu-Yorican Soul), 1994; I Am The Black Gold of The Sun (as Nu-Yorican Soul), 1996; What A Sensation (as Kenlou), 1996; To Be In Love, 1997; Brasilian Beat, 1998. *Address:* c/o Strictly Rhythm, 920 Broadway 1403, New York, USA.

VEGA Suzanne Nadine; b. 11 July 1959, Santa Monica, California, USA. Singer; Songwriter; Musician (guitar). m. Mitchell Froom, 17 March 1995. *Education:* High School For The Performing Arts, New York; Barnard College, New York. *Career:* Folk singer, songwriter, 1982–; Began performing at Greenwich Village; World-wide concerts include: Royal Albert Hall, London, 1986; Prince's Trust Benefit Concert, Wembley Arena, 1986; Carnegie Hall, New York, 1987; Cambridge Folk Festival, 1991; Woody Guthrie Tribute, Central Park, New York, 1992; Berloni Foundation concert (for leukemia patients), Modena, Italy, 1992. *Recordings:* Albums: Suzanne Vega, 1985; Solitude Standing, 1987; Days of Open Hand, 1991; 99.9°F, 1992; In Concert, 1993; Nine Objects of Desire, 1996; Hit singles include: Marlene On The Wall, 1986; Luka, 1987; Tom's Diner, 1987; Book of Dreams, 1990; 99.9°F, 1992; Blood Makes Noise, 1992; When Heroes Go Down, 1993; Book and A Cover, 1998; Contributions to: Deadicated (Grateful Dead tribute album), 1991; Tom's Album, 1991; Pavarotti and Friends, 1993; Tower of Strength (Leonard Cohen tribute album), 1995. *Honours:* Grammy, Art Direction, 1990; Other Nominations; MTV Award, Best Female Video, Luka, 1988. *Current Management:* AGF Entertainment Ltd, 30 W 21st St, New York, NY 10010, USA.

VEJSLEV Jakob; b. 25 July 1957, Copenhagen, Denmark. Musician (guitar); Composer. m. Astrid Dyssegaard, 24 July 1987, 1 s. *Musical*

Education: Self-taught. *Career:* Played harmonica from age 13; Guitar, 1975–; Full-time guitarist with several groups and musicians (free jazz, fusion, latin, rock), Copenhagen, 1977–; Composed jazz, classical music, worked with own trio and duo, 1985–; Moved to Norway to work as composer, musician and music teacher, 1992-. *Compositions:* Flute quartet in 8 movements, 1992; Trio (trombone, violin and marimba), 1993; Piece for 10 instruments, 1994. *Recordings:* News: Stereo Magasin; Arranger, soloist: Håndslag Til Frank, 1987; Arranger, soloist: Til Dine Ojnes Åndmusik, 1990. *Memberships:* Danish Jazz, Beat and Folk Composer Asscn; KODA (Danish Composers Copyright Asscn); Norwegian Jazz Asscn. *Leisure interest:* Artist. *Current Management:* Warner Chappell.

VEJSLEV Tony; b. 25 Oct. 1926, Copenhagen, Denmark. Composer; Singer; Musician (guitar). m. Benthe Kolding, 19 Oct. 1954, 1 s. *Education:* Teacher. *Musical Education:* Self-taught. *Career:* Concerts in Denmark; Radio broadcasts, 1938–; Television appearances, 1949-. *Recordings:* Tony Vejslev Synger, 1983; Haandslag Til Frank, 1988; Til Dine Oejnes Aaandemusik, 1990; 50 Danske Viser Og Sange, 1993; Old Poems – New Songs, 2001. *Publications:* 19 Jaegerviser 1953, 1967; 26 Viser, 1987; Fem Farum Digte, 1988; 18 Danske Sange, 1990. *Honours:* KODA; Dansk Musikraad; Scholarships. *Membership:* Danish Jazz, Beat and Folk Authors; Prize of Honour, Danish Jazz, Beat and Folk Authors, 1998. *Leisure interests:* Travel; Literature. *Current Management:* Olafssongs, Paarupvej 44, Græsted, Denmark. *E-mail:* fo@olafssongs.dk.

VELGHE Rudy; b. 4 Jan. 1960, Oudenaarde, Belgium. Violin; Nyckelharpa; Guitar; Composer; Arranger. *Education:* Licence Degree, History, Rug-State University Ghent, Belgium. *Career:* Professional Musician, 1987–; Founder Member, Celtic band, Orion; Composed and arranged music for different short films and TV programmes; Performed in many shows on radio and TV/BRT, RTB, BBC, Irish Radio; Studio musician, with many artists. *Compositions:* Wailing Reel; Restless Home; Shores of Marsannay; Reel of Notes. *Recordings:* Histoires de Rue; 1990; Blue Room; Restless Home; Dao Dezi; About to Go. *Current Management:* VZW Worm Productions ASBL, 136 Chaussée de Wemmel, 1090 Brussels, Belgium.

VELOSO Caetano Emanuel Vianna Telles; b. 7 Aug. 1942, Santa Amaro da Purificação, Bahia, Brazil. Vocalist, Musician (guitar), Songwriter. *Career:* Won a lyric competition in mid 1960s with Um Dia; Signed to the Philips label; Part of MPB (Musica Popular Brasileira) new wave of young artists along with artists such as Gal Costa and Gilberto Gil; Experimental nature of Veloso's music was not favoured by the military dictatorship, resulting in arrest, 1968; Two months in prison before going into exile in London; Returned to Brazil, 1972; His great knowledge of old Brazilian songs led to him reviving the careers of older musicians, including Luiz Gonzaga; Hosted a TV show with Chico Buarque in 1980s. *Recordings include:* Albums: Domingo, 1967; Caetano Veloso, 1967; Atrás do Trio Eléctrico, 1969; Caetano E Chico – Ao Vivo Na Bahia, 1972; Araçá Azul, 1973; Jóia, 1975; Doces Barbaros, 1976; Bicho, 1977; Maria Bethania and Caetano Veloso Ao Vivo, 1978; Cinema Transcendental, 1979; Outras Palavaras, 1981; Cores Nomes, 1982; Uns, 1983; Velo, 1984; Caetano, 1987; Estrangeiro, 1989; Muito, 1990; Circulado, 1992; Tropicália 2, 1994; Fina Estampa En Vivo, 1995; Divina Estampa, 1996; Tieta Do Agresta, 1997; Livros, 1998; Noites Do Norte, 2001. *Honours:* Latin Grammy Award, Best MPB Album, Livros, 2000; Grammy Award, Best World Music Album, Livros, 2000. *Address:* c/o Universal Do Brasil Ltda, PO Box 37133, 22622–970 Rio de Janeiro, RJ, Brazil. *Internet:* www.caetanoveloso.com.br.

VENIER Glauco; b. 8 Sept. 1962, Sedegliano, Udine, Italy. Musician (piano); Composer. *Education:* Berklee College of Music, Boston, Massachusetts, 1991; Graduated, Performance Major in Organ, Conservatory of Music, Udine, Italy, 1985; Studied privately with Franco D'Andrea, Enrico Rava, Hal Crook, Ray Santisi, George Garzone. *Career:* Private Piano Instructor, Udine, 1985–90; Music Educator, several grammar schools, 1985–90; Educator, Conservatory of Music, Gorizia, Italy, 1993–98; Performed with: Kenny Wheeler, Lee Konitz, Jack Walrath, Enrico Rava, Paolo Fresu, Valery Ponomarev, Flavio Boltro, Hal Crook, George Garzone, Massimo Urbani, Stefano Di Battista, Gianni Basso, Chriss Speed, Matt Garrison, Abe Laboriel Jr. *Recordings include:* Massimo De Mattia, Poesie Pour Pasolini, 1993, The Silent Drama, 1995; Enrica Bacchia, Ancora, 1995; Monografie By New Age (compilation), 1996; Diego Sandrin, Millionaire, 1996; Tamara Obrovac, Triade, 1996; Enzo Pietropaoli, Stolen Songs, 1998; Fondazione Luigi Bon, Il Vieli, Il Dragon e Il Cavalir, Music for Fairytale By Glauco Venier, 1998; Klaus Gesing and Glauco Venier Play Bach, 2000; Ides of March (with Lee Konitz), 2001; Gorizia (with Kenny Wheeler), 2001. *Honours:* Semifinalist, Martial Solal Piano Jazz Competition, Paris, 1989; Finalist, Thelonious Monk Piano Jazz Competition, Washington, 1989; Berklee College of Music Achievement Scholarship, 1991; Best Group, Glauco Venier Trio, Jazz Festival in Vienne, France, 1997. *Leisure interests:* Riding Vespa scooter; Soccer. *Current Management:* Orpheus Management, via Giberti, Verona, Italy. *Address:* Via Castelliere No. 6, Gradisca di Sedegliano, Udine, Italy. *E-mail:* orpheus@serenacom.net.

VENTO Joseph; b. 16 Dec. 1926, Los Angeles, California, USA. Composer; Conductor; Band Leader. *Education:* Composition, Film-Scoring, Psychology, University of South Califonia; Optometry, Philosophy, Fresno State College; Piano, composition, Juilliard School; Conducting, New England Conservatory of Music. *Career:* Debut: Accordion Solo, Radio KFI, Los Angeles, The William Tell Overture, 10 years old, 1937; Films, Counterpoint, Man's Favorite Sport, This Earth is Mine, The Competition, Guide for a Married Man, Made in Paris, Girl Happy, Those Lips Those Eyes. *Compositions:* The Three Suns; I Can't Forget; Our Love is Gone; City of The Angles; Sacro Sanctum; Warsaw Connection; Sarah Suite; Ole Joe, 1997; Joes Bach, 1997. *Recordings:* Artist of The Three Suns, Twilight Time; Joe Vento Golden Hits, Vol. I and II; Surfside Records; Bells of Christmas; The Best of Joe Vento; The Best of The Three Suns; Film Soundtrack, True Friends. *Publications:* I Can't Forget, 1939; City of The Angels, 1968; Sacro Sanctum, 1979; Love Is Gone, 1995; Edulerp III, 1995. Contributions to: Midi'ing in Music Composition, Moorpark College, 1991; Nurturing Music in the Nineties. *Honour:* Best Accordionist Grand Prize, 1939. *Memberships:* ASCAP; ASMAC; AFofM, New York and Los Angeles; NARAS; American Academy of Sciences; Disabled American Veterans, SR, CDR; Music Teachers National Asscn, USA. *Leisure interests:* Oceanography; Forestry; The environment. *Current Management:* S V Enterprises. *Address:* 419 Mark Dr., Simi, CA 93065, USA.

VERA Billy; b. 28 May 1944, Riverside, California, USA. Singer; Actor; Songwriter; Prod.; Music Historian. m. (1) Barbara, Jan. 1966, (2) Rosalee, 30 April 1988, 1 s., 1 d. *Education:* 1 year, Fordham University, Bronx, New York. *Musical Education:* Self-taught. *Career:* Concerts: Peppermint Lounge, New York City, 1963; Apollo Theater, 2 times, 1968; Dick Cavett Show, 1968; Steve Allen Show, 1969; NYC Academy of Music, 13 times, 1972–75; Madison Square Garden, 1972; Howard Theater, Washington DC, 1979; Johnny Carson Show, 9 times, 1986–89; Films: Buckaroo Banzai; Blind Date; The Doors; Television: Wise Guy; Alice; Scarecrow and Mrs King; Knot's Landing. *Compositions:* Recorded by: Ricky Nelson: Mean Old World; Barbara Lewis: Make Me Belong To You; Dolly Parton: I Really Got The Feeling; Bonnie Raitt: Papa Come Quick. *Recordings:* Storybook Children, 1967; With Pen In Hand, 1968; I Can Take Care of Myself, 1981; At This Moment, 1987; Out of the Darkness, 1994; Oh What A Night, 1996. *Publications:* Liner notes to over 200 historical albums. *Honours:* Gold Prize, Tokyo Music Festival, 1981; ASCAP Award, 1987; Star on Hollywood Walk of Fame, 1988; George Peabody Award for Excellence in Broadcasting, 1994. *Membership:* Trustee, Rhythm and Blues Foundation; ASCAP; AFTRA; SAG; AFofM. *Leisure interest:* Record Collector. *Current Management:* Danny Robinson Agency for the Performing Arts. *Address:* 9200 Sunset Blvd, Los Angeles, CA 90069, USA. *Internet:* www.billyvera.com.

VERA Stephane; b. 11 May 1965, Paris, France. Musician (drums). *Education:* 1 year Right University, World Music. *Musical Education:* Boulogne Conservatory, Jazz-Rock School. *Career:* Gilbert Becaud; Dany Brillant; Jeane Manson; Vivian Reed; David Koven; I Muvrini; Karim Kacel; Eric Lelann; Ultra Marine; Angelique Kidjo; Jacky Quartz; Idrissa Diop; Yvan Dautin; Georges Macintosh. *Recordings with:* Dany Brillant; Jacky Quartz; Imurvine; Karim Kacel; Richard Bona, Scenes from My Life, 1999; Film: Le Nouveau Monde, 1994. *Publications:* Drummer's Magazine, Paris; VAC Magazine. *Memberships:* SACEM; SPEDIDAM; SDRM. *Leisure interests:* Swimming; Tennis; Films; Music. *Current Management:* Marouani Charley, Becaud's agent; Ginibrej. *Address:* 27 rue D'Herblay, 78700 Conflans, Ste Honorine, France.

VEREEN Ben; Singer; Actor; Entertainer. *Career:* Broadway productions include: The Chimney Man in musical, Jelly's Last Jam, 1993; Sweet Charity; Hair; Jesus Christ Superstar; Pippin; Grind; I'm Not Rappaport; A Christmas Carol, 1995; One-man show, concert tours, throughout US including Las Vegas; Atlantic City; Lake Tahoe; Also Europe; Asia; Caribbean Islands; Television includes: The Fresh Prince of Bel Air; The Nanny; New York Undercover; Star Trek – The Next Generation; Intruders; They Are Among Us; Silk Stockings; Own series, Tenspeed and Brownshoe, 1980; JJ Starbuck; Booker; Louis Armstrong – Chicago Style; Roots; Ben Vereen: His Roots; The Jesse Owens Story; Ellis Island; All That Jazz; Funny Lady; In demand speaker on lecture circuit; Formed organization, Celebrities For a Drug Free America, 1991; Currently developing performing arts center, Chicago; Appears on Once Upon A Forest, 1993. *Honours include:* Israel's Humanitarian Award, 1978; NAACP, Image Award, 1978; 1979; Eleanor Roosevelt Humanitarian Award, 1983; Victory Award, 1990; Tony for Best Actor, Pippin; American Guild of Variety Artists: Entertainer of The Year; Rising Star; Song and Dance Star; Hon. Doctorates: Emerson College, Boston; St Francis College, Brooklyn; Columbia College, Chicago. *Address:* c/o Stan Scotland, JKE Services, 404 Park Ave S, 10th Floor, New York, NY 10016, USA.

VERHAEREN Gert J M; b. 30 July 1973, Neerpelt, Belgium. Singer; Songwriter; Musician (Guitar, Bass Guitar; Sequencer). *Musical Education:* Self-taught, Guitar, Bass Guitar, Sequencer. *Career:* Main concerts with

band named Ivy: 1996: Zeezicht, Antwerp, Belgium; Geuseltpop Festival, Maastricht, The Netherlands; Electric Ladyland Festival, Maarheze, The Netherlands; Airpop-Festival, Heerlen, The Netherlands; 1997: Absolutely Free Festival, Ghent, Belgium; with band named Supergum: 1997: Support act for The Paranoiacs, Overpelt, Belgium; 1998: Absolutely Free Festival, Ghent, Belgium; Eurorock Festival, Neerpelt, Belgium; Hangarock Festival, Lo-reninge, Belgium. *Recordings:* with band named Ivy: Bo(o)s(e); Goozehand; Liquid Courage; Watermelon; with band named Supergum: Airplane; Eating Bullets; Last Song; Local Hero; Indecision; Airplane (engineless); Bitch!; Doctor Y; Surfin' Suspect. *Publications:* with band named Supergum: 3 CD singles: Airplane, 1997; Local Hero, 1998; Bitch, 1999. *Honour:* Finalist, Rock Competition, Het Licht Van Eindhoven, Eindhoven, The Netherlands, 1996. *Membership:* SABAM. *Leisure interests:* Listening to lots of music; Attending concerts; Recording and mixing songs. *Current Management:* Kattestraat 17, 3900 Overpelt, Belgium.

VERITY John; b. Bradford, Yorkshire, England. Vocalist; Musician (guitar); Record Prod. m. Karen, 10 Dec. 1994, 2 s., 1 d. (from previous relationships). *Musical Education:* Self-taught. *Career:* Guitarist, various groups, 1960's; Leader, John Verity Band, 1969–73; Support tours with: Jimi Hendrix; Canned Heat; Janis Joplin; Lead vocalist, Argent, 1973–76; Member, Phoenix; Charlie; John Coghlan's Diesel Band; Numerous concerts world-wide, including: Fender Stratocaster 40th Anniversary Concert, Manchester, 1994; Strat Pack, Australia Day, London, Hippodrome, 1995; Built own recording studio; Full time record producer; Producer, guitarist, vocalist, Saxon; John Parr; Motörhead; Ringo Starr; Russ Ballard; Tank; The Zombies; Colin Blunstone. *Recordings:* Albums: with Verity/John Verity Band: John Verity Band, 1972; Interrupted Journey, 1983; Truth of The Matter, 1985; Rock Solid, 1989; Hold Your Head Up, 1994; with Argent: Circus, 1975; Counterpoints, 1975; Hold Your Head Up, 1978; with Phoenix: Phoenix, 1976; In Full View, 1979; with Charlie: Good Morning America, 1981. *Memberships:* MRCS; PRS. *Leisure interest:* Music. *Current Management:* Verity Associates. *Address:* 5A Greta Heath, Burton-In-Lonsdale, via Carnforth, Lancashire LA6 3LH, England.

VERLAINE Tom, (Thomas Miller); b. 13 Dec. 1949, New Jersey, USA. Singer; Musician (guitar). *Career:* Member, The Neon Boys; Goo Goo; Founder member, Television, 1973–78; Solo artiste, 1979–; Reformed Television, 1991–; Glastonbury Festival, 1992; European Festivals, Japanese and US tours, 1992. *Recordings:* Albums: with Television: Marquee Moon, 1978; Adventure, 1979; The Blow Up, 1990; Television, 1993; Solo albums: Tom Verlaine, 1979; Dreamtime, 1981; Words From The Front, 1982; Cover, 1984; Flash Light, 1987; Warm and Cool, 1992; The Miller's Talc, 1996; Singles: with Television: Marquee Moon, 1977; Prove It, 1977; Other recordings: Guitarist, Hey Joe, Patti Smith, 1974. *Honour:* Rolling Stone Magzine Critics Award, Comeback of The Year, Television, 1993. *Current Management:* Basement Music, 6 Pembridge Rd, London W11 3HL, England.

VERLY François; b. 5 April 1958, Paris, France. Jazz Musician (piano, tablas, drums, percussion). 1 d. *Education:* BEPC-Bac D. *Career:* Many concerts on television and radio; World tours, jazz festivals: Canada; Mexico; Colombia; Ecuador; India; Hong Kong; Europe; East Europe; Africa; Plays with Michel Portal, David Friedman and Martial Solal. *Recordings with:* Andy Emler, National French Jazz Orchestra, 1986, 1987; Marc Ducret; Antoine Hérvé; Padovani; Denis Badault; Fawsi Al Aiedy; Nguyen Lê. *Honours:* First prize, Percussion, Creteil, 1978; First Prize, piano solist, Défense, 1986. *Leisure interests:* Nature; Ecology; Solidarity with minorities. *Current Management:* Opus 31, 78 rue Chateaubriand, 34070 Montpelier, France.

VERNEY Frannie; b. 14 May 1963, Buckinghamshire, England. Vocalist; Arranger; Composer; Musician (piano, percussion). *Musical Education:* Grade VIII piano, 1975; Purcell School for Young Musicians; GSMD Diploma in Jazz and Studio Music, 1994. *Career:* Radio appearances include: BBC Radio 5, BBC Radio Scotland, Newstalk AM; Tours throughout Europe; Repeat performances at prestigious Jazz venues throughout Britain including: Jazz Cafe, Royal Festival Hall Foyer, Bull's Head Barnes, Chicken Shed Theatre, Jazz Club Ascot, Edinburgh Festival Fringe, West Wales Jazz Festival, Vortez Jazz Club, Covent Garden Festival, Cork International Jazz Festival, Greenwich and Docklands Jazz Festival; Performs original and arranged Jazz Fusion material with her band, The Big Idea; Bandleader and Promoter of successful party band, Happy Feet, who have played all over Britain and in Europe at numerous venues including: Cumberland Hotel, London, RAC Club, Epsom, St Anton am Arlberg, Austria; Also performs as Soloist, with duos, performs, writes and arranges for smaller bands and acapella groups. *Memberships:* PRS; MCPS; BASCA; Musicians' Union. *Leisure interests:* Aromatherapy; Photography; Restaurant (director); Patron of British Museum; Travel. *Address:* Epicurean Music, London, England.

VERNHETTES Dan (Daniel); b. 20 May 1942, Paris, France. Musician (trumpet); Vocalist. m. Lill, 1965. *Musical Education:* Self-taught cornet,

1959-. *Career:* Main early influence, King Oliver; Interest developed in trumpeters of Swing era, most recently in music from New Orleans; Founder, Jazz O'Maniacs, 1966; Cornet player, bandleader, Six Cats, 1990–93; Member, Eddie Louis' Multicolor Fanfare, 1991–93; Leader, second trumpet, Swing Feeling (30s-40s jazz orchestra), 1992; Currently, trumpet player, singer, bandleader, Vintage Jazzmen (New Orleans-style sextet), 1992; Also, member, Olivier Franc orchestra, specialising in music of Sidney Bechet; Formed Brother D Blue Band, 1999. *Recordings include:* Various records, 1960s; Vintage Jazzmen, 1995; Swing Feeling with Screamin' Jay Hawkins and Spanky Wilson, 1995; 1 CD, Swing Feeling Live in Langen, 1998; 2 CDs: Vintage Jazzmen and Reverend Garrett and Brian Lewis; 1 live CD: Vintage Jazzmen; 1 live CD, Vintage Jazzmen, 1999. *Honours:* Prix Sidney Bechet De L'Académie de Jazz, 1997. *Current Management:* Compact, IVRY. *Address:* 45 rue Roger Buessard, 94200 Ivry-Sur-Seine, France.

VERNON Mike; b. 20 Nov. 1944, Harrow, Middlesex, England. Record Prod.; Songwriter. 2 d. *Education:* Croydon College of Art. *Career:* Production Assistant, then Staff Producer, Decca Record Company, 1962–66; Founder, producer, Blue Horizon Label, 1966; Editor, R & B Monthly (early Blues Fanzine); Independent record producer, 1968; Formed Indigo Records, 1992; Became Code Blue (through East/West), 1994; Artists included Sherman Robertson, The Hoax, Jay Owens, Bo Diddley, John Primer and Eric Bibb; Headed Blueside Label, 1998. *Recordings:* As producer: Singles include: with Fleetwood Mac: Albatross; Need Your Love So Bad; Man of The World; with David Bowie: The Laughing Gnome; with Focus: Hocus Pocus; Sylvia; with Bloodstone: Natural High; with Roachford: Family Man; Albums by numerous artistes include: Level 42; John Mayall's Bluesbreakers; David Bowie; Fleetwood Mac; Focus; Ten Years After; Savoy Brown; Rocky Sharpe and The Replays; Edwin Starr; Dr Feelgood; Sherman Robertson; Jimmy Witherspoon; Climax Blues Band; Joe Cocker; Danza Invisible; Renaud Hantson; Candye Kane; Eugene Bridges; Jerry McCain; Six Was Nine; Bo Diddley. *Honours:* 10 Gold records; 6 Silver; WC Handy Award, 1987–88. *Memberships:* Associate Mem., Re-Pro; PRS. *Current Management:* Worlds End (America) Inc, 183 N Martel Ave, Suite 270, Los Angeles, CA 90036.

VERSAILLES Fred; b. 15 June 1958, Versailles, France. Prod.; Composer. m. Line Alloet, 1984, 2 d. *Education:* University of Nantere, Economics. *Recordings:* NTM, first single: Le Monde De Demain; Albums: Authentik; Incontrolables; Native; Paris Groove Up; Dis Bonjour A La Dame. *Honours:* Victoire de la Musique, France, for: Native, 1994. *Membership:* Co-manager, Zbing Publishing. *Address:* 16 rue de Saint Denis, 95160 Montmorency, France.

VESALA Edward; b. 15 Jan. 1945. Musician (percussion); Composer. *Career:* Member, Tuohi Quartet, Montreux Jazz Festival, 1971; Joined Jan Garbarek's trio, 1972; Played jazz workshops, festivals throughout Europe; Worked with Tomasz Stanko, Stanko-Vesala Quartet, 1974–78; Solo percussionist, Finland and Europe, including Prague and Le Mans Jazz festivals; Teacher, Helsinki Theatre College; Bandleader, current group Sound and Fury. *Compositions include:* Music for Shakespeare's plays; Aleksis Kivi's Seven Brothers; National epic, Kalevala. *Recordings:* Albums: Solo: Nan Madol; Heavy Life; with Sound and Fury: Lumi; Ode To The Death of Jazz; Invisible Storm; Nordic Gallery. *Honours:* Best Jazz Ensemble, (with Tuohi Quartet), Montreux Jazz Festival, 1971; Yrjö Awards, Finnish Jazz Federation, 1972, 1980. *Address:* Seilimäki 25 C, 02180 Espoo, Finland.

VEYS Luc; Accordion; Spoons. *Musical Education:* Classical Education Piano; Private lessons accordion; Self-taught spoons. *Career:* Dranouter Festival, 1995; Gooik Festival 2002, 1997; De Brakke Grond, Amsterdam, Netherlands, 1997; Labadoux Festival, 1997; Den Ekster, 1996, 1997; Paulus Festival, Ostend, 1997; Sloanthe Festival, 1997; Foleys Irish Pub, Ghent; National radio (Radio 1, De Groote Boodschap) and several regional radio and television appearances. *Compositions:* Jumpin' the Fences – Dirty Wally; Friend's Sadness; Something To Fear; Shut the Pub; A Whistler's Wedding. *Recordings:* Tales From the Great Whiskey Book, CD, 1996. *Honours:* Government Medal for Flute, 1986; Second Place, Youth Soloist Festival, Flute, 1986; Finale, Westtalent, 1995. *Membership:* Volksmuziekfederatie, Belgium. *Leisure interest:* Music. *Current Management:* KAFT Producties, Akkerwindelaan 20, 8791 Beveren-Leie, Belgium. *Address:* Derudder Peter, Barrierestraat 49, 8940 Wervik, Belgium.

VIBSKOV Per (Nielsen); b. 23 May 1962, Viborg, Denmark. Composer; Prod.; Musician (bass). *Musical Education:* Self-taught. *Career:* Bass player with: Peyote, 1978–85; Rosegarden, 1986; Janes Rejoice, 1986–87; TAO, 1988–; Bayou Brothers, 1990–94; Bass player, producer, Home Sweet Home, 1994–; Bass fiddle player with Luksus, 1996–; Roskilde Festival, 1998. *Recordings:* with Peyote: For Sent Igen, 1984; with Janes Rejoice: Wievs To Keep, 1987; with TAO: Senor Maski, 1995; with Home Sweet Home: Divine, 1996. *Honours:* Prize for application, Efterslaegten, 1994. *Membership:* Danish Jazz, Beat, and Folk Authors. *Leisure interests:*

Theology; Yachting. *Address:* Viktoriagade 10 ITV, Copenhagen V, Denmark.

VICH Michal; b. 5 Nov. 1952, Prague, Czechoslovakia. Singer; Musician (guitar); High School Dir. m. Vera Vichova, 3 March 1977, 1 d. *Education:* School of Economics, Prague. *Musical Education:* Prague Musical School; J Jezek Conservatoire, guitar and voice studies. *Career:* Musician, recital group Vpred; Member, artistic group, The Prague Five; Film music for the films of T Vorel, including: Olda's Party, 1988; Kour, musical, 1990; La Serra, opera, Prague, 1994; Songs for the Children. *Compositions:* Kour, film soundtrack, 1990; La Serra, opera score, 1994. *Recordings:* Kour, film soundtrack, 1990; La Serra, opera, 1994; Albums: Monday Tells To Tuesday, 1995; Oh, The Sails, Where Are They? (with members of the Czech Philharmonic Orchestra), 1997. *Publications:* Books for children: Monday Tells to Tuesday, 1995; Oh, The Sails, Where Are They?, 1996. *Honour:* Oh, The Sails, Where Are They? selected as one of the best books of the year, 1996. *Memberships:* The Protective Syndicate of Authors (Czech Republic). *Leisure interest:* Sport. *Address:* 252 62 Unetice 84, Okr Prague Za'pad, Czech Republic.

VICKHOFF Björn Ture; b. 9 May 1946, Växjö, Sweden. Singing Songwriter (Guitar). m. Eva-Marie Vickhoff, 1 s., 1 d. *Education:* MA, Gothenburg University. *Musical Education:* Individual Musician Degree, Gothenburg University. *Career:* Kosmiskt Eko, an opus for TV (music, lyrics and performance); Film music to Samtidigt en Fredag; TV-serie music to Flykten; Appearances in Scandinavian TV and radio. *Recordings:* LP: Fiskdikt Och Fågelsäng; Riv Alla Stängsel, with Göteborgs Visgrupp, Kosmiskt Eko, with Åke Parmerud; Huset vid Havet, Än Finns Det Tid, CD: Fantastico. *Publication:* Än Finns Det Tid, with Ulf Marken, anthology with environmental songs; Música Popular Brazileira, an academic thesis. *Honours:* STIM Award; Gothenburg City Award; Art Society Award. *Memberships:* SKAP; SAMI; Musikcentrum Väst; Yrkestrubadurernas Förening; Visans Vänner. *Leisure interests:* Canoeing and fishing. *Address:* Björn Vickhoff, Småkullav 23, 424 70 Olofstorp, Sweden.

VICKREY Dan; b. 26 Aug. 1966, Walnut Creek, California, USA. Musician (Guitar). *Career:* Member, Counting Crows; Numerous headlining tours and TV appearances including MTV. *Recordings:* Singles: Round Here, 1994; Mr Jones, 1994; Rain King, 1994; Angels of the Silence (live), 1996; Albums: August and Everything After, 1993; Recovering the Satellites, 1996; Across a Wire: Live in New York, 1998; Long December, 1999; Daylight Fading, 1999.

VIDAL Jacques Henri; b. 13 Oct. 1949, Athis-Mons, France. Musician (double bass); Composer; Teacher. m. 13 April 1993, 1 s. *Musical Education:* National Versailles Academy of Music. *Career:* Formation of Christian Vander's group, Magma, 1970; Leader, Trijoums, 1976; Tour, France, with American drummer Philly Joe Jones, 1977; Played with guitarist Frederic Sylvestre, 1978; Jacques Vidal Quintet (Michel Graillier, piano, Florin Niculescu, violin, Frederic Sylvestre, guitar, Simon Goubert, drums), 1995; Television series as musician/actor. *Compositions:* Music for theatre. *Recordings:* Return, with Christian Escoudé and A Romano, 1979; Be Bop, Pepper Adams and B Altschul, 1979; Live A L'Olympia, J P Debarbat, 1979; A Live In Paris, Glenn Ferris, 1980; Rencontre, J P Debarbat, 1981; Music Band, Teddy Lasry, 1983; Under The Magnolias, Richard Raux, 1989; with Frederic Sylvestre: Premier Grand Cru with J L Chautemps, 1980; 2 Plus, with Eric Lelann, 1982; Hommages, with Eric Lelann, A Jean-Marie, 1983; Trio Live, S Huchard, 1986; Capricorne, 1989; As bandleader: Bass For Ever, 1995; News of Bop, Jacques Vidal Quintet, 1995. *Memberships:* SACEM; SACD; ADAMI. *Address:* 2 Bis Cité Popincourt, 75011 Paris, France.

VIDOVIC Ana; b. 8 Nov. 1980, Karlovac, Croatia. Musician (Guitar). *Education:* Music Academy, Zagreb. *Career:* Performing Solo and With Orchestras In Great Music Centres, Warsaw, Vienna, Salzburg, Budapest, Tel Aviv, Paris, London, Oslo, Aarhus, Bergen, Rome, Bari, Vaduz, Copenhagen; Has Had A Television Documentary Made About Her. *Recordings:* 3 CDs, Sony, 1993; London BGS Records, 1996; Croatia Records, 1998. *Address:* Donja Jelsa 61, HR 470–00 Karlovac, Croatia.

VIG Butch; Record Prod.; Musician (drums). *Career:* Record producer, various artists; Musician, with group Spooner; Founder, group Garbage. *Recordings:* with Garbage: Album: Garbage; Singles: Vow, 1995; Subhuman, 1995; Queer, 1995; Only Happy When It Rains, 1995; Stupid Girl, 1996; As producer: Nevermind, Nirvana; Siamese Dream, Smashing Pumpkins; Remixes for: U2; Nine Inch Nails; House of Pain; Depeche Mode; Ash; Chainsaw Kittens. *Current Management:* SOS Management, 106 Cleveland St, London W1 5DP, England.

VILLEGER André Franucin Raymond; b. 12 Aug. 1945, Rosny L/Bois, France. Musician (saxophone). 1 s., 1 d. *Musical Education:* Self-taught. *Career:* Festivals: Nice; Antibes; Paris; Marciac; Saragosse; London; Madrid; Carthage; Bayonne; Trinidad; Fort De France. *Recordings:* Albums: Something To Live For, 1986; A Villeger Connections, 1991; Also appears: with Claude Bolling: Jazz Gala; Live at the Meridien; Bolling Plays Ellington; Tone Parallel to Harlem. *Honours:* Prix Sidney Bechet 1973 (Academie Du Jazz). *Membership:* Los Angeles Jazz Society. *Leisure interests:* Gardening; Astronomy. *Address:* 28 rue du Gibet, 95100 Argenteuil, France.

VINCENT Amanda; b. 20 Jan. 1958, Perth, Australia. Musician (keyboards). *Education:* BMus, major, composition. *Musical Education:* University of Western Australia. *Career:* Tours with: Eurogliders, UK, USA, Philippines, Australia, 1980–87; Tim Finn, Australia, New Zealand, 1986; The Thompson Twins, UK, Ireland, USA, Canada, 1987; Boy George, UK, Europe, Australia, 1987–93; Jenny Morris, UK, Europe, Australia supporting Prince, 1990; Gang of Four, UK, USA, Canada, 1991; Billy Bragg, Australia, New Zealand, Japan, 1992; Black, UK, Turkey, 1993; Yazz, UK, 1994. *Compositions include:* Music for Strollers, ballet, Human Veins dance theatre, Canberra, 1980; Music, Fields of Fire, ABC TV, 1987; Music, The Collector, cinema and television, 1994; Music for TV documentary: The Feelgood Factor, 1995. *Recordings:* with Tim Finn: Escapade, 1983; Les Patterson Saves The World (soundtrack), 1987; with Eurogliders: Pink Suit Blue Day, 1981; This Island, 1983; Absolutely, 1985; with Jenny Morris: Animal Magic, 1986; Body and Soul, 1987; Shiver, 1989; with Boy George: Clause 28 (single), 1988; Boyfriend, 1989; High Hat, 1988; Tense Nervous Headache, 1988; Don't Try This At Home, 1991; Spiritual High, Moodswings featuring Chrissie Hynde, (single) 1991. *Honours:* 1 Platinum, 2 Gold albums, 1 Gold single; Second Prize, New York Film, TV awards, video: Heaven, Euroglider (single), 1985; Best Single, Heaven, Australia, 1985. *Memberships:* PRS; MCPS; Musicians' Union. *Leisure interests:* Film (studying film composition, International Film School); Psychotherapy; Writing; West African art and culture. *Address:* Flat 5, 15A Cricklewood Broadway, London, NW2 3JX, England.

VINCENT Eric; b. 27 June 1946, Force, France. Singer; Guitarist; Violinist. m. 4 March 1987. *Education:* Conservatory. *Career:* Performed in more than 120 countries: Brooklyn Auditorium, New York, USA; World Congress Center, Atlanta, USA; Opera Manaus, Brasil; National Folk Festival of Adelaide, Australia; Theatre Municipal Manoi, Viet Nam. *Compositions:* CD: Un Pays Quelquepart; Luca; Harmoniques; Voyage Pour L'Immediat; Haiti Kimbe. *Recordings:* Operation Boule De Neige; Je Suis Fatigue. *Publications:* Cest Comme Ça, 1987; Iles, 1987; Reflets France, 1992; Sans Borne, 1990. *Memberships:* SCPP; SACEM; ADAMI; SPEDIDAM. *Leisure interests:* Chess; Windsurfing; Tennis. *Address:* Madura, 11 bd de la Bastille, 75012, Paris, France.

VINCENT Julian Francis Vincent; b. 19 Jan. 1943, London, England. University Prof. m. Elizabeth May, 22 June 1968, 1 d. *Education:* MA, Cambridge University; PhD, DSc, Sheffield University. *Career:* Concerts at Purcell Room as Solo Recitalist; Appearances at 100 Club; TV appearances for BBC, ITV and Radio RTE, with tenor banjo; Organizer, Reading Banjo Festival, 1983-. *Recordings:* Stomp Off, Tenor Banjo with Paramount Theatre Orchestra. *Publications:* Banjoists' Broadsheet, journal. *Address:* 93 Redhatch Dr., Earley, Reading RG6 5QN, England.

VINDING Mads; b. 7 Dec. 1948, Copenhagen, Denmark. Musician (bass). *Career:* Professional at age 16; House bass player, Montmartre jazz club, Copenhagen; Worked with many jazz masters including: Herbie Hancock, Wayne Shorter, Stan Getz, Gary Burton, Hank Jones, Dexter Gordon, Bob Brookmeyer, Ben Webster, Benny Goodman, Dizzy Gillespie, Quincy Jones, Johnny Griffin, Eddie 'Lockjaw' Davis, Gerry Mulligan, Tony Williams, Ed Thigpen, Sir Roland Hanna, Dollar Brand, Clark Terry, Monty Alexander and Toots Thielemans. *Recordings:* Numerous albums include: Solo albums: Danish Design, 1974; The Kingdom (Where Nobody Dies), 1997; with Ed Thigpen: Action-Re-Action, 1974; Mr Taste, 1991; with Tony Williams and Wlodek Gulgowsky, Pop-Workshop, 1974; with Kai Winding: Trombone Summit, 1980; with Doug Raney: Guitar Guitar Guitar, 1985; with Dexter Gordon and Herbie Hancock: Cinema Jazz, 1986; The Other Side of Midnight, 1986; with Hanne Boel and Jorgen Emborg: Shadow of Love, 1987; with Roland Hanna and Jesper Thilo: This Time It's Real, 1987; with Thomas Clausen Trio: She Touched Me, 1988; Psalm, 1995; with Sven Asmussen: Fiddler Supreme, 1989; with Thomas Clausen Trio and Gary Burton: Cafe Noir, 1991; Flowers and Trees, 1992; with Danish Radio Big Band: Endangered Species, 1993; with Trine Lise Væring: When I Close My Eyes, 1996; with Jesper Thilo: Jesper Thilo Meets Thomas Clausen, 1997; with Bob Brookmeyer: Old Friends, 1998; with Great Jazz Trio: Great Standards Vols 1–5, 1998; Other albums with Duke Jordan; Johnny Griffin; Ernie Wilkins; Kenny Drew; Hank Jones. *Address:* Bogevej 8, 3500 Voerlose, Denmark.

VINTON Bobby (Stanley Robert); b. 16 April 1935, Canonsburg, Pennsylvania, USA. Singer. *Career:* Played trumpet with The Tempos; Formed own band; Became solo singer, 1962–; Sold over 30m. records world-wide; Actor, films Surf Party; Big Jake; The Train Robbers; Numerous television appearances including host of weekly variety show, 1975–78; Major concerts include: The Biggest Show of Stars For 1960, with Chubby Checker and Brenda Lee; Dick Clark's Caravan of Stars, US tour,

1961; New Zealand tour with Gene Pitney, 1962; Carnegie Hall, 1974; Opened The Bobby Vinton Blue Velvet Theater, Branson, Missouri, 1993. *Recordings:* US No. 1 singles: Roses Are Red; Blue Velvet; There! I've Said It Again; Numerous other hits include: Blue On Blue; My Heart Belongs To Only You; Clinging Vine; L-O-N-E-L-Y; I Love How You Love Me; Coming Home Soldier; Every Day of My Life; My Melody of Love; Blue Velvet (No. 2, UK), re-issued owing to television commercial, 1990; Albums: Roses Are Red, 1962; Bobby Vinton Sings The Big Ones, 1963; Blue Velvet, 1963; Bobby Vinton's Greatest Hits, 1964; Tell Me Why, 1964; Bobby Vinton Sings For Lonely Nights, 1965; Satin Pillows and Careless, 1966; Please Love Me Forever, 1968; Take Good Care of My Baby, 1968; I Love How You Love Me, 1969; Vinton, 1969; Bobby Vinton's Greatest Hits of Love, 1970; My Elusive Dreams, 1970; Every Day of My Life, 1972; Sealed With A Kiss, 1972; Bobby Vinton's All-Time Greatest Hits, 1972; Melodies of Love, 1974; Bobby Vinton Sings The Golden Decade of Love, 1975; Heart of Hearts, 1975; The Bobby Vinton Show, 1976; The Name of Love, 1977; Timeless, 1990; Duet with George Burns on album, As Time Goes By, 1993; A Very Merry Christmas, 1994; Kissin' Christmas, 1995; Branson City Limits, 1998. *Honours include:* Bobby Vinton Day, Chicago, 1975; Hon. citizen, Chicago, City's Certificate of Merit, 1975: Hon. doctorate of Music, Duquesne University, 1978; Several Gold discs.

VIRTANEN Heikki; b. 4 Sept. 1953, Finland. Musician (bass). *Musical Education:* Studied contrabass and Musicology. *Career:* Member, jazz-rock group, Tasavallen Presidentti, early 70s; Concerts with Juhani Aaltonen; Jarmo Savolainen; Severi Pyysalo; Jukkis Uotila, 1980s-; Bass player, Conjunto Baron (with Seppo Paakkunainen); Bassist for Olli Ahvenlahti, backing singer Vesa-Matti Loiri on Olli Ahvenlahti's compositional projects. *Honour:* Yrjö Award, Finnish Jazz Federation, 1987. *Address:* Töölöntorinkatu 7, 00260 Helsinki, Finland.

VISKINDE Peter; b. 14 Nov. 1953, Copenhagen, Denmark. Musician (guitar); Composer. m. Susan Kjeldsen, 23 June 1992, 2 s., 2 d. *Career:* Musician, 1974–; Member of groups Buffalo; Hualsospillemandene; Malurt Doraz; Also recorded as solo artist. *Recordings:* Two albums with Buffalo; Two albums with Hualsospillemandene; Seven albums with Malurt; Five solo albums, 1986, 1993, 1994, 1998 and 2000; Seven albums with Big Fat Snake, 1991–2000. *Membership:* DJBFA. *Current Management:* Aarhus Musikkontor, Mindegade 10, 8000 Aarhus C, Denmark.

VITEK Pavel; b. 30 Sept. 1962, Olomouc, Czech Republic. Singer; Actor; Composer; Lyrics Author. *Musical Education:* Academy of Musical Art (Faculty of Dramatic Art); Conservatoire, Musical Singing. *Career:* Theatre Musicals: Pop Festival, 1984; Gypsies Go To Heaven, 1986; Some Like It Hot, 1987; Dracula, 1995–; TV Films: Creation of the World, 1988; About 100 various TV shows including own recital, To Find My World, 1988; Many video clips; Radio: 1994–96; Own talk show on radio frequence 1. *Compositions:* Scent of Your Skin, 1992; This Time I Love You Much Better, lyrics, 1993; Garden of Wishes, 1994; Amen With You, 1995; Heaven Full of Stars, lyrics, 1995. *Recordings:* Albums: She's Got Her Day, 1988; Scent of Your Skin, 1992; Garden of Wishes, 1994; Lucky Star, 1995; Dracula, 1996. *Honours:* Second Prize, OIRT Festival Budapest, 1988; Prize of Finland, The Midnight Sun Song Festival, 1992. *Memberships:* Czech Asscn of Authors; Intergram. *Leisure interests:* Fine Arts; Beautiful Cars; Antiques; Gardening; Good Wine. *Current Management:* Nota Bene Musical Londy'nska' 53, Prague 2, 12000, Czech Republic. *Address:* Pavel Vitek, Nota Bene Musical, Londy'nska' 53, 12000 Prague 2, Czech Republic.

VOLCKE Ivan; Musician. *Musical Education:* Self-taught Guitar, Vocals, Badhan, Brass Pedals. *Career:* Member, Group The Swingshift; Dranouter Festival, 1995; Den Ekster, 1996, 1997; Labadoux, 1997; Paulus Festival, 1997; Sloanthe Festival, 1997; Gooik Festival 2002, 1997; De Brakke Grond, Amsterdam, 1997; Foleys Irish Pub, Ghent; Radio 1 De Groote Boodschap; Several Regional Radio and Television Appearances. *Compositions:* Jumpin The Fences; Dirty Wally; Friends Sadness; Something to Fear; Shut the Pub; A Whistler's Wedding. *Recording:* Tales From the Great Whiskey Book, 1996. *Honours:* Government Medal, Flute, 1986; Second Place, Youth Soloist Festival, 1986; Finale, Westtalent, 1995. *Membership:* Volksmuziekfederatie, Belgium. *Leisure interest:* Music. *Current Management:* KAFT Productions, Akkerwindelaan 20, 8791 Beveren-Leie, Belgium. *Address:* c/o Barrierestraat 49, 8940 Wervik, Belgium.

VOLCY Jean-Marc; b. 29 Jan. 1966, Anse Royal, Seychelles. Cultural Officer; Musician (Guitar; Banjo; Percussion); Singer. m. Eudoxie Volcy, 4 d. *Musical Education:* Degree in Voice Training; Self-taught Banjo and Guitar. *Career:* TV appearance, RFO, Reunion Island, 1994; Festival des Flaurallis Reunion Island, 1994; Radio appearance, RFI Bamako, 1993; MBF, 1995, 1996, 1997. *Compositions:* Musical Director, Three, musical play, 1995, 1996, 1997. *Recordings:* Debut album, sound track Sanmoi Swar Lo Zil St Pierre; Oeselwa and Sega of Seychelles. *Publications:* Debut album, Vandreni Sen and Musique Traditionelle Des Seychelles. *Honours:* Winner, Grand Prix D'Afrique Decouvert Des RFI, 1993; Winner, Festival Creole Song Contest, 1993, 1996. *Leisure interests:* Cooking; Traditional

Music; Watching videos. *Address:* Volcy c/o NAC, National Arts Council Mahe, Seychelles.

VOLKSORKEST Brabants; b. Nov. 1978. *Career:* Concerts, Television and Radio appearances, Belgium, Netherlands, Germany, France, Spain, Italy, Denmark, England, Ireland, Czechoslovakia, Hungary, Canada, USSR (Russia, Moldavia, Armenia, Mari Republic, Chuvash Republic); Mali, Kenya, Uganda, Cuba, Brazil. *Recordings include:* Brabantse Volksmuziek; Volksmuziek uit Brabant en de Kempen; Volksmuziek uit Brabant en de Vlaamse gewesten; Flemish Folk Music, Vol. 1 and Vol. 2; Rozenland; De Liedboeken, Vol. 1 and Vol. 2; Belgian Folk Music; Le Printemps de la Cornemuse; Harbalorifa: 25 jaar Omroep Brabant; Café B. *Honours:* La Cithare d'Argent (Paris 1979); Europa Preis für Volkskunst, 1989. *Current Management:* Egide Vissenaekens.

VOLLENWEIDER Andreas; b. 4 Oct. 1953, Zurich, Switzerland. Musician (Harp, Multi-instrumentalist). m. Beata, 27 Oct. 1973, 2 s., 1 d. *Career:* Composer of numerous musical productions for theatre, films and ballets; Alvin Atley Company on world tour with ballet based on own music. *Compositions:* Ace Verde, anthem of European Peace Movement, 1983; Pearls and Tears, anthem in black townships of South Africa, 1990. *Recordings:* Behind the Gardens; Caverna Magica; White Winds; Down to the Moon; Dancing with the Lion; Book of Roses; Eolian Minstrel; Live; Kryptos; Pavarotti and Friends II. *Honours:* Edison Award, 1983; Grammy Award, 1987; World Music Award, 1992. *Address:* Impact Music Inc, Zollikerstr 144, 8008 Zurich, Switzerland.

VOLLMER Brian Joseph; b. 30 June 1955, Kitchener, Ontario, Canada. Vocalist. m. Lynda Cowgill, 10 Aug. 1991, 1 d. *Musical Education:* Bel canto method of singing. *Career:* Vocalist, heavy rock group Helix; Several tours with Helix to Europe; Tours, North America; Appearances numerous TV shows, MTV. *Recordings:* Albums: White Lace and Black Leather, 1978; Breaking Loose, 1979; No Rest For The Wicked, 1982; Walking The Razor's Edge, 1984; Long Way To Heaven, 1985; Wild In The Streets, 1988; Back For Another Taste, 1990; It's A Business Doing Pleasure, 1992; Half Alive, 1998; Best of Helix: Deep Cuts, 1999. *Honours:* 2 nominations Canadian Juno Award; Heavy Metal Video of Year, Running Wild In The 21st Century. *Current Management:* William Seip Management. *Address:* 52 Terrence St, London, ON N52 1C4, Canada.

VOROS George Ladislaus; b. 5 March 1958, Swaziland. Musician (drums); Drum Teacher. *Musical Education:* Grade 8 Music Theory, Royal Schools; Military Band Certificate. *Career:* Member, South African bands: Neil Solomon; E'Void; Wozani; Numerous South African television appearances and sessions; Worked with Jimmy James and The Vagabonds, UK; Member, Stu Page Band, UK; Television: Stars In Your Eyes; Private drum studio, The Drum Workshop, 5 years. *Recordings:* The Love We Can Share, World Vision (charity single); Album: Come and Dance, Wozani. *Publications:* Book on drums, practice and performance, endorsed by Virgil Donati, Steve White and others. *Honours:* Best British Country Band, Stu Page Band, 1994. *Membership:* Musicians' Union (registered teacher). *Leisure interest:* Tai Chi Chuan. *Address:* Hayter and Shone Ltd Music Publishers, 19 Grove Hill, South Woodford, London E18 2JB, England.

VRAIT-WRIGHT Silvi; b. 28 April 1951, Kehra, Estonia. Singer; Music Teacher; English Teacher; Actress. 1 s. *Education:* Tartu University, Estonia, graduate, English, Philology, Language, Literature, 1974. *Musical Education:* Children's Music School, piano. *Career:* Lead singer, Fix (Estonia), 1976–83; Solo artist, 1983–; Rock opera; Porgy and Bess (Bess) by George Gershwin; Television specials: Light and Shade; Silvi and Her Friends; Silvi Vrait Sings, Eurovision Song Contest, 1994. *Recordings:* Albums: Silvi Vrait, 1985; Embrace, 1988; English Children's Songs; Single: Like The Sea, 1994; Album: Cosy and Warm, 1994. *Leisure interests:* Tallinn ZONTA club; Astrology; Painting. *Current Management:* Rock Hotel Management. *Address:* Astangu 22–61, 00035 Tallinn, Estonia.

VRIENDS Peter; b. 31 Oct. 1963, Rotterdam, The Netherlands. Midi Instruments. *Musical Education:* Self-educated. *Career:* Co-owner, record company essential dance music; Co-owner, record company basic beat recordings; Owner and Engineer, recording studio; Producing own compositions; Producing productions for third parties, mixing great variety of dance mix albums. *Compositions:* Pot of Gold; Joy; Love; Follow Your Heart; Emotional Travellogue, album. *Honour:* Best House Record of the Year, Benelux, Pot of Gold, 1991. *Memberships:* SENA; IFPI, Stermra, Buma. *Leisure interests:* Diving (scuba); Travelling; Theatre; Movies; Sports. *Address:* Essential Dance Music BV, Nieuwe Binnenweg 19, 3014 GB Rotterdam, The Netherlands.

VUJICA Matija; b. 19 July 1963, Metkovic, Croatia. Singer. *Education:* Faculty of Economics, Zagreb. *Musical Education:* Private piano lessons. *Career:* Vocalist with group Gracia, 1990–; Concerts, tours and rock festivals all over Croatia, Austria, Germany, Slovenia and Sweden; Many television and radio appearances. *Recordings:* Hit singles: Rolana; Zaplesimo; Albums: Gracia; Vrijeme Snova (Time of Dreams); Jer Tu Ima Neki Crni Vrag (Black Devil Spies Upon Us All); Dancetheria; Forte Forte. *Publications:* Croatian Awards: Ethno Dance Award 1994; Most Original Look, 1994. *Membership:* Croatian Musical Union (HGU). *Leisure interests:* Fashion; Design.

VUKAN George; b. 21 Aug. 1941, Budapest, Hungary. Composer; Musician. *Education:* Liszt Academy of Music; Medical University Budapest. *Career:* Concerts include Classical and Jazz, with his trio and solo; Guest artist, all around Europe; Played with Philly Joe Jones, Clifford Jordan, Linda Hopkins, Annette Lowman, Frank Foster, Clarck Terry, Kenny Wheeler; Played with his creative art Jazz trio in Sevilla at World Expo; Composer; Conductor, Ferenc Liszt, Ferenc Erkel Chamber Orchestras, Hungarian Symphonica Orchestra; Written music for more than 140 films, three ballets, opera, symphonic works, concertos, chamber music compositions, 150 psalms, music to theatrical performances, television, radio and films; Pianist member, founder, quartet, 1997-. *Compositions:* Missa Ad Dominum Jesum Christum. *Honours:* Include, Hilikon Prize, 1957; Press Award Montreux, 1968; Composer Award of The Hungarian Record Producing Company, 1970; Balàzs Bèla Prize, 1978; Artist Prize of The Hungarian Radio, 1981; Erkel Ferene Prize, 1991; Lyra Prize, Little Cross of Hungarian Republic, 1996. *Address:* Határör UT 19/B 8, 1122 Budapest, Hungary.

VUVU J L; b. 12 Dec. 1968, Uige, Angola. Musician (keyboards); Songwriter. 2 s. *Education:* Car mechanic. *Career:* Street musician in Zaire (as Abute Bango Likonga); Club musician in Angola (as Parisien J L); Tour of Zaire; Residency in Cafe Rio; Now relocated to UK as dance musician. *Recordings:* Debut album being recorded, own compositions. *Publications:* Listed in Zairians and Angolans. *Membership:* Musicians' Union. *Current Management:* Basky-Capitao, Love Life M P M. *Address:* 82A Plashet Rd, Plaistow, London, E1 0RQ, England.

VYVÉRE Pascale; b. 31 May 1966, Brussels; Belgium. Singer; Composer; Songwriter; Musician (Piano, Accordion); Actress. *Musical Education:* Fine Arts Degree; Musical Theory, Harmony, Piano, Song Writing, Singing and Performing Lessons. *Career:* Festivals: Botanique, Brussels, 1993, 1994, 1997; Francofolies, Spa, 1994, 1997; Festival De Marne, 1993, 1999; Chorus Des Hauts-De-Seine, 1994; Many concerts in France, Belgium and Switzerland; Roles in: Chants De Femmes, Film, R Olivier, 1994; La Voix Humaine, J Cocteau, 1996; La Dame De Chez Maxim, G Feydeau, 1996; Les Poules, 1997–99; Les Miroirs d'Ostende, P Willems, 1998, 2000; Les Feux de Babel, 1998–99. *Compositions:* Words and/or music of many French songs. *Recordings:* Single: Solo, 1994; Contributor, album: J G Coulange, Enfin Seul, 1994; Solo album: Je Vous Attends, 1997. *Honours:* Prize Sentier Des Halles and Prize Adiam-92, Tremplin Chorus Hauts-De-Seine, 1993; Prize Auditeurs France-Inter/RTBF/RSR, 1994. *Membership:* SABAM, Brussels. *Current Management:* Tango, ASBL, 5 Av Des Vanneaux, 1420 Braine-L'Alleud, Belgium.

W

WADE Terri (Teresa); b. 3 March 1957, Staffordshire, England. Singer; Entertainer. m. David Bryan, 6 Oct. 1987, 1 s. *Education:* College of Further Education. *Career:* Sang for Mecca, Top Rank Dance bands; Touring bands, session work for local studios; Career as Terri Wade, 1980–; Television: Walk on parts: Crossroads; Keynotes; Sky Star Search; New Faces, 1986; Hippodrome, London; Stringfellows to promote Single Girl; Interviewed on radio stations all over country; Performed over 1,000 live shows. *Recordings:* Light, 1982; Single Girl, 1985, number 11 (Gay Top 20). *Honours:* Best Vocalist, NSSCEP, 1986, South Skeffs, 1990. *Memberships:* Musicians' Union; Equity. *Leisure interests:* Tennis; Squash; Table Tennis. *Current Management:* Ray Stanton Entertainments. *Address:* 294 Ash Bank Rd, Werrington, Stoke-on-Trent ST9 OJS, England.

WAGER Henrik Rickard; b. 14 March 1969, Manchester, England. Singer. *Musical Education:* Birmingham University; Birmingham Conservatoire. *Career:* Founder member, Brave New World, 1992–93; Ascension, 1993–94; Singer with The Flying Pickets; Performed on Warning Tour, 1994; 5 Alive In '95 Tour; Director, Inner Sactum Studio; Inner Sanctum Productions; Director of Ulum Jingle Shed. *Memberships:* Musicians' Union; Equity. *Leisure interests:* Dance, modern and jazz.

WAGHORN Gary; b. 9 May 1949, Chatham, Kent, England. Musician (guitar, banjo). m. Linda Evans, 15 Aug. 1970, 1 d. *Career:* Lead guitarist for Bonnie Tyler; Lead guitarist, vocalist, Slack Alice; Lead guitarist, backing vocals, Mountain Child. *Recordings:* Album: Diamond Cut, Bonnie Tyler; 6 singles with Bonnie Tyler; Single: Night Pilots, Mountain Child. *Memberships:* PRS; Musicians' Union. *Leisure interests:* Music; Reading.

WAGNER Bill (William); b. 12 Feb. 1920, Warsaw, Indiana, USA. Record Prod.; Trumpet Arranger. m. Vicki, 23 May 1942, 2 d. *Education:* Mechanical Engineering, Purdue University; Pilot, US Air Force. *Career:* Personal Manager for The Four Freshmen; Pete Christlieb; Cavanaugh; Si Zentner; Vicki McClure; Faunda Hinton; Michael Dees; Sandy Graham; Over 100 record dates for: Serenade In Blue, USAF Band, Washington DC. *Compositions:* 5 jingles (musak); Airmen of Note, USAF Band. *Recordings:* Producer of over 1,000 records to date with various artistes include: 23 albums, The Four Freshmen; 2 albums, Sandy Graham; 3 albums, Page Cavanaugh, 1989; John Klemmer: Priceless Jazz, 1999. *Memberships:* NARAS; AFTRA; AGMA. *Leisure interests:* Bridge; Reading; Music; Golf. *Address:* 14343 Addison St, #221, Sherman Oaks, CA 91423, USA.

WAGNER Heribert; b. 24 Dec. 1952, Vienna, Austria. Musician (Violin); Composer. 1 s. *Education:* Violin, since aged 7; Conservatory of Vienna and Enschede, Netherlands. *Career:* WDR-TV appearance, Live from Berlin Jazz Festival; Dutch TV, NL3, Jazz uit het BIM-Huis; North Sea Festival, The Hague; Montreux Jazz Festival; Jazzfest Wien; Nürnberg Ost-West; Nancy Jazz Pulsations; Stuttgarter Jazztage. *Compositions:* Gaia, a Story for Jazzgroup and Symphony Orchestra, Donemus, Amsterdam; Homage; 5; Ballad for a Lonesome Guy Somewhere on This Earth; Horizontal Curve. *Recordings:* LP, To Be Continued, with New Association; CD, Four Wheel Drive, with New Association. *Honour:* Jaromir Prize, Netherlands, 1988. *Memberships:* BUMA; BIM; NTR. *Current Management:* Art in Music. *Address:* Altingstraat 38, The Hague, Netherlands.

WAGNER Kurt; b. 1958, Bethseda, Maryland, USA. Vocalist; Musician (guitar); Songwriter. *Education:* Art School, Memphis, Tennessee, USA. *Career:* Lead vocalist and main songwriter of loose collective known as Lambchop; One of the main bands in the alternative country or Americana movement, their music mixes country, soul, folk and jazz; Brought up in Nashville, went to art school in Memphis and spent time in Montana before returning to Nashville; Formed Posterchild, 1986; Act renamed Lambchop owing to existence of another band The Poster Children, 1992. *Recordings:* Albums: with Lambchop: I Hope You're Sitting Down/Jack's Tulips, 1994; How I Quit Smoking, Hank, 1996; Thriller, 1997; What Another Man Spills, 1998; Nixon, 2000; Is A Woman, 2002; with Josh Rouse: Chester, 1999; features on: Salesman and Bernadette, Vic Chesnutt, 1998; Kathleen Lague, Kathleen Lague, 1999.

WAGNER Windy; b. 6 Dec. 1971, Los Angeles, CA, USA. Vocalist. *Career:* Vocals for Walt Disney Records, Baywatch, Fame LA, Various Television Commercials. *Recordings:* Vocals On Trine Rein; Walt Disney Records; T Braxton. *Honours:* Los Angeles Music Award, Best Female Vocalist. *Memberships:* SAG; AFTRA; LA Singers United. *Current Management:* Kelly Coleman Esq. *Address:* PO Box 17551, Beverley Hills, CA 90209, USA.

WAGONER Porter; b. 12 Aug. 1930, West Plains, Missouri, USA. Country Singer; Songwriter. *Career:* Worked at radio station; Cast member, television series Ozark Jubilee; Recording artist, 1954; Regular member, Grand Ole Opry, 1957–; Television series with own band The Wagonmasters, 1960s-70s; Co-host with singers Norma Jean, Dolly Parton; Regular recording partnership with Dolly Parton, 1967–74; Regular tours and concerts with All-Girls Band. *Recordings:* 81 Country hit singles include: A Satisfied Mind (US Country No. 1); Eat Drink and Be Merry; Your Old Love Letters; Sorrow On The Rocks; Misery Loves Company (US Country No. 1); The Green Green Grass of Home (later recorded by Tom Jones and Elvis Presley); The Cold Hard Facts of Life; The Carroll County Accident; Duets with Dolly Parton: The Last Thing On My Mind; Just Someone I Used To Know; Daddy Was An Old Time Preacher Man; If Teardrops Were Pennies; Please Don't Stop Loving Me (US Country No. 1); Albums include: A Satisfied Mind, 1956; A Slice of Life, 1962; Old Log Cabin For Sale, 1965; The Thin Man From West Plains, 1965; The Bottom of The Bottle, 1968; Howdy Neighbour Howdy, 1970; The Farmer, 1973; Porter, 1977; Today, 1979; Natural Wonder, 1982; One For The Road, 1983; Porter Wagoner, 1986; with Norma Jean: Porter Wagoner Show, 1963; In Person, 1964; Live – On The Road, 1966; with Dolly Parton: Just Between You and Me, 1968; Just The Two of Us, 1969; Always, Always, 1969; Porter Wayne and Dolly Rebecca, 1970; Once More, 1971; The Right Combination, 1972; Together Always, 1972; Love and Music, 1973; We Found It, 1973; Porter 'N' Dolly, 1974; Say Forever You'll Be Mine, 1975; Porter Wagoner and Dolly Parton, 1980. *Honours include:* CMA Awards: Vocal Group of The Year, 1968; Vocal Duo of the Year, 1970, 1971. *Address:* c/o Porter Wagoner Enterprises, PO Box 290785, Nashville, TN 37229, USA.

WAGSTAFF Paul (Wags); b. 28 Dec. 1964, Stockport, Cheshire, England. Musician (Guitar). *Career:* Member, Black Grape; Numerous tours and festival appearances including Tribal Gathering and Reading festivals, 1997. *Recordings:* Singles: Reverend Black Grape, 1995; England's Irie, 1996; Fat Neck, 1996; Get Higher, 1997; Marbles, 1998; Albums: It's Great When You're Straight... Yeah, 1995; Stupid, Stupid, Stupid, 1997.

WAHLBERG Ulf; b. 11 April 1951, Stockholm, Sweden. Prod.; Musician (Keyboards). m. Catherina, 1 s., 2 d. *Musical Education:* Five years Piano; Two years music. *Career:* Ola Hakansson, The Group Secret Service, 1979; Producer, 1979-. *Compositions:* Som Stormen River Oppet Hav; Heden. *Recordings:* Secret Service; Freestyle; Susan Alfvengren; Magnum Bonum; Martin. *Publications:* Popcorn; Jukebox. *Honours:* Swedish Grammy as Producer, 1986. *Memberships:* STIM; SAMI; SKAP. *Leisure interests:* Sailing; Travel. *Current Management:* XTC Productions AB, PO Box 2065 12502 Alvsjo, Sweden.

WAILER Bunny, (Neville O'Riley Livingston); b. Kingston, Jamaica. Singer; Songwriter. *Career:* Harmony singer, songwriter, and occasional lead singer, reggae group Bob Marley and the Wailers, 1960s and 1970s; Solo recording artist, on own Solomonic record label, 1974-. *Recordings:* Albums include: with the Wailers: Catch A Fire; Burnin'; Solo albums: Blackheart Man; Protest; Struggle; In A Fathers House; Bunny Wailer Sings The Wailers; Tribute To The Hon. Robert Nesta Marley; Rock 'n' Groove; Hook Line and Sinker; Roots Radics Rockers Reggae; Marketplace; Bunny Wailer Live; Roots Man Skanking; Rule Dancehall; Liberation; Gumption; Hall of Fame: A Tribute to Bob Marley's 50th, 1995; Complete Bob Marley and the Wailers, 1998; with Bob Marley: Rock to the Rock, 1999. *Address:* c/o Performers of the World, 8901 Melrose Ave, Second Floor, West Hollywood, CA 90069, USA.

WAINWRIGHT Loudon III; b. 5 Sept. 1946, Chapel Hill, North Carolina, USA. Singer; Songwriter; Musician (guitar). m. Kate McGarrigle, 2 c., divorced 1977. *Education:* Studied acting, Carnegie Mellon University, Pittsburgh. *Career:* Singer, folk clubs, New York and Boston, 1968; Recording artiste, 1969–; Founding member of Spinal Tap, turned down opportunity to join Steely Dan; Concerts include: Support to Everly Brothers, UK; Cambridge Folk Festival, 1972; Royal Festival Hall, 1992; Television includes: The Jasper Carrot Show; Original musician/sidekick on David Letterman Show; Conan O'Brien; Compositions for ABC Nightline; Several episodes, M.A.S.H.; Episode of Soldier Soldier; Own show for BBC Scotland, Loudon and Co; Stage performances: The Birthday Party; Pump Boys and Dinettes; Caryl Churchill's Owners at the Young Vic; Films: The Slugger's Wife; Jacknife; 28 Days; Radio: NPR in USA continues to commission topical songs on events and individuals in the news. *Compositions include:* Dead Skunk; Your Mother and I; I wish I was a Lesbian; YK2; Glad To See You've Got Religion; The Man Who Couldn't Cry; Swimming Song; Motel Blues; Be Careful, There's A Baby In The House; The Picture, 1992; Dreaming, 1995. *Recordings:* Albums: Loudon

Wainwright III, 1970; Album II, 1971; Album III, 1972; Attempted Moustache, 1974; Unrequited, 1975; T-Shirt, 1976; Final Exam, 1978; A Live One, 1979; Fame and Wealth, 1983; I'm Alright, 1985; More Love Songs, 1986; Therapy, 1989; History, 1992; Career Moves, 1993; Grown Man, 1996; Little Ship, 1998; Social Studies, 1999. *Honours:* Grammy nominations, 1985, 1986. *Current Management:* Mike Kappus, The Rosebud Agency, PO Box 170429, San Francisco, CA 94117, USA.

WAINWRIGHT Rufus; b. 22 July 1973, Rhinebeck, New York, USA. Vocalist; Musician (piano); Songwriter. *Education:* Millbrook School. *Musical Education:* McGill University, studied classical music, 1991. *Career:* Son of Kate McGarrigle and Loudon Wainwright III; Sang backing vocals on tour with mother and aunt (folk duo Kate and Anna McGarrigle), 1980s; Dropped out of university to perform own songs in and around Montréal; Cut demo, 1997; Signed record deal with DreamWorks; Tours North America, Britain and Europe. *Compositions:* I'm A-Runnin'; Millbrook; Cigarettes and Chocolate Milk. *Recordings:* Rufus Wainwright, 1998; Poses, 2001. *Current Management:* Ron Stone, Gold Mountain Entertainment. *Address:* c/o DreamWorks Records, 9268 W Third St, Beverly Hills, CA 90210, USA. *Internet:* www.rufuswainwright.com.

WAITE John; b. 4 July 1955, England. Singer; Songwriter; Musician (bass, harmonica). *Career:* Member, The Babys, 1976–81; Solo artiste, 1981–; Singer, Bad English, 1989–91. *Recordings:* Albums: with The Babys: The Babys, 1976; Broken Heart, 1977; Head First, 1978; Union Jacks, 1980; On The Edge, 1980; Anthology, 1981; Solo albums: Ignition, 1982; No Brakes, 1984; Mask of Smiles, 1985; Rovers Return, 1987; The Essential, 1991; Temple Bar (USA only), 1995; with Bad English: Bad English, 1989; Backlash, 1991; Solo: The King Biscuit Flower Hour, 1999; These Times are Hard for Lovers; with Ian McDonald, Driver's Eyes, 1999; Singles: Solo: Missing You (No. 1, USA); Change; with Bad English: When I See You Smile (No. 1, USA). *Current Management:* Gold Mountain Entertainment. *Address:* 120 W 44th St, Suite 704, New York, NY 10036, USA.

WAITS Tom; b. 7 Dec. 1949, Pamona, California, USA. Singer; Songwriter; Musician (piano, accordion); Actor. m. Kathleen Brennan, 31 Dec. 1981, 1 s., 1 d. *Career:* Recording artist, 1973–; Concerts include: Ronnie Scott's jazz club, 1976; London Palladium, 1979; The Black and White Night – Roy Orbison and Friends, 1987; Actor, films including: Paradise Alley; Wolfen; Stone Boy; One From The Heart; The Outsiders; Rumblefish; The Cotton Club; Down By Law; Cold Feet; The Fisher King; At Play In The Fields of The Lord; Queen's Logic; Bram Stoker's Dracula; Coffee and Cigarettes. *Compositions include:* Ol' 55, The Eagles, 1974; Angel Wings, Rickie Lee Jones, 1983; Downtown Train, Rod Stewart, 1990; One From The Heart (film soundtrack), 1981; Co-writer (with wife), musical Frank's Wild Years, 1986; Score, Alice In Wonderland, Hamburg, 1992. *Recordings:* Albums: Closing Time, 1973; The Heart of Saturday Night, 1974; Nighthawks At The Diner, 1975; Small Change, 1976; Foreign Affairs, 1977; Blue Valentine, 1978; Heartattack and Vine, 1980; One From The Heart, 1982; The Asylum Years – Bounced Check, 1983; Anthology, 1983; Swordfishtrombones, 1983; Raindogs, 1985; Frank's Wild Years, 1987; Big Time, 1988; Stay Awake, 1988; Bone Machine, 1992; Black Rider, 1993; Mule Variations, 1999. *Contributions to:* Lost In The Stars, 1984; Stay Awake, 1988; Night On Earth (film soundtrack), 1992. *Honours:* Academy Award nomination, One From The Heart, 1982; Grammy Award, Best Alternative Music, Bone Machine, 1993.

WAKEFIELD MILLSAPS Wilma; b. 13 Feb. 1949, Monroe Co, Tennessee, USA. Singer; Songwriter; Musician (guitar). m. Bill Millsaps, 13 Nov. 1967, 1 s., 1 d. *Musical Education:* Apprenticed under Tommy Scott. *Career:* Travelled extensively across USA with husband Bill Millsaps and their Snowbird Mountain Band; Appears twice weekly on satellite TV on Snowbird Mountain Bluegrass. *Recordings:* Albums include: Legendary Friends of The Snowbird Mountain Band, with John Hartford, Uncle Josh Graves, Benny Martin, others. *Publications:* Bluegrass Unlimited, by Dr Ivan Tribe, 1992. *Memberships:* BMI; IBMA. *Leisure interests:* Hiking; Photography; Genealogy. *Current Management:* Bill Millsaps. *Address:* PO Box 85, Robbinsville, NC 28771, USA.

WAKEMAN Adam; b. 11 March 1974, Windsor, Berkshire, England. Musician (keyboards); Vocalist; Musical Dir. *Musical Education:* All 8 practical and theory Associated Board exams, 1993–94. *Career:* Toured most of Europe, America, South America, UK with Wakeman band alongside father, Rick, 1995; Performing Musical Director with Cirque Surreal, touring UK. *Recordings:* Albums include: Wakeman with Wakeman; No Expense Spared; Romance of a Victorian Age; The Official Bootleg; Tapestries, 1995; Vignettes, 1996; Return to the Centre of the Earth, 1999; Solo albums include: Soliloquy; 100 Years Overtime; Real World Trilogy, 1997; 1 track on Yes tribute album with new band Jeronimo Road. *Honours:* Keyboard magazine, Readers Poll in Best New Talent Category, 1994. *Memberships:* Musicians' Union; PRS. *Leisure interests:* Golf; Cycling. *Current Management:* Jeronimo Road Management, Felmersham Hall Studios, One The Row, The High Rd, Felmersham,

Bedfordshire MK43 7HP, England. *Address:* Bajonor House, 2 Bridge St, Peel, Isle of Man.

WAKEMAN Dusty; b. 31 Aug. 1953, Houston, Texas, USA. Musician (bass guitar); Record Prod.; Engineer. m. Szu Wang, 5 April 1986. *Education:* University of Texas. *Musical Education:* Studied with Jamie Faunt. *Career:* Mixer, engineer, bassist, numerous recordings, 1986–; Bassist, Michelle Shocked British tour, 1989. *Recordings:* Mixer, engineer, producer, bassist on albums by: Dwight Yoakam; Rosie Flores; Lucinda Williams; Buck Owens; Michelle Shocked; Los Lobos; Jackson Browne; Wynton Marsalis; Tom Russell; Ralph Stanley; American Pie. *Honours:* 2 Grammy Awards: Cryin', Roy Orbison/kd lang, 1987; Ain't That Lonely Yet, Dwight Yoakam, 1993. *Current Management:* Bonnie Simmons. *Address:* PO Box 5895, Berkeley, CA 94705, USA.

WAKEMAN Rick; b. 18 May 1949, London, England. Musician (keyboards). *Career:* Member, UK progressive rock group Yes, 1971–74, 1976–80, 1990; International concerts include: Yesshows '91 – Round The World in 80 Dates tour, 1991; Film: Yessongs, 1973; Solo artiste, 1974–. *Compositions include:* Score for Phantom of The Opera, 1991. *Recordings:* Albums: with Yes: Fragile, 1971; Yessongs, 1973; Tales From Topographic Oceans, 1973; Going For The One, 1977; Union, 1991; Yesstory, 1991; Solo albums: The Six Wives of Henry VIII, 1973; Journey To The Centre of The Earth, 1974; The Myths and Legends of King Arthur and The Knights of The Round Table, 1975; White Rock, 1976; No Earthly Connections, 1976; Criminal Record, 1977; Rhapsodies, 1979; 1984, 1981; Beyond The Planets, 1984; The Gospels, 1987; Soundtrack to 1982 World Cup film Golé!, 1983; Themes, 1998; A Tribute to the Beatles, 1998; Natural World Trilogy, 1999; Selections from Journey to he Centre of the Earth, 1999; Preludes to a Century, 2000; as Anderson Bruford Wakeman Howe: Anderson Bruford Wakeman Howe, 1989. *Honours include:* Gold Ticket, Madison Square Garden, 1978. *Current Management:* BDA, Bryson House, Chiltern Rd, Culceth, Warrington, Cheshire WA3 4LL, England.

WALDEN Chris; b. 10 Oct. 1966, Hamburg, Germany. Composer; Arranger (Trumpet). m. Beate Walden, 15 March 1996, 1 s., 1 d. *Education:* Music University, Cologne, 1988–93; MA Composition, 1994. *Career:* Feature Films, Schtonk, 1992; Ein Mann Fuer Jede Tonart, 1992; Lilien in der Bank, 1992; Engel Ohne Fluegel, 1993; Late Show, 1998; 20 TV Movies; Director, German Movie Award Show, 1995–98. *Compositions:* Ticino, suite for big band; A Deadly Vision, suite for symphony orchestra; Opus 3, for orchestra. *Recordings:* Smokie, 1994' Ticino, 1995; Harlem Gospel Singers, 1998. *Honours:* Ernst Fischer Prizes, 1993, 1997. *Memberships:* GEMA; ASCAP; SCL. *Leisure interest:* Sailing. *Current Management:* Alan Davis, Legal Representation. *Address:* 8491 Sunset Blvd No. 340, Los Angeles, CA 90069, USA.

WALDEN John 'White Boy'; b. 23 Oct. 1948, London, England. Musician (harmonica); Blues singer. m. Natalie Marjory Gellineau, 26 Dec. 1982, 1 s., 1 d. *Musical Education:* Self-taught; Influenced by Sonny Boy Williamson and Little Walter Jacobs. *Career:* Took up harmonica when child; Started to play blues aged 13 with Bespoke Tailor Unit; Several European tours with John Walden Workshop, late 1960s; Madison Blues Band, 1990s; Reformed John Walden's Blues Band, 1997. *Recordings:* Many sessions, soundtracks, commercials; John Walden's Blues Band, CD, 1997. *Honour:* Acknowledged as one of the World's best blues harmonica players; Medal Winner, European Harp (Harmonica) Festival, Trossingham, Germany, 1996. *Membership:* Musicians' Union. *Leisure interests:* Music; Photography; Bonsai; Fish-keeping; Reading; Computers. *Address:* 90 Shooters Hill Rd, Blackheath, London SE3 8RL, England.

WALDEN Myron; b. 18 Oct. 1973, Miami, Florida, USA. Musician (alto saxophone); Songwriter; Arranger. *Education:* La Guardia High School of Music and Art; Harlem School of the Arts. *Musical Education:* Manhattan School of Music. *Career:* Performed and recorded with Ron Carter; Benny Golson; Winard Harper; Eddie Henderson; Kevin Hays; Mulgrew Miller. *Recordings:* Night Watch, Winard Harper; Be Yourself, Ravi Coltrane; Brian Blade; Phil Woods; Akilli, Ravi Coltrane; Bop, Carl Allen and Vincent Herring. *Honours:* Young and Upcoming Artist, Yamaha Corporation, 1990; Saxophonist of The Year, Harlem School of The Arts. *Current Management:* c/o Preston Powell, Jazzateria Inc, 112 W 72nd St, #2F, New York, NY 10023, USA.

WALDEN Narada Michael; b. 23 April 1952, Kalamazoo, Michigan, USA. Singer; Musician (drums, keyboards); Record Prod.; Songwriter. m. Anukampa Coles. *Education:* West Michigan University, 1970–72. *Career:* Drummer, with John McLaughlin, 1974–76; President, Perfection Light Productions, 1976–; Recording artist, songwriter, producer, 1976–; Board of Directors, Bay Area Music Awards, San Francisco, 1992. *Recordings:* Solo albums: Garden of Love Light, 1977; I Cry, I Smile, 1978; Awakening, 1979; The Dance of Life, 1979; Victory, 1980; Confidence, 1982; Looking At You, Looking At Me, 1983; The Nature of Things, 1985; Divine Emotion, 1985; with John McLaughlin: Apocalypse, 1974; Visions of The Emerald Beyond, 1975; Inner Worlds, 1976; Other recordings as musician: Teaser, Tom

Bolin, 1975; Wired, Jeff Beck, 1976; My Spanish Heart, Chick Corea, 1976; Jaco Pastorius, Jaco Pastorius, 1976; Black Market, Weather Report, 1976; Loading Zone, Roy Buchanan, 1977; Velvet Darkness, Allan Holdsworth, 1977; Exposure, Robert Fripp, 1979; Oneness, Santana, 1979; Clarke Duke Project 2, Stanley Clarke, 1983; Patti Austin, Patti Austin, 1984; Teaser, Angela Bofill, 1984; Who's Zoomin' Through, Aretha Franklin, 1985; Through The Storm, Aretha Franklin, 1989; As musician and producer: Hero, Clarence Clemons, 1985; While The City Sleeps, George Benson, 1986; As producer: with Sister Sledge: Love Somebody Today, 1980; All American Girls, 1981; Rose is Still a Rose, Aretha Franklin, 1998; Ladies and Gentleman, George Micheal, 1998; Definitive Collection, Angela Bofill, 1999; Best of Bond... James Bond, 1999; Love Songs, Jefferson Airplane, 2000; with Whitney Houston: Whitney Houston, 1985; I'm Your Baby Tonight, 1990. *Honours:* NARAS Award: Songwriter of The Year, 1986; Grammy, 1986; ASCAP Awards: Producer of the Year; Songwriter of the Year; Publisher of the Year, 1987; Billboard Magazine: Producer of the Year, 1986, 1987.

WALDEN Natan; b. 3 Nov. 1947, Bystrzyca, Klodska, Poland. Musician (bass, keyboards); Composer. m. Ewa Kryger-Walden, 5 Jan. 1974, 1 s., 1 d. *Musical Education:* MFA, Music Education, Lund University, Sweden, 1982; Music Producer Degree, Malmö Academi of Music, Sweden, 1985. *Career:* Poland: Nastolatki (Teenagers); Bassplayer with legendary singer, Niemen; USA: Live work, studio work commercials with Billy Cobham and Valerie Simpson; Sweden: Studio work, theatre-musical, Röda Orm; Animalen; Blood Brothers; TV and live works with Toots Thielemans; Nestor Marconi; Lill Babs, Eurovision Song Contest; Musical Director, many TV shows on Swedish TV; Many theme songs for TV serials, Sköna Söndag; Vem Tar Vem; Helt Apropa; In Denmark: The Most; Bassplayer, in live concert versions of a musical Chees; with 3 different orchestras: Danish Radio Orchestra; Odense Symphonic Orchestra; Sonderjisk Symphonic Orchestra. *Honours:* Golden Rose Montreux for music production of The Prize; Finalist for Outstanding Achievement in Popular Arts; International Emmy Awards, 1987. *Membership:* Swedish Society of Popular Music Composers. *Current Management:* Wiktor Kubiak Management. *Address:* 14 Henrietta St, London WC2, England.

WALICKI Peter Englundh; b. 4 Feb. 1950, Denmark. Musician (Drums, Keyboards); Songwriter; Singer. m. Hanne Jakobsen, 11 May 1974, 1 s., 1 d. *Education:* Music Teacher, Danish Music School. *Career:* Scool Band, 1960; Doctor Phill, 1967; Several Dance bands on DFDs, 1971; Golden Diamond, 1980; Grethe Ingmann and Sunset, 1984; A/S Rockompagniet, 1985; Hit the Hay, 1996; A/S Rockkompagniet, 1998. *Compositions:* Ann Mari, 1975; Habet Er Gront, 1977; Dancing Dynamite, 1996. *Recordings:* Ann Mari, 1975; Habet Er Gront, 1977; A/S Rockkompagniet Several Songs, 1985–98; Nikki Hokey, 1982; Mooreen, 1982. *Publication:* TV Show, Rock Palazt, ZDF Germany with Joe Bank's Rock Medicine Show, 1986. *Memberships:* KODA; NBC; DMF. *Leisure interests:* Composing; Computers. *Current Management:* Strike Records, own company. *Address:* Peter Englundh Walicki, Lysholm Alle 64, 4690, Haslev, Denmark.

WALKER Billy; b. Ralls, Texas, USA. Musician (guitar); Singer. m. Bettie, 6 Feb. 1978. *Career:* Toured with Elvis Presley, Texas, 1954; Performances include: Hollywood Bowl; Las Vegas; Hee Haw; Nashville Now; Crook and Chase; Grand Ole Opry Show, 1960–; Music City Tonight; Yesteryear; The Nashville Network; The Statler Brothers; Jimmy Dean Show; Dick Clark's American Bandstand; Billy Walker's Country Carnival, 3 years; 32 State Fairs; Tours: Austria; Bermuda; England; Guam; Hawaii; Ireland; Italy; Japan; Korea; Philippines; Japan; Spain; Sweden; Switzerland; Germany. *Recordings:* Over 100 chart records; 32 Top 10 hits; No. 1 hit singles: Funny How Time Slips Away; Charlie's Shoes; Cross The Brazos At Waco; A Million and One; When A Man Loves A Woman; Sing Me A Love Song Too Baby; Also: She Goes Walking Through My Mind; In Del Rio; Gone Our Endless Love; Curtains On The Window; Come A Little Bit Closer; Word Games; If I'm Losing You; Don't Stop In My World; Adam's Side (most requested wedding song, USA); Latest album: Larger Than Life. *Publications:* Larger Than Life (autobiography), 1998. *Leisure interests:* Golf; Fishing. *Current Management:* Bettie Crook, Artist Management. *Address:* PO Box 618, Hendersonville, TN 37077–0618, USA.

WALKER Clay (Ernest Clayton Jr); b. 9 Aug. 1969, Beaumont, Texas, USA. Country vocalist; Musician (guitar); Songwriter. *Musical Education:* Taught guitar by father, aged 9. *Career:* Played bars in local Beaumont, Texas area from age 16 before gigging more extensively in Louisiana, Oklahoma and New Mexico; Spotted by record producer James Stroud while performing as resident singer at Neon Armadillo bar, Beaumont; Stroud helped secure recording contract with Giant Records; Debut single What's It To You became his first No. 1 hit, 1993; Career hiatus when diagnosed with multiple sclerosis (now recovering), 1996; Achieved four platinum albums, two gold albums and has sold over 8m. albums; Has landed a song on Billboard's year-end Top 10 country list for five consecutive years, unmatched by any artist in same period. *Compositions include:* Live Until I Die; Rumor Has It; Who Needs You Baby. *Recordings include:* Rumor Has It, 1997; This Woman and This Man, 1995; Live Until I

Die, 1993; What's It To You, 1993; Dreaming With My Eyes Wide Open, 1994; If I Could Make A Living, 1994; Albums include: Clay Walker, 1993; If I Could Make A Living, 1994; Hypnotise The Moon, 1995; Rumor Has It, 1997; Greatest Hits, 1998; Live Laugh Love, 1999; Say No More, 2001. *Current Management:* c/o The Erv Woolsey Agency, 1000 18th Ave S, Nashville 37212, USA. *Internet:* www.claywalker.com.

WALKER Eddie; b. 31 Oct. 1948, Middlesbrough, England. Singer; Musician (guitar); Songwriter. m. Judith Ann, 22 March 1969, 1 s. *Education:* Charles Trevelyan Technical College, Newcastle. *Career:* Concert, folk festival and club appearances throughout UK, Germany, Belgium, Netherlands, Italy, Austria, Denmark, Slovenia, Croatia, Switzerland, Ireland, Luxembourg, Hong Kong, Bangkok, New Zealand; Television and radio appearances: Tyne Tees TV; BBC Radio 2; BBC Radio Scotland. *Recordings:* Solo albums: Everyday Man, 1977; Castle Cafe, 1981; Red Shoes On My Feet, 1983; Picking My Way, 1985; with guitarist John James: Carolina Shout!, 1990; Sidesteppin, 1993; Live At The Albert Hole!, solo video album, 1996. *Honours:* Winner of Songwriter Competition, Stolen My Heart Away, 1982; Northumbria Trophy for Songwriting, 1975; Slough Arts Festival, Solo Winner, 1977. *Memberships:* PRS; MCPS. *Address:* 33 The Grove, Brookfield, Middlesbrough, Cleveland TS5 8DT, England.

WALKER Junior (Autrey Dewalt II); b. 1942, Blythesville, Arizona, USA. Musician (saxophone); Vocalist. *Career:* Founder, Junior Walker and The All Stars, 1961–; Concerts include: Miami Pop Festival, 1968; Jazz and Blues Festival, Ann Arbor, Michigan, 1972; American Bandstand's 25th Anniversry Special, ABC TV, 1977. *Recordings:* Albums: Shotgun, 1965; Soul Session, 1966; Road Runner, 1966; Home Cookin', 1969; Greatest Hits, 1969; What Does It Take To Win Your Love, 1970; A Gasses, 1970; Rainbow Funk, 1971; Peace and Understanding Is Hard To Find, 1973; Sax Appeal, 1977; Whopper Bopper Show Stopper, 1977; Blow The House Down, 1981; Greatest Hits, 1982; Shake and Fingerpop, 1996; Uno Dos Tres: Latin Jazz Grooves, 1998; Singles: Shot Gun (No. 1, US R & B Chart), 1965; Do The Boomerang, 1965; Shake and Fingerpop, 1965; (I'm A Roadrunner), 1966; How Sweet It Is (To Be Loved By You), 1966; Money (That's What I Want) Part 1, 1966; Pucker Up Buttercup, 1967; Shoot Your Shot, 1967; Come See About Me, 1968; Hip City Pt 2, 1968; Home Cookin', 1969; What Does It Take (To Win Your Love) (No. 1, US R & B), 1969; These Eyes, 1969; Gotta Hold On To This Feeling, 1970; Do You See My Love (For You Growing), 1970; Take Me Girl, I'm Ready, 1971; Walk In The Night, 1972; Way Back Home, 1973; Guest on: Urgent, Foreigner, 1981.

WALKER Mark Robert Thomas; b. 7 March 1962, London, England. Musician (drums); Lyricist; Songwriter; Journalist. m. Claire Cooper, 6 Aug. 1988, 1 s., 2 d. *Education:* BEd Hons. *Career:* Tours with the Tin Gods, UK, Europe; Appeared at Lausanne Festival, Switzerland, 1991; Television: Hangar 17, BBC1; Radio: Live sessions for Capital Radio and GLR with Peachey Keen and World of Leather; TV appearances: House band drummer for the Jack Dee Show; National Lottery Show; Blue Peter; This Morning; Nightfever; London Tonight; The Big Stage and the Esther Show with Rolf Harris; Solo Performer of drum shows and clinics; British tours with Rolf Harris including Glastonbury Festival, 1997–2000; Ireland, 1999; Capetown, South Africa, 2000; Solo performer of The Have-A-Go Drum Show, appearances include GMTV, This Morning; Rhythmsticks 1998, 1999, 2000; Festival Hall; National Music Show, Wembley; BBC Music Live; Mad About Music, Docklands Arena; Duo Drum 'n' Didg, appearances include Rhythmsticks 1999 and Horniman Museum; Drumming in London West End production, Walt Disney's The Lion King. *Recordings:* St Mark's Place, World of Leather (debut album); The Coronation Street Album; Invisible History, Martin, Okasili; Private Party, Akin; Numerous recording sessions with producers Robin Miller; Faney; Colin Fairley; Jeff Foster; Composed theme tune for Airdrum (cartoon series); With Rolf Harris: Albums: Bootleg 1 and 70/30; Single: Christmas in the Sun; Fine Day. *Publications:* The Court of King Rolf – a tribute book to Rolf Harris, 2000; Regular features writer for Rhythm magazine, including series, The Secret Diary of a Session Drummer Aged 33 3/4; The Rudiments of Time; Rhythm Beginners. *Memberships:* Musicians' Union; PAMRA; PAS. *Leisure interests:* Parenthood; Cycling. *Current Management:* Active Entertainment Management. *Address:* 165 Green Lane, London SE9 3SZ, England.

WALKER Scott, (Noel Scott Engel); b. 9 Jan. 1944, Hamilton, Ohio, USA. Singer; Songwriter; Musician (bass). m. Mette Teglbjaerg, divorced, 1 d. *Education:* Fine Arts foundation course. *Musical Education:* Double bass lessons. *Career:* Member, The Routers, 1963; Member, Dalton Brothers, 1964; Member, Walker Brothers, 1965–67; Regular television appearances; Concerts include: British tour with Roy Orbison and Lulu, 1966; British tour with the Troggs, 1966; Far East tour with Yardbirds and Roy Orbison, 1967; British tour with Jimi Hendrix, 1967; Solo artiste, 1967–; British tour, 1968; Weekly show, BBC, 1969; Walker Brothers Reunion, 1975–78. *Recordings:* Albums: with the Walker Brothers: Take It Easy With The Walker Brothers, 1966; Portrait, 1966; Images, 1967; No Regrets, 1976; Lines, 1977; Nite Flights, 1978; After The Lights Go Out, 1990; No Regrets – The Best of The Walker Brothers, 1992; Solo albums: Scott, 1967; Scott 2,

1968; Scott 3, 1969; Scott 4, 1970; Til The Band Comes In, 1971; The Moviegoer, 1972; Any Day Now, 1973; Stretch, 1974; We Had It All, 1974; Scott Walker Plays Jacques Brel, 1981; Climate of Hunter, 1984; Boy Child, 1990; Tilt, 1995; Pola X, 1999; Hit singles: with the Routers: Let's Go, 1963; with The Walker Brothers: Make It Easy On Yourself (No. 1, UK), 1965; My Ship Is Coming In, 1966; The Sun Ain't Gonna Shine Any More, (No. 1, UK) 1966; No Regrets, 1976; Solo: Joanna, 1968; Lights of Cincinnati, 1969. *Current Management:* Negus-Fancey Co, 78 Portland Rd, London W11 4LQ, England.

WALKER SMITH Nicola; b. 18 Feb. 1964, Batley, West Yorkshire, England. Singer. m. Geoff Smith, 16 Sept. 1989, two s. (twins). *Musical Education:* BA Hons, Music, Electronics, Keele University, 1987; MA Music Theatre, Birmingham University, 1988. *Career:* World-wide concert appearances; Television and radio includes: In Tune, BBC Radio 3; Midnight Oil; Music In Our Time; The Late Show, BBC2; Other radio broadcasts world-wide. *Recordings:* Albums: The Garden, 1991; Gas Food Lodging, 1993; Fifteen Wild Decembers, 1995; Black Flowers, with the Geoff Smith Band, 1997; L'imboscata, with Franco Battiato, 1997. *Publications:* American Originals (co-author with Geoff Smith), 1994. *Honours:* Winston Churchill Fellowship, 1992. *Leisure interests:* Gardening; Old English crafts. *Current Management:* Keith Armstrong, Kitchenware, St Thomas' St Stables, Newcastle Upon Tyne NE1 4LE, England. *Address:* 25 Exeter Close, Chippenham, Wiltshire SN14 0YG, England.

WALLACE Angus; b. 7 April 1968, Guilsborough, Northants, England. *Education:* Media Productions, School of Recording, Brixton, London, 1987. *Career:* Own Recording Studio, age 18. *Recordings:* Album tracks for: Love and Rockets; Spiritualized; The Fall; Natasha Atlas (Transglobal Underground); Live Drums, recorded for The Prodigy; I Don't Need a Gun. *Honours:* Ampex Golden Reel Award, 1994; Gold Disc, world-wide sales, Fiend with Violin by The Fall, 1996. *Leisure interests:* Architecture; Travel. *Current Management:* GMM Management, Coton, NN6 8RF, England. *Address:* Far Heath, Guilsborough, Northants, NN6 8RH, England.

WALLACE Robert Andrew; b. 21 Nov. 1951, Glasgow, Scotland. Musician (pipes). 1 s., 1 d. *Career:* Member, folk band Whistlebinkies, 1974–; Appeared on television and radio with RSNO, Scottish Ensemble, John Cage, Yehudhi Menuhin. *Recordings:* 5 albums with Whistlebinkies; Solo albums: Chance Was A Fine Thing, 1982; Piper of Distinction, 1990. *Publications:* Glasgow Collection of Bagpipe Music. *Honours:* Gold Medal, Oban, 1985; Bratach Gorm (Blue Banner), London, 1989. *Memberships:* Musicians' Union; CPA; Piobaireachd Society. *Leisure interests:* Music; Reading.

WALLEME Christophe; b. 1964. Musician (acoustic bass). *Musical Education:* Private lessons with M Kazoran; Hein Van de Guyn; Césarius Alvim; Training with: QUEST; Kenny Barron's rhythm section. *Career:* Member, PRYSM; Manuel Rocheman Trio; David Patois Trio, Quintet; Sarah Lazarus Quartet; Lois Winsberg Quintet; Jean-Pierre Como Quintet; Jean-Loup Longnon Sextet and Big Band; Played numerous clubs, Paris; Festivals, France; Played with: Tom Harrell; Ted Curson; Jean-Loup Longnon; Rick Margitza; Sylvain Beuf; Eric Barret; Richard Galliano; Philip Catherine; Christian Escoudé; N'Guyen Lee; Stephanie Crawford; Walter Davis Jr; Barry Altschul; René Urtreger; Michel Graillier; Alain Jean-Marie; Georges Arvanitas; Jacky Terrasson; Jean-Pierre Como; Denuis Badault; Bob Mover; George Brown; Aldo Romano; Teacher, EDIM, 1986-. *Recordings:* Bop For Sale, Ludovic de Preissac Quintet, 1989; Correspondence, Daniel Beaussier Quartet, 1990; Ciao Mon Coeur, Elizabeth Caumont, 1993; Sanscrit, Daniel Beaussier Quartet, 1993; Impro Primo, Sylvain Beuf Quartet, 1993; Cyclades, Jean-Loup Lognon Big Band, 1994; PRYSM, PRYSM, 1995; Tropic City, Manuel Rocheman Trio, 1995; Express Paris-Rome, Jean-Pierre Como Quintet, 1996; Louis Winsberg Quintet. *Honours:* Solist Award, La Défense National Jazz Contest, 1988; First Prize, Jazz Et Polar Contest, 1991; First Prize, La Défense National Jazz Contest, 1994. *Address:* 16 rue des Eglantines, 91130 Ris-Orangis, France.

WALLER Paul; b. 1961, London, England. Record Prod.; Remixer; Songwriter. 2 s., 1 d. *Recordings for:* Björk; Soul II Soul; Naughty By Nature; Lisa Stansfield; Baby Face; Eric Clapton; Elton John. *Membership:* Musicians' Union. *Current Management:* Paul Kennedy, 1 2 One Management, PO Box 6627, London N22 4JZ, England.

WALLGREN Henrik; b. 10 Sept. 1965, Gothenburg, Sweden. Singer Songwriter. m. Katarina Wallgren, 24 June 1988, 2 d. *Musical Education:* Self-taught. *Career:* Formed ORO, 1990; For Gothenburg Film Festival: Metropolis, 1994; Total King Kong, 1996; Joined Den Fule, 1994; Solo album, 1996. *Compositions:* New Music to Mother Curage, 1994; New Music to Nosferatu, 1995. *Recordings:* Milk and Concrete, 1990; Iron-Storm, 1992; Ragamedon... 2048, 1993; Quake!, 1995; Walk On By, 1996. *Honours:* Grammis, 1993; City of Gothenburg Prize, 1997. *Membership:*

Swedish Composers of Popular Music. *Leisure interest:* Sailing. *Current Management.* Musikcentrum Väst Pjurgardsgatan 13, 414 62 GBG Sweden. *Address:* Pl. 1039, 430 85 Branne, Sweden.

WALLINGER Karl; b. 19 Oct. 1957, Prestatyn, Wales. Vocalist; Musician (multi-instrumentalist); Record Prod.; Arranger; Songwriter. *Career:* Member, groups Quasimodo; Zero Zero; Out; Invisible Body Club; Member, The Waterboys, 1983–86; Founder, World Party, 1986; Concerts include: Launch of Greenpeace – Rainbow Warriors album, with Peter Gabriel, Annie Lennox, Moscow, 1989; Reims Music Festival, France, 1990. *Recordings:* with The Waterboys: Singles: The Whole of The Moon, 1985; with World Party: Ship of Fools, 1987; Is It Like Today, 1993; All I Gave, 1993; Albums: with The Waterboys: A Pagan Place, 1984; This Is The Sea, 1985; with World Party: Private Revolution, 1987; Goodbye Jumbo, 1990; Bang!, 1993; Whole of The Moon: The Music of The Waterboys, 1998. *Honours include:* Q Award, Best Album, Goodbye Jumbo, 1990. *Current Management:* Pure Management, 39 Bolton Gardens, London SW5 0AQ, England.

WALSH Greg; b. England. Record Prod. *Career:* Producer for: Heaven 17; Tina Turner; Chicago; Elkie Brooks; Lucio Battisti; British Lions; Trainspotting; Ron. *Honours:* Grammy Nomination, Album of the Year, 1984. *Current Management:* Gary Davison, The Liaison and Promotion Co. *Address:* 70 Gloucester Pl., London WH1 3HL, England.

WALSH Joe; b. 20 Nov. 1947, Wichita, Kansas, USA. Singer; Musician (guitar, keyboards); Record Prod. *Education:* Kent (Ohio) State University. *Career:* Member, James Gang; Solo artiste, and with own group Barnstorm, 1971–; Member, The Eagles, 1976–81; Tour of Australia, New Zealand, Japan, 1976; 2 US tours, 1977; 2 European tours, 1977; Canadian tour, 1978; Self-nominated for Vice-President, 2 US presidential campaigns; Joined with the Eagles for the Hell Freezes Over tour and album, world tour spanning 3 years and 5 countries. *Recordings:* Albums: with The James Gang: Yer Album, 1969; James Gang Rides Again, 1970; Thirds, 1971; Live In Concert, 1971; with The Eagles: Hotel California (No. 1, USA), 1976; The Long Run (No. 1, USA), 1979; Eagles Live, 1980; Solo/with Barnstorm: Barnstorm, 1972; The Smoker You Drink..., 1973; So What, 1974; You Can't Argue With A Sick Mind, 1976; But Seriously Folks, 1978; There Goes The Neighbourhood, 1981; You Bought It, You Name It, 1983; The Confessor, 1985; Got Any Gum, 1987; Ordinary Average Guy, 1991; Songs For A Dying, 1992; Look What I Did! – The Joe Walsh Anthology, 1995; Robocop (soundtrack), 1995; Look What I Did!: The Joe Walsh Anthology, 1995; Greatest Hits: Little Did He Know, 1997; 20th Century Masters Millennium Collection, 2000; with Ringo Starr: Vertical Man, 1998; with Randy Newman: Guilty: 30 Years of Randy Newman; Hit singles: with The Eagles: Hotel California (No. 1, USA), 1977; Life In The Fast Lane, 1977; Heartache Tonight (No. 1, USA), 1979: The Long Run, 1980; Seven Bridges Road, 1981. *Honours:* Grammy Awards: Records of The Year, Hotel California, 1978; Best Vocal Arrangement, New Kid In Town, 1978; Best Rock Vocal Performance, Heartache Tonight, 1980; American Music Awards: Favourite Pop/Rock Album, 1977, 1981; Favourite Pop/Rock Band, 1981. *Leisure interests:* Amateur radio; Synthesizers. *Current Management:* David Spero Management. *Address:* 1679 S Belvoir Blvd, Cleveland, OH 44121, USA.

WALSH Peter; b. England. Record Prod. *Career:* Producer for: Simple Minds; China Crisis; Boomtown Rats; Alphaville; The Church; Scott Walker; Peter Gabriel; Miguel Bose. *Current Management:* Gary Davison, The Liaison and Promotion Co. *Address:* 70 Gloucester Pl., London W1H 3HL, England.

WALSH Steve; b. 1951, St Joseph, Missouri, USA. Vocalist; Musician (keyboards); Songwriter. *Career:* Member, US rock group, Kansas, 1972–80; 1986–; Also solo artiste. *Recordings:* Albums: with Kansas: Kansas, 1974; Songs For America, 1975; Masque, 1975; Leftoverture, 1976; Point of No Return, 1977; Two For The Show, 1978; Monolith, 1979; Audio-Visions, 1980; Power, 1986; In The Spirit of Things, 1988; At the Tower Theatre in Philadelphia, 1998; Solo album: Schemer Dreamer. *Honour:* UNICEF Deputy Ambassador of Goodwill, 1978. *Current Management:* Entertainment Services Unltd. *Address:* Main St Plaza 1000, Suite 303, Voorhess, NJ 08043, USA.

WALTER Rémy; b. 1 Sept. 1964, Paris, France. Singer; Actor; Record Prod. 1 d. *Musical Education:* Exam as an arranger (SACEM). *Career:* Producer, 1986–; First International success: Etienne by Guesh Patti; Producer, 20 singles and 7 albums; Formed own record label; Actor in 6 films, 1979. *Recordings:* Albums include: Ziskakan: Kasasnicola; Rosina de Peira: Anveit; Pascal Mathieu: En Attendant Des Jours Pires; A3: Les Fous Du Large; Clément Masdonoar: Anastasia; First solo album: Face To The Ground, 1995. *Honours:* Clément Masdonoar: Anastasia, Best World Music Record of Year, Le Monde, 1990. *Memberships:* GRAF; SACEM. *Leisure interests:* Surfing; Snowboarding; Skateboarding. *Current Management:* Safta Jaffery. *Address:* 1 Prince of Wales Passage, 117 Hampstead Rd, London NW1 3EF, England.

WALTERS Dez; b. 1 Oct. 1948, Llysfaen, North Wales. Musician (guitar, banjo); Songwriter; Vocalist. 3 d. *Musical Education:* Self-taught. *Career:* Began, early teens in rock band; Worked playing country music in: Middle East; America; Canada; Europe; Backing musician and support act to: Billie Jo Spears: Jim Glaser; Ronnie Prophet; UK and European tours; Song in film: Too Young To Die; 3 songs appeared on STV Show, 1994, 1995; Various radio stations, UK. *Compositions:* Writer, most of own material. *Recordings:* Here's Looking At You; Wide Brimmed and Legless, 1995; Ladies Man; Totally Covered, 2001; videos: Choice Cuts, 2000; Live In Tuscon, 2001. *Honours:* Nomination, Best British Country Album, Wide Brimmed and Legless, 1995; Scotland's No. 1 Country Band, 1994, 1995; Various awards, country clubs nationwide. *Memberships:* Equity; Musicians' Union. *Leisure interests:* Reading; Motor racing; Travel; Music (general).

WALTERS Hannelore Liesemarie (Fil); b. 31 Jan. 1970, Dartford, Kent, England. Singer; Songwriter; Lyricist. *Musical Education:* Studied violin, aged 9–12; Currently learning piano. *Career:* Member, various bands from age 16; Singer, songwriter, lyricist, Back To The Planet, 6 years; Appearances radio and television; Signed to London Records, 1993; Continuous concerts, England, Europe, 6 years; Festivals include: Glastonbury; Phoenix; Reading. *Recordings:* 2 cassettes, 1991; 1992; Albums: Mind and Soul Collaborators, 1993; Messages After The Bleep, 1994. *Leisure interests:* Painting; Computers (music); Reading; Swimming. *Current Management:* Westbury Music Ltd. *Address:* 8 Roberts Rd, Belvedere, Kent DA17 6NP, England.

WANDALL Marietta; b. 21 Nov. 1956, Copenhagen, Denmark. Jazz Musician (piano); Composer; Music Teacher. m. Kristian Sparre Andersen, 5 Nov. 1988, 2 d. *Musical Education:* Private teachers; University of Copenhagen; Mainly self-taught. *Career:* Played piano, synthesizer in jazz ensembles, including Crystal Quintet (with Marylin Mazur); Concerts in Denmark, Norway, Finland; Solo pianist at several Copenhagen Jazz Festivals; Duo concerts with Chris Poole (flute); Jazz duo with Hanne Romer (saxophone), 1980–; Numerous appearances on Danish radio and television; Piano teacher in digital piano-lab. *Recordings:* with Hanne Romer: Akijava, 1990; Ametyst, 1994. *Address:* C F Richsvej, 101 C, 2000 Frederiksberg, Denmark.

WANGFORD Hank (Samuel Hutt); b. 15 Nov. 1940, Wangford, Suffolk, England. Country Singer; Musician (guitar); Doctor. *Education:* Medicine, Cambridge University. *Career:* Became singer, London pub circuit, 1976–; Founder, Sincere Management; Sincere Products; Presenter, 2 country music television series, Channel 4; Stage show, Radio Wang; Also Senior Medical Officer, Family Planning Clinic, London. *Recordings:* Chicken Rhythm; Cowboys Stay On Longer; Albums: Live Hank Wangford, 1982; Hank Wangford, 1985; Rodeo Radio, 1985; Stormy Horizons, 1990; Hard Shoulder To Cry On, 1993. *Publication:* Author (as Sam Hutt): Hank Wangford Vol. III – The Middle Years, 1989. *Current Management:* FAB, 132 Liverpool Rd, London N1 1LA, England.

WARD Bill; b. 5 May 1948, Birmingham, England. Musician (drums). *Career:* Drummer, UK heavy rock group Black Sabbath (formerly Earth), 1967–80, 1983; Concerts include: Hollywood Music Festival, 1970; Madison Square Garden, New York, 1975. *Recordings:* Albums; Black Sabbath, 1970; Paranoid, 1970; Master of Reality, 1971; Black Sabbath, Vol. 4, 1972; Sabbath Bloody Sabbath, 1974; Sabotage, 1975; We Sold Our Souls For Rock 'n' Roll, 1976; Technical Ecstacy, 1976; Never Say Die, 1978; Heaven and Hell, 1980; Live At Last, 1980; Born Again, 1983; Black Sabbath, Reunion, 1998; Solo Album: Two Hands Clapping, 1999 Singles: Evil Woman, 1970; Paranoid, 1970; Iron Man, 1972; Never Say Die, 1978; Hard Road, 1978; Neon Knights, 1980.

WARD John Robert; b. 28 June 1964, Halesworth, Suffolk, England. Singer/Songwriter; Musician (Guitar, Bodhran, Bass Guitar, Harmonica). m. Lynne, 3 Feb. 1996, 1 s., 1 d. *Education:* Lowestoft College. *Career:* Bass Player, Singer in rock and pop bands, 1980's; Full Time Acoustic Singer/ Songwriter, 1988–; TV appearance at Cambridge Folk Festival; Elected, Folk Section, Committee of Musicians Union; Times feature and interview, 1996. *Recordings:* The Shrinking World, album, 1988; Water on the Shore, CD, 1992; Billy Bragg and Friends, contributor 1996; Waking Dreams, CD, 1998. *Memberships:* PRS; PPL; PAMRA; Musicians' Union. *Leisure interests:* Photography; Natural history; Cookery. *Address:* PO Box 59, Lowestoft, Suffolk NR33 8EA, England.

WARE Martyn; Musician; Record Prod. *Career:* Founder member, Human League; Founder member, Heaven 17; World-wide tours, numerous television and concert appearances; Independent Record Producer. *Recordings:* Albums: All Heaven 17 albums; Council Collective EP, Paul Weller; Private Dancer, Tina Turner; The Hardline According To. . ., Terence Trent D'Arby; I Say I Say I Say, Erasure; Reproduction, Travelog, Human League; Musta, Sanna Kurki-Suonio; Simply the Best, Tina Turner; Singles: Let's Stay Together, Tina Turner; Sign Your Name, Dance Little Sister, Wishing Well, Terence Trent D'Arby; Always, Run To

The Sun, Erasure; Lover, Back In My Life, Joe Roberts; Numerous singles with: Heaven 17; Scritti Politti; Lena Fiagbe; Alison Moyet; Urban Cookie Collective; Pauline Henry; Human League. *Current Management:* Stephen Budd Management. *Address:* 109B Regents Park Rd, London NW1 8UR, England.

WARE Nicholas Stewart; b. 5 April 1963, Burnham, Buckinghamshire, England. Project Man., Videoconferencing. *Musical Education:* O Level Music, High Wycombe Music CTRE, Baritone and alto saxophone, bass guitar. *Career:* Bucks Cyjo, 1982–88; Herman Nush Windtunnel Experience, 1988–89; Saxophonist, musical director, arranger, soul/blues band Straight Eight, 1990–; Bucks Symphonic Ensemble, 1990–94. *Recordings:* Session recording with No No Fear, 1987, 1989, 1990; with Orbitone: All Day; Set Me Free; Optimism; with Straight Eight: It's A Cover Up (album), 1991. *Leisure interests:* Motorcycling; Painting; Jiving. *Address:* 9 Rectory Court, High Wycombe, Buckinghamshire HP13 7DH, England.

WARINER Steve; b. 25 Dec. 1954, Noblesville, Indiana, USA. Musician (bass); Songwriter; Singer. *Career:* Bass player with Dottie West; Bob Luman; Chet Atkins; Solo artiste, 1978–. *Compositions include:* I'm Already Taken, Conway Twitty; Several songs recorded by Bob Luman. *Recordings:* US Country No. 1 hits: All Roads Lead To You; Some Fools Never Learn; You Can Dream On Me; Love's Highway; Small Town Girl; Lynda; The Weekend; Duets include: The Hand That Rocks The Cradle, with Glen Campbell; That's How You Know When Love's Right, with Nicolette Larson; Albums: Steve Wariner, 1982; Midnight Fire, 1983; One Good Night Deserves Another, 1985; Life's Highway, 1985; Down In Tennessee, 1986; It's A Crazy World, 1987; I Should Be With You, 1988; I Got Dreams, 1989; I Am Ready, 1991; Drive, 1993; No More Mr Nice Guy, 1996; Christmas Memories, 1998; Burnin' the Roadhouse Down, 1998; Two Teardrops, 1999; Loser Wins; Plano Texas Girl; Where Did I Go Wrong; with: T Graham Brown, Wine into Water, 1998; Clint Black, D'Lectrified, 1999; Kieth Urban, 1999. *Honour:* CMA Vocal Event Award, Restless, 1991. *Address:* Steve Wariner Productions, 1103 16th Ave S, Nashville, TN 37212, USA.

WARNES Jennifer; b. 1947, Seattle, Washington, USA. Singer. *Career:* Singer, 1967–; Theatre appearance, Hair, Los Angeles, 1968. *Recordings:* Albums: I Can Remember Everything, 1968; See Me, Feel Me, Touch Me, Heal Me, 1969; Jennifer, 1972; Shot Through The Heart, 1979; The Best Of. . ., 1982; Famous Blue Raincoat, 1987; Just Jennifer, 1992; The Hunter, 1992; Also featured on: The Mason Williams Ear Show, Mason Williams, 1967; Everbody's Angel, Tanita Tikaram, 1991; For Our Children, with Jackson Browne, 1991; Singles include: Right Time of The Night, 1978; I Know A Heartache When I See One, 1979; It Goes Like It Goes, 1980; Up Where We Belong, duet with Joe Cocker, for film An Officer and A Gentleman (No. 1, USA), 1982; All The Right Moves, for film All The Right Moves, 1983; (I've Had) The Time of My Life, duet with Bill Medley, for film Dirty Dancing (No. 1, USA), 1987; Albums include: Shot Through the Heart, 1979; The Best of Jennifer Warnes, 1982; Famous Blue Raincoat, 1987; with Chris Hillman: Like a Hurricane, 1998; with Michael Martin Murphy: Wildfire 1972–84, 1998; with Jim Billie: Alligator Tales, 1998. *Honours:* Academy Awards: It Goes Like It Goes, 1980; Up Where We Belong, 1983; (I've Had) The Time of My Life, 1988; (all for Best Original Song); Academy Award nomination, One More Hour, 1981; Grammy Awards: Best Pop Performances, Up Where We Belong, 1983; (I've Had) The Time of My Life, 1987. *Current Management:* Donald Miller, 1246 Kling St, Studio City, CA 91604, USA.

WARREN Diane; b. 1956, California, USA. Songwriter. *Education:* Film Studies, Cal State University. *Compositions include:* If I Could Turn Back Time, Cher; Solitaire, Laura Brannigan; If You Asked Me To, Celine Dion; I Get Weak, Belinda Carlisle; Rhythm of The Night, Debarge; Look Away, Chicago; Who Will You Run To, Michael Bolton; When I'm Back On My Feet Again, Michael Bolton; Not A Dry Eye In The House, Meat Loaf; Also composed for Gloria Estefan, Al Green, Olivia Newton-John, Roy Orbison, Joe Cocker, Christina Aguilera. *Honours include:* ASCAP Songwriter of the Year, 1990, 1991, 1993; Billboard Singles Publishers of the Year, 1990, 1993; ASCAP Voice of Music Award, 1995.

WARREN (Robert) Huw; b. 18 May 1962, Swansea, West Glamorgan, Wales. Musician (piano, accordion, keyboards); Composer. *Musical Education:* Studied classical piano and cello at young age; Degree in Music, London. *Career:* Crosses many genre boundaries including: Jazz; Folk; Contemporary Classical; World Music; Early musical experiences included playing organ in working men's clubs, South Wales; Moved to London to study for a music degree, 1980; Involved with the British experimental music scene and London jazz musicians; Collaborated with musicians from: Brazil; Democratic Republic of the Congo; Iran; Indian sub-continent; Began long-running collaboration with June Tabor, late 1980s; Co-founder: Perfect Houseplants (with Mark Lockheart and Dudley Phillips); Collaborations include: Billy Bragg; Christine Tobin; The Orlando Consort; Mose Se Fan Fan (African guitarist). *Compositions:*

commissions include: Riot for Piano Circus; Steamboat Bill Jr (new score for the Buster Keaton film); Music for a production of Jean Cocteau's Monologues, Lyric Theatre, London. *Recordings:* Albums: A Barrel Organ Far From Home, 1997; Infinite Riches In A Little Room, 2000; with Perfect Houseplants: Perfect Houseplants, 1993; Clec, 1995; Snap Clatter, 1997; Extempore (with Orlando Consort), 1998; New Folk Songs, 2000; with June Tabor: Some Other Time, 1989; Aqaba Topic, 1990; Angel Tiger, 1992; Against The Streams, 1994; Aleyn, 1997; A Quiet Eye, 2000; Rosa Mundi, 2001; with Maddy Prior and June Tabor: No More To The Dance, 1988; features on: Through Rose Coloured Glasses, Mark Lockheart, 1998; Mirmama, Eddi Reader, 1992; Busy Listening, Steve Arguelles, 1994; Entertainment USA, Billy Jenkins, 1994; Tales From The Sun, Tim Garland, 1995; Mayfest 95, Billy Jenkins and the Fun Horns of Berlin, 1995; Aililiu, Christine Tobin, 1995; Yell of The Gazelle, Christine Tobin, 1996; East Meets West 95, Billy Jenkins and the Fun Horns of Berlin, 1996; Circuits, Steve Arguelles, 1998; House of Women, Christine Tobin, 1998. *Internet:* www.huwwarren.com.

WARWICK (Marie) Dionne; b. 12 Dec. 1940, East Orange, New Jersey, USA. Singer. m. Bill Elliott, deceased, 2 s. *Education:* Hartt College of Music, Hartford, Connecticut. *Musical Education:* MA, Music. *Career:* Singer, gospel groups The Drinkard Singers; The Gospelaires; Solo singer, 1962–; Association with songwriters Bacharach and David, originally as demo and backing singer, 1961–72; Numerous concerts, tours and benefit shows world-wide; Television includes: Top of The Pops; Thank Your Lucky Stars; Ready Steady Goes Live!; The Bacharach Sound; It's What's Happening Baby; The Divine Dionne Warwick; Ed Sullivan Show; Host, Solid Gold, 1980, 1984–86; Host, A Gift of Music, 1981; Sisters In The Name of Love, 1986; Dionne and Friends, 1990; Actress, film Slaves, 1969. *Recordings:* Albums: Presenting Dionne Warwick, 1964; Make Way For Dionne Warwick, 1964; The Sensitive Sound of Dionne Warwick, 1965; Dionne Warwick In Paris, 1966; Here Where There Is Love, 1967; On Stage and In The Movies, 1967; The Windows of The World, 1967; Valley of The Dolls, 1968; Promises Promises, 1969; Soulful, 1969; Dionne, 1972; From Within, 1972; Just Being Myself, 1973; Then Came You, 1975; Track of The Cat, 1976; A Man and A Woman, with Isaac Hayes, 1977; No Night So Long, 1980; Hot, Live and Otherwise, 1981; Friends In Love, 1982; Heartbreaker, 1982; So Amazing, 1983; Without Your Love, 1985; Reservations For Two, 1987; Dionne Warwick Sings Cole Porter, 1990; Friends Can Be Lovers, 1993; Aquarela Do Brazil, 1995; Hits from Stage and Screen, 1997; Dionne Sings Dionne, 1998; Numerous compilation albums; Hit singles include: Anyone Who Had A Heart, 1964; Walk On By, 1964; A Message To Michael, 1966; Alfie, 1967; I Say A Little Prayer, 1967; Do You Know The Way To San José, 1968; This Girl's In Love With You, 1969; I'll Never Fall In Love Again, 1970; Then Came You, with The Spinners (No. 1, USA), 1974; I'll Never Love This Way Again, 1979; Heartbreaker, with Barry Gibb (No. 2, UK), 1982; All The Love In The World, 1983; That's What Friends Are For (AIDS charity record), with Stevie Wonder, Gladys Knight, Elton John (No. 1, USA), 1985; Featured on numerous film soundtracks including: A House Is Not A Home, 1964; What's New Pussycat?, 1965; Valley of The Dolls, 1968; The April Fools, 1969; Slaves, 1969; The Love Machine, 1971; After You, 1980; The Woman In Red, 1984; Contributor, charity records: We Are The World, USA For Africa, 1985; Forgotten Eyes, 1990; Lift Up Every Voice and Sing, 1990; That's What Friends Are For, 1993; Sunny Weather Lover, 1993; What the World Needs Now, 1998. *Honours:* Top Selling Female Artist, NARM, 1964; Grammy Awards: Best Female Pop Vocal Performance, 1969, 1970, 1980; Best Contemporary Vocal Performance, 1971; Best Female R & B Vocal Performance, 1980; Best Pop Performance, Duo or Group, 1987; Song of The Year, 1987; Star on Hollywood's Walk of Fame, 1985; NAACP Key of Life Award, 1990; CORE Humanitarian Award, 1992; Nosotros Golden Eagle Humanitarian Award, 1992; Award from City of New York for contributions to AIDS research, 1987; DIVA Award, 1992; Platinum and Gold discs. *Address:* c/o Brokaw Company, 9255 Sunset Blvd, Suite 804, Los Angeles, CA 90069, USA.

WARWICK Ricky; b. Belfast, Northern Ireland. Vocalist; Rock Musician (guitar). m. Vanessa Warwick. *Career:* Member, New Model Army, Def Leppard; Founder member, UK heavy rock group The Almighty, 1988–; Major concerts include: Monsters of Rock Festival, Castle Donington, UK, 1982. *Recordings:* Albums: with The Almighty: Blood Fire and Love, 1989; Blood Fire and Live, 1990; Soul Destruction, 1991; Powertrippin', 1993; Crank, 1995; Just Add Life, 1996; with Def Leppard, 1999; Hit single: Free 'N' Easy, 1991. *Current Management:* Triple T Management Co, 21 Napier Pl., London W14 8LG, England.

WASHBURN Dan; b. 28 May 1956, Coburg, Ontario, Canada. Singer; Songwriter; Musician (bass). m. Jane, 15 Dec. 1984, 3 s., 1 d. *Career:* Lead singer, South Mountain, 1992; Concerts, as lead singer and bassist, South Mountain: Netherlands; Germany; Switzerland; Belgium; Canada; Appeared with: Marty Stuart; Waylon Jennings; Toby Keith; Merle Haggard; Prairie Oyster; Various television shows in above mentioned countries; Appeared, CCMA Awards Show, 1993. *Recordings:* Played on soundtrack for Into The Fire, 1990; South Mountain album: Where There's

A Will, 1995; Session bassist, singer, many Canadian country, folk, blues albums. *Memberships:* AFofM; Canadian Country Music Asscn. *Leisure interests:* Fishing with his children; Flying model radio-controlled airplanes. *Current Management:* Katherine Faint, Agent, Savannah Music Group. *Address:* 768 Chamberlain St, Peterborough, ON K9J 4M3, Canada.

WASTIE Heather Ann; b. 18 Oct. 1955, Stourbridge, England. Vocalist; Musician (keyboards, recorder); Lyricist; Songwriter; Poet. m. Mark Edward Wastie. *Education:* Birmingham University. *Career:* Community Musician, Animateur: Special needs groups and schools; Member of alchemy linking Medieval music with maths; Composer-in-residence, Lichfield Mysteries; AOR group Moulin Ridge. *Leisure interests:* Cycling; Walking; Canal Boating; Crosswords. *Address:* 20 Cedarwood Rd, Dudley, DY3 2JD, England.

WATERHOUSE David Boyer; b. 13 July 1936, Harrogate. University Prof.; Musician (Piano, Highland Bagpipes). m. Naoko Matsubara, 1 s. *Education:* MA, King's College, Cambridge, 1963; LRAM, 1956, Piano pupil of M Denny (pupil of Tobias Matthay), Highland Bagpipes with P/M John Wilson. *Career:* Research Assistant, Cambridge Institute of Criminology, 1959–60; Research Fellow, Center for Asian Arts, University of Washington, 1964–66; Assistant Professor, 1966–70, Associate Professor, 1970–75, Professor, 1975-, Department of East Asian Studies; Consultant to numerous museums, publishers on Asian art and other subjects; Solo performance of Highland bagpipes, ensemble with the 48th Highlanders of Canada. *Publications include:* Harunobu and his Age: The Development of Colour Printing in Japan, 1964; Japanese Woodblock Prints from the J Bruce Varcoe Collection, 1976; Early Japanese prints in the Philadelphia Museum of Art, 1983; Dance of India, editor, 1998; Numerous contributions to books including The New Grove Dictionary of Music and Musicians, 2001; Encyclopaedia of Music in Canada, 1992; Numerous articles including those on Japanese music, Buddhist music and Highland bagpipes. *Memberships include:* International Council for Traditional Music; Pipers' Society of Ontario; Pipes and Drums Asscn, 48th Highlanders of Canada; Fellow, Royal Society of Canada; Fellow, Royal Asiatic Society; Society for Asian Music, USA; Society for Ethnomusicology, USA; Toyo Ongaku Gakkai, Japan;. *Address:* 324 Coral Terrace, Oakville, ON L6J 4C4, Canada.

WATERMAN Pete; b. 15 Jan. 1947. Songwriter; Record Prod.; Record Co Exec. *Career:* Soul DJ; Promoter, record producer and remixer, for artistes including Adrian Baker; Susan Cadogan; Member, group, Agents Aren't Aeroplanes, 1984; Member, songwriting and production team Stock/Aitken/ Waterman (SAW), with Matt Aitken and Mike Stock, 1984–93; Founder, own PWL record label, 1988; Founder, 3 record labels, PWL America, PWL Continental, PWL Black, 1991-. *Recordings:* Albums: Hit Factory, 1987; Hit Factory Vol. 2, 1988; Hit Factory Vol. 3, 1989; The Best of Stock, Aitken and Waterman, 1990; Hit singles: As co-writer, producer: You Spin Me Round, Dead Or Alive (No. 1, UK), 1984; So Macho, Sinitta, 1986; Respectable, Mel and Kim (No. 1, UK), 1987; Never Gonna Give You Up, Rick Astley, 1987; with Kylie Minogue: I Should Be So Lucky (No. 1, 12 countries), 1988; Got To Be Certain, 1988; The Locomotion, 1988; Hand On Your Heart, 1989; Better The Devil You Know, 1990; Rhythm of Love, 1993; 50+1, 1998; with Steps: Steptacular, 2000; Also recordings for: Jason Donovan; Divine; Hazell Dean; Sonia; Brother Beyond; Big Fun; Donna Summer. *Current Management:* PWL Management International, 4–7 The Vineyard, off Sanctuary St, London SE1 1QL, England.

WATERS Peter Russell; b. 4 Aug. 1953, Broken Hill, Australia. Musician (Concert Pianist; Jazz Pianist). m. Sybille Waters, 29 Aug. 1997, 1 d. *Education:* Piano studies in Adelaide with Rolland May and Clemens Leske, and in London with Peter Walfisch. *Career:* Concert Pianist, Salzburg Gestival with Gundula Janowitz; Solo and duo recitals with Janowitz in Paris, Vienna, Berlin, London, Lyon, Rome, Stockholm, Cologne, Frankfurt, Munich, Zurich and numerous festivals; Bach Festival Schaffhausen, 1985; Numerous tours, live concerts and recordings in Europe and South America, 1992–; Musical Director, Solo Pianist, exchange project with St Petersburg and Switzerland; Solo tour with Orchestre de Lille, 1997; Formed Treya Quartet with Sardinian Trumpeter Paolo Fresu. *Recordings:* CD, Gates Beyond, music of John Adams, Ravel and Satie; Treya Quartet plays Gabriel Fauré. *Honour:* ABC FM Best Classical Recording in Australia, for Gates Beyond, 1997. *Membership:* Tonkünstlerverein, Switzerland; World Wildlife Fund. *Leisure interests:* T'ai chi; Swimming; Reading Shantideva. *Current Management:* Jacqui Howard. *Address:* Rothalde 333, 9055 Bühler, Switzerland.

WATERS Roger; b. 6 Sept. 1944, Great Bookham, Surrey, England. Vocalist; Musician (bass); Composer. *Education:* Regent Street Polytechnic, London. *Career:* Founder member, Pink Floyd, 1965–83; Performances include: Rome International Pop Festival, 1968; Hyde Park, London, 1968; Bath Festival, 1970; Montreux Festival, 1971; Knebworth Festival, 1975; Films: Pink Floyd Live At Pompeii, 1972; The

Wall, 1982; Solo artiste, 1984–; Performance of The Wall, Berlin, 1990; Guitar Legends, Seville, Spain, 1991. *Recordings:* Albums: Piper At The Gates of Dawn, 1967; A Saucerful of Secrets, 1968; More (film soundtrack), 1969; Ummagumma, 1969; Meddle, 1971; Relics, 1971; Obscured By Clouds, 1972; The Dark Side of The Moon (No. 1, USA), 1973; Wish You Were Here (No. 1, UK and USA), 1975; Animals, 1976; The Wall (No. 1, USA), 1979; The Final Cut, 1983; Solo albums: Music From The Body (film soundtrack), 1970; The Pros and Cons of Hitch Hiking, 1984; When The Wind Blows, 1986; Radio KAOS, 1987; The Wall – Live In Berlin, 1990; Amused To Death, 1992; Also appears on: Vagabond Ways, Marianne Faithfull, 1999; Madcap Laughs, Syd Barrett, 1999; Legend of 1900, 1999; Singles include: See Emily Play, 1967; Another Brick In The Wall (No. 1, USA and UK), 1979; Run Like Hell, 1980; When The Tigers Break Free, 1982; Not Now John, 1983; Solo: 5.01 AM (The Pros and Cons of Hitch-Hiking), 1984; Radio Waves, 1987; The Tide Is Turning (After Live Aid), 1988. *Honours include:* with Pink Floyd: Silver Clef Award, Nordoff-Robbins Music Therapy Centre, 1980; Ivor Novello Award, Outstanding Contribution To British Music, 1992.

WATERSON Norma, (Norma Christine Carthy); b. 15 Aug. 1939, Kingston-upon-Hull, Humberside, England. Vocalist. m. Martin Carthy. *Career:* Member of seminal folk group The Watersons (line-up included sister Lal, brother Mike and husband Martin Carthy), 1960s; Toured with daughter Eliza Carthy, Lal Waterson and Lal's daughter Maria as the Waterdaughters, 1980s; Formed another family band Waterson: Carthy (including Norma, Martin Carthy and daughter Eliza), 1990s; Released first solo album, a well-received collection of contemporary songs (in contrast to mostly traditional live material), 1996; Third solo album Bright Shiny Morning more representative of usual repertoire. *Recordings:* Albums: with The Watersons: New Voices, Frost and Fire, 1965; Watersons, A Yorkshire Garland, 1966; For Pence and Spice Ale, 1975; Sound Sound Your Instruments, 1977; Greenfields, 1981; with Lal Waterson: A True Hearted Girl, 1977; with Waterson-Carthy: Waterson-Carthy, 1994; Common Tongue, 1997; Broken Ground, 1999; solo: Norma Waterson, 1996; The Very Thought of You, 1999; Bright Shiny Morning, 2000. *Honours:* Mercury Music Prize, nominee, Norma Waterson, 1996.

WATES Matt (Matthew James); b. 1964. Musician (saxophone, flute, clarinet); Composer. *Musical Education:* Berklee College of Music, 1988. *Career:* Jazz musician, arranger and composer; Recorded with: Roadside Picnic; PAZ; Sax Appeal; NYJO; The Michael Garrick Big Band; Recorded three albums, including many orignal compositions, as leader of The Matt Wates Sextet; Appeared with many top jazz musicians including: Bucky Pizzarelli; Humphrey Lyttelton; Georges Arvanitas; Helen Shapiro; John Colianni; Don Weller; Bobby Wellins; Dusko Goykevich; Duncan Lamont; Ian Shaw; Norma Winston; Peter King. *Recordings:* Albums: with Matt Wates Sextet: Relaxin' At The Cat, 1993; Two, 1996; Smallbill's Garage, 1999; with PAZ: Dancing In The Park, 1995; Samba, Samba, 2000; Laying Eggs, 2001; with Itchy Fingers: Full English Breakfast, 1993; with Roadside Picnic: La Famille, 1995; features on: Meteors Close At Hand, Michael Garrick, 1995; Mellow Mania, Liz Fletcher, 1997; Live In The Park, Liz Fletcher, 1999. *Honours:* BT British Jazz Awards: Rising Star Award, 1997; Alto Saxophone nominee, 1997–2001; Best Small Group, Matt Wates Sextet, 2001. *E-mail:* mattwates@hotmail.com.

WATKINS Tienne Tenese, (T-Boz); b. 26 April 1970, Des Moines, Iowa, USA. Singer. *Career:* Began as singer in Church choir; Member, TLC; Main singer and head of band business; Acting role, Tionne in film Belly, 1998; Owner, companies, Shee Inc and Grunge Girl Music; Released solo song Touch Myself for soundtrack for film Fled; Co-Owner, line of clothes, Grungy Glamorous; Author, book of poetry. *Recordings:* Singles: Get It Up, 1993; Creep, 1994; Waterfalls, 1995; Red Light Special, 1995; Diggin on You, 1995; No Scrubs, 1999; Unpretty, 1999; Albums: Crazysexycool, 1994; Fan Mail, 1999. *Honours:* One of 50 Most Beautiful People, People Magazine, 1995; 2 Grammy Awards, Best R & B Performance by Duo/Group; Best R & B Album, for Crazysexycool; 2 Lady of Soul Awards; 2 Billboard Music Awards; 3 Soul Train Awards; Blockbuster Entertainment Award; 4 MTV Music Video Awards, for Waterfalls.

WATSON Andy; b. 20 June 1958, Enfield, England. Session Musician (guitar). m. Pam Watson, 20 Aug. 1983. *Education:* Crawley and Swindon Technical College. *Musical Education:* London College of Music; Royal College of Music; Leeds College of Music. *Career:* Sessions for YTV; BBC; Channel 4; Royal Philharmonic Orchestra; West End Shows: Joseph and The Amazing Technicolour Dreamcoat; Les Miserables; Sunset Boulevard; Anything Goes; Ross Mitchell Band and Singers. *Recordings:* Solo album: Sweeping Statement, 1989. *Publications:* Author, Join The Dots column, Guitarist magazine. *Honours:* Associate, Royal College of Music; Graduate, Leeds College of Music. *Memberships:* Musicians' Union; PRS; MCPS. *Address:* Chelmsford, Essex, England.

WATSON Bobby Jr (Robert Michael); b. 23 Aug. 1953, Lawrence, USA. Musician (alto saxophone); Composer; Bandleader. m. Pamela Watson, 11 Sept. 1976, 1 s., 1 d. *Musical Education:* BM, Theory and Composition,

University of Miami. *Career:* Musical director with Art Blakey and The Jazz Messengers, 1977–81; Member, Leads Horizon, 1980–; Alto with Zahir Batin, 1980–; Alto with Art Blakey and The Jazz Messengers, 1981–; Alto with Mickey Bass Quartet, 1981–; Member, 28th Street Saxophone Quartet, 1983–; Lead alto with Panama Francis and The Savoy Sultans, 1983–; Lead alto with The Duke's Men, 1987–; Performs with Charlie Mingus Epitaph Project, 1989–; Alto with Smithsonian Jazz Masterworks Orchestra, 1982; Lead alto, Carnegie Hall Jazz Orchestra, 1992; Premiered Tailor Made big band, 1993; Tours: Brazil; Europe; Japan; Canada; North America; Caribbean; Italy; Netherlands; Scotland; Germany; England; Cyprus; Every major jazz festival in Europe; Own publishing company, Lafiya Music, 1979–; Record label, New Note Records, 1983-. *Compositions:* Over 100. *Recordings include:* As leader: Post-Motown Bop; No Question About It; The Inventor; The Year of The Rabbit; Love Remains; Round Trip; All Because of You; Gumbo; Jewel; Recordings with artists including: Bill Cosby; Art Blakey and The Jazz Messengers; 29th Street Quartet; Duke Ellington; Charlie Mingus; Cornelius Kreusch. *Honours include:* Recipient of National Endowment Composers Grant, 1980; Downbeat Critics Poll Wins: Best Alto Saxophonist, 1989–92; Jazz Musician of the Year, 1990. *Leisure interests:* Fishing; Bowling; Table tennis. *Current Management:* Timothy Patterson, Split Second Timing. *Address:* 104 W 70th St, Apt 11C, New York, NY 10024, USA.

WATSON (Gary) Gene; b. 11 Oct. 1943, Palestine, Texas. Country vocalist; Songwriter; Musician (guitar). *Career:* Formed first band, Gene Watson and the Other Four, with brothers and cousins, Houston, Texas, aged 14; Debut single Autumn In June on Wide World Records; Also recorded for Stoneway Records; Country chart debut, Bad Water, on Resco Records, 1975; Signed to Capitol, 1975; Nearly 50 Billboard country chart singles on labels including: Capitol; MCA; Epic; Warner Bros; Continues to record on independent labels and tour with own band, the Farewell Party Band. *Recordings include:* Love In The Hot Afternoon, 1975; Paper Rosie, 1977; Should I Come Home (Or Should I Go Crazy), 1979; Fourteen Carat Mind, 1981; You're Out Doing What I'm Here Doing Without, 1983; Albums: Love In The Hot Afternoon, 1975; Should I Come Home, 1979; Sometimes I Get Lucky, 1983. *Leisure interests:* Automobiles. *Address:* c/o Adams and Green Entertainment Agency, 2011 Masters Lane, Missouri City, TX 77459, USA.

WATSON Jamie; b. 3 June 1954, Canada. Recording Engineer; Prod.; Musician (guitar, drums, keyboards). m. Beverley Watson, 29 March 1990. *Education:* George Watsons College; Edinburgh Art College. *Musical Education:* Self-taught. *Career:* Member, Solos; Major British tour support to The Tourists, 1979; Currently owns and runs Chamber Recording Studio in Edinburgh. *Recordings:* Singles: Talking Pictures, Solos; Single by Persian Rugs; Album and other records on various independent labels. *Memberships:* PRS; MCPS. *Leisure interests:* Playing football; Reading; Live music. *Address:* 120A W Granton Rd, Edinburgh EH5 1PF, Scotland.

WATSON Jeff; b. 4 Nov. 1959, Sacramento, California, USA. Musician (guitar); Singer; Writer; Record Prod.; Sound Engineer. *Career:* Guitarist, US rock group, Night Ranger, 1982–91; Guitarist, Mothers Army; Television appearances include: American Bandstand (4 times); Solid Gold; Tours world-wide; 10m. albums sold. *Recordings:* Albums: with Night Ranger: Dawn Patrol, 1982; Midnight Madness, 1983; Seven Wishes, 1985; Big Life, 1987; Man In Motion, 1988; Live In Japan, 1990; Seven, 1998; Solo: Lone Ranger, 1992; Around The Sun, 1999; with Steve Morse: Southern Steel; with Chris Isaak: San Francisco Days; Forever Blue; with Mothers Army: Mothers Army I and II; 3 No. 1 videos with Night Ranger. *Honours:* Multiple Platinum and Gold albums. *Memberships:* BMI; AFTRA; JASRAC. *Leisure interests:* Water skiing; Scrabble. *Current Management:* Bruce Cohn Management, 15140 Sonoma Hwy, Glenellen, CA 93442, USA. *Address:* 120 Sunnyside, #149 Mill Valley, CA 94941, USA.

WATT Ben; b. 6 Dec. 1962. Musician (guitars, keyboards); Vocalist. Songwriter. *Education:* Hull University. *Career:* Solo artiste, 1981–82; Formed duo, Everything But The Girl, with singer Tracey Thorn, 1983–; Appearances include: Regular British tours, 1984–; World Tour 1990, including Japan; Friends of the Earth Benefit Concerts; Red Hot and Dance AIDS Benefit Concert, 1991; UK and US Tours, 1993–95; World Tour, 1996–97, including Japan and Australasia. *Compositions:* Writer, co-writer with Tracey Thorn, of own material for duo and solo work. *Recordings:* Albums: Solo album: North Marine Drive, 1983; with Everything But The Girl: Eden, 1984; Everything But The Girl (USA only), 1984; Love Not Money, 1985; Baby, The Stars Shine Bright, 1986; Idlewild, 1988; The Language of Life, 1990; World-wide, 1991; Essence and Rare (Japan only), 1992; Acoustic, 1992 (USA only); Home Movies – Best of Everything But The Girl, 1993; Amplified Heart, 1994; Walking Wounded, 1996; Temperamental, 1999; with Deep Dish: future of the Future, 1998; Junk Science, 1999; With Splendour, Splendour, 1999; with Next Best Thing, Next Best Thing, 2000; Singles include: Everything But The Girl: Each and Every One, 1984; Come On Home, 1986; I Don't Want To Talk About It, 1988; Missing, 1995; Walking Wounded, 1996; Wrong, 1996.

Current Management: JFD Management, 106 Dalling Rd, London W6 0JA, England.

WATTS Andy; b. Macclesfield, England. Musician (shawn, Flemish bagpipes, clarinet, recorders, curtal); Vocalist. *Education:* History of Music, Cambridge University. *Musical Education:* Guildhall School of Music and Drama; Royal Conservatory, The Hague, Netherlands. *Career:* Recorder teacher; Freelance musician with early music groups; Musical Director, Medieval Players; Baroque and classical bassoon with: The Orchestra of The Age of The Enlightenment; The English Baroque Soloists; The Academy of Ancient Music; Teacher, baroque bassoon, Royal Academy of Music; Founder member, The Carnival Band, 1984–; Appearances include: Glasgow Cathedral; Birmingham Symphony Hall; Barbican Centre; Arts theatres and centres; Plays material from: Sweden; Croatia; USA; Bolivia; Spain; UK; France. *Recordings include:* Album with Maddy Prior: Christmas Carols. *Current Management:* c/o Jim McPhee, Acorn Entertainments. *Address:* Winterfold House, 46 Woodfield Rd, Kings Heath, Birmingham B13 9UJ, England.

WATTS Charlie; b. 2 June 1941, Islington, London, England. Musician (drums). *Career:* Member, Blues Incorporated; Member, Rolling Stones, 1962–; Numerous tours and concerts include: National Jazz and Blues Festival, 1963; First British tour, 1963; Group Scene British tour, 1964; Debut US tour, 1964; Free concert, Hyde Park, 1969; Free concert, Altamont Speedway, 1969; Knebworth Festival, 1976; Steel Wheels North American Tour, 1989; Films include: Ladies and Gentlemen The Rolling Stones, 1976; Let's Spend The Night Together, 1983; Co-founder, record label, Rolling Stones Records, 1971. *Recordings:* Albums include: The Rolling Stones, 1965; The Rolling Stones No 2, 1965; Out of Our Heads, 1965; Aftermath, 1966; Between The Buttons, 1967; Their Satanic Majesties Request, 1967; Beggar's Banquet, 1968; Let It Bleed, 1969; Get Yer Ya-Ya's Out, 1969; Sticky Fingers, 1971; Exile On Main Street, 1972; Goat's Head Soup, 1973; It's Only Rock and Roll, 1974; Black and Blue, 1976; Some Girls, 1978; Emotional Rescue, 1980; Tattoo You, 1981; Still Life, 1982; Steel Wheels, 1989; Flashpoint, 1991; Stripped, 1995; Long Ago and Far Away, 1996; Hit singles include: It's All Over Now; Little Red Rooster; Get Off of My Cloud; (I Can't Get No) Satisfaction; 19th Nervous Breakdown; Ruby Tuesday; Jumping Jack Flash; Honky Tonk Women; Let's Spend The Night Together; Brown Sugar; Miss You; Start Me Up; Emotional Rescue; Harlem Shuffle; Going To A Go-Go; Paint It Black; Angie; Undercover of The Night; She's So Cold. *Honours:* with Rolling Stones include: Silver Clef, Nordoff-Robbins Therapy, 1982; Grammy Award, Lifetime Achievement Award, 1986; Inducted into Rock and Roll Hall of Fame, 1989; Q Award, Best Live Act, 1990; Ivor Novello Award, Outstanding Contribution to British Music, 1991. *Current Management:* Rupert Loewenstein, 2 King St, London SW1Y 6QL, England.

WATTS Trevor Charles; b. 26 Feb. 1939, York, Yorkshire, England. Musician (alto, soprano saxophones). 2 s., 1 d. *Musical Education:* Self-taught. *Career:* Founder member, Spontaneous Music Ensemble; Amalgam; Moiré Music; Toured with Drum Orchestra in New Zealand; Burma; India; Caribbean; USA; Canada; Venezuela; Mexico; Botswana; South Africa; Lesotho; Colombia; Ecuador; Bolivia; Malaysia, China; First group to play Burma for 10 years; Arte Television show, 1994; Collaborated with traditional musicians, Khartoum International Festival, Sudan, 1996; Collaborations with Afro-Venezuelan Barlovento musicians, 1992, 1995; Toured in Cameroon, West Africa. *Compositions:* Bracknell Festival Commission: Mr Sunshine, 1984. *Recordings:* with M M Drum Ork: A Wider Embrace; with Moiré Music: With One Voice; with Moiré Music Trio: Intakt, 1995; with Moiré Music, CD: Live at the Athens Concert Hall, 2000. *Publications:* Music Outside, Ian Carr, 1973; Leonard Feathers Encyclopaedia of Jazz. *Memberships:* PRS; MCPS; Musicians' Union; PAMRA. *Leisure interests:* Music; Gardening. *Address:* Moire Music, 20 Collier Rd, Hastings, East Sussex TN34 3JR, England. *E-mail:* moire@wattsgood.freeserve.co.uk.

WAVERLY Josie; b. USA. Entertainer. m., 2 s. *Musical Education:* Church. *Career:* Plays 150–180 dates a year, with band: Genuine Country; Appearances with country artists including: John Michael Montgomery; Lorrie Morgan; Tracy Lawrence; Charlie Daniels; Randy Travis; Neal McCoy; John Anderson; Sawyer Brown; Doug Stone. *Recordings:* CD and cassette: Who Cries This Time. *Honours:* Citizen of The Year. *Memberships:* CMA; ASCAP; BMI; NAFE. *Leisure interests:* Baking; Dude ranches; Travel; Shops. *Current Management:* Nancy Carroll Agency. *Address:* PO Box 19468, Sarasota, FL 34276, USA.

WAY Bryan Douglas; b. 20 Jan. 1953, Cornerbrook, Newfoundland, Canada. Singer; Songwriter. 1 s., 1 d. *Education:* Academic, English Literature. *Musical Education:* Self-taught. *Career:* Appearances: Oprey North; Tommy Hunter Show; Ronnie Prophet Show; Global TV; Day By Day Show; Country Music Showcase; Mountain Festival; Hiram Walker Canadian Songwriter Tour. *Compositions:* Goodbye To The Rain, recorded by Roger Whittaker; Your Memory Lays Down With Me, recorded by James Owen Bush; End of Money, written and recorded by Bryan Way, played on

70 European radio stations. *Publications:* Country Music News; Billboard; Canadian Composer. *Memberships:* CCMA (Canadian Country Music Asscn); NSAI (Nashville Songwriters' Asscn International). *Leisure interests:* Golf; Cooking; Fine Art. *Current Management:* Penelope Talent Agency; Suzanne Gaudette Management; Publisher: Songcraft Communications. *Address:* 20 Gamble Ave, Suite 105, Toronto, ON M4K 2G9, Canada.

WAY Pete; Musician (bass). *Career:* Founder member, UFO, 1969–83; Founder member, Waysted, 1983–88; Rejoined UFO, 1991–; UK and world-wide tours with both bands. *Recordings:* Albums: with UFO: UFO, 1971; UFO 2 – Flying, 1971; Live In Japan, 1972; Phenomenon, 1974; Face It, 1975; No Heavy Pettin', 1976; Lights Out, 1977; Obsession, 1978; Strangers In The Night, 1979; No Place To Run, 1980; The Wild, The Willing and The Innocent, 1981; Mechanix, 1982; High Stakes and Dangerous Men, 1992; with Waysted: Vices, 1983; The Good The Bad The Waysted, 1985.

WAYBILL Fee, (John Waldo); b. 17 Sept. 1950, Omaha, Nebraska, USA. Singer. *Education:* Drama student. *Career:* Lead singer, The Tubes, 1972–; Regular international tours and concerts including: Knebworth Festival (with Frank Zappa and Peter Gabriel), 1978; KUPD U-Fest, Phoenix, 1993; Band appeared in film Xanadu, 1980. *Recordings:* Albums: Read My Lips, 1984; Don't Be Scared by These Hands, 1996; With The Tubes: The Tubes, 1975; Young and Rich, 1976; The Tubes Now, 1977; What Do You Want From Live, 1978; Remote Control, 1979; Completion Backwards Principle, 1981; TRASH (Tubes Rarities and Smash Hits), 1982; Inside Outside, 1983; Love Bomb, 1986; Solo album, Read My Lips, 1984; Singles: White Punks On Dope, 1975; Don't Touch Me There, 1976; Prime Time, 1979; I Don't Want To Anymore, 1981; She's A Beauty, 1983; Tip of My Tongue, 1983; The Monkey Time, 1983; Piece By Piece, 1985; Other recordings: Richard Marx, Richard Marx, 1988; Contributor, film soundtrack Nobody's Perfect, 1990. *Address:* c/o Geoffrey Blumenauer Artists, 11846 Balboa Blvd, Suite 204, Granada Hills, CA 91344, USA.

WAYNE Jeff; b. New York, New York, USA. Composer; Arranger. *Education:* Journalism Graduate. *Musical Education:* Juilliard School of Music, New York; Trinity College of Music, London. *Career:* Member, The Sandpipers, 1960s; Arranger, The Righteous Brothers; Composer for TV commercials, 1970s; Producer, musical director, David Essex, 1970s. *Compositions include:* A Tale of Two Cities, 1969. *Recordings:* War of The Worlds, 1978; War of The Worlds: Highlights, 1981; Spartacus, 1992; Contributor, Beyond The Planets, Rick Wakeman and Kevin Peek, 1984.

WAYNE John Phil; b. 14 July 1946, West Kensington, London, England. International Concert Musician (guitar, keyboards, bass, drums); Vocalist; Actor. Partner, Ludivine Blondin, Jan. 1989, 1 d. *Education:* Radio Telegraphy for Planes and Ships (HMS). *Musical Education:* Private tuition, 1 year; Guitar, piano, self-taught. *Career:* Sideman with Wild Bill Davis; David Bowie; Tom Jones; John Littleton; Stéphane Grappelli; 5 days with Count Basie; Solo artist and Trio, 1975; Arranger, replaced Quincy Jones for a year, 1978; Conducted The Paris Opera Musicians; Solo concerts: Most international festivals and concerts (jazz); Tours: Africa; Europe; Television, radio, newspapers, magazines, world-wide; Played with: Shirley Bassey; Memphis Slim; Babik Reinhardt; Christian Escoude; Militia Battlefield; Willy Mabon; Sugar Blue; Vic Pitts; Jerome Van Jones; Bruce Grant; Sangoma Everett; Jack Greg; Yos Zoomer; Business: Longsongs Music Ltd. *Recordings:* Let's Rock, 1968; Nunchaku, 1974; Nostalgia, 1980; Broadway By Night, 1981; 1981 Guitar Solo, 1981; John Phil Wayne Live In Europe, 1986; Fairy Queen, 1987; Heavy Metal of The '90s, 1991; Express X, 1992; Trio Compilation, 1995; Solo Compilations, 1995; Music for films, 1970-. *Honours:* Godfather of the International Monte Carlo Racing Car; Twice Best Jazz Guitarist, First Prize Jazz, USA, 1980–82. *Memberships:* PRS; MCPS; Musicians' Union; SACEM; SGVA; Steam Train Companies. *Leisure interests:* CFV Touristic steam train (France); Wrestling. *Current Management:* Longsongs Music Ltd, 21–23 Greenwich Market, London SE10 9HZ, England.

WAZIMBO (Benfica Humberto Carlos); b. 1948, Chibuto, Mozambique. Vocalist; Songwriter. *Career:* Member: The Silverstars, 1964; The Geiziers; Grupo Radio Mocambique, 1975; Orchestra Marrabenta Star de Mocambique, lead vocalist, 1979; Song, Nwahulwana, used in Microsoft commercial and film The Pledge, 2001. *Recordings:* with Orchestre Marrabenta Star de Mocambique: Independence, 1985; Marrabenta Piquenique, 1996; solo: Makweru, 1997; Nwahulwana, 2001. *E-mail:* records@piranha.de. *Internet:* www.piranha.de.

WEATHERALL Andrew (Andy); b. 6 April 1963, Windsor, Berkshire, England. Prod.; Remixer; DJ. *Career:* Began DJ career at Danny Rampling's Shoom club night; Remixed Primal Scream's Loaded and went on to produce their Mercury Music Prize-winning Screamadelica album; Co-founder: Boy's Own fanzine; Founder: Sabres of Paradise; Emissions Audio Output; Rotter's Golf Club Recordings; Collaborations: Terry Farley; Keith Tenniswood; Jagz Kooner; Member: Bocca Juniors; Sabres of Paradise; Two Lone Swordsmen; Remixed: Texas; Primal Scream;

Future Sound of London; My Bloody Valentine; The Orb. *Recordings:* Albums: Sabresonic (with Sabres of Paradise), 1993; Haunted Dancehall (with Sabres of Paradise), 1994; Stay Down (with Two Lone Swordsmen), 1998; Tiny Reminders (with Two Lone Swordsmen), 2001; Singles: Raise (with Bocca Juniors), 1990; Smokebelch (with Sabres of Paradise), 1993; Wilmot (with Sabres of Paradise), 1994; Rico's Helly (with Two Lone Swordsmen), 1996; A Bag of Blue Sparks (with Two Lone Swordsmen), 1998. *Address:* c/o Warp Records, Spectrum House, 32–34 Gordon House Rd, London, NW5 1LP, England.

WEAVER Blue; b. 11 March 1947, Cardiff, Wales. Prod.; Musician (keyboards). m. Ann, 24 June, 1 d. *Musical Education:* Piano Lessons; Cardiff College of Music and Drama. *Career:* Keyboard player, Amen Corner, tours with artists including Jimi Hendrix, Pink Floyd, Hermans Hermits, The Nice, Status Quo, 1965–70; Member, The Stawbs, 1970–73; Also session work included: T Rex; Lou Reed; Family; Alice Cooper; Graeme Edge (Moody Blues); Member, Mott The Hoople, US tour supported by Queen, first rock band to play Broadway, 1973–74; Also played keyboards for Streetwalkers; Member, Ian Hunter/Mick Ronson Band, European tour, 1974–75; US resident, member Bee Gees, 1975–82; Keyboard player, co-producer, co-writer, 6 consecutive No. 1 records, USA; Also session work; Returned to London, 1982; Played keyboards, produced, programmed computers for artists including: Pet Shop Boys; Art of Noise; Stevie Wonder; Miguel Bose; Duran Duran; Propaganda; The Damned; Billy Ocean; Swing Out Sister; Five Star; Own digital studio; Tutor, popular music, Westminster University, London. *Compositions include:* Co-wrote songs for Bee Gees; Commercials include jingles for Labatts, music for Volkswagen; Videos; Film soundtracks for Palace Pictures. *Recordings with:* Amen Corner; Strawbs, 1970–73; Get It On, T Rex; Mott The Hoople Live; Berlin, Lou Reed; Bee Gees, 1974–82; Keyboards on albums by: Chicago; Stephen Stills; Neil Young; McGuinn Clark Hillman; The Osmonds; John Cougar Mellencamp; KC and Sunshine Band, 1999. *Honours:* Emmy, music on Calder Racetrack; BMI 2m. performance song co-written with Barry Gibb: Our Love. *Memberships:* PRS; BMI; BASCA; Musicians' Union; Re-Pro. *Address:* 12 South Parade, Bedford Park, London W4 1JU, England.

WEBB Eric Loder; b. 27 May 1921, Bedford, Bedfordshire, England. Musican (bass, guitar, steel guitar). m. 2 s., 1 d. *Musical Education:* Self-taught. *Career:* Wartime: Ralph Readers Gang Shows; Own band: Beginners Please, 1947; BBC Radio, 1948; Showtime, BBC, 1949; Geraldo Orchestra, Bermudiana Hotel, Bermuda, 1960–70. *Membership:* Musicians' Union. *Leisure interests:* Genealogy; Cycling. *Current Management:* Colin Bryant Entertainments, Poole, Dorset, England. *Address:* Cuckoo Cottage, Green Bottom, Colehill, Wimborne, Dorset BH21 2LW, England.

WEBB Sarah Anne; b. 1971. Vocalist. *Career:* Singer, D-Influence; Concerts include: Support to Prince and Michael Jackson; British tour, 1995; Television appearances include: Later With Jools Holland (with Björk), BBC2, 1995. *Recordings include:* Singles: I'm The One, 1990; Midnite, 1995; Waiting, 1995; Albums: Good 4 We, 1992; Prayer and Unity, 1995; Backing vocalist on album Seal, Seal, 1994. *Current Management:* The Third Rail, 70 Hurlingham Rd, London SW6 3RQ, England.

WEBBER Mark; b. 14 Sept. 1970, Chesterfield, Derbyshire, England. Musician (Guitar). *Career:* Member, Pulp; Numerous tours, TV appearances and festival appearances; Contributed track to film soundtrack for Mission Impossible, 1996. *Recordings:* Little Girl (With the Blue Eyes), 1985; My Legendary Girlfriend, 1990; O.U. (Gone, Gone), 1992; Lipgloss, 1993; Do You Remember the First Time, 1994; The Sisters EP, 1994; Common People, 1995; Disco 2000, 1995; Mis-Shapes/Sorted for E's and Wizz, 1995; Help the Aged, 1998; This is Hardcore, 1998; Albums: Freaks, 1987; Separations, 1992; His 'N' Hers, 1994; Masters of the Universe: Pulp on Fire 1985–86, 1995; Different Class, 1995; Countdown 1985–87, 1996; This is Hardcore, 1998.

WEBBER Stephen; b. 14 April 1958. Composer; Prod.; Prof.; Musician (Guitar). m. Susan Matthews, 1 Aug. 1981, 2 d. *Education:* BM, University of North Texas; MM, WKU; Guitar Studies with Sharon Isbin, Aspen, and John Johns, Vanderbilt. *Career:* Owner, Mid South Recording Studios, 1987–94; Professor of Record Production and Music Production for TV and Film, Berklee College of Music, 1994–; Music Director, Americana, 1997–; Music Director, National Tour, off Broadway, Cotton Patch Gospel; Bandleder, Stephen Webber Swing Band. *Compositions:* Zoetrobics, produced and conducted soundtrack at Lucasfilm's Skywalker ranch; I'm in the Truth Business, documentary; TV series theme music, Art Hysteria and Integrated Science. *Recordings:* As Guitarist: Timeless, 1988; Hymns, 1990; Cumberland Consort, 1992; Angel Christmas, 1994; Producer: He Calms the Storm in Me, Brenda Stuart, 1992; No Solid Ground, Donna Carey, 1993; Kevin Gallagher, 1994; Manhattan Guitar Duo, 1997. *Publications:* Interview with George Martin for Mix magazine, 1996; Active Monitor Comparison Study, Cover story, Electronic Musician, 1997; Riverdance feature for Mix, 1997. *Honours:* Outstanding New

Leader Award, Berklee College of Music, 1995; Emmy Award, Outstanding Achievement, Individual Excellence/Composer, Southern region, 1997. *Memberships:* NARAS; AES; AFM; GFA. *Leisure interest:* Bach to the Future: One-man show for schools on music technology. *Current Management:* Willow Shade Records.

WEBER Eberhard; b. 22 Jan. 1940, Stuttgart, Germany. Musician (bass guitar, double bass). m. Maja, 28 June 1968. *Musical Education:* Studied violincello; Self-taught, double bass. *Career:* Member: Dave Pike Set, 1972–73; Volker Kriegel Spectrum, 1973–75; Eberhard Weber Colours, 1975–81; United Jazz and Rock Ensemble, 1975–87; Collaborations include: Jan Garbarek, 1982–; Kate Bush; Monty Alexander; Pat Metheny; Stephane Grapelli; World-wide solo performances; Composer of music for TV and film, 1975–;. *Recordings:* The Colours of Chloe, 1973; Yellow Fields, 1975; The Following Morning, 1976; Silent Feet, 1977; Fluid Rustle, 1978; Little Movements, 1980; Later That Evening, 1982; Chorus, 1984; Works, 1985; Orchestra, 1988, Pendulum, 1993; Endless Days, 2001. *Honours:* German Phono Academy Awards: Artist of the Year; Record of the Year, Colours of Chloe, 1975. *Membership:* Union of German Jazz Musicians (UDJ). *Current Management:* Bremme and Hohensee, Hauptstrasse 25, 69117 Heidelberg, Germany. *Internet:* www.bremme-hohensee.de/weber_e.htm.

WECKL Dave; b. 8 Jan. 1960, St Louis, MO, USA. Drums. m. Joyce, 6 May 1989, 1 d. *Education:* 2 Years Jazz Studies Program, Marching Bands College. *Career:* Stage: Simon and Garfunkel, Paul Simon, Chick Corea, Brecker Bros, Michel Camit, Mike Stern, Dave Weckl Band; TV: Tonight Show with Chick Corea; Arsenio Hill Show with Chick Corea; Mag: On covers of Modern Drummer Jazz Is and Downbeat. *Compositions:* Co-writer, 4 solo records. *Recordings:* with Chick Corea Elektric Band; Robert Plant (Honey Drippers); Diana Ross (Swept Away); Dave Grusin; Chick Corea Akoustic Band; Solo Albums: Rhythm of the Soul, 1998; Synergy, 1999. *Publications:* Instructional – On Warner Bros, 1988; Back to Basics, Next Step, 1989; Working It Out, I and II, 1994; The Ultimate Play Along, I and II, 1994, 1995. *Honours:* Grammy, Chick Corea Akoustic Band, 1988; Best Electric Jazz Drummer, Modern Drummer, 1987–92. *Leisure interests:* Auto/Kart Racing; Swimming. *Current Management:* Ron Moss Management Agency. *Address:* 2635 Griffith Park Blvd, LA, CA 90039, USA.

WEEDON Bert; b. 10 May 1920, East Ham, London, England. Musician (guitar); Guitar Tutor. *Career:* Session musician, 1950s–; Member, touring groups of Django Reinhardt; Stéphane Grappelli; Featured soloist, Mantovani; Played with numerous artistes including: Ted Heath; Jimmy Shand; Leader, own quartet, 1956; Television appearances: Residency, 5 O'Clock Club, ITV; Subject, This Is Your Life, 1992; Radio appearances: 3 shows per week, BBC Show Band; Guitar tutor, 1950s–; Play In A Day tutor books once used by Eric Clapton, George Harrison, Pete Townsend. *Recordings:* Guitar Boogie Shuffle (No. 1, UK), 1959; Apache, 1960; Numerous albums include: King Size Guitar, 1960; The Romantic Guitar of Bert Weedon, 1970; Rockin At The Roundhouse, 1971; The Gentle Guitar of Bert Weedon, 1975; 22 Guitar Greats, 1976; Guitar Favourites, 1983; Mr Guitar, 1984; Once More With Feeling, 1988; Encore!, 1990; Featured musician, hundreds of records by artists including: Marty Wilde; Cliff Richard; Adam Faith; Billy Fury; Tommy Steele; Laurie London; Alma Cogan; Dicky Valentine; Frank Sinatra; Rosemary Clooney, 1950s–. *Publications:* Numerous guitar tuition books, courses, videos, including: Play In A Day (2m. copies sold, most successful guitar tutor book ever); Play Every Day.

WEEKES Alan Noel; b. 25 Dec. 1958, London, England. Musician (guitar); Tutor; Composer. 1 s. *Musical Education:* Guildhall School of Music and Drama, Post-graduate. *Career:* Founder member, pop band La Famille; Original member, Jazz Warriors; Television appearances include: Channel 4 club mix; Black On Black; Party At The Palace; Top of The Pops; Switch; Pebble Mill; The White Room; Late Show; Tours: Japan; West Indies; First Lucia Jazz Festival; Africa; Europe with Jazz Jamaica and Sound Advice. *Composition:* Composer, performer, Breath (series of music commissioned by Arts Council), Shaw Theatre, 1992; Just a Dream, album, 1996. *Recordings:* with Sugar Minot; Carol Thompson; Trevor Walters; Jean Adebambo; Jacky Mitto; Janet Kay; Art Blakey and Dick Heckstall-Smith; Courtney Pine; Recent recordings with: Jazz Jamaica; Byron Wallen's Sound Advice; Jazz Warriors. *Membership:* Musicians' Union. *Leisure interests:* Fitness; Reading; Photography. *Address:* 65 Clinger Court, Hoxton St, London N1 5DF, England.

WEEKS Clifford M.; b. New York City, USA. Arranger; Composer; Musician (trombone); Teacher. 1 s., 1 d. *Education:* CAGS in Educational Administration, Boston State College, 1977. *Musical Education:* Professional Diploma in Arranging and Composition, Berklee College of Music, 1962; Bachelor of Music (magna cum laude), 1963, Master of Music, 1975, Boston Conservatory of Music. *Career:* Teacher, Assistant Principal, Adminstrative Assistant and Cluster Co-ordinator in Boston public schools; Conductor, All-City Jazz band and college jazz bands; Musical Arranger,

Greater Bostonians and various professional artists. *Compositions:* Triptych For Tuba and Piano; Four jazz/stage band compositions. *Recording:* Triptych For Tuba and Piano, recorded by Karl Megules, 1975. *Honours:* Fellow, Boston University; Omega Man of the Year, Omega Psi Phi Fraternity, 1972. *Leisure interests:* Athletic workouts at the gym. *Address:* 20 Fells Ave, Medford, MA 02155, USA.

WEIDNER Tim; Mix Engineer; Engineer; Programmer. *Career:* Worked with Seal on the Spacejam Soundtrack; Worked with Trevor Horn for The Art of Noise and Seal. *Recordings:* Tina Turner, Wildest Dreams; Seal, Seal I, Seal II, Human Being, Kiss From a Rose (Engineer), Prayer For the Dying (Engineer, Programmer), Future Love Paradise (Engineer); Janet Jackson and Luther Vandross, Best Things in Life Are Free (Engineer, Remixer); Mike Oldfield, Tubular Bells II (Engineer, Mixed, Programmer), 1992; Shara Nelson, I Fell (Engineer, Mixed); Brand New Heavies, Back To Love (Engineer, Mixed); Sweetback; Art of Noise: Seduction of Claude Debussy, 1999; Frames, Dance the Devil, 1999; Genesis: Turn it on Again: The Hits, 1999. *Honour:* Grammy Nomination, 1995. *Address:* SARM Productions, SP2 Holdings Ltd, The Blue Building, 42/46 St Luke's Mews, London W11 1DG, England.

WEILAND Scott; b. Cleveland, USA. Vocalist. *Career:* Member, Stone Temple Pilots; Numerous headlining tours and television appearances. *Recordings:* Singles: Sex Type Thing, 1992; Plush, 1993; Vasoline, 1994; Interstate Love Song, 1994; Trippin' on a Hole in a Paper Heart, 1996; Big Bang Baby, 1996; Albums: Core, 1992; Live, 1992; Purple Ltd, 1994; Purple, 1994; Tiny Music... Songs from the Vatican Gift Shop, 1996.

WELCH Ed; b. 22 Oct. 1947, Oxford, England. Composer; Arranger; Musician (piano). m. Jane, April 13 1968, 2 s., 1 d. *Education:* Trinity College London. *Musical Education:* Music Scholar, Trinity College of Music, London, GTCL, LTCL, Mus Ed. *Career:* Staff arranger, plugger, orchestrator, United Artists Music, 1967–76; Freelance composer, 1977–; Guest conductor with all major British Orchestras; Musical Director for television series. *Compositions:* 250 recorded songs; 3 musicals; over 200 television themes, incidentals, including: Films: The Thirty Nine Steps, 1974; The Snow Goose, 1976; Television: Shillingbury Tales, 1980; Blockbusters, 1983; Catchphrase, 1985; TV AM News, 1986; Knightmare, 1986; $64000?, 1989; Jim Henson's Animal Show (all music), 1994; The National Lottery, 1994; Wolves Witches Giants, 1995. *Memberships:* BASCA; PRS; Musicians' Union; BAFTA Jury. *Leisure interests:* Cricket; Farming; Reading; Travel. *Address:* c/o Welcome Music Ltd, Redhills, Stokenham, Nr Kingsbridge, Devon TQ7 2SS, England.

WELCH Gillian Howard; b. 1968, California, USA. Vocalist; Musician (guitar, banjo); Songwriter. m. David Rawlings. *Musical Education:* Berklee School of Music, Boston, Massachusetts. *Career:* Born into a musical family (parents scored the music for TV comedy The Carol Burnett Show); Listened to bluegrass and early country music as a child and, whilst studying at Berklee, began performing in this style along with her own material as part of a duo with fellow student David Rawlings; Heard by T-Bone Burnett whilst performing in Nashville; He produced the duo's Revival album, 1996; Featured solo on film soundtracks including: O Brother Where Art Thou?; Down From The Mountain; Songcatcher; The Horse Whisperer; Appeared on Dwight Yoakam and Gram Parsons tribute albums; Guested on albums by: Mark Knopfler; Ryan Adams; Nanci Griffiths; Steve Earle; Songs recorded by artists including: Ryan Adams; Cindy Church; Christine Collister; Emmylou Harris; Alison Krauss; Union Station. *Recordings:* Albums: Revival, 1996; Hell Among The Yearlings, 1996; Time (The Revelator), 2001; features on: Gringo Honeymoon, Robert Earl Keen, 1994; Horse Whisperer OST, 1998; Other Voices Too, Nanci Griffiths, 1998; Beneath My Wheels, Kevin Welch, 1999; Mountain, Steve Earle and Del McCoury, 1999; Swing Set, Ani DiFranco, 2000; O Brother Where Art Thou? OST, 2000; Heartbreaker, Ryan Adams, 2000; Sailing To Philadelphia, Mark Knopfler, 2000; Rich From The Journey, Kimmie Rhodes, 2000; Sebastapol, Jay Farrar, 2001; Down From The Mountain OST, 2001. *Honours:* Grammy Awards: Best Contemporary Folk Album nominee, Time (The Revelator); Best Collaboration with Vocals nominee, Didn't Leave Anybody But The Baby (with Emmylou Harris and Alison Krauss), 2002.

WELCH Justin Stephen; b. 4 Dec. 1972, Nuneaton. Musician (Drummer). *Career:* Drummer With Psychedelic Rockers Spitfire; Joined Justine Frischmann, 1992; Formed Band, Elastica, 1992; Toured Extensively World-wide; Television Performances Included Top of The Pops. *Recordings:* Album, Elastica; EP, Elastica; Album, The Menace. *Honours:* Nomination For Brit Award; NME Readers Award for Best New Band, 1994. *Current Management:* Chris Morrison, CMO Management International Ltd, Unit 32 Ransomes Dock, 35–37 Parkgate Rd, London SW11 4NP.

WELCH Sean; b. 12 April 1965, Enfield, England. Musician (Bass). *Career:* Member, The Beautiful South. *Recordings:* Singles: Song For Whoever, 1989; My Book EP, 1990; One Last Love Song, 1992; Prettiest Eyes, 1994; Everybody's Talkin', 1994; Rotterdam (Or Anywhere); Don't Marry Her; Liar's Bar, 1997; Perfect 10, 1998; Dumb, 1999; Albums: Welcome To The Beautiful South, 1989; Choke, 1990; 0898, 1992; Miaow, 1994; Carry On Up the Charts: The Best of The Beautiful South, 1994; Blue Is The Colour, 1996; Quench, 1998.

WELDEN Judy Ann; b. 1 April, 1938, Buffalo Valley, Pennsylvania, USA. Singer; Songwriter; Promoter; Musician (Piano). m. William Blecha, 28 Dec. 1983, 1 s., 2 d. *Education:* Voice and piano lessons. *Career:* Singer, songwriter and entertainer; Member of numerous bands; Owner, 2 record labels; Performed at festivals in many countries. *Compositions:* Too Old Blues; Woman of the 90's; Hurry Up Sunrise; I'm Hittin' The Road; Love Conquers All; Shelter in the Rain. *Recordings include:* Come on Home; Fishin' For A New Love; You Are There For Me; Daddy's Army Whistle; Every Day's A Holiday; Confusion, What's The Solution; Grandma's Quilts; Grace; Chasing A Dream. *Publication:* 68 Unforgettable Days in Europe, 1998. *Honours:* First Place Vocal Award, 1990; Hollywood Song Jubilee, 1992; Woman of the Year in Arts, 1998; Most Promising Female Vocalist, New Gospel Division, 1999; Modern Country Album of the Year, Judy Welden Country Hits, 1999; Female International Recording Artist of the Year, 1999; American Horizon Award, 1999; Horizon Co-Writer Award (Best of Texas), Grandma's Quilts and Confusion (What's The Solution), with Terrance Alan and Mia Heylen, 1999; ICMAG, Promoter of the Year, Artist of the 20th Century, Hall of Fame, 2000. *Memberships:* CGMA; DCDJA; ECMA; ICMAG; LSSCMA. *Leisure interests:* Reading; Swimming; Plays; Cycling; Walking. *Current Management:* Well Done Promotions. *Address:* 692 SE Port St Lucie Blvd, Port St Lucie, FL 34984, USA.

WELDING Paul Daniel; b. 14 May 1971, St Helens, England. Record Prod.; Remixer. *Musical Education:* Self-taught. *Career:* Dance music record producer; Various radio appearances on local stations; 2 appearances on television; Remixes for major record companies and also DJ at The Opera House, Toronto, Canada. *Recordings:* 3 record releases: Void 1 and 2; Rebound; Various remixes including: Sounds of Blackness; Crystal Waters; Lisa M. *Membership:* Musicians' Union. *Leisure interests:* Photography; DJ; Art. *Current Management:* John Slater, Ken Grogan, Deep Management. *Address:* 85 Central Dr., Haydock, St Helens W11 0JE, England.

WELDON Joel; b. 1958. Singer; Songwriter. m. 1986–95, 1 s., 1 d. *Career:* Major touring artist in contemporary Christian music. *Recordings:* Mistaken Identity, 1985; Terror and Love, 1987; Pure Adventure, 1988; Wisdom Street, 1989; Cross The World, 1990; Catch Fire America, 1991; Rock It, 1993; Rise Up America, 1994. *Current Management:* Brian A Mayes, BMP Artist Management.

WELDON Shelly; b. 22 Sept. 1960, London, England. Singer; Entertainer; Musician (piano, keyboard, guitar); Writer. *Education:* Pitman's College, London. *Musical Education:* Advanced studies with Professor Dora Zafransky, Hon Professor, Trinity College of Music. *Career:* Two tours, Sweden; Swedish television and radio broadcasts, 1982, 1983; Writer, producer, presenter, Capitol Radio, 1982; Personal appearance, before HM The Sultan of Oman, 1983; Radio Tross, Amsterdam, 1984; Norwegian tour, radio broadcasts, 1985; Dorchester Hotel, London, 1987–88; Featured session singer, Heathrow Hotels, London; Winner, Alternative Eurovision Song Contest, London Newstalk Radio, with If Heaven Is A Kiss Away (own lyric), 1995; Live TV, 1996; Channel 5 TV, 1997; Talent Channel, 1997. *Compositions include:* Lyricist, While There's A Song To Sing (composer, Marie Francis), signature tune for tenor Wynford Evans, programmes, BBC Radio 2, 1993; Granada TV, 1998. *Recordings include:* The Touch of Love, 1983; Album: Shelly At The Sheraton, 1983; Let the Bells Ring, 1996. *Honours:* Presented to HRH Princess Alexandra, for highest single donation to Kingston Hospital Scanner Appeal, 1994; Lenny Beige, BBC Choice, 2000. *Memberships:* British Equity; Musicians' Union; PRS. *Leisure interests:* Philately; Writing children's stories; Walking; Dancing; Reading. *Address:* c/o British Equity, Guild House, Upper St Martin's Lane, London WC2H 9EG, England.

WELLER Martin William Charles; b. 28 Oct. 1961, Bristol, England. Singer; Songwriter; Musician (guitar); Arranger. 1 d. *Education:* City and Guilds, Industrial heating and Welding. *Musical Education:* Guitar and singing lessons. *Career:* Support to: Benny Gallagher; Isaac Guillory; Clive Gregson; Counterfeit Stones; Tours include: UK; France; Germany; Cyprus; Television appearances include: Cable TV; London Weekend Television; Local radio includes: Eclipse; Mercury; London News Radio. *Compositions:* Many unpublished. *Recordings:* Singles: The Good Die Young, 1984; Maggie, 1990. *Honours:* Finalist, Hammersmith Rock Festival, 1985; Selected to play German Festival, 1995. *Membership:* Musicians' Union. *Leisure interests:* Snooker; Golf; Badminton; Squash; Skiing; Music.

WELLER Paul; b. 25 May 1958, Woking, Surrey, England. Singer; Songwriter; Musician (guitar, piano). m. Dee C Lee, Dec. 1986. *Career:* Founder, singer, guitarist, The Jam, 1976–82; Concerts include: Reading

Festival, 1978; Great British Music Festival, 1978; Pink Pop Festival, 1980; Loch Lomond Festival, 1980; Founder, The Style Council, 1983–89; Appearances include: Miners benefit concert, Royal Albert Hall, London, 1984; Live Aid, Wembley Arena, 1985; Film: JerUSAlem, 1987; Founder, The Paul Weller Movement, 1990; Solo artiste, 1990–; UK and international tours; Phoenix Festival, 1995; T In The Park Festival, Glasgow, 1995; Own record label, Freedom High. *Compositions include:* My Ever Changing Moods; Shout To The Top; The Walls Come Tumbling Down; Have You Ever Had It Blue, for film Absolute Beginners; It Didn't Matter; Wanted; Sunflower; Wild Wood; The Weaver. *Recordings:* Albums: with the Jam: In The City, 1977; This Is The Modern World, 1977; All Mod Cons, 1978; Setting Sons, 1979; Sound Affects, 1980; The Gift, 1982; Dig The New Breed, 1982; Snap!, 1983; Greatest Hits, 1991; Extras, 1992; Live Jam, 1993; with Style Council: Introducing The Style Council, 1983; Café Bleu, 1984; Our Favourite Shop, 1985; Home and Abroad, 1986; The Cost of Loving, 1987; Confessions of a Pop Group, 1988; The Singular Adventures of The Style Council, 1989; Here's Some That Got Away, 1993; Solo albums: Paul Weller, 1992; Wild Wood, 1993; Live Wood, 1994; Stanley Road, 1995; Heavy Soul, 1997; Helioscentric, 2000; EPs and Singles: Broken Stones, 1998; Brushed, 1998; Friday Street, 1998; Mermaids, 1998; Brand New Start, 1999; Wild Wood (remixes), 1999; Hung Up, 1999. *Honours include:* Ivor Novello Award; BRIT Awards: Best Male Artist, 1995, 1996. *Current Management:* Solid Bond Management, 45–53 Sinclair Rd, London W14 0NS, England.

WELLER Timothy James; b. 30 Dec. 1969, Tunbridge Wells, Kent, England. Musician (drums, percussion). m. Aliza Colman, 28 Nov. 1992. *Education:* University of London, Kings College. *Musical Education:* Drummers Collective (New York); Bob Armstrong (London). *Career:* Tours with: McKoy; Federation; Eddie Floyd; Ashley Flowers; Colin John; Performed with: Izit; Zeke Manyika; Jerry Dammers; Roger Beaujolais; Maxi Jazz; Daniel Walker; Giles Martin. *Recordings:* Original soundtracks for: The Confessional (David Puttnam), 1995; Johnny and The Dead (LWT), 1995; Albums, singles with: Teenie Hodges; Zeke Manyika and Jalal; McKoy; Paul Reid. *Honours:* Drummer of The Year, Joe Hubbards School, Pearl Drums, 1993. *Leisure interest:* Keep Fit. *Current Management:* Sound Advice Management. *Address:* C104, Faircharm Trading Estate, 10 Creekside, London SE8 3DX, England.

WELLINGS Clive; b. 20 Sept. 1953, Burton Upon Trent, England. Musician (drums); Massage Therapist. *Education:* BA Hons. *Musical Education:* Self-taught, with help from Steve York, Paul Whiteside, Jon Hiseman. *Career:* Drummer for: Nasty Sandwich; Midnight Sun, Bracknell Jazz Festival, 1978; Hydra; The Fabulous Falling Angels; The Royal Monkeys; Lacewing Bomber, support to Great White, 1987; The Young Outlawz; Wild Angel; Lipstick Daggers; Twisted; Secret Society; Also various session recordings. *Recordings:* with Lacewing Bomber: Feelin' Electric; with The Fabulous Falling Angels: Unsung Heroes. *Membership:* Musicians' Union. *Leisure interests:* Graphic art; Rambling; Photography. *Current Management:* 1A Musical Promotions. *Address:* 76 Hamilton Rd, Reading, Berkshire RG1 5RD, England.

WELLINGS George; b. 13 Jan. 1941, Wolverhampton, Staffordshire, England. Musician (saxophones, clarinets, flutes). m. Maureen Glenn, 23 Dec. 1967, 1 d. *Career:* In backing orchestras for many American and British stars including: Johnny Mathis; Jack Jones; Four Tops; O'Jays; Englebert Humperdinck; Gene Pitney; Shirley Bassey; Matt Munro; Pat Boone; Variety artistes include: Morecombe and Wise; Bruce Forsythe; Des O'Connor. *Membership:* Musicians' Union. *Leisure interests:* Golf; Fly-fishing.

WELLMAN Samuel Edison; b. 15 May 1951, Anderson, Indiana, USA. Prof.; Composer; Musician (Piano). m. Deborah Eileen Moyer, 12 June 1971, 4 s., 2 deceased, 3 d. *Education:* BA, Music Education, Lenoir Rhyne College; MM, Music Theory, DM, Composition, Florida State University. *Career:* College Professor, Warner Southern College, Lake Wales, Florida, 1974–92, Liberty University, Lynchburg, Virginia, 1992–; Concert Pianist and Accompanist; Church Pianist and Organist, 1962-. *Compositions:* Over 730 works. *Publications:* Four American Pieces, 1991; Anna Magdalena Revisited, 1993; Hometown, USA, 1997; Hymn Favourites, 1997. *Honour:* Commissioned Composer, Florida State Music Teachers Asscn, 1989. *Memberships:* American Composers Alliance; Music Teachers National Asscn; American Music Center. *Leisure interests:* Travel; Hiking; Reading. *Address:* 125 Temple Circle, Lynchburg, VA 24502, USA.

WELLS Kitty, (Muriel Ellen Deason); b. 30 Aug. 1919, Nashville, Tennessee, USA. Singer. m. Johnnie Wright, 30 Oct. 1937, 1 s., 2 d. *Career:* Founder member, the Deason Sisters, 1935–37; Regular radio programme, Nashville; Later billed as Johnnie Wright and The Harmony Girls, then the Tennessee Mountain Boys; Took name Kitty Wells, 1943; Solo recording artist, 1949–; Became member of Grand Ole Opry, 1951; Extensive world-wide tours, 1950s-70s; Toured as The Kitty Wells and Johnny Wright Family Show, 1963–; Hosted own television show, 1969–; First UK appearance, Wembley Festival, 1974. *Recordings:* Over 80

country hits; US Country No. 1 singles include: It Wasn't God Who Made Honky Tonk Angels, 1952; One By One (with Red Foley), 1954; Heartbreak USA, 1961; Albums include: Solo: Country Hit Parade, 1956; After Dark, 1959; Queen of Country Music, 1962; Kitty Wells, 1966; Country Heart, 1969; Your Love Is The Way, 1970; Pledging My Love, 1971; I've Got Yesterday, 1972; Sincerely, 1972; Yours Truly, 1973; Forever Young, 1974; with Red Foley: Golden Favourites, 1961; Together Again, 1967; with Johnnie Wright: We'll Stick Together, 1969; Heartwarming Gospel Songs, 1972; Christmas with Kitty Wells, 1996; Country Spotlight, 1996, Queen of Country, 1996; with Roy Drusky: Kitty Wells and Roy Drusky, 1987; Various compilations. *Honours include:* Female Country Artiste, Billboard, 1953–65; Inducted into Country Music Hall of Fame, 1976; Named Queen of Country Music, 1952; First female country singer to have No. 1 record, 1952. *Current Management:* Wright's Enterprises, 240 Old Hickory Blvd, Madison, TN 37115, USA.

WELLS Robert Henry Arthur; b. 7 April 1962, Stockholm, Sweden. Composer; Musician (Piano and Vocal). Engaged to Maria Sköld. *Education:* Adolf Fredriks Music School, 1969–78; Academy of Music, 1978–82; Private piano lessons, 1969–78. *Career:* Professionally working in Scandinavia and Russia, 1987–; Toured with different bands and singers, 1977–87; Featuring in major TV-shows; Played for Swedish Royalties several times; Concerts and TV performances in USA and Canada, 1998–99. *Recordings:* Upp Pa Berget, 1987; The Way I Feel, 1988; Rhapsody in Rock I, 1989; Rhapsody in Rock II, 1990; Norman Vs Wells, 1991; Rhapsody in Rock III, 1993; Nordic Rhapsody, 1996; Boogie Woogie Norman and Wells, 1996; Rhapsody In Rock Complete, 1998. *Honours:* Gold Record, 1998. *Leisure interests:* Golf; Jogging. *Address:* Gurtman and Murtha, 450 Seventh Ave, New York, NY 10123, USA.

WELSFORD Andy Wells; b. 14 March 1959, Bristol, England. Musician (drums). 1 d. *Education:* Technical college. *Musical Education:* Self-taught. *Career:* Drummer with Meat Loaf, 1985–86; March Violets, 1987; Romeo's Daughter, 1989; Then Jerico, 1994; World tours, television and radio appearances, videos; Sessions for Roxette; Whitney Houston; John Parr; Dee Lewis; Daniel Weaver; Andy Leek. *Recordings:* 2 albums, Romeo's Daughter; 1 track, album, Meat Loaf; 1 album, Then Jerico. *Current Management:* Grahame Perkins, Session Connection, B & H Musicians. *Address:* 20 Clementina Rd, London E10 7LS, England.

WELTY Ron; b. 1 Feb. 1971, Long Beach, California, USA. Musician (drums). m. Erica, 1 s. *Education:* California trade school, Electronics graduate. *Career:* Played alto saxophone and drums in high school bands; Previously FQX band member; Joined The Offspring, 1987; Privately pressed single took over 2 years to sell 1,000 copies, 1987; Signed to independent labels, Nemesis and Epitaph, for 1988–95 releases; Major US breakthrough following heavy MTV/radio play rotation, 1994; Accused of betraying punk roots when signing to Columbia after dispute with former label, 1996; Consolidated world-wide success by scoring UK No. 1 hit single, 1999; Live shows include: Woodstock festival, 1999; KROQ Weenie Roast, 2000; European tour, 2001; Band gave lucky fan $1m. in Offspring prize draw, 2000; Drummer with side-project group Spinning Fish, 1990-. *Recordings:* Albums: The Offspring, 1989; Ignition, 1992; Smash!, 1994; Ixnay On The Hombre, 1997; Americana, 1998; Conspiracy of One, 2000; Singles: I'll Be Waiting, 1987; Baghdad EP, 1988; Come Out and Play (Keep 'Em Separated), Self-Esteem, 1994; Gotta Get Away, 1995; All I Want, Gone Away, 1997; Pretty Fly (For A White Guy), 1998; Why Don't You Get A Job?, The Kids Aren't Alright, She's Got Issues, 1999; Original Prankster, 2000; Want You Bad, Million Miles Away, 2001. *Honours:* Over 9m copies of Smash album sold world-wide, best selling independent record of all time. *Current Management:* Jim Guerinot, Rebel Waltz Management, 31652 Second Ave, Laguna Beach, CA 92651, USA. *Internet:* www.offspring.com.

WELZ Joey, (Joseph Welzant); b. 17 March 1940, Baltimore, Maryland, USA. Singer; Musician (piano); Record Prod.; Record Co Exec. 1 s., 1 d. *Education:* Degree in Broadcasting, Harford College, 1978. *Musical Education:* Self-taught. *Career:* Pianist, Bill Haley and the Comets, 1960s-80s; Played with Beatles; Link Wray; Roy Buchanan; Reformed Original Comets, 1981; Numerous world-wide tours and television appearances; A & R executive, Canadian American Records, 1966–70; Palmer Records, Detroit, 1971–73; Music City Records, Nashville, 1974–81; Caprice Records, Pennsylvania, 1982–4; President, Caprice International Records, 1984–; Canadian American Records, 1989–; President/owner, Rock Mill Studios, Pennsylvania, 1990–. *Compositions include:* Hey Little Moonbeam; Baby Let Your Head Hang Down; Candle In The Wind; Forever; Everyday For The Rest of My Life; Universal Love; One Stormy Love; In The Middle of The Night Time; Hey Baby; Life on Mars, 1997; Your Love Means Everything, with Amy Beth; A Ring Between Us, with Amy Beth; Rang-a-Tang Boogie. *Recordings:* Over 100 singles and 75 albums; Hits include: One Way Ticket; 16 Ways; Where Would I Be; Rock-A-Billy; Shake Rattle and Roll; Summertime Blues; Blue Collar Love; Last Kiss; Lonesome Traveller; Forever and A Day; Spanish Rose From Mexico; Summer Place, 1996; You Don't Own Me, 1997. *Honours:* 5 Grammy Nominations; Top 25 Rock Pianist, Keyboard Magazine, 3 times; One of

Top Rock Pianists, DIB, London, 1971; Country Rock Pioneer Award; EIA Award, Most Promising Country Male Vocalist; CMA Award, Video of Year, 1993; Independent Country Male Vocalist of Year; Legendary Performer of Year; Songwriter of Year; Inductee and Gold Charter Mem., Rock and Roll Hall of Fame. *Memberships:* ASCAP. *Leisure interests:* Pool; Yo-Yos. *Current Management:* Caprice International Records. *Address:* PO Box 808, Lititz, PA 17543, USA.

WENER Louise; b. Ilford, Essex, England. Singer; Songwriter. *Education:* Politics and English degree, Manchester University. *Career:* Lead singer, Sleeper, 1993–; Support tours with: Blur; Manic Street Preachers; Major concerts include: Heineken Festival, Leeds, 1995; T In The Park, Glasgow, 1995; Glastonbury Festival, 1995; Feile Festival, Ireland, 1995; Milton Keynes Bowl (with REM, The Cranberries, Radiohead), 1995; Also toured in Japan; Television includes: Later With... Britpop Now, BBC2, 1995; Tours: with Elvis Costello, 1996; Brixton Academy, 1996–97; Milton Keynes Bowl, 1996. *Compositions:* What Do I Do Now?, 1995; Sale of The Century, 1996; Nice Guy Eddie, 1996; She's A Good Girl, 1997. *Recordings:* Albums: Smart, 1995; It Girl, 1996; Pleased To Meet You, 1997; Singles: Inbetweener; What Do I Do Now?; Vegas; Delicious. *Honours:* Gold Disc, 1996; Platinum Disc, 1996. *Memberships:* PRS; MU; PAMRA. *Current Management:* Geoff Wener, Big Brother Management, 15 Pratt Mews, London NW1 0AD, England.

WENNIKE Ole B; b. 15 May 1958, Copenhagen, Denmark. Musician; Composer. 1 s. *Musical Education:* Self-taught. *Career:* Founder, Copenhagen Based The Sandmen, 1985–92, support gigs in Copenhagen for Nico, Jeffrey Lee Pierce, Long Ryders, 1985–86; USA Tour, 1989, London's Borderline, 1989; Founder, Copenhagen Based Nerve, 1995, support gigs in Copenhagen for David Bowie. *Compositions:* Western Blood, House in the Country, Heart of Steel, 1989; 5 mins Past Loneliness, Can't Cry No More, 1993; Slave Song, 1994. *Recordings:* The Sandmen Albums: Western Blood, 1988; Sleepy Head, 1993; In the House of Secrets, 1994; Nerve Album: Speedfreak Jive, 1996. *Honours:* Danish Grammy, 1993; Gold Record, Denmark. *Leisure interest:* Movies. *Current Management:* Rock-On APS. *Address:* Rosenörns Alle 6, 4Tv, 1634 Copenhagen V, Denmark.

WENTZEL Magni; b. 28 June 1945, Oslo, Norway. Musician (classical guitar); Jazz Vocalist. m. 28 April 1976, 1 s. *Musical Education:* Private teachers, Norway and abroad. *Recordings:* As guitarist: with Radio Symphony Orchestra: Concierto de Aranjuez; with Art Farmer: My Wonderful One; with Roger Kelleway and Red Mitchell: New York Nights; with Roger Kelleway and Niels H O Pedersen: Come Away With Me. *Honours:* Gamling Prize. *Membership:* Norsk Musikerforbund (Norwegian Musicians' Union). *Leisure interests:* Reading; Biology; Astrophysics; Grammar. *Current Management:* Den Norske Jazzscene and Diane Mitchell. *Address:* Neubrggt 6 A, 0367 Oslo, Norway.

WÉRGLER Arne Niels; b. 30 Oct. 1943, Copenhagen, Denmark. Singer; Songwriter. m. Asa Didriksen, 27 May 1989, 2 d. *Career:* Singer and songwriter; President, The Danish Society for Jazz, Rock and Folk Composers. *Address:* Danish Society for Jazz, Rock and Folk Composers, Gråbrodretorv 16, 1154 Copenhagen K, Denmark.

WERMAN Thomas Ehrlich; b. 2 March 1945, Newton, Massachusetts, USA. Record Prod.; Musician (guitar, percussion). m. 25 Aug. 1968, 1 s., 2 d. *Education:* BA, Columbia College; MBA Columbia Business School. *Career:* A & R Epic Records, 1970–82; Senior Vice-President, A & R Elektra Records, 1982; Independent producer, 1983–; Signed: REO Speedwagon; Ted Nugent; Cheap Trick; Molly Hatchet; Boston; The Producers; Mother's Finest. *Recordings:* Produced: Ted Nugent; Cheap Trick; Molly Hatchet; Twisted Sister; Jeff Beck; Poison; Mötley Crüe; Kix; LA Guns; Jason and the Scorchers; Lita Ford; Gary Myrick; The Supersuckers. *Honours:* 13 RIAA Platinum records, 9 Gold records. *Membership:* NARAS. *Leisure interests:* Running; Golf. *Address:* 11818 Laurel Hills Rd, Studio City, CA 91604, USA.

WERNICK Peter, (Dr Banjo); b. 25 Feb. 1946, New York, USA. Musician (banjo); Author; Teacher; Music Asscn Exec. m. Joan (Nondi) Leonard, 29 June 1974, 1 s. *Education:* BA, Columbia College, 1966; PhD Sociology, Columbia University, 1973. *Career:* Country Cooking, Ithaca, New York, 1970–76; Rambling Drifters, Denver, Colorado, 1976–78; Hot Rize, Boulder, Colorado, 1978–90; Pete Wernick's Live Five, 1992–; US and international tours with Hot Rize; Appeared on Austin City Limits; Grand Ole Opry; Nashville Now; Prairie Home Companion; President, IBMA (International Bluegrass Association). *Recordings:* Writer, performer, No. 1 hit songs: Ruthie; Just Like You; Albums: Solo albums: On A Roll; Dr Banjo Steps Out; with Hot Rize: Untold Stories; Take It Home; Traditional Ties; In Concert; with Five Live: I Tell You What!. *Publications:* Bluegrass Banjo, 1974; Bluegrass Song Book, 1976; How to Make a Band Work, 1991; Acutab Transcriptions, Vol. I, 1996; I Tell You What, 1996; with Tony Trischka: Early Years, 1998; with Marshall Wilborn: Brass and Piano, 1999; Choice Picks, 2000. *Honours:* IBMA Entertainer of The Year with Hot Rize, 1989; Grammy Nomination, Hot Rize album, 1990. *Memberships:* President IBMA; ASCAP; NARAS. *Leisure interests:* Sports coaching; Basketball; Homemaking. *Current Management:* Keith Case Associates, Nashville, Tennessee. *Address:* 59 Music Sq. W, Nashville, TN 37203, USA.

WERTICO Paul David; b. 5 Jan. 1953, Chicago, Illinois, USA. Musician (drums, percussion); Instructor and Clinician. m. Barbara Ungerleider, 22 Aug. 1986, 1 d. *Education:* 2 years at College; Scholarship, Western Illinois University. *Musical Education:* Self-taught drummer. *Career:* Member, Pat Metheny Group, 1983–; Tours include: US and world-wide tours as clinician, 1986–; North American tours with the Simon and Bard Group, 1980–82; world-wide tours with the Pat Metheny Group, 1983–; Tour of Argentina, with Pat Metheny, Ernie Watts and Charlie Haden, 1986; Also California, Japan and Hong Kong apperances, 1988; Tour of Japan with Special EFX, 1991; Tour of Germany and Poland with the Paul Wertico Trio, 1994; Member, Pat's Secret Story Band, performing in 18 countries world-wide; Tour of Denmark with the Niels Lan Doky Band, 1999; Performed with numerous jazz artists including: Larry Coryell; Lee Konitz; Herbie Mann; Terry Gibbs; Buddy DeFranco; Lew Tabakin; Art Porter; Jaco Pastorius; Chico Freeman; Ron Carter; Alan Pasqua; Ramsey Lewis; Dave Liebman; Eddie Harris; Sam Rivers; Bob Mintzer; Jay McShann. *Recordings include:* Albums: Solo/bandleader: The Yin and The Yout; Live in Warsaw!; Don't Be Scared Anymore; as co-leader: Earwax Control; Spontaneous Composition; 2 LIVE; BANG!; The Sign of Four; Union; State of The Union; with Pat Metheny/Pat Metheny Group: First Circle, 1984; Still Life (Talking), 1987; Letter From Home, 1989; Secret Story, 1992; The Road To You, 1993; We Live Here, 1995; Quartet, 1996; Imaginary Day, 1997; Appeared on three Pat Metheny videos; Film soundtrack The Falcon and the Snowman, with Pat Metheny; Albums with artists including: Paul Winter; Kurt Elling; John Moulder; Bobby Lewis; Ken Nordine; Ellen McIlwaine; Jerry Goodman; Terry Callier; Niels Lan Doky. *Publications:* Columnist, Drums and Drumming magazine; DRUM! magazine; Drum Tracks magazine; Modern Drummer magazine; Contributor, Thinking In Jazz; Instructional videos on drumming and percussion: Fine Tuning Your Performance; Sound Work of Drumming. *Honours:* 8 Grammy Award winning albums with Pat Metheny/Pat Metheny Group, (three for Best Jazz Fusion Performance, four for Best Contemporary Jazz Performance), one Grammy Award for Best Rock Instrumental and one Grammy Award Nomination for Best Pop Instrumental Performance; Three Grammy Award Nominations for albums with Kurt Elling; One Grammy Award Nomination for album with Paul Winter; NARAS Outrageous Recording Award, 1990; NAIRD Best Rock Record Award, with Ellen McIlwaine, 1981; Fourth in Electric Jazz Drummer Reader's Poll, Modern Drummer Magazine, 1997; Fusion Drummer of the Year, DRUM! Magazine Reader's Poll, 1997; Second in Electric Jazz Drummer, Reader's Poll, Modern Drummer Magazine, 1998; Best Electric Group (Pat Metheny Group), Reader's Poll, Downbeat Magazine, 1997–99. *Memberships:* Chicago Federation of Musicians; National Academy of Recording Arts and Sciences, Broadcast Music Inc (BMI), Harry Fox Agency Inc. *Leisure interests:* Steam Locomotives and Model Rainroading. *Current Management:* Ungerleider Artist Management. *Address:* 8728 N Drake, Skokie, IL 60076, USA.

WEST Harry; b. 11 June 1926, Lee County, Virginia, USA. Singer; Musician (mandolin, banjo, guitar, other stringed instruments). m. Jeanie West, 31 July 1951, 3 s., 1 d. *Career:* Husband and wife vocal/instrumental duet, 1951–; Perform old time gospel and traditional songs at revivals, homecomings, festivals, fiddlers conventions and local functions including Asheville North Carolina Mountain Dance and Music Festival, 1950s-60s, also recent years; Many recordings. *Address:* PO Box 321, Granite Quarry, NC 28072, USA.

WEST Jeanie; b. 24 Aug. 1933, Lower Homony, Buncombe County, North Carolina, USA. Singer; Musician (guitar). m. Harry West, 31 July 1951, 3 s., 1 d. *Career:* Husband and wife vocal/instrumental duet, 1951–; Playing old gospel and traditional songs at revivals, homecomings, festivals, fiddlers conventions, local functions including Asheville North Carolina Mountain Dance and Folk Music Festival, 1950s-60s, and recent years; Many recordings. *Address:* PO Box 321, Granite Quarry, NC 28072, USA.

WEST Leslie, (Leslie Weinstein); b. 22 Oct. 1945, Queens, New York, USA. Musician (guitar). *Career:* Guitarist, Vagrants; Founder member, US rock group Mountain, 1968–85; Concerts include: Woodstock Festival, 1970; European tour, support to Deep Purple, 1985; Also recorded as West, Bruce, Laing (with Jack Bruce, Corky Laing), 1974; Track Nantucket Sleighride used as theme for TV series, World In Action, UK. *Recordings:* Albums: Mountain Climbing, 1979; Nantucket Sleighride, 1971; Flowers of Evil, 1971; The Road Goes On Forever – Mountain Live, 1972; Best Of..., 1973; Twin Peaks, 1974; Avalanche, 1974; Go For Your Life, 1975; Dodgin' the Dirt, 1994; Over The Top, 1995; As Phat as It Gets, 1999, Sessions, 1999. *Address:* c/o Skyline Music, PO Box 31, Lancaster, NH 03584, USA.

WEST Steve; b. 1967, Richmond, Virginia, USA. Musician (Drums). *Career:* Joined Pavement, 1992; Numerous headlining tours; Appeared in cartoon Space Ghost Coast to Coast, 1997. *Recordings:* Singles: Trigger Cut, 1992; Cut Your Hair, 1994; Gold Soundz, 1994; Range Life, 1995; Rattled by La Rush, 1995; Father to a Sister of Thought, 1995; Pacific Trim EP, 1996; Stereo, 1997; Shady Lane EP, 1997; Spit on a Stranger, 1999; Albums: Slanted and Enchanted, 1992; Crooked Rain, Crooked Rain, 1994; Wowee Zowee, 1995; Brighten the Corners, 1997; Terror Twilight, 1999.

WESTBROOK Kate (Katherine Jane); b. Guildford, Surrey, England. Singer; Songwriter; Librettist; Painter. m. (1) 1 s., 2 d., (2) Mike Westbrook, 23 Sept. 1976. *Education:* Bath Academy of Art; Reading University; London University, Institute of Education. *Musical Education:* Self-taught. *Career:* Joined Mike Westbrook Brass Band, 1974; Mike Westbrook Orchestra, 1979; formed Westbrook and Company, 1998; Tours: Europe; Far East; Australia; Canada; Co-author with Mike Westbrook of theatre, dance pieces including: The Ass, 1985; Pier Rides, 1986; London Bridge Is Broken Down, 1987; Platterback, 1998; Jago (opera), 2000; Played role of Anna in Seven Deadly Sins, by Brecht/Weill, with LSO, Barbican, London, 1989–90; Sang Big Band Rossini, Royal Albert Hall, Proms, 1992; Good Friday 1663, television opera, libretto by Helen Simpson, C4 TV, 1995; Soloist, KlangWettReligion with Heribert Leuchter's Lux Orchestra, Germany, 2001; Exhibitions of paintings in UK and USA, Europe and Australia, 1963-. *Compositions:* with Kate Westbrook Ensemble: Revenge Suite, Bloomsbury Festival, 1985; with Kate Westbrook and the Skirmishers; Even/Uneven, 1994; Nijinska (music by Errolyn Wallen), 1998. *Recordings include:* Solo album: Goodbye Peter Lorre, 1992; Duo with Mike Westbrook, Stage Set, 1996; Love Or Infatuation, 1997; Bar Utopia, with Mike Westbrook Orchestra, 1997; The Orchestra of Smith's Academy, 1998; Glad Day, 1999; Platterback, 1999. *Honours:* Diaspason d'Or, Goodbye Peter Lorre; Also for Love For Sale with The Westbrook Trio, 1992. *Membership:* Musicians' Union; PRS; SACEM. *Current Management:* MYOM. *E-mail:* janinka@myom.fsnet.co.uk.

WESTBROOK Mike (Michael John David); b. 21 March 1936, High Wycombe, Buckinghamshire, England. Composer; Musician (piano); Bandleader. m. Katherine Jane (Kate), 23 Sept. 1976, 1 s., 1 d. (by previous marriage). *Education:* NDD, Plymouth College of Art; ATD, Hornsey College of Art. *Musical Education:* Self-taught. *Career:* Formed first band, Plymouth Art School, 1958; Led groups including: Mike Westbrook Brass Band, 1973–; Mike Westbrook Orchestra, 1974–; The Westbrook Trio, 1982–; Kate Westbrook/Mike Westbrook Duo, 1995–; Westbrook and Company, 1998–; Tours: Britain; Europe; Australia; Singapore; Hong Kong; Canada; New York. *Compositions:* Music for theatre, opera, dance, radio, television, films. *Recordings include:* Marching Song, 1967; Metropolis, 1969; Tyger (A celebration of William Blake), 1971; Citadel/Room 315, 1974; The Westbrook Blake, 1980; On Duke's Birthday, 1984; Love For Sale, 1986; Big Band Rossini, 1987; Off Abbey Road, 1988; Bean Rows and Blues Shots, 1991; Coming Through Slaughter, 1994; Bar Utopia, 1995; Blues For Terenzi; Cable Street Blues, 1997; The Orchestra of Smith's Academy, 1998; Classical Blues, 2001; Television score: Caught On A Train, 1980; Cinema: Moulin Rouge, 1990; Concert works with Kate Westbrook: The Cortege, 1979; London Bridge Is Broken Down, 1987; Measure For Measure, 1992; Music theatre with Kate Westbrook include: Mama Chicago, 1978; Westbrook Rossini, 1984; The Ass, 1985; Pier Rides, 1987; Quichotte, 1989; Good Friday 1663, (TV opera), 1995; Stage Set, 1996; Love or Infatuation, 1997; Platterback, 1998, Jago (opera), 2000; Chanson Irresponsable, 2001. *Honour:* OBE, 1988. *Memberships:* Musicians' Union; Duke Ellington Society. *Leisure interest:* Walking by the Erme Estuary. *Current Management:* Mind Your Own Music. *Address:* Brent House, Holbeton, Nr Plymouth, Devon PL8 1LX, England. *E-mail:* janinka@myom.fsnet.co.uk. *Internet:* www.westbrookjazz.co.uk.

WESTERGAAD MADSEN Dicte (Benedicte); b. 9 Sept. 1966, Denmark. Singer; Songwriter; Musician. *Career:* Formed band Her Personal Pain, 1989; Numerous Danish club tours, including Roskilde Festival, 1991, 1994, 1997, 2000; Popkomm, Germany, 1997; Sopot Festival, Poland, 1997; Actress in film Smukke Dreng (Beautiful Boy), 1992; Lead Actress in play by Hotel Pro Forma, 1998. *Recordings:* with Her Personal Pain: 6 songs on Secrets II Live, 1990; 1 song (You Can't Always Get What You Want) on Rock Love and Understanding, (Amnesty International), 1991; Songs From Cinema Cafe, 1992; Solo albums: Between Any Four Walls, 1994; Voodoo Vibe, 1996; 1 song (Machinery) on Gaa Ikke Over Sporet (Don't Pass the Trail, Danish National Railways), 1997; This Is Cool, 2000. *Honours:* Grammy, Best New Name, 1992. *Current Management:* Aarhus Musikkontor. *Address:* Åarhus Musikkontor, Aps – Skole Bakken 7, 8000 Åarhus C, Denmark.

WESTERGAARD Torben; b. 9 Oct. 1960, Aarhus, Denmark. Musician (Bass Guitar); Composer. *Education:* Musicians' Institute, Los Angeles; New School, New York. *Career:* Plays in own groups and freelance work in many music styles, Jazz, Brazilian, Pop, Funk, Latin; Studio Musician. *Recordings:* Own albums: What I Miss, 1990; Brazilian Heart, 1996. *Honour:* Outstanding Bass Player of the Year, Musicians' Institute, 1985. *Membership:* DJBFA. *Current Management:* B M Productions. *Address:* Ragnhildsgade 74 2th, 2100 Copenhagen, Denmark.

WESTFALL-KING Carmen Sigrid; b. 24 Aug. 1962, Burlington, Ontario, Canada. Singer; Songwriter; Musician (guitar). m. Kenny King, 27 May 1989, 1 d. *Musical Education:* Recording Arts. *Career:* Television apperances include: Tommy Hunter Show, CBC Canada; Global TV Network; Opened concerts for Vince Gill; Waylon Jennings; Mary Chapin Carpenter; Michelle Wright; Dan Seals; Kitty Wells. *Recordings:* Your Old Girlfriend; You're An Angel; I Wanna Hear It From You; Talk Around Town (all Top 10, Canada). *Honours:* Big Country Awards, Outstanding New Artist, 1989. *Memberships:* SOCAN; CCMA. *Leisure interests:* Clothing Design; Sewing; Horses. *Current Management:* Jerry Knight. *Address:* 1050 Barnardo Ave, Peterborough, ON K9H 5X2, Canada.

WESTFIELD Steve; b. 2 May 1965, Massachusetts, USA. Singer; Songwriter; Musician (guitar). *Education:* University of Massachusetts. *Career:* Singer, songwriter, guitarist, Pajama Slave Dancers, 1981–; Singer, songwriter, guitarist, Steve Westfield Slow Band, 1993–; Tour, Europe, Sebadoit, 1995–96. *Recordings:* with Pajama Slave Dancers: All You Can Eat, 1982; Problems of Sects, 1983; Blood, Sweat and Beers, 1984; Pajama Beach Party, 1984; Heavy Petting Zoo, 1985; Full Metal Underpants, 1989; It Came From The Barn, 1996; It's Heartbreak the Sells, 1999; with Steve Westfield Slow Band: Mangled, 1994; Reject Me... First, 1996; Underwhelmed, 1998. *Current Management:* c/o Andy Doherty, 63 Endicott St #9, Boston, MA 02113, USA.

WESTWOOD Elizabeth Rose; b. 29 Nov. 1963, Washington DC, USA. Musician. *Education:* Art School, Washington DC. *Career:* Singer with Westworld; Radio and television appearances includes Top of The Pops; Tours; Singer in Moondogg. *Recordings:* Albums with Westworld: Where The Action Is; Beat Box Rock 'n' Roll; Movers and Shakers. *Memberships:* PRS; Musicians' Union. *Leisure interests:* Painting; Travel. *Current Management:* Proper Management. *Address:* 93 Rivington St, London EC1, England.

WESTWOOD Tim; b. 3 Oct. 1967, London, England. DJ. *Career:* Rap DJ for radio and clubs including: Pirate radio, LWR and Kiss FM, 1984–87; Capital FM, 1987–94; Presenter and producer of the Radio 1 Rap Show and producer of the Radio 1 Reggae Dancehall Nite Show, BBC Radio 1, 1994-. *Recordings:* Owner, Justice Productions, independent TV and radio production company for Radio 1 Rap Show and Radio 1 Reggae Show; Producer, General Levi and London Posse. *Honours:* Sony Radio Award, Best Specialist Music Programme, 1990–91, 1996, 1999. *Membership:* Radio Academy. *Current Management:* Justice Production. *Address:* PO Box 689, London SW6 6HW, England.

WETTON John; b. 12 June 1949, Derby, England. Singer; Songwriter; Musician (bass, keyboards). m. Jill Briggs, 10 July 1987. *Education:* Bournemouth College. *Musical Education:* Brother Robert, organist, choirmaster. *Career:* Member, Family, 1971–72; King Crimson, 1973–75; Roxy Music, 1975; Uriah Heep, 1976; UK, 1978–79; Solo artiste, 1980; Member, Asia, 1982–91; Solo artiste, 1991-. *Recordings:* with Family: Fearless, 1971; Bandstand, 1972; with King Crimson: Larks Tongues In Aspic, 1973; Starless and Bible Black, 1974; Red, 1974; USA, 1975; Night Watch, 1998; Collectors' King Crimson, Vol. 1; with Roxy Music: Viva!, 1976; with UK: UK, 1978; Danger Money, 1979; Live Roxy Music Album, 1999; with Asia: Asia, 1982; Alpha, 1983; Astra, 1985; Then and Now, 1990; Solo album: Battle Lines, 1994; Chasing The Deer, 1998; Live in Tokyo, 1998; Monkey Business, 1999; Arkangel, 1999. *Honours:* 2 Grammy Nominations; 3 ASCAP Awards; 40 Gold and Platinum discs. *Memberships:* PRS; National Academy of Songwriters; ASCAP. *Leisure interests:* Horse riding; Skiing; Reading. *Current Management:* Carr/Sharpe Entertainment. *Address:* 9320 Wilshire Blvd, Suite 200, Beverly Hills, CA 90212, USA.

WETTRE Petter; b. 11 Aug. 1967, Sandefjord, Norway. Musician (saxophone). 1 s. *Musical Education:* Berklee College of Music, Boston, USA, 1989–92. *Career:* Several Norwegian tours with Nordic Jazz Quartet and Petter Wettre Quartet; Appeared at Konigsberg Jazz Festival with Petter Wettre Quartet, 1993; Oslo Jazz Festival, 1994; Recorded for Norwegian National Broadcasting 2 times; Appeared on several TV shows including: Amandas How; Tawde P; Melody Grand Prix; Freelance musician with artists including: Shirley Bassey; Magui Wenjzel; Lilh Babs; Jon Eberson; Jon Christensen; Several commercials for Norwegian radio and TV; Also runs various clinics and workshops; Currently member of: Petter Wettre Quartet, Horns For Hire, All Stars, and Oystein Sevags. *Recordings include:* Works with Jan Werner; Stephen Ackles; The Stavanger Gospel Choir. *Honour:* Outstanding Achievement Award, Berklee College of Music. *Address:* Bergliotsveg 1B, 0575 Oslo, Norway.

WHARTON Darren Dean; Musician (keyboards, guitar); Vocalist; Songwriter. *Career:* Keyboard player with Phil Lynott, 1980; Member, Thin Lizzy, 1981–83; Concerts include: Tours of UK; Scandinavia; Europe; Japan; Reading Rock Festival, 1983; Monsters of Rock Festival, Germany, 1983; Founder member, Dare, 1987–91. *Recordings:* Albums with Thin Lizzy: Chinatown, 1980; Adventures of Thin Lizzy, 1981; Renegade, 1981; Thunder and Lightning, 1983; The Boys Are Back In Town, 1983; Thin Lizzy Live, 1992; Wild One: The Very Best of Thin Lizzy, 1996; with Dare: Out of The Silence, 1988; Blood From Stone, 1991; with Phil Lynott: Solo In Soho, 1980.

WHEATLEY Martin Russell; b. 29 Aug. 1958, London, England. Musician. m. Angela, 3 s. *Education:* BA, Colchester College; MA, University College, London. *Career:* Broadcasts on Radio and Television, BBC and Commercial; Concert Appearances at the Purcell Room and Queen Elizabeth Hall; Extensive Touring of Canada, USA, including Hawaii; Specialist in acoustic fretted instruments playing in authentic early styles, jazz, blues, ragtime, Hawaiian. *Recordings:* New Orleans Hop Scop Blues, with Bent Persson and Alain Marquet; Charleston Mad, with Neville Dickie; Syncopated Jamboree, I Like To Do Things For You, The Henderson Project, Harlem's Arabian Nights, all with Keith Nichols; with Hula Bluebirds: Stowaways In Paradise. *Leisure interests:* Cricket; Old Cars; Letterpress Printing.

WHEELER Tim; b. 4 Jan. 1977, Downpatrick, Northern Ireland. Musician (Guitar); Vocalist. *Career:* Founder Member, Ash; Early releases on indie label; Secured record deal; Support slots to Suede, Dinosaur Jr and Elastic; Headline tours and TV appearances; Festival dates in UK; Record deal and tour of USA; Performed tracks for film A Life Less Ordinary, 1997. *Recordings:* Singles: Jack Names the Planets, 1994; Petrol, 1994; Uncle Pat, 1994; Girl From Mars; Goldfinger; Oh Yeah; Kung Fu, 1995; A Life Less Ordinary, 1997; Jesus Says, 1998; Albums: Trailer, 1994; 1977, 1996; Live At The Wireless, 1997; Nu-Clear Sounds, 1998.

WHELAN Bill, (William Michael Joseph Weldon); b. 1950, Ireland. Composer. *Career:* Toured and recorded with Planxty for 2 years; Composer in residence at the Yeats festival, Abbey Theatre, Dublin; Collaborations include: Andy Irvine; The Dubliners; Kate Bush; Soundtracks include: Lamb (co-written with Van Morrison); Some Mother's Son, 1996; Dancing At Lughnasa. *Compositions include:* The Seville Suite, 1992; The Spirit of Mayo, 1993; Riverdance, 1995; Music for 15 Yeats International Theatre Festival plays in Dublin. *Honours:* Riverdance single stayed at number 1 for 18 weeks in Ireland, went platinum in the USA and Ireland; Grammy Award, Best Musical Show Album, Riverdance, 1997; Laurence Olivier Award nomination for HMS Pinafore adaptation; Billboard Award, Top World Music Artist, 1996 and 1997. *Internet:* www.billwhelan.com.

WHELAN Gavan; Musician (Drums). *Career:* Founder Member, James, 1983–; Numerous tours, festival dates and television appearances. *Recordings:* Singles: Jimone; James II; Hymn from a Village; Come Home; Sit Down; Albums: Stutter, 1986; Strip-Mine, 1987; One Man Clapping, live, 1989; Gold Mother, 1990.

WHILE Christine Mills; b. 22 Dec. 1955, Barrow-in-Furness, England. Singer; Musician (guitar); Songwriter. m. Joe While, 18 Oct. 1974, divorced 1993, 1 s., 1 d. *Musical Education:* Self-taught. *Career:* Lead vocalist: The Albion Band, 1993–97; Duo with Julie Matthews; Tours: UK; USA; Australia; Europe; Numerous television and radio appearances; Performed at Cambridge and Edmonton festivals. *Compositions:* 100 Miles, 1992; Young Man Cut Down In His Prime, co-written with Julie Matthews, 1996; The Light In My Mother's Eye, 1999. *Recordings:* Albums: Solo album (own compositions): Look At Me Now; Blue Moon On The Rise (EP), with Julie Matthews: In The Big Room, 1996; Piecework, 1997; Higher Potential, 1999; Stages (live), 2000; with the Albion Band: Acousticity; Albion Heart. *Honours:* BBC Folk Award nominations: Best Song, The Light In My Mother's Eye; Best Duo or Band. *Memberships:* MCPS; PRS; Musicians' Union. *Leisure interests:* Gardening; Films; Reading; Socializing. *Current Management:* Blue Moon Music. *Address:* PO Box 291, Southport, PR8 3GY, England.

WHITAKER Michael Whiteley; b. 26 May 1948, Ploughley, Oxfordshire, England. Musician (keyboards, harmonica, percussion); Vocalist. m. Helen, 15 Aug. 1969, 2 s. *Musical Education:* Newcastle College of Arts and Technology School of Music. *Career:* Member of Halfbreed; European tour with Leo Sayer; British tour with Curved Air; Television and radio apppearances: Tube; Geordie Scene; In Concert, BBC Radio 1. *Recordings:* 4 albums; 2 releases for North East labels; 12 singles. *Publications:* Out Now (Rock fanzine). *Memberships:* PRS; Equity; Musicians' Union. *Leisure interests:* Snooker; Supporter of Newcastle United Football Club; Reading. *Current Management:* Bill Dixon Agency. *Address:* 58 Hedley St, Gosforth, Newcastle Upon Tyne NE3 1DL, England.

WHITE Adam Peter; b. 22 Sept. 1948, Bristol, England. Journalist. *Career:* Reporter, news editor, Music Week, 1974–77; International Editor, Billboard, 1978–80; Managing Editor, Billboard, 1981–83; Editor-in-Chief, Billboard, 1983–85; New York Bureau Chief, Radio and Records, 1985–88; London correspondent, Rolling Stone, 1988–89; International Editor-In-Chief, Billboard, 1989–. *Publications:* The Billboard Book of Gold and Platinum Hits, 1990; Co-author, The Billboard Book of No 1 Rhythm and Blues Hits, 1993. *Address:* Billboard, Endeavour House, 189 Shaftesbury Ave, London WC2H 8TJ, England.

WHITE Alan; b. 26 May 1972, London, England. Musician (Drums). *Career:* Joined Oasis, 1995; Numerous headlining tours, television appearances and festival dates. *Recordings:* Singles: Wonderwall; Roll With It; Champagne Supernova; Don't Look Back in Anger; D'You Know What I Mean; Stand By Me; All Around the World; Albums: Be Here Now, 1997; The Masterplan, boxed set, 1999.

WHITE Andrew Nathaniel III; b. 6 Sept. 1942, Washington, District of Columbia, USA. Musician (saxophone, oboe, English horn, bass); Recording Engineer; Composer; Arranger; Conductor; Musicologist; Lecturer; Publisher; Impresario. m. Jocelyne H J Uhl. *Education:* BMus Music Theory, Howard University, Washington, 1964. *Career:* Jazz saxophonist, JFK Quintet, 1960–64, New Jazz Trio, 1965–66; Oboist, English horn player, Center of Creative and Performing Arts, 1965–67; Principal oboe and English horn, American Ballet Theater, 1968–70; Electric bassist, Stevie Wonder and Motown Records, 1968–70; Fifth Dimension, 1970–76; Weather Report (recordings), 1970–73; The Jupiter Hair Company, 1971–; Solo debut, Carnegie Hall, 1974; Jazz saxophonist, Elvin Jones, 1980–81; Beaver Harris, 1983-. *Compositions include:* Concerto, 1963; Concertina, 1963; Shepherd Song, 1963; Andrew With Strings, 1987; A Jazz Concerto (5 versions), 1988. *Recordings:* 42 self-produced recordings. *Publications include:* Saxophone Transcriptions – The Works of John Coltrane, 14 vols; The Eric Dolphy Series Limited; The Charlie Parker Collection, 4 vols; The Andrew White Transcription Series; Big Band Series; Small Band Series; Andy's Song Book; Chamber Music Series; Saxophone Recital Series; Saxophone Etudes; Saxophone Trios, Quartets, Quintets; 2 Symphonies For 8 Saxophones; 4 Jazz Duets; 4 Jazz Trio Sonatas; 12 Jazz Miniatures; Books on improvisation, professionalism, practice, transcription, jazz education, self-production, Coltrane's music; 5 comedy books; Autobiography, Everybody Loves The Sugar – The Book, 2001; Contributor, numerous articles to trade journals; Staff writer, Saxophone Journal. *Honours include:* Numerous study grants; Conductor, Dean Dixon Memorial Award, 1984; Washington Area Music Asscn Award, 1985. *Memberships include:* International Double Reed Society; Pi Kappa Lambda. *Current Management:* Andrew's Musical Enterprises Inc. *Address:* 4830 South Dakota Ave NE, Washington, DC 20017, USA.

WHITE Andy; b. 28 May 1962, Belfast, Ireland. Singer; Songwriter; Guitar; Bass. m. Christine, 26 Aug. 1995, 1 s. *Education:* Degree in English, Robinson College, Cambridge. *Recordings:* Religious Persuasion, 1985; Rave on Andy White, 1986; Kiss the Big Stone, 1988; Himself, 1990; Out There, 1992; Destination Beautiful, 1994; Teenage, 1996; andywhite.compilation, 1998; Speechless, 2000; Andy White, 2001; With Liam Ó Maonlaí and Tim Finn as ALT: Altitude, 1995; Bootleg, 1995. *Publications:* The Music of What Happens, 1998. *Honour:* Hot Press Irish Songwriter of the Year, 1993. *Current Management:* c/o Madeleine Seiler, 5 Wellington Gardens, Oakley Rd, Dublin 6, Ireland.

WHITE Barry; b. 12 Sept. 1944, Galveston, Texas, USA. Singer; Musician (keyboards, drums). *Career:* Singer with The Upfronts and The Majestics; Drummer, road manager, for Earl Nelson, 1966; Manager, producer, Love Unlimited, 1968; Solo singer (originally as Barry Lee), 1965–; Founder, own production company, Soul Unlimited Productions; Television appearances include: Late Night With David Letterman; Arsenio Hall Show; Major concerts include: First Annual Gospel Festival, Jerusalem, 1983; Regular world-wide tours. *Recordings:* Albums: with Love Unlimited: Love Unlimited, 1972; Under The Influence Of..., 1974; Rhapsody In White, 1974; Together Brothers (soundtrack), 1974; Solo: I've Got So Much To Give, 1973; Stone Gon', 1974; Can't Get Enough (No. 1, USA), 1974; Just Another Way To Say I Love You, 1975; Let The Music Play, 1976; Is This Whatcha Wont?, 1976; Barry White Sings For Someone Your Love, 1977; Barry White The Man, 1978; The Man, 1979; The Message Is Love, 1979; I Love To Sing The Songs I Sing, 1979; Barry White's Sheet Music, 1981; Change, 1982; Heart and Soul, 1985; The Right Night and Barry White, 1987; The Man Is Back!, 1990; Love Is The Icon, 1994; Staying Power, 1999; What a Groove, 1999; My Musical Bouget, 1999; Hit singles include: with Love Unlimited: Walkin' In The Rain With The One I Love, 1972; Solo: I'm Gonna Love You Just A Little More Baby, 1973; Can't Get Enough of Your Love Babe (No. 1, USA), 1974; You're The First The Last My Everything (No. 1, UK), 1974; What Am I Gonna Do With You?, 1975; You See The Trouble With Me, 1976; It's Ecstasy When You Lay Down Next To Me, 1977; Just The Way You Are, 1979; Sho' You Right, 1987; Staying Power, 1999. *Honours:* American Music Award, Favourite Male Soul/R & B Artist, 1976; Hon. degree, Recording Arts and Sciences, UCLA, 1980; Grammy Award Best Traditional R & B Vocal; Grammy Award, Best Male R & B

Vocal. *Current Management:* SDM Management, 740 N La Brea Ave, First Floor, Los Angeles, CA 90038, USA.

WHITE Freddie; b. 22 Sept. 1951, Cobh, Cork, Ireland. Singer; Songwriter; Musician (guitar). m. Ann O'Sullivan, 31 March 1979, 1 s., 1 d. *Musical Education:* Self-taught. *Career:* Concerts: Olympia Theatre; National Concert Hall; National Stadium; Television appearances: Late Late Show; Pat Kenny Show; Kelly Show; Live At Three. *Recordings:* Albums: Freddie White, 1979; Do You Do, 1981; Long Distance Runner, 1985; Close To You, 1991; Straight Up, 1993. *Honours:* Hot Press, Best Folk Specialist, 1981. *Membership:* PRS. *Leisure interest:* Reading. *Current Management:* Madeleine Seiler. *Address:* 5 Wellington Gardens, Dublin 6, Ireland.

WHITE Melvyn Arthur; b. 1 Dec. 1963, Norwich, England. Musician (bass guitar). m. Amanda Ross, 5 Dec. 1992, 2 s. *Musical Education:* Self-taught. *Career:* Broadland Radio, 1985; Radio Manchester, 1991; Supported Jools Holland, 1991; Member, group Law; Supported Nils Lofgren and Steve Marriott. *Recordings:* Only One Night Away, Gospel Truth, 1988; Jackie Dee, Law, 1990. *Honours:* UK Band of Year, Runner up, with Law, 1991. *Membership:* Musicians Union. *Leisure interests:* Song writing; Photography; Running. *Address:* 16 Marsh Rd Upton, Nr Acle, Norwich, Norfolk NR13 6BS, England.

WHITE Peter; b. 20 Sept. 1954, Luton, Bedfordshire, England. Musician; Composer. *Musical Education:* Self-taught. *Career:* 20 years, Al Stewart; Tours, recordings, with Basia; Solo tours, recordings, 1990-. *Recordings:* Reveillez-Vous, 1990; Excusez-Moi, 1991; Promenade, 1993; Caravan of Dreams, 1996; Songs of the Season, 1997; Perfect Moment, 1998; With Al Stewart: Year of The Cat, 1974; Time Passages, 1978; Midnight Rocks, 1980; With Basia: Time and Tide, 1987; London Warsaw New York, 1990; The Sweetest Illusion, 1994; Basia, 1998; With Shippen Wise; Standing Outside In The Rain, 1990; With Roberto Perera: In the Mood, 1999. *Honours:* BMI Adult Contemporary Song of The Year, Time Passages, 1978. *Memberships:* BMI; AFofM. *Leisure interests:* Reading biographies; Cycling. *Current Management:* Chapman and Co Management. *Address:* PO Box 15906, North Hollywood, CA 91615, USA.

WHITE Snowy (Terence Charles); b. 3 March 1948, Devon, England. Musician (guitar); Vocalist. *Career:* Guitarist with Peter Green; Guitarist with Pink Floyd (touring band); Thin Lizzy, 1979–81; Tours, Europe, UK, Japan, US, Australia, 1979–81; Solo artiste, 1982-. *Recordings:* Albums: with Thin Lizzy: Chinatown, 1980; Renegade, 1981; Adventures of Thin Lizzy, 1981; Solo: White Flames, 1984; Snowy White, 1985; That Certain Thing, 1987; Change My Life, 1991; Little Wing, 1998; Melting, 1999; Singles: with Thin Lizzy: Chinatown; Killers Live (EP); Solo: Bird of Paradise.

WHITE Tony Joe; b. Oak Grove, Louisiana, USA. Songwriter. *Career:* Toured with rock bands including Creedence Clearwater Revival, 1970s; Toured extensively throughout Europe, including shows with Joe Cocker and Eric Clapton, 1991–92. *Compositions:* Rainy Night in Georgia; Produced hits for: Tina Turner, Joe Cocker, Etta James, Waylon Jennings, John Anderson, Isaac Hayes, Roy Orbison, Kris Kristofferson, Charlie Rich, Chet Atkins, Hank Williams Jr, Jessi Colter, Christine McVie, Ray Charles, Aretha Franklin and Wild Cherry. *Recordings:* Polk Salad Annie; For Ole Times Sake; I've Got a Thing About You, Baby; The Path of a Decent Groove; Lake Placid Blues, album; with Kerouac: Kicks Joy Darkness, 1997. *Honour:* Nominated for Rhythm and Blues Album, Nashville Music Awards. *Current Management:* RD World-wide Management BV, Keizersgracht 683, Amsterdam 1017 DW, Netherlands.

WHITE Will; Musician. *Career:* Member of Propellerheads, with Alex Gifford. *Recordings:* Albums: Bang On!, 1997; Decksandrumsandrockandroll, 1998; Singles: On Her Majesty's Secret Service (with Shirley Bassey), 1997; Dive, 1997; Take California (EP), 1997; Spybreak (EP), 1997; History Repeating (with Shirley Bassey), 1997. *Address:* c/o Wall of Sound, Office 3, 9 Thorpe Close, London W10 5XL, England.

WHITEHEAD Alan; b. 24 July 1945, Oswestry, Shropshire, England. Man.; Agent; Musician (drums). m. Louise Burton, 17 Dec. 1978, divorced, 2 s. *Career:* Drummer, Marmalade, 1967–78; 14 Hit records, Marmalade; Started own company, disco act promotion, 1979; Founder, manager, Mel and Kim (4 major hit records); dance group Body Check; robotic acts: Arbie The Robot; Adam and Eve; magician Marc Oberon; Bought out by Mecca Leisure, 1985; Current owner, largest Glamour Shows agency in Europe, including: The Sunday Sport Roadshow; The Dreamboys, 1988–; Touring girl roadshows: Europe; The Far East; Japan; Australia; Currently managing artists in partnership with Ben Findon and Steve Rowland. *Recordings:* Marmalade, 14 hit songs including: Loving Things; Wait For Me Mary Ann; Ob-La-Di Ob-La-Da; Baby Make It Soon; Reflections of My Life; Rainbow; Cousin Norman; Ra Dancer; Back On the Road; Falling Apart At The Seams. *Honours:* Pop Group of The Year, 1968; Various Gold

discs. *Memberships:* British Institute of Management; Fellow, The Agents Asscn. *Leisure interests:* Tennis; Scuba-diving; Collecting American cars. *Address:* 1 Wellington Dr., Welwyn Garden City, Herts, AL7 2NL, England.

WHITEHEAD Tim; b. 12 Dec. 1950, Liverpool, England. Jazz Musician (saxophone). m. Linda Jones, 26 June 1978, 2 s., 2 d. *Musical Education:* Self-taught. *Career:* Member, Loose Tubes (modern jazz orchestra), 1984–89; Founder, Tim Whitehead Quartet, Tim Whitehead Band; Regular recordings on BBC radio, including Appleby Jazz Festival, 1995; Numerous tours, concerts include: Brecon Jazz Festival, 1992; London Jazz Festival, 1994; PORI International Jazz Festival, Finland, 1995; Regular appearances at Ronnie Scott's Club, London; Television apperances include: Wogan, BBC TV, 1986, 1987; Bath Festival, BBC2 TV, 1987; with Loose Tubes, New Years Day, Granada TV, 1988; 30 Years of PORI, Finnish TV, 1995; Also performed, toured, broadcast with: Ian Carr's Nucleus; Graham Collier; Jim Mullen's Meantime; Breakfast Band; Woodworks; Martin Drew Quartet. *Composition:* Nine Sketches for Solo Saxophone, 1996; Soundtracks; Heart and Soul. *Recordings:* with Tim Whitehead Band: English People, 1983; Decision, 1988; with Tim Whitehead Quartet: Authentic, 1991; Silence Between Waves, 1994, 1995; Personal Standards, 1999; with Loose Tubes: Loose Tubes; Delightful Precipice; Open Letter; Other recordings include: Water's Edge, Breakfast Band; Firedance, Richard Bailey; Pictures of You, Harry Beckett; Aural Sculpture, The Stranglers; Live In London, Maria Muldaur; Permission, with Pete Fairclough, Mike Walker and Dudley Phillips, 1997; with Colin Riley: Tides, 2001. *Honours:* Young Jazz Musician, 1977; Arts Council Commission, Silence Between Waves, GLA, 1992; Commissioned by Jazz Umbrella/Arts Council to compose Nine Sketches for Solo Saxophone for London Jazz Festival on the South Bank, 1996; BBC Music Magazine, Critics' Choice of the Year, Personal Standards; Andrew Milne Award for Jazz, Soundtracks, 1998; Peter Whittingham Award Tides (with Colin Riley), 2000. *Membership:* Chairperson, Co-founder, Jazz Umbrella (London Jazz Musicians Cooperative). *Leisure interests:* Painting; Parenting. *Current Management:* Basho Music, 18 Linhope St, London, NW1 6HT, England. *Address:* 5 Willowbank, Ham, Richmond, Surrey, England. *Internet:* www.timwhitehead.co.uk.

WHITEHOUSE Cedric John; b. 24 March 1944, Walsall, West Midlands, England. Musician (guitar). m. Peggy Whitehouse, 27 Feb. 1987, 2 d. *Musical Education:* A Level Music. *Career:* Session guitarist, 1971–; Television shows include: Golden Shot; New Faces, 1974–80; Pebble Mill at One; Radio sessions include: BBC Radio Orchestras, 1974–76; Radio 2; Archers, 1975–76; Writing, producing artists, and television commercials, 1980–95. *Recordings:* About 1000 television shows as session guitarist; Current production work includes: Ruby Turner (Gershwin Album); Howard McCrary; Chaka Khan. *Honours:* Mecca Bandleader of the Year, 1976, 1977, 1978; Carl Alan Award, 1981. *Membership:* Musicians' Union. *Leisure interests:* Horses; Music. *Address:* Pool House, Pirton, Worcs, England.

WHITFIELD George William; b. 29 Feb. 1964, Worcester, England. Musician (accordion); Vocalist. *Education:* Warwick University. *Musical Education:* Self-taught. *Career:* Accordion player, vocalist with Pressgang, 1988; Solo appearances; Work with outcast band, WOB, Steve Hunt; Pressgang played 180 concerts: England (including Glastonbury Festival); Germany; Belgium; France; Wales; US (including SXSW Festival), 1994. *Recordings:* with Pressgang: Rogues, 1989; Albums: with Pressgang: Burning Boats, 1994; with Outcast Band: Devil's Road, 1993; Steve Hunt: Head The Heart and The Hand, 1993. *Memberships:* Musicians' Union; PRS. *Leisure interest:* Informal musical sessions. *Current Management:* Vox Pop, Reading, England; Berlin Consert, Max Biere Strasse, Berlin, Germany. *Address:* c/o Vox Pop, 1 Donnington Gardens, Reading, Berks, England.

WHITFIELD Mark Adrian; b. 6 Oct. 1966, New York, New York, USA. Musician (guitar). 2 s. *Musical Education:* BMus, Berklee College of Music, Boston. *Career:* Appearances include: The Tonite Show; Good Morning America; The Today Show; CNN Showbiz Today; CBS Sunday Morning. *Recordings:* Albums: The Marksman; Patrice; Mark Whitfield; True Blue; Seventh Avenue Stroll; Forever Love; Take the Ride. *Publication:* Mark Whitfield Guitar Transcriptions. *Honour:* Hon. Mayor of Baton Rouge, Louisiana, USA. *Current Management:* Paul Tannen. *Address:* 38 Laurel Ledge Court, Stamford, CT 06903, USA.

WHITMAN Slim, (Otis Dewey Whitman Jr); b. 20 Jan. 1924, Tampa, Florida, USA. Singer; Musician (guitar). m. Geraldine Crist, 1941, 1 s. *Career:* Recording artist, 1949–; Weekly appearances on Louisiana Hayride radio show; Joined in 1955 with regular appearances on Grand Ole Opry; Film appearance, Disc Jockey Jamboree, 1957; Recorded 25th Anniversary concert, Empire Theatre, Liverpool, England, 1973; Toured with son Byron, 1977–; First Country and Western singer to headline the London Palladium, 1956; Celebrated 50 years in showbusiness in 1998. *Recordings:* Hit singles include: Love Song of The Waterfall; Indian Love Call (No. 1, UK, 11 weeks), 1955; China Doll; Cattle Call; Tumbling

Tumbleweeds; Serenade; Happy Anniversary; Numerous albums include: Slim Whitman Sings and Yodels, 1954; Slim Whitman, 1958; Once In A Lifetime, 1961; A Lonesome Heart, 1967; Slim, 1969; 25th Anniversary Concert, 1973; The Very Best of Slim Whitman (No. 1, UK), 1976; Home On The Range, 1977; Red River Valley (No. 1, UK), 1977; Ghost Riders In The Sky, 1978; Just For You, 1980; Songs I Love To Sing, 1980; Mr Songman, 1981; Till We Meet Again, 1981; Country Songs, City Hits, 1982; Angeline, 1984; Magic Moments (with Byron Whitman), 1990; Cow Poke, 1992; Traditional Country, with Byron Whitman, 1999. *Honours:* BCMA, Best International Male Vocalist, 1978–80. *Address:* c/o Tessier-Marsh Talent, 505 Canton Pass, Madison, TN 37115, USA.

WHITMORE Andrew David; b. 31 March 1962, Coventry, England. Prod.; Musician (keyboards); Studio player. m. 27 Sept. 1988, 1 s., 1 d. *Musical Education:* Grade 8 piano; Grade 5 cello; Grade 5 theory. *Career:* Member, Terence Trent D'Arby band, keyboard player; Now accomplished programmer, producer. *Composition:* Co-wrote with Peter Andre, No 1 single, Flava, 1996. *Recordings:* Albums: MN8 (production); East 17; Paris Paris, Malcolm McLaren; Peter Andre, 3 tracks, Natural album; Kavana Productions, 3 tracks; S-Man Classics: The Essential Sanchez, 1998; Barrington Levy, Living Dangerously (synthesizer and drums), 1998. *Memberships:* PRS; MCPS. *Leisure interests:* Diving; Water skiing; Jet skiing. *Current Management:* Stephen Budd Management. *Address:* 39 Greystoke Parr Terrace, Ealing, London W5 1JL, England.

WHITTAKER Roger; b. 22 March 1936, Nairobi, Kenya. Singer; Whistler; Musician (guitar); Songwriter. *Education:* Medicine; Biology; Biochemistry. *Career:* Former teacher and part-time folk singer; Recording artist, 1961–; Television includes: This and That, Ulster TV; Own series, BBC TV; Concerts include: Knokke Music Festival, Belgium, 1967; Launched UNESCO songwriting competition, 1975; World-wide record sales exceed 40m. Copies. *Recordings:* Singles include: Mexican Whistler (No. 1 throughout Europe), 1967; The Leavin' (Durham Town), 1969; I Don't Believe In If Anymore, 1970; New World In The Morning, 1971; The Last Farewell (over 11m. copies sold), 1975; The Skye Boat Song, with Des O'Connor, 1986; Over 70 albums, including compilations and special German language recordings, 1965–. *Publication:* So Far So Good, with Natalie Whittaker. *Honours include:* B'nai B'rith Humanitarian Award, 1975. *Current Management:* Tembo Entertainments. *Address:* 223 Regent St, London W1R 7DB, England.

WHITWAM Jan Barry; b. 21 July 1946, Prestbury, Cheshire, England. Musician (percussion, guitar). m. Anne Patricia, 19 Jan. 1987, 1 s., 1 d. *Musical Education:* 2 years drum tuition. *Career:* Original member, Herman's Hermits, 31 years; 75 major US tours with Herman's Hermits; 20 World tours; Numerous major concerts including Royal Command Performance; Television appearances: Top of The Pops; Ready Steady Go (UK); Danny Kay; Dean Martin; Jackie Gleason; Merv Griffin; Ed Sullivan; Hullabaloo; Shindig (USA); Film appearances: Hold On, 1966; Mrs Brown You've Got A Lovely Daughter, 1967. *Recordings:* 23 hit singles, UK; 24 hit singles, USA; Best-selling records in world, 1965; 60m. records sold to date. *Honours:* NME Award winner; Keys to 25 cities, USA; 8 Gold albums; 9 Gold singles. *Memberships:* Musicians' Union; Equity. *Leisure interests:* Golf; Sailing; Gardening; Watersports. *Current Management:* Barry Whitwam Management. *Address:* 26 S Park Rd, Gatley, Cheadle, Cheshire SK8 4AN, England.

WHYTE Gordon; b. 22 May 1971, Glasgow, Scotland. Freelance Musician (keyboards, guitar, bodhran); Vocalist; Songwriter. *Education:* Master of Engineering (MEng), 1993; Strathclyde University, Glasgow. *Career:* Session work for: Rick Wakeman; Noel Richards; Ian White; Established Leader of Christian Worship for conferences and festivals, including: Spring Harvest; Greenbelt; Carberry Festivals; Songwriting partnership with Susan Lennartson established 1994. *Recordings:* Debut album with Susan Lennartson: Wind of Life, 1995. *Membership:* Musicians Christian Fellowship (MCF). *Leisure interest:* Exploring potential of spiritual and emotional healing through music. *Current Management:* Gordon Whyte. *Address:* 31 Dunchurch Rd, Paisley PA1 3JW, England.

WICKENS Paul (Wix); b. 27 March 1956, Chelmsford, Essex, England. Record Prod.; Musician (keyboards). m. Margo Buchanan, 31 Jan. 1992. *Musical Education:* O and A Level Music; Piano grades. *Career:* Recorded with: The Pretenders; Dave Stewart; Mike and The Mechanics; Celine Dion; Nik Kershaw; Boy George; Status Quo; Alison Moyet; John Hiatt; The The; Prefab Sprout; The Kane Gang; Performed live with: Joni Mitchell; Jon Bon Jovi; Ry Cooder; The Kane Gang; The Chieftains; Bob Dylan; Jim Diamond; Worked with Paul McCartney, 5 albums, 2 world tours including Maracana Stadium, Brazil (record breaking concert), 1989–; Production credits include: The Kane Gang; Jim Diamond; The Big Dish; Freddie McGregor; Mel Garside; Carmel; Tasmin Archer, including Sleeping Satellite, No. 1, UK charts. *Membership:* Musicians' Union; PRS; MCPS; MPG. *Leisure interests:* Sport; Classic cars. *Current Management:* The Producers. *Address:* 45–53 Sinclair Rd, London W14 ONS, England.

WICKHAM Steve; b. 28 Oct. 1960, Dublin, Ireland. Musician (violin). m. (1) Barbara Kernal, (2) Heidi Ansell, Aug. 1996. *Musical Education:* College of Music. *Career:* With U2, tour Ireland, European dates, 1982; Television touring: the Waterboys, 1986–89; Touring and Television: Texas Kellys, 1990–92. *Compositions:* Score for Abbey Theatre production of Caoineadh Art O'Laoghaire, 1998. *Recordings:* Elvis Costello: Spike, 1988; Texas Kellys, 1992; Waterboys: This Is The Sea Fisherman's Blues, 1987; Room To Roam, 1989; U2: War, 1982; Sinead O'Connor: The Lion and Lion Cobra, 1987; Karl Wallinger, World Party, 1988; Sharon Shannon, 1991; Sweet White Water, Deirdre Cunningham, 1991. *Publications:* Sofa So Good, 1991. *Honours:* Hot Press Musician of the Year, 1986. *Membership:* IMRO. *Leisure interests:* Cycling; Fishing; Golf. *Current Management:* Traci Gordon.

WIDMARK Anders; b. 25 Nov. 1963, Uppsala, Sweden. Pianist; Composer. *Musical Education:* Royal Academy of Music, Stockholm. *Career:* Professional pianist, 1986–; Collaborated with Stockholm Jazz Orchestra, The Swedish Radio Jazz Orchestra, Eddie Harris, Bob Brookmeyer, Clark Terry, Rebecka Törnqvist, Bengt-Arne Wallin; Soloist, performances with Sundsvall Symphony Orchestra and Uppsala Chamber Soloists; The Uppsala Stadsteater, composing music for plays, 1 year. *Recordings:* Solo Albums: Sylvesters sista resa, 1991; Anders Widmark and the Soul Quartet, 1993; Holly Hannah, 1994; Freewheelin', 1995; Anders Widmark, 1996; Anders Widmark Trio – Psalmer, 1997; Contributor: Dreams, Bob Brookmeyer and Stockholm Jazz Orchestra, 1989; A Night Like This, Rebecka Törnqvist, 1993; Obsession! Live at Fasching, Egil Bop Johansen, 1994; Quel Bordel, Christian Falk, 1999. *Memberships:* STIM; SKAP. *Current Management:* NW Produktion, Björngardsgatan 9A, 11852 Stockholm, Sweden. *Address:* Karlsborgsvagen 10, 121 50, Johanneshov, Sweden.

WIEDLIN Jane; b. 20 May 1958, Oconomowoc, Wisconsin, USA. Vocalist; Musician (guitar); Songwriter. *Career:* Founder member, US all-female group the Go-Gos (formerly The Misfits), 1978–84; Numerous international tours; Solo artist, 1985–93; Member, reformed Go-Gos, 1994–. *Compositions include:* Our Lips Are Sealed (co-writer with Terry Hall). *Recordings:* Albums: with the Go-Gos: Beauty and The Beat (No. 1, USA), 1981; Vacation, 1982; Talk Show, 1984; Greatest, 1991; Return To The Valley of The Go-Gos, 1994; Contributor, Tame Yourself (Animal Rights benefit album), 1991; Solo albums: Jane Wiedlin, 1985; Fur, 1988; Tangled, 1990; Very Best of Jane Wiedlin, 1993; Singles: with the Go-Gos: Our Lips Are Sealed, 1981; We Got The Beat (No. 2, US), 1982; Beauty and The Beat, 1982; Solo: Blue Kiss, 1986; Inside A Dream, 1988; Rush Hour, 1988; World on Fire, 1990; The Whole World Lost Its Head, 1995. *Address:* c/o Gold Mountain Entertainment, Suite 450, 3575 Cahvenga Blvd W, Los Angeles, CA 90068, USA.

WIENEUSKI Matthew; b. 20 Sept. 1965, London, England. Composer; Filmmaker; Musician (saxophone, flute). *Education:* Bristol University, English degree. *Career:* European tour, 1993; Japan, 1994; Screenplays: Hardcore Nation; The Kabbalist of Lincoln. *Compositions:* D*votions; The Garden of Earthly Delights. *Recordings:* Albums under D*note: Babel; Criminal Justice. *Membership:* PRS. *Address:* Dorado Records, 76 Brewer St, London W1R 3PH, England.

WIGGS Josephine Miranda Cordelia; b. 26 Feb. 1963, Letchworth, Hertfordshire, England. Musician (bass guitar); Composer. *Education:* BA, Hons, London; MA, Philosophy, Sussex. *Musical Education:* Studied cello, 6 years. *Career:* Bass player and backing vocalist with Perfect Disaster, 1987–90; Bass, vocals, guitar, cello, drums, with The Breeders, 1990–; Bass player with Ultra Vivid Scene, US tour, 1990; Honey Tongue (solo project with Jon Mattock, Spacemen 3, Spiritualized), 1992–. *Recordings:* with Perfect Disaster: Asylum Road, 1988; Up, 1989; Heaven Scent, 1990; with Breeders: Pod, 1990; Last Splash, 1993; Nude Nudes, Honey Tongue, 1992. *Publication:* Breeders Digest, official Fanclub newsletter. *Honours:* Platinum Award for US sales, Last Splash; NME Brit Awards Best Single, for Cannonball, 1993. *Leisure interest:* Needlepoint. *Current Management:* Janet Billig, Manage This, 154 W 57th St, #828, New York, NY 10019, USA. *Address:* Fairfield House, Biggleswade, Bedfordshire SG18 0AA, England.

WIGGS Pete; b. 15 May 1966, Reigate, Surrey, England. Musician (Keyboards, Programming). *Career:* Formed Saint Etienne; Worked with several guest vocalists; Joined by Sarah Cracknell; Released single with Tim Burgess of the Charlatans, 1993; Support slot on Oasis tour, 1994; Worked with Etienne Daho, 1995; Work remixed by Aphex Twin, Chemical Brothers and others; Launched own label Emidisc. *Recordings include:* Singles: Only Love Can Break Your Heart, 1990; Kiss and Make Up, 1990; Nothing Can Stop Us, 1991; Filthy, 1991; Fingertips, 1991; Heartspin, 1991; Journey To The Centre of Love, 1991; He Is Cola, 1991; Join Our Club, 1992; Blade's Love Machine, 1992; Avenue, 1992; You're In A Bad Way, 1993; I Was Born on Christmas Day, with Tim Burgess, 1993; Pale Movie, 1994; Like A Motorway, 1994; Hug My Soul, 1994; Reserection, 1995; He's On The Phone, 1995; Gone, 1996; Anymore, 1996; Angel/Burnt

Out Car, 1996; Goldie, 1997; Sylvie, 1998; Albums: Foxbase Alpha, 1991; So Tough, 1993; You Need A Mess of Help To Stand Alone, compilation album, 1993; Tiger Bay, 1994; Fairytales from Saint Etienne, compilation album, 1995; Too Young To Die, singles compilation album, 1995; Casino Classics, remix album, 1996; Lipslide, 1997; Good Humor, 1998.

WILBER Bob, (Robert Sage); b. 15 March 1928, New York City, USA. Bandleader; Composer; Arranger; Writer; Musician (clarinet, soprano, alto, tenor saxophones). m. Joanne Horton, 2 s., 1 d. *Education:* BA, State University, New York. *Musical Education:* Juilliard, Eastman, Manhattan schools; Teachers: Sidney Bechet; Lennic Tristano; Leon Russianoff. *Career:* Subbed for Sidney Bechet, Nice Festival, 1948; Also leading bands at Savoy, Storyville clubs, Boston; Played with: Bobby Hackett; Benny Goodman; Jack Teagarden; Eddie Condon; Founding member, World's Greatest Jazz Band, 1969; Began Soprano Summit with Kenny Davern, 1973–78; Reformed as Summit Reunion, 1990; Performed, recorded with jazz artists including: Duke Ellington; Billy Strayhorn; Louis Armstrong; Sidney Bechet; Performed, presented Carnegie Hall Tribute to Benny Goodman; Premiered orchestral version of Duke Ellington's Queens Suite; Toured with Bechet Legacy Band; Helped organize New York jazz Repertory Company; Director, Smithsonian Jazz Repertory Ensemble; Leads big band in Benny Goodman re-creations; Musical Director: The Cotton Club; Soloist, Pittsburgh, Baltimore, Colorado Symphony Orchestras; Recorded chamber music by Brahms, Beethoven, Mozart. *Compositions:* The Piscean Suite; Portraits In Jazz. *Recordings:* Over 1,500 titles include: Saxophones on: Horns A-Plenty; Nostalgia. *Publications:* Autobiography: Music Was Not Enough, 1987. *Honours:* Grammy Award, music for film: The Cotton Club, 1985; Hon. Doctorate of Music, Hamilton College, 1998. *Memberships:* ASCAP; Rotary; Senior Statesman of Jazz. *Leisure interests:* Tennis; Travel; Theatre; Reading.

WILDE Danny; Singer; Songwriter; Musician. *Career:* Member, Great Buildings; The Rembrandts, 1991–; Also solo artiste. *Recordings:* Solo Albums: Danny Wilde; Any Man's Hunger; The Boyfriend; With The Rembrandts: Rembrandts, 1991; Untitled, 1992; LP, 1995; Spin This!, 1998; Singles: That's Just The Way It Is Baby; Johnny Have You Seen Her?; I'll Be There For You (theme for television series Friends), 1995. *Current Management:* Mogul Entertainment Group. *Address:* 9744 Wilshire Blvd, Suite 305, Beverly Hills, CA 90212, USA.

WILDE Kim, (Kim Smith); b. 18 Nov. 1960, Chiswick, London, England. Singer. *Education:* Art school. *Career:* Backing singer to father Marty; Solo artiste, 1980–; Sold 6m. discs world-wide in 18 months, 1981–82; AIDS benefit concert, Wembley, 1987; Support to Michael Jackson, Bad world tour, 1988; Performed at World Music Awards, Monaco, 1992. *Recordings:* Albums: Kim Wilde, 1981; Select, 1982; Catch As Can Can, 1983; Teases and Dares, 1984; The Very Best of Kim Wilde, 1985; Another Step, 1986; Close, 1988; Love Moves, 1990; Love Is, 1992; The Singles Collection 1981–93, 1993; Now and Forever, 1995; Breaking Away, 1995; The Gold Collection, 1996; Original Gold, 1999; Hit singles include: Kids In America, 1981; Chequered Love, 1981; Water On Glass, 1981; Cambodia, 1981; View From The Bridge, 1982; Rage To Love, 1985; You Keep Me Hangin' On (No. 1, USA), 1986; Another Step (Closer To You), duet with Junior, 1987; Say You Really Want Me, 1987; Rockin' Around The Christmas Tree, with Mel Smith (for Comic Relief), 1987; You Came, 1988; Never Trust A Stranger, 1988; Four Letter Word, 1988; Love Is Holy, 1992; If I Can't Have You, 1994. *Contributions to:* Rock The World charity record, 1990; Let It Be, Ferry Aid (Zeebrugge ferry disaster benefit). *Honours:* BRIT Award, Best British Female Artist, 1983; Played female lead in West End production of Pete Townshend's Tommy, 1996. *Current Management:* Big M Productions. *Address:* Big M House, 1 Stevenage Rd, Knebworth, Herts SG3 6AN, England.

WILDE Marty, (Reginald Smith); b. 15 April 1939, Greenwich, London, England. Singer. m. Joyce Baker, 2 Dec. 1959, 2 s., 2 d. *Career:* Performed as Reg Patterson, and with The Hound Dogs; Changed name, with backing group The Wildcats, 1957; Television appearances include: Off The Record, 1957; Oh Boy!, ITV, 1958; Host, Boy Meets Girls, 1959; Group Scene 1964, Regular British tours, including Group Scene 1964, with Rolling Stones, 1964; Formed the Wilde Three, vocal trio, with Justin Haywood, 1965; Rock 'n' Roll Road Show, British tour with Bert Weedon, 1977; AIDS benefit, with son Ricky and daughter Kim, Wembley, 1987; Film appearances: The Helions, 1961; What A Crazy World, 1964; Theatre: Bye Bye Birdie, London production, 1961. *Compositions include:* Co-writer (with Ronnie Scott), Ice In The Sun, Status Quo; Jesamine, The Casuals; Co-writer (with Ricky Wilde), Kim Wilde, 1981–. *Recordings:* Albums: Diversions, 1969; Good Rocking, Now and Then, 1973; Solid Gold, 1994; It's Been Nice, 1996; Born To Rock 'n' Roll, 1999; Hit singles include: Endless Sleep, 1958; Donna, 1959; A Teenager In Love, 1959; Sea of Love, 1959; Bad Boy, 1960; Little Girl, 1961; Rubber Ball, 1961; Jezebel, 1963. *Current Management:* Joyce Wilde. *Address:* Thatched Rest, Queen Hoo Lane, Tewin, Hertfordshire AL6 0LT, England.

WILDER Alan; b. 1 June 1959, London, England. *Career:* Joined Depeche Mode, 1982; Numerous world tours including Pasadena Rose Bowl, California; TV and radio appearances world-wide; Left band, 1995. *Recordings:* Singles: Leave in Silence, 1982; Meaning of Love, 1982; Love in Itself, 1983; Everything Counts, 1983; Get the Balance Right, 1983; Blasphemous Rumours, 1984; Master and Servant, 1984; Shake the Disease, 1985; It's Called a Heart, 1985; Stripped, 1986; Question of Lust, 1986; Never Let Me Down Again, 1987; I Want You Know, 1988; Behind the Wheel, 1988; People are People, 1988; Personal Jesus, 1989; Enjoy the Silence, 1990; Policy of Truth, 1990; Heavens in Motion, 1990; A Heart, 2990; But Not Tonight, 1990; World in My Eyes, 1990; A Question of Time, 1991; Condemnation, 1993; Walking in My Shoes, 1993; One Caress, 1993; In Your Room, 1994; Albums: Construction Time Again, 1983; Some Great Reward, 1984; Catching Up With Depeche Mode, 1985; Black Celebration, 1986; Music for the Masses, 1987; Violator, 1990; Songs of Faith and Devotion, 1993; Depeche Mode, 1995.

WILDHORN Frank N; b. 29 Nov. 1958, New York, USA. Composer; Prod. 1 s. *Education:* College. *Career:* Long-term relationship with Warner Brothers Pictures to develope and compose both musical feature-length animated films and live-action projects; Creative Director of Atlantic Theatre. *Recordings:* Theatrical productions of: Jekyll and Hyde; The Scarlet Pimpernel; Victor/Victoria; Svengali; The Civil War; Over 200 songs. *Publications:* Song books: Jekyll and Hyde (romantic highlights and The Gothic Musical Thriller; The Scarlet Pimpernel; Linda Eder's albums: Linda Eder; So Much More; Something to Believe In; A Little Bit of Heaven (single); Jung, Gift, 1998; Scarlet Pimpernel, Encore, 1999; Broadway in Love, 2000. *Honours:* Numerous Platinum, Gold discs; ASCAP writing awards. *Memberships:* ASCAP; NAS; DGA; WGA. *Leisure interests:* Son; Sports. *Current Management:* Mark Shimmel Management, 8899 Beverly Blvd, Suite #100, Los Angeles, CA 90048, USA.

WILFRIED (Scheutz); b. 24 June 1950, Bad Goisern, Austria. Singer; Actor. m. Marina, 15 April 1982, 1 s. *Education:* Trades Academy, English, French studies. *Career:* Three No. 1 hits in Austria; 17 hits (studio); One live double LP and CD; Tours in Austria, Germany, France; About 10 films in major roles. *Recordings:* Run Rabbit Run; Highdelbeeren; Ziwui Ziwui; Mary Oh Mary; Ikarus; Television, film music: St Benedikt. *Leisure interests:* Mountainbiking; Snow Boarding.

WILK Bradley; b. 1968, Portland, Oregon, USA. Musician (Drums). *Career:* Member, Rage Against the Machine; Obtained major label record deal; Involvement in various causes including Fairness and Accuracy in Reporting, Rock for Choice and Refuse and Resist; Numerous tours including Lollapalooza; Tour with Wu Tang Clan; Contribution to soundtrack for film Godzilla, 1998. *Recordings:* Singles: Freedom, 1994; Bombtrack Plus Live, 1994; People of the Sun EP, 1997; Albums: Rage Against the Machine, 1992; Evil Empire, 1996.

WILKIE Chris; b. 25 Jan. 1973, Gateshead, England. Songwriter; Musician (Guitar). *Career:* Member of British popgroup, Dubstar. *Compositions:* Anywhere; Just A Girl; I Will Be Your Girlfriend; Can't Tell Me; It's Clear; When You Say Goodbye; Wearchest; Week In, Week Out. *Recordings:* Stars; Not So Manic Now; Dubstar; Cathedral Park; Anxious; Albums: Disgraceful, 1995; Goodbye, 1997. *Honour:* Gold Disc for Disgraceful, album, 1996. *Current Management:* Stevo Pearce, Some Bizarre. *Address:* 124 New Bond St, London, W1Y 9AE, England.

WILKINS Keith Allen; b. 12 Sept. 1974, Farmington Hills, Michigan, USA. Musician (drums, clarinet); Lyricist. *Musical Education:* 1 year Music Business Management; 4 years clarinet; 1 year drum class. *Career:* Studio drummer, lyricist, consulting manager; Wrote 2 songs with Donn Hecht, 1994; Collaborated with many musicans; Drummer in local concerts; Guest, television show, Dave's Garage. *Compositions:* Always, 1993; Hard Promises, 1993; News For You Baby, 1993; Everytime I Cry, 1995; Together, 1995; Good Lovin' Gone Bad, 1995; You're A Part of Me, 1996; Could It Be You, 1996; Down By The Ocean Shore, 1996; They'll Come A' Runnin', 1996; Magic Moment, 1996. *Recordings:* Music of America, 1993; Hollywood Gold, 1993; America Sings, 1995. *Publications:* Lock and Load magazine, 1993; Stars magazine, 1995; Jam magazine, 1995. *Honours:* Songwriter's Guild of America, Composer and Lyricist Certificate, 1999; Music Business Seminars Ltd, Diploma in Music Business Management, 1999. *Memberships:* Charter mem., Rock 'N' Roll Hall of Fame and Museum; BMI; Nashville Songwriters Asscn International (NSAI); South West Virginia Songwriters Asscn (SVSA); Memphis Songwriters Asscn (MSA); Songwriters Guild of America (SGA); Florida Music Asscn (FMA); National Academy of Songwriters (NAS); Songwriters of Wisconsin (SOW); Rock Out Censorship (ROC); Central Florida Musicians Asscn; American Federation of Musicians (AFofM); The National Academy of Recording Arts and Sciences Inc; Housequake Recording Studios. *Leisure interests:* Travel; Drawing; Writing; Going to the beach. *Address:* KAM Lyric Writing, 11124 64th Terrace N, Seminole, FL 33772, USA.

WILKINS Mark Thomas; b. 14 Dec. 1956, Seattle, Washington, USA. Music Organization Exec. *Education:* BA Education, 2 teaching credentials, CSULA. *Musical Education:* Sherwood Oaks Experimental College, LACC, CSULA. *Career:* Member, Quincy Jones Workshops; Head of Promotion, Mystic Records, 1983–90; Founder, Affiliated Independent Record Labels (AIR Co), and International Record Promotion (IRP), 1990–93; Co-founder, CEO, Independent Network (Indy Net), 1993–; CEO, IMRA; AIM, ILTPA. *Recordings:* with Mandrill: Love Attack; with Bandit: 1 World 1 People. *Publications:* Soundtrack Mag; Author: Music Biz 411 (USA); 411 International (Europe, Asia); The Right Way To Run A Record Label, 1996; Forms and Contracts For Success, 1996; International Success In The Music Business, 1996. *Honours:* Innovations In Music. *Memberships:* Founder, CEO, The Independent Network; Vice President, Independent Music Asscn (IMA); Co-founder, Independent Music Retailer's Asscn (IMRA); Independent Live Talent Presenter's Asscn (ILTPA); Asscn of Independent Media (AIM). *Leisure interests:* Computers; The law; Writing; Travel.

WILKINSON Alan James; b. 22 Aug. 1954, Ilford, Essex, England. Musician (soprano, alto, baritone saxophones). Vocalist. Partner, Gina Southgate. *Education:* BA Hons Degree Fine Art, Leeds Polytechnic, 1975–78. *Musical Education:* Self-taught; Guitar, from age 13; Saxophone, 1978-. *Career:* Joined Crow, with Matthew Coe (a.k.a. Xero Slingsby), drummer Paul Hession, 1978; Art Bart and Fargo with Hession (toured in Europe), 1979; Trio with Akemi Kuniyoshi and Hession, 1982; Tour, Europe with drummer Steve Hubback; Duo with Hession, played 10th Free Music Festival, Antwerp and Netherlands, 1983; Art Initiative, Eindhoven; Started Termite Club, Leeds; Derek Bailey's Company, 1987; Italy, 1988, 1993; Sound Symposium, St Johns, Newfoundland, with Hession, Wilkinson, Fell, 1994; Radio 3, Jazz Today, 1987; Mixing It, 1993; CBC: Two New Hours, 1994. *Recordings:* with Hession, Wilkinson, Fell: Bogey's, 1991; foom! foom!, 1992; The Horrors of Darmstadt, 1994; The Saxophone Phenomenon, 1992; with John Law Quartet: Exploded on Impact, 1992; Live solo recordings: Seedy Boy, 1994. *Publications:* Featured in: Penguin Guide To Jazz On CD; Guinness Encyclopedia of Popular Music. *Honours:* Several ACGB and ACE touring and study awards, 1985–95; LAB travel grant, 1994. *Memberships:* Musicians' Union; Director London Musicians Collective. *Leisure interests:* Concerts; Cinema; Walking; Cycling; Socializing; Eating; Cooking; Travel. *Address:* 36 Arbor Court, Queen Elizabeth's Walk, London N16 0QU, England.

WILKINSON Gary; Record Prod. *Recordings:* Records Produced and Remixed: Fire Island; Farley and Heller; The Farm; Sunscreen; Janet Jackson; Roach Motel; Jimmy Somerville; Happy Mondays; M People; Pet Shop Boys; Run DMC; U2; *Recordings:* As Remixer/Producer: Inspiral Carpets, Life, 1990; The Farm, Spartacus, 1991; New Order, Regret, 1993; One Dove, Morning Dove White, 1993; Kylie Minogue, Confide in Me, 1994; Janet Jackson, Runaway, 1995; Michael Jackson, Blood on the Dance Floor, 1997; Sneaker Pimps, Spin Spin Sugar, 1997; Glasgow Gangster, Deeva Feeva, 1999. *Current Management:* One Management Ltd, 43 St Alban's Ave, London W4 5JS, England.

WILKINSON Peter; b. 9 May 1969, Liverpool, England. Musician (Bass). *Career:* Member, Cast; Early tours supporting Elvis Costello and Oasis; Numerous headlining tours; Festival appearances; TV and radio appearances. *Recordings:* Singles: Finetime, 1995; Alright, 1995; Free Me; Live the Dream, 1998; Guiding Star, 1998; Sandstorm, 1998; Walkaway, 1998; Albums: All Change, 1995; Mother Nature Calls, 1997.

WILLIAM-OLSSON Staffan; b. 13 Dec. 1959, Gothenburg, Sweden. Jazz Musician (guitar); Composer; Arranger. 1 d. *Career:* Member, Norwegian hard-rock group Sons of Angels, 1989–91; Tours, USA, UK, Germany; Band disbanded, 1991; Now working with Norwegian soul/jazz group The Real Thing. *Recordings:* Albums: with Sons of Angels: Sons of Angels, 1990; with The Real Thing: The Real Thing, 1992; The Real Thing In New York, 1993; A Perfect Match, 1994; Shades of Blue, 1996; Contribution to: Jukka Linkola, Pegasos, 1996. *Address:* Eikev 5, 1181 Oslo, Norway.

WILLIAMS Andy (Howard Andrew); b. 3 Dec. 1928, Wall Lake, Iowa, USA. Singer. *Career:* Member, quartet with his three brothers; Own US radio shows; Backed Bing Crosby in film Going My Way, 1944; Other film appearances: Kansas City Kitty, 1944; I'd Rather Be Rich, 1964; Worked as The Williams Brothers, with Kay Thompson (pianist, singer), 1947–48; Solo singer, 1952–; Featured artist, Tonight Show, 2 years; Own weekly variety show, 1962–71. *Recordings:* Albums include: Moon River and Other Great Movie Themes; Days of Wine and Roses; The Wonderful World of Andy Williams; Dear Heart; Born Free; Love Andy; Honey; Happy Heart; Home Loving Man; Love Story; Solitaire; The Way We Were; Reflections; Greatest Love Classics; Christmas Album; Under Paris Skies; Branson City Limits; Singles include: Canadian Sunset; Butterfly; I Like Your Kind of Love (duet with Peggy Powers); Lips of Wine; Are You Sincere; Promise Me Love; The Hawaiian Wedding Song; Lonely Street; The Village of St Bernadette; Can't Get Used To Losing You; Hopeless; A Fool Never Learns; (Where Do I Begin) Love Story; Solitaire; Almost There.

WILLIAMS Brad; b. 13 April 1968, Clatterbridge, England. Musician (guitar, bass, keyboards); Vocalist; Prod.; Programmer. *Musical Education:* Self-taught. *Career:* Musician, 17 years; Performer, 12 years; Recording artist, 10 years; Teacher, 9 years; Exodus 1992 British tour supporting Mike Peters and The Poets of Justice; Subsequent recording and touring as guitarist in his band; Live performance, interview, regular airplay, Wirral Community Radio, 1995; Interview, Mersey Community Radio, 1995. *Recordings:* Over 50 original compositions by Mike Peters; The Next Sound You Hear, 1991; Upon a Jazz Top: Christmas Holiday Series, 1999. *Membership:* Musicians' Union. *Leisure interests:* Music; Cycling; Reading. *Address:* c/o Paul Brown, The Image Business Ltd, Orleans House, Edmund St, Liverpool L3 9NG, England.

WILLIAMS Claude; b. 22 Feb. 1908, Muskogee, Oklahoma, USA. Jazz Musician (violin, guitar). *Career:* Musician for 77 years; Played with: Charlie Parker; Lester Young; Mary Lou Williams; Oklahoma Blue Devils; The Pettifords Band; Andy Kirk; Don Byas; Buddy Tate; Lloyd Cole; Nat King Cole; Count Basie; Jay McShann; Sir Roland Hanna; Grady Tate; Ruth Brown; Bill Easley; Earl May; First recorded guitarist with Basie, 1936; Musician and bandleader, 1960s-70s; Concerts included Newport in New York; Monterey Festival; Played in Black and Blue, Paris and New York, 1980's; World-wide tours and concerts including: Carnegie Hall; President Clinton inaugural events, 1992; Jazz festivals at New Orleans; Monterey; Newport; Jazz Triumph, Puerto Rico; Master of The Folk Violin US Tour, 1994–95. *Recordings include:* Swing Time In New York; Man From Muskogee (with Jay McShann); Call For The Fiddler; Live At J's, Vols 1 and 2; King of Kansas City; Swingin' the Blues; Recorded and toured with Statesmen of Jazz (including Milt Hinton, Benny Waters, Jane Jarvis), 1994–95; Featured soloist, Lincoln Center Jazz Orchestra, directed by Wynton Marsalis, 1995. *Honours:* Best Guitarist of Year, Downbeat, 1936; First Inductee, Oklahoma Jazz Hall of Fame; Charlie Christian Jazz Award, Black Liberated Arts Inc (only recipient ever), 1994; Distinguished Achievement Award, Amherst University, 1995. *Current Management:* Russ Dantzler, Hot Jazz Management. *Address:* Suite 4FW, 328 W 43rd St, New York, NY 10036, USA.

WILLIAMS Dar, (Dorothy Snowden); b. 19 April 1967, Mount Kisco, New York, USA. Vocalist; Musician (guitar); Songwriter. *Education:* Wesleyan University, Connecticut, BA in Theatre and Religion. *Career:* Has had material recorded by Joan Baez; Active in environmental issues and set up Snowden Environmental Trust. *Recordings:* Albums: I Have No History, 1990; All My Heroes Are Dead, 1991; The Honesty Room, 1993; Mortal City, 1996; End of Summer, 1997; Cry Cry Cry (with Lucy Kaplansky and Richard Shindell), 1998; The Green World, 2000; Out There Live, 2001; features on Gone From Danger (with Joan Baez), 1997; Badlands – Bruce Springsteen Tribute, 2000. *Current Management:* c/o AGF Entertainment, 30 W 21st St, Seventh Floor New York, NY 10010–6905, USA.

WILLIAMS (David) Paul (Gifford), (Terry Day); b. 3 Sept. 1940, Kingston, Surrey, England. Composer; Music Prod. m. Rosalind Anne Burns, 3 Sept. 1965, 1 s., 2 d. *Education:* MA, Cambridge University. *Musical Education:* Royal College of Music; Jesus College, Cambridge. *Career:* BBC Senior Producer, 1980; Sony Award winner, McCartney, BBC series, 1988; Composer for film, television; Worked with Phil Manzanera on Nowomowa album, 1988; TV music, House of Gristle, BBC TV, 1994; BBC TV Out of This World, 1994; Mysteries, BBC TV, 1997–98; Growing Places, BBC TV, 1999. *Compositions:* Over 1,200 published for television, films. *Recordings:* 22 albums. *Honours:* 3 Sony radio awards, 1988, 1990, 1992; Stemra Award, Netherlands, 1994. *Memberships:* BACS; PRS; Musicians' Union. *Leisure interests:* Music; Golf. *E-mail:* paul@paulwilliamsmusic.com.

WILLIAMS Deniece, (Deniece Chandler); Vocalist. *Career:* Solo gospel/ soul singer; Joined Stevie Wonder's backing group, Wonderlove; Recording artiste, including many duets with Johnny Mathis; Recorded first gospel album 1988. *Compositions:* Numerous including songs recorded by: Merry Clayton; The Emotions; The Whispers; Frankie Valli. *Recordings:* Albums: This Is Niecy, 1976; I'm So Proud, 1983; Let's Hear It For The Boy, 1984; Hot On The Trail, 1986; Water Under The Bridge, 1987; So Glad I Know, 1988; As Good As It Gets, 1989; Special Love, 1989; Lullabies to Dreamland, 1991; Love Solves It All, 1996; This Is My Song, 1998; Singles: Free, 1990; Why You Wanna Do Me, 1996; Great Is Thy Faithfulness, 1996. *Address:* c/o Pyramid Entertainment Group, 89 Fifth Ave, Seventh Floor, New York, NY 10003, USA.

WILLIAMS Don; b. 27 May 1939, Floydada, Texas, USA. Songwriter; Singer; Musician (guitar). *Career:* Member, Strangers Two; Pozo-Seco Singers; Solo artiste, 1971–; Film appearances: W W and The Dixie Dancekings; Smokey and The Bandit 2. *Recordings:* Albums: with the Poco-Seco Singers: Time, 1966; I Can Make It With You, 1967; Shades of Time, 1968; Solo albums: Don Williams Vols 1–3, 1973, 1974; You're My Best Friend, 1975; Harmony, 1976; Visions, 1977; Country Boy, 1977; Expressions, 1978; Portrait, 1979; I Believe In You, 1980; Especially For You, 1981; Listen To The Radio, 1982; Yellow Moon, 1983; Cafe Carolina,

1984; New Moves, 1986; Traces, 1987; One Good Well, 1989; As Long As I Have You, 1989; True Love, 1990; Currents, 1992; I've Got a Winner in You, 1993; Lord I Hope This Day Is Good, 1993; I Turn the Page, 1998; Various compilations; Singles include: Amanda; The Shelter of Your Eyes; I Recall A Gypsy Woman; You're My Best Friend; Tulsa Time; Till The Rivers All Run Dry; Some Broken Hearts Never Mend; Lay Down Beside Me; I Believe In You; If I Needed You (duet with Emmylou Harris); Good Ol' Boys Like Me; An Evening with Don Williams, Best of Live, 1994; Borrowed Tales, 1995; Flatlands, 1996; Pretty Little Baby Child, 1998. *Address:* c/o Don Williams Productions, PO Box 160206, Nashville, TN 37216, USA.

WILLIAMS Doug; b. 22 Oct. 1950, Chicago, USA. Singer; Bass Guitarist. 3 d. *Career:* Powerhouse, 1975–76; My Old School, 1985; Missing in Action; Marcia Hines Band; Renee Geyer Band; Hip Hop, 1988; Duffhead, 1990; The Black Mass, 1992; The Rockmelons, 1992; D Williams and the Black Mass, 1993. *Compositions:* Feel So Good, 5 Track EP, 1993; Stronger Together (The Rockmelons), lead vocals; Love is Gonna Bring You Home (The Rockmelons), lead vocals; Doug Williams L R Mix, 2000; 2 track EP, Walking on Thin Ice, second track (original) Fall into Love, 2000. *Recordings:* The Rockmelons, lead vocals; Form One Planet; My Island Home; Peter Andre; Kate Cebereno, backing vocals; Grace Knight, backing vocals; Swoop, backing vocals. *Honours:* Chosen to sing to President Bill Clinton, Australia, 1996. *Membership:* APRA, Australia. *Current Management:* Milly Petriella, Playworks Entertainment Management. *Address:* PO Box 448, Crows Nest, NSW 2065, Australia.

WILLIAMS Geoffrey; b. 25 April 1964, London, England. Songwriter; Singer; Musician (guitar). *Compositions:* Songs for Beverly Hills 90210 album; Eternal; Colour Me Badd; The Drop, album, 1997. *Recordings:* Albums: The Drop, 1997; Lost in Dinosaur World, 1997; Prisoner of Love, 1997; Singles: It's Not a Love Thing, 1992; Drive, EP, 1996; I Guess I Will Always Love You, 1996; Sex Life, 1997; Deliver Me Up, 1997. *Membership:* Musicians' Union. *Current Management:* Hands On Management. *Address:* 3 Lambton Pl., London W11 2SH, England.

WILLIAMS J Owen; b. 1 Feb. 1959, Ireland. Singer; Songwriter; Musician (acoustic guitar). *Musical Education:* Irish traditional music. *Career:* Glastonbury Festival, 1992, 1993; Milan, Turin festivals, Italy, 1992, 1993; Live radio sessions for Greater London Radio (GLR); London gig residency. *Recordings:* Albums: Ribbonmen, 1991; Sean One Shoe, 1994. *Memberships:* Musicians' Union; PRS. *Leisure interests:* History; Poetry. *Current Management:* Freddie Daniels, Runaway Music. *Address:* 18c Alwyne Pl., Islington, London N1 2NL, England.

WILLIAMS John; b. 8 Feb. 1932, New York, New York, USA. Composer. *Education:* Studied Music, UCLA and Juilliard School, New York. *Career:* Pianist, Columbia Pictures; Jazz Pianist, working with Henry Mancini on television scores; Worked solo on television soundtracks before progressing to film scores; Work with orchestras includes the American Film Orchestra, Boston Pops Orchestra, Cincinnati Pops, London Symphony Orchestra, Movin' Dream Orchestra, National Philharmonic Orchestra; Has also worked with the Chieftains, Ray Conniff, Sally Harmon and others. *Recordings include:* Jaws, 1975; Close Encounters of the Third Kind, 1977; The Empire Strikes Back, 1980; Indiana Jones and the Temple of Doom, 1984; 1941, 1989; Born on the Fourth of July, 1989; Indiana Jones and the Last Crusade, 1989; Hook, 1991; Stars Wars Trilogy, 1991; Jurassic Park, 1993; The Reivers, 1995; Nixon, 1996; John Williams Plays the Movies, 1996; Land of the Giants, 1997; The Lost World: Jurassic Park, 1997; Lost in Space, 1997; Time Tunnel, 1997; Music from the Star Wars Saga, 1999; Compilation albums include: Themes from Academy Award Winners; Over the Rainbow: Songs from the Movies, 1992; The Classic Film Music of Schindler's List, 1995; John Williams Conducting the Boston Pops, 1996; The Hollywood Sound, 1997; From Sousa to Spielberg; Best of John Williams, 1998. *Honours include:* Five Academy Awards for Best Music, Original Score; Six BAFTA Awards; Three Golden Globes; 16 Grammy Awards; 36 Academy Award nominations overall; 14 Golden Globe nominations.

WILLIAMS John Charles; b. 8 Feb. 1941, Hammersmith, London. Composer; Arranger; Musician. m. Frances Margaret, 3 s., 1 d. *Education:* Acton Technical College, 1957–59. *Career:* Leader, Resident Big Band, Marquee Club, London, 1961–63; Formed Octet, 1969 and Big Band, 1973; Ensembles include saxophone quartet Changing Face, 1976–78, Trio Spectrum, 1985, Baritone Band, 1985; Played and recorded with Keith Tippett, Alan Cohen, Don Rendell; Instituted annual Summer Music Festival, Shropshire. *Compositions:* Four pieces for Jazz Soloists and Orchestra; Out of Focus; When Summers End Is Nighing; Tenorama, 2001. *Recordings:* Year of The Buffalo; Spotlite; Five Housman Settings and other jazz works; with John Williams' Baritone Band: Spotlite. *Membership:* Musicians Union. *Leisure interest:* Walking. *Current Management:* All Electric Theatre Productions, Unit 6, 94 Charlton Rd, Andover, Hants SP10 3JY, England. *Address:* Leasowes Bank Farm, Ratlinghope, Shrewsbury SY5 0SW, England.

WILLIAMS Leroy Anthony; b. 4 Sept. 1962, London, England. Musician (drums, percussion). 1 s. *Career:* Played with: Five Star; Level 42; Simple Minds; Talk Talk; Hi Tension; Aswad. *Recordings:* There's A Reason, Hi Tension. *Membership:* Musicians' Union. *Leisure interests:* Collecting classic sports cars. *Current Management:* Session Connection. *Address:* 12c Parkfield Cres., Harrow, Middlesex HA2 6JZ, England.

WILLIAMS Linda; b. 7 July 1947, Anniston, Alabama, USA. Musician (guitar, banjo, mouth harp); Singer; Songwriter. m. Robin Williams, 2 June 1973. *Education:* BA Michigan State University. *Musical Education:* Piano lessons. *Career:* Began together, 1973; Worked with Garrison Keillor's Home Companion, as semi-regulars, 1975–; Numerous appearances, Grand Ole Opry, Nashville, Tennessee; Numerous television appearances include: Austin City Limits; Disney Specials; TNN Shows; Played all major festivals in USA, Canada; Two tours: Europe, UK; Carnegie Hall, 1987. *Compositions:* Songs recorded by: Emmylou Harris; Tom T Hall; George Hamilton IV; Holly Near; Tim and Molly O'Brien; The Seldom Scene. *Recordings:* 14 albums including, Devil of a Dream; Close As We Can Get. *Publications:* Song Book of Original Pieces, Vol. 1, 1979. *Honours:* Peabody Award, Broadcasting, for work on a Prairie Home Companion, 1980. *Memberships:* Country Music Asscn; International Bluegrass Music Asscn; The Folk Alliance. *Leisure interests:* Gardening; Listening to music; Reading; Golf.

WILLIAMS Marcus Christian; b. 25 Oct. 1965, Rochdale, England. Musician (bass guitar). *Education:* Art College, 1 year. *Musical Education:* Self-taught. *Career:* Tours: with Julian Cope in UK, Europe and Japan; with The Mighty Lemon Drops in UK (twice), Europe and USA and Canada (3 times); with Blue Aeroplanes in UK and Europe; with The Madonnas in UK; with Kirsty MacColl in UK, USA and Canada; Various appearances on television, radio and at festivals, with artists including Nick Heywood; Alison Moyet; Terry Wogan. *Recordings:* 4 albums with The Mighty Lemon Drops; 2 albums with Blue Aeroplanes; 1 album with Hectors House; Played on 2 Lisa Stansfield albums; Contributions to: Don Diego, This Must Be Heaven, 1998, Isaac Curry, Lavender Bull, 1998, James Bignon, On the Other Side of Through, 1998, Heaven Belongs to You, 1999, as drummer; Various singles and sessions. *Memberships:* Musicians' Union; PRS. *Leisure interests:* Cooking; Horticulture; Reading; History; Geography; Drink. *Address:* 5 Dralda House, Keswick Rd, London SW15 2JL, England.

WILLIAMS Mason; b. 24 Aug. 1938, Abilene, Texas, USA. Composer; Writer; Performer; Musician (guitar); Singer. m. (1), 1 d., (2), (3) Kate, 23 Feb. 1993. *Education:* Music major, Oklahoma City University, 3 years. *Career:* College student/folk singer, 1959–61; US Navy, 1962–63; Hollywood folksinger, songwriter, sideman, 1964–65; Television Writer, Smothers Brothers, Andy Williams, Glenn Campbell and Petula Clark, 1966–69; Musical performances at clubs, concerts, festivals, symphony orchestra, television, 1972–; Current concerts: Mason Williams and Friends, Symphonic Bluegrass, of Time and Rivers Flowing, X-Mas and Pop Shows. *Recordings:* 3 Folk, 1960–63; 6 Folk Anthologies and Them Poems, 1963–65; 5 Warner Bros LPs, 1968–71; Classical Gas, hit single, 1968; Albums: Fresh Fish, 1978; Of Time and Rivers Flowing, 1984; Classical Gas with Mannheim Steamroller, Pop, 1987; A Gift of Song, CD X-Mas, 1992; Of Time and Rivers Flowing, CD, 1996. *Publications:* The Mason Williams Reading Matter, 1969; Flavors, 1971; The FCC Report, 1969; The Music of Mason Williams, 1992; 14 limited editions. *Honours:* 2 Grammys; 3 Grammy Nominations; 2 Emmy nominations; 1 Emmy; 1 Writers Guild Award, 1 Nomination; Hon. DMus, Oklahoma City University, 1995; University of Oregon, Distinguished Service Award, 1999; State of Oregon, Musicians Laureate, 2000. *Memberships:* AFofM; AFTRA; WGAW; NARAS; NAS; SGA. *Leisure interests:* Flyfishing; Art projects. *Address:* PO Box 5105, Eugene, OR 97405, USA.

WILLIAMS Melanie Joy; b. 28 Oct. 1964, London, England. Singer; Songwriter. *Education:* Languages; English; History. *Career:* Television appearances: Top of The Pops; The Word; The Beat; Lily Savage; Passion; The O-Zone. *Recordings:* Albums: Temper Temper; Human Cradle, 1995; Singles: Ain't No Love; Everyday Thang, 1994; You Are Everything, 1995. *Honours:* Silver disc (UK); Gold disc (Australia). *Memberships:* Musicians Union; Equity. *Leisure interests:* Meditation; Alternative Therapies; Camping; Horseriding; Animals. *Current Management:* Paul Craig, Sound Management. *Address:* 222 Lambolle Pl., London, NW3 4PG, England.

WILLIAMS Mervyn; b. 8 May 1957, St James, Jamaica. Audio Engineer. Fiancée, Kaye Troy E Janagalee, 1 s., 2 d. *Musical Education:* Aquarius recording studio, studios overseas. *Career:* Several tours with Burning Spear. *Recordings:* with Jimmy Cliff; Burning Spear; Beres Hammond; Vocalist on Tiger, Ras Portraits, 1997. *Honour:* Jamaica Federation of Music (JFM). *Membership:* MFM. *Leisure interests:* Dominoes; Basketball; Cricket; All sports. *Address:* 3 Tunbridge Dr., Kingston 19, Jamaica.

WILLIAMS Michelle; b. 1 Dec. 1980, Rockford, Illinois, USA. Vocalist. *Career:* Joined Destiny's Child group, February 2000; Numerous TV and live performances including tour with Christina Aguilera, 2000; Appeared at United We Stand concert, USA, 2001; Released solo gospel album, 2002. *Recordings:* Albums: Survivor, 8 Days of Christmas, 2001; solo: From My Heart To You, 2002; Singles: Independent Women (from Charlie's Angels OST), 2000; Survivor, Bootylicious, Emotion, 8 Days of Christmas, 2001. *Honours:* Independent Women reached the largest audience in the USA's history of monitored airplay (over 140m. radio listeners in 1 week). *Address:* c/o Mathew Knowles, Music World Entertainment, 9898 Bissonnet, Suite 625, Houston, TX 77036, USA. *Internet:* www.destinyschild.com.

WILLIAMS Otis Clayborn; b. 30 Oct. 1941, Texarkana, Texas, USA. Singer; Songwriter; Prod. m. 28 Jan. 1982, 1 d. *Career:* Member, Temptations; Television specials; Motown revue tours; Countless tours. *Recordings:* 51 albums (31 gold and platinum records). *Publications:* Temptations, life story written by Otis Williams. *Honours:* Rock 'n' Roll Hall of Fame; Star On Hollywood Boulevard; 31 Gold, Platinum records. *Membership:* ASCAP. *Leisure interests:* Writing songs; Reading; Walking out; Shopping. *Current Management:* William Morris, Star Direction Management. *Address:* 9255 Sunset Blvd, Suite 610, Los Angeles, CA 90069, USA.

WILLIAMS Pharrell; b. Virginia, USA. Prod.; Remixer. *Career:* Formed The Neptunes production duo with school friend Chad Hugo; One of the most successful production teams, 2000–01; Produced: Jay-Z; Kelis; Britney Spears; Mystikal; Formed recording act N.E.R.D. (Nobody Ever Really Dies), 2001; Collaborations: Kelis; Usher; Ol' Dirty Bastard; Ludacris. *Recordings:* Albums: In Search Of... (with N.E.R.D.), 2001; Singles: Lapdance (with N.E.R.D.), 2001. *Honours:* Source Award, Producer of The Year, The Neptunes, 2001. *Address:* c/o Virgin, 304 Park Ave S, Fifth Floor, New York, USA.

WILLIAMS Philip; b. 18 Oct. 1962, England. Musician (bass guitar); Vocalist. *Education:* BEC in Business. *Musical Education:* Diploma in Jazz and Light Music, Chichester. *Career:* Tours and various television appearances including, Kim Wilde; Walk On Fire; Curtis Stigers; Jordinaires; Greg Parker; Tony Hadley; Gary Barlow; Rick Wakeman; Vonda Shepherd. *Membership:* Musicians' Union. *Leisure interests:* Squash; Swimming. *Current Management:* Session Connection. *Address:* 62 New Rd, Staines, Middlesex TW18 3DA, England.

WILLIAMS (Randall) Hank Jr; b. 26 May 1949, Shreveport, Louisiana, USA. Country Singer; Musician. m. Mary Jane Williams, 2 s., 3 d. *Career:* Performer since aged 8; Debut appearance Grand Ole Opry, 1960; Recording debut aged 14; Recorded with father Hank Williams; Connie Francis; Toured with band, the Cheatin' Hearts; Recorded as Luke The Drifter, 1960s-70s; Career halted by mountaineering accident, 1975–77. *Recordings:* 64 albums include: Your Cheatin' Heart (film soundtrack), 1964; Living Proof, 1974; Hank Williams Jr and Friends, 1976; 14 Greatest Hits, 1976; One Night Stands, 1977; The New South, 1977; Family Tradition, 1979; Rowdy, 1981; Hank Live, 1987; Born To Boogie, 1987; Pure Hank, 1991; Maverick, 1992; Out of Left Field, 1993; Hog Wild, 1995; Wham Bam Sam, 1996; Stormy, 1999; Singles include: Long Lonesome Blues; Standing In The Shadows (US Country No. 1); All My Rowdy Friends (Have Settled Down), 1981; Recorded with numerous artists including: Ray Charles; Willie Nelson; John Lee Hooker; Johnny Cash; Reba McEntire; Huey Lewis; Tom Petty; Waylon Jennings; George Jones; George Thorogood; Travis Tritt. *Publication:* Living Proof (with Michael Bane). *Honours include:* 5 Entertainer Awards for country music; Youngest songwriter to win BMI citation, age 16; Emmy, Monday Night Football theme, ABC, 1990; Grammy Award, There's A Tear In My Bear, 1990; Gold Medal, International Film and TV Festival, New York; Platinum and Gold albums. *Memberships:* BMI; ASCAP; NEA; CMA; NARAS; ACM; AMA; AFTRA; SAG. *Current Management:* Merle Kilgore Management, 2 Music Circle S, Nashville, TN 37203, USA.

WILLIAMS Robbie (Robert Peter); b. 13 Feb. 1974, Stoke-on-Trent, Staffordshire, England. Singer. *Career:* Member, UK all-male vocal group Take That, 1990–95; Solo artiste, 1995–; Television includes: Take That and Party, C4, 1993; Take That Away documentary, BBC2, 1993; Take That In Berlin, 1994. *Recordings:* Albums: Take That and Party, 1992; Everything Changes, 1993; Greatest Hits, 1996; Solo albums: Life Thru A Lens, 1997; I've Been Expecting You, 1998; Sing When You're Winning, 2000; Swing When You're Winning, 2001; Hit singles: with Take That: It Only Takes A Minute, 1992; I Found Heaven, 1992; A Million Love Songs, 1992; Could It Be Magic, 1993; Why Can't I Wake Up With You, 1993; Love Ain't Here Anymore, 1994; Solo hit singles: Freedom, 1996; Old Before I Die, 1997; Lazy Days, 1997; South of the Border, 1997; Angels, 1997; Let Me Entertain You, 1998; No Regrets, 1998; Kids, duet with Kylie Minogue, 2000; Supreme, 2000; UK No. 1 hits: with Take That: Pray, 1993; Relight My Fire (with Lulu), 1993; Babe, 1993; Everything Changes, 1994; Sure, 1994; Back For Good, 1995; Never Forget, 1995; Solo: Millennium, 1998; Strong, 1999; She's The One/It's Only Us, 1999; Rock DJ, 2000; Eternity/ The Road To Mandalay, 2001; Somethin' Stupid, duet with Nicole Kidman,

2001; I've Been Expecting You, 1998; Millenium, 1998; Let Me Entertain You, 1998; No Regrets, 1999; She's The One/It's Only Us, 1999; Strong, 1999. *Publications:* Numerous videos, books, magazines. *Honours include:* 7 Smash Hit Awards, 1992, 1 in 1996; BRIT Award, Best British Single, 1994, 1996, 1999, 2000, 2001; Best British Male Solo Artist, 1999, 2001; MTV Award, Best Male, 1998; Smash Hits, Best Male, 1998. *Memberships:* Equity; Musicians' Union; MCPS; PRS; ADAMI; GVC; AURA. *Leisure interests:* Football; Music; Backgammon. *Current Management:* IE Music Ltd. *Address:* 59A Chesson Rd, London W14 9QS, England.

WILLIAMS Robin; b. 16 March 1947, Charlotte, North Carolina, USA. Musician (guitar, banjo, mouth harp); Singer; Songwriter. m. Linda, 2 June 1973. *Education:* BA, Presbyterian College. *Career:* Solo artiste, 1969–73; Began with Linda (wife), 1973; Worked with Garrison Keillor's Prairie Home Companion, as semi-regulars, 1975–; Numerous appearances: Grand Ole Opry, Nashville, Tennessee; Numerous television appearances include: Austin City Limits; Disney Specials; TNN Shows; Played all major festivals in USA, Canada; Toured Europe, UK, 2 times, played Carnegie Hall, 1987. *Recordings:* 14 albums, lates, Devil of Dream; Appears on: My Life, with Iris Dement, 1993; Songs recorded by Emmylou Harris; Tom T Hall; George Hamilton IV; Holly Near; Tim and Molly O'Brien; The Seldom Scene. *Publications:* Song Book of original pieces, Vol. I, 1979. *Honours:* Peabody Award for Broadcasting, for work on Prairie Home Companion, 1980. *Membership:* Country Music Asscn; International Bluegrass Music Asscn; The Folk Alliance. *Leisure interests:* Gardening; Listening to music; Reading; Golf. *Current Management:* Music Tree. *Address:* 1414 Pennsylvania Ave, Pittsburgh, PA 15233, USA.

WILLIAMS Tim; b. 11 Aug. 1948, California, USA. Songwriter; Musician (Multi Instrumentalist). m. Johanne Deleevw, 2 s. *Career:* Coffee Houses; Concerts; Signed with Epic Records, 1968. *Compositions:* My Heart Can't Take Another Rodeo; Trying to Rope the Wind; Au Contraire Mon Frere. *Recordings:* Blues Full Circle, 1969; Writing This Song, 1977; Enough to be Remembered, 1982; Riverboat Rendezvous, 1995; Indigo Incidents, 1997. *Honours:* Magazine Awards; Betty Mitchell Theatre Award. *Leisure interests:* Collecting Pre-World War II String Instruments. *Current Management:* Cayuse Music. *Address:* 833 17th Ave SE, Calgary, AB T2G 1J2, Canada.

WILLIAMS Victoria Ann; b. 23 Dec. 1958, Shreveport, Louisiana, USA. Singer; Songwriter; Musician (guitar, banjo, dulcimer, piano, mandolin, harmonica). m. Mark Olson, 22 Dec. 1993. *Education:* 2 years' college. *Musical Education:* Some music theory, college; Piano aged 8–10. *Career:* Solo recording artiste, 1987–; Appearances include: Tonight Show with Johnny Carson; Also with Jay Leno; David Letterman with Dave Pirman; Today Show; Good Morning America; Dave Stewart Show; Politically Incorrect, Comedy Channel; MTV Host twice. *Recordings:* Albums: Happy Come Home, 1987; Swing The Statue, 1990; Sweet Relief (compilation of own compositions recorded by artists including Lou Reed, Michael Penn, Evan Dando, Lucinda Williams, Michelle Shock, Jay Hawks, Michael Scott, Maria McKee; Pearl Jam, Soul Asylum), 1993; Loose, 1994; This Moment Live In Toronto, with the Loose Band, 1995; Gas, Food and Lodging (film soundtrack), 1995; Lilith Compilation, from tour, 1997; Musings of a Creek Dipper, 1998; The Original Harmony Ridge Creek Dippers, 1998; Pacific Coast Rambler, 1998; Zola and the Tulip Tree, 1999; Water to Drink, 2000. *Memberships:* US Musicians' Union; AFTRA; SAG. *Leisure interests:* Dogs, horses and mules; Swimming; Hiking; Biking; Painting. *Current Management:* Danny Heaps, PO Box 23, Pioneertown, CA 92268, USA.

WILLIAMSON Astrid; b. 28 Nov. 1968, Shetland Islands, Scotland. Musician (piano, guitar); Singer. *Musical Education:* BA Hons Music, Royal Scottish Academy. *Career:* British tour with Suede; Support to Bryan Ferry; Melody Maker tour. *Recordings:* with Hope Blister, Smile's OK, 1998; with Electronic: Vivid Pt. 2; Late at Night Pt. 1 and 2, 1999. *Leisure interest:* Knitting. *Current Management:* Nick Moore, Splash Management. *Address:* 328 Grays Inn Rd, Kings Cross, London WC1X 8BZ, England.

WILLIAMSON Cris; b. 15 Feb. 1947, Deadwood, South Dakota, USA. Singer; Songwriter; Musician (keyboards, guitar). *Education:* BA, University of Denver. *Musical Education:* 7 years piano, 7 years voice. *Career:* Performances include 3, Carnegie Hall, New York (2 sell-outs); Newport Folk Festival; 25 years touring include Europe; Australia; Russia; Several documentary scores; 3 film scores; Play, Blue Fish Cove (Last Summer Of), feature song, Don't Lose Heart. *Recordings:* Albums: Artistry of Cris Williamson, 1963; The World Around Cris Williamson, 1965; Cris Williamson, Ampex, 1971; The Changer and The Changed, 1974; Live Dream, 1977; Strange Paradise, 1978; Lumiere, 1981; Blue Rider, 1982; Meg and Cris at Carnegie Hall, 1983; Portrait, 1983; Prairie Fire, 1984; Snow Angel, 1985; Wolf Moon, 1988; Country Blessed, 1989; The Best of Cris Williamson, 1990; Circle of Friends, 1991; Postcards From Paradise, (with Tret Fure), 1993; Between The Covers (with Tret Fure); Radio Quiet, 1999. *Honours:* Parents Choice Award, Lumiere, 1982; Cable Car Award, Outstanding Recording Artist, 1983; 1990; City and County of San

Francisco, State of California Honour Award, Outstanding Performer and Musician, 1988. *Memberships:* AFofM; AFTRA. *Leisure interest:* Horses. *Current Management:* Tam Martin, Beachfront Bookings. *Address:* PO Box 970, Marcola, OR 97454–0970, USA.

WILLIAMSON Harry; b. 12 May 1950, Ilfracombe, Devon, England. Composer; Musician (guitar); Prod. Divorced, 1 d. *Education:* Physics, London University. *Musical Education:* Chorister at Exeter Cathedral; seventh grade piano and guitar. *Career:* Collaborated with Anthony Phillips (Genesis), 2 albums; Worked with Gong and Mother Gong, including tours USA, Europe, 1979–; Currently part of Far From The Madding Crowd, with Australian singer Liz Van Dort. *Compositions include:* Nuclear Waste, featuring Sting. *Recordings:* with Sphynx: Xitintoday; with Anthony Phillips: Tarka (No. 1, New Music Charts), 1988; The Gypsy Suite; 12 albums with Mother Gong/Gong; Far From The Madding Crowd. *Honours:* Best Independent Producer, USA, 1986. *Memberships:* PRS; MCPS; Musicians' Union. *Leisure interests:* Swimming; Tennis; Holistic science; Woodwork. *Address:* PO Box 2237, St Kilda West, Melbourne, Victoria 3182, Australia.

WILLIAMSON John Robert; b. 1 Nov. 1945, Victoria, Australia. Singer; Songwriter. *Career:* One of Australia's leading singer/songwriters, in a career spanning over 30 years and selling over 2m. Albums; Creative works: 23 albums; Designer of four distinctive Australian flags. *Honours:* 4 Golden Guitars for Album of Yr; 7 Golden Guitars for Biggest Selling Album of Year; 2 Golden Guitars for Male Vocalist of Year; 2 Golden Guitars for Song of Year; 2 Golden Guitars for Heritage Award; 1 Golden Guitar for Video Clip of Year; Indicted to Roll of Renown, 1997; From the Tamworth Songwriter's Asscn: Songmaker Award, 1986; Children's Song of the Year for 'Bushtown' (The Lawnmower Song), 1996; Children's Song of the Year for 'Kitchy Kitchy Koo', 1997; Further awards since 1986 including: NZ Professional Country Music Recording Industry's vote for Best Australian Act; 4 MO Awards for Best Male Country Performer of Previous Years; 2 MO Awards for Best Country Performer; 2 MO Awards for Most Sucessful Attraction of Year; 2 ARIA Awards for Best Australian Country Record, Variety Club Entertainer of Year; Advance Australia Award for contribution to Arts and Environment; Ambassadorship from Advance Australia Foundation; AM (Mem. of the Gen Div of the Order of Aust) for services to Australian Country Music and for stimulating conservation awareness. *Memberships:* Australian Conservation Foundation; Salvation Army; Bush Heritage Fund; Australian National Museum; Country Music Asscn of Australia; Landcare Australia. *Address:* PO Box 399, Epping, NSW 2121, Australia.

WILLIAMSON (John Robert) Graeme; b. Montréal, Québec, Canada. Musician (guitar); Singer; Songwriter. m. Iris Jamieson, 10 June 1995. *Education:* MA, Glasgow University. *Musical Education:* Self-taught. *Career:* Frequent live television CBC (national) television and local television, 1984–85; Radio: Live concert broadcasts and tours, Canada; Retired from live performance, 1985. *Compositions:* Might As Well Be On Mars; Every Man and Every Woman Is A Star; Let Your Light Shine; Rubber Girl. *Recordings:* 3 tracks, album, 1970; Albums with Pukka Orchestra: Pukka Orchestra, 1984; Dear Harry, 1993; Palace of Memory, 1986. *Honours:* Casby Award (Canada), 1984. *Membership:* SOCAN (Canada). *Leisure interest:* Travel. *Address:* 38 Victoria Crescent Rd, Glasgow G12 9DE, Scotland.

WILLIS Gary Glen; b. 28 March 1957, Longview, Texas, USA. Musician (electric bass); Composer. m. Pamela Nichols, 11 April 1991. *Musical Education:* Kiljore Jr College; East Texas State University; North Texas State University. *Career:* Co-founder, co-leader of Tribal Tech, with Scott Henderson, 1983–; Annual tours: USA; Europe; South America; Performed, recorded with: Allan Holdsworth; Wayne Shorter; Hubert Laws. *Recordings:* Albums: Tribal Tech; Spears, 1985; Dr Hee, 1987; Nomad, 1989; Tribal Tech, 1991; Illicit, 1992; Face First, 1993; Reality Check, 1995; No Sweat, 1997; Bent, 1998. *Publications:* Instructional Video: Progressive Basics, 1991; Book: Lessons With The Greats For Bass, 1995. *Leisure interests:* Tennis; Mountain Biking.

WILLOUGHBY Brian; b. 20 Sept. 1949, Glenarm, County Antrim, Northern Ireland. Musician (guitar). m. Christina Onesti, 9 Aug. 1986. *Education:* Degree, French, Spanish and Italian. *Musical Education:* Self-taught. *Career:* Guitarist for: Mary Hopkin; Joe Brown; Roger Whittaker; New World; Brian Connolly; Jim Diamond; The Monks; The Strawbs. *Recordings:* Albums with: Monty Python; The Strawbs; Dave Cousins/ Brian Willoughby; Nanci Griffith; Numerous sessions with other artistes. *Publications:* Guitar reviews, Musicians Only. *Honours:* Gold album, The Monks. *Memberships:* Musicians' Union; Institute of Linguists. *Leisure interests:* Guitar collecting; Car and motorcycle maintenance; Swimming. *Address:* 6 Hall Rd, Isleworth, Middlesex TW7, England.

WILLS Mark, (Daryl Mark Williams); b. 8 Aug. 1973, Cleveland, Tennessee, USA. Country vocalist. *Career:* Won Buckboard Country Music Showcase talent show at 17, leading to regular spot; Continued

there for five years, augmented by demo work in Atlanta area and, eventually, demo work in Nashville; Secured deal with Mercury Records after being spotted at a Buckboard show by songwriter Carson Chamberlain and writer/performer Keith Stegall; The pair produced moderately successful self-titled debut album, 1996; Continued to sell consistently, making regular visits to Billboard singles and albums chart; Took unusual step of covering contemporary R & B hits, Brian McKnight's Back At One and Brandy's Almost Doesn't Count, on Permanently album, 2000. *Recordings include:* Jacob's Ladder, 1996; Places I've Never Been, 1997; I Do (Cherish You), Don't Laugh At Me, 1998; Wish You Were Here, She's In Love, 1999; Back At One, 2000; Albums include: Mark Wills, 1996; Wish You Were Here, 1998; Permanently, 2000; Loving Every Minute, 2001. *Address:* c/o The Country Music Asscn, Nashville, Tennessee, USA. *Internet:* www.markwills.com.

WILSON Allan; b. 5 Sept. 1949, London, England. Conductor. m. 25 Jan. 1986, 2 d. *Musical Education:* State University of New York; Studied trumpet, composition, conducting, London's Royal Academy of Music. *Career:* Teacher, Conducting, orchestral training, State University of New York; Lecture recitals, Britain; USA; Canada; Appearances as trumpet player; Specialist conductor, film soundtrack music; Film credits include: by Colin Towns: The Puppet Master; Fellow Traveller; Wolves of Willoughby Chase; Bellman and True; Knights and Emeralds; by Chris Young: The Dark Half; Hellbound: Hellraiser II; by Basil Polidouris: Lassie; by Loek Dikker: Body Parts; Television music includes: by Colin Towns: Clarissa; Capital City; The Fifteen Streets; Blind Justice. *Recordings include:* Conductor: Many film soundtracks; Classical works by Mozart, Holst, Wagner, with orchestras and ensembles such as: National Studio Orchestra; London Wind Ensemble; Munich Symphony Orchestra; Hungarian State Orchestra; The Mercury Players; Festival Brass of London; Symphonie-Orchester Graunke. *Current Management:* Soundtrack Music Management. *Address:* 22 Ives St, Chelsea, London SW3 2ND, England.

WILSON Ann; b. 19 June 1951, San Diego, California, USA. Singer. 1 d. *Career:* Member, groups Ann Wilson and The Daybreaks; Bordersong; The Army; Renamed White Heart; Later became Heart, 1974–; UK debut, London, 1976; Regular US and international tours with artistes including Queen; Tears For Fears; Michael Bolton; Cheap Trick; Black Crowes; Concerts include: California Jam II Festival, 1978; Bread and Roses Festival, 1981; Benefit concert for local environmental groups, Seattle, 1990; Benefit for Seattle centre for victims of child abuse, 1992; Also member of side project The Lovemongers; Performed with Alice In Chains, animal rights benefit concert, Los Angeles, 1992. *Recordings:* Albums: with Heart: Dreamboat Annie, 1975; Little Queen, 1977; Magazine, 1978; Dog and Butterfly, 1978; Bebe Le Strange, 1980; Private Audition, 1982; Passionworks, 1983; Heart (No. 1, USA), 1985; Bad Animals, 1987; Brigade, 1990; Rock The House Live!, 1991; Desire Walks On, 1993; The Road Home, 1996; Hit singles include: Magic Man, 1976; Barracuda, 1977; Straight On, 1978; Tell It Like It Is, 1981; How Can I Refuse, 1984; What About Love?, 1985; Never, 1985; These Dreams (No. 1, USA), 1986; Nothin' At All, 1986; If Looks Could Kill, 1986; Alone (No. 1, USA), 1987; Who Will You Run To, 1987; There's The Girl, 1988; What About Love, 1988; All I Wanna Do Is Make Love To You, 1990; Stranded, 1990; Will You Be There (In The Morning), 1993; Solo single: The Best Man In The World, from film The Golden Child, 1987; Duet with Robin Zander: Surrender To Me, from film Tequila Sunrise, 1989; with The Lovermongers: Battle of Evermore, from film Singles, 1992; Albums: Whirlygig, 1997; Here is Christmas, 1998; Guest vocalist, Sap (EP), Alice In Chains, 1992; Contributions to: Heats, Smoke, 1998; Renaissance Album, 1998; Love Shouldn't Hurt, 1998; Golden Child, 1998. *Current Management:* Borman Entertainment Inc, 1250 Sixth St, Suite 401, Santa Monica, CA 90401, USA.

WILSON Brian; b. 20 June 1942, Inglewood, California, USA. Musician (bass, keyboards); Singer; Composer. *Career:* Founder member, the Beach Boys, 1961–; Retired from live performance, to concentrate on composing and recording, 1964–; Appearances include: Australian tour, 1964; Headlines Million Dollar Party, Honolulu, 1964; US tour, 1964; Established Brother Records label, 1967; Concert at International Center, Honolulu, 1967; Plays with Beach Boys, Whiskey-A-Go-Go, Los Angeles, 1970; Filmed for NBC Special, 1976; Presenter, Don Kirshner's Second Annual Rock Music Awards, Hollywood, 1976; 15th Anniversary Beach Boys show, 1976; Rejoins band for US concerts, 1989; Solo appearance, China Club, Hollywood, 1991; Documentaries include: Prime Time Live, ABC, 1991; I Just Wasn't Made For These Times, BBC, 1995. *Compositions:* Many hit songs include: Caroline No; Co-writer, California Girls; Good Vibrations; Fun Fun Fun. *Recordings:* Albums include: Surfin' Safari, 1962; Surfer Girl, 1963; Little Deuce Coupe, 1963; Shut Down Vol. 2, 1964; All Summer Long, 1964; Surfin' USA, 1965; Beach Boys Party, 1966; Pet Sounds, 1966; Beach Boys Today!, 1966; Smile, 1967; Surfer Girl, 1967; Smiley Smile, 1967; Wild Honey, 1968; 15 Big Ones, 1976; The Beach Boys Love You, 1977; Solo albums: Brian Wilson, 1988; I Just Wasn't Made For These Times, 1995; Contributor, vocals for film soundtrack Shell Life; Singles include: Surfin' USA; Surfer Girl; Little Deuce Coupe; In My Room;

I Get Around; When I Grow Up To Be A Man; Dance Dance Dance; Producer: Help Me Rhonda; Barbara Ann; Sloop John B; God Only Knows; Good Vibrations; Wouldn't It Be Nice; Friends; Do It Again; I Can Hear Music; Brian Wilson, 1988; Sweet Insanity, 1990; I Just Wasn't Made for These Times, 1995; Orange Crate Art, 1995; Imagination, 1998. *Honours include:* Rock and Roll Hall of Fame, 1988; Special Award of Merit, 1988. *Current Management:* Elliott Lott, Boulder Creek Entertainment Corp, 4860 San Jacinto Circle W, Fallbrook, CA 92028, USA.

WILSON Brian Scott; b. 12 Nov. 1962, Massachusetts, USA. Composer; Conductor; Musician (Jazz Pianist). m. Ruth, 1 s. *Education:* BMus, New England Conservatory; MA, University of Chicago; DMus, University of Arizinia. *Career:* Professor of Music, Composer in Residence, Hartwick College, NY, 1992–; Faculties, Hartwick College Summer Music Festival and Institute in Oneonta. *Recordings:* Orchestral, My Mother's Irises; Wandering The River; The First Sea Shell; The Flat Top Roof; Symphony No. 1, Desert Scenes; Symphony No. 2, Modes of Transportation; Band, Fastfare; Melting Pot; Choral, Jabberwocky; Three Songs of Nature; Joy; Wings; Chamber Music Including, The Avanti Feels Glued to the Road; Sentiments; Tuba Cat Fanfare; The Season; Avinu Malkaynu; Musicals including, The Birds; Speak of The 20's; The Knights; Operas including, Agamemnon; incidental music to Medea; The Bachal. *Honours:* Include, Winner of the International Trombone Asscn Composition Competition, 1998; Fellowship to Composers Conference Center for New Music, Duquesne University; James Madison Flute Choir Composition Competition Prize; ASCAP Distribution Award; Nominated Best Music Director; Phi mu Alpha's Orpheus Award. *Memberships:* Include, American Composers Forum; American Music Center; ASCAP; College Band Directors National Asscn; Conductors Guild; Kappa Kappa Psi; Phi Mu Alpha; Pi Kappa Lambda. *Leisure interest:* Travel. *Address:* 1 Tilton Ave, Oneonta, NY 13820, USA.

WILSON Cassandra; b. Jackson, Mississippi, USA. Jazz Singer. *Musical Education:* Listening to father, Herman B Fowlkes, jazz musician. *Career:* Started playing guitar aged 6; Songwriting at 12; Solo performer as folk and blues singer, turned to jazz; Regular collaborations with saxophonist Steve Coleman; Signed to Blue Note Records. *Recordings:* Albums include: Point of View, 1986; Days Aweigh, 1987; Blue Skies, 1988; Jumpworld, 1990; She Who Weeps, 1991; Blue Light 'Til Dawn, 1993; New Moon Daughter, 1996; Blue Moon Rendezvous, 1998; Traveling Miles, 1999; Also featured vocalist on other artist's works. *Current Management:* Dream Street Management, 1460 Fourth St, Suite 205, Santa Monica, CA 90401, USA.

WILSON Damian Augustine Howitt; b. 11 Oct. 1969, Guildford, Surrey, England. Singer; Songwriter. *Recordings:* Albums: with Landmarq: Solitary Witness, 1992; Infinity Parade, 1993; The Vision Pit, 1995; with Threshold: Wounded Land, 1993; with LaSalle, 1994; Contributions to: Tribute to the Late Joseph T, 1996. *Honours:* Best Vocalist, Classic Rock Society, 1993.

WILSON Dennis Edward; b. 22 July 1952, Greensboro, North Carolina, USA. Musician (trombone). m. Rebecca Elvert, 12 July 1986, 1 s. *Musical Education:* MusB in Education, Berklee College of Music, Boston, 1974. *Career:* Trombonist, Musical director, Lionel Hampton Orchestra, 1974–76; Teacher, Choral director, NY schools, 1976–77; Trombonist arranger, Count Basie Orchestra, 1977–87; Music production manager, Count Basie Enterprises, 1987–; Trombonist, arranger, Frank West Orchestra, 1990–; Also arranger, conductor, Manhattan Transfer, Blee Blop Blues, 1985; Trombonist, Dizzy Gillespie Orchestra, 1988; Creator, executive producer, Count Basie Orchestra Big Band Festival. *Honour:* Grammy Nomination, Manhattan Transfer, 1985. *Membership:* National Asscn of Jazz Educators.

WILSON Gerald Stanley; b. 4 Sept. 1918, Shelby, Mississippi, USA. Musician (trumpet, piano); Arranger; Composer; Orchestrator; Bandleader. m. Josefina Villaseñor, 4 Sept. 1950, 1 s., 3 d. *Musical Education:* Cass Tech, Detroit, Michigan, USA; Private Tutorial. *Career:* Local bands, Detroit; Joined Jimmie Lunceford Orchestra, as trumpeter, arranger, 1939–42; Moved to Los Angeles; Arranger, trumpeter, Les Hite, Benny Carter, Phil Moore; World War II, Joined Count Basie band, trumpeter, arranger, 1948–49; Trumpeter for Dizzy Gillespie, 1949; Arranged for artists including: Ella Fitzgerald; Nancy Wilson; Ray Charles; Bobby Darin; Dinah Washington; Carmen McRae; Sarah Vaughn; Benny Goodman; Cab Calloway; The Platters; Eartha Kitt; Billy Eckstine; Jean Luc Ponty; Performed, with Al Hirt, Carnegie Hall, 1965; Musical director, Redd Foxx Variety series, 1978; Leader, composer, arranger, own orchestra; Member, faculty, University of California, Los Angeles; Festivals include: Chicago Jazz, 1994; Playboy Jazz, 1995. *Compositions include:* Royal Suite In Seven Movements; Imagine My Frustration, featured Broadway hit: Sophisticated Ladies; Piece for symphony orchestra, 1972; filmscores include: Where The Boys Are, 1960; Love Has Many Faces, 1960; Paco, 1964; Viva Tirado (recorded by El Chicano), no 1, 1968. *Recordings include:* Lomelin, 1981; Jessica, 1982; Calafia, 1984; Jenna, 1989; State Street Sweet, 1994; Suite Memories, 1996; Theme

from Monterey, 1998. *Honours:* 2 Grammy nominations, 1963, 1964; American Jazz Masters Fellowship Grant, 1990; Paul Robeson Award; Music archived by Library of Congress, Washington DC. *Memberships:* AFM; NARAS; ASMAC; Los Angeles Jazz Society; Board Governors, National Academy, Recording Arts and Sciences.

WILSON Joe Lee; b. 22 Dec. 1935, Bristow, Oklahoma, USA. Jazz Singer; Composer; Musician (guitar, piano, percussion). m. Jill Carlyon Christopher, 13 Dec. 1976, 2 d. *Musical Education:* Piano lessons age 5–10; Sang Baptist Gospel church, age 5–16; Major in voice, Los Angeles Conservatory of Music, 1955; City College, 1956–58. *Career:* Played with: Sonny Rollins; Freddie Hubbard; Lee Morgan; Jackie MacLean; Roy Brooks; Pharoah Sanders; Frank Foster; The Collective Black Artists' Ensemble; Roy Haynes; Milt Jackson; Rashied Ali; Miles Davis; Archie Shepp; Innovator, the Jazz Loft Movement, 1973–78; Organized Live Loft Festivals; Appeared Newport New York Jazz Festival, 1973; Numerous television shows include: Showcase '68, NBC-TV; DJ, broadcasting live jazz scenes; Leader, own jazz band; Travelled to Europe; Middle East; Africa; Far East; Played Ronnie Scott's, 1978; Clubs, concerts, festivals, France, England; Humphrey Lyttelton's BBC Radio programme; Special guest, Satchmo concert, Royal Festival Hall; Tonight In Town, BBC1 TV; Performed with Dizzy Gillespie, Marciac Festival, 1986. *Compositions:* Nice and Easy; Come and See; The Shadow; Lyrics to Milestones; Blues Ain't Nothing; Sphirlov; Children's Suite – Makes You Feel You're Real. *Recordings:* Albums: Living High Off Nickels and Dimes; Mr Joe Lee Wilson In The Great City; Without A Song; What Would It Be Without You; Things Gotta Change, Archie Shepp; Secrets From The Sun; Shout For Trane; with Archie Shepp: A Touch of The Blues; Cry of My People; The Shadow; Acid Rain. *Honours:* 5 Downbeat magazine awards; ASCAP Song award; NBC Showcase winner, 1968. *Leisure interests:* Tai Chi Chu'an; Antiques and stones; Fishing; Dowsing laylines; Cooking original recipes. *Address:* 41 rue St Louis En l'Ile; 75004 Paris, France.

WILSON Mari; b. 29 Sept. 1957, London, England. Singer. *Musical Education:* Self-taught. *Career:* Six hit singles, hit album, 1981–84; Television and concert tours: UK; Europe; USA; with 12 piece band the Wilsations; Jazz/pop career includes: Regular Ronnie Scott's Clubs appearances; Theatre, television, radio, DJ on Greater London Radio; Theatre acting: Sweet Charity; Chainsaw Manicure. *Recordings:* Hit singles: Just What I've Always Wanted, 1982; Cry Me A River, 1983; Theme tune to Dance With A Stranger, 1984; Albums: Show People, 1983; The Rhythm Romance, 1992. *Honours:* Nomination, Best British Female Artist, 1982. *Memberships:* Musicians' Union; Equity; PRS; MCPS. *Leisure interests:* Writing; Working out; Swimming; Spiritual reading; Cooking. *Current Management:* Music: BPR, 36 Como St, Romford, Essex RM7 7DR, England; Acting: Macfarlane Chard Associates, 7/8 Little Turnstile, London WC1V 7DX, England.

WILSON Mary; b. 3 June 1944, Greenville, Mississippi, USA. Singer; Entertainer. m. Pedro A Ferrer, 11 May 1973, 2 s. (1 deceased), 1 d. *Musical Education:* Glee Club and Choir in High School; Professional vocal lessons, 1970–92. *Career:* Member, Supremes, 1961–77; World tours; 15 appearances on Ed Sullivan Show; Only American act with 5 consecutive number 1 hits; 12 number 1 hits; Broke record for sales; Broke racial barriers for blacks and women; Epitomized the Motown Sound. *Recordings:* Where Did Our Love Go, 1964; Baby Love, 1964; Come See About Me, 1964; Stop! In The Name of Love, 1965; Back In My Arms Again, 1965; I Hear A Symphony, 1965; My World Is Empty Without You, 1965; You Can't Hurry Love, 1966; You Keep Me Hangin' On, 1966; Love Is Here and Now You're Gone, 1967; The Happening, 1967; Reflections, 1967; Love Child, 1968; I'm Gonna Make You Love Me (with the Temptations), 1968; Someday We'll Be Together, 1969; Up The Ladder To The Roof, 1970; Stoned Love, 1970; River Deep Mountain High (with the Four Tops), 1970; Nathan Jones, 1971; Floy Joy, 1972; Solo: Red Hot, 1979; Walk The Line, 1992; U, 1995. *Publications:* Dreamgirl: My Life As A Supreme, 1986; Supreme Faith: Someday We'll Be Together, 1990. *Honours:* Star, Hollywood Walk of Fame; Inductee, Rock 'N' Roll Hall of Fame, 1988; Several awards, recording recognition from music industry; Organizations include NAACP. *Leisure interests:* Cooking; Skiing; Tennis; Reading; Dancing; Bowling. *Current Management:* Duryea Entertainment. *Address:* 54 Danbury Rd, Suite 367, Ridgefield, CT 06877, USA.

WILSON Nancy; b. 16 March 1954, San Francisco, California, USA. Singer; Musician (guitar). m. Cameron Crowe. *Career:* Member, Bordersong; Solo folk singer; Member, US rock group Heart, 1974–; UK debut, London, 1976; Regular US and international tours with artists including Queen; Tears For Fears; Michael Bolton; Black Crowes; Cheap Trick; Major concerts include: California Jam II Festival, 1978; Bread and Roses Festival, Berkeley, 1981; Benefit concert for local environmental groups, Seattle, 1990; Also member, side project The Lovemongers; Film appearances: Fast Times At Ridgemount High; The Wild Life. *Recordings:* Albums: Dreamboat Annie, 1975; Little Queen, 1977; Magazine, 1978; Dog and Butterfly, 1978; Bebe Le Strange, 1980; Private Audition, 1982; Passionworks, 1983; Heart (No. 1, USA), 1985; Bad Animals, 1987;

Brigade, 1990; Rock The House Live!, 1991; Desire Walks On, 1993; The Road Home, 1996; Hit singles: Magic Man, 1976; Barracuda, 1977; Straight On, 1978; Tell It Like It Is, 1981; How Can I Refuse, 1983; What About Love?, 1985; Never, 1985; These Dreams (No. 1, USA), 1986; Nothin' At All, 1986; If Looks Could Kill, 1986; Alone (No. 1, USA), 1987; Who Will You Run To, 1987; There's The Girl, 1987; What About Love, 1988; All I Wanna Do Is Make Love To You, 1990; Stranded, 1990; Will You Be There (In The Morning), 1993; Duet with Mike Reno: Almost Paradise, from film Footloose, 1984; with the Lovermongers: Battle of Evermore, from film Singles, 1992; Albums: Here is Christmas, 1998; Whirlygig, 1998; Contributions to: Simpsons, Yellow Album (vocals), 1998; Golden Child, Golden Child, 1998. *Current Management:* Borman Entertainment Inc, 1250 Sixth St, Suite 401, Santa Monica, CA 90401, USA.

WILSON Peter, (Emerson Peters); b. 28 July 1956, Newport, Isle of Wight, England. Musician (piano); Composer; Arranger; Teacher. *Musical Education:* Royal Artillery Band, 1972–77; City of Leeds College of Music, 1977–78; Trinity College of Music, London, 1978–82. *Career:* Keyboards for Helen Shapiro and Neil Reid including television and radio; Freelance pianist, ballet, dance, cocktail, bands, 1982–; First keyboards for Robin Cousins tour of UK, Electric Ice, 1984; First keyboards for rock opera, Jeanne, and musical, Judy, 1985; Keyboards for Bruce Forsyth, Val Doonican, Michael Barrymore, other cabaret acts, 1985–; Teacher, Blackheath Conservatoire of Music, 1981–83; Member, Tower Hamlets Strings Project, 1981–92; Teacher, Arts Educational College, 1983–85; Director, Greenwich Strings Project, 1993-. *Compositions:* Overture and suite for string orchestra; 1 Symphony for string orchestra, 2 horns and oboe; The Pirate Suite for strings and piano; The Wild West Suite for strings and piano; 3 piano suites, 1 piano sonata and many small pieces. *Publications:* Stringpops; Ragtime Preludes; Go Canon Go; Palm Court Trios; Fanfares; The 2001 Piano Collection. *Honours:* 2 awards of The Van Someren-Godfrey Gold Medal, Royal Artillery Band; Hannah Brooke Prize for piano at TCM; Scholarship at TCM, 1981–82; LTCL, LGSM, AMusTCL. *Memberships:* Musicians' Union; Radio Society of Great Britain. *Leisure interests:* Amateur radio (call sign G0NGP); Model Making; Badminton; Reading; Walking. *Address:* 74 Coleraine Rd, Blackheath, London SE3 7PE, England.

WILSON Reuben; b. 9 April 1935, Mounds, Oklahoma, USA. Musician (Hammond B3 Organ). *Career:* Tour with Guru and Jazzmatazz II, 1995. *Recordings:* Ronnie's Bonnie; Inner City Blues; We're In Love; Walk On By; On Broadway; Love Bug; Groovy Situation; Blue Mode; Set Us Free; Cisco Kid; Bad Stuff; Sweet Life; Gotta Get Your Own; Straight No Chaser; The Lost Grooves; Giant Steps; Hot Rod; Blue Breaks Vol. 2; Orange Peel; Shades of Red; Hip Hop Bop! NY Funkies; Live at SOB's; Organ Donor; Organic Grooves II; Down With It; Sampled Recordings: Hand On The Torch: I Got It Goin' On, US3; Ill Matic: Memory Lane: NAS; Inner City Blues; Tribe Called Quest. *Current Management:* c/o Preston Powell, Jazzateria Inc. *Address:* 112 W 72nd St, #2F, New York, NY 10023, USA.

WILSON Roger; b. 22 July 1961, Leicester, England. Folk Musician; Songwriter. Divorced, 1 d. *Education:* BA, Graphic Design. *Career:* Solo, 1986–; Urban Folk, 1990–; Touring with the House Band, 1995–98; Wood, Wilson, Carthy, 1997-. *Compositions:* Ultrasound, The Zakynthos Jig; Payday; Indian Tea; Sick of the Working Life; Many Re-workings of Folk Songs Including Hey Joe; Delia; Fair and Tender Lovers; Ramble Away, Two Sisters. *Recordings:* The Palm of your Hand; Stark Naked; Wood, Wilson, Carthy; Urban Folk Volumns I and II; Rockall; October Song. *Leisure interests:* Golf; Chess; Music; Tennis; Gardening. *Address:* 71 Lothair road, Leicester, LE2 7QE, England.

WIMBISH Doug; b. 22 Sept. 1956, Hartford, Connecticut, USA. Musician (Bass). *Career:* Joined Living Colour, 1993. *Recordings:* Singles: Leave It Alone, 1993; Nothingness, 1993; Ausländer, 1993; Bi, 1993; Sunshine of Your Love, 1994; Albums: Stain, 1993; Pride, 1995.

WINDRICH Erik Rudolph; b. 5 Feb. 1960, Netherlands. Singer; Songwriter; Musician (multi-instrumentalist). 2 d., 2 step-s., 1 step-d. *Education:* University entrance (South Africa). *Career:* Evoid, 1982–86; Campus tour, 1984; Operation Hunger, Ellis Park Stadium, South Africa, 1985; Gold selling debut album, 3 hit singles, 1987–90; European tours; Regional radio UK, with The Vision Thing, 1992–; Work in progress with Ear Productions. *Compositions:* with Evoid: Shadows; Taximan; I Am A Fadget; with The Vision Thing: Fist In The Air; Wyah; Brother Sistem. *Recordings:* with Evoid: Evoid; Here Comes The Rot; A Space In Which To Create; with The Vision Thing: The Vision Thing. *Honours:* Sarie Award, South Africa, 1984. *Memberships:* SAMRO; PRS; PPL; Musicians' Union; COBRA. *Leisure interests:* Reading; Swimming; Cycling. *Current Management:* Sack The Management. *Address:* PO Box 572, Harrow, Middlesex HA1 3XA, England.

WINK Josh, (Joshua Winkelman, Winx, Size 9, Winc); b. Philadelphia, Pennsylvania, USA. Prod.; Remixer; DJ. *Career:* After meeting King Britt, duo recorded Tribal Confusion for Strictly Rhythm label; Co-founder: Ovum

Records (with King Britt); World-wide DJ with club residencies in Philadelphia, New York and London; Collaborations: King Britt; Ursula Rucker; Remixed: Slam; Mood II Swing; Moby. *Recordings:* Singles: Tribal Confusion (as E-Culture), 1991; I'm Ready (as Size 9), Hypnotizin', Higher State of Consciousness, Don't Laugh (as Winx), 1995; Thoughts of a Tranced Love, 1996; How's Your Evening So Far? (with Lil' Louis), 2000. *Current Management:* Elite Music Management, PO Box 3261, Brighton, East Sussex, England BN2 4WA.

WINN Tony Ellis; b. 15 Aug. 1949, Ilford, Essex, England. Singer; Songwriter; Performance Poet; Musician (guitar, banjo). m. Rebecca Jane Stewart, 30 May 1987, 2 s. *Career:* Member, 2 touring bands; Currently mainly solo performances at folk clubs, festivals, arts centres around UK; Appearances include: TV AM; Live local radio performances; Recordings played on local and national radio; Formed new band Mamwf, 1995. *Recordings:* Albums: Between Venus and Mars; Short Stories; Solo Album: Mice On A Cheese; Singles: Motorway Maniac/Rubbish; Shadows In The Night/Secretly Admiring You. *Memberships:* Musicians' Union. *Leisure interests:* Amateur theatre; Gardening; Home. *Current Management:* Freefall Records, 21 London Rd, Kelvedon, Essex CO5 9AR, England.

WINSTON George; b. 1949, Hart, Michigan, USA. Solo Musician (piano, guitar). *Career:* Solo piano, guitar concerts; Producer, recordings by Hawaiian slack key guitarists for Dancing Cat Records. *Recordings:* Solo piano albums: Ballads and Blues, 1972; Autumn, 1980; Winter Into Spring, 1982; December, 1982; Summer, 1991; Forest, 1994; Soundtracks: The Velveteen Rabbit (solo piano with narration by Meryl Streep), 1985; Sadako and The Thousand Paper Cranes (solo guitar with narration by Liv Ullmann) 1995; Linus and Lucy The Music of Vince Guaraldi, 1996; Plains, 1999. *Current Management:* Dancing Cat Productions, Inc. *Address:* PO Box 639, Santa Cruz, CA 95061, USA.

WINTER Edgar; b. 28 Dec. 1946, Beaumont, Texas, USA. Musician (multi-instrumentalist); Composer. m. Monica Winter, 23 March 1979. *Musical Education:* Self-taught. *Career:* Member, various groups: Black Plague; Johnny Winter's group (brother); Founder, White Trash, 1971; Founder, the Edgar Winter Group, 1972; Session musician with: Meat Loaf, Dan Hartman, Bette Midler, Tina Turner, 1981-. *Recordings:* Albums: with Johnny Winter: Second Winter, 1970; Johnny Winter And..., 1970; with White Trash: Edgar Winter's White Trash, 1971; Roadwork, 1972; with the Edgar Winter Group: They Only Come Out At Night, 1973; Shock Treatment, 1974; The Edgar Winter Group With Rick Derringer, 1975; Recycled, 1977; The Edgar Winter Album, 1979; Standing On Rock, 1981; Solo album: Entrance, 1975; Jasmine Nightdreams, 1975; Not a Kid Anymore, 1994; The Real Deal, 1996; Live in Japan, 1998; Winter Blues, 1999; Singles include: with White Trash: Keep Playin' That Rock and Roll!; I Can't Turn You Loose; with the Edgar Winter Group: Frankenstein; Free Ride; Hangin' Around; River's Risin'; Easy Street. *Honours:* Grammy Award Nomination. *Leisure interest:* Music. *Current Management:* Hooker Enterprises International, 5958 Bosch Dr., Malibu, CA 90265, USA.

WINTER Johnny (John Dawson III); b. 23 Feb. 1944, Beaumont, Texas, USA. Singer; Songwriter; Musician (guitar, harmonica); Record Prod. *Career:* Member, various bands, including Black Plague; Gene Terry and the Downbeats; Founder, leader, own band, 1968–; Appearances include: Newport '69 Festival, 1969; Newport Jazz Festival, 1969; Texas International Pop Festival, Dallas, 1969; Atlanta International Pop Festival, 1970; Royal Albert Hall, 1970; Bath Festival, 1970; San Francisco Blues Festival, 1987; Riverwalk Blues Fest, Fort Lauderdale, 1988; Highway 61 Revisited, 1992; Live In NYC '97, New York, 1997. *Recordings:* Albums: The Progressive Blues Experiment, 1969; Johnny Winter, 1969; The Johnny Winter Story, 1969; Second Winter, 1970; Johnny Winter And/Live, 1971; Nothin' But The Blues, 1977; White Hot and Blue, 1978; Raisin' Cain, 1980; Guitar Slinger, 1984; Serious Business, 1985; Third Degree, 1985; Winter of '88, 1988; Let Me In, 1991; with Edgar Winter (brother): Entrance, 1970; White Trash, 1971; Roadwork, 1972; Jasmine Nightdreams, 1975; Together, 1976; Together Live, 1977; with Muddy Waters: Hard Again, 1977; I'm Ready, 1977; King Bee, 1980; Guest musician, Mr Lucky, John Lee Hooker, 1991; Live In NYC '97, 1998. *Honours:* Gold disc, Johnny Winter and – Live, 1974. *Memberships:* BMI; Musicians' Union. *Current Management:* Slatus Management, 208 E 51st St, New York, NY 10022, USA.

WINTER Paul Theodore; b. 31 Aug. 1939, Altoona, Pennsylvania, USA. Musician (saxophone); Composer; Bandleader; Recording Artist. m. Chez Liley, 1 Sept. 1991. *Education:* BA, English composition, Northwestern University. *Musical Education:* Private studies with John Monti, Joe Allard. *Career:* Concert, recording artist, 1961–; Performed 2,300 concerts, 37 countries; Recorded 31 albums; Paul Winter Sextet won Intercollegiate Jazz Festival, 1961; State Department tour, 23 Latin American countries, 1962; Founded Paul Winter Consort, 1967; Founded Living Music Records, 1980; Played numerous environmental events including Global Forum, Oxford, 1988; Global Forum, Moscow, 1990;

Earth Summit, Rio, 1992; Global Forum, Kyoto, 1993. *Recordings include:* The Paul Winter Sextet, 1961; Jazz Meets the Bossa Nova, 1962; Jazz Premiere. Washington, 1963, NewJazz on Campus, 1963, Jazz Meets the Folk Song, 1963; The Song of Ipanema, 1963; Rio, 1963; The Winter COnsort, 1968; Something in the Wind, 1969; Road, 1970; Icarus, 1972; Common Ground, 1977; Callings, 1980; Earth Mass, 1981; Sunsinger, 1983; Concert for the Earth, 1984; Canyon, 1985; Wintersong, 1986; Whales Alive, 1987; Earthbeat, 1988; Wolf Eyes, 1989; Earth: Voices of a Planet, 1990; Solstice Live, 1992; Spanish Angel, 1993; Prayer For The Wild Things, 1994; Canyon Lullaby, 1997; Brazilian Days, 1998; Celtic Solstice, 1999. *Honours include:* Grammy Awards, 1993, 1994, 1999; Global 500 Award, United Nations; Award of Excellence from UN's Environmental Programme; Joseph Wood Krutch Medal, US Humane Society; Alumni Merit Award, Northwestern University, 1996; Hon. DHL, Juniata College; Governor's Distinguished Arts Award, State of Pennsylvania. *Current Management:* International Music Network, 2 Main St, Fourth Floor, Gloucester, MA 01930, USA. *Address:* Living Music, PO Box 72, Litchfield, CT 06759, USA.

WINTERHART Paul; b. 19 Sept. 1971, London, England. Musician (Drums). *Career:* Joined The Objects of Desire; Became The Kays and then Kula Shaker; Numerous TV appearances and live festival gigs. *Recordings:* Singles: Tattva, 1996; Hey Dude, 1996; Govinda, 1996; Hush, 1997; Sound of Drums, 1998; Albums: K, 1996; Peasants, Pigs and Astronauts, 1999.

WINTHER Jens; b. 29 Oct. 1960, Næstved, Denmark. Musician (trumpet); Composer; Bandleader. m. Trine Ulla Abildgård, 2 s., 2 d. *Musical Education:* Self-taught. *Career:* with Ernie Wilkins: Almost Big Band, 1980; Solo trumpeter, Danish Radio Big Band, 1982–89; Moved to New York to join a two-year Jazz Composers Workshop and played with groups and musicians including: Toshiko Akoishi Band, Eddie Palmieri, Kenny Barron, Max Roach, Tito Puente, Marie Bauza Orchestra, George Mraz, Xavier Cugat Orchestra, 1989–91; Major projects (writing and playing) for Danish Radio Big Band; Own music played with WDR, SWR, HR, NDR, RIAS, big bands in Germany, Finland, Sweden, Norway; Fulltime Composer and Trumpet Soloist, 1991-. *Compositions:* The Beginning, Now, The Future, Beyond, 1996; The Four Elements, 1996 Facing The Sun, 1998; Angels for choir and big band, 1998; The Eagle, 1999; Pluto and Beyond, 2001. *Recordings:* JW/Danish Radio Big Band, 1991; with JW Group: Scorpio Dance with Al Foster, 1991; The Planets, 1995; The 4 Elements, big band composition, 1996, CD, 1997; Pieces for symphony orchestra; The 4 Elements, 1998; The Escape, 1998; with Jens Winther Trio, Standards, 2000. *Honours:* International Competition of Jazz Themes in Monaco, First Prize, 1990, 1991, 1996, Second Prize, 1988, 1997; Grammy for Best Danish Jazz Recording of the Year, 1996; Award Danish National Arts Foundation, 1998. *Membership:* DJBFA. *Leisure interests:* Theosophy; Meditation; Diving. *Address:* Sotoften 6B, 2680 Solrod Strand, Denmark.

WINWOOD Muff (Mervyn); b. 15 June 1943, Birmingham, England. Musician (bass); Music Co Exec. *Career:* Folk/blues soloist; Member, Muff-Woody Jazz Band (with brother Steve); Rhythm and Blues Quartet; Member, Spencer Davis Group, 1963–67; Concerts include: National Jazz and Blues Festival, 1965, 1966; Grand Gala du Disques, Amsterdam, 1966; British tours with: The Rolling Stones, 1965; The Who, 1966; The Hollies, 1967; Management Executive, West End Promotions; Executive, CBS Records; Currently Managing Director, Sony Soho Square (S²) Records, London. *Recordings:* Albums: Their First LP, 1966; The Second Album, 1966; Autumn '66, 1966; Singles include: Strong Love, 1965; Keep On Running (No. 1, UK), 1966; Somebody Help Me (No. 1, UK), 1966; Gimme Some Lovin', 1966; I'm A Man, 1967; Producer, Steve Winwood: 20th Century Masters, album, 1999. *Honour:* Carl Alan Award, Most Outstanding Group, 1966. *Current Management:* Sony Soho Square Records, 10 Great Marlborough St, London W1V 2LP, England.

WINWOOD Steve; b. 12 May 1948, Birmingham, Warwickshire, England. Musician (keyboards, guitar); Vocalist. *Career:* Founder member, Spencer Davis Group, 1963–67; Performances include: National Jazz and Blues Festival, 1965, 1966; Grand Gala du Disques, Amsterdam, 1966; British tours with The Rolling Stones, 1965; The Who, 1966; The Hollies, 1967; Traffic, 1967–68; Blind Faith, 1969; Concerts include: Hyde Park, 1969; Madison Square Garden, 1969; Rejoined Traffic, 1970–75; Concerts include: Zurich Rock Festival, 1968; Hollywood Festival, 1970; Headliners, Reading Festival, 1973; Solo artiste, 1977–; ARMS benefit concert, Royal Albert Hall, 1983; US tour, with Robert Cray, 1991. *Recordings:* Albums: with The Spencer Davis Group: Their First LP, 1966; The Second Album, 1966; Autumn '66, 1966; with Traffic: Mr Fantasy, 1968; Traffic, 1968; John Barleycorn Must Die, 1970; The Low Spark of High Heeled Boys, 1972; When The Eagle Flies, 1974; with Blind Faith: Blind Faith (No. 1, UK and USA), 1969; Solo albums: Steve Winwood, 1977; Arc of a Diver, 1981; Talking Back To The Night, 1982; Back In The High Life, 1986; Refugees of The Heart, 1990; Junction Seven, 1997; Singles include: with Spencer Davis Group: Keep On Running (No. 1, UK), 1966; Somebody Help Me,

1966; Gimme Some Lovin', 1966; I'm A Man, 1967; with Traffic: Paper Sun, 1967; Hole In My Shoe, 1967; Solo: Freedom Overspill, 1986; Roll With It, 1989; One and Only Man, 1990; I Will Be Here, 1991; Reach for the Light, 1995; Spy in the House of Love, 1997; Solo include: Higher Love, 1986; The Finer Things, 1987; Valerie, 1987; Roll With It (No. 1, USA), 1988; Don't You Know What The Night Can Do, 1988; Holding On, 1989; One and Only Man, 1989. *Honours include:* Grammy Awards: Record of the Year, Best Pop Vocal Performance, Higher Love, 1987; Gold discs. *Address:* Helter Skelter, Third Floor, 18 Bond St, Brighton BN1 1RD, England.

WIRE Nicky, (Nicky Jones); b. 20 Jan. 1969, Tredegar, Gwent, Wales. Musician (Bass). *Career:* Member, Manic Street Preachers. *Recordings:* Singles: New Art Riot EP, 1990; You Love Us, 1991; Motorcycle Emptiness, 1992; Theme From M.A.S.H., 1992; From Despair To Where, 1993; La Tristessa Durera, 1993; Roses In The Hospital, 1993; She Is Suffering, 1994; A Design for Life, 1996; Everything Must Go, 1996; If You Tolerate This Your Children Will Be Next, 1998; The Everlasting, 1998; You Stole The Sun From My Heart, 1999; Tsunami, 1999; Albums: Generation Terrorists, 1992; Gold Against The Soul, 1993; The Holy Bible, 1994; Everything Must Go, 1996; This Is My Truth, Tell Me Yours, 1998.

WISE Denny; b. 12 Sept. 1947, Bedford, Bedfordshire, England. Bandleader; Vocalist; Musician; Composer. m. Teresa Wise, 16 Aug. 1955, 1 s., 1 d. *Education:* Intermediate, Leicester Collge of Art and Technology. *Musical Education:* Piano and vocal lessons. *Career:* Radio appearances include: BBC; Capital Radio; Local stations; Television appearances in Germany. *Recordings:* Wise One; Time; with Marian Davies, A Toast To Gilbert O'Sullivan (Denny Wise Sings). *Publications:* Wise One; Love In The Night; Where Did We Go Wrong. *Memberships:* Musicians' Union; Variety and Allied Entertainments Council. *Leisure interests:* Music; Swimming; Sport; Reading. *Current Management:* Denny Wise Organisation. *Address:* 65 Shawley Way, Epsom Downs, Surrey KT18 5PD, England.

WISEFIELD Laurence Mark (Laurie); b. London, England. Musician (guitar, electric and acoustic, slide, banjo); Vocalist; Songwriter. m. Patricia France Rousseau, 26 May 1986. *Musical Education:* Self-taught. *Career:* Formed group Home, 1971–73; Joined Al Stewart Band, 1973; Member, group Wishbone Ash, 1974–86; Joined Tina Turner Band, 1987; Solo performance, Night of the Guitars; Tours: Joe Cocker, Night Calls tour; Tom Jones Show; Roger Chapman Band, 1991; Eros Ramazzotti, 1994; 14 month world tour with Tina Turner, Break Every Rule Tour, including live album, video, Christmas special, Live In Rio, numerous television appearances. *Recordings:* 3 albums with Home, 1971–73; 9 studio albums, 2 live albums, with Wishbone Ash; Live album with Tina Turner; Albums: Night of Guitars; UNO, Roger Chapman. *Honours:* Platinum, Gold albums. *Memberships:* Musicians' Union; PRS; MCPS; PAMRA. *Leisure interests:* Martial arts. *Address:* c/o Loz Ltd, 56 Forest Court, Snaresbrook, London E11 1PL, England.

WISEMAN Debbie; b. 10 May 1963, London, England. Composer; Conductor. m. Tony Wharmby, 21 Sept. 1987. *Education:* Saturday Exhibitioner, Trinity College of Music, 1977–81; Kingsway Princeton/ Morley College, 1979–81; GGSM, Guildhall School of Music and Drama, 1984. *Career:* Freelance composer and conductor. *Compositions:* Music for film and television productions including: Wilde; Tom and Viv; Haunted; The Guilty; Lighthouse; Warriors; Female Perversions; The Dying of The Light; The Good Guys; The Upper Hand; The Churchills; The Second Russian Revolution; Little Napoleons; Children's Hospital; What Did You Do In The War, Auntie?; The Cuban Missile Crisis; Vet's School; The Missing Postman; Tom's Midnight Garden; My Uncle Silas, 2001; Othello, 2001. *Recordings:* Wilde; Tom and Viv; Haunted; Lighthouse; Special performance of original composition with The Debbie Wiseman Collection, St John's Smith Square, London, 1989; Wilde, 1997; Featured works on BBC Radio 3 series The Music Machine and Every Note Paints A Picture; Tom's Midnight Garden; Absolute Truth; The Fairy Tales of Oscar Wilde. *Honours:* David Taylor Memorial Prize, Trinity College of Music, 1981; Television and Radio Industries Club Award for TV Theme Music of the Year (The Good Guys), 1993; Nominated for Rank Film Laboratories Award for Creative Originality, 1994; Women in Film and Television Awards; Ivor Novello Award Nomination, 1996, Royal Television Society Award Nomination, 1996, for Death of Yugoslavia; Wilde nominated for an Ivor Novello Award, 1998; Royal Television Society Award, Warriors, 2000. *Memberships:* Performing Right Society; British Academy of Film and Television Arts; Musicians' Union; British Academy of Composers and Songwriters. *Leisure interest:* Snooker. *Current Management:* Music Makers International, Crest House, 102–104 Church Rd, Teddington, Middlesex, England.

WISNIAK Alain; b. 23 Sept. 1947, Boulogne, Seine, France. Composer; Arranger; Prod. m. Mariline Raichenbach, 25 March 1975, 1 s., 1 d. *Musical Education:* Marguerite Long piano school; Harmony with André Hodeir. *Career:* Musician for sessions and tours with major French pop artists. *Recordings:* Show theme for television series Maguy; Producer, composer,

Cerrone's Supernature album; Soundtracks for films: La Femme Publique; L'Année Des Méduses; On Peut Toujours Rever; Victoire De La Musique, 1992; Medaille De La SACEM. *Memberships:* Sociétaire Définitif; SACEM. *Leisure interest:* Catamaran sailing. *Current Management:* Tralala Music, 14 Blvd Emile Augier, 75116 Paris, France. *Address:* 16 rue Paira, 92190 Meudon, France.

WITHERS Bill; b. 4 July 1938, Slab Fork, West Virginia, USA. Singer; Songwriter. m. Denise Nicholas. *Career:* Began work with Ford, IBM, Lockheed Aircraft Corporation; Recording artiste, 1970–; Appearances include: British tour, 1988; Summer Jazz Explosion '92, 1992; Valley Forge Music Fair, 1992; 2 tribute concerts for Eddie Kendricks, organized by Bobby Womack, California, 1992. *Recordings:* Albums: Just As I Am, 1971; Still Bill, 1972; Bill Withers Live At Carnegie Hall, 1973; The Best of Bill Withers, 1975; Making Music, 1975; Naked and Warm, 1976; Menagerie, 1977; 'Bout Love, 1979; Bill Withers Greatest Hits, 1981, 1988; Watching You, Watching Me, 1985; Ain't No Sunshine, 1997; Top Bill, 1999; Singles include: Ain't No Sunshine, 1971; Grandma's Hands, 1971; Lean On Me (No. 1, USA), 1972; Use Me, 1972; with Grover Washington: Just The Two of Us, 1981; with Ralph McDonald: In The Name of Love, 1984; Lovely Day, 1988. *Honours:* Grammy Awards: Best R & B Song, 1982, 1988; Gold discs for: Still Bill, 1972; Menagerie, 1977; Lean On Me, 1987. *Address:* c/o Associated Booking Corporation, 1995 Broadway, Suite 501, New York, NY 10023, USA.

WITHERS Pick; b. 4 April 1948, Leicester, England. Musician (Drums). *Career:* Member, Dire Straits; Obtained major label deal and subsequent management contract; Support slot on Talking Heads European Tour, 1978; Numerous headlining tours and TV appearances; Left band, 1982. *Recordings:* Singles: Sultans of Swing, 1978; Making Movies, 1980; Albums: Sultans of Swing, 1978; Communiqué, 1979; Making Movies, 1980; Love Over Gold, 1982.

WITTER Rick; b. 23 Nov. 1972, Stockport, Cheshire, England. Singer. *Career:* Two Top of The Pops appearances; Reading Festival; Four British tours; Three European tours; Roskilde '95 (Denmark); Sellout Far East tours; Various appearances on music programmes; MTV live concert; Extensive press coverage. *Recordings:* Singles: Mark/Casino Girl; Dolphin; Speakeasy; Ocean Pie; Disco Down; Devil in Your Shoes; She Left Me on Friday; Heroes; Albums: Change Giver, 1995; Maximum High, 1996; Let It Ride, 1998. *Honours:* Gold disc, 25,000 sales: Changegiver. *Memberships:* PRS; Musicians' Union. *Leisure interests:* Smoking; Sleeping; Music. *Current Management:* Cut Throat Management; Polydor. *Address:* PO Box 77, Coventry CV7 9Y2, England.

WITTMAN William; b. 16 Sept. 1952, Richmond-on-Thames, Surrey, England. Record Prod. m. Barbara Solomon, 23 Aug. 1975, 1 s. *Career:* Mixer, record producer, New York, 1978–87; RCA Records, 1987–90; CBS Records, 1990-. *Recordings:* As producer include: with Cyndi Lauper: She's So Unusual, 1982; Hat Full of Stars, 1992; 12 Deadly Cyns, 1995; with Graham Parker: Steady Nerves, 1985; Passion Is No Ordinary Word, 1993; with Fixx: Calm Animals, 1988; Ink, 1991. *Membership:* NARAS.

WOBBLE Jah, (John Wardle); b. London, England. Musician (bass). *Career:* Member, Public Image Ltd (PIL), 1978–80; Founder, Human Condition; Jah Wobble's Invaders of The Heart. *Composition:* The River, Ku-cheng concerto performed by the Royal Liverpool Philharmonic Orchestra. *Recordings:* Albums: with PIL: Public Image Ltd, 1978; Metal Box, 1979; Second Edition, 1980; Solo: Take Me to God, 1994; Heaven and Earth, 1995; The Inspiration of William Blake, 1996; Requiem, 1997; Umbra Sumus, 1998; Celtic Poets, 1998; Deep Space, 1999. *Current Management:* c/o 30 Hertz, PO Box 11177, London E2 0DS, England.

WOIWOD Bill (William); b. 27 Oct. 1919, London, England. Musician (clarinet, bass clarinet, flute, alto flute, piccolo). m. Joan Jenner, 8 July 1950. *Musical Education:* Trinity College; Guildhall School of Music; London College of Music. *Career:* Featured soloist, Edmundo Ros LA Orchestra, 26 years; 9 concert tours, Scandinavia; Royal Command Performance, 1962; State Visit of Queen, 1956; 3 seasons, Monte Carlo; tours Japan, Okinawa, Singapore; 81 television appearances, including 9 abroad; 904 BBC broadcasts. *Recordings:* 118 for Edmundo Ros Orchestra, Decca Studios; Teacher of woodwind for: ILEA, 15 years; Havering and Essex, 10 years; Brentwood School, 12 years. *Leisure interests:* Golf; Model making; Playing organ.

WOLANIN Vincent M; b. 13 Dec. 1947, Philadelphia, Pennsylvania, USA. Prod. and Management Exec. m. Illona Koch Dove, 27 July 1981, 2 d. *Education:* BS Philadelphia University, 1969; Grad school, Union College, 1971. *Musical Education:* Accordion, piano. *Career:* President/CEO Topnotch Entertainment Corp; Holds musical trademarks for Studiolive Sound TM, Thoughts TM, Topnotch; Founder, Topnotch Music, Records; Former Professional Athlete; Creator, Executive Producer, Supercollossal TM Show; Head, TopNotch Management Company. *Recordings:* Producer, Breaking Through album, 1995; Producer, Angry Room, Lyndal's Burning;

Producer, Lingerie, Natalia. *Publications:* Created ads for Spin Magazine, April, May, 1996. *Honours:* Gold and Platinum discs for various albums and records; Platinum disc: Holy Water, Bad Company; Gold discs: Dangerous Age, Bad Company; Here ComesTrouble, Bad Company; Exposed, Vince Neil, Japan, 1993; Silver disc, for Breakin' Through, 1996. *Memberships:* NARM (National Asscn of Recording Merchandises) NARAS (National Academy Recording Arts/Science); Grammy Voting Member. *Leisure interests:* Golf; Racquetball (former professional). *Current Management:* Topnotch Entertainment Corp, Topnotch Music and Records. *Address:* PO Box 1515, Sanibel Island, FL 33957–1515, USA.

WOLFSON Mark; b. 1 Sept. 1951, Chicago, Illinois, USA. Record Prod.; Sound Engineer; Songwriter. *Career:* Record Production, Sound Engineer, Artist Development; Clients include: Natalie Cole; Jane Child; Stone Temple Pilots; Kimberly Bass; Producer: Film soundtracks; Television music. *Recordings:* (As producer) with UB40: Something Wild; with Talking Heads: Stop Making Sense; Also producer for Jane Child; School of Fish; Stone Temple Pilots; Natalie Cole; Sound Engineer for: Sir Mix-A-Lot; Talking Heads; Smokey Robinson; Ice-T; Natalie Cole; Thelma Houston; Phil Everly; Melle Mel; Kim Carnes; Celia Cruz; Jane Child; Michael Des Barres; Film soundtracks include: Philadelphia; Silence of The Lambs; That Thing You Do; 12 Bucks; Police Academy; Police Academy III; Down and Out In Beverly Hills; K2; Television commercials include: Burger King; Coors; Toyota; 7 Up; Pizza Hut; Circle K. *Honours:* 25 Multi-Platinum, Platinum and Gold Records. *Membership:* NARAS. *Leisure interests:* Travel; Horses. *Address:* 11684 Ventura Blvd, Suite 134 Studio City, CA 91604, USA.

WOLLO Erik; b. 6 Jan. 1961, Norway. Composer; Prod.; Musician (guitar, synthesizer). 1 s. *Career:* Professional artist, 1980–; Rock, jazz, classical music; Music for film, theatre, ballets, multimedia; Mostly electronic/synthesizer music, also strings, woodwinds, orchestra; Producer other artists; Building own Wintergarden Studio. *Compositions:* Formations, 1982; Buteo Buteo, 1986; Eb Brottsjo, 1986; Solar, 1986; Windows, 1988; Pre sense, 1990; Vidder, 1992; Cairns, 1992; Music for ballet: Pyramider, 1986; Jeg Dromte, 1992; Music for theatre: Motspillerne, 1988, 1991; Aldri Verden, 1992; Fossegrimen, 1992; Abiriels Love, music for theatre, 1996; Maunushymnen, 1997. *Recordings:* Albums: Where It All Begins, 1983; Dreams of Pyramids, 1984; Traces, 1985; Silver Beach, 1986; Images of Light, 1990; Solstice, 1992; Fossegrimen, 1995; Albums with other artists: Celeste: Design By Music, 1984; Wiese/Wollo/Waring: Trio, 1984; New Music Composer's Group: In Real Time, 1992; Transit, 1996; Dimension D, Exile, 1997; Solo album: Guitar Nova, 1998. *Memberships:* NOPA; Ny Musikk. *Leisure interest:* Mountain climbing. *Current Management:* Monumental Records. *Address:* Blomsterveien 10, 1636 Fredrikstad, Norway.

WOLSTENHOLME Chris Tony; b. 2 Dec. 1978. Musician (bass guitar). *Career:* Spent pre-teen years in Manchester, England; Formed group Gothic Plague in adopted hometown of Teignmouth, aged 13; Group became Fixed Penalty then Rocket Baby Dolls before finally settling on name Muse; Released two 1,000-copy EPs on UK independent label Dangerous; Signed to Madonna's US label Maverick following lauded UK In The City '98 and New York CMJ festival appearances; Rapid rise to fame followed; Live shows include: Ill-fated Woodstock '99 US festival; Headline slots at UK's Leeds, Reading and T In The Park festivals, 2000; European tours, 2001. *Recordings:* Albums: Showbiz, 1999; Origin of Symmetry, 2001; Singles: Muse EP, 1998; Muscle Museum EP, Uno, Cave, 1999; Sunburn, Unintended, 2000; Plug In Baby, New Born, Bliss, Hyper Music/Feeling Good, 2001. *Honours:* NME Award, Best Newcomer, 2000; Kerrang! Award, Best British Band, 2001. *Current Management:* Taste Media/SJP Management, 263 Putney Bridge Rd, London, SW15 2PU, England. *Internet:* www.muse-official.com.

WOMACK Bobby; b. 4 March 1944, Cleveland, Ohio, USA. Singer; Songwriter; Musician (guitar). m. Barbara Cooke, 1965, divorced 1970. *Career:* Member, The Womack Brothers (later known as The Valentinos); Support to James Brown, US tour, 1962; Guitarist, Sam Cooke, 1960; Session work, 1965; Solo artiste, 1968–; Regular UK and US tours; Concerts include: New Orleans Jazz Festival, 1992. *Compositions include:* It's All Over Now (UK No. 1 for Rolling Stones); Numerous songs for Wilson Pickett including: 634–5789; I'm A Midnight Mover; I'm In Love. *Recordings:* Albums: Fly Me To The Moon, 1968; The Womack Live, 1971; Communication, 1972; Understanding, 1972; Across 110th Street, 1973; Facts of Life, 1974; Looking For Love Again, 1974; Bobby Womack's Greatest Hits, 1974; I Don't Know What The World Is Coming to, 1975; Safety Zone, 1976; BW Goes C&W, 1976; Home Is Where The Heart Is, 1976; Pieces, 1978; Roads of Life, 1979; The Poet, 1981; The Poet II, 1984; So Many Rivers, 1985; Womagic, 1987; The Last Soul Man, 1987; Lookin' For A Love (1968–75), 1993; I Still Love You, 1993; I Wanna Make Love To You, 1993; Soul Seduction Supreme, 1994; Back To My Roots, 1999; Traditions, 1999; Producer, Now Look, Ron Wood, 1974; Contributor, Sun City, Artists Against Apartheid, 1985; Dirty Work, The Rolling Stones, 1986; Coast To Coast, Paul Shaffer, 1989; Nearly Human, Todd Rundgren,

1989; Guitarist on recordings by artists including: King Curtis; Ray Charles; Wilson Pickett; Joe Tex; Aretha Franklin; Dusty Springfield; Janis Joplin; Singer, duets with Patti Labelle; Altrina Grayson; Shirley Brown; Lulu. *Address:* c/o Nick Cowan, Bobby Womack and Co, 9595 Wilshire Blvd #502, Beverly Hills, CA 90210, USA.

WOMACK Lee Ann; b. 19 Aug. 1966, Jacksonville, Texas, USA. Country vocalist. m. Jason Sellers, 1990, divorced. *Education:* South Plains Jr College, Levelland, Texas. *Musical Education:* Bellmont University, Nashville. *Career:* Joined college band Country Caravan; After studying music business at Bellmont University, worked as intern at MCA Records in A & R department; Became a parent after marriage to fellow country singer Jason Sellers; Started to write songs, perform at artist showcases and sing on demo sessions; Signed by Tree Publishing in Nashville, 1995; Wrote material with Bill Anderson, Mark Wright, Ed Hill and husband Sellers; Signed by MCA Records, 1996; Self-titled album produced first country chart entry Never Again Again, highly praised for its adherence to a hardcore country sound; Subsequent recordings moved away from strict traditional approach, but were critically well-received and chart success continued for remainder of the decade; Recorded I Hope You Dance with backing vocals from Sons of The Desert, 2000; Song charted internationally, becoming career record; Lyrical content inspired a best-selling book celebrating the joy of living and the possibility of dreams; Disowns hit dance remix of track. *Recordings include:* The Fool, You've Got To Talk To Me, 1997; Albums include: Lee Ann Womack, 1997. *Honours:* CMA Awards: Single of the Year, Song of the Year, I Hope You Dance, 2000; Female Vocalist of the Year, 2001. *Address:* c/o The Country Music Asscn, Nashville, Tennessee, USA. *Internet:* www.leeannwomack.com.

WONDER Stevie, (Steveland Morris); b. 13 May 1950, Saginaw, Michigan, USA. Singer; Musician (multi-instrumentalist); Composer. m. Syreeta Wright, 1970, divorced, 3 c. *Education:* Michigan State School for the Blind, 1963–68. *Musical Education:* Self-taught harmonica, piano. *Career:* Motown recording artist (initially as Stephen Judkins), 1963–70; Founder, president, music publishing company, Black Bull Music Inc; Founder, Wonderdirection Records Inc; Taurus Productions; Numerous concerts include: Midem Festival, France, 1974; Night of The Hurricane II (hurricane relief concert), Houston, 1976; Peace Sunday, Rose Bowl, 1982; Nelson Mandela's Birthday Tribute, Wembley, 1988; Film appearances include: Bikini Beach, 1964; Muscle Beach Party, 1964. *Compositions include:* Lovin' You, Minnie Riperton, 1975. *Recordings:* Hit singles include: Fingertips Part 2 (No. 1, USA), 1963; Uptight (Everything's Alright), 1966; I Was Made To Love Her, 1967; For Once In My Life, 1968; My Cherie Amour, 1969; Yester-Me, Yester-You, Yesterday, 1969; Signed Sealed Delivered I'm Yours, 1970; Superstition (No. 1, USA), 1973; You Are The Sunshine of My Life (No. 1, USA), 1973; Higher Ground, 1974; Living For The City, 1974; You Haven't Done Nothin' (No. 1, USA), 1974; Boogie On Reggae Woman, 1975; I Wish (No. 1, USA), 1977; Sir Duke (No. 1, USA), 1977; Master Blaster, 1980; Lately, 1981; Happy Birthday, 1981; Ebony and Ivory, duet with Paul McCartney (No. 1, USA and UK), 1982; I Just Called To Say I Love You (No. 1, USA and UK), 1984; Part-Time Lover, 1985; Don't Drive Drunk, 1985; Get It, 1988; Keep Our Love Alive, 1990; Gotta Have You, 1991; Fun Day, 1991; These Three Words, 1991; For Your Love, 1995; Tomorrow Robins Will Sing, 1995; Treat Myself, 1995; Kiss Away Your Tears, 1996; Albums include: The 12 Year Old Genius, 1963; Up Tight Everything's Alright, 1966; Down To Earth, 1967; I Was Made To Love Her, 1967; Greatest Hits, 1968; For Once In My Life, 1969; My Cherie Amour, 1969; Signed Sealed and Delivered, 1969; Greatest Hits Vol. 2, 1971; Music of My Mind, 1972; Talking Book, 1972; Innervisions, 1973; Fulfillingness' First Finale, 1974; Songs In The Key of Life, 1976; Journey Through The Secret Life of Plants, 1979; Hotter Than July, 1980; Woman In Red (soundtrack), 1984; Love Songs, 1984; In Square Circle, 1985; Characters, 1987; Music From The Music Jungle Fever (soundtrack), 1991; Conversation Peace, 1995; Natural Wonder, 1996; Contributor, I Feel For You, Chaka Khan, 1984; There Must Be An Angel, The Eurythmics, 1985; That's What Friends Are For, Dionne Warwick and Friends, 1986; Hallelujah!, Quincy Jones, 1992. *Honours include:* Numerous Grammy Awards, including Lifetime Achievement Award, 1990; Edison Award, 1973; NARM Presidential Award, 1975; Inducted into Songwriters Hall of Fame, 1983; Numerous American Music Awards, including Special Award of Merit, 1982; Academy Award, Best Song, 1984; Gold Ticket, Madison Square Garden, 1986; Soul Train Heritage Award, 1987; Inducted into Rock 'n' Roll Hall of Fame, 1989; Nelson Mandela Courage Award, 1991; IAAAM Diamond Award for Excellence, 1991; Lifetime Achievement Award, National Academy of Songwriters, 1992; NAACP Image Award, 1992; Numerous other charity and civil rights awards. *Current Management:* Stevland Morris Music, 4616 Magnolia Blvd, Burbank, CA 91505, USA.

WOOD Jeffrey; b. 5 Sept. 1950, Chicago, Illinois, USA. Record Prod.; Recording Artist; Composer. m. Carine F Verheyen, 16 Nov. 1992. *Education:* BA, University of Illinois. *Musical Education:* 12 years piano and composition, Helen Beidel. *Career:* Produced over 30 major recording artists including: Luka Bloom; The Housemartins; The Origin; Pauline

Black. *Recordings include:* Twist of Destiny; The Surrendering Room; 3 feature film soundtracks. *Current Management:* Steve Moir Company. *Address:* 46 Hillside Ave, Mill Valley, CA 94941, USA.

WOOD Michael Stefan; b. 12 April 1954, Hyde, Cheshire, England. Head of Music and Expressive Arts Faculty, School. m. Anita Jane, 25 May 1991. *Musical Education:* Music at University of Hertfordshire, recorder with Evelyn Nallen, guitar/lute, Ian Gammie. *Career:* Formed folk band: The Brighthelmstones, 1969; Semi finalists National Folk Rock Fest, 1972; Album, 1971; Co-founded Wilbury Jam, 1977; Folk/cabaret in band play guitars, mandolin, banjo, recorder, clarinet, violin, trombone, horn; Played Krummhorn as part of Drake Anniversary, TVS, 1988; Similar, BBC radio, 1988. *Recordings:* Album: Brighthelmstones, 1971; Wilbury Jam: A Good Spread, 1980; A Second Helping, 1991. *Honours:* Dip Mus LTCL (Performers Recorder) LLCM ALCM. *Membership:* Musicians' Union. *Leisure interests:* Walking; Watching war films; Conducting orchestras. *Address:* 52 Chanctonbury Rd, Burgess Hill, West Sussex RH15 9EY, England.

WOOD Patte; b. 29 Jan. 1949, Seattle, Washington, USA. Musician (Piano); Arts Admin. *Education:* Studies in Piano Performance, Harpsichord and Music Theory, 1956–75; BA, Music, San Jose State University, 1972; Studies in Fine Art Administration, 1979–81, Fine Art Photography, 1978–89; MA Candidate, 1997-. *Career:* Instructor, Piano Performance and Accompanist, San Francisco Bay Area, 1965–76; Administrative Director, Stanford University Center for Computer Research in Music and Acoustics, 1984–95; Visiting Scholar, Stanford University, 1995–99; Director, Blue Ridge Association for Community, Culture, Art and Technology, Eagle Rock, Virginia, 1999–; Solo Performances at festivals and concerts; Coproducer, numerous music projects; Consultant for numerous musical conferences. *Publications:* Early History of the Center for Computer Research in Music and Acoustics, 1988; Conversations with John Robinson Pierce, 1991; Interview with French composer Jean-Claude Risset, 1992–98, forthcoming. *Honours:* National Piano Auditions, Outstanding and Superior Grades, 1956–66, International Standing, Superior Grade, 1967. *Memberships:* International Computer Music Asscn; Bay Area New Music Coalition, 1986–90; ICMA Commission Awards Selection Panel, 1992; Officer, Board of Directors, ICMA, 1992–2000; Advisory Board, Electronic Music Foundation, 1995. *Address:* 572 Poorhouse Rd, Lexington, VA 24450, USA.

WOOD Paul, (Paul Richard Woodcock); b. 16 Nov. 1964, Romford, Essex, England. Vocalist. *Career:* Played with The Ray Ward Trio; Worked with artists including: Don Lusher; George Chisholm; Kenny Ball; Terry Lightfoot; Appeared at venues including: Pizza Express; Cafe Loire; Royal Festival Hall; Royal Ascot; Various radio and television includes: 2 hour radio broadcast from The Film Festival Hall, Cannes, France; Currently with Glenn Miller Memorial Orchestra, 1987–; Concert tours in France, Switzerland, Spain, Italy, Germany, Belgium, Austria, including Sporting Club, Monte Carlo, before Prince Rainier and Princess Caroline; Works regularly with various bands on the Continent; Played many Liberation Concerts; Spa Belgium; Toulon, France; Lille (25,000 people); Nice Jazz Festivals. *Recordings:* 4 albums with Glenn Miller Orchestra include: Recorded Live The Sporting Club Monte Carlo; 2 albums with Lex Van Wel and His Swing Orchestra. *Honours:* Freedom of The City of London. *Memberships:* Musicians' Union; The Coda Club. *Leisure interests:* Collecting antiquarian books; Rolls Royce models. *Current Management:* Lex Van Wel, PO Box 1436, 5602 BK Eindhoven, Netherlands.

WOOD Ron; b. 1 June 1947, Hillingdon, London, England. Musician (guitar, bass). 1 s. *Career:* Musician, Jeff Beck Group, 1967–69; Concerts include: National Jazz and Blues Festival, 1967, 1968; Newport Jazz Festival, 1969; Member, The Faces, 1969–75; Reading Jazz Festival, 1972; Buxton Festival, 1974; Member, The Rolling Stones, 1975–; US tour, 1975; Knebworth Festival, 1976; The Band's Last Waltz Farewell Concert, San Francisco, 1976; Film, Ladies and Gentlemen, The Rolling Stones, 1977; Played Knebworth Festival as The New Barbarians (with Keith Richards), 1979; Live Aid, JFK Stadium, Philadelphia, 1985; Played with Bo Diddley as the Gunslingers; Tours: North America, 1987; Japan, 1988; Germany, Italy, Spain, 1988; Sang at Bob Dylan 30th Anniversary Tribute, Madison Square Garden, 1992. *Recordings:* Albums with The Faces: First Step, 1970; Long Player, 1971; A Nod's As Good As A Wink... To A Blind Horse, 1971; Coast To Coast Overture and Beginners, 1974; with The Rolling Stones: Made In The Shade, 1975; Black and Blue, 1976; Love You Live, 1977; Emotional Rescue, 1980; Tattoo You, 1981; Still Life, 1982; Undercover, 1983; Dirty Work, 1986; Steel Wheels, 1989; Solo: I've Got My Own Album to Do; Now Look; Mahoney's Last Stand; 1234; Live at the Ritz; Slide on This; Slide on Live; Singles: with The Faces: Stay With Me, 1972; Cindy Incidentally, 1973; Pool Hall Richard, 1974; You Can Make Me Dance Or Sing Or Everything, 1974; with The Rolling Stones: Fool To Cry, 1976; Miss You (No. 1, USA), 1978; Emotional Rescue, 1980; Start Me Up, 1981; Going To a Go-Go; Undercover of The Night; Dancing In The Street (No. 1, UK), 1985; Mixed Emotions,

1989. *Honours include:* Silver Clef, Nordoff-Robbins Music Therapy, 1982; Madison Square Garden Hall of Fame, 1984; Grammy, Lifetime Achievement Award, 1986; Ivor Novello, Outstanding Contribution To British Music, 1991. *Current Management:* Rupert Loewenstein, 2 King St, London SW1Y 6QL, England.

WOOD Roy; b. 8 Nov. 1947, Birmingham, England. Singer; Musician (guitar). *Career:* Member, Mike Sheridan and the Nightriders; Singer, guitarist, The Move, 1966–72; Appearances include National Jazz and Blues Festival, 1966; 14-Hour Technicolour Dream, with Pink Floyd, Alexandra Palace, 1967; Isle of Wight Festival, 1968; Founder member, Electric Light Orchestra (ELO), 1971–72; Founder, lead singer, Wizzard, 1972–75; Concerts include: London Rock 'n' Roll Festival, 1972; Reading Festival, 1972; Also formed The Wizzo Band; The Helicopters; Writer, producer, various artists including Darts, 1977; Performed at Heartbeat '86 benefit concert, 1986; Cropredy Festival, 1995. *Compositions include:* Night of Fear; I Can Hear The Grass Grow; Blackberry Way; Hello Susie; See My Baby Jive. *Recordings:* UK Top 10 singles include: with The Move: Night of Fear, 1967; I Can Hear The Grass Grow, 1967; Flowers In The Rain (first song ever played on BBC Radio 1), 1967; Fire Brigade, 1968; Blackberry Way (No. 1, UK); Hello Susie, 1969; Brontosaurus, 1970; California Man, 1972; with ELO: 10538 Overture, 1972; with Wizzard: Ball Park Incident, 1973; See My Baby Jive (No. 1, UK), 1973; Angel Fingers (No. 1, UK); I Wish It Could Be Christmas Every Day, 1973; Rock 'n' Roll Winter, 1974; Are You Ready To Rock, 1975; Solo singles include: Dear Elaine; Forever; Going Down The Road; Oh What A Shame; Albums with The Move: Move, 1968; Shazam, 1970; Looking On, 1970; Message From The Country, 1971; with ELO: Electric Light Orchestra, 1972; with Wizzard: Wizzard Brew, 1973; Introducing Eddy and The Falcons, 1974; with The Wizzo Band: On The Road Again, 1977; Super Active Wizzo, 1977; Solo albums: Boulders, 1973; Mustard, 1976; Starting Up, 1987; Various compilation albums; Contributor, Arrested (album of Police covers by various artists and the Royal Philharmonic Orchestra), 1983. *Address:* RO-LO Productions, 35 Dillotford Ave, Coventry CV3 5DR, England.

WOODLEY Mark Kenneth; b. 5 Sept. 1953, Brantford, Ontario, Canada. Songwriter; Musician (piano); Vocalist; Motivator. m. Elaine, 18 June 1977, 1 s., 2 d. *Education:* Leadership Training. *Career:* Toured through Canada, USA, UK, 1981–; National television in Canada. *Recordings:* Taken By Force, Image 7, 1987; More Like You, Image 7, 1985; Breaking Ground, Listen, 1981; Edify The Church, 1991. *Honours:* Nominated to International Airplay Award, 1995. *Memberships:* SOCAN; GMA. *Leisure interests:* Skiing; Long-distance running; Aviation. *Current Management:* YES International Inc. *Address:* 7 Painters Rd, RR7, Brantford, ON N3T 5L9, Canada.

WOODRUFF Bob; b. 14 March 1961, Suffern, New York, USA. Singer; Songwriter; Musician (guitar, drums). *Career:* Television appearances include: Music City Tonight, Nashville Network; TNN Country News; Inside Country, Ontario, Canada; The Road, Tribune Entertainment; Country Road Frutigen, Switzerland. *Recordings:* Albums: Dreams and Saturday Nights, 1994; Desire Road, 1997; Singles: Alright, 1994; Hard Liquor Cold Women Warm Beer, 1994. *Honours:* Charleston International Film Festival Silver Award, Best Country Music Video, for Alright, 1994. *Memberships:* CMA; NARAS; AFTRA; AFofM. *Leisure interests:* Reading the classics and musical biographies; Skateboarding; 1960s 'muscle cars'. *Current Management:* Jim Della Croce Management, 1229 17th Ave S, Nashville, TN 37212, USA.

WOODS John William; b. 23 July 1967, Cheltenham. *Career:* Ektos; Quest; Universe; Bristol Exposure; Pandemonium; Vibes Alive; Sutra; Obsession; Obsessed; Hyperbolic; Pleasuredome; Kinetic; Tick Tock; Own Record Label, Junkie Vinyl. *Recordings:* Tear'in My Love Apart; Funky Man; Seatrching For A Beat; Drive Me Crazy; Just Be Good; Hidden Dreams. *Memberships:* MCPS; PRS; PPL. *Leisure interest:* Music. *Address:* 18A High St, Shirehampton, Bristol, BS11 0DX, England.

WOODS Philip Wells; b. 2 Nov. 1931, Springfield, Massachusetts, USA. Muscian (Alto Saxophone, Clarinet); Composer. m. Jill Goodwin, 20 Dec. 1985, 1 s., 2 d. *Education:* Lessons with Harvey Larose, Springfield; Manhattan School, New York, 1948; Juilliard Conservatory, 1948–52. *Career:* Appearances with Benny Goodman, Buddy Rich, Quincy Jones, Thelonious Monk, Michel Legrand, Dizzy Gillespie and others; Appearing with own bands, Phil Woods Quintet, Phil Woods Little Big Band, Phil Woods Big Band; Featured, soundtracks of films including It's My Turn; Bandleader, Composer, Arranger and Soloist. *Compositions include:* Three Improvizations for Saxophone Quartet; Sonata for Alto and Piano; Rights of Swing; The Sun Suite; Fill the Woods with Light; I Remember; Deer Head Sketches. *Recordings include:* Images, with Michel Legrand, 1976; I Remember, Phil Woods Quartet, 1979; Dizzy Gillespie Meets Phil Woods Quintet; Evolution, Phil Woods Little Big Band; An Affair to Remember, Phil Woods Quintet; The Rev and I, with Johnny Griffin; Elsa, 1998; Porgy and Bess, 1999. *Honours:* Down Beat Magazine New Star Award, 1956, Critics' Poll Winner, alto saxophone, 1975–79, 1981–90, 1992, Readers' Poll

Winner, alto saxophone, 1976–95; Grammy Award, Images with Michel Legrand, 1976, for More Live, Phil Woods Quartet, 1982, 1983; National Asscn of Jazz Educators Poll Winner, alto saxophone, 1987, Phil Woods Quintet, 1987; East Stroudsburg University Hon. Degree, 1994; Induction into American Jazz Hall of Fame, 1994. *Memberships:* Delaware Water Gap Celebration of the Arts; Board of Directors, Al Cohn Memorial Jazz Collection; American Federation of Musicians; International Asscn of Jazz Educators. *Leisure interests:* Computer games; Reading; Educational TV. *Address:* PO Box 278, Delaware Water Gap, PA 18327, USA.

WOODWARD Keren; b. 2 April 1961, Bristol, Somerset, England. Singer. *Career:* Worked at BBC; Singer, all-girl group Bananarama, 1981–; Performances include: BRIT Awards, 1988. *Recordings:* Albums: Deep Sea Skiving, 1983; Bananarama, 1984; True Confessions, 1986; The Greatest Hits Collection, 1988; Please Yourself, 1993; Singles include: Really Sayin' Somethin', 1982; Na Na Hey Hey Kiss Him Goodbye, 1983; Cruel Summer, 1983; Robert De Niro's Waiting, 1984; Cruel Summer (featured in film The Karate Kid), 1984; Venus (No. 1, USA), 1986; I Heard A Rumour, 1987; Love In The First Degree, 1987; I Want You Back, 1988; Nathan Jones, 1988; Help! (with comedy duo French and Saunders), 1989; Preacher Man, 1991; Long Train Running, 1991; Movin' On, 1992; More More More, 1993; with Fun Boy Three: It Ain't What You Do, It's The Way That You Do It, 1982; Contributor: Do They Know It's Christmas, Band Aid (Ethiopian famine relief), 1984; Let It Be, Ferry Aid (Zeebrugge ferry disaster benefit), 1987; Rock The World, benefit album, 1990.

WOOLEY Sheb (Shelby F); b. 10 April 1921, Eric, Oklahoma, USA. Actor; Musician (fiddle, harmonica, acoustic guitar); Songwriter; Comedian. m. Linda S Dotson, 30 Dec. 1985, 2 d. *Career:* Over 80 major films, including: High Noon; Outlaw; Josie Wales; War Wagon; Rio Bravo; Rocky Mountain; Giant; Television appearances include: Original cast member, Hee Haw; Rawhide, 7 years; American Bandstand; Mod Squad; Murder She Wrote; Hootnanny Hoot; The Lone Ranger; Ed Sullivan Show. *Recordings:* Hit singles include: The Purple People Eater (100m. sales including covers); That's My Pa; Are You Satisfied; Sweet Chile; White Lightnin'; as Ben Colder: Fifteen Beers Ago; Almost Persuaded; Harper Valley PTA. *Honours:* CMA Comedian of the Year, 1968; 2 Golden Boot Awards; 7 Western Heritage Awards, 1966–; Second fastest selling record ever, The Purple People Eater. *Memberships:* ASCAP; CMA; NARAS; ROPE; ACM; AFM; SAG; AFTRA. *Leisure interests:* Sailing; Dominos; Cards. *Current Management:* Linda Dotson, Circuit Rider Talent and Management. *Address:* 123 Walton Ferry Rd, Hendersonville, TN 37075–3616, USA.

WOOLWAY Colin; b. 24 Jan. 1959, London, England. Musician (drums); Teacher. m. Lucy MacArthur, 22 July 1995. *Career:* Theatre tours: Godspell; Rocky Horror Show; 1978–80; English tour with The Enid, 1984; with Suzi Quatro: 5 Australian tours, 2 Japan tours, Russian tour, constant television appearances, 1985–93; Top Clinician for Zildjan Cymbals; Clinician for Sonor Drums, teaching at Drumsense studio. *Publications:* Drumsense, Vols 1–3, (drum tutors); 4 musician joke books. *Leisure interest:* Cartoonist. *Current Management:* Hayter and Shone, Publisher. *Address:* Flat 8, Highview House, 1 Highview Rd, Upper Norwood, London SE19 3SS, England.

WORLLEDGE Terry; b. 31 Jan. 1945, Essex, England. Musician (guitar, harmonica); Singer; Songwriter; Prod.; Engineer. m. Jean, 10 Oct. 1964, 2 d. *Musical Education:* Self-taught. *Career:* Member, Country Shack; Member, Jackson Queen; Numerous appearances, Wembley Country Music Festival; Television and radio appearances: BBC; ITV; Radio: BBC Radio 2. *Recordings:* Albums include: with Country Shack: Your Country Needs You; Portrait; Which Way Is Gone?; BBC Compilation album: 20 Country Greats; with Jackson Queen: Jackson Queen (EP); On The Rewind. *Honours:* British Country Music Asscn, Most Promising Act, 1980; Radio 2 Country Club, Best Band during 3 years as producer. *Memberships:* Musicians' Union; BCMA; PRS; PAMRA. *Leisure interest:* Motor racing. *Address:* Pipers, Maypole Rd, Tiptree, Essex CO5 0EP, England.

WORRALL Sean; b. 6 June 1966, Leicester, England. Artist; Record Label Owner; Magazine Editor; Concert Promoter; Singer; Musician (bass player); Fashion Designer. *Education:* West Surrey College of Art. *Career:* Editor, Organ Magazine; Toured extensively; Many radio, television appearances; Several album covers, videos. *Recordings:* Sophie Magic, Angel Cage; Late Developer, Rhatigan; Bullseye, Cardiacs; Redoubtable, Deathblanket, Goosebumps. *Publications:* Organ Magazine; Organ Videozine. *Honours:* The Golden Bassoon for Services to Punk Rock, 1994. *Membership:* The Yous Family. *Address:* Unit 205, The Old Gramophone Works, 326 Kensal Rd, London W10 5BZ, England.

WORTLEY Barry George; b. 19 May 1951, Norwich, Norfolk, England. Musician (drummer, guitar); Vocalist. m. Susan Read, 4 Oct. 1986, 5 s. *Musical Education:* School. *Career:* Member: The Aytons, 1966–68; Norma and The Shade of Pale, 1968–71; Edentree (touring comedy/showband), 1972–75; Fresh 1975–; Winner, ITV's New Faces, 1978; (name changed to Monte Carlo for last 12 of Song For Europe and Dooley's Tour Support

Band, name returned to Fresh); Currently a trio working functions and summer seasons. *Recordings:* Valentino; Win A Few, Lose A Few; Home Again. *Honours:* Music Award, Ljubljana Song Festival, Yugoslavia, 1979. *Membership:* Musicians' Union. *Leisure interests:* Golf; Snooker; Odd pint of real ale. *Current Management:* Anglia Artistes, Nicky Walker Entertainments and Leisure Services. *Address:* 105 Netherwood Green, Norwich, Norfolk NR1 2RJ, England.

WORTLEY J; b. 5 June 1971, Grimsby, Lincolnshire, England. Singer; Songwriter; Musician (guitar). *Musical Education:* Self-taught. *Career:* Joined Illustrious Gy, 1989; Signed to Arista Records, 1991; Toured with Squeeze in UK; Appeared: Going Live (BBC); Several ITV programmes; Played live, Steve Wright In The Afternoon, BBC Radio 1; Recently signed with MCA, as Giant Icicles. *Recordings:* Singles: Twenty Questions; Anytime At All; I'm Very; Album: No No No. *Membership:* Musicians' Union. *Leisure interests:* Keen Footballer. *Current Management:* J Cooke, Fatcat Management. *Address:* 81 Harley House, Marylebone Rd, London NW1 5HT, England.

WRAIGHT Jeffrey Charles; b. 17 Aug. 1954, West Sussex, England. Musician (keyboards, bass guitar); Vocalist; Arranger; Composer; Musical Dir; Co Dir, Entertainments Agency and Management. *Musical Education:* A Level Music; Early piano lessons but mainly self-taught; Studied with Cyril Winn. *Career:* Accompanied many modern jazz artists, 1973–79; Experimental free jazz workshop, Reading, 1977–79; Television broadcasts from Bracknell Jazz Festival, 2 years running, Soulstice, Funk Jazz group recording with Tony Visconti; Founder member of early Punk group Billy and the Conquerors; Joined big band on QEII, 1979, became band leader of own band on the same ship; Several television appearances; Worked with: The Batchelors; Bob Monkhouse; Tommy Dorsey Orchestra; Peter Gordeno; Joe Loss; Faith Brown; Elaine Delmar; Lorna Dallas; Started business venture in 1983 becoming Heartrate Entertainments, 1989–; Keyboard player, vocalist, arrangements for A Tribute To The Blues Brothers, London West End, 1992; Musical Director, and rewriter of show, 1994–. *Recordings include:* Soulstice, Tony Visconti; Several live sessions by Pendulum; Some recordings for BBC TV and Radio including several Blues Brothers appearances. *Publication:* Critique on the music of Miles Davis (in preparation). *Honour:* John Dankworth Award for Best Instrumentalist Under 25 (Piano), 1977. *Leisure interests:* Computer Music; Computer Studies. *Current Management:* Heartrate Entertainments. *Address:* 3 Seacroft, 9 Lansdowne Rd, Worthing, Sussex BN11 4NA, England.

WRAY John; b. 16 Jan. 1943, Ramshaw, England. Co Dir; Musician (keyboards). m. Karen Anne Western, 9 July 1986, 1 s., 1 d. *Musical Education:* Private tuition. *Career:* Owner, Spennymoor Variety Club; Band leader, John Ray Set; Director, Air Entertainments Agency; Producer, tours: Simply The Best; Reach Out. *Recordings:* Owner, Bullseye Recording Studios. *Leisure interests:* Flying; Swimming; Cooking. *Current Management:* Air Entertainments. *Address:* 17 Clyde Terrace, Spennymoor, Co Durham DL16 7SE, England.

WRAY Walter; b. 7 Feb. 1959, Portsmouth, Hampshire, England. Singer; Songwriter; Musician (guitar). m. Joanne Redfearn, 1 April 1989, 1 d. *Education:* Sheffield University. *Musical Education:* Guitar and piano lessons, BA dual Hons, Music/English. *Career:* Two albums with band Junk; Joined rock band King Swamp, 1988; 2 albums, and tours of USA and Europe; Currently solo artist. *Recordings:* Albums: with Junk: Cuckooland, 1986; Drop City Souvenirs, 1987; with King Swamp: King Swamp, 1988; Wiseblood, 1990; Solo: Foxgloves and Steel Strings, 1992. *Memberships:* Musicians' Union; PRS. *Leisure interests:* Family. *Current Management:* JFD Management, 106 Dalling Rd, Hammersmith, London W6 0JA, England.

WRETZKY D'Arcy; b. 1 May 1968, South Haven, Michigan, USA. Musician (Bass). *Career:* Member, Smashing Pumpkins; Early tours supporting Jane's Addiction, Red Hot Chili Peppers, Pearl Jam; Numerous headlining tours; Many TV appearances and radio sessions; Left band, 1999. *Recordings:* Singles: Lull EP, 1992; Today, 1994; Cherub Rock EP, 1994; Disarm, 1994; I Am One EP, 1994; Bullet with Butterfly Wings, 1995; Thirty Three, 1996; Zero EP, 1996; End is the Beginning is the End, 1997; Perfect, 1998; Albums: Gish, 1991; Siamese Dream, 1993; Mellon Collie and the Infinite Sadness, 1995; Adore, 1998.

WRIGHT Chely; b. 25 Oct. 1970, Kansas City, Missouri, USA. Country vocalist; Musician (guitar). *Career:* Formed own band County Line; Moved to Branson, Missouri, securing a job singing on the Ozark Jubilee before finishing high school; Moved to Nashville and landed a job impersonating country artists by age 18; Signed to Mercury after coming to the attention of producer Harold Shedd; Records performed moderately until move to MCA Records, 1997; Let Me In album gave first real taste of success on both country singles and album charts; Turned further away from traditional country sound heard in earlier work and recordings have become more sophisticated and uptown, culminating in the complex

Never Love You Enough, 2001; Latterly has been recording and writing with friend and fellow artist Brad Paisley, including the hit duet Hard To Be A Husband – Hard To Be A Wife. *Recordings include:* Single White Female, It Was, 2000; Hard To Be A Husband – Hard To Be A Wife (with Brad Paisley), 2001; Albums include: Right In The Middle of It, 1996; Let Me In, 1997; Single White Female, 1999; Never Love You Enough, 2001. *Honours:* ACM, Top New Female Vocalist, 1995. *Address:* c/o The Country Music Asscn, Nashville, Tennessee, USA. *Internet:* www.chely.com.

WRIGHT David; b. 2 Feb. 1958, Colombo, Sri Lanka. Local Government Officer. m. Nicola, 4 July 1987, 2 s. *Education:* Degree, Environmental Sciences. *Musical Education:* Self-taught. *Career:* Solo performer and with band The Thomas Wright Affair; Live performance, BBC Radio Bristol, Somerset Sound, 1993; Canny Wizard Stage, Glastonbury, 1994, 1995; Castle Park Stage, Bristol Sound City, 1995; Mean Fiddler, Acoustic Room, London, 1996, 1997. *Compositions:* Kathy's Eyes, 1996; Sign Your Life Away, 1996; Eastern Promise, 1996. *Recordings:* Self-produced albums: Fags Out Chaps We're Going In, Thomas Wright Affair, 1993; Solo demo album: Intimate, 1996; Solo CD, Kathy's Eyes, 1996. *Honours:* Glastonbury Festival Canny Wizard Stage, 1994, 1995; Radio 1 FM Park Stage for Bristol Sound City, 1995; Ashton Court Festival, Bristol, 1995, 1998. *Memberships:* PRS; PAMRA; Musicians' Union. *Leisure interests:* Football; Tennis. *Address:* PO Box 743, Bristol BS99 5GU, England.

WRIGHT Dennis; b. 12 Dec. 1926, Rochdale, Lancashire, England. Musician (drums); Arranger. m. Auidrey Elsie Jones, 8 Sept. 1986, 4 s. *Musical Education:* George Evans arranging course; Glenn Miller booklet. *Career:* Played radio broadcast, 1947; Further broadcasts Rink Ballroom, Sunderland; Own trio accompanied artists at Wetherals Night Club, Sunderland, include: Bobby Bennett; Donald Peers; Mike Sarne; Lance Percival; Bertice Reading; Bill Pertwee; Frankie Vaughn (big band); Valerie Masters; Vince Hill; Lena Martell; Dorothy Squires; Dick Emery. *Recordings:* Newcastle broadcast, 1947; Local band, Henfield, Sussex, recorded. *Leisure interest:* Music. *Current Management:* Sunrise Management, Forest Green, Dorking, Surrey, England.

WRIGHT Eugene Joseph; b. 29 May 1923, Chicago, Illinois, USA. Musician (bass); Composer. m. Jacqueline Winters, 29 May 1945, divorced 1954, 1 s., 1 d., m. (2) Phyllis Lycett, 10 Aug. 1962. *Education:* Tilden Tech, Chicago, 1938. *Career:* Bandleader, Dukes of Swing Orchestra, 1943–46; Bassist with: Count Basie Orchestra; Gene Ammons/Sonny Stitt Quintet; Buddy DeFranco; Red Norvo; Arnett Cobb; Cal Tjader; Dave Brubeck; Monty Alexander, 1947–72; Billie Holiday, US and European tours, 1954; Duo, Money Tree, 1975–86; Bandleader, Eugene J Wright Ensemble, 1986–; Private music teacher, 1969–; Performed with B. B. King Blues Band, Linda Hopkins International Jazz Festival, Switzerland, 1988; Performed with Dave Brubeck Quartet, US State Dinner (for Presidents Reagan and Gorbachev), Moscow, 1988. *Publications:* Bass Solos; Modern Music For Bass; Jazz Giants. *Honours:* Playboy Jazz Poll Award, 1964–66; Outstanding Voluntary Service Award, Los Angeles Human Relations Commission, 1988. *Memberships:* NARAS; AFofM. *Leisure interests:* Gardening; Bowling; Cycling. *Address:* c/o Dukes of Swing Record Company, Hollywood, California, USA.

WRIGHT Finbar; b. 26 Sept. 1959, Kinsale, Co Cork, Ireland. Tenor singer. m. Angela, 23 Nov. 1990, 1 s., 1 d. *Education:* BD; HDE. *Musical Education:* Studied with Ileana Cotrubas and Veronica Dunne. *Career:* Australian Tour, performed with Melbourne Symphony Orchestra, Spring 1994; Performed with Montserrat Caballe, Dublin, 1993; USA tour, Spring 1995. *Compositions:* Blackwind, 1998. *Recordings:* Albums: Because; Whatever You Believe; Live Tribute To John McCormack; Lift The Wings; I Give My Heart; Another Season. *Honours:* IRMA Best MOR Artist, 1992; IRMA Best Male Artist, 1993. *Membership:* IMRO. *Current Management:* Mattie Fox Management, Derryneel, Baillinalee, County Longford, Ireland.

WRIGHT Michelle; b. Chatham, Ontario, Canada. Singer; Songwriter; Musician (Guitar). *Musical Education:* Self-taught guitar. *Career:* Radio: Grand Ole Opry Debut, 1992; TV: Tonight Show with Jay Leno, 1992; The Women of Country; Prime the CBC Specials, Michelle, 1991; Songs and Secrets, 1996; Co-Host, TNN Music City News Awards, 1994; Host, 1995; CCMA Awards Show; ACM and CMA Awards Shows, 1992–96. *Recordings:* Do Right By Me, 1988; Michelle Wright, 1990; Now and Then, 1992; The Reasons Why, 1994; The Power of Peace, 1996; Star of Wonder, 1996; For Me It's You, 1996; Singles: One Good Man, 1994; Nobody's Girl, 1996. *Honours include:* Top Female Vocalist, 1989; Top Female Vocalist, 1991; Artist of the Year, 1991; Top Country Single, Take It Like a Man, 1992; Top Female Vocalist, 1993; Artist of the Year, 1993; Top Country Album, Now and Then, 1993; Top Country Single, He Would Be Sixteen, 1993; Top Female Vocalist, 1994; Top Female Vocalist, 1995; Hon. Spokesperson for Special Olympics, 1996. *Memberships:* National Academy of Recording Arts and Sciences, Academy of Country Music; Country Music Asscn; Canadian Country Music Asscn; Canadian Academy of Recording Arts and Sciences.

Current Management: Savannah Music, 209 10th Ave S, Suite 528, Nashville, TN 37203, USA.

WRIGHT Nod (Alexander James); b. 14 June 1966, Hertfordshire, England. Musician (drums, percussion, guitar, keyboards). *Education:* North Herts College. *Career:* Member, Fields of The Nephilim, now known as Rubicon; Numerous European tours; 2 American tours; Reading Festival, 1987, 1988; Loralei Festival (Germany); Chart show videos; Top of The Pops; BBC Radio Live; Drums and Percussion. *Recordings:* Fields of The Nephilim Discography, 1984–91; Rubicon, 1992–95; Co-wrote, produced, albums: The Nephilim; Elizium; Revelations; What Starts Ends; Room 101. *Honours:* Best Album and Band, Melody Maker Readers Poll. *Memberships:* PRS; Musicians' Union; BPI. *Leisure interest:* Writing other material. *Address:* 57 Regent St, Stotfold, Herts SG5 4EA, England.

WRIGHT Rick; b. 28 July 1943, London, England. Musician (keyboards). *Career:* Member, Pink Floyd, 1965–80; 1986–; Performances include: Rome International Pop Festival, 1968; Hyde Park, London, 1968; Bath Festival, 1970; Montreux Festival, 1971; Knebworth Festival, 1975; Films: Pink Floyd Live At Pompeii, 1972. *Recordings:* Albums: Piper at the Gates of Dawn, 1967; A Saucerful of Secrets, 1968; More (film soundtrack), 1969; Zabriskie Point, (film soundtrack), 1969; Ummagumma, 1969; Atom Heart Mother, 1970; Relics, 1971; Meddle, 1971; Obscured By Clouds, 1972; The Dark Side of The Moon, 1973; Wish You Were Here (No. 1, UK and USA), 1975; Animals, 1976; The Wall (No. 1, USA), 1979; A Momentary Lapse of Reason, 1987; The Delicate Sound of Thunder, 1988; Shine On, 1992; The Division Bell, 1994; Pulse, 1995; Solo: Wet Dream, 1977; As Zee (with Dee Harris): Identity, 1984; Solo: Broken China, 1996; Singles include: See Emily Play, 1967; Another Brick In The Wall, 1979; Run Like Hell, 1980; When The Tigers Break Free, 1982; Learning To Fly, 1987; On The Turning Away, 1987; 1 Slip, 1988. *Honours:* Best Group Video, MTV Music Awards, 1988; Ivor Novello Award, Outstanding Contribution To British Music, 1992; Rock and Roll Hall of Fame, 1995. *Current Management:* Steve O'Rourke, EMKA Productions Ltd, 43 Portland Rd, Holland Park, London W11 4LJ, England.

WRIGHT Steve, (Simon Neale Railton); b. 6 Feb. 1962, Newcastle-Upon-Tyne, England. Musician (guitar); Music Teacher; Composer; Sound Recording Engineer; Singer. *Musical Education:* BA Honours Music, Anglia Polytechnic University; BA Music, Open University. *Career:* Guitarist, songwriter with heavy metal bands Atomkraft and Blitzkrieg, 1986–88; Guitarist with Anglia Jazz Orchestra, 1990–93; Appearances: Claremont Jazz Festival; Los Angeles, 1991; Umbria Jazz Festival, with students from Berklee College of Music, 1992. *Membership:* Musicians' Union. *Leisure interests:* Saturday League amateur football; Cinema; Fitness; Travel. *Address:* 15 Simonside View, Ponteland, Newcastle-upon-Tyne, NE20 9TF, England.

WRIGHT Tony; b. Bradford, Yorkshire, England. Singer. *Career:* Singer, UK rock group Terrovision (formerly the Spoilt Bratz), 1986–; Support tours with The Ramones; Motörhead; Television apperances include: Top of The Pops. *Recordings:* Albums: Formaldehyde, 1993; How To Make Friends and Influence People, 1994; Regular Urban Survivors, 1996; Singles: Oblivion, 1994; Middleman, 1994; Pretend Best Friend, 1994; Alice What's The Matter, 1994; Some People Say, 1995; Perseverance, 1996. *Current Management:* JPR Management, The Power House, 70 Chiswick High Rd, London W4 1SY, England.

WYATT Robert; b. 28 Jan. 1945, Bristol, England. Composer; Singer. m. Alfreda Benge, 26 July 1974, 1 s. *Career:* Featured in full-length profile, Catalan Television, mid-1980s; Various radio programmes, Europe, USA; Several recordings own pieces including: Old Rottenhat, solo CD; EPS, Box set of Mini-CDs. *Compositions:* Heaps of Sheeps, with Alfreda Benge, 1997; September 9th; Alien; Out of Season; A Sunday in Madrid. *Recordings:* Matching Mole/Little Red Record; Rock Bottom; Ruth Is Stranger Than Richard; Dondestan (with poems by Alfreda Benge), compilation, mid-80s; Shleep, CD, 1997; Hapless Child, with Mike Mantler and Carla Bley, 1976. *Publications:* MW, with J M Marchetti. *Honours:* Grand Prix Du Disque, Academie Charles Cros. *Memberships:* PRS; MCPS; Musicians' Union; PAMRA. *Leisure interest:* Sitting around in cafes. *Address:* Hannibal/Ryko.

WYKES Debsey; b. 21 Dec. 1960, London, England. Singer; Songwriter; Musician (bass). *Career:* Six years with all girl band Dolly Mixture; Support tours with The Undertones, Bad Manners, The Jam, Dexy's Midnight Runners; Films: Dolly Mixture documentary, director Simon West, 1983; Backing vocals, Saint Etienne, 2 years; British tours, European tour, US tour; Television includes: Top of The Pops; Something Else; The Word; Later With Jools Holland; The Beat; Glastonbury; Radio sessions: Dolly Mixture, John Peel session, Radio 1, 1979; Kid Jensen session, 1981, 1982. *Recordings:* 4 singles, 1980–83; Double album: Demonstration Tapes, 1983, re-released 1995; with Captain Sensible: 6 singles include: Happy Talk (No. 1, UK charts), 1982; with Coming Up Roses: I Said Ballroom (Mini-album);

Various backing vocals: Saint Etienne; Duetted on: Who Do You Think You Are?

WYMAN Bill, (William George Perks); b. 24 Oct. 1936, Lewisham, London, England. Musician (bass). m. (1) Diane Cory, 1959, divorced, 1 s., (2) Mandy Smith, 1989, divorced 1991, m. (3) Suzanne Accosta, 1993, 3 d. *Career:* Member, The Rolling Stones, 1962–93; Owner: WGW Holdings; Ripple Productions; Ripple Records; Ripple Music; WGW Enterprises; Wytel Music; KJM Nominees; Sticky Fingers Restaurant; Numerous Rolling Stones tours and concerts 1963–90; ARMS Tour, UK and USA, 1983. *Recordings:* Albums include: The Rolling Stones, 1964; The Rolling Stones, No 2, 1965; Out of Our Heads, 1965; Aftermath, 1966; Between The Buttons, 1967; Their Satanic Majesties Request, 1967; Beggar's Banquet, 1968; Let It Bleed, 1969; Get Yer Ya-Ya's Out, 1969; Sticky Fingers, 1971; Exile On Main Street, 1972; Goat's Head Group, 1973; It's Only Rock and Roll, 1974; Black and Blue, 1976; Some Girls, 1978; Emotional Rescue, 1980; Still Life, 1982; Primitive Cool, 1987; Steel Wheels, 1989; Flashpoint, 1991; solo: Stone Alone; Monkey Grip; Bill Wyman; Digital Dreams; Struttin' Our Stuff; Anyway the Wind Blows; Double Bill, 2001; Blues Odyssey, 2001; Singles include: Come On; I Wanna Be Your Man; Get Off of My Cloud; 19th Nervous Breakdown; Let's Spend The Night Together; It's All Over Now; Little Red Rooster; (I Can't Get No) Satisfaction; Jumping Jack Flash; Honky Tonk Women; Brown Sugar; Miss You; Ruby Tuesday; Paint It Black; Going To A Go-Go; Emotional Rescue; It's Only Rock 'n' Roll; Harlem Shuffle; Start Me Up; Angie; Undercover of The Night; Harlem Shuffle; solo: (Si Si) Je Suis Un Rock Star. *Publications:* Stone Alone – The Story of a Rock and Roll Band (with Ray Coleman), 1990; Wymna Shoots Chagall, 2000. *Honours include:* Silver Clef Award, Nordoff-Robbins Music Therapy, 1982; Grammy Lifetime Achievement Award, 1986; Inducted into Rock and Roll Hall of Fame, 1989; Q Award, Best Live Act, 1990; Ivor Novello Awards, Outstanding Contribution To British Music, 1991. *Address:* c/o Ripple Productions, 344 Kings Rd, London SW3 5UR, England. *Internet:* www.billwyman.com.

WYNENS Rene; b. 21 Aug. 1954, Bouwel, Belgium. Musician (drums); Television and Film Figuration. m. Helsen Anita, 6 Sept. 1974, 1 s. *Education:* Private lessons, by drummer Jan Cuyvers and Academie of Music Herentals. *Career:* Figuration in different professional films: Brylcream Boulevard; Karakter; Elixir d'Anvers; Gastons War; Left Luggage; Sono Pazzo Di Iris Blond; De Bal; Lijmen Het Been; Iedereen Beroemd; Music Clip For Nova Star; Different television productions for several TV stations and production houses; TV soaps: Wittekerke; Familie; Levensgevaar; Vennebos; Dokters; Gaston Berghmansshow '98 I and II; De Kampioenen; Engeltjs; Sitcom with Walter Baele; Founder, drummer and contact person of rock and roll/beatgroup, Big Problem. *Recordings:* Album CD, Big Problem 1; Album CD, Big Problem Rockers Look Out; Album CD, Big Problem Look Out Again. *Memberships:* Belgian Drumclub; Dutch Slagwerkkrant; Modern Drummer. *Current Management:* Big Problem, PO Box 27, 2200 Herentals, Belgium.

WYNNE Michael Alexander; b. West Kirby, Merseyside, England. Composer; Songwriter; Record Prod.; Arranger; Musician (electric, acoustic guitars, mandolin, banjo). *Education:* BA, Newcastle University. *Musical Education:* Self-taught. *Career:* Part-time recording, live work, with Irish group Flynn and Wynne; Tours include Holland, Germany, Singapore; Worked in Karachi, 1989; Producer, live all-star show, and pop album, singer Mohammed Ali Shiakhi; Also film score composition; Producer, dance album, New York, 1993; Television apperance with band Posh Monkeys, UK. *Compositions:* Composed musical Baby and 3 Devils. *Recordings:* Shiakhi Speaks (Karachi); The Wise Guys (Abbey Road). *Membership:* Musicians' Union; PRS; BASCA. *Leisure interests:* Active pursuits; Philosophy. *Address:* c/o Wilson Barca, 13–14 Dean St, London W1V 5AH, England.

WYNONNA (Wynonna Judd); b. 1966. Country Singer; Musician. *Career:* Member, Country duo, The Judds, with mother Naomi, 1984–90; Solo artiste, billed as Wynonna, 1991–; Most successful country duo, as the Judds, with 15m. album sales; Undefeated, all 3 major US Country Awards, 8 consecutive years; Co-founder, booking agency Pro-Tours, 1988. *Recordings include:* Singles: Had A Dream For The Heart, 1983; Mama He's Crazy, 1984; Why Not Me, 1984; Girls' Night Out, 1985; Rockin' With The Rhythm of The Rain, 1986; Let Me Tell You About Love, 1989; Love Can Build A Bridge, 1990; No One Else on Earth, 1992; My Strongest Weakness, 1992; Only Love, 1993; Healing, 1994; Rock Bottom, 1994; When Love Starts Talkin', 1997; Love Like That, 1999; Can't Nobody Love You Like I Do..., 1999; Albums include: with The Judds: The Judds, 1984; Why Not Me?, 1985; Rockin' With The Rhythm of The Rain, 1986; Heartland, 1987; Greatest Hits, 1988; River of Time, 1989; Love Can Build A Bridge, 1990; The Judds Collection, 1991; The Essential, 1996; Solo albums: Wynnona, 1992; Tell Me Why, 1993; Revelations, 1996; The Other Side, 1997; New Day Dawning, 2000. *Honours:* 7 Grammy Awards; 4 ACM Awards, Best Duet, 1984–89; 3 CMA Awards, Best Vocal Duo, 1988–91. *Current Management:* William Morris. *Address:* c/o The Judd House, 325 Bridge St, Franklin, TN 37064, USA.

WYSOCKI Jon; b. 17 Jan. 1971, Northampton, Massachusetts, USA. Musician (drums). *Career:* Invited to join Staind rock group by friend and guitarist Mike Mushok; First gig with band, 1995; Released self-financed debut album, 1996; Album sold 4,000 copies; Discovered by Fred Durst, 1997; Signed to Flip/Elektra; Presented to rock cognoscenti at Limp Bizkit gold record party for Three Dollar Bill Y'All $, 1998; Major breakthrough with unscheduled smash US No. 1 radio hit Outside; Appeared on bill for Korn-founded Family Values tours, 1999, 2001; Headlined MTV's Return of the Rock tour, 2000. *Recordings:* Albums: Tormented, 1996; Dysfunction, 1999; Break The Cycle, 2001; Singles: Mudshovel, Just Go, 1999; Home, Outside, 2000; It's Been Awhile, Fade, 2001. *Honours:* Break The Cycle certified quadruple platinum by RIAA; It's Been Awhile topped Billboard Modern Rock Singles Chart for record-equalling 16 weeks; VH-1 Award, Your Song Kicked Ass But Was Played Too Damn Much prize, 2001. *Address:* c/o The Firm, Inc, 9100 Whilshire Blvd, Suite 400W, Beverly Hills, CA 90212, USA. *Internet:* www.staind.com.

X

X (CROSS) Alan; b. 8 March 1958, London, England. Prod.; Writer; Musician (keyboards). *Education:* BA; Diploma Architecture Pt III Professional. *Musical Education:* Grade 5 Theory; Self-taught. *Career:* Founder member, band Chakk; Signed to MCA Records/Publishing, 1985; Signed solo publishing deal with Warner Chappell; Now writing and producing; International DJ; Writing film sound-track music. *Recordings:* Set Me Free, Clubland; So In Love/Real Deal, Judy Cheeks. *Leisure interests:* Swimming; Photography. *Current Management:* XTRAX. *Address:* PO Box 966, London SE11 5SA, England.

XIMENES Charlson Pedro Vasconcelos; b. 8 May 1965, Sao Caitano, Pernambuco, Brazil. Performer; Songwriter; Musician (guitar, bass, drums, saxophone); Vocalist. *Musical Education:* Songwriting, Music in the Making, Music History, Morley College, London. *Career:* Radio broadcasts include: Radio Bitury; Belo Jardim; Garanhuns Difusora; 97.7 São Paulo, Brazil; WMRZ Radio Miami, USA; Television appearances: Belezinha The Clown TV Show; Brazil tour with Universitaria TV crew. *Recordings:* with Flying Squad (Esquadrilha Da Fumaça): Tora Tora Tora, 1984; with Deja Vu: Black Angel, 1987; Love Me Tonite, 1988; Collision Course, 1998; Never Around (with Nando Lynch), 2000. *Honours:* Amateur Theatre Background Music Award, Brazil, 1980; Second Prize, Northeastern Popular Music Festival, Belo Jardim Pe, Brazil. *Membership:* Musicians' Union. *Leisure interests:* Reading; Night-clubbing. *Current Management:* Aqua Records. *Address:* 434 Devon Mansions, Tooley St, London SE1 2XJ, England.

Y

YA KID K (Manuela Kamosi); b. Zaire. Rapper. *Career:* Moved to Belgium, aged 11; Member, Antwerp-based rap group Fresh Beat; Member, Technotronik; Rapping partnership with MC Eric. *Recordings:* Albums: with Technotronik: Pump Up The Jam, 1990; Trip On This – Remixes, 1990; Body To Body, 1991; Singles: Pump Up The Jam (No. 2, UK); Get Up (Before The Night Is Over); This Beat Is Technotronik; Rockin' Over The Beat; with Hi Tek: Spin That Wheel, 1990. *Current Management:* ARS Productions. *Address:* Singel 5, 2550 Kontich, Belgium.

YAGNIK Alka; b India. Vocalist. *Career:* Indian film playback singer; Musically trained from an early age; All India Radio artist in Calcutta; Won a Sugam Sangeet award, aged 11; Sang a few lines in film Payal Ki Jhankar, 1979; First full song on film was a duet with Amit Kumar, Hum Tum Rahenge, in Hamari Bahu Alka but the film was delayed; First release was Mere Angne Mein from Laawaris, 1981; Sang regularly for most of the top directors throughout the 1980s; Became established as one of the top playback singers with massive hit Ek Do Teen, 1988. *Recordings:* soundtracks include: Mera Jawaab, 1985; Biwi Ho To Aisi, Qayamat Se Qayamat Tak, Tezaab, 1988; 100 Days, Saajan, Afsana Pyar Ka, Akayla, 1991; Deewana, Khiladi, Raju Ban Gaya Gentleman, 1992; Darr, Hum Hain Rahi Pyaar Ke, Anari, 1993; Akele Hum Akele Tum, Barsaat, Coolie No 1, Karan Arjun, 1995; Gupt, Ishq, Judaai, Pardes, Yes Boss, 1997; China-Gate, Ghulam, 1998; Baadshah, Dil Kya Kare, Dillagi, Hum Aapke Dil Mein Rehte..., Hum Dil De Chuke Sanam, Hum Saath-Saath Hain, Jaanam Sanjha Karo, Taal, 1999; Champion, Deewane, Dulhan Hum Le Jayenge, Har Dil Jo Pyar Karega, Josh, Kahin Pyaar Na Ho Jaaye, Kaho Naa... Pyaar Hai, Refugee, 2000; Albela, Bas Itna Sa Khwaab Hai, Choori Choori Chupke Chupke, Daman, Dil Chahta Hai, Ek Rishtaa – The Bond of Love, Kasoor, Lagaan, One 2 Ka 4, Pyaar Ishq Aur Mohabbat, Pyaar Tune Kya Kiya, Rahul, Yaadein, 2001. *Honours:* 4 Filmfare Awards; 2 National Awards.

YAMAKOSHI Brian Seiji; b. 29 Dec. 1957, Chicago, Illinois, USA. Musician (koto – Japanese harp); Composer. *Education:* Middlesex Polytechnic, Semester At Sea, Arizona State University. *Musical Education:* Music theory, guitar, piano, and koto training. *Career:* Television appearances: Numerous in Japan; Concon C'est Nous (France); NHK Television and radio, Japan; BBC Radio. *Recordings:* Snowflake, Peter Gabriel; Akiko Yano, Akira Inoue; World Diary, with Tony Levin, Manu Katché, Shanker. *Memberships:* ASCAP; JASRAC; SACEM. *Leisure interests:* Skiing; Swimming; Windsurfing; Reading. *Current Management:* Ms Naoto Tsunoi.

YANG Mu; b. 16 Aug. 1949, Fuzhou, China. Ethnomusicologist. *Musical Education:* BA and Diploma in Musicology, Central Conservatory of Music, Beijing, China, 1983; PhD, Ethnomusicology, University of Queensland, Australia, 1990. *Career:* Violinist, Composer, Conductor, 1971–78; Music Editor and Programme Producer, China's National Broadcasting Service, Beijing, 1983–85; Sessional Lecturer, Project Director, Research Fellow in Ethnomusicology, Monash University, Melbourne, 1990–95; Visiting Fellow, Australian National University, Canberra, 1995–98; Research Fellow, Northern Territory University; Australia, 1999–2002. *Publications:* Chinese Musical Instruments: An Introduction, 1993; Articles in Music Research (Beijing), Musicology Australia, Ethnomusicology, International Journal of Music Education, Yearbook for Traditional Music, Asian Music, Journal of the Central Conservatory of Music (Beijing). *Honour:* Jaap Kunst Prize, Society for Ethnomusicology, USA, 1998. *Memberships:* Society for Ethnomusicology; International Council of Traditional Music; Musicological Society of Australia; Asscn for Chinese Music Research, USA. *Address:* School of Southeast Asian and Australian Studies, Northern Territory University, Darwin, NT 0909, Australia.

YANKOVIC 'Weird' Al (Alfred); b. 23 10 1959, Lynwood, California, USA. Musician (accordion); Songwriter; Performer; Actor. *Education:* BA, Architecture, California Polytechnic San Luiz Obispo, California. *Musical Education:* Accordion lessons. *Career:* As Weird Al, 15 years of successful parodies of pop classics; Concert appearances; Television and radio appearances: including own Showtime and MTV specials; 3 best-selling home videos; Film: UHF, 1989. *Recordings include:* Ricky, 1983; Weird Al Yankovic In 3-D, 1984; Dare To Be Stupid, 1985; Polka Party, 1986; Fat (parody of Michael Jackson: Bad), 1988; Greatest Hits, 1988; Peter and The Wolf, 1988; UHF- Soundtrack, 1989; Off The Deep End, featuring the hit Smells Like Nirvana, 1992; The Food Album, 1993; Apalooza, 1993; Bad Hair Day, 1996; Running with Scissors, 1999. *Publications:* The Authorized Al, autobiography by Al Yankovic and Tino Insana, 1985. *Honours:* Grammy Awards: Best Comedy Recording: Eat It, 1984; Best Video: Fat, 1988. *Membership:* NARAS; BMI; AFofM. *Leisure interests:* Eating; Sleeeping; Watching television; Films; Concerts. *Current Management:* Jan Levey, Imaginary Entertainment. *Address:* 923 Westmount Dr., Los Angeles, CA 90069, USA.

YANNI (Yanni Chryssomallis); b. 1955, Kalamata, Greece. Composer; Musician (keyboards). *Education:* Psychology degree, Minnesota. *Career:* Keyboard player with US progressive rock group Chameleon; Composer, leader, own orchestra; Recent concerts include: The Acropolis, Athens, 1993; Royal Albert Hall, London, 1995; Taj Mahal, India, 1997; Forbidden City, China, 1997. *Recordings:* Albums include: Keys To Imagination, 1986; Out of Silence, 1987; Chameleon Days, 1988; Niki Nana, 1989; Reflections of Passion, 1990; In Celebration of Life, 1991; Dare To Dream, 1992; Yanni – Live At The Acropolis, 1993; Tribute, 1997; If I Could Tell You, 2000. *Honours:* 2 Grammy Awards. *Current Management:* CPRA Inc, 1712 Cypress Row Dr., West Palm Beach, FL 33411, USA.

YARLING Nicole; b. 31 July 1957, Brooklyn, NY, USA. Musician (Violin, Vocals). m. John Yarling. *Education:* BA, Baruch College; MA, Columbia University; Private Instruction in Violin, Composition and Arranging. *Career:* Freelance, Formed Ensemble Strings, 1981–84; Formed R & B Rock Band Little Nicky and the Slicks, 1985; Featured Soloist with Jimmy Yarling, 1990–94; Walden Wood Concert, 1993; Tribute to Ella Fitzgerald, 1997; JVC – Jazz Festival, 1998. *Recordings:* Strings Attached, 1984; Little Nicky and the Slicks, 1988; Fruitcakes, 1994; Afro Blue Band, 1997; N Yarling, 1999. *Memberships:* AFTRA. *Current Management:* John Levy Enterprises, 1828 Coolidge Ave, Altadena, CA 91001, USA. *Address:* 690 Siesta Key Circle #2018, Deerfield Beach, Florida 33441, USA.

YARROW Peter; b. 31 May 1938, New York, USA. Singer; Songwriter; Film and Television Prod. *Career:* Member, Peter Paul and Mary, 1960–; Television specials: 25th Anniversary Special, PBS, 1985; A Holiday Celebration, PBS, 1988; Peter Paul and Mommy Too, PBS, 1993; Co-founder, Kerrville Folk Festival, Texas; Founding member, board of directors, Newport Folk Festival; Television Specials, Lifelines, PBS, 1995. *Compositions:* Author/co-author songs include: Puff The Magic Dragon; Light One Candle; Day Is Done; The Great Mandala; Torn Between Two Lovers. *Recordings:* 16 albums with Peter Paul and Mary; 4 solo albums. *Honours:* Allard K Lowenstein Award (for Human Rights, Peace and Freedom); Vista Citizen Action Leadership Award; Kate Wolf Memorial Award, The World Folk Music Asscn; Grammy Awards, 1962, 1963, 1969; Emmy Nominations, 1979, 1993, 1996. *Memberships:* Board of Directors: Center for Global Education, North American Congress on Latin America, Friends of Vista. *Current Management:* Walk Street Management. *Address:* 1639 B Electric Ave, Venice, CA 90291, USA.

YASINITSKY Gregory Walter; b. 3 Oct. 1953, San Francisco, California, USA. Composer; Musician (saxophone); Educator. m. Ann Marie Kelley, 15 Jan. 1977, 1 d. *Musical Education:* AA Music, College San Mateo, 1973; San Francisco State University, BM, Composition, 1976, MA, 1978; DMA, Composition, Eastman School of Music, Rochester, New York, 1995; Composition studies: Joseph Schwantner; Wayne Peterson; Lou Harrison; Samuel Adler; Robert Morris; Saxophone studies with Ramon Ricker, Joe Henderson, Donald Carroll, James Matheson, Jerry Vejmola. *Career:* Professor of Music, Co-ordinator, Jazz Studies, Washington State Univesity, 1982–; Lecturer in Music, San Jose State University, 1978–82; San Francisco State University, 1977–81; Lecturer, Jazz Studies, 1977–80; Principal saxophonist, Spokane Symphony, 1991–; Orchestral saxophonist with: San Francisco Symphony; Oakland Symphony; Cabrillo Festival Orchestra; Performances as jazz saxophonist with: Sarah Vaughan; Lionel Hampton; Stan Getz; Clark Terry; Louis Bellson; Randy Brecker; Tom Harrell; Gary Burton; Mark Isham; Art Lande; Performances, clinics, workshops throughout USA, Canada, Japan, Europe. *Compositions:* Over 90 works published. *Publications:* Articles for: Jazz Educators Journal; Band World; New Ways; Aftertouch; Saxophone Symposium. *Honours:* Mullen Award Excellence in Teaching, Washington State University, 1989; Jazz Fellowship, US National Endowment for the Arts, 1986; ASCAP Special Awards for Composition, 1986-. *Memberships:* ASCAP; IAJE; MENC. *Leisure interest:* Cooking. *Address:* NW 485 Robert St, Pullman, WA 99163, USA.

YATES Mark (Sark); b. 4 April 1968. Musician (Guitar). *Career:* Joined Spoilt Bratz with Shutty, Leigh Marklew and Tony Wright; Renamed as Terrorvision; Major label deal, 1991; Support slot to Ramones; Numerous headlining tours and TV appearances. *Recordings:* Singles: My House, 1993; Oblivion, 1994; Pretend Best Friend, 1994; Alice, What's The Matter, 1994; Bad Actress, 1996; Perseverance, 1996; Easy, 1996; Moonage Daydream, 1997; Josephine, 1998; Tequila, 1999; Albums: My House,

1993; Formaldehyde, 1993; How to Win Friends and Influence People, 1994; Regular Urban Survivors, 1996; Shaving Peaches, 1998.

YEARWOOD Trisha; b. Georgia, USA. Country Singer. *Education:* Belmont University. *Career:* Session singer, Nashville, 1985–; Discovered by, support tours with Garth Brooks, 1991. *Recordings:* Albums: Trisha Yearwood, 1991; Hearts In Armor, 1992; The Song Remembers When, 1993; The Sweetest Gift, 1994; Thinking About You, 1995; Everybody Knows, 1996; Song Book (A Collection of Hits), 1997; Where Your Road Leads, 1997; Real Live Woman, 2000; Backing vocals, No Fences, Garth Brooks; Tower of Strength (Leonard Cohen tribute album), 1995. *Honours:* Best New Country Artist, American Music Award, 1991; Country Music Asscn, Female Vocalist of The Year, 1997; British Country Music Award, Female Vocalist of The Year, 1997; Grammy Awards for: Best Country Vocal Collaboration; Best Female Country Performance, 1998; Academy of Country Music Award, Top Female Vocalist, 1998; Country Music Asscn Award, Female Vocalist of The Year, 1998. *Current Management:* Force Inc. *Address:* 1505 16th Ave S, Nashville, TN 37212, USA.

YEN Wen-Hsiung; b. 26 June 1934, Tainan, Taiwan. Musician (Piano, Erhu). m. Yuan Yuan, 6 Jan. 1961, 3 s. *Education:* BA, National Taiwan Normal University; MA, Chinese Culture University; MA, University of California at Los Angeles, PhD, candidate; Cultural Doctorate, Philosophy and Music, World University; Studied Piano with Qing-Yan Zhou, Fu-Mei Lee, Composition with Paul Chihara Hsu and Chang-Houei. *Career:* Radio appearance, Taiwan, 1967, 1990; TV appearance, Channel 62, 1992; Leading Chinese Music Orchestra of Southern California, for An Evening of Chinese Music and Dance; Professor and Instructor, colleges and universities; Video, with Chinese American Musicians' Association of Southern California; Video, Chinese Performing Arts Association of America. *Publications:* Taiwan Folk Songs, Vol. I, 1967, Vol. II, 1969; A Dictionary of Chinese Music, 1967; A Collection of Wen-Hsiung Yen's Songs, 1968, Vol. II, 1987; Chinese Musical Culture and Folk-songs, 1989. *Honours:* Outstanding Teacher, Confucius Commemorative Day Ceremony, Los Angeles, 1984; National Tainan Normal University Alumni Asscn of Southern California. *Memberships:* Overseas Chinese Affairs Commission; International Council for Traditional Music; Society for Ethnomusicology; Society for Asian Music. *Leisure interests:* Walking; Tai chi chuan; Attending concerts. *Address:* 482 Los Altos Ave, Arcadia, CA 91007, USA.

YEO Oscar, (Port); b. 28 June 1929, London, England. Musician (drums); Vocalist; Graphic designer. m. Gay Clarke, 16 Sept. 1964, 2 s. *Musical Education:* Private violin tuition as child; Self-taught since. *Career:* Known as Port, pre-1960; Founder member, Eric Silk's Southern Jazz Band; Broadcasts include: Albert Hall, Festival Hall concerts, include Festival of Britain, 1950–54; Freelanced music; Graphic design to 1959; Professional musician until 1963; Semi-professional, 1963-. *Membership:* Musicians' Union (Gold card holder). *Leisure interests:* Walking; Dogs; Classic cars; Jazz concerts. *Address:* Bray, Berkshire, England.

YEOH Nicola Beng Ean; b. 24 May 1973, London, England. Musician (Piano); Composer; Arranger; Band Leader. *Musical Education:* A Level Music, Centre Young Musicians Weekend Arts College. *Career:* Courtney Pine Band, 1991–94; Neneh Cherry, 1993; The Roots, 1994; Eddie Harris, 1996; Jools Holland, TV Show, Later, 1993; Arsenio Hall, show, USA, 1993; Infinitum, own band, featuring Keith Le Blanc and Michael Mondesir, Radio 3 Broadcast, 1993; Composer in Residence for NYJOS, 1998–99; Commission of Quiet Freedom, 1998. *Compositions:* Commissioned: Six as 1, 1996; Speechmix X-ploration, 1997; Be-Bop, 1997; Entwined, for pianist Joanna MacGregor, 1997; Infinitum, Big Band, 12 piece, 1997; Common Denominator, commissioned by LAB, 1998; Two Rainbows, 1998; 4 Pieces for Cello and Piano, commissioned by Norfolk and Norwich Jazz Festival, 1999. *Recording:* Red, Hot and Cool, with The Roots and Roy Ayers. *Honour:* Montreux Jazz Piano Competition, semi-finalist, 1999. *Memberships:* PRS; PAMRA; MU. *Leisure interests:* Swimming; Cycling; Learning languages. *Current Management:* Beng Ean Productions, 1 Rodney House, Donegal St, London N1 9QF. *Address:* 67 Dyne Rd, London, NW6 7DR, England.

YERNJAKIAN Lilit; b. 8 Feb. 1950, Yerevan, Armenia. Musician (Piano); Musicologist. m. V Gasparian, 2 s. *Education:* Yerevan State Conservatory, 1968–73. *Publications:* Traditional Genres of Monody and The Present, 1987; Armenian Musicians, 1990; Mythopoetic Sources of Ashoog Dastgahus, 1994; From The History of Armenian-Persian Musical Ties, Yerevan, 1991; Hymn to the Sun, Yerevan, 1998. *Memberships:* Union of Composers of Armenia. *Leisure interest:* Tennis. *Address:* Nalbanian St N47 Ap 19a, 375025 Yerevan, Armenia.

YETNIKOFF Walter R; b. 11 Aug. 1933, Brooklyn, New York, USA. Record Co Exec. m. June Yetnikoff, 24 Nov. 1957, 2 s. *Education:* BA, Brooklyn College, New York Bar, 1953; LLB, Columbia University, 1956. *Career:* Lawyer, New York, 1958–61; Attorney, CBS Records, 1961–65; General attorney, CBS Group, 1965–69; Vice President, International

Division, CBS, 1969–71; President, CBS International, 1971–75; President, CBS Group, 1975-. *Membership:* International Federation of Producers of Phonographs and Videograms.

YOAKAM Dwight; b. 23 Oct. 1956, Pikeville, Kentucky, USA. Country Singer; Musician (guitar); Songwriter. *Education:* History and Philosophy, Ohio University. *Career:* Country singer, 1978–; Also played with Los Lobos; Concerts include: UK and US tours; Tours with Buck Owens; Farm Aid VI, Indiana, 1993. *Recordings:* Albums: Guitars, Cadillacs, 1986; Hillbilly Deluxe, 1987; Buenas Noches From A Lonely Room, 1988; Just Looking For A Hit, 1989; If There Was A Way, 1990; La Croix D'Amour, 1992; This Time, 1993; Gone, 1996; Under the Covers, 1997; Come on Christmas, 1997; A Long Way Home, 1998; La Croix d'Amour, 1999; Singles: Honky Tonk Man, 1986; Guitars, Cadillacs, 1986; Little Sister, 1987; Streets of Bakersfield, duet with Buck Owens, (No. 1, USA Country charts), 1988; Always Late (With Your Kisses), 1988; I Sang Dixie (No. 1, USA Country charts), 1989; Suspicious Minds, from film soundtrack, Honeymoon In Vegas, 1992; Fast As You Can, 1993; Dwight Live, 1995; These Arms, 1998. *Honours:* 5 Platinum discs; One Multi Platinum disc; One Gold disc; Academy of Country Music, Best New Male Artist, 1986; Music City News Country Award, Best Vocal Collaboration, with Buck Owens, 1988. *Current Management:* Borman Entertainment, 1250 Sixth St, Suite 401, Santa Monica, CA 90401, USA.

YOGESWARAN Manickam; b. 3 March 1959, Sri Lanka. Vocalist; Musician (South Indian flute, drums). *Education:* Accountancy (CIMA). *Musical Education:* Learnt by Guru-Sisya method. *Career:* Concert vocalist, musician, Indo-pop Music; Lead singer, Dissidenten, European tours, 1993–; Concerts include Commonwealth Institute, 1992; Paris Music Festival, 1993; Music Guimet, Paris, 1994; Music Festival, Madras, India, 1995; Visiting Lecturer for Music Workshop Skills, Goldsmiths College, University of London, England. *Recordings:* Background score, documentary Serendipity; 7 albums, 1990–94; Singer, Duets With Automobiles (Shobana Jeyasing Dance Company); Romance With Footnotes; Tamil Classics, CD. *Publications:* Currently compiling video: South Indian Drumming. *Honours:* Kalai Mamani, London Sri Murugan Temple; Suranaya Devan, Oslo Music Asscn; Regular Appearances in the December Music Festival, Madras, 1994-. *Membership:* Musicians' Union. *Leisure interests:* Nature; Yoga; Exercise; Teaching. *Address:* 29 Firdene, Tolworth, Surrey KT5 9QQ, England.

YORKE Thom; Vocalist; Musician. *Career:* Singer, Radiohead; Also designer of record sleeves; Support to REM, US tour, 1995; Milton Keynes Bowl, 1995. *Recordings:* Albums: Pablo Honey, 1993; The Bends, 1995; Singles: Creep, 1993; My Iron Lung, 1994; High and Dry, 1995; Fake Plastic Trees, 1995; Just, 1995; Street Spirit (Fade Out), 1996; Contributor, Help (Bosnia Relief Album), 1995; guest vocalist with Drugstore on White Magic for Lovers, and El President, 1998; with Velvet Goldmine, 1998; MTV's 120 Minutes Live, 1998. *Honours:* BRIT Nomination, Best British Group, 1996. *Current Management:* Courtyard Management, 21 The Nursery, Sutton Courtenay, Abingdon, Oxon OX14 4UA, England.

YOUNG Angus; b. 31 March 1959, Glasgow, Scotland. Rock Musician (guitar). *Career:* Guitarist, heavy rock group AC/DC, 1973–; Numerous tours world-wide; Major concerts include: Reading Rock Festival, 1978; Monsters of Rock Festival, Castle Donington, 1981, 1984; European rock festivals, Hungary, Switzerland, Belgium, Germany, 1991; Concert, Moscow, 1991; Over 80m. albums sales to date. *Recordings:* Singles include: Rock 'n' Roll Damnation, 1978; Highway To Hell, 1979; Touch Too Much, 1980; Rock 'n' Roll Ain't Noise Pollution, 1980; You Shook Me All Night Long, 1980; Back In Black, 1981; Let's Get It Up, 1982; For Those About To Rock (We Salute You), 1982; Guns For Hire, 1983; Nervous Shakedown, 1984; Shake Your Foundations, 1986; Who Made Who, 1986; Heatseeker, 1988; Thunderstruck, 1990; Moneytalks, 1990; Are You Ready, 1991; That's The Way I Wanna Rock 'n' Roll, 1993; Big Gun (used in film The Last Action Hero), 1993; Hard As A Rock, 1995; Albums: High Voltage, 1975; TNT, 1975; High Voltage, 1975; Dirty Deeds Done Cheap, 1976; Let There Be Rock, 1977; Powerage, 1978; If You Want Blood You've Got It, 1978; Highway To Hell, 1979; Back In Black, 1980; For Those About To Rock (We Salute You), 1981; Flick of The Switch, 1983; Fly On The Wall, 1985; Who Made Who, 1986; Blow Up Your Video, 1988; The Razor's Edge, 1990; Live, 1992; Ballbreaker, 1995; Private Parts, 1997; Bonfire, 1997. *Current Management:* Hard To Handle Management, 1133 Broadway, Suite 1301, New York, NY 10010, USA.

YOUNG Jesse Colin, (Perry Miller); b. 11 Nov. 1944, New York City, New York, USA. Singer; Musician (guitar, bass). *Career:* Began as folk singer, New York; Founder member The Youngbloods, 1965–72; Appearances include: Sky River Rock Festival; Lighter Than Air Fair, 1968; Solo career, 1973–; Appeared, No Nukes, Madison Square Garden, New York, with Bruce Springsteen, Doobie Brothers, Jackson Browne, 1979. *Compositions include:* Get Together, recorded by Dave Clark Five, 1970. *Recordings:* Albums with The Youngbloods: The Youngbloods, 1967; Earth Music, 1967; Elephant Mountain, 1969; Best of The Youngbloods,

1970; Rock Festival, 1970; Ride The Wind, 1971; Good 'n' Dusty, 1971; Sunlight, 1971; High On A Ridgetop, 1972; Get Together, 1972; Solo albums: The Soul of a City Boy, 1964; Youngblood, 1964; Song For Juli, 1973; Light Shine, 1974; Songbirds, 1974; On The Road, 1974; Love On The Wing, 1974; American Dreams, 1978. *Current Management:* Skyline Music, PO Box 31, Lancaster, NH 03584, USA.

YOUNG John; b. 31 May 1956, Romford, Essex, England. Musician (keyboards); Songwriter. *Musical Education:* Head Chorister, Liverpool Metropolitan Cathedral; Grade VIII Piano; A Level Music. *Career:* Tours: Uli Jon Roth – Electric Sun world tour, 1985; Robin George, UK, 1986; Roy Wood, UK, Asia, Europe, 1987–90; Paul Rodgers and Kenny Jones (billed as The Law), UK, 1991; Bonnie Tyler world tour, 1994–; Also member, MTV band, 1988. *Recordings:* Albums by Batisti; Steeleye Span; Various unsigned artists including own Project Cathedral, 1986–89; Crime of Passion, John Wetton, 1994; Live album, 1995; Current projects: Brand X album and solo album. *Publication:* Currently making tuition video with Robin Lumley. *Membership:* PRS. *Current Management:* The Control Group. *Address:* Chapel Mews, 68 Crewe Rd, Alsager, Cheshire ST7 2HA, England.

YOUNG Neil; b. 12 Nov. 1945, Toronto, Ontario, Canada. Singer; Songwriter; Musician (guitar). m. Pegi Young, 1 s., 1 d. *Career:* Lead singer, The Squires; Co-founder, Buffalo Springfield (with Stephen Stills), 1966–69; Support to Rolling Stones, Hollywood Bowl, 1966; CAFF Charity concert, 1967; Support tours to Steve Miller Band, 1967; Iron Butterfly, 1968; Solo artiste, with own backing group, Crazy Horse, 1969–; Joined Crosby Stills and Nash, to become Crosby Stills Nash and Young, 1969–74; Tours include: US tour, 1969; Support to Rolling Stones, 1969; European tour, 1970; European tour with Booker T and the MGs, 1993; US tour with Pearl Jam, 1995; Major concerts include: Royal Festival Hall, 1973; The Last Waltz (the Band's Farewell Concert), 1976; Miami Music Festival, 1977; Live Aid, Philadelphia, 1985; Farm Aid II, 1987; Nelson Mandela – An International Tribute, Wembley, 1990; Farm Aid V, 1992; Bob Dylan's 30th Anniversary concert, Madison Square Garden, 1992; Reading Festival, 1995; Writer, director, films: Rust Never Sleeps (also recorded soundtrack), 1979; Human Highway, 1982; Subject of documentary film, Journey Through The Past, 1973. *Recordings:* include: 3 albums with Buffalo Springfield; with Crosby Stills Nash and Young: Deja Vu, 1970; Four Way Street, 1971; So Far, 1974 (all US No. 1's); with Stills/Young Band: Long May You Run, 1970; Solo/with Crazy Horse: Neil Young, 1969; Everybody Knows This Is Nowhere, 1969; After The Goldrush, 1970; Crazy Horse, 1971; Loose 1972; Harvest, 1972; Journey Through The Past, 1972; Time Fades Away, 1973; On The Beach, 1974; Tonight's The Night, 1975; Zuma, 1975; American Stars and Bars, 1977; Decade, 1978; Crazy Moon, 1978; Comes A Time, 1978; Hawks and Doves, 1979; Live Rust, 1980; Re-ac-tor, 1981; Trans, 1983; Everybody's Rockin', 1983; Old Ways, 1985; Landing On Water, 1986; Life, 1987; This Note's For You, 1988; American Dream, 1988; Eldorado, 1989; Freedom, 1989; Ragged Glory, 1990; Left For Dead, 1990; Weld, 1991; Harvest Moon, 1992; Lucky Thirteen, 1993; Unplugged, 1993; Sleeps With Angels, 1994; Mirror Ball, 1995; Dead Man – Music From and Inspired By The Motion Picture, 1996; Broken Arrow, 1996; Year of The Horse, 1997; Crazy Moon and Bonus Tracks, 1997. *Honours include:* Grammy Award, Best New Artists (with Crosby Stills Nash and Young), 1970; Melody Maker Poll Winner, Best International Group, 1971; MTV Video Award, 1989; Rolling Stone Critics Award, Best Album, 1989; Bay Area Music Award, Outstanding Album, 1993; Q Award, Best Live Act, 1993. *Current Management:* Elliot Roberts, Lookout Management, 1460 Fourth St, Suite 210, Santa Monica, CA 90401, USA.

YURKOVICH Richard; b. 8 June 1947, Neillsville, WI, USA. Musician (Accordion). m. Gabrielle Reyzer, 2 s. *Education:* Private Accordian Lessons. *Career:* Weekly Radio Show; Guest Appearances on Local Television; 2 Musican Tours; Owner, Manager, RY Recording Studio. *Recordings:* 20 Folk Albums. *Membership:* BMI. *Leisure interests:* Hunting; Sporting Events. *Current Management:* RY Productions, N10060 Fisher Ave, Willard, WI 54493, USA.

Z

ZABALA Fernando; b. 19 April 1962, Madrid, Spain. Promoter. *Education:* Lawyer. *Musical Education:* Saxophone player. *Career:* Promoter in Spain for: U2; Bruce Springsteen; Whitney Houston; REM; Michael Jackson; Pink Floyd; Tina Turner; Bryan Adams; Bon Jovi; Mike Oldfield; Paul McCartney; Dire Straits; Joe Cocker; Simply Red; Keith Richards; Red Hot Chili Peppers; Cirque Du Soliel; David Copperfield; Current manager of Radio Tarifa, Joaquin Ruiz. *Publications:* Guiá De La Música-El Pais, Año De Rock. *Membership:* APCI (International Concert Promoters Asscn). *Leisure interests:* Skiing; Squash; Football. *Address:* Sold Out, Alcalá 114–6B, 28009 Madrid, Spain.

ZAMFIR Gheorghe; b. Romania. Musician (pan-pipes). *Career:* World's leading pan-pipe player; Recording artist, traditional folk music, 1974; Pan-pipe versions, pop, classical and religious tunes. *Recordings:* Numerous albums include: L'Alouette, 1978; Impressions, 1978; In Paris, 1981; Zamfir, 1981; Lonely Shepherd, 1982; Music For The Millions, 1983; Romance, 1984; Atlantis, 1985; By Candlelight, 1986; Beautiful Dreams, 1988; Images, 1989; Singles include: Doina De Jale, theme to BBC series, The Light of Experience, 1976; Theme from De Verlaten Mijn, with James Last, 1979.

ZAMORA Tye; b. 30 May 1977, Artesia, California, USA. Musician (bass guitar). *Career:* Played with local bands NOW, UVOD, The Color Red, Carpet; Stank Toof, Tyemus; Member: Alien Ant Farm, 1996–; Self-financed independent LP released to acclaim, 1999; Signed to Papa Roach's New Noize label; Second album released in conjunction with DreamWorks label, leading to major international breakthrough, 2000–01. *Recordings:* Albums: Greatest Hits, 1999; ANThology, 2001; Singles: $100 EP, 1996; Love Songs EP, 1998; Movies, Smooth Criminal, 2001. *Honours:* L.A. Music Award, Best Independent Album, 1999. *Address:* c/o New Noize, 2022 Cliff Dr #123, Santa Barbara, CA 93109, USA. *E-mail:* info@newnoize.com. *Internet:* www.alienantfarm.com.

ZANDER Robin; b. 23 Jan. 1953, Rockford, Illinois, USA. Singer; Musician (guitar). *Career:* Founder member, singer, guitarist, Cheap Trick, 1969–; Concerts include: California Music Festival, 1979; Reading Festival, 1979; Montreux Rock Festival, 1988; US tour with Robert Plant, 1988; US tour with Kiss, 1988; US tour with Heart, 1990. *Recordings:* albums: Cheap Trick, 1977; In Color, 1977; Heaven Tonight, 1978; Cheap Trick At Budokan, 1979; Dream Police, 1979; Found All The Parts, 1980; All Shook Up, 1980; One On One, 1982; Next Positions Please, 1983; Standing On The Edge, 1985; The Doctor, 1986; Lap of Luxury, 1988; Busted, 1990; The Greatest Hits, 1991; Solo album: Robin Zander, 1993; with Shudder to Think: First Love, Last Rites, 1998; with Posies: Amazing Disgrace, 1999; Singles include: I Want You To Want Me, 1979; Voices, from film soundtrack Roadie, 1980; Stop This Game, 1980; If You Want My Love, 1982; Mighty Wings, from film soundtrack Top Gun, 1986; Ghost Town, 1988; Never Had A Lot To Lose, 1990; Surrender To Me, duet with Ann Wilson, from film soundtrack Tequila Sunrise, 1990; Can't Stop Falling Into Love, 1990. *Current Management:* Ken Adamany Associates, 1818 Parmenter St, Suite 202, Middleton, WI 53562, USA.

ZANKLAN; b. 22 Aug. 1966, Atchoukpa, Benin. Percussionist. *Education:* Benin National Gendarmerie. *Career:* National Television Programme ORIRE, 1998; Television LC2 First Anniversary, 1998; Radio Atlantique FM, 1998; Radio Golfe FM, 1998. *Compositions:* Sotie; Ohovive; Repos; Mi N'Danase; Gbehobada; Sorcier; ata N'De Kuku. *Recordings:* Album, Ohovive. *Honours:* Prize of The Most Experienced Singer In Lomé, 1996. *Memberships:* BUBEDRA; UMC. *Leisure interests:* Music; Reading; Sports. *Address:* PO Box 1135 Porto-Novo, Benin.

ZANNOU Guy Dossa; b. 15 June 1962, Porto-Novo, Benin. Musician (guitar); Singer. m. Blandine Ayi, 2 s., 1 d. *Career:* Appearances on Beninoise radio and TV including Coup de Pouce, Stars' Music; Participated in shows with famous African stars including François Louga, Aïcha Koné, Aurlus Mabélé, Afia Mala, Gadji Céli; Musical arrangements for Beninoise artists; Band Leader for Suka-Siko. *Compositions:* Corruption; Ce sera la Fête; Time is Money. *Recording:* Corruption. *Memberships:* Local Union of Pop; Musicians' Local Asscn of Artists for Environment; Secretary General, National Federation of Artists' Asscn. *Leisure interest:* Table tennis. *Current Management:* Z Plus Productions. *Address:* 01 PO Box 447, Porto-Novo, Benin.

ZAPPELLINI Marino; b. 17 May 1955, Bourges, France. Musician (saxophone, flute); Composer; Actor. *Education:* Master of Music, University of Paris. *Musical Education:* Jazz Improvisation, Harmony, Berklee School of Music, Boston, USA; Music info and Midi techniques, AFDAS; Electro-acoustic music, GMEN, GRM; Jazz professional, AFDAS;

Theatre production, AFDAS. *Career:* Professional musician, 1978–; Leader, Madzano Quartet; Actor, theatre: Du Vent Dans Les Branches De Sassafras; Actor, film: 10 Seconds; Film director and composer, films: Le Onzième Comandment; 10 Seconds; Saxophone improvisation, orchestra, with MJC Marcel Cachin de Romainville, 1988–; Administrator, Artistic director, L'association loi 1901, Big Band Paris Est; Worked with numerous artistes including: Mama Bea Tiekelski; Toure Kunda; Antoine Tome; Urban Sax; Pierre Henri; Bernard Lubat; Gérard Marais; Mico Nissim; Corazon Rebelde; Pajaro Canzani; Salif Keita; Ousmane Kouyate; Kaba Mane; Manfila Kante; Carlos Nasciomiento; Gery Burtin; Organizer, tours for artists from: Africa; UK; Spain; Portugal; Italy; Producer, publisher and promoter, recordings; Agent for shows in France and internationally; Administration for Big Band Paris Est; Tours; Mozambique; Antilles; Algeria; Gabon; UK; Spain; Portugal; Switzerland; Numerous European festivals. *Recordings:* Au Printemps de Bourges, Mama Bea; Mandinka Dong, Toure Kunda; L'Amour Titant, Antoine Tome; with Urban Sax: Urban Sax II; Urban Sax III; Les Noces Alchymiques, Pierre Henry; Kunga Kungaké, Kaba Mane; Madzano Live Concert; Corazon Rebelde; Pajaro Canzani; Kabe Mane. *Memberships:* Admin, Cultural division, SPEDIDAM; Mem., Jazz Commission, SNAM; Jazz Players Union (UMJ). *Leisure interests:* Sport; Fishing. *Address:* 81 rue Saint Maur, 75011 Paris, France.

ZAWINUL Joe (Josef Erich); b. 7 July 1932, Vienna, Austria. Jazz Musician (piano, synthesizer); Songwriter. *Musical Education:* Vienna Conservatory; Berklee College of Music, Boston, 1959. *Career:* Local session musician, dance, radio orchestras, 1950s; House pianist for Polydor Records; Played with Hans Koller; Maynard Ferguson; Dinah Washington; Cannonball Adderley; Miles Davis, 1961–71; Formed jazz/rock group Weather Report with Wayne Shorter, 1970–86; Solo artiste, 1985–; Leader, own groups Weather Update; Zawinul Syndicate. *Recordings:* Solo albums: Rise and Fall, 1968; Zawinul, 1970; Dialects, 1986; with Zawinul Syndicate: The Immigrants, 1988; Black Water, 1989; World Tour Live, 1998; To You with Love, 1998; with Weather Report: Weather Report, 1971; I Sing The Body Electric, 1972; Sweetnighter, 1973; Mysterious Traveller, 1974; Tail Spinnin', 1975; Black Market, 1976; Heavy Weather, 1977; Mr Gone, 1978; 8:30, 1979; Night Passages, 1980; Weather Report, 1982; Procession, 1983; Domino Theory, 1984; Sportin' Life, 1985; This Is This, 1986; Heavy Weather – The Collection, 1990; with Cannonball Adderley: Mercy Mercy Mercy, 1966; with Miles Davis: In A Silent Way, 1969; Witches Brew, 1970; Live Evil, 1972; Big Fun, 1974; Circle In The Round, 1979; Also recorded with: Tim Hardin; Eddie Harris; Quincy Jones. *Honours:* Mercy Mercy Mercy (as songwriter), 1967.

ZÉ Tom, (Antonio José Santana Martins); b. 11 Oct. 1936, Irará, Bahia, Brazil. Composer; Singer; Arranger; Actor. m. Neusa S Martins, 14 Feb. 1970, 1 s. *Musical Education:* University of Bahia, Music School; Higher Courses, 1962–67; Studied composition and structure with Ernst Widmer; History of Music with Professor H J Koellreuter; Cello with Piero Bastianelli; Counterpoint with Yulo Brandao; Piano and Guitar studies. *Career:* Tropicalist Movement, 1967; MoMA, New York, Latin American Artists of 20th Century, Concert, 1993; Opened London International Festival of Theatre, Queen Elizabeth Hall, London, England, 1993; Walker Art Center, USA, 1993; Lincoln Center, New York and Avery Fisher Hall, 1996; Jazz Festivals in USA, Canada and Europe; Only Connect, Barbican Centre Festival, London, 2001; Stage acting roles include: Arena Canta Bahia, by Augusto Boal, 1965; Rocky Horror Show, directed by Rubens Correia, 1975; Film appearances include: Sábado, by Ugo Giogetti, 1994; Mater Dei, by Vinícius Mainardi, 2001. *Recordings:* Sao Benedito, 1965; Tropicália, 1968; Todosos Olhos, 1973; Estudanddo o Samba, 1976; The Best of Tom Zé, 1990; The Hips of Tradition, 1993; Fabrication Defect, 1999. *Honours:* Festival Composer to Composer, Telluride Institute, USA; Down Beat magazine awards: Third place (Readers Poll), Fourth place (Critics Poll), for album The Best of Tom Zé, 1991; Billboard Top Alternative Album, 1991; Music Festival, TV Record: First place, Golden Viola and Silver Sabiá (song São São Paulo, Meu Amor), 1968; Fourth place (song 2001); Award for best lyrics; APCA, Best Composer, 1999; Multicultural Estadão (São Paulo) prize, 2001. *Memberships:* US: BMI; RZO; Brazil: Abramus; Fermata; Arlequim; Irará Edições Musicais. *Leisure interests:* Football; Mythology; Literature. *Address:* Rua Dr Homem de Mello 717, 05007–002 São Paulo, SP, Brazil.

ZECIC Drazen; b. 24 July 1967, Split, Croatia. m. Bozena Poljak, 29 Aug. 1992, 2 d. *Education:* Hotel Management. *Musical Education:* Self-educated. *Career:* Concerts: Croatia, including Sports Arena, Split, 1993, 1994; Tours: Canada; Australia; US; Germany; Switzerland; Italy; Television: HTV-Croatia; Local television in Australia and Canada. *Recordings:* Zagrli Me Nocas Jace, 1990; Govore Mi Mnogi Ljudi, 1993; Boem U Dusi, 1995. *Honours:* Spilt Fest-Croatia, Composer I Award, 1992;

Melodije Jadrana-Cro/Grand Prix, Singer, Composer, 1993; Cardinal Stepinac Fest -Croatia, Composer I Award, 1993. *Memberships:* Croatian Musicians' Union; HGU. *Leisure interests:* Swimming; Sailing; Football. *Address:* Croatia Records, Medugorska 61, 41000 Zagreb, Croatia.

ZELENKA Karel; b. 27 May 1946, Prague, Czech Republic. Musician (Alto and Tenor Trombone). *Education:* Studied, Prague Conservatory and Academy of Arts, Prague, Graduated, 1976. *Career:* Prague Jazz Club Reduta; Berlin Jazz Club; Lucerna Hall in Prague; Warzsaw Jazz Club, Poland. *Recordings:* Poste Restante, CD; Prague Big Band, Lucerna Hall Roth; Anniversary Concert, CD. *Membership:* The Prague Big Band. *Address:* Cimelicka 960/7, 142 00 Prague 4, Czech Republic.

ZENDER Stuart; b. 18 March 1974, Philadelphia, Pennsylvania, USA. Musician (Bass). 1 child. *Career:* Member, Jamiroquai; Numerous tours and TV appearances; Left band, 1998. *Recordings:* Singles: When You Gonna Learn, 1993; Emergency on Planet Earth, 1994; Space Cowboy EP, 1995; Cosmic Girl, 1996; Light Years, 1996; Alright, 1997; Deeper Underground, 1998; High Times, 1998; Albums: Emergency on Planet Earth, 1993; Travelling Without Moving, 1996. *Honours:* Gold and Platinum Albums; Numerous MTV Video Music Awards.

ZEPHANIAH Benjamin Obadiah Iqbal; b. 15 April 1958, Birmingham, England. Poet; Writer; Musician; Vocalist. *Career:* Acting: Didn't You Kill My Brother, 1987; Farendg, 1989; Radio Presenter: A Night with Benjamin Zephaniah, Radio 4, 1996; Newham United, Radio 4, 1998; Stage Plays: Playing the Right Tune, 1985; Job Rocking, 1987; Delirium (dance), 1987; Streetwise, 1990; Mickey Tekka, 1991; Radio: Hurricane Dub, 1989; Our Teacher's Gone Crazy, 1990; Dread Poets Society, 1991; Radio plays: Listen To Your Parents, 2000. *Recordings:* Dub Ranting EP, 1982; Rasta, LP, 1983; Big Boys Don't Make Girls Cry, single, 1984; Free South Africa, single, 1986; Us and Dem, LP, 1990; Crisis, single, 1992; Back to Our Roots, LP, 1995; Belly of the Beast, LP, 1996; Contributor to: Thin Red Line, 1999; Dancing Tribes, single (with Back To Base), 1999; Illegal (with Swayzak), 2000. *Honours:* BBC Young Playwright's Award; Hon. Doctorate, Arts and Humanities, University of North London, 1998; Hon. Doctorate, Literature, University of West of England, 1999. *Memberships:* Musicians' Union; Equity; Performing Rights Society; ALCS. *Leisure interests:* Martial arts; Numismatics. *Current Management:* Sandra Boyce Management. *Address:* PO Box 673, East Ham, London E6 3QD, England.

ZEVON Warren; b. 24 Jan. 1947, Chicago, Illinois, USA. Singer; Musician (guitar, piano); Songwriter. *Career:* Folk singer, 1969; Writer for commercials; Musician with Everly Brothers and Phil Everly, 1970–73; Solo artiste, 1973–; Member, Hindu Love Gods (with members of R.E.M.), 1990. *Compositions include:* When Johnny Strikes Up The Band; Hasten Down The Wind; Werewolves of London; Poor Poor Pitiful Me; Play It All Night Long. *Recordings:* Albums: Zevon – Wanted Dead Or Alive, 1969; Warren Zevon, 1976; Excitable Boy, 1978; Bad Luck Streak In Dancing School, 1980; Stand In The Fire, 1981; The Envoy, 1982; Sentimental Hygiene, 1987; Quiet Normal Life, 1988; Transverse City, 1989; Mr Bad Example, 1991; Learning To Flinch, 1993; Mutineer, 1995; Life'll Kill Ya, 2000; with Don Henley; I Can't Stand Still, 1982; with Phil Everly: Star Spangled Springer, 1973; Mystic Line, 1975; with Everly Brothers: Stories We Could Tell, 1972; with Hindu Love Gods: Hindu Love Gods, 1990. *Current Management:* Peter Asher Management.

ZGUROVA Kalinka Kaneva; b. 25 Sept. 1945, Debelt, Bourgas District, Bulgaria. Folk Singer. m. Stefan Kanev, 30 Aug. 1976, 1 s. *Career:* Debut, First National Singing Competition, Gramatikovo, 1960; Concert tours in Europe, Asia, America and Africa. *Recordings:* Over 350 recorded songs on Bulgarian National Radio, Bulgarian TV, cassettes and CDs. *Honours:* Grammy Award, with Mystery of Bulgarian Voices Folk Ensemble; Numerous Bulgarian and international awards and distinctions. *Address:* 27 Belmeken Str, Pavlovo, Sofia, Bulgaria.

ZHAO Jia-Zi; b. 30 Aug. 1934, Jiangsu, China. Musicologist. m. Si-Jie Xu, March 1959, 1 s., 1 d. *Education:* Shanghai Conservatory of Music, 1956–61. *Career:* Research Scholar, Music University of New Delhi, Indian Art Centre, Madras Ethnomusicology Research Institute, 1986–88; Head, Institute of Music Research, Shanghai Conservatory of Music; Full-time Supervisor of Doctorate students; Deputy Director, World Ethnomusicological Association; Deputy Director, Oriental Music Association. *Publications:* The Music of Asia; Ethnic Music of Asian Countries; Collection of Writings, Music of Shen Zhi-Bai; Indian Music around the period of Sui and Tang Dynasty; Rabindranath Tagore and his Music; Gamelan Music in Java and Bali; Comparative Study of Indian and Chinese Ancient Music; Comparative Study of Wu Dan-Qi Shen and Qi Tiao Bei. *Memberships:* Chinese Musician Asscn; Life Mem., Indian Musicological Society; Singapore Asscn for Asian Studies; Australian-Chinese Writers' Asscn, Queensland Branch; International Council for Traditional Music, USA; Asian-Pacific Society of Ethnomusicology. *Leisure interest:* Photography. *Address:* 6 Garden Court, The Ave, Sunnybank Hills, Brisbane, Qld 4109, Australia.

ZIEGLER Michael; b. 7 Nov. 1962, Copenhagen, Denmark. Musician. 1 s., 2 d. *Musical Education:* Self-taught. *Career:* Hotel Hunger Released the Album This is Where the Fun Starts in the USA and Canada, 1989; Opened the Orange Stage at Roskilde Festival, 1990; EBU Rock Festival, Ireland and Berlin, 1992. *Compositions:* This is Where the Fun Starts, 1989; Waiting For Alice, 1992; Frankie My Dear I Dont Give A Dam, 1994; Mars Needs Guitars, 1995; Happy Hour, 1996. *Recordings:* This is Where the Fun Starts, 1989; Waiting for Alice, 1992; Frankie My Dear I Dont Give a Dam, 1994; Mars Needs Guitars, 1995; Happy Hour, 1996. *Memberships:* Danish Artists Union; DPA. *Leisure interests:* Computers; Football. *Current Management:* Mardal Management.

ZIEGLER Pablo; b. 2 Sept. 1944, Buenos Aires, Argentina. Musician (Piano); Composer; Arranger. m. Sandra Sicbert, 10 Oct. 1977, 1 s., 1 d. *Education:* Buenos Aires University, not completed; Classical Music, Music Conservatory of Buenos Aires. *Career:* Astor, Piazzolla, New Tango Quintet, Piano Player, 1978–88; Montreaux Jazz Festival, North Sea Jazz Festival and Nice Jazz Festival; Summer Stage Central Park; Solo Performer: Lincoln Center, Saint Martin in the Field Cathedral. *Compositions:* Milonga in the Wind; La Conexion Portena Album. *Recordings:* with Piazzolla Quintet: Live in Montreaux; Live in Wien; Be As Zero Hour; Symphonic Tango; Los Tangueros; with Quintet for New Tango: Tango Romance, 1998; Asfalto: Street Tango, 1998; Quintet for New Tango, 1999. *Honours:* Arlequin 1992 National Prize; Hon. Citizen of New Orleans City. *Membership:* ASCAP. *Leisure interests:* Sailing; Fishing; Scuba Diving. *Current Management:* Santa Fe World, Music Agency, 609 Onate Pl., Santa Fe, NM 87501, USA. *Address:* Tucuman, 1455 8 C (CP 1050), Buenos Aires, Argentina.

ZIMMER Hans; b. 1957, Frankfurt, Germany. Film Composer; Record Prod. 1 d. *Compositions:* Film scores include: Green Card; Driving Miss Daisy; Pacific Heights; Backdraft; Rain Man; Regarding Henry; Thelma and Louise; My Beautiful Laundrette. *Recordings:* Crimson Tide, 1995; Beyond Rangoon, 1995.

ZIMMERMANN André François; b. 19 Jan. 1965, Fort de France, Martinique. Musician (piano); Composer. *Musical Education:* Music school; Conservatory; Sessions. *Career:* Appearances on TV France; Concerts as soloist, duos, trios, big bands include: Bucharest, 1990; with the Big Band de Jazz, Metabetchouan, Canada; International Festival of Brasov, Transylvania, 1990; Festivals at Mulhouse; Nitting; Avoriaz; Piano solo, St Louis, France, 1991; Teacher, School of Music, Sundgau-Alsace. *Compositions:* Theatre: Les Estivants, Gorki, 1986; La Mouette, Chekov, 1990; Derrière les 7 Papiers Peints, Wilfred Grote, with Haute Alsace, 1990; Un Chapeau de Paille d'Italy, Labiche, 1991; Children's pieces (2 selections for piano and orchestra); Music for flute and strings; Composition for regional cinema. *Recordings:* Album: Jazz Conceptions, music for popular songs. *Leisure interest:* Art. *Address:* 22 rue de Spechbach, 68720 Illfurth, France.

ZIMOLKA Ales; b. 7 April 1963, Jihlava, Czech Republic. Drummer. m. Lenka Zimolková, 8 Oct. 1988. *Education:* Business Academy; Piano, guitar, Basic Art School; Private lessons, drums, Prague, Prague Conservatory. *Career:* Member, many rock group bands, 1978–89; Member of band, Harley's John, 1990–95; Member of bands, Zoo, TMA, Little Big Company, Los Vobos, 1995–; Many video and studio recordings. *Recordings:* Ballads L, Irish ballads, 1996; Los Vobos: Cerné Díza (Black Hole), 1996; Zoo, 1997; Zome Country albums, 1996–97; Zoo: Good Morning, 1998. *Honours:* 3 times Winner, Czech Radio Top 10, Harleys, 1991. *Leisure interests:* Sport; Literature; Sleeping. *Address:* Jicínská 29, 130 00 Prague 3, Czech Republic.

ZLOKIC Jasna; b. 15 March 1955, Vela Luka, Croatia. Economist. m. Boris Zlokic, 25 June 1977, 1 s. *Musical Education:* Guitar lessons. *Career:* First public performance aged 10; Amateur career sustained until first solo album, 1980; Highly successful solo career, 1980-. *Recordings:* Single: Krugovi Na Vodi, 1980; Albums: Pusti Me Da Prodem, 1983; Skitnica, 1984; Ja Sam Ti Jedini Drug, 1985; Vjeruj Mi, 1986; Kad Odu Svi, 1987; Lutajuce Srce, 1988; Vrijeme Je Uz Nas, 1989; Tiho Sviraj Pjesmu Ljubavnu, 1990; Bez Predaha, 1992; Nisam Ti Se Tugo Nadala, 1994; Ja Zivjet Cu Za Dane Radosti, 1995. *Honours:* Zagreb Fest, Grand Prix, 1984, 1988; Split Musical Festival Award, 1982, 1984, 1987, 1993, 1994; MESAM Awards, Female Singer of the Year, 1984, 1988; Sarajevo Festival, 1988; Bratislava Festival, 1985; Madeira Festival, 1988. *Membership:* HGU (Hrvatska Glazbena Unija). *Leisure interests:* Swimming; Skiing; Tennis. *Current Management:* Boris Zlokic. *Address:* Laurenciceva 8A, 41000 Zagreb, Croatia.

ZOLA (Thuthukani Bonginkosi Dlamini); b. 1976, South Africa. Vocalist. *Education:* Jabulani Technical High, South Africa. *Career:* Stage named after Zola, suburb of Soweto; Early acting roles included youth series Teens On A Tightrope; Starred as Papa Action in TV series Yizo Yizo 2, 2001; Followed by meteoric rise to fame as kwaito/rap/hip-hop music artist; Has own TV talk show Take 5/Zola On 5. *Recordings:* Albums:

Umdlwembe (Stray Dog), 2001; Singles: Ghetto Fabulous (from Yizo Yizo OST), 2001. *Honours:* Metro FM Music Awards: Album of The Year; Artist of The Year; Song of The Year, 2001. *E-mail:* lance@ghettoruff.co.za.

ZOLOTHUHIN Adrian Dimitri; b. 22 July 1970, Middlesbrough, Cleveland, England. Musician (guitar); Arranger; Prod. *Musical Education:* BMus (tonmeister), University of Surrey. *Career:* Guitarist, Kabak; Concerts: Ashcroft Theatre; Spencer House; St James' Palace; National Portrait Gallery; Guitarist, World of Leather; Concerts: Marquee; Garage; Subterrania; Borderline; Television: What's That Noise, BBC TV; Radio: BBC GLR, various sessions. *Recordings:* St Mark's Place, World of Leather, 1994; Guitar, producer: Russian Party, World of Leather, 1994; Guitar, arranger, Blow, as solo artist on album: Bachology, 1995. *Address:* 110 Grove Ave, Hanwell, London W7 3ES, England.

ZORN John; b. 2 Sept. 1953, New York City, USA. Musician (saxophone, keyboards); Composer. *Career:* Associated with the avant garde tradition, performing with numerous artists including Wayne Horvitz and David Moss; Works performed world-wide; Compositions commissioned by groups including the New York Philharmonic Orchestra, Brooklyn Philharmonic, Bayerische Staasoper, WDR Orchestra Köln, American Composers Orchestra, Stephen Drury and The Kronos Quartet. *Compositions:* Christabel, 1972; Conquest of Mexico, 1973; Mikhail Zoetrope, 1974; Lacrosse, 1977; Hockey, 1978; Fencing, 1978; The Book of Heads, 1978; Pool, 1979; Archery, 1979; Track and Field, 1980; Locus Solus, 1982; Sebastopol, 1983; Rugby, 1983; Cobra, 1984; Xu Feng, 1985; Godard, 1985; Spillane, 1986; Hu Die, 1986; Ruan Lingyu, 1987; Hwang Chin-ee, 1988; Cat O'Nine Tails, 1988; Qûê Trân, 1988; For Your Eyes Only, 1989; Bézique, 1989; Torture Garden, 1990; Grand Guignol, 1990; Dead Man, 1990; Elegy, 1991; Leng Teh'e, 1991; Carny, 1992; Memento Mori, 1992; Kristallnacht, 1992; Absinthe, 1992; Angelus Novus, 1993; Masada, 1993–97; The Sand's Share, 1994; Redbird, 1995; Dark River, 1995; Aporias, 1995; Music For Children, 1996; Duras, 1996; Kol Nidre, 1996; Orchestra Variations, 1996; Etant Donnés, 1997; Shibboleth, 1997; Cycles du Nord, 1998; Rituals, 1998; Recent recordings include: Downtown Lullaby, 1998; Circle Maker, 1998; Bribe, 1998; Masada Live in Jerusalem, 1999; The String Quartets, 1999; Lacrosse, 2000.

ZULFIKARPSIC Bojan; b. 2 Feb. 1968, Belgrade, Serbia. Musician (piano). m. Marie Chevallier, Aug. 1993, 1 s. *Career:* Played with: Henri Texier; Michel Portal; Leader, Bojan Z Quartet; Concerts include: Banlieues Bleues Festival; Halle That Jazz Festival; London Jazz Festival; Jazz Across The Border, Berlin; Auditorium des Halles, Paris; Radio France, 1995. *Recordings:* with Bojan Z Quartet: Bojan Z Quartet, 1994; with Henri Texier's Azur Quartet: Indian's Week, 1993; Mad Nomad. *Honours:* First prize for composition: Concours de la Defense, 1993. *Current Management:* Laurence Voiturier, Artalent. *Address:* 15 Passage de la Main d'Or, 75011 Paris, France.

ZURBACH Cyril, (Zebra); b. 24 Aug. 1974, Paris, France. Composer; Musician (Guitars, Bass); Sound Engineer; Editor. *Education:* School of Filmmaking, Paris; Art and Cinema, Musicology, University of St Denis. *Career:* TV Signature, France Supervision, 1997; Composer and Writer; Sound Designer, films and TV. *Recordings:* Sound Assistant: Quiet Times, Tommy Carpet; J'Attends, J'Apprends, Nicoletta; Epique Epoque, Alain Goldstein. *Membership:* SALEM. *Leisure interests:* Cinema; Video art; Music on Internet. *Current Management:* Zebra Production. *Address:* 57 Blvd Soult, 75012 Paris, France.

ZURSTRASSEN Pirly; b. 15 April 1958, Heusy, Belgium. Musician (Piano), Composer. m. Bouhon Janine, 1 s., 1 d. *Education:* Conservatoire De Verviers; Seminaire De Jazz De Liege; Classe D'Improvisation Du Conservatoire Royal De Liege. *Career:* Many Compositions for theatre, television and dance; Teacher, Jazz Harmony, Jazz Composition, Royal Conservatory, Brussels. *Recordings:* 'H' Septet: Hautes Fagnes; 'H Septet: Horizons Azur; Zurstrassew/Stokart Duo. *Honours:* Saxe Best Young Musician, 1988; Prix Andre Grosjean, 1993. *Membership:* Lundis D'Hortense. *Address:* 4 Wayai, B 4845 Sart, Belgium.

ZWILGMEYER Kalle; b. 29 Oct. 1937, Porsgrunn, Norway. Folksinger; Songwriter; Translator; Guitar. *Education:* University Degree in History and Geography. *Musical Education:* Self-taught guitar. *Career:* Programme Leader, numerous folk-song programmes, Norwegian radio and TV; Appearances in great many radio and TV programmes, Nordic countries; Many tours in Scandinavia and as Member of Nordic groups: Polarkvartetten; Viser På Vandring; Nordenom; Kalmarunionen; Nordiska Visensemblen; 3 Vise-menn and 1 Svenske; Appearances in folk music festivals; Working for connection between folksingers in The Baltic States and the Nordic countries. *Recordings:* Graverende Bevis, 1987; Fra Lofoten Til Arkipelagos, 1991. *Publications:* Vise Og Gitar, 1977; Bli Dus Med Gitaren, 1978; Viser Som Ringer I Vann, 1980; Songtexts published in more than 20 song books. *Honour:* Vispramen Storkens Minne (Swedish Folksingers Prize), 1983; Nordic folksinger prize, Liv, 1989. *Memberships:* TONO; NOPA ang Gramart, Norway; DANSK, DJBEA, Denmark. *Leisure interests:* Gathering folksingers from all Nordic countries in Skagen, Denmark (first weekend in February every year) and in Greece (May). *Address:* Foderstofgården 76, 3600 Frederikssund, Denmark. *E-mail:* kallezwilgmeyer@hotmail.com.

APPENDIX A: RECORD COMPANIES

Andorra

Limitada de Producciones SL: Ciutat Consuegra 12, 2°, Edif. Orió, Andorra La Vella; Admin. JOAN DELTELL PORTA.

Argentina

AIM (Arco Iris Musical): Avda Santa Fé 4910, 4°, Of. B, 1425 Buenos Aires; tel. and fax (11) 4775-2343; e-mail aimcontenidos@aol.com; Dir-Gen. OSVALDO BERMOLEN.

Barca Discos Srl: Avda Santa Fé 1780, 11°, Of. 1102, 1060 Buenos Aires; Dir ELIO BARBEITO.

Clan Dilo Music: Casilla Correo 123 La Plata, 1900 Buenos Aires; Pres. GIORGIO DI LORENZO.

D Cipa Diaz Colodrero: Avda Paseo Colón 524, Of. 1, 1063 Buenos Aires; Dir-Gen. MARÍA ANTONIA DIAZ COLODRERO.

Del Cielito Records: Laprida 1898, 4°, Of. B, 1425 Buenos Aires; Dir GUSTAVO GAUVRY.

Discos Melopea SA: Jean Jaurés 444, 1215 Buenos Aires; Pres. FÉLIX FRANCISCO NEBBIA.

Epsa Electrical Products SAIC: México 2835, 1223 Buenos Aires; Pres. LAURA ROMA CASELLA.

Esther M Soto Ciclo 3: Estados Unidos 629, 1101 Buenos Aires; Contact ESTHER M SOTO.

Kralendijk Producciones: Sánchez de Bustamente 444, 5°, Dpto 1, 1173 Buenos Aires; Pres. ALEJANDRO SOLIGNAC.

Main Records SA: Tucumán 1673, 3° 6, 1050 Buenos Aires; Pres. ALEJANDRO AMADORI.

Musidisc Europe Sudamerica SAIC: Güemes 4418, 1° A, 1425 Buenos Aires; Pres. JIMMY OLSZEVICKI.

OM Records: Colombia 1727 Valantín Alsina, 1822 Buenos Aires; Pres. OSCAR MEIDVILLA.

Polygram Discos SA: Avda Córdoba 1345, 14°, 1055 Buenos Aires; Man. Dir RUBÉN APRILE.

Rave On SA: Uruguay 546 2 6, 1015 Buenos Aires; Pres. BERNADO BERGERET.

Australia

ABC Music: Level 3, John Mellion Bldg, 10A Campbell St, Artamon, NSW 2065; tel. (2) 9950-3996; fax (2) 9950-3989; e-mail hodson.clive@abc.net.au; Head of Music CLIVE HODSON.

Acid Jazz Australia Pty Ltd: Suite 73, 380 Wattle St, Ultimo, NSW 2007; Dirs CAROLYN SMEE, MARK LOVETT.

Akaba Records Pty Ltd: Level 5, 14 Martin Pl., Sydney, NSW 2000; Exec. Dir JAMES R G BELL.

Anabasis: PO Box 437, Kew, VIC 3101; Man. GINA LUCA VELOCI.

Au-Go-Go: 349 Little Bourke St, Melbourne, VIC 3000; Dirs GRETA MOON, BRUCE MILNE.

BIB Productions Pty Ltd: 356 Swan St, Richmond, VIC 3121; CEO MIKE BRADY.

Big Rock Pty Ltd: PO Box 273, Dulwich Hill, NSW 2203; A & R Man. CHRIS TURNER.

Black Market Music: 172 Roden St, West Melbourne, VIC 3003; Man. ELLY MANTZARIS.

BMG Australia Ltd: 194 Miller St, North Sydney, NSW 2060; Man. Dir MICHAEL SMELLIE.

BMG Music Pty Ltd: 194 Miller St, N Sydney, NSW 2060; tel. (2) 9900-7888; fax (2) 9955-4825; internet www.click2music.com.au; Man. Dir EOL ST JOHN.

Broad Music Pty Ltd: 56 Winborne Rd, Brookvale, NSW 2100; Man. Dir KEN BROAD.

CAAMA Music (Central Australian Aboriginal Media Association): 101 Todd St, Alice Springs, NT 0870; tel. (8) 8952-9205; fax (8) 8952-9212; e-mail musicmgr@caama.com.au; internet www.caama.com.au; Music Man. GILLIAN HARRISON.

Central Station Records: 81 Market St, South Melbourne, VIC 3205; Man. Dir GUISEPPE PALUMBO.

CMC (Christian Marketing Communications): Unit 9, 147 Marshalltown Rd, Grovedale, VIC 3216; Gen. Man. ALAN KENNEDY.

Colossal Records: 14–16 Wilson Ave, Brunswick, VIC 3056; Man. Dir DOMENIC LOPRETE.

Creative Vibes: 8/40 Victoria St, Potts Point, NSW 2011; Man. Dirs GORDON HENDERSON, PETER PASQUAL, HEIDI PASQUAL.

Dino Music Pty Ltd: PO Box 242, Purmont, NSW 2009; Man. Dir JOHN HARPER.

Diverse System Music: PO Box 1161, Fitzroy North, VIC 3068; Man. Dir TONY GREENE.

Dog Meat Records: PO Box 2366 V, Melbourne, VIC 3001; Man. Dir DAVID LAING.

Dolphin Music Group Pty Ltd: 23 Darvall St, Balmain, NSW 2041; Chair. BARRY CHAPMAN.

East West Records: 39–47 Albany St, Crows Nest, NSW 2065; Man. Dir CHRIS HANLON.

EMI Music Australia: 98–100 Glover St, Cremore, NSW 2090; Man. Dir DAVID SNELL.

Emily Rocords: PO Box 405, Hamilton, Brisbane, QLD 4007; Label Man. MARK HANLON.

Empire Records & Publishing: 23–25A Johnston St, Collingwood, VIC 3066; tel. (3) 9417-7707; fax (3) 9417-5294; e-mail info@empirerecords.com.au; internet www.empirerecords.com.au; Label Man. PAUL HIGGINS.

Fellaheen: PO Box A537, Sydney South, NSW 2000; A & R and Asst Man. Dir ADAM YEE.

Festival Records Pty Ltd: 63–79 Miller St, Pyrmont, NSW 2009; Chair. ALLAN HELY.

Half a Cow Records: PO Box 1100, Strawberry Hills, NSW 2012; tel. (2) 6345-3235; fax (2) 6345-3298; e-mail haclabel@mpx.com.au; internet www.halfacow.com.au; Owner NIC DALTON.

Image Music Group Pty Ltd: 19 Johnston St, Port Melbourne, VIC 3207; Man. Dir JOHN MCDONALD.

Integrity Music Pty Ltd: 120 Herries St, Toowoomba, QLD 4350; Gen. Man. MARK FREEMAN.

J Albert & Son P/L Albert Productions: 9 Rangers Rd, Neutral Bay, NSW 2089; Gen. Man. FIFA RICCOBONO.

Kriminal Rekords: Suite 314, Prudential Bldg, 2 Queen St, Brisbane, QLD 4000; CEO ALAN MADDAMS.

Larrakin Entertainment Pty Ltd: Unit 4, 809–821 Botany Rd, Rosebery, NSW 2018; Man. Dir WARREN FAHEY.

Lavender Music: 5/159 Arthurton Rd, Northcote, VIC 3070; Partners MADELEN RAYNER, BARBARA YOUNG.

MCA Music Entertainment Inc (Australia): PO Box 899, Crows Nest, NSW 2065; Man. Dir PAUL KRIGE.

Mint Records Pty Ltd: PO Box 210, Blackheath, NSW 2785; Contact CHARLES L NAUDI.

Modern Invasion Music: Unit 2, 14 Spink St, Gardenvale, VIC 3185; Man. DANIEL JANECKA.

MRA Enterainment Group: 39 Gosford St, Mt Gravatt, QLD 4122; Man. Dir RAY HARTLEY.

Mushroom Exports Pty Ltd: 55 Danks St, Port Melbourne, VIC 3207; Man. Dir SCOTT MURPHY.

Mushroom Records Pty Ltd: 9 Dundas Lane, Albert Park, VIC 3206; Chair. MICHAEL GUDINSKI.

Music World: PO Box 1462, Milton Centre 4064; Man. Dir HOGHTON HUGHES.

Natural Symphonies: 10 Broughton St, Camden, NSW 2570; Creative Dir IAN O'HARE.

New World Productions: 151 Boundary St, Bardon, QLD 4065; Man. Dir ANDREW WATSON.

Newmarket Music: 393–395 Macaulay Rd, Kensington, VIC 3031; National Sales Man. LEN MCQUALTER.

Odessa–Mama Records: 557a North Rd, Ormond, VIC 3204; Man. Dir DAVID FAIMAN.

One Movement Records: Suite 335, 410 Elizabeth St, Surry Hills, NSW 2010; Label Man. MATT HAYWARD.

Opulent Music Entertainment: PO Box 270, 48 David Cres., Bundoora, VIC 3083; Man. Dir ANTHONY CHIDIAC.

Origin Recordings: PO Box 3265, Sydney, NSW 2001; Man. Dir PHILIP MORTLOCK.

Outlaw Records: 62 Thompson St, Darlinghurst, NSW 2010; Dir DAVID CAPLICE.

Phonogram/Polygram Records Australia: Unit C, 110 McEvoy St, Alexandria, NSW 2015; Man. Dir TIM DELANEY.

Pickwick Australia Pty Ltd: 2/111 Queensbridge St, South Melbourne, VIC 3205; Publicity Man. LOUISE BEDFORD.

Pinewood Records and Promotions: 3 Hessel Pl., Emu Heights, NSW 2750; tel. (2) 6742-1543; fax (2) 6742-0249; e-mail ianb@pinewoodrecords.com.au; internet www.pinewoodrecords.com.au; Man. Dir IAN B MACLEOD.

Possum Music Pty Ltd: 2 /27 Wongala Cres., Beecroft, NSW 2119; Man. Dir PHILIP ISRAEL.

Rascal Records Pty Ltd: PO Box 146, Glenside, SA 5064; Dir CAROLYN COMBE.

Ravenswood / Foghorn Records: 64 Wattle St, Ultimo, NSW 2007; Man. Dir BOB ARMSTRONG.

Republic Records: 9 Knox St, Chippendale, NSW 2008; Man. Dir VICKI GORDON.

Request Records: 15 High Peak Pl., Lesmurdie, WA 6076; Proprietor JOHN GREEN.

Roadrunner Records (Australia) Pty Ltd: 24 High St, Northcote, VIC 3070; Label Man. BOB STEVENSON.

Round Records: 42 Breaker St, St Morris, SA 5068; Contact TERRY BRADFORD.

Rubber Records: 59 Victoria Ave, Albert Park, VIC 3206; Man. Dir DAVID VODICKA.

Rufus Records: PO Box 116, Paddington, NSW 2021; Pres. TIM DUNN.

Sandstock Music Pty Ltd: PO Box 557, Charlestown, NSW 2290; Man. Dir JILL GARTRELL.

Servant Communications: PO Box 2020, Launceston, Tasmania 7250; Pres. KEVIN N HOOPER.

Shock / Shagpile / Thrust Records: 24 High St, Northcote, VIC 3070; Label Man. DAVID WILLIAMS.

Sirius Music: 70 Toorak Rd, South Yarra, VIC 3141; Dirs STEPHEN ROBINSON, ADRIAN MARCHESANI.

Sonart Music Vision: PO Box 691, Brookvale, NSW 2100; Man. Dir LES HODGE.

Sony Music Australia Ltd: 11–19 Hargrave St, East Sydney, NSW 2010; Man. Dir DENIS HANDLIN.

Terra Australia Records: Suite 223, 161 Military Rd, Neutral Bay, NSW 2089; Contact ALEX SVENCIS.

Time-Life Australia Pty Ltd: Level 6, 61 Lavender St, Milsons Point, NSW 2061; Chair. & Man. Dir BONITA L BOEZEMAN.

Vampire Records: PO Box 669, Epping, NSW 1710; tel. (2) 9876-3239; fax (2) 9617-0199; e-mail vampire@vampire.com.au; internet www.vampire.com.au; Man. Dir DANNY KALEDA.

Vicious Vinyl: 7B Baxter St, Frankston, VIC 3199; International Affairs ANDY VAN.

Virgin Records Australia Pty Ltd: 98–100 Glover St, Cremorne, NSW 2090; Dir of Operations MICHAEL MANOS.

Warner Music Australia Pty Ltd: 39–47 Albany St, Crows Nest, NSW 2065; Chair. BRIAN HARRIS.

Word Australia: 142 Canterbury Rd, Kilsyth, VIC 3137; Product & Marketing Man. WENDY MOULTON.

Austria

Aardvarks Music: Nachtigallenstr 18, 5023 Salzburg; Man. Dir MICHAEL WAGNER.

ATS Records: Breitenau 7, 4591 Molln; tel. (0) 7584-2454; fax (0) 7584-2424; e-mail office@ats-records.com; internet www.ats-records.com; Man. Dir REINHARD BRUNNER.

Banananas Records: Pebalstrasse 31/1, 8700 Leoben; Man. Dir KLAUS KATZIANKA.

Cactus Records: Nibelungering 1, 3423 St Andrä-Wördern; Man. Dir HANS HARTEL.

Christmas Records: Reinhard-Machold str 47/3, 8075 Graz; Dir ALEXANDER REHAK.

Doremi Records: Spundag 5/6, 1210 Vienna; Dir EMAD SAYYAH.

Edition Rossori/Pate Records: Hietzinger Hauptstr 94, 1130 Vienna; tel. (1) 8762400; fax (1) 8795464; e-mail office@poppate.com; internet www.paterecords.com; Man. Dir MARIO ROSSORI.

EMI Austria: Webgasse 43, 1060 Vienna; Man. Dir HANS REINISCH.

EMP: Weinitzenstr 1, 8045 Graz; Man. Dir EGON HINZ.

European Music Project: Reinhard-Machold str 47/3, 8075 Hart/Graz; Dir ALEXANDER REHAK.

Extraplatte GmbH: PO Box 2, 1094 Vienna; tel. (1) 310-1084; fax (1) 310-0324; e-mail info@extraplatte.at; internet www.extraplatte.at; Man. Dir HARALD QUENDLER.

FIPS Records: Schöpfergasse 3, 1120 Vienna; tel. (1) 8122189; fax (1) 8136878; e-mail fips.records@aon.at; Gen. Man. GUNTHER PFEIFFER.

Frizzey Records: Hauptstr 13, 6522 Prutz; Man. Dir FRIEDRICH GREIF.

Gash: Raaberbahngasse 21/4/5, 1100 Vienna; Man. Dir EDI EHN.

Gig Records: Fuehrichgasse 8, 1010 Vienna; Man. Dir MARCUS SPIEGEL.

Goblin Records: Dr Theodor Kornerstr, 3100 St Polte; Label Man. INGRID MANGOLD.

Honk Music and Records: Hormayrgasse 3/25, 1170 Vienna; tel. and fax (1) 486-4287; internet www.sra.at/sr/comps/7196.htm; Man. Dir JIVI HONK.

Operator: Brauhausgasse 14, 3003 Gablitz; Man. Dir ERWIN KIENNAUST.

PolyGram GmbH: Edelsinnstr 4, PO Box 85, 1120 Vienna; Asst Man. Dir ULLA PFEIFFER.

SBF Records: Molln 129, 4591 Molln; Man. Dir MANFRED PRENTNER.

Sony Music Austria: Erlachgasse 134–140, 1101 Vienna; Man. Dir MARTIN PAMMER.

Ton Art: Hietzinger Hauptstr 130, 1130 Vienna; Man. Dir ALEXANDER MUNKAS.

TP Records: Reinhard-Machold str 47/3, 8075 Hart/Graz; Dir ALEXANDER REHAK.

Video & Tontechnik: Hoechsterstr 47, 6850 Dornbirn; Man. Dir MANFRED MÄSER.

Belarus

Beloton Records: Shrader str 8–15, Vitebsk 210015; Dir VLADIMIR SARTCHENKO.

Belgium

3Rioart Vzw Maoisch Theater Productions: Juliaandillenstr 22, 2018 Antwerp; Dir SANDY NYS.

A L C Productions: Ave Eugène Ysaye 47, 1070 Brussels; Label Man. ALEXANDER LOUVET.

Alora Music: Villegas de Clercamp 13, 1853 Grimbergen; Man. Dir BERT BURM.

Amor Et Psyche Productions: Allee du Cloître 43, 1050 Brussels; Man. LAURENT JADOT.

Arcade Music Company: rue de Wand 209–213, 1020 Brussels; Gen. Man. RICHARD DEDAPER.

ARS Productions: Single 5, 2550 Kontich; Man. Dir PATRICK BUSSCHOTS.

Baltic NV: Rederijkersstraat 82, 2610 Wilrijk-Antwerp; tel. (3) 828-4084; fax (3) 829-1068; e-mail info@baltic.be; internet www.baltic.be; Man. Dir BEN GYSELINCK.

Big Time International: Kloosterstraat 54, 3900 Overpelt; Man. Dir JOS BORREMANS.

BMG Ariola Belgium: François Riga Sq. 30 B 8, 1030 Brussels; Man. Dir DERK JOLINK.

Boom!: Bergensesteenweg 19, 1500 Halle; tel. (0) 2360-2851; internet www.jpvan.be; Man. Dir J P VAN.

Byte Records: Schriekbos n5, 2980 Zoersel; Man. Dir JEAN-PAUL DE COSTER.

Caracol Music Sprl Group: 5 rue du Cheneau, 6120 Ham-sur-Heure; Gen. Man. TIMOTHY HAGELSTEIN.

Carbon 7: 23 Ave Général Eisenhower, 1030 Brussels; tel. (2) 242-9703; fax (2) 245-3885; e-mail carbon7records@compuserve.com; Dir GUY SEGERS.

Clip Records: Rozemarijnstraat 12, 9300 Aalst; Man. Dir JOE BOGART.

Commedia VZW: Fonteinstraat 19, 8000 Bruges; Man. Dir CHERRY DERYOKE.

Crammed Discs: rue de Général Patton 43, 1050 Brussels; Man. Dir MARC HOLLANDER.

Dexon Sprl: 41 rue Cité de L'Enfance, 6001 Marcinelle; Man. DELFOSSE PIERRE.

Disques du Crepuscle: 15 Galerie du Roi, 1000 Brussels; Man. Dir MICHEL DUVAL.

Emergency! Records: rue Ferdinand Bernier 38, 1060 Brussels; Man. Dir MARC DEBOUVIER.

EMI Belgium: Kolonel Bourgstraat 128, 1040 Brussels; Man. Dir GUY BRULEZ.

Franc'Amour: rue Paul Emile Janson 9, 1050 Brussels; Man. Dir CHRISTINE JOTTARD.

Hautregard Recording Sc: 119 Route De Veaviers, 4650 Herue; Public Relations THIERAY STEINBRECHER.

Insane Music: 2 Grand rue, 6183 Trazegnies; Contact ALAIN NEFFE.

Loft Records: Kloosterstraat 54, 3900 Overpelt; Man. Dir JOS BORREMANS.

Madagascar Records: Krijgsbaan 240, 2070 Zwyndrecht; tel. (3) 253-1480; fax (3) 253-1496; e-mail madagascar@pandora.be; internet www.kkrecords.be; Man. Dir JOSEF VERBRUGGEN.

Mag SA: Ave Louise 65, 1050 Brussels; Man. Dir PIERRE PIRONT.

Mixz Productions: Berchemlei 198, 2140 Borgerhout; Man. Dir KOEN TILLIC.

MMD SA: rue Fernand Bernier 38, 1060 Brussels; Man. Dir PLASTIC BERTRAND.

Music & Words Belgium: Europalaan 7, 8970 Poperinge; Pres. HANS PETERS.

Myron Records: Bergstraat 13, 1560 Hoeilaart; Man. Dir LEON LAMAL.

Parsifal bvba: Gulden Vlieslaan 67, 8000 Bruges; Contact NICO A MERTENS.

Play It Again Sam: rue de Veeweyde 90, 1070 Brussels; Man. Dir JAN HUBLAU.

Play That Beat: rue Fernand Bernier 38, 1060 Brussels; Man. Dir MARC DEBOUVIER.

PolyGram Belgium: Roodebeek Ave 30, 1040 Brussels; Man. Dir BERT CLOECKAERT.

Private Life/ Noise Records: 13 rue Villegas de Clercamp, 1853 Strombeek-Bever; Man. Dir OLIVIER VERHAEGHE.

Punch: rue de Lausanne 37, 1060 Brussels; Man. Dir ALEXANDRE SABOUNDJIAN.

Rainbow Records & Music: Herentaesesteenweg 20A, 2220 Heist-Op-Den Berg; tel. (0) 1524-4950; fax (0) 1524-1470; Contact KATHLEEN GOSSENS.

Rainland: 9 rue Paul-Emile Janson, 1050 Brussels; Man. Dir CHRISTINE JOTTARD.

Rox Records: Marie Henrieet Laan 71, 1700 Dilbeck; Man. Dir MARIO GUCCI.

Sawdust Alley: Ave Circulaire 144b, 1180 Brussels; Man. Dir CALVIN OWENS.

Selection & B Sharp Records: 24 Gachardstreet, 1050 Brussels; Gen. Man. PIERRE PLETINCKX.

Smash Productions/Now Discs: Charles Quint 34B–5, 1080 Brussels; Man. Dir MICHEL NACHTERGAELE.

Sony Music Belgium: Evenepoelstraat 9, 1040 Brussels; Man. Dir PATRICK DECAM.

Target Records: Oordegemsesteenweg, 1050 Brussels; Contact CLAUDINE SARLET.

Team for Action (T4A): Ave Oscar van Goibtsnoven 45B, 1180 Brussels; Man. Dir CLAUDE MARTIN.

Tempo (Top Entertainment Editions): Krijgslaan 61, 9000 Gent; Gen. Man. LUC STANDAERT.

Tessa Records Rock Label: Dennenlaan 13, 9160 Lokeren; tel. and fax (09) 3489836; Pres./Owner MARC DE BLOCK.

Virgin Belgium NV: Blvd General Wahis 41, 1030 Brussels; Man. Dir DIRK DE VRIES.

Warner Music Belgium: Lambermontlaan 79, 1030 Brussels; Man. Dir TED SIKKINK.

Witlof: Leernsesteenweg 168, 9800 Deinze; Dir JEAN TANT.

Bolivia

Discolandia Dueri & Cia Ltda: Potosí 920, 1°, 422 La Paz; Proprietor MIRIAM DUERI.

Producciones Gum Prodisco: Plaza Alonso de Mendoza 500, Edif. Santa Anita Of. 8, 13733 La Paz; Dir-Gen. GERMÁN URQUIDI NAVRIC.

Brazil

Caipirapirs Produçoes Artisticas Ltda: Avda das Aguas Marinhas 157 Pg Petrópolis, 07600-00 São Paulo, SP; Gen. Man. PABLO OSSIPOFF.

Estudio Eldorado Ltda: Rua Pires da Mota 820–830, 01529 São Paulo, SP; Exec. Dir JOÃO LARA MESQUITA.

Paradox Music: Rua Dr Pinto Ferraz 58, Vila Mariana, 04117-040 São Paulo, SP; Dir SILVIO ARNALDO CALIGARIS.

Planet Music: Avda Rebouças 2315, 04501-30 São Paulo, SP; Pres. CARLOS BRANCO.

Bulgaria

AVA Records: 10/83 Bassanovitch str, 9010 Varna; Man. Dir ANATOLY VAPIROV.

Balkanton Records: 6 Haidoushka Polyana str, 1612 Sofia; tel. (2) 952-0373; fax (2) 952-6090; e-mail balkanton@yahoo.com; Man. Dir VENTSISLAV BOZHINOV.

Denis Records: 25 Shipka str, 1504 Sofia; Man. Dir DANIEL RIZOV.

DS Music: 17 Mizia str, 1124 Sofia; Dirs LUBOMIR VELEV, IVAN VULKOV.

Kings Records: 37 Hristo Botev Blvd, 1000 Sofia; Man. Dir VALENTIN MARKOV.

Mega Music Ltd: 2 Trapezitza str, 1000 Sofia; Man. Dir DORA TCHERNKVA.

Riva Sound Records Ltd: Fl 3, 103 Maria Luiza Blvd, 1202 Sofia; tel. (2) 310060; fax (2) 317128; e-mail office@rivasound.com; internet www.rivasound.com; Man. Dir RUMEN BONCHEV.

Canada

A&M/Island Records: 1345 Denison St, Markham, ON L3R 5V2; Promotion RANDY WELLS.

Alert Music: 305–41 Britain St, Toronto ON M5A 1R7; Promotion KATHY MEISLER.

Ambassador Music: DVPO 43029, Calgary, AB T2J 5C6; A & R Man. WAYNE CHAULK.

Attic Music Group: 102 Atlantic Ave, Toronto, ON M6K 1X9; Pres. ALEXANDER MAIR.

Audiogram: 822 rue Sherbrooke Est, Montréal, QC H2L 1K4; Chair. MICHEL BELANGER.

BMG Music Canada Inc: 150 John St, 6th Floor, Toronto, ON M5V 3C3; Contact DAVID BENDETH.

Boomtown Music: PO Box 265, Station C, Toronto, ON M6S 3P4; Head of A & R KEVIN LEFLAR.

Botany Park Records & Music Publishing Co: 361 Walter Dr., Keswick, ON L4P 3A8; Pres. MARLAINE RENNOCKS.

Chacra Alternative Music Inc: 3155 Halpern, St Laurent, QC H4S 1P5; tel. (514) 335-0245; fax (514) 335-5037; e-mail info@chacramusic.com; internet www.chacramusic.com; Pres. BOB CHACRA.

Contagious Records: PO Box 183, 905 Croydon Ave, Winnipeg, MB R3M 3S7; Contact ROMAN PANCHYSHYN.

Current/Rage Records and Management: 4 Bowden St, Toronto, ON M4K 2X2; Pres. GERRY YOUNG.

Distribution Fusion III: 5455 Paré #101, Montréal, QC H4P 1P7; National Promotions NADINE CAMPBELL.

DMT Records: Suite 11714, 113th Ave, Edmonton, AB T5G 0J8; Pres. DANNY MAKARM.

Duke Street Records: 121 Logan Ave, Toronto, ON M4M 2M9; Public Relations ANDY HERMANT.

Ed Preston Enterprises Inc: 192 Tweedsdale Cres., Oakville, ON L6L 4P7; tel. (905) 827-8095; fax (905) 827-8095; Pres. & Gen. Man. ED PRESTON.

EMC Records of Canada: 189 Scugog St, Bowmanville, ON L1C 3J9; Contact PAUL ANDREW SMITH.

EMI Music Canada: 3109 American Dr., Mississauga, ON L4V 1B2; Public Relations LIZ MCELHERAN.

Festival Records: 3271 Main St, Vancouver, BC V5V 3M6; Public Relations VALDINE CIWKO.

Forte Records and Productions Inc: 320 Spadina Rd, Toronto, ON M5R 2V6; Contact DAWNA ZEEMAN.

Fringe Product: PO Box 670, Station A, Toronto, ON M5W 1G2; Gen. Man. ANGUS MACKAY.

Heaven Bent Music Corp: 11 Hopewell Cres., Hamilton, ON L8J 1P3; Gen. Man. KATHIE PIETRON.

Heritage Music: 1111 Davis Dr., Unit 1, Suite 247, Newmarket, ON L34 7V1; tel. (416) 989-0372; fax (416) 989-0414; Contact JACK BOSWELL.

Hi-Bias Records Inc: 49 Beckett Ave, Toronto, ON M6L 2B3; Dir NICK FIORUCCI.

Hypnotic Records: 96 Spadina Ave, 9th Floor, Toronto, ON M5V 2J6; Contact DARYN BARRY.

Icedrum Records: PO Box 2310, Station A, Sudbury, ON P3A 4S8; Contact JAMES HUNT.

Inner Music: 65 Front St W, Units 116–165, Toronto, ON M5J 1E6; Contact STEVE HOLT.

Intrepid Music: 93 Hazelton Ave, 3rd Floor, Toronto, ON M5R 2E1; Public Relations ANDY MCLEAN.

Joe-Radio: Suite 8, 299 Lesmill Rd, Toronto, ON M3B 2U1; Contact CHRISTINE RODWAY.

John H Lennon Music Ltd: 1235 Bay St, Suite 400, Toronto, ON M5R 3K4; Pres. JOHN LENNON; Man. Dir LENNY MOORE.

Justin Time Records Inc: 5455 Paré #101, Montréal, QC H4P 1P7; National Promotions NADINE CAMPBELL.

KSM Records: 2305 Vista Court, Coquitlam, BC V3J 6W2; Pres. DAVID LONDON.

LA Records: PO Box 1096 Hudson, QC J0P 1V0; tel. (450) 458-2819; e-mail la_records@excite.com; internet www.radiofreedom.com; Prod. MICHAEL LENGIES.

LCDM Entertainment: 2–19 Victoria Ave W, Weston ON M9N 1E3; Public Relations/Promotion L C DIMARCO.

Les Disques Passeport Inc: PO Box 529, Succursale Beaubien, Montréal, QC H2G 3E2; Public Relations MARC RACINE.

Les Disques Rubicon: 835 A Querbes, Outremont, QC H2V 3X1; Contact GILLES BEDARD.

Magnum Records: 8607 128 Ave, Edmonton, AB T5E 0G3; tel. (780) 476-8230; fax (780) 472-2584; Contact BILL MAXIM.

Margaree Sound: 225 The Lake Driveway, West Ajax, ON L1S 5A3; Pres. & CEO RUSSELL DAIGE.

Master Factory: Suite 11714, 113th Ave, Edmonton, AB T5G 0J8; Pres. GERRY DERE.

MCA Records Canada: 2450 Victoria Park Ave, Willowdale, ON M2J 4A2; Promotion BILL BANHAM.

Murder Records: 1588 Grandville St, Halifax, NS B3J 1X1; Promotion COLIN MACKENZIE.

MUSINFO Publishing Group Inc: 2504 Mayfair Ave, Montréal, QC H4B 2C8; tel. (514) 484-5419; fax (514) 484-9948; e-mail musinfo@musinfo.com; internet www.musinfo.com; Pres./Owner JEHAN V VALIQUET.

Nightlife Records: 2533A Yonge St, Toronto, ON M4P 2H9; Contact JOEY CEE.

Oasis Productions Limited: 76 Cadorna Ave, Toronto, ON M4J 3X1; Vice-Pres. RON KORB.

PolyGram Records of Canada: 1345 Denison St, Markham, ON L3R 5V2; Contact BOB ANSELL.

Quantum Records: 170A Baldwin St, Toronto, ON M5T 1L8; Contact MIKE ALYANAK.

Quinlan Road Ltd: PO Box 933, Stratford, ON N5A 7M3; Controller BILL BRUCE; Contact LOREENA MCKENNIT.

RDR Music Group: 299 Lesmill Rd, Suite 8, Toronto, ON M3B 2U1; Pres. JOE WOOD.

Record Peddler Distribution: 621 Yonge St, Toronto, ON M4Y 1Z5; Pres. BEN HOFFMAN.

Resort Records: 14 Sumach St, Toronto, ON M5A 1J4; Pres. JOE BAMFORD.

Roto Noto: 148 Erin Ave, Hamilton, ON L8K 4W3; Promotion ELAINE DOMSY.

Sam Cat Records: 8 Woodlands Rd, St Albert, AB T8N 3L9; tel. and fax (780) 460-7460; e-mail fun@peterandmary.net; Contact PETER JANSEN; Also organizes the Earth Day Festival.

Savannah Music Inc: 123 Applefield Dr., Scarborough, ON M1P 3Y5; Dir of Canadian Operations BILL CARRUTHERS.

Scratch Records: PO Box 5381, Whitehorse, YK Y1A 4Z2; Prod. DANIEL JANKE.

Skylark Records: 3964 W 18th Ave, Vancouver, BC V6S 1B7; Contact GEORGE LAVEROCK.

Slak Productions: 9 Hector Ave, Toronto, ON M6G 3G2; tel. (416) 588-6751; fax (416) 588-6751; e-mail akussin@sympatico.ca; Pres. AL KUSSIN.

Sony Music Entertainment Canada: 1121 Leslie St, North York, ON M3C 2J9; Imports Man. JOHN ELLIS THOMSON.

Sound Solutions: 5905 Thimens, St Laurent, QC H4S 1V8; Public Relations/Promotion FRANK TRIMARCHI.

Sparwood Music Productions: PO Box 270, Bentley, AB T0C 0J0; Man. DICK DAMRON.

Spinner Music Group Inc: Third Floor, 68 Water St, Vancouver, BC V6B 1A4; Pres. KEN SPENCE; Man. Dir WOLFGANG BURANDT.

Stony Plain Records: PO Box 861, Edmonton, AB T5J 2I8; tel. (780) 468-6423; fax (780) 465-8941; e-mail info@stonyplainrecords.com; internet www.stonyplainrecords.com; Pres. HOLGER PETERSON.

Sunnydays Records: 6263 28th Ave, Rosemont, Montréal, QC H1T 3H8; Talent Search/Man. FADEL CHIDIAC.

Tembo Music Canada Inc: 284 Church St, Oakville, ON L6J 7N2; Contact J EDWARD PRESTON.

The Sunshine Group: 275 Selkirk Ave, Winnipeg, MB R2W 2L5; Man. NESS MICHAELS.

Third Wave Productions Ltd: PO Box 563, Gander, NF A1V 2E1; Pres. R ARCHIBALD BONNELL.

Unidisc Music Inc: 57B Hymus Blvd, Pointe Claire, QC H9R 4T2; Pres. GEORGE CUCUZZELLA.

Virgin Music Canada: Rundle House, 514 Jarvis St, Toronto, ON M4Y 2H6; Public Relations CAROLE MACDONALD.

Warner Music Canada: 1810 Birchmount Rd, Scarborough, ON M1P 2J1; Promotion RANDY STARK.

Windchime Records: 99 Ivy St, Toronto, ON M4L 2H8; Contact TERRY WATADA.

Chile

Alerce Producciones Fonográficas SA: Jorge Washington 380 Nuñoa, Santiago; Gen. Man. GLORIA TRUMPER.

BMG Chile SA: Avda 11 de Septiembre 2353, 3°, Providencia, Santiago; Gen. Man. EDGARDO LARRAZABAL.

Calipso: Thompson 3450, Estación Central, Santiago; Man. HUGO ASCUETA NORAMBUENA.

Ediciones Musicales Fermata Ltda: Ebro 2751, Of. 609, Las Condes 41, Santiago; Gen. Man. ELIANA CISTERNAS.

China (Taiwan)

BMG Music Taiwan Inc: 17F, 216, Section 2, Tun-Hua South Rd, Taipei; tel. (2) 2708-1830; fax (2) 2755-0821; internet www.click2music.com.tw; Man. Dir REN REN; CEO KATE SU.

Chiang Huat Co / Around The World Music: 3/F 278 Chung Hsiao East Rd, Section 4, Taipei; Prod. MS HSIU HUA HO.

Decca Records Taiwan Ltd: 12/Fl No. 112 Chung Hsiao East Rd, Section 1, Taipei; Man. Dir DENVER CHANG.

EMI (Taiwan) Ltd: 2nd Floor, No. 12, 10 Alley 321 Lane, Hsing-Ming Rd, Taipei; Man. Dir HUNG TIK.

K & D Music Entertainment Inc: 6F No. 63, Po-Ai Rd, Taipei; Sr Man. Dir TOM UEND.

Polygram Records Ltd: 5F 99 Nankang Rd, Section 3, Nankang District, Taipei; Man. Dir MICHAEL HWANG.

Renaissance Records Co Ltd: No 12, Lane 13, Kwang Fu South Rd, Taipei; Pres. BOB CHEN.

Rock Records and Tapes: 5F, No. 3, Lane 240, Kwang Fu S Rd, Taipei; Pres. SAM C T DUANN.

Sony Music Entertainment (Taiwan) Ltd: 8th Fl, No. 35, Lane 11, Kwang-Fu North Rd, Taipei; Man. Dir MATTHEW ALLISON.

Colombia

Ava Limitada: Carrera 54, 75–45, PO Box 50–804, Barranquilla; Proprietor TONY FORTOU.

BMG / Ariola de Colombia SA: Calle 67, 7–94, 12°, Santafé de Bogotá, DC; Dir-Gen. FRANCISCO VILLANUEVA.

Compañia Colombiana de Discos SA (Codiscos): Carrera 67, 1, Sur 92 Guayabal, 1428 Medellín; Pres. CÉSAR VALLEJO.

Discos Dago: C / 33AA, 81–25, Medellín; Pres. DARIO GÓMEZ ZAPATA.

Discos Philips: Calle 13, 51–39, 4282 Santafé de Bogotá, DC; Commercial Man. MARTÍN WOWGEMUNT.

G&M Es Musica: Calle 114, 6A–92, Of. 419, Zona D Cundinamarca, Santafé de Bogotá, DC; Gen. Man. JAVIER GARCÍA M.

Croatia

Adam Records: Anke Butorac 12, 52000 Pula; Man. Dir DARIO MATOSEVIC.

Crno Bijeli Svijet: Avenija Marina Drzica BB, 41000 Zagreb; Man. Dir BRANKO PAIC.

Croatia Records: Medjugorska 61, 10000 Zagreb; Dir of International Business Affairs DJORDJE KEKIC.

Denyken Music: Senoina 1, 41000 Zagreb; Man. Dir DENIS MUJAVDZIC.

Esnaf: Gunduliceva 29, 41000 Zagreb; Man. Dir HUSEIN HASANEFENDIC.

Jazzette Records: Vukovar Ave 35, Zagreb; Vice-Pres. KOLYA PETROVIC.

Koncept VD: Trg Bana Josipa Jelacica 5, 41000 Zagreb; Man. ZVONMIR BENCIC.

Skalinada: Dubrovacka 23, 58000 Split; Dir ZDENKO RUNJIC.

TRIP: Argentinska 3, 10000 Zagreb; A & R Man. ALEKSANDAR DRAGAS.

Tutico: Veprinacka 16, 10000 Zagreb; Dir ZRINKO TUTIC.

Cuba

Artex SA: 5a Ave, 8010, Miramar, Havana; Gen. Man. TONY PINELLI.

Caribe Productions Inc: Ave 17, 18401 Municipio Playa, Havana; Pres. FEDERICO GARCÍA ANTONIO.

Egrem: Calle 18, 105, Entre 1 y 3, Miramar, Havana; Dir-Gen. JULIO BALLESTER.

The Czech Republic

BMG Ariola (Czech Republic): Hellichova 5, Prague 1; Man. Dir CAP PETR.

Bonton Music: Ostrov-Stvanice 858, 170 21 Prague 7; Man. Dir VISEK PAVEL.

Indies Records: Mildy Horakove 25, 602 00 Brno; Man. Dir PALES MILAN.

Marco Music: Sokolskà 8, 70100 Ostrava 1; Man. Dir KRASNY DENEK.

Monitor—EMI Ltd: Kova'rova 39, 15500 Prague 5, Stodulky; Man. Dir VLADIMIR KOCANDRLE.

Popron: U Lanové Dràhy 3, Prague 1; Man. Dir ALYNSKY ZDENEK.

Denmark

BMG Genlyd Grammofon Denmark: Overgarden Neden Vandet 17/2, 1414 Copenhagen K; Man. Dir DIETMAR GLODDE.

Cloudland: Skt Jørgens Allé 7 O, G6 1th, 1615 Copenhagen; Man. Dir SIMON SHEIKA.

Cope Records: Oehlenschlaegersgade 28, 1663 Copenhagen V; tel. 7020-0037; e-mail sales@coperecords.com; internet www.coperecords.com.

ELAP Music A/S: Bransagervej 2–10, 9490 Pandrup; Promotion STEFFEN LUND NIELSEN.

EMI Music Denmark: Vognmagergade 10, 1120 Copenhagen K; Man. Dir MICHAEL RITTO.

Foenix Music APS: Sonder Alle 12, 8000 Aarhus C; Man. Dir OLE KJAER.

Forlaget Kragen (Craw Records): Christians Brygge 3, 1219 Copenhagen K; tel. 3313-5800; fax 3313-5804; e-mail sun@dafo.dk; Administration Dir SVEND NIELSEN.

Iceberg Records: Ronne Alle 78A, 8600 Silkeborg; Man. Dir MANFRED ZÄHRINGER.

Kavan Music Scandinavia: Klokkestobervef 39, 8800 Viborg; Man. KARL AAGE JENSEN.

Kick Music ApS: Energivej 42 B, 2750 Ballerup; Man. Dir MICHAEL QUVANG.

Klepto Records & Publishing: Langdries 4, 9450 Haaltert; Man. Dir WILFRIED BRITS.

Mega Scandinavia A/S: Indiakaj 1, 2100 Copenhagen Ø; Vice-Pres. CAI LEITNER; Dir of A & R and Marketing JESPER BAN.

Olafssongs: Paarupves 44, 3230 Graested; tel. 4839-2259; fax 4839-1629; e-mail fo@olafssongs.dk; internet www.olafssongs.dk; Pres. FINN OLAFSSON.

Olga Musik ApS: Boleetvej 4, 8680 Ry; Man. Dir BIRGER HANSEN.

Olufsen Records: Uraniavej 12, 1878 Frederiksberg C; fax 3321-4502; Man. Dir PETER OLUFSEN.

Pineapple Records ApS: Frodesgade 74, 6700 Esbjerg; Man. Dir HELGE ENGELBRECHT.

Polygram-Sonet Denmark: Emdrupvej 115A, 2400 Copenhagen NV; A & R Man. DAVID ROWLEY.

Rock Owl Records: Tagensvej 204, 2400 Copenhagen; Man. Dir KIM KOFOD.

Sony Music Denmark: Vognmagergade 10, 1120 Copenhagen; Man. Dir STEEN SORGENFREI.

Steeplechase Productions: PO Box 35, Slots Aleen 16, 2930 Klampenborg; Man. Dir NILS WINTHER.

Storyville: Dortheavej 39, 2400 Copenhagen NV; Man. Dir KARL EMIL KNUDSEN.

Street Dance Records ApS: Vestergade 17, 1456 Copenhagen K; Man. Dir PETER LARSEN.

Sundance/Stunt Records: Havnegade 41, 1050 Copenhagen K; tel. 3333-8720; fax 3333-8730; e-mail sundance@sundance.dk; internet www.sundance.dk; Man. Dir PETER LITTAUER.

Virgin Denmark: Ny Vestergade 7 B, 1471 Copenhagen K; Man. Dir HENRIETTE BLIX.

Warner Music Denmark: Antoinettevej 2, 2500 Valby/Copenhagen; Man. Dir FINN WORK.

Zing Zing Music Production: Kirkegaardsstraede 3, 9000 Aalborg; Man. Dir BIRGITTE RODE.

Ecuador

Fabrica Ecuatoriana de Discos SA: Km 7.5, Via a la Costa, 09018 56 Guayaquil; Pres. FRANCISCO FERAUD AROCA.

Estonia

Forte: PO Box 472, 0090 Tallinn; Man. Dir MART MARIPUU.

Salumusik: Tondi 17a, Tallinn; Man. Dir MADIS SALUM.

Fiji

Procera Music Co Ltd: PO Box 10272, Suva; Man. Dir ANILESH CHANDRA.

South Pacific Recordings Ltd: PO Box 17, Nadi; tel. 670-0478; fax 670-2193; e-mail spr@is.com.fj; internet sprfiji.com; Man. Dir RAVINDRA PATEL.

Finland

Aani Records: Aholantie 43, 03150, Huhmari; Man. Dir TAPANI RINNE.

Amigo Musik Finland: Cygnaeuksenkatu 12, 00100 Helsinki; Man. Dir MARTTI HEIKKINEN.

Bad Vagum: PO Box 362, 90101 Oulu; Man. Dir KARI HEIKONEN.

Bluebird Music/Blue Bubble Records: Arinatie 8, 00370 Helsinki; Man. Dir NIKO NORDSTRÖM.

Bluelight Records: PO Box 153, 00171 Helsinki; Man. Dir MIKA MYYRYLÄINEN.

BMG/Ariola Finland: PO Box 173, Vattuniemenranta 2, 00211 Helsinki; Man. Dir KUUSI MAIJA.

EMI Finland: Arinatie 6 E, PO Box 28, 00371 Helsinki; Man. Dir H PUHAKKA.

Evidence/Dig It/Fazer Records: PO Box 169, 02101 Espoo; Label Man. PIA LOUHIVOURI.

Gaga Goodies: PO Box 47, 13211 Hämeenlinna; Man. Dir KARI HELENIUS.

Goofin' Records: PO Box 63, 01601 Vantaa; Man. Dir PETE HAKONEN.

Hiljaiset Levyt Records: PO Box 211, 33201 Tampere; e-mail hiljaiset@hiljaiset.sci.fi; internet www.hiljaiset.com; Man. Dir JUKKA JUNTTILA.

Megamania Music: Hämeentie 6 A 1, 00530 Helsinki; Man. Dir ATTE BLOM.

MIPU Music: PO Box 15, 82300 Rääkkylä; Man. Dir HEIKKI KEMPAINEN.

Olarin Musiikki Oy: PO Box 20, 02211 Espoo; tel. (9) 881-3227; e-mail olarinmusiikki@olarinmusiikki.fi; internet www.olarinmusiikki.fi; Man. Dir TIMO NÄRVÄINEN.

Poko Records: PO Box 483, 33101 Tampere; Man. PERTTI PALKOAHO.

Polarvox: Arinatie 2 A, 00370 Helsinki; Man. Dir LEENA JUURANTO.

PolyGram Finland: Vattuniemenranta 2, PO Box 172, 00211 Helsinki; Man. Dir GUGI KOKLJUSCHKIN.

Pro Records: P Hesperiankatu 9 A 7, 00260 Helsinki; Contact EERO KOIVISTOINEN.

Real Art: Pursimiehenkatu 26 i, 00150 Helsinki; Man. Dir PASI ERVI.

Rockadillo: PO Box 35, 33201 Tampere; Man. Dir TAPIO KORJUS.

Sähkö Recordings: Perämiehenkatu 11, 00150, Helsinki; Contact TOMMI GRÖNLUND.

Siboney/Love Records: Hämeentie 6 A 1, 00530 Helsinki; Man. Dir SINI PERHO.

Sony Music Finland: PO Box 12, 02171 Espoo; Man. Dir ANTTI HOLMA.

Spinefarm Records: Elimäenkatu 12–16 D, 5th Floor, 00510 Helsinki; Man. Dir RIKU PAAKKONEN.

Strawberry Records: PO Box 17, 01351 Vantaa; Man. Dir PASI KOSTIAINEN.

Stupido Twins Records: PO Box 301, 00121 Helsinki; Head of Public Relations JOOSE BERGLUND.

Syrene Music: Saarnitie 14a, 00780 Helsinki; tel. (9) 385-7939; fax (9) 385-7349; e-mail jukka.linkola@syrenemusic.fi; internet www.fimic.fi; Contact JUKKA LINKOLA; Man. Dir MARITA LINKOLA.

WEA/Warner Music Finland: Melkonkatu 28 E, 00210 Helsinki; Man. Dir MARITA KAASALAINEN.

Zen Garden: PO Box 76, 00501, Helsinki; Man. Dir KARI HYNNINEN.

France

AB Disques: 144 Ave du Pdt Wilson, 93210 La Plaine St Denis; Chair. JEAN-MICHEL FAVA.

Airplay Records: 39 rue de la Rochefoucauld, 92100 Boulogne; Head of Marketing JEAN-MICHEL DOUE.

Ariola: 2 rue des Quatre Fils, 75003, Paris; Label Man. NATHALIE MERCENIER.

Atoll Music: 18/20 rue du Borrego, 75020 Paris; Chair. CHARLES IBGUI.

Auvidis: PO Box 21, 47 Ave Paul Vaillant Couturier, 94251 Genitilly Cédex; Chair. LOUIS BRICARD.

AYAA Disques: PO Box 167, 51056 Reims Cédex; Owner DENIS THIEBLEMONT.

Baya: 18 rue de Reuilly, 75012 Paris; Man. Dir FRANÇIS KERTEKIAN.

Black Et Noir Records: 4 rue Valdemaine, 49100 Angers; Head of Promotion PACO.

Boucherie Productions: 15 Bis rue du Plateau, 75019 Paris; Dir NATALI LUC.

Carrere Music: 27 rue de Suresne, 75008 Paris; Gen. Man. MICHAEL WIJNEN.

Celine Music: 44 rue de Miromesnil, 75008 Paris; Contact VLINE BUGGY.

Celluloid: 50 rue Stendahl, 75020 Paris; Contact GILBERT CASTRO.

Cobalt: 145 rue de Ménilmontant, 75020 Paris; tel. 1 47 97 69 99; fax 1 47 97 65 44; e-mail cobalt@africolor.com; internet www.africolor.com; Man. Dir PHILIPPE CONRATH.

Columbia / Epic Records: 131 Ave de Wagram, 75017 Paris; Dirs OLIVIER MONTFORT, LAURENCE LE NY.

Declic Communication: 45 rue St Sebastein, 75011 Paris; Chair. ERIC BASSET.

Delabel: 3 rue des Minimes, 75003 Paris; Chair. EMMANUEL DE BURETEL.

Delphine Productions: 150 Bvd Haussman, 75008 Paris; Chair. PAUL DE SENNEVILLE.

Dixie Frog: 218 rue du Faubourg St Denis, 75010 Paris; Chair. PHILIPPE LANGLOIS.

EMI France: 37 rue Camille Desmoulins, 92133 Issy Les Moulineaux; Chair. GILBERT OHAYON.

EPM: 188 Blvd Voltaire, 75011 Paris; Chair. FRANÇOIS DACLA.

Eric Taffoureau Productions/Valotte Records International: 138 rue Nationale, PO Box 46, 75013 Paris; tel. 1 45 83 45 00; fax 1 45 83 45 00; internet www.francemp3.com; Dir ERIC TAFFOUREAU.

F Communications: 11 rue de Clichy, 75003 Paris; Prime Minister ERIC NORAND.

FGL: 25 Blvd Arago, 75013 Paris; Man. Dir THIERRY WOLF.

Francis Dreyfus Music: 26 Ave Kléber, 75116 Paris; Chair. FRANCIS DREYFUS.

GRRR: 134 rue d'Estienne d'Orves, 92140 Clamart, France; Contact JEAN-JACQUES BIRGE.

Happy Music: 38 rue Voltaire, 92800 Puteaux; Label Man. FRÉDÉRICK GITEAU.

Island/Barclay: 16 rue des Fossés St Jacques, 75005 Paris; Man. Dir PASCAL NEGRE.

Karmel Music: 73 rue de Turbigo, 75003 Paris; Gen. Dir EDWARD APRAHAMIAN.

Larsen Records & Fanzine: 116 rue Du Crey, 73230 St Alban Leysse; tel. 4 79 70 14 64; fax 4 79 70 14 64; e-mail slushyruin@larsen.asso.fr; internet www.larsen.asso.fr; Contact DENIS OLIVERES.

Made In Heaven: 6 rue Rémy de Gourmont, 75019 Paris; Label Man. MATHIAS JEANNIN.

Mango: 20 rue Des Fossés St Jacques, 75005 Paris; Chair. PHILIPPE CONSTANTIN.

MCA Music Entertainment SA: 65 rue D'Anjou, 75008 Paris; Asst to the Pres. VICKI RUMMLER.

MSI SA: Baudrin, Labastide Castel Amouroux, 47250 Bouglon; Contact PIERRE-EMMANUEL GILBERT.

Musea: 68 La Tinchotte, 57117 Retonfey; Pres. BERNARD GUEFFIER.

Musidisc: PO Box 190, 3/5 rue de Albert Vatimesnil, 92300 Levallois-Perret; Chair. FRANÇOIS GRANDCHAMP.

Mute France: 17 rue Soyer, 92200 Neuilly; Public Relations HELENE LEMOINE.

Ness Music: 35 rue Petit, 75019 Paris; Dir NESSIM SAROUSSI.

PEM Claude Martinez: 59 Bvd Exelmans, 75016 Paris; Chair. CLAUDE MARTINEZ.

Phonogram: 20 rue des Fossés St Jacques, 75005 Paris Cédex 05; Man. Dir YVES BIGOT.

Polydor: 22 rue des Fossés St Jacques, 75005 Paris; Gen. Man. BRUNO GERENTES.

Polygram France: 20 rue des Fossés St Jacques, 75005 Paris; Chair. ALFREDO GANGOTENA.

RCA Records: 17 rue Soyer, 92200 Neuilly; Gen. Man. ANTOINE CHOUCHANI.

Remark Records: 89 rue de la Boétie, 75008 Paris; Chair. MARC LUMBROSO.

Roadrunner: 3–5 rue de Albert Vatimesnil, 92300 Levallois-Perret; Label Man. STÉPHANE SAUNIER.

Rosebud Records: 10/12 rue Jean Guy, 35000 Rennes; Chair. ALAN GAC.

RRose Selavy: PO Box 521, 35006 Rennes Cédex; Company Sec. OLIVIER MELLANO.

Scorpio Music: 12 Ave George V, 75008 Paris; Pres. HENRI BELOLO.

Sephora–La Musique de la Vie (Dept of Gam International SA): 6 Pl. Jean-Paul Sartre, 51170 Fismes; Man. MARC BRUNET.

Sidonie: 31 rue François 1er, 75008 Paris; Chair. CHRISTAIN DULCY.

Skydog / Kind of Groove: 32 Ave Claude Vellefaux, 75010 Paris; PDG MARC ZERMATI.

Sony Music France: 131 Ave de Wagram, 75017 Paris; Chair. PAUL-RENÉ ALBERTINI.

Top Records: 17 Ave du Président Wilson, 75116 Paris; Label Man. ALAIN BELOLO.

Topomic Music: 26 rue L M Nordmann, 92250 La Garenne-Colombes; Pres. PIERRE JAUBERT.

Vinilkosmo: c/o Eurokka, Esperanto Rok Asocio, 31450 Donneville; Dir FLOREAL MARTORELL.

Virgin France: 11 Pl. des Vosges, 75004 Paris; Chair. EMMANUEL DE BURETEL.

Vogue: 2 rue des Quatre Fils, 75003 Paris; Chair. FABRICE NATAF.

Warner Music France / WEA Music: 102 Ave du Prsident Kennedy, 75116 Paris; Chair. MARCO-ANTONIO BIGNOTTI.

XIII Bis Music Group: 34 rue Eugene Flachat, 75017 Paris; Man. Dir LAURENT DREUX-LEBLANC; Music Dir BRIAN RAWLING.

Germany

Arcade Deutschland: Kaiser Wilhelm Ring 17, 40505 Düsseldorf; Man. Dir SYLVIAN JONKERGOW.

Ata Tak Records: Kölner str 226 F, 40227 Düsseldorf; tel. (211) 782-2329; internet www.atatak.com; Dir FRANK FENSTERMACHER.

Bellaphon Records: Mainzer Landstr 87–89, 60329 Frankfurt; Chair. JUTTA ZIZANOVIC-RIEDEL.

BMG Ariola Munich: Steinhauserstr 1–3, 81677 Munich; Man. Dir THOMAS STEIN.

Century Media Records: Bissenkamp 11–13, 44135 Dortmund; Man. Dir ROBERT KAMPF.

CMP Records: PO Box 1129, 52368 Kreuzau; Man. Dir ULRICH KURT RATTAY.

Comma Records & Tapes: PO Box 2148, 63243 Neu-Isenburg; Dir ROLAND BAUER.

Crosscut Records: PO Box 10 65 24, 2800 Bremen; Man. Dir DETEVV HOEGEN.

EastWest Records GmbH: Heussweg 25, 20255 Hamburg; Artist Marketing Dir BORIS LOEHE.

EMI Records: Maarweg 149, PO Box 30 03 29, 50825 Cologne; Man. Dir HELMUT FEST.

Enemy Productions Inc: #2 Edward Schmid str 28, 81541 Munich; Pres. MICHAEL KNUTH.

Exile Records: Lintuperstr 39, 12305 Berlin; Man. Dir TED BAXTER.

Garbitowski: Metzer str 30, 50677 Cologne; Owner & Dir JÜRGEN GARBITOWSKI.

Global Records: Nederlingerstr 21, 80638 Munich; Man. Dir PETER KIRSTEN.

Grover Records: PO Box 3072, 48016 Münster; e-mail info@grover.de; internet www.grover.de; Man. Asst REINHILD SANDER.

Hansa Musik Produktion: Wittelbachstr 18, 10707 Berlin; Man. Dir ANDRÉ SELLENEIT.

Hyperium Records GmbH: PO Box 910127, 90259 Nürnberg; Gen. Man. OLIVER RÖSCH.

Intercord: Aixhiemer str 26, 70619 Stuttgart; International Label Man. PETER CADERA.

Jaro Medien GmbH: Bismarckstr 83, 28293 Bremen; Man. Dir ULRICH BALSS.

Jupiter Records: Hoechlstr 2, 81675 Munich; Man. Dir JOACHIM NEUBAUER.

Logic Records: Strahlenbergerstr 125A, 63067 Offenbach; Man. Dir MATTHIAS MARTINSOHN.

M A D Fuesgen/Nickel GBR: Hagelberger str 48, 10965 Berlin; Owner UTE FUESGEN.

Messidor Musik GmbH: Kleine Bockenheimer str 10–12, 60313 Frankfurt; Man. Dir GOETZ WOERNER.

Modern Music: Kurfuersten str 23, 10785 Berlin; International Man. BIRGIT NIELSEN.

Obsession Records: Mosel str 24, 50674 Cologne; Pres. CORDULA SCHÜTTEN.

Orgasm Records: Obertor str 6, 35792 Löhnberg; Label Man. ERICH KNODT.

Perfect Beat: Industriestr 37, 33034 Brakel; Man. Dir DIETER SCHUBERT.

Play It Again Sam (Germany): Spaldingstr 74, 20097 Hamburg; Man. Dir MARK CHUNG.

PolyGram Germany: Glockengiesserwall 3, PO Box 10 49 09, 20095 Hamburg; Chair. WOLF GRAMATKE.

Rough Trade Germany: Eickeler str 25, 44561 Herne; Contact CARSTEN STRICKER.

Sony Music Entertainment Germany: PO Box 10 19 60, Bleichstr 64, 60313 Frankfurt; Man. RÜDIGER FLIEGE.

SPV GmbH: PO Box 1147, 30537 Hanover; Gen. Man. MANFRED SCHUTZ.

Sub Pop Germany: Gruener Weg 25, 37688 Beverungen; Man. Dir REINHARD HOLSTEIN.

Subway Records: Vohwinkeler str 154, 42329 Wuppertal; Man. Dir MICHAEL SCHUSTER.

Synthetic Product Records: PO Box 690441, 30613 Hanover; Contact LORENZ MACKE.

TGM Musikverlag Nietsch, Green, Kleinhammer: Max Beer str 25, 10119 Berlin; CEO TIM GREEN.

TRITT Records: Siegener str 6, 65936 Frankfurt; Owner NILS SELZER.

TRIXX Musikproduktion GmbH: Prinzessinnen str 16, 10969 Berlin; Studio Man. KLAUS KNAPP.

Vielklang Musikproduktion GmbH: Forster str 4/5, 10999 Berlin; Man. Dir JOERG FUKKING.

Virgin Germany: Herzogstr 64, 80803 Munich; International Label Man. MICHAEL BINDERNAGEL.

Warner Music Germany: Hallerstr 40, 20146 Hamburg; Man. HANS BARTH.

Westpark Music: PO Box 260 227, Rathenauplatz 4, 50515 Cologne; tel. (221) 247-644; fax (221) 231-819; e-mail westparkmusic@aop.com; internet www.westparkmusic.com; Pres. ULLI HETSCHER.

Greece

Akti: 311 Mesogheion St, 15231 Athens; Head of Promotion ELENI MAVROVOUNIOTI.

Ano Kato Records: PP Germanou St 19, 54622 Salonica; Man. Dir GEORGE TSAKALIDES.

BMG Ariola Greece: Mesogheion 230 and Perikleous 1, Holargos, 15561 Athens; Man. Dir MILTOS KARATZAS.

Hitch Hyke Records: Kosma Balanou St 5, 11636 Athens; Man. Dir HANNELORE THOSPANN.

Iptamenoi Diski (Flying Discs): 24 Korytsas St, Papagou, 15669 Athens; Man. Dir THEO MANIKAS.

Lyra: Zalokosta St 4, 10671 Athens; Man. Dir PANAGIOTIS MARAVELIAS.

Minos—EMI: 245–247 Mesogheion Ave, 15451 Athens; Chair. MAKIS MATSAS.

Pegasus Records: Odiseos Androutsou St 3–5, 15772 Athens; Man. Dir PETROS KOUTSOUMBAS.

Penguin Ltd: 58 Lambrou Katsuni St, 11471 Athens; Gen. Man. P STAVROSKI.

Polygram Greece: Mesogheion Ave 296, 15510 Athens; Man. Dir VICOTR ANTIPPAS.

Sony Music Entertainment Greece: 311 Mesogheion St, 15231 Athens; Man. Dir DIMITRIS YARMENITIS.

Virgin Records Greece: 557 Mesogheion Ave, 15344 Athens; Man. Dir YANNIS PETRIDIS.

WEA Greece: 319 Mesogheion Ave, 15231 Athens; Man. Dir ION STAMBOULIS.

Wipe Out Records: PO Box 80512, 18510 Piraeus; tel. and fax (10) 494-4488; e-mail wipeout@atenet.gr; internet www.wipeout.gr; Man. Dir THEO KRITHARIS.

Greenland

ULO—Greenlandic Music: PO Box 184, 3911 Sisimiut; Production Man. KARSTEN SOMMER.

Hong Kong

BMG Hong Kong Ltd: 11/F Peninsula Office Tower, 18 Middle Rd, Tsimshatsui, Kowloon; Contact STEVE BEAVER.

HNH International Ltd: 8/F Kai It Bldg, 58 Pak Tai St, Tokwawan, Kowloon; Man. Dir KLAUS HEYMANN.

Polygram Records Ltd: 1503 Garley Bldg, 233–239 Nathan Rd, Kowloon; Man. Dir DOUGLAS CHAN.

Rock In Music Ltd: Room A, 24/F Haven Commercial Bldg, 8 Tsing Fung St, Causeway Bay; tel. 2807-1297; fax 2806-3204; Gen. Man. KEITH YIP.

Schtung Records Ltd: Top Floor, 2 Kennedy Rd; Man. Dir MORTON WILSON.

Sony Music Entertainment (Hong Kong) Ltd: 4/F Acme Bldg, 22–28 Nanking St, Kowloon; Contact PETER CHIU.

Virgin/EMI (Hong Kong) Ltd: Room 3201–7 Shell Tower, Times Sq., 1 Matheson St, Causeway Bay; Man. Dir HERMAN HO.

Warner Music Hong Kong Ltd: 12/f Peninsula Office Tower, 18 Middle Rd, Tsimshatsui, Kowloon; Man. Dir PACO WONG.

Wing Hang Record Trading Co Ltd: Flat A, 21/F, Lung Shing Industrial Centre, 142–148 Texaco Rd, Tsuen Wan NT; Man. Dir TANG PING HANG; Chief Marketing Exec. WINNIE TANG.

Hungary

Alt Product: 5002 Szolnok, PO Box 76; Man. Dir BELA PAP.

Bahia Records: Baross u 6, 1088 Budapest; A & R Man. CSABA HAJNOCZY.

BMG Hungary: szt Istvàn Park 16, 1137 Budapest; Man. Dir JÀNOS KALLUS.

EMI—Quint Records: Terez krt 19, 1067 Budapest; Man. Dir JENÖ BORS.

HMK Records: Lovag u 2, 1075 Budapest; Man. Dir VOJISLAV NESIC.

Hungaroton Gong: Vörösmarty tér 1, 1051 Budapest; A & R Mans LASZLO BENKÖ, ATTILA HOTH.

LP Records: Bajscy Zsilinsky u 62, 1054 Budapest; Man. Dir NORBERT LAPIS.

Newsis Records: Villàlyi ùt 107, 1118 Budapest; Man. Dir ROBERT MANDEL.

Polygram Hungary Ltd: Steindl Imre u 12, 1054 Budapest; Man. Dir LASZLO KEGEOUS.

Record Express Ltd: Kunigunda ut 41/B, 1037 Budapest; tel. (1) 437-1800; fax (1) 437-1899; e-mail meszaros@recordexpress.hu; internet www.recordexpress.hu; Man. Dir ATTILA SCHNEIDER; International Affairs BARBARA MÉSZAROS.

Rosza Records: Maros u 29, 1122 Budapest; Man. Dir ISTVAN ROSZA.

Sony Music Hungary: Ponty u 7, 1011 Budapest; Man. Dir MALCOLM CARRUTHERS.

T3 Records: PO Box 8, 1922 Budapest; Man. Dir PETER GYÖRGY.

Trottel Records: Hunyadi 4, 1011 Budapest; Man. Dir TAMÀS RUPASZOV.

Warner Music Hungary: Hüvösvölgyi ùt 54 III EP, 1021 Budapest; Man. Dir ISTVAN JOOZ.

Iceland

Bo Haldorson Productions: PO Box 5445, Pverholt 26, 105 Reykjavik; Man. Dir BO HALDORSON.

Platonic: Skeifan 17, 108 Reykjavík; Man. Dir HILMAR ÖRN HILMARSSON.

Skifan Hf: Skeifan 17, 108 Reykjavík; Man. Dir THORVALDUR THORSTEINSSON.

Smekkleysa / Bad Taste: PO Box 710, 121 Reykjavík; Man. Dir ASMUNDUR JONSSON.

Spor HF: Nýbýlavegur 4, PO Box 320, 202 Kópavogur; Man. Dir STEINAR BERG ISLEIFSSON.

Indonesia

Jeka Records: Jalan Jembatan Tiga, 38 Blok B-13, Jakarta 14440; Dir SOFYAN ALI.

Metro Utama Raya Electronics Industry: PO Box 4920/JKTF, Jakarta 11049; Export Man. MISS LISNAWATI.

Polygram Records, PT Suara Sentral Sejati: Kapuk Utara 89, Jakarta 14460; Man. Dir ANTHONY SHIH.

RIS Music Wijaya International (BMG): Mangga Dua Plaza, Komplek Agung Sedaya Blok D/11, Jakarta 10730; Man. Dir EFFENDY WIDJAJA.

Sony Music, PT Indo Semar Sakti: JI Jelambar Ilir 2, Jakarta 1460; Dir DR SUNTONO.

Tira Wahari Lestari (BASF): Tira Bldg 5th Floor, Jl Hr Rasuna Said Kav, B-3 Jakarta Selatan; Sales Man. JOHANNES HARDIMAN.

Ireland

Ainm Music: 5–6 Lombard St East, Dublin 2; tel. and fax (1) 677-8701; e-mail fstubbs@ainm-music.com; internet www.ainm-music.com; CEO FRANK STUBBS.

Aquarhythms Ltd: 15 Upper Mount St, Dublin 2; Label Man. ANN POMERANT.

AX-S Records: 26 Mount Eagle View, Leopardstown Heights, Dublin 18; Man. Dir PETER JONES.

Beaumex Music: Unit 45, Western Rockway Business Centre, Lower Ballymount Rd, Walkinstown, Dublin 12; Dir CATHAL TULLY.

Beautiful Records: Ballyloughan, Bagnelstown, Co Carlow; Man. Dir KIERAN CONNORS.

BMG Ireland: Grafton Bldgs, 34 Grafton St, Dublin 2; tel. 677-9006; fax 677-9204; internet www.click2music.ie; Man. Dir FREDDIE MIDDLETON; Marketing Man. KATHRYN MASON.

Celtic Heartbeat Ltd: 30/32 Sir John Rogerson's Quay, Dublin 2; Label Man. AISLING MEEHAN.

Claddagh Records: Dame House, Dame St, Dublin 2; Production Man. TOM SHERLOCK.

Cross Border Media Ltd: 10 Deer Park, Ashbourne, Co Meath; Contact OLIVER SWEENEY.

Dabble Music: The Elms, Richmond Ave South, Dartry, Dublin 6; CEO PETER BLACKBYRNE.

Danceline Records: 267 Crodaun Forest Park, Celbridge, Co Kildare; Contact PETER MCCLUSKEY.

Dara Records: Unit 4, Great Ship St, Dublin 8; Man. Dir JOE O'REILLY, PAUL O'REILLY.

Dino Entertainment: Dino House, 12 Malborough Court, Malborough St, Dublin 1; A & R Man. SUSAN DUNNE.

EMI Records (Ireland) Ltd: EMI House, 1 Ailesbury Rd, Ballsbridge, Dublin 4; Man. Dir WILLIE KAVANAGH.

Goya Records: Thompson House, McCurtain St, Cork City; PRO PAUL MCDERMOTT.

Grapevine /Solid Records: Alexandra House, Earlsfort Centre, Earlsfort Terrace, Dublin 2; Man. Dir PETER KENNY; Label Man. JANINE NALLEN.

Green Linnet Records: 17 Lower Baggot St, Dublin 2; Contact AMY GARVEY.

Harmac Music Ltd: 67 Amiens St, Dublin 1; Man. Dir BRENDAN HARVEY.

Hazel Music: Dublin Rd, Monasterevin, Co Kildare; Man. Dir JOHN KELLY.

Independent Records: The Factory, 35A Barrow St, Dublin 4; Contact DAVE O'GRADY.

K-Tel Ireland Ltd/Celtic Collections: 30–32 Sir John Rogerson's Quay, Dublin 2; tel. (1) 679-0667; fax (1) 679-0668; e-mail celticc@indigo.ie; internet www.celtic-collections.com; CEO SHARON BROWNE.

Lodge Records: Ballinclea Rd, Co Dublin; International Man. PAT DEMPSEY.

Lunar / Unicorn Records: 5–6 Lombard St East, Dublin 2; Contact BRIAN MOLLOY, JUDY CARDIFF; Marketing Man. GRAHAM MOLLOY.

MCA Records Ireland: 30–32 Sir John Rogerson's Quay, Dublin 2; Gen. Man. DAVE PENNEFATHER.

Mother Records: 30–32 Sir John Rogerson's Quay, Dublin 2; Contact ELVA TARPEY.

Polygram Records Ireland: 9 Whitefriars, Aungiers St, Dublin 2; Man. Dir PAUL KEOGH.

Preplay Records: c/o The Galway Arts Centre, 47 Dominick St, Galway; Man. Dir PHILIP GRAY.

Rivervalley Records Ltd: Shruthaun, Baltinglass, Co Wicklow; Man. Dir FIONA JOYCE.

Round Tower Music: 48 Downside, Skerries, Co Dublin; Dir CLIVE HUDSON.

RSE Records: 11–13 Station Rd, Raheny, Dublin 5; Dirs RAYMOND J SMYTH, BREIDE P SMYTH.

Rut Records: c/o The Galway Arts Centre, 47 Dominick St, Galway; Man. Dir PHILIP GRAY.

Sony Music Ireland Ltd: Unit 2, Carriglea Industrial Estate, Naas Rd, Dublin 2; Man. Dir JOHN SHEEHAN.

Tara Music Company Ltd: 8 Anne's Lane, Dublin 2; Man. Dir JOHN COOK.

Virgin Records Ireland: 1 Ailesbury Rd, Ballsbridge, Dublin 4; Public Relations JOSEPHINE NESTOR.

Warner Music (Ireland) Ltd: Alexandra House, Earlsfort Centre, Earlsfort Terrace, Dublin 2; Man. Dir DENNIS WOODS.

Whirling Discs Ltd: Cairns Hill, Aughamore, Co Sligo; Man. Dir BRIAN MCDONAGH.

Italy

A Tempo Srl: Via Filipo Turati 12, 50136 Florence; Man. Dir PIERO BORRI.

Abraxas Srl: Via Guglielmo Marconi 106, 50131 Florence; Man. Dir SIMONE FRINGUELLI.

Ala Bianca Group Srl: Via G Mazzoni 34/36, 41100 Modena; Gen. Man. TONI VERONA.

AND Recommended Records Italia: Via Decembrio 26, 20137 Milan; Man. Dir ALBERTO CROSTA.

Artis/Cramps Records: Via False 33, 36050 Monteviale (Vicenze); Man. Dir ALFREDO TISOCCO.

Baby Records: Via Timavo 34, 20124 Milan; Man. Dir MONICA DAHL.

Blindness Inc: Rain 10, 39040 Cortaccia; Man. Dir GIOVANNETTI REINHOLD.

Blu Bus: Via Consolata 5, 11100 Aosta; Man. Dir SERGIO MILANI.

BMG Ariola Italy: Via di San Alessandro 7, 00131 Rome; Man. Dir FRANCO REALI.

Cave Canem/Spray Records: Via Saline 8/C, 65013 Marina di Citta San Angelo; Man. Dir BELFINO DE LEONARDIS.

Clac Records: Via Salvatore di Giacomo 73, 00142 Rome; Mans MASSIMO CALABRESE, PIERO CALABRESE.

Contempo Records: Corso de'Tintori 6/18r, 50122 Florence; International Label Man. SEBASTIAN KOCH.

EMI Italy: Via Bergamo 315, 21042 Caronno Pertusella (Milan); International Man. NICO SPINOSA.

Flying Records: Via R Ruggiero 16D, 80125 Naples; Man. Dir FLAVIO ROSSI.

FMA Edizioni Musicali E Discografiche Srl: Via Boccaccio N 47, 20123 Milan; Pres. MARIO ALLIONE.

I Soulzionisti: Largo dell'Olgiata, 15-1s 59 3/2, 00123 Rome; Man. Dir STEFANO BONAGURA.

Interbeat: Via A Straedella 174, 00124 Rome; International Label Man. LUIGI FEDELE.

Kaleidoscopic Music Srl: Viale Manzoni 52, Cerveteri, 00052 Rome; Contact ROBBIE ZEE.

Kindergarten Records: Via Panicale 9, 50123 Florence; Man. Dir FABRIZIO FEDERIGHI.

Klang Records: Via Valle Viola 35, 00141 Rome; Man. Dir MASSIMO BERNARDI.

L M Records Crotalo Ed Mus: Via Del Pino 71, 48100; Man. Dir LUIGI MAZZESI.

Materiali Sonori: Via Trieste 35, 52027 San Giovanni Valdarno; International Label Man. ARLO BIGAZZI.

Minus Habens Records: Via Giustino Fortunato 8/N, 70125 Bari; Owner IVAN IUSCO.

Musica Maxima Magnetica: PO Box 2280, 50110 Florence; tel. (0571) 559000; fax (0571) 959745; e-mail mmm@penteres.it; internet www.musicamaximamagnetica.com; Man. Dir LUCIANO DARI.

New Tone Records: Via Principi d' Acaia 28, 10138 Turin; International Label Man. BEPE GREPI.

Nuova Durium Srl: Piazza Mirabello 1, 20121 Milan; Asst Man. FRANCESCO PICCARREDA.

Polygram Italia: Via Carlo Tenca 2, 20124 Milan; Man. Dir STEFANO SENARDI.

Recordthings: Zona Archives, Box 1486, 50122 Florence.

Reform Records: Via Cosenza 5, 20137 Milan; Label Man. ALBERTO LAPRIS; A & R International FRAN SICCARDI.

Robi Droli Snc: Strada Roncaglia 16, 15040 San Germano (AL); Man. Dir BEPPE GREPPI.

Sentemo Records: Via Calstorta Vecchia 21 A, 31040 Cessalto (Treviso); International Label Man. PAOLO BOARATO.

Sony Music Italy: Via Amedei 9, 20123 Milan; Man. Dir FRANCO CABRINI.

Studiotianta—Fortuna Records: Via Cernaia 3, 14031 Calliano; Gen. Man. MASSIMO VISENTIN.

Virgin Italy: Via Porpora 26, 20131 Milan; Man. Dir LUIGI MANTOVANI.

Vizio Records: Via Festaz 52, 11100 Aoste; Man. Dir FRANCSECO BATTISTI.

Vox Pop/Crazy Mannequin: Via Bergognone 31, 20144 Milan; Man. Dir CARLO ALBERTOLI.

Warner Music / WEA Italiana: Via Milani 16, 20090 Redecescio Segrate (Milan); Man. Dir MARCO ANTONIO BIGNOTTI.

Zion: Via Latini 5, 24032 Calalziocorte (BG); Man. Dir CAMERONI SLIVIA.

Japan

BMG Victor Inc: 1-3-9 Shibuya, Shibuya-ku, Tokyo 150; Pres. OSAMU SATO.

East West Japan: 3-1-2 Kita-Aoyama, Minato-ku, Tokyo 107; Pres. TAKASHI KAMIDE.

JVC Victor Entertainment Inc: 26-18 Jingu-Mae, 4-Chome, Shibuya-ku, Tokyo 150; Pres. JUN DEGUCHI.

MCA Victor Inc: 9F JBP Oval, 5-52-2 Jingu-Mae, Shibuya-ku, Tokyo 150; Pres. HIROYUKI IWATA.

Nippon Columbia Co Ltd (Denon): 14-14-4 Chome, Akasaka, Minato-ku, Tokyo 107; Dir TOSHIKIKO HIRAHARA.

Nippon Phonogram Co Ltd: Wako Bldg, 4-8-5 Roppongi, Minato-ku, Tokyo 106; CEO ALEX ABRAMOFF.

Polydor / Polygram K K: 1-8-4 Ohashi 1-Chome, Meguro-ku, Tokyo 153; Pres. TAKEO KASAHARA.

Pony Canyon Inc: 2-1-1 Irifune, Chuo-ku, Tokyo 104; Gen. Man. of International A & R TATSUO OZU; Asst Gen. Man. KAZ SAITO.

Seven Gods Productions: Suite 403, Mejidori Bldg, 2-3-21 Kabukicho Shimjulou-lou, Tokyo 160-0021; tel. (3) 5292-5551; fax (3) 5292-5552; e-mail benten@jk9.so-net.no.jp; internet www.sister.co.jp; Pres. HIROSHI ASADA.

Shinko Music Publishing Co Ltd: 2–1 Ogawamachi, Kanda, Chiyoda-ku, Tokyo 101; Pres. SHOICHI KUSANO.

Sony Music Entertainment (Japan) Inc: PO Box 5208, Tokyo International, Tokyo 100-31; Pres. SHUGO MATSUO.

Victor Entertainment Inc (JVC): 4-26-18 Jingumae, Shibuya-Ku, Tokyo 150; International Operations AYA OHI.

Warner Music Japan Inc: 3-1-2 Kita-Aoyama, Minato-ku, Tokyo 107; Chair. RYUZO KOSUGI.

Republic of Korea

BMG (Han Kook) Music Co Ltd: 3rd Floor, BaekRim Bldg, 823–33 Yuksam-dong, Kangnam-ku, Seoul; Man. Dir SEUNG DOO PARK.

Columbia / Epic Music (Korea) Inc: 2nd Floor, Doosung Bldg, 77–2 Sadang-dong, Dongjak-ku, Seoul 156 090; Man. Dir YEOUEL YOON.

EMI—Kemongsa Music Ltd: 9th Fl, Kemongmunhwa Centre Bldg, 772 Yuksam-dong, Kangnam-ku, Seoul 135 080; Pres. LEE KWAN-CHOI.

Korea Music Co: 724–43 Yuksam-dong, Kangnam-ku, Seoul 135 080; Contact DUK-JOO LEE.

Nices A & R International Entertainment, Business Division, Samsung Electronics: 19th Fl, Ahtae Bldg, 1337–20, Seocho 2-dong, Seocho-Ku, Seoul 137-072; Man. KWANG WOO NAM.

Polygram Ltd: 3rd Fl, Sungsoo Bldg, 284–9 2-ka Sungsoo-dong, Sungdong-ku, Seoul; Man. Dir DAVID LEE.

Seoul Music Inc: 3F Jung-Nam Bldg, 721–39 Yuksam-dong, Kang-Nam-Ku, Seoul; Pres. YONG-IL LEE.

Seoul Records Inc: 2nd Floor, Hankook Glass Bldg, 45–1 Yoido-dong, Youngdeungpo-ku, Seoul 150 010; Contact HONG-KYUN SHIN.

Sony Music: 98519 Bangbae-dong, Seocho-ku, Seoul; Contact YUN YEO UL.

Warner Music Korea Ltd: 5th Floor, Eunsung Bldg, 601–18 Yuksum-dong, Kangnam-Ku, Seoul 135-080; Man. Dir JONATHAN S PARK.

Lithuania

Blue Baltic Records: Arhcitektu 79, 2049 Vilnius; Man. Dir ALGIS PIGAGA.

BNA Music: Gedimino Ave 2, 2001 Vilnius; Pres. ARTURAS ZUOKAS.

Bomba: Zygimantu 6, 2001 Vilnius; Gen. Dir RIMAS ALISAUSKAS.

Zona Records: Seskines 79, 2010 Vilnius; Man. Dir GIEDRUS KLIMKEVICUS.

Luxembourg

Intercommunication: 275 Rote d'Arlon, 8001 Strassen; Man. ALEX FELTEN.

Joybringer: 27 rue Victor Hugo, 4583 Differdange; Contact ANDRE DEPIENNE.

Malaysia

BMG Malaysia Sdn Bhd: 133–1 Jalan Segambut, Kuala Lumpur 51200; Man. Dir FRANKIE CHEAH.

EMI (Malaysia) Sdn Bhd: Suite 10.01 10th Floor, Exchange Sq., Off Jalem Semantan, Damansara Heights, 50490 Kuala Lumpur; Man. Dir BEH SUAT PHENG.

Musico Sdn Bhd: Rm 3901, China Insurance Bldg, 174 Jalan Tuanku Abdul Rahman, Kuala Lumpur; Pres. BOB WEISS.

Noize Records: 17 Jalan Yap Kwan Seng, Kuala Lumpur 50450; Contact GEORGE LOURDES.

Polygram Malaysia Records Sdn Bhd: 83–87 Jalan Kampung Pandan, Taman Maluri, Kuala Lumpur 55100; Man. Dir ERIC YEO.

Sony Music Entertainment (Malaysia): C16 & C17 Jalan Ampang, Utama 1/1, Taman Ampang Utama, 68000 Ampang; tel. (3) 4252-3233; fax (3) 4252-2235; e-mail rickloh@sonymusic.com.my; internet www.sonymusic.com.my; Man. DIR RICK LOH.

Warner Music Malaysia: 9th Floor, Mui Plaza, Jalan P Ramlee, 50250 Kuala Lumpur; Man. Dir ANTHONY F FERNANDES.

Mexico

Compañía Fonográfica Internacional SA/IM Discos & Cassettes: Sanctorum 86-B Col. Argentina, 11230 México, DF; tel. (55) 5399-2434; fax (55) 5399-2630; e-mail jmorales@imdiscos.com; internet www.imdiscos.com; Dir-Gen. JOSÉ I. MORALES BETANCOURT.

Discos Continental: Poniente 75, 160 Col. 16 de Septiembre, 11810 México, DF; Pres. MARCO ANTONIO LUGA.

EMI Music Mexico: Rio Tigris, 33 Col. Cuauhtémac, 06500 México, DF; Pres. MARIO RUIZ.

Maple Audiosistemas: Priv. Alberto Barocio, 3 Circuito Ingeniero, 53100 México, DF; Pres. DAVID ROJAS DE AVILA.

Musica de Mexico: Ignacio Esteva 26-A, 11850 México, DF; Proprietor DARIO ANTONIO ZORZANO.

Organización Latino Internacional: Avda Insurgentes Sur 953-202, Col. Nápoles, 03810 México, DF; Dir-Gen. TONY MÉNDEZ.

Polygram Discos SA: Avda Miguel Angel de Quevedo 531, Col. Romero de Torreros, 04310 México, DF; Dir-Gen. FRANCISCO BESTARD.

Producciones Fonograficas: Adolfo Prieto 1649, 1°, Col. del Valle-Benito Juárez, 03100 México, DF; Dir-Gen. BERNADO YANCELSON.

Suite Sync de Mexico: Prolongación Tajin, 900 Col. Emperadores, 03320 México, DF; Dir GERARDO SUÁREZ.

The Netherlands

Ala Bianca Benelux: Zonnelaan 13, 1217 ND Hilversum; Man. Dir H LESSING.

Artists and Business: PO Box 64, 1200 AB Hilversum; Man. Dir BOUDEWYN VAN BAVEL.

Basic Beat: Nieuwe Binnenweg 54, 3015 BB Rotterdam; Man. Dir RON HOFLAND.

BMG The Netherlands BV: Laaporsveld 63, 1213 VB Hilversum; Man. Dir D STURM.

Brinker Media: PO Box 1276, 1400 Bussum; tel. (35) 603-5368; fax (35) 693-4877; e-mail studio@brinkermedia.com; internet www.brinkermedia.com; Man. Dir ERIC VAN DEN BRINK.

Brinkman Records BV: Vlietberg 5–45, 6576 JB Ooy; Man. Dir FRED MAESSEN.

CNR Music Holland: Brinklaan 109, 1404 GA Bussum; Gen. Man. LEON TEN HENGEL.

Corazong Records: Langeweid 7, 1831 BL Koedyk; tel. and fax (72) 561-5857; e-mail info@corazong.com; internet www.corazong.com; Pres. EVERT WILBRINK.

Count Orlok Music: PO Box 2738, 3000 CS Rotterdam; Contact JOHNNY ZUIDHOF.

Djax Records: PO Box 2408, 5600 CK Eindhoven; Man. Dir SASKIA SLEGERS.

EMI Music Holland BV: Bronsteenweg 49, 2101 AB Heemstede; Man. Dir HENNIE VAN KUIJEREN.

Essential Dance Music BV: Nieuwe Binnenweg 19, 3014 GB Rotterdam; Man. Dirs P BOERTJE, P VRIENDS.

Hotsound: Pleinweg 242 A-d, 3083 EZ Rotterdam; Man. Dir ERIK VAN VLIET.

Lana Lane Records: Faas Eliaslaan 13, 3742 AR Baarn; Man. Dir GERRY VAN DER ZWAARD.

Lower East Side Records: Govert Flickstraat 285, 1073 CA Amsterdam; Man. Dir JEROEN FLAMMAN.

Mascot Records: PO Box 231, 2650 AE Berkel; Man. Dir ED VAN ZIJL.

MMS Group of Companies: PO Box 55559, 1007 NB Amsterdam; Vice-Pres. of A & R JELLE BAKKER.

Music & Words: PO Box 1160, 3430 BD Nieuwegein; tel. (30) 606-7674; fax (30) 606-7225; e-mail info@musicwords.nl; internet www.musicwords.nl; Pres HANS PETERS, LIESBETH PUTS.

Play It Again Sam BV: Ampèrestraat 10, 1221 GJ Hilversum; tel. (35) 646-3030; fax (35) 646-3035; e-mail play.it@pias.nl; internet www.pias.com; Man. Dir LEO VAN SCHAICK.

Replay Records: Herenweg 9, 2465 AA Rijnsaterwoude; tel. (172) 507450; fax (172) 507642; e-mail info@catmusic.nl; internet www.catmusic.nl; Man. Dir AART MOL.

Roadrunner Records: Bijdorp 2, 1181 MZ Amstelveen; Man. Dir CEES WESSELS.

Semaphore: PO Box 213, 1740 AE Schagen; Label Man. MARCEL PAUVORT.

Sony Music Entertainment Holland: Herenweg 115, 2105 MG Heemstede; Label Man. GERARD RUTTE.

Staalplaat: PO Box 11453, 1001 GC Amsterdam; Man. Dir GEENT JAN HOBIJN.

Via Records: PO Box 2277, 1200 JV Hilversum; Label Man. JOS HAIJER.

Virgin Benelux: Melkpad 29, 1217 KA Hilversum; Label Man. REMMELT VAN BEYERSBERGEN.

Warner Music Netherlands BV: Noorderweg 68, 1221 AB Hilversum; International Man. MICHIEL TEN VEEN.

Windham Hill Europe: Oude Enghweg 24, 1217 JD Hilversum; Gen. Man. FRANK VAN HOUTEN.

Zodiac Records: Rozengracht 228, 1016 SZ Amsterdam; Man. Dir GERT VAN VEEN.

BMG Music New Zealand Ltd: 3rd Floor, Altos House, Cnr Newton Rd/ Abbey St, Newton; Gen. Man. MORRIE SMITH.

Deepgrooves Entertainment: PO Box 5404, Wellesley St, Auckland; Contact KANE MASSEY.

EMI Music New Zealand: PO Box 864, Auckland; tel. (9) 356-1570; fax (9) 366-7221; internet www.emimusic.co.nz; Man. Dir CHRIS CADDICK.

Flying Nun Records Ltd & Flying In Distribution: PO Box 677, Auckland; Gen. Man. LESLEY PARRS.

Gateway Productions: PO Box 6735, Wellesley St, Auckland; Man. GREG HENWOOD.

Gecko Records: 38A Glenmall Pl., Glen Eden, Auckland; Man. ANDREW DIXON.

Hark Records: 564 Victoria St, Hamilton; Man. Dir GRANT HISLOP.

Kiwi Pacific Records International Ltd: PO Box 826, Wellington; Production Man. M F VINCENT.

Metro Marketing Ltd: 45 Mackelvie St, Ponsonby, Auckland; Man. Dir GRAEME PETHIG.

Mushroom Records: 2nd Floor, ASB Chambers, 138 Queen St, Auckland; Contact SANDII RICHES.

Onset Offset: Cashel Chambers, 224 Cashel St, Christchurch; Contact EMILIE DOBINSON.

Pagan Records: PO Box 47-290, Ponsonby, Auckland; Dirs TREVOR REEKIE, SHERYL MORRIS.

Rattle Records: PO Box 4187, Auckland; Man. Dir KEITH HILL.

Someone Up There Records: 39 Kensington Ave, Mt Eden, Auckland 4; Dirs KEVIN ADAIR, DARLENE ADAIR.

Sony Music Entertainment (New Zealand) Ltd: Level One, 103 Carlton Gore Rd, Newmarket, Auckland; tel. (9) 979-5330; fax (9) 979-5337; internet www.sonymusic.co.nz; Man. Dir MICHAEL GLADING.

Sun Pacific Music Co: 49 Murdoch Rd, Grey Lynn; Mans MICHAEL DONNELLY, BERNARD GRIFFIN.

Tangata Records: PO Box 3679, Shortland St, Auckland; A & R Dir NEIL CRUICKSHANK.

Virgin Records New Zealand: 9th Floor, Baycorp House, 15 Hopetoun St, Ponsonby, Auckland; tel. (9) 356-1580; fax (9) 379-9964; internet www.virginmusic.co.nz; Man. Dir CHRIS CADDICK.

Warner Music New Zealand Ltd: 7th Floor, Babbage House, 15 Hopetoun St, Ponsonby, Auckland; Contact JAMES SOUTHGATE.

Yellow Bike Records: PO Box 586, Palmerston North; Co-ordinators CLAIRE PANNELL, DAVE WHITE.

Yellow Eye Music: 33 Fortune St, Dalmore, Dunedin; tel. 3473-9426; fax 3473-9700; e-mail simon@yelloweye.co.nz; internet www.yelloweye.co.nz; Partner SIMON VARE.

Norway

Arne Bendiksen Records AS: Jornstadsvn. 62, 1360 Nesbru; tel. 6678-4778; fax 6679-0630; e-mail arnebend@online.no; Man. Dir ARNE BENDIKSEN.

Blue Wolf Productions: PO Box 98, 3671 Notodden; Man. Dir ARILD REINERTSEN.

Busk Records: Fredbo Alle 14, PO Box 471, 3903 Porsgrunn; Man. Dir TERJE WELLE BUSK.

CIA Productions: Waldemar Thranesgate 55 B, 0173 Oslo; Administration Dir CAROLINE ASPLIN.

CNR NonStop AS: Sandakervn. 24C, 0401 Oslo; Man. Dir OLE VIDAR LIEN.

Continental Records: Sunbyjordet 4, 2051 Jessheim; Man. Dir BARRY MATHESON.

Crema AS: Nedre Vollgt 3, 0158 Oslo; Man. Dir ARVE SIGVALDSEN.

Curling Legs Productions DA: PO Box 5298, Majorst UA, 0303 Oslo; Man. KNUT VAERHES.

DAT O/S: 9520 Guovdageaidnu; tel. 7848-6772; fax 7848-6788; e-mail dat@dat.net; internet www.dat.net; Contact PER L BOINE.

dbut internautics: PO Box 9415 Valerenga, 0610 Oslo; Dir PER PLATOW.

EMI Norsk AS: Karl Johansgt. 12 J, PO Box 492 Sentrum, 0105 Oslo; Man. Dir JAN OSTLI.

Enjoy Records: Tidemansgt. 1, 0266 Oslo; Man. Dir JIMMY JAMES.

Gemini Records: Nils Hansensvej 13, PO Box 13, Bryn, 0611 Oslo; Man. Dir BJORN PETERSEN.

Grammofon AS Electra: St Halvardsgt. 33, 0192 Oslo; Man. Dir OYVIND DALSRUD.

Grappa Records AS: Akersgata 7, 0158 Oslo; tel. 2335-8000; fax 2335-8001; e-mail info@grappa.no; internet www.grappa.no; Man. Dir HELGE WESTBYE.

Heilo: PO Box 2645 Solli, 0302 Oslo; Man. HALVARD KVALE.

Hot Club Records: PO Box 5202, Majorstua, 0302 Oslo; Man. Dir/Prod. JON LARSEN.

Hypertonia World Enterprises: PO Box 4307 Nygardstangen, 5028 Bergen; Man. JAN BRUUN.

Idut: Iggaldas, 9710 Inore, Billefjord; Gen. Man. ÅGE PERSEN.

Jeps AS: Mandalsgt. 5, 0190 Olso; Man. Dir HAVARD HANSTEEN.

LA Music AS: Skolebakken 14, 1435 Krakstad; Man. Dir LILLIAN ASKELAND.

Lynor AS: Bergtorasvn. 74, PO Box 4086 Kongsgard, 4602 Kristiansand S; Man. Dir LIVAR HOLLAND.

Majorselskapet: Rosenborggt. 19, PO Box 5949 Majorstua, 0308 Oslo; International Label Man. TROND AMLIE.

MCA Music Entertainment Norway AS: Parkvn. Blvd, PO Box 2702 Solli, 0204 Oslo; Gen. Man. PETTER SINGSAAS.

MTG Productions: PO Box 2500, 3003 Drammen; tel. 2411-8470; e-mail mtg@mtg.as; internet www.mtg.as; Man. Dir LARRY BRINGSSORD.

Nidelven Grammofon AS: Hogreina 432, 7079 Flatasen; Man. Dir PER ADLOFSEN.

Nor Wave/Norsk Gram: PO Box 4603, Valentinlyst., 7002 Trondheim; Man. Dir GUNNAR NORDVIK.

Nor-CD: Kongens gate 16, 0153 Oslo; tel. 2233-4144; fax 2233-4143; e-mail norcd@norcd.no; internet www.norcd.no; Man. Dir KARL SEGLEM.

Norsk Lyd & Bilde/Norwegian Sound & Vision: Rute 598, 2760 Brandbu; Dirs ODD ERIK, ELI KRISTIN HAGEN.

Notabene Records AS: Bogstanvn. 31 B, 0366 Oslo; Man. Dir OLE A SORLI.

Odin: Tollbugt. 28, 0157 Oslo; tel. 2335-8180; fax 2335-8181; e-mail norsk@jazzforum.no; internet www.jazzforum.no; Man. Dir TONE MARTINSEN.

Olso Records: Harald Romckes Vei 37, 0286 Oslo; Man. LARS BORKE,.

Origo Sound: Ospelia 8, 1900 Fetsund; Man. Dir HARALD LERVIK.

Polygram Norway: PO Box 2645 Solli, Drammensvn 82 B, 0203 Oslo; International Label Man. PETTER SINGSAAS.

Prima Music AS: Storgt. 38, PO Box 4697 Sofienberg, 0506 Oslo; Man. Dir BJORN SKJENNUM.

Progress Records: Gregusgt. 9, 7002 Trondheim; Man. Dir JENS PETTER WIIG.

Rage Records: PO Box 4721 Sofienberg, 0506 Oslo; Man. Dir RINO FROSTAD.

Rec 90: PO Box 1291, 5001 Bergen; Man. Dir TORFINN ANDERSEN.

Revolution Records: PO Box 6005, 7003 Trondheim; Man. Dir DIESEL DAHL.

Scandinavian Records: Dronningensgt. 8B, PO Box 517 Sentrum, 0105 Oslo; Man. Dir KAI ROGER OTTESEN.

Sonet Distribution: Drammensvg. 88 B, PO Box 2645 Solli, 0203 Oslo; tel. 2254-1400; fax 2243-0570; e-mail gronn.rune@umusic.com; Distribution Man. RUNE GRONN.

Sony Music Norway: PO Box 134, Okern, 0509 Oslo; tel. 2288-0000; fax 2264-4133; e-mail firmapost@sonymusic.no; internet www.sonymusic.no; Man. Dir RUNE HAGBERG.

Spesial Laboratoriet: Braavallagt. 25 B, 5500 Haugesund; Dir TORGRIM EIDE.

Truels Brodtkorb: PO Box 2645 Solli, 0271 Oslo; Head of Marketing TRUELS BRODTKORB.

Tvers Forlag AS: Hasseln. 47 Ottestad, 2301 Hamar; Man. Dir ARNOLD BORUD.

Virgin Records Norway: Karljohansgt. 12 J, 0101 Oslo; Man. Dir GYRO LEIRA.

Voices of Wonder: Thv. Meyersgt. 33, 0555 Oslo; Contact PER THOMAS LUND, KETIL SVEEN.

Warner Music Norway: Maridalsveden 87 B, 0403 Oslo; Label Mans STEEN BRODTKROB, JONNY STYVE.

Peru

Discos Hispanos Del Peru SA: Esquilache, 179 San Isidro, Lima 27; Gen. Man. JAVIER CASTAÑEDA.

Discos Independientes SA: Avda Arenales 2586, Lima 14; Pres. SAMIR GIHA.

El Virrey Industrias Musicales SA: Avda República de Panamá, 355 San Isidro, Lima 1; Dir WILAN KAFKA.

Iempsa SA: Avda Guillermo Dansey 1247, PO Box 67, Lima 1; Dir NILO MARCHAND.

The Philippines

A&W Records: 2nd Fl, Vergel de Dios Bldg, 530 Evangelista St, Quiapo, Manila; Gen. Man. WILLIE J, VILLAR.

BMG Records (Pilipinas) Inc: 3F, Equitable Bank Bldg, 898 Aurora Blvd, cor Stanford Sts, Cubao, Quezon City; Man. Dir RUDY Y TEE.

DD International Recording Corporation: 363 P Casal St, Quiapo, Manila 1001; Chair. & Pres. DEMY A QUIRINO JR.

Ivory Records: 2/F Quadstar Bldg, Ortigas Ave, Greenhills, San Juan, Metro Manila; Pres. ANTONIO OCAMPO.

Platinum Records: Unit 15, Town & Country Arcade, Marcos Highway, Cainta, Rizal; Pres. ELI BALBOA.

Solar Records Inc: 2nd Floor, Roman Santos Bdlg, Plaza Lacson, Santa Cruz, Manila; Pres. MAURO MANALANGSANG.

Universal Records: 135 P, Sevilla St, Cnr 3rd Ave, Grace Park, Kalookan City, Metro Manila; Vice-Pres. RAMON CHUAYING.

Warner Music Philippines Inc: 4th Fl, Ma. Danile Bldg, 470 MH Del Pilar Corner, San Andres St, Malate, Manila; Man. Dir MA-AN HONTIVEROS.

Poland

Abrakadabra SA: Sportoaw 5 M 36, 05-400 Otwock; Chair. ANTONI ROSZCZUK.

Artson: Nowogrodzka 49, 00-695 Warsaw; Man. Dir MAREK PIORO.

BMG International Poland: Dygasinskiego 10, 01-603 Warsaw; Man. Dir POITR NAGLOWSKI.

Digiton: Aleje Jerozolimskie 29 Apt 3, 00-508 Warsaw; Man. Dir LYSZARD MARCINIAK.

Elbo Phonographic Enterprise: Ul. Moniuszki 10 m 54, 00-009 Warsaw; Man. Dir BOGUSLAW BORYSIUK.

Inter Sonus: Al 3 Maja 2 m 5, 00-391 Warsaw; Man. Dir RYGZARD ADAMUS.

Lion Records: Rejtana 3, 01-800 Warsaw; Man. Dir PIOTR GRYGLEWICZ.

Loud Out Records: U. Zielna 45/30, 00-108 Warsaw; Man. Dir ANDRZEJ MACKIEWICZ.

MJM Music: Ul. Grochowska 341 bud 28, 03-822 Warsaw; Man. Dir GRZEGORZ STABEUSZ.

Polmark: Konrada 30, 01-922 Warsaw; Man. Dir TADEUSZ KRASNODEBSKI.

Polonia Records Ltd: Ul. Jana Pawla II 18m 13, 00-116 Warsaw; Man. Dir STANISLAW SOBOLA.

Polskie Nagrania: Goleszowska 6, 01-249 Warsaw; Man. Dir ALEKSANDER OLASZEWSKI.

Polton Music Distribution: Ul Dantyszka 8, 02-054 Warsaw; Pres. JAN CHOONAUCI.

PUP Metal Mind Productions: Sleligiewicza 8/21, 40-044 Katowice; Man. Dir TOMASZ DZIUBINSKI.

Selles Records: Ul Jagielska 43, 02-886 Warsaw; Owner/Man. Dir TOMASZ BIELSKI.

SONIC sp.200: Mscislawska 6, 01-647 Warsaw; tel. (22) 833-3782; fax (22) 833-5784; e-mail sonic@sonicrecords.pl; Man. Dir MAREK PRONIEWICZ.

Sound Pol: Bitny Warsawskiej, 1920 R 14/88, 02-366 Warsaw; Man. Dir KAJETAN SLONINA.

SPV Poland: Ul. Twardowska 3, 01-810 Warsaw; Man. Dir IGOR KURONSKI.

Veriton Records: Bobrowiecka 1, 00-278 Warsaw; Dir GRAZYNA SOLINSKA.

Zic-Zac Music Company: Sulkowskiego 9, 01-602 Warsaw; Man. Dir MAREK KOSCIKIEWICZ.

ZPR Inc–United Entertainment Enterprises Inc: Senatorska 13/15, 00 075 Warsaw; Pres./CEO ZBIGNIEW BENBENEK; Artists & Marketing Man. ANNA KAROLICKA.

Portugal

Ama Romanta: R Coelho da Rocha 46, 1 Dto, 1200 Lisbon; Man. Dir JOAO PESTE.

Ananana: PO Box 21671, 1137 Lisbon; Man. Dir FRED SONSEN.

Andante-Discos Musica E Som Lda: Avda da Boavista, 1471 Loja 8, 4100 Porto; Pres. JEAN PIERRE JONGENELEN.

BMG Ariola Portugal: Edif. Infante D Henrique, Rua Joao Chagas 53 A, 1495 Lisbon; Man. Dir TOZE BRITO.

Dark Records: PO Box 142, 2830 Barreiro Codex; Man. Dir PEDRO CRUZ.

Discos Belter Lda: Constituiça 74, 4200 Porto; Contact ANTONIO FIGUEIREDO.

Discossete: Rua Dr Faria Vasconcolos 4A, 1900 Lisbon; Man. Dir HELENA CARDINALLI.

Edisom: Rua Manuel F Andrade 6B, 1500 Lisbon; Man. Dir CARLOS FERREIRA.

Eltatu Editor: R Rodrigo Da Fonseca, 182 4E, 1070 Lisbon; Dir ANTONIO DOS SANTOS; Label Man. MARTA FERREIRA.

EMI Portugal: Rua de Cruz dos Poias 111, 1200 Lisbon; Man. Dir DAVID FERREIRA.

Farol Musica: Alto do Couto, Arnazéns I, 2735 Cacém; Dirs ANTONIO GUIMARÁES, FERNANDO JÚRICE.

Fast 'N' Loud: PO Box 13037, 1019 Lisbon Codex; Commercial Dir FILIPE MARQUES.

Independent Records: Rua do Jardim, 598-4405 Valadares, Porto; Dir FRANCISCO PINHO.

Johnny Blue: Rua da Madalena 90 3?, 1100 Lisbon; Dir MIGUEL SANTOS.

Megamusica: Representação e Distribuição Lda; PO Box 13, 2775 Carcavelos; tel. (21) 446-1400; fax (21) 446-1409; e-mail megamusica@mail.telepac.pt MAN. DIR; José Eduardo Santos.

Monasterium Records: PO Box 1078, 2670 Santo Antonio Dos Cavaleiros; Man. Dir DUARTE PICOTO.

Morgana Records: PO Box 845, 2840 Seixal; Man. Dir DUARTE DIONISIO.

MTM: PO Box 30072, 1321 Lisbon Codex; Man. Dir HUGO MOUTINHO.

Musica Alternativa: Pra das Roicadas n 37 RcE, 2700 Amadora; Man. Dir SAMUEL LOPES.

Polygram Portugal: Rua Prof Reinaldo dos Santos, 12-D, 1500 Lisbon; Man. Dir RODRIGO MARIN.

Sony Musica Portugal: Rua Juliao Quintinha 11, 1500 Lisbon; Head of Public Relations PAOLO BISMARK.

Strauss Musica e Video SA: Rua Adelaide Cabete 3A, 1500 Lisbon; Admin. ARMANDO MARTINS.

Vidisco: N13 1D, Ave Bombeiros Voluntarios Pontinha, 1675 Lisbon; Man. Dir ARTUR ANTUNES.

Warner Music Portugal Lda: Rua D Constantino de Bragança, 26 1400 Lisbon; International Product Co-ordinate XANA TAYLOR.

Romania

Astra 22 Adv Ag: Str Turda 122, BL 39, ScA, Et 6, Ap 30, Sector 1, Bucharest; Pres. VERTAN ADRIANA.

Electrecord S A: Blvd Timisoara 94, Sector 6, 78702 Bucharest; Gen. Dir GRIGORE PETREANU.

Romagram Music Ltd: 8 Aviator Mircea Zorileanu str, Sector 1, 70242 Bucharest; Chair. JOEY DE ALVARE.

Tilt and Partners: 202 A Splaiul Independentei str, Sector 6, 77208 Bucharest; Man. Dir GUISEPPE ROSSI.

Toji Productions: 9 Piata Romana, C/40, Sector 1, 70167 Bucharest; Man. Dir NICU ALIFANTIS.

Russia

Alien Records: Bolshaya Serpukhovskaya 44, Moscow; Man. Dir OLEG KURBATKIN.

Aprelevka Sound Inc: Arbat 44, 121 002 Moscow; Man. Dir GRIGORY FIGLIN.

Feelee Record Company: 27 Novozavadskaya str, 121 309 Moscow; Man. Dir IGOR TONKIKH.

Gala Records: Staraya Basmannaya 27–22, 121 309 Moscow; Dir BORIS TZIGMAN.

Lad Records: Dimitrova 39, 117 040 Moscow; Chair. FELIX PEREPELOV.

Russky Disc: Stankevicha 8, 103 009 Moscow; Man. Dir JURY PAROL.

SNC Records: Krymsky Val 9, 117 049 Moscow; Man. Dir ALEXEY UGRINOVITCH.

St Petersburg Label: B Sampsoniyevsky Pr. 57, 194 044 St Petersburg; Dir LYDIA COBRINA.

Syntex: B Spasskaya 33–10, 129 010 Moscow; Chair. ALEXANDER KUTIKOV.

Tau Product: PO Box 377, 117 333 Moscow; Chair. ANDREI BOGDANOV.

Vist: Triokhprudny Per. 4, 103 031 Moscow; Gen. Man. VLADIMIR OLETSKY.

Zolotaya Dolina Co: Ismaelovsky Proiezd 14/1/34, 105 037 Moscow; Contact EUGENI GREKHOV.

Singapore

EMI (Singapore): 213 Henderson Rd, 04–015 Henderson Industrial Park, Singapore; Man. Dir DAVID WEE.

Form Pte Ltd: Block 994, Bendemeer Rd 02–01, Singapore; Company Dir ANG CHOON BENG.

Hype Records Pte Ltd: 221 Henderson Rd, Suite 02–04 Henderson Bldg, Singapore 159557; tel. 375-3787; fax 275-2757; e-mail hype@hyperecords.com; internet www.hyperecords.com; Administration Man. MELVIS YIP.

Polygram Records Pte Ltd: 23 Genting Rd, 04–01 Chevalier House, Singapore 1334; Man. Dir ERIC YEO.

Sony Music Entertainment (Singapore) Pte Ltd: 601 Sims Dr., 02–07, Singapore 887382; Man. Dir TERENCE PHUNG.

Warner Music Singapore Pte Ltd: 10 Anson Rd, No. 12-06/07/08, International Plaza, Singapore; Man. Dir PETER LAU.

White Cloud Record Pte Ltd: 246 MacPherson Rd, #05-01, Betime Bldg, Singapore 348578; tel. 741-7178; fax 741-9233; e-mail whitecloud@pacific.net.sg; Man. Dir HENG SER PIAH.

Slovenia

Dallas: Kersnikova 4, 61000 Ljubljana; Man. Dir GORAN LISICA.

Front Rock: PO Box 48, 62000 Maribor; Man. DUJAN HEDL.

Matrix Music: Hranilniska 6, 61000 Ljubljana; Man. Dir PRIMOZ PECOUNIK.

RTV Slovania Records & Tapes: Dalmatinova 10, 61000 Ljubljana; Label Man. IVO UMEK.

SKUC—AFK: Kersnikova 4, 61000 Ljubljana; Man. Dir MITJA PREZELJ.

Zavod Za Umetnisko in Kulturno Produkcijo: Kersnikova 4, 61000 Ljubljana; Man. Dir MONIKA SKABERNE.

South Africa

Ahoy Records: PO Box 5984, Johannesburg 2000; Contact BLONDIE MAKHENE.

BMG Records Africa (Pty) Ltd: PO Box 5894 Johannesburg 2000; tel. (001) 242-3000; fax (001) 242-3030; internet click2music.co.sa; Man. Dir of Records KEITH LISTER; Man. Dir of Publishing PETER VEE.

Brettian Productions: PO Box 96395, Brixton 2019; Contact CLIVE RISKO.

Cap Records: 134 Unie Ave, Lyttelton 0157; Contact GRAHAM ABRAHAMS.

CCP Record Co (Pty) Ltd: PO Box 112564, Johannesburg 2000; Contact BARRY GUY.

Cornerstone Records: 175 Nicolette St, Meyerspark 0184; Contact ANDREW CARTWRIGHT.

CSR Records: PO Box 7578 Johannesburg 2000; Contact CHRIS GHELAKIS.

David Gresham Record Co (Pty) Ltd: PO Box 46020, Orange Grove 2119; Owner DAVID GRESHAM.

Eagle Records: PO Box 11112, Marine Parade 4056; Contact JEAN SNYMAN.

EMI South Africa/Virgin Records: PO Box 11254, Johannesburg 2000; Contact MIKE EDWARDS.

Gazania Records: PO Box 569, Vredendal 8160; Contact HC VISSER.

Gold Dust Records (Pty) Ltd: 9 9th Ave, Houghton 2198; Contact PHIL HOLLIS.

Hit City Records: PO Box 156, Crown Mines 2025; Contact JILL GALANKIS.

Inhouse Records: PO Box 15, Bassonia 2061; Contact PHILLIP NEL.

Kalawa Records: 232 Louis Botha Ave, Orange Grove 2192; Contact DON LAKA.

Maranatha Record Co: PO Box 32823, Glenstantia 0010; Contact LUKIE CARLESON.

Mike Fuller Music Records (Pty) Ltd: PO Box 66254, Broadway 2020; Proprietor MIKE FULLER.

Natal Records: 20B Church Rd, Westville, Durban 3630; Contact DON CLARKE.

Phase 2 Records: PO Box 48321, Roosevelt Park 2129; Contact TERRY FAIRWEATHER.

Rampant Records: PO Box 192, Halfway House 1685; Contact GREG NEFDT.

RPM Record Co (Pty) Ltd: PO Box 2807, Johannesburg 2000; Contact IRVING SCHLOSBERG.

Shifty Records: PO Box 5894, Johannesburg 2000; Contact LLOYD ROSS.

Stave Record Productions: PO Box 1854, Pinegowrie 2123; Contact ROBERT SCHRODER.

Tequila Records: PO Box 391405, Bramley, Johannesburg 2018; Contact DAVID ALEXANDER.

To The Edge Records: PO Box 5012, Weltevreden Park 1715; Exec. Prod. LEON RETIEF.

Trio Records (Pty) Ltd: PO Box 33283, Jeppsetown 2042; Contact GAVIN GIBB.

TSOP Record Co: 84 Retief St, Pretoria West 0183; Contact MM MPYE.

Vusa Records: PO Box 423, Milnerton 7435; Contact MYNIE GROVE.

Spain

Alleluia Records: Rambla Catalunya 10, 08006 Barcelona; Man. Dir REYES TORIO.

Avispa SL: c/o Jeronima Llorente 74, 28039 Madrid; International Dept MARGARITA ABRANTE GUERRA.

AZ Productions: Riera de Argentona, s/n, 08300 Nataro (Barcelona); International Dept PERE-LLUIS PONT.

Bat Discos, SA: Sagunto 2, 28010 Madrid; Gen. Man. JORGE E GOMEZ DIAZ.

B-Core: Marques de Sentmenat 72, interior 3a, 08029 Barcelona; tel. and fax (9) 3419-7883; e-mail bcore@bcoredisc.com; internet www.bcore.com; Man. Dir JORDI LLANSAMA.

CDR Praktik: Alcade Mostoles 41, 08026 Barcelona; Man. Dir ERNEST CASAL.

Crab Ediciones Musicales SA: Sagunto 2, 28010 Madrid; Gen. Man. JORGE E GOMEZ DIAZ.

Disc Medi: Argentona 3–5 Bajos, 08024 Barcelona; Dir ALEX ESLAVA.

Elephant Records: PO Box 331, 28203 Las Rozas; Man. Dir LUIS CALVO.

Esese & Co: Llacuna 162, 08018 Barcelona; Man. Dir SERGI SOLIS.

Fabrica Magnética: Dr Fourquet 31, 28012 Madrid; Man. Dir SERVANDO CARBALLAR.

Fonomusic Distrimusic: Garcia de Paredes 12, 28010 Madrid; Contact VALENTIN LADREDO.

Goo Records: Bailen 3 1, 48003 Bilbao; Man. Dir ESTIBALIZ HERNANDEZ.

GSG—Grup de Serveis Guilleries: Granja Baró, Ctra de la Guixa, km 2, 08500 Barcelona; Administration JORDI COSTA; Management IGNASI PLA; Production JOAN CAPDEVILA.

Lakota SA: Guadalmina Alta, Calle 21 Casa 631, San Pedro de Alcantara, Marbella, 29670 Malaga; Man. Dir CARLO CAVICCHI.

Liquid Records: Gomis 42, 08023 Barcelona; Man. Dir PETER EICHENBERG.

More Discos / Boy Records: Industria 132, 08025 Barcelona; Man. Dir ANA MORAN.

New Music Ediciones Musicales SA: PO Box 9.046, 28060 Madrid; Gen. Man. GERHARD HALTERMANN.

On The Rock—Caroline: Rossello 336, 08025 Barcelona; Man. Dir ENRIC PADASCOLL.

PDI: Passeig de Gracia 74 3 1, 08008 Barcelona; International Label Man. GERHARD HALTERMANN.

Polygram Iberica: Suero de Quinones 38, 28002 Madrid; Contact ELENA GOROSTIZA, ENRIQUE PRIETO.

Por Caridad Producciones: La Palma 72 3, 28015 Madrid; Man. Dir M JOSÉ MARTIN.

Radiation Records: Nicolas Alicorta 2, 48080 Bilbao; Man. Dir UNDI FRESNEDO.

Salseta Discos: Diputacio 180 5C, 08011 Barcelona; Man. Dir SALVADOR ESCRIVA.

Siesta Records: Sta Cruz de Marcenado 31 6, 28015 Madrid; International Man. JOAQUIN GARCIA.

Subterfuge Records: Augusto Figueroa 21 4, 28080 Madrid; Man. Dir CARLOS GALAN.

Tram Cat: Amigo 26 4, 08021 Barcelona; Man. Dir TONI ORO.

Urantia Records: Rossello 227, 08008 Barcelona; Man. Dir RAMON BERTRAN.

Victoria Ediciones Musicales SA: Narvaez 14, 28009 Madrid; Man. Dir GERHARD HALTERMANN.

Walkaria Records: Pl. Morron 16, 10002 Caceres; Man. Dir VICTOR GUILLEN.

Warner Music Spain: Aribau 282–284 5 4, 08006 Barcelona; Head of Promotion LUCAS HOLTEN.

Sweden

Amalthea Records: PO Box 271, 18523 Waxholm; Man. Dir TORGNY SJÖÖ.

Atlantis Grammofon AB: Karlbergsvagen 57, 11335 Stockholm; Man./Owner JAN HANSSON.

Birdsnest Records: Kolsvagatan 4, 73133 Köping; Man. Dir PER GRANBERG.

Blitz Records AB: PO Box 347, 10126 Stockholm 1; Man. Dir WOLFGANG JEDLICZKA.

BMG Ariola Sweden: PO Box 1026, 17221 Sundbyberg; Man. Dir HANS BREITHOLZ.

Borderline: Gamlestadsvägen 1, 41502 Gothenburg; Man. Dir PÄR MALMSTEDT.

BORG Music Int: PO Box 6082, 20011 Malmö; Chair. BJÖRN GÄRDSBY.

Burning Heart: Kolsvagatan 4, 73133 Köping; Man. Dir PETER AHLQUIST.

Business Record Concept (BRC): PO Box 7083, 63007 Eskilstuna; Dir PETER ROZENBACHS.

Caprice Records: PO Box 1225, 11182 Stockholm; Man. Dir KJELL SÖDERQVIST.

Einnicken Records: Eskilsgatan 11A, 63356 Eskilstuna; tel. 1612-1553; e-mail einnicken@spray.se; Financial Man. STEFAN WISTRAND.

EMI Sweden: PO Box 1289, Tritonvägen 17, 17125 Solna; Label Man. PER ERIK HOTTI.

Empire Records: Vintergatan 2, 17230 Sundbyberg; Man. Dir CHRISTER WEDIN.

Energy Records AB: Vastergatan 23, 21121 Malmö; Contact HÅKAN EHRNST.

Fifty/Fifty Records: PO Box 14096, 63014 Eskilstuna; A & R PETER TORSÉN.

Four Leaf Clover Records: PO Box 1231, 17226 Sundbyberg; Dir LARS SAMUELSON.

Frequent Frenzy Records: PO Box 6009, 10231 Stockholm; Man. Dir DAGGAN STAMENKOVIC.

Gazell Music AB: Tappvägen 24, PO Box 20055, 16102 Bromma; Dir DAG HAEGGQVIST.

Gothenburg Records: Gammlestan 2, 41507 Gothenburg; Man. Dir JOHN BALLARD.

H Lime Records: Kvangärdesgatan 36 B, 63355 Eskilstuna; International Man. MAGNUS BÅCKSTRÖM.

Hawk Records: PO Box 8061, 10420 Stockholm; Man. Dir BJÖRN HÅKANSON.

House of Kicks Distribution: PO Box 2140, 10314 Stockholm; Dir ROGER REINHOLD.

HSM Records: PO Box 1122, 22104 Lund; Man. Dir ULF LUNDWALL.

Last Buzz Record Co: Husargatanis, 41122 Gothenburg; Prod. HÅKAN FORSHULT.

Lush Records: Landsvägsgatan 11, 41304 Gothenburg; Owner RALPH STERN-PETTERSSON.

M & A Music Art: Simrishamnsgatan 20A, 21423 Malmö; Man. Dir ANDREAS LARSSON.

Mega Records: Ske Pargatan 8, 11452 Stockholm; Head of Promotion BRITA JUNGBERG.

MNW Independent Label Representation: Industrivägen 1, 17148 Solna; Asst Dir TOMAS SUNMO.

MVG Records: PO Box 271, 18523 Waxholm; International Man. LINA BECKMANN.

Noble Art Records: PO Box 78, 445 22 Bohus; A & R Man. MAGNUS CORNELIUS.

NonStop Records: PO Box 7273, 40235 Gothenburg; Man. Dir PETER KAGERLAND.

Nordic Soundlab: PO Box 31, 53221 Skara; Man. Dir LASSE HOLM.

North of No South (NONS) Records: Sotiehemsv 45, 90738 Umeå; Man. Dir ROBERT NORSTEN.

Planet Records: Torggatan 15, 17154 Solna; Chair. MATS OLSSON.

Polygram Records Sweden: PO Box 20510, 16102 Bromma; Man. Dir LENART BACKMAN.

Rainbow Music: Höstvägen 5, 17140 Solna / Stockholm; Man. Dir STURE HALLBERG.

Real Time Music: Wennerbergsgatan 1, 11258 Stockholm; Man. ALLAN GUTHEIM.

Roligan Records: Gotabergsgatan 2, Box 53045, 40014 Gothenburg; Man. Dir JASPER KUMBERG.

Sidelake: Trädgardsgatan 23, 85172 Sundsvall; Man. Dir ANDERS MELIN.

Silence: PO Box 271, 18523 Waxholm; Man. Dir EVA WILKE.

Sonet Music: PO Box 20105, 16102 Bromma; Man. Dir BÖRGE ENGEN.

Sony Music Sweden: PO Box 20037, 16102 Bromma; Man. Dir STEFAN KLINTEBERG.

Step One: Katrinebergsvgen 2, 10074 Stockholm; Man. Dir JÖRGEN SIGFRIDSSON.

Stockholm Records: PO Box 20504, 16102 Bromma; Gen. Man. ERIC HASSELQVIST.

Strawberry Songs: PO Box 157, 63103 Eskilstuna; Man. Dir HANS LINDELL.

Swedish Prime Time Records: PO Box 250 32, 75025 Upsala; Man. Dir DAG CARLSSON.

Tempo Records: PO Box 231 49, 10435 Stockholm; Man. Dir PETER HARTZELL.

Triple / Lionheart Records: Götgatan 81, 11662 Stockholm; Man. Dir ROBERT LJUNGGREN.

Virgin Records Sweden: PO Box 1291, 17125 Solna; Man. Dir ANDERS HJELMSTORP.

Warner Music Sweden: PO Box 1228, 16428 Kista; Man. MARTEN AGLANDER.

Zakana Records: Skolgatan 73A, 90330 Umeå; Man. Dir MIKAEL REINHOLDSSON.

Switzerland

150 BPM Records: Steinhauserstr 21, 6330 Cham; A & R Man. HANS RAYMONDAZ.

Atina Records GmbH: Hafnarstr 23, 8005 Zürich; Owner/Man. Dir ANITA TIZIANI.

Black Cat: Faellendenstrase 20, 8124 Maur; Man. Dir HILI HEILINGER.

BMG Ariola Switzerland: Letzigraben 89, 8047 Zürich; Dir GUIDO VENDRAMINI.

Brambus Records: PO Box 44, 7004 Chur; Dir PAUL ROSTETTER.

Dircom: Fausses-Brayes 19, 2000 Neuchatel; Pres. JOEL DESAULES.

Dirty Alternative Beat: rue de O'Ale 35, POB 225, 1000 Lausanne 17; Contact T LERESCHE.

Disques Cellier: Aiguemont 26, rue du Bourg de Plait, 1605 Chexbres; Dirs MARCEL CELLIER, CATHERINE CELLIER.

Editions Cellier: Aiguemont 26, rue du Bourg de Plait, 1071 Chexbres; tel. (21) 946-1649; fax (21) 946-3533; e-mail ccellier@merging.com; internet ulliherkenhoff.freepage.de/cellier.html; Contacts MARCEL CELLIER, CATHERINE CELLIER.

Face Music: Dorfstr 29/1, 8800 Thalwil; e-mail face.music@bluewin.ch; internet www.music.ch/face/; Dir ALBI WETHLI.

Grooveline AG: Laubenhof, 6300 Zug; Man. Dir ERMIN TREVISAN.

Lux-Noise: PO Box 3212, 5001 Aarau; Man. Dir MICHAEL HEDIGER.

Noise Product Switzerland: CP 363, 1213 Petit Lancy 1; Label Man. ALBAN CHAPERON.

NSS Records: Fahrweidstr 81 A, 8651 Fahrweid; Contact MICHEL F HUWILER.

Off Course Records: PO Box 241, 8025 Zürich; Man. Dir URS STEIGER.

Phonag AG: Zürcherstr 77, 8041 Winterthur; Man. Dir PETER FREI.

Pick Records: Brunnwiesenstr 26, 8049 Zürich; Chair. ANTON PETERER.

Sony Music Switzerland: Oberneuhofstr 6, 6340 Bahr; Man. MIRCO VAIZ.

Steinblatt Music: Via Vicari 18, 6900 Lugano; Man. Dir MARCO ANTOGNINI.

Turicaphon AG: Turicaphonstr 31, 8616 Riedikon; Man. Dir HANS OESTREICHER.

Viteka Music Production: PO Box 173, Ringstr 14, 8600 Dübendorf / Zürich; Chair. WILLY VITEKA.

Warner Music Switzerland: Ave Chilton 70, 1820 Montreux; Man. Dir CHARLES NOBS.

Thailand

BMG Music: 18/F Vanissa Bdlg, Soi Chidlom, Pleonchit Rd, Patumwam, Bangkok 10110; Man. Dir STEVEN TAN.

EMI (Thailand) Ltd: 1091/183 New Petchburi Rd, Makkasa, Phayathai, Bangkok 10400; Gen. Man. VICHART JIRATHIYUT.

Giant Records: 61/123 Taveemit Soi 9, Rama IX Rd, Asoke-Din Daeng, Huay-Kwang, Bangkok 10310; Contact KRAISAK OCHAREON.

Grammy Records: 59/1 Soi Prom Pong, Sukhumvit 39, Sukhumvit Rd, Prakanong, Bangkok 10110; Man. Dir PAIBOON DAMRONG CHAITAM.

Michael Record Co Ltd: 52/17–18 Moo 8, Orn-Nuch Rd, Suanluang, Bangkok 10250; Man. Dir CHOKECHAI JARUWATEE.

Polygram (Far East Bangkok Enterprises): 21 115–116 Royal City Ave, Rama IX Rd, Huay Kwang, Bangkok 10310; Man. Dir JERRY SIM.

Sony Music Entertainment (Thailand) Ltd: 1091/184–5 New Petchburi Rd, Payathai, Bangkok 10400; Gen. Man. PETER GAN.

Warner Music Thailand: 143 Sukhumvit 62/1, Sukhumvit Rd, Prakhanong, Bangkok 10250; Man. Dir WASANA SILPIKUL.

Turkey

Hades Records: Gazi cd, Reisul Kuttap Sk, Peken Ap 50/B, 81160 Baglarbasi, Istanbul; Dir VOLKAN OLGUN.

Jazz Records & Publishing: Atlamatasi Caddesi 5, Serilen, 34470 Unkapani, Istanbul; Pres. YASAR DEMIRTURK.

MMY: IMC 6, Blok 6437, 34470 Unkapani Istanbul; Pres. YESIL GIRESUNLU.

RKD Ltd: Ferah Sok Ferah Apt 1, 19–9 Nisantasi, Istanbul; tel. (212) 241-3411; fax (212) 231-9673; e-mail rkdltd@lxir.com; internet www.akustamusic.com; Man. Dir ARMAGAN AK.

Ukraine

Audio Ukraine: Laboratorny Provulok 7A, 252 133 Kiev; Man. Dir YURI GONCHARUK.

Komora: Dav 22, NEC, Hlushkova Ave 1, 252 085 Kiev; Interpreter IVAN CHUIGOUK.

Leva: Kostyushka str 18, 290 000 Lviv; Man. Dir IGOR KRYTOVITCH.

NAC: Gorkok str 47, 252 005 Kiev; Man. Dir VOLODYMYR LAGODNY.

The United Kingdom

4AD: 15 Alma Rd, London SW18 1AA; Man. Dir IVOR WATTS-RUSSELL.

A&M Records: 136–140 New Kings Rd, London SW6 4LZ; Man. Dir OSMAN ERLAP.

Abbey Records: 4 Newtec Pl., Magdalen Rd, Oxford, Oxon OX4 1RE; Press Officer PETER BROMLEY.

Ace Records: 46–50 Steele Rd, London NW10 7AS; Man. Dir TED CAROLL.

Acid Jazz Records: 11 Greek St, London WC1V 5LE; Man. Dir EDWARD PILLER.

Active Records: Rockfield Studios, Amberley Court, Monmouth, Gwent NP5 4ET; tel. (1600) 712449; fax (1600) 714421; e-mail rockfieldstudios@compuserve.com; internet www.rockfieldstudios.com; Dir KINGSLEY WARD.

AKR Records: Waterside Penthouse, 156 High St, Brentford, Middx TW8 8JA; Man. Dir KEVIN MORAN.

Almo Sounds: 3 Heathmans Rd, London SW6 4TJ; Contact MERCEDES LUIS FUENTES.

Alphabet Records: 253 Camberwell New Rd, London SE5 0TH; Contact MARK WALMESLEY.

Alternative Tentacles Records: 64 Mountgrove Rd, London N5 2LT; Label Man. BRIDGET CLAY.

Anagram Records: Bishops Park House, 25–29 Fulham High St, London SW6 3JH; Label Man. ADAM VELASCO.

Anxious: Devonshire House, 2/4 The Broadway, London N8 9SN; Man. Dir TONY QUINN.

Arista Records: Cavendish House, 423 New Kings Rd, London SW6 4RN; Gen. Man. MARK WILLIAMS.

Ariwa Sounds Ltd: 34 Whitehorse Lane, South Norwood, London SE25 6RE; Man. Dir NEIL FRASER.

Arrival Records: 39 Leyton Rd, Harpenden, Herts AL5 2JB; Man. Dir DAVID BLAYLOCK.

Astranova: Unit 306, Canalot Production Studios, 222 Kensal Rd, London W10 5BN; Dir SCOTT HILL.

Atomic Records: 32 Neal St, London WC2H 9PS; Contact MICK NEWTON.

Avex UK: 22 Soho Sq., London W1V 5FJ; Dir PHIL FRANCE.

Awesome Records: 59 Moore Park Rd, London SW6 2HA; Man. Dir FALCON STUART.

Bad Habits Music Group: PO Box 111, London W13 0ZH; Man. Dir JOHN S RUSHTON.

Bearcat Records: PO Box 94, Derby DE22 1XA; Contact CHRIS HALL.

Beat Goes On Records: PO Box 22, Bury St Edmunds, Suffolk IP28 6XQ; Label Man. MICHAEL GOTT.

Beatfarm Recordings: Studio C, Chelsea Studios, 416 Fulham Rd, London SW6 1HP; Owner MARCO PERRY.

Beechwood Music Ltd: Littleton House, Littleton Rd, Ashford, Middlesex TW15 1UU; tel. (1784) 423214; fax (1784) 251245; e-mail info@beechwoodmusic.co.uk; internet www.beechwoodmusic.co.uk; Contact CHET SELWOOD.

Big Bear Music: PO Box 944, Edgbaston, Birmingham B16 8UT; tel. (121) 4547020; fax (121) 4549996; e-mail admin@bigbearmusic.com; internet www.bigbearmusic.com; Man. Dir JIM SIMPSON.

Big Cat (UK) Records Ltd: PO Box 3074, 3rd Floor, Devonshire House, Barley Mow Passage, London W4 4ZN; Label Man. TIM VASS.

Big Life Records: 15 Little Portland St, London W1N 5DE; Chair. JAZZ SUMMERS.

Blackout Records: 253 Camberwell New Rd, London SE5 0TH; Contact MARK WALMESLEY.

Blanco y Negro: 66 Golborne Rd, London W10 5PS; tel. (20) 8960 9888; fax (20) 8968 6715; e-mail james@roughtraderecords.com; internet www.roughtraderecords.com; Man. Dir GEOFF TRAVIS.

Blueprint: PO Box 5, Derwentside, Co Durham DH9 7HR; Label Man. ROB AYLING.

BMG (UK) / RCA Records: Bedford House, 69–79 Fulham High St, London SW6 3JW; Chair. JOHN PRESTON.

Bobb Records: 12 Waterford Rd, Ashley, New Milton, Hants BH25 5BH; Dirs MIKE PRESTON, ANDREA PRESTON.

Brilliant Records: 19 Ford Sq., London E1 2HS; Man. Dir FRAZER HENRY.

BSC Records: 23 Corbyn St, London N4 3BY; Dirs ANDY MONOYOS, GORDON ELLINGTON.

Bulldog Records: PO Box 130, Hove, East Sussex BN3 6QU; Dir of International Operations STEVE LEWIS.

Buzz Records: 192 Glasgow Rd, Perth PH2 0NA, Scotland; Man. Dir DAVE ARCARI.

Caritas Records: 28 Dalrymple Cres., Edinburgh EH9 2NX, Scotland; tel. (131) 6673633; fax (131) 6673633; e-mail caritas-records@caritas-music.co.uk; internet www.caritas-music.co.uk; Man. Dir JAMES DOUGLAS.

Carlton Records: The Waterfront, Elstree Rd, Elstree, Herts WD6 3BS; A & R Dir JOHN HOWARD.

Carrera Recordings Ltd: Westco House, Pensarn Business Park, Abergele, Clwyd LL22 7SF, Wales; Contact PAUL WHITE.

Castle Communications: Unit 29, Barwell Business Park, Leatherhead Rd, Chessington, Surrey KT9 2NY; Chair. TERRY SHAND.

Charley Records Ltd: 156–166 Ilderton Rd, London SE15 1NT; Founder JEAN LUC YOUNG.

Check Records: Stewart House, Hillbottom Rd, Sands Industrial Estate, High Wycombe, Bucks HP12 4HJ; A & R Copyrite Dept CATHRINE LEE.

Chimera Records Ltd: 41 Rosebank, Holyport Rd, London SW6 6LQ; Man. Dir SADIA SADIA.

China Records: 111 Frithville Gardens, London W12 7JG; Contact RACHEL SPEERS.

Circle Sound Services: Circle House, 14 Waveney Close, Bicester, Oxon OX6 8GP; Proprietor JOHN WILLETT.

Columbia Records: 10 Great Marlborough St, London W1V 2LP; Man. Dir KIP KRONES.

Confidential Records: 127 Dewsbury Rd, Ossett, West Yorkshire WF5 9PA; Dir NEV BARKER.

Cooking Vinyl: 3 Park Mews, 213 Kilburn Lane, London W10 4BQ; A & R NEIL ARMSTRONG.

Deconstruction: Bedford House, 69–79 Fulham High St, London SW6 3JW; Man. Dirs KEITH BLACKHURST, PETE HADFIELD.

Dedicated Records: 36A Notting Hill Gate, London W11 3JQ; Man. Dir DOUG D'ARCY.

Demi Monde Records & Publishing: Foel Studio, Llanfair, Caereinion, Powys SY21 0DS, Wales; tel. (1938) 810758; fax (1938) 810758; e-mail dave.anderson@dial.pipex.com; internet www.demimonde.co.uk; Man. Dir DAVE ANDERSON.

Dick Bros Record Co Ltd: The Main House, Spittalrig Farm, Nr Haddington EH41 3SU, Scotland; Contact JEREMY LAWSON.

Direct Heat Records: PO Box 1345, Worthing, West Sussex BN14 7FB; tel. and fax (1903) 202426; e-mail dhm@happyvibes.co.uk; internet www.happyvibes.co.uk; Man. Dir MIKE PAILTHORPE.

Dorado Records Ltd: 76 Brewer St, London W1R 3PH; Man. Dir OLLIE BUCKWELL.

Down To Jam Records: 112A-B Westbourne Grove, Chepstow Rd, London W2 5RU; Man. Dir PAUL MOORE.

East West Records: Electric Lighting Station, 46 Kensington Court, London W8 5DP; tel. (20) 7938-5500; fax (20) 7368-4910; Man. Dir CHRISTIAN TATTERSFIELD.

Echo Label: 13 Bramley Rd, London W10 6SP; Man. Dir STEVE LEWIS.

Ember Records: PO Box 130, Hove, East Sussex BN3 6QU; tel. (1273) 550088; fax (1273) 540969; e-mail jskruger@tkogroup.com; internet www.tkogroup.com; Chair. of the Board JEFFREY KRUGER.

EMI Records Group: EMI House, 43 Brook Green, London W6 7EF; Contact DAVID HUGHES.

Engine Records: 253 Camberwell New Rd, London SE5 0TH; Contact MARK WALMESLEY.

Epic Records: 10 Great Marlborough St, London W1V 2LP; Man. Dir ROB STRINGER.

Equity Records: 112A–B Westbourne Grove, Chepstow Rd, London W2 5RU; Man. Dir PAUL MOORE.

Esprit Music Ltd: Unit 306, Canalot Production Studios, 222 Kensal Rd, London W10 5BN; Dir TONY WARREN.

Fair Oaks Entertainment: PO Box 19, Ulverston, Cumbria CA12 9TF; Proprietor/Man. J G LIVINGSTONE.

Fat Boy Records: PO Box 130, Hove, East Sussex BN3 6QU; Operations Man. PETER HAZLEDINE.

Fellside Recordings: 15 Banklands, Workington, Cumbria CA14 3EW; Partner PAUL ADAMS.

Fire Records: 21A Maury Rd, London N16 7BP; A & R Dept DAVE BARKER, JON EYDMANN.

First Avenue Records: The Courtyard, 42 Colwith Rd, London W6 9EY; Contact OLIVER SMALLMAN.

FM-Revolver / Heavy Metal Records: 152 Goldthorn Hill, Penn, Wolverhampton, West Midlands WV2 3JA; Man. Dir PAUL BIRCH.

Food Records: 172A Arlington Rd, London NW1 7HL; Contact ELLIE O'READY.

Funki Dred Records Ltd: 36/38 Rochester Pl., London NW1 9JX; A & R H BROWNE.

Go! Discs: 72 Black Lion Lane, London W6 9BE; Man. Dir ANDY MCDONALD.

Grand Records: 107A High St, Canvey Island, Essex SS8 7RF; tel. (1268) 694888; fax (1268) 695009; e-mail grandrecords@aol.com; Contact ANN ADLEY.

Grasmere Records: Suite 3 Bolingbroke House, 332 Brighton Rd, South Croydon, Surrey CR2 6AJ; tel. (20) 8666-0201; fax (20) 8667-0037; Man. Dir BOB BARRATT.

Greentrax Recordings Ltd: Cockenzie Business Centre, Edinburgh Rd, Cockenzie, East Lothian EH32 0XL, Scotland; tel. (1875) 815888; fax (1875) 813545; e-mail iangtrax@aol.com; internet www.greentrax.com; Proprietor IAN D GREEN.

Grenquille Records: Stewart House, Hill Bottom Rd, Sands Industrial Estate, High Wycombe, Bucks HP12 4HJ; International A & R Copyright Lawyer KEITH R PHILLIPS.

GRP Records International: 33 Broadwick St, London W1V 1FR; Contact FRANK HENDRICKS.

Handle Records: Handle House, 1 Albion Pl., Galena Rd, Hammersmith, London W6 0QT; Chair. DAVID WALKER.

Harbourtown Records: PO Box 25, Ulverston, Cumbria LA12 7UN; Man. Dir GORDON JONES.

Hawk Records Ltd: 123–137 York St, Belfast BT15 1AB, Northern Ireland; Man. Dir CHARLIE TOSH.

Headscope: St End Lane, Broadoak, Heathfield, East Sussex TN21 8TU; tel. (1435) 863994; fax (1435) 867027; e-mail ron@geesin.demon.co.uk; internet www.rongeesin.com; Partner RON GEESIN.

Hotshot Records: 29 St Michaels Rd, Leeds LS6 3BG; Man. Dirs D FOSTER, CLIO BRADBURY.

Hut Records: Kensal House, 553–579 Harrow Rd, London W10 4RH; Contact DAVID BOYD.

Indigo Records: 2nd Fl, Twyman House, 31–39 Camden Rd, London NW1 9LF; Contact COLIN NEWMAN.

Inky Blackness: 7 Mornington Terrace, Camden Town, London NW1 7RR; Man. Dir IAN TREGONING.

Iona Records: 27–29 Carnoustie Pl., Scotland St, Glasgow G5 8PH, Scotland; tel. (141) 4201881; fax (141) 4201892; e-mail lismor@lismor.com; internet www.lismor.com; Man. Dir RONNIE SIMPSON.

IRS Records: EMI House, 443 Brook Green, London W6 7EF; Label Man. RICHARD BREEDEN.

Island Records: 22 St Peter's Sq., London W6 9NW; Man. Dir MARC MAROT.

Kinetix: The Black Office, DC Warehouse, Unit 6, Industrial Park, Maple Cross WD3 2AS; Chair. JON SHARP.

Kitchenware: 7 The Stables, St Thomas St, Newcastle-Upon-Tyne, Tyne & Wear NE1 4LE; Man. Dir KEITH ARMSTRONG.

KRL: 9 Watt Rd, Hillington, Glasgow G52 4RY, Scotland; Man. Dir GUS MCDONALD.

Kufe Records Ltd: 154 Rucklidge Ave, Harlesden, London NW10 4PR; tel. (20) 8533-1879; fax (20) 8986-8649; e-mail lindel@kuferecords.com; internet www.kuferecords.com; Man. Dir LINDEL LEWIS.

L'attitude Ltd: First Floor, Ducie House, 37 Ducie St, Manchester M1 2JW; Dirs ANDY DODD, ELLIOT RASHMAN.

Lena Davis, John Bishop Associates: Cotton's Farmhouse, Whiston Rd, Cogenhoe, Northants NN7 1NL; tel. (1604) 891487; fax (1604) 890405; Dir JOHN BISHOP.

Linn Records: Floors Rd, Waterfoot, Eaglesham, Glasgow G76 0EP, Scotland; Label Man. PHILIP HOBBS.

Lismor Recordings Ltd: 27–29 Carnoustie Pl., Scotland St, Glasgow G5 8PH, Scotland; tel. (141) 420-1881; fax (141) 420-1892; e-mail lismor@lismor.com; internet www.lismor.com; Man. Dir RONNIE SIMPSON.

Liverpool Music House Ltd: 51–55 Highfield St, Liverpool L3 6AA; Dir COLIN HALL.

Logic Records: 1st Floor, 34–35 Berwick St, London W1V 3RF; Contact TONY PIERCY.

London Records: PO Box 1422, Chancellors House, Chancellors Rd, London W6 9SG; Man. Dir COLIN BELL.

Luna Park: 81 Harley House, Marylebone Rd, London NW1 5HT; Contact RUSSELL VAUGHT.

MCA Records Ltd: 139 Piccadilly, London W1V 0AX; Deputy Man. Dir JEFF COLEMBO.

Medium Productions Limited: 74 Saint Lawrence Rd, Upminster, Essex RM14 2UW; tel. (7939) 080524; fax (1708) 640291; e-mail info@mediumproductions.co.uk; internet www.mediumproductions.co.uk; Co-Dir DEBI ZORNES.

Mel Bush Organization Ltd: Tanglewood, Arrowsmith Rd, Wimborne, Dorset BHZ1 3BG; tel. (1202) 691891; fax (1202) 691896; e-mail mbobmth@aol.com; Man. Dir MEL BUSH.

Mercury Records: Chancellors House, 72 Chancellors Rd, London W6 9QB; Man. Dir HOWARD BERMAN.

Metro Music Productions: Metro Radio Ltd, Longriggs, Swalwell, Gateshead, Tyne & Wear NE99 1BB; Dir of Music Production JON CRAIG.

Midnight Rock: Grays Farm Barns, Marshside, Kent CT3 4EL; tel. (1227) 860638; fax (1227) 860627; e-mail rockindave@midnightrock.demon.co.uk; internet www.midnightrock.demon.co.uk; Contact DAVE TAYLOR.

Millennium Records: 9 Thorpe Close, Portobello Rd, London W10 5XL; Man. Dir RALPH RUPPERT.

Milltown Productions Ltd: 26 East Parade, Bradford, West Yorkshire BD1 5HD; Prod. IAN SMITH.

Moksha: PO Box 102, London E15 2IIH; Man. Dir CHARLES COLM.

Moving Shadow Records: 1st & 2nd Floors, 17 St Anne's Court, Soho, London W1V 3AW; Label Co-ordinator CAROLINE BUTLER.

Mrs Casey Music: PO Box 296, Aylesbury, Bucks HP19 3TL; Dir STEVE HEAP.

Mushroom Records UK Ltd: 1 Sharrolds Rd, London SW6 7TR; tel. (20) 7343-5678; fax (20) 7343-5656; internet www.mushroomuk.com; Man. Dir KORDA MARSHALL.

Music For Nations: 333 Latimer Rd, London W10 6RA; tel. (20) 8964-9544; fax (20) 8964-5460; e-mail mfn@music-for-nations.co.uk; internet www.music-for-nations.co.uk; Man. Dir ANDY BLACK.

Music of Life & Living Beat Records: 20 Hanway St, London W1P 9DD; Man. Dir CHRIS FRANCE.

Musidisc UK: 32 Queensdale Rd, Holland Park, London W11 4SB; Label Man. JUDITH FISHER.

Mute Records: 429 Harrow Rd, London W10 4RE; Man. Dir DANIEL MILLER.

Nation Records Ltd: 19 All Saints Rd, Notting Hill, London W11 1HE; tel. (20) 7792-8167; fax (20) 7792-2854; e-mail aki@nationrecords.co.uk; internet www.nationrecords.co.uk; Man. Dir AKI NAWAZ.

NIKT Records: Cadillac Ranch, Pencraig Uchaf, Cwm Bach, Whiland, Dyfed SA3 40DT, Wales; tel. (1994) 484466; fax (1994) 484294; e-mail cadillac_ranch@telco4u.net; internet www.nikturner.com; A & R NIK TURNER.

Now and Then: Unit 29, Empress Ind Estate, Anderson Sreet, Wigan, Lancs WN2 2BG; Label Man. MARK ASHTON.

NRG Records: 49 High St, Kingston-Upon-Thames, Surrey KT1 1LQ; Man. Dir ROBERT JONES.

Nude Records: 6 Warren Mews, London W1P 5DJ; Man. Dir SAUL GALPERN.

One Little Indian Records: 250 York Rd, London SW11 3SJ; tel. (20) 8772-7600; fax (20) 8772-7601; e-mail db@indian.co.uk; internet www.indian.co.uk; Man. Dir DEREK BIRKETT.

Outburst Music Ltd: 71 High St East, Wallsend, Tyne and Wear NE 28 7RJ; tel. (191) 2624999; fax (191) 2637082; e-mail mdwood33@aol.com; internet www.geordiestuff.co.uk; Man. Dir DAVE WOOD.

Palace of Fun: 16 Elm View, Huddersfield Rd, Halifax, Yorkshire HX3 0AE; Man. Dir BILL BYFORD.

Park Records: PO Box 651, Oxford OX2 9RB; Man. Dir JOHN DAGNELL.

Perfecto Records: Electric Lighting Station, 46 Kensington Court, London W8 5DP; Contact SPENCER BALDWIN.

Performance Equities Ltd: 112 A & B Westbourne Grove, Chepstow Rd, London W2 5RU; Man. Dir PAUL MOORE.

Permanent Records: 22–23 Brook Mews, London W2 3BW; Man. Dir J LENNARD.

PHAB: High Notes, Sheerwater Ave, Woodham, Weybridge, Surrey KT15 3SD; Contact PHILIP H A BAILEY.

Planet 4: Sun House, 2–4 Little Peter St, Manchester M15 4PS; Man. Dir CHRIS JOYCE.

Plankton Records: 236 Sebert Rd, Forest Gate, London E7 0NP; Sr Partner SIMON LAW.

Play It Again Sam (UK): Suite G, Tech West, 10 Warple Way, London W3 0UE; Gen. Man. PETER DODGE.

Plutonium Records: Stanley House, 15/17 Ladybridge Rd, Cheadle Hulme, Greater Manchester SK8 5BL; Press & Promotions ZOEY FAULKNER.

Pogo Records: Stewart House, Sands Industrial Estate, High Wycombe, Bucks HP12 4HJ; A & R XAVIER LEE.

Pollytone Music: PO Box 124, Ruislip, Middlesex HA4 9BB; tel. (1895) 638584; fax (1895) 624793; e-mail val@pollyton.demon.co.uk; internet www.pollytone.com; Dir VALERIE BIRD.

PolyGram UK: PO Box 1420, 1 Sussex Pl., London W6 9XS; CEO ROGER AIMES.

Positiva: 43 Brook Green, London W6 7EF; tel. (20) 7605-5157; fax (20) 7605-5186; internet www.positivarecords.com; Head of A & R JASON ELLIS.

President Records Limited: Exmouth House, 11 Pine St, London EC1R 0JH; Man. Dir DAVID KASSNER.

Priory Records: Unit 9B, Upper Wingbury Courtyard, Wingrave, Bucks HP22 4LW; Proprietor NEIL COLLIER.

Profile Records Ltd: White Swan House, Bennett St, London W4 2AH; Dir JON SHARP.

PWL International: 222–224 Borough High St, London SE1 1JX; Man. Dir PETER PRICE.

Quinlan Road (UK): 1 Heathgate Pl., 75/87 Agincourt Rd, London NW3 2NT; Gen. Man. IAN BLACKABY.

R & B Division Limited: 34 Salisbury St, London NW8 8QE; tel. (20) 7402-9111; fax (20) 7723-3064; Man. Dir ELIOT M COHEN.

Red Bus Records Ltd: 34 Salisbury St, London NW8 8QE; tel. (20) 7402-9111; fax (20) 7723-3064; e-mail eliot@amimedia.co.uk; internet www.amimedia.co.uk; Man. Dir ELIOT M COHEN.

Red Lightnin' Ltd: The White House, The St, North Lopham, Diss, Norfolk IP22 2LU; tel. (1379) 687693; fax (1379) 687559; e-mail peter@redlightnin.com; internet www.redlightnin.com; Dir PETER SHERTSER; Blues specialist.

Riddle Records: Cadillac Ranch, Pencraig Uchaf, Cum Bach, Whitland, Dyfed SA34 0DT, Wales; e-mail cadillac-ranch@telco4u.net; internet www.nikturner.com; A & R M MENENDES, CHRISTY FRENCH.

Roadrunner Records: Tech West House, Warple Way, London W3 0UL; Gen. Man. MARK PALMER.

Rock 'n' Roll Enterprises: 16 Grove Plce, Penarth CF64 2ND, Wales; tel. (2920) 704279; fax (2920) 709989; e-mail barrett.rocknroll@aimserve.net; Dir PAUL BARRETT.

Rollover Productions: 29 Beethoven St, London W10 4LJ; Man. Dir SEAMUS MORLEY.

Ronnie Scott's Jazz House: Magnum House, High St, Lane End, High Wycombe, Bucks HP14 3JG; Man. Dir DEREK EVERETT.

RooArt Europe: 22a Lambolle Pl., London NW3 4HP; Contact PAUL CRAIG.

Rough Trade Records: 66 Golborne Rd, London W10 5PS; tel. (20) 8960 9888; fax (20) 8968 6715; e-mail james@roughtraderecords.com; internet www.roughtraderecords.com; Man. Dir GEOFF TRAVIS.

RTL Music: Stewart House, Hill Bottom Rd, Sands Industrial Estate, High Wycombe, Bucks HP12 4HJ; Owner/Prod. RON LEE.

Rykodisc Limited: 78 Stanley Gardens, London W3 7SN; Man. Dir IAN MOSS.

Sadia Sadia: 41 Rosebank, Holyport Rd, London SW6 6LQ.

Sain: Caolfan Sain, Llandwrog, Caernarfon, Gwynedd LL54 5TG, Wales; Man. Dir DAFYDD IWAN.

Sambawamba: 6 Handel St, Nottingham, NG3 1JE.

Saxology Records: 49E St Paul's Rd, London N1 2LT; Man. Dir MIKE TANOUSIS.

Saydisc Records: Chipping Manor, The Chipping, Wotton-Under-Edge, Glos GL12 7AD; Partner GEF LUCENA.

Scotdisc Music & Video: BGS Productions Ltd, Newtown St, Kilsyth, Glasgow G65 0JX, Scotland; Marketing Dir DOUGIE STEVENSON.

Seriously Groovy Music Ltd: 3rd Floor, 28 D'Arblay St, Soho, London W1F 8EW; tel. (20) 7439-1947; fax (20) 7734-7540; e-mail seriously.groovy@virgin.net; internet www.seriouslygroovy.com; Dir LORRAINE SNAPE.

Setanta Records: PO Box 4693, London SE5 7XZ; Contact KEITH CULLEN.

Sidestep Records Limited: 9A Dallington St, London EC1V 0BQ; Joint Man. Dir HEDDI GREENWOOD.

Some Bizarre Ltd: 4 Denmark St, London, WC2H 8LP.

Sony Music Entertainment (UK): 10 Great Marlborough St, London W1V 2LP; Chair. PAUL BURGER.

Sony Soho Square (S²): 10 Great Marlborough St, London W1V 2LP; Man. Dir MUFF WINWOOD.

Stamina Management: 47 Prout Grove, London NW10 1PU; Man. Dir PETER GAGE.

Stephen W Tayler: 41 Rosebank, Holyport Rd, London SW6 6LQ; Contact STEPHEN W TAYLER.

Stone Tiger Records: PO Box 4464, London SW19 6XT; Owner LES ROWLEY.

Strange Fruit: 333 Latimer Rd, London W10 6RA; tel. (20) 8964-9544; fax (20) 8964-5460; e-mail sfm@strange-fruit-music.co.uk; internet www.strangefruitrecords.com; Label Man. SUE ARMSTRONG.

Strange Fruit Records: Electron House, Cray Ave, Orpington, Kent BR5 3PN; Gen. Man. BRIAN O'REILLY.

Stress Records: PO Box 89, Slough, Berkshire SL1 8NA; Man. NICK GORDON BROWN.

Swoop Records: Stewart House, Hillbottom Rd, Sands Industrial Estate, High Wycombe, Bucks HP12 4HJ; A & R KATHRINE LE MATT.

SYME International—Hengest Records: 81 Park Rd, Wath-Upon-Dearne, Rotherham, South Yorkshire S63 7LE; tel. (1709) 877920; fax (1709) 873119; e-mail admin@hengest.com; internet www.hengest.com; Product Man. PATSY PRINCE.

Taurus Records: 23 Blackheath Rise, Lewisham, London SE13 7PN; Contact BEVERLEY MILLER.

Tembo Entertainments: PO Box 1655, London W8 5HZ; Contact HOWARD ELSON.

The Brothers Organisation: 74 The Archway, Station Approach, Ranelagh Gardens, London SW6 3UH; Dirs IAN TITCHENER, NICK TITCHENER.

Theobald Dickson Productions Ltd: The Coach House, Swinhope Hall, Swinhope, Lincolnshire LN3 6HT; Man. Dir BERNARD THEOBALD.

Timbre Records Ltd: 93 Brondesbury Rd, London NW6 6RY; Man. Dir DIANE M HINDS.

TKO Licensing Ltd: PO Box 130, Hove, East Sussex BN3 6QU; tel. (1273) 550088; fax (1273) 540969; e-mail warren@tkogroup.com; internet www.tkogroup.com; Head of Licensing WARREN HEAL.

TKO Magnum Music Ltd: Unit 5, Pilot Trading Estate, West Wycombe Rd, High Wycombe, Bucks HP12 3AB; tel. (1494) 450606; fax (1494) 450230; e-mail music@tkomagnum.co.uk; internet www.tkomagnum.co.uk; Joint CEO NIGEL MOLDEN.

Too Pure: 3A Highbury Cres., London N5 1RN.

Trim Top Records: 13 Winton Park, Edinburgh EH10 7EX, Scotland; tel. (1314) 451687; e-mail gerryford@madasafish.com; internet www.gerryford.co.uk; Owner GERRY FORD.

Triple Earth: 24 Foley St, London W1P 7LA; Partner IAIN SCOTT.

Unexploded Persons Bureau: PO Box 6414, London N1 3SA; Co-ordinator RUSSELL WILLES.

Unity Records: John Henry Bldg, 16/24 Brewery Rd, London N7 9NH; Sales & Retail Man. PEPIN CLOUT.

Upbeat Management and Recordings: Sutton Business Centre, Rastmor Way, Wallington, Surrey SM6 7AH; tel. (20) 8773-1223; fax (20) 8669-6752; e-mail beryl@upbeat.co.uk; internet www.upbeat.co.uk; Contact BERYL KORMAN.

Upbeat Recordings Ltd: Sutton Business Centre, Rastmor Way, Wallington, Surrey SM6 7AH; Contact BERYL KORMAN.

Vinyl Japan (UK) Ltd: 281 Camden High St, London NW1 7BX; Man. PATRICK JAMES.

Vinyl Solution: 231 Portobello Rd, London W11 1LT; Contacts ROB TENNANT, ALAIN DE LA MATA, NICK BROWN.

Virgin Records: Kensal House, 553–579 Harrow Rd, London W10 4RH; Chair. KEN BERRY.

Vision Discs: PO Box 92, Gloucester GL4 8HW; Contact VIC COPPERSMITH.

Warner Music (UK)/ WEA Records: The Warner Bldg, 28 Kensington Church St, London W8 4EP; Chair. ROB DICKINS.

Warp Records Ltd: Spectrum House, 32–34 Gordon House Rd, London NW5 1LP; internet www.warprecords.com.

Wolf Records: 83 Brixton Water Lane, London SW2 1PH; tel. (20) 7733-8088; fax (20) 7326-4016; Man. Dir DOMINIQUE BRETHES.

X-Factor Music Group International: PO Box 52, Ilford, Essex IG1 3JT; tel. and fax (20) 8252-1007; e-mail xsquad_uk@yahoo.co.uk; Dir/Prod. RAMESH KANSARA.

XL Recordings: 17–19 Alma Rd, London SW18 1AA; Administration Man. ELISE THEUMA.

Young Guns Productions: 95 Carshalton Park Rd, Carshalton Beeches, Surrey SM5 3SJ; Owner TOM JENNINGS.

Zarg Records: Stewart House, Hillbottom Rd, High Wycombe, Bucks HP12 4HJ; A & R Writer/Prod. RON DICKSON.

Zomba Records: Zomba House, 165–167 Willesden High Rd, London NW10 2SG; Gen. Man. ANDY RICHMOND.

Zoo Bee Records: Suite 6, 1 Cranbourn Alley, Cranbourn St, London WC2H 7AN; Prod. TIM RABJOHNS.

ZTT Records: The Blue Bldg, 42–46 St Lukes Mews, London W11 1DG; Contact CLAIRE LEADBITTER.

The United States of America

(510) Records: 5299 College Ave, Suite E, Oakland, CA 94618; Pres. ELLIOT CAHN.

A & E Music Inc: 13644 S W 142 Ave, Suite D, Miami, FL 33186; Pres. JOE GRANDA.

A & R Records: 900 19th Ave S, Suite 207, Nashville, TN 37212; Owner RUTH STEELE.

A&M Records: 1416 N La Brea Ave, Hollywood, CA 90028; Pres. AL CAFARO.

Aarrow Records: 900 19th Ave S, Suite 207, Nashville, TN 37212; Owner KELLI STEELE; A & R Dir RUTH STEELE.

Airtrax: 273 Chippewa Dr., Columbia, SC 29210-6508.

Alcazar Productions: PO Box 429 South, Main St, Waterbury, VT 05676; Vice-Pres. JENNIFER HARWOOD.

Alexandria House: 3310 West End Ave, 5th Floor, Nashville, TN 37203; Marketing Co-ordinator MICHELLE GUST.

All American Music Group: 808 Wilshire Blvd, Santa Monica, CA 90405; Dir, National Publicity SHERYL NORTHROP.

American Music: 1206 Decatur St, New Orleans, LA 70116; Pres. GEORGE H BUCK JR.

American Recordings: 3500 W Olive Ave, Suite 1550, Burbank, CA 91505.

Antithesis Records: 273 Chippewa Dr., Columbia, SC 29210-6508.

Arista Records: 6 W 57th St, New York, NY 10019; Pres. CLIVE DAVIS.

Artan Records: PO Box 5672, Buena Park, CA 90622-5672; Man. CARMEN ORTIZ.

Ash Music: 116 NE 136 Ave, Portland, OR 97230; A & R JASON CHARLES.

Asil Records: PO Box 790576, Middle Village, NY 11379-0576; Pres. DAN KARPF.

Atlantic Records: 75 Rockefeller Plaza, New York, NY 10019-6907; Co-Chairs AHMET ERTEGUN, DOUG MORRIS.

Audiophile: 1206 Decatur St, New Orleans, LA 70116; Pres. GEORGE H BUCK JR.

Axbar Records: PO Box 12353, San Antonio, TX 78212; tel. (210) 829-1909; e-mail axbar@stic.net; internet www.axbarmusic.com; Prod./Gen. Man. JOE SCATES.

Baker Productions: 311 2nd Ave SW, Cullman, AL 35055; tel. (256) 739-0388; fax (256) 739-7196; e-mail cbaker@bakerproductions.com; internet www.bakerproductions.com; Pres. CHARLES BAKER.

Bar None Records: PO Box 1709, Hoboken, NJ 07030; Pres. TOM PRENDERGAST.

Bell Records International: PO Box 725, Daytona Beach, FL 32115-0725; Vice-Pres. CHARLES VICKERS.

Benson Music Group Inc: 365 Great Circle Rd, Nashville, TN 37228; International Sales JANICE CUTTLER.

Black & Blue Records: Suite 152, 400 D Putnam Pike, Smithfield, RI 02917; Pres. PETER YARMOUTH.

Blaster-Boxx Hits: 519 N Halifax Ave, Dayton Beach, FL 32118; tel. and fax (386) 252-0381; e-mail blasterboxxhits@aol.com; internet www.blasterboxxhits.com; CEO BOBBY LEE CUDE.

Blowin' Smoke Records: 7438 Shoshone Ave, Van Nuys, CA 91406-2340; tel. (818) 881-9888; fax (818) 881-0555; e-mail blowinsmokeband.com; internet www.blowinsmokeband.com; Pres. LARRY WEISBERG.

BME Records: PO Box 76507, Washington, DC 20013; Pres. CARL BENTLEY.

BMG Music / RCA: 1540 Broadway, New York, NY 10036; Chair. MICHAEL DORNEMANN.

Bob Scott Frick Enterprises: 404 Bluegrass Ave, Madison, TN 37115; tel. (615) 865-6380; e-mail bfrick@att.net; Pres. BOB FRICK.

Broken Rekids: PO Box 460402, San Francsico, CA 94146-0402, USA; Pres. JAYDID.

BSW Records: PO Box 2297, Universal City, TX 78148; tel. (210) 599-0022; fax (210) 653-3989; e-mail bswr18@txdirect.net; internet www.bswrecords.com; Pres./CEO FRANK WILLSON.

C & S Productions: PO Box 91492, Anchorage, AK 99509-1492; Partner TIM R CRAWFORD.

C E R Records: 7400 N Adams Rd, North Adams, MI 49262; Pres. CLAUDE E REED.

Cadence Jazz Records: Cadence Bldg, Redwood, NY 13679; Prod. BOB RUSCH.

Camaraderie Music Co: 238 Austin St, Boston, MA 02136-1844; Contact CURT NAIHERSEY.

Capitol Records: 1750 N Vine St, Hollywood, CA 90028; Pres. GARY GERSH.

Caprice International Records: PO Box 808, Lititz, PA 17543; Pres. JOEY WELZ.

Case Entertainment Group Inc (R): 102 East Pikes Peak Ave, Suite 200, Colorado Springs, CO 80903; Contact ROBERT A CASE.

Cat's Voice Productions: PO Box 1361, Sanford, ME 04073-7361; Owner TOM REEVES.

Century Media Records: 2323 W El Segundo Blvd, Hawthorne, CA 90250; tel. (323) 418-1400; fax (323) 418-0118; e-mail mail@centurymedia.com; internet www.centurymedia.com; Vice-Pres./Gen. Man. MARCO BARBIERI.

Cerebral Records: 1236 Laguna Dr., Carlsbad, CA 92008; Pres. LINCOLN KROLL; Publicist CAROL LENO.

Chapel Music Group Inc: 2021 Richard Jones Rd, Suite 180, Nashville, TN 37215; Dir of Marketing HEATHER CAMPBELL.

Chemistry Records Ltd: PO Box 68, Las Vegas, NM 87701; Pres. ROBERT JOHN JONES.

Circle: 1206 Decatur St, New Orleans, LA 70116; Pres. GEORGE H BUCK JR.

Clarity Recordings: PO Box 411407, San Francisco, CA 94141-1407; Pres. ED WOODS.

Confidential Records: 1013 Evelyn Ave, Albany, CA 94706; Pres. JOEL BRANDWEIN.

Convenience: PO Box 66461, AMC O'Hare, IL 60666; Dir JOHN MAZ.

Cosmotone Records: 3350 Highway 6 S, PMB 412, Sugar Land, TX 77478; internet www.marianland.com/music02.html; Pres. RAFAEL BROM.

Creative Improvised Music Projects: Cadence Bldg, Redwood, NY 13679; tel. (315) 287-2852; fax (315) 287-2860; Prod. BOB RUSCH.

CSP Records MC: PO Box 69646, Los Angeles, CA 90096; Dir LARRY KLENO.

Cude & Pickens Music: 519 N Halifax Ave, Daytona Beach, FL 32118; tel. and fax (386) 252-0381; e-mail cudepickenspub@aol.com; internet www.broadwayusa.us; CEO BOBBY LEE CUDE.

Cybortravik Recording & Video Group: 8927 Claycott Dr., Dallas, TX 75243; CEO DAVID C MAY.

DanceFloor Distribution/Echo USA: 95 Cedar Lane, Englewood, NJ 07631; Pres. JEFFREY COLLINS.

Del-Fi Records Inc: PO Box 69188, Los Angeles, CA 90069; Owner & Pres. BOB KEANE.

Diva Entertainment World: 853 Broadway #1516, New York City, NY 10003; Man. Dir MARC KRASNOW.

E & J Records: 1505 Elvis Presley Blvd, Memphis, TN 38106; Exec. Asst LINDA LLOYD.

East West Records America: 75 Rockefeller Plaza, New York, NY 10019-6907; CEO SYLVIA RHONE.

Edensong: PO Box 34, Days Creek, OR 97429; Owner RICK FOSTER.

Elastic Records: PO Box 17598, Anaheim, CA 92817-7598; Owner AMIN GHASHGHAI.

Elektra Records: 75 Rockefeller Plaza, New York, NY 10019-6907; Chair. BOB KRASNOW.

Ember Records: 4501 Connecticut Ave, NW, Suite 905, Washington, DC 20008; CEO MICHAEL COHN.

EMI Records Group: 1290 6th Ave, New York NY 10104; CEO CHARLES KOPPLEMAN.

Enemy Productions Inc: 234 6th Ave, Brooklyn, NY 11215; Pres. MICHAEL KNUTH.

Ernie Bivens Productions: 203 Gates Dr., Hendersonville, TN 37075-4961; Owner/Prod. ERNIE BIVENS.

FAME Recording Studios: PO Box 2527, Muscle Shoals, AL 35662; Studio Man. RODNEY HALL.

Feather Records: PO Box 132, Astor Station, Boston, MA 02123-0132; Co-Owner L PASS.

Five Roses Music Group: 34A Lanier Rd, Studio 1, Jekyll Island, GA 31527; Pres. SAMMIE LEE MARLER.

Flying Heart Records: 4026 NE 12th Ave, Portland, OR 97212; Owner JAN CELT.

Fox Records: PO Box 1027, Neenah, WI 54957-1027; Pres. TONY ANSEMS.

Frank Russell Productions: PO Box 453, Totowa, NJ 07511; Prod. FRANK RUSSELL.

GBS Records: 203 Gates Dr., Hendersonville, TN 37075-4961; Owner/Prod. ERNIE BIVENS.

Geffen/DGC Records: 9130 Sunset Blvd, Los Angeles, CA 90069-6197; Chair. DAVID GEFFEN.

Genius Records: PO Box 481052, Los Angeles, CA 90048; Contact MARCY BLAUSTEIN.

GHB: 1206 Decatur St, New Orleans, LA 70116; Pres. GEORGE H BUCK JR.

Giant Records: 8900 Wilshire Blvd, Suite 200, Beverly Hills, CA 90211; Owner IRVING AZOFF.

Glide Records: PO Box 8243, Calabasas, CA 91372; tel. (818) 883-8407; Proprietor CHO PAQUET.

Gotee Records: 227 Third Ave N, Franklin, TN 37064; Admin. Asst CLAUDIA TAPIA.

Gramophone Records: PO Box 910, Beverly Hills, CA 90213; tel. (310) 557-0534; Gen. Man. LIONEL HOLLAND.

Gray Dot Records: 1991 South Cobb Dr., Marietta, GA 30060; CEO MARTY BUSH.

Greco Holdings Inc: Market St Sq., 33 Wilkes Barre Blvd, Wilkes Barre, PA 18701; Pres./CEO THOM GRECO.

Greener Pastures Records: 70 N 202, Peterborough, NH 03458-1107; Pres. WAYNER GREEN.

Group Productions: 1515 Cascade Ave, Box 481, Loveland, CO 80538; tel. (970) 669-3836; internet www.grouppublishing.com; Contact BRENDA KRAFT.

GRP Records: 555 W 57th St, New York, NY 10019; Pres. LARRY ROSEN.

Grrr Records: 920 W Wilson Ave, Chicago, IL 60640; Publicity/Retail Man. SHELLEY NEEDHAM; Booking Man. DIANE BORDEN.

Hammerhead Records Inc: 41 East University Ave, Champaign, IL 61820; Pres. TODD THORSTENSON.

Hard Hat Records: 519 N Halifax Ave, Daytona Beach, FL 32118; tel. and fax (386) 252-0381; e-mail hardhatrecords@aol.com; internet www.hardhatrecords.com; CEO BOBBY LEE CUDE.

Heartwrite Music: PO Box 1739, Texarkana, AR 75504; Pres. DAVID PATILLO.

High Kite Productions & Publishing: 1245 Elizabeth St, Denver, CO 80206; Prod. (Owner/Pres.) HENRY BROZ ROWLAND.

Higher Octave Music: 23852 Pacific Court Highway, H&C, Suite 385, Malibu, CA 90265; tel. (310) 589-1515; fax (310) 589-1525; internet www.higheroctave.com; Sr Vice-Pres. SCOTT BERGSTEIN.

Hollywood Records: 500 S Buena Vista St, Burbank, CA 91521; CEO WESLEY HEIN.

IKON Records: 212 N 12th St, Suite 3, Philadelphia, PA 19107; Pres. A & R VINCENT KRISHNER.

Imaginary Records: PO Box 66, Whites Creek, TN 37189; Proprietor LLOYD TOWNSEND JR.

Imago Recording Company: 152 W 57th St, 44th Floor, New York, NY 10019; Pres. TERRY ELLIS.

Inferno Records: PO Box 28743, Kansas City, MO 64118; Dir of A & R MARK MURTHA.

Interscope Records: 10900 Wilshire Blvd, 12th Floor, Los Angeles, CA 90024; Label Man. TED FIELD.

Island Records: 400 Lafayette St, New York, NY 10003; Chair. CHRIS BLACKWELL.

Jay Jay Records: 35 NE 62nd St, Miami, FL 33138; Pres. WALTER E JAGIELLO.

Jazzology: 1206 Decatur St, New Orleans, LA 70116; Pres. GEORGE H BUCK JR.

Jin: PO Drawer 10, 238 E Main St, Ville Platte, LA 70586; Pres. FLOYD SOILEAU.

Justice Music Corporation: 11586 Blix St, North Hollywood, CA 91602; Exec. Vice-Pres. MONTE R THOMAS.

Ketter Entertainment: PO Box 740702, San Diego, CA 92174-0702; Pres./ CEO AL KETTER.

King of Kings: PO Box 725, Daytona Beach, FL 32115-0725; Vice-Pres. CHARLES VICKERS.

Krypton Records: PO Box 372, Highland, MI 48357; Pres. DENNIS CYPORYN.

K-Tel International (USA) Inc: 2605 Fernbrook Lane N, Minneapolis, MN 55447-4736; Pres. & CEO MICKEY ELFENBEIN.

L&A Records: PO Box 296, 324 Godwin Ave, Midland Park, NJ 07432; Pres. TONY LOEFFLER.

LA International: PO Box 725, Daytona Beach, FL 32115-0725; Vice-Pres. CHARLES VICKERS.

Landmark Communications Group: PO Box 1444, Hendersonville, TN 37077; Pres. BILL ANDERSON JR.

Lanor Records: PO Box 233, 329 N Main St, Church Point, LA 70525; Owner LEE LAVERGNE.

Liberty Records: 3322 West End Ave, Nashville, TN 37203; Pres. JIMMY BOWEN.

Lifesong Records: PO Box 5807, Englewood, NJ 07631; tel. (201) 969-9990; fax (201) 969-9955; e-mail plcagent@aol.com; Pres. PHILIP S KURNIT.

Light Records: 1207 17th Ave S, #103, Nashville, TN 37212; Gen. Man. ROB WOOLSEY.

Loud Cry Records: PO Box 210270, Nashville, TN 37221-0270; Owner/ Pres. DON SANDERS.

Maiden Music: PO Box 777, Trevilians, VA 23170; Pres. MICHAEL D MOORE.

Mail Order Jazz: 601 Virginia Ave, Tiften, GA 31794; Owner GUS P STATIRAS.

Maison de Soul: PO Drawer 10, 238 E Main St, Ville Platte, LA 70586; Pres. FLOYD SOILEAU.

Map The Planet Records: 228 West 5th St, Kansas City, MO 64105; Project Co-ordinator JOE COMPARATO.

MCA Records: 70 Universal Plaza, Universal City, CA 91608; Chair. AL TELLER.

Mel Carter: PO Box 69646, Los Angeles, CA 90069; tel. and fax (323) 934-4122; e-mail red@mel-carter.com; internet www.mel-carter.com; Artist/ Owner LARRY KLENO.

Mercury Records: Wolrdwide Plaza, 825 8th Ave, New York, NY 10019; Pres. ED ECKSTINE.

Metal Blade Records Inc: 2345 Erringer Rd, Suite 108, Simi Valley, CA 93065; office Man./Mechanical Licensing KIM KELLY.

Mirror Records Inc: 645 Titus Ave, Rochester, NY 14617; Pres. ARMAND SCHAUBROECK.

Mobile Fidelity International: PO Box 8359, Incline Village, NV 89452-8359; Pres. & Exec. Prod. BRAD S MILLER.

Monster Music: 274 Wattis Way, South San Francisco, CA 94080; Gen. Man. THAD WHARTON.

Motown Records: 6255 W Sunset Blvd, 17th Floor, Los Angeles, CA 90028; CEO JHERYL BUSBY.

NAIL Inc: 231 Commercial St, NE, Salem, OR 97301-3411; Pres. MIKE JONES.

Planet Dallas Studios Inc: 3515 Dickason, Dallas, TX 75219; Gen. Man. DEBB ROONEY.

Platinum Gold Productions: 9200 Sunset Blvd, Suite 1220, Los Angeles, CA 90069; Partner STEVE COHEN.

Plug Productions: 273 Chippewa Dr., Columbia, SC 29210-6508; Dir JOHN MACK; Contact RON SPARKS.

Polydor/Atlas: 1416 N La Brea Ave, Los Angeles, CA 90028; Exec. Asst DEANA J SMART.

PolyGram Group: Worldwide Plaza, 825 8th Ave, New York, NY 10019; Pres. RICK DOBBIS.

PPL-MCI Entertainment Group: 10 Universal Plaza, PO Box 8442, Universal City, CA 91618; tel. (818) 506-8533; fax (818) 506-8534; e-mail pplzmi@aol.com; internet www.pplzmi.com; CEO JAESON ST JAMES JARRETT; Man. Dir MAXX DIAMOND.

Pravda Records Inc: 3823 N Southport, Chicago, IL 60613; Man. Dir KENNETH GOODMAN.

Primitech Releases: PO Box 210330, San Francisco, CA 94121; Owner/ Label Man. VICTOR KRAG.

Progressive: 1206 Decatur St, New Orleans, LA 70116; Pres. GEORGE H BUCK JR.

Projekt Records: PO Box 1591, Garden Grove, CA 92642-1591; Gen. Man. SAM.

Pulse Records: PO Box 294, Westerville, OH 43086-0294; Pres./Owner RANDY KETTERING.

Punk Metal Rock Records: PO Box 410099, San Francisco, CA 94141-0099; A & R Head STASH RAVINE.

Quango Music Group Inc: 9744 Wilshire Blvd, Suite 305, Beverly Hills, CA 90212; Pres. GEORGE GHIZ.

Rainforest Records Inc: 8855 SW Holly Lane, Suite 110, Wilsonville, OR 97070; Prod. & CEO RAY WOODS.

Rambunctious Records Inc: c/o Power, Weiss & Kurnit, LLP, 600 Madison Ave, 22nd Floor, New York, NY 10022-1615; Pres. PHILIP S KURNIT.

Randolf Productions Inc: 23181 Verdugo Dr., Suite 106, Laguna Hills, CA 92653; Pres. RANDY RAY.

Relativity Records: 187–07 Henderson Ave, Hollis, NY 11423; Pres. BARRY KORBIN.

Rhino Entertainment: 10635 Santa Monica Blvd, Los Angeles, CA 90025; Pres. RICHARD FOOS.

Rhythms Productions/Tom Thumb Music: PO Box 34485, Los Angeles, CA 90034-0485; Pres. RUTH WHITE.

Rising Son Records International: PO Box 657, Housatonic, MA 01236; Asst DAWN MITCHELL.

Rising Star Records: 52 Executive Park South, Suite 5203, Atlanta, GA 30329; Owner BARBARA TAYLOR.

Rock Dog Records: PO Box 3687, Hollywood, CA 90028; Vice-Pres. of A & R GERRY NORTH.

Rodell Records Inc: PO Box 93457, Hollywood, CA 90093; Pres. ADAM S RODELL.

Rosebud Records: 1030 Villa Pl., Nashville, TN 37212; Pres./Record Prod. FATE VANDERPOOL.

Rotten Records: PO Box 2157, Montclair, CA 91763; A & R Dir DICK SHITELMEYER.

RRRecords: 151 Paige St, Lowell, MA 01852; Owner RON.

Rustron-Whimsong Music Productions: c/o The Whimsy, 1156 Park Lane, West Palm Beach, FL 33417; tel. and fax (561) 478-8315; e-mail safehavenwpb@yahoo.com; Exec. Dir/Owner RUSTY GORDON.

Sabre Productions: PO Box 10147, San Antonio, TX 78210; Prod. E J HENKE.

Salexo Music Co: PO Box 18093, Charlotte, NC 28218-0093; Pres. SAMUEL OBIE.

Schizophonic Records: 231 Commercial St, NE, Salem, OR 97301-3411; Pres. MIKE JONES.

Scooter Records/Scootertunes Inc: PO Box 610166, Dallas, TX 75261; tel. (972) 986-5582; fax (972) 986-5582; e-mail scootune@gte.net; internet www.scootertunes.com; Pres. JANETT BELLAMY; Vice-Pres. GINA BELLAMY.

Scotti Bros Records: 2114 Pico Blvd, Santa Monica, CA 90405; Pres. MYRON ROTH.

Shiro Records Inc: 8228 Sunset Blvd, Suite 108, Los Angeles, CA 90046; Pres. SHIRO GUTZIE.

Sikio Marika Records: 6840 N Maple #157, Fresno, CA 93710; Label Head TYRONE WHITE.

Silent Records: 340 Bryant St, 3rd Floor, San Francisco, CA 94107; Pres. KIM CASCONE.

Songchild Productions: 117 Manor Circle, Myrtle Beach, SC 29575-7201; Artist PAUL SKYLAND.

Southland: 1206 Decatur St, New Orleans, LA 70116; Pres. GEORGE H BUCK JR.

Sovereign Records: 11 Manor House Dr., Dobbs Ferry, NY 10522; tel. and fax (212) 730-4848; e-mail aloftmusic@aol.com; internet www.songandstorypress.com; Pres. RUBY FISHER.

Springhollow Records: PO Box 294, Westerville, OH 43086-0294; Owner/Pres. RANDY KETTERING.

Sunset Promotions of Chicago Inc: 9359 S Kedzie Ave, Box 42807, Evergreen Park, IL 60805; tel. (773) 586-1800; fax (773) 586-1855; e-mail sunsetpromogip@inetmail.att.net; Pres. NEIL J CACCIOTTOLO.

Swallow: PO Drawer 10, 238 E Main St, Ville Platte, LA 70586; Pres. FLOYD SOILEAU.

Syntonic Research Inc: 3405 Barranos Circle, Austin, TX 78731-5711; Sales Man. MICHAEL KRON.

Tar Heel Records: PO Box 1557, West Caldwell, NJ 07007-1557; Pres. TAR HEEL PETE; Vice-Pres. TONY ANSEMS.

Tedesco Tunes: 16020 Lahey St, Granada Hills, CA 91344; Pres. DALE T TEDESCO.

Temple Productions Ltd: 310 E Chicago St, Elgin, IL 60120; Pres. CAESAR F KALINOWSKI.

Terra Nova Recording Company: 853 Broadway, #1516, New York, NY 10003; Pres. MARC KRASNOW; CEO ROBERT MANGOVLEFF.

The Eternal Song Agency: 6326 E Livingston Ave, Reynoldsburg, OH 43068; Pres. LEOPOLD XAVIER CRAWFORD.

Times Square Fantasy Theatre: 519 N Halifax Ave, Daytona Beach, FL 32118; tel. and fax (386) 252-0381; e-mail timessqfntsythtr@aol.com; internet www.timessqfantasytheatre.com; CEO BOBBY LEE CUDE.

TKO Records: 4501 Connecticut Ave, NW, Suite 905, Washington, DC 20008; CEO MICHAEL COHN.

Tranquil Technology Music: PO Box 20463, Oakland, CA 94620; Prod. MICHAEL MANTRA.

Tropicana Records: PO Box 910, Beverly Hills, CA 90213; tel. (310) 557-0534; Gen. Man. G O HERNANDEZ.

Virgin Records: 338 N Foothill Rd, Beverly Hills, CA 90210; Pres. PHIL QUARTARARO.

Vokes Music, Record & Promotion Co: PO Box 12, New Kensington, PA 15068-0012; tel. (724) 335-2775; Pres./Owner HOWARD VOKES.

Warner/Reprise/Sire Records: 3300 Warner Blvd, Burbank, CA 91510; Chair. MO OSTIN.

Woodrich Enterprises Inc: PO Box 38, Lexington, AL 35648; e-mail mernee@msn.com; Pres. WOODY RICHARDSON.

Worship & Praise Records Inc: PO Box 593, Times Sq. Station, New York, NY 10108; Pres./CEO/Exec. Prod. MINISTER MAHAROLD PEOPLES JR.

Zero Hour Records: 1600 Broadway, Number 701, New York, NY 10019; Popmeister SERGE ZERO.

Zippah Recording Studio: PO Box 1790, Brookline, MA 02146; Co-Owner/Prod. PETER WEISS.

Zomba Enterprises Inc: 137–139 W 25th St, New York, NY 10001; Sr Vice-Pres. /Gen. Man. DAVID RENZER.

Venezuela

Discorona CA: Río a Puente Soublette, Edif. Fonodisco PO Box 5995, 1010 Caracas; Pres. EVELIO CORTÉS.

Inversiones Rodven CA: Centro Comercial Concresa, 2°, Of. 422 Prado del Este, 1080 Caracas; Pres. RODOLFO RODRÍGUEZ.

Manoca Records Venezuela SA: Avda San Martin, PB Local 5–6, Resid. Metroplace, 1020 Caracas; Gen. Man. ANGELO NIGRO.

APPENDIX B: MANAGEMENT COMPANIES

Andorra

Espectacles del Principat: Ctra de l'Aldosa, Botiga 2, La Massana; Dir JOAN M ARMENGAL.

Limitada de Producciones SL: Ciutat Consuegra 12, 2°, Edif. Orió, Andorra La Vella; Admin. JOAN DELTELL PORTA.

RIAL Andorra: Avda de Tarragona 24, Andorra La Vella; tel. 860686; fax 866286; e-mail rial@andorra.ad; Man. PASCAL LAIR.

Argentina

Abraxas Producciones Internacionales: Avda Callao 875, 4° H, 1023 Buenos Aires; Dir-Gen. CARLOS PITY YÑURRIGARRO.

Argentina Producciones: Avda Corrientes 1628, 11°G, Of. B, 1042 Buenos Aires; Dir NORBERTO HORACIO BACCON.

CDN Producciones Iberoamericanas: Loyola 1530, 1414 Buenos Aires; Dir-Gen. ESTEBA MELLINO.

Data Pop Rock Comunicación: 25 de Mayo 758, 5°, Of. E, 1002 Buenos Aires; Pres. JUAN CARLOS KOHAN.

Esther M Soto Ciclo 3: Estados Unidos 629, 1101 Buenos Aires; Contact ESTHER M SOTO.

Hector Cavallero Producciones SA: Hipólito Irigoyen 1994, PB 4, 1089 Buenos Aires; Pres. FERNANDO CAVALLERO; Contact HECTOR CAVALLERO.

JC Producciones Srl: Rivadavia 86, 4°, Of. 6, 8300 Neuquen; Pres. JUAN CARLOS ALLENDE.

Juan Carlos Baglieto: Fragata Pte, Sarmiento 1663, Buenos Aires; Man. EDUARDO HAGOPIAN.

Matt Hungo Srl: Tucumán 1455, 5°, Of. A-B, 1050 Buenos Aires; Gen. Man. OMAR ALBERTO LAURIA.

Mediavilla Producciones Srl: Colombia, 1727 Valetin Alsina, 1822 Buenos Aires; Pres. OSCAR MEDIAVILLA.

Ohanian Producciones: Aguilar 2073, 1428 Buenos Aires; Dir ALBERTO OHANIAN.

Poggini & Asociados Srl: Pasteur 250, 1°, Of. C, 1028 Buenos Aires; Man. RODOLFO POGGINI.

Australia

Alan James Management: PO Box 2727, Darwin, NT 0801; fax (8) 8941-1088; e-mail yothuyindi@yothuyindi.com; internet www.yothuyindi.com; Man. ALAN JAMES.

Andrew McManus Management: Suite 1, 3 Smail St, Ultimo, NSW 2007; Man. Dir ANDREW MCMANUS.

B & S Promotions: PO Box 1481, Frankston, VIC 3199; Partners BILL DETTMER, SALLY DETTMER.

Bernie Stahl Entertainments: Parkrise, 5th Floor, 3 Alison St, Surfers Paradise, QLD 4217; Man. Dir BERNIE STAHL; Dir SUZANNE STAHL.

Cranium Management: PO Box 760, Leichhardt, NSW 2040; Man. SKIP BEAUMONT-EDMONDS.

Entertainment Plus: Gordon Pl., Suite 15/24 Little Bourke St, Melbourne, VIC 3000; Man. ANDREW MALOUF.

Feel Management & Tour Co-ordination: 2/54 Bronte Rd, Bondi Junction, NSW 2022; Dir TIM PITTMAN.

Gary Morris Management: PO Box 21, Hawks Nest, NSW 2324; e-mail oils@ozemail.com.au; internet www.midnightoil.com; Contact GARY MORRIS.

Grant Thomas Management: PO Box 176, Potts Point, NSW 2011; Principal GRANT THOMAS.

Ideal Management P/C: PO Box 1037, Caulfield North, Melbourne, VIC 3161; Man. Dir/CEO NATHAN D BRENNER.

International Management Group: 281 Clarence St, Sydney, NSW 2000; Dir of Arts & Entertainment STEPHEN FLINT WOOD.

International Profile Management: Entertainment Pl., PO Box 4, Broadway, QLD 4006; Dir DARREN CLARK.

Isaac Apel Management: 46 Caroline St, South Yarra, VIC 3141; tel. (3) 9820-9081; fax (3) 9820-5448; e-mail kj@iam.com.au; Dir KIM JACOBI.

Jaybee's Entertainment Agency: PO Box 37, Sanctuary Pl., NSW 2540; Man. NARRELL M BROWN.

Julie Hickson Management: 25 Overend St, Brunswick, VIC 3056; Man. JULIE HICKSON.

Kevin Jacobsen Management: Level 1, 98 Glebe Point Rd, Glebe, NSW 2037; Man. Dir KEVIN JACOBSEN.

Lighthouse Promotions: 1st Floor, Cherry Tree, 53 Balmain St, Sandringham VIC 3121; Dir LINDA GEBAR.

Loud & Clear Management Pty Ltd: PO Box 276, Albert Park, VIC 3206; Man. Dir MICHAEL ROBERTS.

Management Only: PO Box 1289, North Sydney, NSW 2059; Man. Dir GARY GRANT.

Mark Bishop Management Pty Ltd: PO Box 123, Kensington, VIC 3031; Man. MARK BISHOP.

McLean's Artist Management: Suite 8, 4 Jacques Ave, Bondi Beach, NSW 2026; Man. Dir CALUM MCLEAN.

Melke (Artist Representation & Media Co-ordination): 158 Raglan St, Mosman, Sydney, NSW 2088; Dir SUE MELKE.

Melody Management: PO Box 598, Coogee, NSW 2034; Dirs MICHAEL MCMARTIN, ELIZABETH MCMARTIN.

MGM (Michael Gudinski Management): 9 Dundas Lane, Albert Park, VIC 3206; Man. Dir MICHAEL GUDINSKI.

Michael Long Management: PO Box 494, Double Bay, NSW 2028; Man. MICHAEL LONG.

Mighty Management: 21 Castle St, Randwick, Sydney, NSW 2031; Man. MICK MAZZONE.

MMA Management International: 351 Crown St, Surry Hills, NSW 2010; Man. SAM EVANS.

Mr Walker's Company: PO Box 2197, St Kilda, VIC 3182; Contact ANDREW WALKER.

Oz Artist Management: PO Box 4074, Doncaster Heights, VIC 3109; Man. JOHN PEROSA.

Oz-X-Press Music: 400 North Rocks Rd, Carlingford, NSW 2118; Man. TRUDI NICHOLLS.

Painters & Dockers Management: PO Box 69, Burnley, Melbourne, VIC 3121; Man. COLIN BUCKLER.

Paisley Management: PO Box 2227, Rose Bay North, NSW 2030; Man. Dir KENT PAISLEY.

Paul Cussen Management: Suite 1, Level 2, 41 Oxford St, Darlinghurst, NSW 2010; Proprietor PAUL CUSSEN.

Peter Rix Management Pty Ltd: PO Box 957, Crows Nest, NSW 1585; tel. (2) 9966-5511; fax (2) 9966-5444; e-mail info@rixman.com.au; Man. Dir PETER RIX.

Phill Shute Management Pty Ltd: PO Box 273, Dulwich Hill, NSW 2203; Man. Dir PHILL SHUTE.

Ralph Carr Management: c/o RCM International Group, 29 Balmain St, Richmond, VIC 1321; Man. Dir RALPH CARR.

Richard East Management Pty Ltd: 20 Leila St, Prahran, VIC 3181; Man. Dir RICHARD EAST.

Russell J White Management: PO Box 325, South Melbourne, VIC 3205; Man. Dir RUSSELL WHITE.

Servant Communications: PO Box 2020, Launceston, Tasmania 7250; Pres. KEVIN N HOOPER.

Smartartists Management: PO Box 2093, St Kilda West, VIC 3182; Man. MICHAEL LYNCH.

Talentworks Pty Ltd: Suite 1A, 663 Victoria St, Abbotsford, VIC 3067; tel. (3) 9429-6933; fax (3) 9428-7433; e-mail mail@talentworks.com.au; Man. Dir GLENN WHEATLEY.

Terry Blamey Management: 329 Monatgue St, Albert Park, VIC 3206; Dir TERRY BLAMEY.

The Neil Clugston Organization: PO Box 387, Glebe, NSW 2037; tel. (2) 9552-3277; fax (2) 9552-3713; e-mail neil@nco.com.au; internet www.nco.com.au; Man. Dir NEIL CLUGSON.

Vicki Watson Management: PO Box 9, Balmain, Sydney, NSW 2041; Dir VICKI WATSON.

Woodruff Management: 128 Bourke St, Woolloomooloo, NSW 2011; Dir JOHN WOODRUFF.

WPA Management: 1st Floor, 411 George St, Fitzroy, VIC 3065; Gen. Man. PETULA BIER.

Yothu Yindi Music Pty Ltd: PO Box 2727, Darwin, NT 0801; fax (8) 8941-1088; e-mail yothuyindi@yothuyindi.com; internet www.yothuyindi.com; Man. ALAN JAMES.

Austria

FF Arts and Media Consultants: Kienmayergasse 47, 1140 Vienna; tel. (1) 923-990-230; fax (1) 923-990-211; e-mail harald.buechel@aon.at; Man. Dir HARALD TH BUECHEL.

Georg Leitner Productions: Hütteldorfstr 259/14, 1140 Vienna; Proprietor GEORG LEITNER.

Hämmerle Barbara & Werner: Harderstr 14, 6972 Fussach; Man. Dirs BARBARA HÄMMERLE, WERNER HÄMMERLE.

Milica: Liebhartstalstr 15/5, 1160 Vienna; Contact MILICA.

RATZ Promotions: Vorachstr 65, 6890 Lustenau; Contact THOMAS RADOVAN.

RGG Management: Favoritstr 52.2.6.18, 1100 Vienna; Man. PETER STEINBACH.

Rock Promotion: Hietzinger Hauptstr 36A, 1130 Vienna; Contact PETER FRÖSTL.

Stein Music Wien: Bernardgasse 39/33, 1070 Vienna; Man. Dir REGINE STEINMETZ.

WOM: PO Box 20, 3105 St Pölten; Contact ALBIN WEGERBAUER.

Belgium

Aril Private Studio: rue de Coron 1, 7040 Bougnies; Man. Dir MARYLIN LELEU.

ARS Management: Singel 5, 2550 Kontich; Man. Dir PATRICK BUSSCHOTS.

Baard & Kale: Brederodestraat 40, 2018 Antwerp; Man. Dir BOB CAMPENAERTS.

Backline: Kammerstraat 19, 9000 Ghent; Man. ROBERT VAN YPER; Bookings Agents SANDRA HEYLEN, LAWRENCE VAN DEN EEDE.

Commedia VZW: Fonteinstraat 19, 8000 Bruges; Man. Dir CHERRY DERYOKE.

Foundation VZW: Fruithoflaan 124, PO Box 11, 2600 Berchem/Antwerp; Dirs PETER VERSTRAEVEN, BERT VAN ROY.

Klepto Management: Leuvensesteenweg 54, 3080 Tervuren; Man. Dir WILFRIED BRITS.

Kras Artists: Leernsesteenweg 168, 9800 Deinze; Dir JEAN TANT.

L&S Agency: PO Box 5, 3800 Sint-Truiden 2; tel. 11671701; fax 11673331; e-mail lsagency@belgacom.net; internet www.lsagency.be; Man. Dir MARK STRAUVEN.

Merlijn: Gulden Vlieslaan 67, 8000 Brugge; Contact NICO A MERTENS.

Music BaM: Lelielaan 11, 2460 Lichtaart; Man. Dir GERT VAN DINGENEN; Asst Man. Dir TOM VAN DINGENEN.

Paperwork: Aarschotsesteenweg 245, 3012 Wilsele; Man. JOHAN P BERCKMANS.

Pyramid International Music: Lepelhoekstraat 26, 9100 Sint-Niklaas; tel. (3) 778-1854; fax (3) 766-8441; e-mail marc@marcdecoen.be; internet www.marcdecoen.be; Man. Dir MARC DE COEN.

Swing Promotions: Beukenlaan 3, 2970 Schilde; Man. WIM GROOS.

Team for Action (T4A): Ave Oscar van Goibtsnoven 45B, 1180 Brussels; Man. Dir CLAUDE MARTIN.

Tempo (Top Entertainment Editions): Krijgslaan 61, 9000 Gent; Gen. Man. LUC STANDAERT.

Tour de Force: rue des Archers 19–21, 1080 Brussels; Man. Dir TON VAN DRAANEN.

TTT: Vriesenhof 22/5, 3000 Leuven; Mans RICK TUBBAX, JOHAN P BERCKMANS.

UBU: rue Van Obberghen 92, 1140 Brussels; Dir PATRICK DUBUCQ.

Western Productions: Kammerstraat 19, 9000 Ghent; Man. ROBERT VAN YPER.

Bolivia

Chelo Music: Tarbo, 118 Santa Cruz, Santa Cruz De La Sierra; Dir SERGIO SERRALE JUSTINIANO.

HR Producciones: Loayza 349, 15°, Dpto 1503, Edifico Loayza, La Paz; Gen. Man. NESTOR HORACIO RASGIDO.

Brazil

Carlindo Soares Promoçoes Artisticas: Rua Castro Menezes 51, Rio de Janiero, RJ; Contact CARLINDO SOARES.

Fred Rossi Eventos e Produçoes: Rua Augusta 2516, Cj 121 Cerqueira César, 01412 100 São Paulo, SP; Dir FRED ROSSI.

MR Comunicaçao Produçao Ltda: PO Box 16692, 03197-970, São Paulo, SP; Dir MÁRIO RONCO.

Bulgaria

Berti: 14 A Skobelevska str, 5300 Gabrovo; Man. Dir PLAMEN TOLEV.

Factor TC: 2 Krakra str, 1504 Sofia; Man. Dir VESELIN TODOROV.

Mega Music Ltd: 2 Trapezitza str, 1000 Sofia; Man. Dir DORA TCHERNKVA.

New Music Agency: Nadejda Bl 634, Apt 14, 1231 Sofia; tel. 9825-6509; fax 2934-4297; e-mail christ@newmusic.bg; internet www.newmusic.bg; Pres. CHRISTO ROUSSANOV.

Canada

Amok Artist Agency: Suite 202, 243 Main St East, Milton, ON L9T 1P1; Contact LORENZ EPPINGER.

Artistic Canadian Entertainers Management Association: 4544 Dufferin St #24, Downsview, ON M3H 5X2; Pres./Consultant RAYMOND A SARE.

Balmur Ltd: 2400–4950 Yonge St, Toronto, ON M2N 6K1; Contact TINTI MOFFAT.

Bamford Group: 14 Sumach St, Toronto, ON M5A 1J4; Pres. JOE BAMFORD.

Brass Ring Productions/Manford Music Inc: PO Box 1266 Station A, Kelowna, BC V1Y 7V8; tel. and fax (250) 763-5502; e-mail manford@telus.net; Pres. BECKY CHAPMAN.

Bruce Allen Talent: 406–68 Water St, Vancouver, BC V6B 1A4; Contact KIM BLAKE.

Current/Rage Records and Management: 4 Bowden St, Toronto, ON M4K 2X2; Pres. GERRY YOUNG.

Donna Kay Music Inc: Ministikwan Lake, PO Box 451, Pierceland, SK S0M 2K0; Contact PAUL S POSPISIL.

Double A Productions: 64 Desbrisay Dr., Bridgewater, NS B4V 3H6; Man. KEN ALEXANDER.

Early Morning Productions: 1365 Yonge St #207, Toronto, ON M4T 2P7; Contact BARRY HARVEY.

Feeling Productions Inc: 500–4 Pl. Laval, Laval, QC H7N 5Y3; Man. RENE ANGELIL.

Finkelstein Management Company Ltd: 301–151 John St, Toronto, ON M5V 2T2; Contact J LANGUEDOC.

Forte Records and Productions Inc: 320 Spadina Rd, Toronto, ON M5R 2V6; Contact DAWNA ZEEMAN.

Gino Empry Entertainment: 315–120 Carlton St, Toronto, ON M5A 4K2; Owner GINO EMPRY.

Ground Swell Productions: 1725 Barrington St, Halifax, NS B3J 2N7; Pres. IAN MCKINNON.

Jones & Co: 1819 Granville St, 4th Floor, Halifax, NS B3J 3R1; Pres. SHERI JONES.

Latitude 45/Arts Promotion Inc: 109 St Joseph Blvd West, Montréal, QC H2T 2P7.

Lazy J Management: PO Box 8085, Saskatoon, SK S7K 4R7; tel. (306) 955-4976; fax (306) 955-4978; e-mail info@oiem.net; internet www.oiem.net; Man. LOUIS O'REILLY.

LCDM Entertainment: 1995 Weston Rd, Box 79564, Weston, ON M9N 3W9; Prod./Artist/Writer L C DI MARCO.

Lou Blair Management Inc: 407–68 Water St, Vancouver, BC V6B 1A4; Contact LOU BLAIR.

Management Trust Ltd: 219 Dufferin St, Suite 309B, Toronto, ON M6K 3J1; Contact SARAH BARKER-TONGE.

Mary Bailey Management: PO Box 546, 4 Al Wende Ave, ON P2N 3J5; Pres. MARY BAILEY.

Pandyamonium/William Tenn Artist Management: 67 Mowat #431, Toronto, ON M6K 3E3; Contact SANDY PANDYA, WILLIAM TENN.

Paquin Entertainment Group: 1067 Sherwin Rd, Winnipeg, MB R3H 0T8; Pres. GILLES PAQUIN.

Popas Management Corp (PMC): 1407 Mount Pleasant Rd, Toronto, ON M4N 2T9; Man. STEVE PROPAS.

Pro Arts Management: Suite 3, 3611 Mavis Rd, Mississauga, ON L5C 1T7; Contact GIL MOORE.

Productions Martin Leclerc Inc: 2220 rue Notre-Dame Ouest, Suite 201, Montréal, QC H3J 2V4; Man. MARTIN LECLERC.

Quinlan Road Ltd: PO Box 933, Stratford, ON N5A 7M3; Controller BILL BRUCE; Contact LOREENA MCKENNITT.

Radius International: PO Box 81, 260 Adelaide St E, Toronto, ON M5A 1N1; tel. (416) 979-5822; fax (416) 979-9886; e-mail radius@interlog.com; Gen. Man. BOB STEVENS; artistic management; music festival consultant.

Regal Recordings Ltd: 2421 Hammond Rd, Mississauga, ON L5K 1T3; Vice-Pres. DOREEN M DAVEY.

Robert Luhtala Management: 869 Broadview Ave, Toronto, ON M4K 4P9; Man. ROBERT LUHTALA.

Savannah Music Inc: 123 Applefield Dr., Scarborough, ON M1P 3Y5; Dir of Canadian Operations BILL CARRUTHERS.

SEG Productions: 3611 Mavis Rd, Mississauga, ON L5C 1T7; Contact CLIFF HUNT.

Showcana Corporation: PO Box #4689, Station C, Calgary, AB T2T 5P1; Pres. ROBERT JAMES CHIN.

SL Feldman & Associates: 1505 W 2nd Ave, Suite 200, Vancouver, BC V6H 3Y4; tel. (604) 734-5945; fax (604) 732-0922; e-mail feldman@slfa.com; internet www.slfa.com; Proprietor SAM L FELDMAN; Sr Vice-Pres. SHAW SALTZBERG.

SRO Management: 189 Carlton St, Toronto, ON M5A 2K7; Contact BOB ROPER.

Star Rise International: 6263 28th Ave, Rosemont, Montréal, QC H1T 3H8; Talent Search/Man. FADEL CHIDIAC.

Swell Music Inc: 46 Mitchell Ave, Toronto, ON M6J 1B9; Contact JEFF ROGERS, SANDY ROGERS.

TKO Entertainment Corp: 1406-1288 Alberni St, Vancouver, BC V5J 3L2; tel. (604) 331-0110; fax (604) 331-0109; Contact PETER KARROLL.

United Artist Productions Worldwide: 224 Beaverbrook St, Winnipeg, MB R3N 1M8; Contact WARREN BROWN.

Val Haas: Suite 1002, 5 Rowntree Rd, Etobicoke, ON M9V 5G9; Man. VAL HAAS.

Vocal Image Productions: 192 Kensington Rd, Charlottetown, PEI C1A 7S3; Man. BERNI WOOD.

Ways and Means Committee: 1971 Sprice Hill Rd, Pickering, ON L1V 1S6; Contact MICHAEL WHITE.

William Seip Management: 1615 Highland Rd, Kitchener, ON N2G 3W5; Contact WILLIAM SEIP.

Chile

Calipso: Thompson 3450, Estación Central, Santiago; Man. HUGO ASCUETA NORAMBUENA.

Galo Producciones: Alameda 171, Of. 807, Santiago; Gen. Man. ALFREDO SAINT-JEAN.

Producciones Macondo Chile Ltda: Alvarez 58 L-6, Viña Del Mar; Man. ALFREDO TRONCOSO.

Providencia Television: Pedro de Valivia 3128 Nuñoa, Santiago; Exec. Dir LUIS VENEGAS.

Ricardo Suarez Daud Y Cia Ltda: La Concepción 81, Of. 405, Providencia, Santiago; Man. RICARDO SUÁREZ DAUD.

Romero & Campbell Producciones: Bombero Nuñez, 385 Barrio Bellavista, Santiago; Dir CARMEN ROMERO QUERO.

China (Taiwan)

Formosa Artist Management: 11F, 215 Fu-Hsin South Rd Sec. 1, Taipei; Gen. Man. CARLOS YUNG-HUI LEE.

Croatia

Crno Bijeli Svijet: Avenija Marina Drzica BB, 41000 Zagreb; Man. Dir BRANKO PAIC.

Music Time: Petreticev Trg 4, 41000 Zagreb; Man. Dir BRANKO KNEZEVIC.

Suput DOO: Novska 41, 41000 Zagreb; Man. Dir BORIS SUPUT.

Tutico: Veprinacka 16, 10000 Zagreb; Dir ZRINKO TUTIC.

Cuba

Agencia Promusic: Avda 3, 1008, Entre 10 y 12 Miramar, 11300 Municipio Playa, Havana; Dir-Gen. JULIO BALLESTER GUZMÁN.

Oficina de Pablo Lilanes: Calle 11, 257 Entre J y I Vedado, Havana; Dir-Gen. ORLANDO HECAHVARRÍA.

Denmark

Buks Booking International: Gunløgsgade 15, 2300 Copenhagen; Dir THOMAS H HANSEN.

Hanne Wilhelm Hansen: Gothersgade 11, 1123 Copenhagen K; Contact HANNE WILHELM HANSEN.

JP Management: Jernbanevej 22, 8660 Skanderborg; Man. Dir J P ANDERSEN.

Mega Scandinavia A/S: Indiakaj 1, 2100 Copenhagen Ø; Vice-Pres. CAI LEITNER; Dir of A & R and Marketing JESPER BAN.

PDH Dansk Musik Formidling: Ny Vestergade 7, 1471 Copenhagen K; Personal Man. OLE DREYER.

TG Management: Badehusvej 1, 9000 Aalborg; Man. JOHN AAGAARD.

Wennick Management: Linnesgade 14A, 1361 Copenhagen K; Man. Dir KJELD WENNICK.

The Dominican Republic

July Mateo Y Associates: Jos Coluene, 10 Alma Rosa, Santo Domingo; Contact JULY MATEO.

Televisa Talents SA: Lea de Castro, 153 Gazcue, Santo Domingo; Dir-Gen. LUIS MEDRANO.

Estonia

Eesti Kontsert: Estonia pst 4, 0001 Tallinn; Dir E MATTISEN.

Estonian Jazz Foundation: PO Box 3641, Viru str 16, 0090 Tallinn; Dir TIIT LAUK.

Makaroy Muusik Management: Regati PST 1–6K, 0019 Tallinn; Man. MARTTI KITSING.

Finland

NEM: PO Box 220, 33201 Tampere; Man. Dir HARRI KARVINEN.

Piikkikasvi Agency: PO Box 145, 00531 Helsinki; Man. Dir KARI PÖSSI.

Rockadillo: PO Box 35, 33201 Tampere; Man. Dir TAPIO KORJUS.

France

3 Comm: 16 Bis rue d'Odessa, 75014 Paris; Dir JEAN-PIERRE LENOIR.

Africa Music International: 15 rue Charles Gounod, 56100 Lorient; tel. and fax 2 97 83 38 75; Vice-Chair. & Sec. GAËLLA TONJÉ-TONJÉ.

Agence Kathoche: 16 rue de Marignan, 75008 Paris; Agent/Dir CATHERINE POENSIN.

Agence Sylvie Dupuy: 27 rue Auguste Delaune, 94800 Villejuif; Man. SYLVIE DUPUY.

Alpha Bravo: 64 Ave Jean Jaurès, 93500 Pantin; Contact DANIEL BORNET.

Bistro Production: 31 rue St Sébastien, 75011 Paris; Man. PATRICE ESKENAZY.

Corida: 120 Blvd, Rochechojart, 75018 Paris; Man. ASSAAD DEBS.

Daniel Bornet Management: 64 Ave Jean Jaurès, 93500 Pantin; Dir DANIEL BORNET.

Do Si La Ba: 159 Chemin Lanussc, 31200 Toulouse; Man. LAWRENCE LARROUY.

Etienne Vanke: 94 Blvd Chaumin, 49000 Angers; Contact ETIENNE VANKE.

Fiesta Latina Homero Cardoso: 51 rue Mirabeau, 94200 Ivry Sur Seine; Promoter HOMERO CARDOSO.

Gafaiti Production: 3 rue de la Haie du Coq, 93300 Aubervilliers; Man. NOURREDINE GAFAITI.

Genevieve Peygrene: 62 rue des Rondeaux, 75020 Paris; Dir GENEVIEVE PEYGRENE.

Infernal: 102 Blvd Henri Barbusse, 93100 Montreuil; Man. LAURENT LEFEBVRE.

IPS Management: 11/13 rue Montlouis, 75001 Paris; Man. ANDRÉ GNIMAGNON.

Le Haut de L'Affiche: 2 Bis rue Hiche, 94130 Nogent Sur Marne; Chair. CLAUDE ABIHSSIRA.

Made In Heaven: 6 rue Rémy de Gourmont, 75019 Paris; Label Man. MATHIAS JEANNIN.

Marouani, Charley and Maurice: 37 rue Marbeuf, 75008 Paris; Mans CHARLEY MAROUANI, MAURICE MAROUANI.

Martine Palmé Management: 33 Bis rue Doudeauville, 75018 Paris; Artist Man. MARTINE PALMÉ.

Meyer Productions: 10 rue de L'Isly, 75008 Paris; Mans OLIVIA MEYER, CHRISTIAN MEYER.

Mondial Management: 64 Bis rue de Paris, 93230 Romainville; Mans GEORGES LANCRY, LISETTE OBYDOL.

Musicomedia: 21 Ave d'Italie, 75013 Paris; Man. GLADYS GABISON.

RA Production: 471 Ave Victor Hugo, 26000 Valence; Man. FRÉDÉRIC LOISON.

Robert Bialek Conseils: 33 rue des Jeuneurs, 75002 Paris; Contact ROBERT BIALEK.

Salam Aleikum Amusements: 2 rue Carpeaux, 75018 Paris; Dir STEPHANE BENHAMOU.

Sixieme Sens: 2 rue du Chemin Vert, 14000 Caen; Contact JEAN MICHEL LEBIGOT.

Talent Sorcier Productions: Parc d'Activité Activa, rue de la Batterie, 67400 Geispolsheim/Strasbourg; Man. RICHARD WALTER.

Tourrillon Sarl: 1/233 rue Barberaisse, 59000 Lille; Agent XAVIER COLLIN.

Utopia Spectacles: 1 rue Niece, 75014 Paris; Dir JACQUES FICHELLE.

VMA: 40 rue François 1er, 75008 Paris; Dir ROSE LEANDRI.

XIII Bis Music Group: 34 rue Eugene Flachat, 75017 Paris; Man. Dir LAURENT DREUX-LEBLANC; Music Dir BRIAN RAWLING.

Germany

Blue Star Promotion Konzertagentur GmbH: Goebenstr 3, 28209 Bremen; Public Relations MICHAEL K GRUSCHE.

Castor Promotions: Dragonerstr 21, 30163 Hanover; Contact ELKE FLEING.

Commissioned Music: Hauptstr 30, 10827 Berlin; tel. (30) 280-7095; e-mail info@blixa-bargeld.com; internet www.blitza-bargeld.com; Man. Dir BLIXA BARGELD.

Double Trouble: Haupstr 30, 10437 Berlin; Man. Dir PETRA HAMMERER.

Falkland Musik Management: Herderstr 16, 44147 Dortmund; Man. Dir THOMAS FALKE.

Freestyle eV: Morgensternsweg 7, 22305 Hamburg; Contact HELMUT HEUER; Music festival and event organisers.

Fun Factory! GmbH: Hermannstadtweg 9, 48151 Münster; Marketing Asst CLAUDIA WEILER.

Kick Musikverlag: Burgunder str 8, 50677 Cologne; Man. Dir GOETZ ELBERTZHAGEN; International Man. LYNDA HILL.

Künstlersekretariat Ott: Moltkestr 18, 79098 Freiburg; Contact DIETER OTT.

Line Up Co: Linden str 52, 50674 Cologne Centrum.

Meduse Live Events: Karlsruher Ring 1A, 76297 Stutensee; tel. (7249) 94650; fax (7249) 952199; e-mail info@medusa-online.de; internet www.medusa-online.de; Contact REINHARD NEROTH.

Music Arts Network: Fichtestr 16, 60316 Frankfurt; Gen. Man. ROBERT LYNG.

Paradise Management International: PO Box 2180, 63243 Neu-Isenburg; Man. Dir RALF KLUG.

Partysanen Music: Skalitzer str 68, 10997 Berlin; Man. Dir ROMA CASLEY.

Playtime Management: Weidengasse 56, 50668 Cologne; Chair. JOCHEN SPERBER.

Rudy Holzhauer Management: Bramfelder Chaussee 238C, 22177 Hamburg; Artist Man. RUDY HOLZHAUER.

That's Entertainment!: Orleanstr 76, 31135 Hildesheim; Man. Dirs FELIX ALMSTADT, JOACHIM FRIEDMANN.

Thomann Künstler Management GmbH: PO Box 1, 96136 Burgebrach; tel. (9546) 9449; fax (9546) 6844; e-mail info@thomann-music.de; internet www.thomann-music.de; Contact JOSEPH THOMANN.

Triple M Management: Schaefflerstr 5, 80333 Munich; Man. Dir MARIO MENDRYCKI.

Greece

Neo Revma: 8 Ainianos str, 10434 Athens; Man. Dir DIMITRIS HELMIS.

Rock Management: PO Box 21526, 55236 Panorama, Thessaloniki; Man. Dir CHRISTOS TERZIDES.

Show Productions: 318 Sygrou Ave, 17673 Kalithea, Athens; Man. Dir KONSTANTINOS ARVANITIS; Public Relations ANTA ARVANTI.

Hong Kong

Aural Fidelity: 3B Cambridge Villa, 8–10 Chancery Lane, Central Hong Kong; Man. Dir JOHN POWTER.

Paciwood Music and Entertainment Ltd: 8 King Tung St, Hammer Hill Rd, Ngau Chi Wan, Kowloon.

Spraylot Music Ltd: Suite A, 15th Floor, Ritz Plaza, 122 Austin Rd, Tsim Sha Tsui, Kowloon; Publishing Exec. PEGGY YU.

Hungary

OB Art Management/Alt Product: PO Box 76, 5002 Szolnok; Man. Dir BELA PAP.

Iceland

Bo Haldorson Productions: PO Box 5445, Pverholt 26, 105 Reykjavík; Man. Dir BO HALDORSON.

Spor HF: Nýbýlavegur 4, PO Box 320, 202 Kópavogur; Man. Dir STEINAR BERG ISLEIFSSON.

Ireland

Bluemedia Ltd: 7 Willow Cres., Riverbank, Anacotty, Limerick; tel. (61) 331276; fax (61) 331277; e-mail bluemedia@eircom.net; internet www.bluemedia.ie; Man. Dir JOE CLARKE.

Brian Molloy: 5–6 Lombard St East, Dublin 2; Contact BRIAN MOLLOY; Marketing Man. GRAHAM MOLLOY.

Connie Lynch: 11 Stockton Green, Castleknock, Dublin 15; Man. CONNIE LYNCH.

Dabble Music: The Elms, Richmond Ave South, Dartry, Dublin 6; CEO PETER BLACKBYRNE.

Denis Desmond Promotions: Top House, Clontarf St, Cork 1; Man. Dir DENIS DESMOND.

Elite Music Management: Oakdale, Roscrea Rd, Templemore, Co Tipperary; Man. TONY O'TOOLE.

Excellent Management: 137 Carrigwood, Firhouse, Dublin 24; Dir NEIL O'SHEA.

Fifty-Seventh Street Ltd: 24 Upper Mount St, Dublin 2; Contacts MAURICE CASSIDY, ELIZABETH REEVES.

HARMONY Music Management Ltd: The Grange, Carbury, Co Kildare; tel. (405) 53005; fax (405) 53224; e-mail infocus@eircom.net; internet www.infocus.ie; Man. Dir JOHN H PICKERING.

Icebreaker Promotions: Emyvale, Co Monaghan; Contact PJ MCKENNA.

Joe McFadden Promotions: 19 Stockton Green, Castleknock, Dublin 15; Man. Dir JOE MCFADDEN.

Mister T Productions: 141 Parnell St, Dublin 1; tel. and fax (1) 878-7623; e-mail mistert@ireland.com; Dir TONIE WALSH.

Muchwood Management: 1 Killiney Court, Seafield Rd, Killiney, Co Dublin; Man. DAVID O'REILLY.

Pat Egan Sound Ltd: Merchant's Court, 24 Merchant's Quay, Dublin 8; Man. Dir PAT EGAN.

Principle Management: 30–32 Sir John Rogerson's Quay, Dublin 2; tel. (1) 677-7330; fax (1) 677-7276; Man. Dir PAUL MCGUINNESS; Contact Sheila Roche.

Real Good Management Ltd: 17 Dame Court, Dublin 2; Dir GERARD KEENAN.

RSE Promotions: 11–13 Station Rd, Raheny, Dublin 5; Dir RAYMOND J SMYTH.

Ryan Management: 6 Danieli Dr., Artane, Dublin 5; Mans NICKY RYAN, ROMA RYAN.

TTMAR: Rear 22 St Stephens Green, Dublin 2; Man. Dir DERMOT MCEVOY.

Underscore Management: Pellestown House, Ashtown Gate, Ashtown, Dublin 15; Man. COLUMB FARRELLY.

Upfront Management: 4 Windmill Lane, Dublin 2; Man. Dir DAVID KAVANAGH.

Westland Entertainment: 35 Westland Sq., Dublin 2; Contact LUCY MCCOLGAN.

Whirling Music Agency: Cairns Hill, Aughamore, Co Sligo; Man. BRIAN MCDONAGH.

Italy

Arci Pisa: Borgo Stretto 72, 56100 Pisa; Man. Dir NICOLA ZACCARDI.

Casi Umani: Piazza Luigi di Savoia 28, 20124 Milan; Man. Dir MARCO CONFORTI.

City Medial Two: Via Premuda 30, 42100 Reggio Emilia; Man. Dir ROBERTO MEGLIOLI.

Dell'Amore Management: Via Zeffirino Re 2, 47023 Cesena; Art Dir FRANCO DELL'AMORE.

Duende Management: Via Vanchiglia 9, 10124 Turin; Man. ETTORE CARETTE.

Giancarlo Passarella: PO Box 86, 50018 Scandicci, Florence; Contact GIANCARLO PASSARELLA.

IRA Transeuropa Management: Via Landucci 38, 50100 Florence; Man. Dir ANNE-MARIE POURCET.

Lion Snc: Via Goldoni 42/A, 30174 Mestre, Venezia; Gen. Man. LUCIANO TREVISAN.

Massimo Maggioni Management: Villoresi 24, 20143 Milan; Man. MASSIMO MAGGIONI.

Mela Di Odessa: Via Gioberti 119, 58015 Orbetello (Grosseto); Man. Dir LORA PALMERINI.

Soggiorno Obbligato Management: Via Delle Viole 17, Vialfiorta, 37020 S, Maria di Negrar (VR); Man. Dir DIEGO ALVERA.

Vitola Dino Management: Via I, Goiran 8, 00195 Rome; Man. Dir LEONARDO VITOLA.

Vu Balle' Vu Management: Via Andreini 2, 40126 Bologna; Man. Dir GIOVANNI VINCI.

Japan

International Management Group: 4th Floor, Moto-Akasaka Kikutei Bldg, 7–18 Moto Akasaka 1-Chome, Minato-ku, Tokyo 107; Contact KAZUO KONDO.

Seven Gods Productions: Suite 403, Mejidori Bldg, 2-3-21 Kabukicho Shimjulou-lou, Tokyo 160-0021; tel. (3) 5292-5551; fax (3) 5292-5552; e-mail benten@jk9.so-net.no.jp; internet www.sister.co.jp; Pres. HIROSHI ASADA.

Shinko Music Publishing Co Ltd: 2–1 Ogawamachi, Kanda, Chiyoda-ku, Tokyo 101; Pres. SHOICHI KUSANO.

Malaysia

Public Performance (Malaysia): 2nd Floor, Wisma Hiap Lee, Jln Segambut, Kuala Lumpur 51200; tel. (3) 6252-5588; fax (3) 6252-1818; e-mail nftan@ppm.org.my; internet www.ppm.org.my; CEO TAN NGIAP FOO.

Mexico

AG Ediciones Musicales SA: Peter 117, Col. Narvate, 03020 México, DF; Man. GERADO FOJO.

Arrabal y Compañía SA: Insurgentes Sur 2388, 5° San Angle, 01000 México, DF; Contact FELIPE VEGA PUENTES.

Organización Latino Internacional: Avda Insurgentes Sur 953-202, Col. Nápoles, 03810 México, DF; Dir-Gen. TONY MÉNDEZ.

Producciones Enrique Guzmán SA: Avda San Bernabé 781, Col. San Jerónimo, 10200 México, DF; Pres. ENRIQUE GUZMÁN.

Producciones Música y Equipos SC: Manuel Acuña 3359-B, Fracc, Monraz Guadalajara, 44670 Jalisco; tel. (33) 3642-6511; fax (33) 642-5360; e-mail roxanadrexel@megared.net.mx; internet www.mana.com.mx; Man. J ULISES CALLEROS RAMOS.

Promesa: Camino a Santa Teresa, 13 Toresa 5-1804, 14110 México, DF; Dir-Gen. IGNACIO RODRÍGUEZ MARTÍNEZ.

RAC Producciones SA: Sierra Gorda 30, 11010 México, DF; tel. (55) 5202-1313; fax (55) 5202-1980; Dir-Gen. ALEJANDRO GARZA.

The Netherlands

ACT: Van Leeuwenhoeksingel 69, 2611 AE Delft; Contact A C RAVEN.

Hans Van Pol Management BV: Utrechtseweg 3g B, 1301 GS Weesp; Pres. HANS W VAN POL.

Home Management: Faas Eliaslaan 13, 3742 AR Baarn; Mans ERIC VAN EERDENBURG, GEERT VAN ITALLIE.

JB Management: Boterstraat 73, 3082 SP Schiedam; Man. Dir JAN BEUNK, RIEN RIETVELD.

Mega Management: PO Box 9242, 1006 AE Amsterdam.

Mojo Management: PO Box 3121, 2601 DC Delft; Man. Dir PAUL VAN MELIS.

Moonshine Management: Langeweid 7, 1831 BL Koedyk; tel. and fax (72) 561-5857; e-mail wilbrink@yahoo.com; internet www.moonshine-management.com; Pres. EVERT WILBRINK.

Music World Management: PO Box 55 55 9, 1007 NB Amsterdam; Man. Dir PAUL COOPS.

Ray Derkzen: Zoutstraat 2, 5612 HW Eindhoven; Man. Dir RAY DERKZEN.

Supersonic Management: PO Box 339, 3500 AH Utrecht; Man. LIZET HOBEYN.

VIP Promotions: Looievsgracht 38, 1016 VS Amsterdam; PD G BEZUIJEN.

New Zealand

Jude Walcott Management: PO Box 55, Paekakariki, Kapiti Coast; Contact JUDE WALCOTT.

McCook Management: 7 Verel St, 2001 Hamilton; Man. Dir JEANNIE MCCOOK.

Showcase Management Ltd: 140 Vanguard St, Nelson; Dir MIKE DUFFIELD.

Spasim Music Management: PO Box 2901, Christchurch; Contacts JEFF SIM, KAREN NEILL.

Spirit Management: Lister Bldg, 9 Victoria St East, Auckland; Man. DANIEL KEIGHLEY.

York Street Management: PO Box 6884, Wellesley St, Auckland; Contact TANYA MOORE.

Norway

Continental AS: PO Box 110, Smestad, 0309 Oslo; tel. 2206-2770; fax 2206-2771; internet www.continentalmusic.net; Man. Dir BARRY MATHESON.

dbut internautics: PO Box 9415 Valerenga, 0610 Oslo; Dir PER PLATOW.

Groovy Management: PO Box 1291, 5001 Bergen; Man. Dir TORFINN ANDERSEN.

Ha-Ha Management: Mandalsgt. 5, 0190 Oslo; Man. Dir HAAVARD HANSTEEN.

Petter Sandberg A/S: Cort Adelersgt 2, 0254 Oslo; Contact JAN SOLLIEN.

Rage Management: PO Box 4721, 0506 Oslo; Man. Dir TORD NAESS.

Ramalama Management and Productions: Bispegt 12, 0191 Oslo; Man. Dir STEINAR VIKAN.

Stageway Management AS: Skuteviksboder 11, 5035 Bergen-Sandviken; Man. WOLL STEINAR.

TS Artist Byra: PO Box 1683, 7002 Trondheim; Man. Dir TERJE STORLI.

Viggo Lund Management: Akersgt. 7, 0158 Oslo; Man. Dir VIGGO LUND.

Wildlife Productions: Ammerudhellinga 74, 0959 Oslo; Man. Dir OYVIND BORGSO.

Peru

Acordes EIRL: Los Paujiles 285 D, Lima 34; Proprietor JULIE FREUNDT LÓPEZ.

Mapa Producciones SA: Jr. Mayta Capac 1380, Jesús María; Man. ALFREDO SAMANIEGO.

Pro Art SA: Diez Canseco 236, Of. 403, Miraflores, Lima 18; Dir-Gen. JORGE FERRAND LANCIOTTI.

Poland

Dzem Agency: PO Box 580, Katowice 2; Contact ENA OTOLINSUA.

Polish Radio Artists Management: Woronicza 17, 00-999 Warsaw; Dir ANDRZEJ HALUCH.

Warsaw Artists Management Ltd: Kazimierzowska 47/5, 02-572 Warsaw; Pres. ANDRZEJ HALUCH.

ZPR Inc–United Entertainment Enterprises Inc: Senatorska 13/15, 00 075 Warsaw; Pres./CEO ZBIGNIEW BENBENEK; Artists & Marketing Man. ANNA KAROLICKA.

Portugal

Companhia das Ideas: Ave Roma 49 5D, 1700 Lisbon; Dir ANTONIO AVELAR PINHO.

Contacto: PO Box 29, 2840 Seixal; Man. Dir DIONISIO DUARTE.

Dimas Mario Management: Rua Serpa Pinto 4A, 2800 Almada; Public Relations ISABEL SILVA.

Encore: Rua S. João da Praça 114 1, 1100 Lisbon; Man. Dir RUI SIMOES.

MS Management: Rua General c. da Silva 10 7, 1500 Lisbon; Man. Dir MANUEL MOURA DOS SANTOS.

MTM: PO Box 30072, 1321 Lisbon Codex; Man. Dir HUGO MOUTINHO.

Regiespectáculo: Alto do Coutão, Armazem I, 2735 Cacém; CEO ANTÓNIO GUIMARÃES.

Terra de Musica: Rua Casimiero Freire 19RC, 1900 Lisbon; Dir FRANCISCO MORGADO.

Uniao Lisbon: Rua B Sabrosa 84 2C, 1900 Lisbon; Dir ANTONIO CUNHA.

Puerto Rico

Producciones Norma Pujals: Ave Condado 57, PO Box 7a, Condado Vilomar, 00907 Condado; Man. NORMA PUJALS.

Producciones Tropical: PO Box 11673, Fernandez Juncos, 00910 San Juan; tel. (787) 728-7428; fax (787) 268-5112; Pres. ANGIE GARCIÁ.

TS Entertainment: PO Box 12004, 00922-2004 San Juan; Dirs LYNN SANTIAGO, RAFAEL TIRADO.

Romania

AMMA: Scara B, Apart 73, Calea Victorei 48/50, Sector 1, 70102 Bucharest; Man. AUREL MITRAN.

Cartianu Ltd: 58 Aviator Traian Vasile str, Sector 1, 78336 Bucharest; Chair. RADU CARTIANU.

Russia

Limelite Management Services: 38B Geylang Lorong 23, Singapore 1438; Operations Man. ERNEST CHEONG.

M&L Art: PO Box 28, 630 011 Novosibirisk; Man. Dir SERGEY BUGEYEV.

Rock-Azia: Pupova 96-268, Barnaul, 656062 Siberia; Contact EUGENE KOLBASHEV.

SNC Management: Krymsky Val 9, 103 045 Moscow; Man. Dir STAS NAMIN.

Slovakia

Martin Sarvas Productions: Jakubovo nám 14, 81109 Bratislava; tel. 2529-25287; fax 2529-21015; e-mail sarvas@hapri.sk; internet www.martinsarvas.sk; Dir MARTIN SARVAS.

Slovenia

Buba Promotion: 40 A Moskriceva, 61000 Ljubljana; Man. Dir DAVID KRZISNIK.

FV-Zavod Za Umetnisko in Kulturno Produkcijo: Kersnikova 4, 61000 Ljubljana; Man. Dir SKABERNE MÓNIKA.

SKUC—AFK: Kersnikova 4, 61000 Ljubljana; Man. Dir MITJA PREZELJ.

Spain

Attraction Management: Genova 3, 28010 Madrid; Man. Dir PACO LOPEZ.

AYA Producciones y Management: Dante 75 Bajos, 08032 Barcelona; Man. Dir JOAQUIN ASCON.

AZ Music & Management: Riera Argentona Sin, 08300 Mataro; Man. Dir BRAULIO PAZ SIMON.

Blac Management: Corcega 257, 08036 Barcelona; Man. Dir JULIO CANO.

BM Management: Mejico 17, 4–4A, 08004 Barcelona; Chair. MONICA GUTIERREZ.

Caturla & Navarro: Angela de la Cruz 24, 28020 Madrid; Dirs JOSÉ CATURLA, J EMILIO NAVARRO.

Chihuahua Management: Sancho Davila, 1 Entreplanta, 28028 Madrid; Man. Dir FLOR MADRID.

Crab Ediciones Musicales SA: Sagunto 2, 28010 Madrid; Gen. Man. JORGE E GOMEZ DIAZ.

Diez Management: Martinez Corrochano 3, 28007 Madrid; Chair. MERCEDES MARTIN.

EMC Management: Carlos Latorre 13, 28039 Madrid; Dir JOAN A SERRA.

GSG—Grup de Serveis Guilleries: Granja Baró, Ctra de la Guixa, km 2, 08500 VIC (Barcelona); Administration JORDI COSTA; Management IGNASI PLA; Production JOAN CAPDEVILA.

Madma S L: Calle Major, 5 Urbanización La Rosaleda, 08727 Sant Fuitos de Bages (Barcelona); Contact FELIX CAMPRUBI I SANTAMANS.

MCM Management: Modesto Lafuento 46 6B, 28003 Madrid; Chair. ISABEL BURGOS.

Oniria International S L: Alzines 3, St Quirze Parc, 08192 St Quirze Del Vallès, Barcelona; Pres. MICHEL HUYGEN; Man. ANTONI BRUNET.

Pino Sagliocco Presenta SL: C/ Quintana 2, 7° 9a, 28008 Madrid; Chair. PINO SAGLIOCCO.

Posto Nove: Muntaner 494 5B, 08022 Barcelona; Contact ALEJANDRO NAVARRO.

RLM Producciones: Jose Maria Cavero 9, Ch A, 28027 Madrid; Man. Dir ROSA LAGARRIGUE.

Sauma & Tumbao: Gral Oraa 37 4, 28006 Madrid; Dir SAUL RODRIGUEZ.

Store Music: Gran Via 28, 3C, 18010 Granada; Man. Dir CARMEN CARNICERO.

WOM Music: Dusai 6, 07001 Palma de Mallorca; Dir JUANJO ARZUBIALDE.

Sweden

AMP: Karlsgatan 9, 252 24 Helsingborg; Man. Dir HASSE JÖNSSON.

Feedback Management: PO Box 558, 631 07 Eskilstuna; Man. Dir MATS OLSSON.

Luger Production: Fredriksgatan 35, 811 33 Sandviken; Man. Dir/Agent OLA BROQUIST; Agents PATRICK FREDRIKSSON, MORGAN JOHANSSON.

Madhouse: PO Box 103 30, 100 55 Stockholm; Man. Dir JON GRAY.

MPA Musicart: Simrishamnsgatan 20A, 214 23 Malmö; Man. Dir ANDREAS LARSSON.

Projektbyrån: Kungsgatan 34, 972 41 Luleå; Man. Dir TOMAS LIND.

RMP Management AB: PO Box 17180, 104 62 Stockholm; Man. Dir STEFAN LIGA.

Siljemark Production: Gärdsvagen 2, 171 52 Solna; Man. JONAS SILJEMARK; Contact LASSE KARLSSON.

Stockhouse: PO Box 74, 182 71 Stocksund; Man. Dir MATS BOKSTRÖM.

Ton Art: PL 8007, 441 91 Alingås; Man. KLAS JOHANSSON.

XTC Productions AB: Ripsavägen 59, 124 51 Bandhagen; Man. Dir ULF WAHLBERG.

Switzerland

Artways Productions: rue des-deux-Gares 6B, PO Box 30, 1800 Vevey; Man. FABRICE LA LUC.

Choc Auditif Management: Route de Genève 17, Le Flon, 1003 Lausanne; Man. DOMINIQUE ROTTET.

Its Time To Management: PO Box 1344, 5610 Wohlen; Man. JEAN-LUC ITTEN.

Just Two Management: Hagenbuchstr 31, 9000 St Gallen; Contact CHRISTOPH HARZENMOSER.

Migration: PO Box 431, 1800 Vevey; tel. (21) 923-6363; fax (21) 923-6362; e-mail hdill@bluewin.ch; internet www.farafina.com; Contact HEINZ DILL.

VIP AG Productions: Schützengasse 30, 8001 Zürich; Man. Dir URS PETER KELLER.

The United Kingdom

140dB Management: The Fan Club 133, Kilburn Lane, London W10 4AN; tel. (20) 8354-2900; fax (20) 8354-2091; e-mail enquiries@14od6.co.uk; internet www.14od6.co.uk; Contact KATRINA BERRY, JUSTIN PRITCHARD.

19 Management Ltd: Unit 32, 35–37 Parkgate Rd, London SW11 4NP; Man. Dir SIMON FULLER.

Acker's International Jazz Agency: 53 Cambridge Mansions, Cambridge Rd, London SW11 4RX; tel. (20) 7978-5885; fax (20) 7978-5882; e-mail pamela@ackersmusicagency.co.uk; internet www.ackersmusicagency.co.uk; Owner PAMELA FRANCES SUTTON.

Acorn Entertainments: Winterfold House, 46 Woodfield Rd, Kings Heath, Birmingham, B13 9UJ; Man. Dir JIM MCPHEE.

Adrian Boss Promotions: 363–365 Harrow Rd, London W9 3NA; Contact ADRIAN BOSS.

AGM UK: 145A Ladbroke Grove, London W10 6HJ; Contact TONY MEILANDT.

ARC Music Management: 63 Blenheim Terrace, London NW8 0EJ; Contact ALEX RUHEMAN.

Arctic King Management: Bank Chambers, 4–6 Church St, Wilmslow, Cheshire SK9 1AU; Contact JOHN KING.

Asgard Management: 125 Parkway, London NW1 7PS; tel. (20) 7387-5090; fax (20) 7387-8740; e-mail pl@asgard.uk.com; Contact PAUL CHARLES.

Atomic Management: 32 Neal St, London WC2H 9PS; Contact MICK NEWTON.

Avalon Management Group Ltd: Queen's House, 1 Leicester Pl., Leicester Sq., London WC2H 7BP; Company Admin. MARC GOODSON.

BA Music Management: PO Box 34351, London NW6 7ZW; tel. (20) 7372-6648; fax (20) 7372-6673; e-mail enquiries@bjornagain.com; internet www.bjornagain.com; Dirs JOHN TYRRELL, ROD LEISSLE.

Bad Habits Music Group: PO Box 111, London W13 0ZH; Man. Dir JOHN S RUSHTON.

Bamn Management: 167 Caledonian Rd, London N1 0SL; Man. Dir STEVE FINAN.

Basement Music: 6 Pembridge Rd, London W11 3HL; Man. Dir JOHN TELFER.

BDA Ltd: Bryson House, Chiltern Rd, Culcheth, Warrington WA3 4LL; tel. (1925) 766655; fax (1925) 765577; e-mail brian.durkin@btinternet.com; Man. Dir BRIAN DURKIN.

Bedlam Management (UK) Ltd: 3rd Floor, Devonshire House, 14 Barley Mow Passage, London W4 4ZN; Contact TIM VASS.

Bernard Lee Management: Moorcroft Lodge, Farleigh Common, Warlingham, Surrey CR6 9PE; Man. Dir BERNARD LEE.

Big Advance Management: 12 Oval Rd, London NW1 7DH; Contact PADDY PRENDERGAST.

Big Bear Music: PO Box 944, Edgbaston, Birmingham B16 8UT; tel. (121) 4547020; fax (121) 4549996; e-mail admin@bigbearmusic.com; internet www.bigbearmusic.com; Man. Dir JIM SIMPSON.

Big Life Management: 15 Little Portland St, London W1N 5DE; Contact JAZZ SUMMERS.

Black Magic Management Ltd: 296 Earls Court Rd, London SW5 9BA; Man. Dir MATAYA CLIFFORD.

Blaylock Management Ltd: 39 Leyton Rd, Harpenden, Herts AL5 2JB; Man. Dir DAVID BLAYLOCK.

Blitz: Edgwarebury Farm, Edgwarebury Lane, Edgware, Middlesex HA8 8QX; Partners SUE HARRIS, CLAIRE POWELL.

Blueprint Management: 134 Lots Rd, London SW10 0RJ; Dirs JOHN GLOVER, MATT GLOVER.

BPR: 36 Como St, Romford, Essex RM7 7DR; tel. (1708) 725330; fax (1708) 725322; internet www.bprmusic.com; Man. BRIAN THEOBALD.

Brave Management: 15 Nottingham Rd, Wandsworth, London SW17 7EA; Man. Dir NETTY WALKER.

Braw Music Management: 76 Pentland Pl., Edinburgh EH10 6HS; Contact KENNY MACDONALD.

Brian Gannon Management: PO Box 106, Rochdale, Lancashire OL16 4HW; Man. Dir BRIAN GANNON.

Brian Reza Management: 416 High Rd, Harrow Weald, Middlesex HA3 6HJ; tel. (20) 8954-3428; fax (20) 8954-3239; Owner BRIAN REZA.

Brian Yeates Associates: Home Farm House, Canwell, Sutton Coldfield, West Midlands B75 5SH; tel. (121) 323-2200; fax (121) 323-2313; e-mail info@brianyeates.co.uk; internet www.brianyeates.co.uk; Contact BRIAN YEATES, ASHLEY YEATES.

Brilliant Artistes: 253 Camberwell New Rd, London SE5 0TH; Contact MARK WALMESLEY.

Brilliant Management: 20 Stamford Brook Ave, London W6 0YD; Contact DEE HARRINGTON.

Bruno Brookes Media and Management Ltd: Denford Mill House, Lower Derford, Hungerford, Berkshire RE17 0UN; Man. Dir BRUNO BROOKES.

Buzz Records: 192 Glasgow Rd, Perth PH2 0NA, Scotland; Man. Dir DAVE ARCARI.

By Eleven: 12 Tideway Yard, 125 Mortlake High St, London SW14 8SN; Man. JILL TAYLOR.

Caromac Music Management: Unit 104, Ducie House, 37 Ducie St, Manchester M1 2JW; Man. CAROLINE ELLERAY.

Century Music Entertainment: PO Box 1008, London W3 8ZW; Pres. JAMES LITTLE.

Chapter 22 Music/Sanctuary Music Management (Birmingham): Suite 114, The Custard Factory, Gibb St, Birmingham B9 4AA; tel. (121) 693-5454; fax (121) 693-5424; e-mail rod.thomson@sanctuarygroup.com; Contact ROD THOMSON.

Charmenko: 46 Spencer Rd, London SE24 0NR; tel. (20) 7274-6618; fax (20) 7737-4712; e-mail nick@charmenko.net; internet www.charmenko.net; Contact NICK HOBBS.

Clive Banks Limited: 1 Glenthorne Mews, 115A Glenthorne Rd, London W6 0LT; tel. (20) 8748-5036; fax (20) 8748-3356; e-mail mail@clivebanks.com; Man. Dir CLIVE BANKS; Contacts SHARON WHEELER, CAROLINE STEWART.

CMC Management: 1st Floor, 50 Bonnington Sq., London SW8 1TQ; Man. Dir CHRIS MOLLOY.

CMO Management (International) Ltd: Unit 32 Ransomes Dock, 35/37 Parkgate Rd, London SW11; Man. Dir CHRIS MORRISON.

Congo Music Ltd: 17A Craven Park Rd, Harlesden, London NW10 8SE; Dirs BYRON LYE-FOOK, ROOT JACKSON.

Courtyard Management: 21 The Nursery, Sutton Courtenay, Abingdon, Oxon OX14 4UA; tel. (1235) 845800; fax (1235) 847692; Mans BRYCE EDGE, CHRIS HUFFORD.

Cromwell Management: 4–5 High St, Huntingdon, Cambs PE29 3TE; tel. (1480) 435600; fax (1480) 356250; e-mail tricvic@lineone.net; Man. Partner VIC GIBBONS.

Cut Throat Management: PO Box 77, Coventry, West Midlands CV7 9YZ; Contact SIMON LAWLER.

Damage Management: 16 Lambton Pl., London W11 2SH; Man. Dir ED BICKNELL.

David Aspden Management: The Coach House, Capel Leyse, South Holmwood, Dorking, Surrey RH5 4LJ; Proprietor DAVID ASPDEN.

David Harper Management: 137 Talgarth Rd, London W14 9DA; Contact DAVID HARPER.

David Jaymes Associates/ D-Management: Suite 223A, Canalot Studios, 222 Kensal Rd, London W10 5BN; Contact DAVID JAYMES.

Derek Block Promotions: Douglas House, 3 Richmond Bldgs, London W1V 5AE; Man. Dir DEREK BLOCK.

Diamond Sounds Music Management: The Fox and Punchbowl, Burfield Rd, Old Windsor, Berkshire SL4 2RD; tel. (1753) 855420; fax (1753) 855420; e-mail samueldsm@aol.com; Man. Dir JULIE SAMUEL.

Direct Heat Management: PO Box 1345, Worthing, West Sussex BN14 7FB; e-mail dhm@happyvibes.co.uk; internet www.happyvibes.co.uk; Man. Dir MIKE PAILTHORPE.

Eastonia Entertainments: Eastonia House, 174 Lisnafin Park, Strabane, Co Tyrene, Northern Ireland; Contact GERRY HARDING.

EC1: 1 Cowcross St, London EC1 6DE; Contact ALEX NIGHTINGALE.

EG Management: 63A Kings Rd, London SW3 4NT; Chair. SAM ADLER.

Eleventh Hour Arts: 113 Cheesemans Terrace, Star Rd, London W14 9XH; Man. Dir DEBBIE GOLT.

Emka Productions: 43 Portland Rd, London W11 4LJ; Contact S O'ROURKE.

Equator Music: 17 Hereford Mansions, Hereford Rd, London W2 5BA; Contact ERNEST CHAPMAN.

Eternal Management: 55 Lark St, Liverpool L17 8UW; Contact JILL THOMPSON.

Europa Jazz Live: 6 Belgrove, Tunbridge Wells, Kent TN1 1YN; tel. (1892) 516722; fax (1892) 536080; e-mail jazz@davidjacobs.f9.co.uk; internet www.tinamay.com; Dir DAVID E JACOBS.

Excellent Management: 50A Waldron Rd, London SW18 3TD; Contact MARK WOOD.

Falcon Stuart Management: 59 Moore Park Rd, London SW6 2HH; Man. Dir FALCON STUART.

Fexborough Ltd: 195 Sandycome Rd, Kew, Surrey TW9 2EW; Man. JOHN KALINOWSKI.

Firebirds: 11 Chavenage, Kingswood, Bristol BS15 4LA; Dir CRAIG DUNN.

First Avenue Management: The Courtyard, 42 Colwith Rd, London W6 9EY; Contact OLIVER SMALLMAN.

Firstars/Talent Bank Management: Bugle House, 21A Noel St, London W1V 3PD; Contact TONY BRINSLEY.

Forward Management: 132 Liverpool Rd, London N1 1LA; Man. Dir ROB CHALLICE.

Friars Management Ltd: 33 Alexander Rd, Aylesbury, Buckinghamshire HP20 2NR; Man. Dir DAVID R STOPPS.

Fruit Management: Unit 104, Saga Centre, 326 Kensal Rd, London W10 5BZ; Mans CAROLINE KILLOURY, DEBBIE SWAINSON.

Gailforce Management Ltd: 30 Ives St, London SW3 2ND; Man. Dir GAIL COLSON; Co-ordinator NORMA BISHOP.

Ganeshe Management: Ganeshe House, Ingleby Dr., Harrow, Middlesex HA1 3LE; Man. Dir HARVEY FROST.

Genius Management: 89A High Rd, London N22 6BB; Contact BRUCE RUFFIN.

Gloria Butler Management: PO Box 2686, Knowle B94 5NQ; Man. GLORIA BUTLER.

GR Management: 974 Pollokshaws Rd, Shawlands, Glasgow G41 2HA, Scotland; Administration Man. ALAN CONNELL.

Hal Carter Organization: 101 Hazelwood Lane, Palmers Green, London N13 5HQ; Man. Dir HAL CARTER.

Hall or Nothing: 8 Poplar Mews, Oxbridge Rd, London W12 7JS; Contact MARTIN HALL.

Handle Artists Management: Handle House, 1 Albion Pl., Galena Rd, Hammersmith, London W6 0QT; Chair. DAVID WALKER.

Harvey Lisberg Associates: Kennedy House, 31 Stamford St, Altrincham, Cheshire WA14 1ES; Contacts HARVEY LISBERG, PHILIP LISBERG.

Hit & Run Music Ltd: 25 Ives St, London SW3 2ND; tel. (20) 7590-2600; fax (20) 7584-5774; e-mail tony@hit-and-run.com; internet www.genesis-music.com; Chair. & Man. Dir TONY SMITH.

Holland-Ford's: 103 Lydyett Lane, Barnton, Northwich, Cheshire CW8 4JT; Proprietor BOB HOLLAND-FORD.

Hopscotch Media Management: 46 Broadwick St, London W1V 1FF; Dir/Partner ALFIE DOSOO.

Huge and Jolly: 56–60 Islington Park St, London N1 1PX; Dir JOLYON BURNHAM.

Hyperactive Music Management: 1 Glenthorne Mews, 115A Glenthorne Rd, Hammersmith, London W6 0LJ; Asst Man. FIONA RIDDICK.

IE Music Ltd: 111 Frithville Gardens, London W12 7JQ; tel. (20) 8600-3400; fax (20) 8600-3401; e-mail info@iemusic.co.uk; internet www.iemusic.co.uk; Dirs TIM CLARK, DAVID ENTHOVEN.

Ignition Management: 8A Wyndham Pl., London W1H 1PP; Contacts MARCUS RUSSELL, ALEC MCKINNEY.

Interaction: 21 Douglas Rd, London NW6 7RN; Contact JOAN MARINDIN.

Interceptor Enterprises: The Greenhouse, 34–38 Provost St, London N1 7NG; Man. CHARLIE CHARLTON.

Interface Management: 37 Oxford Gardens, London W4 3BN; Contact DOUGLAS KEAN.

Invasion Group: 17 Gosfield St, London W1P 7HE; Contact MIKE HEDGE.

Jack Bruce Music: PO Box 2440, Bures, Suffolk CO8 5HY; tel. (1787) 269402; fax (1787) 269473; e-mail margrit@spotsmusic.co.uk; internet www.jackbruce.com; Man. MARGRIT SEYFFER.

Jackie Khan Management: Monroe Studios, 103–105 Holloway Rd, London N7 8LT; Man. Dir JACKIE KHAN.

Jam X Management: PO Box 3836, London NW3 4XF; tel. (1726) 844466; fax (1726) 844608; e-mail julian.able@jamx.co.uk; internet www.jamx.co.uk; Dir JULIAN ABLE.

James Joseph Music Management: 85 Cicada Rd, Wandsworth, London SW18 2PA; Man. Dir JAMES JOSEPH.

Jef Hanlon Management: 1 York St, London W1P 1PZ; tel. (20) 7487-2558; fax (20) 7487-2584; e-mail jhanlon@agents-uk.com; Man. Dir JEF HANLON; Dir ALICE HANLON.

JFD Management: 106 Dalling Rd, London W6 0JA; Contact JASMINE DAINES.

John Ford Promotions: Bradford Court, Bradford St, Digbeth, Birmingham B12 0NS; Owner JOHN FORD.

John Henry Management: The John Henry Bldg, 16/24 Brewery Rd, London N7 4NH; Sales & Retail Man. PEPIN CLOUT.

John Osborne Management: PO Box 173, New Malden, Surrey KT3 3YR; tel. (20) 8949-7730; fax (20) 8949-7798; e-mail john.osb1@btinternet.com; internet www.vibeuk.co.uk; Contact JOHN OSBORNE.

Johnny Lawes Management: 18 All Saints Rd, Unit 8, London W11 1HH; Man. Dir JOHNNY LAWES.

JPR Management: The Power House, 70 Chiswick High Rd, London W4 1SY; Contact JOHN REID.

Jukes Productions Ltd: PO Box 13995, London W9 2FL; tel. (20) 7286-9532; fax (20) 7286-4739; e-mail jukes@easynet.co.uk; internet www.jukesproductions.co.uk; Contact GEOFF JUKES.

Kasevin Rodell: 6 Bowling Green Rd, Cranfield, Bedfordshire MK43 0ET; Partner DIANA RODELL.

Kayam: Laurels Farm, Worstead, Norfolk NR28 9RW; tel. (1692) 536025; fax (1692) 535456; e-mail richard@kayam.co.uk; internet www.kayam.co.uk; Contact RICHARD ABEL.

Ken Spencer Personal Management: 138 Sandy Hill Rd, London, SE18 7BA; tel. and fax (20) 8854-2558; e-mail pagandferret@hotmail.com; Dir KEN SPENCER; Administration PAUL GRIFFITH.

Kitchenware: 7 The Stables, St Thomas St, Newcastle-Upon-Tyne, Tyne & Wear NE1 4LE; Man. Dir KEITH ARMSTRONG.

Lena Davis, John Bishop Associates: Cotton's Farmhouse, Whiston Rd, Cogenhoe, Northants NN7 1NL; tel. (1604) 891487; fax (1604) 890405; Dir JOHN BISHOP.

Les Johnson Management: 55 Rockford Close, Oakenshaw South, Redditch, Worcs B98 7SZ; Les Johnson .

LJE: 32 Willesden Lane, London NW6 7ST; Contact LAURIE JAY.

M D O: The Dawn, Northwood Lane, Bewdley, Worcs DY12 1AS; tel. (1299) 404579; fax (1299) 405079; e-mail themick.mdo@btinternet.com; Contact MICK OWEN.

M Management: 45A Longley Rd, London SW17 9LA; Man. Dir MORT MARRINAN.

Management Connection: Flat 3, Haversham Lodge, Melrose Ave, Willesden Green, London NW2 4JS; tel. (20) 8450-8882; fax (20) 8202-4219; e-mail sharon@thepublicityconnection.com; internet www.thepublicityconnection.com; Man. Dir SHARON CHEVIN.

Mark Dean: Electric Lighting Station, 48 Kensington Church St, London W8 5DP; Man. MARK DEAN.

Maverick Management: The Old Manor House, Station Rd, Thames Ditton, Surrey KT7 0NU; Man. STEIN.

Medium Productions Limited: 74 Saint Lawrence Rd, Upminster, Essex RM14 2UW; tel. (7939) 080524; fax (1708) 640291; e-mail info@mediumproductions.co.uk; internet www.mediumproductions.co.uk; Co-Dir DEBI ZORNES.

Mercenary Music Services: 143 Turks Rd, Radcliffe, Manchester M26 3WW; Production Man. PAUL NAYLOR.

Midnight Rock: Grays Farm Barns, Marshside, Kent CT3 4EL; tel. (1227) 860638; fax (1227) 860627; e-mail rockindave@midnightrock.demon.co.uk; internet www.midnightrock.demon.co.uk; Contact DAVE TAYLOR.

Milltown Productions Ltd: 26 East Parade, Bradford, West Yorkshire BD1 5HD; Prod. IAN SMITH.

Mission Control Management Ltd: Unit 3, Brunel Lock Devt, Cumberland Basin, Bristol BS1 6SE; Man. Dir RICHARD HUTCHISON.

Modernwood Management: Cambridge House, Card Hill, Forest Row RH18 5BA; Dirs MARK WOOD, MICKEY MODERN.

MoHoHo: 149 Gibson Gardens, London N16 7HH; Man. RAY HOGAN.

Moksha: PO Box 102, London E15 2HH; Man. Dir CHARLES COLM.

Money Talks Management: Cadillac Ranch, Pencraig Uchaf, Cwm Bach, Whitland, Dyfed SA34 0DT, Wales; tel. (1994) 484466; fax (1994) 484294; e-mail cadillac_ranch@telco4u.net; internet www.nikturner.com; Dir MOOSE MAGOON; Man. SID MONEY.

Motley Music Ltd: 132 Liverpool Rd, Islington, London N1 1LA; Man. DEBBIE RAWLINGS.

Muirhead Management: Michelin House, 81 Fulham Rd, Chelsea, London SW3 6RD; tel. (20) 7351-5167; fax (870) 1363878; e-mail info@muirheadmanagement.co.uk; internet www.muirheadmanagement.co.uk; CEO DENNIS MUIRHEAD.

NE Music Management: Priory House, 55 Lawe Rd, South Sheilds, Tyne & Wear NE33 2AL; tel. (191) 427-6207; fax (191) 427-6323; e-mail dave@nemproductions.com; internet www.nemproductions.com; Contact DAVE SMITH.

Negus-Fancey Co: 78 Portland Rd, London W11 4LQ; Contact CHARLES NEGUS-FANCEY.

Nigel Martin-Smith Management Ltd: 41 South King St, Manchester M2 6DE; Man. Dir NIGEL MARTIN-SMITH.

Northern Music Company: Cheapside Chambers, 43 Cheapside, Bradford, West Yorkshire BO1 4HP; Man. Dir ANDY FARROW.

One Fifteen: 1 Prince of Orange Lane, Greenwich, London SE10 8JQ; tel. (20) 8293-0999; fax (20) 8293-9525; e-mail mail@onefifteen.com; internet www.onefifteen.com; Man. PAUL LOASBY.

One Management: 43 St Alban's Ave, London W4 5JS; Man. Dir KARIN CLAYTON.

Opal Ltd: 4 Pembridge Mews, London W11 3EQ; Contact CATHERINE DEMPSEY.

Opium (Arts): 49 Portland Rd, London W11 4LJ; tel. (20) 7229-5080; fax (20) 7229-4841; Man. Dir RICHARD CHADWICK.

Palace of Fun: 16 Elm View, Huddersfield Rd, Halifax, Yorkshire HX3 0AE; Man. Dir BILL BYFORD.

Park Promotions: PO Box 651, Oxford OX2 9RB; tel. (1865) 241717; fax (1865) 204556; internet www.parkrecords.com; Man. Dir JOHN DAGNELL.

Part Rock Management: Suite 318, 535 Kings Rd, London SW10 0SZ; Contact STEWART YOUNG.

Paul Crockford Management: 56–60 Islington Park St, London N1; Contact PAUL CROCKFORD.

Pet Shop Boys Partnership: 8 Pembridge Studios, 27A Pembridge Villas, London W11 3EP; Contact JILL WALL.

Pete Hawkins Management: 54 The Ave, West Wickham, Kent BR4 0DY; tel. (20) 8777-9959; fax (20) 8777-9330; e-mail petervhawkins@aol.com; Man. Dir PETE HAWKINS.

PHAB: High Notes, Sheerwater Ave, Woodham, Weybridge, Surrey KT15 3SD; Contact PHILIP H A BAILEY.

Planet 4: Sun House, 2–4 Little Peter St, Manchester M15 4PS; Man. Dir CHRIS JOYCE.

PNG/Worldwide: Westminster Court, 10 Park Rd North, Birmingham, B6 5UJ; Man. JOHN SLATER.

Polar Union: 45–53 Sinclair Rd, London W14 0NS; Contact SARAH THORP.

Pure Management: 39 Bolton Gardens, London SW5 0AQ; Contact STEVE FARGNOLI.

Purple Palace: 34A Flower Lane, Mill Hill, London NW7 2JE; Contact STEPHANIE KAYS.

PWL Management: 4–7 The Vineyard, off Sanctuary St, London SE1 1QL; Gen. Man. SALLY ATKINS.

Queen Productions: 46 Pembridge Rd, London W11 3HN; Contact JIM BEACH.

Quickfire Management: Basement, 19 All Saints Rd, London W11 1HE; Proprietor KATHERINE CANOVILLE.

Quinlan Road (UK): 1 Heathgate Pl., 75/87 Agincourt Rd, London NW3 2NT; Gen. Man. IAN BLACKABY.

Raymond Coffer Management Limited: Suite 1, Hadleigh House, 96 High St, Bushey, Herts WD2 3DE; Man. Dir RAYMOND COFFER.

Real Life: 122 Holland Park Ave, London W11 4UA; Contact PAUL LILLY.

Ricochet: 5 Old Garden Rd, The Lanterns, Bridge Lane, London SW11 3AD; Man. Dir STEPHEN KING.

Riviera Global: 20 Cromwell Mews, London SW7 2JY; Contact JAKE RIVIERA.

Roger Forrester Management: 18 Harley House, London NW1 5H; Man. Dir ROGER FORRESTER.

Rollover Productions: 29 Beethoven St, London W10 4LJ; Man. Dir SEAMUS MORLEY.

Rough Trade Management: 66 Golborne Rd, London W10 5PS; tel. (20) 8960 9888; fax (20) 8968 6715; e-mail pru@roughtraderecords.com; internet www.roughtraderecords.com; Man. Dir GEOFF TRAVIS.

Running Dog Management: Minka, Lower Hampton Rd, Sunbury, Middlesex TW16 5PR; Management Co-ordinator RACHEL MALE.

Rupert Loewenstein: 2 King St, London SW1Y 6QL; Dir CLARE TURNER.

Salamander & Son Music Ltd: 23 Longman Dr., Inverness IV1 1SU, Scotland; Contact HEATHER BUNTING.

Sanctuary Music (Overseas): 1st Floor Ste, The Colonnades, 82 Bishops Bridge Rd, London W2 6BB; Contact ROD SMALLWOOD.

Sandcastle Productions: 236 Sebert Rd, Forest Gate, London E7 0NP; Sr Partner SIMON LAW.

Seb Shelton Management: 13 Lynton Rd, London N8 8SR; Contact SEB SHELTON.

Serious Speakout: 42 Old Compton St, London W1V 5PB; Partners JOHN CUMMING, JOHN ELLSON, DAVID JONES.

Shamrock Music Ltd: 9 Thornton Pl., London W1H 1FG; tel. (20) 7935-9719; fax (20) 7935-0241; e-mail lindy@celtus.demon.co.uk; internet www.folking.com/celtus/; Man. Dir LINDY BENSON.

Sincere Management: Flat B, 6 Bravington Rd, London W9 3AH; tel. (20) 8960-4438; fax (20) 8968-8458; e-mail office@sinman.co.uk; Contacts PETER JENNER, MUSHI JENNER.

So What Arts: 1st Floor, Ducie House, 37 Ducie St, Manchester M1 2JW; Contact ANDY DODD.

Solid Bond Management: Nomis Studios, 45–53 Sinclair Raod, London W14 0NS; Man. JOHN WELLER.

Some Bizarre Ltd: 124 New Bond St, London W1; Prod. STEVO.

SOS Management: 106 Cleveland St, London W1Y 5DP; Contact MEREDITH CORK.

Sound Management Associates: 22A Lambolle Pl., London NW3 4HP; Man. Dir PAUL CRAIG.

Soundtrack Music Management: 22 Ives St, London SW3 2ND; Dirs OLAF WYPER, CAROLYNNE WYPER.

Southwestern Management: 13 Portland Rd, St, Somerset BA16 9PX; tel. (1458) 445186; fax (1458) 841186; e-mail info@sw-management.co.uk; internet www.sw-management.co.uk; Dir CHRIS HANNAM.

Splash Management & Promotions: 328 Gray's Inn Rd, King's Cross, London WC1X 8BZ; Man. Dir NICK MOORE.

Stamina Management: 47 Prout Grove, London NW10 1PU; Man. Dir PETER GAGE.

Startrack Studio & Artist Management: 108B North Western St, Manchester M1 2WS; Studio Man. ROYSTON.

Stephen Budd Management: 109B Regents Park Rd, London NW1 8UR; Man. Dir STEPHEN BUDD.

Sylvantone Promotions: 17 Allerton Grange Way, Leeds LS17 6LP; tel. (113) 268-7788; fax (709) 235-9333; e-mail sylvantore@hotmail.com; Proprietor TONY GOODACRE.

SYME International—Hengest Records: 81 Park Rd, Wath-Upon-Dearne, Rotherham, South Yorkshire S63 7LE; tel. (1709) 877920; fax (1709) 873119; e-mail admin@hengest.com; internet www.hengest.com; Product Man. PATSY PRINCE.

Taurus Records: 23 Blackheath Rise, Lewisham, London SE13 7PN; Contact BEVERLEY MILLER.

Tender Prey Management: 50 Werter Rd, Putney, London SW15 2LJ; tel. (20) 8788-9600; fax (20) 8788-4600; e-mail tanya.rayner@tenderprey.com; Contact RAYNER JESSON, TANYA BUSHNELL.

The Deluxe Corporation: 13Charnhill Cres., Bristol BS16 9JU; tel. (117) 970-2712; fax (117) 970-2713; e-mail info@volumerecords.co.uk; internet www.volumerecords.co.uk; Administration Man. HELEN HAWKEN.

Theobald Dickson Productions Ltd: The Coach House, Swinhope Hall, Swinhope, Lincolnshire LN3 6HT; Man. Dir BERNARD THEOBALD.

TKO Management: PO Box 130, Hove, East Sussex BN3 6QU; tel. (1273) 550088; fax (1273) 540969; e-mail management@tkogroup.com; internet www.tkogroup.com; Contact HOWARD KRUGER.

Tony Denton Promotions Ltd: 19 South Molton Lane, Mayfair, London W1Y 1AQ; Contact SIMON NICHOLLS.

Tracy Carter Management Ltd: WT House, Pilling, Preston, Lancashire PR3 6SJ; Owner WILLIAM TRACY CARTER.

Trinifold Management: 22 Harley House, Marylebone Rd, London NW1 4PR; Man. Dir BILL CURBISHLEY.

TYGER: c/o 19A Bedford Rd, London N15 4HA; Head of Music TIM NOYCE.

UK/LA Management: Bugle House, 21A Noel St, London W1V 3PD; Contact MICHAEL COX.

Value Added Talent (VAT): 1–2 Purley Pl., London N1 1QA; Man. Dir DAN SILVER.

Van Walsum Management Ltd: 4 Addison Bridge Pl., London W14 8XP.

Voodoo Productions: 21 Ruckholt Close, Leyton, London E10 5NX; Contact RITA CAMPBELL.

Waveeffect Limited: 34 Salisbury St, London NW8 8QE; tel. (20) 7402-9111; fax (20) 7723-3064; e-mail satellite_artists@hotmail com; Man. Dir ELIOT M COHEN.

Wedge Music: 63 Grosvenor St, London W1X 9DA; Contact TONY GORDON.

Wilcox Zodiac Organisation: 1099A Finchley Rd, London NW11 0QB; Artist Man. BERT WILCOX.

Wildlife Management: Unit F, 21 Heathmans Rd, London, SW6 4TJ; tel. (20) 7371-7008; fax (20) 7371-7708; Man. Dir IAN MCANDREW.

William Tracey-Carter Management: WT House, Pilling, Preston, Lancs PR3 6SJ; Contact WILLIAM TRACEY-CARTER.

Wolfgang Kuhle Artist Management: PO Box 425, London SW6 3TX; Contact WOLFGANG KUHLE.

Worldchief Ltd: 132 Liverpool Rd, London N1 1LA; Dir STEVE BAKER; Asst SUSIE BLYTH.

X-Factor Music Group International: PO Box 52, Ilford, Essex IG1 3JT; tel. and fax (20) 8252-1007; e-mail xsquad_uk@yahoo.co.uk; Dir/Prod. RAMESH KANSARA.

XL Talent: Studio 7, 27A Pembridge Villas, London W11 3EP; Contact IAN WRIGHT.

The United States of America

A Train Management: PO Box 29242, Oakland, CA 94604; tel. (510) 893-4705; fax (510) 893-4807; e-mail postmaster@a-train.com; Contact AL EVERS.

Ace Productions: PO Box 428, Portland, TN 37148-0428; Pres. JIM CASE.

Addis, Wechsler & Associates: 955 S Carrillo Dr., Los Angeles, CA 90048; Contact NICK WECHSLER.

AEG Management: 1025 16th Ave S, Suite 401, Nashville, TN 37212; CEO MARC OSWALD.

AFG Entertainment: 30 W 21st St, 7th Floor, New York, NY 10010- 6905; Contact RONALD FIERSTEIN.

Aggressive Entertainment: 130 W 57th St, Suite 5A, New York, NY 10019; Man. NICK MOYLE.

Al Bunetta Management: Suite 102A, 33 Music Sq. W, Nashville, TN 37203; Man. AL BUNETTA.

Al Embry International: PO Box 23162, Nashville, TN 37202; Owner/ Pres. AL EMBRY.

All Access Entertainment: 425 Madison Ave, Ste 802, New York, NY 10017; Mans BRIAN DOYLE, RICHARD FLYNN, AMY MCFARLAND.

Alliance Artists Ltd: Ste 220, 3423 Piedmont Rd NE, Atlanta, GA 30305; Contact CHARLIE BRUSCO.

Allman Brothers Band: 18 Tamworth Rd, Waban, MA 02168; Man. BERT HOLMAN.

Ambassador Artist Agency: PO Box 50358, Nashville, TN 37205; tel. (615) 370-4700; fax (615) 661-4344; e-mail wes@ambassadoragency.com; internet www.ambassadoragency.com; Pres. WES YODER.

American Band Management: PO Box 840607, Houston, TX 77284-0607; Pres. JOHN BLOMSTROM SR.

Amethyst Group Ltd: 273 Chippewa Dr., Columbia, SC 29210-6508; Chair. C G BUTLER.

Andon Artists: 79 Farview Farm Rd, W Redding, CT 06896; Owner / Man. ARMA ANDON.

Angelus Entertainment: 9016 Wilshire Blvd, Suite 346, Beverly Hills, CA 90211; Man. PETE ANGELUS.

Art Collins Management: PO Box 561, Pine Bush, NY 12566; Man. ART COLLINS.

Artist Representation & Management: 1257 Arcade St, St Paul, MN 55106; Office Man./Agent ROGER ANDERSON.

Atomic Communications Group: 10553 W Jefferson Blvd, Culver City, CA 90232; CEO GABRIEL LECONTE.

Barron Entertainment: 209 10th Ave S, Suite 232, Nashville, TN 37203; Contact JAY BARRON.

Barry Bergman Management: 350 E 30th St, Ste 4D, New York, NY 10016; Man. BARRY BERGMAN.

Baruck / Consolo Management: 15003 Greenleaf St, Sherman Oaks, CA 91403; Contact JOHN BARUCK, TOM CONSOLO.

Bet-Car Management: 307 Lake St, San Francisco, CA 94118; Contact ORA HARRIS.

Big FD Entertainment: 10801 National Blvd, Suite 530, Los Angeles, CA 90064; Pres. DOUG GOLDSTEIN.

Bill Graham Management: PO Box 429094, San Francisco, CA 94142-9094; Owner BILL GRAHAM.

Bill Sammeth Organization: PO Box 960, Beverly Hills, CA 90213; Pres. BILL SAMMETH.

Bill Thompson Management: 2051 Third St, San Francisco, CA 94107; Man. BILL THOMPSON.

BJM: 250 W 57th St, Suite 603–5, New York, NY 10107; Man. PAUL KORZILIUS.

Blanton/Harrell Entertainment: 2910 Poston Ave, Nashville, TN 37203; Mans MICHAEL BLANTON, DAN HARRELL.

Blowin' Smoke Records: 7438 Shoshone Ave, Van Nuys, CA 91406-2340; tel. (818) 881-9888; fax (818) 881-0555; e-mail blowinsmokeband.com; internet www.blowinsmokeband.com; Pres. LARRY WEISBERG.

BMP Artist Management: PO Box 1703, La Mirada, CA 90637; Contact BRIAN A MAYES.

Bobby Roberts Co: PO Box 3007, Hendersonville, TN 37077; Pres. BOBBY ROBERTS.

Borman Entertainment: 9220 Sunset Blvd, Suite 320, Los Angeles, CA 90069; Pres. GARY BORMAN.

Brock & Associates Management: 201 Seaboard Lane, Franklin, TN 37067; Pres. DARLENE BROCK.

Brokaw Company: 9255 Sunset Blvds, Suite 804, Los Angeles, CA 90069; Mans DAVID BROKAW, SANDY BROKAW, JOEL BROKAW.

Brothers Management Associates: 141 Dunbar Ave, Fords, NJ 08863.

BTB Management Group: PO Box 3509, Westport, CT 06880; Contact DEE ANTHONY, JOSHUA SIMONS.

Budd Carr Co Inc: 9320 Wilshire Blvd, Suite #200, Beverly Hills, CA 90212; Contact MARNI FEENBERG.

Bullet Entertainment: 120 N Victory, Suite 102, Burbank, CA 91052; Contact KARMEN BECK, GARY BIRD.

Bust It Management: 80 Swan Way, Suite 130, Oakland, CA 94621; CEO LOUIS BURRELL.

C & M Productions Management Group: 5114 Albert Dr., Brentwood, TN 37027; tel. (615) 371-5098; fax (615) 371-5317; e-mail rwcotton@mindspring.com; internet www.c-m-production.com; Pres. RONALD COTTON.

C M S Management: 627 Main St, Simpson, PA 18407; Vice-Pres. CARL CANEDY.

C Winston Simone Management: 1790 Broadway, 10th Floor, New York, NY 10019; CEO C WINSTON SIMONE.

Carr-Sharpe Entertainment Servcies: 9320 Wilshire Blvd, Suite 200, Beverly Hills, CA 90212; Partners BUDD CARR, WIL SHARPE.

Columbia Artists Management: 165 W 57th St, New York, NY 10019; Chair. RONALD WILFORD.

Concrete Management: 301 W 53rd St, Suite 11D, New York, NY 10019; Contact ANDY GOULD.

Courage Management: 2899 Agoura Rd, Suite 562, Westlake, CA 91361; Man. JOHN COURAGE.

Craig H Berlin CPA: 1650 Broadway, Suite 510, New York, NY 10019; Principal C BERLIN.

Crossfire Productions: 1209 Baylor St, Austin, TX 78703-4123; Pres. VICKY MOERBE.

Curtis Management: 417 Denny Way, 2nd Floor, Seattle, WA 98109-4934; Contact KELLY CURTIS.

DAS Communications: 83 Riverside Dr., New York, NY 10024; Contacts DAVID SONENBERG, BERNARD ALEXANDER.

David Lefkowitz Management: 3470 19th St, San Francisco, CA 94110; Owner DAVID LEFKOWITZ.

Depth of Field Management: 1501 Broadway, Suite 1304, New York, NY 10036; Pres. DARRYL PITT.

Diamondback-Great Pyramid (Musics): PO Box 170040, San Francisco, CA 94117; Owner JOSEPH BUCHWALD.

Dream Street Management: 1460 Fourth St, Suite 205, Santa Monica, CA 90401; Man. ED GERRARD.

Dynamic Productions Inc: 11410 West Wisconsin Ave, Wauwatosa, WI 53226; Vice-Pres. ARTHUR GREINKE.

Earth Tracks Artists: 4809 Ave N, Suite 286, Brooklyn, NY 11234; Man. Dir DAVID KRINSKY.

East End Management: 8209 Melrose Ave, 2nd Floor, Los Angeles, CA 90046; Man. TONY DIMITRIADES.

Endangered Species Artists Management: PO Box 20469, Columbus Circle Station, New York, NY 10023-1485; Pres. FRED PORTER.

Erv Woolsey Co: 1000 18th Ave S, Nashville, TN 37212; tel. (615) 329-2402; fax (615) 327-4917; e-mail erv@ervwoolsey.com; CEO ERV WOOLSEY.

ESP Management: 888 Seventh Ave, Suite 2904, New York, NY 10106-0001; Pres. BUD PRAGER.

Famous Artist Agency: 1700 Broadway, 5th Floor, New York, NY 10019; Pres. JERRY ADE; Man. DAVID ZEDECK.

Firstars: 3520 Hayden Ave, Culver City, CA 90232; Man. MILES COPELAND.

Fitzgerald-Hartley Company: 50 W Main St, Ventura, CA 93001; Mans LARRY FITZGERLAD, MARK HARTLEY.

Gallin-Morey Associates: 345 N Maple Dr., Suite 300, Beverly Hills, CA 90210; Chair. SANDY GALLIN; Pres. JIM MOREY.

Gold Mountain Entertainment: Suite 450, 3575 Cahuenga Blvd West, Los Angeles, CA 90068; Pres. RON STONE.

Greco Holdings Inc: Market St Sq., 33 Wilkes Barre Blvd, Wilkes Barre, PA 18701; Pres./CEO THOM GRECO.

Grrr Records: 920 W Wilson Ave, Chicago, IL 60640; Publicity/Retail Man. SHELLEY NEEDHAM; Booking Man. DIANE BORDEN.

Hallmark Direction Company: 1905 Broadway, Nashville, TN 37203; Artist Co-ordinator DONNA HYSMITH.

Hard To Handle Management: 640 Lee Rd, Suite 106, Wayne, PA 19087; Contact STEVE BARNETT.

Heart Music Inc: PO Box 160326, Austin, TX 78716-0326; Promotion Dir KAREN BILLER.

Heartwrite Music: PO Box 1739, Texarkana, AR 75504; Pres. DAVID PATILLO.

Herbie Herbert Management: 2051 Third St, San Francisco, CA 94107; Contact HERBIE HERBERT.

HK Management: 8900 Wilshire Blvd, Suite 300, Beverly Hills, CA 90211; Man. HOWARD KAUFMAN.

Imani Entertainment Inc: PO Box 150-139, Brooklyn, NY 11215; Dir GUY ANGLADE.

Industrial Management: 3450 3rd St, 2A Suite 300, San Francisco, CA 94124-1402; Pres. CHRIS COYLE.

J & D Music Services Ltd: 38 West 21 St, 5th Floor, New York, NY 10010-6906; Pres. JEROME HERSHMAN.

Jerry Kravat Entertainment Services (JKES) Inc: 404 Park Ave, New York, NY 10016; Contact STAN SCOTTLAND.

Joe Granda Management: 13644 S W 142 Ave, Suite D, Miami, FL 33186; Pres. JOE GRANDA.

Joseph Buchwald: PO Box 347008, San Francisco, CA 94134; Contact JOSEPH BUCHWALD.

Ken Adamany Associates: 1818 Parmenter St, Suite 202, Middleton, WI 53562; Contact KEN ADAMANY.

Kragen & Co: 1112 N Sherbourne Dr., Los Angeles, CA 90069; Contact KEN KRAGEN.

Kurfirst/Blackwell Entertainment: 601 W 26th St, 11th Floor, New York, NY 10001; tel. (212) 320-3680; fax (212) 320-3689; internet www.kurfirst-blackwellentertainment.com; Pres. GARY KURFIRST.

Landmark Communications Group: PO Box 1444, Hendersonville, TN 37077; Pres. BILL ANDERSON JR.

Legend Artists: 120 W 44th St, Suite 404, New York, NY 10036; Pres. JOE BOYLAND.

Lippman Entertainment: 8900 Wilshire Blvd, Suite 340, Beverly Hills, CA 90211-1906; Contact MICHAEL LIPPMAN, TERRY LIPPMAN.

Lone Wolf Management: PO Box 163390, Austin, TX 78716; Pres. BILL HAM.

Lookout Management: 2644 30th St, 1st Floor, Santa Monica, CA 90405; Contact FRANK GIRONDA, ELIIOT ROBERTS.

Louis Levin Management: 130 W 57th St, Suite 10B, New York, NY 10019; Pres. LOUIS LEVIN.

Madhouse Management: PO Box 15108, Ann Arbor, MI 48106; Contact DOUG BANKER.

Management By Jaffe: 1560 Broadway, Suite 1103, New York, NY 10036; tel. (212) 869-6912; fax (212) 869-7102; e-mail jerjaf@aol.com; internet www.jocymcintyre.com; Pres. JERRY JAFFE.

Management Network: 19430 Ventura Blvd, Suite 205, Sherman Oaks, CA 91403; Contact GERRY TOLMAN.

Mark A Abbattista: 1875 Century Park East, Seventh Floor, Los Angeles, CA 90067; Contact MARK 'ABBA' ABBATTISTA.

Mark Alan Agency: PO Box 21323, St Paul, MN 55121; Pres. MARK ALAN.

Maxine S Harvard Unltd: Commerce Center, 2227 US Highway 1 #251, N Brunswick, NJ 08902; Man. MAXINE S HARVARD.

McFadden Artists: 818 18th Ave S, Nashville, TN 37203; Chairs JACK MCFADDEN, JO MCFADDEN.

McCraw Management: 1830 E Kane Pl., Suite #3, Milwaukee, WI 53202; Man. MARK MCCRAW.

Metropolitan Entertainment: 7 N Mountain Ave, Montclair, NJ 07042; Contact ROBERT KOS.

Mirkin Management: 9061/2 Congress Ave, Austin, TX 78701; Owner JAN MIRKIN.

Moress Nanas Entertainment: 12424 Wilshire Blvd, Suite 840, Los Angeles, CA 90025; Partner HERB NANAS.

Music Man Productions: 568 Snelling Ave N, Suite 106, St Paul, MN 55104; Owners PAUL MANSKE, STEVE YORK.

Music Umbrella: PO Box 1067, Santa Monica, CA 90406; Pres./CEO GLENN H FRIEDMAN.

Niji Management: Suite 307, 18653 Ventura Blvd, Tarzana, CA 91356; Pres. WENDY DIO.

Nippy Inc: 2160 N Central Rd, Fort Lee, NJ 07024-7547; CEO JOHN HOUSTON.

Oasis Management: 3010 E Bloomfield, Phoenix, AZ 85032; Man. GLORIA CAVALERA.

Open Door Management: 15327 Sunset Blvd, Suite 365, Pacific Palisades, CA 90272; Pres. BILL TRAUT.

Panacea Entertainment: 2705 Glendower Ave, Los Angeles, CA 90027; Chair./CEO ERIC GARONER.

Peter Asher Management: 644 N Doheny Dr., Los Angeles, CA 90069; Pres. IRA KOSLOW.

Pilot Management Company: PO Box 23203, Nashville, TN 37202; Pres. JOHNSON BELL.

Platinum Gold Productions: 9200 Sunset Blvd, Suite 1220, Los Angeles, CA 90069; Partner STEVE COHEN.

PPL-MCI Entertainment Group: 10 Universal Plaza, PO Box 8442, Universal City, CA 91618; tel. (818) 506-8533; fax (818) 506-8534; e-mail pplzmi@aol.com; internet www.pplzmi.com; CEO JAESON ST JAMES JARRETT; Man. Dir MAXX DIAMOND.

Precision Management: 825 N King St, Suite A-1, Hampton, VA 23669-2814; Operations Man. CAPPRICCIEO M SCATES.

Premier Artist Services: 1401 University Dr., Suite 305, Coral Springs, FL 33071; Pres. ELIOT H WEISMAN.

Premier Productions: 1909 N Spruce, Wichita, KS 67214; Owner ANTHONY WELCH.

Production Group International: 2200 Wilson Blvd, Suite 200, Arlington, VA 22201; Pres. ED YOE.

Q-Prime Inc: 729 Seventh Ave, 14th Floor, New York, NY 10019; Co-Pres CLIFF BURNSTEIN, PETER MENSCH.

Quango Music Group Inc: 9744 Wilshire Blvd, Suite 305, Beverly Hills, CA 90212; Pres. GEORGE GHIZ.

Quiet Storm Inc: 103 Westward Dr., Miami Springs, FL 33166; Contact CARL C VALLDEJULI.

Ralph Mercado Management: 568 Broadway, Suite 806, New York, NY 10012; Pres. RALPH MERCADO.

REM/Athens Ltd: PO Box 8032, Athens, GA 30603; Contact BERTIS E DOWNS, W JEFFERSON HOLT.

Remington Management Inc: 6602 Harbor Town, Suite 501, Houston, TX 77036; Pres. JANICE D HAYES.

Rick Levy Management: 1881 S Kirkman Rd, 715, Orlando, FL 32811; Pres. RICK LEVY.

Roger Davies Management: 15030 Ventura Blvd, Suite 772, Sherman Oaks, CA 91403; Man. ROGER DAVIES.

Ron Weisner Entertainment: 9200 Sunset Blvd, PH 15, Los Angeles, CA 90069; Man. RON WEISNER.

Rosebud Agency: PO Box 170429, San Francisco, CA 94117; tel. (415) 386-3456; fax (415) 386-0599; e-mail info@rosebudus.com; internet www.rosebudus.com; Pres. MIKE KAPPUS.

Rustron-Whimsong Music Productions: c/o The Whimsy, 1156 Park Lane, West Palm Beach, FL 33417; tel. and fax (561) 478-8315; e-mail safehavenwpb@yahoo.com; Exec. Dir/Owner RUSTY GORDON.

Ruth Blakely Management: 610 Players Court, Nashville, TN 37211; CEO RUTH BLAKELY.

Siddons & Associates: 584 North Larchmont Blvd, Los Angeles, CA 90004; Pres. BILL SIDDONS.

Slatus Management: 208 E 51st St, New York, NY 10022; Man. TEDDY SLATER.

Stiefel Phillips Entertainment: 9720 Wilshire Blvd, 4th Floor, Beverly Hills, CA 90212; Mans ARNOLD STIEFEL, RANDY PHILLIPS.

Stilleto Entertainment: 5443 Beethoven St, Los Angeles, CA 90066; Partners EDNA COLLISON, GARRY KIEF, STEVE WAX.

Surface Entertainment & Management: PO Box 2935, Church St Station, New York, NY 10008; Contact PAM BENINON.

Susan Silver Management: 207 1/2 First Ave S, Suite 300, Seattle, WA 98104; Owner SUSAN SILVER.

Suzi Reynolds & Associates: 200 Rector Pl., Suite 7H, New York, NY 10280; Dir SUZI REYNOLDS.

Talent House: 7211 Santa Monica, Suite 200, Los Angeles, CA 90046; Pres. STACI SLATER.

Ted Kurland Associates: 173 Brighton Ave, Boston, MA 02134; tel. (617) 254-0007; fax (617) 782-3524; e-mail ted@tedkurland.com; internet www.tedkurland.com; Pres. TED KURLAND.

Ten Ten Management: 33 Music Sq. W, Suite 110, Nashville, TN 37203; Pres. BARRY COBURN.

Thames Talent: 45 E Putnam Ave, Greenwich, CT 06830; Man. BRUCE PAYNE.

Third Rail Entertainment: 9169 Sunset Blvd, Los Angeles, CA 90069; Contact BOB CAVALLO.

Top Rock Development Corporation: 6399 Wilshire Blvd, Suite 1001, Los Angeles, CA 90049; Mans DOUG THALER, STEPHANIE GUREVITZ.

Troubadour Entertainment: 5305 Barton Vale Court, Nashville, TN 37211-8404; Pres. TONY LEE.

Turi's Music: 103 Westward Dr., Miami Springs, FL 33166; Contact CARL C VALLDEJULI.

Umpire Entertainment Enterprises: 1507 Scenic Dr., Longview, TX 75604; Pres. JERRY HAYMES.

Up Front Management: 1906 Seward Dr., Pittsburg, CA 94565; CEO CHARLES COKE; Vice-Pres. TERRY PITTS.

Vector Management: PO Box 128037, Nashville, TN 37212; Man. KEN LEVITAN.

Warren Entner Management: 5550 Wilshire Blvd, Suite 302, Los Angeles, CA 90036; Pres. WARREN ENTNER.

Westwood Entertainment Group: 1115 Inman Ave, Suite 330, Edison, NJ 08820-1132; Gen. Man. ELENA PETILLO.

Wolgemath & Hyatt Inc: 8012 Brooks Chapel Rd, Suite 243, Brentwood, TN 37027; Artist Man. JOHN MALLORY.

Woodrich Enterprises Inc: PO Box 38, Lexington, AL 35648; e-mail mernee@msn.com; Pres. WOODY RICHARDSON.

Zane Management: The Land Title Bldg, 100 S Broad St, Suite 630, Philadelphia, PA 19110; tel. (215) 640-9770; fax (215) 640-9769; e-mail lzr@remick-martone.com; internet www.zanemanagement.com; Pres., CEO LLOYD ZANE REMICK.

Uruguay

ABT Producciones: 25 de Mayo 544, 2°, Montevideo; Dir ADOLFO BRUN THIELMAN.

Edmundo Klinger-Garcia Rial Association: Avda Garibaldi 2748, PO Box 203, Montevideo; Dir EDMUNDO KLINGER.

San Martín Producciones: José Enrique Rodó 1661, PO Box 401, 11200 Montevideo; Dir EDUARDO SAN MARTÍN.

Venezuela

Carlos Cassina: Avda Lecuna, Edif. El Tjar 3, PO Box E Parque Central, Caracas; Contact CARLOS CASSINA.

Fonart SA: Avda Caurimare, Ctro Caroní MA, Of. A-26, Col. del Bello Monte, 1041 Caracas; Vice-Pres. ANTONIO SÁNCHEZ G.

Producciones Maria Gómez: PO Box 50 158, 1050 A, Caracas; Dir MARIA GÓMEZ.

Representaciones Billo SA: Avda Paez, Res. Verónica 7°, PO Box C, El Paraiso, Caracas; Pres. AMABLE FRÓMENTE.

Sonia Guedez: Multicentro Empresarial del Este, Edif. Miranda Nucleo A, 4, Of. 47-A, Caracas; Contact SONIA GUEDEZ.

APPENDIX C: BOOKING AGENTS AND PROMOTERS

Andorra

RIAL Andorra: Avda de Tarragona 24, Andorra La Vella; tel. 860686; fax 866286; e-mail rial@andorra.ad; Man. PASCAL LAIR.

Argentina

Abraxas Producciones Internacionales: Avda Callao 875, 4° H, 1023 Buenos Aires; Dir-Gen. CARLOS PITY YÑURRIGARRO.

Aisenberg & Asociados: Juncal 3361, 6°, Of. C, 1425 Buenos Aires; Dir CHICHE AISENBERG.

Dario Arellano Producciones: San Gerónimo 2005, 3000 Santa Fe; Dir DARIO ARELLANO.

Felix Marín & Asociados: Talcahuano 68, 6°, Of. D, 1013 Buenos Aires; Dir FELIX MARÍN.

Fernando Moya Producciones: Heredia 1425, 1427 Buenos Aires; Dir FERNANDO MOYA.

Hector Cavallero Producciones SA: Hipólito Irigoyen 1994, PB 4, 1089 Buenos Aires; Pres. FERNANDO CAVALLERO; Contact HECTOR CAVALLERO.

Kralendijk Producciones: Sánchez de Bustamente 444, 5°, Dpto 1, 1173 Buenos Aires; Pres. ALEJANDRO SOLIGNAC.

Matt Hungo Srl: Tucumán 1455, 5°, Of. A-B, 1050 Buenos Aires; Gen. Man. OMAR ALBERTO LAURIA.

Ohanian Producciones: Aguilar 2073, 1428 Buenos Aires; Dir ALBERTO OHANIAN.

Rock & Pop Internacional: Zapiola 1625, 1427 Buenos Aires; Dir DANIEL GRINBANK.

TM Producciones: Nicaragua 4994, 1425 Buenos Aires; Dir RAÚL FERNÁNDEZ.

Australia

A R E The Entertainment Company: 186 Glen Osmond Rd, Fullarton, SA 5063; Dir MARK DRAPER.

Abracadabra Event Company: 186 Glen Osmond Rd, Fullarton, SA 5063; Dir BRIAN GLEESON.

Adrian Bohm Presents Pty Ltd: 44 Fourth Ave, St Peters, SA 5069; tel. (8) 8363-0212; fax (8) 8363-1231; e-mail promoter@abpresents.com.au; Dir ADRIAN BOHM.

ATA Allstar Artists Pty Ltd: 98 Glebe Point, Glebe, NSW 2037; Dirs TONY BRADY, KEVIN JACOBSEN.

Australian Variety Artists: PO Box 300, Kings Cross, NSW 2011; Agents DEZ DALTON, SUZANNE TERRY.

B & S Promotions: PO Box 1481, Frankston, VIC 3199; Partners BILL DETTMER, SALLY DETTMER.

Cheersquad: PO Box 4153, East Richmond, VIC 3121; Contact WALLY KEMPTON.

Chevy's Entertainment Booking Agency: PO Box 380W, Smithfield West, NSW 2164; tel. and fax (2) 9822-9105; e-mail chevys@zeta.org.au; Man. MARIO J BORG.

Class Entertainment Organization Pty Ltd: PO Box 169, Sutherland, NSW 2232; Man. Dir RON RAGEL.

Entertainers Pty Ltd: 48 Millswood Cr, Millswood, SA 5034; Man. Dir IVAN TANNER.

Feel Management & Tour Co-ordination: 2/54 Bronte Rd, Bondi Junction, NSW 2022; Dir TIM PITTMAN.

Harbour Agency Pty Ltd: 3rd Floor, 63 William St, East Sydney, NSW 2011; Man. Dir SAM RIGHI.

Heart Beat Promotions: 10 Raggatt St, Alice Springs, NT 0870; Man. MATTHEW GUGGISBERG.

International Management Group: 281 Clarence St, Sydney, NSW 2000; Dir of Arts & Entertainment STEPHEN FLINT WOOD.

Jaybee's Entertainment Agency: PO Box 37, Sanctuary Pl., NSW 2540; Man. NARRELL M BROWN.

Lynne James & Associates: PO Box 511, Lane Cove, Sydney, NSW 2060; Man. Dir LYNNE JAMES.

Mario Maicho Promotions Pty Ltd: PO Box 572, North Adelaide, SA 5006; Sec./Tour Co-ordinator MARGARET RUDGE.

Melke (Artist Representation & Media Co-ordination): 158 Raglan St, Mosman, Sydney, NSW 2088; Dir SUE MELKE.

Michael Coppel Presents: 716–718 High St, Armadale, VIC 3143; Man. Dir MICHAEL COPPEL.

Opulent Music Entertainment: PO Box 270, 48 David Cres., Bundoora, VIC 3083; Man. Dir ANTHONY CHIDIAC.

Paul Cussen Management: Suite 1, Level 2, 41 Oxford St, Darlinghurst, NSW 2010; Proprietor PAUL CUSSEN.

Pegasus Event Management Pty Ltd: The Hills Centre, Carrington Rd, Castle Hill, NSW 2154; Man. Dir CHRISTOPHER RIX.

Phill Shute Management Pty Ltd: PO Box 273, Dulwich Hill, NSW 2203; Man. Dir PHILL SHUTE.

Pinewood Records and Promotions: 3 Hessel Pl., Emu Heights, NSW 2750; tel. (2) 6742-1543; fax (2) 6742-0249; e-mail ianb@pinewoodrecords.com.au; internet www.pinewoodrecords.com.au; Man. Dir IAN B MACLEOD.

Premier Artists Pty Ltd: 9 Dundas Lane, Albert Park, VIC 3206; Man. Dir FRANK STIVALA.

Servant Communications: PO Box 2020, Launceston, Tasmania 7250; Pres. KEVIN N HOOPER.

Shawthing Entertainment: Entertainment Pl., PO Box 4, Broadway, QLD 4006; Man. JOHN MAHER.

Sphere Organization: Suite 15/835 Pennant Hills Rd, Carlingford, NSW 2118; tel. (2) 9872-4144; fax (2) 9872-3992; e-mail sphere@sphereorg.com.au; internet www.sphereorg.com.au; Dir/Man. ERIC 'CHUBBY' CARLINI.

Sun Promotions: PO Box 192, West Ryde, Sydney, NSW 2114; Reggae Promoter/Venue Consultant TED VASSELL.

Trading Post Entertainments Agency: PO Box 124, Round Corner, Sydney, NSW 2158; Man. Dir/Booking Agent OWEN ORFORD.

Austria

Austrian International Artist Agency: M Felder str 5, 6900 Bregenz; Man. Dir VIKTOR PAMMINGER.

Live Performance Service: Esteplatz 3/13, 1030 Vienna; Pres. FRITZ THOM.

Memphis Music Concerts: Sleveringerstr 194, 1190 Vienna; Man. Dir WOLFGANG BERGELT.

Milica: Liebhartstalstr 15/5, 1160 Vienna; Contact MILICA.

RATZ Promotions: Vorachstr 65, 6890 Lustenau; Contact THOMAS RADOVAN.

Rock Produktion West: Bregenzerstr 73, 6900 Bregenz; Man. Dir ALEX NUSSBAUMER.

RoCo Management: Huetteldorfer str 257C, 1140 Vienna; Owner ROLAND COLERUS.

Stein Music Wien: Bernardgasse 39/33, 1070 Vienna; Man. Dir REGINE STEINMETZ.

Wien Concerts: Margaretenstr 78, 1050 Vienna; Man. Dir JEFF MAXIAN.

Belarus

Beloton Records: Shrader str 8–15, Vitebsk 210015; Dir VLADIMIR SARTCHENKO.

Belgium

AALN International: PO Box 15, Antwerpen 17, 2018 Antwerp; Man. Dir LUC NUITTEN; Jazz, blues and world music events.

Backline: Kammerstraat 19, 9000 Ghent; Man. ROBERT VAN YPER; Bookings Agents SANDRA HEYLEN, LAWRENCE VAN DEN EEDE.

Boom!: Bergensesteenweg 19, 1500 Halle; tel. (0) 2360-2851; internet www.jpvan.be; Man. Dir J P VAN.

Centre Culturel de la Communaute Francaise Wallonie Bruxelles le Botanique: rue Royale 236, 1210 Brussels; Contact PAUL-HENRI WAUTERS.

CPA (Country Programmers' Association): St Pieterstraat 34/2, 2400 Mol; Pres. ERIC VAN DE MERT.

Euro Promo Music: 5 Sq. de Noville, 1080 Brussels; Chair. HANS PICCINI.

Foundation VZW: Fruithoflaan 124, PO Box 11, 2600 Berchem/Antwerp; Dirs PETER VERSTRAEVEN, BERT VAN ROY.

Kras Artists: Leernsesteenweg 168, 9800 Deinze; Dir JEAN TANT.

L&S Agency: PO Box 5, 3800 Sint-Truiden 2; tel. 11671701; fax 11673331; e-mail lsagency@belgacom.net; internet www.lsagency.be; Man. Dir MARK STRAUVEN.

Les Fruits de la Passion Asbl: Pl. du Nord 3, 4000 Liege; tel. 495546089; fax 42234848; Man. Dir BERNARD HEMBLENNE; Concert promotor.

Merlijn: Gulden Vlieslaan 67, 8000 Brugge; Contact NICO A MERTENS.

Music BaM: Lelielaan 11, 2460 Lichtaart; Man. Dir GERT VAN DINGENEN; Asst Man. Dir TOM VAN DINGENEN.

Paperwork: Aarschotsesteenweg 245, 3012 Wilsele; Man. JOHAN P BERCKMANS.

Pyramid International Music: Lepelhoekstraat 26, 9100 Sint-Niklaas; tel. (3) 778-1854; fax (3) 766-8441; e-mail marc@marcdecoen.be; internet www.marcdecoen.be; Man. Dir MARC DE COEN.

Rainbow Records & Music: Herentaesesteenweg 20A, 2220 Heist-Op-Den Berg; tel. (0) 1524-4950; fax (0) 1524-1470; Contact KATHLEEN GOSSENS.

Show Organisation: Drève du Prophète 23A, 7000 Mons; Man. Dir GEORGE HAYES.

Swing Promotions: Beukenlaan 3, 2970 Schilde; Man. WIM GROOS.

Tour de Force: rue des Archers 19–21, 1080 Brussels; Man. Dir TON VAN DRAANEN.

TTT: Vriesenhof 22/5, 3000 Leuven; Mans RICK TUBBAX, JOHAN P BERCKMANS.

Witlof: Leernsesteenweg 168, 9800 Deinze; Dir JEAN TANT.

Bolivia

HR Producciones: Loayza 349, 15°, Dpto 1503, Edifico Loayza, La Paz; Gen. Man. NESTOR HORACIO RASGIDO.

Bulgaria

Arsis Productions: 15 Tsarigradsko Chausse Blvd, 1220 Sofia; Chair. VELIZAR SOKOLOV.

Mega Music Ltd: 2 Trapezitza str, 1000 Sofia; Man. Dir DORA TCHERNKVA.

New Music Agency: Nadejda Bl 634, Apt 14, 1231 Sofia; tel. 9825-6509; fax 2934-4297; e-mail christ@newmusic.bg; internet www.newmusic.bg; Pres. CHRISTO ROUSSANOV.

Sofia Music Enterprise: 15 Ivan Rilski str, 1000 Sofia; Man. Dir DIMITUR KOVACHEV.

Sofiaconcert Artistic Agency: Volov 3, 1527 Sofia; Man. JEANNA MOLLOVA.

Canada

Am-Can International Talent Inc: 9615 Macleod Trail S, Calgary, AB T2J 0P6; VP Dir of Sales FRANK SCOTT.

Amok Artist Agency: Suite 202, 243 Main St East, Milton, ON L9T 1P1; Contact LORENZ EPPINGER.

August Music: 4 Maple Lead Lane, Aberfoyle, ON N1H 6H9; Gen. Man. PAUL EMBRO.

Bandstand (International Entertainment Agency): PO Box 1010, Simcoe, ON N3Y 5B3; Pres. WAYNE ELLIOT.

Big Time Productions Ltd: 54 Duncombe Dr, Lower Level, Hamilton, ON L9A 2G2; Pres./CEO JOHN BALOGH JR.

BWL Entertainment Connection: 19 Acadia Cres., St Catharines, ON L2P 1H7; Contact BRUCE LILLEY.

Community Box Offices: 1234 W Hastings St, Vancouver, BC V6E 2M4.

ESP—Elwood Saracuse Productions: 720 Spadina Ave, #1702, Toronto, ON M5S 2T9; Pres. ELWOOD SARACUSE.

Festival City Folk Guild: 129 Bedford Dr., Stratford, ON N5A 5J7; Dir BETH BEECH.

Firestar Promotions Inc: PO Box 165, 1896 West Broadway, Vancouver, BC, V6J 1Y9; Pres. FIRESTAR.

Gino Empry Entertainment: 315–120 Carlton St, Toronto, ON M5A 4K2; Owner GINO EMPRY.

Joanne Smale Productions Ltd: 51 Bulwer St, Main Level, Toronto, ON M5T 1A1; Pres. JOANNE SMALE.

KISS Talent Referrals: 19695, 56th Ave, Langley, BC, V3A 3X7; Man./Agent SHANNON M MYERS.

More Than Booking: 1819 Granville St, 4th Floor, Halifax, NS B3J 3R1; Pres. WAYNE O'CONNOR.

Music Company Entertainment: 31 Hamlet Rd, SW, Calgary, AB T2V 3C9; Pres. FRED THOUTENHOOFD.

Nat Raider Productions Inc: 5799 Eldriege Ave, Montréal, QC H4W 2E3; Pres. NAT RAIDER.

Noteable Entertainment Ltd: 940 Brunette Ave, Coquitlam, BC, V3K 1C9; Dir, Country Division DON BUCHANAN.

Productions Martin Leclerc Inc: 2220 rue Notre-Dame Ouest, Suite 201, Montréal, QC H3J 2V4; Man. MARTIN LECLERC.

Regal Recordings Ltd: 2421 Hammond Rd, Mississauga, ON L5K 1T3; Vice-Pres. DOREEN M DAVEY.

Rose Concert Productions Inc: PO Box 23053, London, ON N6A 5N9; Promoter DAVID ROSE.

Showcana Corporation: PO Box #4689, Station C, Calgary, AB T2T 5P1; Pres. ROBERT JAMES CHIN.

Siegel Entertainment Ltd: 101–1648 W 7th Ave, Vancouver, BC, V6J 1S5; tel. (604) 736-3896; fax (604) 736-3464; e-mail siegelent@telus.net; internet www.siegelent.com; Pres. ROBERT SIEGEL.

Silverhawk Publishing: 3073 Cedarbank Rd, Rural Route 11, Peterborough, ON K9J 6Y3; Pres. JIM FREAKE.

SL Feldman & Associates: 1505 W 2nd Ave, Suite 200, Vancouver, BC V6H 3Y4; tel. (604) 734-5945; fax (604) 732-0922; e-mail feldman@slfa.com; internet www.slfa.com; Proprietor SAM L FELDMAN; Sr Vice-Pres. SHAW SALTZBERG.

Sphere Entertainment: 22 Bainsford Rd, Toronto, ON M4L 3N4; Pres. PATRICIA SILVER.

Stella Black Live Music: PO Box 23, St Anne de Belle, QC, H9X 3L4; Pres. STELLA BLACK.

Trick Or Treat Entertainment: 1971 Spruce Hill Rd, Pickering, ON L1V 1S6; Contact KAY WHITE.

Vocal Image Productions: 192 Kensington Rd, Charlottetown, PEI C1A 7S3; Man. BERNI WOOD.

Chile

Best: Jarunska 88, 41000 Zagreb; Man. Dir MIRKO KRAMARIC.

Galo Producciones SA: Hernando de Aguirre, 944 Providencia, Santiago; Gen. Man. ALFREDO SAINT-JEAN.

Geomusica: Paseo Poniente, 4593 El Portal de la Viña, Santiago; Dir CLAUDIO CÁCERAS.

Jazzette: Avenija Vukovar 35, 41000 Zagreb; Man. KOLJA PETROVIC.

Prodin Chile SA: Tomas Andrews 089, Comuna de Providencia, Santiago; Exec. Dir ERNESTO CLAVERIA.

Producciones Macondo Chile Ltda: Alvarez 58 L-6, Viña Del Mar; Man. ALFREDO TRONCOSO.

Ricardo Suarez Daud Y Cia Ltda: La Concepción 81, Of. 405, Providencia, Santiago; Man. RICARDO SUÁREZ DAUD.

Romero & Campbell Producciones: Bombero Nuñez, 385 Barrio Bellavista, Santiago; Dir CARMEN ROMERO QUERO.

T R I P: Argentinska 3, 10000 Zagreb; A & R Man. ALEKSANDAR DRAGAS.

Urban Concert: K Tomislava 30, 42300 Cakovec; Dir TONI SABOL.

Croatia

BJ Promotions: D Cesarica 11, 41000 Zagreb; Man. Dir BORISLAV JANKOVIC.

Croatian Music Art: Trg S, Radica 4, 41000 Zagreb; Man. Dir DAMIR GOSTL.

Promomedia Ltd: Kralja Zvonimira 82, 10 000 Zabreb; Man. Dir MARIJAN CRNARIC.

Denmark

Arte Booking: Hvidkildevej 64, 2400 Copenhagen NV; Man. Dir FIMM THORKILDSEN.

Basement Productions: PO Box 394, 8900 Randers; Man. Dir PETER ASTRUP.

Buks Booking International: Gunløgsgade 15, 2300 Copenhagen; Dir THOMAS H HANSEN.

DKB Concertpromotion Aps: Vester Soegade 44, 1601 Copenhagen V; Man. Dir STEEN MARIBOE.

ET Promotion: Skindergade 8, 1159 Copenhagen K; Man. Dir OLE DREYER.

International Concert Organization: Rosenborggade 1, 1130 Copenhagen K; tel. 3312-2000; fax 3393-2290; e-mail arne@concerts.dk; internet www.concerts.dk; Man. Dir ARNE WORSOE.

Musicline: Livjægergade, 2100 Copenhagen O; Contact NIELS CHRISTENSEN.

PDH Dansk Musik Formidling: Ny Vestergade 7, 1471 Copenhagen K; Personal Man. OLE DREYER.

Rock On International: Raadhusstraede 4A, 1466 Copenhagen K; Man. Dir JOHN ROSING.

Soren Hojberg Booking: Frodesgade 74, 6700 Esbjerg; Man. Dir SOREN HOJBERG.

TG Management: Badehusvej 1, 9000 Aalborg; Man. JOHN AAGAARD.

Ecuador

William's Convention Center: Los Rios, 920 Y Hurtado, 11692 Guayquil; Gen. Man. WILLIAM SAN ANDRÉS.

Estonia

Estonian Jazz Foundation: PO Box 3641, Viru str 16, 0090 Tallinn; Dir TIIT LAUK.

Raivo Pihlak: 2061 Purtse; Owner RAIVO PIHLAK.

Tallinn Rock Club: Sopruse Pst 219-68, 13414 Tallin; tel. 652-4345; fax 656-3157; Man. Dir ANATOLY BELOV.

Tartu Jazzclub: Laulupeo 25, 2400 Tartu; Man. AADU BIRNBAUM.

Fiji

Communications Fiji Ltd: 23 Stewart St, Suva; Man. Dir WILLIAM PARKINSON.

Finland

NEM: PO Box 220, 33201 Tampere; Man. Dir HARRI KARVINEN.

Piikkikasvi Agency: PO Box 145, 00531 Helsinki; Man. Dir KARI PÖSSI.

Rockadillo: PO Box 35, 33201 Tampere; Man. Dir TAPIO KORJUS.

France

Agence Kathoche: 16 rue de Marignan, 75008 Paris; Agent/Dir CATHERINE POENSIN.

Alias: 17 Ave Trudaine, 75009 Paris; Chair. DOMINIQUE REVERT.

Aquitania Editions—Stars: Domaine de Barry, 33690 Sigalens; Dir PRYL ON LATASTE.

Atefact: 13 rue du Howald, 67000 Strasbourg; Dir PATRICK SCHNEIDER.

Blue Line Productions: 5 rue Leon, Giraud, 75019 Paris; Dir MICHEL VAUTROT.

Caramba! Productions: 7 Pl. de Seoul, 75014 Paris; Dir LUC GAURICHON.

Diogene Productions: Le Grand Kerven, 29200 Brest; Dir JACQUES ABALAIN.

Do Si La Ba: 159 Chemin Lanusse, 31200 Toulouse; Man. LAWRENCE LARROUY.

Encore Productions: 8 rue de Mont-Thabor, 75001 Paris; Dir PASCAL BERNARDIN.

Festirock Organisation: Parl Tertiaire Dijon Est, 2 bis rue du Cap Vert, 21800 Quetigny; Pres. G GRAS.

Fiesta Latina Homero Cardoso: 51 rue Mirabeau, 94200 Ivry Sur Seine; Promoter HOMERO CARDOSO.

Francophonie Diffusion: 33 rue du Faubourg, Saint-Antoine, 75011 Paris; Dir MARIE CHRISTINE BLOCH.

Leon: 23 rue des Manguiers, 34070 Montpellier; Mans PHILIPPE MAURIZI, SEAN HERVE MICHEL.

LPI/Isotope Agency: 23 rue Gravette, 31300 Toulouse; Man. JEAN PHILIPPE MORER.

L'Usine: 115 rue Lesage, 51100 Reims; Pres. ALAIN BOUCHERON.

Meyer Productions: 10 rue de L'Isly, 75008 Paris; Mans OLIVIA MEYER, CHRISTIAN MEYER.

Noumatrouff/Fédération Hiéro: 57 rue de la Mertzav, 68100 Mulhouse; Dir LODET-BOISSE SIMON.

Ripost—Le Bocal Association Ripost: 23 Route de Villeflanzy, 41000 Villebarou-Blois; Pres. DENIS TRADEAU.

Salam Aleikum Amusements: 2 rue Carpeaux, 75018 Paris; Dir STEPHANE BENHAMOU.

VMA: 40 rue François 1er; 75008 Paris; Dir ROSE LEANDRI.

Germany

Art Concerts GmbH: Widenmayer str 41, 80538 Munich; Dir FRANZ ABRAHAM.

ASS Concert & Promotion GmbH: PO Box 730225, 22122 Hamburg; Pres MICHAEL BISPING, DIEKR SCHUBERT.

Bizarre Productions GmbH: Buelaustr 8, 20099 Hamburg; Man. Dir CHRISTOPHER BROSCH.

Blue Star Promotion Konzertagentur GmbH: Goebenstr 3, 28209 Bremen; Public Relations MICHAEL K GRUSCHE.

Castor Promotions: Dragonerstr 21, 30163 Hanover; Contact ELKE FLEING.

Freestyle eV: Morgensternsweg 7, 22305 Hamburg; Contact HELMUT HEUER; Music festival and event organisers.

Freibank: Ditmar-Koel str 26, 20459 Hamburg; Dirs MARK CHUNG, KLAUS MAECK.

Harde & Partner: Unter de Linde 20, 80939 Munich; Owner JASMINE HARDE.

Harry Fox: Steinstr 53, 81667 Munich; Contact HARRY FOX.

Hello Concerts GmbH: Philippine-Welser str 6, Rathausplatz, 86150 Augsburg; tel. (0821) 154027; fax (0821) 154020; e-mail mail@helloconcerts.de; internet www.helloconcerts.de; Contacts WALTER CZERMAK, LOTHAR SCHLESSMANN.

Karsten Jahnke Konzertdirektion GmbH: PO Box 130553, Oberstr 14b, 20144 Hamburg; tel. (40) 414-788; fax (40) 443-597; e-mail info@karsten-jahnke.de; internet www.karsten-jahnke.de; Man. & Owner KARSTEN JAHNKE.

Kick Musikverlag: Burgunder str 8, 50677 Cologne; Man. Dir GOETZ ELBERTZHAGEN; International Man. LYNDA HILL.

Kultur in Der Landschaft: Brückstr 16, 76703 Kraichtal; tel. 7251-69471; fax 7251-61571; internet www.kultur-i-d-landschaft.de; Contact BRUNO WALLISCH.

Künstlersekretariat Ott: Moltkestr 18, 79098 Freiburg; Contact DIETER OTT.

M A D Fuesgen/Nickel GBR: Hagelberger str 48, 10965 Berlin; Owner UTE FUESGEN.

Moskito Promotion: PO Box 3072, 48016 Münster; e-mail info@grover.de; internet www.grover.de; Man. Dir OSWALD MÜNNIG.

Music Box GmbH: Rahlstedter str 65, 22149 Hamburg; Man. Dir HUBERTUS BRANZKO.

Musik Komh GmbH: Rottscheidter str 6, 42329 Wuppertal; Head of PR Dept ANDREA ZECH.

Piranha Kultur & Medien Produktion GmbH: Carmer str 11, 10623 Berlin; tel. (30) 318-6140; fax (30) 3186-1410; e-mail womex@womex.com; internet www.womex.com; Man. Dir BORKOWSKY AKBAR.

Synthetic Product Records: PO Box 690441, 30613 Hanover; Contact LORENZ MACKE.

Thomann Künstler Management GmbH: PO Box 1, 96136 Burgebrach; tel. (9546) 9449; fax (9546) 6844; e-mail info@thomann-music.de; internet www.thomann-music.de; Contact JOSEPH THOMANN.

Greece

Anosi: 20 Zan Moreas St, 15232 Halandri Athens; Man. Dir NICK HASSID.

Rock Management: PO Box 21526, 55236 Panorama, Thessaloniki; Man. Dir CHRISTOS TERZIDES.

Show Productions: 318 Sygrou Av, 17673 Kalithea, Athens.

Show Productions: 318 Sygrou Ave, 17673 Kalithea, Athens; Man. Dir KONSTANTINOS ARVANITIS; Public Relations ANTA ARVANTI.

Sound & Vision Music: Militiadou str 9, 10560 Athens; Man. Dir DOZI PANAGIOTOPOULOU.

Hong Kong

Arena Group Ltd: 602 California Tower, 30–32 D'Aguilar St, Central Hong Kong; Contact ALLEN JAPP.

International Management Group: 12/F Sunning Plaza, 10 Hysan Ave, Causeway Bay; Dir MARK COWLEY.

Hungary

Darshan Court Cultural Centre: Krudy Gy u 7, 1088 Budapest; tel. 1266-6139; e-mail darshan@axelero.hu; Contact KAROLY CSONKICS.

Krokodil Kft: Parisi u 6B, 1052 Budapest; Man. Dir LASZLO BESNYÖ.

Multimedia Ltd: Steindl Imre 4 12, 1054 Budapest; Man. Dir LASZLO HEGEDUS.

OB Art Management/Alt Product: PO Box 76, 5002 Szolnok; Man. Dir BELA PAP.

PG Productions: PO Box 8, 5002 Szolnok; Man. Dir PETER PAP.

Purple Concerts: Menyelske u. 11 F/1, 1112 Budapest; Man. Dir MARTON BRADY.

Iceland

Bo Haldorson Productions: PO Box 5445, Pverholt 26, 105 Reykjavík; Man. Dir BO HALDORSON.

Smekkleysa / Bad Taste: PO Box 710, 121 Reykjavík; Man. Dir ASMUNDUR JONSSON.

Spor HF: Nýbýlavegur 4, PO Box 320, 202 Kópavogur; Man. Dir STEINAR BERG ISLEIFSSON.

Indonesia

Art Circle Network: Jl Cut Meutia 5, Jakarta-Pusat; Marketing Dir GUMILANG RAMADHAN.

JEF Production: Jl Setiabudi Tengah 29, Jakarta-Pusat; Contact SOFYAN ALI.

Ono Artists Promotion: Jalan Tebet Barat 1, No. 23, Jakarta 12810; Dir RINNY NOOR.

Ireland

Ackland Productions: 35 Rehoboth Pl., Dublin 8; Dir JODY ACKLAND.

AX-S Records: 26 Mount Eagle View, Leopardstown Heights, Dublin 18; Man. Dir PETER JONES.

Bluemedia Ltd: 7 Willow Cres., Riverbank, Anacotty, Limerick; tel. (61) 331276; fax (61) 331277; e-mail bluemedia@eircom.net; internet www.bluemedia.ie; Man. Dir JOE CLARKE.

Denis Desmond Promotions: Top House, Clontarf St, Cork 1; Man. Dir DENIS DESMOND.

Fifty-Seventh Street Ltd: 24 Upper Mount St, Dublin 2; Contacts MAURICE CASSIDY, ELIZABETH REEVES.

Frontline Promotions: Thompson House, MacCurtain St, Cork City; PRO PAUL MCDERMOTT.

HARMONY Music Management Ltd: The Grange, Carbury, Co Kildare; tel. (405) 53005; fax (405) 53224; e-mail infocus@eircom.net; internet www.infocus.ie; Man. Dir JOHN H PICKERING.

Joe McFadden Promotions: 19 Stockton Green, Castleknock, Dublin 15; Man. Dir JOE MCFADDEN.

Kieran Cavanagh Promotions: 56 Fitzwilliam Sq., Dublin 2; Man. Dir KIERAN CAVANAGH.

Mister T Productions: 141 Parnell St, Dublin 1; tel. and fax (1) 878-7623; e-mail mistert@ireland.com; Dir TONIE WALSH.

Pat Egan Sound Ltd: Merchant's Court, 24 Merchant's Quay, Dublin 8; Man. Dir PAT EGAN.

Project Arts Centre: 39 East Essex St, Dublin 2; Contacts JODY ACKLAND, ANN MARIE WALSH.

RSE Promotions: 11–13 Station Rd, Raheny, Dublin 5; Dir RAYMOND J SMYTH.

Italy

Azelea Promotion: Via Gelio Cassi 36/a, 33053 Latisana (UD); Man. Dir IVAN TRAMONTIN.

Big Mama: Vicolo S Francesco & Ripa, 18 00153 Rome; Man. MARCO TIRIEMMI.

Circuito Giovani Artisti Italiani: Via Assarotti 2, 10122 Torino; Network Sec. LUIGI RATCLIF.

City Medial Two: Via Premuda 30, 42100 Reggio Emilia; Man. Dir ROBERTO MEGLIOLI.

Giancarlo Passarella: Via Salutati 7, 50126 Florence; Contact GIANCARLO PASSARELLA.

Lion Snc: Via Goldoni 42/A, 30174 Mestre, Venezia; Gen. Man. LUCIANO TREVISAN.

Made In Italy Productions: Piazale Clodio 8, 00195 Rome; Man. Dir GEPINO AFELTRA.

Rock Alliance Productions: Via Marrone 20, 33170 Pordenone; Dir CORRADO RIZZOTTO.

Skip Agency: Via Sivori 16–23, 16136 Genova; Man. Dir ROBERTO SARACCO.

Solid Rock: Passarella Giancarlo, Via Salutati 7, 50126 Florence.

Zard Iniziative: Viale Mazzini 6, 00195 Rome; Chair. DAVID ZARD.

Japan

Global Enterprise Co Ltd: 1-15-3 Dogenzaka, Primera Dogenzaka Ste 816, Shibuya-ku, Tokyo 150; Contact OHNO.

Hayashi International Promotion: Aoyama Nozu Bldg 4F, 3-31-20 Jingumae, Shibuya-ku, Tokyo 150; Contact MASSY HAYASHI.

Min-On Concert Association: 1-32-13 Kita-Shinjuku, Shinjuku-ku, Tokyo 169; Contact TERUO NAKAMURA.

Republic of Korea

Big CI Event: 901 Dongbuk Bldg, 45-14 Youido-dong, Youngdeungpo-ku, Seoul 150 010; Contact WON BOCK CHOI.

Cosmos Event Promotion: 401 Seongwon Bldg, 3-1 Pil-dong, 1-ga, Jung-ku, Seoul; Contact SUN CHUL KANG.

Seoul Promotions: UN Mansion, Ste 2 B2, 1035 Shinsa-dong, Yongsan-ku, Seoul; Contact TAE-HYUN LEE.

Luxembourg

Folk Clupp Letzerverg A S B L: PO Box 2745, 1027; Pres. MARCO UHRES.

Promotion 4: PO Box 728, 2017 Luxembourg; Chair. MIKE KOEDINGER.

Real Music: 27 rue Victor Hugo, 4583 Differdange; Contact ANDRE DEPIENNE.

Malaysia

Asia Entertainment Network: 2768–2769 Jalan Changkat Permata, Taman Permata, Ulu Kelang, Kuala Lumpur 53300; Exec. Chair. MIKE BERNIE.

Music City Entertainment Corp: 20 Jalan 20/101, Taman Desa Aman, Cheras, Kuala Lumpur 56100; Man. Dir JOHN CHACKO.

The Netherlands

ACT: Van Leeuwenhoeksingel 69, 2611 AE Delft; Contact A C RAVEN.

Buro Gogo: PO Box 7092, 9701 JB Groningen; tel. (50) 314-4110; (50) 314-0174; e-mail info@burogogo.nl; Agent IGOR MÖNNINK.

DIBA International Concerts: PO Box 37, Westersingel 46, 8600 AA Sneek; tel. (515) 420510; fax (515) 423606; e-mail bauke@diba.nl; internet www.diba.nl; Man. Dir BAUKE ALGERA.

Music World Management: PO Box 55 55 9, 1007 NB Amsterdam; Man. Dir PAUL COOPS.

Orange Artist Promotion: Bezuidenhoutseweg 106, 2594 AZ Den Haag; Man. Dir DIDO SMIT.

Paperclip Agency: PO Box 1519, 6501 BM Nymegen; tel. (24) 323-9322; fax (24) 323-2762; e-mail info@paperclip-agency.com; internet www.paperclip-agency.com; Proprietor ROB BERENDS.

Varke International Promotions: Looiersgracht 38, 1016 VS Amsterdam; Man. GERRIE BEZUIJEN.

New Zealand

Benny Levin Promotions Ltd: PO Box 5564, Auckland; Contact LOUISE HUNTER.

Chamber Music New Zealand: PO Box 6238, Wellington; Gen. Man. ELISABETH AIREY.

Entertainment Venues of New Zealand (EVANZ): Private Bag 3029, Rotorua; tel. (07) 347-2751; fax (07) 347-2816; e-mail nick.dallimore@rdc.gout.nz; internet www.evanz.co.nz; Pres. NICK DALLIMORE.

Pacific Region Entertainment Services: PO Box 25275, Auckland 5; Contact GARY BARTLETT, KEITH GOSLING.

Real Groovy Promotions: 438 Queen St, Auckland; Promotions Man. PAUL ROSE.

Shawthing Entertainment NZ Ltd: 18 Steyne Ave, Plimmerton, Wellington; Man. Dir PHILIPPA BROWNE.

Sons of Thunder: PO Box 509, 4 Dellys Grove, Levin 5500; Man. Dir REGAN CUNLIFFE.

Norway

Major Artist: Rosenborggaten 19, 0308 Oslo 8; Man. JAN PAULSEN.

Norsk Lyd & Bilde/Norwegian Sound & Vision: Rute 598, 2760 Brandbu; Dirs ODD ERIK, ELI KRISTIN HAGEN.

Petter Sandberg A/S: Cort Adelersgt 2, 0254 Oslo; Contact JAN SOLLIEN.

WAPL: Gamle Kongev 16, 0743 Trondheim; Man. Dir KENNETH NYGARD.

Panama

Ache Booking Agency: Calle 2, Casa 213, Zona 5, Nuevo Reparto Panamá, 6373 Panamá; Pres. PABLO YANES.

Peru

Acordes EIRL: Los Paujiles 285 D, Lima 34; Proprietor JULIE FREUNDT LÓPEZ.

In & Out Artists: Avda Larco 930, Of. 702 Miraflores, Lima 18; Pres. ROBERTO BEAUMONT FRAÑOWSKY.

Pro Art SA: Diez Canseco 236, Of. 403, Miraflores, Lima 18; Dir-Gen. JORGE FERRAND LANCIOTTI.

The Philippines

GR Creative Management Services: 7 Washington St, Midland Park Manor II, Greenhills, San Juan, Metro Manilla; Pres. GERLIE RODIS.

Octoarts Entertainments: 108 Panay Ave, Quezon City, Metro Manila; Man. Dir ORLY ILACAD.

Poland

Dzem Agency: PO Box 580, Katowice 2; Contact ENA OTOLINSUA.

Interart Ltd: Ul Pugeta 6, 51-628 Wroclaw; Contact MARGARET SZABLOWSKA.

Kantaro Art Agency: Ul. Polistancov W Ucp 20, 70-110 Szczecin; Owner WITOLD TANCZYNSKI.

Metal Mind Productions Sp Z 00: Szeligiewicza 8/21, 40-044 Katowice; Man. Dir TOMASZ DRIVBINSKI.

Tomasz Bielski Agency: Ul. Krucza 49, 00509 Warsaw; Gen. Man. TOMASZ BIELSKI; Man. Dir KRZYSZTOF WOTOWIEC.

Warsaw Artists Management Ltd: Kazimierzowska 47/5, 02-572 Warsaw; Pres. ANDRZEJ HALUCH.

ZPR Inc–United Entertainment Enterprises Inc: Senatorska 13/15, 00 075 Warsaw; Pres./CEO ZBIGNIEW BENBENEK; Artists & Marketing Man. ANNA KAROLICKA.

Portugal

Concertos de Portugal: Lote 23, Sub Cave Esq, Quinta de so Miguel das Encostas, 2775 Carcavelos/Parede; Contact AFONSO GOMES.

MTM: PO Box 30072, 1321 Lisbon Codex; Man. Dir HUGO MOUTINHO.

Regiespectáculo: Alto do Coutão, Armazem I, 2735 Cacém; CEO ANTÓNIO GUIMARÃES.

Romania

AMMA: Scara B, Apart 73, Calea Victorei 48/50, Sector 1, 70102 Bucharest; Man. AUREL MITRAN.

Artexim: 155 Calea Victorei, Bl D1, Scara 8, Et 2, 71102 Bucharest; Gen. Man. MIHAI CONSTANTINESCU.

Cartianu Ltd: 58 Aviator Traian Vasile str, Sector 1, 78336 Bucharest; Chair. RADU CARTIANU.

Holograf Productions Srl: 26 SF Elefterie str, Sector 5, Bucharest; Man. Dir HORIA MOCULESCU.

Russia

Biz Enterprises: Bolshaya Serpukhovskaya 27, 129 010 Moscow; Man. Dir SERGEY CHISTOPRUDOV.

Fee Lee Promotion: 27 Novozavodskaya str, 121 309 Moscow; Man. Dir IGOR TONKIKH.

Rock-Azia: Pupova 96-268, Barnaul, 656062 Siberia; Contact EUGENE KOLBASHEV.

SAV Entertainment: Milyutinsky Per 15/24, 101 000 Moscow; tel. (095) 925-6422; fax (095) 923-7665; e-mail saven@col.ru; Chair. NADIA SOLOVIEVA.

Singapore

Hype Records Pte Ltd: 221 Henderson Rd, Suite 02–04 Henderson Bldg, Singapore 159557; tel. 375-3787; fax 275-2757; e-mail hype@hyperecords.com; internet www.hyperecords.com; Administration Man. MELVIS YIP.

International Management Group: 50 Cuscaden Rd, 05-02 HPL House, Singapore 1024; Contact BART COLLINS.

Jasper Productions: Unit 157A, 1st Floor, Thomson Rd, Singapore 1130; Contact JIMMY LOH.

Top Ten Entertainment: 400 Orchard Rd, 05-18A Orchard Towers, Singapore 0923; Man. Dir PETER BADER.

Slovenia

BUBA Booking and Promotion: PO Box 38, 40A Moskriceva, 1110 Ljubljana; tel. and fax (1) 542-4411; e-mail buba@moj.net; internet www.ljudmila.org/buba/; Contact IRENA POVSE.

FV-Zavod Za Umetnisko in Kulturno Produkcijo: Kersnikova 4, 61000 Ljubljana; Man. Dir SKABERNE MÓNIKA.

Radio Student: Cesta 27, Aprila 31, Blou 8, 61000 Ljubljana; Music Editor IGOR BASIN.

SKUC—AFK: Kersnikova 4, 61000 Ljubljana; Man. Dir MITJA PREZELJ.

Spain

Artcelona: Regomir 3, 08002 Barcelona; tel. (93) 315-2698; fax (93) 315-2050; e-mail agnes.blot@artcelona.com; internet www.artcelona.com; Dir ANGEL DOMÍNGUEZ.

AZ Productions: Riera de Argentona, s/n, 08300 Nataro (Barcelona); International Dept PERE-LLUIS PONT.

Colectivo Promocion de Jazz: Navarro Reverter 22, 46004 Valencia; Contact JULIO MARTIN.

Diez Management: Martinez Corrochano 3, 28007 Madrid; Chair. MERCEDES MARTIN.

GSG—Grup de Serveis Guilleries: Granja Baró, Ctra de la Guixa, km 2, 08500 VIC (Barcelona); Administration JORDI COSTA; Management IGNASI PLA; Production JOAN CAPDEVILA.

Munster Tourin—Espárrago Rock Productions S L: c/ Reyes Catdlicos 25 Of. 2 Planta, 18001 Granada; Promotion Dir JAVIER GONZALEZ.

Nox Producciones: Gran Via 40, 7-2, 28013 Madrid; Man. GLORIA PARRA.

Pino Sagliocco Presenta SL: C/ Quintana 2, 7° 9a, 28008 Madrid; Chair. PINO SAGLIOCCO.

Posto Nove: Muntaner 494 5B, 08022 Barcelona; Contact ALEJANDRO NAVARRO.

RLM Producciones: Jose Maria Cavero 9, Ch A, 28027 Madrid; Man. Dir ROSA LAGARRIGUE.

Store Music: Gran Via 28, 3C, 18010 Granada; Man. Dir CARMEN CARNICERO.

UADR Marketing: Residencial Coruna 21, Casa 5, 28230 Las Rozas; Dir CARLOS LOPEZ.

Sweden

Ema Telstar: PO Box 1018, 181 21 Lidingö; Man. Dir THOMAS JOHANSSON.

Energy Records AB: Vastergatan 23, 21121 Malmö; Contact HÅKAN EHRNST.

Export Music Sweden (ExMS): PO Box 27 327, 102 54 Stockholm; tel. 8783-8800; fax 8783-9510; e-mail christer@exms.com; internet www.exms.com; Gen. Man. CHRISTER LUNDBLAD.

Fritid & Nöjen: Sandgatan 2, 223 50 Lund; Pres. JULIUS MALMSTRÖM.

Headlne Productions: PO Box 5948, Vasatorget 1, 700 05 Örebro; Man. Dir DENNIS KARLSSON.

Luger Production: Fredriksgatan 35, 811 33 Sandviken; Man. Dir/Agent OLA BROQUIST; Agents PATRICK FREDRIKSSON, MORGAN JOHANSSON.

M & A Music Art: Simrishamnsgatan 20A, 214 23 Malmo; Man. Dir ANDREAS LARSSON.

Projektbyrån: Kungsgatan 34, 972 41 Luleå; Man. Dir TOMAS LIND.

Release Musik & Media: PO Box 7144, 402 33 Gothenburg; Man. Dir LOTTA JANSSON.

RMP Management AB: PO Box 17180, 104 62 Stockholm; Man. Dir STEFAN LIGA.

Siljemark Production: Gärdsvagen 2, 171 52 Solna; Man. JONAS SILJEMARK; Contact LASSE KARLSSON.

Storsjöyran: Storgatan 28, 831 30 Ostersund; Man. Dir STEFAN KAUPPI.

United Stage Production AB: PO Box 9174, 200 39 Malmo; Man. Dir ANDERS LARSSON.

Switzerland

Artways Productions: rue des-deux-Gares 6B, PO Box 30, 1800 Vevey; Man. FABRICE LA LUC.

BAROCK Enterprises: Waldheimstr 17, 3604 Thun; tel. and fax (33) 335-3530; e-mail barock@bluewin.ch; internet www.barock.ch; Contact BEAT AEGLER.

Jazz Willisau: PO Box, 6130 Willisau; tel. (41) 970-2731; fax (41) 970-3231; e-mail troxler@centralnet.ch; internet www.jazzwillisau.ch; Dir NIKLAUS TROXLER; Festival of jazz.

Joker System Agency: PO Box 325, 1000 Lausanne 17; Man. Dir MARC LAMBELET.

L'Agence Marcel Schiess: 12 rue du Premier Mars, 2300 La-Chaux-de-Fonds; Contact MARCEL SCHIESS.

Music Service Adi Weiss AG: Buhlweg 5, PO Box 265, 3072 Ostermandiga 2; tel. (31) 930-1010; fax (31) 930-1015; e-mail roli.roethlisberger@musicservice.ch; internet www.musicservice.ch; Pres. ROLAND RÖTHLISBERGER.

Rocking Chair: PO Box 4, 1800 Vevey 2; Contact NICOLA DE PINTO.

SOFA Agency: PO Box 101, 1707 Fribourg; Contact PASCAL HUNKELER, JACQUES SCHOUWEY.

Swiss Music Edition: PO Box 7851, 6000 Luzern 7; tel. and fax (41) 210-6070; e-mail mail@musicedition.ch; Sec. PETER BITTERLI.

VIP AG Productions: Schützengasse 30, 8001 Zürich; Man. Dir URS PETER KELLER.

Thailand

Music Train: 186 Soi Samarnmitr, Ramkhamhaeng Rd, Prakanong, Bangkok 10250; Man. Dir MR RAYA.

Nititad Entertainment: 1/79–80 Moo-Baan, Shinnaket Soi 10, Ngamwongwarn Rd, Bangken, Bangkok 10210; Man. Dir VICHIAN USVISESSIVAKUL.

Soco Entertainment: 21/9 Saladaeng 1 Silom, Bangkok 10500; Chair. SAM ARMENIO.

Turkey

Imaj Entertainment: Haci Adil Sokak, 4 Aralik No. 2, 80630 Levent, Istanbul; Dir HALE DICELI YAMANOGLU.

Major Musical Productions: Ihlamurdere Cad Misirli Sk, Arda Apt, 80690 Besiktas, Istanbul; Man. Dir EYUP IBLAG.

Most Production: Yildizcicegi Sok 7, Etiler,Istanbul; Chair. MUSTAFA OGUZ.

Pozitif: Istiklal Caddesi 1, Baro Han 611–612, 80080 Beyoglu, Istanbul; Pres. CEM YEGUL.

The United Kingdom

Acker's International Jazz Agency: 53 Cambridge Mansions, Cambridge Rd, London SW11 4RX; tel. (20) 7978-5885; fax (20) 7978-5882; e-mail pamela@ackersmusicagency.co.uk; internet www.ackersmusicagency.co.uk; Owner PAMELA FRANCES SUTTON.

Adastra: 2 Star Row, North Dalton, Driffield, East Yorkshire YO25 9UR; Owner CHRIS WADE.

Aiken Promotions Limited: Marlborough House, 348 Lisburn Rd, Belfast BT9 6GH, Northern Ireland; Contact PETER AIKEN.

Alan James Public Relations: 253 Camberwell New Rd, London SE5 0TH; Man. Dir ALAN JAMES.

Andrew Storr Entertainments: 2 Burn Grange Cottage, Doncaster Rd, Burn Nr Selby, North Yorkshire YO8 8LA; Partner PHIL STORR.

Asgard Management: 125 Parkway, London NW1 7PS; tel. (20) 7387-5090; fax (20) 7387-8740; e-mail pl@asgard.uk.com; Contact PAUL CHARLES.

Asgard Promotions Ltd: 125 Parkway, London NW1 7PS; tel. (20) 7387-5090; fax (20) 7387-8740; e-mail info@asgard-uk.com; Joint Man. Dirs PAUL FENN, PAUL CHARLES.

Autonomous Talent Booking: Unit 301 Alpha Business Centre, 60 South Grove, London E17 7NX; Contact MIKE HINC.

Barry Collings Entertainments: 21A Clifftown Rd, Southend-on-Sea, Essex SS1 1AB; tel. (1702) 330005; fax (1702) 333309; e-mail bcollent@aol.com; internet www.barrycollings.co.uk; Man. Dir BARRY COLLINGS.

BDA Ltd: Bryson House, Chiltern Rd, Culcheth, Warrington WA3 4LL; tel. (1925) 766655; fax (1925) 765577; e-mail brian.durkin@btinternet.com; Man. Dir BRIAN DURKIN.

Bernard Lee Management: Moorcroft Lodge, Farleigh Common, Warlingham, Surrey CR6 9PE; Man. Dir BERNARD LEE.

Big Bear Music: PO Box 944, Edgbaston, Birmingham B16 8UT; tel. (121) 4547020; fax (121) 4549996; e-mail admin@bigbearmusic.com; internet www.bigbearmusic.com; Man. Dir JIM SIMPSON.

Black Magic Management Ltd: 296 Earls Court Rd, London SW5 9BA; Man. Dir MATAYA CLIFFORD.

Blitz: Edgwarebury Farm, Edgwarebury Lane, Edgware, Middlesex HA8 8QX; Partners SUE HARRIS, CLAIRE POWELL.

BPR: 36 Como St, Romford, Essex RM7 7DR; tel. (1708) 725330; fax (1708) 725322; internet www.bprmusic.com; Man. BRIAN THEOBALD.

Brian Rix & Associates: PO Box 100, Ashford, Kent TN24 8AR; Operations Man. SIMON GRANT.

Brian Yeates Associates: Home Farm House, Canwell, Sutton Coldfield, West Midlands B75 5SH; tel. (121) 323-2200; fax (121) 323-2313; e-mail info@brianyeates.co.uk; internet www.brianyeates.co.uk; Contact BRIAN YEATES, ASHLEY YEATES.

Bull-Sheet Music: 18 The Bramblings, Chingford, London E4 6LU; tel. and fax (20) 8529-5807; e-mail irene.bull@btinternet.com; internet www.bull-sheetmusic.co.uk; Man. Dir IRENE BULL.

Burniston Cooke Productions: 69 MacFarlane Rd, London W12 7JY; Contact SIMON COOKE.

Buzz Records: 192 Glasgow Rd, Perth PH2 0NA, Scotland; Man. Dir DAVE ARCARI.

Cadillac Promotions: Cadillac Ranch, Pencraig Uchaf, Cwm Bach, Whitland, Dyfed SA34 0DT; tel. (1994) 484466; fax (1994) 484294; e-mail cadillac_ranch@telco4u.net; internet www.nikturner.com; Man. M MAGOON.

Clear Channel Entertainment (Music) UK Ltd: 1st Floor, Regent Arcade House, 252–260 Regent St, London W1B 3BX; tel. (20) 7009-3333; fax (8707) 493191; e-mail music@clearchannel.co.uk; internet www.uk.cc.com; Man. Dir TIM PARSONS.

Concorde International Artistes: Concorde House, 101 Shpeherds Bush Rd, London W6 7CP; Man. Dir LOUIS PARKER.

Creeme Entertainments: East Lynne, Harper Green Rd, Doe Hey, Farnworth, Bolton BL4 7HT; Partners TOM IVERS, LYNNE IVERS, ANTHONY IVERS.

Cromwell Management: 4–5 High St, Huntingdon, Cambs PE29 3TE; tel. (1480) 435600; fax (1480) 356250; e-mail tricvic@lineone.net; Man. Partner VIC GIBBONS.

D F Concerts Ltd: 272 St Vincent St, Glasgow G2 5RL, Scotland: tel. (141) 566-4998; e-mail admin@dfconcerts.co.uk; internet www.gigsinscotland.com; Dir GEOFF ELLIS.

Dark Blues Management Ltd: 30 Stamford Brook Rd, London W6 0XH; Dir of Business Devt KATE MARTIN.

Dax Entertainments: 48 Fernside Rd, Poole, Dorset BH15 2JJ; tel. (1202) 773103; fax (1202) 681419; e-mail dave.dacosta@ukonline.co.uk; Man. Dir DAVE DACOSTA.

Derek Block Promotions: Douglas House, 3 Richmond Bldgs, London W1V 5AE; Man. Dir DEREK BLOCK.

Deri Promotions: 8 Wick Lane, Felpham, Bognor Regis, West Sussex PO22 8QG; Proprietor R W COOPER.

Devenish Entertainements Ltd: 8 Forthill Rd, Enniskillen, Co Fermanagh BT74 6AW, Northern Ireland; Contact SEAN MCGRADE.

Entertainment Agency Group: 7 Northumberland St, Huddersfield HD1 1RL; Entertainment Exec. LENNY PHILLIP.

Europa Jazz Live: 6 Belgrove, Tunbridge Wells, Kent TN1 1YN; tel. (1892) 516722; fax (1892) 536080; e-mail jazz@davidjacobs.f9.co.uk; internet www.tinamay.com; Dir DAVID E JACOBS.

Fadermusic: Perth Rd, Wood Green, London N22 5QP; Gen. Man. BENGI F-B.

Fair Oaks Entertainment: PO Box 19, Ulverston, Cumbria CA12 9TF; Proprietor/Man. J G LIVINGSTONE.

Fanfare 3000: The Folly, Pinner Hill Rd, Pinner, Middlesex HA5 3YQ; Partners PETER RICHARDSON, PAUL BAXTER.

Fish Krish: 6 Carlton House, 319 West End Lane, London NW6 1RN; Contact FISH KRISH.

Fiveash & Hill Publicity and Promotions: 106 Great Portland St, London W1N 5PE; Partner GRAEME HILL.

Focus Marketing Communications: HMA House, 78 Durham Rd, Wimbledon, London SW20 0TL; Man. Dir BRIAN OLIVER.

Forward Agency Booking: 132 Liverpool Rd, London N1 1LA; Man. Dir ROB CHALLICE.

Garry Brown Associates (International) Ltd: 27 Downs Side, Cheam, Surrey SM2 7EH; tel. (20) 8643-3991; fax (20) 8770-7241; e-mail gbaltd@compuserve.com; Chair. GARRY BROWN.

Gordon Poole Agency Ltd: The Limes, Brockley, Bristol BS48 3BB; tel. (1275) 463222; fax (1275) 462252; e-mail agents@gordonpoole.com; internet www.gordonpoole.com; Man. Dir GORDON POOLE.

Greig Clifford Promotions: 23 Harsfold Rd, Rustington, West Sussex BN16 2QE; Proprietor GRIEG CLIFFORD.

Grosvenor Productions Ltd: The Limes, Brockley, Bristol BS19 3BB; Contact GORDON POOLE.

Hal Carter Organization: 101 Hazelwood Lane, Palmers Green, London N13 5HQ; Man. Dir HAL CARTER.

Harvey Goldsmith Entertainments: The Glassworks, 3–4 Ashland Pl., London W1M 3JH; Man. Dir HARVEY GOLDSMITH.

Helter Skelter (Agency) Ltd: The Plaza, 535 Kings Rd, London SW10 0SZ; tel. (20) 7376-8501; fax (20) 7376-8336; e-mail johnjackson@helterskelter.co.uk; Pres. JOHN JACKSON.

Holland-Ford's: 103 Lydyett Lane, Barnton, Northwich, Cheshire CW8 4JT; Proprietor BOB HOLLAND-FORD.

Hopscotch Media Management: 46 Broadwick St, London W1V 1FF; Dir/Partner ALFIE DOSOO.

Houndog Music Entertainment Agency: 49 Arthurton Rd, Spixworth, Norwich NR10 3QU; tel. and fax (1603) 897789; Proprietor GRAHAM JOHN BAILEY.

I A Entertainment: 44 Top Llan, Glan Conwy, Colwyn Bay, Clwyd LL28 5ND, Wales; Proprietor ANDREW BOGGIE.

International Talent Booking (ITB): 27A Floral St, Covent Garden, London WC2 ED9Q; Man. Dir BARRY DICKENS.

Jean Mills Entertainments: Cox Park Cottage, Cox Park, Gunnislake, Cornwall PL18 9BB; tel. and fax (1822) 832791; e-mail jmillsents@aol.com; Proprietor JEAN MILLS.

Jef Hanlon Management: 1 York St, London W1P 1PZ; tel. (20) 7487-2558; fax (20) 7487-2584; e-mail jhanlon@agents-uk.com; Man. Dir JEF HANLON; Dir ALICE HANLON.

John Boddy Agency: Acro 53 Chalk Hill, Oxhey Village, Watford, Herts, WD1 48Y.

John Ford Promotions: Bradford Court, Bradford St, Digbeth, Birmingham B12 0NS; Owner JOHN FORD.

John Martin Promotions Ltd: 29 Hartfield Rd, London SW19 3SG; Man. Dir JOHN MARTIN.

Kasevin Rodell: 6 Bowling Green Rd, Cranfield, Bedfordshire MK43 0ET; Partner DIANA RODELL.

Kennedy Street Management: Kennedy House, 31 Stamford St, Altrincham, Cheshire WA14 1ES; tel. (161) 941-5151; fax (161) 928-9491; e-mail kse@kennedystreet.com; Dir DANNY BETESH; Production Man. JIM COLSON.

Latin Touch Entertainments: Fatima Community Centre Commonwealth Ave, London W12 7QR; tel. (20) 8740-9020; fax (20) 8740-8903; e-mail orlando@latintouch.com; internet www.latintouch.com; Man. Dir ORLANDO RINCON P.

M D O: The Dawn, Northwood Lane, Bewdley, Worcs DY12 1AS; tel. (1299) 404579; fax (1299) 405079; e-mail themick.mdo@btinternet.com; Contact MICK OWEN.

Matters Musical Limited: The Loft, Rear of 8 West St, Dorking, Surrey RH4 1BL; Dir VICTORIA BURNS.

Max Clifford Associates Limited: Top Floor, 109 New Bond St, London W1Y 9AA; Man. Dir MAX CLIFFORD.

Mean Fiddler: 24–28A HighSt, Harlseden, London NW10 4LX; Man. Dir VINCE POWER.

Mel Bush Organization Ltd: Tanglewood, Arrowsmith Rd, Wimborne, Dorset BHZ1 3BG; tel. (1202) 691891; fax (1202) 691896; e-mail mbobmth@aol.com; Man. Dir MEL BUSH.

Mercenary Music Services: 143 Turks Rd, Radcliffe, Manchester M26 3WW; Production Man. PAUL NAYLOR.

Midland Entertainment & Management Agency: PO Box 259, Coventry CV5 8YU; tel. and fax (2476) 715544; e-mail chrissy@midland-entertainment.com; internet www.midland-entertainment.com; Proprietor CHRISSY PRICE.

Miracle Prestige International Ltd: Bugle House, 21A Noel St, London W1V 3PD; Man. Dir STEVE PARKER.

Mission Control Agency: 63 Lant St, London SE1 1QN; Dir GUY ANDERSON.

Money Talks Agency: Cadillac Ranch, Pencraig Uchaf, Cwm Bach, Whitland, Dyfed SA34 0DT, Wales; tel. (1994) 484466; fax (1994) 484294; e-mail cadillac-ranch@telco4u.net; internet www.nikturner.com; Man. M MAGOON.

Mrs Casey Music: PO Box 296, Aylesbury, Bucks HP19 3TL; Dir STEVE HEAP.

NE Music Management: Priory House, 55 Lawe Rd, South Sheilds, Tyne & Wear NE33 2AL; tel. (191) 427-6207; fax (191) 427-6323; e-mail dave@nemproductions.com; internet www.nemproductions.com; Contact DAVE SMITH.

Norman Jackson Entertainment Agency: 2 Dawlish Rd, Leyton, London E10 6QY; tel. (20) 556-3222; fax (20) 556-3223; Dir RAY GOULD.

NVB Entertainments: 80 Holywell Rd, Studham, Dunstable, Beds LU6 2PD; tel. (1582) 873623; fax (1582) 873618; e-mail nvb_entertainments@hotmail.com; Contact HENRI HARRISON.

Park Promotions: PO Box 651, Oxford OX2 9RB; tel. (1865) 241717; fax (1865) 204556; internet www.parkrecords.com; Man. Dir JOHN DAGNELL.

Paul Barrett Rock 'n' Roll Enterprises: 16 Grove Pl., Penarth, South Glamorgan CF64 2ND, Wales; tel. (2920) 704279; fax (2920) 709989; e-mail barrett.rocknroll@aimserve.net; Dir PAUL BARRETT.

Paul Dainty Corporation (UK) Ltd: 4 Yeomans Row, Knightsbridge, London SW3 2AH; Vice-Pres. PETER LYSTER-TODD.

Pendle Borough Council: Bank House, 61 Albert Rd, Colne, Lancashire BB8 0PB; Arts & Entertainment Man. GARY HOOD.

Phil McIntyre Promotions: 15 Riversway Business Village, Navigation Way, Preston PR2 2YP; Man. Dir PHIL MCINTYRE.

Pollytone Music: PO Box 124, Ruislip, Middlesex HA4 9BB; tel. (1895) 638584; fax (1895) 624793; e-mail val@pollyton.demon.co.uk; internet www.pollytone.com; Dir VALERIE BIRD.

Pomona: 14 Oxford Pl., Rochdale OL16 5LU; Man. Dir MARK JONES.

Primary Talent International Limited: Africa House, 64–78 Kingsway, London WC2B 6PR; Contact PETER MALONEY.

Prime Time: 28 Yonge Park, London N4 3NT; Dir MAGGIE O'CONNOR.

Profile Artists Agency: 141 Railton Rd, London SE24 0LT; Agent SERENA PARSONS.

Prostar: 106 Hillcrest Ave, Toftwood, Dereham, Norfolk NR19 1TD; Proprietor MALCOLM COOK.

Public Eye Communications: Greyhound House, 16 Greyhound Rd, London W6 8NX; New Business Dir ELAINE ROBERTSON.

Purple Palace: 34A Flower Lane, Mill Hill, London NW7 2JE; Contact STEPHANIE KAYS.

Raymond Gubbay Limited: 176a High St, Barnet, Herts EN5 5SZ; Man. Dir RAYMOND GUBBAY.

Real Time: 16/18 Ramillies St, London W1V 1DL; P R Man. CHARLIE INSKIP.

Rock 'n' Roll Enterprises: 16 Grove Plce, Penarth CF64 2ND, Wales; tel. (2920) 704279; fax (2920) 709989; e-mail barrett.rocknroll@aimserve.net; Dir PAUL BARRETT.

Rush Release Ltd: 74 The Archway, Station Approach, Ranelagh Gardens, London SW6 3UH; Gen. Man. JO UNDERWOOD.

Serious Speakout: 42 Old Compton St, London W1V 5PB; Partners JOHN CUMMING, JOHN ELLSON, DAVID JONES.

Sharp End Promotions Ltd: Grafton House, 2–3 Golden Sq., London W1R 3AD; Dir ROBERT LEMON.

Solo: Regent Arcade House, 252–260 Regent St, London W1B 3BX; tel. (20) 7009-3361; fax (870) 7493174; e-mail solo@solo.uk.com; internet www.solo.uk.com; Man. Dir JOHN GIDDINGS.

Sound & Light Productions: Kerrison Hall, 28 Kerrison Rd, London W5 5NW; Dir JAN GOODWIN.

Splash Management & Promotions: 328 Gray's Inn Rd, King's Cross, London WC1X 8BZ; Man. Dir NICK MOORE.

Square Deal Promotions: 56 Kilmuir Rd, Inverness IV3 8EP, Scotland; tel. (1463) 221268; fax (1463) 221268; Proprietor ANN CARMODY.

Steve Allen Entertainments: 60 Broadway, Peterborough, Cambs PE1 1SU; tel. (1733) 569589; fax (1733) 561854; e-mail steve@sallenent.co.uk; internet www.sallenent.co.uk; Proprietor STEVE ALLEN.

Stoneyport Agency: 39 Shandon Cres., Edinburgh EH11 1QF, Scotland; tel. (131) 346-8237; fax (131) 313-2083; e-mail jb@stoneyport.demon.co.uk; internet www.stoneyport.demon.co.uk; Contact JOHN BARROW.

Swamp Agency: PO Box 94, Derby DE22 1XA; Contact CHRIS HALL.

Sylvantone Promotions: 17 Allerton Grange Way, Leeds LS17 6LP; tel. (113) 268-7788; fax (709) 235-9333; e-mail sylvantore@hotmail.com; Proprietor TONY GOODACRE.

Talk Loud P R: 90–92 Great Portland St, London W1N 5PB.

Taurus Records: 23 Blackheath Rise, Lewisham, London SE13 7PN; Contact BEVERLEY MILLER.

The Life Organisation: 62 Argyle St, Birkenhead, Merseyside L41 6AF; Dir J O'CONNOR.

TKO Promotions Ltd: PO Box 130, Hove, East Sussex BN3 6QU; Creative Dir HOWARD KRUGER.

Tony Denton Promotions Ltd: 19 South Molton Lane, Mayfair, London W1Y 1AQ; Contact SIMON NICHOLLS.

Upbeat Management and Recordings: Sutton Business Centre, Rastmor Way, Wallington, Surrey SM6 7AH; tel. (20) 8773-1223; fax (20) 8669-6752; e-mail beryl@upbeat.co.uk; internet www.upbeat.co.uk; Contact BERYL KORMAN.

Vinyl Japan (UK) Ltd: 281 Camden High St, London NW1 7BX; Man. PATRICK JAMES.

WOMAD: The Malt House, Mill Lane, Box, Wiltshire SN14 9PN; Man. Dir THOMAS BROOMAN.

Work Hard P R: 19d Pinfold Rd, London SW16 2SL; tel. (20) 8677-8466; fax (20) 8677-5374; e-mail enquiries@workhardpr.com; internet www.workhardpr.com; Owner ROLAND HYAMS.

The United States of America

A & R European/US Radio Record Promotions: 900 19th Ave S, Suite 207, Nashville, TN 37212; Owners RUTH STEELE, DAVID STEELE.

Aarrow Artist/Writer Development: 900 19th Ave S, Suite 207, Nashville, TN 37212; Owner KELLI STEELE; A & R Dir RUTH STEELE.

Abby Hoffer Enterprises: 223 1/2 E 48th St, New York, NY 10017-1538; Pres. ABBY HOFFER.

Al Embry International: PO Box 23162, Nashville, TN 37202; Owner/Pres. AL EMBRY.

Ambassadors of Praise: PO Box 369, Pearland, TX 77588-0369; Pres. PATRICIA NEDBALEK.

American Band Management: PO Box 840607, Houston, TX 77284-0607; Pres. JOHN BLOMSTROM SR.

American Famous Talent: 816 W Evergreen, Chicago, IL 60622; Pres. RIC BRICAMONTES.

AristoMedia: 1620 16th Ave S, Nashville, TN 37212; Pres./Owner JEFF WALKER.

Artist Representation & Management: 1257 Arcade St, St Paul, MN 55106; Office Man./Agent ROGER ANDERSON.

Barry Agency: PO Box 1414, Maple Grove, MN 55311; Pres. LISA A BARRY.

Bay Concerts: 1906 Seward Dr., Pittsburg, CA 94565; CEO/Pres. CHARLES COKE; Vice-Pres. TERRY PITTS.

Bennett Morgan & Associates Ltd: 1022 Route 370, Wappingers Falls, NY 12590; tel. (845) 227-6065; fax (845) 227-4002; internet www.bennettmorgan.com; Pres. BENNETT MORGAN.

Berkeley Agency: 2608 Ninth St, Berkeley, CA 94710; Agent JIM CASSELL.

Bill Hollingshead Productions Inc: 1720 N Ross St, Santa Ana, CA 92706; Pres. BILL HOLLINGSHEAD.

Blowin' Smoke Records: 7438 Shoshone Ave, Van Nuys, CA 91406-2340; tel. (818) 881-9888; fax (818) 881-0555; e-mail blowinsmokeband.com; internet www.blowinsmokeband.com; Pres. LARRY WEISBERG.

BMI (Butler Music International): 273 Chippewa Dr., Columbia, SC 29210-6508.

Bobby Roberts Co: PO Box 3007, Hendersonville, TN 37077; Pres. BOBBY ROBERTS.

Brad Simon Organization: 122 E 57th St, New York, NY 10022; Pres. BRAD SIMON.

Brentwood Music Publishing Inc: One Maryland Farms, Brentwood, TN 37027; Vice-Pres. of Publishing DALE MATHEWS.

Brothers Management Associates: 141 Dunbar Ave, Fords, NJ 08863.

Buddy Lee Attractions: 38 Music Sq. E, Suite 300, Nashville, TN 37203; tel. (615) 244-4336; fax (615) 726-0429; e-mail tconway@blanash.com; internet www.buddyleeattractions.com; Pres. TONY CONWAY.

Captain Telegram Special Event: 2890 N Andrews Ave, Fort Lauderdale, FL 33311-2514; Pres. ROGER HUGHES.

Cardenas Fernandez & Associates: 1254 N Wells St, Chicago, IL 60610; Pres. HENRY CARDENAS.

Cerebral Records: 1236 Laguna Dr., Carlsbad, CA 92008; Pres. LINCOLN KROLL; Publicist CAROL LENO.

Competitive Edge Public Relations: 9 Music Sq., Suite 240, Nashville, TN 37203; Contact DEBBIE MCCLURE.

Concerted Efforts Inc: PO Box 99, Newtonville, MA 02160; Dir PAUL KAHN.

Creative Artists Agency (CAA): 3310 West End Ave, 5th Floor, Nashville, TN 37203; Contact RON BAIRD.

De Leon Artists: 4031 Panama Court, Piedmont, CA 94611; Agent LUPE DE LEON.

DMR Booking Agency: Suite 250, The Galleries of Syracuse, Syracuse, NY 13202; Owner DAVID REZAK.

Dynamic Directions Inc: 11410 West Wisconsin Ave, Wauwatosa, WI 53226; Vice-Pres. ARTHUR GREINKE.

Events International Inc: PO Box 1560, Honolulu, HI 96806; Pres. DAVID BOOTH.

Famous Artist Agency: 1700 Broadway, 5th Floor, New York, NY 10019; Pres. JERRY ADE; Man. DAVID ZEDECK.

Fate's House of Music: 1030 Villa Pl., Nashville, TN 37212; Pres. FATE VANDERPOOL.

Five Roses Music Group: 34A Lanier Rd, Studio 1, Jekyll Island, GA 31527; Pres. SAMMIE LEE MARLER.

Folklore Inc: 1671 Appian Way, Santa Monica, CA 90401; Contact MITCH GREENHILL.

General Broadcasting Service: 203 Gates Dr., Hendersonville, TN 37075-4961; Owner ERNIE BIVENS.

Geoffrey Blumenauer Artists (GBA): PO Box 343, Burbank, CA 91503; tel. (818) 845-9658; fax (818) 558-3939; e-mail gbatalent@aol.com; Pres. GEOFFREY BLUMENAUER.

Grelo Holdings Inc: Market St Sq., 33 Wilkes Barre Blvd, Wilkes Barre, PA 18701; Pres./CEO THOM GRELO.

Heartfelt Concerts: PO Box 294, Westerville, OH 43086-0294; Pres./Owner RANDY KETTERING.

International Creative Management (ICM): 8943 Wilshire Blvd, Beverly Hills, CA 90211; Contact MUSIC DEPT.

International Creative Management (ICM): 40 W 57th St, New York, NY 10019; Contact MUSIC DEPT.

Jackie Paul Entertainment Group Inc: 559 Wanamaker Rd, Jenkintown, PA 19046; CEO JACKIE PAUL.

Keith Case & Associates: 59 Music Sq. W, Nashville, TN 37203; Owner KEITH CASE.

Landmark Communications Group: PO Box 1444, Hendersonville, TN 37077; Pres. BILL ANDERSON JR.

Laura Grüb Enterprises: 235-4 Lucas Lane, Voorhees, NJ 08043; Pres. LAURA GRÜB-GESCHWINDT.

Living Rock Ministries: 1225 Atlantic Ave, Suite 3, Rochester, NY 14609; Programme & Music Dir PASTOR SAMME PALERMO.

Loud Cry Productions: PO Box 210270, Nashville, TN 37221-0270; Owner/Pres. DON SANDERS.

Marco Music Group: 1620 16th Ave S, Nashville, TN 37212; Pres./Owner JEFF WALKER.

Mark Alan Agency: PO Box 21323, St Paul, MN 55121; Pres. MARK ALAN.

Mazur Publications: PO Box 360, East Windsor, NJ 08520; Publicist MICHAEL MAZUR.

Mia Mind Music: 5001/2 E 84th St, Suite 4B, New York, NY 10028-7368; CEO STEVEN BENTZEL.

Mirkin Management: 9061/2 Congress Ave, Austin, TX 78701; Owner JAN MIRKIN.

Music & Entertainment Division: 2200 Wilson Blvd, Suite 200, Arlington, VA 22201; Pres., Music & Entertainment Division ED YOE.

Music Man Productions: 568 Snelling Ave N, Suite 106, St Paul, MN 55104; Owners PAUL MANSKE, STEVE YORK.

Nancy Carlin Associates: 411 Ferry St, Ste 4, Martinez, CA 94553; Agent NANCY CARLIN.

Nancy Fly Agency: PO Box 90306, Austin, TX 78709-0306; Dir NANCY FLY.

Only New Age Music Inc: 8033 Sunset Blvd, Suite #472, Los Angeles, CA 90046; Pres. SUZANNE DOUCET; Vice-Pres. JAMES BELL.

Pal Productions Co: PO Box 80691, Baton Rouge, LA 70898; Pres. JOHNNY R PALAZZOTTO.

Plug Productions: 273 Chippewa Dr., Columbia, SC 29210-6508; Dir JOHN MACK; Contact RON SPARKS.

PPL-MCI Entertainment Group: 10 Universal Plaza, PO Box 8442, Universal City, CA 91618; tel. (818) 506-8533; fax (818) 506-8534; e-mail pplzmi@aol.com; internet www.pplzmi.com; CEO JAESON ST JAMES JARRETT; Man. Dir MAXX DIAMOND.

Precision Management: 825 N King St, Suite A-1, Hampton, VA 23669-2814; Operations Man. CAPPRICCIEO M SCATES.

Premier Productions: 1909 N Spruce, Wichita, KS 67214; Owner ANTHONY WELCH.

Prince/SF Productions: 1135 Francisco St, Suite 7, San Francisco, CA 94109-1087; Pres. KEN MALUCELLI.

Punk Metal Rock Records: PO Box 410099, San Francisco, CA 94141-0099; A & R Head STASH RAVINE.

Remington Management Inc: 6602 Harbor Town, Suite 501, Houston, TX 77036; Pres. JANICE D HAYES.

Rock Dog Records: PO Box 3687, Hollywood, CA 90028; Vice-Pres. of A & R GERRY NORTH.

Ron Rainey & Associates: 315 S Beverly Dr., Suite 206, Beverly Hills, CA 90212; Man. RON RAINEY.

Rosebud Agency: PO Box 170429, San Francisco, CA 94117; tel. (415) 386-3456; fax (415) 386-0599; e-mail info@rosebudus.com; internet www.rosebudus.com; Pres. MIKE KAPPUS.

S T A R S Productions: 1 Professional Quadrangle, 2nd Floor Suite, Sparta, NJ 07871; Pres. STEPHEN TARKANISH.

Silver Star Productions Inc: 1800 Amberwood Dr., Riverview, FL 33569; tel. (813) 689-3944; fax (813) 685-6899; e-mail marstarrr@aol.com; Pres. MARGORIE SEXTON.

Squad 16: 2632 Boston Rd, PO Box 65, Wilbraham, MA 01095; Contact TOM NAJEMY.

SRO Entertainment Inc: PO Box 10161, Honolulu, HI 96816; Pres. KEN ROSENE.

SRO Productions Inc: 821 Marquette Ave S, Suite 1815, Minneapolis, MN 55402; Pres. LAWRENCE H BERLE.

St John Artists: PO Box 619, Neenah, WI 54957-0619; Owner JON ST JOHN.

Stardate Concerts Inc: 10430 Shady Trail, Suite 104, Dallas, TX 75220; tel. (940) 497-2200; fax (940) 497-6677; e-mail starconkw@cs.com; Pres. RANDY SHELTON.

Surface Entertainment & Management: PO Box 2935, Church St Station, New York, NY 10008; Contact PAM BENINON.

Terrace Entertainment Corp: PO Box 68, Las Vegas, NM 87701; Pres. ROBERT JOHN JONES.

Tone Zone Booking Agency: 939 W Wilson Ave, Chicago, IL 60610; Booking Man. DIANE BORDEN.

Triage International: PO Box 448, New York, NY 10014; Man. BOB WEYERSBERG.

Triangle Talent Inc: 10424 Watterson Trail, Louisville, KY 40299; Agent GARY DEUSNER.

Umpire Entertainment Enterprises: 1507 Scenic Dr., Longview, TX 75604; Pres. JERRY HAYMES.

Vokes Music, Record & Promotion Co: PO Box 12, New Kensington, PA 15068-0012; tel. (724) 335-2775; Pres./Owner HOWARD VOKES.

William Morris Agency: 151 El Camino Dr., Beverly Hills, CA 90212; 1350 Ave of the Americas, New York, NY 10019; 2100 West End Ave, Nashville, TN 31203; Vice-Pres. RICK SHIPP.

Work Horse Productions: PO Box 1001, Kapaa, Kauai, HI 96746; tel. (808) 822-0933; fax (808) 822-7737; e-mail whp@aloha.net; Owner MICHAEL GREGG.

APPENDIX D: MUSIC PUBLISHERS

Andorra

RIAL Andorra: Avda de Tarragona 24, Andorra La Vella; tel. 860686; fax 866286; e-mail rial@andorra.ad; Man. PASCAL LAIR.

Argentina

AIM (Arco Iris Musical): Avda Santa Fé 4910, 4°, Of. B, 1425 Buenos Aires; tel. and fax (11) 4775-2343; e-mail aimcontenidos@aol.com; Dir-Gen. OSVALDO BERMOLEN.

Clan Dilo Music: Casilla Correo 123 La Plata, 1900 Buenos Aires; Pres. GIORGIO DI LORENZO.

Musidisc Europe Sudamerica SAIC: Güemes 4418, 1° A, 1425 Buenos Aires; Pres. JIMMY OLSZEVICKI.

Peermusic Argentina Ediciones Y Producciones SA: Rivadavia 5012, 6°, 1424 Buenos Aires; Pres. ELSA VILLAR.

Australia

Australian Music Publishers Pty Ltd: Level 5, 83 Mount St, North Sydney, NSW 2060; tel. (2) 9925-0765; fax (2) 9925-0521; e-mail srhanson@ozmusicpub.com; Man. Dir STEPHEN HANSON.

Black Pig Publishing: PO Box 2093, St Kilda West, VIC 3182; Man. Dir MICHAEL LYNCH.

Boosey & Hawkes (Australia) Pty Ltd: Unit 12/6, Campbell St, Artarmon, NSW 2064; Man. Dir RICHARD MACKIE.

Bright Spark Songs Pty Ltd: 20 Leila St, Prahran, VIC 3181; Contact TONY MORAN.

Central Australian Aboriginal Media Associates Music: 101 Todd St, Alice Springs NT 0870; Head of Dept RICHARD MICALLEF.

EMI Music Publishing: 1st Floor, 100 Glover St, Cremorne, NSW 2090; Man. Dir JOHN ANDERSON.

Festival Music Publishing Group: 63–79 Miller St, Pyrmont, NSW 2009; Man. Dir BRUCE POWELL.

Grundy Music Pty Ltd: Locked Bag 526, Frenchs Forest, NSW 2086; Sr Consultant Business Affairs J M FOWLER.

Ideal Management P/C: PO Box 1037, Caulfield North, Melbourne, VIC 3161; Man. Dir/CEO NATHAN D BRENNER.

Image Music Group Pty Ltd: 19 Johnston St, Port Melbourne, VIC 3207; Man. Dir JOHN MCDONALD.

Immedia!: PO Box 2977, Sydney, NSW 2001; Man. Partner PHIL TRIPP.

J Albert & Son P/L Albert Productions: 9 Rangers Rd, Neutral Bay, NSW 2089; Gen. Man. FIFA RICCOBONO.

Leosong Music Group: 6th Floor, 350 Kent St, Sydney, NSW 2000; Contact PHILIP WALKER, SUE BOYLAN.

MCA Music Pty Ltd: 23 Pelican St, Darlinghurst, NSW 2010; Man. Dir PETER HEBBES.

MMA Music: 351 Crown St, Surry Hills, NSW 2010; CEO C M MURPHY.

Mushroom Music: 9 Dundas Lane, Albert Park, VIC 3206; Chair. MICHAEL GUDINSKI.

Polygram Music Publishing (Australia) Pty Ltd: 122 McEvoy St, Alexandria, NSW 2015; Man. Dir ROGER GRIERSON.

Rondor Music: 78 Chandos St, St Leonards, NSW 2065; Man. Dir BOB AIRD.

Shock Music Publishing Pty Ltd: 24 High St, Northcote, VIC 3070; Publishing Man. SALLY GALWEY.

Sony Music Publishing Australia: 11–19 Hargrave St, Easy Sydney, NSW 2010; Gen. Man. DAMIAN TROTTER.

Warner Chappell Music: 1 Cassins Ave, North Sydney, NSW 2060; Man. Dir JOHN BROMELL.

Zomba Production Music (Australia) Pty Limited: 25 Burton St, Glebe, NSW 2037; Man. Dir STUART LIVINGSTON.

Austria

ATS Records: Breitenau 7, 4591 Molln; tel. (0) 7584-2454; fax (0) 7584-2424; e-mail office@ats-records.com; internet www.ats-records.com; Man. Dir REINHARD BRUNNER.

Edition Helbing: Kaplanstr 9, 6063 Rum; Man. Dir ELVIRA HARM-DEMATTE.

Edition Musica Musikverlag: Webgasse 43, PO Box 451, 1060 Vienna; Man. Dir FRANZ WALLNER.

Edition Rossori/Pate Records: Hietzinger Hauptstr 94, 1130 Vienna; tel. (1) 8762400; fax (1) 8795464; e-mail office@poppate.com; internet www.paterecords.com; Man. Dir MARIO ROSSORI.

Honk Music and Records: Hormayrgasse 3/25, 1170 Vienna; tel. and fax (1) 486-4287; internet www.sra.at/sr/comps/7196.htm; Man. Dir JIVI HONK.

International Society for Jazz Research: Leonhardstr 15, 8010 Graz; tel. (0) 389-3160; fax (0) 389-3161; e-mail gertrand.steinserger@kug.ac.at; internet www.jazzresearch.org; Contact GERTRAND STEINSERGER; promotes jazz research.

Koch Music Publishing: Gewerbegebeit, PO Box 24, 6600 Höfen; Man. Dir FRANZ KOCH.

Meltemi Music: Hirschstettner str 26/H 13, 1220 Vienna; Man. Dir HORST BICHLER.

Polygram/Antenna Musikverlag Austria: PO Box 85, Edelsinnstr 4, 1122 Vienna; Chair. ADOLF HOFFMANN.

Shamrock: Altwaidhofen 37, 3830 Waidhofen/Thaya; Man. Dir UWE KRANNER.

Stein Music Wien: Bernardgasse 39/33, 1070 Vienna; Man. Dir REGINE STEINMETZ.

Warner/Chappell Musikverlag GmbH: Diefenbachgasse 35, 1150 Vienna; Man. Dir PETER GRUBER.

Belgium

ALC Productions: Ave Eugène Ysaye 47, 1070 Brussels; Label Man. ALEXANDER LOUVET.

Baltic NV: Rederijkersstraat 82, 2610 Wilrijk-Antwerp; tel. (3) 828-4084; fax (3) 829-1068; e-mail info@baltic.be; internet www.baltic.be; Gen. Man. KOEN BOGAERTS.

Boom!: Bergensesteenweg 19, 1500 Halle; tel. (0) 2360-2851; internet www.jpvan.be; Man. Dir J P VAN.

Caracol Music Sprl Group: 5 rue du Cheneau, 6120 Ham-sur-Heure; Gen. Man. TIMOTHY HAGELSTEIN.

Carbon 7: 23 Ave Général Eisenhower, 1030 Brussels; tel. (2) 242-9703; fax (2) 245-3885; e-mail carbon7records@compuserve.com; Dir GUY SEGERS.

Dexon Sprl: 41 rue Cité de L'Enfance, 6001 Marcinelle; Man. DELFOSSE PIERRE.

Editions Confidentielles: 90 rue de Veeweyde, 1070 Brussels; Professional Man. PIET BEKAERT.

EMI Music Publishing Belgium: Eugene Plaskylaan 140 B, 1040 Brussels; Man. GUY VAN HANDENHOVE.

MMD SA: rue Fernand Bernier 38, 1060 Brussels; Man. Dir PLASTIC BERTRAND.

Multi Sound Music Publishing: 24 Gachardstreet, 1050 Brussels; Gen. Man. PIERRE PLETINCKX.

Prestation Music: 24 Gachardstreet, 1050 Brussels; Gen. Man. PIERRE PLETINCKX.

Pyramid International Music: Lepelhoekstraat 26, 9100 Sint-Niklaas; tel. (3) 778-1854; fax (3) 766-8441; e-mail marc@marcdecoen.be; internet www.marcdecoen.be; Man. Dir MARC DE COEN.

RVY Music Publishing: Kammerstraat 19, 9000 Ghent; Man. ROBERT VAN YPER.

T & B Music: Gulden Vlieslaan 67, 8000 Brugge; Contact NICO A MERTENS.

Team for Action (T4A): Ave Oscar van Goibtsnoven 45B, 1180 Brussels; Man. Dir CLAUDE MARTIN.

Tempo (Top Entertainment Editions): Krijgslaan 61, 9000 Gent; Gen. Man. LUC STANDAERT.

Tessa Records Rock Label: Dennenlaan 13, 9160 Lokeren; tel. and fax (09) 3489836; Pres./Owner MARC DE BLOCK.

Witlof: Leernsesteenweg 168, 9800 Deinze; Dir JEAN TANT.

Brazil

Caipirapirs Produçoes Artisticas Ltda: Avda das Aguas Marinhas 157 Pg Petrópolis, 07600-00 São Paulo, SP; Gen. Man. PABLO OSSIPOFF.

Estudio Eldorado Ltda: Rua Pires da Mota 820–830, 01529 São Paulo, SP; Exec. Dir JOÃO LARA MESQUITA.

Paradox Music: Rua Dr Pinto Ferraz 58, Vila Mariana, 04117-040 São Paulo, SP; Dir SILVIO ARNALDO CALIGARIS.

Bulgaria

Arsis Publishing: 15 Tsarigradsko Chausse Blvd, 1220 Sofia; Chair. BORISLAV IVANCHEV.

Balkanton Music Publishing: 6 Haidoushka Polyana str, 1612 Sofia; tel. (2) 952-0373; fax (2) 952-6090; e-mail balkanton@yahoo.com; Man. Dir VENTSISLAV BOZHINOV; Vice-Pres. ANI PAVLOVA.

Mega Music Ltd: 2 Trapezitza str, 1000 Sofia; Man. Dir DORA TCHERNKVA.

Union Media Ltd Record Company: 71A Evlogi Georgiev Blvd 4th Floor, 1142 Sofia; Pres. MARTIN ZACHARIEV.

Union of Bulgarian Composers (UBC): 2 Ivan Vazov St, 1000 Sofia; tel. (2) 988-1560; fax (2) 987-4378; e-mail ubc@mail.bol.bg; internet www.ubc-bg.com; Pres. VICTOR CHUCHKOV.

Canada

Attic Music Group: 102 Atlantic Ave, Toronto, ON M6K 1X9; Pres. ALEXANDER MAIR.

BMG Music Publishing Canada Inc: 150 John St, 6th Floor, Toronto, ON M5V 3C3.

Botany Park Records & Music Publishing Co: 361 Walter Dr., Keswick, ON L4P 3A8; Pres. MARLAINE RENNOCKS.

Brass Ring Productions/Manford Music Inc: PO Box 1266 Station A, Kelowna, BC V1Y 7V8; tel. and fax (250) 763-5502; e-mail manford@telus.net; Pres. BECKY CHAPMAN.

EMI Music Publishing Canada: 300 Richmond St W, 2nd Floor, Toronto, ON M5V 1E6.

G Man Music: 4 Bowden St, Toronto, ON, M4K 2X2; Pres. GERRY YOUNG.

G String Publishing: PO Box 1096, Hudson, QC J0P 1V0; tel. (450) 458-2819; e-mail la_records@excite.com; internet www.radiofreedom.com; Man. MAKA HANNA.

Heaven Bent Music Corp: 11 Hopewell Cres., Hamilton, ON L8J 1P3; Gen. Man. KATHIE PIETRON.

John H Lennon Music Ltd: 1235 Bay St, Suite 400, Toronto, ON M5R 3K4; Pres. JOHN LENNON; Man. Dir LENNY MOORE.

Montina Music: PO Box 702, Snowdon Station, Montréal, QC H3X 3X8; Professional Gen. Man. D LEONARD.

Morning Music Limited: 5200 Dixie Rd, Suite 203, Mississauga, ON L4W 1E4; Pres. MARK ALTMAN.

MUSINFO Publishing Group Inc: 2504 Mayfair Ave, Montréal, QC H4B 2C8; tel. (514) 484-5419; fax (514) 484-9948; e-mail musinfo@musinfo.com; internet www.musinfo.com; Pres./Owner JEHAN V VALIQUET.

PolyGram Music Publishing: 1345 Denison St, Markham, ON L3R 5V2; Vice-Pres./Gen. Man. JOHN REDMOND.

Savannah Music Inc: 123 Applefield Dr., Scarborough, ON M1P 3Y5; Dir of Canadian Operations BILL CARRUTHERS.

Sony Music Publishing: 1121 Leslie St, Don Mills, ON M3C 2J9.

Sparwood Music Productions: PO Box 270, Bentley, AB T0C 0J0; Man. DICK DAMRON.

Spinner Music Group Inc: Third Floor, 68 Water St, Vancouver, BC V6B 1A4; Pres. KEN SPENCE; Man. Dir WOLFGANG BURANDT.

Third Wave Productions Ltd: PO Box 563, Gander, NF A1V 2E1; Pres. R ARCHIBALD BONNELL.

TMP—The Music Publisher: Suite #300, 1670 Bayview Ave, Toronto, ON M4G 3C2; Pres. FRANK DAVIES.

Warner/Chappell Music Canada Ltd: 85 Scarsdale Rd, Unit 101, Don Mills, ON M3B 2R2; Pres. JERRY RENEWYCH; Creative Man. ANNE-MARIE SMITH.

Chile

Ediciones Musicales Fermata Ltda: Ebro 2751, Of. 609, Las Condes 41, Santiago; Gen. Man. ELIANA CISTERNAS.

China (Taiwan)

Polygram Music Publishing Ltd: 5F 99 Nankang Rd, Section 3, Nankang District, Taipei; Contact YVETTE TUNG.

Colombia

BMG Ariola de Colombia SA: Calle 67, 7-94, 12°, Santafé de Bogotá, DC; Dir FRANCISCO VILLANUEVA.

Compañia Colombiana de Discos SA (Codiscos): Carrera 67, 1, Sur 92 Guayabal, 1428 Medellín; Pres. CÉSAR VALLEJO.

Edisdago Ltda: C / 33AA, 81-25, Medellín; Pres. DARIO GÓMEZ ZAPATA.

Promotora Colombiana de Musica Ltda: Carrera 67, 1 Sur 92, Medellín; Man. SYLVIA N ARANGO.

Croatia

Kinel Music: Vinogradska Cesta 3, 41000 Zagreb; Man. Dir MARIO KINEL.

Melody: Rubesi 139 A, 51215 Kastav; Dir ANDREJ BASA.

Skalinada: Dubrovacka 23, 58000 Split; Dir ZDENKO RUNJIC.

Tutico: Veprinacka 16, 10000 Zagreb; Dir ZRINKO TUTIC.

The Czech Republic

Czech Music Information Centre: Besední 3, 118 00 Prague 1; tel. (2) 5731-7424; fax (2) 5731-7424; e-mail his@vol.cz; internet www.musica.cz; Dir MIROSLAV PUDLAK.

Denmark

Cloudland: Skt Jørgens Allé 7 O, G6 1th, 1615 Copenhagen; Man. Dir SIMON SHEIKA.

ELAP Music A/S: Bransagervej 2–10, 9490 Pandrup; Promotion STEFFEN LUND NIELSEN.

EMI Music Publishing Denmark: Gladsaxevej 135, 2860 Soeborg; Man. Dir JOHN RASMUSSEN.

Great Dane Music: c/o Replay Records, Frederikssundvej 60 C, 2400 NV Copenhagen; Man. Dir HENRIK BOETCHER.

Iceberg Music: Ronne Alie 78A, 8600 Silkeborg; Man. Dir MANFRED ZÄHRINGER.

Inhouse Publishing: Vognmagergade 10, 1120 Copenhagen K.

Klepto Records & Publishing: Langdries 4, 9450 Haaltert; Man. Dir WILFRIED BRITS.

Mega Scandinavia A/S: Indiakaj 1, 2100 Copenhagen Ø; Vice-Pres. CAI LEITNER; Dir of A & R and Marketing JESPER BAN.

Olafssongs: Paarupves 44, 3230 Graested; tel. 4839-2259; fax 4839-1629; e-mail fo@olafssongs.dk; internet www.olafssongs.dk; Pres. FINN OLAFSSON.

Pineapple Publishing ApS: Frodesgade 74, 6700 Esbjerg; Man. Dir HELGE ENGELBRECHT.

Sundance/Stunt Records: Havnegade 41, 1050 Copenhagen K; tel. 3333-8720; fax 3333-8730; e-mail sundance@sundance.dk; internet www.sundance.dk; Man. Dir PETER LITTAUER.

Warner Chappell Music Denmark: Anker Heegaardsgade 2, ST TV, 1572 Copenhagen.

Finland

Bluebird Music: Henrikities 5 C, 00370 Helsinki; Man. Dir NIKLAS NORDSTRÖM.

Flamingo Music: Vapaalantie 2, 01650 Vantaa; Man. Dir VEXI SALMI.

Love Kustannus: Hämeentie 6 A 4, 00530 Helsinki; Man. Dir SINI PERHO.

Polarvox: Arinatie 2 A, 00370 Helsinki; Man. Dir LEENA JUURANTO.

Poplandia Music: PO Box 483, 33101 Tampere; Man. Dir KARI HELENIUS.

Taurus Music: PO Box 33, 02431 Masala; Man. Dir ANTERO PÄIVÄIÄNEN.

Warner Chappell Music, Finland: PO Box 126, 00521 Helsinki; tel. (9) 229-560; fax (9) 2295-6600; internet www.warnerchappell.com; A & R TOM FRISK.

Zen Master Publishing: PO Box 35, 33201 Tampere; Man. Dir TAPIO KORJUS.

France

Alpha Bravo: 64 Ave Jean Jaurès, 93500 Pantin; Contact DANIEL BORNET.

BMG Music Publishing France: 10 rue Duphot, 75001 Paris; Dir STÉPHANE BERLOW.

Boucherie Productions: 15 Bis rue du Plateau, 75019 Paris; Dir NATALI LUC.

Caravage: 130 rue Marius Aufan, 92300 Levallois-Perret; Gen. Man. JEAN-PAUL SMETS.

Editions Essex: 5 rue Lincoln, 75008 Paris; Man. Dir RENÉ BOYER.

Editions Fortin: 4 Cité Chaptal, 75009 Paris; Contact MULTRIER FORTIN.

EMI Music Publishing France SA: 20 rue Molitor, 75016 Paris; tel. 1 40 71 32 00; fax 1 40 71 61 80; Dir FABRICE NATAF.

Fairplay (Fair and Square Publishing): 10–12 rue Richer, 75009 Paris; Dir FABRICE ABSIL.

FKO Music: 18 rue de Revilly, 25012 Paris; Man. Dir FRANCIS KERTEKIAN; International Dept GRACE CASTA.

Made In Heaven: 6 rue Rémy de Gourmont, 75019 Paris; Label Man. MATHIAS JEANNIN.

MCA Caravelle France: 35 Blvd Malesherbes, 75008 Paris; Chair. TOM ARENA.

Metisse Music Sarl: 1 Villa Juge, 75015 Paris; Man. Dir PETRA GEHRMANN.

Nouvelles Editions Meridian: 5 rue Lincoln, 75008 Paris; Man. Dir RENÉ BOYER.

Peermusic: 5 rue Lincoln, 75008 Paris; Man. Dir RENÉ BOYER.

Polygram Music: 14 rue Curie, 75005 Paris; Chair. PHILIPPE LERICHOMME.

Promo Sonor International: 30 rue de Saussure, 75017 Paris; Man. Dir JO PUCHEU.

Rondor Music: 32 rue Etienne Marcel, 75002 Paris; Dir HALIT UMAN.

Salam Aleikum Amusements: 2 rue Carpeaux, 75018 Paris; Dir STEPHANE BENHAMOU.

Scorpio Music: 12 Ave George V, 75008 Paris; Pres. HENRI BELOLO.

Skydog / Kind of Groove: 32 Ave Claude Vellefaux, 75010 Paris; PDG MARC ZERMATI.

Société d'Editions Musicales Internationales: 5 rue Lincoln, 75008 Paris; Man. Dir RENÉ BOYER.

Sony Music Publishing France: 131 Ave de Wagram, 75017 Paris; Dir NICOLAS GALIBERT.

Topomic Music: 26 rue L M Nordmann, 92250 La Garenne-Colombes; Pres. PIERRE JAUBERT.

XIII Bis Music Group: 34 rue Eugene Flachat, 75017 Paris; Man. Dir LAURENT DREUX-LEBLANC; Music Dir BRIAN RAWLING.

Germany

AlphaTon Publishing GmbH: Am Haidberg 4, 21465 Wentorf; Contacts JOE RUDOLPH, GERD GERDES.

Ata Tak Records: Kölner str 226 F, 40227 Düsseldorf; tel. (211) 782-2329; internet www.atatak.com; Dir FRANK FENSTERMACHER.

Blanko Musik: Clemens str 75, 80796 Munich; Man. Dir HAGE HEIN; Asst Man. Dir GERHILD MALORNY.

Castor Promotions: Dragonerstr 21, 30163 Hanover; Contact ELKE FLEING.

Edition Metromania / Warner Chappell Germany: Osterstr 36, 30159 Hanover; Man. Dir FRANK BORNEMANN.

Edition Partysanen Publishing: Skalitzer str 68, 10997 Berlin; Man. Dir RONA CASLEY.

EMI Music Publishing Germany GmbH: Alsterufer 1, 20354 Hamburg; Dir ANDREAS KIEL.

Freibank: Ditmar-Koel str 26, 20459 Hamburg; Dirs MARK CHUNG, KLAUS MAECK.

Fun Factory! GmbH: Hermannstadtweg 9, 48151 Münster; Marketing Asst CLAUDIA WEILER.

Garbitowski: Metzer str 30, 50677 Cologne; Owner & Dir JÜRGEN GARBITOWSKI.

Heartpunch Music Publishing & Promotion: Vohwinkeler str 154, 42329 Wuppertal; Man. Dir MICHAEL SCHUSTER.

Kick Musikverlag: Burgunder str 8, 50677 Cologne; Man. Dir GOETZ ELBERTZHAGEN; International Man. LYNDA HILL.

Mainhattan Music Production: Friedrich-Ebert str 48, 63179 Obertshausen; Man. UWE BLOCK.

Moderne Welt Musikproduktions & Vennoskfungs GmbH: Marienbaden str 6/1, 70372 Stuttgart; Man. Dir HENNING TÖGEL.

Music Box GmbH: Rahlstedter str 65, 22149 Hamburg; Man. Dir HUBERTUS BRANZKO.

Musikverlag Progressive GmbH: Bramfelder Chaussee 238c, 22177 Hamburg; Contact RUDY HOLZHAUER.

Polygram Songs Musikverlag Germany: Glockengiesserwall 3, 20095 Hamburg; Man. Dir OS VAN JOOST.

Rolf Budde Musikverlag GmbH: Hohenzollerdamm 54 A, 14199 Berlin; tel. (30) 823-4015; fax (30) 823-7076; e-mail budde@buddemusic.de; internet www.buddemusic.de; Man. Dir DR ROLF BUDDE.

t'Bwana Sound/Big Easy: Schleswigerstr 19, 44145 Dortmund; Contact HELMUT PHILIPPS.

Thomann Künstler Management GmbH: PO Box 1, 96136 Burgebrach; tel. (9546) 9449; fax (9546) 6844; e-mail info@thomann-music.de; internet www.thomann-music.de; Contact JOSEPH THOMANN.

Vielklang Musikproduktion GmbH: Forster str 4/5, 10999 Berlin; Man. Dir MATTHIAS BRÖCKEL.

Westpark Music: PO Box 260 227, Rathenauplatz 4, 50515 Cologne; tel. (221) 247-644; fax (221) 231-819; e-mail westparkmusic@aop.com; internet www.westparkmusic.com; Pres. ULLI HETSCHER.

Greece

Filippos Nakas Mousikos Oikos: 13 Navarinoy St, 10680 Athens; Man. Dir G NAKAS.

General Publishing Company SA: 11 Kriezotou St, 10671 Athens; Man. Dir PANAYIOTIS MARAVELIAS.

Greenland

ULO—Greenlandic Music: PO Box 184, 3911 Sisimiut; Production Man. KARSTEN SOMMER.

Hong Kong

Blue Max Productions: 1st Floor, Kingsfield Mansion, 457–459 King's Rd, North Point; Man. Partner RALPH LISTER.

BMG Music Publishing Hong Kong Ltd: 11/Fl, Peninsula Office Tower, 18 Middle Rd, Tsimshatsui, Kowloon; Gen. Man. IRENE HO.

Cinepoly Music Publishing Co Ltd: 8/F 100 Canton Rd, Tsimshatsui, Kowloon; Publishing Exec. SANDY SUN.

EMI Music Publishing (S E Asia) Ltd: Room 3201-7 Shell Tower, Times Sq., 1 Matherson St, Causeway Bay; Gen. Man. TERESA YIU.

Polygram Music Publishing Hong Kong Ltd: 8F 100 Canton Rd, Kowloon; Pres. NORMAN CHENG.

Sony Music Publishing: 4/F Acme Bldg, 22–28 Nanking St, Yaumati, Kowloon; Gen. Man. ANGELA HON.

Warner Music Publishing Hong Kong Ltd: Room 301–303, Corporation Sq., 8 Lam Lok St, Kowloon Bay, Kowloon; Man. Dir PACO WONG.

Hungary

Edito Musica: Vörösmarty tér 1, 1051 Budapest; Man. Dir ISTVAN HOMOLYA.

Joker: Florian ter 4–5, 1033 Budapest; Man. Dir PETER RADO.

PG Publishing: PO Box 8, 1922 Budapest.

Record Express Ltd: Kunigunda ut 41/B, 1037 Budapest; tel. (1) 437-1800; fax (1) 437-1899; e-mail meszaros@recordexpress.hu; internet www.recordexpress.hu; Man. Dir ATTILA SCHNEIDER; International Affairs BARBARA MÉSZAROS.

Sonic Boom: Iskola U 1, Szentendre; Man. Dir DITMAR LUPFER.

Iceland

Skifan HF: Skiefan 17, 108 Reykjavík; Chair. JON OLAFSSON.

Spor HF: Nýbýlavegur 4, PO Box 320, 202 Kópavogur; Man. Dir STEINAR BERG ISLEIFSSON.

Ireland

Acorn Music Ltd: Roncalli, Claremont Pines, Carrickmines, Dublin 18; Dir BRENDAN GRAHAM.

Aigle Music: 6 Danieli Dr., Artane, Dublin 5; Contact NICKY RYAN, ROMA RYAN.

Ainm Music: 5–6 Lombard St East, Dublin 2; tel. and fax (1) 677-8701; e-mail fstubbs@ainm-music.com; internet www.ainm-music.com; CEO FRANK STUBBS.

Asdee Music: Glenageary Office Park, Glenageary, Co Dublin; Admin. PETER BARDON.

Bardis Music Co Ltd: Glenageary Office Park, Glenageary, Co Dublin; Man. Dir PETER BARDON.

Beann Eadair Music: 48 Downside, Skerries, Co Dublin; Dir CLIVE HUDSON.

Blue Dandelion Publishing: 17 Dame Court, Dublin 2; Contact FRAN COLEMAN.

Brian Molloy: 5–6 Lombard St East, Dublin 2; Contact BRIAN MOLLOY; Marketing Man. GRAHAM MOLLOY.

Bright-Child Productions: The Elms, Richmond Ave South, Dartry, Dublin 6; tel. (1) 496-0970; fax (1) 497-9411; e-mail info@bright-child.com; internet www.bright-child.com; CEO PETER BLACKBYRNE; Dir ROSALEEN DURKIN.

Clannad Music: Film House, 4 Windmill Lane, Dublin 2; Man. Dir DAVID KAVANAGH.

Cló Iar—Chonnachta: Indreabhán, Conamara, Co na Gaillimhe; tel. (91) 593307; fax (91) 593362; e-mail cic@iol.ie; internet www.cic.ie; Marketing & Sales Man. DEIRDRE O'TOOLE.

Coyle and Coyle: 30 Lower Leeson St, Dublin 2; Dir JAMES COYLE.

Danceline Music: 267 Crodaun Forest Park, Celbridge, Co Kildare; Dir PETER MCCLUSKEY.

Emma Music Ltd: 5/6 Lombard St, Dublin 2; Dir MICHAEL O'RIORDAN.

Foxrock Music Productions: Alexandra House, Earlsfort Centre, Earlsfort Terrace, Dublin 2; Man. Dir JOHN JOHN LAPPIN.

Gael Linn Music: 26 Merrion Sq., Dublin 2; Contact MICHAEL WARD.

Hazel Records: Dublin Rd, Monasterevin, Co Kildare; Man. Dir JOHN KELLY.

Jump Music: 19 Stockton Green, Castleknock, Dublin 15; Man. Dir JOE MCFADDEN.

Lunar / Unicorn Records: 5–6 Lombard St East, Dublin 2; Contact BRIAN MOLLOY, JUDY CARDIFF; Marketing Man. GRAHAM MOLLOY.

McGuinness/Whelan Music Publishers: 30/32 Sir John Rogerson's Quay, Dublin 2; Man. Dir BARBARA GALAVAN.

Mother Music Ltd: 30–32 Sir John Rogerson's Quay, Dublin 2; Man. Dir BARBARA GALAVAN.

Mulligan Music Ltd: 75 Sweetmount Ave, Dundrum, Co Dublin; Man. Dir BRIAN O'NEILL.

Music Network: The Coach House, Dublin castle, Dublin 2; tel. (1) 671-9429; fax (1) 671-9430; e-mail info@musicnetwork.ie; internet www.musicnetwork.ie; Information Man. SEAMUS O'REILLY.

Peer Music Ireland Ltd: The Peer Suite, 26–27 Upper Pembroke St, Dublin 2; Contact DARRAGH KETTLE.

Raglan Music: Glenageary Office Park, Glenageary, Co Dublin; Admin. PETER BARDON.

Rosette Music Ltd: 5–6 Lombard St, Dublin 2; tel. (1) 830-1707; fax (1) 830-1981; Dir MICHAEL O'RIORDAN.

RSE Music Publishing: 11–13 Station Rd, Raheny, Dublin 5; Dirs RAYMOND J SMYTH, BREIDE P SMYTH.

The Evolving Music Company Ltd: Alexandra House, Earlsfort Centre, Earlsfort Terrace, Dublin 2; Contact DENIS DESMOND, JOHN J LAPPIN.

Third Floor Ltd: 70 Lower Baggot St, Dublin 2; Man. Dir MAURICE CASSIDY.

Woodtown Music: Dame House, Dame St, Dublin 2; Man. Dir JANE BOLTON.

Italy

Ala Bianca Group Srl: Via G Mazzoni 34/36, 41100 Modena; Gen. Man. TONI VERONA.

BMG Italy: Via di S Alessandro 7, 00131 Rome; Man. Dir MARIO CANTINI.

Crotalo Ed Mus: Via Del Pino 71, 48100 Lido Adriano; Man. Dir LUIGI MAZZESI.

EMI Music Publishing Italia: Via C Ravizza 43–45, 20148 Milan; Man. Dir ANTONIO MARRAPODI.

FMA Edizioni Musicali E Discografiche Srl: Via Boccaccio N 47, 20123 Milan; Pres. MARIO ALLIONE.

General Rock: Viale Manzoni 52, Cerveteri, 00052 Rome; Contact ROBBIE ZEE.

Lion Snc: Via Goldoni 42/A, 30174 Mestre, Venezia; Gen. Man. LUCIANO TREVISAN.

Nuova Durium Srl: Piazza Mirabello 1, 20121 Milan; Asst Man. FRANCESCO PICCARREDA.

Polygram Italia Edizioni: Via Carlo Tenca 2, 20124 Milan; Man. Dir GIANFRANCO REBULLA.

Sony Music Publishing (Italy): Via Amedei 9, 20123 Milan; Chair. FRANCO CABRINI.

Sugar Music Group: Via Quintiliano 40, 20138 Milan; International Business Affairs MONICA DAHL.

Virgin Dicshi Edizioni Musicali: Via Porpora 26, 20131 Milan; Man. Dir LUIGI MONTOVANI.

Warner Chappell Music Italiana: Corso Buenos Aires 79, 20124 Milan; Man. LUIGI BARTOLOTTA.

Japan

Columbia Music Publishing Co: 4-14-14 Akasaka, Minato-ku, Tokyo 107; Man. HAIJIME OGURA.

EMI Music Publishing Co Ltd: Shibuya Mitake Bldg 3F, 1-19-5 Shinuya, Shibuya-ku, Tokyo 150; Man. Dir NAMAHIKO SASAKI.

MCA Panasonic Music Co Ltd: KFI Bdlg 8F, 3-6-20 Kita-Aoyama, Minato-ku, Tokyo 107; Pres. NOBU YOSHINARI.

Shinko Music Publishing Co Ltd: 2–1 Ogawamachi, Kanda, Chiyoda-ku, Tokyo 101; Pres. SHOICHI KUSANO.

Sony Music Publishing: 1-32-12 Higashi, Shibuya-ku, Tokyo 150; Gen. Man. YOSHYUKI ITOH.

Sunkyo Music Co Ltd: 87-6 Torocho 2-Chome, Omiya-City 330; Dir YOUICHI TAKEUCHI.

Warner Chappell Music Japan KK: Nichion Inc, Akasaka Media Bldg, 3-6 Akasaka 5-Chome, Minato-ku, Tokyo 107; Man. Dir MANMORU MURAKAMI.

Republic of Korea

Korea Music Publishing: 325 Nakwon Arcade, 286-4 Nakwon-dong, Jongro-ku, Seoul; Contact EUN-SIK LEE.

Sony Music Entertainment (Korea) Inc: 985-19 Bangbae-dong, Seochu-ku, Seoul; Finance Man. TAE HWAN CHUNG.

Time Recording Inc: 620 Daeha Bldg, 14-11 Yoido-dong, Youngdungpo-ku, Seoul; Pres. N W CHO.

Luxembourg

Joybringer: 27 rue Victor Hugo, 4583 Differdange; Contact ANDRE DEPIENNE.

Promotion 4: PO Box 728, 2017 Luxembourg; Chair. MIKE KOEDINGER.

Radio Music International: Villa Louvigny, 2825 Luxumbourg-Ville; Man. Dir RAY VAN CANT.

Malaysia

BMG Music Publishing Sdn Bhd: 13-1 Jalan Seganmbut, Kuala Lumpur 51200; Man. Dir FRANKIE CHEAH.

Polygram Records Sdn Bhd: 83–87 Jalan Kampung Pandan, Taman Maluri, Kuala Lumpur 55100; Man. Dir ERIC YEO.

Pustaka Muzik EMI (Malaysia): Suite 10.01, 10th Fl, Exchange Sq., off Jln Semantan, Damansara Heights, Kuala Lumpur 50490; Publishing Man. LIMCHENG HOO.

Sony Music Entertainment (Malaysia): C16 & C17 Jalan Ampang, Utama 1/1, Taman Ampang Utama, 68000 Ampang; tel. (3) 4252-3233; fax (3) 4252-2235; e-mail rickloh@sonymusic.com.my; internet www.sonymusic.com.my; Man. Dir RICK LOH.

Mexico

Beechwood de Mexico SA: Río Tigris 33, 06500 México, DF; Dir-Gen. ANTONIO FRITZ.

Compañía Fonográfica Internacional SA/IM Discos & Cassettes: Sanctorum 86-B Col. Argentina, 11230 México, DF; tel. (55) 5399-2434; fax (55) 5399-2630; e-mail jmorales@imdiscos.com; internet www.imdiscos.com; Dir-Gen. JOSÉ I. MORALES BETANCOURT.

Editorial Musical Juventa: Ignacio Esteva 26A, 11850 México, DF; Proprietor DARIO ANTONIO ZORZANO.

Galaxia Musical SA: Leibnitz 130, 11590 México, DF; tel. (55) 5250-0378; fax (55) 5254-5790; internet www.galaxiamusical.com; Dir-Gen. JOSÉ G CRUZ AYALA.

Organización Latino Internacional: Avda Insurgentess Sur 953-202, Col. Nápoles, 03810 México, DF; Dir-Gen. TONY MÉNDEZ.

Polygram Discos SA: Avda Miguel Angel de Quevedo 531, Col. Romero de Torreros, 04310 México, DF; Dir-Gen. FRANCISCO BESTARD.

Produciones Fonograficas SA: Adolfo Prieto 1649, 1°, Col. del Valle, 03100 Benito Juárez, México, DF; Dir-Gen. BERNARDO YANCELSON.

Warner Chappell Music Mexico SA: Avda Ejercito Nacional 209, 3°, Col. Verónica Anzures, 11300 México, DF; Dir-Gen. JESÚS PÉREZ MARTÍN.

The Netherlands

Best Music: Wilhelminaplein 20, 5171 KX Kaatsheuvel; tel. (416) 273270; fax (416) 273270; Man. Dir PETER VAN BEST.

Blue & White Songs: Utrechtseweg 3g B, 1381 9S Weesp; Pres. HANS W VAN POL.

Brinker Media: PO Box 1276, 1400 Bussum; tel. (35) 603-5368; fax (35) 693-4877; e-mail studio@brinkermedia.com; internet www.brinkermedia.com; Man. Dir ERIC VAN DEN BRINK.

CM Songs: Herenweg 9, 2465 AA Rijnsaterwoude; tel. (172) 509853; fax (172) 507642; e-mail info@catmusic.nl; internet www.catmusic.nl; Man. Dir AART MOL.

Dutchy Publishing: Pampuslaan 45, 1382 JM Weesp; Man. Dir XAVIER PILGRIMS DE BIGARD.

EMI Music Publishing: Schapenkamp 8A, 1211 PA Hilversum; Man. Dir ARJEN WITTE.

Moonshine Management: Langeweid 7, 1831 BL Koedyk; tel. and fax (72) 561-5857; e-mail wilbrink@yahoo.com; internet www.moonshine-management.com; Pres. EVERT WILBRINK.

Narada Media: J Penhyweg 2, 1217 JH Hilversum; Dir of European Marketing JAAP HOITINGH.

Peermusic Holland bv: Larenseweg 159, 1221 CL Hilversum; Man. Dir J H M G VAN DÝL.

Pennies From Heaven: PO Box 3121, 2601 DC Delft; Vice-Pres. PAUL VAN MEELIS.

Stichting Conamus: PO Box 929, 1200 AX Hilversum; Gen. Man. J H DE MOL; Press Officer SASKIA BRWNING.

Strengholt Music Group: Flevolaan 41, 1411 KC Naarden; tel. (35) 695-8580; fax (35) 694-0362; e-mail info@strengholt.com; internet www.strengholt.com; Gen. Man. MARK WGNSTEKERS.

Universal Songs Holland: PO Box 2305, 1200 CH Hilversum; Man. Dir BRAM KEIZER.

VIP Promotions: Looievsgracht 38, 1016 VS Amsterdam; PD G BEZUIJEN.

New Zealand

Jayrem Music: PO Box 3101, Ohope, Woorl, 110 Symonds St, Auckland; Gen. Man. PAUL ELLIS.

South Pacific Music Associates Ltd: PO Box 47-088, Ponsonby, Auckland; Man. CLARE CHAMBERS.

Yellow Eye Music: 33 Fortune St, Dalmore, Dunedin; tel. 3473-9426; fax 3473-9700; e-mail simon@yelloweye.co.nz; internet www.yelloweye.co.nz; Partner SIMON VARE.

Norway

Frost Music A/S: PO Box 6062 Etterstad, 0601 Oslo; Man. Dir PHILIP KEVSE.

Late Night Music: PO Box 44, Aserudun 2 Strommen, 2014 Blystadlia; Man. Dir TOM SENNERUD.

Musikk Produksion AS: Kjelsasvn 139 D, 0491 Oslo; Man. Dir HARALD FJELD.

Norsk Musikkforlag A/S: PO Box 1499, Vika, 0016 Oslo; Dir LEIF DRAMSTAD.

Norwegian Songs: PO Box 4329 Torshov, Sandakaervn 24C, 0402 Oslo; Man. Dir AUDUN TYLDEN.

Polygram Publishing Norway: PO Box 2645 Solli, Drammensvn 82B, 0203 Oslo; Man. Dir STEIN G JOHNSEN.

Rec 90: PO Box 1291, 5001 Bergen; Man. Dir TORFINN ANDERSEN.

Sonet Music Norway: PO Box 26 45 Solli, Drammensvn 88 B, 0403 Oslo; Man. Dir TERJE ENGEN.

Peru

Ediciones Musiales Hispanas: Esquilache 179, Lima 27; Gen. Man. CARLOS RENJIPO MERCADO.

The Philippines

BAMI (Bayanihan Music Philippines Inc): PO Box AC 270, 782 Aurora Blvd, Cubao, Quezon City, Manila; Pres. FLORENDO GARCIA.

BMG Music Philippines: 3/F Equitable Banking Corp Bldg, 898 Aurora Blvd, Cubao, Quezon City, Manila; Contact NATHANIEL TAN.

DD International Recording Corporation: 363 P Casal St, Quiapo, Manila 1001; Chair. & Pres. DEMY A QUIRINO JR.

EMI (Eligardi Music Inc): 6/F NIDC Bldg, 259–263 Sen Gil J, Puyat Ave, Makati, Metro Manila; Pres. ELI GARDINER.

Poland

Polonia Records Ltd: Ul. Jana Pawla II 18m 13, 00-116 Warsaw; Man. Dir STANISLAW SOBOLA.

Polskie Nagrania: Goleszowska 6, 01-249 Warsaw; Man. Dir ALEKSANDER OLASZEWSKI.

Polskie Wydawnictwo Muzyczne (PWM): Al Krasinskiego 11A, 31-111 Krakow; Man. Dir JAN BETKOWSKI.

Portugal

BMG Ariola Portugal: Rua Gregório Lopes 1514/2, 1400 Lisbon.

Concertos de Portugal Lda: PO Box 13, 2775 Carcavelos; Dir JOSÉ SILVA.

EMI Songs Portugal: Praca Nuno Rodrigues do Santos 7, 1600 Lisbon.

Farol Musica: Alto do Couto, Arnazéns I, 2735 Cacém; Dirs ANTONIO GUIMARÁES, FERNANDO JÚRICE.

Polygram Discos SA: Rua Prof Reinaldo dos Santos 12-D, 1500 Lisbon; Man. Dir RODRIGO MARIN.

Sony Music Portugal: Rua Juliao Quintinha 11, 1500 Lisbon.

Vidisco Comercio e Industria de Som Lda: Avda Bombeiros Voluntarios 13, 1675 Pontinha; Gen. Man. JOÃO PEDRO JADAUJI.

Warner Chappell Portugal: Rua Dr Constantino de Braganca 26A, 1400 Lisbon.

Romania

Contera AV: Str Turda 122, BL 39, SCA, Et 6 Ap 30, Sect 1 Bucharest; Pres. IORDACHESCU OCTAVIAN.

Russia

Mezhdunarodnaya Kniga: Dimitrova 39, 117 049 Moscow; Man. Dir STANISLAV OSTAPISHIN.

Muzyka Publishers: Neglinnaya 14, 103 031 Moscow; Man. Dir L SIDELNIKOV.

Singapore

EMI Music Publishing Singapore Pte Ltd: 213 Henderson Rd, 04–05 Henderson Industrial Estate, Singapore 0315; CEO DAVID WEE.

Fox Agency International Inc: 391 B, Orchard Rd, Suite 09–10, Tower B, Ngee Ann City, Singapore 0923; Regional Dir FABIAN LEK.

Polygram Music Publishing Pte Ltd: 23 Genting Rd, 04-01 Chevalier House, Singapore 1334; Man. KAREN SIM.

Sony Music Publishing (Pte) Ltd: 601 Sims Dr., 02–07, Singapore 1438; Gen. Man. TERENCE PHUNG.

Warner/Chappell Music Singapore Pte Ltd: 10 Anson Rd #12-06/07/08, International Plaza, Singapore 079903; Publishing Man. LIZ CHEAM.

Slovakia

CS Music: Votrubova 2, 82109 Bratislava; Man. Dir DUSAN TLOLKA.

DMC Disco Box: Ruzinovska 28, 82101 Bratislava; Man. Dir IVAN MALOVEC.

EMI/Monitor Slovakia: Radvanska 1, 81101 Bratislava; Man. Dir PAVOL HAMMEL.

Musica: palisady 36, 81632 Bratislava; Man. Dir F J WALNER.

Polygram Slovakia: Pribinova 25, 81109 Bratislava; Man. Dir PETER RIAVA.

Slovenia

SKUC—AFK: Kersnikova 4, 61000 Ljubljana; Man. Dir MITJA PREZELJ.

South Africa

BMG Records Africa (Pty) Ltd: PO Box 5894 Johannesburg 2000; tel. (001) 242-3000; fax (001) 242-3030; internet click2music.co.sa; Man. Dir of Records KEITH LISTER; Man. Dir of Publishing PETER VEE.

Spain

B-Core: Marques de Sentmenat 72, interior 3a, 08029 Barcelona; tel. and fax (9) 3419-7883; e-mail bcore@bcoredisc.com; internet www.bcore.com; Man. Dir JORDI LLANSAMA.

Blanco Y Negro: Amigo 14–16, 08021 Barcelona; Man. Dir SITO MANOVENT.

Canciones del Mundo: Magallanes 25, 28015 Madrid; Man. Dir LUIS REGATERO.

Crab Ediciones Musicales SA: Sagunto 2, 28010 Madrid; Gen. Man. JORGE E GOMEZ DIAZ.

Doctor Music Publishing: Alcala 114-6B, 28009 Madrid; Dir LUCIA CARDENES.

Ediciones Musicales Warner Bros SA: Lopez de Hoyos 42, 28006 Madrid; Man. Dir INIGO ZABALA.

Epoca Music: Joanot Martorell 15, 08203 Barcelona; Man. Dir LEN ROY CARVALHO.

GSG—Grup de Serveis Guilleries: Granja Baró, Ctra de la Guixa, km 2, 08500 Barcelona; Administration JORDI COSTA; Management IGNASI PLA; Production JOAN CAPDEVILA.

Huygen Corp: Alzines 3, St Quirze Parc, 08192 St Quirze del Vallès, Barcelona; Contact MICHEL HUYGEN.

Neuronium Music: Calle Alzines 3, St Quirze Parc, 08192 St Quirze del Vallès, Barcelona; Contact MICHEL HUYGEN.

New Music Ediciones Musicales SA: PO Box 9.046, 28060 Madrid; Gen. Man. GERHARD HALTERMANN.

RLM Producciones: Jose Maria Cavero 9, Ch A, 28027 Madrid; Man. Dir ROSA LAGARRIGUE.

Sintonía, SA: Abdón Terradas 5, 28015 Madrid; tel. (91) 549-2350; fax (91) 543-9690; e-mail clif@sintonia.es; Publisher CLIFTON J WILLIAMS.

Sonifolk Arpafolk: Fernando el Catalico 58, 28015 Madrid; Man. Dir JOSE DE LA FUENTE.

Victoria: Narvaez 14-1A, 28009 Madrid; Gen. Man. GERHARD HALTERMANN.

Vortex Music: Magallanes 25, 28015 Madrid; Man. Dir LUIS REGATERO.

Sweden

BMG Music Publishing Scandinavia: PO Box 1026, Starrbäcksgatan 1, 17121 Sundbyberg; Man. Dir LARS KARLSSON.

EMI Music Publishing Scandinavia AB: PO Box 20509, 161 02 Bromma; Contact NINA SCHRIJVERSHOF.

Energy Records AB: Vastergatan 23, 21121 Malmö; Contact HÅKAN EHRNST.

Gazell Music AB: Tappvägen 24, PO Box 20055, 16102 Bromma; Dir DAG HAEGGQVIST.

MCA Music Sweden: PO Box 55 505, Riddargatan 23 4, 10204 Stockholm.

Misty Music AB: PO Box 10 149, 10055 Stockholm; Man. Dir ANDERS MÖREN.

Mixturen: Frijyrkliga Studieförbundet, Box 479, 10129 Stockholm; Editor TORGNY ERSÉUS.

Out of Time Music: Husargatan 15, 41122 Gothenburg; Prod. HÅKAN FORSHULT.

Real Time Music: Wennerbergsgatan 1, 11258 Stockholm; Man. ALLAN GUTHEIM.

Sonet Music AB: PO Box 20504, Mariehällsvägen 35, 16103 Bromma; Man. Dir INGERMAR BERGMAN.

Stockholm Records: PO Box 20504, 16102 Bromma; Gen. Man. ERIC HASSELQVIST.

Warner Chappell Music Scandinavia AB: PO Box 533, Vendevägen 85 B, 18215 Danderyd; tel. (8) 622-0900; fax (8) 755-1596; internet www.warnerchappell.com; Man. Dir HANS DESMOND.

Switzerland

Check Point Music: Rainweg 6, 8967 Widen; Man. Dir MARTIN SCHEISS.

Dinemec Productions SA: Blvd Helvétique 17, PO Box 893, 1211 Geneva; Man. Dir PAUL SUTIN.

Edition Helbing AG: Pfeaffikerstr 6, 8604 Volgetswil; Man. Dir WILLY VOGT.

Edition Melodie: Brunnwiesenstr 26, 8049 Zürich; Chair. ANTON PETERER.

Editions Cellier: Aiguemont 26, rue du Bourg de Plait, 1071 Chexbres; tel. (21) 946-1649; fax (21) 946-3533; e-mail ccellier@merging.com; internet ulliherkenhoff.freepage.de/cellier.html; Contacts MARCEL CELLIER, CATHERINE CELLIER.

Global Music Swiss: Im Hauel 15, 4147 Aesch; Public Relations SONJA SCHMIDT-MONTFORT.

Hyper Music: Domberweg 12, 4423 Hersberg; Man. Dir P J WASERMAN.

Marion Caravatti Music (MCM): Hochwachstr 27A, 8400 Winterthur; Chair. MARION CARAVATTI.

Migration: PO Box 431, 1800 Vevey; tel. (21) 923-6363; fax (21) 923-6362; e-mail hdill@bluewin.ch; internet www.farafina.com; Contact HEINZ DILL.

Turicaphon AG: Turicaphonstr 31, 8616 Riedikon; Man. Dir HANS OESTREICHER.

VIP AG Productions: Schützengasse 30, 8001 Zürich; Man. Dir URS PETER KELLER.

Viteka Music Production: PO Box 173, Ringstr 14, 8600 Dübendorf / Zürich; Chair. WILLY VITEKA.

Thailand

BMG Music: 18/F Vanissa Bdlg, Soi Chidlom, Pleonchit Rd, Patumwam, Bangkok 10110; Man. Dir STEVEN TAN.

Song Music Publishing: 1091, 185-5 New Petchburi Rd, Payathai, Bangkok 10400; Gen. Man. PETER GAN.

Turkey

Jazz Records & Publishing: Atlamatasi Caddesi 5, Serilen, 34470 Unkapani, Istanbul; Pres. YASAR DEMIRTURK.

Topkapi Music: Mesrutiyet Caddesi 113, Ece Han Kat 2, 80050 Tepebasi, Istanbul; Dir MEHMET ARMAN.

Ukraine

Muzychna Ukraina: Pushkinska St 32, 252 004 Kiev; Man. Dir MYKOLA LYNNYK.

Ukrainian Musical Information Centre: Richkova St 4, 252 135 Kiev; Man. Dir SERGIY GALUZIN.

The United Kingdom

Acuff-Rose Music Ltd: 25 James St, London W1M 6AA; Gen. Man. TONY PETERS.

Amphonic Music Ltd: Kerchesters, Waterhouse Lane, Kingswood, Tadworth, Surrey KT20 6HT; Dir ERICA DALE.

Associated Music International Ltd: 34 Salisbury St, London NW8 8QE; tel. (20) 7402-9111; fax (20) 7723-3064; e-mail eliot@amimedia.co.uk; internet www.amimedia.co.uk; Man. Dir ELIOT M COHEN.

Bad Habits Music Group: PO Box 111, London W13 0ZH; Man. Dir JOHN S RUSHTON.

Barn Dance Publications Ltd: 62 Beechwood Rd, South Croydon, Surrey CR2 0AA; Man. DEREK JONES.

Barry Collings Music: 15 Claremont Rd, Westcliff On Sea, Essex SS0 7DX; Man. Dir BARRY COLLINGS.

Big Bear Music: PO Box 944, Edgbaston, Birmingham B16 8UT; tel. (121) 4547020; fax (121) 4549996; e-mail admin@bigbearmusic.com; internet www.bigbearmusic.com; Man. Dir JIM SIMPSON.

Black Magic Management Ltd: 296 Earls Court Rd, London SW5 9BA; Man. Dir MATAYA CLIFFORD.

BMG Music Publishing Limited: Bedford House, 69–79 Fulham High St, London SW6 3JN; Man. Dir PAUL CURRAN.

Boosey & Hawkes Music Publishers: 295 Regents St, London W1R 8JH; Man. Dir R A FELL.

Brilliant Music: 19 Ford Sq., London E1 2HS; Man. Dir FRAZER HENRY.

Brothers Organization: 74 The Archway, Station Approach, Ranelagh Gardens, London SW6 3UH; Dirs IAN TITCHENER, NICK TITCHENER.

Bucks Music Ltd: Onward House, 11 Uxbridge St, London W8 7TQ; tel. (20) 7221-4275; fax (20) 7229-6893; e-mail info@bucksmusicgroup.co.uk; internet www.bucksmusicgroup.com; Man. Dir SIMON PLATZ.

Bulk Music Ltd: 9 Watt Rd, Hillington, Glasgow G52 4RY, Scotland; Dir ISOBEL WAUGH.

Bushranger Music: 86 Rayleigh Rd, Hutton, Brentwood, Essex CM13 1BH; Man. Dir KATHY LISTER.

Campbell Connelly & Co Ltd: 8/9 Frith St, London W1V 5TZ; Head of Copyright KEVIN WHITE.

Carlin Music Corporation: Ironbridge House, 3 Bridge Approach, London NW1 8BD; tel. (20) 7734-3251; fax (20) 7439-2391; e-mail daisie@carlinmusic.com; CEO DAVID JAPP.

Charly Publishing Limited: 156–166 Ilderton Rd, London SE15 1NT; Dir JAN FRIEDMANN.

Chrysalis Music Ltd: The Chrysalis Bldg, 13 Barmley Rd, London W10 6SP; tel. (20) 7465-6169; fax (20) 7229-4498; e-mail jeremy.lascelles@chrysalis.com; internet www.chrysalis.com; CEO JEREMY LASCELLES.

Congo Music Ltd: 17A Craven Park Rd, Harlesden, London NW10 8SE; Dirs BYRON LYE-FOOK, ROOT JACKSON.

Cornish Legend Music: 153 Vauxhall St, The Barbican, Plymouth PL4 0DF, Devon; Partner NICK STRACHAN.

Cramer Music: 23 Garrick St, London WC2E 8AX; Contact PETER MAXWELL.

Cwmni Cyhoeddi Gwynn Cyf: Y Gerlan Heol Y Dwr, Penygroes, Caernarfon, Gwynedd LL54 6LR, Wales; tel. (1286) 881797; fax (1286) 882634; Contact WENDY JONES.

Dance Music: 7 Mornington Terrace, Camden Town, London NW1 7RR; Man. Dir IAN TREGONING.

Demi Monde Records & Publishing: Foel Studio, Llanfair, Caereinion, Powys SY21 0DS, Wales; tel. (1938) 810758; fax (1938) 810758; e-mail dave.anderson@dial.pipex.com; internet www.demimonde.co.uk; Man. Dir DAVE ANDERSON.

Demon Music Ltd: Canal House, Stars Estate, Transport Ave, Brentford, Middlesex TW8 9HF; James Bedbrook.

EMI Music Publishing: 127 Charing Cross Rd, London WC2H 0EA; Man. Dir PETER REICHARDT.

Endomorph Music Publishing: 29 St Michaels Rd, Leeds LS6 3BG; Man. Dir DAVE FOSTIN.

Equity Records: 112A–B Westbourne Grove, Chepstow Rd, London W2 5RU; Man. Dir PAUL MOORE.

Eschenbach Editions: 28 Dalrymple Cres., Edinburgh EH9 2NX, Scotland; tel. (131) 6673633; fax (131) 6673633; e-mail eschenbach@caritas-music.co.uk; internet www.caritas-music.co.uk; Man. Dir JAMES DOUGLAS.

Express Music (London) Ltd: The Studio, Yew Tree Farm, Charing Heath, Kent TN27 0AU; Man. Dir S JACKSON.

Fair Oaks Entertainment: PO Box 19, Ulverston, Cumbria CA12 9TF; Proprietor/Man. J G LIVINGSTONE.

Friendly Overtures Ltd: 345 West Wycombe Rd, High Wycombe, Bucks HP12 4AD; Creative Dir MICHAEL BATORY.

Global Chrysalis Music Publishing Co Ltd: The Chrysalis Bldg, 13 Bramley Rd, London W10 6SP; tel. (20) 7465-6203; fax (20) 7465-6318; internet www.chrysalis.com; Gen. Man. PETER KNIGHT JR.

Grade One Music: 34 Salisbury St, London NW8 8QE; tel. (20) 7402-9111; fax (20) 7723-3064; Man. Dir ELIOT COHEN.

Gramavision: 329 Latimer Rd, London W10 6RA; tel. (20) 8960-3311; fax (20) 8960-4334; Gen. Man. ANDY CHILDS.

Grian Music: Cockenzie Business Centre, Edinburgh Rd, Cockenzie, East Lothian EH32 0XL, Scotland; tel. (1875) 815888; fax (1875) 813545; e-mail iangtrax@aol.com; internet www.greentrax.com; Proprietor IAN D GREEN.

Harbourtown Music: PO Box 25, Ulverston, Cumbria LA12 7UN; Man. Dir GORDON JONES.

Hit & Run Music Ltd: 25 Ives St, London SW3 2ND; tel. (20) 7590-2600; fax (20) 7584-5774; e-mail tony@hit-and-run.com; internet www.genesis-music.com; Chair. & Man. Dir TONY SMITH.

Howard Jones Music Ltd: 33 Alexander Rd, Aylesbury, Bucks HP20 2NR; Admin. DAVID R STOPPS.

Jermaine Springer Publishing: PO Box 8969, London SE9 4ZB; Dir JERMAINE SPRINGER.

John Fiddy Music: Fruit Farm House, Foxton, Cambridge CB2 6RT; Admin. CHERYL KENNY.

Josef Weinberger Ltd: 12–14 Mortimer St, London W1N 7RD; Promotion & Marketing SEAN GRAY.

Kassner Associated Publishers Limited: Exmouth House, 11 Pine St, London EC1R 0JH; Man. Dir DAVID KASSNER.

Kinetix: The Black Office, DC Warehouse, Unit 6, Industrial Park, Maple Cross WD3 2AS; Chair. JON SHARP.

Lee Music: Stewart House, Hillbottom Rd, Sands Industrial Estate, High Wycombe, Bucks HP12 4HJ; International A & R and Company Lawyer KEITH PHILLIPS.

Maecenas Europe Publishers: 5 Bushey Close, Old Barn Lane, Kenley, Surrey CR8 5AU; Sales Man. ALAN KIRK.

Maran Steele Music: Ellemford Farmhouse, Duns TD11 3SG, Scotland; Man. Dir HUNTER STEELE.

MCA Music: Elsinore House, 77 Fulham Palace Rd, London W6 8JA; Man. Dir PAUL CONNOLLY.

Mcasso Music Productions Ltd: 9 Carnaby St, London W1V 1PG; Prod. LISA MCCAFFERY.

Metro Music Publishers Ltd: Longriggs, Swalwell, Gateshead, Tyne & Wear NE99 1BB; Dir of Music Production JON CRAIG.

Moggie Music Limited: 101 Hazelwood Lane, Palmers Green, London N13 5HQ; Man. Dir HAL CARTER.

Moksha: PO Box 102, London E15 2HH; Man. Dir CHARLES COLM.

Moving Shadow Records: 1st & 2nd Floors, 17 St Anne's Court, Soho, London W1V 3AW; Label Co-ordinator CAROLINE BUTLER.

Muirhead Music: Michelin House, 81 Fulham Rd, Chelsea, London SW3 6RD; tel. (20) 7351-5167; fax (870) 1363878; e-mail info@muirheadmanagement.co.uk; internet www.muirheadmanagement.co.uk; CEO DENNIS MUIRHEAD.

Music Collection International Ltd: 36–38 Caxton Way, Watford, Hertfordshire WD1 8UF; Marketing Dir DANNY KEENE.

Music Copyright Solutions PLC: 32 Lexington St, London W1F 0LQ; tel. (20) 7255-8777; fax (20) 7255-8778; e-mail info@mcs.music.com; internet www.mcsmusic.com; CEO BRIAN SCHOLFIELD.

Park Records: PO Box 651, Oxford OX2 9RB; Man. Dir JOHN DAGNELL.

Peermusic (UK) Ltd: Peer House, 8–14 Verulam St, London WC1X 8LZ; Man. Dir NIGEL ELDERTON.

Performance Equities Ltd: 112 A & B Westbourne Grove, Chepstow Rd, London W2 5RU; Man. Dir PAUL MOORE.

Phantom Publishing: 59 Moore Park Rd, London SW6 2HA; Man. Dir FALCON STUART.

Pink Floyd Music Publishers: 27 Noel St, London W1V 3RD; Dir PETER BARNES.

Pollytone Music: PO Box 124, Ruislip, Middlesex HA4 9BB; tel. (1895) 638584; fax (1895) 624793; e-mail val@pollyton.demon.co.uk; internet www.pollytone.com; Dir VALERIE BIRD.

PolyGram International Music Publishing: 8 St James Sq., London SW1Y 4JU; CEO DAVID HOCKMAN.

R T L Music: Stewart House, Hill Bottom Rd, Sands Industrial Estate, High Wycombe HP12 4HJ; Owner & Prod. RON LEE.

Rive Droite UK Ltd: 166 Upper Richmond Rd, London SW15 2SH; Music Dir BRIAN RAWLING.

Robert Kingston (Music) Ltd: c/o Music Sales, 5–9 Faith St, London W1V 5TZ; tel. (20) 7434-0066.

Rondor Music: Rondor House, 10A Parsons Green, London SW6 4TW; Man. Dir STUART HORNALL.

Rykomusic Ltd: 329 Latimer Rd, London W10 6RA; tel. (20) 8960-3311; fax (20) 8960-4334; Gen. Man. PAUL LAMBDEN.

S W Music (UK): 48 Fernside Rd, Poole, Dorset BH15 2JJ; tel. (1202) 773103; fax (1202) 681419; e-mail dave.dacosta@ukonline.co.uk; Man. Dir DAVE DACOSTA.

Satellite Music Limited: 34 Salisbury St, London NW8 8QE; tel. (20) 7402-9111; fax (20) 7723-3064; e-mail satellite_artists@hotmail.com; Man. Dir ELIOT M COHEN.

Scotford Music: 13 Winton Park, Edinburgh EH10 7EX, Scotland; tel. (1314) 451687; e-mail gerryford@madasafish.com; internet www.gerryford.co.uk; Proprietor GERRY FORD.

Sea Dream Music: 236 Sebert Rd, Forest Gate, London E7 0NP; Sr Partner SIMON LAW.

Seriously Groovy Music Ltd: 3rd Floor, 28 D'Arblay St, Soho, London W1F 8EW; tel. (20) 7439-1947; fax (20) 7734-7540; e-mail seriously.groovy@virgin.net; internet www.seriouslygroovy.com; Dir LORRAINE SNAPE.

Songs for Today Inc: PO Box 130, Hove, East Sussex BN3 6QU; tel. (1273) 550088; fax (1273) 540969; e-mail publishing@tkogroup.com; internet www.tkogroup.com; Dir of Administration ROLAND ROGERS.

Sony Music Publishing: 13 Great Marlborough St, London W1V 2LP; Man. Dir BLAIR MCDONALD.

Soundtrack Music Publishing: 22 Ives St, London SW3 2ND; Contact OLAF WYPER.

Studio G Ltd: Ridgway House, Great Brington, Northampton NN7 4JA; tel. (1604) 770511; fax (1604) 770022; e-mail library@studiog.co.uk; internet www.studiog.co.uk; Man. Dir JOHN GALE.

Sylvantone Music: 17 Allerton Grange Way, Leeds LS17 6LP; tel. (113) 2687788; fax (709) 2359333; e-mail sylvantore@hotmail.com; Proprietor TONY GOODACRE.

TKO Music Publishing Ltd: PO Box 130, Hove, East Sussex BN3 6QU; tel. (1273) 550088; fax (1273) 540969; e-mail publishing@tkogroup.com; internet www.tkogroup.com; Dir of Administration ROLAND ROGERS.

Tonecolor Ltd: The Studio, Yew Tree Farm, Charing Heath, Kent TN27 0AU; Man. Dir S JACKSON.

Unity Music Publishing: John Henry Bldg, 16/24 Brewery Rd, London N7 9NH; Sales & Retail Man. PEPIN CLOUT.

Universal Songs Ltd: 14 Montpelier Villas, Brighton BN1 3DG; tel. (1273) 771488; e-mail ptubbs@naeamar.co.uk; internet www.pierretubbs.uk; Contact PIERRE TUBBS.

Vinyl Japan (UK) Ltd: 281 Camden High St, London NW1 7BX; Man. PATRICK JAMES.

Warlock Music Ltd: 329 Latimer Rd, London, W10 6RA; tel. (20) 8960-3311; fax (20) 8960-4334; Gen. Man. PAUL LAMBDON.

Warner Chappell Music: 129 Park St, London W1Y 3FA; Man. Dir ED HEINE.

Whole Armor/Full Armor: PO Box 130, Hove, East Sussex BN3 6QU; tel. (1273) 550088; fax (1273) 540969; e-mail publishing@tkogroup.com; internet www.tkogroup.com; Dir of Administration ROLAND ROGERS.

Windswept Pacific: 27 Queensdale Pl., London W11 4SQ; Contact DEBBIE MILES.

Wolf Records: 83 Brixton Water Lane, London SW2 1PH; tel. (20) 7733-8088; fax (20) 7326-4016; Man. Dir DOMINIQUE BRETHES.

Wot Films & Music: Suite 3, 44 Mortimer St, London W1N 7DG; Prod. JACKIE THOMAS.

Zomba Music Publishers: Zomba House, 165–167 Willesden High Rd, London NW10 2SG; Man. Dir STEVEN HOWARD.

The United States of America

Another Amethyst Song: 273 Chippewa, Columbia, SC 29210-6508.

Arista Music Publishing: 8370 Wilshire Blvd, 3rd Floor, Beverly Hills, CA 90211; Contact JUDY HICKS.

Ashleigh Publishing: PO Box 76507, Washington DC 20013; Pres. CARL BENTLEY.

Axbar Records: PO Box 12353, San Antonio, TX 78212; tel. (210) 829-1909; e-mail axbar@stic.net; internet www.axbarmusic.com; Prod./Gen. Man. JOE SCATES.

Bekool Music Group: 23 Music Sq. East, #101, Nashville, TN 37203; Pres. PAT MCKOOL.

Benson Music Group Inc: 365 Great Circle Rd, Nashville, TN 37228; International Sales JANICE CUTTLER.

Betty Jane/Josie Jane Music Pub Co: 7400 N Adams Rd, North Adams, MI 49262; Pres. CLAUDE E REED.

Bivens Music: 203 Gates Dr., Hendersonville, TN 37075-4961; Owner ERNIE BIVENS.

Bloozy Publishing: 542 Prospect Ave #1, Brooklyn, NY 11215; Contact MICHAEL STEVENS.

BMG Music Publishing: 1 Music Circle N, Nashville, TN 37203; Contact HENRY HURT.

Bob Scott Frick Enterprises: 404 Bluegrass Ave, Madison, TN 37115; tel. (615) 865-6380; e-mail bfrick@att.net; Pres. BOB FRICK.

Bob White Music Inc: 212 Morrison St, McMinnville, TN 37110; Pres. & CEO THOMAS B VAUGHN.

Cactus & Winnebago Music Publishing: PO Box 1027, Neenah, WI 54957-1027; Pres. TONY ANSEMS.

Carl Fischer Inc: 62 Cooper Sq., New York, NY 10003; Vice-Pres. of Publishing LAUREN KEISER.

Cat's Voice Productions: PO Box 1361, Sanford, ME 04073-7361; Owner TOM REEVES.

Cavet-Vanderpool Publ/BMI: 1030 Villa Pl., Nashville, TN 37212; Pres. VERA CAVET VANDERPOOL.

Center for The Queen of Peace: 3350 Highway 6 S, Suite 412, Sugar Land, TX 77478; internet www.marianland.com; Dir RAFAEL BROM.

Cerebral Records: 1236 Laguna Dr., Carlsbad, CA 92008; Pres. LINCOLN KROLL; Publicist CAROL LENO.

Chapel Music Group Inc: 2021 Richard Jones Rd, Suite 180, Nashville, TN 37215; Dir of Marketing HEATHER CAMPBELL.

Charisma Music Publishing Co Inc: 1841 Broadway, Suite 411, New York, NY 10023; Pres. JULIE LIPSIVS.

Christmas and Holiday Music: 3517 Warner Blvd, Suite 4, Burbank, CA 91505-4636; Pres. JUSTIN WILDE.

Cosmotone Records: 3350 Highway 6 S, PMB 412, Sugar Land, TX 77478; internet www.marianland.com/music02.html; Pres. RAFAEL BROM.

Cude & Pickens Music: 519 N Halifax Ave, Daytona Beach, FL 32118; tel. and fax (386) 252-0381; e-mail cudepickenspub@aol.com; internet www.broadwayusa.us; CEO BOBBY LEE CUDE.

DanceFloor Distribution/Echo USA: 95 Cedar Lane, Englewood, NJ 07631; Pres. JEFFREY COLLINS.

De Stijl Music (BMI): PO Box 170206, San Francisco, CA 94117-0206.

Disney Music Publishing Group: 350 S Buena Vista St, Burbank, CA 91521; Vice-Pres. SUSAN BORGESON.

Diva Entertainment World: 853 Broadway #1516, New York City, NY 10003; Man. Dir MARC KRASNOW.

Edensong: PO Box 34, Days Creek, OR 97429; Owner RICK FOSTER.

EMI/Virgin Music: 827 N Hilldale Ave, West Hollywood, CA 90069; Vice-Pres. SUSAN COLLINS.

Energy Productions Inc: 234 6th Ave, Brooklyn, NY 11215; Pres. MICHAEL KNUTH.

Eternal Song Agency: 6326 E Livingston Ave, Reynoldsburg, OH 43068; Pres. LEOPOLD XAVIER CRAWFORD.

FAME Recording Studios: PO Box 2527, Muscle Shoals, AL 35662; Studio Man. RODNEY HALL.

Faniork Music BMI: 23797 Via Irana Valencia, CA 91355; Owner DON LEE.

Fiesta City Publishers: PO Box 5861, Santa Barbara, CA 93150-5861; Pres. FRANK E COOKE.

Five Roses Music Group: 34A Lanier Rd, Studio 1, Jekyll Island, GA 31527; Pres. SAMMIE LEE MARLER.

Five Star Music Inc: 40 Music Sq. E, Nashville, TN 37203; Contact GUY PARKER.

Flat Town Music Co: PO Drawer 10, 238 E Main St, Ville Platte, LA 70586; Pres. FLOYD SOILEAU.

Folklore Inc: 1671 Appian Way, Santa Monica, CA 90401; Contact MITCH GREENHILL.

GBS Music: 203 Gates Dr., Hendersonville, TN 37075-4961; Owner ERNIE BIVENS.

Gramophone Music Co: PO Box 921, Beverly Hills, CA 90213; Gen. Man. O BERLINER.

Group Productions: 1515 Cascade Ave, Box 481, Loveland, CO 80538; tel. (970) 669-3836; internet www.grouppublishing.com; Contact BRENDA KRAFT.

Hall of Fame Music Co: PO Box 921, Beverly Hills, CA 90213; Gen. Man. O BERLINER.

Heartbeat Music: PO Box 294, Westerville, OH 43086-0294; Pres./Owner RANDY KETTERING.

Heartwrite Music: PO Box 1739, Texarkana, AR 75504; Pres. DAVID PATILLO.

Hidden Pun Music Inc: 1841 Broadway, Suite 411, New York, NY 10023; Pres. JULIE LIPSIVS.

High Kite Productions & Publishing: 1245 Elizabeth St, Denver, CO 80206; Prod. (Owner/Pres.) HENRY BROZ ROWLAND.

Jon Music, BMI: PO Box 233, 329 N Main St, Church Point, LA 70525; Owner LEE LAVERGNE.

Justice Music Corporation: 11586 Blix St, North Hollywood, CA 91602; Exec. Vice-Pres. MONTE R THOMAS.

Ketter Entertainment: PO Box 740702, San Diego, CA 92174-0702; Pres./CEO AL KETTER.

Lieber & Stoller Music Publishers: 9000 Sunset Blvd, Suite 1107, Los Angeles, CA 90069; Gen. Man. RANDY POE.

Lipservices: 9 Prospect Park W, Room 14B, Brooklyn, NY 11215-1741; tel. (718) 638-2815; fax (718) 638-0842; e-mail ezclear@mindspring.com; Pres. JULIE LIPSIVS.

Little Big Town Music: 803 18th Ave South, Nashville, TN 37203; Pres. WENDY BOMAR.

Loud Cry Music Pub Co: PO Box 210270, Nashville, TN 37221-0270; Owner/Pres. DON SANDERS.

Metrostar Music: PO Box 5807, Englewood, NJ 07631; tel. (201) 969-9990; fax (201) 969-9955; e-mail plcagent@aol.com; Gen. Man. PHILIP S KURNIT.

MNM Music Group Inc: 1410 2nd St, Suite 300, Santa Monica, CA 90401; Pres. NICK MARTINELLI.

Moller Digital Publishing: 17176 Grand Ave, Lake Elsinore, CA 92530; Sales Man. IRMA MOLLER.

More Brand Music Publishing, BMI: PO Box 1027, Neenah, WI 54957-1027; Pres. RITA ANSEMS.

Music Sales Corporation: 257 Park Ave S, 20th Floor, New York, NY 10010; tel. (212) 254-2100; fax (212) 254-2013; internet www.musicsales.com; Pres. BARRIE EDWARDS.

Namax Music Publishing: PO Box 24162, Richmond, VA 23224; e-mail namaxmusic@aol.com; Pres. NANETTE BROWN.

Pal Productions Co: PO Box 80691, Baton Rouge, LA 70898; Pres. JOHNNY R PALAZZOTTO.

Pathway Music dba: PO Box 2250, Cleveland, TN 37320-2250; Co-ordinator of Music CHARLES TOWLER; Copyright Supervisor CONNIE CALDWELL.

Peermusic: 8159 Hollywood Blvd, Los Angeles, CA 90069; COO/Sr Vice-Pres. KATHY SPANBERGER.

Peermusic: 810 Seventh Ave, New York, NY 10019; COO/Sr Vice-Pres. KATHY SPANBERGER.

PKM Music: PO Box 5807, Englewood, NJ 07631; tel. (201) 969-9990; fax (201) 969-9955; e-mail plcagent@aol.com; Partner PHILIP S KURNIT.

Platinum Gold Productions: 9200 Sunset Blvd, Suite 1220, Los Angeles, CA 90069; Partner STEVE COHEN.

PolyGram Music Publishing Group: Worldwide Plaza, 825 8th Ave, New York, NY 10019; Creative Dirs RANDY SABISTON, DWAYNE ALEXANDER.

PPL-MCI Entertainment Group: 10 Universal Plaza, PO Box 8442, Universal City, CA 91618; tel. (818) 506-8533; fax (818) 506-8534; e-mail pplzmi@aol.com; internet www.pplzmi.com; CEO JAESON ST JAMES JARRETT; Man. Dir MAXX DIAMOND.

Pravda Records Inc: 3823 N Southport, Chicago, IL 60613; Man. Dir KENNETH GOODMAN.

Quango Music Group Inc: 9744 Wilshire Blvd, Suite 305, Beverly Hills, CA 90212; Pres. GEORGE GHIZ.

Rising Star Music Publishers: 52 Executive Park South, Suite 5203, Atlanta, GA 30329; Editor PAT NUGENT.

Rondor Music International: 360 N La Cienega Blvd, Los Angeles, CA 90048; Man. CANDI BROWN.

Rustron Music Publishers: c/o The Whimsy, 1156 Park Lane, West Palm Beach, FL 33417; tel. (561) 686-1354; e-mail safehavenwpb@yahoo.com; Exec. Dir RUSTY GORDON.

Set A Record Publishing: 720 North Roosevelt St, Cherokee, IA 51012; Man. FRANK GALLAGHER.

Shawnee Press Inc: 49 Waring Dr., Delaware Water Gap, PA 18327; Dir of Sales DENNIS BELL.

Sikio Marika Records: 6840 N Maple #157, Fresno, CA 93710; Label Head TYRONE WHITE.

Single Kick Music: PO Box 8243, Calabasas, CA 91372; tel. (818) 883-8407; Proprietor CHO PAQUET.

Songs for Today: 15 Rolling Way, New City, NY 10956-6912; tel. (845) 634-8282; fax (845) 634-5888; e-mail publishing@tkogroup.com; CEO MICHAEL COHN.

Sony Music Publishing: 666 5th Ave, PO Box 4451, New York, NY 10101-4451; Dir of Creative Affairs PATI DEVRIES.

Spencer Ministries: 2225 Amoy West Rd, Mansfield, OH 44903; Exec. Dir DAVID CONNER.

Sublime Music: 15 Rolling Way, New City, NY 10956-6912; tel. (202) 966-3280; fax (202) 364-1367; e-mail publishing@tkogroup.com; internet www.tkogroup.com; CEO MICHAEL COHN.

Sunset Promotions of Chicago Inc: 9359 S Kedzie Ave, Box 42807, Evergreen Park, IL 60805; tel. (773) 586-1800; fax (773) 586-1855; e-mail sunsetpromogip@inetmail.att.net; Pres. NEIL J CACCIOTTOLO.

Tedesco Tunes: 16020 Lahey St, Granada Hills, CA 91344; Pres. DALE T TEDESCO.

Terra Nova Recording Company: 853 Broadway, #1516, New York, NY 10003; Pres. MARC KRASNOW; CEO ROBERT MANGOVLEFF.

The Music Umbrella: PO Box 1067, Santa Monica, CA 90406; Pres./CEO GLENN H FRIEDMAN.

TKO Publishing Inc: 15 Rolling Way, New City, NY 10956-6912; tel. (845) 634-8282; fax (845) 634-5888; e-mail publishing@tkogroup.com; Admin. M A COHN.

Tranquil Technology Music: PO Box 20463, Oakland, CA 94620; Prod. MICHAEL MANTRA.

TurnerSong: 4263 San Jose Blvd, Jacksonville, FL 32207-6342; Partner LEE TURNER.

ViRay Publishing, BMI/Kerryray Publishing: 22432 Bayberry, Mission Viejo, CA 92692; Pres. RANDY RAY.

Warner Chappell Music Inc: 10585 Santa Monica Blvd, Los Angeles, CA 90025-4950; Sr Vice-Pres. RICK SHOEMAKER.

Westwood Entertainment Group: 1115 Inman Ave, Suite 330, Edison, NJ 08820-1132; Gen. Man. ELENA PETILLO.

Wilcom Publishing: PO Box 4456, West Hills, CA 91308; tel. and fax (661) 285-8032; e-mail info@wilcompublishing.com; internet www.wilcompublishing.com; Owner WILLIAM CLARK.

Windswept Holdings LLC: 9320 Wilshire Blvd, Suite 200, Beverly Hills, CA 90212; tel. (310) 550-1500; fax (310) 247-0195; internet www.windsweptpacific.com; CEO EVAN R MEDOW.

Woodrich Enterprises Inc: PO Box 38, Lexington, AL 35648; e-mail mernee@msn.com; Pres. WOODY RICHARDSON.

Xmas Music: PO Box 828, Hollywood, CA 90028; Pres. RANDALL PAUL.

Zettitalia Music International: PO Box 8442, Universal City, CA 91618; tel. (818) 506-8533; fax (818) 506-8534; e-mail zettworks@aol.com; internet www.pplzmi.com; Pres./CEO SUZETTE CUSEO-JARRETT.

Zomba Enterprises Inc: 137–139 W 25th St, New York, NY 10001; Sr Vice-Pres./Gen. Man. DAVID RENZER.

Venezuela

Distribuidora Sonografica CA: Dolores a Pte Soublette, Edif. Centro Empresarial Sur 4, Qta. Crespo, Caracas; Gen. Man. GUILLERMO URBANO MIJARES.

APPENDIX E: MUSIC FESTIVALS AND EVENTS

Australia

Adelaide Fringe Festival: Lion Arts Centre, Cnr N Terrace & Morphett St, Adelaide, SA 5000; tel. (8) 8100-2000; fax(8) 8100-2020; e-mail buzz@adelaidefringe.com.au; internet www.adelaidefringe.com.au; Artistic Dir KAREN HADFIELD; Australia's largest fringe festival, held February–March.

Big Day Out: 212 Palmer St, East Sydney, NSW 2010; National alternative music event, held annually in January.

Brisbane Biennial International Music Festival: Level 2, 75 Grey St, South Brisbane, QLD 4101; CEO NICHOLAS HEYWARD; Next festival will take place from May to June.

Brisbane's World of Music Festival: 120 Main St, Kangaroo Point, QLD4169; Dir CHRISTOPHER BOWEN; World Music festival, Held at end of October.

East Coast Blues Festival: PO Box 97, Byron Bay, NSW 2481; Dir Co Prod. KEVEN OXFORD; Festival of Blues & Roots music held each Easter.

Festival of Perth: 3 Crawley Ave, Crawley, WA 6009; Dir DAVID BLENKINSOP; Multi-arts festival held February–March.

Highfield Music Festival: c/o B & S Promotions, Bears Choice Music & Entertainment, PO Box 1481 Frankston, VIC 3199; Partners BILL DETTMER, SALLY DETTMER; Festival co-ordinators providing live to music to venues.

Melbourne Music Festival: 62–74 Pickles St, S Melbourne, VIC 3205; Exec. Prod. DOBE NEWTON; Australia's largest contemporary music festival; held in February.

Moomba Festival: 117 Sturt St, S Melbourne, VIC 3205; Dirs BOB BURTON, MARIA KATSONIS; Australia's largest outdoor festival; held annually in mid-March.

Port Fairy Folk Festival: PO Box 1252, Geelong, VIC 3220; tel. (3) 5225-1232; fax (3) 5225-1211; e-mail pfff@portfairyfolkfestival.com; internet www.portfairyfolkfestival.com; Festival Dir JAMIE MCKEW; Nation's premier world and folk music event.

Sydney Festival: Level II, 31 Market St, Sydney, NSW 2000; Festival Dir ANTHONY STEEL.

Tamworth Country Music Festival: Tamworth City Council, PO Box 555, Tamworth, NSW 2340; Annual Country Music festival held in January, incorporating the Golden Guitar Awards.

WOMADelaide: c/o Arts Projects Australia, 12 King William Rd, Unley SA 5061; tel. (8) 8271-1488; fax (8) 8271-9905; e-mail apadmin@artsprojects.com.au; internet www.artsprojectsaustralia.com.au; Event Dir IAN SCOBIE; Biennial three-day music festival; part of international World of Music, Arts and Dance, WOMAD, network.

Austria

Artclub Festival Imst: PO Box 9, 6460 Imst; A & R Man. ARIN SCHROTT; Open air rock festival.

Kultodrom: Mistelhach; Contact OTMAR BIRINGER; Held 14–16 June.

Rock At The Border: Weitaer str 104, 3950 Gmünd; Chair. GERARD SIMON; Open-air rock festival held in the second week of August.

Sommer Rock Festival: Hauptstr 140, 7203 Wiesen; Chair. EWALD TARTAR; Open-air pop and indie music festival, held on last weekend of July.

Sunsplash Festival: Hauptstr 140, 7203 Wiesen; Chair. EWALD TARTAR; Open-air reggae festival held on the last weekend of August.

Transmitter: ImSohl 1, 6845 Hohenems; Dir BERNHARD AMANN; Avant-garde festival held in the first week of July.

Belgium

AALN International: PO Box 15, Antwerpen 17, 2018 Antwerp; Man. Dir LUC NUITTEN; Jazz, blues and world music events.

Belga Jazz Festival: c/o Jazzronaute, 34 rue Africaine, 1050 Brussels; Man. JEAN-MICHEL DE BIE; Jazz and blues festival held October–November.

Belgium Rhythm 'N' Blues Festival: c/o Breakaway Vzw, Deusterstraat 11A, PO Box 2, 3990 Peer; tel. (11) 611125; fax (11) 611126; e-mail brbf@break-away.be; Man. Dir LOUIS VANHOEF; R & B festival held in July.

Boogietown Festival: Fruithoflaan 124, PO Box 11, 2600 Berchem, Antwerp; Dirs PETER VERSTRAELEN, FREDERIC MARECHAL; Blues Festival held in May every year.

Dour Music Festival: 10 rue du Marché, 7370 Dour; Man. Dir CARLO DI ANTONIO; Pop music festival featuring rock, pop and rap.

European Forum of Worldwide Music Festivals: Jan Frans Willemsstraat 10, 2530 Boechout; Sec. PATRICK DE GROOTE.

Jazz A Liege: 18 Blvd d'Avroy, 4000 Liege; Chair. JEAN-MARIE PETERKEN; Jazz festival held in May.

Leffinge Leuren: c/o Leernsestwg 168, 9800 Deimze; Dir JEAN TANT; International festival featuring all styles of music, held in September.

Marktrock: PO Box 21, 3000 Louvain 1; Man. Dir OMER HOYELAERTS; Festival of rock, pop and blues music with 10 stages.

Nandrin Rock Festival: 10 rue de Fort, 1060 Brussels; Chair. PILIPPE DECOSTER.

On The Rox: Kleine Gentstraat 46, 9051 Ghent SDW; Man. Dir CHRIS VERLEYEN; International rock festival.

Schrikkelpop Festival: Fruithoflaan 12G, Bus 11, 2600 Berchem, Antwerp; Dirs PETER VERSTRAELEN, JOHAN PELGRIMS; Alternative Music festival held in early August.

Sfinks Festival: J F Willemsstraat 10, 2530 Boechout; Dir PATRICK DE GROOTE; Annual worldwide music festival; held in July.

Torhout-Werchter: Beverlaat 3, 3118 Werchter; Chair. HERMAN SCHUEREMANS; International rock festival held on the first weekend of July.

Bulgaria

Bourgas Blues Festival: Leten Teater, Studio Goresht Piasak, 8000 Bourgas; Dir ROUMEN YANEV; Open-air blues festival held in August.

Country Festival Society 'Costar': 23 Metodi Popov str, 1113 Sofia; Pres. CONSTANTIN BAHAROV.

Sofia Country Festival: 23 Metodi Popov str, 1113 Sofia; Man. DECHO TARALEZHKOV; Leading International Country Music festival.

Varna Folk Festival: Varna Municipality, Culture Dept, 43 Osmi Primorski Polk, Varna 9000; International Folk Festival; held in August.

Varna Jazz Festival: Varna Municipality, Culture Dept, 43 Osmi Primorski Polk, Varna 9000; International Jazz Festival; held July–August.

Canada

Beaches International Jazz Festival: 1976A Queen St E, Toronto, ON M4L 1H8; tel. (416) 698-2152; fax (416) 698-2064; e-mail beachesjazz@rogers.com; internet www.beachesjazz.com; Pres. LIDO CHILELLI; Week long festival held in July.

Big Valley Jamboree: 1042 Winnipeg St, Regina, SK S4R 8P8; Exec. Prod. ALAN VINET; Country Music festival.

Calgary International Jazz Festival: PO Box 2735 Station M, Calgary, AB T2P 3C2; Two-day outdoor event.

Canadian Music Festival: c/o Chart Toppers, 106-5397 Eglinton Ave W, Toronto ON M9C 5K6; Event featuring Canadian artists.

Du Maurier Ltd Downtown Jazz Festival: 366 Adelaide St E, Suite #230, Toronto, Ontario M5A 3X9; Dir of Marketing & Communications BOB MCCULLOUGH; Annual jazz festival held in June–July.

Edmonton Folk Festival: PO Box 4130, Edmonton, AB T6E 4T2; Four-day music festival held annually in August.

Festival International de Jazz de Montréal: 822 Sherbrook E, Montréal, QC H2L 1K4; Largest Jazz festival in North America, held in July.

Folk on the Rocks: PO Box 326, Yellowknife, NWT X1A 2N7; tel. (867) 920-7806; fax (867) 873-6535; e-mail fotr@ssimicro.com; internet www.folkontherocks.com; Exec. Festival Dir TRACEY BRYANT; Annual four-day summer music festival held on the third weekend in July.

JUNO Awards: c/o CARAS, 124 Merton St, 3rd Floor, Toronto, ON M4S 2Z2; Annual awards for outstanding Canadian achievement in the field of recorded music.

Mariposa Folk Festival: 786 Dundas St E, Toronto, ON M4M 1R1; Traditional and Contemporary Folk festival.

Mill Race Festival of Traditional Folk Music: PO Box 22148, Galt Central PO, Cambridge, ON N1R 8E3; tel. (519) 621-7135; e-mail mill_race@yahoo.com; internet www.millracefolksociety.com; Chair/Artistic Dir BRAD MCEWEN; Festival of traditional folk music and dance.

Music West: #306, 21 Water St, Vancouver, BC V6B 1A1; Prod. MAUREEN JACK; Annual music conference and festival held in May.

Musicfest Canada: 200, 1400 1st St, SW, Calgary, AB T2R 0V8; Exec. Dir JIM HOWARD; National music festival.

Ottawa International Jazz Festival: PO Box 3104 Station D, Ottawa, ON K1P 6H7; Jazz festival with emphasis on Canadian talent.

Sam Cat Records: 8 Woodlands Rd, St Albert, AB T8N 3L9; tel. and fax (780) 460-7460; e-mail fun@peterandmary.net; Contact PETER JANSEN; Also organizes the Earth Day Festival.

St Jean-Baptiste Festival: Société des mélomanes (Canada) Inc, 1056 Burnaby St, Suite 201, Vancouver, BC V6E 1N7; Dir EUGÈNE EVANS.

Summerfolk Music & Crafts Festival: PO Box 521, Oven Sound, ON N4K 5R1; Promotion Co-ordinator LINDA ASHLEY; Festival held the third weekend of August every year.

Under The Volcano Festival of Art & Social Change: #21552, 1850 Commercial Dr., Vancouver, BC V5N 4A0; Co-ordinating Collective Member IRWIN OOSTINDIE; Annual music and arts event held since 1990.

Vancouver Folk Music Festival: PO Box 381, 916 W Broadway, Vancouver, BC V5Z 1K7; Gen. Man. BRENT GIBSON; Four day folk/world music festival held in Jericho Beach Park.

Winnipeg Folk Festival: 203–211 Bannatyne Ave, Winnipeg, MB R3B 1B7; tel. (204) 231-0096; fax (204) 231-0076; e-mail info@winnipegfolkfestival.ca; internet www.winnipegfolkfestival.ca; Artistic Dir RICK FENTON; Folk music festival takes place during second weekend in July.

Wye Marsh Festival: Music Committee, Wye Marsh Wildlife Centre, PO Box 100, Midland, ON L4R 4K6; Contact MUSIC COMMITTEE; Annual wildlife festival which includes a folk music component.

Croatia

B P Club Jazz Festivals: Teslina 7, Zagreb; Contact BOŠKO PETROVIC; Two annual jazz festivals.

Croatian Festival of Pop Music—Split: c/o Dalmaciakoncert, Trg Republike 1/11, 58000 Split; Man. Dir IVICA VRKIC; Pop Festival held in July.

HTF: c/o Croatian Television, Prisavlje 3, 10000 Zagreb; tel. 9822-7652; fax 1634-3646; e-mail a.kostadinov@hrt.hr; Prod. ALEKSANDAR KOSTADINOV; National contest for Eurovision Song Contest and music shows.

ZagrebFest: c/o Alta, Berislaviceva 9, HDS, 41000 Zagreb; Man. Dir DRAGO DIKLIC; Pop Festival held in mid-December.

Denmark

Aarhus International Jazz Festival: Thomas Jensens Alle, 8000 C Aarhus; internet www.jazzfest.dk; tel. 8940-9191; fax 8940-9199; e-mail mail@aarhusfestival.dk; internet www.aarhusfestival.dk; Head of Programmes Section ANNITA HORNSLET; Festival held at the end of August or beginning of September.

Copenhagen Jazz Festival: Kjled Langes Gade 4A, 1367 K Copenhagen; e-mail info@jazzfestival.dk; internet www.jazzfestival.dk; Man. BODIL JACOBSEN; Festival of Jazz, Blues and World Music held in July.

Esbjerg 60's Festival: SHB—Soeren Hoejberg Booking ApS, Frodesgade 74, 6700 Esbjerg; Man. Dir SOEREN HOEJBERG; One day festival taking place in Spring.

Esbjerg Open Air: SHB—Soeren Hoejberg Booking ApS, Frodesgade 74, 6700 Esbjerg; Man. Dir SOEREN HOEJBERG; One day open air festival held in August.

Esbjerg Rock Festival: SHB—Soeren Hoejberg Booking ApS, Frodesgade 74, 6700 Esbjerg; Man. Dir SOEREN HOEJBERG; Open air festival held on the first weekend of June.

Images of Africa: Copenhagen; Contact LENE THIESEN; Held June–July.

Midtfyns Festival: Laessoegade 78 st, 5230 M Odense; Man. Dir NINA FAERGEREMANN; Rock, Pop and Folk Music festival held in June–July.

Roskilde Festival: Havsteensvej 11, 4000 Roskilde; tel. 4636-6613; fax 4632-6613; e-mail bigbox@roskilde-festival.dk; internet www.roskilde-festival.dk; Gen. Man. LEIF SKOV; Four-day music festival.

Skagen Festival: PO Box 33, 9990 Skagen; tel. 9844-4969; fax 9844-6377; e-mail peer.andersen@wanadoo.dk; internet www.skagenfestival.dk; Programme Dir PEER LØGSTED ANDERSEN.

Skanderborg Festival: c/o J P Management, Jernbanevej 22, 8660 Skanderborg; Man. Dir J P ANDERSEN; Festival of Folk, Pop, Jazz and Rock music held in August.

Tivoli Festival: Vesterbrogade 3, DK 1630 Copenhagen V.

Tønder Festival Foundation: Vestergade 80, 6270 Tønder; Festival Dir CARSTEN PANDURO; Folk music festival since 1975.

Estonia

Ollefestival: PO Box 2907, Tallina Peapostkontor, Tatari 23, 0090 Tallinn; Promoter LAURI VIIKNA; Pop Music festival held late June–early July.

Pärnu Jazz: Papiniidu 50, 3600 Pärnu; Festival Dir TIIT LAUK; International beachtown summer festival held in July.

Rock Summer Festival: PO Box 3333, Regati Pst 1-6K, 0019 Tallinn; Man. MARTTI KITSING; Rock festival, held in July.

Tartu Jazz: Laulupeo 25, 2400 Tartu; Festival Arena Man. AADU BIRNBAUM; International outdoor festival of traditional and modern jazz held in mid-July.

Tartu Rock Festival: Laulupeo 25, 2400 Tartu; Festival Arena Man. AADU BIRNBAUM; Outdoor festival, mainly Estonian artists with some foreign guest musicians.

Tudengijazz: PO Box 3641, 0090 Tallinn; Man. REIMO UNT; International student jazz festival held in February.

Finland

April Jazz Espoo: Ahertajantie 6 B, 02100 Espoo; Contact MARTTI LAPPAIAINEN; International indoors jazz festival, with special focus on vocal and big band jazz; held in April.

Baltic Jazz: Kålabacksvågen 1, 25900 Taalintehdas; Contact MAGI KULLA; National and international swing and traditional jazz event held in July.

EloJazz&Blues: Kaislatie 9 M 2, 90160 Oulu; Contact KARI KESTI; National outdoors and indoors jazz festival held in late July, covering all styles.

Etinosoi!: Helsinki; Contact ANU LAAKKONEN; Held in November.

Finnish National Jazz Days: PO Box 54, 00101 Helsinki; Contact FINNISH JAZZ FEDERATION; Annual national jazz festival involving all styles; held in a different town each year (recently held in Helsinki and Jyväskylä); held in November.

Global Music Centre: Mikkolantie 17, 00640 Helsinki; Dir ANU LAAKKONEN.

Helsinki Festival: Rauhankatu 7 E, 00170 Helsinki; Artistic Dir ESA-PEKKA SALONEN; Festival of Jazz, Pop, Rock and Ethnic music; held August–September.

Imatra Big Band Festival: PO Box 22, 55101 Imatra; National and international outdoors/indoors festival of all jazz styles, with special interest in big band music; held June–July.

Jazz at the Market Place: Vesijärvenkatu 20, 15140 Lahti; Contact MARTTI PEIPPO; National outdoor jazz festival held in mid-August.

Jazz on the Beach: Kauppakatu 23, 92100 Raahe; Contact PERTTI KINNUNEN; National and international outdoors/indoors festival featuring all jazz styles; held late July.

KaamosJazz (Jazz Under Northern Lights): 99695 Tankavaara; tel. (16) 626-158; fax (16) 626-261; Contact KAUKO LAINONEN; National indoors jazz festival held in late November.

Kainuu Jazz Spring: Kalliokatu 7, 87100 Kajaani; Contact UNTO TOMIAINEN; International indoors event with all jazz styles, held in May.

Kaustinen Folk Music Festival: Kaustinen; Contact JYRKI HEISKANEN; Held in July.

Keitele Jazz: Humpinkatu 4 A, 44120 Äänekoski; Contact KALEVI PLATTONEN; All jazz styles featured in a national and international event held in July.

Kerava Jazz: Asemantie 4, 04200 Kerava; tel. (9) 2949-2005; fax (9) 2949-2082; e-mail mavno.kahranaho@pp.inet.fi; internet personal.inet.fi/yhdistys/keravajazz/; Contact KERAVA CITY CULTURAL BUREAU; International modern and contemporary jazz festival; held in early June.

Nummirock: 61910 Nummijärvi; Rock festival held midsummer.

Pori International Jazz Festival: Pohjoisranta 11, 28100 Pori; tel. (2) 626-2200; fax (2) 626-2225; e-mail jyrki.kangas@porijazz.fi; internet www.porijazz.fi; Contact JYRKI KANGAS; International open-air event held in July; all jazz, rhythm 'n' blues and rock styles.

Provinssirock: PO Box 180, 60101 Seinäjoki; tel. (6) 421-2700; fax (6) 414-8622; e-mail info@provinssirock.fi; internet www.provinssirock.fi; Rock festival held in early June.

Ruisrock: Uudenmaankatu 1, 20500 Turku; Contact TURKU MUSIC FESTIVAL FOUNDATION; Rock festival staged by the sea in Turku and has attendance figures close to 25,000; held in mid-summer.

Ruska-Swing: Oy Yleisradio Ab, PL 64, 98101 Kemijärvi; Contact PEKKA LINTULA; National swing and traditional jazz event held in September.

Tampere Jazz Happening: Tullikamarinaukio 2, 33100 Tampere; tel. (3) 3146-6136; fax (3) 223-0121; e-mail music@tampere.fi; internet www.tampere.fi/jazz/; Contact ANNAMAIJA SAARELA; International contemporary and modern jazz indoor festival held in October–November.

Turku Jazz Festival: Uudenmaankatu 1, 20500 Turku; Contact RAINER KOSKI; National and international festival, with mainly contemporary jazz styles, held in March.

Ylläs Jazz Blues: 95970 Äkäslompolo; Contact PIRKKO HIETANIEMI; All jazz and rhythm 'n' blues styles; national and international acts featured; held in February.

France

Africolor: 145 rue de Ménilmontant, 75020 Paris; tel. 1 47 97 69 99; fax 1 47 97 65 44; e-mail africolor@africolor.com; internet www.africolor.com; Artistic Dir PHILIPPE CONRATH; Music festival focused on music from Western Africa and Indian Ocean; held in December.

Banlieues Blues: 9 Ave Berlioz, 93270 Sevran; Dir JACQUES PORNON; Jazz and blues events throughout Paris in March and April.

Carnavalorock: 9 rue Galis Bizoin, 22000 St Brieuc; Chair. SAM BURLOT; Festival held in April–May.

Festival 'Synthèse' International Festival of Electronic Music and Creations of Bourges: Institut International de Musique Electroacoustique, PO Box 39, 18001 Bourges Cédex; tel. 2 48 20 41 87; fax 2 48 20 45 51; e-mail administration@ime-bourges.org; internet www.gmeb.fr; Artistic Dirs FRANÇOISE BARRIERE; Christian Clozier.

Festival d'Ete de Nantes/Musique Sur L'ile: rue de l'évêché, 44000 Nantes; tel. 2 40 08 01 00; fax 2 40 48 12 64; e-mail contact@festival-ete-nantes.asso.fr; internet www.festival-ete-nantes.asso.fr; Contact BERTRAND DE LAPORTE; Festival of world music; held in July.

Festival International de Guitares de Vittel: PO Box 698, Porte de la Craffe, 54043 Nancy; Contact MARC LEONARD; Guitar festival held in June.

Festival International de Jazz Antibes: Office du Tourisme, 11 Pl. de Gaulle, 06000 Antibes; Dir JEAN-PIERRE GONZÁLEZ; Open-air Jazz festival held in July.

Festival National de Blues: c/o Association Clin d'Oreille, Hotel de Ville, 71200 Le Creusot; Pres. RENEE CERRUTI; Artistic Dir EMILIO ARMILLES; Annual festival held in July in Burgundy.

Fiesta des Suds: Latinissimo, PO Box 121, 13473 Marseille; Dir FLORENCE CHASTANIER.

Jazz A Manosque: Service Culturel, Hotel de Ville, 04100 Manosque; Directeur M GERARD OLLIVIER; Ten-day festival held in the second fortnight in July.

Le Lieu Unique—CRDC: PO Box 21304, 2 rue de la Biscuiterie, 44013 Nantes Cédex 01; tel. 2 51 82 15 00; fax 2 40 20 20 12; e-mail info@lelieuunique.com; internet www.lelieuunique.com; Dir JEAN BLAISE; Musical Curator KITTY HARTL; popular music and video events and festivals.

Les 24 Heures de l'Insa: Amicale des élèves INSA, Bâtiment B2, Ave de Rangueil, 31077 Toulouse; tel. 5 62 17 00 79; fax 5 62 17 75 97; e-mail amicale@etud.insa-tlse.fr; Contact RENAUD POINCLOUX; Annual student festival held in May.

Les Nuits Atypiques: Langon; Contact PATRICK LAVAUD; Held July–August.

Musiques Métisses: Angouléme; Contact CHRISTIAN MOUSSET; Held 22–26 May.

Nice Jazz Festival: c/o Nice Jazz Productions, 7 Pl. de Seoul, 75014 Paris; Dir LUC GAVRICHON; Annual Jazz festival held in July.

Octob'rock: 115 reu Lesage, 5110 Reims; Pres. ALAIN BOUCHERON; Organizer and Promoter of concerts including the Rock Festival held in October.

Pro Jazz: 10 avenue des 27 Martyrs, 78400 Chatou; Pres. PIERRE DIEUZEY.

Rock 'n' Solex: c/o Amicale de Eleves INSA, 20 Ave des Buttes de Coësmes, 35043 Rennes Cédex; Pres. NICOLAS ORHON; Organizer of the Rennes two-day rock festival.

Germany

Afrika Festival: Würzburg; Contact STEFAN OSCHMANN; Held in May.

Alandia Jazz: c/o Nachtigallensteg 3, 23611 Bad Schwartau; tel. 451-27705; fax 451-26491; e-mail alandia.jazz@aland.net; internet www.alandiajazz.aland.fi; Contact CHRISTER MÖRN; National and international jazz festival; held in July.

Berlin Independence Days: Köpenicker str 6, 10997 Berlin; Contacts MICHAEL BETZ; Held in October.

Freestyle eV: Morgensternsweg 7, 22305 Hamburg; Contact HELMUT HEUER; Music festival and event organisers.

Heimatklänge: Berlin; Contact BORKOWKSY AKBAR; Held in July–August.

Leipziger Rockfestival: Tollweg 42, 04289 Leipzig; Man. Dir EDGAR BERGMANN; Annual rock festival held in June.

Music Factory: Rottscheidter str 6, 42329 Wuppertal; Head PR Dept ANDREA ZECH; Organizer of music fairs.

Musikmesse/Pro Light and Sound: Messe Frankfurt GmbH, Ludwig-Erhard-Anlage 1, 60327 Frankfurt; tel. (69) 7575-6452; fax (69) 7575-6613; e-mail wilhelm-p.hosenseidl@messefrankfurt.com; Brand Devt Man. WILHELM-PETER HOSENSEIDL; International trade fairs for musical instruments and sheet music, light, sound and event technology.

Popkomm: Rottscheidter str 6, 42329 Wuppertal; Head of PR Dept ANDREA ZECH; Organizer of music fairs.

Rheinkultur: PO Box 201303, Moltkestr. 41, 53173 Bonn; Prod. SABINE FUNK; Germany's largest open-air festival, held in late June–early July.

Tanz & Folkfest: Stadt Rudolstadt, Kulturburo, Markt 7, 07407 Rudolstadt; tel. (3672) 412-651; fax (3672) 412-796; e-mail tffrudolstadt@saale-net.de; internet www.rudolstadt.de; Contact PETER UHLMANN; Held on the first weekend in July.

Greece

Athens Festival: Voukourestiou 1, 10564 Athens; Man. Dir DIMOS VRATSANOS; International festival held in July–August.

Mediterranean Music Festival: 2 Kritis St, 15562 Holargos, Athens; Public Relations MARILENA KOUSSOULOU; World Music festival held every two years.

Hungary

Diaksziget: Lonyay u 18/B, 1093 Budapest; A & R Man. KARLY GERENDAI; International festival held in July–August.

Island Festival: c/o Sziget Kulturális Szervezö Iroda, Ul 18/B Lónyay, 1093 Budapest; Foreign Affairs Man. MATTHEW BRAGHINI; Festival held in the third week of August each year.

Kalaka Folk Festival: Miskolo; Contact CSABA LÖKÖS; Held in July.

Taban: Bem Rakpart 6, 1014 Budapest; Contact ARANKA MARKA; Rock, folk and blues festival.

Womufe: Villanyi ut 107, 1118 Budapest; Contact ROBERT MANDEL; World music event held in May–June in Budapest.

Ireland

Bacardi Plugged Band Competition: Hot Press, 13 Trinity St, Dublin 2; tel. (1) 241-1500; fax (1) 241-1538; e-mail jachay@iol.ie; internet www.hotpress.com; Project Co-ordinator JACKIE HAYDEN; National band competition.

Boyle Arts Festival: Great Meadow, Boyle, Co Roscommon; Co-ordinator FERGUS D AHERN; Held in last week of July to first week in August each year.

Cork Jazz Festival: 18 Stephen's Lane, Upper Mount St, Dublin 2; Contact JACK MCGOURAN; Jazz festival with Irish and international acts held in October.

Drogheda Samba Festival: The Droichead Arts Centre, Drogheda, Co Louth; Contact KIERAN GALLAGHER; Festival of Afro-Brazilian music including performances, workshops and carnival; held in July each year.

Feakle Traditional Music Week: Maghera, Caher, Feakle, Co Clare; Chair. PAT HAYES; Festival of traditional music, song and dance from East Clare.

Feile Seamus Ennis: Finglas Art Centre, Art Squad, Unit 14B Main Shopping Centre, Finglas, Dublin 11; Chairperson MARY MCDERMOTT; Workshops and summer school promoting artists past and present in traditional music.

Galway Arts Festival: Black Box Theatre, Galway; tel. (91) 509700; fax (91) 562655; e-mail info@gaf.iol.ie; internet www.galwayartsfestival.ie; Man. FERGAL MCGRATH; Arts Festival held in July.

Hot Press Music Seminars: 13 Trinity St, Dublin 2; tel. (1) 241-1500; fax (1) 241-1538; e-mail jachay@iol.ie; internet www.hotpress.com; Seminar Co-ordinator JACKIE HAYDEN; A series of seminars explaining the basic of the music industry to musicians etc.

Mary From Dungloe International Festival: Festival Office, Main St, Dungloe, Co Donegal; Festival Dir COLM CROFFY; 10 music festivals held late July to early August each year; various concerts during the year.

Monaghan Rhythm & Blues Festival: The Arts Office, Market House, Monaghan; tel. (47) 71114; fax (47) 71113; e-mail harvestblues@eircom.net; internet www.harvestblues.net; Contact SAMHAIRLE MAC CONGHAIL; Annual rhythm and blues festival held on the first weekend of September; other annual concerts of popular music.

Sligo Arts Festival: Model Arts, The Mall, Sligo; Contact DANNY KIRRANE; Arts festival held at the end of May, with world music, street events and theatre.

Israel

Israel Festival: PO Box 4409, Jerusalem 91044; Festival of performing arts including music, dance and theatre; held in May–June.

Italy

Arezzo Wave: via Masaccio 14, 52100 Arezzo; tel. (0575) 911005; fax (0575) 911038; e-mail info@arezzowave.com; internet www.arezzowave.com; Man. Dir MAURO VALENTI; European rock festival held in the first week of July.

Bassano Jazz: Via Sonda 21, 36061 Bassano del Grapa; Man. Dir GIOVANNI MAYER; Jazz and progressive music.

Corridonia Jazz Festival: Antonello Andreaniu di Coop Ephemeria, P'zza 30 Aprile, 62100 Macerata; Jazz festival held in July.

Cremona Rock: c/o Centro Musicale Il Cascinetto, Via Maffi 2, 26100 Cremona; Annual Italian rock festival in early June.

Festambiente: Via Tripoli 27, 58100 Grosseto; Cultural Section Resp MICHELA PRESTA; Ecological festival.

Magna Grecia Rock: Via Cavour, 96100 Siracuse; International festival held annually in Sicily.

Rockin' Umbria: Via Della Viola 1, 06100 Perugia; Man. Dir SERGIO PIAZZOLI; International music festival.

Voci E Suoni Del Mediterraneo: Gibellina; Contact POMPEO BENINCASA; Held August–September.

World Music Festival: Rome; Contact PIETRO CARLI; Held in August.

The Netherlands

12th Music Meeting: Nijmegen; Contact WIM WESTERVELD; Held in November.

Befrydings Festival: Grote Kerkstraat 14, Dg11E6 Leeuwarden; Contact SJOERD CUPERUS; Festival programming and production.

Dunya Festival: Rotterdam; Contact MARTIN VAN GINKEL; Held 1–2 June.

Dynamo Open Air Festival: Juliusstraat 45, 5621 GC Rotterdam; Man. Dir M. KANTERS; Largest heavy rock festival in Europe.

Frysk Festival: Grote Kerkstraat 14, DG 1146 Leeuwarden; Contact SJOERD CUPERUS.

Metropolis Festival: PO Box 131, 3000 AC Rotterdam; Man. Dir CORINNE LAMPEN; Pop festival for young up-and-coming bands; held in early July.

Music and Harmony: Oude Enghweg 24, 1217 JD Hilversum; Contact P M V DOOREN; Organizer of international musical instruments fair in Jaarbeurs-Utrecht; held at the beginning of September.

North Sea Jazz Festival: PO Box 3325, 2601 DH Delft; tel. (15) 214-8900; fax (15) 214-8393; e-mail tejo@northseajazz.nl; internet www.northseajazz.nl; Festival Dir T VAN DEN HOEK; Largest indoor Jazz festival in Europe.

PinkPop: PO Box 117, 6160 AC Geleen; Contact JAN SMEETS; International pop festival.

World Roots Festival: Amsterdam; Contact FRANS GOOSSENS; Held in June.

New Zealand

Bay of Islands Country Rock Festival: PO Box 355 Kerikeri Bay of Islands; tel. (9) 404-1063; fax (9) 404-1065; e-mail maysplace@actrix.co.nz; internet www.country-rock.co.nz; Contact SHIRLEY MAY; Annual country music festival held on the second weekend in May.

Bay of Islands Jazz & Blues Festival: PO Box 355 Kerikeri Bay of Islands; tel. (9) 404-1063; fax (9) 404-1065; e-mail maysplace@actrix.co.nz; Contact SHIRLEY MAY; Annual jazz and blues event, held on second weekend in August.

Fringe Festival: 6 Majoribanks St, Mt Victoria; Dir TRACY MEDLAND; New Zealand's largest open-access fringe festival.

International Music Expo: PO Box 25046, St Heliers, Auckland; Contact ROB EADY; Annual trade event held in September.

New Zealand International Festival of the Arts: PO Box 10113, Wellington; Exec. Dir CARLA VAN ZON; Largest arts event in the country, held alternate years.

Tarankai Festival of the Arts: PO Box 4251, New Plymouth; Festival Dir ROGER KING; Three week long festival held on alternate years in March.

Norway

Førde Folk Music Festival: PO Box 395, 6801 Førde; tel. 5772-1940; fax 5772-1941; e-mail info@fordefestival.no; internet www.fordefestival.no; Contact HILDE BJØRKUM; Held in July.

Glopperock: PO Box 222, 6860 Sandane; Man. Dir REMI TYSTAD; Rock festival held in June.

Kalvöyafestivalen: Karl Johansgaten 8, 0154 Oslo 1; Man. PAUL KARLSEN; International festival held at the end of June.

Molde International Jazz Festival: PO Box 211, 3671 Notodden; Man. Dir EINAR GJENDEM; Major Jazz festival in July.

Notodden Blues Festival: PO Box 211, 3671 Notodden; Promoter ESPEN FJELLE; Blues festival; held in early August.

Poland

Folk Blues Fair: Poznan; Contact DIONIZY PIATKOWSKI; Held in early March.

Jazz on Odra Festival: c/o Interart Ltd, ul. Pugeta 6, 51-628 Wroclaw; Contact MARGARET SZABLOWSKA.

Odjazdy: ALMA–ART, ul. Teatralna 9, 40-003 Katowice; Dir BOGDAN MARCINKOWSKI; Festival of rock and independent music; held in mid-November at Spodek Hall.

Piknik Country: Grojecka 75, 01 094 Warsaw; Man. EWA DABROWSKA; Country Music festival held in July.

Sopot International Music Festival: Ul. Kosciuzki 61, 81703 Sopot; Contact WOJCIECH KORZENIEWSKI; International Song Contest.

Stage Song Festival: Arts and Culture Centre, Rynek-Ratusz 24, 50-101 Wroclaw; Artistic Dir ROMAN KOLAKOWSKI; Presentation of Polish musical theatre highlights of the season; promoting young actors through competition; concerts by prominent guest performers from abroad.

Warsaw Summer Jazz Days: E Plater 49, 0125 Warsaw; Contact MARIUSZ ADAMIAK; Jazz event held in June.

Winter Rock Festival: ALMA–ART, ul. Teatralna 9, 40-003 Katowice; Dir BOGDAN MARCINKOWSKI; Rock music festival for Polish and foreign bands; 23 February at Spodek Hall.

Romania

Golden Stag: Etaj 4, cam 412, Calea Dorobanti 101, Sector 1, Bucharest; Gen. Man. DUMITRI MOROSANU; International music festival.

Slovakia

Rock Pop Bratislava: Jakubovo nam 12, 81499 Bratislava; Dir PAVEL DANEK; Major rock and pop festival.

Slovenia

Druga Godba: Ljubljana; Contact BOGDAN BENIGAR; Held in early June.

Festival Ljubljana: Trg Francoske Revolucije 1–2, 61000 Ljubljana; Man. Dir VLADIMIR VAJDA; Open-air event from June to September.

No Border Jam Festival: Front Rock, PO Box 48, 62000 Marilor; tel. (41) 832736; fax (26) 476381; e-mail frontrock@iname.com; Man. DUSAN HEDL; Annual international punk, rock, pop, ethno, garage festivals held in June and October.

Spain

Barcelona Jazz Festival: Ronda Sant Pere, 33 Principal, 08010 Barcelona; tel. (934) 817040; fax (934) 817041; e-mail theproject@the-project.net; internet www.the-project.net; Man. Dir TITO RAMONEDA; Jazz festival in October–November.

Espárrago Rock Festival: c/o Reyes, Catolicos 25, Of. 2 Planta, 18001 Granada; Promotion Dir JAVIER GONZALEZ.

Guitar Festival of Cordoba: Avda Gran Capitan, No. 3, 14008 Córdoba; Production Man. ANA LINARES BUENO; Concerts of Classical, Flamenco, Pop, Rock and Antique music.

Madrid Jazz Festival: Navarro Reverter 22, 46004 Valencia; A & R JULIO MARTIN; Jazz festival held in June and July.

Pirineos Sur: Huesca; Contact LUIS CALVO; Held July–August.

WOMAD in Caceres: TBA, Caceres; Contact THOMAS BROOMAN.

Sweden

Dala Rock: PO Box 12, 77621 Hedemora; Man. Dir PUTTE BROLUND; Festival held in July, featuring Swedish and international artists.

Falun Folk Music Festival: Falun; Contact MAGNUS BÄCKSTRÖM; Held in July.

Festival Sjöslaget: c/o Projektbyrån, Kungsgatan 34, 97241 Luleå; Man. Dir TOMAS LIND.

Gothenburg All Star Festival: World Trade Centre, Box 5264, 40225 Gothenburg; A & R Man. MAGNUS ERIKSON; Major rock festival with international acts.

Hultsfred Festival: PO Box 170, 57724 Hultsfred; tel. 4956-9500; fax 4956-9550; e-mail gunnar.lagerman@rockparty.se; internet www.rockparty.se; Man. Dir GUNNAR LAGERMAN.

Kalott Jazz & Blues: Hallituskatu 9, 95400 Tornio-Haaparanta; Contact TORNIO CITY CULTURAL BUREAU; National and international festival of all jazz styles and blues; held late June.

Re Orient Festival: Stockholm; Contact JONAS ELVERSTIG; Held in June.

The Arvika Festival: PO Box 99, 671 23 Arvika; tel. 5701-2199; fax 5701-2112; e-mail arvikafestivalen@galaxen.se; internet www.galaxen.se; Mans BJÖRN SERRANDER, TOMAS FÄNDRIKS; Rock and indie music festival held in July.

Switzerland

Caribana Festival: rue de la combe 4, 1260 Nyon; Co-ordinator TONY LERCH; Music festival over four days covering rock, folk, tropical, rap and acid jazz.

Estival Jazz Lugano: 6992 Vernate; e-mail info@estivaljazz.ch; internet www.estivaljazz.ch; Man. ANDREAS WYDEN; Free open air jazz festival.

Jazz Willisau: PO Box, 6130 Willisau; tel. (41) 970-2731; fax (41) 970-3231; e-mail troxler@centralnet.ch; internet www.jazzwillisau.ch; Dir NIKLAUS TROXLER; Festival of jazz.

Montreux Jazz Festival: CP 126, CH 1820 Montreux-Territet; Artistic Dir CLAUDE NOBS; Annual festival held in July consisting of jazz, pop, rock, blues, and soul; 2 halls and 5 off-stages; Workshops.

Turkey

Istanbul International Jazz Festival: Istiklal Caddesi 146, Luvr Apt Beyoglu, 80070 Istanbul; Jazz festival held June–July.

Ukraine

Beatlesmania Music Festival: Independent Artist's Agency, Ljubchenko & Co, Room 7, Mietrostrojevskaja St 5, 320128 Dniepropetrovsk; Dir VALERI LJUBCHENKO; Annual music festival.

Dirate of the All-Ukrainian Festival of Independent Music Alternative: Culture Foundation, Lesva Kur-Basa str 4, 290007 Lviv; Dir YOURY GREKH; Vice Dir RUSLAN KOSHIV; Held in September.

Kharkov Assemblies International Music Festival: Institute of Musicology, Soviet Ukraine Sq. 20 #9, 310003 Kharkov; Dir GRIGORY HANSBURG.

Musica Pura Europae Festival: R Eideman str 2–16, 310112 Kharkiv; Man. SERGEY MYASOEDOV; International music festival dealing with European neofolk & independent rock music.

Rock Fest Bee: c/o Independent Artists Agency Ljubchenko & Co, Room 7, Mietrostrojevskaja St 5, 320128 Dniepropetrovsk; Dir VALERI LJUBCHENKO; Annual music festival.

'Tavria Games' International Festival: 36V, Lesi Ukrainki Blvd, 252133, Kiyiv; Gen. Dir NIKOLAY BAGRAEV; Organizers of the Tavria Games International Festival since 1992.

Teenwave: c/o Independent Artist Agency Ljubchenko & Co, Room 7, Mietrostrojevskaja St 5, 320128 Dniepropetrovsk; Dir VALERI LJUBCHENKO; International teenage song festival.

The United Kingdom

Aberdeen Alternative Festival: 10 Belmont St, Aberdeen AB1 1JE, Scotland; Dir DUNCAN HENDRY; Annual arts festival held each October, combining culture of north-east Scotland with international music, comedy, drama and dance.

Appalachian and Bluegrass Music Festival: Ulster-American Folk Park, Castletown, Omagh, Co Tyrone; Head of Museum Services JOHN A WALSH.

Bath International Music Festival: Linley House, 1 Pierrepont Pl., Bath BA1 1JY; Artistic Dir TIM JOSS; Held May–June.

Belfast Folk Festival: Students Union, University Rd, Belfast BT17 1PR, Northern Ireland; Contact NOEL DEVLIN; Irish and international festival.

Beverley Folk Festival: 2 Star Row, N Dalton, Driffield, E Yorks YO25 9UR; tel. (1377) 217569; fax (1377) 217754; e-mail chris@adastey.demon.co.uk; internet www.adastey.demon.co.uk; Dir CHRIS WADE; Annual festival specialising in folk, roots and related music; held third weekend in June.

Birkenhead Guitar Festival of Great Britain: Dept Leisure Servcies & Tourism, Westminster House, Birkenhead, Wirral L41 5FN; Festival Dir RON SMITH; Held 9–17 November.

Birmingham International Jazz Festival: PO Box 944, Edgbaston, Birmingham B16 8UT; tel. (121) 454-7020; fax (121) 454-9996; e-mail festival@bigbearmusic.com; internet www.bigbearmusic.com; Dir JIM SIMPSON; Held in early July.

Bracknell Festival: South Hill Park, Ringmead, Bracknell, Berks RG12 7PA; tel. (1344) 484858; fax (1344) 411427; e-mail festival@southhillpark.org.uk; internet www.southhillpark.org.uk; Festival Dir SIMON CHATTERTON; Music and arts festival.

Brecon Jazz: Jazz Festival Offices, Watton Chambers, Brecon, Powys LD3 7EF, Wales; Festival Co-ordinator DEBORAH PARRY; Held in August.

Cambridge Folk Festival: The Guildhall, Cambridge CB2 3QJ; tel. (1223) 457512; fax (1223) 457529; e-mail eddieb@cambridge.gov.uk; internet www.cam-folkfest.co.uk; Promotions Officer EDDIE BARCAN; Folk festival with programme including folk, blues and country.

Cheltenham International Festival of Music: Town Hall, Imperial Sq., Cheltenham, Glos GL50 1QA; Festival Organiser KIM SARGEANT; Held during July.

City of London Festival: Bishopsgate Hall, 230 Bishopsgate, London EC2M 4HW; tel. (20) 7377-0540; fax (20) 7377-1972; e-mail admin@colf.org; internet www.colf.org; Gen. Man. KATHRYN MCDOWELL; Arts Festival; Held in June–July.

Cropredy Music Festival: c/o Fairport Convention, PO Box 37, Banbury, Oxon OX16 8YN; Contact DAVID PEGG; Organizers of the Cropredy Music Festival.

Cross Rhythms: PO Box 183, Plymouth, PL3 4YN; Admin. JONATHAN BELLAMY; Annual festival.

Edinburgh International Festival: 21 Market St, Edinburgh EH1 1BW, Scotland; Man. Dir MIKE HART; International Arts Festival of music, theatre and dance.

Fleadh: 18 High St, Harlesden, London NW10 4LP; tel. (20) 8961-5490; fax (20) 8961-5743; internet www.meanfiddler.com; Chair. VINCE POWER; Man. Dir MELVIN BENN; Irish and Scottish folk festival held in Finsbury Park.

Glasgow International Jazz Festival: 18 Albion St, Merchant City, Glasgow G1 1LH, Scotland; Festival Dir DEREK GORMAN; 10-day jazz festival; held late June–early July.

Glastonbury Festival: Worthy Farm, Pilton, Shepton Mallet, Somerset; Man. Dir MICHAEL EAVIS; One of the United Kingdom's leading international music events, held in June.

Great British Rhythm and Blues Festival: Bank House, 61 Albert Rd, Colne, Lancashire BB8 0PB; Arts & Entertainment Man. GARY HOOD.

Greenbelt Festival: The Greenhouse, Hillmarton Rd, London N7 9JE; Contact MARTIN EVANS; International festival held in August.

Greenwich Festival: Festival Office, 6 College Approach, Greenwich, London SE10 9HY; Festival Co-ordinator SOPHIE ELLIOTT; Held May–June.

Heineken Music Big Top: Toll House Studios, Cambridge Cottages, Kew Gardens, Surrey TW9 3AY; Man. Dir MIKE EDDOWES; International events held in various British cities throughout the summer.

International Festival of Folk Arts: Sidmouth, Devon; Contact STEVE HEAP; Held in early August.

Jersey Jazz Festival: 131 Quennevais Park, St Brelade, Jersey; Contact ERNIE ROSCOUET; Held in April.

London Cajun Music Festival: 41 Gillam Way, Rainham, Essex RM13 7HS; Chair. ERLING HAGLAND; Festival of Cajun music and dance.

London Jazz Festival: c/o Serious Speakout, 42 Old Compton St, London W1V 5PB; Contacts DAVID JONES, JOHN CUMMING, JOHN ELLSON; Annual jazz festival held in May.

Monsters of Rock Festival: 16 Birmingham Rd, Walsall, West Midlands WS1 2NA; Man. Dir MAURICE JONES; The United Kingdom's leading Heavy Metal festival, held annually in August.

North Wales Bluegrass Festival: Woodstock, Llanrwst Rd, Glan Conwy, Conwy LL28 5SR, Wales; tel. and fax (1492) 580454; e-mail northwalesbluegrass@hotmail.com; internet www.northwalesbluegrass.co.uk; Festival Organizers JOHN LES, GILL

WILLIAMS; Three-day international bluegrass music festival; held in the first week of July.

Notting Hill Carnival: 332 Ladbroke Grove, London W10 5AH; Man. Dir ELAINE SPENCER; Street carnival and international music event, held in August.

Oliver Cromwell Jazz Festival: 125 Sandwell St, Highgate, Walsall, West Midlands, WS1 3EG; Festival Organiser ALAN BUCKLEY; Largest traditional three-day Jazz Festival in the United Kingdom; held last weekend in June.

Phoenix Festival: PO Box 1707, London NW10; Man. Dir VINCE POWER; International indie music festival, held in Stratford in July.

Portobello Jazz Week: c/o Eleventh Hour Arts, 113 Cheesemans Terrace, Star Rd, London W14 9XH; Man. Dir DEBBIE GOLT.

Pyramid Productions: Cadillac Ranch, Pencraig Uchaf, Cwm Bach, Whitland, Dyfed SA34 0DT; tel. (1994) 484466; fax (1994) 484294; e-mail cadillac_ranch@telco4u.net; internet www.nikturner.com; Dir S M STEIN.

Reading Rock Festival: 18 High St, Harlesden, London NW10 4LP; tel. (20) 8961-5490; fax (20) 8961-5743; internet www.meanfiddler.com; Chair. VINCE POWER; Man. Dir MELVIN BENN; British rock and pop festival, held over three days in August.

Soho Jazz Festival: 29 Romily St, London W1V 6HP; Artistic Dir PETER BOIZE OATES; Held in first week of October.

Stanford in the Vale Folk Festival: 1 Membury Way, Grove, Wantage, Oxon OX12 0BP.

T-in-the-Park Festival/Big Day Out Ltd: 272 St Vincent St, Glasgow G2 5RL, Scotland: tel. (141) 566-4998; e-mail admin@dfconcerts.co.uk; internet www.gigsinscotland.com; Dir GEOFF ELLIS.

Warwick Folk Festival: 13 Styvechale Ave, Earlsdon, Coventry CV5 6DW; Admin. FRANCES DIXON; Annual festival providing concerts, dances, workshops, crafts, displays of traditional and contemporary folk arts.

Winchester Folk Festival: 44 Peverells Wood Ave, Chandlers Ford, Hampshire SO53 3BW; Press Officer ANNE SUTHERLAND; Annual festival of traditional dance, music and song held on the last weekend in April.

Woburn Festival: Kilnside, Harvest Hill, Bourne End, Bucks SL8 5JJ; Sec. KATE BOOTH; Jazz Festival; Held throughout October.

WOMAD: Mill Side, Mill Lane, Box, Wiltshire SN13 8PN; tel. (1225) 743188; fax (1225) 743481; e-mail thomas.brooman@realworld.co.uk; internet www.womad.org; Artistic Dir THOMAS BROOMAN; Worldwide festival co-ordination and production; festival held in July.

The United States of America

American Classic Music Festivals: 4243 E Piedras Dr. Ste. 155, San Antonio, TX 78228; Festival Organiser RICK DILLARD.

CMJ Music Marathon & Music Fest: 11 Middle Neck Rd, Suite 400, Great Neck, NY 11021; Exec. Prod. JOANNE ABBOT GREEN; 3 days and 4 nights of panels, workshops and live music showcases promoting the discovery and development of new music.

Cultural Initiative Inc: PO Box 1672, Washington, DC 20013-1672; Dir TIMOTHY JONES; Annual Hip-hop music conference.

Foundations Forum Inc: 1133 Broadway, Suite 1220, New York, NY 10010; Vice-Pres. KEVIN KEENAN; Annual music event since 1988 of showcases, exhibits, screenings, parties etc.

Independent Label Festival: 600 South Michigan Ave, Chicago, IL 60605; Exec. Dir LEOPOLDO LASTRE; A music industry convention featuring panels, workshops, trade show and showcases; held in late July.

Independent Music Seminar: PO Box 99090, San Diego, CA 92169; Annual independent music event.

Jazz Times Convention: 7961 Eastern Ave, #303, Silver Spring, MD 20910; Associate Publisher LEE MERGNER; Music industry convention.

Mobile Jazz Festival: 555 Broadcast Dr., Mobile, AL 36606; Festival Organiser: BOB SPIELMANN.

MusicFest: 231 Harrison Dr., Denver, CO 80206; Songwriters trade event and conference.

NAIRD Convention: 1000 Maplewood Dr., Suite 211, Maple Shade, NJ 08052; Contact HOLLY CASS; Convention for Independent record labels held in May.

New Music Seminar: 632 Broadway, 9th Floor, New York, NY 10012; Contact MARK JOSEPHSON; International music business convention.

New Orleans Jazz & Heritage Festival: 1205 N Rampart St, New Orleans, LA 70116.

Ravinia Jazz Festival: Chicago Symphony Center, 400 Iris Lane, Highland Park, IL 60035; tel. (847) 266-5143; fax (847) 432-3758; e-mail jzzz5@aol.com; internet www.ravinia.org; Festival Organiser PENNY TYLER.

Songwriters Expo: PO Box 93759, Hollywood, CA 90093; Contact DAN KIMPEL; Annual Songwriters conference.

South by Southwest Music and Media Conference: PO Box 4999, Austin, TX 78765; Man. Dir ROLAND SWENSON; Annual conference held in March for members of the music industry.

Talent Search America: 273 Chippewa Dr., Columbia, SC 29210-6508; Contact TALENT DIR; International songwriting and lyric writing contests.

Tri-C Jazz Festival: Cuyahoga Community College, 2900 Community College Ave, Cleveland, OH 44115; Festival Organiser DR THOMAS HORNING.

Undercurrents: PO Box 94040, Cleveland, OH 44101-6040; tel. (216) 571-4141; e-mail music@undercurrents.com; internet www.undercurrents.com; Dir JOHN LATIMER; Annual international music conference, trade shows and showcase.

Wichita Jazz Festival Inc: PO Box 47231, Wichita, KS 67201; Festival Dir DEE STARKEY.

APPENDIX F: MUSIC ORGANIZATIONS

Argentina

Asociación Argentina de Interpretes (AADI): Avda Belgrano 3655, 1210 Buenos Aires.

Asociación de Representantes Artisticos (ADRA): Sarmiento 1848, 1°C, 1044 Buenos Aires.

Camara Argentina de la Música: Tucumán 1748, 2°, Of. 4, 1050 Buenos Aires.

Camara Argentina de Productores e Indus de Fonogramas y sus Reproduc (CAPIF): Avda Corrientes 1628, 5°H, 1042 Buenos Aires.

Consejo Argentino de la Música: Casilla de Correo 5532, Correo Central, 1000 Buenos Aires.

Fundacion Encuentros Internacionales de Música Contemporánea: Casilla de Correo 1008, Correo Central, 100 Buenos Aires.

Sindicato Argentino de Músicos (SADEM): Avda Belgrano 3655, 1210 Buenos Aires.

Sociedad Argentina de Autores y Compositores de Música (SADAIC): Lavalle 1547, 1048 Buenos Aires.

Sociedad General de Autores de la Argentina (ARGENTORES): Pacheco de Melo 1820, 1126 Buenos Aires.

Sociedad General de Autores y Editores (SGAE): Uruguay 775, 4° A, 1015 Buenos Aires.

Australia

Australasian Christian Broadcasters: PO Box 2020, Launceston, Tasmania 7250; Pres. KEVIN N HOOPER.

Australasian Mechanical Copyright Owners Society Ltd (AMCOS): 14th Floor, 56 Berry St, North Sydney, NSW 2060; Company Sec. BRITTEN SUTCLIFFE.

Australasian Performing Rights Association (APRA) Ltd: Locked Bag 3665, St Leonards, NSW 2065; tel. (2) 9935-7900; fax (2) 9935-7999; e-mail apra@apra.com.au; internet www.apra.com.au; CEO BRETT COTTLE.

Australian Contemporary Music Development Company Ltd (AUSMUSIC): PO Box 307, Port Melbourne, Victoria 3207; Exec. Dir PETE STEEDMAN.

Australian Copyright Council: 3/245 Chalmers St, Redfern, NSW 2016; CEO LIBBY BAULCH.

Australian Entertainment Industry Association Ltd: PO Box 423, Crows Nest, NSW 2065; Pres. NIGEL LAMPE.

Australian Music Association Inc: PO Box 6306, St Kilda Rd, Melbourne, VIC 3004; CEO ROB WALKER.

Australian Music Examinations Board: 5th Floor, 175 Flinders Lane, Melbourne 3000; tel. (3) 9650-2833; fax (3) 9650-6954; e-mail ceo@ameb.net; internet www.ameb.edu.au; CEO KATE LEWIS.

Australian Music Manager's Forum (AMMF): PO Box 109, Surry Hills, NSW 2010; Co-Chairpersons MICHAEL MCMARTIN, JOHN WOODRUFF.

Australian Music Publishers Association,Ltd: 56 Berry St, 14th Floor, North Sydney, NSW 2060.

Australian Music Retailers Association (AMRA): PO Box W333, Warringah Mall, NSW 2100; Chair. BARRY BULL.

Australian Record Industry Association (ARIA) Ltd: 8th Floor, 263 Clarence St, Sydney, NSW 2000; tel. (2) 9267-7996; fax (2) 9267-7962; e-mail aria@aria.com.au; internet www.aria.com.au; CEO STEPHEN PEACH.

Australian Songwriters Association: PO Box 123, Surry Hills, VIC 3127; Pres. MIKE BOWEN.

Australian Women's Contemporary Music Inc: 9 Knox St, Chippendale, NSW 2008; Pres. VICKI GORDON.

Central Australian Aboriginal Media Association (CAAMA): 99–101 Todd St, Alice Springs, NT 0871; Gen. Man. OWEN COLE.

Country Music Association of Australia (CCMA): PO Box 298, Tamworth, NSW 2340; CEO G M ELLIS.

Export Music Australia (EMA) Ltd: 9th Floor, 263 Clarence St, Sydney NSW 2000; Co-ordinator DONNA CHAPMAN.

International Society for Contemporary Music (Australian Section): c/o University of Sydney Music Dept, Sydney, NSW 2006.

Music Industry Advisory Council: PO Box 9839, Canberra, ACT 2601; Contact IAN JAMES.

Musicians' Union of Australia: Suite 506, 3 Smail St, Ultimo, NSW 2007; Federal Sec. JOHN MCAULIFFE.

Musicological Society of Australia Inc: PO Box 2404, Canberra, ACT 2601; National Sec. JAKI KANE.

National Indigenous Arts Advocacy Association Inc (NIAAA): Suite 401, Level 4, 60–62 Foveaux St, Surry Hills, NSW 2010; Exec. Dir BRONWYN BANCROFT.

Phonographic Performance Co. of Australia (PPCA) Ltd: 9th Floor, 263 Clarence St, Sydney, NSW 2000; tel. (2) 9267-7877; fax (2) 9264-5589; e-mail ppca@ppca.com.au; internet www.ppca.com.au; CEO STEPHEN PEACH.

Push Inc: 66 Cecil St, Fitzroy 3065; Exec. Dir PAUL SLADDIN.

Society of Australian Songwriters Inc: PO Box 290, Leichardt, NSW 2040; Pres. THOMAS POLAND.

Songwriters, Composers and Lyricists Association Inc (SCALA): PO Box 228, Kensington Park, SA 5068; tel. (08) 8431-4063; fax (08) 8332-1013; e-mail scala@senet.com.au/~scala; Pres. ROBERT CHILDS.

Tasmusic: Level 2, 34 Brisbane St, Launceston, TAS 7250; tel. (3) 6331-4470; fax (3) 6331-0227; e-mail info@tasmusic.com.au; internet www.tasmusic.com.au; Man. MARTIN STUART.

Venue Management Association: 100 St Kilda Rd, Melbourne, NSW 3004; Membership Sec. SHANE HEWITT.

Austria

AIM: Seitenberggasse 50–54, 1160 Vienna; Chair. FRANK GOLISCHEWSKI.

AKM: Baumannstr. 8–10, 1030 Vienna; Chair. GERHARD WIMBERGER.

Art Institut Wien: PO Box 101, 1043 Vienna; Chair. GREGOR JASCH.

Austria Top 30: Habsburgergasse 6-8/18, 1010 Vienna; Man. Dir FRANZ MEDWENITSCH.

Austrian Music Producers (AMP): PO Box 2, 1094 Vienna; Pres. GUENTER MENSCHIK.

Austro-Mechana: Baumannstr 8–10, 1030 Vienna; tel. (1) 71787; fax (1) 712-7136; e-mail office@aume.at; Chair. DIETER KAUFMANN; Gen. Man. HELMUT STEINMETZ.

IFPI: Habsburgergasse 6-8/18, 1010 Vienna; Chair. FRANZ MEDWENITSCH.

IGV: Siebenbrunnengasse 20/1, 1050 Vienna; Chair. ANDREAS EGGER.

International Music Centre (IMZ): Lothringerstr 20, 130 Vienna; Chair. AVRIL MACRORY.

LSG: Habsburgergasse 6-8/18, 101 Vienna; Man. Dir PAUL FÜRST.

Musiker-Komponisten Autorengilde (MKAG): Hofgasse 2/13, 1050 Vienna; tel. (1) 544-5599; fax (1) 545-6510; e-mail info@musikergilde.at; internet www.musikergilde.at; Chair. PETER PAUL SKREPEK; musicians' union.

Musikverleger Union: Baumannstr 8–10, 1030 Vienna; Chair. JOHANN JURANEK.

Österreichischer Komponistenbund (ÖKM): Ungargasse 9/2, 1030 Vienna.

Österreichishe Tonmeistervereinigung: Natterergasse 4, 2361 Laxenburg; Pres. WOLFGANG FRITZ.

Verwertungsgesellschaft Bild Und Ton (VBT): Habsburgergasse 6-8/18, 1010 Vienna; Man. Dir FRANZ MEDWENITSCH.

Belgium

ACOD Cultuur/Sector Musiek: Fontainasplein 9–11, 1000 Brussels; Sec. LAURETTE MUYLAERT.

Artist Service Vzw/ASBL: PO Box 1, 8460 Oudenburg; tel. (59) 332116; fax (59) 331672; e-mail artist-service@village.uunet.be; internet gallery.uunet.be/artist-service/; Pres. JEAN-PAUL STEENMANS.

Association Belge du Spectacle: Ave Bel Air 36, 1180 Brussels; Pres. MICHEL HALLIWELL.

Association Diffusion Musique Belge (ADIBUMEL): rue d'Arlon 75–77, 1040 Brussels; Contact FRANZ CONSTANT.

Ateliers Chanson: rue PE Janson 9, 1050 Brussels; Chair. MICHEL VAN MUYLEM.

Belgian Association of Recording Studios: rue Moorslede 77, 1020 Brussels; Chair. ERWIN VERAECKE.

Belgian Music Publishers Association: Fernand Neuraystraat 8, 1060 Brussels; Pres. ROLAND KRUGER.

Beroepsvereniging Van Belgische Impresario's (BVBI): Kammerstraat 19, 9000 Ghent; Sec. ROBERT VAN YDER.

CMCFB: Local 4 M 24, Blvd Reyers 52, 1044 Brussels; Chair. ROBERT WANGERMEE.

Country And Western Association Belgium: Nutstraat 18, 3830 Wellen; Chair. WILLIAM MAGNANI.

De Bazuin Vzw: Pauwenlaan 23, 3583 Paal-Beringen; tel. (11) 431778; Pres. LOUIS TIELENS.

European Forum of Worldwide Music Festivals: Jan Frans Willemsstraat 10, 2530 Boechout; Sec. PATRICK DE GROOTE.

European Music Office: 126 rue Franklin, 1040 Brussels; Gen. Sec. J F MICHEL.

Flanders Music Service: Stationsteenweg 238B, 2560 Nijlen; Man. Dir FRANCIS THIJS.

SABAM: rue d'Arlon 75–77, 1040 Brussels; Chair. VICTOR LEGLEY.

Belgium

SIMIM: Pl. de l'Alma 3 B5, 1200 Brussels; tel. (02) 7758210; fax (02) 7758211; e-mail simim@simim.be; Man. Dir VINCENT VAN NÉLE; Defence of music producers' rights.

Union Professionelle des Producteurs Independants (UPPI): rue Gachard 24, 1050 Brussels; Pres. PIERRE PLATINCKX.

Union Royale des Editeurs de Musique: Fernand Neuraystraat 8, 1060 Brussels; Pres. ROLAND KRUGER.

URADEX: rue d'Arlon 75–77, 1040 Brussels.

Wallonie-Bruxelles Musique: rue Marche aux Herbes 61, 4 etage, 1000 Brussels; Co-ordinator PATRICK PRINTZ.

Bolivia

Asociación Boliviana de Radiodifusoras (ASBORA): Avda Sánchez Lima, 2278 Casilla 5324, La Paz.

Educación Radiofónica de Bolivia (ERBOL): Ballivia, 1323, 4° Casilla 5946, La Paz.

Brazil

Associação Brasileira de Emissoras de Radio E Televisao (ABERT): Mezanino do Hotel Nacional Salas 5–8, 04280, 70322 Brasília, DF.

Associação Brasileira dos Produtores de Discos: Rua Sao José 90, Gr 1406/10, 22021 Rio de Janeiro, RJ.

Instituto Brasileiro de Arte e Cultura: Rua de Imprensa 16, 20030 Rio de Janeiro, RJ.

Sindicato dos Músicos Profissionals do Estado de São Paulo: Largo Paissandu, São Paulo, SP.

Sindicato Nac. de Empresas de Agenciamento: Produção de Eventos (SINAPREM); Avda Iparanga, 877, 13°, 01039 São Paulo, SP.

Sociedada Brasileira de Música Contemporânea: SQS 105, Bloco B, Ap 506, 70344-020 Brasília, DF.

Sociedada Independente de Compositores & Autores Musicals: Largo Paissandú 51, 10th, 11th and 16th Floors, 01034 São Paulo, SP.

Uniao Brasileira de Compositores: Rua Visconde de Inhaúma 107, 20091 Rio de Janeiro, RJ.

Uniao dos Músicos do Brasil: Avda Rio Branco 185, Rio de Janeiro, RJ.

Bulgaria

BAZI: 15 Tsarigradsko Chausse Blvd, 1220 Sofia; Man. DORA CHERNEVA.

Jusautor: Pl. Bulgaria 1, 1463 Sofia; Dir-Gen. JANA MARKOVA.

Musicautor: 6 Rajcho Dimchev, 1000 Sofia; Chair. KONSTANTIN DRAGNEV.

Podkrepa: 2 Angel Kunchev str, 1000 Sofia; Chair. ASEN GARGOV.

Pop-Rock Federation: Liulin Bl. 210, Vh A, 1343 Sofia; Chair. CHAVDAR CHENDOV.

Union of Bulgarian Composers (UBC): 2 Ivan Vazov St, 1000 Sofia; tel. (2) 988-1560; fax (2) 987-4378; e-mail ubc@mail.bol.bg; internet www.ubc-bg.com; Pres. VICTOR CHUCHKOV.

Canada

Alberta Recording Industries Association: #208, 10136-100 St, Edmonton, AB T5J 0P1; Exec. Asst CHARLOTTE BOWMAN.

American Federation of Musicians of the United States and Canada, Canadian Office: 75 The Donway West, Suite 1010, Don Mills, ON M3C 2E9; tel. (416) 391-5161; fax (416) 391-5165; e-mail afmcan@afm.org; internet www.afm.org; Vice-Pres. (Canada) DAVID J JANDRISCH.

BC Country Music Association: 177 W 7 Ave, 4th Floor, Vancouver BC V5Y 1L8.

Black Music Association of Canada: 59 Chester Hill Rd, Toronto, ON M4K 1X4; Pres. DANIEL CAUDEIRON.

Caledonia Folk Club: 23 Buchanan Dr., Caledonia, ONN3W 1H1; Organiser BILL CRAWFORD.

Canadian Academy of Recording Arts and Sciences (CARAS): 124 Merton St, 3rd Floor, Toronto, ON M4S 2Z2; Exec. Dir DAISY FALLE.

Canadian Amateur Musicians: PO Box 353, Westmount, QC H3Z 2T5; Dir-Gen. BARRY CRAGO.

Canadian Association for Music Therapy: c/o Wilfrid Laurier University, 75 University Ave W, Waterloo, ON N2L 3C5; Admin. Co-ordinator LYNDA TRACY.

Canadian Association of Artists' Managers: 117 Ava Rd, Toronto, ON M6C 1W2.

Canadian Country Music Association (CCMA): 127-3800 Steeles Ave W, Woadbridge, ON L4L 4G9; Exec. Dir SHEILA HAMILTON.

Canadian Disc Jockey Association Inc: National Office, 3148 Kingston Rd, Suite 209-300, Scarborough, ON M1M 1P4; National Pres. & CEO DENNIS E HAMPSON.

Canadian Independent Record Producers Association (CIRPA): 114 Front St W, Suite 202, Toronto, ON M5J 2L7; Exec. Dir BRIAN CHATER.

Canadian Music Centre: 20 St Joseph St, Toronto, ON M4Y 1J9.

Canadian Music Publishers Association: 320–56 Wellesley St W, Toronto, ON M5S 2S3.

Canadian Musical Reproduction Rights Agency Ltd: 56 Wellesley St West, Suite 320, Toronto, ON M5S 2S4; Gen. Man. DAVID BASKIN.

Canadian Recording Industry Association: 1255 Yonge St, Suite 300, Toronto, ON M4T 1W6; Pres. BRIAN ROBERTSON.

Canadian Society for Traditional Music: PO Box 4232, Sta C, Calgary, Alberta, T2T 5N1; Membership Co-Sec. JOHN LEEDER.

Coastal Jazz and Blues Society: 435 West Hastings St, Vancouver, BC V6B 1L4; Exec. Dir ROBERT KERR.

Country Music Foundation of Canada: 8607 128 Ave, Edmonton, AB T5E 0G3; tel. (780) 476-8230; fax (780) 472-2584; Contact BILL MAXIM; Museum of country music.

Federation of Canadian Music Festivals: 1034 Chestnut Ave, Moose Jaw, SK S6H 1A6.

Foundation to Assist Canadian Talent on Records: 125 George St, 2nd Floor, Toronto, ON, M5A 2N4; Exec. Dir HEATHER SYM.

Georgian Bay Folk Society: PO Box 521, Owen Sound, ON N4K 5R1; Promotion Co-ordinator LINDA ASHLEY.

Music Industries Association of Canada (MIAC): 109–1210 Sheppard Ave E, North York, ON M2K 1E3.

Northern Praise Ministries Inc: PO Box 61015, Oakville, ON L6J 7P5; Founder/Admin. MICHELLE SIM.

Pacific Music Industry Association: 400-177 W 7th Ave, Vancouver, BC V5Y 1L8; Exec. Dir ELLIE O'DAY.

Photo-Connect: 244–423 King St West, Hamilton, ON L8P 4Y1; Pres. & CEO KIRBY ELLIS.

Société des Mélomanes (Canada) Inc: 1056 Burnaby St, Suite 201, Vancouver, BC V6E 1N7; Dir Factotum EUGÈNE EVANS.

Society for Reproduction Rights of Authors, Composers and Publishers in Canada (SODRAC): 759 Victoria Sq., Suite 420, Montréal, QC H2Y 2J7; tel. (514) 845-3268; fax (514) 845-3401; e-mail sodrac@sodrac.com; internet www.sodrac.com; Gen. Man. CLAUDETTE FORTIER.

Society of Composers, Authors & Music Publishers in Canada (SOCAN): 41 Valleybrook Dr., Don Mills, ON M3B 2S6.

Toronto Downtown Jazz Society: 366 Adelaide St SE Sutie #230, Toronto, Ontario M5A 3X9; Dir of Marketing & Communications BARB MCCULLAUGH.

Toronto Musicians' Association: 101 Thorncliffe Park Dr., Toronto, ON M4H 1M2; Sec. MARK TETREAULT.

Chile

Asociación de Radiodifusores de Chile (ARCHI): Pasaje Matte, 957, Of. 801, Santiago.

Asociación Nacional de Compositores: Almirante Moritt 453, Santiago.

Instituto de Música: Universidad Católica de Chile, Jaime Guzman E 3 300, Santiago.

Sociedad Chilena del Derecho de Autor (SCD): San Antonio, 427, 2°, Santiago.

China (Taiwan)

ARCO (The Association of Recording Copyright Owners of ROC): 3F, No. 95, Sec 4, Nanking East Rd, Taipei; Exec. Dir ROBIN LEE.

IFPI Members Foundation in Taiwan: 3F, No. 95, Sec 4, Nanking East Rd, Taipei; Sec.-Gen. ROBIN LEE.

Colombia

Asociación Colombiana de Músicos Profesionales: Calles 17, 10–16, Of. 607, Santafé de Bogotá, DC.

Asociación des Artistas de Colombia: Calle 13, 9–63, Interior 104, PO Box 24627, Santafé de Bogotá, DC.

Centro de Documentación Musical—Instituto Colombiano de Cultura: Calle 11, 5–51, 2nd Floor, Santafé de Bogotá, DC.

Instituto Colombiano de Cultura—Colcultura: Calle 11, 5–51, 2nd Floor, Santafé de Bogotá, DC.

Sociedad de Autores y Compositores de Colombia: Carrera 19, 40–72, PO Box 6482, Santafé de Bogotá, DC.

Croatia

Croatian Authors Agency: Preradoviceva 25, 41000 Zagreb; Man. ZELJKA MODRUSAC-RANOGAJEC.

Croatian Composers Society: Berislaviceva 9, 41000 Zagreb; Man. Dir OZREN KANCELJAK.

Croatian Musicians Union: PP 560, Gruška 10, 41001 Zagreb; Chair. PAOLO SFECI; Sec.-Gen. SINIŠA DORONJGA.

Music Information Centre: Kneza Mislava 18, 41000 Zagreb; Man. Dir JAGODA MARTINCEVIC.

Cuba

Centro de Información y Promoción de la Música Cubana Odilio Urfé: Calle 17 esq. a E, Vedado, Havana.

Centro de Investigación y Desarrollo de la Música Cubana: Calle G, No. 505 e/21 y 23, Vedado, Havana.

Centro Nacional de Derecho de Autor: Calle Línea No. 365 (altos), esp a G, Vedado, Havana.

Centro Nacional de Música de Concierto: Calle Línea No. 365, esq a G, Vedado, Havana.

Centro Nacional de Música Popular: Avda 1 ra. e/10 y 12, Playa, Havana.

Editora Musical de Cuba: San Rafael No. 104, esq a Consulado, Centro Habana, Havana.

Empresa de Grabaciones y Ediciones Musicales: Campanario No. 315, e/Neptuno y San Miguel, Centro Habana, Havana.

Instituto Cubano de la Música: Calle 15 No. 452, esq a F Vedado, Havana.

Unión de Escritores y Artistas de Cuba (Music Section): Calle 17 No. 351, esq a H, Vedado, Havana.

The Czech Republic

Association of Musicians and Musicologists: Maltézské nám. 1, 118 00 Prague 1.

Authors Association of Protection for Rights on Musical Works: Cs. armády 20, 160 56 Prague 6.

Czech Music Fund: Besední 3, 118 00 Prague 1.

Czech Music Information Centre: Besední 3, 118 00 Prague 1; tel. (2) 5731-7424; fax (2) 5731-7424; e-mail his@vol.cz; internet www.musica.cz; Dir MIROSLAV PUDLAK.

Czech Music Society: Radlická 99, Smíchov, 150 00 Prague 5; tel. (2) 5155-2382; fax (2) 5155-2453; e-mail czechmusiksoc@hotmail.com; Pres. MÍLA SMETÁCKOVÁ.

Guild of Czech Composers and Concert Artists: Valdstejnske nam. 1, 100 00 Prague 1; Pres. JAN SEIDEL.

IFPI CR: Senovazne nam 23, 112 82 Prague 1; Sec. & CEO VRATISLAV SAFAR.

International Federation of Phonogram and Videogram Producers (Czech Section): Gorkého nam. 23, 112 82 Prague 1.

International Music Council (National Committee): Valdstejnske nám. 1, Prague 1.

International Society for Contemporary Music (Czechoslovak Section): Na Brezince 22, 150 00 Prague 5.

Ochranny Svaz Autorsky (OSA): Cs. Armady 20, 160 56 Prague 6; Pres. PETR JANDA.

Society for Jazz: Janáckovo nábr. 59, Smíchov, 150 00 Prague 5.

Union of Authors and Interpreters: Skroupova nám 9, 130 00 Prague 3.

Denmark

Association of Rock/Jazz Clubs in Denmark (SAMSPIL): Graven 25 A, 8000 Aarhus C; Chair. PALLE SKOV; Sec Leader RIKKE SINDING.

Danish Association of Jazz and Rock Amateurs (FAJABEFA): Musiskkens Hus, Enghavevej 40 sal, 1674 Copenhagen V; Contact JACOB KRAGH.

Danish Jazz Association: Kjeld Langesgade 4A, 1367 Copenhagen K; Chair. FRANS BAK.

Danish Jazz Federation: Nytorv 3, 3, 1450 Copenhagen K; tel. 3345-4300; fax 3345-4311; e-mail info@dkjazz.dk; internet www.dkjazz.dk.

Danish Music Council: Vesterbrogade 24 4, 1620 Copenhagen V; Chair. LARS GRUNTH.

Danish Music Information Centre: Gräbrødretorv 16, 1154 Copenhagen K; Chair. JORGEN ARNSTED.

Danish Rock Council (ROSA): Karetmagergaarden, Graven 25 A, 8000 Aarhus C; Chair. GUNNAR MADSEN.

Dansk Folkemindesamling (Danish Folklore Archives): Christians Brygge 3, 1219 Copenhagen K; Administration Dir SVEND NIELSEN.

Danske Jazz Beat Og Folkemusik Autorer (DJBFA): Gräbrødretrov 16, 1154 Copenhagen K; Chair. TORBEN KJAER.

Den Rytmiske Konsulentitjeneste: Kjeld Langesgade 4A, 1367 Copenhagen K; Chair. NILLER WISCHMANN.

Foreningen Danmarks Folkeminder (Danish Folklore Society): Christians Brygge 3, 1219 Copenhagen K; Administration Dir SVEND NIELSEN.

GRAMEX: Reventlowsgade 8/1, 1651 Copenhagen V; Dir BJORN JUELL-SUNDBYE.

IFPI Denmark: Store Strandstraede 20 st, 1255 Copenhagen K; Chair. STEFAN FRYLAND.

Jazz Centret/Jazzkontakten: Borupvej 66, 4683 Rönnede; tel. 5671-1749; e-mail jazzpar@mail.tele.dk; internet www.jazzpar.dk; Man. Dir CIM MEYER; Awards the annual international JAZZPAR Prize.

KIM (Women In Music): c/o Conservatory of Music, Niels Brocksgade 1, 1574 Copenhagen V; Chair. TOVE KRAG.

KODA: Maltegaardsvej 24, 2820 Gentofte; Chair. HENRIK LUND.

MXP—Danish Music Export and Promotion: Sondervej 56, 5700 Svendborg; Music Consultant/CEO MIKAEL HØJRIS.

Nordisk Copyright Bureau (NCB): PO Box 3064, 1021 Copenhagen K; Administration Exec. KURT HVIID MIKKELSEN.

Rhythmic Music Conservatory: Dr Priemesvej 3, 1854 Frederiksberg C; Dir ERIK MOSEHOLM.

Estonia

Estonian Jazz Foundation: PO Box 3641, Viru str 16, 0090 Tallinn; Dir TIIT LAUK.

Tallinn Zeppelin Club: PO Box 3526, Tallinn 0090; Club Consultant PETER ZELUIKO.

VAAP: Toompuiestee 7, 0101 Tallinn.

Fiji

Fiji Composers Association: PO Box 2371, Government Bldgs, Suva; Vice-Pres. SERU SEREVI.

Fiji Musicans' Association: PO Box 364, Loutoka; Vice-Pres. DANNY COSTELLO JR.

Fiji Performing Right Association Limited: PO Box 15061, 170 Renwick Rd, Suva; Chair. SAIMONE VUATALEVU.

Finland

AFRB: Italahdenkatu 22 BC, 00210 Helsinki.

Finnish Big Band Association: Makslahdenkatu 1 C, 02140 Espoo; Contact RISTO OINAALA.

Finnish Folk and Country Music Society: PO Box 181, 00531 Henlsinki; Contact JIHANI AALTO.

Finnish Jazz and Pop Archive: Rajasampaanranta 2, 00560 Helsinki.

Finnish Jazz Archives: Pihlajatie 43 A, 00270 Helsinki.

Finnish Jazz Federation: PO Box 54, 00101 Helsinki; tel. (9) 757-2077; fax (9) 757-2067; e-mail info@jazzfin.com; internet www.jazzfin.com; Exec. Man. TIMO VAHASILTA.

Finnish Music Information Centre: Lauttasaarentie 1, 00200 Helsinki; tel. (9) 6810-1313; fax (9) 682-0770; e-mail info@mic.teosto.fi; internet www.fimic.fi; Contact JARI MUIKKU.

Finnish Music Publishers Association: Lastenkodinkatu 7, 00180 Helsinki; tel. (9) 5860-870; fax (9) 5860-8755; e-mail info@musiikkikustantajat.fi; internet www.musiikkikustantajat.fi; Man. Dir PEKKA SIPILÄ.

Finnish Musicians' Union: Pieni Roobertinkatu 16, 00120 Helsinki; tel. (9) 6803-4073; fax (9) 6803-4087; e-mail raimo.vikstrom@musicfinland.com; internet www.musicfinland.com/sml/; Pres. RAIMO VIKSTROM.

Global Music Centre: Mikkolantie 17, 00640 Helsinki; Dir ANU LAAKKONEN.

GRAMEX: Hietaniemenkatu 15/A/12, 00100 Helsinki; Dir JUKKA NISKANEN.

Musikkikustantajatorg: Hietaniemenkatu 2, 00100 Helsinki; Man. Dir MINNA AALTO-SETÄLÄ.

Rock Musicians Association: Uudenmaankatu 36/F/34, 00120 Helsinki; Chair. NISSILA PEKKA.

Society of Finnish Composers: Runeberginkatu 15/A/11, 00100 Helsinki.

Teosto: Lauttasaarentie 1, 00200 Helsinki; Man. Dir JAAKKO FREDMAN.

France

ADAMI: 10A rue de la Paix, 75002 Paris; Contact MARIE-JEANNE PERALDI.

ANARLP: PO Box 174, 10005 Troyes Cédex; Pres. GUY CAPET.

BIEM: 56 Ave Kleber, 75116 Paris; Pres. JEAN LOUP TOURNIER.

Bureau Export de la Musique Française: 27 rue du Docteur Lancereaux, 75008 Paris; Exec. Dir MARIE AGNES BEAU.

Centre Information et Ressources pour les Musiques Actuelles (IRMA): 22 rue Soleillet, 75020 Paris Cédex 20; tel. 1 43 15 11 11; fax 1 43 15 11 10; e-mail info@irma.asso.fr; internet www.irma.asso.fr; Dir BERNARD BATZEN.

Centre Musical et Creatif de Nancy: 92 Grande rue, PO Box 698, 54063 Nancy Cédex; Teaching Dir HANS J KULLOCK.

Centre National d'Action Musicale (CENAM): 11–13 rue de l'Escaut, 75019 Paris; Dir DOMINQUE PONSARD.

CISAC: 1 rue Keppler, 75116 Paris; Sec.-Gen. JEAN ALEXIS ZIEGLER.

Collectif HASK: 9 Ave Pasteur, 93100 Montreuil; Contact HUBERT DUPONT.

Comite National De La Musique (CNM): 91 rue Jouffroy d'Abbans, 75017 Paris; tel. and fax 1 42 27 07 31; Gen. Sec. J MASSON FORESTIER.

Concours de Piano Jazz Martial Solal: Acanthes—Concours Internationaux de la Ville de Paris, 3 rue des Couronnes, 75020 Paris; tel. 1 40 33 45 35; fax 1 40 33 45 38; e-mail civp@acanthes.com; internet www.civp.com; Gen. Delegate CLAUDE SAMUEL; International jazz piano competition held in late September; first prize of 70,000 French francs and engagements at a number of festivals.

CSDEM: 62 rue Blanche, 75009 Paris; Pres. JEAN DAVOUST.

Eurokka (Esperanto-Rok-Asocio): 31450 Donneville; Dir FLORÉAL MARTORELL.

Ferarock: PO Box 4015, 31028 Toulouse Cédex; Pres. FRANÇOISE DUVAL.

FNAMU: 41 Bis Quai de la Loire, 75019 Paris; Man. Dir CATHERINE LESAGE.

Fondation Pour La Creation Musicale (FCM): 141 rue Lafayette, 75010 Paris; Dir BRUNO RONY.

French Studios Association (ASF): 30 rue Henri Barbusse, 75005 Paris; Dir JEAN LOUIS RIZET.

Institut du Monde Arabe: 1 rue des Fosses Saint-Bernard, 75236 Paris; Programme Dir for Music, Dance & Theatre MOHAMED METALSI.

Institut International de Musique Electroacoustique: PO Box 39 18001 Bourges Cédex; Dirs FRANÇOISE BARRIÈRE, CHRISTIAN CLOZIER; Sec.-Gen. CATHARINA KROLING.

International Confederation of Music Publishers: 47 rue de Turbigo, 75003 Paris; tel. 1 42 72 38 99; fax 1 42 72 38 05; e-mail 101374.25@compuserve.com; internet www.icmp-ciem.org; Contact JENNY VACHER.

Le Lieu Unique—CRDC: PO Box 21304, 2 rue de la Biscuiterie, 44013 Nantes Cédex 01; tel. 2 51 82 15 00; fax 2 40 20 20 12; e-mail info@lelieuunique.com; internet www.lelieuunique.com; Dir JEAN BLAISE; Musical Curator KITTY HARTL; popular music and video events and festivals.

MIDEM Organization: 179 Ave Victor Hugo, 75116 Paris; CEO XAVIER ROY.

SACEM/SDRM: 225 Ave Charles de Gaulle, 92521 Neuilly-sur-Seine Cédex; Pres. GERARD CALVI.

SCPP: 159 Charles de Gaulle, 92200 Neuilly-sur-Seine; Pres. RENE GUITTAN.

SIPLACDA: 255 rue Saint-Honoré, 75001 Paris; Pres. JOËLLE FEAUVEAU.

SNAAL: 17 rue Brey, 75017 Paris; Pres. ROLAND BERTIN.

SPEDIDAM: 8 rue Bremontier, 75017 Paris; Pres. MAURICE HUSSON.

Syndicat Francais des Artistes-Interpretes (SFA): 21 bis rue Victor Masse, 75009 Paris; Exec. Dir FRANCOIS PARROT.

Syndicat National de L'Edition Phonographique (SNEP): 27 rue du Docteur Lancereaux, 75008 Paris; Man. HERVE RONY.

Syndicat National des Artistes Musiciens (SNAM): 14–16 rue des Lilas, 75019 Paris; tel. 1 42 02 30 80; fax 1 42 02 34 01; e-mail snamf@free.fr; Pres. RAYMOND SILVAND.

Syndicat National des Auteurs et Compositeurs (SNAC): 80 rue Taitbout, 75442 Paris Cédex 9; Pres. ANTOINE DUHAMEL.

Germany

Bundesverband Der Phonographischen Wirtschaft eV (BPW): Grelckstr 36, 20257 Hamburg 1; Contact PETRA DENZEN.

Deutsche Bibliothek/Deutsches Musikarchiv Berlin: PO Box 4502 29, 12172 Berlin; Library Dir DR HEINZ LANSKE.

Deutsche Disc Jockey Organisation: Kaiser Friedrich Allee 1–3, 52074 Aachen; Contact KLAUS QUIRINI.

Deutsche Landesgruppe der IFPI eV: Grelckstr 36, 22529 Hamburg; Head of Public Relations ELMAR KRUSE.

Deutsche Phono-Akademie: Grelckstr 36, 22529 Hamburg; Contact HARTMUTH BENDER.

Deutscher Musikverleger Verband (DMV): Freidrich Wilhelm str 31, 53113 Bonn; Pres. MAJA MARIA REIS.

Deutscher Rock und Pop Musikerverband eV: Kolberger str 30, 21339 Luenburg; tel. (4131) 233-030; fax (4131) 233-0315; e-mail info@drmv.de; internet www.drmv.de; Chair. OLE SEELENMEYER.

Deutscher Tonkunstlerverband e.V (DTKV): Linprunstr, 16 Rgb 80335 Munchen.

European Association of Concert Agents: Sülzgürtel 86, 50937 Cologne; Contact ANDREAS BRAUN.

Gesellschaft für musikalische Aufführungs und mechanische Vervielfältigungsrechte—GEMA: Rosenheimer str 11, 81667 Munich; tel. (89) 4800-3421; fax (89) 4800-3424; e-mail pr@gema.de; internet www.gema.de; Dir of Communications DR HANS-HERWIG GEYER.

GVL: Heimhuder str 5, 20148 Hamburg; Man. Dir ROLF DUENNWALD.

IDKV (German Concert Promoter and Artists Agents Association): PO Box 202364, 20216 Hamburg; Pres. & Gen. Man. JENS MICHOW.

Internationaler Arbeitskries für Musik eV: PO Box 410236, 34064 Kassel.

MusikKomm GmbH: Rottscheider str 6, 42329 Wuppertal; Man. Dir ULI GROSSMASS.

Verband der Deutschen Konzertdirekionen eV: Liebigstr 39, 80538 Munich.

Warehouse: Linden str 52, 50674 Cologne.

Zentrum für Musik & Kommunikations-Tech.: Rottscheider str 6, 42329 Wuppertal; Man. Dir DIETER GORNY.

Greece

AEPI: Deligani 14, 106 83 Athens; Pres. MIMIS TRAIFORIS.

IFPI Greece: Aghia Paraskevi 63, 152 34 Halandri, Athens; Sec. MILTOS KARADSAS.

International Music Council (Greek Section): Mitropoleos 38, 105 63 Athens; Pres. DEMETRE MICHAELIDES.

Panhellenic Musicians' Union: 10 Sapfous str, 10553 Athens; Pres. T. ATHINEOS; Gen. Sec. G. LAMBRIANIDIS.

Hong Kong

Composers and Authors Society of Hong Kong (CASH) Ltd: 18/F Universal Trade Centre, 3 Arbuthnot Rd, Central Hong Kong; Contact LESLIE CHING.

Hong Kong Composers Guild: c/o Music Dept, Chung Chi College, Chinese University, Shatin, New Territories; Contact CHAN WING WAH.

IFPI (Hong Kong Group): 22/F Gitic Centre, 28 Queen's Rd East, Wanchai, Hong Kong; Chief Sec. PATRICK WONG.

Music Publishers Association: 11/F Peninsula Office Tower, 18 Middle Rd, Kowloon; Contact DAVID LOITERTON.

Hungary

Gewerkschaft für Musik und Tanzkünstler: Gorkij Fasor 38, PO Box 8, 1406 Budapest; Sec. LÁSZLÓ GYIMESI.

Hungarian Music Council: PO Box 47, 1364 Budapest.

Hungarian Music Society: Vörösmarty tér 1, 1051 Budapest; Pres. ZSOLT DURKÓ.

Institute for Musicology of the Hungarian Academy of Sciences: Táncsics Mihály utca 7, 1014 Budapest; Asst Dir TIBOR TALLIÁN.

Mahasz (IFPI): Regiposta u 13, 1052 Budapest; Man. Dir AGNES MUSINGER.

Musicians Trade Union: Gorkij Fasor 38, 1068 Budapest; Pres. SANOR SOLYOM NAGY.

Society of Hungarian Commercial Radios: Steindl Ihre u 12, 1054 Budapest; Pres. LASZLO HEGEOUS.

Iceland

Association of Light Composers and Songwriters: Háteigsvegur 28, 105 Reykjavík.

Iceland Music Information Centre: Sidumuli 34, 108 Reykjavík; Man. ASTA HRÖNN.

Icelandic Composers Society: Laufásvegur 40, 101 Reykjavík.

Icelandic Musicians' Union: Laufásvegur 40, Reykjavík; Gen. Sec. ASGEIR H. STEINGRIMSSON.

IFPI Iceland: Kringlan 4, PO Box 3360, 123 Reykjavík; Chair. STEINAR BERG ISLEIFSSON.

International Society for Contemporary Music: Laufásvegur 40, 101 Reykjavík.

Jazzvakning: PO Box 31, 121 Reykjavík.

Reykjavík Music Society: Garoastraeti 17, 101 Reykjavík.

Society of Icelandic Musicians: Dalsel 8, Reykjavík.

STEF: Laufásvegur 40, 101 Reykjavík; Gen. Man. EIREKUR TOMASSON.

Union of Authors and Copyright Owners: Laufásvegur 40, 101 Reykjavík.

Indonesia

Indonesian Society of Composers and Arrangers: Komp Mangga Dua Plaza, Blok J, no. 30, Jl Mangga Dua raya, Jakarta Utara; Chair. SAKIKIN ZUCHRA.

Ireland

An Chomhairle Ealaion (The Arts Council): 70 Merrion Sq., Dublin 2; tel. (1) 618-0200; fax (1) 676-1302; e-mail dermot@artscouncil.ie; Artform Dir DERMOT MCLAUGHLIN.

Association of Independent Record Retailers: 5 Cope St, Dublin 2; Pres. BRIAN O'KELLY.

Association of Irish Composers: Copyright House, Pembroke Row, Lower Baggot St, Dublin 2; Contact MAURA EATON.

Association of Irish Festival Events (AOIFE): Administration Office, Rear 32 Upper Main St, Arklow, Co Wicklow; National Sec. VICTOR RYAN.

British Institute of Jazz Studies: 17 The Chase, Crowthorne, Berkshire RG45 6HT; Sec. GRAHAM LANGLEY.

Cork Music Resource Co-Op: Unit 12, Thompson's Bldg, McCurtain St, Cork; Administration Dir ANGELA DORCRAN.

Federation of Music Collectives: The Temple Bar Music Centre, Cyred St North, Temple Bar, Dublin 2; Contact ANGELA DORGAN.

Folk Music Society of Ireland: 15 Henrietta St, Dublin 1.

IFPI Ireland: 26 Merrion Sq., Dublin 2; Chair. PAUL KEOGH.

Independent Radio and Television Commission (IRTC): Marine House, Clanwilliam Pl., Dublin 2; Contact LYNNE SCANLAN.

International Songwriters' Association (ISA): PO Box 46, Limerick City, Limerick; Man. Dir JAMES LIDDANE.

Irish Association of Songwriters and Composers (IASC): Ballinclea Lodge, Ballinclea Rd, Killiney, Co Dublin; Chair. KEITH DONALD.

Irish Bluegrass Music Club: 86 Barton Rd East, Dublin 14; Contact CAROL HAWKINS.

Irish Federation of Musicians and Associated Professions: 63 Lower Gardiner St, Dublin 1; Pres. RICHARD GLYNN.

Irish Federation of the Phonographic Industry (IFPI): 9 Whitefriars, Aungier St, Dublin 2; Chair. PAUL KEOGH; Sec. RIOBAIRD MACGORIAN.

Irish Music Rights Organisation Ltd (IMRO): Copyright House, Pembroke Row, Lower Baggot St, Dublin 2; CEO HUGH DUFFY.

Irish Traditional Music Archive: 63 Merrion Sq., Dublin 2; tel. (1) 661-9699; fax (1) 662-4585; internet www.itma.ie; Dir NICHOLAS CAROLAN.

Mechanical Copyright Protection Society (Ireland) Ltd (MCPS): Copyright House, Pembroke Row, Lower Baggot St, Dublin 2; Gen. Man. VICTOR FINN.

Music Base: 44 East Essex St, Dublin 2; Youth Arts Devt Officer GREG MCATEER.

Music Network: The Coach House, Dublin castle, Dublin 2; tel. (1) 671-9429; fax (1) 671-9430; e-mail info@musicnetwork.ie; internet www.musicnetwork.ie; Information Man. SEAMUS O'REILLY.

Music Publishers Association of Ireland (MPAI): Copyright House, Pembroke Row, Lower Baggot St, Dublin 2; tel. (1) 676-6940; fax (1) 661-1316; Pres. MICHAEL O'RIORDAN; Sec. JOHN LAPPIN.

Music Retailers of Ireland: 5 Cope St, Dublin 2; Exec. Member BRIAN O KELLY.

Oifig an Cheoil (The Music Office): Teo Cuilin, Dingle, Co. Kerry; Contact JOAN MAGUIRE.

Performing Rights Society: Copyright House, Pembroke Row, Lower Baggot St, Dublin 2; Contact PAULA MCDERMOTT.

Phonographic Performance (Ireland) Ltd (PPI): PPI House, 1 Corrig Ave, Dun Laoghaire. Co Dublin; CEO DICK DOYLE.

Republic of Ireland Music Publishers Association (RIMPA): Copyright House, Pembroke Row, Lower Baggot St, Dublin 2; Sec. JOHN J LAPPIN.

Israel

Independent Musicians Union: 6 Malkei Yisrael Sq., 64591 Tel Aviv; tel. (3) 695-9355; fax (3) 696-3528; e-mail eilam@netvision.net.il; Chair. DANY GOTTFRIED.

International Music Council (Israeli Section): Ministry of Science, Culture and Sport, Kanfei nesharim 22, 91342 Jerusalem; tel. (2) 560-1741; fax (2) 560-1568; e-mail raaya@most.gov.il; internet www.most.gov.il; Chief Officer, Music Dept RAAYA SIMRAN.

International Society for Contemporary Music (Israeli Section): c/o Israel Composers' League, PO Box 45068, 61450 Tel Aviv.

Israel Composers' League: PO Box 45068, 61450 Tel Aviv; Chair. MANACHEM ZUR.

Israel Music Institute (IMI): PO Box 3004, 61030 Tel Aviv; tel. (3) 524-4645; fax (3) 524-5276; e-mail musicinst@bezeqint.net; Dir PAUL LANDAU.

Jerusalem Music Centre: Mishkanot Sha'ananim, Jerusalem; Dir BENNY GAL-ED.

Jeunesses Musicales Israel: 19 Achad Ha'am St, Tel Aviv 65151.

Music Information Centre of Israel: PO Box 3004, 61030 Tel Aviv; tel. (3) 524-6475; fax (3) 524-5276; e-mail musicinst@bexeqint.net; Dir PAUL LANDAU.

National Council for Culture and Arts: 16 Hanatziv St, 67018 Tel Aviv; Chief Officer DAVID SINAI.

Society of Authors, Composers and Music Publishers in Israel (ACUM): 9 Tuval St, PO Box 1704; Ramatgan 52117; tel. (3) 611-3400; fax (3) 612-2629; e-mail acum@acum.org.il; Chair. NAOMI SHEMER.

Union of Musicians: Histradut Bldg, 93 Arlozorof St, 62098 Tel Aviv; Gen. Sec. ARYEH LEVANON.

Italy

AMI: via Montenapoleone 20, 20121 Milan; Chair. ROBERTO DE LUCA.

Associazione dei Fonografici Italiani (AFI): via Vittor Pisani 10, 20124 Milan; Pres. GUIDO RIGNANO.

Associazione di Informatica Musicale Italiana (AIMI): c/o La Biennale di Venezia, Settore Musica, San Marco, Ca Giustinian, 30124 Venice.

Associazione Italiana Degli Editori di Musica (AIDEM): via Enrico Toti 4, 20123 Milan; Pres. MAURIZIO CORECHA.

Associazione Italiana Operatori Musicali (ASSIOM): c/o Centro di Ricerca e Sperimentazione per la Didattica Musicale, Villa La Torraccia, via delle Fontanelle 24, 50016 San Domenico di Fiesolo (FI).

Associazione Nazionale Musicisti di Jazz (ANMJ): via Vallerozzi 77, 53100 Sienna; Chair. GIORGIO GASLINI.

Bluegrass & Country Music Association of Italy: PO Box 1733, 20101 Milan; Pres. MAURIZIO FAULISI.

CIDIM—National Music Committee of Italy (IMC—UNESCO): via Vittoria Colonna 18, 00193 Rome.

Editori Musicali Associati (EMA): Piazza del Liberty 2, 20121 Milan; Pres. ADRIANO SOLARO.

Federazione Industria Musicale Italiana (FIMI): Largo Augusto 3, 20122 Milan; Pres. FRANCO REALI.

Federazione Italiana dei Compositori de Musica Contemporanea: via Cavalieri di Vittorio Veneto 34, 56121 Cascina (PI).

Federazione Italiana della Musica (FEDERMUSICA): via Vittor Piasni 10, 20124 Milan.

FILIS: Piazza Sallustio 24, 00187 Rome; Gen. Sec. MASSIMO BORDINI.

IMAIE: Piazza Sallusto 28, 00187 Rome; Chair. ANGELI OTELLO.

International Association for the Study of Popular Music (IASPM), Italian Section: c/o Il Giornale della Musica, corso Vittorio Emanuelle II n 198 bis, 10138 Turin.

International Dance Organization (IDO): via Bronzino 117, 50142 Florence.

Istituto Italiano per la Storia della Musica: via Vittoria 6, 00187 Rome.

Italian Braodcasting Association: via della Moscova 38A, 20121 Milan; Pres. RICCARDO FAUSONE.

Laboratorio Musicale Periferico: via Pratese 48/a, 50145 Firenze; Pres. ROBERTO BUONI.

SIAE: Viale della Letteratura 30, 00144 Rome; Pres. ROMAN VLAD.

Sindacato Nazionale Musicisti (SNM): via Pinelli 100, 10144 Turin.

Società Italiana Musica Contemporanea (SIMC): via F Juvara 11, 21029 Milan.

UNCLA: Galleria del Corso 4, 20122 Milan; Sec.-Gen. ARMANDO CARNADELLI.

Unione Editori di Musica Italiani (UNEMI): via Teulada 52, 00195 Rome; Pres. LUCIANO VILLEVILLE BIDERI.

Unione Nazionale Editori di Musica Italiani (UNEMI): via Teulada 52, 00195 Rome.

Japan

Concert Managers' Association of Japan: Mitoko Bldg, 6-2-4 Akasaka, Minato-ku, Tokyo 107; Chair. NAOYASU KAJIMOTO.

Federation of Music Producers Japan: Jingumae Wada Bdlg, Shibuya-ku, Tokyo 150; Pres. TAKESHI HOSOKAWA.

Japan Association of Music Enterprises: 4F Koyanagi Bldg 1-7 Ginza, Chuo-ku, Toyko 104; Contact AKITOMO TANABE.

Japan Audio Society: 3F Mori Bldg, 1-14-34 Jingumae, Shibuya-ku, Tokyo 150; Chair. HEITARO NAKAJIMA.

Japan Council of Performers Organizations (Geidankyo): 11F Tokyo Opera City Tower, 3-20-2 Nishishinjuku, Shinjuku-ku, Tokyo 163-14; PR SAMUEL SHU. MASUYAMA.

Japan International League of Artists: 2-3-16-607 Shinjuku, Shinkjku-ku, Tokyo 160; Chief Officer KAZUHIKO HATTORI.

Japanese Composers Society: Ogawa Bldg, 3-7-15 Akasaka, Minato-ku, Tokyo 107.

Japanese Society for Rights of Authors, Composers & Publishers (JASRAC): 1-7-13 Nishishimbashi, Minato-ku, Tokyo 105; Pres. RAY NAKANISHI.

Music Publishers Association of Japan: 7F Daiichi Nanou Bldg, 2-21-2 Nishi Shinbashi, Minato-ku, Tokyo 105; Pres. MISA WATANABE.

Musicians' Union of Japan: Showa Bldg, 2nd Floor, 4-8 Udagawa-cho, Shibuya-ku, Tokyo 150; Sec.-Gen. KAZUHARU SATO.

Recording Industry Association of Japan (RIAJ): 2F Kobiki Bldg, 7-16-3 Giaza, Chao-ku 104; tel. (3) 3541-4411; fax (3) 3541-4460; internet www.riaj.or.jp; Chair. ISAMU TOMITSUKA.

Union of Tokyo Music Business People: 3F Diar Inoue Bldg, 1-6-6 Akasaka, Mianto-ku, Tokyo 107; Chair. MASAKASU SUNADOI.

Republic of Korea

Asian Composers' League (Korean Committee): PO Box 874, Seoul 110 062; Dir SUNG-JAE LEE.

IFPI: 5 Floor, Kumseok Bldg, 1574-14 Seocho-dong, Seocho-ku, Seoul 137 070; Contact KIM SEH WON.

Korea Music Copyright Association (KOMCA): 2-4F, Samjeon Bldg, 236-3 Nonhyeon-dong, Kangnam-ku, Seoul 135 010; Pres. SEOG-WAN GIM.

Korea Performers' Association: 6 Floor, Yeil B/D, 60 Chungshin-dong, Chongro-ku, Seoul; Contact YUN TONG WOONG.

Music Association of Korea: 1-117 Dongsoong-dong, Chongro-ku, Seoul; Pres. SANG-HYUN CHO.

Luxembourg

SACEM: 46 rue Goethe, 1637 Luxembourg; Contact PIERRE NEUEN.

Malaysia

IFPI: 137-1/139-1 1st Floor, Wisma Hiap lee, Jln Segambut, Kuala Lumpur 51200; Gen. Man. TAN NGIAP FOO.

Mexico

AMPROFON: Francisco Petrarca 223–503, Chapultepec Morales, 11560 México, DF.

Camara Nacional de la Industria de Radio y Televisión (CIRT): Avda Horacio, 1013 Col. Polanco, 11550 México, DF; Pres. RAUL ARECHINA ESPINOZA; Gen. Man. CÉSAR HERNÁNDEZ ESPEJO.

Dirección de Normas de Radiodifusión: Eugenia, 197, 1° Col. Vértiz Narvarte, 03020 México, DF; Dir ALFONSO AMILPAS.

Dirección General de Telecomunicaciones: Lázaro Cárdenas, 567, 11°, ala norte Navarte, 03020 México, DF; Dir CARLOS LARA SUMANO.

National Traditional Country Music Association of Mexico: Esq Américas, Fracc, Reforma, Veracruz.

Sociedad de Autores y Compositores de Música (SACM): Mayorazgo 129, 03330 México, DF.

The Netherlands

BUMA (Composers Rights Society): PO Box 725, 1180 AS Amstelveen; Chair. GERARD VAN LAAR.

BVPOP: PO Box 63107, 1005 LC Amsterdam; Chair. ANDREA STEINMETZ.

Conamus Foundation: PO Box 929, Vaartweg 32, 1200 AX Hilversum; tel. (35) 621-8748; fax (35) 621-2750; e-mail info@conamus.nl; internet www.conamus.nl; Man. Dir JERNEY KAAGMAN.

Genootschap van Nederlandse Componisten (GENECO): PO Box 16463, 1001 RN, Amsterdam; tel. and fax (20) 622-7022; e-mail info@geneco.nl; internet www.geneco.nl; Sec. C H MACKAY.

Gong: Kerkweg 41, 3603 CL Maarssen; Contact MICHAEL LAMBRECHSTEN.

Hard Disc (Association of Hard Rock DJs): Arkplein 103, 1826 DM Alkmaar; Pres. GUS VAN SUNTENMAARTENSDIJK.

International Federation of Popular Music Publishers (IFPMP): Eikbosserweg 181, 1213 RX Hilversum; Sec.-Gen. COR SMIT.

Mega Top 50: PO Box 483, 1200 AL Hilversum; Man. Dir SIEB KROESKE.

Nederlandse Toonkunstenaarsbond (NTB): Herengracht 272, 1016 BW Amsterdam; Chair. MICHIEL DE STERKE.

Nederlandse Vereniging van Producenten en Importeurs (NVPI): Albertus Perkstraat 36, 1217 NT Hilversum; tel. (35) 625-4411; fax (35) 625-4410; e-mail info@nupi.nl; internet www.nupi.nl; Man. Dir P R C SOLLEVELD.

NVGD: Die Noord 3, 1452 PS Ilpendam; Chair. J F T HOTZENBOSCH.

Osgood and Morley Clip/Music Video Production: Utrechtseweg 39 B, 1301 gs Weesp; Prod. HANS W.VAN POL.

PALM: Vaartweg 32, 1217 SV Hilversum; Chair. CEES SCHRAMA.

Royal Society for Music History of the Netherlands (KVNM): PO Box 1514, 3500 BM Utrecht; Pres. DR J M M VAN GEMERT; Sec. DR A J WESTER.

SENA: PO Box 113, 1200 AC Hilversum; tel. (35) 625-1700; fax (35) 628-0971; e-mail sena@sena.nl; internet www.sena.nl; Man. of International Affairs NATALIE LOOP.

STEMRA (Mechanical Rights Society): PO Box 725, 1180 AS Amstelveen; Chair. GERARD VAN LAAR.

UNIM: Eikbosserweg 181, 1213 JE Hilversum; Chair. GUUS JANSEN JR.

Vecta: PO Box 49, 1394 ZG Nederhorst Den Berg; Chair. M HANSON.

New Zealand

Australasian Mechanical Copyright Owners Society Ltd (New Zealand Branch Officer) (AMCOS): PO Box 36795, Parnell, Auckland; Gen. Man. (NZ) JANICE GILES.

Composers Association of New Zealand (CANZ): PO Box 4065, Wellington; Pres. DENISE HULFORD.

Independent Music Producers and Performers Associations (IMPPA): PO Box 68-593, Newton, Auckland; Chair. JEFF CLARKSON.

New Zealand Composers Foundation Ltd: 11–13 Broderick Rd, Johnsonville, Wellington; Chair. ASHLEY HEENAN.

New Zealand Country Music Association: PO Box 602, Wakatane; Sec. LINDA MITA.

New Zealand Jazz Foundation: 18 Motueka St, Ngaio, Wellington; Pres. JOHN CRAWFORD.

New Zealand Music Centre: 15 Brandon St, Wellington; Chair. MERWYN NORRISH.

New Zealand Music Information Bureau Inc.: Carnegie Centre, 110 Moray Pl., Dunedin; Man. Dir JOHN KITTO.

New Zealand Musicians' Union: Private Bag 68-914, Newton, Auckland; tel. (9) 834-3382; fax (9) 834-5897; e-mail peter@sfwu.org.nz; internet www.sfwu.org.nz; Sec. PETER SHANNON.

NZ On Air: PO Box 9744, Wellington; tel. (4) 382-9524; fax (4) 382-9546; e-mail kiwihits@nzonair.govt.nz; internet www.nzonair.govt.nz; Music Man. BRENDAN SMYTH.

Phonographic Performances (NZ) Ltd (PPNZ): 6th Floor, Courtenay Chambers Bldg, 15 Courtenay Pl., Wellington; Chair. TERENCE O'NEILL-JOYCE.

Recording Industry Association of New Zealand (RAINZ): 6th Floor, Courtenay Chambers Bldg, 15 Courtenay Pl., Wellington; Chair. TERENCE O'NEILL-JOYCE.

Norway

DENIF: PO Box 365, 1701 Sarpsborg; Chair. PER LANGSHOLT.

Foreningen Norskeplateselkaper (FONO): Rosenborggate 19, 0356 Oslo; Chair. JAN PAULSEN.

Gramo: Osterhaus 6T, 27, 0183 Oslo; Exec. Dir JON MARTIN GRAN.

IFPI Norge: Sandakervelen 52, 0477 Oslo; tel. 2222-1788; fax 2222-1768; e-mail ifpi.sekretariat@ifpi.no; internet www.ifpi.no; Dir SAEMUND FISKVIK.

Norsk Forening For Opphavsrett: PO Box 9171, 0134 Oslo.

Norsk Jazzarkiv: Toftesgate 69, 0552 Oslo; Dir FINN KRAMER-JOHANSEN.

Norsk Musiker Og Musikkpedagogforening (NMM): PO Box 210, 4301 Sandnes; Man. HARALD BJØRGAN.

Norsk Musikerforbund: Youngsgate 11, 0181 Oslo; Man. Dir TORE NORDVIK.

Norsk Rockforbund/Norwegian Rock Association: PO Box 8892 Youngstorget, 0028 Oslo; Man. Dir ØYSTEIN RONANDER.

Norske Populaerautorer (NOPA): Toyenbekken 21, PO Box 9171 Gronland, 0134 Oslo; Chair. SIGURD JANSEN.

Norwegian Jazz Association: Tollbugt. 28, 0157 Oslo; tel. 2335-8180; fax 2335-8181; e-mail norsk@jazzforum.no; internet www.jazzforum.no; Man. TONE MARTINSEN.

Norwegian Music Information Centre: Toftesgate 69, 0552 Oslo; Contact HILDE HOLBACK HANSSEN.

Norwegian Society of Composers: PO Box 9171 Gronland, 0134 Oslo; Chair. HAKON BERGE.

Tono: PO Box 9171, Gronland, 0134 Oslo; tel. 2205-7200; fax 2205-7250; e-mail tono@tono.no; internet www.tono.no; Man. CATO STRÖM.

The Philippines

Filipino Society of Composers, Authors and Publishers Inc (FILSCAP): 1365 E Rodriguez Sr Ave, Quezon City, Metro Manila; tel. (2) 721-3903; fax (2) 722-9450; internet www.filscap.com.ph; Chair. GEORGE CANSECO.

Philippine Association of the Recording Industry: 1020 Soliven Bldg, EDSA, San Juan, Metro Manila; tel. (2) 722-8014; fax (2) 725-0786; Pres. DANILO OLIVARES.

Poland

Association of Polish Musicians (SPAM): Ul. Krucza 24–26, 00 526 Warsaw; Pres. EUGENIUSZ SASIADEK.

Country Music Association of Poland: Ul. Grójecka 75, 02 094 Warsaw; Vice-Pres. JERZY GLUSZYK; Contact EWA DABROWSKA.

IFPI Poland: Ul. Czarnieckiego 5/2, 01 511 Warsaw; Dir BIANKA KORTLAN.

Polish Composers Union (ZKP): Rynek Starego Miasta 27, 00-272 Warsaw; Pres. ANDRZEJ CHODKOWSKI.

Polish Jazz Society: Ul. Chmielna 20, 00 020 Warsaw; Chair. HENRYK MAJEWSKI.

Polish Music Centre: Fredry 8, 00-097 Warsaw; Man. BARBARA ZWOLSKA-STESZEWSKA.

Society of Authors (ZAIKS): Hipoteczna 2, 00 950 Warsaw; Chair. TADEUSZ MAKLAKIEWICZ.

Stomur/Association of Entertainment Musicians: Ul. Lwowska 13, 00 660 Warsaw; Chair. MACIEJ CZARNECKI.

Union of Lyric Writers and Composers of Light Music (ZAKR): Hipoteczna 2, 00 950 Warsaw; Chair. TADEUSZ MAKLAKIEWICZ.

Zwiazek Producentow Audio-Video/Polish Society of the Phonographic Industry (ZPAV): Ul. Kruczkowskiego 12 m 2, 00-380 Warsaw; tel. (22) 622-9219; fax 625-1661; e-mail biuro@2pav.pl; internet www.zpav.pl; Man. Dir MAREK STASZEWSKI.

Portugal

Associação Fonografica Portuguesa (AFP): Augusto das Santos, 2/2, 1000 Lisbon; Pres. DANIEL DE SOUSA.

Conselho Portugues da Musica: Rua Rosa Araújo, 6, 3°, 1200 Lisbon.

Instituto de Comunicacoes de Portugal (ICP): Avda José Malhoa, Lote 1683, 1000 Lisbon; Chair. FERNANDO MENDES.

Sindicato dos Musicos: Avda D Carlos I 72-2°, 1200 Lisbon; Pres. JOSÉ TRISTÃO NUNES NOGUEIRA.

Sociedade Portuguesa de Autores: Avda Duque de Loulé, 31, 1050 Lisbon; Pres. LUIZ FRANCISCO REBELLO.

Romania

Institut de Etnografie Si Folclor C Brailoiu: Str Al Obregria Nr 3, Bloc M2, Ap 73, Sector 4, 75571 Bucharest; Contact CONSTANTA CRISTESCU.

National Complex Astra Museum: 11 Piata Mica, Sibiu 2400; tel. (69) 218-195; fax (69) 218-060; e-mail astra@sbx.logicnet.ro; internet www.romquest.com/astra; Gen. Dir CORNELIU BUCUR; museum of traditional and folk music.

Union des Musiciens Professionnels: Str Franklin Nr1, Sect 1, 70149 Bucharest; Contact STEFAN GHEORGHIU.

Union of Composers and Musicians: Calea Victorei 141, Sect 1, 70149 Bucharest; Chair. ADRAIN IORGULESCU.

Russia

International Music Council: Ul. Nyezhdanova str 8, 103 009 Moscow; Contact BORIS DIMENTMAN.

International Union of Musicians: Ul. Gertsena 14/2, 103 009 Moscow; Pres. IRINA ARKHIPOVA.

Moscow Jazz Agency (MJA): Ul. Nyezhdanova str 8–10, 103 009 Moscow; Chair. YURII SAULSKY.

Russian Phonographic Association: Krymsky Val 7, 117 418 Moscow; Man. ALEXEY UGRINOVICH.

Union of Composers of Russia: Ul. Nyezhdanova 8, 103 009 Moscow; Contact YEVGENI KRIVOJEV.

VAAP (Copyright Agency): Bolshaya Bronnaya 6A, 103 670 Moscow; Chair. NIKOLAJ TCHETVERKIOV.

Singapore

Composers and Authors Society of Singapore Ltd (COMPASS): 11-A Bukit Pasoh Rd, Singapore 089825; Gen. Man. EDMUND LAM.

IFPI (South East Asia Ltd): 1 Marine Parade Central, #12-01 Parkway Builders' Centre, Singapore 1544; Deputy Regional Dir, S E Asia LEONG MAY SEEY.

Music Publishers (S) Ltd: 1 Marine Parade Central, #12-01 Parkway Builders' Centre, Singapore 1544; Admin. Exec. LARAINE SOH.

Musicians & Singers Association: Block 3, 03-628 Rochor Centre, Rochor Rd, Singapore 0718; Chief Officer STEPHEN GOMEZ.

Singapore Phonogram & Videogram Association (SPVA): 1 Marine Parade Central, #12-01 Parkway Builders' Centre, Singapore 1544; Admin. Exec. LARAINE SOH.

Slovakia

Association of Country Music: Jakubovo nam 12, 81109 Bratislava; Chair. PETER GASPAR.

Disco Club Mix (DMC): Klincova 12, 821-08 Bratislava; Man. IGOR MALOVEC.

Slovak Jazz Society: Jakubovo nam 12, 81109 Bratislava; Contact PETER LIPA.

Slovensky Ochranny Zvaz Autorsky (SOZA): Kollarovo nam 20, 81327 Bratislava; Pres. JULIUS KINCEK.

Union of Authors and Interpreters: Jakubovo nam 12, 81109 Bratislava; Dir JAN BALAZ.

South Africa

Association of the South African Music Industry: PO Box 367, Randburg 2125, Johannesburg; CEO DES DUBERY.

Dramatic, Artistic, and Literary Rights Organization Ltd (DALRO): PO Box 9292, Johannesburg; Man. Dir GIDEON ROSS.

Foundation for the Creative Arts: PO Box 91122, Auckland Park 2006; Exec. Man. HERMAN VAN NIEKERK.

South African Music Rights Organization Ltd (SAMRO): PO Box 9292, Johannesburg 2000; Man. Dir GIDEON ROSS.

South African Musicians Union: PO Box 5837, Johannesburg 2000; Pres. HOWARD BELLING.

South African Recording Rights Association Ltd (SARRAL): PO Box 4378, Johannesburg 2000; Chief Officer GEORGE HARDIE.

South African Society of Music Teachers: PO Box 5318, Walmer 6065.

Spain

AEDEM: Paseo de la Castellana 93, 28046 Madrid; Pres. JUAN MARQUEZ.

AFYVE/IFPI Spain: c/ Pedro Muguruza 8 entreplanta izquierda, 28036 Madrid; Dir-Gen. CARLOS GRANDE.

AIE: c/ Principe de Vergara 9, bajo derecha, 28001 Madrid; Pres. LUIS COBOS.

Associacio Musics de Jazz: Gran Via 410-4, 08015 Barcelona; Sec. ANGEL PERIERA.

Centro para la Difusión de la Música Contemporánea (CDMC): Santa Isabel 52, 28012 Madrid.

Instituto de Bibliografica Musical: Penulas 12, 12p 28071 Madrid; Pres. JACINTO TORRES MULAS.

Sindicato Profesional de Músicos Españoles (SPME): c/Veneras 9-1°, 28013 Madrid; Gen. Sec. JACINTO BERZOSA ARROYO.

Sociedad de Conciertos: Atlamira 3, 03002 Alicante; Dir MARGARITA BERENGER.

Sociedad Española de Musicologica (SEM): Canos del Peral 7, 28013 Madrid; Pres. ISMAEL FERNANDEZ DE LA CUESTA.

Sociedad General de Autores de España (SGAE): Fernando VI 4, 28004 Madrid; Pres. MANUEL GUTIERREZ ARAGÓN.

Sweden

DMC Sweden: PO Box 295, 101 25 Stockholm; Contact PER STAVBORG.

Folkparkenas Nöjesservice: PO Box 171 94, 104 62 Stockholm; Chair. BJÖRN ERIKSSON.

Föreningen Svenska Kompositörer Ave Populärmusik (SKAP): Sandhamnsgatan 79, Box 27327, 10254 Stockholm; Chair. HAAKAN ELMGUIST; Contact INGERED LINDBERG.

Föreningen Svenska Tonsättare (FST): PO Box 27 237, 102 54 Stockholm; Chair. STEN HANSON.

IFPI Sweden: PO Box 1008, 171 21 Solna; Chair. EDDIE LANDQUIST.

Nordic Music Committee (NOMUS): Nybrokajen 11, 111 48 Stockholm; tel. 8407-1600; e-mail gen.secr@novens.org; Sec.-Gen. BO BYDBERG.

Rockfile Sweden HB: PO Box 558, 631 07 Eskilstuna; Man. Dir HANS LINDELL.

Society of Swedish Composers: PO Box 27 327, 102 54 Stockholm.

Svensk Impressarieförening (SVIMP): Villawagen 25A, 19146 Sollentuna; tel. 8661-3800; fax 8665-1795; e-mail knut.rutenborg@ema.se; internet www.ema.se; Chair. ASA INGMAN.

Svensk Musik/Swedish Music Information Centre: PO Box 27 327, 102 54 Stockholm; Chair. ROLAND SANDBERG.

Swedish Artists' and Musicians' Interest Organization (SAMI): Döbelnsgatan 3, 111 40 Stockholm; tel. 8453-3400; fax 8453-3440; e-mail hans.sami.se; internet www.sami.se; Man. Dir HANS LINDSTRÖM.

Swedish Music Publishers Association (SMFF): PO Box 27 327, 102 54 Stockholm; tel. (8) 783-8965; fax (8) 663-4963; e-mail carl.lindencrona@smff.se; internet www.smff.sc; Man. Dir CARL LINDENCICNA.

Swedish Musicians Union/Svenska Musiker Förbundet: PO Box 43, Tegneratan 4, 101 20 Stockholm; Contact HAKAN HILLERSTRÖM.

Swedish Performing Rights Society (STIM): PO Box 27 327, 102 54 Stockholm; Gen. Man. GUNNAR PETRI.

Switzerland

Association of Swiss Concert Agents: 7 rue de la Fontaine, 1211 Geneva; Pres. JACK YFAR.

Association of Swiss Musicians: Ave du Grammont 11 bis, Case Postale 177, 1000 Lausanne 13; Gen. Sec. HÉLÈNE PETITPIERRE.

European Association of Music Festivals: c/o Centre Européen de la Culture Villa Moynier, 122 rue de Lausanne, 1211 Geneva; Sec. DR HENRY SIEGWART.

Federation of International Music Competitions: 104 rue de Carouge, 1205 Geneva.

Fondation Suisa Pour la Musique: rue de l'Hôpital 22, PO Box 2331, 2001 Neuchatel; tel. (32) 725-2536; fax (32) 724-0472; e-mail info@fondation-suisa.ch; internet www.fondation-suisa.ch; Pres. JEAN BALISSAT; Dir CLAUDE DELLEY.

IFPI Switzerland: Toblerstr 76a, 8044 Zurich; tel. (1) 252-5866; fax (1) 252-6167; internet www.ifpi-schwiez.ch; Dir PETER VOSSELER.

International Society for Contemporary Music: c/o Association of Swiss Musicians, Ave du Grammont 11 bis, Case Postale 177, 1000 Lausanne 13.

Schweizer Zentralband Musikhandels (SZM): Zeughausgasse 9, PO Box 238, 6301 Zug; Pres. ERIKA HUG.

Schweizerischer Musikverband (SMV): Hotelgasse 1, 300 Bern 7; Pres. HEINZ MARTI.

Suisa (Performing Rights Society of Switzerland): Bellariastr 82, 8038 Zürich; Man. FABIO HUGEL.

Suisa Music Foundation (Music Information Centre): Passage Maxmililien-de-Meuron 4, PO Box 409, 2001 Neuchâtel; Man. Dir P LIECHTI.

SVMM: PO Box, 8616 Riedikon /Uster; Pres. WILLY VITEKA.

Swiss Association of Professional Musicians: Elisabethenstr 2, 4051 Basel.

Swiss Society for Musical Research: PO Box 231, 4020 Basel.

Swiss Society for Popular Music: c/o SUISA, Bellariastr 82, 8038 Zürich.

VSM: Zeughausgasse 9, PO Box 238, 6301 Zug; Pres. EDMUND SCHOENBERGER.

VSSF: Zeughausgasse 9, PO Box 238, 6301 Zug; Pres. DANIEL BAER.

Thailand

Thai Composers Association (TCA): 107–108 Siripong Rd, Sao Chingcha, Samranrat, Bangkok 10200.

Turkey

MESAM: Kuyulu Bostan Sokak Kristal Plas Apt, Nisantasi, Istanbul.

MUYAP (Muzik Yapimlari Dernegi): IMC 6, Blok 6437, 34470 Unkapani, Istanbul; Contact YASAR KEKEVA.

Ukraine

Broken Barricades: Tchernovoarmiyska 17B, 252 003 Kiev; Man. SERGIY KALYTA.

Dirate of the All-Ukrainian Festival of Independent Music Alternative: Culture Foundation, Lesva Kur-Basa str 4, 290007 Lviv; Dir YOURY GREKH; Vice Dir RUSLAN KOSHIV; Held in September.

Independent Artist's Agency 'Ljubchenko & Co': Room 7, Mietrostrojevskaja St 5, 320128 Dniepropetrovsk; Dir VALERI LJUBCHENKO.

Institute of Musicology: Institute of Musicology, Soviet Ukraine Sq., 20 # 9, 310003 Kharkov; Dir GRIGORY HANSBURG.

Musical Information Agency IRA: PO Box 83, 326 840 Novoya Kakhovka/Kherson; Man. IRYNA TSYGIPA.

Producers Centre Rock Academy: Khreschatyk 6, 252 001 Kiev; Man. Dir MYKOLA DRIK..

The United Kingdom

Agents' Association (GB): 54 Keyes House, Dolphin Sq., London SW1V 3NA; Gen. Sec. IVAN BIRCHALL.

Alchemea—The London College of Professional Audio Engineering and Production: The Windsor Centre, 2–18 Britannia Row, The Angel Islington, London N1 8QH; College Dir CLAUDE CAMILLERI.

American Society of Composers, Authors and Publishers (ASCAP): 8 Cork St, London W1X 1PB; Contact KAREN CROWLEY.

Association of Music Industry Accountants (AMIA): Becket House, 1 Lambeth Rd, London SE1 7EU; Sec. NICKI DAVIES.

Association of Professional Recording Services Ltd (APRS): 2 Windsor Sq., Reading, Berkshire RG1 2TH; CEO MARK BROAD.

Association of United Recording Artists (Aura): Flat B, 6 Bravington St, London W9 3AH; Contact PETER JENNER.

Belfast Jazz Society: 18 Lyndhurst Dr., Belfast B13 3PA, Northern Ireland; Administration GEORGE CHAMBERS.

Black Music Industry Association: 146 Manor Park Rd, Harlesden, London NW10 4JP; Contact KWAKU LUTTERFOOT.

British Academy of Songwriters, Composers & Authors (BASCA): The Penthouse, 4 Brook St, Mayfair, London W1Y 1AA; Chair. GUY FLETCHER.

British Archive of Country Music: 163 The Gateway, Marine Parade, Dover CT16 1LS, Kent; Man. Dir DAVID BARNES.

British Association of Concert Agents: 26 Wadham Rd, London SW15 2LR; Pres. DAVID SIGALL.

British Association of Record Dealers (BARD): Premier House, Hinton Rd, Bournemouth, Dorset BH1 2EF; Dir-Gen. BOB LEWIS.

British Country Music Association: PO Box 240, Harrow, Middlesex HA3 7PH; tel. (1273) 559750; fax (1273) 559750; e-mail thebcma@yahoo.com; Chair. JIM MARSHALL.

British Phonographic Industry (BPI): 25 Saville Row, London W1X 1AA; Dir-Gen. JOHN DEACON; Gen. Man. PETER SCAPING.

Broadcast Music Incorporated (BMI): 84 harley House, Marylebone Rd, London NW1 5HN; Dir (United Kingdom) CHRISTIAN ULF-HANSEN.

Celfyddydau Mari Arts: Studio 4, Model House Craft and Design Centre, The Bullring, Llantrisant, Rhondda Cynon Taf, Wales CF72 8EB; Co-ordinator MICK TEMS.

Christian Copyright Licensing Ltd: PO Box 1339, Eastbourne, East Sussex BN21 4YF; United Kingdom Church & Schools Representative CHRIS WILLIAMS.

Club Gwerin Llantrisant Folk Club: 1 Ty Clwyta Cottages, Cross Inn, Llantrisant, Rhondda Cynon Taf, Wales CF72 8AZ; tel. and fax (1443) 226892; e-mail folkclub@folkwales.org.uk; internet www.folkwales.org.uk; Sec. MICK TEMS.

Commercial Radio Companies Association (CRCA): 77 Shaftesbury Ave, London W1V 7AD; tel. (20) 7306-2603; fax (20) 7470-0062; e-mail info@crea.co.uk; internet www.crea.co.uk; CEO PAUL BROWN.

Country Music Association (CMA): 3rd Floor, 18 Golden Sq., London W1R 3AG; European Operations Co-ordinator BOBBI BOYCE; Dir (United Kingdom/Ireland) DAVID BOWER.

C-Thru Music Ltd: 6 Pleasant Row, Woodford, Northamptonshire NN14 4HP; tel. (1832) 733214; internet www.c-thru-music.com; Contact ANDREW LLEWELLYN.

Friends of the Upton Jazz Festival: Court Cottage, Lockeridge Lane, Upton-Upon-Severn, WR8 0RP; tel. (1684) 593794; Sec. PAUL LAWRENCE.

Guild of International Songwriters and Composers (GISC): Sovereign House, 12 Trewartha Rd, Parr Sands, Penzance, Cornwall TR20 9ST; tel. (1736) 762826; fax (1736) 763328; e-mail

songmag@aol.com; internet www.songwriters-guild.co.uk; Gen. Sec. CAROLE A JONES.

Guild of Recording Producers, Dirs and Engineers (Re-Pro): 68 Cleveland Gardens, Barnes, London SW13 0AH; Contact JACKIE DACOSTA.

Incorporated Society of Musicians: 10 Stratford Pl., London W1C 1AA; tel. (20) 7629-4413; fax (20) 7408-1538; e-mail membership@ism.org; internet www.ism.org; CEO NEIL HOYLE.

International Artist Managers' Association (IAMA): 4 Addison Bridge Pl., London, W14 8XP.

International Federation of the Phonographic Industry (IFPI): 54 Regent St, London W1R 5PJ; Chair. DAVID FINE; Dir-Gen. NIC GARNETT.

International Managers Forum (IMF): 134 Lots Rd, London SW10 0RJ; Gen. Sec. JAMES FISHER.

International Music Markets (IMM) Ltd: 245 Old Marylebone Rd, London NW1 5QT; Gen. Man. PHIL GRAHAM.

International Society of European Songwriters and Composers (SESAC): Gresham House, 53 Clarendon Rd, Watford, Herts WD1 1LA; Chair. WAYNE BICKERTON.

Jazz Action: 1 Portrush Close, Darlington, County Durham DL1 3HU; Devt Officer ADRIAN TILBROOK.

Jazz Educaton Trust: 1 Fox Glove Close, Ringmer, East Sussex BN8 5PB; Dir ADRIAN KENDON.

Jazz North West: 2A Church St, Malpas, Cheshire SY14 8NZ; Dir NICK PURNELL.

Jazz Services: 1st Floor, 132 Southwark St, London SE1 0SW; tel. (20) 7928-9089; fax (20) 7401-6870; e-mail admin@jazzservices.org.uk; internet www.jazzservices.org.uk; Contact CELIA WOOD.

Mechanical Copyright Protection Society Ltd (MCPS): Elgar House, 41 Streatham High Rd, London SW16 1ER; CEO JOHN HUTCHINSON.

Millward Brown Market Research Ltd: Olympus Ave, Tachbrook Park, Warwick CV34 6RJ; Charts Dir BOB BARNES.

Music Industry Human Rights Association: 192 Chiswick Village, London W4 3DG.

Music Industry Research Organization (MIRO): 8th Floor, Ludgate House, 245 Blackfriars Rd, London SE1 9UR; Editor LEE FISHER.

Music Publishers Association (MPA): 3rd Floor, Strandgate, 18–20 York Bldgs, London WC2 6JU; CEO SARAH FOULDER.

Musicians Benevolent Fund: 16 Ogle St, London W1P 8JB; Sec. to the Fund HELEN FAULKNER.

Musicians' Union (MU): 60–62 Clapham Rd, London SW9 0JJ; Gen. Sec. DENNIS SCARD.

National Entertainment Agents Council: PO Box 112, Seaford, East Sussex BN25 2DQ; tel. (1323) 492488; fax (1323) 492234; e-mail info@neac.org.uk; internet www.neac.org.uk; Gen. Sec. CHRIS BRAY.

Nordoff Robbins Music Therapy: 55 Fulham High St, London SW6 3JJ; Chair. ANDREW MILLER.

North West Composers' Association: Stanway Rd, Whitefield, Manchester M45 8EG; tel. (161) 766-5950; Treasurer GEOFFREY KIMPTON; Sec. COLIN BAYLISS.

Northern Ireland Musicians' Association: 525 Antrim Rd, Belfast BT15 3BS; Gen. Sec. HENRY C. HAMILTON.

North-West Musicians Collective: 6C Shipquay St, Derry, Northern Ireland BT48 6DN; Co-ordinators JOHN O'NEILL, SEAN PEMBERTON.

OVC Ltd: 34 Salisbury St, London NW8 8QE; tel. (20) 7402-9111; fax (20) 7723-3064; e-mail ovcmedia@hotmail com; internet www.ovcmedia.com; Man. Dirs JOANNE COHEN, PETER SULLIVAN.

Performing Artists Media Rights Association (PAMRA): 4th Floor, 80 Borough High St, London SE1 1LR; CEO ANN RAWCLIFFE-KING; Dir BENNY GALLAGHER.

Performing Rights Society (PRS): 29–33 Berners St, London W1P 4AA; CEO JOHN HUTCHINSON; Membership Dir JOHN SWEENEY.

Phonographic Performance Ltd (PPL): 1 Upper James St, London W1R 3HG; CEO CHARLES ANDREWS; Man. Dir JOHN LOVE.

Publicity Connection: Flat 3, Haversham Lodge, Melrose Ave, Willesden Green, London NW2 4JS; tel. (20) 8450-8882; fax (20) 8202-4219; e-mail sharon@thepublicityconnection.com; internet www.thepublicityconnection.com; Man. Dir SHARON CHEVIN.

Radio Academy: 5 Marklet Pl., London W1N 7AH; tel. (20) 7255-2010; fax (20) 7255-2029; e-mail info@radioacademy.org; internet www.radioacademy.org; CEO JOHN BRADFORD.

Radio Advertising Bureau (RAB): 77 Shaftesbury Ave, London W1V 7AD; Dir DOUGLAS MCARTHUR.

Radio Authority: Holbrook House, 14 Great Queen St, London WC2B 5DG; Chair. SIR PETER GIBBINGS; Contact MARION SHELLEY.

Red Bus Music (International) Ltd: 34 Salisbury St, London NW8 8QE; tel. (20) 7402-9111; fax (20) 7723-3064; internet www.amimedia.co.uk; Man. Dir ELIOT M COHEN.

Regional Promoters Association (RPA): The Leadmill, 6–7 Leadmill Rd, Sheffield S1 4SE; tel. (114) 2212860; fax (114) 2212848; e-mail rupert@leadmill.co.uk; internet www.leadmill.co.uk; Contact RUPERT DELL.

Scottish Music Information Centre: 1 Bowmont Gardens, Glasgow G12 9LR.

South West Jazz: Exeter and Devon Arts Centre, Bradninch Pl., Gandy St, Exeter EX4 3LS; Regional Devt Officer KEVIN BUCKLAND.

The Official UK Charts Company: 3rd Floor, Century House, 100 Oxford St, London W1N 9LD; tel. (20) 7436-3000; fax (20) 7436-8000; e-mail info@theofficialcharts.com; internet www.theofficialcharts.com; Chart Dir OMAR MASKATIYA.

Variety and Light Entertainment Council: 54 Keyes House, Dolphin Sq., London SW1V 3NA; tel. (20) 7834-0515; fax (20) 7821-0261; e-mail association-uk.com; internet www.agents-uk.com; Joint Secretaries KENNETH EARLE, CHRISTINE PAYNE.

Video Performance Ltd (VPL): 1 Upper James St, London W1R 3HG; CEO CHARLES ANDREWS.

Vocem Electric Voice Theatre: 39 Birnam Rd, London N4 3LJ.

Welsh Jazz Society Ltd: 26 The Balcony, Castle Arcade, Cardiff, South Glamorgan CF10 1BY; tel. (2920) 340591; fax (2920) 665160; e-mail jazzwale@cs.com; internet www.jazzwales.org.uk; Dir BRIAN HENNESSEY.

Whistlebinkies: 13 Lawrence St, Glasgow G11 5HH; Contact EDDIE MCGUIRE.

Women in Music: BAC, Lavender Hill, Battersea, London SW11 5TF; Admin. Dir LOLITA RATCHFORD.

The United States of America

Academy of Country Music (ACM): 6255 Sunset Blvd, Suite 923, Hollywood, CA 90028; Pres. FRED REISER.

Affiliated Independent Record Companies (AIRC): PO Box 241648, Los Angeles, CA 90024; Pres. M WILKES.

American Federation of Musicians: 1501 Broadway, Suite 600, New York, NY 10036; Pres. MARK MASSAGLI.

American Federation of Television and Radio Artists (AFTRA): 260 Madison Ave, New York, NY 10016; Exec. Dir BRUCE YORK.

American Mechanical Rights Agency Inc (AMRA): 333 South Tamiami Trail, Suite 295, Venice, FL 34285; Chief Officer PATRICIA BENTE.

American Musicians' Union: 8 Tobin Court, Dumont, NJ 07628; Pres. BEN INTORRE.

American Society of Composers, Authors and Publishers (ASCAP): 1 Lincoln Plaza, New York, NY 10023; Pres. MARILYN BERGMAN.

American Society of Music Arrangers & Composers (ASMAC): PO Box 17840, Encino, CA 91416; tel. (818) 994-4661; fax (818) 994-6181; e-mail properimage2000@earthlink.net; internet www.asmac.org; Pres. JOHN CLAYTON; Sec. BONNIE JANOFSKY.

Audio Engineering Society: 60 East 42nd St, Lincoln Bldg, Room 2520, New York, NY 10165; Dir DONALD PLUNKETT.

Black Rock Coalition: PO Box 1054, Cooper Station, New York, NY 10276; Pres. BRUCE MACK.

Broadcast Music Inc (BMI): 320 W 57th St, New York, NY 10019; Pres. FRANCES PRESTON.

Chorus America: 1156 15th St, NW Suite 310, Washington, DC 20005; Exec. Dir MAURICE STAPLES.

Company of Fifers and Drummers: PO Box 525, Ivoryton, CT 06443; Archivist ED OLSON.

Composers Guild: PO Box 586, Framington, UT 84025; Pres. RUTH GATRELL.

Concerts for the Environment: 126 N 3rd St, Suite 305, Minneapolis, MN 55401; Exec. Dir MICHAEL MARTIN.

Country Music Association (CMA): 4 Music Circle S, Nashville, TN 37203; Exec. Dir ED BENSON.

CSP Records MC: PO Box 69646, Los Angeles, CA 90096; Dir LARRY KLENO.

GAVIN: 140 2nd St, 2nd Floor, San Francisco, CA 94105; CEO DAVID DALTON.

Gospel Music Association: 7 Music Circle North, Nashville, TN 37203; Exec. Dir BRUCE KOBLISH.

Guitar and Accessories Marketing Association: 38 W 21st St, 5th Floor, New York, NY 10010-6906; Pres. JEROME HERSHMAN.

Guitar Foundation of America: PO Box 1240, Calremont, CA 91711; e-mail gunnar@cyberg8t.com; internet www.guitarfoundation.org; Exec. Dir GUNNAR EISEL.

Hawaiian Academy of Recording Arts (HARA): PO Box 821, Honolulu, 96808; Contact BONNI RYDER.

Independent Music Association: 10 Spruce Rd, Saddle River, NJ 07456; Contact DON KULAK.

Independent Network (East Coast Office): PO Box 609, Ringwood, NJ 07456.

Independent Network (West Coast Office): PO Box 241648 Los Angeles, CA 90024; CEO M WILKINS.

Institute of Recording Arts & Sciences: PO Box 22653, Nashville, TN 37202; Founder & Admin. DAVID MATHES.

International Association of Electronic Keyboard Manufacturers: 38 W 21st St, 5th Floor, New York, NY 10010-6906; Pres. JEROME HERSHMAN.

International Bluegrass Music Association (IBMA): 207 East Second St, Owensboro, KY 42303.

Jazz Foundation of America: 1200 Broadway, Suite 7D, New York, NY 10001; Promotions Dir RUSS DANTZLER.

Long Island Songwriters' Association Inc (LISA): PO Box 395, Holbrook, NY 11741; Pres./Exec. Dir ERWIN K COCHRAN.

Mel Carter: PO Box 69646, Los Angeles, CA 90069; tel. and fax (323) 934-4122; e-mail red@mel-carter.com; internet www.mel-carter.com; Artist/Owner LARRY KLENO.

Mexican Network International: 235-4 Lucas Lane, Voorhees, NJ 08043; Pres./Founder LAURA GRÜB-GESCHWINDT.

Music Association of America: 224 King St, Englewood, NJ 07631; Exec. Dir GEORGE STRUM.

Music Distributors Association: 38 West 21 St, 5th Floor, New York, NY 10010-6906; Pres. JEROME HERSHMAN.

Music Educators National Conference: 1806 Robert Fulton Dr., Reston, VA 22091-4348; Exec. Dir JOHN J MAHLMANN.

Music Publishers' Association of the United States: 711 Third Ave, New York, NY 10017.

Musicians Contact Service: 7315 Sunset Blvd D, Hollywood, CA 90046; Contact STERLING HAUG.

NAIRD: 1000 Maplewood Dr., Suite 211, Maple Shade, NJ 08052; Exec. Dir HOLLY CASS.

Nashville Entertainment Association: PO Box 121948, Nashville, TN 37212-1948; Exec. Dir SHERRY BOND.

Nashville Songwriters Association International (NSAI): 15 Music Sq. West, Nashville, TN 37203; Exec. Dir PAT ROGERS.

National Academy of Popular Music: 885 Second Ave, 26th Floor, New York, NY 10017-2201; Dir BOB LEONE.

National Academy of Recording Arts & Sciences Inc (NARAS): 2 Music Circle S, Nashville, TN 37203.

National Academy of Songwriters (NAS): 6381 Hollywood Blvd, Suite 780, Hollywood, CA 90028; Exec. Dir DAN KIRKPATRICK.

National Association of Band Instrument Manufacturers: 38 West 21 St, 5th Floor, New York, NY 10010-6906; Pres. JEROME HERSHMAN.

National Association of Recording Merchandisers (NARM): 11 Eves Dr., Suite 140, Marlton, NJ 08053; Exec. Vice-Pres. PAM HOROWITZ.

National Coalition Against Censorship: 275 Seventh Ave, New York, NY 10001; Exec. Dir LEANNE KATZ.

National Council of Music Importers and Exporters: 38 W 21st St, 5th Floor, New York, NY 10010-6906; Pres. JEROME HERSHMAN.

National Music Publishers' Association: 711 Third Ave, 8th Floor, New York, NY 10017; Public Relations Man. MARGARET O'KEEFFE.

Northern California Songwriters Association: 855 Oak Grove Ave, Suite #211, Menlo Park, CA 94025; Exec. Dir IAN CROMBIE.

Publishers' Licensing Corporation: PO Box 5807, Englewood, NJ 07631; tel. (201) 969-9990; fax (201) 969-9955; e-mail plcagent@aol.com; Pres. PHILIP S KURNIT.

Recording Industry Association of America (RIAA): 1020 19th St NW, Suite 200, Washington, DC 20096; Vice-Pres., Member Services JOHN H GANOE.

Rhythm and Blues Rock and Roll Society Inc: PO Box 1949, New Haven, CT 06510; tel. (203) 924-1079; Dir BILL NOLAN.

Rock And Roll Hall of Fame: 1290 Sixth Ave, New York, NY 10104; Exec. Dir SUSAN EVANS.

Rock Out Censorship (ROC): PO Box 147, Jewett, OH 43986; Co-Founder/Editor JOHN WOODS.

SESAC: 55 Music Sq. East, Nashville, TN 37203.

Songwriters Guild of America: 6430 Sunset Blvd, Suite 705, Hollywood, CA 90028; tel. (323) 462-1108; fax (323) 462-5430; e-mail lasga@aol.com; internet www.songwriters.org; West Coast Dir B AARON MEZA.

Songwriters of Wisconsin International—SOWI: PO Box 1027, Neenah, WI 54957-1027; tel. (920) 725-5129; fax (920) 720-0195; e-mail sowtoner@aol.com; Pres. TONY ANSEMS.

Talent Search America: 273 Chippewa Dr., Columbia, SC 29210-6508; Contact TALENT DIR; International songwriting and lyric writing contests.

Tennessee Film, Entertainment and Music Commission: Rachel Jackson Bldg, 320 6th Ave, No, Nashville, TN 37243-0790; Exec. Dir MARSHA BLACKBURN.

Tennessee Songwriters Association (TSA): PO Box 2664, Hendersonville, TN 37075; Contact JIM SYLVIS.

Texas Music Office, Office of the Governor: PO Box 13246, Austin, TX 78711; Dir CASEY MONAHAN.

Women in Music Business Association: 20 Music Sq. W #200, Nashville, TN 37203; Dir CATHERINE MASTERS.

Women In Music National Network: 31121 Mission Blvd, Suite 123, Hayward, CA 94544; Chair. KAREN JACKSON.

Uruguay

Asociación General de Autores del Uruguay (AGADU): Canelones, 1122, 11100 Montevideo; Pres. ANTONIO ITALIANO.

Asociación Uruguay de Músicos: Calle Maldonado 983, CP 11100 Montevideo; Pres. ALFONSO CORONEL.

Sociedad Uruguay de Interpretes: Canelones 1090, Montevideo; Pres. JOSÉ MARIA LORENZO.

Sociedad Uruguay de Música Contemporánea: Casilla de Correo 1328, Montevideo; Pres. DIEGO LEGRAND.

Venezuela

Sociedad de Autores y Compositores de Venezuela: Edif. Vam, Entrada Oeste 9°, Avda Andrés Bello, Caracas.